ç *ch* in German *ich:* a (j) sound as in *yes,* said without voice; similar to the first sound in *huge.*

β *b* in Spanish *Habana:* a voiced fricative sound similar to (v), but made by the two lips.

ʎ *ll* in Spanish *llamar, gl* in Italian *consiglio:* similar to the (lj) sequence in *million,* but with the tongue tip lowered and the sounds said simultaneously.

ɥ *u* in French *lui:* a short (y).

ɲ *gn* in French *vigne,* Italian *gnocchi,* *ñ* in Spanish *España:* similar to the (nj) sequence in *onion,* but with the tongue tip lowered and the two sounds said simultaneously.

ɣ *g* in Spanish *luego:* a weak (g) made with voiced friction.

Length

The symbol ː denotes length and is shown together with certain vowel symbols when the vowels are typically long.

Stress

Three grades of stress are shown in the transcriptions by the presence or absence of marks placed immediately *before* the affected syllable. Primary or strong stress is shown by ˈ, while secondary or weak stress is shown by ˌ. Unstressed syllables are not marked. In *photographic* (ˌfəʊtəˈgræfɪk), for example, the first syllable carries secondary stress and the third primary stress, while the second and fourth are unstressed.

List of Abbreviations

abbrev.	abbreviation
adj.	adjective
adv.	adverb(ial)
approx.	approximate(ly)
Austral.	Australian
Brit.	British
C	century (e.g. C14 = 14th century)
°C	degrees Celsius
cap.	capital
cf.	compare
conj.	conjunction
E	east(ern)
e.g.	for example
esp.	especially
est.	estimate
etc.	et cetera
fem.	feminine
foll.	followed
ft.	feet
i.e.	that is
in.	inches
interj.	interjection
intr.	intransitive
IPA	International Phonetic Alphabet
km	kilometres
masc.	masculine
N	north(ern)
n.	noun
NE	northeast(ern)
no.	number
NW	northwest(ern)
N.Z.	New Zealand
p.	page
pl.	plural
Pop.	population
pp.	pages
prep.	preposition(al)
pron.	pronoun
pt.	point
RP	Received Pronunciation
S	south(ern)
S. African	South African
Scot.	Scottish
SE	southeast(ern)
sing.	singular
sq.	square
SW	southwest(ern)
tr.	transitive
U.S.	United States
vb.	verb
vol.	volume
W	west(ern)
wt.	weight

COLLINS DICTIONARY OF THE ENGLISH LANGUAGE

General Consultant

J. M. Sinclair
Professor, Department of English Language and Literature
University of Birmingham

Special Consultants

SCOTTISH ENGLISH
A. J. Aitken
Department of English Language
University of Edinburgh
Editor, *Dictionary of the Older Scottish Tongue*

CARIBBEAN ENGLISH
S. R. R. Allsopp
Co-ordinator, Caribbean Lexicography Project
University of the West Indies
Barbados

INDIAN ENGLISH
R. K. Bansal
Professor, Department of Phonetics and Spoken English
Central Institute of English and Foreign Languages
Hyderabad

PRONUNCIATION
A. C. Gimson
Professor, Department of Phonetics and Linguistics
University College
University of London

CANADIAN AND IRISH ENGLISH
R. J. Gregg
Professor, Department of Linguistics
University of British Columbia

EAST AFRICAN ENGLISH
J. Kalema
Department of Linguistic Science
University of Reading

SOUTH AFRICAN ENGLISH
L. W. Lanham
Professor, Department of Phonetics and General Linguistics
University of the Witwatersrand

BRITISH REGIONAL ENGLISH, URBAN DIALECTS
Harold Orton
Professor Emeritus, Department of English
University of Leeds

WEST AFRICAN ENGLISH
J. Spencer
Director, Institute of Modern English Language Studies
University of Leeds

AUSTRALIAN ENGLISH
G. A. Wilkes
Challis Professor of English Literature
University of Sydney

W. S. Ramson
Reader in English
Australian National University

COLLINS DICTIONARY OF THE ENGLISH LANGUAGE

Patrick Hanks
EDITOR

Thomas Hill Long
MANAGING EDITOR

Laurence Urdang
EDITORIAL DIRECTOR

Collins
London & Glasgow

First Published 1979

Reprinted and updated 1979, 1980 (twice), 1981, 1982, 1983 (twice), 1984

Standard ISBN 0 00 433078-1
Indexed ISBN 0 00 433080-3

Computer data file designed and prepared for typesetting
by Laurence Urdang Associates Ltd., Aylesbury

Computer typeset by Oriel Computer Services Ltd., Oxford

Manufactured in the United States of America
by Rand McNally & Company
for William Collins Sons & Co. Ltd.
PO Box, Glasgow G4 0NB

NOTE

Entered words that we have reason to believe constitute trademarks have been designated as such. However, neither the presence nor absence of such designation should be regarded as affecting the legal status of any trademark.

CONTENTS

STAFF AND CONTRIBUTORS

Patrick Hanks
EDITOR

Thomas Hill Long
MANAGING EDITOR

Laurence Urdang
EDITORIAL DIRECTOR

GENERAL CONTRIBUTORS

Paul Procter
Chief Defining Editor

Della Summers
Deputy Defining Editor

Alan Dingle
William Gould
Christopher Hotten
John Huggins
Bernard James
Catherine Limm
Lucy Liddell
Edwin Riddell
Michael Scherk
Clare Vickers
Eileen Williams
John D. Wright

CONTENT EDITORS

Barbara Barrett
Jonathan Hunt
Catherine Hutton
Martin Manser
Judith Ravenscroft
Mary Shields
Maurice Waite
Judith Wardman
Rosalind Williams

SCIENCE CONTRIBUTORS

Alan Isaacs
Chief Science Editor

Elizabeth Martin
Deputy Science Editor

Edward R. Brace
John Daintith
Martin Elliott
Anthony Lee
Stephanie Pain
Valerie H. Pitt
Stella E. Stiegeler

PRONUNCIATION CONTRIBUTORS

Carolyn Herzog
Chief Pronunciation Editor

Judith Scott
William Gould
Jill Douglas Graham
Hope Liebersohn
Vera Steiner

ETYMOLOGY CONTRIBUTORS

Thomas Hill Long
Chief Etymologist

Yvonne Shorthouse
Eva Wagner

COMPUTER SYSTEMS AND OPERATIONS

Barry Evans
Data Processing Manager

Allistair Bywater
Jeremy Knight

KEYBOARDING STAFF

Jessica Scholes
Chief Keyboarder

Elizabeth Bonham
Julie Cox
Margaret Davis
Mandy Durham
Margaret Hobbs
Hazel Lee
Diane Mabe
Sandra McQueen
Gwyneth Shaw

SECRETARIAL AND CLERICAL STAFF

Brenda Bradbury
Dreda Burnard
Hazel Hall
Linda Harvey
Lesley Ledingham
Carole Putman

Special Contributors

AUSTRALIAN ENGLISH
Steve Higgs
B.Sc.
Melbourne Grammar School

MALAYSIAN ENGLISH
U Yong-ee
B.Sc., M.B.A.

PIDGINS AND CREOLES
Loreto Todd
The School of English
University of Leeds

URBAN DIALECT (ABERDEEN)
John D. McClure
Department of English
University of Aberdeen

URBAN DIALECT (BELFAST)
Michael V. Barry
Department of English
Queen's University of Belfast

URBAN DIALECT (BIRMINGHAM)
Clive Upton
Institute of Dialect and Folklife Studies
University of Leeds

URBAN DIALECT (BRADFORD AND LEEDS)
Stanley Ellis
Department of English
University of Leeds

URBAN DIALECT (BRISTOL)
Geoffrey Woodruff
Bristol

URBAN DIALECT (DUBLIN)
Angela M. Lucas
Department of English
University College, Dublin

URBAN DIALECT (GLASGOW)
M. K. C. MacMahon
Department of Linguistics and Phonetics
University of Glasgow

URBAN DIALECT (LIVERPOOL)
Gerald Knowles
Department of English
Queen's University of Belfast

URBAN DIALECT (LONDON)
M. Beaten
Department of English
University of Lancaster
Martyn F. Wakelin
Royal Holloway College
University of London

URBAN DIALECT (MANCHESTER)
Pauline Duncan
Sedgley Park College, Manchester
Peter Wright
Department of Modern Languages
University of Salford

URBAN DIALECT (NEWPORT)
David Parry
Department of English
University College, Swansea

URBAN DIALECT (THE NORTHEAST)
M. J. Shields
Jarrow
Co. Durham

URBAN DIALECT (SWANSEA)
Melvyn J. Davies
Department of English
University College, Swansea

URBAN DIALECT (SHEFFIELD)
J. D. A. Widdowson
Department of English Language
University of Sheffield
Ena Wright
Sheffield

AERONAUTICS
T. C. Wooldridge
T.Eng. (L.E.I.),
A.F.S.L.A.E.T.

ARCHITECTURE; CIVIL ENGINEERING
Bruce Martin
M.A., A. A. Dip. (Hons),
F.R.I.B.A., M.S.I.A.

LAW
Richard Latham
Barrister-at-Law

LINGUISTICS AND GRAMMAR
Lloyd Humberstone
M.A.

METALLURGY
Stanley White
Ph.D., Dip. Met.,
A.S.M.B.

MILITARY AND NAUTICAL TERMS
Cmdr. I. Johnston
R.N.

PLANTS
Sandra Holmes
M.A., M.I.Biol.

PRINTING
C. H. Parsons
B.Sc., Dip. Chem. Eng.
Laurence Chizlett
B.Sc., M.I.O.P.

PHILOSOPHY
Christopher Sion
M.A.

PSYCHOLOGY
Eric Taylor
M.A., M.B., M.R.C.P.(U.K.),
M.R.C.Psych.

RAILWAYS
James Barnes
M.A., LL.B.

RELIGIOUS TERMS
David Bourke Ph.D.
Rev. Canon D. W. Gundry
Chancellor of Leicester Cathedral

TOOLS
N. J. Smail
Associate of the Institute of Marine Engineers

Other Contributors

Jane Bartholomew ANIMALS
Jenny Baster COOKERY; CLOTHING AND FASHION; TEXTILES
Denise Bown PLACE NAMES
Ron Brown JAZZ
Daphne Butler CHEMISTRY
Christopher L. Clarke HOROLOGY
Brian Dalgleish METALLURGY
Carolyn Eardley ANTIQUES; FURNITURE; TEXTILES
R. J. Edwards PSYCHOLOGY
Dennis Exton FILMS, T.V., AND RADIO
Ian Fuller PSYCHOLOGY
C. Gallon PLANTS
Cherry McDonald-Taylor EDUCATION; LIBRARY SCIENCE
David Martin PSYCHOLOGY
Mary Marshall CARDS; DANCING AND BALLET
Peter Miller SPORTS
Stewart Murray METALLURGY
Serena Penman ART
H. G. Procter PSYCHOLOGY
David H. Shaw ENGINEERING
Brian Street ANTHROPOLOGY
Andrew Treacher PSYCHOLOGY
Ralph Tyler FILMS, T.V., AND RADIO; LITERATURE; MYTHOLOGY; THEATRE; BIOGRAPHIES
Jennifer Wearden ARCHAEOLOGY
Irene Wise BIOCHEMISTRY

Publisher's Foreword

This completely new and original English dictionary is one of the most important books ever published by Collins. It contains some 3 000 000 words and 162 000 references—more than any other single volume dictionary of British English in general use. *Collins English Dictionary* is, in fact, the first major English-language dictionary on a scale substantially greater than any dictionary in the "concise" category to be originated in Britain since the publication of the *Shorter Oxford Dictionary* in 1933.

Its origins date back 10 years to when Collins asked Laurence Urdang, formerly Managing Editor of the *Random House Dictionary of the English Language* and many other major reference works, to take on the task of creating the dictionary. He assembled in Aylesbury, England, a strong team of more than 20 full-time lexicographers, led by Patrick Hanks, Thomas Hill Long, and Alan Isaacs, all of whom had many years of experience in reference-book compiling.

We thought it was essential that the dictionary should cover all the spoken and written English that is likely to be required by any but the most highly specialized users, with enough space for clear and helpful definitions. We have also included many biographical and geographical entries and an exceptionally wide range of scientific and technical terms, in order to provide a truly comprehensive and useful dictionary. Great care was taken to represent as fully as possible many varieties of national and regional usage, so as to ensure that the scope of this English dictionary would be fully international. Clearly, all this would have been impossible in a book of "concise" length, but we found that this new, convenient-sized volume would accommodate the necessary text of approximately 3 000 000 words.

For the first time in a major dictionary of this kind, computer technology has been used from the inception of the work. This has made it possible to survey every field of human activity subject by subject, defining technical as well as everyday vocabulary in an exceptionally short time. Specialist and general defining editors, pronunciation editors, etymologists, and other contributors were all enabled to work in parallel and then their contributions were sorted into their proper places by computer.

Some 200 people have taken part in this complex operation. It remains only for me to thank them all for making this book such a significant development in British-originated dictionaries of the English language.

JAN COLLINS

Glasgow

February 1979

Editorial Preface

In a decade that has seen more lexicographical activity worldwide than the preceding century the first question arising from the publication of a new dictionary is, Why another dictionary? The immediate response is that we must keep pace with the language, which is in a state of ever-changing flux.

But, in fact, there are two reasons that go deeper than that. The first is the development, especially since the Second World War, of English as the most important language in the world. Today, English is the *lingua franca* not only of science, technology, commerce, and diplomacy, but of culture as well. The English-speaking peoples are voracious consumers of film, drama, literature, television—of every possible manifestation of the printed and spoken word.

The other reason is that, for the first time since the structuralist theories of language were set forth and codified in the first half of the twentieth century, linguists have begun to turn their attention to meaning, to semantics, and, more recently, to semiotics.

Both of these influences are reflected in *Collins English Dictionary*. The first can be seen in the careful attention paid to the selection of headwords from America, Australia, New Zealand, the Caribbean, South Africa, and other parts of the world where English is spoken as a native language, as well as to the enormous number of words borrowed from foreign languages in the past 40 years. The second influence is reflected in the arrangement of the definitions and other information. Both of these are fully described in the Guide to the Use of the Dictionary and the other articles that follow it.

In the thousands of days that have gone into the preparation of the *Dictionary*, no one showed greater enthusiasm and support for the project than Jan Collins, Chairman of Collins. For his close editorial involvement, we are also most grateful to William McLeod, Publishing Manager of Collins's Reference Book Department. With their aid, every effort has been made to ensure that *Collins English Dictionary* will provide its users with the best and most up-to-date guide to the English language throughout the world.

LAURENCE URDANG

Aylesbury, Bucks

February 1979

different semantic areas clearly numbered: see 7.2 *

varieties of English labelled

jug (dʒʌg) *n.* **1.** a vessel for holding or pouring liquids, usually having a handle and a spout or lip. U.S. equivalent: **pitcher. 2.** *Austral.* such a vessel used as a kettle: *an electric jug.* **3.** *U.S.* a large vessel with a narrow mouth. **4.** Also called: **jug+ful.** the amount of liquid held by a jug. **5.** *Brit. informal.* a glass of alcoholic drink, esp. beer. **6.** a slang word for **jail.** ~*vb.* **jugs, jug+ging, jugged. 7.** to stew or boil (meat, esp. hare) in an earthenware container. **8.** (*tr.*) *Slang.* to put in jail. [C16: probably from *Jug,* nickname from girl's name *Joan*]

inflected forms: see 3

inflected forms: see 3

ju+gal ('dʒu:gᵊl) *adj.* **1.** of or relating to the zygomatic bone. ~*n.* **2.** Also called: **jugal bone.** other names for **zygomatic bone.** [C16: from Latin *jugālis* of a yoke, from *jugum* a yoke]

ju+gate ('dʒu:geɪt, -gɪt) *adj.* (esp. of compound leaves) having parts arranged in pairs. [C19: from New Latin *jugātus* (unattested), from Latin *jugum* a yoke]

jug band *n.* a small group playing folk or jazz music, using empty jugs that are played by blowing across their openings to produce bass notes.

up-to-date word list

foreign words: see 2.6

Ju+gend+stil *German.* ('ju:gᵊnt,ʃti:l) *n.* another name for **art nouveau.** [from *Jugend* literally: youth, name of illustrated periodical that first appeared in 1896, + *Stil* STYLE]

acronyms: see 7.8

JUGFET ('dʒʌgfɛt) *n. acronym for* junction-gate field-effect transistor; a type of field-effect transistor in which the semiconductor gate region or regions form one or more p-n junctions with the conduction channel. Compare **IGFET.**

thorough scientific and technical coverage

jugged hare *n.* a stew of hare cooked in an earthenware pot or casserole.

jug+ger+naut ('dʒʌgə,nɔ:t) *n.* **1.** any terrible force, esp. one that destroys or that demands complete self-sacrifice. **2.** *Brit.* a very large lorry for transporting goods by road, esp. one that travels throughout Europe.

field labels: see 6.5

Jug+ger+naut ('dʒʌgə,nɔ:t) *n. Hinduism.* **1.** a crude idol of Krishna worshipped at Puri and throughout Orissa and Bengal. At an annual festival the idol is wheeled through the town on a gigantic chariot and devotees are supposed to have formerly thrown themselves under the wheels in the hope of going straight to paradise. **2.** a form of Krishna miraculously raised by Brahma from the state of a crude idol to that of a living god. [C17: from Hindi *Jagannath,* from Sanskrit *Jagannātha* lord of the world (that is, Vishnu, chief of the Hindu gods), from *jagat* world + *nātha* lord]

useful encyclopedic information

jug+gins ('dʒʌgɪnz) *n. Brit. informal.* a silly fellow. [C19: special use of the surname *Juggins*]

helpful usage labels: see 6.3

jug+gle ('dʒʌgᵊl) *vb.* **1.** to throw and catch (several objects) continuously so that most are in the air all the time, as an entertainment. **2.** to arrange or manipulate (facts, figures, etc.) so as to give a false or misleading picture. **3.** (*tr.*) to keep (several activities) in progress, esp. with difficulty. ~*n.* **4.** an act of juggling. [C14: from Old French *jogler* to perform as a jester, from Latin *joculārī* to jest, from *jocus* a jest] —'**jug+gler·y** *n.*

parts of speech: see 4

jug+gler ('dʒʌglə) *n.* **1.** a person who juggles, esp. a professional entertainer. **2.** a person who fraudulently manipulates facts or figures.

ju+glan+da+ceous (,dʒu:glæn'deɪʃəs) *adj.* of, relating to, or belonging to the *Juglandaceae,* a family of trees that includes walnut and hickory. [C19: via New Latin from Latin *juglans* walnut, from *ju-,* shortened from *Jovi-* of Jupiter + *glans* acorn]

pronunciations in IPA: see 2

Ju+go+sla+vi+a (,ju:gəʊ'slɑ:vɪə) *n.* a variant spelling of **Yugoslavia.** —'**Ju+go+,slav** *or* ,**Ju+go+'sla+vi+an** *adj., n.*

jug+u+lar ('dʒʌgjʊlə) *adj.* **1.** of, relating to, or situated near the throat or neck. **2.** of, having, or denoting pelvic fins situated in front of the pectoral fins: *a jugular fish.* ~*n.* **3.** short for **jugular vein.** [C16: from Late Latin *jugulāris,* from Latin *jugulum* throat]

senses in order of current usage: see 7.3

jug+u+lar vein *n.* any of three large veins of the neck that return blood to the heart from the head and face.

jug+u+late ('dʒʌgjʊ,leɪt) *vb.* (*tr.*) *Rare.* to check (a disease) by extreme measures or remedies. [C17 (in the obsolete sense: kill by cutting the throat of): from Latin *jugulāre,* from *jugulum* throat, from *jugum* yoke] —,**jug+u+'la+tion** *n.*

derived forms: see 12

ju+gum ('dʒu:gəm) *n.* **1.** a small process at the base of each forewing in certain insects by which the forewings are united to the hindwings during flight. **2.** *Botany.* a pair of opposite leaflets. [C19: from Latin, literally: YOKE]

Ju+gur+tha (dʒu:'gɜ:θə) *n.* died 104 B.C., king of Numidia (?112–104), who waged war against the Romans (the **Jugurthine War,** 112–105) and was defeated and executed.

juice (dʒu:s) *n.* **1.** any liquid that occurs naturally in or is secreted by plant or animal tissue: *the juice of an orange; digestive juices.* **2.** *Informal.* **a.** fuel for an engine, esp. petrol. **b.** electricity. **c.** alcoholic drink. **3. a.** vigour or vitality. **b.** essence or fundamental nature. [C13: from Old French *jus,* from Latin] —'**juice+less** *adj.*

lettered senses: see 7.2

juice ex+trac+tor *n.* a kitchen appliance, usually operated by electricity, for extracting juice from fruits and vegetables. U.S. equivalent: **juicer.**

phrasal verbs entered as headwords: see 5.6.6

juice up *vb.* (*tr., adv.*) **1.** *U.S. slang.* to make lively: *to juice up a party.* **2.** (*often passive*) to cause to be drunk: *he got juiced up on Scotch last night.*

juic·y ('dʒu:sɪ) *adj.* **juic·i+er, juic·i·est. 1.** full of juice. **2.** provocatively interesting; spicy: *juicy gossip.* **3.** *Slang.* voluptuous or seductive: *she's a juicy bit.* **4.** *Chiefly U.S.* profitable: *a juicy contract.* —'**juic·i+ly** *adv.* —'**juic·i+ness** *n.*

examples of typical use: see 7.1.5

Juiz de Fo·ra (*Portuguese* 'ʒwiz di 'fɔra) *n.* a city in SE Brazil, in Minas Gerais state on the Rio de Janeiro–Belo Horizonte railway: textiles. Pop.: 218 832 (1970).

ju+jit+su, ju+jut+su, *or* **jiu+jut+su** (dʒu:'dʒɪtsu:) *n.* the traditional Japanese system of unarmed self-defence perfected by

variant spellings: see 1.6

* *References are to numbered sections of the Guide to the Use of the Dictionary, pp. x ff.*

cal system, device, or circuit. **2.** the quality or condition of such a network. ~*adj.* **3.** used in wiring.

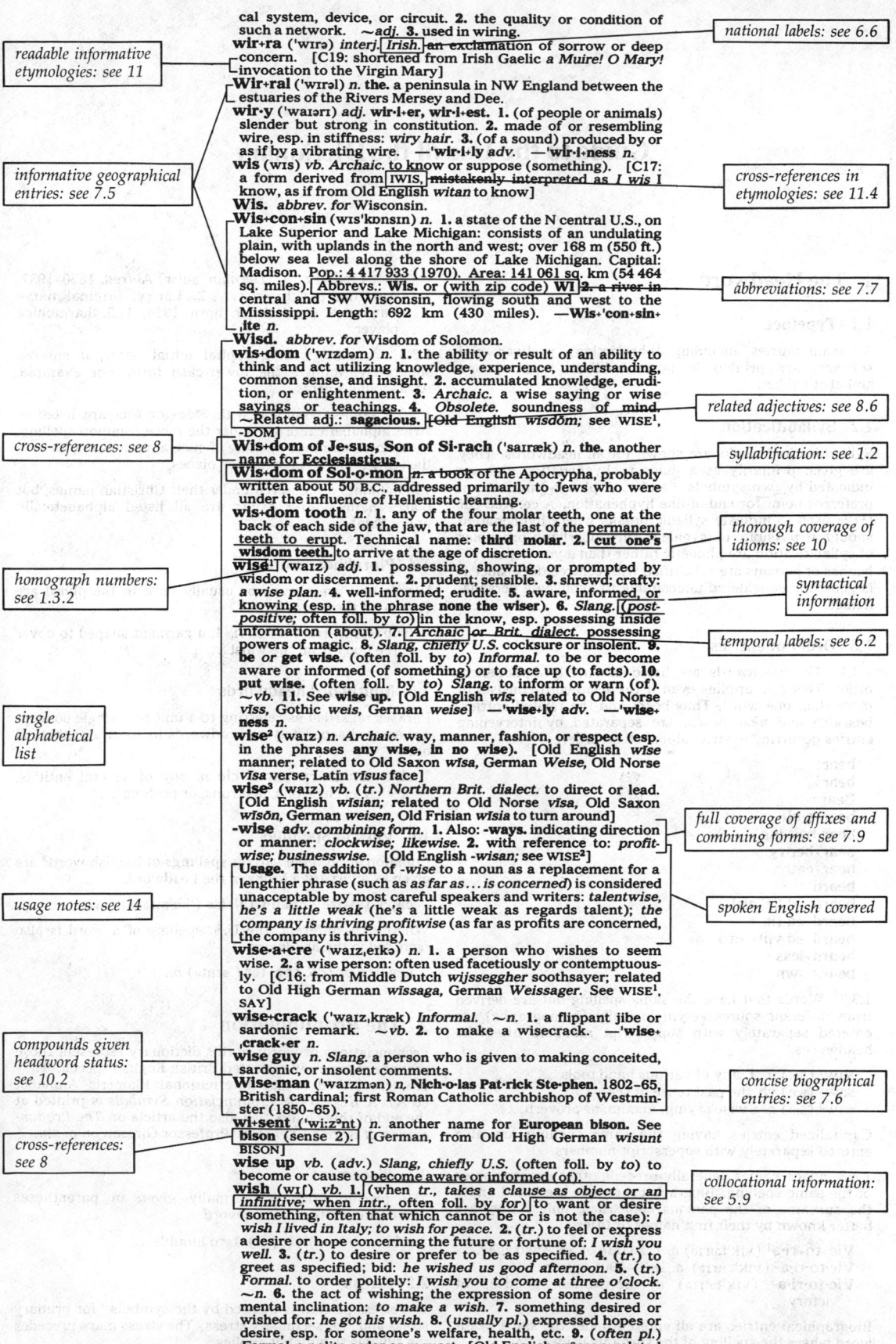

national labels: see 6.6

wir·ra ('wɪrə) *interj. Irish.* an exclamation of sorrow or deep concern. [C19: shortened from Irish Gaelic *a Muire! O Mary!* invocation to the Virgin Mary]

readable informative etymologies: see 11

Wir·ral ('wɪrəl) *n.* **the.** a peninsula in NW England between the estuaries of the Rivers Mersey and Dee.

wir·y ('waɪərɪ) *adj.* **wir·i·er, wir·i·est. 1.** (of people or animals) slender but strong in constitution. **2.** made of or resembling wire, esp. in stiffness: *wiry hair.* **3.** (of a sound) produced by or as if by a vibrating wire. —'**wir·i·ly** *adv.* —'**wir·i·ness** *n.*

informative geographical entries: see 7.5

wis (wɪs) *vb. Archaic.* to know or suppose (something). [C17: a form derived from IWIS, mistakenly interpreted as *I wis* I know, as if from Old English *witan* to know]

cross-references in etymologies: see 11.4

Wis. *abbrev. for* Wisconsin.

Wis·con·sin (wɪs'kɒnsɪn) *n.* **1.** a state of the N central U.S., on Lake Superior and Lake Michigan: consists of an undulating plain, with uplands in the north and west; over 168 m (550 ft.) below sea level along the shore of Lake Michigan. Capital: Madison. Pop.: 4 417 933 (1970). Area: 141 061 sq. km (54 464 sq. miles). Abbrevs.: **Wis.** or (with zip code) **WI 2.** a river in central and SW Wisconsin, flowing south and west to the Mississippi. Length: 692 km (430 miles). —**Wis·'con·sin·,ite** *n.*

abbreviations: see 7.7

Wisd. *abbrev. for* Wisdom of Solomon.

wis·dom ('wɪzdəm) *n.* **1.** the ability or result of an ability to think and act utilizing knowledge, experience, understanding, common sense, and insight. **2.** accumulated knowledge, erudition, or enlightenment. **3.** *Archaic.* a wise saying or wise sayings or teachings. **4.** *Obsolete.* soundness of mind. ~Related adj.: **sagacious.** [Old English *wīsdōm*; see WISE[1], -DOM]

related adjectives: see 8.6

cross-references: see 8

Wis·dom of Je·sus, Son of Si·rach ('saɪræk) *n.* **the.** another name for **Ecclesiasticus.**

syllabification: see 1.2

Wis·dom of Sol·o·mon *n.* a book of the Apocrypha, probably written about 50 B.C., addressed primarily to Jews who were under the influence of Hellenistic learning.

wis·dom tooth *n.* **1.** any of the four molar teeth, one at the back of each side of the jaw, that are the last of the permanent teeth to erupt. Technical name: **third molar. 2. cut one's wisdom teeth.** to arrive at the age of discretion.

thorough coverage of idioms: see 10

homograph numbers: see 1.3.2

wise[1] (waɪz) *adj.* **1.** possessing, showing, or prompted by wisdom or discernment. **2.** prudent; sensible. **3.** shrewd; crafty: *a wise plan.* **4.** well-informed; erudite. **5.** aware, informed, or knowing (esp. in the phrase **none the wiser**). **6.** *Slang.* (*postpositive;* often foll. by *to*) in the know, esp. possessing inside information (about). **7.** *Archaic or Brit. dialect.* possessing powers of magic. **8.** *Slang, chiefly U.S.* cocksure or insolent. **9. be or get wise.** (often foll. by *to*) *Informal.* to be or become aware or informed (of something) or to face up (to facts). **10. put wise.** (often foll. by *to*) *Slang.* to inform or warn (of). ~*vb.* **11.** See **wise up.** [Old English *wīs*; related to Old Norse *vīss*, Gothic *weis*, German *weise*] —'**wise·ly** *adv.* —'**wise·ness** *n.*

syntactical information

temporal labels: see 6.2

single alphabetical list

wise[2] (waɪz) *n. Archaic.* way, manner, fashion, or respect (esp. in the phrases **any wise, in no wise**). [Old English *wīse* manner; related to Old Saxon *wīsa*, German *Weise*, Old Norse *vīsa* verse, Latin *vīsus* face]

wise[3] (waɪz) *vb. (tr.) Northern Brit. dialect.* to direct or lead. [Old English *wīsian*; related to Old Norse *vīsa*, Old Saxon *wīsōn*, German *weisen*, Old Frisian *wīsia* to turn around]

full coverage of affixes and combining forms: see 7.9

-wise *adv. combining form.* **1.** Also: **-ways.** indicating direction or manner: *clockwise; likewise.* **2.** with reference to: *profitwise; businesswise.* [Old English *-wīsan*; see WISE[2]]

usage notes: see 14

spoken English covered

Usage. The addition of *-wise* to a noun as a replacement for a lengthier phrase (such as *as far as ... is concerned*) is considered unacceptable by most careful speakers and writers: *talentwise, he's a little weak* (he's a little weak as regards talent); *the company is thriving profitwise* (as far as profits are concerned, the company is thriving).

wise·a·cre ('waɪz,eɪkə) *n.* **1.** a person who wishes to seem wise. **2.** a wise person: often used facetiously or contemptuously. [C16: from Middle Dutch *wijsseggher* soothsayer; related to Old High German *wīssaga*, German *Weissager*. See WISE[1], SAY]

wise·crack ('waɪz,kræk) *Informal.* ~*n.* **1.** a flippant jibe or sardonic remark. ~*vb.* **2.** to make a wisecrack. —'**wise·,crack·er** *n.*

compounds given headword status: see 10.2

wise guy *n. Slang.* a person who is given to making conceited, sardonic, or insolent comments.

Wise·man ('waɪzmən) *n.* **Nich·o·las Pat·rick Ste·phen.** 1802–65, British cardinal; first Roman Catholic archbishop of Westminster (1850–65).

concise biographical entries: see 7.6

wi·sent ('wi:zᵊnt) *n.* another name for **European bison.** See **bison** (sense 2). [German, from Old High German *wisunt* BISON]

cross-references: see 8

wise up *vb. (adv.) Slang, chiefly U.S.* (often foll. by *to*) to become or cause to become aware or informed (of).

collocational information: see 5.9

wish (wɪʃ) *vb.* **1.** (when *tr., takes a clause as object or an infinitive;* when *intr.,* often foll. by *for*) to want or desire (something, often that which cannot be or is not the case): *I wish I lived in Italy; to wish for peace.* **2.** *(tr.)* to feel or express a desire or hope concerning the future or fortune of: *I wish you well.* **3.** *(tr.)* to desire or prefer to be as specified. **4.** *(tr.)* to greet as specified; bid: *he wished us good afternoon.* **5.** *(tr.) Formal.* to order politely: *I wish you to come at three o'clock.* ~*n.* **6.** the act of wishing; the expression of some desire or mental inclination: *to make a wish.* **7.** something desired or wished for: *he got his wish.* **8.** (*usually pl.*) expressed hopes or desire, esp. for someone's welfare, health, etc. **9.** (*often pl.*) *Formal.* a polite order or request. [Old English *wȳscan*; related

Guide to the Use of the Dictionary

1 The Headword

1.1 Typeface

All main entries, including abbreviations, prefixes, and suffixes, are printed in large boldface type in one alphabetical list.

1.2 Syllabification

Syllabification breaks are shown for all headwords. They are given primarily as a guide to hyphenation and are indicated by two symbols: · and +. A plus (+) indicates a preferred point for end-of-line hyphenation. A centred dot (·) is used to indicate syllabic breaks where hyphenation should, if possible, be avoided. The underlying principles of syllabification are phonetic rather than etymological. Names of persons are syllabified with centred dots, since it is generally considered undesirable to hyphenate personal names.

1.3 Order of entries

1.3.1 The headwords are listed in strictly alphabetical order. This rule applies even if the headword consists of more than one word. Thus **bear**[1] and the related entries, **bearable** and **bear down,** are separated by intervening entries occurring in strict alphabetical order:

bear[1]
bear[2]
Bear
bear+a·ble
bear-bait·ing
bear+ber·ry
bear+cat
beard
beard+ed liz+ard
beard+ed tit
beard+ed vul+ture
beard+less
bear down

1.3.2 Words that have the same spelling but are derived from different sources etymologically (homographs) are entered separately with superscript numbers after the headwords.

saw[1] (sɔː) *n.* **1.** any of various hand tools....
saw[2] (sɔː) *vb.* the past tense of **see**[1].
saw[3] (sɔː) *n.* a wise saying, maxim, or proverb....

Capitalized entries having the same spelling are also entered separately with superscript numbers.

1.3.3 Place names generally precede other proper names of the same spelling. Biographical entries are listed under the surname of the persons concerned, unless they are better known by their first names or titles.

Vic+to+ri·a[1] (vɪk'tɔːrɪə) *n.* **1.** a state of SE Australia....
Vic·to·ri·a[2] (vɪk'tɔːrɪə) *n.* 1819–1901, queen....
Vic·to·ri·a[3] (vɪk'tɔːrɪə) *n.* the Roman goddess of victory....

Biographical entries are all entered under the same headword where the spelling of the surname is identical.

Ad·ler ('ædlə) *n.* **1.** (*German* 'adlər) **Al·fred.** 1870–1937, Austrian psychiatrist.... **2. Lar·ry,** original name *Lawrence Cecil Adler.* born 1914, U.S. harmonica player.

1.3.4 A word with a capital initial letter, if entered separately, follows the lower-case form. For example, **Arras** follows **arras.**

1.3.5 Names beginning with **Mac-** or **Mc-** are listed in strict alphabetical order under the more common spelling. If the more common spelling of such a name is not known, the reader should look in both places.

1.3.6 Saints are entered under their Christian names, but places named after saints are all listed alphabetically under **Saint.**

1.4 Plural headwords

Words that are always or usually used in the plural are entered in the plural form.

trou+sers ('traʊzəz) *pl. n.* **1.** a garment shaped to cover the body from the waist....

1.5 Multiword headwords

Phrases regarded as referring to a unit or a single concept are entered separately as headwords in strict alphabetical order.

el+e·men+ta+ry par+ti+cle *n.* any of several entities, such as electrons, neutrons, or protons....

1.6 Variant spellings

Common acceptable variant spellings of English words are given as alternative forms of the headword.

cap·i+tal+ize *or* **cap·i+tal+ise** ('kæpɪtəˌlaɪz) *vb.*...

Where it is different, the U.S. spelling of a word is also recorded in the headword.

cen+tre *or U.S.* **cen+ter** ('sɛntə) *n.*...

2 The Pronunciation

Pronunciations of words in this dictionary represent those that are common in educated British English speech. They are transcribed in the International Phonetic Alphabet (IPA). A *Key to the Pronunciation Symbols* is printed at the end of this Guide. See also the article on *The Pronunciation of British English* by Professor Gimson on p. xix.

2.1 Placement

The pronunciation is normally given in parentheses immediately after the headword.

a·base (ə'beɪs) *vb.* (*tr.*) **1.** to humble....

2.2 Stress

The stress pattern is marked by the symbols ' for primary stress and ˌ for secondary stress. The stress mark precedes the syllable to which it applies.

2.3 Variant pronunciations

When a headword has an acceptable variant pronunciation or stress pattern, the variant is given by repeating only the syllable or syllables that change.

ab·do·men ('æbdəmən, æb'dəʊ-) *n.* **1.** the region of the body....

2.4 U.S. pronunciation

U.S. pronunciation, not normally represented in this dictionary, is shown for a few words where it is greatly different from the usual British pronunciation. In general, such U.S. pronunciations are given only where they are not predictable by application of rules governing the relationship of British and American vowel quality, stress, pronunciation of orthographic *r*, etc.

no·men·cla·ture (nəʊ'mɛnklətʃə; *U.S.* 'nəʊmən,kleɪtʃər) *n.* the terminology....

2.5 Naturalized foreign words and phrases

A word or phrase of recent foreign origin that is regarded as having been accepted into English is printed in large boldface roman type and is given an anglicized pronunciation followed by a foreign pronunciation.

poste res·tante ('pəʊst rɪ'stænt; *French* pɔst rɛs'tɑ̃:t) *n....*

2.6 Foreign words and phrases

Foreign words or phrases are otherwise printed in boldface italic type and are given foreign-language pronunciations only.

haut monde *French.* (o'mɔ̃d) *n....*

2.7 Foreign proper names

Foreign proper names, chiefly place names and biographies, are printed in large boldface roman type. If they do not have widely accepted conventional English pronunciations, they are given only foreign-language pronunciations.

Mi·laz·zo (*Italian* mi'lattso) *n.* a port in NE Sicily....

In biographical entries, a language label in the pronunciation of the main entry word may be assumed to apply to given names as well, unless otherwise stated.

Prae·to·ri·us (*German* prɛ'to:riʊs) *n.* **Mi·cha·el** ('mɪça,e:l). 1571–1621, German composer....

2.8 Pronunciation of inflections

When an inflected form has a widely different pronunciation from that of the headword, the relevant parts are shown after the inflection.

in·dex ('ɪndɛks) *n. pl.* **·dex·es** *or* **·di·ces** (-dɪ,si:z). **1.** an alphabetical list....

2.9 Pronunciations with different parts of speech

When two or more parts of speech of a word have different pronunciations, the pronunciations are shown in parentheses before the relevant group of senses.

rec·ord *n.* ('rɛkɔ:d). **1.** an account in permanent form... ~*vb.* (rɪ'kɔ:d). (*mainly tr.*) **18.** to set down in some permanent form....

2.10 Pronunciation of individual senses

If one sense of a headword has a different pronunciation from that of the rest, that pronunciation is given in parentheses after the sense number.

con·jure ('kʌndʒə) *vb.* **1.** (*intr.*) to practise conjuring or be a conjuror. **2.** (*intr.*) to call upon supposed supernatural forces by spells and incantations. **3.** (*tr.*) (kən'dʒʊə). to appeal earnestly or strongly to: *I conjure you to help me....*

3 Inflected Forms

Inflected forms of nouns, verbs, and adjectives are shown immediately after the part-of-speech label if they are irregular or, in certain cases, if they are regular but might cause confusion.

3.1 Regular inflections

Regular inflections are not shown. They are formed as follows:

3.1.1 *nouns.* Regular plurals are formed by the addition of *-s* (e.g. *pencils, monkeys*) or, in the case of nouns ending in *-s, -x, -z, -ch,* or *-sh,* by the addition of *-es* (e.g. *losses*).

3.1.2 *verbs.* In regularly inflected verbs: (1) the third person singular of the present tense is formed by the addition of *-s* to the infinitive (e.g. *plays*) or, for verbs ending in *-s, -x, -z, -ch,* or *-sh,* by the addition of *-es* (e.g. *passes, reaches*); (2) the past tense and past participle are formed by the addition of *-ed* to the infinitive (e.g. *played*); (3) the present participle is formed by the addition of *-ing* to the infinitive (e.g. *playing*). Verbs that end in a consonant plus *-e* (e.g. *locate, snare*) regularly lose the final *-e* before the addition of *-ed* and *-ing.*

3.1.3 *adjectives.* The regular comparative and superlative degrees of adjectives are formed by adding *-er* and *-est,* respectively, to the base (e.g. *short, shorter, shortest*). Adjectives that end in a consonant plus *-e* regularly lose the *-e* before *-er* and *-est* (e.g. *fine, finer, finest*).

3.2 Irregular and unfamiliar inflections

Inflected forms are shown for the following:

3.2.1 Nouns and verbs whose inflections involve a change in internal spelling.

goose (gu:s) *n., pl.* **geese....**
drive (draɪv) *vb.,* **drives, driv·ing, drove, driv·en....**

3.2.2 Nouns, verbs, and adjectives that end in a consonant plus *y,* where *y* is changed to *i* before inflectional endings.

au·gu·ry ('ɔ:gjʊrɪ) *n., pl.* **·ries....**

3.2.3 Nouns having identical singular and plural forms.

sheep (ʃi:p) *n., pl.* **sheep....**

3.2.4 Nouns that closely resemble others that form their plurals differently.

mon·goose ('mɒŋ,gu:s) *n., pl.* **·goos·es....**

3.2.5 Nouns that end in *-ful, -o,* and *-us.*

hand·ful ('hænd,fʊl) *n., pl.* **·fuls....**
to·ma·to (tə'mɑ:təʊ; *U.S.* tə'meɪtəʊ) *n., pl.* **·toes....**
pro·spec·tus (prə'spɛktəs) *n., pl.* **·tus·es....**

3.2.6 Nouns whose plurals are not regular English inflections.

ba·sis ('beɪsɪs) *n., pl.* **·ses** (-si:z)....

3.2.7 Plural nouns whose singulars are not regular English forms.

bac·te·ri·a (bæk'tɪərɪə) *pl. n., sing.* **·ri·um** (-rɪəm)....

3.2.8 Nouns whose plurals have regular spellings but involve a change in pronunciation.

house *n.* (haʊs), *pl.* **hous·es** ('haʊzɪz)....

3.2.9 Multiword nouns when it is not obvious which word takes a plural inflection.

at·tor·ney-at-law *n., pl.* **at·tor·neys-at-law....**

3.2.10 Latin names of constellations whose genitive forms are used in referring to individual stars, with *Alpha, Beta,* etc.

Li+bra ('li:brə) *n., Latin genitive* **Li+brae** ('li:bri:)....

3.2.11 Adjectives that change their roots to form comparatives and superlatives.

good (gʊd) *adj.,* **bet+ter, best....**

3.2.12 Adjectives and verbs that double their final consonant before adding endings.

fat (fæt) *adj.* **fat+ter, fat+test....**
con+trol (kən'trəʊl) *vb.* **+trols, +trol+ling, +trolled....**

3.2.13 Verbs and adjectives that end in a vowel plus *e.*

ca+noe (kə'nu:)... ~*vb.* **+noes, +noe+ing, +noed....**
free (fri:) *adj.* **fre+er, fre+est....** ~*vb.* **frees, free+ing, freed....**

4 Parts of Speech

A part-of-speech label in italics precedes the account of the sense or senses relating to that part of speech.

4.1 Standard parts of speech

The following parts of speech, with abbreviations as shown, are standard in all widely taught forms of English grammar and need no further explanation:
adjective (*adj.*), adverb (*adv.*), conjunction (*conj.*), interjection (*interj.*), noun (*n.*), preposition (*prep.*), pronoun (*pron.*), verb (*vb.*).

4.2 Less traditional parts of speech

Certain other less traditional parts of speech have been adopted in this dictionary. They are as follows:

4.2.1 *determiners.* Such words as *that, this, my, his,* etc., which used to be classed as demonstrative and possessive adjectives and/or pronouns, have been classified in this dictionary as determiners.
The label *determiner* also replaces the traditional classification for words like *the, a, some, any,* as well as the numerals, and possessives such as *my* and *your.* Many determiners can have a pronoun function without change of meaning, and this is indicated as in the following example:

some (sʌm; *unstressed* səm) *determiner....* **2. a.** an unknown or unspecified quantity or amount of: *there's some rice on the table; he owns some horses.* **b.** (*as pronoun; functioning as sing. or pl.*): *we'll buy some....*

4.2.2 *sentence connectors.* This description replaces the traditional classification of certain words, such as *therefore* and *however,* as adverbs or conjunctions. These words link sentences together in continuous discourse rather in the manner of conjunctions; however, they are not confined to the first position in a clause as conjunctions are.

4.2.3 *sentence substitutes.* Sentence substitutes comprise words such as *yes, no, perhaps, definitely,* and *maybe.* They can stand as meaningful utterances by themselves. They are distinguished in this dictionary from interjections such as *ouch, ah, damn,* etc., which are expressions of emotional reaction rather than meaningful utterances.

4.3 Words used as more than one part of speech

If a word can be used as more than one part of speech, the account of the senses of one part of speech is separated from the others by a swung dash.

lure (luə) *vb.* (*tr.*)... **2.** *Falconry.* to entice (a hawk or falcon) from the air to the falconer by a lure. ~*n.* **3.** a person or thing that lures....

5 Descriptive, Grammatical, and Contextual Information

5.1 Adjectives and Determiners

Some adjectives and determiners are restricted by usage to a particular position relative to the nouns they qualify. This is indicated by the following labels:

5.1.1 *postpositive* (used predicatively or after the noun, but not before the noun):

a·blaze (ə'bleɪz) *adj.* (*postpositive*), *adv.* **1.** on fire; burning....

5.1.2 *immediately postpositive* (always used immediately following the noun qualified and never used predicatively):

ga+lore (gə'lɔ:) *determiner.* (*immediately postpositive*) *Informal.* in great numbers or quantity: *there were daffodils galore in the park....*

5.1.3 *prenominal* (used before the noun, and never used predicatively):

chief (tʃi:f)... ~*adj.* **4.** (*prenominal*) **a.** most important; principal. **b.** highest in rank or authority....

5.2 Intensifiers

Adjectives and adverbs that perform an exclusively intensifying function, with no addition of meaning, are described as (intensifier) without further explanation.

bloom+ing ('blu:mɪŋ) *adv., adj. Brit. informal.* (intensifier): *a blooming genius; blooming painful....*

5.3 Conjunctions

Conjunctions are divided into two classes, marked by the following labels placed in parentheses:

5.3.1 *coordinating.* Coordinating conjunctions connect words, phrases, or clauses that perform an identical function and are not dependent on each other. They include *and, but,* and *or.*

5.3.2 *subordinating.* Subordinating conjunctions introduce clauses that are dependent on a main clause in a complex sentence. They include *where, until,* and *before.*

5.3.3 Some conjunctions, such as *while* and *whereas,* can function as either coordinating or subordinating conjunctions.

5.4 Singular and plural labelling of nouns

5.4.1 If a particular sense of a noun is generally found in the plural form, this fact is noted in the phrase "*often pl.*"

fly[1] (flaɪ) *vb....* **21.** (*often pl.*) Also called: **fly front.** a closure that conceals a zip, buttons, or other fastening....

5.4.2 If a noun is entered in its plural form but is also found occasionally in the singular, this fact is noted in the words "*sometimes sing.*"

wits (wɪts) *pl. n.* **1.** (*sometimes sing.*) the ability to reason and act, esp. quickly....

5.4.3 Headwords and senses that are apparently plural in form but that take a singular verb, etc., are marked "*functioning as sing.*"

phys+ics ('fɪzɪks) *n.* (*functioning as sing.*) **1.** the branch of science....

5.4.4. Headwords and senses that appear to be singular, such as collective nouns, but that take a plural verb, etc., are marked "*functioning as pl.*"

cat+tle ('kætᵊl) *n.* (*functioning as pl.*) **1.** bovid mammals of the tribe *Bovini....*

5.4.5 Headwords and senses that may take either a

singular or a plural verb, etc., are marked "*functioning as sing. or pl.*"

bel·lows ('bɛləuz) *n.* (*functioning as sing. or pl.*) **1.** Also called: **pair of bellows.** an instrument consisting of an air chamber....

5.5 Modifiers

A noun that is commonly used with adjectival force is labelled *modifier.*

5.5.1 If the sense of the modifier is strictly inferable from the sense of the noun, the modifier is shown without further explanation, with an example to illustrate its use.

den·im ('dɛnɪm) *n. Textiles* **1. a.** a hard-wearing twill-weave cotton fabric used for trousers, work clothes, etc. **b.** (*as modifier*): *a denim jacket....*

5.5.2 If the sense of the modifier is not inferable from the sense of the noun, or if it is related to more than one of the noun senses, an account of its meaning and/or usage is given separately.

key[1] (ki:) *n....* **24.** (*modifier*) of great importance: *a key issue....*

5.6 Verbs

5.6.1 When a sense of a verb (*vb.*) is restricted to transitive use, it is labelled (*tr.*); if it is intransitive only, it is labelled (*intr.*). If all the senses of a verb are either transitive or intransitive, the appropriate label appears before the first numbered sense and is not repeated. Absence of a label is significant: it indicates that the sense may be used both transitively and intransitively.

The account of the meaning of a verb is given without subdivision into separate groupings for transitive and intransitive senses. Instead, each sense is worded so as to take account of its transitivity or intransitivity.

If nearly all the senses of a verb are transitive, the label (*mainly tr.*) appears immediately before the first numbered sense. This indicates that, unless otherwise labelled, any given sense of the verb is transitive. An individual sense may then be labelled (*also intr.*) to show that it is both transitive and intransitive, or it may be labelled (*intr.*) to show that it is intransitive only.

carry ('kærɪ) *vb....*(*mainly tr.*) **1.** (*also intr.*) to take or bear (something) from one place to another: *to carry a baby in one's arms.* **2.** to transfer for consideration; take: *he carried his complaints to her superior....* **27.** (*intr.*) (of a ball, projectile, etc.) to travel through the air or reach a specified point: *his first drive carried to the green....*

Similarly, all the senses of a verb may be labelled (*mainly intr.*) and the labels (*also tr.*) and (*tr.*) introduced before individual senses as required.

The labels (*usually tr.*) and (*usually intr.*) may be used at the beginning of a particular sense to indicate that the sense is usually but not always transitive or intransitive.

wind[2] (waɪnd) *vb....* **5.** (*usually intr.*) to move or cause to move in a sinuous, spiral, or circular course: *the river winds through the hills....*

5.6.2 When a sense of a verb covers both transitive and intransitive uses, a direct object that is typical of the class of direct objects taken by the verb in its transitive uses may be shown in parentheses. The parentheses should be ignored in order to obtain the intransitive sense.

act (ækt) *vb....* **11.** to perform (a part or role) in a play....

5.6.3 When the object of the transitive sense of a verb constitutes the subject of the intransitive sense, the account of its meaning is styled as follows:

fire (faɪə)... ~*vb.* **25.** to discharge (a firearm or projectile) or (of a firearm, etc.) to be discharged....

5.6.4 When the intransitive equivalent of the transitive sense of a verb functions with a preposition, an equivalent preposition is given in parentheses in the account of the meaning.

dif·fer·en·ti·ate (ˌdɪfəˈrɛnʃɪˌeɪt) *vb....* **2.** (when *intr.*, often foll. by *between*) to perceive, show, or make a difference (in or between); discriminate.

5.6.5 **Copulas**

A verb that takes a complement is labelled *copula.*

seem (si:m) *vb.* (may take an infinitive) **1.** (*copula*) to appear to the mind or eye; look....

5.6.6. **Phrasal verbs**

Verbal constructions consisting of a verb and a preposition or a verb and an adverbial particle are given headword status if the meaning of the phrasal verb cannot be deduced from the separate meanings of the verb and the particle. These phrasal verbs are usually informal in register and often idiomatic in meaning.

5.6.6.1 Phrasal verbs are labelled to show four possible distinctions:

a transitive verb with an adverbial particle (*tr., adv.*); a transitive verb with a preposition (*tr., prep.*); an intransitive verb with an adverbial particle (*intr., adv.*); an intransitive verb with a preposition (*intr., prep.*):

turn on... **1.** (*tr., adv.*)...to cause (something) to operate by turning a knob, etc.: *to turn on the light.*

take for... **1.** (*tr., prep.*)...to consider or suppose to be, esp. mistakenly: *the fake coins were taken for genuine; who do you take me for?*

play up... **3.** (*intr., adv.*) (of a machine, etc.) to function erratically: *the car is playing up again.*

turn on... **2.** (*intr., prep.*) to depend or hinge on: *the success of the party turns on you.*

As with the labelling of other verbs, the absence of a label is significant. If there is no label (*tr.*) or (*intr.*), the verb may be used either transitively or intransitively. If there is no label (*adv.*) or (*prep.*), the particle may be either adverbial or prepositional.

5.6.6.2 Any noun, adjective, or modifier formed from a phrasal verb is entered under the phrasal-verb headword. In some cases, where the noun or adjective is more common than the verb, the phrasal verb is entered after the noun/adjective form:

break·a·way ('breɪkəˌweɪ) *n.* **1. a.** loss or withdrawal of a group of members from an association, club, etc. **b.** (*as modifier*): *a breakaway faction....* ~*vb.* **break a·way.** (*intr., adv.*)... **4.** to withdraw or secede.

5.6.6.3 A cross-reference is given at the main verb when related phrasal verbs are entered as headwords but are separated from it by more than five intervening entries.

fit[1] (fɪt) *vb....* ~See also **fit in, fit out, fit up.** [C14: probably from Middle Dutch *vitten*...]

5.7 Capitalization

When a particular sense of a word usually has an initial capital letter or, in the case of a capitalized headword, an initial lower-case letter, this is noted by the words "*sometimes not cap.,*" "*often cap.,*" etc.

5.8 Words used in combination

Where a word occurs frequently in hyphenated combination with another word, this is stated and an example is given.

armed[2] (ɑ:md) *adj.* **a.** having an arm or arms. **b.** (*in combination*): *long-armed; one-armed.*

For affixes and combining forms, see 7.9 below.

5.9 Collocational information

If a word or sense is usually or often followed or preceded by a particular word, this is noted by a phrase such as "often preceded by *the*" or "usually foll. by *up*" before the appropriate sense. Only the commonest such collocations are recorded in this dictionary.

> **ice** (aɪs)... *vb.* **8.** (often foll. by *up, over,* etc.) to form or cause to form ice; freeze....

If the word "the" always occurs with the particular headword or sense, it is shown in boldface after the part-of-speech label or sense number.

5.10 Negatives

When a word or phrase usually occurs with a negating word, the phrase "*used with a negative*" or "*usually used with a negative*" precedes the appropriate sense.

> **budge**[1] (bʌdʒ) *vb.* (*usually used with a negative*) **1.** to move, however slightly: *the car won't budge.*

6 Restrictive Labels and Phrases

6.1 Placement

6.1.1 If a particular sense requires a label indicating restriction of use as to appropriateness, connotation, subject field, etc., an italicized label is placed immediately before the account of the relevant meaning. Occasionally a phrase in roman type, placed in parentheses before the account of the meaning, is used for an equivalent purpose.

> **take off** *vb.* (*adv.*)... **3.** *Informal.* to set out or cause to set out on a journey: *they took off for Spain....*

6.1.2 If a label applies to all senses of one part of speech, it is placed after the part-of-speech label.

> **re·pair**[2] (rɪˈpɛə) *vb.* (*intr.*) **1.** (usually foll. by *to*) to go (to a place).... ~*n. Archaic.* **4.** the act of going or returning. **5.** a haunt or resort....

6.1.3 If a label applies to all senses of a headword, it is placed immediately after the pronunciation (or inflections).

> **con**[1] (kɒn) *Slang.* ~*n.* **1. a.** short for **confidence trick. b.** (*as modifier*): *con man.* ~*vb.* **cons, con·ning, conned. 2.** (*tr.*) to swindle or defraud.

6.2 Temporal labels

6.2.1 *Archaic.* This label denotes a word or sense that is no longer in common use but may be found in literary works or used to impart a historical colour to contemporary writing.

6.2.2 *Obsolete.* This label denotes a word or sense that is no longer in use. In specialist or technical fields the label often implies that the term has been superseded.

6.2.3 The word "formerly" is placed in parentheses before a sense or set of senses when the practice, concept, etc., being described, rather than the word itself, is obsolete or out-of-date.

6.3 Usage labels

6.3.1 *Slang.* This refers to words or senses that are racy or extremely informal. The appropriate contexts in which slang is used are restricted: it is appropriate, for example, among members of a particular social group or those engaging in a particular activity, such as a sporting activity. Slang words are inappropriate in formal speech or writing.

6.3.2 *Informal.* This label applies to words or senses that may be widely used, especially in conversation, letter-writing, etc., but that are not common in formal writing. Such words are subject to fewer contextual restrictions than slang words.

6.3.3 *Taboo.* This label applies to words that are not acceptable in polite use. The reader is advised to avoid the use of such words if he wishes to be sure of avoiding giving offence.

6.3.4 A number of other usage labels, such as *Ironic, Facetious,* and *Euphemistic,* are used where appropriate.

6.3.5 *Not standard.* This label is given to words or senses that are frequently encountered but widely regarded as incorrect and therefore avoided by careful speakers and writers.

6.4 Connotative labels

6.4.1 *Derogatory.* This implies that the connotations of a word are unpleasant with intent on the part of the speaker or writer.

6.4.2 *Offensive.* This label indicates that a word might be regarded as offensive by the person described or referred to, even if the speaker uses the word without any malicious intention.

6.5 Subject-field labels

A number of italicized labels are used to indicate that a word or sense is used in a particular specialist or technical field.
Subject-field labels are given either in full (e.g. *Astronomy, Banking, Ethics*) or only slightly abbreviated, so that the full label may be easily understood.

6.6 National and regional labels

6.6.1 Words or senses restricted to or associated with a particular country or region are labelled accordingly. The following labels are the ones most frequently used: *Austral.* (Australian), *Brit.* (British), *Canadian, Caribbean, Irish, N.Z.* (New Zealand), *S. African, Scot.* (Scottish), *U.S.* (United States).

6.6.2 The label "*Brit.*" is used mainly to distinguish a particular word or sense from its North American equivalent or to identify a term or concept that does not exist in North American English. In such cases the *Brit.* word may sometimes also be found to be acceptable in Australian, New Zealand, or some other regional variety of English. The U.S. equivalent may then be given in boldface type after the appropriate numbered sense. In the same way, senses and terms labelled "*U.S.*" may be acceptable in Canada, the Caribbean, and in other varieties of English. The meaning of such terms is accounted for by a cross-reference to the *Brit.* equivalent where such an equivalent exists.

> **blue-eyed boy** *n. Informal, chiefly Brit.* the favourite or darling of a person or group. Usual U.S. equivalent: **fair-haired boy.**
> **fair-haired boy** *n.* the usual U.S. name for **blue-eyed boy.**

6.6.3 Regional dialects (*Northern Brit. dialect, New England dialect,* etc.) have been specified as precisely as possible, even at the risk of overrestriction, in order to give the reader an indication of the appropriate regional flavour.

6.7 Trademarks

Where an entry is believed by the editors to be a proprietary name, it has been labelled "*Trademark.*" However, neither the presence nor the absence of such a label should be taken as affecting the legal status of a proprietary name.
If a word that is understood by the editors to be now in the public domain originated as a trademark, this information is given in the etymology.

7 The Account of the Meaning

7.1 Wording

7.1.1 The meaning of each headword in this dictionary is explained in one or more "definitions," together with information about context, collocation, and other relevant facts. The editors have given as much or as little information as they have judged necessary to explain the meaning of the term. No artificial rules for defining technique have been set that might obscure or eliminate important aspects of meaning.

7.1.2 The definitions are written in lucid English prose, and every word used in explaining a meaning is itself an entry in the dictionary, except for the New Latin words used for the taxonomy of plants and animals (see section 7.4.2 below) and certain scientific compound words, the meaning of which is deducible from the combining forms of which they are made up.

7.1.3 Generally, the account of each sense is so worded that it may be substituted for the headword in any appropriate collocation. However, this practice has not been followed where it has seemed more useful to give an account of the word's syntactic function, usage, etc.

> **thank** (θæŋk) *vb.* (*tr.*) **1.** to convey feelings of gratitude to....
>
> **ouch**[1] (aʊtʃ) *interj.* an exclamation of sharp sudden pain.

7.1.4 Each numbered sense is worded as far as possible so as to explain the headword alone, regardless of context. Thus, where reference is made to a collocational restriction, the collocational word is either ignored or is represented by an appropriate equivalent word in parentheses.

> **a·bound** (əˈbaʊnd) *vb.* (*intr.*)... **2.** (foll. by *with* or *in*) to be plentifully supplied (with); teem (with): *the gardens abound with flowers....*

7.1.5 Example sentences and phrases illustrating the use of a sense are given at the end of many definitions.

7.2 Numbering of senses

7.2.1 Where a headword has more than one sense, an account of each sense is given separately and each account is numbered in order to avoid confusion.

7.2.2 In certain cases numbered definitions have been subdivided into parts, marked **a., b., c.,** etc. These subdivisions are used for the following purposes:

7.2.2.1 To show the use of a word as a different part of speech without change of meaning.

> **beige** (beɪʒ) *n.* **1. a.** a very light brown, sometimes with a yellowish tinge, similar to the colour of undyed wool. **b.** (*as adj.*) *beige gloves....*

7.2.2.2 To show a very slight variation in sense, especially in certain technical fields:

> **back+fire** (ˌbækˈfaɪə)... ~*n.* **4.** (in an internal-combustion engine) **a.** an explosion of unburnt gases in the exhaust system. **b.** a premature explosion in a cylinder or inlet manifold....

7.2.2.3 To show that a restrictive label, such as *Archaic* or *Informal,* applies to a number of senses:

> **ver·y** (ˈvɛrɪ)... **4.** *Archaic.* **a.** real or true; genuine: *the very living God.* **b.** lawful: *the very vengeance of the gods....*

7.2.2.4 To number the senses of an idiom. See section 10.1.3 below.

7.3 Order of senses

7.3.1 As a general rule, where a headword has more than one sense, the first sense given is the one most common in current usage.

> **com+plex+ion** (kəmˈplɛkʃən) *n.* **1.** the colour and general appearance of a person's skin, esp. of the face. **2.** aspect, character, or nature: *the general complexion of a nation's finances.* **3.** *Obsolete.* **a.** the temperament of a person....

7.3.2 Where the editors consider that a current sense is the "core meaning," in that it illuminates the meaning of other senses, the core meaning may be placed first.

> **think** (θɪŋk) *vb.* **think+ing, thought. 1.** (*tr.; may take a clause as object*) to consider, judge, or believe: *he thinks my ideas impractical....* **2.** (*intr.;* often foll. by *about*) to exercise the mind as in order to make a decision; ponder. **3.** (*intr.*) to be capable of conscious thought: *man is the only animal that thinks.*

7.3.3 Subsequent senses are arranged so as to give a coherent account of the meaning of a headword. If a word is used as more than one part of speech, all the senses of each part of speech are grouped together in a single block. Within a part-of-speech block, closely related senses are grouped together; technical senses generally follow general senses; archaic and obsolete senses follow technical senses; idioms and fixed phrases are generally placed last.

7.4 Scientific and technical definitions

7.4.1 *Units, physical quantities, formulas, etc.* In accordance with the recommendations of the International Standards Organization, all scientific measurements are expressed in SI units (*Système International d'Unités*). Measurements and quantities in more traditional units are often given as well as SI units.

7.4.2 *Plants and animals.* When the scientific (Latin) names of phyla, divisions, classes, orders, families, genera, and species are used in definitions, they are printed in italic type and all except the specific name have an initial capital letter. Taxonomic information is always given.

> **moss** (mɒs) *n.* **1.** any bryophyte of the class *Musci,* typically growing in dense mats on trees....
>
> **cap·y+ba+ra** (ˌkæpɪˈbɑːrə) *n.* the largest rodent: a pig-sized amphibious hystricomorph, *Hydrochoerus hydrochaeris,...*

7.5 Place names

7.5.1 If a place has more than one name, the main entry is given at the name most common in present-day English-language contexts, with a cross-reference at other names. Thus, the main entry for the capital of Bavaria is at **Munich,** with a cross-reference at **München.** By contrast, the main entry for **Livorno** is given at that spelling rather than at **Leghorn,** an anglicized form that has now fallen into disuse. The name in the local language or languages is always given, and if no current anglicized name exists, the name chosen for main entry is generally that of the language of the current administrative authorities. Thus, the main entry is at **Brno,** with a cross-reference at **Brünn.** Historical names of importance are also given, with dates where these can be ascertained.

> **Par+is**[1] (ˈpærɪs; *French* paˈri) *n....* Ancient name: **Lutetia.**
>
> **Vol+go+grad** (*Russian* vəlgaˈgrat; *English* ˈvɒlgəˌgræd) *n....* Former names: **Tsaritsyn** (until 1925), **Stalingrad** (1925–61).

7.5.2 Statistical information about places has been obtained from the most up-to-date and reliable sources available. Population figures have been compiled from the most recent census available at the time of going to press. The date of the census is always given. Where no census figure is available, the most reliable recent estimate has been given, with a date.

Que·bec (kwɪˈbɛk, kə-, kɛ-) *n.* **1.** a province in E Canada:... Pop.: 6 234 445 (1976)....

Green·land (ˈgriːnlənd) *n.* the largest island in the world.... Pop.: 54 000 (1975 UN est.).

7.6 Biographical entries

7.6.1 Biographical entries are entered separately from and immediately following place names of the same spelling. They are entered at the surname of the subject or at his title if that is the name by which he is better known.

7.6.2 Original names, pseudonyms, nicknames, etc., are given in italics (without syllabification or pronunciation). Names or parts of names not commonly used are indicated in parentheses and are not syllabified.

Arm·strong (ˌɑːmˈstrɒŋ) *n.* **1. (Daniel) Lou·is,** nickname *Satchmo,* 1900–71, U.S. jazz trumpeter....

El·i·ot (ˈɛlɪət) *n.*... **3. T(homas) S(tearns).** 1888–1965, British poet, dramatist, and critic, born in the U.S....

7.6.3 If the headword is a family name, titles (if they exist) are printed in roman type after the given names.

Rus·sell (ˈrʌsᵊl) *n.* **1. Ber·trand Ar·thur Wil·liam,** 3rd Earl Russell. 1872–1970, English philosopher....

If the headword is a title, the family name is printed in boldface type along with the given names.

Mel·bourne[2] (ˈmɛlbən) *n.* **Wil·liam Lamb,** 2nd Viscount. 1779–1848; Whig prime minister (1834; 1835–41)....

7.7 Abbreviations and symbols

Abbreviations and symbols are entered as headwords in the main alphabetical list.

7.8 Acronyms

Words formed from the initial letters of the name of an organization, a scientific term, etc., but pronounced as a word (acronyms) are treated as entries in the appropriate alphabetical place.

NATO (ˈneɪtəʊ) *n. acronym for* North Atlantic Treaty Organization, an international organization composed of the U.S., Canada, Iceland, Britain, and 11 other European countries....

7.9 Affixes and combining forms

Prefixes (e.g. **in-**[1], **pre-**, **sub-**), suffixes (e.g. **-able, -ation, -ity**), and combining forms (e.g. **psycho-, -iatry**) have been entered as headwords if they are still used freely to produce new words in English.

8 Cross-references

8.1 Placement

The main entry is always given at the most common spelling or form of the word. Cross-reference entries refer to this main entry. Thus the entry for **deoxyribonucleic acid** cross-refers to **DNA,** where the full explanation is given.

8.2 Numbered cross-references

If a cross-reference entry applies to a particular sense of a headword, the number of the sense in question is given.

al·ka·net (ˈælkəˌnɛt) *n.*... **3.** any of certain hairy blue-flowered Old World plants of the boraginaceous genus *Anchusa* (or *Pentaglottis*), such as *A. sempervirens* of Europe. See also **bugloss** (sense 2). **4.** another name for **puccoon** (sense 1)....

8.3 Comparisons

Cross-references introduced by the words "See also" or "Compare" refer the reader to additional information elsewhere in the dictionary. If the cross-reference is preceded by a boldface swung dash, it applies to all the senses of the headword that have gone before it, unless otherwise stated. If there is no swung dash, the cross-reference applies only to the sense immediately preceding it.

8.4 Variant spellings

Variant spellings (e.g. **esthetic,** a variant spelling of **aesthetic**) are generally entered as cross-references if their place in the alphabetical list is more than ten entries distant from the main entry.

8.5 Alternative names

Alternative names are printed in boldface type and introduced by the words "Also" or "Also called." If the alternative name is preceded by a boldface swung dash, it applies to the entire entry.

8.6 Related adjectives

Certain nouns of Germanic origin have related adjectives that are derived from Latin or French. For example, *mural* (from Latin) is an adjective related in meaning to *wall.* Such adjectives are shown in a number of cases after the sense (or part-of-speech block) to which they are related.

wall (wɔːl) *n.* **1. a.** a vertical construction made of stone, brick, wood, etc.... Related adj.: **mural.**...

9 Hidden Entries

Entries within the account of the sense of a headword (hidden entries) are usually phrases composed of the headword plus a modifier.

law of ther·mo·dy·nam·ics *n.* any of three principles governing the relationships between different forms of energy. The **first law of thermodynamics** (law of conservation of energy) states....

10 Idioms

10.1 Placement

10.1.1 Verbal and certain other idioms are given as separate senses of the key word in the idiom, generally at the end of the appropriate part-of-speech block of the key word.

ground[1] (graʊnd) *n.*... **21. break new ground.** to do something that has not been done before....

10.1.2 When an idiom is closely related in meaning to a particular sense, it is usually entered immediately following that sense.

wing (wɪŋ) *n.*... **15.** the space offstage to the right or left of the acting area in a theatre. **16. in** *or* **on the wings.** ready to step in when needed....

10.1.3 Where an idiom has more than one sense, the senses are entered separately and numbered **a., b., c.,** etc.

10.2 Noun phrases

Fixed noun phrases and certain other idioms are given full headword status.

dark horse *n.* **1.** a competitor in a race or contest about whom little or nothing is known....

10.3 Fixed phrases

Words and senses that occur only or mainly in fixed collocations are styled as follows:

kith (kɪθ) *n.* one's friends and acquaintances (esp. in the phrase **kith and kin**).

11 The Etymology

11.1 Placement and selection

Etymologies are placed in square brackets after the account of the meaning. They are given for all headwords except those that are derivative forms (consisting of a base word and a suffix or prefix), compound words, inflected forms, and proper names. Thus, the headword **manage** has been given an etymology but the related headwords **manageable** (equivalent to *manage* plus the suffix *-able*), **management** (*manage* plus *-ment*), **manager** (*manage* plus *-er*[1]), **manageress** (*manager* plus *-ess*), etc., do not have etymologies. Inflected forms such as **saw**[2] (the past tense of *see*) and obvious compounds such as **mothball** are not given an etymology. Many headwords, such as **enlighten** and **prepossess**, consist of a prefix and a base word and are not accompanied by etymologies since the essential etymological information is shown for the component parts, all of which are entered in the dictionary as headwords in their own right (in this instance, **en-**[1], **light**[1], **-en**[1] and **pre-**, **possess**).

11.2 Information given in etymologies

The purpose of the etymologies is to trace briefly the history of the word back from the present day, through its first recorded appearance in English, to its origin, often in some source language other than English. The etymologies show the history of the word both in English (wherever there has been significant change in form or sense) and in its pre-English source languages. Since records of both Latin and Ancient Greek exist, it is usually possible to show the actual Latin or Greek form of the source of an English word. In the case of English words of Germanic origin, cognate forms in one or more Germanic languages are shown. These cognate forms are words from the same (lost) Germanic originals, and the chief cognate languages cited are Old Norse, Swedish, Danish, German, Dutch, and Old Saxon.

11.3 Dating

The etymology records the first known occurrence (a written citation) of a word in English. Words first appearing in the language during the Middle English period or later are dated by century, abbreviated C.

man·tis.... [C17: New Latin, from Greek: prophet, alluding to its praying posture]

This indicates that there is a written citation for *mantis* in the seventeenth century, when the word was in use as a New Latin term in the scientific vocabulary of the time. The absence of a New Latin or Greek form in the etymology means that the form of the word was the same in those languages as in English.

Native words from Old English are not dated, written records of Old English being comparatively scarce, but are simply identified as being of Old English origin.

mar (mɑː) *vb.* **mars, mar·ring, marred**.... [Old English *merran;* compare Old Saxon *merrian* to hinder, Old Norse *merja* to bruise]

11.4 Wording of etymologies

The etymologies are intended to be readable and understood by the general reader; accordingly, technical symbols and abbreviations have generally been avoided, with the exception of a few conventional abbreviations such as C for century and *n.* and *vb.* for *noun* and *verb.* All the languages and linguistic terminology used in the etymologies are entries in their own right in the dictionary. Words printed in SMALL CAPITALS refer the reader to other headwords where relevant or additional information, either in the definition text or in the etymology, may be found.

11.5 Biographical information

Words formed from a person's name are etymologized and brief biographical details are given for the person in question.

Mo·ho·ro·vi·čić dis·con·ti·nu·i·ty.... [C20: named after Andrija *Mohorovičić* (1857–1936), Yugoslav geologist]

12 Derived Words or Run-on Entries

Words derived from a base word by the addition of suffixes such as *-ly, -ness,* etc., are entered in boldface type immediately after the etymology or after the last definition if there is no etymology. The meanings of such words may be deduced from the meanings of the suffix and the headword.

13 Listed Entries

In English many words are formed by adding productive prefixes such as *non-*, *over-*, *pre-*, *un-*, etc., to existing words. In most cases, the meanings of these words are obvious. Such words are listed alphabetically, without further explanation of the meaning, at the foot of the appropriate page.

14 Usage Notes

A brief note introduced by the label **Usage** has been added at the end of a number of entries in order to comment on matters of usage. These comments are based on the observed practice or preference of the majority of educated speakers and writers.

ain't (eɪnt) *Not standard. contraction of* am not, is not, are not, have not, *or* has not: *I ain't seen it.*
Usage. Although the interrogative form *ain't I?* would be a natural contraction of *am not I?*, it is generally avoided in spoken English and never used in formal English.

Pronunciation Key

The symbols used in the pronunciation transcriptions are those of the International Phonetic Alphabet. The following consonant symbols have their usual English values: *b, d, f, h, k, l, m, n, p, r, s, t, v, w, z.* The remaining symbols and their interpretations are listed in the tables below.

English Sounds

ɑː as in *father* ('fɑːðə), *alms* (ɑːmz), *clerk* (klɑːk), *heart* (hɑːt), *sergeant* ('sɑːdʒənt)

æ as in *act* (ækt), *Caedmon* ('kædmən), *plait* (plæt)

aɪ as in *dive* (daɪv), *aisle* (aɪl), *guy* (gaɪ), *might* (maɪt), *rye* (raɪ)

aɪə as in *fire* (faɪə), *buyer* (baɪə), *liar* (laɪə), *tyre* (taɪə)

aʊ as in *out* (aʊt), *bough* (baʊ), *crowd* (kraʊd), *slouch* (slaʊtʃ)

aʊə as in *flour* (flaʊə), *cower* (kaʊə), *flower* (flaʊə), *sour* (saʊə)

ɛ as in *bet* (bɛt), *ate* (ɛt), *bury* ('bɛrɪ), *heifer* ('hɛfə), *said* (sɛd), *says* (sɛz)

eɪ as in *paid* (peɪd), *day* (deɪ), *deign* (deɪn), *gauge* (geɪdʒ), *grey* (greɪ), *neigh* (neɪ)

ɛə as in *bear* (bɛə), *dare* (dɛə), *prayer* (prɛə), *stairs* (stɛəz), *where* (wɛə)

g as in *get* (gɛt), *give* (gɪv), *ghoul* (guːl), *guard* (gɑːd), *examine* (ɪg'zæmɪn)

ɪ as in *pretty* ('prɪtɪ), *build* (bɪld), *busy* ('bɪzɪ), *nymph* (nɪmf), *pocket* ('pɒkɪt), *sieve* (sɪv), *women* ('wɪmɪn)

iː as in *see* (siː), *aesthete* ('iːsθiːt), *evil* ('iːvᵊl), *magazine* (ˌmægə'ziːn), *receive* (rɪ'siːv), *siege* (siːdʒ)

ɪə as in *fear* (fɪə), *beer* (bɪə), *mere* (mɪə), *tier* (tɪə)

j as in *yes* (jɛs), *onion* ('ʌnjən), *vignette* (vɪ'njɛt)

ɒ as in *pot* (pɒt), *botch* (bɒtʃ), *sorry* ('sɒrɪ)

əʊ as in *note* (nəʊt), *beau* (bəʊ), *dough* (dəʊ), *hoe* (həʊ), *slow* (sləʊ), *yeoman* ('jəʊmən)

ɔː as in *thaw* (θɔː), *broad* (brɔːd), *drawer* (drɔːə), *fault* (fɔːlt), *halt* (hɔːlt), *organ* ('ɔːgən)

ɔɪ as in *void* (vɔɪd), *boy* (bɔɪ), *destroy* (dɪ'strɔɪ)

ʊ as in *pull* (pʊl), *good* (gʊd), *should* (ʃʊd), *woman* ('wʊmən)

uː as in *zoo* (zuː), *do* (duː), *queue* (kjuː), *shoe* (ʃuː), *spew* (spjuː), *true* (truː), *you* (juː)

ʊə as in *poor* (pʊə), *skewer* ('skjʊə), *sure* (ʃʊə)

ə as in *potter* ('pɒtə), *alone* (ə'ləʊn), *furious* ('fjʊərɪəs), *nation* ('neɪʃən), *the* (ðə)

ɜː as in *fern* (fɜːn), *burn* (bɜːn), *fir* (fɜː), *learn* (lɜːn), *term* (tɜːm), *worm* (wɜːm)

ʌ as in *cut* (kʌt), *flood* (flʌd), *rough* (rʌf), *son* (sʌn)

ʃ as in *ship* (ʃɪp), *election* (ɪ'lɛkʃən), *machine* (mə'ʃiːn), *mission* ('mɪʃən), *pressure* ('prɛʃə), *schedule* ('ʃɛdjuːl), *sugar* ('ʃʊgə)

ʒ as in *treasure* ('trɛʒə), *azure* ('æʒə), *closure* ('kləʊʒə), *evasion* (ɪ'veɪʒən)

tʃ as in *chew* (tʃuː), *nature* ('neɪtʃə)

dʒ as in *jaw* (dʒɔː), *adjective* ('ædʒɪktɪv), *lodge* (lɒdʒ), *soldier* ('səʊldʒə), *usage* ('juːsɪdʒ)

θ as in *thin* (θɪn), *strength* (strɛŋθ), *three* (θriː)

ð as in *these* (ðiːz), *bathe* (beɪð), *lather* ('lɑːðə)

ŋ as in *sing* (sɪŋ), *finger* ('fɪŋgə), *sling* (slɪŋ)

ᵊ indicates that the following consonant (*l* or *n*) is syllabic, as in *bundle* ('bʌndᵊl) and *button* ('bʌtᵊn).

Foreign Sounds

The symbols above are also used to represent foreign sounds where these are similar to English sounds. However, certain common foreign sounds require symbols with markedly different values, as follows:

a *a* in French *ami* ·German *Mann,* Italian *pasta:* a sound between English (æ) and (ɑː), similar to the vowel in Northern English *cat* or London *cut.*

e *é* in French *été, eh* in German *sehr, e* in Italian *che:* a sound similar to the first part of the English diphthong (eɪ) in *day* or to the Scottish vowel in *day.*

ɔ *o* in Italian *no,* French *bonne,* German *Sonne:* a vowel resembling English (ɒ), but with a higher tongue position and more rounding of the lips.

o *o* in French *rose,* German *so,* Italian *voce:* a sound between English (ɔː) and (uː) with closely rounded lips, similar to the Scottish vowel in *so.*

y *u* in French *tu, ü* in German *über* or *fünf:* a sound made with a tongue position similar to that of English (iː) but with closely rounded lips.

ø *eu* in French *deux, ö* in German *schön:* a sound made with the tongue position of (e) but with closely rounded lips.

œ *œu* in French *œuf, ö* in German *zwölf:* a sound made with a tongue position similar to that of English (ɛ) but with open rounded lips.

~ above a vowel indicates nasalization, as in French *un* (œ̃), *bon* (bɔ̃), *vin* (vɛ̃), *blanc* (blɑ̃).

x *ch* in Scottish *loch,* German *Buch, j* in Spanish *Juan.*

ç *ch* in German *ich:* a (j) sound as in *yes,* said without voice; similar to the first sound in *huge.*

β *b* in Spanish *Habana:* a voiced fricative sound similar to (v), but made by the two lips.

ʎ *ll* in Spanish *llamar, gl* in Italian *consiglio:* similar to the (lj) sequence in *million,* but with the tongue tip lowered and the sounds said simultaneously.

ɥ *u* in French *lui:* a short (y).

ɲ *gn* in French *vigne,* Italian *gnocchi, ñ* in Spanish *España:* similar to the (nj) sequence in *onion,* but with the tongue tip lowered and the two sounds said simultaneously.

ɣ *g* in Spanish *luego:* a weak (g) made with voiced friction.

Length

The symbol ː denotes length and is shown together with certain vowel symbols when the vowels are typically long.

Stress

Three grades of stress are shown in the transcriptions by the presence or absence of marks placed immediately *before* the affected syllable. Primary or strong stress is shown by ', while secondary or weak stress is shown by ˌ. Unstressed syllables are not marked. In *photographic* (ˌfəʊtə'græfɪk), for example, the first syllable carries secondary stress and the third primary stress, while the second and fourth are unstressed.

The Pronunciation of British English

by A. C. Gimson

The Origins

English has been spoken in Britain for some fourteen centuries. During this time, it has undergone such fundamental changes (affecting grammar, vocabulary, and pronunciation) that the speech of an inhabitant of the London region of the 7th century would be totally unintelligible to the modern Londoner. The earliest form of English, brought by Germanic invaders from the 5th century onwards, is known as *Old English* and extends up to about the 11th century. This general term itself embraces a number of separate dialects deriving from the different geographical origins of the invaders. It was the West-Saxon form of the South and the Southwest of the country that ultimately became regarded as a standard language, and it is in this form that most of the extant texts are written. From about the 7th century, Old English began to be written with the Latin alphabet, probably introduced into England by Irish missionaries. The Latin alphabet was, however, inadequate to express the more complex phonological system of the dialects of Old English. New letters, such as "æ," were added to indicate a value between that of Italian *e* and *a;* digraphs, such as 'th,' had to be used for consonant sounds that were unknown in Italian. Although there was a good deal of agreement about the orthography to be applied to the Old English sound system, there are in the texts of the period considerable variations in spelling forms as between one dialect and another and also between scribes. In fact, English has had a standardized form of spelling for not much more than two hundred years, the present apparent inconsistencies in our orthography reflecting the historical development of the language.

It can be said that the next major influence on our language—that of the French dominance from the 11th century onwards—affected spelling more than pronunciation (although it added enormously to our stock of words). During this period of *Middle English* (roughly 1100–1450), English remained the language of the people, but French was used by the aristocracy as well as in administrative and legal proceedings. It was not until the end of this era that English became re-established as the language used by all sections of society. By then, various French spelling forms had been taken over, e.g. *u* was replaced by *ou* in a word like *house* because of the different value attributed to *u* in French borrowings; and the *ch* sound of a word like *chin* (originally spelt with *c*) took on the French spelling of words such as *chamber.* By the time of Chaucer, the language began to look more like modern English and would be to a large extent intelligible to the modern ear.

In the following period, *Early Modern English* (1450–1600), the pronunciation of the language became increasingly similar to that of today. A modern Londoner would have little difficulty in understanding the speech used in the plays performed at Shakespeare's *Globe,* although it would make a somewhat rustic impression on his ear. Nevertheless, he would notice that there was still considerable variation in the spelling forms used, to some extent in printed works (where the styles depended upon the conventions adopted by individual printers) but more particularly in the handwritten letters of individuals (who continued to spell largely according to their own phonetic principles and thus provided us with a good deal of information about contemporary pronunciation). It is not until the end of the 18th century that English began to sound more completely like the language we speak today. What is more, with the appearance of the great dictionaries of that century, the orthography was standardized into a form almost identical with our present one. However, even in the last two centuries, there have been notable pronunciation changes, which demonstrate that the sound system of the language is constantly undergoing evolution. The ambiguities of spelling that reflect fourteen centuries of linguistic history remain to puzzle the native user and to frustrate the foreign learner.

The Present Situation

With so many influences at work on the language for so long, it is hardly surprising that the pronunciation of English in Britain today presents an extremely complex picture. It is possible to discern three main causes for variation, relating to the speaker's regional origin, his place in society, and his generation.

Elements of regional differences of pronunciation are evident today, to such an extent that a Cockney and a Glaswegian may still have serious difficulties of communication in speech. Englishmen are still readily able to identify the part of the country from which a person comes simply by listening to his speech, despite the fears of those who predict that dialect forms will soon disappear completely. Indeed, these regional forms of speech are often related to gross statements of regional prejudice—the Southerner who regards the speech of the Northerner as over-blunt, and the Northerner who characterizes the speaker with a Southern accent as affected. Dialect differences of pronunciation are therefore still important both for reasons of intelligibility and also in social terms. It is worth remarking too that, of all the various accents of British English, that of the London region has developed most rapidly, the speech of the other regions remaining closer to the historical origins of the language.

But the pronunciation of English in Britain has also a more purely social significance. As has been stated, at one time the upper classes would speak French whereas the rest of the people spoke English. In more recent centuries, when English was in universal use, there emerged different types of pronunciation in any region relating to the speaker's position in society, e.g. the popular speech forms of the working man, full of the historical characteristics of the region, as opposed to the pronunciation used by the professional and upper classes, which was modified towards a general standard. It can be said that the notion of a socially prestigious standard of pronunciation arose explicitly in the 16th century, when grammarians began to recommend that the only acceptable form of pronunciation was that used in London and at the Court, i.e. the speech of educated people in the Southeast of England. Such a notion of standard pronunciation, based on social criteria, became increasingly accepted during the next three centuries, so that in the middle of the 19th century the philologist Alexander J. Ellis was able to characterize it as "received pronunciation"—a term which is used to this day (often in an abbreviated form as RP). A century ago, persons of the ruling classes would pronounce English in the same way wherever they lived in Britain. This form of pronunciation had the advantage, therefore, of being widely intelligible. Moreover, it was important for the ambitious, who might wish to move upwards in society, to change their pronunciation. This was the sociolinguistic climate in which Bernard Shaw wrote his *Pygmalion*, a play which had a greater social significance at the time of its first production than it can possibly have now. In the first half of this century, this standard was adopted as a model by more and more of the population, despite vigorous opposition from a number of interests, notably the Poet Laureate, Robert Bridges, and his Society for Pure English, who advocated a standard based on a more Northern type. It was on the grounds of wide intelligibility that, in the 1930s, the BBC decided to adopt "received pronunciation" as the form to be used by announcers. Indeed, the British public became so accustomed to this style of speech that they were suspicious of any attempt by the BBC to introduce news readers with a regional pronunciation. Moreover, the broadcasting media exposed more and more of the population to the Southern-based standard, with the result that a greater number of people began to use it, at least in a modified form.

Within the last twenty-five years, however, a considerable change of attitude seems to have taken place. The social divisions in the country have become noticeably less rigid, and the movement between classes has become easier. In particular, the young tend to reject the former "received" pronunciation as the voice of outmoded authority, preferring new speech-styles related to their own culture, such as the popular speech of London and Liverpool, as well as non-British accents such as those of America and Australia. It is too early to say whether this reaction by the young will have lasting consequences for the line of development of the traditional standard. But it is already clear that it is no longer possible to define the standard form as simply the variety of speech used by a particular section of society, since in a diluted form its use is more widespread than was the case even fifty years ago. It is no longer thought of as the "best" pronunciation, but as one which has advantages on account of its wide intelligibility; it is for this reason that it remains the form taught to foreign learners, although it is not the simplest system for them to acquire. It continues to have as its basis the speech of the London region, but, being no longer socially determined, must rely for definition on phonetic and phonological criteria. In the remarks on the sound system given below, 20 vowels and 24 consonants are listed. In addition, certain characteristics of usage identify the accent, e.g. different vowels are used in *cat* and *calm*; the vowels of *cot* and *caught* are distinguished; the vowel of *book* is the same as that in *good* rather than that in *food*; an *r* is not pronounced in words like *farm*, despite the spelling, nor is the final *g* sounded in *sing*, etc. Other characteristics are of a more phonetic kind, i.e. are concerned with the quality of the sounds, e.g. the vowels of *day* and *go* are clearly diphthongal, though the more open onset typical of Cockney is excluded; the two *l* sounds of *little* have different qualities, the first being "clear" and the second "dark," thus excluding some Scottish accents where both are "dark" and some Irish accents where both tend to be "clear," etc.

Nevertheless, even when a theoretical basis for the standard has been decided upon, account has to be taken of changes in pronunciation, especially in respect of vowels, reflected in the speech of different generations. Thus, older speakers (and those with conservative attitudes to life) use the vowel of *saw* in words like *off, cloth* and *cross*, rather than that of *hot*, which is of almost universal currency amongst the younger generation. Consonantal change is typified by the treatment of words beginning with *wh-*, such as *where, which* as opposed to *wear, witch*. The distinction between such pairs began to be lost, on a large scale, in the London region as early as the 18th century. Today, it may be regarded as an optional extra to the system (often advocated by elocutionists) but almost totally abandoned by the young. The pronunciation shown in this dictionary represents the form used by the middle generations, avoiding the archaisms of the old and the possibly ephemeral eccentricities of the young.

It will be clear from what has been said that there remains a great diversity in the pronunciation of English in Britain, reflecting differences of region, social class, and generation. It is possible that modern facility of communication, in all its senses, is levelling out some of the extreme forms of pronunciation which even a century ago led to lack of intelligibility. But complete standardization is unlikely to be achieved. However far we proceed along the road to a standard pronunciation, there will always remain slight differences as between one individual and another, and between the various speech styles which an individual will use in different situations.

The Sound System

The infinite number of sounds produced in speaking a language can be reduced for linguistic purposes to a finite set of distinctive terms known as *phonemes*. Thus, the meaningful oppositions illustrated by the English series *seat, sit, set, sat*, etc., demonstrate the operation of vowel phonemes; similarly, *pin, tin, kin, bin, fin*, etc., exemplify the distinctive use of consonant phonemes. The realization of a phoneme may differ considerably according to its situation, e.g. the /p/ of *pin* is different from the /p/ of *nip*; the sound of /l/ in *leaf* differs from that in *feel*. But these differences of phonetic quality, of which the speaker is usually unaware, do not distinguish meaning. A phoneme may therefore be regarded as the smallest linguistic unit that can bring about a change of meaning. It should be noted, however, that English tolerates a certain degree of variability in the incidence of phonemes in particular words, even within the standard pronunciation, e.g. the short or long vowel in *room*. This dictionary recommends the form that has the most extensive current usage and is most widely understood. It is not a form which is intrinsically "better" than any other nor can it be thought of as synonymous with "educated": many highly educated people speak in a way that is easily identifiable as regional, e.g. with a type of Scottish, Northern, Southwestern, or even Cockney English.

(a) Vowels

The standard Southern English form of pronunciation operates with 20 basic vowel phonemes:

5 long vowels: /iː/ *feed*, /uː/ *food*, /ɑː/ *calm*, /ɔː/ *saw*, /ɜː/ *bird* (where : indicates length)

7 short vowels: /ɪ/ *bit*, /ɛ/ *bet*, /æ/ *bat*, /ʌ/ *bud*, /ɒ/ *hot*, /ʊ/ *foot*; and the unstressed vowel /ə/ as in the first syllable of *above*

8 diphthongs: /eɪ/ *late*, /aɪ/ *five*, /ɔɪ/ *boy*, /əʊ/ *home*, /aʊ/ *house*, /ɪə/ *dear*, /ɛə/ *fair*, /ʊə/ *poor*

Notes:

(i) The length of so-called long vowels and diphthongs varies considerably. Thus, the /iː/ sound of *seat* is very much shorter than those in *seed* and *sea*; the diphthong in *plate* is shorter than those in *played* or *play*. In such cases, the duration of the vowel is a prime cue in distinguishing between a pair like *seat* and *seed*—more important than the final consonants. The actual length of long vowels and diphthongs is conditioned by the type of syllable closure involved: when a "voiceless" consonant (e.g. /s/ or /t/) closes the syllable, the long vowel or diphthong is much shorter than when it is followed by "voiced" consonant (e.g. /z/ or /d/) or when it is in an open syllable (e.g. in *see*). The result is that, in fact, the shortened "long" /iː/ of *seat* may be no longer than the short /ɪ/ of *sit*.

(ii) The vowels /iː, ɪ, uː, ʊ/ are traditionally paired as long and short. However, the difference of quality between /iː/ and /ɪ/ and between /uː/ and /ʊ/ is more important than that of length. In an opposition such as *bead—bid*, both length and quality operate as distinctive features; but, as was noted above, *seat* and *sit* exhibit an opposition which relies entirely upon a quality difference. In this dictionary, the notations /iː/-/ɪ/ and /uː/-/ʊ/ indicate the quality distinction by means of different symbols.

(iii) /ɪ/ frequently occurs in unstressed syllables, e.g. in *pocket, waited, savage,* etc. However, there is a tendency for the traditional /ɪ/ to be replaced by /ə/ in many cases, e.g. in words like *hopeless, goodness, secret,* etc. This use of /ə/, characteristic of regional forms of English, is extended by some even to cases like *boxers* v. *boxes,* where a meaningful opposition is lost. In this dictionary, the use of /ɪ/ in such cases, typical of the middle generations of English speakers, is retained.

(iv) Considerable variation between the use of /juː/ and /uː/ is found in words like *lurid, revolution, suit,* and the prefix *super-*. The /j/-less form, which is increasingly common in such cases, is the first form given in this dictionary.

(v) Similarly, it is possible to use /æ/ or /ɑː/ in the prefix *trans-* (e.g. *translation*) or the suffix *-graph* (e.g. *telegraph*). The most common forms, shown in the dictionary, are /æ/ for the prefix and /ɑː/ for the suffix.

(vi) The old-fashioned /ɔː/ in words like *off, cloth, cross,* is abandoned in favour of /ɒ/.

(vii) Since the distinction between *pour* and *paw* is now rarely made, /ɔː/ is shown in both.

(viii) The sequences /aɪə, aʊə/ as in *tyre, tower* have, for at least a century, been reduced to /aə/ or /ɑː/, so that for many speakers the opposition is lost. Since this merger is by no means completely established in the language, the full forms /aɪə, aʊə/ are retained.

(ix) Certain monosyllables, having a grammatical function, e.g. *and, was, for,* have different pronunciations according to whether or not they carry stress, e.g. stressed /ænd, wɒz, fɔː/, unstressed /ən(d), wəz, fə/. The citation (stressed) form is given first in the dictionary, although in normal discourse the weaker form has a much higher frequency of occurrence.

(b) Consonants

There are 24 consonant phonemes:

/p/ *pin,* /t/ *tin,* /k/ *kin*
/b/ *bay,* /d/ *day,* /g/ *gay*
/tʃ/ *choke,* /dʒ/ *joke*
/m/ *some,* /n/ *sun,* /ŋ/ *sung*
/r/ *red,* /l/ *led*
/f/ *fine,* /v/ *vine,* /θ/ *thing,* /ð/ *this*
/s/ *seal,* /z/ *zeal,* /ʃ/ *shoe,* /ʒ/ *measure,* /h/ *hat*
/w/ *wet,* /j/ *yet*

Notes:

(i) Some consonant phonemes have a restricted distribution, e.g. /ŋ/ occurs only in syllable-final positions; /ʒ/ occurs typically only in medial positions. In the case of words borrowed comparatively recently from French, such as *prestige, beige, camouflage,* both /ʒ/ and /dʒ/ are possible, the more common form being given in the dictionary.

(ii) Words ending in *r,* e.g. *father, far,* have no /r/ in the pronunciation when a consonant or a pause follows. However, it is normal for a "linking" /r/ to be pronounced when a vowel follows, e.g. in *father and mother, far off.* (This usage is extended by many speakers to cases where no *r* exists in the spelling, e.g. *the idea*/r/ *of it.*)

(iii) Variant pronunciations occur in words like *issue* (/sj/ or /ʃ/), *actual* (/tj/ or /tʃ/). The commonest form is given.

(iv) /l/ and /n/, in particular, are frequently sounded as syllabic, without an accompanying vowel. Such cases are shown with raised ᵊ, e.g. *mutton* /ˈmʌtᵊn/.

(c) Stress

What is here referred to as "stress," for the sake of brevity, is in English a complex of several factors, including stress (i.e. intensity for the speaker and loudness for the listener), pitch, quality (some sounds being more prominent to the listener than others), and length. The effect of this combination of factors is to render a syllable more or less prominent amongst its neighbours. The situation of the stressed syllable has always been an important feature of English pronunciation both in the word and in connected speech. Indeed, there are some pairs of words that are distinguished entirely or mainly by the placing of the stress-accent, e.g. *insult* (*vb.*) v. *insult* (*n.*), *object* (*vb.*) v. *object* (*n.*). In short words, there is usually only one stress-accent, e.g. *over* and *above.* This is shown by placing ˈ before the stressed syllable, e.g. /ˈəʊvə/ and /əˈbʌv/. However, in addition to this type of primary (tonic) stress, there may occur secondary stresses, e.g. *consideration,* where the secondary stress on *-sid-* is shown by ˌ before the syllable, e.g. /kənˌsɪdəˈreɪʃən/.

The stress patterns given in the dictionary will always be those of the isolate, predicative forms, although in the case of double stressed words and compounds there may be a shift of primary and secondary stressing when the word or compound is used attributively, e.g. *afternoon* (predicative) /ˌ--ˈ-/; but attributive in *afternoon tea* /ˌ---ˈ-/.

Finally, as was the case with vowels and, to a lesser extent, with consonants, word stress patterns are liable to change in time; e.g. *character* was once stressed on the second syllable, whereas now the first syllable carries the stress-accent. Today, some instability of stressing may be observed in certain words, e.g. *controversy* (ˈkɒntrəˌvɜːsɪ, kənˈtrɒvəsɪ). There are also stressing variants that are characteristic of regional forms of English, e.g. Scottish English *realize* with /-ˈ-/ rather than the Southern /ˈ--/. As with the sounds, the most common Southern form is given.

Selected Bibliography

G. F. Arnold, *Stress in English Words* (North Holland Publishing Co.), 1957.

A. Campbell, *Old English Grammar* (Oxford University Press), 1959.

E. J. Dobson, *English Pronunciation 1500–1700* (Oxford University Press), 1957.

A. C. Gimson, *An Introduction to the Pronunciation of English* (Edward Arnold), 2nd edition 1970.

D. Jones, *The Pronunciation of English* (Cambridge University Press), 4th edition 1956.

D. Jones, *An English Pronouncing Dictionary,* ed. A. C. Gimson (Dent), 14th edition 1977.

R. Kingdon, *Groundwork of English Stress* (Longman), 1958.

H. C. Wyld, *A History of Modern Colloquial English* (Blackwell), 3rd edition 1936.

The Development of English as a World Language

The Making of English

by David Brazil

Over the last five hundred years, the English language, formerly the language of a mere five or six million people living within the confines of the British Isles, has expanded to become the everyday speech of over three hundred million. Among the results of this expansion is the present status of English as the mother tongue of most of the inhabitants of the vast ethnically diverse society of the United States of America and as the most important second language of some fifty millions in Southern Asia and in a number of new nations of Africa. The expansion has, however, for all practical purposes been a feature of the most recent of the three major phases of development into which linguistic scholarship customarily divides the recorded history of the language. Although our principal concern here is with that geographical extension that has led to the label "English" being applied to many simultaneously existing varieties round the world, we can achieve a proper perspective only if we consider briefly the historical dimension of its variation.

"New English" or "Modern English," which has been so pre-eminently an article for export, is distinguished from the earlier variety, "Middle English," and the latter in turn from the still earlier "Old English." The three periods are separated by two watersheds, one associated historically with the Norman Conquest of the English, and the other with those complex developments to which historians apply the terms Renaissance and Reformation. After the Norman Conquest and again during the Renaissance there occurred marked accelerations in the process of change that all living language is subject to. The response of the language to historical pressures resulted on each occasion in the emergence of a form significantly different from that which preceded it, so that Old English must now be learned by the native speaker of English as a foreign language, and Middle English, the language of Chaucer and Langland, is today fully intelligible only to the specialist scholar.

Old English was the language of the heathen invaders who began to appear along the Eastern coast of Britain in the third century A.D., and who, after the withdrawal of the Roman legions, settled all but the West and North, where a Celtic language continued to be used. As Angles, Saxons, and Jutes, they spoke different dialects of a common Germanic tongue, and their geographical disposition in the new land, the Jutes in the Southeast, the Saxons in Wessex, and the two major divisions of the Angles in the Midlands and the North, set up at the outset many of the regional differences that still persist in the popular speech of the British Isles.

The earliest written records date from after the Christian conversion of the English instigated by Pope Gregory in 597. By then, the warlike habits of the English had, for the most part, given way to agricultural pursuits, and one can create a pleasant, if somewhat romanticized, picture of the agrarian life from a stock of words that are often spoken of approvingly as "short," "simple," and Anglo-Saxon—e.g. *man* and *child; eat, drink,* and *sleep; love* and *hate; land, harvest,* and *crops.*

Old English had a facility, comparable with that of modern German, for meeting the need for new vocabulary by compounding existing words: *daisy* is picturesquely derived from "day's eye" and *nostril* from "nose hole." But the conversion to Christianity created needs that were not supplied from indigenous resources, and the Latin of the new clerics provided the first large-scale acquisition of foreign loans we know of. Apart from words of obvious ecclesiastical significance, like *priest, monk, hymn, altar,* and *candle,* others like *master* and *grammar, plaster* and *fever,* reflect the Church's commitment to learning and medical care.

The arrival of the Vikings, who, until King Alfred's victory in 878, threatened to subjugate the newly Christianized English, resulted in further augmentation of the vocabulary. But the language they spoke, which had a strong influence upon the speech of the Danelaw, the area lying to the northeast of a line drawn from Chester to London, was closely related to English. The results of its admixture were more subtle and elusive. Pairs of words, differentiated by a single sound, like *skirt* and *shirt, whole* and *hale,* have survived. Instead of a technical vocabulary associated with a new field of interest or endeavour, we have Old Norse borrowings that are every bit as commonplace as native Old English words: *husband, ugly, call, want,* and, most surprisingly, the pronouns *they, them,* and *their* to go alongside Old English *he, him,* and *her.*

When William, Duke of Normandy, defeated the English king at Hastings in 1066, he inaugurated a period of rule by French-speaking kings and of pervasive domination by a nobility whose interests were predominantly in things French. Until King John lost the last of the major continental possessions in 1205, Norman-French was the language of the Court, of business, and of lay culture, while Latin remained the ecclesiastical language. English was virtually reduced to the role of a patois. When its use was revived in educated circles in the thirteenth century, it had undergone radical change, some of which can be directly related to the long break in the literary tradition.

The elaborate inflection system that had been a feature of Old English, manifested, for instance, in the six different forms of the noun *stan* (stone), may well have been undergoing simplification in the spoken language before the Norman Conquest. Absence of the conservative influence of the written form would undoubtedly accelerate the process: although some vestiges of inflectional endings survive until after Chaucer's time, Middle English is essentially without this refinement. Another change was largely due to the fact that the French-trained scribes, who now replaced those of the Old English tradition, introduced new orthographical conventions and in so doing were responsible for much of the inconsistency for which modern English spelling is notorious. (Cf. Professor Gimson's comments, *The Pronunciation of British English,* p. xix.) New characters—k, g, q, v, w, and z—were brought into use. The two pronunciations of Old English "c" could now be differentiated, as in the modern spelling of *king* (from *cyning*) and *choose* (from *ceosan*). But the retention of "c" in words like *cat,* and its use to represent /s/ in *nice* have left us with confusing results: *king, can, cent, sent.* The characteristic Old English letters ð and þ were gradually replaced by *th,* and the loss of ȝ resulted in the sound it represented (a sound that was itself subsequently lost) being spelt as *gh* in words like *night, daughter,* and *laugh.* Finally, because of the similarity of a number of characters such as *u, v, n, m,* and *w* in the

Carolingian script used by the scribes, *u* was replaced by *o* in many words like *come, son,* and *wonder.*

But by far the most noticeable feature of English, as it came to be re-established after the period of the supremacy of French, was the very large number of French words that had been absorbed into the common stock. Many of these have been sorted by scholars into sets that correspond with activities in which the indigenous English speakers are thought to have played little active part. They include much of the modern vocabulary of government and law, of ecclesiastical and military matters, of art, learning, and medicine, and words that reflect a preoccupation with fashion, polite social life, and refined feeding habits. A measure of the degree of assimilation of the new French words is the extent to which they occurred in derivatives, taking English endings as in *gently* and *gentleness,* and forming compounds with English nouns as in *gentleman.* Generally, however, the accession of loan words was accompanied by a marked decline in the facility of the language for creating new, self-explanatory compounds, a practice that was not revived extensively until the nineteenth century, when scientific and technological advances generated new needs.

A characteristic of Middle English was its very considerable regional variation. Contemporary writers testify that the speech of one area was frequently unintelligible to inhabitants of another. Amid the dialectal confusion, it is possible to distinguish five major areas: the North extending as far as the Humber, the East and West Midlands, together extending from the Humber to the Thames, the South, and Kent. The end of the fourteenth century saw the rise of Standard English, a result largely of the commercial supremacy of the East Midlands. In particular, the growing importance of London as a political, judicial, social, and intellectual centre led to the elevation of one particular variety of the East Midland dialect, namely London English, to a position of prestige that it has enjoyed ever since. It was this dialect that would be used overwhelmingly when the invention of printing opened up unprecedented possibilities for the dissemination of the written word.

The printing press was one of the factors that, around 1500, resulted in the second great change in English. The need and the possibility of what we can properly think of as mass circulation placed a high premium on the use of the vernacular. As in other parts of Europe, the latter made incursions into territories in which Latin had formerly held sway: law, medicine, and religion in particular. And one aspect of the revival of interest in classical antiquity was the very considerable translating activity that gave Shakespeare, for instance, with his "little Latin and less Greek," access to much of the classical heritage. Engagement with Latin and Greek had effects upon English—upon both vocabulary and grammar. The effects on vocabulary were more immediately noticeable and led to a further large accession of new words, often learned and polysyllabic, which, when carried to excess, earned contemporary castigation as "ink-horn" terms. In this way, the classical experience may be said to have been a potent instrument of change. Its effect upon grammar, though less immediate, was, by contrast, conservative.

The increasing use of English in more scholarly contexts after 1500 resulted in misgivings about its ability to survive. Compared with the fixity and predictability of Ciceronian Latin—by now a well and truly "dead" language—it seemed all too subject to change. The desire to "fix" English, so that matter expressed in it would have the same chances of survival as that expressed in the ancient languages, led to attempts by grammarians to legislate for the user; the basis of their legislation was, understandably, the well-known syntax of Latin. A similar concern for durability and respectability underlay the new preoccupation with orthography. Early spelling reformers, especially printers, sought to replace the largely idiosyncratic practices that had sufficed in the pre-printing era with a common system that seemed to them to be more consistently related to the sound system. They were not helped in this enterprise—an enterprise that, incidentally, has continued to exercise the minds of language teachers ever since—by the fact that some of the sounds were themselves currently undergoing major changes. A complex process that led to an altered distribution of all the long vowels of English, known to philologists as the Great Vowel Shift, began in the latter part of the Middle English period but was not completed until after Shakespeare's time. For his audiences *Rome* and *room, raisin* and *reason* had similar pronunciations.

In bringing this sketch of the development of English to the beginning of the Modern English period, we have already reached the stage where its internal history and its external history react upon each other. The astonishing—and, as some thought, excessive—openness of English to new vocabulary resulted in the adoption of words not only from every major European language, but also from the more exotic languages of remoter lands to which it was now being carried. In the following paragraphs we note something of the effect of local languages and conditions upon the speech of English-speaking settlers not only in vocabulary, but in grammar and pronunciation also. An important aspect of the more recent development of British English has been its absorption of features from the new regional varieties to which geographical dispersion gave rise. Since no account of language development, however brief, can legitimately omit reference to attitudes, we must recognize that this last tendency has by no means always been welcomed by purists. And if a desire to protect the home-grown product from the effects of outside interference is questionable, the wish to prescribe standards for the much greater number of people who speak English outside the British Isles is even more so.

In the various forms that Standard English now takes there are, in fact, only very slight differences in grammar, and the variations in pronunciation—the numerous local accents—represent no insuperable barrier to intelligibility, however forcibly they may impress themselves upon the listener. As for vocabulary, there is a central core of ordinary, most frequently used words shared by all types of the standard language; and there is also a shared lexicon of highly specialized and technical terms. Between these two lies a considerable body of moderately common words and idioms, and it is here that the major national and local distinctions are to be found: Americanisms, Australianisms, Scotticisms, and so on, all having their own peculiarities of usage.

The differences and distinctions obtaining in the use of English around the world seem hardly likely to wither away. Present conditions seem rather to indicate a gradual increase, and common sense suggests willing acceptance of them as natural and interesting aspects of the language and of the individualities of the people who use it.

English Around the World

by A. J. Aitken, S. R. R. Allsopp, R. K. Bansal, D. Brazil, R. J. Gregg, L. W. Lanham, T. H. Long, Harold Orton, J. M. Sinclair, John Spencer, Loreto Todd, and G. A. Wilkes

The Regional Dialects of England

The question of the existence of a standard pronunciation of English has been the occasion for controversy nowhere more than in the context of discussions of the local and social varieties of the language that coexist within England. Before World War II many believed that a standard form did exist but that it was a class dialect rather than a regional one, flourishing in the public schools, the older universities, the law courts, the higher ranks of the armed forces and the civil service, the BBC, and of course the Royal Court. Having a well-recognized sound system, it was also characterized by the use of a pleasing voice quality, a rhythmical unhurried speech tempo, and a good articulation that was not staccato or too precise and lacked a glottal stop or any trace of regional intonation. This they called "Received Pronunciation" or RP.

Between the World Wars, linguistic historians recognized the existence of modified forms of RP. Having penetrated into the provinces, the socially prestigious speech of London and the Home Counties was modified by local speech habits, which differed from county to county and even from town to town. These modified varieties have since achieved much greater prominence and standing, partly through changed attitudes to English used in broadcasts and partly through the emergence of an influential group from the provincial grammar schools and universities, who have been inclined to resent the stigmatization of their own regional accents. A widely held belief that any pronunciation is good provided it is intelligible and appropriate to its geographical context has also perhaps helped, though a reaction, in the form of a returning preference for RP, is now discernible.

The sounds of RP vary in their realizations within acceptable limits. They also undergo changes. Recently these changes have been less extensive and have been rather obscured by phonological features of educated London English. Nevertheless, the traditional long /ɔː/ before /s/, /f/, and /θ/, as in *cross, off,* and *cloth,* has now given way to the more open vowel /ɒ/; the long /ɑː/ that developed before the same sounds, as in *pass, path,* and *chaff,* has been extended by some speakers to other words such as *plastic, mass,* and *raffia;* the *-ing* of present participles and verbal nouns (*hunting, shooting*) has recovered its /ŋ/; and initial *wh-,* as in *white,* often persists as /hw/.

Among modern trends that seem definitely attributable to the influence of London English is the treatment of the vowels /ɛ/ and /æ/, which, in words like *set* and *sat,* may sound very similar. Many young people in the public eye tend in their speech to retract /æ/ to a type of /a/ similar to a sound long assumed to characterize Northern and Midland English. In so doing they reduce the distinction from the /ʌ/ of *hut,* a sound very similar in quality to /a/. Other London traits involve the pronunciation of /əʊ/ in *boat* rather like /u/, the diphthongization of /iː/ and /uː/, as in *feet* and *boot,* and the representation of /aʊ/ in *mouse* and /aɪ/ in *mice* with an advanced and a retracted first element respectively.

Some of the sounds that serve to differentiate the regional dialects of England can be traced back to Old English. Initial *wh-* is still a vigorous /hw/ in Northumbrian speech; in South Lancashire and the West Midlands a characteristic /g/ ends word like *ring* and *long;* in Northumberland /l/ is clear (like the first *l* in *little*) in all positions, while further south it becomes darker (like the second *l* in *little*) until it almost becomes /u/ in the Home Counties. In the eastern part of the country /r/ before a consonant disappears or is faintly articulated (*farm, fort*), in the south and west it is pronounced with the tongue turned back or reverted, and in Northumbria it is characteristically "throaty" (the Northumberland burr). The pronunciation of the *u* of *cup* and *bun* as /ʊ/, as in standard English *pull,* is a trait commonly found in dialects of much of the north of England (except for the extreme northeast). The absence of initial /h/ is frequently assumed to characterize regional dialects generally; it is, however, still preserved in the extreme north, in East Anglia and Essex, and in Somerset and Wiltshire.

Historical factors have conditioned the lexicon and grammar of the modified forms of standard English as well as their sounds. Many educated northerners do not hesitate to use local vernacular items like *beck, burn,* and *gill* (streams). *Bonny* and *canny* (agreeable) are frequently encountered, as are *body* (a person), *lad, lass, pikelet* (a crumpet), and *scallion* (a spring onion). The word stock of large parts of Northern England, the East Midlands, and East Anglia was greatly enriched as a result of the Viking invasions. Local words like *band* (string), *lop* (flea), *nay, sile, stoop* (a post), and *teem* (pour) come from this source. The ubiquity of *bairn* is due to its double descent from both the Old English and the Old Norse word for *child.* The extent of the choice that may be provided by dialectal variants can be illustrated by the variety of the terms *drawing room, front room, lounge, parlour,* and *sitting room;* and tea may be *made, brewed, mashed, scalded,* or *steeped.*

Dialect usages characteristic of the regions also seem sometimes to spread into varieties of the language that are nearer to high prestige forms. Educated Northerners may use expressions like *I'll be away then; I want this letter posting; The dog wants out;* and *The boy got wrong off* (was punished by) *his father.*

Local historical dialects in England are disappearing faster than ever before, regional peculiarities of pronunciation being supplanted by the sounds of RP or of one of its locally modified varieties. Provincial vocabulary seems, however, more likely to survive, except for the names of things that have themselves become obsolete, such as terms relating to equipment used for thatching, harvesting, or blacksmithing.

The English of Scotland

Until the seventeenth century the national literary and spoken language of Scotland was the northern English dialect known as Older Scots, the ancestor of the modern dialects of the Lowlands, but with the accession of the Stuarts to the English throne in 1603 this began to give way to Standard English as the language of writing. The use of something approximating to educated Standard English as the spoken language of polite society began a little later. But this new Scottish English was shaped and modified by the native Scots that the gentry and intelligentsia had previously spoken. The distinctiveness of the Scots variety of present-day Standard English is attributable to this underlying native tradition.

Its peculiarities include the free use of a very considerable body of Scots vocabulary. Many words associated with special cultural features of Scottish society, like *laird, kirk, ceilidh,* and *Hogmanay,* are as likely to be used by anyone who writes or talks of Scotland as they are by a Scotsman and are hardly to be considered peculiarities of Scottish usage. Neither are the many Scotticisms that have passed into general English usage, largely through the influence of Burns, Scott, and Carlyle, such as *cuddle, eerie, gloaming,* and *greed* (all from Old English) and *clan, pet, slogan,* and *whisky* (from Gaelic). More peculiarly Scottish are those native locutions with which speakers are apt to pepper their English, especially when adopting an informal or explicitly Scottish role: *He's a right old sweetiewife; It's back to auld claes* (old clothes) *and parritch* (porridge) *tomorrow; like a hen on a het* (hot) *girdle;* or similarly used "couthy" words like *dreich, peeliewally,* and *scunner.* But in addition to such obvious and deliberate Scotticisms, most Scottish speakers of English also employ usages the Scottishness of which they may be scarcely aware of: *Is that you away then?* (Are you about to leave?); *I put her gas at a peep* (I deflated her); *to come up one's back* (occur to one), and, of course, the ubiquitous preposition *outwith.*

The grammar of spoken Scottish English has one or two minor rules of its own, such as the avoidance of *isn't* and *won't,* for which *'s not* and *'ll not* are regularly substituted, and the use of the form *mines* in *that's mines.*

The variety is most Scottish, however, in its pronunciation. Characteristic forms are /lɛnθ/ and /strɛnθ/ (for *length* and *strength*), and /lʊdʒ/ and /lʊdʒər/ (for *lodge* and *lodger*); the "full" pronunciation of items like *raspberry, Wednesday,* and *tortoise;* and disyllabic versions of words like *elm, burn,* and *whirl.* Many sounds, particularly the vowels and *wh-, r,* and *l,* have special Scottish pronunciations, and there is an extra consonant, /x/, heard in words like *loch, Buchan,* and *Brechin.* Whereas *aunt* and *ant* are usually pronounced alike, *oar, or,* and *awe,* which are indistinguishable in the speech of London and certain other kinds of English, are quite distinct in Scots.

Scottish English is exceptional among other kinds of

English in having no true long vowels: the vowel in *seed* and *seat* is short. On the other hand, there is marked lengthening of certain vowels in particular positions: the verb *close* ending with /z/ has a much longer vowel than the adjective *close* which ends in /s/. Related to this is the long diphthong in words like *five* and *rise*, which can be compared with the short diphthong in *fife* and *rice*. This last phenomenon, which is observable also in Ulster Scots (Scotch-Irish standard speech), can be shown to result from sound changes occurring around the year 1600.

Apart from the educated Scottish English to which the foregoing notes apply, many other types exist, particularly among rural speakers, who have additional dialect features in their pronunciations. Working-class people in Glasgow and Edinburgh also have features that are widely regarded, by speakers who do not have them, as debased or slovenly. They include pronunciation habits like the tendency to replace non-initial /p/, /k/, or /t/ by the glottal stop, and special usages of vocabulary and grammar: *You'll be away to the bingo, eh, no?; She's awfie tatty-peelin* (stuck up); *I shouldnae never went.* At the other extreme are the varieties of Scottish speech that have been strongly influenced by the RP of the Scottish gentry and by broadcasting, of which the "Morningside" and "Kelvinside" types are regarded by many Scots as comical. Yet another set of distinguishing features separates the "Highland English" and "Island English" from all these dialects, which share a typically Lowland provenance. The most important of such features are those that derive from speech habits originally native to Scottish Gaelic and from the fact that English was for long a "school-book" language in the Highlands and Islands.

The influence of the earlier Celtic tongue is by and large less noticeable in the English used in Wales. However, its effect on Irish English merits greater attention.

Irish English

All the varieties of English currently heard in Ireland have their origins in the Elizabethan period. The English that developed in the Pale around Dublin at that time is frequently called Anglo-Irish. It was based mainly on the northwest Midland dialects of England. This was the type of English that, encroaching everywhere on the native Gaelic, spread south and west and as far north as the Ulster border. The survival of Gaelic dialects there stopped its advance and separated it from a northern version of Anglo-Irish, which had similarly originated in the English Midlands but entered Ireland by way of Belfast and the Lagan valley. The differences that are nowadays observable between the northern and southern dialects arise for the most part from differences in the substratum of Gaelic speech.

Similarities include many characteristically Irish vocabulary items that are widely distributed throughout the whole island: *blarney, galore, slug* (swig, drink), *smithereens*, and *twig* (to understand, find out) are all of Gaelic origin. Some of the special vocabulary—*banshee* and *keen* (lament for the dead), for instance—is naturally related to Irish folk culture and has thus attained wider currency. Syntactic peculiarities shared by North and South are exemplified in: *He is just after finishing his work; She has a desperate cold on her; I have a terrible drooth* (drought) *on me* (I am very thirsty); *I wonder will she go.* All these arise from a literal translation of the Gaelic. Among the distinctive phonological features is the universal retention of final and preconsonantal /r/, which has a semi-vocalic articulation that seems to have arisen in Elizabethan times. Irish English further agrees in giving the lateral /l/ a "bright" or "clear" resonance as in French. "Pure" long vowels generally occur where many other varieties of English have diphthongs: thus /de:/ is preferred to /deɪ/ as a pronunciation of *day*, and /go:/ to /gəʊ/ for *go*. The vowel in words like *pat* or *mat* is pronounced with the tongue lower in the mouth than in most other regional types. The slight lip-rounding observable everywhere in the Irish English vowel in words like *putt* is paralleled in some Northern English dialects.

Northern Anglo-Irish was considerably influenced by its contacts with Lowland Scottish dialects that were introduced into Ulster during the Jacobean period. The influence has been sufficiently strong to give rise to the expression *Scotch Irish*, used originally in North America to distinguish all types of Ulster accents from the so-called southern Irish brogue. Much of the distinctive vocabulary of the North is of Scottish origin. It includes *byre* (cow house), *corn* (oats), *dander* or *danner* (stroll), *lift* (steal), and *mind* (remember). Ulster speakers resemble some Scots also in pronouncing words like *too* or *prove* with a very advanced central vowel somewhat like that in the French word *tu*.

The southern variety is often distinguished from that of the north by the use of a different dialectal form, or set of forms, for a particular notion. Thus the concept "left-handed"—including all the social and superstitious implications proper to the Irish environment—is expressed by *clootie, flyuggy*, etc., in the north, but by *kittagh, kittogue*, etc., in the south. The most conspicuous pronunciation trait of the south is the treatment of the fricatives /θ/ and /ð/, a dental variety of /t/ or /d/ being used at the beginning of words like *thin* and *then*. These sounds are, however, quite distinct from the alveolar /t/ and /d/ that are regularly used in *tin* and *den*. Ulster speakers normally have the usual English fricatives.

An interesting feature of the English of most parts of Ireland is the survival of pronunciations characteristic of earlier stages in the development of the language in England. We can instance /te:/ (*tea*), /'de:sənt/ (*decent*), /kürs/ (*course*), /'lɑ:ndrɪ/ (*laundry*), and /'so:dʒər/ (*soldier*).

American English

The development of English in the United States may be traced in three historical stages. The first of these, the colonial period, dates from the settlement of Jamestown in 1607 (followed shortly, in 1620, by the arrival of the Puritans in New England) to about 1790, the date of the ratification of the Constitution of an independent United States. The settlers in Virginia and New England spoke a seventeenth-century English that was predominantly that of the southern counties of England. Although regional dialects never developed the distinctive characteristics they have in England, some of the local variation that does exist can be traced to this time. Subsequent settlement of the Middle Atlantic States was influenced by the ideals of William Penn, and the population of these areas, in particular colonial Pennsylvania, was less uniformly Anglo-Saxon in origin. The presence there of a large number of immigrants from Ulster and, after an agreement made with Penn in 1683, of Palatinate Germans, has been a factor of continuing linguistic significance.

The second stage of development runs from 1790 to about the time of the Civil War (1860). This period saw two important developments. There was an expansion southwards and westwards from the thirteen original Atlantic colonies, across the Appalachian Mountains that had temporarily confined them, and on to the Pacific. In addition, new waves of immigrants arrived, this time from Ireland, after the famine of 1845, and from Germany after 1848. At the end of this period, the population was still predominantly British by origin, as it had been at the beginning, but it now included a higher proportion of other Northern European immigrants.

The most recent phase, from about 1860 to the present, witnessed massive immigration from southern Europe and from the Slavonic countries. This last development seems to have had little effect on American English with the exception of New York and its environs, where certain influences on speech and vocabulary are discernible.

The first of these three periods is responsible for certain archaisms that survive in American English. Forms like *gotten* (the past participle of *get*), *sick*, with its general instead of its restrictive sense, and *I guess* meaning *I suppose*, exemplify this linguistic conservatism, the latter having been standard in England as early as the fourteenth century. Such evidences of conservatism are, however, far less representative than developments that show the facility of the language for innovation. Contemporary American speech differs as much from the language of the colonists as modern British English differs from the seventeenth- and eighteenth-century speech of England.

The vocabulary of American English began to change at first contact with the new environment. Words were borrowed from Indians and from other Europeans, and native English words were adapted to new meanings. From the Indian languages came a number of words for flora and fauna and other terms relating to Indian life: *canoe, caucus, hickory, hominy, moccasin, opossum, pecan, raccoon, skunk, squash* (a vegetable marrow), *tapioca*, and *toboggan*. From Dutch settlers the colonists borrowed *boss, cookie*, and *coleslaw*, and from the French *chowder* and *bureau*. Perhaps the most famous example of an existing English word being borrowed for a new use is *corn*, a development that occurred when the adjective was dropped from the colonists' original phrase, *Indian corn*. The term *maize* entered British English as a Spanish loan word at the same time as the specialized use of *corn* was becoming established in America.

The pattern of settlement in the seventeenth and eighteenth centuries has left its mark on the dialects of present-day America. Three large speech areas are conventionally distinguished: *Northern* (New England and New York State), *Midland* (Pennsylvania and New Jersey and along the Blue Ridge mountains south to Georgia), and *Southern* (southern Delaware and Virginia along the Atlantic coast and west to the foothills in the Carolinas and Georgia). Within these large areas, eighteen dialects have been identified. Discussion of the sound patterns of American English involves reference not only to the way they differ from British English but also consideration of how the dialects—at least the three major ones—differ from each other.

The retention of final and preconsonantal /r/, which tends to be dropped in Britain, for instance, is characteristic of Midland American but is not a feature of Eastern New England or of all Southern dialects. Another feature of American speech, sometimes wrongly assumed to characterize all dialects, is the vowel /æ/ in such words as *fast, laugh, grass*, etc. In Eastern New England and Virginia, a so-called broad *a* /ɑ/ is often used, the quality of which more closely resembles that of the comparable vowel in southern British English. A distinction that does hold between British English and most American English is in the treatment of *o*, which American English tends to make unrounded as /ɑ/ in such words as *rob, stop*, and *hop*. This, like the use of /iː/ in *either* and *neither*, is a survival of the pronunciation that was current in Britain at the time of colonization. Finally, we may note the tendency, which has increased in America in recent years, to pronounce words like *duke, new*, and *Tuesday* with /uː/ instead of /juː/, in sharp contrast with British usage.

Two further characteristics that differentiate much American speech from British may be noted. One is that the Northern American dialects have less variety in pitch-pattern. The second is the preservation of the secondary accent in polysyllabic words, especially those ending in *-ory, -ary*, or *-ery*. The contrast with British pronunciation in *ordinary, dictionary, secretary, temporary*, etc., is noticeable in all American speech.

Many specific differences between American and British English were listed by H. L. Mencken in *The American Language* (first edition 1919). Since the publication of that book, various influences have operated to reduce these differences, among them films, radio, television, and the growth since the 1950s and 1960s of an international youth culture grounded in a common popular music (rock). Most often, resulting changes have been in favour of terminology originating in America. Nevertheless, much of the diversity represented by Mencken's list still exists:

US	UK
apartment	flat
baby carriage	pram
broiled (meat)	grilled
candy	sweets
cookie	biscuit
cotton (absorbent)	cotton wool
daylight-saving time	summer time
druggist	chemist
elevator	lift
instalment plan	hire purchase
oatmeal (boiled)	porridge
second floor	first floor
sidewalk	pavement
spigot (*or* faucet)	tap
suspenders (men's)	braces
undershirt	vest *or* singlet
water heater	geyser
checkers (game)	draughts
deck (cards)	pack
gasoline, gas	petrol
hood (car)	bonnet
intermission (theatre)	interval
legal holiday	bank holiday
vacation	holiday
windshield (car)	windscreen

Finally, there are minor differences between preferred spellings. Among them are the American preference for *-er* in *center, fiber*, and *theater; -or* in *honor, color, humor; -se* instead of *-ce* in *defense* and *offense;* and undoubled intervocalic consonants in certain words such as *jeweler, marvelous*, and *traveling*. The majority of these differences are traceable to the lexicographer Noah Webster's interest in spelling reform. Although his earlier writings on the subject argued for radical changes based on phonetic spelling, he gradually modified his view. The system used in his *American Dictionary* (1828) was adopted in America and accounts for most of the distinguishing features of modern American orthography.

Canadian English

The early history of Canadian English resembles that of American English. In the early days of settlement the language used was that of contemporary Britain. Features have persisted from this time, supplying a conservative element in present-day speech. Innovations, subsequently made in response to the new environment, led to differentiation that eventually produced a distinctive brand of English that is said to sound like American to Britons and like British to Americans. After the War of American Independence a political boundary separating Canada from the United States encouraged linguistic differentiation. Since then, the continuous contacts to the south on the one hand and the uninterrupted flow of immigrants to Canada from Britain on the other have maintained cultural and linguistic links with both countries.

Many additions to the lexicon resulted from the contacts the Canadians made with the various indigenous Indian and Eskimo peoples, as well as the languages of other groups of settlers from many parts of the Old World. In pioneer days they borrowed many words from Canadian French: *bateau* (flat-bottomed riverboat), *brulé* (area of forest destroyed by fire), *coureur de bois, habitant* (a French Canadian, esp. a farmer), *mush* (a command to sled dogs, from French *marche!*), *charivari* or *shivaree*, and *snye* (side channel of a river, from Canadian French *chenail*). More recent borrowings from Canadian French include *anglophone* and *francophone* (referring respectively to English and French speakers and *tuque* (a long knitted woollen cap, as worn by skiers).

From the native Indian languages came many terms, including the following ultimately from Algonquian sources in Eastern and Central Canada: *babiche* (thongs of rawhide), *bogan*, otherwise *pokelogan* or *logan* (a sluggish sidestream), *carcajou, caribou, kinninnick, muskeg, pemmican*, and *totem*. The contributions of the languages of British Columbia frequently came in through the Chinook Jargon, an Indian-based trade or contact language current in pioneer days west of the Rockies and as far north as the Yukon. Among them were: *chuck* (a body of water), *klahanie* (the great outdoors), *mowitch* (deer), and *tillicum* (friend). The Tlingit language has contributed *hooch,* shortened from *hootchinoo,* which has now passed into general English. From Eskimo Canadian English acquired *anorak, Innuit* (Eskimo), *komatik, malamute, mukluk, Nanook, parka, igloo,* and *kayak.*

Educated Canadian English probably still reflects the spoken norms of the eighteenth century to a large extent. It shares with Midland American the conservative habit of articulating final and preconsonantal /r/. Another early feature is the voicing of medial /t/ in words like *better, patio,* and *little* (/'bɛdər/, /'pædiˌou/, /'lɪdᵊl/); and yet another is the loss of /t/ following /n/, as in *winter* /'wɪnər/ and *Toronto* /'trɑnou/.

The Canadian vocalic system is on the whole very similar to that of General American, but has normally only ten vowels, as illustrated in the following series of words: *beet, bit, bait, bet, bat, bought, butt, boat, boot.* The tenth vowel, that of *pull,* is in contrast with that in *pool* (which is the same as that in *boot*). The words *cot* and *caught* usually rhyme in Canada.

Most characteristic, however, is the Canadian treatment of diphthongs. Speakers in England and the U.S. have generally only one type of diphthong in words like *rye, ride,* and *right,* namely /aɪ/. Canadians agree for the first two items, but have a different diphthong, [əi], for the third, which occurs in all such cases where the following consonant is voiceless, for instance *ripe, hike, life,* and *ice.* Similarly, in words like *now, loud,* and *lout,* Canadian English resembles other types in having /au/ for the first two, but differs in having [ʌu] for the last.

Americans will also notice that the choice of vowel is different in *docile,* /'dousəɪl/ not /'dɒsᵊl/, and in *lever,* /'liːvər/ not /'lɛvər/. Britons, on the other hand, will notice the use of /'mɪsᵊl/ instead of /'mɪsaɪl/ for *missile.*

English of the Caribbean

The history of the English language in the Caribbean dates from the settlement of St. Christopher (St. Kitts) in 1624 and Barbados in 1627. The core of Caribbean English is British English. Modified by the African background of many of its speakers since that first settlement, it has also been subjected to the linguistic influences of French, Spanish, Dutch, and Asian Indian. Portuguese and Chinese have also left their marks. In more recent times, the nearness of the United States, its economic prestige, its cinema and broadcasting, and its black ethnic and cultural sympathies have produced further considerable effects.

All these ingredients mix to produce local varieties at the social bottom of a continuum, the top end of which is the national form of the standard language we may call *Caribbean English,* the variety aspired to by educated speakers. Vocabulary items show the effect of these many influences well. They include survivals from British dialects such as *fig* (a segment of an orange), *gie* (give), and *kerfuffle;* older English words (*glebe land, proven*); and everyday expressions whose use may be related to the influence of the Anglican Church (*beforetime, bounden duty, whosoever*). From African sources have come such items as *ackee, bakra, kokobeh,* and *Quashi,* and many calques (literal translations) based on African substructures, such as *cut one's eye on, day-clean,* and *force-ripe.* Many plant and animal names are of Amerindian origin (*cassava, manatee,* etc.). European elements other than those of British English include, from French, *crapaud* and *dasheen* (from *chou de Chine*), while *pannier* replaces *basket* in many areas. From Dutch come *mawger* and *paal,* and from Spanish *mamaguy* and *mustee* (from *mestizo*). The postslavery immigrations of workers have introduced many Hindu, Muslim, and Chinese terms to do with food, clothing, etc. (*dhoti, chow mein*). Other recent acquisitions have come from informal American English.

The Caribbean life style and culture have produced lexical and idiomatic forms of their own: *Berbice chair, jump-up* (a celebration or dance), *good hair,* etc. Some are now international: *calypso, reggae, steel band, obeah, Rastafarian.* Moreover, in the Caribbean some standard English words take on different meanings. *Breakfast,* among older people, means the midday meal; *bath* and *bathe* refer chiefly to showering; *galvanize* is used as a noun meaning corrugated iron sheeting; and *wares* regularly means crockery.

The pronunciation of Caribbean English is remarkable for its characteristically wide-ranging intonation patterns, probably the result of early phonological influences from African languages. A peculiarity of the distribution of stress in relation to pitch treatment is illustrated in the pronunciation of a word like *biscuit,* which often is pronounced with the main stress on the first syllable (as in standard English) but with a higher pitch level in the second. A few of the many distinguishing segmental features may be singled out. There are fewer vowels and diphthongs than in standard English. The vowel in *fat* is /a/, intermediate between the RP pronunciation of *a* in *fat* and *father.* The RP diphthongs in *bare, beer,* and *bait* are replaced by the same pure vowel /eː/. The vowels in *hot* and *fall* are more open than their RP counterparts. The ending *-ing* is pronounced /ɪn/, and forms of /t/ and /d/ replace the fricatives /θ/ and /ð/.

Non-standard Caribbean English is a form of creole, noticed in more detail at the end of this article. In it, inflections and tense distinctions may be abandoned, and this, combined with functional shifts in syntax, results in sentences like: *de two son tek de fader car go Georgetown las' night* (the two sons took their father's car and went to Georgetown last night); *dey unfairin you* (they're cheating you). Echoic interjections abound, and language at all levels is enlivened by gestures.

The English of Australia and New Zealand

The types of English spoken in Australia and New Zealand have much in common, chiefly because of links in the histories of the two countries, their geographical propinquity, and the continual close contact that has existed between them. Yet the two varieties are distinct from each other in certain details of pronunciation and vocabulary.

The settlement established in New South Wales in 1788 inherited the language of England, Scotland, Ireland, and Wales, including its dialect forms, but Australian English soon began to take a different direction. This was partly because of the new vocabulary supplied by the environment, partly because existing words acquired new senses and applications, and partly because some words, especially those from dialect, survived in Australia after they fell into disuse in Britain. The first source of the new vocabulary was the aboriginal languages, which were responsible for the names of various animals (*kangaroo, dingo, wallaby, wombat,* and the mythical *bunyip*), of birds (*brolga, corella*), of fish (*barramundi, morwong*), of trees (*kurrajong, belah*), of natural features (*billabong, bombora*), and of some artefacts (*waddy, dillybag, gunyah*). Some of these terms, like *boomerang,* have become part of international English.

Another source of Australian vocabulary was the convict system itself, which gave new meaning to words like *assignment* and *special.* The argot of the convicts introduced such words as *shake* in the sense of "steal" and *scale* in the sense of "defraud." Various English dialects were the sources for terms regarded as Australian in origin, such as *dinkum* in the sense of "authentic" or "genuine," *cobber, larrikin, bowyangs, wowser, barrack, bodger, barney, dunny, skerrick,* and *sollicker.*

With the extension of settlement, new terms naturally arose to describe new conditions, and the occupations of rural Australia had a marked effect on vocabulary. *Spinney, coppice,* and *dell* were replaced by more appropriate terms such as *outback, backblocks,* and *back country,* with *stockman, boundary rider,* and *squatter* for those who inhabited such regions. The sheep or cattle *station, pastoral* management, *rouseabout, wood-and-water joey, sundowner* or *remittance man, swagman,* and *bushranger* also originated in rural or bush life.

The gold discoveries of the mid-nineteenth century brought an influx of immigrants and the terminology of another industry, producing terms like *mullock, fossick, nuggety,* and *duffer.* The immigrants from North America brought some terms that became established as Australianisms—by adoption, not origin—especially *digger* (for any miner) and the expressions *up a gumtree* and *stir the possum.* The influx of Chinese gave currency to the derogatory term *Chow.*

A distinctive language of city life was slower to emerge. What passed as "Sydney" and "Australian" slang in the 1890s was still predominantly English. An exception might be found in a handful of terms with criminal associations, like *bludger, drum* (for brothel), *keep nit,* and later *standover,* but even these are in the nature of extensions of existing words. Most of the "rhyming slang" heard in Australia even now is English rather than Australian. Instances of Australian inventions in this field are rare: *on one's pat* for "alone" (Pat Malone), *babbler* for "cook" (babbling brook), *oscar* for "cash" (Oscar Asche, the actor), and more recently *septic* for "Yank" (septic tank).

Of the words with social or nationalistic overtones, the most interesting is *pommy.* Although its origin is uncertain, immigrants from England in the earlier nineteenth century were already being called *jimmygrants,* or *jimmies* for short. Before the first World War *jimmygrant* had become associated with *pomegranate,* and Xavier Herbert in his autobiography *Disturbing Element* recalls in his childhood jeering at newly arrived migrants in heavy British clothing: "Jimmygrants, Pommygranates, Pommies!" It has never been a favourable term.

World War II was responsible for more additions to Australian English. Some of them, like *choco* (for "chocolate soldier") or *munga* (for food) were revivals from the past, but experience in new theatres of war gave rise to *troppo* (nervously affected by conditions in the tropics) and *jungle juice* (improvised alcoholic drink). *To come the raw prawn,* in the sense of seeking an advantage, trying to impose on someone, dates from the war years, as do *earbasher* and *spinebasher,* with *jack up* for a collective refusal of orders and *pull your head in* for "come off it."

The formation of words by abbreviation, often to produce a diminutive ending in *-ie* or *-o,* is a common feature of Australian English. The *bottle-o* and the *milko* go back to the turn of the century, as does the *rabbit-o.* The *schoolie,* the *postie,* and the *trammie* were established by the 1920s, though the habit of taking a *sickie* has grown since, and the *hostie* had to wait the development of commercial aviation. In Australia the abbreviation *super* can refer to the superintendent on a station, to superphosphate, or to superannuation benefits, and a *semi* can be a semi-detached house, a semi-trailer, or a semi-final in a sporting competition.

Some misunderstandings can arise from the way in which Australian English has drawn away from British English, when words held in common have come to denote different things. The *never never* in Australia refers to regions remote from settlement, not to hire purchase. A *spell* is an interval of rest, not another turn of work. A *scallop* in Australia is not only a shellfish and a dress-making term, but also a flat slice of potato cooked in batter. *Maggoty* means angry or irritated; *snags* are sausages. A *theatre* is commonly a "picture theatre," or what is elsewhere a *cinema.* A *radiator* may be a portable electric fire, not a fixed heating system. To be *crook* is to be ill, not dishonest. *Hooray* has the meaning of "goodbye."

In New Zealand—in which, incidentally, a Scottish linguistic element survives in the predominantly Scottish settlement of Otago—borrowings from the languages of the indigenous populations have been even more numerous than those adopted in Australia. This is a consequence of the Maori's readier adaptation to European social institutions. New Zealand's pattern of settlement by separate groupings of free settlers has resulted in a degree of regional conservation, which contrasts with the dialectal homogeneity of Australia, the result of the mobility of the work force during the gold rush and subsequent seasonal employment.

Differences in the vocabularies reflect differences in the two countries: *bush* has a different significance in the two countries because of dissimilarities in flora and terrain; *farm,* respectable enough in New Zealand, implies *smallholding* in Australia. *Football* in New Zealand usually implies rugby, while in Australia it means rugby league or soccer or, especially in Victoria and South Australia, *Australian rules.*

A pronunciation feature that distinguishes both Australian and New Zealand English from British varieties is the treatment of /ɑː/ in words like *part,* the tongue being brought further forward than for the corresponding RP vowel. In New Zealand only, a point of divergence is found in the pronunciation of /ɪ/ in *pit,* for which the tongue is more retracted and slightly lower in the mouth than it is in Australia. What is popularly known as "the Australian accent" (designated Broad Australian by phoneticians) is most readily identified by six sounds:

/eɪ/ as in *praise.* In Broad Australian this tends towards /ʌɪ/, so that *praise* may be heard (though not by another speaker of Broad Australian) as *prize.*

/əʊ/ as in *dough.* This tends towards /ʌʊ/ in Broad Australian.

/iː/ as in *me.* This tends towards the diphthong /əɪ/.

/uː/ as in *boot.* This tends towards the diphthong /əʊ/.

/aɪ/ as in *buy.* This tends towards /ɑɪ/, so that *buy* may be heard as *boy.*

/aʊ/ as in *house.* This tends towards /æʊ/, sometimes with nasalization.

English in Africa

English as a mother tongue was not fully and firmly established on the African continent until the 19th century. Notably instrumental in this process were the 1820 settlers, a group of some four thousand British colonists who took up residence along the eastern borders of the Cape colony. They were a heterogeneous group representing several social and regional British dialects, but within two generations a distinctive South African English had emerged, in which the original speech variations had coalesced into a more or less uniform dialect characterized particularly by speech habits derived from those of the working and lower middle classes of Southeast England, especially London. For example, the tongue positions for the vowels /æ/ and /ɛ/, being higher and more advanced than they are for RP, reflect even in present-day South African English a feature of later 18th-century London pronunciation that is also evident in the semiliterate phonetic spellings of early colonists: *yis* for *yes, kittle* for *kettle, eksel* for *axle.*

These early colonists adapted themselves to their new environment by borrowing from the already implanted Dutch (later Afrikaans) language and to a lesser extent from the indigenous Bantu languages and Khoisan (Hottentot, etc.).

The early efforts of educators were vigorously in the direction of inculcating the grammar and usage prescribed by the middle-class doctrine of correctness that prevailed in late eighteenth- and nineteenth-century Britain. The grammar of South African English differs little, therefore, from the standard southern British form of the language. In vocabulary and usage the more picturesque colloquialisms and slang words disappeared early on, as did those socially stigmatized features of pronunciation that were probably present in the speech of the settlers.

The industrial changes consequent upon the discovery of gold and diamonds significantly changed linguistic attitudes during the late nineteenth and early twentieth centuries. In the new mining and industrial cities, a high social value was placed upon the RP of the British middle classes, to the detriment of both South African English and other British dialects. This attitude, characteristic of urban rather than rural society, continued to prevail among the most influential groups until World War II. Since then, South African English, which had been preserved in the rural areas of its origin, has once again been heard in all sections of society.

Generally, however, rural society was and has remained predominantly Afrikaaner. Since the 1920s, the contact between speakers of English and speakers of Afrikaans has resulted in further vocabulary acquisitions, like *platteland* and *verkrampte;* and pronunciation change such as the rendering of *sin* and *did* with a vowel like the second one of *enter* are probably due to the same cause. The influence of Afrikaans grammar is evident in locutions like *Will you come with?* and *I will throw you with a stone* (I will hit you with a stone). The influence of Bantu and other indigenous African languages has continued to be comparatively weak.

In addition to the one and three-quarter million Whites and some half million Indians who use English as a mother tongue in South Africa, several million Africans and Afrikaans-speaking Whites employ it competently as a second language. The Indian population share with the latter groups a distinctive dialect and accent, which makes its own contribution to the richness and vitality of South African English.

West Africa is the first of the regions considered so far in which the chief importance of English is associated with its status as a second language. It has this status for many speakers in Gambia, Liberia, Sierra Leone, Ghana, Nigeria, and Cameroon. (These states are themselves interspersed between other West African countries that were formerly French colonies and in which French is a lingua franca.) In the first five of these states English is the sole medium of education beyond the first few years of primary school, the main administrative and legislative language, the medium for journalism and broadcasting, and the vehicle for science, technology, large-scale business, and international communication. In the western sector of the Republic of Cameroon it fulfils a similar range of functions, sharing them with French elsewhere in that country. The whole of West Africa is extremely fragmented linguistically, several hundred indigenous languages being in use in the area. In consequence, English serves as a lingua franca for mobile educated West Africans both within and between these states. It is, therefore, *de facto,* if not always *de jure,* a national language for each of them and for their combined population of nearly 100 millions.

Historically, English was first used along the West African coast as a contact language between English traders and the Africans with whom they had dealings. The first recorded instance of West Africans being taught English was in 1554, when an English merchant from Bristol took back five inhabitants of the Guinea coast to learn the language, later returning with them to act as interpreters. As the slave trade increased in the seventeenth and eighteenth centuries, a pidginized variety of English developed along the coast, used not only between European and African but also among the Africans themselves. Freed slaves were settled in Freetown (Sierra Leone) from the end of the eighteenth century, and in Liberia they brought with them a creolized English developed in the slave plantations of the New World. Pidginized and creolized forms continue to be used today alongside standard English. The spread of the western type of education through missionary effort and colonial rule from the nineteenth century onwards gradually extended literacy in English, encouraged the use of the standard form, and gave it high prestige.

Some of the terms peculiar to West African English have resulted from calques or loan translations, especially those for institutions or objects of a traditional kind, as for instance *outdooring,* the traditional ceremony of naming a baby on its first appearance out of doors, practised particularly in Ghana. Others are compounds such as *palm wine,* the drink produced by tapping the palm tree, or *head-tie,* a cloth tied in traditional fashion on the heads of women. Some common English words have special collocations and senses: *on seat* means available for consultation, and is normally used of officials; *been-to,* used either as a noun or attributively, signifies someone who has studied in England. Words borrowed from local languages include *kente,* a handwoven cloth from Ghana. Many words in colloquial use have come from pidginized English: *chop* (food or to eat), *pass* (to serve drinks or food), *pickin* (small child—from Portuguese), etc.

The pronunciation of English in West Africa is variable, depending on the degree to which the phonetic imprint of the first language has been eradicated. There is thus as yet no stable, homogeneous pronunciation. Such general phonetic characteristics as have begun to emerge are mainly distinctive prosodic features relating to syllabification and rhythm.

English is so extensively used in West Africa that slang and colloquial idioms are constantly created and local languages drawn upon for special use. In its written form, however, the language tends to conform to the norms of standard English. Only in Liberia, which has a long history of contact with the United States, is the American variety preferred to the British.

As an expanding second language, the future development of West African English and the processes whereby it accommodates itself to local needs seem unlikely to follow precisely the pattern of change and adaptation observed among native English-speaking communities. While colloquial English is likely to be marked in varying degrees by the continuing contact with African languages and pidginized English, formal and written usage may be expected to conform to internationally accepted norms, except where creative demands or special semantic needs force the language to extend its resources in particular situations.

The present status of English elsewhere on the African continent can usually be related to the availability or non-availability of an indigenous language enjoying sufficiently general currency to serve as a lingua franca. In Zambia, for instance, a survey conducted in 1970–71 by the local broadcasting service identified eleven different language groups; in this situation English serves as the language of education and public life in spite of objections by Zambian teachers, academics, and publicists. By contrast, the linguistically homogeneous state of Lesotho, though ranking English as a second official language, uses Sesotho for many official and semi-official purposes, including its national newspapers. In Malawi, although Chichewa is used as a lingua franca by the majority of the population, English holds a prestigious position among an educated minority. The government of Tanzania has actively promoted the replacement of English by Swahili for all public matters since 1974. In neighbouring Kenya, the very firmly established role of English as a school subject and as a gateway to professional preferment will probably make a similar policy more difficult to implement.

The linguistic complexity that results from the needs—often conflicting ones—for effective communication and the satisfaction of national aspirations makes it difficult to identify particular varieties of English in these countries. It means also that any useful attempt to relate distinctive features, whether of lexis, grammar, or pronunciation, to historical development or the influence of local languages is far beyond the scope of such an introductory article as this.

English in Asia

The situation in Asia is no easier to describe in summary terms, although the use of English in Asia, as in Africa, is best established in those areas that were formerly part of the British Empire. In the nineteenth century English became the medium of higher education, the language of administration, and the lingua franca among the educated population of the whole of the Indo-Pakistan subcontinent. Since the end of British rule in 1947 it has been in competition, to differing degrees, with Hindi in India, with Urdu in Pakistan and, more recently, with Bengali in Bangladesh. In India it has retained the status of associate official language and is still widely used by educated people. In Pakistan it is the language in which the business of government, the higher courts of law, and higher academic studies are normally conducted. Since the political separation of Bangladesh from Pakistan, the teaching and use of English in the former has declined sharply, partly because it is no longer necessary as a link between the two areas of what was formerly a single Muslim state.

The English of India itself shares a number of features with the versions in use in the neighbouring states, all of which resulted ultimately from the influence of the British Raj. Its special vocabulary includes on the one hand words from Indian languages commonly used in English-language books, journals, and newspapers published in India and on the other words that relate particularly to Indian contexts or that have acquired a special form of meaning in India. In the first category are words having mythological, philosophical, or religious reference: *Buddha, Ram, Shiva, yoga,* etc. Others are concerned with political activity (*bandh, hartal, Naxalite, satyagraha*), sociology (*adivasi, Harijan, Sarvodaya, Swadeshi*), clothing (*dhoti, sari*), administration (*Panchayat, Pradesh, Zila*), titles (*mahatma, sahib, sardar*), food (*dal, puree, pan*) and music (*sarangi, tabla*). In the second category are, firstly, words like *Anglo-Indian, Aryan, betel, cardamom, caste, chariot, chilli,* and *turban,* and secondly, words and phrases like *Akademi, basic education, Gandhi cap, Congress, gazetted officer, mass leave,* and *quarters.*

The pronunciation of English in India differs from other varieties very considerably. Here, only some of the more noticeable differences can be indicated. For example, vowel length is not maintained consistently. Words like *cot* and *caught* are pronounced alike; the vowels in the two syllables of a word like *butter* have a similar pronunciation; pairs like *shot/short, coat/court,* and *shut/shirt* are distinguished only by the presence of /r/ in the second.

There are also differences in the distribution of stress as between Indian English and British varieties. This affects both the occurrence of stressed syllables within words and the way stress is related to word classes: grammatical words like articles, pronouns, auxiliary verbs, and prepositions are sometimes stressed while content words may lack stress. A feature related to this is the intonation pattern, which often imposes different groupings of sentence constituents from those that a speaker of British English would expect, and distributes the emphasis among words in a way that can sound confusing. Another related feature is the tendency for unstressed syllables to retain their "full" value instead of being reduced to /ə/ or /ɪ/.

Indian speakers often use a weak /ʊ/ for both /v/ and /w/. /p/, /t/, and /k/ are always unaspirated. Dental forms of aspirated /t/ and unaspirated /d/ replace the fricatives /θ/ and /ð/ in words like *thin* and *then,* while the sounds /t/ and /d/ are sometimes retroflex.

Grammatical divergences can be illustrated by the following example from Indian English: *They want that the number should be fixed* (They want the number to be fixed). *Would* is often used where standard usage would have *will,* and there are characteristic differences in the use of the definite article.

Further east, English has an important role in Malaysia and Singapore. In the latter its increasing use in higher education is recognized in the emphasis on bilingualism in schools. In Malaysia its use is still widespread, in spite of its being officially superseded by Bahasa Malaysia as the language used in government offices and official correspondence. The popular tendency to lump together the English of Singapore with that of, for instance, Kuala Lumpur, is probably an oversimplification. Research yet to be undertaken is likely to reveal systematic differences due to the predominant Chinese and Malaysian influences respectively. Vocabulary differences reflect cultural differences—as for example the Chinese custom of giving *red packets* at the Chinese New Year. English is also important as a language of business and administration in Hong Kong, and as a second language in Japan and the Philippines. In the latter two countries the influence of American English may be detected, in contrast with the countries where English is a legacy of the British Empire.

Creoles and Pidgins

English is in fact now used as a lingua franca of business, science, and sport almost everywhere in the world, whether or not it is spoken as a native language. Its status as a world language has been developing for several centuries, and in the process many exotic varieties, widely different from the native tongue of London, have grown up in places where the influence of the source country has been slight. One such language is Neo-Melanesian, the official language of Papua New Guinea, which is in origin an English pidgin, although to the casual listener its English antecedents are no longer apparent.

A pidgin is a trade or vehicular language of limited vocabulary and structure. It arises to facilitate communication between people with no common language, drawing its vocabulary almost exclusively from a single language. There are two types of pidgin: the first is *restricted pidgin,* a minimal contact language like Korean "Bamboo English" that dies out when contact ceases; the second, *developed pidgin* like Cameroon pidgin, remains in existence after the removal of the contact that initiated it and becomes a lingua franca between indigenous peoples with no mutually intelligible language. The latter type may eventually become the mother tongue of the community and so acquire the status *creole.*

The above process accounts for one of the ways in which a creole may arise. The other is when communities with mutually intelligible languages are kept apart, as was the case with African Negroes in the Americas, who were separated to prevent insurrection. In this situation the community resorts to a pidgin as the only viable lingua franca, and this then becomes a creole.

All the pidgins and creoles examined to date share certain characteristics. They are syntactically simpler than the languages upon which they are based: inflections are minimal, distinctions being made by varying word order; reduplication is common (Jamaica Creole *small-small,* Neo-Melanesian *talk-talk*), as is serial verb structure, giving sentences like this from Cameroon pidgin: *dat chief he woman go start begin teach he.*

Creoles and pidgins based on English exist in all six continents and can be divided into two main groups: *Atlantic* varieties, showing certain West African features, and *Pacific* varieties, related to the English used, especially in the late nineteenth and early twentieth centuries, on the China Coast. While most of the vocabulary comes from English, it also includes Portuguese words such as *savvy* and *piccaninny,* which have passed into standard English.

Selected Bibliography

A. C. Baugh, *A History of the English Language* (Routledge), 3rd edition 1978.

G. L. Brook, *English Dialects* (André Deutsch), 1963.

W. Nelson Francis, *The Structure of American English* (Oxford University Press), 1958.

Otto Jespersen, *Growth and Structure of the English Language* (Basil Blackwell), 9th edition 1956.

L. W. Lanham and K. Prinsloo, *Language and Communication Studies in South Africa* (Oxford University Press), 1978.

Angus McIntosh, *Introduction to a Survey of Scottish Dialects* (Thomas Nelson), 1961.

A. M. Marckwardt, *American English* (Oxford University Press), 1958.

J. Spencer (ed.), *The English Language in West Africa* (Longman), 1971.

Barbara M. H. Strang, *A History of English* (Methuen), 1970.

G. W. Turner, *The English Language in Australia and New Zealand* (Longman), revised edition 1972.

Meaning and Grammar

by Patrick Hanks

"What do you mean?"
"What does this word mean?"
"What is meaning?"

Such questions are often heard—and they provoke a great variety of answers. Since dictionaries are often consulted for an answer, we may add the questions, "By what authority does the lexicographer make his assertions about the words entered in his dictionary? What is the character of these assertions? What can the dictionary user reasonably expect by way of an account of meanings from a dictionary?"

To get answers to such questions, we need to have some insight into the nature of language and have a working hypothesis, at least, about the relations between language and various worlds of existence outside language—that is, the physical universe, the world of everyday life, the many worlds of fictional writing, the worlds of academic study, and so on. It is also necessary to examine some relationships within the world of language itself, especially the relationship between word and sentence and that between the individual speaker and the community as a whole.

Evidence and Intuition

One problem confronting investigators into such questions is what research techniques to use. The traditional technique for the analysis of language is the examination of printed texts—an ancient tradition still hallowed in lexicography. Clearly, the published literature of a language represents a corpus of sentences uttered by and, presumably, therefore acceptable to native speakers. Many grammarians and lexicographers have based all their work on the analysis of written texts (or believe or claim that they have). This has yielded a great deal of valuable information about language: lists of words that undeniably exist in various languages, accounts of some generally observed rules of syntax and morphology in such languages, and other patterns and norms. However, if it is relied on as the sole research technique, the analysis of printed texts has at least one serious drawback: it fosters the impression that a language is a more fixed, homogeneous phenomenon than it is, and that "correct" and "incorrect" and "acceptable" and "unacceptable" utterances can be clearly distinguished. Investigation of spoken language suggests that the dividing line is by no means clear-cut. One man's meat is another man's poison: what one may regard as correct, another frowns upon (even among writers upon language). Textual analysis is an inadequate technique to account for matters of detail in variations in grammatical practice or opinion from one speaker or writer to another, and it has failed even more seriously to account for the nature of meaning, which seems always to elude us. The comparison of large numbers of tape recordings to establish patterns and norms is open to the same objection. It is in fact the very search for patterns and norms itself that causes problems when we examine matters of detail in language—and the meanings of words are all matters of detail. Every time we try to establish a sound basis for a general theory of meaning, it seems to slip away from us like a wraith. One reason for this is that the subject is bedevilled with logical and binary structures imposed on it by its investigators: plurality, redundancy, and analogy are frowned upon, discounted, or ignored.

Among the most interesting developments in post-Chomskyan linguistics are those that promote a re-examination of the relationship between the speech of the individual and a language as a whole. A language is made up of a great number of individual speakers and writers, all of whom have slightly different versions of the language in their heads. Some recent researchers have therefore concentrated their attention on the intuition of the native speaker—by which the researcher usually means himself. Of course, pronouncements on this basis have no universal validity—but that is precisely the point. Examination of one's own intuitions provides no definite answers, but it provokes some interesting questions and has suggested at least one important insight, previously understated—namely the great variation in matters of detail between one speaker and another within a single speech community.

In the investigation of transformational-generative grammar after Chomsky, investigators have found a large grey area between grammatical and ungrammatical sentences, both from one individual to another and within the speech of a single individual.

No native speaker of English is likely to utter or find acceptable the sentence *"The man are good"—but what about, "He don't sing too good"? This actually comes from a native speaker of English, the difference between it and "He doesn't sing very well" being one of *register* (in this case, class dialect). Variations in grammatical acceptability also occur within a single register in a language, and within the speech of a single individual from one time to another. The sentence "When else should I have come?" is regarded by some native speakers of English as perfectly acceptable, by others as ungrammatical or wrong; others regard it as acceptable but awkward, while still others have regarded it as "wrong" or "awkward" one day, and as "right" or "acceptable" some time later. The fact is that individual rules of acceptability differ from person to person and from time to time. It is impossible to draw a precise demarcation between grammatical and ungrammatical sentences, for reasons that have to do with the shortcomings of linguistic performance when compared with competence and with the nature of memory in the brain of the individual. The same difficulty applies even more conspicuously to the attempt to say what is the "correct" meaning of a word.

Structures in the Brain

Consideration of the speech of individuals may provoke us to inquire further where and how language is stored and generated, physically, in the individual person. The answer, of course, is that it is stored and generated in his brain. But where? How? The mechanisms of speech production—phonetics and phonology—have been exhaustively studied. The neurological processes and structures that lie behind speech production, writing, and understanding spoken and written language are less well understood. In years to come, no doubt, neurophysiology will join phonetics as an "indispensable foundation" for the study of language. But at present it remains a daunting subject for laymen, although there are now available some lucid accounts of the current state of knowledge of the nature of the brain—in particular, by Colin Blakemore and Steven Rose, on which this article draws with gratitude.

It is worth reminding ourselves of the character and order of magnitude of the brain: "There are more than

10 000 million nerve cells in the human brain. Each cubic inch of the cerebral cortex receives on its surface an average of several thousand terminals from the fibres of other cells.... Neurons communicate with each other by sending brief bursts of electrical pulses along their fibres. The pulses don't vary in size, but only in the frequency of their bursts, which can be up to 1000 impulses in a second." (Colin Blakemore)

Among other things, the brain performs an analytic or interpretive function, which can operate with great selectivity. Witness, for example, the ability that most of us have to concentrate on hearing one voice clearly against a general background of equally loud or louder noise, as at a party. This selectivity applies to other functions as well, and some of them are crucial to language. For language to work at all, the brain must, on being presented with a piece of language, search through its memories, seeking to match each word in the new context with similar words in similar contexts stored in the memory. In other words, the meaning of a word for each individual is his ability to match the word rapidly with subconscious memories of previous encounters with the word, including memories of all sorts of aspects of the contexts in which it was encountered.

Speech production is generally associated with a particular area of the brain—the left prefrontal lobe. Just behind it is an area normally associated with interpretation of spoken and written language. However, the brain is an extremely versatile organ: functions normally performed by one particular area can sometimes be taken over by another area in the event of brain damage. This is especially true if the brain damage occurs in childhood. We should, therefore, treat with caution the contention that the "deep structure" of grammar is determined by hereditary characteristics. It is equally plausible that what is inherited is simply a brain big enough and powerful enough to respond to and disentangle stimuli as complex as those of language, whatever form they may take, and to mimic such stimuli by generating corresponding ones of its own. In other words, the infant brain may have a vast unprogrammed potential—more powerful by several orders of magnitude than a computer—which can do any of a number of things, depending on what it is stimulated by its environment to do. Certainly it is a finite structure and it has limitations and characteristics, some of which are determined by its links with other organs of the body (muscles, sense receptors, etc.), while others have not yet been discovered. But it is not necessarily the case that any aspect of the generative mechanism of speech is inherited. Language can be satisfactorily accounted for by the inheritance of a powerful brain, plus suitable stimuli—such as the presence of a language-using mother and other speaking humans. Compare the linguistic capabilities of a deaf-mute child brought up in human society with the absence of linguistic capabilities in so-called "wolf children"—those who have been abandoned in infancy and have somehow survived and been captured later on. It seems that in all human children after the age of about seven the ability to acquire language is no longer present if it has not already been exercised. The brain has devoted itself to other things, in response to other stimuli.

One thing that the brain of every normal human being does, from birth, is to store within itself representations of experiences through which the individual has lived. This is long-term memory. When activated by the firing of a series of electrical pulses, this store can give the individual person the sensation of "remembering"—that is, to a limited extent, of "reliving" past experiences. The details of the physical structure of memory are an unresolved question for research. What is undeniable is that long-term memory exists, and just as it can be "connected up" to the areas of the brain that function as consciousness, it can also be connected up to other areas of the brain—including the areas that control speech generation. To understand the relationship between meaning and grammar in language, we need to examine the relationship between memory and the generative processes of speech and language.

Meaning and Memory

In an article entitled "Meaning and Memory" (1976), Dwight Bolinger attacks what he describes as "the prevailing reductionism" in linguistics. He challenges the view that the linguist's job is "to construct a one-piece model to account for everything" and he goes on to draw attention to one aspect of recent work in linguistics on collocations: for no convincing reason immediately apparent to a linguistic analyst, words are not used as freely and interchangeably as we might expect. Instead, it is possible to invent all sorts of contexts for many (if not all) words in which it *ought* to be possible to use them, given their meaning and part of speech as described by dictionaries—but in fact they sound wrong, unacceptable, ungrammatical. The suggestion is that such uses simply fail to correspond closely enough to utterances previously encountered by each of us—and that both grammatical acceptability and the meaning of words for each of us is therefore closely allied with an aspect of memory (not conscious recall, but storage). The grammar of sentences is part of a process in which pieces of prefabricated language—phrases, words, and bound forms—are drawn out of the memory and strung together in speech or writing. The insertion of appropriate speech elements into slots to generate sentences is going on all the time a person is speaking—but it is, nevertheless, a far rarer event than previously supposed. The fluency of a speaker depends on the availability of fairly large prefabricated strings of language in his memory, which accounts for the frequency of some collocations and the paucity of others in the observed utterances of language. It also depends on his ability to reject unwanted memories and trains of thought that a particular word may bring with it out of store, in order to continue with his original theme.

As a person goes through life, he encounters a huge number of experiences of language. If he encounters and pays attention to a piece of language in circumstances that predispose him to regard it as acceptable (e.g., from a parent, a respected teacher, a television pundit, or from a printed book), he will store it in his memory as acceptable. If it is stigmatized or uttered by someone whom he does not respect, he will store it as unacceptable. When other pieces of language are encountered in less commanding circumstances, they are compared with those that the person has already encountered and judged to be correct or incorrect, good usage or bad usage. In this way a store of memories of collocations and contexts is built up that grows ever vaster as the speaker grows older—a store that includes many experiences of being told or of reading that certain usages are "right" and others are "wrong." From this store the person's own utterances are generated. One person may generate a sentence piece by piece from components; another (or the same person at a later date) may generate the very same sentence as a connected string from memory. The whole business is messier, less analysable, more analogical than the clean, neat, binary, logical structures beloved of mathematically minded grammarians. In investigating so fluid a phenomenon as language, there is a danger of mistaking a structure imposed by the observer for something inherent in the phenomenon being observed.

A person's utterances may also fall short of his intentions or his capabilities; they should therefore be used cautiously when cited as evidence. A wise dictionary comments only on collocational restrictions that are extremely widespread throughout the speech community: the lexicographer's pronouncements about the grammar of words may be set aside by any speaker at any time (if he is dealing with a living language). The reaction signal in the brain of a reader or hearer that tells him that a piece of language is incorrect may be switched off at any time by a simple contextual redefinition: "Ah, but this is poetry"—or "Ah, but this is by that most idiosyncratic of writers, James Joyce."

Bolinger says that "I bear them love" (as contrasted with "the love I bear them") is an unacceptable use, for him and others, of the verb *to bear.* But if a major living poet were to use it, the rhythm being right, the sentence would probably become acceptable to him as to others in quite a short time.

The Meaning of Words

The apparent fixedness of the printed page should not blind us to the truly fluid, unstable, uncertain nature of meaning in living, natural language. Wide variations in interpretations of the meaning of words occur in day-to-day spoken language. However, the printed page plays an important role in determining what people mean by words. A literature such as that of the English language, with its great glories and extraordinary range, influences and helps to determine the speech of every succeeding speaker of the language, precisely because of the relationship between experience, memory, and sentence generation that we have been discussing. The language of every person is influenced and to some extent determined by what he reads and, indirectly, by what his friends, family, and acquaintances read, as well as by all the other experiences of his life in which language is used.

Meaning, experience, context, and memory are inextricably interwoven in our brains, and because the experiences of each one of us are different the details of the meanings of our words are likewise different. A problem that scholars have in constructing a detailed general theory of semantics is that, while it might be theoretically possible to describe the full semantics of a particular person at a particular moment in his life (although no-one has yet suggested a practical method of doing so), this would be of illustrative value only; when we get down to details, the semantics of every person is different from that of every other person. There is, however, a great deal that can be said about the ways in which experiences and words fit together.

Each of us carries in his head a model of the world as he knows it, built up out of memories of experiences. Words are both part of this model (being themselves experiences that we have had) and they are processes that can be generated to describe aspects of the model (or for any of a number of other purposes). After being generated, they can themselves be laid down as components in the model.

The meaning of a word in the brain of a speaker consists of an extraordinarily large store of experiences of previous exposure to and use of that word. Such memories are not necessarily available for conscious recall. The conscious mind has very little to do with determining meaning. The memories can be of all sorts—the place in which the word was encountered, changes in the person's sensory perceptions and emotional state at the time, and so on, but chief among them are memories of perceptions of some "reality," some mode of existence or universe of discourse, in which the word figured in some way as a label for some part of the experience. A person assimilates new words, with their meanings, into his vocabulary, in many cases by "inferencing": a person guesses the meaning of an unfamiliar word from the context of life and familiar words by which it is surrounded. Moreover, language works in such a way that the labelling function of a word may be to label other words, which are themselves labels for other labels, and so on. Sometimes, the context in which the word is remembered is explicitly one in which the meaning of it was being explained by use of other words.

A single memory is sufficient by itself to account for the meaning of, say, *triskaidekaphobia*. Of the few people who ever encounter such a word, some will subsequently "know what it means"; others will not. Of those who know, nearly all will be able consciously to recall one or more explicit experiences of being told, in words, that it means fear of the number thirteen. Such words are semantically shallow. But how are we to account for the meaning of such words as *break, good, to,* etc. ("semantically deep" words), in terms of memory alone?

The meaning of such words for an individual person starts off in the same way as that of *triskaidekaphobia,* but whereas he may remember quite clearly all the circumstances in which he learned the meaning of that rare word—the person who used it, the place where the discussion took place, and so on, as well as the explanation—the infant speaker is exposed to a welter of different circumstances in which, say, *good* is used. Before long he discards, seals off, or does not store as memories at all those aspects of each context of hearing *good* that are not strongly reinforced. What is left is the meaning and syntax of *good* for that particular person. Reinforcement may be of two kinds: a strong, attention-demanding stimulus on one particular occasion or a series of stimuli having common features—for example, a sense of pleasure or satisfaction at times when *good* is mentioned.

Words fulfil a dual function: they both *refer* (i.e., have meaning), which could be described as an instinctive procedure by the individual human being involving comparison of context with memory, and *relate,* which is the grammatical activity of binding together the words in the sentence in certain relations one to another. The distinction between referring and relating is not a hard and fast one; some words may be seen as performing more of a relating function; others more of a referring function. Thus, English prepositions and particles such as *in, the,* or *to* tend to serve the grammar more than the meaning. They are sometimes described as "grammar words," "form words," or "function words." The English verbal infinitive marker *to,* for example, serves to record the verb status of the word that follows and, often, some aspect of its relation to the rest of the sentence. But does it have any more distinctly "meaningful" function? Probably not. By the time the child has learned to use the verbal infinitive marker, he has already heard it used with countless different verbs, in such a variety of contexts that the only common feature is the subsequent presence of a verb. However, the question of the extent to which *to* means "to" (motion towards) in the language of English speakers is more complex. Many English speakers may well acquire a deep-buried belief that the verbal infinitive has, obscurely, something to do with motion towards—a belief that is not shared by speakers of, say, Greek, in which this coincidence does not occur.

Similarly, most prepositions have a basic directional or other relational meaning in the physical world, but a very large number of the actual uses of these prepositions have no such meaning, while different languages choose different prepositions to express similar relations among words. This is a well-known trap for language learners. There simply is no reason to explain why *in Shakespeare* should translate into French as *chez Shakespeare* and German as *bei Shakespeare,* whereas *in the country* translates as *à la campagne* and *auf dem Lande,* and *in the box* translates as *dans la boîte* and *in der Schachtel.* It is just that these are the particular words laid down in the memories of English, French, and German speakers to generate such collocations. In other languages, the relations are expressed by other means—for example, by inflections that change the form of the noun and that vary depending on the class of the noun.

Before leaving this topic, we ought to note that the term *word* is used quite loosely here. A more precise term would be *lexeme,* which would include both phrases and combining forms that do not occur as independent words. Lexical meaning may be stored (in such a way as to defy further analysis) in a phrase consisting of more than one word, or it may be stored in a unit that is smaller than a word. Idioms, such as *a pretty kettle of fish, blue blood,* and *bury the hatchet,* and many phrasal verbs, such as *take off* and *put up with,* defy sensible analysis into constituent elements, while bound forms such as *semi-, un-,* and *psycho-* clearly have meaning in their own right, although they are not used independently.

A useful model of language must include a distinction between the grammar of sentences, the meaning of sentences, the grammar of words, and the meaning of words.

The distinction between "the grammar of words" and "the grammar of sentences" could be described as one between calls on memory, in which words are stored with their grammatical collocations, and the operation of generative, rule-governed procedures in the brain to create new sentences. However, it would be a bold undertaking to attempt to tell from examining a sentence how much of it was generated from individual components and how much was drawn from memory. The proportions are different from person to person and, for an individual person, from one utterance to another. There might be some symptoms, interpretable if one knew the individual, such as speed of utterance—but it is difficult to see how such an investigation could be pursued scientifically.

Many of the utterances we make consist of repetitions of previously uttered sentences and phrases, pulled wholesale and ready-made out of store. In so far as the generative procedures of language are put into operation at all, they follow rules, probably quite few in number, which it is the business of grammarians to describe and which govern processes that go on in the areas of the brain involved in generating speech and writing. The rules are either inherited or, more probably, built up by the brain by some process of analogy that is not yet fully understood. The generative procedures call on the store of memories about his language that a person has, and one and the same utterance may be made up of different proportions of items drawn from memory and the operation of generative rules. The rules are all optional, not obligatory, in the sense that even the "obligatory" rules of grammar may be superseded by the input of a ready-made piece of language (which may or may not contain within itself exceptions to the rules that an individual person observes in his own generative grammar).

A further useful distinction is one between the grammar of sentences and the meaning of sentences. Considered from the point of view of meaning, sentences consist of strings of language put together under some stimulus that makes the speaker want to speak or the writer write. The meaning of a sentence or utterance is closely connected with the life context in which it is uttered, and the words in it have meaning by virtue of the speaker's (or writer's) previous experience of contexts in which they have been uttered.

Commensurability

So far we have concentrated on the language of the individual—but what is the relationship between the meaning of a word for the individual and its meaning in the community at large?

When different people use a word they do not all mean the same thing by it. The more extensive the investigation of the vocabulary of individuals, the more discrepancies and differences are revealed. The difference between understanding one's next-door neighbour and understanding a foreign language is one of degree, not a difference in kind. Anybody who cares to assemble a group of his friends may explore with them what they understand by the meaning of a randomly selected list of common words. Before long, differences will start to emerge. Perhaps some people will become angry or contemptuous that others do not accept or understand the "true" meaning of the words; others may try to hide their idiosyncrasies and conform to the majority view. Sooner or later, someone will reach for a dictionary to settle a dispute.

But how can the dictionary help? Why should we assume that the meaning of words, as recorded by dictionaries, is fixed? Why do people so often assume that there are "true" and "false" meanings of words? And by what authority does the lexicographer make his statements? Why should the user take any notice of them?

One answer is that man is a social animal, and language is the instrument of his sociability. Language could not work at all unless everybody assented to the proposition that when a person says something, both speaker and hearer(s) mean the same thing by the utterance. This assent is a stronger, more deeply rooted thing than an act of conscious volition: it is a biological necessity. It is a reflection of the way that man has evolved, just as the construction of webs reflects the way that spiders have evolved. And very often, for practical purposes, speakers and hearers *do* mean the same thing: the differences are glossed over; different people find that they can recall similar experiences prompted by the words in question; usually a group of several people will respond in similar ways to the same utterance. There would be no point in writing this article if I did not assent to the proposition that somebody somewhere will understand what I mean by it. To assume otherwise would be to deny man's power to communicate within his own species—as he so patently and successfully does.

We assume that the meaning of words is fixed because we have to. We must discard the notion that there is such a thing as the "true meaning" of a word, but we may usefully speak of "core meaning," to the extent that experiences of the contexts of a word—and not just linguistic contexts—have features in common, whether in the memory of a single speaker or in the memories of all the members of a group or community.

There is a further important distinction to be made. We must not mistake an act of social consent, necessary for the conduct of human society, for some external force imposed by language itself or by a world that lies outside the human individual. There is no inherent property of words or of what they refer to that makes them mean the same thing for speaker and hearer. The apparent homogeneity or commensurability of meaning in a speech community is a constantly repeated act of social consent among its members. The paradoxical fact is that commensurability of meaning may be an illusion, but it is an illusion that has to be sustained if language is to go on serving its purpose. For this reason, human beings devote enormous amounts of time and energy to the attempt to impose and preserve commensurability of meaning. The meaning of words as used by children is constantly corrected by adults; many of the processes of education have the effect of imposing very similar experiences of meaning on a number of individuals: we read the same books, are taught the same versions of history and science, and so on. Linguists are too often inclined to undervalue the efforts of uniformists and conformists. When children start to "assert themselves" as they grow up, very rarely does this self-assertion take the form of isolated, independent actions; instead, adolescents tend to discard the values of their parents for those of their peers. In language, this process can be seen quite clearly in the form of the constant search by each succeeding generation for a new general adjective of approbation: *a-one, top-hole, ripping, fabulous, fantastic, cool, groovy, far-out, radical,* and so on.

The reader who has a clear picture of what meaning really is will be in a better position to make full use of his dictionary. He will not expect it to achieve the impossible (for example, to distinguish between "correct" and "incorrect" meanings) and he will be more tolerant of the idiosyncrasies of other speakers. One of the chief roles of a dictionary in the community is to sum up in a few carefully chosen words the principal contextual aspects of each word in the language, as accepted by the majority of members (at any rate, respected members) of a speech community. By "contextual" is meant contexts both of language and of life. How is this done?

For many years now, scholarly lexicographers have been energetically disclaiming any right to speak prescriptively about the meaning of words and have been passing the onus back to the community as a whole—or, at least, to the educated or published segment of it: "Words mean," says the lexicographer, "whatever *you*, the writers of the language, have chosen to make them mean." Since speech is so ephemeral and meaning in speech so unstable, lexicographers tend to concentrate on the evidence offered by the published works of "the best authors." This is not necessarily a bad thing, if by "the best authors" is meant those who are widely read by others and whose writing is therefore influential in determining the speech patterns of their successors—ourselves and our children, heirs to the common fortune of the English language and literary tradition. However, it is not by itself an adequate foundation for a dictionary of the contemporary language.

There are many kinds of dictionary, among them those based on historical principles and those, like the present work, that attempt to describe the current, living language. The English-speaking community is indeed fortunate in having available the magnificent 12-volume *Oxford English Dictionary*, together with its new supplement edited by R. W. Burchfield. This great work contains a documented history of a huge number of words, and it is the model for all subsequent historical dictionaries of other languages, other cultures. It was compiled on historical principles, and as a general rule the earliest sense of each word is therefore placed first, regardless of whether it is still current.

Works on a more modest scale, however, run the risk of misleading their users if they place obsolete or archaic meanings first. For example, the reader unaware of the underlying historical principles might be puzzled—or even misled into thinking the word an obsolete one—by an explanation of the noun *size* that reads "an assize (*obs.*): a portion of food and drink (*obs.*): an allowance (*obs.*): bigness: magnitude." Other dictionaries compromise—for example, by sticking to historical order unless the sense is obsolete. Another account of the meaning of *size* begins: "Relative bigness, dimensions, magnitude," which seems to imply that current senses are placed first. However, comparing the entry for *juggle* in the same work, we find that it begins: "*v. & v.i.* Perform conjuring tricks; perform feats of dexterity." Here, the historical principle seems to reassert itself. And at *conjure* another rather literary or old-fashioned sense, "Appeal solemnly to (person *to* do)," is placed first. It is always difficult to tell whether a particular sense has become obsolete until at least a century after the event. However, historical principles and even modified historical principles do not seem to be conducive to an arrangement that is most likely to help the reader who wishes to know what a word means (as opposed to what it meant once).

In this dictionary, the reader may be sure that the sense offered in first place is a current one unless the word itself is obsolete. Each entry may be regarded as a proposition or series of propositions, in which the lexicographer offers the reader a short account of the meaning(s) or role(s) assigned to the word in the language of the community at large, in so far as he is able to determine them from his reading, research, and discussions. In this dictionary, each sense is numbered. This is a device to help the reader follow the account of the meaning of a complex word and to grasp distinctions being made by the lexicographer. It is not suggested that the numbering of senses corresponds to any universal pattern outside the world of the dictionary. Prominence may be given to the word's context-labelling function in relation to the world we live in, or to the particular universe of discourse in which the word characteristically occurs, or to the syntactic function of the word in relation to other words, or to its characteristic register, dialect, or level of usage, or to some combination of these, or to some other feature entirely. If the summary account is well written and the words used in it are well chosen, reflecting the common reading and common judgment of the people interested in the particular subject(s) in which the word may occur, the dictionary fulfils its function. It records senses and uses of each word that are acceptable in the community as a whole.

The dictionary is a device of social integration. For this reason, the lexicographer must be widely read; he must have a deep understanding of the terms he is defining, based on an extensive reading of the literature in which those terms occur. A vast citation file is no substitute for the judgment of the lexicographer. The proliferation of specialized terminologies in the modern world makes it necessary that a dictionary nowadays be compiled by a team of lexicographers, each working within his own field of competence and each subject to checks by his colleagues on accuracy and comprehensibility. These are the principles on which this dictionary has been compiled.

Selected Bibliography

Raven I. McDavid, Jr., and Audrey R. Duckert (eds.), *Lexicography in English* (New York Academy of Sciences), 1973. See in particular papers by Bolinger, Mathiot, G. Lakoff, and Quine.

Dwight Bolinger, "Meaning and Memory" (in *Forum Linguisticum* 1:1), 1976.

Colin Blakemore, *Mechanics of the Mind* (Cambridge University Press), 1976.

Steven Rose, *The Conscious Brain* (revised edition, Penguin Books), 1976.

Noam Chomsky, *Syntactic Structures* (Mouton, The Hague), 1957.

Noam Chomsky, *Aspects of the Theory of Syntax* (Massachusetts Institute of Technology), 1965.

John Lyons, *Semantics* (Cambridge University Press), 1977.

Richard Robinson, *Definition* (Oxford University Press), revised edition 1954.

P. F. Strawson, "On Referring" (in *Mind*, vol. 59), 1950.

John R. Searle, *Speech Acts* (Cambridge University Press), 1969.

Ludwig Wittgenstein, *Philosophical Investigations* (Basil Blackwell), 1953.

A

a *or* **A** (eɪ) *n., pl.* **a's, A's,** *or* **As. 1.** the first letter and first vowel of the modern English alphabet. **2.** any of several speech sounds represented by this letter, in English as in *take, bag, calm, shortage,* or *cobra.* **3.** Also called: **alpha.** the first in a series, esp. the highest grade or mark, as in an examination. **4. from A to Z.** from start to finish; from beginning to end.

a[1] (ə; *emphatic* eɪ) *determiner.* (*indefinite article;* used before an initial consonant. Compare **an**[1]) **1.** used preceding a singular countable noun, if the noun is not previously specified or known: *a dog; a terrible disappointment.* **2.** used preceding a proper noun to indicate that a person or thing has some of the qualities of the one named: *a Romeo; a Shylock.* **3.** used preceding a noun or determiner of quantity: *a cupful; a dozen eggs; a great many; to read a lot.* **4.** used preceding a noun indicating a concrete or abstract thing capable of being divided: *half a loaf; a quarter of a minute.* **5.** (preceded by *once, twice, several times,* etc.) each or every; per: *once a day; fifty pence a pound.* **6.** a certain; one: *to change policy at a stroke; a Mr. Jones called.* **7.** (preceded by *not*) any at all: *not a hope.* ~Compare **the**[1].

a[2] (ə) *vb.* an informal or dialect word for **have:** *they'd a said if they'd known.*

a[3] (ə) *prep.* (usually linked to the preceding noun) an informal form of **of:** *sorta sad; a kinda waste.*

a[4] *symbol for:* **1.** acceleration. **2.** atto-.

A *symbol for:* **1.** *Music.* **a.** a note having a frequency of 440 hertz (**A above middle C**) or this value multiplied or divided by any power of 2; the sixth note of the scale of C major. **b.** a key, string, or pipe producing this note. **c.** the major or minor key having this note as its tonic. **2.** a human blood type of the ABO group, containing the A antigen. **3.** (in Britain) a major arterial road: *the A3 runs from London to Portsmouth.* **4.** (in Britain) **a.** a film certified for viewing by anyone, but which contains material that some parents may not wish their children to see. **b.** (*as modifier*): *an A film.* **5.** mass number. **6.** *Cards.* ace. **7.** argon (now superseded by **Ar**). **8.** ampere(s). **9.** Also: **at.** ampere-turn. **10.** absolute (temperature). **11.** (in circuit diagrams) ammeter. **12.** area. **13.** (*in combination*) atomic: *an A-bomb; an A-plant.* ~**14.** *international car registration for* Austria.

Å *symbol for* angstrom unit.

a. *abbrev. for:* **1.** acre(s) or acreage. **2.** alto. **3.** amateur. **4.** answer. **5.** are(s) (metric measure of land).

A. *abbrev. for:* **1.** acre(s) or acreage. **2.** America(n). **3.** answer.

a', aa, *or* **aw** (ɔ:) *adj. Scot.* variant of **all.**

a-[1] *or before a vowel* **an-** *prefix.* not; without; opposite to: *atonal; asocial.* [from Greek *a-, an-* not, without]

a-[2] *prefix.* **1.** on; in; towards: *afoot; abed; aground; aback.* **2.** *Literary or archaic.* (*used before a present participle*) in the act or process of: *come a-running; go a-hunting.* **3.** in the condition or state of: *afloat; alive; asleep.*

A1, A-1, *or* **A-one** ('eɪ'wʌn) *adj.* **1.** in good health; physically fit. **2.** *Informal.* first class; excellent. **3.** (of a vessel) with hull and equipment in first-class condition.

A4 *n.* **a.** a standard paper size, 297 × 210 mm. **b.** (*as adj.*): *an A4 book.*

A5 *n.* **a.** a standard paper size (half A4), 210 × 148 mm. **b.** (*as adj.*): *A5 notepaper.*

a·a ('ɑ:ɑ:) *n.* a volcanic rock consisting of angular blocks of lava with a very rough surface. [Hawaiian]

AA *abbrev. for:* **1.** Alcoholics Anonymous. **2.** anti-aircraft. **3.** (in Britain) Automobile Association. ~*symbol for:* **4.** (in Britain) a film that may not be publicly shown to a child under fourteen.

A.A.A. *abbrev. for:* **1.** *Brit.* Amateur Athletic Association. **2.** *U.S.* Automobile Association of America.

Aa·chen ('ɑ:kən; *German* 'a:xᵊn) *n.* a city and spa in West Germany, in North Rhine-Westphalia: the northern capital of Charlemagne's empire. Pop.: 241 362 (1974 est.). French name: **Aix-la-Chapelle.**

Aal+borg *or* **Ål+borg** (*Danish* 'ɔlbɔr) *n.* a city and port in Denmark, in N Jutland. Pop.: 154 582 (1974 est.).

Aa·le+sund (*Norwegian* 'o:ləˌsʊn) *n.* a variant spelling of **Ålesund.**

aa·li·i (ɑ:'li:i:) *n.* a bushy sapindaceous shrub, *Dodonaea viscosa,* of Australia, Hawaii, Africa, and tropical America, having small greenish flowers and sticky foliage. [Hawaiian]

Aalst (a:lst) *n.* the Flemish name for **Alost.**

Aal·to (*Finnish* 'ɑ:ltɔ) *n.* **Al·var** ('alvar). 1898–1976, Finnish architect and furniture designer, noted particularly for his public and industrial buildings, in which wood is much used. He invented bent plywood furniture (1932).

AAM *abbrev. for* air-to-air missile.

A & M *abbrev. for:* **1.** Agricultural and Mechanical. **2.** Ancient and Modern (hymn book).

A & R *abbrev. for* artists and repertoire.

Aar·au (*German* 'a:raʊ) *n.* a town in N Switzerland, capital of Aargau canton: capital of the Helvetic Republic from 1798 to 1803. Pop.: 16 881 (1970).

aard+vark ('ɑ:dˌvɑ:k) *n.* a nocturnal mammal, *Orycteropus afer,* the sole member of its family (*Orycteropodidae*) and order (*Tubulidentata*). It inhabits the grasslands of Africa, has long ears and snout, and feeds on termites. Also called: **ant bear.** [C19: from obsolete Afrikaans, from *aarde* earth + *varken* pig]

aard+wolf ('ɑ:dˌwʊlf) *n., pl.* **+wolves.** a nocturnal mammal, *Proteles cristatus,* that inhabits the plains of southern Africa and feeds on termites and insect larvae: family *Hyaenidae* (hyenas), order *Carnivora* (carnivores). [C19: from Afrikaans, from *aarde* earth + *wolf* wolf]

Aar+gau (*German* 'a:rgaʊ) *n.* a canton in N Switzerland. Capital: Aarau. Pop.: 433 284 (1970). Area: 1404 sq. km (542 sq. miles). French name: **Argovie.**

Aar+hus *or* **År+hus** (*Danish* 'ɔrhu:s) *n.* a city and port in Denmark, in E Jutland. Pop.: 187 342 (1970).

Aa·ron ('ɛərən) *n. Old Testament.* the first high priest of the Israelites, brother of Moses (Exodus 4:14).

Aa·ron+ic (ɛə'rɒnɪk) *adj.* **1.** of or relating to Aaron, his family, or the priestly dynasty initiated by him. **2.** of or relating to the Israelite high priesthood. **3.** of or relating to the priesthood in general. **4.** *Mormon Church.* denoting or relating to the second order of the Mormon priesthood.

Aa·ron's beard *n.* another name for **rose of Sharon** (sense 1).

Aa·ron's rod *n.* **1.** the rod used by Aaron in performing a variety of miracles in Egypt. It later blossomed and produced almonds (Numbers 17). **2.** a widespread Eurasian scrophulariaceous plant, *Verbascum thapsus,* having woolly leaves and tall erect spikes of yellow flowers.

A'asia *abbrev. for* Australasia.

AB a human blood type of the ABO group, containing both the A antigen and the B antigen.

A.B. *abbrev. for:* **1.** Also: **a.b.** able-bodied seaman. **2.** (in the U.S.) Bachelor of Arts.

Ab (æb) *or* **Av** (æv) *n.* the eleventh month of the civil year and the fifth of the ecclesiastical year in the Jewish calendar, falling approximately in July and August. [from Hebrew, from Akkadian *abu*]

ab-[1] *prefix.* away from; off; outside of; opposite to: *abnormal; abaxial; aboral.* [from Latin *ab* away from]

ab-[2] *prefix.* denoting a cgs unit of measurement in the electromagnetic system: *abvolt.* [abstracted from ABSOLUTE]

ab·a ('æbə) *n.* **1.** a type of cloth from Syria, made of goat hair or camel hair. **2.** a sleeveless outer garment of such cloth. [from Arabic]

A.B.A. *abbrev. for:* **1.** (in Britain) Amateur Boxing Association. **2.** American Booksellers Association.

a·bac (ˌeɪbæk) *n.* another name for **nomogram.** [C20: from French, from Latin ABACUS]

ab·a+ca ('æbəkə) *n.* **1.** a Philippine plant, *Musa textilis,* related to the banana: family *Musaceae.* Its leafstalks are the source of Manila hemp. **2.** another name for **Manila hemp.** [via Spanish from Tagalog *abaká*]

a·back (ə'bæk) *adv.* **1. taken aback. a.** startled or disconcerted. **b.** *Nautical.* (of a vessel or sail) having the wind against the forward side so as to prevent forward motion. **2.** *Rare.* towards the back; backwards. [Old English *on bæc* to the back]

ab+ac+ti+nal (æb'æktɪnᵊl) *adj. Zoology.* (of organisms showing radial symmetry) situated away from or opposite to the mouth; aboral. —**ab+'ac+ti+nal+ly** *adv.*

ab·a+cus ('æbəkəs) *n., pl.* **+ci** (-ˌsaɪ) *or* **+cus·es. 1.** a counting device that consists of a frame holding rods on which a specific number of beads are free to move. Each rod designates a given denomination, such as units, tens, hundreds, etc., in the decimal system, and each bead represents a digit or a specific number of digits. **2.** *Architect.* the flat upper part of the capital of a column. [C16: from Latin, from Greek *abax* board covered with sand for tracing calculations, from Hebrew *ābhāq* dust]

Ab·a+dan (ˌæbə'dɑ:n) *n.* a port in SW Iran, on an island in the Shatt-al-Arab delta. Pop.: 312 000 (1973 est.).

A·bad+don (ə'bædᵊn) *n.* **1.** the Devil (Revelation 9:11). **2.** (in rabbinical literature) a part of Gehenna; Hell. [Hebrew: literally, destruction]

a·baft (ə'bɑ:ft) *Nautical.* ~*adv., adj.* (*postpositive*) **1.** closer to the stern than to another place on a vessel: *with the wind abaft.* ~*prep.* **2.** behind; aft of: *abaft the mast.* [C13: *on baft; baft* from Old English *beæftan,* from *be* by + *æftan* behind]

A·ba+kan (*Russian* aba'kan) *n.* a city in the S Soviet Union, capital of the Khakass AR, at the confluence of the Yenisei and Abakan Rivers. Pop.: 116 000 (1975 est.).

ab·a+lo+ne (ˌæbə'ləʊnɪ) *n.* any of various edible marine gastropod molluscs of the genus *Haliotis,* having an ear-shaped shell that is perforated with a row of respiratory holes. The shells are used for ornament or decoration. Also called: **ear shell.** See also **ormer.** [C19: from American Spanish *abulón;* origin unknown]

ab+amp ('æbˌæmp) *n.* short for **abampere.**

ab+am+pere (æb'æmpɛə) *n.* the cgs unit of current in the electromagnetic system; the constant current that, when flowing through two parallel straight infinitely long conductors 1 centimetre apart, will produce a force between them of 2 dynes per centimetre: equivalent to 10 amperes. Abbrev.: **abamp.**

a·ban+don (əˈbændən) *vb.* (*tr.*) **1.** to forsake completely; desert; leave behind: *to abandon a baby; drivers had to abandon their cars.* **2.** to give up completely: *to abandon a habit; to abandon hope.* **3.** to yield control of or concern in; relinquish: *to abandon office.* **4.** to give up (something begun) before completion: *to abandon a job; the game was abandoned.* **5.** to surrender (oneself) to emotion without restraint. **6.** to give (insured property that has suffered partial loss or damage) to the insurers in order that a claim for a total loss may be made. ~*n.* **7.** freedom from inhibitions, restraint, concern, or worry: *she danced with abandon.* [C14: *abandounen* (vb.), from Old French, from *a bandon* under one's control, in one's power, from *a* at, to + *bandon* control, power] —**aˈban+don+ment** *n.*

a·ban+doned (əˈbændənd) *adj.* **1.** deserted: *an abandoned windmill.* **2.** forsaken: *an abandoned child.* **3.** unrestrained; uninhibited.

a·ban·don·ee (əˌbændəˈniː) *n. Law.* a person to whom something is formally relinquished, esp. an insurer having the right to salvage a wreck.

à bas *French.* (a ˈba) down with!

a·base (əˈbeɪs) *vb.* (*tr.*) **1.** to humble or belittle (oneself, etc.). **2.** to lower or reduce, as in rank or estimation. [C15: *abessen,* from Old French *abaissier* to make low. See BASE[2]] —**aˈbase+ment** *n.*

a·bash (əˈbæʃ) *vb.* (*tr.; usually passive*) to cause to feel ill at ease, embarrassed, or confused; make ashamed. [C14: via Norman French from Old French *esbair* to be astonished, from *es-* out + *bair* to gape, yawn] —**a·bash+ed+ly** (əˈbæʃɪdlɪ) *adv.* —**aˈbash+ment** *n.*

a·bate (əˈbeɪt) *vb.* **1.** to make or become less in amount, intensity, degree, etc.: *the storm has abated.* **2.** (*tr.*) *Law.* **a.** to remove, suppress, or terminate (a nuisance). **b.** to suspend or extinguish (a claim or action). **c.** to annul (a writ). **3.** (*intr.*) *Law.* (of a writ, legal action, etc.) to become null and void. **4.** (*tr.*) to subtract or deduct, as part of a price. [C14: from Old French *abatre* to beat down, fell]

a·bate+ment (əˈbeɪtmənt) *n.* **1.** diminution or alleviation; decrease. **2.** suppression or termination: *the abatement of a nuisance.* **3.** the amount by which something is reduced, such as the cost of an article. **4.** *Property law.* a decrease in the payment to legatees when the assets of the estate are insufficient to meet all payments in full. **5.** *Property law.* (formerly) a wrongful entry on land by a stranger who takes possession after the death of the owner and before the heir has entered into possession.

ab·a+tis *or* **ab+at+tis** (ˈæbətɪs, ˈæbətiː) *n. Fortifications.* a rampart of felled trees placed with their branches outwards. [C18: from French, from *abattre* to fell]

a·ba+tor (əˈbeɪtə) *n. Law.* a person who effects an abatement.

A bat+ter·y *n. U.S.* a low-voltage battery for supplying power to heat the cathode of a thermionic valve. Compare **B battery, C battery.**

ab+at+toir (ˈæbəˌtwɑː) *n.* another name for **slaughterhouse.** [C19: French, from *abattre* to fell]

ab+ax+i·al (æbˈæksɪəl) *adj.* facing away from the axis, as the surface of a leaf. Compare **adaxial.**

Ab·ba (ˈæbə) *n.* **1.** *New Testament.* father (used of God). **2.** a title given to bishops and patriarchs in the Syrian, Coptic, and Ethiopian Churches. [from Aramaic]

ab+ba+cy (ˈæbəsɪ) *n., pl.* **+cies.** the office, term of office, or jurisdiction of an abbot or abbess. [C15: from Church Latin *abbātia,* from *abbāt-* ABBOT]

Ab·bas·id (ˈæbəˌsɪd, əˈbæsɪd) *n.* **a.** any caliph of the dynasty that ruled the Muslim empire from Baghdad (750–1258) and claimed descent from Abbas, uncle of Mohammed. **b.** (*as modifier*): *the Abbasid dynasty.*

ab+ba+tial (əˈbeɪʃəl) *adj.* of or relating to an abbot, abbess, or abbey. [C17: from Church Latin *abbātiālis,* from *abbāt-* ABBOT; see -AL[1]]

ab·bé (ˈæbeɪ; *French* aˈbe) *n.* **1.** a French abbot. **2.** a title used in addressing any other French cleric, such as a priest.

ab+bess (ˈæbɪs) *n.* the female superior of a convent. [C13: from Old French, from Church Latin *abbātissa*]

Abbe+vill+i·an (æbˈvɪlɪən, -jən) *Archaeol.* ~*n.* **1.** the period represented by Lower Palaeolithic European sites containing the earliest hand axes, dating from the Mindel glaciation. See also **Acheulian.** ~*adj.* **2.** of or relating to this period. [C20: after *Abbeville,* France, where the stone tools were discovered]

ab+bey (ˈæbɪ) *n.* **1.** a building inhabited by a community of monks or nuns governed by an abbot or abbess. **2.** a church built in conjunction with such a building. **3.** such a community of monks or nuns. [C13: via Old French *abeie* from Church Latin *abbātia* ABBACY]

Ab+bey The·a+tre *n.* an influential theatre in Dublin (opened 1904): associated with it were Synge, Yeats, Lady Gregory, and O'Casey. It was closed by fire in 1951 and reopened in 1966.

ab+bot (ˈæbət) *n.* the superior of an abbey of monks. [Old English *abbod,* from Church Latin *abbāt-* (stem of *abbas*), ultimately from Aramaic *abbā* ABBA] —**ˈab+bot+ˌship** *or* **ˈab+bot+cy** *n.*

abbrev. *or* **abbr.** *abbrev. for* abbreviation.

ab+bre+vi+ate (əˈbriːvɪˌeɪt) *vb.* (*tr.*) **1.** to shorten (a word or phrase) by contraction or omission of some letters or words. **2.** to shorten (a speech or piece of writing) by omitting sections, paraphrasing, etc. **3.** to cut short; curtail. [C15: from the past participle of Late Latin *abbreviāre,* from Latin *brevis* brief] —**ab+ˈbre+vi·ˌa+tor** *n.*

ab+bre+vi·a·tion (əˌbriːvɪˈeɪʃən) *n.* **1.** a shortened or contracted form of a word or phrase used in place of the whole. **2.** the process or result of abbreviating.

ABC[1] *n.* **1.** (*often pl. in U.S.*) the alphabet. **2.** (*pl. in U.S.*) the rudiments of a subject. **3.** an alphabetical guide to a subject.

ABC[2] *abbrev. for:* **1.** (of weapons or warfare) atomic, biological, and chemical. **2.** Australian Broadcasting Commission. **3.** American Broadcasting Company.

ab+cou+lomb (æbˈkuːlɒm) *n.* the cgs unit of electric charge in the electromagnetic system; the charge per second passing any cross section of a conductor through which a steady current of 1 abampere is flowing: equivalent to 10 coulombs.

Abd-el-Krim (ˌæbdɛlˈkrɪm) *n.* 1882–1963, Moroccan chief who led revolts against Spain and France, surrendered before their combined forces in 1926, but later formed the North African independence movement.

Ab·di·as (æbˈdaɪəs) *n. Bible.* the Douay form of **Obadiah.**

ab+di+cate (ˈæbdɪˌkeɪt) *vb.* to renounce (a throne, power, responsibility, rights, etc.), esp. formally. [C16: from the past participle of Latin *abdicāre* to proclaim away, disclaim] —**ab+di·ca·ble** (ˈæbdɪkəbᵊl) *adj.* —**ˌab+di+ˈca+tion** *n.* —**ab+dic·a+tive** (æbˈdɪkətɪv) *adj.* —**ˈab+di+ˌca+tor** *n.*

ab+do+men (ˈæbdəmən, æbˈdəʊ-) *n.* **1.** the region of the body of a vertebrate that contains the viscera other than the heart and lungs. In mammals it is separated from the thorax by the diaphragm. **2.** the front or surface of this region; belly. **3.** (in arthropods) the posterior part of the body behind the thorax, consisting of up to ten similar segments. [C16: from Latin; origin obscure] —**ab+dom·i+nal** (æbˈdɒmɪnᵊl) *adj.* —**ab+ˈdom·i·nal+ly** *adv.*

ab+dom·i+nous (æbˈdɒmɪnəs) *adj. Rare.* having a large belly.

ab+du+cens nerve (æbˈdjuːsənz) *n.* either of the sixth pair of cranial nerves, which supply the lateral rectus muscle of the eye. [see ABDUCENT]

ab+du+cent (æbˈdjuːsᵊnt) *adj.* (of a muscle) abducting. [C18: from Latin *abdūcent-, abdūcens* leading away, from *abdūcere,* from *ab-* away + *dūcere* to lead, carry]

ab+duct (æbˈdʌkt) *vb.* (*tr.*) **1.** to remove (a person) by force or cunning; kidnap. **2.** (of certain muscles) to pull away (a leg, arm, etc.) from the median axis of the body. Compare **adduct.** [C19: from the past participle of Latin *abdūcere* to lead away] —**ab+ˈduc+tion** *n.* —**ab+ˈduc+tor** *n.*

Ab·dul-Ha·mid II (ˈæbdʊl ˈhæmɪd) *n.* 1842–1918, sultan of Turkey (1876–1909), deposed by the Young Turks, noted for his brutal suppression of the Armenian revolt (1894–96).

a·beam (əˈbiːm) *adv., adj.* (*postpositive*) at right angles to the length and directly opposite the centre of a vessel or aircraft. [C19: A-[2] + BEAM]

a·be·ce·dar+i·an (ˌeɪbiːsiːˈdɛərɪən) *n.* **1.** a person who is learning the alphabet or the rudiments of a subject. ~*adj.* **2.** alphabetically arranged. [C17: from Late Latin *abecedarius,* from the letters *a, b, c, d*]

a·bed (əˈbɛd) *adv. Archaic.* in bed.

A·bed·ne·go (əˈbɛdnɪˌgəʊ) *n. Old Testament.* one of Daniel's three companions who, together with Shadrach and Meshach, was miraculously saved from destruction in Nebuchadnezzar's fiery furnace (Daniel 3:12–30).

A·bel (ˈeɪbᵊl) *n.* the second son of Adam and Eve, a shepherd, murdered by his brother Cain (Genesis 4:1–8).

Ab·e·lard (ˈæbəˌlɑːd) *n.* **Pe·ter.** French name *Pierre Abélard.* 1079–1142, French scholastic philosopher and theologian whose works include *Historia Calamitatum* and *Sic et Non* (1121). His love for Heloise is recorded in their correspondence.

a·bele (əˈbiːl, ˈeɪbᵊl) *n.* another name for **white poplar.** [C16: from Dutch *abeel,* ultimately related to Latin *albus* white]

A·be·li·an group (əˈbiːlɪən) *n.* a mathematical group that is commutative: if *a* and *b* are members of an Abelian group then *ab* = *ba.* [C19: named after Niels Henrik *Abel* (1802–29), Norwegian mathematician]

a·bel+mosk (ˈeɪbᵊlˌmɒsk) *n.* a tropical bushy malvaceous plant, *Hibiscus abelmoschus,* cultivated for its yellow-and-crimson flowers and for its musk-scented seeds, which yield an oil used in perfumery. Also called: **musk mallow.** [New Latin, from Arabic *abu'l misk* father of musk]

Ab+e·o+ku+ta (ˌæbɪəʊˈkuːtə) *n.* a town in W Nigeria, capital of Ogun state. Pop.: 253 000 (1975 est.).

Ab+er+dare (ˌæbəˈdɛə) *n.* a mining town in South Wales, in N Mid Glamorgan. Pop.: 37 760 (1971).

Ab+er+deen[1] (ˌæbəˈdiːn) *n.* **1.** a city in NE Scotland, administrative centre of Grampian region on the North Sea: centre for processing North Sea oil and gas; university (1494). Pop.: 209 831 (1976 est.). **2.** (until 1975) a county of NE Scotland, now part of Grampian region. —**Ab+er+do+ni·an** (ˌæbəˈdəʊnɪən) *n., adj.*

Ab·er·deen[2] (ˌæbəˈdiːn) *n.* **George Ham·il·ton-Gor·don,** 4th Earl of. 1784–1860, British statesman. He was foreign secretary under Wellington (1828) and Peel (1841–46); became prime minister of a coalition ministry in 1852 but was compelled to resign after mismanagement of the Crimean War (1855).

Ab+er+deen An+gus *n.* a black hornless breed of beef cattle originating in Scotland.

ab+er+neth·y (ˌæbəˈnɛθɪ) *n.* a crisp unleavened biscuit. [C19: perhaps named after Dr. John *Abernethy* (1764–1831), English surgeon interested in diet]

ab+er+rant (æˈbɛrənt) *adj.* **1.** deviating from the normal or usual type, as certain animals from the group in which they are classified. **2.** behaving in an abnormal or untypical way. **3.** deviating from truth, morality, etc. [rare before C19: from the present participle of Latin *aberrāre* to wander away] —**ab+'er+rance** *or* **ab+'er+ran+cy** *n.*

ab+er+ra+tion (ˌæbəˈreɪʃən) *n.* **1.** deviation from what is normal, expected, or usual. **2.** departure from truth, morality, etc. **3.** a lapse in control of one's mental faculties. **4.** *Optics.* a defect in a lens or mirror that causes the formation of either a distorted image (see **spherical aberration**) or one with coloured fringes (see **chromatic aberration**). **5.** *Astronomy.* the apparent displacement of a celestial body due to the motion of the observer with the earth.

Ab+er+yst+wyth (ˌæbəˈrɪstwɪθ) *n.* a resort and university town in Wales, on Cardigan Bay. Pop.: 10 680 (1971).

a·bet (əˈbɛt) *vb.* **a·bets, a·bet+ting, a·bet+ted.** (*tr.*) to assist or encourage, esp. in crime or wrongdoing. [C14: from Old French *abeter* to lure on, entice, from *beter* to bait] —**a·'bet+ment** *or* **a·'bet+tal** *n.* —**a·'bet+tor** *or* **a·'bet+ter** *n.*

a·bey+ance (əˈbeɪəns) *n.* **1.** (usually preceded by *in* or *into*) a state of being suspended or put aside temporarily. **2.** (usually preceded by *in*) *Law.* an indeterminate state of ownership, as when the person entitled to an estate has not been ascertained. [C16–17: from Anglo-French, from Old French *abeance* expectation, literally a gaping after, a reaching towards] —**a·'bey+ant** *adj.*

ab+far+ad (æbˈfærəd, -əd) *n.* the cgs unit of capacitance in the electromagnetic system; the capacitance of a capacitor having a charge of 1 abcoulomb and a potential difference of 1 abvolt between its conductors: equivalent to 10^9 farads.

ab+hen+ry (æbˈhɛnrɪ) *n., pl.* **+ries.** the cgs unit of inductance in the electromagnetic system; the inductance that results when a rate of change of current of 1 abampere per second generates an induced emf of 1 abvolt: equivalent to 10^{-9} henry.

ab+hor (əbˈhɔː) *vb.* **+hors, +hor+ring, +horred.** (*tr.*) to detest vehemently; find repugnant; reject. [C15: from Latin *abhorrēre* to shudder at, shrink from, from *ab-* away from + *horrēre* to bristle, shudder] —**ab+'hor+rer** *n.*

ab+hor+rence (əbˈhɒrəns) *n.* **1.** a feeling of extreme loathing or aversion. **2.** a person or thing that is loathsome.

ab+hor+rent (əbˈhɒrənt) *adj.* **1.** repugnant; loathsome. **2.** (when *postpositive*, foll. by *of*) feeling extreme aversion or loathing (for): *abhorrent of vulgarity.* **3.** (usually *postpositive* and foll. by *to*) conflicting (with): *abhorrent to common sense.* —**ab+'hor+rent+ly** *adv.*

A·bib (*Hebrew* ɑˈbiːb) *n. Judaism.* the month of Nisan in the ancient Hebrew calendar (Exodus 13:4). [Hebrew *ābhībh* ear of grain, hence the month when grain was fresh]

a·bide (əˈbaɪd) *vb.* **a·bides, a·bid+ing, a·bode** *or* **a·bid+ed. 1.** (*tr.*) to tolerate; put up with. **2.** (*tr.*) to accept or submit to; suffer: *to abide the court's decision.* **3.** (*intr.*; foll. by *by*) **a.** to comply (with): *to abide by the decision.* **b.** to remain faithful (to): *to abide by your promise.* **4.** (*intr.*) to remain or continue. **5.** (*intr.*) *Archaic.* to dwell. **6.** (*tr.*) *Archaic.* to await in expectation. **7.** (*tr.*) *Archaic.* to withstand or sustain; endure: *to abide the onslaught.* [Old English *ābīdan*, from *a-* (intensive) + *bīdan* to wait, bide] —**a·'bid+ance** *n.* —**a·'bid+er** *n.*

a·bid+ing (əˈbaɪdɪŋ) *adj.* permanent; enduring: *an abiding belief.* —**a·'bid+ing+ly** *adv.*

A·bid+jan (ˌæbɪˈdʒɑːn; *French* abidˈʒɑ̃) *n.* the capital of the Ivory Coast: a port on the Gulf of Guinea. Pop.: 282 000 (1964 est.).

ab·i·et+ic ac·id (ˌæbɪˈɛtɪk) *n.* a yellowish powder occurring naturally as a constituent of rosin and used in lacquers, varnishes, and soap. Formula: $C_{19}H_{29}COOH$; melting pt.: 173°C. [C19 *abietic*, from Latin *abiēt-*, from *abiēs* silver fir (the acid originally being extracted from the resin)]

ab·i·gail (ˈæbɪˌgeɪl) *n.* (*sometimes cap.*) *Archaic.* a lady's maid. [C17: after the name of a lady's maid in Beaumont and Fletcher's play, *The Scornful Lady* (1610)]

Ab·i·gail (ˈæbɪˌgeɪl) *n. Old Testament.* the woman who brought provisions to David and his followers and subsequently became his wife (I Samuel 25:1–42).

Ab·i·lene (ˈæbəˌliːn) *n.* a city in central Texas. Pop.: 89 653 (1970).

a·bil·i·ty (əˈbɪlɪtɪ) *n., pl.* **·ties. 1.** possession of the qualities required to do something; necessary skill, competence, or power: *the ability to cope with a problem.* **2.** considerable proficiency; natural capability: *a man of ability.* **3.** (*pl.*) special talents. [C14: from Old French from Latin *habilitās* aptitude, handiness, from *habilis* ABLE]

Ab+ing+don (ˈæbɪŋdən) *n.* a market town in S England, in Oxfordshire. Pop.: 18 596 (1971).

ab in·i·ti·o *Latin.* (æb ɪˈnɪʃɪˌəʊ) from the start.

a·bi·o·gen·e·sis (ˌeɪbaɪəʊˈdʒɛnɪsɪs) *n.* the hypothetical process by which living organisms arise from inanimate matter: formerly thought to explain the origin of microorganisms. Also called: **spontaneous generation, autogenesis.** Compare **biogenesis.** [C19: New Latin, from A-[1] + BIO- + GENESIS] —ˌ**a·bi·o·ge·'net·ic** *adj.* —**a·bi·og·e·nist** (ˌeɪbaɪˈɒdʒɪnɪst) *n.*

a·bi·o·sis (ˌeɪbaɪˈəʊsɪs) *n.* absence of life. [C20: from A-[1] + Greek *biōsis* a way of living] —**a·bi·ot·ic** (ˈeɪbaɪˌɒtɪk) *adj.*

ab+ir+ri+tant (æbˈɪrɪtənt) *adj.* **1.** relieving irritation. ~*n.* **2.** any drug or agent that relieves irritation.

ab+ir+ri+tate (æbˈɪrɪˌteɪt) *vb.* (*tr.*) *Med.* to soothe or relieve irritation.

ab+ject (ˈæbdʒɛkt) *adj.* **1.** utterly wretched or hopeless. **2.** miserable; forlorn; dejected. **3.** indicating humiliation; submissive: *an abject apology.* **4.** contemptible; despicable; servile: *an abject liar.* [C14 (in the sense: rejected, cast out): from Latin *abjectus* thrown or cast away, from *abjicere*, from *ab-* away + *jacere* to throw] —**ab+'jec+tion** *n.* —**'ab+ject+ly** *adv.* —**'ab+ject+ness** *n.*

ab+jure (əbˈdʒʊə) *vb.* (*tr.*) **1.** to renounce or retract, esp. formally, solemnly, or under oath. **2.** to abstain from or reject. [C15: from Old French *abjurer* or Latin *abjurāre* to deny on oath] —ˌ**ab+ju+'ra+tion** *n.* —**ab+'jur+er** *n.*

Ab+khaz (æbˈkɑːz) *n.* **1.** (*pl.* **+khaz**) a member of a Georgian people living east of the Black Sea. **2.** the language of this people, belonging to the North Caucasian family.

Ab+khaz Au·ton·o+mous So+vi+et So+cial+ist Re+pub+lic *n.* an administrative division of the S Soviet Union, in the NW Georgian SSR between the Black Sea and the Caucasus Mountains: a subtropical region, with mountains rising over 3900 m (13 000 ft.). Capital: Sukhumi. Pop.: 486 959 (1970). Area: 8600 sq. km (3320 sq. miles). Also called: **Ab+kha+zi·a** (æbˈkɑːzɪə).

abl. *abbrev. for* ablative.

ab+lac+ta+tion (ˌæblækˈteɪʃən) *n.* **1.** the weaning of an infant. **2.** the cessation of milk secretion in the breasts.

ab+late (æbˈleɪt) *vb.* (*tr.*) to remove by ablation. [C20: back formation from ABLATION]

ab+la+tion (æbˈleɪʃən) *n.* **1.** the surgical removal of an organ, structure, or part. **2.** the melting or wearing away of an expendable part, such as the heat shield of a space re-entry vehicle on passing through the earth's atmosphere. **3.** the wearing away of a rock or glacier. [C15: from Late Latin *ablatiōn-*, from Latin *auferre* to carry away, remove]

ab+la+tive (ˈæblətɪv) *Grammar.* ~*adj.* **1.** (in certain inflected languages such as Latin) denoting a case of nouns, pronouns, and adjectives indicating the agent in passive sentences or the instrument, manner, or place of the action described by the verb. ~*n.* **2. a.** the ablative case. **b.** a word or speech element in the ablative case.

ab+la+tive ab+so+lute *n.* an absolute construction in Latin grammar in which a head noun and a modifier in the ablative case function as a sentence modifier; for example, *hostibus victis*, "the enemy having been beaten"

ab+la+tor (æbˈleɪtə) *n.* the heat shield of a space vehicle, which melts or wears away during re-entry into the earth's atmosphere. [C20: from ABLATION]

ab+laut (ˈæblaʊt; *German* ˈaplaʊt) *n. Linguistics.* vowel gradation, esp. in Indo-European languages. See **gradation** (sense 5). [German, coined 1819 by Jakob Grimm from *ab* off + *Laut* sound]

a·blaze (əˈbleɪz) *adj.* (*postpositive*), *adv.* **1.** on fire; burning. **2.** brightly illuminated. **3.** emotionally aroused.

a·ble (ˈeɪbᵊl) *adj.* **1.** (*postpositive*) having the necessary power, resources, skill, time, opportunity, etc., to do something: *able to swim.* **2.** capable; competent; talented: *an able teacher.* **3.** *Law.* qualified, competent, or authorized to do some specific act. [C14: ultimately from Latin *habilis* easy to hold, manageable, apt, from *habēre* to have, hold + *-ilis* -ILE]

-a·ble *suffix forming adjectives.* **1.** capable of, suitable for, or deserving of (being acted upon as indicated): *enjoyable; pitiable; readable; separable; washable.* **2.** inclined to; given to; able to; causing: *comfortable; reasonable; variable.* [via Old French from Latin *-ābilis, -ībilis*, forms of *-bilis*, adjectival suffix] —**-a·bly** *suffix forming adverbs.* —**-a·bil·i·ty** *suffix forming nouns.*

a·ble-bod·ied *adj.* physically strong and healthy; robust.

a·ble-bod·ied sea+man *n.* an ordinary seaman, esp. one in the merchant navy, who has been trained in certain skills. Also: **able seaman.** Abbrev.: **A.B., a.b.**

a·ble rat+ing *n.* (esp. in the Royal Navy) a rating who is qualified to perform certain duties of seamanship.

a·bloom (əˈbluːm) *adj.* (*postpositive*) in flower; blooming.

ab+lu+tion (əˈbluːʃən) *n.* **1.** the ritual washing of a priest's hands or of sacred vessels. **2.** (*often pl.*) the act of washing (esp. in the phrase **perform one's ablutions**). **3.** (*pl.*) *Military informal.* latrines. [C14: ultimately from Latin *ablūere* to wash away] —**ab+'lu+tion+ar·y** *adj.*

a·bly (ˈeɪblɪ) *adv.* in a competent or skilful manner.

ABM *abbrev. for* antiballistic missile.

ab+ne+gate (ˈæbnɪˌgeɪt) *vb.* (*tr.*) to deny to oneself; renounce (privileges, pleasure, etc.). [C17: from Latin *abnegāre* to deny] —ˌ**ab+ne+'ga+tion** *n.* —**'ab+ne+ˌga+tor** *n.*

Ab+ney lev+el (ˈæbnɪ) *n.* a surveying instrument consisting of a spirit level and a sighting tube, used to measure the angle of inclination of a line from the observer to another point. [C20: named after W. de W. *Abney*, died 1920, English scientist]

ab+nor+mal (æbˈnɔːməl) *adj.* **1.** not normal; deviating from the usual or typical; extraordinary. **2.** *Informal.* odd in behaviour or appearance; strange. [C19: AB-[1] + NORMAL, replacing earlier *anormal* from Medieval Latin *anormalus*, a blend of Late Latin *anōmalus* ANOMALOUS + Latin *abnormis* departing from a rule] —**ab+'nor+mal+ly** *adv.*

ab+nor+mal+i·ty (ˌæbnɔːˈmælɪtɪ) *n., pl.* **·ties. 1.** an abnormal feature, event, etc. **2.** a physical malformation; deformity. **3.** deviation from the typical or usual; irregularity.

ab+nor+mal psy+chol+o·gy *n.* the study of behaviour patterns that diverge widely from generally accepted norms, esp. those of a pathological nature.

Ab·o (ˈæbəʊ) *n., pl.* **Ab·os.** (*sometimes not cap.*) *Austral. informal, often derogatory.* **a.** short for **Aborigine. b.** (*as modifier*): *an Abo reserve.*

Å·bo (ˈoːbuː) *n.* the Swedish name for **Turku.**

a·board (əˈbɔːd) *adv., adj.* (*postpositive*), *prep.* **1.** on, in, onto, or into (a ship, train, aircraft, etc.). **2.** *Nautical.* alongside (a vessel). **3. all aboard!** (*interj.*) a warning to passengers to board a vehicle, ship, etc.

a·bode^{1} (ə'bəʊd) *n.* a place in which one lives; one's home. [C17: n. formed from ABIDE]

a·bode^{2} (ə'bəʊd) *vb.* a past tense and past participle of **abide.**

ab+ohm (æb'əʊm, 'æbˌəʊm) *n.* the cgs unit of resistance in the electromagnetic system: equivalent to 10^{-9} ohm.

a·boi+deau ('æbəˌdəʊ) *or* **a·boi+teau** ('æbəˌtəʊ) *n., pl.* **+deaus, +deaux** (-ˌdəʊz) *or* **+teaus, +teaux** (-ˌtəʊz). (in the Canadian Maritimes) **1.** a dyke with a sluice gate that allows flood water to drain off while keeping the sea water out. **2.** a sluice gate in a dyke. [Canadian French]

a·bol+ish (ə'bɒlɪʃ) *vb.* (*tr.*) to do away with (laws, regulations, customs, etc.); put an end to. [C15: from Old French *aboliss-* (lengthened stem of *abolir*), ultimately from Latin *abolēre* to destroy] **—a'bol+ish+a·ble** *adj.* **—a'bol+ish+er** *n.* **—a'bol+ish+ment** *n.*

ab·o+li+tion (ˌæbə'lɪʃən) *n.* **1.** the act of abolishing or the state of being abolished; annulment. **2.** (*often cap.*) (in British territories) the ending of the slave trade (1807) or the ending of slavery (1833): accomplished after a long campaign led by William Wilberforce. **3.** (*often cap.*) (in the U.S.) the emancipation of the slaves, accomplished by the Emancipation Proclamation issued in 1863 and ratified in 1865. [C16: from Latin *abolitio,* from *abolēre* to destroy] **—ˌab·o+'li+tion+ar·y** *adj.* **—ˌab·o+'li+tion+ism** *n.* **—ˌab·o+'li+tion+ist** *n., adj.*

ab·o+ma+sum (ˌæbə'meɪsəm) *n.* the fourth and last compartment of the stomach of ruminants, which receives and digests food from the psalterium and passes it on to the small intestine. [C18: New Latin, from AB-^{1} + *omāsum* bullock's tripe]

A-bomb *n.* short for **atom bomb.**

a·bom·i+na·ble (ə'bɒmɪnəbᵊl) *adj.* **1.** offensive; loathsome; detestable. **2.** *Informal.* very bad, unpleasant, or inferior: *abominable weather; abominable workmanship.* [C14: from Latin *abōminābilis,* from *abōminārī* to ABOMINATE] **—a'bom·i+na·bly** *adv.*

a·bom·i+na·ble snow+man *n.* a large legendary manlike or apelike creature, alleged to inhabit the Himalayan Mountains. Also called: **yeti.** [a translation of Tibetan *metohkangmi,* from *metoh* foul + *kangmi* snowman]

a·bom·i+nate (ə'bɒmɪˌneɪt) *vb.* (*tr.*) to dislike intensely; loathe; detest. [C17: from the past participle of Latin *abōminārī* to regard as an ill omen, from *ab-* away from + *ōmin-,* from OMEN] **—a'bom·i+ˌna+tor** *n.*

a·bom·i+na+tion (əˌbɒmɪ'neɪʃən) *n.* **1.** a person or thing that is disgusting or loathsome. **2.** an action that is vicious, vile, etc. **3.** intense loathing or disgust.

a·bon+dance (*French* abɔ̃'dɑ̃:s) *n. Cards.* a variant spelling of **abundance** (sense 6).

à bon mar+ché *French.* (a bɔ̃ mar'ʃe) *adv.* at a bargain price.

ab+o·ral (æb'ɔ:rəl) *adj. Zoology.* away from or opposite the mouth.

ab·o+rig·i+nal (ˌæbə'rɪdʒɪnᵊl) *adj.* existing in a place from the earliest known period; indigenous; autochthonous. **—ˌab·o+'rig·i+nal+ly** *adv.*

Ab·o+rig·i+nal (ˌæbə'rɪdʒɪnᵊl) *adj.* **1.** of, relating to, or characteristic of the Aborigines of Australia. *~n.* **2.** another word for an Australian **Aborigine.**

ab·o+rig·i+ne (ˌæbə'rɪdʒɪnɪ) *n.* an original inhabitant of a country or region who has been there from the earliest known times. [C16: back formation from *aborigines,* from Latin: inhabitants of Latium in pre-Roman times, probably representing some tribal name but associated in folk etymology with *ab origine* from the beginning]

Ab·o+rig·i+ne (ˌæbə'rɪdʒɪnɪ) *n.* **1.** Also called: **native Australian,** (Austral.) **native,** (Austral.) **Black.** a member of a dark-skinned hunting and gathering people who were living in Australia when European settlers arrived. Often shortened to **Abo. 2.** any of the languages of this people. See also **Australian** (sense 3).

a·born+ing (ə'bɔ:nɪŋ) *adv. U.S.* while being born, developed, or realized (esp. in the phrase **die aborning**). [C20: from A-^{2} + *borning,* from BORN]

a·bort (ə'bɔ:t) *vb.* **1.** to terminate or cause to terminate pregnancy before the fetus is viable. **2.** (*intr.*) to fail to come to completion; go wrong. **3.** (*tr.*) to interrupt the development of. **4.** (*intr.*) to give birth to a dead or nonviable fetus. **5.** (of a space flight, military operation, etc.) to fail or terminate prematurely. **6.** (*intr.*) (of an organism or part of an organism) to fail to develop into the mature form. [C16: from Latin *abortāre,* from the past participle of *aborīrī* to miscarry, from *ab-* wrongly, badly + *orīrī* to appear, arise, be born]

a·bor+ti+cide (ə'bɔ:tɪˌsaɪd) *n.* **1.** the destruction of a fetus; feticide. **2.** a drug or agent that kills a fetus.

a·bor+ti+fa+cient (əˌbɔ:tɪ'feɪʃənt) *adj.* **1.** causing abortion. *~n.* **2.** a drug or agent that causes abortion.

a·bor+tion (ə'bɔ:ʃən) *n.* **1.** an operation or other procedure to terminate pregnancy before the fetus is viable. **2.** the premature termination of pregnancy by spontaneous or induced expulsion of a nonviable fetus from the uterus. **3.** the products of abortion; an aborted fetus. **4.** the arrest of development of an organ. **5.** a failure to develop to completion or maturity: *the project proved an abortion.* **6.** a person or thing that is deformed. **—a'bor+tion+al** *adj.*

a·bor+tion+ist (ə'bɔ:ʃənɪst) *n.* a person who performs abortions, esp. illegally.

a·bor+tive (ə'bɔ:tɪv) *adj.* **1.** failing to achieve a purpose; fruitless. **2.** (of organisms) imperfectly developed; rudimentary. **3.** causing abortion; abortifacient.

ABO sys+tem *n.* a system for classifying human blood on the basis of the presence or absence of two antigens in the red cells: there are four such blood types (A, B, AB, and O).

A·bou+kir Bay *or* **A·bu+kir Bay** (ˌæbu:'kɪə) *n.* a bay on the N coast of Egypt, where the Nile enters the Mediterranean: site of the Battle of the Nile (1798), in which Nelson defeated the French fleet. Arabic name: **Abu Qîr.**

a·bou+li·a (ə'bu:lɪə, -'bju:-) *n.* a variant spelling of **abulia.**

a·bound (ə'baʊnd) *vb.* (*intr.*) **1.** to exist or occur in abundance; be plentiful: *a swamp in which snakes abound.* **2.** (foll. by *with* or *in*) to be plentifully supplied (with); teem (with): *the gardens abound with flowers; the fields abound in corn.* [C14: via Old French from Latin *abundāre* to overflow, from *undāre* to flow, from *unda* wave]

a·bout (ə'baʊt) *prep.* **1.** relating to; concerning; on the subject of. **2.** near or close to. **3.** carried on: *I haven't any money about me.* **4.** on every side of; all the way around. **5.** active in or engaged in: *she is about her business.* **6.** (*foll. by an infinitive*) ready to or intending to: often used to form an immediate future verb: *he was about to jump.* *~adv.* **7.** approximately; near in number, time, degree, etc.: *about 50 years old.* **8.** nearby. **9.** here and there; from place to place; in no particular direction: *walk about to keep warm.* **10.** all around; on every side. **11.** in or to the opposite direction: *he turned about and came back.* **12.** in rotation or revolution: *turn and turn about.* **13.** used in informal phrases to indicate understatement: *I've had just about enough of your insults; it's about time you stopped.* **14.** *Archaic.* in circumference; around. *~adj.* **15.** (*predicative*) active; astir after sleep: *up and about.* [Old English *abūtan, onbūtan* on the outside of, around, from ON + *būtan* outside]

a·bout-ship *vb.* **-ships, -ship·ping, -shipped.** (*intr.*) *Nautical.* to manoeuvre a vessel onto a new tack.

a·bout turn *or U.S.* **a·bout face** *interj.* **1.** a military command to a formation of men to reverse the direction in which they are facing. *~n.* **a·bout-turn** *or U.S.* **a·bout-face. 2.** a complete change or reversal, as of opinion, attitude, direction, etc. *~vb.* **a·bout-turn** *or U.S.* **a·bout-face. 3.** (*intr.*) to perform an about-turn.

a·bove (ə'bʌv) *prep.* **1.** on top of or higher than; over: *the sky above the earth.* **2.** greater than in quantity or degree: *above average in weight.* **3.** superior to or prior to: *to place honour above wealth.* **4.** too honourable or high-minded for: *above petty gossiping.* **5.** too respected for; beyond: *above suspicion; above reproach.* **6.** too difficult to be understood by: *the talk was above me.* **7.** louder or higher than (other noise): *I heard her call above the radio.* **8.** in preference to: *I love you above all others.* **9.** north of: *which town lies just above London?* **10.** upstream from. **11. above all.** most of all or most important. **12. above and beyond.** in addition to. **13. above oneself.** presumptuous or conceited. *~adv.* **14.** in or to a higher place: *the sky above.* **15. a.** in a previous place (in something written). **b.** (*in combination*)*: the above-mentioned clause.* **16.** higher in rank or position. **17.** in or concerned with heaven: *seek the things that are above.* *~n.* **18. the above.** something that is above or previously mentioned. *~adj.* **19.** mentioned or appearing in a previous place (in something written). [Old English *abufan,* from *a-* on + *bufan* above]

a·bove board *adj.* (**aboveboard** *when prenominal*), *adv.* in the open; without dishonesty, concealment, or fraud.

ab o·vo *Latin.* (æb 'əʊvəʊ) from the beginning. [literally: from the egg]

Abp. *or* **abp.** *abbrev. for* archbishop.

abr. *abbrev. for:* **1.** abridged. **2.** abridgment.

ab+ra·ca+dab+ra (ˌæbrəkə'dæbrə) *interj.* **1.** a spoken formula, used esp. by conjurors. *~n.* **2.** a word used in incantations, etc., considered to possess magic powers. **3.** gibberish; nonsense. [C17: from Latin: magical word used in certain Gnostic writings, perhaps related to Greek *Abrasax,* a Gnostic deity]

a·brade (ə'breɪd) *vb.* (*tr.*) to scrape away or wear down by friction; erode. [C17: from Latin *abrādere* to scrape away, from AB- + *rādere* to scrape] **—a'bra+dant** *n.* **—a'brad+er** *n.*

A·bra·ham ('eɪbrəˌhæm, -həm) *n.* **1.** *Old Testament.* the first of the patriarchs, the father of Isaac and the founder of the Hebrew people (Genesis 11–25). **2. Abraham's bosom.** the place where the just repose after death (Luke 16:22).

a·bran+chi+ate (ə'bræŋkɪɪt, -ˌeɪt) *or* **a·bran+chi·al** *adj. Zoology.* having no gills. [C19: A-^{1} + BRANCHIATE]

a·bra+sion (ə'breɪʒən) *n.* **1.** the process of scraping or wearing down by friction. **2.** a scraped area or spot; graze. **3.** *Geography.* the effect of mechanical erosion of rock, esp. a river bed, by rock fragments scratching and scraping it; wearing down. Compare **attrition** (sense 3), **corrasion.** [C17: from Medieval Latin *abrāsiōn-,* from the past participle of Latin *abrādere* to ABRADE]

a·bra+sive (ə'breɪsɪv) *n.* **1.** a substance or material such as sandpaper, pumice, or emery, used for cleaning, grinding, smoothing, or polishing. *~adj.* **2.** causing abrasion; grating; rough. **3.** irritating in manner or personality; causing tension or annoyance.

a·brax+as (ə'bræksəs) *n.* an ancient charm composed of Greek letters: originally believed to have magical powers and inscribed on amulets, etc., but from the second century A.D. personified by Gnostics as a deity, the source of divine emanations. [from Greek: invented word]

ab·re·act (ˌæbrɪ'ækt) *vb.* (*tr.*) *Psychoanal.* to alleviate (emotional tension) through abreaction.
ab·re·ac·tion (ˌæbrɪ'ækʃən) *n. Psychoanal.* the release and expression of emotional tension associated with repressed ideas by bringing those ideas into consciousness.
a·breast (ə'brɛst) *adj.* (*postpositive*) **1.** alongside each other and facing in the same direction. **2.** (foll. by *of* or *with*) up to date (with); fully conversant (with).
a·bri (æ'brɪ) *n.* a shelter or place of refuge, esp. in wartime. [French, from Latin *apricum* an open place]
a·bridge (ə'brɪdʒ) *vb.* (*tr.*) **1.** to reduce the length of (a written work) by condensing or rewriting. **2.** to curtail; diminish. **3.** *Archaic.* to deprive of (privileges, rights, etc.). [C14: via Old French *abregier* from Late Latin *abbreviāre* to shorten] —**a·'bridg·a·ble** *or* **a·'bridge·a·ble** *adj.* —**a·'bridg·er** *n.*
a·bridg·ment *or* **a·bridge·ment** (ə'brɪdʒmənt) *n.* **1.** a shortened version of a written work. **2.** the act of abridging or state of being abridged.
a·broach (ə'brəutʃ) *adj.* (*postpositive*) (of a cask, barrel, etc.) tapped; broached. [C14: from Old French *abrochier* from a- to + *brochier* to BROACH]
a·broad (ə'brɔːd) *adv.* **1.** to or in a foreign country or countries. ~*adj.* (*postpositive*) **2.** (of news, rumours, etc.) in general circulation; current. **3.** out in the open. **4.** over a wide area. **5.** *Archaic.* in error. [C13: from A-[2] + BROAD]
ab·ro·gate ('æbrəuˌgeɪt) *vb.* (*tr.*) to cancel or revoke formally or officially; repeal; annul. [C16: from Latin *abrogātus* repealed, from AB-[1] + *rogāre* to propose (a law)] —ˌ**ab·ro·'ga·tion** *n.* —'**ab·ro·ˌga·tor** *n.*
ab·rupt (ə'brʌpt) *adj.* **1.** sudden; unexpected. **2.** brusque or brief in speech, manner, etc.; curt. **3.** (of a style of writing or speaking) making sharp transitions from one subject to another; disconnected. **4.** precipitous; steep. **5.** *Botany.* shaped as though a part has been cut off; truncate. **6.** *Geology.* (of strata) cropping out suddenly. [C16: from Latin *abruptus* broken off, from AB-[1] + *rumpere* to break] —**ab·'rupt·ly** *adv.* —**ab·'rupt·ness** *n.*
ab·rup·tion (ə'brʌpʃən) *n.* a breaking off of a part or parts from a mass. [C17: from Latin *abruptio*; see ABRUPT]
A·bruz·zi (*Italian* a'bruttsi) *n.* a region of S central Italy, between the Apennines and the Adriatic: separated from the former administrative region **Abruzzi e Molise** in 1965. Capital: Aquila. Pop.: 1 163 334 (1971). Area: 10 794 sq. km (4210 sq. miles).
Ab·sa·lom ('æbsələm) *n. Old Testament.* the third son of David, who rebelled against his father and was eventually killed by Joab (II Samuel 15–18).
ab·scess ('æbsɛs, -sɪs) *n.* **1.** a localized collection of pus formed as the product of inflammation and often caused by bacteria. ~*vb.* **2.** (*intr.*) to form such a collection of pus. [C16: from Latin *abscessus* a going away, a throwing off of bad humours, hence an abscess, from *abscēdere* to go away] —'**ab·scessed** *adj.*
ab·scise (æb'saɪz) *vb.* to separate by abscission. [C17: from Latin *abscīsus*, from *abscīdere* to cut off]
ab·scis·sa (æb'sɪsə) *n., pl.* **·scis·sas** *or* **·scis·sae** (-'sɪsiː). the horizontal or *x*-coordinate of a point in a two-dimensional system of Cartesian coordinates. It is the distance from the *y*-axis measured parallel to the *x*-axis. Compare **ordinate** (sense 1). [C17: New Latin, originally *linea abscissa* a cut-off line]
ab·scis·sion (æb'sɪʒən, -'sɪʃ-) *n.* **1.** the separation of leaves, branches, flowers, and bark from plants by the formation of an abscission layer. **2.** the act of cutting off. [C17: from Latin *abscissiōn-*, from AB-[1] + *scissiō* a cleaving]
ab·scis·sion lay·er *n.* a layer of parenchyma cells, bounded on both sides by cork, that is formed at the base of fruit, flower, and leaf stems and under bark before abscission. As the parenchyma disintegrates the organ becomes separated from the plant.
ab·scond (əb'skɒnd) *vb.* (*intr.*) to run away secretly, esp. to avoid prosecution or arrest after stealing something. [C16: from Latin *abscondere* to hide, put away, from *abs-* AB-[1] + *condere* to stow] —**ab·'scond·er** *n.*
ab·seil ('æbsaɪl) *vb.* (*intr.*) **1.** *Mountaineering.* to descend a steep slope or vertical drop by a rope secured from above and coiled around one's body or through karabiners attached to one's body in order to control the speed of descent. **2.** to descend by rope from a helicopter. ~*n.* **3.** an instance or the technique of abseiling. ~Also called: **rappel.** [C20: from German *abseilen* to descend by a rope, from *ab-* down + *Seil* rope]
ab·sence ('æbsəns) *n.* **1.** the state of being away. **2.** the time during which a person or thing is away. **3.** the fact of being without something; lack. [C14: via Old French from Latin *absentia*, from *absēns* a being away]
ab·sent *adj.* ('æbsənt). **1.** away or not present. **2.** lacking; missing. **3.** inattentive; absent-minded. ~*vb.* (æb'sɛnt). **4.** (*tr.*) to remove (oneself) or keep away. [C14: from Latin *absent-*, stem of *absēns*, present participle of *abesse* to be away] —**ab·'sent·er** *n.*
ab·sen·tee (ˌæbsən'tiː) *n.* **a.** a person who is absent. **b.** (*as modifier*): *an absentee voter.*
ab·sen·tee·ism (ˌæbsən'tiːɪzəm) *n.* persistent absence from work, school, etc.
ab·sen·tee land·lord *n.* a landlord who does not live in or near a property from which he draws an income.
ab·sen·te re·o (æb'sɛntɪ 'riːəu) *Law.* in the absence of the defendant. [Latin: literally: the defendant being absent]
ab·sent·ly ('æbsəntlɪ) *adv.* in an absent-minded or preoccupied manner; inattentively.
ab·sent-mind·ed *adj.* preoccupied; forgetful; inattentive. —ˌ**ab·sent-'mind·ed·ly** *adv.* —ˌ**ab·sent-'mind·ed·ness** *n.*
ab·sent with·out leave *Military.* the full form of **A.W.O.L.**
ab·sinthe *or* **ab·sinth** ('æbsɪnθ) *n.* **1.** a potent green alcoholic drink, technically a gin, originally having high wormwood content. **2.** another name for **wormwood** (the plant). [C15: via French and Latin from Greek *apsinthion* wormwood]
ab·sinth·ism ('æbsɪnˌθɪzəm) *n. Pathol.* a diseased condition resulting from excessive drinking of absinthe.
ab·sit o·men *Latin.* ('æbsɪt 'əumɛn) may the presentiment not become real or take place. [literally: may the (evil) omen be absent]
ab·so·lute ('æbsəˌluːt) *adj.* **1.** complete; perfect. **2.** free from limitations, restrictions, or exceptions; unqualified: *an absolute choice.* **3.** having unlimited authority; despotic: *an absolute ruler.* **4.** undoubted; certain: *the absolute truth.* **5.** not dependent on, conditioned by, or relative to anything else; independent: *an absolute term in logic; the absolute value of a quantity in physics.* **6.** pure; unmixed: *absolute alcohol.* **7.** (of a grammatical construction) syntactically independent of the main clause, as for example the construction *Joking apart* in the sentence *Joking apart, we'd better leave now.* **8.** *Grammar.* (of a transitive verb) used without a direct object, as the verb *intimidate* in the sentence *His intentions are good, but his rough manner tends to intimidate.* **9.** *Grammar.* (of an adjective) used as a noun, as for instance *young* and *aged* in the sentence *The young care little for the aged.* **10.** *Physics.* **a.** (*postpositive*) (of a pressure measurement) not relative to atmospheric pressure: *the pressure was 5 bar absolute.* Compare **gauge** (sense 16). **b.** denoting absolute or thermodynamic temperature. **11.** *Maths.* **a.** Also: **numerical** (sense 4b.). (of a value) having a magnitude but no sign. **b.** (of a constant) never changing in value. **c.** (of an inequality) unconditional. **d.** (of a term) not containing a variable. **12.** *Law.* (of a court order or decree) coming into effect immediately and not liable to be modified; final. See **decree absolute. 13.** *Law.* (of a title to property, etc.) not subject to any encumbrance or condition. ~*n.* **14.** something that is absolute. [C14: from Latin *absolūtus* unconditional, freed from, from *absolvere.* See ABSOLVE]
Ab·so·lute ('æbsəˌluːt) *n.* (*sometimes not cap.*) **1.** *Philosophy.* **a.** the ultimate basis of reality. **b.** that which is totally unconditioned, unrestricted, pure, perfect, or complete. **2.** (in the philosophy of Hegel) that towards which all things evolve dialectically.
ab·so·lute al·co·hol *n.* a liquid containing at least 99 per cent of pure ethanol by weight.
ab·so·lute ceil·ing *n.* the maximum height above sea level, usually measured in feet or metres, at which an aircraft can maintain horizontal flight. Compare **service ceiling.**
ab·so·lute hu·mid·i·ty *n.* the humidity of the atmosphere expressed as the number of grams of water contained in 1 cubic metre of air. Compare **relative humidity.**
ab·so·lute·ly (ˌæbsə'luːtlɪ) *adv.* **1.** in an absolute manner, esp. completely or perfectly. **2.** (*sentence substitute*) yes; certainly; unquestionably.
ab·so·lute mag·ni·tude *n.* the magnitude a given star would have if it were situated at a distance of 10 parsecs (32.6 light years) from the earth.
ab·so·lute ma·jor·i·ty *n.* a majority of over 50 per cent, such as the total number of votes or seats obtained by a party that beats the combined opposition. Compare **relative majority.**
ab·so·lute mon·ar·chy *n.* a monarchy without constitutional limits. Compare **constitutional monarchy.**
ab·so·lute mu·sic *n.* music that is not designed to depict or evoke any scene or event. Compare **programme music.**
ab·so·lute pitch *n.* **1.** the ability to identify or to reproduce the pitch of a note. **2.** the exact pitch of a note determined by vibration per second. ~Also called (not in technical usage): **perfect pitch.**
ab·so·lute tem·per·a·ture *n.* another name for **thermodynamic temperature.**
ab·so·lute u·nit *n.* **1.** a unit of measurement forming part of the electromagnetic cgs system, such as an abampere or abcoulomb. **2.** a unit of measurement forming part of a system of units that includes a unit of force defined so that it is independent of the acceleration of free fall.
ab·so·lute val·ue *n.* **1.** the magnitude of a real number or quantity regardless of its sign. The absolute value of $-x$ is written $|-x|$. **2.** Also called: **modulus.** the positive square root of the sum of the squares of the real and imaginary parts of a complex number: $|4 + 3i| = +\sqrt{(4^2 + 3^2)} = 5$.
ab·so·lute vis·cos·i·ty *n.* a full name for **viscosity,** used to distinguish it from kinematic viscosity and specific viscosity.
ab·so·lute ze·ro *n.* the lowest temperature theoretically attainable, at which the particles constituting matter would be at rest; the zero of thermodynamic temperature; zero on the International Practical Scale of Temperature: equivalent to −273.15°C or −459.67°F.
ab·so·lu·tion (ˌæbsə'luːʃən) *n.* **1.** the act of absolving or the state of being absolved; release from guilt, obligation, or punishment. **2.** *Christianity.* **a.** a formal remission of sin pronounced by a priest in the sacrament of penance. **b.** the prescribed form of words granting such a remission. [C12: from Latin *absolūtiōn-* acquittal, forgiveness of sins, from *absolvere* to ABSOLVE] —**ab·sol·u·to·ry** (æb'sɒljutərɪ, -trɪ) *adj.*
ab·so·lut·ism ('æbsəluːˌtɪzəm) *n.* **1.** the principle or practice of

a political system in which unrestricted power is vested in a monarch, dictator, etc.; despotism. **2.** *Philosophy.* the doctrine of the existence of an absolute or nonrelative being. **3.** *Theol.* an uncompromising form of the doctrine of predestination.

ab·solve (əb'zɒlv) *vb.* (*tr.*) **1.** (usually foll. by *from*) to release from blame, sin, punishment, obligation, or responsibility. **2.** to pronounce not guilty; acquit; pardon. [C15: from Latin *absolvere* to free from, from AB-[1] + *solvere* to make loose] —**ab'solv·a·ble** *adj.* —**ab'solv·er** *n.*

ab·so·nant ('æbsənənt) *adj. Archaic.* discordant or inharmonious. [C16: Medieval Latin, from Latin AB-[1] + *sonant-*, from *sonāns* sounding. Compare CONSONANT]

ab·sorb (əb'sɔ:b, -'zɔ:b) *vb.* (*tr.*) **1.** to soak or suck up (liquids). **2.** to engage or occupy (the interest, attention, or time) of (someone); engross. **3.** to receive or take in (the energy of an impact). **4.** *Physics.* to take in all or part of incident radiated energy and retain it without reflection or transmission. **5.** to take in or assimilate; incorporate. **6.** to accept and find a market for (goods, etc.). **7.** to pay for as part of a commercial transaction: *the distributor absorbed the cost of transport.* **8.** *Chem.* to undergo or cause to undergo a process in which one substance, usually a liquid or gas, permeates into or is dissolved by a liquid or solid: *porous solids absorb water; hydrochloric acid absorbs carbon dioxide.* ~Compare **adsorb.** [C15: via Old French from Latin *absorbēre* to suck, swallow, from AB-[1] + *sorbēre* to suck] —**ab,sorb·a'bil·i·ty** *n.* —**ab'sorb·a·ble** *adj.*

ab·sorb·ance (əb'sɔ:bəns, -'zɔ:-) *n. Physics.* **a.** the logarithm to base ten of internal transmittance. **b.** another term for **transmission density.**

ab·sorbed (əb'sɔ:bd, -'zɔ:bd) *adj.* engrossed; deeply interested. —**ab·sorb·ed·ly** (əb'sɔ:bɪdlɪ, -'zɔ:-) *adv.*

ab·sor·be·fa·cient (əb,sɔ:bɪ'feɪʃənt, -,zɔ:-) *Med.* ~*n.* **1.** a medicine or other agent that promotes absorption. ~*adj.* **2.** causing or promoting absorption.

ab·sorb·ent (əb'sɔ:bənt, -'zɔ:-) *adj.* **1.** able to absorb. ~*n.* **2.** a substance that absorbs. —**ab'sorb·en·cy** *n.*

ab·sorb·ent cot·ton *n.* the usual U.S. term for **cotton wool** (sense 1).

ab·sorb·er (əb'sɔ:bə, -'zɔ:-) *n.* **1.** a person or thing that absorbs. **2.** *Physics.* a material, esp. in a nuclear reactor, that absorbs radiation or causes it to lose energy.

ab·sorb·ing (əb'sɔ:bɪŋ, -'zɔ:b-) *adj.* occupying one's interest or attention; engrossing; gripping. —**ab'sorb·ing·ly** *adv.*

ab·sorp·tance (əb'sɔ:ptəns, -'zɔ:p-) *or* **ab·sorp·tion fac·tor** *n. Physics.* a measure of the ability of an object or surface to absorb radiation, equal to the ratio of the absorbed flux to the incident flux. For a plate of material the ratio of the flux absorbed between the entry and exit surfaces to the flux leaving the entry surface is the **internal absorptance.** Symbol: α Compare **reflectance, transmittance.** [C20: ABSORPTION + -ANCE]

ab·sorp·tion (əb'sɔ:pʃən, -'zɔ:p-) *n.* **1.** the process of absorbing or the state of being absorbed. **2.** *Physiol.* **a.** normal assimilation by the tissues of the products of digestion. **b.** the process of taking up various gases, fluids, drugs, etc., through the mucous membranes or skin. [C16: from Latin *absorptiōn-*, from *absorbēre* to ABSORB] —**ab'sorp·tive** *adj.*

ab·sorp·tion spec·trum *n.* the characteristic pattern of dark lines or bands that occurs when electromagnetic radiation is passed through an absorbing medium into a spectroscope. The same pattern occurs as coloured lines or bands in the emission spectrum of that medium.

ab·sorp·tiv·i·ty (,æbsɔ:p'tɪvɪtɪ, -zɔ:p-) *n. Physics.* a measure of the ability of a material to absorb radiation, equal to the internal absorptance of a homogeneous plate of the material under conditions in which the path of the radiation has unit length and the boundaries of the plate have no influence.

ab·squat·u·late (æb'skwɒtjʊ,leɪt) *vb.* (*intr.*) to leave; decamp. [C19: humorous formation as if from Latin]

ab·stain (əb'steɪn) *vb.* (*intr.*; usually foll. by *from*) **1.** to choose to refrain: *he abstained from alcohol.* **2.** to refrain from voting, esp. in a committee, legislature, etc. [C14: via Old French from Latin *abstinēre*, from *abs-* AB-[1] + *tenēre* to hold, keep] —**ab'stain·er** *n.*

ab·ste·mi·ous (əb'sti:mɪəs) *adj.* moderate or sparing, esp. in the consumption of alcohol or food; temperate. [C17: from Latin *abstēmius*, from *abs-* AB-[1] + *tēm-*, from *tēmētum* intoxicating drink] —**ab'ste·mi·ous·ly** *adv.*

ab·sten·tion (əb'stɛnʃən) *n.* **1.** a voluntary decision not to act; the act of refraining or abstaining. **2.** the act of withholding one's vote. [C16: from Late Latin *abstentiōn-*, from Latin *abstinēre.* See ABSTAIN] —**ab'sten·tious** *adj.*

ab·ster·gent (əb'stɜ:dʒənt) *adj.* cleansing or scouring. [C17: from Latin *abstergent-*, *abstērgens* wiping off, from *abs-* away, off + *tergēre* to wipe]

ab·sti·nence ('æbstɪnəns) *n.* **1.** the act or practice of refraining from some action or from the use of something, esp. alcohol. **2.** *Chiefly R.C. Church.* the practice of refraining from specific kinds of food or drink, esp. from meat, as an act of penance. [C13: via Old French from Latin *abstinentia*, from *abstinēre* to ABSTAIN]

ab·stract *adj.* ('æbstrækt). **1.** having no reference to material objects or specific examples; not concrete. **2.** not applied or practical; theoretical. **3.** hard to understand; recondite; abstruse. **4.** *Fine arts.* characterized by geometric, formalized, or otherwise nonrepresentational qualities. ~*n.* ('æbstrækt). **5.** a condensed version of a piece of writing, speech, etc.; summary. **6.** an abstract term or idea. **7.** an abstract painting, sculpture, etc. **8. in the abstract.** without reference to specific circumstances or practical experience. ~*vb.* (æb'strækt). (*tr.*) **9.** to think of (a quality or concept) generally without reference to a specific example; regard theoretically. **10.** ('æbstrækt). (*also intr.*) to summarize or epitomize. **11.** to remove or extract. **12.** *Euphemistic.* to steal. [C14 (in the sense: extracted): from Latin *abstractus* drawn off, removed from (something specific), from *abs-* AB-[1] + *trahere* to draw]

ab·stract·ed (æb'stræktɪd) *adj.* **1.** lost in thought; preoccupied. **2.** taken out or separated; extracted. —**ab'stract·ed·ly** *adv.* —**ab'stract·ed·ness** *n.*

ab·stract ex·pres·sion·ism *n.* a school of painting in New York in the 1940s that combined the spontaneity of expressionism with abstract forms in unpremeditated, apparently random, compositions. See also **action painting, tachisme.**

ab·strac·tion (æb'strækʃən) *n.* **1.** absence of mind; preoccupation. **2.** the process of formulating generalized ideas or concepts by extracting common qualities from specific examples. **3.** an idea or concept formulated in this way: *good and evil are abstractions.* **4.** an abstract painting, sculpture, etc. **5.** the act of withdrawing or removing. —**ab'strac·tive** *adj.* —**ab'strac·tive·ly** *adv.*

ab·strac·tion·ism (æb'strækʃə,nɪzəm) *n.* the theory and practice of the abstract, esp. of abstract art. —**ab'strac·tion·ist** *n.*

ab·stract noun *n.* a noun that refers to an abstract concept. Compare **concrete noun.**

ab·stract of ti·tle *n. Property law.* a summary of the ownership of land, showing the original grant, conveyances, and any incumbrances.

ab·stric·tion (æb'strɪkʃən) *n.* the separation and release of a mature spore from a sporophore by the formation of a septum. This process occurs in some fungi. [C17: from Latin AB-[1] + *strictio* a binding, from *stringere* to bind]

ab·struse (əb'stru:s) *adj.* not easy to understand; recondite; esoteric. [C16: from Latin *abstrūsus* thrust away, concealed, from *abs-* AB-[1] + *trūdere* to thrust] —**ab'struse·ly** *adv.* —**ab'struse·ness** *n.*

ab·surd (əb'sɜ:d) *adj.* **1.** at variance with reason; incongruous; ridiculous. **2.** ludicrous. [C16: via French from Latin *absurdus* dissonant, senseless, from AB-[1] (intensive) + *surdus* dull-sounding, indistinct] —**ab'surd·i·ty** *or* **ab'surd·ness** *n.* —**ab'surd·ly** *adv.*

A·bu-Bekr (ə,bu:'bɛkə) *or* **A·bu-Bakr** (ə,bu:'bækə) *n.* 573–634 A.D., father-in-law of Mohammed; the first caliph of Islam.

Ab·u Dha·bi ('æbu: 'dɑ:bɪ) *n.* a sheikdom of SE Arabia, on the S coast of the Persian Gulf: the chief sheikdom and capital of the United Arab Emirates, consisting principally of the port of Abu Dhabi and a desert hinterland; contains major oilfields. Pop.: 65 000 (1972 est.). Area: about 10 360 sq. km (4000 sq. miles).

A·bu·kir (,æbu:'kɪə) *n.* a variant spelling of **Aboukir.**

a·bu·li·a *or* **a·bou·li·a** (ə'bu:lɪə, -'bju:-) *n. Psychiatry.* a loss of will power. [C19: New Latin, from Greek *aboulia* lack of resolution, from A-[1] + *boulē* will] —**a'bu·lic** *adj.*

a·bun·dance (ə'bʌndəns) *n.* **1.** a copious supply; great amount. **2.** fullness or benevolence: *from the abundance of my heart.* **3.** degree of plentifulness. **4.** *Chem.* the extent to which an element occurs in the earth's crust or some other specified environment: expressed in parts per million or as a percentage. **5.** *Physics.* the ratio of the number of atoms of a specific isotope in a mixture of isotopes of an element to the total number of atoms present: often expressed as a percentage: *the abundance of neon-22 in natural neon is 8.82 per cent.* **6.** Also: **abondance.** a call in solo whist undertaking to make nine tricks. **7.** affluence. [C14: via Old French from Latin *abundantia*, from *abundāre* to ABOUND]

a·bun·dant (ə'bʌndənt) *adj.* **1.** existing in plentiful supply. **2.** (*postpositive*; foll. by *in*) having a plentiful supply (of). **3.** (of a chemical element or mineral) occurring to an extent specified in relation to other elements or minerals in the earth's crust or some other specified environment. **4.** (of an isotope) occurring to an extent specified in relation to other isotopes in a mixture of isotopes. [C14: from Latin *abundant-*, present participle of *abundāre* to ABOUND] —**a'bun·dant·ly** *adv.*

ab ur·be con·di·ta *Latin.* (æb 'ɜ:bɪ 'kɒndɪtə) the full form of **A.U.C.**

a·buse *vb.* (ə'bju:z). (*tr.*) **1.** to use incorrectly or improperly; misuse. **2.** to maltreat. **3.** to speak insultingly or cruelly to; revile. **4.** (*reflexive*) to masturbate. ~*n.* (ə'bju:s). **5.** improper, incorrect, or excessive use; misuse. **6.** maltreatment of a person; injury. **7.** insulting, contemptuous, or coarse speech. **8.** an evil, unjust, or corrupt practice. **9.** *Archaic.* a deception. [C14 (vb.): via Old French from Latin *abūsus*, past participle of *abūtī* to misuse, from AB-[1] + *ūtī* to USE] —**a'bus·er** *n.*

Ab·u Sim·bel (,æbu: 'sɪmbᵊl) *n.* a former village in S Egypt: site of two temples of Rameses II, which were moved to higher ground (1966–67) before the area behind the Aswan High Dam was flooded. Also called: **Ipsambul.**

a·bu·sive (ə'bju:sɪv) *adj.* **1.** characterized by insulting or coarse language. **2.** characterized by maltreatment. **3.** incorrectly used; corrupt. —**a'bu·sive·ly** *adv.* —**a'bu·sive·ness** *n.*

a·but (ə'bʌt) *vb.* **a·buts, a·but·ting, a·but·ted.** (usually foll. by *on, upon,* or *against*) to adjoin, touch, or border on (something) at one end. [C15: from Old French *abouter* to join at the ends, border on; influenced by *abuter* to touch at an end, buttress] —**a'but·tal** *n.*

a·bu·ti·lon (ə'bju:tɪlən) *n.* any shrub or herbaceous plant of the malvaceous genus *Abutilon*, such as the flowering maple, that have snowy white, yellow, or red flowers. [C18: New Latin from Arabic]

a·but·ment (ə'bʌtmənt) *or* **a·but·tal** *n.* **1.** the state or process of abutting. **2. a.** something that abuts. **b.** the thing on which something abuts. **c.** the point of junction between them. **3.** *Architect., civil engineering.* a construction that takes the thrust of an arch or vault or supports the end of a bridge.
a·but·tals (ə'bʌtᵊlz) *pl. n. Property law.* the boundaries of a plot of land where it abuts against other property.
a·but·ter (ə'bʌtə) *n. Property law.* the owner of adjoining property.
a·buzz (ə'bʌz) *adj.* (*postpositive*) humming, as with conversation, activity, etc.; buzzing.
ab·volt ('æb,vəʊlt) *n.* the cgs unit of potential difference in the electromagnetic system; the potential difference between two points when work of 1 erg must be done to transfer 1 abcoulomb of charge from one point to the other: equivalent to 10^{-8} volt.
ab·watt ('æb,wɒt) *n.* the cgs unit of power in the electromagnetic system, equal to the power dissipated when a current of 1 abampere flows across a potential difference of 1 abvolt: equivalent to 10^{-7} watt.
a·by *or* **a·bye** (ə'baɪ) *vb.* **a·bys** *or* **a·byes, a·by·ing, a·bought.** (*tr.*) *Archaic.* to pay the penalty for; redeem. [Old English *ābycgan* to pay for, atone for, from *bycgan* to buy]
A·by·dos (ə'baɪdəs) *n.* **1.** an ancient town in central Egypt: site of many temples and tombs. **2.** an ancient Greek colony on the Asiatic side of the Dardanelles (Hellespont): scene of the legend of Hero and Leander.
a·bysm (ə'bɪzəm) *n.* an archaic word for **abyss.** [C13: via Old French from Medieval Latin *abysmus* ABYSS]
a·bys·mal (ə'bɪzməl) *adj.* **1.** immeasurable; very great: *abysmal stupidity.* **2.** *Informal.* extremely bad: *an abysmal film.* —**a·'bys·mal·ly** *adv.*
a·byss (ə'bɪs) *n.* **1.** a very deep or unfathomable gorge or chasm. **2.** anything that appears to be endless or immeasurably deep, such as time, despair, or shame. **3.** hell or the infernal regions conceived of as a bottomless pit. [C16: via Late Latin from Greek *abussos* bottomless (as in the phrase *abussos limnē* bottomless lake), from A-[1] + *bussos* depth]
a·bys·sal (ə'bɪsəl) *adj.* **1.** at or belonging to the depths or floor of the ocean. **2.** *Geology.* another word for **plutonic.**
Ab·ys·sin·i·a (,æbɪ'sɪnɪə) *n.* a former name for **Ethiopia.** —**,Ab·ys·'sin·i·an** *adj., n.*
Ab·ys·sin·i·an cat *n.* a variety of cat with a long body and a short brown coat with black or dark brown markings.
Ac *the chemical symbol for* actinium.
a.c. *abbrev. for* (in prescriptions) ante cibum. [Latin: before meals]
AC *abbrev. for* alternating current. Compare **DC.**
A.C. *abbrev. for:* **1.** ante Christum. [Latin: before Christ] **2.** Air Corps. **3.** athletic club.
a/c *Book-keeping. abbrev. for:* **1.** account. **2.** account current.
a·ca·cia (ə'keɪʃə) *n.* **1.** any shrub or tree of the tropical and subtropical mimosaceous genus *Acacia,* having compound or reduced leaves and small yellow or white flowers. See also **wattle** (sense 4). **2. false acacia.** another name for **locust** (senses 2, 3). **3. gum acacia.** another name for **gum arabic.** [C16: from Latin, from Greek *akakia,* perhaps related to *akē* point]
ac·a·deme ('ækə,di:m) *n. Literary.* **1.** any place of learning, such as a college or university. **2. the grove(s) of Academe.** the academic world. [C16: first used by Shakespeare in *Love's Labour's Lost* (1588); see ACADEMY]
ac·a·dem·i·a (,ækə'di:mɪə) *n.* the academic world.
ac·a·dem·ic (,ækə'dɛmɪk) *adj.* **1.** belonging or relating to a place of learning, esp. a college, university, or academy. **2.** of purely theoretical or speculative interest: *an academic argument.* **3.** excessively concerned with intellectual matters and lacking experience of practical affairs. **4.** conforming to set rules and traditions; conventional: *an academic painter.* **5.** *Chiefly U.S.* relating to studies such as languages, philosophy, and pure science, rather than technical or professional studies. ~*n.* **6.** a member of a college or university. —**,ac·a·'dem·i·cal·ly** *adv.*
ac·a·dem·i·cals (,ækə'dɛmɪkᵊlz) *pl. n.* another term for **academic dress.**
ac·a·dem·ic dress *n.* formal dress, usually comprising cap, gown, and hood, worn by university staff and students.
a·cad·e·mi·cian (ə,kædə'mɪʃən, ,ækədə-) *n.* a member of an Academy (sense 2).
ac·a·dem·i·cism (,ækə'dɛmɪ,sɪzəm) *or* **a·cad·e·mism** (ə'kædə,mɪzəm) *n.* adherence to rules and traditions in art, literature, etc.; conventionalism.
a·cad·e·my (ə'kædəmɪ) *n., pl.* **·mies. 1.** an institution or society for the advancement of literature, art, or science. **2.** a school for training in a particular skill or profession: *a military academy.* **3.** a secondary school, esp. a private one. **4.** (in Scotland) a fee-paying secondary day school. [C16: via Latin from Greek *akadēmeia* name of the grove where Plato taught, named after the legendary hero *Akadēmos*]
A·cad·e·my (ə'kædəmɪ) *n.* **the. 1. a.** the grove or garden near Athens where Plato taught in the late fourth century B.C. **b.** the school of philosophy founded by Plato. **c.** the members of this school and their successors. **2.** short for the **French Academy, Royal Academy,** etc.
A·ca·di·a (ə'keɪdɪə) *n.* **1. a.** the Maritime Provinces of Canada. **b.** the French-speaking areas of these provinces. **2.** (formerly) a French colony in the present-day Maritime Provinces: ceded to Britain in 1713. ~French name: **A·ca·die** (aka'di).
A·ca·di·an (ə'keɪdɪən) *adj.* **1.** denoting or relating to Acadia or its inhabitants. ~*n.* **2.** any of the early French settlers in Nova Scotia, many of whom were deported to Louisiana in the 18th century. See also **Cajun.**
ac·a·jou ('ækə,ʒu:) *n.* **1.** a type of mahogany used by cabinet-makers in France. **2.** a less common name for **cashew.** [C18: via French from Portuguese *acajú,* from Tupi]
ac·a·leph ('ækə,lɛf) *n. Obsolete.* any of the coelenterates of the former taxonomic group *Acalephae,* which included the jellyfishes. [C18: from New Latin, from Greek *akalēphē* a sting]
ac·an·tha·ceous (,ækən'θeɪʃəs) *adj.* **1.** of or relating to the *Acanthaceae,* a mainly tropical and subtropical family of flowering plants that includes the acanthus. **2.** having spiny or prickly outgrowths.
a·can·thine (ə'kænθaɪn, -θi:n) *adj.* **1.** of or resembling an acanthus. **2.** decorated with acanthus leaves.
a·can·tho- *or before a vowel* **a·canth-** *combining form.* indicating a spine or thorn: *acanthocephalan.* [New Latin from Greek *akanthos* thorn plant, from *akantha* thorn]
a·can·tho·ceph·a·lan (ə,kænθəʊ'sɛfələn) *n.* **1.** any of the parasitic wormlike invertebrates of the phylum *Acanthocephala,* the adults of which have a spiny proboscis and live in the intestines of vertebrates. ~*adj.* **2.** of, relating to, or belonging to the *Acanthocephala.*
a·can·thoid (ə'kænθɔɪd) *adj.* resembling a spine; spiny.
ac·an·thop·ter·yg·i·an (,ækən,θɒptə'rɪdʒɪən) *adj.* **1.** of, relating to, or belonging to the *Acanthopterygii,* a large group of teleost fishes having spiny fin rays. The group includes most saltwater bony fishes. ~*n.* **2.** any fish belonging to the *Acanthopterygii.* ~Compare **malacopterygian.** [C19: from New Latin *Acanthopterygii,* from ACANTHO- + Greek *pterúgion* fin]
a·can·thous (ə'kænθəs) *adj.* another term for **spinous.**
a·can·thus (ə'kænθəs) *n., pl.* **·thus·es** *or* **·thi** (-θaɪ). **1.** any shrub or herbaceous plant of the genus *Acanthus,* native to the Mediterranean region but widely cultivated as ornamental plants, having large spiny leaves and spikes of white or purplish flowers: family *Acanthaceae.* See also **bear's-breech. 2.** a carved ornament based on the leaves of the acanthus plant, esp. as used on the capital of a Corinthian column. [C17: New Latin, from Greek *akanthos,* from *akantha* thorn, spine]
a cap·pel·la (ɑ: kə'pɛlə) *adj., adv. Music.* without instrumental accompaniment. [Italian: literally, according to (the style of the) chapel]
A·ca·pul·co (,ækə'pʊlkəʊ; *Spanish* ,aka'pulko) *n.* a port and resort in SW Mexico, in Guerrero state. Pop.: 352 673 (1975 est.). Official name: **A·ca·pul·co de Juá·rez** (*Spanish* ðe 'xwares).
ac·a·ri·a·sis (,ækə'raɪəsɪs) *n.* infestation of the hair follicles and skin with acarids, esp. mites. [C19: New Latin. See ACARUS, -IASIS]
ac·a·rid ('ækərɪd) *or* **a·car·i·dan** (ə'kærɪdᵊn) *n.* **1.** any of the small arachnids of the order *Acarina* (or *Acari*), which includes the ticks and mites. ~*adj.* **2.** of or relating to the order *Acarina.* [C19: from ACARUS]
ac·a·roid ('ækə,rɔɪd) *adj.* resembling a mite or tick. [C19: see ACARUS, -OID]
ac·a·roid gum *or* **res·in** *n.* a red alcohol-soluble resin that exudes from various species of grass tree, esp. *Xanthorrhoea hastilis,* and is used in varnishes, for coating paper, etc. Also called: **gum accroides.** [C19 *acaroid,* of uncertain origin (apparently not related to ACARUS)]
ac·a·rol·o·gy (,ækə'rɒlədʒɪ) *n.* the study of mites and ticks.
a·car·pel·lous *or U.S.* **a·car·pel·ous** (eɪ'kɑ:pələs) *adj.* (of flowers) having no carpels.
a·car·pous (eɪ'kɑ:pəs) *adj.* (of plants) producing no fruit. [from Greek *akarpos,* from A-[1] + *karpos* fruit]
ac·a·rus ('ækərəs) *n., pl.* **·ri** (-,raɪ). any of the free-living mites of the widely distributed genus *Acarus,* several of which, esp. *A. siro,* are serious pests of stored flour, grain, etc. [C17: New Latin, from Greek *akari* a small thing, a mite]
ACAS ('eɪkæs) *n.* (in Britain) *acronym for* Advisory Conciliation and Arbitration Service.
a·cat·a·lec·tic (æ,kætə'lɛktɪk) *Prosody.* ~*adj.* **1.** having the necessary number of feet or syllables, esp. having a complete final foot. ~*n.* **2.** a verse having the full number of syllables. [C16: via Late Latin from Greek *akatalēktikos.* See A-[1], CATALECTIC]
a·cau·dal (eɪ'kɔ:dᵊl) *or* **a·cau·date** *adj. Zoology.* having no tail.
a·cau·les·cent (,ækɔ:'lɛsᵊnt) *adj.* having no visible stem or a very short one.
acc. *abbrev. for:* **1.** *Commerce.* acceptance. **2.** accompanied. **3.** according. **4.** *Book-keeping.* account. **5.** *Grammar.* accusative.
Ac·cad ('ækæd) *n.* a variant spelling of **Akkad.**
ac·cede (æk'si:d) *vb.* (*intr.;* usually foll. by *to*) **1.** to assent or give one's consent; agree. **2.** to enter upon or attain (to an office, right, etc.): *the prince acceded to the throne.* **3.** *International law.* to become a party (to an agreement between nations, etc.), as by signing a treaty. [C15: from Latin *accēdere* to approach, agree, from *ad-* to + *cēdere* to go, yield] —**ac·'ced·ence** *n.* —**ac·'ced·er** *n.*
accel. *abbrev. for* accelerando.
ac·cel·er·an·do (æk,sɛlə'rændəʊ) *Music.* ~*adj., adv.* **1.** becoming faster. ~*n., pl.* **·dos. 2.** an increase in speed. [Italian]
ac·cel·er·ant (æk'sɛlərənt) *n. Chem.* another name for **accelerator** (sense 3). [C20: from Latin from *accelerāns,* present participle of *accelerāre* to go faster]
ac·cel·er·ate (æk'sɛlə,reɪt) *vb.* **1.** to go, occur, or cause to go or occur more quickly; speed up. **2.** (*tr.*) to cause to happen

sooner than expected. **3.** (*tr.*) to increase the velocity of (a body, reaction, etc.); cause acceleration. [C16: from Latin *accelerātus,* from *accelerāre* to go faster, from *ad-* (intensive) + *celerāre* to hasten, from *celer* swift] —**ac·'cel·er·a·ble** *adj.* —**ac·'cel·er·a·tive** *or* **ac·'cel·er·a·to·ry** *adj.*

ac·cel·er·a·tion (æk,sɛlə'reɪʃən) *n.* **1.** the act of accelerating or the state of being accelerated. **2.** the rate of increase of speed or the rate of change of velocity. Symbol: *a*

ac·cel·er·a·tion of free fall *n.* the acceleration of a body falling freely in a vacuum in the earth's gravitational field: the standard value is 9.806 65 metres per second per second or 32.174 feet per second per second. Symbol: *g* Also called: **acceleration due to gravity, acceleration of gravity.**

ac·cel·er·a·tor (æk'sɛlə,reɪtə) *n.* **1.** a device for increasing speed, esp. a pedal for controlling the fuel intake in a motor vehicle; throttle. **2.** Also called (not in technical usage): **atom smasher.** *Physics.* a machine for increasing the kinetic energy of subatomic particles or atomic nuclei and focusing them on a target. **3.** *Chem.* a substance that increases the speed of a chemical reaction, esp. one that increases the rate of vulcanization of rubber or the rate of development in photography; catalyst.

ac·cel·er·om·e·ter (æk,sɛlə'rɒmɪtə) *n.* an instrument for measuring acceleration, esp. of an aircraft or rocket.

ac·cent *n.* ('æksənt). **1.** the relative prominence of a spoken or sung syllable, esp. with regard to stress or pitch. Compare **pitch**[1] (sense 26), **stress** (sense 2). **2.** a mark (such as ', ˌ, ˊ, or ˋ) used in writing to indicate the stress or prominence of a syllable. Such a mark may also be used to indicate that a written syllable is to be pronounced, esp. when such pronunciation is not usual, as in *turnèd.* **3.** any of various marks or symbols conventionally used in writing certain languages to indicate the quality of a vowel, or for some other purpose, such as differentiation of homographs. See **acute** (sense 9), **grave**[2] (sense 5), **circumflex. 4.** (in some languages, such as Chinese) any of the tones that have phonemic value in distinguishing one word from another. Compare **tone** (sense 7). **5.** rhythmical stress in verse or prose. **6.** *Music.* **a.** stress placed on certain notes in a piece of music, indicated by a symbol printed over the note concerned. **b.** the rhythmical pulse of a piece or passage, usually represented as the stress on the first beat of each bar. See also **syncopation. 7.** *Maths.* **a.** a superscript symbol used to distinguish between variables represented by the same letter, as in *a*′, *a*″. **b.** a superscript symbol indicating the first or a higher derivative of a variable, as in *y*′, the second derivative. **8.** either of two superscript symbols indicating a specific unit, such as feet (′), inches (″), minutes of arc (′), or seconds of arc (″). **9.** the characteristic mode of pronunciation of a person or group, esp. one that betrays social or geographical origin. **10.** a distinctive characteristic of anything, such as taste, pattern, style, etc. **11.** particular attention or emphasis: *an accent on learning.* **12.** a strongly contrasting detail: *a blue rug with red accents.* ~*vb.* (æk'sɛnt). (*tr.*) **13.** to mark with an accent in writing, speech, music, etc. **14.** to lay particular emphasis or stress on. [C14: via Old French from Latin *accentus,* from *ad-* to + *cantus* chant, song. The Latin is a rendering of Greek *prosōidia* a song sung to music, the tone of a syllable]

ac·cen·tor (æk'sɛntə) *n.* any small sparrow-like songbirds of the genus *Prunella,* family *Prunellidae,* which inhabit mainly mountainous regions of Europe and Asia. See also **hedge sparrow.**

ac·cen·tu·al (æk'sɛntʃʊəl) *adj.* **1.** of, relating to, or having accents; rhythmical. **2.** *Prosody.* of or relating to verse based on the number of stresses in a line rather than on the number of syllables. Compare **quantitative.** —**ac·'cen·tu·al·ly** *adv.*

ac·cen·tu·ate (æk'sɛntʃʊ,eɪt) *vb.* (*tr.*) to stress or emphasize. —**ac·,cen·tu·'a·tion** *n.*

ac·cept (ək'sɛpt) *vb.* (*mainly tr.*) **1.** to take or receive (something offered). **2.** to give an affirmative reply to: *to accept an invitation.* **3.** to take on the responsibilities, duties, etc., of: *he accepted office.* **4.** to tolerate or accommodate oneself to. **5.** to consider as true or believe in (a philosophy, theory, etc.): *I cannot accept your argument.* **6.** (*may take a clause as object*) be willing to grant or believe: *you must accept that he lied.* **7.** to receive with approval or admit, as into a community, group, etc. **8.** *Commerce.* to agree to pay (a bill, draft, shipping document, etc.), esp. by signing. **9.** to receive as adequate, satisfactory, or valid. **10.** to receive, take, or hold (something applied, inserted, etc.). **11.** *Archaic.* (*intr.;* sometimes foll. by *of*) to take or receive an offer, invitation, etc. [C14: from Latin *acceptāre,* from *ad-* to + *capere* to take] —**ac·'cept·er** *n.*

ac·cept·a·ble (ək'sɛptəbᵊl) *adj.* **1.** satisfactory; adequate. **2.** pleasing; welcome. **3.** tolerable. —**ac·,cept·a·'bil·i·ty** *or* **ac·'cept·a·ble·ness** *n.* —**ac·'cept·a·bly** *adv.*

ac·cept·ance (ək'sɛptəns) *n.* **1.** the act of accepting or the state of being accepted or acceptable. **2.** favourable reception; approval. **3.** (often foll. by *of*) belief (in) or assent (to). **4.** *Commerce.* **a.** a formal agreement by a debtor to pay a draft, bill, etc. **b.** the document so accepted. Compare **bank acceptance, trade acceptance. 5.** *Contract law.* words or conduct by which a person signifies his assent to the terms and conditions of an offer or agreement.

ac·cept·ant (ək'sɛptənt) *adj.* receiving willingly; receptive.

ac·cep·ta·tion (,æksɛp'teɪʃən) *n.* the accepted meaning, as of a word, phrase, etc.

ac·cept·ed (ək'sɛptɪd) *adj.* commonly approved or recognized; customary; established. —**ac·'cept·ed·ly** *adv.*

ac·cep·tor (ək'sɛptə) *n.* **1.** *Commerce.* the person or organization on which a draft or bill of exchange is drawn after liability has been accepted, usually by signature. **2.** Also called: **acceptor impurity.** *Electronics.* an impurity, such as gallium, added to a semiconductor material to increase its p-type conductivity by increasing the number of holes in the semiconductor. Compare **donor** (sense 5). **3.** *Chem.* the atom or group that does not supply electrons in a semipolar bond. **4.** *Electronics.* a circuit tuned to accept a particular frequency.

ac·cess ('æksɛs) *n.* **1.** the act of approaching or entering. **2.** the state or condition of being approachable or easy to enter. **3.** the right or privilege to approach, reach, enter, or make use of something. **4.** a way or means of approach or entry. **5.** (*modifier*): designating programmes made by the general public as distinguished from those made by professional broadcasters: *access television.* **6.** a sudden outburst or attack, as of rage or disease. ~*vb.* **7.** (*tr.*) *Computer technol.* **a.** to obtain or retrieve (information) from a storage device. **b.** to place (information) in a storage device. See also **direct access, sequential access.** [C14: from Old French or from Latin *accessus* an approach, from *accēdere* to ACCEDE]

ac·ces·sa·ry (ək'sɛsərɪ) *n., pl.* **·ries.** *Law.* a less common spelling of **accessory.** —**ac·'ces·sa·ri·ly** *adv.* —**ac·'ces·sa·ri·ness** *n.*

ac·ces·si·ble (ək'sɛsəbᵊl) *adj.* **1.** easy to approach, enter, or use. **2. accessible to.** likely to be affected by; open to; susceptible to. **3.** obtainable; available. —**ac·,ces·si·'bil·i·ty** *n.* —**ac·'ces·si·bly** *adv.*

ac·ces·sion (ək'sɛʃən) *n.* **1.** the act of entering upon or attaining to an office, right, condition, etc. **2.** an increase due to an addition. **3.** an addition, as to a collection. **4.** *Property law.* **a.** an addition to land or property by natural increase or improvement. **b.** the owner's right to the increased value of such land. **5.** *International law.* the formal acceptance of a convention or treaty. **6.** agreement; consent. **7.** a less common word for **access** (sense 1). ~*vb.* **8.** (*tr.*) to make a record of (additions to a collection). —**ac·'ces·sion·al** *adj.*

ac·ces·sion num·ber *n. Library science.* the number given to record a new addition to a collection.

ac·ces·so·ry (ək'sɛsərɪ) *n., pl.* **·ries. 1.** a supplementary part or object, as of a car, appliance, etc. **2.** (*often pl.*) a small accompanying item of dress, esp. of women's dress. **3.** (formerly) a person involved in a crime although absent during its commission, either a person who incites or encourages or otherwise assists the planning of a crime (**accessory before the fact**) or a person who knowingly conceals, comforts, or assists after the commission of a crime (**accessory after the fact**). ~*adj.* **4.** supplementary; additional; subordinate. **5.** assisting in or having knowledge of an act, esp. a crime. —**ac·ces·so·ri·al** (,æksɛ'sɔːrɪəl) *adj.* —**ac·'ces·so·ri·ly** *adv.* —**ac·'ces·so·ri·ness** *n.*

ac·ces·so·ry fruit *n.* another name for **pseudocarp.**

ac·ces·so·ry nerve *n.* either one of the eleventh pair of cranial nerves, which supply the muscles of the head, shoulders, larynx, and pharynx and the viscera of the abdomen and thorax.

ac·cess road *n.* a road providing a means of entry into a region or of approach to another road, esp. a motorway.

ac·cess time *n. Computer technol.* the time required to retrieve a piece of stored information.

ac·ciac·ca·tu·ra (ɑː,tʃɑːkɑː'tʊərə) *n., pl.* **·ras** *or* **·re** (-reɪ, -riː). **1.** a small grace note melodically adjacent to a principal note and played simultaneously with or immediately before it. **2.** (in modern music) a very short appoggiatura. [C18: literally: a crushing sound]

ac·ci·dence ('æksɪdəns) *n.* inflectional morphology; the part of grammar concerned with changes in the form of words by internal modification or by affixation, for the expression of tense, person, case, number, etc. [C15: from Latin *accidentia* accidental matters, hence inflections of words, from *accidere* to happen. See ACCIDENT]

ac·ci·dent ('æksɪdənt) *n.* **1.** an unforeseen event or one without an apparent cause. **2.** anything that occurs unintentionally or by chance; chance; fortune: *I met him by accident.* **3.** a misfortune or mishap, esp. one causing injury or death. **4.** a material quality that is not an essential part of something (as opposed to *substance*). **5.** Also called: **adjunct.** *Logic.* a nonessential attribute or characteristic of something. **6.** *Geology.* a surface irregularity in a natural formation, esp. in a rock formation or a river system. **7.** *Archaic.* an inflected form of a word. [C14: via Old French from Latin *accident-* chance, happening, from the present participle of *accidere* to befall, happen, from *ad-* to + *cadere* to fall]

ac·ci·den·tal (,æksɪ'dɛntᵊl) *adj.* **1.** occurring by chance, unexpectedly, or unintentionally. **2.** nonessential; incidental. **3.** *Music.* denoting sharps, flats, or naturals that are not in the key signature of a piece. ~*n.* **4.** an incidental, nonessential, or supplementary circumstance, factor, or attribute. **5.** *Music.* a symbol denoting that the following note is a sharp, flat, or natural that is not a part of the key signature. —**,ac·ci·'den·tal·ly** *adv.*

ac·ci·dent in·sur·ance *n.* insurance providing compensation for accidental injury or death.

ac·ci·dent-prone *adj.* liable to become involved in accidents.

ac·ci·die ('æksɪdɪ) *or* **a·ce·di·a** *n.* spiritual sloth; apathy; indifference. [in use C13 to C16 and revived C19: via Late Latin from Greek *akēdia,* from A-[1] + *kēdos* care]

ac·cip·i·ter (æk'sɪpɪtə) *n.* any hawk of the genus *Accipiter,* typically having short rounded wings and a long tail. [C19: New Latin, from Latin: hawk]

ac·cip·i·trine (æk'sɪpɪ,traɪn, -trɪn) *adj.* **1.** Also: **ac·cip·i·tral**

(æk'sɪpɪtrəl). of, relating to, or resembling a hawk; rapacious. **2.** of, relating to, or belonging to the subfamily *Accipitrinae,* which includes the hawks.

ac+claim (ə'kleɪm) *vb.* **1.** (*tr.*) to acknowledge publicly the excellence of (a person, act, etc.). **2.** to salute with cheering, clapping, etc.; applaud. **3.** (*tr.*) to acknowledge publicly that (a person) has (some position, quality, etc.): *they acclaimed him king.* ~*n.* **4.** an enthusiastic shout of welcome, approval, etc. [C17: from Latin *acclāmāre* to shout at, shout applause, from *ad-* to + *clamāre* to shout] —**ac+'claim+er** *n.*

ac+cla+ma+tion (ˌæklə'meɪʃən) *n.* **1.** an enthusiastic reception or exhibition of welcome, approval, etc. **2.** an expression of approval by a meeting or gathering through shouts or applause. **3. by acclamation. a.** by an overwhelming majority without a ballot. **b.** *Canadian.* (of an election or electoral victory) without opposition: *he won by acclamation.* —**ac+clam·a+to·ry** (ə'klæmətərɪ, -trɪ) *adj.*

ac+cli+ma+tize, ac+cli+ma+tise (ə'klaɪməˌtaɪz), *or* **ac+cli+mate** (ə'klaɪmɪt, 'æklɪˌmeɪt) *vb.* to adapt or become accustomed to a new climate or environment. —**ac+'cli+ma+ˌtiz+a·ble, ac+'cli+ma+ˌtis+a·ble,** *or* **ac+'cli+mat+a·ble** *adj.* —**ac+ˌcli+ma+ti+'za+tion, ac+ˌcli+ma+ti+'sa+tion,** *or* **ˌac+cli+'ma+tion** *n.* —**ac+'cli+ma+ˌtiz+er** *or* **ac+'cli+ma+ˌtis+er** *n.*

ac+cliv+i+ty (ə'klɪvɪtɪ) *n., pl.* **·ties.** an upward slope, esp. of the ground. Compare **declivity.** [C17: from Latin *acclīvitās,* from *acclīvis* sloping up, steep] —**ac+'cliv·i+tous** *or* **ac+cli+vous** (ə'klaɪvəs) *adj.*

ac+co+lade ('ækəˌleɪd, ˌækə'leɪd) *n.* **1.** strong praise or approval; acclaim. **2.** an award or honour. **3.** the ceremonial gesture used to confer knighthood, originally an embrace, now a touch on the shoulder with a sword. **4.** a rare word for **brace** (sense 7). **5.** *Architect.* a curved ornamental moulding, esp. one having the shape of an ogee arch. [C17: via French and Italian from Vulgar Latin *accollāre* (unattested) to hug; related to Latin *collum* neck]

ac+com+mo+date (ə'kɒməˌdeɪt) *vb.* **1.** (*tr.*) to supply or provide, esp. with lodging or board and lodging. **2.** (*tr.*) to oblige or do a favour for. **3.** to adjust or become adjusted; adapt. **4.** (*tr.*) to bring into harmony; reconcile. **5.** (*tr.*) to allow room for; contain. **6.** (*tr.*) to lend money to. [C16: from Latin *accommodāre* to make fit, from *ad-* to + *commodus* having the proper measure] —**ac+'com+mo+ˌda+tive** *adj.*

ac+com+mo+dat+ing (ə'kɒməˌdeɪtɪŋ) *adj.* willing to help; kind; obliging. —**ac+'com+mo+ˌdat+ing+ly** *adv.*

ac+com+mo+da+tion (əˌkɒmə'deɪʃən) *n.* **1.** adjustment, as of differences or to new circumstances; adaptation, settlement, or reconciliation. **2.** lodging or board and lodging. **3.** something fulfilling a need, want, etc.; convenience or facility. **4.** *Physiol.* the automatic or voluntary adjustment of the thickness of the lens of the eye for far or near vision. **5.** willingness to help or oblige. **6.** *Commerce.* a loan, usually made as an act of favour by a bank before formal credit arrangements are agreed.

ac+com+mo+da+tion ad+dress *n.* an address on letters, etc., to a person or business that does not wish or is not able to receive post at a permanent or actual address.

ac+com+mo+da+tion bill *n. Commerce.* a bill of exchange cosigned by a guarantor: designed to strengthen the acceptor's credit.

ac+com+mo+da+tion lad+der *n. Nautical.* a flight of stairs or a ladder for lowering over the side of a ship for access to and from a small boat, pier, etc.

ac+com+pa+ni+ment (ə'kʌmpənɪmənt, ə'kʌmpnɪ-) *n.* **1.** something that accompanies or is served or used with something else. **2.** something inessential or subsidiary that is added, as for ornament or symmetry. **3.** *Music.* a subordinate part for an instrument, voices, or an orchestra.

ac+com+pa+nist (ə'kʌmpənɪst, ə'kʌmpnɪst) *or U.S.* (*sometimes*) **ac+com+pa+ny+ist** (ə'kʌmpəniːɪst) *n.* a person who supplies a musical accompaniment.

ac+com+pa+ny (ə'kʌmpənɪ, ə'kʌmpnɪ) *vb.* **+nies, +ny+ing, +nied.** **1.** (*tr.*) to go along with, so as to be in company with or escort. **2.** (*tr.*; foll. by *with*) to supplement: *he accompanied his tirade with gestures.* **3.** (*tr.*) to occur, coexist, or be associated with. **4.** to provide a musical accompaniment for (a soloist, etc.). [C15: from Old French *accompaignier,* from *compaing* COMPANION] —**ac+'com+pa+ni+er** *n.*

ac+com+plice (ə'kɒmplɪs, ə'kʌm-) *n.* a person who has helped another in committing a crime. [C15: from *a complice,* interpreted as one word. See COMPLICE]

ac+com+plish (ə'kɒmplɪʃ, ə'kʌm-) *vb.* (*tr.*) **1.** to manage to do; achieve. **2.** to conclude successfully; complete. [C14: from Old French *acomplir* to complete, ultimately from Latin *complēre* to fill up. See COMPLETE] —**ac+'com+plish+a·ble** *adj.* —**ac+'com+plish+er** *n.*

ac+com+plished (ə'kɒmplɪʃt, ə'kʌm-) *adj.* **1.** successfully completed; achieved. **2.** expert; proficient.

ac+com+plish+ment (ə'kɒmplɪʃmənt, ə'kʌm-) *n.* **1.** the act of carrying out or achieving. **2.** something achieved or successfully completed. **3.** (*often pl.*) skill or talent. **4.** (*often pl.*) social grace, style, and poise.

ac+cord (ə'kɔːd) *n.* **1.** agreement; conformity; accordance (esp. in the phrase **in accord with**). **2.** consent or concurrence of opinion. **3. with one accord.** unanimously. **4.** pleasing relationship between sounds, colours, etc.; harmony. **5.** a settlement of differences, as between nations; compromise. **6. of one's own accord.** voluntarily. ~*vb.* **7.** to be or cause to be in harmony or agreement. **8.** (*tr.*) to grant; bestow. [C12: via Old French from Latin *ad-* to + *cord-*, stem of *cor* heart] —**ac+'cord+a·ble** *adj.* —**ac'cord+er** *n.*

ac+cord+ance (ə'kɔːdəns) *n.* **1.** conformity; agreement; accord (esp. in the phrase **in accordance with**). **2.** the act of granting; bestowal: *accordance of rights.*

ac+cord+ant (ə'kɔːdᵊnt) *adj.* (*usually postpositive* and foll. by *with*) in conformity or harmony. —**ac+'cord+ant+ly** *adv.*

ac+cord+ing (ə'kɔːdɪŋ) *adj.* **1.** (foll. by *to*) in proportion; in relation. **2.** (foll. by *to*) on the report (of); as stated (by). **3.** (foll. by *to*) in conformity (with); in accordance (with). **4.** (foll. by *as*) depending (on whether). **5.** *Not standard.* dependent on: *it's all according where you want to go.*

ac+cord+ing+ly (ə'kɔːdɪŋlɪ) *adv.* **1.** in an appropriate manner; suitably. ~ **2.** (*sentence connector*) consequently.

ac+cor+di+on (ə'kɔːdɪən) *n.* **1.** a portable box-shaped instrument of the reed organ family, consisting of metallic reeds that are made to vibrate by air from a set of bellows controlled by the player's hands. Notes are produced by means of studlike keys. **2.** short for **piano accordion.** [C19: from German *Akkordion,* from *Akkord* harmony, chord] —**ac+'cor+di+on+ist** *n.*

ac+cor+di+on pleats *pl. n.* tiny knife pleats.

ac+cost (ə'kɒst) *vb.* **1.** (*tr.*) to approach, stop, and speak to (a person), as to ask a question, confront with a crime, solicit sexually, etc. ~*n.* **2.** *Rare.* a greeting. [C16: from Late Latin *accostāre* to place side by side, from Latin *costa* side, rib] —**ac+'cost+a·ble** *adj.*

ac+couche+ment *French.* (akuʃ'mã; *English* ə'kuːʃmənt) *n.* childbirth or the period of confinement. [C19: from *accoucher* to put to bed, to give birth. See COUCH]

ac+cou+cheur *French.* (aku'ʃœːr) *or* (*fem.*) ***ac+cou+cheuse*** (aku'ʃœːz) *n.* an obstetrician or midwife. [literally: one who is present at the bedside]

ac+count (ə'kaʊnt) *n.* **1.** a verbal or written report, description, or narration of some occurrence, event, etc. **2.** an explanation of conduct, esp. one made to someone in authority. **3.** ground; basis; consideration (often in the phrases **on this (that, every, no,** *etc.*) **account, on account of**). **4.** importance, consequence, or value: *of little account.* **5.** assessment; judgment. **6.** profit or advantage: *to turn an idea to account.* **7.** part or behalf (only in the phrase **on one's** *or* **someone's account**). **8.** *Finance.* **a.** a business relationship between a bank, department store, stockbroker, etc., and a depositor, customer, or client permitting the latter certain banking or credit services. **b.** the sum of money deposited at a bank. **c.** the amount of credit available to the holder of an account. **d.** a record of these. **9.** a statement of monetary transactions with the resulting balance. **10.** (on the London Stock Exchange) the period, ordinarily of a fortnight's duration, in which transactions take place and at the end of which settlements are made. **11.** *Book-keeping.* a chronological list of debits and credits relating to a specified asset, liability, expense, or income of a business and forming part of the ledger. **12.** *Chiefly U.S.* **a.** a regular client or customer, esp. a firm that purchases commodities on credit. **b.** an area of business assigned to another: *they transferred their publicity account to a new agent.* **13. call** (*or* **bring**) **to account. a.** to insist on explanation. **b.** to rebuke; reprimand. **c.** to hold responsible. **14. give a good** (**bad,** *etc.*) **account of oneself.** to perform well (badly, etc.): *he gave a poor account of himself in the examination.* **15. on account. a.** on credit. **b.** Also: **to account.** as partial payment. **16. on account of.** (*prep.*) because of; by reason of. **17. take account of** *or* **take into account.** to take into consideration; allow for. **18. settle** *or* **square accounts with. a.** to pay or receive a balance due. **b.** to get revenge on (someone). **19.** See **bank account** or **credit account.** ~*vb.* **20.** (*tr.*) to consider or reckon: *he accounts himself poor.* [C13: from Old French *acont,* from *conter, compter* to COUNT[1]]

ac+count+a·ble (ə'kaʊntəbᵊl) *adj.* **1.** responsible to someone or for some action; answerable. **2.** able to be explained. —**ac+ˌcount+a·'bil+i+ty** *n.* —**ac+'count+a·bly** *adv.*

ac+count+an+cy (ə'kaʊntənsɪ) *n.* the profession or business of an accountant.

ac+count+ant (ə'kaʊntənt) *n.* a person concerned with the maintenance and audit of business accounts and the preparation of consultant reports in tax and finance.

ac+count day *n.* (on the London Stock Exchange) the day on which deliveries and payments relating to transactions made during the preceding account are made.

ac+count for *vb.* (*intr., prep.*) **1.** to give reasons for (an event, act, etc.). **2.** to make or provide a reckoning of (expenditure, payments, etc.). **3.** to be responsible for destroying, killing, or putting (people, aircraft, etc.) out of action.

ac+count+ing (ə'kaʊntɪŋ) *n.* the skill or practice of maintaining and auditing accounts and preparing reports on the assets, liabilities, etc., of a business.

ac+count pay+a·ble *n. Accounting, U.S.* a current liability account showing amounts payable by a firm to suppliers for purchases of materials, stocks, or services on credit.

ac+count re+ceiv+a·ble *n. Accounting, U.S.* a current asset account showing amounts payable to a firm by customers who have made purchases of goods and services on credit.

ac+cou+ple+ment (ə'kʌpᵊlmənt) *n.* a timber joist or beam that serves as a tie or support. [C15: French, from *accoupler,* from Latin *copulāre* to COUPLE]

ac+cou+tre *or U.S.* **ac+cou+ter** (ə'kuːtə) *vb.* (*tr.; usually passive*) to provide with military equipment. [C16: from Old French *accoustrer* to equip with clothing, ultimately related to Latin *consuere* to sew together]

ac+cou+trement *or U.S.* **ac+cou+terment** (ə'kuːtrəmənt) *n.* **1.** equipment worn by soldiers in addition to their clothing and weapons. **2.** (*usually pl.*) clothing, equipment, etc.; trappings: *the accoutrements of war.*

Ac+cra (ə'krɑː) *n.* the capital of Ghana, a port on the Gulf of Guinea: built on the site of three 17th-century trading fortresses founded by the English, Dutch, and Danish. Pop.: 564 194 (1970).

ac·cred·it (əˈkrɛdɪt) *vb.* (*tr.*) **1.** to ascribe or attribute. **2.** to give official recognition to; sanction; authorize. **3.** to certify or guarantee as meeting required standards. **4.** (often foll. by *at* or *to*) **a.** to furnish or send (an envoy, etc.) with official credentials. **b.** to appoint (someone) as an envoy, etc. **5.** to believe. [C17: from French *accréditer*, from the phrase *mettre à crédit* to put to CREDIT] —**ac·ˌcred·i·ˈta·tion** *n.*

ac·cres·cent (æˈkrɛsᵊnt) *adj. Botany.* (of a calyx or other part) continuing to grow after flowering. [C18: from Latin *accrēscere* to continue to grow, from *crēscere* to grow]

ac·crete (əˈkriːt) *vb.* **1.** to grow or cause to grow together; be or become fused. **2.** (*tr.*) to make or become bigger, as by addition. ~*adj.* **3.** (of plant organs) grown together. [C18: back formation from ACCRETION]

ac·cre·tion (əˈkriːʃən) *n.* **1.** any gradual increase in size, as through growth or external addition. **2.** something added, esp. extraneously, to cause growth or an increase in size. **3.** the growing together of normally separate plant or animal parts. **4.** *Pathol.* **a.** abnormal union or growing together of parts; adhesion. **b.** a mass of foreign matter collected in a cavity. **5.** *Law.* an increase in the share of a beneficiary in an estate, as when a co-beneficiary fails to take his share. [C17: from Latin *accretiō* increase, from *accrēscere.* See ACCRUE] —**ac·ˈcre·tive** *or* **ac·ˈcre·tion·ar·y** *adj.*

Ac·cring·ton (ˈækrɪŋtən) *n.* a town in NW England, in SE Lancashire. Pop.: 36 838 (1971).

ac·crue (əˈkruː) *vb.* ·**crues,** ·**cru·ing,** ·**crued.** (*intr.*) **1.** to increase by growth or addition, esp. (of capital) to increase by periodic addition of interest. **2.** (often foll. by *to*) to fall naturally (to); come into the possession (of); result (for). **3.** *Law.* (of a right or demand) to become capable of being enforced. [C15: from Old French *accreue* growth, ultimately from Latin *accrēscere* to increase, from *ad-* to, in addition + *crēscere* to grow] —**ac·ˈcru·ment** *or* **ac·ˈcru·al** *n.*

acct. *Book-keeping. abbrev. for* account.

ac·cul·tur·ate (əˈkʌltʃəˌreɪt) *vb.* (*tr.*) (of a cultural or social group) to assimilate the cultural traits of another group. [C20: from AD- + CULTURE + -ATE[1]] —**ac·ˌcul·tur·ˈa·tion** *n.*

ac·cum·bent (əˈkʌmbənt) *adj.* **1.** *Botany.* (of plant parts and plants) lying against some other part or thing. **2.** a rare word for **recumbent.** [C18: from Latin *accumbere* to recline] —**ac·ˈcum·ben·cy** *n.*

ac·cu·mu·late (əˈkjuːmjʊˌleɪt) *vb.* to gather or become gathered together in an increasing quantity; amass; collect. [C16: from Latin *accumulātus,* past participle of *accumulāre* to heap up, from *cumulus* a heap] —**ac·ˈcu·mu·la·ble** *adj.* —**ac·ˈcu·mu·la·tive** *adj.* —**ac·ˈcu·mu·la·tive·ly** *adv.* —**ac·ˈcu·mu·la·tive·ness** *n.*

ac·cu·mu·la·tion (əˌkjuːmjʊˈleɪʃən) *n.* **1.** the act or process of collecting together or becoming collected. **2.** something that has been collected, gathered, heaped, etc. **3.** *Finance.* **a.** the continuous growth of capital by retention of interest or earnings. **b.** (in computing the yield on a bond purchased at a discount) the amount that is added to each yield to bring the cost of the bond into equality with its par value over its life. Compare **amortization** (sense 2). **4.** the taking of a first and an advanced university degree simultaneously.

ac·cu·mu·la·tion point *n. Maths.* another name for **limit point.**

ac·cu·mu·la·tor (əˈkjuːmjʊˌleɪtə) *n.* **1.** Also called: **battery, storage battery.** a rechargeable device for storing electrical energy in the form of chemical energy, consisting of one or more separate secondary cells. **2.** *Horse racing, Brit.* a collective bet, esp. on four or more races, in which the stake and winnings on each successive race are carried forward to become the stake on the next, so that both stakes and winnings accumulate progressively so long as the bet continues to be a winning one. **3. a.** a register in a calculator and the possible associated electrical circuits in which figures are stored and arithmetical operations performed on them. **b.** a location in a computer store in which arithmetical results are produced.

ac·cu·ra·cy (ˈækjʊrəsɪ) *n., pl.* ·**cies. 1.** faithful measurement or representation of the truth; correctness; precision. **2.** *Physics, chem.* the degree of agreement between a measured value and the standard or accepted value for that measurement. **3.** *Maths.* the number of significant figures used or appearing in a number.

ac·cu·rate (ˈækjərɪt) *adj.* **1.** faithfully representing or describing the truth. **2.** showing a negligible or permissible deviation from a standard: *an accurate ruler.* **3.** without error; precise; meticulous. [C16: from Latin *accūrātus,* past participle of *accūrāre* to perform with care, from *cūra* care] —ˈ**ac·cu·rate·ly** *adv.* —ˈ**ac·cu·rate·ness** *n.*

ac·curs·ed (əˈkɜːsɪd, əˈkɜːst) *or* **ac·curst** (əˈkɜːst) *adj.* **1.** under or subject to a curse; doomed. **2.** (*prenominal*) hateful; detestable; execrable. [Old English *ācursod,* past participle of *ācursian* to put under a CURSE] —**ac·curs·ed·ly** (əˈkɜːsɪdlɪ) *adv.* —**ac·ˈcurs·ed·ness** *n.*

ac·cus·al (əˈkjuːzᵊl) *n.* another word for **accusation.**

ac·cu·sa·tion (ˌækjʊˈzeɪʃən) *n.* **1.** an allegation that a person is guilty of some fault, offence, or crime; imputation. **2.** a formal charge brought against a person stating the crime that he is alleged to have committed.

ac·cu·sa·tive (əˈkjuːzətɪv) *adj.* **1.** *Grammar.* denoting a case of nouns, pronouns, and adjectives in inflected languages that is used to identify the direct object of a finite verb, of certain prepositions, and for certain other purposes. See also **objective** (sense 5). **2.** another word for **accusatorial.** ~*n.* **3.** *Grammar.* **a.** the accusative case. **b.** a word or speech element in the accusative case. [C15: from Latin; in grammar, from the phrase *cāsus accūsātīvus* accusative case, a mistaken translation of Greek *ptōsis aitiatikē* the case indicating causation. See ACCUSE] —**ac·cu·sa·ti·val** (əˌkjuːzəˈtaɪvᵊl) *adj.* —**ac·ˈcu·sa·tive·ly** *adv.*

ac·cu·sa·to·ri·al (əˌkjuːzəˈtɔːrɪəl) *or* **ac·cu·sa·to·ry** (əˈkjuːzətərɪ, -trɪ, ˌækjʊˈzeɪtərɪ) *adj.* **1.** containing or implying blame or strong criticism. **2.** *Law.* denoting criminal procedure in which the prosecutor is distinct from the judge and the trial is conducted in public. Compare **inquisitorial** (sense 3).

ac·cuse (əˈkjuːz) *vb.* to charge (a person or persons) with some fault, offence, crime, etc.; impute guilt or blame. [C13: via Old French from Latin *accūsāre* to call to account, from *ad-* to + *causa* lawsuit] —**ac·ˈcus·er** *n.* —**ac·ˈcus·ing·ly** *adv.*

ac·cused (əˈkjuːzd) *n.* (preceded by *the*) *Law.* the defendant or defendants appearing on a criminal charge.

ac·cus·tom (əˈkʌstəm) *vb.* (*tr.;* usually foll. by *to*) to make (oneself) familiar (with) or used (to), as by practice, habit, or experience. [C15: from Old French *acostumer,* from *costume* CUSTOM]

ac·cus·tomed (əˈkʌstəmd) *adj.* **1.** usual; customary. **2.** (*postpositive;* foll. by *to*) used or inured (to). **3.** (*postpositive;* foll. by *to*) in the habit (of): *accustomed to walking after meals.*

Ac·cu·tron (ˈækjuːˌtrɒn) *n. Trademark.* a type of watch in which the balance wheel and hairspring are replaced by a tuning fork kept in vibration by a tiny internal battery.

AC/DC *adj. Slang.* (of a person) bisexual. [C20: humorous reference to electrical apparatus that is adaptable for ALTERNATING CURRENT and DIRECT CURRENT]

ace (eɪs) *n.* **1.** any die, domino, or any of four playing cards with one spot. **2.** a single spot or pip on a playing card, die, etc. **3.** *Tennis.* **a.** a winning serve that the opponent fails to reach. **b.** any winning serve. **4.** *Golf, chiefly U.S.* a hole in one. **5.** a fighter pilot accredited with destroying many enemy aircraft. **6.** *Informal.* an expert or highly skilled person: *an ace at driving.* **7. an ace up one's sleeve** *or* **an ace in the hole.** a hidden and powerful advantage. ~*adj.* **8.** *Informal.* superb; excellent. ~*vb.* **9.** (*tr.*) *Tennis.* to serve an ace against. **10.** *Golf.* to play (a hole) in one stroke. [C13: via Old French from Latin *as* a unit, perhaps from a Greek variant of *heis* one]

ACE (eɪs) *n.* (in Britain) *acronym for* Advisory Centre for Education; a private organization offering advice on schools to parents.

-a·ce·a *suffix forming plural proper nouns.* denoting animals belonging to a class or order: *Crustacea* (class); *Cetacea* (order). [New Latin, from Latin, neuter plural of *-āceus* -ACEOUS]

-a·ce·ae *suffix forming plural proper nouns.* denoting plants belonging to a family: *Liliaceae; Ranunculaceae.* [New Latin, from Latin, feminine plural of *-āceus* -ACEOUS]

a·ce·di·a (əˈsiːdɪə) *n.* another word for **accidie.**

A·cel·da·ma (əˈsɛldəmə) *n. New Testament.* the place near Jerusalem that was bought with the 30 pieces of silver paid to Judas for betraying Jesus (Matthew 27:8; Acts 1:19). [C14: from Aramaic *haqēl demā* field of blood]

a·cel·lu·lar (eɪˈsɛljʊlə) *adj. Biology.* not made up of or containing cells.

a·cen·tric (eɪˈsɛntrɪk) *adj.* **1.** without a centre. **2.** not on centre; eccentric.

-a·ceous *suffix forming adjectives.* relating to, belonging to, having the nature of, or resembling: *herbaceous; larvaceous.* [New Latin, from Latin *-āceus* of a certain kind; related to *-āc, -āx,* adjectival suffix]

a·ceph·a·lous (əˈsɛfələs) *adj.* **1.** having no head or one that is reduced and indistinct, as certain insect larvae. **2.** having or recognizing no ruler or leader. [C18: via Medieval Latin from Greek *akephalos.* See A-[1], -CEPHALOUS]

ac·er·ate (ˈæsəˌreɪt, -rɪt) *adj.* another word for **acerose.** [C19: from Latin *ācer* sharp + -ATE[1]]

ac·er·bate (ˈæsəˌbeɪt) *vb.* (*tr.*) **1.** to embitter or exasperate. **2.** to make sour or bitter. [C18: from Latin *acerbātus,* past participle of *acerbāre* to make sour]

a·cer·bic (əˈsɜːbɪk) *adj.* harsh, bitter, or astringent; sour. [C17: from Latin *acerbus* sour, bitter]

a·cer·bi·ty (əˈsɜːbɪtɪ) *n., pl.* ·**ties. 1.** vitriolic or embittered speech, temper, etc. **2.** sourness or bitterness of taste.

ac·er·ose (ˈæsəˌrəʊs, -ˌrəʊz) *or* **ac·er·ous** *adj.* shaped like a needle, as pine leaves. [C18: from Latin *acerōsus* full of chaff (erroneously used by Linnaeus as if derived from *ācer* sharp)]

a·cer·vate (əˈsɜːvɪt, -ˌveɪt) *adj. Botany.* growing in heaps or clusters. [C19: from Latin *acervātus,* from *acervāre* to heap up, from *acervus* a heap] —**a·ˈcer·vate·ly** *adv.*

a·ces·cent (əˈsɛsᵊnt) *adj.* slightly sour or turning sour. [C18: from Latin *acēscent-,* from *acēscere* to become sour, from *ācer* sharp] —**a·ˈces·cence** *or* **a·ˈces·cen·cy** *n.*

ac·e·tab·u·lum (ˌæsɪˈtæbjʊləm) *n., pl.* ·**la** (-lə). **1.** the deep cuplike cavity on the side of the hipbone that receives the head of the thighbone. **2.** a round muscular sucker in flatworms, leeches, and cephalopod molluscs. [Latin: vinegar cup, hence a cuplike cavity, from *acētum* vinegar + *-abulum,* suffix denoting a container]

ac·e·tal (ˈæsɪˌtæl) *n.* **1.** a colourless volatile liquid used as a solvent and in perfumes. Formula: $CH_3CH(OC_2H_5)_2$. **2.** any organic compound containing the group $-CH(OR_1)OR_2$, where R_1 and R_2 are other organic groups. [C19: from German *Azetal,* from ACETO- + ALCOHOL]

ac·et·al·de·hyde (ˌæsɪˈtældɪˌhaɪd) *n.* a colourless volatile pungent liquid, miscible with water, used in the manufacture of organic compounds and as a solvent and reducing agent. Formula: CH_3CHO.

ac+et+am+ide (ˌæsɪˈtæmaɪd, əˈsɛtɪˌmaɪd) *or* **ac+et+am+id** (ˌæsɪˈtæmɪd, əˈsɛtɪmɪd) *n.* a white or colourless soluble deliquescent crystalline compound, used in the manufacture of organic chemicals. Formula: CH_3CONH_2. [C19: from German *Azetamid*, from ACETO- + AMIDE]

ac+et+an·i+lide (ˌæsɪˈtænɪˌlaɪd) *or* **ac+et+an·i+lid** (ˌæsɪˈtænɪlɪd) *n.* a white crystalline powder used in the manufacture of dyes and rubber and as an analgesic in medicine. Formula: $C_6H_5NHCOCH_3$. [C19: from ACETO- + ANILINE + -IDE]

ac+e·tate (ˈæsɪˌteɪt) *n.* **1.** any salt or ester of acetic acid, containing the monovalent ion CH_3COO^- or the group CH_3COO-. **2.** (*modifier*) consisting of, containing, or concerned with the group CH_3COO-: *acetate group or radical.* **3.** short for **acetate rayon** *or* **cellulose acetate.** [C19: from ACETIC + -ATE[1]] —ˈ**ac+e·tat+ed** *adj.*

ac+e·tate ray+on *n.* a synthetic textile fibre made from cellulose acetate. Also called: **acetate.**

a·ce·tic (əˈsiːtɪk, əˈsɛt-) *adj.* of, containing, producing, or derived from acetic acid or vinegar. [C19: from Latin *acētum* vinegar]

a·ce·tic ac·id *n.* a colourless pungent liquid, miscible with water, widely used in the manufacture of acetic anhydride, vinyl acetate, plastics, pharmaceuticals, dyes, etc. Formula: CH_3COOH. See also **glacial acetic acid, vinegar.**

a·ce·tic an+hy+dride *n.* a colourless pungent liquid used in the manufacture of cellulose and vinyl acetates for synthetic fabrics. Formula: $(CH_3CO)_2O$.

a·cet·i+fy (əˈsɛtɪˌfaɪ) *vb.* **+fies, +fy+ing, +fied.** to become or cause to become acetic acid or vinegar. —**a·ˌcet·i+fi+ˈca+tion** *n.* —**a·ˈcet·i·ˌfi+er** *n.*

ac·e·to- *or before a vowel* **ac·et-** *combining form.* containing an acetyl group or derived from acetic acid: *acetone.* [from Latin *acētum* vinegar]

ac+e·tom+e·ter (ˌæsɪˈtɒmɪtə) *n.* a device for measuring the concentration of acetic acid in a solution, esp. in vinegar.

ac+e·tone (ˈæsɪˌtəʊn) *n.* a colourless volatile flammable pungent liquid, miscible with water, used in the manufacture of chemicals and as a solvent and thinner for paints, varnishes, and lacquers. Formula: CH_3COCH_3. [C19: from German *Azeton*, from ACETO- + -ONE] —**ac+e·ton+ic** (ˌæsɪˈtɒnɪk) *adj.*

ac+e·tone bod·y *n.* another name for **ketone body.**

a·ce·to+phe+net·i·din (əˌsiːtəʊfəˈnɛtɪdɪn) *n.* another name for **phenacetin.**

ac+e·tous (ˈæsɪtəs, əˈsiː-) *or* **ac+e·tose** (ˈæsɪˌtəʊs, -ˌtəʊz) *adj.* **1.** containing, producing, or resembling acetic acid or vinegar. **2.** tasting like vinegar. [C18: from Late Latin *acētōsus* vinegary, from *acētum* vinegar]

a·ce·tum (əˈsiːtəm) *n.* **1.** another name for **vinegar.** **2.** a solution that has dilute acetic acid as solvent. [Latin]

ac+e·tyl (ˈæsɪˌtaɪl, əˈsiːtaɪl) *n.* (*modifier*) of, consisting of, or containing the monovalent group CH_3CO-: *acetyl group or radical.* [C19: from ACET(IC) + -YL] —**ac+e·tyl+ic** (ˌæsɪˈtɪlɪk) *adj.*

a·cet·y+late (əˈsɛtɪˌleɪt) *vb.* **1.** (*tr.*) to introduce an acetyl group into (a chemical compound). **2.** (*intr.*) (of a chemical compound) to gain or suffer substitution of an acetyl group. —**a·ˌcet·y+ˈla+tion** *n.*

ac+e·tyl+cho+line (ˌæsɪtaɪlˈkəʊliːn, -lɪn) *n.* a chemical substance secreted at the ends of many nerve fibres, esp. in the autonomic nervous system, and responsible for the transmission of nervous impulses. Formula: $C_7H_{17}NO_3$.

a·cet·y+lene (əˈsɛtɪˌliːn) *n.* **1.** Also called: **ethyne.** a colourless soluble flammable gas used in the manufacture of organic chemicals and in cutting and welding metals. Formula: C_2H_2. **2.** another name for **alkyne.** —**a·cet·y+len+ic** (əˌsɛtɪˈlɛnɪk) *adj.*

a·cet·y+lide (əˈsɛtɪˌlaɪd) *n.* any of a class of carbides in which the carbon is present as a diatomic divalent ion. They are formally derivatives of acetylene.

ac+e·tyl+sal·i·cyl+ic ac·id (ˌæsɪtaɪlˌsælɪˈsɪlɪk, əˈsiːtaɪl-) *n.* the chemical name for **aspirin.**

ace·y·deuc·y (ˈeɪsɪˈdjuːsɪ) *n.* a form of backgammon.

A.C.G.I. *abbrev. for* Associate of the City and Guilds Institute.

A·chae·a (əˈkiːə) *or* **A·cha·ia** (əˈkaɪə) *n.* **1.** a department of Greece, in the N Peloponnese. Capital: Patras. Pop.: 239 859 (1971). Area: 3209 sq. km (1239 sq. miles). Modern Greek name: **Akhaïa.** **2.** a province of ancient Greece, in the N Peloponnese on the Gulf of Corinth: enlarged as a Roman province in 27 B.C.

A·chae+an (əˈkiːən) *or* **A·chai·an** (əˈkaɪən) *n.* **1.** a member of a principal Greek tribe in the Mycenaean era. **2.** a native or inhabitant of the later Greek province of Achaea. ~*adj.* **3.** of or relating to Achaea or the Achaeans.

A·chae+an League *n.* a confederation of Achaean cities formed in the early third century B.C., which became a political and military force in Greece, directed particularly against Macedonian domination of the Peloponnesus.

A·chae·me·nid (əˈkiːmənɪd, əˈkɛm-) *n., pl.* **A·chae·me·nids, Ach·ae·men·i·dae** (ˌækɪˈmɛnɪˌdiː), *or* **Ach·ae·men·i·des** (ˌækɪˈmɛnɪˌdiːz). any member of a Persian dynasty of kings, including Cyrus the Great, that ruled from about 550 to 331 B.C., when Darius III was overthrown by Alexander the Great. [from Greek, after *Akhaimenēs*, name of the founder]

A·cha·tes (əˈkeɪtiːz) *n.* a loyal friend. [from the name of Aeneas' faithful companion in Virgil's *Aeneid*]

ache (eɪk) *vb.* (*intr.*) **1.** to feel, suffer, or be the source of a continuous dull pain. **2.** to suffer mental anguish. ~*n.* **3.** a continuous dull pain. [Old English *ācan* (vb.), *æce* (n.), Middle English *aken* (vb.), *ache* (n.). Compare BAKE, BATCH] —ˈ**ach+ing+ly** *adv.* —ˈ**ach·y** *adj.*

Ach·e·lo·us (ˌækɪˈləʊəs) *n. Classical myth.* a river god who changed into a snake and a bull while fighting Hercules but was defeated when Hercules broke off one of his horns.

a·chene *or* **a·kene** (əˈkiːn) *n.* a dry one-seeded indehiscent fruit with the seed distinct from the fruit wall. It may be smooth, as in the buttercup, or feathery, as in clematis. [C19: from New Latin *achaenium* that which does not yawn or open, from A-[1] + Greek *khainein* to yawn] —**a·ˈche·ni·al** *or* **a·ˈke·ni·al** *adj.*

A·cher+nar (ˈeɪkəˌnɑː) *n.* the brightest star in the constellation Eridanus, visible only in the S hemisphere. Visual magnitude: 0.6; spectral type: B5; distance: 66 light years. [from Arabic *ākhīr al-nahr*, literally: end of the river, alluding to the star's location in the constellation]

Ach+er+on (ˈækəˌrɒn) *n. Greek myth.* **1.** one of the rivers in Hades over which the souls of the dead were ferried by Charon. Compare **Styx.** **2.** the underworld or Hades.

A·cheu+li·an *or* **A·cheu+le·an** (əˈʃuːlɪən, -jən) *Archaeol.* ~*n.* **1.** (in Europe) the period in the Lower Palaeolithic following the Abbevillian, represented by the use of soft hammerstones in hand axe production made of chipped stone, bone, antler, or wood. The Acheulian dates from the Riss glaciation. **2.** (in Africa) the period represented by every stage of hand axe development. ~*adj.* **3.** of or relating to this period. [C20: after *St. Acheul*, town in northern France]

à che+val *French.* (a ʃəˈval) (of a bet, esp. in roulette) made on two numbers, cards, etc. [literally: on horseback]

a·chieve (əˈtʃiːv) *vb.* **1.** to bring to a successful conclusion; accomplish; attain. **2.** (*tr.*) to gain as by hard work or effort: *to achieve success.* [C14: from Old French *achever* to bring to an end, from the phrase *a chef* to a head, to a conclusion] —**a·ˈchiev+a·ble** *adj.* —**a·ˈchiev+er** *n.*

a·chieve+ment (əˈtʃiːvmənt) *n.* **1.** something that has been accomplished, esp. by hard work, ability, or heroism. **2.** successful completion; accomplishment. **3.** *Heraldry.* a less common word for **hatchment.**

a·chieve+ment age *n. Psychol.* the age at which a child should be able to perform a standardized test successfully. Compare **mental age.**

a·chieve+ment quo+tient *n. Psychol.* a measure of ability derived by dividing an individual's achievement age by his actual age. Abbrev.: **AQ**

a·chieve+ment test *n. Psychol.* a test designed to measure the effects that learning and teaching have on individuals.

A·chil·les (əˈkɪliːz) *n. Greek myth.* Greek hero, the son of Peleus and the sea goddess Thetis: in the *Iliad* the foremost of the Greek warriors at the siege of Troy. While he was a baby his mother plunged him into the river Styx making his body invulnerable except for the heel by which she held him. After slaying Hector, he was killed by Paris who wounded him in the heel. —**Ach+il+le·an** (ˌækɪˈliːən) *adj.*

A·chil·les heel *n.* a small but fatal weakness.

A·chil·les ten+don *n.* the fibrous cord that connects the muscles of the calf to the heelbone.

Ach+ill Is+land (ˈækɪl) *n.* an island in Ireland, off the W coast of Co. Mayo. Area: 3133 sq. km (1210 sq. miles). Pop.: 3598 (1966).

A·chit·o·phel (əˈkɪtəˌfɛl) *n. Bible.* the Douay spelling of **Ahithophel.**

ach+la+myd+e·ous (ˌækləˈmɪdɪəs) *adj.* (of flowers such as the willow) having neither petals nor sepals.

a·chlor+hy+dri·a (ˌeɪklɔːˈhaɪdrɪə) *n.* a marked reduction or virtual absence of free hydrochloric acid from the gastric juice. [C20: New Latin; see A-[1], CHLORO-, HYDRO-]

a·chon+drite (eɪˈkɒndraɪt) *n.* a rare stony meteorite that consists mainly of silicate minerals and has the texture of igneous rock but contains no chondrules. Compare **chondrite.** —**a·chon+drit+ic** (ˌeɪkɒnˈdrɪtɪk) *adj.*

a·chon+dro+pla+si·a (eɪˌkɒndrəʊˈpleɪzɪə) *n.* a skeletal disorder, characterized by failure of normal conversion of cartilage into bone, that begins during fetal life and results in dwarfism. [C20: New Latin; see A-[1], CHONDRO-, -PLASIA] —**a·chon+dro+plas+tic** (eɪˌkɒndrəʊˈplæstɪk) *adj.*

ach+ro+mat (ˈækrəˌmæt) *or* **ach+ro+mat+ic lens** *n.* a lens designed to bring light of two chosen wavelengths to the same focal point, thus reducing chromatic aberration. Compare **apochromat.**

ach+ro+mat+ic (ˌækrəˈmætɪk) *adj.* **1.** without colour. **2.** capable of reflecting or refracting light without chromatic aberration. **3.** *Cytology.* **a.** not staining with standard dyes. **b.** of or relating to achromatin. **4.** *Music.* **a.** involving no sharps or flats. **b.** another word for **diatonic.** —ˌ**ach+ro+ˈmat·i+cal+ly** *adv.* —**a·chro+ma+tism** (əˈkrəʊməˌtɪzəm) *or* **a·chro+ma+tic+i+ty** (əˌkrəʊməˈtɪsɪtɪ) *n.*

ach+ro+mat+ic col+our *n. Physics.* colour, such as white, black, and grey, that is devoid of hue. See **colour** (sense 2).

a·chro+ma+tin (əˈkrəʊmətɪn) *n.* the material of the nucleus of a cell that does not stain with basic dyes. Compare **chromatin.**

a·chro+ma+tize *or* **a·chro+ma+tise** (əˈkrəʊmətaɪz) *vb.* (*tr.*) to make achromatic; to remove colour from. —**a·ˌchro+ma+ti+ˈza+tion** *or* **a·ˌchro+ma+ti+ˈsa+tion** *n.*

a·chro+ma+tous (əˈkrəʊmətəs) *adj.* having little or no colour or less than is normal.

a+chro+mic (əˈkrəʊmɪk) *or* **a·chro+mous** *adj.* colourless.

ach·y-fi (ˌaxəˈviː, ˌʌx-) *interj. Welsh dialect.* an expression of disgust or abhorrence. [Welsh, probably from *ach, achy* general exclamation of disgust + *fi* I, me]

a·cic·u+la (əˈsɪkjʊlə) *n., pl.* **+lae** (-ˌliː). a needle-shaped part, such as a spine, prickle, or crystal. [C19: New Latin, diminutive of *acus* needle] —**a'cic·u+lar** *adj.*

a·cic·u+late (ə'sɪkjʊlɪt, -ˌleɪt) *or* **a·cic·u+lat+ed** *adj.* **1.** having aciculae. **2.** marked with or as if with needle scratches.

a·cic·u+lum (ə'sɪkjʊləm) *n., pl.* **+lums** *or* **+la** (-lə). a needle-like bristle that provides internal support for the appendages (chaetae) of some polychaete worms. [C19: New Latin; see ACICULA]

ac·id ('æsɪd) *n.* **1.** any substance that dissociates in water to yield a sour corrosive solution containing hydrogen ions, having a pH of less than 7, and turning litmus red. See also **Lewis acid. 2.** a sour-tasting substance. **3.** a slang name for **LSD. 4. put the acid on (someone).** *Austral. informal.* to apply pressure to someone, usually when seeking a favour. *~adj.* **5.** *Chem.* **a.** of, derived from, or containing acid: *an acid radical.* **b.** being or having the properties of an acid: *sodium bicarbonate is an acid salt.* **6.** sharp or sour in taste. **7.** cutting, sharp, or hurtful in speech, manner, etc.; vitriolic; caustic. **8.** (of igneous rocks) having a silica content of more than two thirds the total and containing at least one tenth quartz. **9.** *Metallurgy.* of or made by a process in which the furnace or converter is lined with an acid material: *acid steel.* [C17 (first used by Francis Bacon): from French *acide* or Latin *acidus,* from *acēre* to be sour or sharp] —**'ac+id+ly** *adv.* —**'ac+id+ness** *n.* —**'ac+id·y** *adj.*

ac·id drop *n.* a boiled sweet with a sharp taste.

ac·id-fast *adj.* (of bacteria and tissues) resistant to decolorization by mineral acids after staining.

ac·id-form·ing *adj.* **1.** (of an oxide or element) yielding an acid when dissolved in water or having an oxide that forms an acid in water; acidic. **2.** (of foods) producing an acid residue following digestion.

ac·id-head *n. Slang.* a person who uses LSD.

a·cid+ic (ə'sɪdɪk) *adj.* **1.** another word for **acid. 2.** (of an oxide) yielding an acid in aqueous solution.

a·cid·i+fy (ə'sɪdɪˌfaɪ) *vb.* **+fies, +fy+ing, +fied.** to convert into or become acid. —**a'cid·i+ˌfi+a·ble** *adj.* —**aˌcid·i+fi+'ca+tion** *n.* —**a'cid·i+ˌfi+er** *n.*

ac·i+dim+e·ter (ˌæsɪ'dɪmɪtə) *n.* **1.** any instrument for determining the amount of acid in a solution. **2.** another name for **acidometer.** —**ac·i+di+met+ric** (ˌæsɪdə'mɛtrɪk) *or* **ˌac·i+di+'met+ri+cal** *adj.*

ac·i+dim+e·try (ˌæsɪ'dɪmɪtrɪ) *n.* the determination of the amount of acid present in a solution, measured by an acidimeter or by volumetric analysis. —**ac·i+di+met+ric** (ˌæsɪdɪ'mɛtrɪk) *or* **ˌac·i+di+'met+ri+cal** *adj.* —**ˌac·i+di+'met+ri+cal+ly** *adv.*

a·cid·i·ty (ə'sɪdɪtɪ) *n., pl.* **·ties. 1.** the quality or state of being acid. **2.** the amount of acid present in a solution, often expressed in terms of pH. **3.** another name for **hyperacidity.**

ac·i+dom+e·ter (ˌæsɪ'dɒmɪtə) *n.* a type of hydrometer for measuring the relative density of an acid solution, esp. the acid in a battery. Also called: **acidimeter.**

ac·i+do+phil ('æsɪdəʊˌfɪl, ə'sɪdə-) *or* **ac·i+do+phile** ('æsɪdəʊˌfaɪl, ə'sɪdə-) *adj. also* **ac·i+do+phil+ic** (ˌæsɪdəʊ'fɪlɪk, əˌsɪdə-) *or* **ac·i+doph·i+lous** (ˌæsɪ'dɒfɪləs). **1.** (of cells or cell contents) easily stained by acid dyes. **2.** (of microorganisms) growing well in an acid environment. *~n.* **3.** an acidophil organism. [C20: see ACID, -PHILE]

ac·i+doph·i+lus milk (ˌæsɪ'dɒfɪləs) *n. Med.* milk fermented by bacteria of the species *Lactobacillus acidophilus,* used in treating disorders of the gastrointestinal tract.

ac·i+do+sis (ˌæsɪ'dəʊsɪs) *n.* a condition characterized by an abnormal increase in the acidity of the blood and extracellular fluids. —**ac·i+dot+ic** (ˌæsɪ'dɒtɪk) *adj.*

ac·id rock *n.* a type of rock music characterized by electronically amplified bizarre instrumental effects. [C20: from ACID (LSD), alluding to its supposed inspiration by drug-induced states of consciousness]

ac·id soil *n.* a soil that gives a pH reaction of below 7.2, found especially in cool moist areas where soluble bases are leached away.

ac·id test *n.* a rigorous and conclusive test to establish worth or value: *the play passed the critic's acid test.* [C19: from the testing of gold with nitric acid]

a·cid·u+late (ə'sɪdjʊˌleɪt) *vb.* (*tr.*) to make slightly acid or sour. [C18: ACIDULOUS + -ATE[1]] —**aˌcid·u+'la+tion** *n.*

a·cid·u·lous (ə'sɪdjʊləs) *or* **a·cid·u+lent** *adj.* **1.** rather sour. **2.** sharp or sour in speech, manner, etc.; acid. [C18: from Latin *acidulus* sourish, diminutive of *acidus* sour]

ac·id val·ue *n.* the number of milligrams of potassium hydroxide required to neutralize the free fatty acid in one gram of a fat, oil, resin, etc.

ac·i+er+ate ('æsɪəˌreɪt) *vb.* (*tr.*) to change (iron) into steel. [C19: from French *acier* steel, from Latin *aciēs* sharpness] —**ˌac·i+er+'a+tion** *n.*

ac·i+nac·i+form (ˌæsɪ'næsɪˌfɔːm) *adj.* (of leaves) shaped like a scimitar; curved. [C19: via Latin *acinacēs,* from Greek *akinakēs* short sword, ultimately from Iranian + -FORM]

a·cin·i+form (ə'sɪnɪˌfɔːm) *adj.* shaped like a bunch of grapes. [C19: from New Latin *aciniformis;* see ACINUS]

ac·i+nus ('æsɪnəs) *n., pl.* **+ni** (-ˌnaɪ). **1.** *Anatomy.* any of the terminal saclike portions of a compound gland. **2.** *Botany.* any of the small drupes that make up the fruit of the blackberry, raspberry, etc. **3.** *Botany.* a collection of berries, such as a bunch of grapes. [C18: New Latin, from Latin: grape, berry] —**a·cin+ic** (ə'sɪnɪk), **'ac·i+nous,** *or* **'ac·i+nose** *adj.*

A·cis ('eɪsɪs) *n. Greek myth.* a Sicilian shepherd and the lover of the nymph Galatea. In jealousy, Polyphemus crushed him with a huge rock, and his blood was turned by Galatea into a river.

ack-ack ('ækˌæk) *n. Military.* **1. a.** anti-aircraft fire. **b.** (*as modifier*): *ack-ack guns.* **2.** anti-aircraft arms. [C20: British signalling code term for AA, abbreviation of *anti-aircraft*]

ack·ee *or* **ak·ee** ('ækiː) *n.* **1. a.** a sapindaceous tree, *Blighia sapida,* native to tropical Africa and cultivated in the West Indies for its fruit, edible when cooked. **b.** the red pear-shaped fruit of this tree. **2.** a sapindaceous tree, *Melicoccus bijugatus,* that grows on some Caribbean islands and is valued for its timber and edible fruit. **3.** the green tough-skinned berry of this tree. [C18: of African origin]

ac+knowl+edge (ək'nɒlɪdʒ) *vb.* (*tr.*) **1.** (*may take a clause as object*) to recognize or admit the existence, truth, or reality of. **2.** to indicate recognition or awareness of, as by a greeting, glance, etc. **3.** to express appreciation or thanks for: *to acknowledge a gift.* **4.** to make the receipt of known to the sender: *to acknowledge a letter.* **5.** to recognize, esp. in legal form, the authority, rights, or claims of. [C15: probably from earlier *knowledge,* on the model of Old English *oncnāwan,* Middle English *aknowen* to confess, recognize] —**ac+'knowl+edge+a·ble** *adj.* —**ac+'knowl+edg+er** *n.*

ac+knowl+edg+ment *or* **ac+knowl+edge+ment** (ək'nɒlɪdʒmənt) *n.* **1.** the act of acknowledging or state of being acknowledged. **2.** something done or given as an expression of thanks, as a reply to a message, etc. **3.** (*pl.*) an author's statement acknowledging his use of the works of other authors, usually printed at the front of a book.

a·clin+ic line (ə'klɪnɪk) *n.* another name for **magnetic equator.** [C19 *aclinic,* from Greek *aklinēs* not bending, from A-[1] + *klinein* to bend, lean]

ac·me ('ækmɪ) *n.* the culminating point, as of achievement or excellence; summit; peak. [C16: from Greek *akmē*]

ac·ne ('æknɪ) *n.* a chronic skin disease common in adolescence, involving inflammation of the sebaceous glands and characterized by pustules on the face, neck, and upper trunk. [C19: New Latin, from a misreading of Greek *akmē* eruption on the face. See ACME]

ac+node ('ækˌnəʊd) *n.* a point whose coordinates satisfy the equation of a curve although it does not lie on the curve; an isolated point. The origin is an acnode of the curve $y^2 + x^2 = x^3$. [C19: from Latin *acus* a needle + NODE] —**ac+'no+dal** *adj.*

Ac·ol ('ækᵊl) *n. Bridge.* a popular British bidding system favouring light opening bids and a flexible approach. [C20: named after a club in Acol Road, London]

ac·o+lyte ('ækəˌlaɪt) *n.* **1.** a follower or attendant. **2.** *Christianity.* an officer who attends or assists a priest. [C16: via Old French and Medieval Latin from Greek *akolouthos* a follower]

A·con+ca+gua (*Spanish* akon'kaɣwa) *n.* a mountain in W Argentina: the highest peak in the Andes and in the W Hemisphere. Height: 6960 m (22 835 ft.).

ac·o+nite ('ækəˌnaɪt) *or* **ac·o+ni+tum** (ˌækə'naɪtəm) *n.* **1.** any of various N temperate plants of the ranunculaceous genus *Aconitum,* such as monkshood and wolfsbane, many of which are poisonous. Compare **winter aconite. 2.** the dried poisonous root of many of these plants, sometimes used as a narcotic and analgesic. [C16: via Old French or Latin from Greek *akoniton* aconite, monkshood] —**ac·o+nit+ic** (ˌækə'nɪtɪk) *adj.*

A·çô+res (ə'sorɪʃ) *n.* the Portuguese name for (the) **Azores.**

a·corn ('eɪkɔːn) *n.* the fruit of the oak tree, consisting of a smooth thick-walled nut in a woody scaly cuplike base. [C16: variant (through influence of *corn*) of Old English *æcern* the fruit of a tree, acorn; related to Gothic *akran* fruit, yield]

a·corn bar+na+cle *or* **shell** *n.* any of various barnacles, such as *Balanus balanoides,* that live attached to rocks and have a volcano-shaped shell from the top of which protrude feathery food-catching appendages (cirri).

a·corn valve *or U.S.* **tube** *n.* a small electronic valve, approximately acorn-shaped with small closely-spaced electrodes, used in ultrahigh-frequency applications.

a·corn worm *n.* any of various small burrowing marine animals of the genus *Balanoglossus* and related genera, having an elongated wormlike body with an acorn-shaped eversible proboscis at the head end: subphylum *Hemichordata* (hemichordates).

a·cot·y+le·don (əˌkɒtɪ'liːdᵊn) *n.* any plant, such as a fern, moss, or fungus, that does not possess cotyledons. —**aˌcot·y+'le·don+ous** *adj.*

a·cou+chi *or* **a·cou+chy** (ə'kuːʃɪ) *n., pl.* **+chis** *or* **+chies.** any of several South American rodents of the genus *Myoprocta,* closely related to the agoutis but much smaller, with a white-tipped tail: family *Dasyproctidae.* [C19: via French from a native name in Guiana]

a·cous+tic (ə'kuːstɪk) *or* **a·cous+ti+cal** *adj.* **1.** of or related to sound, the sense of hearing, or acoustics. **2.** designed to respond to, absorb, or control sound: *an acoustic tile.* **3.** (of a musical instrument or recording) without electronic amplification: *an acoustic bass; acoustic guitar.* [C17: from Greek *akoustikos,* from *akouein* to hear] —**a'cous+ti+cal+ly** *adv.*

a·cous+tic fea+ture *n. Phonetics.* any of the acoustic components or elements present in a speech sound and capable of being experimentally observed, recorded, and reproduced.

a·cous+ti+cian (ˌæku'stɪʃən) *n.* an expert in acoustics.

a·cous+tic nerve *n.* either one of the eighth pair of cranial nerves, which supply the cochlea and semicircular canals of the internal ear and contribute to the sense of hearing.

a·cous+tic pho+net+ics *n.* the branch of phonetics concerned with the acoustic properties of human speech. Compare **articulatory phonetics.**

a·cous·tics (əˈkuːstɪks) *n.* **1.** (*functioning as sing.*) the scientific study of sound and sound waves. **2.** (*functioning as pl.*) the characteristics of a room, auditorium, etc., that determine the fidelity with which sound can be heard within it.

acpt. *Commerce. abbrev. for* acceptance.

ac·quaint (əˈkweɪnt) *vb.* (*tr.*) **1.** (foll. by *with* or *of*) to make (a person) familiar or conversant (with); inform (of). **2.** (foll. by *with*) *Chiefly U.S.* to introduce (to); bring into contact (with). [C13: via Old French and Medieval Latin from Latin *accognitus*, from *accognōscere* to know perfectly, from *ad-* (intensive) + *cognōscere* to know]

ac·quaint·ance (əˈkweɪntəns) *n.* **1.** a person with whom one has been in contact but who is not a close friend. **2.** knowledge of a person or thing, esp. when slight. **3. make the acquaintance of.** to come into social contact with. **4.** those persons collectively whom one knows. —**acˈquaint·ance·ˌship** *n.*

ac·quaint·ed (əˈkweɪntɪd) *adj.* (*postpositive*) **1.** (sometimes foll. by *with*) on terms of familiarity but not intimacy. **2.** (foll. by *with*) having knowledge or experience (of); familiar (with).

ac·qui·esce (ˌækwɪˈɛs) *vb.* (*intr.; often foll. by in or to*) to comply (with); assent (to) without protest. [C17: from Latin *acquiēscere* to remain at rest, agree without protest, from *ad-* at + *quiēscere* to rest, from *quiēs* QUIET] —**ˌac·qui·ˈes·cence** *n.* —**ˌac·qui·ˈes·cent** *adj.* —**ˌac·qui·ˈes·cent·ly** *adv.*

ac·quire (əˈkwaɪə) *vb.* (*tr.*) to get or gain (something, such as an object, trait, or ability), esp. more or less permanently. [C15: via Old French from Latin *acquīrere*, from *ad-* in addition + *quaerere* to get, seek] —**acˈquir·a·ble** *adj.* —**acˈquire·ment** *n.* —**acˈquir·er** *n.*

ac·quired char·ac·ter·is·tic *n.* a characteristic of an organism resulting from increased use or disuse of an organ or the effects of the environment. See also **Lamarckism.**

ac·quired taste *n.* **1.** a liking for something that is at first considered unpleasant. **2.** the thing so liked.

ac·qui·si·tion (ˌækwɪˈzɪʃən) *n.* **1.** the act of acquiring or gaining possession. **2.** something acquired. **3.** a person or thing of special merit added to a group. **4.** *Astronautics.* **a.** the re-establishment of communications between a spacecraft and a ground control station after a temporary blackout. **b.** the process of locating a spacecraft, satellite, etc., esp. by radar, in order to gather tracking and telemetric information. [C14: from Latin *acquīsītiōn-*, from *acquīrere* to ACQUIRE]

ac·quis·i·tive (əˈkwɪzɪtɪv) *adj.* inclined or eager to acquire things, esp. material possessions or ideas: *an acquisitive mind.* —**acˈquis·i·tive·ly** *adv.* —**acˈquis·i·tive·ness** *n.*

ac·quit (əˈkwɪt) *vb.* **·quits, ·quit·ting, ·quit·ted.** (*tr.*) **1.** (foll. by *of*) **a.** to free or release (from a charge of crime). **b.** to pronounce not guilty. **2.** (foll. by *of*) to free or relieve (from an obligation, duty, responsibility, etc.). **3.** to repay or settle (something, such as a debt or obligation). **4.** to perform (one's part); conduct (oneself). [C13: from Old French *aquiter*, from *quiter* to release, free from, QUIT] —**acˈquit·ter** *n.*

ac·quit·tal (əˈkwɪtᵊl) *n.* **1.** *Criminal law.* the deliverance and release of a person appearing before a court on a charge of crime, as by a finding of not guilty. **2.** a discharge or release from an obligation, duty, debt, etc.

ac·quit·tance (əˈkwɪtəns) *n.* **1.** a release from or settlement of a debt, etc. **2.** a record of this, such as a receipt.

a·cre (ˈeɪkə) *n.* **1.** a unit of area used in certain English-speaking countries, equal to 4840 square yards or 4046.86 square metres. **2.** (*pl.*) **a.** land, esp. a large area. **b.** *Informal.* a large amount: *he has acres of space in his room.* [Old English *æcer* field, acre; related to Old Norse *akr*, German *Acker*, Latin *ager* field, Sanskrit *ajra* field]

A·cre *n.* **1.** (ˈɑːkrə). a territory of W Brazil: mostly unexplored tropical forests; acquired from Bolivia in 1903. Capital: Rio Branco. Pop.: 215 299 (1970). Area: 148 026 sq. km (57 153 sq. miles). **2.** (ˈeɪkə, ˈɑːkə). a city and port in N Israel, strategically situated on the **Bay of Acre** in the E Mediterranean: taken and retaken during the Crusades (1104, 1187, 1191, 1291), taken by the Turks (1517), by Egypt (1832), and by the Turks again (1839). Pop.: 34 400 (1972). Old Testament name: **Ac·cho** (ɑːˈkəʊ). Arabic name: **'Ak·ka** (ɑːˈkɑː). Hebrew name: **'Ak·ko** (ɑːˈkəʊ).

a·cre·age (ˈeɪkərɪdʒ) *n.* land area in acres.

a·cred (ˈeɪkəd) *adj.* (*usually in combination*) having acres of land: *a many-acred farm; a well-acred nobleman.*

a·cre-foot *n., pl.* **-feet.** the volume of water that would cover an area of 1 acre to a depth of 1 foot: equivalent to 43 560 cubic feet or 1233.5 cubic metres.

a·cre-inch *n.* the volume of water that would cover an area of 1 acre to a depth of 1 inch; one twelfth of an acre-foot: equivalent to 3630 cubic feet or 102.8 cubic metres.

ac·rid (ˈækrɪd) *adj.* **1.** unpleasantly pungent or sharp to the smell or taste. **2.** sharp or caustic, esp. in speech or nature. [C18: from Latin *ācer* sharp, sour; probably formed on the model of ACID] —**a·crid·i·ty** (əˈkrɪdɪtɪ) *or* **ˈac·rid·ness** *n.* —**ˈac·rid·ly** *adv.*

ac·ri·dine (ˈækrɪˌdiːn) *n.* a colourless crystalline solid used in the manufacture of dyes. Formula: $C_{13}H_9N$.

ac·ri·fla·vine (ˌækrɪˈfleɪvɪn, -viːn) *n.* a brownish or orange-red powder used in medicine as an antiseptic and bacteriostat. Formula: $C_{14}H_{14}N_3Cl$. [C20: from ACRIDINE + FLAVIN]

ac·ri·fla·vine hy·dro·chlor·ide *n.* a red crystalline water-soluble solid substance obtained from acriflavine and used as an antiseptic. Also called: **flavine.**

Ac·ri·lan (ˈækrɪˌlæn) *n. Trademark.* an acrylic fibre or fabric, characterized by strength, softness, and crease-resistance and used for clothing, upholstery, carpets, etc.

ac·ri·mo·ny (ˈækrɪmənɪ) *n., pl.* **·nies.** bitterness or sharpness of manner, speech, temper, etc. [C16: from Latin *ācrimōnia*, from *ācer* sharp, sour] —**ac·ri·mo·ni·ous** (ˌækrɪˈməʊnɪəs) *adj.* —**ˌac·ri·ˈmo·ni·ous·ly** *adv.* —**ˌac·ri·ˈmo·ni·ous·ness** *n.*

ac·ro- *combining form.* **1.** denoting something at a height, summit, top, tip, beginning, or end: *acropolis; acrogen.* **2.** denoting an extremity of the human body: *acromegaly.* [from Greek *akros* extreme, topmost]

ac·ro·bat (ˈækrəˌbæt) *n.* **1.** an entertainer who performs acts that require skill, agility, and coordination, such as tumbling, swinging from a trapeze, or walking a tightrope. **2.** *Informal.* a person noted for his frequent and rapid changes of position or allegiances: *a political acrobat.* [C19: via French from Greek *akrobatēs* acrobat, one who walks on tiptoe, from ACRO- + *bat-*, from *bainein* to walk] —**ˌac·ro·ˈbat·ic** *adj.* —**ˌac·ro·ˈbat·i·cal·ly** *adv.*

ac·ro·bat·ics (ˌækrəˈbætɪks) *n.* **1.** (*functioning as pl.*) the skills or feats of an acrobat. **2.** (*functioning as sing.*) the art of an acrobat. **3.** (*functioning as pl.*) any activity requiring agility and skill: *mental acrobatics.*

ac·ro·car·pous (ˌækrəʊˈkɑːpəs) *adj.* (of ferns, mosses, etc.) having the reproductive parts at the tip of a stem. [C19: from New Latin, from Greek *akrokarpos*]

ac·ro·dont (ˈækrəˌdɒnt) *adj.* **1.** (of the teeth of some reptiles) having no roots and being fused at the base to the margin of the jawbones. See also **pleurodont** (sense 1). **2.** having acrodont teeth. [C19: from ACRO- + -ODONT]

ac·ro·drome (ˈækrəˌdrəʊm) *adj.* (of the veins of a leaf) running parallel to the edges of the leaf and fusing at the tip. Also: **a·crod·ro·mous** (əˈkrɒdrəməs).

ac·ro·gen (ˈækrədʒən) *n.* any flowerless plant, such as a fern or moss, in which growth occurs from the tip of the main stem. —**ac·ro·gen·ic** (ˌækrəˈdʒɛnɪk) *or* **a·crog·e·nous** (əˈkrɒdʒɪnəs) *adj.* —**aˈcrog·e·nous·ly** *adv.*

a·cro·le·in (əˈkrəʊlɪɪn) *n.* a colourless or yellowish flammable poisonous pungent liquid used in the manufacture of resins and pharmaceuticals. Formula: $CH_2{:}CHCHO$. [C19: from Latin *ācer* sharp + *olēre* to smell + -IN]

ac·ro·lith (ˈækrəlɪθ) *n.* (esp. in ancient Greek sculpture) a wooden, often draped figure with only the head, hands, and feet in stone. [C19: via Latin *acrolithus* from Greek *akrolithos* having stone extremities] —**ˌac·ro·ˈlith·ic** *adj.*

ac·ro·meg·a·ly (ˌækrəʊˈmɛgəlɪ) *n.* a chronic disease characterized by enlargement of the bones of the head, hands, and feet. It is caused by excessive secretion of growth hormone by the pituitary gland. Compare **gigantism.** [C19: from French *acromégalie*, from ACRO- + Greek *megal-*, stem of *megas* big] —**ac·ro·me·gal·ic** (ˌækrəʊmɪˈgælɪk) *adj., n.*

a·cro·mi·on (əˈkrəʊmɪən) *n., pl.* **·mi·a** (-mɪə). the outermost edge of the spine of the shoulder blade. [C17: New Latin, from Greek *akrōmion* the point of the shoulder, from ACRO- + *ōmion*, diminutive of *ōmos* shoulder]

a·cron·y·chal, a·cron·y·cal, *or U.S.* **a·cron·i·cal** (əˈkrɒnɪkᵊl) *adj.* occurring at sunset: *the star has an acronychal rising.* [C16: from Greek *akronychos* at sunset, from ACRO- + *nykh-*, *nyx* night] —**aˈcron·y·chal·ly, aˈcron·y·cal·ly,** *or U.S.* **aˈcron·i·cal·ly** *adv.*

ac·ro·nym (ˈækrənɪm) *n.* a word formed from the initial letters of a group of words; for example, *UNESCO* for the *United Nations Educational, Scientific, and Cultural Organization.* [C20: from ACRO- + ONYM] —**ˌac·ro·ˈnym·ic** *or* **a·cron·y·mous** (əˈkrɒnɪməs) *adj.*

a·crop·e·tal (əˈkrɒpɪtᵊl) *adj.* (of leaves and flowers) produced in order from the base upwards so that the youngest are at the apex. Compare **basipetal.**

ac·ro·pho·bi·a (ˌækrəˈfəʊbɪə) *n.* abnormal fear or dread of being at a great height. [C19: from ACRO- + -PHOBIA] —**ˌac·ro·ˈpho·bic** *adj.*

a·crop·o·lis (əˈkrɒpəlɪs) *n.* the citadel of an ancient Greek city. [C17: from Greek, from ACRO- + *polis* city]

A·crop·o·lis (əˈkrɒpəlɪs) *n.* the citadel of Athens on which the Parthenon and the Erechtheum stand.

ac·ro·spire (ˈækrəˌspaɪə) *n.* the first shoot developing from the plumule of a germinating grain seed. [C17: from obsolete *akerspire*, from *aker* EAR² + *spire* sprout, SPIRE¹; the modern form is influenced by ACRO-]

a·cross (əˈkrɒs) *prep.* **1.** from one side to the other side of. **2.** on or at the other side of. ~*adv.* **3.** from one side to the other. **4.** on or to the other side. [C13 *on croice, acros*, from Old French *a croix* crosswise]

a·cross-the-board *adj.* **1.** (of salary increases, taxation cuts, etc.) affecting all levels or classes equally. **2.** *Horse racing, chiefly U.S.* designating a bet in which equal amounts are staked on the same contestant to win or to come second or third in a race.

a·cros·tic (əˈkrɒstɪk) *n.* **a.** a number of lines of writing, such as a poem, certain letters of which form a word, proverb, etc. A **single acrostic** is formed by the initial letters of the lines, a **double acrostic** by the initial and final letters, and a **triple acrostic** by the initial, middle, and final letters. **b.** the word, proverb, etc., so formed. **c.** (*as modifier*): *an acrostic sonnet.* [C16: via French from Greek *akrostikhis*, from ACRO- + *stikhos* line of verse, STICH] —**aˈcros·ti·cal·ly** *adv.*

a·cro·ter (əˈkrəʊtə, ˈækrətə) *n. Architecture.* a plinth bearing a statue, etc., at either end or at the apex of a pediment. [C18: from French, from Latin *acroterium*, from Greek *akrōtērion* summit, from *akros* extreme]

a·cryl·ic (əˈkrɪlɪk) *adj.* **1.** of, derived from, or concerned with acrylic acid. ~*n.* **2.** short for **acrylic resin.** [C20: from ACROLEIN + -YL + -IC]

a·cryl·ic ac·id *n.* a colourless corrosive pungent liquid, miscible with water, used in the manufacture of acrylic resins. Formula: CH_2:CHCOOH.

a·cryl·ic fi·bre *n.* a textile fibre, such as Orlon or Acrilan, produced from acrylonitrile.

a·cryl·ic res·in *n.* any of a group of polymers or copolymers of acrylic acid, its esters, or amides, used as synthetic rubbers, textiles, paints, adhesives, and as plastics such as Perspex.

ac·ry·lo·ni·trile (ˌækrɪləʊ'naɪtraɪl) *n.* a colourless liquid that is miscible with water and has toxic fumes: used in the manufacture of acrylic fibres and resins, rubber, and thermoplastics. Formula: CH_2:CHCN. [C20: from ACRYLIC + NITRILE]

ac·ry·lyl ('ækrɪlɪl) *n.* (*modifier*) of, consisting of, or containing the monovalent group CH_2:CHCO-: *acrylyl group or radical.*

a/cs pay. *abbrev. for* accounts payable.

a/cs rec. *abbrev. for* accounts receivable.

act (ækt) *n.* **1.** something done or performed; a deed. **2.** the performance of some physical or mental process; action. **3.** (*cap. when part of a name*) the formally codified result of deliberation by a legislative body; a law, edict, decree, statute, etc. **4.** (*often pl.*) a formal written record of transactions, proceedings, etc., as of a society, committee, or legislative body. **5.** a major division of a dramatic work. **6. a.** a short performance of skill, a comic sketch, dance, etc., esp. one that is part of a programme of light entertainment. **b.** those giving such a performance. **7.** an assumed attitude or pose, esp. one intended to impress. **8.** *Philosophy.* an occurrence effected by a human agent as opposed to one that is determined. Compare **event** (sense 4). ~*vb.* **9.** (*intr.*) to do something; carry out an action. **10.** (*intr.*) to function in a specified way; operate; react: *his mind acted quickly.* **11.** to perform (a part or role) in a play, etc. **12.** (*tr.*) to present (a play, etc.) on stage. **13.** (*intr.;* usually foll. by *for* or *as*) to be a substitute (for); function in place (of). **14.** (*intr.;* foll. by *as*) to serve the function or purpose (of): *the glass acted as protection.* **15.** (*intr.*) to conduct oneself or behave (as if one were): *she usually acts like a lady; she was acting tired.* **16.** (*intr.*) to behave in an unnatural or affected way. **17.** (*copula*) to pose as; play the part of: *to act the fool.* **18.** (*copula*) to behave in a manner appropriate to (esp. in the phrase **act one's age**). **19.** (*copula*) *Not standard.* to seem or pretend to be: *to act tired.* ~See also **act on, act out, act up.** [C14: from Latin *actus* a doing, performance, and *actum* a thing done, from the past participle of *agere* to do] —**'act·a·ble** *adj.* —ˌ**act·a·'bil·i·ty** *n.*

A.C.T. *abbrev. for* Australian Capital Territory.

Ac·tae·on (æk'tiːən, 'æktɪən) *n. Greek myth.* a hunter of Boeotia who, having accidentally seen Artemis bathing, was turned into a stag and torn apart by his own hounds.

actg. *abbrev. for* acting.

ACTH *n.* adrenocorticotropic hormone; a polypeptide hormone, secreted by the anterior lobe of the pituitary gland, that stimulates growth of the adrenal gland and the synthesis and secretion of corticosteroids. It is used in treating rheumatoid arthritis, allergic and skin diseases, and many other disorders. Also called: **corticotrophin.**

ac·tin ('æktɪn) *n.* a protein in muscle that exists in both globular and fibrous forms and associates with myosin to form the complex protein actomyosin. [C20: from ACT + -IN]

ac·ti·nal ('æktɪnᵊl, æk'taɪnᵊl) *adj.* **1.** of or denoting the oral part of a radiate animal, such as a jellyfish, sea anemone, or sponge, from which the rays, tentacles, or arms grow. **2.** possessing rays or tentacles, as a jellyfish. [C19: see ACTINO-, -AL[1]] —**'ac·ti·nal·ly** *adv.*

act·ing ('æktɪŋ) *adj.* (*prenominal*) **1.** taking on duties temporarily, esp. as a substitute for another: *the acting president.* **2.** operating or functioning: *an acting order.* **3.** intended for stage performance; provided with directions for actors: *an acting version of "Hedda Gabler."* ~*n.* **4.** the art or profession of an actor.

ac·tin·i·a (æk'tɪnɪə) *n., pl.* **·tin·i·ae** (-'tɪnɪˌiː) *or* **·tin·i·as.** any sea anemone of the genus *Actinia,* which are common in rock pools. [C18: New Latin, literally: things having a radial structure. See ACTINO-, -IA]

ac·tin·ic (æk'tɪnɪk) *adj.* (of radiation) producing a photochemical effect. [C19: from ACTINO- + -IC] —**ac·'tin·i·cal·ly** *adv.* —**'ac·tin·ˌism** *n.*

ac·ti·nide ('æktɪˌnaɪd) *n.* a member of the actinide series. Also called: **actinon.** [C19: from ACTINO- + -IDE]

ac·ti·nide se·ries *n.* a series of 15 radioactive elements with increasing atomic numbers from actinium to lawrencium.

ac·tin·i·form (æk'tɪnɪˌfɔːm) *adj.* another word for **actinoid.** [C20: from ACTINO- + -FORM]

ac·tin·i·um (æk'tɪnɪəm) *n.* a radioactive element of the actinide series, occurring as a decay product of uranium. It is used as an alpha-particle source and in neutron production. Symbol: Ac; atomic no.: 89; half-life of most stable isotope, ^{227}Ac: 22 years; relative density: 10.07; melting pt.: 1050°C; boiling pt.: 3200°C (est.). [C19: New Latin, from ACTINO- + -IUM]

ac·tin·i·um se·ries *n.* a radioactive series that starts with actinium-235 and ends with lead-207.

ac·ti·no- *or before a vowel* **ac·tin-** *combining form.* **1.** indicating a radial structure: *actinomorphic.* **2.** indicating radioactivity or radiation: *actinometer.* [from Greek *aktino-,* from *aktis* beam, ray]

ac·tin·o·chem·is·try (æk,tɪnəʊ'kɛmɪstrɪ) *n.* another name for **photochemistry.**

ac·ti·noid ('æktɪˌnɔɪd) *adj.* having a radiate form, as a sea anemone or starfish.

ac·tin·o·lite (æk'tɪnəˌlaɪt) *n.* a green mineral of the amphibole group consisting of calcium magnesium iron silicate. Formula: $Ca_2(Mg,Fe)_5Si_8O_{22}(OH)_2$. [C19: from ACTINO- (from the radiating crystals in some forms) + -LITE]

ac·ti·no·mere ('æktɪnəʊˌmɪə) *n.* another name for **antimere.**

ac·ti·nom·e·ter (ˌæktɪ'nɒmɪtə) *n.* an instrument for measuring the intensity of radiation, esp. of the sun's rays. —**ac·ti·no·met·ric** (ˌæktɪnəʊ'mɛtrɪk) *or* ˌ**ac·ti·no·'met·ri·cal** *adj.* —ˌ**ac·ti·'nom·e·try** *n.*

ac·ti·no·mor·phic (ˌæktɪnəʊ'mɔːfɪk) *or* **ac·ti·no·mor·phous** *adj. Botany.* (esp. of a flower) having radial symmetry, as buttercups; capable of being cut vertically through the axis in any of two or more planes so that the two cut halves are mirror images of each other. See also **zygomorphic.**

ac·ti·no·my·cete (ˌæktɪnəʊmaɪ'siːt) *n.* any microorganism of the group *Actinomycetes,* usually regarded as filamentous bacteria.

ac·ti·no·my·cin (ˌæktɪnəʊ'maɪsɪn) *n.* any of several toxic antibiotics obtained from bacteria of the genus *Streptomyces,* used in treating some cancers.

ac·ti·no·my·co·sis (ˌæktɪnəʊmaɪ'kəʊsɪs) *n.* a fungal disease of cattle, sometimes transmitted to man, characterized by a swelling of the affected part, most often the jaw. Nontechnical name: **lumpy jaw.** —**ac·ti·no·my·cot·ic** (ˌæktɪnəʊmaɪ'kɒtɪk) *adj.*

ac·ti·non ('æktɪˌnɒn) *n.* **1.** a radioisotope of radon that is a decay product of radium. Symbol: An or ^{219}Rn; atomic no.: 86; half-life: 3.92s. **2.** another name for **actinide.** [C20: New Latin, from ACTINIUM + -ON]

ac·tin·o·pod (æk'tɪnəˌpɒd) *n.* any protozoan of the subclass *Actinopoda,* such as a radiolarian or a heliozoan, having stiff radiating pseudopodia.

ac·ti·no·ther·a·py (ˌæktɪnəʊ'θɛrəpɪ) *n.* another name for **radiotherapy.**

ac·ti·no·u·ra·ni·um (ˌæktɪnəʊjʊ'reɪnɪəm) *n.* the isotope of uranium that has a mass number of 235.

ac·ti·no·zo·an (ˌæktɪnəʊ'zəʊən) *n., adj.* another word for **anthozoan.**

ac·tion ('ækʃən) *n.* **1.** the state or process of doing something or being active; operation. **2.** something done, such as an act or deed. **3.** movement or posture during some physical activity. **4.** activity, force, or energy: *a man of action.* **5.** (*usually pl.*) conduct or behaviour. **6.** *Law.* **a.** a legal proceeding brought by one party against another, seeking redress of a wrong or recovery of what is due; lawsuit. **b.** the right to bring such proceeding. **7.** the operating mechanism, esp. in a piano, gun, watch, etc. **8.** the force applied to a body: *the reaction is equal and opposite to the action.* **9.** the way in which something operates or works. **10.** *Physics.* **a.** a property of a system expressed as twice the mean kinetic energy of the system over a given time interval multiplied by the time interval. **b.** the product of work or energy and time, usually expressed in joule seconds: *Planck's constant of action.* **11.** the events that form the plot of a story, film, play, or other composition. **12.** *Military.* **a.** a minor engagement. **b.** fighting at sea or on land: *he saw action in the war.* **13.** *Informal.* the profits of an enterprise or transaction (esp. in the phrase **a piece of the action**). **14.** *Slang.* the main activity, esp. social activity. ~*interj.* **15.** a command given by a film director to indicate that filming is to begin. See also **cue**[1] (senses 1, 8). [C14 *accioun,* ultimately from Latin *āctiōn-,* stem of *āctiō,* from *agere* to do, act]

ac·tion·a·ble ('ækʃənəbᵊl) *adj. Law.* affording grounds for legal action. —**'ac·tion·a·bly** *adv.*

ac·tion paint·ing *n.* a development of abstract expressionism evolved in the 1940s, characterized by broad vigorous brush strokes and accidental effects of thrown, smeared, dripped, or spattered paint. Also called: **tachisme.** See also **abstract expressionism.**

ac·tion po·ten·tial *n.* a localized change in electrical potential, from −70 mV to +30 mV, that occurs across a nerve fibre during transmission of a nerve impulse.

ac·tion re·play *n.* the rerunning of a small section of a television film or tape of a match or other sporting contest, often in slow motion. U.S. name: **instant replay.**

ac·tion sta·tions *pl. n. Military.* **1.** the positions taken up by individuals in preparation for or during a battle. ~*interj.* **2.** a command to take up such positions. **3.** *Informal.* a warning to get ready for something.

Ac·ti·um ('æktɪəm) *n.* a town of ancient Greece that overlooked the naval battle in 31 B.C. at which Octavian's fleet under Agrippa defeated that of Mark Antony and Cleopatra.

ac·ti·vate ('æktɪˌveɪt) *vb.* (*tr.*) **1.** to make active or capable of action. **2.** *Physics.* to make radioactive. **3.** *Chem.* **a.** to increase the rate of (a reaction). **b.** to treat (a substance, such as carbon or alumina) so as to increase powers of adsorption. **4.** to purify (sewage) by aeration. **5.** *U.S. military.* to create, mobilize, or organize (a unit). —ˌ**ac·ti·'va·tion** *n.* —**'ac·ti·ˌva·tor** *n.*

ac·ti·vat·ed a·lu·mi·na *n.* a granular highly porous and adsorptive form of aluminium oxide, used for drying gases and as an oil-filtering material and catalyst.

ac·ti·vat·ed car·bon *n.* a porous highly adsorptive form of carbon used to remove colour or impurities from liquids and gases, in the separation and extraction of chemical compounds, and in the recovery of solvents. Also called: **activated charcoal, active carbon.**

ac·ti·vat·ed sludge *n.* a mass of aerated precipitated sewage added to untreated sewage to bring about purification by hastening bacterial decomposition.

ac+tive ('æktɪv) *adj.* **1.** in a state of action; moving, working, or doing something. **2.** busy or involved: *an active life.* **3.** physically energetic. **4.** exerting influence; effective: *an active ingredient.* **5.** *Grammar.* **a.** denoting a voice of verbs used to indicate that the subject of a sentence is performing the action or causing the event or process described by the verb, as *kicked* in *The boy kicked the football.* Compare **passive** (sense 5). **b.** another word for **nonstative. 6.** being fully engaged in military service (esp. in the phrase **on active service**). **7.** (of a volcano) erupting periodically; not extinct. Compare **dormant** (sense 3), **extinct** (sense 3). **8.** *Astronomy.* (of the sun) exhibiting a large number of sunspots, solar flares, etc., and a marked variation in intensity and frequency of radio emission. Compare **quiet** (sense 7). **9.** *Commerce.* producing or being used to produce profit, esp. in the form of interest: *active balances.* **10.** *Electronics.* **a.** containing a source of power: *an active network.* **b.** capable of amplifying a signal or controlling some function: *an active component; an active communication satellite.* ~*n.* **11.** *Grammar.* **a.** the active voice. **b.** an active verb. **12.** *Chiefly U.S.* a member of an organization who participates in its activities. [C14: from Latin *āctīvus.* See ACT, -IVE] —**'ac+tive+ly** *adv.* —**'ac+tive+ness** *n.*

ac+tive list *n. Military.* a list of officers available for full duty.

ac+tive serv+ice *or esp. U.S.* **ac+tive du·ty** *n.* military duty in an operational area.

ac+tiv+ism ('æktɪ,vɪzəm) *n.* a policy of taking direct and often militant action to achieve an end, esp. a political or social one. —**'ac+tiv+ist** *n.*

ac+tiv+i·ty (æk'tɪvɪtɪ) *n., pl.* **·ties. 1.** the state or quality of being active. **2.** lively action or movement. **3.** any specific deed, action, pursuit, etc.: *recreational activities.* **4.** the number of disintegrations of a radioactive substance in a given unit of time, usually expressed in curies or disintegrations per second. **5. a.** the capacity of a substance to undergo chemical change. **b.** the effective concentration of a substance in a chemical system. The **absolute activity** of a substance B, λ_B, is defined as $\exp(\mu_B/RT)$ where μ_B is the chemical potential.

act of con+tri+tion *n. Theol.* a short prayer of penitence.

act of faith *n. Theol.* an act that demonstrates or tests a person's religious beliefs.

act of God *n. Law.* a sudden and inevitable occurrence caused by natural forces and not by the agency of man, such as a flood, earthquake, or a similar catastrophe.

act of war *n.* an aggressive act, usually employing military force, which constitutes an immediate threat to peace.

ac+to+my·o+sin (,æktəʊ'maɪəsɪn) *n.* a complex protein in skeletal muscle that is formed by actin and myosin and which, when stimulated, shortens to cause muscle contraction.

act on *or* **up·on** *vb. (intr., prep.)* **1.** to regulate one's behaviour in accordance with (advice, information, etc.). **2.** to have an effect on (illness, a part of the body, etc.).

Ac·ton[1] ('æktən) *n.* a district of the London borough of Ealing.

Ac·ton[2] ('æktən) *n.* **1. John Em·er·ich Ed·ward Dal·berg,** 1st Baron Acton. 1834–1902, English historian: a proponent of Christian liberal ethics and adviser of Gladstone. **2.** his grandfather, Sir **John Fran·cis Ed·ward.** 1736-1811, European naval commander and statesman: admiral of Tuscany (1774–79) and Naples (1779 onwards) and chief minister of Naples (1779–1806).

ac+tor ('æktə) *or (fem.)* **ac+tress** ('æktrɪs) *n.* **1.** a person who acts in a play, film, broadcast, etc. **2.** *Informal.* a person who puts on a false manner in order to deceive others (often in the phrase **bad actor**).

act out *vb. (adv.)* **1.** *(tr.)* to reproduce (an idea, former event, etc.) in actions, often by mime. **2.** *Psychiatry.* to express unconsciously (a repressed impulse or experience) in overt behaviour.

Acts of the A·pos+tles *n.* the fifth book of the New Testament, describing the development of the early Church from Christ's ascension into heaven to Paul's sojourn at Rome. Often shortened to **Acts.**

A.C.T.U. *abbrev. for* Australian Council of Trade Unions.

ac+tu·al ('æktʃʊəl) *adj.* **1.** existing in reality or as a matter of fact. **2.** real or genuine. **3.** existing at the present time; current. **4.** (usually preceded by *your*) *Brit. informal, often facetious.* (intensifier): *that music's by your actual Mozart, isn't it?* [C14 *actuel* existing, from Late Latin *āctuālis* relating to acts, practical, from Latin *āctus* ACT]

Usage. The excessive use of *actual* and *actually* should be avoided. They are unnecessary in sentences such as *in actual fact, he is forty-two,* and *he did actually go to the play but did not enjoy it.*

ac+tu+al+i·ty (,æktʃʊ'ælɪtɪ) *n., pl.* **·ties. 1.** true existence; reality. **2.** *(sometimes pl.)* a fact or condition that is real.

ac+tu+al+ize *or* **ac+tu+al+ise** ('æktʃʊə,laɪz) *vb. (tr.)* **1.** to make actual or real. **2.** to represent realistically. —**,ac+tu+al+i+'za+tion** *or* **,ac+tu+al+i+'sa+tion** *n.*

ac+tu+al+ly ('æktʃʊəlɪ) *adv.* **1. a.** as an actual fact; really. **b.** *(as sentence modifier)*: *actually, I haven't seen him.* **2.** at present. **3.** *Informal.* a parenthetic filler used to add slight emphasis: *I don't know, actually.*

ac+tu+ar·y ('æktʃʊərɪ) *n., pl.* **+ar·ies.** a statistician, esp. one employed by insurance companies to calculate risks, policy premiums and dividends, and annuity rates. [C16 (meaning: registrar): from Latin *āctuārius* one who keeps accounts, from *actum* public business, and *acta* documents, deeds. See ACT, -ARY] —**ac+tu+ar·i+al** (,æktʃʊ'ɛərɪəl) *adj.*

ac+tu+ate ('æktʃʊ,eɪt) *vb. (tr.)* **1.** to put into action or mechanical motion. **2.** to motivate or incite into action: *actuated by unworthy desires.* [C16: from Medieval Latin *actuātus,* from *actuāre* to incite to action, from Latin *āctus* ACT] —**,ac+tu·'a+tion** *n.* —**'ac+tu·,a+tor** *n.*

act up *vb. (intr., adv.) Informal.* to behave in a troublesome way: *the engine began to act up.*

a·cu+i·ty (ə'kju:ɪtɪ) *n.* keenness or acuteness, esp. in vision or thought. [C15: from Old French, from Latin *acūtus* ACUTE]

a·cu+le·ate (ə'kju:lɪɪt, -,eɪt) *or* **a·cu+le·at+ed** *adj.* **1.** cutting; pointed. **2.** having prickles or spines, as a rose. **3.** having a sting, as bees, wasps, and ants. [C17: from Latin *acūleātus;* see ACULEUS]

a·cu+le·us (ə'kju:lɪəs) *n.* **1.** a prickle or spine, such as the thorn of a rose. **2.** a sting or ovipositor. [C19: from Latin, diminutive of *acus* needle]

ac·u+men ('ækjʊ,mɛn, ə'kju:mən) *n.* the ability to judge well; keen discernment; insight. [C16: from Latin: sharpness, from *acuere* to sharpen, from *acus* needle] —**a·'cu+mi+nous** *adj.*

a·cu+mi+nate *adj.* (ə'kju:mɪnɪt, -,neɪt). **1.** narrowing to a sharp point, as some types of leaf. ~*vb.* (ə'kju:mɪ,neɪt). **2.** *(tr.)* to make pointed or sharp. [C17: from Latin *acūmināre* to sharpen; see ACUMEN] —**a·,cu+mi+'na+tion** *n.*

ac·u+punc+ture ('ækjʊ,pʌŋktʃə) *n.* the insertion of the tips of needles into the skin at specific points for the purpose of treating various disorders by stimulating nerve impulses. Originally Chinese, this method of treatment is practised in many parts of the world. Also called: **stylostixis.** [C17: from Latin *acus* needle + PUNCTURE]

a·cut+ance (ə'kju:tᵊns) *n.* a physical rather than subjective measure of the sharpness of a photographic image.

a·cute (ə'kju:t) *adj.* **1.** penetrating in perception or insight. **2.** sensitive to details; keen. **3.** of extreme importance; crucial. **4.** sharp or severe; intense: *acute pain; an acute drought.* **5.** having a sharp end or point. **6.** *Maths.* **a.** (of an angle) less than 90°. **b.** (of a triangle) having all its interior angles less than 90°. **7.** (of a disease) **a.** arising suddenly and manifesting intense severity. **b.** of relatively short duration. Compare **chronic** (sense 2). **8.** *Phonetics.* **a.** (of a vowel or syllable in some languages with a pitch accent, such as ancient Greek) spoken or sung on a higher musical pitch relative to neighbouring syllables or vowels. **b.** of or relating to an accent (´) placed over vowels, denoting that the vowel is pronounced with higher musical pitch (as in ancient Greek), with certain special quality (as in French), etc. Compare (for a. and b.) **grave**[2] (sense 5), **circumflex.** ~*n.* **9.** an acute accent. [C14: from Latin *acūtus,* past participle of *acuere* to sharpen, from *acus* needle] —**a·'cute+ly** *adv.* —**a·'cute+ness** *n.*

a·cute ac+cent *n.* the diacritical mark (´), used in the writing system of some languages to indicate that the vowel over which it is placed has a special quality (as in French *été*) or that it receives the strongest stress in the word (as in Spanish *hablé*).

a·cute arch *n.* another name for **lancet arch.**

A.C.W. *abbrev. for* aircraftwoman.

a·cy+clic (eɪ'saɪklɪk, eɪ'sɪklɪk) *adj.* **1.** *Chem.* not cyclic; having an open chain structure. **2.** *Botany.* having flower parts arranged in a spiral rather than a whorl.

a·cyl ('eɪsaɪl) *n.* **1.** *(modifier)* of, denoting, or containing the monovalent group of atoms RCO-: *acyl group or radical; acyl substitution.* **2.** an organometallic compound in which a metal atom is directly bound to an acyl group. [C20: from ACID + -YL]

ad[1] (æd) *n.* short for **advertisement.**

ad[2] (æd) *n. Tennis, U.S.* short for **advantage.** Brit. word: **van.**

AD *Military. abbrev. for* active duty.

A.D. (indicating years numbered from the supposed year of the birth of Christ) *abbrev. for* anno Domini: *70* A.D. Compare **B.C.** [Latin: in the year of the Lord]

Usage. In strict usage, A.D. is only employed with specific years: *he died in 1621* A.D., but *he died in the 17th century* (and not *the 17th century* A.D.). Formerly the practice was to write A.D. preceding the date (A.D. *1621*), and it is also strictly correct to omit *in* when A.D. is used, since this is already contained in the meaning of the Latin *anno Domini* (in the year of Our Lord), but this is no longer general practice. B.C. is used with both specific dates and indications of the period: *Heraclitus was born about 540* B.C.; *the battle took place in the fourth century* B.C.

ad- *prefix.* **1.** to; towards: *adsorb; adverb.* **2.** near; next to: *adrenal.* [from Latin: to, towards. As a prefix in words of Latin origin, *ad-* became *ac-, af-, ag-, al-, an-, acq-, ar-, as-,* and *at-* before *c, f, g, l, n, q, r, s,* and *t,* and became *a-* before *gn, sc, sp, st*]

-ad[1] *suffix forming nouns.* **1.** a group or unit (having so many parts or members): *triad.* **2.** an epic poem concerning (the subject indicated by the stem): *Dunciad.* [via Latin from Greek *-ad-* (plural, *-ades*), originally forming adjectives; names of epic poems are all formed on the model of the *Iliad*]

-ad[2] *suffix forming adverbs.* denoting direction towards a specified part in anatomical descriptions: *cephalad.* [from Latin *ad* (preposition) to, towards]

a·dac+ty+lous (eɪ'dæktɪləs) *adj.* possessing no fingers or toes. [C19: from A-[1] + DACTYL + -OUS]

ad+age ('ædɪdʒ) *n.* a traditional saying that is accepted by many as true or partially true; proverb. [C16: via Old French from Latin *adagium;* related to *āio* I say]

a·da+gi·o (ə'dɑ:dʒɪ,əʊ; *Italian* a'dadʒo) *Music.* ~*adj., adv.* **1.** slow. ~*n., pl.* **+gi·os 2.** a movement or piece to be performed slowly. **3.** *Ballet.* a slow section of a pas de deux. [C18: Italian, from *ad* at + *agio* ease]

Ad·am[1] ('ædəm) *n.* **1.** *Old Testament.* the first man, created by God: the progenitor of the human race (Genesis 2–3). **2. not know (someone) from Adam.** to fail to be acquainted with someone. **3. the old Adam.** the evil supposedly inherent in human nature. **4. Adam's ale** *or* **wine.** water.

Ad·am[2] ('ædəm) *n.* **1. Rob·ert.** 1728–92, Scottish architect and furniture designer. Assisted by his brother, **James,** 1730–94, he emulated the harmony of classical and Italian Renaissance architecture. *~adj.* **2.** in the neoclassical style made popular by Robert Adam.

Ad·am-and-Eve *n.* another name for **puttyroot.**

ad·a·mant ('ædəmənt) *adj.* **1.** unyielding; inflexible. **2.** unbreakable; impenetrable. *~n.* **3.** any extremely hard or apparently unbreakable substance. **4.** a legendary stone said to be impenetrable, often identified with the diamond or loadstone. [Old English: from Latin *adamant-*, stem of *adamas,* from Greek; literal meaning perhaps: unconquerable, from A-[1] + *daman* to tame, conquer]

ad·a·man·tine (ˌædə'mæntaɪn) *adj.* **1.** having the lustre of a diamond. **2.** *Rare.* another word for **adamant.**

Ad·a·ma·wa (ˌædə'mɑːwə) *n.* a small group of languages of W Africa, spoken chiefly in E Nigeria, N Cameroon, the Central African Republic, and N Zaïre, forming a branch of the Niger-Congo family.

Ad·am·ite ('ædəˌmaɪt) *n.* **1.** a human being. **2.** a nudist, esp. a member of an early Christian sect who sought to imitate Adam. **—Ad·am·it·ic** (ˌædə'mɪtɪk) *adj.*

Ad·ams[1] ('ædəmz) *n.* a mountain in SW Washington, in the Cascade Range. Height: 3751 m (12 307 ft.).

Ad·ams[2] ('ædəmz) *n.* **1. John.** 1735–1826, second president of the U.S. (1797–1801); U.S. ambassador to Great Britain (1785–88); helped draft the Declaration of Independence (1776). **2. John Couch.** 1819–92, English astronomer who deduced the existence and position of the planet Neptune. **3. John Quin·cy,** son of John Adams. 1767–1848, sixth president of the U.S. (1825–29); secretary of state (1817–25). **4. Sam·u·el.** 1722–1803, American revolutionary leader; one of the organizers of the Boston Tea Party; a signatory of the Declaration of Independence.

Ad·am's ap·ple *n.* the visible projection of the thyroid cartilage of the larynx at the front of the neck.

ad·ams·ite ('ædəmˌzaɪt) *n.* a yellow poisonous crystalline solid that readily sublimes. It is used as a tear gas; diphenylaminechlorarsine. Formula: $C_6H_4AsClNHC_6H_4$; relative density: 1.65; melting pt.: 195°C; boiling pt.: 410°C. [C20: named after Roger *Adams* (born 1899), American chemist]

Ad·am's-nee·dle *n.* a North American liliaceous plant, *Yucca filamentosa,* that has a tall woody stem, stiff pointed leaves, and large clusters of white flowers arranged in spikes. It is cultivated as an ornamental plant. See also **Spanish bayonet.**

Ad·ams-Stokes syn·drome *n.* another term for **heart block.** [C19: named after R. *Adams* (1791–1875) and W. *Stokes* (1804–78), Irish physicians]

A·da·na ('ædənə) *n.* a city in S Turkey, capital of Adana province. Pop.: 475 384 (1975). Also called: **Seyhan.**

a·dapt (ə'dæpt) *vb.* **1.** (often foll. by *to*) to adjust (someone or something, esp. oneself) to different conditions, a new environment, etc. **2.** (*tr.*) to fit, change, or modify to suit a new or different purpose: *to adapt a play for use in schools.* [C17: from Latin *adaptāre,* from *ad-* to + *aptāre* to fit, from *aptus* APT] **—a·'dapt·a·ble** *adj.* **—a·ˌdapt·a·'bil·i·ty** *or* **a·'dapt·a·ble·ness** *n.* **—a·'dap·tive** *adj.*

ad·ap·ta·tion (ˌædəp'teɪʃən, ˌædæp-) *n.* **1.** the act or process of adapting or the state of being adapted; adjustment. **2.** something that is produced or created by adapting something else. **3.** something that is changed or modified to suit new conditions or needs. **4.** *Biology.* an inherited or acquired modification in organisms that makes them better suited to survive and reproduce in a particular environment.

a·dapt·er *or* **a·dap·tor** (ə'dæptə) *n.* **1.** a person or thing that adapts. **2.** any device for connecting two parts, esp. ones that are of different sizes or have different mating fitments. **3. a.** a plug used to connect an electrical device to a mains supply when they have different types of terminals. **b.** a device used to connect several electrical appliances to a single mains socket.

a·dap·tive ra·di·a·tion *n.* the development of many different forms from an originally homogeneous group of animals as a result of the increase of the original stock and its spread and adaptation to different environments. This type of evolution occurred in the Tertiary mammals and the Mesozoic reptiles.

A·dar (*Hebrew* a'dar) *n.* the sixth month of the civil year and the twelfth of the ecclesiastical year in the Jewish calendar, falling approximately in February and March.

A·dar She·ni (*Hebrew* ʃe'niː) *n. Judaism.* the month of Adar in leap years when an intercalary month, Adar Rishon, is inserted between Shebat and Adar. [Hebrew: Adar the Second]

ad·ax·i·al (æd'æksɪəl) *adj.* facing towards the axis, as the surface of a leaf that faces the stem. Compare **abaxial.**

A.D.C. *abbrev. for:* **1.** aide-de-camp. **2.** analog-digital converter.

add (æd) *vb.* **1.** to combine (two or more numbers or quantities) by addition. **2.** (*tr.;* foll. by *to*) to increase (a number or quantity) by another number or quantity using addition. **3.** (*tr.;* often foll. by *to*) to join (something) to something else in order to increase the size, quantity, effect, or scope; unite (with): *to add insult to injury.* **4.** (*intr.;* foll. by *to*) to have an extra and increased effect (on): *her illness added to his worries.* **5.** (*tr.*) to say or write further. **6.** (*tr.;* foll. by *in*) to include. *~*See also **add up.** [C14: from Latin *addere,* literally: to put to, from *ad-* to + *-dere* to put]

add. *abbrev. for:* **1.** addendum. **2.** addition. **3.** additional. **4.** address.

Ad·dams ('ædəmz) *n.* **Jane.** 1860–1935, U.S. social reformer, feminist, and pacifist, who founded Hull House, a social settlement in Chicago: Nobel peace prize 1931.

ad·dax ('ædæks) *n.* a large light-coloured antelope, *Addax nasomaculatus,* having ribbed loosely spiralled horns and inhabiting desert regions in N Africa: family *Bovidae,* order *Artiodactyla.* [C17: Latin, from an unidentified ancient N African language]

add·ed sixth *n.* a chord much used esp. in jazz, consisting of a triad with an added sixth above the root. Also called: **added sixth chord.** Compare **sixth chord.**

ad·dend ('ædɛnd, ə'dɛnd) *n.* any of a set of numbers that form a sum. Compare **augend.** [C20: short for ADDENDUM]

ad·den·dum (ə'dɛndəm) *n., pl.* **·da** (-də). **1.** something added; an addition. **2.** a supplement or appendix to a book, magazine, etc. **3.** the radial distance between the inner and outer pitch circles of a screw thread. **4.** the radial distance between the pitch circle and tip of a gear tooth. [C18: from Latin, literally: a thing to be added, neuter gerundive of *addere* to ADD]

ad·der[1] ('ædə) *n.* **1.** Also called: **viper.** a common viper, *Vipera berus,* that is widely distributed in Europe, including Britain, and Asia and is typically dark greyish in colour with a black zigzag pattern along the back. **2.** any of various similar venomous or nonvenomous snakes. *~*See also **puff adder.** [Old English *nǣdre* snake; in Middle English *a naddre* was mistaken for *an addre,* whence the modern form; related to Old Norse *nathr,* Gothic *nadrs*]

add·er[2] ('ædə) *n.* a person or thing that adds.

ad·der's-meat *n.* another name for the **greater stitchwort** (see **stitchwort**).

ad·der's-mouth *n.* any of various orchids of the genus *Malaxis* that occur in all parts of the world except Australia and New Zealand and have clusters of small usually greenish flowers. See also **bog orchid.**

ad·der's-tongue *n.* **1.** any of several terrestrial ferns of the genus *Ophioglossum,* esp. *O. vulgatum,* that grow in the N hemisphere and have a narrow spore-bearing body that sticks out like a spike from the leaf: family *Ophioglossaceae.* **2.** another name for **dogtooth violet.**

ad·dict *vb.* (ə'dɪkt). **1.** (*tr.; usually passive;* often foll. by *to*) to cause (someone or oneself) to become dependent (on something, esp. a narcotic drug). *~n.* ('ædɪkt). **2.** a person who is addicted, esp. to narcotic drugs. **3.** *Informal.* a person who is devoted to something: *a jazz addict.* [C16 (as adj. and as vb.; n. use C20): from Latin *addictus* given over, from *addīcere* to give one's assent to, from *ad-* to + *dīcere* to say]

ad·dic·tion (ə'dɪkʃən) *n.* the condition of being abnormally dependent on some habit, esp. compulsive dependency on narcotic drugs.

ad·dic·tive (ə'dɪktɪv) *adj.* of, relating to, or causing addiction.

add·ing ma·chine *n.* a mechanical device, operated manually or electrically, for adding and often subtracting, multiplying, and dividing. Compare **calculating machine.**

Ad·ding·ton ('ædɪŋtən) *n.* **Hen·ry,** 1st Viscount Sidmouth. 1757–1844, English statesman; prime minister (1801–04) and home secretary (1812–21).

Ad·dis Ab·a·ba ('ædɪs 'æbəbə) *n.* the capital of Ethiopia, on a central plateau 2400 m (8000 ft.) above sea level: founded in 1887; became capital in 1896. Pop.: 1 161 267 (1975 est.).

Ad·di·son ('ædɪsᵊn) *n.* **Jo·seph.** 1672–1719, English essayist and poet who, with Richard Steele, founded *The Spectator* (1711–14) and contributed most of its essays, including the *de Coverley Papers.*

Ad·di·son's dis·ease *n.* a disease characterized by deep bronzing of the skin, anaemia, and extreme weakness, caused by underactivity of the adrenal glands. Also called: **adrenal insufficiency.** [C19: named after Thomas *Addison* (1793–1860), English physician who identified it]

ad·di·tion (ə'dɪʃən) *n.* **1.** the act, process, or result of adding. **2.** a person or thing that is added or acquired. **3.** a mathematical operation in which the sum of two numbers or quantities is calculated. Usually indicated by the symbol +. **4.** *Chiefly U.S.* a part added to a building or piece of land; annexe. **5.** *Obsolete.* a title following a person's name. **6. in addition.** (*adv.*) also; as well; besides. **7. in addition to.** (*prep.*) besides; as well as. [C15: from Latin *additiōn-*, from *addere* to ADD]

ad·di·tion·al (ə'dɪʃənᵊl) *adj.* added or supplementary.

ad·di·tive ('ædɪtɪv) *adj.* **1.** characterized or produced by addition; cumulative. *~n.* **2.** any substance added to something to improve it, prevent deterioration, etc. [C17: from Late Latin *additīvus,* from *addere* to ADD]

ad·dle[1] ('ædᵊl) *vb.* **1.** to make or become confused or muddled. **2.** to make or become rotten. *~adj.* **3.** (*in combination*) indicating a confused or muddled state: *addle-brained; addle-pated.* [C18 (vb.), back formation from *addled,* from C13 *addle* rotten, from Old English *adela* filth; related to dialect German *Addel* liquid manure]

ad·dle[2] ('ædᵊl) *vb. Northern English dialect.* to earn (money or one's living). [C13 *addlen,* from Old Norse *ōthlask* to gain possession of property, from *ōthal* property]

ad·dress (ə'drɛs) *n.* **1.** the conventional form by which the location of a building is described. **2.** the written form of this, as on a letter or parcel, preceded by the name of the person or organization for whom it is intended. **3.** the place at which someone lives. **4.** a speech or written communication, esp. one of a formal nature. **5.** skilfulness or tact. **6.** *Archaic.* manner or style of speaking or conversation. **7.** *Computer technol.* a number giving the location of a piece of stored information. See also **direct access. 8.** *Brit. government.* a statement of the opinions or wishes of either or both Houses of Parliament that is sent to the sovereign. **9.** the alignment or position of a part, component, etc., that permits correct assembly or fitting. **10.** *Rare.* the act of dispatching or directing a ship. **11.** (*usually pl.*) expressions of affection made by a man in courting a woman. ~*vb.* **+dress·es, +dress+ing; +dressed** *or* **+drest.** (*tr.*) **12.** to mark (a letter, parcel, etc.) with an address. **13.** to speak to, refer to in speaking, or deliver a speech to. **14.** (used reflexively; foll. by *to*) **a.** to speak or write to: *he addressed himself to the chairman.* **b.** apply oneself to: *he addressed himself to the task.* **15.** to direct (a message, warning, etc.) to the attention of. **16.** to consign or entrust (a ship or a ship's cargo) to a factor, merchant, etc. **17.** to adopt a position facing (the ball in golf, a partner in a dance, the target in archery, etc.). **18.** an archaic word for **woo.** [C14 (in the sense: to make right, adorn) and C15 (in the modern sense: to direct words): via Old French from Vulgar Latin *addrictiāre* (unattested) to make straight, direct oneself towards, from Latin *ad-* to + *dīrectus* DIRECT] **—ad+'dress+er** *or* **ad+'dres+sor** *n.*

ad+dress·ee (ˌædrɛ'si:) *n.* a person or organization to whom a letter, parcel, etc., is addressed.

Ad+dres+so+graph (ə'drɛsəʊˌgrɑ:f, -ˌgræf) *n. Trademark.* a machine for addressing envelopes, etc.

ad+duce (ə'dju:s) *vb.* (*tr.*) to cite (reasons, examples, etc.) as evidence or proof. [C15: from Latin *addūcere* to lead or bring to] **—ad+'duce+a·ble** *or* **ad+'duc+i·ble** *adj.* **—ad+'du+cent** *adj.* **—ad+duc+tion** (ə'dʌkʃən) *n.*

ad+duct (ə'dʌkt) *vb.* (*tr.*) (of a muscle) to draw or pull (a leg, arm, etc.) towards the median axis of the body. Compare **abduct** (sense 2). [C19: from Latin *addūcere;* see ADDUCE] **—ad+'duc+tion** *n.*

ad+duc+tor (ə'dʌktə) *n.* a muscle that adducts.

add up *vb.* (*adv.*) **1.** to find the sum (of). **2.** (*intr.*) to result in a correct total. **3.** (*intr.*) *Informal.* to make sense. **4.** (*intr.;* foll. by *to*) to amount to.

-ade *suffix forming nouns.* a sweetened drink made of various fruits: *lemonade; limeade.* [from French, from Latin *-āta* made of, feminine past participle of verbs ending in *-āre*]

Ad+e·laide ('ædɪˌleɪd) *n.* the capital of South Australia: **Port Adelaide,** 11 km (7 miles) away on St. Vincent Gulf, handles the bulk of exports. Pop.: 899 300 (1975 est.).

A·dé·lie Coast ('ædɪlɪ; *French* ade'li) *n.* a part of Antarctica, between Wilkes Land and George V Land: under French sovereignty. Also called: **Adélie Land.**

a·demp+tion (ə'dɛmpʃən) *n. Property law.* the failure of a specific legacy, as by a testator disposing of the subject matter in his lifetime. [C16: from Latin *ademptiōn-* a taking away, from *adimere* to take away, take to (oneself), from *ad-* to + *emere* to buy, take]

A·den ('eɪdᵊn) *n.* **1.** the main port and capital of Southern Yemen, on the N coast of the **Gulf of Aden**, an arm of the Indian Ocean at the entrance to the Red Sea: formerly an important port of call on shipping routes to the East. Pop.: 264 326 (1973 est.). **2.** a former British colony and protectorate on the S coast of the Arabian Peninsula: became the People's Republic of Southern Yemen in 1967. Area: 195 sq. km (75 sq. miles).

A·den·au·er (*German* 'a:dəˌnaʊər) *n.* **Kon·rad** ('kɔnra:t). 1876–1967, German statesman; chancellor of West Germany (1949–63).

ad+e·nec+to+my (ˌædə'nɛktəmɪ) *n., pl.* **+mies. 1.** surgical removal of a gland. **2.** another name for **adenoidectomy.** [C19: from ADENO- + -ECTOMY]

ad+e·nine ('ædənɪn, -ˌni:n, -ˌnaɪn) *n.* a purine base present in animal and plant tissues as a constituent of the nucleic acids DNA and RNA and of certain coenzymes; 6-aminopurine. Formula: $C_5H_5N_5$; melting pt.: 360–365°C.

ad+e·ni+tis (ˌædə'naɪtɪs) *n.* inflammation of a gland or lymph node. [C19: New Latin, from ADENO- + -ITIS]

ad·e·no- *or before a vowel* **ad·en-** *combining form.* gland or glandular: *adenoid; adenology.* [New Latin, from Greek *adēn* gland]

ad+e·no+car+ci+no+ma (ˌædɪnəʊˌkɑ:sɪ'nəʊmə) *n., pl.* **+mas** *or* **+ma+ta** (-mətə). **1.** a malignant tumour originating in glandular tissue. **2.** a malignant tumour with a glandlike structure.

ad+e·no+hy+poph·y+sis (ˌædɪnəʊhaɪ'pɒfɪsɪs) *n.* the anterior lobe of the pituitary gland. Compare **neurohypophysis.**

ad+e·noid ('ædɪˌnɔɪd) *adj.* **1.** of or resembling a gland. **2.** of or relating to lymphoid tissue, as that found in the lymph nodes, spleen, tonsils, etc. **3.** of or relating to the adenoids. [C19: from Greek *adenoeidēs.* See ADENO-, -OID]

ad+e·noi·dal (ˌædɪ'nɔɪdᵊl) *adj.* **1.** having the nasal tones or impaired breathing of one with enlarged adenoids. **2.** another word for **adenoid** (for all senses).

ad+e·noid+ec+to+my (ˌædɪnɔɪ'dɛktəmɪ) *n., pl.* **+mies.** surgical removal of the adenoids.

ad+e·noids ('ædɪˌnɔɪdz) *pl. n.* a mass of lymphoid tissue at the back of the throat behind the uvula: when enlarged it often restricts nasal breathing, esp. in young children. Technical name: **pharyngeal tonsil.**

ad+e·no+ma (ˌædɪ'nəʊmə) *n., pl.* **+mas** *or* **+ma+ta** (-mətə). **1.** a tumour, usually benign, occurring in glandular tissue. **2.** a tumour having a glandlike structure.

a·den·o+sine (æ'dɛnəˌsi:n, ˌædɪ'nəʊsi:n) *n. Biochem.* a nucleoside formed by the condensation of adenine and ribose. It is present in all living cells in a combined form, as in ribonucleic acids. Formula: $C_{10}H_{13}N_5O_4$. [C20: a blend of ADENINE + RIBOSE]

a·den·o+sine tri+phos+phate *n.* the full name of **ATP.**

ad+e·no+vi+rus (ˌædɪnəʊ'vaɪrəs) *n.* any of a group of viruses that may cause upper respiratory diseases in man. Compare **enterovirus, myxovirus.**

a·dept *adj.* (ə'dɛpt). **1.** very proficient in something requiring skill or manual dexterity. **2.** skilful; expert. ~*n.* ('ædɛpt). **3.** a person who is skilled or proficient in something. [C17: from Medieval Latin *adeptus,* from Latin *adipiscī* to attain, from *ad-* to + *apiscī* to attain] **—a·'dept+ly** *adv.* **—a·'dept+ness** *n.*

ad+e·quate ('ædɪkwɪt) *adj.* able to fulfil a need or requirement without being abundant, outstanding, etc. [C17: from Latin *adaequāre* to equalize, from *ad-* to + *aequus* EQUAL] **—ad+e·qua+cy** ('ædɪkwəsɪ) *n.* **—'ad+e·quate+ly** *adv.*

à deux *French.* (a 'dø) *adj., adv.* of or for two persons.

ad+here (əd'hɪə) *vb.* (*intr.*) **1.** (usually foll. by *to*) to stick or hold fast. **2.** (foll. by *to*) to be devoted (to a political party, cause, religion, etc.); be a follower (of). **3.** (foll. by *to*) to follow closely or exactly: *adhere to the rules.* [C16: via Medieval Latin *adhērēre* from Latin *adhaerēre* to stick to] **—ad+'her+ence** *n.*

ad+her+ent (əd'hɪərənt) *n.* **1.** (usually foll. by *of*) a supporter or follower. ~*adj.* **2.** sticking, holding fast, or attached.

ad+he+sion (əd'hi:ʒən) *n.* **1.** the quality or condition of sticking together or holding fast. **2.** ability to make firm contact without skidding or slipping. **3.** attachment or fidelity, as to a political party, cause, etc. **4.** an attraction or repulsion between the molecules of unlike substances in contact: distinguished from *cohesion.* **5.** *Pathol.* abnormal union of structures or parts. **6.** *Rare.* concurrence; assent. [C17: from Latin *adhaesiōn-* a sticking. See ADHERE]

ad+he+sive (əd'hi:sɪv) *adj.* **1.** able or designed to adhere; sticky: *adhesive tape.* **2.** tenacious or clinging. ~*n.* **3.** a substance used for sticking objects together, such as glue, cement, or paste. **—ad+'he+sive+ly** *adv.* **—ad+'he+sive+ness** *n.*

ad+hib+it (əd'hɪbɪt) *vb.* (*tr.*) *Rare.* **1.** to administer or apply. **2.** to affix; attach. [C16: from Latin *adhibēre* to bring to, from *ad-* to + *habēre* to have, hold] **—ad+hi+bi+tion** (ˌædhɪ'bɪʃən) *n.*

ad hoc (æd 'hɒk) *adj., adv.* for a particular purpose only: *an ad hoc decision; an ad hoc committee.* [Latin, literally: to this]

ad ho+mi+nem *Latin.* (æd 'hɒmɪˌnɛm) *adj., adv.* directed against a person rather than against his arguments. [literally: to the man]

ad·i·a+bat+ic (ˌædɪə'bætɪk, ˌeɪ-) *adj.* **1.** (of a thermodynamic process) taking place without loss or gain of heat. ~*n.* **2.** a curve on a graph representing the changes in two characteristics (such as pressure and volume) of a system undergoing an adiabatic process. [C19: from Greek *adiabatos* not to be crossed, impassable (to heat), from A-[1] + *diabatos* passable, from *dia-* across + *bainein* to go]

ad·i+aph+or+ism (ˌædɪ'æfəˌrɪzəm) *n.* a Christian Protestant theological theory that certain rites and actions are matters of indifference in religion since not forbidden by the Scriptures. [C19: see ADIAPHOROUS] **—ˌad·i·'aph·o+rist** *n.* **—ˌad·i·ˌaph·o+'ris+tic** *adj.*

ad·i+aph·o+rous (ˌædɪ'æfərəs) *adj. Med.* having no effect for good or ill, as a drug or placebo. [C17: from Greek *adiaphoros* indifferent, from A-[1] + *diaphoros* different]

ad·i·a+ther+man+cy (ˌædɪə'θɜ:mənsɪ) *n.* another name for **athermancy. —ˌad·i·a+'ther+ma+nous** *adj.*

a·dieu (ə'dju:; *French* a'djø) *interj., n. pl.* **a·dieus** *or* **a·dieux** (ə'dju:z; *French* a'djø). goodbye; farewell. [C14: from Old French, from *a* to + *dieu* God]

A·di·ge (*Italian* 'a:didʒe) *n.* a river in N Italy, flowing southeast to the Adriatic. Length: 354 km (220 miles).

ad in+fi+ni+tum (æd ˌɪnfɪ'naɪtəm) *adv.* without end; endlessly; to infinity. Abbrev.: **ad inf.** [Latin]

ad in+ter+im (æd 'ɪntərɪm) *adj., adv.* for the meantime; for the present: *ad interim measures.* ~Abbrev.: **ad int.** [Latin]

a·di·os (ˌɑ:dɪ'ɒs; *Spanish* a'ðjos) *interj.* goodbye; farewell. [literally: to God]

ad·i+po+cere (ˌædɪpəʊ'sɪə) *n.* a waxlike fatty substance formed during the decomposition of corpses. Nontechnical name: **grave-wax.** [C19: via French from New Latin *adiposus* fat (see ADIPOSE) + French *cire* wax] **—ad·i·poc+er+ous** (ˌædɪ'pɒsərəs) *adj.*

ad·i+pose ('ædɪˌpəʊs, -ˌpəʊz) *adj.* **1.** of, resembling, or containing fat; fatty. ~*n.* **2.** animal fat. [C18: from New Latin *adiposus,* from Latin *adeps* fat]

ad·i+pose fin *n.* a posterior dorsal fin occurring in the salmon and related fishes.

Ad·i+ron+dack Moun+tains (ˌædɪ'rɒndæk) *or* **Ad·i+ron+dacks** *pl. n.* a mountain range in NE New York State. Highest peak: Mount Marcy, 1629 m (5344 ft.).

ad·it ('ædɪt) *n.* an almost horizontal shaft into a mine, for access or drainage. [C17: from Latin *aditus* an approach, from *adīre,* from *ad-* towards + *īre* to go]

A·di+va+si ('ɑ:dɪˌvɑ:sɪ) *n.* a member of any of the aboriginal peoples of India. [Sanskrit, from *adi* beginning + *vasi* dweller]

adj. *abbrev. for:* **1.** *Maths.* adjacent. **2.** adjective. **3.** adjunct. **4.** adjourned. **5.** *Insurance, banking, etc.* adjustment. **6.** Also: **adjt.** adjutant.

ad+ja+cent (ə'dʒeɪsᵊnt) *adj.* **1.** being near or close, esp. having a common boundary; adjoining; contiguous. ~*n.* **2.** the side lying between a specified angle and a right angle in a right-angled triangle. [C15: from Latin *adjacēre* to lie next to, from *ad-* near + *jacēre* to lie] —**ad·'ja·cen·cy** *n.* —**ad·'ja·cent·ly** *adv.*

ad·jec·tive ('ædʒɪktɪv) *n.* **1. a.** a word imputing a characteristic to a noun or pronoun. **b.** (*as modifier*): *an adjective phrase.* Abbrev.: **adj.** ~*adj.* **2.** additional or dependent. **3.** (of law) relating to court practice and procedure, as opposed to the principles of law dealt with by the courts. Compare **substantive** (sense 7). [C14: from Late Latin *adjectīvus* attributive, from *adjicere* to throw to, add, from *ad-* to + *jacere* to throw; in grammatical sense, from the Latin phrase *nōmen adjectīvum* attributive noun] —**ad·jec·ti·val** (ˌædʒɪk'taɪvᵊl) *adj.*

ad·join (ə'dʒɔɪn) *vb.* **1.** to be next to (an area of land, etc.). **2.** (*tr.;* foll. by *to*) to join; affix or attach. [C14: via Old French from Latin *adjungere,* from *ad-* to + *jungere* to join]

ad·join·ing (ə'dʒɔɪnɪŋ) *adj.* being in contact; connected or neighbouring.

ad·joint ('ædˌdʒɔɪnt) *n. Maths.* another name for **Hermitian conjugate.**

ad·journ (ə'dʒɜ:n) *vb.* **1.** (*intr.*) (of a court, etc.) to close at the end of a session. **2.** to postpone or be postponed, esp. temporarily or to another place. **3.** (*tr.*) to put off (a problem, discussion, etc.) for later consideration; defer. **4.** (*intr.*) *Informal.* **a.** to move elsewhere: *let's adjourn to the kitchen.* **b.** to stop work. [C14: from Old French *ajourner* to defer to an arranged day, from *a-* to + *jour* day, from Late Latin *diurnum,* from Latin *diurnus* daily, from *diēs* day] —**ad·'journ·ment** *n.*

adjt. *abbrev. for* adjutant.

ad·judge (ə'dʒʌdʒ) *vb.* (*tr.; usually passive*) **1.** to pronounce formally; declare: *he was adjudged the winner.* **2. a.** to determine judicially; judge. **b.** to order or pronounce by law; decree: *he was adjudged bankrupt.* **c.** to award (costs, damages, etc.). **3.** *Archaic.* to sentence or condemn. [C14: via Old French from Latin *adjūdicāre.* See ADJUDICATE]

ad·ju·di·cate (ə'dʒu:dɪˌkeɪt) *vb.* **1.** (when *intr.,* usually foll. by *upon*) to decide (an issue) judicially; pass or sit in judgment. **2.** (*tr.*) *Chess.* to determine the likely result of (a game) by counting relative value of pieces, positional strength, etc. **3.** (*intr.*) to serve as a judge or arbiter, as in a competition. [C18: from Latin *adjūdicāre* to award something to someone, from *ad-* to + *jūdicāre* to act as a judge, from *jūdex* judge] —**adˌju·di·'ca·tion** *n.*

ad·junct ('ædʒʌŋkt) *n.* **1.** something incidental or not essential that is added to something else. **2.** a person who is subordinate to another. **3.** *Grammar.* **a.** part of a sentence other than the subject or the predicate. **b.** part of a sentence that may be omitted without making the sentence ungrammatical; a modifier. **4.** *Logic.* another name for **accident** (sense 5). ~*adj.* **5.** added or connected in a secondary or subordinate position; auxiliary. [C16: from Latin *adjunctus,* past participle of *adjungere* to ADJOIN] —**ad·junc·tive** (ə'dʒʌŋktɪv) *adj.* —**'ad·junct·ly** *adv.*

ad·jure (ə'dʒʊə) *vb.* (*tr.*) **1.** to command, often by exacting an oath; charge. **2.** to appeal earnestly to. [C14: from Latin *adjūrāre* to swear to, from *ad-* to + *jūrāre* to swear, from *jūs* oath] —**ad·ju·ra·tion** (ˌædʒʊə'reɪʃən) *n.* —**ad·'jur·a·to·ry** *adj.* —**ad·'jur·er** *or* **ad·'ju·ror** *n.*

ad·just (ə'dʒʌst) *vb.* **1.** (*tr.*) to alter slightly, esp. to achieve accuracy; regulate: *to adjust the television.* **2.** to adapt, as to a new environment, etc. **3.** (*tr.*) to put into order. **4.** (*tr.*) *Insurance.* to determine the amount payable in settlement of (a claim). [C17: from Old French *adjuster,* from *ad-* to + *juste* right, JUST] —**ad·'just·a·ble** *adj.* —**ad·'just·a·bly** *adv.* —**ad·'just·er** *n.*

ad·just·ment (ə'dʒʌstmənt) *n.* **1.** the act of adjusting or state of being adjusted. **2.** a control for regulating: *the adjustment for volume is beside the speaker.*

ad·ju·tant ('ædʒətənt) *n.* **1.** an officer who acts as administrative assistant to a superior officer. **2.** short for **adjutant bird.** [C17: from Latin *adjūtāre* to AID] —**'ad·ju·tan·cy** *n.*

ad·ju·tant bird *or* **stork** *n.* either of two large carrion-eating storks, *Leptoptilos dubius* or *L. javanicus,* which are closely related and similar to the marabou and occur in S and SE Asia.

ad·ju·tant gen·er·al *n., pl.* **ad·ju·tants gen·er·al. 1.** *Brit. Army.* **a.** the head of a department of the general staff. **b.** a general's executive officer. **2.** *U.S. Army.* the adjutant of a military unit with general staff.

ad·ju·vant ('ædʒəvənt) *adj.* **1.** aiding or assisting. ~*n.* **2.** something that aids or assists; auxiliary. [C17: from Latin *adjuvāns,* present participle of *adjuvāre,* from *juvāre* to help]

Ad·ler *n.* **1.** (*German* 'adlər) **Al·fred** ('alfre:t). 1870–1937, Austrian psychiatrist, noted for his descriptions of overcompensation and inferiority feelings. **2.** ('ædlə). **Lar·ry,** original name *Lawrence Cecil Adler.* born 1914, U.S. harmonica player. —**Ad·ler·i·an** (æd'lɪərɪən) *adj.*

ad-lib (æd'lɪb) *vb.* **-libs, -lib·bing, -libbed. 1.** to improvise and deliver spontaneously (a speech, musical performance, etc.). ~*adj.* (**ad lib** when predicative) **2.** improvised; impromptu. ~*adv.* **ad lib. 3.** spontaneously; freely. ~*n.* **4.** an improvised performance, often humorous. [C18: short for Latin *ad libitum,* literally: according to pleasure] —**ad-'lib·ber** *n.*

ad li·tem *Latin.* (æd 'laɪtɛm) *adj.* (esp. of a guardian) appointed for a lawsuit.

Adm. *abbrev. for:* **1.** Admiral. **2.** Admiralty.

ad·man ('ædˌmæn, -mən) *n., pl.* **·men.** *Informal.* a person who works in advertising.

ad·mass ('ædmæs) *n.* the section of the public that is susceptible or responsive to advertising, publicity, etc. [C20: from AD[1] + MASS]

ad·meas·ure (æd'mɛʒə) *vb.* **1.** to measure out (land, etc.) as a share; apportion. **2.** (*tr.*) to determine the dimensions, capacity, weight, and other details of (a vessel), as for an official registration, documentation, or yacht handicap rating. [C14 *amesuren,* from Old French *amesurer,* from *mesurer* to MEASURE; the modern form derives from AD- + MEASURE] —**ad·'meas·ure·ment** *n.*

Ad·me·tus (æd'mi:təs) *n. Greek myth.* a king of Thessaly, one of the Argonauts, who was married to Alcestis.

ad·min ('ædmɪn) *n. Informal.* short for **administration.**

ad·min·i·cle (æd'mɪnɪkᵊl) *n. Law.* something contributing to prove a point without itself being complete proof. [C16: from Latin *adminiculum* support]

ad·min·is·ter (əd'mɪnɪstə) *vb.* (*mainly tr.*) **1.** (*also intr.*) to direct or control (the affairs of a business, government, etc.). **2.** to put into execution; dispense: *administer justice.* **3.** (when *intr.,* foll. by *to*) to give or apply (medicine, assistance, etc.) as a remedy or relief. **4.** to apply formally; perform: *to administer extreme unction.* **5.** to supervise or impose the taking of (an oath, etc.). **6.** to manage or distribute (an estate, property, etc.). [C14 *amynistre* via Old French from Latin *administrare,* from *ad-* to + *ministrāre* to MINISTER]

ad·min·is·trate (əd'mɪnɪˌstreɪt) *vb.* to manage or direct (the affairs of a business, institution, etc.).

ad·min·is·tra·tion (ədˌmɪnɪ'streɪʃən) *n.* **1.** management of the affairs of an organization, such as a business or institution. **2.** the duties of an administrator. **3.** the body of people who administer an organization. **4.** the conduct of the affairs of government. **5.** term of office: often used of presidents, governments, etc. **6.** the executive branch of government along with the public service; the government as a whole. **7.** (*often cap.*) *Chiefly U.S.* the political executive, esp. of the U.S.; the government. **8.** *Chiefly U.S.* a government board, agency, authority, etc. **9.** *Property law.* **a.** the conduct or disposal of the estate of a deceased person. **b.** the management by a trustee of an estate subject to a trust. **10.** something administered, such as a sacrament, oath, or medical treatment. —**ad·'min·is·tra·tive** *adj.* —**ad·'min·is·tra·tive·ly** *adv.*

ad·min·is·tra·tor (əd'mɪnɪˌstreɪtə) *n.* **1.** a person who administers the affairs of an organization, official body, etc. **2.** *Property law.* a person authorized to manage an estate, esp. when the owner has died intestate or without having appointed executors. —**adˌmin·is·'tra·trix** *fem. n.*

ad·mi·ra·ble ('ædmərəbᵊl) *adj.* deserving or inspiring admiration; excellent. —**'ad·mi·ra·bly** *adv.*

ad·mi·ral ('ædmərəl) *n.* **1.** the supreme commander of a fleet or navy. **2.** Also called: **admiral of the fleet, fleet admiral.** a naval officer of the highest rank, equivalent to general of the army or field marshal. **3.** a senior naval officer entitled to fly his own flag. See also **rear admiral, vice admiral. 4.** *Chiefly Brit.* the master of a fishing fleet. **5.** any of various nymphalid butterflies, esp. the red admiral or white admiral. [C13 *amyral,* from Old French *amiral* emir, and from Medieval Latin *admīrābilis* (the spelling with *d* probably influenced by *admīrābilis* admirable); both from Arabic *amīr* emir, commander, esp. in the phrase *amīr-al* commander of, as in *amīr-al-bahr* commander of the sea] —**'ad·mi·ral·ˌship** *n.*

ad·mi·ral·ty ('ædmərəltɪ) *n., pl.* **·ties. 1.** the office or jurisdiction of an admiral. **2. a.** jurisdiction over naval affairs. **b.** (*as modifier*): *admiralty law.*

Ad·mi·ral·ty Board *n.* **the.** a department of the British Ministry of Defence, responsible for the administration and planning of the Royal Navy.

Ad·mi·ral·ty House *n.* the official residence of the governor general of Australia, in Sydney.

Ad·mi·ral·ty Is·lands *pl. n.* a group of about 40 volcanic and coral islands in the SW Pacific, part of Papua New Guinea, in the Bismarck Archipelago: main island: Manus. Pop.: 20 647 (1966). Area: about 2000 sq. km (800 sq. miles). Also called: **Admiralties.**

Ad·mi·ral·ty mile *n.* another name for **nautical mile.**

Ad·mi·ral·ty Range *n.* a mountain range in Antarctica, on the coast of Victoria Land, northwest of the Ross Sea.

ad·mi·ra·tion (ˌædmə'reɪʃən) *n.* **1.** pleasurable contemplation or surprise. **2.** a person or thing that is admired: *she was the admiration of the court.* **3.** *Archaic.* wonder.

ad·mire (əd'maɪə) *vb.* (*tr.*) **1.** to regard with esteem, respect, approval, or pleased surprise. **2.** *Archaic.* to wonder at. [C16: from Latin *admīrāri* to wonder at, from *ad-* to, at + *mīrāri* to wonder, from *mīrus* wonderful] —**ad·'mir·ing·ly** *adv.*

ad·mis·si·ble (əd'mɪsəbᵊl) *adj.* **1.** able or deserving to be considered or allowed. **2.** deserving to be admitted or allowed to enter. **3.** *Law.* (esp. of evidence) capable of being or bound to be admitted in a court of law. —**adˌmis·si·'bil·i·ty** *or* **ad·'mis·si·ble·ness** *n.*

ad·mis·sion (əd'mɪʃən) *n.* **1.** permission to enter or the right, authority, etc., to enter. **2.** the price charged for entrance. **3.** acceptance for a position, office, etc. **4.** a confession, as of a crime, mistake, etc. **5.** an acknowledgment of the truth or validity of something. [C15: from Latin *admissiōn-,* from *admittere* to ADMIT] —**ad·'mis·sive** *adj.*

ad·mit (əd'mɪt) *vb.* **·mits, ·mit·ting, ·mit·ted.** (*mainly tr.*) **1.** (*may take a clause as object*) to confess or acknowledge (a crime, mistake, etc.). **2.** (*may take a clause as object*) to concede (the truth or validity of something). **3.** to allow to enter; let in. **4.** (foll. by *to*) to allow participation (in) or the right to be part (of): *to admit to the profession.* **5.** (when *intr.,* foll. by *of*) to allow (of); leave room (for). **6.** (*intr.*) to give access: *the door admits onto the lawn.* [C14: from Latin *admittere* to let come or go to, from *ad-* to + *mittere* to send]

ad·mit·tance (əd'mɪtᵊns) *n.* **1.** the right or authority to enter. **2.** the act of giving entrance. **3.** the reciprocal of impedance, usually measured in reciprocal ohms or siemens. It can be expressed as a complex quantity, the real part of which is the conductance and the imaginary part the susceptance. Symbol: *y*

ad+mit+ted+ly (əd'mɪtɪdlɪ) *adv.* (*sentence modifier*) willingly conceded: *admittedly I am afraid.*

ad+mix (əd'mɪks) *vb.* (*tr.*) *Rare.* to mix or blend. [C16: back formation from obsolete *admixt*, from Latin *admīscēre* to mix with]

ad+mix+ture (əd'mɪkstʃə) *n.* **1.** a less common word for **mixture. 2.** anything added in mixing; ingredient.

ad+mon+ish (əd'mɒnɪʃ) *vb.* (*tr.*) **1.** to reprove firmly but not harshly. **2.** to advise to do or against doing something; warn; caution. [C14: via Old French from Vulgar Latin *admonestāre* (unattested), from Latin *admonēre* to put one in mind of, from *monēre* to advise] —**ad+'mon+ish+er** *or* **ad+'mon+i+tor** *n.* —**ad+mo+ni+tion** (ˌædmə'nɪʃən) *n.* —**ad+'mon+i+to+ry** *adj.*

ad+nate ('ædneɪt) *adj. Botany.* growing closely attached to an adjacent part or organ. [C17: from Latin *adnātus*, a variant form of *agnātus* AGNATE]

ad nau+se+am (æd 'nɔːzɪˌæm, -sɪ-) *adv.* to a disgusting extent. [Latin: to (the point of) nausea]

ad+nom+i+nal (əd'nɒmɪnᵊl) *Grammar.* ~*n.* **1.** a word modifying a noun. ~*adj.* **2.** of or relating to an adnoun.

ad+noun ('ædnaʊn) *n.* an adjective used as a noun; absolute adjective. [C18: from Latin *ad* to + NOUN, formed on the model of ADVERB]

a+do (ə'duː) *n.* bustling activity; fuss; bother; delay (esp. in the phrases **without more ado, with much ado**). [C14: from the phrase *at do* a to-do, from Old Norse *at* to (marking the infinitive) + DO[1]]

a+do+be (ə'dəʊbɪ) *n.* **1. a.** a sun-dried brick used for building. **b.** (*as modifier*): *an adobe house.* **2.** a building constructed of such bricks. **3.** the clayey material from which such bricks are made. [C19: from Spanish]

a+do+be flat *n. Chiefly U.S.* a gently sloping clayey plain formed by a short-lived stream or flood water.

ad+o+les+cence (ˌædə'lɛsəns) *n.* the period in human development that occurs between the beginning of puberty and adulthood. [C15: via Old French from Latin *adolēscentia*, from *adolēscere* to grow up, from *alēscere* to grow, from *alēre* to feed, nourish]

ad+o+les+cent (ˌædə'lɛsᵊnt) *adj.* **1.** of or relating to adolescence. **2.** *Informal.* behaving in an immature way; puerile. ~*n.* **3.** an adolescent person.

Ad+o+nai (ˌædɒ'naɪ, -'neɪaɪ) *n. Judaism.* a name for God. [C15: from Hebrew: lord; compare ADONIS]

A+don+ic (ə'dɒnɪk) *adj.* **1.** (in classical prosody) of or relating to a verse line consisting of a dactyl (¯˘˘) followed by a spondee (¯¯) or by a trochee (¯˘), thought to have been first used in laments for Adonis. **2.** of or relating to Adonis. ~*n.* **3.** an Adonic line or verse.

A+do+nis (ə'dəʊnɪs) *n.* **1.** *Greek myth.* a handsome youth loved by Aphrodite. Killed by a wild boar, he was believed to spend part of the year in the underworld and part on earth, symbolizing the vegetative cycle. **2.** a handsome young man. [C16: from Latin, via Greek *Adōnis* from Phoenician *adōni* my lord, a title of the god Tammuz; related to Hebrew ADONAI]

a+dopt (ə'dɒpt) *vb.* (*tr.*) **1.** *Law.* to bring (a person) into a specific relationship, esp. to take (another's child) as one's own child. **2.** to choose and follow (a plan, technique, etc.). **3.** to take over (an idea, etc.) as if it were one's own. **4.** to take on; assume: *to adopt a title.* **5.** to accept (a report, etc.). [C16: from Latin *adoptāre* to choose for oneself, from *optāre* to choose] —**a+'dop+tion** *n.*

a+dopt+ed (ə'dɒptɪd) *adj.* having been adopted; fostered: *an adopted child.* Compare **adoptive.**

a+dop+tive (ə'dɒptɪv) *adj.* due to adoption; foster: *an adoptive parent.* Compare **adopted.**

a+dor+a+ble (ə'dɔːrəbᵊl) *adj.* **1.** very attractive; charming; lovable. **2.** *Becoming rare.* deserving or eliciting adoration. —**a+'dor+a+bly** *adv.*

ad+o+ra+tion (ˌædə'reɪʃən) *n.* **1.** deep love or esteem. **2.** the act of worshipping.

a+dore (ə'dɔː) *vb.* **1.** (*tr.*) to love intensely or deeply. **2.** to worship (a god) with religious rites. **3.** (*tr.*) *Informal.* to like very much: *I adore chocolate.* [C15: via French from Latin *adōrāre*, from *ad-* to + *ōrāre* to pray] —**a+'dor+er** *n.* —**a+'dor+ing+ly** *adv.*

a+dorn (ə'dɔːn) *vb.* (*tr.*) **1.** to decorate: *she adorned her hair with flowers.* **2.** to increase the beauty, distinction, etc., of. [C14: via Old French from Latin *adōrnāre*, from *ōrnāre* to furnish, prepare] —**a+'dorn+ment** *n.*

A+do+wa ('ɑːdʊˌwɑː) *n.* a variant spelling of **Aduwa.**

ADP *n. Biochem.* adenosine diphosphate; a nucleotide derived from ATP with the liberation of energy that is then used in the performance of muscular work.

A.D.P. *abbrev. for* automatic data processing.

A+dras+tus (ə'dræstəs) *n. Greek myth.* a king of Argos and leader of the Seven against Thebes of whom he was the sole survivor.

ad rem *Latin.* (æd 'rɛm) *adj., adv.* to the point; without digression: *to reply ad rem; an ad rem discussion.*

ad+re+nal (ə'driːnᵊl) *adj.* **1.** on or near the kidneys. **2.** of or relating to the adrenal glands or their secretions. ~*n.* **3.** an adrenal gland. [C19: from AD- (near) + RENAL]

ad+re+nal gland *n.* an endocrine gland at the anterior end of each kidney. Its medulla secretes adrenaline and noradrenaline and its cortex secretes several steroid hormones. Also called: **suprarenal gland.**

A+dren+a+lin (ə'drɛnəlɪn) *n. Trademark.* a brand of **adrenaline.**

a+dren+a+line (ə'drɛnəlɪn, -ˌliːn) *n.* a hormone that is secreted by the adrenal medulla in response to stress and increases heart rate, pulse rate, and blood pressure, and raises the blood levels of glucose and lipids. It is extracted from animals or synthesized for such medical uses as the treatment of asthma. Chemical name: aminohydroxyphenylpropionic acid; formula: $C_9H_{13}NO_3$. U.S. name: **epinephrine.**

ad+re+nal in+suf+fi+cien+cy *n.* another name for **Addison's disease.**

ad+ren+er+gic (ˌædrə'nɜːdʒɪk) *adj.* releasing or activated by adrenaline or an adrenaline-like substance. [C20: ADRENALINE + Greek *ergon* work]

a+dre+no+cor+ti+co+trop+ic (əˌdriːnəʊˌkɔːtəkəʊ'trɒpɪk) *or* **a+dre+no+cor+ti+co+troph+ic** (əˌdriːnəʊˌkɔːtəkəʊ'trɒfɪk) *adj.* stimulating the adrenal cortex.

a+dre+no+cor+ti+co+trop+ic hor+mone *n.* the full name of **ACTH.**

A+dri+an ('eɪdrɪən) *n.* **Ed+gar Doug+las,** Baron Adrian. 1889-1977, English physiologist, noted particularly for his research into the function of neurons: shared with Sherrington the Nobel prize for medicine (1932).

A+dri+an IV *n.* original name *Nicholas Breakspear.* ?1100–59, the only English pope (1154–59).

A+dri+an+o+ple (ˌeɪdrɪə'nəʊpᵊl) *or* **A+dri+a+nop+o+lis** (ˌeɪdrɪə'nɒpəlɪs) *n.* former names of **Edirne.**

A+dri+at+ic (ˌeɪdrɪ'ætɪk) *adj.* **1.** of or relating to the Adriatic Sea, or to the inhabitants of its coast or islands. ~*n.* **2. the.** short for the **Adriatic Sea.**

A+dri+at+ic Sea *n.* an arm of the Mediterranean between Italy and Yugoslavia.

a+drift (ə'drɪft) *adj.* (*postpositive*), *adv.* **1.** floating without steering or mooring; drifting. **2.** without purpose; aimless. **3.** *Informal.* off course or amiss: *the project went adrift.*

a+droit (ə'drɔɪt) *adj.* **1.** skilful or dexterous. **2.** quick in thought or reaction. [C17: from French *à droit* according to right, rightly] —**a+'droit+ly** *adv.* —**a+'droit+ness** *n.*

ad+sci+ti+tious (ˌædsɪ'tɪʃəs) *adj.* added or supplemental; additional. [C17: from Latin *adscītus* admitted (from outside), from *adscīscere* to admit, from *scīscere* to seek to know, from *scīre* to know] —**ˌad+sci+'ti+tious+ly** *adv.*

ad+scrip+tion (əd'skrɪpʃən) *n.* a less common word for **ascription.**

ad+sorb (əd'sɔːb, -'zɔːb) *vb.* to undergo or cause to undergo a process in which a substance, usually a gas, accumulates on the surface of a solid forming a thin film, often only one molecule thick: *to adsorb hydrogen on nickel; oxygen adsorbs on tungsten.* Compare **absorb** (sense 8). [C19: AD- + *-sorb* as in ABSORB] —**ad+'sorb+a+ble** *adj.* —**ad+ˌsorb+a+'bil+i+ty** *n.* —**ad+'sorp+tion** *n.*

ad+sorb+ate (əd'sɔːbeɪt, -bɪt, -'zɔː-) *n.* a substance that has been or is to be adsorbed on a surface.

ad+sor+bent (əd'sɔːbənt, -'zɔː-) *adj.* **1.** capable of adsorption. ~*n.* **2.** a material, such as activated charcoal, on which adsorption can occur.

ad+su+ki bean (æd'suːkɪ, -'zuː-) *n.* a variant spelling of **adzuki bean.**

ad+u+lar+i+a (ˌædjʊ'lɛərɪə) *n.* a white or colourless glassy variety of orthoclase in the form of prismatic crystals. It occurs in metamorphic rocks and is a minor gemstone. Formula: $KAlSi_3O_8$. [C18: via Italian from French *adulaire*, after *Adula*, a group of mountains in Switzerland]

ad+u+late ('ædjʊˌleɪt) *vb.* (*tr.*) to flatter or praise obsequiously. [C17: back formation from C15 *adulation*, from Latin *adūlārī* to flatter] —**ˌad+u+'la+tion** *n.* —**'ad+u+ˌla+tor** *n.* —**ad+u+la+to+ry** (ˌædjʊ'leɪtərɪ, 'ædjʊˌleɪtərɪ) *adj.*

A+dul+la+mite (ə'dʌləˌmaɪt) *n.* a person who has withdrawn from a political group and joined with a few others to form a dissident group. [C19: originally applied to members of the British House of Commons who withdrew from the Liberal party (1866); alluding to the cave of *Abdullam* in the Bible, to which David and others fled (1 Samuel 22: 1–2)]

a+dult ('ædʌlt, ə'dʌlt) *adj.* **1.** having reached maturity; fully developed. **2.** of or intended for mature people: *adult education; adult films.* ~*n.* **3.** a person who has attained maturity; a grownup. **4.** a mature fully grown animal or plant. **5.** *Law.* a person who has attained the age of legal majority (18 years for most purposes). Compare **infant.** [C16: from Latin *adultus*, from *adolēscere* to grow up, from *alēscere* to grow, from *alēre* to feed, nourish] —**a+'dult+hood** *n.*

a+dul+ter+ant (ə'dʌltərənt) *n.* **1.** a substance or ingredient that adulterates. ~*adj.* **2.** adulterating.

a+dul+ter+ate *vb.* (ə'dʌltəˌreɪt). **1.** (*tr.*) to debase by adding inferior material: *to adulterate milk with water.* ~*adj.* (ə'dʌltərɪt, -ˌreɪt). **2.** adulterated; debased or impure. **3.** a less common word for **adulterous.** [C16: from Latin *adulterāre* to corrupt, commit adultery, probably from *alter* another, hence to approach another, commit adultery] —**a+ˌdul+ter+'a+tion** *n.* —**a+'dul+ter+ˌa+tor** *n.*

a+dul+ter+er (ə'dʌltərə) *or* (*fem.*) **a+dul+ter+ess** *n.* a person who has committed adultery. [C16: originally also *adulter*, from Latin *adulter*, back formation from *adulterāre* to ADULTERATE]

a+dul+ter+ine (ə'dʌltərɪn, -ˌriːn, -ˌraɪn) *adj.* **1.** of or made by adulteration; fake. **2.** conceived in adultery: *an adulterine child.*

a+dul+ter+ous (ə'dʌltərəs) *adj.* **1.** of, characterized by, or inclined to adultery. **2.** an obsolete word for **adulterate** (sense 2). —**a·'dul·ter·ous·ly** *adv.*

a·dul·ter·y (ə'dʌltərɪ) *n., pl.* **·ter·ies.** voluntary sexual intercourse between a married man or woman and partner other than the legal spouse. [C15 *adulterie,* altered (as if directly from Latin *adulterium*) from C14 *avoutrie,* via Old French from Latin *adulterium,* from *adulter,* back formation from *adulterāre.* See ADULTERATE]

ad·um·bral (æd'ʌmbrəl) *adj. Usually poetic.* shadowy. [C19: from AD- (in the sense: in) + Latin *umbra* shadow]

ad·um·brate ('ædʌm,breɪt) *vb. (tr.)* **1.** to outline; give a faint indication of. **2.** to foreshadow. **3.** to overshadow; obscure. [C16: from Latin *adumbrātus* represented only in outline, from *adumbrāre* to cast a shadow on, from *umbra* shadow] —**,ad·um·'bra·tion** *n.* —**ad·um·bra·tive** (æd'ʌmbrətɪv) *adj.* —**ad·'um·bra·tive·ly** *adv.*

a·dust (ə'dʌst) *adj. Archaic.* **1.** dried up or darkened by heat; burnt or scorched. **2.** gloomy or melancholy. [C14 (in the sense: gloomy): from Latin *adūstus,* from *adūrere* to set fire to, from *ūrere* to burn]

A·du·wa *or* **A·do·wa** ('ɑːdʊ,wɑː) *n.* a town in N Ethiopia: Emperor Menelik II defeated the Italians here in 1896. Pop.: 16 430 (1971 est.). Italian name: **A·du·a** (a'dua).

adv. *abbrev. for:* **1.** adverb. **2.** adverbial. **3.** adversus. [Latin: against] **4.** advertisement. **5.** advocate.

ad val. *abbrev. for* ad valorem.

ad va·lo·rem (æd və'lɔːrəm) *adj., adv.* (of taxes) in proportion to the estimated value of the goods taxed. Abbrev.: **ad val.** [from Latin]

ad·vance (əd'vɑːns) *vb.* **1.** to go or bring forward in position. **2.** (foll. by *on*) to move (towards) in a threatening manner. **3.** (*tr.*) to present for consideration; suggest. **4.** to bring or be brought to a further stage of development; improve; further. **5.** (*tr.*) to cause (an event) to occur earlier. **6.** (*tr.*) to supply (money, goods, etc.) beforehand, either for a loan or as an initial payment. **7.** to increase (a price, value, rate of occurrence, etc.) or (of a price, etc.) to be increased. **8.** (*intr.*) to improve one's position; be promoted: *he advanced rapidly in his job.* **9.** (*tr.*) *Archaic.* to promote in rank, status, or position. ~*n.* **10.** forward movement; progress in time or space. **11.** improvement; progress in development. **12.** *Commerce.* **a.** the supplying of commodities or funds before receipt of an agreed consideration. **b.** the commodities or funds supplied in this manner. **c.** (*as modifier*): *an advance supply.* **13.** Also called: **advance payment.** a money payment made before it is legally due. **14.** increase in price, value, rate of occurrence, etc. **15.** a less common word for **advancement** (sense 1). **16. in advance. a.** beforehand: *payment in advance.* **b.** (foll. by *of*) ahead in time or development: *ideas in advance of the time.* **17.** (*modifier*) forward in position or time: *advance booking; an advance warning.* [C15 *advauncen,* altered (on the model of words beginning with Latin *ad-*) from C13 *avauncen,* via Old French from Latin *abante* from before, from *ab-* away from + *ante* before] —**ad·'vanc·er** *n.* —**ad·'vanc·ing·ly** *adv.*

ad·vanced (əd'vɑːnst) *adj.* **1.** being ahead in development, knowledge, progress, etc.: *advanced studies.* **2.** having reached a comparatively late stage: *a man of advanced age.* **3.** ahead of the times: *advanced views on religion.*

ad·vanced gas-cooled re·ac·tor *n.* a nuclear reactor using carbon dioxide as the coolant, graphite as the moderator, and ceramic uranium dioxide cased in stainless steel as the fuel. Abbrev.: **AGR**

ad·vance guard *n.* **1.** a military unit sent ahead of an advancing formation to ensure its progress, etc. **2.** Also called: **advanced guard.** another name for **avant-garde.**

ad·vance·ment (əd'vɑːnsmənt) *n.* **1.** promotion in rank, status, etc.; preferment. **2.** a less common word for **advance** (senses 10, 11). **3.** *Property law.* the transfer during the life of a testator of money or property to a person (usually a child) to which the person is entitled.

ad·vance poll *n. Canadian.* (in an election) a poll held prior to election day to permit voters who expect to be absent then to cast their ballots.

ad·vanc·es (əd'vɑːnsɪz) *pl. n.* (*sometimes sing.;* often foll. by *to* or *towards*) personal overtures made in an attempt to become friendly, gain a favour, etc.

ad·van·tage (əd'vɑːntɪdʒ) *n.* **1.** (often foll. by *over* or *of*) superior or more favourable position or power: *he had an advantage over me because of his experience.* **2.** benefit or profit (esp. in the phrase **to one's advantage**). **3.** *Tennis.* **a.** the point scored after deuce. **b.** the resulting state of the score. **4. take advantage of. a.** to make good use of. **b.** to impose upon the weakness, good nature, etc., of; abuse. **c.** to seduce. **5. to advantage.** to good effect: *he used his height to advantage at the game.* **6. you have the advantage of me.** you know me but I do not know you. ~*vb.* **7.** (*tr.*) to put in a better position; favour. [C14 *avantage* (later altered to *advantage* on the model of words beginning with Latin *ad-*), from Old French *avant* before, from Latin *abante* from before, away. See ADVANCE]

ad·van·ta·geous (,ædvən'teɪdʒəs) *adj.* producing advantage. —**,ad·van·'ta·geous·ly** *adv.* —**,ad·van·'ta·geous·ness** *n.*

ad·vec·tion (əd'vɛkʃən) *n.* the transference of heat energy in a horizontal stream of gas, esp. of air. [C20: from Latin *advectiō* conveyance, from *advehere,* from *ad-* to + *vehere* to carry]

ad·vent ('ædvɛnt, -vənt) *n.* an arrival or coming, esp. one which is awaited. [C12: from Latin *adventus,* from *advenīre,* from *ad-* to + *venīre* to come]

Ad·vent ('ædvɛnt, -vənt) *n. Christianity.* the season including the four Sundays preceding Christmas.

Ad·vent·ist ('ædvɛntɪst, 'ædvən-) *n.* a member of any of the Christian groups, such as the **Seventh Day Adventists,** that hold that the Second Coming of Christ is imminent.

ad·ven·ti·ti·a (,ædvɛn'tɪʃɪə, -'tɪʃə) *n.* the outermost covering of an organ or part, esp. the outer coat of a blood vessel. [C19: New Latin, from the neuter plural of Latin *adventīcius;* see ADVENTITIOUS]

ad·ven·ti·tious (,ædvɛn'tɪʃəs) *adj.* **1.** added or appearing accidentally or unexpectedly. **2.** (of a plant or animal part) developing in an abnormal position, as a root that grows from a stem. [C17: from Latin *adventīcius* coming from outside, from *adventus* a coming] —**,ad·ven·'ti·tious·ly** *adv.*

Ad·vent Sun·day *n.* the first of the four Sundays of Advent, and the one that falls nearest to November 30.

ad·ven·ture (əd'vɛntʃə) *n.* **1.** a risky undertaking of unknown outcome. **2.** an exciting or unexpected event or course of events. **3.** a hazardous financial operation; commercial speculation. **4.** *Obsolete.* **a.** danger or misadventure. **b.** chance. ~*vb.* **5.** to take a risk or put at risk. **6.** (*intr.;* foll. by *into, on, upon*) to dare to go or enter (into a place, dangerous activity, etc.). **7.** to dare to say (something): *he adventured his opinion.* [C13 *aventure* (later altered to *adventure* after the Latin spelling), via Old French ultimately from Latin *advenīre* to happen to (someone), arrive] —**ad·'ven·ture·ful** *adj.*

ad·ven·ture play·ground *n. Brit.* a playground for children that contains building materials, discarded industrial parts, etc., used by the children to build with, hide in, climb on, etc.

ad·ven·tur·er (əd'vɛntʃərə) *or* (*fem.*) **ad·ven·tur·ess** *n.* **1.** a person who seeks adventure, esp. one who seeks success or money through daring exploits. **2.** a person who seeks money or power by unscrupulous means. **3.** a speculator.

ad·ven·tur·ism (əd'vɛntʃə,rɪzəm) *n.* recklessness, esp. in politics and finance. —**ad·'ven·tur·ist** *n.*

ad·ven·tur·ous (əd'vɛntʃərəs) *adj.* **1.** Also: **ad·ven·ture·some.** daring or enterprising. **2.** dangerous; involving risk. —**ad·'ven·tur·ous·ly** *adv.*

ad·verb ('æd,vɜːb) *n.* **a.** a word or group of words that serves to modify a whole sentence, a verb, another adverb, or an adjective; for example, *easily, probably, very,* and *happily* respectively in the sentence *They could probably easily envy the very happily married couple.* **b.** (*as modifier*): *an adverb marker.* Abbrev.: **adv.** [C15–C16: from Latin *adverbium* adverb, literally: added word, a translation of Greek *epirrhēma* a word spoken afterwards]

ad·ver·bi·al (æd'vɜːbɪəl) *n.* **1.** a word or group of words playing the grammatical role of an adverb, such as *in the rain* in the sentence *I'm singing in the rain.* ~*adj.* **2.** of or relating to an adverb or adverbial.

ad·ver·sar·y ('ædvəsərɪ) *n., pl.* **·sar·ies. 1.** a person or group that is hostile to someone; enemy. **2.** an opposing contestant in a game or sport. [C14: from Latin *adversārius,* from *adversus* against. See ADVERSE]

ad·ver·sa·tive (əd'vɜːsətɪv) *Grammar.* ~*adj.* **1.** (of a word, phrase, or clause) implying opposition or contrast. *But* and *although* are adversative conjunctions introducing adversative clauses. ~*n.* **2.** an adversative word or speech element.

ad·verse ('ædvɜːs, æd'vɜːs) *adj.* **1.** antagonistic or inimical; hostile: *adverse criticism.* **2.** unfavourable to one's interests: *adverse circumstances.* **3.** contrary or opposite in direction or position: *adverse winds.* **4.** (of leaves, flowers, etc.) facing the main stem. Compare **averse** (sense 2). [C14: from Latin *adversus* opposed to, hostile, from *advertere* to turn towards, from *ad-* to, towards + *vertere* to turn] —**ad·'verse·ly** *adv.* —**ad·'verse·ness** *n.*

ad·verse pos·ses·sion *n. Property law.* the occupation or possession of land by a person not legally entitled to it. If continued unopposed for a period specifed by law, such occupation extinguishes the title of the rightful owner.

ad·ver·si·ty (əd'vɜːsɪtɪ) *n., pl.* **·ties. 1.** distress; affliction; hardship. **2.** an unfortunate event or incident.

ad·vert[1] (əd'vɜːt) *vb.* (*intr.;* foll. by *to*) to draw attention (to); refer (to). [C15: from Latin *advertere* to turn one's attention to. See ADVERSE]

ad·vert[2] ('ædvɜːt) *n. Brit. informal.* short for **advertisement.**

ad·vert·ence (əd'vɜːtəns) *or* **ad·vert·en·cy** *n.* heedfulness or attentiveness. —**ad·'vert·ent** *adj.* —**ad·'vert·ent·ly** *adv.*

ad·ver·tise *or U.S.* (*sometimes*) **ad·ver·tize** ('ædvə,taɪz) *vb.* **1.** to present or praise (goods, a service, etc.) to the public, esp. in order to encourage sales. **2.** to make (something, such as a vacancy, article for sale, etc.) publicly known, as to possible applicants, buyers, etc.: *to advertise a job.* **3.** (*intr.;* foll. by *for*) to make a public request (for), esp. in a newspaper, etc.: *she advertised for a cook.* **4.** *Obsolete.* to warn; caution. [C15: from a lengthened stem of Old French *avertir,* ultimately from Latin *advertere* to turn one's attention to. See ADVERSE] —**'ad·ver·,tis·er** *n.*

ad·ver·tise·ment *or U.S.* (*sometimes*) **ad·ver·tize·ment** (əd'vɜːtɪsmənt, -tɪz-) *n.* any public notice, as a printed display in a newspaper, short film on television, announcement on radio, etc., designed to sell goods, publicize an event, etc. Shortened forms: **ad, advert.**

ad·ver·tis·ing *or U.S.* (*sometimes*) **ad·ver·tiz·ing** ('ædvə,taɪzɪŋ) *n.* **1.** the action or practice of drawing public attention to goods, services, events, etc., as by the distribution of printed notices, broadcasting, etc. **2.** the business that specializes in creating such publicity. **3.** advertisements collectively; publicity.

ad·vice (əd'vaɪs) *n.* **1.** recommendation as to appropriate choice of action; counsel. **2.** (*sometimes pl.*) formal notification of facts, esp. when communicated from a distance.

[C13 *avis* (later *advise*), via Old French from a Vulgar Latin phrase based on Latin *ad* to, according to + *vīsum* view (hence: according to one's view, opinion)]

ad·vis·a·ble (əd'vaɪzəbᵊl) *adj.* worthy of recommendation; prudent; sensible. —**ad·'vis·a·bly** *adv.*

ad·vise (əd'vaɪz) *vb.* (*when tr., may take a clause as object or an infinitive*) **1.** to offer advice (to a person or persons); counsel: *he advised the king; to advise caution; he advised her to leave.* **2.** (*tr.;* sometimes foll. by *of*) to inform or notify. **3.** (*intr.;* foll. by *with*) *Chiefly U.S., obsolete in Brit.* to consult or discuss. [C14: via Old French from Vulgar Latin *advīsāre* (unattested) to consider, from Latin *ad-* to + *visāre* (unattested), from *vīsere* to view, from *vidēre* to see]

Usage. *Advise* is often used in the same sense as *inform: as we advised you in our last communication, the order is being dealt with.* This use is accepted and common in business correspondence. Careful users of English prefer *inform, notify,* or *tell* in general English: *when he returned home, the police informed him* (not *advised him*) *that his car had been stolen.*

ad·vised (əd'vaɪzd) *adj.* resulting from deliberation. See also **ill-advised, well-advised.** —**ad·vis·ed·ly** (əd'vaɪzɪdlɪ) *adv.*

ad·vise·ment (əd'vaɪzmənt) *n. Chiefly U.S., archaic in Brit.* consultation; deliberation.

ad·vis·er or **ad·vi·sor** (əd'vaɪzə) *n.* **1.** a person who advises. **2.** *Education.* a person responsible for advising students on academic matters, career guidance, etc. **3.** *Brit. education.* a subject specialist who advises heads of schools on current teaching methods and facilities.

ad·vi·so·ry (əd'vaɪzərɪ) *adj.* giving advice; empowered to make recommendations: *an advisory body.*

ad·vo·caat ('ædvəʊˌkɑː, -ˌkɑːt, 'ædvə-) *n.* a liqueur having a raw egg base. [C20: Dutch, from *advocatenborrel,* from *advocaat* ADVOCATE (n.) + *borrel* drink]

ad·vo·ca·cy ('ædvəkəsɪ) *n., pl.* **-cies.** active support, esp. of a cause.

ad·vo·cate *vb.* ('ædvəˌkeɪt). **1.** (*tr.; may take a clause as object*) to support or recommend publicly; plead for or speak in favour of. ~*n.* ('ædvəkɪt, -ˌkeɪt). **2.** a person who upholds or defends a cause; supporter. **3.** a person who intercedes on behalf of another. **4.** a person who pleads his client's cause in a court of law. See also **barrister, solicitor, counsellor. 5.** *Scottish law.* the usual word for **counsel.** [C14: via Old French from Latin *advocātus* legal witness, advocate, from *advocāre* to call as witness, from *vocāre* to call] —**ˌad·vo·'ca·to·ry** *adj.*

Ad·vo·cate De·pute *n.* a Scottish law officer with the functions of public prosecutor.

ad·vo·ca·tion (ˌædvə'keɪʃən) *n. Scottish and papal law.* the transfer to itself by a superior court of an action pending in a lower court.

ad·vo·ca·tus di·ab·o·li *Latin.* (ˌædvə'kɑːtəs daɪ'æbəˌlaɪ) *n.* another name for the **devil's advocate.**

ad·vow·son (əd'vaʊzᵊn) *n. English ecclesiastical law.* the right of presentation to a vacant benefice. [C13: via Anglo-French and Old French from Latin *advocātiōn-* the act of summoning, from *advocāre* to summon]

advt. *abbrev. for* advertisement.

A·dy·gei or **A·dy·ghe** ('ɑːdɪˌgeɪ, ˌɑːdɪ'geɪ, ˌɑːdɪ'gɛ) *n.* **1.** (*pl.* **-gei, -geis** or **-ghe, -ghes**) a member of a Circassian people of the Northwest Caucasus. **2.** the Circassian language.

A·dy·gei Au·ton·o·mous Re·gion *n.* an administrative division of the SW Soviet Union, bordering on the Caucasus Mountains: chiefly agricultural. Capital: Maikop. Pop.: 385 644 (1970). Area: 7600 sq. km (2934 sq. miles).

ad·y·na·mi·a (ˌædɪ'neɪmɪə) *n.* loss of vital power or strength, esp. as the result of illness; weakness or debility. [C19: New Latin, from A-¹ + *-dynamia,* from Greek *dunamis* strength, force] —**ad·y·nam·ic** (ˌædɪ'næmɪk) *adj.*

ad·y·tum ('ædɪtəm) *n., pl.* **-ta** (-tə). the most sacred place of worship in an ancient temple from which the laity was prohibited. [C17: Latin, from Greek *aduton* a place not to be entered, from A-¹ + *duein* to enter]

adze or *U.S.* **adz** (ædz) *n.* a heavy hand tool with a steel cutting blade attached at right angles to a wooden handle, used for dressing timber. [Old English *adesa,* of unknown origin]

A·dzhar Au·ton·o·mous So·vi·et So·cial·ist Re·pub·lic (ə'dʒɑː) *n.* an administrative division of the S Soviet Union, in the SW Georgian SSR on the Black Sea: part of Turkey from the 17th century until 1878; mostly mountainous, reaching 2805 m (9350 ft.), with a subtropical coastal strip. Capital: Batumi. Pop.: 309 768 (1970). Area: 3000 sq. km (1160 sq. miles). Also called: **A·dzha·ri·a** (ə'dʒɑːrɪə).

ad·zu·ki bean (æd'zuːkɪ) or **ad·su·ki bean** *n.* **1.** a papilionaceous plant, *Phaseolus angularis,* that has yellow flowers and pods containing edible brown seeds and is widely cultivated as a food crop in China and Japan. **2.** the seed of this plant. [*adzuki,* from Japanese: red bean]

æ or **Æ** **1.** a digraph in Latin representing either a native diphthong, as in *æquus,* or a Greek *αι* (*ai*) in Latinized spellings, as in *Æschylus:* now usually written *ae,* or *e* in some words, such as *demon.* **2.** a ligature used in Old and early Middle English to represent the vowel sound of *a* in *cat.* **3.** a ligature used in modern phonetic transcription also representing the vowel sound *a* in *cat.*

A.E. or **AE** *n.* the pen name of (George William) **Russell.**

ae. *abbrev. for* aetatis. [Latin: at the age of; aged]

A.E.A. (in Britain) *abbrev. for* Atomic Energy Authority.

A.E. & P. *abbrev. for* Ambassador Extraordinary and Plenipotentiary.

A.E.C. (in the U.S.) *abbrev. for* Atomic Energy Commission.

ae·ci·o·spore ('iːsɪəˌspɔː) *n.* any of the spores produced in an aecium of the rust fungi, which spread to and infect the primary host. [C20: from AECIUM + SPORE]

ae·ci·um ('iːsɪəm) or **ae·cid·i·um** (iː'sɪdɪəm) *n., pl.* **-ci·a** (-sɪə) or **-cid·i·a** (-'sɪdɪə). a globular or cup-shaped structure in some rust fungi in which aeciospores are produced. [C19: New Latin, from Greek *aikia* injury (so called because of the damage the fungi cause)]

a·e·des (eɪ'iːdiːz) *n.* any mosquito of the genus *Aedes* (formerly *Stegomyia*) of tropical and subtropical regions, esp. *A. aegypti,* which transmits yellow fever and dengue. [C20: New Latin, from Greek *aēdēs* unpleasant, from A-¹ + *ēdos* pleasant]

ae·dile or *U.S.* (*sometimes*) **e·dile** ('iːdaɪl) *n.* a magistrate of ancient Rome in charge of public works, games, buildings, and roads. [C16: from Latin *aedīlis* concerned with buildings, from *aedēs* a building]

Ae·ë·tes (iː'iːtiːz) *n. Greek myth.* a king of Colchis, father of Medea and keeper of the Golden Fleece.

Ae·ge·an (iː'dʒiːən) *adj.* **1.** of or relating to the Aegean Sea or Islands. **2.** of or relating to the Bronze Age civilization of Greece, Asia Minor, and the Aegean Islands.

Ae·ge·an Is·lands *pl. n.* the islands of the Aegean Sea, including the Cyclades, Dodecanese, Euboea, and Sporades. The majority are under Greek administration.

Ae·ge·an Sea *n.* an arm of the Mediterranean between Greece and Turkey.

Ae·ge·us (iː'dʒiːuːs, 'iːdʒɪəs) *n. Greek myth.* an Athenian king and father of Theseus.

Ae·gi·na (iː'dʒaɪnə) *n.* **1.** an island in the Aegean Sea, in the Saronic Gulf. Area: 85 sq. km (33 sq. miles). **2.** a town on the coast of this island: a city-state of ancient Greece. **3. Gulf of.** another name for the **Saronic Gulf.** ~Greek name: **Aiyina.**

Ae·gir ('iːdʒɪə) *n. Norse myth.* the god of the sea.

ae·gis or *U.S.* (*sometimes*) **e·gis** ('iːdʒɪs) *n.* **1.** sponsorship or protection; auspices (esp. in the phrase **under the aegis of**). **2.** *Greek myth.* the shield of Zeus, often represented in art as a goatskin. [C18: from Latin, from Greek *aigis* shield of Zeus, perhaps related to *aig-,* stem of *aix* goat]

Ae·gis·thus (iː'dʒɪsθəs) *n. Greek myth.* a cousin to and the murderer of Agamemnon, whose wife Clytemnestra he had seduced. He usurped the kingship of Mycenae until Orestes, Agamemnon's son, returned home and killed him.

Ae·gos·pot·a·mi (ˌiːgəs'pɒtəˌmaɪ) *n.* a river of ancient Thrace that flowed into the Hellespont. At its mouth the Spartan fleet under Lysander defeated the Athenians in 405 B.C., ending the Peloponnesian War.

ae·gro·tat ('aɪgrəʊˌtæt, 'iː-; iː'grəʊtæt) *n.* **1.** (in British and certain other universities) a certificate allowing a candidate to pass an examination although he has missed part of it through illness. **2.** a degree obtained in such circumstances. [C19: Latin, literally: he is ill]

Ae·gyp·tus (iː'dʒɪptəs) *n. Greek myth.* a king of Egypt and twin brother of Danaüs.

Æl·fric ('ælfrɪk) *n.* called *Grammaticus.* ?955–?1020, English abbot, writer, and grammarian.

-ae·mi·a, -hae·mi·a, or *U.S.* **-e·mi·a, -he·mi·a** *n. combining form.* denoting blood, esp. a specified condition of the blood in names of diseases: *leucaemia.* [New Latin, from Greek *-aimia,* from *haima* blood]

Ae·ne·as (ɪ'niːəs) *n. Classical myth.* a Trojan prince, the son of Anchises and Aphrodite, who escaped the sack of Troy and sailed to Italy via Carthage and Sicily. After seven years, he and his followers established themselves near the site of the future Rome.

Ae·ne·as Sil·vi·us or **Syl·vi·us** ('sɪlvɪəs) *n.* the literary name of **Pius II.**

Ae·ne·id (ɪ'niːɪd) *n.* an epic poem in Latin by Virgil relating the experiences of Aeneas after the fall of Troy, written chiefly to provide an illustrious historical background for Rome.

a·e·ne·ous (eɪ'iːnɪəs) *adj. Rare.* of a lustrous bronze colour. [C19: from Latin *aēneus* of bronze, from *aes* bronze]

Ae·o·li·an or **E·o·li·an** (iː'əʊlɪən) *n.* **1.** a member of a Hellenic people who settled in Thessaly and Boeotia and colonized Lesbos and parts of the Aegean coast of Asia Minor. ~*adj.* **2.** of or relating to this people or their dialect of Ancient Greek; Aeolic. **3.** of or relating to Aeolus. **4.** denoting or relating to an authentic mode represented by the ascending natural diatonic scale from A to A: the basis of the modern minor key. See also **Hypo-.**

ae·o·li·an harp *n.* a stringed instrument that produces a musical sound when a current of air or wind passes over the strings. Also called: **wind harp.**

Ae·o·li·an Is·lands *pl. n.* another name for the **Lipari Islands.**

Ae·ol·ic or **E·ol·ic** (iː'ɒlɪk, iː'əʊlɪk) *adj.* **1.** of or relating to the Aeolians or their dialect. ~*n.* **2.** one of four chief dialects of Ancient Greek, spoken chiefly in Thessaly, Boeotia, and Aeolis. Compare **Arcadic, Doric, Ionic.**

ae·ol·i·pile (iː'ɒlɪˌpaɪl) *n.* a device illustrating the reactive forces of a gas jet: usually a spherical vessel mounted so as to rotate and equipped with angled exit pipes from which steam within it escapes. [C17: from Latin *aeolipilae* balls of AEOLUS or *aeolīpylae* gates of AEOLUS]

Ae·o·lis ('iːəlɪs) or **Ae·o·li·a** (iː'əʊlɪə) *n.* the ancient name for the coastal region of NW Asia Minor, including the island of Lesbos, settled by the Aeolian Greeks (about 1000 B.C.)

ae·o·lo·trop·ic (ˌiːələʊ'trɒpɪk) *adj.* a less common word for **anisotropic.** [C19: from Greek *aiolos* fickle + -TROPIC]

Ae·o·lus ('iːələs, iː'əʊləs) *n. Greek myth.* **1.** the god of the winds. **2.** the founding king of the Aeolians in Thessaly.

ae·on *or U.S.* **e·on** (ˈi:ən, ˈi:ɒn) *n.* **1.** an immeasurably long period of time; age. **2.** *Geology.* the longest division of geological time, comprising two or more eras. **3.** (*often cap.*) *Gnosticism.* one of the powers emanating from the supreme being and culminating in the demiurge. [C17: from Greek *aiōn* an infinitely long time]

ae·o·ni·an *or* **e·o·ni·an** (i:ˈəʊnɪən) *adj. Literary.* everlasting.

ae·py+or+nis (ˌi:pɪˈɔ:nɪs) *n.* any of the large extinct flightless birds of the genus *Aepyornis*, remains of which have been found in Madagascar. [C19: New Latin, from Greek *aipus* high + *ornis* bird]

aer- *combining form.* variant of **aero-** before a vowel.

aer+ate (ˈɛəreɪt) *vb.* (*tr.*) **1.** to charge (a liquid) with a gas, esp. carbon dioxide, as in the manufacture of effervescent drink. **2.** to expose to the action or circulation of the air, so as to purify. —**aer·ˈa+tion** *n.* —**ˈaer·a+tor** *n.*

aer·i- *combining form.* variant of **aero-**.

aer+i·al (ˈɛərɪəl) *adj.* **1.** of, relating to, or resembling air. **2.** existing, occurring, moving, or operating in the air: *aerial cable car; aerial roots of a plant.* **3.** ethereal; light and delicate. **4.** imaginary; visionary. **5.** extending high into the air; lofty. **6.** of or relating to aircraft: *aerial combat.* ~*n.* **7.** Also called: **antenna.** the part of a radio or television system having any of various shapes, such as a dipole, Yagi, long-wire, or vertical aerial, by means of which radio waves are transmitted or received. [C17: via Latin from Greek *aērios*, from *aēr* air]

aer·i·al+ist (ˈɛərɪəˌlɪst) *n. Chiefly U.S.* a trapeze artist or tightrope walker.

aer+i·al lad+der *n.* the U.S. term for **turntable ladder.**

aer+i·al per+spec·tive *n.* (in painting and drawing) a means of indicating relative distance in terms of a gradation of clarity, tone, and colour, esp. blue. Also called: **atmospheric perspective.**

aer+i·al ping+pong *n. Austral., facetious.* Australian Rules football.

aer·ie (ˈɛərɪ, ˈɪərɪ) *n.* a variant spelling (esp. U.S.) of **eyrie.**

aer·i+form (ˈɛərɪˌfɔ:m) *adj.* **1.** having the form of air; gaseous. **2.** unsubstantial.

aer·i+fy (ˈɛərɪˌfaɪ) *vb.* **+fies, +fy+ing, +fied. 1.** to change or cause to change into a gas. **2.** to mix or combine with air. —**ˌaer·i+fi+ˈca+tion** *n.*

aer·o (ˈɛərəʊ) *n.* (*modifier*) of or relating to aircraft or aeronautics: *an aero engine.*

aer·o-, aer·i-, *or before a vowel* **aer-** *combining form.* **1.** denoting air, atmosphere, or gas: *aerodynamics.* **2.** denoting aircraft: *aeronautics.* [ultimately from Greek *aēr* air]

aer·o+bal+lis+tics (ˌɛərəʊbəˈlɪstɪks) *pl. n.* the ballistics of projectiles dropped, launched, or fired from aircraft.

aer·o+bat+ics (ˌɛərəʊˈbætɪks) *pl. n.* spectacular or dangerous manoeuvres, such as loops or rolls, performed in an aircraft or glider; stunt flying. [C20: from AERO- + (ACRO)BATICS]

aer+obe (ˈɛərəʊb) *or* **aer·o+bi·um** (ɛəˈrəʊbɪəm) *n., pl.* **+obes** *or* **·o+bi·a** (-ˈəʊbɪə). an organism that requires free oxygen or air for respiration. Compare **anaerobe.** [C19: from AERO- + Greek *bios* life. Compare MICROBE]

aer·o+bic (ɛəˈrəʊbɪk) *adj.* **1.** (of an organism or process) depending on free oxygen or air. **2.** of or relating to aerobes. ~Compare **anaerobic.**

aer·o+bi+ol·o·gy (ˌɛərəʊbaɪˈɒlɪdʒɪ) *n.* the study of airborne microorganisms, spores, etc., esp. those causing disease. —**ˌaer·o+bi·o+ˈlog·i+cal** *adj.* —**ˌaer·o+bi·o+ˈlog·i+cal+ly** *adv.* —**ˌaer·o+bi+ˈol·o+gist** *n.*

aer·o+bi·o+sis (ˌɛərəʊbaɪˈəʊsɪs) *n.* life in the presence of free oxygen. —**aer·o+bi·o+tic** (ˌɛərəʊbaɪˈɒtɪk) *adj.*

aer·o+do+net+ics (ˌɛərəʊdəˈnɛtɪks) *n.* (*functioning as sing.*) the study of soaring or gliding flight, esp. the study of gliders. [C20: from Greek *aerodonetos* tossed in the air, from AERO- + *donetos*, past participle of *donein* to toss]

aer·o+drome (ˈɛərəˌdrəʊm) *or U.S.* **air+drome** (ˈɛəˌdrəʊm) *n. Brit.* a landing area, esp. for private aircraft, that is usually smaller than an airport.

aer·o+dy+nam+ics (ˌɛərəʊdaɪˈnæmɪks) *n.* (*functioning as sing.*) the study of the dynamics of gases, esp. of the forces acting on a body passing through air. Compare **aerostatics** (sense 1). —**ˌaer·o+dy+ˈnam+ic** *adj.* —**ˌaer·o+dy+ˈnam·i+cal+ly** *adv.*

aer·o+dyne (ˈɛərəʊˌdaɪn) *n.* any heavier-than-air machine, such as an aircraft, that derives the greater part of its lift from aerodynamic forces. [C20: back formation from AERODYNAMIC; see DYNE]

aer·o+em+bo+lism (ˌɛərəʊˈɛmbəˌlɪzəm) *n.* the presence in the tissues and blood of nitrogen bubbles, caused by an abrupt and substantial reduction in atmospheric pressure. See **decompression sickness.**

aer·o en+gine *n.* an engine for powering an aircraft.

aer·o+foil (ˈɛərəʊˌfɔɪl) *or U.S.* **air+foil** (ˈɛəˌfɔɪl) *n. Brit.* a surface, such as an aileron, wing, or tailplane, that is designed to produce lift or to control an aircraft in flight.

aer·o+gel (ˈɛərəˌdʒɛl) *n.* a colloid that has a continuous solid phase containing dispersed gas.

aer·o+gram *or* **aer·o+gramme** (ˈɛərəˌɡræm) *n.* **1.** Also called: **air letter.** an air-mail letter written on a single sheet of lightweight paper that folds and is sealed to form an envelope. **2.** another name for **radiotelegram.**

aer+og+ra+phy (ɛəˈrɒɡrəfɪ) *n.* the description of the character of the atmosphere.

aer·o+lite (ˈɛərəˌlaɪt) *n.* a stony meteorite consisting of silicate minerals.

aer+ol·o·gy (ɛəˈrɒlədʒɪ) *n.* the study of the atmosphere, including its upper layers. —**aer·o+lo+gic** (ˌɛərəˈlɒdʒɪk) *or* **ˌaer·o+ˈlog·i+cal** *adj.* —**aer+ˈol·o·gist** *n.*

aer·o+me·chan+ic (ˌɛərəʊmɪˈkænɪk) *n.* **1.** an aircraft mechanic. ~*adj.* **2.** of or relating to aeromechanics.

aer·o+me·chan+ics (ˌɛərəʊmɪˈkænɪks) *n.* (*functioning as sing.*) the mechanics of gases, esp. air. —**ˌaer·o+me·ˈchan·i+cal** *adj.*

aer·o+me·te+or·o+graph (ˌɛərəʊˈmi:tɪərəˌɡrɑ:f, -ˌɡræf) *n. Chiefly U.S.* an aircraft instrument that records temperature, humidity, and atmospheric pressure.

aer+om·e+ter (ɛəˈrɒmɪtə) *n.* an instrument for determining the mass or density of a gas, esp. air. —**aer·o+met+ric** (ˌɛərəˈmɛtrɪk) *adj.*

aer+om·e·try (ɛəˈrɒmɪtrɪ) *n.* another name for **pneumatics.**

aeron. *abbrev. for:* **1.** aeronautics. **2.** aeronautical.

aer·o+naut (ˈɛərəˌnɔ:t) *n.* a person who flies in a lighter-than-air craft, esp. the pilot or navigator.

aer·o+nau+ti+cal (ˌɛərəˈnɔ:tɪkəl) *adj.* of or relating to aeronauts or aeronautics. —**ˌaer·o+ˈnau+ti+cal+ly** *adv.*

aer·o+nau+ti+cal en+gi+neer+ing *n.* the branch of engineering concerned with the design, production, and maintenance of aircraft. —**aer·o+nau+ti+cal en+gi+neer** *n.*

aer·o+naut+ics (ˌɛərəˈnɔ:tɪks) *n.* (*functioning as sing.*) the study or practice of all aspects of flight through the air.

aer·o+neu+ro+sis (ˌɛərəʊnjʊˈrəʊsɪs) *n.* a functional disorder of aeroplane pilots characterized by anxiety and various psychosomatic disturbances, caused by insufficient oxygen at high altitudes and the emotional tension of flying.

aer·o+pause (ˈɛərəˌpɔ:z) *n.* the region of the upper atmosphere above which aircraft cannot fly.

aer·o+pha+gi·a (ˌɛərəˈfeɪdʒɪə, -dʒə) *n.* spasmodic swallowing of air, sometimes occurring in hysteria.

aer·o+pho+bi·a (ˌɛərəˈfəʊbɪə) *n.* an abnormal fear of draughts of air. —**ˌaer·o+ˈpho+bic** *adj.*

aer·o+phyte (ˈɛərəˌfaɪt) *n.* another name for **epiphyte.**

aer·o+plane (ˈɛərəˌpleɪn) *or U.S.* **air+plane** (ˈɛəˌpleɪn) *n. Brit.* a heavier-than-air powered flying vehicle with fixed wings. [C19: from French *aéroplane*, from AERO- + Greek *-planos* wandering, related to PLANET]

aer·o+plane cloth *or* **fab+ric** *n.* **1.** a strong fabric made from cotton, linen, and nylon yarns, used for some light aircraft fuselages and wings. **2.** a similar lightweight fabric used for clothing. ~Also called: **aircraft fabric.**

aer·o+plane spin *n.* a wrestling attack in which a wrestler lifts his opponent onto his shoulders and spins around, leaving the opponent dizzy.

aer·o+sol (ˈɛərəˌsɒl) *n.* **1.** a colloidal dispersion of solid or liquid particles in a gas; smoke or fog. **2.** a substance, such as a paint, polish, or insecticide, dispensed from a small metal container by a propellant under pressure. **3.** Also called: **air spray.** such a substance together with its container. [C20: from AERO- + SOL(UTION)]

aer·o+space (ˈɛərəˌspeɪs) *n.* **1.** the atmosphere and space beyond. **2.** (*modifier*) of or relating to rockets, missiles, space vehicles, etc., that fly or operate in aerospace: *the aerospace industry.*

aer·o+sphere (ˈɛərəˌsfɪə) *n.* the entire atmosphere surrounding the earth.

aer·o+stat (ˈɛərəˌstæt) *n.* a lighter-than-air craft, such as a balloon. [C18: from French *aérostat*, from AERO- + Greek *-statos* standing] —**ˌaer·o+ˈstat+ic** *or* **ˌaer·o+ˈstat·i·cal** *adj.*

aer·o+stat+ics (ˌɛərəˈstætɪks) *n.* (*functioning as sing.*) **1.** the study of gases in equilibrium and bodies held in equilibrium in gases. Compare **aerodynamics. 2.** the study of lighter-than-air craft, such as balloons.

aer·o+sta+tion (ˌɛərəˈsteɪʃən) *n.* the science of operating lighter-than-air craft.

aer·o+ther+mo+dy+nam+ics (ˌɛərəʊˌθɜ:məʊdaɪˈnæmɪks) *n.* (*functioning as sing.*) the study of the exchange of heat between solids and gases, esp. of the heating effect on aircraft flying through the air at very high speeds. —**ˌaer·o+ˌther+mo+dy+ˈnam+ic** *adj.*

ae+ru+go (ɪˈru:ɡəʊ) *n.* (esp. of old bronze) another name for **verdigris.** [C18: from Latin, from *aes* copper, bronze] —**ae+ru+gin+ous** (ɪˈru:dʒɪnəs) *adj.*

aer·y[1] (ˈɛərɪ, ˈeɪərɪ) *adj. Poetic.* **1.** a variant spelling of **airy. 2.** lofty, insubstantial, or visionary. [C16: via Latin from Greek *aērios*, from *aēr* AIR]

aer·y[2] (ˈɛərɪ, ˈɪərɪ) *n., pl.* **aer·ies.** a variant spelling of **eyrie.**

Aes·chi·nes (ˈi:skəˌni:z) *n.* ?389–?314 B.C., Athenian orator; the main political opponent of Demosthenes.

Aes·chy·lus (ˈi:skələs) *n.* ?525–?456 B.C., Greek dramatist, regarded as the father of Greek tragedy. Seven of his plays are extant, including *Seven Against Thebes, Prometheus Bound,* and the trilogy of the *Oresteia.*

Aes+cu+la+pi+an (ˌi:skjʊˈleɪpɪən) *adj.* of or relating to Aesculapius or to the art of medicine.

Aes·cu·la·pi·us (ˌi:skjʊˈleɪpɪəs) *n.* the Roman god of medicine or healing. Greek counterpart: **Asclepius.**

Ae·sir (ˈeɪsɪə) *n.* the chief gods of Norse mythology dwelling in Asgard. [Old Norse, literally: gods]

Ae·sop (ˈi:sɒp) *n.* ?620–564 B.C. Greek author of fables in which animals are given human characters and used to satirize human failings. —**Ae·ˈsop·i·an** *or* **Ae·ˈsop+ic** *adj.*

aes+the+si·a *or U.S.* **es+the+si·a** (i:sˈθi:zɪə) *n.* the normal ability to experience sensation, perception, or sensitivity. [C20: back formation from ANAESTHESIA]

aes+thete *or U.S.* **es+thete** (ˈi:sθi:t) *n.* a person who has or who affects a highly developed appreciation of beauty, esp. in poetry and the visual arts. [C19: back formation from AESTHETICS]

aes+thet+ic (iːsˈθɛtɪk, ɪs-), **aes+thet·i+cal** *or U.S.* (*sometimes*) **es+thet+ic, es+thet·i·cal** *adj.* **1.** connected with aesthetics or its principles. **2. a.** relating to pure beauty rather than to other considerations. **b.** artistic or relating to good taste: *an aesthetic consideration.* —**aes+ˈthet·i+cal+ly** *or U.S.* (*sometimes*) **es+ˈthet·i·cal+ly** *adv.*

aes+the+ti+cian *or U.S.* (*sometimes*) **es+the+ti+cian** (ˌiːsθɪˈtɪʃən, ˌɛs-) *n.* a student of aesthetics.

aes+thet·i+cism *or U.S.* (*sometimes*) **es+thet·i·cism** (iːsˈθɛtɪˌsɪzəm, ɪs-) *n.* **1.** the doctrine that aesthetic principles are of supreme importance and that works of art should be judged accordingly. **2.** sensitivity to beauty, esp. in art, music, literature, etc.

aes+thet+ics *or U.S.* (*sometimes*) **es+thet+ics** (iːsˈθɛtɪks, ɪs-) *n.* (*functioning as sing.*) **1.** the branch of philosophy concerned with the study of such concepts as beauty, taste, etc. **2.** the study of the rules and principles of art.

aes+ti+val *or U.S.* **es+ti+val** (iːˈstaɪvᵊl, ˈɛstɪ-) *adj. Rare.* of or occurring in summer. [C14: from French, from Late Latin *aestīvālis,* from Latin *aestās* summer]

aes+ti+vate *or U.S.* **es+ti+vate** (ˈiːstɪˌveɪt, ˈɛs-) *vb.* (*intr.*) **1.** to pass the summer. **2.** (of animals such as the lungfish) to pass the summer or dry season in a dormant condition. Compare **hibernate.** [C17: from Latin *aestīvātus,* from *aestīvāre* to stay during the summer, from *aestās* summer] —**ˈaes+ti+ˌva+tor** *or U.S.* **ˈes+ti+ˌva+tor** *n.*

aes+ti+va+tion *or U.S.* **es+ti+va+tion** (ˌiːstɪˈveɪʃən, ˌɛs-) *n.* **1.** the act or condition of aestivating. **2.** the arrangement of the parts of a flower bud, esp. the sepals and petals.

aet. *or* **aetat.** *abbrev. for* aetatis. [Latin: at the age of]

Æth·el·bert (ˈæθəlˌbɜːt) *n.* a variant spelling of **Ethelbert.**

Æth·el·red (ˈæθəlˌrɛd) *n.* a variant spelling of **Ethelred.**

ae·ther (ˈiːθə) *n.* a variant spelling of **ether** (senses 3–5).

ae·the+re·al (ɪˈθɪərɪəl) *n.* a variant spelling of **ethereal** (senses 1, 2, 3). —**ae·the+re·al+i·ty** (ɪˌθɪərɪˈælɪtɪ) *n.* —**ae·ˈthe+re·al+ly** *adv.*

ae·ti+ol·o·gy *or U.S.* **e·ti+ol·o·gy** (ˌiːtɪˈɒlədʒɪ) *n., pl.* **·gies. 1.** the philosophy or study of causation. **2.** the study of the causes of diseases. **3.** the cause of a disease. [C16: from Late Latin *aetiologia,* from Greek *aitiologia,* from *aitia* cause] —**ae·ti·o+log·i·cal** *or U.S.* **e·ti·o+log·i·cal** (ˌiːtɪəˈlɒdʒɪkᵊl) *adj.* —**ˌae·ti·o+ˈlog·i·cal+ly** *or U.S.* **ˌe·ti·o+ˈlog·i+cal+ly** *adv.* —**ˌae·ti+ˈol·o·gist** *or U.S.* **ˌe·ti+ˈol·o·gist** *n.*

Aet+na (ˈɛtnə) *n.* the Latin name for Mount **Etna.**

Ae·to+li·a (iːˈtəʊlɪə) *n.* a mountainous region forming a department of W central Greece, north of the Gulf of Patras: a powerful federal state in the third century B.C. Chief city: Missolonghi. Pop. (with Acarnania): 228 719 (1971). Area: 5390 sq. km. (2081 sq. miles).

A.E.U. (in Britain) *abbrev. for* Amalgamated Engineering Union.

Af. *abbrev. for* Africa(n).

a.f. *abbrev. for* audio frequency.

A.F. *abbrev. for* Anglo-French.

A/F (in auction catalogues, etc.) *abbrev. for* as found.

A.F.A.M. *abbrev. for* Ancient Free and Accepted Masons.

a·far (əˈfɑː) *adv.* **1.** at, from, or to a great distance. ~*n.* **2.** a great distance (esp. in the phrase **from afar**). [C14 *a fer,* altered from earlier *on fer* and *of fer;* see A-², FAR]

A·fars and the Is+sas (ˈɑːfɑːz, ˈiːsɑːs) *n.* **Territory of the.** a former French territory in E Africa (1946–77), now the independent republic of Djibouti. Former name (until 1967): **French Somaliland.**

AFB *abbrev. for* (U.S.) Air Force Base.

A.F.C. *abbrev. for:* **1.** Air Force Cross. **2.** Association Football Club. **3.** automatic flight control. **4.** automatic frequency control.

a·feard *or* **a·feared** (əˈfɪəd) *adj.* (*postpositive*) an archaic or dialect word for **afraid.** [Old English *āfǣred,* from *afǣran* to frighten, from *fǣran* to FEAR]

a·fe·brile (æˈfiːbraɪl, eɪ-) *adj.* without fever.

af+fa·ble (ˈæfəbᵊl) *adj.* **1.** showing warmth and friendliness; kindly; mild; benign. **2.** easy to converse with; approachable; amicable. [C16: from Latin *affābilis* easy to talk to, from *affārī* to talk to, from *ad-* to + *fārī* to speak; compare FABLE, FATE] —**ˌaf+fa·ˈbil+i·ty** *n.*

af+fair (əˈfɛə) *n.* **1.** a thing to be done or attended to; matter; business: *this affair must be cleared up.* **2.** an event or happening: *a strange affair.* **3.** (*qualified by an adjective or descriptive phrase*) something previously specified, esp. a man-made object; thing: *our house is a tumbledown affair.* **4.** a sexual relationship between two people who are not married to each other. [C13: from Old French, from *à faire* to do]

af+faire *French.* (aˈfɛːr) *n.* a love affair.

af+faire d'hon+neur *French.* (afɛr dɔˈnœːr) *n., pl.* ***af+faires d'hon+neur*** (afɛr dɔˈnœːr). a duel.

af+fairs (əˈfɛəz) *pl. n.* **1.** personal or business interests: *his affairs were in disorder.* **2.** matters of public interest: *current affairs.*

af+fect¹ *vb.* (əˈfɛkt). (*tr.*) **1.** to act upon or influence, esp. in an adverse way: *damp affected the sparking plugs.* **2.** to move or disturb emotionally or mentally: *her death affected him greatly.* **3.** (of pain, disease, etc.) to attack. ~*n.* (ˈæfɛkt, əˈfɛkt). **4.** *Psychol.* the emotion associated with an idea or set of ideas. See also **affection.** [C17: from Latin *affectus,* past participle of *afficere* to act upon, from *ad-* to + *facere* to do]

af+fect² (əˈfɛkt) *vb.* (*mainly tr.*) **1.** to put on an appearance or show of; make a pretence of: *to affect ignorance.* **2.** to imitate or assume, esp. pretentiously: *to affect an accent.* **3.** to have or use by preference: *she always affects funereal clothing.* **4.** to adopt the character, manner, etc., of: *he was always affecting the politician.* **5.** (of plants or animals) to live or grow in: *penguins affect an arctic climate.* **6.** to incline naturally or habitually towards: *falling drops of liquid affect roundness.* [C15: from Latin *affectāre* to strive after, pretend to have; related to *afficere* to AFFECT¹]

af+fec+ta+tion (ˌæfɛkˈteɪʃən) *n.* **1.** an assumed manner of speech, dress, or behaviour, esp. one that is intended to impress others. **2.** (often foll. by *of*) deliberate pretence or false display: *affectation of nobility.* [C16: from Latin *affectātiōn-* an aiming at, striving after, from *affectāre;* see AFFECT²]

af+fect+ed¹ (əˈfɛktɪd) *adj.* (*usually postpositive*) **1.** deeply moved, esp. by sorrow or grief: *he was greatly affected by her departure.* **2.** changed, esp. detrimentally. [C17: from AFFECT¹ + -ED²]

af+fect+ed² (əˈfɛktɪd) *adj.* **1.** behaving, speaking, etc., in an artificial or assumed way, esp. in order to impress others. **2.** feigned: *affected indifference.* **3.** *Archaic.* inclined; disposed. [C16: from AFFECT² + -ED²] —**af+ˈfect+ed+ly** *adv.* —**af+ˈfect+ed+ness** *n.*

af+fect+ing (əˈfɛktɪŋ) *adj.* evoking feelings of pity, sympathy, or pathos; moving. —**af+ˈfect+ing+ly** *adv.*

af+fec+tion (əˈfɛkʃən) *n.* **1.** a feeling of fondness or tenderness for a person or thing; attachment. **2.** (*often pl.*) emotion, feeling, or sentiment: *to play on a person's affections.* **3.** *Pathol.* any disease or pathological condition. **4.** *Psychol.* any form of mental functioning that involves emotion. See also **affect¹. 5.** the act of affecting or the state of being affected. **6.** *Archaic.* inclination or disposition. [C13: from Latin *affectiōn-* disposition, from *afficere* to AFFECT¹] —**af+ˈfec+tion+al** *adj.* —**af+ˈfec+tion+al+ly** *adv.*

af+fec+tion+ate (əˈfɛkʃənɪt) *adj.* having or displaying tender feelings, affection, or warmth: *an affectionate mother; an affectionate letter.* —**af+ˈfec+tion+ate+ly** *adv.*

af+fec+tive (əˈfɛktɪv) *n.* **1.** *Psychol.* relating to affects. ~*adj.* **2.** concerned with or arousing the emotions or affection. —**af+fec+tiv+i·ty** (ˌæfɛkˈtɪvɪtɪ) *or* **af+ˈfec+tive+ness** *n.*

af+fen+pin+scher (ˈæfənˌpɪnʃə) *n.* a small wire-haired breed of dog of European origin, having tufts of hair on the muzzle. [German, literally: monkey-terrier, so called because its face resembles a monkey's]

af+fer+ent (ˈæfərənt) *adj.* bringing or directing inwards to a part or an organ of the body, esp. towards the brain or spinal cord. Compare **efferent.** [C19: from Latin *afferre* to carry to, from *ad-* to + *ferre* to carry]

af+fet+tu·o+so (æˌfɛtʃuːˈəʊsəʊ) *adj., adv. Music.* with feeling. [C18: from Italian]

af+fi+ance (əˈfaɪəns) *vb.* **1.** (*tr.*) to bind (a person or oneself) in a promise of marriage; betroth. ~*n.* **2.** *Archaic.* a solemn pledge, esp. a marriage contract. [C14: via Old French from Medieval Latin *affīdāre* to trust (oneself) to, from *fīdāre* to trust, from *fīdus* faithful]

af+fi+ant (əˈfaɪənt) *n. U.S. law.* a person who makes an affidavit. [C19: Old French, from *affier* to trust to, from Medieval Latin *affīdāre;* see AFFIANCE]

af+fiche *French.* (aˈfiʃ) *n.* a poster or advertisement, esp. one drawn by an artist, as for the opening of an exhibition. [C18: from *afficher* to post]

af+fi+da+vit (ˌæfɪˈdeɪvɪt) *n. Law.* a declaration in writing made upon oath before a person authorized to administer oaths. [C17: from Medieval Latin, literally: he declares on oath, from *affīdāre* to trust (oneself) to; see AFFIANCE]

af+fil·i+ate *vb.* (əˈfɪlɪˌeɪt). **1.** (*tr.;* foll. by *to* or *with*) to receive into close connection or association (with a larger body, group, organization, etc.); adopt as a member, branch, etc. **2.** (foll. by *with*) to associate (oneself) or be associated, esp. as a subordinate or subsidiary; bring or come into close connection: *he affiliated himself with the Union.* ~*n.* (əˈfɪlɪɪt, -ˌeɪt). **3. a.** a person or organization that is affiliated with another. **b.** (*as modifier*): *an affiliate member.* [C18: from Medieval Latin *affīliātus* adopted as a son, from *affīliāre,* from Latin *fīlius* son] —**af+ˌfil·i·ˈa+tion** *n.*

af+fil·i·a+tion or+der *n. Law.* an order made by a magistrates' court that a man adjudged to be the father of an illegitimate child shall contribute a specified periodic sum towards the child's maintenance.

af+fil·i·a+tion pro+ceed+ings *pl. n.* legal proceedings, usually initiated by an unwed mother, claiming legal recognition that a particular man is the father of her child, often associated with a claim for financial support.

af+fine (ˈæfaɪn) *adj. Maths.* of, characterizing, or involving a transformation that has a combination of single transformations, such as translation, rotation, and reflection in an axis. [C16: via French from Latin *affīnis* bordering on, related]

af+fined (əˈfaɪnd) *adj.* closely related; connected.

af+fin+i·ty (əˈfɪnɪtɪ) *n., pl.* **·ties. 1.** a natural liking, taste, or inclination for a person or thing. **2.** the person or thing so liked. **3.** a close similarity in appearance or quality; inherent likeness. **4.** relationship by marriage or by ties other than of blood, as by adoption. Compare **consanguinity. 5.** similarity in structure, form, etc., between different animals, plants, or languages. **6.** *Chem.* **a.** the force holding atoms together in a molecule; chemical attraction. **b.** a measure of the tendency of a chemical reaction to take place expressed in terms of the free energy change. Symbol: *A* [C14: via Old French from Latin *affīnitāt-* connected by marriage, from *affīnis* bordering on, related] —**af+ˈfin·i+tive** *adj.*

af+firm (əˈfɜːm) *vb.* (*mainly tr.*) **1.** (*may take a clause as object*) to declare to be true; assert positively. **2.** to uphold, confirm, or ratify. **3.** (*intr.*) *Law.* to make an affirmation. [C14: via Old French from Latin *affirmāre* to present (something) as firm or fixed, assert, from *ad-* to + *firmāre* to make FIRM] —**af+ˈfirm+er** *or* **af+ˈfirm+ant** *n.*

af+fir+ma+tion (ˌæfəˈmeɪʃən) *n.* **1.** the act of affirming or the state of being affirmed. **2.** a statement of the existence or truth of something; assertion. **3.** *Law.* a solemn declaration permitted on grounds of conscientious objection to taking an oath.

af+firm·a+tive (əˈfɜːmətɪv) *adj.* **1.** confirming or asserting something as true or valid: *an affirmative statement.* **2.** indicating agreement or assent: *an affirmative answer.* **3.** *Logic.* (of a proposition) affirming the truth of the predicate, as in the propositions *all living birds have feathers; some men are married.* Compare **negative** (sense 12). ~*n.* **4.** a positive assertion. **5.** a word or phrase stating agreement or assent, such as *yes* (esp. in the phrase **answer in the affirmative**). **6.** *Logic.* a proposition that affirms the truth of the predicate. **7.** **the affirmative.** *Chiefly U.S.* the side in a debate that supports the proposition. ~ **8.** *sentence substitute. Military, etc.* a signal codeword used to express assent or confirmation. —**af+ˈfirm·a+tive+ly** *adv.*

af+fix *vb.* (əˈfɪks). (*tr.; usually foll. by to or on*) **1.** to attach, fasten, join, or stick: *to affix a poster to the wall.* **2.** to add or append: *to affix a signature to a document.* **3.** to attach or attribute (guilt, blame, etc.). ~*n.* (ˈæfɪks). **4.** a linguistic element added to a word or root to produce a derived or inflected form: *-ment* in *establishment* is a derivational affix; *-s* in *drowns* is an inflectional affix. See also **prefix, suffix, infix. 5.** something fastened or attached; appendage. [C15: from Medieval Latin *affixāre*, from *ad-* to + *fixāre* to FIX] —**af+fix·a+tion** (ˌæfɪkˈseɪʃən) *or* —**af+fix+ture** (əˈfɪkstʃə) *n.*

af+fla+tus (əˈfleɪtəs) *n.* an impulse of creative power or inspiration, esp. in poetry, considered to be of divine origin (esp. in the phrase **divine afflatus**). [C17: Latin, from *afflātus*, from *afflāre* to breathe or blow on, from *flāre* to blow]

af+flict (əˈflɪkt) *vb.* (*tr.*) to cause suffering or unhappiness to; distress greatly. [C14: from Latin *afflictus*, past participle of *afflīgere* to knock against, from *flīgere* to knock, to strike] —**af+ˈflic+tive** *adj.*

af+flic+tion (əˈflɪkʃən) *n.* **1.** a condition of great distress, pain, or suffering. **2.** something responsible for physical or mental suffering, such as a disease, grief, etc.

af+flu+ence (ˈæfluəns) *n.* **1.** an abundant supply of money, goods, or property; wealth. **2.** *Rare.* abundance or profusion.

af+flu+ent (ˈæfluənt) *adj.* **1.** rich; wealthy. **2.** abundant; copious. **3.** flowing freely. ~*n.* **4.** a tributary stream. [C15: from Latin *affluent-*, present participle of *affluere* to flow towards, from *fluere* to flow]

af+flux (ˈæflʌks) *n.* a flowing towards a point: *an afflux of blood to the head.* [C17: from Latin *affluxus*, from *fluxus* FLUX]

af+ford (əˈfɔːd) *vb.* **1.** (preceded by *can, could,* etc.) to be able to do or spare something, esp. without incurring financial difficulties or without risk of undesirable consequences: *we can afford to buy a small house; I can afford to give you one of my chess sets; we can't afford to miss this play.* **2.** to give, yield, or supply: *the meeting afforded much useful information.* [Old English *geforthian* to further, promote, from *forth* FORTH; the Old English prefix *ge-* was later reduced to *a-*, and the modern spelling (C16) is influenced by words beginning *aff-*]

af+for+est (əˈfɒrɪst) *vb.* (*tr.*) to plant trees on; convert into forested land. [C15: from Medieval Latin *afforestāre*, from *forestis* FOREST] —**af+ˌfor+est·ˈa+tion** *n.*

af+fran+chise (əˈfræntʃaɪz) *vb.* (*tr.*) to release from servitude or an obligation. [C15: from Old French *afranchiss-*, a stem of *afranchir*, from *franchir* to free; see FRANK[1]] —**af+ˈfran+chise+ment** *n.*

af+fray (əˈfreɪ) *n.* **1.** *Law.* a fight, noisy quarrel, or disturbance between two or more persons in a public place. ~*vb.* **2.** (*tr.*) *Archaic.* to frighten. [C14: via Old French from Vulgar Latin *exfridāre* (unattested) to break the peace; compare German *Friede* peace]

af+freight+ment (əˈfreɪtmənt) *n.* a contract hiring a ship to carry goods. [C19: from French *affréter* to charter a ship, from *fret* FREIGHT]

af+fri+cate (ˈæfrɪˌkɪt) *n.* a composite speech sound consisting of a stop and a fricative articulated at the same point, such as the sound written *ch*, as in *chair.* [C19: from Latin *affricāre* to rub against, from *fricāre* to rub; compare FRICTION]

af+fric·a+tive (əˈfrɪkətɪv, ˈæfrəˌkeɪ-) *n.* **1.** another word for **affricate.** ~*adj.* **2.** of, relating to, or denoting an affricate.

af+fright (əˈfraɪt) *Archaic or poetic.* ~*vb.* **1.** (*tr.*) to frighten. ~*n.* **2.** a sudden terror. [Old English *āfyrhtan*, from *a-*, a prefix indicating the beginning or end of an action + *fyrhtan* to FRIGHT]

af+front (əˈfrʌnt) *n.* **1.** a deliberate insult. ~*vb.* (*tr.*) **2.** to insult, esp. openly. **3.** to offend the pride or dignity of. **4.** *Obsolete.* to confront defiantly. [C14: from Old French *afronter* to strike in the face, from Vulgar Latin *affrontāre* (unattested), from the Latin phrase *ad frontem* to the face]

af+fu+sion (əˈfjuːʒən) *n.* the baptizing of a person by pouring water onto his head. Compare **aspersion** (sense 3), **immersion.** [C17: from Late Latin *affūsiōn-* a pouring upon, from *affundere*, from *fundere* to pour]

Afg. *or* **Afgh.** *abbrev. for* Afghanistan.

af+ghan (ˈæfgæn, -gən) *n.* **1.** a knitted or crocheted wool blanket or shawl, esp. one with a geometric pattern. **2.** a sheepskin coat, often embroidered and having long fur trimming around the edges.

Af+ghan (ˈæfgæn, -gən) *or* **Af+ghan·i** (æfˈgænɪ, -ˈgɑː-) *n.* **1.** a native, citizen, or inhabitant of Afghanistan. **2.** another name for **Pashto** (the language). ~*adj.* **3.** denoting or relating to Afghanistan, its people, or their language.

Af+ghan hound *n.* a tall graceful breed of hound with a long silky coat.

af+ghan·i (æfˈgɑːnɪ) *n.* the standard monetary unit of Afghanistan, divided into 100 puls.

Af+ghan·i+stan (æfˈgænɪˌstɑːn, -ˌstæn) *n.* a republic in central Asia: became independent in 1919; invaded by Russia (1979); generally arid and mountainous, with the Hindu Kush range rising over 7500 m (25 000 ft.) and fertile valleys of the Amu Darya, Helmand, and Kabul Rivers. Languages: Pashto and Tadzhik. Religion: Muslim. Currency: afghani. Capital: Kabul. Pop.: 18 796 000 (1974 UN est.). Area: 657 500 sq. km (250 000 sq. miles).

a·fi+cio+na+do (əˌfɪʃjəˈnɑːdəʊ; *Spanish* aˌfiθjoˈnaðo) *n., pl.* **+dos** (-dəʊz; *Spanish* -ðos). **1.** an ardent supporter or devotee: *a jazz aficionado.* **2.** a devotee of bullfighting. [Spanish, from *aficionar* to arouse affection, from *afición* AFFECTION]

a·field (əˈfiːld) *adv., adj.* (*postpositive*) **1.** away from one's usual surroundings or home (esp. in the phrase **far afield**). **2.** off the subject; away from the point (esp. in the phrase **far afield**). **3.** in or to the field, esp. the battlefield.

a·fire (əˈfaɪə) *adv., adj.* (*postpositive*) **1.** on fire; ablaze. **2.** intensely interested or passionate: *he was afire with enthusiasm for the new plan.*

a·flame (əˈfleɪm) *adv., adj.* (*postpositive*) **1.** in flames; ablaze. **2.** deeply aroused, as with passion: *he was aflame with desire.* **3.** (of the face) red or inflamed.

af+la+tox+in (ˌæfləˈtɒksɪn) *n.* a toxin produced by the fungus *Aspergillus flavus* growing on peanuts, maize, etc., thought to cause liver disease (esp. cancer) in man. [C20: from *A(spergillus) fla(vus)* + TOXIN]

AFL-CIO *abbrev. for* American Federation of Labor and Congress of Industrial Organizations; a federation of independent American trade unions formed by the union of these two groups in 1955.

a·float (əˈfləʊt) *adj.* (*postpositive*), *adv.* **1.** floating. **2.** aboard ship; at sea. **3.** covered with water; flooded. **4.** aimlessly drifting: *afloat in a sea of indecision.* **5.** in circulation; afoot: *nasty rumours were afloat.* **6.** free of debt; solvent.

a·flut+ter (əˈflʌtə) *adj.* (*postpositive*), *adv.* in or into a nervous or excited state.

A.F.M. *abbrev. for* Air Force Medal.

a·foot (əˈfʊt) *adj.* (*postpositive*), *adv.* **1.** in circulation or operation; astir: *mischief was afoot.* **2.** on or by foot.

a·fore (əˈfɔː) *adv., prep., conj.* an archaic or dialect word for **before.**

a·fore+men+tioned (əˈfɔːˌmɛnʃənd) *adj.* (*usually prenominal*) (chiefly in legal documents) stated or mentioned before or already.

a·fore+said (əˈfɔːˌsɛd) *adj.* (*usually prenominal*) (chiefly in legal documents) spoken of or referred to previously.

a·fore+thought (əˈfɔːˌθɔːt) *adj.* (*immediately postpositive*) premeditated (esp. in the phrase **malice aforethought**).

a·fore+time (əˈfɔːˌtaɪm) *adv. Archaic.* formerly.

a for+ti·o+ri (eɪˌfɔːtɪˈɔːraɪ, -rɪ, ɑː-) *adv.* for a stronger, more convincing, or more certain reason: *if Britain cannot afford a space programme, then, a fortiori, neither can India.* [Latin]

a·foul (əˈfaʊl) *adv., adj.* (*postpositive*) **1.** (usually foll. by *of*) in or into a state of difficulty, confusion, or conflict (with). **2.** (often foll. by *of*) into an entanglement or collision (with) (often in the phrase **run afoul of**): *the boat ran afoul of a steamer.*

Afr. *abbrev. for* Africa(n).

a·fraid (əˈfreɪd) *adj.* (*postpositive*) **1.** (often foll. by *of*) feeling fear or apprehension; frightened: *he was afraid of cats.* **2.** reluctant (to do something), as through fear or timidity: *he was afraid to let himself go.* **3.** (often foll. by *that;* used to lessen the effect of an unpleasant statement) regretful: *I'm afraid that I shall have to tell you to go.* [C14 *affraied*, past participle of AFFRAY (to frighten)]

af+reet *or* **af+rit** (ˈæfriːt, əˈfriːt) *n. Arabian myth.* a powerful evil demon or giant monster. [C19: from Arabic *ʻifrīt*]

a·fresh (əˈfrɛʃ) *adv.* once more; once again; anew.

Af+ri+ca (ˈæfrɪkə) *n.* the second largest of the continents, on the Mediterranean in the north, the Atlantic in the west, and the Red Sea, Gulf of Aden, and Indian Ocean in the east. The Sahara Desert divides the continent unequally into North Africa (an early centre of civilization, in close contact with Europe and W Asia, now inhabited chiefly by Arabs) and Africa south of the Sahara (relatively isolated from the rest of the world until the 19th century and inhabited chiefly by Negro peoples). It was colonized mainly in the 18th and 19th centuries by Europeans and now comprises chiefly independent nations. The largest lake is Lake Victoria and the chief rivers are the Nile, Niger, Congo, and Zambezi. Pop.: 346 015 000 (1969 est.). Area: about 30 300 000 sq. km (11 700 000 sq. miles).

Af+ri+can (ˈæfrɪkən) *adj.* **1.** denoting or relating to Africa or any of its peoples, languages, nations, etc. ~*n.* **2.** a native, inhabitant, or citizen of any of the countries of Africa. **3.** a member or descendant of any of the peoples of Africa, esp. a Negro.

Af+ri+can+ism (ˈæfrɪkəˌnɪzəm) *n.* something characteristic of Africa or Africans, esp. a characteristic feature of an African language when introduced into a non-African language.

Af+ri+can+ist (ˈæfrɪkənɪst) *n.* a person specializing in the study of African affairs or culture.

Af+ri+can+ize *or* **Af+ri+can+ise** (ˈæfrɪkəˌnaɪz) *vb.* (*tr.*) to make

African, esp. to give control of (policy, government, etc.) to Africans. —ˌ**Af·ri·can·i·'za·tion** *or* ˌ**Af·ri·can·i·'sa·tion** *n.*

Af·ri·can lil·y *n.* a liliaceous plant, *Agapanthus africanus,* of southern Africa, having rounded clusters of blue or white funnel-shaped flowers.

Af·ri·can ma·hog·a·ny *n.* **1.** any of several African trees of the meliaceous genus *Khaya,* esp. *K. ivorensis,* that have wood similar to that of true mahogany. **2.** the wood of any of these trees, used for furniture, etc. **3.** any of various other African woods that resemble true mahogany.

Af·ri·can vi·o·let *n.* any of several tropical African plants of the genus *Saintpaulia,* esp. *S. ionantha,* cultivated as house plants, with violet, white, or pink flowers and hairy leaves: family *Gesneriaceae.*

Af·ri·kaans (ˌæfrɪ'kɑːns, -'kɑːnz) *n.* an official language of all the Republic of South Africa, closely related to Dutch and Flemish. Also called: **South African Dutch, Taal.** [C20: from Dutch: African]

Af·ri·kan·der *or* **Af·ri·can·der** (ˌafrɪ'kændə, ˌæf-) *n.* **1.** a breed of humped-back beef cattle originally raised in southern Africa. **2.** a southern African breed of fat-tailed sheep. **3.** a former name for an **Afrikaner.** [C19: from South African Dutch, formed on the model of *Hollander*]

Af·ri·ka·ner (ˌafrɪ'kɑːnə, ˌæf-) *n.* a White native of the Republic of South Africa whose mother tongue is Afrikaans. See also **Boer.**

Af·ri·ka·ner·dom (ˌafrɪ'kɑːnədəm, ˌæf-) *n.* (in South Africa) Afrikaner nationalism based on pride in the Afrikaans language and culture, conservative Calvinism, and a sense of heritage as pioneers.

Af·ri·ka·ner·ize *or* **Af·ri·ka·ner·ise** (ˌafrɪ'kɑːnəˌraɪz, ˌæf-) *vb.* (*tr.*) *Chiefly S. African.* to make (a person) Afrikaans in attitudes, language, etc. —ˌ**Af·ri·ka·ner·i·'za·tion** *or* ˌ**Af·ri·ka·ner·i·'sa·tion** *n.*

af·rit ('æfriːt, ə'friːt) *n.* a variant spelling of **afreet.**

Af·ro ('æfrəʊ) *n., pl.* **·ros.** a hair style in which the hair is shaped into a wide frizzy bush, popular esp. among Negroes. [C20: independent use of AFRO-]

Af·ro- ('æfrəʊ-) *combining form.* indicating Africa or African: *Afro-Asiatic.*

Af·ro-A·mer·i·can *n.* **1.** an American Negro. *~adj.* **2.** denoting or relating to American Negroes, their history, or their culture.

Af·ro-A·sian *adj.* of or relating to both Africa and Asia, esp. as part of the Third World.

Af·ro-A·si·at·ic *n.* **1.** Also called: **Semito-Hamitic.** a family of languages of SW Asia and N Africa, consisting of the Semitic, ancient Egyptian, Berber, Cushitic, and Chadic subfamilies. *~adj.* **2.** denoting, belonging to, or relating to this family of languages.

Af·ro-chain *n.* (in the Caribbean) a large chain necklace with a central pendant: usually worn with a dashiki by men.

Af·ro-comb *n.* (in the Caribbean) a hand-shaped comb with long metal teeth used in tending an Afro.

Af·ro-Cu·ban *adj.* of or relating to a type of jazz influenced by Cuban variants of African rhythms. Compare **Cu·bop.**

af·ror·mo·si·a (ˌæfrɔː'məʊzɪə) *n.* a hard teaklike wood obtained from tropical African trees of the leguminous genus *Pericopsis.* [C20: from AFRO- + *Ormosia* (genus name)]

aft (ɑːft) *adv., adj. Chiefly nautical.* towards or at the stern or rear: *the aft deck; aft of the engines.* [C17: perhaps a shortened form of earlier ABAFT]

af·ter ('ɑːftə) *prep.* **1.** following in time; in succession to: *after dinner; time after time.* **2.** following in space; behind: *they entered one after another.* **3.** in pursuit or search of: *chasing after a thief; he's only after money.* **4.** concerning: *to inquire after his health.* **5.** considering: *after what you have done, you shouldn't complain.* **6.** next in excellence or importance to: *he ranked Jonson after Shakespeare.* **7.** in imitation of; in the manner of: *a statue after classical models.* **8.** in accordance with or in conformity to: *a man after her own heart.* **9.** with a name derived from: *Mary was named after her grandmother.* **10.** *U.S.* past (the hour of): *twenty after three.* **11. after all. a.** when everything is considered: *after all, why worry about it?* **b.** in spite of expectations, efforts, etc.: *he won the race after all!* **12. after you.** please go, enter, etc., before me. *~adv.* **13.** at a later time; afterwards. **14.** coming afterwards; in pursuit. **15.** *Nautical.* further aft; sternwards. *~conj.* **16.** (*subordinating*) at a time later than that at which: *he came after I had left.* *~adj.* **17.** *Nautical.* further aft: *the after cabin.* [Old English *æfter;* related to Old Norse *aptr* back, *eptir* after, Old High German *aftar*]

af·ter·birth ('ɑːftəˌbɜːθ) *n.* the placenta and fetal membranes expelled from the uterus after the birth of offspring.

af·ter·bod·y ('ɑːftəˌbɒdɪ) *n., pl.* **·bod·ies.** any discarded part that continues to trail a satellite, rocket, etc., in orbit.

af·ter·brain ('ɑːftəˌbreɪn) *n.* a nontechnical name for **myelencephalon.**

af·ter·burn·er ('ɑːftəˌbɜːnə) *n.* **1.** a device in the exhaust system of an internal-combustion engine for removing or rendering harmless potentially dangerous components in the exhaust gases. **2.** a device placed in the jet pipe of an aircraft jet engine to produce afterburning.

af·ter·burn·ing ('ɑːftəˌbɜːnɪŋ) *n.* **1.** Also called: **reheat.** a process in which additional fuel is ignited in the exhaust gases of a jet engine to produce additional thrust. **2.** irregular burning of fuel in a rocket motor after the main burning has ceased. **3.** persistence of combustion in an internal-combustion engine, either in an incorrect part of the cycle or after the ignition has been switched off.

af·ter·care ('ɑːftəˌkɛə) *n. Med.* the care of a patient recovering from a serious illness or operation.

af·ter·damp ('ɑːftəˌdæmp) *n.* a poisonous gas, consisting mainly of carbon monoxide, formed after the explosion of firedamp in coal mines. See also **white damp.**

af·ter·deck ('ɑːftəˌdɛk) *n. Nautical.* the unprotected deck behind the bridge of a ship.

af·ter·ef·fect ('ɑːftərɪˌfɛkt) *n.* **1.** any result occurring some time after its cause. **2.** *Med.* any delayed response to a stimulus or agent. Compare **side effect.**

af·ter·glow ('ɑːftəˌgləʊ) *n.* **1.** the glow left after a light has disappeared, such as that sometimes seen after sunset. **2.** the glow of an incandescent metal after the source of heat has been removed. **3.** *Physics.* luminescence persisting in a gas discharge after the source of power has been removed. **4.** a trace, impression, etc., of past emotion, brilliance, etc.

af·ter·heat ('ɑːftəˌhiːt) *n.* the heat generated in a nuclear reactor after it has been shut down, produced by residual radioactivity in the fuel elements.

af·ter·im·age ('ɑːftərˌɪmɪdʒ) *n.* a sustained or renewed sensation, esp. visual, after the original stimulus has ceased. Also called: **aftersensation.**

af·ter·life ('ɑːftəˌlaɪf) *n.* life after death or at a later time in a person's lifetime.

af·ter·math ('ɑːftəˌmɑːθ, -ˌmæθ) *n.* **1.** signs or results of an event or occurrence considered collectively, esp. of a catastrophe or disaster: *the aftermath of war.* **2.** *Agriculture.* a second mowing or crop of grass from land that has already yielded one crop earlier in the same year. [C16: AFTER + *math* a mowing, from Old English *mæth*]

af·ter·most ('ɑːftəˌməʊst) *adj.* closer or closest to the rear or (in a vessel) the stern; last.

af·ter·noon (ˌɑːftə'nuːn) *n.* **1. a.** the period of the day between noon and evening. **b.** (*as modifier*): *afternoon tea.* **2.** a middle or later part: *the afternoon of life.*

af·ter·noons (ˌɑːftə'nuːnz) *adv. Informal.* during the afternoon, esp. regularly.

af·ter·pains ('ɑːftəˌpeɪnz) *pl. n.* cramplike pains caused by contraction of the uterus after childbirth.

af·ter·piece ('ɑːftəˌpiːs) *n.* a brief usually comic dramatic piece presented after a play.

af·ters ('ɑːftəz) *n.* (*functioning as sing. or pl.*) *Brit. informal.* dessert; sweet.

af·ter·sen·sa·tion ('ɑːftəsɛnˌseɪʃən) *n.* another word for **afterimage.**

af·ter·shaft ('ɑːftəˌʃɑːft) *n. Ornithol.* a secondary feather arising near the base of a contour feather.

af·ter·shave lo·tion ('ɑːftəˌʃeɪv) *n.* a lotion, usually styptic and perfumed, for application to the face after shaving. Often shortened to **aftershave.**

af·ter·shock ('ɑːftəˌʃɒk) *n.* one of a series of minor tremors occurring after the main shock of an earthquake.

af·ter·taste ('ɑːftəˌteɪst) *n.* **1.** a taste that lingers on after eating or drinking. **2.** a lingering impression or sensation.

af·ter·thought ('ɑːftəˌθɔːt) *n.* **1.** a comment, reply, etc., that occurs to one after the opportunity to deliver it has passed. **2.** an addition to something already completed.

af·ter·wards ('ɑːftəwədz) *or* **af·ter·ward** *adv.* after an earlier event or time; subsequently. [Old English *æfterweard, æfteweard,* from AFT + WARD]

af·ter·word ('ɑːftəˌwɜːd) *n.* an epilogue or postscript in a book, etc.

af·ter·world ('ɑːftəˌwɜːld) *n.* a world inhabited after death.

Ag *the chemical symbol for* silver. [from Latin *argentum*]

A.G. *abbrev. for:* **1.** Adjutant General. **2.** Attorney General. **3.** Aktiengesellschaft. [German: joint-stock company]

a·ga *or* **a·gha** ('ɑːgə) *n.* (in the Ottoman Empire) **1.** a title of respect, often used with the title of a senior position. **2.** a military commander. [C17: Turkish, literally: lord]

A·ga·dir (ˌægə'dɪə) *n.* a port in SW Morocco, which became the centre of an international crisis (1911), when a gunboat arrived to protect German interests. Britain issued a strong warning to Germany but the French negotiated and war was averted. In 1960 the town was virtually destroyed by an earthquake, about 10 000 people being killed. Pop.: 61 192 (1971).

a·gain (ə'gɛn, ə'geɪn) *adv.* **1.** another or second time; once more; anew: *he had to start again.* **2.** once more in a previously experienced or encountered place, state, or condition: *he is ill again; he came back again.* **3.** in addition to the original amount, quantity, etc. (esp. in the phrases **as much again; half as much again**). **4.** (*sentence modifier*) on the other hand: *he might come and then again he might not.* **5.** besides; also: *she is beautiful and, again, intelligent.* **6.** *Archaic.* in reply; back: *he answered again to the questioning voice.* **7. again and again.** continuously; repeatedly. **8.** (*used with a negative*) *Caribbean.* any more; any longer: *I don't eat pumpkin again.* ~ **9.** *sentence connector.* moreover; furthermore: *again, it could be said that he is not dead.* [Old English *ongegn* opposite to, from A-^{2} + *gegn* straight]

a·gainst (ə'gɛnst, ə'geɪnst) *prep.* **1.** opposed to; in conflict or disagreement with: *they fought against the legislation.* **2.** standing or leaning beside or in front of: *a ladder against the wall.* **3.** coming in contact with: *the branches of a tree brushed against the bus.* **4.** in contrast to: *silhouettes are outlines against a light background.* **5.** having an adverse or unfavourable effect on: *the economic system works against small independent companies.* **6.** as a protection from or means of defence from the adverse effects of: *a safeguard against contaminated water.* **7.** in exchange for or in return for. **8.** *Now rare.* in preparation for: *he gave them warm clothing against their journey through the night.* **9. as against.** as opposed to or as compared with: *he had two shots at him this time as against only one last time.* [C12 *ageines*, from *again*, *ageyn*, etc., AGAIN + *-es* genitive ending; the spelling with *-t* (C16) was probably due to confusion with superlatives ending in *-st*]

A·ga Khan[1] (ˈɑːgə ˈkɑːn) *n.* the hereditary title of the head of the Ismaili Islamic sect.

A·ga Khan[2] (ˈɑːgə ˈkɑːn) *n.* Prince **Sa·drud·din** (səˈdruːdɪn). born 1933, Iranian international civil servant; United Nations High Commissioner for Refugees (1965–77).

A·ga Khan IV *n.* Prince **Ka·rim** (kəˈriːm). born 1936, spiritual leader of the Ismaili sect of Muslims since 1957.

a·gal·loch (əˈgælək) *n.* another name for **eaglewood.** [C17: from Greek *agallokhon*]

ag·a·ma (ˈægəmə, əˈgæmə) *n.* **1.** any small terrestrial lizard of the genus *Agama*, which inhabit warm regions of the Old World: family *Agamidae*. **2.** Also called: **agamid** (ˈægəmɪd, əˈgæmɪd). any other lizard of the family *Agamidae*, which occur in the Old World and Australia and show a wide range of habits and diversity of structure. [C19: Carib]

Ag·a·mem·non (ˌægəˈmɛmnɒn) *n. Greek myth.* a king of Mycenae who led the Greeks at the siege of Troy. On his return home he was murdered by his wife Clytemnestra and her lover Aegisthus. See also **Menelaus.**

a·gam·ete (əˈgæmiːt) *n.* a reproductive cell, such as the merozoite of some protozoans, that develops into a new form without fertilization. [C19: from Greek *agametos* unmarried; see A-[1], GAMETE]

a·gam·ic (əˈgæmɪk) *adj.* asexual; occurring or reproducing without fertilization. [C19: from Greek *agamos* unmarried, from A-[1] + *gamos* marriage] —**aˈgam·i·cal·ly** *adv.*

ag·a·mo·gen·e·sis (ˌægəməʊˈdʒɛnɪsɪs) *n.* asexual reproduction, such as fission or parthenogenesis. [C19: AGAMIC + GENESIS] —**ag·a·mo·ge·net·ic** (ˌægəməʊdʒəˈnɛtɪk) *adj.* —**ˌag·a·mo·geˈnet·i·cal·ly** *adv.*

A·ga·ña (əˈgɑːnjə) *n.* the capital of the Pacific island of Guam, on its W coast. Pop.: 2119 (1970).

ag·a·pan·thus (ˌægəˈpænθəs) *n.* any African liliaceous plant of the genus *Agapanthus*, esp. the African lily, with rounded clusters of blue or white flowers. [C19: New Latin, from Greek *agapē* love + *anthos* flower]

a·gape (əˈgeɪp) *adj.* (*postpositive*) **1.** (esp. of the mouth) wide open. **2.** very surprised, expectant, or eager, esp. as indicated by a wide open mouth. [C17: A-[2] + GAPE]

A·ga·pe (ˈægəpɪ) *n. Christianity.* **1.** Christian love, esp. as contrasted with erotic love; charity. **2.** a communal meal in the early Church taken in commemoration of the Last Supper; love feast. [C17: Greek *agapē* love]

a·gar (ˈeɪgə) *n.* a complex gelatinous carbohydrate obtained from seaweeds, esp. those of the genus *Gelidium*, used as a culture medium for bacteria, a laxative, in food, etc. Also called: **agar-agar.** [C19: Malay]

ag·a·ric (ˈægərɪk, əˈgærɪk) *n.* **1.** any saprophytic basidiomycetous fungus of the family *Agaricaceae*, having gills on the underside of the cap. The group includes the edible mushrooms and poisonous forms such as the fly agaric. **2.** the dried spore-producing bodies of certain fungi, esp. *Polyphorus officinalis* (or *Boletus laricis*), formerly used in medicine. [C16: via Latin *agaricum*, from Greek *agarikon*, perhaps named after *Agaria*, a town in Sarmatia] —**a·gar·i·ca·ceous** (əˌgærɪˈkeɪʃəs) *adj.*

A·gar·ta·la (ˈʌgətəˌlɑː) *n.* a city in NE India, capital of the state of Tripura. Pop.: 100 264 (1971).

ag·ate (ˈægɪt) *n.* **1.** an impure microcrystalline form of quartz consisting of a variegated, usually banded chalcedony, used as a gemstone and in making pestles and mortars, burnishers, and polishers. Formula: SiO_2. **2.** a playing marble of this quartz or resembling it. **3.** *Printing.* the U.S. name for **ruby** (sense 5). [C16: via French from Latin *achātēs*, from Greek *akhatēs*]

ag·ate line *n. U.S.* a measure of advertising space, one column wide and one fourteenth of an inch deep. Sometimes shortened to **line.**

ag·ate·ware (ˈægɪtˌwɛə) *n.* ceramic ware made to resemble agate or marble.

a·ga·ve (əˈgeɪvɪ, ˈægeɪv) *n.* any plant of the genus *Agave* native to tropical America with tall flower stalks rising from thick fleshy leaves: family *Agavaceae*. Some species are the source of fibres such as sisal or of alcoholic beverages such as pulque and tequila. See also **century plant.** [C18: New Latin, from Greek *agauē*, feminine of *agauos* illustrious, probably alluding to the height of the plant]

AGC *abbrev. for* automatic gain control.

agcy. *abbrev. for* agency.

age (eɪdʒ) *n.* **1.** the period of time that a person, animal, or plant has lived or is expected to live: *the age of a tree; what age was he when he died? the age of a horse is up to thirty years.* **2.** the period of existence of an object, material, group, etc.: *the age of this table is 200 years.* **3. a.** a period or state of human life: *he should know better at his age; she had got beyond the giggly age.* **b.** (*as modifier*): *age group.* **4.** the latter part of life. **5. a.** a period of history marked by some feature or characteristic; era. **b.** (*cap. when part of a name*): *the Middle Ages; the Space Age.* **6.** generation: *the Edwardian age.* **7.** *Geology, palaeontol.* **a.** a period of the earth's history distinguished by special characteristics: *the age of reptiles.* **b.** the period during which a stage of rock strata is formed; a subdivision of an epoch. **8.** *Myth.* any of the successive periods in the legendary history of man, which were, according to Hesiod, the golden, silver, bronze, heroic, and iron ages. **9.** (*often pl.*) *Informal.* a relatively long time: *she was an age washing her hair; I've been waiting ages.* **10.** *Psychol.* the level in years that a person has reached in any area of development, such as mental or emotional, compared with the normal level for his chronological age. See also **achievement age, mental age.** **11. age before beauty.** (often said humorously when yielding precedence) older people take precedence over younger people. **12. of age.** adult and legally responsible for one's actions (usually at 18 or 21 years). ~*vb.* **ag·es, age·ing** *or* **ag·ing, aged.** **13.** to grow or make old or apparently old; become or cause to become old or aged. **14.** to begin to seem older: *to have aged a lot in the past year.* **15.** *Brewing.* to mature or cause to mature. [C13: via Old French from Vulgar Latin *aetatīcum* (unattested), from Latin *aetās*, ultimately from *aevum* lifetime; compare AEON]

-age *suffix forming nouns.* **1.** indicating a collection, set, or group: *acreage; baggage.* **2.** indicating a process or action or the result of an action: *haulage; passage; breakage.* **3.** indicating a state, condition, or relationship: *bondage; parentage.* **4.** indicating a house or place: *orphanage.* **5.** indicating a charge or fee: *postage.* **6.** indicating a rate: *dosage; mileage.* [from Old French, from Late Latin *-āticum*, noun suffix, neuter of *-āticus*, adjectival suffix, from *-ātus* -ATE-[1] + *-icus* -IC]

a·ged (ˈeɪdʒɪd) *adj.* **1. a.** advanced in years; old. **b.** (*as collective n.* preceded by *the*): *the aged.* **2.** of, connected with, or characteristic of old age. **3.** (eɪdʒd). (*postpositive*) having the age of: *a woman aged twenty.* **4.** *Geography.* having reached an advanced stage of erosion.

a·gee *or* **a·jee** (əˈdʒiː) *adj. Scot. and Brit. dialect.* awry, crooked, or ajar. [C19: A-[2] + GEE[1]]

age har·den·ing *n.* the hardening of metals by spontaneous structural changes over a period of time. See also **precipitation hardening.**

age·less (ˈeɪdʒlɪs) *adj.* **1.** apparently never growing old. **2.** timeless; eternal: *an ageless quality.*

A·gen (*French* aˈʒɛ̃) *n.* a market town in SW France, on the Garonne river. Pop.: 35 839 (1975).

a·gen·cy (ˈeɪdʒənsɪ) *n., pl.* **·cies.** **1.** a business or other organization providing a specific service: *an employment agency.* **2.** the place where an agent conducts business. **3.** the business, duties, or functions of an agent. **4.** action, power, or operation: *the agency of fate.* **5.** intercession or mediation. **6.** *Chiefly U.S.* one of the administrative organizations of a government. [C17: from Medieval Latin *agentia*, from Latin *agere* to do]

a·gen·da (əˈdʒɛndə) *n.* **1.** (*functioning as sing.*) a schedule or list of items to be attended to. Also: **a·gen·dum.** **2.** (*functioning as pl.*) matters to be attended to, as at a meeting of a committee. Also: **a·gen·das, a·gen·dums.** [C17: Latin, literally: things to be done, from *agere* to do]

a·gen·e·sis (eɪˈdʒɛnɪsɪs) *n.* **1.** (of an animal or plant) imperfect development. **2.** impotence or sterility. —**a·ge·net·ic** (ˌeɪdʒəˈnɛtɪk) *adj.*

a·gent (ˈeɪdʒənt) *n.* **1.** a person who acts on behalf of another person, group, business, government, etc.; representative. **2.** a person or thing that acts or has the power to act. **3.** a phenomenon, substance, or organism that exerts some force or effect: *a chemical agent.* **4.** the means by which something occurs or is achieved; instrument: *wind is an agent of plant pollination.* **5.** a person representing a business concern, esp. a travelling salesman. **6.** *Brit.* short for **estate agent.** **7.** short for **secret agent.** [C15: from Latin *agent-*, noun use of the present participle of *agere* to do] —**a·gen·tial** (eɪˈdʒɛnʃəl) *adj.*

a·gent-gen·er·al *n., pl.* **a·gents-gen·er·al.** a representative in London of a Canadian province or an Australian state.

a·gen·tive (ˈeɪdʒəntɪv) *or* **a·gen·tial** (eɪˈdʒɛnʃəl) *Grammar.* ~*adj.* **1.** (in some inflected languages) denoting a case of nouns, etc., indicating the agent described by the verb. **2.** (of a speech element) indicating agency: *"-er" in "worker" is an agentive suffix.* ~*n.* **3. a.** the agentive case. **b.** a word or element in the agentive case.

a·gent of pro·duc·tion *n.* another name for **factor of production.**

a·gent pro·vo·ca·teur *French.* (aˈʒɑ̃ prɔvɔkaˈtœːr) *n., pl.* ***a·gents pro·vo·ca·teurs*** (aˈʒɑ̃ prɔvɔkaˈtœːr). a secret agent employed to provoke suspected persons to commit illegal acts and so be discredited or liable to punishment.

age of con·sent *n.* the age at which a person, esp. a female, is considered legally competent to consent to marriage or sexual intercourse.

Age of Rea·son *n.* (usually preceded by *the*) the 18th century in W Europe. See also **Enlightenment.**

age-old *or* **age-long** *adj.* very old or of long duration; ancient.

ag·er·a·tum (ˌædʒəˈreɪtəm) *n.* any tropical American plant of the genus *Ageratum*, such as *A. houstonianum* and *A. conyzoides*, which have thick clusters of purplish-blue flowers. [C16: New Latin, via Latin from Greek *agēraton* that which does not age, from A-[1] + *gērat-*, stem of *gēras* old age; the flowers of the plant remain vivid for a long time]

ag·ger (ˈædʒə) *n.* an earthwork or mound forming a rampart, esp. in a Roman military camp. [C14: from Latin *agger* a heap, from *ad-* to + *gerere* to carry, bring]

ag·gior·na·men·to *Italian.* (adˌdʒornaˈmɛnto) *n., pl.* ***·ti*** (-ti). *R.C. Church.* the process of bringing up to date methods, ideas, etc.

ag·glom·er·ate *vb.* (əˈglɒməˌreɪt). **1.** to form or be formed into a mass or cluster; collect. ~*n.* (ə'glɒmərɪt, -ˌreɪt). **2.** a confused mass. **3.** a volcanic rock consisting of angular fragments within a groundmass of lava. Compare **conglomerate** (sense 2). ~*adj.* (ə'glɒmərɪt, -ˌreɪt). **4.** formed into a mass. [C17: from Latin *agglomerāre,* from *glomerāre* to wind into a ball, from *glomus* ball, mass] —**ag+ˌglom+er·'a+tion** *n.* —**ag+'glom+er·a+tive** *adj.*

ag+glu+ti+nate *vb.* (ə'glu:tɪˌneɪt). **1.** to cause to adhere, as with glue. **2.** *Linguistics.* to combine or be combined by agglutination. **3.** (*tr.*) to cause (bacteria, red blood cells, etc.) to clump together. ~*adj.* (ə'glu:tɪnɪt, -ˌneɪt). **4.** united or stuck, as by glue. [C16: from Latin *agglūtināre* to glue to, from *gluten* glue] —**ag+ˌglu+ti+na·'bil+i·ty** *n.* —**ag+'glu+ti+na·ble** *adj.* —**ag+'glu+ti+nant** *adj.*

ag+glu+ti+na+tion (əˌglu:tɪ'neɪʃən) *n.* **1.** the act or process of agglutinating. **2.** the condition of being agglutinated; adhesion. **3.** a united mass or group of parts. **4.** *Linguistics.* the building up of words from component morphemes in such a way that these undergo little or no change of form or meaning in the process of combination.

ag+glu+ti+na+tive (ə'glu:tɪnətɪv) *adj.* **1.** tending to join or capable of joining. **2.** Also: **agglomerative.** *Linguistics.* denoting languages, such as Hungarian, whose morphology is characterized by agglutination. Compare **analytic** (sense 3), **synthetic** (sense 3), **polysynthetic.**

ag+glu+ti+nin (ə'glu:tɪnɪn) *n.* an antibody that causes agglutination. [C19: AGGLUTINATE + -IN]

ag+glu+tin·o+gen (ˌæglʊ'tɪnədʒən) *n.* an antigen that reacts with or stimulates the formation of a specific agglutinin. [C20: from AGGLUTINATE + -GEN]

ag+grade (ə'greɪd) *vb.* (*tr.*) to build up the level of (any land surface) by the deposition of sediment. Compare **degrade** (sense 4). —**ag+grad·a+tion** (ˌægrə'deɪʃən) *n.*

ag+gran+dize *or* **ag+gran+dise** ('ægrənˌdaɪz, ə'grændaɪz) *vb.* (*tr.*) **1.** to increase the power, wealth, prestige, scope, etc., of. **2.** to cause (something) to seem greater; magnify; exaggerate. [C17: from Old French *aggrandiss-,* long stem of *aggrandir* to make bigger, from Latin *grandis* GRAND; the ending *-ize* is due to the influence of verbs ending in *-ise, -ize*] —**ag+gran+dize+ment** *or* **ag+gran+dise+ment** (ə'grændɪzmənt) *n.* —**'ag+gran+ˌdiz+er** *or* **'ag+gran+ˌdis+er** *n.*

ag+gra+vate ('ægrəˌveɪt) *vb.* (*tr.*) **1.** to make (a disease, situation, problem, etc.) worse or more severe. **2.** *Informal.* to annoy; exasperate. [C16: from Latin *aggravāre* to make heavier, from *gravis* heavy] —**ˌag+gra+'va+tion** *n.*

Usage. The use of *aggravate* and *aggravation* for *annoy* and *annoyance* is usually avoided in formal English.

ag+gre+gate *adj.* ('ægrɪgɪt, -ˌgeɪt). **1.** formed of separate units collected into a whole; collective; corporate. **2.** (of fruits and flowers) composed of a dense cluster of carpels or florets. ~*n.* ('ægrɪgɪt, -ˌgeɪt). **3.** a sum or assemblage of many separate units; sum total. **4.** *Geology.* a rock, such as granite, consisting of a mixture of minerals. **5.** the sand, etc., mixed with cement and water to make concrete. **6. in the aggregate.** taken as a whole. ~*vb.* ('ægrɪˌgeɪt). **7.** to combine or be combined into a body, etc. **8.** (*tr.*) to amount to (a number). [C16: from Latin *aggregāre* to add to a flock or herd, attach (oneself) to, from *grex* flock] **'ag+gre+gate+ly** *adv.* —**ˌag+gre+'ga·tion** *n.* —**ag+gre+ga+tive** ('ægrɪˌgeɪtɪv) *adj.*

ag+gress (ə'grɛs) *vb.* (*intr.*) to attack first or begin a quarrel. [C16: from Medieval Latin *aggressāre* to attack, from Latin *aggredī* to attack, approach]

ag+gres+sion (ə'grɛʃən) *n.* **1.** an attack or harmful action, esp. an unprovoked attack by one country against another. **2.** any offensive activity, practice, etc.: *an aggression against personal liberty.* **3.** *Psychol.* a hostile or destructive mental attitude or behaviour. [C17: from Latin *aggression-,* from *aggrēdi* to attack] —**ag+gres+sor** (ə'grɛsə) *n.*

ag+gres+sive (ə'grɛsɪv) *adj.* **1.** quarrelsome or belligerent: *an aggressive remark.* **2.** assertive; vigorous: *an aggressive businessman.* —**ag+'gres+sive+ly** *adv.*

ag+grieve (ə'gri:v) *vb.* (*tr.*) **1.** (*often impersonal or passive*) to grieve; distress; afflict: *it aggrieved her much that she could not go.* **2.** to injure unjustly, esp. by infringing a person's legal rights. [C14 *agreven,* via Old French from Latin *aggravāre* to AGGRAVATE] —**ag+griev+ed+ly** (ə'gri:vɪdlɪ) *adv.*

ag+gro ('ægrəʊ) *n. Brit. slang.* aggressive behaviour, esp. by youths in a gang. [C20: from AGGRAVATION]

a·gha ('ɑ:gə) *n.* a variant spelling of **aga.**

a·ghast (ə'gɑ:st) *adj.* (*postpositive*) overcome with amazement or horror. [C13 *agast,* from Old English *gæstan* to frighten. The spelling with *gh* is on the model of GHASTLY]

ag+ile ('ædʒaɪl) *adj.* **1.** quick in movement; nimble. **2.** mentally quick or acute. [C15: from Latin *agilis,* from *agere* to do, act] —**'ag+ile+ly** *adv.* —**a·gil+i·ty** (ə'dʒɪlɪtɪ) *n.*

Ag+in+court ('ædʒɪnˌkɔ:t; *French* aʒɛ̃'ku:r) *n.* a battle fought in 1415 near the village of Agincourt, N France: a decisive victory for English longbowmen under Henry V over French forces vastly superior in number.

ag·i·o ('ædʒɪəʊ) *n.* **1. a.** the difference between the nominal and actual values of a currency. **b.** the charge payable for conversion of the less valuable currency. **2.** a percentage payable for the exchange of one currency into another. **3.** an allowance granted to compensate for differences in currency values, as on foreign bills of exchange. **4.** an informal word for **agiotage.** [C17: from Italian, literally: ease]

ag·io+tage ('ædʒətɪdʒ) *n.* **1.** the business of exchanging currencies. **2.** speculative dealing in stock exchange securities or foreign exchange. [C19: French, from AGIO]

a·gist (ə'dʒɪst) *vb.* (*tr.*) *Law.* **1.** to care for and feed (cattle or horses) for payment. **2.** to assess and charge (land or its owner) with a public burden, such as a tax. [C14: from Old French *agister,* from *gister* to lodge, ultimately from Latin *jacēre* to lie down]

ag·i+tate ('ædʒɪˌteɪt) *vb.* **1.** (*tr.*) to excite, disturb, or trouble (a person, the mind or feelings); worry. **2.** (*tr.*) to cause to move vigorously; shake, stir, or disturb. **3.** (*intr.; often foll. by for or against*) to attempt to stir up public opinion for or against something. **4.** (*tr.*) to discuss or debate in order to draw attention to or gain support for (a cause, etc.): *to agitate a political cause.* [C16: from Latin *agitātus,* from *agitāre* to move to and fro, set into motion, from *agere* to act, do] —**ˌag·i+'ta+tion** *n.*

a·gi+ta+to (ˌædʒɪ'tɑ:təʊ) *adj., adv. Music.* in an agitated manner.

ag·i+ta+tor ('ædʒɪˌteɪtə) *n.* **1.** a person who agitates for or against a cause, etc. **2.** a device, machine, or part used for mixing, shaking, or vibrating a material.

ag·it+prop ('ædʒɪtˌprɒp) *n.* **1.** (*often cap.*) a bureau of the Central Committee of the Communist Party of the Soviet Union, in charge of agitation and propaganda on behalf of Communism. **2.** any promotion of political agitation and propaganda, esp. of a Communist nature. [C20: short for Russian *Agitpropbyuro*]

A·glai·a (ə'glaɪə) *n. Greek myth.* one of the three Graces. [Greek: splendour, from *aglaos* splendid]

a·gleam (ə'gli:m) *adj.* (*postpositive*) glowing; gleaming.

ag+let ('æglɪt) *or* **ai·glet** *n.* **1.** a metal sheath or tag at the end of a shoelace, ribbon, etc. **2.** a variant spelling of **aiguillette. 3.** any ornamental pendant. [C15: from Old French *aiguillette* a small needle]

a·gley (ə'gleɪ, ə'gli:) *adj. Scot.* awry. [from *gley* squint]

a·glim+mer (ə'glɪmə) *adj.* (*postpositive*) glimmering.

a·glit+ter (ə'glɪtə) *adj.* (*postpositive*) sparkling; glittering.

a·glow (ə'gləʊ) *adj.* (*postpositive*) glowing.

A.G.M. *abbrev. for* annual general meeting.

ag·ma ('ægmə) *n. Phonetics.* the symbol (ŋ), used to represent a velar nasal consonant, as in *long* (lɒŋ) or *tank* (tæŋk).

ag+mi+nate ('ægmɪnɪt, -ˌneɪt) *adj.* gathered or clustered together. [C19: from Latin *agmen* a moving throng]

ag+nail ('ægˌneɪl) *n.* another name for **hangnail.**

ag+nate ('ægneɪt) *adj.* **1.** related by descent from a common male ancestor. **2.** related in any way; cognate. ~*n.* **3.** a male or female descendant by male links from a common male ancestor. [C16: from Latin *agnātus* born in addition, added by birth, from *agnāsci,* from *ad-* in addition + *gnāsci* to be born] —**ag+nat+ic** (æg'nætɪk) *adj.* —**ag+'na+tion** *n.*

Ag·nes ('ægnɪs) *n.* **Saint.** ?292–?304 A.D., Christian child martyr under Diocletian. Feast day: Jan. 21.

Ag·ni ('ʌgnɪ) *n. Hinduism.* the god of fire, one of the three chief deities of the Vedas. [Sanskrit: fire]

ag+no+men (æg'nəʊmɛn) *n., pl.* **+nom·i+na** (-'nɒmɪnə). **1.** the fourth name or second cognomen occasionally acquired by an ancient Roman. See also **cognomen, nomen, praenomen. 2.** another word for **nickname.** [C18: from Late Latin, from *ad-* in addition to + *nōmen* name] —**ag+nom·i·nal** (æg'nɒmɪnᵊl) *adj.*

ag+nos+tic (æg'nɒstɪk) *n.* **1.** a person who holds that only material phenomena can be known and knowledge of a Supreme Being, ultimate cause, etc., is impossible. ~*adj.* **2.** of or relating to agnostics. [C19: coined 1869 by T. H. Huxley from A-[1] + GNOSTIC] —**ag+'nos+ti+cism** *n.*

Ag+nus De·i ('ægnʊs 'deɪɪ) *n. Christianity.* **1.** the figure of a lamb bearing a cross or banner, emblematic of Christ. **2.** a chant beginning with these words or a translation of them, forming part of the Roman Catholic Mass or sung as an anthem in the Anglican liturgy. **3.** a wax medallion stamped with a lamb as emblem of Christ and blessed by the pope. [Latin: Lamb of God]

a·go (ə'gəʊ) *adv.* in the past: *five years ago; long ago.* [C14 *ago,* from Old English *āgān* to pass away]

Usage. The use of *ago* with *since* (*it's ten years ago since he wrote the novel*) is redundant and is therefore avoided in careful English. *Ago* should be followed by *that: it was ten years ago that he wrote the novel.*

a·gog (ə'gɒg) *adj.* (*postpositive*) highly impatient, eager, or curious. [C15: perhaps from Old French *en gogues* in merriments, origin unknown]

à go·go (ə 'gəʊˌgəʊ) *adj., adv. Informal.* as much as one likes; galore: *champagne à gogo.* [C20: from French]

-a·gogue *or esp. U.S.* **-a·gog** *n. combining form.* **1.** indicating a person or thing that leads or incites to action: *pedagogue; demagogue.* **2.** denoting a substance that stimulates the secretion of something: *galactagogue.* [via Late Latin from Greek *agōgos* leading, from *agein* to lead] —**-a·gog·ic** *adjective combining form.* —**-a·go·gy** *noun combining form.*

ag·on ('ægəʊn, -gɒn) *n., pl.* **a·go+nes** (ə'gəʊni:z). (in ancient Greece) a festival at which competitors contended for prizes. Among the best known were the Olympic, Pythian, Nemean, and Isthmian Games. [C17: Greek: contest, from *agein* to lead]

a·gone (ə'gɒn) *adv.* an archaic word for **ago.**

a·gon+ic (ə'gɒnɪk, eɪ'gɒnɪk) *adj.* forming no angle. [C19: from Greek *agōnos,* from A-[1] + *gōnia* angle]

a·gon+ic line *n.* an imaginary line on the surface of the earth connecting points of zero magnetic declination.

ag·o+nist ('ægənɪst) *n.* **1.** any muscle that is opposed in action by another muscle. Compare **antagonist. 2.** a competitor, as in an agon. [C17: from Greek *agōn* AGON]

ag·o+nis+tic (ˌægə'nɪstɪk) *adj.* **1.** striving for effect; strained. **2.** eager to win in discussion or argument; competitive. [C17: via Late Latin from Greek *agōnistikos,* from *agōn* contest]

ag·o+nize *or* **ag·o+nise** ('ægəˌnaɪz) *vb.* **1.** to suffer or cause to suffer agony. **2.** (*intr.*) to make a desperate effort; struggle; strive. [C16: via Medieval Latin from Greek *agōnizesthai* to contend for a prize, from *agōn* AGON] —'**ag·o+ˌniz+ing+ly** *or* '**ag·o+ˌnis+ing+ly** *adv.*

ag·o+ny ('ægənɪ) *n., pl.* **+nies. 1.** acute physical or mental pain; anguish. **2.** the suffering or struggle preceding death. **3. pile, put,** *or* **turn on the agony.** *Brit. informal.* to exaggerate one's distress for sympathy or greater effect. [C14: via Late Latin from Greek *agōnia* struggle, from *agōn* contest]

ag·o+ny col+umn *n. Brit. informal.* a newspaper column devoted to advertisements relating esp. to personal problems.

ag·o+ra[1] ('ægərə) *n., pl.* **+rae** (-riː, -raɪ) *or* **+ras.** (*often cap.*) **a.** the marketplace in Athens, used for popular meetings, or any similar place of assembly in ancient Greece. **b.** the meeting itself. [from Greek, from *agorein* to gather]

ag·o+ra[2] (ˌægə'rɑː) *n., pl.* **+rot** (-'rɒt). an Israeli monetary unit worth one hundredth of a pound. [Hebrew, from *āgōr* to collect]

ag·o+ra+pho+bi·a (ˌægərə'fəʊbɪə) *n.* an abnormal dread of open spaces. —ˌ**ag·o+ra+'pho+bic** *adj., n.*

A·gos·ti·ni (*Italian* agos'tiːni) *n.* **Gia·co·mo** ('dʒɑːkomo). born 1944, Italian racing motorcyclist: world champion (500 cc. class) 1966–72; (350 cc. class) 1968–74.

a·gou+ti (ə'guːtɪ) *n., pl.* **+tis** *or* **+ties. 1.** any hystricomorph rodent of the genus *Dasyprocta,* of Central and South America and the West Indies: family *Dasyproctidae.* Agoutis are agile and long-legged, with hooflike claws, and are valued for their meat. **2.** a pattern of fur in certain rodents, characterized by irregular stripes. [C18: via French and Spanish from Guarani]

agr. *or* **agric.** *abbrev. for:* **1.** agricultural. **2.** agriculture. **3.** agricultur(al)ist.

AGR *abbrev. for* advanced gas-cooled reactor.

A·gra ('ɑːgrə) *n.* a city in N India, in W Uttar Pradesh on the Jumna River: a capital of the Mogul empire until 1658; famous for its Mogul architecture, esp. the Taj Mahal. Pop.: 591 917 (1971).

a·graffe *or U.S.* (*sometimes*) **a·grafe** (ə'græf) *n.* **1.** a fastening consisting of a loop and hook, formerly used in armour and clothing. **2.** a metal cramp used to connect stones. [C18: from French, from *grafe* a hook]

A·gram ('ɑːgram) *n.* the German name for **Zagreb.**

a·gran+u·lo+cy+to·sis (əˌgrænjʊləʊsaɪ'təʊsɪs) *n.* a serious and sometimes fatal illness characterized by a marked reduction of leucocytes, usually caused by hypersensitivity to certain drugs. [C20: New Latin; see A-[1], GRANULE, -CYTE, -OSIS]

ag+ra+pha ('ægrəfə) *pl. n.* sayings of Jesus not recorded in the canonical Gospels. [Greek: things not written, from A-[1] + *graphein* to write]

a·graph·i·a (ə'græfɪə) *n.* loss of the ability to write, resulting from a brain lesion. [C19: New Latin, from A-[1] + Greek *graphein* to write]

a·grar+i·an (ə'grɛərɪən) *adj.* **1.** of or relating to land or its cultivation or to systems of dividing landed property. **2.** of or relating to rural or agricultural matters. **3.** (of plants) growing wild. ~*n.* **4.** a person who favours the redistribution of landed property. [C16: from Latin *agrārius,* from *ager* field, land] —**a·'grar+i·an+ism** *n.*

a·gree (ə'griː) *vb.* **a·grees, a·gree+ing, a·greed.** (*mainly intr.*) **1.** (often foll. by *with*) to be of the same opinion; concur. **2.** (*also tr.;* when *intr.,* often foll. by *to;* when *tr., takes a clause as object or an infinitive*) to give assent; consent: *she agreed to go home; I'll agree to that.* **3.** (*also tr.;* when *intr.,* foll. by *on* or *about;* when *tr., may take a clause as object*) to come to terms (about); arrive at a settlement (on). **4.** (foll. by *with*) to be similar or consistent; harmonize; correspond. **5.** (foll. by *with*) to be agreeable or suitable (to one's health, temperament, etc.). **6.** *Grammar.* to undergo agreement. **7.** (*tr.; takes a clause as object*) to concede or grant; admit: *they agreed that the price was too high.* [C14: from Old French *agreer,* from the phrase *a gre* at will or pleasure]

a·gree+a·ble (ə'griːəb^əl) *adj.* **1.** pleasing; pleasant. **2.** prepared to consent. **3.** (foll. by *to* or *with*) in keeping; consistent: *salaries agreeable with current trends.* **4.** (foll. by *to*) to one's liking: *the terms were not agreeable to him.* —**a·'gree+a·ble+ness** *n.* —**a·'gree+a·bly** *adv.*

a·greed (ə'griːd) *adj.* determined by common consent: *the agreed price.*

a·gree+ment (ə'griːmənt) *n.* **1.** the act of agreeing. **2.** a settlement, esp. one that is legally enforceable; covenant; treaty. **3.** a contract or document containing such a settlement. **4.** the state of being of the same opinion; concord; harmony. **5.** the state of being similar or consistent; correspondence; conformity. **6.** *Grammar.* the determination of the inflectional form of one word by some grammatical feature, such as number or gender, of another word, esp. one in the same sentence. Also called: **concord.** [C14: from Old French]

a·gres+tal (ə'grɛstəl) *adj.* (of uncultivated plants such as weeds) growing on cultivated land.

a·gres+tic (ə'grɛstɪk) *adj.* **1.** rural; rustic. **2.** unpolished; uncouth. [C17: from Latin *agrestis,* from *ager* field]

ag+ri+busi+ness ('ægrɪˌbɪznɪs) *n.* the various businesses collectively that process, distribute, and support farm products. [C20: from AGRI(CULTURE) + BUSINESS]

agric. *or* **agr.** *abbrev. for:* **1.** agricultural. **2.** agriculture. **3.** agricultur(al)ist.

A·gric·o·la (ə'grɪkələ) *n.* **1. Geor·gi·us** ('dʒɔːdʒɪəs), original name *Georg Bauer.* 1494–1555, German mineralogist, metallurgist, and author, commonly regarded as the father of mineralogy. **2. Gnae·us Ju·li·us** ('niːəs 'dʒuːlɪəs) 40–93 A.D., Roman general; governor of Britain who advanced Roman rule north to the Firth of Forth.

ag+ri+cul+ture ('ægrɪˌkʌltʃə) *n.* the science or occupation of cultivating land and rearing crops and livestock; farming; husbandry. [C17: from Latin *agricultūra,* from *ager* field, land + *cultūra* CULTURE] —ˌ**ag+ri+'cul+tur+al** *adj.* —ˌ**ag+ri+'cul+tur+al+ly** *adv.* —ˌ**ag+ri+'cul+tur+ist** *or* ˌ**ag+ri+'cul+tur+al+ist** *n.*

A·gri+gen+to (*Italian* agri'dʒɛnto) *n.* a town in Italy, in SW Sicily: site of six Greek temples. Pop.: 49 213 (1971). Former name (until 1927): **Girgenti.**

ag+ri+mo+ny ('ægrɪmənɪ) *n.* **1.** any of various temperate rosaceous plants of the genus *Agrimonia,* which have compound leaves, long spikes of small yellow flowers, and bristly burlike fruits. **2.** any of several other plants, such as hemp agrimony. [C15: altered from *egrimonie* (C14), via Old French from Latin *agrimōnia,* variant of *argemōnia* from Greek *argemōnē* poppy]

A·grip·pa (ə'grɪpə) *n.* **Mar·cus Vip·sa·ni·us** ('mɑːkəs vɪp'seɪnɪəs). 63–12 B.C., Roman general: chief adviser and later son-in-law of Augustus.

Ag·rip·pi·na (ˌægrɪ'piːnə) *n.* **1.** called *the Elder. c.* 14 B.C.–33 A.D., Roman matron: granddaughter of Augustus: wife of Germanicus, mother of Caligula and Agrippina the Younger. **2.** called *the Younger.* 15–59 A.D., mother of Nero, who put her to death after he became emperor.

ag·ro- *combining form.* denoting fields, soil, or agriculture: *agronomy.* [from Greek *agros* field]

ag+ro+bi+ol+o·gy (ˌægrəʊbaɪ'ɒlədʒɪ) *n.* the science of plant growth and nutrition in relation to agriculture. —**ag+ro+bi·o+log·i·cal** (ˌægrəʊˌbaɪə'lɒdʒɪk^əl) *adj.* —ˌ**ag+ro+bi+'ol+o·gist** *n.*

a·grol+o·gy (ə'grɒlədʒɪ) *n.* the scientific study of soils and their potential productivity. —**ag+ro+log·i·cal** (ˌægrə'lɒdʒɪk^əl) *adj.*

agron. *abbrev. for* agronomy.

ag+ro+nom+ics (ˌægrə'nɒmɪks) *n.* (*functioning as sing.*) the branch of economy dealing with the distribution, management, and productivity of land. —ˌ**ag+ro+'nom+ic** *or* ˌ**ag+ro+'nom+i+cal** *adj.*

a·gron·o+my (ə'grɒnəmɪ) *n.* the science of cultivation of land, soil management, and crop production. —**a·'gron·o+mist** *n.*

ag+ros+tol+o·gy (ˌægrə'stɒlədʒɪ) *n.* the branch of botany concerned with the study of grasses. [C19: from Greek *agrōstis* a type of grass + -LOGY]

a·ground (ə'graʊnd) *adv., adj.* (*postpositive*) on or onto the ground or bottom, as in shallow water.

ag+ryp+not+ic (ˌægrɪp'nɒtɪk) *adj.* **1.** inducing, relating to, or characterized by insomnia. ~*n.* **2.** a drug or agent that induces insomnia. [C20: from Greek *agrupnos* wakeful, from *agrein* to pursue + *hupnos* sleep]

agt. *abbrev. for:* **1.** agent. **2.** agreement.

a·guar+dien+te *Spanish.* (aɣwar'ðjente) *n.* any inferior brandy or similar spirit, esp. from Spain, Portugal, or South America. [C19: Spanish: burning water]

A·guas+ca+lien+tes (*Spanish* ˌaɣwaska'ljentes) *n.* **1.** a state in central Mexico. Pop.: 338 142 (1970). Area: 6472 sq. km (2499 sq. miles). **2.** a city in central Mexico, capital of Aguascalientes state, about 1900 m (6200 ft.) above sea level, with hot springs. Pop.: 221 538 (1975 est.).

a·gue ('eɪgjuː) *n.* **1.** malarial fever with successive stages of fever and chills. **2.** a fit of shivering. [C14: from Old French (*fievre*) *ague* acute fever; see ACUTE]

a·gue+weed ('eɪgjuːˌwiːd) *n.* **1.** a North American gentianaceous plant, *Gentiana quinquefolia,* that has clusters of pale blue-violet or white flowers. **2.** another name for **boneset.**

A·gul+has (ə'gʌləs) *n.* **Cape.** a headland in South Africa, the southernmost point of the African Continent.

ah (ɑː) *interj.* an exclamation expressing pleasure, pain, sympathy, etc., according to the intonation of the speaker.

a.h. *abbrev. for* ampere-hour.

A.H. (indicating years in the Muslim system of dating, numbered from the Hegira (622 A.D.)) *abbrev. for* anno Hegirae. [Latin]

a·ha (ɑː'hɑː) *interj.* an exclamation expressing triumph, surprise, etc., according to the intonation of the speaker.

A·hab ('eɪhæb) *n. Old Testament.* the king of Israel from approximately 869 to 850 B.C. and husband of Jezebel: rebuked by Elijah (I Kings 16:29–22:40).

A·has·u·e·rus (əˌhæzjuː'ɪərəs) *n. Old Testament.* a king of ancient Persia and husband of Esther, generally identified with Xerxes.

a·head (ə'hɛd) *adj.* **1.** (*postpositive*) in front; in advance. ~*adv.* **2.** at or in the front; in advance; before. **3.** onwards; forwards: *go straight ahead.* **4. ahead of. a.** in front of; at a further advanced position than. **b.** *Stock exchange.* in anticipation of: *the share price rose ahead of the annual figures.* **5.** *Informal.* **be ahead.** to have an advantage; be winning: *ahead on points.* **6. get ahead.** to advance or attain success.

a·hem (ə'hɛm) *interj.* a clearing of the throat, used to attract attention, express doubt, etc.

a·him+sa (ɑː'hɪmsɑː) *n.* (in Hindu, Buddhist, and Jainist philosophy) the law of reverence for, and nonviolence to, every form of life. [Sanskrit, from A-[1] + *himsā* injury]

a·his+tor·i·cal (ˌeɪhɪs'tɒrɪkəl) *or* **a·his+tor+ic** *adj.* not related to history; not historical.

A·hith·o·phel (ə'hɪθəˌfɛl) *or* **A·chit·o·phel** *n. Old Testament.* a member of David's council, who became one of Absalom's advisers in his rebellion and hanged himself when his advice was overruled (II Samuel 15:12–17:23).

Ah+med·a+bad *or* **Ah+mad·a+bad** ('ɑːmədəˌbɑːd) *n.* a city in

W India, capital of Gujarat state: famous for its mosque. Pop.: 1 585 544 (1971).
Ah+med+na+gar *or* **Ah+mad+na+gar** (ˌɑːməd'nʌgə) *n.* a city in W India, in Maharashtra: formerly one of the kingdoms of Deccan. Pop.: 118 236 (1971).
A ho+ri+zon *n.* the top layer of a soil profile, usually dark coloured and containing humus, from which the soluble salts have been leached. See **B horizon, C horizon.**
a·hoy (ə'hɔɪ) *interj. Nautical.* a hail used to call a ship or to attract attention.
AHQ *abbrev. for* Army Headquarters.
Ah·ri·man ('ɑːrɪmən) *n. Zoroastrianism.* the supreme evil spirit and diabolical opponent of Ormazd.
A·hu·ra Maz·da (ə'hʊərə 'mæzdə) *n. Zoroastrianism.* another name for **Ormazd.**
Ah+ve+nan+maa ('ɑhvɛnɑmmɑː) *n.* the Finnish name for the **Åland Islands.**
Ah+waz (ɑː'wɑːz) *or* **Ah+vaz** (ɑː'vɑːz) *n.* a town in SW Iran, on the Karun River. Pop.: 302 000 (1973 est.).
a·i ('ɑːɪ) *n., pl.* **a·is.** another name for **three-toed sloth** (see **sloth** (sense 1)). [C17: from Portuguese, from Tupi]
A.I. *abbrev. for* artificial insemination.
A.I.A. *abbrev. for* Associate of the Institute of Actuaries.
A.I.C.C. *abbrev. for* All India Congress Committee: the national assembly of the Indian National Congress.
aid (eɪd) *vb.* **1.** to give support to (someone to do something); help or assist. **2.** (*tr.*) to assist financially. ~*n.* **3.** assistance; help; support. **4.** a person, device, etc., that helps or assists: *a teaching aid.* **5.** (in medieval Europe; in England after 1066) a feudal payment made to the king or any lord by his vassals, usually on certain occasions such as the marriage of a daughter or the knighting of an eldest son. **6. in aid of.** *Brit. informal.* in support of; for the purpose of. [C15: via Old French *aidier* from Latin *adjūtāre* to help, from *juvāre* to help] —**'aid+er** *n.*
A.I.D. *abbrev. for:* **1.** acute infectious disease. **2.** artificial insemination (by) donor. **3.** Agency for International Development.
Ai·dan ('eɪdᵊn) *n.* **Saint.** died 651 A.D. Irish missionary in Northumbria, who founded the monastery at Lindisfarne (635).
aide (eɪd) *n.* **1.** short for **aide-de-camp. 2.** an assistant.
aide-de-camp *or* **aid-de-camp** ('eɪd də 'kɒŋ) *n., pl.* **aides-de-camp** *or* **aids-de-camp.** a military officer serving as personal assistant to a senior. Abbrev.: **A.D.C., ADC, a.d.c.** [C17: from French: camp assistant]
aide-mé·moire *French.* (ɛd me'mwaːr; *English* 'eɪd mɛm'wɑː) *n., pl.* ***aides-mé·moire*** (ɛd me'mwaːr; *English* 'eɪdz mɛm'wɑː). a memorandum or summary of the items of an agreement, etc. [from *aider* to help + *mémoire* memory]
Ai·din ('aɪdɪn) *n.* a variant spelling of **Aydin.**
A.I.F. *abbrev. for* Australian Imperial Force.
ai·glet ('eɪglɪt) *n.* a variant of **aglet.**
ai·grette *or* **ai·gret** ('eɪgrɛt, eɪ'grɛt) *n.* **1.** a long plume worn on hats or as a headdress, esp. one of long egret feathers. **2.** an ornament or piece of jewellery in imitation of a plume of feathers.
ai·guille (eɪ'gwiːl, 'eɪgwiːl) *n.* **1.** a rock mass or mountain peak shaped like a needle. **2.** an instrument for boring holes in rocks or masonry. [C19: French, literally: needle]
ai·guil+lette (ˌeɪgwɪ'lɛt) *n.* **1.** a metal tip or tag on loops of ornamental braid on military uniforms. **2.** a variant of **aglet.**
A.I.H. *abbrev. for* artificial insemination (by) husband.
ai·kid·o ('aɪkɪdəʊ) *n.* a Japanese system of self-defence employing similar principles to judo. [from Japanese, from *ai* to harmonize + *ki* control, breath + *do* way]
ai·ko·na ('aɪkɔːnə) *interj. S. African.* an informal word expressing strong negation. [from Zulu]
ail (eɪl) *vb.* **1.** (*tr.*) to trouble; afflict. **2.** (*intr.*) to feel unwell. [Old English *eglan* to trouble, from *egle* troublesome, painful, related to Gothic *agls* shameful]
ai·lan+thus (eɪ'lænθəs) *n., pl.* **+thus·es.** an E Asian simaroubaceous deciduous tree, *Ailanthus altissima,* planted in Europe and North America, having pinnate leaves, small greenish flowers, and winged fruits. Also called: **tree of heaven.** [C19: New Latin, from Amboinese *ai lanto* tree (of) the gods]
ai·ler+on ('eɪləˌrɒn) *n.* a flap hinged to the trailing edge of an aircraft wing to provide lateral control, as in a bank or roll. [C20: from French, diminutive of *aile* wing]
ail+ing ('eɪlɪŋ) *adj.* unwell, esp. over a long period.
ail+ment ('eɪlmənt) *n.* a slight but often persistent illness.
ai·lu+ro+phile (aɪ'lʊərəˌfaɪl) *n.* a person who likes cats. [C20: facetious coinage from Greek *ailuros* cat + -PHILE] —**ai·lu+ro+phil·i·a** (aɪˌlʊərə'fɪlɪə) *n.*
ai·lu+ro+phobe (aɪ'lʊərəˌfəʊb) *n.* a person who dislikes or is afraid of cats. [C20: from Greek *ailuros* cat + -PHOBE]
aim (eɪm) *vb.* **1.** to point (a weapon, missile, etc.) or direct (a blow) at a particular person or object; level. **2.** (*tr.*) to direct (satire, criticism, etc.) at a person, object, etc. **3.** (*intr.;* foll. by *at* or an infinitive) to propose or intend: *we aim to leave early.* **4.** (*intr.;* often foll. by *at* or *for*) to direct one's efforts or strive (towards): *to aim at better communications; to aim high.* ~*n.* **5.** the action of directing something at an object. **6.** the direction in which something is pointed; line of sighting (esp. in the phrase **to take aim**). **7.** the object at which something is aimed; target. **8.** intention; purpose. [C14: via Old French *aesmer* from Latin *aestimāre* to ESTIMATE]
aim+less ('eɪmlɪs) *adj.* having no goal, purpose, or direction. —**'aim+less+ly** *adv.* —**'aim+less+ness** *n.*
ain[1] (eɪn) *determiner.* a Scot. word for **own.**
a·in[2] ('ɑːjɪn) *n.* a variant spelling of **ayin.**
Ain (*French* ɛ̃) *n.* **1.** a department in E central France, in Rhône-Alpes region. Capital: Bourg. Pop.: 386 943 (1975). Area: 5785 sq. km (2256 sq. miles). **2.** a river in E France, rising in the Jura Mountains and flowing south to the Rhône. Length: 190 km (118 miles).
ain't (eɪnt) *Not standard. contraction of* am not, is not, are not, have not, *or* has not: *I ain't seen it.*
Usage. Although the interrogative form *ain't I?* would be a natural contraction of *am not I?,* it is generally avoided in spoken English and never used in formal English.
Ain+tab (aɪn'tɑːb) *n.* the former name (until 1921) of **Gaziantep.**
Ai·nu ('aɪnuː) *n.* **1.** (*pl.* **·nus** *or* **·nu**) a member of the aboriginal people of Japan, now mostly intermixed with Mongoloid immigrants whose skin colour is more yellowish. **2.** the language of this people, of no known relationships, still spoken in parts of Hokkaido and elsewhere. [Ainu: man]
aï·o·li (aɪ'əʊlɪ, eɪ-) *n.* garlic mayonnaise. [from French *ail* garlic]
air (ɛə) *n.* **1.** the mixture of gases that forms the earth's atmosphere. At sea level dry air has a density of 1.226 kilograms per sq. metre and consists of 78.08 per cent nitrogen, 20.95 per cent oxygen, 0.93 per cent argon, 0.03 per cent carbon dioxide, with smaller quantities of ozone and inert gases; water vapour varies between 0 and 4 per cent and in industrial areas sulphur gases may be present as pollutants. **2.** the space above and around the earth; sky. Related adj.: **aerial. 3.** breeze; slight wind. **4.** public expression; utterance: *to give air to one's complaints.* **5.** a distinctive quality: *an air of mystery.* **6.** a person's distinctive appearance, manner, or bearing. **7.** *Music.* **a.** a simple tune for either vocal or instrumental performance. **b.** another word for **aria. 8.** transportation in aircraft (esp. in the phrase **by air**). **9.** an archaic word for **breath** (senses 1-3). **10. clear the air.** to rid a situation of tension or discord by settling misunderstandings, etc. **11. give (someone) the air.** *Slang.* to reject or dismiss (someone). **12. in the air. a.** in circulation; current. **b.** in the process of being decided; unsettled. **13. into thin air.** leaving no trace behind. **14. on** (*or* **off**) **the air.** (not) in the act of broadcasting or (not) being broadcast on radio or television. **15. take the air.** to go out of doors, as for a short walk or ride. **16. up in the air. a.** uncertain. **b.** *Informal.* agitated or excited. **17. walk** (*or* **tread**) **on air.** to feel elated. **18.** (*modifier*) *Astrology.* of or relating to a group of three signs of the zodiac, Gemini, Libra, and Aquarius. Compare **earth** (sense 10), **fire** (sense 24), **water** (sense 12). ~*vb.* **19.** to expose or be exposed to the air so as to cool or freshen; ventilate: *to air a room.* **20.** to expose or be exposed to warm or heated air so as to dry: *to air linen.* **21.** (*tr.*) to make known publicly; display; publicize: *to air one's opinions.* [C13: via Old French and Latin from Greek *aēr* the lower atmosphere]
A·ïr ('ɑːɪə) *n.* a mountainous region of N central Niger, in the Sahara, rising to 1500 m (5000 ft.): a former native kingdom. Area: about 77 700 sq. km (30 000 sq. miles). Also called: **Asben, Azbine.**
A.I.R. *abbrev. for* All India Radio.
air a·lert *n. Military.* **1.** the condition in which combat aircraft are airborne and ready for an operation. **2.** a signal to prepare for this.
air bag *n.* a safety device in a car, consisting of a bag that inflates automatically in an accident and prevents the passengers from being thrown forwards.
air base *n.* a centre from which military aircraft operate. Also called: **air station.**
air bed *n.* an inflatable mattress.
air blad+der *n.* **1.** *Ichthyol.* an air-filled sac, lying above the alimentary canal in bony fishes, that regulates buoyancy at different depths by a variation in the pressure of the air. Also called: **swim bladder. 2.** any air-filled sac, such as one of the bladders of seaweeds.
air+boat ('ɛəˌbəʊt) *n.* another name for **swamp boat.**
air+borne ('ɛəˌbɔːn) *adj.* **1.** conveyed by or through the air. **2.** (of aircraft) flying; in the air.
air brake *n.* **1.** a brake operated by compressed air, esp. in heavy vehicles and trains. **2.** an articulated flap or small parachute for reducing the speed of an aircraft. Also called: **dive brake. 3.** a rotary fan or propeller connected to a shaft to reduce its speed.
air+brick ('ɛəˌbrɪk) *n. Chiefly Brit.* a brick with holes in it, put into the wall of a building for ventilation.
air bridge *n. Brit.* a link by air transport between two places, esp. two places separated by a stretch of sea.
air+brush ('ɛəˌbrʌʃ) *n.* an atomizer for spraying paint or varnish by means of compressed air.
air+burst ('ɛəˌbɜːst) *n.* the explosion of a bomb, shell, etc., in the air.
air+bus ('ɛəˌbʌs) *n.* an airliner operated over short distances.
air chief mar+shal *n.* a senior officer of the Royal Air Force and certain other air forces, of equivalent rank to admiral in the Royal Navy.
air com+mo+dore *n.* a senior officer of the Royal Air Force and certain other air forces, of equivalent rank to brigadier in the Army.
air-con·di·tion *vb.* (*tr.*) to apply air conditioning to.
air con+di·tion+ing *n.* a system or process for controlling the temperature and sometimes the humidity and purity of the air in a house, etc. —**air con+di·tion+er** *n.*
air-cool *vb.* (*tr.*) to cool (an engine, etc.) by a flow of air. Compare **water-cool.**

air cor·ri·dor *n.* an air route along which aircraft are allowed to fly.
air cov·er *n.* **a.** the support of military forces by additional airborne units. **b.** the aircraft providing this. Also called: **air support.**
air·craft ('ɛəˌkrɑːft) *n., pl.* ·**craft.** any machine capable of flying by means of buoyancy or aerodynamic forces, such as a glider, helicopter, or aeroplane.
air·craft car·ri·er *n.* a warship built with an extensive flat deck space for the launch and recovery of aircraft.
air·craft cloth *or* **fab·ric** *n.* variants of **aeroplane cloth.**
air·craft·man ('ɛəˌkrɑːftmən) *n., pl.* ·**men.** a serviceman of the most junior rank in the RAF. ~'**air·craft·ˌwom·an** *fem. n.*
air·crew ('ɛəˌkruː) *n.* the crew of an aircraft.
air cur·tain *n.* an air stream across a doorway to exclude draughts, etc.
air cush·ion *n.* **1.** an inflatable cushion, usually made of rubber or plastic. **2.** the pocket of air that supports a hovercraft. **3.** a form of pneumatic suspension consisting of an enclosed volume of air. See also **air spring.**
air cyl·in·der *n.* a cylinder containing air, esp. one fitted with a piston and used for damping purposes.
Air·drie ('ɛədrɪ) *n.* a burgh and town in W central Scotland, E of Glasgow: coal and iron industries. Pop.: 37 736 (1971).
air·drome ('ɛəˌdrəʊm) *n.* the U.S. name for **aerodrome.**
air·drop ('ɛəˌdrɒp) *n.* **1.** a delivery of supplies, troops, etc., from an aircraft by parachute. ~*vb.* ·**drops,** ·**drop·ping,** ·**dropped. 2.** (*tr.*) to deliver (supplies, etc.) by an airdrop.
air-dry *vb.* **-dries, -dry·ing, -dried.** (*tr.*) to dry by exposure to the air.
Aire (ɛə) *n.* a river in N England rising in the Pennines and flowing southeast mainly through West Yorkshire to the Ouse. Length: 112 km (70 miles).
Aire·dale ('ɛəˌdeɪl) *n.* a large rough-haired tan-coloured breed of terrier characterized by a black saddle-shaped patch on the back. Also called: **Airedale terrier.** [C19: name of a district in Yorkshire]
air em·bo·lism *n.* another name for **aeroembolism.**
air·field ('ɛəˌfiːld) *n.* a landing and taking-off area for aircraft, usually with permanent buildings.
air·flow ('ɛəˌfləʊ) *n.* the flow of air in a wind tunnel or past a moving aircraft, car, train, etc.; airstream.
air·foil ('ɛəˌfɔɪl) *n.* the U.S. name for **aerofoil.**
air force *n.* **1. a.** the branch of a nation's armed services primarily responsible for military aircraft. **b.** (*as modifier*): *an air-force base.* **2.** a formation in the U.S. and certain other air forces larger than an air division but smaller than an air command.
air·frame ('ɛəˌfreɪm) *n.* the body of an aircraft, excluding its engines.
air gas *n.* another name for **producer gas.**
air·glow ('ɛəˌgləʊ) *n.* the faint light from the upper atmosphere in the night sky, esp. in low latitudes.
air gun *n.* a gun discharged by means of compressed air.
air·head ('ɛəˌhɛd) *n. Military, chiefly U.S.* an area secured in hostile territory of sufficient size to allow the continuous supply of troops and equipment by air.
air hole *n.* **1.** a hole that allows the passage of air, esp. for ventilation. **2.** a section of open water in a frozen surface. **3.** a less common name for **air pocket** (sense 1).
air host·ess *n.* a stewardess on an airliner.
air·i·ly ('ɛərɪlɪ) *adv.* **1.** in a jaunty or high-spirited manner. **2.** in a light or delicate manner.
air·i·ness ('ɛərɪnɪs) *n.* **1.** the quality or condition of being fresh, light, or breezy. **2.** lightness of heart; gaiety.
air·ing ('ɛərɪŋ) *n.* **1. a.** exposure to air or warmth, as for drying or ventilation. **b.** (*as modifier*): *airing cupboard.* **2.** an excursion in the open air. **3.** exposure to public debate.
air-in·take *n.* **1. a.** an opening in an aircraft through which air is drawn, esp. for the engines. **b.** the amount of air drawn in. **2.** the part of a carburettor or similar device through which air enters an internal-combustion engine. **3.** any opening, etc., through which air enters.
air jack·et *n.* **1.** an air-filled envelope or compartment surrounding a machine or part to reduce the rate at which heat is transferred to or from it. Compare **water jacket. 2.** a less common name for **life jacket.**
air·less ('ɛəlɪs) *adj.* **1.** lacking fresh air; stuffy or sultry. **2.** devoid of air. —'**air·less·ness** *n.*
air let·ter *n.* another name for **aerogram** (sense 1).
air·lift ('ɛəˌlɪft) *n.* **1.** the transportation by air of passengers, troops, cargo, etc., esp. when other routes are blocked. ~*vb.* **2.** (*tr.*) to transport by an airlift.
air·line ('ɛəˌlaɪn) *n.* **1. a.** a system or organization that provides scheduled flights for passengers or cargo. **b.** (*as modifier*): *an airline pilot.* **2.** a hose or tube carrying air under pressure. **3.** *Chiefly U.S.* a beeline.
air·lin·er ('ɛəˌlaɪnə) *n.* a large passenger aircraft.
air·lock ('ɛəˌlɒk) *n.* **1.** a bubble in a pipe causing an obstruction or stoppage to the flow. **2.** an airtight chamber with regulated air pressure used to gain access to a space that has air under pressure.
air mail *n.* **1.** the system of conveying mail by aircraft. **2.** mail conveyed by aircraft. ~*adj.* **air-mail. 3.** of, used for, or concerned with air mail. ~*vb.* **air-mail. 4.** (*tr.*) to send by air mail.
air·man ('ɛəmən) *n., pl.* ·**men.** an aviator, esp. one serving in the armed forces. —'**air·ˌwom·an** *fem. n.*
air mar·shal *n.* **1.** a senior Royal Air Force officer of equivalent rank to a vice admiral in the Royal Navy. **2.** a Royal Australian Air Force officer of the highest rank.
air mass *n.* a large body of air having characteristics of temperature, moisture, and pressure that are approximately uniform horizontally.
air mile *n.* another name for **nautical mile** (sense 1).
air-mind·ed *adj.* interested in or promoting aviation or aircraft. —'**air-mind·ed·ness** *n.*
Air Of·fic·er *n.* an officer in the Royal Air Force above the rank of Group Captain.
air·plane ('ɛəˌpleɪn) *n.* the U.S. name for **aeroplane.**
air plant *n.* another name for **epiphyte.**
air pock·et *n.* **1.** a localized region of low air density or a descending air current, causing an aircraft to suffer an abrupt decrease in height. **2.** any pocket of air that prevents the flow of a liquid or gas, as in a pipe.
air·port ('ɛəˌpɔːt) *n.* a landing and taking-off area for civil aircraft, usually with surfaced runways and aircraft maintenance and passenger facilities.
air pow·er *n.* the strength of a nation's air force.
air pump *n.* a device for pumping air in or out of something.
air raid *n.* **a.** an attack by hostile aircraft or missiles. **b.** (*as modifier*): *an air-raid shelter.*
air-raid ward·en *n.* a member of a civil defence organization responsible for enforcing regulations, etc., during an air attack.
air ri·fle *n.* a rifle discharged by compressed air.
airs (ɛəz) *pl. n.* affected manners intended to impress others (esp. in the phrases **give oneself airs, put on airs**).
air sac *n.* **1.** any of the membranous air-filled extensions of the lungs of birds, which increase the efficiency of gaseous exchange in the lungs. **2.** any of the thin-walled extensions of the tracheae of insects having a similar function.
air scoop *n.* a device fitted to the surface of an aircraft to provide air pressure or ventilation from the airflow.
Air Scout *n.* a scout belonging to a scout troop that specializes in flying, gliding, etc. See **Scout.**
air·screw ('ɛəˌskruː) *n. Brit.* an aircraft propeller.
air-sea res·cue *n.* an air rescue at sea.
air shaft *n.* a shaft for ventilation, esp. in a mine or tunnel.
air·ship ('ɛəˌʃɪp) *n.* a lighter-than-air self-propelled craft. Also called: **dirigible.**
air·sick ('ɛəˌsɪk) *adj.* sick or nauseated from travelling in an aircraft. —'**air·ˌsick·ness** *n.*
air sock *n.* another name for **windsock.**
air·space ('ɛəˌspeɪs) *n.* the atmosphere above the earth or part of the earth, esp. the atmosphere above a country deemed to be under its jurisdiction.
air·speed ('ɛəˌspiːd) *n.* the speed of an aircraft relative to the air in which it moves. Compare **groundspeed.**
air spray *n.* another name for **aerosol** (sense 3).
air spring *n. Mechanical engineering.* an enclosed pocket of air used to absorb shock or sudden fluctuations of load.
air sta·tion *n.* an airfield, usually smaller than an airport but having facilities for the maintenance of aircraft.
air·stream ('ɛəˌstriːm) *n.* **1.** a wind, esp. at a high altitude. **2.** a current of moving air.
air·strip ('ɛəˌstrɪp) *n.* a cleared area for the landing and taking off of aircraft; runway. Also called: **landing strip.**
airt (ɛət) *or* **airth** (ɛəθ) *n. Scot.* a direction or point of the compass, esp. the direction of the wind. [C14: from Scots Gaelic *aird* point of the compass, height]
air ter·mi·nal *n. Brit.* a building in a city from which air passengers are taken by road or rail to an airport.
air·tight ('ɛəˌtaɪt) *adj.* **1.** not permitting the passage of air either in or out. **2.** having no weak points; invulnerable: *an airtight argument.*
air-to-air *adj.* operating between aircraft in flight.
air traf·fic *n.* **1.** the organized movement of aircraft within a given space. **2.** the passengers, cargo, or mail carried by aircraft.
air-traf·fic con·trol *n.* an organization that determines the altitude, speed, and direction at which planes fly in a given area, giving instructions to pilots by radio.
air tur·bine *n.* a small turbine driven by compressed air, esp. one used as a starter for engines.
air valve *n.* **1.** a device for controlling the flow of air in a pipe. **2.** a valve for exhausting air from a fluid system, esp. from a central-heating installation. See also **bleed valve.**
air ves·i·cle *or* **cav·i·ty** *n.* **1.** a large air-filled intercellular space in some aquatic plants. **2.** a large intercellular space in a leaf into which a stoma opens.
air vice-mar·shal *n.* **1.** a senior Royal Air Force officer of equivalent rank to a rear admiral in the Royal Navy. **2.** a Royal Australian Air Force officer of the second highest rank.
air·waves ('ɛəˌweɪvz) *pl. n. Informal.* radio waves used in radio and television broadcasting.
air·way ('ɛəˌweɪ) *n.* **1.** an air route, esp. one that is fully equipped with emergency landing fields, navigational aids, etc. **2.** a passage for ventilation, esp. in a mine.
air·wor·thy ('ɛəˌwɜːðɪ) *adj.* (of an aircraft) safe to fly.
air·y ('ɛərɪ) *adj.* **air·i·er, air·i·est. 1.** abounding in fresh air. **2.** spacious or uncluttered. **3.** of or relating to air. **4.** weightless and insubstantial: *an airy gossamer.* **5.** light and graceful in movement. **6.** buoyant and gay; lively. **7.** visionary; fanciful: *airy promises; airy plans.* **8.** having no material substance: *airy spirits.* **9.** high up in the air; lofty. **10.** performed in the air; aerial. **11.** *Informal.* nonchalant; superficial.

air·y-fair·y ('ɛərɪ'fɛərɪ) *adj.* **1.** *Informal.* fanciful and unrealistic: *an airy-fairy scheme.* **2.** delicate to the point of being insubstantial; light. [C19: from Tennyson's poem *Lillian* (1830), where the central figure is described as "Airy, fairy Lillian"]

A·i·sha *or* **A·ye·sha** ('ɑːiːˌʃɑː) *n.* ?613–678 A.D., the favourite wife of Mohammed; daughter of Abu Bekr.

aisle (aɪl) *n.* **1.** a passageway separating seating areas in a theatre, church, etc.; gangway. **2.** a lateral division in a church flanking the nave or chancel. **3. (rolling) in the aisles.** *Informal.* (of an audience) overcome with laughter. [C14 *ele* (later *aile, aisle,* through confusion with *isle* (island)), via Old French from Latin *āla* wing] —**aisled** *adj.* —'**aisle+less** *adj.*

Aisne (eɪn; *French* ɛn) *n.* **1.** a department of NE France, in Picardy region. Capital: Laon. Pop.: 549 372 (1975). Area: 7428 sq. km (2897 sq. miles). **2.** a river in N France, rising in the Argonne Forest and flowing northwest and west to the River Oise: scene of several battles during World War I. Length: 282 km (175 miles).

ait (eɪt) *or* **eyot** *n. Brit. dialect.* an islet, esp. in a river. [Old English *ȳgett* small island, from *ieg* ISLAND]

aitch (eɪtʃ) *n.* the letter *h* or the sound represented by it: *he drops his aitches.* [C16: a phonetic spelling]

aitch+bone ('eɪtʃˌbəʊn) *n.* **1.** the rump bone or floor of the pelvis in cattle. **2.** a cut of beef from or including the rump bone. [C15 *hach-boon,* altered from earlier *nache-bone, nagebone* (*a nache* mistaken for *an ache, an aitch;* compare ADDER); *nache* buttock, via Old French from Late Latin *natica,* from Latin *natis* buttock]

Ait·ken ('eɪtkɪn) *n.* **1. Rob·ert Grant.** 1864–1951, U.S. astronomer who discovered over three thousand double stars. **2. Wil·liam Max·well.** See **Beaverbrook.**

Aix-en-Pro·vence (*French* ɛks ɑ̃ prɔ'vɑ̃ːs) *n.* a city and spa in SE France: the medieval capital of Provence. Pop.: 114 014 (1975). Also called: **Aix.**

Aix-la-Cha·pelle (*French* ɛks la ʃa'pɛl) *n.* the French name for **Aachen.**

Aí+yi+na ('ejina) *n.* transliteration of the Modern Greek name for **Aegina.**

A.J.A. *abbrev. for* Australian Journalists' Association.

A·jac+cio (ə'dʒætsɪˌəʊ, -'dʒeɪ-) *n.* the capital of Corsica, a port on the W coast. Pop.: 44 659 (1968).

a·jar[1] (ə'dʒɑː) *adj.* (*postpositive*), *adv.* (esp. of a door or window) slightly open. [C18: altered form of obsolete *on char,* literally: on the turn; *char,* from Old English *cierran* to turn]

a·jar[2] (ə'dʒɑː) *adj.* (*postpositive*) not in harmony. [C19: altered form of *at jar* at discord. See JAR[2]]

A·jax ('eɪdʒæks) *n. Greek myth.* **1.** the son of Telamon; a Greek hero of the Trojan War who killed himself in vexation when Achilles' armour was given to Odysseus. **2.** called *Ajax the Lesser,* a Locrian king, a swift-footed Greek hero of the Trojan War.

A.J.C. *abbrev. for* Australian Jockey Club.

Aj+mer (ʌdʒ'mɪə) *n.* a city in NW India, in Rajasthan: textile centre. Pop.: 262 851 (1971).

A·kad+e·mi (ə'kɑːdəmɪ) *n.* (in India) a learned society.

A·kan ('ɑːkɑːn) *n.* **1.** (*pl.* **·kan** *or* **·kans**) a member of a people of Ghana and the E Ivory Coast. **2.** the language of this people, having two chief dialects, Fanti and Twi, and belonging to the Kwa branch of the Niger-Congo family.

Ak·bar ('ækbɑː) *n.* called *Akbar the Great.* 1542–1605, Mogul emperor of India (1556–1605), who extended the Mogul empire to include N India.

A·ke+la (ɑː'keɪlə) *n. Brit.* the adult leader of a pack of Cub Scouts. U.S. equivalent: **Den Mother.** [C20: after a character in Kipling's *The Jungle Book* (1894–95), who is the leader of a wolfpack]

a·kene (ə'kiːn) *n.* a variant spelling of **achene.**

A·kha·ï·a (ˌaka'ia) *n.* transliteration of the modern Greek name for **Achaea.**

a·kha+ra (ə'kɑːrɑː) *n.* (in India) a gymnasium.

Ak·he·na·ten *or* **Ak·he·na·ton** (ˌækə'nɑːtᵊn) *n.* original name *Amenhotep IV.* died ?1358 B.C., king of Egypt, of the 18th dynasty; he moved his capital from Thebes to Tell El Amarna and introduced the cult of Aten.

Akh·ma·to·va (*Russian* ax'matəvə) *n.* **An·na** ('annə). pseudonym of *Anna Gorenko.* 1889–1966, Russian poetess: noted for her concise and intensely personal lyrics.

Ak·i·hi·to (ˌækɪ'hiːtəʊ) *n.* born 1933, crown prince of Japan.

a·kim+bo (ə'kɪmbəʊ) *adj.* (*postpositive*), *adv.* with hands on hips and elbows projecting outwards. [C15: *in kenebowe,* literally: in keen bow, that is, in a sharp curve]

a·kin (ə'kɪn) *adj.* (*postpositive*) **1.** related by blood; of the same kin. **2.** (often foll. by *to*) having similar characteristics, properties, etc.

Ak+kad *or* **Ac+cad** ('ækæd) *n.* **1.** a city on the Euphrates in N Babylonia, the centre of a major empire and civilization (2360–2180 B.C.). Ancient name: **Agade. 2.** an ancient region lying north of Babylon, from which the Akkadian language and culture is named.

Ak+ka·di·an *or* **Ac+ca+di·an** (ə'kædɪən, ə'keɪ-) *n.* **1.** a member of an ancient Semitic people who lived in central Mesopotamia in the second millennium B.C. **2.** the extinct language of this people, belonging to the E Semitic subfamily of the Afro-Asiatic family. ~*adj.* **3.** of or relating to this people or their language.

Ak+ker+man (*Russian* akɪr'man) *n.* the former name (until 1946) of **Byelgorod-Dnestrovski.**

Ak+mo+linsk (*Russian* ak'mɔlinsk) *n.* the former name (until 1961) of **Tselinograd.**

Ak+ron ('ækrən) *n.* a city in NE Ohio. Pop.: 261 520 (1973 est.).

Ak+sum *or* **Ax·um** ('ɑːksʊm) *n.* an ancient town in N Ethiopia, in Tigré province: capital of the Aksumite Empire (1st to 6th centuries A.D.). According to tradition, the Ark of the Covenant was brought here from Jerusalem.

Ak+tyu+binsk (*Russian* ak'tjuːbinsk) *n.* an industrial city in the Soviet Union, in the Kazakh SSR. Pop.: 175 000 (1975 est.).

A·ku+re (ə'kuːre) *n.* a city in SW Nigeria, capital of Ondo state: agricultural trade centre. Pop.: 71 106 (1963).

ak+va+vit ('ɑːkvɑːˌviːt) *n.* a variant spelling of **aquavit.**

Al *the chemical symbol for* aluminium.

AL *international car registration for* Albania.

al. *abbrev. for* alcohol *or* alcoholic.

A.L. *or* **AL** *abbrev. for* Anglo-Latin.

-al[1] *suffix forming adjectives.* of; related to; connected with: *functional; sectional; tonal.* [from Latin *-ālis*]

-al[2] *suffix forming nouns.* the act or process of doing what is indicated by the verb stem: *rebuttal; recital; renewal.* [via Old French *-aille, -ail,* from Latin *-ālia,* neuter plural used as substantive, from *-ālis* -AL[1]]

-al[3] *suffix forming nouns.* **1.** indicating an aliphatic aldehyde containing six or more carbon atoms: *hexanal.* **2.** (*not used systematically*) indicating any aldehyde: *salicylal.* **3.** indicating a pharmaceutical product: *phenobarbital.* [shortened from ALDEHYDE]

a·la ('eɪlə) *n., pl.* **a·lae** ('eɪliː). **1.** *Zoology.* a wing or flat winglike process or structure, such as a part of some bones and cartilages. **2.** *Botany.* a winglike part, such as one of the wings of a sycamore seed or one of the flat petals of a sweet pea flower.

à la (ɑː lɑː, æ lə; *French* a la) *prep.* **1.** in the manner or style of. **2.** as prepared in (a particular place) or by or for (a particular person). [C17: from French, short for *à la mode de* in the style of]

Ala. *abbrev. for* Alabama.

Al·a+bam·a (ˌælə'bæmə) *n.* **1.** a state of the southeastern U.S., on the Gulf of Mexico: consists of coastal and W lowlands crossed by the Tombigbee, Black Warrior, and Alabama Rivers, with parts of the Tennessee Valley and Cumberland Plateau in the north; noted for producing cotton and white marble. Capital: Montgomery. Pop.: 3 444 165 (1970). Area: 131 333 sq. km (50 708 sq. miles). Abbrevs.: **Ala.** or (with zip code) **AL 2.** a river in Alabama, flowing southwest to the Mobile and Tensaw Rivers. Length: 507 km (315 miles). —ˌ**Al·a+'bam+i·an** *adj.*

al·a+bas+ter ('æləˌbɑːstə, -ˌbæstə) *n.* **1.** a fine-grained usually white, opaque, or translucent variety of gypsum used for statues, vases, etc. **2.** a variety of hard semitranslucent calcite, often banded like marble. ~*adj.* **3.** of or resembling alabaster. [C14: from Old French *alabastre,* from Latin *alabaster,* from Greek *alabastros*] —ˌ**al·a+'bas+trine** *adj.*

à la carte (ɑː lɑː 'kɑːt, æ lə; *French* a la 'kart) *adj., adv.* **1.** (of a menu or a section of a menu) having dishes listed separately and individually priced. Compare **table d'hôte. 2.** (of a dish) offered on such a menu. [C19: from French, literally: according to the card]

a·lack (ə'læk) *or* **a·lack·a·day** (ə'lækəˌdeɪ) *interj.* an archaic or poetic word for **alas.** [C15: from *a* ah! + *lack* loss, LACK]

a·lac+ri·ty (ə'lækrɪtɪ) *n.* liveliness or briskness. [C15: from Latin *alacritās,* from *alacer* lively] —**a·'lac+ri+tous** *adj.*

A·la Dağ *or* **A·la Dagh** (*Turkish* ɑ'lɑ dɑː) *n.* **1.** the E part of the Taurus Mountains, in SE Turkey, rising over 3600 m (12 000 ft.). **2.** a mountain range in E Turkey, rising over 3300 m (11 000 ft.). **3.** a mountain range in NE Turkey, rising over 3000 m (10 000 ft.).

A·lad·din (ə'lædɪn) *n.* (in *The Arabian Nights' Entertainments*) a poor youth who obtains a magic lamp and ring, with which he summons genies who grant his wishes.

A·la+gez *or* **A·la+göz** (ˌala'gœz) *n.* the Turkish name for **Aragats.**

A·la+go+as (*Portuguese* ˌala'goas) *n.* a state in NE Brazil, on the Atlantic coast. Capital: Maceió. Pop.: 1 588 109 (1970). Area: 30 776 sq. km (11 031 sq. miles).

A·lai (ɑː'laɪ) *n.* a mountain range in the S Soviet Union, in the SW Kirghiz SSR, running from the Tien Shan range in China into the Tadzhik SSR. Average height: 4800 m (16 000 ft.), rising over 5850 m (19 500 ft.).

A·lain-Four·nier (*French* alɛ̃ fur'nje) *n.* pen name of *Henri-Alban Fournier.* 1886–1914, French novelist; author of *Le Grand Meaulnes* (1913; translated as *The Lost Domain,* 1959).

à la king (ɑː lɑː 'kɪŋ, æ lə) *adj.* (*usually postpositive*) cooked in a cream sauce with mushrooms and green peppers.

al·a+me·da (ˌælə'meɪdə) *n. Chiefly southwestern U.S.* a public walk or promenade lined with trees, often poplars.

Al·a+mein ('æləˌmeɪn) *n.* see **El Alamein.**

Al·a+mo ('æləˌməʊ) *n.* **the.** a mission in San Antonio, Texas, the site of a siege and massacre in 1836 by Mexican forces under Santa Anna of a handful of American rebels fighting for Texan independence from Mexico.

à la mode (ɑː lɑː 'məʊd, æ lə; *French* a la 'mɔd) *adj.* **1.** fashionable in style, design, etc. **2.** (of meats) braised with vegetables in wine. **3.** *Chiefly U.S.* (of desserts) served with ice cream. [C17: from French: according to the fashion]

a·la+mode ('æləˌməʊd) *n.* a soft light silk used for shawls and dresses, esp. in the 19th century. See also **surah.**

Al·an·brooke ('ælənˌbrʊk) *n.* **1st Viscount,** title of *Alan Francis*

Brooke. 1883–1963, British field marshal; chief of Imperial General Staff (1941–46).

Å·land Is+lands ('ɑːlənd, 'ɔːlənd; *Swedish* 'oːland) *pl. n.* a group of over 6000 islands under Finnish administration, in the Gulf of Bothnia. Capital: Mariehamn. Pop.: 21 500 (1968). Finnish name: **Ahvenanmaa.**

al·a+nine ('æləˌniːn, -ˌnaɪn) *n.* a sweet-tasting aliphatic amino acid that occurs in many proteins and has several isomeric forms; aminoproprionic acid. Formula: $CH_3CH(NH_2)COOH$. [C19: from German *Alanin,* from AL(DEHYDE) + *-an-* (euphonic infix) + *-in* -INE²]

a·lan+nah (ə'lænə) *interj. Irish.* my child: used as a term of address or endearment. [from Irish Gailic *a leanbh*]

a·lap (ə'lɑːp) *n.* Indian vocal music without words.

a·lar ('eɪlə) *adj.* relating to, resembling, or having wings or alae. [C19: from Latin *āla* a wing]

A·lar·cón (*Spanish* ˌalar'kon) *n.* **Pe·dro An·to·nio de** ('peðro an'tonjo ðe). 1833–91, Spanish novelist and short-story writer, noted for his humorous sketches of rural life, esp. in *The Three-Cornered Hat* (1874).

Al·a·ric ('ælərɪk) *n.* ?370–410 A.D., king of the Visigoths, who served under the Roman emperor Theodosius I but later invaded Greece and Italy, capturing Rome in 410.

a·larm (ə'lɑːm) *vb.* (*tr.*) **1.** to fill with apprehension, anxiety, or fear. **2.** to warn about danger; alert. ~*n.* **3.** fear or terror aroused by awareness of danger; fright. **4.** apprehension or uneasiness: *the idea of failing filled him with alarm.* **5.** a noise, signal, etc., warning of danger. **6.** any device that transmits such a warning: *a burglar alarm.* **7. a.** the device in an alarm clock that triggers off the bell or buzzer. **b.** short for **alarm clock. 8.** *Archaic.* a call to arms. **9.** *Fencing.* a warning or challenge made by stamping the front foot. [C14: from Old French *alarme,* from Old Italian *all'arme* to arms; see ARM²] —**a·'larm+ing** *adj.* —**a·'larm+ing+ly** *adv.*

a·larm clock *n.* a clock with a mechanism that sounds at a set time: used esp. for waking a person up.

a·larm+ist (ə'lɑːmɪst) *n.* **1.** a person who alarms or attempts to alarm others needlessly or without due grounds. **2.** a person who is easily alarmed. ~*adj.* **3.** characteristic of an alarmist. —**a·'larm+ism** *n.*

a·lar+um (ə'lærəm, -'lɑːr-, -'lɛər-) *n.* **1.** *Archaic.* an alarm, esp. a call to arms. **2.** (used as a stage direction, esp. in Elizabethan drama) a loud disturbance or conflict (esp. in the phrase **alarums and excursions**). [C15: variant of ALARM]

a·lar·y ('eɪlərɪ, 'æ-) *adj.* of, relating to, or shaped like wings. [C17: from Latin *ālārius,* from *āla* wing]

a·las (ə'læs) *interj.* an exclamation of grief, compassion, or alarm. [C13: from Old French *ha las!* oh wretched!; *las* from Latin *lassus* weary]

Alas. *abbrev. for* Alaska.

A·las+ka (ə'læskə) *n.* **1.** the largest state of the U.S., in the extreme northwest of North America: the aboriginal inhabitants are Eskimos; the earliest White settlements were made by the Russians. It is mostly mountainous and volcanic, rising over 6000 m (20 000 ft.), with the Yukon basin in the central region; large areas are covered by tundra; it has important mineral resources (chiefly coal, oil, and natural gas). Capital: Willow South. Pop.: 302 173 (1970). Area: 1 518 859 sq. km (586 432 sq. miles). Abbrevs.: **Alas.** or (with zip code) **AK 2. Gulf of.** the N part of the Pacific, between the Alaska Peninsula and the Alexander Archipelago. —**A·'las+kan** *adj., n.*

A·las+ka High+way *n.* a road extending from Dawson Creek, British Columbia, to Fairbanks, Alaska: built by the U.S. Army (1942). Length: 2452 km (1523 miles). Also called: **Alcan Highway.**

A·las+ka Pen+in+su+la *n.* an extension of the mainland of SW Alaska between the Pacific and the Bering Sea, ending in the Aleutian Islands. Length: about 644 km (400 miles).

A·las+ka Range *n.* a mountain range in S central Alaska. Highest peak: Mount McKinley, 6090 m (20 300 ft.).

a·late ('eɪleɪt) *adj.* having wings or winglike extensions. [C17: from Latin *ālātus,* from *āla* wing]

alb (ælb) *n. Christianity.* a long white linen vestment with sleeves worn by priests and others. [Old English *albe,* from Medieval Latin *alba (vestis)* white (clothing)]

Alb. *abbrev. for* Albania(n).

Al·ba (*Spanish* 'alβa) *n.* see (Duke of) **Alva.**

Al+ba+ce·te (*Spanish* ˌalβa'θete) *n.* a city in SE Spain. Pop.: 93 233 (1970).

al+ba+core ('ælbəˌkɔː) *n.* a tunny, *Thunnus alalunga,* occurring mainly in warm regions of the Atlantic and Pacific. It has very long pectoral fins and is a valued food fish. Also called: **long-fin tunny.** [C16: from Portuguese *albacor,* from Arabic *al-bakrah,* from *al* the + *bakr* young camel]

Al·ba Lon+ga ('ælbə 'lɒŋgə) *n.* a city of ancient Latium, southeast of modern Rome: the legendary birthplace of Romulus and Remus.

Al+ba+ni·a (æl'beɪnɪə) *n.* a republic in SE Europe, on the Balkan Peninsula: became independent in 1912 after more than four centuries of Turkish rule; established as a republic (1946) under Communist rule. It is generally mountainous, rising over 2700 m (9000 ft.), with extensive forests. Language: Albanian. Currency: lek. Capital: Tirana. Pop.: 2 322 600 (1973). Area: 28 749 sq. km (11 100 sq. miles). Official name: **Socialist People's Republic of Albania.**

Al+ba+ni·an (æl'beɪnɪən) *n.* **1.** the official language of Albania: of uncertain relationship within the Indo-European family, but thought to be related to ancient Illyrian. **2. a.** a native, citizen, or inhabitant of Albania. **b.** a native speaker of Albanian. ~*adj.* **3.** of or relating to Albania, its people, or their language.

Al+ba+ny ('ɔːlbənɪ) *n.* **1.** a city in E New York State, on the Hudson River: the state capital. Pop.: 111 373 (1973 est.). **2.** a river in central Canada, flowing east and northeast to James Bay. Length: 982 km (610 miles).

al+ba+ta (æl'beɪtə) *n.* a variety of German silver consisting of nickel, copper, and zinc. [C19: from Latin, literally: clothed in white, from *albus* white]

al+ba+tross ('ælbəˌtrɒs) *n.* **1.** any large oceanic bird of the genera *Diomedea* and *Phoebetria,* family *Diomedeidae,* of cool southern oceans: order *Procellariiformes* (petrels). They have long narrow wings and are noted for a powerful gliding flight. See also **wandering albatross. 2.** *Golf.* a score of three strokes under par for a hole. [C17: from Portuguese *alcatraz* pelican, from Arabic *al-ghattās,* from *al* the + *ghattās* white-tailed sea eagle; influenced by Latin *albus* white]

al+be+do (æl'biːdəʊ) *n.* the ratio of the intensity of light reflected from an object, such as a planet, to that of the light it receives from the sun. [C19: from Church Latin: whiteness, from Latin *albus* white]

al+be+it (ɔːl'biːɪt) *conj.* even though. [C14 *al be it,* that is, although it be (that)]

Al+be+marle Sound ('ælbəˌmɑːl) *n.* an inlet of the Atlantic in NE North Carolina. Length: about 96 km (60 miles).

Al·bé·niz (*Spanish* al'βeniθ) *n.* **I·sa·ac** (ˌisa'ak). 1860–1909, Spanish composer; noted for piano pieces inspired by folk music, such as the suite *Iberia.*

Al·ber·ich (*German* 'albərɪç) *n.* (in medieval German legend) the king of the dwarfs and guardian of the treasures of the Nibelungs.

al+bert ('ælbət) *n.* **1.** a kind of watch chain usually attached to a waistcoat. **2.** *Brit.* a standard size of notepaper, 6 × 3⅞ inches. [C19: named after Prince ALBERT]

Al+bert¹ ('ælbət) *n.* **Lake.** a lake in E Africa, between Zaïre and Uganda in the Great Rift Valley, 660 m (2200 ft.) above sea level: a source of the Nile, fed by the Victoria Nile, which leaves as the Albert Nile. Area: 5345 sq. km (2064 sq. miles). Official name: **Lake Mobutu.**

Al·bert² ('ælbət) *n.* **Prince.** full name *Albert Francis Charles Augustus Emmanuel of Saxe-Coburg-Gotha.* 1819–61, Prince Consort of Queen Victoria of England.

Al·bert I *n.* **1.** *c.* 1255–1308, king of Germany (1298–1308). **2.** 1875–1934, king of the Belgians (1909–34). **3.** called *Albert the Bear. c.* 1100–70. German military leader: first margrave of Brandenburg.

Al+ber+ta (æl'bɜːtə) *n.* a province of W Canada: mostly prairie, with the Rocky Mountains in the southwest. Capital: Edmonton. Pop.: 1 838 037 (1976). Area: 661 188 sq. km (255 285 sq. miles). Abbrev.: **Alta.**

Al+bert Ed+ward *n.* a mountain in SE New Guinea, in the Owen Stanley Range. Height: 3993 m (13 100 ft.).

Al·ber·ti (*Italian* al'bɛrti) *n.* **Le·on Bat·tis·ta** (le'ɔn bat'tiːsta). 1404–72, Italian Renaissance architect, painter, writer, and musician; among his architectural designs are the façades of Sta. Maria Novella at Florence and S. Francesco at Rimini.

al+bert+ite ('ælbəˌtaɪt) *n.* a black solid variety of bitumen that has a conchoidal fracture and occurs in veins in oil-bearing strata. [C19: named after *Albert* county, New Brunswick, Canada, where it is mined]

Al·ber·tus Mag·nus (æl'bɜːtəs 'mægnəs) *n.* **Saint.** original name *Albert, Count von Böllstadt.* ?1193–1280, German scholastic philosopher; teacher of Thomas Aquinas and commentator on Aristotle. Feast day: Nov. 15.

al+bes+cent (æl'bɛsᵊnt) *adj.* shading into, growing, or becoming white. [C19: from Latin *albēscere* to grow white, from *albus* white] —**al·'bes+cence** *n.*

Al·bi (*French* al'bi) *n.* a town in S France: connected with the Albigensian heresy and the crusade against it. Pop.: 49 456 (1975).

Al+bi+gen+ses (ˌælbɪ'dʒɛnsiːz) *pl. n.* members of a Manichean sect that flourished in S France from the 11th to the 13th century. [from Medieval Latin: inhabitants of Albi, from *Albiga* ALBI] —ˌ**Al+bi+'gen+si·an** *adj.* —ˌ**Al+bi+'gen+si·an+ism** *n.*

al+bi+no (æl'biːnəʊ) *n., pl.* **+nos. 1.** a person with congenital absence of pigmentation in the skin, eyes, and hair. **2.** any animal or plant that is deficient in pigment. [C18: via Portuguese from Spanish, from *albo* white, from Latin *albus*] —**al+bin+ic** (æl'bɪnɪk) *or* ˌ**al+bin+'is+tic** *adj.* —**al+bi+nism** ('ælbɪˌnɪzəm) *n.* —**al+bi+not+ic** (ˌælbɪ'nɒtɪk) *adj.*

Al·bi·no·ni (*Italian* ˌalbi'noːni) *n.* **To·ma·so** (to'maːzo). 1671–1750, Italian composer and violinist. He wrote concertos and over 50 operas.

Al·bi·nus (æl'biːnəs) *n.* another name for **Alcuin.**

Al+bi+on ('ælbɪən) *n. Archaic or poetic.* Britain or England. [C13: from Latin, of Celtic origin]

al+bite ('ælbaɪt) *n.* a white, bluish-green, or reddish-grey widely occurring feldspar mineral of the plagioclase series consisting of an aluminium silicate of sodium. It is used in the manufacture of glass and ceramics and as a gemstone. Formula: $NaAlSi_3O_8$. [C19: from Latin *albus* white] —**al+bit+ic** (æl-'bɪtɪk) *adj.*

Al·boin ('ælbɔɪn, -bəʊɪn) *n.* died 573 A.D., king of the Lombards (565–73); conqueror of N Italy.

Å+borg (*Danish* 'ɔlbɔr) *n.* a variant spelling of **Aalborg.**

al+bum ('ælbəm) *n.* **1.** a book or binder consisting of blank pages, pockets, or envelopes for keeping photographs, stamps, autographs, drawings, poems, etc. **2.** a booklike holder containing sleeves for gramophone records. **3.** one or more long-playing records released as a single item. **4.** *Chiefly Brit.* an anthology, usually large and illustrated. [C17: from Latin: blank tablet, from *albus* white]

al+bu+men ('ælbjʊmɪn, -mɛn) *n.* **1.** the white of an egg; the nutritive and protective gelatinous substance, mostly an albumin, that surrounds the yolk. **2.** a rare name for **endosperm. 3.** a variant spelling of **albumin.** [C16: from Latin: white of an egg, from *albus* white]

al+bu+me·nize *or* **al+bu+me·nise** (æl'bju:mɪ,naɪz) *vb.* (*tr.*) to coat with a solution containing albumen or albumin.

al+bu+min *or* **al+bu+men** ('ælbjʊmɪn) *n.* any of a group of simple water-soluble proteins that are coagulated by heat and are found in blood plasma, egg white, etc. [C19: from ALBUMEN + -IN]

al+bu+mi+nate (æl'bju:mɪ,neɪt) *n. Now rare.* any of several substances formed from albumin by the action of acid or alkali.

al+bu+mi+noid (æl'bju:mɪ,nɔɪd) *adj.* **1.** resembling albumin. ~*n.* **2.** another name for **scleroprotein.**

al+bu+mi+nous (æl'bju:mɪnəs) *adj.* of or containing albumin.

al+bu+mi+nu+ri·a (æl,bju:mɪ'njʊərɪə) *n. Pathol.* the presence of albumin in the urine. Also called: **proteinuria.**

al+bu+mose ('ælbjʊ,məʊs, -,məʊz) *n.* the U.S. name for **proteose.** [C19: from ALBUMIN + -OSE[2]]

Al+bu+quer+que[1] ('ælbə,kɜ:kɪ) *n.* a city in central New Mexico, on the Rio Grande. Pop.: 243 751 (1970).

Al·bu·quer·que[2] ('ælbə,kɜ:kɪ; *Portuguese* ,albu'kɛrkə) *n.* **A·fon·so de** (ə'fõsu də). 1453–1515, Portuguese navigator, who established Portuguese colonies in the East by conquering Goa, Ceylon, Malacca, and Ormuz.

al+bur+num (æl'bɜ:nəm) *n.* a former name for **sapwood.** [C17: from Latin: sapwood, from *albus* white]

Al+bu+ry ('ɔ:bərɪ, -brɪ) *n.* a city in SE Australia, in S central New South Wales, on the Murray River: commercial centre of an agricultural region. Pop.: 32 250 (1975 est.).

Al·cae·us (æl'sɪəs) *n.* 7th century B.C., Greek lyric poet who wrote hymns, love songs, and political odes.

al+ca+hest ('ælkə,hɛst) *n.* a variant spelling of **alkahest.**

Al+ca+ic (æl'keɪɪk) *adj.* **1.** of or relating to a metre used by the poet Alcaeus, consisting of a strophe of four lines each with four feet. ~*n.* **2.** (*usually pl.*) verse written in the Alcaic form. [C17: from Late Latin *Alcaicus* of ALCAEUS]

al+caide (æl'keɪd; *Spanish* al'kaiðe) *n.* (in Spain and Spanish America) **1.** the commander of a fortress or castle. **2.** the governor of a prison. [C16: from Spanish, from Arabic *al-qā'id* the captain, commander, from *qād* to give orders]

al+cal+de (æl'kældɪ; *Spanish* al'kalde) *or* **al+cade** (æl'keɪd) *n.* (in Spain and Spanish America) the mayor or chief magistrate in a town. [C17: from Spanish, from Arabic *al-qādī* the judge, from *qadā* to judge]

Al+can High+way ('ælkæn) *n.* another name for the **Alaska Highway.**

Al+ca+traz ('ælkə,træz) *n.* an island in W California, in San Francisco Bay: a federal prison until 1963.

al+ca+zar (,ælkə'zɑ:; *Spanish* al'kaθar) *n.* any of various palaces or fortresses built in Spain by the Moors. [C17: from Spanish, from Arabic *al-qasr* the castle]

Al+ca+zar de San Juan ('ælkə,zɑ:; *Spanish* al'kaθar) *n.* a town in S central Spain: associated with Cervantes and Don Quixote. Pop.: 26 963 (1970).

Al·ces·tis (æl'sɛstɪs) *n. Greek myth.* the wife of king Admetus of Thessaly. To save his life, she died in his place, but was rescued from Hades by Hercules.

al+che+mist ('ælkəmɪst) *n.* a person who practises alchemy.

al+che+mize *or* **al+che+mise** ('ælkə,maɪz) *vb.* (*tr.*) to alter (an element, metal, etc.) by alchemy; transmute.

al+che+my ('ælkəmɪ) *n., pl.* **+mies. 1.** the pseudoscientific predecessor of chemistry that sought a method of transmuting base metals into gold, an elixir to prolong life indefinitely, a panacea or universal remedy, and an alkahest or universal solvent. **2.** a power like that of alchemy: *her beauty had a potent alchemy.* [C14 *alkamye,* via Old French from Medieval Latin *alchimia,* from Arabic *al-kīmiyā',* from *al* the + *kīmiyā'* transmutation, from Late Greek *khēmeia* the art of transmutation] —**al+chem+ic** (æl'kɛmɪk), **al+'chem·i+cal,** *or* **,al+chem+'is+tic** *adj.*

al+che+rin+ga (,ælt∫ə'rɪŋgə) *n.* (in the mythology of Australian Aboriginal peoples) a mythical Golden Age of the past. Also called: **al+che·ra** ('ælt∫ərə), **dreamtime.** [from a native Australian language, literally: dream-time]

Al·ci·bi·a·des (,ælsɪ'baɪə,di:z) *n.* 450–404 B.C., Athenian statesman and general in the Peloponnesian war: brilliant, courageous, and unstable, he defected to the Spartans in 415, but returned and led the Athenian victories at Abydos (411) and Cyzicus (410). —**,Al+ci+,bi·a+'de·an** *adj.*

Al·ci·des (æl'saɪdi:z) *n.* another name for **Hercules**[1].

al+ci+dine ('ælsɪ,daɪn) *adj.* of, relating to, or belonging to the *Alcidae,* a family of sea birds including the auks, guillemots, puffins, and related forms. [C20: from New Latin *Alcidae,* from *Alca* type genus]

Al·cin·o·üs (æl'sɪnəʊəs) *n.* (in Homer's *Odyssey*) a Phaeacian king at whose court the shipwrecked Odysseus told of his wanderings. See also **Nausicaä.**

Alc·man ('ælkmən) *n.* 7th century B.C., Greek lyric poet.

Alc·me·ne (ælk'mi:nɪ) *n. Greek myth.* the mother of Hercules by Zeus who visited her in the guise of her husband, Amphitryon.

Al·cock ('ɔ:lkɒk) *n.* Sir **John Wil·liam.** 1892–1919, English aviator who with A.W. Brown made the first flight across the Atlantic (1919).

al+co+hol ('ælkə,hɒl) *n.* **1.** a colourless flammable liquid, the active principle of intoxicating drinks, produced by the fermentation of sugars, esp. glucose, and used as a solvent and in the manufacture of organic chemicals. Formula: C_2H_5OH. Also called: **ethanol, ethyl alcohol. 2.** a drink or drinks containing this substance. **3.** *Chem.* any one of a class of organic compounds that contain one or more hydroxyl groups bound to carbon atoms that are not part of an aromatic ring. The simplest alcohols have the formula ROH, where R is an alkyl group. Compare **phenol** (sense 2). See also **diol, triol.** [C16: via New Latin from Medieval Latin, from Arabic *al-kuhl* powdered antimony; see KOHL]

al+co+hol+ic (,ælkə'hɒlɪk) *n.* **1.** a person affected by alcoholism. ~*adj.* **2.** of, relating to, containing, or resulting from alcohol.

al+co+hol+ic+i+ty (,ælkəhɒ'lɪsɪtɪ) *n.* the strength of an alcoholic liquor.

Al+co+hol+ics A·non·y+mous *n.* an association of alcoholics who try, esp. by mutual assistance, to overcome alcoholism.

al+co+hol+ism ('ælkəhɒ,lɪzəm) *n.* **1.** continual heavy consumption of alcoholic drink. **2.** a physiological disorder resulting from this.

al+co+hol+ize *or* **al+co+hol+ise** ('ælkəhɒ,laɪz) *vb.* (*tr.*) to turn into alcoholic drink, as by fermenting or mixing with alcohol. —**,al+co+,hol·i+'za+tion** *or* **,al+co+,hol·i+'sa+tion** *n.*

al+co+hol+om+e·ter (,ælkəhɒ'lɒmɪtə) *n.* an instrument, such as a specially calibrated hydrometer, for determining the percentage of alcohol in a liquid.

Al+co+ran *or* **Al+ko+ran** (,ælkɒ'rɑ:n) *n.* another name for the **Koran.** —**,Al+co+'ran+ic** *or* **,Al+ko+'ran+ic** *adj.*

Al·cott ('ɔ:lkət) *n.* **Lou·i·sa May.** 1832–88, U.S. novelist, noted for her children's books, esp. *Little Women* (1869).

al+cove ('ælkəʊv) *n.* **1.** a recess or niche in the wall of a room, as for a bed, books, etc. **2.** any recessed usually vaulted area, as in a garden wall. **3.** any covered or secluded spot, such as a summerhouse. [C17: from French *alcôve,* from Spanish *alcoba,* from Arabic *al-qubbah* the vault, arch]

Al·cuin ('ælkwɪn) *or* **Al·bi·nus** *n.* 735–804 A.D., English scholar and theologian; friend and adviser of Charlemagne.

Al·cy·o·ne[1] (æl'saɪənɪ) *n. Greek myth.* **1.** the daughter of Aeolus and wife of Ceyx, who drowned herself in grief for her husband's death. She was transformed into a kingfisher. See also **Ceyx.** Also called: **Halcyone. 2.** one of the Pleiades.

Al+cy·o+ne[2] (æl'saɪənɪ) *n.* the brightest star in the Pleiades, located in the constellation Taurus.

Ald. *or* **Aldm.** *abbrev. for* Alderman.

Al+dab+ra (æl'dæbrə) *n.* an island group in the Indian Ocean: part of the British Indian Ocean Territory (1965–76); now adminstratively part of the Seychelles.

Al+dan (*Russian* al'dan) *n.* a river in the Soviet Union in the SE Yakut ASSR, rising in the **Aldan Mountains** and flowing north and west to the Lena River. Length: about 2700 km (1700 miles).

Al+deb·a+ran (æl'dɛbərən) *n.* a binary star, one component of which is a red giant, the brightest star in the constellation Taurus. It is situated close to the star cluster Hyades. Visual magnitude: 1.06; spectral type: K5; distance: 55 light years. [C14: via Medieval Latin from Arabic *al-dabarān* the follower (of the Pleiades)]

al+de+hyde ('ældɪ,haɪd) *n.* **1.** any organic compound containing the group -CHO. Aldehydes are oxidized to carboxylic acids and take part in many addition reactions. **2.** (*modifier*) consisting of, containing, or concerned with the group -CHO: *aldehyde group or radical.* [C19: from New Latin *al(cohol) dehyd(rogenātum)* dehydrogenated alcohol] —**al+de+hyd+ic** (,ældə'hɪdɪk) *adj.*

al den+te *Italian.* (al 'dɛnte) *adj.* (of a pasta dish) cooked so as to be firm when eaten. [literally: to the tooth]

al+der ('ɔ:ldə) *n.* **1.** any N temperate betulaceous shrub or tree of the genus *Alnus,* having toothed leaves and conelike fruits. The bark is used in dyeing and tanning and the wood for bridges, etc. because it resists underwater rot. **2.** any of several similar trees or shrubs. ~Compare **elder**[2]. [Old English *alor;* related to Old High German *elira,* Latin *alnus*]

al+der buck+thorn *n.* a Eurasian rhamnaceous shrub, *Frangula alnus,* with small greenish flowers and black berry-like fruits.

al+der fly *n.* any of various neuropterous insects of the widely distributed group *Sialoidea,* such as *Sialis lutaria,* that have large broad-based hind wings, produce aquatic larvae, and occur near water.

al+der+man ('ɔ:ldəmən) *n., pl.* **+men. 1.** (in England and Wales until 1974) one of the senior members of a local council, elected by other councillors. **2.** (in the U.S., Canada, etc.) a member of the governing body of a municipality. **3.** *History.* a variant spelling of **ealdorman.** ~Abbrevs. (for senses 1, 2): **Ald., Aldm.** [Old English *aldormann,* from *ealdor* chief (comparative of *eald* OLD) + *mann* MAN] —**al+der+man+ic** (,ɔ:ldə'mænɪk) *adj.* —**'al+der+man+ry** *n.* —**'al+der+man+,ship** *n.*

Al+der+mas+ton ('ɔ:ldə,mɑ:stən) *n.* a village in S England, in Berkshire southwest of Reading: site of the Atomic Weapons Research Establishment and starting point of the Aldermaston marches (1958–63), organized by the Campaign for Nuclear Disarmament.

Al+der+ney ('ɔ:ldənɪ) *n.* one of the Channel Islands, in the English Channel: separated from the French coast by a dangerous tidal channel (the **Race of Alderney**). Pop.: 1686 (1971). Area: 8 sq. km (3 sq. miles).

Al+der+shot ('ɔ:ldə,∫ɒt) *n.* a town in S England, in Hampshire: site of a large military camp. Pop.: 33 311 (1971).

Al+dine ('ɔ:ldaɪn, -di:n) *adj.* **1.** relating to Aldus Manutius or to his editions of the classics. ~*n.* **2.** a book printed by the Aldine press. **3.** any of the several typefaces designed by Aldus Manutius.

Al+dis lamp ('ɔ:ldɪs) *n.* a portable lamp used to transmit Morse code. [C20: originally a trademark, after A. C. W. *Aldis*, its inventor]

al+dol ('ældɒl) *n.* **1.** a colourless or yellowish oily liquid, miscible with water, used in the manufacture of rubber accelerators, as an organic solvent, in perfume, and as a hypnotic and sedative. Formula: $CH_3CHOHCH_2CHO$. **2.** any organic compound containing the group $-CHOHCH_2CHO$. **3.** (*modifier*) consisting of, containing, or concerned with the group $-CHOHCH_2CHO$: *aldol group or radical.* [C19: from ALD(EHYDE) + -OL]

al+dose ('ældəʊs, -dəʊz) *n.* a sugar that contains the aldehyde group or is a hemiacetal. [C20: from ALD(EHYDE) + -OSE[2]]

al+dos+te·rone (æl'dɒstəˌrəʊn) *n.* the principal mineralocorticoid secreted by the adrenal cortex. A synthesized form is used in the treatment of Addison's disease. [C20: from ALD(EHYDE) + -O- + STER(OL) + -ONE]

ald+ox+ime (æl'dɒksi:m) *n.* an oxime formed by reaction between hydroxylamine and an aldehyde.

Al·dridge-Brown·hills ('ɔ:ldrɪdʒ 'braʊnˌhɪlz) *n.* a town in central England, in N West Midlands: formed by the amalgamation of neighbouring towns in 1966; coalmining. Pop.: 88 475 (1971).

al+drin ('ɔ:ldrɪn) *n.* a brown to white poisonous crystalline solid, more than 95 per cent of which consists of the compound $C_{12}H_8Cl_6$, which is used as an insecticide. Melting pt.: 105°C. [C20: named after K. *Alder* (1902–58) German chemist]

Al·dus Ma·nu·ti·us ('ɔ:ldəs mə'nju:ʃɪəs) *n.* 1450–1515, Italian printer, noted for his fine editions of the classics. He introduced italic type.

ale (eɪl) *n.* **1.** an alcoholic drink made by fermenting a cereal, esp. barley, originally differing from beer by being unflavoured by hops. **2.** *U.S.* such a drink made by the top-fermentation process. Compare **beer. 3.** *Chiefly Brit.* another word for **beer.** [Old English *alu, ealu;* related to Old Norse *öl,* Old Saxon *alofat*]

a·le·a+to+ry ('eɪlɪətərɪ, -trɪ) *or* **a·le·a+to+ric** (ˌeɪlɪə'tɒrɪk) *adj.* **1.** dependent on chance. **2.** (esp. of a musical composition) involving elements chosen at random by the performer. [C17: from Latin *āleātōrius,* from *āleātor* gambler, from *ālea* game of chance, dice, of uncertain origin]

al·ec *or* **al+eck** ('ælɪk) *n. Austral. slang.* a stupid person; silly fool.

ale+cost ('eɪlˌkɒst) *n.* another name for **costmary.**

A·lec·to (ə'lɛktəʊ) *n. Greek myth.* one of the three Furies; the others are Megaera and Tisiphone.

a·lee (ə'li:) *adv., adj.* (*postpositive*) *Nautical.* on or towards the lee: *with the helm alee.* Compare **aweather.**

al+e·gar ('eɪlɪgə, 'æ-) *n.* malt vinegar. [C14: from ALE + VINEGAR]

ale+house ('eɪlˌhaʊs) *n.* an archaic or dialect name for **pub.**

Al·e·khine ('ælɪˌki:n; *Russian* al'jɛxɪn) *n.* **Al·ex·an·der.** 1892–1946, Russian chess player who lived in France; world champion (1927–35, 1937–46).

A·le·ksan+dro+pol (*Russian* alɪksan'drɔpəlj) *n.* the former name (from 1837 until after the Revolution) of **Leninakan.**

A·le·ksan+drovsk (*Russian* alɪ'ksandrəfsk) *n.* the former name (until 1921) of **Zaporozhye.**

A·le·mán (*Spanish* ˌale'man) *n.* **Ma·te·o** (ma'teo). 1547–?1614, Spanish novelist, author of the picaresque novel *Guzmán de Alfarache* (1599).

Al·e·man+ni (ˌælə'mɑ:nɪ) *n.* a West Germanic people who settled in the 4th century A.D. between the Rhine, the Main, and the Danube. [C18: from Latin, of Germanic origin; related to Gothic *alamans* a totality of people]

Al+e·man+nic (ˌælə'mænɪk) *n.* **1. a.** the group of High German dialects spoken in Alsace, Switzerland, and SW Germany. **b.** the language of the ancient Alemanni, from which these modern dialects have developed. See also **Old High German.** ~*adj.* **2.** of or relating to the Alemanni, their speech, or the High German dialects descended from it. [C18: from Late Latin *Alamannicus,* of Germanic origin]

A·lem·bert, d' (*French* dalã'bɛ:r) *n.* **Jean Le Rond** (ʒã lə 'rõ). 1717–83, French mathematician, physicist, and rationalist philosopher, noted for his contribution to Newtonian physics in *Traité de Dynamique* (1743) and for his collaboration with Diderot in editing the *Encyclopédie.*

a·lem+bic (ə'lɛmbɪk) *n.* **1.** an obsolete type of retort used for distillation. **2.** anything that distils or purifies. [C14: from Medieval Latin *alembicum,* from Arabic *al-anbīq* the still, from Greek *ambix* cup]

a·lem+bi·cat+ed (ə'lɛmbɪˌkeɪtɪd) *adj.* (of a literary style) excessively refined; precious. **—a·ˌlem+bi+'ca+tion** *n.*

A·len+çon (*French* alã'sõ) *n.* a town in NW France: early lace-manufacturing centre. Pop.: 34 666 (1975).

A+len+çon lace *n.* an elaborate lace worked on a hexagonal mesh and used as a border, or a machine-made copy of this.

a·leph ('ɑ:lɪf; *Hebrew* 'alɛf) *n.* the first letter in the Hebrew alphabet (א) articulated as a glottal stop and transliterated with a superior period (˙). [Hebrew: ox]

a·leph-null *or* **a·leph-ze·ro** *n.* the smallest infinite cardinal number; the cardinal number of the set of positive integers. Symbol: $\aleph_0$.

A·lep+po (ə'lɛpəʊ) *n.* an ancient city in NW Syria: industrial and commercial centre. Pop.: 639 428 (1970). French name: **A·lep** (a'lɛp). Arabic name: **Ha+leb** (hɑ:'lɛb).

A·lep+po gall *n.* a type of nutgall occurring in oaks in W Asia and E Europe.

a·lert (ə'lɜ:t) *adj.* (*usually postpositive*) **1.** vigilantly attentive: *alert to the problems.* **2.** brisk, nimble, or lively. ~*n.* **3.** an alarm or warning, esp. a siren warning of an air raid. **4.** the period during which such a warning remains in effect. **5. on the alert. a.** on guard against danger, attack, etc. **b.** watchful; ready: *on the alert for any errors.* ~*vb.* (*tr.*) **6.** to warn or signal (troops, police, etc.) to prepare for action. **7.** to warn of danger, an attack, etc. [C17: from Italian *all'erta* on the watch, from *erta* lookout post, from *ergere* to build up, from Latin *ērigere;* see ERECT] **—a·'lert+ly** *adv.* **—a·'lert+ness** *n.*

-a·les *suffix forming plural proper nouns.* denoting plants belonging to an order: *Rosales; Filicales.* [New Latin, from Latin, plural of *-ālis* -AL]

A·les+san+dri·a (*Italian* ˌales'sandrja) *n.* a town in NW Italy, in Piedmont. Pop.: 103 474 (1975 est.).

Å·le+sund *or* **Aa·le+sund** (*Norwegian* 'o:ləˌsʊn) *n.* a port and market town in W Norway, on an island between Bergen and Trondheim: fishing and sealing fleets. Pop.: 39 145 (1970).

a·le·thic (ə'li:θɪk) *adj. Logic.* **a.** of or relating to such philosophical concepts as truth, necessity, possibility, contingency, etc. **b.** designating the branch of modal logic that deals with the formalization of these concepts. [C20: from Greek *alētheia* truth]

al·eu+rone (ə'lʊərən, -ˌrəʊn) *or* **al·eu+ron** (ə'lʊərɒn, -rən) *n.* an albuminoid protein that occurs in the form of storage granules in plant cells, esp. in seeds such as maize. [C19: from Greek *aleuron* flour]

Al+eut (æ'lu:t, 'æli:ˌu:t) *n.* **1.** a member of a people inhabiting the Aleutian Islands and SW Alaska, related to the Eskimos. **2.** the language of this people, related to Eskimo. [from Russian *aleút,* probably of Chukchi origin]

A·leu+tian (ə'lu:ʃən) *adj.* **1.** of, denoting, or relating to the Aleutian Islands, the Aleuts, or their language. ~*n.* **2.** another word for **Aleut.**

A·leu+tian Is+lands *n.* a chain of over 150 volcanic islands, extending southwestwards from the Alaska Peninsula between the N Pacific and the Bering Sea.

A lev+el *n. Brit.* the advanced level of a subject taken for General Certificate of Education **(G.C.E.)**, in schools usually taken two years after O level.

al+e·vin ('ælɪvɪn) *n.* a young fish, esp. a young salmon or trout. [C19: from French, from Old French *alever* to rear (young), from Latin *levāre* to raise]

ale+wife ('eɪlˌwaɪf) *n., pl.* **+wives.** a North American fish, *Pomolobus pseudoharengus,* similar to the herring *Clupea harengus:* family *Clupeidae* (herrings). [C19: perhaps an alteration (through influence of *alewife,* that is, a large rotund woman, alluding to the fish's shape) of French *alose* shad]

Al·ex·an·der (ˌælɪg'zɑ:ndə) *n.* **Har·old (Rupert Leofric George),** Earl Alexander of Tunis. 1891–1969, British field marshal in World War II, who organized the retreat from Dunkirk and commanded the victories of North Africa (1943) and Sicily and Italy (1944–45); governor general of Canada (1946–52); British minister of defence (1952–54).

Al·ex·an·der I *n.* **1.** *c.* 1080–1124, king of Scotland (1107–24), son of Malcolm III. **2.** 1777–1825, tsar of Russia (1801–25), who helped defeat Napoleon and formed the Holy Alliance (1815).

Al·ex·an·der II *n.* **1.** 1198–1249, king of Scotland (1214–49), son of William I. **2.** 1818–81, tsar of Russia (1855–81), son of Nicholas I, who emancipated the serfs (1861). He was assassinated by the Nihilists.

Al·ex·an·der III *n.* **1.** 1241–86, king of Scotland (1249–86), son of Alexander II. **2.** original name *Orlando Bandinelli.* died 1181, pope (1159–81), who excommunicated Barbarossa. **3.** 1845–94, tsar of Russia (1881–94), son of Alexander II.

Al·ex·an·der VI *n.* original name *Rodrigo Borgia.* 1431–1503, pope (1492–1503): noted for his extravagance and immorality as well as for his patronage of the arts; father of Cesare and Lucrezia Borgia, with whom he is said to have committed incest.

Al+ex+an+der Ar+chi+pel·a+go *n.* a group of over 1000 islands along the coast of SE Alaska.

Al+ex+an+der I Is+land *n.* an island of Antarctica, west of Palmer Land, in the Bellingshausen Sea. Length: about 378 km (235 miles).

Al·ex·an·der Nev·ski ('nɛvskɪ, 'nɛf-; *Russian* 'njɛfskij) *n.* **Saint.** ?1220–63, Russian prince and military leader, who defeated the Swedes at the River Neva (1240) and the Teutonic knights at Lake Peipus (1242).

al+ex+an+ders (ˌælɪg'zɑ:ndəz) *n.* **1.** a biennial umbelliferous plant, *Smyrnium olusatrum,* native to S Europe, with dense umbels of yellow-green flowers and black fruits. **2. golden alexanders.** an umbelliferous plant, *Zizia aurea,* of North America, having yellow flowers in compound umbels. [Old English, from Medieval Latin *alexandrum,* probably (through association in folk etymology with *Alexander* the Great) changed from Latin *holus atrum* black vegetable]

Al·ex·an·der the Great *n.* 356–323 B.C., king of Macedon, who conquered Greece (336), Egypt (331), and the Persian Empire (328), and founded Alexandria.

Al·ex·an·dra (ˌælɪg'zɑ:ndrə) *n.* 1844–1925, queen consort of Edward VII of England.

Al+ex+an+dret+ta (ˌælɪgzɑ:n'drɛtə) *n.* the former name of **Iskenderun.**

Al+ex+an+dri·a (ˌælɪg'zændrɪə, -'zɑ:n-) *n.* the chief port of Egypt, on the Nile Delta: cultural centre of ancient times, founded by Alexander the Great (332 B.C.). Pop.: 2 259 000 (1974 est.). Arabic name: **El Iskandariyah.**

Al+ex+an+dri·an (ˌælɪg'zændrɪən, -'zɑːn-) *adj.* **1.** of or relating to Alexandria in Egypt. **2.** of or relating to Alexander the Great. **3.** relating to the Hellenistic philosophical, literary, and scientific ideas that flourished in Alexandria in the last three centuries B.C. **4.** (of writers, literary works, etc.) erudite and imitative rather than original or creative. *~n.* **5.** a native or inhabitant of Alexandria.

Al+ex+an+drine (ˌælɪg'zændraɪn, -drɪn, -'zɑːn-) *Prosody.* *~n.* **1.** a line of verse having six iambic feet, usually with a caesura after the third foot. *~adj.* **2.** of, characterized by, or written in Alexandrines. [C16: from French *alexandrin,* from *Alexandre* title of 15th-century poem written in this metre]

al+ex+an+drite (ˌælɪg'zændraɪt) *n.* a green variety of chrysoberyl used as a gemstone. [C19: named after ALEXANDER I of Russia; see -ITE[1]]

A·le·xan+droú+po+lis (*Greek* ˌalɛksan'ðrupɔlis) *n.* a port in NE Greece, in W Thrace. Pop.: 22 995 (1971). Former name (until the end of World War I): **Dedéagach.**

a·lex·i·a (ə'lɛksɪə) *n.* a disorder of the central nervous system characterized by impaired ability to read. Nontechnical name: **word blindness.** Compare **aphasia.** [C19: from New Latin, from A-[1] + Greek *lexis* speech; influenced in meaning by Latin *legere* to read]

a·lex+in (ə'lɛksɪn) *n. Immunol.* a former word for **complement** (sense 9). [C19: from German, from Greek *alexein* to ward off] **—a·lex+in+ic** (ˌælɪk'sɪnɪk) *adj.*

a·lex·i+phar+mic (əˌlɛksɪ'fɑːmɪk) *Med.* *~adj.* **1.** acting as an antidote. *~n.* **2.** an antidote. [C17: from Greek *alexipharmakon* antidote, from *alexein* to avert + *pharmakon* drug]

A·lex·is Mi·khai·lo·vich (ə'lɛksɪs mɪ'kaɪləˌvɪtʃ) *n.* 1629–76, tsar of Russia (1645–76); father of Peter the Great.

A·lex·i·us I Com·ne·nus (ə'lɛksɪəs; kɒm'niːnəs) *n.* 1048–1118, ruler of the Byzantine Empire (1081–1118).

al+fal+fa (æl'fælfə) *n.* a papilionaceous plant, *Medicago sativa,* of Europe and Asia, having compound leaves with three leaflets and clusters of small purplish flowers. It is widely cultivated for forage and used as a commercial source of chlorophyll. Also called: **lucerne.** [C19: from Spanish, from Arabic *al-fasfasah,* from *al* the + *fasfasah*]

Al Fat+ah (æl 'fætə) *n.* See **Fatah.**

Al·fie·ri (*Italian* al'fjɛːri) *n.* Count **Vit·to·rio** (vit'tɔːrjo). 1749–1803, Italian dramatist and poet, noted for his classical tragedies and political satires.

al+fil·a·ri·a *or* **al+fil·e·ri·a** (ˌælfɪ'lɛərɪə) *n.* a geraniaceous plant, *Erodium cicutarium,* native to Europe, with finely divided leaves and small pink or purplish flowers. It is widely naturalized in North America and is used as fodder. Also called: **pin clover.** [via American Spanish from Spanish *alfilerillo,* from *alfiler* pin, from Arabic *al-khilāl* the thorn]

Al·fon·so XIII (*Spanish* al'fonso) *n.* 1886–1941, king of Spain (1886–1931), who was forced to abdicate on the establishment of the republic in 1931.

al+for+ja (æl'fɔːdʒə) *n. Southwestern U.S.* a saddlebag made of leather or canvas. [C17: from Spanish, from Arabic *al-khurj* the saddlebag]

Al·fred the Great ('ælfrɪd) *n.* 849–99, king of Wessex (871–99) and overlord of England, who defeated the Danes and encouraged learning and writing in English.

al+fres+co (æl'frɛskəʊ) *adj., adv.* in the open air. [C18: from Italian: in the cool]

alg. *abbrev. for* algebra *or* algebraic.

Alg. *abbrev. for* Algeria(n).

al+gae ('ældʒiː) *pl. n., sing.* **al·ga** ('ælgə). unicellular or multicellular plants, occurring in fresh or salt water or moist ground, that have chlorophyll and other pigments but lack true stems, roots, and leaves. The group includes the seaweeds, diatoms, and spirogyra. See also **thallophyte.** [C16: from Latin, plural of *alga* seaweed, of uncertain origin] **—al+gal** ('ælgəl) *adj.*

al+gar+ro+ba *or* **al+ga+ro+ba** (ˌælgə'rəʊbə) *n.* **1.** another name for **mesquite** or **carob. 2.** the edible pod of these trees. [C19: from Spanish, from Arabic *al* the + *kharrūbah* CAROB]

al+ge+bra ('ældʒɪbrə) *n.* **1.** a branch of mathematics in which arithmetical operations and relationships are generalized by using symbols to represent members of specified sets of numbers. **2.** a system of logical notation in which variables represent propositions and symbols represent the relations, such as conjunction or disjunction, between them. [C14: from Medieval Latin, from Arabic *al-jabr* the bone-setting, reunification, mathematical reduction] **—al+ge+bra+ist** (ˌældʒɪ'breɪɪst) *n.*

al+ge+bra+ic (ˌældʒɪ'breɪɪk) *or* **al+ge+bra·i+cal** *adj.* **1.** of or relating to algebra: *an algebraic expression.* **2.** using or relating to finite numbers, operations, or relationships. **—ˌal+ge+'bra·i+cal+ly** *adv.*

al+ge+bra+ic num+ber *n.* **1.** any positive or negative real number. **2.** any number that is a root of a polynomial equation having rational coefficients.

Al+ge+ci+ras (ˌældʒɪ'sɪrəs; *Spanish* ˌalxe'θiras) *n.* a port and resort in SW Spain, on the Strait of Gibraltar: scene of a conference of the Great Powers in 1906. Pop.: 81 662 (1970).

Al·ger ('ældʒə) *n.* **Ho·ra·ti·o.** 1834–99, U.S. author of adventure stories for boys, including *Ragged Dick* (1867).

Al+ge+ri·a (æl'dʒɪərɪə) *n.* a republic in NW Africa, on the Mediterranean: became independent in 1962, after more than a century of French rule; consists chiefly of the N Sahara Desert, with the Atlas Mountains in the north, and contains rich deposits of oil and natural gas. Official language: Arabic; French also widely spoken. Religion: Muslim. Currency: dinar. Capital: Algiers. Pop.: 14 431 000 (1973 est.). Area: about 2 382 800 sq. km (920 000 sq. miles). French name: **Al+gé+rie** (alʒe'ri). **—Al+'ge+ri·an** *or* **Al+ge+rine** ('ældʒəˌriːn) *adj., n.*

al+ge+rine (ˌældʒə'riːn) *n.* a soft striped woollen cloth.

-al·gi·a *n. combining form.* denoting pain or a painful condition of the part specified: *neuralgia; odontalgia.* [from Greek *algos* pain] **—-al·gic** *adj. combining form.*

al+gi+cide ('ældʒɪˌsaɪd) *n.* any substance that kills algae.

al+gid ('ældʒɪd) *adj. Med.* chilly or cold. [C17: from Latin *algidus,* from *algēre* to be cold] **—al+'gid·i·ty** *n.*

Al+giers (æl'dʒɪəz) *n.* the capital of Algeria, an ancient port on the Mediterranean; up to 1830 a centre of piracy. Pop.: 903 533 (1966). Arabic name: **Al-Je·za·ir** (ˌældʒɛ'zɑːɪə). French name: **Al+ger** (al'ʒe).

al+gin ('ældʒɪn) *n.* alginic acid or one of its esters or salts, esp. the gelatinous solution obtained as a by-product in the extraction of iodine from seaweed, used in mucilages and for thickening jellies.

al+gi+nate ('ældʒɪˌneɪt) *n.* a salt or ester of alginic acid.

al+gin+ic ac·id (æl'dʒɪnɪk) *n.* a white or yellowish powdery polysaccharide having marked hydrophilic properties. Extracted from kelp, it is used mainly in the food and textile industries and in cosmetics and pharmaceuticals. Formula: $(C_6H_8O_6)_n$; molecular wt.: 32 000–250 000.

al·go- *combining form.* denoting pain: *algometer; algophobia.* [from Greek *algos* pain]

al+goid ('ælgɔɪd) *adj.* resembling or relating to algae.

Al+gol ('ælgɒl) *n.* the second brightest star in Perseus, the first known eclipsing binary. Visual magnitude: 2.2–3.5; period: 68.8 hours; spectral type (brighter component): B8. [C14: from Arabic *al ghūl* the GHOUL]

ALGOL ('ælgɒl) *n.* a computer programming language designed for mathematical and scientific purposes, in which algorithms can be expressed unambiguously; a high-level language. Compare **FORTRAN, PL/1, COBOL.** [C20: *alg(orithmic) o(riented) l(anguage)*]

al+go+lag+ni·a (ˌælgə'lægnɪə) *n.* a perversion in which sexual pleasure is gained from the experience or infliction of pain. See also **sadism, masochism. —ˌal+go+'lag+nic** *adj.* **—ˌal+go+'lag+nist** *n.*

al+gol+o·gy (æl'gɒlədʒɪ) *n.* the branch of botany concerned with the study of algae. **—al+go+log·i·cal** (ˌælgə'lɒdʒɪkəl) *adj.* **—ˌal+go+'log·i·cal+ly** *adv.* **—al+'gol·o·gist** *n.*

al+gom+e·ter (æl'gɒmɪtə) *n.* an instrument for measuring sensitivity to pressure **(pressure algometer)** or to pain. **—al+'gom+e·try** *n.*

Al+gon+ki·an (æl'gɒŋkɪən) *n., adj.* **1.** an obsolete term for **Proterozoic. 2.** a variant spelling of **Algonquian.**

Al+gon+qui·an (æl'gɒŋkɪən, -kwɪ-) *or* **Al+gon+ki·an** *n.* **1.** a family of North American Indian languages whose speakers ranged over an area stretching from the Atlantic between Newfoundland and Delaware to the Rocky Mountains, including Micmac, Mahican, Ojibwa, Fox, Blackfoot, Cheyenne, and Shawnee. **2.** (*pl.* **·ans** *or* **·an**) a member of any of the North American Indian peoples that speak one of these languages. *~adj.* **3.** denoting, belonging to, or relating to this linguistic family or its speakers.

Al+gon+quin (æl'gɒŋkɪn, -kwɪn) *or* **Al+gon+kin** (æl'gɒŋkɪn) *n.* **1.** (*pl.* **+quins, +quin** *or* **+kins, +kin**) a member of a North American Indian people formerly living along the St. Lawrence and Ottawa Rivers in Canada. **2.** the language of this people, a dialect of Ojibwa. *~n., adj.* **3.** a variant spelling of **Algonquian.** [C17: from Canadian French, earlier written as *Algoumequin;* perhaps related to Micmac *algoomaking* at the fish-spearing place]

Al+gon+quin Park *n.* a provincial park in S Canada, in E Ontario, containing over 1200 lakes. Area: 7100 sq. km (2741 sq. miles).

al+go+pho+bi·a (ˌælgə'fəʊbɪə) *n. Psychiatry.* an acute fear of experiencing or witnessing bodily pain.

al+gor ('ælgɔː) *n. Med.* chill. [C15: from Latin]

al+go+rism ('ælgəˌrɪzəm) *n.* **1.** the Arabic or decimal system of counting. **2.** the skill of computation using any system of numerals. **3.** another name for **algorithm.** [C13: from Old French *algorisme,* from Medieval Latin *algorismus,* from Arabic *al-khuwārizmi,* from the name of abu-Ja'far Mohammed ibn-Mūsa *al-Khuwārizmi,* ninth-century Persian mathematician] **—ˌal+go+'ris+mic** *adj.*

al+go+rithm ('ælgəˌrɪðəm) *n.* any method or procedure of computation, usually involving a series of steps as in long division. Also called: **algorism.** [C17: changed from ALGORISM, through influence of Greek *arithmos* number] **—ˌal+go+'rith+mic** *adj.* **—ˌal+go+'rith+mi+cal+ly** *adv.*

Al+ham+bra (æl'hæmbrə) *n.* a citadel and palace in Granada built for the Moorish kings during the 13th and 14th centuries: noted for its rich ornamentation. **—Al+ham+bresque** (ˌælhæm'brɛsk) *adj.*

Al Ha·sa (ɑːl 'hɑːsə) *n.* a province in E Saudi Arabia, in Nejd on the Persian Gulf: site of the first discovery of oil in Saudi Arabia (near Ad Dammam in 1933). Chief town: Al Hufuf. Pop.: 500 000 (1961 est.). Area: 106 708 sq. km (41 200 sq. miles).

Al Hu+fuf *or* **Al Ho+fuf** (æl hʊ'fuːf) *n.* a town in E Saudi Arabia: a trading centre with nearby oilfields and oases. Pop.: 100 000 (1970 est.).

A·li ('ɑːlɪː) *n.* **1.** ?600–661 A.D., fourth caliph of Islam (656–61 A.D.), considered the first caliph by the Shiites: cousin and son-in-law of Mohammed. **2. Mehemet.** See **Mehemet Ali.**

a·li·as ('eɪlɪəs) *adv.* **1.** at another time or place known as or named: *Dylan, alias Zimmerman.* ~*n., pl.* **·as·es. 2.** an assumed name. [C16: from Latin *aliās* (adv.) otherwise, at another time, from *alius* other]
A·li Ba·ba ('ælɪ 'bɑːbə) *n.* (in *The Arabian Nights' Entertainments*) a poor woodcutter who discovers that the magic words "open sesame" will open the doors of the cave containing the treasure of the Forty Thieves.
al·i·bi ('ælɪˌbaɪ) *n., pl.* **·bis. 1.** *Law.* **a.** a defence by an accused person that he was elsewhere at the time the crime in question was committed. **b.** the evidence given to prove this. **2.** *Informal.* an excuse. ~*vb.* **3.** (*tr.*) to provide with an alibi. [C18: from Latin *alibī* elsewhere, from *alius* other + *-bī* as in *ubī* where]
al·i·ble ('æləbᵊl) *adj. Archaic.* nourishing; nutritive. [C17: from Latin *alibilis* nutritious, from *alere* to nourish]
Al·i·can·te (ˌælɪ'kæntɪ) *n.* a port in SE Spain: commercial centre. Pop.: 184 716 (1970).
Al·ice-in-Won·der·land *adj.* fantastic; irrational. [C20: alluding to the absurdities of Wonderland in Lewis Carroll's book]
Al·ice Springs *n.* a town in Australia, in the Northern Territory, in the Macdonnell Ranges: capital of the former territory of Central Australia. Pop.: 13 400 (1975 est.). Former name (until 1933): **Stuart.**
al·i·cy·clic (ˌælɪ'saɪklɪk, -'sɪk-) *adj.* (of an organic compound) having essentially aliphatic properties, in spite of the presence of a ring of carbon atoms. [C19: from German *alicyclisch*, from ALI(PHATIC) + CYCLIC]
al·i·dade ('ælɪˌdeɪd) *or* **al·i·dad** ('ælɪˌdæd) *n.* **1.** a surveying instrument used in plane-tabling for drawing lines of sight on a distant object and taking angular measurements. **2.** the upper rotatable part of a theodolite, including the telescope and its attachments. [C15: from French, from Medieval Latin *allidada*, from Arabic *al-'idāda* the revolving radius of a circle]
al·ien ('eɪljən, 'eɪlɪən) *n.* **1.** a person owing allegiance to a country other than that in which he lives; foreigner. **2.** any being or thing foreign to the environment in which it now exists: *an alien from another planet.* ~*adj.* **3.** unnaturalized; foreign. **4.** having foreign allegiance: *alien territory.* **5.** unfamiliar; strange: *an alien quality in a work of art.* **6.** (*postpositive* and foll. by *to*) repugnant or opposed (to): *war is alien to his philosophy.* ~*vb.* **7.** (*tr.*) *Rare.* to transfer (property, etc.) to another. [C14: from Latin *aliēnus* foreign, from *alius* other] —**al·ien·age** ('eɪljənɪdʒ, 'eɪlɪə-) *n.*
al·ien·a·ble ('eɪljənəbᵊl, 'eɪlɪə-) *adj. Law.* (of property) transferable to another owner. —ˌ**al·ien·a·'bil·i·ty** *n.*
al·ien·ate ('eɪljəˌneɪt, 'eɪlɪə-) *vb.* (*tr.*) **1.** to cause (a friend, sympathizer, etc.) to become indifferent, unfriendly, or hostile; estrange. **2.** to turn away; divert: *to alienate the affections of a person.* **3.** *Law.* to transfer the ownership of (property, title, etc.) to another person. —'**al·ien·ˌa·tor** *n.*
al·ien·a·tion (ˌeɪljə'neɪʃən, ˌeɪlɪə-) *n.* **1.** a turning away; estrangement. **2.** the state of being an outsider or the feeling of being isolated, as from society. **3.** *Psychiatry.* a state in which a person's feelings are inhibited so that eventually both the self and the external world seem unreal. **4.** *Law.* **a.** the transfer of property, as by conveyance or will, into the ownership of another. **b.** the right of an owner to dispose of his property.
al·ien·ee (ˌeɪljə'niː, ˌeɪlɪə-) *n. Law.* a person to whom a transfer of property is made.
al·ien·ism ('eɪljəˌnɪzəm, 'eɪlɪə-) *n. Obsolete.* the study and treatment of mental illness.
al·ien·ist ('eɪljənɪst, 'eɪlɪə-) *n.* **1.** *U.S.* a psychiatrist who specializes in the legal aspects of mental illness. **2.** *Obsolete.* a person who practises alienism.
al·ien·or ('eɪljənə, 'eɪlɪə-) *n. Law.* a person who transfers property to another.
al·i·form ('ælɪˌfɔːm, 'eɪlɪ-) *adj.* wing-shaped; alar. [C19: from New Latin *āliformis*, from Latin *āla* a wing]
A·li·garh (ˌɑːlɪ'gɜː, ˌælɪ-) *n.* a city in N India, in W Uttar Pradesh, with a famous Muslim university (1920). Pop.: 252 314 (1971).
a·light[1] (ə'laɪt) *vb.* **a·lights, a·light·ing, a·light·ed** *or* **a·lit.** (*intr.*) **1.** (usually foll. by *from*) to step out (of) or get down (from): *to alight from a taxi.* **2.** to come to rest; settle; land: *a thrush alighted on the wall.* [Old English *ālīhtan*, from A-[2] + *līhtan* to make less heavy, from *līht* LIGHT[2]]
a·light[2] (ə'laɪt) *adj.* (*postpositive*), *adv.* **1.** burning; on fire. **2.** illuminated; lit up. [Old English *ālīht* lit up, from *ālīhtan* to light up; see LIGHT[1]]
a·light·ing gear *n.* another name for **undercarriage** (sense 1).
a·lign (ə'laɪn) *vb.* **1.** to place or become placed in a line. **2.** to bring (components or parts, such as the wheels of a car) into proper or desirable coordination or relation. **3.** (*tr.*; usually foll. by *with*) to bring (a person, country, etc.) into agreement or cooperation with the policy, etc. of another person or group. [C17: from Old French *aligner*, from *à ligne* into line]
a·lign·ment (ə'laɪnmənt) *n.* **1.** arrangement in a straight line. **2.** the line or lines formed in this manner. **3.** alliance or union with a party, cause, etc. **4.** proper or desirable coordination or relation of components. **5.** a ground plan of a railway, motor road, etc. **6.** *Archaeol.* an arrangement of one or more ancient rows of standing stones, of uncertain significance.
a·like (ə'laɪk) *adj.* (*postpositive*) **1.** possessing the same or similar characteristics: *they all look alike to me.* ~*adv.* **2.** in the same or a similar manner, way, or degree: *they walk alike.* [Old English *gelīc*; see LIKE[1]]
al·i·ment *n.* ('ælɪmənt). **1.** something that nourishes, supports, or sustains the body or mind. **2.** *Scot. law.* another term for **alimony.** ~*vb.* ('ælɪˌmɛnt). **3.** (*tr.*) *Obsolete.* to support or sustain. [C15: from Latin *alimentum* food, from *alere* to nourish] —**al·i·'men·tal** *adj.*
al·i·men·ta·ry (ˌælɪ'mɛntərɪ, -trɪ) *adj.* **1.** of or relating to nutrition. **2.** providing sustenance or nourishment. **3.** *Scot. law.* free from the claims of creditors: *an alimentary trust.*
al·i·men·ta·ry ca·nal *n.* the tubular passage extending from the mouth to the anus, through which food is passed and digested.
al·i·men·ta·tion (ˌælɪmɛn'teɪʃən) *n.* **1.** nourishment. **2.** sustenance; support. —ˌ**al·i·'men·ta·tive** *adj.*
al·i·mo·ny ('ælɪmənɪ) *n. Law.* an allowance paid under a court order by one spouse to another when they are separated, either before or after divorce. See also **maintenance.** [C17: from Latin *alimōnia* sustenance, from *alere* to nourish]
a·line (ə'laɪn) *vb.* a rare spelling of **align.** —**a·'line·ment** *n.* —**a·'lin·er** *n.*
A·li Pa·sha ('ɑːliː 'pɑːʃə) *n.* called *the Lion of Janina.* 1741–1822, Turkish pasha and ruler of Albania (1787–1820), who was deposed and assassinated after intriguing against Turkey.
al·i·ped ('ælɪˌpɛd) *adj.* **1.** (of bats and similar animals) having the digits connected by a winglike membrane. ~*n.* **2.** an aliped animal. [C19: from Latin *ālipēs* having winged feet, from *āla* wing + -PED]
al·i·phat·ic (ˌælɪ'fætɪk) *adj.* (of an organic compound) not aromatic, esp. having an open chain structure, such as alkanes, alkenes, and alkynes. [C19: from Greek *aleiphat-*, *aleiphar* oil]
al·i·quant ('ælɪkwənt) *adj. Maths.* of, signifying, or relating to a quantity or number that is not an exact divisor of a given quantity or number: *5 is an aliquant part of 12.* Compare **aliquot** (sense 1). [C17: from New Latin, from Latin *aliquantus* somewhat, a certain quantity of]
al·i·quot ('ælɪˌkwɒt) *adj.* **1.** *Maths.* of, signifying, or relating to an exact divisor of a quantity or number: *3 is an aliquot part of 12.* Compare **aliquant. 2.** consisting of equal quantities: *the sample was divided into five aliquot parts.* ~*n.* **3.** an aliquot part. [C16: from Latin: several, a few]
a·lit (ə'lɪt) *vb.* a rare past tense and past participle of **alight**[1].
a·li·un·de (ˌeɪlɪ'ʌndɪ) *adv., adj.* from a source extrinsic to the matter, document, or instrument under consideration: *evidence aliunde.* [Latin: from elsewhere]
a·live (ə'laɪv) *adj.* (*postpositive*) **1.** (of people, animals, plants, etc.) living; having life. **2.** in existence; active: *they kept hope alive; the tradition was still alive.* **3.** (*immediately postpositive and usually used with a superlative*) of those living; now living: *the happiest woman alive.* **4.** full of life; lively: *she was wonderfully alive for her age.* **5.** (usually foll. by *with*) animated: *a face alive with emotion.* **6.** (foll. by *to*) aware (of); sensitive (to). **7.** (foll. by *with*) teeming (with): *the mattress was alive with fleas.* **8.** *Electronics.* another word for **live**[2] (sense 10). **9. alive and kicking.** (of a person) active and lively. **10. look alive! a.** hurry up! **b.** pay attention! [Old English *on līfe* in LIFE] —**a·'live·ness** *n.*
a·liz·a·rin (ə'lɪzərɪn) *n.* a brownish-yellow powder or orange-red crystalline solid used as a dye and in the manufacture of other dyes. Formula: $C_6H_4(CO)_2C_6H_2(OH)_2$. [C19: probably from French *alizarine*, probably from Arabic *al-'asārah* the juice, from *'asara* to squeeze]
alk. *abbrev. for* alkali.
al·ka·hest *or* **al·ca·hest** ('ælkəˌhɛst) *n.* the hypothetical universal solvent sought by alchemists. [C17: apparently coined by Paracelsus on the model of Arabic words]
al·ka·li ('ælkəˌlaɪ) *n., pl.* **·lis** *or* **·lies. 1.** *Chemistry.* a soluble base or a solution of a base. **2.** a soluble mineral salt that occurs in arid soils and some natural waters. [C14: from Medieval Latin, from Arabic *al-qili* the ashes (of the plant saltwort)]
al·kal·ic (æl'kælɪk) *adj.* **1.** (of igneous rocks) containing large amounts of alkalis, esp. caustic soda and caustic potash. **2.** another word for **alkaline.**
al·ka·li flat *n.* an arid plain encrusted with alkaline salts derived from the streams draining into it.
al·ka·li·fy ('ælkəlɪˌfaɪ, æl'kæl-) *vb.* **·fies, ·fy·ing, ·fied.** to make or become alkaline.
al·ka·li met·al *n.* any of the monovalent metals lithium, sodium, potassium, rubidium, caesium, and francium, belonging to group 1A of the periodic table. They are all very reactive and electropositive.
al·ka·lim·e·ter (ˌælkə'lɪmɪtə) *n.* **1.** an apparatus for determining the concentration of alkalis in solution. **2.** an apparatus for determining the quantity of carbon dioxide in carbonates. —**al·ka·li·met·ric** (ˌælkəlɪ'mɛtrɪk) *adj.*
al·ka·lim·e·try (ˌælkə'lɪmɪtrɪ) *n.* determination of the amount of alkali or base in a solution, measured by an alkalimeter or by volumetric analysis.
al·ka·line ('ælkəˌlaɪn) *adj.* having the properties of or containing an alkali.
al·ka·line earth *n.* **1.** Also called: **alkaline earth metal.** any of the divalent electropositive metals beryllium, magnesium, calcium, strontium, barium, and radium, belonging to group 2A of the periodic table. **2.** an oxide of one of the alkaline earth metals.
al·ka·lin·i·ty (ˌælkə'lɪnɪtɪ) *n.* **1.** the quality or state of being alkaline. **2.** the amount of alkali or base in a solution, often expressed in terms of pH.
al·ka·li soil *n.* a soil that gives a pH reaction of 8.5 or above, found esp. in dry areas where the soluble salts, esp. of sodium,

have not been leached away but have accumulated in the B horizon of the soil profile.

al+ka+lize or **al+ka+lise** ('ælkəˌlaɪz) *vb.* (*tr.*) to make alkaline. —'al+ka+ˌliz+a·ble or 'al+ka+ˌlis+a·ble *adj.*

al+ka+loid ('ælkəˌlɔɪd) *n.* any of a group of nitrogenous basic compounds found in plants, typically insoluble in water and physiologically active. Common examples are morphine, strychnine, and quinine.

al+ka+lo+sis (ˌælkə'ləʊsɪs) *n.* an abnormal increase in alkalinity of the blood and extracellular fluids.

al+kane ('ælkeɪn) *n.* **a.** any saturated aliphatic hydrocarbon with the general formula C_nH_{2n+2}. **b.** (*as modifier*): *alkane series.* Also called: **paraffin.**

al+ka+net ('ælkəˌnɛt) *n.* **1.** a European boraginaceous plant, *Alkanna tinctoria,* the roots of which yield a red dye. **2.** the dye obtained from this plant. Also called: **anchusin, alkannin. 3.** any of certain hairy blue-flowered Old World plants of the boraginaceous genus *Anchusa* (or *Pentaglottis*), such as *A. sempervirens* of Europe. See also **bugloss. 4.** another name for **puccoon** (sense 1). [C14: from Spanish *alcaneta,* diminutive of *alcana* henna, from Medieval Latin *alchanna,* from Arabic *al* the + *hinnā'* henna]

al+kene ('ælki:n) *n.* **a.** any unsaturated aliphatic hydrocarbon with the general formula C_nH_{2n}. **b.** (*as modifier*): *alkene series.* Also called: **olefine.**

Alk+maar (*Dutch* 'alkma:r) *n.* a city in the W Netherlands, in North Holland. Pop.: 60 375 (1973 est.).

Al+ko+ran or **Al+co+ran** (ˌælkɒ'rɑ:n) *n.* a less common name for the **Koran.**

al+ky or **al+kie** ('ælkɪ) *n., pl.* **·kies.** *Slang, chiefly U.S. and Austral.* a heavy drinker or alcoholic.

al+kyd res+in ('ælkɪd) *n.* any synthetic resin made from a dicarboxylic acid, such as phthalic acid, and diols or triols: used in paints and adhesives.

al+kyl ('ælkɪl) *n.* **1.** (*modifier*) of, consisting of, or containing the monovalent group C_nH_{2n+1}: *alkyl group or radical.* **2.** an organometallic compound, such as tetraethyl lead, containing an alkyl group bound to a metal atom. [C19: from German, from *Alk(ohol)* ALCOHOL + -YL]

al+kyl·a+tion (ˌælkɪ'leɪʃən) *n.* **1.** the replacement of a hydrogen atom in an organic compound by an alkyl group. **2.** the addition of an alkane hydrocarbon to an alkene in producing high-octane fuels.

al+kyne ('ælkaɪn) *n.* **a.** any unsaturated aliphatic hydrocarbon that has a formula of the type C_nH_{2n-2}. **b.** (*as modifier*): *alkyne series.* Also called: **acetylene.**

all (ɔ:l) *determiner.* **1. a.** the whole quantity or amount of; totality of: *all the rice; all interested parties.* **b.** (*as pronoun; functioning as sing. or pl.*): *is that all there are? all of it is nice; all are welcome.* **2.** every one of a class: *all men are mortal.* **3.** the greatest possible: *in all earnestness.* **4.** any whatever: *to lose all hope of recovery; beyond all doubt.* **5. above all.** most important. **6. after all.** in spite of everything: *it's only a game, after all.* **7. all but.** almost; nearly: *all but dead.* **8. all of.** no less or smaller than:. *she's all of thirteen years.* **9. all over. a.** finished; at an end: *the affair is all over between us.* **b.** over the whole area (of something); everywhere (in, on, etc.): *all over England.* **c.** *Informal.* typically; representatively (in the phrase **that's me (you, him, us, them,** *etc.*) **all over**). **d.** unduly effusive towards. **e.** *Sports.* in a dominant position over. **10. all in.** exhausted; tired out. **11. all in all. a.** everything considered: *all in all, it was a great success.* **b.** the object of one's attention or interest: *you are my all in all.* **12. all that.** *Informal.* (intensifier; used in negative sentences and often implying a comparison with some norm or standard): *she's not all that intelligent.* **13. all the.** (foll. by a comparative adjective or adverb) so much (more or less) than otherwise: *we must work all the faster now.* **14. and all.** *Brit. informal.* as well; too: *and you can take that smile off your face and all.* **15. and all that.** *Informal.* **a.** and similar or associated things; etcetera: *coffee, tea, and all that will be served in the garden.* **b.** used as a filler or to make what precedes more vague: in this sense, it often occurs with concessive force: *she was sweet and pretty and all that, but I still didn't like her.* **16. as all that.** as one might expect or hope: *she's not as pretty as all that, but she has a personality.* **17. at all. a.** (*used with a negative or in a question*) in any way whatsoever or to any extent or degree: *I didn't know that at all.* **b.** even so; anyway: *I'm surprised you came at all.* **18. be all for.** *Informal.* be strongly in favour of. **19. for all. a.** in so far as; to the extent that: *for all anyone knows, he was a baron.* **b.** notwithstanding: *for all my pushing, I still couldn't move it.* **20. for all that.** in spite of that: *he was a nice man for all that.* **21. in all.** altogether: *there were five of them in all.* ~*adv.* **22.** (in scores of games) apiece; each: *the score at half time was three all.* ~*n.* **23.** (preceded by *my, your, his,* etc.) (one's) complete effort or interest: *to give your all; you are my all.* **24.** totality or whole. [Old English *eall;* related to Old High German *al,* Old Norse *allr,* Gothic *alls* all]

all- *combining form.* variant of **allo-** before a vowel.

al·la bre+ve ('ælə 'breɪvɪ; *Italian* 'alla 'bre:ve) *n.* **1.** a musical time signature indicating two or four minims to a bar. ~*adj., adv.* **2.** twice as fast as normal. Musical symbol: ¢ [C19: literally: (according) to the breve]

Al·lah ('ælə) *n. Islam.* the principal Muslim name for God; the one Supreme Being. [C16: from Arabic, from *al* the + *Ilāh* god; compare Hebrew *elōah*]

Al+lah·a+bad (ˌæləhə'bæd, -'bɑ:d) *n.* a city in N India, in SE Uttar Pradesh at the confluence of the Ganges and Jumna Rivers: Hindu pilgrimage centre. Pop.: 490 622 (1971).

all-A·mer·i·can *U.S.* ~*adj.* **1.** representative of the whole of the United States. **2.** composed exclusively of American members. **3.** (of a person) typically American.

Al·lan-a-Dale (ˌælənə'deɪl) *n.* (in English balladry) a member of Robin Hood's band who saved his sweetheart from an enforced marriage and married her himself.

al+lan+ite ('æləˌnaɪt) *n.* a rare black or brown mineral consisting of the hydrated silicate of calcium, aluminium, iron, cerium, lanthanum, and other rare earth minerals. It occurs in granites and other igneous rocks. Formula: $(Ca,Ce,La,Na)_2(Al,Fe,Be,Mn,Mg)_3(SiO_4)_3(OH)$. [C19: named after T. *Allan* (1777–1833), English mineralogist]

al+lan+toid (ə'læntɔɪd) *adj.* **1.** relating to or resembling the allantois. **2.** *Botany.* shaped like a sausage. ~*n.* **3.** another name for **allantois.** [C17: from Greek *allantoeidēs* sausage-shaped, from *allas* sausage + -OID] —**al+lan+toi+dal** (ˌælən'tɔɪdəl) *adj.*

al+lan+to+is (ˌælən'təʊɪs, ə'læntɔɪs) *n.* a membranous sac growing out of the ventral surface of the hind gut of embryonic reptiles, birds, and mammals. It combines with the chorion to form the mammalian placenta. [C17: New Latin, irregularly from Greek *allantoeidēs* sausage-shaped, ALLANTOID] —**al+lan+to+ic** (ˌælən'təʊɪk) *adj.*

al·la pri+ma ('ɑ:lɑ: 'pri:mə) *adj.* (of a painting) painted with a single layer of paint, in contrast to paintings built up layer by layer. [C19: from Italian: at once]

al+lar+gan+do (ˌɑ:lɑ:'gændəʊ) *Music.* ~*adj., adv.* to be slowed down considerably. [Italian, from *allargare* to make slow or broad]

all-a·round *adj.* (*prenominal*) the U.S. equivalent of **all-round.**

al+lay (ə'leɪ) *vb.* **1.** to relieve (pain, grief, etc.) or be relieved. **2.** (*tr.*) to reduce (fear, anger, etc.). [Old English *ālecgan* to put down, from *lecgan* to LAY[1]]

All Black *n.* a member of the international Rugby Union football team of New Zealand. [so named because of the players' black strip]

all clear *n.* **1.** a signal, usually a siren, indicating that some danger, such as an air raid, is over. **2.** an indication that obstacles are no longer present; permission to proceed: *he received the all clear on the plan.*

al+le+ga+tion (ˌælɪ'geɪʃən) *n.* **1.** the act of alleging. **2.** an unproved statement or assertion, esp. one in an accusation.

al+lege (ə'lɛdʒ) *vb.* (*tr.; may take a clause as object*) **1.** to declare in or as if in a court of law; state without or before proof: *he alleged malpractice.* **2.** to put forward (an argument or plea) for or against an accusation, claim, etc. **3.** *Archaic.* to cite or quote, as to confirm. [C14 *aleggen,* ultimately from Latin *allēgāre* to despatch on a mission, from *lēx* law]

al+leged (ə'lɛdʒd) *adj.* (*prenominal*) **1.** stated or described to be such; presumed: *the alleged murderer.* **2.** dubious: *an alleged miracle.* —**al+leg+ed+ly** (ə'lɛdʒɪdlɪ) *adv.*

Al+le+ghe+ny Moun+tains (ˌælɪ'geɪnɪ) or **Al+le+ghe+nies** *pl. n.* a mountain range in Pennsylvania, Maryland, Virginia, and West Virginia: part of the Appalachian system; rising from 600 m (2000 ft.) to over 1440 m (4800 ft.).

al+le+giance (ə'li:dʒəns) *n.* **1.** loyalty, as of a subject to his sovereign or of a citizen to his country. **2.** (in feudal society) the obligations of a vassal to his liege lord. See also **fealty, homage** (sense 2). [C14: from Old French *ligeance,* from *lige* LIEGE]

al+le+gor·i·cal (ˌælɪ'gɒrɪkəl) or **al+le+gor+ic** *adj.* used in, containing, or characteristic of allegory. —ˌ**al+le+'gor·i·cal+ly** *adv.*

al+le+go+rize or **al+le+go+rise** ('ælɪgəˌraɪz) *vb.* **1.** to transform (a story, narrative, fable, etc.) into or compose in the form of allegory. **2.** (*tr.*) to interpret allegorically. —ˌ**al+le+ˌgor·i+'za+tion** or ˌ**al+le+ˌgor·i+'sa+tion** *n.*

al+le+go+ry ('ælɪgərɪ) *n., pl.* **+ries. 1.** a poem, play, picture, etc., in which the apparent meaning of the characters and events is used to symbolize a deeper moral or spiritual meaning. **2.** the technique or genre that this represents. **3.** use of such symbolism to illustrate truth or a moral. **4.** anything used as a symbol or emblem. [C14: from Old French *allegorie,* from Latin *allēgoria,* from Greek, from *allēgorein* to speak figuratively, from *allos* other + *agoreuein* to make a speech in public, from *agora* a public gathering] —'**al+le+go+rist** *n.*

al+le+gret+to (ˌælɪ'grɛtəʊ) *Music.* ~*adj., adv.* **1.** quickly or briskly. ~*n., pl.* **+tos. 2.** a piece or passage to be performed in this manner. [C19: diminutive of ALLEGRO]

al+le+gro (ə'leɪgrəʊ, -'lɛg-) *Music.* ~*adj., adv.* **1.** quickly; in a brisk lively manner. ~*n., pl.* **+gros. 2.** a piece or passage to be performed in this manner. [C17: from Italian: cheerful, from Latin *alacer* brisk, lively]

al+lele (ə'li:l) *n.* any of two or more genes that have the same relative position on homologous chromosomes and are responsible for alternative characteristics, such as smooth or wrinkled seeds in peas. Also called: **al+le+lo+morph** (ə'li:ləˌmɔ:f). See also **multiple alleles.** [C20: from German *Allel,* shortened from *allelomorph,* from Greek *allēl-* one another + *morphē* form] —**al+'lel+ic** *adj.* —**al+'lel+ism** *n.*

al+le+lu·ia (ˌælɪ'lu:jə) *interj.* **1.** praise the Lord! Used more commonly in liturgical contexts in place of *hallelujah.* ~*n.* **2.** a song of praise to God. [C14: via Medieval Latin from Hebrew *hallelūyāh*]

al+le+mande ('ælɪmænd; *French* al'mã:d) *n.* **1.** the first movement of the classical suite, composed in a moderate tempo in a time signature of four-four. **2.** any of several German dances. **3.** a figure in a quadrille or a square dance. [C17: from French *danse allemande* German dance]

Al+len[1] ('ælən) *n.* **1. Bog of.** a region of peat bogs in central

Ireland, west of Dublin. Area: over 10 sq. km (3.75 sq. miles). **2. Lough.** a lake in Ireland, in county Leitrim.

Al·len[2] ('ælən) *n.* **1. E·than.** 1738–89, American soldier during the War of Independence who led the Green Mountain Boys of Vermont. **2. Wood·y.** original name *Allen Stewart Konigsberg.* born 1935, U.S. film comedian, screenwriter, and director: his films include *Bananas* (1971), *Play it again, Sam* (1973), *Sleeper* (1973), and *Annie Hall* (1977), which he also directed.

Al·len·by ('ælənbɪ) *n.* **Ed·mund Hen·ry Hyn·man,** 1st Viscount Allenby. 1861–1936, British field marshal who commanded British forces in Palestine in World War I; high commissioner in Egypt (1919–25).

Al·len·de (*Spanish* a'ʎende) *n.* **Sal·va·dor** (ˌsalβa'ðor). 1908–73, Chilean Marxist politician; president of Chile from 1970 until 1973, when the army seized power and he was killed.

Al+len+town ('ælənˌtaʊn) *n.* a city in E Pennsylvania, on the Lehigh River. Pop.: 108 655 (1973 est.).

Al+lep+pey ('ʌləpɪ) *n.* a port in S India, in Kerala on the Malabar Coast. Pop.: 160 166 (1971).

al+ler+gen ('ælәˌdʒɛn) *n.* any substance, usually a protein, capable of inducing an allergy. —ˌ**al+ler+'gen+ic** *adj.*

al+ler+gic (ə'lɜ:dʒɪk) *adj.* **1.** of, relating to, having, or caused by an allergy. **2.** (*postpositive;* foll. by *to*) *Informal.* having an aversion (to): *he's allergic to work.*

al+ler+gist ('ælədʒɪst) *n.* a physician skilled in the diagnosis and treatment of diseases or conditions caused by allergy.

al+ler+gy ('ælədʒɪ) *n., pl.* **+gies. 1.** a hypersensitivity to a substance that causes the body to react to any contact with that substance. Hay fever is an allergic reaction to pollen. **2.** *Informal.* aversion: *he has an allergy to studying.* [C20: from German *Allergie* (indicating a changed reaction), from Greek *allos* other + *ergon* activity]

al+le+thrin (æ'lɛθrɪn) *n.* a clear viscous amber-coloured liquid used as an insecticide and synergist. Formula: $C_{19}H_{26}O_3$; relative density: 1.005. [C20: from ALL(YL) + (PYR)ETHRIN]

al+le+vi+ate (ə'li:vɪˌeɪt) *vb.* (*tr.*) to make (pain, sorrow, etc.) easier to bear; lessen; relieve. [C15: from Late Latin *alleviāre* to mitigate, from Latin *levis* light] —**al+ˌle+vi+'a+tion** *n.* —**al+'le+vi+a+tive** *adj.* —**al+'le+vi+ˌa+tor** *n.*

al+ley[1] ('ælɪ) *n.* **1.** a narrow lane or passage, esp. one between or behind buildings; back street. **2.** See **bowling alley. 3.** *Tennis, chiefly U.S.* the space between the singles and doubles sidelines. **4.** a walk in a park or garden, esp. one lined with trees or bushes. **5. up** (*or* **down**) **one's alley.** *Slang.* suited to one's abilities or interests. [C14: from Old French *alee,* from *aler* to go, ultimately from Latin *ambulāre* to walk]

al+ley[2] ('ælɪ) *n.* a large playing marble. [C18: shortened and changed from ALABASTER]

al+ley cat *n. U.S.* a homeless cat that roams in back streets.

al·ley+way ('ælɪˌweɪ) *n.* a narrow passage; alley.

all-fired *Slang, chiefly U.S.* ~*adj.* **1.** (*prenominal*) excessive; extreme. ~*adv.* **2.** (intensifier): *don't be so all-fired sure of yourself!*

all-fly·ing tail *n.* a type of aircraft tailplane in which the whole of the tailplane is moved for control purposes.

All Fools' Day *n.* another name for **April Fools' Day** (see **April fool**).

all fours *n.* **1.** both the arms and legs of a person or all the legs of a quadruped (esp. in the phrase **on all fours**). **2.** another name for **seven-up.**

all hail *interj.* an archaic greeting or salutation. [C14, literally: all health (to someone)]

All+hal+lows (ˌɔ:l'hæləʊz) *n.* **1.** a less common term for **All Saints' Day. 2. Allhallows Eve.** a less common name for **Halloween.**

All+hal+low+tide (ˌɔ:l'hæləʊˌtaɪd) *n.* the season of All Saints' Day (Allhallows).

all+heal ('ɔ:lˌhi:l) *n.* any of several plants reputed to have healing powers, such as selfheal and valerian.

al+li+a+ceous (ˌælɪ'eɪʃəs) *adj.* **1.** of or relating to *Allium,* a genus of liliaceous plants that have a strong onion or garlic smell and often have bulbs. The genus occurs in the N hemisphere and includes onion, garlic, leek, chive, and shallot. **2.** tasting or smelling like garlic or onions. [C18: from Latin *allium* garlic; see -ACEOUS]

al+li+ance (ə'laɪəns) *n.* **1.** the act of allying or state of being allied; union; confederation. **2.** a formal agreement or pact, esp. a military one, between two or more countries to achieve a particular aim. **3.** the countries involved in such an agreement. **4.** a union between families through marriage. **5.** affinity or correspondence in qualities or characteristics. **6.** *Botany.* a taxonomic category consisting of a group of related families; subclass. [C13: from Old French *aliance,* from *alier* to ALLY]

al+lied (ə'laɪd, 'ælaɪd) *adj.* **1.** joined, as by treaty, agreement, or marriage; united. **2.** of the same type or class; related.

Al+lied ('ælaɪd) *adj.* of or relating to the Allies.

Al+lier (*French* a'lje) *n.* **1.** a department of central France, in Auvergne region. Capital: Moulins. Pop.: 386 489 (1975). Area: 7382 sq. km (2879 sq. miles). **2.** a river in S central France, rising in the Cévennes and flowing north to the Loire. Length: over 403 km (250 miles).

al+lies ('ælaɪz) *n.* the plural of **ally.**

Al+lies ('ælaɪz) *pl. n.* **1.** (in World War I) the powers of the Triple Entente (France, Russia, and Britain) together with the nations allied with them. **2.** (in World War II) the countries that fought against the Axis and Japan. The main Allied powers were Britain and the Commonwealth countries, the U.S., the Soviet Union, France, and Poland. See also **Axis.**

al+li+ga+tor ('ælɪˌgeɪtə) *n.* **1.** a large crocodilian, *Alligator mississipiensis,* of the southern U.S., having powerful jaws and sharp teeth and differing from the crocodiles in having a shorter and broader snout: family *Alligatoridae* (alligators and caymans). **2.** a similar but smaller species, *A. sinensis,* occurring in China near the Yangtse River. **3.** any crocodilian belonging to the family *Alligatoridae.* **4.** any of various tools or machines having adjustable toothed jaws, used for gripping, crushing, or compacting. [C17: from Spanish *el lagarto* the lizard, from Latin *lacerta*]

al+li+ga+tor pear *n.* another name for **avocado.**

al+li+ga+tor pep+per *n. Chiefly W. African.* **1.** a tropical African zingiberaceous plant, *Amomum melegueta,* having red or orange spicy seed capsules. **2.** the capsules or seeds of this plant, used as a spice.

all-im·por·tant *adj.* crucial; vital.

all in *adj.* **1.** (*postpositive*) *Slang.* completely exhausted; tired out. ~*adv., adj.* **(all-in** *when prenominal*). **2. a.** with all expenses or costs included in the price: *the flat is twenty pounds a week all in.* **b.** (*prenominal*): *the all-in price is thirty pounds.* **3.** (of wrestling) freestyle.

all-in·clu·sive *adj.* including everything; comprehensive.

al+lit+er+ate (ə'lɪtəˌreɪt) *vb.* **1.** to contain or cause to contain alliteration. **2.** (*intr.*) to speak or write using alliteration.

al+lit+er·a+tion (əˌlɪtə'reɪʃən) *n.* the use of the same consonant (**consonantal alliteration**) or of a vowel, not necessarily the same vowel (**vocalic alliteration**), at the beginning of each word or each stressed syllable in a line of verse, as in *around the rock the ragged rascal ran.* [C17: from Medieval Latin *allīterātiō* (from Latin *litera* letter), on the model of *obliterātiō* OBLITERATION] —**al+'lit+er·a+tive** *adj.*

al+li·um ('ælɪəm) *n.* any liliaceous plant of the genus *Allium,* such as the onion, garlic, shallot, leek, and chive. [C19: from Latin: garlic]

all-night *adj.* open or lasting all night: *an all-night show.*

al·lo- *or before a vowel* **all-** *combining form.* indicating difference, variation, or opposition: *allopathy; allomorph; allophone; allonym.* [from Greek *allos* other, different]

Al+lo·a ('æləʊə) *n.* a town in E central Scotland, in Central region. Pop.: 14 110 (1971).

al+lo+cate ('æləˌkeɪt) *vb.* (*tr.*) **1.** to assign or allot for a particular purpose. **2.** a less common word for **locate** (sense 2). [C17: from Medieval Latin *allocāre,* from Latin *locāre* to place, from *locus* a place] —**'al+lo+ˌcat+a·ble** *adj.*

al+lo+ca+tion (ˌælə'keɪʃən) *n.* **1.** the act of allocating or the state of being allocated. **2.** a part that is allocated; share. **3.** *Accounting, Brit.* a system of dividing overhead expenses between the various departments of a business.

al+loch+tho+nous (ə'lɒkθənəs) *adj.* (of rocks, deposits, etc.) found in a place other than where they or their constituents were formed. Compare **autochthonous** (sense 1).

al+lo+cu+tion (ˌælə'kju:ʃən) *n. Rhetoric.* a formal or authoritative speech or address, esp. one that advises, informs, or exhorts. [C17: from Late Latin *allocūtiō,* from Latin *alloquī* to address, from *loquī* to speak]

al+lo+di·al (ə'ləʊdɪəl) *adj.* **1.** (of land) held as an allodium. **2.** (of tenure) characterized by or relating to the system of holding land in absolute ownership: *the allodial system.* **3.** (of people) holding an allodium.

al+lo+di·um (ə'ləʊdɪəm) *or* **al+lod** ('ælɒd) *n., pl.* **+lo+di·a** (-'ləʊdɪə) *or* **+lods.** *History.* lands held in absolute ownership, free from such obligations as rent or services due to an overlord. Also: **alodium.** [C17: from Medieval Latin, from Old German *allōd* (unattested) entire property, from *al-* ALL + *-ōd* property; compare Old High German *ōt,* Old English *eād* property]

al+log·a+my (ə'lɒgəmɪ) *n.* cross-fertilization in flowering plants. —**al+'log·a+mous** *adj.*

al+lo+graph ('æləˌgrɑ:f) *n.* **1.** a document written by a person who is not a party to it. **2.** a signature made by one person on behalf of another. Compare **autograph. 3.** *Linguistics.* any of the written symbols that constitute a single grapheme: m *and* M *are allographs in the Roman alphabet.* —**al+lo+graph+ic** (ˌælə'græfɪk) *adj.*

al+lom+er+ism (ə'lɒməˌrɪzəm) *n.* similarity of crystalline structure in substances of different chemical composition. —**al+'lom+er+ous** *adj.*

al+lom+e+try (ə'lɒmɪtrɪ) *n.* **1.** the study of the growth of part of an organism in relation to the growth of the entire organism. **2.** a change in proportion of any of the parts of an organism that occurs during growth. —**al+lo+met+ric** (ˌælə'mɛtrɪk) *adj.*

al+lo+morph ('æləˌmɔ:f) *n.* **1.** *Linguistics.* any of the phonological representations of a single morpheme. For example, the final (s) and (z) sounds of *bets* and *beds* are allomorphs of the English noun-plural morpheme. **2.** any of two or more different crystalline forms of a chemical compound, such as a mineral. —ˌ**al+lo+'mor+phic** *adj.*

al+lo+mor+phism (ˌælə'mɔ:fɪzəm) *n.* variation in the crystalline form of a chemical compound.

al+lo+nym ('ælənɪm) *n.* a name, often one of historical significance or that of another person, assumed by a person, esp. an author.

al+lo+path ('æləˌpæθ) *or* **al+lop·a+thist** (ə'lɒpəθɪst) *n.* a person who practises or is skilled in allopathy.

al+lop·a+thy (ə'lɒpəθɪ) *n.* the usual method of treating disease, by inducing a condition different from the cause of the disease. Compare **homeopathy.** —**al+lo+path+ic** (ˌælə'pæθɪk) *adj.* —ˌ**al+lo+'path·i+cal+ly** *adv.*

al+lo+pat+ric (ˌælə'pætrɪk) *adj.* (of biological speciation or species) taking place or existing in areas that are geographically isolated from one another. Compare **sympatric.** [C20: from ALLO- + *-patric,* from Greek *patris* native land] —ˌ**al+lo+'pat+ri+cal+ly** *adv.*

al+lo+phane ('ælə,feɪn) *n.* a variously coloured amorphous mineral consisting of hydrated aluminium silicate and occurring in cracks in some sedimentary rocks. [C19: from Greek *allophanēs* appearing differently, from ALLO- + *phainesthai* to appear]

al+lo+phone ('ælə,fəʊn) *n.* any of several speech sounds that are regarded as contextual or environmental variants of the same phoneme. In English the aspirated initial (p) in *pot* and the unaspirated (p) in *spot* are allophones of the phoneme /p/. —**al+lo+phon+ic** (ˌælə'fɒnɪk) *adj.*

al+lo+plasm ('ælə,plæzəm) *n. Biology.* part of the cytoplasm that is specialized to form cilia, flagella, and similar structures. —ˌ**al+lo+'plas+mic** *adj.*

al+lo+pu+ri+nol (ˌæləʊ'pjʊərəˌnɒl) *n.* a synthetic drug that reduces blood levels of uric acid and is administered orally in the treatment of gout. Formula: $C_5H_4N_4O$. [C20: from ALLO- + PURINE + -OL]

al+lot (ə'lɒt) *vb.* **+lots, +lot+ting, +lot+ted.** (*tr.*) **1.** to assign or distribute (shares, etc.). **2.** to designate for a particular purpose: *money was allotted to cover expenses.* **3.** (foll. by *to*) apportion: *we allotted two hours to the case.* [C16: from Old French *aloter,* from *lot* portion, LOT]

al+lot+ment (ə'lɒtmənt) *n.* **1.** the act of allotting; apportionment. **2.** a portion or amount allotted. **3.** *Brit.* a small piece of usually public land rented by an individual for cultivation.

al+lo+trope ('ælə,trəʊp) *n.* any of two or more physical forms in which an element can exist: *diamond and graphite are allotropes of carbon.*

al+lot+ro+py (ə'lɒtrəpɪ) *or* **al+lot+ro+pism** *n.* the existence of an element in two or more physical forms. The most common elements having this property are carbon, sulphur, and phosphorus. —**al+lo+trop+ic** (ˌælə'trɒpɪk) *adj.* —ˌ**al+lo+'trop+i+cal+ly** *adv.*

all'ot+ta+va (æl ə'tɑːvə) *adj., adv. Music.* to be played an octave higher or lower than written. Symbol: 8va [Italian: at the octave]

al+lot+tee (əlɒt'iː) *n.* a person to whom something is allotted.

all-out *Informal.* ~*adj.* **1.** using one's maximum powers: *an all-out effort.* ~*adv.* **all out. 2.** to one's maximum effort or capacity: *he went all out on the home stretch.*

all-o·ver *adj.* covering the entire surface.

al+low (ə'laʊ) *vb.* **1.** (*tr.*) to permit (to do something); let. **2.** (*tr.*) to set aside: *five hours were allowed to do the job.* **3.** (*tr.*) to let enter or stay: *they don't allow dogs.* **4.** (*tr.*) to acknowledge or concede (a point, claim, etc.). **5.** (*tr.*) to let have; grant: *he was allowed few visitors.* **6.** (*intr.;* foll. by *for*) to take into account: *allow for delays.* **7.** (*intr.;* often foll. by *of*) to permit; admit: *a question that allows of only one reply.* **8.** (*tr.; may take a clause as object*) *U.S. dialect.* to assert; maintain. **9.** (*tr.*) *Archaic.* to approve; accept. [C14: from Old French *alouer,* from Late Latin *allaudāre* to extol, influenced by Medieval Latin *allocāre* to assign, ALLOCATE]

al+low+a·ble (ə'laʊəbəl) *adj.* permissible; admissible. —**al+'low+a·bly** *adv.*

al+low+ance (ə'laʊəns) *n.* **1.** an amount of something, esp. money or food, given or allotted usually at regular intervals. **2.** a discount, as in consideration for something given in part exchange or to increase business; rebate. **3.** a portion set aside to compensate for something or to cover special expenses. **4.** admission; concession. **5.** the act of allowing; sanction; toleration. **6.** something allowed. **7. make allowances** (*or* **allowance).** (usually foll. by *for*) **a.** to take mitigating circumstances into account in consideration (of). **b.** to allow (for). ~*vb.* (*tr.*) **8.** to supply (something) in limited amounts.

Al+lo+way ('ælə,weɪ) *n.* a village in Scotland, south of Ayr: birthplace of Robert Burns.

al+low+ed+ly (ə'laʊɪdlɪ) *adv.* (*sentence modifier*) by general admission or agreement; admittedly.

al+loy *n.* ('ælɔɪ, ə'lɔɪ). **1.** a metallic material, such as steel, brass, or bronze, consisting of a mixture of two or more metals or of metallic elements with nonmetallic elements. Alloys often have physical properties markedly different from those of the pure metals. **2.** something that impairs the quality or reduces the value of the thing to which it is added. ~*vb.* (ə'lɔɪ). (*tr.*) **3.** to add (one metal or element to another metal or element) to obtain a substance with a desired property. **4.** to debase (a pure substance) by mixing with an inferior element. **5.** to diminish or impair. [C16: from Old French *aloi* a mixture, from *aloier* to combine, from Latin *alligāre,* from *ligāre* to bind]

al+loyed junc+tion *n.* a semiconductor junction used in some junction transistors and formed by alloying metal contacts, functioning as emitter and collector regions, to a wafer of semiconductor that acts as the base region. Compare **diffused junction.**

all-pur·pose *adj.* useful for many things: *an all-purpose gadget.*

all right *adj.* (*postpositive except in slang use*), *adv.* **1.** adequate; satisfactory. **2.** unharmed; safe. **3. all-right.** *U.S. slang.* **a.** acceptable: *an all-right book.* **b.** reliable: *an all-right guy.* ~*adv.* **4.** very well: used to express assent. **5.** satisfactorily; adequately: *the car goes all right.* **6.** without doubt: *he's a bad one, all right.* ~Also (not standard): **alright.**

all-round *adj.* **1.** efficient in all respects, esp. in sport; versatile: *an all-round player.* **2.** comprehensive; many-sided; not narrow: *an all-round education.*

all-round·er *n.* a versatile person, esp. in a sport.

All Saints' Day *n.* a Christian festival celebrated on Nov. 1 to honour all the saints.

all+seed ('ɔːlˌsiːd) *n.* any of several plants that produce many seeds, such as knotgrass.

all-sorts *pl. n.* a mixture, esp. a mixture of liquorice sweets.

All Souls' Day *n. R.C. Church.* a day of prayer (Nov. 2) for the dead in purgatory.

all+spice ('ɔːlˌspaɪs) *n.* **1.** a tropical American myrtaceous tree, *Pimenta officinalis,* having small white flowers and aromatic berries. **2.** the whole or powdered seeds of this berry used as a spice, having a flavour said to resemble a mixture of cinnamon, cloves, and nutmeg. ~Also called: **pimento.**

all-star *adj.* (*prenominal*) consisting of star performers.

all-time *adj.* (*prenominal*) *Informal.* unsurpassed in some respect at a particular time: *an all-time record.*

Usage. *All-time* is an imprecise superlative and is avoided by careful writers as being superfluous: *his high jump was a record* (not *an all-time record*).

all told (*sentence modifier*) taking every one into account; in all: *we were seven all told.*

al+lude (ə'luːd) *vb.* (*intr.;* foll. by *to*) to refer indirectly: *he often alluded to his life in the army.* [C16: from Latin *allūdere,* from *lūdere* to sport, from *lūdus* a game]

al+lure (ə'lʊə) *vb.* **1.** (*tr.*) to entice or tempt (someone) to a person or place or to a course of action; attract. ~*n.* **2.** attractiveness; appeal: *the cottage's allure was its isolation.* [C15: from Old French *alurer,* from *lure* bait, LURE] —**al+'lur+er** *n.* —**al+'lure+ment** *n.*

al+lur+ing (ə'lʊərɪŋ) *adj.* enticing; fascinating; attractive. —**al+'lur+ing+ly** *adv.*

al+lu+sion (ə'luːʒən) *n.* **1.** the act of alluding. **2.** a passing reference; oblique or obscure mention. [C16: from Late Latin *allūsiō,* from Latin *allūdere* to sport with, ALLUDE]

al+lu+sive (ə'luːsɪv) *adj.* containing or full of allusions. —**al+'lu+sive+ly** *adv.* —**al+'lu+sive+ness** *n.*

al+lu+vi·al (ə'luːvɪəl) *adj.* **1.** of or relating to alluvium. ~*n.* **2.** another name for **alluvium. 3.** *Austral.* alluvium containing any heavy mineral, esp. gold.

al+lu+vi·al fan *or* **cone** *n.* a fan-shaped accumulation of silt, sand, gravel, and boulders deposited by fast-flowing mountain rivers when they reach flatter land.

al+lu+vi·on (ə'luːvɪən) *n.* **1. a.** the wash of the sea or of a river. **b.** an overflow or flood. **c.** matter deposited as sediment; alluvium. **2.** *Law.* the gradual formation of new land, as by the recession of the sea or deposit of sediment on a riverbed. [C16: from Latin *alluviō* an overflowing, from *luere* to wash]

al+lu+vi·um (ə'luːvɪəm) *n., pl.* **+vi·ums** *or* **+vi·a** (-vɪə). a fine-grained fertile soil consisting of mud, silt, and sand deposited by flowing water on flood plains, in river beds, and in estuaries. [C17: from Latin; see ALLUVION]

al·ly *vb.* (ə'laɪ), **+lies, +ly+ing, +lied.** (usually foll. by *to* or *with*) **1.** to unite or be united, esp. formally, as by treaty, confederation, or marriage. **2.** (*tr.; usually passive*) to connect or be related, as through being similar or compatible. ~*n.* ('ælaɪ, ə'laɪ), *pl.* **·lies. 3.** a country, person, or group allied with another. **4.** a plant, animal, substance, etc., closely related to another in characteristics or form. [C14: from Old French *alier* to join, from Latin *alligāre* to bind to, from *ligāre* to bind]

al+lyl ('ælaɪl, 'ælɪl) *n.* (*modifier*) of, consisting of, or containing the monovalent group CH_2:CHCH$_2$-: *allyl group or radical; allyl resin.* [C19: from Latin *allium* garlic + -YL; first distinguished in a compound isolated from garlic]

al+lyl al+co+hol *n.* a colourless pungent poisonous liquid used in the manufacture of resins, plasticizers, and other organic chemicals. Formula: CH_2:CHCH$_2$OH; relative density: 0.85; melting pt.: –129°C; boiling pt.: 96.9°C.

al+lyl res+in *n.* any of several thermosetting synthetic resins made by polymerizing esters of allyl alcohol with a dibasic acid. They are used as adhesives.

al+lyl sul+phide *n.* a colourless liquid that smells like garlic and is used as a flavouring. Formula: $(CH_2:CHCH_2)_2S$; relative density: 0.888; boiling pt.: 139°C.

all+you ('ɔːlˌjuː, 'ɔːˌjʊ) *pron.* (*used in addressing more than one person*) *Caribbean informal.* all of you.

Al·ma-A·ta (*Russian* al'ma a'ta) *n.* a city in the S Soviet Union, the capital of the Kazakh SSR. Pop.: 836 000 (1975 est.). Former name (until 1927): **Verny.**

Al+ma+da (*Portuguese* al'maðə) *n.* a city in S central Portugal, on the S bank of the Tagus estuary opposite Lisbon: statue of Christ 110 m (360 ft.) high, erected 1959. Pop.: 108 150 (1970).

Al+ma+dén (*Spanish* ˌalma'ðen) *n.* a town in S Spain: rich cinnabar mines, worked since Roman times. Pop.: 10 910 (1970).

Al Ma+di+nah (ˌæl mæ'diːnə) *n.* the Arabic name for **Medina.**

Al+ma+gest ('ælmə,dʒɛst) *n.* **1.** a work on astronomy compiled by Ptolemy in the 2nd century A.D. containing a description of the geocentric system of the universe and a star catalogue. **2.** (*sometimes not cap.*) any of various similar medieval treatises on astrology, astronomy, or alchemy. [C14: from Old French, from Arabic *al-majisti,* from *al* the + *majisti,* from Greek *megistē* greatest (treatise)]

al+ma ma+ter ('ælmə 'mɑːtə, 'meɪtə) *n.* (*often caps.*) one's school, college, or university. [C17: from Latin: bountiful mother]

al+ma+nac ('ɔːlmə,næk) *n.* a yearly calendar giving statistical information on events and phenomena, such as the phases of the moon, times of sunrise and sunset, tides, anniversaries, etc. Also (archaic): **almanack.** [C14: from Medieval Latin *almanachus,* perhaps from Late Greek *almenikhiaka*]

al+man+dine ('ælmənˌdɪn, -ˌdaɪn) *n.* a deep violet-red garnet that consists of iron aluminium silicate and is used as a gemstone. Formula: $Fe_3Al_2(SiO_4)_3$. [C17: from French, from Medieval Latin *alabandīna,* from *Alabanda,* ancient city of Asia Minor where these stones were cut]

Al Man+sû+rah (ˌæl mæn'sʊərə) *n.* a variant spelling of **El Mansura.**

Al Marj (æl 'mɑːdʒ) *n.* an ancient town in N Libya: founded in about 550 B.C. Pop.: 10 645 (1969 est.). Italian name: **Barce.**

Al·ma-Tad·e·ma ('ælmə 'tædɪmə) *n.* Sir **Law·rence.** 1836–1912, Dutch-English painter of studies of Greek and Roman life.

Al+me+lo (*Dutch* 'ɑlməloː) *n.* a city in the E Netherlands, in Overijssel province. Pop.: 59 821 (1973 est.).

al+me+mar (æl'miːmɑː) *n. Judaism.* (in Ashkenazic usage) the raised platform in a synagogue on which the reading desk stands. Also called: **bema, bimah.** [from Hebrew, from Arabic *al-minbar* the pulpit, platform]

Al+me+rí·a (*Spanish* ˌalme'ria) *n.* a port in S Spain. Pop.: 114 510 (1970).

al+might·y (ɔːl'maɪtɪ) *adj.* **1.** all-powerful; omnipotent. **2.** *Informal.* (intensifier): *an almighty row.* ~*adv.* **3.** *Informal.* (intensifier): *an almighty loud bang.* —**al+'might·i·ly** *adv.* —**al+'might·i·ness** *n.*

Al+might·y (ɔːl'maɪtɪ) *n.* **the.** another name for **God.**

Al+mo+hade ('ælməˌheɪd, -ˌheɪdiː) *or* **Al+mo+had** ('ælməˌhæd) *n., pl.* **+hades** *or* **hads.** a member of a group of puritanical Muslims, originally Berbers, who arose in S Morocco in the 12th century as a reaction against the corrupt Almoravides and who ruled Spain and all Maghrib from about 1147 to after 1213. [from Arabic *al-muwahhid*]

al+mond ('ɑːmənd) *n.* **1.** a small widely cultivated rosaceous tree, *Prunus amygdalus,* that is native to W Asia and has pink flowers and a green fruit containing an edible nutlike seed. **2.** the oval-shaped nutlike edible seed of this plant, which has a yellowish-brown shell. **3.** (*modifier*) made of or containing almonds: *almond cake.* **4. a.** a pale yellowish-brown colour. **b.** (*as adj.*)*: almond wallpaper.* **5.** Also called: **almond green. a.** a yellowish-green colour. **b.** (*as adj.*)*: an almond skirt.* **6.** anything shaped like an almond nut. [C13: from Old French *almande,* from Medieval Latin *amandula,* from Latin *amygdala,* from Greek *amugdalē*]

al·mond-eyed *adj.* having narrow oval eyes.

al+mon+er ('ɑːmənə) *n.* **1.** *Brit.* a trained hospital social worker responsible for the welfare of patients. **2.** (formerly) a person who distributes alms or charity on behalf of a household or institution. [C13: from Old French *almosnier,* from *almosne* alms, from Vulgar Latin *alemosina* (unattested), from Late Latin *eleēmosyna;* see ALMS]

al+mon+ry ('ɑːmənrɪ) *n., pl.* **+ries.** *History.* the house of an almoner, usually the place where alms were given. [C15: from Old French *almosnerie;* see ALMONER, ALMS]

Al+mo+ra+vide (æl'mɔːrəˌvaɪd) *or* **Al+mo+ra+vid** (æl'mɔːrəvɪd) *n.* a member of a fanatical people of Berber origin and Islamic faith, who founded an empire in N Africa that spread over much of Spain in the 11th century A.D. [from Arabic *al-murābitūn* the holy ones]

al+most ('ɔːlməʊst) *adv.* little short of being; very nearly.

alms (ɑːmz) *pl. n.* charitable donations of money or goods to the poor or needy. [Old English *ælmysse,* from Late Latin *eleēmosyna,* from Greek *eleēmosunē* pity; see ELEEMOSYNARY]

alms+house ('ɑːmzˌhaʊs) *n.* **1.** *Brit.* a privately supported house offering accommodation to the aged or needy. **2.** *Chiefly Brit.* another name for **poorhouse.**

alms+man ('ɑːmzmən) *or* (*fem.*) **alms+wom·an** *n., pl.* **+men** *or* **+wom·en.** *Archaic.* a person who gives or receives alms.

al+mu+can+tar *or* **al+ma+can+tar** (ˌælmə'kæntə) *n.* **1.** a circle on the celestial sphere parallel to the horizontal plane. **2.** an instrument for measuring altitudes. [C14: from French, from Arabic *almukantarāt* sundial]

al+muce ('ælmjuːs) *n.* a fur-lined hood or cape formerly worn by members of certain religious orders, more recently by canons of France. [C15: from Old French *aumusse,* from Medieval Latin *almucia,* of unknown origin]

Al+ni+co ('ælnɪˌkəʊ) *n. Trademark.* an alloy of aluminium, nickel, and cobalt, used to make permanent magnets.

a·lo+di·um (ə'ləʊdɪəm) *n., pl.* **+di·a** (-dɪə). a variant spelling of **allodium.** —**a·'lo+di·al** *adj.*

al·oe ('æləʊ) *n., pl.* **·oes. 1.** any plant of the liliaceous genus *Aloe,* chiefly native to southern Africa, with fleshy spiny-toothed leaves and red or yellow flowers. **2. American aloe.** another name for **century plant.** [C14; from Latin *aloē,* from Greek] —**al·o·e·tic** (ˌæləʊ'ɛtɪk) *adj.*

al·oes ('æləʊz) *n.* (*functioning as sing.*) **1.** Also called: **aloes wood.** another name for **eaglewood. 2. bitter aloes.** a bitter purgative drug made from the leaves of several species of aloe.

a·loft (ə'lɒft) *adv., adj.* (*postpositive*). **1.** in or into a high or higher place; up above. **2.** *Nautical.* in or into the rigging of a vessel. [C12: from Old Norse *ā lopt* in the air; see LIFT, LOFT]

a·lo+ha (ə'ləʊə, ɑː'ləʊhɑː) *n., interj.* a Hawaiian word for **hello** or **goodbye.**

al·o+in ('æləʊɪn) *n.* a bitter crystalline compound derived from various species of aloe and used medicinally as a laxative. [C19: from ALOE + -IN]

a·lone (ə'ləʊn) *adj.* (*postpositive*), *adv.* **1.** apart from another or others; solitary. **2.** without anyone or anything else: *one man alone could lift it.* **3.** without equal; unique: *he stands alone in the field of microbiology.* **4.** to the exclusion of others; only: *she alone believed him.* **5. leave** *or* **let alone.** to refrain from annoying or interfering with. **6. leave** *or* **let well (enough) alone.** to be content with the state of things as they are. **7. let alone.** even less: *he can't afford beer, let alone whisky.* [Old English *al one,* literally: all (entirely) one]

a·long (ə'lɒŋ) *prep.* **1.** over or for the length of, esp. in a more or less horizontal plane: *along the road.* ~*adv.* **2.** continuing over the length of some specified thing. **3.** in accompaniment; together with some specified person or people: *he says he'd like to come along.* **4.** forward: *the horse trotted along at a steady pace.* **5.** to a more advanced state: *he got the work moving along.* **6. along with.** accompanying; together with: *consider the advantages along with the disadvantages.* [Old English *andlang,* from *and-* against + *lang* LONG[1]; compare Old Frisian *andlinga,* Old Saxon *antlang*]

Usage. See at **plus.**

a·long+shore (əˌlɒŋ'ʃɔː) *adv., adj.* (*postpositive*) close to, by, or along a shore.

a·long+side (ə'lɒŋˌsaɪd) *prep.* **1.** (often foll. by *of*) along the side of; along beside: *alongside the quay.* ~*adv.* **2.** along the side of some specified thing: *come alongside.*

a·loof (ə'luːf) *adj.* distant, unsympathetic, or supercilious in manner, attitude, or feeling. [C16: from A-[1] + *loof,* variant of LUFF] —**a·'loof+ly** *adv.* —**a·'loof+ness** *n.*

al·o·pe·ci·a (ˌælə'piːʃɪə) *n.* loss of hair, esp. on the head; baldness. [C14: from Latin, from Greek *alōpekia,* originally: mange in foxes, from *alōpēx* fox]

A·lost (*French* a'lɔst) *n.* a town in central Belgium, in East Flanders province. Pop.: 46 659 (1970). Flemish name: **Aalst.**

a·loud (ə'laʊd) *adv., adj.* (*postpositive*) **1.** in a normal voice; not in a whisper. **2.** in a spoken voice; not silently. **3.** *Archaic.* in a loud voice.

a·low (ə'ləʊ) *adv., adj.* (*postpositive*) *Nautical.* in or into the lower rigging of a vessel, near the deck.

alp (ælp) *n.* a high mountain. ~See also **Alps.** [C14: back formation from *Alps*]

A.L.P. *abbrev. for* Australian Labor Party.

al+pac·a (æl'pækə) *n.* **1.** a domesticated cud-chewing artiodactyl mammal, *Lama pacos,* closely related to the llama and native to South America: family *Camelidae.* Its dark shaggy hair is a source of wool and cloth. **2.** the wool or cloth obtained from this animal. **3.** a glossy fabric simulating this, used for linings, etc. [C18: via Spanish from Aymara *allpaca*]

al·pen+glow ('ælpənˌgləʊ) *n.* a reddish light on the summits of snow-covered mountain peaks at sunset or sunrise. [partial translation of German *Alpenglühen,* from *Alpen* ALPS + *glühen* to GLOW]

al·pen+horn ('ælpənˌhɔːn) *n.* another name for **alphorn.**

al·pen+stock ('ælpənˌstɒk) *n.* a stout stick with an iron tip used by hikers, mountain climbers, etc. [C19: from German, from *Alpen* ALPS + *Stock* STICK]

Alpes-de-Haute-Pro+vence (*French* alp də ot prɔ'vɑ̃ːs) *n.* a department of SE France in Provence-Côte-d'Azur region. Capital: Digne. Pop.: 115 697 (1975). Area: 6988 sq. km (2725 sq. miles). Former name: **Basses-Alpes.**

Alpes Ma+ri+times (*French* alp mari'tim) *n.* a department of the SE corner of France in Provence-Côte-d'Azur region. Capital: Nice. Pop.: 823 731 (1975). Area: 4298 sq. km (1676 sq. miles).

al+pes+trine (æl'pɛstrɪn) *adj.* (of plants) growing at high altitudes; subalpine. [C19: from Medieval Latin *alpestris,* from Latin *Alpēs* the Alps]

al+pha ('ælfə) *n.* **1.** the first letter in the Greek alphabet (Α, α), a vowel transliterated as *a.* **2.** *Brit.* the highest grade or mark, as in an examination. **3.** (*modifier*) **a.** involving or relating to helium nuclei: *an alpha particle.* **b.** relating to one of two or more allotropes or crystal structures of a solid: *alpha iron.* **c.** relating to one of two or more isomeric forms of a chemical compound, esp. one in which a group is attached to the carbon atom to which the principal group is attached. [via Latin from Greek, of Phoenician origin; related to Hebrew *āleph,* literally: ox]

Al+pha ('ælfə) *n.* (*foll. by the genitive case of a specified constellation*) usually the brightest star in a constellation: *Alpha Centauri.*

al+pha and o·me·ga *n.* **1.** the first and last, a phrase used in Revelation 1:8 to signify God's eternity. **2.** the basic reason or meaning; most important part.

al+pha+bet ('ælfəˌbɛt) *n.* **1.** a set of letters or other signs used in a writing system, usually arranged in a fixed order, each letter or sign being used to represent one or sometimes more than one phoneme in the language being transcribed. **2.** any set of symbols or characters, esp. one representing sounds of speech. **3.** basic principles or rudiments, as of a subject. [C15: from Late Latin *alphabētum,* from Greek *alphabētos,* from the first two letters of the Greek alphabet; see ALPHA, BETA]

al+pha+bet·i·cal (ˌælfə'bɛtɪkᵊl) *or* **al+pha+bet+ic** *adj.* **1.** in the conventional order of the letters or symbols of an alphabet. **2.** of, characterized by, or expressed by an alphabet. —**ˌal+pha+'bet·i·cal+ly** *adv.*

al+pha+bet+ize *or* **al+pha+bet+ise** ('ælfəbəˌtaɪz) *vb.* (*tr.*) **1.** to arrange in conventional alphabetical order. **2.** to express by an alphabet. —**ˌal+pha+bet·i·'za+tion** *or* **ˌal+pha+bet·i·'sa+tion** *n.* —**'al+pha+bet+ˌiz·er** *or* **'al+pha+bet+ˌis+er** *n.*

Al+pha Cen+tau+ri (sɛn'tɔːrɪ) *n.* a binary star that is the brightest in the constellation Centaurus and is the second nearest star to the sun. Visual magnitude: 0.0 (A), 1.4 (B); spectral type: G4 (A), K1 (B); distance from earth: 4.3 light years. Also called: **Rigil Kent.** See also **Proxima.**

al+pha i·ron *n.* a magnetic allotrope of iron that is stable below 910°C; ferrite.

al+pha+nu+mer+ic (ˌælfənjuːˈmɛrɪk) *or* **al+pha+mer+ic** *adj.* (of a character set, code, or file of data) consisting of alphabetical and numerical symbols. —ˌ**al+pha+nu+ˈmer·i·cal+ly** *or* ˌ**al+pha+ˈmer·i·cal+ly** *adv.*

al+pha par+ti+cle *n.* a helium nucleus, containing two neutrons and two protons, emitted during some radioactive transformations.

al+pha priv·a·tive *n.* (in Greek grammar) the letter alpha (or *an-* before vowels) used as a negative or privative prefix. It appears in English words derived from Greek, as in *atheist, anaesthetic.*

al+pha ray *n.* ionizing radiation consisting of a stream of alpha particles.

al+pha rhythm *or* **wave** *n. Physiol.* the normal bursts of electrical activity from the cerebral cortex of a drowsy or inactive person, occurring at a frequency of 8 to 12 hertz and detectable with an electroencephalograph. See also **brain wave.**

Al·phe·us (ælˈfiːəs) *n. Greek myth.* a river god, lover of the nymph Arethusa. She changed into a spring to evade him, but he changed into a river and mingled with her.

Al+phon+sus (ælˈfɒnsəs) *n.* a crater in the SE quadrant of the moon, about 112 kilometres in diameter, in which volcanic activity has been observed.

alp+horn (ˈælpˌhɔːn) *or* **al·pen+horn** *n. Music.* a wind instrument used in the Swiss Alps, consisting of a very long tube of wood or bark with a cornet-like mouthpiece. [C19: from German *Alpenhorn:* Alps horn]

al+pho+sis (ælˈfəʊsɪs) *n. Pathol.* absence of skin pigmentation, as in albinism. [C19: from New Latin, from Greek *alphos* leprosy]

al+pine (ˈælpaɪn) *adj.* **1.** of or relating to high mountains. **2.** (of plants) growing on mountains above the limit for tree growth. **3.** connected with or used in mountaineering. **4.** *Skiing.* of or relating to events such as the slalom and downhill.

Al+pine (ˈælpaɪn) *adj.* **1.** of or relating to the Alps or their inhabitants. **2.** *Geology.* of or relating to an episode of mountain building in the Tertiary period during which the Alps were formed.

al+pin+ist (ˈælpɪnɪst) *n.* a mountain climber. —ˈ**al+pin+ism** *n.*

Alps (ælps) *pl. n.* **1.** a mountain range in S central Europe, extending over 1000 km (650 miles) from the Mediterranean coast of France and NW Italy through Switzerland, N Italy, and Austria to NW Yugoslavia. Highest peak: Mont Blanc, 4807 m (15 771 ft.). **2.** a range of mountains in the NW quadrant of the moon, which is cut in two by a straight fracture, the **Alpine Valley.**

al+read·y (ɔːlˈrɛdɪ) *adv.* **1.** by or before a stated or implied time: *he is already here.* **2.** at a time earlier than expected: *is it ten o'clock already?*

al+right (ɔːlˈraɪt) *adv. Not standard.* a variant spelling of **all right.**

A.L.S. *abbrev. for* autograph letter signed.

Al+sace (ælˈsæs; *French* alˈzas) *n.* a region and former province of NE France, between the Vosges mountains and the Rhine: famous for its wines. Area: 8296 sq. km (3203 sq. miles). Ancient name: **Alsatia.** German name: **Elsass.**

Al·sace-Lor·raine *n.* an area of NE France, comprising the modern regions of Alsace and Lorraine: under German rule 1871–1919 and 1940–44. Area: 14 522 sq. km (5607 sq. miles). German name: **Elsass-Lothringen.**

Al+sa+tia (ælˈseɪʃə) *n.* **1.** the ancient name for **Alsace. 2.** an area around Whitefriars, London, in the 17th century, which was a sanctuary for criminals and debtors.

Al+sa+tian (ælˈseɪʃən) *n.* **1.** a large wolflike breed of dog often used as a guard or guide dog and by the police. U.S. name: **German shepherd. 2.** a native or inhabitant of Alsace. **3.** (in the 17th century) a criminal or debtor who took refuge in the Whitefriars area of London. ~*adj.* **4.** of or relating to Alsace or its inhabitants.

al+sike (ˈælsaɪk, -sɪk, ˈɔːl-) *n.* a clover, *Trifolium hybridum,* native to Europe and Asia but widely cultivated as a forage crop. It has trifoliate leaves and pink or whitish flowers. Also called: **alsike clover.** [C19: named after *Alsike,* Sweden]

Al Si+rat (ˌæl sɪˈræt) *n. Islam.* **1.** the correct path of religion. **2.** the razor-edged bridge by which all who enter paradise must pass. [from Arabic: the road, from Latin *via strāta* paved way]

al·so (ˈɔːlsəʊ) *adv.* (*sentence modifier*) **1.** in addition; as well; too. ~ **2.** *sentence connector.* besides; moreover. [Old English *alswā;* related to Old High German *alsō,* Old Frisian *alsa;* see ALL, SO[1]]

al·so-ran *n.* **1.** a contestant, horse, etc., failing to finish among the first three in a race. **2.** *Informal.* an unsuccessful person; loser or nonentity.

alt (ælt) *Music.* ~*adj.* **1.** (esp. of vocal music) high in pitch. **2.** of or relating to the octave commencing with the G above the top line of the treble staff. ~*n.* **3. in alt.** in the octave directly above the treble staff. [C16: from Provençal, from Latin *altus* high, deep]

alt. *abbrev. for:* **1.** alternate. **2.** altitude. **3.** alto.

Alta. *abbrev. for* Alberta.

Al+ta+ic (ælˈteɪɪk) *n.* **1.** a family of languages of Asia and SE Europe, consisting of the Turkic, Mongolic, and Tungusic branches or subfamilies. See also **Ural-Altaic.** ~*adj.* **2.** denoting, belonging to, or relating to this linguistic family or its speakers.

Al+tai Moun+tains (ɑːlˈtaɪ) *pl. n.* a mountain system of central Asia, in W Mongolia, W China, and the S Soviet Union. Highest peak: Belukha, 4506 m (14 783 ft.).

Al+tair (ˈæltɛə) *n.* the brightest star in the constellation Aquilla. Visual magnitude: 0.9; spectral type: A5; distance: 15.7 light years. [Arabic, from *al* the + *tā'ir* bird]

Al+ta+mi+ra (*Spanish* ˌaltaˈmira) *n.* a cave in N Spain, SW of Santander, noted for Old Stone Age wall drawings.

al+tar (ˈɔːltə) *n.* **1.** a raised place or structure where sacrifices are offered and religious rites performed. **2.** (in Christian churches) the communion table. **3.** a step in the wall of a dry dock upon which structures supporting a vessel can stand. **4. lead to the altar.** *Informal.* to marry. [Old English, from Latin *altāria* (plural) altar, from *altus* high]

al+tar boy *n. R.C. Church, Church of England.* a boy serving as an acolyte.

al·tar+piece (ˈɔːltəˌpiːs) *n.* a work of art set above and behind an altar; a reredos.

alt+az·i+muth (ælˈtæzɪməθ) *n.* an instrument for measuring the altitude and azimuth of a celestial body by the horizontal and vertical rotation of a telescope. [C19: from ALT(ITUDE) + AZIMUTH]

Alt+dorf (*German* ˈaltˌdɔrf) *n.* a town in central Switzerland, capital of Uri canton: setting of the William Tell legend. Pop: 8647 (1970).

Alt·dor·fer (*German* ˈaltˌdɔrfər) *n.* **Al·brecht** (ˈalbrɛçt). ?1480–?1538, German painter and engraver: one of the earliest landscape painters.

al+ter (ˈɔːltə) *vb.* **1.** to make or become different in some respect; change. **2.** (*tr.*) *Informal, chiefly U.S.* a euphemistic word for **castrate** or **spay.** [C14: from Old French *alterer,* from Medieval Latin *alterāre* to change, from Latin *alter* other] —ˈ**al+ter+a·ble** *adj.* —ˈ**al+ter+a·bly** *adv.* —ˌ**al+ter+a·ˈbil+i·ty** *n.*

al+ter·a·tion (ˌɔːltəˈreɪʃən) *n.* **1.** an adjustment, change, or modification. **2.** the act of altering or state of being altered.

al+ter·a·tive (ˈɔːltərətɪv) *adj.* **1.** likely or able to produce alteration. **2.** (of a drug) able to restore normal health. ~*n.* **3.** a drug that restores normal health.

al+ter+cate (ˈɔːltəˌkeɪt) *vb.* (*intr.*) to argue, esp. heatedly; dispute. [C16: from Latin *altercārī* to quarrel with another, from *alter* other]

al+ter+ca+tion (ˌɔːltəˈkeɪʃən) *n.* an angry or heated discussion or quarrel; argument.

al+tered chord *n. Music.* a chord in which one or more notes are chromatically changed by the introduction of accidentals.

al+ter e·go (ˈæltər ˈiːgəʊ, ˈɛgəʊ) *n.* **1.** a second self. **2.** a very close and intimate friend. [Latin: other self]

al+ter+nant (ɔːlˈtɜːnənt) *adj.* alternating. [C17: from French, from Latin *alternāre* to ALTERNATE]

al+ter+nate *vb.* (ˈɔːltəˌneɪt). **1.** (often foll. by *with*) to occur or cause to occur successively or by turns: *day and night alternate.* **2.** (*intr.;* often foll. by *between*) to swing repeatedly from one condition, action, etc., to another: *he alternates between success and failure.* **3.** (*tr.*) to interchange regularly or in succession. **4.** (*intr.*) (of an electric current, voltage, etc.) to reverse direction or sign at regular intervals, usually sinusoidally, the instantaneous value varying continuously. **5.** (*intr.;* often foll. by *for*) *Theatre.* to understudy another actor or actress. ~*adj.* (ɔːlˈtɜːnɪt). **6.** occurring by turns: *alternate feelings of love and hate.* **7.** every other or second one of a series: *he came to work on alternate days.* **8.** being a second or further choice; alternative. **9.** *Botany.* **a.** (of leaves, flowers, etc.) arranged singly at different heights on either side of the stem. **b.** (of parts of a flower) arranged opposite the spaces between other parts. Compare **opposite** (sense 4). ~*n.* (ˈɔːltənɪt, ɔːlˈtɜːnɪt). **10.** *U.S.* a person who substitutes for another in his absence; stand-in. [C16: from Latin *alternāre* to do one thing and then another, from *alternus* one after the other, from *alter* other]

al+ter+nate an+gles *pl. n.* two angles at opposite ends and on opposite sides of a transversal cutting two lines.

al+ter+nate+ly (ɔːlˈtɜːnɪtlɪ) *adv.* in an alternating sequence or position.

al+ter+nat+ing cur+rent *n.* a continuous electric current that reverses direction sinusoidally with a frequency independent of the characteristics of the circuit through which it flows. Abbrev.: **a.c.** Compare **direct current.**

al+ter+nat·ing-gra·di·ent fo+cus+ing *n. Physics.* a method of focusing beams of charged particles in high-energy accelerators, in which a series of magnetic or electrostatic lenses alternately converge and diverge the beam, producing a net focusing effect and thus preventing the beam from spreading.

al+ter+na+tion (ˌɔːltəˈneɪʃən) *n.* **1.** successive change from one condition or action to another and back again repeatedly. **2.** *Logic.* another name for **disjunction** (sense 3).

al+ter+na+tion of gen+er·a+tions *n.* the production within the life cycle of an organism of alternating asexual and sexual reproductive forms. It occurs in many plants and lower animals. Also called: **metagenesis, heterogenesis, digenesis, xenogenesis.**

al+ter+na+tive (ɔːlˈtɜːnətɪv) *n.* **1.** a possibility of choice, esp. between two things, courses of action, etc. **2.** either of such choices: *we took the alternative of walking.* ~*adj.* **3.** presenting a choice, esp. between two possibilities only. **4.** (of two things) mutually exclusive. **5.** *Logic.* another word for **disjunctive** (sense 3). —**al+ˈter+na+tive+ly** *adv.* —**al+ˈter+na+tive+ness** *n.*

al+ter+na+tor (ˈɔːltəˌneɪtə) *n.* an electrical machine that generates an alternating current.

al·thae·a *or U.S.* **al·the·a** (æl'θi:ə) *n.* **1.** any Eurasian plant of the malvaceous genus *Althaea,* such as the hollyhock, having tall spikes of showy white, yellow, or red flowers. **2.** another name for **rose of Sharon** (sense 2). [C17: from Latin *althaea,* from Greek *althaia* marsh mallow (literally: healing plant), from Greek *althein* to heal]

Al·thing ('ælθɪŋ) *n.* the bicameral parliament of Iceland.

alt·horn ('ælt,hɔ:n) *n.* a valved brass musical instrument belonging to the saxhorn or flügelhorn families.

al·though (ɔ:l'ðəʊ) *conj.* (*subordinating*) despite the fact that; even though: *although she was ill, she worked hard.*

al·ti- *combining form.* indicating height or altitude: *altimeter.* [from Latin *altus* high]

al·tim·e·ter (æl'tɪmɪtə, 'æltɪ,mi:tə) *n.* an instrument that indicates height above sea level, esp. one based on an aneroid barometer and fitted to an aircraft.

al·tim·e·try (æl'tɪmɪtrɪ) *n.* the science of measuring altitudes, as with an altimeter. —**al·ti·met·ri·cal** (,æltɪ'mɛtrɪkᵊl) *adj.* —**,al·ti·'met·ri·cal·ly** *adv.*

Al·ti·pla·no (*Spanish* ,alti'plano) *n.* a plateau of the Andes, covering two thirds of Bolivia and extending into S Peru: contains Lake Titicaca. Height: 3000 m (10 000 ft.) to 3900 m (13 000 ft.).

al·tis·si·mo (æl'tɪsɪ,məʊ) *adj.* **1.** (of music) very high in pitch. **2.** of or relating to the octave commencing on the G lying an octave above the treble clef. ~*n.* **3. in altissimo.** in the octave commencing an octave above the treble clef. [Italian, literally: highest]

al·ti·tude ('æltɪ,tju:d) *n.* **1.** the vertical height of an object above some chosen level, esp. above sea level; elevation. **2.** *Maths.* the perpendicular distance from the base of a figure to the opposite vertex. **3.** Also called: **elevation.** *Astronomy, navigation.* the angular distance of a celestial body from the horizon measured along the vertical circle passing through the body. Compare **azimuth** (sense 1). **4.** *Surveying.* the angle of elevation of a point above the horizontal plane of the observer. **5.** (*often pl.*) a high place or region. [C14: from Latin *altitūdō,* from *altus* high, deep] —**,al·ti·'tu·di·nal** *adj.*

al·to ('æltəʊ) *n., pl.* **·tos. 1.** the lowest female voice, usually having a range approximately from F a fifth below middle C up to D a ninth above it. **2.** the highest adult male voice; countertenor. **3.** a singer with such a voice. Compare **contralto. 4.** another name for **viola**[1] (sense 1). **5.** a flute, saxophone, etc., that is the third or fourth highest instrument in its group. ~*adj.* **6.** denoting a flute, saxophone, etc., that is the third or fourth highest instrument in its group. [C18: from Italian: high, from Latin *altus*]

al·to- *combining form.* high: *altocumulus; altostratus.* [from Latin *altus* high]

al·to clef *n.* the clef that establishes middle C as being on the third line of the staff. Also: **viola clef.** See also **C clef.**

al·to·cu·mu·lus (,æltəʊ'kju:mjʊləs) *n., pl.* **·li** (-laɪ). a globular cloud at an intermediate height of about 2400 to 6000 metres (8000 to 20 000 feet).

al·to·geth·er (,ɔ:ltə'gɛðə, 'ɔ:ltə,gɛðə) *adv.* **1.** with everything included: *altogether he owed me sixty pounds.* **2.** completely; utterly; totally: *he was altogether mad.* **3.** on the whole: *altogether it was a very good party.* ~*n.* **4. in the altogether.** *Informal.* naked.

al·to horn *n.* another term for **althorn.**

Al·to·na (æl'təʊnə; *German* 'altona) *n.* a port in N West Germany: part of Hamburg since 1937.

al·to-re·lie·vo *or* **al·to-ri·lie·vo** (,æltəʊrɪ'li:vəʊ) *n., pl.* **·vos.** another name for **high relief.** [C18: from Italian]

al·to·stra·tus (,æltəʊ'streɪtəs, -'strɑ:-) *n., pl.* **·ti** (-taɪ). a layer cloud at an intermediate height of about 2400 to 6000 metres (8000 to 20 000 feet).

al·tri·cial (æl'trɪʃəl) *adj.* **1.** (of young birds after hatching) naked, blind, and dependent on the parents for food. ~*n.* **2.** an altricial bird, such as a pigeon. ~Compare **precocial.** [C19: from New Latin *altriciālis,* from Latin *altrix* a nurse, from *alere* to nourish]

Al·trin·cham ('ɔ:ltrɪŋəm) *n.* a residential town in NW England, in Greater Manchester. Pop.: 40 752 (1971).

al·tru·ism ('æltru:,ɪzəm) *n.* the principle or practice of unselfish concern for the welfare of others. Compare **egoism.** [C19: from French *altruisme,* from Italian *altrui* others, from Latin *alterī,* plural of *alter* other] —**'al·tru·ist** *n.* —**,al·tru·'is·tic** *adj.* —**,al·tru·'is·ti·cal·ly** *adv.*

ALU *Computer technol. abbrev. for* arithmetical and logical unit.

al·u·del ('æljʊ,dɛl) *n. Chem.* a pear-shaped vessel, open at both ends, formerly used with similar vessels for collecting condensates, esp. of subliming mercury. [C16: via Old French from Spanish, from Arabic *al-uthāl* the vessel]

al·u·la ('æljʊlə) *n., pl.* **·lae** (-li:). another name for **bastard wing.** [C18: New Latin: a little wing, from Latin *āla* a wing] —**'al·u·lar** *adj.*

al·um ('æləm) *n.* **1.** Also called: **potash alum.** a colourless soluble hydrated double sulphate of aluminium and potassium used in the manufacture of mordants and pigments, in dressing leather and sizing paper, and in medicine as a styptic and astringent. Formula: $KAl(SO_4)_2.12H_2O$. **2.** any of a group of isomorphic double sulphates of a monovalent metal or group and a trivalent metal. Formula: $XY(SO_4)_2.12H_2O$, where X is monovalent and Y is trivalent. [C14: from Old French, from Latin *alūmen*]

alum. *abbrev. for* aluminium.

a·lu·mi·na (ə'lu:mɪnə) *n.* another name for **aluminium oxide.** [C18: from New Latin, plural of Latin *alūmen* ALUM]

a·lu·mi·nate (ə'lu:mɪneɪt) *n.* a salt of the ortho or meta acid forms of aluminium hydroxide containing the ions AlO_2^- or AlO_3^{3-}.

a·lu·mi·nif·er·ous (ə,lu:mɪ'nɪfərəs) *adj.* containing or yielding aluminium or alumina.

al·u·min·i·um (,æljʊ'mɪnɪəm) *or U.S.* **a·lu·mi·num** (ə'lu:mɪnəm) *n.* a light malleable ductile silvery-white metallic element that resists corrosion; the third most abundant element in the earth's crust (8.1 per cent), occurring only as a compound, principally in bauxite. It is used, esp. in the form of its alloys, in aircraft parts, kitchen utensils, etc. Symbol: Al; atomic no.: 13; atomic wt.: 26.981; valency: 3; relative density: 2.699; melting pt.: 660.2°C; boiling pt.: 2467°C.

a·lu·min·i·um hy·drox·ide *n.* a white crystalline powder derived from bauxite and used in the manufacture of glass and ceramics, aluminium and its salts, and in dyeing. Formula: $Al(OH)_3$ or $Al_2O_3.3H_2O$.

a·lu·min·i·um ox·ide *n.* a white or colourless insoluble powder occurring naturally as corundum and used in the production of aluminium and its compounds, abrasives, glass, and ceramics. Formula: Al_2O_3. Also called: **alumina.** See also **activated alumina.**

a·lu·min·i·um sul·phate *n.* a white crystalline salt used in the paper, textile, and dyeing industries and in the purification of water. Formula: $Al_2(SO_4)_3$.

a·lu·mi·nize *or* **a·lu·mi·nise** (ə'lu:mɪ,naɪz) *vb.* (*tr.*) to cover with aluminium or aluminium paint.

a·lu·mi·no·ther·my (ə,lu:mɪnəʊ'θɜ:mɪ) *n.* a process for reducing metallic oxides using finely divided aluminium powder. The mixture of aluminium and oxide is ignited, causing the aluminium to be oxidized and the metal oxide to be reduced to the metal. Also called: **thermite process.**

a·lu·mi·nous (ə'lu:mɪnəs) *adj.* **1.** resembling aluminium. **2.** another word for **aluminiferous.** —**a·lu·mi·nos·i·ty** (ə,lu:mɪ'nɒsɪtɪ) *n.*

a·lum·nus (ə'lʌmnəs) *or* (*fem.*) **a·lum·na** (ə'lʌmnə) *n., pl.* **·ni** (-naɪ) *or* **·nae** (-ni:). *Chiefly U.S.* a graduate of a school, college, etc. [C17: from Latin: nursling, pupil, foster-son, from *alere* to nourish]

al·um·root ('æləm,ru:t) *n.* **1.** any of several North American plants of the saxifragaceous genus *Heuchera,* having small white, reddish, or green bell-shaped flowers and astringent roots. **2.** the root of such a plant.

A·lun·dum (ə'lʌndəm) *n. Trademark.* a hard material composed of fused alumina, used as an abrasive and a refractory.

al·u·nite ('æljʊ,naɪt) *n.* a white, grey, or reddish mineral consisting of hydrated aluminium sulphate. It occurs in volcanic igneous rocks and is a source of potassium and aluminium compounds. Formula: $KAl_3(SO_4)_2(OH)_6$. [C19: from French *alun* alum (from Latin *alūmen*) + -ITE[1]]

Al·va *or* **Al·ba** (*Spanish* 'alβa) *n.* **Duke of,** title of *Fernando Alvarez de Toledo.* 1508–82, Spanish general and statesman who suppressed the Protestant revolt in the Netherlands (1567–72) and conquered Portugal (1580).

al·ve·o·lar (æl'vɪələ, ,ælvɪ'əʊlə) *adj.* **1.** *Anatomy.* of, relating to, or resembling an alveolus. **2.** denoting the part of the jawbone containing the roots of the teeth. **3.** (of a consonant) articulated with the tongue in contact with the projecting part of the jawbone immediately behind the upper teeth. ~*n.* **4.** an alveolar consonant, such as the speech sounds written *t, d,* and *s* in English.

al·ve·o·late (æl'vɪəlɪt, -,leɪt) *adj.* **1.** having many alveoli. **2.** resembling the deep pits of a honeycomb. [C19: from Late Latin *alveolātus* forming a channel, hollowed, from Latin: ALVEOLUS] —**,al·ve·o·'la·tion** *n.*

al·ve·o·lus (æl'vɪələs) *n., pl.* **·li** (-,laɪ). **1.** any small pit, cavity, or saclike dilation, such as a honeycomb cell. **2.** any of the sockets in which the roots of the teeth are embedded. **3.** any of the tiny air sacs in the lungs at the end of the bronchioles, through which oxygen is taken into the blood. [C18: from Latin: a little hollow, diminutive of *alveus*]

al·vine ('ælvɪn, -vaɪn) *adj. Obsolete.* of or relating to the intestines or belly. [C18: from Latin *alvus* belly]

al·ways ('ɔ:lweɪz, -wɪz) *adv.* **1.** without exception; on every occasion; every time: *he always arrives on time.* **2.** continually; repeatedly. **3.** in any case: *you could always take a day off work.* **4. for always.** *Informal.* for ever; without end: *our marriage is for always.* ~Also (archaic): **al·way.** [C13 *alles weiss,* from Old English *ealne weg,* literally: all the way; see ALL, WAY]

a·lys·sum ('ælɪsəm) *n.* any widely cultivated herbaceous garden plant of the genus *Alyssum,* having clusters of small yellow or white flowers: family *Cruciferae* (crucifers). See also **sweet alyssum.** [C16: from New Latin, from Greek *alusson,* from *alussos* (adj.) curing rabies, referring to the ancient belief in the plant's healing properties]

am (æm; *unstressed* əm) *vb.* (used with *I*) a form of the present tense (indicative mood) of **be.** [Old English *eam;* related to Old Norse *em,* Gothic *im,* Old High German *bim,* Latin *sum,* Greek *eimi,* Sanskrit *asmi*]

Am *the chemical symbol for* americium.

AM *or* **am** *abbrev. for* amplitude modulation.

Am. *abbrev. for* America(n).

a.m. *or* **A.M.** (indicating the time period from midnight to midday) *abbrev. for* ante meridiem. [Latin: before noon] Compare **p.m.**

A.M. *abbrev. for:* **1.** associate member. **2.** Albert Medal. **3.** (in the U.S.) Master of Arts.
A.M.A. *abbrev. for* American Medical Association.
am·a+da+vat (ˌæmədəˈvæt) *n.* another name for **avadavat.**
am·a+dou (ˈæməˌduː) *n.* a spongy substance made from certain fungi, such as *Polyporus* (or *Fomes*) *fomentarius* and related species, used as tinder to light fires and in medicine to stop bleeding. [C18: from French, from Provençal: lover, from Latin *amātor,* from *amāre* to love; so called because it readily ignites]
A·ma+ga+sa+ki (əˌmɑːgəˈsɑːkɪ) *n.* an industrial city in Japan, in W Honshu, on Osaka Bay. Pop.: 537 781 (1974 est.).
a·mah (ˈɑːmə, ˈæmə) *n.* (in the East, esp. formerly) a nurse or maidservant. [C19: from Portuguese *ama* nurse, wet nurse]
a·main (əˈmeɪn) *adv. Archaic or poetic.* with great strength, speed, or haste. [C16: from A-[2] + MAIN[1]]
Am·a+lek+ite (əˈmæləˌkaɪt) *n. Old Testament.* a member of a nomadic tribe descended from Esau (Genesis 36:12), dwelling in the desert between Sinai and Canaan and hostile to the Israelites: they were defeated by Saul and destroyed by David (I Samuel 15–30).
a·mal+gam (əˈmælgəm) *n.* **1.** an alloy of mercury with another metal, esp. with silver: *dental amalgam.* **2.** a rare white metallic mineral that consists of silver and mercury and occurs in deposits of silver and cinnabar. **3.** a blend or combination. [C15: from Medieval Latin *amalgama,* of obscure origin]
a·mal+gam+ate (əˈmælgəˌmeɪt) *vb.* **1.** to combine or cause to combine; unite. **2.** to alloy (a metal) with mercury.
a·mal+gam·a·tion (əˌmælgəˈmeɪʃən) *n.* **1.** the action or process of amalgamating. **2.** the state of being amalgamated. **3.** a method of extracting precious metals from their ores by treatment with mercury to form an amalgam. **4.** *Commerce.* another word for **merger** (sense 1).
A·mal·the·a (ˌæmælˈθiːə) *n. Greek myth.* **a.** a nymph who brought up the infant Zeus on goat's milk. **b.** the goat itself. Also: **Amaltheia.**
am·a+ni+ta (ˌæməˈnaɪtə) *n.* any of various saprophytic agaricaceous fungi constituting the genus *Amanita,* having white gills and a broken membranous ring (volva) around the stalk. The genus includes several highly poisonous species, such as death cap, destroying angel, and fly agaric. [C19: from Greek *amanitai* (plural) a variety of fungus]
a·man·u·en+sis (əˌmænjʊˈɛnsɪs) *n., pl.* **+ses** (-siːz). a person employed to take dictation or to copy manuscripts. [C17: from Latin *āmanuensis,* from the phrase *servus ā manū* slave at hand (that is, handwriting)]
A·ma+pá (*Portuguese* ˌəmaˈpa) *n.* a territory of N Brazil, on the Amazon delta. Capital: Macapá. Pop.: 114 359 (1970). Area: 143 716 sq. km (55 489 sq. miles).
am·a+ranth (ˈæməˌrænθ) *n.* **1.** *Poetic.* an imaginary flower that never fades. **2.** any of numerous tropical and temperate plants of the genus *Amaranthus,* having tassel-like heads of small green, red, or purple flowers: family *Amaranthaceae.* See also **love-lies-bleeding, tumbleweed, pigweed** (sense 1). [C17: from Latin *amarantus,* from Greek *amarantos* unfading, from A-[1] + *marainein* to fade]
am·a+ran+tha+ceous (ˌæmərænˈθeɪʃəs) *adj.* of, relating to, or belonging to the *Amaranthaceae* (or *Amarantaceae*), a family of tropical and temperate herbaceous or shrubby flowering plants that includes the amaranths and cockscomb.
am·a+ran+thine (ˌæməˈrænθaɪn) *adj.* **1.** of a dark reddish-purple colour. **2.** of or resembling the amaranth.
am·a+relle (ˈæməˌrɛl) *n.* a variety of sour cherry that has pale red fruit and colourless juice. Compare **morello.** [C20: from German, from Medieval Latin *amārellum,* from Latin *amārus* bitter; compare MORELLO]
Am·a+ril+lo (ˌæməˈrɪləʊ) *n.* an industrial city in NW Texas. Pop.: 129 808 (1973 est.).
am·a+ryl+li+da+ceous (ˌæməˌrɪlɪˈdeɪʃəs) *adj.* of, relating to, or belonging to the *Amaryllidaceae,* a tropical and subtropical family of widely cultivated flowering plants having bulbs and including the amaryllis, snowdrop, narcissus, and daffodil.
am·a+ryl+lis (ˌæməˈrɪlɪs) *n.* **1.** Also called: **belladonna lily.** an amaryllidaceous plant, *Amaryllis belladonna,* native to southern Africa and having large lily-like reddish or white flowers. **2.** any of several related plants. [C18: from New Latin, from Latin: named after AMARYLLIS]
Am·a+ryl+lis (ˌæməˈrɪlɪs) *n.* (in pastoral poetry) a name for a shepherdess or country girl.
a·mass (əˈmæs) *vb.* **1.** (*tr.*) to accumulate or collect (esp. riches, etc.). **2.** to gather in a heap; bring together. [C15: from Old French *amasser,* from *masse* MASS] **—a·ˈmass+er** *n.*
am·a+teur (ˈæmətə, -tʃə, -ˌtjʊə; ˌæməˈtɜː) *n.* **1.** a person who engages in an activity, esp. a sport, as a pastime rather than professionally or for gain. **2.** an athlete or sportsman. **3.** a person unskilled in or having only a superficial knowledge of a subject or activity. **4.** a person who is fond of or admires something. **5.** (*modifier*) consisting of or for amateurs: *an amateur event.* ~*adj.* **6.** amateurish; not professional or expert: *an amateur approach.* [C18: from French, from Latin *amātor* lover, from *amāre* to love] **—ˈam·a+teur+ism** *n.*
am·a+teur+ish (ˈæmətərɪʃ, -tʃər- -ˌtʃʊər-; ˌæməˈtɜːrɪʃ) *adj.* lacking professional skill or expertise. **—ˈam·a+teur+ish+ly** *adv.* **—ˈam·a+teur+ish+ness** *n.*
A·ma·ti (*Italian* aˈmaːti) *n.* **1.** a family of Italian violin makers, active in Cremona in the 16th and 17th centuries, esp. **Ni·co·lò** (nikoˈlɔ), 1596–1684, who taught Guarneri and Stradivari. **2.** a violin or other stringed instrument made by any member of this family.
am·a+tive (ˈæmətɪv) *adj.* a rare word for **amorous.** [C17: from Medieval Latin *amātīvus,* from Latin *amāre* to love] **—ˈam·a+tive+ly** *adv.* **—ˈam·a+tive+ness** *n.*
am·a+tol (ˈæməˌtɒl) *n.* an explosive mixture of ammonium nitrate and TNT, used in shells and bombs. [C20: from AM(MONIUM) + (TRINITRO) TOL(UENE)]
am·a+to+ry (ˈæmətərɪ) *or* **am·a+to+ri·al** *adj.* of, relating to, or inciting sexual love or desire. [C16: from Latin *amātōrius,* from *amāre* to love]
am·au+ro+sis (ˌæmɔːˈrəʊsɪs) *n. Pathol.* blindness, esp. when occurring without observable damage to the eye. [C17: via New Latin from Greek: darkening, from *amauroun* to dim, darken] **—am·au+rot+ic** (ˌæmɔːˈrɒtɪk) *adj.*
a·maut *or* **a·mowt** (əˈmaʊt) *n. Canadian.* a hood on an Eskimo woman's parka for carrying a child. [from Eskimo]
a·maze (əˈmeɪz) *vb.* (*tr.*) **1.** to fill with incredulity or surprise; astonish. **2.** an obsolete word for **bewilder.** ~*n.* **3.** an archaic word for **amazement.** [Old English *āmasian;* see MAZE]
a·maze+ment (əˈmeɪzmənt) *n.* **1.** incredulity or great astonishment; complete wonder or surprise. **2.** *Obsolete.* bewilderment or consternation.
a·maz+ing (əˈmeɪzɪŋ)) *adj.* causing wonder or astonishment: *amazing feats.* **—a·ˈmaz+ing+ly** *adv.*
am·a+zon (ˈæməzᵊn) *n.* any of various tropical American parrots of the genus *Amazona,* such as *A. farinosa* (green amazon), having a short tail and mainly green plumage.
Am·a+zon[1] (ˈæməzᵊn) *n.* **1.** *Greek myth.* one of a race of women warriors of Scythia near the Black Sea. **2.** one of a legendary tribe of female warriors of South America. **3.** (*often not cap.*) any tall, strong, or aggressive woman. [C14: via Latin from Greek *Amazōn,* of uncertain origin] **—Am·a+zo+ni·an** (ˌæməˈzəʊnɪən) *adj.*
Am·a+zon[2] (ˈæməzᵊn) *n.* a river in South America, rising in the Peruvian Andes and flowing east through N Brazil to the Atlantic: in volume, the largest river in the world; navigable for 3700 km (2300 miles). Length: over 6440 km (4000 miles). Area of basin: over 5 827 500 sq. km (2 250 000 sq. miles). **—Am·a+zo+ni·an** (ˌæməˈzəʊnɪən) *adj.*
am·a+zon ant *n.* any of several small reddish ants of the genus *Polyergus,* esp. *P. rufescens,* that enslave the young of other ant species.
A·ma+zo+nas (ˌæməˈzəʊnəs) *n.* a state of W Brazil, consisting of the central Amazon basin: vast areas of unexplored tropical rain-forest. Capital: Manaus. Pop.: 955 235 (1970). Area: 1 542 277 sq. km (595 474 sq. miles).
am·a+zon+ite (ˈæməzəˌnaɪt) *n.* a green variety of microcline used as a gemstone. Formula: $KAlSi_3O_8$. Also called: **Amazon stone.**
am+bage (ˈæmbɪdʒ) *n., pl.* **am+bag·es** (ˈæmbɪdʒɪz, æmˈbeɪdʒiːz). *Archaic.* (*often pl.*) circuitous, secret, or tortuous paths, ways, thoughts, etc. [C14: via Old French from Latin *ambāges* a going around, from *ambi-* around + *agere* to lead] **—am+ba+gious** (æmˈbeɪdʒəs) *adj.*
Am+ba+la (əmˈbɑːlə) *n.* a city in N India, in Haryana: site of archaeological remains of a prehistoric Indian civilization. Pop.: 102 493 (1971).
am+ba+ry *or* **am+ba+ri** (æmˈbɑːrɪ) *n., pl.* **+ries** *or* **+ris. 1.** a tropical Asian malvaceous plant, *Hibiscus cannabinus,* that yields a fibre similar to jute. **2.** the fibre derived from this plant. ~Also called: **kenaf.** [C20: from Hindi *ambārī*]
am+bas+sa+dor (æmˈbæsədə) *n.* **1.** short for **ambassador extraordinary and plenipotentiary;** a diplomatic minister of the highest rank, accredited as permanent representative to another country or sovereign. **2. ambassador extraordinary.** a diplomatic minister of the highest rank sent on a special mission. **3. ambassador plenipotentiary.** a diplomatic minister of the first rank with treaty-signing powers. **4. ambassador-at-large.** *U.S.* an ambassador with special duties who may be sent to more than one government. **5.** an authorized representative or messenger. [C14: from Old French *ambassadeur,* from Italian *ambasciator,* from Old Provençal *ambaisador,* from *ambaisa* (unattested) mission, errand; see EMBASSY] **—am+ˈbas+sa+dress** *fem. n.* **—am+bas+sa+dor+i·al** (æmˌbæsəˈdɔːrɪəl) *adj.* **—am+ˈbas+sa+dor+ˌship** *n.*
am+ber (ˈæmbə) *n.* **1. a.** a yellow or yellowish-brown hard translucent fossil resin derived from extinct coniferous trees that occurs in Tertiary deposits and often contains trapped insects. It is used for jewellery, ornaments, etc. **b.** (*as modifier*): *an amber necklace.* **2. a.** a medium to dark brownish-yellow colour, often somewhat orange, similar to that of the resin. **b.** (*as adj.*): *an amber dress.* **3.** an amber traffic light used as a warning between red and green. [C14: from Medieval Latin *ambar,* from Arabic *ʽanbar* ambergris]
am+ber+gris (ˈæmbəˌgriːs, -grɪs) *n.* a waxy substance consisting mainly of cholesterol secreted by the intestinal tract of the sperm whale and often found floating in the sea: used in the manufacture of perfumes. [C15: from Old French *ambre gris* grey amber]
am+ber+jack (ˈæmbəˌdʒæk) *n.* any of several large carangid fishes of the genus *Seriola,* esp. *S. dumerili,* with golden markings when young, occurring in tropical and subtropical Atlantic waters. [C19: from AMBER + JACK[1]]
am+ber+oid (ˈæmbəˌrɔɪd) *or* **am+broid** *n.* a synthetic amber made by compressing pieces of amber and other resins together at a high temperature.
am+bi- *combining form.* indicating both: *ambidextrous; ambivalence; ambiversion.* [from Latin: round, on both sides, both, from *ambo* both; compare AMPHI-]
am+bi+dex+trous (ˌæmbɪˈdɛkstrəs) *adj.* **1.** equally expert with

each hand. **2.** *Informal.* highly skilled or adept. **3.** underhanded; deceitful. —**am·bi·dex·ter·i·ty** (ˌæmbɪdɛkˈstɛrɪtɪ) *or* ˌ**am·bi·ˈdex·trous·ness** *n.* —ˌ**am·bi·ˈdex·trous·ly** *adv.*

am·bi·ence *or* **am·bi·ance** (ˈæmbɪəns; *French* ãˈbjã:s) *n.* the atmosphere of a place. [C19: from French *ambiance,* from *ambiant* surrounding; see AMBIENT]

am·bi·ent (ˈæmbɪənt) *adj.* of or relating to the immediate surroundings: *the ambient temperature was 15°C.* [C16: from Latin *ambiēns* going round, from *ambīre,* from AMBI- + *īre* to go]

am·bi·gu·i·ty (ˌæmbɪˈgju:ɪtɪ) *n., pl.* **·ties. 1.** vagueness or uncertainty of meaning. **2.** an instance of this, as in the sentence *they are cooking apples.* **3.** an ambiguous phrase, statement, etc.

am·big·u·ous (æmˈbɪgjʊəs) *adj.* **1.** having more than one possible interpretation or meaning. **2.** difficult to understand or classify; obscure. [C16: from Latin *ambiguus* going here and there, uncertain, from *ambigere* to go around, from AMBI- + *agere* to lead, act] —**am·ˈbig·u·ous·ly** *adv.* —**am·ˈbig·u·ous·ness** *n.*

am·bit (ˈæmbɪt) *n.* **1.** scope or extent. **2.** limits, boundary, or circumference. [C16: from Latin *ambitus* a going round, from *ambīre* to go round, from AMBI- + *īre* to go]

am·bi·tion (æmˈbɪʃən) *n.* **1.** strong desire for success, achievement, or distinction. **2.** something so desired; goal; aim. [C14: from Old French, from Latin *ambitiō* a going round (of candidates), a striving to please, from *ambīre* to go round; see AMBIT]

am·bi·tious (æmˈbɪʃəs) *adj.* **1.** having a strong desire for success or achievement; wanting power, money, etc. **2.** necessitating extraordinary effort or ability: *an ambitious project.* **3.** (often foll. by *of*) having a great desire (for something or to do something). —**am·ˈbi·tious·ly** *adv.* —**am·ˈbi·tious·ness** *n.*

am·biv·a·lence (æmˈbɪvələns) *or* **am·biv·a·len·cy** *n.* the simultaneous existence of two opposed and conflicting attitudes, emotions, etc. —**am·ˈbiv·a·lent** *adj.*

am·bi·vert (ˈæmbɪˌvɜ:t) *n. Psychol.* a person who is intermediate between an extravert and an introvert. —**am·bi·ver·sion** (ˌæmbɪˈvɜ:ʃən) *n.*

am·ble (ˈæmbᵊl) *vb.* (*intr.*) **1.** to walk at a leisurely relaxed pace. **2.** (of a horse) to move slowly, lifting both legs on one side together. **3.** to ride a horse at an amble or leisurely pace. ~*n.* **4.** a leisurely motion in walking. **5.** a leisurely walk. **6.** the ambling gait of a horse. [C14: from Old French *ambler,* from Latin *ambulāre* to walk] —**ˈam·bler** *n.*

am·blyg·o·nite (æmˈblɪgəˌnaɪt) *n.* a white or greyish mineral consisting of lithium aluminium fluophosphate in triclinic crystalline form. It is a source of lithium. Formula: $LiAl(PO_4)(F,OH)$. [C16: from Greek *amblugōnios,* from *amblus* blunt + *gōnia* angle; referring to the obtuse angles in its crystals]

am·bly·o·pi·a (ˌæmblɪˈəʊpɪə) *n.* impaired vision with no discernible damage to the eye or optic nerve. [C18: New Latin, from Greek *ambluōpia,* from *amblus* dull, dim + *ōps* eye] —**am·bly·op·ic** (ˌæmblɪˈɒpɪk) *adj.*

am·bo (ˈæmbəʊ) *n., pl.* **·bos.** either of two raised pulpits from which the gospels and epistles were read in early Christian churches. [C17: from Medieval Latin, from Greek *ambōn* raised rim, pulpit]

am·bo·cep·tor (ˈæmbəʊˌsɛptə) *n.* an immune body formed in the blood during infection or immunization that serves to link the complement to the antigen. [C20: from Latin *ambō* both (see AMBI-) + (RE)CEPTOR]

Am·boi·na (æmˈbɔɪnə) *n.* **1.** an island in Indonesia, in the Moluccas. Capital: Amboina. Area: 1000 sq. km (386 sq. miles). **2.** Also called: **Am·bon** (ˈɑ:mbɔ:n). a port in the Moluccas, the capital of Amboina Island.

Am·boise (*French* ãˈbwa:z) *n.* a town in NW central France, on the River Loire: famous castle, a former royal residence. Pop.: 8000 (1968 est.).

am·boy·na *or* **am·boi·na** (æmˈbɔɪnə) *n.* the mottled curly-grained wood of an Indonesian papilionaceous tree, *Pterocarpus indicus,* used in making furniture.

am·broid (ˈæmbrɔɪd) *n.* a variant spelling of **amberoid.**

Am·brose (ˈæmbrəʊz) *n.* **Saint.** ?340–397 A.D., bishop of Milan; built up the secular power of the early Christian Church; also wrote music and Latin hymns. Feast day: Dec. 7. —**Am·ˈbro·si·an** *adj.*

am·bro·si·a (æmˈbrəʊzɪə) *n.* **1.** *Classical myth.* the food of the gods, said to bestow immortality. Compare **nectar** (sense 2). **2.** anything particularly delightful to taste or smell. **3.** another name for **beebread. 4.** any of various herbaceous plants constituting the genus *Ambrosia,* mostly native to America but widely naturalized: family *Compositae* (composites). The genus includes the ragweeds. [C16: via Latin from Greek: immortality, from *ambrotos,* from A-¹ + *brotos* mortal] —**am·ˈbro·si·al** *or* **am·ˈbro·si·an** *adj.* —**am·ˈbro·si·al·ly** *adv.*

am·bro·si·a bee·tle *n.* any of various small beetles of the genera *Anisandrus, Xyleborus,* etc., that bore tunnels into solid wood, feeding on fungi growing in the tunnels: family *Scolytidae* (bark beetles).

am·bro·type (ˈæmbrəʊˌtaɪp) *n. Photog.* an early type of glass negative that could be made to appear as a positive by backing it with black varnish or paper. [C19: from Greek *ambrotos* immortal + -TYPE; see AMBROSIA]

am·bry (ˈæmbrɪ) *or* **aum·bry** (ˈɔ:mbrɪ) *n., pl.* **·bries. 1.** a recessed cupboard in the wall of a church near the altar, used to store sacred vessels, etc. **2.** *Obsolete.* a small cupboard or other storage space. [C14: from Old French *almarie,* from Medieval Latin *almārium,* from Latin *armārium* chest for storage, from *arma* arms]

ambs·ace *or* **ames·ace** (ˈeɪmzˌeɪs, ˈæmz-) *n.* **1.** double ace, the lowest throw at dice. **2.** bad luck. [C13: from Old French *ambes as,* both aces; *as* from Latin: unit]

am·bu·lac·rum (ˌæmbjʊˈleɪkrəm) *n., pl.* **·ra** (-rə). any of five radial bands on the ventral surface of echinoderms, such as the starfish and sea urchin, on which the tube feet are situated. [C19: from Latin: avenue, from *ambulāre* to walk] —ˌ**am·bu·ˈlac·ral** *adj.*

am·bu·lance (ˈæmbjʊləns) *n.* a motor vehicle designed to carry sick or injured people. [C19: from French, based on (*hôpital*) *ambulant* mobile or field (hospital), from Latin *ambulāre* to walk]

am·bu·lance chas·er *n. U.S. slang.* a lawyer who seeks to encourage and profit from the lawsuits of accident victims. —**am·bu·lance chas·ing** *n.*

am·bu·lant (ˈæmbjʊlənt) *adj.* **1.** moving about from place to place. **2.** *Med.* another word for **ambulatory** (sense 3).

am·bu·late (ˈæmbjʊˌleɪt) *vb.* (*intr.*) to wander about or move from one place to another. [C17: from Latin *ambulāre* to walk, AMBLE] —ˌ**am·bu·ˈla·tion** *n.*

am·bu·la·to·ry (ˌæmbjʊˈleɪtərɪ) *adj.* **1.** of, relating to, or designed for walking. **2.** changing position; not fixed. **3.** Also: **ambulant.** able to walk. **4.** *Law.* (esp. of a will) capable of being altered or revoked. ~*n., pl.* **·ries. 5.** *Architect.* **a.** an aisle running around the east end of a church, esp. one that passes behind the sanctuary. **b.** a place for walking, such as an aisle or a cloister.

am·bus·cade (ˌæmbəˈskeɪd) *n.* **1.** an ambush. ~*vb.* **2.** to ambush or lie in ambush. [C16: from French *embuscade,* from Old Italian *imboscata,* probably of Germanic origin; compare AMBUSH]

am·bush (ˈæmbʊʃ) *n.* **1.** the act of waiting in a concealed position in order to launch a surprise attack. **2.** a surprise attack from such a position. **3.** the concealed position from which such an attack is launched. **4.** the person or persons waiting to launch such an attack. ~*vb.* **5.** to lie in wait (for). **6.** (*tr.*) to attack suddenly from a concealed position. [C14: from Old French *embuschier* to position in ambush, from *em-* IM- + *-buschier,* from *busche* piece of firewood, probably of Germanic origin; see BUSH¹]

A.M.D.G. *abbrev. for* ad majorem Dei gloriam (the Jesuit motto). [Latin: to the greater glory of God]

a·me·ba (əˈmi:bə) *n., pl.* **·bae** (-bi:) *or* **·bas.** the usual U.S. spelling of **amoeba.** —**a·ˈme·bic** *adj.*

a·meer (əˈmɪə) *n.* **1.** a variant spelling of **emir. 2.** (formerly) the ruler of Afghanistan; amir.

a·me·lio·rate (əˈmi:ljəˌreɪt) *vb.* to make or become better; improve. [C18: from MELIORATE, influenced by French *améliorer* to improve, from Old French *ameillorer* to make better, from *meillor* better, from Latin *melior*] —**a·me·lio·ra·ble** (əˈmi:ljərəbᵊl) *adj.* —**a·ˈme·lio·rant** *n.* —**a·ˈme·lio·ra·tive** *adj.* —**a·ˈme·lio·ˌra·tor** *n.*

a·me·lio·ra·tion (əˌmi:ljəˈreɪʃən) *n.* **1.** the act or an instance of ameliorating or the state of being ameliorated. **2.** something that ameliorates; an improvement. **3.** Also called: **elevation.** *Linguistics.* (of the meaning of a word) a change from pejorative to neutral or positively pleasant. The word *nice* has achieved its modern meaning by amelioration from the earlier sense *foolish, silly.*

a·men (ˌeɪˈmɛn, ˌɑ:ˈmɛn) *interj.* **1.** So be it! A term used at the end of a prayer or religious statement. ~*n.* **2.** the use of the word *amen,* as at the end of a prayer. **3. say amen to.** to give assent to. [C13: via Late Latin via Greek from Hebrew *āmēn* certainly]

A·men, A·mon, *or* **A·mūn** (ˈɑ:mən) *n. Egyptian myth.* a local Theban god, having a ram's head and symbolizing life and fertility, identified by the Egyptians with the national deity Amen-Ra.

a·me·na·ble (əˈmi:nəbᵊl) *adj.* **1.** open or susceptible to suggestion; likely to listen, cooperate, etc. **2.** accountable for behaviour to some authority; answerable. **3.** capable of being or liable to be tested, judged, etc. [C16: from Anglo-French, from Old French *amener* to lead up, from Latin *mināre* to drive (cattle), from *minārī* to threaten] —**a·ˌme·na·ˈbil·i·ty** *or* **a·ˈme·na·ble·ness** *n.* —**a·ˈme·na·bly** *adv.*

a·men cor·ner *n.* **the.** *U.S.* the part of a church, usually to one side of the pulpit, occupied by people who lead the responsive amens during the service.

a·mend (əˈmɛnd) *vb.* (*tr.*) **1.** to improve; change for the better. **2.** to remove faults from; correct. **3.** to alter or revise (legislation, a constitution, etc.) by formal procedure. [C13: from Old French *amender,* from Latin *ēmendāre* to EMEND] —**a·ˈmend·a·ble** *adj.* —**a·ˈmend·er** *n.*

a·mend·a·to·ry (əˈmɛndətərɪ, -trɪ) *adj. U.S.* serving to amend; corrective.

a·mend·ment (əˈmɛndmənt) *n.* **1.** the act of amending; correction. **2.** an addition, alteration, or improvement to a motion, document, etc.

a·mends (əˈmɛndz) *n.* recompense or compensation given or gained for some injury, insult, etc.: *to make amends.* [C13: from Old French *amendes* fines, from *amende* compensation, from *amender* to EMEND]

A·men·ho·tep III (ˌæmɛnˈhəʊtɛp) *or* **A·men·hot·pe III** (ˌæmɛnˈhɒtpɪ) *n.* Greek name *Amenophis.* ?1411–?1375 B.C., Egyptian pharaoh who expanded Egypt's influence by peaceful diplomacy and erected many famous buildings.

Am·en·ho·tep IV *or* **Am·en·hot·pe IV** *n.* the original name of **Akhenaten.**

a·men+i·ty (əˈmiːnɪtɪ) *n., pl.* **·ties. 1.** (*often pl.*) a useful or pleasant facility or service: *a swimming pool was just one of the amenities.* **2.** the fact or condition of being pleasant or agreeable. **3.** (*usually pl.*) a social courtesy or pleasantry. [C14: from Latin *amoenitās* pleasantness, from *amoenus* agreeable]

a·men+or+rhoe·a *or esp. U.S.* **a·men+or+rhe·a** (æˌmɛnəˈrɪə, eɪ-) *n.* abnormal absence of menstruation. [C19: from A-[1] + MENO- + -RRHOEA]

A·men-Ra (ˌɑːmənˈrɑː) *n. Egyptian myth.* the sun-god; the principle deity during the period of Theban hegemony.

a men+sa et tho+ro (eɪ ˈmɛnsə ɛt ˈθɔːrəʊ) *adj. Law.* denoting or relating to a form of divorce in which the parties remain married but do not cohabit: abolished in England in 1857. [Latin: from table and bed]

am+ent[1] (ˈæmənt, ˈeɪmənt) *n.* another name for **catkin.** Also called: **amentum.** [C18: from Latin *āmentum* strap, thong] **—ˌam+en+ˈta·ceous** *adj.* **—ˌam+en+ˈtif+er+ous** *adj.*

a·ment[2] (æˈmɛnt, ˈeɪmənt) *n. Psychiatry.* a mentally deficient person. [C19: from Latin *āment-, āmens* without mind; see AMENTIA]

a·men+tia (əˈmɛnʃə) *n.* severe mental deficiency, usually congenital. Compare **dementia.** [C14: from Latin: insanity, from *āmēns* mad, from *mēns* mind]

Amer. *abbrev. for* America(n).

a·merce (əˈmɜːs) *vb.* (*tr.*) *Obsolete.* **1.** *Law.* to punish by a fine. **2.** to punish with any arbitrary penalty. [C14: from Anglo-French *amercier,* from Old French *à merci* at the mercy (because the fine was arbitrarily fixed); see MERCY] **—a·ˈmerce+a·ble** *adj.* **—a·ˈmerce+ment** *n.* **—a·ˈmerc+er** *n.*

A·mer·i·ca (əˈmɛrɪkə) *n.* **1.** short for the **United States of America. 2.** Also called: **the Americas.** the American continent, including North, South, and Central America. [C16: from *Americus,* Latin form of *Amerigo;* see VESPUCCI]

A·mer·i+can (əˈmɛrɪkən) *adj.* **1.** of or relating to the United States of America, its inhabitants, or their form of English. **2.** of or relating to the American continent. **3.** *Rare.* of or relating to the American Indians. *~n.* **4.** a native or citizen of the U.S. **5.** a native or inhabitant of any country of North, Central, or South America. **6.** the English language as spoken or written in the United States.

A·mer·i+ca+na (əˌmɛrɪˈkɑːnə) *n.* objects, such as books, documents, relics, etc., relating to America, esp. in the form of a collection.

A·mer·i+can al·oe *n.* another name for **century plant.**

A·mer·i+can Beau+ty *n.* a variety of hybrid perennial rose bearing large long-stemmed purplish-red flowers.

A·mer·i+can cha+me·le·on *n.* another name for **anole.**

A·mer·i+can cheese *n.* a type of smooth hard white or yellow cheese similar to a mild Cheddar.

A·mer·i+can cloth *n.* a glazed or waterproofed cotton cloth.

A·mer·i+can ea·gle *n.* another name for **bald eagle,** esp. when depicted as the national emblem of the U.S.

A·mer·i+can Ex+pe+di+tion+ar·y Forc·es *pl. n.* the troops sent to Europe by the U.S. during World War I.

A·mer·i+can Fed+er·a+tion of La+bor *n.* the first permanent national labour movement in America, founded in 1886. It amalgamated with the Congress of Industrial Organizations in 1955. See also **AFL-CIO.**

A·mer·i+can foot+ball *n.* **1.** a team game similar to rugby, with 11 players on each side. Forward passing is allowed and planned strategies and formations for play are decided during the course of the game. **2.** the oval-shaped inflated ball used in this game.

A·mer·i+can In+di·an *n.* **1.** Also called: **Indian, Red Indian, Amerindian.** a member of any of the indigenous peoples of North, Central, or South America, having Mongoloid affinities, notably straight black hair and a yellow to brown skin. *~adj.* **2.** of or relating to any of these peoples, their languages, or their cultures.

A·mer·i+can In+di·an Move+ment *n.* a militant movement or grouping of American Indians, organized in 1968 to combat discrimination, injustice, etc. Abbrev.: **AIM.**

A·mer·i+can+ism (əˈmɛrɪkəˌnɪzəm) *n.* **1.** a custom, linguistic usage, or other feature peculiar to or characteristic of the United States, its people, or their culture. **2.** loyalty to the United States, its people, customs, etc.

A·mer·i+can+ist (əˈmɛrɪkənɪst) *n.* a person who studies some aspect of America, such as its history or languages.

A·mer·i+can+ize *or* **A·mer·i+can+ise** (əˈmɛrɪkəˌnaɪz) *vb.* to make or become American in outlook, attitudes, etc. **—A·ˌmer·i+can·i+ˈza+tion** *or* **A·ˌmer·i+can·i+ˈsa+tion** *n.* **—A·ˈmer·i+can+ˌiz+er** *or* **A·ˈmer·i+can+ˌis+er** *n.*

A·mer·i+can plan *n. U.S.* a hotel rate in which the charge includes meals. Compare **European plan.**

A·mer·i+can Rev+o+lu+tion *n.* the usual U.S. term for **War of American Independence.**

A·mer·i+can Sa+mo·a *n.* the part of Samoa administered by the U.S. Capital: Pago Pago. Pop.: 27 769 (1970). Area: 197 sq. km (76 sq. miles).

A·mer·i+can Stand+ard Ver+sion *n.* a revised version of the Authorized (King James) Version of the Bible, published by a committee of American scholars in 1901.

A·mer·i+can tryp·a+no+so+mi·a+sis *n. Pathol.* another name for **Chagas' disease.**

A·mer·i·ca's Cup *n.* an international yachting trophy, first won by the schooner *America* in 1851 and since then held as a challenge trophy by the New York Yacht Club.

am+er·i·ci·um (ˌæməˈrɪsɪəm) *n.* a white metallic transuranic element artificially produced from plutonium. It is used as an alpha-particle source. Symbol: Am; atomic no.: 95; half-life of most stable isotope, ^{243}Am: 7.4×10^3 years; valency: 3,4,5, or 6; relative density: 13.67; melting pt.: 995°C; boiling pt.: 2607°C (est.).

A·mer·i·go Ve·spuc·ci (*Italian* ˌameˈriːgo vesˈputtʃi) *n.* See **Vespucci.**

Am+er+in·di·an (ˌæməˈrɪndɪən) *n. also* **Am+er+ind** (ˈæmərɪnd), *adj.* another word for **American Indian.** **—ˌAm+er+ˈin·dic** *adj.*

A·mers+foort (*Dutch* ˈaːmərsˌfoːrt) *n.* a town in the central Netherlands, in E Utrecht province. Pop.: 79 876 (1973 est.).

ames+ace (ˈeɪmzˈeɪs, ˈæmz-) *n.* a variant spelling of **ambsace.**

am+e·thyst (ˈæmɪθɪst) *n.* **1.** a purple or violet transparent variety of quartz used as a gemstone. Formula: SiO_2. **2.** a purple variety of sapphire; oriental amethyst. **3.** the purple colour of amethyst. [C13: from Old French *amatiste,* from Latin *amethystus,* from Greek *amethustos,* literally: not drunken, from A-[1] + *methuein* to make drunk; referring to the belief that the stone could prevent intoxication] **—am+e·thys+tine** (ˌæmɪˈθɪstaɪn) *adj.*

am+e·tro+pi·a (ˌæmɪˈtrəʊpɪə) *n.* loss of ability to focus images on the retina, caused by an imperfection in the refractive function of the eye. [C19: New Latin, from Greek *ametros* unmeasured (from A-[1] + *metron* measure) + *ōps* eye]

Am·for·tas (æmˈfɔːtəs) *n.* (in medieval legend) the leader of the knights of the Holy Grail.

Am+ha+ra (æmˈhɑːrə) *n.* **1.** a province of NW Ethiopia: formerly a kingdom. Capital: Gondar. Area: 197 448 sq. km (76 235 sq. miles). **2.** an inhabitant of the former kingdom of Amhara.

Am+har+ic (æmˈhærɪk) *n.* **1.** the official language of Ethiopia, belonging to the SE Semitic subfamily of the Afro-Asiatic family. *~adj.* **2.** denoting or relating to this language.

Am·herst (ˈæmhɜːst) *n.* **Jef·frey,** 1st Baron Amherst. 1717–97, British general who defeated the French in Canada (1758–60): governor general of British North America (1761–63).

a·mi *French.* (aˈmi) *n.* a male friend.

a·mi+a·ble (ˈeɪmɪəbᵊl) *adj.* having or displaying a pleasant or agreeable nature; friendly. [C14: from Old French, from Late Latin *amīcābilis* AMICABLE] **—ˌa·mi+a·ˈbil+i·ty** *or* **ˈa·mi+a·ble+ness** *n.* **—ˈa·mi+a·bly** *adv.*

am·i·an+thus (ˌæmɪˈænθəs) *n.* any of the fine silky varieties of asbestos. [C17: from Latin *amiantus,* from Greek *amiantos* unsullied, from A-[1] + *miainein* to pollute] **—ˌam·i·ˈan+thine, ˌam·i·ˈan+thoid,** *or* **ˌam·i+an+ˈthoid+al** *adj.*

am·i·ca·ble (ˈæmɪkəbᵊl) *adj.* characterized by friendliness: *an amicable agreement.* [C15: from Late Latin *amīcābilis,* from Latin *amīcus* friend; related to *amāre* to love] **—ˌam·i·ca·ˈbil+i·ty** *or* **ˈam·i+ca·ble+ness** *n.* **—ˈam·i·ca·bly** *adv.*

am+ice[1] (ˈæmɪs) *n. Christianity.* a rectangular piece of white linen worn by priests around the neck and shoulders under the alb or, formerly, on the head. [C15: from Old French *amis,* plural of *amit,* or from Medieval Latin *amicia,* both from Latin *amictus* cloak, from *amicīre* to clothe, from *am-* AMBI- + *iacere* to throw]

am+ice[2] (ˈæmɪs) *n.* another word for **almuce.**

A.M.I.C.E. *abbrev. for* Associate Member of the Institution of Civil Engineers.

A.M.I.Chem.E. *abbrev. for* Associate Member of the Institution of Chemical Engineers.

a·mi·cus cu+ri·ae (æˈmiːkʊs ˈkjʊərɪˌiː) *n., pl.* **a·mi·ci cu·ri·ae** (æˈmiːkaɪ) *Law.* a person not directly engaged in a case who advises the court. [Latin, literally: friend of the court]

a·mid (əˈmɪd) *or* **a·midst** *prep.* in the middle of; among. [Old English *on middan* in the middle; see MID[1]]

am+ide (ˈæmaɪd) *n.* **1.** any organic compound containing the group $-CONH_2$. **2.** (*modifier*) consisting of, containing, or concerned with the group $-CONH_2$: *amide group or radical.* **3.** an inorganic compound having the general formula $M(NH_2)_x$, where M is a metal atom. [C19: from AM(MONIA) + -IDE] **—a·ˈmid+ic** (əˈmɪdɪk) *adj.*

a·mi·do- *combining form.* (in chemistry) indicating the presence of an amide group. [from AMIDE]

Am·i·dol (ˈæmɪdɒl) *n. Trademark.* a grey to colourless soluble crystalline solid that is used as a photographic developer; 2,4-diaminophenol dihydrochloride. Formula: $C_6H_3(NH_2)_2(OH).2HCl$.

a·mid+ships (əˈmɪdʃɪps) *adv., adj.* (*postpositive*) *Nautical.* at, near, or towards the centre of a vessel.

a·mie *French.* (aˈmi) *n.* a female friend.

A.M.I.E.E. (in Britain) *abbrev. for* Associate Member of the Institution of Electrical Engineers.

Am·i·ens (ˈæmɪənz; *French* aˈmjɛ̃) *n.* a city in N France: its Gothic cathedral is the largest church in France. Pop.: 135 992 (1975).

a·mi·go (æˈmiːgəʊ, ə-) *n., pl.* **+gos.** a friend; comrade. [Spanish, from Latin *amicus*]

A.M.I.Mech.E. (in Britain) *abbrev. for* Associate Member of the Institution of Mechanical Engineers.

A·min[1] (æˈmiːn, ɑː-) *n.* **Lake.** the official name for (Lake) **Edward.**

A·min[2] (æˈmiːn, ɑː-) *n.* **I·di** (ˈiːdiː). born 1925, Ugandan soldier; dictator and head of state 1971–78.

a·mine (əˈmiːn, ˈæmɪn) *n.* an organic base formed by replacing one or more of the hydrogen atoms of ammonia by organic groups. [C19: from AM(MONIUM) + -INE[2]]

-a·mine *n. combining form.* indicating an amine: *histamine; methylamine.*

a·mi+no (əˈmaɪnəʊ, -ˈmiː-) *n.* (*modifier*) of, consisting of, or containing the group of atoms $-NH_2$: *amino group or radical; amino acid.*

a·mi·no- *combining form.* indicating the presence of an amino group: *aminobenzoic acid.* [from AMINE]

a·mi+no ac·id *n.* any of a group of organic compounds containing one or more amino groups, $-NH_2$, and one or more carboxyl groups, -COOH. They are the component molecules of proteins.

a·mi+no+ben+zo+ic ac·id (əˌmaɪnəʊbɛnˈzəʊɪk, -ˌmiː-) *n.* a derivative of benzoic acid existing in three isomeric forms, the *para-* form being used in the manufacture of dyes and sunburn preventatives. Formula: $NH_2C_6H_4COOH$.

a·mi+no+phe·nol (əˌmaɪnəʊˈfiːnɒl, -ˌmiː-) *n. Chem.* any of three isomeric forms that are white soluble crystalline solids, used as a dye intermediate (meta- and ortho-), in dyeing hair, fur, and textiles (ortho- and para-), and as a photographic developer (para-). Formula: $C_6H_4NH_2OH$.

a·mi+no+py+rine (əˌmaɪnəʊˈpaɪriːn, -ˌmiː-) *n.* a crystalline compound used to reduce pain and fever. Formula: $C_{13}H_{17}N_3O$.

a·mi+no res+in *n.* any thermosetting synthetic resin formed by copolymerization of amines with aldehydes. Amino resins are used as adhesives and as coatings for paper and textiles. See also **urea-formaldehyde resin, melamine.**

a·mir (əˈmɪə) *n.* **1.** a variant spelling of **emir. 2.** (formerly) the ruler of Afghanistan; ameer. [C19: from Arabic, variant of EMIR] —**a·ˈmir+ate** *adj.*

A·mis (ˈeɪmɪs) *n.* **King·sley.** born 1922, English novelist and poet, noted esp. for his satirical novel *Lucky Jim* (1954).

A·mish (ˈɑːmɪʃ, ˈæ-) *adj.* **1.** of or relating to a U.S. Mennonite sect that traces its origin to Jakob Amman. ~*n.* **2.** the Amish people. [C19: from German *Amisch,* after Jakob *Amman,* 17th-century Swiss Mennonite bishop]

a·miss (əˈmɪs) *adv.* **1.** in an incorrect, inappropriate, or defective manner. **2. take amiss.** to feel offended by. ~*adj.* **3.** (*postpositive*) wrong, incorrect, or faulty. [C13 *a mis,* from *mis* wrong; see MISS[1]]

am·i+to+sis (ˌæmɪˈtəʊsɪs) *n.* an unusual form of cell division in which the nucleus and cytoplasm divide by constriction without the formation of chromosomes; direct cell division. —**am·i+tot+ic** (ˌæmɪˈtɒtɪk) *adj.* —**ˌam·i+ˈtot·i+cal+ly** *adv.*

am+i·ty (ˈæmɪtɪ) *n., pl.* **·ties.** friendship; cordiality. [C15: from Old French *amité,* from Medieval Latin *amīcitās* friendship, from Latin *amīcus* friend]

Am+man (əˈmɑːn) *n.* the capital of Jordan, northeast of the Dead Sea: ancient capital of the Ammonites, rebuilt by Ptolemy in the 3rd century B.C. Pop.: 598 000 (1974 est.). Ancient names: **Rabbath Ammon, Philadelphia.**

am+me·ter (ˈæmˌmiːtə) *n.* an instrument for measuring an electric current in amperes. [C19: AM(PERE) + -METER]

am+mine (ˈæmiːn, əˈmiːn) *n.* a compound that has molecules containing one or more ammonia molecules bound to another molecule, group, or atom by coordinate bonds. Also called: **ammoniate, ammonate.** [C19: from AMM(ONIA) + -INE[2]]

am·mo (ˈæməʊ) *n. Informal.* short for **ammunition.**

am+mo+coete (ˈæməˌsiːt) *n.* the larva of primitive jawless vertebrates, such as the lamprey, that lives buried in mud and feeds on microorganisms. [C19: from New Latin *ammocoetēs,* literally: that lie in sand, from Greek *ammos* sand + *koitē* bed, from *keisthai* to lie]

Am·mon[1] (ˈæmən) *n. Old Testament.* the ancestor of the Ammonites.

Am·mon[2] (ˈæmən) *n. Myth.* the classical name of the Egyptian god Amen, identified by the Greeks with Zeus and by the Romans with Jupiter.

am+mo+nal (ˈæmənᵊl) *n.* an explosive made by mixing TNT, ammonium nitrate, and aluminium powder. [C20: from AMMON(IUM) + AL(UMINIUM)]

am+mo+nate (ˈæməˌneɪt) *n.* another name for **ammine.**

am+mo+ni·a (əˈməʊnɪə, -njə) *n.* **1.** a colourless pungent highly soluble gas mainly used in the manufacture of fertilizers, nitric acid, and other nitrogenous compounds and as a refrigerant and solvent. Formula: NH_3. **2.** short for **aqueous ammonia.** [C18: from New Latin, from Latin (*sal*) *ammōniacus* (sal) AMMONIAC]

am+mo+ni+ac[1] (əˈməʊnɪˌæk) *adj.* a variant of **ammoniacal.**

am+mo+ni+ac[2] (əˈməʊnɪˌæk) *n.* a strong-smelling gum resin obtained from the stems of the N Asian umbelliferous plant *Dorema ammoniacum* and formerly used as an expectorant, stimulant, perfume, and in porcelain cement. Also called: **gum ammoniac.** [C14: from Latin *ammōniacum,* from Greek *ammōniakos* belonging to Ammon (apparently the gum resin was extracted from plants found in Libya near the temple of Ammon)]

am+mo+ni·a+cal (ˌæməˈnaɪəkᵊl) *adj.* of, containing, using, or resembling ammonia. Also: **ammoniac.**

am+mo+ni·a so+lu+tion *n.* another name for **ammonium hydroxide.**

am+mo+ni+ate (əˈməʊnɪˌeɪt) *vb.* **1.** to unite or treat with ammonia. ~*n.* **2.** another name for **ammine.** —**am+ˌmo+ni·ˈa+tion** *n.*

am+mon+ic (əˈmɒnɪk, əˈməʊnɪk) *adj.* of or concerned with ammonia or ammonium compounds. —**am+ˈmon·i+cal** *adj.*

am+mon·i+fy (əˈmɒnɪˌfaɪ, əˈməʊnɪ-) *vb.* **+fies, +fy+ing, +fied.** to treat or impregnate with ammonia or a compound of ammonia. —**am+ˌmon·i+fi+ˈca+tion** *n.*

am+mo+nite[1] (ˈæməˌnaɪt) *n.* **1.** any extinct marine cephalopod mollusc of the order *Ammonoidea,* which were common in Mesozoic times and had a coiled partitioned shell. Their closest modern relative is the pearly nautilus. **2.** the shell of any of these animals, commonly occurring as a fossil. [C18: from New Latin *Ammōnītēs,* from Medieval Latin *cornū Ammōnis,* literally: horn of Ammon] —**am+mo+nit+ic** (ˌæməˈnɪtɪk) *adj.*

am+mo+nite[2] (ˈæməˌnaɪt) *n.* **1.** an explosive consisting mainly of ammonium nitrate with smaller amounts of other substances, such as TNT. **2.** a nitrogenous fertilizer made from animal wastes. [C20: from AMMO(NIUM) + NI(TRA)TE]

Am+mo+nites (ˈæməˌnaɪts) *n. Old Testament.* a nomadic tribe living east of the Jordan: a persistent enemy of the Israelites.

am+mo+ni·um (əˈməʊnɪəm, -njəm) *n.* (*modifier*) of, consisting of, or containing the monovalent group NH_4- or the ion NH_4^+: *ammonium compounds.*

am+mo+ni·um car+ba+mate *n.* a white soluble crystalline compound produced by reaction between dry ammonia and carbon dioxide and used as a nitrogen fertilizer. Formula: $(NH_4)CO_2NH_2$.

am+mo+ni·um car+bon+ate *n.* **1.** an unstable pungent soluble white powder that is a double salt of ammonium bicarbonate and ammonium carbamate: used in the manufacture of baking powder, smelling salts, and ammonium compounds. Formula: $(NH_4)HCO_3.(NH_4)CO_2NH_2$. **2.** an unstable substance that is produced by treating this compound with ammonia. Formula: $(NH_4)_2CO_3$.

am+mo+ni·um chlo+ride *n.* a white soluble crystalline solid used chiefly as an electrolyte in dry batteries and as a mordant and soldering flux. Formula: NH_4Cl. Also called: **sal ammoniac.**

am+mo+ni·um hy+drox+ide *n.* a colourless pungent solution of ammonia and water, containing ammonium and hydroxyl ions and used in the manufacture of rayon, rubber, and plastics, in photography, in pharmaceuticals, and as a household cleanser. Formula: NH_4OH. Also called: **ammonia solution, aqua ammoniae.**

am+mo+ni·um ni+trate *n.* a colourless highly soluble crystalline solid used mainly as a fertilizer and in explosives and pyrotechnics. Formula: NH_4NO_3.

am+mo+ni·um sul+phate *n.* a white soluble crystalline solid used mainly as a fertilizer and in water purification. Formula: $(NH_4)_2SO_4$.

am+mu+ni+tion (ˌæmjʊˈnɪʃən) *n.* **1.** any projectiles, such as bullets, rockets, etc., that can be discharged from a weapon. **2.** bombs, missiles, chemicals, biological agents, nuclear materials, etc., capable of use as weapons. **3.** any means of defence or attack, as in an argument. [C17: from obsolete French *amunition,* by mistaken division from earlier *la munition;* see MUNITION]

am+ne+si·a (æmˈniːzɪə) *n.* partial or total loss of memory. [C19: via New Latin from Greek: forgetfulness, probably from *amnēstia* oblivion; see AMNESTY] —**am+ne+si+ac** (æmˈniːzɪˌæk) *or* **am+ne+sic** (æmˈniːsɪk, -zɪk) *adj., n.*

am+nes+ty (ˈæmnɪstɪ) *n., pl.* **+ties. 1.** a general pardon, esp. for offences against a government. **2.** a period during which a law is suspended to allow offenders to admit their crime without fear of prosecution. **3.** *Law.* a pardon granted by the Crown and effected by statute, effective for a limited period of time. ~*vb.* **+ties, +ty+ing, +tied. 4.** (*tr.*) to overlook or forget (an offence). [C16: from Latin *amnēstia,* from Greek: oblivion, from *amnēstos* forgetting, from A-[1] + *-mnēstos,* from *mnasthai* to remember]

am+ni·o+cen+te·sis (ˌæmnɪəʊsɛnˈtiːsɪs) *n., pl.* **·ses** (-siːz). removal of some amniotic fluid for therapeutic or diagnostic purposes.

am+ni+on (ˈæmnɪən) *n., pl.* **+ni+ons** *or* **+ni+a** (-nɪə). the innermost of two membranes (see also **chorion**) enclosing an embryonic reptile, bird, or mammal. [C17: via New Latin from Greek: a little lamb, from *amnos* a lamb] —**am+ni+ot+ic** (ˌæmnɪˈɒtɪk) *adj.*

a·moe+ba *or U.S.* **a·me·ba** (əˈmiːbə) *n., pl.* **+bae** (-biː) *or* **+bas.** any protozoan of the order *Amoebida,* esp. any of the genus *Amoeba,* able to change shape because of the movements of cell processes (pseudopodia): class *Sarcodina.* They live in fresh water or soil or as parasites in man and animals. [C19: from New Latin, from Greek *amoibē* change, from *ameibein* to change, exchange] —**a·ˈmoe+bic** *or U.S.* **a·ˈme·bic** *adj.*

am+oe·bae·an *or* **am+oe·be·an** (ˌæmɪˈbiːən) *adj. Prosody.* of or relating to lines of verse dialogue that answer each other alternately.

am+oe·bi·a+sis (ˌæmɪˈbaɪəsɪs) *n., pl.* **+ses** (-ˌsiːz). infection, esp. of the intestines, caused by the parasitic amoeba *Endamoeba histolytica.*

a·moe+bic dys+en+ter·y *n.* inflammation of the intestines caused by the parasitic amoeba *Endamoeba histolytica.*

a·moe+bo+cyte *or U.S.* **a·me·bo+cyte** (əˈmiːbəˌsaɪt) *n.* any amoeboid cell found in the blood and body fluids. Some kinds, such as the phagocytic white blood cell, can engulf foreign particles.

a·moe+boid *or U.S.* **a·me·boid** (əˈmiːbɔɪd) *adj.* of, related to, or resembling amoebae.

a·mok (əˈmʌk, əˈmɒk) *n., adv.* a variant spelling of **amuck.**

A·mon (ˈɑːmən) *n. Egyptian myth.* a variant spelling of **Amen.**

a·mong (əˈmʌŋ) *or* **a·mongst** *prep.* **1.** in the midst of: *he lived among the Indians.* **2.** to each of: *divide the reward among yourselves.* **3.** in the group, class, or number of: *ranked among the greatest writers.* **4.** taken out of (a group): *he is only one among many.* **5.** with one another within a group; by the joint action of: *a lot of gossip among the women employees; decide it among yourselves.* [Old English *amang,* contracted from *on*

gemang in the group of, from ON + *gemang* crowd; see MINGLE, MONGREL]
Usage. See at **between.**

a·mon·til·la·do (əˌmɒntɪˈlɑːdəʊ) *n.* a medium dry Spanish sherry, not as pale in colour as a fino. [C19: from Spanish *vino amontillado* wine of *Montilla,* town in Spain]

a·mor·al (æˈmɒrəl, eɪ-) *adj.* **1.** having no moral quality; non-moral. **2.** without moral standards or principles. —**a·mo·ral·i·ty** *n.* (ˌæmɒˈrælɪtɪ, ˌeɪmɒ-) *n.* —**a·ˈmor·al·ly** *adv.*
Usage. *Amoral* is frequently and incorrectly used where *immoral* is meant. In careful usage, however, *immoral* is applied to that which infringes moral rules and *amoral* is only used of that to which considerations of morality are irrelevant or of persons who lack any moral code.

a·mo·ret·to (ˌæməˈrɛtəʊ) *or* **a·mo·ri·no** (ˌæmɔːˈriːnəʊ) *n., pl.* **·ret·ti** (-ˈrɛtɪ) *or* **·ri·ni** (-ˈriːnɪ). (esp. in painting) a small chubby naked boy representing a cupid. Also called: **putto.** [C16: from Italian, diminutive of *Amore* Cupid, from Latin *Amor* Love]

am·o·rist (ˈæmərɪst) *n.* a lover or a writer about love.

am·o·ro·so (ˌæməˈrəʊsəʊ) *adj., adv.* **1.** *Music.* lovingly. ~*n.* **2.** a rich sweetened sherry of a dark colour. [from Italian and Spanish: AMOROUS]

am·o·rous (ˈæmərəs) *adj.* **1.** inclined towards or displaying love or desire. **2.** in love. **3.** of or relating to love. [C14: from Old French, from Medieval Latin *amōrōsus,* from Latin *amor* love] —**ˈam·o·rous·ly** *adv.* —**ˈam·o·rous·ness** *n.*

a·mor pa·tri·ae *Latin.* (ˈæmɔː ˈpætrɪˌiː) *n.* love of one's country; patriotism.

a·mor·phous (əˈmɔːfəs) *adj.* **1.** lacking a definite shape; formless. **2.** of no recognizable character or type. **3.** (of chemicals, rocks, etc.) not having a crystalline structure. [C18: from New Latin, from Greek *amorphos* shapeless, from A-[1] + *morphē* shape] —**a·ˈmor·phism** *n.* —**a·ˈmor·phous·ly** *adv.* —**a·ˈmor·phous·ness** *n.*

a·mor·ti·za·tion *or* **a·mor·ti·sa·tion** (əˌmɔːtaɪˈzeɪʃən) *n.* **1. a.** the process of amortizing a debt. **b.** the money devoted to amortizing a debt. **2.** (in computing the redemption yield on a bond purchased at a premium) the amount that is subtracted from the annual yield. Compare **accumulation** (sense 3b). —**a·mor·tize·ment** *or* **a·mor·tise·ment** (əˈmɔːtɪzmənt) *n.*

a·mor·tize *or* **a·mor·tise** (əˈmɔːtaɪz) *vb.* (*tr.*) **1.** *Finance.* to liquidate (a debt, mortgage, etc.) by instalment payments or by periodic transfers to a sinking fund. **2.** to write off (a wasting asset) by annual transfers to a sinking fund. **3.** *Property law.* (formerly) to transfer (lands, etc.) in mortmain. [C14: from Medieval Latin *admortizāre,* from Old French *amortir* to reduce to the point of death, ultimately from Latin *ad* to + *mors* death] —**a·ˈmor·tiz·a·ble** *or* **a·ˈmor·tis·a·ble** *adj.*

A·mos (ˈeɪmɒs) *n.* *Old Testament.* **1.** a Hebrew prophet of the 8th century B.C. **2.** the book containing his oracles.

a·mount (əˈmaʊnt) *n.* **1.** extent; quantity; supply. **2.** the total of two or more quantities; sum. **3.** the full value, effect, or significance of something. **4.** a principal sum plus the interest on it, as in a loan. ~*vb.* **5.** (*intr.;* usually foll. by *to*) to be equal or add up in effect, meaning, or quantity. [C13: from Old French *amonter* to go up, from *amont* upwards, from *a* to + *mont* mountain (from Latin *mōns*)]

a·mour (əˈmʊə) *n.* a love affair, esp. a secret or illicit one. [C13: from Old French, from Latin *amor* love]

a·mour-pro·pre *French.* (amuːrˈprɔpr) *n.* self-respect.

a·mowt (əˈmaʊt) *n.* a variant spelling of **amaut.**

A·moy (əˈmɔɪ) *n.* **1.** a port in SE China, in Fukien province on **Amoy Island,** at the mouth of the Chiu-lung River opposite Taiwan: one of the first treaty ports opened to European trade (1842). Pop.: 224 300 (1953). Modern Chinese name: **Hsiamen. 2.** the dialect of Chinese spoken in Amoy, Taiwan, and elsewhere: a Min dialect.

amp. *abbrev. for:* **1.** amperage. **2.** ampere.

AMP *abbrev. for* adenosine monophosphate.

am·pe·lop·sis (ˌæmpɪˈlɒpsɪs) *n.* any woody vine of the vitaceous genus *Ampelopsis,* of tropical and subtropical Asia and America. [C19: from New Latin, from Greek *ampelos* grapevine]

am·per·age (ˈæmpərɪdʒ) *n.* the strength of an electric current measured in amperes, esp. the rated current of an electrical component or device.

am·pere (ˈæmpɛə) *n.* **1.** the basic SI unit of electric current; the constant current that, when maintained in two parallel conductors of infinite length and negligible cross section placed 1 metre apart in a vacuum, produces a force of 2×10^{-7} newton per metre between them. 1 ampere is equivalent to 1 coulomb per second. **2.** a former unit of electric current (**international ampere**); the current that, when passed through a solution of silver nitrate, deposits silver at the rate of 0.001118 gram per second. 1 international ampere equals 0.999835 ampere. ~Abbrev.: **amp.** Symbol: A [C19: named after A. M. AMPÈRE]

Am·père (ˈæmpɛə; *French* ɑ̃ˈpɛːr) *n.* **An·dré Ma·rie** (ɑ̃ˈdre maˈri). 1775–1836, French physicist and mathematician, who made major discoveries in the fields of magnetism and electricity.

am·pere-hour *n.* a practical unit of quantity of electricity; the quantity that flows in one hour through a conductor carrying a current of one ampere. 1 ampere-hour is equivalent to 3600 coulombs.

am·pere-turn *n.* a unit of magnetomotive force; the magnetomotive force produced by a current of 1 ampere passing through one complete turn of a coil. 1 ampere-turn is equivalent to $4\pi/10$ or 1.257 gilberts.

am·per·sand (ˈæmpəˌsænd) *n.* the character (&), meaning *and: John Brown & Co.* [C19: shortened from *and per se and,* that is, the symbol & by itself (represents) *and*]

am·phet·a·mine (æmˈfɛtəˌmiːn, -mɪn) *n.* a synthetic colourless volatile liquid used medicinally, mainly for its stimulant action on the central nervous system, although it also stimulates the sympathetic nervous system. It can have unpleasant or dangerous side effects and drug dependence can occur; 1-phenyl-2-aminopropane. Formula: $C_6H_5CH_2CH(NH_2)CH_3$. [C20: from A(LPHA) + M(ETHYL) + PH(ENYL) + ET(HYL) + AMINE]

am·phi- *prefix of nouns and adjectives.* **1.** on both sides; at both ends; of both kinds: *amphipod; amphitrichous; amphibious.* **2.** around: *amphibole.* [from Greek]

am·phi·ar·thro·sis (ˌæmfɪɑːˈθrəʊsɪs) *pl. n.,* **·ses** (-siːz). *Anatomy.* a type of articulation permitting only slight movement, as between the vertebrae of the backbone. [C19: from AMPHI- + Greek *arthrōsis* articulation, from *arthron* a joint]

am·phi·as·ter (ˈæmfɪˌæstə) *n.* *Cytology.* the structure that occurs in a cell undergoing mitosis, consisting of a spindle with an aster at each end. [C19: from AMPHI- + New Latin *aster;* see ASTER]

am·phib·i·an (æmˈfɪbɪən) *n.* **1.** any cold-blooded vertebrates of the class *Amphibia,* typically living on land but breeding in water. Their aquatic larvae (tadpoles) undergo metamorphosis into the adult form. The class includes the newts and salamanders, frogs and toads, and caecilians. **2.** a type of aircraft able to land and take off from both water and land. **3.** any vehicle able to travel on both water and land. ~*adj.* **4.** another word for **amphibious. 5.** of, relating to, or belonging to the class *Amphibia.*

am·phi·bi·ot·ic (ˌæmfɪbaɪˈɒtɪk) *adj.* having an aquatic larval form and a terrestrial adult form, as amphibians.

am·phib·i·ous (æmˈfɪbɪəs) *adj.* **1.** able to live both on land and in the water, as frogs, toads, etc. **2.** designed for operation on or from both water and land. **3.** relating to military forces and equipment organized for operations launched from the sea against an enemy shore. **4.** having a dual or mixed nature. [C17: from Greek *amphibios,* literally: having a double life, from AMPHI- + *bios* life] —**am·ˈphib·i·ous·ly** *adv.* —**am·ˈphib·i·ous·ness** *n.*

am·phi·blas·tu·la (ˌæmfɪˈblæstjʊlə) *n.* the free-swimming larva of certain sponges, which consists of a hollow spherical mass of cells some of which have flagella.

am·phi·bole (ˈæmfɪˌbəʊl) *n.* any of a large group of minerals consisting of the silicates of calcium, iron, magnesium, sodium, and aluminium, usually in the form of long slender dark-coloured crystals. Members of the group, including hornblende, actinolite, and tremolite, are common constituents of igneous rocks. [C17: from French, from Greek *amphibolos* uncertain; so called from the large number of varieties in the group]

am·phib·o·lite (æmˈfɪbəˌlaɪt) *n.* a metamorphic rock consisting mainly of amphibole and plagioclase.

am·phi·bol·o·gy (ˌæmfɪˈbɒlədʒɪ) *or* **am·phib·o·ly** (æmˈfɪbəlɪ) *n., pl.* **·gies** *or* **·lies.** ambiguity of expression, esp. when due to a grammatical construction, as in *save rags and waste paper.* [C14: from Late Latin *amphibologia,* ultimately from Greek *amphibolos* ambiguous; see AMPHIBOLE, -LOGY] —**ˌam·phi·ˈbol·ic** *or* **am·phib·o·lous** (æmˈfɪbələs) *adj.* —**am·phib·o·log·i·cal** (æmˌfɪbəˈlɒdʒɪkᵊl) *adj.* —**am·ˌphib·o·ˈlog·i·cal·ly** *adv.*

am·phi·brach (ˈæmfɪˌbræk) *n.* *Prosody.* a metrical foot consisting of a long syllable between two short syllables (˘¯˘). Compare **cretic.** [C16: from Latin, from Greek *amphibrakhus,* literally: both ends being short, from AMPHI- + *brakhus* short] —**ˌam·phi·ˈbrach·ic** *adj.*

am·phi·chro·ic (ˌæmfɪˈkrəʊɪk) *or* **am·phi·chro·mat·ic** (ˌæmfɪkrəʊˈmætɪk) *adj.* producing two colours, one on reacting with an acid, the other on reacting with a base.

am·phi·coe·lous (ˌæmfɪˈsiːləs) *adj.* (of the vertebrae of most fishes and some amphibians) concave at the anterior and posterior ends. [C19: from AMPHI- + Greek *koilos* hollow]

am·phic·ty·on (æmˈfɪktɪən) *n.* a delegate to an amphictyonic council. [C16: back formation from *amphictyons,* from Greek *amphiktiones* neighbours, from AMPHI- + *ktizein* to found]

am·phic·ty·o·ny (æmˈfɪktɪənɪ) *n., pl.* **·nies.** (in ancient Greece) a religious association of states for the maintenance of temples and the cults connected with them. —**am·phic·ty·on·ic** (æmˌfɪktɪˈɒnɪk) *adj.*

am·phi·dip·loid (ˌæmfɪˈdɪplɔɪd) *n.* a hybrid plant in which the chromosome number is the sum of the chromosome numbers of both parental species.

am·phi·go·ry (ˈæmfɪgərɪ) *or* **am·phi·gou·ri** (ˈæmfɪˌgʊərɪ) *n., pl.* **·ries** *or* **·ris.** a piece of nonsensical writing in verse or, less commonly, prose. [C19: from French *amphigouri,* of unknown origin] —**am·phi·gor·ic** (ˌæmfɪˈgɒrɪk) *adj.*

am·phim·a·cer (æmˈfɪməsə) *n.* *Prosody.* another word for **cretic.** [C16: from Latin *amphimacrus,* from Greek *amphimakros* both ends being long, from AMPHI- + *makros* long]

am·phi·mix·is (ˌæmfɪˈmɪksɪs) *n., pl.* **·mix·es** (-ˈmɪksiːz). true sexual reproduction, esp. the fusion of gametes from two organisms. Compare **apomixis.** [C19: from AMPHI- + Greek *mixis* a blending, from *mignunai* to mingle] —**am·phi·mic·tic** (ˌæmfɪˈmɪktɪk) *adj.*

am·phi·ox·us (ˌæmfɪˈɒksəs) *n., pl.* **·ox·i** (-ˈɒksaɪ) *or* **·ox·us·es.** another name for the **lancelet.** [C19: from New Latin: both ends being sharp, from AMPHI- + Greek *oxus* sharp]

am·phi·pod (ˈæmfɪˌpɒd) *n.* **1.** any marine or freshwater crustacean of the order *Amphipoda,* such as the sand hoppers, in which the body is laterally compressed: subclass *Malacostraca*. ~*adj.* **2.** of, relating to, or belonging to the *Amphipoda*.

am+phip+ro+style (æm'fɪprəˌstaɪl, ˌæmfɪ'prəʊstaɪl) *adj.* (esp. of a classical temple) having a set of columns at both ends but not at the sides. —**am+ˌphip+ro+'sty+lar** *adj.*

am+phi+pro+tic (ˌæmfɪ'prəʊtɪk) *adj.*, another word for **amphoteric.**

am+phis+bae+na (ˌæmfɪs'bi:nə) *n., pl.* **+nae** (-ni:) *or* **+nas. 1.** any worm lizard of the genus *Amphisbaena*. **2.** *Classical myth.* a poisonous serpent having a head at each end and able to move forwards or backwards. [C16: via Latin from Greek *amphisbaina,* from *amphis* both ways + *bainein* to go] —**ˌam+phis+'bae+nic** *adj.*

am+phi+sty+lar (ˌæmfɪ'staɪlə) *adj.* (esp. of a classical temple) having a set of columns at both ends or at both sides.

am+phi+the·a+tre *or U.S.* **am+phi+the·a+ter** ('æmfɪˌθɪətə) *n.* **1.** a building, usually circular or oval, in which tiers of seats rise from a central open arena, as in those of ancient Rome. **2.** a place where contests are held; arena. **3.** any level circular area of ground surrounded by higher ground. **4. a.** the first tier of seats in the gallery of a theatre. **b.** any similarly designated seating area in a theatre. **5.** a lecture room in which seats are tiered away from a central area. —**am+phi+the·at+ric** (ˌæmfɪθɪ'ætrɪk) *or* **ˌam+phi+the·'at+ri+cal** *adj.* —**ˌam+phi+the·'at+ri+cal+ly** *adv.*

am+phi+the·ci·um (ˌæmfɪ'θi:sɪəm) *n., pl.* **+ci·a** (-sɪə). the outer layer of cells of the embryo of mosses and liverworts that develops into the outer parts of the spore-bearing capsule. [C19: from New Latin, from AMPHI- + Greek *thēkion* a little case, from *thēkē* case]

am+phit+ri+cha (æm'fɪtrɪkə) *n.* bacteria that have flagella at both ends. [C20: from AMPHI- + *-tricha,* from Greek *thrix* hair] —**am+'phit+ri+chous** *adj.*

Am·phi·tri·te (ˌæmfɪ'traɪtɪ) *n. Greek myth.* a sea goddess, wife of Poseidon and mother of Triton.

am+phit+ro+pous (æm'fɪtrəpəs) *adj.* (of a plant ovule) partially inverted so that the base and the micropyle at the apex are the same distance from the funicle.

Am·phit·ry·on (æm'fɪtrɪən) *n. Greek myth.* the grandson of Perseus and husband of Alcmene.

am+pho+ra ('æmfərə) *n., pl.* **+pho+rae** (-fəˌri:) *or* **+pho+ras.** an ancient Greek or Roman two-handled narrow-necked jar for oil, wine, etc. [C17: from Latin, from Greek *amphoreus,* from AMPHI- + *phoreus* bearer, from *pherein* to bear]

am+pho+ter+ic (ˌæmfə'tɛrɪk) *adj. Chem.* able to function as either a base or an acid. Also: **amphiprotic.** [C19: from Greek *amphoteros* each of two (from *amphō* both) + -IC]

am+ple ('æmpəl) *adj.* **1.** more than sufficient; abundant: *an ample helping.* **2.** large in size, extent, or amount: *of ample proportions.* [C15: from Old French, from Latin *amplus* spacious] —**'am+ple+ness** *n.*

am+plex·i·caul (æm'plɛksɪˌkɔ:l) *adj.* (of some sessile leaves, stipules, etc.) having an enlarged base that encircles the stem. [C18: from New Latin *amplexicaulis,* from Latin *amplectī* to embrace + *caulis* stalk]

am+pli+fi+ca+tion (ˌæmplɪfɪ'keɪʃən) *n.* **1.** the act or result of amplifying. **2.** material added to a statement, story, etc., in order to expand or clarify it. **3.** a statement, story, etc., with such additional material. **4.** *Electronics.* **a.** the increase in strength of an electrical signal or sound by means of an amplifier. **b.** another word for **gain**[1] (sense 13).

am+pli+fi+er ('æmplɪˌfaɪə) *n.* **1.** an electronic device used to increase the strength of the current or voltage signal fed into it. **2.** such a device used for the amplification of sound in a radio, record player, etc. **3.** *Photog.* an additional lens for altering the focal length of a camera lens. **4.** a person or thing that amplifies.

am+pli+fy ('æmplɪˌfaɪ) *vb.* **+fies, +fy+ing, +fied. 1.** (*tr.*) to increase in size, extent, effect, etc., as by the addition of extra material; augment; enlarge; expand. **2.** *Electronics.* to produce amplification of (electrical signals, sound, etc.); increase the amplitude of (signals, etc.). **3.** (*tr.*) *U.S.* to exaggerate. **4.** (*intr.*) to expand or enlarge a speech, narrative, etc. [C15: from Old French *amplifier,* ultimately from Latin *amplificāre* to enlarge, from *amplus* spacious + *facere* to make] —**'am+pli+ˌfi+a+ble** *adj.*

am+pli+tude ('æmplɪˌtju:d) *n.* **1.** greatness of extent; magnitude. **2.** abundance or copiousness. **3.** breadth or scope, as of the mind. **4.** the maximum displacement from the zero or mean position of a periodic motion or curve. **5.** *Astronomy.* the angular distance along the horizon measured from true east or west to the point of intersection of the vertical circle passing through a celestial body. **6.** Also called: **argument.** *Maths.* (of a complex number) the angle that the vector representing the complex number makes with the positive horizontal axis. [C16: from Latin *amplitūdō* breadth, from *amplus* spacious]

am+pli+tude mod·u+la+tion *n.* **1.** one of the principal methods of transmitting radio audio, visual, or other types of information using radio waves, the relevant signal being superimposed onto a radio-frequency carrier wave. The frequency of the carrier wave remains unchanged but its amplitude is varied in accordance with the amplitude of the input signal. Abbrev.: **AM, am.** Compare **frequency modulation. 2.** a wave that has undergone this process.

am+ply ('æmplɪ) *adv.* more than sufficiently; fully; generously: *he was amply rewarded.*

am+poule ('æmpu:l, -pju:l) *or* (*esp. U.S.*) **am+pule** *n. Med.* a small glass vessel in which liquids for injection are hermetically sealed.

am+pul+la (æm'pʊlə) *n., pl.* **+pul+lae** (-'pʊli:). **1.** *Anatomy.* the dilated end part of certain ducts or canals, such as the end of a uterine tube. **2.** *Christianity.* **a.** a vessel for containing the wine and water used at the Eucharist. **b.** a small flask for containing consecrated oil. **3.** a Roman two-handled bottle for oil, wine, or perfume. [C16: from Latin, diminutive of AMPHORA] —**am+pul+la+ceous** (ˌæmpʊ'leɪʃəs) *or* **ˌam+pul+'la+ceal** *adj.* —**am+pul+lar** (æm'pʊlə) *or* **am+pul+lar+y** (æm'pʊlərɪ) *adj.*

am+pu+tate ('æmpjʊˌteɪt) *vb. Surgery.* to remove (all or part of a limb, esp. an arm or leg). [C17: from Latin *amputāre,* from *am-* around + *putāre* to trim, prune] —**ˌam+pu+'ta+tion** *n.* —**'am+pu+ˌta+tor** *n.*

am+pu+tee (ˌæmpjʊ'ti:) *n.* a person who has had a limb amputated.

Am+ra+va+ti (æm'rɑ:vətɪ) *n.* a town in central India, in NE Maharashtra: cotton centre. Pop.: 193 636 (1971). Former name: **Am+rao+ti** ('æmˌrɑ:ətɪ, 'ʌm-).

am+ri+ta *or* **am+ree+ta** (æm'ri:tə) *n. Hindu myth.* **1.** the ambrosia of the gods that bestows immortality. **2.** the immortality it confers. [from Sanskrit *amrta* immortal, from *a-* without + *mrta* death]

Am+rit+sar (æm'rɪtsə) *n.* a city in India, in NW Punjab: centre of the Sikh religion; site of a massacre in 1919 of unarmed supporters of Indian self-government by British troops. Pop.: 407 628 (1971).

Am+ster+dam (ˌæmstə'dæm; *Dutch* ˌɑmstər'dɑm) *n.* the commercial capital of the Netherlands, a major industrial centre and port on the IJsselmeer, connected with the North Sea by canal: built on about 100 islands within a network of canals. Pop.: 764 382 (1974 est.).

amt. *abbrev. for* amount.

amu *abbrev. for* atomic mass unit.

a·muck (ə'mʌk) *or* **a·mok** *n.* **1.** a state of murderous frenzy, originally observed among Malays. ~*adv.* **2. run amuck.** to run about with or as if with a frenzied desire to kill. [C17: from Malay *amoq* furious assault]

A·mu Dar+ya (*Russian* a'mu dar'ja) *n.* a river in central Asia, rising in the Pamirs and flowing northwest through the Hindu Kush and across Turkmenistan and Uzbekistan to its delta in the Aral Sea: forms much of the boundary between Afghanistan and the Soviet Union. Length: 2400 km (1500 miles). Ancient name: **Oxus.**

am·u·let ('æmjʊlɪt) *n.* a trinket or piece of jewellery worn as a protection against evil; charm. [C17: from Latin *amulētum,* of unknown origin]

A·mūn ('ɑ:mən) *n. Egyptian myth.* a variant spelling of **Amen.**

A·mund·sen (*Norwegian* 'a:mʊnsən) *n.* **Ro·ald** ('rɔald). 1872–1928, Norwegian explorer and navigator, who was the first man to reach the South Pole (1911).

A·mund·sen Sea ('ɑ:mʊndsən) *n.* a part of the South Pacific Ocean, in Antarctica off Byrd Land.

A·mur (ə'mʊə) *n.* a river in NE Asia, rising in N Mongolia as the Argun and flowing southeast, then northeast to the Sea of Okhotsk: forms the boundary between Manchuria and the Soviet Union. Length: about 4350 km (2700 miles).

a·muse (ə'mju:z) *vb.* (*tr.*) **1.** to keep pleasantly occupied; entertain; divert. **2.** to cause to laugh or smile. [C15: from Old French *amuser* to cause to be idle, from *muser* to MUSE]

a·muse+ment (ə'mju:zmənt) *n.* **1.** something that amuses, such as a game or other pastime. **2.** a mechanical device used for entertainment, as at a fair. **3.** the act of amusing or the state or quality of being amused.

a·muse+ment ar+cade *n. Brit.* a covered area having coin-operated game machines.

a·muse+ment park *n.* an open-air entertainment area consisting of stalls, side shows, etc.

a·mus+ing (ə'mju:zɪŋ) *adj.* mildly entertaining; pleasantly diverting; causing a smile or laugh. —**a·'mus+ing+ly** *adv.*

a·myg+da+la (ə'mɪgdələ) *n., pl.* **+lae** (-ˌli:). *Anatomy.* an almond-shaped part, such as a tonsil. [C16: from Medieval Latin: ALMOND]

a·myg+da+late (ə'mɪgdəlɪt, -ˌleɪt) *adj.* relating to, having, or bearing almonds.

a·myg+dale (ə'mɪgdeɪl) *n.* an oval vesicle in a volcanic rock, formed from a bubble of escaping gas, that has become filled with a light-coloured mineral, such as quartz. Also called: **amygdule.** [C19: from Greek: ALMOND]

a·myg+da+lin (ə'mɪgdəlɪn) *n.* a white soluble bitter-tasting crystalline glycoside extracted from bitter almonds and used as an expectorant. Formula: $C_6H_5CHCNOC_{12}H_{21}O_{10}$.

a·myg+da+line (ə'mɪgdəlɪn, -ˌlaɪn) *adj.* **1.** *Anatomy.* of or relating to a tonsil. **2.** of or resembling almonds.

a·myg+da+loid (ə'mɪgdəˌlɔɪd) *n.* **1.** a volcanic igneous rock containing amygdales. ~*adj.* **2.** having the shape of an almond. **3.** a less common form of **amygdaloidal** (sense 1).

a·myg+da+loi+dal (əˌmɪgdə'lɔɪdəl) *adj.* **1.** (of a volcanic rock) containing amygdales. **2.** a less common form of **amygdaloid** (sense 2).

am·yl ('æmɪl) *n.* (*modifier*) (*no longer in technical usage*) of, consisting of, or containing any of eight isomeric forms of the monovalent group C_5H_{11}-: *amyl group or radical.* See also **pentyl.** [C19: from Latin: AMYLUM]

am·y+la+ceous (ˌæmɪ'leɪʃəs) *adj.* of or resembling starch.

am·yl ac+e·tate *n.* another name (no longer in technical usage) for **pentyl acetate.**

am·yl al+co+hol *n.* a colourless flammable liquid existing in eight isomeric forms that is used as a solvent and in the manufacture of organic compounds and pharmaceuticals. Formula: $C_5H_{11}OH$.

am+yl+ase ('æmɪˌleɪz) *n.* any of several enzymes that hydrolyse starch and glycogen to simple sugars, such as glucose. They are present in saliva.

am+yl+ene ('æmɪˌliːn) *n.* another name (no longer in technical usage) for **pentene.**

am·yl ni+trite *n.* a yellowish unstable volatile fragrant liquid used in medicine as a vasodilator and in perfumes. Formula: $(CH_3)_2CHCH_2CH_2NO_2$.

am·y·lo- *or before a vowel* **am·yl-** *combining form.* indicating starch: *amylolysis; amylase.* [from Latin: AMYLUM]

am·y+loid ('æmɪˌlɔɪd) *n.* **1.** *Pathol.* a complex protein resembling starch, deposited in tissues in some degenerative diseases. **2.** any substance resembling starch. ~*adj.* **3.** starch-like.

am·y+lol·y+sis (ˌæmɪ'lɒlɪsɪs) *n.* the conversion of starch into sugar.

am·y+lo+pec+tin (ˌæmɪləʊ'pɛktɪn) *n.* the major component of starch (about 80 per cent), consisting of branched chains of glucose units. It is insoluble and gives a red-brown colour with iodine. Compare **amylose.**

am·y+lop+sin (ˌæmɪ'lɒpsɪn) *n.* an enzyme of the pancreatic juice that converts starch into sugar; pancreatic amylase. [C19: from AMYLO(LYSIS) + (PE)PSIN]

am+yl+ose ('æmɪˌləʊz, -ləʊs) *n.* the minor component (about 20 per cent) of starch, consisting of long unbranched chains of glucose units. It is soluble in water and gives an intense blue colour with iodine. Compare **amylopectin.**

am·y+lum ('æmɪləm) *n.* another name for **starch** (sense 1). [Latin, from Greek *amulon* fine meal, starch, from *amulos* not ground at the mill, from A-[1] + *mulē* mill]

a·my·o+to+ni·a (ˌeɪmaɪə'təʊnɪə) *n.* another name for **myotonia.**

Am·y+tal ('æmɪˌtæl) *n. Trademark.* a crystalline compound used as a sedative and hypnotic; amobarbital.

an[1] (æn; *unstressed* ən) *determiner.* (*article*) a form of **a**[1], used before an initial vowel and sometimes before an initial *h: an old car; an elf; an historic moment.* [Old English *ān* ONE]

an[2] *or* **an'** (æn; *unstressed* ən) *conj.* (*subordinating*) an obsolete word for **if.** See **and** (sense 9).

An *the chemical symbol for* actinon.

An (ɑːn) *n. Myth.* the Sumerian sky god. Babylonian counterpart: **Anu.**

an. *abbrev. for* anno. [Latin: in the year]

A.N. *abbrev. for* Anglo-Norman.

an- *or before a consonant* **a-** *prefix.* not; without: *anaphrodisiac.* [from Greek]

-an, -e·an, *or* **-i·an** *suffix.* **1.** (*forming adjectives and nouns*) belonging to or relating to; a person belonging to or coming from: *European.* **2.** (*forming adjectives and nouns*) typical of or resembling; a person typical of: *Elizabethan.* **3.** (*forming adjectives and nouns*) adhering to or following; an adherent of: *Christian.* **4.** (*forming nouns*) a person who specializes or is expert in: *dietician; phonetician.* [from Latin *-ānus,* suffix of adjectives]

a·na[1] ('eɪnə, 'ɑːnə) *adv. Pharmacol.* (of ingredients in a prescription) in equal quantities. Abbrev.: **aa.** [C16: via Medieval Latin from Greek: of every one similarly]

an·a[2] ('ɑːnə) *n.* **1.** a collection of reminiscences, sketches, etc., of or about a person or place. **2.** an item of or for such a collection. [C18: independent use of -ANA]

an·a- *or before a vowel* **an-** *prefix.* **1.** up; upwards: *anadromous.* **2.** again: *anagram.* **3.** back; backwards: *anatropous.* [from Greek *ana*]

-a·na *or* **-i·a·na** *suffix forming nouns.* denoting a collection of items, esp. anecdotes or bibliographical items, on a certain individual or place: *Shakespeariana; Americana.* [New Latin, from Latin *-āna,* literally: matters relating to, neuter plural of *-ānus;* see -AN]

an·a+bae+na (ˌænə'biːnə) *n., pl.* **+nas.** any freshwater alga of the genus *Anabaena,* sometimes occurring in drinking water, giving it a fishy taste and smell. [New Latin, from Greek *anabainein* to shoot up, go up, from ANA- + *bainein* to go; so called because they rise to the surface at intervals]

an·a+ban+tid (ˌænə'bæntɪd) *n.* **1.** any of various spiny-finned fishes constituting the family *Anabantidae* and including the fighting fish, climbing perch, and gourami. See also **labyrinth fish.** ~*adj.* **2.** of, relating to, or belonging to the family *Anabantidae.*

An·a+bap+tist (ˌænə'bæptɪst) *n.* **1.** a member of any of various 16th-century Protestant movements that rejected infant baptism, insisted that adults be rebaptized, and sought to establish Christian communism. **2.** a member of a later Protestant sect holding the same doctrines, esp. with regard to baptism. ~*adj.* **3.** of or relating to these movements or sects or their doctrines. [C16: from Ecclesiastical Latin *anabaptista,* from *anabaptīzāre* to baptize again, from Late Greek *anabaptizein;* see ANA-, BAPTIZE] —ˌ**An·a+'bap+tism** *n.*

an·a+bas ('ænəˌbæs) *n.* any of several labyrinth fishes of the genus *Anabas,* esp. the climbing fish. [C19: from New Latin, from Greek *anabainein* to go up; see ANABAENA]

a·nab·a+sis (ə'næbəsɪs) *n., pl.* **+ses** (-ˌsiːz). **1.** the march of Cyrus the Younger and his Greek mercenaries from Sardis to Cunaxa in Babylonia in 401 B.C., described by Xenophon in his *Anabasis.* Compare **katabasis. 2.** any military expedition, esp. one from the coast to the interior. [C18: from Greek: a going up, ascent, from *anabainein* to go up; see ANABAENA]

an·a+bat+ic (ˌænə'bætɪk) *adj. Meteorol.* (of air currents) rising upwards, esp. up slopes. Compare **katabatic.** [C19: from Greek *anabatikos* relating to ascents, from *anabainein* to go up; see ANABASIS]

an·a+bi·o+sis (ˌænəbaɪ'əʊsɪs) *n.* a return to life after apparent death; resuscitation. [C19: via New Latin from Greek, from *anabioein* to come back to life, from ANA- + *bios* life] —**an·a+bi+ot+ic** (ˌænəbaɪ'ɒtɪk) *adj.*

an·a+bleps ('ænəˌblɛps) *n., pl.* **+bleps.** any of various cyprinodont fishes constituting the genus *Anableps,* which includes the four-eyed fishes. [New Latin, literally: one who looks up, from Greek, from *anablepein* to look up]

an·a+bol+ic ster+oid (ˌænə'bɒlɪk) *n.* any of a group of synthetic steroid hormones (androgens) used to stimulate muscle and bone growth for athletic or therapeutic purposes.

a·nab·o+lism (ə'næbəˌlɪzəm) *n.* a metabolic process in which complex molecules are synthesized from simpler ones with the storage of energy; constructive metabolism. Compare **catabolism.** [C19: from ANA- + (META)BOLISM] —**an·a+bol+ic** (ˌænə'bɒlɪk) *adj.*

a·nab·o+lite (ə'næbəˌlaɪt) *n.* a product of anabolism. —**a·nab·o+lit+ic** (əˌnæbə'lɪtɪk) *adj.*

a·na+branch ('ɑːnəˌbrɑːntʃ) *n.* a stream that leaves a river and enters it again further downstream. [C19: from *ana(stomosing) branch*]

an·a+car+di·a+ceous (ˌænəˌkɑːdɪ'eɪʃəs) *adj.* of, relating to, or belonging to the *Anacardiaceae,* a chiefly tropical family of trees and shrubs many of which have edible drupes. The family includes the cashew, mango, pistachio, and sumach. [C19: from New Latin *Anacardiāceae,* from ANA- + Greek *kardia* heart; so called from the shape of the top of the fruit stem]

a·nach·o+rism (ə'nækəˌrɪzəm) *n.* a geographical misplacement; something located in an incongruous position. Compare **anachronism.** [C19: from ANA- + *khōros* place]

an·a+chron+ic (ˌænə'krɒnɪk) *or* **an·a+chron·i+cal** *adj.* out of chronological order or out of date. [C19: see ANACHRONISM] —ˌ**an·a+'chron·i+cal+ly** *adv.*

a·nach+ro+nism (ə'nækrəˌnɪzəm) *n.* **1.** the representation of an event, person, or thing in a historical context in which it could not have occurred or existed. **2.** a person or thing that belongs or seems to belong to another time. [C17: from Latin *anachronismus,* from Greek *anakhronismos* a mistake in chronology, from *anakhronizein* to err in a time reference, from ANA- + *khronos* time] —**a·ˌnach+ro+'nis+tic** *adj.* —**a·ˌnach+ro+'nis+ti+cal+ly** *adv.*

an·a+cli+nal (ˌænə'klaɪnᵊl) *adj.* (of valleys and similar formations) progressing in a direction opposite to the dip of the surrounding rock strata. [C19: see ANA-, -CLINE]

an·a+clit+ic (ˌænə'klɪtɪk) *adj. Psychoanal.* of or relating to relationships that are characterized by the strong dependence of one person on others or another. [C20: from Greek *anaklitos* for leaning upon; see ANA-, -CLINE] —**an·a+cli+sis** (ˌænə'klaɪsɪs) *n.*

an·a+co+lu+thi·a (ˌænəkə'luːθɪə) *n. Rhetoric.* lack of grammatical sequence, esp. within a single sentence. —ˌ**an·a+co+'lu+thic** *adj.*

an·a+co+lu+thon (ˌænəkə'luːθɒn) *n., pl.* **+tha** (-θə). *Rhetoric.* a construction that involves the change from one grammatical sequence to another within a single sentence; an example of anacoluthia. [C18: from Late Latin, from Greek *anakolouthon,* from *anakolouthos* not consistent, from AN- + *akolouthos* following]

an·a+con+da (ˌænə'kɒndə) *n.* a very large nonvenomous arboreal and semiaquatic snake, *Eunectes murinus,* of tropical South America, which kills its prey by constriction: family *Boidae* (boas). [C18: probably changed from Sinhalese *henakandayā* whip snake, from *hena* lightning + *kanda* stem; originally referring to a snake of Sri Lanka]

an·a+cous+tic (ˌænə'kuːstɪk) *adj.* unable to support the propagation of sound; soundless.

A·nac·re·on (ə'nækrɪˌɒn, -ən) *n.* ?572–?488 B.C., Greek lyric poet, noted for his short songs celebrating love and wine.

A·nac+re·on+tic (əˌnækrɪ'ɒntɪk) (*sometimes not cap.*) ~*adj.* **1.** in the manner of Anacreon. **2.** (of verse) in praise of love or wine; amatory or convivial. ~*n.* **3.** an Anacreontic poem. —**A·ˌnac+re·'on+ti+cal+ly** *adv.*

an·a+cru+sis (ˌænə'kruːsɪs) *n., pl.* **+ses** (-siːz). **1.** *Prosody.* one or more unstressed syllables at the beginning of a line of verse. **2.** *Music.* **a.** an unstressed note or group of notes immediately preceding the strong first beat of the first bar. **b.** another word for **upbeat.** [C19: from Greek *anakrousis* prelude, from *anakrouein* to strike up, from ANA- + *krouein* to strike] —**an·a+crus+tic** (ˌænə'krʌstɪk) *adj.*

an·a+dem ('ænəˌdɛm) *n. Poetic.* a garland for the head. [C17: from Latin *anadēma* wreath, from Greek *anadēma,* from *anadein* to wreathe, from ANA- + *dein* to bind]

an·a+di+plo+sis (ˌænədɪ'pləʊsɪs) *n. Rhetoric.* repetition of the words or phrase at the end of one sentence, line, or clause at the beginning of the next. [C16: via Latin from Greek: repetition, from *anadiploun* to double back, from ANA- + *diploun* to double]

a·nad+ro+mous (ə'nædrəməs) *adj.* (of fishes such as the salmon) migrating up rivers from the sea in order to breed. Compare **catadromous.** [C18: from Greek *anadromos* running upwards, from ANA- + *dromos* a running]

A·na+dyr (*Russian* a'nadirj) *n.* **1.** a town in the Soviet Union, in NE Siberia at the mouth of the Anadyr River. Pop.: 7703 (1970). **2.** a mountain range in the Soviet Union, in NE Siberia, rising over 1500 m (5000 ft.). **3.** a river in the Soviet Union, rising in mountains on the Arctic Circle, south of the Anadyr Range, and flowing east to the Gulf of Anadyr. Length: 725 km (450 miles). **4. Gulf of.** an inlet of the Bering Sea, off the coast of the NE Soviet Union.

a·nae·mi·a or *U.S.* **a·ne·mi·a** (əˈniːmɪə) *n.* **1.** a deficiency in the number of red blood cells or in their haemoglobin content, resulting in pallor, shortness of breath, and lack of energy. **2.** lack of vitality or vigour. **3.** pallid complexion. [C19: from New Latin, from Greek *anaimia* lack of blood, from AN- + *haima* blood]

a·nae·mic or *U.S.* **a·ne·mic** (əˈniːmɪk) *adj.* **1.** relating to or suffering from anaemia. **2.** pale and sickly looking; lacking vitality.

an+aer+obe (ænˈɛərəʊb) or **an+aer·o·bi·um** (ˌænɛəˈrəʊbɪəm) *n., pl.* **+obes** or **·o·bi·a** (-ˈəʊbɪə). an organism that does not require free oxygen or air for respiration. Compare **aerobe.**

an+aer·o+bic (ˌænɛəˈrəʊbɪk) *adj.* **1.** (of an organism or process) requiring the absence of or not dependent on the presence of free oxygen or air. **2.** of or relating to anaerobes. ~Compare **aerobic.** —ˌ**an+aer·ˈo+bi+cal+ly** *adv.*

an+aes+the+si·a or *U.S.* **an+es+the+si·a** (ˌænɪsˈθiːzɪə) *n.* **1.** local or general loss of bodily sensation, esp. of touch, as the result of nerve damage or other abnormality. **2.** loss of sensation, esp. of pain, induced by drugs: called **general anaesthesia** when consciousness is lost and **local anaesthesia** when only a specific area of the body is involved. **3.** a general dullness or lack of feeling. [C19: from New Latin, from Greek *anaisthēsia* absence of sensation, from AN- + *aisthēsis* feeling]

an+aes+the+si+ol+o·gy or *U.S.* **an+es+the+si+ol+o·gy** (ˌænɪsˌθiːzɪˈɒlədʒɪ) *n.* the U.S. name for **anaesthetics.**

an+aes+thet+ic or *U.S.* **an+es+thet+ic** (ˌænɪsˈθɛtɪk) *n.* **1.** a substance that causes anaesthesia. ~*adj.* **2.** causing or characterized by anaesthesia.

an+aes+thet+ics (ˌænɪsˈθɛtɪks) *n.* (*functioning as sing.*) the science, study, and practice of anaesthesia and its application. U.S. name: **anesthesiology.**

a·naes+the+tist (əˈniːsθətɪst) *n.* **1.** *Brit.* a qualified doctor specializing in the administration of anaesthetics. U.S. name: **anesthesiologist. 2.** *U.S.* a person qualified to administer anaesthesia, often a nurse or someone other than a physician. Compare **anesthesiologist.**

a·naes+the+tize, a·naes+the+tise, or *U.S.* **a·nes+the+tize** (əˈniːsθəˌtaɪz) *vb.* (*tr.*) to render insensible to pain by administering an anaesthetic. —**a·ˌnaes+the+ti+ˈza+tion, a·ˌnaes+the+ti+ˈsa+tion,** or *U.S.* **a·ˌnes+the+ti+ˈza+tion** *n.*

an·a·glyph (ˈænəˌglɪf) *n.* **1.** *Photog.* a stereoscopic picture consisting of two images of the same object, taken from slightly different angles, in two complementary colours, usually red and cyan (green-blue). When viewed through spectacles having one red and one cyan lens, the images merge to produce a stereoscopic sensation. **2.** anything cut to stand in low relief, such as a cameo. [C17: from Greek *anagluphē* carved in low relief, from ANA- + *gluphē* carving, from *gluphein* to carve] —ˌ**an·a+ˈglyph+ic,** ˌ**an·a+ˈglyph·i·cal** or **an·a·glyp·tic** (ˌænəˈglɪptɪk), ˌ**an·a+ˈglyp+ti+cal** *adj.* —**a·nag+ly+phy** (əˈnægləfɪ, ˈænəˌglɪfɪ) *n.*

an·a+glyp+ta (ˌænəˈglɪptə) *n.* a type of thick embossed wallpaper. [C19: originally a trademark, from Greek *anagluptos;* see ANAGLYPH]

an+ag+nor·i+sis (ˌænəgˈnɒrɪsɪs) *n., pl.* **+ses** (-ˌsiːz). (in Greek tragedy) the recognition or discovery by the protagonist of the identity of some character or the nature of his own predicament, which leads to the resolution of the plot; denouement. [from Greek: recognition]

an·a+go+ge or **an·a+go+gy** (ˈænəˌgɒdʒɪ) *n.* **1.** allegorical or spiritual interpretation, esp. of sacred works such as the Bible. **2.** *Christianity.* allegorical interpretation of the Old Testament as typifying or foreshadowing subjects in the New Testament. [C18: via Late Latin from Greek *anagōgē* a lifting up, from *anagein,* from ANA- + *agein* to lead] —**an·a+gog+ic** (ˌænəˈgɒdʒɪk) or ˌ**an·a+ˈgog·i+cal** *adj.* —ˌ**an·a+ˈgog·i+cal+ly** *adv.*

an·a+gram (ˈænəˌgræm) *n.* a word or phrase the letters of which can be rearranged into another word or phrase. [C16: from New Latin *anagramma,* shortened from Greek *anagrammatismos,* from *anagrammatizein* to transpose letters, from ANA- + *gramma* a letter] —**an·a·gram+mat+ic** (ˌænəgrəˈmætɪk) or ˌ**an·a·gram+ˈmat·i·cal** *adj.* —ˌ**an·a·gram+ˈmat·i·cal+ly** *adv.*

an·a+gram+ma+tize or **an·a+gram+ma+tise** (ˌænəˈgræməˌtaɪz) *vb.* to arrange into an anagram. —ˌ**an·a+ˈgram+ma+ˌtism** *n.* —ˌ**an·a+ˈgram+ma+tist** *n.*

An·a+heim (ˈænəˌhaɪm) *n.* a city in SW California: site of Disneyland. Pop.: 186 842 (1973 est.).

a·nak ku+ching (ˈana ˈkuːtʃɪŋ) *n.* the Malaysian name for the **chevrotain.** [from Malay: small cat]

a·nal (ˈeɪnəl) *adj.* **1.** of, relating to, or near the anus. **2.** *Psychoanal.* **a.** relating to a stage of psychosexual development during which the child's interest is concentrated on the anal region and excremental functions. **b.** designating personality traits in the adult, such as orderliness, meanness, stubbornness, etc., due to fixation at the anal stage of development. Compare **oral** (sense 7). [C18: from New Latin *ānālis;* see ANUS] —ˈ**a·nal+ly** *adv.*

anal. *abbrev. for:* **1.** analogous. **2.** analogy. **3.** analysis. **4.** analytic.

a·nal ca+nal *n.* the terminal part of the rectum forming the passage to the anus.

a·nal+cite (æˈnælsaɪt; ˈænəlˌsaɪt, -sɪt) or **a·nal+cime** (æˈnælsɪm, -saɪm, -siːm) *n.* a white, grey, or colourless zeolite mineral consisting of hydrated sodium aluminium silicate in cubic crystalline form. Formula: $NaAlSi_2O_6.H_2O$. [C19: from Greek *analkimos* weak (from AN- + *alkimos* strong, from *alkē* strength) + -ITE[1]]

an·a+lects (ˈænəˌlɛkts) or **an·a+lec+ta** (ˌænəˈlɛktə) *pl. n.* selected literary passages from one or more works. [C17: via Latin from Greek *analekta,* from *analegein* to collect up, from *legein* to gather] —ˌ**an·a+ˈlec+tic** *adj.*

an·a+lem+ma (ˌænəˈlɛmə) *n., pl.* **+mas** or **+ma+ta** (-mətə). a graduated scale shaped like a figure eight that indicates the daily declination of the sun. [C17: from Latin: sundial, pedestal of sundial, from Greek *analēmma* pedestal, from *analambanein* to support] —**an·a+lem+mat+ic** (ˌænəlɛˈmætɪk) *adj.*

an·a+lep+tic (ˌænəˈlɛptɪk) *adj.* **1.** (of a drug, etc.) restorative or invigorating. ~*n.* **2.** a restorative remedy or drug. [C17: from New Latin *analēpticus,* from Greek *analēptikos* stimulating, from *analambanein* to take up; see ANALEMMA]

a·nal fin *n.* a median ventral unpaired fin, situated between the anus and the tail fin in fishes, that helps to maintain stable equilibrium.

an+al+ge·si·a (ˌænəlˈdʒiːzɪə, -sɪə) or **an+al+gi·a** (ænˈældʒɪə) *n.* inability to feel pain. [C18: via New Latin from Greek: insensibility, from AN- + *algēsis* sense of pain]

an+al+ge+sic (ˌænəlˈdʒiːzɪk, -sɪk) *adj.* **1.** of or causing analgesia. ~*n.* **2.** a substance that produces analgesia.

a·nal in·ter+course *n.* a form of sexual intercourse in which the penis is inserted into the anus rather than the vagina.

an·a+log com+put+er *n.* a mechanical, electrical, or electronic computer that performs arithmetical operations by using some variable physical quantity, such as voltage, to represent numbers. It is used in monitoring systems, simulation processes, etc., but is less accurate than a digital computer.

an·a·log-dig·it·al con+vert+er *n.* a device converting the output of an analog computer into its digital representation so that it can be fed into a digital computing system. Abbrev.: **A.D.C.**

a·nal·o+gize or **a·nal·o+gise** (əˈnæləˌdʒaɪz) *vb.* **1.** (*intr.*) to make use of analogy, as in argument; draw comparisons. **2.** (*tr.*) to make analogous or reveal analogy in.

a·nal·o+gous (əˈnæləgəs) *adj.* **1.** similar or corresponding in some respect. **2.** *Biology.* (of organs and parts) having the same function but different evolutionary origin: *the paddle of a whale and the fin of a fish are analogous.* Compare **homologous** (sense 4). **3.** *Linguistics.* formed by analogy: *an analogous plural.* [C17: from Latin *analogus,* from Greek *analogos* proportionate, from ANA- + *logos* speech, ratio] —**a·ˈnal·o+gous+ly** *adv.* —**a·ˈnal·o+gous+ness** *n.*

an·a+logue or *U.S.* (*sometimes*) **an·a+log** (ˈænəˌlɒg) *n.* **1.** something analogous to something else. **2.** *Biology.* an analogous part or organ.

a·nal+o·gy (əˈnælədʒɪ) *n., pl.* **·gies. 1.** agreement or similarity, esp. in a certain limited number of features or details. **2.** a comparison made to show such a similarity: *to draw an analogy between an atom and the solar system.* **3.** *Biology.* the relationship between analogous organs or parts. **4.** *Logic, maths.* a form of reasoning in which a similarity between two or more things is inferred from a known similarity between them in other respects. **5.** *Linguistics.* imitation of existing models or regular patterns in the formation of words, inflections, etc.: *a child may use "sheeps" as the plural of "sheep" by analogy with "dog," "dogs," "cat," "cats," etc.* [C16: from Greek *analogia* ratio, correspondence, from *analogos* ANALOGOUS] —**an·a·log·i·cal** (ˌænəˈlɒdʒɪkəl) or ˌ**an·a+ˈlog+ic** *adj.* —ˌ**an·a+ˈlog·i·cal+ly** *adv.* —**a·ˈnal·o·gist** *n.*

an+al+pha+bet+ic (ˌænælfəˈbɛtɪk, ænˌæl-) *adj.* **1.** not in alphabetic order. ~*n., adj.* **2.** a less common word for **illiterate.** [C20: from Greek *analphabētos;* see AN-, ALPHABET] —ˌ**an+al+pha+ˈbet·i·cal+ly** *adv.*

a·nal·y+sand (əˈnælɪˌsænd) *n.* any person who is undergoing psychoanalysis. [C20: from ANALYSE + *-and,* on the model of *multiplicand*]

an·a+lyse or *U.S.* **an·a+lyze** (ˈænəˌlaɪz) *vb.* **1.** (*tr.*) to examine in detail in order to discover meaning, essential features, etc. **2.** (*tr.*) to break down into components or essential features: *to analyse a financial structure.* **3.** (*tr.*) to make a mathematical, chemical, grammatical, etc., analysis of. **4.** another word for **psychoanalyse.** [C17: back formation from ANALYSIS] —ˌ**an·a+ˈlys+a·ble** or *U.S.* ˌ**an·a+ˈlyz+a·ble** *adj.* —ˌ**an·a+ly+ˈsa+tion** or *U.S.* ˌ**an·a+ly+ˈza+tion** *n.* —ˈ**an·a+ˌlys+er** or *U.S.* ˈ**an·a+ˌlyz+er** *n.*

a·nal·y+sis (əˈnælɪsɪs) *n., pl.* **+ses** (-ˌsiːz) **1.** the division of a physical or abstract whole into its constituent parts to examine or determine their relationship or value. Compare **synthesis** (sense 1). **2.** a statement of the results of this. **3.** short for **psychoanalysis. 4.** *Chem.* **a.** the decomposition of a substance into its elements, radicals, or other constituents in order to determine the kinds of constituents present (**qualitative analysis**) or the amount of each constituent (**quantitative analysis**). **b.** the result obtained by such a determination. **5.** *Linguistics.* the use of word order together with word function to express syntactic relations in a language, as opposed to the use of inflections. Compare **synthesis** (sense 4). **6.** *Maths.* the branch of mathematics principally concerned with the methods and concepts of algebra and calculus. **7.** *Philosophy.* (in the writings of Kant) the separation of a concept from another that contains it. Compare **synthesis** (sense 6). **8. in the last, final,** *or* **ultimate analysis.** after everything has been given due consideration. [C16: from New Latin, from Greek *analusis,* literally: a dissolving, from *analuein,* from ANA- + *luein* to loosen]

a·nal·y·sis of var·i+ance *n. Statistics.* a technique for analysing the total variation of a set of observations as measured by the variance of the observations multiplied by their number.

a·nal·y+sis si+tus *n.* a former name for **topology** (sense 2).

an·a+lyst (ˈænəlɪst) *n.* **1.** a person who analyses or is skilled in analysis. **2.** short for **psychoanalyst.**

an·a·lyt·ic (ˌænəˈlɪtɪk) *or* **an·a·lyt·i·cal** *adj.* **1.** relating to analysis. **2.** capable of or given to analysing: *an analytic mind.* **3.** Also: **isolating.** *Linguistics.* denoting languages, such as Chinese, whose morphology is characterized by analysis. Compare **synthetic** (sense 3), **agglutinative** (sense 2), **polysynthetic. 4.** *Logic.* (of a proposition) necessarily true by reference to meaning alone, being independent of fact or experience, as in *all spinsters are unmarried.* Compare **synthetic** (sense 4), **a priori. 5.** Also called: **regular, holomorphic.** *Maths.* (of a function of a complex variable) having a derivative at each point of its domain. [C16: via Late Latin from Greek *analutikos* from *analuein* to dissolve, break down; see ANALYSIS] —ˌ**an·a·ˈlyt·i·cal·ly** *adv.*

an·a·lyt·i·cal ge·om·e·try *n.* the branch of geometry that uses algebraic notation and analysis to locate a geometric point in terms of a coordinate system; coordinate geometry.

an·a·lyt·ic psy·chol·o·gy *n.* a school of psychoanalysis founded by Jung as a result of disagreements with Freud. See also **archetype, collective unconscious.**

A·nam (æˈnæm, ˈænæm) *n.* a variant spelling of **Annam.**

A·nam·bra (əˈnæmbrə) *n.* a state of S Nigeria, formed in 1976 from part of East-Central State. Capital: Enugu. Pop.: 2 469 000 (1976 est.). Area: 21 189 sq. km (8179 sq. miles).

an·am·ne·sis (ˌænæmˈniːsɪs) *n., pl.* **·ses** (-siːz). **1.** the ability to recall past events; recollection. **2.** the case history of a patient. [C17: via New Latin from Greek, from *anamimnēskein* to recall, from *mimnēskein* to call to mind] —**an·am·nes·tic** (ˌænæmˈnɛstɪk) *adj.* —ˌ**an·am·ˈnes·ti·cal·ly** *adv.*

an·a·mor·phic (ˌænəˈmɔːfɪk) *adj.* of, relating to, or caused by anamorphosis or anamorphism.

an·a·mor·phism (ˌænəˈmɔːfɪzəm) *n.* metamorphism of a rock in which complex minerals are formed from simpler ones.

an·a·mor·pho·scope (ˌænəˈmɔːfəˌskəʊp) *n.* an optical device, such as a cylindrical lens, for correcting an image that has been distorted by anamorphosis.

an·a·mor·pho·sis (ˌænəˈmɔːfəsɪs, -mɔːˈfəʊsɪs) *n., pl.* **·ses** (-ˌsiːz). **1.** *Optics.* **a.** an image or drawing distorted in such a way that it becomes recognizable only when viewed in a specified manner or through a special device. **b.** the process by which such images or drawings are produced. **2.** the evolution of one type of organism from another by a series of gradual changes. [C18: from Greek, from *anamorphoun* to transform, from *morphē* form, shape]

an·an·drous (ænˈændrəs) *adj.* (of flowers) having no stamens. [C19: from Greek *anandros,* lacking males, from AN- + *anēr* man]

An·a·ni·as (ˌænəˈnaɪəs) *n.* **1.** *New Testament.* a Jewish Christian of Jerusalem who was struck dead for lying (Acts 5). **2.** a liar.

an·an·thous (ænˈænθəs) *adj.* (of higher plants) having no flowers. [C19: from Greek *ananthēs,* from AN- + *anthos* flower]

an·a·paest *or* **an·a·pest** (ˈænəpɛst, -ˌpiːst) *n. Prosody.* a metrical foot of three syllables, the first two short, the last long (˘˘¯). [C17: via Latin from Greek *anapaistos* reversed, (that is, a dactyl reversed), from *anapaiein,* from *ana-* back + *paiein* to strike] —ˌ**an·a·ˈpaes·tic** *or* ˌ**an·a·ˈpes·tic** *adj.*

an·a·phase (ˈænəˌfeɪz) *n.* **1.** the third stage of mitosis, during which the chromatids separate and migrate towards opposite ends of the spindle. See also **prophase, metaphase, telophase. 2.** the corresponding stage of the first division of meiosis. [C19: from ANA- + PHASE]

a·naph·o·ra (əˈnæfərə) *n.* **1.** *Rhetoric.* the repetition of a word or phrase at the beginning of successive clauses. **2.** *Grammar.* the use of a word such as a pronoun to avoid repetition of a word or words, as for example *one* in *He offered me a drink but I didn't want one.* [C16: via Latin from Greek: repetition, from *anapherein,* from ANA- + *pherein* to bear] —**a·ˈnaph·o·ral** *or* **an·a·pho·ric** (ˌænəˈfɒrɪk) *adj.* —ˌ**an·a·ˈphor·i·cal·ly** *adv.*

an·aph·ro·dis·i·ac (ˌænæfrəˈdɪzɪˌæk) *adj.* **1.** tending to lessen sexual desire. ~*n.* **2.** an anaphrodisiac drug. —ˌ**an·aph·ro·ˈdis·i·a** *n.*

an·a·phy·lax·is (ˌænəfɪˈlæksɪs) *n.* extreme sensitivity to an injected antigen, esp. a protein, following a previous injection. [C20: from ANA- + (PRO)PHYLAXIS] —ˌ**an·a·phy·ˈlac·tic** *adj.* —ˌ**an·a·phy·ˈlac·ti·cal·ly** *adv.*

an·a·pla·si·a (ˌænəˈpleɪsɪə) *n.* reversion of plant or animal cells to a simpler less differentiated form.

an·a·plas·tic (ˌænəˈplæstɪk) *adj.* **1.** of or relating to anaplasia. **2.** relating to plastic surgery.

an·a·plas·ty (ˈænəˌplæstɪ) *n. Surgery.* another name for **plastic surgery.**

an·ap·tyx·is (ˌænæpˈtɪksɪs) *n., pl.* **·tyx·es** (-ˈtɪksiːz). the insertion of a short vowel between consonants in order to make a word more easily pronounceable. [C19: via New Latin from Greek *anaptuxis,* from *anaptussein* to unfold, from ANA- + *ptussein* to fold] —**an·ap·tyc·tic** *or* (ˌænæpˈtɪktɪk) ˌ**an·ap·ˈtyc·ti·cal** *adj.*

A·na·pur·na (ˌænəˈpʊənə) *n.* a variant spelling of **Annapurna.**

an·arch (ˈænɑːk) *n. Archaic.* an instigator or personification of anarchy.

an·ar·chism (ˈænəˌkɪzəm) *n.* **1.** *Political theory.* a doctrine advocating the abolition of government. **2.** the principles or practice of anarchists.

an·ar·chist (ˈænəkɪst) *n.* **1.** a person who advocates the abolition of government and a social system based on voluntary cooperation. **2.** a person who causes disorder or upheaval. —ˌ**an·ar·ˈchis·tic** *adj.*

an·ar·chy (ˈænəkɪ) *n.* **1.** general lawlessness and disorder, esp. when thought to result from an absence or failure of government. **2.** the absence or lack of government. **3.** the absence of any guiding or uniting principle; disorder; chaos. **4.** the theory or practice of political anarchism. [C16: from Medieval Latin *anarchia,* from Greek *anarkhia,* from *anarkhos* without a ruler, from AN- + *arkh-* leader, from *arkhein* to rule] —**an·ar·chic** (ænˈɑːkɪk) *or* **an·ˈar·chi·cal** *adj.* —**an·ˈar·chi·cal·ly** *adv.*

an·ar·thri·a (ænˈɑːθrɪə) *n. Pathol.* loss of the ability to speak coherently. [C19: New Latin, from Greek *anarthros* lacking vigour, from AN- + *arthros* joint]

an·ar·throus (ænˈɑːθrəs) *adj.* **1.** (of a noun) used without an article. **2.** having no joints or articulated limbs. [C19: from Greek *anarthros,* from AN- + *arthros* joint, definite article] —**an·ˈar·throus·ly** *adv.* —**an·ˈar·throus·ness** *n.*

an·a·sar·ca (ˌænəˈsɑːkə) *n. Pathol.* a generalized accumulation of serous fluid within the subcutaneous connective tissue, resulting in oedema. [C14: from New Latin, from ANA- (puffed up) + Greek *sarx* flesh] —ˌ**an·a·ˈsar·cous** *adj.*

An·a·sta·si·a (ˌænəˈstɑːzɪə, -ˈsteɪ-) *n.* **Grand Duchess.** 1901–?1918, daughter of Tsar Nicholas II, believed to have been executed by the Bolsheviks in 1918, although several women subsequently claimed to be her.

an·as·tig·mat (æˈnæstɪgˌmæt, ˌænəˈstɪgmæt) *n.* a lens or system of lenses designed to be free of astigmatism.

an·as·tig·mat·ic (ˌænəstɪgˈmætɪk) *adj.* (of a lens or optical device) not astigmatic. Also: **stigmatic.**

a·nas·to·mose (əˈnæstəˌməʊz) *vb.* to join (two parts of a blood vessel, etc.) by anastomosis.

a·nas·to·mo·sis (əˌnæstəˈməʊsɪs) *n., pl.* **·ses** (-siːz). **1.** a natural connection between two tubular structures, such as blood vessels. **2.** the surgical union of two hollow organs or parts that are normally separate. [C16: via New Latin from Greek: opening, from *anastomoun* to equip with a mouth, from *stoma* mouth] —**a·nas·to·mot·ic** (əˌnæstəˈmɒtɪk) *adj.*

a·nas·tro·phe (əˈnæstrəfɪ) *n. Rhetoric.* another term for **inversion** (sense 3). [C16: from Greek, from *anastrephein* to invert]

anat. *abbrev. for:* **1.** anatomical. **2.** anatomy.

an·a·tase (ˈænəˌteɪz) *n.* a rare blue or black mineral that consists of titanium oxide in tetragonal crystalline form and occurs in veins in igneous rocks. Formula: TiO_2. Also called: **octahedrite.** [C19: from French, from Greek *anatasis* an extending (referring to the length of the crystals), from *anateinein* to stretch out]

a·nath·e·ma (əˈnæθəmə) *n., pl.* **·mas. 1.** a detested person or thing: *he is anathema to me.* **2.** a formal ecclesiastical curse of excommunication or a formal denunciation of a doctrine. **3.** the person or thing so cursed. **4.** a strong curse; imprecation. [C16: via Church Latin from Greek: something accursed, dedicated (to evil), from *anatithenai* to dedicate, from ANA- + *tithenai* to set]

a·nath·e·ma·tize *or* **a·nath·e·ma·tise** (əˈnæθɪməˌtaɪz) *vb.* to pronounce an anathema (upon a person, etc.); curse. —**a·ˌnath·e·ma·ti·ˈza·tion** *or* **a·ˌnath·e·ma·ti·ˈsa·tion** *n.*

An·a·to·li·a (ˌænəˈtəʊlɪə) *n.* the Asian part of Turkey, occupying the peninsula between the Black Sea, the Mediterranean, and the Aegean: consists of a plateau, largely mountainous, with salt lakes in the interior. Historical name: **Asia Minor.**

An·a·to·li·an (ˌænəˈtəʊlɪən) *adj.* **1.** of or relating to Anatolia or its inhabitants. **2.** denoting, belonging to, or relating to an ancient family of languages related to the Indo-European family and including Hittite. ~*n.* **3.** this family of languages, sometimes regarded as a branch of Indo-European. **4.** a native or inhabitant of Anatolia.

an·a·tom·i·cal (ˌænəˈtɒmɪkᵊl) *adj.* of or relating to anatomy. —ˌ**an·a·ˈtom·i·cal·ly** *adv.*

an·a·tom·i·cal snuff·box *n.* the triangular depression on the back of the hand between the thumb and the index finger.

a·nat·o·mist (əˈnætəmɪst) *n.* an expert in anatomy.

a·nat·o·mize *or* **a·nat·o·mise** (əˈnætəˌmaɪz) *vb.* (*tr.*) **1.** to dissect (an animal or plant). **2.** to examine in minute detail. —**a·ˌnat·o·mi·ˈza·tion** *or* **a·ˌnat·o·mi·ˈsa·tion** *n.* —**a·ˈnat·o·ˌmiz·er** *or* **a·ˈnat·o·ˌmis·er** *n.*

a·nat·o·my (əˈnætəmɪ) *n., pl.* **·mies. 1.** the science concerned with the physical structure of animals and plants. **2.** the physical structure of an animal or plant or any of its parts. **3.** a book or treatise on this subject. **4.** dissection of an animal or plant. **5.** any detailed analysis: *the anatomy of a crime.* **6.** *Informal.* the human body. [C14: from Latin *anatomia,* from Greek *anatomē,* from *anatemnein* to cut up, from ANA- + *temnein* to cut]

a·nat·ro·pous (əˈnætrəpəs) *adj.* (of a plant ovule) inverted during development by a bending of the stalk (funicle) attaching it to the carpel wall. Compare **orthotropous.** [C19: from ANA- (inverted) + -TROPOUS]

a·nat·to (əˈnætəʊ) *n., pl.* **·tos.** a variant spelling of **annatto.**

An·ax·ag·o·ras (ˌænækˈsægərəs) *n.* ?500–428 B.C., Greek philosopher who maintained that all things were composed of minute particles arranged by an eternal intelligence.

A·nax·i·man·der (əˌnæksɪˈmændə) *n.* 611–547 B.C., Greek philosopher, astronomer, and mathematician who believed the first principle of the world to be the Infinite.

An·ax·im·e·nes (ˌænækˈsɪməˌniːz) *n.* 6th century B.C., Greek philosopher who believed air to be the primary substance.

an·bur·y (ˈænbərɪ) *n., pl.* **·bur·ies. 1.** a soft spongy tumour occurring in horses and oxen. **2.** a disease of cruciferous plants, esp. root crops, in which the roots are clubbed. [C16: of uncertain origin]

-ance *or* **-an·cy** *suffix forming nouns.* indicating an action, state or condition, or quality: *utterance; hindrance; resem-*

blance. Compare **-ence.** [via Old French from Latin *-antia;* see -ANCY]

an+ces+tor ('ænsɛstə) *n.* **1.** (*often pl.*) a person from whom another is directly descended, esp. someone more distant than a grandparent; forefather. **2.** an early type of animal or plant from which a later, usually dissimilar, type has evolved. **3.** a person or thing regarded as a forerunner of a later person or thing: *the ancestor of the modern camera.* [C13: from Old French *ancestre,* from Late Latin *antecēssor* one who goes before, from Latin *antecēdere;* see ANTECEDE] **—'an+ces+tress** *fem. n.*

an+ces+tral (æn'sɛstrəl) *adj.* of, inherited from, or derived from ancestors. **—an+'ces+tral+ly** *adv.*

an+ces+try ('ænsɛstrɪ) *n., pl.* **+tries. 1.** lineage or descent, esp. when ancient, noble, or distinguished. **2.** ancestors collectively.

An·chi·ses (æn'kaɪsi:z) *n. Classical myth.* a Trojan prince and father of Aeneas. In the *Aeneid,* he is rescued by his son at the fall of Troy and dies in Sicily.

an+chor ('æŋkə) *n.* **1.** any of several devices, usually of steel, attached to a vessel by a cable and dropped overboard so as to grip the bottom and restrict the vessel's movement. **2.** an object used to hold something else firmly in place: *the rock provided an anchor for the rope.* **3.** a source of stability or security: *religion was his anchor.* **4.** a metal cramp, bolt, or similar fitting, esp. one used to make a connection to masonry. **5.** *Sport.* **a.** the rear person in a tug-of-war team. **b.** short for **anchor man. 6. at anchor.** (of a vessel) anchored. **7. cast, come to,** *or* **drop anchor.** to anchor a vessel. **8. weigh anchor.** to haul in an anchor. **9. ride at anchor.** to be anchored. **10. drag anchor.** (of a vessel) to be subjected to such strain, esp. by wind or waves, as to cause the anchor to lose hold on the bottom. *~vb.* **11.** to use an anchor to hold (a vessel) in one place. **12.** to fasten or be fastened securely; fix or become fixed firmly. [Old English *ancor,* from Latin *ancora,* from Greek *ankura;* related to Greek *ankos* bend; compare Latin *uncus* bent, hooked]

an+chor+age ('æŋkərɪdʒ) *n.* **1.** the act of anchoring. **2.** any place where a vessel is anchored. **3.** a place designated for vessels to anchor. **4.** a fee imposed for anchoring. **5.** anything used as an anchor. **6.** a source of security or strength. **7.** something that supplies a secure hold for something else.

An+chor+age ('æŋkərɪdʒ) *n.* the largest city in Alaska, a port in the south, at the head of Cook Inlet. Pop.: 48 029 (1970).

an+cho+rite ('æŋkə,raɪt) *n.* a person who lives in seclusion, esp. a religious recluse; hermit. [C15: from Medieval Latin *anchorīta,* from Late Latin *anachōrēta,* from Greek *anakhōrētēs,* from *anakhōrein* to retire, withdraw, from *khōra* a space] **—'an+cho+ress** *fem. n.*

an+chor man *n.* **1.** *Sport.* the last person in a team to compete, esp. in a relay race. **2.** (in broadcasting) a person in a central studio who links up and maintains contact with various outside camera units, reporters, etc.

an+chor ring *n.* a ring made from an iron bar of circular cross-section.

an+cho+vet·a (,æntʃə'vɛtə) *n.* a small anchovy, *Cetengraulis mysticetus,* of the American Pacific, used as bait by tuna fishermen. [C20: Spanish, diminutive of *anchova* ANCHOVY]

an+cho+vy ('æntʃəvɪ) *n., pl.* **+vies** *or* **+vy.** any of various small marine food fishes of the genus *Engraulis* and related genera, esp. *E. encrasicolus* of S Europe: family *Clupeidae* (herrings). They have a salty taste and are often canned or made into a paste or essence. [C16: from Spanish *anchova,* perhaps ultimately from Greek *aphuē* small fish]

an+cho+vy pear *n.* a West Indian tree, *Grias cauliflora,* bearing edible fruit that taste like the mango: family *Lecythidaceae.*

an+chu+sa (æŋ'kju:sə) *n.* any Eurasian plant of the boraginaceous genus *Anchusa,* having rough hairy stems and leaves and blue flowers. See also **alkanet** (sense 3), **bugloss.** [C18: from Latin]

an+chu+sin (æŋ'kju:sɪn) *n.* another name for **alkanet** (sense 2).

an+chy+lose ('æŋkɪ,ləʊz) *vb.* a variant spelling of **ankylose. —,an+chy+'lo+sis** *n.* **—an+chy+lot+ic** (,æŋkɪ'lɒtɪk) *adj.*

an+cien ré+gime *French.* (ãsjɛ̃ re'ʒim) *n., pl.* ***an+ciens ré+gimes*** (ãsjɛ̃ re'ʒim). **1.** the political and social system of France before the Revolution of 1789. **2.** a former or outdated regime. [literally: old regime]

an+cient[1] ('eɪnʃənt) *adj.* **1.** dating from very long ago: *ancient ruins.* **2.** very old; aged. **3.** of the far past, esp. before the collapse of the Western Roman Empire (476 A.D.). Compare **medieval, modern. 4.** *Law.* having existed since before the time of legal memory. **5. ancient light.** a right to the access of light through a window, recognized at law when it has been enjoyed for 20 years or more without interruption. *~n.* **6.** (*often pl.*) a member of a civilized nation in the ancient world, esp. a Greek, Roman, or Hebrew. **7.** (*often pl.*) one of the classical authors of Greek or Roman antiquity. **8.** *Archaic.* an old man. [C14: from Old French *ancien,* from Vulgar Latin *anteanus* (unattested), from Latin *ante* before] **—'an+cient+ness** *n.*

an+cient[2] ('eɪnʃənt) *n. Archaic.* **1.** a flag or other banner; standard. **2.** a standard-bearer; ensign. [C16: changed from ENSIGN through the influence of ANCIENT[1]]

An+cient Greek *n.* the Greek language from the earliest records to about 300 B.C., the chief dialect areas of which were Aeolic, Arcadic, Doric, and Ionic (including Attic). Compare **Koine, Late Greek, Medieval Greek.**

an+cient his+to+ry *n.* **1.** the history of the **ancient world,** from the earliest known civilizations to the collapse of the Western Roman Empire in 476 A.D.. **2.** *Informal.* a recent event or fact sufficiently familiar to have lost its pertinence.

an+cient+ly ('eɪnʃəntlɪ) *adv.* in ancient times.

An+cient of Days *n. Old Testament.* God (Daniel 7:9).

an+cil+lar·y (æn'sɪlərɪ) *adj.* **1.** subsidiary. **2.** auxiliary; supplementary: *ancillary services.* *~n., pl.* **+lar·ies. 3.** a subsidiary or auxiliary thing or person: *the company has an ancillary abroad.* [C17: from Latin *ancillāris* concerning maidservants, from *ancilla,* diminutive of *ancūla* female servant]

an+cip·i+tal (æn'sɪpɪtᵊl) *or* **an+cip·i+tous** (æn'sɪpɪtəs) *adj. Biology.* flattened and having two edges: *ancipital stems.* [C18: from Latin *anceps* two-headed]

An+co+hu+ma (,æŋkəʊ'u:mə) *n.* one of the two peaks of (Mount) **Sorata.**

an+con ('æŋkɒn) *or* **an+cone** ('æŋkəʊn) *n., pl.* **an+con·es** (æŋ'kəʊni:z). **1.** *Architect.* a projecting bracket or console supporting a cornice. **2.** a former technical name for **elbow.** [C18: from Greek *ankōn* a bend] **—an+co+nal** (æŋ'kəʊnᵊl) *or* **an+co+ne·al** (æŋ'kəʊnɪəl) *adj.*

An+co+na (*Italian* aŋ'ko:na) *n.* a port in Central Italy, on the Adriatic, capital of the Marches region: founded by Greeks from Syracuse in about 390 B.C. Pop.: 107 213 (1975 est.).

-an·cy *suffix forming nouns.* variant of **-ance,** indicating condition or quality: *expectancy, poignancy.*

an+cy+los+to+mi·a+sis (,ænsɪ,lɒstə'maɪəsɪs), **an+ky+los+to+mi·a+sis,** *or* **an+chy+los+to+mi·a+sis** *n.* infestation of the human intestine with blood-sucking hookworms, causing progressive anaemia. Also called: **hookworm disease.** [from New Latin, from *Ancylostoma* genus of hookworms, from Greek *ankulos* hooked, crooked + *stoma* mouth]

and (ænd; *unstressed* ənd, ən) *conj.* (*coordinating*) **1.** along with; in addition to: *boys and girls.* **2.** as a consequence: *he fell down and cut his knee.* **3.** afterwards: *we pay the man and go through that door.* **4.** (preceded by *good* or *nice*) (intensifier): *the sauce is good and thick.* **5.** plus: *two and two equals four.* **6.** used to join identical words or phrases to give emphasis or indicate repetition or continuity: *better and better; we ran and ran; it rained and rained.* **7.** used to join two identical words or phrases to express a contrast between instances of what is named: *there are jobs and jobs.* **8.** *Informal.* used in place of *to* in infinitives after verbs such as *try, go,* and *come: try and see it my way.* **9.** an obsolete word for **if:** *and it please you.* Informal spellings: **an', 'n, 'n'.** *~n.* **10.** (*usually pl.*) an additional matter or problem (esp. in the phrase *ifs, ands, or buts*). [Old English *and;* related to Old Frisian *anda,* Old Saxon *ande,* Old High German *anti,* Sanskrit *atha*]

Usage. See at **to.**

And. *international car registration for* Andorra.

-and *or* **-end** *suffix forming nouns.* indicating a person or thing that is to be dealt with in a specified way: *analysand; dividend; multiplicand.* [from Latin gerundives ending in *-andus, -endus*]

An+da+lu+si·a (,ændə'lu:zɪə) *n.* a region of S Spain, on the Mediterranean and the Atlantic, with the Sierra Morena in the north, the Sierra Nevada in the southeast, and the Guadalquivir River flowing over fertile lands between them; a centre of Moorish civilization. Area: about 87 280 sq. km (33 700 sq. miles). Spanish name: **An+da+lu+cí·a** (,andalu'θia).

an+da+lu+site (,ændə'lu:saɪt) *n.* a grey, pink, or brown hard mineral consisting of aluminium silicate in orthorhombic crystalline form. It occurs in metamorphic rocks and is used as a refractory and as a gemstone. Formula: Al_2SiO_5.

An+da+man and Nic·o+bar Is+lands ('ændəmən; 'nɪkəʊ,bɑ:) *pl. n.* a territory of India, in the E Bay of Bengal, consisting of two groups of over 200 islands. Capital: Port Blair. Pop.: 115 133 (1971). Area: 8140 sq. km (3143 sq. miles).

An+da+man Is+lands *pl. n.* a group of islands in the E Bay of Bengal, part of the Indian territory of the Andaman and Nicobar Islands. Area: 6475 sq. km (2500 sq. miles).

An+da+man Sea *n.* part of the Bay of Bengal, between the Andaman and Nicobar Islands and the Malay Peninsula.

an+dan+te (æn'dæntɪ) *Music.* *~adj., adv.* **1.** at a moderately slow tempo; walking pace. *~n.* **2.** a passage or piece to be performed in this manner. [C18: from Italian, from *andare* to walk, from Latin *ambulāre*]

an+dan+ti+no (,ændæn'ti:nəʊ) *Music.* *~adj., adv.* **1.** slightly faster, or slightly slower, than andante. *~n., pl.* **+nos. 2.** a passage or piece to be performed in this manner. [C19: diminutive of ANDANTE]

AND cir+cuit *or* **gate** (ænd) *n. Computer technol.* a logic circuit having two or more input wires and one output wire that has a high-voltage output signal if and only if all input signals are at a high voltage simultaneously: used extensively as a basic circuit in computers. Compare **OR circuit, NOR circuit.** [C20: so named because the action performed on electrical signals is similar to the operation of the conjunction *and* in logical constructions]

An+de·an (æn'di:ən, 'ændɪən) *adj.* of, relating to, or resembling the Andes.

An+der+lecht (*Flemish* 'ɑndərlɛxt) *n.* a town in central Belgium, a suburb of Brussels. Pop.: 103 796 (1970).

An·der·sen ('ændəsᵊn) *n.* **Hans Chris·tian.** 1805–75, Danish author of fairy tales, including *The Ugly Duckling, The Tin Soldier,* and *The Snow Queen.*

An·der·sen Nex·ø *n.* See (Martin Andersen) **Nexø.**

An+der+son[1] ('ændəsᵊn) *n.* a river in N Canada, in the Northwest Territories, rising in lakes north of Great Bear Lake and flowing west and north to the Beaufort Sea. Length: about 580 km (360 miles).

An·der·son[2] ('ændəsᵊn) *n.* **1. Carl Da·vid.** born 1905, U.S. physicist, who discovered the positron in cosmic rays (1932): Nobel prize for physics 1936. **2. E·liz·a·beth Gar·rett.** 1836–

1917, English physician and feminist: a campaigner for the admission of women to the professions. **3. Mar·i·an.** born 1902, U.S. contralto, the first Negro permanent member of the Metropolitan Opera Company, New York.

An·ders·sen ('ændəsᵊn) *n.* **A·dolf** ('a:dɔlf). 1818–79, German chess player: noted for the incisiveness of his combination play.

An·des ('ændi:z) *n.* a major mountain system of South America, extending for about 7250 km (4500 miles) along the entire W coast, with several parallel ranges or cordilleras and many volcanic peaks: rich in minerals, including gold, silver, copper, iron ore, and nitrates. Average height: 3900 m (13 000 ft.). Highest peak: Aconcagua, 6850 m (22 835 ft.).

an·de·sine ('ændɪˌzi:n, -zɪn) *n.* a rare feldspar mineral of the plagioclase series consisting of an aluminium silicate of sodium and calcium. Formula: $NaAlSi_3O_8.CaAl_2Si_2O_8$. [C19: from the ANDES (where it is found) + -INE[1]]

an·de·site ('ændɪˌzaɪt) *n.* a fine-grained grey volcanic rock consisting of plagioclase feldspar, esp. andesine, amphibole, and pyroxene. [C19: from ANDES + -ITE[1]]

An·dhra Pra·desh ('ændrə prɑ:'dɛʃ) *n.* a state of SE India, on the Bay of Bengal: formed in 1953 from parts of Madras and Hyderabad states. Capital: Hyderabad. Pop.: 43 502 708 (1971). Area: about 274 540 sq. km (106 000 sq. miles).

and·i·ron ('ændˌaɪən) *n.* either of a pair of decorative metal stands in a hearth for supporting logs. [C14: from Old French *andier,* of unknown origin; influenced by IRON]

An·di·zhan (*Russian* andi'ʒan) *n.* a city in the SW Soviet Union, in the E Uzbek SSR. Pop.: 215 000 (1975 est.).

and/or *conj.* (*coordinating*). used to join terms when either one or the other or both is indicated: *passports and/or other means of identification.*

Usage. *And/or* is not universally accepted as being appropriate in good usage outside legal and commercial contexts. It is never used by careful writers and speakers where *or* is meant: *he must bring his car or his bicycle* (not *his car and/or his bicycle*).

An·dor·ra (æn'dɔ:rə) *n.* a mountainous coprincipality in SW Europe, between France and Spain: according to tradition, given independence by Charlemagne in the ninth century for helping to fight the Moors; under the joint sovereignty of the president of France and the Spanish bishop of Urgel since 1278. Languages: Catalan, French, and Spanish. Religion: Roman Catholic. Currency: French franc and Spanish peseta. Capital: Andorra la Vella. Pop.: 20 550 (1971). Area: 453 sq. km (175 sq. miles). Official name: **Valleys of Andorra.** —**An·'dor·ran** *adj., n.*

An·dor·ra La Ve·lla (*Spanish* an'dorra la 'beʎa) *n.* the capital of Andorra, situated in the west of the principality. Pop.: 2000 (1971). French name: **An·dorre la Vieille** (ãdɔr la 'vjɛj).

an·dra·dite ('ændrəˌdaɪt) *n.* a yellow, green, or brownish-black garnet that consists of calcium iron silicate and is used as a gemstone. Formula: $Ca_3Fe_2(SiO_4)_3$. [C19: named after J. B. d'*Andrada* e Silva (1763–1838), Brazilian mineralogist; see -ITE[1]]

An·drás·sy (æn'dræsɪ; *Hungarian* 'ɔndra:ʃi) *n.* Count **Gyu·la** ('djulɔ). 1823–90, Hungarian statesman; the first prime minister of Hungary under the Dual Monarchy of Austria-Hungary (1867).

An·dré ('ɑ:ndreɪ, 'ændrɪ) *n.* **John.** 1751–80, British major who was hanged as a spy for conspiring with Benedict Arnold during the War of American Independence.

An·dre·a del Sar·to (*Italian* an'drɛ:a del 'sarto) *n.* See **Sarto.**

An·dre·a·nof Is·lands (ˌændrɪ'ɑ:nɒf) *pl. n.* a group of islands in the central Aleutian Islands, Alaska. Area: 3710 sq. km (1432 sq. miles).

An·dre·ot·ti (*Italian* andre'ɔtti) *n.* **Giu·lio** ('dʒu:ljo). born 1919, Italian statesman; prime minister of Italy (1972–73; since 1976).

An·drew ('ændru:) *n. New Testament.* one of the twelve apostles of Jesus; the brother of Peter; patron saint of Scotland. Feast day: Nov. 30.

An·drewes ('ændru:z) *n.* **Lanc·e·lot.** 1555–1626, English bishop and theologian.

An·drews ('ændru:z) *n.* **Thom·as.** 1813–85, Irish physical chemist, noted for his work on the liquefaction of gases.

An·drić (*Serbo-Croat* 'andritʃ) *n.* **I·vo** ('i:vɔ). 1892–1975, Yugoslav novelist; author of *The Bridge on the Dvina* (1945): Nobel prize for literature 1961.

an·dro- *or before a vowel* **andr-** *combining form.* **1.** male; masculine: *androsterone.* **2.** (in botany) stamen or anther: *androecium.* [from Greek *anēr* (genitive *andros*) man]

An·dro·cles ('ændrəˌkli:z) *or* **An·dro·clus** ('ændrəkləs) *n.* (in Roman legend) a slave whose life was spared in the arena by a lion from whose paw he had once extracted a thorn.

an·dro·clin·i·um (ˌændrə'klɪnɪəm) *n., pl.* **-clin·i·a** (-'klɪnɪə). another name for **clinandrium.** [C19: New Latin, from ANDRO- + *-clinium,* from Greek *klinē* slope; see CLINO-]

an·droe·ci·um (æn'dri:sɪəm) *n., pl.* **-ci·a** (-sɪə). the stamens of a flowering plant collectively. [C19: from New Latin, from ANDRO- + Greek *oikion* a little house] —**an·'droe·ci·al** *adj.*

an·dro·gen ('ændrədʒən) *n.* any of several steroids, produced as hormones by the testes or made synthetically, that promote development of male sexual organs and male secondary sexual characteristics. —**an·dro·gen·ic** (ˌændrə'dʒɛnɪk) *adj.*

an·drog·e·nous (æn'drɒdʒɪnəs) *adj. Biology.* producing only male offspring.

an·dro·gyne ('ændrəˌdʒaɪn) *n.* another word for **hermaphrodite.** [C17: from Old French, via Latin from Greek *androgunos,* from *anēr* man + *gunē* woman]

an·drog·y·nous (æn'drɒdʒɪnəs) *adj.* **1.** *Botany.* having male and female flowers in the same inflorescence, as plantain. **2.** having male and female characteristics; hermaphrodite.

an·droid ('ændrɔɪd) *n.* **1.** (in science fiction) a robot resembling a human being. ~*adj.* **2.** resembling a human being. [C18: from Late Greek *androeidēs* manlike; see ANDRO-, -OID]

An·dro·ma·che (æn'drɒməkɪ) *n. Greek myth.* the wife of Hector.

An·drom·e·da[1] (æn'drɒmɪdə) *n. Greek myth.* the daughter of Cassiopeia and wife of Perseus, who saved her from a sea monster.

An·drom·e·da[2] (æn'drɒmɪdə) *n., Latin genitive* **An·drom·e·dae** (æn'drɒmɪˌdi:). a constellation in the N hemisphere lying between Cassiopeia and Pegasus, the three brightest stars being of the second magnitude. It contains the **Andromeda Galaxy,** a spiral galaxy 2.2 million light years away.

An·dros ('ændrɒs) *n.* **1.** an island in the Aegean Sea, the northernmost of the Cyclades: long famous for wine. Capital: Andros. Pop.: 10 457 (1971). Area: about 311 sq. km (120 sq. miles). **2.** an island in the N West Indies, the largest of the Bahamas. Pop.: 8845 (1970). Area: 4144 sq. km (1600 sq. miles).

an·dro·sphinx ('ændrəˌsfɪŋks) *n., pl.* **-sphinx·es** *or* **-sphin·ges** (-ˌsfɪndʒi:z). a sphinx having the head of a man.

an·dros·ter·one (æn'drɒstəˌrəʊn) *n.* an androgenic steroid hormone produced in the testes. Formula: $C_{19}H_{30}O_2$.

-an·drous *adj. combining form.* (in botany) indicating number or type of stamens: *diandrous.* [from New Latin *-andrus,* from Greek *-andros,* from *anēr* man]

-an·dry *n. combining form.* indicating number of husbands: *polyandry.* [from Greek *-andria,* from *anēr* man]

And·va·ri (æn'dwɑ:rɪ) *n. Norse myth.* a dwarf who possessed a treasure hoard, which was robbed by Loki.

ane (eɪn) *determiner, pron., n.* a Scot. word for **one.**

-ane *suffix forming nouns.* indicating an alkane hydrocarbon: *hexane.* [coined to replace *-ene, -ine,* and *-one*]

a·near (ə'nɪə) *Archaic.* ~*prep.* **1.** near. ~*adv.* **2.** nearly.

an·ec·dot·age ('ænɪkˌdəʊtɪdʒ) *n.* **1.** anecdotes collectively. **2.** *Humorous.* talkative or garrulous old age.

an·ec·dote ('ænɪkˌdəʊt) *n.* a short usually amusing account of an incident, esp. a personal or biographical one. [C17: from Medieval Latin *anecdota* unpublished items, from Greek *anekdotos* unpublished, from AN- + *ekdotos* published, from *ekdidonai,* from *ek-* out + *didonai* to give] —ˌ**an·ec·'do·tal** *or* ˌ**an·ec·'dot·ic** *adj.* —ˌ**an·ec·'do·tal·ist** *or* '**an·ec**ˌ**dot·ist** *n.*

an·e·cho·ic (ˌænɪ'kəʊɪk) *adj.* having a low degree of reverberation: *an anechoic recording studio.*

an·e·lace ('ænəˌleɪs) *n.* a variant spelling of **anlace.**

a·nele (ə'ni:l) *vb.* (*tr.*) *Archaic.* to anoint, esp. to give extreme unction to. [C14 *anelen,* from *an-* (from Old English *an-* ON) + *elen* to anoint (from *ele* oil, from Latin *oleum*)]

a·ne·mi·a (ə'ni:mɪə) *n.* the usual U.S. spelling of **anaemia.** [C19: from New Latin, from Greek *anaimia* lack of blood]

a·ne·mic (ə'ni:mɪk) *adj.* the usual U.S. spelling of **anaemic.**

a·ne·mo- *combining form.* indicating wind: *anemometer; anemophilous.* [from Greek *anemos* wind]

a·nem·o·chore (ə'ni:məʊˌkɔ:) *n.* a plant in which the fruits or seeds are dispersed by wind.

a·nem·o·graph (ə'nɛməʊˌgrɑ:f) *n.* a self-recording anemometer. —**a·nem·o·graph·ic** (əˌnɛməʊ'græfɪk) *adj.* —**a**ˌ**nem·o·'graph·i·cal·ly** *adv.*

an·e·mog·ra·phy (ˌænɪ'mɒgrəfɪ) *n. Meteorol.* the technique of recording wind measurements.

an·e·mol·o·gy (ˌænɪ'mɒlədʒɪ) *n.* the study of winds.

an·e·mom·e·ter (ˌænɪ'mɒmɪtə) *n.* **1.** Also called: **wind gauge.** an instrument for recording the speed and often the direction of winds. **2.** any instrument that measures the rate of movement of a fluid. —**an·e·mo·met·ric** (ˌænɪmɒ'mɛtrɪk) *adj.* —ˌ**an·e·mo·'met·ri·cal** *adj.*

an·e·mom·e·try (ˌænɪ'mɒmɪtrɪ) *n. Meteorol.* the technique of measuring wind speed and direction.

a·nem·o·ne (ə'nɛmənɪ) *n.* any ranunculaceous woodland plant of the genus *Anemone* of N temperate regions, such as the white-flowered *A. nemorosa* (**wood anemone** or **windflower**). Some cultivated anemones have lilac or pale blue flowers. See also **pasque flower.** Compare **sea anemone** (an animal). [C16: via Latin from Greek: wind-flower, from *anemos* wind]

a·nem·o·ne fish *n.* any of various damselfishes of the genus *Amphiprion,* such as *A. percula* (clown anemone fish), that usually live closely associated with sea anemones.

an·e·moph·i·lous (ˌænɪ'mɒfɪləs) *adj.* (of flowering plants such as grasses) pollinated by the wind. Compare **entomophilous.** —ˌ**an·e·'moph·i·ly** *n.*

a·nem·o·scope (ə'nɛməˌskəʊp) *n. Meteorol.* any device that shows the presence and direction of a wind.

a·nent (ə'nɛnt) *prep. Archaic or Scot.* concerning; about. [Old English *on efen,* literally: on even (ground)]

an·er·gy ('ænədʒɪ) *n.* **1.** lack of energy. **2.** *Immunol.* diminution or lack of immunity to an antigen. [from New Latin *anergia,* from AN- + Greek *ergon* work] —**a·ner·gic** (æ'nɜ:dʒɪk) *adj.*

an·er·oid ba·rom·e·ter ('ænəˌrɔɪd) *n.* a device for measuring atmospheric pressure without the use of fluids. It consists of a partially evacuated metal chamber, the thin corrugated lid of which is displaced by variations in the external air pressure. This displacement is magnified by levers and made to operate a pointer. [C19 *aneroid,* from French, from AN- + Greek *nēros* wet + -OID]

an·es·the·si·a (ˌænɪsˈθiːzɪə) *n.* the usual U.S. spelling of **anaesthesia.**

an·es·the·si·ol·o·gist *or* **an·aes·the·si·ol·o·gist** (ˌænɪsˌθiːzɪˈɒlədʒɪst) *n.* the U.S. name for an **anaesthetist;** in the U.S., a qualified doctor specializing in the administration of anaesthesia. Compare **anesthetist.**

an·es·thet·ic (ˌænɪsˈθɛtɪk) *n., adj.* the usual U.S. spelling of **anaesthetic.**

an·es·the·tist (əˈniːsθətɪst) *n.* (in the U.S.) a person qualified to administer anaesthesia, often a nurse or someone other than a physician. Compare **anesthesiologist.**

an·es·trus (ænˈiːstrəs) *n.* a variant spelling (esp. U.S.) of **anoestrus.** —**anˈes·trous** *adj.*

an·e·thole (ˈænɪˌθəʊl) *n.* a white water-soluble crystalline substance with a liquorice-like odour, used as a flavouring and a sensitizer in the processing of colour photographs. Formula: $CH_3CH{:}CHC_6H_4OCH_3$. [C19: from Latin *anēthum* dill, anise, from Greek *anēthon*]

A·ne·to (*Spanish* aˈneto) *n.* **Pi·co de** (ˈpiko ðe). a mountain in N Spain, near the French border: the highest in the Pyrenees. Height: 3404 m (11 168 ft.).

an·eu·ploid (ˈænjʊˌplɔɪd) *adj.* **1.** (of polyploid cells or organisms) having a chromosome number that is not an exact multiple of the haploid number, caused by one chromosome set being incomplete. ~*n.* **2.** a cell or individual of this type. ~Compare **euploid.**

an·eu·rin (əˈnjʊərɪn) *n.* a less common name for **thiamine.** [C20: from A(NTI-) + (POLY)NEUR(ITIS) + (VITAM)IN]

an·eu·rysm *or* **an·eu·rism** (ˈænjəˌrɪzəm) *n.* a sac formed by abnormal dilation of the weakened wall of a blood vessel. [C15: from Greek *aneurusma,* from *aneurunein* to dilate, from *eurunein* to widen] —**ˌan·euˈrys·mal, ˌan·euˈris·mal, ˌan·eu·rysˈmat·ic,** *or* **ˌan·eu·risˈmat·ic** *adj.* —**ˌan·euˈrys·mal·ly, ˌan·euˈris·mal·ly, ˌan·eu·rysˈmat·i·cal·ly,** *or* **ˌan·eu·risˈmat·i·cal·ly** *adv.*

a·new (əˈnjuː) *adv.* **1.** over again; once more. **2.** in a different way; afresh. [Old English *of nīwe;* see OF, NEW]

an·frac·tu·os·i·ty (ˌænfræktʃʊˈɒsɪtɪ) *n.* **1.** the condition or quality of being anfractuous. **2.** a winding, circuitous, or intricate passage, surface, process, etc.

an·frac·tu·ous (ænˈfræktʃʊəs) *adj.* characterized by twists and turns; convoluted. [C17: from Late Latin *anfractuōsus,* from Latin *anfractus* a digression, literally: a bending]

An·ga·ra (*Russian* angaˈra) *n.* a river in the S Soviet Union, in Siberia, flowing from Lake Baikal north and west to the Yenisei River: important for hydroelectric power. Length: about 2100 km (1300 miles).

An·garsk (*Russian* anˈgarsk) *n.* an industrial city in the SE Soviet Union, in the southern RSFSR northwest of Irkutsk. Pop.: 228 000 (1975 est.).

an·ga·ry (ˈæŋgərɪ) *n. International law.* the right of a belligerent state to use the property of a neutral state or to destroy it if necessary, subject to payment of full compensation to the owners. [C19: from French *angarie,* from Late Latin *angaria* enforced service, from Greek *angareia* office of a courier, from *angaros* courier, of Persian origin]

an·gel (ˈeɪndʒəl) *n.* **1.** *Theol.* one of a class of spiritual beings attendant upon God. In medieval angelology they are divided by rank into nine orders: seraphim, cherubim, thrones, dominations (or dominions), virtues, powers, principalities (or princedoms), archangels, and angels. **2.** a divine messenger from God. **3.** a guardian spirit. **4.** a conventional representation of any of these beings, depicted in human form with wings. **5.** *Informal.* a person, esp. a woman, who is kind, pure, or beautiful. **6.** *Informal.* an investor in a venture, esp. a backer of a theatrical production. **7.** Also called: **angel-noble.** a former English gold coin with a representation of the archangel Michael on it, first minted in Edward IV's reign. **8.** *Informal.* an unexplained signal on a radar screen. [Old English, from Late Latin *angelus,* from Greek *angelos* messenger]

an·gel cake *or esp. U.S.* **an·gel food cake** *n.* a very light sponge cake made without egg yolks.

An·ge·le·no (ˌændʒəˈliːnəʊ) *n., pl.* **·nos.** a native or inhabitant of Los Angeles.

An·gel Falls *n.* a waterfall in SE Venezuela, on the Caroni River. Height (probably the highest in the world): 979 m (3211 ft.).

an·gel·fish (ˈeɪndʒəlˌfɪʃ) *n., pl.* **·fish** *or* **·fish·es. 1.** any of various small tropical marine percoid fishes of the genus *Pomacanthus* and related genera, which have a deep flattened brightly coloured body and brushlike teeth: family *Chaetodontidae.* See also **butterfly fish. 2.** Also called: **scalare.** a South American cichlid, *Pterophyllum scalare,* of the Amazon region, having a compressed body and large dorsal and anal fins: a popular aquarium fish. **3.** another name for **angel shark.**

an·gel·ic (ænˈdʒɛlɪk) *adj.* **1.** of or relating to angels. **2.** *Informal.* resembling an angel in beauty, purity, power, etc. —**anˈgel·i·cal** *adj.* —**anˈgel·i·cal·ly** *adv.*

an·gel·ic·a (ænˈdʒɛlɪkə) *n.* **1.** Also called: **archangel.** any tall umbelliferous plant of the genus *Angelica,* having compound leaves and clusters of small white or greenish flowers, esp. *A. archangelica,* the aromatic seeds, leaves, and stems of which are used in medicine and cookery. **2.** the candied stems of this plant, used for decorating and flavouring sweet dishes. [C16: from Medieval Latin (*herba*) *angelica* angelic herb]

An·gel·ic Doc·tor *n.* an epithet of Saint Thomas Aquinas.

An·ge·li·co (*Italian* anˈdʒɛːliko) *n.* **Fra** (fra) original name *Guido di Pietro;* monastic name *Fra Giovanni da Fiesole.* ?1400–1455, Italian fresco painter and Dominican friar.

An·gell (ˈeɪndʒəl) *n.* Sir **Nor·man.** original name *Ralph Norman Angell Lane.* 1874–1967, English writer, pacifist, and economist, noted for his work on the economic futility of war, *The Great Illusion* (1910): Nobel peace prize 1933.

an·gel·ol·o·gy (ˌeɪndʒəˈlɒlədʒɪ) *n.* a doctrine or theory treating of angels.

an·gel shark *or* **fish** *n.* any of several sharks constituting the family *Squatinidae,* such as *Squatina squatina,* that have very large flattened pectoral fins and occur in the Atlantic and Pacific Oceans. Also called: **monkfish.**

an·gels-on-horse·back *n. Brit.* a savoury of oysters wrapped in bacon slices and served on toast.

an·gel's tears *n.* (*functioning as sing.*) another name for **moonflower** (sense 2).

An·ge·lus (ˈændʒɪləs) *n. R.C. Church.* **1.** a series of prayers recited in the morning, at midday, and in the evening, commemorating the Annunciation and Incarnation. **2.** the bell (**Angelus bell**) signalling the times of these prayers. [C17: Latin, from the phrase *Angelus domini nuntiavit Mariae* the angel of the Lord brought tidings to Mary]

an·ger (ˈæŋgə) *n.* **1.** a feeling of great annoyance or antagonism as the result of some real or supposed grievance; rage; wrath. ~*vb.* (*tr.*) **2.** to make angry; enrage. [C12: from Old Norse *angr* grief; related to Old English *enge,* Old High German *engi* narrow, Latin *angere* to strangle]

An·gers (*French* ɑ̃ˈʒe) *n.* a city in W France, on the River Maine. Pop.: 142 966 (1975).

An·ge·vin (ˈændʒɪvɪn) *n.* **1.** a native or inhabitant of Anjou. **2.** *History.* a member of the Plantagenet royal line descended from Geoffrey, Count of Anjou, esp. one of the kings of England from Henry II to Richard II (1154–1216). ~*adj.* **3.** of or relating to Anjou or its inhabitants. **4.** of or relating to the Plantagenet kings of England between 1154 and 1216.

an·gi·na (ænˈdʒaɪnə) *n.* **1.** any disease marked by painful attacks of spasmodic choking, such as Vincent's angina and quinsy. **2.** short for **angina pectoris.** [C16: from Latin: quinsy, from Greek *ankhonē* a strangling] —**anˈgi·nal** *adj.* —**an·gi·nose** (ænˈdʒaɪnəʊs, -nəʊz) *or* **anˈgi·nous** *adj.*

an·gi·na pec·to·ris (ˈpɛktərɪs) *n.* a sudden intense pain in the chest, often accompanied by feelings of suffocation, caused by momentary lack of adequate blood supply to the heart muscle. Sometimes shortened to **angina.** [C18: New Latin: angina of the chest]

an·gi·o- *or before a vowel* **an·gi-** *combining form.* indicating a blood or lymph vessel; seed vessel: *angiology; angiosperm; angioma.* [from Greek *angeion* vessel]

an·gi·ol·o·gy (ˌændʒɪˈɒlədʒɪ) *n.* the branch of medical science concerned with the blood vessels and the lymphatic system.

an·gi·o·ma (ˌændʒɪˈəʊmə) *n., pl.* **·mas** *or* **·ma·ta** (-mətə). a tumour consisting of a mass of blood vessels (**haemangioma**) or a mass of lymphatic vessels (**lymphangioma**). —**ˌan·giˈom·a·tous** *adj.*

an·gi·o·sperm (ˈændʒɪəˌspɜːm) *n.* any seed-bearing plant of the division *Angiospermae,* in which the ovules are enclosed in an ovary, which develops into the fruit after fertilization; any flowering plant. Compare **gymnosperm.** —**ˌan·gi·oˈsper·mous** *adj.*

Ang·kor (ˈæŋkɔː) *n.* a large area of ruins in NW Cambodia, containing **Angkor Thom** (tɔːm), the capital of the former Khmer Empire, and **Angkor Wat** (wɒt), a three-storey temple, which were overgrown with dense jungle from the 14th to 19th centuries.

Angl. *abbrev. for* Anglican.

an·gle[1] (ˈæŋgəl) *n.* **1.** the space between two straight lines that diverge from a common point or between two planes that extend from a common line. **2.** the shape formed by two such lines or planes. **3.** the extent to which one such line or plane diverges from another, measured in degrees or radians. **4.** an angular projection or recess; corner. **5.** standpoint; point of view: *look at the question from another angle; the angle of a newspaper article.* **6.** *Informal.* a selfish or devious motive or purpose. **7.** See **angle iron.** ~*vb.* **8.** to move in or bend into angles or an angle. **9.** (*tr.*) to produce (an article, statement, etc.) with a particular point of view. **10.** (*tr.*) to present, direct, or place at an angle. **11.** (*intr.*) to turn or bend in a different direction: *the path angled sharply to the left.* [C14: from French, from Old Latin *angulus* corner]

an·gle[2] (ˈæŋgəl) *vb.* (*intr.*) **1.** to fish with a hook and line. **2.** (often foll. by *for*) to attempt to get: *he angled for a compliment.* ~*n.* **3.** *Obsolete.* any piece of fishing tackle, esp. a hook. [Old English *angul* fishhook; related to Old High German *ango,* Latin *uncus,* Greek *onkos*]

An·gle (ˈæŋgəl) *n.* a member of a West Germanic people from N Germany who invaded and settled large parts of E and N England in the 5th and 6th centuries A.D. [from Latin *Anglus,* from Germanic (compare ENGLISH), an inhabitant of *Angul,* a district in Schleswig (now *Angeln*), a name identical with Old English *angul* hook, ANGLE[2], referring to its shape]

an·gle brack·et *n.* either of a pair of brackets having the shapes < and >.

an·gle i·ron *n.* **1.** Also called: **angle, angle bar.** an iron or a steel structural bar that has an L-shaped cross section. **2.** any piece of iron or steel forming an angle, esp. a right angle.

an·gle of at·tack *n.* the acute angle between the chord line of an aerofoil and the undisturbed relative airflow. Also called: **angle of incidence.**

an·gle of bank *n.* the angle between the lateral axis of an aircraft in flight and the horizontal.

an·gle of de·vi·a·tion *n.* the angle between the direction of the refracted ray and the direction of the incident ray when a ray of light passes from one medium to another.

an·gle of dip *n.* the full name for **dip** (sense 29).

an·gle of in·ci·dence *n.* **1.** the angle that a line or beam of radiation makes with a line perpendicular to the surface at the point of incidence. **2.** another name for **angle of attack. 3.** Also called: **rigging angle of incidence.** the angle between the chord line of an aircraft wing or tailplane and the aircraft's longitudinal axis.

an·gle of re·flec·tion *n.* the angle that a beam of reflected radiation makes with the normal to a surface at the point of reflection.

an·gle of re·frac·tion *n.* the angle that a refracted beam of radiation makes with the normal to the surface between two media at the point of refraction.

an·gle of re·pose *n.* the maximum angle to the horizontal at which rocks, soil, etc., will remain without sliding.

an·gle plate *n.* a steel structural plate, esp. one in the shape of a right-angled triangle, used to connect structural members and stiffen frameworks.

an·gler ('æŋglə) *n.* **1.** a person who fishes with a rod and line. **2.** *Informal.* a person who schemes or uses devious methods to secure an advantage. **3.** Also called: **angler fish.** any spiny-finned fish of the order *Pediculati* (or *Lophiiformes*). They live at the bottom of the sea and typically have a long spiny movable dorsal fin with which they lure their prey.

An·gle·sey ('æŋgᵊlsɪ) *n.* an island and, until 1974, a county of N Wales, now part of Gwynedd, separated from the mainland by the Menai Strait. Pop.: 59 705 (1971). Area: 714 sq. km (276 sq. miles).

an·gle·site ('æŋgᵊlˌsaɪt) *n.* a white or grey secondary mineral consisting of lead sulphate in orthorhombic crystalline form. It occurs in lead-ore deposits and is a source of lead. Formula: $PbSO_4$. [C19: from ANGLESEY, where it was first found]

an·gle·worm ('æŋgᵊlˌwɜːm) *n.* an earthworm used as bait by anglers.

An·gli·a ('æŋglɪə) *n.* a Latin name for **England.**

An·gli·an ('æŋglɪən) *adj.* **1.** of or relating to the Angles or to the Anglian dialects of Old English. ~*n.* **2.** the group of Old and Middle English dialects spoken in the Midlands and the north of England, divided into Mercian and Northumbrian. See also **Kentish, West Saxon.** ~See also **East Anglia.**

An·gli·can ('æŋglɪkən) *adj.* **1.** denoting or relating to the Anglican communion. ~*n.* **2.** a member of the Church of England or one of the Churches in full communion with it. [C17: from Medieval Latin *Anglicānus*, from *Anglicus* English, from Latin *Anglī* the Angles]

An·gli·can Church *n.* any Church of the Anglican Communion or the Anglican Communion itself.

An·gli·can Com·mun·ion *n.* a group of Christian Churches including the Church of England, the Church of Ireland, the Episcopal Church in Scotland, the Church in Wales, the Episcopal Church in the U.S., and certain other Churches, all of which are in full communion with each other.

An·gli·can·ism ('æŋglɪkəˌnɪzəm) *n.* the doctrine and practice of the Church of England and other Anglican Churches.

An·gli·ce ('æŋglɪsɪ) *adv.* in English: *Roma, Anglice Rome.* [from Medieval Latin]

An·gli·cism ('æŋglɪˌsɪzəm) *n.* **1.** a word, phrase, or idiom peculiar to the English language, esp. as spoken in England. **2.** an English attitude, mannerism, custom, etc. **3.** the fact or quality of being English.

An·gli·cist ('æŋglɪsɪst) *or* **An·glist** *n. Rare.* an expert in or student of English literature or language.

an·gli·cize, an·gli·cise ('æŋglɪˌsaɪz), *or* **an·gli·fy** ('æŋglɪˌfaɪ) ~*vb.* **·ciz·es, ·ciz·ing, ·cized, ·cis·es, ·cis·ing, ·cised** *or* **·fies, ·fy·ing, ·fied.** (*sometimes cap.*) to make or become English in outlook, attitude, form, etc. —ˌ**an·gli·ci·'za·tion** *or* ˌ**an·gli·ci·'sa·tion** *n.*

an·gling ('æŋglɪŋ) *n.* **a.** the art or sport of catching fish with a rod and line and a baited hook or other lure, such as a fly; fishing. **b.** (*as modifier*): *an angling contest.*

An·glo- ('æŋgləʊ-) *combining form.* denoting English or England: *Anglo-Saxon.* [from Medieval Latin *Anglii*]

An·glo-A·mer·i·can *adj.* **1.** of or relating to relations between England and the United States or their peoples. ~*n.* **2.** *Chiefly U.S.* an inhabitant or citizen of the United States who was or whose ancestors were born in England.

An·glo-Cath·o·lic *adj.* **1.** of or relating to a group within the Church of England or the Anglican Communion that emphasizes the Catholic elements in its teaching and practice. ~*n.* **2.** a member of this group. —**An·glo-Ca·thol·i·cism** *n.*

An·glo-French *adj.* **1.** of or relating to England and France. **2.** of or relating to Anglo-French. ~*n.* **3.** the Norman-French language of medieval England.

An·glo-In·di·an *adj.* **1.** of or relating to England and India. **2.** denoting or relating to Anglo-Indians. **3.** (of a word) introduced into English from an Indian language. ~*n.* **4.** a person of mixed British and Indian descent. **5.** an Englishman who lives or has lived for a long time in India.

An·glo-I·rish *n.* **1.** (preceded by *the; functioning as pl.*) the inhabitants of Ireland of English birth or descent. **2.** the English language as spoken in Ireland. ~*adj.* **3.** of or relating to the Anglo-Irish. **4.** of or relating to English and Irish. **5.** of or relating to the English language as spoken in Ireland.

An·glo·ma·ni·a (ˌæŋgləʊ'meɪnɪə) *n.* excessive respect for English customs, etc. —ˌ**An·glo·'ma·ni·ac** *n.*

An·glo-Nor·man *adj.* **1.** *History.* relating to the Norman conquerors of England, their society, or their language. ~*n.* **2.** *History.* a Norman inhabitant of England after 1066. **3.** the Anglo-French language.

An·glo·phile ('æŋgləʊfɪl, -ˌfaɪl) *or* **An·glo·phil** *n.* a person having admiration for England or the English. —**An·glo·phil·i·a** (ˌæŋgləʊ'fɪlɪə) *n.* —**An·glo·phil·i·ac** (ˌæŋgləʊ'fɪlɪˌæk) *or* **An·glo·phil·ic** (ˌæŋgləʊ'fɪlɪk) *adj.*

An·glo·phobe ('æŋgləʊˌfəʊb) *n.* a person who hates or fears England or its people. —ˌ**An·glo·'pho·bi·a** *n.*

An·glo·phone ('æŋgləˌfəʊn) *n.* **1.** a person who speaks English, esp. a native speaker. ~*adj.* **2.** speaking English.

An·glo-Sax·on *n.* **1.** a member of any of the West Germanic tribes (Angles, Saxons, and Jutes) that settled in Britain from the 5th century A.D. and were dominant until the Norman conquest. **2.** the language of these tribes. See **Old English. 3.** any White person whose native language is English and whose cultural affiliations are those common to Britain and the U.S. **4.** *Informal.* plain blunt English, esp. English containing taboo words. ~*adj.* **5.** forming part of the Germanic element in Modern English: *"forget" is an Anglo-Saxon word.* **6.** of or relating to the Anglo-Saxons or the Old English language. **7.** of or relating to the White Protestant culture of Britain and the U.S. **8.** *Informal.* (of English speech or writing) plain and blunt.

An·go·la (æŋ'gəʊlə) *n.* a republic in SW Africa, on the Atlantic: includes the enclave of Cabinda, north of the River Congo; a Portuguese colony from 1575 until its independence in 1975. It consists of a narrow coastal plain with a large fertile plateau in the east. Currency: kwanza. Capital: Luanda. Pop.: 5 673 046 (1970). Area: 1 246 693 sq. km (481 351 sq. miles). —**An·'go·lan** *adj., n.*

an·go·ra (æŋ'gɔːrə) *n.* (*sometimes cap.*) **1. a.** the long soft hair of the outer coat of the Angora goat or the fur of the Angora rabbit. **b.** yarn, cloth, or clothing made from this hair. **c.** a material made to resemble this yarn or cloth. **d.** (*as modifier*): *an angora sweater.* See also **mohair. 2.** *Austral. slang.* an idiot; fool.

An·go·ra *n.* **1.** (æŋ'gɔːrə, 'æŋgərə). the former name (until 1930) of **Ankara. 2.** (æŋ'gɔːrə). short for **Angora cat, Angora goat,** or **Angora rabbit.**

An·go·ra cat *n.* a former long-haired variety of cat, similar to the Persian.

An·go·ra goat *n.* a breed of domestic goat with long soft hair.

An·go·ra rab·bit *n.* a breed of rabbit with long usually white silky hair.

An·go·stu·ra (*Spanish* ˌaŋgo'stura) *n.* the former name (1764–1846) for **Ciudad Bolívar.**

an·gos·tu·ra bark (ˌæŋgə'stjʊərə) *n.* the bitter aromatic bark of certain South American rutaceous trees of the genus *Cusparia* or *Galipea,* used to make angostura bitters and formerly used medicinally to reduce fever.

an·gos·tu·ra bit·ters *pl. n.* (*often cap.*) *Trademark.* a bitter aromatic tonic, used as a flavouring in alcoholic drinks.

An·gra do He·ro·ís·mo (*Portuguese* 'ɜ̃ŋgrə ðu i'rwiʒmu) *n.* a port in the Azores, on Terceira Island. Pop.: 40 362 (1970).

an·gry ('æŋgrɪ) *adj.* **·gri·er, ·gri·est. 1.** feeling or expressing annoyance, animosity, or resentment; enraged. **2.** suggestive of anger: *angry clouds.* **3.** severely inflamed: *an angry sore.* —'**an·gri·ly** *adv.*

an·gry young man *n.* **1.** (*often cap.*) one of several British novelists and playwrights of the 1950s who shared a hostility towards the established traditions and ruling elements of their country. **2.** any similarly rebellious person or group.

angst (æŋst; *German* aŋst) *n.* an acute but nonspecific sense of anxiety or remorse. [German]

ang·strom ('æŋstrʌm, -strəm) *n.* a unit of length equal to 10^{-10} metre, used principally to express the wavelengths of electromagnetic radiations. It is equivalent to 0.1 nanometre. Symbol: Å or A Also called: **angstrom unit.** [C20: named after Anders J. ÅNGSTRÖM]

Ång·ström ('æŋstrəm; *Swedish* 'ɔŋstrœm) *n.* **An·ders Jo·nas** ('andərs 'juːnas). 1814–74, Swedish physicist, noted for his work on spectroscopy and solar physics.

An·guil·la (æŋ'gwɪlə) *n.* an island in the West Indies, in the Leeward Islands: part of the British territory of St. Kitts-Nevis-Anguilla. Pop.: 5500 (1970 est.); area: 90 sq. km (35 sq. miles).

an·guil·li·form (æŋ'gwɪlɪˌfɔːm) *adj.* having the shape or form of an eel. [C17: from Latin *anguilla* eel, diminutive of *anguis* snake]

an·guine ('æŋgwɪn) *adj.* of, relating to, or similar to a snake. [C17: from Latin *anguīnus,* from *anguis* snake]

an·guish ('æŋgwɪʃ) *n.* **1.** extreme pain or misery; mental or physical torture; agony. ~*vb.* **2.** to afflict or be afflicted with anguish. [C13: from Old French *angoisse* a strangling, from Latin *angustia* narrowness, from *angustus* narrow]

an·gu·lar ('æŋgjʊlə) *adj.* **1.** lean or bony. **2.** awkward or stiff in manner or movement. **3.** having an angle or angles. **4.** placed at an angle. **5.** measured by an angle or by the rate at which an angle changes. [C15: from Latin *angulāris,* from *angulus* ANGLE[1]] —'**an·gu·lar·ly** *adv.* —'**an·gu·lar·ness** *n.*

an·gu·lar ac·cel·er·a·tion *n.* the rate of change of angular velocity.

an·gu·lar·i·ty (ˌæŋgjʊ'lærɪtɪ) *n., pl.* **·ties. 1.** the condition of being angular. **2.** an angular form or shape.

an·gu·lar mo·men·tum *n.* the product of the momentum of a rotating body and its distance from the axis of rotation.

an·gu·lar ve·loc·i·ty *n.* the velocity of a body rotating about a fixed point measured as the rate of change of the angle subtended at that fixed point by the path of the body. Symbol: ω

an+gu+late *adj.* ('æŋgjʊlɪt, -ˌleɪt). **1.** having angles or an angular shape. ~*vb.* ('æŋgjʊˌleɪt). **2.** to make or become angular. [C18: from Late Latin *angulāre* to make angled, from Latin *angulus* ANGLE[1]] —'**an+gu+ˌlat+ed** *adj.*

an+gu+la+tion (ˌæŋgjʊ'leɪʃən) *n.* **1.** an angular formation. **2.** the precise measurement of angles.

An+gus ('æŋgəs) *n.* (until 1975) a county of E Scotland, now part of Tayside region.

An·gus Og (əʊg) *n. Irish myth.* the god of love and beauty.

ang+wan+ti+bo (æŋ'gwæntɪˌbəʊ) *n., pl.* **+bos.** a rare gold-coloured prosimian primate, *Arctocebus calabarensis,* having digits that are specialized as a pair of pincers for climbing: family *Lorisidae* (lorises). Also called: **golden potto.** [C19: from Efik]

An+halt (*German* 'anhalt) *n.* a former state of central Germany, now part of West Germany.

an+he+dral (æn'hi:drəl) *n.* the downward inclination of an aircraft wing in relation to the lateral axis. Compare **dihedral** (sense 3).

an+hin+ga (æn'hɪŋgə) *n.* another name for **darter** (the bird). [C18: via Portuguese from Tupi]

An+hwei ('æn'weɪ) *n.* a province of E China, crossed by the Yangtze River. Capital: Hofei. Pop.: 35 000 000 (1967–71 est.). Area: 13 986 sq. km (54 000 sq. miles).

an+hy+dride (æn'haɪdraɪd, -drɪd) *n.* **1.** a compound that has been formed from another compound by dehydration. **2.** a compound that forms an acid or base when added to water. **3.** any organic compound containing the group -CO.O.CO- formed by removal of one water molecule from two carboxyl groups. [C19: from ANHYDR(OUS) + -IDE]

an+hy+drite (æn'haɪdraɪt) *n.* a glassy colourless to grey mineral consisting of anhydrous calcium sulphate in orthorhombic crystalline form, found in sedimentary rocks. Formula: $CaSO_4$. [C19: from ANHYDR(OUS) + -ITE[1]]

an+hy+drous (æn'haɪdrəs) *adj.* containing no water, esp. no water of crystallization. [C19: from Greek *anudros;* see AN-, HYDRO-]

a·ni ('ɑ:nɪ) *n., pl.* **a·nis.** any of several gregarious tropical American birds of the genus *Crotophaga:* family *Cuculidae* (cuckoos). They have a black plumage, long square-tipped tail, and heavily hooked bill. [Spanish *aní,* from Tupi]

An·i·ak+chak (ˌænɪ'æktʃæk) *n.* an active volcanic crater in SW Alaska, on the Alaska Peninsula: the largest explosion crater in the world. Height: 1347 m (4420 ft.). Diameter: 9 km (6 miles).

an+i·con+ic (ˌænaɪ'kɒnɪk) *adj.* (of images of deities, symbols, etc.) not portrayed in a human or animal form. [C19: from AN- + ICONIC]

an·il ('ænɪl) *n.* a leguminous West Indian shrub, *Indigofera suffruticosa:* a source of indigo. Also called: **indigo.** [C16: from Portuguese, from Arabic *an-nīl,* the indigo, from Sanskrit *nīla* dark blue]

an+ile ('ænaɪl, 'eɪnaɪl) *adj.* of or like a feeble old woman. [C17: from Latin *anīlis,* from *anus* old woman] —**a·nil+i·ty** (ə'nɪlɪtɪ) *n.*

an·i+line ('ænɪlɪn, -ˌli:n) *n.* a colourless oily pungent poisonous liquid used in the manufacture of dyes, plastics, pharmaceuticals, and explosives. Formula: $C_6H_5NH_2$. Also called: **phenylamine.**

an·i+line dye *n.* any synthetic dye originally made from raw materials, such as aniline, found in coal tar.

a·ni+lin+gus (ˌeɪnɪ'lɪŋgəs) *n.* sexual stimulation involving oral contact with the anus. [C20: from *ani-* ANUS + *-lingus,* as in CUNNILINGUS]

anim. *abbrev. for* animato.

an·i+ma ('ænɪmə) *n.* (in Jungian psychology) **a.** the inner personality, which is in communication with the unconscious. **b.** the feminine principle as present in the male unconscious. See also **animus.** [Latin: air, breath, spirit, feminine of ANIMUS]

an·i+mad+ver+sion (ˌænɪmæd'vɜ:ʃən) *n.* **1.** criticism or censure. **2.** a carefully considered observation.

an·i+mad+vert (ˌænɪmæd'vɜ:t) *vb. (intr.)* **1.** (usually foll. by *on* or *upon*) to comment with strong criticism (upon); make censorious remarks (about). **2.** to make an observation or comment. [C16: from Latin *animadvertere* to notice, pay attention, from *animus* mind + *advertere* to turn to, from *vertere* to turn]

an·i+mal ('ænɪməl) *n.* **1.** *Zoology.* any living organism characterized by voluntary movement, the possession of cells with noncellulose cell walls and specialized sense organs enabling rapid response to stimuli, and the ingestion of complex organic substances such as plants and other animals. **2.** any mammal, esp. any mammal except man. **3.** a brutish person. **4.** *Facetious.* a person or thing (esp. in the phrase **no such animal**). ~*adj.* **5.** of or relating to animals: *animal products; an animal characteristic.* **6.** of or relating to the physical needs or desires; carnal; sensual. [C14: from Latin *animal* (n.), from *animālis* (adj.) living, breathing; see ANIMA]

an·i+mal+cule (ˌænɪ'mælkju:l) *or* **an·i+mal+cu+lum** (ˌænɪ'mælkjʊləm) *n., pl.* **+cules** *or* **+cu+la** (-kjʊlə). a microscopic animal such as an amoeba or rotifer. [C16: from New Latin *animalculum* a small ANIMAL] —ˌ**an·i+'mal+cu+lar** *adj.*

an·i+mal hus+band+ry *n.* the science of breeding, rearing, and caring for farm animals.

an·i+mal+ism ('ænɪməˌlɪzəm) *n.* **1.** satisfaction of or preoccupation with physical matters; sensuality. **2.** the doctrine or belief that man lacks a spiritual nature. **3.** a trait or mode of behaviour typical of animals. —'**an·i+mal+ist** *n.*

an·i+mal+i·ty (ˌænɪ'mælɪtɪ) *n.* **1.** the animal side of man, as opposed to the intellectual or spiritual. **2.** the fact of being or having the characteristics of an animal.

an·i·mal+ize *or* **an·i·mal+ise** ('ænɪməˌlaɪz) *vb. (tr.)* to rouse to brutality or sensuality or make brutal or sensual. —ˌ**an·i+mal·i+'za+tion** *or* ˌ**an·i·mal·i·'sa+tion** *n.*

an·i·mal king+dom *n.* a category of living organisms comprising all animals. Compare **plant kingdom, mineral kingdom.**

an·i·mal mag+net+ism *n.* **1.** *Sometimes facetious.* the quality of being attractive, esp. to members of the opposite sex. **2.** *Obsolete.* hypnotism.

an·i+mal starch *n.* a less common name for **glycogen.**

an·i+mate *vb.* ('ænɪˌmeɪt). *(tr.)* **1.** to give life to or cause to come alive. **2.** to make gay or lively; enliven. **3.** to encourage or inspire. **4.** to impart motion to; move to action or work. **5.** to record on film so as to give movement to: *an animated cartoon.* ~*adj.* ('ænɪmɪt). **6.** being alive or having life. **7.** gay, spirited, or lively. [C16: from Latin *animāre* to fill with breath, make alive, from *anima* breath, spirit] —'**an·i·ˌmat+ed+ly** *adv.*

an·i+mat+ed car+toon *n.* a film produced by photographing a series of gradually changing drawings, etc., which give the illusion of movement when the series is projected rapidly.

an·i·ma+tion (ˌænɪ'meɪʃən) *n.* **1.** liveliness; vivacity. **2.** the condition of being alive. **3. a.** the techniques used in the production of animated cartoons. **b.** a variant of **animated cartoon.**

an·i·ma+tism ('ænɪməˌtɪzəm) *n.* the belief that inanimate objects have consciousness.

a·ni+ma+to (ˌænɪ'mɑ:təʊ) *adj., adv. Music.* lively; animated. [Italian]

an·i·ma+tor *or* **an·i·mat+er** ('ænɪˌmeɪtə) *n.* an artist who produces animated cartoons.

an·i·mé ('ænɪˌmeɪ, -mɪ) *n.* any of various resins, esp. that obtained from the tropical American leguminous tree *Hymenaea courbaril.* [French: of uncertain origin]

an·i+mism ('ænɪˌmɪzəm) *n.* **1.** the belief that natural objects, phenomena, and the universe itself possess souls. **2.** (in the philosophies of Plato and Pythagoras) the hypothesis that there is an immaterial force that animates the universe. [C19: from Latin *anima* vital breath, spirit] —'**an·i+mist** *n.* —**an·i+mis+tic** (ˌænɪ'mɪstɪk) *adj.*

an·i+mos+i·ty (ˌænɪ'mɒsɪtɪ) *n., pl.* **·ties.** a powerful and active dislike or hostility; enmity. [C15: from Late Latin *animōsitās,* from Latin *animōsus* spirited, from ANIMUS]

an·i+mus ('ænɪməs) *n.* **1.** intense dislike; hatred; animosity. **2.** motive, intention, or purpose. **3.** (in Jungian psychology) the masculine principle present in the female unconscious. See also **anima.** [C19: from Latin: mind, spirit]

an+i+on ('ænˌaɪən) *n.* a negatively charged ion; an ion that is attracted to the anode during electrolysis. Compare **cation.** [C19: from ANA- + ION] —**an·i+on+ic** (ˌænaɪ'ɒnɪk) *adj.*

an+ise ('ænɪs) *n.* a Mediterranean umbelliferous plant, *Pimpinella anisum,* having clusters of small yellowish-white flowers and liquorice-flavoured seeds (see **aniseed**). [C13: from Old French *anis,* via Latin from Greek *anison*]

an·i+seed ('ænɪˌsi:d) *n.* the liquorice-flavoured aromatic seeds of the anise plant, used medicinally for expelling intestinal gas and in cookery as a flavouring, esp. in cakes. Also called: **anise.**

an+is·ei+ko+ni·a (ˌænaɪsaɪ'kəʊnɪə) *n.* a visual defect in which the shape and size of an object seen by one eye differs from that seen by the other eye. [C20: New Latin, from ANISO- + Greek *eikon* image] —ˌ**an+is·ei+'kon+ic** *adj.*

an·i+sette (ˌænɪ'zɛt, -'sɛt) *n.* a liquorice-flavoured liqueur made from aniseed. [C19: from French; see ANISE, -ETTE]

an·i·so- *or before a vowel* **an·is-** *combining form.* not equal: *anisogamy.* [New Latin, from Greek *anisos;* see AN-, ISO-]

an+i·so+dac+tyl (ænˌaɪsəʊ'dæktɪl, ˌænaɪ-) *adj. also* **an+i+so+dac+ty+lous. 1.** (of the feet of passerine birds) having the first toe directed backwards and the other three toes directed forwards. ~*n.* **2.** a bird having this type of feet.

an·i+sog·a+my (ˌænaɪ'sɒgəmɪ) *n.* a type of sexual reproduction in which the gametes are dissimilar, either in size alone or in size and form. —ˌ**an·i·'sog·a·mous** *adj.*

an·i+sole ('ænɪˌsəʊl) *n.* a colourless pleasant-smelling liquid used as a solvent and vermicide and in perfume and flavouring. Formula: $C_6H_5OCH_3$; relative density: 0.996; melting pt.: -37.5°C; boiling pt.: 155°C. [C19: from ANISE + -OLE]

an+i·som+er+ous (ˌænɪ'sɒmərəs) *adj.* (of flowers) having floral whorls that differ in the number of their parts. Compare **isomerous** (sense 2).

an+i·so+met+ric (ænˌaɪsəʊ'mɛtrɪk) *adj.* **1.** not isometric; having unsymmetrical parts or unequal measurements. **2.** (of a crystal) having unequal axes.

an+i·so+me·tro+pi·a (ænˌaɪsəʊmə'trəʊpɪə, ˌænaɪ-) *n.* an imbalance in the power of the two eyes to refract light.

an+i·so+trop+ic (ænˌaɪsəʊ'trɒpɪk, ˌænaɪ-) *adj.* **1.** not isotropic; having different physical properties in different directions: *anisotropic crystals.* **2.** (of a plant) responding unequally to an external stimulus in different parts of the plant. —**an+ˌi·so+'trop·i·cal+ly** *adv.* —**an+i·sot+ro+py** (ˌænaɪ'sɒtrəpɪ) *n.*

An+jou (*French* ɑ̃'ʒu) *n.* a former province of W France, in the Loire valley: a medieval countship from the tenth century, belonging to the English crown from 1154 until 1204; annexed by France in 1480.

An+ka+ra ('æŋkərə) *n.* the capital of Turkey, an ancient city in the Anatolian highlands: first a capital in the 3rd century B.C., in the Celtic kingdom of Galatia. Pop.: 1 701 004 (1975). Ancient name: **Ancyra.** Former name (until 1930): **Angora.**

an·ker·ite ('æŋkə,raɪt) *n.* a greyish to brown mineral that resembles dolomite and consists of a carbonate of calcium, magnesium, and iron. Formula: $(Ca,Mg,Fe)CO_3$. [C19: named after M. J. *Anker* (died 1843), Austrian mineralogist]

ankh (æŋk) *n.* a tall cross with a loop on the top, symbolizing eternal life: often appearing in Egyptian personal names, such as Tutankhamen. Also called: **ansate cross, crux ansata.** [from Egyptian *'nh* life, soul]

An·king ('ɑ:n'kɪŋ) *n.* a city in E China, capital of Anhwei province, on the Yangtze River: famous seven-storeyed pagoda. Pop.: 105 300 (1953).

an·kle ('æŋkᵊl) *n.* **1.** the joint connecting the leg and the foot. See **talus**[1]. **2.** the part of the leg just above the foot. [C14: from Old Norse; related to German, Dutch *enkel*, Latin *angulus* ANGLE[1]]

an·kle·bone ('æŋkᵊl,bəʊn) *n.* the nontechnical name for **talus**[1].

an·kle sock *n.* (*often pl.*) *Brit.* a short sock coming up to the ankle. U.S. term: **anklet.**

an·klet ('æŋklɪt) *n.* **1.** an ornamental chain worn around the ankle. **2.** the U.S. word for **ankle sock.**

an·kus ('æŋkəs) *n., pl.* **·kus** *or* **·kus·es.** a stick used, esp. in India, for goading elephants. [from Hindi]

an·ky·lo·saur ('æŋkɪləʊ,sɔ:) *n.* any of various quadrupedal herbivorous ornithischian dinosaurs constituting the suborder *Ankylosauria*, which were most abundant in upper Cretaceous times and had a very heavily armoured tanklike body. [C20: from New Latin, from Greek *ankulos* crooked + -SAUR]

an·ky·lose *or* **an·chy·lose** ('æŋkɪ,ləʊs, -,ləʊz) *vb.* (of bones in a joint, etc.) to fuse or stiffen by ankylosis.

an·ky·lo·sis *or* **an·chy·lo·sis** (,æŋkɪ'ləʊsɪs) *n.* abnormal adhesion or immobility of the bones in a joint, as by a direct joining of the bones, a fibrous growth of tissues within the joint, or surgery. [C18: from New Latin, from Greek *ankuloun* to crook] —**an·ky·lot·ic** *or* **an·chy·lot·ic** (,æŋkɪ'lɒtɪk) *adj.*

an·ky·los·to·mi·a·sis (,æŋkɪ,lɒstə'maɪəsɪs) *n.* a variant spelling of **ancylostomiasis.**

an·lace ('ænlɪs) *or* **an·e·lace** ('ænə,leɪs) *n.* a medieval short dagger with a broad tapering blade. [C13: of unknown origin]

an·la·ge ('æn,lɑ:gə) *n., pl.* **·gen** (-gən) *or* **·ges.** another word for **primordium.** [German: predisposition, layout]

ann. *abbrev. for:* **1.** annals (periodical publications). **2.** annual. **3.** annuity.

an·na ('ænə) *n.* a former Indian copper coin, worth one sixteenth of a rupee. [C18: from Hindi *ānā*]

An·na·ba ('ænəbə) *n.* a port in NE Algeria: site of the Roman city of Hippo Regius. Pop.: 152 006 (1966). Former name: **Bône.**

an·na·berg·ite ('ænə,bɜ:gaɪt) *n.* a rare green secondary mineral consisting of hydrated nickel arsenate in monoclinic crystalline form. Formula: $Ni_3(AsO_4)_2.8H_2O$. Also called: **nickel bloom.** [C19: named after *Annaberg* in Saxony, where it was discovered; see -ITE[1]]

an·nal ('ænᵊl) *n.* the recorded events of one year. See also **annals.**

an·nals ('ænᵊlz) *pl. n.* **1.** yearly records of events, generally in chronological order. **2.** history or records of history in general. **3.** regular reports of the work of a society, learned body, etc. [C16: from Latin (*librī*) *annālēs* yearly (books), from *annus* year] —'**an·nal·ist** *n.* —,**an·nal·'is·tic** *adj.*

An·nam *or* **A·nam** (æ'næm, 'ænæm) *n.* a former kingdom (3rd cent.–1428), empire (1428–1884), and French protectorate (1884–1945) of E Indochina: now part of Vietnam.

An·na·mese (,ænə'mi:z) *adj.* **1.** of or relating to Annam. ~*adj., n.* **2.** a former word for **Vietnamese.**

An·nap·o·lis (ə'næpəlɪs) *n.* the capital of Maryland, near the mouth of the Severn River on Chesapeake Bay: site of the U.S. Naval Academy. Pop.: 29 592 (1970).

An·nap·o·lis Roy·al *n.* a town in SE Canada in W Nova Scotia on an arm of the Bay of Fundy: the first settlement in Canada (1605). Pop.: 758 (1971). Former name (until 1710): **Park Royal.**

An·na·pur·na *or* **A·na·pur·na** (,ænə'pʊənə) *n.* a massif of the Himalayas, in Nepal. Highest peak: 8078 m (26 502 ft.).

Ann Ar·bor (æn 'ɑ:bə) *n.* a city in SE Michigan: seat of the University of Michigan. Pop.: 104 791 (1973 est.).

an·nates ('ænεɪts, -əts) *pl. n. R.C. Church.* the first year's revenue of a see, an abbacy, or a minor benefice, paid to the pope. [C16: plural of French *annate*, from Medieval Latin *annāta*, from Latin *annus* year]

an·nat·to *or* **a·nat·to** (ə'nætəʊ) *n., pl.* **·tos.** **1.** a small tropical American tree, *Bixa orellana*, having red or pinkish flowers and pulpy seeds that yield a dye: family *Bixaceae*. **2.** the yellowish-red dye obtained from the pulpy outer layer of the coat of the seeds of this tree, used for colouring fabrics, butter, varnish, etc. [from Carib]

Anne (æn) *n.* **1. Princess.** born 1950, daughter of Elizabeth II of England; noted also as a horsewoman. **2. Queen.** 1665–1714, queen of Great Britain and Ireland (1702–14), daughter of James II, and the last of the Stuart monarchs. **3. Saint.** (in Christian tradition) the mother of the Virgin Mary. Feast day: July 26.

an·neal (ə'ni:l) *vb.* **1.** to temper or toughen (something) by heat treatment. **2.** to subject to or undergo some physical treatment, esp. heating, that removes internal stress, crystal defects, and dislocations. **3.** (*tr.*) to toughen or strengthen (the will, determination, etc.). **4.** (often foll. by *out*) *Physics.* to disappear or cause to disappear by a rearrangement of atoms: *defects anneal out at different temperatures.* ~*n.* **5.** an act of annealing. [Old English *onǣlan*, from ON + *ǣlan* to burn, from *āl* fire] —**an·'neal·er** *n.*

Anne Bo·leyn *n.* See (Anne) **Boleyn.**

Anne·cy (*French* an'si) *n.* **1.** a city and resort in E France, on Lake Annecy. Pop.: 54 954 (1975). **2. Lake.** a lake in E France, in the Alps.

an·ne·lid ('ænəlɪd) *n.* **1.** any worms of the phylum *Annelida*, in which the body is divided into segments both externally and internally. The group includes the earthworms, lugworm, ragworm, and leeches. ~*adj.* **2.** of, relating to, or belonging to the *Annelida*. [C19: from New Latin *Annelida*, from French *annelés*, literally: the ringed ones, from Old French *annel* ring, from Latin *ānellus*, from *ānulus* ring] —**an·nel·i·dan** (ə'nεlɪdən) *n., adj.*

Anne of Aus·tri·a *n.* 1601–66, wife of Louis XIII of France and daughter of Philip III of Spain: regent of France (1643–61) for her son Louis XIV.

Anne of Bo·he·mi·a *n.* 1366–94, queen consort of Richard II of England.

Anne of Cleves (kli:vz) *n.* 1515–57, the fourth wife of Henry VIII of England, whose marriage (1540) was annulled after six months.

an·nex *vb.* (æ'nεks). (*tr.*) **1.** to join or add, esp. to something larger; attach. **2.** to add territory by conquest or occupation. **3.** to add or append as a condition, warranty, etc. **4.** to appropriate without permission. ~*n.* ('ænεks). **5.** a variant spelling (esp. U.S.) of **annexe.** [C14: from Medieval Latin *annexāre*, from Latin *annectere* to attach to, from *nectere* to join] —**an·'nex·a·ble** *adj.*

an·nex·a·tion (,ænɪk'seɪʃən, -εk-) *n.* **1.** the act of annexing, esp. territory, or the condition of being annexed. **2.** something annexed. —,**an·nex·'a·tion·al** *adj.* —,**an·nex·'a·tion·ism** *n.* —,**an·nex·'a·tion·ist** *n.*

an·nexe *or esp. U.S.* **an·nex** ('ænεks) *n.* **1.** an extension to a main building. **2.** something added or annexed, esp. a supplement to a document.

an·ni·hi·late (ə'naɪə,leɪt) *vb.* (*tr.*) **1.** to destroy completely; extinguish. **2.** *Informal.* to defeat totally, as in debate or argument. [C16: from Late Latin *annihilāre* to bring to nothing, from Latin *nihil* nothing] —**an·ni·hil·a·ble** (ə'naɪələbᵊl) *adj.* —**an·'ni·hi·la·tive** *adj.* —**an·'ni·hi·,la·tor** *n.*

an·ni·hi·la·tion (ə,naɪə'leɪʃən) *n.* **1.** total destruction. **2.** the act of annihilating. **3.** the destruction of a particle and its antiparticle when they collide. The energy equivalent of the interacting masses is converted into one or more photons of **annihilation radiation.**

an·ni·ver·sa·ry (,ænɪ'vɜ:sərɪ) *n., pl.* **·ries.** **1.** the date on which an event occurred in some previous year: *a wedding anniversary.* **2.** the celebration of this. ~*adj.* **3.** of or relating to an anniversary. **4.** recurring every year, esp. on the same date. [C13: from Latin *anniversārius* returning every year, from *annus* year + *vertere* to turn]

An·ni·ver·sa·ry Day *n.* another name for **Australia Day.**

an·no Dom·i·ni ('ænəʊ 'dɒmɪ,naɪ, -,ni:) the full form of **A.D.** [Latin: in the year of our Lord]

an·no reg·ni *Latin.* ('ænəʊ 'rεgnaɪ) in the year of the reign.

an·no·tate ('ænəʊ,teɪt, 'ænə-) *vb.* to supply (a written work, such as an ancient text) with critical or explanatory notes. [C18: from Latin *annotāre*, from *nota* mark] —'**an·no·,tat·a·ble** *adj.* —'**an·no·,ta·tive** *adj.* —'**an·no·,ta·tor** *n.*

an·no·ta·tion (,ænəʊ'teɪʃən, ,ænə-) *n.* **1.** the act of annotating. **2.** a note added in explanation, etc., esp. of some literary work.

an·nounce (ə'naʊns) *vb.* **1.** (*tr.; may take a clause as object*) to make known publicly; proclaim. **2.** (*tr.*) to declare the arrival of: *to announce a guest.* **3.** (*tr.; may take a clause as object*) to reveal to the mind or senses; presage: *the dark clouds announced rain.* **4.** (*intr.*) to work as an announcer, as on radio or television. **5.** *U.S.* to make known (one's intention to run as a candidate): *to announce for the presidency.* [C15: from Old French *anoncer*, from Latin *annuntiāre*, from *nuntius* messenger]

an·nounce·ment (ə'naʊnsmənt) *n.* **1.** a public statement. **2.** a brief item or advertisement, as in a newspaper. **3.** a formal printed or written invitation. **4.** the act of announcing.

an·nounc·er (ə'naʊnsə) *n.* a person who announces, esp. one who reads the news, introduces programmes, etc., on radio or television.

an·no ur·bis con·di·tae *Latin.* ('ænəʊ 'ɜ:bɪs 'kɒndɪ,ti:) the full form of **A.U.C.**

an·noy (ə'nɔɪ) *vb.* **1.** to irritate or displease. **2.** to harass with repeated attacks. [C13: from Old French *anoier*, from Late Latin *inodiāre* to make hateful, from Latin *in odiō* (*esse*) (to be) hated, from *odium* hatred] —**an·'noy·er** *n.*

an·noy·ance (ə'nɔɪəns) *n.* **1.** the feeling of being annoyed. **2.** the act of annoying. **3.** a person or thing that annoys.

an·nu·al ('ænjʊəl) *adj.* **1.** occurring, done, etc., once a year or every year; yearly: *an annual income.* **2.** lasting for a year: *an annual subscription.* ~*n.* **3.** a plant that completes its life cycle in one year. Compare **perennial** (sense 3), **biennial** (sense 3). **4.** a book, magazine, etc., published once every year. [C14: from Late Latin *annuālis*, from Latin *annuus* yearly, from *annus* year] —'**an·nu·al·ly** *adv.*

an·nu·al par·al·lax *n.* See under **parallax** (sense 2).

an·nu·al ring *n.* a ring of wood indicating one year's growth, seen in the transverse section of stems and roots of woody plants growing in temperate climates.

an·nu·i·tant (ə'nju:ɪtənt) *n.* a person in receipt of or entitled to an annuity.

an·nu·i·ty (əˈnjuːɪtɪ) *n., pl.* **·ties. 1.** a fixed sum payable at specified intervals, esp. annually, over a period, such as the recipient's life, or in perpetuity, in return for a premium paid either in instalments or in a single payment. **2.** the right to receive or the duty to pay such a sum. [C15: from French *annuité*, from Medieval Latin *annuitās*, from Latin *annuus* ANNUAL]

an·nul (əˈnʌl) *vb.* **·nuls, ·nul·ling, ·nulled.** (*tr.*) to make (something, esp. a law or marriage) void; cancel the validity of; abolish. [C14: from Old French *annuller*, from Late Latin *adnullāre* to bring to nothing, from Latin *nullus* not any; see NULL] —**an·ˈnul·la·ble** *adj.*

an·nu·lar (ˈænjʊlə) *adj.* ring-shaped; of or forming a ring. [C16: from Latin *annulāris*, from *annulus*, *ānulus* ring] —**an·nu·lar·i·ty** (ˌænjʊˈlærɪtɪ) *n.* —ˈ**an·nu·lar·ly** *adv.*

an·nu·lar e·clipse *n.* an eclipse of the sun in which the moon does not cover the entire disc of the sun, so that a ring of sunlight surrounds the darkened moon. Compare **total eclipse, partial eclipse.**

an·nu·lar lig·a·ment *n. Anatomy.* any of various ligaments that encircle a part, such as the wrist, ankle, or trachea.

an·nu·late (ˈænjʊlɪt, -ˌleɪt) *adj.* having, composed of, or marked with rings. [C19: from Latin *ānulātus*, from *ānulus* a ring] —ˈ**an·nu·ˌlat·ed** *adj.*

an·nu·la·tion (ˌænjʊˈleɪʃən) *n.* **1.** the formation of rings. **2.** a ringlike formation or part.

an·nu·let (ˈænjʊlɪt) *n.* **1.** *Architect.* a moulding in the form of a ring, as at the top of a column adjoining the capital. **2.** *Heraldry.* a ring-shaped device on a shield; hollow roundel. **3.** a little ring. [C16: from Latin *ānulus* ring + -ET]

an·nul·ment (əˈnʌlmənt) *n.* **1.** a formal invalidation, as of a marriage, judicial proceeding, etc. **2.** the act of annulling.

an·nu·lose (ˈænjʊˌləʊs, -ˌləʊz) *adj.* (of earthworms, crustaceans, and similar animals) having a body formed of a series of rings; segmented. [C19: from New Latin *annulōsus*; see ANNULUS]

an·nu·lus (ˈænjʊləs) *n., pl.* **·li** (-ˌlaɪ) *or* **·lus·es. 1.** the area between two concentric circles. **2.** a ring-shaped part, figure, or space. [C16: from Latin, variant of *ānulus* ring]

an·nun·ci·ate (əˈnʌnsɪˌeɪt, -ʃɪ-) *vb.* (*tr.*) a less common word for **announce.** —**an·ˌnun·ci·ˈa·tion** *n.* —**an·nun·ci·a·tive** (əˈnʌnsɪətɪv, -ʃətɪv) *or* **an·nun·ci·a·to·ry** (əˈnʌnsɪətərɪ, -ʃə-) *adj.*

An·nun·ci·a·tion (əˌnʌnsɪˈeɪʃən) *n.* **1. the.** *New Testament.* the announcement of the Incarnation by the angel Gabriel to the Virgin Mary (Luke 1:26–38). **2.** Also called: **Annunciation Day.** the festival commemorating this, held on March 25 (Lady Day).

an·nun·ci·a·tor (əˈnʌnsɪˌeɪtə) *n.* **1.** a device that gives a visual indication as to which of a number of electric circuits has operated, such as an indicator in a hotel showing in which room a bell has been rung. **2.** a device giving an audible signal indicating the position of a train. **3.** a less common word for **announcer.**

an·nus mi·ra·bi·lis *Latin.* (ˈænʊs mɪˈræbɪlɪs) *n., pl.* ***an·ni mi·ra·bi·les*** (ˈænaɪ mɪˈræbɪliːz). a year of wonders, catastrophes, or other notable events.

a·no·a (əˈnəʊə) *n.* the smallest of the cattle tribe *Anoa depressicornis*, having small straight horns and inhabiting the island of Celebes in Indonesia. Compare **tamarau.** [from a native name in Celebes]

an·ode (ˈænəʊd) *n.* **1.** the positive electrode in an electrolytic cell. **2.** Also called (esp. U.S.): **plate.** the positively charged electrode in an electronic valve or tube. **3.** the negative terminal of a primary cell. Compare **cathode.** [C19: from Greek *anodos* a way up, from *hodos* a way; alluding to the movement of the current to or from the positive pole] —**an·od·al** (eɪˈnəʊdᵊl) *or* **an·od·ic** (əˈnɒdɪk) *adj.*

an·o·dize *or* **an·o·dise** (ˈænəˌdaɪz) *vb.* to coat (a metal, such as aluminium or magnesium) with a protective oxide film by electrodeposition.

an·o·dyne (ˈænəˌdaɪn) *n.* **1.** a drug that relieves pain; analgesic. **2.** anything that alleviates mental distress. ~*adj.* **3.** capable of relieving pain or distress. [C16: from Latin *anōdynus*, from Greek *anōdunos* painless, from AN- + *odunē* pain]

an·oes·trus *or U.S.* **an·es·trus** (ænˈiːstrəs) *n.* a period of sexual inactivity between two periods of oestrus in many mammals. [C20: New Latin; see AN-, OESTRUS] —**an·ˈoes·trous** *or U.S.* **an·ˈes·trous** *adj.*

a·noint (əˈnɔɪnt) *vb.* (*tr.*) **1.** to smear or rub over with oil or an oily liquid. **2.** to apply oil to as a sign of consecration or sanctification in a sacred rite. [C14: from Old French *enoint*, from *enoindre*, from Latin *inunguere*, from IN-[2] + *unguere* to smear with oil] —**a·ˈnoint·er** *n.* —**a·ˈnoint·ment** *n.*

a·nole (əˈnəʊl) *n.* any small arboreal tropical American insectivorous lizards of the genus *Anolis*, such as *A. carolinensis* (**green anole**): family *Iguanidae* (iguanas). They are able to change the colour of their skin. Also called: **American chameleon.** [C18 *annolis*, from French *anolis*, from Carib *anoli*]

a·nom·a·lis·tic month *n.* the interval between two successive passages of the moon through perigee; 27.55455 days.

a·nom·a·lis·tic year *n.* the interval between two successive passages of the earth through perihelion; 365.25964 mean solar days.

a·nom·a·lous (əˈnɒmələs) *adj.* deviating from the normal or usual order, type, etc.; irregular, abnormal, or incongruous. [C17: from Late Latin *anōmalus*, from Greek *anōmalos* uneven, inconsistent, from AN- + *homalos* even, from *homos* one and the same] —**a·ˈnom·a·lous·ly** *adv.* —**a·ˈnom·a·lous·ness** *n.*

a·nom·a·ly (əˈnɒməlɪ) *n., pl.* **·lies. 1.** something anomalous. **2.** deviation from the normal or usual order, type, etc.; irregularity. **3.** *Astronomy.* the angle between a planet, the sun, and the previous perihelion of the planet. —**a·ˌnom·a·ˈlis·tic** *adj.* —**a·ˌnom·a·ˈlis·ti·cal·ly** *adv.*

an·o·mie *or* **an·o·my** (ˈænəʊmɪ) *n. Sociol.* lack of social or moral standards in an individual or society. [from Greek *anomia* lawlessness, from A-[1] + *nomos* law] —**a·nom·ic** (əˈnɒmɪk) *adj.*

a·non (əˈnɒn) *adv. Archaic or literary.* **1.** in a short time; soon. **2. ever and anon.** now and then. [Old English *on āne*, literally: in one, that is, immediately]

anon. *abbrev. for* anonymous.

an·o·nym (ˈænənɪm) *n.* **1.** a less common word for **pseudonym. 2.** an anonymous person or publication.

a·non·y·mous (əˈnɒnɪməs) *adj.* **1.** from or by a person, author, etc., whose name is unknown or withheld: *an anonymous letter.* **2.** having no known name. **3.** lacking individual characteristics; unexceptional. [C17: via Late Latin from Greek *anōnumos*, from AN- + *onoma* name] —**an·o·nym·i·ty** (ˌænəˈnɪmɪtɪ) *n.* —**a·ˈnon·y·mous·ly** *adv.* —**a·ˈnon·y·mous·ness** *n.*

a·noph·e·les (əˈnɒfɪˌliːz) *n., pl.* **·les.** any of various mosquitoes constituting the genus *Anopheles*, some species of which transmit the malaria parasite to man. [C19: via New Latin from Greek *anōphelēs* useless, from AN- + *ōphelein* to help, from *ophelos* help]

a·no·rak (ˈænəˌræk) *n.* a warm waterproof hip-length jacket usually with a hood, originally worn in polar regions, but now worn for any outdoor activity. [from Eskimo *ánorâq*]

an·o·rex·i·a (ˌænɒˈrɛksɪə) *n.* loss of appetite. [C17: via New Latin from Greek, from AN- + *orexis* appetite]

an·o·rex·i·a ner·vo·sa (nɜːˈvəʊsə) *n. Psychiatry.* a psychological disorder characterized by fear of becoming fat and refusal of food, leading to debility and even death.

an·or·thic (ænˈɔːθɪk) *adj.* another word for **triclinic.** [C19: from AN- + ORTHO- + -IC]

an·or·thite (ænˈɔːθaɪt) *n.* a rare feldspar mineral of the plagioclase series that consists of an aluminium silicate of calcium and occurs in volcanic regions, esp. in Italy and Japan. Formula: $CaAl_2Si_2O_8$. [C19: from AN- + ORTHO- + -ITE[1]] —**an·or·thit·ic** (ˌænɔːˈθɪtɪk) *adj.*

an·or·tho·site (ænˈɔːθəˌsaɪt) *n.* a coarse-grained plutonic igneous rock consisting almost entirely of plagioclase feldspar. [C19: from French *anorthose* (see AN-, ORTHO-) + -ITE[1]]

an·os·mi·a (ænˈɒzmɪə, -ˈɒs-) *n. Pathol.* loss of the sense of smell, usually as the result of a lesion of the olfactory nerve, disease in another organ or part, or obstruction of the nasal passages. [C19: from New Latin, from AN- + Greek *osmē* smell, from *ozein* to smell] —**an·os·mat·ic** (ˌænɒzˈmætɪk) *or* **an·ˈos·mic** *adj.*

an·oth·er (əˈnʌðə) *determiner.* **1. a.** one more; an added: *another chance.* **b.** (*as pronoun*): *help yourself to another.* **2. a.** a different; alternative: *another era from ours.* **b.** (*as pronoun*): *to try one path, then another.* **3. a.** a different example of the same sort: *another Beethoven.* **b.** (*as pronoun*): *we got rid of one loafer, but I think this new man's another.* **4. another place.** the other House of Parliament (used in the House of Commons to refer to the House of Lords and vice versa).

A.N. Oth·er *n. Brit.* an unnamed person: used in team lists, etc., to indicate a place that remains to be filled.

A·nouilh (*French* aˈnuj) *n.* **Jean** (ʒã). born 1910, French dramatist, noted for his reinterpretations of Greek myths: his works include *Eurydice* (1942), *Antigone* (1944), and *Becket* (1959).

an·ox·ae·mi·a *or U.S.* **an·ox·e·mi·a** (ˌænɒkˈsiːmɪə) *n.* a deficiency in the amount of oxygen in the arterial blood. [C19: from New Latin, from AN- + OX(YGEN) + -AEMIA] —**ˌan·ox·ˈae·mic** *or U.S.* **ˌan·ox·ˈe·mic** *adj.*

an·ox·i·a (ænˈɒksɪə) *n.* **1.** lack or absence of oxygen. **2.** a deficiency of oxygen in tissues and organs. Compare **hypoxia.** [C20: from AN- + OX(YGEN) + -IA] —**an·ˈox·ic** *adj.*

an·sate (ˈænseɪt) *adj.* having a handle or handle-like part. [C19: from Latin *ansātus*, from *ansa* handle]

An·schluss (ˈænʃlʊs) *n.* a political or economic union, esp. the annexation of Austria by Nazi Germany (1938). [German: from *anschliessen* to join]

An·selm (ˈænsɛlm) *n.* **Saint.** 1033–1109, Italian Benedictine monk; archbishop of Canterbury (1093–1109): one of the founders of scholasticism; author of *Cur Deus Homo?* (*Why did God become Man?*). Feast day: Aug. 21.

an·ser·ine (ˈænsəˌraɪn, -rɪn) *or* **an·ser·ous** (ˈænsərəs) *adj.* **1.** of or resembling a goose. **2.** of, relating to, or belonging to the subfamily *Anserinae*, which includes geese, swans, and certain ducks: family *Anatidae*, order *Anseriformes.* **3.** silly; foolish. [C19: from Latin *anserīnus*, from *anser* goose]

An·ser·met (*French* ãsɛrˈmɛ) *n.* **Er·nest** (ɛrˈnɛst). 1883–1969, Swiss orchestral conductor; principal conductor of Diaghilev's Ballet Russe.

An·shan (ˌænˈʃæn) *n.* **1.** a city in NE China, in Liaoning province. Pop.: 1 050 000 (1970 est.). **2.** an ancient city and region in Persia, associated with Elam.

an·swer (ˈɑːnsə) *n.* **1.** a reply, either spoken or written, as to a question, request, letter, or article. **2.** a reaction or response in the form of an action: *drunkenness was his answer to disappointment.* **3.** a solution, esp. of a mathematical problem. **4.** *Law.* **a.** a party's written reply to his opponent's interrogatories. **b.** (in divorce law) the respondent's written reply to the petition. **5.** a musical phrase that follows the subject of a fugue, reproducing it a fifth higher or a fourth lower. ~*vb.* **6.**

(when *tr.*, *may take a clause as object*) to reply or respond (to) by word or act: *to answer a question; he answered; to answer the door; he answered that he would come.* **7.** (*tr.*) to reply correctly to; solve or attempt to solve: *I could answer only three questions.* **8.** (*intr.*; usually foll. by *to*) to respond or react (to a stimulus, command, etc.): *the steering answers to the slightest touch.* **9.** (*tr.*) to pay off (a debt, obligation, etc.); discharge. **10.** (when *intr.*, often foll. by *for*) to meet the requirements (of); be satisfactory (for); serve the purpose (of): *this will answer his needs; this will answer for a chisel.* **11.** (when *intr.*, foll. by *to*) to match or correspond (esp. in the phrase **answer** (or **answer to**) **the description**). **12.** (*tr.*) to give a defence or refutation of (a charge) or in (an argument). [Old English *andswaru* an answer; related to Old Frisian *ondser*, Old Norse *andsvar*; see SWEAR]

an·swer·a·ble ('ɑːnsərəbᵊl) *adj.* **1.** (*postpositive*; foll. by *for* or *to*) responsible or accountable: *answerable for someone's safety; answerable to one's boss.* **2.** able to be answered. —ˌ**an·swer·a·'bil·i·ty** *or* '**an·swer·a·ble·ness** *n.* —'**an·swer·a·bly** *adv.*

an·swer back *vb.* (*adv.*) to reply rudely to (a person, esp. someone in authority) when one is expected to remain silent.

an·swer for *vb.* (*intr., prep.*) **1.** to be liable or responsible for (a person's actions, behaviour, etc.). **2.** to vouch for or speak on behalf of (a person). **3.** to suffer or atone for (one's wrongdoing).

ant (ænt) *n.* **1.** any small social insect of the widely distributed hymenopterous family *Formicidae*, typically living in highly organized colonies of winged males, wingless sterile females (workers), and fertile females (queens), which are winged until after mating. See also **army ant, fire ant, slave ant, wood ant.** Related adj.: **formic. 2. white ant.** another name for a **termite. 3. have ants in one's pants.** *Slang.* to be restless or impatient. [Old English *ǣmette*; related to Old High German *āmeiza*, Old Norse *meita*; see EMMET] —'**ant·like** *adj.*

ant. *abbrev. for* antonym.

an't *Chiefly Brit.* **1.** (ɑːnt). a rare variant spelling of **aren't. 2.** (eɪnt). *Dialect.* a variant spelling of **ain't.**

ant- *prefix.* variant of **anti-:** *antacid.*

-ant *suffix forming adjectives and nouns.* causing or performing an action or existing in a certain condition; the agent that performs an action: *pleasant; claimant; deodorant; protestant; servant.* [from Latin *-ant*, ending of present participles of the first conjugation]

an·ta ('æntə) *n., pl.* **an·tae** ('æntiː). *Architect.* a pilaster attached to the end of a side wall or sometimes to the side of a doorway.

An·ta·buse ('æntəˌbjuːs) *n. Trademark.* a drug used in the treatment of alcoholism that acts by inducing nausea following ingestion of alcohol; tetraethylthiuram disulphide.

ant·ac·id (ænt'æsɪd) *n.* **1.** a substance used to treat acidity, esp. in the stomach. ~*adj.* **2.** having the properties of this substance.

An·tae·us (æn'tiːəs) *n. Greek myth.* an African giant who was invincible as long as he touched the ground, but was lifted into the air by Hercules and crushed to death.

an·tag·o·nism (æn'tægəˌnɪzəm) *n.* **1.** openly expressed and usually mutual opposition. **2.** the inhibiting or nullifying action of one substance or organism on another. **3.** *Physiol.* the normal opposition between certain muscles.

an·tag·o·nist (æn'tægənɪst) *n.* **1.** an opponent or adversary, as in a contest, drama, sporting event, etc. **2.** any muscle that opposes the action of another. Compare **agonist. 3.** a drug that neutralizes or counteracts the effects of another drug. Compare **synergist** (sense 1).

an·tag·o·nis·tic (ænˌtægə'nɪstɪk) *adj.* **1.** in active opposition. **2.** mutually opposed. —**an·ˌtag·o·'nis·ti·cal·ly** *adv.*

an·tag·o·nize *or* **an·tag·o·nise** (æn'tægəˌnaɪz) *vb.* (*tr.*) **1.** to make hostile; annoy or irritate. **2.** to act in opposition to or counteract. [C17: from Greek *antagōnizesthai*, from ANTI- + *agōnizesthai* to strive, from *agōn* contest] —**an·'tag·o·ˌniz·a·ble** *or* **an·'tag·o·ˌnis·a·ble** *adj.* —**an·ˌtag·o·ni·'za·tion** *or* **an·ˌtag·o·ni·'sa·tion** *n.*

An·ta·ki·ya (ˌæntɑː'kiːjə) *n.* the Arabic name for **Antioch.**

An·ta·kya (ɑn'tɑkjɑ) *n.* the Turkish name for **Antioch.**

ant·al·ka·li (ænt'ælkəˌlaɪ) *n., pl.* **·lis** *or* **·lies.** a substance that neutralizes alkalis, esp. one used to treat alkalosis. —**ant·al·ka·line** (ænt'ælkəˌlaɪn, -lɪn) *adj., n.*

An·tal·ya (*Turkish* ɑn'tɑljɑ) *n.* a port in SW Turkey, on the **Gulf of Antalya.** Pop.: 130 774 (1975).

An·ta·na·na·ri·vo (ˌæntəˌnænə'riːvəʊ) *n.* another name for **Tananarive.**

Ant·arc·tic (ænt'ɑːktɪk) *n.* **1. the.** Also called: **Antarctic Zone.** Antarctica and the surrounding waters. ~*adj.* **2.** of or relating to the south polar regions. [C14: via Latin from Greek *antarktikos*; see ANTI-, ARCTIC]

Ant·arc·ti·ca (ænt'ɑːktɪkə) *n.* a continent around the South Pole: consists of an ice-covered plateau, 1800–3000 m (6000 ft. to 10 000 ft.) above sea level, and mountain ranges rising to 4500 m (15 000 ft.) with some volcanic peaks; average temperatures all below freezing and human settlement is confined to research stations.

Ant·arc·tic Ar·chi·pel·a·go *n.* the former name of the **Palmer Archipelago.**

Ant·arc·tic Cir·cle *n.* the imaginary circle around the earth, parallel to the equator, at latitude 66° 32′ S.

Ant·arc·tic O·cean *n.* the sea surrounding Antarctica, consisting of the most southerly parts of the Pacific, Atlantic, and Indian Oceans.

Ant·arc·tic Pen·in·su·la *n.* the largest peninsula of Antarctica, between the Weddell Sea and the Pacific: consists of Graham Land in the north and the Palmer Peninsula in the south. Former name (until 1964): **Palmer Peninsula.**

An·tar·es (æn'tɛəriːz) *n.* the brightest star in the constellation Scorpius. It is a variable binary star whose main component, a red supergiant, is associated with a fainter green component. Visual magnitude: 1.2 (red), 6.8 (green); spectral type: MO (red); distance: 250 light years. [from Greek *Antarēs*, literally: simulating Mars (in colour), from ANTI- + *Arēs* Mars]

ant bear *n.* another name for **aardvark.** See **anteater** (sense 1).

ant bird *n.* any of various dull-coloured South American passerine birds of the family *Formicariidae*, such as *Hylophylax naevioides* (spotted ant bird), that typically feed on ants. Also called: **bush-shrike, ant thrush.**

ant cow *n.* an insect, esp. an aphid, that excretes a sweet honey-like substance that is collected and eaten by ants.

an·te ('æntɪ) *n.* **1.** the gaming stake put up before the deal in poker by the players. **2.** *Informal, chiefly U.S.* a sum of money representing a person's share, as in a syndicate. ~*vb.* **·tes, ·te·ing; ·ted** *or* **·teed. 3.** to place (one's stake) in poker. **4.** (usually foll. by *up*) *Informal, chiefly U.S.* to pay.

an·te- *prefix.* before in time or position; previous to; in front of: *antedate; antechamber.* [from Latin]

ant·eat·er ('æntˌiːtə) *n.* **1.** any toothless edentate mammal of the family *Myrmecophagidae* of Central and South America, esp. *Myrmecophaga tridactyla* (or **jubata**) **(ant bear), having a long tubular snout used for eating termites. See also tamandua. 2. scaly anteater.** another name for **pangolin. 3. spiny anteater.** another name for **echidna. 4. banded anteater. another name for numbat.**

an·te·bel·lum (ˌæntɪ'bɛləm) *adj.* of or during the period before a war, esp. the American Civil War: *the antebellum South.* [Latin *ante bellum*, literally: before the war]

an·te·cede (ˌæntɪ'siːd) *vb.* (*tr.*) to go before, as in time, order, etc.; precede. [C17: from Latin *antecēdere*, from *cēdere* to go]

an·te·ced·ence (ˌæntɪ'siːdᵊns) *n.* **1.** precedence; priority. **2.** *Astronomy.* retrograde motion.

an·te·ced·ent (ˌæntɪ'siːdᵊnt) *n.* **1.** an event, circumstance, etc., that happens before another. **2.** *Grammar.* a word or phrase to which a pronoun refers. In the sentence "People who live in glass houses shouldn't throw stones," *people* is the antecedent of *who.* **3.** *Logic.* the first proposition in a conditional, such as *John was born in Wales* in *if John was born in Wales then he is British.* **4.** *Maths.* an obsolescent name for **numerator** (sense 1). ~*adj.* **5.** preceding in time or order; prior.

an·te·ced·ents (ˌæntɪ'siːdᵊnts) *pl. n.* **1.** ancestry. **2.** a person's past history.

an·te·cham·ber ('æntɪˌtʃeɪmbə) *n.* another name for **anteroom.** [C17: from Old French, from Italian *anticamera*; see ANTE-, CHAMBER]

an·te·choir ('æntɪˌkwaɪə) *n.* the part of a church in front of the choir, usually enclosed by screens, tombs, etc.

an·te·date *vb.* ('æntɪˌdeɪt, ˌæntɪ'deɪt). (*tr.*) **1.** to be or occur at an earlier date than. **2.** to affix a date to (a document, etc.) that is earlier than the actual date. **3.** to assign a date to (an event, etc.) that is earlier than its previously assigned date. **4.** to cause to occur sooner. ~*n.* ('æntɪˌdeɪt) **5.** an earlier date.

an·te·di·lu·vi·an (ˌæntɪdɪ'luːvɪən, -daɪ-) *adj.* **1.** belonging to the ages before the biblical Flood (Genesis 7, 8). **2.** old-fashioned or antiquated. ~*n.* **3.** an antediluvian person or thing. [C17: from ANTE- + Latin *dīluvium* flood]

an·te·fix ('æntɪˌfɪks) *n., pl.* **·fix·es** *or* **·fix·a** (-ˌfɪksə). a carved ornament at the eaves of a roof to hide the joint between the tiles. [C19: from Latin *antefixa* (things) fastened in front, from *figere* to FIX] —**an·te·fix·al** (ˌæntɪ'fɪksəl) *adj.*

an·te·lope ('æntɪˌləʊp) *n., pl.* **·lopes** *or* **·lope. 1.** any bovid mammal of the subfamily *Antilopinae*, of Africa and Asia. They are typically graceful, having long legs and horns, and include the gazelles, springbok, impala, gerenuk, blackbuck, and dik-diks. **2.** any of various similar bovids of Africa and Asia. **3. American antelope.** another name for **pronghorn.** [C15: from Old French *antelop*, from Medieval Latin *antalopus*, from Late Greek *antholops* a legendary beast]

an·te·me·rid·i·an (ˌæntɪmə'rɪdɪən) *adj.* before noon; in the morning. [C17: from Latin *antemerīdiānus*; see ANTE-, MERIDIAN]

an·te me·rid·i·em ('æntɪ mə'rɪdɪəm) the full form of **a.m.** [Latin, from ANTE- + *merīdiēs* midday]

an·te-mor·tem *adj., adv.* (esp. in legal or medical contexts) before death. [Latin]

an·te·na·tal (ˌæntɪ'neɪtᵊl) *adj.* **1.** occurring or present before birth; during pregnancy. ~*n.* **2.** Also called: **prenatal.** *Informal.* an examination during pregnancy. —ˌ**an·te·'na·tal·ly** *adv.*

an·ten·na (æn'tɛnə) *n.* **1.** (*pl.* **·nae** (-niː)). one of a pair of mobile appendages on the heads of insects, crustaceans, etc., that are often whiplike and respond to touch and taste but may be specialized for swimming or attachment. **2.** (*pl.* **·nas**) another name for **aerial** (sense 7). [C17: from Latin: sail yard, of obscure origin] —**an·'ten·nal** *or* **an·'ten·na·ry** *adj.*

an·ten·nule (æn'tɛnjuːl) *n.* one of a pair of small mobile appendages on the heads of crustaceans in front of the antennae, usually having a sensory function. [C19: from French, diminutive of ANTENNA]

an·te·pen·di·um (ˌæntɪ'pɛndɪəm) *n., pl.* **·di·a** (-dɪə). a covering hung over the front of an altar. [C17: from Medieval Latin, from Latin ANTE- + *pendēre* to hang]

an·te·pe·nult (ˌæntɪpɪ'nʌlt) *n.* the third last syllable in a word.

[C16: shortened from Latin (*syllaba*) *antepaenultima;* see ANTE-, PENULT]

an·te·pe·nul·ti·mate (ˌæntɪpɪˈnʌltɪmɪt) *adj.* **1.** third from last. ~*n.* **2.** anything that is third from last.

an·te·ri·or (ænˈtɪərɪə) *adj.* **1.** situated at or towards the front. **2.** earlier in time. **3.** *Zoology.* of or near the head end. **4.** *Botany.* (of part of a flower or leaf) situated farthest away from the main stem. ~Compare **posterior.** [C17: from Latin, comparative of *ante* before] —**an·te·ri·or·i·ty** (ænˌtɪərɪˈɒrɪtɪ) *n.*

an·te·room (ˈæntɪˌruːm, -ˌrʊm) *n.* a room giving entrance to a larger room, often used as a waiting room.

an·te·type (ˈæntɪˌtaɪp) *n.* an earlier form; prototype.

an·te·ver·sion (ˌæntɪˈvɜːʃən) *n.* abnormal forward tilting of a bodily organ, esp. the uterus.

an·te·vert (ˌæntɪˈvɜːt) *vb.* (*tr.*) to displace (an organ or part) by tilting forward. [C17: from Latin *antevertere* to go in front, from *vertere* to turn]

ant·he·li·on (æntˈhiːlɪən, ænˈθiː-) *n., pl.* **·li·a** (-lɪə). **1.** a faint halo sometimes seen in polar or high altitude regions around the shadow of an object cast onto a thick cloud bank or fog. **2.** a white spot occasionally appearing on the parhelic circle at the same height as and opposite to the sun. [C17: from Late Greek, from *anthēlios* opposite the sun, from ANTE- + *hēlios* sun]

ant·he·lix (æntˈhiːlɪks, ænˈθɪː-) *or* **an·ti·he·lix** *n., pl.* **·hel·i·ces** (-ˈhiːlɪsiːz) *or* **·he·lix·es.** *Anatomy.* a prominent curved fold of cartilage just inside the outer rim of the external ear.

an·thel·min·tic (ˌænθɛlˈmɪntɪk) *or* **an·thel·min·thic** (ˌænθɛlˈmɪnθɪk) *n. Med.* another name for **vermifuge.**

an·them (ˈænθəm) *n.* **1.** a song of loyalty or devotion, as to a nation or college: *a national anthem.* **2.** a musical composition for choir, usually set to words from the Bible, sung as part of a church service. **3.** a religious chant sung antiphonally. [Old English *antemne,* from Late Latin *antiphōna* ANTIPHON]

an·the·mi·on (ænˈθiːmɪən) *n., pl.* **·mi·a** (-mɪə). a floral design, used esp. in ancient Greek and Roman architecture and decoration, usually consisting of honeysuckle, lotus, or palmette leaf motifs. [from Greek: a little flower, from *anthos* flower]

an·ther (ˈænθə) *n.* the terminal part of a stamen consisting of two lobes each containing two sacs in which the pollen matures. [C18: from New Latin *anthēra,* from Latin: a remedy prepared from flowers, from Greek, from *anthēros* flowery, from *anthos* flower] —**ˈan·ther·al** *adj.*

an·ther·id·i·um (ˌænθəˈrɪdɪəm) *n., pl.* **·i·a** (-ɪə). the male sex organ of algae, fungi, mosses, and ferns, which produces antherozoids. [C19: from New Latin, diminutive of *anthēra* ANTHER] —**ˌan·ther·ˈid·i·al** *adj.*

an·ther·o·zo·id (ˌænθərəˈzəʊɪd, -ˈzɔɪd) *n.* one of many small male gametes produced in an antheridium. [C19: see ANTHER, ZO(O)ID]

an·the·sis (ænˈθiːsɪs) *n.* the process of flowering in plants. [C19: via New Latin from Greek: full bloom, from *anthein* to bloom, from *anthos* flower]

ant hill *n.* a mound of soil, leaves, etc., near the entrance of an ants' nest, carried and deposited there by the ants while constructing the nest.

an·tho- *combining form.* denoting a flower: *anthophore; anthotaxy; anthozoan.* [from Greek *anthos*]

an·tho·cy·a·nin (ˌænθəʊˈsaɪənɪn) *or* **an·tho·cy·an** (ˌænθəʊˈsaɪən) *n.* any of a class of water-soluble glycosidic pigments, esp. those responsible for the red and blue colours in flowers. They are closely related to vitamins E and P. [C19: from ANTHO- + *-cyanin,* from Greek *kuanos* dark blue]

an·tho·di·um (ænˈθəʊdɪəm) *n., pl.* **·di·a** (-dɪə). *Botany.* another name for **capitulum** (sense 1). [C19: from New Latin, from Greek *anthōdēs* flower-like, from *anthos* flower + *-ōdēs* -OID]

an·thol·o·gize *or* **an·thol·o·gise** (ænˈθɒləˌdʒaɪz) *vb.* (*tr.*) to compile or put into an anthology.

an·thol·o·gy (ænˈθɒlədʒɪ) *n., pl.* **·gies. 1.** a collection of literary passages or works, esp. poems, by various authors. **2.** any printed collection of literary pieces, songs, works of art, etc. [C17: from Medieval Latin *anthologia,* from Greek, literally: a flower gathering, from *anthos* flower + *legein* to collect] —**an·tho·log·i·cal** (ˌænθəˈlɒdʒɪkᵊl) *adj.* —**anˈthol·o·gist** *n.*

An·tho·ny (ˈæntənɪ). *n.* **Saint.** ?251–?356 A.D., Egyptian hermit, commonly regarded as the founder of Christian monasticism. Feast day: Jan. 17.

An·tho·ny of Pad·u·a *n.* **Saint.** 1195–1231, Franciscan friar, who preached in France and Italy. Feast day: June 13.

an·tho·phore (ˈænθəʊˌfɔː, -θə-) *n.* an elongation of the receptacle of a flower between the calyx and corolla.

an·tho·tax·y (ˈænθəˌtæksɪ) *n.* the arrangement of flowers on a stem or parts on a flower.

an·tho·zo·an (ˌænθəˈzəʊən) *n.* **1.** any of the solitary or colonial sessile marine coelenterates of the class *Anthozoa,* including the corals, sea anemones, and sea pens, in which the body is in the form of a polyp. ~*adj.* **2.** Also: **actinozoan.** of or relating to the class *Anthozoa.*

an·thra·cene (ˈænθrəˌsiːn) *n.* a colourless tricyclic crystalline solid having a slight blue fluorescence, used in the manufacture of chemicals, esp. diphenylamine and alizarin, and as crystals in scintillation counters. Formula: $C_6H_4(CH)_2C_6H_4$. [C19: from ANTHRAX + -ENE]

an·thra·cite (ˈænθrəˌsaɪt) *n.* a hard jet-black coal that burns slowly with a nonluminous flame giving out intense heat. Fixed carbon content: 86–98 per cent; calorific value: 3.14×10^7–3.63×10^7 J/kg. Also called: **hard coal.** [C19: from Latin *anthracītes* type of bloodstone, from Greek *anthrakitēs* coal-like, from *anthrax* coal, ANTHRAX] —**an·thra·cit·ic** (ˌænθrəˈsɪtɪk) *adj.*

an·thrac·nose (ænˈθræknəʊs) *n.* any of several fungus diseases of plants, such as vines and beans, characterized by oval dark depressed spots on the fruit and elsewhere. [C19: from French, from Greek *anthrax* coal, carbuncle + *nosos* disease]

an·thra·coid (ˈænθrəˌkɔɪd) *adj.* **1.** resembling anthrax. **2.** resembling carbon, coal, or charcoal.

an·thra·qui·none (ˌænθrəkwɪˈnəʊn, -ˈkwɪnəʊn) *n.* a yellow crystalline solid used in the manufacture of dyes, esp. **anthraquinone dyes,** which have excellent colour properties. Formula: $C_6H_4(CO)_2C_6H_4$. [C19: ANTHRA(CENE) + QUINONE]

an·thrax (ˈænθræks) *n., pl.* **·thra·ces** (-θrəˌsiːz). **1.** a highly infectious disease of animals, esp. cattle and sheep, characterized by fever, enlarged spleen and swelling of the throat. It is caused by the bacterium *Bacillus anthracis* and can be transmitted to man. **2.** a pustule or other lesion caused by this disease. [C19: from Late Latin, from Greek: carbuncle]

anthrop. *abbrev. for:* **1.** anthropological. **2.** anthropology.

an·thro·po- *combining form.* indicating man or human: *anthropology; anthropomorphism.* [from Greek *anthrōpos*]

an·thro·po·cen·tric (ˌænθrəpəʊˈsɛntrɪk) *adj.* regarding man as the most important and central factor in the universe. —**ˌan·thro·po·ˈcen·trism** *n.*

an·thro·po·gen·e·sis (ˌænθrəpəʊˈdʒɛnɪsɪs) *or* **an·thro·po·gen·y** (ˌænθrəˈpɒdʒɪnɪ) *n.* the study of the origins of man. —**ˌan·thro·po·ge·ˈnet·ic** *or* **ˌan·thro·po·ˈgen·ic** *adj.*

an·thro·poid (ˈænθrəˌpɔɪd) *adj.* **1.** resembling man. **2.** resembling an ape; apelike. **3.** of or relating to the suborder *Anthropoidea.* ~*n.* **4.** any primate of the suborder *Anthropoidea,* including monkeys, apes, and man. Compare **prosimian.** —**ˌan·thro·ˈpoi·dal** *adj.*

an·thro·poid ape *n.* any primate of the family *Pongidae,* having no tail, elongated arms, and a highly developed brain. The group includes gibbons, orang-utans, chimpanzees, and gorillas.

anthropol. *abbrev. for* anthropology.

an·thro·pol·o·gy (ˌænθrəˈpɒlədʒɪ) *n.* the study of man, his origins, physical characteristics, institutions, religious beliefs, social relationships, etc. See also **cultural anthropology, ethnology, physical anthropology, social anthropology.** —**an·thro·po·log·i·cal** (ˌænθrəpəˈlɒdʒɪkᵊl) *adj.* —**ˌan·thro·po·ˈlog·i·cal·ly** *adv.* —**ˌan·thro·ˈpol·o·gist** *n.*

an·thro·pom·e·try (ˌænθrəˈpɒmɪtrɪ) *n.* the comparative study of sizes and proportions of the human body. —**an·thro·po·met·ric** (ˌænθrəpəˈmɛtrɪk) *or* **ˌan·thro·po·ˈmet·ri·cal** *adj.* —**ˌan·thro·po·ˈmet·ri·cal·ly** *adv.* —**ˌan·thro·ˈpom·e·trist** *n.*

an·thro·po·mor·phic (ˌænθrəpəˈmɔːfɪk) *adj.* **1.** of or relating to anthropomorphism. **2.** resembling the human form.

an·thro·po·mor·phism (ˌænθrəpəˈmɔːfɪzəm) *n.* the attribution of human form or behaviour to a deity, animal, etc. —**ˌan·thro·po·ˈmor·phist** *n.*

an·thro·po·mor·phize *or* **an·thro·po·mor·phise** (ˌænθrəpəˈmɔːfaɪz) *vb.* to attribute or ascribe human form or behaviour to (a god, animal, object, etc.).

an·thro·po·mor·pho·sis (ˌænθrəpəˈmɔːfəsɪs) *n.* transformation into human form.

an·thro·po·mor·phous (ˌænθrəpəˈmɔːfəs) *adj.* **1.** shaped like a human being. **2.** another word for **anthropomorphic.** —**ˌan·thro·po·ˈmor·phous·ly** *adv.*

an·thro·pop·a·thy (ˌænθrəˈpɒpəθɪ) *or* **an·thro·pop·a·thism** *n.* the attribution of human passions, etc., to a deity, object, etc. —**an·thro·po·path·ic** (ˌænθrəpəˈpæθɪk) *adj.*

an·thro·poph·a·gi (ˌænθrəˈpɒfəˌgaɪ) *pl. n., sing.* **·gus** (-gəs). cannibals. [C16: from Latin, from Greek *anthrōpophagos;* see ANTHROPO-, PHAGO-]

an·thro·poph·a·gite (ˌænθrəˈpɒfəˌgaɪt) *n.* a rare word for **cannibal.** —**an·thro·poph·a·gy** (ˌænθrəˈpɒfədʒɪ) *n.* —**an·thro·po·phag·ic** (ˌænθrəpəˈfædʒɪk) *adj.* —**ˌan·thro·ˈpoph·a·gous** *adj.*

an·thro·pos·o·phy (ˌænθrəˈpɒsəfɪ) *n.* the spiritual and mystical teachings of Rudolph Steiner. —**an·thro·po·soph·ic** (ˌænθrəpəʊˈsɒfɪk) *adj.* —**ˌan·thro·ˈpos·o·phist** *n.*

an·thu·ri·um (ænˈθjʊərɪəm) *n.* any of various tropical American aroid plants constituting the genus *Anthurium,* many of which are cultivated as house plants for their showy foliage and their flowers, which have a long-stalked spike surrounded by a flaring heart-shaped white or red bract. [C19: New Latin, from ANTHO- + Greek *oura* a tail]

an·ti (ˈæntɪ) *Informal.* ~*adj.* **1.** opposed to a party, policy, attitude, etc.: *he won't join because he is rather anti.* ~*n.* **2.** an opponent of a party, policy, etc.

an·ti- *prefix.* **1.** against; opposing: *anticlerical; antisocial.* **2.** opposite to: *anticlimax; antimere.* **3.** rival; false: *antipope.* **4.** counteracting, inhibiting, or neutralizing: *antifreeze; antihistamine.* [from Greek *anti*]

an·ti-air·craft (ˌæntɪˈɛəkrɑːft) *n.* (*modifier*) of or relating to defence against aircraft attack: *anti-aircraft batteries.*

an·ti·ar (ˈæntɪˌɑː) *n.* another name for **upas** (senses 1, 2). [from Javanese]

ˌan·ti·a·ˈbra·sion *adj.*
ˌan·ti-ˈal·i·en *adj.*
ˌan·ti-ˌa·ris·to·ˈcrat·ic *adj.*
ˌan·ti·bac·ˈte·ri·al *adj.*
ˌan·ti·bal·ˈlis·tic *adj.*
ˌan·ti·ˈbib·li·cal *adj.*
ˌan·ti-ˈBol·she·vik *n., adj.*
ˌan·ti-ˈBol·she·vism *n.*

an·ti+bar·y·on (ˌæntɪ'bærɪən) *n. Physics.* the antiparticle of any of the baryons.

An+tibes (*French* ã'tib) *n.* a port and resort in SE France, on the Mediterranean: an important Roman town. Pop.: 56 309 (1975).

an·ti+bi·o+sis (ˌæntɪbaɪ'əʊsɪs) *n.* an association between two organisms, esp. microorganisms, that is harmful to one of them.

an·ti+bi+ot+ic (ˌæntɪbaɪ'ɒtɪk) *n.* **1.** any of various chemical substances, such as penicillin, streptomycin, neomycin, and tetracycline, produced by various microorganisms, esp. fungi, or made synthetically and capable of destroying or inhibiting the growth of microorganisms, esp. bacteria. ~*adj.* **2.** of or relating to antibiotics.

an·ti+bod·y ('æntɪˌbɒdɪ) *n., pl.* **+bod·ies.** any of various proteins produced in the blood in response to the presence of an antigen. It combines with the antigen, usually a toxin produced by a bacterium, rendering it harmless. See also **immunoglobulin.**

an+tic ('æntɪk) *n.* **1.** *Archaic.* an actor in a ludicrous or grotesque part; clown; buffoon. ~*adj.* **2.** *Archaic.* fantastic; grotesque. [C16: from Italian *antico* something ancient, or grotesque (from its application to fantastic carvings found in ruins of ancient Rome); see ANTIQUE]

an·ti+cat·a+lyst (ˌæntɪ'kætəlɪst) *n.* **1.** a substance that destroys or diminishes the activity of a catalyst. **2.** another name for **inhibitor** (sense 1).

an·ti+cath+ode (ˌæntɪ'kæθəʊd) *n.* the target electrode for the stream of electrons in a vacuum tube, esp. an x-ray tube.

an·ti+chlor ('æntɪˌklɔː) *n.* a substance used to remove chlorine from a material after bleaching. [C19: from ANTI- + CHLOR(INE)] —**ˌan·ti+chlo+'ris+tic** *adj.*

an·ti+cho+lin+er+gic (ˌæntɪˌkɒlɪ'nɜːdʒɪk) *adj.* **1.** *Physiol.* blocking nerve impulses through the parasympathetic nerves. ~*n.* **2.** *Med.* a drug or agent that blocks these nerve impulses, used esp. to control intestinal spasm.

an·ti+cho+lin+es+ter+ase (ˌæntɪˌkɒlə'nɛstəˌreɪz) *n.* any of a group of substances that inhibit the action of cholinesterase.

An·ti+christ ('æntɪˌkraɪst) *n.* **1.** *New Testament.* the antagonist of Christ, expected by early Christians to appear and reign over the world until overthrown at Christ's Second Coming. **2.** (*sometimes not cap.*) an enemy of Christ or Christianity. —**ˌAn·ti+'chris+tian** *adj.*

an+tic·i+pant (æn'tɪsɪpənt) *adj.* **1.** operating in advance; expectant. ~*n.* **2.** a person who anticipates.

an+tic·i+pate (æn'tɪsɪˌpeɪt) *vb.* (*mainly tr.*) **1.** (*may take a clause as object*) to regard as likely; expect; foresee: *he anticipated that it would happen.* **2.** (*may take a clause as object*) to foresee and act in advance of: *he anticipated the fall in value by selling early.* **3.** to thwart by acting in advance of; forestall: *I anticipated his punch by moving out of reach.* **4.** (*also intr.*) to mention (something) before its proper time: *don't anticipate the climax of the story.* **5.** to make use of in advance of possession: *he anticipated his salary in buying a house.* **6.** to pay (a bill, etc.) before it falls due. **7.** to cause to happen sooner: *the spread of nationalism anticipated the decline of the Empire.* [C16: from Latin *anticipāre* to take before, realize beforehand, from *anti-* ANTE- + *capere* to take] —**an+'tic·i+ˌpa+tor** *n.* —**an+'tic·i+ˌpa+to·ry** *or* **an+'tic·i+pa+tive** *adj.* —**an+'tic·i+ˌpa+to+ri+ly** *or* **an+'tic·i+pa+tive+ly** *adv.*

an+tic·i+pa+tion (ænˌtɪsɪ'peɪʃən) *n.* **1.** the act of anticipating; expectation, premonition, or foresight. **2.** the act of taking or dealing with funds before they are legally available or due. **3.** *Music.* an unstressed, usually short note introduced before a downbeat and harmonically related to the chord immediately following it. Compare **suspension** (sense 11).

an·ti+clas+tic (ˌæntɪ'klæstɪk) *adj. Maths.* (of a surface) having a curvature, at a given point and in a particular direction, that is of the opposite sign to the curvature at that point in a perpendicular direction. Compare **synclastic.**

an·ti+cler·i·cal (ˌæntɪ'klɛrɪkᵊl) *adj.* **1.** opposed to the power and influence of the clergy, esp. in politics. ~*n.* **2.** a supporter of an anticlerical party. —**ˌan·ti+'cler·i·cal+ism** *n.*

an·ti+cli+max (ˌæntɪ'klaɪmæks) *n.* **1.** a disappointing or ineffective conclusion to a series of events, etc. **2.** a sudden change from a serious subject to one that is disappointing or ludicrous. **3.** *Rhetoric.* a descent in discourse from the significant or important to the trivial, inconsequential, etc. —**an·ti+cli+mac+tic** (ˌæntɪklaɪ'mæktɪk) *adj.* —**ˌan·ti+cli+'mac+ti+cal+ly** *adv.*

an·ti+cli+nal (ˌæntɪ'klaɪnᵊl) *adj.* **1.** of, relating to, or resembling an anticline. **2.** *Botany.* of or relating to the plane at right angles to the surface of an organ.

an·ti+cline ('æntɪˌklaɪn) *n.* a formation of stratified rock raised up, by folding, into a broad arch so that the strata slope down on both sides from a common crest. Compare **syncline.**

an·ti+cli+no+ri·um (ˌæntɪklaɪ'nɔːrɪəm) *n., pl.* **+no+ri·a** (-'nɔːrɪə). a vast elongated anticline with its strata further folded into anticlines and synclines.

an·ti+clock+wise (ˌæntɪ'klɒkˌwaɪz) *adv., adj.* in the opposite direction to the rotation of the hands of a clock. U.S. equivalent: **counterclockwise.**

an·ti+co+ag·u+lant (ˌæntɪkəʊ'ægjʊlənt) *adj.* **1.** acting to prevent or retard coagulation, esp. of blood. ~*n.* **2.** an agent that prevents or retards coagulation.

an·ti+co+in+ci+dence (ˌæntɪkəʊ'ɪnsɪdəns) *n.* (*modifier*) of or relating to an electronic circuit that produces an output pulse if one but not both of its input terminals receives a pulse within a specified interval of time. Compare **coincidence** (sense 3).

an·ti+con+vul+sant (ˌæntɪkən'vʌlsənt) *n.* **1.** any of a class of drugs used to relieve convulsions. ~*adj.* **2.** of or relating to this class of drugs.

An·ti-Corn Law League *n.* an organization founded in 1839 by Richard Cobden and John Bright to oppose the Corn Laws, which were repealed in 1846.

An·ti+cos+ti (ˌæntɪ'kɒstɪ) *n.* an island of E Canada in the Gulf of St. Lawrence; part of Quebec. Area: 7881 sq. km (3043 sq. miles).

an+tics ('æntɪks) *pl. n.* absurd or grotesque acts or postures.

an·ti+cy+clone (ˌæntɪ'saɪkləʊn) *n. Meteorol.* a body of moving air of higher pressure than the surrounding air, in which the pressure decreases away from the centre. Winds circulate around the centre in a clockwise direction in the N hemisphere and anticlockwise in the S hemisphere. Also called: **high.** —**an·ti+cy+clon+ic** (ˌæntɪsaɪ'klɒnɪk) *adj.*

an·ti+de+pres+sant (ˌæntɪdɪ'prɛsᵊnt) *n.* **1.** any of a class of drugs used to alleviate depression. ~*adj.* **2.** of or relating to this class of drugs.

an·ti+dote ('æntɪˌdəʊt) *n.* **1.** *Med.* a drug or agent that counteracts or neutralizes the effects of a poison. **2.** anything that counteracts or relieves a harmful or unwanted condition; remedy. [C15: from Latin *antidotum,* from Greek *antidoton* something given as a countermeasure, from ANTI- + *didonai* to give] —**ˌan·ti+'dot+al** *adj.*

an·ti+drom+ic (ˌæntɪ'drɒmɪk) *adj.* **1.** (of nerve fibres) conducting nerve impulses in a direction opposite to normal. **2.** (of plants) showing twining to the left and right in members of the same species.

An+tie+tam (æn'tiːtəm) *n.* a creek in NW Maryland, flowing into the Potomac: scene of a Civil War battle (1862), in which the Confederate forces of General Robert E. Lee were defeated.

an·ti+fe·brile (ˌæntɪ'fiːbraɪl) *adj.* **1.** reducing fever; antipyretic. ~*n.* **2.** an antifebrile agent or drug.

An·ti+fed+er+al+ist (ˌæntɪ'fɛdərəlɪst, -'fɛdrə-) *n.* **1.** *U.S. history.* a person who opposed the ratification of the Constitution in 1789 and thereafter allied with Thomas Jefferson's Antifederal Party, which opposed extension of the powers of the federal Government. **2.** (*often not cap.*) any person who opposes federalism.

an·ti+fer+ro+mag+ne+tism (ˌæntɪˌfɛrəʊ'mægnɪˌtɪzəm) *n. Physics.* the phenomenon exhibited by substances that resemble paramagnetic substances in the value of their relative permeability but that behave like ferromagnetic substances when their temperature is varied. See also **ferrimagnetism.**

an·ti+foul+ing (ˌæntɪ'faʊlɪŋ) *adj.* **1.** (of a paint or other coating) inhibiting the growth of barnacles and other marine organisms on a ship's bottom. ~*n.* **2.** an antifouling paint or other coating.

an·ti+freeze ('æntɪˌfriːz) *n.* a liquid, usually ethylene glycol (ethanediol), added to cooling water to lower its freezing point, esp. for use in an internal-combustion engine.

an·ti+gen ('æntɪdʒən, -ˌdʒɛn) *n.* a substance that stimulates the production of antibodies. [C20: from ANTI(BODY) + -GEN] —**ˌan·ti+'gen+ic** *adj.* —**ˌan·ti+'gen·i·cal+ly** *adv.*

An·tig·o·ne (æn'tɪgənɪ) *n. Greek myth.* daughter of Oedipus and Jocasta, who was condemned to death for cremating the body of her brother Polynices in defiance of an edict of her uncle, King Creon of Thebes.

An·tig·o·nus I (æn'tɪgənəs) *n.* called *Cyclops.* 382–301 B.C., Macedonian general under Alexander the Great; king of Macedon (306–301).

an·ti-G suit *n.* another name for **G-suit.**

An+ti+gua (æn'tiːgə) *n.* an island of the West Indies, one of the Leeward Islands: a former British colony; it became independent in 1981. Capital: St. John's. Pop.: 66 000 (1972 est.). Area: 279 sq. km (108 sq. miles). —**An+'ti+guan** *adj., n.*

an·ti+ha+la+tion (ˌantɪhə'leɪʃən) *n. Photog.* **a.** a process by which light, passing through the emulsion on a film or plate, is not reflected back into it but is absorbed by a layer of dye or pigment, usually on the back of the film, thus preventing halation. **b.** (*as modifier*): *antihalation backing.*

an·ti+he+lix (ˌæntɪ'hiːlɪks) *n., pl.* **+hel·i·ces** (-'hiːlɪsiːz) *or* **+he+lix·es.** a variant spelling of **anthelix.**

an·ti+he+ro ('æntiˌhɪərəʊ) *n., pl.* **+roes.** a central character in a novel, play, etc., who lacks the traditional heroic virtues.

an·ti+his+ta+mine (ˌæntɪ'hɪstəˌmiːn, -mɪn) *n.* any drug that neutralizes the effects of histamine, used esp. in the treatment of allergies.

ˌan·ti-'Bol·she+vist *n.*
ˌan·ti+'cap·i·tal+ist *n., adj.*
ˌan·ti+ˌcap·i·tal+'is+tic *adj.*
ˌan·ti-'Cath·o·lic *adj., n.*
ˌan·ti-Ca·'thol·i·cism *n.*
ˌan·ti+'cen+sor+ship *adj.*
ˌan·ti+'church *adj.*
ˌan·ti+'clas+si·cal *adj.*
ˌan·ti·co+'ag·u+ˌlat+ing *adj.*
ˌan·ti-'Com·mu·nist *n., adj.*
ˌan·ti+con+'scrip+tion *adj.*
ˌan·ti+ˌcon+sti+'tu+tion+al *adj.*
ˌan·ti+cor+'ro+sive *adj.*
ˌan·ti-Dar·'win+i·an *adj., n.*
ˌan·ti-'Dar·win+ism *n.*
ˌan·ti+ˌdem·o+'crat+ic *adj.*
ˌan·ti+ˌdi·u+'ret+ic *adj.*
ˌan·ti-ec·ˌcle·si+'as+ti+cal *adj.*
ˌan·ti-ec·ˌcle·si+'as+ti+cal+ly *adv.*
ˌan·ti-e·'pis·co+pal *adj., n.*
ˌan·ti-e·'ro·sion *adj.*
ˌan·ti-ˌev·o·'lu+tion *adj.*
ˌan·ti-ev·o·'lu+tion+ist *n., adj.*
ˌan·ti+'fac+tion *adj.*
ˌan·ti+'fas+cist *n., adj.*
ˌan·ti-'Freud·i·an *adj., n.*
ˌan·ti+ˌfun+da+'men+tal+ist *n., adj.*
ˌan·ti+'hu+man+ism *n.*
ˌan·ti+'hu+man+ist *adj., n.*
ˌan·ti-im·'pe·ri·al+ism *n.*
ˌan·ti-im·'pe·ri·al+ist *adj., n.*

an·ti·ic·er *n.* a device fitted to an aircraft to prevent the formation of ice. Compare **de-icer.**

an·ti+knock (ˌæntɪˈnɒk) *n.* a compound, such as lead tetraethyl, added to petrol to reduce knocking in the engine.

An·ti-Leb·a·non *n.* a mountain range running north and south between Syria and Lebanon, east of the Lebanon Mountains. Highest peak: Mount Hermon, 279 m (9232 ft.).

an·ti+lep+ton (ˌæntɪˈlɛptɒn) *n. Physics.* the antiparticle of any of the leptons.

An·til+les (ænˈtɪliːz) *pl. n.* **the.** a group of islands in the West Indies consisting of the **Greater Antilles** and the **Lesser Antilles.**

an·ti+log (ˈæntɪˌlɒg) *n.* short for **antilogarithm.**

an·ti+log·a+rithm (ˌæntɪˈlɒgəˌrɪðəm) *n.* a number whose logarithm is the given number: *100 is the antilogarithm of 2.* Often shortened to **antilog.** —ˌ**an·ti+ˌlog·a+ˈrith+mic** *adj.*

an+til·o+gism (ænˈtɪləˌdʒɪzəm) *n.* a triad of propositions consisting of the two premisses of a syllogism and the negation of its conclusion. [C20: from ANTI- + (SYL)LOGISM]

an+til·o·gy (ænˈtɪlədʒɪ) *n., pl.* **·gies.** a contradiction in terms. [C17: from Greek *antilogia*]

an·ti+ma+cas+sar (ˌæntɪməˈkæsə) *n.* a cloth covering the back and arms of chairs, etc., to prevent soiling or as decoration. [C19: from ANTI- + MACASSAR (OIL)]

an·ti+mag+net+ic (ˌæntɪmægˈnɛtɪk) *adj.* of or constructed of a material that does not acquire permanent magnetism when exposed to a magnetic field: *an antimagnetic watch.*

an·ti+ma+lar+i·al (ˌæntɪməˈlɛərɪəl) *adj.* **1.** effective in the treatment of malaria. ~*n.* **2.** an antimalarial drug or agent.

an·ti+masque (ˈæntɪˌmɑːsk) *n.* a comic or grotesque dance, presented between the acts of a masque.

an·ti+mat+ter (ˈæntɪˌmætə) *n.* a hypothetical form of matter composed of antiparticles.

an·ti+mere (ˈæntɪˌmɪə) *n.* a part or organ of a bilaterally or radially symmetrical organism that corresponds to a similar structure on the other side of the axis, such as the right or left limb of a four-legged animal. Also called: **actinomere.** —**an·ti+mer+ic** (ˌæntɪˈmɛrɪk) *adj.* —**an+tim+er+ism** (ænˈtɪməˌrɪzəm) *n.*

an·ti+mis+sile (ˌæntɪˈmɪsaɪl) *adj.* **1.** relating to defensive measures against missile attack: *an antimissile system.* ~*n.* **2.** a defensive missile used to intercept and destroy attacking missiles.

an·ti+mo+ni·al (ˌæntɪˈməʊnɪəl) *adj.* **1.** of or containing antimony. ~*n.* **2.** a drug or agent containing antimony.

an·ti+mo+nic (ˌæntɪˈmɒnɪk) *adj.* of or containing antimony in the pentavalent state.

an·ti+mo+nous (ˈæntɪmənəs) *adj.* of or containing antimony in the trivalent state.

an·ti+mo+ny (ˈæntɪmənɪ) *n.* a toxic metallic element that exists in two allotropic forms and occurs principally in stibnite. The stable form is a brittle silvery-white crystalline metal that is added to alloys to increase their strength and hardness and is used in semiconductors. Symbol: Sb; atomic no.: 51; atomic wt.: 121.75; valency: 3 or 5; relative density: 6.684; melting pt.: 630.5°C; boiling pt.: 1640°C. [C15: from Medieval Latin *antimōnium,* of uncertain origin]

an·ti+mo+nyl (ˈæntɪmənɪl, ænˈtɪm-) *n.* (*modifier*) of, consisting of, or containing the monovalent group SbO-: *an antimonyl group or radical.*

an·ti+mo+ny po+tas+si·um tar+trate *n.* a colourless odourless poisonous crystalline salt used as a mordant for textiles and leather, as an insecticide, and as an anthelmintic. Formula: $K(SbO)C_4H_4O_6$. Also called: **tartar emetic.**

an·ti+neu+tri+no (ˌæntɪnjuːˈtriːnəʊ) *n., pl.* **+nos.** the antiparticle of a neutrino; a particle having the opposite spin to a neutrino.

an·ti+neu+tron (ˌæntɪˈnjuːtrɒn) *n.* the antiparticle of a neutron; a particle having the same mass as the neutron but a magnetic moment of opposite sign.

ant+ing (ˈæntɪŋ) *n.* the placing or rubbing of ants by birds on their feathers. The body fluids of the ants are thought to repel parasites.

an·ti+node (ˈæntɪˌnəʊd) *n.* a point of maximum displacement between two adjacent nodes in a standing wave. —ˌ**an·ti+ˈnod+al** *adj.*

an·ti+no+mi·an (ˌæntɪˈnəʊmɪən) *adj.* **1.** relating to the doctrine that by faith and the dispensation of grace a Christian is released from the obligation of adhering to any moral law. ~*n.* **2.** a member of a Christian sect holding such a doctrine. —ˌ**an·ti+ˈno+mi+an+ism** *n.*

an+tin·o+my (ænˈtɪnəmɪ) *n., pl.* **+mies.** **1.** opposition of one law, principle, or rule to another; contradiction within a law. **2.** *Philosophy.* contradiction existing between two apparently indubitable propositions; paradox. [C16: from Latin *antinomia,* from Greek: conflict between laws, from ANTI- + *nomos* law] —**an·ti+nom+ic** (ˌæntɪˈnɒmɪk) *adj.* —ˌ**an·ti+ˈnom·i+cal+ly** *adv.*

an·ti+nov+el (ˈæntɪˌnɒvᵊl) *n.* a type of prose fiction in which conventional or traditional novelistic elements are rejected. Also called: **anti-roman, nouveau roman.**

an·ti+nu+cle·on (ˌæntɪˈnjuːklɪˌɒn) *n.* an antiproton or an antineutron.

An·ti+och (ˈæntɪˌɒk) *n.* a city in S Turkey, on the Orantes River: ancient commercial centre and capital of Syria (300–64 B.C.); early centre of Christianity. Pop.: 57 900 (1965). Arabic name: **Antakiya.** Turkish name: **Antakya.**

An·ti·o·chus III (ænˈtaɪəkəs) *n.* called *the Great.* 242–187 B.C., king of Syria (223–187), who greatly extended the Seleucid empire but was forced (190) to surrender most of Asia Minor to the Romans.

An·ti·o·chus IV *n.* ?215–164 B.C., Seleucid king of Syria (175–164), who attacked the Jews and provoked the revolt of the Maccabees.

an·ti+ox·i+dant (ˌæntɪˈɒksɪdənt) *n.* any substance that retards deterioration by oxidation, esp. of fats, oils, foods, petroleum products, or rubber.

an·ti+par+al+lel (ˌæntɪˈpærəˌlɛl) *adj.* **1.** *Physics.* parallel but pointing or rotating in opposite directions. **2.** *Maths.* (of two lines) cutting two given lines so that in the quadrilateral formed the interior opposite angles are supplementary.

an·ti+par+ti+cle (ˈæntɪˌpɑːtɪkᵊl) *n.* any of a group of elementary particles that have the same mass as their corresponding particle but have a charge, baryon number, strangeness, and isospin quantum number, I_3, of equal magnitude but opposite sign. When a particle collides with its antiparticle mutual annihilation occurs.

an·ti+pas+to (ˌæntɪˈpɑːstəʊ, -ˈpæs-) *n., pl.* **+tos.** a course of hors d'oeuvres in an Italian meal. [Italian: before food]

An·tip·a·ter (ænˈtɪpətə) *n.* ?398–319 B.C., Macedonian general under Alexander the Great: regent of Macedon (334–323).

an·ti+pa+thet+ic (ænˌtɪpəˈθɛtɪk, ˌæntɪpə-) *or* **an·ti+pa+thet+ic·al** *adj.* (often foll. by *to*) having or arousing a strong aversion. —ˌ**an·ti+pa+ˈthet·i+cal+ly** *adv.*

an+tip·a+thy (ænˈtɪpəθɪ) *n., pl.* **+thies.** **1.** a feeling of intense aversion, dislike, or hostility. **2.** the object of such a feeling. [C17: from Latin *antipathia,* from Greek *antipatheia,* from ANTI- + *patheia* feeling]

an·ti+pe·ri+od+ic (ˌæntɪˌpɪərɪˈɒdɪk) *Med.* ~*adj.* **1.** efficacious against recurring attacks of a disease. ~*n.* **2.** an antiperiodic drug or agent.

an·ti+per·i+stal+sis (ˌæntɪˌpɛrɪˈstælsɪs) *n. Physiol.* contractions of the intestine that force the contents in the opposite direction to the normal.

an·ti+per+son+nel (ˌæntɪˌpɜːsəˈnɛl) *adj.* (of weapons, etc.) designed to cause casualties to personnel rather than to destroy equipment or defences.

an·ti+per+spi+rant (ˌæntɪˈpɜːspərənt) *n.* **1.** an astringent substance applied to the skin to reduce or prevent perspiration. ~*adj.* **2.** reducing or preventing perspiration.

an·ti+phlo+gis+tic (ˌæntɪfləˈdʒɪstɪk) *adj.* **1.** of or relating to the prevention or alleviation of inflammation. ~*n.* **2.** an antiphlogistic agent or drug.

an·ti+phon (ˈæntɪfən) *n.* **1.** a short passage, usually from the Bible, recited or sung as a response after certain parts of a liturgical service. **2.** a psalm, hymn, etc., chanted or sung in alternate parts. **3.** any response or answer. [C15: from Late Latin *antiphōna* sung responses, from Late Greek, plural of *antiphōnon* (something) responsive, from *antiphōnos,* from ANTI- + *phōnē* sound]

an+tiph·o+nal (ænˈtɪfənəl) *adj.* **1.** sung or recited in alternation. ~*n.* **2.** another word for **antiphonary.** —**an+ˈtiph·o+nal+ly** *adv.*

an+tiph·o+nar·y (ænˈtɪfənərɪ) *n., pl.* **+nar+ies.** **1.** a bound collection of antiphons, esp. for use in the divine office. ~*adj.* **2.** of or relating to such a book.

an+tiph·o+ny (ænˈtɪfənɪ) *n., pl.* **+nies.** **1.** the antiphonal singing of a musical composition by two choirs. **2.** any musical or other sound effect that answers or echoes another.

an+tiph+ra+sis (ænˈtɪfrəsɪs) *n. Rhetoric.* the use of a word in a sense opposite to its normal one, esp. for ironic effect. [C16: via Late Latin from Greek, from ANTI- + *phrasis,* from *phrazein* to speak]

an+tip·o+dal (ænˈtɪpədᵊl) *adj.* **1.** of or relating to diametrically opposite points on the earth's surface. **2.** exactly or diametrically opposite.

an·ti+pode (ˈæntɪpəʊd) *n.* the exact or direct opposite.

an+tip·o+des (ænˈtɪpəˌdiːz) *pl. n.* **1.** either or both of two points, places, or regions that are situated diametrically opposite to one another on the earth's surface, esp. the country or region opposite one's own. **2.** the people who live there. **3.** (*often cap.*) **the.** Australia and New Zealand. **4.** (*sometimes functioning as sing.*) the exact or direct opposite. [C16: via Late Latin from Greek, plural of *antipous* having the feet opposite, from ANTI- + *pous* foot] —**an+tip·o·de·an** (ænˌtɪpəˈdiːən) *adj.*

An+tip·o+des (ænˈtɪpəˌdiːz) *pl. n.* **the.** a group of small uninhabited islands in the South Pacific, southeast of and belonging to New Zealand. Area: 62 sq. km (24 sq. miles).

an·ti+pope (ˈæntɪˌpəʊp) *n.* a rival pope elected in opposition to one who has been canonically chosen.

an·ti+pro+ton (ˈæntɪˌprəʊtɒn) *n.* the antiparticle of the proton; a particle having the same mass as the proton but an equal and opposite charge.

ˌ**an·ti+ˈla·bour** *adj.*
ˌ**an·ti+li+ˈtur+gi+cal** *adj.*
ˌ**an·ti+ma+ˌte·ri+al+ˈis+tic** *adj.*
ˌ**an·ti+mi+ˈcro+bi·al** *adj.*
ˌ**an·ti+ˈmil·i+ta+rism** *n.*
ˌ**an·ti+ˈmil·i+ta+rist** *n., adj.*
ˌ**an·ti+ˌmil·i+ta+ˈris+tic** *adj.*
ˌ**an·ti+ˈmod+ern+ist** *n., adj.*
ˌ**an·ti+mo+ˈnar+chic+al** *adj.*
ˌ**an·ti+ˈmo+nar+chist** *adj., n.*
ˌ**an·ti+nar+ˈcot+ic** *adj., n.*
ˌ**an·ti+ˈna+tion+al+ist** *n., adj.*
ˌ**an·ti+ˌna+tion+al+ˈis+tic** *adj.*
ˌ**an·ti+ˈnoise** *adj.*
ˌ**an·ti+ˈpac·i+fist** *n., adj.*
ˌ**an·ti+ˈpath·o+gen** *n.*
ˌ**an·ti+ˌpath·o+ˈgen+ic** *adj.*
ˌ**an·ti+po+ˈlit·i+cal** *adj.*
ˌ**an·ti+ˌpro+hi+ˈbi+tion** *n.*
ˌ**an·ti+ˌpro+hi+ˈbi+tion+ist** *n., adj.*
ˌ**an·ti-ˈProt·es+tant** *adj., n.*
ˌ**an·ti+ˈpu+ri+tan** *n., adj.*
ˌ**an·ti+ˈrad·i+cal** *adj., n.*
ˌ**an·ti+pol+ˈlu+tion** *adj., n.*

an·ti+psy+chi·a+try (ˌæntɪsaɪˈkaɪətrɪ) *n.* an approach to mental disorders that makes use of concepts derived from existentialism, psychoanalysis, and sociological theory.

an·ti+py+ret+ic (ˌæntɪpaɪˈrɛtɪk) *adj.* **1.** preventing or alleviating fever. ~*n.* **2.** an antipyretic remedy or drug. —**an·ti+py+re·sis** (ˌæntɪpaɪˈriːsɪs) *n.*

an·ti+py+rine (ˌæntɪˈpaɪrɪn, -riːn) *n.* a white powder used medicinally to reduce pain and fever. Formula: $C_{11}H_{12}N_2O$.

antiq. *abbrev. for:* **1.** antiquarian. **2.** antiquity.

an·ti+quar+i·an (ˌæntɪˈkwɛərɪən) *adj.* **1.** concerned with the study of antiquities or antiques. ~*n.* **2.** the largest size of handmade drawing paper, 53 × 31 inches. **3.** a less common name for **antiquary.** —ˌ**an·ti+ˈquar·i+an+ism** *n.*

an·ti+quar·y (ˈæntɪkwərɪ) *n., pl.* **+quar·ies.** a person who collects, deals in, or studies antiques, ancient works of art, etc.

an·ti+quate (ˈæntɪˌkweɪt) *vb.* (*tr.*) **1.** to make obsolete or old-fashioned. **2.** to give an old or antique appearance to. [C15: from Latin *antīquāre* to make old, from *antīquus* ancient]

an·ti+quat+ed (ˈæntɪˌkweɪtɪd) *adj.* **1.** outmoded; obsolete. **2.** aged; ancient. —ˈ**an·ti+ˌquat+ed+ness** *n.*

an+tique (ænˈtiːk) *n.* **1. a.** a decorative object, piece of furniture, or other work of art created in an earlier period, that is collected and valued for its beauty, workmanship, and age. **b.** (*as modifier*): *an antique shop.* **2.** any object made in an earlier period. **3. the.** the style of ancient art, esp. Greek or Roman art, or an example of it. **4.** *Printing.* a family of typefaces having all lines of nearly equal thickness. ~*adj.* **5.** made in or in the style of an earlier period. **6.** of or belonging to the distant past, esp. of or in the style of ancient Greece or Rome. **7.** *Informal.* old-fashioned; out-of-date. **8.** *Archaic.* aged or venerable. **9.** (of paper) not calendered or coated; having a rough surface. ~*vb.* **10.** (*tr.*) to give an antique appearance to. [C16: from Latin *antīquus* ancient, from *ante* before]

an+tiq+ui·ties (ænˈtɪkwɪtɪz) *pl. n.* remains or relics, such as statues, buildings, or coins, that date from ancient times.

an+tiq+ui·ty (ænˈtɪkwɪtɪ) *n., pl.* **·ties.** **1.** the quality of being ancient or very old: *a vase of great antiquity.* **2.** the far distant past, esp. the time preceding the Middle Ages in Europe. **3.** the people of ancient times collectively; the ancients.

an·ti+ra+chit+ic (ˌæntɪrəˈkɪtɪk) *adj.* **1.** preventing or curing rickets. ~*n.* **2.** an antirachitic remedy or agent.

An·ti+re·mon+strant (ˌæntɪrɪˈmɒnstrənt) *n. Dutch Reformed Church.* the party that opposed the Remonstrants.

an+tir+rhi+num (ˌæntɪˈraɪnəm) *n.* any scrophulariaceous plant of the genus *Antirrhinum,* esp. the snapdragon, which have two-lipped flowers of various colours. [C16: via Latin from Greek *antirrhinon,* from ANTI- (imitating) + *rhis* nose; so called from a fancied likeness to an animal's snout]

An·ti+sa+na (*Spanish* ˌantiˈsana) *n.* a volcano in N central Ecuador, in the Andes. Height: 5756 m (18 885 ft.).

an·ti+scor+bu+tic (ˌæntɪskɔːˈbjuːtɪk) *adj.* **1.** preventing or curing scurvy. ~*n.* **2.** an antiscorbutic remedy or agent.

an·ti-Sem·ite *n.* a person who persecutes or discriminates against Jews. —ˌ**an·ti-Se·ˈmit·ic** *adj.* —ˌ**an·ti-Se·ˈmit·i+cal+ly** *adv.* —ˌ**an·ti-ˈSem·i·tism** *n.*

an·ti+sep+sis (ˌæntɪˈsɛpsɪs) *n.* **1.** destruction of undesirable microorganisms, such as those that cause disease or putrefaction. Compare **asepsis. 2.** the state or condition of being free from such microorganisms.

an·ti+sep+tic (ˌæntɪˈsɛptɪk) *adj.* **1.** of, relating to, or affecting antisepsis. **2.** entirely free from contamination. **3.** *Informal.* lacking spirit or excitement; clinical. ~*n.* **4.** an antiseptic agent or substance. —ˌ**an·ti+ˈsep+ti+cal+ly** *adv.*

an·ti+se·rum (ˌæntɪˈsɪərəm) *n., pl.* **·rums** *or* **·ra** (-rə). blood serum containing antibodies against a specific antigen, used to treat or provide immunity to a disease.

an·ti+slav+er·y (ˌæntɪˈsleɪvərɪ) *adj.* opposed to slavery, esp. Negro slavery.

an·ti+so+cial (ˌæntɪˈsəʊʃəl) *adj.* **1.** avoiding the company of other people; unsociable. **2.** contrary or injurious to the interests of society in general. —ˌ**an·ti+ˈso+cial+ly** *adv.*

an·ti+spas+mod+ic (ˌæntɪspæzˈmɒdɪk) *adj.* **1.** preventing or arresting spasms. ~*n.* **2.** an antispasmodic drug.

an·ti+stat+ic (ˌæntɪˈstætɪk) *adj.* (of a substance, textile, etc.) retaining sufficient moisture to provide a conducting path, thus avoiding the effects of static electricity.

An·tis·the·nes (ænˈtɪsθəˌniːz) *n.* ?445–365 B.C., Greek philosopher, founder of the Cynic school, who taught that the only good was virtue, won by self-control and independence from worldly needs.

an+tis+tro+phe (ænˈtɪstrəfɪ) *n.* **1.** (in ancient Greek drama) **a.** the second of two movements made by a chorus during the performance of a choral ode. **b.** the second part of a choral ode sung during this movement. **2.** (in classical prosody) the second of two metrical systems used alternately within a poem. ~See **strophe.** [C17: via Late Latin from Greek *antistrophē* an answering turn, from ANTI- + *strophē* a turning] —**an·ti+stroph+ic** (ˌæntɪˈstrɒfɪk) *adj.* —ˌ**an·ti+ˈstroph·i+cal+ly** *adv.*

an·ti+tank (ˌæntɪˈtæŋk) *adj.* designed to immobilize or destroy armoured vehicles: *antitank weapons.*

an+tith+e·sis (ænˈtɪθɪsɪs) *n., pl.* **·ses** (-ˌsiːz). **1.** the exact opposite. **2.** contrast or opposition. **3.** *Rhetoric.* the juxtaposition of contrasting ideas, phrases, or words so as to produce an effect of balance, such as *my words fly up, my thoughts remain below.* **4.** *Philosophy.* the second stage in the **Hegelian dialectic.** [C15: via Latin from Greek: a setting against, from ANTI- + *tithenai* to place]

an·ti+thet·i+cal (ˌæntɪˈθɛtɪkəl) *or* **an·ti+thet+ic** *adj.* **1.** of the nature of antithesis. **2.** directly contrasted.

an·ti+tox+in (ˌæntɪˈtɒksɪn) *n.* **1.** an antibody that neutralizes a toxin. **2.** blood serum that contains a specific antibody. —ˌ**an·ti+ˈtox+ic** *adj.*

an·ti+trades (ˈæntɪˌtreɪdz) *pl. n.* winds in the upper atmosphere blowing in the opposite direction from and above the trade winds.

an+tit+ra+gus (ænˈtɪtrəgəs) *n., pl.* **+gi** (-ˌdʒaɪ). a cartilaginous projection of the external ear opposite the tragus. [C19: from New Latin, from Greek *antitragos;* see ANTI-, TRAGUS]

an·ti+trust (ˌæntɪˈtrʌst) *n.* (*modifier*) *Chiefly U.S.* regulating or opposing trusts, monopolies, cartels, or similar organizations, esp. in order to prevent unfair competition.

an·ti+tus+sive (ˌæntɪˈtʌsɪv) *adj.* **1.** alleviating or suppressing coughing. ~*n.* **2.** an antitussive drug.

an·ti+type (ˈæntɪˌtaɪp) *n.* **1.** a person or thing that is foreshadowed or represented by a type or symbol, esp. a character or event in the New Testament prefigured in the Old Testament. **2.** an opposite type. —**an·ti+typ+ic** (ˌæntɪˈtɪpɪk) *or* ˌ**an·ti+ˈtyp·i+cal** *adj.* —ˌ**an·ti+ˈtyp·i+cal+ly** *adv.*

an·ti+ven+in (ˌæntɪˈvɛnɪn) *n.* an antitoxin that counteracts a specific venom, esp. snake venom. [C19: from ANTI- + VEN(OM) + -IN]

an·ti+world (ˈæntɪˌwɜːld) *n.* a hypothetical or supposed world or universe composed of antimatter.

ant+ler (ˈæntlə) *n.* one of a pair of bony outgrowths on the heads of male deer and some related species of either sex. The antlers are shed each year and grow more branches as the animal ages. [C14: from Old French *antoillier,* from Vulgar Latin *anteoculare* (unattested) (something) in front of the eye]

ant+ler moth *n.* a European noctuid moth, *Cerapteryx* (or *Charaeas*) *graminis,* that has white antler-like markings on the forewings and produces larvae that periodically cause great damage to pastures and grasslands.

Ant+li·a (ˈæntlɪə) *n., Latin genitive* **Ant+li·ae** (ˈæntlɪˌiː). a faint constellation in the S hemisphere close to Hydra and Vela. [C19: from Latin, from Greek: bucket]

ant+li+on (ˈæntˌlaɪən) *n.* **1.** Also called: **antlion fly.** any of various neuropterous insects of the family *Myrmeleontidae,* which typically resemble dragonflies and are most common in tropical regions. **2.** Also called (U.S.): **doodlebug.** the larva of this insect, which has very large jaws and buries itself in the sand to await its prey.

An+to+fa+gas+ta (ˌæntəfəˈgæstə; *Spanish* ˌantofaˈɣasta) *n.* a port in N Chile. Pop.: 149 720 (1975 est.).

An+toi+nette (*French* ɑ̃twaˈnɛt) *n.* See **Marie Antoinette.**

An·to·ni·nus (ˌæntəˈnaɪnəs) *n.* See **Marcus Aurelius Antoninus.**

An·to·ni·nus Pi·us *n.* 86–161 A.D., emperor of Rome (138–161); adopted son and successor of Hadrian.

An·to·ni·o·ni (ˌæntəʊnɪˈəʊnɪ) *n.* **Mi·chel·an·ge·lo** (mikeˈlandʒelo). born 1912, Italian film director; his films include *L'Avventura* (1959), *La Notte* (1961), *Blow Up* (1966), and *Zabriskie Point* (1970).

An·to·ni·us (ænˈtəʊnɪəs) *n.* **Mar·cus** (ˈmɑːkəs). Latin name of (Mark) **Antony.**

an+to+no+ma+si·a (ˌæntənəˈmeɪzɪə) *n. Rhetoric.* **1.** the substitution of a title or epithet for a proper name, such as *his highness.* **2.** the use of a proper name for an idea: *he is a Daniel come to judgment.* [C16: via Latin from Greek, from *antonomazein* to name differently, from *onoma* name] —**an+to+no+mas+tic** (ˌæntənəˈmæstɪk) *adj.* —ˌ**an+to+no+ˈmas+ti+cal+ly** *adv.*

An·to·ny (ˈæntənɪ) *n.* **Mark.** Latin name *Marcus Antonius.* ?83–30 B.C., Roman general who served under Julius Caesar in the Gallic wars and became a member of the second triumvirate (43). He defeated Brutus and Cassius at Philippi (42) but having repudiated his wife for Cleopatra, he was defeated by his brother-in-law Octavian (Augustus) at Actium (31).

an+to+nym (ˈæntənɪm) *n.* a word that means the opposite of another word: *"empty" is an antonym of "full".* [C19: from Greek *antōnumia,* from ANTI- + *onoma* name] —**an+ton·y+mous** (ænˈtɒnɪməs) *adj.*

an+tre (ˈæntə) *n. Rare.* a cavern or cave. [C17: from French, from Latin *antrum,* from Greek *antron*]

An+trim (ˈæntrɪm) *n.* a county of NE Northern Ireland: famous for the Giant's Causeway on the N coast. County town: Belfast. Pop.: 352 549 (1971). Area: 2843 sq. km (1098 sq. miles).

an+trorse (ænˈtrɔːs) *adj. Biology.* directed or pointing upwards or forwards. [C19: from New Latin *antrorsus,* from *antero-* front + *-orsus,* as in Latin *introrsus;* see INTRORSE] —**an+ˈtrorse+ly** *adv.*

an+trum (ˈæntrəm) *n., pl.* **+tra** (-trə). *Anatomy.* a natural cavity, hollow, or sinus, esp. in a bone. [C14: from Latin: cave, from Greek *antron*] —ˈ**an+tral** *adj.*

An+tung (ˈænˈtʊŋ) *n.* a port in E China, in Liaoning province at the mouth of the Yalu River. Pop.: 360 000 (1953).

Ant+werp (ˈæntwɜːp) *n.* **1.** a province of N Belgium. Pop.: 1 559 269 (1975 est.). Area: 2859 sq. km (1104 sq. miles). **2.** a

---

ˌan·ti·ˈra·tion·al *adj.*
ˌan·ti+ˈra·tion+al·ism *n.*
ˌan·ti+re·ˈli·gious *adj.*
ˌan·ti+re·ˈpub·li·can *adj., n.*
ˌan·ti+ˌrev·o+ˈlu·tion·ar·y *adj., n., pl.* +ar·ies.
ˌan·ti+ˈrust *adj.*
ˌan·ti+ˌsci+en+ˈtif+ic *adj.*
ˌan·ti+ˈspir+it+u·al *adj.*
ˌan·ti+ˌsub+ma+ˈrine *adj.*
ˌan·ti+ˈtar+nish+ing *adj.*
ˌan·ti+ˈthe+ism *n.*
ˌan·ti+ˈthe+ist *n.*
ˌan·ti+trin·i+ˈtar+i·an *n.*
ˌan·ti+ˈvi+rus *adj.*
ˌan·ti+viv·i+ˈsec+tion *n.*
ˌan·ti+viv·i+ˈsec+tion+ist *n., adj.*
ˌan·ti+ˈwar *adj.*
ˌan·ti-ˈZi·on+ism *n.*
ˌan·ti-ˈZi·on+ist *n., adj.*

port in N Belgium, capital of Antwerp province, on the River Scheldt: a major European port. Pop.: 224 543 (1970). Flemish name: **Ant+werp+en** ('ɑntwɛrpə). French name: **Anvers.**

A.N.U. *abbrev. for* Australian National University.

A·nu ('ɑːnuː) *n. Babylonian myth.* the sky god.

A·nu·bis (ə'njuːbɪs) *n. Egyptian myth.* a deity, a son of Osiris, who conducted the dead to judgment. He is represented as having a jackal's head and was identified by the Greeks with Hermes.

A·nu+ra+dha+pu+ra (ə'nʊərədəˌpʊərə, ˌʌnʊ'rɑːdə-) *n.* a town in Sri Lanka: ancient capital of Ceylon; site of the sacred bo tree and place of pilgrimage for Buddhists. Pop.: 35 000 (1971).

a·nu+ran (ə'njʊərən) *n.* **1.** any of the vertebrates of the order *Anura* (or *Salientia*), characterized by absence of a tail and very long hind legs specialized for hopping: class *Amphibia* (amphibians). The group includes the frogs and toads. ~*adj.* **2.** of, relating to, or belonging to the order *Anura.* ~Also: **salientian.** [C20: from New Latin *Anura,* from AN- + Greek *oura* tail]

an·u·re·sis (ˌænjʊ'riːsɪs) *n. Pathol.* inability to urinate even though urine is formed by the kidneys and retained in the urinary bladder. Compare **anuria.** [C20: New Latin, from AN- + Greek *ouresis* urination, from *ouron* urine]

an·u+ri·a (ə'njʊərɪə) *n. Pathol.* complete suppression of urine formation, often as the result of a kidney disorder. Compare **anuresis, oliguria.** [C19: from New Latin, from AN- + Greek *ouron* urine]

a·nu+rous (æ'njʊərəs) *adj. Zoology.* lacking a tail; tailless; acaudate. [C19: from AN- + Greek *oura* tail]

a·nus ('eɪnəs) *n.* the excretory opening at the end of the alimentary canal. [C16: from Latin]

An+vers (ɑ̃'vɛr) *n.* the French name for **Antwerp.**

an+vil ('ænvɪl) *n.* **1.** a heavy iron or steel block on which metals are hammered during forging. **2.** any part having a similar shape or function, such as the lower part of a telegraph key. **3.** the fixed jaw of a measurement device against which the piece to be measured is held. **4.** *Anatomy.* the nontechnical name for **incus.** [Old English *anfealt;* related to Old High German *anafalz,* Middle Dutch *anvilte;* see ON, FELT[2]]

anx·i·e·ty (æŋ'zaɪɪtɪ) *n., pl.* **·ties. 1.** a state of uneasiness or tension caused by apprehension of possible future misfortune, danger, etc.; worry. **2.** intense desire; eagerness. **3.** *Psychol.* an intense state of apprehension or worry occurring in a variety of nervous and mental disorders. See also **angst.** [C16: from Latin *anxietas;* see ANXIOUS]

anx+ious ('æŋkʃəs, 'æŋʃəs) *adj.* **1.** worried and tense because of possible misfortune, danger, etc.; uneasy. **2.** fraught with or causing anxiety; worrying; distressing: *an anxious time.* **3.** intensely desirous; eager: *anxious for promotion.* [C17: from Latin *anxius;* related to Latin *angere* to torment; see ANGER, ANGUISH] —**'anx+ious+ly** *adv.* —**'anx+ious+ness** *n.*

an·y ('ɛnɪ) *determiner.* **1. a.** one, some, or several, as specified, no matter how much or many, what kind or quality, etc.: *any cheese in the cupboard is yours; you may take any clothes you like.* **b.** (*as pronoun; functioning as sing. or pl.*): *take any you like.* **2.** (*usually used with a negative*) **a.** even the smallest amount or even one: *I can't stand any noise.* **b.** (*as pronoun; functioning as sing. or pl.*): *don't give her any.* **3.** whatever or whichever; no matter what or which: *any dictionary will do; any time of day.* **4.** an indefinite or unlimited (esp. in the phrases **any amount** or **number**): *any number of friends.* ~*adv.* **5.** (*usually used with a negative*) **a.** (foll. by a comparative adj.) to even the smallest extent: *it isn't any worse now.* **b.** *Not standard.* at all: *he doesn't care any.* [Old English *ǣnig;* related to Old Frisian *ēnig,* Old High German *einag,* Old Norse *einigr* anyone, Latin *ūnicus* unique; see AN[1], ONE]

An+yang ('ɑːn'jɑːŋ) *n.* a town in E China: archaeological site and capital of the Shang dynasty. Pop.: 124 900 (1953).

an·y+bod·y ('ɛnɪˌbɒdɪ, -bədɪ) *pron.* **1.** any person; anyone. **2.** (*usually used with a negative or a question*) a person of any importance: *he isn't anybody in this town.* ~*n., pl.* **+bod·ies. 3.** (often preceded by *just*) any person at random; no matter who.

an·y+how ('ɛnɪˌhaʊ) *adv.* **1.** in any case; at any rate. **2.** in any manner or by any means whatever. **3.** in a haphazard manner; carelessly.

an·y more *or esp. U.S.* **an·y+more** *adv.* any longer; still; now or from now on; nowadays: *he does not work here any more.*

an·y+one ('ɛnɪˌwʌn, -wən) *pron.* **1.** any person; anybody. **2.** (*used with a negative or a question*) a person of any importance: *is he anyone in this town?* **3.** (often preceded by *just*) any person at random; no matter who.

an·y+place ('ɛnɪˌpleɪs) *adv. U.S. informal.* in, at, or to any unspecified place.

an·y+thing ('ɛnɪˌθɪŋ) *pron.* **1.** any object, event, action, etc., whatever: *anything might happen.* ~*n.* **2.** a thing of any kind: *have you anything to declare?* ~*adv.* **3.** in any way: *he wasn't anything like his father.* **4. anything but.** by no means; not in the least: *she was anything but happy.* **5. like anything.** (intensifier; usually euphemistic): *he ran like anything.*

an·y+way ('ɛnɪˌweɪ) *adv.* **1.** in any case; at any rate; nevertheless; anyhow. **2.** in a careless or haphazard manner. **3.** Usually **any way.** in any manner; by any means.

an·y+ways ('ɛnɪˌweɪz) *adv. U.S.* a nonstandard word for **anyway.**

an·y+where ('ɛnɪˌwɛə) *adv.* **1.** in, at, or to any place. **2. get anywhere.** to be successful: *it took three years before he got anywhere.* **3. anywhere from.** any quantity, time, degree, etc., above a specified limit: *he could be anywhere from 40 to 50 years old.*

an·y+wheres ('ɛnɪˌwɛəz) *adv. U.S.* a nonstandard word for **anywhere.**

an·y+wise ('ɛnɪˌwaɪz) *adv. Chiefly U.S.* in any way or manner; at all.

An+zac ('ænzæk) *n.* **1.** (in World War I) a soldier serving with the Australian and New Zealand Army Corps. **2.** (now) any Australian or New Zealand soldier. **3.** the Anzac landing at Gallipoli in 1915.

An+zac Day *n.* 25 April, a public holiday in Australia and New Zealand commemorating the Anzac landing at Gallipoli in 1915.

An+zi·o ('ænzɪˌəʊ; *Italian* 'antsjo) *n.* a port and resort on the W coast of Italy: site of Allied landings in World War II. Pop.: 22 927 (1971).

ANZUS ('ænzəs) *n. acronym for* Australia, New Zealand, and the United States, with reference to the security alliance between them.

A/O *or* **a/o** (accounting, etc.) *abbrev. for* account of.

a.o.b. *or* **A.O.B.** *abbrev. for* any other business.

A-OK *or* **A-o·kay** *adj. Informal, chiefly U.S.* in perfect working order; excellent. [C20: from *a(ll systems) OK*]

A·o·ran+gi (ˌeɪəʊ'ræŋgɪ) *n.* another name for Mount **Cook.**

a·o·rist ('eɪərɪst, 'ɛərɪst) *n. Grammar.* a tense of the verb in classical Greek and in certain other inflected languages, indicating past action without reference to whether the action involved was momentary or continuous. Compare **perfect** (sense 8), **imperfect** (sense 4). [C16: from Greek *aoristos* not limited, from A-[1] + *horistos* restricted, from *horizein* to define] —**ˌa·o·'ris+tic** *adj.* —**ˌa·o·'ris+ti+cal+ly** *adv.*

a·or+ta (eɪ'ɔːtə) *n., pl.* **+tas** *or* **+tae** (-tiː). the main vessel in the arterial network, which conveys oxygen-rich blood from the heart to all parts of the body except the lungs. [C16: from New Latin, from Greek *aortē,* literally: something lifted, from *aeirein* to raise] —**a·'or+tic** *or* **a·'or+tal** *adj.*

A·o·sta (*Italian* a'ɔsta) *n.* a town in NW Italy, in Piedmont: Roman remains. Pop.: 36 906 (1971).

a·ou+dad ('ɑːʊˌdæd) *n.* a wild mountain sheep, *Ammotragus lervia,* of N Africa, having horns curved in a semicircle and long hair covering the neck and forelegs. Also called: **Barbary sheep.** [from French, from Berber *audad*]

ap- *prefix.* variant of **apo-:** *aphelion.*

a.p. *abbrev. for:* **1.** additional premium. **2.** (in prescriptions, etc.) ante prandium. [Latin: before a meal]

A.P. *abbrev. for:* **1.** Air Police. **2.** Associated Press.

a·pace (ə'peɪs) *adv.* quickly; rapidly. [C14: probably from Old French *à pas,* at a (good) pace]

a·pache (ə'pɑːʃ, -'pæʃ; *French* a'paʃ) *n.* a Parisian gangster or ruffian. [from French: APACHE]

A·pach·e (ə'pætʃɪ) *n.* **1.** (*pl.* **A·pach·es** *or* **A·pach·e**) a member of a North American Indian people, formerly nomadic and warlike, inhabiting the southwestern U.S. and N Mexico. **2.** the language of this people, belonging to the Athapascan group of the Na-Dene phylum. [from Mexican Spanish, probably from Zuñi *Apachu,* literally: enemy]

a·pache dance *n.* a fast violent dance in French vaudeville, supposedly between a Parisian gangster and his girl.

ap·a+go+ge (ˌæpə'gəʊdʒɪ) *n.* an indirect proof of a proposition, hypothesis, etc., by showing that its contrary is false, impossible, or absurd. [C18: from Greek *apagōgē* a taking away, from *agein* to lead] —**ap·a+gog+ic** (ˌæpə'gɒdʒɪk) *or* **ˌap·a+'gog·i+cal** *adj.* —**ˌap·a+'gog·i+cal·ly** *adv.*

ap·a+nage ('æpənɪdʒ) *n.* a variant spelling of **appanage.**

a·pa+re·jo *Spanish.* (apa'rexo) *n., pl.* **·jos** (-xos). *Southwestern U.S.* a kind of packsaddle made of stuffed leather cushions. [American Spanish: equipment, from *aparejar* to make ready; see APPAREL]

A·par+ri (æ'pɑːrɪ) *n.* a port in the Philippines, on the N coast of Luzon. Pop.: 40 307 (1970).

a·part (ə'pɑːt) *adj.* (*postpositive*), *adv.* **1.** to pieces or in pieces: *he had the television apart on the floor.* **2.** placed or kept separately or to one side for a particular purpose, reason, etc.; aside (esp. in the phrases **set** *or* **put apart**). **3.** separate in time, place, or position; at a distance: *he stood apart from the group; two points three feet apart.* **4.** not being taken into account; aside: *these difficulties apart, the project ran smoothly.* **5.** individual; distinct; separate: *a race apart.* **6.** separately or independently in use, thought, or function: *considered apart, his reasoning was faulty.* **7. apart from.** (*prep.*) besides; other than. ~See also **take apart, tell apart.** [C14: from Old French *a part* at (the) side]

a·part+heid (ə'pɑːthaɪt, -heɪt) *n.* (in South Africa) the official government policy of racial segregation. [C20: Afrikaans, from *apart* APART + *-heid* -HOOD]

a·part+ment (ə'pɑːtmənt) *n.* **1.** (*often pl.*) any room in a building, usually one of several forming a suite, esp. one that is spacious and well furnished and used as living accommodation, offices, etc. **2. a.** another name (esp. U.S.) for **flat**[2] (sense 1). **b.** (*as modifier*): *apartment building; apartment house.* [C17: from French *appartement,* from Italian *appartamento,* from *appartare* to set on one side, separate]

ap·a+tet+ic (ˌæpə'tɛtɪk) *adj.* of or relating to coloration that disguises and protects an animal. [C19: from Greek *apatētikos* deceitful, from *apateuein* to deceive]

ap·a+thet+ic (ˌæpə'θɛtɪk) *adj.* having or showing little or no emotion; indifferent. [C18: from APATHY + PATHETIC] —**ˌap·a+'thet·i+cal+ly** *adv.*

ap·a+thy ('æpəθɪ) *n.* **1.** absence of interest in or enthusiasm for things generally considered interesting or moving. **2.** absence of emotion. [C17: from Latin, from Greek *apatheia,* from *apathēs* without feeling, from A-[1] + *pathos* feeling]

ap·a·tite ('æpə,taɪt) *n.* a common naturally occurring mineral consisting basically of calcium fluorophosphate or calcium chlorophosphate in hexagonal crystalline form. It is a source of phosphorus and is used in the manufacture of fertilizers. Formula: $Ca_5(F,Cl,OH,\frac{1}{2}CO_3)(PO_4)_3$. [C19: from German *Apatit,* from Greek *apatē* deceit; from its misleading similarity to other minerals]

APC *n.* acetylsalicylic acid, phenacetin, and caffeine; the mixture formerly used in headache and cold tablets.

ape (eɪp) *n.* **1.** any of various primates, esp. those of the family *Pongidae* (see **anthropoid ape**), in which the tail is very short or absent. **2.** (*not in technical use*) any monkey. **3.** an imitator; mimic. **4.** *U.S. informal.* a coarse, clumsy, or rude person. ~*vb.* **5.** (*tr.*) to imitate. [Old English *apa;* related to Old Saxon *ape,* Old Norse *api,* Old High German *affo*] —'**ape**,**like** *adj.*

a·peak (ə'pi:k) *adv., adj. Nautical.* in a vertical or almost vertical position: *with the oars apeak.*

A·pel·doorn ('æpᵊl,dɔ:n; *Dutch* 'a:pəldo:rn) *n.* a town in the Netherlands, in central Gelderland province: nearby is the summer residence of the Dutch royal family. Pop.: 131 768 (1974 est.).

A·pel·les (ə'pɛli:z) *n.* 4th century B.C., Greek painter of mythological subjects, none of whose work survives, his fame resting on the testimony of Pliny and other writers.

ape·man ('eɪp,mæn) *n., pl.* ·**men.** any of various extinct apelike primates thought to have been the forerunners, or closely related to the forerunners, of modern man.

Ap·en·nines ('æpə,naɪnz) *pl. n.* **1.** a mountain range in Italy, extending over 1250 km (800 miles) from the northwest to the southernmost tip of the peninsula. Highest peak: Monte Corno, 2912 m (9554 ft.). **2.** a mountain range lying in the N quadrants of the moon, extending over 950 km along the SE border of the Mare Imbrium and rising to 6200 m.

a·per·çu *French.* (apɛr'sy) *n.* **1.** an outline; summary. **2.** an insight. [from *apercevoir* to PERCEIVE]

a·per·i·ent (ə'pɪərɪənt) *Med.* ~*adj.* **1.** laxative. ~*n.* **2.** a mild laxative. [C17: from Latin *aperīre* to open]

a·pe·ri·od·ic (,eɪpɪərɪ'ɒdɪk) *adj.* **1.** not periodic; not occurring at regular intervals. **2.** *Physics.* **a.** (of a system or instrument) being damped sufficiently to reach equilibrium without oscillation. **b.** (of an oscillation or vibration) not having a regular period. —,**a·pe·ri·'od·i·cal·ly** *adv.* —**a·pe·ri·o·dic·i·ty** (,eɪpɪərɪə'dɪsɪtɪ) *n.*

a·pé·ri·tif (ɑ:,pɛrɪ'ti:f, ə,pɛr-) *n.* an alcoholic drink, esp. a wine, drunk before a meal to whet the appetite. [C19: from French, from Medieval Latin *aperitīvus,* from Latin *aperīre* to open]

ap·er·ture ('æpətʃə) *n.* **1.** a hole, gap, crack, slit, or other opening. **2.** *Physics.* **a.** a usually circular and often variable opening in an optical instrument or device that controls the quantity of radiation entering or leaving it. **b.** the diameter of such an opening. See also **relative aperture.** [C15: from Late Latin *apertūra* opening, from *aperīre* to open]

ap·er·y ('eɪpərɪ) *n., pl.* ·**er·ies.** imitative behaviour; mimicry.

a·pet·al·ous (eɪ'pɛtələs) *adj.* (of flowering plants such as the wood anemone) having no petals. [C18: from New Latin *apetalus,* see A-[1], PETAL] —**a·'pet·al·y** *n.*

a·pex ('eɪpɛks) *n., pl.* **a·pex·es** *or* **a·pi·ces** ('æpɪ,si:z, 'eɪ-). **1.** the highest point; vertex. **2.** the pointed end or tip of something. **3.** a pinnacle or high point, as of a career, etc. **4.** Also called: **solar apex.** *Astronomy.* the point on the celestial sphere, lying in the constellation Hercules, towards which the sun appears to move at a velocity of 7.5 kilometres per second relative to the nearest stars. [C17: from Latin: point]

a·phaer·e·sis *or* **a·pher·e·sis** (ə'fɪərɪsɪs) *n.* the omission of a letter or syllable at the beginning of a word. [C17: via Late Latin from Greek, from *aphairein* to remove]

a·pha·gi·a (ə'feɪdʒɪə) *n. Pathol.* refusal or inability to swallow. [C20: from A-[1] + Greek *phagein* to consume]

aph·a·nite ('æfə,naɪt) *n.* any fine-grained rock, such as a basalt, containing minerals that cannot be distinguished with the naked eye. [C19: from Greek *aphanēs* invisible]

a·pha·si·a (ə'feɪzɪə) *n.* a disorder of the central nervous system characterized by partial or total loss of the ability to communicate, esp. in speech or writing. Compare **alexia.** [C19: via New Latin from Greek, from A-[1] + *-phasia,* from *phanai* to speak]

ap·he·li·on (æp'hi:lɪən, ə'fi:-) *n., pl.* ·**li·a** (-lɪə). the point in its orbit when a planet or comet is at its greatest distance from the sun. Compare **perihelion.** [C17: from New Latin *aphēlium* (with pseudo-Greek ending *-ion*) from AP- + Greek *hēlios* sun] —**ap·'he·li·an** *adj.*

ap·he·li·o·trop·ic (æp,hi:lɪə'trɒpɪk, ə,fi:-) *adj. Biology.* growing in a direction away from the sunlight, as the roots of plants. [C19: see APO-, HELIOTROPIC]

aph·e·sis ('æfɪsɪs) *n.* the gradual disappearance of an unstressed vowel at the beginning of a word, as in *squire* from *esquire.* [C19: from Greek, from *aphienai* to set free, send away] —**a·phet·ic** (ə'fɛtɪk) *adj.* —**a·'phet·i·cal·ly** *adv.*

a·phid ('eɪfɪd) *n.* any of the small homopterous insects of the family *Aphididae,* which feed by sucking the juices from plants. Also called: **plant louse.** See also **greenfly, blackfly.** [C19: back formation from *aphides,* plural of APHIS] —**a·phid·i·an** (ə'fɪdɪən) *adj., n.* —**a·'phid·i·ous** *adj.*

a·phis ('eɪfɪs) *n., pl.* **aph·i·des** ('eɪfɪ,di:z). **1.** any of various aphids constituting the genus *Aphis,* such as the blackfly. **2.** any other aphid. [C18: from New Latin (coined by Linnaeus for obscure reasons)]

a·pho·ni·a (ə'fəʊnɪə) *or* **a·pho·ny** ('æfənɪ) *n.* loss of the voice. [C18: via New Latin from Greek, from A-[1] + *phōnē* sound, voice]

a·phon·ic (ə'fɒnɪk) *adj.* **1.** affected with aphonia. **2.** *Phonetics.* **a.** not representing a spoken sound, as *k* in *know.* **b.** voiceless or devoiced.

aph·o·rism ('æfə,rɪzəm) *n.* a short pithy saying expressing a general truth; maxim. [C16: from Late Latin *aphorismus,* from Greek *aphorismos* definition, from *aphorizein* to define, set limits to, from *horos* boundary] —'**aph·o·rist** *n.*

aph·o·ris·tic (,æfə'rɪstɪk) *adj.* **1.** of, relating to, or resembling an aphorism. **2.** tending to write or speak in aphorisms.

aph·o·rize *or* **aph·o·rise** ('æfə,raɪz) *vb.* (*intr.*) to write or speak in aphorisms.

a·pho·tic (ə'fɒtɪk) *adj.* **1.** characterized by or growing in the absence of light: *an aphotic plant.* **2.** of or relating to the zone of an ocean below about 90m (300 ft.), the lowest level at which photosynthesis can take place. [C20: from A-[1] + *-photic,* from Greek *phōs* light]

aph·ro·dis·i·ac (,æfrə'dɪzɪæk) *n.* **1.** a drug, food, etc., that excites sexual desire. ~*adj.* **2.** exciting or heightening sexual desire. [C18: from Greek *aphrodisiakos,* from *aphrodisios* belonging to APHRODITE]

Aph·ro·di·te (,æfrə'daɪtɪ) *n. Greek myth.* the goddess of love and beauty, daughter of Zeus. Roman counterpart: **Venus.** Also called: **Cytherea.**

aph·tha ('æfθə) *n.* a small ulceration on a mucous membrane, as in thrush, caused by a fungal infection. [C17: via Latin from Greek: mouth-sore, thrush]

a·phyl·lous (ə'fɪləs) *adj.* (of plants) having no leaves. [C19: from New Latin *aphyllus,* from Greek *aphullos,* from A-[1] + *phullon* leaf] —**a·'phyl·ly** *n.*

A·pi·a (æ'pɪə, 'æpɪə) *n.* the capital of Western Samoa, a port on the N coast of Upolu. Pop.: 28 880 (1970 est.).

a·pi·an ('eɪpɪən) *adj.* of, relating to, or resembling bees. [C19: from Latin *apiānus,* from *apis* bee]

a·pi·ar·i·an (,eɪpɪ'ɛərɪən) *adj.* of or relating to the breeding and care of bees.

a·pi·a·rist ('eɪpɪərɪst) *n.* a person who studies or keeps bees.

a·pi·ar·y ('eɪpɪərɪ) *n., pl.* ·**ar·ies.** a place where bees are kept, usually in beehives. [C17: from Latin *apiārium* from *apis* bee]

ap·i·cal ('æpɪkᵊl, 'eɪ-) *adj.* **1.** of, at, or being the apex. **2.** of or denoting a consonant articulated with the tip of the tongue, such as (t) or (d). [C19: from New Latin *apicālis,* from Latin: APEX] —'**ap·i·cal·ly** *adv.*

ap·i·ces ('æpɪ,si:z, 'eɪ-) *n.* a plural of **apex.**

a·pic·u·late (ə'pɪkjʊlɪt, -,leɪt) *adj.* (of leaves) ending in a short sharp point. [C19: from New Latin *apiculātus,* from *apiculus* a short point, from APEX]

a·pi·cul·ture ('eɪpɪ,kʌltʃə) *n.* the breeding and care of bees. [C19: from Latin *apis* bee + CULTURE] —,**a·pi·'cul·tur·al** *adj.* —,**a·pi·'cul·tur·ist** *n.*

a·piece (ə'pi:s) *adv.* for, to, or from each one: *they were given two apples apiece.*

à pied *French.* (a 'pje) *adv., adj.* (*postpositive*) on foot.

Ap·i·e·zon (,æpɪ'eɪzɒn) *adj. Trademark.* designating any of a number of hydrocarbon oils, greases, or waxes, characterized by a low vapour pressure and used in vacuum equipment.

A·pis ('ɑ:pɪs) *n.* (in ancient Egypt) a sacred bull worshipped at Memphis.

ap·ish ('eɪpɪʃ) *adj.* **1.** stupid; foolish. **2.** resembling an ape. **3.** slavishly imitative. —'**ap·ish·ly** *adv.* —'**ap·ish·ness** *n.*

a·piv·or·ous (eɪ'pɪvərəs) *adj.* eating bees: *apivorous birds.* [C19: from Latin *apis* bee + -VOROUS]

a·pla·cen·tal (,eɪplə'sɛntᵊl, ,æplə-) *adj.* (of monotremes and marsupials) having no placenta.

ap·la·nat·ic (,æplə'nætɪk) *adj.* (of a lens or mirror) free from spherical aberration. [C18: from Greek *aplanētos* prevented from wandering, from A-[1] + *planētos,* from *planaein* to wander] —,**ap·la·'nat·i·cal·ly** *adv.*

a·plan·o·spore (ə'pleɪnəʊ,spɔ:) *n.* a nonmotile asexual spore produced by certain algae and fungi. [C20: from A-[1] + Greek *planos* wandering + SPORE]

a·pla·si·a (ə'pleɪzɪə) *n. Pathol.* congenital absence or abnormal development of an organ or part. [C19: New Latin, from A-[1] + *-plasia,* from Greek *plassein* to form]

a·plas·tic (eɪ'plæstɪk) *adj.* **1.** relating to or characterized by aplasia. **2.** failing to develop into new tissue; defective in the regeneration of tissue, as of blood cells: *aplastic anaemia.*

a·plen·ty (ə'plɛntɪ) *adj.* (*postpositive*), *adv.* in plenty.

ap·lite ('æplaɪt) *or* **hap·lite** *n.* a light-coloured fine-grained acid igneous rock with a sugary texture, consisting of quartz and feldspars. [C19: from German *Aplit,* from Greek *haploos* simple + -ITE[1]] —**ap·lit·ic** (æp'lɪtɪk) *or* **hap·'lit·ic** *adj.*

a·plomb (ə'plɒm) *n.* equanimity, self-confidence, or self-possession. [C18: from French: rectitude, uprightness, from *à plomb* according to the plumbline, vertically]

ap·noe·a *or U.S.* **ap·ne·a** (æp'nɪə) *n.* a temporary inability to breathe. [C18: from New Latin, from Greek *apnoia,* from A-[1] + *pnein* to breathe]

A·po ('ɑ:pəʊ) *n.* the highest mountain in the Philippines, on SE Mindanao: active volcano with three peaks. Height: 2954 m (9690 ft.).

ap·o- *or* **ap-** *prefix.* **1.** away from; off: *apogee.* **2.** indicating separation of: *apocarpous.* **3.** indicating a lack or absence of: *apogamy.* **4.** indicating derivation from or relationship to: *apomorphine.* [from Greek *apo* away, off]

Apoc. *abbrev. for:* **1.** Apocalypse. **2.** Apocrypha or Apocryphal.

a·poc·a·lypse (ə'pɒkəlɪps) *n.* **1.** a prophetic disclosure or revelation. **2.** an event of great importance, violence, etc., like the events described in the Apocalypse. [C13: from Late Latin *apocalypsis,* from Greek *apokalupsis,* from *apokaluptein* to disclose, from APO- + *kaluptein* to hide]

A·poc·a·lypse (ə'pɒkəlɪps) *n. Bible.* (in the Vulgate and Douay versions of the Bible) the Book of Revelations.

a·poc·a·lyp·tic (əˌpɒkə'lɪptɪk) *adj.* **1.** outstanding in revelation, prophecy, or significance. **2.** of or like an apocalypse. —**aˌpoc·a·'lyp·ti·cal·ly** *adv.*

ap·o·carp ('æpəˌkɑːp) *n.* an apocarpous gynoecium or fruit.

ap·o·car·pous (ˌæpə'kɑːpəs) *adj.* (of the ovaries of flowering plants such as the buttercup) consisting of separate carpels. Compare **syncarpous.**

ap·o·chro·mat (ˌæpə'krəʊmæt) *or* **ap·o·chro·mat·ic lens** *n.* a lens, consisting of three or more elements of different types of glass, that is designed to bring light of three colours to the same focal point, thus reducing its chromatic aberration. Compare **achromat.**

ap·o·chro·mat·ic (ˌæpəkrə'mætɪk) *adj.* (of a lens) almost free from spherical and chromatic aberration. —**ap·o·chro·ma·tism** (ˌæpə'krəʊməˌtɪzəm) *n.*

a·poc·o·pate (ə'pɒkəˌpeɪt) *vb.* (*tr.*) to omit the final sound or sounds of (a word). —**aˌpoc·o·'pa·tion** *n.*

a·poc·o·pe (ə'pɒkəpɪ) *n.* omission of the final sound or sounds of a word. [C16: via Late Latin from Greek *apokopē,* from *apokoptein* to cut off]

Apocr. *abbrev. for* Apocrypha.

ap·o·crine ('æpəkraɪn, -krɪn) *adj.* denoting a type of glandular secretion in which part of the secreting cell is lost with the secretion, as in mammary glands. Compare **merocrine, holocrine.** [C20: from APO- + *-crine,* from Greek *krinein* to separate]

A·poc·ry·pha (ə'pɒkrɪfə) *n.* **the.** (*functioning as sing. or pl.*) **1.** the 14 books included as an appendix to the Old Testament in the Septuagint and the Vulgate but not included in the Hebrew canon. They are not printed in Protestant versions of the Bible. **2.** *R.C. Church.* another name for the **Pseudepigrapha.** [C14: via Late Latin *apocrypha* (*scripta*) hidden (writings), from Greek, from *apokruptein* to hide away]

a·poc·ry·phal (ə'pɒkrɪfəl) *adj.* **1.** of questionable authenticity. **2.** (*sometimes cap.*) of or like the Apocrypha. **3.** untrue; counterfeit. —**a·'poc·ry·phal·ly** *adv.*

a·poc·y·na·ceous (əˌpɒsɪ'neɪʃəs) *adj.* of, relating to, or belonging to the *Apocynaceae,* a family of mostly tropical flowering plants with latex in their stems, including the dogbane, periwinkle, oleander, and some lianas. [C19: from New Latin *Apocynum* type genus, from Latin: dogbane, from Greek *apokunon,* from *kuōn* dog]

a·po·cyn·thi·on (ˌæpə'sɪnθɪən) *n.* the point at which a spacecraft in lunar orbit is farthest from the moon. Compare **apolune, pericynthion.** [C20: from APO- (away) + *cynthion,* from Latin *Cynthia* goddess of the moon]

ap·o·dal ('æpədᵊl) *adj.* (of snakes, eels, etc.) without feet; having no obvious hind limbs or pelvic fins. [C18: from Greek *apous* from A-[1] + *pous* foot]

ap·o·dic·tic (ˌæpə'dɪktɪk) *or* **ap·o·deic·tic** (ˌæpə'daɪktɪk) *adj.* **1.** unquestionably true by virtue of demonstration. **2.** *Logic.* necessarily true. [C17: from Latin *apodīcticus,* from Greek *apodeiktikos* clearly demonstrating, from *apodeiknunai* to demonstrate] —ˌ**ap·o·'dic·ti·cal·ly** *or* ˌ**ap·o·'deic·ti·cal·ly** *adv.*

a·pod·o·sis (ə'pɒdəsɪs) *n., pl.* **-ses** (-ˌsiːz). *Grammar.* the main clause of a conditional sentence, as *then I would go* in *If he were to ask me, then I would go.* Compare **protasis.** [C17: via Late Latin from Greek: a returning or answering (clause), from *apodidonai* to give back]

ap·o·en·zyme (ˌæpəʊ'ɛnzaɪm) *n.* a protein component that together with a coenzyme forms an enzyme.

a·pog·a·my (ə'pɒgəmɪ) *n.* a type of reproduction, occurring in some ferns, in which the sporophyte develops from the gametophyte without fusion of gametes. —**ap·o·gam·ic** (ˌæpə'gæmɪk) *adj.* —**a·'pog·a·mous** *adj.*

ap·o·gee ('æpəˌdʒiː) *n.* **1.** the point in its orbit around the earth when the moon or an artificial satellite is at its greatest distance from the earth. Compare **perigee. 2.** the highest point. [C17: from New Latin *apogaeum* (influenced by French *apogée*), from Greek *apogaion,* from *apogaios* away from the earth, from APO- + *gaia* earth] —ˌ**ap·o·'ge·an** *adj.*

ap·o·ge·ot·ro·pism (ˌæpədʒɪ'ɒtrəˌpɪzəm) *n.* negative geotropism, as shown by plant stems. [C19: from Greek *apogaios* away from the earth + *tropos* a turn] —**ap·o·ge·o·trop·ic** (ˌæpəˌdʒɪə'trɒpɪk) *adj.*

a·po·lit·i·cal (ˌeɪpə'lɪtɪkᵊl) *adj.* politically neutral; without political attitudes, content, or bias.

A·pol·li·naire (*French* apɔli'nɛːr) *n.* **Guil·laume** (gi'joːm). pen name of *Wilhelm Apollinaris de Kostrowitzki.* 1880–1918, French poet, novelist, and dramatist, regarded as a precursor of surrealism; author of *Alcoöls* (1913) and *Calligrammes* (1918).

A·pol·li·naris (əˌpɒlɪ'nɛərɪs) *n.* an effervescent mineral water. [C19: named after *Apollinarisburg,* near Bonn, Germany]

a·pol·lo (ə'pɒləʊ) *n., pl.* **-los.** a strikingly handsome youth.

A·pol·lo[1] (ə'pɒləʊ) *n. Classical myth.* the god of light, poetry, music, healing, and prophecy: son of Zeus and Leto.

A·pol·lo[2] (ə'pɒləʊ) *n.* any of a series of manned U.S. spacecraft designed to explore the moon and surrounding space. **Apollo 11** made the first moon landing in July 1969.

Ap·ol·lo·ni·an (ˌæpə'ləʊnɪən) *adj.* **1.** of or relating to Apollo or the cult of Apollo. **2.** (*sometimes not cap.*) (in the philosophy of Nietzsche) denoting or relating to the set of static qualities that encompass form, reason, harmony, sobriety, etc. **3.** (*often not cap.*) harmonious; serene; ordered. ~Compare **Dionysian.**

A·pol·lyon (ə'pɒljən) *n. New Testament.* the destroyer, a name given to the Devil (Revelation 9:11). [C14: via Late Latin from Greek, from *apollunai* to destroy totally]

a·pol·o·get·ic (əˌpɒlə'dʒɛtɪk) *adj.* **1.** expressing or anxious to make apology; contrite. **2.** protecting or defending in speech or writing. —**aˌpol·o·'get·i·cal·ly** *adv.*

a·pol·o·get·ics (əˌpɒlə'dʒɛtɪks) *n.* (*functioning as sing.*) **1.** the branch of theology concerned with the defence and rational justification of Christianity. **2.** a defensive method of argument.

ap·o·lo·gi·a (ˌæpə'ləʊdʒɪə) *n.* a formal written defence of a cause or one's beliefs or conduct.

a·pol·o·gist (ə'pɒlədʒɪst) *n.* a person who offers a defence by argument.

a·pol·o·gize *or* **a·pol·o·gise** (ə'pɒləˌdʒaɪz) *vb.* (*intr.*) **1.** to express or make an apology; acknowledge failings or faults. **2.** to defend formally in speech or writing. —**a·'pol·o·ˌgiz·er** *or* **a·'pol·o·ˌgis·er** *n.*

ap·o·logue ('æpəˌlɒg) *n.* an allegory or moral fable. [C17: from Latin, from Greek *apologos*]

a·pol·o·gy (ə'pɒlədʒɪ) *n., pl.* **-gies. 1.** a verbal or written expression of regret or contrition for a fault or failing. **2.** a poor substitute or offering. **3.** another word for **apologia.** [C16: from Old French *apologie,* from Late Latin *apologia,* from Greek: a verbal defence, from APO- + *logos* speech]

ap·o·lune ('æpəˌluːn) *n.* the point in a lunar orbit when a spacecraft is at its greatest distance from the moon. Compare **apocynthion, perilune.** [C20: from APO- + *-lune,* from Latin *lūna* moon]

ap·o·mict ('æpəˌmɪkt) *n.* an organism, esp. a plant, produced by apomixis.

ap·o·mix·is (ˌæpə'mɪksɪs) *n., pl.* **-mix·es** (-'mɪksiːz). any of several types of asexual reproduction, such as parthenogenesis and apogamy, in which fertilization does not take place. Compare **amphimixis.** [C20: New Latin, from Greek APO- + *mixis* a mixing] —ˌ**ap·o·'mic·tic** *adj.*

ap·o·mor·phine (ˌæpə'mɔːfiːn, -fɪn) *n.* a white crystalline alkaloid, derived from morphine but less strong in action, that is used medicinally as an emetic, expectorant, and hypnotic. Formula: $C_{17}H_{17}NO_2$.

ap·o·neu·ro·sis (ˌæpənjʊə'rəʊsɪs) *n., pl.* **-ses** (-siːz). *Anatomy.* a white fibrous sheet of tissue by which certain muscles are attached to bones. [C17: via New Latin from Greek, from *aponeurousthai* to change into a tendon, from *neuron tendon*] —**ap·o·neu·rot·ic** (ˌæpənjʊə'rɒtɪk) *adj.*

ap·o·pemp·tic (ˌæpə'pɛmptɪk) *Archaic.* ~*adj.* **1.** relating to leave-taking or farewell; valedictory. ~*n.* **2.** a speech or poem made on departure. [C18: from Greek *apopemptikos* concerning dismissal, from *apopempein* to dismiss, from *pempein* to send]

a·poph·a·sis (ə'pɒfəˌsɪs) *n. Rhetoric.* the device of mentioning a subject by stating that it will not be mentioned: *I shall not discuss his cowardice or his treachery.* [C17: via Latin from Greek: denial, from APO- + *phanai* to say]

ap·o·phthegm *or* **ap·o·thegm** ('æpəˌθɛm) *n.* a short cryptic remark containing some general or generally accepted truth; maxim. [C16: from Greek *apophthegma,* from *apophthengesthai* to speak one's opinion frankly, from *phthengesthai* to speak] —**ap·o·phtheg·mat·ic** *or* **ap·o·theg·mat·ic** (ˌæpəθɛg'mætɪk) *adj.*

a·poph·y·ge (ə'pɒfɪdʒɪ) *n. Architect.* the outward curve at each end of the shaft of a column, adjoining the base or capital. Also called: **hypophyge.** [C16: from Greek *apophugē,* literally: escape, from *apopheugein* to escape from]

a·poph·yl·lite (ə'pɒfɪˌlaɪt, ˌæpə'fɪlaɪt) *n.* a white, colourless, pink, or green mineral consisting of a hydrated silicate of calcium, potassium, and fluorine in tetragonal crystalline form. It occurs in cracks in volcanic rocks. Formula: $KCa_4FSi_4O_{10}.8H_2O$. [C19: from French, from APO- + Greek *phullon* leaf + -ITE[1]; referring to its tendency to exfoliate]

a·poph·y·sis (ə'pɒfɪsɪs) *n., pl.* **-ses** (-ˌsiːz). **1.** a process, outgrowth, or swelling from part of an animal or plant. **2.** *Geology.* a tapering offshoot from a larger igneous intrusive mass. [C17: via New Latin from Greek *apophusis* a sideshoot, from APO- + *phusis growth*] —**a·poph·y·sate** (ə'pɒfɪsɪt, -seɪt) *adj.* —**a·poph·y·si·al** (ˌæpə'fɪzɪəl) *adj.*

ap·o·plec·tic (ˌæpə'plɛktɪk) *adj.* **1.** of or relating to apoplexy. **2.** *Informal.* furious. ~*n.* **3.** a person having apoplexy. —ˌ**ap·o·'plec·ti·cal·ly** *adv.*

ap·o·plex·y ('æpəˌplɛksɪ) *n.* sudden loss of consciousness, often followed by paralysis, caused by rupture or occlusion of a blood vessel in the brain. [C14: from Old French *apoplexie,* from Late Latin *apoplēxia,* from Greek: from *apoplēssein* to cripple by a stroke, from *plēssein* to strike]

a·port (ə'pɔːt) *adv., adj.* (*postpositive*) *Nautical.* on or towards the port side: *with the helm aport.*

ap·o·se·mat·ic (ˌæpəsɪ'mætɪk) *adj.* (of the coloration of certain distasteful or poisonous animals) characterized by bright conspicuous markings, which predators recognize and learn to avoid; warning. [C19: from APO- + Greek *sēma* sign]

ap·o·si·o·pe·sis (ˌæpəʊˌsaɪə'piːsɪs) *n., pl.* **-ses** (-siːz). *Rhetoric.* the device of suddenly breaking off in the middle of a sentence as if unwilling to continue. [C16: via Late Latin from Greek, from *aposiōpaein* to be totally silent, from *siōpaein* to be silent] —**ap·o·si·o·pet·ic** (ˌæpəʊˌsaɪə'pɛtɪk) *adj.*

a·po·spor·y ('æpəˌspɔ:rɪ) *n. Botany.* development of the gametophyte from the sporophyte without the formation of spores. [C19: from APO- + SPORE + -Y[1]]

a·pos·ta·sy (ə'pɒstəsɪ) *n., pl.* **·sies.** abandonment of one's religious faith, party, a cause, etc. [C14: from Church Latin *apostasia,* from Greek *apostasis* desertion, from *apostanai* to stand apart from, desert]

a·pos·tate (ə'pɒsteɪt, -tɪt) *n.* **1.** a person who abandons his religion, party, cause, etc. ~*adj.* **2.** guilty of apostasy. —**ap·o·stat·i·cal** (ˌæpə'stætɪkᵊl) *adj.*

a·pos·ta·tize *or* **a·pos·ta·tise** (ə'pɒstəˌtaɪz) *vb.* (*intr.*) to forsake or abandon one's belief, faith, or allegiance.

a pos·te·ri·o·ri (eɪ pɒsˌtɛrɪ'ɔ:raɪ, -rɪ, ɑ:) *adj. Logic.* **1.** relating to or involving inductive reasoning from particular facts or effects to a general principle. **2.** derived from or requiring evidence for its validation or support; empirical; open to revision. ~Compare **a priori, synthetic** (sense 4). [C18: from Latin, literally: from the latter (that is, from effect to cause)]

a·pos·til (ə'pɒstɪl) *n.* a marginal note. [C16: from French *apostille,* from Old French *apostiller* to make marginal notes, from Medieval Latin *postilla,* probably from Latin *post illa* (*verba*) after those (words)]

a·pos·tle (ə'pɒsᵊl) *n.* **1.** (*often cap.*) one of the 12 disciples chosen by Christ to preach his gospel. **2.** any prominent Christian missionary, esp. one who first converts a nation or people. **3.** an ardent early supporter of a cause, reform movement, etc. **4.** *Mormon Church.* a member of a council of twelve officials appointed to administer and preside over the Church. [Old English *apostol,* from Church Latin *apostolus,* from Greek *apostolos* a messenger, from *apostellein* to send forth]

A·pos·tles' Creed *n.* a concise statement of Christian beliefs dating from about 500 A.D., traditionally ascribed to the Apostles.

a·pos·tle spoon *n.* a silver spoon with a figure of one of the Apostles on the handle.

a·pos·to·late (ə'pɒstəlɪt, -ˌleɪt) *n.* the office, authority, or mission of an apostle.

ap·os·tol·ic (ˌæpə'stɒlɪk) *adj.* **1.** of, relating to, deriving from, or contemporary with the Apostles. **2.** of or relating to the teachings or practice of the Apostles. **3.** of or relating to the pope regarded as chief successor of the Apostles. —ˌ**ap·os·'tol·i·cal** *adj.* —ˌ**ap·os·'tol·i·cal·ly** *adv.*

ap·os·tol·ic del·e·gate *n. R.C. Church.* a representative of the pope sent to countries that do not have full or regular diplomatic relations with the Holy See.

Ap·os·tol·ic Fa·thers *pl. n.* the Fathers of the early Church who immediately followed the Apostles.

Ap·os·tol·ic See *n.* **1.** *R.C. Church.* the see of the pope regarded as the successor to Saint Peter. **2.** (*often not caps.*) a see established by one of the Apostles.

Ap·os·tol·ic suc·ces·sion *n.* the doctrine that the authority of Christian bishops derives from the Apostles through an unbroken line of consecration.

a·pos·tro·phe[1] (ə'pɒstrəfɪ) *n.* the punctuation mark ' used to indicate the omission of a letter or number, such as *he's* for *he has* or *he is,* also used in English to form the possessive, as in *John's father* and *the houses' chimneys.* [C17: from Late Latin, from Greek *apostrophos* mark of elision, from *apostrephein* to turn away]

a·pos·tro·phe[2] (ə'pɒstrəfɪ) *n. Rhetoric.* a digression from a discourse, esp. an address to an imaginary or absent person or a personification. [C16: from Latin *apostrophē,* from Greek: a turning away, digression] —**ap·o·stroph·ic** (ˌæpə'strɒfɪk) *adj.*

a·pos·tro·phize *or* **a·pos·tro·phise** (ə'pɒstrəˌfaɪz) *vb. Rhetoric.* to address an apostrophe to.

a·poth·e·car·ies' meas·ure *n.* a system of liquid volume measure used in pharmacy in which 60 minims equal 1 fluid drachm, 8 fluid drachms equal 1 fluid ounce, and 20 fluid ounces equal 1 pint.

a·poth·e·car·ies' weight *n.* a system of weights formerly used in pharmacy based on the Troy ounce, which contains 480 grains. 1 grain is equal to 0.065 gram.

a·poth·e·car·y (ə'pɒθɪkərɪ) *n., pl.* **·car·ies.** **1.** an archaic word for **chemist. 2.** *Law.* a chemist licensed by the Society of Apothecaries of London to prescribe, prepare, and sell drugs. [C14: from Old French *apotecaire,* from Late Latin *apothēcārius* warehouseman, from *apothēca,* from Greek *apothēkē* storehouse]

ap·o·the·ci·um (ˌæpə'θi:sɪəm) *n., pl.* **·ci·a** (-sɪə). *Botany.* a cup-shaped structure that contains the asci; a type of ascocarp. [C19: from New Latin, from APO- + Greek *thēkion* a little case] —**ap·o·the·ci·al** (ˌæpə'θi:sɪəl) *adj.*

ap·o·thegm ('æpəˌθɛm) *n.* a variant spelling of **apophthegm.**

ap·o·them ('æpəˌθɛm) *n.* the perpendicular line or distance from the centre of a regular polygon to any of its sides. [C20: from APO- + Greek *thema,* from TITHENAI to place]

a·poth·e·o·sis (əˌpɒθɪ'əʊsɪs) *n., pl.* **·ses** (-si:z). **1.** the elevation of a person to the rank of a god; deification. **2.** glorification of a person or thing. **3.** a glorified ideal. [C17: via Late Latin from Greek: deification, from *theos* god]

a·poth·e·o·size *or* **a·poth·e·o·sise** (ə'pɒθɪəˌsaɪz) *vb.* (*tr.*) **1.** to deify. **2.** to glorify or idealize.

ap·o·tro·pa·ic (ˌæpəʊtrə'peɪɪk) *adj.* preventing or intended to prevent evil. [C19: from Greek *apotropaios* turning away (evil), from *apotrepein;* see APO-, TROPE]

app. *abbrev. for:* **1.** apparatus. **2.** appendix (of a book). **3.** applied. **4.** appointed. **5.** apprentice. **6.** approved. **7.** approximate.

ap·pal *or U.S.* **ap·pall** (ə'pɔ:l) *vb.* **·pals, ·pal·ling, ·palled** *or U.S.* **·palls, ·pal·ling, ·palled.** (*tr.*) to fill with horror; shock or dismay. [C14: from Old French *appalir* to turn pale]

Ap·pa·la·chi·a (ˌæpə'leɪtʃɪə) *n.* a highland region of the eastern U.S., containing the Appalachian Mountains, extending from Pennsylvania to Alabama.

Ap·pa·la·chi·an (ˌæpə'leɪtʃɪən) *adj.* **1.** of, from, or relating to the Appalachian Mountains. **2.** *Geology.* of or relating to an episode of mountain building in the late Palaeozoic era during which the Appalachian Mountains were formed.

Ap·pa·la·chi·an Moun·tains *or* **Ap·pa·la·chi·ans** *pl. n.* a mountain system of E North America, extending from Quebec province in Canada to central Alabama: contains rich deposits of anthracite, bitumen, and iron ore. Highest peak: Mount Mitchell, 2038 m (6684 ft.).

ap·pal·ling (ə'pɔ:lɪŋ) *adj.* causing extreme dismay, horror, or revulsion. —**ap·'pal·ling·ly** *adv.*

Ap·pa·loo·sa (ˌæpə'lu:sə) *n.* a breed of horse, originally from America, typically having a spotted rump. [C19: perhaps from *Palouse,* river in Idaho]

ap·pa·nage *or* **ap·a·nage** ('æpənɪdʒ) *n.* **1.** land or other provision granted by a king for the support of a member of the royal family, esp. a younger son. **2.** a natural or customary accompaniment or perquisite, as to a job or position. [C17: from Old French, from Medieval Latin *appanāgium,* from *appanāre* to provide for, from Latin *pānis* bread]

ap·pa·rat·us (ˌæpə'reɪtəs) *n., pl.* **·rat·us** *or* **·rat·us·es. 1.** a collection of instruments, machines, tools, parts, or other equipment used for a particular purpose. **2.** a machine having a specific function: *breathing apparatus.* **3.** the means by which something operates; organization: *the apparatus of government.* **4.** *Anatomy.* any group of organs having a specific function. [C17: from Latin, from *apparāre* to make ready]

ap·pa·rat·us crit·i·cus ('krɪtɪkəs) *n.* textual notes, list of variant readings, etc., relating to a document, esp. in a scholarly edition of a text. [Latin: critical apparatus]

ap·par·el (ə'pærəl) *n.* **1.** something that covers or adorns, esp. outer garments or clothing. **2.** *Nautical.* a vessel's gear and equipment. ~*vb.* **·els, ·el·ling, ·elled** *or U.S.* **·els, ·el·ing, ·eled. 3.** *Archaic.* (*tr.*) to clothe, adorn, etc. [C13: from Old French *apareillier* to make ready, from Vulgar Latin *apparicu-lāre* (unattested), from Latin *apparāre,* from *parāre* to prepare]

ap·par·ent (ə'pærənt, ə'pɛər-) *adj.* **1.** readily seen or understood; evident; obvious. **2.** (*usually prenominal*) seeming, as opposed to real: *his apparent innocence belied his complicity in the crime.* **3.** *Physics.* as observed but discounting such factors as the motion of the observer, changes in the environment, etc. Compare **true** (sense 9). [C14: from Latin *appārēns,* from *appārēre* to APPEAR] —**ap·'par·ent·ly** *adv.* —**ap·'par·ent·ness** *n.*

ap·par·ent mag·ni·tude *n.* another name for **magnitude** (sense 4).

ap·pa·ri·tion (ˌæpə'rɪʃən) *n.* **1.** an appearance, esp. of a ghost or ghostlike figure. **2.** the figure so appearing; phantom; spectre. **3.** the act of appearing or being visible. [C15: from Late Latin *appāritiō,* from Latin: attendance, from *appārēre* to APPEAR]

ap·par·i·tor (ə'pærɪtə) *n.* an officer who summons witnesses and executes the orders of an ecclesiastical and (formerly) a civil court. [C15: from Latin: public servant, from *appārēre* to APPEAR]

ap·pas·sio·na·to (əˌpæsjə'nɑ:təʊ) *adj., adv. Music.* in an impassioned manner.

ap·peal (ə'pi:l) *n.* **1.** a request for relief, aid, etc. **2.** the power to attract, please, stimulate, or interest: *a dress with appeal.* **3.** an application or resort to another person or authority, esp. a higher one, as for a decision or confirmation of a decision. **4.** *Law.* **a.** the judicial review by a superior court of the decision of a lower tribunal. **b.** a request for such review. **c.** the right to such review. **5.** *Cricket.* a verbal request to the umpire from one or more members of the fielding side to declare a batsman out. **6.** *English law.* (formerly) a formal charge or accusation: *appeal of felony.* ~*vb.* **7.** (*intr.*) to make an earnest request for relief, support, etc. **8.** (*intr.*) to attract, please, stimulate, or interest. **9.** *Law.* to apply to a superior court to review (a case or particular issue decided by a lower tribunal). **10.** (*intr.*) to resort to, as for a decision or confirmation of a decision. **11.** (*intr.*) *Cricket.* to ask the umpire to declare a batsman out. **12.** (*intr.*) to challenge the umpire's or referee's decision. [C14: from Old French *appeler,* from Latin *appellāre* to entreat (literally: to approach), from *pellere* to push, drive] —**ap·'peal·a·ble** *adj.* —**ap·'peal·er** *n.* —**ap·'peal·ing·ly** *adv.*

ap·pear (ə'pɪə) *vb.* (*intr.*) **1.** to come into sight or view. **2.** (*copula; may take an infinitive*) to seem or look: *the evidence appears to support you.* **3.** to be plain or clear, as after further evidence, etc.: *it appears you were correct after all.* **4.** to develop or come into being; occur: *faults appeared during testing.* **5.** to become publicly available; be published: *his biography appeared last month.* **6.** to perform or act: *he has appeared in many London productions.* **7.** to be present in court before a magistrate or judge: *he appeared on two charges of theft.* [C13: from Old French *aparoir,* from Latin *appārēre* to become visible, attend upon, from *pārēre* to appear]

ap·pear·ance (ə'pɪərəns) *n.* **1.** the act or an instance of appearing, as to the eye, before the public, etc. **2.** the outward or visible aspect of a person or thing: *her appearance was stunning; it has the appearance of powdered graphite.* **3.** an outward show; pretence: *he gave an appearance of working* *hard.* **4.** (*often pl.*) one of the outward signs or indications by which a person or thing is assessed: *first appearances are deceptive.* **5.** *Law.* **a.** the formal attendance in court of a party in an action. **b.** formal notice that a party or his legal representative intends to maintain or contest the issue: *to enter an appearance.* **6.** *Philosophy.* **a.** the outward or phenomenal manifestation of things. **b.** the world as revealed by the senses, as opposed to its real nature. Compare **reality** (sense 4). **7. keep up appearances.** to maintain the public impression of well-being or normality. **8. put in** *or* **make an appearance.** to come or attend briefly, as out of politeness. **9. to all appearances.** to the extent that can easily be judged; apparently.

ap+pease (ə'pi:z) *vb.* (*tr.*) **1.** to calm, pacify, or soothe, esp. by acceding to the demands of. **2.** to satisfy or quell (an appetite or thirst, etc.). [C16: from Old French *apaisier,* from *pais* peace, from Latin *pax*] **—ap+'peas+a·ble** *adj.* **—ap+'peas+er** *n.*

ap+pease+ment (ə'pi:zmənt) *n.* **1.** the policy of acceding to the demands of a potentially hostile nation in the hope of maintaining peace. **2.** the act of appeasing.

ap+pel (ə'pɛl; *French* a'pɛl) *n. Fencing.* **1.** a stamp of the foot, used to warn of one's intent to attack. **2.** a sharp blow with the blade made to procure an opening. [from French: challenge]

Ap·pel (*Dutch* 'apəl) *n.* **Ka·rel** ('ka:rəl). born 1921, Dutch abstract expressionist painter.

ap+pel+lant (ə'pɛlənt) *n.* **1.** a person who appeals. **2.** *Law.* the party who appeals to a higher court from the decision of a lower tribunal. *~adj.* **3.** *Law.* another word for **appellate.** [C14: from Old French; see APPEAL]

ap+pel+late (ə'pɛlɪt) *adj. Law.* **1.** of or relating to appeals. **2.** (of a tribunal) having jurisdiction to review cases on appeal and to reverse decisions of inferior courts. [C18: from Latin *appellātus* summoned, from *appellāre* to APPEAL]

ap+pel+la+tion (ˌæpɪ'leɪʃən) *n.* **1.** an identifying name or title. **2.** the act of naming or giving a title to.

ap+pel+la+tive (ə'pɛlətɪv) *n.* **1.** an identifying name or title; appellation. **2.** *Grammar.* another word for **common noun.** *~adj.* **3.** of or relating to a name or title. **4.** (of a proper noun) used as a common noun. **—ap+'pel+la+tive+ly** *adv.*

ap+pel+lee (ˌæpɛ'li:) *n. Law,* a person who is accused or appealed against. [C16: from Old French *apele* summoned; see APPEAL]

ap+pend (ə'pɛnd) *vb.* (*tr.*) **1.** to add as a supplement: *to append a footnote.* **2.** to attach; hang on. [C15: from Late Latin *appendere* to hang (something) from, from Latin *pendere* to hang]

ap+pend+age (ə'pɛndɪdʒ) *n.* **1.** an ancillary or secondary part attached to a main part; adjunct. **2.** *Zoology.* any organ that projects from the trunk of animals such as arthropods. **3.** *Botany.* any subsidiary part of a plant, such as a branch or leaf.

ap+pen+dant (ə'pɛndənt) *adj.* **1.** attached, affixed, or added. **2.** attendant or associated as an accompaniment or result. **3.** a less common word for **pendent. 4.** *Law.* relating to another right. *~n.* **5.** a person or thing attached or added. **6.** *Property law.* a subordinate right or interest, esp. in or over land, attached to a greater interest and automatically passing with the sale of the latter.

ap+pen+di+cec+to+my (əˌpɛndɪ'sɛktəmɪ) *or esp. U.S.* **ap+pen+dec+to+my** (ˌæpən'dɛktəmɪ) *n., pl.* **+mies.** surgical removal of any appendage, esp. the vermiform appendix.

ap+pen+di+ci+tis (əˌpɛndɪ'saɪtɪs) *n.* inflammation of the vermiform appendix.

ap+pen+di+cle (ə'pɛndɪkᵊl) *n.* a small appendage. [C17: from Latin *appendicula;* see APPENDIX]

ap+pen+dic·u+lar (ˌæpən'dɪkjʊlə) *adj.* **1.** relating to an appendage or appendicle. **2.** *Anatomy.* of or relating to the vermiform appendix.

ap+pen+dix (ə'pɛndɪks) *n., pl.* **+dix·es** *or* **+di+ces** (-dɪˌsi:z). **1.** a body of separate additional material at the end of a book, magazine, etc., esp. one that is documentary or explanatory. **2.** any part that is dependent or supplementary in nature or function; appendage. **3.** *Anatomy.* See **vermiform appendix.** [C16: from Latin: an appendage, from *appendere* to APPEND]

Ap+pen+zell (*German* apᵊn'tsɛl, 'apᵊnˌtsɛl) *n.* **1.** a canton of NE Switzerland, divided in 1597 into the Protestant demicanton of **Appenzell Outer Rhodes** and the Catholic demicanton of **Appenzell Inner Rhodes.** Capitals: Herisau and Appenzell. Pop.: 49 023 and 13 124 (1970). Areas: 243 sq. km (94 sq. miles) and 171 sq. km (66 sq. miles) respectively. **2.** a town in NE Switzerland, capital of Appenzell Inner Rhodes demicanton. Pop.: 5217 (1970).

ap+per+ceive (ˌæpə'si:v) *vb.* (*tr.*) **1.** to be aware of perceiving. **2.** *Psychol.* to comprehend by assimilating (a perception) to ideas already in the mind. [C19: from Old French *aperceveir,* from Latin *percipere* to PERCEIVE]

ap+per+cep+tion (ˌæpə'sɛpʃən) *Psychol.* *~n.* **1.** conscious awareness of the act and significance of perception; focused perception, esp. when selective of certain sensory data. **2.** the act or process of apperceiving. **—ˌap+per+'cep+tive** *adj.*

ap+per+tain (ˌæpə'teɪn) *vb.* (*intr.;* usually foll. by *to*) to belong (to) as a part, function, right, etc.; relate (to) or be connected (with). [C14: from Old French *apertenir* to belong, from Late Latin *appertinēre,* from Latin APO- + *pertinēre* to PERTAIN]

ap+pes+tat ('æpɪstæt) *n.* a neural control centre within the hypothalamus of the brain that regulates the sense of hunger and satiety. [C20: from APPE(TITE) + -STAT]

ap+pe+tence ('æpɪtəns) *or* **ap+pe+ten+cy** *n., pl.* **+tenc·es** *or* **+ten+cies. 1.** a natural craving or desire. **2.** a natural or instinctive inclination. **3.** an attraction or affinity. [C17: from Latin *appetentia,* from *appetere* to crave]

ap+pe+tite ('æpɪˌtaɪt) *n.* **1.** a desire for food or drink. **2.** a desire to satisfy a bodily craving, as for sexual pleasure. **3.** (usually foll. by *for*) a desire, liking, or willingness: *a great appetite for work.* [C14: from Old French *apetit,* from Latin *appetītus* a craving, from *appetere* to desire ardently] **—ap+pet·i+tive** (ə'pɛtɪtɪv, 'æpɪˌtaɪtɪv) *adj.*

ap+pe+tiz+er *or* **ap+pe+tis+er** ('æpɪˌtaɪzə) *n.* **1.** a small amount of food or drink taken to stimulate the appetite. **2.** any stimulating foretaste.

ap+pe+tiz+ing *or* **ap+pe+tis+ing** ('æpɪˌtaɪzɪŋ) *adj.* pleasing or stimulating to the appetite; delicious; tasty.

Ap+pi·an Way ('æpɪən) *n.* a Roman road in Italy, extending from Rome to Brindisi: begun in 312 B.C. by Appius Claudius Caecus. Length: about 560 km (350 miles).

ap+plaud (ə'plɔ:d) *vb.* **1.** to indicate approval of (a person, performance, etc.) by clapping the hands. **2.** (*usually tr.*) to offer or express approval or praise of (an action, person, or thing): *I applaud your decision.* [C15: from Latin *applaudere* to clap, from *plaudere* to beat, applaud] **—ap+'plaud+er** *n.* **—ap+'plaud+ing+ly** *adv.*

ap+plause (ə'plɔ:z) *n.* appreciation or praise, esp. as shown by clapping the hands.

ap+ple ('æpᵊl) *n.* **1.** a rosaceous tree, *Malus pumila* (or *Pyrus malus*), widely cultivated in temperate regions in many varieties, having pink or white fragrant flowers and firm rounded edible fruits. **2.** the fruit of this tree, having red, yellow, or green skin and crisp whitish flesh. **3.** the wood of this tree. **4.** any of several unrelated trees that have fruit similar to the apple, such as the custard apple, sugar apple, and May apple. See also **love apple, oak apple, thorn apple. 5. apple of one's eye.** a person or thing that is very precious or much loved. [Old English *æppel;* related to Old Saxon *appel,* Old Norse *apall,* Old High German *apful*]

ap+ple blight *n.* an aphid, *Eriosoma lanigera,* that is covered with a powdery waxy secretion and infests apple trees. Also called: **American blight.**

ap+ple box *n.* an ornamental Australian tree, *Eucalyptus bridgesiana,* having heart-shaped juvenile leaves, large lanceolate adult leaves, and conical fruits. Also called: **apple gum.**

ap+ple but+ter *n.* a jam made from stewed spiced apples.

ap+ple+cart ('æpᵊlˌkɑ:t) *n.* **1.** a cart or barrow from which apples and other fruit are sold in the street. **2. upset the** *or* **one's applecart.** to spoil plans or arrangements.

ap+ple green *n., adj.* (**apple-green** *when prenominal*). **a.** a bright light green or moderate yellowish-green. **b.** (*as adj.*)*: an apple-green carpet.*

Apple Isle *n.* **the.** *Austral. informal.* Tasmania. **—'Ap+ple 'Is+land+er** *n.*

ap·ple+jack ('æpᵊlˌdʒæk) *n.* a brandy made from apples; distilled cider. Also called: **applejack brandy, apple brandy.**

ap+ple mag+got *n.* a fruit fly, *Rhagoletis pomonella,* the larvae of which bore into and feed on the fruit of apple trees: family *Trypetidae.*

ap+ple of dis+cord *n. Greek myth.* a golden apple inscribed "For the fairest." It was claimed by Hera, Athena, and Aphrodite, to whom Paris awarded it, thus beginning a chain of events that led to the Trojan War.

ap·ple-pie bed *n. Brit.* a way of making a bed so as to prevent the person from entering it.

ap·ple-pie or+der *n. Informal.* perfect order or condition.

ap+ple pol+ish+er *n. U.S. slang.* a sycophant; toady.

ap+ples ('æpᵊlz) *n.* **1.** See **apples and pears. 2. she's apples.** *Austral. informal.* all is going well.

ap+ples and pears *pl. n. Cockney rhyming slang.* stairs. Often shortened to **apples.**

ap+ple sauce *n.* **1.** a purée of stewed apples often served with pork. **2.** *U.S. slang.* nonsense; rubbish.

ap·ple+snits ('æpᵊlˌsnɪts) *n. Canadian W coast.* a dish consisting of apple slices. [from German *Apfelschnitzel*]

Ap·ple·ton ('æpᵊltən) *n.* Sir **Ed·ward (Victor).** 1892–1965, English physicist, noted particularly for his research on the ionosphere: Nobel prize for physics 1947.

Ap·ple·ton lay+er *n.* another name for **F region** (of the ionosphere).

ap+pli+ance (ə'plaɪəns) *n.* **1.** a machine or device, esp. an electrical one used domestically. **2.** any piece of equipment having a specific function. **3.** a device fitted to a machine or tool to adapt it for a specific purpose. **4.** another name for a **fire engine.**

ap+pli+ca·ble ('æplɪkəbᵊl, ə'plɪkə-) *adj.* being appropriate or relevant; able to be applied; fitting. **—ˌap+plic+a·'bil+i·ty** *or* **'ap+pli+ca·ble+ness** *n.* **—'ap+pli+ca·bly** *adv.*

ap+pli+cant ('æplɪkənt) *n.* a person who applies, as for a job, grant, support, etc.; candidate. [C15: from Latin *applicāns,* from *applicāre* to APPLY]

ap+pli+ca+tion (ˌæplɪ'keɪʃən) *n.* **1.** the act of applying to a particular purpose or use. **2.** relevance or value: *the practical applications of space technology.* **3.** the act of asking for something: *an application for leave.* **4.** a verbal or written request, as for a job, etc.: *he filed his application.* **5.** diligent effort or concentration: *a job requiring application.* **6.** something, such as a healing agent or lotion, that is applied, esp. to the skin.

ap+plic·a+tive (ə'plɪkətɪv) *adj.* relevant or applicable. **—ap+'plic·a+tive+ly** *adv.*

ap+pli+ca+tor ('æplɪˌkeɪtə) *n.* a device, such as a spatula or rod, for applying a medicine, glue, etc.

ap+pli+ca+to·ry ('æplɪˌkeɪtərɪ) *adj.* suitable for application.

ap+plied (ə'plaɪd) *adj.* related to or put to practical use: *applied mathematics.* Compare **pure** (sense 5).

ap+pli+qué (æ'pli:keɪ) *n.* **1.** a decoration or trimming of one material sewn or otherwise fixed onto another. **2.** the practice of decorating in this way. ~*vb.* **+qués, +qué+ing, +quéd. 3.** (*tr.*) to sew or fix (a decoration) on as an appliqué. [C18: from French, literally: applied]

ap+ply (ə'plaɪ) *vb.* **+plies, +ply+ing, +plied. 1.** (*tr.*) to put to practical use; utilize; employ. **2.** (*intr.*) to be relevant, useful, or appropriate. **3.** (*tr.*) to cause to come into contact with; put onto. **4.** (*intr.*; often foll. by *for*) to put in an application or request. **5.** (*tr.*; often foll. by *to*) to devote (oneself, one's efforts) with diligence. **6.** (*tr.*) to bring into operation or use: *the police only applied the law to aliens.* **7.** (*tr.*) to refer (a word, epithet, etc.) to a person or thing. [C14: from Old French *aplier,* from Latin *applicāre* to attach to] —**ap+'pli+er** *n.*

ap+pog+gia+tu+ra (əˌpɒdʒə'tʊərə) *n., pl.* **+ras** *or* **+re** (-rɛ). *Music.* an ornament consisting of a nonharmonic note (short or long) preceding a harmonic one either before or on the stress. See also **acciaccatura** (sense 2). [C18: from Italian, literally: a propping, from *appoggiare* to prop, support]

ap+point (ə'pɔɪnt) *vb.* (*mainly tr.*) **1.** (*also intr.*) to assign officially, as for a position, responsibility, etc.: *he was appointed manager.* **2.** to establish by agreement or decree; fix: *a time was appointed for the duel.* **3.** to prescribe or ordain: *laws appointed by tribunal.* **4.** *Property law.* to nominate (a person), under a power granted in a deed or will, to take an interest in property. **5.** to equip with necessary or usual features; furnish: *a well-appointed hotel.* [C14: from Old French *apointer* to put into a good state, from *a point* in good condition, literally: to a POINT] —**ap+'point+er** *n.*

ap+poin+tee (əpɔɪn'ti:, ˌæp-) *n.* **1.** a person who is appointed. **2.** *Property law.* a person to whom property is granted under a power of appointment.

ap+poin+tive (ə'pɔɪntɪv) *adj. Chiefly U.S.* relating to or filled by appointment: *an appointive position.*

ap+point+ment (ə'pɔɪntmənt) *n.* **1.** an arrangement to meet a person or be at a place at a certain time. **2.** the act of placing in a job or position. **3.** the person who receives such a job or position. **4.** the job or position to which such a person is appointed. **5.** (*usually pl.*) a fixture or fitting. **6.** *Property law.* nomination to an interest in property under a deed or will.

ap+poin+tor (ə'pɔɪntə, əpɔɪn'tɔ:) *n. Property law.* a person to whom a power to nominate persons to take property is given by deed or will. See also **power of appointment.**

Ap+po+mat+tox (ˌæpə'mætəks) *n.* **1.** a village in central Virginia where the Confederate army under Robert E. Lee surrendered to Ulysses S. Grant's Union forces on April 9, 1865, effectively ending the American Civil War.

ap+por+tion (ə'pɔ:ʃən) *vb.* (*tr.*) to divide, distribute, or assign appropriate shares of; allot proportionally: *to apportion the blame.* —**ap+'por+tion+a+ble** *adj.* —**ap+'por+tion+er** *n.*

ap+por+tion+ment (ə'pɔ:ʃənmənt) *n.* **1.** the act of apportioning. **2.** *U.S. government.* the proportional distribution of the seats in a legislative body, esp. the House of Representatives, on the basis of population.

ap+pos·a+ble (ə'pəʊzəbəl) *adj.* **1.** capable of being apposed or brought into apposition. **2.** *Anatomy.* another word for **opposable** (sense 2).

ap+pose (ə'pəʊz) *vb.* (*tr.*) **1.** to place side by side or near to each other. **2.** (usually foll. by *to*) to place (something) near or against another thing. [C16: from Old French *apposer,* from *poser* to put, from Latin *pōnere*]

ap+po+site ('æpəzɪt) *adj.* well suited for the purpose; appropriate; apt. [C17: from Latin *appositus* placed near, from *appōnere,* from *pōnere* to put, place] —**'ap+po+site+ly** *adv.* —**'ap+po+site+ness** *n.*

ap+po+si+tion (ˌæpə'zɪʃən) *n.* **1.** a putting into juxtaposition. **2.** a grammatical construction in which a word, esp. a noun phrase, is placed after another to modify its meaning. **3.** *Biology.* growth in the thickness of a cell wall by the deposition of successive layers of material. Compare **intussusception** (sense 2). —**ˌap+po+'si+tion+al** *adj.*

ap+pos·i+tive (ə'pɒzɪtɪv) *adj.* **1.** *Grammar.* **a.** standing in apposition. **b.** another word for **nonrestrictive. 2.** of or relating to apposition. ~*n.* **3.** an appositive word or phrase. —**ap+'pos·i+tive+ly** *adv.*

ap+prais+al (ə'preɪzəl) *or* **ap+praise+ment** *n.* **1.** an assessment or estimation of the worth, value, or quality of a person or thing. **2.** a valuation of property or goods.

ap+praise (ə'preɪz) *vb.* (*tr.*) **1.** to assess the worth, value, or quality of. **2.** to make a valuation of, as for taxation purposes. [C15: from Old French *aprisier,* from *prisier* to PRIZE[2]] —**ap+'prais+a+ble** *adj.* —**ap+'prais+er** *n.* —**ap+'prais+ing+ly** *adv.* —**ap+'prais+ive** *adj.* —**ap+'prais+ive+ly** *adv.*

ap+pre+ci+a+ble (ə'pri:ʃɪəbəl, -ʃəbəl) *adj.* sufficient to be easily seen, measured, or noticed. —**ap+'pre+ci+a+bly** *adv.*

ap+pre+ci+ate (ə'pri:ʃɪˌeɪt, -sɪ-) *vb.* (*mainly tr.*) **1.** to feel thankful or grateful for: *to appreciate a favour.* **2.** (*may take a clause as object*) to take full or sufficient account of: *to appreciate a problem.* **3.** to value highly: *to appreciate Shakespeare.* **4.** (*usually intr.*) to raise or increase in value. [C17: from Medieval Latin *appretiāre* to value, prize, from Latin *pretium* PRICE] —**ap+'pre+ci+ˌa+tor** *n.*

ap+pre+ci+a+tion (əˌpri:ʃɪ'eɪʃən, -sɪ-) *n.* **1.** thanks or gratitude. **2.** assessment of the true worth or value of persons or things. **3.** perceptive recognition of qualities, as in art. **4.** an increase in value, as of goods or property. **5.** a written review of a book, etc., esp. when favourable.

ap+pre+ci+a+tive (ə'pri:ʃɪətɪv, -ʃə-) *or* **ap+pre+cia+to+ry** *adj.* feeling, expressing, or capable of appreciation. —**ap+'pre+ci+a+tive+ness** *n.* —**ap+'pre+ci+a+tive+ly** *or* **ap+'pre+ci+a+to+ri+ly** *adv.*

ap+pre+hend (ˌæprɪ'hɛnd) *vb.* **1.** (*tr.*) to arrest and escort into custody; seize. **2.** to perceive or grasp mentally; understand. **3.** to await with fear or anxiety; dread. [C14: from Latin *apprehendere* to lay hold of]

ap+pre+hen+si+ble (ˌæprɪ'hɛnsɪbəl) *adj.* capable of being comprehended or grasped mentally. —**ˌap+pre+ˌhen+si·'bil+i+ty** *n.* —**ˌap+pre+'hen+si+bly** *adv.*

ap+pre+hen+sion (ˌæprɪ'hɛnʃən) *n.* **1.** fear or anxiety over what may happen. **2.** the act of capturing or arresting. **3.** the faculty of comprehending; understanding. **4.** a notion or conception.

ap+pre+hen+sive (ˌæprɪ'hɛnsɪv) *adj.* **1.** fearful or anxious. **2.** able to learn or understand quickly. **3.** (usually *postpositive* and foll. by *of*) perceptive or appreciative. —**ˌap+pre+'hen+sive+ly** *adv.* —**ˌap+pre+'hen+sive+ness** *n.*

ap+pren+tice (ə'prɛntɪs) *n.* **1.** someone who works for a skilled or qualified person in order to learn a trade or profession, esp. for a recognized period. **2.** any beginner or novice. ~*vb.* **3.** (*tr.*) to take, place, or bind as an apprentice. [C14: from Old French *aprentis,* from Old French *aprendre* to learn, from Latin *apprehendere* to APPREHEND] —**ap+'pren+tice+ˌship** *n.*

ap+pressed (ə'prɛst) *adj.* pressed closely against, but not joined to, a surface: *leaves appressed to a stem.* [C18: from Latin *appressus,* from *apprimere,* from *premere* to press]

ap+prise *or* **ap+prize** (ə'praɪz) *vb.* (*tr.*; often foll. by *of*) to make aware; inform. [C17: from French *appris,* from *apprendre* to teach; learn; see APPREHEND]

ap+pro ('æprəʊ) *n.* an informal shortening of **approval:** *on appro.*

ap+proach (ə'prəʊtʃ) *vb.* **1.** to come nearer in position, time, quality, character, etc., to (someone or something). **2.** (*tr.*) to make advances to, as with a proposal, suggestion, etc. **3.** (*tr.*) to begin to deal with: *to approach a problem.* **4.** (*tr.*) *Rare.* to cause to come near. ~*n.* **5.** the act of coming towards or drawing close or closer. **6.** a close approximation. **7.** the way or means of entering or leaving; access. **8.** (*often pl.*) an advance or overture to a person. **9.** a means adopted in tackling a problem, job of work, etc. **10.** Also called: **approach path.** the course followed by an aircraft preparing for landing. **11.** Also called: **approach shot.** *Golf.* a shot made to or towards the green after a tee shot. [C14: from Old French *aprochier,* from Late Latin *appropiāre* to draw near, from Latin *prope* near]

ap+proach+a+ble (ə'prəʊtʃəbəl) *adj.* **1.** capable of being approached; accessible. **2.** (of a person) friendly. —**ap+ˌproach+a·'bil+i+ty** *or* **ap+'proach+a+ble+ness** *n.*

ap+pro+bate ('æprəˌbeɪt) *vb.* (*tr.*) **1.** *Scot. law.* to accept as valid. **2. approbate and reprobate.** *Scot. law.* to accept part of a document and reject those parts unfavourable to one's interests. **3.** *Chiefly U.S.* to sanction officially. [C15: from Latin *approbāre* to approve, from *probāre* to test]

ap+pro+ba+tion (ˌæprə'beɪʃən) *n.* **1.** commendation; praise. **2.** official recognition or approval. **3.** an obsolete word for **proof.** —**'ap+pro+ˌba+tive** *or* **'ap+pro+ˌba+to+ry** *adj.*

ap+pro+pri+ate *adj.* (ə'prəʊprɪɪt). **1.** right or suitable; fitting. **2.** *Rare.* particular; own: *they had their appropriate methods.* ~*vb.* (ə'prəʊprɪˌeɪt). (*tr.*) **3.** to take for one's own use, esp. illegally or without permission. **4.** to put aside (funds, etc.) for a particular purpose or person. [C15: from Late Latin *appropriāre* to make one's own, from Latin *proprius* one's own; see PROPER] —**ap+'pro+pri+a+ble** *adj.* —**ap+'pro+pri+ate+ly** *adv.* —**ap+'pro+pri+ate+ness** *n.* —**ap+'pro+pri·ˌa+tor** *n.*

ap+pro+pri·a+tion (əˌprəʊprɪ'eɪʃən) *n.* **1.** the act of setting apart or taking for one's own use. **2.** a sum of money set apart for a specific purpose, esp. by a legislature.

ap+prov+al (ə'pru:vəl) *n.* **1.** the act of approving. **2.** formal agreement; sanction. **3.** a favourable opinion; commendation. **4. on approval.** (of articles for sale) for examination with an option to buy or return.

ap+prove[1] (ə'pru:v) *vb.* **1.** to consider fair, good, or right; commend (a person or thing). **2.** (*tr.*) to authorize or sanction. **3.** (*tr.*) *Obsolete.* to demonstrate or prove by trial. [C14: from Old French *aprover,* from Latin *approbāre* to approve, from *probāre* to test, PROVE]

ap+prove[2] (ə'pru:v) *vb.* (*tr.*) *Law.* to improve or increase the value of (waste or common land), as by enclosure. [C15: from Old French *approuer* to turn to advantage, from *prou* advantage]

ap+proved school *n.* a former name for **community home.**

approx. *abbrev. for* approximate(ly).

ap+prox·i+mal (ə'prɒksɪməl) *adj. Anatomy.* situated side by side; close together: *approximal teeth or fillings.*

ap+prox·i+mate *adj.* (ə'prɒksɪmɪt). **1.** almost accurate or exact. **2.** inexact; rough; loose: *only an approximate fit.* **3.** much alike; almost the same. **4.** near; close together. ~*vb.* (ə'prɒksɪˌmeɪt). **5.** (usually foll. by *to*) to come or bring near or close; be almost the same (as). [C15: from Late Latin *approximāre,* from Latin *proximus* nearest, from *prope* near] —**ap+'prox·i+mate+ly** *adv.* —**ap+'prox·i+ma+tive** *adj.*

ap+prox·i+ma+tion (əˌprɒksɪ'meɪʃən) *n.* **1.** the process or result of making a rough calculation, estimate, or guess: *he based his conclusion on his own approximation of the fuel consumption.* **2.** an imprecise or unreliable record or version: *an approximation of what really happened.* **3.** *Maths.* an inexact number, relationship, or theory that is sufficiently accurate for a specific purpose.

ap+pulse (ə'pʌls) *n.* a very close approach of two celestial bodies so that they are in conjunction but no eclipse or occultation occurs. [C17: from Latin *appulsus* brought near, from *appellere* to drive towards, from *pellere* to drive] —**ap+'pul+sive** *adj.* —**ap+'pul+sive+ly** *adv.*

ap+pur+te+nance (ə'pɜːtɪnəns) *n.* **1.** a secondary or less significant thing or part. **2.** (*pl.*) accessories or equipment. **3.** *Property law.* a minor right, interest, or privilege which passes when the title to the principal property is transferred. [C14: from Anglo-French *apurtenance*, from Old French *apartenance*, from *apartenir* to APPERTAIN]

ap+pur+te+nant (ə'pɜːtɪnənt) *adj.* **1.** relating, belonging, or accessory. ~*n.* **2.** another word for **appurtenance.**

Apr. *abbrev. for* April.

a·prax·i·a (ə'præksɪə) *n.* a disorder of the central nervous system characterized by apparent loss of the memory of how to make certain purposeful muscular movements. [C19: via New Latin from Greek: inactivity, from A-[1] + *praxis* action] —**a+'prax+ic** *or* **a+'prac+tic** *adj.*

a·près-ski (ˌæpreɪ'skiː) *n.* **a.** social activity following a day's skiing. **b.** (*as modifier*): *an après-ski outfit.* [French, literally: after ski]

a·pri+cot ('eɪprɪˌkɒt) *n.* **1.** a rosaceous tree, *Prunus armeniaca*, native to Africa and W Asia, but widely cultivated for its edible fruit. **2.** the downy yellow juicy edible fruit of this tree, which resembles a small peach. [C16: earlier *apricock*, from Portuguese (*albricoque*) or Spanish, from Arabic *al-birqūq* the apricot, from Late Greek *praikokion*, from Latin *praecox* early-ripening; see PRECOCIOUS]

A·pril ('eɪprəl) *n.* the fourth month of the year, consisting of 30 days. [C14: from Latin *Aprīlis*, probably of Etruscan origin]

A·pril fool *n.* an unsuspecting victim of a practical joke or trick traditionally performed on the first of April (**April Fools' Day** *or* **All Fools' Day**).

a pri·o·ri (eɪ praɪ'ɔːraɪ, ɑː prɪ'ɔːrɪ) *Logic.* ~*adj.* **1.** relating to or involving deductive reasoning from a general principle to the expected facts or effects. **2.** known to be true independently of or in advance of experience of the subject matter; requiring no evidence for its validation or support. ~Compare **a posteriori, analytic** (sense 4). [C18: from Latin, literally: from the previous (that is, from cause to effect)] —**a·pri+or+i·ty** (ˌeɪpraɪ'ɒrɪtɪ) *n.*

a·pri+or+ism (eɪ'praɪəˌrɪzəm) *n.* the doctrine that knowledge is based on a priori ideas.

a·pron ('eɪprən) *n.* **1.** a protective or sometimes decorative or ceremonial garment worn over the front of the body and tied around the waist. **2.** the part of a stage extending in front of the curtain line; forestage. **3.** a hard-surfaced area in front of or around an aircraft hangar, terminal building, etc., upon which aircraft can stand. **4.** a continuous conveyor belt composed of metal slats linked together. **5.** a protective plate screening the operator of a machine, artillery piece, etc. **6.** a ground covering of concrete or other material used to protect the underlying earth from water erosion. **7.** a panel or board between a window and a skirting in a room. **8.** *Geology.* a sheet of sand, gravel, etc., deposited at the front of a moraine. **9.** *Golf.* the part of the fairway leading onto the green. **10.** *Machinery.* the housing for the lead screw gears of a lathe. **11.** another name for **skirt** (sense 3). **12. tied to someone's apron strings.** dependent on or dominated by someone, esp. a mother or wife. ~*vb.* **13.** (*tr.*) to protect or provide with an apron. [C16: mistaken division (as if *an apron*) of earlier *a napron*, from Old French *naperon* a little cloth, from *nape* cloth, from Latin *mappa* napkin]

a·pron stage *n.* a stage that projects into the auditorium so that the audience sit on three sides of it.

ap+ro+pos (ˌæprə'pəʊ) *adj.* **1.** appropriate; pertinent. ~*adv.* **2.** appropriately or pertinently. **3.** by the way; incidentally. **4. apropos of.** (*prep.*) with regard to; in respect of. [C17: from French *à propos* to the purpose]

apse (æps) *n.* **1.** Also called: **apsis.** a domed or vaulted semicircular or polygonal recess, esp. at the east end of a church. **2.** *Astronomy.* another name for **apsis** (sense 1). [C19: from Latin *apsis*, from Greek: a fitting together, arch, from *haptein* to fasten] —**ap+si+dal** (æp'saɪdᵊl, 'æpsɪdᵊl) *adj.*

ap+sis ('æpsɪs) *n., pl.* **ap+si+des** (æp'saɪdiːz, 'æpsɪˌdiːz). **1.** Also called: **apse.** either of two points lying at the extremities of an eccentric orbit of a planet, satellite, etc., such as the aphelion and perihelion of a planet or the apogee and perigee of the moon. The **line of apsides** connects two such points and is the principal axis of the orbit. **2.** another name for **apse** (sense 1). [C17: via Latin from Greek; see APSE] —**ap+si+dal** (æp'saɪdᵊl, 'æpsɪdᵊl) *adj.*

apt (æpt) *adj.* **1.** suitable for the circumstance or purpose; appropriate. **2.** (*postpositive;* foll. by an infinitive) having a tendency (to behave as specified). **3.** having the ability to learn and understand easily; clever (esp. in the phrase **an apt pupil**). [C14: from Latin *aptus* fitting, suitable, from *apere* to fasten] —**'apt+ly** *adv.* —**'apt+ness** *n.*

apt. *pl.* **apts.** *abbrev. for* apartment.

APT *abbrev. for* Advanced Passenger Train.

ap+ter+al ('æptərəl) *adj.* **1.** (esp. of a classical temple) not having columns at the sides. **2.** (of a church) having no aisles. [C19: from Greek *apteros* wingless; see APTEROUS]

ap+ter+ous ('æptərəs) *adj.* **1.** (of insects) without wings, as silverfish and springtails. **2.** without winglike expansions, as some plant stems, seeds, and fruits. [C18: from Greek *apteros* wingless, from A-[1] + *pteron* wing]

ap+ter+yg+i·al (ˌæptə'rɪdʒɪəl) *adj.* (of eels, certain insects, etc.) lacking such paired limbs as wings or fins. [C20: from New Latin *apteryx* wingless creature; see APTEROUS]

ap+ter+yx ('æptərɪks) *n.* another name for **kiwi** (the bird). [C19: from New Latin: wingless creature; see APTEROUS]

ap+ti+tude ('æptɪˌtjuːd) *n.* **1.** inherent or acquired ability. **2.** ease in learning or understanding; intelligence. **3.** the condition or quality of being apt. [C15: via Old French from Late Latin *aptitūdō*, from Latin *aptus* APT]

ap+ti+tude test *n.* a test designed to assess a person's ability to do a particular type of work.

Ap·u·lei·us (ˌæpjʊ'liːəs) *n.* **Lu·ci·us** ('luːsɪəs). 2nd century A.D. Roman writer, noted for his romance *The Golden Ass.*

A·pu+lia (ə'pjuːljə) *n.* a region of SE Italy, on the Adriatic. Capital: Bari. Pop.: 3 493 265 (1971). Area: 19 223 sq. km (7422 sq. miles). Italian name: **Puglia.**

A·pu+re (*Spanish* a'pure) *n.* a river in W Venezuela, rising in the Andes and flowing east to the Orinoco. Length: about 676 km (420 miles).

Ap·u·ri+mac (ˌæpuː'riːmæk) *n.* a river in S Peru, rising in the Andes and flowing northwest into the Urubamba River. Length: about 885 km (550 miles).

A·pus ('eɪpəs) *n., Latin genitive* **Ap·o+dis** ('æpədɪs). a constellation in the S hemisphere situated near Musca and Octans. [New Latin, from Greek *apous*, literally: footless, from A-[1] + *pous* foot]

ap·y+re+tic (ˌæpaɪ'rɛtɪk) *adj.* without fever. [C19: from A-[1] + Greek *puretos* fever]

AQ *abbrev. for* achievement quotient.

aq. *or* **Aq.** *abbrev. for:* **1.** aqua. [Latin: water] **2.** aqueous.

Aq·a+ba *or* **Ak·a+ba** ('ækəbə) *n.* **1.** the only port in Jordan, in the southwest, on the **Gulf of Aqaba.** Pop.: 10 000 (1964 est.).

aq·ua ('ækwə) *n., pl.* **aq·uae** ('ækwiː) *or* **aq·uas. 1.** water: used in compound names of certain liquid substances (as in **aqua regia**) or solutions of substances in water (as in **aqua ammoniae**), esp. in the names of pharmacological solutions. ~*adj.* **2.** short for **aquamarine** (the colour). [Latin: water]

aq·ua am+mo+ni·ae (ə'məʊnɪˌiː) *n. Rare.* another name for **ammonium hydroxide.** [New Latin]

aq·ua+cul+ture ('ækwəˌkʌltʃə) *n.* the cultivation of marine organisms for human consumption or use.

aq·ua for+tis ('fɔːtɪs) *n.* an obsolete name for **nitric acid.** [C17: from Latin, literally: strong water]

aq·ua+lung ('ækwəˌlʌŋ) *n.* breathing apparatus used by divers, etc., consisting of an oxygen mask attached to a cylinder strapped to the back.

aq·ua+ma+rine (ˌækwəmə'riːn) *n.* **1.** a pale greenish-blue transparent variety of beryl used as a gemstone. **2. a.** a pale blue to greenish-blue colour. **b.** (*as adj.*): *an aquamarine dress.* [C19: from New Latin *aqua marīna*, from Latin: sea water (referring to the gem's colour)]

aq·ua+naut ('ækwənɔːt) *n.* **1.** a person who lives and works underwater. **2.** a person who swims or dives underwater. [C20: from AQUA + *-naut*, as in ASTRONAUT]

aq·ua+pho+bi·a (ˌækwə'fəʊbɪə) *n.* an abnormal fear of water, esp. because of the possibility of drowning. Compare **hydrophobia** (sense 2).

aq·ua+plane ('ækwəˌpleɪn) *n.* **1.** a single board on which a person stands and is towed by a motorboat at high speed, as in water skiing. ~*vb.* (*intr.*) **2.** to ride on an aquaplane. **3.** (of a motor vehicle travelling at high speeds in wet road conditions) to rise up onto a thin film of water between the tyres and road surface so that actual contact with the road is lost.

aq·ua re+gi·a ('riːdʒɪə) *n.* a yellow fuming corrosive mixture of one part nitric acid and three to four parts hydrochloric acid, used in metallurgy for dissolving metals, including gold. Also called: **nitrohydrochloric acid.** [C17: from New Latin: royal water; referring to its use in dissolving gold, the royal metal]

aq·ua+relle (ˌækwə'rɛl) *n.* **1.** a method of watercolour painting in transparent washes. **2.** a painting done in this way. [C19: from French] —ˌ**aq·ua+'rel+list** *n.*

aq·ua+rist ('ækwərɪst) *n.* **1.** the curator of an aquarium. **2.** a person who studies aquatic life.

a·quar+i·um (ə'kwɛərɪəm) *n., pl.* **a·quar+i·ums** *or* **a·quar·i·a** (ə'kwɛərɪə). **1.** a tank, bowl, or pool in which aquatic animals and plants are kept for pleasure, study, or exhibition. **2.** a building housing a collection of aquatic life, as for exhibition. [C19: from Latin *aquārius* relating to water, on the model of VIVARIUM]

A·quar+i·us (ə'kwɛərɪəs) *n., Latin genitive* **A·quar·i·i** (ə'kwɛərɪˌaɪ). **1.** *Astronomy.* a zodiacal constellation in the S hemisphere lying between Pisces and Capricorn on the ecliptic. **2.** *Astrology.* **a.** Also called: the **Water Carrier.** the eleventh sign of the zodiac, symbol ♒, having a fixed air classification and ruled by the planets Saturn and Uranus. The sun is in this sign between about Jan. 20 and Feb. 18. **b.** a person born during a period when the sun is in this sign. ~*adj.* **3.** *Astrology.* born under or characteristic of Aquarius. ~Also (for senses 2b, 3): **A·quar+i·an** (ə'kwɛərɪən). [Latin]

aq·ua+show ('ækwəˌʃəʊ) *or U.S.* **aq·ua+cade** *n.* an exhibition of swimming and diving, often accompanied by music.

a·quat+ic (ə'kwætɪk, ə'kwɒt-) *adj.* **1.** growing, living, or found in water. **2.** *Sport.* performed in or on water. ~*n.* **3.** a marine animal or plant. [C15: from Latin *aquāticus*, from *aqua* water]

a·quat+ics (ə'kwætɪks, ə'kwɒt-) *pl. n.* sports or pastimes performed in or on the water.

aq·ua+tint ('ækwəˌtɪnt) *n.* **1.** a technique of etching copper with acid to produce an effect resembling the flat tones of wash or watercolour. **2.** an etching made in this way. ~*vb.* **3.** (*tr.*) to etch (a block, etc.) in aquatint. [C18: from Italian *acqua tinta:* dyed water]

aq·ua+vit ('ækwəˌvɪt) *n.* a grain- or potato-based spirit from the

Scandinavian countries, flavoured with aromatic seeds and spices, esp. caraway. Also: **akvavit.** [from Scandinavian; see AQUA VITAE]

aq·ua vi·tae ('vi:taɪ, 'vaɪti:) *n.* an archaic name for **brandy.** [Medieval Latin: water of life]

aq·ue·duct ('ækwɪˌdʌkt) *n.* **1.** a conduit used to convey water over a long distance. **2.** a structure, often a bridge, that carries such a conduit or a canal across a valley or river. **3.** a channel in an organ or part of the body, esp. one that conveys a natural body fluid. [C16: from Latin *aquaeductus,* from *aqua* water + *dūcere* to convey]

a·que·ous ('eɪkwɪəs, 'ækwɪ-) *adj.* **1.** of, like, or containing water. **2.** (of rocks, deposits, etc.) formed from material laid down in water. [C17: from Medieval Latin *aqueus,* from Latin *aqua* water]

a·que·ous am·mo·ni·a *n.* a solution of ammonia gas in water forming **ammonium hydroxide.** Sometimes shortened to **ammonia.**

a·que·ous hu·mour *n. Physiol.* the watery fluid within the eyeball between the cornea and the lens.

a·qui·cul·ture ('eɪkwɪˌkʌltʃə, 'ækwɪ-) *n.* another name for **hydroponics.** —**'aq·ui·ˌcul·tur·ist** *n.* —**'aq·ui·ˌcul·tur·al** *adj.*

aq·ui·fer ('ækwɪfə) *n.* a deposit or rock, such as a sandstone, containing water that can be used to supply wells.

Aq·ui·la[1] ('ækwɪlə, ə'kwɪlə) *n., Latin genitive* **Aq·ui·lae** ('ækwɪˌli:). a constellation lying in the Milky Way close to Cygnus and situated on the celestial equator. The brightest star is Altair. [from Latin: eagle]

Aq·ui·la[2] ('ækwɪlə; *Italian* 'a:kwila) *or* **l'Aq·ui·la** *n.* a city in central Italy, capital of Abruzzi region. Pop.: 60 131 (1971). Official name: **A·qui·la de·gli A·bruz·zi** ('deʎi a'bruttsi).

aq·ui·le·gi·a (ˌækwɪ'li:dʒɪə) *n.* another name for **columbine**[1]. [C19: from Medieval Latin, of uncertain origin]

Aq·ui·le·ia (ˌækwɪ'li:ə) *n.* a town in NE Italy, at the head of the Adriatic: important Roman centre, founded in 181 B.C. Pop.: 3041 (1971).

aq·ui·line ('ækwɪˌlaɪn) *adj.* **1.** (of a nose) having the curved or hooked shape of an eagle's beak. **2.** of or resembling an eagle. [C17: from Latin *aquilīnus,* from *aquila* eagle]

A·qui·nas (ə'kwaɪnəs) *n.* **Saint Thom·as.** 1225–74, Italian theologian, scholastic philosopher, and Dominican friar, whose works include *Summa contra Gentiles* (1259–64) and *Summa Theologiae* (1267–73), the first attempt at a comprehensive theological system. See also **Thomism.**

Aq·ui·taine (ˌækwɪ'teɪn; *French* aki'tɛn) *n.* a region of SW France on the Bay of Biscay: a former Roman province and medieval duchy. It is generally flat in the west, rising to the slopes of the Massif Central in the northeast and the Pyrenees in the south; mainly agricultural. Ancient name: **Aquitania.**

Ar *the chemical symbol for* argon.

ar. *abbrev. for:* **1.** arrival. **2.** arrive(s).

Ar. *abbrev. for:* **1.** Arabia(n). **2.** Also: **Ar** Arabic. **3.** Aramaic.

a.r. *abbrev. for* anno regni. [Latin: in the year of the reign]

A.R. *abbrev. for* Autonomous Region.

-ar *suffix forming adjectives.* of; belonging to; like: *linear; polar; minuscular.* [via Old French *-er* from Latin *-āris,* replacing *-ālis* (-AL[1]) after stems ending in *l*]

A·ra ('ɑ:rə) *n., Latin genitive* **A·rae** ('ɑ:ri:). a constellation in the S hemisphere near Scorpius. [from Latin: altar]

A.R.A. (in Britain) *abbrev. for* Associate of the Royal Academy.

Ar·ab ('ærəb) *n.* **1.** a member of a Semitic people originally inhabiting Arabia, who spread throughout the Middle East, N Africa, and Spain during the seventh and eighth centuries A.D. **2.** a small lively intelligent breed of horse, mainly used for riding. **3.** See **street Arab. 4.** (*modifier*) of or relating to the Arabs: *the Arab nations.* [C14: from Latin *Arabs,* from Greek *Araps,* from Arabic *'Arab*]

Arab. *abbrev. for:* **1.** Arabia(n). **2.** Arabic.

ar·a·besque (ˌærə'bɛsk) *n.* **1.** *Ballet.* a classical position in which the dancer has one leg raised behind and both arms stretched out in one of several conventional poses. **2.** *Music.* a piece or movement with a highly ornamented or decorated melody. **3.** *Arts.* **a.** a type of curvilinear decoration in painting, metalwork, etc., with intricate intertwining leaf, flower, animal, or geometrical designs. **b.** a design of flowing lines. ~*adj.* **4.** designating, of, or decorated in this style. [C18: from French, from Italian *arabesco* in the Arabic style]

A·ra·bi·a (ə'reɪbɪə) *n.* a great peninsula of SW Asia, between the Red Sea and the Persian Gulf: consists chiefly of a desert plateau, with mountains rising over 3000 m (10 000 ft.) in the west and scattered oases; includes the present-day countries of Saudi Arabia, Yemen, Southern Yemen, Oman, Bahrain, Qatar, and the United Arab Emirates. Area: about 2 600 000 sq. km (1 000 000 sq. miles).

A·ra·bi·an (ə'reɪbɪən) *adj.* **1.** of or relating to Arabia or the Arabs. ~*n.* **2.** another word for an **Arab.**

A·ra·bi·an cam·el *n.* a domesticated camel, *Camelus dromedarius,* having one hump on its back and used as a beast of burden in the hot deserts of N Africa and SW Asia. See also **dromedary.** Compare **Bactrian camel.**

A·ra·bi·an Des·ert *n.* **1.** a desert in E Egypt, between the Nile, the Gulf of Suez, and the Red Sea: mountainous parts rise over 1800 m (6000 ft.). **2.** the desert area of the Arabian Peninsula, esp. in the north.

A·ra·bi·an Nights' En·ter·tain·ment *n.* **The.** a collection of oriental folk tales dating from the tenth century. Often shortened to **the Arabian Nights.** Also called: **the Thousand and One Nights.**

A·ra·bi·an Sea *n.* the NW part of the Indian Ocean, between Arabia and India.

Ar·a·bic ('ærəbɪk) *n.* **1.** the language of the Arabs, spoken in a variety of dialects; the official language of Algeria, Egypt, Iraq, Jordan, the Lebanon, Libya, Morocco, Saudi Arabia, the Sudan, Syria, Tunisia, Yemen and Southern Yemen. It is estimated to be the native language of some 75 million people throughout the world. It belongs to the Semitic subfamily of the Afro-Asiatic family of languages and has its own alphabet, which has been borrowed by certain other languages such as Urdu. ~*adj.* **2.** denoting or relating to this language, any of the peoples that speak it, or the countries in which it is spoken.

Ar·a·bic nu·mer·al *n.* one of the numbers 1,2,3,4,5,6,7,8,9,0 (opposed to *Roman numerals*).

a·rab·i·nose (ə'ræbɪˌnəuz, -ˌnəus) *n.* a pentose sugar in plant gums, esp. of cedars and pines. It is used as a culture medium in bacteriology. Formula: $C_5H_{10}O_5$. [C19: from *arabin* (from (GUM) ARAB(IC) + -IN) + -OSE[2]]

Ar·ab·ist ('ærəbɪst) *n.* a student or expert in Arabic culture, language, history, etc.

ar·a·ble ('ærəbəl) *adj.* **1.** (of land) being or capable of being tilled for the production of crops. **2.** of, relating to, or using such land: *arable farming.* ~*n.* **3.** arable land or farming. [C15: from Latin *arābilis* that can be ploughed, from *arāre* to plough]

Ar·ab League *n.* the league of independent Arab states formed in 1945 to further cultural, economic, military, political, and social cooperation.

Ar·a·by ('ærəbɪ) *n.* an archaic or poetic name for **Arabia.**

A·ra·ca·jú (*Portuguese* ˌaraka'ʒu) *n.* a port in E Brazil, capital of Sergipe state. Pop.: 179 512 (1970).

a·ra·ceous (ə'reɪʃəs) *adj.* another word for **aroid** (sense 1). [C19: from New Latin *Arāceae;* see ARUM]

A·rach·ne (ə'ræknɪ) *n. Greek myth.* a maiden changed into a spider for having presumptuously challenged Athena to a weaving contest. [from Greek *arakhnē* spider]

a·rach·nid (ə'ræknɪd) *n.* any terrestrial chelicerate arthropod of the class *Arachnida,* characterized by simple eyes and four pairs of legs. The group includes the spiders, scorpions, ticks, mites, and harvestmen. [C19: from New Latin *Arachnida,* from Greek *arakhnē* spider] —**a·'rach·ni·dan** *adj., n.*

a·rach·noid (ə'ræknɔɪd) *n.* **1.** the middle of the three membranes (see **meninges**) that cover the brain and spinal cord. **2.** another name for **arachnid.** ~*adj.* **3.** of or relating to the middle of the three meninges. **4.** *Botany.* consisting of or covered with soft fine hairs or fibres. **5.** of or relating to the arachnids.

Ar·ad ('æræd) *n.* a city in W Rumania, on the Mures River: became part of Rumania after World War I, after belonging successively to Turkey, Austria, and Hungary. Pop.: 145 968 (1974 est.).

Ar·a·fat ('ærəfæt) *n.* **Yas·ser** ('jæsə). born 1929, Palestinian leader; co-founder of Al Fatah (1956) and leader since 1968 of the Palestine Liberation Organization.

Ar·a·fu·ra Sea (ˌærə'fuərə) *n.* a part of the W Pacific Ocean, between N Australia and SW New Guinea.

A·ra·gats (*Russian* ˌara'gats) *n.* **Mount.** a volcanic mountain in the Soviet Union, in the NW Armenian SSR. Height: 4095 m (13 435 ft.). Turkish name: **Alagez.**

Ar·a·gon[1] ('ærəgən) *n.* a region of NE Spain: independent kingdom from the 11th century until 1479, when it was united with Castile to form modern Spain. Area: 47 609 sq. km (18 382 sq. miles). —**Ar·a·go·nese** (ˌærəgə'ni:z) *n., adj.*

A·ra·gon[2] (*French* ˌara'gɔ̃) *n.* **Louis** (lwi). 1897–1982, French poet, essayist, and novelist; an early surrealist, later a committed Communist. His works include the verse collections *Le Crève-Coeur* (1941) and *Les Yeux d'Elsa* (1942) and the series of novels *Le Monde réel* (1933–44).

a·rag·o·nite (ə'rægəˌnaɪt) *n.* a colourless or white rare mineral that consists of calcium carbonate in orthorhombic crystalline form and is found in deposits from hot springs. Formula: $CaCO_4$. [C19: from ARAGON[1] + -ITE[1]]

A·ra·guai·a *or* **A·ra·guay·a** (ˌɑ:rə'gwaɪə) *n.* a river in central Brazil, rising in S central Mato Grosso state and flowing north to the Tocantins River. Length: over 1771 km (1100 miles).

ar·ak ('ærək) *n.* a variant spelling of **arrack.**

A·rak (æ'rɑ:k, ə'ræk) *n.* a town in central Iran. Pop.: 72 087 (1966). Former name: **Sultanabad.**

A·ra·kan Yo·ma (ˌɑ:rɑ:'kɑ:n 'jəumɑ:) *n.* a mountain range in Burma, between the Irrawaddy River and the W coast: forms a barrier between Burma and India; teak forests.

A·raks (a'raks) *n.* the Russian name for the **Aras** (River).

a·ra·li·a·ceous (əˌreɪlɪ'eɪʃəs) *adj.* of, relating to, or belonging to the *Araliaceae,* a chiefly tropical family of trees, shrubs, or woody climbers having small clusters of whitish or greenish flowers. The family includes the ivy and ginseng. [C19: from New Latin *Aralia* (genus), of uncertain origin]

Ar·al Sea ('ærəl) *n.* the fourth largest lake in the world, in the SW Soviet Union east of the Caspian Sea: shallow and saline. Area: about 64 750 sq. km (25 000 sq. miles). Also called: **Lake Aral.**

A·ram ('ɛəræm, -rəm) *n.* the biblical name for ancient Syria. —**Ar·a·mae·an** *or* **Ar·a·me·an** (ˌærə'mi:ən) *n., adj.*

Aram. *abbrev. for* Aramaic.

Ar·a·ma·ic (ˌærə'meɪɪk) *n.* **1.** an ancient language of the Middle East, still spoken in parts of Syria and the Lebanon, belonging to the NW Semitic subfamily of the Afro-Asiatic family. Originally the speech of Aram, in the fifth century B.C. it spread to become the lingua franca of the Persian empire. See also

Biblical Aramaic. ~*adj.* **2.** of, relating to, or using this language.

Ar·an ('ærən) *adj.* **1.** of or relating to the Aran Islands. **2.** made of thick undyed wool with its natural oils retained: *an Aran sweater.*

a·ra·ne·id (ə'reɪnɪɪd) *n.* any of numerous arachnids constituting the order *Araneae* (or *Araneida*), which comprises the spiders. [C19: from New Latin *Araneida,* from Latin *arānea* spider]

Ar·an Is·lands *pl. n.* a group of three islands in the Atlantic, off the W coast of Ireland: Aranmore or Inishmore (the largest), Inishmaan, and Inisheer. Pop.: 1612 (1966). Area: 46 km (18 sq. miles).

A·rany (*Hungarian* 'ɒrɒnj) *n.* **Já·nos** ('ja:noʃ). 1817–82, Hungarian epic poet, ballad writer, and scholar.

A·rap·a·ho (ə'ræpəˌhəʊ) *n.* **1.** (*pl.* ·**hos** *or* ·**ho**) a member of a North American Indian people of the Plains, now living chiefly in Oklahoma and Wyoming. **2.** the language of this people, belonging to the Algonquian family.

ar·a·pai·ma (ˌærə'paɪmə) *n.* a very large primitive freshwater teleost fish, *Arapaima gigas,* that occurs in tropical South America and can attain a length of 4.5 metres (15 feet) and a weight of 200 kilograms (440 lbs): family *Osteoglossidae.* [via Portuguese from Tupi]

Ar·a·rat ('ærəˌræt) *n.* an extinct volcanic mountain massif in E Turkey: two main peaks; **Great Ararat** 5155 m (16 916 ft.), said to be the resting place of Noah's Ark after the Flood (Genesis 8:4), and **Little Ararat** 3914 m (12 843 ft.).

ar·a·ro·ba (ˌærə'rəʊbə) *n.* **1.** a Brazilian leguminous tree, *Andira araroba.* **2.** Also called: **Goa powder.** a bitter yellow powder obtained from cavities in the wood of this tree, used in medicine to treat skin ailments. See also **chrysarobin.** [from Portuguese, probably from Tupi, from *arara* parrot + *yba* tree]

A·ras (æ'ræs) *n.* a river rising in mountains in Turkish Armenia and flowing east to the Caspian Sea: forms part of the border between the Soviet Union and Turkey and Iran. Length: about 1100 km (660 miles). Ancient name: **Araxes.** Russian name: **Araks.**

Ar·au·ca·ni·a (ˌærɔ:'keɪnɪə; *Spanish* ˌarau'kanja) *n.* a region of central Chile, inhabited by Araucanian Indians.

Ar·au·ca·ni·an (ˌærɔ:'keɪnɪən) *n.* **1.** a South American Indian language of no known relationships, spoken in Chile and W Argentina. **2.** a member of the people who speak this language. ~*adj.* **3.** of or relating to this people or their language.

ar·au·ca·ri·a (ˌærɔ:'kɛərɪə) *n.* any tree of the coniferous genus *Araucaria* of South America, Australia, and Polynesia, such as the monkey puzzle and bunya-bunya. [C19: from New Latin (*arbor*) *Araucaria* (tree) from *Arauco,* a province in Chile]

Ar·a·wak·an (ˌærə'wækən) *n.* **1.** a family of American Indian languages found throughout NE South America. ~*adj.* **2.** of or relating to the peoples speaking these languages.

A·rax·es (ə'ræksi:z) *n.* the ancient name for **Aras.**

ar·ba·lest *or* **ar·ba·list** ('ɑ:bəlɪst) *n.* a large medieval crossbow, usually cocked by mechanical means. [C11: from Old French *arbaleste,* from Late Latin *arcuballista,* from Latin *arcus* bow + BALLISTA]

Ar·be·la (ɑ:'bi:lə) *n.* an ancient city in Assyria, near which the **Battle of Arbela** took place (331 B.C.), in which Alexander the Great defeated the Persians. Modern name: **Erbil.**

Ar·bil ('ɑ:bɪl) *n.* a variant spelling of **Erbil.**

ar·bi·ter ('ɑ:bɪtə) *n.* **1.** a person empowered to judge in a dispute; referee; arbitrator. **2.** a person having complete control of something. [C15: from Latin, of obscure origin] —'**ar·bi·tress** *fem. n.*

ar·bi·trage ('ɑ:bɪˌtrɑ:ʒ, 'ɑ:bɪtrɪdʒ) *n. Finance.* **a.** the purchase of currencies, securities, or commodities in one market for immediate resale in others in order to profit from unequal prices. **b.** (*as modifier*): *arbitrage operations.* [C15: from French, from *arbitrer* to ARBITRATE] —**ar·bi·tra·geur** (ˌɑ:bɪtræ'ʒɜ:) *n.*

ar·bi·tral ('ɑ:bɪtrəl) *adj.* of or relating to arbitration.

ar·bit·ra·ment (ɑ:'bɪtrəmənt) *n.* **1.** the decision or award made by an arbitrator upon a disputed matter. **2.** the power or authority to pronounce such a decision. **3.** another word for **arbitration.**

ar·bi·trar·y ('ɑ:bɪtrərɪ) *adj.* **1.** founded on or subject to personal whims, prejudices, etc.; capricious. **2.** having only relative application or relevance; not absolute. **3.** (of a government, ruler, etc.) despotic or dictatorial. **4.** *Maths.* not representing any specific value: *an arbitrary constant.* **5.** *Law.* (esp. of a penalty or punishment) not laid down by statute; within the court's discretion. ~*n., pl.* ·**trar·ies.** **6.** *Printing.* a less common name for **peculiar** (sense 4). [C15: from Latin *arbitrārius* arranged through arbitration, uncertain] —'**ar·bi·trar·i·ly** *adv.* —'**ar·bi·trar·i·ness** *n.*

ar·bi·trate ('ɑ:bɪˌtreɪt) *vb.* **1.** to settle or decide (a dispute); achieve a settlement between parties. **2.** to submit to or settle by arbitration. [C16: from Latin *arbitrāri* to give judgment; see ARBITER] —'**ar·bi·tra·ble** *adj.* —'**ar·bi**ˌ**tra·tor** *n.*

ar·bi·tra·tion (ˌɑ:bɪ'treɪʃən) *n.* **1.** *Law.* the hearing and determination of a dispute by an impartial referee selected or agreed upon by the parties concerned. **2.** *International law.* the procedure laid down for the settlement of international disputes.

ar·bi·tress ('ɑ:bɪtrɪs) *n.* a female arbitrator.

Ar·blay, d' ('dɑ:bleɪ; *French* dar'blɛ) *n.* **Ma·dame.** the married name of (Fanny) **Burney.**

ar·bor[1] ('ɑ:bə) *n.* the U.S. spelling of **arbour.**

ar·bor[2] ('ɑ:bə) *n.* **1.** a rotating shaft in a machine or power tool on which a milling cutter or grinding wheel is fitted. **2.** a rotating shaft or mandrel on which a workpiece is fitted for machining. **3.** *Foundry.* a part, piece, or structure used to reinforce the core of a mould. [C17: from Latin: tree, mast]

ar·bor·a·ceous (ˌɑ:bə'reɪʃəs) *adj. Literary.* **1.** resembling a tree. **2.** wooded.

ar·bor·e·al (ɑ:'bɔ:rɪəl) *adj.* **1.** of, relating to, or resembling a tree. **2.** living in or among trees: *arboreal monkeys.*

ar·bo·re·ous (ɑ:'bɔ:rɪəs) *adj.* **1.** thickly wooded; having many trees. **2.** another word for **arborescent.**

ar·bo·res·cent (ˌɑ:bə'rɛsᵊnt) *adj.* having the shape or characteristics of a tree. —ˌ**ar·bo·'res·cence** *n.*

ar·bo·re·tum (ˌɑ:bə'ri:təm) *n., pl.* ·**ta** (-tə) *or* ·**tums.** a place where trees or shrubs are cultivated for their scientific or educational interest. [C19: from Latin, from *arbor* tree]

ar·bor·i·cul·ture ('ɑ:bərɪˌkʌltʃə) *n.* the cultivation of trees or shrubs, esp. for the production of timber. —ˌ**ar·bor·i·'cul·tur·al** *adj.* —ˌ**ar·bor·i·'cul·tur·ist** *n.*

ar·bor·ist ('ɑ:bərɪst) *n.* a specialist in the cultivation of trees.

ar·bor·i·za·tion *or* **ar·bor·i·sa·tion** (ˌɑ:bəraɪ'zeɪʃən) *n.* a branching treelike appearance in certain fossils and minerals.

ar·bor vi·tae ('ɑ:bɔ: 'vi:taɪ, 'vaɪti:) *n.* any of several Asian and North American evergreen coniferous trees of the genera *Thuja* and *Thujopsis,* esp. *Thuja occidentalis,* having tiny scalelike leaves and egglike cones. See also **red cedar.** [C17: from New Latin, literally: tree of life]

ar·bour ('ɑ:bə) *n.* **1.** a leafy glade or bower shaded by trees, vines, shrubs, etc., esp. when trained about a trellis. **2.** *Obsolete.* an orchard, garden, or lawn. [C14 *erber,* from Old French *herbier,* from Latin *herba* grass]

Ar·broath (ɑ:'brəʊθ) *n.* a port and resort in E Scotland, in Tayside region: scene of Robert I's declaration of independence in 1320. Pop.: 22 585 (1971).

Ar·buth·not (ɑ:'bʌθnɒt) *n.* **John.** 1667–1735, Scottish physician and satirist: author of *The History of John Bull* (1712) and, with others, of the *Memoirs of Martinus Scriblerus* (1741).

ar·bu·tus (ɑ:'bju:təs) *n., pl.* ·**tus·es.** **1.** any of several temperate ericaceous shrubs of the genus *Arbutus,* esp. the strawberry tree of S Europe. They have clusters of white or pinkish flowers, broad evergreen leaves, and strawberry-like berries. **2.** See **trailing arbutus.** [C16: from Latin; related to *arbor* tree]

arc (ɑ:k) *n.* **1.** something curved in shape. **2.** part of an unbroken curved line. **3.** a luminous discharge that occurs when an electric current flows between two electrodes or any other two surfaces separated by a small gap and a high potential difference. **4.** *Astronomy.* a circular section of the apparent path of a celestial body. ~*vb.* **arcs, arc·ing, arced** *or* **arcs, arck·ing, arcked.** **5.** (*intr.*) to form an arc. ~*adj.* **6.** *Maths.* specifying an inverse trigonometric function: usually written **arcsin, arccos, arctan,** etc., or sometimes $\sin^{-1}$, $\cos^{-1}$, $\tan^{-1}$, etc. [C14: from Old French, from Latin *arcus* bow, arch]

ar·cade (ɑ:'keɪd) *n.* **1.** a set of arches and their supporting columns. **2.** a covered and sometimes arched passageway, usually with shops on one or both sides. **3.** a building, or part of a building, with an arched roof. [C18: from French, from Italian *arcata,* from *arco,* from Latin *arcus* bow, arch]

Ar·ca·di·a (ɑ:'keɪdɪə) *n.* **1.** a department of Greece, in the central Peloponnese. Pop.: 11 263 (1971). Area: 4367 sq. km (1686 sq. miles). **2.** Also (poetic): **Ar·ca·dy** ('ɑ:kədɪ). the traditional idealized rural setting of Greek and Roman bucolic poetry and later in the literature of the Renaissance.

Ar·ca·di·an (ɑ:'keɪdɪən) *adj.* **1.** of or relating to Arcadia or its inhabitants, esp. the idealized Arcadia of pastoral poetry. **2.** rustic or bucolic: *a life of Arcadian simplicity.* ~*n.* **3.** an inhabitant of Arcadia. **4.** a person who leads or prefers a quiet simple rural life. —**Ar·'ca·di·an·ism** *n.*

Ar·cad·ic (ɑ:'keɪdɪk) *adj.* **1.** of or relating to the Arcadians or to their dialect of Ancient Greek. ~*n.* **2.** one of four chief dialects of Ancient Greek; the dialect spoken by the Arcadians. Compare **Aeolic, Doric, Ionic.**

ar·ca·na (ɑ:'keɪnə, -'kɑ:-) *n.* either of the two divisions (the **minor arcana** and the **major arcana**) of a pack of tarot cards.

ar·cane (ɑ:'keɪn) *adj.* requiring secret knowledge to be understood; mysterious; esoteric. [C16: from Latin *arcānus* secret, hidden, from *arcēre* to shut up, keep safe] —**ar·'cane·ly** *adv.* —**ar·'cane·ness** *n.*

ar·ca·num (ɑ:'keɪnəm) *n., pl.* ·**na** (-nə). **1.** (*sometimes pl.*) a profound secret or mystery known only to initiates. **2.** a secret of nature sought by alchemists. [C16: from Latin; see ARCANE]

ar·ca·ture ('ɑ:kətʃə) *n.* **1.** a small-scale arcade. **2.** a set of blind arches attached to the wall of a building as decoration.

arc-bou·tant *French.* (ar bu'tã) *n., pl.* ***arcs-bou·tants*** (ar bu'tã). another name for **flying buttress.**

arc fur·nace *n.* a furnace in which the charge is heated by an electric arc.

arch[1] (ɑ:tʃ) *n.* **1.** a curved structure, normally in the vertical plane, that spans an opening. **2.** Also called: **archway.** a structure in the form of an arch that serves as a gateway. **3.** something curved like an arch. **4. a.** any of various parts or structures of the body having a curved or archlike outline, such as the transverse portion of the aorta (**arch of the aorta**) or the raised bony vault formed by the tarsal and metatarsal bones (**arch of the foot**). **b.** one of the basic patterns of the human fingerprint, formed by several curved ridges one above the other. Compare **loop**[1] (sense 9a.), **whorl** (sense 3). ~*vb.* **5.** (*tr.*) to span (an opening) with an arch. **6.** to form or cause to form an arch or a curve resembling that of an arch: *the cat arched its back.* **7.** (*tr.*) to span or extend over: *the bridge arched the flooded stream.* [C14: from Old French *arche,* from Vulgar Latin *arca* (unattested), from Latin *arcus* bow, ARC]

arch[2] (ɑːtʃ) *adj.* **1.** (*prenominal*) chief; principal; leading: *his arch rival.* **2.** (*prenominal*) very experienced; expert: *an arch criminal.* **3.** knowing or superior: *an arch look.* **4.** mischievous or cunning: *an arch child.* [C16: independent use of ARCH-] —**'arch·ly** *adv.* —**'arch·ness** *n.*

arch. *abbrev. for:* **1.** archaic. **2.** archaism. **3.** archery. **4.** archipelago. **5.** architect. **6.** architectural. **7.** architecture.

Arch. *abbrev. for* Archbishop.

arch- *or* **ar·chi-** *combining form.* **1.** chief; principal; of highest rank: *archangel; archbishop; archduke.* **2.** eminent above all others of the same kind; extreme: *archenemy; archfiend; archfool.* [ultimately from Greek *arkhi-*, from *arkhein* to rule]

-arch *n. combining form.* leader; ruler; chief: *patriarch; monarch; heresiarch.* [from Greek *-arkhēs,* from *arkhein* to rule; compare ARCH-]

Ar·chae·an *or esp. U.S.* **Ar·che·an** (ɑː'kiːən) *adj.* of or relating to the highly metamorphosed rocks formed in the early Precambrian era.

ar·chae·o- *or* **ar·che·o-** *combining form.* indicating ancient or primitive time or condition: *archaeology; archaeopteryx.* [from Greek *arkhaio-*, from *arkhaios*, from *arkhein* to begin]

archaeol. *abbrev. for* archaeology.

ar·chae·ol·o·gy *or* **ar·che·ol·o·gy** (ˌɑːkɪ'ɒlədʒɪ) *n.* the study of man's past by scientific analysis of the material remains of his cultures. See also **prehistory, protohistory.** [C17: from Late Latin *archaeologia,* from Greek *arkhaiologia* study of what is ancient, from *arkhaios* ancient (from *arkhē* beginning)] —**ar·chae·o·log·i·cal** *or* **ar·che·o·log·i·cal** (ˌɑːkɪə'lɒdʒɪkᵊl) *adj.* —ˌ**ar·chae·o·'log·i·cal·ly** *or* ˌ**ar·che·o·'log·i·cal·ly** *adv.* —ˌ**ar·chae·'ol·o·gist** *or* ˌ**ar·che·'ol·o·gist** *n.*

ar·chae·o·mag·net·ism *or* **ar·che·o·mag·net·ism** (ˌɑːkɪəʊ'mægnɪˌtɪzəm) *n.* an archaeological technique for dating certain clay objects by measuring the extent to which they have been magnetized by the earth's magnetic field.

ar·chae·op·ter·yx (ˌɑːkɪ'ɒptərɪks) *n.* any of several extinct primitive birds constituting the genus *Archaeopteryx,* esp. *A. lithographica,* which occurred in Jurassic times and had teeth, a long tail, well-developed wings, and a body covering of feathers. [C19: from ARCHAEO- + Greek *pterux* winged creature]

ar·chae·or·nis (ˌɑːkɪ'ɔːnɪs) *n.* an extinct primitive Jurassic bird, formerly placed in the genus *Archaeornis* but now thought to be a species of archaeopteryx. [C19: New Latin, from ARCHAEO- + Greek *ornis* bird]

Ar·chae·o·zo·ic *or esp. U.S.* **Ar·che·o·zo·ic** (ˌɑːkɪə'zəʊɪk) *adj.* **1.** of or formed in the early Precambrian era. ~*n.* **2.** the earlier of two divisions of the Precambrian era, during which the earliest forms of life are assumed to have appeared. Compare **Proterozoic.**

ar·cha·ic (ɑː'keɪɪk) *adj.* **1.** belonging to or characteristic of a much earlier period; ancient. **2.** out of date; antiquated: *an archaic prison system.* **3.** (of idiom, vocabulary, etc.) characteristic of an earlier period of a language and not in ordinary use. [C19: from French *archaïque,* from Greek *arkhaïkos,* from *arkhaios* ancient, from *arkhē* beginning, from *arkhein* to begin] —**ar·'cha·i·cal·ly** *adv.*

ar·cha·ism ('ɑːkɪˌɪzəm, -keɪ-) *n.* **1.** the adoption or imitation of something archaic, such as a word or an artistic or literary style. **2.** an archaic word, expression, style, etc. [C17: from New Latin *archaismus,* from Greek *arkhaïsmos,* from *arkhaizein* to model one's style upon that of ancient writers; see ARCHAIC] —**'ar·cha·ist** *n.* —ˌ**ar·cha·'is·tic** *adj.*

ar·cha·ize *or* **ar·cha·ise** ('ɑːkɪˌaɪz, -keɪ-) *vb.* (*tr.*) to give an archaic appearance or character to, as by the use of archaisms. —**'ar·cha·ˌiz·er** *or* **'ar·cha·ˌis·er** *n.*

arch·an·gel ('ɑːkˌeɪndʒəl) *n.* **1.** *Theol.* a principal angel, a member of the order ranking immediately above the angels in medieval angelology. **2.** another name for **angelica** (sense 1). **3. yellow archangel.** a Eurasian herbaceous plant, *Galeobdolon luteum* (or *Lamium galeobdolon*), that occurs in woodlands and has yellow helmet-shaped flowers: family *Labiatae* (labiates). **4.** a bronze-coloured breed of domestic pigeon with black markings. —**arch·an·gel·ic** (ˌɑːkæn'dʒɛlɪk) *adj.*

Arch·an·gel ('ɑːkˌeɪndʒəl) *n.* a port in the NW Soviet Union, on the Dvina River: major centre for the timber trade and White Sea fisheries. Pop.: 376 000 (1975 est.). Russian name: **Arkhangelsk.**

arch·bish·op ('ɑːtʃ'bɪʃəp) *n.* a bishop of the highest rank. Abbrev.: **abp., Abp., Arch., Archbp.**

arch·bish·op·ric ('ɑːtʃ'bɪʃəprɪk) *n.* **1.** the rank, office, or jurisdiction of an archbishop. **2.** the area governed by an archbishop.

Archbp. *abbrev. for* archbishop.

Archd. *abbrev. for:* **1.** archdeacon. **2.** archduke.

arch·dea·con ('ɑːtʃ'diːkən) *n.* **1.** an Anglican clergyman ranking just below a bishop and having supervisory duties under the bishop. **2.** a clergyman of similar rank in other Churches.

arch·dea·con·ry ('ɑːtʃ'diːkənrɪ) *n., pl.* **·ries. 1.** the office, rank, or duties of an archdeacon. **2.** the residence of an archdeacon.

arch·di·o·cese (ˌɑːtʃ'daɪəˌsiːs, -sɪs) *n.* the diocese of an archbishop. —**arch·di·oc·e·san** (ˌɑːtʃdaɪ'ɒsɪsᵊn) *adj.*

arch·du·cal ('ɑːtʃ'djuːkᵊl) *adj.* of or relating to an archduke, archduchess, or archduchy.

arch·duch·ess ('ɑːtʃ'dʌtʃɪs) *n.* **1.** the wife or widow of an archduke. **2.** (since 1453) a princess of the Austrian imperial family, esp. a daughter of the Austrian emperor.

arch·duch·y ('ɑːtʃ'dʌtʃɪ) *n., pl.* **·duch·ies.** the territory ruled by an archduke or archduchess.

arch·duke ('ɑːtʃ'djuːk) *n.* a chief duke, esp. (since 1453) a prince of the Austrian imperial dynasty.

Ar·che·an (ɑː'kiːən) *adj.* a variant spelling (esp. U.S.) of **Archaean.**

arched (ɑːtʃt) *adj.* **1.** provided with or spanned by an arch or arches. **2.** shaped like an arch; curved.

ar·che·go·ni·um (ˌɑːkɪ'gəʊnɪəm) *n., pl.* **·ni·a** (-nɪə). a female sex organ, occurring in mosses, ferns, and evergreen trees, that produces a single egg cell in its swollen base. [C19: from New Latin, from Greek *arkhegonos* original parent, from *arkhe-* chief, first + *gonos* seed, race] —ˌ**ar·che·'go·ni·ate** *adj.*

arch·en·e·my ('ɑːtʃ'ɛnɪmɪ) *n., pl.* **·mies. 1.** a chief enemy. **2.** (*often cap.;* preceded by *the*) the devil.

ar·chen·ter·on (ɑː'kɛntəˌrɒn) *n.* the cavity within an embryo at the gastrula stage of development that eventually becomes the digestive cavity. [C19: from Greek *arkhē* beginning + *enteron* intestine] —**ar·chen·ter·ic** (ˌɑːkən'tɛrɪk) *adj.*

ar·che·ol·o·gy (ˌɑːkɪ'ɒlədʒɪ) *n.* a variant spelling of **archaeology.**

Ar·che·o·zo·ic (ˌɑːkɪə'zəʊɪk) *adj.* a variant spelling (esp. U.S.) of **Archaeozoic.**

arch·er ('ɑːtʃə) *n.* a person skilled in the use of a bow and arrow. [C13: from Old French *archier,* from Late Latin *arcārius,* from Latin *arcus* bow]

Arch·er[1] ('ɑːtʃə) *n.* **the.** the constellation Sagittarius, the ninth sign of the zodiac.

Arch·er[2] ('ɑːtʃə) *n.* **Wil·liam.** 1856–1924, Scottish critic and dramatist: made the first English translations of Ibsen.

arch·er·fish ('ɑːtʃəˌfɪʃ) *n., pl.* **·fish** *or* **·fish·es.** any freshwater percoid fish of the family *Toxotidae* of S and SE Asia and Australia, esp. *Toxotes jaculatrix,* that catch insects by spitting water at them.

ar·cher·y ('ɑːtʃərɪ) *n.* **1.** the art or sport of shooting with bows and arrows. **2.** archers or their weapons collectively.

Arch·es ('ɑːtʃɪz) *pl. n.* **Court of.** *Church of England.* the court of appeal of the Province of Canterbury, formerly held under the arches of Bow Church.

ar·che·spore ('ɑːkɪˌspɔː) *or* **ar·che·spo·ri·um** (ˌɑːkɪ'spɔːrɪəm) *n., pl.* **·spores** *or* **·spo·ri·a** (-'spɔːrɪə). *Botany.* the cell or group of cells in a sporangium that gives rise to spores. —ˌ**ar·che·'spo·ri·al** *adj.*

ar·che·type ('ɑːkɪˌtaɪp) *n.* **1.** a perfect or typical specimen. **2.** an original model or pattern; prototype. **3.** *Psychoanal.* one of the inherited mental images postulated by Jung as the content of the collective unconscious. **4.** a constantly recurring symbol or motif in literature, painting, etc. [C17: from Latin *archetypum* an original, from Greek *arkhetupon,* from *arkhetupos* first-moulded; see ARCH-, TYPE] —**'ar·che·ˌtyp·al** *or* **ar·che·typ·i·cal** (ˌɑːkɪ'tɪpɪkᵊl) *adj.* —ˌ**ar·che·'typ·al·ly** *or* ˌ**ar·che·'typ·i·cal·ly** *adv.*

arch·fiend (ˌɑːtʃ'fiːnd) *n.* (*often cap.*) **the.** the chief of fiends or devils; Satan.

ar·chi- *combining form.* variant of **arch-.**

ar·chi·carp ('ɑːkɪˌkɑːp) *n.* a female reproductive structure in ascomycetous fungi that consists of a cell or hypha and develops into the ascogonium.

ar·chi·di·ac·o·nal (ˌɑːkɪdaɪ'ækənᵊl) *adj.* of or relating to an archdeacon or his office.

ar·chi·di·ac·o·nate (ˌɑːkɪdaɪ'ækənɪt) *n.* the office, term of office, or area of jurisdiction of an archdeacon.

ar·chi·e·pis·co·pal (ˌɑːkɪɪ'pɪskəpᵊl) *adj.* of or associated with an archbishop.

ar·chi·e·pis·co·pate (ˌɑːkɪɪ'pɪskəpɪt, -ˌpeɪt) *or* **ar·chi·e·pis·co·pa·cy** (ˌɑːkɪɪ'pɪskəpəsɪ) *n.* the rank, office, or term of office of an archbishop.

ar·chil ('ɑːtʃɪl) *n.* a variant spelling of **orchil.**

Ar·chi·lo·chi·an (ˌɑːkɪ'ləʊkɪən) *adj.* denoting or relating to Archilochus or his verse, esp. the iambic trimeters or trochaic tetrameters used by him.

Ar·chil·o·chus (ɑː'kɪləkəs) *n.* 7th century B.C., Greek poet of Paros, notable for using his own experience as subject matter.

ar·chi·mage ('ɑːkɪˌmeɪdʒ) *n.* a great magician or wizard. [C16: from ARCHI- + *mage,* from Latin *magus* magician]

ar·chi·man·drite (ˌɑːkɪ'mændraɪt) *n. Greek Orthodox Church.* the head of a monastery or a group of monasteries. [C16: from Late Latin *archimandrīta,* from Late Greek *arkhimandritēs,* from ARCHI- + *mandra* monastery]

Ar·chi·me·des[1] (ˌɑːkɪ'miːdiːz) *n.* ?287–212 B.C., Greek mathematician and physicist of Syracuse, noted for his work in geometry, hydrostatics, and mechanics. —**Ar·chi·me·de·an** (ˌɑːkɪ'miːdɪən, -mɪ'diːən) *adj.*

Ar·chi·me·des[2] (ˌɑːkɪ'miːdiːz) *n.* a walled plain in the NE quadrant of the moon, about 80 kilometres in diameter.

Ar·chi·me·des' prin·ci·ple *n.* a law of physics stating that the apparent loss in weight of a body immersed in a fluid is equal to the weight of the displaced fluid.

Ar·chi·me·des' screw *or* **Ar·chi·me·de·an screw** *n.* an ancient type of water-lifting device making use of a spiral passage in an inclined cylinder. The water is raised when the spiral is rotated.

ar·chine (ɑː'ʃiːn) *n.* a Russian unit of length equal to about 71 cm. [from Russian *arshin,* of Turkic origin]

ar·chi·pel·a·go (ˌɑːkɪ'pɛlɪˌgəʊ) *n., pl.* **·gos** *or* **·goes. 1.** a group of islands. **2.** a sea studded with islands. [C16 (meaning: the Aegean Sea): from Italian *arcipelago,* literally: the chief sea (perhaps originally a mistranslation of Greek *Aigaion pelagos* the Aegean Sea), from ARCHI- + *pelago* sea, from Latin *pelagus,* from Greek *pelagos*] —**ar·chi+pe·lag+ic** (ˌɑːkɪpəˈlædʒɪk) *or* **ar·chi+pe+la·gi·an** (ˌɑːkɪpəˈleɪdʒɪən) *adj.*

Ar·chi·pen·ko (*Russian* arˈxipɪnkə) *n.* **A·le·ksan·dr Por·fir·ye·vich** (alɪˈksandʳr parˈfirjɪvitʃ). 1887–1964, Russian sculptor and painter, in the U.S. after 1923, whose work is characterized by economy of form.

ar·chi+pho+neme (ˈɑːkɪˌfəuniːm, ˌɑːkɪˈfəuniːm) *n. Phonetics.* an abstract linguistic unit representing two or more phonemes when the distinction between these has been neutralized: conventionally shown by a capital letter within slashes, as /T/ for /t/ and /d/ in German *Rat* and *Rad.*

ar·chi+plasm (ˈɑːkɪˌplæzəm) *n.* a variant spelling of **archoplasm.** —ˌ**ar·chi+ˈplas+mic** *adj.*

archit. *abbrev. for* architecture.

ar·chi+tect (ˈɑːkɪˌtɛkt) *n.* **1.** a person qualified to design and supervise the construction of buildings. **2.** a person similarly qualified in another form of construction: *a naval architect.* **3.** any planner or creator: *the architect of the expedition.* [C16: from French *architecte,* from Latin *architectus,* from Greek *arkhitektōn* director of works, from ARCHI- + *tektōn* workman; related to *tekhnē* art, skill]

ar·chi+tec+ton+ic (ˌɑːkɪtɛkˈtɒnɪk) *adj.* **1.** denoting, relating to, or having architectural qualities. **2.** *Metaphysics.* of or relating to the systematic classification of knowledge. [C16: from Late Latin *architectonicus* concerning architecture; see ARCHITECT] —ˌ**ar·chi+tec+ˈton·i+cal+ly** *adv.*

ar·chi+tec+ton+ics (ˌɑːkɪtɛkˈtɒnɪks) *n.* (*functioning as sing.*) **1.** the science of architecture. **2.** *Metaphysics.* the scientific classification of knowledge.

ar·chi+tec+ture (ˈɑːkɪˌtɛktʃə) *n.* **1.** the art and science of designing and supervising the construction of buildings and similar structures. **2.** a style of building or structure: *Gothic architecture.* **3.** buildings or structures collectively. **4.** the structure or design of anything: *the architecture of the universe.* —ˌ**ar·chi+ˈtec+tur+al** *adj.* —ˌ**ar·chi+ˈtec+tur+al+ly** *adv.*

ar·chi+trave (ˈɑːkɪˌtreɪv) *n. Architect.* **1.** the lowest part of an entablature that bears on the columns. **2.** a moulding around a doorway, window opening, etc. [C16: via French from Italian, from ARCHI- + *trave* beam, from Latin *trabs*]

ar+chives (ˈɑːkaɪvz) *pl. n.* **1.** a collection of records of or about an institution, family, etc. **2.** a place where such records are kept. [C17: from Late Latin *archīvum,* from Greek *arkheion* repository of official records, from *arkhē* government] —**ar+ˈchiv+al** *adj.*

ar·chi+vist (ˈɑːkɪvɪst) *n.* a person in charge of archives, their collection, and cataloguing.

ar·chi+volt (ˈɑːkɪˌvəult) *n. Architect.* **1.** a moulding around an arch, sometimes decorated. **2.** the under surface of an arch. [C18: from Italian *archivolto;* see ARC, VAULT¹]

ar+chon (ˈɑːkɒn, -kən) *n.* (in ancient Athens) one of the nine chief magistrates. [C17: from Greek *arkhōn* ruler, from *arkhein* to rule] —**ˈar+chon+ˌship** *n.*

ar+cho+plasm (ˈɑːkəˌplæzəm) *or* **ar·chi+plasm** *n.* the protoplasmic material surrounding the centrosome, formerly thought to be involved in the formation of the asters and spindle during mitosis. —ˌ**ar+cho+ˈplas+mic** *adj.*

arch+priest (ˈɑːtʃˈpriːst) *n. Ecclesiast.* **1.** (formerly) a chief assistant to a bishop, performing many of his sacerdotal functions during his absence. **2.** a senior priest. —**ˈarch+ˈpriest+ˌhood** *or* **ˈarch+ˈpriest+ˌship** *n.*

archt. *abbrev. for* architect.

arch+way (ˈɑːtʃˌweɪ) *n.* a passageway or entrance under an arch or arches.

-ar·chy *n. combining form.* government; rule: *anarchy; monarchy.* [from Greek *-arkhia;* see -ARCH] —**-ar·chic** *adj. combining form.* —**-ar·chist** *n. combining form.*

arc light *n.* a light source in which an arc between two electrodes, usually carbon, produces intense white illumination. Also called: **arc lamp.**

A.R.C.M. *abbrev. for* Associate of the Royal College of Music.

arc·o·graph (ˈɑːkəˌgrɑːf, -ˌgræf) *n. Geom.* an instrument used for drawing arcs without using a central point. Also called: **cyclograph.**

A.R.C.S. *abbrev. for* Associate of the Royal College of Science.

arc+tic (ˈɑːktɪk) *adj.* **1.** of or relating to the Arctic: *arctic temperatures.* **2.** *Informal.* cold; freezing: *the weather at Christmas was arctic.* ~*n.* **3.** *U.S.* a high waterproof overshoe with buckles. **4.** (*modifier*) designed or suitable for conditions of extreme cold: *arctic clothing.* [C14: from Latin *arcticus,* from Greek *arktikos* northern, literally: pertaining to (the constellation of) the Bear, from *arktos* bear]

Arc+tic (ˈɑːktɪk) *n.* **1. the.** Also called: **Arctic Zone.** the regions north of the Arctic Circle. ~*adj.* **2.** of or relating to the regions north of the Arctic Circle.

arc+tic char *n.* a char, *Salvelinus alpinus,* that occurs in northern and arctic seas.

Arc+tic Cir+cle *n.* the imaginary circle round the earth, parallel to the equator, at latitude 66° 32′ N.

arc+tic fox *n.* a fox, *Alopex lagopus,* of arctic regions, whose fur is dark grey in the summer and white in the winter. See also **blue fox.**

Arc+tic O·cean *n.* the ocean surrounding the North Pole, north of the Arctic Circle. Area: about 14 100 000 sq. km (5 440 000 sq. miles).

arc+tic tern *n.* a black-capped tern, *Sterna paradisea,* that breeds in the Arctic and then migrates as far south as the Antarctic.

Arc+to+gae·a (ˌɑːktəˈdʒiːə) *n.* a zoogeographical area comprising the Palaearctic, Nearctic, Oriental, and Ethiopian regions. Compare **Neogaea, Notogaea.** —ˌ**Arc+to+ˈgae·an** *adj.*

Arc+tu+rus (ɑːkˈtjuərəs) *n.* the brightest star in the constellation Boötes: a red giant. Visual magnitude: 0.24; spectral type: KO; distance: 36 light years. [C14: from Latin, from Greek *Arktouros,* from *arktos* bear + *ouros* guard, keeper] —**Arc+ˈtu+ri·an** *adj.*

ar+cu+ate (ˈɑːkjuːɪt, -ˌeɪt) *adj.* shaped or bent like an arc or bow: *arcuate leaves; arcuate fibres of the cerebrum.* Also: **arcuated.** [C17: from Latin *arcuāre,* from *arcus* ARC] —**ˈar+cu+ate+ly** *adv.*

ar+cu·a+tion (ˌɑːkjuˈeɪʃən) *n.* **1.** the use of arches or vaults in buildings. **2.** an arrangement of arches. [C17: from Late Latin *arcuātiō* arch, from Latin *arcuāre* to curve]

ar+cus se+ni+lis (ˈɑːkəs sɪˈnaɪlɪs) *n.* an opaque circle around the cornea of the eye, often seen in elderly people. [Latin: senile bow]

arc weld+ing *n.* a technique in which metal is welded by heat generated by an electric arc struck between two electrodes or between one electrode and the metal workpiece. —**arc weld+er** *n.*

-ard *or* **-art** *suffix forming nouns.* indicating a person who does something, esp. to excess, or is characterized by a certain quality: *braggart; drunkard; dullard.* [via Old French from Germanic *-hard* (literally: hardy, bold), the final element in many Germanic masculine names, such as *Bernhard* Bernard, *Gerhart* Gerard, etc.]

ar+deb (ˈɑːdɛb) *n.* a unit of dry measure used in Egypt and other Middle Eastern countries. In Egypt it is approximately equal to 0.195 cubic metres. [C19: from Arabic *ardabb,* from Greek *artabē* a Persian measure]

Ar+dèche (*French* arˈdɛʃ) *n.* a department of S France, in Rhône-Alpes region. Capital: Privas. Pop.: 263 790 (1975). Area: 5556 sq. km (2167 sq. miles).

Ar+den (ˈɑːdᵊn) *n.* **Forest of.** a region of N Warwickshire, part of a former forest: scene of Shakespeare's *As You Like It.*

Ar+dennes (ɑːˈdɛn; *French* arˈdɛn) *n.* **1.** a department of NE France, in Champagne-Ardenne region. Capital: Mézières. Pop.: 317 139 (1975). Area: 5253 sq. km (2049 sq. miles). **2. the.** a wooded plateau in SE Belgium, Luxembourg, and NE France: scene of heavy fighting in both World Wars.

ar+dent (ˈɑːdᵊnt) *adj.* **1.** expressive of or characterized by intense desire or emotion; passionate: *ardent love.* **2.** intensely enthusiastic; eager: *an ardent longing.* **3.** glowing, flashing, or shining: *ardent eyes.* **4.** *Rare.* burning: *an ardent fever.* [C14: from Latin *ārdēre* to burn] —**ˈar+den+cy** *n.* —**ˈar+dent+ly** *adv.*

ar+dent spir+its *pl. n.* spirits, such as rum, whisky, etc.

ar+dour *or U.S.* **ar+dor** (ˈɑːdə) *n.* **1.** feelings of great intensity and warmth; fervour. **2.** eagerness; zeal. **3.** *Rare.* burning heat. [C14: from Old French *ardour,* from Latin *ārdor,* from *ārdēre* to burn]

ar+du+ous (ˈɑːdjuːəs) *adj.* **1.** requiring great physical or mental effort; difficult to accomplish; strenuous. **2.** hard to endure; harsh: *arduous conditions.* **3.** hard to overcome or surmount; steep or difficult: *an arduous track.* [C16: from Latin *arduus* steep, difficult] —**ˈar+du+ous+ly** *adv.* —**ˈar+du+ous+ness** *n.*

are¹ (ɑː; *unstressed* ə) *vb.* the plural form of the present tense (indicative mood) of **be** and the singular form used with *you.* [Old English *aron,* second person plural of *bēon* to BE]

are² (ɑː) *n.* a unit of area equal to 100 sq. metres or 119.599 sq. yards; one hundredth of a hectare. [C19: from French, from Latin *ārea* piece of ground; see AREA]

ar·e·a (ˈɛərɪə) *n.* **1.** any flat, curved, or irregular expanse of a surface. **2. a.** the extent of a two-dimensional surface enclosed within a specified boundary or geometric figure: *the area of Ireland; the area of a triangle.* **b.** the two-dimensional extent of the boundary of a closed plane or curved surface: *the area of a sphere.* **3.** a section, portion, or part: *an area of the body; an area of the sky.* **4.** region; district; locality: *a mountainous area.* **5.** a part or section, as of a building, town, etc., having some specified function or characteristic: *reception area; commercial area; slum area.* **6.** the range, extent, or scope of anything. **7.** a subject field or field of study. **8.** any unoccupied or unused flat open piece of ground. **9.** the ground on which a building stands, or the ground surrounding a building. **10.** *Anatomy.* any of the various regions of the cerebral cortex. **11.** *Computer technol.* any part of a computer memory assigned to store data of a specified type. [C16: from Latin: level ground, open space for play, threshing-floor; related to *ārēre* to be dry] —**ˈar+e·al** *adj.*

ar·e·a code *n. U.S.* a three-digit number prefixed to an individual telephone number: used in making long-distance calls.

ar·e·a+way (ˈɛərɪəˌweɪ) *n.* **1.** a passageway between parts of a building or between different buildings. **2.** Also called **area.** a sunken area, usually enclosed, giving light, air, and sometimes access to a cellar or basement.

ar+e·ca (ˈærɪkə, əˈriːkə) *n.* any of various tall palms of the genus *Areca,* which are native to SE Asia and have white flowers and orange or red egg-shaped nuts. [C16: from Portuguese, from Malayalam *adekka*]

a·reg (əˈrɛg) *n.* a plural of **erg**².

a·re·na (əˈriːnə) *n.* **1. a.** an enclosure or platform, usually surrounded by seats on all sides, in which sports events, contests, entertainments, etc., are performed: *a boxing arena.* **b.** (*as modifier*): *arena stage.* **2.** the central area of an ancient Roman amphitheatre, in which gladiatorial contests and other spectacles were held. **3.** a sphere or scene of conflict or intense activity: *the political arena.* [C17: from Latin *harēna* sand, place where sand was strewn for the combats]

ar·e·na·ceous (ˌærɪˈneɪʃəs) *adj.* **1.** (of sedimentary rocks and deposits) composed of sand or sandstone. Compare **argillaceous** and **rudaceous. 2.** (of plants) growing best in a sandy soil. [C17: from Latin *harēnāceus* sandy, from *harēna* sand]

a·re·na the·a·tre *n.* another term for **theatre-in-the-round.**

ar·e·nic·o·lous (ˌærɪˈnɪkələs) *adj.* growing or living in sand or sandy places: *arenicolous plants.* [C19: from Latin *harēna* sand + *colere* to inhabit]

ar·e·nite (ˈærəˌnaɪt, əˈriː-) *n.* any arenaceous rock; a sandstone. [C20: from Latin *harēna* sand + -ITE[1]] —**ar·e·nit·ic** (ˌærəˈnɪtɪk) *adj.*

aren't (ɑːnt) **1.** *contraction of* are not. **2.** *Informal, chiefly Brit.* (used in interrogative sentences) *contraction of* am not.

ar·e·og·ra·phy (ˌɛərɪˈɒɡrəfɪ) *n.* the description of the physical features, such as the surface, atmosphere, etc., of the planet Mars. [C19: from Greek *Areos* Mars + -GRAPHY]

a·re·o·la (əˈrɪələ) *n., pl.* **-lae** (-ˌliː) *or* **-las. 1.** *Biology.* a space outlined on a surface, such as an area between veins on a leaf or on an insect's wing. **2.** *Anatomy.* any small circular area, such as the pigmented ring around the human nipple or the inflamed area surrounding a pimple. [C17: from Latin: diminutive of AREA] —**a·ˈre·o·lar** *or* **a·re·o·late** (əˈrɪəlɪt, -ˌleɪt) *adj.* —**a·re·o·la·tion** (əˌrɪəˈleɪʃən) *n.*

Ar·e·op·a·gus (ˌærɪˈɒpəɡəs) *n.* **1. a.** the hill to the northwest of the Acropolis in Athens. **b.** (in ancient Athens) the judicial council whose members (Areopagites) met on this hill. **2.** *Literary.* any high court. [via Latin from Greek *Areiopagus*, contracted from *Areios pagos*, hill of Ares] —**Ar·e·op·a·gite** (ˌærɪˈɒpədʒaɪt) *n.*

A·re·qui·pa (ˌærɪˈkiːpə; *Spanish* ˌareˈkipa) *n.* a city in S Peru, at an altitude of 2250 m (7500 ft.): founded in 1540 on the site of an Inca city. Pop.: 302 316 (1972).

Ar·es (ˈɛəriːz) *n. Greek myth.* the god of war, born of Zeus and Hera. Roman counterpart: **Mars.**

a·rête (əˈreɪt) *n.* a sharp ridge found in mountainous regions that separates two cirques or glacial valleys. [C19: from French: fishbone, backbone (of a fish), ridge, sharp edge, from Latin *arista* ear of corn, fishbone]

ar·e·thu·sa (ˌærɪˈθjuːzə) *n.* a North American orchid, *Arethusa bulbosa*, having one long narrow leaf and one rose-purple flower fringed with yellow.

Ar·e·thu·sa (ˌærɪˈθjuːzə) *n. Greek myth.* a nymph who was changed into a spring on the island of Ortygia to escape the amorous advances of the river god Alpheus.

Ar·e·ti·no (*Italian* ˌareˈtiːno) *n.* **Pie·tro** (ˈpjɛːtro). 1492–1556, Italian satirist, poet, and dramatist, noted for his satirical attacks on leading political figures.

A·rez·zo (əˈrɛtsəʊ; *Italian* aˈrettsɔ) *n.* a city in central Italy, in E Tuscany. Pop.: 87 128 (1971).

Arg. *abbrev. for* Argentina.

ar·gal (ˈɑːɡəl) *n.* another name for **argol.**

ar·ga·li (ˈɑːɡəlɪ) *or* **ar·gal** *n., pl.* **·ga·li** *or* **·gals.** a wild sheep, *Ovis ammon*, inhabiting semidesert regions in central Asia: family *Bovidae*, order *Artiodactyla*. It is the largest of the sheep, having massive horns in the male, which may almost form a circle. [C18: from Mongolian]

Ar·gand di·a·gram (ˈɑːɡænd) *n. Maths.* a diagram consisting of two perpendicular axes, the real axis (*x*-axis) and the imaginary axis (*y*-axis), on which a complex number $z = x + iy$ can be represented as a point. [C19: named after Jean-Robert *Argand* (1768–1822), French mathematician]

ar·gent (ˈɑːdʒənt) *n.* **a.** an archaic or poetic word for **silver. b.** (*as adj.; often postpositive, esp. in heraldry*): *a bend argent.* [C15: from Old French, from Latin]

Ar·gen·teuil (*French* arʒɑ̃ˈtœj) *n.* a suburb of Paris, with a convent (656) that became famous when Héloïse was abbess (12th century). Pop.: 103 141 (1975).

ar·gen·tic (ɑːˈdʒɛntɪk) *adj. Chem.* of or containing silver in the divalent or trivalent state.

ar·gen·tif·er·ous (ˌɑːdʒənˈtɪfərəs) *adj.* containing or bearing silver.

Ar·gen·ti·na (ˌɑːdʒənˈtiːnə) *n.* a republic in southern South America: colonized by the Spanish from 1516 onwards; gained independence in 1816 and became a republic in 1852; consists chiefly of subtropical plains and forests (the Chaco) in the north, temperate plains (the pampas) in the central parts, the Andes in the west, and an infertile plain extending to Tierra del Fuego in the south (Patagonia); an important meat producer. Language: Spanish. Religion: Roman Catholic. Currency: peso. Capital: Buenos Aires. Pop.: 23 362 204 (1970). Area: 2 776 653 sq. km (1 072 067 sq. miles). Also called: **the Argentine.**

ar·gen·tine (ˈɑːdʒənˌtaɪn) *adj.* **1.** of, relating to, or resembling silver. ~*n.* **2.** any of various small marine salmonoid fishes, such as *Argentina sphyraena*, that constitute the family *Argentinidae* and are characterized by a long silvery body.

Ar·gen·tine (ˈɑːdʒənˌtiːn, -ˌtaɪn) *n.* **1. the.** another name for **Argentina. 2.** a native or inhabitant of Argentina. ~*adj.* **3.** of or relating to Argentina. ~Also (for senses 2, 3): **Ar·gen·tin·e·an** (ˌɑːdʒənˈtɪnɪən).

ar·gen·tite (ˈɑːdʒənˌtaɪt) *n.* a dark grey mineral that consists of silver sulphide, usually in cubic crystalline forms, and occurs in veins, often with native silver. It is found esp. in Mexico, Nevada, and Saxony and is an important source of silver. Formula: Ag_2S.

ar·gen·tous (ɑːˈdʒɛntəs) *adj. Chem.* of or containing silver in the monovalent state.

ar·gen·tum (ɑːˈdʒɛntəm) *n.* an obsolete name for **silver.** [Latin]

ar·gil (ˈɑːdʒɪl) *n.* clay, esp. potters' clay. [C16: from Latin *argilla* white clay, from Greek *argillos*]

ar·gil·la·ceous (ˌɑːdʒɪˈleɪʃəs) *adj.* (of sedimentary rocks and deposits) composed of very fine-grained material, such as clay, shale, etc. Compare **arenaceous** (sense 1) and **rudaceous.**

ar·gil·lif·er·ous (ˌɑːdʒɪˈlɪfərəs) *adj.* containing or yielding clay: *argilliferous rocks.*

ar·gil·lite (ˈɑːdʒɪˌlaɪt) *n.* any argillaceous rock, esp. a hardened mudstone. [C18: from Latin *argilla* clay (from Greek *argillos*) + -ITE[1]] —**ar·gil·lit·ic** (ˌɑːdʒɪˈlɪtɪk) *adj.*

ar·gi·nine (ˈɑːdʒɪˌnaɪn) *n.* an essential bitter-tasting amino acid of plant and animal proteins, necessary for nutrition. Its absence from the diet leads to a reduced production of spermatozoa; 2-amino-5-guanidopentanoic acid. Formula: $H_2NC(:NH)NH(CH_2)_3CHNH_2COOH$. [C19: from German *Arginin*, of uncertain origin]

Ar·give (ˈɑːdʒaɪv, -ɡaɪv) *adj.* **1.** (in Homer, Virgil, etc.) of or relating to the Greeks besieging Troy, esp. those from Argos. **2.** of or relating to Argos or Argolis. **3.** a literary word for **Greek.** ~*n.* **4.** an ancient Greek, esp. one from Argos or Argolis.

ar·gle-bar·gle (ˌɑːɡəlˈbɑːɡəl) *n.* another word for **argy-bargy.**

Ar·go[1] (ˈɑːɡəʊ) *n. Greek myth.* the ship in which Jason sailed in search of the Golden Fleece.

Ar·go[2] (ˈɑːɡəʊ) *n., Latin genitive* **Ar·gus** (ˈɑːɡəs). an extensive constellation in the S hemisphere now subdivided into the smaller constellations of **Puppis, Vela, Carina,** and **Pyxis.** Also called: **Argo Navis.**

ar·gol (ˈɑːɡɒl) *or* **ar·gal** *n.* crude potassium hydrogen tartrate, deposited as a crust on the sides of wine vats. [C14: from Anglo-French *argoil*, of unknown origin]

Ar·go·lis (ˈɑːɡəlɪs) *n.* **1.** a department and ancient region of Greece, in the NE Peloponnese. Pop.: 88 698 (1971). Area: 2261 sq. km (873 sq. miles). **2. Gulf of.** an inlet of the Aegean Sea, in the E Peloponnese.

ar·gon (ˈɑːɡɒn) *n.* an extremely unreactive colourless odourless element of the rare gas series that forms almost 1 per cent (by volume) of the atmosphere. It is used in electric lights. Symbol: Ar; atomic no.: 18; atomic wt.: 39.95; density: 1.78 kg/m^3; freezing pt.: -189.2°C; boiling pt.: -185.7°C. [C19: from Greek, from *argos* idle, inactive, from A-[1] + *ergon* work]

Ar·go·naut (ˈɑːɡəˌnɔːt) *n.* **1.** *Greek myth.* one of the heroes who sailed with Jason in quest of the Golden Fleece. **2.** a person who took part in the Californian gold rush of 1849. **3.** another name for the **paper nautilus.** [C16: from Greek *Argonautēs*, from *Argō* the name of Jason's ship + *nautēs* sailor] —ˌ**Ar·go·ˈnaut·ic** *adj.*

Ar·gonne (ˈɑːɡɒn; *French* arˈɡɔn) *n.* **The.** a wooded region of NE France: scene of major battles in both World Wars.

ar·go·non (ˈɑːɡəˌnɒn) *n.* another name for **inert gas.** [C20: from ARGON + -ON (indicating an inert gas)]

Ar·gos (ˈɑːɡɒs, -ɡəs) *n.* an ancient city in SE Greece, in the NE Peloponnese: one of the oldest Greek cities, it dominated the Peloponnese in the 7th century B.C. Pop.: 19 878 (1971).

ar·go·sy (ˈɑːɡəsɪ) *n., pl.* **-sies.** *Archaic or poetic.* a large abundantly laden merchant ship, or a fleet of such ships. [C16: from Italian *Ragusea* (*nave*) (ship) of Ragusa]

ar·got (ˈɑːɡəʊ) *n.* slang or jargon peculiar to a particular group, esp. (formerly) a group of thieves. [C19: from French, of unknown origin] —**ar·got·ic** (ɑːˈɡɒtɪk) *adj.*

Ar·go·vie (arɡɔˈvi) *n.* the French name for **Aargau.**

ar·gu·a·ble (ˈɑːɡjʊəbəl) *adj.* **1.** capable of being disputed; doubtful. **2.** capable of being supported by argument; plausible. —ˈ**ar·gu·a·bly** *adv.*

ar·gue (ˈɑːɡjuː) *vb.* **·gues, ·gu·ing, ·gued. 1.** (*intr.*) to quarrel; wrangle: *they were always arguing until I arrived.* **2.** (*intr.; often foll. by* for *or* against) to present supporting or opposing reasons or cases in a dispute; reason. **3.** (*tr.; may take a clause as object*) to try to prove by presenting reasons; maintain. **4.** (*tr.; often passive*) to debate or discuss: *the case was fully argued before agreement was reached.* **5.** (*tr.*) to persuade: *he argued me into going.* **6.** (*tr.*) to give evidence of; suggest: *her looks argue despair.* [C14: from Old French *arguer* to assert, charge with, from Latin *arguere* to make clear, accuse; related to Latin *argūtus* clear, *argentum* silver] —ˈ**ar·gu·er** *n.*

ar·gu·fy (ˈɑːɡjʊˌfaɪ) *vb.* **·fies, ·fy·ing, ·fied.** *Facetious or dialect.* to argue or quarrel, esp. over something trivial.

ar·gu·ment (ˈɑːɡjʊmənt) *n.* **1.** a quarrel; altercation. **2.** a discussion in which reasons are put forward in support of and against a proposition, proposal, or case; debate: *the argument on birth control will never be concluded.* **3.** (*sometimes pl.*) a point or series of reasons presented to support or oppose a proposition. **4.** a summary of the plot or subject of a book, etc. **5.** *Logic.* **a.** a process of deductive or inductive reasoning in which the conclusion can be shown to be true or false. **b.** the term present in both premisses of a syllogism but absent from its conclusion. **6.** *Maths.* **a.** another name for **independent variable** of a function. **b.** another name for **amplitude** (sense 6) of a complex number.

ar·gu·men·ta·tion (ˌɑːɡjʊmɛnˈteɪʃən) *n.* **1.** the process of reasoning methodically. **2.** a less common word for **argument** (senses 2, 3).

ar·gu·men·ta·tive (ˌɑːɡjʊˈmɛntətɪv) *adj.* **1.** given to arguing; contentious. **2.** characterized by argument; controversial. —ˌ**ar·gu·ˈmen·ta·tive·ly** *adv.* —ˌ**ar·gu·ˈmen·ta·tive·ness** *n.*

ar·gu·men·tum *Latin.* (ˌɑːɡjʊˈmɛntʊm) *n., pl.* **-ta** (-tə). an argument, proof, or series of reasons in support or refutation of a proposition. [Latin: argument]

Ar·gus ('ɑːgəs) *n.* **1.** *Greek myth.* a giant with a hundred eyes who was made guardian of the heifer Io. After he was killed by Hermes his eyes were transferred to the peacock's tail. **2.** a vigilant person; guardian.

Ar·gus-eyed *adj.* keen-sighted; observant; vigilant.

ar+gus pheas+ant *n.* either of two pheasants, *Argusianus argus* (great argus) or *Rheinardia ocellata* (crested argus), occurring in SE Asia and Indonesia. The males have very long tails marked with eyelike spots.

ar·gy-bar·gy ('ɑːdʒɪ'bɑːdʒɪ) *n., pl.* **-bar·gies.** *Brit. informal.* a wrangling argument or verbal dispute. Also called: **argle-bargle.** [C19: from Scottish, compound based on dialect *argle*, probably from ARGUE]

ar+gyle (ɑː'gaɪl) *adj.* **1.** made of knitted or woven material with a diamond-shaped pattern of two or more colours. ~*n.* **2.** (*often pl.*) a sock made of this. [C20: after Campbell of *Argyle* (Argyll), the pattern being an adaptation of the tartan of this clan]

Ar+gyll (ɑː'gaɪl) *or* **Ar+gyll+shire** *n.* (until 1975) a county of W Scotland, now part of Strathclyde region.

Ar+gy+rol ('ɑːdʒɪˌrɒl, ɑː'dʒɪərɒl) *n. Trademark.* a dark brown compound of silver and a protein, used medicinally as a local antiseptic.

Ar+hat ('ɑːhət) *n.* a Buddhist, esp. a monk who at death passes to nirvana. Compare **Bodhisattva.** [from Sanskrit: worthy of respect, from *arhati* he deserves]

År+hus (*Danish* 'ɔrhuːs) *n.* a variant spelling of **Aarhus.**

a·ri·a ('ɑːrɪə) *n.* an elaborate accompanied song for solo voice from a cantata, opera, or oratorio. See also **da capo.** [C18: from Italian: tune, AIR]

Ar·i·ad·ne (ˌærɪ'ædnɪ) *n. Greek myth.* daughter of Minos and Pasiphaë: she gave Theseus the thread with which he found his way out of the Minotaur's labyrinth.

Ar·i·an ('ɛərɪən) *adj.* **1.** of, relating to, or characterizing Arius or Arianism. ~*n.* **2.** an adherent of Arianism. ~*adj., n.* **3.** a variant spelling of **Aryan.**

-ar·i·an *suffix forming nouns.* indicating a person or thing that advocates, believes, or is associated with something: *vegetarian; millenarian; librarian.* [from Latin *-ārius* -ARY + -AN]

Ar·i+an+ism ('ɛərɪəˌnɪzəm) *n. Theol.* the doctrine of Arius, pronounced heretical at the Council of Nicaea, which asserted that Christ was not of one substance with the Father, but a creature raised by the Father to the dignity of Son of God.

A·ri+ca (ə'riːkə; *Spanish* a'rika) *n.* a port in extreme N Chile: awarded to Chile in 1929 after the lengthy Tacna-Arica dispute with Peru; outlet for Bolivian and Peruvian trade. Pop.: 112 300 (1975 est.). See also **Tacna-Arica.**

ar·id ('ærɪd) *adj.* **1.** having little or no rain; dry; parched with heat. **2.** devoid of interest. [C17: from Latin *āridus*, from *ārēre* to be dry] —**a·rid+i·ty** (ə'rɪdɪtɪ) *or* **'ar+id+ness** *n.* —**'ar+id+ly** *adv.*

A·riège (*French* a'rjɛːʒ) *n.* a department of SW France, in Midi-Pyrenees region. Capital: Foix. Pop.: 141 436 (1975). Area: 4903 sq. km (1912 sq. miles).

ar·i+el ('ɛərɪəl) *n.* an Arabian gazelle, *Gazella arabica* (or *dama*). [C19: from Arabic *aryal*]

Ar·i+el ('ɛərɪəl) *n.* the third largest of the five satellites of Uranus and the second nearest to the planet.

Ar·ies ('ɛəriːz) *n., Latin genitive* **A·ri+e·tis** (ə'raɪɪtɪs). **1.** *Astronomy.* a small zodiacal constellation in the N hemisphere lying between Taurus and Pisces on the ecliptic and having a second-magnitude star. **2.** *Astrology.* **a.** Also called: the **Ram.** the first sign of the zodiac, symbol ♈, having a cardinal fire classification, ruled by the planet Mars. The sun is in this sign between about March 21 and April 19. **b.** a person born during the period when the sun is in this sign. ~*adj.* **3.** *Astrology.* born under or characteristic of Aries. ~Also (for senses 2b., 3): **Ar+i·en** ('ɛərɪən). [C14: from Latin: ram]

ar·i·et+ta (ˌærɪ'ɛtə; *Italian* ari'etta) *or* **ar·i+ette** (ˌærɪ'ɛt) *n., pl.* **+et+tas, +et+te** (-'ette), *or* **+ettes.** a short relatively uncomplicated aria. [C18: from Italian, diminutive of ARIA]

a·right (ə'raɪt) *adv.* correctly; rightly; properly.

ar·il ('ærɪl) *n.* an appendage on certain seeds, such as those of the yew and nutmeg, developed from or near the funicle of the ovule and often brightly coloured and fleshy. [C18: from New Latin *arillus*, from Medieval Latin *arilli* raisins, pips of grapes] —**'ar+il+ˌlate** *adj.*

ar+il+lode ('ærɪˌləʊd) *n.* a structure in certain seeds, such as the nutmeg, that resembles an aril but is developed from the micropyle of the ovule. [C19: from ARIL + -ODE[1]]

Ar·i+ma+the·a *or* **Ar·i+ma+thae·a** (ˌærɪmə'θiːə) *n.* a town in ancient Palestine: location unknown.

A·rim·i+num (ə'rɪmɪnəm) *n.* the ancient name of **Rimini.**

a·ri+ose ('ɑːrɪˌəʊs, 'æ-; ˌɑːrɪ'əʊs, ˌæ-) *adj. Rare.* melodic or songlike. [C18: from Italian ARIOSO]

a·ri·o+so (ˌɑːrɪ'əʊzəʊ, 'æ-) *n. Music.* a recitative with the lyrical quality of an aria. [C18: from Italian, from ARIA]

A·ri·o·sto (*Italian* a'rjɔsto) *n.* **Lu·do·vi·co** (ˌludo'viːko). 1474–1533, Italian poet, famous for his romantic epic *Orlando Furioso* (1516).

a·rise (ə'raɪz) *vb.* **a·ris·es, a·ris·ing, a·rose, a·ris+en.** (*intr.*) **1.** to come into being; originate. **2.** (foll. by *from*) to spring or proceed as a consequence; result. **3.** to get or stand up, as from a sitting, kneeling, or lying position. **4.** to come into notice. **5.** to move upwards; ascend. [Old English *ārīsan*; related to Old Saxon *arīsan*, Old High German *irrīsan*; see RISE]

a·ris+ta (ə'rɪstə) *n., pl.* **+tae** (-tiː). **1.** a stiff bristle such as the awn of some grasses and cereals. **2.** a bristle-like appendage on the antennae of some insects. [C17: from Latin: ear of corn, fishbone] —**a·'ris+tate** *adj.*

Ar·is·tae·us (ˌærɪ'stiːəs) *n. Greek myth.* a son of Apollo and Cyrene: protector of herds and fields.

Ar+is+tar+chus (ˌærɪ'stɑːkəs) *n.* a crater in the NE quadrant of the moon, having a diameter of about 37 kilometres, which is the brightest formation on the moon.

Ar·is·tar·chus of Sa+mos *n.* 3rd century B.C., Greek astronomer who anticipated Copernicus in advancing the theory that the earth revolves around the sun.

Ar·is·tar·chus of Sam·o+thrace *n.* ?220–?150 B.C., Greek scholar: librarian at Alexandria, noted for his edition of Homer.

A·ris·ti·des (ˌærɪ'staɪdiːz) *n.* called *the Just.* ?530–?468 B.C., Athenian general and statesman, who played a prominent part in the Greek victories over the Persians at Marathon (490), Salamis (480), and Plataea (479).

Ar·is·tip·pus (ˌærɪ'stɪpəs) *n.* ?435–?356 B.C., Greek philosopher who believed pleasure to be the highest good and founded the Cyrenaic school.

ar+is+toc+ra+cy (ˌærɪ'stɒkrəsɪ) *n., pl.* **+cies.** **1.** government by the best citizens. **2.** a privileged class of people usually of high birth; the nobility. **3.** such a class as the ruling body of a state. **4.** government by such a class. **5.** a state governed by such a class. **6.** a class of people considered to be outstanding in a sphere of activity. [C16: from Late Latin *aristocratia*, from Greek *aristokratia* rule by the best-born, from *aristos* best; see -CRACY]

a·ris+to+crat ('ærɪstəˌkræt) *n.* **1.** a member of the aristocracy; a noble. **2.** a person who has the manners or qualities of a member of a privileged or superior class. **3.** a person who advocates aristocracy as a form of government.

a·ris+to+crat+ic (ˌærɪstə'krætɪk) *adj.* **1.** relating to or characteristic of aristocracy or an aristocrat. **2.** elegant or stylish in appearance and behaviour. —**ˌa·ris+to+'crat·i·cal·ly** *adv.*

Ar·is·toph·a·nes (ˌærɪ'stɒfəˌniːz) *n.* ?448–?380 B.C., Greek comic dramatist, who satirized leading contemporary figures such as Socrates and Euripides. Eleven of his plays are extant, including *The Clouds, The Frogs, The Birds,* and *Lysistrata.*

Ar+is+to+te·li·an (ˌærɪstə'tiːlɪən) *adj.* **1.** of or relating to Aristotle or his philosophy. ~*n.* **2.** a follower of Aristotle.

Ar+is+to+te·li·an log+ic *n.* **1.** traditional or classical logic, esp. as opposed to modern or symbolic logic. **2.** logical method relying on the theory of syllogism, which considers the form of propositions regardless of their content. **3.** the logical method of Aristotle, esp. as developed in the Middle Ages.

Ar·is·to·tle[1] ('ærɪˌstɒtᵊl) *n.* 384–322 B.C., Greek philosopher; pupil of Plato, tutor of Alexander the Great, and founder of the Peripatetic school at Athens; author of works on logic, ethics, politics, poetics, rhetoric, biology, zoology, and metaphysics. His works influenced Muslim philosophy and science and medieval scholastic philosophy.

Ar+is+tot+le[2] ('ærɪˌstɒtᵊl) *n.* a prominent crater in the NW quadrant of the moon about 83 kilometres in diameter.

a·rith+me+tic *n.* (ə'rɪθmətɪk) **1.** the branch of mathematics concerned with numerical calculations, such as addition, subtraction, multiplication, division, and also involution and evolution. **2.** one or more calculations involving numerical operations. **3.** knowledge of or skill in using arithmetic: *his arithmetic is good.* ~*adj.* (ˌærɪθ'mɛtɪk), *also* **a·rith+met·i+cal.** **4.** of, related to, or using arithmetic. [C13: from Latin *arithmētica*, from Greek *arithmētikē*, from *arithmein* to count, from *arithmos* number] —**a·ˌrith+me·'ti·cian** *n.*

a·rith+me+tic mean *n.* the average value of a set of integers, terms, or quantities, expressed as their sum divided by their number: *the arithmetic mean of 3, 4, and 8 is 5.* Often shortened to **mean.** Also called: **average.** Compare **geometric mean.**

a·rith+me+tic pro+gres+sion *n.* a sequence of numbers or quantities, each term of which differs from the succeeding term by a constant amount, such as 3,6,9,12. Compare **geometric progression.**

-ar·i·um *suffix forming nouns.* indicating a place for or associated with something: *aquarium; planetarium; solarium.* [from Latin *-ārium*, neuter of *-ārius* -ARY]

Ar·i·us ('ɛərɪəs) *n.* ?250–336 A.D., Greek Christian theologian, originator of the doctrine of Arianism.

Ariz. *abbrev. for* Arizona.

Ar·i+zo+na (ˌærɪ'zəʊnə) *n.* a state of the southwestern U.S.: consists of the Colorado plateau in the northeast, including the Grand Canyon, divided from desert in the southwest by mountains rising over 3750 m (12 500 ft.). Capital: Phoenix. Pop.: 1 772 482 (1970). Area: 293 750 sq. km (113 417 sq. miles). Abbrevs.: **Ariz.** or (with zip code) **AZ**

Ar·ju·na ('ɑːdʒʊnə) *n. Hindu myth.* the most important of the five princes in the *Mahabharata.* Krishna served as his charioteer in the battle with the Kauravas.

ark (ɑːk) *n.* **1.** the vessel that Noah built and in which he saved himself, his family, and a number of animals and birds during the Flood (Genesis 6–9). **2. out of the ark.** *Informal.* very old; out of date. **3.** a place or thing offering shelter or protection. **4.** *Dialect.* a chest, box, or coffer. [Old English *arc*, from Latin *arca* box, chest]

Ark (ɑːk) *n. Judaism.* **1.** Also called: **Ark of the Covenant.** the most sacred symbol of God's presence among the Hebrew people, carried in their journey from Sinai to the Promised Land (Canaan) and eventually enshrined in the holy of holies of the Temple in Jerusalem. **2.** Also called: **Holy Ark.** a receptacle for the scrolls of the Law usually kept in the place of honour of a synagogue.

Ark. *abbrev. for* Arkansas.

Ar+kan+sas ('ɑːkənˌsɔː) *n.* **1.** a state of the southern U.S.: mountainous in the north and west, with the alluvial plain of the Mississippi in the east; has the only diamond mine in the U.S.; the chief U.S. producer of bauxite. Capital: Little Rock. Pop.: 1 923 295 (1970). Area: 134 537 sq. km (51 945 sq. miles). Abbrevs.: **Ark.** or (with zip code) **AR** **2.** a river in the S central U.S., rising in central Colorado and flowing east and southeast to join the Mississippi in Arkansas. Length: 2335 km (1450 miles).

Ar+khan+gelsk (ar'xangɪlsk) *n.* the Russian name for **Archangel.**

ar+kose ('ɑːkəʊs) *n.* a sandstone consisting of grains of feldspar and quartz cemented by a mixture of quartz and clay minerals. [C19: from French]

Ark·wright ('ɑːkraɪt) *n.* Sir **Rich·ard.** 1732–92, English cotton manufacturer: inventor of the spinning frame (1769) which produced cotton thread strong enough to be used as a warp.

Arl+berg (*German* 'arlˌbɛrk) *n.* a mountain pass in W Austria: a winter sports region. Height: 1802 m (5910 ft.).

Arles (ɑːlz; *French* arl) *n.* **1.** a city in SE France, on the Rhône: Roman amphitheatre. Pop.: 50 345 (1975). **2. Kingdom of.** a kingdom in SE France which had dissolved by 1378: known as the Kingdom of Burgundy until about 1200.

Ar+ling+ton ('ɑːlɪŋtən) *n.* a county of N Virginia: site of **Arlington National Cemetery.**

Ar+lon (*French* ar'lɔ̃) *n.* a town in SE Belgium, capital of Luxembourg province. Pop.: 13 745 (1970).

arm[1] (ɑːm) *n.* **1.** (in man) either of the upper limbs from the shoulder to the wrist. Related adj.: **brachial. 2.** the part of either of the upper limbs from the elbow to the wrist; forearm. **3. a.** the corresponding limb of any other vertebrate. **b.** an armlike appendage of some invertebrates. **4.** an object that covers or supports the human arm, esp. the sleeve of a garment or the side of a chair, sofa, etc. **5.** anything considered to resemble an arm in appearance, position, or function, esp. something that branches out from a central support or larger mass: *an arm of the sea; the arm of a record player.* **6.** an administrative subdivision of an organization: *an arm of the government.* **7.** power; authority: *the arm of the law.* **8.** any of the specialist combatant sections of a military force, such as cavalry, infantry, etc. **9.** *Nautical.* See **yardarm. 10.** *Sport, esp. ball games.* ability to throw or pitch: *he has a good arm.* **11. arm in arm.** with arms linked. **12. at arm's length.** at a distance; away from familiarity with or subjection to another. **13. in the arms of Morpheus.** sleeping. **14. with open arms.** with great warmth and hospitality: *to welcome someone with open arms.* ~*vb.* **15.** (*tr.*) *Archaic.* to walk arm in arm with. [Old English; related to German *Arm,* Old Norse *armr* arm, Latin *armus* shoulder, Greek *harmos* joint] —**'arm+less** *adj.* —**'arm+ˌlike** *adj.*

arm[2] (ɑːm) *vb.* **1.** to equip with weapons as a preparation for war. **2.** (*tr.*) to provide (a person or thing) with something that strengthens, protects, or increases efficiency: *he armed himself against the cold.* **3.** (*tr.*) to activate a fuse so that it will explode at the required time. **4.** (*tr.*) *Nautical.* to pack arming into (a sounding lead). ~*n.* **5.** (*usually pl.*) a weapon, esp. a firearm. [C14: (n.) back formation from *arms,* from Old French *armes,* from Latin *arma;* (vb.) from Old French *armer* to equip with arms, from Latin *armāre,* from *arma* arms, equipment]

Arm. *abbrev. for:* **1.** Armenia(n). **2.** Armoric.

ar+ma+da (ɑː'mɑːdə) *n.* a large number of ships or aircraft. [C16: from Spanish, from Medieval Latin *armāta* fleet, armed forces, from Latin *armāre* to provide with arms]

Ar+ma+da (ɑː'mɑːdə) *n.* (usually preceded by *the*) See the **Spanish Armada.**

ar+ma+dil+lo (ˌɑːmə'dɪləʊ) *n., pl.* **+los. 1.** any edentate mammal of the family *Dasypodidae* of Central and South America and S North America, such as *Priodontes giganteus* (**giant armadillo**). They are burrowing animals, with peglike rootless teeth and a covering of strong horny plates over most of the body. **2. fairy armadillo.** another name for **pichiciego.** [C16: from Spanish, diminutive of *armado* armed (man), from Latin *armātus* armed; compare ARMADA]

Ar+ma+ged+don (ˌɑːmə'gɛdᵊn) *n.* **1.** *New Testament.* the place (possibly to be identified with Megiddo in N Palestine) designated in Revelation 16:16 as the scene of the final battle between the kings of the earth at the end of the world. **2.** a catastrophic and extremely destructive conflict, esp. World War I viewed as this. [C19: from Late Latin *Armagedōn,* from Greek, from Hebrew *har megiddōn,* mountain district of *Megiddo,* site of various battles in the Old Testament]

Ar+magh (ɑː'mɑː) *n.* **1.** a county of S Northern Ireland. County town: Armagh. Pop.: 133 196 (1971). Area: 1266 sq. km (489 sq. miles). **2.** a town in S Northern Ireland, county town of Co. Armagh: seat of Roman Catholic and Protestant archbishops. Pop.: 12 297 (1971).

Ar+ma+gnac ('ɑːmənˌjæk) *n.* a dry brown brandy distilled in the French district of Gers. [from *Armagnac,* the former name of this region]

ar+ma+ment ('ɑːməmənt) *n.* **1.** the weapon equipment of a military vehicle, ship, or aircraft. **2.** a military force raised and armed ready for war. **3.** preparation for war involving the production of equipment and arms. [C17: from Latin *armāmenta* utensils, from *armāre* to equip]

ar+ma+men+tar+i+um (ˌɑːməmɛn'tɛərɪəm) *n., pl.* **+i+ums** *or* **·i·a** (-ɪə). the items that comprise the material and equipment used by a physician in his professional practice.

ar+ma+ture ('ɑːmətjʊə) *n.* **1.** a revolving structure in an electric motor or generator, wound with the coils that carry the current. **2.** any part of an electric machine or device that vibrates under the influence of a magnetic field or within which an electromotive force is induced. **3.** Also called: **keeper.** a soft iron or steel bar placed across the poles of a permanent magnet to close the magnetic circuit. **4.** such a bar placed across the poles of an electromagnet to transmit mechanical force. **5.** *Sculpture.* a framework to support the clay or other material used in modelling. **6.** the protective outer covering of an animal or plant. **7.** *Archaic.* armour. [C15: from Latin *armātūra* armour, equipment, from *armāre* to furnish with equipment; see ARM[2]]

arm+band ('ɑːmˌbænd) *n.* a band of material worn round the arm, such as one bearing an identifying mark, etc., or a black one indicating mourning.

arm+chair ('ɑːmˌtʃɛə) *n.* **1.** a chair, esp. an upholstered one, that has side supports for the arms or elbows. **2.** (*modifier*) taking no active part; lacking practical experience; theoretical: *an armchair strategist.* **3.** (*modifier*) participated in away from the place of action or in the home: *armchair theatre.*

Arm+co ('ɑːmkəʊ) *n. Trademark.* a metal safety barrier erected at the side of motor-racing circuits, esp. on corners.

armed[1] (ɑːmd) *adj.* **1.** equipped with or supported by arms, armour, etc. **2.** prepared for conflict or any difficulty.

armed[2] (ɑːmd) *adj.* **a.** having an arm or arms. **b.** (*in combination*): *long-armed; one-armed.*

armed forc·es *pl. n.* the military forces of a nation or nations, including the army, navy, air force, marines, etc.

Ar+me+ni·a (ɑː'miːnɪə) *n.* **1.** a region of W Asia, now divided among the Soviet Union, Turkey, and Iran: formerly a kingdom, with origins in the 12th century B.C. **2.** a town in central Colombia: centre of a coffee-growing district. Pop.: 135 615 (1973).

Ar+me+ni·an (ɑː'miːnɪən) *n.* **1.** a native or inhabitant of Armenia or an Armenian-speaking person elsewhere. **2.** the language of the Armenians: an Indo-European language probably belonging to the Thraco-Phrygian branch, but containing many non-Indo-European elements. **3.** an adherent of the Armenian Church or its doctrines. ~*adj.* **4.** of or relating to Armenia, its inhabitants, their language, or the Armenian Church.

Ar+me+ni·an Church *n.* the national Church of Armenia, founded in the early fourth century A.D., the dogmas and liturgy of which are similar to those of the Orthodox Church.

Ar+me+ni·an So+vi+et So+cial+ist Re+pub+lic *n.* an administrative division of the S Soviet Union, bordering on Iran in the south and Turkey in the west: mountainous, rising over 4000 m (13 000 ft.). Capital: Yerevan. Pop.: 2 491 873 (1970). Area: 229 800 sq. km (11 490 sq. miles).

Ar+men+tières ('ɑːmənˌtɪəz; *French* armɑ̃'tjɛːr) *n.* a town in N France: site of battles in both World Wars. Pop.: 27 473 (1975).

armes par+lantes (*French* arm par'lɑ̃ːt) *pl. n. Heraldry.* arms using devices to illustrate the name of the bearers, such as a rose and a wall to illustrate the name *Rosewall.* [literally: speaking arms]

ar+met ('ɑːmɛt) *n.* a close-fitting medieval visored helmet with a neck guard. [C16: from Old French, from Old Spanish *almete,* from Old French HELMET]

arm+ful ('ɑːmfʊl) *n., pl.* **+fuls.** the amount that can be held by one or both arms.

arm+hole ('ɑːmˌhəʊl) *n.* the opening in an article of clothing through which the arm passes and to which a sleeve is often fitted.

ar+mi+ger ('ɑːmɪdʒə) *n.* **1.** a person entitled to bear heraldic arms, such as a sovereign or nobleman. **2.** a squire carrying the armour of a medieval knight. [C16: from Medieval Latin: squire, from Latin: armour-bearer, from *arma* arms + *gerere* to carry, bear] —**ar+mig+er+ous** (ɑː'mɪdʒərəs) *adj.*

ar+mil+lar·y ('ɑːmɪlərɪ, ɑː'mɪlərɪ) *adj.* of or relating to bracelets. [C17: from New Latin *armillaris,* from Latin *armilla* bracelet]

ar+mil+lar·y sphere *n.* a model of the celestial sphere consisting of rings representing the relative positions of the celestial equator, ecliptic, etc., used by early astronomers for determining the positions of stars.

arm+ing ('ɑːmɪŋ) *n.* **1.** the act of taking arms or providing with arms. **2.** *Nautical.* a greasy substance, such as tallow, packed into the recess at the bottom of a sounding lead to pick up samples of sand, gravel, etc., from the bottom.

Ar+min·i+an (ɑː'mɪnɪən) *adj.* **1.** denoting, relating to, or believing in the Christian Protestant doctrines of Jacobus Arminius, published in 1610, which rejected absolute predestination and insisted that the sovereignty of God is compatible with free will in man. These doctrines deeply influenced Wesleyan and Methodist theology. ~*n.* **2.** a follower of such doctrines. —**Ar+'min·i+an+ˌism** *n.*

Ar+min·i·us (ɑː'mɪnɪəs) *n.* **Ja·co·bus** (dʒə'kəʊbəs). original name *Jacob Harmensen.* 1560–1609, Dutch Protestant theologian.

ar+mip·o·tent (ɑː'mɪpətənt) *adj. Literary.* strong in arms or war. [C14: from Latin *armipotēns,* from *arma* arms + *potēns* powerful, from *posse* to be able] —**ar+'mip·o+tence** *n.*

ar+mi+stice ('ɑːmɪstɪs) *n.* an agreement between opposing armies to suspend hostilities in order to discuss peace terms; truce. [C18: from New Latin *armistitium,* from Latin *arma* arms + *sistere* to stop, stand still]

Ar+mi+stice Day *n.* the anniversary of the signing of the armistice that ended World War I, on Nov. 11, 1918, now kept on Remembrance Sunday. See also **Remembrance Sunday.** U.S. name: **Veterans Day.**

arm+let ('ɑːmlɪt) *n.* **1.** a small arm, as of a lake, the sea, etc. **2.** a band or bracelet worn round the arm for ornament, identification, etc. **3.** a very short sleeve on a garment.

ar+moire (ɑːmˈwɑː) *n.* a large cabinet, originally used for storing weapons. [C16: from French, from Old French *armaire,* from Latin *armārium* chest, closet; see AMBRY]

ar+mor (ˈɑːmə) *n.* the U.S. spelling of **armour.**

ar+mo+ri+al (ɑːˈmɔːrɪəl) *adj.* **1.** of or relating to heraldry or heraldic arms. ~*n.* **2.** a book of coats of arms.

Ar+mor·i+ca (ɑːˈmɒrɪkə) *n.* an ancient name for Brittany. —**Ar+ˈmor·i+can** *n., adj.*

ar+mor·y (ˈɑːmərɪ) *n., pl.* **+mor·ies. 1.** *Rare.* another name for **heraldry. 2.** the usual U.S. spelling of **armoury.** —**ˈar+mor+ist** *n.*

ar+mour *or U.S.* **ar+mor** (ˈɑːmə) *n.* **1.** any defensive covering, esp. that of metal, chain mail, etc., worn by medieval warriors to prevent injury to the body in battle. **2.** the protective metal plates on a tank, warship, etc. **3.** *Military.* armoured fighting vehicles in general. **4.** any protective covering, such as the shell of certain animals. **5.** *Nautical.* the watertight suit of a diver. **6.** heraldic insignia; arms. ~*vb.* **7.** (*tr.*) to equip or cover with armour. [C13: from Old French *armure,* from Latin *armātūrā* armour, equipment]

ar·mour-bear·er *n. History.* a retainer who carried the arms or armour of a warrior.

ar+moured *or U.S.* **ar+mored** (ˈɑːməd) *adj.* **1.** having a protective covering, such as armour or bone. **2.** comprising units making use of armoured vehicles: *an armoured brigade.* **3.** (of glass) toughened.

ar+moured car *n.* **1.** *Military.* a fast lightly armed and armoured vehicle, mainly used for reconnaissance. **2.** any vehicle strengthened by armoured plate, esp. a security van for transporting cash and valuables.

ar+mour+er *or U.S.* **ar+mor+er** (ˈɑːmərə) *n.* **1.** a person who makes or mends arms and armour. **2.** a person employed in the maintenance of small arms and weapons in a military unit.

ar+mour plate *n.* a tough heavy steel, usually containing chromium, nickel, and molybdenum and often hardened on the surface, used for protecting warships, tanks, etc.

ar+moury *or U.S.* **ar+mor·y** (ˈɑːmərɪ) *n., pl.* **+mour·ies** *or* **+mor·ies. 1.** a secure place for the storage of weapons. **2.** a building in which training in the use of arms and drill takes place. **3.** a place where arms are made. **4.** armour generally; military supplies.

arm+pit (ˈɑːmˌpɪt) *n.* the small depression beneath the arm where it joins the shoulder. Technical name: **axilla.**

arm+rest (ˈɑːmˌrɛst) *n.* the part of a chair, sofa, etc., that supports the arm. Sometimes shortened to **arm.**

arms (ɑːmz) *pl. n.* **1.** weapons collectively. See also **small arms. 2.** military exploits: *prowess in arms.* **3.** the official heraldic symbols of a family, state, etc., including a shield with distinctive devices, and often supports, a crest, or other insignia. **4. bear arms. a.** to carry weapons. **b.** to serve in the armed forces. **c.** to have a coat of arms. **5. in** *or* **under arms.** armed and prepared for war. **6. lay down one's arms.** to stop fighting; surrender. **7. present arms.** *Military.* **a.** a position of salute in which the rifle is brought up to a position vertically in line with the body, muzzle uppermost and trigger guard to the fore. **b.** the command for this drill. **8. take (up) arms.** to prepare to fight. **9. to arms!** arm yourselves! **10. up in arms.** indignant; prepared to protest strongly. [C13: from Old French *armes,* from Latin *arma;* see ARM[2]]

arms race *n.* the continuing attempt by two or more nations each to have available to it more and more powerful weapons than the other(s).

Arm·strong (ˈɑːmˌstrɒŋ) *n.* **(Daniel) Lou·is,** nickname *Satchmo.* 1900–71, U.S. jazz trumpeter and bandleader.

ar+mure (ˈɑːmjʊə) *n.* a silk or wool fabric with a small cobbled pattern. [C19: from French: ARMOUR]

ar·my (ˈɑːmɪ) *n., pl.* **·mies. 1.** the military land forces of a nation. **2.** a military unit usually consisting of two or more corps with supporting arms and services. **3.** (*modifier*) of, relating to, or characteristic of an army: *army rations.* **4.** any large body of people united for some specific purpose. **5.** a large number of people, animals, etc.; multitude. [C14: from Old French *armee,* from Medieval Latin *armāta* armed forces; see ARMADA]

ar·my ant *n.* any of various mainly tropical American predatory ants of the subfamily *Dorylinae,* which live in temporary nests and travel in vast hordes preying on other animals. Also called: **legionary ant.** See also **driver ant.**

Ar·my List *n. Brit.* an official list of all serving commissioned officers of the army and reserve officers liable for recall.

ar·my worm *n.* **1.** the caterpillar of a widely distributed noctuid moth, *Leucania unipuncta,* which travels in vast hordes and is a serious pest of cereal crops in North America. **2.** any of various similar caterpillars.

Arne (ɑːn) *n.* **Thom·as (Augustine).** 1710–78, English composer, noted for his setting of Shakespearean songs and for his song *Rule Britannia.*

Arn+hem (ˈɑːnəm) *n.* a city in the E Netherlands, capital of Gelderland province, on the Rhine: site of a World War II battle. Pop.: 126 955 (1974 est.).

Arn+hem Land *n.* a region of N Australia, in the N Northern Territory: mainly a reserve for Aborigines.

ar+ni+ca (ˈɑːnɪkə) *n.* **1.** any N temperate or arctic plant of the genus *Arnica,* typically having yellow flowers: family *Compositae* (composites). **2.** the tincture of the dried flower heads of any of these plants, esp. *A. montana,* used in treating bruises. [C18: from New Latin, of unknown origin]

Ar·nim (*German* ˈarnɪm) *n.* **Ach·im von** (ˈaxɪm fɔn). 1781–1831, German romantic poet. He published, with Clemens Brentano, the collection of folk songs, *Des Knaben Wunderhorn* (1805–08).

Ar·no (ˈɑːnəʊ) *n.* a river in central Italy, rising in the Apennines and flowing through Florence and Pisa to the Ligurian Sea. Length: about 240 km (150 miles).

Ar+nold[1] (ˈɑːnᵊld) *n.* a town in N central England, in S Nottinghamshire. Pop.: 33 254 (1971).

Ar·nold[2] (ˈɑːnᵊld) *n.* **1. Mal·colm.** born 1921, English composer, esp. of orchestral works in a traditional idiom. **2. Mat·thew.** 1822–88, English poet, essayist, and literary critic, noted particularly for his poems *Sohrab and Rustum* (1853) and *Dover Beach* (1867), and for his *Essays in Criticism* (1865) and *Culture and Anarchy* (1869). **3.** his father, **Thom·as.** 1795–1842, English historian and educationalist, headmaster of Rugby School, noted for his reforms in public-school education.

ar+oid (ˈærɔɪd, ˈɛər-) *adj.* **1.** Also: **araceous.** of, relating to, or belonging to the *Araceae,* a family of plants having small flowers massed on a spadix surrounded by a large petaloid spathe. The family includes arum, calla, and anthurium. ~*n.* **2.** any plant of the *Araceae.* [C19: from New Latin *Arum* type genus + -OID; see ARUM]

a·roint thee *or* **ye** (əˈrɔɪnt) *interj. Archaic.* away! begone! [C17: of unknown origin]

a·ro·ma (əˈrəʊmə) *n.* **1.** a distinctive usually pleasant smell, esp. of spices, wines, and plants. **2.** a subtle pervasive quality or atmosphere. [C18: via Latin from Greek: spice]

ar·o·mat+ic (ˌærəˈmætɪk) *adj.* **1.** having a distinctive, usually fragrant smell. **2.** (of an organic compound) having an unsaturated ring containing alternating double and single bonds, esp. containing a benzene ring; exhibiting aromaticity. Compare **aliphatic.** ~*n.* **3.** something, such as a plant or drug, giving off a fragrant smell. —**ˌar·o+ˈmat·i·cal+ly** *adv.*

ar·o·ma+tic+i·ty (əˌrəʊməˈtɪsɪtɪ) *n.* **1.** the property of certain planar cyclic conjugated molecules, esp. benzene, of behaving like unsaturated molecules and undergoing substitution reactions rather than addition. **2.** the quality or state of having an aroma.

a·ro+ma+tize *or* **a·ro+ma+tise** (əˈrəʊməˌtaɪz) *vb.* **1.** (*tr.*) to make aromatic. **2.** to convert (an aliphatic compound) to an aromatic compound. —**a·ˌro+ma+ti+ˈza+tion** *or* **a·ˌro+ma+ti+ˈsa+tion** *n.*

a·rose (əˈrəʊz) *vb.* the past tense of **arise.**

a·round (əˈraʊnd) *prep.* **1.** surrounding, encircling, or enclosing: *a band around her head.* **2.** on all or most sides of: *to look around one.* **3.** on or outside the circumference or perimeter of: *the stands around the racecourse.* **4.** situated at various points in: *a lot of shelves around the house.* **5.** from place to place in: *driving around Ireland.* **6.** somewhere in or near: *to stay around the house.* **7.** making a circuit or partial circuit about: *the ring road around the town.* **8.** reached by making a partial circuit about something: *the shop around the corner.* **9.** revolving round a centre or axis: *the earth's motion around its axis.* **10.** so as to have a basis in: *the story is built around a good plot.* **11.** approximately in: *it happened around 1957, I think.* ~*adv.* **12.** on all or most sides: *the garden is fenced all around; the crowd gathered around.* **13.** on or outside the circumference or perimeter: *the racing track is two miles around.* **14.** in all directions from a point of reference: *he owns the land for ten miles around.* **15.** to all members of a group: *pass the food around.* **16.** in the vicinity, esp. restlessly but idly: *to wait around; stand around.* **17.** here and there; in no particular place or direction: *to sleep around.* **18.** in rotation or revolution: *the wheels turn around.* **19.** by a circuitous route: *the road to the farm goes around by the pond.* **20.** to a specific place: *she came around to see me.* **21.** *Informal.* (of people) active and prominent in a particular area or profession: *some pop stars are around for only a few years.* **22.** *Informal.* present in some place (the exact location being inexact): *he's around here somewhere.* **23.** *Informal.* in circulation; available: *that type of phone has been around for some years now.* **24.** *Informal.* to many places, so as to have gained considerable experience, often of a worldly or social nature: *he gets around; I've been around.* [C17 (rare earlier): from A-[2] + ROUND]

Usage. In adverbial and prepositional senses *round* is now regarded by most speakers and writers of British English as a less formal variant of *around,* although historically it is the better established form. In American English, *around* has almost completely replaced *round* in these senses, except in a few fixed phrases such as *all year round.*

a·rouse (əˈraʊz) *vb.* **1.** (*tr.*) to evoke or elicit (a reaction, emotion, or response); stimulate. **2.** to awaken from sleep. —**a·ˈrous·al** *n.* —**a·ˈrous+er** *n.*

Arp (*French* arp) *n.* **Jean** (ʒɑ̃) *or* **Hans** (hans). 1887–1966, Alsatian sculptor, painter, and poet, cofounder of the Dada movement in Zurich, noted particularly for his abstract organic sculptures based on natural forms.

Ar·pád (ˈɑːpɑːd) *n.* died 907 A.D., Magyar chieftain who conquered Hungary in the late ninth century.

ar+peg+gi·o (ɑːˈpɛdʒɪəʊ) *n., pl.* **+gi·os. 1.** a chord whose notes are played in rapid succession rather than simultaneously. **2.** an ascending and descending figuration used in practising the piano, voice, etc. [C18: from Italian, from *arpeggiare* to perform on the harp, from *arpa* HARP]

ar+pent (ˈɑːpənt; *French* arˈpɑ̃) *n.* a former French unit of area, approximately equal to one acre, still used in parts of Canada. [C16: from Old French, probably from Late Latin *arepennis* half an acre, of Gaulish origin; related to Middle Irish *airchenn* unit of land measure]

ar+que+bus (ˈɑːkwɪbəs) *or* **har+que+bus** *n.* a portable long-barrelled gun dating from the 15th century: fired by a wheel-lock or matchlock. Also: **hackbut, hagbut.** [C16: via Old French *harquebuse* from Middle Dutch *hakebusse,* literally: hook gun, from *hake* hook + *busse* box, gun, from Late Latin *busis* box]

arr. *abbrev. for:* **1.** arranged (by). **2.** arrival. **3.** arrive(d).

ar·rack *or* **ar·ak** ('ærək) *n.* a coarse spirit distilled in various Eastern countries from grain, rice, sugar cane, etc. [C17: from Arabic *'araq* sweat, sweet juice, liquor]

ar·raign (ə'reɪn) *vb.* **1.** (*tr.*) to bring (a prisoner) before a court to answer an indictment. **2.** (*tr.*) to call to account; complain about; accuse. [C14: from Old French *araisnier* to speak, accuse, from A-[2] + *raisnier,* from Vulgar Latin *ratiōnāre* (unattested) to talk, argue, from Latin *ratiō* a reasoning] —**ar'raign·er** *n.* —**ar'raign·ment** *n.*

Ar·ran ('ærən) *n.* an island off the SW coast of Scotland, in the Firth of Clyde. Pop.: 3567 (1971). Area: 427 sq. km (165 sq. miles).

ar·range (ə'reɪndʒ) *vb.* **1.** (*tr.*) to put into a proper, systematic, or decorative order. **2.** (*tr.; may take a clause as object or an infinitive*) to arrive at an agreement or understanding about; settle. **3.** (when *intr.,* often foll. by *for;* when *tr., may take a clause as object or an infinitive*) to make plans or preparations in advance (for something): *we arranged for her to be met.* **4.** (*tr.*) to adapt (a musical composition) for performance in a different way, esp. on different instruments. **5.** (*tr.*) to adapt (a play, etc.) for broadcasting. **6.** (*intr.;* often foll. by *with*) to come to an agreement. [C14: from Old French *arangier,* from A-[2] + *rangier* to put in a row, RANGE] —**ar'range·a·ble** *adj.* —**ar'rang·er** *n.*

ar·range·ment (ə'reɪndʒmənt) *n.* **1.** the act of arranging or being arranged. **2.** the form in which things are arranged: *he altered the arrangement of furniture in the room.* **3.** a thing composed of various ordered parts; the result of arranging: *a flower arrangement.* **4.** (*often pl.*) a preparatory measure taken or plan made; preparation. **5.** an agreement or settlement; understanding. **6.** an adaptation of a piece of music for performance in a different way, esp. on different instruments from those for which it was originally composed. **7.** an adaptation (of a play, etc.) for broadcasting.

ar·rant ('ærənt) *adj.* utter; out-and-out: *an arrant fool.* [C14: variant of ERRANT (wandering, vagabond); sense developed from its frequent use in phrases like *arrant thief* (hence: notorious)] —**'ar·rant·ly** *adv.*

ar·ras ('ærəs) *n.* a wall hanging, esp. of tapestry.

Ar·ras ('ærəs; *French* a'rɑːs) *n.* a town in N France: formerly famous for tapestry; severely damaged in both World Wars. Pop.: 50 396 (1975).

ar·ray (ə'reɪ) *n.* **1.** an impressive display or collection. **2.** an orderly or regular arrangement, esp. of troops in battle order. **3.** *Poetic.* rich clothing; apparel. **4.** *Maths.* a sequence of numbers or symbols in a specified order. **5.** *Maths.* a set of numbers or symbols arranged in rows and columns, as in a determinant or matrix. **6.** *Electronics.* an arrangement of aerials spaced to give desired directional characteristics, used esp. in radar. **7.** *Law.* a panel of jurors. **8.** the arming of military forces. ~*vb.* (*tr.*) **9.** to dress in rich attire; adorn. **10.** to arrange in order, esp. troops for battle; marshal. **11.** *Law.* to draw up (a panel of jurors). [C13: from Old French *aroi* arrangement, from *arayer* to arrange, of Germanic origin; compare Old English *arǣdan* to make ready] —**ar'ray·al** *n.*

ar·rears (ə'rɪəz) *n.* **1.** (*sometimes sing.*) Also called: **arrearage.** something outstanding or owed. **2. in arrears** *or* **arrear.** late in paying a debt or meeting an obligation. [C18: from obsolete *arrear* (adv.) behindhand, from Old French *arere,* from Medieval Latin *adretrō,* from Latin *ad* to + *retrō* backwards]

ar·rest (ə'rɛst) *vb.* (*tr.*) **1.** to deprive (a person) of liberty by taking him into custody, esp. under lawful authority. **2.** to seize (a ship) under lawful authority. **3.** to slow or stop the development or progress of (a disease, growth, etc.). **4.** to catch and hold (one's attention, sight, etc.). **5. arrest judgment.** *Law.* to stay proceedings after a verdict, on the grounds of error or possible error. ~*n.* **6.** the act of taking a person into custody, esp. under lawful authority. **7.** the act of seizing and holding a ship under lawful authority. **8.** the state of being held, esp. under lawful authority: *under arrest.* **9.** Also called: **ar·res·ta·tion** (ˌærɛs'teɪʃən). the slowing or stopping of the development or progress of something. **10.** the stopping or sudden cessation of motion of something: *a cardiac arrest.* [C14: from Old French *arester,* from Vulgar Latin *arrestāre* (unattested), from Latin *ad* at, to + *restāre* to stand firm, stop]

ar·rest·a·ble (ə'rɛstəb^{ə}l) *adj.* **1.** liable to be arrested. **2.** (of an offence) such that an offender may be arrested without a warrant.

ar·rest·er (ə'rɛstə) *n.* **1.** a person who arrests. **2.** a thing that stops or checks motion, esp. a mechanism of wires for slowing aeroplanes as they land on an aircraft carrier.

ar·rest·ing (ə'rɛstɪŋ) *adj.* attracting attention; striking. —**ar'rest·ing·ly** *adv.*

ar·rest·ment (ə'rɛstmənt) *n. Scot. law.* the seizure of money or property to prevent a debtor paying one creditor in advance of another.

ar·rest of judg·ment *n. Law.* a stay of proceedings after a verdict, on the grounds of error or possible error.

Ar·re·tine ware *n.* another term for **Samian ware** (sense 2).

Ar·re·ti·um (æ'riːtɪəm, -'rɛt-) *n.* the ancient Latin name of **Arezzo.** —**Ar·re·tine** ('ærɪˌtaɪn) *adj.*

Ar·rhe·ni·us (*Swedish* a're:nius) *n.* **Svan·te Au·gust** ('svantə 'august). 1859–1927, Swedish chemist and physicist, noted for his work on the theory of electrolytic dissociation: Nobel prize for chemistry 1903.

ar·rhyth·mi·a (ə'rɪðmɪə) *n.* any variation from the normal rhythm in the heartbeat. [C19: New Latin, from Greek *arrhuthmia,* from A-[1] + *rhuthmos* RHYTHM]

ar·rière-ban (*French* arjɛr'bɑ̃) *n.* **1.** (in medieval France) a summons to the king's vassals to do military service. **2.** the vassals so assembled for military service. [C16: from French, changed from Old French *herban* call to arms, of Germanic origin; compare Old High German *heriban,* from *heri* army + *ban* summons, BAN[2]]

ar·rière-pen·sée *French.* (arjɛrpɑ̃'se) *n.* an unrevealed intention; mental reservation. [C19: literally: behind thought]

Ar Ri·mal (ɑːr rɪ'mɑːl) *n.* another name for **Rub' al Khali.**

ar·ris ('ærɪs) *n., pl.* **·ris** *or* **·ris·es.** a sharp edge at the meeting of two surfaces at an angle with one another, as at two adjacent sides of a stone block. [C17: apparently from Old French *areste* beard of grain, sharp ridge; see ARÊTE]

ar·ri·val (ə'raɪv^{ə}l) *n.* **1.** the act or time of arriving. **2.** a person or thing that arrives or has arrived. **3.** the reaching of a condition or objective.

ar·rive (ə'raɪv) *vb.* (*intr.*) **1.** to come to a certain place during or after a journey; reach a destination. **2.** to agree upon; reach: *to arrive at a decision.* **3.** to occur eventually: *the moment arrived when pretence was useless.* **4.** *Informal.* (of a baby) to be born. **5.** *Informal.* to attain success or gain recognition. [C13: from Old French *ariver,* from Vulgar Latin *arrīpāre* (unattested) to land, reach the bank, from Latin *ad* to + *rīpa* riverbank] —**ar'riv·er** *n.*

ar·ri·ve·der·ci *Italian.* (ˌarrive'dertʃi) *interj.* goodbye.

ar·ri·visme (ˌæriː'viːzmə; *French* ari'vism) *n.* unscrupulous ambition.

ar·ri·viste (ˌæriː'viːst; *French* ari'vist) *n.* a person who is unscrupulously ambitious. [French: see ARRIVE, -IST]

ar·ro·ba (ə'rəʊbə) *n.* **1.** a unit of weight, approximately equal to 11 kilograms, used in some Spanish-speaking countries. **2.** a unit of weight, approximately equal to 15 kilograms, used in some Portuguese-speaking countries. **3.** a liquid measure used in some Spanish-speaking countries with different values, but in Spain used as a wine-measure, approximately equal to 16 litres. [C16: from Spanish, from Arabic *ar-rub'* the quarter (of a quintal)]

ar·ro·gant ('ærəgənt) *adj.* having or showing an exaggerated opinion of one's own importance, merit, ability, etc.; conceited; overbearingly proud: *an arrogant teacher; an arrogant assumption.* [C14: from Latin *arrogāre* to claim as one's own; see ARROGATE] —**'ar·ro·gance** *n.* —**'ar·ro·gant·ly** *adv.*

ar·ro·gate ('ærəˌgeɪt) *vb.* **1.** (*tr.*) to claim or appropriate for oneself presumptuously or without justification. **2.** (*tr.*) to attribute or assign to another without justification. [C16: from Latin *arrogāre,* from *rogāre* to ask] —**ˌar·ro'ga·tion** *n.* —**ar·rog·a·tive** (ə'rɒgətɪv) *adj.* —**'ar·ro·ˌga·tor** *n.*

ar·ron·disse·ment (*French* arɔ̃dis'mɑ̃) *n.* (in France) **1.** the largest administrative subdivision of a department. **2.** a municipal district of certain large cities, esp. Paris. [C19: from *arrondir* to make round, from AB-[1] + *-rondir* from *rond* ROUND]

ar·row ('ærəʊ) *n.* **1.** a long slender pointed weapon, usually having feathers fastened at the end as a balance, that is shot from a bow. **2.** any of various things that resemble an arrow in shape, function, or speed, such as a sign or symbol indicating direction or position. [Old English *arwe;* related to Old Norse *ör,* Gothic *arhvazna,* Latin *arcus* bow, ARCH[1]]

ar·row·head ('ærəʊˌhɛd) *n.* **1.** the pointed tip of an arrow, often removable from the shaft. **2.** something that resembles the head of an arrow in shape, such as a triangular decoration on garments used to reinforce joins. **3.** any aquatic herbaceous plant of the genus *Sagittaria,* esp. *S. sagittifolia,* having arrow-shaped aerial leaves and linear submerged leaves: family *Alismataceae.*

ar·row·root ('ærəʊˌruːt) *n.* **1.** a white-flowered West Indian plant, *Maranta arundinacea,* whose rhizomes yield an easily digestible starch: family *Marantaceae.* **2.** the starch obtained from this plant. **3.** any of several other plants whose rhizomes or roots yield starch.

ar·rows ('ærəʊz) *pl. n. Brit.* an informal name for **darts.**

ar·row·wood ('ærəʊˌwʊd) *n.* any of various trees or shrubs, esp. certain viburnums, having long straight tough stems formerly used by North American Indians to make arrows.

ar·row·worm ('ærəʊˌwɜːm) *n.* any small marine invertebrate of the genus *Sagitta,* having an elongated transparent body with fins and prehensile oral bristles: phylum *Chaetognatha* (chaetognaths).

ar·roy·o (ə'rɔɪəʊ) *n., pl.* **·os.** *Chiefly southwestern U.S.* a stream or brook. [C19: from Spanish, probably related to Latin *arrūgia* shaft in a goldmine]

Ar·ru Is·lands ('ɑːruː) *pl. n.* a variant spelling of **Aru Islands.**

arse (ɑːs) *or U.S.* **ass** *n. Taboo.* **1.** the buttocks. **2.** the anus. **3.** a stupid person; fool. **4.** *Slang.* sexual intercourse. **5.** *Austral. slang.* effrontery; cheek. ~Also called (for senses 2, 3): **arse·hole** ('ɑːsˌhəʊl).

arse *or U.S.* **ass a·bout** *or* **a·round** *vb.* (*intr., adv.*) *Taboo slang.* to play the fool; act stupidly, esp. in an irritating manner.

arse lick·er ('ɑːsˌlɪkə) *or U.S.* **ass lick·er** *n. Taboo slang.* a person who curries favour. —**'arse-ˌlick·ing** *or U.S.* **'ass-ˌlick·ing** *adj., n.*

ar·se·nal ('ɑːsən^{ə}l) *n.* **1.** a store for arms, ammunition, and other military items. **2.** a workshop or factory that produces munitions. **3.** a store of anything regarded as weapons: *an arsenal of destructive arguments.* [C16: from Italian *arsenale* dockyard, from Arabic *dār sinā'ah,* from *dār* house + *sinā'ah* manufacture]

ar·se·nate ('ɑːsəˌneɪt, -nɪt) *n.* a salt or ester of arsenic acid.

ar·se·nic *n.* ('ɑːsnɪk). **1.** a toxic metalloid element, existing in several allotropic forms, that occurs principally in realgar and orpiment and as the free element. It is used in transistors, lead-based alloys, and high-temperature brasses. Symbol: As; atomic no.: 33; atomic wt.: 74.92; valency: 3 or 5; relative density: 5.73 grey; melting pt.: 817°C at a pressure of 3MN/m^2 (grey); sublimes at 613°C (grey). **2.** a nontechnical name for **arsenic trioxide.** ~*adj.* (ɑː'sɛnɪk). **3.** of or containing arsenic, esp. in the pentavalent state. [C14: from Latin *arsenicum,* from Greek *arsenikon* yellow orpiment, from Syriac *zarnīg* (influenced in form by Greek *arsenikos* virile)]

ar·se·nic ac·id *n.* a white poisonous soluble crystalline solid used in the manufacture of arsenates and insecticides. Formula: H_3AsO_4.

ar·sen·i·cal (ɑː'sɛnɪkᵊl) *adj.* **1.** of or containing arsenic. ~*n.* **2.** a drug or insecticide containing arsenic.

ar·se·nic tri·ox·ide *n.* a white poisonous powder used in the manufacture of glass and as an insecticide, rat poison, and weedkiller. Formula: As_2O_3.

ar·se·nide ('ɑːsəˌnaɪd) *n.* a compound in which arsenic is the most electronegative element.

ar·se·ni·ous (ɑː'siːnɪəs) *or* **ar·sen·ous** ('ɑːsɪnəs) *adj.* of or containing arsenic in the trivalent state.

ar·se·nite ('ɑːsɪˌnaɪt) *n.* a salt or ester of arsenous acid.

ar·se·no·py·rite (ˌɑːsɪnəʊ'paɪraɪt, ɑːˌsɛnə-) *n.* a white or grey metallic mineral consisting of a sulphide of iron and arsenic in monoclinic crystalline form: an ore of arsenic. Formula: FeAsS. Also called: **mispickel.**

ar·sine ('ɑːsiːn) *n.* a colourless poisonous gas used in the manufacture of organic compounds, to dope transistors, and as a military poisonous gas. Formula: AsH_3.

ar·sis ('ɑːsɪs) *n., pl.* **·ses** (-siːz). (in classical prosody) the long syllable or part on which the ictus falls in a metrical foot. Compare **thesis** (sense 6). [C18: via Late Latin from Greek, from *airein* to raise]

A.R.S.M. (in Britain) *abbrev. for* Associate of the Royal School of Mines.

ars no·va ('ɑːz 'nəʊvə) *n.* a style of music of the 14th century, characterized by great freedom and variety of rhythm and melody contrasted with the strictness of the music of the 13th century. [Latin, literally: new art]

ar·son ('ɑːsᵊn) *n. Criminal law.* the act of intentionally or recklessly setting fire to another's property or to one's own property for some improper reason. [C17: from Old French, from Medieval Latin *ārsiō,* from Latin *ārdēre* to burn; see ARDENT] —**'ar·son·ist** *n.*

ars·phen·a·mine (ɑːs'fɛnəmɪn, -ˌmiːn) *n.* a drug containing arsenic, formerly used in the treatment of syphilis and related infections.

ars po·e·ti·ca (ɑːz pəʊ'ɛtɪkə) *n.* the art of poetry.

ars·y-vers·y (ˌɑːsɪ'vɜːsɪ) *adv. Slang.* **1.** backwards or upside down. **2.** in reverse. [C16: from ARSE + Latin *versus* turned, modelled on compounds like *hurly-burly*]

art[1] (ɑːt) *n.* **1. a.** the creation of works of beauty or other special significance. **b.** (*as modifier*): *an art movement.* **2.** the exercise of human skill (as distinguished from *nature*). **3.** imaginative skill as applied to representations of the natural world or figments of the imagination. **4. a.** the products of man's creative activities; works of art collectively, esp. of the visual arts, sometimes also music, drama, dance, and literature. **b.** (*as modifier*): *an art gallery.* See also **arts, fine art. 5.** excellence or aesthetic merit of conception or execution as exemplified by such works. **6.** any branch of the visual arts, esp. painting. **7. a.** any field using the techniques of art to display artistic qualities: *advertising art.* **b.** (*as modifier*): *an art film.* **8.** *Journalism.* photographs or other illustrations in a newspaper, etc. **9.** method, facility, or knack: *the art of threading a needle; the art of writing letters.* **10.** the system of rules or principles governing a particular human activity: *the art of government.* **11.** artfulness; cunning. **12. get something down to a fine art.** to become highly proficient at something through practice. [C13: from Old French, from Latin *ars* craftsmanship]

art[2] (ɑːt) *vb. Archaic.* (used with the pronoun *thou*) a singular form of the present tense (indicative mood) of **be.** [Old English *eart,* part of *bēon* to BE]

art. *abbrev. for:* **1.** article. **2.** artificial. **3.** Also: **arty.** artillery.

-art *suffix forming nouns.* variant of **-ard.**

Ar·taud (*French* ar'to) *n.* **An·to·nin** (ɑ̃tɔ'nɛ̃). 1896–1948, French stage director and dramatist, whose concept of the theatre of cruelty is expounded in *Manifeste du théâtre de la cruauté* (1932) and *Le Théâtre et son double* (1938).

Ar·ta·xerx·es I (ˌɑːtə'zɜːksiːz) *n.* died 425 B.C., king of Persia (465–425): son of Xerxes I.

Ar·ta·xerx·es II *n.* died ?358 B.C., king of Persia (?404–?358). He defeated his brother Cyrus the Younger at Cunaxa (401).

Art Dec·o ('dɛkəʊ) *n.* **a.** a style of interior decoration, jewellery, architecture, etc., at its height in the 1930s and characterized by geometrical shapes, stylized natural forms, and symmetrical utilitarian designs adapted to mass production. **b.** (*as modifier*): *an Art-Deco carpet.* [C20: shortened from *art décoratif,* after the *Exposition des arts décoratifs* held in Paris in 1925]

ar·te·fact *or U.S.* **ar·ti·fact** ('ɑːtɪˌfækt) *n.* **1.** something made or given shape by man, such as a tool or a work of art, esp. an object of archaeological interest. **2.** *Cytology.* a structure seen in tissue after death, fixation, staining, etc., that is not normally present in the living tissue. [C19: from Latin phrase *arte factum,* from *ars* skill + *facere* to make]

ar·tel (ɑː'tɛl) *n.* **1.** (in the Soviet Union) a cooperative union or organization, esp. of producers, such as peasants. **2.** (in pre-revolutionary Russia) a quasi-cooperative association of people engaged in the same activity. [from Russian *artel',* from Italian *artieri* artisans, from *arte* work, from Latin *ars* ART[1]]

Ar·te·mis ('ɑːtɪmɪs) *n. Greek myth.* the virgin goddess of the hunt and the moon: the twin sister of Apollo. Roman counterpart: **Diana.** Also called: **Cynthia.**

ar·te·mi·si·a (ˌɑːtɪ'miːzɪə) *n.* any herbaceous perennial plant of the genus *Artemisia,* of the N hemisphere, such as mugwort, sagebrush, and wormwood: family *Compositae* (composites). [C14: via Latin from Greek, probably from *Artemis* ARTEMIS]

ar·te·ri·al (ɑː'tɪərɪəl) *adj.* **1.** of, relating to, or affecting an artery or arteries: *arterial disease.* **2.** denoting or relating to the usually bright red reoxygenated blood returning from the lungs or gills that circulates in the arteries. **3.** being a major route, esp. one with many minor branches: *an arterial road.* —**ar·'te·ri·al·ly** *adv.*

ar·te·ri·al·ize *or* **ar·te·ri·al·ise** (ɑː'tɪərɪəˌlaɪz) *vb.* (*tr.*) **1.** to change (venous blood) into arterial blood by replenishing the depleted oxygen. **2.** to vascularize (tissues). **3.** to provide with arteries. —**ar·ˌte·ri·al·i·'za·tion** *or* **ar·ˌte·ri·al·i·'sa·tion** *n.*

ar·te·ri·o- *combining form.* artery or arteries: *arteriosclerosis.* [from Greek; see ARTERY]

ar·te·ri·ole (ɑː'tɪərɪˌəʊl) *n. Anat.* any of the small subdivisions of an artery that form thin-walled vessels ending in capillaries. [C19: from New Latin *arteriola,* from Latin *artēria* ARTERY]

ar·te·ri·o·scle·ro·sis (ɑːˌtɪərɪəʊsklɪ'rəʊsɪs) *n., pl.* **·ses** (-siːz). a pathological condition of the circulatory system characterized by thickening and loss of elasticity of the arterial walls. Nontechnical name: **hardening of the arteries.** —**ar·te·ri·o·scle·rot·ic** (ɑːˌtɪərɪəʊsklɪ'rɒtɪk) *adj.*

ar·te·ri·o·ve·nous (ɑːˌtɪərɪəʊ'viːnəs) *adj.* of, relating to, or affecting an artery and a vein.

ar·te·ri·tis (ˌɑːtə'raɪtɪs) *n. Pathol.* inflammation of an artery.

ar·ter·y ('ɑːtərɪ) *n., pl.* **·ter·ies. 1.** any of the tubular thick-walled muscular vessels that convey oxygenated blood from the heart to various parts of the body. Compare **pulmonary artery, vein. 2.** a major road or means of communication in any complex system. [C14: from Latin *artēria,* related to Greek *aortē* the great artery, AORTA]

ar·te·sian well (ɑː'tiːzɪən, -ʒən) *n.* a well sunk through impermeable strata into strata receiving water from an area at a higher altitude than that of the well, so that there is sufficient pressure to force water to flow upwards. [C19: from French *artésien,* from Old French *Arteis* Artois, old province, where such wells were common]

art·ful ('ɑːtfʊl) *adj.* **1.** cunning or tricky. **2.** skilful in achieving a desired end. **3.** *Archaic.* characterized by skill or art. **4.** *Archaic.* artificial. —**'art·ful·ly** *adv.* —**'art·ful·ness** *n.*

ar·thral·gia (ɑː'θrældʒə) *n. Pathol.* pain in a joint. —**ar·'thral·gic** *adj.*

ar·thri·tis (ɑː'θraɪtɪs) *n.* inflammation of a joint or joints characterized by pain and stiffness of the affected parts, caused by gout, rheumatic fever, etc. See also **rheumatoid arthritis.** [C16: via Latin from Greek: see ARTHRO-, -ITIS] —**ar·thrit·ic** (ɑː'θrɪtɪk) *adj., n.*

ar·thro- *or before a vowel* **arthr-** *combining form.* indicating a joint: *arthritis; arthropod.* [from Greek *arthron*]

ar·thro·mere ('ɑːθrəˌmɪə) *n.* any of the segments of the body of an arthropod. —**ar·thro·mer·ic** (ˌɑːθrə'mɛrɪk) *adj.*

ar·thro·pod ('ɑːθrəˌpɒd) *n.* any invertebrate of the phylum *Arthropoda,* having jointed limbs, a segmented body, and an exoskeleton made of chitin. The group includes the crustaceans, insects, arachnids, and centipedes. —**ar·throp·o·dous** (ɑː'θrɒpədəs) *or* **ar·'throp·o·dal** *adj.*

ar·thro·spore ('ɑːθrəˌspɔː) *n.* **1.** a sporelike cell of ascomycetous fungi and some algae produced by a breaking of the hyphae. **2.** a resting sporelike cell produced by some bacteria. —**ˌar·thro·'spor·ic** *or* **ˌar·thro·'spor·ous** *adj.*

Ar·thur ('ɑːθə) *n.* **1.** a legendary king of the Britons in the sixth century A.D., who led Celtic resistance against the Saxons: possibly based on a historical figure; represented as leader of the Knights of the Round Table at Camelot. **2. Ches·ter Al·an.** 1830–86, 21st president of the U.S. (1881–85).

Ar·thu·ri·an (ɑː'θjʊərɪən) *adj.* of or relating to King Arthur and his Knights of the Round Table.

ar·tic (ɑː'tɪk) *n. Informal.* short for **articulated lorry.**

ar·ti·choke ('ɑːtɪˌtʃəʊk) *n.* **1.** Also called: **globe artichoke.** a thistle-like Eurasian plant, *Cynara scolymus,* cultivated for its large edible flower head containing many fleshy scalelike bracts: family *Compositae* (composites). **2.** the unopened flower head of this plant, which can be cooked and eaten. **3.** See **Jerusalem artichoke.** [C16: from Italian *articiocco,* from Old Spanish *alcarchofa,* from Arabic *al-kharshūf*]

ar·ti·cle ('ɑːtɪkᵊl) *n.* **1.** one of a class of objects; item: *an article of clothing.* **2.** an unspecified or previously named thing, esp. a small object: *he put the article on the table.* **3.** a distinct part of a subject or action. **4.** a written composition on a subject, often being one of several found in a magazine, newspaper, etc. **5.** *Grammar.* a kind of determiner, occurring in many languages including English, that lacks independent meaning but may serve to indicate the specificity of reference of the noun phrase with which it occurs. See also **definite article, indefinite article. 6.** a clause or section in a written document such as a treaty, contract, statute, etc. **7.** (*often cap.*) *Christianity.* See **article of faith, Thirty-nine Articles. 8.** *Archaic.* a topic or subject. ~*vb.* (*tr.*) **9.** to bind by a written contract, esp. one that governs a period of training: *an articled clerk in a solici-*

tor's office. **10.** *Archaic.* to accuse. [C13: from Old French, from Latin *articulus* small joint, from *artus* joint]

ar+ti+cle of faith *n.* **1.** *Christianity.* any of the clauses or propositions into which a creed or other statement of doctrine is divided. **2.** a deeply held belief.

ar+ti+cles of as+so+ci+a+tion *pl. n.* **1.** the constitution and regulations of a registered company as required by the British Companies Acts. **2.** the document containing these.

Ar+ti+cles of Con+fed+er+a+tion *pl. n.* the agreement made by the original 13 states in 1777 establishing a confederacy to be known as the United States of America; replaced by the Constitution of 1788.

Ar+ti+cles of War *pl. n.* **1.** the disciplinary and legal procedures by which the naval and military forces of Great Britain were bound before the 19th century. **2.** the regulations of the U.S. army, navy, and air force until the Uniform Code of Military Justice replaced them in 1951.

ar+tic·u+lar (ɑːˈtɪkjʊlə) *adj.* of or relating to joints or to the structural components in a joint. [C15: from Latin *articulāris* concerning the joints, from *articulus* small joint; see ARTICLE]

ar+tic·u+late *adj.* (ɑːˈtɪkjʊlɪt). **1.** able to express oneself fluently and coherently: *an articulate lecturer.* **2.** having the power of speech. **3.** distinct, clear, or definite; well-constructed: *an articulate voice; an articulate document.* **4.** *Zoology.* (of arthropods and higher vertebrates) possessing joints or jointed segments. *~vb.* (ɑːˈtɪkjʊˌleɪt). **5.** to speak or enunciate (words, syllables, etc.) clearly and distinctly. **6.** (*tr.*) to express coherently in words. **7.** (*intr.*) *Zoology.* to be jointed or form a joint. **8.** to be separated into jointed segments. [C16: from Latin *articulāre* to divide into joints; see ARTICLE] **—ar+ˈtic·u+late+ly** *adv.* **—ar+ˈtic·u+late+ness** *or* **ar+ˈtic·u+la+cy** *n.*

ar+tic·u+lat+ed lor+ry *n.* a large lorry made in two separate sections, a tractor and a trailer, connected by a pivoted bar. U.S. name: **trailer truck.**

ar+tic·u+la+tion (ɑːˌtɪkjʊˈleɪʃən) *n.* **1.** the act or process of speaking or expressing in words. **2. a.** the process of articulating a speech sound. **b.** the sound so produced, esp. a consonant. **3.** the act or the state of being jointed together. **4.** the form or manner in which something is jointed. **5.** *Zoology.* **a.** a joint such as that between bones or arthropod segments. **b.** the way in which jointed parts are connected. **6.** *Botany.* the part of a plant at which natural separation occurs, such as the joint between leaf and stem. **7.** a joint or jointing. **—ar+ˈtic·u+la+to+ry** *adj.*

ar+tic·u+la+tor (ɑːˈtɪkjʊˌleɪtə) *n.* **1.** a person or thing that articulates. **2.** *Phonetics.* any vocal organ that takes part in the production of a speech sound. Such organs are of two types: those that can move, such as the tongue, lips, etc. (**active articulators**), and those that remain fixed, such as the teeth, the hard palate, etc. (**passive articulators**).

ar+tic·u+la+to+ry pho+net+ics *n.* the branch of phonetics concerned with the production of speech sounds. Compare **acoustic phonetics.**

ar+ti+fact (ˈɑːtɪˌfækt) *n.* a variant spelling of **artefact.**

ar+ti+fice (ˈɑːtɪfɪs) *n.* **1.** a clever expedient; ingenious stratagem. **2.** crafty or subtle deception. **3.** skill; cleverness. **4.** a skilfully contrived device. **5.** *Obsolete.* craftsmanship. [C16: from Old French, from Latin *artificium* skill, from *artifex* one possessed of a specific skill, from *ars* skill + *-fex,* from *facere* to make]

ar+tif·i+cer (ɑːˈtɪfɪsə) *n.* **1.** a skilled craftsman. **2.** a clever or inventive designer. **3.** a serviceman trained in mechanics.

ar+ti+fi+cial (ˌɑːtɪˈfɪʃəl) *adj.* **1.** produced by man; not occurring naturally: *artificial materials of great strength.* **2.** made in imitation of a natural product, esp. as a substitute; not genuine: *artificial cream.* **3.** pretended; assumed; insincere: *an artificial manner.* **4.** lacking in spontaneity; affected: *an artificial laugh.* **5.** *Biology.* relating to superficial characteristics not based on the interrelationships of organisms: *an artificial classification.* [C14: from Latin *artificiālis* belonging to art, from *artificium* skill, ARTIFICE] **—ar+ti+fi+ci+al+i+ty** (ˌɑːtɪˌfɪʃɪˈælɪtɪ) *n.* **—ˌar+ti+ˈfi+cial+ly** *adv.*

ar+ti+fi+cial feel *n.* a system, used in aircraft that have fully powered control surfaces, providing the pilot with simulated aerodynamic forces on the controls.

ar+ti+fi+cial ho+ri+zon *n.* **1.** Also called: **gyro horizon.** an aircraft instrument, using a gyroscope, that indicates the aircraft's attitude in relation to the horizontal. **2.** *Astronomy.* a level reflecting surface, such as one of mercury, that measures the altitude of a celestial body as half the angle between the body and its reflection.

ar+ti+fi+cial in+sem+i+na+tion *n.* introduction of spermatozoa into the vagina or uterus by means other than sexual union. See **AID, AIH.**

ar+ti+fi+cial+ize *or* **ar+ti+fi+cial+ise** (ˌɑːtɪˈfɪʃəˌlaɪz) *vb.* (*tr.*) to render artificial.

ar+ti+fi+cial kid+ney *n. Med.* a mechanical apparatus for performing haemodialysis.

ar+ti+fi+cial lan+guage *n.* an invented language, esp. one intended as an international medium of communication or for use with computers. Compare **natural language.**

ar+ti+fi+cial res+pi+ra+tion *n.* **1.** any of various methods of restarting breathing after it has stopped, by manual rhythmic pressure on the chest, mouth-to-mouth breathing, etc. **2.** any method of maintaining respiration artificially, as by use of an iron lung.

ar+til+ler·y (ɑːˈtɪlərɪ) *n.* **1.** cannon or any mounted guns of higher calibre than machine guns. **2.** troops or military units specializing in using such guns. **3.** the science dealing with the use of guns. **4.** devices for discharging heavy missiles, such as catapults or slings. [C14: from Old French *artillerie,* from *artillier* to equip with weapons, of uncertain origin]

ar+til·ler·y+man (ɑːˈtɪlərɪmən) *n., pl.* **+men.** a serviceman who serves in an artillery unit.

ar+til+ler·y plant *n.* any of various tropical urticaceous plants of the genus *Pilea,* such as *P. microphylla,* all having stamens that discharge their pollen explosively.

ar+ti·o+dac+tyl (ˌɑːtɪəʊˈdæktɪl) *n.* **1.** any placental mammal of the order *Artiodactyla,* having hooves with an even number of toes; an even-toed ungulate. The order includes pigs, hippopotamuses, camels, deer, cattle, and antelopes. *~adj.* **2.** of, relating to, or belonging to the order *Artiodactyla.* **—ˌar+ti·o+ˈdac+ty+lous** *adj.*

ar+ti+san (ˈɑːtɪˌzæn, ˌɑːtɪˈzæn) *n.* **1.** a skilled workman; craftsman. **2.** *Obsolete.* an artist. [C16: from French, from Old Italian *artigiano,* from *arte* ART[1]]

art+ist (ˈɑːtɪst) *n.* **1.** a person who practises or is skilled in an art, esp. painting, drawing, or sculpture. **2.** a person who displays in his work qualities required in art, such as sensibility and imagination. **3.** a person whose profession requires artistic expertise, esp. a designer: *a commercial artist.* **4.** a person skilled in some task or occupation: *an artist at bricklaying.* **5.** *Obsolete.* an artisan. **6.** *U.S. and Austral. slang.* a person devoted to or proficient in something: *a booze artist; a con artist.* **—ar+ˈtis+tic** *adj.* **—ar+ˈtis+ti+cal+ly** *adv.*

ar+tiste (ɑːˈtiːst; *French* arˈtist) *n.* **1.** an entertainer, such as a singer or dancer. **2.** a person who is highly skilled in some occupation: *a hair artiste.*

art+ist+ry (ˈɑːtɪstrɪ) *n.* **1.** artistic workmanship, ability, or quality. **2.** artistic pursuits. **3.** great skill.

art+less (ˈɑːtlɪs) *adj.* **1.** free from deceit: *an artless manner.* **2.** natural or simple; unpretentious: *artless elegance.* **3.** without art or skill. **4.** naive or awkward: *an artless remark.* **5.** ignorant, uneducated, or uncultured. **—ˈart+less+ly** *adv.* **—ˈart+less+ness** *n.*

art mu+sic *n.* music written by a composer rather than passed on by oral tradition. Compare **folk music.**

Art Nou+veau (ˈɑː nuːˈvəʊ; *French* ar nuˈvo) *n.* **a.** a style of art and architecture of the 1890s, characterized by swelling sinuous outlines and stylized natural forms, such as flowers and leaves. **b.** (*as modifier*): *an Art-Nouveau mirror.* [French, literally: new art]

Ar+tois (*French* arˈtwa) *n.* a former province of N France.

art pa+per *n.* a high-quality type of paper having a smooth coating of china clay or similar substance on it.

arts (ɑːts) *pl. n.* **1. a. the.** imaginative, creative, and nonscientific branches of knowledge considered collectively, esp. as studied academically. **b.** (*as modifier*): *an arts degree.* **2.** See **fine art.** **3.** cunning or crafty actions or plots; schemes.

art un+ion *n. Austral.* a lottery for prizes of cash or goods.

art+work (ˈɑːtˌwɜːk) *n.* all the original nontextual matter in a publication, esp. the illustrations.

art·y (ˈɑːtɪ) *adj.* **art·i+er, art·i+est.** *Informal.* having an ostentatious or affected interest in or desire to imitate artists or artistic standards. **—ˈart·i+ness** *n.*

A·ru+ba (əˈruːbə; *Dutch* ɑˈryːbaː) *n.* an island in the West Indies, in the Netherlands Antilles off the NW coast of Venezuela. Chief town: Oranjestad. Pop.: 61 293 (1972 est.). Area: about 181 sq. km (70 sq. miles).

A·ru Is+lands (ˈɑːruː) *pl. n.* a group of islands in Indonesia, in the SW Moluccas. Area: about 8500 sq. km (3300 sq. miles).

ar·um (ˈɛərəm) *n.* **1.** any plant of the aroid genus *Arum,* of Europe and the Mediterranean region, having arrow-shaped leaves and a typically white spathe. See also **cuckoopint.** **2. arum lily.** another name for **calla** (sense 1). [C16: from Latin, variant of *aros* wake-robin, from Greek *aron*]

A·ru+na+chal Pra+desh (ˌɑːrəˈnɑːkəl prəˈdɛʃ) *n.* a union territory of NE India, formed in 1972 from the former North East Frontier Agency. Capital: Shillong. Pop.: 467 511 (1971). Area: 81 426 sq. km (31 756 sq. miles).

Ar+un+del (ˈærəndəl) *n.* a town in S England, in West Sussex: 11th-century castle. Pop.: 2382 (1971).

a·run+di+na+ceous (əˌrʌndɪˈneɪʃəs) *adj. Botany.* resembling a reed. [C17: from Latin *harundināceus,* from *harundō* a reed]

a·rus+pex (əˈrʌspɛks) *n., pl.* **+pi+ces** (-pɪˌsiːz). a variant spelling of **haruspex.**

A·ru+wi+mi (ˌɑːruːˈwiːmɪ) *n.* a river in NE Zaïre, rising near Lake Albert as the Ituri and flowing west into the River Congo (Zaïre). Length: about 1288 km (800 miles).

ar·vo (ˈɑːvəʊ) *n. Austral. informal.* afternoon.

-a·ry *suffix.* **1.** (*forming adjectives*) of; related to; belonging to: *cautionary; rudimentary.* **2.** (*forming nouns*) **a.** a person connected with or engaged in: *missionary.* **b.** a thing relating to; a place for: *commentary; aviary.* [from Latin *-ārius, -āria, -ārium*]

Ar·y+an *or* **Ar·i+an** (ˈɛərɪən) *n.* **1.** (in Nazi ideology) a Caucasian of non-Jewish descent, esp. of the Nordic type. **2.** a member of any of the peoples supposedly descended from the Indo-Europeans, esp. a speaker of an Iranian or Indic language in ancient times. *~* **3.** *adj.* of, relating to, or characteristic of an Aryan or Aryans. *~adj., n.* **4.** *Archaic.* Indo-European. [C19: from Sanskrit *ārya* of noble birth]

Ar·y+an+ize *or* **Ar·y+an+ise** (ˈɛərɪəˌnaɪz) *vb.* (*tr.*) (in Nazi ideology) to purge (politics and society) of all non-Aryan elements or people; make characteristically Aryan.

ar·yl (ˈærɪl) *n.* **1.** (*modifier*) *Chem.* of, consisting of, or containing an aromatic group: *aryl group or radical.* **2.** an organometallic compound in which a metal atom is bound to an aryl or molecule. [C20: from AR(OMATIC) + -YL]

ar·y·te·noid *or* **ar·y·tae·noid** (ˌærɪˈtiːnɔɪd) *adj. also* **ar·y·te·noid·al. 1.** denoting either of two small cartilages of the larynx that are attached to the vocal cords. **2.** denoting any of three small muscles of the larynx that narrow the space between the vocal cords. ~*n.* **3.** an arytenoid cartilage or muscle. [C18: from New Latin *arytaenoïdes*, from Greek *arutainoeidēs* shaped like a ladle, from *arutaina* ladle]

as[1] (æz; *unstressed* əz) *conj.* (*subordinating*) **1.** (often preceded by *just*) while; when; at the time that: *he caught me as I was leaving.* **2.** in the way that: *dancing as only she can.* **3.** that which; what: *I did as I was told.* **4.** (of) which fact, event, etc. (referring to the previous statement): *to become wise, as we all know, is not easy.* **5. as it were.** in a way; so to speak; as if it were really so. **6. as you were. a.** a military command to return to the previous position. **b.** a statement to withdraw something just said. **7.** since; seeing that: *as you're in charge here, you'd better tell me where to wait.* **8.** in the same way that: *he died of cancer, as his father had done.* **9.** in spite of the extent to which: *intelligent as you are, I suspect you will fail.* **10.** for instance: *capital cities, as London.* ~*prep., conj.* **11. a.** used correlatively before an adjective or adverb and before a noun phrase or a clause to indicate identity of extent, amount, etc.: *she is as heavy as her sister; she is as heavy now as she used to be.* **b.** used with this sense after a noun phrase introduced by *the same: the same height as her sister.* ~*prep.* **12.** in the role of; being: *as his friend, my opinions are probably biased.* **13. as for** *or* **to.** with reference to: *as for my past, I'm not telling you anything.* **14. as from** *or* (*U.S.*) **of.** *Formal.* (in expressions of time) from: *fares will rise as from January 11.* **15. as if** *or* **though.** as it would be if: *he talked as if he knew all about it.* **16. as (it) is.** in the existing state of affairs: *as it is, I shall have difficulty finishing all this work, without any more.* **17. as per.** See **per** (sense 3). **18. as regards.** See **regard** (sense 6). **19. as such.** See **such** (sense 3). **20. such as.** See **such** (sense 5). **21. as was.** in a previous state. **22. as well.** See **well** (sense 12). **23. as yet.** up to now; so far. [Old English *alswā* likewise; see ALSO]

as[2] (æs) *n.* **1.** an ancient Roman unit of weight approximately equal to 1 pound troy (373 grams). **2.** the standard monetary unit and copper coin of ancient Rome. [C17: from Latin *ās* unity, probably of Etruscan origin]

As *symbol for:* **1.** *Chemistry.* arsenic. **2.** altostratus.

AS *abbrev. for:* **1.** Also: **A.S.** Anglo-Saxon. **2.** antisubmarine.

As. *abbrev. for:* **1.** Asia(n). **2.** Asiatic.

A.S.A. *abbrev. for:* **1.** (in Britain) Amateur Swimming Association. **2.** (in the U.S.) American Standards Association.

ASA/BS *abbrev.* an expression of the speed of a photographic film, given as 0.8/*E*, where *E* is the exposure of a point 0.1 density units above the fog level on the characteristic curve of a particular sensitized material. Compare **DIN.** [C20: from *American Standards Association/British Standard*]

as·a·foet·i·da *or* **as·a·fet·i·da** (ˌæsəˈfɛtɪdə) *n.* a bitter resin with an unpleasant onion-like smell, obtained from the roots of some umbelliferous plants of the genus *Ferula:* formerly used to treat flatulence, hysteria, etc. [C14: from Medieval Latin, from *asa* gum (compare Persian *azā* mastic) + Latin *foetidus* evil-smelling, FETID]

A·san·te·he·ne (æˈʃæntɪˌhɛnɪ) *n.* the ruler of the Ashanti people of Ghana.

as·a·ra·bac·ca (ˌæsərəˈbækə) *n.* a perennial evergreen Eurasian plant, *Asarum europaeum*, having kidney-shaped leaves and a single brownish flower: family *Aristolochiaceae.*

as·a·rum (ˈæsərəm) *n.* the dried strong-scented root of the wild ginger plant: a flavouring agent and source of an aromatic oil used in perfumery, formerly used in medicine. [C19: via New Latin from Latin: hazelwort, from Greek *asaron*]

As·ben (æsˈbɛn) *n.* another name for **Aïr** (region of the Sahara).

as·bes·tos (æsˈbɛstɒs, -təs) *n.* **a.** any of the fibrous amphibole and serpentine minerals, esp. chrysotile and tremolite, that are incombustible and resistant to chemicals. It is widely used in the form of fabric or board as a heat-resistant structural material. **b.** (*as modifier*): *asbestos matting.* [C14 (originally applied to a mythical stone the heat of which could not be extinguished): via Latin from Greek: from *asbestos* inextinguishable, from A-[1] + *sbennunai* to extinguish] —**as·ˈbes·tine** *adj.*

as·bes·to·sis (ˌæsbɛsˈtəʊsɪs) *n.* inflammation of the lungs resulting from chronic inhalation of asbestos particles.

Asc. *Astrology. abbrev. for* Ascendant.

As·ca·ni·us (æˈskeɪnɪəs) *n. Roman myth.* the son of Aeneas and Creusa; founder of Alba Longa, mother city of Rome. Also called: **Iulus.**

as·ca·ri·a·sis (ˌæskəˈraɪəsɪs) *n.* infestation of the intestines with the roundworm *Ascaris lumbricoides,* causing abdominal pain, nausea and vomiting, weight loss, etc.

as·ca·rid (ˈæskərɪd) *n.* any parasitic nematode worm of the family *Ascaridae,* such as the common roundworm of man and pigs. [C14: from New Latin *ascaridae,* from Greek *askarides,* plural of *askaris*]

as·cend (əˈsɛnd) *vb.* **1.** to go or move up (a ladder, hill, slope, etc.); mount; climb. **2.** (*intr.*) to slope or incline upwards. **3.** (*intr.*) to rise to a higher point, level, degree, etc. **4.** to follow (a river) upstream towards its source. **5.** to trace (a genealogy, etc.) back in time. **6.** to sing or play (a scale, arpeggio, etc.) from the lower to higher notes. **7. ascend the throne.** to become king or queen. [C14: from Latin *ascendere,* from *scandere*]

as·cend·an·cy, as·cend·en·cy (əˈsɛndənsɪ) *or* **as·cend·ance, as·cend·ence** *n.* the condition of being dominant, esp. through superior economic or political power.

as·cend·ant *or* **as·cend·ent** (əˈsɛndənt) *adj.* **1.** proceeding upwards; rising. **2.** dominant, superior, or influential. **3.** *Botany.* another term for **ascending.** ~*n.* **4.** *Rare.* an ancestor. **5.** a position or condition of dominance, superiority or control. **6.** *Astrology.* (*sometimes cap.*) **a.** a point on the ecliptic that rises on the eastern horizon at a particular moment and changes as the earth rotates on its axis. **b.** the sign of the zodiac containing this point. **7. in the ascendant.** increasing in influence, prosperity, etc.

as·cend·er (əˈsɛndə) *n.* **1.** *Printing.* **a.** the part of certain lower-case letters, such as *b* or *h,* that extends above the body of the letter. **b.** any letter having such a part. **2.** a person or thing that ascends.

as·cend·ing (əˈsɛndɪŋ) *adj.* **1.** moving upwards; rising. **2.** *Botany.* sloping or curving upwards: *the ascending stem of a vine.*

as·cen·sion (əˈsɛnʃən) *n.* **1.** the act of ascending. **2.** *Astronomy.* the rising of a star above the horizon. —**as·ˈcen·sion·al** *adj.*

As·cen·sion[1] (əˈsɛnʃən) *n. New Testament.* the passing of Jesus Christ from earth into heaven (Acts 1:9).

As·cen·sion[2] (əˈsɛnʃən) *n.* an island in the S Atlantic, northwest of St. Helena: uninhabited until claimed by Britain in 1815. Pop.: 1231 (1971). Area: 88 sq. km (34 sq. miles).

As·cen·sion Day *n. Christianity.* the 40th day after Easter, when the Ascension of Christ into heaven is celebrated.

As·cen·sion·tide (əˈsɛnʃənˌtaɪd) *n.* the ten days from Ascension Day to the day before Whit Sunday.

as·cent (əˈsɛnt) *n.* **1.** the act of ascending; climb or upward movement: *the ascent of hot gases.* **2.** an upward slope; incline or gradient. **3.** movement back through time, as in tracing of earlier generations (esp. in the phrase **line of ascent**).

as·cer·tain (ˌæsəˈteɪn) *vb.* (*tr.*) **1.** to determine or discover definitely. **2.** *Archaic.* to make certain. [C15: from Old French *acertener* to make certain] —ˌ**as·cer·ˈtain·a·ble** *adj.* —ˌ**as·cer·ˈtain·a·bly** *adv.* —ˌ**as·cer·ˈtain·ment** *n.*

as·ce·sis (əˈsiːsɪs) *n., pl.* **·ses** (-siːz). the exercise of self-discipline. [C19: from Greek, from *askeîn* to exercise]

as·cet·ic (əˈsɛtɪk) *n.* **1.** a person who practises great self-denial and austerities and abstains from worldly comforts and pleasures, esp. for religious reasons. **2.** (in the early Christian Church) a monk. ~*adj. also* **as·ˈcet·i·cal. 3.** rigidly abstinent or abstemious; austere. **4.** of or relating to ascetics or asceticism. **5.** intensely rigorous in religious austerities. [C17: from Greek *askētikos,* from *askētēs,* from *askeîn* to exercise] —**as·ˈcet·i·cal·ly** *adv.*

as·cet·i·cism (əˈsɛtɪˌsɪzəm) *n.* **1.** the behaviour, discipline, or outlook of an ascetic, esp. of a religious ascetic. **2.** the principles of ascetic practices, esp. in the early Christian Church. **3.** *Theol.* the theory and system of ascetic practices.

Asch (æʃ) *n.* **Sho·lem** (ˈʃəʊləm). 1880–1957, U.S. writer, born in Poland, who wrote in Yiddish. His works include biblical novels.

A·schaf·fen·burg (*German* aˈʃafənˌbʊrk) *n.* a city in central West Germany, on the River Main in Bavaria: seat of the Imperial Diet (1447); ceded to Bavaria in 1814. Pop.: 55 100 (1970).

As·cham (ˈæskəm) *n.* **Rog·er.** ?1515–68, English humanist writer and classical scholar: tutor to Queen Elizabeth I.

as·ci (ˈæsaɪ, ˈæskaɪ) *n.* plural of **ascus.**

as·cid·i·an (əˈsɪdɪən) *n.* **1.** any minute marine invertebrate animal of the class *Ascidiacea,* such as the sea squirt, the adults of which are degenerate and sedentary: subphylum *Tunicata* (tunicates). **2. ascidian tadpole.** the free-swimming larva of an ascidian, having a tadpole-like tail containing the notochord and nerve cord. ~*adj.* **3.** of, relating to, or belonging to the *Ascidiacea.*

as·cid·i·um (əˈsɪdɪəm) *n., pl.* **·cid·i·a** (-ˈsɪdɪə). part of a plant that is shaped like a pitcher, such as the modified leaf of the pitcher plant. [C18: from New Latin, from Greek *askidion* a little bag, from *askos* bag]

ASCII (ˈæskiː) *n. acronym for* American standard code for information interchange: a computer code for representing alphanumeric characters.

as·ci·tes (əˈsaɪtiːz) *n., pl.* **as·ci·tes.** *Pathol.* accumulation of serous fluid in the peritoneal cavity. [C14: from Latin: a kind of dropsy, from Greek *askitēs,* from *askos* wineskin] —**as·cit·ic** (əˈsɪtɪk) *adj.*

as·cle·pi·a·da·ceous (æˌskliːpɪəˈdeɪʃəs) *adj.* of, relating to, or belonging to the *Asclepiadaceae,* a family of mostly tropical and subtropical flowering plants, including the milkweed and swallowwort, having pollen in the form of a waxy mass (pollinium). [C19: from New Latin *Asclēpias* genus name, from Latin, from Greek *asklēpias,* named after ASCLEPIUS]

As·cle·pi·a·de·an (æˌskliːpɪəˈdiːən) *Prosody.* ~*adj.* **1.** of or relating to a type of classical verse line consisting of a spondee, two or three choriambs, and an iamb. ~*n.* **2.** Also called: **Asclepiad.** an Asclepiadean verse. [C17: via Latin from Greek *Asklēpiadēs* (about 270 B.C.), who invented the verse form]

As·cle·pi·us (əˈskliːpɪəs) *n. Greek myth.* a god of healing; son of Apollo. Roman counterpart: **Aesculapius.**

as·co- *combining form.* indicating a bladder or ascus: *ascomycete.* [from Greek *askos* bladder]

as·co·carp (ˈæskəˌkɑːp) *n.* (in some ascomycetous fungi) a globular structure containing the asci. See **apothecium, perithecium.**

as·co·go·ni·um (ˌæskəˈgəʊnɪəm) *n., pl.* **·ni·a** (-nɪə). a female reproductive body in some ascomycetous fungi in which, after fertilization, the asci develop.

As·co·li Pi·ce·no (*Italian* ˈaskoli piˈtʃɛːno) *n.* a town in E central Italy, in the Marches: capital of the Roman province of Picenum; site of the massacre of all its Roman citizens in the Social War in 90 B.C. Pop.: 55 053 (1971). Latin name: **Asculum Picenum.**

as+co+my+cete (ˌæskəmaɪˈsiːt) *n.* any fungus of the class *Ascomycetes,* in which the spores (ascospores) are formed inside a club-shaped cell (ascus). The group includes yeast, penicillium, aspergillus, truffles, and certain mildews. —**ˌas+co+my+ˈce·tous** *adj.*

a·scor+bic ac·id (əˈskɔːbɪk) *n.* a white crystalline vitamin present in plants, esp. citrus fruits, tomatoes, and green vegetables. A deficiency in the diet of man leads to scurvy. Formula: $C_6H_8O_6$. Also called: **vitamin C.**

as+co+spore (ˈæskəˌspɔː) *n.* one of the spores (usually eight in number) that are produced in an ascus.

as+cot (ˈæskət) *n.* a cravat with wide square ends, usually secured with an ornamental stud. [C20: named after ASCOT, where it was probably first worn]

As+cot (ˈæskət) *n.* a horse race meeting held at Ascot, Berkshire, esp. **Royal Ascot,** a four-day meeting held in June: one of the chief events of the English racing year.

as+cribe (əˈskraɪb) *vb.* (*tr.*) **1.** to credit or assign, as to a particular origin or period: *to ascribe parts of a play to Shakespeare.* **2.** to attribute as a quality; consider as belonging to: *to ascribe beauty to youth.* [C15: from Latin *ascrībere* to enrol, from *ad* in addition + *scrībere* to write] —**as+ˈcrib+a·ble** *adj.*

as+crip+tion (əˈskrɪpʃən) *or* **ad+scrip+tion** (ədˈskrɪpʃən) *n.* **1.** the act of ascribing. **2.** a statement ascribing something to someone, esp. praise to God. [C16: from Latin *ascrīptiō,* from *ascrībere* to ASCRIBE]

as+cus (ˈæskəs) *n., pl.* **as·ci** (ˈæsaɪ, ˈæskaɪ). a saclike structure that produces (usually) eight ascospores during sexual reproduction in ascomycetous fungi such as yeasts and mildews. [C19: from New Latin, from Greek *askos* bag]

as+dic (ˈæzdɪk) *n.* another name for an **echo sounder.** [C20: from *A(nti-)S(ubmarine) D(etection) I(nvestigation) C(ommittee)*]

-ase *suffix forming nouns.* indicating an enzyme: *oxidase.* [abstracted from DIASTASE]

A.S.E.A.N. *abbrev. for* Association of Southeast Asian Nations.

a·se+i·ty (eɪˈsiːɪtɪ) *n. Philosophy.* existence derived from itself, having no other source. [C17: from Medieval Latin *aseitas,* from Latin *ā* from + *sē* oneself]

a·sep+al+ous (æˈsɛpələs) *adj.* (of a plant or flower) having no sepals.

a·sep+sis (əˈsɛpsɪs, eɪ-) *n.* **1.** the state of being free from living pathogenic organisms. **2.** the methods of achieving a germ-free condition. —**a·ˈsep+tic** *adj.*

a·sex·u·al (eɪˈseksjʊəl, æ-) *adj.* **1.** having no apparent sex or sex organs. **2.** (of reproduction) not involving the fusion of male and female gametes, as in vegetative reproduction, fission, and budding. —**a·ˌsex·u+ˈal+i·ty** *n.* —**a·ˈsex·u·al+ly** *adv.*

As+gard (ˈæsgɑːd) *or* **As+garth** (ˈæsgɑːθ) *n. Norse myth.* the dwelling place of the principal gods, the Aesir.

ash[1] (æʃ) *n.* **1.** the nonvolatile products and residue formed when matter is burnt. **2.** any of certain compounds formed by burning. See **soda ash. 3.** fine particles of lava thrown out by an erupting volcano. **4.** a light silvery grey colour, often with a brownish tinge. [Old English *æsce;* related to Old Norse, Old High German *aska,* Gothic *azgō,* Latin *aridus* dry]

ash[2] (æʃ) *n.* **1.** any oleaceous tree of the genus *Fraxinus,* esp. *F. excelsior* of Europe and Asia, having compound leaves, clusters of small greenish flowers, and winged seeds. **2.** the close-grained durable wood of any of these trees, used for tool handles, etc. **3.** any of several trees resembling the ash, such as the mountain ash. [Old English *æsc;* related to Old Norse *askr,* Old Saxon, Old High German *ask,* Lithuanian *uosis*]

ash[3] (æʃ) *n.* the digraph *æ,* as in Old English, representing a front vowel approximately like that of the *a* in Modern English *hat.* The character is also used to represent this sound in the International Phonetic Alphabet.

a·shamed (əˈʃeɪmd) *adj.* (*usually postpositive*) **1.** overcome with shame, guilt, or remorse. **2.** (foll. by *of*) suffering from feelings of inferiority or shame in relation to (a person, thing, or deed). **3.** (foll. by *to*) unwilling through fear of humiliation, shame, etc. [Old English *āscamod,* past participle of *āscamian* to shame, from *scamu* SHAME] —**a·sham+ed+ly** (əˈʃeɪmɪdlɪ) *adv.*

A·shan+ti (əˈʃæntɪ) *n.* **1.** an administrative region of central Ghana: former native kingdom, suppressed by the British in 1900 after four wars. Capital: Kumasi. Pop.: 1 477 397 (1970). Area: 24 390 sq. km (9417 sq. miles). **2.** a native or inhabitant of Ashanti. **3.** a former name for **Twi** (the language).

ash blond *n.* **1. a.** a very light blond colour. **b.** (*as adj.*): *ash-blond hair.* **2.** a person whose hair is this colour.

ash can *n.* a U.S. word for **dustbin.** Also called: **garbage can, ash bin, trash can.**

Ash Can School *n.* a group of U.S. painters including Robert Henri and later George Bellows, founded in 1907, noted for their depiction of the sordid aspects of city life.

Ash·croft (ˈæʃkrɒft) *n.* Dame **Peg·gy.** born 1907, English actress.

Ashe (æʃ) *n.* **Ar·thur (Robert).** born 1943, U.S. tennis player: U.S. champion 1968; Wimbledon champion 1975.

ash+en[1] (ˈæʃən) *adj.* **1.** drained of colour; pallid. **2.** consisting of or resembling ashes. **3.** of a pale greyish colour.

ash+en[2] (ˈæʃən) *adj.* of, relating to, or made from the ash tree or its timber.

Ash·er (ˈæʃə) *n.* the son of Jacob and ancestor of one of the 12 tribes of Israel.

ash·es (ˈæʃɪz) *pl. n.* **1.** ruins or remains, as after destruction or burning: *the city was left in ashes.* **2.** the remains of a human body after cremation.

Ash·es (ˈæʃɪz) *pl. n.* **the.** a cremated cricket stump constituting a trophy competed for by England and Australia in test cricket.

ash·et (ˈæʃɪt) *n. Scot. and northern English dialect.* a shallow oval dish or large plate. [C16: from French *assiette*]

Ash+ford (ˈæʃfəd) *n.* a market town in SE England in central Kent. Pop.: 35 560 (1971).

Ash+ke+na+zi (ˌæʃkəˈnɑːzɪ) *n., pl.* **+zim** (-zɪm). **1.** (*modifier*) of or relating to the Jews of Germany and E Europe. **2.** a Jew of German or E European descent. **3.** the pronunciation of Hebrew used by these Jews. Compare **Sephardi.** [C19: Late Hebrew, from Hebrew *Ashkenaz,* the son of Gomer (Genesis 10:3; I Chronicles 1:6), a descendant of Noah through Japheth, and hence taken to be identified with the ancient Ascanians of Phrygia and, in the medieval period, the Germans]

ash+key (ˈæʃkiː) *n.* the winged fruit of the ash.

Ash+kha+bad (*Russian* aʃxaˈbat) *n.* a city in the SW Soviet Union, capital of the Turkmen SSR. Pop.: 289 000 (1975 est.).

ash+lar *or* **ash+ler** (ˈæʃlə) *n.* **1.** a block of hewn stone with straight edges for use in building. **2.** Also called: **ashlar veneer.** a thin dressed stone with straight edges, used to face a wall. **3.** masonry made of ashlar. [C14: from Old French *aisselier* crossbeam, from *ais* board, from Latin *axis* axletree; see AXIS[1]]

ash+lar+ing (ˈæʃlərɪŋ) *n.* **1.** ashlars collectively. **2.** a number of short upright boards forming the wall of a garret, cutting off the acute angle between the rafters and the floor.

a·shore (əˈʃɔː) *adv.* **1.** towards or onto land from the water: *we swam ashore.* ~*adj.* (*postpositive*), *adv.* **2.** on land, having come from the water: *a day ashore before sailing.*

ash+plant (ˈæʃˌplɑːnt) *n.* a walking stick made from an ash sapling.

ash+ram (ˈæʃrəm, ˈɑːʃ-) *n.* **1.** a religious retreat or community where a Hindu holy man lives. **2.** a house that provides accommodation for destitute people. [from Sanskrit *āśrama,* from *ā-* near + *śrama* religious exertion]

Ash·ton (ˈæʃtən) *n.* Sir **Fred·e·rick.** born 1906, British ballet dancer and choreographer. His ballets include *Façade* (1931), to music by Walton, *La Fille mal gardée* (1960), *The Dream* (1964), and *A Month in the Country* (1976).

Ash·ton-un·der-Lyne (ˈæʃtən, ˈlaɪn) *n.* a town in NW England, in Greater Manchester. Pop.: 48 865 (1971).

Ash·to·reth (ˈæʃtəˌrɛθ) *n. Old Testament.* an ancient Semitic fertility goddess, identified with Astarte and Ishtar.

ash+tray (ˈæʃˌtreɪ) *n.* a receptacle for tobacco ash, cigarette butts, etc.

Ash·ur (ˈæʃʊə) *n.* a variant spelling of **Assur.**

Ash·ur·ba·ni·pal (ˌæʃʊəˈbɑːnɪˌpæl) *or* **As·sur·ba·ni·pal** *n.* died ?626 B.C., king of Assyria (?668–?626): son of Esarhaddon. He built the magnificent palace and library at Nineveh.

Ash Wednes+day *n.* the first day of Lent, named from the practice of Christians of placing ashes on their heads.

ash·y (ˈæʃɪ) *adj.* **ash·i·er, ash·i+est. 1.** of a pale greyish colour; ashen. **2.** consisting of, covered with, or resembling ash.

ʻA·si (ˈæsɪ) *n.* the Arabic name for the **Orontes.**

A·sia (ˈeɪʃə, ˈeɪʒə) *n.* the largest of the continents, bordering on the Arctic Ocean, the Pacific Ocean, the Indian Ocean, and the Mediterranean and Red Seas in the west. It includes the large peninsulas of Asia Minor, India, Arabia, and Indo-China and the island groups of Japan, Indonesia, the Philippines, and Ceylon; contains the mountain ranges of the Hindu Kush, Himalayas, Pamirs, Tien Shan, Urals, and Caucasus, the great plateaus of India, Iran, and Tibet, vast plains and deserts, and the valleys of many large rivers including the Mekong, Irrawaddy, Indus, Ganges, Tigris, and Euphrates. Pop.: 2 052 000 000 (1968 est.). Area: 44 391 162 sq. km (17 139 445 sq. miles).

A·sia Mi+nor *n.* the historical name for **Anatolia.**

A·sian (ˈeɪʃən, ˈeɪʒən) *adj.* **1.** of or relating to Asia or to any of its peoples or languages. ~*n.* **2.** a native or inhabitant of Asia or a descendant of one.

Usage. *Asian* is used in formal writing as a noun indicating a person from Asia. The use of the word *Asiatic* in this sense is regarded by some people as offensive.

A·sian flu *n.* a type of influenza recurring in worldwide epidemics, caused by a virus (A2 strain or subsequent antigenic variants), which apparently originated in China in 1957.

A·si+at+ic (ˌeɪʃɪˈætɪk, -zɪ-) *n., adj.* another name for **Asian.**

A·si+at+ic bee+tle *n.* a Japanese scarabaeid beetle, *Anomala orientalis,* introduced into Hawaii and the northeastern U.S.: a serious pest of sugar cane and cereal crops by destroying the roots.

A·si+at+ic chol+er·a *n.* another name for **cholera.**

a·side (əˈsaɪd) *adv.* **1.** on or to one side: *they stood aside to let him pass.* **2.** out of hearing; in or into seclusion: *he took her aside to tell her of his plan.* **3.** away from oneself: *he threw the book aside.* **4.** out of mind or consideration: *he put aside all fears.* **5.** in or into reserve: *to put aside money for old age.* **6.** **aside from.** (*prep.*) *Chiefly U.S.* **a.** besides: *he has money aside from his possessions.* **b.** except for: *he has nothing aside from the clothes he stands in.* Compare **apart** (sense 7). ~*n.* **7.** something spoken by an actor, intended to be heard by the audience, but not by the others on stage. **8.** any confidential statement spoken in undertones. **9.** a digression.

as·i·nine ('æsɪˌnaɪn) *adj.* **1.** obstinate or stupid. **2.** resembling an ass. [C16: from Latin *asinīnus*, from *asinus* ASS[1]] —'**as·i·ˌnine·ly** *adv.* —**as·i·nin·i·ty** (ˌæsɪ'nɪnɪtɪ) *n.*

A.S.I.O. *abbrev. for* Australian Security Intelligence Organization.

A·sir (æ'sɪə) *n.* a region of SW Saudi Arabia, on the Red Sea: under Turkish rule until 1933. Pop.: about 1 000 000 (1970 est.). Area: 103 600 sq. km (40 000 sq. miles).

-asis *suffix forming nouns.* a variant of **-iasis.**

ask (ɑːsk) *vb.* **1.** (often foll. by *about*) to put a question (to); request an answer from: *she asked (him) about God.* **2.** (*tr.*) to inquire about: *she asked him the time of the train; she asked the way.* **3.** (*tr.*) to direct or put (a question). **4.** (*may take a clause as object or an infinitive;* often foll. by *for*) to make a request or demand: *she asked (him) for information; they asked for a deposit.* **5.** (*tr.*) to demand or expect (esp. in the phrases **ask a lot of, ask too much of**). **6.** (*tr.*) Also: **ask out, ask over.** to request (a person) politely to come or go to a place; invite: *he asked her to the party.* **7.** (*tr.*) to need; require: *the job asks both time and patience.* **8.** (*tr.*) *Archaic.* to proclaim (marriage banns). ~See also **ask after, ask for.** [Old English *āscian;* related to Old Frisian *āskia*, Old Saxon *ēscon*, Old High German *eiscōn*] —'**ask·er** *n.*

Ask (ɑːsk) *n. Norse myth.* the first man, created by the gods from an ash tree.

ask af·ter *vb.* (*prep.*) to make enquiries about the health of (someone): *he asked after her mother.*

a·skance (ə'skæns) *or* **a·skant** (ə'skænt) *adv., adj.* **1.** with an oblique glance. **2.** with doubt or mistrust. [C16: of unknown origin]

as·ka·ri (as'kariː) *n.* (in East Africa) a soldier or policeman. [C19: from Arabic: soldier]

a·skew (ə'skjuː) *adv., adj.* at an oblique angle; towards one side; awry.

ask for *vb.* (*prep.*) **1.** to try to obtain by requesting: *he asked for help.* **2.** (*intr.*) *Informal.* to behave in a provocative manner that is regarded as inviting (trouble, etc.): *she's asking for trouble; you're asking for it.*

ask·ing price *n.* the price suggested by a seller but usually considered to be subject to bargaining.

Ask·ja ('ɑːskjə) *n.* a volcano in E central Iceland: active in 1961; largest crater in Iceland. Height: 1510 m (4954 ft.). Area of crater: 88 sq. km (34 sq. miles).

a·slant (ə'slɑːnt) *adv.* **1.** at a slant. ~*prep.* **2.** at a slant across or athwart.

a·sleep (ə'sliːp) *adj.* (*postpositive*) **1.** in or into a state of sleep. **2.** in or into a dormant or inactive state. **3.** (of limbs, esp. when the blood supply to them has been restricted) numb; lacking sensation. **4.** *Euphemistic.* dead.

ASLEF ('æzlɛf) *n.* (in Britain) *acronym for* Associated Society of Locomotive Engineers and Firemen.

a·slope (ə'sləʊp) *adv., adj.* (*postpositive*) sloping.

A.S.M. *abbrev. for* air-to-surface missile.

As·ma·ra (æs'mɑːrə) *n.* a city in Ethiopia: capital of Eritrea. Pop.: 317 950 (1975 est.).

As·mo·de·us (æs'məʊdɪəs, ˌæsməʊ'diːəs) *n.* (in Jewish demonology) prince of the demons. [via Latin *Asmodaeus*, from Avestan *Aēsma-daēva*, spirit of anger]

As·nières (*French* a'njɛːr) *n.* a suburb of Paris, on the Seine. Pop.: 75 679 (1975).

A·so ('ɑːsəʊ) *n.* a group of five volcanic cones in Japan on central Kyushu, one of which, Naka-dake, has the largest crater in the world, between 16 km (10 miles) and 24 km (15 miles) in diameter. Highest cone: 1592 m (5223 ft.). Also called: **A·so·san** (ˌɑːsəʊ'sɑːn).

a·so·cial (eɪ'səʊʃəl) *adj.* **1.** avoiding contact; not gregarious. **2.** unconcerned about the welfare of others. **3.** hostile to society or social practices.

A·so·ka (ə'səʊkə, ə'ʃəʊ-) *n.* died 232 B.C., Indian emperor (?273–232 B.C.), who elevated Buddhism to the official state religion.

asp[1] (æsp) *n.* **1.** the venomous snake, probably *Naja haje* (Egyptian cobra), that caused the death of Cleopatra and was formerly used by the Pharaohs as a symbol of their power over life and death. See also **uraeus. 2.** Also called: **asp viper.** a viper, *Vipera aspis*, that occurs in S Europe and is very similar to but smaller than the adder. **3. horned asp.** another name for **horned viper.** [C15: from Latin *aspis*, from Greek]

asp[2] (æsp) *n.* an archaic name for the **aspen.** [Old English *æspe;* related to Old Norse *ösp*, Old High German *aspa*]

as·par·a·gine (ə'spærəˌdʒiːn, -dʒɪn) *n.* a nonessential amino acid obtained mainly from asparagus, potatoes, and beetroot. Formula: $NH_2COCH_2CH(NH_2)COOH$. [C19: from French, from Latin *asparagus* ASPARAGUS + -INE[2]]

as·par·a·gus (ə'spærəgəs) *n.* **1.** any Eurasian liliaceous plant of the genus *Asparagus*, esp. the widely cultivated *A. officinalis*, having small scaly or needle-like leaves. **2.** the succulent young shoots of *A. officinalis*, which may be cooked and eaten. **3. asparagus fern.** a fernlike species of asparagus, *A. plumosus*, native to southern Africa. [C15: from Latin, from Greek *asparagos*, of obscure origin]

as·par·tic ac·id (ə'spɑːtɪk) *n.* a nonessential amino acid occurring naturally in sugar cane and sugar beet; aminosuccinic acid. Formula: $COOHCH_2CH(NH_2)COOH$. [C19: from ASPAR(AGUS) + -IC]

A·spa·si·a (ə'speɪzɪə) *n.* 5th century B.C., Greek courtesan; mistress of Pericles.

as·pect ('æspɛkt) *n.* **1.** appearance to the eye; visual effect: *the physical aspect of the landscape.* **2.** a distinct feature or element in a problem, situation, etc.; facet: *to consider every aspect of a problem.* **3.** the way in which a problem, idea, etc., may be considered: *to consider a problem from every aspect.* **4.** a facial expression; manner of appearing: *a severe aspect.* **5.** a position facing a particular direction; outlook: *the southern aspect of a house.* **6.** a view in a certain direction: *a good aspect of the village from the tower.* **7.** a surface that faces in a given direction: *the ventral aspect of a fish.* **8.** *Astrology.* any of several specific angular distances between two planets or a planet and the Ascendant or Midheaven measured, from the earth, in degrees along the ecliptic. **9.** *Grammar.* a category of verbs or verbal inflections that expresses such features as the continuity, repetition, or completedness of the action described. Compare **perfective** (sense 2), **progressive** (senses 8, 10). **10.** *Archaic.* glance or gaze. [C14: from Latin *aspectus* a sight, from *aspicere*, from *ad-* to, at + *specere* to look]

as·pect ra·ti·o *n.* **1.** the ratio of the width of a televised picture to its height. **2.** the ratio of the span of an aerofoil to its mean chord.

as·pec·tu·al (æ'spɛktjʊəl) *adj.* of or relating to grammatical aspect.

as·pen ('æspən) *n.* **1.** any of several trees of the salicaceous genus *Populus*, such as *P. tremula* of Europe, in which the leaves are attached to the stem by long flattened stalks so that they quiver in the wind. Archaic name: **asp.** ~*adj.* **2.** *Archaic, chiefly literary.* trembling. [Old English *æspe;* see ASP[2]]

as·per ('æspə) *n.* a Turkish monetary unit, formerly a silver coin, worth 1/120 of a piastre. [from Turkish, ultimately from Latin: rough, harsh]

As·per·ges (æ'spɜːdʒiːz) *n. R.C. Church.* **1.** a short rite preceding Mass, in which the celebrant sprinkles those present with holy water to the accompaniment of the chant *Asperges me, Domine.* **2.** the chant opening with these words. [C16: from Latin *Asperges (me hyssopo)* Thou shalt purge (me with hyssop)]

as·per·gil·lo·sis (æˌspɜːdʒɪ'ləʊsɪs) *n., pl.* **-ses** (-siːz). a rare fungal infection, esp. of the mucous membranes or lungs, caused by various species of *Aspergillus.* [C19: from New Latin, from ASPERGILLUS]

as·per·gil·lum (ˌæspə'dʒɪləm) *or* **as·per·gill** ('æspədʒɪl) *n., pl.* **-gil·la** (-'dʒɪlə), **-gil·lums,** *or* **-gills.** another term for **aspersorium** (sense 2). [C17: from New Latin *aspergillum*, from Latin *aspergere*, from *spargere* to sprinkle]

as·per·gil·lus (ˌæspə'dʒɪləs) *n., pl.* **-gil·li** (-'dʒɪlaɪ). any ascomycetous fungus of the genus *Aspergillus*, having chains of spores attached like bristles to a club-shaped stalk: family *Aspergillaceae.* [C19: from New Latin: *aspergillum (from its similar appearance)*]

as·per·i·ty (æ'spɛrɪtɪ) *n., pl.* **·ties. 1.** roughness or sharpness of temper. **2.** roughness or harshness of a surface, sound, taste, etc. **3.** a condition hard to endure; affliction. [C16: from Latin *asperitās*, from *asper* rough]

as·perse (ə'spɜːs) *vb.* (*tr.*) **1.** to spread false rumours about; defame. **2.** *Rare.* to sprinkle, as with water in baptism. [C15: from Latin *aspersus*, from *aspergere* to sprinkle] —**as·'pers·er** *n.* —**as·'per·sive** *adj.* —**as·'per·sive·ly** *adv.*

as·per·sion (ə'spɜːʃən) *n.* **1.** a disparaging or malicious remark; slanderous accusation (esp. in the phrase **cast aspersions (on)**). **2.** the act of defaming. **3.** *Rare.* the act of sprinkling, esp. of water in baptism.

as·per·so·ri·um (ˌæspə'sɔːrɪəm) *n., pl.* **-ri·a** (-rɪə). *R.C.Church.* **1.** a basin containing holy water with which worshippers sprinkle themselves. **2.** Also called: **aspergillum.** a perforated instrument used to sprinkle holy water.

as·phalt ('æsfælt, -fɔːlt) *n.* **1.** any of several black semisolid substances composed of bitumen and inert mineral matter. They occur naturally in parts of America and as a residue from petroleum distillation: used as a waterproofing material and in paints, dielectrics, and fungicides. **2.** a mixture of this substance with gravel, used in road-surfacing and roofing materials. **3.** (*modifier*) containing or surfaced with asphalt. ~*vb.* **4.** (*tr.*) to cover with asphalt. [C14: from Late Latin *aspaltus*, from Greek *asphaltos*, probably from A-[1] + *sphallein* to cause to fall; referring to its use as a binding agent] —**as·'phal·tic** *adj.*

as·phal·tite (æs'fæltaɪt) *n.* any of various naturally occurring hydrocarbons that resemble asphalt but have a higher melting point.

as·pho·del ('æsfəˌdɛl) *n.* **1.** any of various S European liliaceous plants of the genera *Asphodelus* and *Asphodeline*, having clusters of white or yellow flowers. Compare **bog asphodel. 2.** any of various other plants, such as the daffodil. **3.** an unidentified flower of Greek legend, probably a narcissus, said to cover the Elysian fields. [C16: from Latin *asphodelus*, from Greek *asphodelos*, of obscure origin]

as·phyx·i·a (æs'fɪksɪə) *n.* lack of oxygen in the blood due to restricted respiration; suffocation. If severe enough and prolonged, it causes death. [C18: from New Latin, from Greek *asphuxia* a stopping of the pulse, from A-[1] + *sphuxis* pulse, from *sphuzein* to throb] —**as·'phyx·i·al** *adj.*

as·phyx·i·ant (æs'fɪksɪənt) *adj.* **1.** causing asphyxia. ~*n.* **2.** anything that causes asphyxia: *carbon monoxide is an asphyxiant.*

as·phyx·i·ate (æs'fɪksɪˌeɪt) *vb.* to cause asphyxia in or undergo asphyxia; smother; suffocate. —**as·ˌphyx·i·'a·tion** *n.* —**as·'phyx·i·ˌa·tor** *n.*

as·pic[1] ('æspɪk) *n.* a savoury jelly based on meat or fish stock, used as a relish or as a mould for meat, vegetables, etc. [C18: from French: aspic (jelly), ASP[1]; variously explained as referring to its colour or coldness as compared to that of the snake]

as·pic[2] ('æspɪk) *n.* an archaic word for **asp**[1]. [C17: from

French, from Old Provençal *espic* spike, from Latin *spīca,* head (of flower); compare SPIKENARD]

as+pic[3] ('æspɪk) *n.* either of two species of lavender, *Lavandula spica* or *L. latifolia,* that yield an oil used in perfumery: family *Labiatae* (labiates). [C16: from Old French, variant of *aspe* ASP[2]]

as+pi+dis+tra (ˌæspɪ'dɪstrə) *n.* any Asian plant of the liliaceous genus *Aspidistra,* esp. *A. lurida,* a popular house plant with long tough evergreen leaves and small brownish flowers. [C19: from New Latin, from Greek *aspis* shield, on the model of *Tupistra* genus of liliaceous plants]

As+pin+wall ('æspɪnˌwɔːl) *n.* the former name of **Colón.**

as+pir+ant ('æspɪrənt, ə'spaɪərənt) *n.* **1.** a person who aspires, as to a high position. *~adj.* **2.** aspiring or striving.

as+pi+rate *vb.* ('æspɪˌreɪt). (*tr.*) **1.** *Phonetics.* **a.** to articulate (a stop) with some force, so that breath escapes with audible friction as the stop is released. **b.** to pronounce (a word or syllable) with an initial *h.* **2.** to draw in or remove by inhalation or suction, esp. to suck (air or fluid) from a body cavity or to inhale (fluid) into the lungs after vomiting. *~n.* ('æspɪrɪt). **3.** *Phonetics.* **a.** a stop pronounced with an audible release of breath. **b.** the glottal fricative represented in English and several other languages as *h.* *~adj.* ('æspɪrɪt). **4.** *Phonetics.* (of a stop) pronounced with a forceful and audible expulsion of breath.

as+pi+ra+tion (ˌæspɪ'reɪʃən) *n.* **1.** strong desire to achieve something, such as success. **2.** the aim of such desire. **3. a.** the act of breathing. **b.** a breath. **4.** *Phonetics.* **a.** the pronunciation of a stop with an audible and forceful release of breath. **b.** the friction of the released breath. **c.** an aspirated consonant. **5.** removal of air or fluid from a body cavity by suction. **6.** *Med.* the sucking of fluid or foreign matter into the air passages of the body. **—as+pir·a+to·ry** (ə'spaɪrətərɪ, -trɪ; 'æspɪˌreɪtərɪ, -trɪ) *adj.*

as+pi+ra+tor ('æspɪˌreɪtə) *n.* a device employing suction, such as a jet pump or one for removing fluids from a body cavity.

as+pire (ə'spaɪə) *vb.* (*intr.*) **1.** (usually foll. by *to* or *after*) to yearn (for) or have a powerful or ambitious plan, desire, or hope (to do or be something): *to aspire to be a great leader.* **2.** to rise to a great height. [C15: from Latin *aspīrāre* to breathe upon, from *spīrāre* to breathe] **—as+'pir+er** *n.* **—as+'pir+ing** *adj.*

as+pi+rin ('æsprɪn) *n., pl.* **+rin** *or* **+rins. 1.** a white crystalline compound widely used in the form of tablets to relieve pain, fever, and colds and to reduce inflammation. Formula: $CH_3COOC_6H_4COOH$. Chemical name: **acetylsalicylic acid. 2.** a tablet of aspirin. [C19: from German, from *A(cetyl)* + *Spir(säure)* spiraeic acid (modern salicylic acid); see also SPIRAEA, + -IN]

a·squint (ə'skwɪnt) *adv., adj.* (*postpositive*) with a glance from the corner of the eye, esp. a furtive one. [C13: perhaps from Dutch *schuinte* slant, of obscure origin]

As·quith ('æskwɪθ) *n.* **Her·bert Hen·ry,** 1st Earl of Oxford and Asquith. 1852–1928, British statesman; prime minister (1908–16); leader of the Liberal Party (1908–26).

ass[1] (æs) *n.* **1.** either of two perissodactyl mammals of the horse family (*Equidae*), *Equus asinus* (**African wild ass**) or *E. hemionus* (**Asiatic wild ass**). They are hardy and sure-footed, having longer ears than the horse. **2.** (*not in technical use*) the domesticated variety of the African wild ass; donkey. **3.** a foolish or ridiculously pompous person. [Old English *assa,* probably from Old Irish *asan,* from Latin *asinus;* related to Greek *onos* ass]

ass[2] (æs) *n.* **1.** the usual U.S. word for **arse. 2.** *U.S. slang, offensive.* sexual intercourse or a woman considered sexually (esp. in the phrase **piece of ass**). [Old English *ærs;* see ARSE]

As·sad ('asad) *n.* **Haf·e·zal** ('hafɛzal). born 1928, Syrian statesman and general; president of Syria since 1971.

as+sa+gai ('æsəˌgaɪ) *n., pl.* **+gais.** a variant spelling of **assegai.**

as+sai[1] (æ'saɪ) *adv. Music.* (usually preceded by a musical direction) very much: *allegro assai.* [Italian: enough]

as+sai[2] (æ'saɪ) *n.* **1.** any of several Brazilian palm trees of the genus *Euterpe,* esp. *E. edulis,* that have small dark purple fleshy edible fruit. **2.** a beverage made from the fruit of this tree. [via Brazilian Portuguese from Tupi]

as+sail (ə'seɪl) *vb.* (*tr.*) **1.** to attack violently; assault. **2.** to criticize or ridicule vehemently, as in argument. **3.** to beset or disturb: *his mind was assailed by doubts.* **4.** to encounter with the intention of mastering: *to assail a problem; to assail a difficult mountain ridge.* [C13: from Old French *asalir,* from Vulgar Latin *assalīre* (unattested) to leap upon, from Latin *assilīre,* from *salīre* to leap] **—as+'sail+a·ble** *adj.* **—as+'sail+er** *n.* **—as+'sail+ment** *n.*

as+sail+ant (ə'seɪlənt) *n.* a person who attacks another, either physically or verbally.

as+sam ('asam) *n.* (in Malaysia) tamarind as used in cooking. **Assam ikan** is a dish of fish cooked with tamarind. [from Malay *asam* sour]

As+sam (æ'sæm) *n.* a state of NE India, situated in the central Brahmaputra valley: tropical forest, with the heaviest rainfall in the world; produces large quantities of tea. Capital: Shillong. Pop.: 14 957 542 (1971). Area: about 220 150 sq. km (85 000 sq. miles).

As+sa+mese (ˌæsə'miːz) *n., pl.* **+mese. 1.** the state language of Assam, belonging to the Indic branch of the Indo-European family and closely related to Bengali. **2.** a native or inhabitant of Assam. *~adj.* **3.** of or relating to Assam, its people, or their language.

as+sas+sin (ə'sæsɪn) *n.* a murderer, esp. one who kills a prominent political figure. [C16: from Medieval Latin *assassīnus,* from Arabic *hashshāshīn,* plural of *hashshāsh* one who eats HASHISH]

As+sas+sin (ə'sæsɪn) *n.* a member of a secret sect of Muslim fanatics operating in Persia and Syria from about 1090 to 1256, murdering their victims, usually Crusaders.

as+sas+si+nate (ə'sæsɪˌneɪt) *vb.* (*tr.*) **1.** to murder (a person, esp. a public or political figure), usually by a surprise attack. **2.** to ruin or harm (a person's reputation, etc.) by slander. **—as+ˌsas+si+'na+tion** *n.*

as+sas+sin bug *n.* any long-legged predatory, often blood-sucking, insect of the heteropterous family *Reduviidae.*

as+sault (ə'sɔːlt) *n.* **1.** a violent attack, either physical or verbal. **2.** *Law.* an intentional or reckless act that causes immediate and unlawful violence to another. Compare **battery. 3. a.** the culmination of a military attack, closing at close quarters. **b.** (*as modifier*): *assault troops.* **4.** rape. *~vb.* (*tr.*) **5.** to make an assault upon. **6.** to rape or attempt to rape. [C13: from Old French *asaut,* from Vulgar Latin *assaltus* (unattested), from *assalīre* (unattested) to leap upon; see ASSAIL] **—as+'sault+er** *n.* **—as+'saul+tive** *adj.*

as+sault and bat+ter·y *n. Criminal law.* a threat of attack to another person followed by actual attack, which need amount only to touching with hostile intent.

as+say *vb.* (ə'seɪ). **1.** to subject (a substance, such as silver or gold) to chemical analysis, as in the determination of the amount of impurity. **2.** (*tr.*) to attempt (something or to do something). **3.** (*tr.; may take a clause as object*) to test, analyse, or evaluate: *to assay the significance of early childhood experience.* *~n.* (ə'seɪ, 'æseɪ). **4. a.** an analysis, esp. a determination of the amount of metal in an ore or the amounts of impurities in a precious metal. **b.** (*as modifier*): *an assay office.* **5.** a substance undergoing an analysis. **6.** a written report on the results of an analysis. **7.** a test. **8.** *Archaic.* an attempt. [C14: from Old Northern French *assai;* see ESSAY] **—as+'say+a·ble** *adj.* **—as+'say+er** *n.*

as+se+gai *or* **as+sa+gai** ('æsəˌgaɪ) *n., pl.* **+gais. 1.** a southern African cornaceous tree, *Curtisia faginea,* the wood of which is used for making spears. **2.** a sharp light spear, esp. one made of this wood. [C17: from Portuguese *azagaia,* from Arabic *az zaghāyah,* from *al* the + *zaghāyah* assegai, from Berber]

as+sem+blage (ə'sɛmblɪdʒ) *n.* **1.** a number of things or persons assembled together; collection; assembly. **2.** a list of dishes served at a meal or the dishes themselves. **3.** the act or process of assembling or the state of being assembled. **4.** (ˌæsəm'blɑːʒ). a three-dimensional work of art that combines various objects into an integrated whole.

as+sem+ble (ə'sɛmbəl) *vb.* **1.** to come or bring together; collect or congregate. **2.** to fit or join together (the parts) of (something, such as a machine): *to assemble the parts of a kit.* **3.** to run (a computer program) that converts a set of symbolic data, usually in the form of specific single-step instructions, into machine language. [C13: from Old French *assembler,* from Vulgar Latin *assimulāre* (unattested) to bring together, from Latin *simul* together] **—as+'sem+bler** *n.*

as+sem+blé *French.* (asɑ̃'ble) *n. Ballet.* a sideways leap in which the feet come together in the air in preparation for landing. [literally: brought together]

as+sem+bler (ə'sɛmblə) *n.* a computer program that converts a set of symbolic data, usually in the form of specific single-step instructions, into machine language. Compare **compiler** (sense 2).

as+sem+bly (ə'sɛmblɪ) *n., pl.* **+blies. 1.** a number of people gathered together, esp. for a formal meeting held at regular intervals. **2.** the act of assembling or the state of being assembled. **3.** the process of putting together a number of parts to make a machine or other product. **4.** *Machinery.* a group of mating components before or after fitting together. **5.** *Military.* **a.** a signal for personnel to assemble, as by drum, bugle, etc. **b.** (*as modifier*): *an assembly area.*

As+sem+bly (ə'sɛmblɪ) *n., pl.* **+blies.** the lower chamber in various American state legislatures. See also **House of Assembly, legislative assembly, National Assembly.**

as+sem+bly line *n.* a sequence of machines, tools, operations, workers, etc., in a factory, arranged so that at each stage a further process is carried out.

as+sem·bly+man (ə'sɛmblɪmən) *n., pl.* **+men.** (*sometimes cap.*) a member of an assembly, esp. a legislature.

As+sen (*Dutch* 'ɑsə) *n.* a city in the N Netherlands, capital of Drenthe province. Pop.: 42 410 (1973 est.).

as+sent (ə'sɛnt) *n.* **1.** agreement, as to a statement, proposal, etc.; acceptance. **2.** hesitant agreement; compliance. **3.** sanction. *~vb.* (*intr.;* usually foll. by *to*) **4.** to agree or express agreement. **5.** *Archaic.* to concede. [C13: from Old French *assenter,* from Latin *assentīrī,* from *sentīre* to think]

as+sen+ta+tion (ˌæsɛn'teɪʃən) *n.* servile or hypocritical agreement.

as+sen+ti·ent (ə'sɛnʃɪənt) *adj.* **1.** approving or agreeing. *~n.* **2.** a person who assents.

as+sen+tor (ə'sɛntə) *n. Brit. government.* any of the eight voters legally required to endorse the nomination of a candidate in a parliamentary or local election in addition to the nominator and seconder.

as+sert (ə'sɜːt) *vb.* (*tr.*) **1.** to insist upon (rights, claims, etc.). **2.** (*may take a clause as object*) to state categorically; declare. **3.** to put (oneself) forward in an insistent manner. [C17: from Latin *asserere* to join to oneself, from *serere* to join] **—as+'sert+er** *or* **as+'ser+tor** *n.* **—as+'sert+i·ble** *adj.*

as+ser+tion (ə'sɜːʃən) *n.* **1.** a positive statement, usually made without an attempt at furnishing evidence. **2.** the act of asserting.

as·ser·tive (əˈsɜːtɪv) *adj.* given to making assertions or bold demands; dogmatic or aggressive. —**asˈser·tive·ly** *adv.* —**asˈser·tive·ness** *n.*

as·sess (əˈsɛs) *vb.* (*tr.*) **1.** (foll. by *at*) to estimate the value of (income, property, etc.) for taxation purposes: *the estate was assessed at three thousand pounds.* **2.** to determine the amount of (a fine, tax, damages, etc.). **3.** to impose a tax, fine, etc., on (a person or property). **4.** to judge the worth, importance, etc., of; evaluate. [C15: from Old French *assesser,* from Latin *assidēre* to sit beside, from *sedēre* to sit] —**asˈsess·a·ble** *adj.*

as·sess·ment (əˈsɛsmənt) *n.* **1.** an amount determined as payable. **2.** a valuation set on taxable property, income, etc. **3.** evaluation; estimation. **4.** the act of assessing.

as·ses·sor (əˈsɛsə) *n.* **1.** a person who values property for taxation. **2.** a person who estimates the value of damage to property for insurance purposes. **3.** a person with technical expertise called in to advise a court on specialist matters. **4.** a person who shares another's position or rank, esp. in an advisory capacity. —**as·ses·so·ri·al** (ˌæsɛˈsɔːrɪəl) *adj.*

as·set (ˈæsɛt) *n.* anything valuable or useful: *experience is their main asset.* [C19: back formation from ASSETS]

as·sets (ˈæsɛts) *pl. n.* **1.** *Accounting.* the property and claims against debtors that a business enterprise may apply to discharge its liabilities. Assets may be fixed, current, liquid, or intangible and are shown balanced against liabilities. Compare **liabilities. 2.** *Law.* the property available to an executor or administrator for settlement of the debts and payment of legacies of a deceased person's estate. **3.** any property owned by a person or firm. [C16 (in the sense: enough to discharge one's liabilities): via Anglo-French from Old French *asez* enough, from Vulgar Latin *ad satis* (unattested), from Latin *ad* up to + *satis* enough]

as·set-strip·ping *n. Commerce.* the practice of taking over a failing company at a low price and then selling the assets piecemeal. —**ˈas·set-ˌstrip·per** *n.*

as·sev·er·ate (əˈsɛvəˌreɪt) *vb.* (*tr.*) to assert or declare emphatically or solemnly. [C18: from Latin *assevērāre* to do (something) earnestly, from *sevērus* SEVERE] —**asˌsev·er·ˈa·tion** *n.*

As·shur (ˈæʃʊə) *n.* a variant spelling of **Assur.**

as·sib·i·late (əˈsɪbɪˌleɪt) *vb. Phonetics.* **1.** (*intr.*) (of a speech sound) to be changed into a sibilant. **2.** (*tr.*) to pronounce (a speech sound) with or as a sibilant. [C19: from Late Latin *assībilāre* to hiss at, from *sībilāre* to hiss; see SIBILANT] —**asˌsib·iˈla·tion** *n.*

as·si·du·i·ty (ˌæsɪˈdjuːɪtɪ) *n., pl.* **·ties. 1.** constant and close application. **2.** (*often pl.*) devoted attention.

as·sid·u·ous (əˈsɪdjʊəs) *adj.* **1.** hard-working; persevering: *an assiduous researcher.* **2.** undertaken with perseverance and care: *assiduous editing.* [C16: from Latin *assiduus* sitting down to (something), from *assidēre* to sit beside, from *sedēre* to sit] —**asˈsid·u·ous·ly** *adv.* —**asˈsid·u·ous·ness** *n.*

as·sign (əˈsaɪn) *vb.* (*mainly tr.*) **1.** to select for and appoint to a post, etc.: *to assign an expert to the job.* **2.** to give out or allot (a task, problem, etc.): *to assign advertising to an expert.* **3.** to set apart (a place, person, time, etc.) for a particular function or event: *to assign a day for the meeting.* **4.** to attribute to a specified cause, origin, or source; ascribe: *to assign a stone cross to the Vikings.* **5.** to transfer (one's right, interest, or title to property) to someone else. **6.** (*also intr.*) *Law.* (formerly) to transfer (property) to trustees so that it may be used for the benefit of creditors. **7.** *Military.* to allocate (men or materials) on a permanent basis. Compare **attach.** ~*n.* **8.** *Law.* a person to whom property is assigned; assignee. [C14: from Old French *assigner,* from Latin *assignāre,* from *signāre* to mark out] —**asˈsign·a·ble** *adj.* —**asˌsign·a·ˈbil·i·ty** *n.* —**asˈsign·a·bly** *adv.* —**asˈsign·er** *n.*

as·sig·nat (ˈæsɪgˌnæt, ˌæsɪˈnjɑː; *French* asiˈnja) *n. French history.* the paper money issued by the Constituent Assembly in 1789, backed by the confiscated land of the Church and the émigrés. [C18: from French, from Latin *assignātum* something appointed; see ASSIGN]

as·sig·na·tion (ˌæsɪgˈneɪʃən) *n.* **1.** a secret or forbidden arrangement to meet, esp. one between lovers. **2.** the act of assigning; assignment. **3.** *Law, chiefly Scot.* another word for **assignment.** [C14: from Old French, from Latin *assignātiō* a marking out; see ASSIGN]

as·sign·ee (ˌæsaɪˈniː) *n.* **1.** *Law.* a person to whom some right, interest, or property is transferred. **2.** *Austral. history.* a convict who had undergone assignment.

as·sign·ment (əˈsaɪnmənt) *n.* **1.** something that has been assigned, such as a mission or task. **2.** a position or post to which a person is assigned. **3.** the act of assigning or state of being assigned. **4.** *Law.* **a.** the transfer to another of a right, interest, or title to property, esp. personal property: *assignment of a lease.* **b.** the document effecting such a transfer. **c.** the right, interest, or property transferred. **5.** *Law.* (formerly) the transfer, esp. by an insolvent debtor, of property in trust for the benefit of his creditors. **6.** *Austral. history.* a system (1789–1841) whereby a convict could become the unpaid servant of a freeman.

as·sign·or (ˌæsɪˈnɔː) *n. Law.* a person who transfers or assigns property.

as·sim·i·late (əˈsɪmɪˌleɪt) *vb.* **1.** (*tr.*) to learn (information, a procedure, etc.) and understand it thoroughly. **2.** (*tr.*) to absorb (food) and incorporate it into the body tissues. **3.** (*intr.*) to become absorbed, incorporated, or learned and understood. **4.** (usually foll. by *into* or *with*) to bring or come into harmony; adjust or become adjusted: *the new immigrants assimilated easily.* **5.** (usually foll. by *to* or *with*) to become or cause to become similar. **6.** (usually foll. by *to*) *Phonetics.* to change (a consonant) or (of a consonant) to be changed into another under the influence of one adjacent to it: (*n*) *often assimilates to* (ŋ) *before* (*k*), *as in "include".* [C15: from Latin *assimilāre* to make one thing like another, from *similis* like, SIMILAR] —**asˈsim·i·la·ble** *adj.* —**asˈsim·i·la·bly** *adv.* —**asˌsim·iˈla·tion** *n.* —**asˈsim·i·la·tive** *or* **asˈsim·i·la·to·ry** *adj.* —**asˈsim·iˌla·tor** *n.* —**asˈsim·i·la·tive·ly** *adv.*

As·sin·i·boine (əˈsɪnɪˌbɔɪn) *n.* a river in W Canada, rising in E Saskatchewan and flowing southeast and east to the Red River at Winnipeg. Length: over 860 km (500 miles).

As·si·si (*Italian* asˈsiːzi) *n.* a town in central Italy, in Umbria: birthplace of St. Francis, who founded the Franciscan religious order here in 1208. Pop.: 24 002 (1971).

as·sist (əˈsɪst) *vb.* **1.** to give help or support to (a person, cause, etc.); aid. **2.** to work or act as an assistant or subordinate to (another). **3.** *Ice hockey.* to help (a teammate) to score, as by passing the puck. **4.** (*intr.; foll. by at*) *Archaic.* to be present; attend. ~*n.* **5.** *U.S.* the act of helping; aid; assistance. **6.** *Baseball.* the act of a player who throws or deflects a batted ball in such a way that a team is enabled to put out an opponent. **7.** *Ice hockey.* a pass of the puck that enables a teammate to score. [C15: from French *assister* to be present, from Latin *assistere* to stand by, from *sistere* to cause to stand, from *stāre* to stand] —**asˈsist·er** *n.*

as·sis·tance (əˈsɪstəns) *n.* **1.** help; support. **2.** the act of assisting. **3.** *Brit. informal.* See **national assistance.**

as·sis·tant (əˈsɪstənt) *n.* **1. a.** a person who assists, esp. in a subordinate position. **b.** (*as modifier*): *assistant manager.* ~*adj.* **2.** *Archaic.* helpful or useful as an aid.

as·sis·tant pro·fes·sor *n. U.S.* a university teacher lower in rank than an associate professor.

As·siut (æˈsjuːt) *n.* a variant spelling of **Asyut.**

as·size (əˈsaɪz) *n.* **1.** (in the U.S.) **a.** a sitting of a legislative assembly or administrative body. **b.** an enactment or order of such an assembly. **2.** *English history.* a trial or judicial inquest, the writ instituting such inquest, or the verdict. **3.** *Scot. law.* **a.** trial by jury. **b.** another name for **jury.** [C13: from Old French *assise* session, from *asseoir* to seat, from Latin *assidēre* to sit beside; see ASSESS]

as·siz·es (əˈsaɪzɪz) *pl. n.* (formerly in England and Wales) the sessions, usually held four times a year, of the principal court in each county, exercising civil and criminal jurisdiction, attended by itinerant judges: replaced in 1971 by crown courts.

assn. *abbrev. for* association.

assoc. *abbrev. for:* **1.** associate(d). **2.** association.

as·so·ci·ate *vb.* (əˈsəʊʃɪˌeɪt, -sɪ-). (usually foll. by *with*) **1.** (*tr.*) to link or connect in the mind or imagination: *to associate Christmas with fun.* **2.** (*intr.*) to keep company; mix socially: *to associate with writers.* **3.** (*intr.*) to form or join an association, group, etc. **4.** (*tr.; usually passive*) to consider in conjunction; connect: *rainfall is associated with humidity.* **5.** (*tr.*) to bring (a person, esp. oneself) into friendship, partnership, etc. **6.** (*tr.; often passive*) to express agreement or allow oneself to be connected (with): *Bertrand Russell was associated with the peace movement.* ~*n.* (əˈsəʊʃɪɪt, -ˌeɪt, -sɪ-). **7.** a person joined with another or others in an enterprise, business, etc.; partner; colleague. **8.** a companion or friend. **9.** something that usually accompanies another thing; concomitant: *hope is an associate to happiness.* **10.** a person having a subordinate position in or admitted to only partial membership of an institution, association, etc. ~*adj.* (əˈsəʊʃɪɪt, -ˌeɪt, -sɪ-). (*prenominal*) **11.** joined with another or others in an enterprise, business, etc.; having equal or nearly equal status: *an associate director.* **12.** having partial rights and privileges or subordinate status: *an associate member.* **13.** accompanying; concomitant. [C14: from Latin *associāre* to ally with, from *sociāre* to join, from *socius* an ally] —**asˈso·ci·a·ble** *adj.* —**asˈso·ci·a·tor** *n.* —**asˈso·ci·a·to·ry** *adj.* —**asˈso·ci·ate·ˌship** *n.*

as·so·ci·at·ed state·hood *n.* the semi-independent political status of various former British colonies in the Caribbean since 1967, by which Britain retains responsibility for defence and some aspects of foreign affairs. The **associated states** are Antigua, Dominica, Grenada, St. Kitts-Nevis-Anguilla, St. Lucia, and St. Vincent.

as·so·ci·ate pro·fes·sor *n. U.S.* a university teacher lower in rank than a full professor but higher than an assistant professor.

as·so·ci·a·tion (əˌsəʊsɪˈeɪʃən, -ʃɪ-) *n.* **1.** a group of people having a common purpose or interest; a society or club. **2.** the act of associating or the state of being associated. **3.** friendship or companionship: *their association will not last.* **4.** a mental connection of ideas, feelings, or sensations: *association of revolution with bloodshed.* **5.** *Psychol.* the mental process of linking events so that the recurrence of one event automatically recalls the other. See also **free association. 6.** *Chem.* the formation of groups of molecules and ions, esp. in liquids, held together by weak chemical bonds. **7.** *Ecology.* a group of similar plants that grow in a uniform environment and contain one or more dominant species.

as·so·ci·a·tion foot·ball *n.* **1.** a more formal name for **soccer. 2.** *Austral.* Australian Rules played in a football association rather than a league.

as·so·ci·a·tion·ism (əˌsəʊsɪˈeɪʃəˌnɪzəm) *n. Psychol.* a theory that all mental activity is based on connections between basic mental events, such as sensations and feelings.

as·so·ci·a·tive (əˈsəʊʃɪətɪv) *adj.* **1.** of, relating to, or causing association or union. **2.** *Maths, logic.* **a.** being independent of the grouping of numbers, symbols, or terms within a given set, as in conjunction or in an expression such as $(2 \times 3) \times 4 = 2 \times (3 \times 4)$. **b.** referring to this property: *the associative laws of arithmetic.*

as+soil (ə'sɔɪl) *vb.* (*tr.*) *Archaic.* **1.** to absolve; set free. **2.** to atone for. [C13: from Old French *assoldre,* from Latin *absolvere* to ABSOLVE]

as+so+nance ('æsənəns) *n.* **1.** the use of the same vowel sound with different consonants or the same consonant with different vowels in successive words or stressed syllables, as in a line of verse. Examples are *time* and *light* or *mystery* and *mastery.* **2.** partial correspondence; rough similarity. [C18: from French, from Latin *assonāre* to sound, from *sonāre* to sound] —**'as+so+nant** *adj., n.* —**as+so+nan+tal** (ˌæsə'næntᵊl) *adj.*

as+sort (ə'sɔːt) *vb.* **1.** (*tr.*) to arrange or distribute into groups of the same type; classify. **2.** (*intr.;* usually foll. by *with*) to fit or fall into a class or group; match. **3.** (*tr.*) to supply with an assortment of merchandise. **4.** (*tr.*) to put in the same category as others; group. **5.** (*intr.;* usually foll. by *with*) *Rare.* to keep company; consort. [C15: from Old French *assorter,* from *sorte* SORT] —**as+'sort·a+tive** *or* **as+'sort+ive** *adj.* —**as+'sort·a+tive+ly** *adv.* —**as+'sort+er** *n.*

as+sort+ed (ə'sɔːtɪd) *adj.* **1.** consisting of various kinds mixed together; miscellaneous: *assorted sweets.* **2.** arranged in sorts; classified: *assorted categories.* **3.** matched; suited (esp. in the combinations **well-assorted, ill-assorted**).

as+sort+ment (ə'sɔːtmənt) *n.* **1.** a collection or group of various things or sorts. **2.** the act of assorting.

ASSR *abbrev. for* Autonomous Soviet Socialist Republic.

asst. *abbrev. for* assistant.

as+suage (ə'sweɪdʒ) *vb.* (*tr.*) **1.** to soothe, moderate, or relieve (grief, pain, etc.). **2.** to give relief to (thirst, appetite, etc.); satisfy. **3.** to pacify; calm. [C14: from Old French *assouagier,* from Vulgar Latin *assuāviāre* (unattested) to sweeten, from Latin *suāvis* pleasant; see SUAVE] —**as+'suage+ment** *n.* —**as+'suag+er** *n.* —**as+sua+sive** (ə'sweɪsɪv) *adj.*

As+suan *or* **As+souan** (ɑːs'wɑːn) *n.* variant spellings of **Aswan.**

as+sume (ə'sjuːm) *vb.* (*tr.*) **1.** (*may take a clause as object*) to take for granted; accept without proof; suppose: *to assume that someone is sane.* **2.** to take upon oneself; undertake or take on or over (a position, responsibility, etc.): *to assume office.* **3.** to pretend to; feign: *he assumed indifference, although the news affected him deeply.* **4.** to take or put on; adopt: *the problem assumed gigantic proportions.* **5.** to appropriate or usurp (power, control, etc.); arrogate: *the revolutionaries assumed control of the city.* **6.** *Christianity.* (of God) to take up (the soul of a believer) into heaven. [C15: from Latin *assūmere* to take up, from *sūmere* to take up, from SUB- + *emere* to take] —**as+'sum+a·ble** *adj.* —**as+'sum+er** *n.*

as+sumed (ə'sjuːmd) *adj.* **1.** false; fictitious: *an assumed name.* **2.** taken for granted: *an assumed result.* **3.** usurped; arrogated: *an assumed authority.*

as+sum+ing (ə'sjuːmɪŋ) *adj.* expecting too much; presumptuous; arrogant.

as+sump+sit (ə'sʌmpsɪt) *n. Law.* (before 1875) an action to recover damages for breach of an express or implied contract or agreement that was not under seal. [C17: from Latin, literally: he has undertaken, from *assūmere* to ASSUME]

as+sump+tion (ə'sʌmpʃən) *n.* **1.** the act of taking something for granted or something that is taken for granted. **2.** an assuming of power or possession of something. **3.** arrogance; presumption. **4.** *Logic.* a minor premiss. [C13: from Latin *assūmptiō* a taking up, from *assūmere* to ASSUME] —**as+'sump+tive** *adj.* —**as+'sump+tive+ly** *adv.*

As+sump+tion (ə'sʌmpʃən) *n. Christianity.* **1.** the taking up of the Virgin Mary (body and soul) into heaven when her earthly life was ended. **2.** the feast commemorating this, celebrated by Roman Catholics on Aug. 15.

As·sur, A·sur ('æsə), **As·shur,** *or* **A·shur** ('æʃʊə) *n.* **1.** the supreme national god of the ancient Assyrians, chiefly a war god, whose symbol was an archer within a winged disc. **2.** one of the chief cities of ancient Assyria, on the River Tigris about 100 km (60 miles) downstream from the present-day city of Mosul.

as+sur+ance (ə'ʃʊərəns) *n.* **1.** a statement, assertion, etc., intended to inspire confidence or give encouragement: *she was helped by his assurance that she would cope* **2.** a promise or pledge of support: *he gave an assurance of nelp when needed.* **3.** freedom from doubt; certainty: *his assurance about his own superiority infuriated her.* **4.** forwardness; impudence. **5.** *Chiefly Brit.* insurance providing for certainties such as death as contrasted with fire or theft.

As·sur·ba·ni·pal (ˌæsʊə'bɑːnɪˌpæl) *n.* a variant of **Ashurbanipal.**

as+sure (ə'ʃʊə) *vb.* (*tr.; may take a clause as object*) **1.** to cause to feel sure or certain; convince: *to assure a person of one's love.* **2.** to promise; guarantee: *he assured us that he would come.* **3.** to state positively or with assurance. **4.** to make (an event) certain; ensure. **5.** *Chiefly Brit.* to insure against loss, esp. of life. **6.** *Property law.* another word for **convey.** [C14: from Old French *aseürer* to assure, from Medieval Latin *assēcūrāre* to secure or make sure, from *sēcūrus* SECURE] —**as+'sur+a·ble** *adj.* —**as+'sur+er** *n.*

as+sured (ə'ʃʊəd) *adj.* **1.** made certain; sure; guaranteed. **2.** self-assured. **3.** *Chiefly Brit.* insured, esp. by a life assurance policy. ~*n. Chiefly Brit.* **4. a.** the beneficiary under a life assurance policy. **b.** the person whose life is insured. —**as+sur+ed+ly** (ə'ʃʊərɪdlɪ) *adv.* —**as+'sur+ed+ness** *n.*

as+sur+gent (ə'sɜːdʒənt) *adj.* (of leaves, stems, etc.) curving or growing upwards; rising. [C16: from Latin *assurgere* to rise up, from *surgere* to rise] —**as+'sur+gen+cy** *n.*

Assyr. *abbrev. for* Assyrian.

As+syr·i·a (ə'sɪrɪə) *n.* an ancient kingdom of N Mesopotamia: it established an empire that stretched from Egypt to the Persian Gulf, reaching its greatest extent between 721 and 633 B.C. Its chief cities were Assur and Nineveh.

As+syr·i·an (ə'sɪrɪən) *n.* **1.** an inhabitant of ancient Assyria. **2.** the extinct language of the Assyrians, belonging to the E Semitic subfamily of the Afro-Asiatic family and regarded as a dialect of Akkadian. ~*adj.* **3.** of, relating to, or characteristic of the ancient Assyrians, their language, or culture.

As+syr·i+ol+o·gy (əˌsɪrɪ'ɒlədʒɪ) *n.* the study of the culture, history, and archaeological remains of ancient Assyria. —**As+ˌsyr·i+'ol·o+gist** *n.*

A.S.T. *abbrev. for* Atlantic Standard Time.

a·sta+ble (eɪ'steɪbᵊl) *adj.* **1.** not stable. **2.** *Electricity.* capable of oscillating between two states.

A·staire (ə'stɛə) *n.* **Fred.** born 1899, U.S. dancer, whose films include *Top Hat* (1935).

As·tar·te (æ'stɑːtɪ) *n.* a fertility goddess worshipped by the Phoenicians: identified with Ashtoreth of the Hebrews and Ishtar of the Babylonians and Assyrians.

a·stat+ic (æ'stætɪk, eɪ-) *adj.* **1.** not static; unstable. **2.** *Physics.* **a.** having no tendency to assume any particular position or orientation. **b.** (of a galvanometer) having two mutually compensating magnets arranged so that the instrument is independent of the earth's magnetic field. [C19: from Greek *astatos* unsteady; see A-^{1}, STATIC] —**a·'stat·i+cal+ly** *adv.* —**a·'stat·i+ˌcism** *n.*

as+ta+tine ('æstəˌtiːn, -tɪn) *n.* a radioactive element of the halogen series: a decay product of uranium and thorium that occurs naturally in minute amounts and is artificially produced by bombarding bismuth with alpha particles. Symbol: At; atomic no.: 85; half-life of most stable isotope, ^{210}At: 8.3 hours; valency: 1,3,5, or 7. [C20: from Greek *astatos* unstable (see ASTATIC) + -INE^2]

as+ter ('æstə) *n.* **1.** any plant of the genus *Aster,* having white, blue, purple, or pink daisy-like flowers: family *Compositae* (composites). Compare **golden aster. 2. China aster.** a related Chinese plant, *Callistephus chinensis,* widely cultivated for its showy brightly coloured flowers. **3.** *Cytology.* a group of radiating cytoplasmic threads that surrounds the centrosome before and during mitosis. [C18: from New Latin, from Latin *aster* star, from Greek]

-as·ter *suffix forming nouns.* a person or thing that is inferior or bears only a poor resemblance to what is specified: *poetaster.* [from Latin: suffix indicating imperfect resemblance]

as+te+ri+at+ed (æ'stɪərɪˌeɪtɪd) *adj.* (of a crystal, esp. a gemstone) exhibiting a star-shaped figure in transmitted or reflected light.

as+ter+isk ('æstərɪsk) *n.* **1.** a star-shaped character (*) used in printing or writing to indicate a cross-reference to a footnote, an omission, etc. **2. a.** (in historical linguistics) this sign used to indicate an unattested reconstructed form. **b.** (in descriptive linguistics) this sign used to indicate that an expression is ungrammatical or in some other way unacceptable. ~*vb.* **3.** (*tr.*) to mark with an asterisk. [C17: from Late Latin *asteriscus* a small star, from Greek *asteriskos,* from *astēr* star]

as+ter+ism ('æstəˌrɪzəm) *n.* **1.** three asterisks arranged in a triangle (⁂ or ⁂), to draw attention to the text that follows. **2.** a starlike effect seen in some minerals and gemstones when viewed by reflected or transmitted light. **3.** a cluster of stars or a constellation. [C16: from Greek *asterismos* arrangement of constellations, from *astēr* star]

a·stern (ə'stɜːn) *Nautical.* ~*adv., adj.* (*postpositive*) **1.** at or towards the stern. **2.** with the stern first: *full speed astern!* **3.** aft of the stern of a vessel.

a·ster+nal (æ'stɜːnᵊl, eɪ-) *Anatomy.* ~*adj.* **1.** not connected or joined to the sternum. **2.** lacking a sternum.

as+ter+oid ('æstəˌrɔɪd) *n.* **1.** Also called: **minor planet.** any of numerous small celestial bodies that move around the sun mainly between the orbits of Mars and Jupiter. Their diameters range from 670 kilometres (Ceres) to less than one kilometre. **2.** Also: **as+ter·oi·de·an** (ˌæstə'rɔɪdɪən). any echinoderm of the class *Asteroidea;* a starfish. ~*adj. also* **as+ter·oi·dal** (ˌæstə'rɔɪdᵊl). **3.** of, relating to, or belonging to the class *Asteroidea.* **4.** shaped like a star. [C19: from Greek *asteroeidēs* starlike, from *astēr* a star]

as+the·ni·a (æs'θiːnɪə) *or* **as+the+ny** ('æsθənɪ) *n. Pathol.* an abnormal loss of strength; debility. [C19: via New Latin from Greek *astheneia* weakness, from A-^{1} + *sthenos* strength]

as+then+ic (æs'θɛnɪk) *adj.* **1.** of, relating to, or having asthenia; weak. **2.** (in constitutional psychology) referring to a physique characterized by long limbs and a small trunk: claimed to be associated with a schizoid personality. See also **somatotype.** ~*n.* **3.** a person having long limbs and a small trunk.

as+the+no+pi·a (ˌæsθɪ'nəʊpɪə) *n.* a technical name for **eyestrain.** [C19: from New Latin, from Greek *asthenēs* weak (from A-^{1} + *sthenos* strength) + *ōps* eye] —**as+the+nop+ic** (ˌæsθɪ'nɒpɪk) *adj.*

as+then·o·sphere (əs'θiːnəˌsfɪə, -'θɛn-) *n.* a zone of the earth's crust below the lithosphere, thought to yield readily to the pressure of subsiding land, allowing the compensating elevation of a less dense region. See also **isostasy.** [C20: from *astheno-,* from Greek *asthenēs* weak + SPHERE]

asth+ma ('æsmə) *n.* a respiratory disorder, often of allergic origin, characterized by difficulty in breathing, wheezing, and a sense of constriction in the chest. [C14: from Greek: laborious breathing, from *azein* to breathe hard]

asth·mat·ic (æs'mætɪk) *adj.* **1.** of, relating to, or having asthma. ~*n.* **2.** a person who has asthma. —**asth'mat·i·cal·ly** *adv.*

As·ti ('æstɪ) *n.* a town in NW Italy: famous for its sparkling wine (**Asti spumante**). Pop.: 76 048 (1971).

as·tig·mat·ic (ˌæstɪg'mætɪk) *adj.* **1.** of, relating to, having, correcting, or corrected for astigmatism. ~*n.* **2.** a person who has astigmatism. [C19: from A-[1] + Greek *stigmat-*, *stigma* spot, focus; see STIGMA] —ˌ**as·tig'mat·i·cal·ly** *adv.*

a·stig·ma·tism (ə'stɪgməˌtɪzəm) *or* **a·stig·mi·a** (ə'stɪgmɪə) *n.* **1.** a defect of a lens resulting in the formation of distorted images; caused by the curvature of the lens being different in different planes. **2.** faulty vision resulting from astigmatism of the lens of the eye.

a·stil·be (ə'stɪlbɪ) *n.* any perennial saxifragaceous plant of the genus *Astilbe* of E Asia and North America: cultivated for their ornamental pink or white flowers. [C19: New Latin, from Greek: not glittering, from A-[1] + *stilbē*, from *stilbein* to glitter; referring to its inconspicuous individual flowers]

a·stir (ə'stɜː) *adj.* (*postpositive*) **1.** awake and out of bed. **2.** in motion; on the move.

A.S.T.M.S. (in Britain) *abbrev. for* Association of Scientific, Technical, and Managerial Staffs.

As·to·lat ('æstəʊˌlæt) *n.* a town in Arthurian legend: location unknown.

a·stom·a·tous (æ'stɒmətəs, -'stəʊ-) *adj.* **1.** (of animals) having no mouth. **2.** (of plants) having no stomata.

As·ton ('æstən) *n.* **Fran·cis Wil·liam.** 1877–1945, English physicist and chemist, who developed the first mass spectograph, using it to investigate the isotopic structures of elements: Nobel prize for chemistry 1922.

as·ton·ied (ə'stɒnɪd) *adj. Archaic.* stunned; dazed. [C14: from *astonyen* to ASTONISH]

a·ston·ish (ə'stɒnɪʃ) *vb.* (*tr.*) to fill with amazement; surprise greatly. [C15: from earlier *astonyen* (see ASTONIED), from Old French *estoner*, from Vulgar Latin *extonāre* (unattested) to strike with thunder, from Latin *tonāre* to thunder] —**a'ston·ish·ing** *adj.* —**a'ston·ish·ing·ly** *adv.*

a·ston·ish·ment (ə'stɒnɪʃmənt) *n.* **1.** extreme surprise; amazement. **2.** a cause of amazement.

As·tor ('æstə) *n.* **1. John Ja·cob,** 1st Baron Astor of Hever. 1886–1971, British proprietor of *The Times* (1922–66). **2.** Viscountess **Nan·cy Witch·er Lang·horne** ('wɪtʃə 'læŋˌhɔːn). 1879–1964, British politician, born in the U.S.; the first woman to sit in the British House of Commons.

As·to·ri·a (ə'stɔːrɪə) *n.* a port in NW Oregon, near the mouth of the Columbia River: founded as a fur-trading post in 1811 by John Jacob Astor. Pop.: 10 244 (1970).

a·stound (ə'staʊnd) *vb.* (*tr.*) to overwhelm with amazement and wonder; bewilder. [C17: from *astoned* amazed, from Old French *estoné*, from *estoner* to ASTONISH] —**a'stound·ing·ly** *adv.*

astr. *or* **astron.** *abbrev. for:* **1.** astronomer. **2.** astronomical. **3.** astronomy.

a·strad·dle (ə'strædᵊl) *adj.* **1.** (*postpositive*) with a leg on either side of something. ~*prep.* **2.** astride.

as·tra·gal ('æstrəgᵊl) *n.* **1.** *Architect.* **a.** Also called: **bead.** a small convex moulding, usually with a semicircular cross section. **b.** a moulding having the form of a string of beads. **2.** *Furniture.* a glazing-bar, esp. in a bookcase. **3.** *Anatomy.* the ankle or ankle bone. [C17: from Latin *astragalus*, from Greek *astragalos* ankle bone, hence, small round moulding]

a·strag·a·lus (æ'strægələs) *n., pl.* **·li** (-ˌlaɪ). *Anatomy.* another name for **talus.** [C16: via New Latin from Latin: ASTRAGAL]

as·tra·khan (ˌæstrə'kæn, -'kɑːn) *n.* **1.** a fur, usually black or grey, made of the closely curled wool of lambs from Astrakhan. **2.** a cloth with curled pile resembling this. **3.** (*modifier*) made of such fur or cloth: *an astrakhan collar.*

As·tra·khan (ˌæstrə'kæn, -'kɑːn; *Russian* 'astrəxənj) *n.* a city in the S Soviet Union, on the delta of the Volga River, 21 m (70 ft.) below sea level. Pop.: 452 000 (1975 est.).

as·tral ('æstrəl) *adj.* **1.** relating to, proceeding from, consisting of, or resembling the stars: *an astral body.* **2.** *Biology.* of or relating to the aster occurring in dividing cells. **3.** *Theosophy.* denoting or relating to a supposed supersensible substance believed to form the material of a second body for each person, taking the form of an aura discernible to certain gifted individuals. [C17: from Late Latin *astrālis*, from Latin *astrum* star, from Greek *astron*] —'**as·tral·ly** *adv.*

as·tra·pho·bi·a *or* **as·tro·pho·bi·a** (ˌæstrə'fəʊbɪə) *n.* an exaggerated fear of thunder and lightning. [C20: see ASTRO-, -PHOBIA] —ˌ**as·tra'pho·bic** *or* ˌ**as·tro'pho·bic** *adj.*

a·stray (ə'streɪ) *adj.* (*postpositive*), *adv.* **1.** out of the correct path or direction. **2.** out of the right, good, or expected way; into error. [C13: from Old French *estraie* roaming, from *estraier* to STRAY]

as·trict (ə'strɪkt) *vb. Archaic.* to bind, confine, or constrict. [C16: from Latin *astrictus* drawn closely together, from *astringere* to tighten, from *stringere* to bind] —**as'tric·tion** *n.* —**as'tric·tive** *adj.* —**as'tric·tive·ly** *adv.*

a·stride (ə'straɪd) *adj.* (*postpositive*) **1.** with a leg on either side. **2.** with the legs far apart. ~*prep.* **3.** with a leg on either side of. **4.** with a part on both sides of; spanning.

as·trin·gent (ə'strɪndʒənt) *adj.* **1.** severe; harsh. **2.** sharp or invigorating. **3.** causing contraction of body tissues, checking blood flow, or restricting secretions of fluids; styptic. ~*n.* **4.** an astringent drug. [C16: from Latin *astringēns* drawing together; see ASTRICT] —**as'trin·gen·cy** *or* **as'trin·gence** *n.* —**as'trin·gent·ly** *adv.*

as·tro- *combining form.* **1.** indicating a heavenly body, star, or star-shaped structure: *astrology; astrocyte.* **2.** indicating outer space: *astronautics.* [from Greek, from *astron* star]

as·tro·bi·ol·o·gy (ˌæstrəʊbaɪ'ɒlədʒɪ) *n.* the branch of biology that investigates the possibility of life on other planets.

as·tro·bot·a·ny (ˌæstrəʊ'bɒtənɪ) *n.* the branch of botany that investigates the possibility that plants grow on other planets.

as·tro·com·pass (ˌæstrəʊ'kʌmpəs) *n.* a navigational instrument for giving directional bearings from the centre of the earth to a particular star. It is carried in long-range aircraft, ships, spacecraft, etc.

as·tro·cyte ('æstrəʊˌsaɪt) *n.* any of the star-shaped cells in the tissue supporting the brain and spinal cord (neuroglia).

as·tro·dome ('æstrəˌdəʊm) *n.* a transparent dome on the top of an aircraft, through which observations can be made, esp. of the stars. Also called: **astrohatch.**

as·tro·dy·nam·ics (ˌæstrəʊdaɪ'næmɪks) *n.* (*functioning as sing.*) the study of the motion of natural and artificial bodies in space.

as·tro·ge·ol·o·gy (ˌæstrəʊdʒɪ'ɒlədʒɪ) *n.* the study of the structure, composition, and history of other planets and other bodies in the solar system.

as·troid ('æstrɔɪd) *n. Maths.* a hypocycloid having four cusps. [C19: from ASTRO- + -OID]

astrol. *abbrev. for:* **1.** astrologer. **2.** astrological. **3.** astrology.

as·tro·labe ('æstrəˌleɪb) *n.* an instrument used by early astronomers to measure the altitude of stars and planets and also as a navigational aid. It consists of a graduated circular disc with a movable sighting device. Compare **sextant.** [C13: via Old French and Medieval Latin from Greek, from *astrolabos* (adj.), literally: star-taking, from *astron* star + *lambanein* to take]

as·trol·o·gy (ə'strɒlədʒɪ) *n.* **1.** the study of the motions and relative positions of the planets, sun, and moon, interpreted in terms of human characteristics and activities. **2.** the primitive study of celestial bodies, which formed the basis of astronomy. [C14: from Old French *astrologie*, from Latin *astrologia*, from Greek, from *astrologos* (originally: astronomer); see ASTRO-, -LOGY] —**as'trol·o·ger** *or* **as'trol·o·gist** *n.* —**as·tro·log·i·cal** (ˌæstrə'lɒdʒɪkᵊl) *adj.* —ˌ**as·tro'log·i·cal·ly** *adv.*

as·trom·e·try (ə'strɒmɪtrɪ) *n.* the branch of astronomy concerned with the measurement of the position and motion of celestial bodies. —**as·tro·met·ric** (ˌæstrə'mɛtrɪk) *or* ˌ**as·tro'met·ri·cal** *adj.*

as·tro·naut ('æstrəˌnɔːt) *n.* a person trained for travelling in space. [C20: from ASTRO- + *-naut* from Greek *nautēs* sailor, on the model of *aeronaut*]

as·tro·nau·tics (ˌæstrə'nɔːtɪks) *n.* (*functioning as sing.*) the science and technology of space flight. —ˌ**as·tro'nau·tic** *or* ˌ**as·tro'nau·ti·cal** *adj.* —ˌ**as·tro'nau·ti·cal·ly** *adv.*

as·tro·nav·i·ga·tion (ˌæstrəʊnævɪ'geɪʃən) *n.* another term for **celestial navigation.** —ˌ**as·tro'nav·iˌga·tor** *n.*

as·tron·o·mer (ə'strɒnəmə) *n.* a scientist who studies astronomy.

as·tro·nom·i·cal (ˌæstrə'nɒmɪkᵊl) *or* **as·tro·nom·ic** *adj.* **1.** enormously large; immense. **2.** of or relating to astronomy. —ˌ**as·tro'nom·i·cal·ly** *adv.*

as·tro·nom·i·cal tel·e·scope *n.* any telescope designed and mounted for use in astronomy. Such telescopes usually form inverted images. See **Cassegrainian telescope, Newtonian telescope, equatorial telescope.**

as·tro·nom·i·cal u·nit *n.* a unit of distance used in astronomy equal to the mean distance between the earth and the sun. 1 astronomical unit is equivalent to 1.495×10^{11} metres or about 9.3×10^{7} miles.

as·tro·nom·i·cal year *n.* another name for **solar year.** See **year** (sense 4).

as·tron·o·my (ə'strɒnəmɪ) *n.* the scientific study of the individual celestial bodies (excluding the earth) and of the universe as a whole. Its various branches include astrometry, astrodynamics, cosmology, and astrophysics. [C13: from Old French *astronomie*, from Latin *astronomia*, from Greek; see ASTRO-, -NOMY]

as·tro·pho·tog·ra·phy (ˌæstrəʊfə'tɒgrəfɪ) *n.* the photography of celestial bodies used in astronomy. —**as·tro·pho·to·graph·ic** (ˌæstrəʊˌfəʊtə'græfɪk) *adj.*

as·tro·phys·ics (ˌæstrəʊ'fɪzɪks) *n.* (*functioning as sing.*) the branch of physics concerned with the physical and chemical properties, origin, and evolution of the celestial bodies. —ˌ**as·tro'phys·i·cal** *adj.* —ˌ**as·tro'phys·i·cist** *n.*

as·tro·sphere ('æstrəˌsfɪə) *n. Cytology.* **1.** another name for **centrosome. 2.** Also called: **attraction sphere.** the part of the aster excluding the centrosome.

As·tu·ri·as (æ'stʊərɪˌæs) *n.* a region and former kingdom of NW Spain, consisting of a coastal plain and the Cantabrian Mountains: a Christian stronghold against the Moors (8th to 13th centuries); rich mineral resources.

as·tute (ə'stjuːt) *adj.* having insight or acumen; perceptive; shrewd. [C17: from Latin *astūtus* cunning, from *astus* (n.) cleverness] —**as'tute·ly** *adv.* —**as'tute·ness** *n.*

As·ty·a·nax (æ'staɪəˌnæks) *n. Greek myth.* the young son of Hector and Andromache, who was hurled from the walls of Troy by the Greeks.

a·sty·lar (æ'staɪlə, eɪ-) *adj. Architect.* without columns or pilasters. [C19: from A-[1] + Greek *stulos* pillar]

A·sun·ción (*Spanish* ˌasun'sjon) *n.* the capital and chief port of Paraguay, on the Paraguay River, 1530 km (950 miles) from the Atlantic. Pop.: 387 676 (1972 est.).

a·sun·der (ə'sʌndə) *adv., adj.* (*postpositive*) **1.** in or into parts or pieces; apart: *to tear asunder.* **2.** *Archaic.* in or into a position apart or separate. [Old English *on sundran* apart; see SUNDER]

A·sur ('æsə) *n.* a variant spelling of **Assur.**

As+wan (ɑːs'wɑːn) *n.* an ancient town in SE Egypt, on the Nile, just below the First Cataract. Pop.: 246 000 (1974 est.). Ancient name: **Syene.** Also: **Assuan, Assouan.**

As+wan High Dam *n.* a dam on the Nile forming a reservoir (Lake Nasser) extending 480 km (300 miles) from the First to the Third Cataracts: opened in 1971, it was built 6 km (4 miles) upstream from the old **Aswan Dam** (built in 1902 and twice raised). Height of dam: 109 m (365 ft.).

a·swarm (ə'swɔːm) *adj.* (*postpositive*) filled, esp. with moving things; swarming: *flower beds aswarm with bees.*

a·syl+lab+ic (ˌæsɪ'læbɪk, ˌeɪ-) *adj.* not functioning in the manner of a syllable.

a·sy+lum (ə'saɪləm) *n.* **1.** an institution for the shelter, treatment, or confinement of individuals, esp. a mental hospital (formerly termed **lunatic asylum**). **2.** a safe or inviolable place of refuge, esp. as formerly offered by the Christian Church to criminals, outlaws, etc.; sanctuary (often in the phrase **give asylum to**). **3.** shelter; refuge. **4.** *International law.* refuge afforded to a person whose extradition is sought by a foreign government: *political asylum.* [C15: via Latin from Greek *asulon* refuge, from *asulos* that may not be seized, from A-^{1} + *sulon* right of seizure]

a·sym+met+ric (ˌæsɪ'mɛtrɪk, ˌeɪ-) *or* **a·sym+met+ri+cal** *adj.* **1.** not symmetrical; lacking symmetry; misproportioned. **2.** *Chem.* **a.** (of a molecule) having its atoms and radicals arranged unsymmetrically. **b.** (of a carbon atom) attached to four different atoms or radicals so that stereoisomerism results. **3.** *Logic, maths.* (of a relation) altered in meaning or value if the related terms are interchanged, as in *John is the father of David.* —ˌ**a·sym+'met+ri+cal+ly** *adv.*

a·sym+met+ric time *n.* musical time consisting of an odd number of beats in each bar divided into uneven combinations, such as 3 + 2, 4 + 3, 2 + 3 + 2, etc.

a·sym+me+try (æ'sɪmɪtrɪ, eɪ-) *n.* lack or absence of symmetry in spatial arrangements or in mathematical or logical relations.

a·symp+to+mat+ic (æˌsɪmptə'mætɪk, eɪ-) *adj.* (of a disease or suspected disease) without symptoms; providing no subjective evidence of existence. —**a·ˌsymp+to+'mat·i+cal+ly** *adv.*

as+ymp+tote ('æsɪmˌtəʊt) *n.* a straight line that is closely approached by a plane curve so that the perpendicular distance between them decreases to zero as the distance from the origin increases to infinity. [C17: from Greek *asumptōtos* not falling together, from A-^{1} + SYN + *ptōtos* inclined to fall, from *piptein* to fall]

as+ymp+tot+ic (ˌæsɪm'tɒtɪk) *or* **as+ymp+tot·i+cal** *adj.* **1.** of or referring to an asymptote. **2.** (of a function, series, formula, etc.) approaching a given value or condition, as a variable or an expression containing a variable approaches a limit, usually infinity. —ˌ**as+ymp+'tot·i+cal+ly** *adv.*

a·syn+chro+nism (æ'sɪŋkrəˌnɪzəm, eɪ-) *n.* a lack of synchronism; occurrence at different times. —**a·'syn+chro+nous** *adj.* —**a·'syn+chro+nous+ly** *adv.*

as+yn+det+ic (ˌæsɪn'dɛtɪk) *adj.* **1.** (of a catalogue or index) without cross references. **2.** (of a linguistic construction) having no conjunction, as in *I came, I saw, I conquered.* —ˌ**as+yn+'det·i+cal+ly** *adv.*

a·syn+de·ton (æ'sɪndɪtən) *n., pl.* **-de·ta** (-dɪtə). **1.** the omission of a conjunction between the parts of a sentence. **2.** an asyndetic construction. Compare **syndeton.** [C16: from New Latin, from Greek *asundeton,* from *asundetos* unconnected, from A-^{1} + *sundein* to bind together]

A·syut *or* **As+siut** (æ'sjuːt) *n.* an ancient city in central Egypt, on the Nile. Pop.: 197 200 (1974 est.). Ancient Greek name: **Lycopolis.**

at^{1} (æt) *prep.* **1.** used to indicate location or position: *are they at the table? staying at a small hotel.* **2.** towards; in the direction of: *looking at television; throwing stones at windows.* **3.** used to indicate position in time: *come at three o'clock.* **4.** engaged in; in a state of (being): *children at play; stand at ease; he is at his most charming today.* **5.** (in expressions concerned with habitual activity) during the passing of (esp. in the phrase **at night**): *he used to work at night.* **6.** for; in exchange for: *it's selling at four pounds.* **7.** used to indicate the object of an emotion: *angry at the driver; shocked at his behaviour.* **8. where it's at.** *Slang.* the real place of action. [Old English *æt;* related to Old Norse *at* to, Latin *ad* to]

at^{2} (ɑːt, æt) *n., pl.* **at.** a Laotian monetary unit worth one hundredth of a kip. [from Thai]

At **1.** *the chemical symbol for* astatine. **2.** Also: **A** *abbrev. for* ampere-turn.

at. *abbrev. for:* **1.** (unit of pressure) atmosphere. **2.** atomic.

A·ta+ca+ma Des+ert (*Spanish* ˌata'kama) *n.* a desert region along the W coast of South America, mainly in N Chile: a major source of nitrates.

a·tac+tic (eɪ'tæktɪk) *adj. Chem.* (of a polymer) having random sequence of the stereochemical arrangement of groups on carbon atoms in the chain; not stereospecific.

at·a+ghan ('ætəˌgæn) *n.* a variant of **yataghan.**

At·a·hual·pa (ˌætə'wɑːlpə) *or* **At·a·ba·li·pa** (ˌætə'bɑːlɪpə) *n.* ?1500–33, the last Inca emperor of Peru (1525–33), who was put to death by the Spanish under Pizarro.

At·a·lan·ta (ˌætə'læntə) *n. Greek myth.* a maiden who agreed to marry any man who could defeat her in a running race. She lost to Hippomenes when she paused to pick up three golden apples that he had deliberately dropped.

at·a+man ('ætəmən) *n., pl.* **+mans.** an elected leader of the Cossacks; hetman. [from Russian, from Polish *hetman,* from German *Hauptmann* (literally: head man)]

at·a+rac+tic (ˌætə'ræktɪk) *or* **at·a+rax+ic** (ˌætə'raksɪk) *adj.* **1.** able to calm or tranquillize. ~*n.* **2.** an ataractic drug.

at·a+rax·i·a (ˌætə'ræksɪə) *or* **at·a+rax·y** ('ætəˌræksɪ) *n.* calmness or peace of mind; emotional tranquillity. [C17: from Greek: serenity, from *ataraktos* undisturbed, from A-^{1} + *tarassein* to trouble]

At·a·türk ('ætəˌtɜːk) *n.* **Ke·mal** (kɛ'mɑːl). original name *Mustafa Kemal.* 1881–1938, Turkish general and statesman; founder of the Turkish republic and president of Turkey (1923–38), who westernized and secularized the country.

at·a+vism ('ætəˌvɪzəm) *n.* **1.** the recurrence in a plant or animal of certain primitive characteristics that were present in an ancestor but have not occurred in intermediate generations. **2.** reversion to a former or more primitive type. [C19: from French *atavisme,* from Latin *atavus* strictly: great-grandfather's grandfather, probably from *atta* daddy + *avus* grandfather] —**'at·a·vist** *n.* —ˌ**at·a+'vis+tic** *or* **at·a+vic** (ə'tævɪk) *adj.* —ˌ**at·a+'vis+ti+cal+ly** *adv.*

a·tax·i·a (ə'tæksɪə) *or* **a·tax·y** (ə'tæksɪ) *n. Pathol.* lack of muscular coordination. [C17: via New Latin from Greek: lack of coordination, from A-^{1} + *-taxia,* from *tassein* to put in order] —**a·'tax+ic** *or* **a·'tac+tic** *adj.*

At+ba+ra ('ætbərə, æt'bɑː-) *n.* **1.** a town in NE Sudan. Pop.: 64 326 (1973). **2.** a river in NE Africa, rising in N Ethiopia and flowing through E Sudan to the Nile at Atbara. Length: over 800 km (500 miles).

A.T.C. *abbrev. for:* **1.** air traffic control. **2.** (in Britain) Air Training Corps.

ate (ɛt, eɪt) *vb.* the past tense of **eat.**

A·te ('eɪtɪ, 'ɑːtɪ) *n. Greek myth.* a goddess who makes men blind so that they will blunder into guilty acts. See also **hubris.** [C16: via Latin from Greek *atē* a rash impulse]

-ate^{1} *suffix.* **1.** (*forming adjectives*) possessing; having the appearance or characteristics of: *fortunate; palmate; Latinate.* **2.** (*forming nouns*) a chemical compound, esp. a salt or ester of an acid: *carbonate; stearate.* **3.** (*forming nouns*) the product of a process: *condensate.* **4.** forming verbs from nouns and adjectives: *hyphenate; rusticate.* [from Latin *-ātus,* past participial ending of verbs ending in *-āre*]

-ate^{2} *suffix forming nouns.* denoting office, rank, or a group having a certain function: *episcopate; electorate.* [from Latin *-ātus,* suffix (fourth declension) of collective nouns]

at+e·lec+ta+sis (ˌætə'lɛktəsɪs) *n.* **1.** failure of the lungs to expand fully at birth. **2.** collapse of the lung or a part of the lung, usually caused by bronchial obstruction. [C19: New Latin, from Greek *atelēs* imperfect + *ektasis* extension]

at+el+ier ('ætəlˌjeɪ; *French* atə'lje) *n.* an artist's studio or workshop. [C17: from Old French *astelier* workshop, from *astele* chip of wood, from Latin *astula* splinter, from *assis* board]

a tem+po (ɑː 'tɛmpəʊ) *Music.* ~*adj., adv.* **1.** to the original tempo. ~*n.* **2.** a passage thus marked. ~Also: **tempo primo.** [Italian: in (the original) time]

A·ten *or* **A·ton** ('ɑːtᵊn) *n.* (in ancient Egypt) the solar disc worshipped as the sole god in the reign of Akhenaten.

Ath·a+bas+ka *or* **Ath·a+bas+ca** (ˌæθə'bæskə) *n.* **1. Lake.** a lake in W Canada, in NW Saskatchewan and NE Alberta. Area: about 7770 sq. km (3000 sq. miles). **2.** a river in W Canada, rising in the Rocky Mountains and flowing northeast to Lake Athabaska. Length: 1230 km (765 miles).

Ath·a+mas ('æθəˌmæs) *n. Greek myth.* a king of Orchomenus in Boeotia; the father of Phrixus and Helle by his first wife Nephele, whom he deserted for Ino.

Ath·a+na+sian Creed (ˌæθə'neɪʃən) *n. Christianity.* a profession of faith widely used in the Western Church which, though formerly attributed to Athanasius, probably originated in Gaul between 381 and 428 A.D.

Ath·a·na·sius (ˌæθə'neɪʃəs) *n.* **Saint.** ?296–373 A.D., patriarch of Alexandria who championed Christian orthodoxy against Arianism. Feast day: May 2. —ˌ**Ath·a+'na+sian** *adj.*

Ath·a+pas+can, Ath·a+pas+kan (ˌæθə'pæskən) *or* **Ath·a+bas+can, Ath·a+bas+kan** (ˌæθə'bæskən) *n.* **1.** a group of North American Indian languages belonging to the Na-Dene phylum, including Apache and Navaho. **2.** a speaker of one of these languages. [from Cree *athapaskaaw* scattered grass or reeds]

A·thar·va-Ve·da (ə'tɑːvə'veɪdə) *n. Hinduism.* the fourth and latest Veda, largely consisting of priestly spells and incantations.

a·the+ism ('eɪθɪˌɪzəm) *n.* **1.** the doctrine or belief that there is no God or that the assertion of his existence is meaningless. **2.** rejection of belief in God or gods. **3.** *Archaic.* behaviour or attitudes regarded as evil or sinful; godlessness. [C16: from French *athéisme,* from Greek *atheos* godless, from A-^{1} + *theos* god] —**'a·the+ist** *n., adj.* —ˌ**a·the+'is+tic** *or* ˌ**a·the+'is+ti+cal** *adj.* —ˌ**a·the+'is+ti+cal+ly** *adv.*

ath+el+ing ('æθəlɪŋ) *n.* (in Anglo-Saxon England) a prince of any of the royal dynasties. [Old English *ætheling,* from *æthelu* noble family + -ING^{3}; related to Old High German *adaling,* Old Norse *öthlingr*]

Ath·el·stan ('æθəlstən) *n.* ?895–939 A.D., king of Wessex and Mercia (924–939 A.D.), who extended his kingdom to include most of England.

a·th+e·mat+ic (ˌæθɪ'mætɪk) *adj.* **1.** *Music.* not based on themes. **2.** *Linguistics.* (of verbs) having a suffix attached immediately to the stem, without an intervening vowel.

A·the·na (ə'θiːnə) *or* **A·the·ne** (ə'θiːnɪ) *n. Greek myth.* a virgin goddess of wisdom, practical skills, and prudent warfare. She was born, fully armed, from the head of Zeus. Also called: **Pallas Athena, Pallas.** Roman counterpart: **Minerva.**

ath·e·nae·um *or U.S.* **ath·e·ne·um** (ˌæθɪˈniːəm) *n.* **1.** an institution for the promotion of learning. **2.** a building containing a reading room or library, esp. one used by such an institution. [C18: from Late Latin, from Greek *Athēnaion* temple of Athene, frequented by poets and teachers]

Ath·e·nae·um *or U.S. (sometimes)* **Ath·e·ne·um** (ˌæθɪˈniːəm) *n.* **1.** (in ancient Greece) a building sacred to the goddess Athena, esp. the Athenian temple that served as a gathering place for the learned. **2.** (in imperial Rome) the academy of learning established near the Forum about 135 A.D. by Hadrian.

A·the·ni·an (əˈθiːnɪən) *n.* **1.** a native or inhabitant of Athens. ~*adj.* **2.** of or relating to Athens.

Ath·ens (ˈæθɪnz) *n.* the capital of Greece, in the southeast near the Saronic Gulf: became capital after independence in 1834; ancient city-state, most powerful in the 5th century B.C.; contains the hill citadel of the Acropolis. Pop.: 867 023 (1971). Greek name: **A·thi·nai** (aˈθine).

a·ther·man·cy (æˈθɜːmənsɪ) *n.* an inability to transmit radiant heat or infrared radiation. Also called: **adiathermancy.** [C19: from Greek *athermantos* not heated, from A-[1] + *thermainein* to heat, from *thermē* heat; compare DIATHERMANCY]

a·ther·ma·nous (æˈθɜːmənəs) *adj.* capable of stopping radiant heat or infrared radiation.

ath·er·o·ma (ˌæθəˈrəʊmə) *n., pl.* **·mas** *or* **·ma·ta** (-mətə). *Pathol.* a fatty deposit on or within the inner lining of an artery, often causing an obstruction to the blood flow. [C18: via Latin from Greek *athērōma* tumour full of matter resembling gruel, from *athēra* gruel] —**ath·er·om·a·tous** (ˌæθəˈrɒmətəs, -ˈrəʊ-) *adj.*

ath·er·o·scle·ro·sis (ˌæθərəʊsklɪəˈrəʊsɪs) *n., pl.* **·ses** (-siːz). a degenerative disease of the arteries characterized by patchy thickening of the inner lining of the arterial walls, caused by deposits of fatty material; a form of arteriosclerosis. See **atheroma.** [C20: from New Latin, from Greek *athēra* gruel (see ATHEROMA) + SCLEROSIS] —**ath·er·o·scle·rot·ic** (ˌæθərəʊsklɪəˈrɒtɪk) *adj.*

a·thirst (əˈθɜːst) *adj. (postpositive)* **1.** (often foll. by *for*) having an eager desire; longing. **2.** *Archaic.* thirsty.

ath·lete (ˈæθliːt) *n.* **1.** a person trained to compete in sports or exercises involving physical strength, speed, or endurance. **2.** a person who has a natural aptitude for physical activities. **3.** *Chiefly Brit.* a competitor in track and field events. [C18: from Latin via Greek *athlētēs,* from *athlein* to compete for a prize, from *athlos* a contest]

ath·lete's foot *n.* a fungal infection of the skin of the foot, esp. between the toes and on the soles. Technical name: **dermatophytosis interdigitale.**

ath·let·ic (æθˈlɛtɪk) *adj.* **1.** physically fit or strong; muscular or active. **2.** of, relating to, or suitable for an athlete or for athletics. **3.** of or relating to a person with a muscular and well-proportioned body. See also **somatotype.** —**ath·ˈlet·i·cal·ly** *adv.* —**ath·ˈlet·i·cism** *n.*

ath·let·ics (æθˈlɛtɪks) *n.* **1. a.** track and field events. **b.** (*as modifier*): *an athletics meeting.* **2.** sports or exercises engaged in by athletes. **3.** the theory or practice of athletic activities and training.

ath·let·ic sup·port *n.* a more formal term for **jockstrap.**

ath·o·dyd (ˈæθəʊˌdaɪd) *n.* another name for **ramjet.** [C20: from *a(ero)-th(erm)ody(namic) d(uct)*]

at-home *n.* **1.** a social gathering in a person's home. **2.** another name for **open day.**

Ath·os (ˈæθɒs, ˈeɪ-) *n.* **Mount.** a department of NE Greece, in Macedonia: autonomous since 1927; inhabited by Greek Orthodox Basilian monks in 20 monasteries founded in the tenth century. Administrative centre: Karyai. Pop.: 1732 (1971).

a·thwart (əˈθwɔːt) *adv.* **1.** transversely; from one side to another. ~*prep.* **2.** across the path or line of (esp. a ship). **3.** in opposition to; against. [C15: from A-[1] + THWART]

a·thwart·ships (əˈθwɔːtˌʃɪps) *adv. Nautical.* from one side to the other of a vessel at right angles to the keel.

-at·ic *suffix forming adjectives.* of the nature of the thing specified: *problematic.* [from French *-atique,* from Greek *-atikos*]

a·tilt (əˈtɪlt) *adv., adj. (postpositive)* **1.** in a tilted or inclined position. **2.** *Archaic.* in or as if in a joust.

-a·tion *suffix forming nouns.* indicating an action, process, state, condition, or result: *arbitration; cogitation; hibernation; moderation.* Compare **-ion, -tion.** [from Latin *-ātiōn-,* suffix of abstract nouns, from *-ātus* -ATE[1] + *-iōn-* -ION]

-a·tive *suffix forming adjectives.* of, relating to, or tending to: *authoritative; decorative; informative.* [from Latin *-ātīvus,* from *ātus* -ATE[1] + *īvus* -IVE]

At·kin·son (ˈætkɪnsᵊn) *n.* Sir **Har·ry Al·bert.** 1831–92, New Zealand statesman, born in England: prime minister of New Zealand (1876–77; 1883–84; 1887–91).

At·lan·ta (ətˈlæntə) *n.* a city in N Georgia: the state capital. Pop.: 451 123 (1973 est.).

At·lan·te·an (ˌætlænˈtiːən) *adj.* **1.** *Literary.* of, relating to, or like Atlas; extremely strong. **2.** of or connected with Atlantis.

at·lan·tes (ətˈlæntiːz) *n.* the plural of **atlas** (sense 4).

At·lan·tic (ətˈlæntɪk) *n.* **1. the.** short for the **Atlantic Ocean.** ~*adj.* **2.** of or relating to or bordering the Atlantic Ocean. **3.** of or relating to Atlas or the Atlas Mountains. [C15: from Latin *Atlanticus,* from Greek *(pelagos) Atlantikos* (the sea) of Atlas (so called because it lay beyond the Atlas Mountains)]

At·lan·tic Char·ter *n.* the joint declaration issued by F. D. Roosevelt and Winston Churchill on Aug. 14, 1941, consisting of eight principles to guide a postwar settlement.

At·lan·tic Cit·y *n.* a resort in SE New Jersey on Absecon Beach, an island on the Atlantic coast. Pop.: 47 859 (1970).

At·lan·tic In·tra·coast·al Wa·ter·way *n.* a system of inland and coastal waterways along the Atlantic coast of the U.S. from Cape Cod to Florida Bay. Length: 2495 km (1550 miles).

At·lan·tic O·cean *n.* the world's second largest ocean, bounded in the north by the Arctic, in the south by the Antarctic, in the west by North and South America, and in the east by Europe and Africa. Greatest depth: 9220 m (30 246 ft.). Area: about 81 585 000 sq. km (31 500 000 sq. miles).

At·lan·tic Prov·in·ces *pl. n.* another name for the **Maritime Provinces** of Canada.

At·lan·tic Stand·ard Time *n.* the local time used in eastern Canada.

At·lan·tis (ətˈlæntɪs) *n.* (in ancient legend) a continent said to have sunk beneath the Atlantic Ocean west of the Straits of Gibraltar.

at·las (ˈætləs) *n.* **1.** a collection of maps, usually in book form. **2.** a book of charts, graphs, etc., illustrating aspects of a subject: *an anatomical atlas.* **3.** *Anatomy.* the first cervical vertebra, attached to and supporting the skull in man. Compare **axis**[1] (sense 3). **4.** (*pl.* **at·lan·tes**) *Architect.* another name for **telamon. 5.** a standard size of drawing paper, 26 × 17 inches. [C16: via Latin from Greek; first applied to maps, from depictions of Atlas supporting the heavens in 16th-century collections of maps]

At·las (ˈætləs) *n.* **1.** *Greek myth.* a Titan compelled to support the sky on his shoulders as punishment for rebelling against Zeus. **2.** a U.S. intercontinental ballistic missile, also used in launching spacecraft.

At·las Moun·tains *pl. n.* a mountain system of N Africa, between the Mediterranean and the Sahara Desert. Highest peak: Mount Toubkal, 4165 m (13 664 ft.).

At·li (ˈɑːtlɪ) *n. Norse legend.* a king of the Huns who married Gudrun for her inheritance and was slain by her after he killed her brothers.

atm. *abbrev. for:* **1.** atmosphere (unit of pressure). **2.** atmospheric.

at·man (ˈɑːtmən) *n. Hinduism.* **1.** the personal soul or self; the thinking principle as manifested in consciousness. **2.** Brahman considered as the Universal Soul, the great Self or Person that dwells in the entire created order. [from Sanskrit *ātman* breath; compare Old High German *ātum* breath]

at·mo- *combining form.* air or vapour: *atmometer; atmosphere.* [via New Latin from Greek *atmos* vapour]

at·mol·y·sis (ætˈmɒlɪsɪs) *n., pl.* **·ses** (-ˌsiːz). a method of separating gases that depends on their differential rates of diffusion through a porous substance.

at·mom·e·ter (ætˈmɒmɪtə) *n.* an instrument for measuring the rate of evaporation of water into the atmosphere. Also called: **evaporimeter** or **evaporometer.** —**at·ˈmom·e·try** *n.*

at·mos·phere (ˈætməsˌfɪə) *n.* **1.** the gaseous envelope surrounding the earth or any other celestial body. See also **troposphere, stratosphere, mesosphere,** and **ionosphere. 2.** the air or climate in a particular place: *the atmosphere was thick with smoke.* **3.** a general pervasive feeling or mood: *an atmosphere of elation.* **4.** the prevailing tone or mood of a novel, symphony, painting, or other work of art. **5.** a special mood or character associated with a place. **6.** any local gaseous environment or medium: *an inert atmosphere.* **7.** Abbrev.: **at.** or **atm.** a unit of pressure; the pressure that will support a column of mercury 760 mm high at 0°C at sea level. 1 atmosphere is equivalent to 101 325 newtons per square metre or 14.72 pounds per square inch. —ˌ**at·mos·ˈpher·ic** *or* ˌ**at·mos·ˈpher·i·cal** *adj.* —ˌ**at·mos·ˈpher·i·cal·ly** *adv.*

at·mos·pher·ic per·spec·tive *n.* another term for **aerial perspective.**

at·mos·pher·ic pres·sure *n.* the pressure exerted by the atmosphere at the earth's surface. It has an average value of 1 atmosphere.

at·mos·pher·ics (ˌætməsˈfɛrɪks) *pl. n.* **1.** electrical disturbances produced in the atmosphere by natural causes such as lightning. **2.** radio interference, heard as crackling or hissing in receivers, caused by electrical disturbance.

at. no. *abbrev. for* atomic number.

at·oll (ˈætɒl, əˈtɒl) *n.* a circular coral reef or string of coral islands surrounding a lagoon. [C17: from *atollon,* native name in the Maldive Islands]

at·om (ˈætəm) *n.* **1. a.** the smallest quantity of an element that can take part in a chemical reaction. **b.** this entity as a source of nuclear energy: *the power of the atom.* See also **atomic structure. 2.** the hypothetical indivisible particle of matter postulated by certain ancient philosophers as the fundamental constituent of matter. See also **atomism. 3.** a very small amount or quantity; minute fragment: *to smash something to atoms; there is not an atom of truth in his allegations.* [C16: via Old French and Latin, from Greek *atomos* (n.), from *atomos* (adj.) that cannot be divided, from A-[1] + *temnein* to cut]

at·om bomb *or* **a·tom·ic bomb** *n.* a type of bomb in which the energy is provided by nuclear fission. Uranium-235 and plutonium-239 are the isotopes most commonly used in atom bombs. Also called: **A-bomb, fission bomb.** Compare **fusion bomb.**

a·tom·ic (əˈtɒmɪk) *adj.* **1.** of, using, or characterized by atomic bombs or atomic energy: *atomic warfare.* **2.** of, related to, or comprising atoms: *atomic hydrogen.* **3.** extremely small; minute. —**a·ˈtom·i·cal·ly** *adv.*

a·tom·ic age *n.* **the.** the current historical period, initiated by the development of the first atomic bomb towards the end of World War II and now marked by a balance of power between nations possessing the hydrogen bomb and the growing use of nuclear power as a source of energy.

a·tom·ic clock *n.* an extremely accurate clock in which an electrical oscillator is controlled by the natural vibrations of an atomic or molecular system such as caesium or ammonia.

a·tom·ic cock·tail *n.* an aqueous solution of radioactive substance, such as sodium iodide, administered orally as part of the treatment for cancer.

a·tom·ic en·er·gy *n.* another name for **nuclear energy.**

A·tom·ic En·er·gy Au·thor·i·ty *n.* (in Britain) a government body established in 1954 to control research and development in atomic energy. Abbrev.: **AEA**

A·tom·ic En·er·gy Com·mis·sion *n.* (in the U.S.) a federal board established in 1946 to administer and develop domestic atomic energy programmes. Abbrev.: **AEC**

a·tom·ic heat *n.* the product of an element's atomic weight and its specific heat (capacity).

at·o·mic·i·ty (ˌætəˈmɪsɪtɪ) *n.* **1.** the state of being made up of atoms. **2.** the number of atoms in the molecules of an element. **3.** a less common name for **valency.**

a·tom·ic mass *n. Chem.* **1.** the mass of an isotope of an element in atomic mass units. **2.** See **relative atomic mass.**

a·tom·ic mass u·nit *n.* a unit of mass used to express atomic and molecular weights that is equal to one twelfth of the mass of an atom of carbon-12. It is equivalent to 1.66×10^{-27} kg. Abbrev.: **AMU** Also called: **unified atomic mass unit, dalton.**

a·tom·ic num·ber *n.* the number of protons in the nucleus of an atom of an element. Abbrev.: **at. no.** Symbol: *Z* Also called: **proton number.**

a·tom·ic pile *n.* the original name for a **nuclear reactor.**

a·tom·ic pow·er *n.* another name for **nuclear power.**

a·tom·ic struc·ture *n.* the concept of an atom as a central positively charged nucleus consisting of protons and neutrons surrounded by a number of electrons. The number of electrons is equal to the number of protons: the whole entity is thus electrically neutral.

a·tom·ic the·o·ry *n.* **1.** any theory in which matter is regarded as consisting of atoms, esp. that proposed by John Dalton postulating that elements are composed of atoms that can combine in definite proportions to form compounds. **2.** the current concept of the atom as an entity with a definite structure. See **atomic structure.**

a·tom·ic vol·ume *n.* the atomic weight (relative atomic mass) of an element divided by its density.

a·tom·ic weight *n.* the ratio of the average mass per atom of an element to one-twelfth the mass of an atom of carbon-12. Abbrev.: **at. wt.** Also called: **relative atomic mass.**

Usage. Until 1961 *atomic weights* were based on the mass of an atom of oxygen-16. The carbon-12 atom is now the usual basis of calculations and *relative atomic mass* is the preferred term for the new atomic weights.

at·om·ism (ˈætəˌmɪzəm) *n.* **1.** an ancient philosophical theory that the ultimate constituents of the universe are atoms. See also **Democritus, Lucretius. 2.** *Psychol.* the theory that experiences and mental states are composed of elementary units. —**ˈat·om·ist** *n., adj.* —**ˌat·om·ˈis·tic** *or* **ˌat·om·ˈis·ti·cal** *adj.* —**ˌat·om·ˈis·ti·cal·ly** *adv.*

at·om·ize *or* **at·om·ise** (ˈætəˌmaɪz) *vb.* **1.** to separate or be separated into free atoms. **2.** to reduce (a liquid or solid) to fine particles or spray or (of a liquid or solid) to be reduced in this way. **3.** to destroy by weapons, esp. nuclear weapons. —**ˌat·om·i·ˈza·tion** *or* **ˌat·om·i·ˈsa·tion** *n.*

at·om·iz·er *or* **at·om·is·er** (ˈætəˌmaɪzə) *n.* a device for reducing a liquid to a fine spray, such as the nozzle used to feed oil into a furnace or an enclosed bottle with a fine outlet used to spray perfumes or medicines.

at·om smash·er *n. Physics.* the nontechnical name for **accelerator** (sense 2).

at·o·my[1] (ˈætəmɪ) *n., pl.* **·mies.** *Archaic.* **1.** an atom or minute particle. **2.** a minute creature. [C16: from Latin *atomī* atoms, but used as if singular; see ATOM]

at·o·my[2] (ˈætəmɪ) *n., pl.* **·mies.** an obsolete word for **skeleton.** [C16: from mistaken division of ANATOMY (as if *an atomy*)]

A·ton (ˈɑːtᵊn) *n.* a variant spelling of **Aten.**

a·ton·al (eɪˈtəʊnᵊl, æ-) *adj. Music.* having no established key. Compare **tonal** (sense 2). —**a·ˈton·al·ism** *n.* —**a·ˈton·al·ly** *adv.*

a·to·nal·i·ty (ˌeɪtəʊˈnælɪtɪ, ˌæ-) *n.* **1.** absence of or disregard for an established musical key in a composition. **2.** the principles of composition embodying this and providing a radical alternative to the diatonic system. ~Compare **tonality.**

a·tone (əˈtəʊn) *vb.* **1.** (*intr.;* foll. by *for*) to make amends or reparation (for a crime, sin, etc.). **2.** (*tr.*) to expiate: *to atone a guilt with repentance.* **3.** *Obsolete.* to be in or bring into agreement. [C16: back formation from ATONEMENT] —**a·ˈton·a·ble** *or* **a·ˈtone·a·ble** *adj.* —**a·ˈton·er** *n.*

a·tone·ment (əˈtəʊnmənt) *n.* **1.** satisfaction, reparation, or expiation given for an injury or wrong. **2.** (*often cap.*) *Christian theology.* **a.** the reconciliation of man with God through the life, sufferings, and sacrificial death of Christ. **b.** the sufferings and death of Christ. **3.** *Christian Science.* the state in which the attributes of God are exemplified in man. **4.** *Obsolete.* reconciliation or agreement. [C16: from Middle English phrase *at onement* in harmony]

a·ton·ic (eɪˈtɒnɪk, æ-) *adj.* **1.** (of a syllable, word, etc.) carrying no stress; unaccented. **2.** *Pathol.* relating to or characterized by atony. ~*n.* **3.** an unaccented or unstressed syllable, word, etc., such as *for* in *food for thought.* [C18: from Latin *atonicus,* from Greek *atonos* lacking tone; see ATONY] —**at·o·nic·i·ty** (ˌætəˈnɪsɪtɪ, ˌeɪtəʊ-) *n.*

at·o·ny (ˈætənɪ) *n.* **1.** *Pathol.* lack of normal tone or tension, as in muscles; abnormal relaxation of a muscle. **2.** *Phonetics.* lack of stress or accent on a syllable or word. [C17: from Latin *atonia,* from Greek: tonelessness, from *atonos* slack, from A-[1] + *tonos* TONE]

a·top (əˈtɒp) *adv.* **1.** on top; at the top. ~*prep.* **2.** on top of; at the top of.

-a·tor *suffix forming nouns.* a person or thing that performs a certain action: *agitator; escalator; radiator.* [from Latin *-ātor;* see -ATE[1], -OR[1]]

-a·to·ry *suffix forming adjectives.* of, relating to, characterized by, or serving to: *circulatory; exploratory; migratory; explanatory.* [from Latin *-ātōrius;* see -ATE[1], -ORY[2]]

ATP *n.* adenosine triphosphate; a nucleotide found in the mitochondria of all plant and animal cells. It is the major source of energy for cellular reactions, this energy being released during its conversion to ADP. Formula: $C_{10}H_{16}N_5O_{13}P_3$.

at·ra·bil·ious (ˌætrəˈbɪljəs) *or* **at·ra·bil·i·ar** *adj. Rare.* irritable. [C17: from Latin *ātra bīlis* black bile, from *āter* black + *bīlis* BILE] —**ˌat·ra·ˈbil·ious·ness** *n.*

A·tre·us (ˈeɪtrɪˌuːs, ˈeɪtrɪəs) *n. Greek myth.* a king of Mycenae, son of Pelops, father of Agamemnon and Menelaus, and member of the family known as the **A·tre·ids** (ˈeɪtrɪɪdz).

a·tri·o·ven·tric·u·lar (ˌeɪtrɪəʊvɛnˈtrɪkjʊlə) *adj. Anatomy.* of, relating to, or affecting both the atria and the ventricles of the heart: *atrioventricular disease.* [C19: from *atrio-,* from New Latin *atrium* heart chamber (see ATRIUM) + VENTRICULAR]

a·trip (əˈtrɪp) *adj.* (*postpositive*) *Nautical.* (of an anchor) no longer caught on the bottom; tripped; aweigh.

a·tri·um (ˈeɪtrɪəm, ˈɑː-) *n., pl.* **a·tri·a** (ˈeɪtrɪə, ˈɑː-). **1.** the open main court of a Roman house. **2.** a court in front of an early Christian or medieval church, esp. one flanked by colonnades. **3.** *Anatomy.* a cavity or chamber in the body, esp. the upper chamber of each half of the heart. [C17: from Latin; related to *āter* black, perhaps originally referring to the part of the house that was blackened by smoke from the hearth] —**ˈa·tri·al** *adj.*

a·tro·cious (əˈtrəʊʃəs) *adj.* **1.** extremely cruel or wicked; ruthless: *atrocious deeds.* **2.** horrifying or shocking: *an atrocious road accident.* **3.** *Informal.* very bad; detestable: *atrocious writing.* [C17: from Latin *ātrōx* dreadful, from *āter* black] —**a·ˈtro·cious·ly** *adv.* —**a·ˈtro·cious·ness** *n.*

a·troc·i·ty (əˈtrɒsɪtɪ) *n., pl.* **·ties.** **1.** behaviour or an action that is wicked or ruthless. **2.** the fact or quality of being atrocious. **3.** (*usually pl.*) acts of extreme cruelty, esp. against prisoners or civilians in wartime.

at·ro·phy (ˈætrəfɪ) *n., pl.* **·phies.** **1.** a wasting away of an organ or part, or a failure to grow to normal size as the result of disease, faulty nutrition, etc. **2.** any degeneration or diminution, esp. through lack of use. ~*vb.* **·phies, ·phy·ing, ·phied. 3.** to waste away or cause to waste away. [C17: from Late Latin *atrophia,* from Greek, from *atrophos* ill-fed, from A-[1] + *-trophos* from *trephein* to feed] —**a·troph·ic** (əˈtrɒfɪk) *adj.*

at·ro·pine (ˈætrəˌpiːn, -pɪn) *or* **at·ro·pin** (ˈætrəpɪn) *n.* a poisonous alkaloid obtained from the deadly nightshade, having an inhibitory action on the autonomic nervous system. It is used medicinally in preanaesthetic medication and to treat peptic ulcers, biliary and renal colic, etc. Formula: $C_{17}H_{23}NO_3$. [C19: from New Latin *atropa* deadly nightshade, from Greek *atropos* unchangeable, inflexible; see ATROPOS]

At·ro·pos (ˈætrəˌpɒs) *n. Greek myth.* the one of the three Fates who severs the thread of life. [Greek, from *atropos* that may not be turned, from A-[1] + *-tropos* from *trepein* to turn]

att. *abbrev. for:* **1.** attached. **2.** attorney.

at·ta·boy (ˈætəˌbɔɪ) *interj. Slang, chiefly U.S.* an expression of approval or exhortation.

at·tach (əˈtætʃ) *vb.* (*mainly tr.*) **1.** to join, fasten, or connect. **2.** (*reflexive or passive*) to become associated with or join, as in a business or other venture: *he attached himself to the expedition.* **3.** (*intr.;* foll. by *to*) to be inherent (in) or connected (with): *responsibility attaches to the job.* **4.** to attribute or ascribe: *to attach importance to an event.* **5.** to include or append, esp. as a condition: *a proviso attaches to the contract.* **6.** (*usually passive*) *Military.* to place on temporary duty with another unit. **7.** to appoint officially. **8.** *Law.* to arrest or take (a person, property, etc.) with lawful authority. **9.** *Obsolete.* to seize. [C14: from Old French *atachier* to fasten, changed from *estachier* to fasten with a stake, from *estache* STAKE] —**at·ˈtach·a·ble** *adj.* —**at·ˈtach·er** *n.*

at·ta·ché (əˈtæʃeɪ; *French* ataˈʃe) *n.* **1.** a specialist attached to a diplomatic mission: *military attaché.* **2.** *Brit.* a junior member of the staff of an embassy or legation. [C19: from French: someone attached (to a mission), from *attacher* to ATTACH]

at·ta·ché case *n.* a small flat rectangular briefcase used for carrying documents, papers, etc.

at·tached (əˈtætʃt) *adj.* **1.** (foll. by *to*) fond (of); full of regard (for): *he was very attached to the old lady.* **2.** married, engaged, or associated in an exclusive sexual relationship: *it's no good dancing with her, she's already attached.*

at·tach·ment (əˈtætʃmənt) *n.* **1.** a means of securing; a fastening. **2.** (often foll. by *to*) affection or regard (for); devotion (to): *attachment to a person or to a cause.* **3.** an object to be attached, esp. a supplementary part: *an attachment for an electric drill.* **4.** the act of attaching or the state of being attached. **5. a.** the arrest of a person for disobedience to a court order. **b.** the lawful seizure of property and placing of it under control of a court. **c.** a writ authorizing such arrest or seizure. **6.** *Law.* the binding of a debt in the hands of a garnishee until its disposition has been decided by the court.

at·tack (əˈtæk) *vb.* **1.** to launch a physical assault (against) with or without weapons; begin hostilities (with). **2.** (*intr.*) to take the initiative in a game, sport, etc.: *after a few minutes, the team began to attack.* **3.** (*tr.*) to direct hostile words or writings at; criticize or abuse vehemently. **4.** (*tr.*) to turn one's mind or energies vigorously to (a job, problem, etc.). **5.** (*tr.*) to begin to injure or affect adversely; corrode, corrupt, or infect: *rust attacked the metal.* **6.** (*tr.*) to attempt to rape. ~*n.* **7.** the act or an instance of attacking. **8.** strong criticism or abuse: *an unjustified attack on someone's reputation.* **9.** an offensive move in a game, sport, etc. **10.** commencement of a task, etc. **11.** any sudden and usually severe manifestation of a disease or disorder: *a heart attack; an attack of indigestion.* **12.** **the attack.** *Ball games.* the players in a team whose main role is to attack the opponents' goal or territory. **13.** *Music.* decisiveness in beginning a passage, movement, or piece. **14.** an attempted rape. [C16: from French *attaquer,* from Old Italian *attaccare* to attack, attach, from *estaccare* to attach, from *stacca* STAKE; compare ATTACH] —**atˈtack·a·ble** *adj.* —**atˈtack·er** *n.*

at·tain (əˈteɪn) *vb.* **1.** (*tr.*) to achieve or accomplish (a task, goal, aim, etc.). **2.** (*tr.*) to reach or arrive at in space or time: *to attain old age.* **3.** (*intr.;* often foll. by *to*) to arrive (at) with effort or exertion: *to attain to glory.* [C14: from Old French *ateindre,* from Latin *attingere* to reach, from *tangere* to touch] —**atˈtain·a·ble** *adj.* —**at,tain·a·ˈbil·i·ty** *or* **atˈtain·a·ble·ness** *n.*

at·tain·der (əˈteɪndə) *n.* **1.** (formerly) the extinction of a person's civil rights resulting from a sentence of death or outlawry on conviction for treason or felony. See also **bill of attainder.** **2.** *Obsolete.* dishonour. ~Archaic equivalent: **at·tain·ture** (əˈteɪntʃə). [C15: from Anglo-French *attaindre* to convict, from Old French *ateindre* to ATTAIN]

at·tain·ment (əˈteɪnmənt) *n.* an achievement or the act of achieving; accomplishment.

at·taint (əˈteɪnt) *vb.* (*tr.*) *Archaic.* **1.** to pass judgment of death or outlawry upon (a person); condemn by bill of attainder. **2.** to dishonour or disgrace. **3.** to accuse or prove to be guilty. **4.** (of sickness) to affect or strike (somebody). ~*n.* **5.** a less common word for **attainder.** **6.** a dishonour; taint. [C14: from Old French *ateint* convicted, from *ateindre* to ATTAIN]

at·tar (ˈætə), **ot·to** (ˈɒtəʊ), *or* **ot·tar** (ˈɒtə) *n.* an essential oil from flowers, esp. the damask rose, used pure or as a base for perfume: *attar of roses.* [C18: from Persian *'atir* perfumed, from *'itr* perfume, from Arabic]

at·tem·per (əˈtɛmpə) *vb.* (*tr.*) *Archaic.* **1.** to modify by blending; temper. **2.** to moderate or soothe. **3.** to accommodate or bring into harmony. —**atˈtem·per·ment** *n.*

at·tempt (əˈtɛmpt) *vb.* (*tr.*) **1.** to make an effort (to do something) or to achieve (something); try. **2.** to try to surmount (an obstacle). **3.** to try to climb: *they will attempt the north wall of the Eiger.* **4.** *Archaic.* to attack. **5.** *Archaic.* to tempt. ~*n.* **6.** an endeavour to achieve something; effort. **7.** a result of an attempt or endeavour. **8.** an attack, esp. with the intention to kill: *an attempt on his life.* [C14: from Old French *attempter,* from Latin *attemptāre* to strive after, from *tentāre* to try] —**atˈtempt·a·ble** *adj.* —**atˈtempt·er** *n.*

At·ten·bor·ough (ˈætᵊnbᵊrə) *n.* Sir **Rich·ard.** born 1923, English film actor and producer.

at·tend (əˈtɛnd) *vb.* **1.** to be present at (an event, meeting, etc.). **2.** (when *intr.,* foll. by *to*) to give care; minister. **3.** (when *intr.,* foll. by *to*) to pay attention; listen. **4.** (*tr.; often passive*) to accompany or follow: *a high temperature attended by a severe cough.* **5.** (*intr.;* foll. by *on* or *upon*) to follow as a consequence (of). **6.** (*intr.;* foll. by *to*) to devote one's time; apply oneself: *to attend to the garden.* **7.** (*tr.*) to escort or accompany. **8.** (*intr.;* foll. by *on* or *upon*) to wait (on); serve; provide for the needs (of): *to attend on a guest.* **9.** (*tr.*) *Archaic.* to wait for; expect. **10.** (*intr.*) *Obsolete.* to delay. [C13: from Old French *atendre,* from Latin *attendere* to stretch towards, from *tendere* to extend] —**atˈtend·er** *n.*

at·tend·ance (əˈtɛndəns) *n.* **1.** the act or state of attending. **2.** the number of persons present: *an attendance of 5000 at the festival.* **3.** *Obsolete.* attendants collectively; retinue.

at·tend·ance al·low·ance *n. Brit.* extra money paid under the National Insurance scheme to an invalid who has to have full-time nursing attendance.

at·tend·ance cen·tre *n. Brit.* a place at which young offenders are required to attend regularly instead of going to prison.

at·tend·ant (əˈtɛndənt) *n.* **1.** a person who accompanies or waits upon another. **2.** a person employed to assist, guide, or provide a service for others, esp. for the general public: *a lavatory attendant.* **3.** a person who is present. **4.** a logical consequence or natural accompaniment: *hatred is often an attendant of jealousy.* ~*adj.* **5.** being in attendance. **6.** associated; accompanying; related: *attendant problems.*

at·ten·tion (əˈtɛnʃən) *n.* **1.** concentrated direction of the mind, esp. to a problem or task. **2.** consideration, notice, or observation: *a new matter has come to our attention.* **3.** detailed care or special treatment: *to pay attention to one's appearance.* **4.** (*usually pl.*) an act of consideration, courtesy, or gallantry indicating affection or love: *attentions given to a lover.* **5.** the motionless position of formal military alertness, esp. in drill when an upright position is assumed with legs and heels together, arms to the sides, head and eyes facing to the front. **6.** *Psychol.* the act of concentrating on any one of a set of objects or thoughts. See also **selective attention.** ~*interj.* **7.** the order to be alert or to adopt a position of formal military alertness. [C14: from Latin *attentiō,* from *attendere* to apply the mind to; see ATTEND]

at·ten·tive (əˈtɛntɪv) *adj.* **1.** paying attention; listening carefully; observant. **2.** (*postpositive;* often foll. by *to*) careful to fulfil the needs or wants (of); considerate (about): *she was always attentive to his needs.* —**atˈten·tive·ly** *adv.* —**atˈten·tive·ness** *n.*

at·ten·u·ant (əˈtɛnjuənt) *adj.* **1.** causing dilution or thinness, esp. of the blood. ~*n.* **2.** an attenuant drug or agent.

at·ten·u·ate *vb.* (əˈtɛnjuˌeɪt). **1.** to weaken or become weak; reduce in size, strength, density, or value. **2.** to make or become thin or fine; extend. **3.** (*tr.*) to make (a pathogenic bacterium, virus, etc.) less virulent, as by culture in special media or exposure to heat. ~*adj.* (əˈtɛnjuɪt, -ˌeɪt). **4.** diluted, weakened, slender, or reduced. **5.** *Botany.* tapering gradually to a point. [C16: from Latin *attenuāre* to weaken, from *tenuis* thin]

at·ten·u·a·tion (əˌtɛnjuˈeɪʃən) *n.* **1.** the act of attenuating or the state of being attenuated. **2.** the loss of energy suffered by radiation as it passes through matter, esp. as a result of absorption or scattering.

at·ten·u·a·tor (əˈtɛnjuˌeɪtə) *n.* **1.** *Physics.* any device designed to reduce the power of a wave without distorting it. **2.** a person or thing that attenuates.

at·test (əˈtɛst) *vb.* **1.** (*tr.*) to affirm the correctness or truth of. **2.** (when *intr.,* usually foll. by *to*) to witness (an act, event, etc.) or bear witness (to an act, event, etc.) as by signature or oath. **3.** (*tr.*) to make evident; demonstrate: *his life of luxury attests his wealth.* **4.** (*tr.*) to provide evidence for: *the marks in the ground attested the presence of a fossil.* [C16: from Latin *attestārī* to prove, from *testārī* to bear witness, from *testis* a witness] —**atˈtest·a·ble** *adj.* —**atˈtest·ant, atˈtest·er** *or esp. in legal usage* **atˈtes·tor, atˈtes·ta·tor** *n.* —**at·tes·ta·tion** (ˌætɛˈsteɪʃən) *n.*

at·test·ed (əˈtɛstɪd) *adj. Brit.* (of cattle, etc.) certified to be free from a disease, esp. from tuberculosis.

Att. Gen. *or* **Atty. Gen.** *abbrev. for* Attorney General.

at·tic (ˈætɪk) *n.* **1.** a space or room within the roof of a house. **2.** *Architect.* a storey or low wall above the cornice of a classical façade. [C18: special use of ATTIC, from the use of Attic-style pilasters to adorn the façade of the top storey]

At·tic (ˈætɪk) *adj.* **1.** of or relating to Attica, its inhabitants, or the dialect of Greek spoken there, esp. in classical times. **2.** (*often not cap.*) classically elegant, simple, or pure: *an Attic style.* ~*n.* **3.** the dialect of Ancient Greek spoken and written in Athens: the chief literary dialect of classical Greek. See also **Ionic.**

At·ti·ca (ˈætɪkə) *n.* a department of E central Greece: in ancient times the territory of Athens. Capital: Athens. Pop.: 2 303 051 (1971). Area: 3776 sq. km (1458 sq. miles).

At·ti·cism (ˈætɪˌsɪzəm) *n.* **1.** the idiom or character of the Attic dialect of Ancient Greek, esp. in the Hellenistic period. **2.** an elegant, simple, and clear expression. —**ˈAt·ti·cist** *n.*

At·tic or·der *n.* a low pilaster of any order set into the cornice of a building.

At·tic salt *or* **wit** *n.* refined incisive wit.

At·til·a (əˈtɪlə) *n.* ?406–453 A.D., king of the Huns, who devastated much of the Roman Empire, invaded Gaul in 451 A.D., but was defeated by the Romans and Visigoths at Châlons-sur-Marne.

at·tire (əˈtaɪə) *vb.* **1.** (*tr.*) to dress, esp. in fine elegant clothes; array. ~*n.* **2.** clothes or garments, esp. if fine or decorative. [C13: from Old French *atirier* to put in order, from *tire* row; see TIER[1]]

At·tis (ˈætɪs) *n. Classical myth.* a youth of Phrygia, loved by the goddess Cybele. In a jealous passion she caused him to go mad, whereupon he castrated himself and died.

at·ti·tude (ˈætɪˌtjuːd) *n.* **1.** mental view or disposition, esp. as it indicates opinion or allegiance. **2.** a theatrical pose created for effect (esp. in the phrase **strike an attitude**). **3.** a position of the body indicating mood or emotion. **4.** the orientation of an aircraft's axes in relation to some plane, esp. the horizontal. See also **axis**[1] (sense 1). **5.** the orientation of a spacecraft in relation to its direction of motion. **6.** *Ballet.* a classical position in which the body is upright and one leg raised and bent behind. [C17: from French, from Italian *attitudine* disposition, from Late Latin *aptitūdō* fitness, from Latin *aptus* APT] —**ˌat·tiˈtu·di·nal** *adj.*

at·ti·tu·di·nize *or* **at·ti·tu·di·nise** (ˌætɪˈtjuːdɪˌnaɪz) *vb.* (*intr.*) to adopt a pose or opinion for effect; strike an attitude. —**ˌat·tiˈtu·di·ˌniz·er** *or* **ˌat·tiˈtu·di·ˌnis·er** *n.*

Att·lee (ˈætlɪ) *n.* **Clem·ent Rich·ard,** 1st Earl Attlee. 1883–1967, British statesman; prime minister (1945–51); leader of the Labour party (1935–55). His government instituted the welfare state, with extensive nationalization.

attn. *abbrev. for* attention.

at·to- *prefix.* denoting 10^{-18}: *attotesla.* Symbol: a [from Norwegian, Danish *atten* eighteen]

at·torn (əˈtɜːn) *vb.* **1.** (*intr.*) *Law.* to acknowledge a new owner of land as one's landlord. **2.** (*intr.*) *Feudal history.* to transfer allegiance or do homage to a new lord. **3.** (*tr.*) *Rare.* to transfer. [C15: from Old French *atourner* to direct to, from *tourner* to TURN] —**atˈtorn·ment** *n.*

at·tor·ney (əˈtɜːnɪ) *n.* **1.** a person, esp. a lawyer, appointed or empowered to act for another. **2.** **letter of attorney.** a less common term for **power of attorney.** [C14: from Old French *atourné,* from *atourner* to direct to; see ATTORN] —**atˈtor·ney·ˌship** *n.*

at+tor·ney-at-law *n., pl.* **at+tor·neys-at-law.** *Law.* **1.** *Now chiefly U.S.* a lawyer qualified to represent in court a party to a legal action. **2.** *Brit. obsolete.* a solicitor.
at+tor+ney gen+er+al *n., pl.* **at+tor+neys gen+er+al** *or* **at+tor+ney gen+er+als. 1.** a country's chief law officer and senior legal adviser to its government. **2.** (in the U.S.) the chief law officer and legal adviser of a state government. **3.** (in some states of the U.S.) a public prosecutor.
At+tor+ney Gen+er+al *n.* **1.** (in the United Kingdom except Scotland) the senior law officer and chief legal counsel of the Crown: a member of the government and of the House of Commons. **2.** (in the U.S.) the chief law officer and legal adviser to the Administration: head of the Department of Justice and member of the cabinet.
at+tract (ə'trækt) *vb.* (*mainly tr.*) **1.** to draw (notice, a crowd of observers, etc.) to oneself by conspicuous behaviour or appearance (esp. in the phrase **attract attention**). **2.** (*also intr.*) to exert a force on (a body) that tends to cause an approach or oppose a separation: *the gravitational pull of the earth attracts objects to it.* **3.** to possess some property that pulls or draws (something) towards itself: *jam attracts wasps.* **4.** (*also intr.*) to exert a pleasing, alluring, or fascinating influence (upon); be attractive (to). [C15: from Latin *attrahere* to draw towards, from *trahere* to pull] **—at+'tract+a·ble** *adj.* **—at+'trac+tor** *or* **at+'tract+er** *n.*
at+tract+ant (ə'træktənt) *n.* a substance that attracts, esp. a chemical (**sex attractant**) produced by an insect and attracting insects of the same species. See also **pheromone.**
at+trac+tion (ə'trækʃən) *n.* **1.** the act, power, or quality of attracting. **2.** a person or thing that attracts or is intended to attract. **3.** a force by which one object attracts another, such as the gravitational or magnetic force. **4.** a change in the form of one linguistic element caused by the proximity of another element. Compare **assimilation.**
at+trac+tion sphere *n.* another name for **astrosphere** (sense 2).
at+trac+tive (ə'træktɪv) *adj.* **1.** appealing to the senses or mind through beauty, form, character, etc. **2.** arousing interest: *an attractive opportunity.* **3.** possessing the ability to draw or pull: *an attractive force.* **—at+'trac+tive+ly** *adv.* **—at+'trac+tive+ness** *n.*
attrib. *abbrev. for:* **1.** attribute. **2.** attributive.
at+trib+ute *vb.* (ə'trɪbju:t). **1.** (*tr.; usually foll. by to*) to regard as belonging (to), produced (by), or resulting (from); ascribe (to): *to attribute a painting to Picasso.* ~*n.* ('ætrɪˌbju:t). **2.** a property, quality, or feature belonging to or representative of a person or thing. **3.** an object accepted as belonging to a particular office or position. **4.** *Grammar.* **a.** an adjective or adjectival phrase. **b.** an attributive adjective. **5.** *Logic.* the property, quality, or feature that is affirmed or denied concerning the subject of a proposition. [C15: from Latin *attribuere* to associate with, from *tribuere* to give] **—at+'trib+ut+a·ble** *adj.* **—at+'trib+ut+er** *or* **at+'trib·u·tor** *n.* **—at+trib·u+tion** (ˌætrɪ'bju:ʃən) *n.*
at+trib·u·tive (ə'trɪbjʊtɪv) *adj.* **1.** relating to an attribute. **2.** *Grammar.* (of an adjective or adjectival phrase) preceding the noun modified. Compare **predicative.** ~*n.* **3.** an attributive adjective. **—at+'trib·u·tive+ly** *adv.* **—at+'trib·u·tive+ness** *n.*
at+tri+tion (ə'trɪʃən) *n.* **1.** the act of wearing away or the state of being worn away, as by friction. **2.** constant wearing down to weaken or destroy (often in the phrase **war of attrition**). **3.** *Geography.* the grinding down of rock particles by friction during transportation by water, wind, or ice. Compare **abrasion** (sense 3), **corrasion. 4.** *Theol.* sorrow for sin arising from fear of damnation, esp. as contrasted with contrition, which arises purely from love of God. [C14: from Late Latin *attrītiō* a rubbing against something, from Latin *atterere* to weaken, from *terere* to rub] **—at+'tri+tion+al** *adj.* **—at+tri+tive** (ə'traɪtɪv) *adj.*
At·tu ('ætu:) *n.* the westernmost of the Aleutian Islands, off the coast of SW Alaska: largest of the Near Islands.
at+tune (ə'tju:n) *vb.* (*tr.*) **1.** to adjust or accustom (a person or thing); acclimatize. **2.** to tune (a musical instrument).
atty. *abbrev. for* attorney.
A.T.V. (in Britain) *abbrev. for* Associated Television.
a·tween (ə'twi:n) *prep.* an archaic word for **between.**
at. wt. *abbrev. for* atomic weight.
a·typ·i·cal (eɪ'tɪpɪkᵊl) *adj.* not typical; deviating from or not conforming to type. **—a·'typ·i·cal+ly** *adv.*
Au *the chemical symbol for* gold. [from New Latin *aurum*]
A.U. *or* **a.u.** *abbrev. for:* **1.** angstrom unit. **2.** astronomical unit.
au·bade (*French* o'bad) *n.* **1.** a song or poem appropriate to or greeting the dawn. **2.** a romantic or idyllic prelude or overture. ~Compare **serenade.** [C19: from French, from Old Provençal *aubada* (unattested), from *auba* dawn, ultimately from Latin *albus* white]
Aube (*French* o:b) *n.* **1.** a department of N central France, in Champagne-Ardenne region. Capital: Troyes. Pop.: 292 325 (1975). Area: 6026 sq. km (2350 sq. miles). **2.** a river in N central France, flowing northwest to the Seine. Length: about 225 km (140 miles).
au·berge (*French* o'bɛrʒ) *n.* an inn or tavern. [C17: from French, from Old Provençal *alberga,* of Germanic origin; compare Old Saxon *heriberga* army shelter]
au·ber+gine ('əʊbəˌʒi:n) *n.* **1.** a tropical Old World solanaceous plant, *Solanum melongena,* widely cultivated for its egg-shaped typically dark purple fruit. U.S. name: **eggplant. 2.** the fruit of this plant, which is cooked and eaten as a vegetable. **3. a.** a dark purple colour. **b.** (*as adj.*): *an aubergine dress.* [C18: from French, from Catalan *alberginia,* from Arabic *al-bādindjān,* ultimately from Sanskrit *vatin-ganah,* of obscure origin]
Au·ber+vil+liers (*French* obɛrvi'lje) *n.* an industrial suburb of Paris, on the Seine. Pop.: 72 997 (1975). Former name: **No·tre-Dame-des-Ver·tus** (*French* nɔtr dam de vɛr'ty).
Au·brey ('ɔ:brɪ) *n.* **John.** 1626–97, English antiquary and author, noted for his vivid biographies of his contemporaries, *Brief Lives* (edited 1898).
au·brie+tia *or* **au·bre+tia** (ɔ:'bri:ʃə) *n.* any trailing purple-flowered plant of the genus *Aubrietia,* native to European mountains but widely planted in rock gardens: family *Cruciferae* (crucifers). [C19: from New Latin, named after Claude *Aubriet,* 18th-century French painter of flowers and animals]
au·burn ('ɔ:bᵊn) *n.* **a.** a moderate reddish-brown colour. **b.** (*as adj.*): *auburn hair.* [C15 (originally meaning: blond): from Old French *alborne* blond, from Medieval Latin *alburnus* whitish, from Latin *albus* white]
Au·bus+son (*French* oby'sɔ̃) *adj.* denoting or relating to carpets or tapestries of a type made in and near Aubusson in Creuse department, France, esp. flat-woven carpets.
A.U.C. *abbrev. for:* **1.** (indicating years numbered from the founding of Rome, taken as 753 B.C.) **a.** ab urbe condita. **b.** anno urbis conditae. **2.** Australian Universities Commission.
Auck+land ('ɔ:klənd) *n.* the chief port of New Zealand, in the northern part of North Island: former capital of New Zealand (1840–65). Pop.: 152 600 (1974 est.).
Auck+land Is+lands *n.* a group of six uninhabited islands, south of New Zealand. Area: 611 sq. km (234 sq. miles).
au cou+rant *French.* (o ku'rã) *adj.* up-to-date, esp. in knowledge of current affairs. [literally: in the current]
auc+tion ('ɔ:kʃən) *n.* **1.** a public sale of goods or property, esp. one in which prospective purchasers bid against each other until the highest price is reached. Compare **Dutch auction. 2.** the competitive calls made in bridge and other games before play begins, undertaking to win a given number of tricks if a certain suit is trumps. **3.** See **auction bridge.** ~*vb.* **4.** (*tr.;* often foll. by *off*) to sell by auction. [C16: from Latin *auctiō* an increasing, from *augēre* to increase]
auc+tion bridge *n.* a variety of bridge, now generally superseded by contract bridge, in which all the tricks made score towards game.
auc+tion+eer (ˌɔ:kʃə'nɪə) *n.* **1.** a person who conducts an auction by announcing the lots and controlling the bidding. ~*vb.* **2.** (*tr.*) to sell by auction.
auc+to+ri·al (ɔ:k'tɔ:rɪəl) *adj.* of or relating to an author. [C19: from Latin *auctor* AUTHOR]
aud. *abbrev. for:* **1.** audit. **2.** auditor.
au·da+cious (ɔ:'deɪʃəs) *adj.* **1.** recklessly bold or daring; fearless. **2.** impudent or presumptuous. [C16: from Latin *audāx* bold, from *audēre* to dare] **—au·'da+cious+ly** *adv.* **—au·'da+cious+ness** *or* **au·dac+i·ty** (ɔ:'dæsɪtɪ) *n.*
Aude (*French* o:d) *n.* a department of S France on the Gulf of Lions, in Languedoc-Roussillon region. Capital: Carcassonne. Pop.: 279 003 (1975). Area: 6342 sq. km (2473 sq. miles).
Au·den ('ɔ:dᵊn) *n.* **W**(**ystan**) **H**(**ugh**). 1907–73, English poet, dramatist, critic, and librettist, noted for his lyric and satirical poems and for plays written in collaboration with Christopher Isherwood.
au·di·ble ('ɔ:dɪbᵊl) *adj.* perceptible to the hearing; loud enough to be heard. [C16: from Late Latin *audibilis,* from Latin *audīre* to hear] **—ˌau·di·'bil+i·ty** *or* **'au·di·ble+ness** *n.* **—'au·di·bly** *adv.*
au·di+ence ('ɔ:dɪəns) *n.* **1.** a group of spectators or listeners, esp. at a public event such as a concert or play. **2.** the people reached by a book, film, or radio or television programme. **3.** the devotees or followers of a public entertainer, lecturer, etc.; regular public. **4.** an opportunity to put one's point of view, such as a formal interview with a monarch or head of state. [C14: from Old French, from Latin *audientia* a hearing, from *audīre* to hear]
au·dile ('ɔ:dɪl, 'ɔ:daɪl) *Psychol.* ~*n.* **1.** a person who possesses a faculty for auditory imagery that is more distinct than his visual or other imagery. ~*adj.* **2.** of or relating to such a person. [C19: from AUD(ITORY) + -ILE]
au·di·o ('ɔ:dɪˌəʊ) *n.* **1.** (*modifier*) of or relating to sound or hearing: *audio frequency.* **2.** (*modifier*) relating to or employed in the transmission, reception, or reproduction of sound. **3.** (*modifier*) of, concerned with, or operating at audio frequencies. ~Compare **video.** [C20: independent use of AUDIO-]
au·di·o- *combining form.* indicating hearing or sound: *audiometer; audiovisual.* [from Latin *audīre* to hear]
au·di·o fre+quen+cy *n.* a frequency in the range 50 hertz to 20 000 hertz. A sound wave of this frequency would be audible to the human ear.
au·di·o+gen+ic (ˌɔ:dɪəʊ'dʒɛnɪk) *adj.* caused or produced by sound or an audio frequency: *an audiogenic epileptic fit.*
au·di+ol+o·gy (ˌɔ:dɪ'ɒlədʒɪ) *n.* the scientific study of hearing, often including the treatment of persons with hearing defects. **—au·di·o·log·i·cal** (ˌɔ:dɪə'lɒdʒɪkᵊl) *adj.* **—ˌau·di·o+'log·i·cal+ly** *adv.* **—ˌau·di+'ol·o·gist** *n.*
au·di+om+e·ter (ˌɔ:dɪ'ɒmɪtə) *n.* an instrument for testing the intensity and frequency range of sound that is capable of detection by the human ear. **—au·di·o+met+ric** (ˌɔ:dɪəʊ'mɛtrɪk) *adj.* **—ˌau·di·o+'met+ri+cal+ly** *adv.* **—ˌau·di+'om·e·trist** *n.* **—ˌau·di+'om+e·try** *n.*
au·di·o+phile ('ɔ:dɪəʊˌfaɪl) *n.* a person who has a great interest in high-fidelity sound reproduction.
au·di·o+typ·ist ('ɔ:dɪəʊˌtaɪpɪst) *n.* a typist trained to type from a dictating machine. **—'au·di·o+ˌtyp·ing** *n.*

au·di·o+vis·u·al (ˌɔːdɪəʊˈvɪzjʊəl, -ʒʊəl) *adj.* (esp. of teaching aids) involving or directed at both hearing and sight: *the language class had new audiovisual equipment.* —ˌ**au·di·o+ˈvis·u·al+ly** *adv.*

au·di+phone (ˈɔːdɪˌfəʊn) *n.* a type of hearing aid consisting of a diaphragm that, when placed against the upper teeth, conveys sound vibrations to the inner ear.

au·dit (ˈɔːdɪt) *n.* **1. a.** an inspection, correction, and verification of business accounts by a qualified accountant. **b.** (*as modifier*): *audit report.* **2.** *U.S.* an audited account. **3.** *Archaic.* a hearing. ~*vb.* **4.** to inspect, correct, and certify (accounts, etc.). **5.** *U.S.* to attend (classes, etc.) as an auditor. [C15: from Latin *audītus* a hearing, from *audīre* to hear]

au·di+tion (ɔːˈdɪʃən) *n.* **1.** a test at which a performer or musician is asked to demonstrate his ability for a particular role, etc. **2.** the act, sense, or power of hearing. ~*vb.* **3.** to judge by means of or be tested in an audition. [C16: from Latin *audītiō* a hearing, from *audīre* to hear]

au·di+tor (ˈɔːdɪtə) *n.* **1.** a person qualified to audit accounts. **2.** a person who hears or listens. **3.** *U.S.* a registered student who attends a class that is not an official part of his course of study. [C14: from Old French *auditeur,* from Latin *audītor* a hearer] —ˌ**au·di+ˈto+ri+al** *adj.*

au·di+to+ri·um (ɔːdɪˈtɔːrɪəm) *n., pl.* **+to+ri·ums** *or* **+to+ri·a** (-ˈtɔːrɪə). **1.** the area of a concert hall, theatre, etc., in which the audience sits. **2.** *U.S.* a building for public gatherings or meetings. [C17: from Latin: a judicial examination, from *audītōrius* concerning a hearing; see AUDITORY]

au·di+to·ry (ˈɔːdɪtərɪ, -trɪ) *adj. also* **au·di+tive** (ˈɔːdɪtɪv). **1.** of or relating to hearing, the sense of hearing, or the organs of hearing. ~*n.* **2.** an archaic word for **audience** or **auditorium.** [C14: from Latin *audītōrius* relating to hearing, from *audīre* to hear]

Au·du·bon (ˈɔːdəˌbɒn) *n.* **John James.** 1785–1851, U.S. naturalist and artist, noted particularly for his paintings of birds in *Birds of America* (1827–38).

Au·er (*German* ˈauər) *n.* **Karl** (karl), Baron von Welsbach. 1858–1929, Austrian chemist who discovered the cerium-iron alloy used for flints in cigarette lighters and invented the incandescent gas mantle.

A.U.E.W. (in Britain) *abbrev. for* Amalgamated Union of Engineering Workers.

au fait *French.* (o ˈfɛ; *English* əʊ ˈfeɪ) *adj.* fully informed; in touch or expert. [C18: literally: to the point]

Auf+klä+rung *German.* (ˈaufˌklɛːrʊŋ) *n.* the Enlightenment, esp. in Germany.

au fond *French.* (o ˈfɔ̃) *adv.* fundamentally; essentially. [literally: at the bottom]

auf Wie+der+seh+en *German.* (auf ˈviːdərˌzeːən) *interj.* goodbye, until we see each other again.

aug. *abbrev. for* augmentative.

Aug. *abbrev. for* August.

Au·ge·an (ɔːˈdʒiːən) *adj.* extremely dirty or corrupt. [C16: after *Augeas;* see AUGEAN STABLES]

Au·ge·an sta+bles *pl. n. Greek myth.* the stables, not cleaned for 30 years, where King Augeas kept 3000 oxen. Hercules diverted the River Alpheus through them and cleaned them in a day.

au·gend (ˈɔːdʒɛnd, ɔːˈdʒɛnd) *n.* a number to which another number, the addend, is added. [from Latin *augendum* that is to be increased, from *augēre* to increase]

au·ger (ˈɔːgə) *n.* **1.** a hand tool with a bit shaped like a corkscrew, for boring holes in wood. **2.** a larger tool of the same kind for boring holes in the ground. [C15: *an augur,* resulting from mistaken division of earlier *a nauger,* from Old English *nafugār* nave (of a wheel) spear (that is, tool for boring hubs of wheels), from *nafu* NAVE + *gār* spear; see GORE[2]]

Au·ger ef+fect (ˈaugə) *n.* the emission of an electron instead of a photon by an excited ion as a result of a vacancy being filled in an inner electron shell. [C20: named after Pierre *Auger* (born 1899), French physicist]

aught[1] *or* **ought** (ɔːt) (*used with a negative or in conditional or interrogative sentences or clauses*) *Archaic or literary.* ~*pron.* **1.** anything at all; anything whatever (esp. in the phrase **for aught I know**). ~*adv.* **2.** *Brit. dialect.* in any least part; to any degree. [Old English *āwiht,* from *ā* ever, AY[1] + *wiht* thing; see WIGHT[1]]

aught[2] *or* **ought** (ɔːt) *n.* a less common word for **nought** (zero).

au·gite (ˈɔːgaɪt) *n.* a common black or dark green glassy mineral of the pyroxene group that consists of a silicate of calcium, magnesium, aluminium, and iron in monoclinic crystalline form. Formula: (Ca,Mg,Fe,Al)(Si,Al)O_3. [C19: from Latin *augītēs,* from Greek, from *augē* brightness] —**au+git+ic** (ɔːˈgɪtɪk) *adj.*

aug+ment *vb.* (ɔːgˈmɛnt). **1.** to make or become greater in number, amount, strength, etc.; increase. **2.** (*tr.*) *Music.* to increase (a major or perfect interval) by a semitone. Compare **diminish** (sense 3). **3.** (*tr.*) (in Greek and Sanskrit grammar) to prefix a vowel or diphthong to (a verb) to form a past tense. ~*n.* (ˈɔːgmɛnt). **4.** (in Greek and Sanskrit grammar) a vowel or diphthong prefixed to a verb to form a past tense. [C15: from Late Latin *augmentāre* to increase, from *augmentum* growth, from Latin *augēre* to increase] —**aug+ˈment+a·ble** *adj.* —**aug+ˈmen+tor** *or* **aug+ˈment+er** *n.*

aug+men+ta+tion (ˌɔːgmɛnˈteɪʃən) *n.* **1.** the act of augmenting or the state of being augmented. **2.** the amount by which something is increased. **3.** *Music.* the presentation of a subject of a fugue, in which the note values are uniformly increased. Compare **diminution** (sense 2).

aug+ment·a+tive (ɔːgˈmɛntətɪv) *adj.* **1.** tending or able to augment. **2.** *Grammar.* **a.** denoting an affix that may be added to a word to convey the meaning *large* or *great;* for example, the suffix *-ote* in Spanish, where *hombre* means man and *hombrote* big man. **b.** denoting a word formed by the addition of an augmentative affix. ~*n.* **3.** *Grammar.* an augmentative word or affix. ~Compare (for senses 2, 3) **diminutive.** —**aug+ˈment·a+tive+ly** *adv.*

aug+ment+ed (ɔːgˈmɛntɪd) *adj.* **1.** *Music.* (of an interval) increased or expanded from the state of being perfect or major by the raising of the higher note or the dropping of the lower note by one semitone: *C to G is a perfect fifth, but C to G sharp is an augmented fifth.* Compare **diminished** (sense 2). **2.** *Music.* **a.** denoting a chord based upon an augmented triad: *an augmented seventh chord.* **b.** denoting a triad consisting of the root plus a major third and an augmented fifth. **c.** (*postpositive*) (esp. in jazz) denoting a chord having as its root the note specified: *D augmented.* **3.** having been increased, esp. in number: *an augmented orchestra.*

au gra+tin (*French* o graˈtɛ̃) *adj.* covered and cooked with browned breadcrumbs and sometimes cheese. [French, literally: with the grating]

Augs+burg (*German* ˈauksˌburk) *n.* a city in S West Germany, in Bavaria: founded by the Romans in 14 B.C.; site of the diet that produced the **Peace of Augsburg** (1555), which ended the struggles between Lutherans and Catholics in the Holy Roman Empire and established the principle that each ruler should determine the form of worship in his lands. Pop.: 256 908 (1974 est.). Roman name: **Augusta Vindelicorum.**

au·gur (ˈɔːgə) *n.* **1.** Also called: **auspex.** (in ancient Rome) a religious official who observed and interpreted omens and signs to help guide the making of public decisions. **2.** any prophet or soothsayer. ~*vb.* **3.** to predict (some future event), as from signs or omens. **4.** (*tr.; may take a clause as object*) to be an omen (of); presage. **5.** (*intr.*) to foreshadow future events to be as specified; bode: *this augurs well for us.* [C14: from Latin: a diviner, perhaps from *augēre* to increase] —**au·gur+al** (ˈɔːgjʊrəl) *adj.* —ˈ**au·gur+ship** *n.*

au·gu+ry (ˈɔːgjʊrɪ) *n., pl.* **+ries.** **1.** the art of or a rite conducted by an augur. **2.** a sign or portent; omen.

au·gust (ɔːˈgʌst) *adj.* **1.** dignified or imposing: *an august presence.* **2.** of noble birth or high rank: *an august lineage.* [C17: from Latin *augustus;* related to *augēre* to increase] —**au·ˈgust+ly** *adv.* —**au·ˈgust+ness** *n.*

Au·gust (ˈɔːgəst) *n.* the eighth month of the year, consisting of 31 days. [Old English, from Latin, named after the emperor AUGUSTUS]

Au+gus+ta (ɔːˈgʌstə) *n.* a port in S Italy, in E Sicily. Pop.: 44 794 (1971).

Au·gus+tan (ɔːˈgʌstən) *adj.* **1.** characteristic of, denoting, or relating to the Roman emperor Augustus Caesar, his period, or the poets, notably Virgil, Horace, and Ovid, writing during his reign. **2.** of, relating to, or characteristic of any literary period noted for refinement and classicism, esp. the late 17th century in France (the period of the dramatists Corneille, Racine, and Molière) or the 18th century in England (the period of Swift, Pope, and Johnson, much influenced by Dryden). ~*n.* **3.** an author in an Augustan Age. **4.** a student of or specialist in Augustan literature.

Au·gus·tine (ɔːˈgʌstɪn) *n.* **1. Saint.** 354–430 A.D., one of the Fathers of the Christian Church; bishop of Hippo in North Africa (396–430), who profoundly influenced both Catholic and Protestant theology. His most famous works are *Confessions,* a spiritual autobiography, and *De Civitate Dei,* a vindication of the Christian Church. Feast day: Aug. 28. **2. Saint.** died 604 A.D., Roman monk, who converted the English to Christianity; became the first archbishop of Canterbury (601–604). Feast day: May 28. **3.** a member of an Augustinian order.

Au·gus+tin+i·an (ˌɔːgəˈstɪnɪən) *adj.* **1.** of or relating to Saint Augustine of Hippo, his doctrines, or any of the Christian religious orders founded on his doctrines. ~*n.* **2.** a member of any of several religious orders, such as the **Augustinian Canons, Augustinian Hermits,** and **Austin Friars,** which are governed by the rule of Saint Augustine. **3.** a person who follows the doctrines of Saint Augustine.

Au·gus·tus (ɔːˈgʌstəs) *n.* original name *Gaius Octavianus;* after his adoption by Julius Caesar (44 B.C.) known as *Gaius Julius Caesar Octavianus.* 63 B.C.–14 A.D., Roman statesman, a member of the second triumvirate (43 B.C.). After defeating Mark Antony at Actium (31 B.C.), he became first emperor of Rome, adopting the title Augustus (27 B.C.).

au jus (*French* o ˈʒy) *adj.* (of meat) served in its own gravy. [French, literally: with the juice]

auk (ɔːk) *n.* **1.** any of various diving birds of the family *Alcidae* of northern oceans having a heavy body, short tail, narrow wings, and a black-and-white plumage: order *Charadriiformes.* See also **great auk, razorbill.** **2. little auk.** Also called: **dovekie.** a small short-billed auk, *Plautus alle,* abundant in Arctic regions. [C17: from Old Norse *ālka;* related to Swedish *alka,* Danish *alke*]

auk+let (ˈɔːklɪt) *n.* any of various small auks of the genera *Aethia* and *Ptychoramphus.*

au lait (əʊ ˈleɪ; *French* o ˈlɛ) *adj.* prepared or served with milk. [French, literally: with milk]

auld (ɔːld) *adj.* a Scot. word for **old.**

auld lang syne (ˈɔːld læŋ ˈsaɪn, -ˈzaɪn) *n.* old times; times past, esp. those remembered with affection or nostalgia. [Scottish, literally: old long since]

au·lic (ˈɔːlɪk) *adj. Rare.* relating to a royal court. [C18: from

Latin *aulicus,* from Greek *aulikos* belonging to a prince's court, from *aulē* court]
Au·lic Coun·cil *n.* a council, founded in 1498, of the Holy Roman Emperor. It functioned mainly as a judicial body.
Au·lis ('ɔːlɪs) *n.* an ancient town in E central Greece, in Boeotia: traditionally the harbour from which the Greeks sailed at the beginning of the Trojan war.
au na·tu·rel *French.* (o natyˈrɛl) *adj., adv.* **1.** naked; nude. **2.** uncooked or plainly cooked. [literally: in (a) natural (condition)]
aunt (ɑːnt) *n.* (*often cap., esp. as a term of address*) **1.** a sister of one's father or mother. **2.** the wife of one's uncle. **3.** a term of address used by children for any woman, esp. for a friend of the parents. **4. my (sainted) aunt!** an exclamation of surprise or amazement. [C13: from Old French *ante,* from Latin *amita* a father's sister]
aunt·ie *or* **aunt·y** ('ɑːntɪ) *n., pl.* **·ies.** a familiar or diminutive word for **aunt.**
aunt·ie man *n. Caribbean informal.* an effeminate or homosexual male.
Aunt Sal·ly ('sælɪ) *n., pl.* **·lies.** *Brit.* **1.** a figure of an old woman's head, typically with a clay pipe, used in fairgrounds and fêtes as a target for balls or other objects. **2.** any person who is a target for insults or criticism. **3.** something set up as a target for disagreement or attack.
au pair (əʊ 'pɛə; *French* o 'pɛːr) *n.* **1. a.** a young foreigner, usually a girl, who undertakes housework in exchange for board and lodging, esp. in order to learn the language. **b.** (*as modifier*): *an au pair girl.* **2.** a young person who lives temporarily with a family abroad in exchange for a reciprocal arrangement with his or her own family. *~vb.* **3.** (*intr.*) to work as an au pair. *~adv.* **4.** as an au pair: *she worked au pair in Greece.* [C20: from French: on an equal footing]
au·ra ('ɔːrə) *n., pl.* **au·ras** *or* **au·rae** ('ɔːriː). **1.** a distinctive air or quality considered to be characteristic of a person or thing. **2.** any invisible emanation, such as a scent or odour. **3.** *Pathol.* a phenomenon, such as noises in the ears or flashes of light, that immediately precedes an attack, esp. of epilepsy. **4.** (in parapsychology) an invisible emanation produced by and surrounding a person or object: alleged to be discernible by individuals of supernormal sensibility. [C18: via Latin from Greek: breeze]
au·ral[1] ('ɔːrəl) *adj.* of or relating to the sense or organs of hearing; auricular. [C19: from Latin *auris* ear] **—'au·ral·ly** *adv.*
au·ral[2] ('ɔːrəl) *adj.* of or relating to an aura.
Au·rang·zeb *or* **Au·rung·zeb** ('ɔːrəŋˌzɛb) *n.* 1618–1707, Mogul emperor of Hindustan (1658–1707), whose reign marked both the height of Mogul prosperity and the decline of its power through the revolts of the Mahrattas.
au·rar ('ɔːrɑː) *n.* the plural of **eyrir.**
au·re·ate ('ɔːrɪɪt, -ˌeɪt) *adj.* **1.** covered with gold; gilded. **2.** of a golden colour. **3.** (of a style of writing or speaking) excessively elaborate or ornate; florid. [C15: from Late Latin *aureātus* gilded, from Latin *aureus* golden, from *aurum* gold] **—'au·re·ate·ly** *adv.* **—'au·re·ate·ness** *n.*
Au·re·li·an (ɔːˈriːlɪən) *n.* Latin name *Lucius Domitius Aurelianus.* ?212–275 A.D., Roman emperor (270–275), who conquered Palmyra (273) and restored political unity to the Roman Empire.
Au·re·li·us (ɔːˈriːlɪəs) *n.* See **Marcus Aurelius Antoninus.**
au·re·ole ('ɔːrɪˌəʊl) *or* **au·re·o·la** (ɔːˈriːələ) *n.* **1.** (esp. in paintings of Christian saints and the deity) a border of light or radiance enveloping the head or sometimes the whole of a figure represented as holy. **2.** a less common word for **halo. 3.** another name for **corona** (sense 2). [C13: from Old French *auréole,* from Medieval Latin (*corōna*) *aureola* golden (crown), from Latin *aureolus* golden, from *aurum* gold]
Au·re·o·my·cin (ˌɔːrɪəʊˈmaɪsɪn) *n. Trademark.* a brand of **chlortetracycline.**
au·re·us ('ɔːrɪəs) *n., pl.* **au·re·i** ('ɔːrɪˌaɪ). a gold coin of the Roman Empire. [Latin: golden; see AUREATE]
au re·voir *French.* (o rəˈvwaːr) *interj.* goodbye. [literally: to the seeing again]
au·ric ('ɔːrɪk) *adj.* of or containing gold in the trivalent state. [C19: from Latin *aurum* gold]
Au·ric (*French* ɔˈrik) *n.* **Georges** (ʒɔrʒ). born 1899, French composer; one of *les Six.* His works include ballet and film music.
au·ri·cle ('ɔːrɪkᵊl) *n.* **1. a.** the upper chamber of the heart; atrium. **b.** a small sac in the atrium of the heart. **2.** Also called: **pinna.** *Anat.* the external part of the ear. **3.** Also called: **auricula.** *Biology.* an ear-shaped part or appendage, such as that occurring at the base of some leaves. [C17: from Latin *auricula* the external ear, from *auris* ear] **—'au·ri·cled** *adj.*
au·ric·u·la (ɔːˈrɪkjʊlə) *n., pl.* **·lae** (-ˌliː) *or* **·las. 1.** Also called: **bear's-ear.** a widely cultivated alpine primrose, *Primula auricula,* with leaves shaped like a bear's ear. **2.** another word for **auricle** (sense 3). [C17: from New Latin, from Latin: external ear; see AURICLE]
au·ric·u·lar (ɔːˈrɪkjʊlə) *adj.* **1.** of, relating to, or received by the sense or organs of hearing; aural. **2.** shaped like an ear. **3.** of or relating to an auricle of the heart. **4.** (of feathers) occurring in tufts surrounding the ears of owls and similar birds. *~n.* **5.** (*usually pl.*) an auricular feather. **—au'ric·u·lar·ly** *adv.*
au·ric·u·late (ɔːˈrɪkjʊlɪt, -ˌleɪt) *or* **au·ric·u·lat·ed** *adj.* **1.** having ears. **2.** *Botany.* having ear-shaped parts or appendages. **3.** Also: **au·ri·form** ('ɔːrɪˌfɔːm). shaped like an ear; auricular. **—au'ric·u·late·ly** *adv.*

au·rif·er·ous (ɔːˈrɪfərəs) *adj.* (of rock) containing gold; gold-bearing. [C18: from Latin *aurifer* gold-bearing, from *aurum* gold + *ferre* to bear]
Au·ri·ga (ɔːˈraɪgə) *n., Latin genitive* **Au·ri·gae** (ɔːˈraɪdʒiː). a conspicuous constellation in the N hemisphere between the Great Bear and Orion, at the edge of the Milky Way. It contains the first magnitude star Capella and the binary star **Epsilon Aurigae,** which is the largest known star. [Latin: charioteer]
Au·rig·na·cian (ˌɔːrɪgˈneɪʃən) *adj.* of, relating to, or produced during a flint culture of the Upper Palaeolithic type characterized by the use of bone and antler tools, pins, awls, etc., and also by cave art and evidence of the beginnings of religion. [C20: from French *Aurignacien,* after *Aurignac,* France, in the Pyrenees, near which is the cave where remains were discovered]
Au·riol (*French* ɔˈrjɔl) *n.* **Vin·cent** (vɛ̃ˈsɑ̃). 1884–1966, French statesman; president of the Fourth Republic (1947–54).
au·rist ('ɔːrɪst) *n.* an ear specialist.
au·rochs ('ɔːrɒks) *n., pl.* **·rochs.** a recently extinct member of the cattle tribe, *Bos primigenius,* that inhabited forests in N Africa, Europe, and SW Asia. It had long horns and is thought to be one of the ancestors of modern cattle. Also called: **urus.** [C18: from German, from Old High German *ūrohso,* from *ūro* bison + *ohso* OX]
au·ro·ra (ɔːˈrɔːrə) *n., pl.* **·ras** *or* **·rae** (-riː). **1.** an atmospheric phenomenon consisting of bands, curtains, or streamers of light, usually green, red, or yellow, that move across the sky, esp. in polar regions. It is caused by collisions between air molecules and charged particles from the sun that are trapped in the earth's magnetic field. **2.** *Poetic.* the dawn. [C14: from Latin: dawn; see EAST] **—au'ro·ral** *adj.* **—au'ro·ral·ly** *adv.*
Au·ro·ra[1] (ɔːˈrɔːrə) *n.* **1.** the Roman goddess of the dawn. Greek counterpart: **Eos. 2.** the dawn or rise of something.
Au·ro·ra[2] (ɔːˈrɔːrə) *n.* another name for **Maewo.**
au·ro·ra aus·tra·lis (ɒˈstreɪlɪs) *n.* (*sometimes cap.*) the aurora seen around the South Pole. Also called: **southern lights.** [New Latin: southern aurora]
au·ro·ra bo·re·al·is (ˌbɔːrɪˈeɪlɪs) *n.* (*sometimes cap.*) the aurora seen around the North Pole. Also called: **northern lights.** [C17: New Latin: northern aurora]
aur·ous ('ɔːrəs) *adj.* of or containing gold, esp. in the monovalent state. [C19: apparently from French *aureux,* from Late Latin *aurōsus* gold-coloured, from Latin *aurum* gold]
au·rum ('ɔːrəm) *n. Obsolete.* gold. [C16: Latin: gold]
AUS *international car registration for* Australia.
Aus. *abbrev. for:* **1.** Australia(n). **2.** Austria(n).
Ausch·witz ('aʊʃvɪts) *n.* the German name for **Oświęcim.**
aus·cul·tate ('ɔːskəlˌteɪt) *vb.* to examine (a patient) by means of auscultation. **—'aus·cul·ˌta·tor** *n.*
aus·cul·ta·tion (ˌɔːskəlˈteɪʃən) *n.* **1.** the diagnostic technique in medicine of listening to the various internal sounds made by the body, usually with the aid of a stethoscope. **2.** the act of listening. [C19: from Latin *auscultātiō* a listening, from *auscultāre* to listen attentively; related to Latin *auris* ear] **—aus·cul·ta·to·ry** (ɔːˈskʌltətərɪ) *or* **aus·cul·ta·tive** (ɔːˈskʌltətɪv, ˈɔːskəlˌteɪtɪv) *adj.*
aus·form·ing ('aʊsˌfɔːmɪŋ) *n.* a treatment to strengthen hard steels, prior to quenching, in which the specimen is plastically deformed while it is in the austenite temperature range. [C20: from AUS(TENITIC) + (DE)FORM]
Aus·gleich *German.* ('aʊsglaɪç) *n.* the agreement (1867) that established the Dual Monarchy of Austria-Hungary. [German: levelling out, from *aus* OUT + *gleichen* to be similar]
Au·so·ni·us (ɔːˈsəʊnɪəs) *n.* **Dec·i·mus Mag·nus** ('dɛsɪməs 'mægnəs). ?310–?395 A.D., Latin poet, born in Gaul.
aus·pex ('ɔːspɛks) *n., pl.* **aus·pi·ces** ('ɔːspɪˌsiːz). *Roman history.* another word for **augur** (sense 1). [C16: from Latin: observer of birds, from *avis* bird + *specere* to look]
aus·pi·cate ('ɔːspɪˌkeɪt) *vb.* (*tr.*) *Archaic.* to begin.
aus·pice ('ɔːspɪs) *n., pl.* **·pic·es** (-pɪsɪz). **1.** (*usually pl.*) patronage or guidance (esp. in the phrase **under the auspices of**). **2.** (*often pl.*) a sign or omen, esp. one that is favourable. [C16: from Latin *auspicium* augury from birds; see AUSPEX]
aus·pi·cious (ɔːˈspɪʃəs) *adj.* **1.** favourable or propitious. **2.** *Archaic.* prosperous or fortunate. **—aus'pi·cious·ly** *adv.* **—aus'pi·cious·ness** *n.*
Aus·sie ('ɒzɪ) *n.* an informal word for **Australian** or (rare) **Australia.**
Aust. *abbrev. for:* **1.** Australia(n). **2.** Austria(n).
Aus·ten ('ɒstɪn, 'ɔː-) *n.* **Jane.** 1775–1817, English novelist, noted particularly for the insight and delicate irony of her portrayal of middle-class families. Her completed novels are *Sense and Sensibility* (1811), *Pride and Prejudice* (1813), *Mansfield Park* (1814), *Emma* (1816), *Northanger Abbey* (1818), and *Persuasion* (1818).
aus·ten·ite ('ɔːstəˌnaɪt) *n.* **1.** a solid solution of carbon in face-centred cubic gamma iron, usually existing above 723°C. **2.** the gamma phase of iron, stabilized at low temperatures by the addition of such elements as nickel. [C20: named after Sir William C. Roberts-Austen (1843–1902), English metallurgist] **—aus·ten·it·ic** (ˌɔːstəˈnɪtɪk) *adj.*
aus·ten·it·ic stain·less steel *n.* an alloy of iron, usually containing 18 per cent of nickel and 8 per cent of chromium, used where corrosion resistance, heat resistance, or nonmagnetic properties are required.
Aus·ter ('ɔːstə) *n. Poetic.* the south wind.
aus·tere (ɒˈstɪə) *adj.* **1.** stern or severe in attitude or manner: *an austere schoolmaster.* **2.** grave, sober, or serious: *an austere expression.* **3.** self-disciplined, abstemious, or ascetic: *an*

austere life. **4.** severely simple or plain: *an austere design.* [C14: from Old French *austère,* from Latin *austērus* sour, from Greek *austēros* astringent; related to Greek *hauein* to dry] —**aus+'tere+ly** *adv.* —**aus+'tere+ness** *n.*

aus+ter+i·ty (ɒ'stɛrɪtɪ) *n., pl.* **·ties. 1.** the state or quality of being austere. **2.** (*often pl.*) an austere habit, practice, or act. **3. a.** reduced availability of luxuries and consumer goods, esp. when brought about by government policy. **b.** (*as modifier*): *an austerity budget.*

Aus+ter+litz ('ɔ:stəlɪts) *n.* a town in central Czechoslovakia, in Moravia: site of Napoleon's victory over the Russian and Austrian armies in 1805. Pop.: 4747 (1972 est.). Czech name: **Slavkov.**

Aus+tin[1] ('ɒstɪn) *n.* a city in central Texas, on the Colorado River: state capital since 1845. Pop.: 291 214 (1973 est.).

Aus·tin[2] ('ɒstɪn, 'ɔ:-) *n.* **John.** 1790–1859, English jurist, whose book *The Province of Jurisprudence Determined* (1832) greatly influenced legal theory and the English legal system.

aus+tral ('ɔ:strəl) *adj.* of or coming from the south: *austral winds.* [C14: from Latin *austrālis,* from *auster* the south wind]

Austral. *abbrev. for:* **1.** Australasia. **2.** Australia(n).

Aus+tral+a·sia (ˌɒstrə'leɪzɪə) *n.* **1.** Australia, New Zealand, and neighbouring islands in the S Pacific Ocean. **2.** (loosely) the whole of Oceania. —ˌ**Aus+tral+'a·si·an** *adj., n.*

Aus+tral·i·a (ɒ'streɪlɪə) *n.* the smallest continent and largest island in the world, situated between the Indian Ocean and the Pacific: a former British colony, now an independent member of the Commonwealth; consists chiefly of a low plateau, mostly arid in the west, with the basin of the Murray River and the Great Dividing Range in the east and the Great Barrier Reef off the NE coast. Language: English. Currency: dollar. Capital: Canberra. Pop.: 13 546 200 (1976). Area: 7 686 845 sq. km (2 967 894 sq. miles).

Aus+tral·i·a Day *n.* a public holiday in Australia, commemorating the landing of the British in 1788: observed on the first Monday after January 26.

Aus+tral+i·an (ɒ'streɪlɪən) *n.* **1.** a native or inhabitant of Australia. **2.** the form of English spoken in Australia. **3.** a linguistic phylum consisting of the languages spoken by the Aborigines of Australia. ~*adj.* **4.** of, relating to, or characteristic of Australia, the Australians, or their form of English. **5.** of, relating to, or belonging to the phylum of languages spoken by the Australian Aborigines. **6.** of or denoting a zoogeographical region consisting of Australia, New Zealand, Polynesia, New Guinea, and the Moluccas.

Aus+tral+i·a+na (ɒˌstreɪlɪ'ɑ:nə) *n.* objects, such as books, relics, etc., considered to be typical of Australia, esp. in the form of a collection.

Aus+tral+i·an Alps *n.* a mountain range in SE Australia, in E Victoria and SE New South Wales. Highest peak: Mount Kosciusko, 2195 m (7316 ft.).

Aus+tral+i·an Ant+arc+tic Ter+ri+to·ry *n.* the area of Antarctica, other than Adélie Land, that is administered by Australia, lying south of latitude 60°S and between longitudes 45°E and 160°E.

Aus+tral+i·an Cap·i·tal Ter+ri+to·ry *n.* a territory of SE Australia, within New South Wales: consists of two exclaves, one containing Canberra, the capital of Australia, and one at Jervis Bay. Pop.: 197 600 (1976). Area: 2432 sq. km (939 sq. miles). Former name: **Federal Capital Territory.**

Aus+tral·i+an+ism (ɒ'streɪlɪəˌnɪzəm) *n.* **1.** the Australian national character or spirit. **2.** loyalty to Australia, its political independence, culture, etc. **3.** a linguistic usage, custom, or other feature peculiar to or characteristic of Australia, its people, or their culture.

Aus+tral·i+an+ize *or* **Aus+tral·i+an+ise** (ɒ'streɪlɪəˌnaɪz) *vb.* (esp. of a new immigrant) to adopt or cause to adopt Australian habits and attitudes; integrate into Australian society.

Aus+tral+i·an Rules *n.* (*functioning as sing.*) a game resembling rugby football, played in Australia between teams of 18 men each on an oval pitch, with a ball resembling a large rugby ball. Players attempt to kick the ball between posts (without crossbars) at either end of the pitch, scoring six points for a goal (between the two main posts) and one point for a behind (between either of two outer posts and the main posts). They may punch or kick the ball and run with it provided that they bounce it every ten yards. Also called: **national code.**

Aus+tral+i·an ter+ri+er *n.* a small wire-haired breed of terrier similar to the cairn.

Aus+tral Is+lands ('ɔ:strəl) *pl. n.* another name for the **Tubuai Islands.**

aus+tra+lite ('ɒstrəˌlaɪt) *n.* a small piece of dark glassy meteorite found in Australia.

Aus+tra+loid ('ɒstrəˌlɔɪd) *adj.* **1.** denoting, relating to, or belonging to a racial group that includes the Australian Aborigines and certain other peoples of southern Asia and the Pacific islands, characterized by dark skin, flat retreating forehead, and medium stature. ~*n.* **2.** any member of this racial group.

aus+tra+lo·pith·e·cine (ˌɒstrələʊ'pɪθɪˌsi:n) *n.* **1.** any of various extinct apelike primates of the genus *Australopithecus* and related genera, remains of which have been discovered in southern and E Africa. Some species are estimated to be over 4.5 million years old. See also **zinjanthropus.** ~*adj.* **2.** of or relating to any of these primates. [C20: from New Latin *Australopithecus,* from Latin *austrālis* southern, AUSTRAL + Greek *pithēkos* ape]

Aus+tral+orp ('ɒstrəˌlɔ:p) *n.* a heavy black breed of domestic fowl laying brown eggs. [shortened from *Austral(ian Black) Orp(ington)*]

Aus+tra+sia (ɒ'streɪʒə, -ʃə) *n.* the eastern region of the kingdom of the Merovingian Franks that had its capital at Metz and lasted from 511 A.D. until 814 A.D. It covered the area now comprising NE France, Belgium, and western Germany.

Aus+tri·a ('ɒstrɪə) *n.* a republic in central Europe: ruled by the Hapsburgs from 1282 to 1918; formed a dual monarchy with Hungary in 1867 and became a republic in 1919; contains part of the Alps, the Danube basin in the east, and extensive forests. Language: German. Religion: chiefly Roman Catholic. Currency: schilling. Capital: Vienna. Pop.: 7 545 000 (1974 est.). Area: 83 849 sq. km (32 374 sq. miles). German name: **Österreich.** —**'Aus+tri·an** *adj., n.*

Aus·tri·a-Hun·ga·ry *n.* the Dual Monarchy established in 1867, consisting of what are now Austria, Hungary, Czechoslovakia, and parts of Poland, Rumania, Yugoslavia, the Ukraine, and Italy. The empire was broken up after World War I. —ˌ**Aus·tro-Hun·'gar+i·an** *adj.*

Aus·tro-[1] ('ɒstrəʊ-) *combining form.* southern: *Austro-Asiatic.* [from Latin *auster* the south wind]

Aus·tro-[2] ('ɒstrəʊ-) *combining form.* Austrian: *Austro-Hungarian.*

Aus·tro-As·i·at·ic *n.* a hypothetical phylum or superfamily of languages that would consist of Malayo-Polynesian together with Mon-Khmer, certain Indian languages, Papuan, etc.

Aus+tro+ne·sia (ˌɒstrəʊ'ni:ʒə, -ʃə) *n.* the islands of the central and S Pacific, including Indonesia, Melanesia, Micronesia, and Polynesia.

Aus+tro+ne·sian (ˌɒstrəʊ'ni:ʒən, -ʃən) *adj.* **1.** of or relating to Austronesia, its peoples, or their languages. ~*n.* **2.** another name for **Malayo-Polynesian.**

aut- *combining form.* variant of **auto-** before a vowel.

au·ta·coid ('ɔ:təˌkɔɪd) *n. Physiol.* any natural internal secretion, esp. one that exerts an effect similar to a drug. [C20: from AUTO- + Greek *akos* cure + -OID]

au·tar+chy ('ɔ:tɑ:kɪ) *n., pl.* **+chies. 1.** unlimited rule; autocracy. **2.** self-government; self-rule. [C17: from Greek *autarkhia,* from *autarkhos* autocratic; see AUTO-, -ARCHY] —**au·'tar+chic** *or* **au·'tar+chi+cal** *adj.*

au·tar+ky *or* **au·tar+chy** ('ɔ:tɑ:kɪ) *n., pl.* **+kies** *or* **+chies. 1.** (esp. of a political unit) a system or policy of economic self-sufficiency aimed at removing the need for imports. **2.** an economically self-sufficient country. [C17: from Greek *autarkeia,* from *autarkēs* self-sufficient, from AUTO- + *arkein* to suffice] —**au·'tar+kic** *or* **au·'tar+chic** *adj.* —**'au·tar+kist** *n.*

au·te·cious (ɔ:'ti:ʃəs) *adj.* a variant spelling of **autoecious.**

aut+e·col·o·gy (ˌɔ:tɪ'kɒlədʒɪ) *n.* the ecological study of an individual organism or species. Compare **synecology.** —ˌ**aut+ec·o·'log·i·cal** *adj.*

au·teur (ɔ:'tɜ:) *n.* a film director, esp. one considered as having a dominant creative role. [French: author]

auth. *abbrev. for:* **1.** author. **2.** authority. **3.** authorized.

au·then+tic (ɔ:'θɛntɪk) *adj.* **1.** of undisputed origin or authorship; genuine: *an authentic signature.* **2.** accurate in representation of the facts; trustworthy; reliable: *an authentic account.* **3.** (of a deed or other document) duly executed, any necessary legal formalities having been complied with. **4.** *Music.* **a.** (of a mode as used in Gregorian chant) commencing on the final and ending an octave higher. **b.** (of a cadence) progressing from a dominant to a tonic chord. Compare **plagal.** [C14: from Late Latin *authenticus* coming from the author, from Greek *authentikos,* from *authentēs* one who acts independently, from AUTO- + *hentēs* a doer] —**au·'then+ti·cal+ly** *adv.* —**au+then+tic·i·ty** (ˌɔ:θɛn'tɪsɪtɪ) *n.*

au·then+ti·cate (ɔ:'θɛntɪˌkeɪt) *vb.* (*tr.*) **1.** to establish as genuine or valid. **2.** to give authority or legal validity to. —**au·ˌthen+ti·'ca+tion** *n.* —**au+'then+ti·ˌca+tor** *n.*

au·thor ('ɔ:θə) *or* (*fem.*) **au·thor+ess** *n.* **1.** a person who composes a book, article, or other written work. Related adj.: **auctorial. 2.** a person who writes books as a profession; writer. **3.** the writings of such a person: *reviewing a postwar author.* **4.** an originator or creator: *the author of this plan.* ~*vb. Not standard.* **5.** to write or originate. [C14: from Old French *autor,* from Latin *auctor* author, from *augēre* to increase] —**au+tho+ri·al** (ɔ:'θɔ:rɪəl) *adj.*

au·thor·i·tar·i·an (ɔ:ˌθɒrɪ'tɛərɪən) *adj.* **1.** favouring, denoting, or characterized by strict obedience to authority. **2.** favouring, denoting, or relating to government by a small elite with wide powers. **3.** despotic; dictatorial; domineering. ~*n.* **4.** a person who favours or practises authoritarian policies. —**au·ˌthor·i+'tar·i·an+ism** *n.*

au·thor·i·ta·tive (ɔ:'θɒrɪtətɪv) *adj.* **1.** recognized or accepted as being true or reliable: *an authoritative article on drugs.* **2.** exercising or asserting authority; commanding: *an authoritative manner.* **3.** possessing or supported by authority; official: *an authoritative communiqué.*—**au·'thor·i+ta+tive+ly** —**au·'thor·i+ta+tive+ness** *n.*

au·thor+i·ty (ɔ:'θɒrɪtɪ) *n., pl.* **·ties. 1.** the power or right to control, judge, or prohibit the actions of others. **2.** (*often pl.*) a person or group of people having this power, such as a government, police force, etc. **3.** a position that commands such a power or right (often in the phrase **in authority**). **4.** such a power or right delegated, esp. from one person to another; authorization: *she has his authority.* **5.** the ability to influence or control others: *a man of authority.* **6.** an expert or an authoritative written work in a particular field: *he is an authority on Ming china.* **7.** evidence or testimony: *we have it on his authority that she is dead.* **8.** confidence resulting from great expertise: *the violinist lacked authority in his cadenza.* **9.** (*cap. when part of a name*) a public board or corporation exercising governmental authority in administering some enterprise: *Independent Broadcasting Authority.* **10.** *Law.* **a.** a judicial decision, statute, or rule of law that establishes a principle; precedent. **b.** legal permission granted to a person to perform a specified act.

au·thor+ize *or* **au·thor+ise** ('ɔ:θə,raɪz) *vb.* (*tr.*) **1.** to confer authority upon (someone to do something); empower. **2.** to permit (someone to do or be something) with official sanction: *a dealer authorized by a manufacturer to retail his products.* —**,au·thor·i+'za+tion** *or* **,au·thor·i+'sa+tion** *n.* —**'au·thor+,iz+er** *or* **'au·thor+,is+er** *n.*

Au·thor+ized Ver+sion *n.* **the.** an English translation of the Bible published in 1611 under James I. Also called: **King James Version, King James Bible.**

au·thor+ship ('ɔ:θə,ʃɪp) *n.* **1.** the origin or originator of a written work, plan, etc.: *a book of unknown authorship.* **2.** the profession of writing books.

Auth. Ver. *abbrev. for* Authorized Version (of the Bible).

au·tism ('ɔ:tɪzəm) *n. Psychiatry.* abnormal self-absorption, usually affecting children, characterized by lack of response to people and actions and limited ability to communicate: children suffering from autism often do not learn to speak. —**au·tis+tic** *adj.*

au·to ('ɔ:təʊ) *n., pl.* **·tos.** *U.S. informal.* **a.** short for **automobile. b.** (*as modifier*): *auto parts.*

auto. *abbrev. for:* **1.** automatic. **2.** automobile. **3.** automotive.

au·to- *or sometimes before a vowel* **aut-** *combining form.* **1.** self; same; of or by the same one: *autobiography.* **2.** acting from or occurring within; self-caused: *autohypnosis.* **3.** self-propelling; automatic: *automobile.* [from Greek *autos* self]

au·to+an·ti+bod·y (,ɔ:təʊ'æntɪ,bɒdɪ) *n., pl.* **+bod·ies.** an antibody reacting with an antigen that is a part of the organism in which the antibody is formed.

au·to+bahn ('ɔ:tə,bɑ:n) *n.* a German motorway.

au·to+bi·o·graph·i·cal (,ɔ:tə,baɪə'græfɪkᵊl) *adj.* **1.** of or concerned with one's own life. **2.** of or relating to an autobiography. —**,au·to+,bi·o+'graph·i·cal+ly** *adv.*

au·to+bi+og+ra+phy (,ɔ:təʊbaɪ'ɒgrəfɪ, ,ɔ:tə-) *n., pl.* **+phies.** an account of a person's life written or otherwise recorded by that person. —**,au·to+bi+'og+ra+pher** *n.*

au·to+cade ('ɔ:təʊ,keɪd) *n. U.S.* another name for **motorcade.**

au·to+ca+tal·y+sis (,ɔ:təʊkə'tælɪsɪs) *n., pl.* **+ses** (-,si:z). the catalysis of a chemical reaction in which the catalyst is one of the products of the reaction.

au·to+ceph·a+lous (,ɔ:təʊ'sɛfələs) *adj.* **1.** (of an Eastern Christian Church) governed by its own national synods and appointing its own patriarchs or prelates. **2.** (of a bishop) independent of any higher governing body. —**au·to+ce·phal+ic** (,ɔ:təʊsɪ'fælɪk) *adj.* —**,au·to+'ceph·a+ly** *n.*

au·to+chang+er ('ɔ:təʊ,tʃeɪndʒə) *n.* **1.** a device in a record player that enables a small stack of records to be dropped automatically onto the turntable one at a time and played separately. **2.** a record player with such a device.

au·toch+thon (ɔ:'tɒkθən, -θɒn) *n., pl.* **+thons** *or* **+tho+nes** (-θə,ni:z). **1.** (*often pl.*) one of the earliest known inhabitants of any country; aboriginal. **2.** an animal or plant that is native to a particular region. [C17: from Greek *autokhthōn* from the earth itself, from AUTO- + *khthōn* the earth]

au·toch+tho+nous (ɔ:'tɒkθənəs), **au·toch+thon+ic** (,ɔ:tɒk'θɒnɪk), *or* **au·toch+tho+nal** *adj.* **1.** (of rocks, deposits, etc.) found where they and their constituents were formed. Compare **allochthonous. 2.** inhabiting a place or region from earliest known times; aboriginal. —**au·'toch+thon+ism** *or* **au·'toch+tho+ny** *n.* —**au·'toch+tho+nous+ly** *adv.*

au·to+clave ('ɔ:tə,kleɪv) *n.* **1.** a strong sealed vessel used for chemical reactions at high pressure. **2.** an apparatus for sterilizing objects (esp. surgical instruments) or for cooking by means of steam under pressure. ~*vb.* **3.** (*tr.*) to put in or subject to the action of an autoclave. [C19: from French AUTO- + *-clave,* from Latin *clāvis* key]

au·to+cor+re+la+tion (,ɔ:təʊ,kɒrɪ'leɪʃən) *n. Statistics.* the condition occurring when successive items in a series are correlated so that their covariance is not zero and they are not independent. Also called: **serial correlation.**

au·toc+ra+cy (ɔ:'tɒkrəsɪ) *n., pl.* **+cies. 1.** government by an individual with unrestricted authority. **2.** the unrestricted authority of such an individual. **3.** a country, society, etc., ruled by an autocrat.

au·to+crat ('ɔ:tə,kræt) *n.* **1.** a ruler who possesses absolute and unrestricted authority. **2.** a domineering or dictatorial person. —**,au·to+'crat+ic** *adj.* —**,au·to+'crat·i+cal+ly** *adv.*

au·to+cross ('ɔ:təʊ,krɒs) *n.* a form of motor sport in which cars race over a half-mile circuit of rough grass. See also **motocross, rallycross.**

au·to+cue ('ɔ:təʊ,kju:) *n.* an electronic television prompting device whereby a prepared script, unseen by the audience, is enlarged line by line for the speaker. U.S. name (trademark): **Teleprompter.**

au·to+cy+cle ('ɔ:təʊ,saɪkᵊl) *n. Obsolete.* a bicycle powered or assisted by a small engine.

au·to-da-fé (,ɔ:təʊdə'feɪ) *n., pl.* **au·tos-da-fé. 1.** *History.* a ceremony of the Spanish Inquisition including the pronouncement and execution of sentences passed on sinners or heretics. **2.** the burning to death of people condemned as heretics by the Inquisition. [C18: from Portuguese, literally: act of the faith]

au·to+di+dact ('ɔ:təʊ,daɪdækt) *n.* a person who is self-taught. —**,au·to+di+'dact+ic** *adj.*

au·to+dyne re+cep+tion ('ɔ:tə,daɪn) *n.* reception of radio signals by a superheterodyne receiver in which the circuit generating the beating oscillation also performs other functions such as amplification or detection.

au·toe+cious *or U.S.* (*sometimes*) **au·te+cious** (ɔ:'ti:ʃəs) *adj.* (of parasites, esp. the rust fungi) completing the entire life cycle on a single species of host. Compare **heteroecious.** —**au·'toe+cism** *or U.S.* (*sometimes*) **au·'te+cism** *n.*

au·to+e·rot·i+cism (,ɔ:təʊɪ'rɒtɪ,sɪzəm) *or* **au·to+er·o+tism** (,ɔ:təʊ'ɛrə,tɪzəm) *n. Psychol.* the arousal and use of one's own body as a sexual object, as through masturbation. —**,au·to+e·'rot+ic** *adj.*

au·tog·a+my (ɔ:'tɒgəmɪ) *n.* **1.** self-fertilization in flowering plants. **2.** a type of sexual reproduction, occurring in some protozoans, in which the uniting gametes are derived from the same cell. —**au·'tog·a+mous** *or* **au·to+gam+ic** (,ɔ:tə'gæmɪk) *adj.*

au·to+gen+e·sis (,ɔ:təʊ'dʒɛnɪsɪs) *or* **au·tog+e·ny** (ɔ:'tɒdʒɪnɪ) *n.* another word for **abiogenesis.** —**au·to+ge·net+ic** (,ɔ:təʊdʒɪ'nɛtɪk) *adj.*

au·tog+e·nous (ɔ:'tɒdʒɪnəs) *adj.* **1. a.** originating within the body. Compare **heterogenous. b.** denoting a vaccine made from bacteria obtained from the patient's own body. **2.** self-generated; self-produced. **3.** (of a joint between two parts) achieved without flux, adhesive, or solder: *autogenous welding.* —**au·'tog+e·nous+ly** *adv.*

au·to+gi+ro *or* **au·to+gy+ro** (,ɔ:təʊ'dʒaɪ,rəʊ) *n., pl.* **+ros.** a self-propelled aircraft supported in flight mainly by unpowered rotating horizontal blades. Also called: **gyroplane.** Compare **helicopter.** [C20: originally a trademark]

au·to+graft ('ɔ:tə,grɑ:ft) *n. Surgery.* a tissue graft obtained from one part of a patient's body for use on another part.

au·to+graph ('ɔ:tə,grɑ:f) *n.* **1. a.** a handwritten signature, esp. that of a famous person. **b.** (*as modifier*): *an autograph album.* **2.** a person's handwriting. **3. a.** a book, document, etc., handwritten by its author; original manuscript; holograph. **b.** (*as modifier*) : *an autograph letter.* ~*vb.* **4.** (*tr.*) to write one's signature on or in; sign. **5.** to write with one's own hand. —**au·to+graph+ic** (,ɔ:tə'græfɪk) *or* **,au·to+'graph·i+cal** *adj.* —**,au·to+'graph·i+cal+ly** *adv.*

au·tog+ra+phy (ɔ:'tɒgrəfɪ) *n.* **1.** the writing of something in one's own handwriting; something handwritten. **2.** the precise reproduction of an illustration or of writing.

Au·to+harp ('ɔ:təʊ,hɑ:p) *n. Trademark.* a zither-like musical instrument used in country-and-western music, equipped with button-controlled dampers that can prevent selected strings from sounding, thus allowing chords to be played. It is plucked with the fingers or a plectrum.

au·to+hyp+no+sis (,ɔ:təʊhɪp'nəʊsɪs) *n. Psychol.* the process or result of self-induced hypnosis. —**au·to+hyp+not+ic** (,ɔ:təʊhɪp'nɒtɪk) *adj.* —**,au·to+hyp+'not·i+cal+ly** *adv.*

au·toi+cous (ɔ:'tɔɪkəs) *adj.* (of plants, esp. mosses) having male and female reproductive organs on the same plant. [C19: from AUTO- + Greek *oikos* dwelling]

au·to+im+mune (,ɔ:təʊɪ'mju:n) *adj.* (of a disease) caused by the action of antibodies produced against substances normally present in the body. —**,au·to+im+'mun+i+ty** *n.*

au·to+in·fec+tion (,ɔ:təʊɪn'fɛkʃən) *n.* infection by a pathogenic agent already within the body or infection transferred from one part of the body to another.

au·to+in·oc·u+la+tion (,ɔ:təʊɪ,nɒkjʊ'leɪʃən) *n.* the inoculation of microorganisms (esp. viruses) from one part of the body into another, usually in the form of a vaccine.

au·to+in·tox·i+ca+tion (,ɔ:təʊɪn,tɒksɪ'keɪʃən) *n.* self-poisoning caused by absorption of toxic products originating within the body. Also called: **autotoxaemia.**

au·to+i·on·i+za+tion *or* **au·to+i·on·i+sa+tion** (,ɔ:təʊ,aɪənaɪ'zeɪʃən) *n. Physics.* the process in which the decay of excited atoms or molecules results in emission of electrons, rather than photons.

au·to+ki+net+ic (,ɔ:təʊkɪ'nɛtɪk, -kaɪ-) *adj.* automatically self-moving.

au·to+ki+net+ic phe+nom+en+on *n. Psychol.* the apparent movement of a fixed point of light when observed in a darkened room. The effect is produced by small eye movements for which the brain is unable to compensate, having no other reference points.

au·to+load+ing ('ɔ:təʊ,ləʊdɪŋ) *adj.* self-loading.

Au·tol·y·cus[1] (ɔ:'tɒlɪkəs) *n.* a crater in the NW quadrant of the moon about 38 kilometres in diameter and 3000 metres deep.

Au·tol·y·cus[2] (ɔ:'tɒlɪkəs) *n. Greek myth.* a thief who stole cattle from his neighbour Sisyphus and prevented him from recognizing them by making them invisible.

au·to+lyse *or U.S.* **au·to+lyze** ('ɔ:tə,laɪz) *vb. Biochem.* to undergo or cause to undergo autolysis.

au·to+ly+sin (,ɔ:tə'laɪsɪn, ɔ:'tɒlɪ-) *n.* any agent that produces autolysis.

au·tol·y+sis (ɔ:'tɒlɪsɪs) *n.* the destruction of cells and tissues of an organism by enzymes produced by the cells themselves. —**au·to+lyt+ic** (,ɔ:tə'lɪtɪk) *adj.*

au·to+mat ('ɔ:tə,mæt) *n.* **1.** Also called: **vending machine.** a machine that automatically dispenses goods such as cigarettes, when money is inserted. **2.** *Chiefly U.S.* an area or room, sometimes having restaurant facilities, where food and other goods are supplied from vending machines.

au·tom·a·ta (ɔ:'tɒmətə) *n.* a plural of **automaton.**

au·to+mate ('ɔ:tə,meɪt) *vb.* to make (a manufacturing process, factory, etc.) automatic, or (of a manufacturing process, etc.) to be made automatic.

au·to·mat·ic (ˌɔːtəˈmætɪk) *adj.* **1.** performed from force of habit or without conscious thought; lacking spontaneity; mechanical: *an automatic smile.* **2. a.** (of a device, mechanism, etc.) able to activate, move, or regulate itself. **b.** (of an act or process) performed by such automatic equipment. **3.** (of the action of a muscle, gland, etc.) involuntary or reflex. **4.** occurring as a necessary consequence: *promotion is automatic after a year.* **5.** (of a firearm) utilizing some of the force of each explosion to eject the empty shell, replace it with a new one, and fire continuously until release of the trigger. Compare **semiautomatic** (sense 2). ~*n.* **6.** an automatic firearm. **7.** a motor vehicle having automatic transmission. **8.** a machine that operates automatically. [C18: from Greek *automatos* acting independently; see AUTOMATON] —ˌ**au·to·ˈmat·i·cal·ly** *adv.* —**au·to·ma·tic·i·ty** (ˌɔːtəʊməˈtɪsɪtɪ) *n.*

au·to·mat·ic da·ta pro·ces·sing *n.* data processing performed by automatic electromechanical devices. Abbrevs.: **A.D.P., ADP, a.d.p.** Compare **electronic data processing.**

au·to·mat·ic gain con·trol *n.* control of a radio receiver in which the gain varies inversely with the magnitude of the input, thus maintaining the output at an approximately constant level. Abbrev.: **AGC.**

au·to·mat·ic pi·lot *n.* a device that automatically maintains an aircraft on a preset course. Also called: **autopilot.**

au·to·mat·ic trans·mis·sion *n.* a transmission system in a motor vehicle, usually incorporating a fluid clutch, in which the gears change automatically.

au·to·mat·ic type·set·ting *n.* another name for **computer typesetting.**

au·to·ma·tion (ˌɔːtəˈmeɪʃən) *n.* **1.** the use of methods for controlling industrial processes automatically, esp. by electronically controlled systems, often reducing manpower. **2.** the extent to which a process is so controlled.

au·tom·a·tism (ɔːˈtɒməˌtɪzəm) *n.* **1.** the state or quality of being automatic; mechanical or involuntary action. **2.** *Philosophy.* the theory that all the activities of men and animals are controlled by unconscious physical and physiological processes. **3.** *Psychol.* the performance of actions such as sleepwalking, without conscious knowledge or control. **4.** the suspension of consciousness sought or achieved by certain artists and writers to allow free flow of uncensored thoughts. —**au·ˈtom·a·tist** *n.*

au·tom·a·tize *or* **au·tom·a·tise** (ɔːˈtɒməˌtaɪz) *vb.* to make (a process, etc.) automatic or (of a process, etc.) to be made automatic. —**au·ˌtom·a·ti·ˈza·tion** *or* **au·ˌtom·a·ti·ˈsa·tion** *n.*

au·tom·a·ton (ɔːˈtɒməˌtɒn, -tᵊn) *n., pl.* **-tons** *or* **-ta** (-tə). **1.** a mechanical device operating under its own hidden power; robot. **2.** a person who acts mechanically or leads a routine monotonous life. [C17: from Latin, from Greek, from *automatos* spontaneous] —**au·ˈtom·a·tous** *adj.*

au·to·mo·bile (ˈɔːtəməˌbiːl) *n. Formal.* a car (sense 1). —**au·to·mo·bil·ist** (ˌɔːtəməˈbiːlɪst, -ˈməʊbɪlɪst) *n.*

au·to·mo·tive (ˌɔːtəˈməʊtɪv) *adj.* **1.** relating to motor vehicles. **2.** self-propelling.

au·to·nom·ic (ˌɔːtəˈnɒmɪk) *adj.* **1.** occurring involuntarily or spontaneously. **2.** of or relating to the autonomic nervous system. **3.** Also: **autonomous.** (of plant movements) occurring as a result of internal stimuli. —ˌ**au·to·ˈnom·i·cal·ly** *adv.*

au·to·nom·ic nerv·ous sys·tem *n.* the section of the nervous system of vertebrates that controls the involuntary actions of the smooth muscles, heart, and glands.

au·ton·o·mous (ɔːˈtɒnəməs) *adj.* **1.** (of a community, country, etc.) possessing a large degree of self-government. **2.** of or relating to an autonomous community. **3.** independent of others. **4.** *Philosophy.* governed by its own principles. **5.** *Biol.* existing as an organism independent of other organisms or parts. **6.** a variant spelling of **autonomic** (sense 3). [C19: from Greek *autonomos* living under one's own laws, from AUTO- + *nomos* law] —**au·ˈton·o·mous·ly** *adv.*

au·ton·o·my (ɔːˈtɒnəmɪ) *n., pl.* **-mies. 1.** the right or state of self-government, esp. when limited. **2.** a state, community, or individual possessing autonomy. **3.** freedom to determine one's own actions, behaviour, etc. **4.** *Philosophy.* the doctrine that the individual human will is governed only by its own principles and laws. [C17: from Greek *automomia* freedom to live by one's own laws; see AUTONOMOUS] —**au·ˈton·o·mist** *n.*

au·to·phyte (ˈɔːtəˌfaɪt) *n.* an autotrophic plant, such as any green plant. —**au·to·phyt·ic** (ˌɔːtəˈfɪtɪk) *adj.* —ˌ**au·to·ˈphyt·i·cal·ly** *adv.*

au·to·pi·lot (ˌɔːtəˈpaɪlət, -təʊ-) *n.* short for **automatic pilot.**

au·to·pis·ta (ˌɔːtəˈpiːstə) *n.* a Spanish motorway. [from Spanish: auto(mobile) track]

au·to·plas·ty (ˈɔːtəˌplæstɪ) *n.* surgical repair of defects by grafting or transplanting tissue from the patient's own body. —ˌ**au·to·ˈplas·tic** *adj.*

au·top·sy (ɔːˈtɒpsɪ, ˈɔːtəp-) *n., pl.* **-sies. 1.** Also called: **necropsy, postmortem examination.** dissection and examination of a dead body to determine the cause of death. **2.** an eye witness observation. **3.** any critical analysis. [C17: from New Latin *autopsia*, from Greek: seeing with one's own eyes, from AUTO- + *opsis* sight]

au·to·put (ˈɔːtəʊˌpʊt) *n.* a Yugoslavian motorway. [from Serbo-Croat: auto(mobile) road]

au·to·ra·di·o·graph (ˌɔːtəʊˈreɪdɪəˌgrɑːf, -ˌgræf) *n.* a photograph showing the distribution of a radioactive substance in a specimen. The photographic plate is exposed by radiation from the specimen. Also called: **radioautograph.** —**au·to·ra·di·o·graph·ic** (ˌɔːtəʊˌreɪdɪəˈgræfɪk) *adj.* —**au·to·ra·di·og·ra·phy** (ˌɔːtəʊˌreɪdɪˈɒgrəfɪ) *n.*

au·to-rick·shaw (ˈɔːtəʊˈrɪkʃɔː) *n.* (in India) a light three-wheeled vehicle driven by a motorcycle engine.

au·to·ro·ta·tion (ˌɔːtəʊrəʊˈteɪʃən) *n.* the continuous rotation of a symmetrical body in an airflow, such as that of the rotor blades of a helicopter in an unpowered descent.

au·to·route (ˈɔːtəʊˌruːt) *n.* a French motorway.

au·to·some (ˈɔːtəˌsəʊm) *n.* any chromosome that is not a sex chromosome. —ˌ**au·to·ˈso·mal** *adj.*

au·to·sta·bil·i·ty (ˌɔːtəʊstəˈbɪlɪtɪ) *n.* the property of being stable either as a result of inherent characteristics or of built-in devices.

au·to·stra·da (ˈɔːtəʊˌstrɑːdə) *n.* an Italian motorway.

au·to·sug·ges·tion (ˌɔːtəʊsəˈdʒestʃən) *n.* a process of suggestion in which the person unconsciously supplies or consciously attempts to supply the means of influencing his own behaviour or beliefs. —ˌ**au·to·sug·ˈges·tive** *adj.*

au·to·tim·er (ˈɔːtəʊˌtaɪmə) *n.* a device for turning an electric cooker on and off automatically at times predetermined by advance setting.

au·tot·o·mize *or* **au·tot·o·mise** (ɔːˈtɒtəˌmaɪz) *vb.* to cause (a part of the body) to undergo autotomy.

au·tot·o·my (ɔːˈtɒtəmɪ) *n., pl.* **-mies.** the casting off by an animal of a part of its body, to facilitate escape when attacked. —**au·to·tom·ic** (ˌɔːtəˈtɒmɪk) *adj.*

au·to·tox·ae·mi·a *or U.S.* **au·to·tox·e·mi·a** (ˌɔːtəʊtɒkˈsiːmɪə) *n.* another name for **autointoxication.**

au·to·tox·in (ˌɔːtəˈtɒksɪn) *n.* any poison or toxin formed in the organism upon which it acts. See **autointoxication.** —ˌ**au·to·ˈtox·ic** *adj.*

au·to·trans·form·er (ˌɔːtəʊtrænsˈfɔːmə) *n.* a transformer in which all or part of the winding is common to both primary and secondary circuits.

au·to·troph·ic (ˌɔːtəˈtrɒfɪk) *adj.* (of organisms such as green plants) capable of manufacturing complex organic nutritive compounds from simple inorganic sources such as carbon dioxide, water, and nitrates. Compare **heterotrophic.**

au·to·type (ˈɔːtəˌtaɪp) *n.* **1.** a photographic process for producing prints in black and white, using a carbon pigment. **2.** an exact copy of a manuscript, etc.; facsimile. —**au·to·typ·ic** (ˌɔːtəˈtɪpɪk) *adj.* —ˈ**au·to·ˌtyp·y** *n.*

au·tox·i·da·tion (ɔːˌtɒksɪˈdeɪʃən) *n. Chem.* **a.** oxidation by exposure to atmospheric oxygen. **b.** oxidation that will only occur when another oxidation reaction is taking place in the same system.

au·tumn (ˈɔːtəm) *n.* **1.** (*sometimes cap.*) **a.** Also called (esp. U.S.): **fall.** the season of the year between summer and winter, astronomically from the September equinox to the December solstice in the N hemisphere and from the March equinox to the June solstice in the S hemisphere. **b.** (*as modifier*): *autumn leaves.* **2.** a period of late maturity, esp. one followed by a decline. [C14: from Latin *autumnus*, perhaps of Etruscan origin]

au·tum·nal (ɔːˈtʌmnᵊl) *adj.* of, occurring in, or characteristic of autumn. —**au·ˈtum·nal·ly** *adv.*

au·tum·nal e·qui·nox *n.* **1.** the time at which the sun crosses the plane of the equator away from the relevant hemisphere, making day and night of equal length. It occurs about Sept. 23 in the N hemisphere (March 21 in the S hemisphere) **2.** *Astronomy.* the point on the celestial sphere, lying in the constellation of Virgo, at which the ecliptic intersects the celestial equator.

au·tumn cro·cus *n.* a liliaceous plant, *Colchicum autumnale,* of Europe and N Africa having pink or purplish autumn flowers. Also called: **meadow saffron.** Compare **saffron.**

au·tun·ite (ˈɔːtəˌnaɪt) *n.* a yellowish fluorescent radioactive mineral consisting of a hydrated calcium uranium phosphate in tetragonal crystalline form. It is found in uranium ores. Formula: $Ca(UO_2)_2(PO_4)_2.10\text{–}12H_2O$.

Au·vergne (əʊˈvɛən, əʊˈvɜːn; *French* oˈvɛrɲ) *n.* a region of S central France: largely mountainous, rising over 1800 m (6000 ft.).

aux. *abbrev. for* auxiliary.

aux·a·nom·e·ter (ˌɔːksəˈnɒmɪtə) *n.* an instrument that measures the linear growth of plant shoots. [C19: from Greek *auxanein* to increase + -METER]

Aux Cayes (əʊ ˈkeɪ; *French* o ˈkaj) *n.* the former name of **Les Cayes.**

aux·e·sis (ɔːgˈziːsɪs, ɔːkˈsiː-) *n.* growth in animal or plant tissues resulting from an increase in cell size without cell division. [C16: via Latin from Greek: increase, from *auxein* to increase, grow]

aux·il·ia·ries (ɔːgˈzɪljərɪz, -ˈzɪlə-) *pl. n.* foreign troops serving another nation; mercenaries.

aux·il·ia·ry (ɔːgˈzɪljərɪ, -ˈzɪlə-) *adj.* **1.** secondary or supplementary. **2.** supporting. **3.** *Nautical.* (of a sailing vessel) having an engine: *an auxiliary sloop.* ~*n., pl.* **-ries. 4.** a person or thing that supports or supplements; subordinate or assistant. **5.** *Nautical.* **a.** a sailing vessel with an engine. **b.** the engine of such a vessel. **6.** *Navy.* a vessel such as a tug, hospital ship, etc., not used for combat. [C17: from Latin *auxiliārius* bringing aid, from *auxilium* help, from *augēre* to increase, enlarge, strengthen]

aux·il·ia·ry note *n. Music.* a nonharmonic note occurring between two harmonic notes.

aux·il·ia·ry pow·er u·nit *n.* an additional engine fitted to an aircraft to operate when the main engines are not in use.

aux·il·ia·ry verb *n.* a verb used to indicate the tense, voice, mood, etc., of another verb where this is not indicated by inflection, such as English *will* in *he will go, was* in *he was eating* and *he was eaten, do* in *I do like you,* etc.

aux+in ('ɔ:ksɪn) *n.* any of various plant hormones, such as indoleacetic acid, that promote growth and control fruit and flower development. Synthetic auxins are widely used in agriculture and horticulture. [C20: from Greek *auxein* to grow]

aux·o·chrome ('ɔ:ksəˌkrəʊm) *n.* a group of atoms that can be attached to a chromogen to convert it into a dye.

Av (æv) *n. Hebrew.* a variant spelling of **Ab.**

av. *abbrev. for:* **1.** average. **2.** avoirdupois.

Av. *or* **av.** *abbrev. for* avenue.

a.v. *or* **A/V** *abbrev. for* ad valorem.

A.V. *abbrev. for* Authorized Version (of the Bible).

a-v, A-V, *or* **AV** *abbrev. for* audiovisual.

av·a+da+vat (ˌævədə'væt) *or* **am·a+da+vat** (ˌæmədə'væt) *n.* either of two Asian weaverbirds of the genus *Estrilda,* esp. *E. amandava,* having a red plumage: often kept as cage birds. [C18: from *Ahmadabad,* Indian city from which these birds were brought to Europe]

a·vail (ə'veɪl) *vb.* **1.** to be of use, advantage, profit, or assistance (to). **2. avail oneself of.** to make use of to one's advantage. ~*n.* **3.** use or advantage (esp. in the phrases **of no avail, to little avail**). [C13 *availen,* from *vailen,* from Old French *valoir,* from Latin *valēre* to be strong, prevail] —**a·'vail+ing+ly** *adv.*

a·vail+a·ble (ə'veɪləbᵊl) *adj.* **1.** obtainable or accessible; capable of being made use of; at hand. **2.** *U.S. politics, derogatory.* suitable for public office, usually as a result of having an inoffensive character: *Smith was a particularly available candidate.* **3.** *Archaic.* advantageous. —**a·ˌvail+a·'bil+i·ty** *or* **a·'vail+a·ble+ness** *n.* —**a·'vail+a·bly** *adv.*

av·a+lanche ('ævəˌlɑ:ntʃ) *n.* **1. a.** a fall of large masses of snow and ice down a mountain. **b.** a fall of rocks, sand, etc. **2.** a sudden or overwhelming appearance of a large quantity of things: *an avalanche of letters.* **3.** *Physics.* a group of ions produced by a single ion as a result of a collision with some other form of matter. ~*vb.* **4.** to come down overwhelmingly (upon). [C18: from French, by mistaken division from *la valanche,* from *valanche,* from (northwestern Alps) dialect *lavantse;* related to Old Provençal *lavanca,* of obscure origin]

Av·a+lon ('ævəˌlɒn) *n. Celtic myth.* an island paradise in the western seas: in Arthurian legend it is where King Arthur was taken after he was mortally wounded. [from Medieval Latin *insula avallonis* island of Avalon, from Old Welsh *aballon* apple]

Av·a+lon Pen+in+su+la *n.* a large peninsula of Newfoundland, between Trinity and Placentia Bays. Area: about 10 000 sq. km (4000 sq. miles).

a·vant-garde (ˌævɒŋ'gɑ:d; *French* avɑ̃'gard) *n.* **1.** those artists, writers, musicians, etc., whose techniques and ideas are markedly experimental or in advance of those generally accepted. ~*adj.* **2.** of such artists, etc., their ideas, or techniques. **3.** radical; daring. [from French: VANGUARD] —**ˌa·vant-'gard·ism** *n.* —**ˌa·vant-'gard·ist** *n.*

A·var ('eɪvɑ:, 'ævɑ:) *n.* a member of a people of unknown origin in E Europe from the sixth to the early 9th century A.D.: crushed by Charlemagne around 800.

av·a+rice ('ævərɪs) *n.* extreme greed for riches; cupidity. [C13: from Old French, from Latin *avaritia,* from *avārus* covetous, from *avēre* to crave] —**ˌav·a·'ri+cious** *adj.* —**ˌav·a·'ri+cious+ly** *adv.*

a·vast (ə'vɑ:st) *interj. Nautical.* stop! cease! [C17: perhaps from Dutch *hou'vast* hold fast]

av·a+tar ('ævəˌtɑ:) *n.* **1.** *Hinduism.* the manifestation of a deity, notably Vishnu, in human, superhuman, or animal form. **2.** a visible manifestation or embodiment of an abstract concept; archetype. [C18: from Sanskrit *avatāra* a going down, from *avatarati* he descends, from *ava* down + *tarati* he passes over]

a·vaunt (ə'vɔ:nt) *interj. Archaic.* go away! depart! [C15: from Old French *avant!* forward! from Late Latin *ab ante* forward, from Latin *ab* from + *ante* before]

avdp. *abbrev. for* avoirdupois.

a·ve ('ɑ:vɪ, 'ɑ:veɪ) *interj.* welcome or farewell. [Latin]

A·ve ('ɑ:vɪ) *n. R.C. Church.* **1.** short for **Ave Maria. 2.** the time for the Angelus to be recited, so called because of the threefold repetition of the Ave Maria in this devotion. **3.** the beads of the rosary used to count the number of Ave Marias said. [C13: from Latin: hail!]

Ave. *or* **ave.** *abbrev. for* avenue.

Ave+bur·y ('eɪvbərɪ) *n.* a village in Wiltshire, near Stonehenge: site of an extensive neolithic stone circle.

A·vei+ro (*Portuguese* ə'vəiru) *n.* a port in N central Portugal, on the **Aveiro lagoon:** ancient Roman town; linked by canal with the Atlantic Ocean. Pop.: 51 709 (1970). Ancient name: **Talabriga.**

A·ve+lla+ne+da (*Spanish* aˌveja'neda) *n.* a city in E Argentina, an industrial suburb of Buenos Aires. Pop.: 329 626 (1960).

A·ve Ma+ri·a (mə'ri:ə) *n. R.C. Church.* a prayer to the Virgin Mary, based on the salutations of the angel Gabriel (Luke 1:28) and Elisabeth (Luke 1:42) to her; Hail Mary. [C14: from Medieval Latin: hail, Mary!]

a·venge (ə'vɛndʒ) *vb.* (*usually tr.*) to inflict a punishment in retaliation for (harm, injury, etc.) done to (a person or persons); take revenge for or on behalf of: *to avenge a crime; to avenge a murdered friend.* [C14: from Old French *avengier,* from *vengier,* from Latin *vindicāre;* see VENGEANCE, VINDICATE] —**a·'veng+er** *n.*

av+ens ('ævɪnz) *n., pl.* **+ens.** (*functioning as sing.*) **1.** any of several temperate or arctic rosaceous plants of the genus *Geum,* such as *G. rivale* **(water avens),** which has a purple calyx and orange-pink flowers. See also **herb bennet. 2. mountain avens.** a trailing evergreen white-flowered rosaceous shrub, *Dryas octopetala,* that grows on mountains in N temperate regions. [C15: from Old French *avence,* from Medieval Latin *avencia* variety of clover]

Av+en+tine ('ævɪnˌtaɪn, -tɪn) *n.* one of the seven hills on which Rome was built.

a·ven+tu+rine, a·ven+tu+rin (ə'vɛntjʊrɪn), *or* **a·van+tu+rine** (ə'væntjʊrɪn) *n.* **1.** a dark-coloured glass, usually green or brown, spangled with fine particles of gold, copper, or some other metal. **2.** Also called: **sunstone.** a light-coloured translucent variety of orthoclase feldspar containing reddish-gold particles of iron compounds. **3.** a variety of quartz containing red or greenish particles of iron oxide or mica: a gemstone. [C19: from French, from Italian *avventurina,* from *avventura* chance; so named because usually found by accident; see ADVENTURE]

av+e·nue ('ævɪˌnju:) *n.* **1. a.** a broad street, often lined with trees. **b.** (*cap. as part of a street name*) a road, esp. in a built-up area: *Shaftesbury Avenue.* **2.** a main approach road, as to a country house. **3.** a way bordered by two rows of trees: *an avenue of oaks.* **4.** a line of approach: *explore every avenue.* [C17: from French, from *avenir* to come to, from Latin *advenīre,* from *venīre* to come]

a·ver (ə'vɜ:) *vb.* **a·vers, a·ver+ring, a·verred.** (*tr.*) **1.** to state positively; assert. **2.** *Law.* to allege as a fact or prove to be true. [C14: from Old French *averer,* from Medieval Latin *adverāre,* from Latin *vērus* true] —**a·'ver+ment** *n.*

av+er+age ('ævərɪdʒ, 'avrɪdʒ) *n.* **1.** the typical or normal amount, quality, degree, etc.: *above average in intelligence.* **2.** Also called: **arithmetic mean.** the result obtained by adding the numbers or quantities in a set and dividing the total by the number of members in the set: *the average of 3, 4, and 8 is 5.* **3.** (of a continuously variable ratio, such as speed) the quotient of the differences between the initial and final values of the two quantities that make up the ratio: *his average over the journey was 30 miles per hour.* **4.** *Maritime law.* **a.** a loss incurred or damage suffered by a ship or its cargo at sea. **b.** the equitable apportionment of such loss among the interested parties. **5.** (*often pl.*) *Stock exchange.* a simple or weighted average of the prices of a selected group of securities computed in order to facilitate market comparisons. **6. on (the** *or* **an) average.** usually; typically: *on average, he goes twice a week.* ~*adj.* **7.** usual or typical. **8.** mediocre or inferior: *his performance was only average.* **9.** constituting a numerical average: *the average age; an average speed.* **10.** approximately typical of a range of values: *the average contents of a matchbox.* ~*vb.* **11.** (*tr.*) to obtain or estimate a numerical average of. **12.** (*tr.*) to assess the general quality of. **13.** (*tr.*) to perform or receive a typical number of: *to average eight hours work a day.* **14.** (*tr.*) to divide up proportionately: *they averaged the profits among the staff.* **15.** (*intr.*) to amount to or be on average: *the children averaged 15 years of age.* **16.** (*intr.*) *Stock exchange.* to purchase additional securities in a holding whose price has fallen **(average down)** or risen **(average up)** in anticipation of a speculative profit after further increases in price. [C15: *averay* loss arising from damage to ships or cargoes (shared equitably among all concerned, hence the modern sense), from Old Italian *avaria,* ultimately from Arabic *awār* damage, blemish] —**'av+er+age+ly** *adv.*

av+er+age de+vi·a+tion *n. Statistics.* another name for **mean deviation.**

A·ver+no (*Italian* a'vɛrno) *n.* a crater lake in Italy, near Naples: in ancient times regarded as an entrance to hell. Latin name: **A·ver+nus** (ə'vɜ:nəs). [from Latin, from Greek *aornos* without birds, from A-^{1} + *ornis* bird; referring to the legend that the lake's sulphurous exhalations killed birds]

A·ver·ro·ës (ə'vɛrəʊˌi:z) *n.* Arabic name *ibn-Rushd.* 1126–88, Arab philosopher and physician in Spain, noted particularly for his attempts to reconcile Aristotelian philosophy with Islamic religion, which profoundly influenced Christian scholasticism.

Av+er+ro+ism (ˌævə'rəʊɪzəm, ə'vɛrəʊ-) *n.* the teachings of Averroës. —**ˌAv+er+'ro+ist** *n.* —**ˌAv+er+ro+'is+tic** *adj.*

a·verse (ə'vɜ:s) *adj.* **1.** (*postpositive;* usually foll. by *to*) opposed, disinclined, or loath. **2.** (of leaves, flowers, etc.) turned away from the main stem. Compare **adverse** (sense 4). [C16: from Latin *āversus,* from *āvertere* to turn from, from *vertere* to turn] —**a·'verse+ly** *adv.* —**a·'verse+ness** *n.*

Usage. *To* is the preposition now normally used with *averse* (*he was averse to giving any assistance*), although *from* is often used with *averse* and *aversion* and was at one time considered to be grammatically correct.

a·ver+sion (ə'vɜ:ʃən) *n.* **1.** (usually foll. by *to* or *for*) extreme dislike or disinclination; repugnance. **2.** a person or thing that arouses this: *he is my pet aversion.*

a·ver+sion ther·a·py *n. Psychiatry.* a method of suppressing an undesirable habit, such as excessive smoking, by causing the subject to associate an unpleasant effect, such as an electric shock or nausea, with the habit, etc.

a·ver+sive (ə'vɜ:sɪv) *adj.* tending to dissuade or repel. —**a·'ver+sive+ly** *adv.*

a·vert (ə'vɜ:t) *vb.* (*tr.*) **1.** to turn away or aside: *to avert one's gaze.* **2.** to ward off; prevent from occurring: *to avert danger.* [C15: from Old French *avertir,* from Latin *āvertere;* see AVERSE] —**a·'vert+i·ble** *or* **a·'vert+a·ble** *adj.*

A·ves ('eɪvi:z) *pl. n.* the class of vertebrates comprising the birds. See **bird**^{1} (sense 1). [pl. of Latin *avis* bird]

A·ves+ta (ə'vɛstə) *n.* a collection of sacred writings of Zoroastrianism, including the Songs of Zoroaster.

A·ves+tan (ə'vɛstən) *or* **A·ves+tic** (ə'vɛstɪk) *n.* **1.** the oldest recorded language of the Iranian branch of the Indo-European family; the language of the Avesta. Formerly called: **Zend.** ~*adj.* **2.** of or relating to the Avesta or its language.

A·vey·ron (*French* avɛ'rɔ̃) *n.* a department of S France in Midi-Pyrenees region. Capital: Rodez. Pop.: 289 352 (1975). Area: 8771 sq. km (3421 sq. miles).

avg. *abbrev. for* average.

a·vi·an ('eɪvɪən) *adj.* of, relating to, or resembling a bird. [C19: from Latin *avis* bird]

a·viar·y ('eɪvjərɪ) *n., pl.* **a·viar·ies.** a large enclosure in which birds are kept. [C16: from Latin *aviārium*, from *aviārius* concerning birds, from *avis* bird]

a·vi·ate ('eɪvɪˌeɪt) *vb.* to pilot or fly in an aircraft.

a·vi·a·tion (ˌeɪvɪ'eɪʃən) *n.* **1. a.** the art or science of flying aircraft. **b.** the design, production, and maintenance of aircraft. **2.** *U.S.* military aircraft collectively. [C19: from French, from Latin *avis* bird]

a·vi·a·tion med·i·cine *n.* the branch of medicine concerned with the effects on man of flight in the earth's atmosphere. Compare **space medicine.**

a·vi·a·tor ('eɪvɪˌeɪtə) *n. Old-fashioned.* the pilot of an aeroplane or airship; flier. —'**a·vi·ˌa·trix** *or* '**a·vi·ˌa·tress** *fem. n.*

Av·i·cen·na (ˌævɪ'sɛnə) *n.* Arabic name *ibn-Sina.* 980–1037, Arab philosopher and physician whose philosophical writings, which combined Aristotelianism with neo-Platonist ideas, greatly influenced scholasticism, and whose medical work *Qanun* was the greatest single influence on medieval medicine.

a·vi·cul·ture ('eɪvɪˌkʌltʃə) *n.* the keeping and rearing of birds. —ˌ**a·vi·'cul·tur·ist** *n.*

av·id ('ævɪd) *adj.* **1.** very keen; enthusiastic: *an avid reader.* **2.** (*postpositive*; often foll. by *for* or *of*) eager (for); desirous (of); greedy (for): *avid for revenge.* [C18: from Latin *avidus*, from *avēre* to long for; compare AVARICIOUS] —'**av·id·ly** *adv.* —**a·vid·i·ty** (ə'vɪdɪtɪ) *or* '**av·id·ness** *n.*

av·i·din ('ævɪdɪn, ə'vɪdɪn) *n.* a protein, found in egg-white, that combines with biotin to form a stable compound that cannot be absorbed, leading to a biotin deficiency in the consumer. [C20: from AVID + (BIOT)IN; from its characteristic avidity for biotin]

A·vie·more (ˌævɪ'mɔː) *n.* a winter sports resort in Scotland, in the Cairngorm Mountains.

a·vi·fau·na (ˌeɪvɪ'fɔːnə) *n.* all the birds in a particular region. —ˌ**a·vi·'fau·nal** *adj.*

A·vi·gnon (*French* avi'ɲɔ̃) *n.* a city in SE France, on the Rhône: seat of the papacy (1309–77); famous 12th-century bridge, now partly destroyed. Pop.: 93 024 (1975).

Á·vi·la (*Spanish* 'aβila) *n.* a city in central Spain: 11th-century granite walls and Romanesque cathedral. Pop.: 30 983 (1970).

a·vi·on·ics (ˌeɪvɪ'ɒnɪks) *n.* (*functioning as sing.*) the science and technology of electronics applied to aeronautics and astronautics. [C20: from *avi(ation electr)onics*] —ˌ**a·vi·'on·ic** *adj.*

a·vir·u·lent (æ'vɪrʊlənt) *adj.* (esp. of bacteria) not virulent.

a·vit·a·min·o·sis (æˌvɪtəmɪn'əʊsɪs, ˌævɪˌtæmɪ'nəʊsɪs) *n., pl.* **-ses** (-siːz). any disease caused by a vitamin deficiency in the diet.

av·i·zan·dum (ˌævɪ'zændəm) *n. Scot. law.* a private consideration by a judge. [from Medieval Latin, from *avizare* to consider; see ADVISE]

Av·lo·na (æv'ləʊnə) *n.* the ancient name for **Vlorë.**

A.V.M. (in Britain) *abbrev. for* Air Vice-Marshal.

avn. *abbrev. for* aviation.

av·o·ca·do (ˌævə'kɑːdəʊ) *n., pl.* **·dos. 1.** a tropical American lauraceous tree, *Persea americana*, cultivated for its fruit. **2.** the pear-shaped fruit of this tree, having a leathery green or blackish skin, a large stony seed, and a greenish-yellow edible pulp. ~Also called: **avocado pear, alligator pear.** [C17: from Spanish *aguacate*, from Nahuatl *ahuacatl* testicle, alluding to the shape of the fruit]

av·o·ca·tion (ˌævə'keɪʃən) *n. Archaic.* **1.** a minor occupation undertaken as a diversion. **2.** a person's regular job or vocation. [C17: from Latin *āvocātiō* a calling away, diversion from, from *āvocāre* to distract, from *vocāre* to call]

av·o·cet *or* **av·o·set** ('ævəˌsɛt) *n.* any of several long-legged shore birds of the genus *Recurvirostra*, such as the European *R. avosetta*, having black-and-white plumage and a long slender upward-curving bill: family *Recurvirostridae*, order *Charadriiformes.* [C18: from French *avocette*, from Italian *avocetta*, of uncertain origin]

A·vo·ga·dro (ˌævə'gɑːdrəʊ; *Italian* ˌavo'gaːdro) *n.* **A·me·de·o** (ˌame'dɛːo), *Conte di Quaregna.* 1776–1856, Italian physicist, noted for his work on gases.

A·vo·ga·dro con·stant *or* **num·ber** *n.* the number of atoms or molecules in a mole of a substance, equal to 6.022 52 × 10^{23} per mole. Symbol: *L* or N_A.

A·vo·ga·dro's law *or* **hy·poth·e·sis** *n.* the principle that equal volumes of all gases contain the same number of molecules at the same temperature and pressure.

a·void (ə'vɔɪd) *vb.* (*tr.*) **1.** to keep out of the way of. **2.** to refrain from doing. **3.** to not allow to happen: *to avoid damage to machinery.* **4.** *Law.* to make (a plea, contract, etc.) void; invalidate; quash. **5.** *Obsolete.* to expel. **6.** *Obsolete.* to depart from. [C14: from Anglo-French *avoider*, from Old French *esvuidier*, from *vuidier* to empty, VOID] —**a·'void·a·ble** *adj.* —**a·'void·a·bly** *adv.* —**a·'void·er** *n.*

a·void·ance (ə'vɔɪdəns) *n.* **1.** the act of keeping away from or preventing from happening. **2.** *Law.* **a.** the act of annulling or making void. **b.** the countering of an opponent's plea with fresh evidence. **3.** *Ecclesiastical law.* the state of a benefice having no incumbent.

avoir. *abbrev. for* avoirdupois.

av·oir·du·pois *or* **av·oir·du·pois weight** (ˌævədə'pɔɪz, ˌævwɑːdjuː'pwɑː) *n.* a system of weights used in many English-speaking countries. It is based on the pound, which contains 16 ounces or 7000 grains. 100 pounds (U.S.) or 112 pounds (Brit.) is equal to 1 hundredweight and 20 hundredweights equals 1 ton. [C14: from Old French *aver de peis* goods of weight]

A·von[1] ('eɪvᵊn) *n.* **1.** (since 1974) a county of SW England, comprising areas that were formerly parts of N Somerset and Gloucestershire. Administrative centre: Bristol. Pop.: 920 200 (1976 est.). Area: 1336 sq. km (516 sq. miles). **2.** a river in central England, rising in Northamptonshire and flowing southwest through Stratford-upon-Avon to the River Severn at Tewkesbury. Length: 154 km (96 miles). **3.** a river in SW England, rising in Gloucestershire and flowing south and west through Bristol to the Severn estuary at **Avonmouth.** Length: 120 km (75 miles). **4.** a river in S England, rising in Wiltshire and flowing south to the English Channel. Length: about 96 km (60 miles).

A·von[2] ('eɪvᵊn) *n.* **Earl of.** title of (Anthony) **Eden.**

a·vouch (ə'vaʊtʃ) *vb.* (*tr.*) *Archaic.* **1.** to vouch for; guarantee. **2.** to acknowledge. **3.** to assert. [C16: from Old French *avochier* to summon, call on, from Latin *advocāre*; see ADVOCATE] —**a·'vouch·ment** *n.*

a·vow (ə'vaʊ) *vb.* (*tr.*) **1.** to state or affirm. **2.** to admit openly. **3.** *Law, rare.* to justify or maintain (some action taken). [C13: from Old French *avouer* to confess, from Latin *advocāre* to appeal to, call upon; see AVOUCH, ADVOCATE] —**a·'vow·a·ble** *adj.* —**a·'vow·al** *n.* —**a·vowed** (ə'vaʊd) *adj.* —**a·vow·ed·ly** (ə'vaʊɪdlɪ) *adv.* —**a·'vow·er** *n.*

a·vul·sion (ə'vʌlʃən) *n.* **1.** a forcible tearing away or separation of a bodily structure or part, either as the result of injury or as an intentional surgical procedure. **2.** *Law.* the sudden removal of soil from one person's land to that of another, as by flooding. [C17: from Latin *āvulsiō*, from *āvellere* to pluck away, from *vellere* to pull, pluck]

a·vun·cu·lar (ə'vʌŋkjʊlə) *adj.* **1.** of or concerned with an uncle. **2.** resembling an uncle; friendly, helpful. [C19: from Latin *avunculus* (maternal) uncle, diminutive of *avus* grandfather]

a·vun·cu·late (ə'vʌŋkjʊlɪt) *n.* **1.** the custom in some societies of assigning rights and duties to a maternal uncle concerning his sister's son. ~*adj.* **2.** of, relating to, or governed by this custom.

aw[1] (ɔː) *adj. Scot.* a variant spelling of **a'** (all).

aw[2] (ɔː) *interj. Informal, chiefly U.S.* an expression of disapproval, commiseration, or appeal.

a.w. *abbrev. for* all water (shipping).

a·wait (ə'weɪt) *vb.* **1.** (*tr.*) to wait for; expect. **2.** (*tr.*) to be in store for. **3.** (*intr.*) to wait, esp. with expectation. **4.** (*tr.*) *Obsolete.* to wait for in order to ambush.

a·wake (ə'weɪk) *vb.* **a·wakes, a·wak·ing; a·woke** *or* **a·waked; a·wok·en** *or* **a·waked. 1.** to emerge or rouse from sleep; wake. **2.** to become or cause to become alert. **3.** (usually foll. by *to*) to become or make aware (of): *to awake to reality.* **4.** Also: **awaken.** (*tr.*) to arouse (feelings, etc.) or cause to remember (memories, etc.). ~*adj.* (*postpositive*) **5.** not sleeping. **6.** (sometimes foll. by *to*) lively or alert. [Old English *awacian, awacan*; see WAKE[1]]

Usage. See at **wake**[1].

a·ward (ə'wɔːd) *vb.* (*tr.*) **1.** to give (something due), esp. as a reward for merit: *to award prizes.* **2.** *Law.* to declare to be entitled, as by decision of a court of law or an arbitrator. ~*n.* **3.** something awarded, such as a prize or medal: *an award for bravery.* **4.** *Law.* **a.** the decision of an arbitrator. **b.** a grant made by a court of law, esp. of damages in a civil action. [C14: from Anglo-Norman *awarder*, from Old Northern French *eswarder* to decide after investigation, from *es-* EX-[1] + *warder* to observe; see WARD] —**a·'ward·a·ble** *adj.* —**a·ˌward·'ee** *n.* —**a·'ward·er** *n.*

a·ward wage *n.* (in Australia) statutory minimum pay. Sometimes shortened to **award.**

a·ware (ə'wɛə) *adj.* **1.** (*postpositive*; foll. by *of*) having knowledge; cognizant: *aware of his error.* **2.** informed of current developments: *politically aware.* [Old English *gewær*; related to Old Saxon, Old High German *giwar* Latin *verērī* to be fearful; see BEWARE, WARY] —**a·'ware·ness** *n.*

a·wash (ə'wɒʃ) *adv., adj.* (*postpositive*) *Nautical.* **1.** at a level even with the surface of the sea. **2.** washed over by the waves.

a·way (ə'weɪ) *adv.* **1.** from a particular place; off: *to swim away.* **2.** in or to another, usual, or proper place: *to put toys away.* **3.** apart; at a distance: *to keep away from strangers.* **4.** out of existence: *the music faded away.* **5.** indicating motion, displacement, transfer, etc., from a normal or proper place, from a person's own possession, etc.: *to turn one's head away; to give away money.* **6.** indicating activity that is wasteful or designed to get rid of something: *to sleep away the hours.* **7.** continuously: *laughing away; fire away.* **8. away with.** a command for a person to go or be removed: *away with you; away with him to prison!* **9. far** (**or out**) **and away.** by far: *far and away the biggest meal he'd ever eaten.* ~*adj.* (*usually postpositive*) **10.** not present: *away from school.* **11.** distant: *he is a good way away.* **12.** having started; released: *he was away before sunrise; bombs away!* **13.** (*also prenominal*) *Sport.* played on an opponent's ground: *an away game.* **14.** *Golf.* (of a ball or player) farthest from the hole. **15.** *Baseball.* (of a player) having been put out. **16.** *Horse racing.* relating to the outward portion or first half of a race. ~*n.* **17.** *Sport.* a game played or won at an opponent's ground. ~*interj.* **18.** an expression of dismissal. [Old English *on wea* on way]

awe (ɔː) *n.* **1.** overwhelming wonder, admiration, respect, or dread. **2.** *Archaic.* power to inspire fear or reverence. ~*vb.* **3.** (*tr.*) to inspire with reverence or dread. [C13: from Old Norse *agi;* related to Gothic *agis* fear, Greek *akhesthai* to be grieved] —**'awe·less** *or U.S.* **'aw·less** *adj.*

a·weath·er (ə'wɛðə) *adv., adj.* (*postpositive*) *Nautical.* towards the weather: *with the helm aweather.* Compare **alee.**

a·weigh (ə'weɪ) *adj.* (*postpositive*) *Nautical.* (of an anchor) no longer hooked into the bottom; hanging by its rode.

awe-in·spir·ing *adj.* causing or worthy of admiration or respect; amazing or magnificent.

awe·some ('ɔːsəm) *adj.* inspiring or displaying awe. —**'awe·some·ly** *adv.* —**'awe·some·ness** *n.*

awe-strick·en *or* **awe-struck** *adj.* overcome or filled with awe.

aw·ful ('ɔːfʊl) *adj.* **1.** nasty or ugly. **2.** *Archaic.* inspiring reverence or dread. **3.** *Archaic.* overcome with awe; reverential. ~*adv.* **4.** *Not standard.* (intensifier): *an awful cold day.* [C13: see AWE, -FUL] —**'aw·ful·ness** *n.*

aw·ful·ly ('ɔːfəlɪ, 'ɔːflɪ) *adv.* **1.** in an unpleasant, bad, or reprehensible manner. **2.** *Informal.* (intensifier): *I'm awfully keen to come.* **3.** *Archaic.* so as to express or inspire awe.

a·wheel (ə'wiːl) *adv.* on wheels.

a·while (ə'waɪl) *adv.* for a brief period.

awk·ward ('ɔːkwəd) *adj.* **1.** lacking dexterity, proficiency, or skill; clumsy; inept: *the new recruits were awkward in their exercises.* **2.** ungainly or inelegant in movements or posture. **3.** unwieldy; difficult to use: *an awkward implement.* **4.** embarrassing: *an awkward moment.* **5.** embarrassed: *he felt awkward about leaving.* **6.** difficult to deal with; requiring tact: *an awkward situation; an awkward customer.* **7.** dangerous or difficult: *an awkward ascent of the ridge.* **8.** *Obsolete.* perverse. [C14: *awk,* from Old Norse *öfugr* turned the wrong way round + -WARD] —**'awk·ward·ly** *adv.* —**'awk·ward·ness** *n.*

awl (ɔːl) *n.* a pointed hand tool with a fluted blade used for piercing wood, leather, etc. See also **bradawl.** [Old English *ǣl;* related to Old Norse *alr,* Old High German *āla,* Dutch *aal,* Sanskrit *ārā*]

awl·wort ('ɔːl,wɜːt) *n.* a small stemless aquatic plant, *Subularia aquatica,* of the N hemisphere, having slender sharp-pointed leaves and minute submerged white flowers: family *Cruciferae* (crucifers).

awn (ɔːn) *n.* any of the bristles growing from the flowering parts of certain grasses and cereals. [Old English *agen* ear of grain; related to Old Norse *ögn* chaff, Gothic *ahana,* Old High German *agana,* Greek *akōn* javelin] —**awned** *adj.* —**'awn·less** *adj.*

awn·ing ('ɔːnɪŋ) *n.* a roof of canvas or other material supported by a frame to provide protection from the weather, esp. one placed over a doorway or part of a deck of a ship. [C17: of uncertain origin]

a·woke (ə'wəʊk) *vb.* a past tense or (now rare or dialectal) past participle of **awake.**

A.W.O.L. *or* **AWOL** (*when acronym* 'eɪwɒl) *adj. Military.* absent without leave; absent from one's post or duty without official permission but without intending to desert.

a·wry (ə'raɪ) *adv., adj.* (*postpositive*) **1.** with a slant or twist to one side; askew. **2.** away from the appropriate or right course; amiss. [C14 *on wry;* see A-[1], WRY]

A.W.U. *abbrev. for* Australian Workers' Union.

ax. *abbrev. for* axiom.

axe *or U.S.* **ax** (æks) *n., pl.* **ax·es. 1.** a hand tool with one side of its head forged and sharpened to a cutting edge, used for felling trees, splitting timber, etc. See also **hatchet. 2. an axe to grind. a.** an ulterior motive. **b.** a grievance. **c.** a pet subject. **3. the axe.** *Informal.* **a.** dismissal, esp. from employment; the sack (esp. in the phrase **get the axe**). **b.** *Brit.* severe cutting down of expenditure, esp. the removal of unprofitable sections of a public service. **4.** *U.S. slang.* any musical instrument. ~*vb.* (*tr.*) **5.** to chop or trim with an axe. **6.** *Informal.* to dismiss (employees), restrict (expenditure or services), or terminate (a project, etc.). [Old English *æx;* related to Old Frisian *axa,* Old High German *acchus,* Old Norse *öx,* Latin *ascia,* Greek *axinē*]

axe-break·er *n. Austral.* an Australian oleaceous tree, *Notelaea longifolia,* yielding very hard timber.

ax·el ('æksəl) *n. Skating.* a jump in which the skater takes off from the forward outside edge of one skate, makes one and a half turns in the air, and lands on the backward outside edge of the other skate. [C20: named after *Axel* Paulsen (d. 1938), Norwegian skater]

a·xen·ic (eɪ'ziːnɪk) *adj.* (of a biological culture or culture medium) free from undesirable microorganisms; uncontaminated. [C20: see A-[1], XENO-, -IC]

ax·es[1] ('æksiːz) *n.* the plural of **axis**[1].

ax·es[2] ('æksɪz) *n.* the plural of **axe.**

ax·i·al ('æksɪəl) *adj.* **1.** relating to, forming, or characteristic of an axis. **2.** situated in, on, or along an axis. —**,ax·i·'al·i·ty** *n.* —**'ax·i·al·ly** *adv.*

ax·i·al flow com·pres·sor *n.* a device for compressing a gas by accelerating it tangentially by means of bladed rotors, to increase its kinetic energy, and then diffusing it through static vanes (stators), to increase its pressure.

ax·i·al skel·e·ton *n.* the bones that together comprise the skull and the vertebral column.

ax·il ('æksɪl) *n.* the angle between the upper surface of a branch or leaf stalk and the stem from which it grows. [C18: from Latin *axilla* armpit]

ax·ile ('æksɪl, -saɪl) *adj. Botany.* of, relating to, or attached to the axis: *axile placentation.*

ax·il·la (æk'sɪlə) *n., pl.* **·lae** (-liː). **1.** the technical name for the **armpit. 2.** the area on the undersurface of a bird's wing corresponding to the armpit. [C17: from Latin: armpit]

ax·il·lar·y (æk'sɪlərɪ) *adj.* **1.** of, relating to, or near the armpit. **2.** *Botany.* growing in or related to the axil: *an axillary bud.* ~*n., pl.* **·lar·ies. 3.** Also called: **ax·il·lar** (æk'sɪlə, 'æksɪlə). (*usually pl.*) one of the feathers growing from the axilla of a bird's wing.

ax·i·ol·o·gy (,æksɪ'ɒlədʒɪ) *n. Philosophy.* **1.** the theory of values. **2.** the study of moral or aesthetic value judgments. [C20: from Greek *axios* worthy] —**ax·i·o·log·i·cal** (,æksɪə'lɒdʒɪkᵊl) *adj.* —**,ax·i·o·'log·i·cal·ly** *adv.* —**,ax·i·'ol·o·gist** *n.*

ax·i·om ('æksɪəm) *n.* **1.** a generally accepted proposition or principle, sanctioned by experience; maxim. **2.** a universally established principle or law that is not a necessary truth: *the axioms of politics.* **3.** *Logic, maths.* a self-consistent self-evident statement that is a universally accepted truth resting on intuition rather than experience and forming the basis of reasoning. [C15: from Latin *axiōma* a principle, from Greek, from *axioun* to consider worthy, from *axios* worthy]

ax·i·o·mat·ic (,æksɪə'mætɪk) *or* **ax·i·o·mat·i·cal** *adj.* **1.** relating to or resembling an axiom; self-evident. **2.** containing maxims; aphoristic. —**,ax·i·o·'mat·i·cal·ly** *adv.*

ax·is[1] ('æksɪs) *n., pl.* **ax·es** ('æksiːz). **1.** a real or imaginary line about which a body, such as an aircraft, can rotate or about which an object, form, composition, or geometrical construction is symmetrical. **2.** one of two or three reference lines used in coordinate geometry to locate a point in a plane or in space. **3.** *Anatomy.* the second cervical vertebra. Compare **atlas** (sense 3). **4.** *Botany.* the main central part of a plant, typically consisting of the stem and root, from which secondary branches and other parts develop. **5.** an alliance between a number of states to coordinate their foreign policy. **6.** Also called: **principal axis.** *Optics.* the line of symmetry of an optical system, such as the line passing through the centre of a lens. **7.** *Geology.* an imaginary line along the crest of an anticline or the trough of a syncline. **8.** *Crystallog.* one of three lines passing through the centre of a crystal and used to characterize its symmetry. [C14: from Latin: axletree, earth's axis; related to Greek *axōn* axis]

ax·is[2] ('æksɪs) *n., pl.* **ax·is·es.** any of several S Asian deer of the genus *Axis,* esp. *A. axis.* They typically have a reddish-brown white-spotted coat and slender antlers. [C18: from Latin: Indian wild animal, of uncertain identity]

Ax·is ('æksɪs) *n.* **a. the.** the alliance of Nazi Germany, Fascist Italy, and Japan, established in 1936 and lasting until their defeat in World War II. **b.** (*as modifier*)*: the Axis powers.*

ax·le ('æksəl) *n.* a bar or shaft on which a wheel, pair of wheels, or other rotating member revolves. [C17: from Old Norse *öxull;* related to German *Achse;* see AXIS[1]]

ax·le·tree ('æksəl,triː) *n.* a bar fixed across the underpart of a wagon or carriage that has rounded ends on which the wheels revolve.

Ax·min·ster car·pet ('æks,mɪnstə) *n.* a type of patterned carpet with a cut pile. Often shortened to **Axminster.** [after *Axminster,* in Devon, where such carpets are made]

ax·o·lotl ('æksə,lɒtᵊl) *n.* **1.** any of several aquatic salamanders of the North American genus *Ambystoma,* esp. *A. mexicanum* (**Mexican axolotl**), in which the larval form (including external gills) is retained throughout life under natural conditions (see **neoteny**): family *Ambystomidae.* **2.** any of various other North American salamanders in which neoteny occurs or is induced. [C18: from Nahuatl, from *atl* water + *xolotl* servant, doll]

ax·on ('æksɒn) *or* **ax·one** ('æksəʊn) *n.* the long threadlike extension of a nerve cell that conducts nerve impulses from the cell body. Compare **dendrite.** [C19: via New Latin from Greek: axis, axle, vertebra] —**'ax·on·al** *adj.*

ay[1] (eɪ) *interj. Archaic, poetic.* an expression of misery or surprise. [C12 *ai,* from Old Norse *ei;* related to Old English *ā* always, Latin *aevum* an age, Greek *aiōn*]

ay[2] *or* **aye** (eɪ) *adv. Archaic, poetic.* ever; always.

A·ya·cu·cho (*Spanish* ,aja'kutʃo) *n.* a city in SE Peru: nearby is the site of the battle (1824) that won independence for Peru. Pop.: 26 400 (1970 est.).

a·yah ('aɪə) *n.* (in the East, Africa, and other parts of the former British Empire) a maidservant, nursemaid, or governess. [C18: from Hindi *āyā,* from Portuguese *aia,* from Latin *avia* grandmother]

a·ya·huas·ca (,aɪə'wɑːskə) *n.* a Brazilian plant, *Banisteriopsis caapi,* that has winged fruits and yields a powerful hallucinogenic alkaloid sometimes used to treat certain disorders of the central nervous system: family *Malpighiaceae.* [C20: from Quechua]

a·ya·tol·lah (,aɪə'tɒlə) *n.* one of a class of Shiite Islamic religious leaders in Iran. [via Persian from Arabic, from *aya* creation + ALLAH]

Ay·cliffe ('eɪklɪf) *n.* a town in Co. Durham: founded as a new town in 1947. Pop.: 20 190 (1971).

Ay·din *or* **Ai·din** ('aɪdɪn) *n.* a town in SW Turkey: an ancient city of Lydia. Pop.: 50 551 (1970). Ancient name: **Tralles.**

aye *or* **ay** (aɪ) *sentence substitute.* **1.** yes: archaic or dialectal except in voting by voice. **2. aye aye. a.** an expression of compliance, esp. used by seamen. **b.** *Brit.* an expression of amused surprise, esp. at encountering something that confirms one's suspicions, expectations, etc. ~*n.* **3. a.** a person who votes in the affirmative. **b.** an affirmative vote. ~Compare **nay.** [C16: probably from pronoun *I,* expressing assent]

aye-aye ('aɪ,aɪ) *n.* a rare nocturnal arboreal prosimian primate of Madagascar, *Daubentonia madagascariensis,* related to the lemurs: family *Daubentoniidae.* It has long bony fingers and rodent-like incisor teeth adapted for feeding on insect larvae and bamboo pith. [C18: from French, from Malagasay *aiay,* probably of imitative origin]

Ayer (ɛə) *n.* Sir **Al·fred Jules.** born 1910, English positivist philosopher, noted particularly for his antimetaphysical work *Language, Truth, and Logic* (1936).

Ayers Rock (ɛəz) *n.* the world's largest monolith, in the Northern Territory of Australia. Height: 330 m (1100 ft.). Base circumference: 9 km (5.6 miles).

A·ye·sha ('ɑ:i:,ʃɑ:) *n.* a variant spelling of **Aisha.**

a·yin *or* **a·in** ('ɑ:jɪn; *Hebrew* 'aji:n) *n.* the 16th letter in the Hebrew alphabet (ע), originally a pharyngeal fricative, that is now silent and transliterated by a centred period (·). [Hebrew]

Ayles+bur·y ('eɪlzbərɪ, -brɪ) *n.* a town in SE central England, administrative centre of Buckinghamshire. Pop.: 38 499 (1971).

Ay+ma+ra (,aɪmə'rɑ:) *n.* **1.** (*pl.* **+ras** *or* **+ra**) a member of a South American Indian people of Bolivia and Peru. **2.** the language of this people, probably related to Quechua. [from Spanish *aimará,* of American Indian origin] **—,Ay+ma+'ran** *adj.*

Ay·mé (*French* ɛ'me) *n.* **Mar·cel** (mar'sɛl). 1902–67, French writer: noted for his light and witty narratives.

Ayr (ɛə) *n.* **1.** a port in SW Scotland, in Strathclyde region. Pop.: 47 884 (1971). **2.** (until 1975) a county of SW Scotland, now part of Strathclyde region.

Ayr+shire ('ɛəʃɪə, -ʃə) *n.* any one of a hardy breed of brown and white dairy cattle.

A·yub Khan (aɪ'ju:b 'kɑ:n) *n.* **Mo·ham·med.** 1907–74, Pakistani field marshal; president of Pakistan (1958–69).

A·yur+ve·da ('ɑ:jʊ,veɪdə, -,vi:də) *n.* *Hinduism.* an ancient medical treatise on the art of healing and prolonging life, sometimes regarded as a fifth Veda. [from Sanskrit, from *āyur* life + *veda* knowledge] **—,A·yur+'ve·dic** *adj.*

A·yut+tha+ya (ɑ:'ju:təjə) *n.* a city in S Thailand, on the Chao Phraya River: capital of the country until 1767; noted for its canals and ruins. Pop.: 501 000 (1970). Also: **A·yudh+ya** (ɑ:'ju:djə), **A·yu+thi·a** (ɑ:'ju:θɪə).

az. *abbrev. for* azimuth.

az·a- *or before a vowel* **az-** *combining form.* denoting the presence of nitrogen, esp. a nitrogen atom in place of a -CH group or an -NH group in place of a $-CH_2$ group: *azathioprine.* [C20: from AZ(O)- + *-a-*]

a·zal·ea (ə'zeɪljə) *n.* any ericaceous plant of the group *Azalea,* formerly a separate genus but now included in the genus *Rhododendron:* cultivated for their showy pink or purple flowers. [C18: via New Latin from Greek, from *azaleos* dry; from its supposed preference for a dry situation]

a·zan (ɑ:'zɑ:n) *n.* *Islam.* the call to prayer five times a day, usually by a muezzin from a minaret. [from Arabic *adhān,* from *adhina* to proclaim, invite; see MUEZZIN]

A·za·ña (*Spanish* a'θaɲa) *n.* **Ma·nuel** (ma'nwel). 1880–1940, Spanish statesman; president of the Spanish Republic (1936–39) until overthrown by Franco.

az·a·thi·o+prine (,æzə'θaɪə,pri:n) *n.* a synthetic drug that suppresses the normal immune responses of the body and is administered orally during and after organ transplantation and also in certain types of anaemia and rheumatoid arthritis. Formula: $C_9H_7N_7O_2S$. [C20: from AZA- + THIO- + P(U)RINE]

A·za+zel (ə'zeɪzəl, 'æzə,zɛl) *n.* **1.** *Old Testament.* a desert demon to whom the scapegoat bearing the sins of Israel was sent out once a year on the Day of Atonement (Leviticus 16:1–28). **2.** (in later Jewish and Gnostic writings and in Muslim tradition) a prince of demons.

Az+bine (æz'bi:n) *n.* another name for **Aïr.**

a·zed·a+rach (ə'zɛdə,ræk) *n.* **1.** the astringent bark of the chinaberry tree, formerly used as an emetic and cathartic. **2.** another name for **chinaberry** (sense 1). [C18: from French *azédarac,* from Persian *āzād dirakht,* from *āzād* free, noble + *dirakht* tree]

a·ze·o+trope (ə'zi:ə,trəʊp) *n.* a mixture of liquids that boils at a constant temperature, at a given pressure, without change of composition. [C20: from A-[1] + *zeo-,* from Greek *zein* to boil + -TROPE] **—a·ze·o+trop+ic** (,eɪzɪə'trɒpɪk) *adj.*

A·zer+bai+jan (,æzəbaɪ'dʒɑ:n) *n.* a mountainous region of NW Iran, separated from Soviet Azerbaijan by the Aras River: divided administratively into **Eastern Azerbaijan** and **Western Azerbaijan.** Capitals: Tabriz and Rezaiyeh. Pop.: 3 600 000 (1977 est.).

A·zer+bai+ja+ni (,æzəbaɪ'dʒɑ:nɪ) *n.* **1.** (*pl.* **+ni** *or* **+nis**) a native or inhabitant of Azerbaijan. **2.** the language of this people, belonging to the Turkic branch of the Altaic family.

A·zer+bai+jan So+vi+et So+cial+ist Re+pub+lic *n.* an administrative division of the S Soviet Union, on the Caspian Sea in the east: consists of dry subtropical steppes around the Aras and Kura Rivers, surrounded by the Caucasus; contains the extensive Baku oilfields. Capital: Baku. Pop.: 5 117 081 (1970). Area: 86 600 sq. km (33 430 sq. miles).

az+ide ('eɪzaɪd) *n.* **1.** any compound containing the monovalent group N_3^- or the monovalent ion N_3. **2.** (*modifier*) consisting of, containing, or concerned with the group N_3^- or the ion N_3: *azide group or radical.*

A·zi·ki·we (,ɑ:zi:'ki:weɪ) *n.* **Nnam·di** (ən'næmdɪ). born 1904, Nigerian statesman; first president of Nigeria (1963–66).

A·zil+i·an (ə'zɪlɪən) *n.* **1.** a Palaeolithic culture of Spain and SW France that can be dated to the 10th millennium B.C., characterized by flat bone harpoons and schematically painted pebbles. ~*adj.* **2.** of or relating to this culture. [C19: named after Mas d'*Azil,* France, where artefacts were found]

az·i+muth ('æzɪməθ) *n.* **1.** *Astronomy, navigation.* the angular distance usually measured clockwise from the south point of the horizon in astronomy or from the north point in navigation to the intersection with the horizon of the vertical circle passing through a celestial body. Compare **altitude** (sense 3). **2.** *Surveying.* the horizontal angle of a bearing clockwise from a standard direction, such as north. [C14: from Old French *azimut,* from Arabic *as-sumūt,* plural of *as-samt* the path, from Latin *semita* path] **—az·i·muth+al** (,æzɪ'mʌθəl) *adj.* **—,az·i+'muth+al+ly** *adv.*

az·i+muth+al pro+jec+tion *n.* another term for **zenithal projection.**

az+ine ('eɪzi:n, -zɪn) *n.* any organic compound having a six-membered ring containing at least one nitrogen atom. See also **diazine, triazine.**

Az·na·vour (*French* azna'vu:r) *n.* **Charles** (ʃarl). original name *Varenagh Aznavourian.* born 1924, French singer and film actor.

az·o ('eɪzəʊ, 'æ-) *adj.* of, consisting of, or containing the divalent group -N:N-: *an azo group or radical.* See also **diazo.** [independent use of AZO-]

az·o- *or before a vowel* **az-** *combining form.* indicating the presence of an azo group: *azobenzene.* [from French *azote* nitrogen, from Greek *azōos* lifeless, from A-[1] + *zōē* life]

az·o+ben+zene (,eɪzəʊ'bɛnzi:n, -bɛn'zi:n) *n.* **1.** a yellow or orange crystalline solid used mainly in the manufacture of dyes. Formula: $C_6H_5N{:}NC_6H_5$. **2.** any organic compound that is a substituted derivative of azobenzene.

az·o dye *n.* any of a class of artificial dyes that contain the azo group. They are usually red, brown, or yellow and are obtained from aromatic amines.

a·zo·ic (ə'zəʊɪk, eɪ-) *adj.* without life; characteristic of the ages that have left no evidence of life in the form of organic remains. [C19: from Greek *azōos* lifeless; see AZO-]

az+ole ('eɪzəʊl, ə'zəʊl) *n.* **1.** an organic five-membered ring compound containing one or more atoms in the ring, the number usually being specified by a prefix: *diazole; triazole.* **2.** a less common name for **pyrrole.** [from AZO- + -OLE, on the model of *diazole*]

a·zon+al soil (eɪ'zəʊnəl) *n.* soil that has a profile determined predominantly by factors other than local climate and vegetation. Azonal soils include some mountain, alluvial, marine, glacial, wind-blown, and volcanic soils. Compare **intrazonal soil, zonal soil.**

A·zores (ə'zɔ:z) *pl. n.* **the.** three groups of volcanic islands in the N Atlantic, forming the Portuguese districts of Angra do Heroísmo, Horta, and Ponta Delgada: achieved partial autonomy (1976). Capital: Ponta Delgada (on São Miguel). Pop.: 336 100 (1970). Area: 2300 sq. km (888 sq. miles). Portuguese name: **Açôres.**

A·zo·rín (*Spanish* aθo'rin) *n.* pen name of *José Martínez Ruiz.* 1874–1967, Spanish writer: noted for his stories of the Spanish countryside.

az+ote ('eɪzəʊt, ə'zəʊt) *n.* an obsolete name for **nitrogen.** [C18: from French, from Greek *azōtos* ungirded, intended for Greek *azōos* lifeless]

az·o+te·mi·a (,æzə'ti:mɪə) *n.* *Pathol.* uraemia. [C20: see AZOTE, -EMIA] **—az·o+te·mic** (,æzə'ti:mɪk) *adj.*

az+oth ('æzɒθ) *n.* **1.** the alchemical name for **mercury,** regarded as the first principle of all metals. **2.** the panacea postulated by Paracelsus. [from Arabic *az-zā'ūq* the mercury]

a·zot+ic (eɪ'zɒtɪk) *adj.* of, containing, or concerned with nitrogen.

az·o+tize *or* **az·o+tise** ('eɪzə,taɪz) *vb.* a less common word for **nitrogenize.**

a·zo+to+bac+ter (ə'zəʊtəʊ,bæktə) *n.* any bacterium of the family *Azotobacteriaceae,* important in nitrogen fixation in the soil. [New Latin; see AZOTE, BACTERIA]

A·zov ('ɑ:zɒv) *n.* **Sea of.** a shallow arm of the Black Sea, to which it is connected by the Kerch Strait: almost entirely landlocked; fed chiefly by the River Don. Area: about 37 500 sq. km (14 500 sq. miles).

Az·rael ('æzreɪl, -rɪəl) *n.* (in Jewish and Islamic angelology) the angel who separates the soul from the body at death.

Az+tec ('æztɛk) *n.* **1.** a member of a Mexican Indian people who established a great empire, centred on the valley of Mexico, that was overthrown by Cortés and his followers in the early 16th century. **2.** the language of the Aztecs. See also **Nahuatl.** ~*adj. also* **Az+tec+an. 3.** of, relating to, or characteristic of the Aztecs, their civilization, or their language. [C18: from Spanish *Azteca,* from Nahuatl *Aztecatl,* from *Aztlan,* their traditional place of origin, literally: near the cranes, from *azta* cranes + *tlan* near]

az+ure ('æʒə, -ʒʊə, 'eɪ-) *n.* **1.** a deep blue, occasionally somewhat purple, similar to the colour of a clear blue sky. **2.** *Poetic.* a clear blue sky. ~*adj.* **3.** of the colour azure; serene. **4.** (*usually postpositive*) *Heraldry.* of the colour blue. [C14: from Old French *azur,* from Old Spanish, from Arabic *lāzaward* lapis lazuli, from Persian *lāzhuward*]

az+ur+ite ('æʒʊ,raɪt) *n.* a deep-blue secondary mineral consisting of hydrated basic copper carbonate in monoclinic crystalline form. It is used as an ore of copper and as a gemstone. Formula: $Cu_3(OH)_2(CO_3)_2$.

az·y+gous ('æzɪgəs) *adj.* *Biology.* developing or occurring singly. [C17: via New Latin from Greek *azugos,* from A-[1] + *zugon* YOKE]

B

b *or* **B** (biː) *n., pl.* **b's, B's,** *or* **Bs. 1.** the second letter and first consonant of the modern English alphabet. **2.** a speech sound represented by this letter, usually a voiced bilabial stop, as in *bell.* **3.** Also: **beta.** the second in a series, esp. the second highest grade in an examination.

B *symbol for:* **1.** *Music.* **a.** a note having a frequency of 493.88 hertz (**B above middle C**) or this value multiplied or divided by any power of 2; the seventh note of the scale of C major. **b.** a key, string, or pipe producing this note. **c.** the major or minor key having this note as its tonic. **2.** the supporting or less important of two things: *the B side of a record.* **3.** a human blood type of the ABO group, containing the B antigen. **4.** (in Britain) a secondary road. **5.** *Chem.* boron. **6.** magnetic flux density. **7.** *Chess.* bishop. **8.** (on Brit. pencils, signifying degree of softness of lead) black: *B; 2B; 3B.* Compare **H** (sense 5). **9.** Also: **b** *Physics.* bel. **10.** *Physics.* baryon number. ~**11.** *international car registration for* Belgium.

b. *or* **B.** *abbrev. for:* **1.** *Music.* bass *or* basso. **2.** (on maps, etc.) bay. **3.** balboa. **4.** belga. **5.** (*cap.*) Bible. **6.** bolivar. **7.** book. **8.** born. **9.** (*not cap.*) *Cricket.* **a.** bowled. **b.** bye. **10.** breadth. **11.** (*cap.*) British.

B- (of U.S. military aircraft) *abbrev. for* bomber: *B-52.*

Ba *the chemical symbol for* barium.

Ba (bɑː) *n. Egyptian myth.* the soul, represented as a bird with a human head.

B.A. *abbrev. for:* **1.** Bachelor of Arts. **2.** British Academy. **3.** British Association (for the Advancement of Science).

B.A.A. *abbrev. for* British Airports Authority.

baa (bɑː) *vb.* **baas, baa+ing, baaed. 1.** (*intr.*) to make the cry of a sheep; bleat. ~*n.* **2.** the cry made by sheep.

Baa·der-Mein·hof Gang (*German* ˈbaːdər ˈmaɪnhoːf) *n.* **the.** a group of West German guerrillas dedicated to the violent overthrow of capitalist society; named after its leading members, Andreas Baader (1943–77) and Ulrike Meinhof (1934–76). See also **Red Brigades.**

Baal (bɑːl) *n.* **1.** any of several ancient Semitic fertility gods. **2.** *Phoenician myth.* the sun god and supreme national deity. **3.** (*sometimes not cap.*) any false god or idol. [from Hebrew *báʿal* lord, master]

Baal+bek (ˈbɑːlbɛk) *n.* a town in E Lebanon: an important city in Phoenician and Roman times; extensive ruins. Pop.: 15 000 (1973 est.). Ancient name: **Heliopolis.**

Baal Shem Tov *or* **Baal Shem Tob** (bɑːl ˈʃɛm tɒv, ˈʃɑːm) *n.* original name *Israel ben Eliezer.* ?1700–60, Jewish religious leader, teacher, and healer in Poland: founder of modern Hasidism.

baas (bɑːs) *n.* a South African word for **boss:** used by Africans and Coloureds in addressing European managers or overseers. [C17: from Afrikaans, from Middle Dutch *baes* master; see BOSS[1]]

baas+kap *or* **baas+skap** (ˈbɑːsˌkap) *n.* (*sometimes cap.*) (in South Africa) control by Whites of non-Whites. [from Afrikaans, from BAAS + *-skap* -SHIP]

Bab (bɑːb) *n.* **the.** title of *Mirza Ali Mohammed.* 1819–50, Persian religious leader: founded Babism; executed as a heretic of Islam. [from Persian *bāb* gate, from Arabic]

ba·ba (ˈbɑːbɑː; *French* baˈba) *n.* a small cake of leavened dough, sometimes mixed with currants and usually soaked in rum (**rum baba**). [C19: from French, from Polish, literally: old woman]

Ba·bar (ˈbɑːbə) *n.* a variant spelling of **Baber.**

ba+bas+su (ˌbɑːbəˈsuː) *n.* a Brazilian palm tree, *Orbignya martiana* (or *O. speciosa*), having hard edible nuts that yield an oil used in making soap, margarine, etc. [from Portuguese *babaçú,* from a native Amerindian word]

Bab·bage (ˈbæbɪdʒ) *n.* **Charles.** 1792–1871, English mathematician and inventor, who built a calculating machine that anticipated the modern electronic computer.

bab+bitt (ˈbæbɪt) *vb.* (*tr.*) to line (a bearing) or face (a surface) with Babbitt metal or a similar soft alloy.

Bab·bitt (ˈbæbɪt) *n. U.S. derogatory.* a narrow-minded and complacent member of the middle class. [C20: after George *Babbitt,* central character in the novel *Babbitt* (1922) by Sinclair Lewis] —**ˈBab+bitt+ry** *n.*

Bab·bitt met+al *n.* any of a number of alloys originally based on tin, antimony, and copper but now often including lead: used esp. in bearings. Sometimes shortened to **Babbitt.** [C19: named after Isaac *Babbitt* (1799–1862), American inventor]

bab+ble (ˈbæbəl) *vb.* **1.** to utter (words, sounds, etc.) in an incoherent or indistinct jumble. **2.** (*intr.*) to talk foolishly, incessantly, or irrelevantly. **3.** (*tr.*) to disclose (secrets, confidences, etc.) carelessly or impulsively. **4.** (*intr.*) (of streams, birds, etc.) to make a low murmuring or bubbling sound. **5.** (*intr.*) *Scot.* to snivel; blubber. ~*n.* **6.** incoherent or foolish speech; chatter. **7.** a murmuring or bubbling sound. [C13: compare Dutch *babbelen,* Swedish *babbla,* French *babiller* to prattle, Latin *babulus* fool; probably all of imitative origin] —**ˈbab+ble+ment** *n.*

bab+bler[1] (ˈbæblə) *n.* **1.** a person who babbles. **2.** any of various insect-eating birds of the Old World tropics and subtropics that have a loud incessant song: family *Muscicapidae* (warblers, thrushes, etc.).

bab+bler[2] *n. Austral. slang.* a cook or chef. [C20: from *babbling brook,* rhyming slang for *cook*]

babe (beɪb) *n.* **1.** a baby. **2.** *Informal.* a naive, gullible, or unsuspecting person (often in the phrase **a babe in arms**). **3.** *Slang, chiefly U.S.* a girl or young woman.

Ba+bel[1] (ˈbeɪbəl) *n.* **1.** *Old Testament.* **a.** Also called: **Tower of Babel.** a tower presumptuously intended to reach from earth to heaven, the building of which was frustrated when Jehovah confused the language of the builders (Genesis 11:1–10). **b.** the city, probably Babylon, in which this tower was supposedly built. **2.** (*often not cap.*) **a.** a confusion of noises or voices. **b.** a scene of noise and confusion. [from Hebrew *Bābhél,* from Akkadian *Bāb-ilu,* literally: gate of God]

Ba+bel[2] (*Russian* ˈbabɪl) *n.* **I·saak Em·ma·nu·i·lo·vich** (ɪˈsak imənuˈiləvitʃ). 1894–1941, Russian short-story writer, whose works include *Stories from Odessa* (1924) and *Red Cavalry* (1926).

Bab el Man+deb (ˈbæb ɛl ˈmændɛb) *n.* a strait between SW Arabia and E Africa, connecting the Red Sea with the Gulf of Aden.

Ba·ber, Ba·bar, *or* **Ba·bur** (ˈbɑːbə) *n.* original name *Zahir ud-Din Mohammed.* 1483–1530, founder of the Mogul Empire: conquered India in 1526.

Ba·beuf (*French* baˈbœf) *n.* **Fran·çois No·ël** (frɑ̃swa nɔˈɛl). 1760–97, French political agitator: plotted unsuccessfully to destroy the Directory and establish a communistic system.

Ba·bi (ˈbɑːbɪ) *n.* **1.** a disciple of the Bab. **2.** another word for **Babism.**

ba+biche (bɑːˈbiːʃ) *n. Canadian.* thongs or lacings of rawhide. [C19: from Canadian French, of Algonquian origin]

ba·bies'-breath *n.* a variant of **baby's-breath.**

bab·i·ru+sa (ˌbɑːbɪˈruːsə) *n.* a wild pig, *Babyrousa babyrussa,* inhabiting marshy forests in Indonesia. It has an almost hairless wrinkled skin and enormous curved canine teeth. [C17: from Malay, from *bābī* hog + *rūsa* deer]

Bab+ism (ˈbɑːbɪzəm) *n.* a pantheistic Persian religious sect, founded in 1844 by the Bab, forbidding polygamy, concubinage, begging, trading in slaves, and indulgence in alcohol and drugs. Compare **Bahaism.**

ba+boon (bəˈbuːn) *n.* any of several medium-sized omnivorous Old World monkeys of the genus *Papio* (or *Chaeropithecus*) and related genera, inhabiting open rocky ground or wooded regions of Africa. They have an elongated muzzle, large teeth, and a fairly long tail. See also **hamadryas, gelada.** [C14 *babewyn* gargoyle, later, baboon, from Old French *babouin,* from *baboue* grimace; related to Old French *babine* a thick lip]

ba+bu (ˈbɑːbuː) *n.* (in India) a title or form of address more or less equivalent to *Mr.,* placed before a person's full name or after his first name. [Hindi, literally: father]

ba+bul (bɑːˈbuːl, ˈbɑːbuːl) *n.* any of several mimosaceous trees of the genus *Acacia,* esp. *A. arabica* of N Africa and India, which bear small yellow flowers and are a source of gum arabic, tannin, and hardwood. [from Persian *babūl;* related to Sanskrit *babbūla*]

Ba·bur (ˈbɑːbə) *n.* a variant spelling of **Baber.**

ba+bush+ka (bəˈbuːʃkə) *n.* a headscarf tied under the chin, worn by Russian peasant women. [Russian: grandmother, from *baba* old woman]

ba·by (ˈbeɪbɪ) *n., pl.* **·bies. 1. a.** a newborn or recently born child; infant. **b.** (*as modifier*): *baby food.* **2.** the youngest or smallest of a family or group. **3. a.** a newborn or recently born animal. **b.** (*as modifier*): *baby rabbits.* **4.** *Usually derogatory.* an immature person. **5.** *Slang.* a young woman or sweetheart: often used as a term of address expressing affection. **6.** *Slang.* a project of personal concern. **7. be left holding the baby.** to be left with the responsibility. **8. throw the baby out with the bath water.** to lose the essential element by indiscriminate rejection. ~*adj.* **9.** (*prenominal*) comparatively small of its type: *a baby grand* (*piano*). ~*vb.* **·bies, +by+ing, +bied. 10.** (*tr.*) to treat with love and attention. [C14: probably childish reduplication; compare MAMA, PAPA] —**ˈba+by+hood** *n.* —**ˈba+by+ish** *adj.*

ba·by bo·nus *n. Canadian informal.* family allowance.

Ba·by-bounc·er *n. Trademark.* a seat on springs suspended from a door frame, etc., in which a baby may be placed for exercise.

ba·by bug+gy *n.* **1.** *Brit.* a kind of child's light pushchair. **2.** *U.S. informal.* a pram.

ba·by car+riage *n.* the U.S. name for **pram[1].**

ba·by-face *n.* **1.** a smooth round face like a baby's. **2.** a person with such a face.

Bab·y·lon (ˈbæbɪlən) *n.* **1.** the chief city of ancient Mesopotamia: first settled around 3000 B.C. See also **Hanging Gardens of Babylon. 2.** any place of exile. **3.** any city of depravity and luxury. **4.** *Derogatory.* (in Protestant polemic) the Roman Catholic Church, regarded as the seat of luxury and corruption. [via Latin and Greek from Hebrew *Bābhel;* see BABEL[1]]

Bab·y+lo+ni·a (ˌbæbɪˈləʊnɪə) *n.* the southern kingdom of ancient Mesopotamia: a great empire from about 2200–538 B.C., when it was conquered by the Persians.

Bab·y+lo+ni·an (ˌbæbɪˈləʊnɪən) *n.* **1.** an inhabitant of ancient Babylon or Babylonia. **2.** the extinct language of Babylonia, belonging to the E Semitic subfamily of the Afro-Asiatic family: a dialect of Akkadian. ~*adj.* **3.** of, relating to, or characteristic of ancient Babylon or Babylonia, its people, or their language. **4.** decadent or depraved.

Bab·y+lo+ni·an cap+tiv+i·ty *n.* **1.** the exile of the Jews in Babylonia from 597 to about 538 B.C. **2.** the exile of the seven popes in Avignon (1309–77).

ba·by's-breath *or* **ba·bies'-breath** *n.* **1.** a tall Eurasian caryophyllaceous plant, *Gypsophila paniculata,* bearing small white or pink fragrant flowers. **2.** any of several other plants, such as the grape hyacinth and certain bedstraws, that have small scented flowers.

ba·by-sit *vb.* **-sits, -sit·ting, -sat.** (*intr.*) to act or work as a baby-sitter.

ba·by-sit·ter *n.* a person who takes care of a child or children while the parents are out.

ba·by snatch+er *n. Informal.* **1.** a person who steals a baby from its pram. **2.** someone who marries or has an affair with a much younger person.

ba·by talk *n.* **1.** the speech of very young children learning to talk. **2.** an adult's imitation of this.

ba·by tooth *n.* another term for **milk tooth.**

Ba·by-walk·er *n. Trademark.* a light frame on casters or wheels to help a baby learn to walk. U.S. equivalent: **go-cart.**

bac+ca+lau+re+ate (ˌbækəˈlɔːrɪɪt) *n.* **1.** the university degree of Bachelor of Arts, Bachelor of Science, etc. **2.** *U.S.* a farewell sermon delivered at the commencement ceremonies in many colleges and universities. [C17: from Medieval Latin *baccalaureātus,* from *baccalaureus* advanced student, alteration of *baccalārius* BACHELOR; influenced in folk etymology by Latin *bāca* berry + *laureus* laurel]

bac+ca+rat (ˈbækəˌrɑː, ˌbækəˈrɑː; *French* bakaˈra) *n.* a card game in which two or more punters gamble against the banker. [C19: from French *baccara,* of unknown origin]

bac+cate (ˈbækeɪt) *adj. Botany.* **1.** like a berry in form, texture, etc. **2.** bearing berries. [C19: from Latin *bāca* berry]

Bac+chae (ˈbækiː) *pl. n.* the priestesses or female devotees of Bacchus. [Latin, from Greek *Bakkhai,* plural of *Bakkhē* priestess of BACCHUS]

bac+cha+nal (ˈbækənᵊl) *n.* **1.** a follower of Bacchus. **2.** a drunken and riotous celebration. **3.** a participant in such a celebration; reveller. ~*adj.* **4.** of or relating to Bacchus. [C16: from Latin *Bacchānālis;* see BACCHUS]

bac+cha+na+li·a (ˌbækəˈneɪlɪə) *pl. n.* **1.** (*often cap.*) orgiastic rites associated with Bacchus. **2.** any drunken revelry. —**ˌbac+cha+ˈna+li·an** *adj., n.*

bac+chant (ˈbækənt) *or* (*fem.*) **bac+chan+te** (bəˈkæntɪ) *n., pl.* **bac+chants, bac+chan+tes** (bəˈkæntɪz) *or* (*fem.*) **bac+chan+tes.** **1.** a priest, priestess, or votary of Bacchus. **2.** a drunken reveller. [C17: from Latin *bacchāns,* from *bacchārī* to celebrate the BACCHANALIA]

Bac+chic (ˈbækɪk) *adj.* **1.** of or relating to Bacchus. **2.** (*often not cap.*) riotously drunk.

bac+chi·us (bæˈkaɪəs) *n., pl.* **+chi·i** (-ˈkaɪaɪ). *Prosody.* a metrical foot of one short syllable followed by two long ones (˘¯¯). Compare **dactyl.** [C16: from Latin, from Greek *Bakkheios* (*pous*) a Bacchic (foot)]

Bac·chus (ˈbækəs) *n.* (in ancient Greece and Rome) a god of wine and giver of ecstasy, identified with Dionysus. [C15: from Latin, from Greek *Bakkhos;* related to Latin *bāca* small round fruit, berry]

bac+cif+er+ous (bækˈsɪfərəs) *adj.* bearing berries. [C17: from Latin *bācifer,* from *bāca* berry + *ferre* to bear]

bac+ci+form (ˈbæksɪˌfɔːm) *adj. Botany.* shaped like a berry.

bac+civ+or+ous (bækˈsɪvərəs) *adj.* feeding on berries.

bac+cy (ˈbækɪ) *n.* a Brit. informal name for **tobacco.**

bach (bætʃ) *n.* **1.** *N.Z.* a second or holiday house, esp. at the seaside. ~*vb. also* **batch. 2.** *Austral.* to live as a bachelor.

Bach (*German* bax) *n.* **1. Jo·hann Chris·tian** (ˈjoːhan ˈkrɪstjan), 11th son of J. S. Bach, called *the English Bach.* 1735–82, German composer, resident in London from 1762. **2. Jo·hann Chri·stoph** (ˈkrɪstɔf). 1642–1705, German composer: wrote oratorios, cantatas, and motets, some of which were falsely attributed to J. S. Bach, of whom he was a distant relative. **3. Jo·hann Se·bas·tian** (zeˈbastjan). 1685–1750, German composer: church organist at Arnstadt (1703–07) and Mühlhausen (1707–08); court organist at Weimar (1708–17); musical director for Prince Leopold of Köthen (1717–28); musical director for the city of Leipzig (1728–50). His output was enormous and displays great vigour and invention within the northern European polyphonic tradition. His works include nearly 200 cantatas and oratorios, settings of the *Passion according to St. John* (1723) and *St. Matthew* (1729), the six *Brandenburg Concertos* (1720–21), the 48 preludes and fugues of the *Well-tempered Clavier* (completed 1744), and the *Mass in B Minor* (1733–38). **4. Karl** (or **Carl**) **Phil·ipp E·ma·nu·el** (karl ˈfiːlɪp eˈmaːnʊeːl), 3rd son of J. S. Bach. 1714–88, German composer, chiefly of symphonies, keyboard sonatas, and church music. **5. Wil·helm Frie·de·mann** (ˈvɪlhɛlm ˈfriːdəman), eldest son of J. S. Bach. 1710–84, German composer: wrote nine symphonies and much keyboard and religious music.

Bach·a·rach (ˈbækəræk) *n.* **Burt.** born 1928, U.S. composer of popular songs.

bach+e·lor (ˈbætʃələ, ˈbætʃlə) *n.* **1. a.** an unmarried man. **b.** (*as modifier*): *a bachelor flat.* **2. a.** a person who holds the degree of Bachelor of Arts, Bachelor of Science, etc. **b.** the degree itself. **3.** Also called: **bachelor-at-arms.** (in the Middle Ages) a young knight serving a great noble. **4. bachelor seal.** a young male seal, esp. a fur seal, that has not yet mated. [C13: from Old French *bacheler* youth, squire, from Vulgar Latin *baccalāris* (unattested) farm worker, of Celtic origin; compare Irish Gaelic *bachlach* peasant] —**ˈbach+e·lor+hood** *n.*

bach+e·lor girl *n.* a young unmarried woman, esp. one who is self-supporting.

Bach+e·lor of Arts *n.* **1.** a degree conferred on a person who has successfully completed his undergraduate studies, usually in a branch of the liberal arts or humanities. **2.** a person who holds this degree.

Bach+e·lor of Sci+ence *n.* **1.** a degree conferred on a person who has successfully completed his undergraduate studies in a branch of the sciences. **2.** a person who holds this degree.

bach·e·lor's-but·tons *n.* (*functioning as sing. or pl.*) any of various plants of the daisy family with button-like flower heads, esp. a double-flowered buttercup.

Bach trum+pet (bax) *n.* a modern small three-valved trumpet for playing clarino passages in Bach's music.

ba+cil+lar·y (bəˈsɪlərɪ) *or* **ba+cil+lar** (bəˈsɪlə) *adj.* **1.** of, relating to, or caused by bacilli. **2.** Also: **ba+cil+li+form** (bəˈsɪlɪˌfɔːm). shaped like a short rod.

ba+cil+lus (bəˈsɪləs) *n., pl.* **+cil+li** (-ˈsɪlaɪ). **1.** any rod-shaped bacterium, such as a clostridium bacterium. Compare **coccus** (sense 1), **spirillum** (sense 1). **2.** any of various rodlike spore-producing bacteria constituting the family *Bacillaceae,* esp. of the genus *Bacillus.* [C19: from Latin: a small staff, from *baculum* walking stick]

bac·i+tra+cin (ˌbæsɪˈtreɪsɪn) *n.* an antibiotic used mainly in treating bacterial skin infections: obtained from the bacterium *Bacillus subtilis.* [C20: BACI(LLUS) + *-trac-* from Margaret *Tracy* (born 1936), American girl in whose blood *Bacillus subtilis* was found; see -IN]

back[1] (bæk) *n.* **1.** the posterior part of the human body, extending from the neck to the pelvis. **2.** the corresponding or upper part of an animal. **3.** the spinal column. **4.** the part or side of an object opposite the front. **5.** the part or side of anything less often seen or used: *the back of a carpet; the back of a knife.* **6.** the part or side of anything that is furthest from the front or from a spectator: *the back of the stage.* **7.** the convex part of something: *the back of a hill; the back of a ship.* **8.** something that supports, covers, or strengthens the rear of an object. **9.** *Ball games.* **a.** a mainly defensive player behind a forward. **b.** the position of such a player. **10.** the part of a book to which the pages are glued or that joins the covers. **11.** *Mining.* **a.** the side of a passage or layer nearest the surface. **b.** the earth between that level and the next. **12.** the upper surface of a joist, rafter, slate, tile, etc., when in position. Compare **bed** (sense 12). **13. at one's back.** behind, esp. in support or pursuit. **14. at the back of one's mind.** not in one's conscious thoughts. **15. behind one's back.** without one's knowledge; secretly or deceitfully. **16. break one's back** *or* (*Taboo*) **balls.** to overwork or work very hard. **17. break the back of.** to complete the greatest or hardest part of (a task). **18. (flat) on one's back.** incapacitated, esp. through illness. **19. get off someone's back.** *Informal.* to stop criticizing or pestering someone. **20. have on one's back.** to be burdened with. **21. put one's back into.** to devote all one's strength to (a task). **22. put** (*or* **get**) **someone's back up.** to annoy someone. **23. see the back of.** to be rid of. **24. back of beyond. a. the.** a very remote place. **b.** *Austral.* in such a place (esp. in the phrase **out back of beyond**). **25. turn one's back on. a.** to turn away from in anger or contempt. **b.** to refuse to help; abandon. **26. with one's back to the wall.** in a difficult or desperate situation. ~*vb.* (*mainly tr.*) **27.** (*also intr.*) to move or cause to move backwards. **28.** to provide support, money, or encouragement for (a person, enterprise, etc.). **29.** to bet on the success of: *to back a horse.* **30.** to provide with a back, backing, or lining. **31.** to provide with a music accompaniment: *a soloist backed by an orchestra.* **32.** to provide a background for; be at the back of: *mountains back the town.* **33.** to countersign or endorse. **34.** *Archàic.* to mount the back of. **35.** (*intr.;* foll. by *on* or *onto*) to have the back facing (towards): *the house backs onto a river.* **36.** (*intr.*) (of the wind) to change direction in an anticlockwise direction. Compare **veer**[1] (sense 3a.). **37.** *Nautical.* to position (a sail) so that the wind presses on its opposite side. **38. back and fill. a.** *Nautical.* to manoeuvre the sails by alternately filling and emptying them of wind to navigate in a narrow place. **b.** to vacillate in one's opinion. ~*adj.* (*prenominal*) **39.** situated behind: *a back lane.* **40.** of the past: *back issues of a magazine.* **41.** owing from an earlier date: *back rent.* **42.** *Chiefly U.S.* remote: *a back road.* **43.** moving in a backward direction: *back current.* **44.** *Phonetics.* of, relating to, or denoting a vowel articulated with the tongue retracted towards the soft palate, as for the vowels in English *hard, fall, hot, full, fool.* ~*adv.* **45.** at, to, or towards the rear; away from something considered to be the front; backwards; behind. **46.** in, to, or towards the original starting point, place, or condition: *to go back home; put the book back; my headache has come back.* **47.** in or into the past: *to look back on one's childhood.* **48.** in reply, repayment, or retaliation: *to hit someone back; pay back a debt; to answer back.* **49.** in check: *the dam holds back the water.* **50.** in concealment; in reserve: *to keep something back; to hold back information.* **51. back and forth.**

to and fro. **52. back to front. a.** in reverse. **b.** in disorder. ~See also **back down, back out, back up.** [Old English *bæc;* related to Old Norse *bak,* Old Frisian *bek,* Old High German *bah*]

back[2] (bæk) *n.* a large tub or vat, esp. one used by brewers. [C17: from Dutch *bak* tub, cistern, from Old French *bac,* from Vulgar Latin *bacca* (unattested) vessel for liquids]

back+ache ('bæk,eɪk) *n.* an ache or pain in one's back.

back+bench·er ('bæk'bɛntʃə) *n. Brit., Austral., etc.* a member of Parliament who does not hold office in the government or opposition.

back+bend ('bæk,bɛnd) *n.* a gymnastic exercise in which the trunk is bent backwards until the hands touch the floor.

back+bite ('bæk,baɪt) *vb.* **+bites, +bit+ing, bit; bit+ten** *or* **bit.** to talk spitefully about (an absent person). —'**back+,bit·er** *n.*

back+blocks ('bæk,blɒks) *pl. n. Austral.* sparsely populated areas in the remote interior. —'**back+,block** *adj.* —'**back+,block+er** *n.*

back+board ('bæk,bɔːd) *n.* **1.** a board that is placed behind something to form or support its back. **2.** a board worn to straighten or support the back, as after surgery. **3.** (in basketball) a flat upright surface supported on a high frame, under which the basket is attached.

back boil+er *n.* a tank or series of pipes at the back of a fireplace for heating water. U.S. name: **water back.**

back+bone ('bæk,bəʊn) *n.* **1.** a nontechnical name for **spinal column. 2.** something that resembles the spinal column in function, position, or appearance. **3.** strength of character; courage. **4.** the main or central mountain range of a country or region. **5.** *Printing.* a less common name for **spine** (sense 4). **6.** *Nautical.* the main longitudinal members of a vessel, giving structural strength.

back+break·er ('bæk,breɪkə) *n.* **1.** a wrestling hold in which a wrestler uses his knee or shoulder as a fulcrum to bend his opponent's body backwards. **2.** *Informal.* an extremely arduous task.

back+break·ing ('bæk,breɪkɪŋ) *adj.* demanding great effort; exhausting.

back+chat ('bæk,tʃæt) *n. Informal.* the act of answering back, esp. impudently.

back+cloth ('bæk,klɒθ) *or* **back+drop** *n.* a large painted curtain hanging at the back of a stage set.

back+comb ('bæk,kəʊm) *vb.* to comb the under layers of (the hair) towards the roots to give more bulk to a hair style. Also: **tease.**

back coun+try *n. Austral.* sparsely populated areas.

back+court ('bæk,kɔːt) *n.* **1.** *Tennis, chiefly U.S.* the part of the court between the service line and the baseline. **2.** (in various court games) the area nearest the back boundary line.

back+cross ('bæk,krɒs) *vb.* **1.** to mate (a hybrid of the first generation) with one of its parents. ~*n.* **2.** the offspring so produced. **3.** the act or process of backcrossing.

back+date (,bæk'deɪt) *vb.* (*tr.*) to make effective from an earlier date: *the pay rise was backdated to August.*

back door *n.* **1.** a door at the rear or side of a building. **2.** a means of entry to a job, position, etc., that is secret, underhand, or obtained through influence.

back down *vb.* **1.** (*intr., adv.*) to withdraw an earlier claim. **2.** (*tr.*) *Rowing.* to cause (a boat) to move backwards by pushing rather than pulling on the oars. ~*n.* **back+down. 3.** abandonment of an earlier claim.

backed (bækt) *adj.* **a.** having a back or backing. **b.** (*in combination*): *high-backed; black-backed.*

back end *n. Northern English dialect.* autumn. [from the phrase *the back end of the year*]

back+er ('bækə) *n.* **1.** a person who gives financial or other support. **2.** a person who bets on a competitor or contestant.

back+fill ('bæk,fɪl) *vb.* **1.** (*tr.*) to refill an excavated trench, esp. (in archaeology) at the end of an investigation. ~*n.* **2.** the soil used to do this.

back+fire (,bæk'faɪə) *vb.* (*intr.*) **1.** (of an internal-combustion engine) to emit a loud noise as a result of an explosion in the inlet manifold or exhaust system. **2.** to fail to have the desired or expected effect: *his plans backfired on him.* **3.** to start a controlled fire in order to halt an advancing forest or prairie fire by creating a barren area. ~*n.* **4.** (in an internal-combustion engine) **a.** an explosion of unburnt gases in the exhaust system. **b.** a premature explosion in a cylinder or inlet manifold. **5.** a controlled fire started to create a barren area that will halt an advancing forest or prairie fire.

back for+ma+tion *n.* **1.** the unwitting invention of a new word on the assumption that a familiar word is derived from it. The verbs *edit* and *burgle* in English were so created from *editor* and *burglar.* **2.** a word formed by this process.

back four *n. Soccer.* the defensive players in many modern team formations: usually two fullbacks and two centre backs.

back+gam+mon ('bæk,gæmən, bæk'gæmən) *n.* **1.** a game for two people played on a board with pieces moved according to throws of the dice. **2.** the most complete form of win in this game. [C17: BACK + *gammon,* variant of GAME]

back green *or* **back·ie** ('bɑːkɪ) *n. Edinburgh dialect.* a yard at the back of a house.

back+ground ('bæk,graʊnd) *n.* **1.** the part of a scene or view furthest from the viewer. **2. a.** an inconspicuous or unobtrusive position (esp. in the phrase **in the background**). **b.** (*as modifier*): *a background influence.* **3.** *Art.* **a.** the plane or ground in a picture upon which all other planes or forms appear superimposed. **b.** the parts of a picture that appear most distant. Compare **foreground, middle distance. 4.** a person's social class, education, training, or experience. **5. a.** the social, historical, or technical circumstances that lead up to or help to explain something: *the background to the French Revolution.* **b.** (*as modifier*): *background information.* **6. a.** a low level of sound, lighting, etc., whose purpose is to be an unobtrusive or appropriate accompaniment to something else, such as a social activity, conversation, or the action of a film. **b.** (*as modifier*): *background music.* **7.** Also called: **background radiation.** *Physics.* low-intensity radiation from small amounts of radio isotopes in soil, air, building materials, etc. **8.** *Electronics.* **a.** unwanted effects, such as noise, occurring in a measuring instrument, electronic device, etc. **b.** (*as modifier*): *background interference.*

back+hand ('bæk,hænd) *n.* **1.** *Tennis, squash, etc.* **a.** a stroke made across the body with the back of the hand facing the direction of the stroke. **b.** (*as modifier*): *a backhand return.* **2.** the side on which backhand strokes are made. **3.** handwriting slanting to the left. ~*adv.* **4.** with a backhand stroke. ~*vb.* (*tr.*) **5.** *Sport.* to play (a shot) backhand.

back+hand+ed (,bæk'hændɪd) *adj.* **1.** (of a blow, shot, stroke, etc.) performed with the arm moving across the body. **2.** double-edged; equivocal: *a backhanded compliment.* **3.** (of handwriting) slanting to the left. **4.** (of a rope) twisted in the opposite way from the normal right-handed direction. ~*adv.* **5.** in a backhanded manner. —**,back+'hand+ed+ly** *adv.* —**,back+'hand+ed+ness** *n.*

back+hand+er ('bæk,hændə) *n.* **1.** a backhanded stroke or blow. **2.** *Informal.* an indirect attack. **3.** *Slang.* a bribe.

back+ing ('bækɪŋ) *n.* **1.** support given to a person, cause, or enterprise. **2.** a body of supporters. **3.** something that forms, protects, supports, or strengthens the back of something. **4.** *Theatre.* a scenic cloth or flat placed behind a window, door, etc., in a set to mask the offstage space. **5.** musical accompaniment, esp. for a pop singer.

back+ing store *n.* a computer storage device, such as a disk, drum, or magnetic tape, that has a larger capacity but longer access time than a computer memory.

back+lash ('bæk,læʃ) *n.* **1.** a reaction or recoil between interacting worn or badly fitting parts in a mechanism. **2.** the excessive play between such parts. **3.** a sudden and adverse reaction, esp. to a political or social development: *the White backlash to the Black Power movement.*

back+less ('bæklɪs) *adj.* (of a dress) low-cut at the back.

back list *n.* a publisher's previously published books that are still available.

back+log ('bæk,lɒg) *n.* **1.** an accumulation of uncompleted work, unsold stock, etc., to be dealt with. **2.** *Chiefly U.S.* a large log at the back of a fireplace.

back mark+er *n.* a competitor who is at the back of a field in a race.

back mat+ter *n.* the parts of a book, such as the index and appendixes, that follow the main text. Also called: **end matter.**

back+most ('bæk,məʊst) *adj.* furthest back.

back num+ber *n.* **1.** an issue of a newspaper, magazine, etc., that appeared on a previous date. **2.** *Informal.* a person or thing considered to be old-fashioned.

back o' Bourke (bɜːk) *adv. Austral.* in a remote or backward place. [from *Bourke,* a town in New South Wales]

back out *vb.* (*intr., adv.;* often foll. by *of*) to withdraw (from an agreement, etc.).

back pack *n.* **1.** *Chiefly U.S.* a rucksack or knapsack. **2.** a pack carried on the back of an astronaut, containing oxygen cylinders, essential supplies, etc.

back pass+age *n.* the rectum.

back-ped·al *vb.* **-ped·als, -ped·al·ling, -ped·alled** *or U.S.* **-ped·als, -ped·al·ing, -ped·aled.** (*intr.*) **1.** to turn the pedals of a bicycle backwards. **2.** to retract or modify a previous opinion, principle, etc. **3.** *Boxing.* to take backward steps.

back pro+jec+tion *n.* a method of projecting pictures onto a translucent screen so that they are viewed from the opposite side, used esp. in films to create the illusion that the actors in the foreground are moving. Also called: **background projection.**

back rest *n.* a support for the back of something.

Back Riv+er *n.* a river in N Canada, rising in the Northwest Territories and flowing northeast to the Arctic Ocean. Length: about 966 km (600 miles).

back room *n.* **a.** a place where research is done, esp. secret research in wartime. **b.** (*as modifier*): *back-room boys.*

Backs (bæks) *pl. n.* **the.** the grounds between the River Cam and certain Cambridge colleges.

back saw *n.* a small handsaw stiffened along its upper edge by a metal section.

back scat+ter *n. Physics.* **1.** the scattering of radiation, such as x-rays or alpha-particles, by the atoms of the medium through which it passes, a proportion of this radiation emerging from the surface through which it entered. **2.** the radiation so scattered.

back+scratch+er ('bæk,skrætʃə) *n.* **1.** an implement with a long handle, used for scratching one's own back. **2.** *Informal.* a person who provides a service, corporate or public money etc., for another, in order to receive a similar service or reward in return.

back seat *n.* **1.** a seat at the back, esp. of a vehicle. **2.** *Informal.* a subordinate or inconspicuous position (esp. in the phrase **take a back seat**).

back-seat driv+er *n. Informal.* **1.** a passenger in a car who offers unwanted advice to the driver. **2.** a person who offers advice on or tries to direct matters that are not his concern.

back+sheesh ('bækʃiːʃ) *n.* a variant spelling of **baksheesh.**

back+side (ˌbæk'saɪd) *n.* **1.** the back of something. **2.** *Informal.* the buttocks.
back+sight ('bækˌsaɪt) *n.* **1.** the sight of a rifle nearer the stock. **2.** *Surveying.* a reading taken looking backwards to a previously occupied station. Compare **foresight** (sense 4).
back slang *n.* a type of slang in which words are spelled and, as far as possible, pronounced backwards.
back-slap·ping *adj.* energetically jovial; hearty.
back+slide ('bækˌslaɪd) *vb.* **+slides, +slid+ing, +slid; +slid** *or* **+slid+den.** (*intr.*) to lapse into bad habits or vices from a state of virtue, religious faith, etc. —**'back+ˌslid+er** *n.*
back+space ('bækˌspeɪs) *vb.* **1.** to move a (typewriter carriage, etc.) backwards. ~*n.* **2.** a typewriter key that can effect such a movement.
back+spin ('bækˌspɪn) *n. Sport.* a backward spinning motion imparted to a ball to minimize its bounce. Compare **topspin.**
back+stage (ˌbæk'steɪdʒ) *adv.* **1.** behind the part of the theatre in view of the audience; in the dressing rooms, wings, etc. **2.** towards the rear of the stage. ~*adj.* **3.** situated backstage. **4.** *Informal.* away from public view.
back+stairs ('bæk'stɛəz) *pl. n.* **1.** a secondary staircase in a house, esp. one originally for the use of servants. ~*adj. also* **back+stair. 2.** underhand: *backstairs gossip.*
back+stay ('bækˌsteɪ) *n.* **1.** *Nautical.* a stay leading aft from the upper part of a mast to the deck or stern. **2.** *Machinery.* a supporting piece or arresting part. **3.** anything that supports or strengthens the back of something, such as leather covering the back seam of a shoe.
back+stitch ('bækˌstɪtʃ) *n.* **1.** a strong sewing stitch made by starting the next stitch at the middle or beginning of the preceding one. ~*vb.* **2.** to sew using this stitch.
back stop *n.* **1.** *Sport.* a screen or fence to prevent balls leaving the playing area. **2.** a block or catch to prevent excessive backward movement, such as one on the sliding seat of a rowing boat.
back straight *n.* a straight part of a circuit, esp. of an athletics track, furthest from the finishing point.
back+street ('bækˌstri:t) *n.* **1.** a street in a town remote from the main roads. **2.** (*modifier*) denoting illicit activities regarded as likely to take place in such a street: *a backstreet abortion.*
back stretch *n.* a horse-racing term for **back straight.**
back+stroke ('bækˌstrəʊk) *n.* **1.** Also called: **back crawl.** *Swimming.* **a.** a stroke performed on the back, using backward circular strokes of each arm and flipper movements of the feet. **b.** (*as modifier*): *the backstroke champion.* **2.** a return stroke or blow. **3.** *Chiefly U.S.* a backhanded stroke. **4.** *Bell-ringing.* the upward movement of the bell rope as the bell swings back and forth. Compare **handstroke.** ~*vb.* **5.** (*intr.*) to swim the backstroke.
back+swept ('bækˌswɛpt) *adj.* **1.** slanting backwards. **2.** another word for **sweptback.**
back+sword ('bækˌsɔ:d) *n.* **1.** another name for **broadsword. 2.** Also called: **back+swords+man.** a person who uses the back-sword. **3.** a fencing stick with a basket-like protective hilt.
back-to-back *adj.* (*usually postpositive*) **1.** facing in opposite directions, often with the backs touching. **2.** *Chiefly Brit.* (of urban houses) built so that their backs are adjacent or separated only by a narrow alley. **3.** *Informal.* consecutive. ~*n.* **4.** a house or terrace built in back-to-back style.
back+track ('bækˌtræk) *vb.* (*intr.*) **1.** to return by the same route by which one has come. **2.** to retract or reverse one's opinion, action, policy, etc.
back up *vb.* (*adv.*) **1.** (*tr.*) to support or assist. **2.** (*intr.*) *Cricket.* (of a nonstriking batsman) to move down the wicket in readiness for a run as a ball is bowled. **3.** (of water) to accumulate. **4.** *Printing.* to print the second side of (a sheet). **5.** *Computer technol.* to make a copy of (a data file), esp. for storage in another place as a security copy. **6.** (*intr.*, usually foll. by *on*) *Austral.* to repeat an action immediately. ~*n.* **back+up.** *Chiefly U.S.* **7.** a support or reinforcement. **8. a.** a reserve or substitute. **b.** (*as modifier*): *backup troops.* **9.** the overflow from a blocked drain or pipe.
back-up light *n.* a U.S. name for **reversing light.**
back+veld ('bækfɛlt, -vɛlt) *n. S. African informal.* a remote sparsely populated rural area. [Afrikaans, from *back* BACK[1] + *velt* field] —**'back+veld+er** *n.*
back+ward ('bækwəd) *adj.* **1.** (*usually prenominal*) directed towards the rear: *a backward glance.* **2.** retarded in physical, material, or intellectual development: *backward countries; a backward child.* **3. a.** of or relating to the past; conservative or reactionary. **b.** (*in combination*): *backward-looking.* **4.** reluctant or bashful: *a backward lover.* ~*adv.* **5.** a variant of **backwards.** —**'back+ward+ly** *adv.* —**'back+ward+ness** *n.*
back+ward·a+tion (ˌbækwə'deɪʃən) *n.* **1.** (on the London Stock Exchange) postponement, usually speculative, of delivery by a seller of securities until the next settlement period. **2.** the fee paid by the seller to the purchaser for such postponement. ~Compare **contango.**
back+wards ('bækwədz) *or* **back+ward** *adv.* **1.** towards the rear. **2.** with the back foremost. **3.** in the reverse of usual order or direction. **4.** to or towards the past. **5.** into a worse state: *the patient was slipping backwards.* **6.** towards the point of origin. **7. bend, lean,** *or* **fall over backwards.** *Informal.* to make a special effort, esp. in order to please. **8. know backwards.** *Brit. informal.* to understand completely.
back+wash ('bækˌwɒʃ) *n.* **1.** a dashing movement of water, such as that of retreating waves. Compare **swash. 2.** water washed backwards by the motion of oars or other propelling devices. **3.** the backward flow of air set up by an aircraft's engines. **4.** a condition resulting from a previous event; repercussion. ~*vb.* **5.** (*tr.*) to remove oil from (combed wool).
back+wa·ter ('bækˌwɔ:tə) *n.* **1.** a body of stagnant water connected to a river. **2.** water held or driven back, as by a dam, flood, or tide. **3.** an isolated, backward, or intellectually stagnant place or condition. ~*vb.* **back wa+ter. 4.** (*intr.*) to reverse the direction of a boat, esp. to push the oars of a rowing boat.
back+woods ('bækwʊdz) *pl. n.* **1.** *Chiefly U.S.* partially cleared, sparsely populated forests. **2.** any remote sparsely populated place. **3.** (*modifier*) of, from, or like the backwoods. **4.** (*modifier*) uncouth; rustic.
back+woods+man ('bækˌwʊdzmən) *n., pl.* **+men. 1.** a person from the backwoods. **2.** *U.S. informal.* an uncouth or rustic person. **3.** *Brit. informal.* a peer who rarely attends the House of Lords.
back yard *n.* **1.** a yard at the back of a house, etc. **2. in one's own back yard.** close at hand.
bac+la+va ('bɑ:kləˌvɑ:) *n.* a variant spelling of **baklava.**
Ba+co+lod (bə'kɒləd) *n.* a town in the Philippines, on the NW coast of Negros Island. Pop.: 196 492 (1975 est.).
ba+con ('beɪkən) *n.* **1.** meat from the back and sides of a pig, dried, salted, and usually smoked. **2. bring home the bacon.** *Informal.* **a.** to achieve success. **b.** to provide material support. **3. save one's bacon.** *Brit. informal.* to escape from a dangerous or difficult situation. [C12: from Old French *bacon,* from Old High German *bahho;* related to Old Saxon *baco;* see BACK[1]]
Ba·con ('beɪkən) *n.* **1. Fran·cis,** Baron Verulam, Viscount St. Albans. 1561–1626, English philosopher, statesman, and essayist; described the inductive method of reasoning: his works include *Essays* (1625), *The Advancement of Learning* (1605), and *Novum Organum* (1620). **2. Fran·cis.** born 1909, Irish painter, noted for his distorted, richly coloured human figures, dogs, and carcasses. **3. Rog·er.** ?1214–92, English Franciscan monk, scholar, and scientist: stressed the importance of experiment, demonstrated that air is required for combustion, and first used lenses to correct vision. His *Opus Majus* (1266) is a compendium of all the sciences of his age. —**Ba+co+ni·an** (beɪ'kəʊnɪən) *adj., n.*
ba·con-and-eggs *n.* another name for **bird's-foot trefoil.**
ba+con+er ('beɪkənə) *n.* a pig that weighs between 83 and 101 kg, from which bacon is cut.
bact. *abbrev. for* bacteria(l).
bac+te+rae+mi·a *or U.S.* **bac+te+re+mi·a** (ˌbæktə'ri:mɪə) *n. Pathol.* the presence of bacteria in the blood.
bac+te+ri·a (bæk'tɪərɪə) *pl. n., sing.* **+ri·um** (-rɪəm). a large group of typically unicellular microorganisms, usually classified as plants. Most bacteria are parasites (many of which cause disease) or saprophytes and reproduce by fission. [C19: plural of New Latin *bacterium,* from Greek *baktērion,* literally: a little stick, from *baktron* rod, staff] —**bac+'te+ri+al** *adj.* —**bac+'te+ri+al+ly** *adv.*
bac+te+ri·a bed *n.* a layer of sand or gravel used to expose sewage effluent, in its final stages, to air and the action of microorganisms. Compare **filter bed** (sense 1).
bac+te+ri·al plaque *n.* another term for **dental plaque.**
bac+te+ri+cide (bæk'tɪərɪˌsaɪd) *n.* a substance able to destroy bacteria. —**bac+ˌte+ri+'cid+al** *adj.*
bac+te+rin ('bæktərɪn) *n.* a vaccine prepared from bacteria.
bac·te·ri·o-, bac·te·ri-, *or sometimes before a vowel* **bac·ter-** *combining form.* indicating bacteria or an action or condition relating to bacteria: *bacteriology; bactericide; bacteroid.* [New Latin, from BACTERIA]
bacteriol. *abbrev. for:* **1.** bacteriological. **2.** bacteriology.
bac+te+ri+ol+o·gy (bækˌtɪərɪ'ɒlədʒɪ) *n.* the branch of science concerned with the study of bacteria. —**bac+te+ri·o·log·i·cal** (bækˌtɪərɪə'lɒdʒɪkᵊl) *adj.* —**bac+ˌte+ri+o+'log·i·cal+ly** *adv.* —**bac+ˌte+ri+'ol·o·gist** *n.*
bac+te+ri+ol·y+sis (bækˌtɪərɪ'ɒlɪsɪs) *n.* the destruction of bacteria, esp. by antibodies. —**bac+te+ri+o+lyt+ic** (bækˌtɪərɪə'lɪtɪk) *adj.*
bac+te+ri·o+phage (bæk'tɪərɪəˌfeɪdʒ) *n.* a virus that is parasitic in a bacterium and multiplies within its host, which is destroyed when the new viruses are released. Often shortened to **phage.** —**bac+te+ri·o+phag+ic** (bækˌtɪərɪə'fædʒɪk) *adj.* —**bac+te+ri+oph·a·gous** (bækˌtɪərɪ'ɒfəgəs) *adj.*
bac+te+ri+o+sta+sis (bækˌtɪərɪəʊ'steɪsɪs, -'stæsɪs) *n., pl.* **+sta+ses** (-'steɪsi:z, -'stæsi:z). inhibition of the growth and reproduction of bacteria, esp. by the action of a chemical agent. —**bac+te+ri+o+stat+ic** (bækˌtɪərɪəʊ'stætɪk) *adj.* —**bac+ˌte+ri+o+'stat·i·cal+ly** *adv.*
bac+te+ri+um (bæk'tɪərɪəm) *n.* singular of **bacteria.**
bac+ter+oid ('bæktəˌrɔɪd) *adj.* **1.** resembling a bacterium. ~*n.* **2.** any rodlike bacterium of the genus *Bacteroides,* occurring in the gut of man and animals.
Bac+tri·a ('bæktrɪə) *n.* an ancient country of SW Asia, between the Hindu Kush mountains and the Oxus River: forms the present district of Balkh in N Afghanistan. —**'Bac+tri·an** *adj., n.*
Bac+tri·an cam+el *n.* a two-humped camel, *Camelus bactrianus,* used as a beast of burden in the cold deserts of central Asia. Compare **Arabian camel.**
ba+cu+li+form (bə'kju:lɪˌfɔ:m, 'bækju:-) *adj. Biology.* shaped like a rod: *baculiform fungal spores.* [C19: from *baculi-,* from Latin *baculum* walking stick + -FORM]
bac·u+lum ('bækjʊləm) *n., pl.* **+la** (-lə) *or* **+lums.** a bony support in the penis of certain mammals, esp. the carnivores. [C20: New Latin, from Latin: stick, staff]

bad[1] (bæd) *adj.* **worse, worst. 1.** not good; of poor quality; inadequate; inferior: *bad workmanship; bad soil; bad light for reading.* **2.** (often foll. by *at*) lacking skill or talent; incompetent: *a bad painter; bad at sports.* **3.** (often foll. by *for*) harmful: *bad air; smoking is bad for you.* **4.** immoral; evil: *a bad life.* **5.** naughty; mischievous; disobedient: *a bad child.* **6.** rotten; decayed; spoiled: *a bad egg.* **7.** severe; intense: *a bad headache.* **8.** incorrect; wrong; faulty: *bad pronunciation.* **9.** ill or in pain (esp. in the phrase **feel bad**). **10.** regretful, sorry, or upset (esp. in the phrase **feel bad about**). **11.** unfavourable; distressing: *bad news; a bad business.* **12.** offensive; unpleasant; disagreeable: *bad language; bad temper.* **13.** not valid or sound; void: *a bad cheque.* **14.** not recoverable: *a bad debt.* **15. go from bad to worse.** to deteriorate even more. **16. go bad.** to putrefy; spoil. **17. in a bad way.** *Informal.* **a.** seriously ill, through sickness or injury. **b.** in trouble of any kind. **18. in someone's bad books.** See **book** (sense 16). **19. make the best of a bad job.** to manage as well as possible in unfavourable circumstances. **20. not bad** *or* **not so bad.** *Informal.* passable; fair; fairly good. **21. not half bad.** *Informal.* very good. **22. too bad.** *Informal.* (often used dismissively) regrettable. **23.** *Slang.* (chiefly U.S. Negro usage, also found in jazz contexts) good; fine. ~*n.* **24.** unfortunate or unpleasant events collectively (often in the phrase **take the bad with the good**). **25.** an immoral or degenerate state (often in the phrase **go to the bad**). **26.** the debit side of an account: *£200 to the bad.* **27. in bad with.** *Informal.* out of favour with. ~*adv.* **28.** *Not standard.* badly: *to want something bad.* [C13: probably from *bæd-*, as the first element of Old English *bǣddel* hermaphrodite, *bǣdling* sodomite] —**'bad+dish** *adj.* —**'bad+ness** *n.*
Usage. See at **good.**

bad[2] (bæd) *vb.* a variant spelling of **bade.**

Ba+da+joz ('bædəˌhɒz; *Spanish* ˌbaðaˈxoθ) *n.* a city in SW Spain: strategically positioned near the frontier with Portugal. Pop.: 101 110 (1970).

Ba+da+lo+na (*Spanish* ˌbaðaˈlona) *n.* a port in NE Spain: an industrial suburb of Barcelona. Pop.: 162 888 (1970).

bad blood *n.* a feeling of intense hatred or hostility; enmity.

bad+der+locks ('bædəˌlɒks) *n.* a seaweed, *Alaria esculenta,* that has long brownish-green fronds and is eaten in parts of N Europe. [C18: of unknown origin]

bad+die *or* **bad+dy** ('bædɪ) *n., pl.* **+dies.** *Informal.* a bad character in a story, film, etc., esp. an opponent of the hero.

bade (bæd, beɪd) *or* **bad** *vb.* the past tense of **bid.**

Ba+den ('ba:dən) *n.* a former state of West Germany, now part of Baden-Württemberg.

Ba·den-Ba·den *n.* a spa in SW West Germany, in Baden-Württemberg. Pop.: 36 900 (1970).

Ba·den-Pow·ell ('beɪdən 'pəʊəl, 'paʊəl) *n.* **Rob·ert Ste·phen·son Smyth** (smɪθ, smaɪθ), 1st Baron Baden-Powell. 1857–1941, British general, noted for his defence of Mafeking (1899–1900) in the Boer War; founder of the Boy Scouts (1908) and (with his sister Agnes) the Girl Guides (1910).

Ba·den-Würt·tem+berg (*German* 'ba:dən 'vyrtəmˌbɛrk) *n.* a state of SW West Germany. Capital: Stuttgart. Pop.: 8 895 048 (1970). Area: 35 742 sq. km (13 800 sq. miles).

badge (bædʒ) *n.* **1.** a distinguishing emblem or mark worn to signify membership, employment, achievement, etc. **2.** any revealing feature or mark. [C14: from Norman French *bage;* related to Anglo-Latin *bagia*]

badg+er ('bædʒə) *n.* **1.** any of various stocky omnivorous musteline mammals of the subfamily *Melinae,* such as *Meles meles* (**Eurasian badger**), occurring in Europe, Asia, and North America: order *Carnivora* (carnivores). They are typically large burrowing animals, with strong claws and a thick coat striped black and white on the head. Compare **ferret badger, hog badger. 2. honey badger.** another name for **ratel.** ~*vb.* **3.** (*tr.*) to pester or harass. [C16: variant of *badgeard,* probably from BADGE (from the white mark on its forehead) + -ARD]

Bad Go+des+berg (*German* ba:t 'go:dəsbɛrk) *n.* the official name for **Godesberg.**

bad·i·nage ('bædɪˌnɑ:ʒ) *n.* playful or frivolous repartee or banter. [C17: from French, from *badiner* to jest, banter, from Old Provençal *badar* to gape]

Bad Lands *pl. n.* a deeply eroded barren region of SW South Dakota and NW Nebraska.

bad+lands ('bædˌlændz) *pl. n.* any deeply eroded barren area.

bad+ly ('bædlɪ) *adv.* **worse, worst. 1.** poorly; defectively; inadequately: *the chair is badly made.* **2.** unfavourably; unsuccessfully; unfortunately: *our scheme worked out badly.* **3.** severely; gravely: *he was badly hurt.* **4.** incorrectly or inaccurately: *to speak German badly.* **5.** improperly; naughtily; wickedly: *to behave badly.* **6.** without humanity; cruelly: *to treat badly.* **7.** very much (esp. in the phrases **need badly, badly in need of, want badly**). **8.** regretfully: *he felt badly about it.* **9. badly off.** poor; impoverished. ~*adj.* **10.** (*postpositive*) *Northern English dialect.* ill; poorly.

bad+man ('bædˌmæn) *n., pl.* **+men.** *Chiefly U.S.* a hired gunman, outlaw, or criminal.

bad+min+ton ('bædmɪntən) *n.* **1.** a game played with rackets and a shuttlecock, which is hit back and forth across a high net. **2.** Also called: **badminton cup.** a long refreshing drink of claret with soda water and sugar.

bad-mouth *vb.* (*tr.*) *U.S. slang.* to speak unfavourably about.

bad news *n. Slang.* someone or something regarded as undesirable: *he's bad news around here.*

Ba·do·glio (*Italian* ba'dɔʎʎo) *n.* **Pie·tro** ('pjɛ:tro). 1871–1956, Italian marshal; premier (1943–44) following Mussolini's downfall: arranged an armistice with the Allies (1943).

Bae·da ('bi:də) *n.* Latin name of **Bede.**

Bae+de+ker ('beɪdɪkə) *n.* **1.** any of a series of travel guidebooks issued by the German publisher Karl Baedeker (1801–59) or his firm. **2.** any guidebook.

Bae+de+ker raid *n. Informal.* one of the German air raids in 1942 on places of cultural and historical importance in England.

bael ('beɪəl) *n.* **1.** a spiny Indian rutaceous tree, *Aegle marmelos.* **2.** the edible thick-shelled fruit of this tree. [C17: from Hindi *bel*]

Bae·yer (*German* 'baɪər) *n.* **Jo·hann Frie·drich Wil·helm A·dolf von** ('jo:han 'fri:drɪç 'vɪlhɛlm 'a:dɔlf fɔn). 1835–1917, German chemist, noted for the synthesis of indigo: Nobel prize for chemistry 1905.

Ba·ez (baɪ'ɛz) *n.* **Joan.** born 1941, U.S. rock and folk singer, guitarist, and songwriter, noted for the pure quality of her voice and for her committed pacifist and protest songs.

Baf+fin Bay ('bæfɪn) *n.* part of the Northwest Passage, situated between Baffin Island and Greenland. [named after William *Baffin,* 17th-century English navigator]

Baf+fin Is+land *n.* the largest island of the Canadian Arctic, between Greenland and Hudson Bay. Pop.: about 2000. Area: 476 560 sq. km (184 000 sq. miles). [see BAFFIN BAY]

baf+fle ('bæfəl) *vb.* (*tr.*) **1.** to perplex; bewilder; puzzle. **2.** to frustrate (plans, efforts, etc.). **3.** to check, restrain, or regulate (the flow of a fluid or the emission of sound or light). **4.** to provide with a baffle. **5.** *Obsolete.* to cheat or trick. ~*n.* **6.** Also called: **baffle board, baffle plate.** a plate or mechanical device designed to restrain or regulate the flow of a fluid, the emission of light or sound, or the distribution of sound, esp. in a loudspeaker or microphone. [C16: perhaps from Scottish dialect *bachlen* to condemn publicly] —**'baf+fle+ment** *n.* —**'baf+fler** *n.* —**'baf+fling+ly** *adv.*

bag (bæg) *n.* **1.** a flexible container with an opening at one end. **2.** Also called: **bagful.** the contents of or amount contained in such a container. **3.** any of various measures of quantity, such as a bag containing 1 hundredweight of coal. **4.** a piece of portable luggage. **5.** short for **handbag. 6.** anything that hangs loosely, sags, or is shaped like a bag, such as a loose fold of skin under the eyes or the bulging part of a sail. **7.** any pouch or sac forming part of the body of an animal, esp. the udder of a cow. **8.** *Hunting.* the quantity of quarry taken in a single hunting trip or by a single hunter. **9.** *Derogatory slang.* an ugly or bad-tempered woman or girl (often in the phrase **old bag**). **10.** *Slang.* a measure of marijuana, heroin, etc., in folded paper. **11.** *Slang.* a person's particular taste, field of skill, interest, activity, etc.: *blues is his bag.* **12. bag and baggage.** *Informal.* **a.** with all one's belongings. **b.** entirely. **13. a bag of bones.** a lean creature. **14. in the bag.** *Slang.* almost assured of succeeding or being obtained. **15. the (whole) bag of tricks.** *Informal.* every device; everything. ~*vb.* **bags, bag+ging, bagged. 16.** (*tr.*) to put into a bag. **17.** to bulge or cause to bulge; swell. **18.** (*tr.*) to capture or kill, as in hunting. **19.** (*tr.*) to catch, seize, or steal. **20.** (*intr.*) to hang loosely; sag. **21.** (*tr.*) *Brit. informal.* to reserve or secure the right to do or to have something: *he bagged the best chair.* **22.** (*tr.*) *Austral. slang.* to criticize; disparage. [C13: probably from Old Norse *baggi;* related to Old French *bague* bundle, pack, Medieval Latin *baga* chest, sack, Flemish *bagge*]

Ba+gan+da (bə'gændə, -'gɑ:n-) *n.* (*functioning as pl.*) a Negroid people of E Africa living chiefly in Uganda. See also **Ganda, Luganda.**

ba+gasse (bə'gæs) *n.* **1.** the dry pulp remaining after the extraction of juice from sugar cane or other similar plants: used as fuel, for making fibreboard, paper, etc. **2.** Also called: **megass, megasse.** a type of paper made from bagasse fibres. [C19: from French, from Spanish *bagazo* dregs, refuse, from *baga* husk, from Latin *bāca* berry]

bag·a+telle (ˌbægə'tɛl) *n.* **1.** something of little value or significance; trifle. **2.** a board game in which balls are struck into holes, with pins as obstacles; pinball. **3.** another name for **bar billiards. 4.** a short light piece of music, esp. for piano. [C17: from French, from Italian *bagattella,* from (dialect) *bagatta* a little possession, from *baga* a possession, probably from Latin *bāca* berry]

Bag+dad (bæg'dæd) *n.* a variant spelling of **Baghdad.**

Bage·hot ('bædʒət) *n.* **Wal·ter.** 1826–77, English economist and journalist: editor of *The Economist;* author of *The English Constitution* (1867), *Physics and Politics* (1872), and *Lombard Street* (1873).

ba+gel *or* **bei+gel** ('beɪgəl) *n.* a hard ring-shaped bread roll, characteristic of Jewish baking. [from Yiddish *beygel,* ultimately from Old High German *boug* ring]

bag+gage ('bægɪdʒ) *n.* **1. a.** suitcases, bags, etc., packed for a journey; luggage. **b.** *Chiefly U.S.* (*as modifier*): *baggage car.* **2.** an army's portable equipment. **3.** *Informal, old-fashioned.* **a.** a pert young woman. **b.** an immoral woman or prostitute. [C15: from Old French *bagage,* from *bague* a bundle, perhaps of Scandinavian origin; compare Old Norse *baggi* BAG]

bag+ging ('bægɪŋ) *n.* coarse woven cloth; sacking.

bag+gy[1] ('bægɪ) *adj.* **+gi+er, +gi+est.** (of clothes) hanging loosely; puffed out. —**'bag+gi+ly** *adv.* —**'bag+gi+ness** *n.*

bag+gy[2] ('bægɪ) *n., pl.* **+gies.** a variant spelling of **bagie.**

bagh (bɑ:g) *n.* (in India and Pakistan) a garden. [Urdu]

Bagh+dad *or* **Bag+dad** (bæg'dæd) *n.* the capital of Iraq, on the River Tigris: capital of the Abbasid Caliphate (762–1258). Pop.: 2 183 760 (1970 est.).

Bagh+lan (bæg'lɑ:n) *n.* a city in NE Afghanistan: sugar refining. Pop.: 110 874 (1973 est.).

ba+gie (ˈbeɪɡɪ) *or* **bag+gy** *n., pl.* **+gies.** *Northumbrian dialect.* a turnip. [perhaps from RUTABAGA]

bag+man (ˈbæɡmən) *n., pl.* **+men. 1.** *Brit. informal.* a travelling salesman. **2.** *U.S. slang.* a person who collects or distributes money for racketeers. **3.** *Austral.* a tramp or swagman, esp. one on horseback.

bag+nette (ˈbæɡnɛt) *n.* a variant of **baguette** (sense 3).

bagn·io (ˈbɑːnjəʊ) *n., pl.* **·ios. 1.** a brothel. **2.** *Obsolete.* an oriental prison for slaves. **3.** *Obsolete.* an Italian or Turkish bathhouse. [C16: from Italian *bagno,* from Latin *balneum* bath, from Greek *balaneion*]

bag+pipe (ˈbæɡˌpaɪp) *n.* (*modifier*) of or relating to the bagpipes. [C14: probably a translation of Low German *sakpīpe;* see SACK[1], PIPE[1]; related to Dutch *zakpijpe*]

bag+pipes (ˈbæɡˌpaɪps) *pl. n.* any of a family of musical wind instruments in which sounds are produced in reed pipes supplied with air from a bag inflated either by the player's mouth, as in the **Irish bagpipes** or **Highland bagpipes** of Scotland, or by arm-operated bellows, as in the **Northumbrian bagpipes.**

bags (bæɡz) *pl. n.* **1.** *Informal.* a lot; a great deal. **2.** short for **Oxford bags. 3.** *Brit. informal.* any pair of trousers. ~*interj.* **4.** Also: **bags I.** *Children's slang, Brit.* an indication of the desire to do, be, or have something.

ba+guette *or* **ba+guet** (bæˈɡɛt) *n.* **1.** a small gem cut as a long rectangle. **2.** the shape of such a gem. **3.** *Architect.* a small moulding having a semicircular cross section. **4.** a narrow French stick loaf. [C18: from French, from Italian *bacchetta* a little stick, from *bacchio* rod, from Latin *baculum* walking stick]

Ba+gui·o (ˈbæɡɪˌəʊ) *n.* a city in the N Philippines, on N Luzon: summer capital of the Republic. Pop.: 84 538 (1970).

bag+wash (ˈbæɡˌwɒʃ) *n. Old-fashioned.* **1.** a laundry that washes clothes without drying or pressing them. **2.** the clothes so washed.

bag+wig (ˈbæɡˌwɪɡ) *n.* an 18th-century wig with hair pushed back into a bag.

bag+worm (ˈbæɡˌwɜːm) *n.* **1.** the larva of moths of the family *Psychidae,* which typically constructs and inhabits a protective case of silk covered with grass, leaves, etc. **2. bagworm moth.** any moth of the family *Psychidae.*

bah (bɑː, bæ) *interj.* an expression of contempt or disgust.

ba+ha+dur (bəˈhɑːdə) *n.* (*often in combination*) a title formerly conferred by the British on distinguished Indians. [C18: from Hindi *bahādur* hero, from Persian: valiant]

Ba+ha·i (bəˈhɑːɪ) *n.* **1.** an adherent of Bahaism. ~*adj.* **2.** of or relating to Bahaism. [from Persian *bahā'ī,* literally: of glory, from *bahā' u'llāh* glory of God, from Arabic]

Ba+ha+ism (bəˈhɑːɪzəm) *n.* a religious system founded in 1863 by Baha'ullah, based on Babism and emphasizing the value of all religions and the spiritual unity of all mankind. —**Ba+'ha+ist** *or* **Ba+'ha+ite** *adj., n.*

Ba+ha+mas (bəˈhɑːməz) *or* **Ba+ha+ma Is+lands** *pl. n.* **The.** a group of over 700 coral islands (about 20 of which are inhabited) in the West Indies: a British colony from 1783 until 1964; an independent nation within the Commonwealth since 1973. Language: English. Currency: Bahamian dollar. Capital: Nassau. Pop.: 175 192 (1970). Area: 11 406 sq. km (4404 sq. miles). —**Ba+ha+mi·an** (bəˈheɪmɪən, -ˈhɑː-) *adj., n.*

Ba+ha+sa In+do+ne·si·a (bɑːˈhɑːsə) *n.* the official language of Indonesia: developed from the form of Malay formerly widely used as a trade language in SE Asia.

Ba·ha'·ul·lah (ˌbɑːhɑːˈʊlə) *n.* title of *Mirza Hosein Ali.* 1817–92, Persian religious leader: originally a Shiite Muslim, later a disciple of the Bab: founder of Bahaism.

Ba+hi·a (bəˈhiːə; *Portuguese* baˈia) *n.* a state of E Brazil, on the Atlantic coast. Capital: Salvador. Pop.: 7 493 470 (1970). Area: about 562 000 sq. km (217 000 sq. miles).

Ba+hí·a Blan+ca (*Spanish* baˈia ˈblaŋka) *n.* a port in E Argentina. Pop.: 175 000 (1970).

Ba+hi·a de los Co+chi+nos (baˈia ðe los koˈtʃinos) *n.* the Spanish name of **Bay of Pigs.**

Bah+rain *or* **Bah+rein** (bɑːˈreɪn) *n.* an independent sheikdom on the Persian Gulf, consisting of several islands: under British protection until the declaration of independence in 1971. It has large oil reserves. Language: Arabic. Religion: Muslim. Currency: dinar. Capital: Manama. Pop.: 243 000 (1974 UN est.). Area: 600 sq. km (232 sq. miles). —**Bah+'rai+ni** *or* **Bah+'rei+ni** *adj., n.*

baht (bɑːt) *n., pl.* **bahts** *or* **baht.** the standard monetary unit of Thailand, divided into 100 satangs.

ba+hu+vri+hi (ˌbɑːhuːˈvriːhiː) *n. Linguistics.* **1.** a class of compound words consisting of two elements the first of which is a specific feature of the second. **2.** a compound word of this type, such as *hunchback, bluebell, highbrow.* [from Sanskrit *bahuvrīhi,* itself this type of compound, from *bahu* much + *vrīh* rice]

Bai+kal (baɪˈkɑːl, -ˈkæl) *n.* **Lake.** a lake in the S Soviet Union, in SE Siberia: the largest freshwater lake in Eurasia and the deepest in the world. Greatest depth: over 1500 m (5000 ft.). Area: about 33 670 sq. km (13 000 sq. miles).

bail[1] (beɪl) *Law.* ~*n.* **1.** a sum of money by which a person is bound to take responsibility for the appearance in court of another person or himself, forfeited if the person fails to appear. **2.** the person or persons so binding themselves; surety. **3.** the system permitting release of a person from custody where such security has been taken: *he was released on bail.* **4. jump bail** *or* (*formal*) **forfeit bail.** to fail to appear in court to answer to a charge. **5. stand** *or* **go bail.** to act as surety (for someone). ~*vb.* (*tr.*) **6.** (often foll. by *out*) to release or obtain the release of (a person) from custody, security having been made. ~See also **bale out.** [C14: from Old French: custody, from *baillier* to hand over, from Latin *bāiulāre* to carry burdens, from *bāiulus* carrier, of obscure origin]

bail[2] *or* **bale** (beɪl) *vb.* (often foll. by *out*) to remove (water) from (a boat). [C13: from Old French *baille* bucket, from Latin *bāiulus* carrier] —**'bail+er** *or* **'bal+er** *n.*

bail[3] (beɪl) *n.* **1.** *Cricket.* either of two small wooden bars placed across the tops of the stumps to form the wicket. **2.** *Agriculture.* **a.** a partition between stalls in a stable or barn, for horses. **b.** a portable dairy house built on wheels or skids. **3.** *Austral.* a framework in a cowshed used to secure the head of a cow during milking. ~*vb.* **4.** See **bail up.** [C18: from Old French *baile* stake, fortification, probably from Latin *baculum* stick]

bail[4] *or* **bale** (beɪl) *n.* **1.** the semicircular handle of a kettle, bucket, etc. **2.** a semicircular support for a canopy. **3.** a movable bar on a typewriter that holds the paper against the platen. [C15: probably of Scandinavian origin; compare Old Norse *beygja* to bend]

bail+a·ble (ˈbeɪləbᵊl) *adj. Law.* **1.** eligible for release on bail. **2.** admitting of bail: *a bailable offence.*

bail bond *n.* a document in which a prisoner and one or more sureties guarantee that the prisoner will attend the court hearing of the charges against him if he is released on bail.

Baile Átha Cli+ath (blɔːˈkliː) *n.* the Irish Gaelic name for **Dublin.**

bail·ee (beɪˈliː) *n. Contract law.* a person to whom goods are entrusted under a contract of bailment.

bai+ley (ˈbeɪlɪ) *n.* the outermost wall or court of a castle. [C13: from Old French *baille* enclosed court, from *bailler* to enclose, from Late Latin *bājulāre* to bear (something heavy); see BAIL[3]]

Bai·ley (ˈbeɪlɪ) *n.* **Na·than** *or* **Na·than·iel.** died 1742, English lexicographer: compiler of *An Universal Etymological English Dictionary* (1721–27), on which Dr. Johnson's dictionary was based.

Bai·ley bridge *n.* a temporary bridge made of prefabricated steel parts that can be rapidly assembled. [C20: named after Sir Donald *Bailey* (born 1901), its English designer]

bail·ie (ˈbeɪlɪ) *n.* **1.** (in Scotland) a municipal magistrate. **2.** an obsolete or dialect spelling of **bailiff.** [C13: from Old French *bailli,* from earlier *baillif* BAILIFF]

bail+iff (ˈbeɪlɪf) *n.* **1.** *Brit.* the agent or steward of a landlord or landowner. **2.** a sheriff's officer who serves writs and summonses, makes arrests, and ensures that the sentences of the court are carried out. **3.** *Chiefly Brit.* (formerly) a high official having judicial powers. **4.** *Chiefly U.S.* an official having custody of prisoners appearing in court. [C13: from Old French *baillif,* from *bail* custody; see BAIL[1]]

bail·i·wick (ˈbeɪlɪwɪk) *n.* **1.** *Law.* the area over which a bailiff has jurisdiction. **2.** a person's special field of interest, authority, or skill. [C15: from BAILIE + WICK]

Bail+ly (ˈbeɪlɪ) *n.* one of the largest craters on the moon, about 293 kilometres in diameter, lying in the SE quadrant.

bail+ment (ˈbeɪlmənt) *n.* **1.** *Contract law.* a contractual delivery of goods in trust to a person for a specific purpose. **2.** *Criminal law.* the act of granting bail.

bail+or (ˈbeɪlə, beɪˈlɔː) *n. Contract law.* a person who delivers goods to another under a contract of bailment.

bails+man (ˈbeɪlzmən) *n., pl.* **+men.** *Rare.* a person who stands bail for another; surety.

bail up *vb.* (*adv.*) *Austral.* **1.** to confine (a cow) or (of a cow) to be confined by the head in a bail. See **bail**[3]. **2.** (*tr.*) (of a bushranger) to tie up or hold under guard in order to rob. **3.** (*intr.*) to submit to robbery without offering resistance. **4.** (*tr.*) *Informal.* to accost or detain, esp. in conversation; buttonhole.

Bai+ly's beads *n.* the brilliant points of sunlight that appear briefly around the moon, just before and after a total eclipse. [C19: named after Francis *Baily* (died 1844), English astronomer who described them]

bain+ite (ˈbeɪnaɪt) *n.* a mixture of iron and iron carbide found in incompletely hardened steels, produced when austenite is transformed at temperatures between the pearlite and martensite ranges. [C20: named after Edgar C. *Bain* (1891–1971), American physicist; see -ITE[1]]

bain-ma·rie *French.* (bɛ̃maˈri) *n., pl.* ***bains-ma·rie*** (bɛ̃maˈri). a vessel for holding hot water, in which sauces and other dishes are gently cooked. [C19: from French, from Medieval Latin *balneum Mariae,* literally: bath of Mary, inaccurate translation of Medieval Greek *kaminos Marios,* literally: furnace of *Miriam,* alleged author of a treatise on alchemy]

Bai+ram (baɪˈræm, ˈbaɪræm) *n.* either of two Muslim festivals, one (**Lesser Bairam**) falling at the end of Ramadan, the other (**Greater Bairam**) 70 days later at the end of the Islamic year. [from Turkish *bayrām*]

Baird (bɛəd) *n.* **John Lo·gie** (ˈləʊɡɪ). 1888–1946, Scottish engineer: inventor of a 240-line mechanically scanned system of television, replaced in 1935 by a 405-line electrically scanned system.

bairn (bɛən) *n. Scot.* a child. [Old English *bearn;* related to *bearm* lap, Old Norse, Old High German *barn* child]

Bairns·fa·ther (ˈbɛənzˌfɑːðə) *n.* **Bruce.** 1888–1959, English cartoonist, born in India: best known for his cartoons of the war in the trenches during World War I.

bait[1] (beɪt) *n.* **1.** something edible, such as soft bread paste, worms, pieces of meat, etc., fixed to a hook or in a trap to attract fish or animals. **2.** an enticement; temptation. **3.** a variant spelling of **bate**[4]. **4.** *Northern Brit. dialect.* food, esp. a packed lunch. **5.** *Archaic.* a short stop for refreshment during a journey. ~*vb.* **6.** (*tr.*) to put a piece of food on or in (a hook or trap). **7.** (*tr.*) to persecute or tease. **8.** (*tr.*) to entice; tempt. **9.** (*tr.*) to set dogs upon (a bear, etc.). **10.** (*tr.*) *Archaic.* to feed (a horse), esp. during a break in a journey. **11.** (*intr.*) *Archaic.* to stop for rest and refreshment during a journey. [C13: from Old Norse *beita* to hunt, persecute; related to Old English *bǣtan* to restrain, hunt, Old High German *beizen*]

bait[2] (beɪt) *vb.* (*intr.*) *Falconry.* a variant spelling of **bate**[2].

baize (beɪz) *n.* **1.** a woollen fabric resembling felt, usually green, used mainly for the tops of billiard tables. ~*vb.* **2.** (*tr.*) to line or cover with such fabric. [C16: from Old French *baies*, plural of *baie* baize, from *bai* reddish brown, BAY[5], perhaps the original colour of the fabric]

Ba·ja Cal·i·for·nia ('baha) *n.* **1.** a state of NW Mexico, in the N part of the Lower California peninsula. Capital: Mexicali. Pop.: 856 773 (1970). Area: about 71 500 sq. km (27 600 sq. miles). **2.** the Spanish name for **Lower California.**

Ba·ja Ca·li·for·nia Sur *n.* a state of NW Mexico, in the S part of the Lower California peninsula. Capital: La Paz. Pop.: 128 019 (1970). Area: about 72 500 sq. km (28 000 sq. miles).

Ba·jan ('beɪdʒən) *Caribbean informal.* ~*n.* **1.** a native of Barbados. ~*adj.* **2.** of or relating to Barbados or its inhabitants. [C20: variant of *Badian,* a shortened form of *Barbadian*]

bake (beɪk) *vb.* **1.** (*tr.*) to cook by dry heat in or as if in an oven. **2.** (*intr.*) to cook bread, pastry, etc., in an oven. **3.** to make or become hardened by heat. **4.** (*intr.*) *Informal.* to be extremely hot, as in the heat of the sun. ~*n.* **5.** *U.S.* a party at which the main dish is baked. **6.** a batch of things baked at one time. **7.** *Scot.* a kind of biscuit. **8.** *Caribbean.* a small flat fried cake. [Old English *bacan;* related to Old Norse *baka,* Old High German *bahhan* to bake, Greek *phōgein* to parch, roast]

bake·ap·ple ('beɪkˌæpᵊl) *n. Canadian.* the fruit of the cloudberry.

baked A·las·ka *n.* a dessert consisting of cake covered with ice cream, with a meringue topping.

baked beans *pl. n.* haricot beans, baked and tinned in tomato sauce.

bake·house ('beɪkˌhaus) *n.* another word for **bakery.**

Ba·ke·lite ('beɪkəˌlaɪt) *n. Trademark.* any one of a class of thermosetting resins used as electric insulators and for making plastic ware, telephone receivers, etc. [C20: named after L. H. *Baekeland* (1863–1944), Belgian-born U.S. inventor; see -ITE[1]]

bak·er ('beɪkə) *n.* **1.** a person whose business or employment is to make or sell bread, cakes, etc. **2.** a portable oven.

Ba·ker ('beɪkə) *n.* **1.** Sir **Ben·ja·min.** 1840–1907, English engineer who, with Sir John Fowler, designed and constructed much of the London underground railway, the Forth Railway Bridge, and the first Aswan Dam. **2.** Dame **Jan·et.** born 1933, English mezzo-soprano. **3.** Sir **Sam·u·el White.** 1821–93, English explorer: discovered Lake Albert (1864).

bak·er's doz·en *n.* thirteen. [from the bakers' former practice of giving thirteen rolls where twelve were requested, to protect themselves against accusations of giving light weight]

bak·er·y ('beɪkərɪ) *n., pl.* **·er·ies. 1.** Also called: **bakehouse.** a room or building equipped for baking. **2.** a shop in which bread, cakes, etc., are sold.

Bake·well tart ('beɪkwɛl) *n. Brit.* an open tart having a pastry base and a layer of jam and filled with almond-flavoured sponge cake. [named after *Bakewell,* Derbyshire]

bak·ing pow·der *n.* any of various powdered mixtures that contain sodium bicarbonate, starch (usually flour), and one or more slightly acidic compounds, such as cream of tartar: used in baking as a substitute for yeast.

bak·la·va *or* **bac·la·va** ('bɑːkləˌvɑː) *n.* a rich cake of Middle Eastern origin consisting of thin layers of pastry filled with nuts and honey. [from Turkish]

bak·ra ('bækrə) *Caribbean.* ~*n., pl.* **·ra** *or* **·ras. 1.** a White person, esp. one from Britain. ~*adj.* **2.** (of people) White, esp. British. [of African origin]

bak·sheesh *or* **back·sheesh** ('bækʃiːʃ) (in some Eastern countries, esp. formerly) ~*n.* **1.** money given as a tip, a present, or alms. ~*vb.* **2.** to give such money to (a person). [C17: from Persian *bakhshīsh,* from *bakhshīdan* to give; related to Sanskrit *bhaksati* he enjoys]

Bakst (*Russian* bakst) *n.* **Le·on Ni·ko·la·ye·vich** (lɪ'ɔn nika'lajɪvitʃ). 1866–1924, Russian painter and stage designer, noted particularly for his richly coloured sets for Diaghilev's *Ballet Russe* (1909–21).

Ba·ku (*Russian* ba'ku) *n.* a port in the S Soviet Union, on the Caspian Sea: the capital of the Azerbaijan SSR: important for its extensive oilfields. Pop.: 851 547 (1970).

Ba·ku·nin (*Russian* ba'kunin) *n.* **Mi·kha·il** (mixa'il). 1814–76, Russian anarchist and writer: a prominent member of the First International, expelled from it after conflicts with Marx.

BAL *abbrev. for* British anti-lewisite. See **dimercaprol.**

bal. *Book-keeping. abbrev. for* balance.

Bal·a ('bælə) *n.* **Lake.** a narrow lake in Gwynedd: the largest natural lake in Wales. Length: 6 km (4 miles).

Ba·laam ('beɪlæm) *n. Old Testament.* a Mesopotamian diviner who, when summoned to curse the Israelites, prophesied future glories for them instead, after being reproached by his ass (Numbers 22–23).

Bal·a·cla·va hel·met (ˌbælə'klɑːvə) *n.* a close-fitting woollen hood that covers the ears, as originally worn by soldiers in the Crimean War.

Ba·la·ki·rev (*Russian* ba'lakirɪf) *n.* **Mi·ly A·lex·e·ye·vich** ('milij alɪk'sjejɪvitʃ). 1837–1910, Russian composer, whose works include two symphonic poems, two symphonies, and many arrangements of Russian folk songs.

Bal·a·kla·va *or* **Bal·a·cla·va** (ˌbælə'klɑːvə; *Russian* bəla'klavə) *n.* a small port in the SW Soviet Union, in S Crimea: scene of an inconclusive battle (1854), which included the charge of the Light Brigade, during the Crimean War.

bal·a·lai·ka (ˌbælə'laɪkə) *n.* a plucked musical instrument, usually having a triangular body and three strings: used chiefly for Russian folk music. [C18: from Russian]

bal·ance ('bæləns) *n.* **1.** a weighing device, generally consisting of a horizontal beam pivoted at its centre, from the ends of which two pans are suspended. The substance to be weighed is placed in one pan and known weights are placed in the other until the beam returns to the horizontal. See also **microbalance. 2.** an imagined device for events, actions, motives, etc., in relation to each other (esp. in the phrases **weigh in the balance, hang in the balance**). **3.** a state of equilibrium. **4.** something that brings about such a state. **5.** equilibrium of the body; steadiness: *to lose one's balance.* **6.** emotional stability; calmness of mind. **7.** harmony in the parts of a whole: *balance in an artistic composition.* **8.** the act of weighing factors, quantities, etc., against each other. **9.** the power to influence or control: *he held the balance of power.* **10.** something that remains or is left: *let me have the balance of what you owe me.* **11.** *Accounting.* **a.** equality of debit and credit totals in an account. **b.** a difference between such totals. **12.** *Chem.* the state of a chemical equation in which the number, kind, electrical charges, etc., of the atoms on opposite sides are equal. **13.** a balancing movement. **14.** short for **spring balance. 15. on balance.** after weighing up all the factors. **16. strike a balance.** to make a compromise. ~*vb.* **17.** (*tr.*) to weigh in or as if in a balance. **18.** (*intr.*) to be or come into equilibrium. **19.** (*tr.*) to bring into or hold in equilibrium. **20.** (*tr.*) to assess or compare the relative weight, importance, etc., of. **21.** (*tr.*) to act so as to equalize; be equal to. **22.** (*tr.*) to compose or arrange so as to create a state of harmony. **23.** (*tr.*) to bring (a chemical or mathematical equation) into balance. **24.** (*tr.*) *Accounting.* **a.** to compute the credit and debit totals of (an account) in order to determine the difference. **b.** to equalize the credit and debit totals of (an account) by making certain entries. **c.** to settle or adjust (an account) by paying any money due. **25.** (*intr.*) (of a business account, balance sheet, etc.) to have the debit and credit totals equal. **26.** to match or counter (one's dancing partner or his or her steps) by moving towards and away from him or her. [C13: from Old French, from Vulgar Latin *bilancia* (unattested), from Late Latin *bilanx* having two scalepans, from BI-[1] + *lanx* scale] —**'bal·ance·a·ble** *adj.*

Bal·ance ('bæləns) *n.* **the.** the constellation Libra, the seventh sign of the zodiac.

bal·ance of na·ture *n.* the stable state in which natural communities of animals and plants exist, maintained by adaptation, competition, and other interactions between members of the community and their nonliving environment.

bal·ance of pay·ments *n.* the difference over a given time between total payments to foreign nations, arising from imports of goods and services and transfers abroad of capital, interest, grants, etc., and total receipts from foreign nations, arising from exports of goods and services and transfers from abroad of capital, interest, grants, etc.

bal·ance of pow·er *n.* **1.** the distribution of power among countries so that no one nation can seriously threaten the fundamental interests of another. **2.** any similar distribution of power or influence.

bal·ance of trade *n.* the difference in value between total exports and total imports of goods. Also called: **visible balance.** Compare **invisible balance.**

bal·anc·er ('bælənsə) *n.* **1.** a person or thing that balances. **2.** *Entomol.* another name for **haltere.**

bal·ance sheet *n.* a statement that shows the financial position of a business enterprise at a specified date by listing the asset balances and the claims on such assets.

bal·ance wheel *n.* a wheel oscillating against the hairspring of a timepiece, thereby regulating its beat.

Bal·an·chine ('bælənˌtʃiːn, ˌbælən'tʃiːn) *n.* **George.** 1904–83, born in Russia, U.S. choreographer.

bal·as ('bæləs, 'beɪ-) *n.* a red variety of spinel, used as a gemstone. Also called: **balas ruby.** [C15: from Old French *balais,* from Arabic *bālakhsh,* from *Badhakhshān,* region in Afghanistan where the gem is found]

bal·a·ta ('bælətə) *n.* **1.** a tropical American sapotaceous tree, *Manilkara bidentata,* yielding a latex-like sap. **2.** a rubber-like gum obtained from this sap: used as a substitute for gutta-percha. [from American Spanish, of Carib origin]

Ba·la·ton (*Hungarian* 'bɔlɔton) *n.* **Lake.** a large shallow lake in W Hungary. Area: 689 sq. km (266 sq. miles).

Bal·bo (*Italian* 'balbo) *n.* **I·ta·lo** ('iːtaˌlo). 1896–1940, Italian Fascist politician and airman: minister of aviation (1929–33).

bal·bo·a (bæl'bəuə) *n.* the standard currency unit of Panama, divided into 100 centesimos.

Bal·bo·a[1] (bæl'bəuə; *Spanish* bal'βoa) *n.* **Vas·co Nú·ñez de** ('basko 'nuɲeθ ðe). ?1475–1519, Spanish explorer, who discovered the Pacific Ocean in 1513.

Bal·bo·a[2] (bæl'bəuə; *Spanish* bal'βoa) *n.* a port at the Pacific end of the Panama Canal: the administrative centre of the Canal Zone. Pop.: 2569 (1970).

bal·brig·gan (bæl'brɪgən) *n.* **1.** a knitted unbleached cotton fabric. **2.** (*often pl.*) underwear made of this. [C19: from *Balbriggan,* Ireland, where it was originally made]

bal·co·ny ('bælkənɪ) *n., pl.* **·nies. 1.** a platform projecting from the wall of a building with a balustrade or railing along its outer edge, often with access from a door or window. **2.** a gallery in a theatre or auditorium, above the dress circle. **3.** *U.S.* the dress circle in a theatre or auditorium. [C17: from Italian *balcone,* probably from Old High German *balko* beam; see BALK] —**'bal+co+nied** *adj.*

bald (bɔːld) *adj.* **1.** having no hair or fur, esp. (of a man) having no hair on all or most of the scalp. **2.** lacking natural growth or covering. **3.** plain or blunt: *a bald statement.* **4.** bare or simple; unadorned. **5.** Also: **bald+faced.** (of certain birds and other animals) having white markings on the head and face. **6.** (of a tyre) having a worn tread. [C14 *ballede* (literally: having a white spot); related to Danish *bældet,* Greek *phalaros* having a white spot] —**'bald+ish** *adj.* —**'bald+ly** *adv.* —**'bald+ness** *n.*

bal+da+chin, bal+da+quin ('bɔːldəkɪn), *or* **bal+da+chi+no** (ˌbɔːldə'kiːnəʊ) *n.* **1.** a richly ornamented silk and gold brocade. **2.** a canopy of fabric or stone over an altar, shrine, or throne in a Christian church or carried in Christian religious processions over an object of veneration. [Old English *baldekin,* from Italian *baldacchino,* literally: stuff from Baghdad, from *Baldacco* Baghdad, noted for its brocades]

bald cy+press *n.* another name for **swamp cypress.**

bald ea·gle *n.* a large eagle, *Haliaeetus leucocephalus,* of North America, having a white head and tail, a yellow bill, and dark wings and body. It is the U.S. national bird (see also **American eagle**).

Bal·der ('bɔːldə) *n. Norse myth.* a god, son of Odin and Frigg, noted for his beauty and sweet nature. He was killed by a bough of mistletoe thrown by the blind god Höd, misled by the malicious Loki.

bal+der+dash ('bɔːldəˌdæʃ) *n.* stupid or illogical talk; senseless rubbish. [C16: of unknown origin]

bald+head ('bɔːldˌhɛd) *n.* a person with a bald head.

bald+head·ed (ˌbɔːld'hɛdɪd) *adj.* **1.** having a bald head. **2. go baldheaded.** (usually foll. by *into, for,* or *at*) *Informal.* to act impetuously without regard to the consequences.

bald+ing ('bɔːldɪŋ) *adj.* somewhat bald or becoming bald.

bald+mon·ey ('bɔːldˌmʌnɪ) *n.* another name for **spignel.**

bald+pate ('bɔːldˌpeɪt) *n.* **1.** a person with a bald head. **2.** another name for the **American wigeon** (see **wigeon** (sense 2)).

bal+dric ('bɔːldrɪk) *n.* a wide silk sash or leather belt worn over the right shoulder to the left hip for carrying a sword, etc. [C13: from Old French *baudrei,* of Frankish origin]

Bald·win ('bɔːldwɪn) *n.* **1. James (Arthur).** born 1924, U.S. writer, whose works include the novel *Go Tell it on the Mountain* (1954). **2. Stan·ley,** 1st Earl Baldwin of Bewdley. 1867–1947, British Conservative statesman: prime minister (1923–24, 1924–29, 1932–37).

Bald·win I *n.* 1058–1118, crusader and first king of Jerusalem (1100–18), who captured Acre (1104), Beirut (1109), and Sidon (1110).

bale[1] (beɪl) *n.* **1.** a large bundle, esp. of a raw or partially processed material, bound by ropes, wires, etc., for storage or transportation: *bale of hay.* **2.** *U.S.* 500 pounds of cotton. **3.** a group of turtles. ~*vb.* **4.** to make (hay, etc.) into a bale or bales. ~See also **bale out.** [C14: probably from Old French *bale,* from Old High German *balla* BALL[1]] —**'bal+er** *n.*

bale[2] (beɪl) *n. Archaic.* **1.** evil; injury. **2.** woe; suffering; pain. [Old English *bealu;* related to Old Norse *böl* evil, Gothic *balwa,* Old High German *balo*]

bale[3] (beɪl) *vb.* a variant spelling of **bail**[2]. —**'bal+er** *n.*

bale[4] (beɪl) *n.* a variant spelling of **bail**[4].

Bâle (bɑːl) *n.* the French name for **Basel.**

Bal+e·ar+ic Is+lands (ˌbælɪ'ærɪk) *pl. n.* a group of islands in the W Mediterranean, consisting of Majorca, Minorca, Ibiza, Formentera, Cabrera, and 11 islets: a province of Spain. Capital: Palma, on Majorca. Pop.: 532 946 (1970). Area: 5012 sq. km (1935 sq. miles). Spanish name: **Ba+le·a+res** (bale'ares).

ba+leen (bə'liːn) *n.* whalebone. [C14: from Latin *bālaena* whale; related to Greek *phalaina* whale]

ba+leen whale *n.* another name for **whalebone whale.**

bale+fire ('beɪlˌfaɪə) *n. Archaic.* **1.** a bonfire. **2.** a beacon fire. **3.** a funeral pyre. [C14 *bale,* from Old English *bǣl* pyre; related to Old Norse *bāl* flame, pyre, Sanskrit *bhāla* brightness]

bale+ful ('beɪlfʊl) *adj.* **1.** harmful, menacing, or vindictive. **2.** dejected. —**'bale+ful+ly** *adv.* —**'bale+ful+ness** *n.*

Ba·len·cia·ga (*Spanish* balen'θjaɣa) *n.* **Cris·tó·bal** (kris'toβal). 1895–1972, Spanish couturier.

bale out *or* **bail out** *vb.* (*adv.*) **1.** (*intr.*) to make an emergency parachute jump from an aircraft. **2.** (*tr.*) *Informal.* to help (a person, organization, etc.) out of a predicament: *the government baled the company out.* **3.** (*intr.*) *Informal.* to escape from a predicament.

bal+er ('beɪlə) *n.* an agricultural machine for making bales of hay, etc. Also called: **baling machine.**

Bal·four ('bælfɔː, -fə, -fʊə) *n.* **Ar·thur James,** 1st Earl of Balfour. 1848–1930, British Conservative statesman: prime minister (1902–05); foreign secretary (1916–19).

Bal·four Dec+la+ra+tion *n.* the statement made by Arthur Balfour in 1917 of British support for the setting up of a national home for the Jews in Palestine, provided that the rights of "existing non-Jewish communities" in Palestine could be safeguarded.

Ba·li ('bɑːlɪ) *n.* an island in Indonesia, east of Java: mountainous, rising over 3000 m (10 000 ft.). Capital: Singaradja. Pop.: 2 217 000 (1974 est.). Area: 5558 sq. km (2146 sq. miles).

bal·i+bun+tal (ˌbælɪ'bʌntᵊl) *n.* **1.** closely woven fine straw, used for making hats in the Philippines. **2.** a hat of this straw. [C20: changed from *Baliuag buntal,* from *Baliuag* in the Philippines, where such hats were made]

Ba+lik+pa+pan (ˌbɑːlɪk'pɑːpɑːn) *n.* a city in Indonesia, on the SE coast of Borneo. Pop.: 137 340 (1971).

Ba+li+nese (ˌbɑːlɪ'niːz) *adj.* **1.** of or relating to Bali, its people, or their language. ~*n.* **2.** (*pl.* **+nese**) a native or inhabitant of Bali. **3.** the language of the people of Bali, belonging to the Malayo-Polynesian family.

Ba·li·ol *or* **Bal·li·ol** ('beɪlɪəl) *n.* **John de.** 1249–1315, king of Scotland (1292–96): defeated and imprisoned by Edward I of England (1296).

balk *or* **baulk** (bɔːk, bɔːlk) *vb.* **1.** (*intr.;* usually foll. by *at*) to stop short, esp. suddenly or unexpectedly; jib: *the horse balked at the jump.* **2.** (*intr.;* foll. by *at*) to turn away abruptly; recoil: *he balked at the idea of murder.* **3.** (*tr.*) to thwart, check, disappoint, or foil: *he was balked in his plans.* **4.** (*tr.*) to avoid deliberately: *he balked the question.* **5.** (*tr.*) to miss unintentionally. ~*n.* **6.** a roughly squared heavy timber beam. **7.** a timber tie beam of a roof. **8.** an unploughed ridge to prevent soil erosion or mark a division on common land. **9.** an obstacle; hindrance; disappointment. **10.** *Baseball.* an illegal motion by a pitcher towards the plate or towards the base when there are runners on base, esp. without delivering the ball. ~See also **baulk.** [Old English *balca;* related to Old Norse *bálkr* partition, Old High German *balco* beam] —**'balk+er** *or* **'baulk+er** *n.*

Bal+kan ('bɔːlkən) *adj.* of, denoting, or relating to the Balkan States or their inhabitants, the Balkan Peninsula, or the Balkan Mountains.

Bal+kan+ize *or* **Bal+kan+ise** ('bɔːlkəˌnaɪz) *vb.* (*tr.*) to divide (a territory) into small warring states. —**ˌBal+kan·i+'za+tion** *or* **ˌBal+kan·i+'sa+tion** *n.*

Bal+kan Moun+tains *pl. n.* a mountain range extending across Bulgaria from the Black Sea to the Yugoslav border. Highest peak: Mount Botev, 2376 m (7793 ft.).

Bal+kan Pen+in+su+la *n.* a large peninsula in SE Europe, between the Adriatic and Aegean Seas.

Bal+kan States *pl. n.* the countries of the Balkan Peninsula: Yugoslavia, Rumania, Bulgaria, Albania, Greece, and the European part of Turkey. Also called: **the Balkans.**

Balkh (bɑːlk) *n.* a district of N Afghanistan, corresponding to ancient Bactria. Chief town: Mazar-i-Sharif.

Bal+khash (*Russian* bal'xaʃ) *n.* **Lake.** a salt lake in the SW Soviet Union, in SE Kazakhstan: fed by the Ili River. Area: about 1800 sq. km (7000 sq. miles).

Bal·kis ('bælkɪs) *n.* the name in the Koran of the queen of **Sheba.**

balk·y *or* **baulk·y** ('bɔːkɪ, 'bɔːlkɪ) *adj.* **balk·i+er, balk·i+est** *or* **baulk·i+er, baulk·i+est.** inclined to stop abruptly and unexpectedly: *a balky horse.* —**'balk·i+ly** *or* **'baulk·i+ly** *adv.* —**'balk·i+ness** *or* **'baulk·i+ness** *n.*

ball[1] (bɔːl) *n.* **1.** a spherical or nearly spherical body or mass: *a ball of wool.* **2.** a round or roundish body, either solid or hollow, of a size and composition suitable for any of various games, such as football, golf, billiards, etc. **3.** a ball propelled in a particular way in a sport: *a high ball.* **4.** any of various rudimentary games with a ball: *to play ball.* **5.** *Cricket.* a single delivery of the ball by the bowler to the batsman. **6.** *Baseball.* a single delivery of the ball by a pitcher outside certain limits and not swung at by the batter. **7. a.** a solid nonexplosive projectile for a firearm, cannon, etc. Compare **shell** (sense 6). **b.** such projectiles collectively. **8.** any more or less rounded part or protuberance: *the ball of the foot.* **9.** *Taboo slang.* a testicle. See **balls. 10.** *Vet. science.* another word for **bolus. 11.** *Horticulture.* the hard mass of roots and earth removed with the rest of the plant during transplanting. **12. ball of muscle.** *Austral.* a very strong, fit, or forceful person. **13. have the ball at one's feet.** to have the chance of doing something. **14. keep the ball rolling.** to maintain the progress of a project, plan, etc. **15. on the ball.** *Informal.* alert; informed. **16. play ball.** *Informal.* to cooperate. **17. start** *or* **set the ball rolling.** to set a project, plan, etc., in motion; start. **18. the ball is in your court.** you are obliged to make the next move. ~*vb.* (*tr.*) **19.** to make, form, wind, etc., into a ball or balls: *to ball wool.* [C13: from Old Norse *böllr;* related to Old High German *balla,* Italian *palla,* French *balle*]

ball[2] (bɔːl) *n.* **1.** a social function for dancing, esp. one that is lavish or formal. **2.** *Informal, chiefly U.S.* a very enjoyable time (esp. in the phrase **have a ball**). ~*vb.* **3.** *Taboo slang, chiefly U.S.* to copulate (with). [C17: from French *bal* (n.), from Old French *baller* (vb.), from Late Latin *ballāre* to dance, from Greek *ballizein*]

Ball (bɔːl) *n.* **John.** died 1381, English priest: executed as one of the leaders of the Peasants' Revolt (1381).

bal+lad ('bæləd) *n.* **1.** a narrative song with a recurrent refrain. **2.** a narrative poem in short stanzas of popular origin, originally sung to a repeated tune. **3.** a slow sentimental song, esp. a pop song. [C15: from Old French *balade,* from Old Provençal *balada* song accompanying a dance, from *balar* to dance, from Late Latin *ballāre;* see BALL[2]]

bal+lade (bæ'lɑːd; *French* ba'lad) *n.* **1.** *Prosody.* a verse form consisting of three stanzas and an envoy, all ending with the same line. The first three stanzas commonly have eight or ten lines each and the same rhyme scheme. **2.** *Music.* an instrumental composition, esp. for piano, based on or intended to evoke a narrative.

bal+lad+eer (ˌbælə'dɪə) *n.* a singer of ballads.

bal+lad me+tre *n.* the metre of a ballad stanza.

bal·lad+mon·ger ('bæləd,mʌŋgə) *n.* **1.** (formerly) a seller of ballads, esp. on broadsheets. **2.** *Derogatory.* a writer of mediocre poetry.

bal·lad op·e·ra *n.* an opera consisting of popular tunes to which appropriate words have been set, interspersed with spoken dialogue.

bal·lad·ry ('bælədrɪ) *n.* **1.** ballad poetry or songs. **2.** the art of writing, composing, or performing ballads.

bal·lad stan·za *n.* a four-line stanza, often used in ballads, in which the second and fourth lines rhyme and have three stresses each and the first and third lines are unrhymed and have four stresses each.

Bal·lance ('bæləns) *n.* **John.** 1839–93, New Zealand statesman, born in Northern Ireland: prime minister of New Zealand (1891–93).

ball and chain *n.* **1.** (formerly) a heavy iron ball attached to a chain and fastened to a prisoner. **2.** a heavy restraint. **3.** *Slang.* one's wife.

ball-and-sock·et joint *n.* **1.** a coupling between two rods, tubes, etc., that consists of a spherical part fitting into a spherical socket, allowing free movement and rotation. **2.** Also called: **multiaxial joint.** *Anatomy.* a bony joint, such as the hip joint, in which a rounded head fits into a rounded cavity, allowing a wide range of movement.

Bal·la·rat ('bælə,ræt, ,bælə'ræt) *n.* a town in SE Australia, in S central Victoria: originally the centre of a gold-mining region. Pop.: 58 434 (1971). See also **Eureka Stockade.**

bal·last ('bæləst) *n.* **1.** any dense heavy material, such as lead or iron pigs, used to stabilize a vessel, esp. one that is not carrying cargo. **2.** crushed rock, broken stone, etc., used for the foundation of a road or railway track. **3.** coarse aggregate of sandy gravel, used in making concrete. **4.** anything that provides stability or weight. **5.** *Electronics.* a device for maintaining the current in a circuit. *~vb.* (*tr.*) **6.** to give stability or weight to. [C16: probably from Low German; related to Old Danish, Old Swedish *barlast,* literally: bare load (without commercial value), from *bar* bare, mere + *last* load, burden]

ball bear·ing *n.* **1.** a bearing consisting of a number of hard steel balls rolling between a metal sleeve fitted over the rotating shaft and an outer sleeve held in the bearing housing, so reducing friction between moving parts. **2.** a metal ball, esp. one used in such a bearing.

ball boy *n.* (esp. in tennis) a person who retrieves balls that go out of play.

ball cock *n.* a device for regulating the flow of a liquid into a tank, cistern, etc., consisting of a floating ball mounted at one end of an arm and a valve on the other end that opens and closes as the ball falls and rises.

bal·le·ri·na (,bælə'ri:nə) *n.* **1.** a female ballet dancer. **2.** *U.S.* the principal female dancer of a ballet company. [C18: from Italian, feminine of *ballerino* dancing master, from *ballare* to dance, from Late Latin *ballāre;* see BALL[2]]

bal·let ('bæleɪ, bæ'leɪ) *n.* **1. a.** a classical style of expressive dancing based on precise conventional steps with gestures and movements of grace and fluidity. **b.** (*as modifier*): *ballet dancer.* **2.** a theatrical representation of a story or theme performed to music by ballet dancers. **3.** a troupe of ballet dancers. **4.** a piece of music written for a ballet. [C17: from French, from Italian *balletto,* literally: a little dance, from *ballare* to dance; see BALL[2]] **—bal·let·ic** (bæ'lɛtɪk) *adj.*

bal·let·o·ma·ni·a (,bælɛtəʊ'meɪnɪə) *n.* passionate enthusiasm for ballet. **—bal·'let·o·mane** *n.*

ball·flow·er ('bɔ:l,flaʊə) *n. Architect.* a carved ornament in the form of a ball enclosed by the three petals of a circular flower.

ball game *n.* **1.** any game played with a ball. **2.** *U.S.* a game of baseball. **3.** *U.S. informal.* any activity: *aeronautics is a whole new ball game from what it was in 1903.*

Bal·li·ol ('beɪlɪəl) *n.* See (John de) **Baliol.**

bal·lis·ta (bə'lɪstə) *n., pl.* **·tae** (-ti:). an ancient catapult for hurling stones, etc. [C16: from Latin, ultimately from Greek *ballein* to throw]

bal·lis·tic (bə'lɪstɪk) *adj.* **1.** of or relating to ballistics. **2.** denoting or relating to the flight of projectiles after power has been cut off, moving under their own momentum and the force of gravity. **3.** (of a measurement or measuring instrument) depending on a brief impulse or current that causes a movement related to the quantity to be measured: *a ballistic pendulum.* **—bal·'lis·ti·cal·ly** *adv.*

bal·lis·tic gal·va·nom·e·ter *n. Physics.* a type of galvanometer for measuring surges of current. After deflection the instrument returns slowly to its original reading.

bal·lis·tic mis·sile *n.* a missile that has no wings or fins and that follows a ballistic trajectory when its propulsive power is discontinued.

bal·lis·tics (bə'lɪstɪks) *n.* (*functioning as sing.*) **1.** the study of the flight dynamics of projectiles. **2.** the study of the effects of firing on firearms and their projectiles, either before (**interior ballistics**) or after (**exterior ballistics**) they have left the muzzle.

bal·locks ('bæləks) *pl. n., interj., vb.* a variant spelling of **bollocks.**

ball of fire *n. Informal.* a very lively person.

bal·lo·net (,bælə'nɛt) *n.* an air or gas compartment in a balloon or nonrigid airship, used to control buoyancy and shape. [C20: from French *ballonnet* a little BALLOON]

bal·loon (bə'lu:n) *n.* **1.** an inflatable rubber bag of various sizes, shapes, and colours: usually used as a plaything or party decoration. **2.** a large impermeable bag inflated with a lighter-than-air gas, designed to rise and float in the atmosphere. It may have a basket or gondola for carrying passengers, etc. See also **barrage balloon, hot-air balloon. 3.** a circular or elliptical figure containing the words or thoughts of a character in a cartoon. **4.** *Brit.* **a.** a kick or stroke that propels a ball high into the air. **b.** (*as modifier*): *a balloon shot.* **5.** *Chem.* a round-bottomed flask. **6.** a large rounded brandy glass. **7. when the balloon goes up.** *Informal.* when the action starts. *~vb.* **8.** (*intr.*) to go up or fly in a balloon. **9.** to inflate or be inflated; distend; swell: *the wind ballooned the sails.* **10.** (*tr.*) *Brit.* to propel (a ball) high into the air. [C16 (in the sense: ball, ball game): from Italian dialect *ballone,* from *balla,* of Germanic origin; compare Old High German *balla* BALL[1]] **—bal·'loon·ist** *n.* **—bal·'loon-,like** *adj.*

bal·loon sail *n. Nautical.* a large light bellying sail used in light winds. Compare **spinnaker.**

bal·loon sleeve *n.* a sleeve fitting tightly from wrist to elbow and becoming fully rounded from elbow to shoulder.

bal·loon tyre *n.* a pneumatic tyre containing air at a relatively low pressure and having a wide tread.

bal·loon vine *n.* a tropical tendril-climbing sapindaceous plant, *Cardiospermum halicacabum,* cultivated for its ornamental balloon-like seed capsules.

bal·lot ('bælət) *n.* **1.** the democratic practice of selecting a representative, a course of action, or deciding some other choice by submitting the options to a vote of all qualified persons. **2.** an instance of voting, usually in secret using ballot papers or a voting machine. **3.** a list of candidates standing for office. **4.** the number of votes cast in an election. **5.** *Archaic.* a drawing of lots. *~vb.* **·lots, ·lot·ing, ·lot·ed. 6.** to vote or elicit a vote from: *we balloted the members on this issue.* **7.** (*tr.;* usually foll. by *for*) to select (conscripts, etc.) by lot or ballot. **8.** (*tr.;* often foll. by *for*) to vote or decide (on an issue, etc.). [C16: from Italian *ballotta,* literally: a little ball, from *balla* BALL[1]]

bal·lot box *n.* a box into which ballot papers are dropped after voting.

bal·lot pa·per *n.* a paper used for voting in a ballot, esp. (in a parliamentary or local government election) one having the names of the candidates printed on it.

bal·lotte·ment (bə'lɒtmənt) *n. Med.* a technique of feeling for a movable object in the body, esp. confirmation of pregnancy by feeling the rebound of the fetus following a quick digital tap on the wall of the uterus. [C19: from French, literally: a tossing, shaking, from *ballotter* to toss, from *ballotte* a little ball, from Italian *ballotta;* see BALLOT]

ball·park ('bɔ:l,pɑ:k) *n.* **1.** *U.S.* a stadium used for baseball games. **2.** *U.S. slang.* **a.** approximate range: *in the right ballpark.* **b.** (*as modifier*): *a ballpark figure.*

ball-peen ham·mer *n.* a hammer that has one end of its head shaped in a hemisphere for beating metal, etc.

ball·play·er ('bɔ:l,pleɪə) *n.* **1.** a player, esp. in soccer, with outstanding ability to control the ball. **2.** *U.S.* a baseball player, esp. a professional.

ball·point, ball·point pen ('bɔ:l,pɔɪnt), *or* **ball pen** *n.* a pen having a small ball bearing as a writing point. Also called (Brit.): **Biro.**

ball·room ('bɔ:l,ru:m, -,rʊm) *n.* a large hall for dancing.

ball·room danc·ing *n.* social dancing, popular since the beginning of the 20th century, to dances in conventional rhythms (**ballroom dances**) such as the foxtrot and the quick-step.

balls (bɔ:lz) *Taboo slang.* *~pl.n.* **1.** the testicles. **2. by the balls.** so as to be rendered powerless. **3.** nonsense; rubbish. *~interj.* **4.** an exclamation of strong disagreement, contempt, annoyance, etc.

balls-up *or U.S.* **ball·up** *Taboo slang.* *~n.* **1.** something botched or muddled. *~vb.* **balls up** *or U.S.* **ball up. 2.** (*tr., adv.*) to muddle or botch.

ball valve *n.* a one-way valve consisting of a metal ball fitting into a concave seat over an opening.

bal·ly ('bælɪ) *adj., adv.* (*intensifier*) *Brit. slang.* a euphemistic word for **bloody** (sense 6).

bal·ly·hoo ('bælɪ,hu:) *n. Informal.* **1.** a noisy, confused, or nonsensical situation or uproar. **2.** sensational or blatant advertising or publicity. *~vb.* **·hoos, ·hoo·ing, ·hooed. 3.** (*tr.*) *Chiefly U.S.* to advertise or publicize by sensational or blatant methods. [C19: of uncertain origin]

bal·ly·rag *vb.* **·rags, ·rag·ging, ·ragged.** a variant spelling of **bullyrag.**

balm (bɑ:m) *n.* **1.** any of various oily aromatic resinous substances obtained from certain tropical trees and used for healing and soothing. See also **balsam** (sense 1). **2.** any plant yielding such a substance, esp. the balm of Gilead. **3.** something comforting or soothing: *soft music is a balm.* **4.** any aromatic or oily substance used for healing or soothing. **5.** Also called: **lemon balm.** an aromatic Eurasian herbaceous plant, *Melissa officinalis,* having clusters of small fragrant white two-lipped flowers: family *Labiatae* (labiates). **6.** a pleasant odour. [C13: from Old French *basme,* from Latin *balsamum* BALSAM] **—'balm-,like** *adj.*

bal·ma·caan (,bælmə'kɑ:n) *n.* a man's knee-length loose flaring overcoat with raglan sleeves. [C19: after *Balmacaan,* near Inverness, Scotland]

Bal·main (*French* bal'mɛ̃) *n.* **Pierre Al·ex·andre** (pjɛ:r alɛk'sɑ̃:dr). 1914-82, French couturier.

balm of Gil·e·ad *n.* **1.** any of several trees of the burseraceous genus *Commiphora,* esp. *C. opobalsamum* of Africa and W Asia, that yield a fragrant oily resin (see **balm** (sense 1)). Compare **myrrh** (sense 1). **2.** the resin exuded by these trees. **3.** a North American hybrid female poplar tree, *Populus gileadensis* (or *P. candicans*), with broad heart-shaped leaves. **4.** a fragrant resin obtained from the balsam fir.

Bal·mor·al[1] (bæl'mɒrəl) *n.* **1.** (*sometimes not cap.*) a laced walking shoe. **2.** a 19th-century woollen petticoat, worn showing below the skirt. **3.** Also called: **bluebonnet.** a Scottish brimless hat of dark blue wool with a cockade and plume on one side.

Bal+mor+al² (bælˈmɒrəl) *n.* a castle in NE Scotland, in Grampian region: a private residence of the British sovereign.

Bal+mung (ˈbælmʊŋ) *or* **Bal+munc** (ˈbælmʊŋk) *n.* (in the *Nibelungenlied*) Siegfried's sword.

balm·y (ˈbɑːmɪ) *adj.* **balm·i·er, balm·i·est.** **1.** (of weather) mild and pleasant. **2.** having the qualities of balm; fragrant or soothing. **3.** a variant spelling (esp. U.S.) of **barmy.** —ˈ**balm·i+ly** *adv.* —ˈ**balm·i·ness** *n.*

bal+ne+al (ˈbælnɪəl) *or* **bal+ne+ar·y** (ˈbælnɪərɪ) *adj. Rare.* of or relating to baths or bathing. [C17: from Latin *balneum* bath, from Greek *balaneion*]

bal+ne+ol+o·gy (ˌbælnɪˈɒlədʒɪ) *n.* the branch of medical science concerned with the therapeutic value of baths, esp. those taken with natural mineral waters. [from Latin *balneum* bath] —**bal+ne·o·log·i·cal** (ˌbælnɪəˈlɒdʒɪkᵊl) *adj.* —ˌ**bal+ne+ˈol·o+gist** *n.*

ba+lo+ney *or* **bo+lo+ney** (bəˈləʊnɪ) *n. Informal.* foolish talk; nonsense. [C20: changed from *Bologna* (sausage)]

BALPA (ˈbælpə) *n. acronym for* British Airline Pilots' Association.

bal+sa (ˈbɔːlsə) *n.* **1.** a bombacaceous tree, *Ochroma lagopus*, of tropical America. **2.** Also called: **bal·sa+wood.** the very light wood of this tree, used for making rafts, etc. **3.** a light raft. [C18: from Spanish: raft]

bal+sam (ˈbɔːlsəm) *n.* **1.** any of various fragrant oleoresins, such as balm or tolu, obtained from any of several trees and shrubs and used as a base for medicines and perfumes. **2.** any of various similar substances used as medicinal or ceremonial ointments. **3.** any of certain aromatic resinous turpentines. See **Canada balsam.** **4.** any plant yielding balsam. **5.** any of several balsaminaceous plants of the genus *Impatiens*, esp. *I. balsamina*, cultivated for its brightly coloured double flowers. **6.** anything healing or soothing. [C15: from Latin *balsamum*, from Greek *balsamon*, from Hebrew *bāšām* spice; see BALM] —**bal+sam+ic** (bɔːlˈsæmɪk) *adj.* —ˈ**bal+sam·y** *adj.*

bal+sam ap+ple *n.* an ornamental cucurbitaceous vine, *Momordica balsamina*, of the Old World tropics, with yellow flowers and orange egg-shaped fruits.

bal+sam fir *n.* a fir tree, *Abies balsamea*, of NE North America, that yields Canada balsam. Also called: **balsam, Canada balsam.** See also **balm of Gilead.**

bal+sam+if+er+ous (ˌbɔːlsəˈmɪfərəs) *adj.* yielding or producing balsam.

bal+sa+mi+na+ceous (ˌbɔːlsəmɪˈneɪʃəs) *adj.* of, relating to, or belonging to the *Balsaminaceae*, a family of flowering plants, including balsam and touch-me-not, that have irregular flowers and explosive capsules.

bal+sam pop+lar *n.* a poplar tree, *Populus balsamifera*, of NE North America, having resinous buds and broad heart-shaped leaves. See also **tacamahac.**

bal+sam spruce *n.* either of two North American coniferous trees of the genus *Picea*, *P. pungens* (the blue spruce) or *P. engelmanni.*

Balt (bɔːlt) *n.* a member of any of the Baltic-speaking peoples of the Baltic States.

Balt. *abbrev. for* Baltic.

Bal+tha+zar¹ (ˈbælθəˌzɑː, bælˈθæzə) *n.* a wine bottle holding the equivalent of sixteen normal bottles (approximately 416 ounces).

Bal·tha·zar² (ˈbælθəˌzɑː, bælˈθæzə) *n.* one of the Magi, the others being Caspar and Melchior.

Bal+tic (ˈbɔːltɪk) *adj.* **1.** denoting or relating to the Baltic Sea or the Baltic States. **2.** of, denoting, or characteristic of Baltic as a group of languages. ~*n.* **3.** a branch of the Indo-European family of languages consisting of Lithuanian, Latvian, and Old Prussian. **4.** short for **Baltic Sea. 5.** Also called: **Baltic Exchange.** a commodities exchange in the City of London.

Bal+tic Sea *n.* a sea in N Europe, connected with the North Sea by the Skaggerak, Kattegat, and Öresund; shallow, with low salinity and small tides.

Bal+tic Shield *n.* the wide area of ancient rock in Scandinavia. Also called: **Scandinavian Shield.** See **shield** (sense 7).

Bal+tic States *pl. n.* the formerly independent republics of Estonia, Latvia, and Lithuania, which became constituent republics of the Soviet Union in 1940.

Bal+ti+more¹ (ˈbɔːltɪˌmɔː) *n.* **Lord.** See (Sir George) **Calvert.**

Bal+ti+more² (ˈbɔːltɪˌmɔː) *n.* a port in N Maryland, on Chesapeake Bay. Pop.: 877 838 (1973 est.).

Bal+ti+more o+ri+ole *n.* a North American oriole, *Icterus galbula*, the male of which has orange and black plumage.

Bal·to-Sla·von+ic *or* **Bal·to-Sla·vic** *n.* a hypothetical subfamily of Indo-European languages consisting of Baltic and Slavonic. It is now generally believed that similarities between them result from geographical proximity rather than any special relationship.

Ba+lu+chi (bəˈluːtʃɪ) *or* **Ba+lo+chi** (bəˈləʊtʃɪ) *n.* **1.** (*pl.* **+chis** *or* **+chi**) a member of a Muslim people living chiefly in coastal Pakistan and Iran. **2.** the language of this people, belonging to the West Iranian branch of the Indo-European family. ~*adj.* **3.** of or relating to Baluchistan, its inhabitants, or their language.

Ba+lu+chi+stan (bəˈluːtʃɪˌstɑːn, -ˌstæn) *n.* **1.** a mountainous region of SW Asia, in SW Pakistan and SE Iran. **2.** a province of SW Pakistan: a former territory of British India (until 1947). Capital: Quetta.

bal+us+ter (ˈbæləstə) *n.* **1.** any of a set of posts supporting a rail or coping. ~*adj.* **2.** (of a shape) swelling at the base and rising in a concave curve to a narrow stem or neck: *a baluster stem on a goblet.* [C17: from French *balustre*, from Italian *balaustro* pillar resembling a pomegranate flower, ultimately from Greek *balaustion*]

bal+us+trade (ˈbæləˌstreɪd) *n.* an ornamental rail or coping with its supporting set of balusters. [C17: from French, from *balustre* BALUSTER]

Bal·zac (ˈbælzæk; *French* balˈzak) *n.* **Ho·no·ré de** (ɔnɔˈre də). 1799–1850, French novelist: author of a collection of novels under the general title *La Comédie humaine*, including *Eugénie Grandet* (1833), *Le Père Goriot* (1834), and *La Cousine Bette* (1846).

Bam·a+ko (ˌbæməˈkəʊ) *n.* the capital of Mali, in the south, on the River Niger. Pop.: 196 800 (1972 est.).

Bam+ba+ra (bɑːmˈbɑːrə) *n.* **1.** (*pl.* **+ra** *or* **+ras**) a member of a Negroid people of W Africa living chiefly in Mali and by the headwaters of the River Niger in Guinea. **2.** the language of this people, belonging to the Mande branch of the Niger-Congo family.

Bam+berg (ˈbæmbɜːg; *German* ˈbambɛrk) *n.* a town in S West Germany, in the north of present-day Bavaria: seat of independent prince-bishops of the Holy Roman Empire (1007–1802). Pop.: 70 400 (1970).

bam+bi+no (bæmˈbiːnəʊ) *n., pl.* **+nos** *or* **+ni** (-niː). **1.** *Informal.* a young child, esp. an Italian one. **2.** a representation of the infant Jesus. [C18: from Italian]

bam+boo (bæmˈbuː) *n.* **1.** any tall treelike tropical or semitropical fast-growing grass of the genus *Bambusa*, having hollow woody-walled stems with ringed joints and edible young shoots (**bamboo shoots**). **2.** the stem of any of these plants, used for building, poles, and furniture. **3.** any of various bamboo-like grasses of the genera *Arundinaria, Phyllostachys*, or *Dendrocalamus.* **4.** (*modifier*) made of bamboo: *a bamboo pipe; a bamboo fence.* [C16: probably from Malay *bambu*]

bam+boo cur+tain *n.* (esp. in the 1950s and 1960s) the political and military barrier to communications around the People's Republic of China.

bam+boo+zle (bæmˈbuːzᵊl) *vb.* (*tr.*) *Informal.* **1.** to cheat; mislead. **2.** to confuse. [C18: of unknown origin] —**bam+ˈboo+zler** *n.* —**bam+ˈboo+zle+ment** *n.*

ban¹ (bæn) *vb.* **bans, ban+ning, banned.** **1.** (*tr.*) to prohibit, esp. officially, from action, display, entrance, sale, etc.; forbid: *to ban a book; to ban smoking.* **2.** (*tr.*) (in South Africa) to place (a person suspected of illegal political activity) under a government order restricting his movement and his contact with other people. **3.** *Archaic.* to curse. ~*n.* **4.** an official prohibition or interdiction. **5.** *Law.* an official proclamation or public notice, esp. of prohibition. **6.** a public proclamation or edict, esp. of outlawry. **7.** *Archaic.* public censure or condemnation. **8.** *Archaic.* a curse; imprecation. [Old English *bannan* to proclaim; compare Old Norse *banna* to forbid, Old High German *bannan* to command]

ban² (bæn) *n.* (in feudal England) the summoning of vassals to perform their military obligations. [C13: from Old French *ban*, of Germanic origin; related to Old High German *ban* command, Old Norse *bann* BAN¹]

ban³ (bæn) *n.* a Rumanian monetary unit worth one hundredth of a leu. [from Rumanian, from Serbo-Croatian *bān* lord]

ba+nal (bəˈnɑːl) *adj.* lacking force or originality; trite; commonplace. [C18: from Old French: relating to compulsory feudal service, hence common to all, commonplace, from *ban* BAN²] —**ba+nal+i·ty** (bəˈnælɪtɪ) *n.* —**ba+ˈnal+ly** *adv.*

ba+na+na (bəˈnɑːnə) *n.* **1.** any of several tropical and subtropical herbaceous treelike plants of the musaceous genus *Musa*, esp. *M. sapientum*, a widely cultivated species propagated from suckers and having hanging clusters of edible fruit. **2.** the crescent-shaped fruit of any of these plants. ~Compare **plantain**². [C16: from Spanish or Portuguese, of African origin]

ba+na+na belt *n. Canadian informal.* a region with a warm climate, esp. one in Canada.

Ba+na+na bend+er *n. Austral. informal; offensive.* a native or inhabitant of Queensland. Also called: **Ba+na+na+land+er** (bəˈnɑːnəˌlændə).

ba+na+na oil *n.* **1.** a solution of cellulose nitrate in pentyl acetate or a similar solvent, which has a banana-like smell. **2.** a nontechnical name for **pentyl acetate.**

ba+na+na re+pub+lic *n. Informal.* a small country, esp. in Central America, that is politically unstable and has an economy dominated by foreign interest, usually dependent on one export, such as bananas.

ba+na+nas (bəˈnɑːnəz) *adj. Brit. slang.* crazy.

ba+na+na split *n.* a dish of ice cream and banana cut in half lengthwise, usually topped with syrup, nuts, whipped cream, etc.

Ba+na+ras (bəˈnɑːrəz) *n.* a variant spelling of **Benares.**

Ban+at (ˈbænɪt, ˈbɑːnɪt) *n.* a fertile plain extending through Hungary, Rumania, and Yugoslavia.

ba+nau+sic (bəˈnɔːsɪk) *adj.* merely mechanical; materialistic; utilitarian. [C19: from Greek *banausikos* for mechanics, from *baunos* forge]

Ban+bur·y (ˈbænbərɪ) *n.* a town in central England, in N Oxfordshire. Pop.: 29 216 (1971).

Ban+bur·y cake *n. Brit.* a cake consisting of a pastry base filled with currants, raisins, candied peel, and sugar, with a criss-cross pattern on the top.

banc (bæŋk) *n.* **in banc.** *Law.* sitting as a full court. [from Anglo-French: bench]

band[1] (bænd) *n.* **1.** a company of people having a common purpose; group: *a band of outlaws.* **2.** a group of musicians playing either brass and percussion instruments only (**brass band**) or brass, woodwind, and percussion instruments (**concert band** or **military band**). **3.** a group of musicians who play popular music, jazz, etc., often for dancing. **4.** a group of instrumentalists generally; orchestra. **5.** *Canadian.* a formally recognized group of Indians on a reservation. **6.** *Anthropol.* a division of a tribe; a family group or camp group. **7.** *U.S., Canadian.* a flock or herd. ~*vb.* **8.** (usually foll. by *together*) to unite; assemble. [C15: from French *bande,* probably from Old Provençal *banda,* of Germanic origin; compare Gothic *bandwa* sign, BANNER]

band[2] (bænd) *n.* **1.** a thin flat strip of some material, used esp. to encircle objects and hold them together: *a rubber band.* **2. a.** a strip of fabric or other material used as an ornament or to reinforce clothing. **b.** (*in combination*): *waistband; hairband; hatband.* **3.** a stripe of contrasting colour or texture **4.** a driving belt in machinery. **5.** a range of values that are close or related in number, degree, or quality. **6.** *Physics.* a range of frequencies or wavelengths between two limits. **7.** short for **energy band. 8.** *Computer technol.* one or more tracks on a magnetic disk or drum. **9.** *Anatomy.* any structure resembling a ribbon or cord that connects, encircles, or binds different parts. **10.** the cords, usually of flax or hemp, to which the folded sheets of a book are sewn. **11.** a thin layer or seam of ore. **12.** *Architect.* a strip of flat panelling, such as a fascia or plinth, usually attached to a wall. **13.** a large white collar, sometimes edged with lace, worn in the 17th century. **14.** either of a pair of hanging extensions of the collar, forming part of academic, legal, or (formerly) clerical dress. **15.** (of a gramophone record) another word for **track** (sense 11). **16.** a ring for the finger (esp. in phrases such as **wedding band, band of gold,** etc.). ~*vb.* (*tr.*) **17.** to fasten or mark with a band. **18.** *U.S.* to ring (birds). See **ring**[1] (sense 22). [C15: from Old French *bende,* of Germanic origin; compare Old High German *binda* fillet; see BAND[3]]

band[3] (bænd) *n.* an archaic word for **bond** (senses 1, 3, 4). [C13: from Old Norse *band;* related to Old High German *bant* fetter; see BEND[1], BOND]

Ban·da ('bændə) *n.* **Has·tings Ka·mu·zu** (kæ'muːzuː). born 1906, Malawi statesman. As first prime minister of Nyasaland (since 1963), he led his country to independence (1964) as Malawi: president since 1966.

band+age ('bændɪdʒ) *n.* **1.** a piece of material used to dress a wound, bind a broken limb, etc. **2.** a strip of any soft material used for binding, etc. ~*vb.* **3.** to cover or bind with a bandage. [C16: from French, from *bande* strip, BAND[2]]

ban+dan+na *or* **ban+dan·a** (bæn'dænə) *n.* a large silk or cotton handkerchief or neckerchief. [C18: from Hindi *bāndhnū* tie-dyeing, from *bāndhnā* to tie, from Sanskrit *bandhnāti* he ties]

Ban·da·ra·na·i·ke (ˌbændərə'naɪɪkə) *n.* **1.** Mrs. **Si·ri·ma·vo** (ˌsɪrɪ'mɑːvəʊ). born 1916, prime minister of Sri Lanka, formerly Ceylon (1960–65; 1970–77). **2.** her husband, **Sol·o·mon.** 1899–1959, prime minister of Ceylon (1956–59); assassinated.

Ban+dar Se·ri Be+ga+wan ('bɑːndɑː 'sɛrɪ bə'gɑːwən) *n.* the capital of Brunei. Pop.: 72 481 (1971). Former name: **Brunei.**

Ban+da Sea ('bændə) *n.* a part of the Pacific in Indonesia, between Celebes and New Guinea.

b. and b. *abbrev. for* bed and breakfast.

band+box ('bændˌbɒks) *n.* a lightweight usually cylindrical box used for holding small articles, esp. hats.

ban+deau ('bændəʊ) *n., pl.* **+deaux** (-dəʊz). a narrow band of ribbon, velvet, etc., worn round the head. [C18: from French, from Old French *bandel* a little BAND[2]]

ban+de+ril+la (ˌbændə'riːə, -'riːljə) *n. Bullfighting.* a decorated barbed dart, thrust into the bull's neck or shoulder. [Spanish, literally: a little banner, from *bandera* BANNER]

ban+de+ril+le+ro (ˌbændəriː'ɛərəʊ, -riː'ljɛərəʊ) *n., pl.* **·ros.** a bullfighter's assistant who sticks banderillas into the bull.

ban+de+role, ban+de+rol ('bændəˌrəʊl), *or* **ban+ne+rol** *n.* **1.** a long narrow flag, usually with forked ends, esp. one attached to the masthead of a ship; pennant. **2.** a square flag draped over a tomb or carried at a funeral. [C16: from Old French, from Italian *banderuola,* literally: a little banner, from *bandiera* BANNER]

band-ga·la ('bʌndgəlɑː) *adj.* (in India) (of a coat) closed at the neck. [from Hindi]

bandh *or* **bundh** (bʌnd) *n.* (in India) a general strike. [Hindi, literally: a tying up]

ban+di+coot ('bændɪˌkuːt) *n.* **1.** any agile terrestrial marsupial of the family *Peramelidae* of Australia and New Guinea. They have a long pointed muzzle and a long tail and feed mainly on small invertebrates. **2. bandicoot rat.** Also called: **mole rat.** any of three burrowing rats of the genera *Bandicota* and *Nesokia,* of S and SE Asia: family *Muridae.* ~*vb.* **3.** *Austral.* to dig up (potatoes), leaving the plant intact above the ground. [C18: from Telegu *pandikokku,* from *pandi* pig + *kokku* bandicoot]

ban+dit ('bændɪt) *n., pl.* **+dits** *or* **+dit+ti** (-'dɪtɪ). a robber, esp. a member of an armed gang; brigand. [C16: from Italian *bandito,* literally: banished man, from *bandire* to proscribe, from *bando* edict, BAN[2]] —**'ban+dit+ry** *n.*

Band+jar+ma+sin *or* **Ban+jer+ma+sin** (ˌbændʒə'mɑːsɪn) *n.* a port in Indonesia, in SW Borneo. Pop.: 281 673 (1971).

band+mas·ter ('bændˌmɑːstə) *n.* the conductor of a band.

ban+do+bust *or* **bun+do+bust** ('bʌndəʊbəst) *n.* (in India and Pakistan) arrangements. [Hindi *band-o-bast* tying and binding, from Persian]

ban+do+leer *or* **ban+do+lier** (ˌbændə'lɪə) *n.* a soldier's broad shoulder belt having small pockets or loops for cartridges. [C16: from Old French *bandouliere,* from Old Spanish *bandolera, bandolero* guerrilla, from Catalan *bandoler,* from *bandol* band, from Spanish *bando;* see BAND[1]]

ban+do+line ('bændəˌliːn) *n.* a glutinous hairdressing, used (esp. formerly) to keep the hair in place. [C19: *bando-,* from French BANDEAU + *-line,* from Latin *linere* to smear]

ban+dore (bæn'dɔː, 'bændɔː) *n.* a 16th-century plucked musical instrument resembling a lute but larger and fitted with seven pairs of metal strings. Also called: **pandore, pandora.** [C16: from Spanish *bandurria,* from Late Latin *pandūra* three-stringed instrument, from Greek *pandoura*]

band-pass fil+ter *n. Electronics.* a filter that transmits only those currents having a frequency lying within specified limits. Compare **high-pass filter, low-pass filter.**

band saw *n.* a power-operated saw consisting of an endless toothed metal band running over and driven by two wheels.

bands+man ('bændzmən) *n., pl.* **+men.** a player in a musical band, esp. a brass or military band.

band spec+trum *n.* a spectrum consisting of a number of bands of closely spaced lines that are associated with emission or absorption of radiation by molecules.

band+spread·ing ('bændˌsprɛdɪŋ) *n.* an additional tuning control in some radio receivers whereby a selected narrow band of frequencies can be spread over a wider frequency band, in order to increase selectivity.

band+stand ('bændˌstænd) *n.* a platform for a band, usually out of doors and roofed.

Ban+dung ('bændʊŋ) *n.* a city in Indonesia, in SW Java. Pop.: 1 201 730 (1971).

band+wag·on ('bændˌwægən) *n.* **1.** *U.S.* a wagon, usually high and brightly coloured, for carrying the band in a parade. **2. climb, jump,** *or* **get on the bandwagon.** *Informal.* to join or give support to a party or movement that seems to be assured of success.

band+width ('bændˌwɪdθ) *n.* **1.** the range of frequencies within a given waveband used for a particular radio transmission. **2.** the range of frequencies over which a receiver or amplifier should not differ appreciably from its maximum value.

ban+dy ('bændɪ) *adj.* **+di+er, +di+est. 1.** Also: **bandy-legged.** having legs curved outwards at the knees. **2.** (of legs) curved outwards at the knees. ~*vb.* **+dies, +dy+ing, +died.** (*tr.*) **3.** to exchange (words) in a heated or hostile manner. **4.** to give and receive (blows). **5.** *Informal.* (often foll. by *about*) to circulate (a name, rumour, etc.). **6.** to throw or strike to and fro; toss about. ~*n., pl.* **+dies. 7.** an early form of hockey, often played on ice. **8.** a stick, curved at one end, used in the game of bandy. **9.** an old form of tennis. **10. knock (someone) bandy.** *Austral. informal.* to amaze or astound. [C16: probably from Old French *bander* to hit the ball back and forth at tennis]

ban·dy-ban·dy ('bændɪ'bændɪ) *n., pl.* **-ban·dies.** a small Australian elapid snake, *Vermicella annulata,* ringed with black and yellow.

ban+dy legs *n.* another term for **bow legs.**

bane (beɪn) *n.* **1.** a person or thing that causes misery or distress (esp. in the phrase **bane of one's life**). **2.** something that causes death or destruction. **3. a.** a fatal poison. **b.** (*in combination*): *ratsbane.* **4.** *Archaic.* ruin or distress. [Old English *bana;* related to Old Norse *bani* death, Old High German *bano* destruction, death]

bane+ber·ry ('beɪnbərɪ) *n., pl.* **·ries. 1.** Also called: **herb Christopher** (Brit.), **cohosh** (U.S.). any ranunculaceous plant of the genus *Actaea,* esp. *A. spicata,* which has small white flowers and red or white poisonous berries. **2.** a berry of any of these plants.

bane+ful ('beɪnfʊl) *adj. Archaic.* destructive, poisonous, or fatal. —**'bane+ful+ly** *adv.* —**'bane+ful+ness** *n.*

Banff (bæmf) *n.* **1.** (until 1975) a county of NE Scotland, now part of Grampian region. **2.** (bænf). a town in Canada, in SW Alberta, in the Rocky Mountains: surrounded by **Banff National Park.** Pop.: 3532 (1971).

bang[1] (bæŋ) *n.* **1.** a short loud explosive noise, as of the bursting of a balloon or the report of a gun. **2.** a hard blow or knock, esp. a noisy one; thump: *he gave the ball a bang.* **3.** *Informal.* a startling or sudden effect: *he realized with a bang that he was late.* **4.** *U.S. slang.* thrill; excitement. **5.** *Slang.* an injection of heroin or other narcotic. **6.** *Taboo slang.* an act of sexual intercourse. **7. with a bang.** successfully: *the party went with a bang.* ~*vb.* **8.** to hit or knock, esp. with a loud noise; bump: *to bang one's head.* **9.** to move noisily or clumsily: *to bang about the house.* **10.** to close (a door, window, etc.) or (of a door, etc.) be closed noisily; slam. **11.** (*tr.*) to cause to move by hitting vigorously: *he banged the ball over the fence.* **12.** to make or cause to make a loud noise, as of an explosion. **13.** (*tr.*) *Brit.* **a.** to cause (stock prices) to fall by rapid selling. **b.** to sell rapidly in (a stock market), thus causing prices to fall. **14.** *Taboo slang.* to have sexual intercourse with. **15.** (*intr.*) *Slang.* to inject heroin, etc. **16. bang one's head against a brick wall.** *Informal.* to make no progress. ~*adv.* **17.** with a sudden impact or effect: *bang went his hopes of winning; the car drove bang into a lamp-post.* **18.** precisely: *bang in the middle of the road.* **19. go bang.** to burst, shut, etc., with a loud noise. ~See also **bang up.** [C16: from Old Norse *bang, banga* hammer; related to Low German *bangen* to beat; all of imitative origin]

bang[2] (bæŋ) *n.* **1.** a fringe or section of hair cut straight across the forehead. ~*vb.* (*tr.*) **2.** to cut (the hair) in such a style. **3.** to dock (the tail of a horse, etc.). [C19: probably short for *bangtail* short tail]

bang[3] (bæŋ) *n.* a variant spelling of **bhang.**

Ban·ga·lore (ˌbæŋɡəˈlɔː) *n.* a city in S India, capital of Karnataka state. Pop.: 1 540 741 (1971).
ban·ga·lore tor·pe·do *n.* an explosive device in a long metal tube, used to blow gaps in barbed-wire barriers. [C20: named after BANGALORE, where it was used]
bang·er (ˈbæŋə) *n. Brit.* **1.** *Slang.* a sausage. **2. a.** an old decrepit car. **b.** (*as modifier*): *banger racing.* **3.** a type of firework that explodes loudly.
Bang·ka *or* **Ban·ka** (ˈbæŋkə) *n.* an island in Indonesia, separated from Sumatra by the **Bangka Strait.** Chief town: Pangkalpinang. Area: about 11 914 sq. km (4600 sq. miles).
Bang·kok (ˈbæŋkɒk, bæŋˈkɒk) *n.* the capital and chief port of Thailand, on the Chao Phraya River: became a royal city and the capital in 1782. Pop.: 1 867 297 (1970). Thai name: **Krung Thep** (ˈkrʊŋ ˈteɪp).
Bang·la·desh (ˌbɑːŋɡləˈdɛʃ, ˌbæŋ-) *n.* a republic in S Asia: formerly the Eastern Province of Pakistan; became independent in 1971 after civil war and the defeat of Pakistan by India; consists of the plains and vast deltas of the Ganges and Brahmaputra Rivers: economy based on jute and jute products (over 80 per cent of world production). Language: Bengali. Religion: Muslim. Currency: taka. Capital: Dacca. Pop.: 71 316 517 (1974). Area: 142 797 sq. km (55 126 sq. miles). —ˌ**Bang·la·ˈdesh·i** *adj., n.*
ban·gle (ˈbæŋɡᵊl) *n.* **1.** a bracelet, usually without a clasp, often worn high up round the arm or sometimes round the ankle. **2.** a disc or charm hanging from a bracelet, necklace, etc. [C19: from Hindi *bangrī*]
bang on *adj., adv. Brit. informal.* **1.** with absolute accuracy. **2.** excellent or excellently. ~Also (U.S.): **bang up.**
Ban·gor (ˈbæŋɡɔː, -ɡə) *n.* **1.** a university town in NW Wales, in Gwynedd, on the Menai Strait. Pop.: 14 526 (1971). **2.** a town in SE Northern Ireland, in Co. Down, on Belfast Lough. Pop.: 35 178 (1971).
bang·tail (ˈbæŋˌteɪl) *n.* **1.** a horse's tail cut straight across but not through the bone. **2.** a horse with a tail cut in this way. [C19: from *bangtail* short tail]
bang·tail mus·ter *n. Austral.* a roundup of cattle to be counted, each one having the hairs on its tail clipped as it is counted.
Ban·gui (*French* bãˈɡi) *n.* the capital of the Central African Empire, in the south part, on the Ubangi River. Pop.: 187 000 (1971 est.).
bang up *vb.* (*tr., adv.*) *Prison slang.* to lock up (a prisoner) in his cell, esp. for the night.
Bang·we·u·lu (ˌbæŋwɪˈuːlʊ) *n.* **Lake.** a shallow lake in NE Zambia, discovered by David Livingstone, who died there in 1873. Area: about 9850 sq. km (3800 sq. miles), including swamps.
ba·ni (ˈbɑːnɪ) *n.* the plural of **ban**³ (the Rumanian coin).
ban·ian (ˈbænjən) *n.* a variant spelling of **banyan.**
ban·ish (ˈbænɪʃ) *vb.* (*tr.*) **1.** to expel from a place, esp. by an official decree as a punishment. **2.** to drive away: *to banish gloom.* [C14: from Old French *banir,* of Germanic origin; compare Old High German *ban* BAN¹] —ˈ**ban·ish·ment** *n.*
ban·is·ters (ˈbænɪstəz) *pl. n.* the railing and supporting balusters on a staircase; balustrade.
Ban·ja Lu·ka (*Serbo-Croatian* ˈbaːnja: ˌluːka) *n.* a city in NW central Yugoslavia, on the Vrbas River in Bosnia and Herzegovina: scene of battles between the Austrians and Turks in 1527, 1688, and 1737. Pop.: 89 866 (1971).
Ban·jer·ma·sin (ˌbændʒəˈmɑːsɪn) *n.* a variant spelling of **Bandjarmasin.**
ban·jo (ˈbændʒəʊ) *n., pl.* **·jos** *or* **·joes. 1.** a stringed musical instrument with a long neck (usually fretted) and a circular drumlike body overlaid with parchment, plucked with the fingers or a plectrum. **2.** *Slang.* any banjo-shaped object, esp. a frying pan. **3.** (*modifier*) banjo-shaped: *a banjo clock.* [C18: variant (U.S. Southern pronunciation) of BANDORE] —ˈ**ban·jo·ist** *n.*
Ban·jul (bænˈdʒuːl) *n.* the capital of Gambia, a port at the mouth of the Gambia river. Pop.: 42 687 (1975 est.).
bank¹ (bæŋk) *n.* **1.** an institution offering certain financial services, such as the safekeeping of money, conversion of domestic into and from foreign currencies, lending of money at interest, and acceptance of bills of exchange. **2.** the building used by such an institution. **3.** a small container used at home for keeping money. **4.** the funds held by a gaming house or a banker or dealer in some gambling games. **5.** (in various games) **a.** the stock, as of money, pieces, tokens, etc., on which players may draw. **b.** the player holding this stock. **6.** any supply, store, or reserve, for future use: *a data bank; a blood bank.* ~*vb.* **7.** (*tr.*) to deposit (cash, cheques, etc.) in a bank. **8.** (*intr.*) to transact business with a bank. **9.** (*intr.*) to engage in the business of banking. **10.** (*intr.*) to hold the bank in some gambling games. ~See also: **bank on.** [C15: probably from Italian *banca* bench, money changer's table, of Germanic origin; compare Old High German *banc* BENCH]
bank² (bæŋk) *n.* **1.** a long raised mass, esp. of earth; mound; ridge. **2.** a slope, as of a hill. **3.** the sloping side of any hollow in the ground, esp. when bordering a river: *the left bank of a river is on a spectator's left looking downstream.* **4. a.** an elevated section, rising to near the surface, of the bed of a sea, lake, or river. **b.** (*in combination*): *sandbank; mudbank.* **5. a.** the area around the mouth of the shaft of a mine. **b.** the face of a body of ore. **6.** the lateral inclination of an aircraft about its longitudinal axis during a turn. **7.** Also called: **camber, cant.** a bend on a road or on a railway, athletics, cycling, or other track having the outside built higher than the inside in order to reduce the effects of centrifugal force on vehicles, runners, etc., rounding it at speed. **8.** the cushion of a billiard table. ~*vb.* **9.** (when *tr.*, often foll. by *up*) to form into a bank or mound. **10.** (*tr.*) to border or enclose (a road, etc.) with a bank. **11.** (*tr.;* sometimes foll. by *up*) to cover (a fire) with ashes, fresh fuel, etc., so that it will burn slowly. **12.** to cause (an aircraft) to tip laterally about its longitudinal axis or (of an aircraft) to tip in this way, esp. while turning. **13.** to travel round a bank, esp. at high speed. **14.** (*tr.*) *Billiards.* to drive (a ball) into the cushion. [C12: of Scandinavian origin; compare Old Icelandic *bakki* hill, Old Danish *banke,* Swedish *backe*]
bank³ (bæŋk) *n.* **1.** an arrangement of objects, esp. similar objects, in a row or in tiers: *a bank of dials.* **2. a.** a tier of oars in a galley. **b.** a bench for the rowers in a galley. **3.** *Printing.* lines of type under a headline. **4.** *Telephony.* (in automatic switching) an assembly of fixed electrical contacts forming a rigid unit in a selector or similar device. ~*vb.* **5.** (*tr.*) to arrange in a bank. [C17: from Old French *banc* bench, of Germanic origin; see BANK¹]
Ban·ka (ˈbæŋkə) *n.* a variant spelling of **Bangka.**
bank·a·ble (ˈbæŋkəbᵊl) *adj.* **1.** appropriate for receipt by a bank. **2.** dependable or reliable: *a bankable promise.*
bank ac·cept·ance *n.* a bill of exchange or draft drawn on and endorsed by a bank. Also called: **banker's acceptance.**
bank ac·count *n.* **1.** an account created by the deposit of money at a bank by a customer. **2.** the amount of money credited to a depositor at a bank.
bank an·nu·i·ties *pl. n.* another term for **consols.**
bank bill *or* **draft** *n.* **1.** a bill of exchange drawn by one bank on another. **2.** Also called: **banker's bill.** *U.S.* a bank note.
bank·book (ˈbæŋkˌbʊk) *n.* a book held by depositors at certain banks, in which the bank enters a record of deposits, withdrawals, and earned interest. Also called: **passbook.**
bank card *n.* another name for **banker's card.**
bank clerk *n. Brit.* an employee of a bank. U.S. name: **teller.**
bank dis·count *n.* interest on a loan deducted from the principal amount when the loan is made and based on the loan's face value.
bank·er¹ (ˈbæŋkə) *n.* **1.** a person who owns or is an executive in a bank. **2.** an official or player in charge of the bank in any of various games, esp. gambling games. **3.** a result that has been forecast identically in a series of entries on a football pool coupon.
bank·er² (ˈbæŋkə) *n.* **1.** a fishing vessel of Newfoundland. **2.** a fisherman in such a vessel. **3.** *Austral. informal.* a stream almost overflowing its banks (esp. in the phrase **run a banker**). **4.** Also called: **bank engine.** *Brit.* a locomotive that is used to help a heavy train up a steep gradient.
bank·er³ (ˈbæŋkə) *n.* **1.** a craftsman's workbench. **2.** a timber board used as a base for mixing building materials.
bank·er's card *n.* a card issued by a bank, guaranteeing payment of the cheques of a customer up to a stated value.
bank·er's or·der *n.* another name for **standing order** (sense 1).
bank·et (ˈbæŋkɪt) *n.* a gold-bearing conglomerate found in South Africa. [C19: from Dutch: a kind of almond hardbake, alluding to its appearance]
bank hol·i·day *n.* (in Britain) any of several weekdays on which banks are closed by law and which are observed as national holidays.
bank·ing¹ (ˈbæŋkɪŋ) *n.* the business engaged in by a bank.
bank·ing² (ˈbæŋkɪŋ) *n.* fishing on a sea bank, esp. off the coast of Newfoundland.
bank man·ag·er *n.* a person who directs the business of a local branch of a bank.
bank note *n.* a promissory note, esp. one issued by a central bank, serving as money.
Bank of Eng·land *n.* the central bank of England and Wales, concerned with credit control, determination of the bank rate, and other aspects of government monetary policy.
bank on *vb.* (*intr., prep.*) *Informal.* to expect or rely with confidence on: *you can bank on him always arriving on time.*
bank rate *n.* **1.** a rate of discount fixed by a bank or banks. **2.** (*sometimes caps.*) the minimum rate by which a central bank, such as the Bank of England, is obliged to rediscount bills of exchange and to lend money. See also **minimum lending rate.**
bank-rid·ing *n.* *Skateboarding.* riding along any sloping banked surface.
bank·roll (ˈbæŋkˌrəʊl) *U.S.* ~*n.* **1.** a roll of currency notes. **2.** the financial resources of a person, organization, etc. ~*vb.* **3.** (*tr.*) *Slang.* to provide the capital for; finance.
bank·rupt (ˈbæŋkrʌpt, -rəpt) *n.* **1.** a person adjudged insolvent by a court, his property being transferred to a trustee and administered for the benefit of his creditors. **2.** any person unable to discharge all his debts. **3.** a person whose resources in a certain field are exhausted or nonexistent: *a spiritual bankrupt.* ~*adj.* **4.** adjudged insolvent. **5.** financially ruined. **6.** depleted in resources or having completely failed: *spiritually bankrupt.* **7.** (foll. by *in*) *Brit.* lacking: *bankrupt in intelligence.* ~*vb.* **8.** (*tr.*) to make bankrupt. [C16: from Old French *banqueroute,* from Old Italian *bancarotta,* from *banca* BANK¹ + *rotta* broken, from Latin *ruptus,* from *rumpere* to break]
bank·rupt·cy (ˈbæŋkrʌptsɪ, -rəptsɪ) *n., pl.* **·cies.** the state, condition, or quality of being or becoming bankrupt.
Banks (bæŋks) *n.* **1. Gor·don.** born 1937, English footballer: goalkeeper in the England team 73 times (1963–72). **2.** Sir **Jo·seph.** 1743–1820, English botanist and explorer: circumnavigated the world with James Cook (1768–71).
bank·si·a (ˈbæŋksɪə) *n.* any shrub or tree of the Australian

genus *Banksia,* having long leathery evergreen leaves and dense cylindrical heads of flowers that are often yellowish: family *Proteaceae.* See also **honeysuckle** (sense 3). [C19: New Latin, named after Sir Joseph BANKS]

Banks Is+land *n.* **1.** an island of N Canada, in the Northwest Territories: the westernmost island of the Arctic Archipelago. Area: about 67 340 sq. km (26 000 sq. miles). **2.** an island of W Canada, off British Columbia. Length: about 72 km (45 miles).

bank state+ment *n.* a statement of transactions in a bank account, esp. one of a series sent at regular intervals to the depositor.

ban+lieue *French.* (bɑ̃'ljø) *n.* a suburb of a city.

ban+ner ('bænə) *n.* **1.** a long strip of flexible material displaying a slogan, advertisement, etc., esp. one suspended between two points. **2.** a placard or sign carried in a procession or demonstration. **3.** something that represents a belief or principle: *a commitment to nationalization is the banner of British socialism.* **4.** the flag of a nation, army, etc., used as a standard or ensign. **5.** (formerly) the standard of an emperor, knight, etc. **6.** Also called: **banner headline.** a large headline in a newspaper, etc., extending across the page, esp. the front page. **7.** a square flag, often charged with the arms of its bearer. [C13: from Old French *baniere,* of Germanic origin; compare Gothic *bandwa* sign; influenced by Medieval Latin *bannum* BAN[1], *bannīre* to BANISH] —**'ban+nered** *adj.*

ban+ner+et ('bænərɪt, -əˌrɛt) *n.* (in the Middle Ages) **1.** Also called: **knight banneret.** a knight who was entitled to command other knights and men-at-arms under his own banner. **2.** a title of knighthood conferred by the king for valour on the battlefield. [C14: from Old French *banerete* a small BANNER]

ban+ner+ette *or* **ban+ner+et** (ˌbænə'rɛt) *n.* a small banner. [C13: from Old French *baneret,* from *banere* BANNER]

ban+ne+rol ('bænəˌrəʊl) *n.* a variant spelling of **banderole.**

Ban·nis·ter ('bænɪstə) *n.* **Ro·ger (Gilbert).** born 1929, British athlete: first man to run a mile in under four minutes (1954).

ban+nis+ters ('bænɪstəz) *pl. n.* a variant spelling of **banisters.**

ban+nock ('bænək) *n.* a round flat cake originating in Scotland, made from wheat or barley and sometimes filled with currants, raisins, etc. [Old English *bannuc;* related to Breton *bannach, banne* drop, bit, Cornish *banna* drop]

Ban+nock+burn ('bænəkˌbɜ:n) *n.* a village in central Scotland, south of Stirling: site of a victory (1314) of the Scots, led by Robert the Bruce, over the English.

banns *or* **bans** (bænz) *pl. n.* **1.** the public declaration of an intended marriage, usually formally announced on three successive Sundays in the parish churches of both the betrothed. **2. forbid the banns.** to raise an objection to a marriage announced in this way. [C14: plural of *bann* proclamation; see BAN[1]]

ban+quet ('bæŋkwɪt) *n.* **1.** a lavish and sumptuous meal; feast. **2.** a ceremonial meal for many people, often followed by speeches. ~*vb.* **+quets, +quet+ing, +quet+ed. 3.** (*intr.*) to hold or take part in a banquet. **4.** (*tr.*) to entertain or honour (a person) with a banquet. [C15: from Old French, from Italian *banchetto,* from *banco* a table, of Germanic origin; see BANK[1]] —**'ban+quet+er** *n.*

ban+quette (bæŋ'kɛt) *n.* **1.** (formerly) a raised part behind a parapet. **2.** a footbridge. **3.** *Chiefly U.S.* an upholstered bench. [C17: from French, from Provençal *banqueta,* literally: a little bench, from *banc* bench; see BANK[3]]

bans (bænz) *pl. n.* a variant spelling of **banns.**

ban+sel·a (ban'sɛlə) *n.* a variant spelling of **bonsela.**

ban+shee ('bænʃi:, bæn'ʃi:) *n.* (in Irish folklore) a female spirit whose wailing warns of impending death. [C18: from Irish Gaelic *bean sidhe,* literally: woman of the fairies]

Ban+stead ('bænˌstɛd) *n.* a town in S England, in NE Surrey: a dormitory town for London. Pop.: 44 986 (1971).

bant (bænt) *n. Lancashire dialect.* string. [probably a dialect pronunciation of BAND[2]]

ban+tam ('bæntəm) *n.* **1.** any of various very small breeds of domestic fowl. **2.** a small but aggressive person. **3.** *Boxing.* short for **bantamweight.** [C18: after *Bantam,* village in Java, said to be the original home of this fowl]

ban·tam+weight ('bæntəmˌweɪt) *n.* **1. a.** a professional boxer weighing 112–118 pounds (51–53.5 kg). **b.** an amateur boxer weighing 112–119 pounds (51–54 kg). **c.** (*as modifier*): *the bantamweight champion.* **2.** a wrestler in a similar weight category (usually 115–126 pounds (52–57 kg)).

ban+ter ('bæntə) *vb.* **1.** to speak or tease lightly or jokingly. ~*n.* **2.** light, teasing, or joking language or repartee. [C17: of unknown origin] —**'ban+ter+er** *n.*

Bant·ing ('bæntɪŋ) *n.* Sir **Fred·er·ick Grant.** 1891–1941, Canadian physiologist: discovered the insulin treatment for diabetes with Best and Macleod (1922) and shared the Nobel prize for medicine with Macleod (1923).

bant+ing ('bæntɪŋ) *n. Obsolete.* slimming by avoiding eating sugar, starch, and fat. [after William *Banting* (1797–1878), London undertaker who popularized this diet]

bant+ling ('bæntlɪŋ) *n. Archaic, disparaging.* a young child; brat. [C16: perhaps from German *Bänkling* illegitimate child, from *Bank* bench + -LING[1]]

Ban+toid ('bɑ:ntɔɪd, 'bæn-) *adj.* denoting or relating to languages, esp. in Cameroon and Nigeria, that possess certain Bantu characteristics. See also **Semi-Bantu.**

Ban+tu ('bɑ:ntʊ, 'bæntu:, bæn'tu:) *n.* **1.** a group of languages of Africa, including most of the principal languages spoken from the equator to the Cape of Good Hope, but excluding the Khoisan family: now generally regarded as part of the Benue-Congo branch of the Niger-Congo family. **2.** (*pl.* **+tu** *or* **+tus**) a member of any of the indigenous Negroid peoples who inhabit southern, eastern, and central Africa and speak any of these languages. ~*adj.* **3.** denoting, relating to, or belonging to this group of peoples or to any of their languages. [C19: from Bantu *Ba-ntu* people]

Ban+tu+stan ('bɑ:ntʊˌstɑ:n, ˌbæntʊ'stɑ:n) *n.* (in South Africa) an area reserved for occupation by a Black African people, with limited self-government. Official name: **homeland.**

Ban·ville (*French* bɑ̃'vil) *n.* **Thé·o·dore de** (teɔ'dɔ:r də). 1823–91, French poet, who anticipated the Parnassian school in his perfection of form and command of rhythm.

ban+yan *or* **ban+ian** ('bænjən) *n.* **1.** a moraceous tree, *Ficus benghalensis,* of tropical India and the East Indies, having aerial roots that grow down into the soil forming additional trunks. **2.** a member of the Hindu merchant caste of N and W India. **3.** a loose-fitting shirt, jacket, or robe, worn originally in India. [C16: from Hindi *baniyā,* from Sanskrit *vānija* merchant]

ban+zai ('bɑ:nzaɪ, bɑ:n'zaɪ) *interj.* a patriotic cheer, battle cry, or salutation. [Japanese: literally, (may you live for) ten thousand years]

ban+zai at+tack *n.* a mass attack of troops, without concern for casualties, as practised by the Japanese in World War II.

ba·o+bab ('beɪəʊˌbæb) *n.* a tropical African bombacaceous tree, *Adansonia digitata,* that has a very thick trunk, large white flowers, and a gourdlike fruit with an edible pulp called monkey bread. Also called: **monkey bread tree.** [C17: probably from a native African word]

B.A.O.R. *abbrev. for* British Army of the Rhine.

bap (bæp) *n. Brit.* a soft bread roll. [of unknown origin]

bapt. *abbrev. for:* **1.** baptism. **2.** baptized.

Bapt. *abbrev. for* Baptist.

bap+tism ('bæptɪzəm) *n.* **1.** a Christian religious rite consisting of immersion in or sprinkling with water as a sign that the subject is cleansed from sin and constituted as a member of the Church. **2.** the act of baptizing or of undergoing baptism. **3.** any similar experience of initiation, regeneration, or dedication. —**bap+'tis+mal** *adj.* —**bap+'tis+mal+ly** *adv.*

bap+tism of fire *n.* **1.** a soldier's first experience of battle. **2.** any initiating ordeal or experience. **3.** *Christianity.* the penetration of the Holy Ghost into the human spirit to purify, consecrate, and strengthen it, as was believed to have occurred initially at Pentecost.

Bap+tist ('bæptɪst) *n.* **1.** a member of any of various Christian sects that affirm the necessity of baptism (usually of adults and by immersion) following a personal profession of the Christian faith. **2. the Baptist.** See **John the Baptist.** ~*adj.* **3.** denoting, relating to, or characteristic of any Christian sect that affirms the necessity of baptism following a personal profession of the Christian faith.

bap+tist+ry *or* **bap+tist+er·y** ('bæptɪstrɪ) *n., pl.* **+ries** *or* **+er·ies. 1.** a part of a Christian church in which baptisms are carried out. **2.** a tank in a Baptist church in which baptisms are carried out.

bap+tize *or* **bap+tise** (bæp'taɪz) *vb.* **1.** *Christianity.* to immerse (a person) in water or sprinkle water on (a person) as part of the rite of baptism. **2.** (*tr.*) to give a name to; christen. **3.** (*tr.*) to cleanse; purify. [C13: from Late Latin *baptīzāre,* from Greek *baptizein,* from *baptein* to bathe, dip]

bar[1] (bɑ:) *n.* **1.** a rigid usually straight length of metal, wood, etc., that is longer than it is wide or thick, used esp. as a barrier or as a structural or mechanical part: *a bar of a gate.* **2.** a solid usually rectangular block of any material: *a bar of soap.* **3.** anything that obstructs or prevents. **4. a.** an offshore ridge of sand, mud, or shingle lying near the shore and parallel to it, across the mouth of a river, bay, or harbour, or linking an island to the mainland. **b.** *U.S.* an alluvial deposit in a stream, river, or lake. **5.** a counter or room where alcoholic drinks are served. **6.** a counter, room, or establishment where a particular range of goods, food, services, etc., are sold: *a coffee bar; a heel bar.* **7.** a narrow band or stripe, as of colour or light. **8.** a heating element in an electric fire. **9.** (in England) the area in a court of law separating the part reserved for the bench and Queen's Counsel from the area occupied by junior barristers, solicitors, and the general public. See also **Bar. 10.** the place in a court of law where the accused stands during his trial: *the prisoner at the bar.* **11.** a particular court of law. **12.** *Brit.* (in the House of Lords and House of Commons) the boundary where nonmembers wishing to address either House appear and where persons are arraigned. **13.** a plea showing that a plaintiff has no cause of action, as when the case has already been adjudicated upon or the time allowed for bringing the action has passed. **14.** anything referred to as an authority or tribunal: *the bar of decency.* **15.** Also called: **measure.** *Music.* **a.** a group of beats that is repeated with a consistent rhythm throughout a piece or passage of music. The number of beats in the bar is indicated by the time signature. **b.** another word for **bar line. 16. a.** *Brit.* insignia added to a decoration indicating a second award. **b.** *U.S.* a strip of metal worn with uniform, esp. to signify rank or as an award for service. **17.** a variant spelling of **barre. 18.** *Football, etc.* See **crossbar. 19.** *Gymnastics.* See **horizontal bar. 20. a.** part of the metal mouthpiece of a horse's bridle. **b.** the space between the horse's teeth in which such a part fits. **21.** either of two horny extensions that project forwards and inwards from the rear of the outer layer of a horse's hoof. **22.** See **crowbar** and **glazing-bar. 23.** *Lacemaking, needlework.* another name for **bride**[2]. **24.** *Heraldry.* an ordinary consisting of a horizontal line across a shield, typically narrower than a fesse, and usually appearing in twos or threes. **25. behind bars.** in prison. **26. won't** (*or*

wouldn't) have a bar of. *Austral. informal.* cannot tolerate; dislike. ~*vb.* **bars, bar·ring, barred.** (*tr.*) **27.** to fasten or secure with a bar: *to bar the door.* **28.** to shut in or out with or as if with barriers: *to bar the entrances.* **29.** to obstruct; hinder: *the fallen tree barred the road.* **30.** (usually foll. by *from*) to prohibit; forbid: *to bar a couple from meeting.* **31.** (usually foll. by *from*) to keep out; exclude: *to bar a person from membership.* **32.** to mark with a bar or bars. **33.** *Law.* to prevent or halt (an action) by showing that the plaintiff has no cause. **34.** to mark off (music) into bars with bar lines. ~*prep.* **35.** except for: *the best recital bar last night's.* **36. bar none.** without exception. [C12: from Old French *barre,* from Vulgar Latin *barra* (unattested) bar, rod, of unknown origin]

bar[2] (bɑː) *n.* a cgs unit of pressure equal to 10^6 dynes per square centimetre. 1 bar is equivalent to 10^5 newtons per square metre. [C20: from Greek *baros* weight]

bar[3] (bɑː) *Southwest Brit. dialect.* ~*n.* **1.** immunity from being caught or otherwise penalized in a game. ~*interj.* **2.** a cry for such immunity. [variant of BARLEY[2]]

Bar (bɑː) *n.* **the. 1.** (in England and elsewhere) barristers collectively. **2.** *U.S.* the legal profession collectively. **3. be called to** *or* **go to the Bar.** *Brit.* to become a barrister. **4. be called within the Bar.** *Brit.* to be appointed as a Queen's Counsel.

bar. *abbrev. for:* **1.** barometer. **2.** barometric. **3.** barrel (container or unit of measure). **4.** barrister.

Bar·ab·bas (bəˈræbəs) *n. New Testament.* a condemned robber who was released at the Passover instead of Jesus (Matthew 27:16).

Bar·a·nof Is·land (ˈbærənɔf) *n.* an island off SE Alaska, in the western part of the Alexander Archipelago. Area: 4162 sq. km (1607 sq. miles).

bar·a·the·a (ˌbærəˈθɪə) *n.* a fabric made of silk and wool or cotton and rayon, used esp. for coats. [C19: of unknown origin]

ba·ra·za (baˈraza) *E. African.* ~*n.* **1.** a place where public meetings are held. **2.** a palaver or meeting. [C19: from Swahili]

barb[1] (bɑːb) *n.* **1.** a subsidiary point facing in the opposite direction to the main point of a fish-hook, harpoon, arrow, etc., intended to make extraction difficult. **2.** any of various pointed parts, as on barbed wire. **3.** a cutting remark; jibe. **4.** any of the numerous hairlike filaments that form the vane of a feather. **5.** a beardlike growth in certain animals. **6.** a hooked hair or projection on certain fruits. **7.** any small cyprinid fish of the genus *Barbus* (or *Puntius*) and related genera, such as *B. conchonius* (**rosy barb**). **8.** (*usually pl.*) any of the small fleshy protuberances beneath the tongue in horses and cattle. **9.** a white linen cloth forming part of a headdress extending from the chin to the upper chest, originally worn by women in the Middle Ages, now worn by nuns of some orders. **10.** *Obsolete.* a beard. ~*vb.* **11.** (*tr.*) to provide with a barb or barbs. [C14: from Old French *barbe* beard, point, from Latin *barba* beard] —**barbed** *adj.*

barb[2] (bɑːb) *n.* a breed of horse of North African origin, similar to the Arab but less spirited. [C17: from French *barbe,* from Italian *barbero* a Barbary (horse)]

barb[3] (bɑːb) *n. Austral.* a black kelpie (see **kelpie**[1]). [C19: named after one that was named *Barb* after a winning racehorse]

Bar·ba·dos (bɑːˈbeɪdəʊs, -dəʊz, -dɒs) *n.* an island in the West Indies, in the E Lesser Antilles: a British colony from 1628 to 1966, now an independent state within the Commonwealth. Language: English. Currency: East Caribbean dollar. Capital: Bridgetown. Pop.: 244 000 (1974 UN est.). Area: 430 sq. km (166 sq. miles). —**Bar·ˈba·di·an** *adj., n.*

bar·bar·i·an (bɑːˈbɛərɪən) *n.* **1.** a member of a primitive or uncivilized people. **2.** a coarse, insensitive, or uncultured person. **3.** a vicious person. ~*adj.* **4.** of an uncivilized culture. **5.** insensitive, uncultured, or brutal. [C16: see BARBAROUS] —**bar·ˈbar·i·an·ism** *n.*

bar·bar·ic (bɑːˈbærɪk) *adj.* **1.** of or characteristic of barbarians. **2.** primitive or unsophisticated; unrestrained. **3.** brutal. [C15: from Latin *barbaricus* foreign, outlandish; see BARBAROUS] —**bar·ˈbar·i·cal·ly** *adv.*

bar·ba·rism (ˈbɑːbəˌrɪzəm) *n.* **1.** a brutal, coarse, or ignorant act. **2.** the condition of being backward, coarse, or ignorant. **3.** a substandard or erroneously constructed or derived word or expression; solecism. **4.** any act or object that offends against accepted taste. [C16: from Latin *barbarismus* error of speech, from Greek *barbarismos,* from *barbaros* BARBAROUS]

bar·bar·i·ty (bɑːˈbærɪtɪ) *n., pl.* **·ties. 1.** the state or condition of being barbaric or barbarous. **2.** a brutal or vicious act. **3.** a crude or unsophisticated quality, style, expression, etc.

bar·ba·rize *or* **bar·ba·rise** (ˈbɑːbəˌraɪz) *vb.* **1.** to make or become barbarous. **2.** to use barbarisms in (language). —ˌ**bar·ba·ri·ˈza·tion** *or* ˌ**bar·ba·ri·ˈsa·tion** *n.*

Bar·ba·ros·sa (ˌbɑːbəˈrɒsə) *n.* the nickname of the Holy Roman Emperor **Frederick I.** See **Frederick Barbarossa.**

bar·ba·rous (ˈbɑːbərəs) *adj.* **1.** uncivilized; primitive. **2.** brutal or cruel. **3.** lacking refinement. [C15: via Latin from Greek *barbaros* barbarian, non-Greek, in origin imitative of incomprehensible speech; compare Sanskrit *barbara* stammering, non-Aryan] —**ˈbar·ba·rous·ly** *adv.* —**ˈbar·ba·rous·ness** *n.*

Bar·ba·ry (ˈbɑːbərɪ) *n.* a region of N Africa, extending from W Egypt to the Atlantic and including the former **Barbary States** of Tripolitania, Tunisia, Algeria, and Morocco.

Bar·ba·ry ape *n.* a tailless macaque, *Macaca sylvana,* that inhabits rocky cliffs and forests in NW Africa and Gibraltar: family *Cercopithecidae,* order *Primates.*

Bar·ba·ry Coast *n.* **the.** the Mediterranean coast of North Africa: a centre of piracy against European shipping from the 16th to the 19th century.

bar·bate (ˈbɑːbeɪt) *adj. Chiefly biology.* having tufts of long hairs; bearded. [C19: from Latin *barba* a beard]

bar·be·cue (ˈbɑːbɪˌkjuː) *n.* **1.** a meal cooked out of doors over an open fire. **2.** a grill or fireplace used in barbecuing. **3.** the food so cooked. ~*vb.* **·cues, ·cu·ing, ·cued.** (*tr.*) **4.** to cook (meat, fish, etc.) on a grill, usually over charcoal and often with a highly seasoned sauce. **5.** *Chiefly U.S.* to cook (meat, etc.) in a highly seasoned sauce. [C17: from American Spanish *barbacoa,* probably from Taino: frame made of sticks]

barbed wire *n.* strong wire with sharply pointed barbs at close intervals. Also called (U.S.): **barbwire.**

barbed-wire grass *n. Austral.* an aromatic grass, *Cymbopogon refractus,* with groups of seed heads resembling barbed wire.

bar·bel (ˈbɑːbᵊl) *n.* **1.** any of several slender tactile spines or bristles that hang from the jaws of certain fishes, such as the catfish and carp. **2.** any of several European cyprinid fishes of the genus *Barbus,* esp. *B. barbus,* that resemble the carp but have a longer body and pointed snout. [C14: from Old French, from Latin *barbus,* from *barba* beard]

bar·bell (ˈbɑːˌbɛl) *n.* a metal rod to which heavy discs are attached at each end for weightlifting exercises.

bar·bel·late (ˈbɑːbɪˌleɪt; bɑːˈbɛlɪt, -eɪt) *adj.* **1.** (of plants or plant organs) covered with barbs, hooks, or bristles. **2.** (of animals) possessing bristles or barbels. [C19: from New Latin *barbellātus,* from *barbella* short stiff hair, from Latin *barbula* a little beard, from *barba* beard]

bar·ber (ˈbɑːbə) *n.* **1.** a person whose business is cutting men's hair and shaving or trimming beards. ~*vb.* (*tr.*) **2.** to cut the hair of. **3.** to shave or trim the beard of. [C13: from Old French *barbeor,* from *barbe* beard, from Latin *barba*]

Bar·ber (ˈbɑːbə) *n.* **Sam·u·el.** 1910-81, U.S. composer: his works include an *Adagio for Strings,* adapted from the second movement of his string quartet No. 1 (1936) and the opera *Vanessa* (1958).

bar·ber·ry (ˈbɑːbərɪ) *n., pl.* **·ries. 1.** any spiny Asian berberidaceous shrub of the genus *Berberis,* esp. *B. vulgaris,* having clusters of yellow flowers and orange or red berries: widely cultivated as hedge plants. **2.** the fruit of any of these plants. [C15: from Old French *berberis,* from Arabic *barbāris*]

bar·ber·shop (ˈbɑːbəˌʃɒp) *n.* **1.** *Now chiefly U.S.* the premises of a barber. **2.** (*modifier*) *U.S.* denoting or characterized by a type of close four-part harmony for male voices, popular in romantic and sentimental songs of the 1920s and 1930s: *a barbershop quartet.*

bar·ber's itch *or* **rash** *n.* any of various fungal infections of the bearded portion of the neck and face. Technical name: **tinea barbae.**

bar·bet (ˈbɑːbɪt) *n.* any small tropical brightly coloured bird of the family *Capitonidae,* having short weak wings and a sharp stout bill with tuftlike feathers at its base: order *Piciformes* (woodpeckers, etc.). [C18: from French, ultimately from Latin *barbātus* bearded, BARBATE]

bar·bette (bɑːˈbɛt) *n.* **1.** (formerly) an earthen platform inside a parapet, from which heavy guns could fire over the top. **2.** an armoured cylinder that protects a turret on a warship. [C18: from French, diminutive of *barbe* a nun's BARB[1], from a fancied similarity between the earthwork around a cannon and this part of a nun's habit]

bar·bi·can (ˈbɑːbɪkən) *n.* **1.** the outwork of a fortified place, esp. to defend a drawbridge. **2.** a watchtower projecting from a fortification. [C13: from Old French *barbacane,* from Medieval Latin *barbacana,* of unknown origin]

bar·bi·cel (ˈbɑːbɪˌsɛl) *n. Ornithol.* any of the minute hooks on the barbules of feathers that interlock with those of adjacent barbules. [C19: from New Latin *barbicella,* literally: a small beard, from Latin *barba* beard]

bar bil·liards *n. Brit.* a table game found in pubs, etc., in which short cues are used to pocket balls into holes scoring various points and guarded by wooden pegs that incur penalties if they are knocked over.

Bar·bi·rol·li (ˌbɑːbəˈrɒlɪ) *n.* Sir **John.** 1899–1970, British conductor of the Hallé Orchestra (1943–68); born in Italy.

bar·bi·tone (ˈbɑːbɪˌtəʊn) *or U.S.* **bar·bi·tal** (ˈbɑːbɪˌtæl) *n.* a long-acting barbiturate used medicinally, usually in the form of the sodium salt, as a sedative or hypnotic. [C20: from BARBIT(URIC ACID) + -ONE]

bar·bi·tu·rate (bɑːˈbɪtjʊrɪt, -ˌreɪt) *n.* a derivative of barbituric acid, such as barbitone or phenobarbitone, used in medicine as a sedative or hypnotic.

bar·bi·tu·ric ac·id (ˌbɑːbɪˈtjʊərɪk) *n.* a white crystalline solid used in the preparation of barbiturate drugs. Formula: $C_5H_4N_2O_3.2H_2O$. Also called: **malonylurea.** [C19: partial translation of German *Barbitursäure,* perhaps from the name *Barbara* + URIC + *Säure* acid]

Bar·bi·zon School (ˈbɑːbɪˌzɒn) *n.* a group of French painters of landscapes of the 1840s, including Théodore Rousseau, Daubigny, Diaz, Corot, and Millet. [C19: from *Barbizon* a village near Paris and a favourite haunt of the painters]

Bar·bu·da (bɑːˈbuːdə) *n.* a coral island in the E West Indies, in the Leeward Islands: a dependency of Antigua. Area: 160 sq. km (62 sq. miles).

bar·bule (ˈbɑːbjuːl) *n.* **1.** a very small barb. **2.** *Ornithol.* any of the minute hairs that project from a barb and in some feathers interlock by hooks and grooves, forming a flat vane. [C19: from Latin *barbula* a little beard, from *barba* beard]

Bar·busse (*French* bar'bys) *n.* **Hen·ri** (ã'ri). 1873–1935, French novelist and poet. His novels include *L'Enfer* (1908) and *Le Feu* (1916), reflecting the horror of World War I.

Bar·ca ('bɑːkə) *n.* the surname of several noted Carthaginian generals, including Hamilcar, Hasdrubal, and Hannibal. —'**Bar·can** *adj.*

bar·ca·role *or* **bar·ca·rolle** ('bɑːkə,rəʊl, -,rɒl; ,bɑːkə'rəʊl) *n.* **1.** a Venetian boat song in a time of six or twelve quaver beats to the bar. **2.** an instrumental composition resembling this. [C18: from French, from Italian *barcarola,* from *barcaruolo* boatman, from *barca* boat; see BARQUE]

Bar·ce ('bartʃe) *or* **Bar·ca** ('barka) *n.* the Italian name for **Al Marj.**

Bar·ce·lo·na (,bɑːsɪ'ləʊnə) *n.* the chief port of Spain, on the NE Mediterranean coast: seat of the Republican government during the Civil War (1936–39); the commercial capital of Spain. Pop.: 1 745 142 (1970). Ancient name: **Barcino.**

B.Arch. *abbrev. for* Bachelor of Architecture.

bar·chan, bar·khan, bar·chane, *or* **bar·kan** (bɑː'kɑːn) *n.* a crescent-shaped shifting sand dune, convex on the windward side and steeper and concave on the leeward.

Bar·clay de Tol·ly ('bɑːklɪ də 'tɒlɪ; *Russian* bar'klai də 'tɔlj) *n.* Prince **Mi·kha·il** (mixa'il). 1761–1818, Russian field marshal: commander in chief against Napoleon in 1812.

Bar·coo Riv·er (bɑː'kuː) *n.* another name for **Cooper's Creek.**

Bar·coo sa·lute *n. Austral. informal.* a movement of the hand to brush flies away from the face.

bard[1] (bɑːd) *n.* **1. a.** (formerly) one of an ancient Celtic order of poets who recited verses about the exploits, often legendary, of their tribes. **b.** (in modern times) a poet who wins a verse competition at a Welsh Eisteddfod. **2.** *Archaic or literary.* any poet, esp. one who writes lyric or heroic verse or is of national importance. [C14: from Scottish Gaelic; related to Welsh *bardd*] —'**bard·ic** *adj.*

bard[2] *or* **barde** (bɑːd) *n.* **1.** a piece of larding bacon or pork fat placed on game or lean meat during roasting to prevent drying out. **2.** an ornamental caparison for a horse. ~*vb.* (*tr.*) **3.** to place a bard on. [C15: from Old French *barde,* from Old Italian *barda,* from Arabic *barda'ah* packsaddle]

Bard (bɑːd) *n.* **the.** an epithet of (William) **Shakespeare.**

bar·dol·a·try (bɑː'dɒlətrɪ) *n. Facetious.* idolatry or excessive admiration of Shakespeare.

Bar·dot (*French* bar'do) *n.* **Bri·gitte** (bri'ʒit) born 1934, French film actress.

bare[1] (bɛə) *adj.* **1.** unclothed; exposed: used esp. of a part of the body. **2.** without the natural, conventional, or usual covering or clothing: *a bare tree.* **3.** lacking appropriate furnishings, etc.: *a bare room.* **4.** unembellished; simple: *the bare facts.* **5.** (*prenominal*) just sufficient; mere: *he earned the bare minimum.* **6. with one's bare hands.** without a weapon or tool. ~*vb.* **7.** (*tr.*) to make bare; uncover; reveal. [Old English *bær;* compare Old Norse *berr,* Old High German *bar* naked, Old Slavonic *bosŭ* barefoot] —'**bare·ness** *n.*

bare[2] (bɛə) *vb. Archaic.* a past tense of **bear**[1].

bare·back ('bɛə,bæk) *or* **bare·backed** *adj., adv.* (of horse-riding) without a saddle.

bare·faced ('bɛə,feɪst) *adj.* **1.** unconcealed or shameless: *a barefaced lie.* **2.** with the face uncovered or shaven. —**bare·fac·ed·ly** ('bɛə,feɪsɪdlɪ) *adv.* —'**bare·,fac·ed·ness** *n.*

bare·foot ('bɛə,fʊt) *or* **bare·foot·ed** *adj., adv.* with the feet uncovered.

ba·rège *French.* (ba'rɛːʒ) *n.* **1.** a light silky gauze fabric made of wool. ~*adj.* **2.** made of such a fabric. [C19: named after *Barèges,* France, where it was originally made]

bare·hand·ed (,bɛə'hændɪd) *adv., adj.* **1.** without weapons, tools, etc. **2.** with hands uncovered.

bare·head·ed (,bɛə'hɛdɪd) *adj., adv.* with head uncovered.

Ba·reil·ly (bə'reɪlɪ) *n.* a city in N India, in N central Uttar Pradesh. Pop.: 296 093 (1971).

bare·ly ('bɛəlɪ) *adv.* **1.** only just; scarcely: *barely enough for their needs.* **2.** *Informal.* not quite; nearly: *barely old enough.* **3.** scantily; poorly: *barely furnished.* **4.** *Archaic.* openly.

Usage. See at **hardly.**

Bar·en·boim ('bærən,bɔɪm) *n.* **Dan·iel.** born 1942, Israeli concert pianist and conductor, born in Argentina.

Bar·ents Sea ('bærənts) *n.* a part of the Arctic Ocean, bounded by Norway, the Soviet Union, and the islands of Novaya Zemlya, Spitsbergen, and Franz Josef Land. [named after Willem *Barents* (1550–97), Dutch navigator and explorer who discovered it in 1596]

bare·sark ('bɛə,sɑːk) *n.* **1.** another word for **berserker.** ~*adv.* **2.** *Archaic.* without armour.

bar fly *n. Informal, chiefly U.S.* a person who frequents bars.

bar·gain ('bɑːgɪn) *n.* **1.** an agreement or contract establishing what each party will give, receive, or perform in a transaction between them. **2.** something acquired or received in such an agreement. **3. a.** something bought or offered at a low price: *a bargain at an auction.* **b.** (*as modifier*): *a bargain basement.* **4. into** *or* (*U.S.*) **in the bargain.** in excess of what has been stipulated; besides. **5. make** *or* **strike a bargain.** to agree on terms. ~*vb.* **6.** (*intr.*) to negotiate the terms of an agreement, transaction, etc. **7.** (*tr.*) to exchange, as in a bargain. **8.** to arrive at (an agreement or settlement). [C14: from Old French *bargaigne,* from *bargaignier* to trade, of Germanic origin; compare Medieval Latin *barcāniāre* to trade, Old English *borgian* to borrow] —'**bar·gain·er** *n.*

bar·gain a·way *vb.* (*tr., adv.*) to lose or renounce (freedom, rights, etc.) in return for something valueless or of little value.

bar·gain for *vb.* (*intr., prep.*) to expect; anticipate (a style of behaviour, change in fortune, etc.): *he got more than he bargained for.*

bar·gain on *vb.* (*intr., prep.*) to rely or depend on (something): *he bargained on her support.*

barge (bɑːdʒ) *n.* **1.** a vessel, usually flat-bottomed and with or without its own power, used for transporting freight, esp. on canals. **2.** a vessel, often decorated, used in pageants, for state occasions, etc. **3.** *Navy.* a boat allocated to a flag officer, used esp. for ceremonial occasions and often carried on board his flagship. **4.** *Informal and derogatory.* any vessel, esp. an old or clumsy one. ~*vb.* **5.** (*intr.;* foll. by *into*) *Informal.* to bump (into). **6.** *Informal.* to push (someone or one's way) violently. **7.** (*intr.;* foll. by *into* or *in*) *Informal.* to interrupt rudely or clumsily: *to barge into a conversation.* **8.** *Sailing.* to bear down on (another boat or boats) at the start of a race. **9.** (*tr.*) to transport by barge. **10.** (*intr.*) *Informal.* to move slowly or clumsily. [C13: from Old French, from Medieval Latin *barga,* probably from Late Latin *barca* a small boat; see BARQUE]

barge·board ('bɑːdʒ,bɔːd) *n.* a board, often decorated with carved ornaments, placed along the gable end of a roof. Also called: **vergeboard.**

barge cou·ple *n.* either of a pair of outside rafters along the gable end of a roof.

barge course *n.* **1.** the overhang of the gable end of a roof. **2.** a course of bricks laid on edge to form the coping of a wall.

bar·gee (bɑː'dʒiː) *or U.S.* **barge·man** ('bɑːdʒmən) *n., pl.* **bar·gees** *or* **barge·men.** a person employed on or in charge of a barge.

barge·pole ('bɑːdʒ,pəʊl) *n.* **1.** a long pole used to propel a barge. **2. not touch with a bargepole.** *Informal.* to refuse to have anything to do with.

bar girl *n. Chiefly U.S.* an attractive girl employed by the management of a bar to befriend male customers and encourage them to buy drinks.

bar graph *n.* a graph consisting of vertical or horizontal bars whose lengths are proportional to amounts or quantities.

Ba·ri ('bɑːrɪ) *n.* a port in SE Italy, capital of Apulia, on the Adriatic coast. Pop.: 376 467 (1975 est.).

bar·ic[1] ('bɛərɪk, 'bærɪk) *adj.* of or containing barium.

bar·ic[2] ('bærɪk) *adj.* of or concerned with weight, esp. that of the atmosphere as indicated by barometric pressure.

ba·ril·la (bə'rɪlə) *n.* **1.** an impure mixture of sodium carbonate and sodium sulphate obtained from the ashes of certain plants, such as the saltworts. **2.** either of two chenopodiaceous plants, *Salsola kali* (or *soda*) or *Halogeton soda,* formerly burned to obtain a form of sodium carbonate. See also **saltwort.** [C17: from Spanish *barrilla,* literally: a little bar, from *barra* BAR[1]]

Bar·ing ('bɛərɪŋ) *n.* **Eve·lyn,** 1st Earl of Cromer. 1841–1917, English administrator. As consul general in Egypt with plenipotentiary powers, he controlled the Egyptian government from 1883 to 1907.

barit. *abbrev. for* baritone.

bar·ite ('bɛəraɪt) *n.* the usual U.S. name for **barytes.** [C18: from BAR(IUM) + -ITE[1]]

bar·i·tone ('bærɪ,təʊn) *n.* **1.** the second lowest adult male voice, having a range approximately from G an eleventh below middle C to F a fourth above it. **2.** a singer with such a voice. **3.** the second lowest instrument in the families of the saxophone, horn, oboe, etc. ~*adj.* **4.** relating to or denoting a baritone: *a baritone part.* **5.** denoting the second lowest instrument in a family: *the baritone horn.* [C17: from Italian *baritono* a deep voice, from Greek *barutonos* deep-sounding, from *barus* heavy, low + *tonos* TONE]

bar·i·um ('bɛərɪəm) *n.* a soft silvery-white metallic element of the alkaline earth group. It is used in bearing alloys and compounds are used as pigments. Symbol: Ba; atomic no.: 56; atomic wt.: 137.34; valency: 2; relative density: 3.5; melting pt.: 725°C; boiling pt.: 1140°C. [C19: from BAR(YTA) + -IUM]

bar·i·um en·e·ma *n.* an injection into the rectum of a preparation of barium sulphate, which is opaque to x-rays, before x-raying the lower alimentary canal.

bar·i·um hy·drox·ide *n.* a white poisonous crystalline solid, used in the manufacture of organic compounds and in the preparation of beet sugar. Formula: $Ba(OH)_2$. Also called: **baryta.**

bar·i·um meal *n.* a preparation of barium sulphate, which is opaque to x-rays, swallowed by a patient before x-ray examination of the upper part of his alimentary canal.

bar·i·um ox·ide *n.* a white or yellowish-white poisonous heavy powder used esp. as a dehydrating agent. Formula: BaO. Also called: **baryta.**

bar·i·um sul·phate *n.* a white insoluble fine heavy powder, used as a pigment, as a filler for paper, rubber, etc., and in barium meals. Formula: $BaSO_4$. Also called: **blanc fixe.**

bark[1] (bɑːk) *n.* **1.** the loud abrupt usually harsh or gruff cry of a dog or any of certain other animals. **2.** a similar sound, such as one made by a person, gun, etc. **3. his bark is worse than his bite.** he is bad-tempered but harmless. ~*vb.* **4.** (*intr.*) (of a dog or any of certain other animals) to make its typical loud abrupt cry. **5.** (*intr.*) (of a person, gun, etc.) to make a similar loud harsh sound. **6.** to say or shout in a brusque, peremptory, or angry tone: *he barked an order.* **7.** *Informal.* to advertise (a show, merchandise, etc.) by loudly addressing passers-by. **8. bark up the wrong tree.** *Informal.* to misdirect one's attention, efforts, etc.; be mistaken. [Old English *beorcan;* related to Lithuanian *burgėti* to quarrel, growl]

bark[2] (bɑːk) *n.* **1.** a protective layer of dead corky cells on the outside of the stems of woody plants. **2.** any of several varieties of this substance that can be used in tanning, dyeing, or in medicine. **3.** an informal name for **cinchona.** ~*vb.* (*tr.*) **4.** to scrape or rub off skin, as in an injury. **5.** to remove the bark or a circle of bark from (a tree or log). **6.** to cover or enclose with bark. **7.** to tan (leather), principally by the tannins in barks. [C13: from Old Norse *börkr;* related to Swedish, Danish *bark,* German *Borke;* compare Old Norse *björkr* BIRCH]

bark[3] (bɑːk) *n.* a variant spelling (esp. U.S.) of **barque.**

bark bee·tle *n.* any small beetle of the family *Scolytidae,* which bore tunnels in the bark and wood of trees, causing great damage. They are closely related to the weevils.

bark cloth *n.* a papery fabric made from the fibrous inner bark of various trees, esp. of the moraceous genus *Ficus* and the leguminous genus *Brachystegia.*

bar·ken·tine *or* **bar·kan·tine** (ˈbɑːkənˌtiːn) *n.* the usual U.S. spellings of **barquentine.**

bark·er[1] (ˈbɑːkə) *n.* **1.** an animal or person that barks. **2.** *Informal.* a person who stands at a show, fair booth, etc., and loudly addresses passers-by to attract customers.

bark·er[2] (ˈbɑːkə) *n.* a person or machine that removes bark from trees or logs or prepares it for tanning.

bar·khan *or* **bar·kan** (bɑːˈkɑːn) *n.* variant spellings of **barchan.**

Bark·ing (ˈbɑːkɪŋ) *n.* a borough of Greater London. Pop.: 153 800 (1976 est.).

bark·ing deer *n.* another name for **muntjac.**

Bar·let·ta (*Italian* barˈletta) *n.* a port in SE Italy, in Apulia. Pop.: 75 728 (1971).

bar·ley[1] (ˈbɑːlɪ) *n.* **1.** any of various erect annual temperate grasses of the genus *Hordeum,* esp. *H. vulgare,* that have short leaves and dense bristly flower spikes and are widely cultivated for grain and forage. **2.** the grain of any of these grasses, used in making beer and whisky and for soups, puddings, etc. See also **pearl barley.** [Old English *bærlīc* (adj.); related to *bere* barley, Old Norse *barr* barley, Gothic *barizeins* of barley, Latin *farīna* flour]

bar·ley[2] (ˈbɑːlɪ) *interj. Brit. dialect.* a cry for truce or respite from the rules of a game. [C19: probably changed from PARLEY]

bar·ley·corn (ˈbɑːlɪˌkɔːn) *n.* **1.** a grain of barley, or barley itself. **2.** an obsolete unit of length equal to one third of an inch.

bar·ley sug·ar *n.* a brittle clear amber-coloured sweet made by boiling sugar, originally with a barley extract.

bar·ley wa·ter *n.* a drink made from an infusion of barley, usually flavoured with lemon or orange.

bar·ley wine *n. Brit.* an exceptionally strong beer.

bar line *or* **bar** *n. Music.* the vertical line marking the boundary between one bar and the next.

barm (bɑːm) *n.* an archaic or dialect word for **yeast.** [Old English *bearm;* related to *beran* to BEAR, Old Norse *barmr* barm, Gothic *barms,* Old High German *barm;* see FERMENT]

bar·maid (ˈbɑːˌmeɪd) *n.* a woman who serves in a pub.

bar·man (ˈbɑːmən) *n., pl.* **·men.** a man who serves in a pub.

barm cake *n. Lancashire dialect.* a round flat soft bread roll.

Bar·me·cide (ˈbɑːmɪˌsaɪd) *or* **Bar·me·cid·al** *adj.* lavish or plentiful in appearance only; illusory; sham: *a Barmecide feast.* [C18: from the name of a prince in *The Arabian Nights* who served empty plates to a beggar, alleging that they held sumptuous food]

bar mitz·vah (bɑː ˈmɪtsvə) *n.* (*sometimes caps.*) *Judaism.* **1.** the ceremony and celebration marking the 13th birthday of a boy, who then assumes his full religious obligations. **2.** the boy himself. [Hebrew: son of the law]

bar·my (ˈbɑːmɪ) *adj.* **·mi·er, ·mi·est.** *Slang.* insane. Also (U.S.): **balmy.** [C16: originally, full of BARM, hence frothing, excited, flighty, etc.]

barn[1] (bɑːn) *n.* **1.** a large farm outbuilding, used chiefly for storing hay, grain, etc., but also for housing livestock. **2.** *U.S.* a large shed for sheltering railroad cars, trucks, etc. **3.** any large building, esp. an unattractive one. [Old English *beren,* from *bere* barley + *ærn* room; see BARLEY[1]]

barn[2] (bɑːn) *n.* a unit of nuclear cross section equal to 10^{-28} square metre. Symbol: b [C20: from BARN[1]; so called because of the relatively large cross section]

Bar·na·bas (ˈbɑːnəbəs) *n. New Testament.* original name: *Joseph.* a Cypriot Levite who supported Saint Paul in his apostolic work (Acts 4:36,37).

bar·na·cle (ˈbɑːnəkᵊl) *n.* **1.** any of various marine crustaceans of the subclass *Cirripedia* that, as adults, live attached to rocks, ship bottoms, etc. They have feathery food-catching cirri protruding from a hard shell. See **acorn barnacle, goose barnacle. 2.** a person or thing that is difficult to get rid of. —**ˈbar·na·cled** *adj.*

bar·na·cle goose *n.* **1.** a N European goose, *Branta leucopsis,* that has a black-and-white head and body and grey wings. **2.** a former name for **brent.**

Bar·nard (ˈbɑːnɑːd) *n.* **1. Chris·tiaan (Neethling).** born 1923, South African surgeon, who performed the first human heart transplant (1967). **2. Ed·ward Em·er·son.** 1857–1923, U.S. astronomer: noted for his discovery of the fifth satellite of Jupiter and his discovery of comets, nebulae, and a red dwarf (1916).

Bar·nar·do (bəˈnɑːdəʊ, bɑː-) *n.* Dr. **Thom·as John.** 1845–1905, British philanthropist, who founded homes for destitute children.

Bar·na·ul (*Russian* bərnaˈul) *n.* a city in the S Soviet Union, in the RSFSR. Pop.: 502 000 (1975 est.).

barn-brack (ˈbɑːnˌbræk) *n. Ulster dialect.* a large muffin with currants in it. [from Irish Gaelic *báirin breac* speckled bread]

barn dance *n.* **1.** *Brit.* a progressive round country dance. **2.** *U.S.* a party with hoedown music and square dancing. **3.** *U.S.* a party featuring country dancing.

barn door *n.* **1.** the door of a barn. **2.** *Informal.* a target so large that it cannot be missed.

Bar·net (ˈbɑːnɪt) *n.* a borough of Greater London: scene of a Yorkist victory (1471) in the Wars of the Roses. Pop.: 305 200 (1976 est.).

bar·ney (ˈbɑːnɪ) *Chiefly Austral. and N.Z. informal.* ~*n.* **1.** a noisy argument. ~*vb.* (*intr.*) **2.** to argue or quarrel. [C19: of unknown origin]

barn owl *n.* any owl of the genus *Tyto,* esp. *T. alba,* having a pale brown and white plumage, long slender legs, and a heart-shaped face: family *Tytonidae.*

Barns·ley (ˈbɑːnzlɪ) *n.* an industrial town in N England, in South Yorkshire. Pop.: 75 330 (1971).

barn·storm (ˈbɑːnˌstɔːm) *vb.* (*intr.*) *Chiefly U.S.* **1.** to tour rural districts putting on shows, esp. theatrical, athletic, or acrobatic shows. **2.** to tour rural districts making speeches in a political campaign. —**ˈbarn·ˌstorm·er** *n.*

barn swal·low *n.* the U.S. name for the common swallow, *Hirundo rustica.* See **swallow**[2].

Bar·num (ˈbɑːnəm) *n.* **P(hineas) T(aylor).** 1810–91, U.S. showman, who created The Greatest Show on Earth (1871) and, with J. A. Bailey, founded the Barnum and Bailey Circus (1881).

barn·yard (ˈbɑːnˌjɑːd) *n.* **1.** a yard adjoining a barn, in which farm animals are kept. **2.** (*modifier*) belonging to or characteristic of a barnyard. **3.** (*modifier*) crude or earthy: *barnyard humour.*

bar·o- *combining form.* indicating weight or pressure: *barometer.* [from Greek *baros* weight; related to Latin *gravis* heavy]

Ba·roc·chio (*Italian* baˈrɔkkjo) *n.* **Gia·co·mo** (ˈdʒaːkomo). See (Giacomo da) **Vignola.**

Ba·ro·da (bəˈrəʊdə) *n.* **1.** a former state of W India, part of Gujarat since 1960. **2.** the former name (until 1976) of **Vadodara.**

bar·o·gram (ˈbærəˌgræm) *n. Meteorol.* the record of atmospheric pressure traced by a barograph or similar instrument.

bar·o·graph (ˈbærəˌgrɑːf, -ˌgræf) *n. Meteorol.* a self-recording aneroid barometer. —**bar·o·graph·ic** (ˌbærəˈgræfɪk) *adj.*

Ba·ro·ja (*Spanish* baˈroxa) *n.* **Pí·o** (ˈpio). 1872–1956, Spanish Basque novelist, who wrote nearly 100 novels, including a series of twenty-two under the general title *Memorias de un Hombre de Acción* (1944–49).

ba·rom·e·ter (bəˈrɒmɪtə) *n.* **1.** an instrument for measuring atmospheric pressure, usually to determine altitude or weather changes. **2.** anything that shows change or impending change: *the barometer of social change.* —**bar·o·met·ric** (ˌbærəˈmɛtrɪk) *or* **ˌbar·o·ˈmet·ri·cal** *adj.* —**ˌbar·o·ˈmet·ri·cal·ly** *adv.* —**ba·ˈrom·e·try** *n.*

bar·o·met·ric pres·sure *n.* atmospheric pressure as indicated by a barometer.

bar·on (ˈbærən) *n.* **1.** a member of a specific rank of nobility, esp. the lowest rank in the British Isles. **2.** (in Europe from the Middle Ages) originally any tenant-in-chief of a king or other overlord, who held land from his superior by honourable service; a land-holding nobleman. **3.** a powerful businessman or financier: *a press baron.* **4.** *English law.* (formerly) the title held by judges of the Court of Exchequer. **5.** short for **baron of beef.** [C12: from Old French, of Germanic origin; compare Old High German *baro* freeman, Old Norse *berjask* to fight]

bar·on·age (ˈbærənɪdʒ) *n.* **1.** barons collectively. **2.** the rank or dignity of a baron.

bar·on·ess (ˈbærənɪs) *n.* **1.** the wife or widow of a baron. **2.** a woman holding the rank of baron in her own right.

bar·on·et (ˈbærənɪt, -ˌnɛt) *n.* (in Britain) a commoner who holds the lowest hereditary title of honour, ranking below a baron. Abbrev.: **Bart.** or **Bt.**

bar·on·et·age (ˈbærənɪtɪdʒ) *n.* **1.** the order of baronets; baronets collectively. **2.** the rank of a baronet; baronetcy.

bar·on·et·cy (ˈbærənɪtsɪ, -ˌnɛt-) *n., pl.* **·cies.** the rank, position, or patent of a baronet.

ba·rong (bæˈrɒŋ) *n.* a broad-bladed cleaver-like knife used in the Philippines. [from Moro; see PARANG]

ba·ro·ni·al (bəˈrəʊnɪəl) *adj.* of, relating to, or befitting a baron or barons.

bar·on of beef *n.* a cut of beef consisting of a double sirloin joined at the backbone.

bar·o·ny (ˈbærənɪ) *n., pl.* **·nies. 1. a.** the domain of a baron. **b.** (in Ireland) a division of a county. **c.** (in Scotland) a large estate or manor. **2.** the rank or dignity of a baron. **3.** a sphere of influence dominated by an industrial magnate or other powerful individual.

ba·roque (bəˈrɒk, bəˈrəʊk) *n.* (*often cap.*) **1.** a style of architecture and decorative art that flourished throughout Europe from the late 16th to the early 18th century, characterized by extensive ornamentation. **2.** a 17th-century style of music characterized by extensive use of the thorough bass and of ornamentation. **3.** any ornate or heavily ornamented style. ~*adj.* **4.** denoting, being in, or relating to the baroque. **5.** (of pearls) irregularly shaped. [C18: from French, from Italian *barroco,* probably from the name of Federigo *Barocci* (1528–1612), Italian painter of this style]

bar·o·scope (ˈbærəˌskəʊp) *n.* any instrument for measuring atmospheric pressure, esp. a manometer with one side open to the atmosphere. —**bar·o·scop·ic** (ˌbærəˈskɒpɪk) *adj.*

bar·o·stat (ˈbærəʊˌstæt) *n.* a device for maintaining constant pressure, such as one used in an aircraft cabin.

Ba·rot·se (bəˈrɒtsɪ) *n.* **1.** (*pl.* **·se** *or* **·ses**) a member of a

Negroid people of central Africa living chiefly in SW Zambia. **2.** the language spoken by this people; Lozi.

ba·rouche (bəˈruːʃ) *n.* a four-wheeled horse-drawn carriage, popular in the 19th century, having a retractable hood over the rear half, seats inside for two couples facing each other, and a driver's seat outside at the front. [C19: from German (dialect) *Barutsche,* from Italian *baroccio,* from Vulgar Latin *birotium* (unattested) vehicle with two wheels, from Late Latin *birotus* two-wheeled, from BI-[1] + *rota* wheel]

Ba·roz·zi (*Italian* baˈrɔttsi) *n.* See (Giacomo da) **Vignola.**

barque *or esp. U.S.* **bark** (bɑːk) *n.* **1.** a sailing ship of three or more masts having the foremasts rigged square and the aftermast rigged fore-and-aft. **2.** *Poetic.* any boat, esp. a small sailing vessel. [C15: from Old French, from Old Provençal *barca,* from Late Latin, of unknown origin]

bar·quen·tine *or* **bar·quan·tine** (ˈbɑːkənˌtiːn) *n.* a sailing ship of three or more masts rigged square on the foremast and fore-and-aft on the others. Usual U.S. spelling: **barkentine.** [C17: from BARQUE + (BRIG)ANTINE]

Bar·qui·si·me·to (*Spanish* ˌbarkisiˈmeto) *n.* a city in NW Venezuela. Pop.: 330 815 (1971).

bar·rack[1] (ˈbærək) *vb.* to house (soldiers, etc.) in barracks.

bar·rack[2] (ˈbærək) *vb. Brit. and Austral. informal.* **1.** to criticize loudly or shout against (a player, team, speaker, etc.); jeer. **2.** (*intr.;* foll. by *for*) to shout support (for). [C19: from northern Irish: to boast]

bar·racks (ˈbærəks) *pl. n.* (*sometimes sing.; when pl., sometimes functions as sing.*) **1.** a building or group of buildings used to accommodate military personnel. **2.** any large building used for housing people, esp. temporarily. **3.** a large and bleak building. [C17: from French *baraque,* from Old Catalan *barraca* hut, of uncertain origin]

bar·ra·coon (ˌbærəˈkuːn) *n.* (formerly) a temporary place of confinement for slaves or convicts, esp. those awaiting transportation. [C19: from Spanish *barracón,* from *barraca* hut, from Catalan]

bar·ra·cou·ta (ˌbærəˈkuːtə) *n.* a large predatory Pacific fish, *Thyrsites atun,* with a protruding lower jaw and strong teeth: family *Gempylidae.* [C17: variant of BARRACUDA]

bar·ra·cu·da (ˌbærəˈkjuːdə) *n., pl.* **·da** *or* **·das.** any predatory marine teleost fish of the mostly tropical family *Sphyraenidae,* esp. *Sphyraena barracuda,* which attacks man. They have an elongated body, strong teeth, and a protruding lower jaw. [C17: from American Spanish, of unknown origin]

bar·rage (ˈbærɑːʒ) *n.* **1.** *Military.* the firing of artillery to saturate an area rather than hit a specific target. **2.** an overwhelming and continuous delivery of something, as words, questions, or punches. **3.** a construction across a watercourse, esp. one to increase the depth of water to assist navigation or irrigation. **4.** *Fencing.* a heat or series of bouts in a competition. ~*vb.* **5.** (*tr.*) to attack or confront with a barrage: *the speaker was barraged with abuse.* [C19: from French, from *barrer* to obstruct; see BAR[1]]

bar·rage bal·loon *n.* one of a number of tethered balloons with cables or net suspended from them, used to deter low-flying air attack.

bar·ra·mun·da (ˌbærəˈmʌndə) *or* **bar·ra·mun·di** (ˌbærəˈmʌndɪ) *n., pl.* **·das, ·da** *or* **·dis, ·dies, ·di.** an edible Australian lungfish, *Neoceratodus forsteri,* having paddle-like fins and a long body covered with large scales. [from a native Australian language]

bar·ran·ca (bəˈræŋkə) *or* **bar·ran·co** (bəˈræŋkəʊ) *n., pl.* **·cas** *or* **·cos.** *Southwestern U.S.* a ravine or precipice. [C19: from Spanish, of uncertain origin]

Bar·ran·qui·lla (*Spanish* ˌbarraŋˈkiʎa) *n.* a port in N Colombia, on the Magdalena River. Pop.: 661 920 (1973).

bar·ra·tor (ˈbærətə) *n.* a person guilty of barratry. [C14: from Old French *barateor,* from *barater* to BARTER]

bar·ra·try *or* **bar·re·try** (ˈbærətrɪ) *n.* **1.** *Criminal law.* the vexatious stirring up of quarrels or bringing lawsuits. **2.** *Maritime law.* a fraudulent practice committed by the master or crew of a ship to the prejudice of the owner or charterer. **3.** *Scot. law.* the crime committed by a judge in accepting a bribe. **4.** the purchase or sale of public or Church offices. [C15: from Old French *baraterie* deception, from *barater* to BARTER] —**ˈbar·ra·trous** *or* **ˈbar·re·trous** *adj.* —**ˈbar·ra·trous·ly** *or* **ˈbar·re·trous·ly** *adv.*

Bar·rault (*French* baˈro) *n.* **Jean-Louis** (ʒɑ̃ˈlwi). born 1910, French actor and director, noted particularly as a mime.

barre *French.* (baːr) *n.* a rail at hip height used for ballet practice.

bar·ré (ˈbæreɪ) *n.* **1.** the act of laying the index finger over some or all of the strings of a guitar, lute, or similar instrument, so that the pitch of each stopped string is simultaneously raised. Compare **capo. 2.** the playing of chords in this manner. ~*vb.* **3.** to execute (chords, etc.) in this manner. ~*adv.* **4.** by using the barré. [from French, from *barrer* BAR[1]]

bar·rel (ˈbærəl) *n.* **1.** a cylindrical container usually bulging outwards in the middle and held together by metal hoops; cask. **2.** Also called: **bar·rel·ful.** the amount that a barrel can hold. **3.** a unit of capacity used in brewing, equal to 36 Imperial gallons. **4.** a unit of capacity used in the oil and other industries, normally equal to 42 U.S. gallons or 35 Imperial gallons. **5.** a thing or part shaped like a barrel, esp. a tubular part of a machine. **6.** the tube through which the projectile of a firearm is discharged. **7.** *Horology.* the cylindrical drum in a watch or clock that is rotated by the mainspring. **8.** the trunk of a four-legged animal: *the barrel of a horse.* **9.** the quill of a feather. **10.** *Informal.* a large measure; a great deal (esp. in the phrases **barrel of fun, barrel of laughter**). **11. over a barrel.** *Informal.* powerless. **12. scrape the barrel.** *Informal.* to be forced to use one's last and weakest resource. ~*vb.* **·rels, ·rel·ling, ·relled** *or U.S.* **·rels, ·rel·ing, ·reled. 13.** (*tr.*) to put into a barrel or barrels. **14.** (*intr.;* usually foll. by *along*) *U.S. informal.* to travel or move very fast. [C14: from Old French *baril,* perhaps from *barre* BAR[1]]

bar·rel-chest·ed *adj.* having a large rounded chest.

bar·rel·house (ˈbærəlˌhaʊs) *n.* **1.** *U.S. informal.* a cheap and disreputable drinking establishment. **2. a.** a vigorous and unpolished style of jazz for piano, originating in the barrelhouses of New Orleans. **b.** (*as modifier*): *barrelhouse blues.*

bar·rel or·gan *n.* **1.** an instrument consisting of a cylinder turned by a handle and having pins on it that interrupt the air flow to certain pipes, thereby playing any of a number of tunes. See also **hurdy-gurdy. 2.** a similar instrument in which the projections on a rotating barrel pluck a set of strings.

bar·rel roll *n.* **1.** a flight manoeuvre in which an aircraft rolls about its longitudinal axis while following a spiral course in line with the direction of flight. ~*vb.* **bar·rel-roll. 2.** (*intr.*) (of an aircraft) to perform a barrel roll.

bar·rel vault *n. Architect.* a vault in the form of a half cylinder. Also called: **wagon vault, tunnel vault.**

bar·ren (ˈbærən) *adj.* **1.** incapable of producing offspring, seed, or fruit; sterile: *a barren tree.* **2.** unable to support the growth of crops, etc.; unproductive; bare: *barren land.* **3.** lacking in stimulation or ideas; dull: *a rather barren play.* **4.** not producing worthwhile results; unprofitable: *a barren period in a writer's life.* **5.** (foll. by *of*) totally lacking (in); devoid (of): *his speech was barren of wit.* [C13: from Old French *brahain,* of uncertain origin] —**ˈbar·ren·ly** *adv.* —**ˈbar·ren·ness** *n.*

Bar·ren Lands *pl. n.* **The.** a region of tundras in N Canada, extending westwards from Hudson Bay: sparsely inhabited, chiefly by Eskimos. Also called: **Barren Grounds.**

bar·rens (ˈbærənz) *pl. n.* (*sometimes sing.*) (in North America) a stretch of usually level land that is sparsely vegetated or barren.

bar·ren·wort (ˈbærənˌwɜːt) *n.* a herbaceous European berberidaceous plant, *Epimedium alpinum,* having red-and-yellow star-shaped flowers.

Bar·rès (*French* baˈrɛs) *n.* **Mau·rice** (mɔˈris). 1862–1923, French novelist, essayist, and politician: a fervent nationalist and individualist.

bar·ret (ˈbærɪt) *n.* a small flat cap resembling a biretta. [C19: from French *barrette,* from Italian *berretta* BIRETTA; compare BERET]

bar·rette (bəˈrɛt) *n.* a clasp or pin for holding women's hair in place. [from French: a little bar, from *barre* BAR[1]]

bar·ri·cade (ˌbærɪˈkeɪd, ˈbærɪˌkeɪd) *n.* **1.** a barrier for defence, esp. one erected hastily, as during street fighting. ~*vb.* (*tr.*) **2.** to erect a barricade across (an entrance, passageway, etc.) or at points of access to (a room, district of a town, etc.): *they barricaded the door.* **3.** (*usually passive*) to obstruct; block: *his mind was barricaded against new ideas.* [C17: from Old French, from *barriquer* to barricade, from *barrique* a barrel, from Spanish *barrica,* from *barril* BARREL] —**ˈbar·ri·ˌcad·er** *n.*

Bar·rie (ˈbærɪ) *n.* Sir **James Mat·thew.** 1860–1937, Scottish dramatist and novelist, noted particularly for his popular children's play *Peter Pan* (1904).

bar·ri·er (ˈbærɪə) *n.* **1.** anything serving to obstruct passage or to maintain separation, such as a fence or gate. **2.** anything that prevents or obstructs passage, access, or progress: *a barrier of distrust.* **3.** anything that separates or hinders union: *a language barrier.* **4. a.** an exposed offshore sand bar separated from the shore by a lagoon. **b.** (*as modifier*): *a barrier beach.* **5.** (*sometimes cap.*) that part of the Antarctic icecap extending over the sea. [C14: from Old French *barriere,* from *barre* BAR[1]]

bar·ri·er cream *n.* a cream used to protect the skin, esp. the hands, from dirt and from the action of oils or solvents.

bar·ri·er reef *n.* a long narrow coral reef near and lying parallel to the shore, separated from it by deep water. See **Great Barrier Reef.**

bar·ring (ˈbɑːrɪŋ) *prep.* unless (something) occurs; except for: *barring rain, the match will be held tomorrow.*

bar·rio *Spanish.* (ˈbarrjo) *n., pl.* ***·rios*** (-rjos). **1.** a Spanish-speaking quarter in a town or city, esp. in the U.S. **2.** a Spanish-speaking community. [from Spanish, from Arabic *barrī* of open country, from *barr* open country]

bar·ris·ter (ˈbærɪstə) *n.* **1.** Also called: **barrister-at-law.** (in England) a lawyer who has been called to the bar and is qualified to plead in the higher courts. Compare **solicitor.** See also **advocate, counsel. 2.** *U.S.* a less common word for **lawyer.** [C16: from BAR[1]]

bar·room (ˈbɑːˌruːm, -ˌrʊm) *n. U.S.* a room or building where alcoholic drinks are served over a counter.

Bar·ros (*Portuguese* ˈbarruʃ) *n.* **João de** (ˈʒwɐ̃ʊ ˈdə). 1496–1570, Portuguese historian: noted for his history of the Portuguese in the East Indies, *Décadas da Ásia* (1552–1615).

bar·row[1] (ˈbærəʊ) *n.* **1.** See **wheelbarrow, handbarrow. 2.** Also called: **bar·row·ful.** the amount contained in or on a barrow. **3.** *Chiefly Brit.* a handcart, typically having two wheels and a canvas roof, used esp. by street vendors. **4.** *Northern English dialect.* concern or business (esp. in the phrases **that's not my barrow, that's just my barrow**). [Old English *bearwe;* related to Old Norse *barar* BIER, Old High German *bāra*]

bar·row[2] (ˈbærəʊ) *n.* a heap of earth placed over one or more prehistoric tombs, often surrounded by ditches. **Long barrows** are elongated Neolithic mounds usually covering stone burial chambers; **round barrows** are Bronze Age, covering cremations in urns. [Old English *beorg;* related to Old Norse *bjarg,* Gothic *bairgahei* hill, Old High German *berg* mountain]

bar·row[3] ('bærəʊ) *n.* a castrated pig. [Old English *bearg;* related to Old Norse *börgr,* Old High German *barug*]

Bar·row ('bærəʊ) *n.* **1.** a river in SE Ireland, rising in the Slieve Bloom Mountains and flowing south to Waterford Harbour. Length: about 193 km (120 miles). **2.** See **Barrow-in-Furness** and **Barrow Point.**

bar·row boy *n. Brit.* a man who sells his wares from a barrow; street vendor.

Bar·row-in-Fur·ness *n.* an industrial town in NW England, in S Cumbria. Pop.: 63 998 (1971).

Bar·row Point *n.* the northernmost tip of Alaska, on the Arctic Ocean.

Bar·ry[1] ('bærɪ) *n.* a port in SE Wales, in South Glamorgan on the Bristol Channel. Pop.: 41 578 (1971).

Bar·ry[2] *n.* **1.** ('bærɪ). Sir **Charles.** 1795–1860, English architect: designer of the Houses of Parliament in London. **2.** (*French* ba'ri) **Com·tesse du.** See **du Barry.**

Bar·ry·more ('bærɪˌmɔː) *n.* a U.S. family of actors, esp. **Eth·el** (1879–1959), **John** (1882–1942), and **Li·o·nel** (1878–1954).

Bar·ry Moun·tains *pl. n.* a mountain range in SE Australia, in E Victoria: part of the Australian Alps.

Bar·sac ('bɑːsæk; *French* ba'sak) *n.* a sweet French white wine produced around the town of Barsac in the Gironde.

bar sin·is·ter *n.* **1.** (*not in heraldic usage*) another name for **bend sinister. 2.** the condition, implication, or stigma of being of illegitimate birth.

Bart. *abbrev. for* Baronet.

bar·tend·er ('bɑːˌtɛndə) *n.* another name (esp. U.S.) for **barman.**

bar·ter ('bɑːtə) *vb.* **1.** to trade (goods, services, etc.) in exchange for other goods, services, etc., rather than for money: *the refugees bartered for food.* **2.** (*intr.*) to haggle over the terms of such an exchange; bargain. ~*n.* **3.** trade by the exchange of goods. [C15: from Old French *barater* to cheat; perhaps related to Greek *prattein* to do] —'**bar·ter·er** *n.*

Barth (*German* bart) *n.* **Karl** (karl). 1886–1968, Swiss Protestant theologian, who stressed man's dependence on divine grace and was a champion of tolerance and ecumenicalism. —**Barth·i·an** ('bɑːtɪən, -θɪən) *adj., n.*

Bar·tho·lin's glands ('bɑːθəlɪnz) *pl. n. Anatomy.* two small reddish-yellow glands, one on each side of the vaginal orifice, that secrete a mucous lubricating substance during sexual stimulation in females. Compare **Cowper's glands.** [named by Caspar *Bartholin* (1655–1738), Danish anatomist, in honour of his father, Thomas]

Bar·thol·o·mew (bɑː'θɒləˌmjuː) *n. New Testament.* one of the twelve apostles (Matthew 10:3).

bar·ti·zan ('bɑːtɪzən, ˌbɑːtɪ'zæn) *n.* a small turret projecting from a wall, parapet, or tower. [C19: variant of *bertisene,* erroneously for *bretising,* from *bretasce* parapet; see BRATTICE] —**bar·ti·zaned** ('bɑːtɪzənd, ˌbɑːtɪ'zænd) *adj.*

Bart·lett *or* **Bart·lett pear** ('bɑːtlɪt) *n.* a variety of pear that has large juicy yellow fruit. [named after Enoch *Bartlett* of Dorchester, Mass., who cultivated it]

Bar·tók ('bɑːtɒk; *Hungarian* 'bɔrtoːk) *n.* **Bé·la** ('beːlɔ). 1881–1945, Hungarian composer, pianist, and collector of folk songs, by which his music was deeply influenced. His works include six string quartets, several piano pieces including *Mikrokosmos* (1926–37), ballets (including *The Miraculous Mandarin,* 1919), and the opera *Bluebeard's Castle* (produced 1918).

Bar·to·lom·me·o (*Italian* ˌbartolom'mɛːo) *n.* **Fra.** original name *Baccio della Porta.* 1472–1517, Italian painter of the Florentine school, noted for his austere religious works.

bar·ton ('bɑːtᵊn) *n. Archaic.* a farmyard. [Old English *beretūn,* from *bere* barley + *tūn* stockade; see TOWN]

Bar·ton ('bɑːtᵊn) Sir **Ed·mund.** 1849–1920, Australian statesman; first prime minister of Australia (1901–03).

Ba·ruch *n.* **1.** (bə'ruːk). **Ber·nard Man·nes** ('mænəs). 1870–1965, U.S. financier and statesman; economic adviser to Presidents Wilson and Roosevelt. **2.** ('bɛərʊk, 'bɑː-). *Bible.* **a.** a disciple of Jeremiah (Jeremiah 32–36). **b.** the book of the Apocrypha said to have been written by him.

bar·y·cen·tre ('bærɪˌsɛntə) *n.* a centre of mass, esp. of the earth-moon system. [C20: from Greek *barus* heavy + CENTRE]

bar·ye ('bærɪ) *n.* a unit of pressure in the cgs system equal to one dyne per square centimetre. 1 barye is equivalent to 1 microbar. [C19: from French, from Greek *barus* heavy]

bar·y·on ('bærɪˌɒn) *n.* any of a class of elementary particles that have a mass greater than or equal to that of the proton, participate in strong interactions, and have a spin of $\frac{1}{2}$. Baryons are either nucleons or hyperons. The **baryon number** is the number of baryons in a system minus the number of antibaryons. [C20: *bary-,* from Greek *barus* heavy + -ON] —ˌ**bar·y·'on·ic** *adj.*

bar·y·sphere ('bærɪˌsfɪə) *n.* the central portion of the earth, thought to consist chiefly of iron and nickel. [C20: from Greek *barus* heavy + SPHERE]

ba·ry·ta (bə'raɪtə) *n.* another name for **barium oxide** or **barium hydroxide.** [C19: New Latin, from Greek *barutēs* weight, from *barus* heavy] —**ba·ryt·ic** (bə'rɪtɪk) *adj.*

ba·ry·tes (bə'raɪtiːz) *n.* a colourless or white mineral consisting of barium sulphate in rhombic crystalline form, occurring in sedimentary rocks and with sulphide ores: a source of barium. Formula: $BaSO_4$. Also called: **barite** (esp. U.S.), **heavy spar.** [C18: from Greek *barus* heavy + *-itēs* -ITE[1]]

bar·y·ton ('bærɪˌtəʊn) *n.* a bass viol with sympathetic strings as well as its six main strings. [C18: from French: BARITONE]

bar·y·tone[1] ('bærɪˌtəʊn) *n.* a less common spelling of **baritone.**

bar·y·tone[2] ('bærɪˌtəʊn) (in ancient Greek) ~*adj.* **1.** having the last syllable unaccented. ~*n.* **2.** a word in which the last syllable is unaccented. ~Compare **oxytone.** [C19: from Greek *barutonos* heavy-sounding, from *barus* heavy + *tonos* TONE]

ba·sal ('beɪsᵊl) *adj.* **1.** at, of, or constituting a base. **2.** of or constituting a foundation or basis; fundamental; essential. —'**ba·sal·ly** *adv.*

ba·sal an·aes·the·si·a *n.* preliminary and incomplete anaesthesia induced to prepare a surgical patient for total anaesthesia with another agent.

ba·sal gan·gli·a *pl. n.* the thalamus together with other closely related masses of grey matter, situated near the base of the brain.

ba·sal met·a·bol·ic rate *n.* the rate at which heat is produced by the body at rest, 12 to 14 hours after eating, measured in kilocalories per square metre of body surface per hour. Abbrev.: **BMR.**

ba·sal me·tab·o·lism *n.* the amount of energy required by an individual in the resting state, for such functions as breathing and circulation of the blood. See **basal metabolic rate.**

bas·alt ('bæsɔːlt) *n.* **1.** a fine-grained dark basic igneous rock consisting of plagioclase feldspar, a pyroxene, and olivine: the most common volcanic rock and usually extrusive. **2.** a form of black unglazed pottery resembling basalt. [C18: from Late Latin *basaltēs,* variant of *basanītēs,* from Greek *basanitēs* touchstone, from *basanos,* of Egyptian origin] —**ba·'sal·tic** *adj.*

ba·salt·ware ('bæsɔːltˌwɛə, 'beɪsɔːlt-) *n.* hard fine-grained black stoneware, made in Europe, esp. in England, in the late 18th century.

bas bleu *French.* (ba 'blø:) *n., pl.* ***bas bleus*** (ba 'blø:). a bluestocking; intellectual woman.

bas·ci·net (ˌbæsɪ'nɛt, 'bæsɪˌnɛt) *n. Armour.* a variant spelling of **basinet.**

bas·cule ('bæskjuːl) *n.* **1.** a bridge with a movable section hinged about a horizontal axis and counterbalanced by a weight. Compare **drawbridge. 2.** a movable roadway forming part of such a bridge: *Tower Bridge has two bascules.* [C17: from French: seesaw, from *bas* low + *cul* rump; see BASE[2], CULET]

base[1] (beɪs) *n.* **1.** the bottom or supporting part of anything. **2.** the fundamental or underlying principle or part, as of an idea, system, or organization; basis. **3. a.** a centre of operations, organization, or supply: *the climbers made a base at 8000 feet.* **b.** (*as modifier*): *base camp.* **4.** a centre from which military activities are coordinated. **5.** anything from which a process, as of measurement, action, or thought, is or may be begun; starting point: *the new discovery became the base for further research.* **6.** the main ingredient of a mixture: *to use rice as a base in cookery.* **7.** a chemical compound that combines with an acid to form a salt and water. A solution of a base in water turns litmus paper blue, produces hydroxyl ions, and has a pH greater than 7. Bases are metal oxides or hydroxides or amines. See also **Lewis base. 8.** a medium such as oil or water in which the pigment is dispersed in paints, inks, etc.; vehicle. **9.** the inorganic material on which the dye is absorbed in lake pigments; carrier. **10.** *Biology.* **a.** the part of an organ nearest to its point of attachment. **b.** the point of attachment of an organ or part. **11.** the bottommost layer or part of anything. **12.** *Architect.* **a.** the lowest division of a building or structure. **b.** the lower part of a column or pier. **13.** another word for **baseline** (sense 2). **14.** the lower side or face of a geometric construction. **15.** *Maths.* the number of units in a counting system that is equivalent to one in the next higher counting place. Any number can be expressed by adding together multiples of increasing integral powers of the base: *in the decimal system* $7.6 = 6 \times 10^{-1} + 7 \times 10^{0}$, *where 10 is the base.* **16.** *Maths.* the number that when raised to a certain power has a logarithm (based on that number) equal to that power: *the logarithm to the base 10 of 1000 is 3.* **17.** *Linguistics.* **a.** a root or stem. **b.** See **base component. 18.** *Electronics.* the region in a transistor between the emitter and collector. **19.** *Photog.* the glass, paper, or cellulose-ester film that supports the sensitized emulsion with which it is coated. **20.** *Heraldry.* the lower part of the shield. **21.** *Jewellery.* the quality factor used in pricing natural pearls. **22.** a starting or finishing point in any of various games. **23.** *Baseball.* any of the four corners of the diamond, which runners have to reach in order to score. **24. get to first base.** *U.S. informal.* to accomplish the first stage in a project or a series of objectives. **25. off base.** *U.S. informal.* wrong or badly mistaken. ~*vb.* **26.** (*tr.;* foll. by *on* or *upon*) to use as a basis (for); found (on): *your criticisms are based on ignorance.* **27.** (often foll. by *at* or *in*) to station, post, or place (a person or oneself). [C14: from Old French, from Latin *basis* pedestal; see BASIS]

base[2] (beɪs) *adj.* **1.** devoid of honour or morality; ignoble; contemptible. **2.** of inferior quality or value. **3.** debased; alloyed; counterfeit: *base currency.* **4.** *English history.* **a.** (of land tenure) held by villein or other ignoble service. **b.** holding land by villein or other ignoble service. **5.** *Archaic.* born of humble parents; plebeian. **6.** *Archaic.* illegitimate. ~*adj., n.* **7.** *Music.* an obsolete spelling of **bass**[1]. [C14: from Old French *bas,* from Late Latin *bassus* of low height, perhaps from Greek *bassōn* deeper] —'**base·ly** *adv.* —'**base·ness** *n.*

base·ball ('beɪsˌbɔːl) *n.* **1.** a team game with nine players on each side, played on a field with four bases connected to form a diamond. The object is to score runs by batting the ball and running round the bases. **2.** the hard rawhide-covered ball used in this game.

base·board ('beɪsˌbɔːd) *n.* **1.** a board functioning as the base of anything. **2.** the usual U.S. word for **skirting board.**

base·born ('beɪsˌbɔːn) *adj. Archaic.* **1.** born of humble parents. **2.** illegitimate. **3.** mean; contemptible.

base·burn·er ('beɪsˌbɜːnə) *n. U.S.* a stove into which coal is automatically fed from a hopper above the fire chamber.

base com·po·nent *n.* the system of rules in a transformational grammar that specify the deep structure of the language.

base hos·pit·al *n. Austral.* a hospital serving a large rural area.

Ba·sel ('bɑːzᵊl) *or* **Basle** (bɑːl) *n.* **1.** a canton of NW Switzerland, divided into the demicantons of **Basel-Land** and **Basel-Stadt.** Pops.: 204 889 and 234 945 (1970). Areas: 427 sq. km (165 sq. miles) and 36 sq. km (14 sq. miles) respectively. **2.** a city in NW Switzerland, capital of Basel canton, on the Rhine: oldest university in Switzerland. Pop.: 195 700 (1975 est.). French name: **Bâle.**

base·less ('beɪslɪs) *adj.* not based on fact; unfounded: *a baseless supposition.* —**'base·less·ly** *adv.* —**'base·less·ness** *n.*

base lev·el *n.* the lowest level to which a land surface can be eroded by streams, which is, ultimately, sea level.

base·line ('beɪsˌlaɪn) *n.* **1.** *Surveying.* a measured line through a survey area from which triangulations are made. **2.** an imaginary line, standard of value, etc., by which things are measured or compared. **3.** a line at each end of a tennis court that marks the limit of play.

base load *n.* the more or less constant part of the total load on an electrical power-supply system. Compare **peak load.**

base·man ('beɪsmən) *n., pl.* **·men.** *Baseball.* a fielder positioned near a base.

base·ment ('beɪsmənt) *n.* **1. a.** a partly or wholly underground storey of a building, esp. the one immediately below the main floor. Compare **cellar. b.** (*as modifier*): *a basement flat.* **2.** the foundation or substructure of a wall or building.

base met·al *n.* any of certain common metals such as copper, lead, zinc, and tin, as distinct from the precious metals, gold, silver, and platinum.

ba·sen·ji (bəˈsɛndʒɪ) *n.* a small smooth-haired breed of dog of African origin having a tightly curled tail and an inability to bark. [from a Bantu language]

base pe·ri·od *n. Statistics.* a neutral period used as a standard for comparison in constructing an index to express a variable factor: 100 is usually taken as the index number for the variable in the base period.

base rate *n. Brit.* the rate of interest used by individual clearing banks as a basis for their lending rates.

ba·ses[1] ('beɪsiːz) *n.* the plural of **basis.**

bas·es[2] ('beɪsɪz) *n.* the plural of **base.**

bash (bæʃ) *Informal.* ~*vb.* **1.** (*tr.*) to strike violently or crushingly. **2.** (*tr.;* often foll. by *in, down,* etc.) to smash, break, etc., with a crashing blow: *to bash a door down.* **3.** (*intr.;* foll. by *into*) to crash (into); collide (with): *to bash into a lamppost.* ~*n.* **4.** a heavy blow, as from a fist. **5.** a party. **6. have a bash.** *Informal.* to make an attempt. [C17: of uncertain origin]

Ba·shan ('beɪʃæn) *n. Old Testament.* a region to the east of the Jordan, renowned for its rich pasture (Deuteronomy 32:14).

ba·shaw (bəˈʃɔː) *n.* **1.** a rare spelling of **pasha. 2.** an important or pompous person.

bash·ful ('bæʃfʊl) *adj.* **1.** disposed to attempt to avoid notice through shyness or modesty; diffident; timid. **2.** indicating or characterized by shyness or modesty. [C16: from *bash,* short for ABASH + -FUL] —**'bash·ful·ly** *adv.* —**'bash·ful·ness** *n.*

bash·i·ba·zouk (ˌbæʃɪbəˈzuːk) *n.* (in the 19th century) one of a group of irregular Turkish soldiers notorious for their brutality. [C19: from Turkish *başıbozuk* irregular soldier, from *bas* head + *bozuk* corrupt]

-bash·ing *n. and adj. combining form. Informal or slang.* **a.** indicating a malicious attack on members of a group: *queer-bashing; union-bashing.* **b.** indicating any of various other activities: *Bible-bashing; spud-bashing; square-bashing.* **—-bash·er** *n. combining form.*

Bash·kir (bæʃˈkɪə) *n.* **1.** (*pl.* **·kir** or **·kirs**) a member of a Mongoloid people of the Soviet Union, living chiefly in the Bashkir ASSR. **2.** the language of this people, belonging to the Turkic branch of the Altaic family and closely related to Tatar.

Bash·kir Au·ton·o·mous So·vi·et So·cial·ist Re·pub·lic *n.* an administrative division of the E central Soviet Union, in the S Urals: established as the first Soviet autonomous republic in 1919; rich mineral resources. Capital: Ufa. Pop.: 3 818 075 (1970). Area: 143 600 sq. km (55 430 sq. miles).

bash up *vb.* (*tr., adv.*) *Brit. slang.* to thrash; beat violently.

ba·sic ('beɪsɪk; *Austral. also* 'bæsɪk) *adj.* **1.** of, relating to, or forming a base or basis; fundamental; underlying. **2.** elementary or simple: *a few basic facts.* **3.** without additions or extras: *basic pay.* **4.** *Chem.* **a.** of, denoting, or containing a base; alkaline. **b.** (of a salt) containing hydroxyl or oxide groups not all of which have been replaced by an acid radical: *basic lead carbonate,* $2PbCO_3.Pb(OH)_2$. **5.** *Metallurgy.* of, concerned with, or made by a process in which the furnace or converter is made of a basic material, such as magnesium oxide. **6.** (of such igneous rocks as basalt) containing less than 50 per cent silica. **7.** *Military.* primary or initial: *basic training.* ~*n.* **8.** (*usually pl.*) a fundamental principle, fact, etc. —**'ba·si·cal·ly** *adv.*

BASIC ('beɪsɪk) *n.* a computer programming language that uses common English terms [C20: *b(eginner's) a(ll-purpose) s(ymbolic) i(nstruction) c(ode)*]

ba·sic ed·u·ca·tion *n.* (in India) education in which all teaching is correlated with the learning of a craft.

ba·sic Eng·lish *n.* a simplified form of English containing a vocabulary of approximately 850 of the commonest English words, intended as an international language.

ba·sic·i·ty (beɪˈsɪsɪtɪ) *n. Chem.* **a.** the state of being a base. **b.** the extent to which a substance is basic.

ba·sic slag *n.* a furnace slag produced in steel-making, containing large amounts of calcium phosphate: used as a fertilizer.

ba·sid·i·o·my·cete (bæˌsɪdɪəʊmaɪˈsiːt) *n.* any fungus of the class *Basidiomycetes,* in which the spores are produced in basidia. The group includes puffballs, smuts, and rusts. [C19: from BASIDI(UM) + -MYCETE] —**baˌsid·i·o·my·ˈcet·ous** *adj.*

ba·sid·i·o·spore (bæˈsɪdɪəʊˌspɔː) *n.* one of the spores, usually four in number, produced in a basidium.

ba·sid·i·um (bæˈsɪdɪəm) *n., pl.* **·i·a** (-ɪə). the structure, produced by basidiomycetous fungi after sexual reproduction, in which spores are formed at the tips of projecting slender stalks. [C19: from New Latin; see BASIS, -IUM]

Ba·sie ('beɪsɪ) *n.* **Wil·liam,** called *Count Basie.* born 1904, U.S. jazz pianist, bandleader, and composer: associated particularly with the polished phrasing and style of big-band jazz.

bas·i·fixed ('beɪsɪˌfɪxt) *adj. Botany.* (of an anther) attached to the filament by its base.

bas·i·fy ('beɪsɪˌfaɪ) *vb.* **·fies, ·fy·ing, ·fied.** (*tr.*) to make basic.

bas·il ('bæzᵊl) *n.* **1.** Also called: **sweet basil.** a Eurasian plant, *Ocimum basilicum,* having spikes of small white flowers and aromatic leaves used as herbs for seasoning: family *Labiatae* (labiates). **2.** Also called: **wild basil.** a European plant, *Satureja vulgaris* (or *Clinopodium vulgare*), with dense clusters of small pink or whitish flowers: family *Labiatae.* **3. basil-thyme.** a European plant, *Acinos arvensis,* having clusters of small violet-and-white flowers: family *Labiatae.* [C15: from Old French *basile,* from Late Latin *basilicum,* from Greek *basilikon,* from *basilikos* royal, from *basileus* king]

Bas·il ('bæzᵊl) *n.* **Saint,** called *the Great.* ?329–379 A.D., Greek patriarch: an opponent of Arianism and one of the founders of monasticism. Feast Day: June 14.

Ba·si·lan (bəˈsiːlɑːn, bæˈsiːlæn) *n.* **1.** a group of islands in the Philippines, SW of Mindanao. **2.** the main island of this group, separated from Mindanao by the **Basilan Strait.** Area: 1282 sq. km (495 sq. miles). **3.** a city on Basilan Island. Pop.: 143 829 (1970).

bas·i·lar ('bæsɪlə) *adj. Chiefly anatomy.* of or situated at a base: *basilar artery* (at the base of the skull). Also: **bas·i·lar·y** ('bæsɪlərɪ, -sɪlrɪ). [C16: from New Latin *basilaris,* from Latin *basis* BASE[1]; compare Medieval Latin *bassile* pelvis]

Ba·sil·don ('bæzɪldən) *n.* a town in SE England, in S Essex: designated a new town in 1955. Pop.: 77 154 (1971).

Ba·sil·i·an (bəˈzɪlɪən) *n.* a monk of the Eastern Christian order of St. Basil, founded in Cappadocia in the 4th century A.D.

ba·sil·i·ca (bəˈzɪlɪkə) *n.* **1.** a Roman building, used for public administration, having a large rectangular central nave with an aisle on each side and an apse at the end. **2.** a rectangular early Christian or medieval church, usually having a nave with clerestories, two or four aisles, one or more vaulted apses, and a timber roof. **3.** a Roman Catholic church having special ceremonial rights. [C16: from Latin, from Greek *basilikē* hall, from *basilikē oikia* the king's house, from *basileus* king; see BASIL] —**baˈsil·i·can** *or* **baˈsil·ic** *adj.*

Ba·si·li·ca·ta (*Italian* baˌziliˈkaːta) *n.* a region of S Italy, between the Tyrrhenian Sea and the Gulf of Taranto. Capital: Potenza. Pop.: 602 389 (1971). Area: 9985 sq. km (3855 sq. miles).

ba·sil·ic vein (bəˈzɪlɪk) *n.* a large vein situated on the inner side of the arm. [C18: from Latin *basilicus* kingly; see BASIL]

bas·i·lisk ('bæzɪˌlɪsk) *n.* **1.** (in classical legend) a serpent that could kill by its breath or glance. **2.** any small arboreal semiaquatic lizard of the genus *Basiliscus* of tropical America: family *Iguanidae* (iguanas). The males have an inflatable head crest, used in display. **3.** (formerly) a large cannon, usually made of brass. [C14: from Latin *basiliscus,* from Greek *basiliskos* royal child, from *basileus* king]

ba·sin ('beɪsᵊn) *n.* **1.** a round container open and wide at the top with sides sloping inwards towards the bottom or base, esp. one in which liquids are mixed or stored. **2.** Also called: **ba·sin·ful.** the amount a basin will hold. **3.** a washbasin or sink. **4.** any partially enclosed or sheltered area where vessels may be moored or docked. **5.** the catchment area of a particular river and its tributaries or of a lake or sea. **6.** a depression in the earth's surface. **7.** *Geology.* a part of the earth's surface consisting of rock strata that slope down to a common centre. [C13: from Old French *bacin,* from Late Latin *bacchīnon,* from Vulgar Latin *bacca* (unattested) container for water; related to Latin *bāca* berry]

bas·i·net *or* **bas·ci·net** ('bæsɪnɪt, -ˌnɛt) *n.* a close-fitting medieval helmet of light steel. [C14: from Old French *bacinet,* a little basin, from *bacin* BASIN]

Ba·sing·stoke ('beɪzɪŋˌstəʊk) *n.* a town in S England, in N Hampshire. Pop.: 52 502 (1971).

ba·si·on ('beɪsɪən) *n. Anatomy.* the midpoint on the forward border of the foramen magnum. [C19: from New Latin, from Latin *basis* BASE]

ba·sip·e·tal (beɪˈsɪpɪtᵊl) *adj.* (of leaves and flowers) produced in order from the apex downwards so that the youngest are at the base. Compare **acropetal.**

ba·sis ('beɪsɪs) *n., pl.* **·ses** (-siːz). **1.** something that underlies, supports, or is essential to something else, esp. an abstract idea. **2.** a principle on which something depends or from which something has issued. [C14: via Latin from Greek: step, from *bainein* to step, go]

bask (bɑːsk) *vb.* (*intr.;* usually foll. by *in*) **1.** to lie in or be exposed to pleasant warmth, esp. that of the sun. **2.** to flourish or feel secure under some benevolent influence or favourable condition. [C14: from Old Norse *bathask* to BATHE]

Bas·ker·ville ('bæskəˌvɪl) *n.* a style of type. [C18: named after John *Baskerville* (1706–1775), English printer]

bas·ket ('bɑːskɪt) *n.* **1.** a container made of interwoven strips of pliable materials, such as cane, straw, thin wood, or plastic, and often carried by means of a handle or handles. **2.** Also called: **bas·ket·ful.** the amount a basket will hold. **3.** something resembling such a container in appearance or function, such as the structure suspended from a balloon. **4.** *Basketball.* **a.** an open horizontal metal hoop fixed to the backboard, through which a player must throw the ball to score points. **b.** a point or points scored in this way. **5.** *Informal.* a euphemism for **bastard** (senses 2, 3). [C13: probably from Old Northern French *baskot* (unattested), from Latin *bascauda* basketwork holder, of Celtic origin]

bas·ket·ball ('bɑːskɪtˌbɔːl) *n.* **1.** a game played by two opposing teams of five men (or six women) each, usually on an indoor court. Points are scored by throwing the ball through an elevated horizontal metal hoop. **2.** the inflated ball used in this game.

bas·ket chair *n.* a chair made of wickerwork; a wicker chair.

bas·ket clause *n.* an all-inclusive or comprehensive clause in a contract.

bas·ket hilt *n.* a hilt fitted to a sword, with a basket-shaped guard to protect the hand. —**'bas·ket-ˌhilt·ed** *adj.*

Bas·ket Mak·er *n.* a member of an early American Indian people of the southwestern U.S., preceding the Pueblo people, known for skill in basket-making.

bas·ket·ry ('bɑːskɪtrɪ) *n.* **1.** the art or practice of making baskets. **2.** baskets collectively.

bas·ket-star *n.* any of several echinoderms of the genus *Gorgonocephalus,* in which long slender arms radiate from a central disc: order *Ophiuroidea* (brittle-stars).

bas·ket weave *n.* a weave of two or more yarns together, resembling that of a basket, esp. in wool or linen fabric.

bas·ket·work ('bɑːskɪtˌwɜːk) *n.* another word for **wickerwork.**

bask·ing shark *n.* a very large plankton-eating shark, *Cetorhinus maximus,* often floating at the sea surface: family *Cetorhinidae.*

Basle (bɑːl) *n.* a variant spelling of **Basel.**

bas mitz·vah (bɑːs 'mɪtsvə) *n.* (*sometimes caps.*) *Judaism.* **1.** (in some congregations) a celebration of a girl's 12th birthday, equivalent to a boy's bar mitzvah. **2.** a girl of this age. ~Also called: **bat mitz·vah** *or* **bath mitz·vah.** [Hebrew, literally: daughter of the commandment]

ba·so·phil ('beɪsəfɪl) *or* **ba·so·phile** *adj. also* **ba·so·phil·ic** (ˌbeɪsə'fɪlɪk). **1.** (of cells or cell contents) easily stained by basic dyes. ~*n.* **2.** a basophil cell, esp. a leucocyte.

Ba·so·tho (bə'suːtuː, -'səʊtəʊ) *n., pl.* **·tho** *or* **·thos.** a member of the subgroup of the Sotho people who chiefly inhabit Lesotho. Former name: **Basuto.**

Ba·so·tho-Qwa·qwa (bə'suːtuː 'kwɑːkwə, -'səʊtəʊ) *n.* a Bantustan in South Africa, in the Orange Free State; the only Bantustan without exclaves. Former name (until 1972): **Basotho-Ba-Borwa.**

Basque (bæsk, bɑːsk) *n.* **1.** a member of a people of unknown origin living around the W Pyrenees in France and Spain. **2.** the language of this people, of no known relationship with any other language. ~*adj.* **3.** relating to, denoting, or characteristic of this people or their language. [C19: from French, from Latin *Vascō* a Basque]

Basque Prov·inc·es *n.* a region of N Spain, comprising the provinces of Álava, Guipúzcoa, and Viscaya: inhabited mainly by Basques, who retained virtual autonomy from the 9th to the 19th century. Pop.: 1 878 636 (1970). Area: about 7250 sq. km (2800 sq. miles).

Bas·ra, Bas·rah ('bæzrə), **Bus·ra,** *or* **Bus·rah** ('bʌsrə) *n.* a port in SE Iraq, on the Shatt-al-Arab. Pop.: 310 950 (1965).

bas-re·lief (ˌbɑːrɪ'liːf, ˌbæs-; 'bɑːrɪˌliːf, 'bæs-) *n.* sculpture in low relief, in which the forms project slightly from the background but no part is completely detached from it. Also called (Italian): **basso rilievo.** [C17: from French, from Italian *basso rilievo* low relief; see BASE², RELIEF]

Bas-Rhin (*French* bɑ 'rɛ̃) *n.* a department of NE France in Alsace region. Capital: Strasbourg. Pop.: 896 185 (1975). Area: 4793 sq. km (1869 sq. miles).

bass¹ (beɪs) *n.* **1.** the lowest adult male voice usually having a range from E a 13th below middle C to D a tone above it. **2.** a singer with such a voice. **3. the bass.** the lowest part in a piece of harmony. See also **thorough bass. 4.** *Informal.* short for **bass guitar, double bass. 5. a.** the low-frequency gain of an audio amplifier, esp. in a record player or tape recorder. **b.** the knob controlling this on such an instrument. ~*adj.* **6.** relating to or denoting the bass: *bass pitch; the bass part.* **7.** denoting the lowest and largest instrument in a family: *a bass clarinet.* [C15 *bas* BASE¹; modern spelling influenced by BASSO]

bass² (bæs) *n.* **1.** any of various sea perches, esp. *Morone labrax,* a popular game fish with one large spiny dorsal fin separate from a second smaller one. See also **sea bass, stone bass. 2.** another name for the **European perch** (see **perch²** (sense 1)). **3.** any of various predatory North American freshwater percoid fishes, such as *Micropterus salmoides* (**largemouth bass**): family *Centrarchidae* (sunfishes, etc.). See also **black bass, rock bass.** [C15: changed from BASE², influenced by Italian *basso* low]

bass³ (bæs) *n.* **1.** another name for **bast. 2.** short for **basswood.**

bass clef (beɪs) *n.* the clef that establishes F a fifth below middle C on the fourth line of the staff. Symbol: 𝄢 Also called: **F clef.**

bass drum (beɪs) *n.* a large shallow drum of low and indefinite pitch. Also called: **gran cassa.**

Bas·sein (bɑː'seɪn) *n.* a city in Burma, on the Irrawaddy delta: a port on the **Bassein River** (the westernmost distributary of the Irrawaddy). Pop.: 133 000 (1969 est.).

Basse-Nor·man·die (*French* bɑs nɔrmã'di) *n.* a region of NW France, on the English Channel: consists of the Cherbourg peninsula in the west rising to the Normandy hills in the east; mainly agricultural.

Bas·sen·thwaite ('bæsᵊnˌθweɪt) *n.* a lake in NW England, in Cumbria near Keswick. Length: 6 km (4 miles).

Basses-Alpes (*French* bɑs 'alp) *n.* the former name for **Alpes-de-Haute-Provence.**

Basses-Py·ré·nées (*French* bɑs pire'ne) *n.* the former name for **Pyrénées (Atlantiques).**

bas·set¹ ('bæsɪt) *n.* a long low smooth-haired breed of hound with short strong legs and long ears. Also called: **basset hound.** [C17: from French, from *basset* short, from *bas* low; see BASE²]

bas·set² ('bæsɪt) *vb.* **·sets, ·set·ing, ·set·ed.** *n.* a less common word for **outcrop.** [C17: perhaps from French: low stool, see BASSET¹]

Basse-Terre ('bæs 'tɛə; *French* bɑs 'tɛːr) *n.* **1.** a mountainous island in the West Indies, in the Leeward Islands, comprising part of Guadeloupe. **2.** a port in W Guadeloupe, on Basse-Terre Island: the capital of the French Overseas Region of Guadeloupe. Pop.: 5800 (1967).

Basse·terre (bæs'tɛə; *French* bɑs'tɛːr) *n.* a port in the West Indies, on St. Kitts in the Leeward Islands: the capital of St. Kitts and of the British Associated State of St. Kitts-Nevis-Anguilla. Pop.: 15 833 (1967).

bas·set horn *n.* an obsolete woodwind instrument of the clarinet family. [C19: probably from German *Bassetthorn,* from Italian *bassetto,* diminutive of BASSO + HORN]

bass gui·tar (beɪs) *n.* an electrically amplified guitar that has the same pitch and tuning as a double bass.

bas·si·net (ˌbæsɪ'nɛt) *n.* a wickerwork or wooden cradle or pram, usually hooded. [C19: from French: little basin, from *bassin* BASIN; associated in folk etymology with French *barcelonnette* a little cradle, from *berceau* cradle]

bass·ist ('beɪsɪst) *n.* a player of a double bass, esp. in a jazz band.

bas·so ('bæsəʊ) *n., pl.* **·sos** *or* **·si** (-sɪ). (esp. in operatic or solo singing) a singer with a bass voice. [C19: from Italian, from Late Latin *bassus* low; see BASE²]

bas·so con·tin·u·o *n.* another term for **thorough bass.** Often shortened to **continuo.** [Italian, literally: continuous bass]

bas·soon (bə'suːn) *n.* **1.** a woodwind instrument, the tenor of the oboe family. Range: about three and a half octaves upwards from the B flat below the bass staff. **2.** an orchestral musician who plays the bassoon. [C18: from French *basson,* from Italian *bassone,* from *basso* deep; see BASE²] —**bas·'soon·ist** *n.*

bas·so pro·fun·do (prəʊ'fʌndəʊ; *Italian* pro'fundo) *n.* (esp. in operatic solo singing) a singer with a very deep bass voice. [Italian, literally: deep bass]

bas·so ri·lie·vo (*Italian* 'basso ri'ljɛːvo) *n., pl.* **·vos.** Italian name for **bas-relief.**

Bass Strait (bæs) *n.* a channel between mainland Australia and Tasmania, linking the Indian Ocean and the Tasman Sea.

bass vi·ol (beɪs) *n.* **1.** another name for **viola da gamba. 2.** *U.S.* a less common name for **double bass** (sense 1).

bass·wood ('bæsˌwʊd) *n.* **1.** any of several North American linden trees, esp. *Tilia americana.* Sometimes shortened to **bass. 2.** the soft light-coloured wood of any of these trees, used for furniture. [C19: from BASS³]

bast (bæst) *n.* **1.** *Botany.* another name for **phloem. 2.** fibrous material obtained from the phloem of jute, hemp, flax, lime, etc., used for making rope, matting, etc. ~Also called: **bass.** [Old English *bæst;* related to Old Norse, Middle High German *bast*]

bas·tard ('bɑːstəd, 'bæs-) *n.* **1.** a person born of unmarried parents; an illegitimate baby, child, or adult. **2.** *Informal, offensive.* an obnoxious or despicable person. **3.** *Informal, often humorous or affectionate.* a person, esp. a man: *lucky bastard.* **4.** *Informal.* something extremely difficult or unpleasant: *that job is a real bastard.* **5.** something irregular, abnormal, or inferior. **6.** a hybrid, esp. an accidental or inferior one. ~*adj.* (*prenominal*) **7.** illegitimate by birth. **8.** irregular, abnormal, or inferior in shape, size, or appearance. **9.** resembling a specified thing, but not actually being such: *a bastard cedar.* **10.** counterfeit; spurious. [C13: from Old French *bastart,* perhaps from *bast* in the phrase *fils de bast* son of the packsaddle (that is, of an unlawful and not the marriage bed), from Medieval Latin *bastum* packsaddle, of uncertain origin] —**'bas·tard·ly** *adj.*

bas·tard·i·za·tion *or* **bas·tard·i·sa·tion** (ˌbɑːstədaɪ'zeɪʃən, ˌbæs-) *n.* **1.** the act of bastardizing. **2.** *Austral.* **a.** an initiation ceremony in a school or military unit, esp. one involving brutality. **b.** brutality or bullying.

bas·tard·ize *or* **bas·tard·ise** ('bɑːstəˌdaɪz, 'bæs-) *vb.* (*tr.*) **1.** to debase; corrupt. **2.** to declare illegitimate.

bas·tard mea·sles *n. Pathol.* an informal name for **rubella.**

bas·tard·ry ('bɑːstədrɪ, 'bæs-) *n. Chiefly Austral.* malicious or cruel behaviour.
bas·tard ti·tle *n.* another name for **half-title** (of a book).
bas·tard wing *n.* a tuft of feathers attached to the first digit of a bird, distinct from the wing feathers attached to the other digits and the ulna. Also called: **alula.**
bas·tard·y ('bɑːstədɪ, 'bæs-) *n.* the condition of being a bastard; illegitimacy.
baste[1] (beɪst) *vb.* (*tr.*) to sew with loose temporary stitches. [C14: from Old French *bastir* to build, of Germanic origin; compare Old High German *besten* to sew with BAST]
baste[2] (beɪst) *vb.* to moisten (meat) during cooking with hot fat and the juices produced. [C15: of uncertain origin]
baste[3] (beɪst) *vb.* (*tr.*) to beat thoroughly; thrash. [C16: probably from Old Norse *beysta*]
bas·ti, bus·tee, *or* **bus·ti** ('bʌstɪ) *n.* (in India) a slum inhabited by poor people. [Urdu: settlement]
Bas·tia ('bɑːstjə) *n.* a port in NE Corsica: the main commercial and industrial town of the island: capital of Haute-Corse department. Pop.: 49 375 (1968).
Bas·tille (bæ'stiːl; *French* ba'stij) *n.* a fortress in Paris, built in the 14th century: a prison until its destruction in 1789, at the beginning of the French Revolution. [C14: from Old French *bastile* fortress, from Old Provençal *bastida,* from *bastir* to build, of Germanic origin; see BASTE[1]]
Bas·tille Day *n.* (in France) an annual holiday on July 14, commemorating the fall of the Bastille.
bas·ti·na·do (ˌbæstɪ'neɪdəʊ) *n., pl.* **·does. 1.** punishment or torture in which the soles of the feet are beaten with a stick. **2.** a blow or beating with a stick. **3.** a stick; cudgel. ~*vb.* **·does, ·do·ing, ·doed. 4.** (*tr.*) to beat (a person) on the soles of the feet. [C16: from Spanish *bastonada,* from *baston* stick, from Late Latin *bastum;* see BATON]
bast·ing ('beɪstɪŋ) *n.* **1.** loose temporary stitches; tacking. **2.** sewing with such stitches.
bas·ti·on ('bæstɪən) *n.* **1.** a projecting part of a rampart, connected by two flanks to the main fortification, esp. one at the angle of a wall. **2.** any fortified place. **3.** a thing or person regarded as upholding or defending an attitude, principle, etc.: *the last bastion of opposition.* [C16: from French, from earlier *bastillon* bastion, from *bastille* BASTILLE]
bast·naes·ite *or* **bast·nas·ite** ('bæstnəˌsaɪt) *n.* a rare yellow to reddish-brown mineral consisting of a carbonate of fluorine and several lanthanide metals. It occurs in association with zinc and is a source of the lanthanides. Formula: $LaFCO_3$. [C19: from Swedish *bastnäsit,* after *Bastnäs,* Sweden, where it was found]
Ba·stogne (bæ'stəʊn; *French* ba'stɔɲ) *n.* a town in SE Belgium: of strategic importance to Allied defences during the Battle of the Bulge; besieged by the Germans during the winter of 1944–45. Pop.: 6816 (1970).
Ba·su·to (bə'suːtəʊ) *n., pl.* **·tos** *or* **·to.** a former name for **Sotho** (senses 3, 4).
Ba·su·to·land (bə'suːtəʊˌlænd) *n.* the former name (until 1966) of **Lesotho.**
bat[1] (bæt) *n.* **1. a.** any of various types of club with a handle, used to hit the ball in certain sports, such as cricket, baseball, or table tennis. **2.** a flat round club with a short handle, resembling a table-tennis bat, used by a man on the ground to guide the pilot of an aircraft when taxiing. **3.** *Cricket.* short for **batsman. 4.** any stout stick, esp. a wooden one. **5.** *Informal.* a blow from such a stick. **6.** *Austral.* a small board used for tossing the coins in the game of two-up. **7.** *U.S. slang.* a drinking spree; binge. **8.** *Slang.* speed; rate; pace: *they went at a fair bat.* **9.** another word for **batting** (sense 1). **10. carry one's bat.** *Cricket.* (of a batsman) to reach the end of an innings without being dismissed. **11. off one's own bat.** of one's own accord; without being prompted by someone else. **12. (right) off the bat.** *U.S. informal.* immediately; without hesitation. ~*vb.* **bats, bat·ting, bat·ted. 13.** (*tr.*) to strike with or as if with a bat. **14.** (*intr.*) *Cricket, etc.* (of a player or a team) to take a turn at batting. ~See also **bat around.** [Old English *batt* club, probably of Celtic origin; compare Gaelic *bat,* Russian *bat*]
bat[2] (bæt) *n.* **1.** any placental mammal of the order *Chiroptera;* any nocturnal mouselike animal flying with a pair of membranous wings (patagia). The group is divided into the *Megachiroptera* (**fruit bats**) and *Microchiroptera* (**insectivorous bats**). **2. blind as a bat.** having extremely poor eyesight. **3. have bats in the** (*or* **one's**) **belfry.** *Informal.* to be mad or eccentric; have strange ideas. [C14 *bakke,* probably of Scandinavian origin; compare Old Norse *ledhrblaka* leather-flapper, Swedish dialect *natt-batta* night bat] —**'bat·like** *adj.*
bat[3] (bæt) *vb.* **bats, bat·ting, bat·ted. 1.** (*tr.*) to wink or flutter (one's eyelids). **2. not bat an eye** (*or* **eyelid**). *Informal.* to show no surprise or concern. [C17: probably a variant of BATE[2]]
Ba·taan (bə'tæn, -'tɑːn) *n.* a peninsula in the Philippines, in W Luzon: scene of the surrender of U.S. and Philippine forces to the Japanese during World War II, later retaken by American forces.
Ba·tan·gas (bə'tæŋgæs) *n.* a port in the Philippines, in SW Luzon. Pop.: 125 304 (1975 est.).
Ba·tan Is·lands (bə'tɑːn) *pl. n.* a group of islands in the Philippines, north of Luzon. Capital: Basco. Pop.: 11 398 (1970). Area: 197 sq. km (76 sq. miles).
bat a·round *vb.* **1.** (*tr., adv.*) *U.S. slang.* to discuss (an idea, proposition, etc.) informally. **2.** (*intr.*) Also: **bat along.** *U.S. slang and Brit. dialect.* to wander or move about.
ba·ta·ta (bə'tɑːtə) *n.* another name for **sweet potato.** [C16: from Spanish, from Taino]
Ba·ta·vi·a (bə'teɪvɪə) *n.* **1.** an ancient district of the Netherlands, on an island at the mouth of the Rhine. **2.** an archaic or literary name for **Holland. 3.** a former name for **Djakarta.** —**Ba·'ta·vi·an** *adj., n.*
batch[1] (bætʃ) *n.* **1.** a group or set of usually similar objects or people, esp. if sent off, handled, or arriving at the same time. **2.** the bread, cakes, etc., produced at one baking. **3.** the amount of a material needed for an operation. **4.** Also called: **batch loaf.** a tall loaf having a close texture and a thick crust on the top and bottom, baked as part of a batch: the sides of each loaf are greased so that they will pull apart after baking to have white crumby sides; made esp. in Scotland and Ireland. [C15 *bache;* related to Old English *bacan* to BAKE; compare Old English *gebæc* batch, German *Gebäck*]
batch[2] (bætʃ) *vb.* a variant spelling of **bach.**
batch pro·cess·ing *n.* a system by which the computer programs of a number of individual users are submitted to the computer as a single batch. Compare **time sharing.**
bate[1] (beɪt) *vb.* **1.** another word for **abate. 2. with bated breath.** holding one's breath in suspense or fear.
bate[2] (beɪt) *vb.* (*intr.*) (of hawks) to jump violently from a perch or the falconer's fist, often hanging from the leash while struggling to escape. [C13: from Old French *batre* to beat, from Latin *battuere;* related to BAT[1]]
bate[3] (beɪt) *vb.* **1.** (*tr.*) to soak (skin or hides) in a special solution to soften them and remove chemicals used in previous treatments. ~*n.* **2.** the solution used. [Old English *bǣtan* to BAIT[1]]
bate[4] (beɪt) *n. Brit. informal.* a bad temper or rage. [C19: from BAIT[1], alluding to the mood of a person who is being baited]
ba·teau (bæ'təʊ; *French* ba'to) *n., pl.* **·teaux** (-təʊz; *French* -'to). a light flat-bottomed boat used on rivers in Canada and the northern U.S. [C18: from French: boat, from Old French *batel,* from Old English *bāt;* see BOAT]
bat·e·leur ea·gle (ˌbætə'lɜː) *n.* an African crested bird of prey, *Terathopius ecaudatus,* with a short tail and long wings: subfamily *Circaetinae,* family *Accipitridae* (hawks, etc.). [C19: from French *bateleur* juggler]
Bates (beɪts) *n.* **H(erbert) E(rnest).** 1905–74, English writer of short stories and novels, which include *The Darling Buds of May* (1958), *A Moment in Time* (1964), and *The Triple Echo* (1970).
Bates·i·an mim·ic·ry ('beɪtsɪən) *n. Zoology.* mimicry in which a harmless species is protected from predators by means of its resemblance to a harmful or inedible species. [C19: named after H. W. *Bates* (1825–92), English naturalist who formulated the hypothesis]
bat·fish ('bætˌfɪʃ) *n., pl.* **·fish** *or* **·fish·es.** any angler of the family *Ogcocephalidae,* having a flattened scaleless body and moving on the sea floor by means of fleshy pectoral and pelvic fins.
bat·fowl ('bætˌfaʊl) *vb.* (*intr.*) to catch birds by temporarily blinding them with light. —**'bat·ˌfowl·er** *n.*
bath[1] (bɑːθ) *n., pl.* **baths** (bɑːðz). **1.** a large container, esp. one made of enamelled iron or plastic, used for washing or medically treating the body. Related adj.: **balneal. 2.** the act or an instance of washing in such a container. **3.** the amount of liquid contained in a bath. **4.** (*usually pl.*) a place having baths or a swimming pool for public use. **5. a.** a vessel in which something is immersed to maintain it at a constant temperature, to process it photographically, electrolytically, etc., or to lubricate it. **b.** the liquid used in such a vessel. ~*vb.* **6.** *Brit.* to wash in a bath. [Old English *bæth;* compare Old High German *bad,* Old Norse *bath;* related to Swedish *basa* to clean with warm water, Old High German *bāen* to warm]
bath[2] (bæθ) *n.* an ancient Hebrew unit of liquid measure equal to about 8.3 Imperial gallons or 10 U.S. gallons. [Hebrew]
Bath (bɑːθ) *n.* a city in SW England, in Avon county on the River Avon: famous for its hot springs; a fashionable spa in the 18th century; Roman remains, notably the baths. Pop.: 84 545 (1971). Latin name: **Aquae Sulis.**
bath bun *n. Brit.* a sweet bun containing spices and dried fruit. [C19: from BATH, where it was originally made]
Bath chair *n.* a wheelchair for invalids, often with a hood.
Bath chap *n.* the lower part of the cheek of a pig, cooked and eaten, usually cold.
bath cube *n.* a cube of soluble scented material for use in a bath.
bathe (beɪð) *vb.* **1.** (*intr.*) to swim or paddle in a body of open water or a river, esp. for pleasure. **2.** (*tr.*) to apply liquid to (skin, a wound, etc.) in order to cleanse or soothe. **3.** to immerse or be immersed in a liquid: *to bathe machine parts in oil.* **4.** *Chiefly U.S.* to wash in a bath. **5.** (*tr.; often passive*) to suffuse: *her face was bathed with radiance.* **6.** (*tr.*) (of water, the sea, etc.) to lap; wash: *waves bathed the shore.* ~*n.* **7.** *Brit.* a swim or paddle in a body of open water or a river. [Old English *bathian;* related to Old Norse *batha,* Old High German *badōn*] —**'bath·er** *n.*
bath·ers ('beɪðəz) *pl. n. Austral.* a swimming costume.
ba·thet·ic (bə'θɛtɪk) *adj.* containing or displaying bathos.
bath·house ('bɑːθˌhaʊs) *n.* a building containing baths, esp. for public use.
bath·ing beaut·y ('beɪðɪŋ) *n.* an attractive girl in a swimming costume. Also called (old-fashioned): **bath·ing belle.**
bath·ing cos·tume ('beɪðɪŋ) *n.* a brief garment worn for swimming or sunbathing.
bath·ing ma·chine ('beɪðɪŋ) *n.* a small hut, on wheels so that

it could be pulled to the sea, used in the 18th and 19th centuries for bathers to change their clothes.
bath+ing suit ('beɪðɪŋ) *n.* **1.** a garment worn for bathing, esp. an old-fashioned one that covers much of the body. **2.** another name (esp. U.S.) for **swimming costume.**
bath·o- *combining form.* variant of **bathy-**: *bathometer.*
bath·o+lith ('bæθəlɪθ) *or* **bath·o+lite** ('bæθəˌlaɪt) *n.* a very large irregular-shaped mass of igneous rock, esp. granite, formed from an intrusion of magma at great depth, esp. one exposed after erosion of less resistant overlying rocks. —ˌ**bath·o+'lith+ic** *or* ˌ**bath·o+'lit+ic** *adj.*
Bath Ol·i+ver *n. Brit.* a kind of unsweetened biscuit. [named after William *Oliver* (1695–1764), a physician at Bath]
ba+thom+e·ter (bə'θɒmɪtə) *n.* an instrument for measuring the depth of water. —**bath·o+met+ric** (ˌbæθə'mɛtrɪk) *adj.* —ˌ**bath·o+'met+ri+cal+ly** *adv.* —**ba+thom+e·try** (bə'θɒmɪtrɪ) *n.*
Ba+tho·ni·an (bə'θəʊnɪən) *adj.* **1.** of or relating to Bath. **2.** *Geology.* of or denoting a stage of the Jurassic system in NW Europe.
ba+thos ('beɪθɒs) *n.* **1.** a sudden ludicrous descent from exalted to ordinary matters or style in speech or writing. **2.** insincere or excessive pathos. **3.** triteness; flatness. **4.** the lowest point; nadir. [C18: from Greek: depth, from *bathus* deep]
bath+robe ('bɑːθˌrəʊb) *n.* **1.** a loose-fitting garment of towelling, for wear before or after a bath or swimming. **2.** *U.S.* a dressing gown.
bath+room ('bɑːθˌruːm, -ˌrʊm) *n.* **1.** a room containing a bath or shower and usually a washbasin and lavatory. **2.** *U.S.* another name for **lavatory.**
bath salts *pl. n.* soluble scented salts for use in a bath.
Bath·she·ba (bæθ'ʃiːbə, 'bæθʃɪbə) *n. Old Testament.* the wife of Uriah, who committed adultery with David and later married him and became the mother of his son Solomon (II Samuel 11–12).
Bath stone *n. Brit.* a kind of limestone used as a building material, esp. at Bath in England.
bath+tub ('bɑːθˌtʌb) *n.* a bath, esp. one not permanently fixed.
Bath+urst ('bæθəst) *n.* **1.** a city in SE Australia, in E New South Wales: scene of a gold rush in 1851. Pop.: 17 550 (1970). **2.** a port in E Canada, in NE New Brunswick: rich mineral resources discovered in 1953. Pop.: 16 674 (1971). **3.** the former name (until 1973) of **Banjul.**
bath·y- *or* **bath·o-** *combining form.* indicating depth: *bathysphere; bathometer.* [from Greek *bathus* deep]
bath·y+al ('bæθɪəl) *adj.* denoting or relating to an ocean depth of between 200 and 2000 metres (about 100 and 1000 fathoms), corresponding to the continental slope.
ba+thym+e·try (bə'θɪmɪtrɪ) *n.* measurement of the depth of an ocean or other large body of water. —**bath·y+met+ric** (ˌbæθɪ'mɛtrɪk) *adj.* —ˌ**bath·y+'met+ri+cal+ly** *adv.*
bath·y+scaph ('bæθɪˌskæf), **bath·y+scaphe** ('bæθɪˌskeɪf, -ˌskæf), *or* **bath·y+scape** *n.* a submersible vessel having a flotation compartment with an observation capsule underneath, capable of reaching ocean depths of over 10 000 metres (about 5000 fathoms). [C20: from BATHY- + *-scaph,* from Greek *skaphē* light boat]
bath·y+sphere ('bæθɪˌsfɪə) *n.* a strong steel deep-sea diving sphere, lowered by cable.
ba+tik *or* **bat+tik** ('bætɪk) *n.* **a.** a process of printing fabric in which parts not to be dyed are covered by wax. **b.** fabric printed in this way. **c.** (*as modifier*): *a batik shirt.* [C19: via Malay from Javanese: painted]
Ba·tis·ta (*Spanish* ba'tista) *n.* **Ful·gen·cio** (ful'xenθjo), full name *Batista y Zaldívar.* 1901–73, Cuban military leader and dictator: president of Cuba (1940–44, 1952–59); overthrown by Fidel Castro.
ba+tiste (bæ'tiːst) *n.* a fine plain-weave cotton fabric: used esp. for shirts and dresses. [C17: from French, from Old French *toile de baptiste,* probably after *Baptiste* of Cambrai, 13th-century French weaver, its reputed inventor]
Bat+ley ('bætlɪ) *n.* a town in N England, in West Yorkshire. Pop.: 42 004 (1971).
bat+man ('bætmən) *n., pl.* **+men.** an officer's personal servant in any of the armed forces. [C18: from Old French *bat, bast,* from Medieval Latin *bastum* packsaddle]
Bat+man ('bætˌmæn) *n.* the secret identity of a civilian character in an American comic strip who assumes a batlike costume in order to fight crime.
bat mitz+vah (bɑːt 'mɪtsvə) *n.* (*sometimes caps.*) a variant spelling of **bas mitzvah.**
ba+ton ('bætɒn; *French* ba'tɔ̃) *n.* **1.** a thin stick used by the conductor of an orchestra, choir, etc., to indicate rhythm or expression. **2.** *Athletics.* **a.** a short bar carried by a competitor in a relay race and transferred to the next runner at the end of each stage. **b.** (*as modifier*): *a baton change.* **3.** a long stick with a knob on one end, carried, twirled, and thrown up and down by a drum major or drum majorette, esp. at the head of a parade. **4.** a staff or club carried by an official as a symbol of authority. **5.** *Heraldry.* a single narrow diagonal line superimposed on all other charges, esp. one curtailed at each end, signifying a bastard line. [C16: from French *bâton,* from Late Latin *bastum* rod, probably ultimately from Greek *bastazein* to lift up, carry]
bâ+ton de com+mande+ment *French.* (batɔ̃ də kɔmɑ̃d'mɑ̃) *n.* an antler object found in Upper Palaeolithic sites from the Aurignacian period onwards, consisting of a rod, often ornately decorated, with a hole through the thicker end. [literally: baton of command, although the object was probably actually used in making shafts for arrows and spears]
Bat+on Rouge ('bætᵊn 'ruːʒ) *n.* the capital of Louisiana, in the SE part on the Mississippi River. Pop.: 289 734 (1973 est.).
ba+tra+chi+an (bə'treɪkɪən) *n.* **1.** any amphibian, esp. a frog or toad. ~*adj.* **2.** of or relating to the frogs and toads. [C19: from New Latin *Batrachia,* from Greek *batrakhos* frog]
bats-in-the-bel·fry *n.* (*functioning as sing.*) **1.** a hairy Eurasian campanulaceous plant, *Campanula trachelium,* with bell-shaped blue-purple flowers. ~*adj.* **2.** *Slang.* mad; demented.
bats+man ('bætsmən) *n., pl.* **+men. 1.** *Cricket., etc.* **a.** a person who bats or whose turn it is to bat. **b.** a player who specializes in batting. **2.** a person on the ground who uses bats to guide the pilot of an aircraft when taxiing. —**'bats+man+ˌship** *n.*
batt (bæt) *n. Textiles.* another word for **batting** (sense 1).
bat+tal+ion (bə'tæljən) *n.* **1.** a military unit comprised of three or more companies or formations of similar size. **2.** (*usually pl.*) any large array. [C16: from French *bataillon,* from Old Italian *battaglione,* from *battaglia* company of soldiers, BATTLE]
bat+tels ('bætᵊlz) *pl. n.* (at Oxford University) the account of a member of a college for board, provisions, and other college expenses. [C16: perhaps from obsolete *battle* to feed, fatten, of uncertain origin]
batte+ment (*French* bat'mɑ̃) *n. Ballet.* extension of one leg forwards, sideways, or backwards, either once or repeatedly.
bat+ten[1] ('bætᵊn) *n.* **1.** a sawn strip of wood used in building to cover joints, provide a fixing for tiles or slates, support lathing, etc. **2.** a long narrow board used for flooring. **3.** a narrow flat length of wood or plastic inserted in pockets of a sail to give it proper shape. **4.** a lath used for holding a tarpaulin along the side of a raised hatch on a ship. ~*vb.* **5.** (*tr.*) to furnish or strengthen with battens. **6. batten down the hatches. a.** to use battens in nailing a tarpaulin over a hatch on a ship to make it secure. **b.** to prepare for action, a crisis, etc. [C15: from French *bâton* stick; see BATON]
bat+ten[2] ('bætᵊn) *vb.* (*intr.*) (usually foll. by *on*) to thrive, esp. at the expense of someone else: *to batten on the needy.* [C16: probably from Old Norse *batna* to improve; related to Old Norse *betr* BETTER, Old High German *bazzen* to get better]
Bat+ten+burg ('bætᵊnˌbɜːg) *n.* an oblong sponge cake divided longitudinally into four square sections, two coloured pink and two yellow, with an outer coating of marzipan. [perhaps named after *Battenberg,* a village in Prussia]
bat+ter[1] ('bætə) *vb.* **1.** to hit (someone or something) repeatedly using heavy blows, as with a club or other heavy instrument; beat heavily. **2.** (*tr.; often passive*) to damage or injure, as by blows, heavy wear, etc. **3.** (*tr.*) to subject (a person, opinion, or theory) to harsh criticism; attack. ~*n.* **4.** printing type or a printing plate that is damaged or worn. **5.** the defective impression produced by such type or such a plate. [C14 *bateren,* probably from *batten* to BAT[1]] —**'bat+ter+er** *n.*
bat+ter[2] ('bætə) *n.* a mixture of flour, eggs, and milk, used to make cakes, pancakes, etc., and to coat certain foods before frying. [C15 *bater,* probably from *bateren* to BATTER[1]]
bat+ter[3] ('bætə) *n. Baseball, etc.* a player who bats.
bat+ter[4] ('bætə) *n.* **1.** the slope of the face of a wall that recedes gradually backwards and upwards. ~*vb.* **2.** (*intr.*) to have such a slope. [C16 (vb.: to incline): of uncertain origin]
bat+ter[5] ('bætə) *n.* a spree or debauch. [C19: of unknown origin]
bat+tered ba·by *n.* **a.** a young child who has sustained serious injuries through mistreatment or violence at the hands of a parent or other adult. **b.** (*as modifier*): *battered-baby syndrome.*
bat+ter+ing ram *n.* (esp. formerly) a large beam used to break down the walls or doors of fortifications.
bat+ter·y ('bætərɪ) *n., pl.* **+ter·ies. 1. a.** two or more primary cells connected together, usually in series, to provide a source of electric current. **b.** short for **dry battery. 2.** another name for **accumulator** (sense 1). **3.** a number of similar things occurring together: *a battery of questions.* **4.** *Criminal law.* unlawful beating or wounding of a person or mere touching in a hostile or offensive manner. See also **assault and battery. 5.** a fortified structure on which artillery is mounted. **6.** a group of guns, missile launchers, searchlights, or torpedo tubes of similar type or size operated as a single entity. **7.** a small tactical unit of artillery. **8.** *Chiefly Brit.* **a.** a large group of cages for intensive rearing of poultry. **b.** (*as modifier*): *battery hens.* **9.** the percussion section in an orchestra. **10.** *Baseball.* the pitcher and the catcher considered together. [C16: from Old French *batterie* beating, from *battre* to beat, from Latin *battuere*]
bat+tik ('bætɪk) *n.* a variant spelling of **batik.**
bat+ting ('bætɪŋ) *n.* **1.** cotton or woollen wadding used in quilts, mattresses, etc. **2.** the action of a person or team that hits with a bat, esp. in cricket or baseball.
bat+tle ('bætᵊl) *n.* **1.** a fight between large armed forces; military or naval engagement; combat. **2.** conflict; contention; struggle: *his battle for recognition.* **3. do, give,** *or* **join battle.** to start fighting. ~*vb.* **4.** (*intr.;* often foll. by *against, for,* or *with*) to fight in or as if in military combat; contend. **5.** to struggle in order to achieve something or arrive somewhere: *he battled through the crowd.* **6.** (*intr.*) *Austral.* to scrape a living, esp. by doing odd jobs. [C13: from Old French *bataile,* from Late Latin *battālia* exercises performed by soldiers, from *battuere* to beat] —**'bat+tler** *n.*
bat+tle-axe *n.* **1.** (formerly) a large broad-headed axe. **2.** *Informal.* an argumentative domineering woman.
bat+tle cruis+er *n.* a heavily armed warship of battleship size but with light armour and capable of high speed.

bat+tle cry *n.* **1.** a shout uttered by soldiers going into battle. **2.** a slogan used to rally the supporters of a campaign, movement, etc.

bat+tle+dore ('bætᵊl,dɔː) *n.* **1.** Also called: **battledore and shuttlecock.** an ancient racket game. **2.** a light racket, smaller than a tennis racket, used for striking the shuttlecock in this game. **3.** (formerly) a wooden utensil used for beating clothes, in baking, etc. ~*vb.* **4.** *Rare.* to hurl or volley (something) back and forth. [C15 *batyldoure,* perhaps from Old Provençal *batedor* a beater, from Old French *battre* to beat, BATTER]

bat+tle fa+tigue *n. Psychol.* a type of mental disorder, characterized by anxiety, depression, and loss of motivation, caused by the stress of active warfare. Also called: **combat fatigue.** See also **shell shock.**

bat·tle+field ('bætᵊl,fiːld) *or* **bat·tle+ground** *n.* the place where a battle is fought; an area of conflict.

bat+tle+ment ('bætᵊlmənt) *n.* a parapet or wall with indentations or embrasures, originally for shooting through. [C14: from Old French *batailles,* plural of *bataille* BATTLE] —'**bat+tle+,ment+ed** *adj.*

bat·tle+piece ('bætᵊl,piːs) *n.* a painting, relief, mosaic, etc., depicting a battle, usually commemorating an actual event.

bat+tle roy+al *n.* **1.** a fight, esp. with fists or cudgels, involving more than two combatants; melee. **2.** a long violent argument.

bat·tle+ship ('bætᵊl,ʃɪp) *n.* **1.** a heavily armoured warship of the largest type. **2.** (formerly) a warship of sufficient size and armament to take her place in the line of battle; ship of the line.

bat+tue (bæ'tuː, -'tjuː; *French* ba'ty) *n.* **1.** the beating of woodland or cover to force game to flee in the direction of hunters. **2. a.** an organized shooting party using this method. **b.** the game disturbed or shot by this method. **3.** indiscriminate slaughter, as of a defenceless crowd. [C19: from French, feminine of *battu* beaten, from *battre* to beat, from Latin *battuere*]

bat+ty ('bætɪ) *adj.* **+ti+er, +ti+est.** *Slang.* **1.** insane; crazy. **2.** odd; eccentric. [C20: from BAT[2]; compare the phrase *have bats in the belfry*]

Ba+tum (bɑː'tuːm) *or* **Ba+tu+mi** (bɑː'tuːmɪ) *n.* a city in the S Soviet Union, in the Georgian SSR: capital of the Adzhar ASSR; a major Black Sea port. Pop.: 114 000 (1975 est.).

bat+wing ('bæt,wɪŋ) *adj.* shaped like the wings of a bat, as a black tie, collar, etc.

bat+wing sleeve *n.* a sleeve of a garment with a deep armhole and a tight wrist.

bat+wom·an ('bætwʊmən) *n., pl.* **+wom·en.** a female servant in any of the armed forces.

bau+ble ('bɔːbᵊl) *n.* **1.** a showy toy or trinket of little value; trifle. **2.** (formerly) a mock staff of office carried by a court jester. [C14: from Old French *baubel* plaything, of obscure origin]

Bau+chi ('baʊtʃɪ) *n.* **1.** a state of N Nigeria: formed in 1976 from part of North-Eastern State; tin mining. Capital: Bauchi. Pop.: 3 239 717 (1976 est.). Area: 17 926 sq. km (6920 sq. miles). **2.** a town in N central Nigeria, capital of Bauchi state. Pop.: 47 200 (1973 est.).

Bau·cis ('bɔːsɪs) *n. Greek myth.* a poor peasant woman who, with her husband Philemon, was rewarded for hospitality to the disguised gods Zeus and Hermes.

baud (bɔːd) *n.* a unit used to measure the speed of telegraphic code transmissions, equal to one unit interval per second. [named after J. M. E. *Baudot* (died 1903), French inventor]

bau+de+kin *or* **bau+di+kin** ('bɔːdɪkɪn) *n. Archaic.* another word for **baldachin** (sense 1).

Bau·de·laire (*French* bo'dlɛːr) *n.* **Charles Pierre** (ʃarl 'pjɛːr). 1821–67, French poet, noted for his macabre imagery; author of *Les fleurs du mal* (1857).

Bau·douin I (*French* bo'dwɛ̃) *n.* born 1930, king of Belgium since 1951.

Bau+haus ('baʊ,haʊs) *n.* **a.** a German school of architecture and applied arts founded in 1919 by Walter Gropius on experimental principles of functionalism and truth to materials. After being closed by the Nazis in 1933, its ideas were widely disseminated by its students and staff, including Kandinsky, Klee, Feininger, Moholy-Nagy, and Mies van der Rohe. **b.** (*as modifier*): *Bauhaus wallpaper.* [German, literally: building house]

bau+hin·i·a (bɔː'hɪnɪə, bəʊ-) *n.* any climbing leguminous plant of the genus *Bauhinia,* of tropical and warm regions, widely cultivated for ornament. [C18: New Latin, named after Jean and Gaspard *Bauhin,* 16th-century French herbalists]

baulk (bɔːk) *n.* **1.** Also called (U.S.): **balk.** *Billiards.* **a.** (in billiards) the space, usually 29 inches deep, between the baulk line and the bottom cushion. **b.** (in baulk-line games) one of the spaces between the cushions and the baulk lines. **c. in baulk.** inside one of these spaces. **2.** *Archaeol.* a strip of earth left between excavation trenches for the study of the complete stratigraphy of a site. ~*vb., n.* **3.** a variant spelling of **balk.**

baulk line *or U.S.* **balk line** *n. Billiards.* **1.** Also called: **string line.** a straight line across a billiard table behind which the cue balls are placed at the start of a game. **2. a.** one of four lines parallel to the cushions dividing the table into a central panel and eight smaller ones (the baulks). **b.** a type of game using these lines as restrictions.

Bau·mé scale (bəʊ'meɪ, 'bəʊmeɪ) *n.* a scale for calibrating hydrometers used for measuring the specific gravity of liquids. 1 degree Baumé is equal to $144.3((s-1)/s)$, where *s* is specific gravity. [C19: named after Antoine *Baumé* (1728–1804), French chemist]

Bau+tzen ('baʊtsən) *n.* a city in SE East Germany: site of an indecisive battle in 1813 between Napoleon's army and an allied army of Russians and Prussians. Pop.: 44 202 (1972 est.).

baux+ite ('bɔːksaɪt) *n.* an amorphous claylike substance consisting of hydrated alumina with iron and other impurities: the chief source of alumina and aluminium and also used as an abrasive and catalyst. Formula: $Al_2O_3.nH_2O$. [C19: from French, from (*Les*) *Baux* in southern France, where it was originally found]

Bav. *abbrev. for* Bavaria(n).

Ba+var·i·a (bə'vɛərɪə) *n.* a state of S West Germany: a former duchy and kingdom; mainly wooded highland, with the Alps in the south. Capital: Munich. Pop.: 10 479 386 (1970). Area: 70 531 sq. km (27 232 sq. miles). German name: **Bayern.** —**Ba+'var+i·an** *adj., n.*

Ba+var+i·an cream *n.* a cold dessert consisting of a rich custard set with gelatine and flavoured in various ways. Also called: **ba+va+rois** (*French* bava'rwa).

baw+bee (bɔː'biː) *n.* **1.** a former Scottish silver coin. **2.** *Scot.* an informal word for **halfpenny.** [C16: named after Alexander Orok of *Sillebawby,* master of the mint from 1538]

baw+cock ('bɔː,kɒk) *n. Archaic.* a fine fellow. [C16: from French *beau coq,* from *beau* handsome + *coq* COCK[1]]

bawd (bɔːd) *n. Archaic.* **1.** a person who runs a brothel, esp. a woman. **2.** a prostitute. [C14: from Old French *baude,* feminine of *baud* merry, of Germanic origin; compare Old High German *bald* BOLD]

bawd+ry ('bɔːdrɪ) *n. Archaic.* obscene talk or language.

bawd·y ('bɔːdɪ) *adj.* **bawd·i·er, bawd·i·est. 1.** (of language, plays, etc.) containing references to sex, esp. to be humorous. ~*n.* **2.** obscenity or eroticism, esp. in writing or drama. —'**bawd·i+ly** *adv.* —'**bawd·i+ness** *n.*

bawd·y+house ('bɔːdɪ,haʊs) *n.* an archaic word for **brothel.**

bawl (bɔːl) *vb.* **1.** (*intr.*) to utter long loud cries, as from pain or frustration; wail. **2.** to shout loudly, as in anger. ~*n.* **3.** a loud shout or cry. [C15: probably from Icelandic *baula* to low; related to Medieval Latin *baulāre* to bark, Swedish *böla* to low; all of imitative origin] —'**bawl+er** *n.*

bawl out *vb.* (*tr., adv.*) *Informal.* to scold loudly.

Bax (bæks) *n.* Sir **Ar·nold** (**Edward Trevor**). 1883–1953, English composer of romantic works, often based on Celtic legends, including the tone poem *Tintagel* (1917).

bay[1] (beɪ) *n.* **1.** a wide semicircular indentation of a shoreline, esp. between two headlands or peninsulas. **2.** an extension of lowland into hills that partly surround it. **3.** *U.S.* an extension of prairie into woodland. [C14: from Old French *baie,* perhaps from Old French *baer* to gape, from Medieval Latin *batāre* to yawn]

bay[2] (beɪ) *n.* **1.** an alcove or recess in a wall. **2.** any partly enclosed compartment, as one in which hay is stored in a barn. **3.** See **bay window. 4.** an area off a road in which vehicles may park or unload, esp. one adjacent to a shop, factory, etc. **5.** a compartment in an aircraft, esp. one used for a specified purpose: *the bomb bay.* **6.** *Nautical.* a compartment in the forward part of a ship between decks, often used as the ship's hospital. **7.** *Brit.* a tracked recess in the platform of a railway station, esp. one forming the terminus of a branch line. [C14: from Old French *baee* gap or recess in a wall, from *baer* to gape; see BAY[1]]

bay[3] (beɪ) *n.* **1.** a deep howl or growl, esp. of a hound on the scent. **2. at bay. a.** (of a person or animal) forced to turn and face attackers: *the dogs held the deer at bay.* **b.** at a distance: *to keep a disease at bay.* **3. bring to bay.** to force into a position from which retreat is impossible. ~*vb.* **4.** (*intr.*) to howl (at) in deep prolonged tones. **5.** (*tr.*) to utter in a loud prolonged tone. **6.** (*tr.*) to drive to or hold at bay. [C13: from Old French *abaiier* to bark, of imitative origin]

bay[4] (beɪ) *n.* **1.** a Mediterranean laurel, *Laurus nobilis.* See **laurel** (sense 1). **2.** any of several magnolias. See **sweet bay** (sense 1). **3.** any of certain other trees or shrubs, esp. bayberry. **4.** (*pl.*) a wreath of bay leaves. See **laurel** (sense 6). [C14: from Old French *baie* laurel berry, from Latin *bāca* berry]

bay[5] (beɪ) *n.* **1. a.** a moderate reddish-brown colour. **b.** (*as adj.*): *a bay horse.* **2.** an animal of this colour, esp. a horse. [C14: from Old French *bai,* from Latin *badius*]

ba+ya+dere (,baɪə'dɪə, -'dɛə) *n.* **1.** a dancing girl, esp. one serving in a Hindu temple. **2.** a fabric or design with horizontal stripes, esp. of a bright colour. ~*adj.* **3.** (of fabric, etc.) having horizontal stripes. [C18: via French from Portuguese *bailadeira* dancing girl, from *bailar* to dance, from Latin *ballāre;* see BALL[2]]

Ba+ya+món (*Spanish* baja'mon) *n.* a city in NE central Puerto Rico, south of San Juan. Pop.: 147 552 (1970).

bay+ard ('beɪəd) *Archaic.* ~*n.* **1.** a bay horse. ~*adj.* **2.** bay-coloured.

Bay+ard[1] ('beɪəd) *n.* a legendary horse that figures prominently in medieval romance.

Ba·yard[2] ('beɪəd; *French* ba'jaːr) *n.* **Che·va·lier de** (ʃəva'lje də), original name *Pierre de Terrail.* ?1473–1524, French soldier, known as *le chevalier sans peur et sans reproche* (the fearless and irreproachable knight).

bay+ber·ry ('beɪbərɪ) *or* **bay** *n., pl.* **·ries. 1.** any of several North American aromatic shrubs or small trees of the genus *Myrica,* that bear grey waxy berries: family *Myricaceae.* See also **wax myrtle. 2.** Also called: **bay rum tree.** a tropical American myrtaceous tree, *Pimenta acris,* that yields an oil used in making bay rum. **3.** the fruit of any of these plants.

Bay+ern ('baɪərn) *n.* the German name for **Bavaria.**

Ba+yeux tap+es·try (*French* ba'jø) *n.* an 11th- or 12th-century tapestry in Bayeux, in NW France, nearly 70.5 metres (231 feet) wide by 50 centimetres (20 inches) high, depicting the Norman conquest of England.

Bayle (*French* bɛl) *n.* **Pierre** (pjɛ:r). 1647–1706, French philosopher and critic, noted for his *Dictionnaire historique et critique* (1697), which profoundly influenced Voltaire and the French Encyclopedists.

bay lynx *n.* another name for **bobcat.**

Bay of Pigs *n.* a bay on the SW coast of Cuba: scene of an unsuccessful invasion of Cuba by U.S.-backed troops (April 17, 1961). Spanish name: **Bahia de los Cochinos.**

bay·o+net ('beɪənɪt) *n.* **1.** a blade for stabbing that can be attached to the muzzle of a firearm. **2.** a type of fastening in which a cylindrical member is inserted into a socket against spring pressure and turned so that pins on its side engage in slots in the socket. ~*vb.* **+net, +net+ing, +net+ed,** *or* **+nets, +net+ting, +net+ted. 3.** (*tr.*) to stab or kill with a bayonet. [C17: from French *baïonnette,* from BAYONNE where it originated]

Ba+yonne (*French* ba'jɔn) *n.* a port in SW France: a commercial centre for the Basque region. Pop.: 44 706 (1975).

bay·ou ('baɪju:) *n.* (in the southern U.S.) a sluggish marshy tributary of a lake or river. [C18: from Louisiana French, from Choctaw *bayuk*]

Bay+reuth (*German* baɪ'rɔɪt) *n.* a city in SE West Germany, in NE Bavaria: home and burial place of Richard Wagner; annual festivals of his music. Pop.: 64 200 (1970).

bay rum *n.* **1.** an aromatic liquid, used in medicines and cosmetics, originally obtained by distilling the leaves of the bayberry tree (*Pimenta acris*) with rum: now also synthesized from alcohol, water, and various oils. **2. bay rum tree.** another name for **bayberry** (sense 2).

Bay Street *n. Canadian.* **1.** the financial centre of Toronto, in which Canada's largest stock exchange is situated. **2.** the financial interests and powers of Toronto.

bay tree *n.* another name for **bay**[4] (sense 1).

bay win+dow *n.* a window projecting from the wall of a building and forming an alcove of a room. Sometimes shortened to **bay.** See also **bow window, oriel.**

bay+wood ('beɪ,wʊd) *n.* the light soft wood of a tropical American mahogany tree, *Swietenia macrophylla,* of the bay region of SE Mexico.

ba+zaar *or* **ba+zar** (bə'zɑ:) *n.* **1.** (esp. in the Orient) a market area, esp. a street of small stalls. **2.** a sale in aid of charity, esp. of miscellaneous secondhand or handmade articles. **3.** a shop where a large variety of goods is sold. [C16: from Persian *bāzār,* from Old Persian *abēcharish*]

ba+zoo (bə'zu:) *n.* a U.S. slang word for **mouth.** [C19: of unknown origin]

ba+zoo+ka (bə'zu:kə) *n.* a portable tubular rocket-launcher that fires a projectile capable of piercing armour: used by infantrymen as a short-range antitank weapon. [C20: named after a pipe instrument invented by Bob Burns (1896–1956), American comedian]

B bat+ter·y *n. U.S.* a battery for supplying a voltage to the anode of a thermionic valve. Compare **A battery, C battery.**

B.B.C. *abbrev. for* British Broadcasting Corporation.

bbl. *abbrev. for* barrel (container or unit of measure).

B.C. *abbrev. for:* **1.** (indicating years numbered back from the supposed year of the birth of Christ) before Christ: *in 54* B.C. *Caesar came.* Compare **A.D. 2.** British Columbia.

Usage. See at **A.D.**

BCD *abbrev. for* binary-coded decimal.

B.C.E. *abbrev. for* Before Common Era (used, esp. by non-Christians, in numbering years B.C.).

BCG Bacillus Calmette-Guérin (anti-tuberculosis vaccine).

B.Ch. *abbrev. for* Bachelor of Surgery. [from Latin *Baccalaureus Chirurgiae*]

B.C.L. *abbrev. for* Bachelor of Civil Law.

B.Com. *abbrev. for* Bachelor of Commerce.

B com+plex *n.* short for **vitamin B complex.**

bd. *abbrev. for:* **1.** board. **2.** *Insurance, finance, etc.* bond. **3.** *Bookbinding.* bound. **4.** bundle.

B.D. *abbrev. for:* **1.** Bachelor of Divinity. **2.** *Commerce.* bills discounted.

B/D *abbrev. for:* **1.** bank draft. **2.** *Commerce.* bills discounted. **3.** Also: **b/d** *Book-keeping.* brought down.

B.D.A. *abbrev. for* British Dental Association.

Bde. *abbrev. for* brigade.

bdel+li·um ('dɛlɪəm) *n.* **1.** any of several African or W Asian trees of the burseraceous genus *Commiphora* that yield a gum resin. **2.** the aromatic gum resin, similar to myrrh, produced by any of these trees. [C16: from Latin, from Greek *bdellion,* perhaps from Hebrew *bĕdhōlah*]

bd.ft. *abbrev. for* board foot.

BDS *international car registration for* Barbados.

bds. *abbrev. for:* **1.** *Bookbinding.* (bound in) boards. **2.** bundles.

B.D.S. *abbrev. for* Bachelor of Dental Surgery.

be (bi:; *unstressed* bɪ) *vb. pres. sing. 1st pers.* **am;** *2nd pers.* **are;** *3rd pers.* **is.** *pres. pl.* **are.** *past sing. 1st pers.* **was;** *2nd pers.* **were;** *3rd pers.* **was.** *past pl.* **were.** *pres. part.* **be+ing.** *past part.* **been.** (*intr.*) **1.** to have presence in the realm of perceived reality; exist; live: *I think, therefore I am; not all that is can be understood.* **2.** (*used in the perfect or past perfect tenses only*) to pay a visit; go: *have you been to Spain?.* **3.** to take place; occur: *my birthday was last Thursday.* **4.** (*copula*) used as a linking verb between the subject of a sentence and its noun or adjective complement or complementing phrase. *be* has no intrinsic meaning of its own but rather expresses the relationship of either essential or incidental equivalence or identity (*John is a man; John is a musician*) or to specify an essential or incidental attribute (*honey is sweet; Susan is angry*). It is also used with an adverbial complement to indicate a relationship of location in space or time (*Bill is at the office; the dance is on Saturday*). **5.** (*takes a present participle*) forms the progressive present tense: *the man is running.* **6.** (*takes a past participle*) forms the passive voice of all transitive verbs and (archaically) certain intransitive ones: *a good film is being shown on television tonight; I am done.* **7.** (*takes an infinitive*) expresses intention, expectation, supposition, or obligation: *the president is to arrive at 9.30; you are not to leave before I say so.* **8.** (*takes a past participle*) forms the perfect or past perfect tense of certain intransitive verbs of motion, such as **go** or **come:** *the last train is gone.* **9. be that as it may.** the facts concerning (something) are of no importance. [Old English *bēon;* related to Old High German *bim* am, Latin *fui* I have been, Greek *phuein* to bring forth, Sanskrit *bhavati* he is]

Be *chemical symbol for* beryllium.

Bé *abbrev. for* Baumé.

be- *prefix forming transitive verbs.* **1.** (*from nouns*) to surround completely; cover on all sides: *befog.* **2.** (*from nouns*) to affect completely or excessively: *bedazzle.* **3.** (*from nouns*) to consider as or cause to be: *befool; befriend.* **4.** (*from nouns*) to provide or cover with: *bejewel.* **5.** (*from verbs*) at, for, against, on, or over: *bewail; berate.* [Old English *be-, bi-,* unstressed variant of *bī* BY]

B.E. *abbrev. for:* **1.** bill of exchange. **2.** (in the U.S.) Board of Education. **3.** Bachelor of Education. **4.** Bachelor of Engineering.

B/E, B.E., *or* **b.e.** *abbrev. for* bill of exchange.

B.E.A. (formerly) *abbrev. for* British European Airways.

beach (bi:tʃ) *n.* **1.** an extensive area of sand or shingle sloping down to a sea or lake, esp. the area between the high and low water marks on a seacoast. Related adj.: **littoral.** ~*vb.* **2.** to run or haul (a boat) onto a beach. [C16: perhaps related to Old English *bæce* river, BECK[2]]

beach ball *n.* a large light brightly coloured ball for playing with on a beach.

Beach+boys ('bi:tʃbɔɪz) *pl. n.* **the.** U.S. singing group (formed 1961): consisting of Brian Wilson (born 1942), Dennis Wilson (born 1944), Carl Wilson (born 1946), Mike Love (born 1941), and Al Jardine (born 1942); noted for their characteristic close harmony. Their recordings include *Surfin' U.S.A.* (1963), *Good Vibrations* (1966), and *Surf's up* (1967; released 1971).

beach bug+gy *n.* a low car, often open and with balloon tyres, for driving on sand. Also called: **dune buggy.**

beach+comb·er ('bi:tʃ,kəʊmə) *n.* **1.** a person who searches shore debris for anything of worth, esp. a vagrant living on a beach. **2.** a long high wave rolling onto a beach.

beach flea *n.* another name for the **sand hopper.**

beach+head ('bi:tʃ,hɛd) *n. Military.* an area on a beach that has been captured from the enemy and on which troops and equipment are landed.

beach·ie ('bi:tʃɪ) *n. Austral. informal.* **1.** a beach fisherman. **2.** a young unemployed vagrant who frequents beaches.

Beach-la-Mar (,bi:tʃlə'mɑ:) *n.* the variety of Neo-Melanesian spoken in the New Hebrides and New Caledonia. Also called: **Bichelamar.** [C19: quasi-French, from BÊCHE-DE-MER (trepang, this being a major trading commodity in the SW Pacific; hence the name was applied to the trading language)]

beach plum *n.* **1.** a rosaceous shrub, *Prunus maritima,* of coastal regions of E North America. **2.** its edible plumlike fruit.

Beach·y Head *n.* a headland in East Sussex, on the English Channel, consisting of chalk cliffs 171 m (570 ft.) high.

bea+con ('bi:kən) *n.* **1.** a signal fire or light on a hill, tower, etc., esp. one used formerly as a warning of invasion. **2.** a hill on which such fires were lit. **3.** a lighthouse, signalling buoy, etc., used to warn or guide ships in dangerous waters. **4.** short for **radio beacon. 5.** a radio or other signal marking a flight course in air navigation. **6.** short for **Belisha beacon. 7.** a person or thing that serves as a guide, inspiration, or warning. ~*vb.* **8.** to guide or warn. **9.** (*intr.*) to shine. [Old English *beacen* sign; related to Old Frisian *bāken,* Old Saxon *bōcan,* Old High German *bouhhan*]

Bea·cons·field ('bi:kənz,fi:ld, 'bɛk-) *n.* **1st Earl of.** title of (Benjamin) **Disraeli.**

bead (bi:d) *n.* **1.** a small usually spherical piece of glass, wood, plastic, etc., with a hole through it by means of which it may be strung with others to form a necklace, etc. **2.** a small drop of moisture: *a bead of sweat.* **3.** a small bubble in or on a liquid. **4.** a small metallic knob acting as the sight of a firearm. **5.** Also called: **astragal.** *Architect., furniture.* a small convex moulding having a semicircular cross section. **6.** *Chem.* a small solid globule made by fusing a powdered sample with borax or a similar flux on a platinum wire. The colour of the globule serves as a test for the presence of certain metals (**bead test**). **7.** *Metallurgy.* a deposit of welding metal on the surface of a metal workpiece, often used to examine the structure of the weld zone. **8.** *R.C. Church.* one of the beads of a rosary. **9. count, say,** *or* **tell one's beads.** to pray with a rosary. ~*vb.* **10.** (*tr.*) to decorate with beads. **11.** to form into beads or drops. [Old English *bed* prayer; related to Old High German *gibet* prayer]

bead+ing ('bi:dɪŋ) *n.* a narrow strip of some material used for edging or ornamentation. Also called: **bead+work** ('bi:d,wɜ:k).

bea+dle ('bi:dᵊl) *n.* **1.** *Brit.* (formerly) a minor parish official who acted as an usher and kept order. **2.** *Judaism.* **a.** a synagogue attendant. **b.** the candle used to kindle the

Hanukkah lights. **3.** an official in certain British universities and other institutions. [Old English *bydel;* related to Old High German *butil* bailiff] —**'bea+dle+ship** *n.*

Bea·dle ('bi:dᵊl) *n.* **George Wells.** born 1903, U.S. biologist, who shared the Nobel prize for medicine in 1958 for his work in genetics.

bea+dle+dom ('bi:dᵊldəm) *n.* petty officialdom.

bead+roll ('bi:d,rəʊl) *n. Archaic.* a list of persons for whom prayers are to be offered.

bead-ru·by *n., pl.* **·bies.** a N temperate liliaceous plant, *Maianthemum canadense,* with small white bell-shaped flowers and small red berries.

beads+man *or* **bedes+man** ('bi:dzmən) *n., pl.* **+men.** *Archaic.* **1.** a person who prays for another's soul, esp. one paid or fed for doing so. **2.** a person kept in an almshouse.

bead·y ('bi:dɪ) *adj.* **bead·i·er, bead·i·est. 1.** small, round, and glittering (esp. in the phrase **beady eyes**). **2.** resembling or covered with beads. —**'bead·i·ly** *adv.* —**'bead·i·ness** *n.*

bea+gle ('bi:gᵊl) *n.* **1.** a small breed of hound resembling a foxhound, often used for hunting hares. **2.** *Archaic.* a person who spies on others. ~*vb.* **3.** *(intr.)* to hunt with beagles, normally on foot. [C15: of uncertain origin]

beak[1] (bi:k) *n.* **1.** the projecting jaws of a bird, covered with a horny sheath; bill. **2.** any beaklike mouthpart in other animals, such as turtles. **3.** *Slang.* a person's nose, esp. one that is large, pointed, or hooked. **4.** any projecting part, such as the pouring lip of a bucket. **5.** *Architect.* the upper surface of a cornice, which slopes out to throw off water. **6.** *Chem.* the part of a still or retort through which vapour passes to the condenser. **7.** *Nautical.* another word for **ram** (sense 5). [C13: from Old French *bec,* from Latin *beccus,* of Gaulish origin] —**beaked** (bi:kt) *adj.* —**'beak+less** *adj.* —**'beak+,like** *adj.* —**'beak·y** *adj.*

beak[2] (bi:k) *n.* a Brit. slang word for **judge, magistrate,** or **headmaster.** [C19: originally thieves' jargon]

beak+er ('bi:kə) *n.* **1.** a cup usually having a wide mouth: *a plastic beaker.* **2.** a cylindrical flat-bottomed container used in laboratories, usually made of glass and having a pouring lip. **3.** the amount a beaker holds. [C14: from Old Norse *bikarr;* related to Old High German *behhāri,* Middle Dutch *bēker* beaker, Greek *bikos* earthenware jug]

Beak+er folk *n.* a prehistoric people thought to have originated in the Iberian peninsula and spread to central Europe and Britain during the second millennium B.C. [named after the beakers found among their remains]

be-all and end-all *n. Informal.* **1.** the ultimate aim or justification: *to provide help for others is the be-all and end-all of this group.* **2.** *Often humorous.* a person or thing considered to be beyond improvement.

beam (bi:m) *n.* **1.** a long thick straight-sided piece of wood, metal, concrete, etc., esp. one used as a horizontal structural member. **2.** any rigid member or structure that is loaded transversely. **3.** the breadth of a ship or boat taken at its widest part, usually amidships. **4.** a ray or column of light, as from a beacon. **5.** a broad smile. **6.** one of the two cylindrical rollers on a loom, one of which holds the warp threads before weaving, the other the finished work. **7.** the main stem of a deer's antler from which the smaller branches grow. **8.** the central shaft of a plough to which all the main parts are attached. **9.** a narrow unidirectional flow of electromagnetic radiation or particles: *a beam of light; an electron beam.* **10.** the horizontal centrally pivoted bar in a balance. **11.** *Informal.* the width of the hips (esp. in the phrase **broad in the beam**). **12. a beam in one's eye.** a fault or grave error greater in oneself than in another person. **13. off (the) beam. a.** not following a radio beam to maintain a course. **b.** *Informal.* wrong, mistaken, or irrelevant. **14. on the beam. a.** following a radio beam to maintain a course. **b.** *Nautical.* opposite the beam of a vessel; abeam. **c.** *Informal.* correct, relevant, or appropriate. ~*vb.* **15.** to send out or radiate (rays of light). **16.** *(tr.)* to divert or aim (a radio signal or broadcast, light, etc.) in a certain direction: *to beam a programme to Tokyo.* **17.** *(intr.)* to smile broadly with pleasure or satisfaction. [Old English *beam;* related to Gothic *bagms* tree, Old High German *boum* tree] —**'beam+less** *adj.* —**'beam+,like** *adj.* —**'beam·y** *adj.*

beam aer+i·al *n.* an aerial system, such as a Yagi aerial, having directional properties.

beam com+pass *n.* an instrument for drawing large circles or arcs, consisting of a horizontal beam along which two vertical legs slide. Also called: **trammel.**

beam-ends *pl. n.* **1.** the ends of a vessel's beams. **2. on her beam-ends.** (of a vessel) heeled over through an angle of 90°. **3. on one's beam-ends. a.** out of resources; destitute. **b.** desperate.

beam hole *n.* a hole in the shield of a nuclear reactor through which a beam of radiation, esp. of neutrons, is allowed to escape for experimental purposes.

beam rid+ing *n.* a method of missile guidance in which the missile steers itself along the axis of a conically scanned microwave beam. —**beam rid+er** *n.*

bean (bi:n) *n.* **1.** any of various papilionaceous plants of the widely cultivated genus *Phaseolus* producing edible seeds in pods. See **French bean, lima bean, scarlet runner, string bean. 2.** any of several other papilionaceous plants that bear edible pods or seeds, such as the broad bean and soya bean. **3.** any of various other plants whose seeds are produced in pods or podlike fruits. **4.** the seed or pod of any of these plants. **5.** *U.S. slang* another word for **head. 6. not have a bean.** *Slang.* to be without money: *I haven't got a bean.* **7. full of beans.** *Informal.* **a.** full of energy and vitality. **b.** *U.S.* mistaken; erroneous. **8. spill the beans.** *Informal.* to disclose something confidential. ~*vb.* **9.** *Chiefly U.S. slang.* *(tr.)* to hit (a person) on the head. [Old English *bēan;* related to Old Norse *baun,* Old Frisian *bāne,* Old High German *bōna* bean]

bean+bag ('bi:n,bæg) *n.* a small cloth bag filled with dried beans and thrown in games.

bean ca+per *n.* a shrub, *Zygophyllum fabago,* of E Mediterranean regions, whose flower buds are eaten as a substitute for capers: family *Zygophyllaceae.*

bean+er·y ('bi:nərɪ) *n., pl.* **+er·ies.** *Informal.* a cheap restaurant.

bean+feast ('bi:n,fi:st) *n. Brit. informal.* **1.** an annual dinner given by employers to employees. **2.** any festive or merry occasion.

bean·ie *or* **bean·y** ('bi:nɪ) *n., pl.* **bean·ies.** *Chiefly U.S.* a round close-fitting hat resembling a skullcap.

bean·o ('bi:nəʊ) *n., pl.* **bean·os.** *Brit. slang.* a celebration, party, or other enjoyable time.

bean+pole ('bi:n,pəʊl) *n.* **1.** a tall stick or pole used to support bean plants. **2.** *Slang.* a tall thin person.

bean sprout *n.* the sprout of newly germinated millet, eaten as a vegetable, esp. in Chinese dishes.

bean tree *n.* any of various trees having beanlike pods, such as the catalpa and carob.

bear[1] (bɛə) *vb.* **bears, bear+ing, bore, borne.** *(mainly tr.)* **1.** to support or hold up; sustain. **2.** to bring or convey: *to bear gifts.* **3.** to take, accept, or assume the responsibility of: *to bear an expense.* **4.** *(past participle* **born** *in passive use)* to give birth to: *to bear children.* **5.** *(also intr.)* to produce by or as if by natural growth: *to bear fruit.* **6.** to tolerate or endure: *she couldn't bear him.* **7.** to admit of; sustain: *his story does not bear scrutiny.* **8.** to hold in the conscious mind or in one's feelings: *to bear a grudge; I'll bear that idea in mind.* **9.** to show or be marked with: *he still bears the scars.* **10.** to transmit or spread: *to bear gossip.* **11.** to render or supply (esp. in the phrase **bear witness**). **12.** to conduct or manage (oneself, the body, etc.): *she bore her head high.* **13.** to have, be, or stand in (relation or comparison): *his account bears no relation to the facts.* **14.** *(intr.)* to move, be located, or lie in a specified direction: *the way bears east.* **15.** to have by right; be entitled to (esp. in the phrase **bear title**). **16. bear a hand.** to give assistance. **17. bring to bear.** to bring into operation or effect: *he brought his knowledge to bear on the situation.* ~See also **bear down, bear off, bear on, bear out, bear up, bear with, born.** [Old English *beran;* related to Old Norse *bera,* Old High German *beran* to carry, Latin *ferre,* Greek *pherein* to bear, Sanskrit *bharati* he carries]

bear[2] (bɛə) *n., pl.* **bears** *or* **bear. 1.** any plantigrade mammals of the family *Ursidae:* order *Carnivora* (carnivores). Bears are typically massive omnivorous animals with a large head, a long shaggy coat, and strong claws. See also **black bear, brown bear, polar bear. 2.** any of various bearlike animals, such as the koala and the ant bear. **3.** a clumsy, churlish, or ill-mannered person. **4.** a teddy bear. **5.** *Stock Exchange.* **a.** a speculator who sells in anticipation of falling prices to make a profit on repurchase. **b.** *(as modifier): a bear market.* Compare **bull**[1] (sense 5). ~*vb.* **bears, bear+ing, beared. 6.** *(tr.)* to lower or attempt to lower the price or prices of (a stock market or a security) by speculative selling. [Old English *bera;* related to Old Norse *bjorn,* Old High German *bero*]

Bear (bɛə) *n.* **the. 1.** the English name for either **Ursa Major (Great Bear)** or **Ursa Minor (Little Bear). 2.** an informal name for **Russia.**

bear+a·ble ('bɛərəbᵊl) *adj.* endurable; tolerable. —**'bear+a·bly** *adv.*

bear-bait·ing *n.* (formerly) an entertainment in which dogs attacked and enraged a chained bear.

bear+ber·ry ('bɛəbərɪ) *n., pl.* **·ries. 1.** a trailing evergreen ericaceous shrub, *Arctostaphylos uva-ursi,* with small pinkish-white flowers, red berries, and astringent leaves. **2. alpine** or **black bearberry.** a related species, *A. alpina* of European mountains, having black berries.

bear+cat ('bɛə,kæt) *n.* another name for **lesser panda** (see **panda** (sense 2)).

beard (bɪəd) *n.* **1.** the hair growing on the lower parts of a man's face. **2.** any similar growth in animals. **3.** a tuft of long hairs in plants such as barley and wheat; awn. **4.** the gills of an oyster. **5.** a barb, as on an arrow or fish-hook. **6.** *Printing.* the part of a piece of type that connects the face with the shoulder. ~*vb. (tr.)* **7.** to oppose boldly or impertinently. **8.** to pull or grasp the beard of. [Old English *beard;* related to Old Norse *barth,* Old High German *bart,* Latin *barba*] —**'beard+ed** *adj.*

beard+ed liz+ard *or* **drag+on** *n.* a large Australian lizard, *Amphibolus barbatus,* having a pouch beneath the jaw that is distended when the animal is threatened. Also called: **jew lizard.**

beard+ed tit *n.* another name for **reedling.**

beard+ed vul+ture *n.* another name for **lammergeier.**

beard+less ('bɪədlɪs) *adj.* **1.** without a beard. **2.** too young to grow a beard; immature. —**'beard+less+ness** *n.*

bear down *vb. (intr., adv.;* often foll. by *on* or *upon)* **1.** to press or weigh down. **2.** to approach in a determined or threatening manner. **3.** (of a vessel) to make an approach (to another vessel, obstacle, etc.) from windward. **4.** (of a woman during childbirth) to exert a voluntary muscular pressure to assist delivery.

Beards·ley ('bɪədzlɪ) *n.* **Au·brey (Vincent).** 1872–98, English illustrator: noted for his stylized black-and-white illustrations, esp. those for Oscar Wilde's *Salome* and Pope's *Rape of the Lock.*

bear+er ('bɛərə) *n.* **1.** a person or thing that bears, presents, or upholds. **2.** a person who presents a note or bill for payment. **3.** (in Africa, India, etc., formerly) **a.** a native carrier, esp. on an expedition. **b.** a native servant. **4.** See **pallbearer. 5.** the holder of a rank, position, office, etc. **6.** (*modifier*) *Finance.* payable to the person in possession: *bearer bonds.*

bear gar·den *n.* **1.** (formerly) a place where bears were exhibited and where bear-baiting took place. **2.** a place or scene of tumult and disorder.

bear hug *n.* **1.** a wrestling hold in which the arms are locked tightly round an opponent's chest and arms. **2.** any similar tight embrace.

bear·ing ('bɛərɪŋ) *n.* **1.** a support, guide, or locating piece for a rotating or reciprocating mechanical part. **2.** (foll. by *on* or *upon*) relevance (to): *it has no bearing on this problem.* **3.** a person's general social conduct, esp. in manners, dress, and behaviour. **4. a.** the act, period, or capability of producing fruit or young. **b.** an amount produced; yield. **5.** the part of a beam or lintel that rests on a support. **6.** anything that carries weight or acts as a support. **7.** the angular direction of a line, point, or course measured from true north or south (**true bearing**), magnetic north or south (**magnetic bearing**), or one's own position. **8.** (*usually pl.*) the position or direction, as of a ship, fixed with reference to two or more known points. **9.** (*usually pl.*) a sense of one's relative position or situation; orientation (esp. in the phrases **lose, get,** *or* **take one's bearings**). **10.** *Heraldry.* **a.** a device or emblem on a heraldic shield; charge. **b.** another name for **coat of arms.**

bear·ing rein *n. Chiefly Brit.* a rein from the bit to the saddle, designed to keep the horse's head in the desired position. Usual U.S. word: **checkrein.**

bear·ish ('bɛərɪʃ) *adj.* **1.** like a bear; rough; clumsy; churlish. **2.** *Stock Exchange.* causing, expecting, or characterized by a fall in prices: *a bearish market.* —**'bear·ish·ly** *adv.* —**'bear·ish·ness** *n.*

Bé·ar·naise (ˌbeɪə'neɪz) *n.* a rich sauce made from egg yolks, lemon juice or wine vinegar, butter, shallots, herbs, and seasoning. [French, from *Béarn* in SW France]

bear off *vb.* (*adv.*) *Nautical.* (of a vessel) to avoid hitting an obstacle, another vessel, etc., by swerving onto a different course.

bear on *vb.* (*intr., prep.*) **1.** to be relevant to; relate to. **2.** to be burdensome to or afflict: *his misdeeds bore heavily on his conscience.*

bear out *vb.* (*tr., adv.*) to show to be true or truthful; confirm: *the witness will bear me out.*

bear's-breech *or* **bear's-breech·es** *n.* a widely cultivated S European acanthus plant, *Acanthus mollis,* having whitish purple-veined flowers.

bear's-ear *n.* another name for **auricula** (sense 1).

bear's-foot *n.* either of two Eurasian hellebore plants, *Helleborus foetidus* or *H. viridis,* having leaves shaped like the foot and claws of a bear.

bear·skin ('bɛəˌskɪn) *n.* **1.** the pelt of a bear, esp. when used as a rug. **2.** a tall helmet of black fur worn by certain regiments in the British Army. **3.** a rough shaggy woollen cloth, used for overcoats.

bear up *vb.* (*intr., adv.*) to endure cheerfully.

bear with *vb.* (*intr., prep.*) to be patient with: *bear with me while I tell you my story.*

bear·wood ('bɛəˌwʊd) *n.* another name for **cascara** (sense 2).

beast (bi:st) *n.* **1.** any animal other than man, esp. a large wild quadruped. **2.** savage nature or characteristics: *the beast in man.* **3.** a brutal, uncivilized, or filthy person. [C13: from Old French *beste,* from Latin *bestia,* of obscure origin]

beast·ings ('bi:stɪŋz) *n.* a U.S. spelling of **beestings.**

beast·ly ('bi:stlɪ) *adj.* **·li·er, ·li·est. 1.** *Informal.* unpleasant; disagreeable; nasty: *beastly weather.* **2.** *Obsolete.* of or like a beast; bestial. ~*adv.* **3.** *Informal.* (intensifier): *the weather is so beastly hot.* —**'beast·li·ness** *n.*

beast of bur·den *n.* an animal, such as a donkey or ox, used for carrying loads.

beat (bi:t) *vb.* **beats, beat·ing, beat; beat·en** *or* **beat. 1.** (when *intr.*, often foll. by *against, on,* etc.) to strike with or as if with a series of violent blows; dash or pound repeatedly (against). **2.** (*tr.*) to punish by striking; flog. **3.** to move or cause to move up and down; flap: *the bird beat its wings heavily.* **4.** (*intr.*) to throb rhythmically; pulsate: *her heart beat fast.* **5.** (*tr.*) to make (one's way) by or as if by blows: *she beat her way out of the crowd.* **6.** (*tr.;* sometimes foll. by *up*) *Cookery.* to stir or whisk (an ingredient or mixture) vigorously. **7.** (*tr.;* sometimes foll. by *out*) to shape, make thin, or flatten (a piece of metal) by repeated blows. **8.** (*tr.*) *Music.* to indicate (pulse or time) by the motion of one's hand, baton, etc., or by the action of a metronome. **9.** (when *tr.*, sometimes foll. by *out*) to produce (a sound or signal) by or as if by striking a drum. **10.** to sound or cause to sound, by or as if by beating: *beat the drums!* **11.** to overcome (an opponent) in a contest, battle, etc. **12.** (*tr.;* often foll. by *back, down, off,* etc.) to drive, push, or thrust. **13.** (*tr.*) to counteract or overcome: *they set off early to beat the rush hour.* **14.** to scour (woodlands, coverts, or undergrowth) so as to rouse game for shooting. **15.** (*tr.*) *Slang.* to puzzle or baffle: *it beats me how he can do that.* **16.** (*intr.*) *Physics.* (of sounds or electrical signals) to combine and produce a pulsating sound or signal. **17.** (*intr.*) *Nautical.* to steer a sailing vessel as close as possible to the direction from which the wind is blowing. **18.** (*tr.*) *U.S. slang.* to cheat or defraud: *he beat his brother out of the inheritance.* **19. beat about the bush.** *Informal.* to be diverted or distracted from the point at issue; avoid the issue. **20. beat a retreat.** to withdraw or depart in haste. **21. beat it.** *Slang.* (*often imperative*) to go away. **22. beat one's brains (out).** *Slang.* to try to find ideas, a solution, etc. **23. beat someone's brains out.** *Slang.* to kill by knocking severely about the head. **24. beat someone to it.** *Informal.* to reach a place or achieve an objective before someone else. **25. beat the bounds. a.** *Brit.* (formerly) to define the boundaries of a parish by making a procession around them and hitting the ground with rods. **b.** to define the scope or limit, as of a topic or discussion. **26. can you beat it** *or* **that?** *Slang.* an expression of utter amazement or surprise. ~*n.* **27.** a stroke or blow. **28.** the sound made by a stroke or blow. **29.** a regular sound or stroke; throb. **30.** an assigned or habitual round or route, as of a policeman or sentry. **31.** the basic rhythmic unit in a piece of music, usually grouped in twos, threes, or fours. **32. a.** pop or rock music characterized by a heavy rhythmic beat. **b.** (*as modifier*): *a beat group.* **33.** *Physics.* one of the regular pulses produced by combining two sounds or electrical signals that have similar frequencies. **34.** *Horology.* the impulse given to the balance wheel by the action of the escapement. **35.** *Prosody.* the accent, stress, or ictus in a metrical foot. **36.** *Nautical.* a course that steers a sailing vessel as close as possible to the direction from which the wind is blowing. **37. a.** the act of scouring for game by beating. **b.** the organized scouring of a particular woodland so as to rouse the game in it. **c.** the woodland where game is so roused. **38.** short for **beatnik. 39.** *Fencing.* a sharp tap with one's blade on an opponent's blade to deflect it. **40.** (*modifier*) (*often cap.*) of, characterized by, or relating to the Beat Generation: *a beat poet; beat philosophy.* ~*adj.* **41.** (*postpositive*) *Slang.* totally exhausted. ~See also **beat down, beat up.** [Old English *bēatan;* related to Old Norse *bauta,* Old High German *bōzan*] —**'beat·a·ble** *adj.*

beat down *vb.* (*adv.*) **1.** (*tr.*) *Informal.* to force or persuade (a seller) to accept a lower price: *I beat him down three pounds.* **2.** (*intr.*) (of the sun) to shine intensely; be very hot.

beat·en ('bi:tᵊn) *adj.* **1.** defeated or baffled. **2.** shaped or made thin by hammering: *a bowl of beaten gold.* **3.** much travelled; well trodden (esp. in the phrase **the beaten track**). **4. off the beaten track. a.** in or into unfamiliar territory. **b.** out of the ordinary; unusual. **5.** (of food) mixed by beating; whipped. **6.** tired out; exhausted. **7.** *Hunting.* (of woods, undergrowth, etc.) scoured so as to rouse game.

beat·er ('bi:tə) *n.* **1.** a person who beats or hammers: *a panel beater.* **2.** an instrument or device used for beating: *a carpet beater.* **3.** a person who rouses wild game

Beat Gen·er·a·tion *n.* (*functioning as sing. or pl.*) members of the generation that came to maturity in the 1950s, whose rejection of the social and political systems of the West was expressed through contempt for regular work, possessions, traditional dress, etc.

be·a·tif·ic (ˌbi:ə'tɪfɪk) *adj.* **1.** displaying great happiness, calmness, etc.: *a beatific smile.* **2.** of, conferring, or relating to a state of celestial happiness. [C17: from Late Latin *beātificus,* from Latin *beātus,* from *beāre* to bless + *facere* to make] —ˌ**be·a·'tif·i·cal·ly** *adv.*

be·at·i·fy (bɪ'ætɪˌfaɪ) *vb.* **·fies, ·fy·ing, ·fied. 1.** (*tr.*) *R.C. Church.* (of the pope) to declare formally that (a deceased person) showed a heroic degree of holiness in his or her life and therefore is worthy of public veneration: the first step towards canonization. **2.** (*tr.*) to make extremely happy. [C16: from Old French *beatifier,* from Late Latin *beātificāre* to make blessed; see BEATIFIC] —**be·at·i·fi·ca·tion** (bɪˌætɪfɪ'keɪʃən) *n.*

beat·ing ('bi:tɪŋ) *n.* **1.** a whipping or thrashing, as in punishment. **2.** a defeat or setback. **3. take some** *or* **a lot of beating.** to be difficult to improve upon.

be·at·i·tude (bɪ'ætɪˌtju:d) *n.* **1.** supreme blessedness or happiness. **2.** an honorific title of the Eastern Christian Church, applied to those of patriarchal rank. [C15: from Latin *beātitūdō,* from *beātus* blessed; see BEATIFIC]

Be·at·i·tude (bɪ'ætɪˌtju:d) *n. New Testament.* any of eight distinctive sayings of Jesus in the Sermon on the Mount (Matthew 5:1-8) in which he declares that the poor, the meek, those that mourn, the merciful, the peacemakers, the pure of heart, those that thirst for justice, and those that are persecuted will, in various ways, receive the blessings of heaven.

Beat·les ('bi:tᵊlz) *pl. n.* **the.** English rock group (1962–70) from Liverpool: comprised John **Lennon,** Paul **McCartney,** George **Harrison,** and Ringo **Starr.** Their hit singles include *Please please me* (1963), *I want to hold your hand* (1964), *Can't buy me love* (1964), *Penny Lane* (1967), and *Hey Jude* (1968); their many albums include *A Hard Day's Night* (film soundtrack, 1964), *Help!* (film soundtrack, 1965), *Revolver* (1966) *Sergeant Pepper's Lonely Hearts Club Band* (1967), *Abbey Road* (1969), and *Let it be* (1970). Much of their material was written by Lennon and McCartney.

beat·nik ('bi:tnɪk) *n.* **1.** a member of the Beat Generation. **2.** *Informal.* any person with long hair and shabby clothes. [C20: from BEAT (n.) + -NIK, by analogy with SPUTNIK]

Be·at·rice ('bi:ətrɪs) *n.* full name *Beatrix Wilhelmina Armgard.* born 1938, queen of the Netherlands from 1980.

Beat·ty ('bi:tɪ) *n.* **Da·vid,** 1st Earl Beatty. 1871–1936, British admiral of the fleet in World War I.

beat up *Informal.* ~*vb.* **1.** (*tr., adv.*) to strike or kick (a person), usually repeatedly, so as to inflict severe physical damage. ~*adj.* **beat-up. 2.** *Chiefly U.S.* worn-out; dilapidated.

beau (bəʊ) *n., pl.* **beaus** (bəʊz) *or* **beaux** (bəʊ, bəʊz). **1.** a lover, sweetheart, or escort of a girl or woman. **2.** a man who is greatly concerned with his clothes and appearance; dandy. [C17: from French, from Old French *biau,* from Latin *bellus* handsome, charming]

Beau·fort scale ('bəʊfət) *n. Meteorol.* an international scale of wind velocities ranging for practical purposes from 0 (calm) to

12 (hurricane force). [C19: after Sir Francis *Beaufort* (1774–1857), English admiral who devised it]

Beau+fort Sea *n.* part of the Arctic Ocean off the N coast of North America.

beau geste *French.* (bo 'ʒɛst) *n., pl.* ***beaux gestes*** (bo 'ʒɛst). a noble or gracious gesture or act, esp. one that is meaningless. [literally: beautiful gesture]

Beau·har·nais (*French* boar'nɛ) *n.* **1. Hor·tense de Eu·gène de** (ɔr'tɑ̃s də ø'ʒɛn də), son of Joséphine. 1781–1824, viceroy of Italy (1805–14) for his stepfather Napoleon I. **2. Hor·tense de,** daughter of Joséphine. 1783–1837, queen of Holland (1806–10) as wife of Louis Bonaparte. **3. Jo·sé·phine de** (ʒoze'fin də). See (Empress) **Josephine.**

beau i·de·al *French.* (bo ide'al) *n., pl.* ***beaux i·de·als*** (bo zide'al). perfect beauty or excellence.

beau+jo+lais ('bəʊʒə,leɪ) *n.* (*sometimes cap.*) a popular fresh-tasting red or white wine from southern Burgundy in France.

Beau·mar·chais (*French* bomar'ʃɛ) *n.* **Pierre Au·gus·tin Ca·ron de** (pjɛːr ogystɛ̃ ka'rɔ̃ də). 1732–99, French dramatist, noted for his comedies *The Barber of Seville* (1775) and *The Marriage of Figaro* (1784).

beau monde ('bəʊ 'mɒnd; *French* bo 'mɔ̃ːd) *n.* the world of fashion and society. [C18: French, literally: fine world]

Beau+mont[1] ('bəʊmɒnt) *n.* a city in SE Texas. Pop.: 112 620 (1973 est.).

Beau·mont[2] ('bəʊmɒnt) *n.* **1. Fran·cis.** 1584–1616, English dramatist, who collaborated with John Fletcher in plays including *The Knights of the Burning Pestle* (1607) and *The Maid's Tragedy* (1611). **2. Wil·liam.** 1785–1853, U.S. surgeon, noted for his pioneering work on digestion.

Beaune (bəʊn) *n.* **1.** a city in E France, near Dijon: an important trading centre for Burgundy wines. Pop.: 19 972 (1975). **2.** a wine produced in this district.

beaut (bjuːt) *Slang, chiefly Austral.* ~*n.* **1.** a person or thing that is outstanding or distinctive. ~*adj., interj.* **2.** good or excellent: an expression of approval.

beau+te+ous ('bjuːtɪəs) *adj.* a poetic word for **beautiful.** —**'beau+te+ous+ly** *adv.* —**'beau+te+ous+ness** *n.*

beau+ti+cian (bjuː'tɪʃən) *n.* a person who works in or manages a beauty salon.

beau+ti+ful ('bjuːtɪfʊl) *adj.* **1.** possessing beauty; aesthetically pleasing. **2.** highly enjoyable; very pleasant: *the party was beautiful.* —**'beau+ti+ful+ness** *n.*

beau+ti+ful+ly ('bjuːtɪflɪ) *adv.* **1.** in a beautiful manner. **2.** *Informal.* (intensifier): *you did beautifully well in the race.*

beau+ti+fy ('bjuːtɪ,faɪ) *vb.* **+fies, +fy+ing, +fied.** to make or become beautiful. —**beau+ti+fi+ca+tion** (,bjuːtɪfɪ'keɪʃən) *n.* —**,beau+ti+'fi+er** *n.*

beau+ty ('bjuːtɪ) *n., pl.* **+ties. 1.** the combination of all the qualities of a person or thing that delight the senses and please the mind. **2.** a very attractive and well-formed girl or woman. **3.** *Informal.* an outstanding example of its kind: *the horse is a beauty.* **4.** *Informal.* an advantageous feature: *one beauty of the job is the short hours.* **5.** *Informal.* a light-hearted and affectionate term of address: *hello, my old beauty!* ~*interj.* **6.** *Austral. slang.* an expression of approval or agreement. [C13: from Old French *biauté,* from *biau* beautiful; see BEAU]

beau+ty queen *n.* an attractive young woman, esp. one who has won a beauty contest.

beau+ty sal+on *or* **par+lour** *n.* an establishment providing women with services to improve their beauty, such as hairdressing, manicuring, facial treatment, and massage.

beau+ty sleep *n. Informal.* sleep, esp. sleep before midnight.

beau+ty spot *n.* **1.** a small dark-coloured patch or spot worn on a lady's face as an adornment or as a foil to her complexion. **2.** a mole or other similar natural mark on the skin. **3.** a place of outstanding beauty.

Beau+vais (*French* bo'vɛ) *n.* a market town in N France, 64 km (40 miles) northwest of Paris. Pop.: 56 725 (1975).

Beau·voir (*French* bo'vwaːr) *n.* **Si·mone de** (si'mɔn də). born 1908, French existentialist novelist and feminist, whose works include *Le sang des autres* (1944), *Le deuxième sexe* (1949), and *Les mandarins* (1954).

beaux (bəʊ, bəʊz) *n.* a plural of **beau.**

beaux-arts (bəʊ'zɑː) *pl. n.* **1.** another word for **fine art. 2.** (*modifier*) relating to the classical decorative style, esp. that of the École des Beaux-Arts in Paris: *beaux-arts influences.* [French]

bea+ver[1] ('biːvə) *n.* **1.** a large amphibious rodent, *Castor fiber,* of Europe, Asia, and North America: family *Castoridae.* It has soft brown fur, a broad flat hairless tail, and webbed hind feet, and constructs complex dams and houses (lodges) in rivers. **2.** the fur of this animal. **3. mountain beaver.** a burrowing rodent, *Aplodontia rufa,* of W North America: family *Aplodontidae.* **4.** a tall hat of beaver fur or a fabric resembling it, worn, esp. by men, during the 19th century. **5.** a woollen napped cloth resembling beaver fur, formerly much used for overcoats, etc. **6.** a greyish- or yellowish-brown. **7.** *Obsolete.* a full beard. **8.** a bearded man. **9.** (*modifier*) having the colour of beaver or made of beaver fur or some similar material: *a beaver lamb coat; a beaver stole.* ~*vb.* **10.** (*intr.;* usually foll. by *away*) *Brit. informal.* to work industriously or steadily. [Old English *beofor;* compare Old Norse *biōrr,* Old High German *bibar,* Latin *fiber,* Sanskrit *babhrú* red-brown]

bea+ver[2] ('biːvə) *n.* a movable piece on a medieval helmet used to protect the lower part of the face. [C15: from Old French *baviere,* from *baver* to dribble]

Bea·ver+board ('biːvə,bɔːd) *n. Trademark.* a stiff light board of compressed wood fibre, used esp. to surface partitions.

Bea·ver·brook ('biːvə,brʊk) *n.* **1st Baron,** title of *William Maxwell Aitken.* 1879–1964, British newspaper proprietor and Conservative politician, born in Canada, whose newspapers included the *Daily Express;* minister of information (1918); minister of aircraft production (1940–41).

be+bee+rine (bə'bɪəriːn, -rɪn) *n.* an alkaloid, resembling quinine, obtained from the bark of the greenheart and other plants. [from German *Bebeerin;* see BEBEERU, -INE[2]]

be+bee+ru (bə'bɪəruː) *n.* another name for **greenheart** (sense 1). [C19: from Spanish *bibirú,* of Carib origin]

Be·bel (*German* 'beːbəl) *n.* **Au·gust** ('aʊgʊst). 1840–1913, German socialist leader: one of the founders of the Social Democratic Party (1869).

Beb+ing+ton ('bɛbɪŋtən) *n.* a town in NW England, in Merseyside: docks and chemical works. Pop.: 61 488 (1971).

be+bop ('biːbɒp) *n.* the full name for **bop**[1] (sense 1). [C20: imitative of the rhythm of the music] —**'be+bop+per** *n.*

be+calmed (bɪ'kɑːmd) *adj.* (of a sailing boat or ship) motionless through lack of wind.

be+came (bɪ'keɪm) *vb.* the past tense of **become.**

be+cause (bɪ'kɒz, -'kəz) *conj.* **1.** (*subordinating*) on account of the fact that; on account of being; since: *because it's so cold we'll go home.* ~ **2. because of.** (*prep.*) on account of; due to: *I lost my job because of her.* [C14 *bi cause,* from *bi* BY + CAUSE]

Usage. See at **reason.**

bec+ca+fi+co (,bɛkə'fiːkəʊ) *n., pl.* **+cos.** any of various European songbirds, esp. warblers of the genus *Sylvia,* eaten as a delicacy in Italy and other countries. [C17: from Italian, from *beccare* to peck + *fico* fig, from Latin *fīcus*]

bé+cha+mel sauce (,beɪʃə'mɛl) *n.* a thick white sauce flavoured with onion and seasonings. [C18: named after the Marquis of *Béchamel,* steward of Louis XIV of France and its inventor]

be+chance (bɪ'tʃɑːns) *vb.* (*intr.*) *Archaic.* to happen (to).

Bé+char (*French* be'ʃaːr) *n.* a city in NW Algeria: an oasis. Pop.: 27 000 (1967). Former name: **Colomb-Béchar.**

bêche-de-mer (,bɛʃdə'mɛə) *n., pl.* **bêches-de-mer** (,bɛʃdə'mɛə) *or* **bêche-de-mer. 1.** another name for **trepang. 2.** See **Beach-la-Mar.** [C19: quasi-French, from earlier English *biche de mer,* from Portuguese *bicho do mar* worm of the sea]

Bech·et ('bɛʃeɪ) *n.* **Sid·ney.** 1897–1959, U.S. jazz soprano saxophonist and clarinettist.

Bech·ua+na (bɛ'tʃwɑːnə; ,bɛtʃʊ'ɑːnə, ,bɛkjʊ-) *n., pl.* **+na** *or* **+nas. 1.** a former name for **Tswana. 2.** a former name for a member of the Bantu people of Botswana.

Bech·ua+na+land (bɛ'tʃwɑːnə,lænd; ,bɛtʃʊ'ɑːnə,lænd, ,bɛkjʊ-) *n.* the former name (until 1966) of **Botswana.**

beck[1] (bɛk) *n.* **1.** a nod, wave, or other gesture or signal. **2. at (someone's) beck and call.** ready to obey (someone's) orders instantly; subject to (someone's) slightest whim. [C14: short for *becnen* to BECKON]

beck[2] (bɛk) *n.* (in N England) a stream, esp. a swiftly flowing one. [Old English *becc,* from Old Norse *bekkr;* related to Old English *bece,* Old Saxon *beki,* Old High German *bah* brook, Sanskrit *bhanga* wave]

beck+et ('bɛkɪt) *n. Nautical.* **1.** a clevis forming part of one end of a sheave, used for securing standing lines by means of a thimble. **2.** a short line with a grommet or eye at one end and a knot at the other, used for securing spars or other gear in place. [C18: of unknown origin]

Beck·et ('bɛkɪt) *n.* **Saint Thom·as.** 1118–70, English prelate; chancellor (1155–62) to Henry II; archbishop of Canterbury (1162–70): murdered following his opposition to Henry's attempts to control the clergy.

beck+et bend *n.* another name for **sheet bend.**

Beck·ett ('bɛkɪt) *n.* **Sam·u·el.** born 1906, Irish dramatist and novelist writing in French and English, whose works portray the human condition as insignificant or absurd in a bleak universe. They include the plays *En attendant Godot* (*Waiting for Godot,* 1952) and *Fin de partie* (*Endgame,* 1957) and the novel *Malone meurt* (*Malone Dies,* 1951): Nobel prize for literature 1969.

Beck·ford ('bɛkfəd) *n.* **Wil·liam.** 1759–1844, English writer and dilettante; author of the oriental romance *Vathek* (1787).

Beck·mann (*German* 'bɛkman) *n.* **Max** (maks). 1884–1950, German expressionist painter.

beck+on ('bɛkən) *vb.* **1.** to summon with a gesture of the hand or head. **2.** to entice or lure. ~*n.* **3.** a summoning gesture. [Old English *bīecnan,* from *bēacen* sign; related to Old Saxon *bōknian;* see BEACON] —**'beck+on+er** *n.*

be+cloud (bɪ'klaʊd) *vb.* (*tr.*) **1.** to cover or obscure with a cloud. **2.** to confuse or muddle: *to becloud the issues.*

be+come (bɪ'kʌm) *vb.* **+comes, +com+ing, +came, +come.** (*mainly intr.*) **1.** (*copula*) to come to be; develop or grow into: *he became a monster.* **2.** (foll. by *of; usually used in a question*) to fall to or be the lot (of); happen (to): *what became of him?* **3.** (*tr.*) (of clothes, etc.) to enhance the appearance of (someone); suit: *that dress becomes you.* [Old English *becuman* to happen; related to Old High German *biqueman* to come to, Gothic *biquiman* to appear suddenly]

be+com+ing (bɪ'kʌmɪŋ) *adj.* **1.** suitable; appropriate. ~*n.* **2.** any process of change. **3.** (in the philosophy of Aristotle) any change from the lower level of potentiality to the higher level of actuality. —**be+'com+ing+ly** *adv.* —**be+'com+ing+ness** *n.*

Bec·que·rel (*French* bɛ'krɛl) *n.* **An·toine Hen·ri** (ɑ̃twan ɑ̃'ri). 1852–1908, French physicist, who discovered the photographic action of the rays emitted by uranium salts and so instigated the study of radioactivity: Nobel prize for physics, 1903.

bed (bɛd) *n.* **1.** a piece of furniture on which to sleep. **2.** the mattress and bedclothes on such a piece of furniture: *an unmade bed.* **3.** sleep or rest: *time for bed.* **4.** any place in which a person or animal sleeps or rests. **5.** *Informal.* a place for sexual intercourse. **6.** *Informal.* sexual intercourse. **7.** a plot of ground in which plants are grown, esp. when considered together with the plants in it: *a flower bed.* **8.** the bottom of a river, lake, or sea. **9.** a part of this used for cultivation of a plant or animal: *oyster beds.* **10.** a layer of crushed rock, gravel, etc., used as a foundation for a road, railway, etc. **11.** a layer of mortar in a masonry wall. **12.** the underside of a brick, tile, slate, etc., when in position. Compare **back** (sense 12). **13.** any underlying structure or part. **14.** a layer of rock, esp. sedimentary rock. **15.** the flat part of a letterpress printing press onto or against which the type forme is placed. **16. a bed of roses.** a situation of comfort or ease. **17. be brought to bed (of).** *Archaic.* to give birth (to). **18. get out of bed on the wrong side.** *Informal.* to be ill-tempered from the start of the day. **19. go to bed. a.** (often foll. by *with*) to have sexual intercourse (with). **b.** *Journalism, printing.* (of a newspaper, magazine, etc.) to go to press; start printing. **20. put to bed. a.** *Journalism.* to finalize work on (a newspaper, magazine, etc.) so that it is ready to go to press. **b.** *Letterpress printing.* to lock up the type forme of (a publication) in the press before printing. **21. take to one's bed.** to remain in bed, esp. because of illness. ~*vb.* **beds, bed+ding, bed+ded. 22.** (usually foll. by *down*) to go to or put into a place to sleep or rest. **23.** (*tr.*) to have sexual intercourse with. **24.** (*tr.*) to place, fix, or sink firmly into position; embed. **25.** *Geology.* to form or be arranged in a distinct layer; stratify. **26.** (*tr.*; often foll. by *out*) to plant in a bed of soil. [Old English *bedd;* related to Old Norse *bethr,* Old High German *betti,* Gothic *badi*]

B.Ed. *abbrev. for* Bachelor of Education.

bed and board *n.* **1.** sleeping accommodation and meals. **2. divorce from bed and board.** *U.S. law.* a form of divorce whereby the parties are prohibited from living together but the marriage is not dissolved.

bed and break+fast *Chiefly Brit. n.* **1.** (in a hotel, boarding house, etc.) overnight accommodation and breakfast. ~*adj.* **2.** *Informal.* (of a stock-exchange transaction) establishing a loss for tax purposes, shares being sold after hours one evening and bought back the next morning when the market opens.

be+daub (bɪˈdɔːb) *vb.* (*tr.*) **1.** to smear all over with something thick, sticky, or dirty. **2.** to ornament in a gaudy or vulgar fashion.

be+daz+zle (bɪˈdæzᵊl) *vb.* (*tr.*) to dazzle or confuse, as with brilliance. —**be+ˈdaz+zle+ment** *n.*

bed+bug (ˈbɛdˌbʌg) *n.* any of several bloodsucking insects of the heteropterous genus *Cimex,* esp. *C. lectularius* of temperate regions, having an oval flattened wingless body and infesting dirty houses: family *Cimicidae.*

bed+cham·ber (ˈbɛdˌtʃeɪmbə) *n.* an archaic word for **bedroom.**

bed+clothes (ˈbɛdˌkləʊðz) *pl. n.* sheets, blankets, and other coverings of a bed.

bed+da·ble (ˈbɛdəbᵊl) *adj.* sexually attractive.

bed+der (ˈbɛdə) *n.* **1.** *Brit.* (at Cambridge University) a college servant employed to keep students' rooms in order. **2.** a plant that may be grown in a garden bed.

bed+ding (ˈbɛdɪŋ) *n.* **1.** bedclothes, sometimes considered together with a mattress. **2.** litter, such as straw, for animals. **3.** something acting as a foundation, such as mortar under a brick. **4.** the arrangement of a mass of rocks into distinct layers; stratification.

bed+ding plant *n.* a plant that may be grown in a garden bed.

Bede (biːd) *n.* **Saint,** called *the Venerable Bede.* ?673–735 A.D., English monk, scholar, historian, and theologian, noted for his Latin *Ecclesiastical History of the English People* (731). Feast day: May 27.

be+deck (bɪˈdɛk) *vb.* (*tr.*) to cover with decorations; adorn.

be+del *or* **be+dell** (ˈbiːdᵊl) *n.* archaic spellings of **beadle** (sense 3).

bedes+man (ˈbiːdzmən) *n., pl.* **+men.** a variant spelling of **beadsman.**

be+dev+il (bɪˈdɛvᵊl) *vb.* **+ils, +il+ling, +illed** *or U.S.* **+ils, +il+ing, +iled.** (*tr.*) **1.** to harass or torment. **2.** to throw into confusion. **3.** to possess, as with a devil. —**be+ˈdev+il+ment** *n.*

be+dew (bɪˈdjuː) *vb.* (*tr.*) to wet or cover with or as if with drops of dew.

bed+fast (ˈbɛdˌfɑːst) *adj.* an archaic word for **bedridden.**

bed+fel·low (ˈbɛdˌfɛləʊ) *n.* **1.** a person with whom one shares a bed. **2.** a temporary ally or associate.

Bed+ford[1] (ˈbɛdfəd) *n.* **1.** a town in SE central England, administrative centre of Bedfordshire, on the River Ouse. Pop.: 73 064 (1971). **2.** short for **Bedfordshire.**

Bed·ford[2] (ˈbɛdfəd) *n.* **Duke of,** title of *John of Lancaster.* 1389–1435, son of Henry IV of England: protector of England and regent of France (1422–35).

Bed+ford cord *n.* a heavy corded cloth, similar to corduroy. [named after BEDFORD[1]]

Bed+ford+shire (ˈbɛdfədˌʃɪə, -ʃə) *n.* a county of S central England: mainly low-lying, with the Chiltern Hills in the south. Administrative centre: Bedford. Pop.: 491 700 (1976 est.). Area: 1232 sq. km (476 sq. miles). Abbrev.: **Beds.**

be+dight (bɪˈdaɪt) *Archaic.* ~*vb.* **+dights, +dight+ing, +dight** *or* **+dight+ed. 1.** (*tr.*) to array or adorn. ~*adj.* **2.** (*past participle of the verb*) adorned or bedecked. [C14: from DIGHT]

be+dim (bɪˈdɪm) *vb.* **+dims, +dim+ming, +dimmed.** (*tr.*) to make dim or obscure.

Bed·i·vere (ˈbɛdɪˌvɪə) *n.* **Sir.** (in Arthurian legend) a knight who took the dying King Arthur to the barge in which he was carried to Avalon.

be+di+zen (bɪˈdaɪzᵊn, -ˈdɪzᵊn) *vb.* (*tr.*) *Archaic.* to dress or decorate gaudily or tastelessly. [C17: from BE- + obsolete *dizen* to dress up, of uncertain origin] —**be+ˈdi+zen+ment** *n.*

bed+lam (ˈbɛdləm) *n.* **1.** a noisy confused place or situation; state of uproar: *his speech caused bedlam.* **2.** *Archaic.* a lunatic asylum; madhouse. [C13 *bedlem, bethlem,* after the Hospital of St. Mary of *Bethlehem* in London]

bed+lam+ite (ˈbɛdləˌmaɪt) *n. Archaic.* a lunatic; insane person.

Bed+ling+ton ter+ri+er (ˈbɛdlɪŋtən) *n.* a large breed of terrier with a thick white fleecy coat. Often shortened to **Bedlington.**

Bed+loe's Is+land (ˈbɛdləʊz) *or* **Bed+loe Is+land** *n.* the former name (until 1956) of **Liberty Island.**

bed mould+ing *n. Architect.* **1.** a moulding in an entablature between the corona and the frieze. **2.** any moulding below a projection.

Bed·ou+in *or* **Bed·u+in** (ˈbɛdʊɪn) *n.* **1.** (*pl.* **+ins** *or* **+in**) a member of any of the nomadic tribes of Arabs inhabiting the deserts of Arabia, Jordan, and Syria, as well as parts of the Sahara. **2.** a wanderer or rover. ~*adj.* **3.** of or relating to the Bedouins. **4.** wandering or roving. [C14: from Old French *beduin,* from Arabic *badāwī,* plural of *badawi,* from *badw* desert]

bed+pan (ˈbɛdˌpæn) *n.* **1.** a shallow vessel placed under a bedridden patient to collect his faeces and urine. **2.** another name for **warming pan.**

bed+plate (ˈbɛdˌpleɪt) *n.* a heavy metal platform or frame to which an engine or machine is attached.

bed+post (ˈbɛdˌpəʊst) *n.* **1.** any of the four vertical supports at the corners of a bedstead. **2. between you and me and the bedpost.** *Informal.* confidentially; in secret.

be+drag+gle (bɪˈdrægᵊl) *vb.* (*tr.*) to make (hair, clothing, etc.) limp, untidy, or dirty, as with rain or mud. —**be+ˈdrag+gled** *adj.*

bed+rail (ˈbɛdˌreɪl) *n.* a rail or board along the side of a bed that connects the headboard with the footboard.

bed+rid+den (ˈbɛdˌrɪdᵊn) *adj.* confined to bed because of illness, esp. for a long or indefinite period. [Old English *bedreda,* from *bedd* BED + *-rida* rider, from *rīdan* to RIDE]

bed+rock (ˈbɛdˌrɒk) *n.* **1.** the solid unweathered rock that lies beneath the loose surface deposits of soil, alluvium, etc. **2.** basic principles or facts (esp. in the phrase **get down to bedrock**). **3.** the lowest point, level, or layer.

bed+roll (ˈbɛdˌrəʊl) *n.* a portable roll of bedding, such as a sleeping bag, used esp. for sleeping in the open.

bed+room (ˈbɛdˌruːm, -ˌrʊm) *n.* **1.** a room furnished with beds or used for sleeping. **2.** (*modifier*) containing references to sex: *a bedroom comedy.*

Beds. *abbrev. for* Bedfordshire.

bed+side (ˈbɛdˌsaɪd) *n.* **a.** the space by the side of a bed, esp. of a sick person. **b.** (*as modifier*): *a bedside lamp; a doctor's bedside manner.*

bed+sit·ter (ˈbɛdˈsɪtə) *n.* a furnished sitting room containing sleeping accommodation and sometimes cooking and washing facilities. Also called: **bedsitting room, bedsit.**

bed+sore (ˈbɛdˌsɔː) *n.* the nontechnical name for **decubitus ulcer.**

bed+spread (ˈbɛdˌsprɛd) *n.* a top cover on a bed over other bedclothes.

bed+stead (ˈbɛdˌstɛd, -stɪd) *n.* the framework of a bed, usually including a headboard and springs but excluding the mattress and other coverings.

bed+straw (ˈbɛdˌstrɔː) *n.* any of numerous rubiaceous plants of the genus *Galium,* which have small white or yellow flowers and prickly or hairy fruits: formerly used as straw for beds. See also **lady's bedstraw.**

bed tea *n.* (in Pakistan) tea served to a guest in bed in the morning.

bed+time (ˈbɛdˌtaɪm) *n.* **a.** the time when one usually goes to bed. **b.** (*as modifier*): *a bedtime story.*

bed+warm·er (ˈbɛdˌwɔːmə) *n.* a metal pan containing hot coals, formerly used to warm a bed.

Bed+worth (ˈbɛdwəθ) *n.* a coal-mining town in central England, in N Warwickshire. Pop.: 40 535 (1971).

bee[1] (biː) *n.* **1.** any hymenopterous insect of the superfamily *Apoidea,* which includes social forms such as the honeybee and solitary forms such as the carpenter bee. See also **bumblebee, mason bee. 2. busy bee.** a person who is industrious or has many things to do. **3. have a bee in one's bonnet.** to be preoccupied or obsessed with an idea. [Old English *bīo;* related to Old Norse *bȳ,* Old High German *bīa,* Dutch *bij,* Swedish *bi*]

bee[2] (biː) *n. Chiefly U.S.* a social gathering for a specific purpose, as to carry out a communal task or hold competitions: *quilting bee; spelling bee.* [perhaps from dialect *bean* neighbourly help, from Old English *bēn* boon]

bee[3] (biː) *n. Nautical.* a small sheave with one cheek removed and the pulley and other cheek fastened flat to a boom or another spar, used for reeving outhauls or stays. [Old English *bēag* related to Old High German *boug* ring, Old Norse *bogi* a bow]

Beeb (biːb) *n.* **the.** an informal name for the **B.B.C.**

bee bee+tle *n.* a European beetle, *Trichodes apiarius,* that is often parasitic in beehives: family *Cleridae.*

bee+bread (ˈbiːˌbrɛd) *n.* a mixture of pollen and nectar prepared by worker bees and fed to the larvae. Also called: **ambrosia.**

beech (biːtʃ) *n.* **1.** any N temperate tree of the genus *Fagus,* esp. *F. sylvatica* of Europe, having smooth greyish bark: family *Fagaceae.* **2.** any tree of the related genus *Nothofagus,* of temperate Australasia and South America. **3.** the hard wood of any of these trees, used in making furniture, etc. **4. copper beech.** a cultivated variety of European beech that has reddish leaves. [Old English *bēce;* related to Old Norse *bók,* Old High German *buohha,* Middle Dutch *boeke,* Latin *fāgus* beech, Greek *phēgos* edible oak] —**'beech+en** *or* **'beech·y** *adj.*

Bee·cham ('bi:tʃəm) *n.* Sir **Thom·as.** 1879–1961, English conductor who did much to promote the works of Delius, Sibelius, and Richard Strauss.

Bee·cher ('bi:tʃə) *n.* **Hen·ry Ward.** 1813–87, U.S. clergyman: a leader in the movement for the abolition of slavery.

beech fern *n.* a fern, *Thelypteris phegopteris,* that grows in damp N temperate woods: family *Polypodiaceae.*

beech+nut ('bi:tʃ,nʌt) *n.* the small brown triangular edible nut of the beech tree. Collectively, the nuts are often termed **beech mast,** esp. when lying on the ground.

bee-eat·er *n.* any insectivorous bird of the family *Meropidae* of tropical and subtropical regions of the Old World, having a long downward-curving bill and long pointed wings and tail: order *Coraciiformes* (kingfishers, etc.).

beef (bi:f) *n.* **1.** the flesh of various bovine animals, esp. the cow, when killed for eating. **2.** (*pl.* **beeves** (bi:vz)) an adult ox, bull, cow, etc., reared for its meat. **3.** *Informal.* human flesh, esp. when muscular. **4.** (*pl.* **beefs**) *Slang.* a complaint. ~*vb.* **5.** (*intr.*) *Slang.* to complain, esp. repeatedly: *he was beefing about his tax.* **6.** (*tr.;* often foll. by *up*) *U.S. slang.* to strengthen; reinforce. [C13: from Old French *boef,* from Latin *bōs* ox; see cow[1]]

beef+bur+ger ('bi:f,bɜ:gə) *n.* a flat fried cake of minced beef; hamburger.

beef+cake ('bi:f,keɪk) *n. Slang.* men displayed for their muscular bodies, esp. in photographs. Compare **cheesecake.**

beef+eat·er ('bi:f,i:tə) *n.* a yeoman warder of the Tower of London.

bee fly *n.* any hairy beelike nectar-eating dipterous fly of the family *Bombyliidae,* whose larvae are parasitic on those of bees and related insects.

beef road *n. Austral.* a road used for transporting cattle.

beef+steak ('bi:f,steɪk) *n.* a piece of beef that can be grilled, fried, etc., cut from any lean part of the animal.

beef strog·a+noff *n.* a dish of slices of beef cooked with onions, mushrooms, and seasonings, served in a sour-cream sauce. [C19: after Count Paul *Stroganoff,* 19th-century Russian diplomat]

beef tea *n.* a drink made by boiling pieces of lean beef: often given to invalids to stimulate the appetite.

beef+wood ('bi:f,wʊd) *n.* **1.** any of various trees that produce very hard wood, esp. the Australian tree *Casuarina equisetifolia* (see **casuarina**), widely planted in warm regions. **2.** the wood of any of these trees.

beef·y ('bi:fɪ) *adj.* **beef·i·er, beef·i·est. 1.** like beef. **2.** *Informal.* muscular; brawny. **3.** *Informal.* fleshy; obese. —**'beef·i+ly** *adv.* —**'beef·i·ness** *n.*

bee glue *n.* another name for **propolis.**

bee+hive ('bi:,haɪv) *n.* **1.** a man-made receptacle used to house a swarm of bees. **2.** a dome-shaped hair style in which the hair is piled high on the head. **3.** a place where busy people are assembled.

bee+hive house *n.* a prehistoric circular building found in various parts of Europe, usually of stone and having a dome-shaped roof.

bee+keep·er ('bi:,ki:pə) *n.* a person who keeps bees for their honey; apiarist.

bee kil+ler *n.* another name for **robber fly.**

bee+line ('bi:,laɪn) *n.* the most direct route between two places (esp. in the phrase **make a beeline for**).

Be·el·ze·bub (bɪ'ɛlzɪ,bʌb) *n.* **1.** *Old Testament.* a god of the Philistines (2 Kings 1:2). **2.** Satan or any devil or demon. [Old English *Belzebub,* ultimately from Hebrew *bá'al zebūb,* literally: lord of flies]

bee moth *n.* any of various pyralid moths, such as the wax moth, whose larvae live in the nests of bees or wasps, feeding on nest materials and host larvae.

been (bi:n, bɪn) *vb.* the past participle of **be.**

been+to ('bi:ntu:, 'bɪntʊ) *W. African informal.* ~*n., pl.* **+tos. 1.** a person who has resided in Britain, esp. during part of his education. ~*adj.* **2.** of, relating to, or characteristic of such a person. [C20: from BEEN + TO]

bee or+chid *n.* a European orchid, *Ophrys apifera,* whose flower resembles a bumble bee in shape and colour.

beep (bi:p) *n.* **1.** a short high-pitched sound, esp. one made by the horn of a car, bicycle, etc., or by electronic apparatus. ~*vb.* **2.** to make or cause to make such a noise. —**'beep+er** *n.*

bee plant *n.* any of various plants much visited by bees for nectar and pollen.

beer (bɪə) *n.* **1.** an alcoholic drink brewed from malt, sugar, hops, and water and fermented with yeast. Compare **ale. 2.** a slightly fermented drink made from the roots or leaves of certain plants: *ginger beer; nettle beer.* **3.** (*modifier*) relating to or used in the drinking of beer: *beer glass; beer mat.* **4.** (*modifier*) in which beer is drunk, esp. (of licensed premises) having a licence to sell beer but not spirits: *beer house; beer cellar; beer garden.* [Old English *beor;* related to Old Norse *bjórr,* Old Frisian *biār,* Old High German *bior*]

beer and skit+tles *n. Informal.* enjoyment or pleasure.

Beer·bohm ('bɪəbəʊm) *n.* Sir **Max.** 1872–1956, English critic, wit, and caricaturist, whose works include *Zuleika Dobson* (1911), a satire on Oxford undergraduates.

Beer+she+ba (bɪə'ʃi:bə) *n.* a town in S Israel: commercial centre of the Negev. In biblical times it marked the southern limit of Palestine. Pop.: 84 100 (1972).

beer-up *n. Austral. slang.* a drinking bout.

beer·y ('bɪərɪ) *adj.* **beer·i·er, beer·i+est. 1.** smelling or tasting of beer. **2.** given to drinking beer. —**'beer·i+ly** *adv.* —**'beer·i+ness** *n.*

bee's knees *n.* **the** (*functioning as sing.*) *Informal.* an excellent or ideally suitable person or thing.

beest+ings, biest+ings *or U.S.* **beast+ings** ('bi:stɪŋz) *n.* (*functioning as sing.*) the first milk secreted by the mammary glands of a cow or similar animal immediately after giving birth; colostrum. [Old English *bӯsting,* from *bēost* beestings; related to Middle Dutch *biest*]

bees+wax ('bi:z,wæks) *n.* **1. a.** a yellowish or dark brown wax secreted by honeybees for constructing honeycombs. **b.** this wax after refining, purifying, etc., used in polishes, ointments, and for modelling. ~*vb.* **2.** (*tr.*) to polish with such wax.

bees+wing ('bi:z,wɪŋ) *n.* **1.** a light filmy crust of tartar that forms in port and some other wines after long keeping in the bottle. **2.** a port or other wine containing beeswing.

beet (bi:t) *n.* **1.** any chenopodiaceous plant of the genus *Beta,* esp. the Eurasian species *B. vulgaris,* widely cultivated in such varieties as the sugar beet, mangel-wurzel, beetroot, and spinach beet. See also **chard. 2.** the leaves of any of several varieties of this plant, which are cooked and eaten as a vegetable. **3. red beet.** the U.S. name for **beetroot.** [Old English *bēte,* from Latin *bēta*]

beet+fly ('bi:t,flaɪ) *n., pl.* **+flies.** a muscid fly, *Pegomyia hyoscyami:* a common pest of beets and mangel-wurzels. Also called: **mangold fly.**

Bee·tho·ven ('beɪtəʊvᵊn) *n.* **Lud·wig van** ('lu:tvɪç fan). 1770–1827, German composer, who greatly extended the form and scope of symphonic and chamber music, bridging the classical and romantic traditions. His works include nine symphonies, 32 piano sonatas, 16 string quartets, five piano concertos, a violin concerto, two masses, the opera *Fidelio* (1805), and choral music.

bee+tle[1] ('bi:tᵊl) *n.* **1.** any insect of the order *Coleoptera,* having biting mouthparts and forewings modified to form shell-like protective elytra. **2.** a game played with dice in which the players draw or assemble a beetle-shaped form. ~*vb.* (*intr.;* foll. by *along, off,* etc.) **3.** *Informal.* to scuttle or scurry; hurry. [Old English *bitela;* related to *bitol* teeth, BIT, *bītan* to BITE]

bee+tle[2] ('bi:tᵊl) *n.* **1.** a heavy hand tool, usually made of wood, used for ramming, pounding, or beating. **2.** a machine used to finish cloth by stamping it with wooden hammers. ~*vb.* (*tr.*) **3.** to beat or pound with a beetle. **4.** to finish (cloth) by means of a beetle. [Old English *bīetel,* from *bēatan* to BEAT; related to Middle Low German *bētel* chisel, Old Norse *beytill* penis]

bee+tle[3] ('bi:tᵊl) *vb.* **1.** (*intr.*) to overhang; jut. ~*adj.* **2.** overhanging; prominent. [C14: perhaps related to BEETLE[1]]

bee·tle-browed *adj.* **1.** having bushy or overhanging eyebrows. **2.** sullen in appearance; scowling.

beet+root ('bi:t,ru:t) *n.* **1.** a variety of the beet plant, *Beta vulgaris,* that has a bulbous dark red root that may be eaten as a vegetable, in salads, or pickled. **2.** the root of this plant. ~U.S. name: **red beet.**

beet sug+ar *n.* the sucrose obtained from sugar beet, identical in composition to cane sugar.

beeves (bi:vz) *n.* the plural of **beef** (sense 2).

bee+zer ('bi:zə) *n. Brit. slang.* **1.** a person or chap. **2.** the nose. [C20: of uncertain origin]

B.E.F. *abbrev. for* British Expeditionary Force.

be+fall (bɪ'fɔ:l) *vb.* **+falls, +fal+ling, +fell, +fall+en.** *Archaic or literary.* **1.** (*intr.*) to take place; come to pass . **2.** (*tr.*) to happen to. **3.** (*intr.;* usually foll. by *to*) to be due, as by right. [Old English *befeallan;* related to Old High German *bifallan,* Dutch *bevallen;* see BE-, FALL]

be+fit (bɪ'fɪt) *vb.* **+fits, +fit+ting, +fit+ted.** (*tr.*) to be appropriate to or suitable for. [C15: from BE- + FIT[1]] —**be+'fit+ting** *adj.* —**be+'fit+ting+ly** *adv.*

be+fog (bɪ'fɒg) *vb.* **+fogs, +fog+ging, +fogged.** (*tr.*) **1.** to surround with fog. **2.** to make confused, vague, or less clear.

be+fool (bɪ'fu:l) *vb.* (*tr.*) **1.** to make a fool of. **2.** *Archaic.* to treat or regard as a fool.

be+fore (bɪ'fɔ:) *conj.* (*subordinating*) **1.** earlier than the time when. **2.** rather than: *he'll resign before he agrees to it.* ~*prep.* **3.** preceding in space or time; in front of; ahead of: *standing before the altar.* **4.** when confronted by: *to withdraw before one's enemies.* **5.** in the presence of: *to be brought before a judge.* **6.** in preference to: *to put friendship before money.* ~*adv.* **7.** at an earlier time; previously; beforehand; in front. [Old English *beforan;* related to Old Frisian *befara,* Old High German *bifora*]

be·fore+hand (bɪ'fɔ:,hænd) *adj.* (*postpositive*), *adv.* early; in advance; in anticipation: *she came an hour beforehand.*

be·fore+time (bɪ'fɔ:,taɪm) *adv. Archaic.* formerly.

be+foul (bɪ'faʊl) *vb.* (*tr.*) to make dirty or foul; soil; defile. —**be+'foul+er** *n.* —**be+'foul+ment** *n.*

be+friend (bɪ'frɛnd) *vb.* (*tr.*) to be a friend to; assist; favour.

be+fud+dle (bɪ'fʌdᵊl) *vb.* (*tr.*) **1.** to confuse, muddle, or perplex. **2.** to make stupid with drink. —**be+'fud+dle+ment** *n.*

beg[1] (bɛg) *vb.* **begs, beg+ging, begged. 1.** (when *intr.,* often foll. by *for*) to solicit (for money, food, etc.), esp. in the street. **2.** to ask (someone) for (something or leave to do something) formally, humbly, or earnestly: *I beg forgiveness; I beg to differ.* **3.** (*intr.*) (of a dog) to sit up with forepaws raised expectantly. **4.** to leave unanswered or unresolved: *to beg a* *point.* **5. beg the question. a.** to evade the issue. **b.** to assume the thing under examination as proved. **6. go begging.** to be unwanted or unused. ~See also **beg off.** [C13: probably from Old English *bedecian;* related to Gothic *bidagwa* BEGGAR]

beg² (bɛg) *n.* a variant spelling of **bey.**

be+gad (bɪˈgæd) *interj. Archaic slang.* an emphatic exclamation. [C18: euphemistic alteration of *by God!*]

be+gan (bɪˈgæn) *vb.* the past tense of **begin.**

be+gat (bɪˈgæt) *vb. Archaic.* a past tense of **beget.**

be+get (bɪˈgɛt) *vb.* **+gets, +get+ting, +got** *or* **+gat; +got+ten** *or* **+got.** (*tr.*) **1.** to father. **2.** to cause or create. [Old English *begietan;* related to Old Saxon *bigetan,* Old High German *pigezzan,* Gothic *bigitan* to find; see BE-, GET] —**be+ˈget+ter** *n.*

beg+gar (ˈbɛgə) *n.* **1.** a person who begs, esp. one who lives by begging. **2.** a person who has no money or resources; pauper. **3.** *Ironic or jocular, chiefly Brit.* fellow: *lucky beggar!* ~*vb.* (*tr.*) **4.** to be beyond the resources of (esp. in the phrase **to beggar description**). **5.** to impoverish; reduce to begging. —**ˈbeg+gar+ˌhood** *or* **ˈbeg+gar+dom** *n.*

beg+gar+ly (ˈbɛgəlɪ) *adj.* meanly inadequate; very poor: *beggarly living conditions.* —**ˈbeg+gar+li+ness** *n.*

beg·gar-my-neigh·bour *n.* **1.** a card game in which one player tries to win all the cards of the other player. **2.** (*modifier*) relating to or denoting an advantage gained by one side at the expense of the other: *beggar-my-neighbour policies.*

beg·gar's-lice *n.* (*functioning as sing.*) **1.** any of several plants, esp. the stickseed, having small prickly fruits that adhere to clothing, fur, etc. **2.** the seed or fruit of any of these plants.

beg·gar-ticks *or* **beg·gar's-ticks** *n.* (*functioning as sing.*) **1.** any of various plants, such as the bur marigold and tick trefoil, having fruits or seeds that cling to clothing, fur, etc. **2.** the seed or fruit of any of these plants.

beg·gar+weed (ˈbɛgəˌwi:d) *n.* any of various leguminous plants of the genus *Desmodium,* esp. *D. purpureum* of the West Indies, grown in the southern U.S. as forage plants and to improve the soil. See also **tick trefoil.**

beg·gar·y (ˈbɛgərɪ) *n.* extreme poverty or need; the condition of being a beggar.

Beg+hard (ˈbɛgəd, bɪˈgɑ:d) *n.* a member of a Christian brotherhood that was founded in Flanders in the 13th century and followed a life based on that of the Beguines.

be+gin (bɪˈgɪn) *vb.* **+gins, +gin+ning, +gan, +gun. 1.** to start or cause to start (something or to do something). **2.** to bring or come into being for the first time; arise or originate. **3.** to start to say or speak. **4.** (*used with a negative*) to have the least capacity (to do something): *he couldn't begin to compete with her.* **5. to begin with.** in the first place. [Old English *beginnan;* related to Old High German *biginnan,* Gothic *duginnan*]

Beg·in (ˈbɛgɪn) *n.* **Me·na·chem** (məˈnɑ:kɪm). born 1913, Israeli statesman, born in Poland. In Palestine after 1942, he became a leader of the militant Zionists; prime minister of Israel since 1977.

be+gin+ner (bɪˈgɪnə) *n.* a person who has just started to do or learn something; novice.

be+gin+ning (bɪˈgɪnɪŋ) *n.* **1.** a start; commencement. **2.** (*often pl.*) a first or early part or stage. **3.** the place where or time when something starts. **4.** an origin; source.

be+gird (bɪˈgɜ:d) *vb.* **+girds, +gird+ing, +girt** *or* **+gird+ed.** (*tr.*) *Poetic.* **1.** to surround; gird around. **2.** to bind. [Old English *begierdan;* see BE-, GIRD]

beg off *vb.* (*intr., adv.*) to ask to be released from an engagement, obligation, etc.

be+gone (bɪˈgɒn) *interj.* go away! [C14: from BE (imperative) + GONE]

be+gon·ia (bɪˈgəʊnjə) *n.* any plant of the genus *Begonia,* of warm and tropical regions, widely cultivated for their ornamental leaves and waxy flowers: family *Begoniaceae.* [C18: New Latin, named after Michel *Bégon* (1638–1710), French patron of science]

be+gor+ra (bɪˈgɔ:rə) *interj.* an emphatic exclamation, regarded as a characteristic utterance of Irishmen. [C19: euphemistic alteration of *by God!*]

be+got (bɪˈgɒt) *vb.* a past tense or past participle of **beget.**

be+got+ten (bɪˈgɒtᵊn) *vb.* a past participle of **beget.**

be+grime (bɪˈgraɪm) *vb.* (*tr.*) to make dirty; soil.

be+grudge (bɪˈgrʌdʒ) *vb.* (*tr.*) **1.** to give, admit, or allow unwillingly or with a bad grace. **2.** to envy (someone) the possession of (something). —**be+ˈgrudg+ing+ly** *adv.*

be+guile (bɪˈgaɪl) *vb.* **+guiles, +guil+ing, +guiled.** (*tr.*) **1.** to charm; fascinate. **2.** to delude; influence by slyness. **3.** (*often foll. by of or out of*) to deprive (someone) of something by trickery; cheat (someone) of. **4.** to pass pleasantly; while away. —**be+ˈguile+ment** *n.* —**be+ˈguil+er** *n.* —**be+ˈguil+ing+ly** *adv.*

Be+guin (ˈbɛgɪn; *French* beˈgɛ̃) *n.* another word for **Beghard.**

be+guine (bɪˈgi:n) *n.* **1.** a dance of South American origin in bolero rhythm. **2.** a piece of music in the rhythm of this dance. **3.** a variant of **biggin.** [C20: from Louisiana French, from French *béguin* flirtation]

Beg+uine (ˈbɛgi:n) *n.* a member of a Christian sisterhood that was founded in Liège in the 12th century, and, though not taking religious vows, followed an austere life. [C15: from Old French, perhaps after *Lambert le Bègue* (the Stammerer), 12th-century priest of Liège, who founded the sisterhood]

be+gum (ˈbeɪgəm) *n.* (esp. in India) a Muslim woman ruler, princess, or lady of high rank, esp. a widow. [C18: from Urdu *begam,* from Turkish *begim;* see BEY]

be+gun (bɪˈgʌn) *vb.* the past participle of **begin.**

be+half (bɪˈhɑ:f) *n.* interest, part, benefit, or respect (only in the phrases **on (someone's) behalf, on** *or U.S.* **in behalf of, in this** (*or* **that**) **behalf**). [Old English *be halfe* from *be* by + *halfe* side; compare Old Norse *af halfu*]

Beh+an (ˈbi:ən) *n.* **Bren·dan.** 1923–64, Irish writer, noted esp. for his plays *The Quare Fellow* (1954) and *The Hostage* (1958) and for an account of his detention as a member of the Irish Republican Army, *Borstal Boy* (1958).

be+have (bɪˈheɪv) *vb.* **1.** (*intr.*) to act or function in a specified or usual way. **2.** to conduct (oneself) in a specified way: *he behaved badly towards her.* **3.** to conduct (oneself) properly or as desired: *the child behaved himself all day.* [C15: see BE-, HAVE]

be+hav+iour *or U.S.* **be+hav+ior** (bɪˈheɪvjə) *n.* **1.** manner of behaving or conducting oneself. **2. on one's best behaviour.** behaving with careful good manners. **3.** *Psychol.* **a.** the aggregate of all the responses made by an organism in any situation. **b.** a specific response of a certain organism to a specific stimulus or group of stimuli. **4.** the action, reaction, or functioning of a machine, chemical substance, etc., under normal or specified circumstances. [C15: from BEHAVE; influenced in form by Middle English *havior,* from Old French *havoir,* from Latin *habēre* to have] —**be+ˈhav+iour+al** *or U.S.* **be+ˈhav+ior+al** *adj.*

be+hav+iour+al sci+ence *n.* the application of scientific methods to the study of the behaviour of organisms.

be+hav+iour+ism *or U.S.* **be+hav+ior+ism** (bɪˈheɪvjəˌrɪzəm) *n.* a school of psychology that regards objective observable aspects of the behaviour of organisms as the only valid subject for study. —**be+ˈhav+iour+ist** *or U.S.* **be+ˈhav+ior+ist** *adj., n.* —**be+ˌhav+iour+ˈis+tic** *or U.S.* **be+ˌhav+ior+ˈis+tic** *adj.*

be+hav+iour ther·a·py *n.* any of various means of treating psychological disorders, such as desensitization, aversion therapy, and instrumental conditioning, that depend on the patient systematically learning new modes of behaviour.

be+head (bɪˈhɛd) *vb.* (*tr.*) to remove the head from; decapitate. [Old English *behēafdian,* from BE- + *heafod* HEAD; related to Middle High German *behoubeten*]

be+held (bɪˈhɛld) *vb.* the past tense and past participle of **behold.**

be+he+moth (bɪˈhi:mɒθ) *n.* **1.** *Old Testament.* a gigantic beast, probably a hippopotamus, described in Job 40:15. **2.** a huge or monstrous person or thing. [C14: from Hebrew *bĕhēmōth,* plural of *bĕhēmāh* beast]

be+hest (bɪˈhɛst) *n.* an authoritative order or earnest request. [Old English *behǣs,* from *behātan;* see BE-, HEST]

be+hind (bɪˈhaɪnd) *prep.* **1.** in or to a position further back than; at the rear of; at the back of. **2.** in the past in relation to: *I've got the exams behind me now.* **3.** late according to; not keeping up with: *running behind schedule.* **4.** concerning the circumstances surrounding: *the reasons behind his departure.* **5.** backing or supporting: *I'm right behind you in your application.* ~*adv.* **6.** in or to a position further back; following. **7.** remaining after someone's departure: *he left his books behind.* **8.** in debt; in arrears: *to fall behind with payments.* ~*adj.* **9.** (*postpositive*) in a position further back; retarded: *the man behind asked me to give you this.* ~*n.* **10.** *Informal.* the buttocks. **11.** *Australian Rules football.* a score of one point made by kicking the ball over the **behind line** between a goalpost and one of the smaller outer posts (**behind posts**). [Old English *behindan*]

be·hind+hand (bɪˈhaɪndˌhænd) *adj.* (*postpositive*), *adv.* **1.** remiss in fulfilling an obligation. **2.** in debt; in arrears. **3.** delayed in development; backward. **4.** late; behind time.

Be+his+tun (ˌbeɪhɪˈstu:n), **Bi+si+tun,** *or* **Bi+su+tun** *n.* a village in W Iran by the ancient road from Ecbatana to Babylon. On a nearby cliff is an inscription by Darius in Old Persian, Elamite, and Babylonian describing his enthronement.

be+hold (bɪˈhəʊld) *vb.* **+holds, +hold+ing, +held.** (often used in the imperative to draw attention to something) *Archaic or literary.* to look (at); observe. [Old English *bihealdan;* related to Old High German *bihaltan,* Dutch *behouden;* see BE-, HOLD] —**be+ˈhold+er** *n.*

be+hold+en (bɪˈhəʊldᵊn) *adj.* indebted; obliged; under a moral obligation. [Old English *behealden,* past participle of *behealdan* to BEHOLD]

be+hoof (bɪˈhu:f) *n., pl.* **+hooves.** *Rare.* advantage or profit. [Old English *behōf;* related to Middle High German *behuof* something useful; see BEHOVE]

be+hove (bɪˈhəʊv) *or U.S.* **be+hoove** (bɪˈhu:v) *vb.* (*tr.; impersonal*) *Archaic.* to be necessary or fitting for: *it behoves me to arrest you.* [Old English *behōfian;* related to Middle Low German *behōven*]

Beh·ring *n.* **1.** (*German* ˈbe:rɪŋ). **E·mil von** (ˈe:mi:l fɔn). 1854–1917, German bacteriologist, who discovered diphtheria and tetanus antitoxins: Nobel prize for medicine 1901. **2.** (ˈbɛrɪŋ, ˈbɛər-). See (Vitus) **Bering.**

Bei·der·becke (ˈbaɪdəˌbɛk) *n.* **Le·on Bis·marcke,** called *Bix.* 1903–1931, U.S. jazz cornettist, composer, and pianist.

beige (beɪʒ) *n.* **1. a.** a very light brown, sometimes with a yellowish tinge, similar to the colour of undyed wool. **b.** (*as adj.*): *beige gloves.* **2.** a fabric made of undyed or unbleached wool. [C19: from Old French, of obscure origin]

bei+gel (ˈbeɪgᵊl) *n.* a variant spelling of **bagel.**

be+ing (ˈbi:ɪŋ) *n.* **1.** the state or fact of existing; existence. **2.** essential nature; self: *she put her whole being into the part.* **3.** something that exists or is thought to exist, esp. something that cannot be assigned to any category: *a being from outer space.* **4.** a person; human being.

Bei+ra (ˈbaɪərə) *n.* a port in E Mozambique: terminus of a transcontinental railway from Lobito, Angola, through Zaïre, Zambia, and Rhodesia. Pop.: 113 770 (1970).

Bei+rut *or* **Bey+routh** (beɪ'ru:t, 'beɪru:t) *n.* the capital of Lebanon, a port on the Mediterranean: part of the Ottoman Empire from the 16th century until 1918; four universities (Lebanese, American, French, and Arab). Pop.: 600 000 (1973 est.).

be+ja+bers (bɪ'dʒeɪbəz) *or* **be+jab+bers** (bɪ'dʒæbəz) *interj.* an exclamation of surprise, emphasis, etc., regarded as a characteristic utterance of Irishmen. [C19: alteration of *by Jesus!*]

Bé·jart (*French* be'ʒa:r) *n.* **Mau·rice.** (mɔ'ris). born 1928, French dancer and choreographer. His choreography is characterized by a combination of classic and modern dance and acrobatics.

be+jew+el (bɪ'dʒu:əl) *vb.* **+els, +el+ling, +elled** *or U.S.* **+els, +el+ing, +eled.** (*tr.*) to decorate with or as if with jewels.

bel (bɛl) *n.* a unit for comparing two power levels, equal to the logarithm to the base ten of the ratio of the two powers. Abbrevs.: **B, b.** See also **decibel.** [C20: named after A. G. BELL]

Bel (beɪl) *n.* (in Babylonian and Assyrian mythology) the god of the earth.

be+la+bour *or U.S.* **be+la+bor** (bɪ'leɪbə) *vb.* (*tr.*) **1.** to beat severely; thrash. **2.** to attack verbally; criticize harshly. **3.** an obsolete word for **labour.**

be+lah *or* **be+lar** ('bi:lɑ:) *n.* an Australian casuarina tree, *Casuarina glauca*, yielding a useful timber.

be+lat+ed (bɪ'leɪtɪd) *adj.* late or too late: *belated greetings.* —**be+'lat+ed+ly** *adv.* —**be+'lat+ed+ness** *n.*

be+lay (bɪ'leɪ) *vb.* **+lays, +lay+ing, +layed.** **1.** *Nautical.* to make fast (a line) by securing to a pin, cleat, or bitt. **2.** (*usually imperative*) *Nautical.* to stop; cease. **3.** *Mountaineering.* to turn (a rope) round an object, piton, etc., to secure (a climber). ~*n.* **4.** *Mountaineering.* a turn of a rope round an object to secure it. [Old English *belecgan;* related to Old High German *bileggen*, Dutch *beleggen*]

be+lay+ing pin *n. Nautical.* a cylindrical, sometimes tapered pin, usually of metal or wood, that fits into a hole in a pin or fife rail: used for belaying.

bel can+to ('bɛl 'kæntəʊ) *n. Music.* **a.** a style of singing characterized by beauty of tone rather than dramatic power. **b.** (*as modifier*): *a bel canto aria.* [Italian, literally: beautiful singing]

belch (bɛltʃ) *vb.* **1.** (*usually intr.*) to expel wind from the stomach noisily through the mouth; eructate. **2.** to expel or be expelled forcefully from inside: *smoke belching from factory chimneys.* **3.** to say (curses, insults, etc.) violently or bitterly. ~*n.* **4.** an act of belching; eructation. [Old English *bialcan;* related to Middle Low German *belken* to shout, Dutch *balken* to bray]

bel+dam *or* **bel+dame** ('bɛldəm) *n.* **1.** *Archaic.* an old woman, esp. an ugly or malicious one; hag. **2.** an obsolete word for **grandmother.** [C15: from *bel-* grand (as in *grandmother*), from Old French *bel* beautiful, from Latin *bellus* + *dam* mother, variant of DAME]

be+lea+guer (bɪ'li:gə) *vb.* (*tr.*) **1.** to trouble persistently; harass. **2.** to lay siege to. [C16: from BE- + LEAGUER[1]]

Be+lém (*Portuguese* be'lẽɪ) *n.* a port in N Brazil, the capital of Pará state, on the Pará River: major trading centre for the Amazon basin. Pop.: 565 097 (1970).

bel+em+nite ('bɛləm,naɪt) *n.* **1.** any extinct marine cephalopod mollusc of the order *Belemnoidea*, related to the cuttlefish. **2.** the long pointed conical internal shell of any of these animals: a common Mesozoic fossil. [C17: from Greek *belemnon* dart]

bel e·sprit *French.* (bɛl ɛ'spri) *n., pl.* ***beaux e·sprits*** (bo zɛ'spri). a witty or clever person. [literally: fine wit]

Bel+fast ('bɛlfɑ:st, bɛl'fɑ:st) *n.* the capital of Northern Ireland, a port on Belfast Lough: became the centre of Irish Protestantism and of the linen industry in the 17th century. Pop.: 360 150 (1971).

Bel+fort (*French* bɛl'fɔ:r) *n.* **1. Territoire de.** a department of E France: the only part of Alsace remaining to France after 1871. Capital: Belfort. Pop.: 131 359 (1975). Area: 608 sq. km (237 sq. miles). **2.** a fortress town in E France: strategically situated in the **Belfort Gap** between the Vosges and the Jura mountains. Pop.: 57 317 (1975).

bel+fry ('bɛlfrɪ) *n., pl.* **+fries.** **1.** the part of a tower or steeple in which bells are hung. **2.** a tower or steeple. Compare **campanile.** **3.** the timber framework inside a tower or steeple on which bells are hung. **4.** (formerly) a movable tower for attacking fortifications. [C13: from Old French *berfrei*, of Germanic origin; compare Middle High German *bercfrit* fortified tower, Medieval Latin *berfredus* tower]

Belg. *or* **Bel.** *abbrev. for:* **1.** Belgian. **2.** Belgium.

bel+ga ('bɛlgə) *n.* a former Belgian monetary unit worth five francs.

Bel+gae ('bɛldʒi:, 'bɛlgaɪ) *n.* an ancient Celtic people who in Roman times inhabited present-day Belgium and N France. —**'Bel+gic** *adj.*

Bel+gian ('bɛldʒən) *n.* **1.** a native, citizen, or inhabitant of Belgium. See also **Fleming[1], Walloon.** ~*adj.* **2.** of, relating to, or characteristic of Belgium or the Belgians. **3.** of or relating to the Walloon French or the Flemish languages.

Bel+gian Con+go *n.* a former name (1908–1960) of **Zaïre.**

Bel+gian hare *n.* a large red breed of domestic rabbit.

Bel+gium ('bɛldʒəm) *n.* a kingdom in NW Europe: at various times under the rulers of Burgundy, Spain, Austria, France, and the Netherlands before becoming an independent kingdom in 1830. It formed the Benelux customs union with the Netherlands and Luxembourg in 1947 and is now a member of the European Economic Community. It consists chiefly of a low-lying region of sand, woods, and heath (the Campine) in the north and west, and a fertile undulating central plain rising to the Ardennes Mountains in the southeast. Languages: French and Flemish. Religion: chiefly Roman Catholic. Currency: franc. Capital: Brussels. Pop.: 9 813 152 (1975 est.). Area: 30 513 sq. km (11 778 sq. miles).

Bel·go·rod-Dnes·trov+ski (*Russian* 'bjɛlgərət dnjɪ'strɔfskij) *n.* a variant spelling of **Byelgorod-Dnestrovski.**

Bel+grade (bɛl'greɪd, 'bɛlgreɪd) *n.* the capital of Yugoslavia, in the E part at the confluence of the Danube and Sava Rivers: became the capital of Serbia in 1878 and of Yugoslavia in 1929. Pop.: 746 105 (1971). Serbo-Croatian name: **Beograd.**

Bel+gra+vi·a (bɛl'greɪvɪə) *n.* a fashionable residential district of W central London, around Belgrave Square.

Be·li·al ('bi:lɪəl) *n.* **1.** a demon mentioned frequently in apocalyptic literature: identified in the Christian tradition with the devil or Satan. **2.** (in the Old Testament and rabbinical literature) worthlessness or wickedness. [C13: from Hebrew *bəlīyya'al*, from *bəlīy* without + *ya'al* worth]

be+lie (bɪ'laɪ) *vb.* **+lies, +ly+ing, +lied.** (*tr.*) **1.** to show to be untrue; contradict. **2.** to misrepresent; disguise the nature of: *the report belied the real extent of the damage.* **3.** to fail to justify; disappoint. [Old English *belēogan;* related to Old Frisian *biliuga*, Old High German *biliugan;* see BE-, LIE[1]] —**be+'li+er** *n.*

be+lief (bɪ'li:f) *n.* **1.** a principle, idea, etc., accepted as true or real, esp. without positive proof. **2.** opinion; conviction. **3.** religious faith. **4.** trust or confidence, as in a person or a person's abilities, probity, etc.

be+lieve (bɪ'li:v) *vb.* **1.** (*tr.; may take a clause as object*) to accept (a statement, supposition, or opinion) as true or real: *I believe God exists.* **2.** (*tr.*) to accept the statement or opinion of (a person) as true. **3.** (*intr.; foll. by in*) to be convinced of the truth or existence (of): *to believe in fairies.* **4.** (*intr.*) to have religious faith. **5.** (*when tr., takes a clause as object*) to think, assume, or suppose: *I believe that he has left already.* **6.** (*tr.; foll. by of; used with can, could, would, etc.*) to think that someone is able to do (a particular action): *I wouldn't have believed it of him.* [Old English *beliefan*] —**be+'liev+a·ble** *adj.* —**be+'liev+a·bly** *adv.* —**be+'liev+er** *n.*

be+like (bɪ'laɪk) *adv. Archaic or dialect.* perhaps; maybe.

Bel·i·sa·ri·us (,bɛlɪ'sɑ:rɪəs) *n.* ?505–565 A.D., Byzantine general under Justinian I. He recovered North Africa from the Vandals and Italy from the Ostrogoths and led forces against the Persians.

Be·li·sha bea+con (bə'li:ʃə) *n.* a flashing light in an orange globe mounted on a post, indicating a pedestrian crossing on a road. [C20: named after Leslie Hore-*Belisha*, British politician]

be+lit+tle (bɪ'lɪtᵊl) *vb.* (*tr.*) **1.** to consider or speak of (something) as less valuable or important than it really is; disparage. **2.** to cause to make small; dwarf. —**be+'lit+tle+ment** *n.* —**be+'lit+tler** *n.* —**be+'lit+tling+ly** *adv.*

Be+li+tung (bɪ'li:tʊŋ) *n.* another name for **Billiton.**

Be+lize (bɛ'li:z) *n.* **1.** a formerly self-governing British colony in Central America, on the Caribbean: site of a Mayan civilization until the 9th century A.D.; colonized by the British 1638; internal self-government 1964; independent 1981. Official language: English; Carib and Spanish are also spoken. Currency: Belize dollar. Capital: Belmopan. Pop.: 122 000 (1969 est.). Area: 22 965 sq. km (8867 sq. miles). Former name (until 1973): **British Honduras.** **2.** a port and the largest city in Belize, on the Caribbean coast: capital until 1973, when it was abandoned as hurricane-prone. Pop.: 33 482 (1966).

bell[1] (bɛl) *n.* **1.** a hollow, usually metal, cup-shaped instrument that emits a musical ringing sound when struck, often by a clapper hanging inside it. **2.** the sound made by such an instrument or device, as for showing the hours or marking the beginning or end of a period of time. **3.** an electrical device that rings or buzzes as a signal. **4.** the bowl-shaped termination of the tube of certain musical wind instruments, such as the trumpet or oboe. **5.** any musical percussion instrument emitting a ringing tone, such as a glockenspiel, one of a set of hand bells, etc. Compare **chime[1]** (sense 3). **6.** *Nautical.* a signal rung on a ship's bell to count the number of half-hour intervals during each of six four-hour watches reckoned from midnight. Thus, one bell may signify 12.30, 4.30, or 8.30 a.m. or p.m. **7.** See **diving bell.** **8.** *Biology.* a structure resembling a bell in shape, such as the corolla of certain flowers or the body of a jellyfish. **9. ring a bell.** to sound familiar; recall to the mind something previously experienced, esp. indistinctly. **10. sound as a bell.** in perfect condition. **11. bell, book, and candle. a.** instruments used formerly in excommunications and other ecclesiastical acts. **b.** *Informal.* the solemn ritual ratification of such acts. ~*vb.* **12.** to be or cause to be shaped like a bell. **13.** (*tr.*) to attach a bell or bells to. [Old English *belle;* related to Old Norse *bjalla*, Middle Low German *bell;* see BELL[2]]

bell[2] (bɛl) *n.* **1.** a bellowing or baying cry, esp. that of a hound or a male deer in rut. ~*vb.* **2.** to utter (such a cry). [Old English *bellan;* related to Old Norse *belja* to bellow, Old High German *bellan* to roar, Sanskrit *bhāsate* he talks; see BELLOW]

Bell (bɛl) *n.* **1. Ac·ton, Cur·rer** ('kʌrə), and **El·lis.** pen names of the sisters Anne, Charlotte, and Emily **Brontë.** **2. Al·ex·an·der Gra·ham.** 1847–1922, U.S. scientist, born in Scotland, who invented the telephone (1876). **3.** Sir **Fran·cis Hen·ry Dil·lon.** 1851–1936, New Zealand statesman; prime minister of New Zealand (1925).

bel+la+don+na (,bɛlə'dɒnə) *n.* **1.** either of two alkaloid drugs, atropine or hyoscyamine, obtained from the leaves and roots of the deadly nightshade. **2.** another name for **deadly nightshade.** [C16: from Italian, literally: beautiful lady; supposed to refer to its use by women as a cosmetic]

bel+la+don+na lil·y *n.* another name for **amaryllis.**

bel+lar+mine ('bɛlɑːˌmiːn) *n.* a large stoneware or earthenware jug for ale or spirits, bearing a bearded mask. [C18: named after Roberto *Bellarmino* (1542–1621), Italian cardinal whom these jugs were intended to caricature]

Bel+la+trix ('bɛlətrɪks) *n.* the third brightest star in the constellation Orion.

Bel·lay (*French* bɛ'lɛ) *n.* **Jo·a·chim du** (ʒɔa'ʃɛ̃ dy). 1522–60, French poet, a member of the Pléiade.

bell+bird ('bɛlˌbɜːd) *n.* **1.** any of several tropical American passerine birds of the genus *Procnias* having a bell-like call: family *Cotingidae* (cotingas). **2.** either of two other birds with a bell-like call: an Australian flycatcher, *Oreoica gutturalis* (**crested bellbird**), or a New Zealand honeyeater, *Anthornis melanura.*

bell-bot·toms *pl. n.* trousers that flare from the knee and have wide bottoms. —**'bell-ˌbot·tomed** *adj.*

bell+boy ('bɛlˌbɔɪ) *n. Chiefly U.S.* a man or boy employed in a hotel, club, etc., to carry luggage and answer calls for service; page; porter. Also called (U.S.): **bellhop.**

bell buoy *n.* a navigational buoy fitted with a bell, the clapper of which strikes when the waves move the buoy.

belle (bɛl) *n.* **1.** a beautiful girl or woman. **2.** the most attractive or admired girl or woman at a place, function, etc. (esp. in the phrase **the belle of the ball**). [C17: from French, feminine of BEAU]

Bel+leau Wood ('bɛləʊ; *French* bɛ'lo) *n.* a forest in N France: site of a battle (1918) in which the U.S. Marines halted a German advance on Paris.

Bel+leek (bə'liːk) *n.* **a.** a kind of thin fragile porcelain with a lustrous glaze. **b.** (*as modifier*): *a Belleek vase.* [after *Belleek,* a town in Northern Ireland where such porcelain is made]

belle é·poque *French.* (bɛl e'pɔk) *n.* the period of comfortable well-established life before World War I. [literally: fine period]

Belle Isle *n.* an island in the Atlantic, at the N entrance to the **Strait of Belle Isle,** between Labrador and Newfoundland. Area: about 39 sq. km (15 sq. miles).

Bel·ler·o·phon (bə'lɛrəˌfɒn) *n. Greek myth.* a hero of Corinth who performed many deeds with the help of the winged horse Pegasus, notably the killing of the monster Chimera.

belles-let·tres (*French* bɛl'lɛtr) *n.* (*functioning as sing.*) literary works, esp. essays and poetry, valued for their aesthetic rather than their informative or moral content. [C17: from French: fine letters]

bel+let+rist (bɛl'lɛtrɪst) *n.* a writer of belles-lettres. —**bel+'let+rism** *n.* —**bel+let+ris+tic** (ˌbɛlɪ'trɪstɪk) *adj.*

bell+flow·er ('bɛlˌflaʊə) *n.* another name for **campanula.**

bell glass *n.* another name for **bell jar.**

bell hea+ther *n.* an ericaceous shrub, *Erica cinerea.* See **heath** (sense 2).

bell+hop ('bɛlˌhɒp) *n. U.S.* another name for **bellboy.**

bel+li+cose ('bɛlɪˌkəʊs, -ˌkəʊz) *adj.* warlike; aggressive; ready to fight. [C15: from Latin *bellicōsus,* from *bellum* war] —**'bel+li+ˌcose+ly** *adv.* —**bel+li+cos+i·ty** (ˌbɛlɪ'kɒsɪtɪ) *n.*

bel+lig+er+ence (bɪ'lɪdʒərəns) *n.* the act or quality of being belligerent or warlike; aggressiveness.

bel+lig+er+en+cy (bɪ'lɪdʒərənsɪ) *n.* the state of being at war.

bel+lig+er+ent (bɪ'lɪdʒərənt) *adj.* **1.** marked by readiness to fight or argue; aggressive: *a belligerent tone.* **2.** relating to or engaged in a legally recognized war or warfare. ~*n.* **3.** a person or country engaged in fighting or war. [C16: from Latin *belliger,* from *bellum* war + *gerere* to wage]

Bel+lings+hau+sen Sea ('bɛlɪŋzˌhaʊzən) *n.* an area of the S Pacific Ocean off the coast of Antarctica.

Bel·li·ni (*Italian* bel'liːni) *n.* **1. Gio·van·ni** (dʒo'vanni). ?1430–1516, Italian painter of the Venetian school, noted for his altarpieces, landscapes, and Madonnas. His father **Jacopo** (?1400–70) and his brother **Gentile** (?1429–1507) were also painters. **2. Vin·cen·zo** (vin'tʃɛntso). 1801–35, Italian composer of operas, esp. *La Sonnambula* (1831) and *Norma* (1831).

Bel+lin+zo+na (*Italian* ˌbellin'tsoːna) *n.* a town in SE central Switzerland, capital of Ticino canton. Pop.: 16 979 (1970).

bell jar *n.* a bell-shaped glass cover used to protect flower arrangements or fragile ornaments or to cover apparatus in experiments, esp. to prevent gases escaping.

bell mag+pie *n.* another name for **currawong.**

bell+man ('bɛlmən) *n., pl.* **+men.** a man who rings a bell, esp. (formerly) a town crier.

bell met+al *n.* an alloy of copper and tin, with some zinc and lead, used in casting bells.

Bel·loc ('bɛlɒk) *n.* **Hi·laire** ('hɪlɛə, hɪ'lɛə). 1870–1953, English poet, essayist, and historian, born in France, noted particularly for his verse for children in *The Bad Child's Book of Beasts* (1896) and *Cautionary Tales* (1907).

Bel·lo·na (bə'ləʊnə) *n.* the Roman goddess of war.

bel+low ('bɛləʊ) *vb.* **1.** (*intr.*) to make a loud deep raucous cry like that of a bull; roar. **2.** to shout (something) unrestrainedly, as in anger or pain; bawl. ~*n.* **3.** the characteristic noise of a bull. **4.** a loud deep sound, as of pain or anger. [C14: probably from Old English *bylgan;* related to *bellan* to BELL²] —**'bel+low+er** *n.*

Bel·low ('bɛləʊ) *n.* **Saul.** born 1915, U.S. novelist, born in Canada. His works include *Dangling Man* (1944), *The Adventures of Augie March* (1953), *Herzog* (1964), and *Humboldt's Gift* (1975): Nobel prize for literature 1976.

bel+lows ('bɛləʊz) *n.* (*functioning as sing. or pl.*) **1.** Also called: **pair of bellows.** an instrument consisting of an air chamber with flexible sides, a means of compressing it, an inlet valve, and a constricted outlet that is used to create a stream of air, as for producing a draught for a fire or for sounding organ pipes. **2.** *Photog.* a telescopic light-tight sleeve, connecting the lens system of some cameras to the body of the instrument. **3.** a flexible corrugated element used as an expansion joint, pump, or means of transmitting axial motion. [C16: from plural of Old English *belig* BELLY]

bel+lows fish *n.* another name for **snipefish.**

bell pull *n.* a handle, rope, or cord pulled to operate a doorbell or servant's bell.

bell punch *n.* a machine that issues or stamps a ticket, etc., ringing a bell as it does so.

bell push *n.* a button pressed to operate an electric bell.

bell-ring·er *n.* **1.** a person who rings church bells. **2.** a person who plays musical handbells. —**'bell-ˌring·ing** *n.*

bell sheep *n. Austral.* a sheep that a shearer is just starting to shear (and which he is allowed to finish) as the bell rings for the end of a work period. Also called: **catch.**

bells of Ire+land *n.* (*functioning as sing.*) an annual garden plant, *Moluccella laevis,* whose flowers have a green cup-shaped calyx: family *Labiatae* (labiates).

bell tent *n.* a cone-shaped tent having a single central supporting pole.

bell+weth·er ('bɛlˌwɛðə) *n.* **1.** a sheep that leads the herd, often bearing a bell. **2.** a leader, esp. one followed blindly.

bell+wort ('bɛlˌwɜːt) *n. U.S.* **1.** any plant of the North American liliaceous genus *Uvularia,* having slender bell-shaped yellow flowers. **2.** another name for **campanula.**

bel+ly ('bɛlɪ) *n., pl.* **+lies. 1.** the lower or front part of the body of a vertebrate, containing the intestines and other abdominal organs; abdomen. **2.** the stomach, esp. when regarded as the seat of gluttony. **3.** a part, line, or structure that bulges deeply: *the belly of a sail.* **4.** the inside or interior cavity of something: *the belly of a ship.* **5.** the front or inner part or underside of something. **6.** the surface of a stringed musical instrument over which the strings are stretched. **7.** the thick central part of certain muscles. **8.** *Tanning.* the portion of a hide or skin on the underpart of an animal. **9.** *Archery.* the surface of the bow next to the bowstring. **10.** an archaic word for **womb** (sense 4). ~*vb.* **+lies, +ly+ing, +lied. 11.** to swell out or cause to swell out; bulge. [Old English *belig;* related to Old High German *balg,* Old Irish *bolg* sack, Sanskrit *barhi* chaff]

bel+ly ache *n.* **1.** an informal term for **stomach ache.** ~*vb.* **bel·ly+ache. 2.** (*intr.*) *Slang.* to complain repeatedly. —**'bel·ly+ˌach·er** *n.*

bel·ly+band ('bɛlɪˌbænd) *n.* a strap around the belly of a draught animal, holding the shafts of a vehicle.

bel·ly+but·ton ('bɛlɪˌbʌtᵊn) *n.* an informal name for the **navel.**

bel+ly dance *n.* **1.** a sensuous and provocative dance of Middle Eastern origin, performed by women, with undulating movements of the hips and abdomen. ~*vb.* **bel·ly-dance. 2.** (*intr.*) to perform such a dance. —**bel+ly danc+er** *n.*

bel+ly flop *n.* **1.** a dive into water in which the body lands horizontally. **2.** another name for **belly landing.** ~*vb.* **bel·ly-flop, -flops, -flop·ping, -flopped. 3.** (*intr.*) to perform a belly flop.

bel+ly+ful ('bɛlɪˌfʊl) *n.* **1.** as much as one wants or can eat. **2.** *Slang.* more than one can tolerate.

bel+ly land+ing *n. Informal.* the landing of an aircraft on its fuselage without use of its landing gear.

bel+ly laugh *n. Informal.* a loud deep hearty laugh.

Bel·mon·do (bɛl'mɒndəʊ; *French* bɛlmɔ̃'dɔ) *n.* **Jean-Paul** (ʒɑ̃ 'pɔl). born 1933, French film actor.

Bel+mo+pan (ˌbɛlmə'pæn) *n.* (since 1973) the capital of Belize, about 50 miles inland: founded in 1970. Pop.: 4000 (1974 est.).

Be·lo Ho+ri+zon+te (*Portuguese* 'bɛlori'zonti) *n.* a city in SE Brazil, the capital of Minas Gerais state. Pop.: 1 232 708 (1970).

be+long (bɪ'lɒŋ) *vb.* (*intr.*) **1.** (foll. by *to*) to be the property or possession (of). **2.** (foll. by *to*) to be a member (of a club, etc.). **3.** (foll. by *to, under, with,* etc.) to be classified (with): *this plant belongs to the daisy family.* **4.** (foll. by *to*) to be a part or adjunct (of): *this top belongs to the smaller box.* **5.** to have a proper or usual place: *that plate belongs in the cupboard.* **6.** *Informal.* to be suitable or acceptable, esp. socially: *although they were rich, they just didn't belong.* [C14 *belongen,* from BE- (intensive) + *longen;* related to Old High German *bilangēn* to reach; see LONG³]

be+long+ing (bɪ'lɒŋɪŋ) *n.* secure relationship; affinity (esp. in the phrase **a sense of belonging**).

be+long+ings (bɪ'lɒŋɪŋz) *pl. n.* (*sometimes sing.*) the things that a person owns or has with him; possessions; effects.

Be+lo+rus+sian (ˌbjɛləʊ'rʌʃən, ˌbɛl-) *n.* a variant spelling of **Byelorussian.** —**ˌBe+lo+'rus+sian** *adj.*

Be+los+tok (bjɪla'stɔk) *n.* transliteration of the Russian name for **Białystok.**

be+lov+ed (bɪ'lʌvɪd, -'lʌvd) *adj.* **1.** dearly loved. ~*n.* **2.** a person who is dearly loved, such as a wife or husband.

Be+lo+vo (*Russian* 'bjɛləvə) *n.* a variant spelling of **Byelovo.**

be+low (bɪ'ləʊ) *prep.* **1.** at or to a position lower than; under. **2.** less than in quantity or degree. **3.** south of. **4.** downstream of. **5.** unworthy of; beneath. ~*adv.* **6.** at or to a lower position or place. **7.** at a later place (in something written): *see below.* **8.** *Archaic.* beneath heaven; on earth or in hell. [C14: *bilooghe,* from *bi* BY + *looghe* LOW¹]

Bel Pa·e·se ('bɛl pɑː'eɪzɪ) *n.* a mild creamy Italian cheese.

Bel·sen ('bɛlsən; *German* 'bɛlzᵊn) *n.* a village in N West Germany: with Bergen, the site of a Nazi concentration camp (1943–45).

Bel·shaz·zar (bɛl'ʃæzə) *n.* the son of Nabonidus; coregent of Babylon with his father for eight years: referred to as king and son of Nebuchadnezzar in the Old Testament (Daniel 5:1, 17; 8:1); described as having received a divine message of doom written on a wall at a banquet (**Belshazzar's Feast**).

belt (bɛlt) *n.* **1.** a band of cloth, leather, etc., worn, usually around the waist, to support clothing, carry tools, weapons, or ammunition, or as decoration. **2.** a narrow band, circle, or stripe, as of colour. **3.** an area, esp. an elongated one, where a specific thing or specific conditions are found; zone: *a belt of high pressure.* **4.** See **seat belt. 5.** a band of flexible material between rotating shafts or pulleys to transfer motion or transmit goods: *a fan belt; a conveyer belt.* **6.** short for **beltcourse** (see **cordon** (sense 4)). **7.** *Informal.* a sharp blow, as with a bat or the fist. **8. below the belt. a.** *Boxing.* below the waist, esp. in the groin. **b.** *Informal.* in an unscrupulous or cowardly way. **9. tighten one's belt.** to take measures to reduce expenditure. **10. under one's belt. a.** (of food or drink) in one's stomach. **b.** in one's possession. **c.** as part of one's experience: *he had a linguistics degree under his belt.* ~*vb.* **11.** (*tr.*) to fasten or attach with or as if with a belt. **12.** (*tr.*) to hit with a belt. **13.** (*tr.*) *Slang.* to give a sharp blow; punch. **14.** (*intr.;* often foll. by *along*) *Slang.* to move very fast, esp. in a car: *belting down the motorway.* **15.** (*tr.*) *Rare.* to mark with belts, as of colour. **16.** (*tr.*) *Rare.* to encircle; surround. [Old English, from Latin *balteus*]

Bel·tane ('bɛlteɪn, -tən) *n.* an ancient Celtic festival with a sacrificial bonfire on May Day. [C15: from Scottish Gaelic *bealltainn*]

belt·course *n.* another name for **cordon** (sense 4).

belt·ing ('bɛltɪŋ) *n.* **1.** the material used to make a belt or belts. **2.** belts collectively. **3.** *Informal.* a beating.

belt man *n. Austral.* the member of a beach lifesaving team who swims out with a line attached to his belt.

belt out *vb.* (*tr., adv.*) *Informal.* to sing loudly or emit (sound, esp. pop music) loudly: *a jukebox belting out the latest hits.*

belt up *vb.* (*adv.*) **1.** *Slang.* to become or cause to become silent; stop talking: often used in the imperative. **2.** to fasten with or be a belt, esp. a seat belt.

belt·way ('bɛlt,weɪ) *n.* the usual U.S. name for a **ring road.**

be·lu·ga (bɪ'luːgə) *n.* **1.** a large white sturgeon, *Acipenser* (or *Huso*) *huso,* of the Black and Caspian Seas: a source of caviar and isinglass. **2.** another name for **white whale.** [C18: from Russian *byeluga,* from *byely* white]

bel·ve·dere ('bɛlvɪ,dɪə, ,bɛlvɪ'dɪə) *n.* a building, such as a summerhouse or roofed gallery, sited to command a fine view. See also **gazebo.** [C16: from Italian: beautiful sight]

B.E.M. *abbrev. for* British Empire Medal.

be·ma, bi·mah, *or* **bi·ma** ('biːmə) *n.* **1.** the speaker's platform in the assembly in ancient Athens. **2.** *Christian Orthodox Church.* a raised area surrounding the altar in a church; the sanctuary. **3.** *Judaism.* a platform in a synagogue from which the Scriptures are read. [C17: via Late Latin, from Greek *bēma,* from *bainein* to go]

Bem·ba ('bɛmbə) *n.* **1.** (*pl.* **-ba** *or* **-bas**) a member of a Negroid people of Africa, living chiefly in Zambia on a high infertile plateau. **2.** the language of this people, belonging to the Bantu group of the Niger-Congo family.

be·mean (bɪ'miːn) *vb.* a less common word for **demean**[1].

be·mire (bɪ'maɪə) *vb.* (*tr.*) **1.** to soil with or as if with mire. **2.** (*usually passive*) to stick fast in mud or mire.

be·moan (bɪ'məʊn) *vb.* to grieve over (a loss, etc.); mourn; lament (esp. in the phrase **bemoan one's fate**). [Old English *bemǣnan;* see BE-, MOAN]

be·muse (bɪ'mjuːz) *vb.* (*tr.*) to confuse; bewilder.

be·mused (bɪ'mjuːzd) *adj.* preoccupied; lost in thought.

ben[1] (bɛn) *Scot.* ~*n.* **1.** an inner room in a house or cottage. ~*prep., adv.* **2.** in; within; inside. ~*adj.* **3.** inner. [Old English *binnan,* from BE- + *innan* inside]

ben[2] (bɛn) *n.* **1.** any of several Asiatic trees of the genus *Moringa,* esp. *M. oleifera* of Arabia and India, whose seeds yield **oil of ben,** used in manufacturing perfumes and cosmetics, lubricating delicate machinery, etc.: family *Moringaceae.* **2.** the seed of such a tree. [C15: from Arabic *bān*]

ben[3] (bɛn) *n. Scot., Irish.* a high mountain peak (esp. in place names): *Ben Lomond.* [C18: from Gaelic *beann*]

Ben·a·dryl ('bɛnədrɪl) *n. Trademark.* an antihistamine drug used in sleeping pills; diphenhydramine. Formula: $C_{17}H_{21}NO$.

be·name (bɪ'neɪm) *vb.* **-names, -nam·ing, -named;** **-named** *or* **-nempt.** (*tr.*) an archaic word for **name** (sense 11). [Old English *benemnan;* see BE-, NAME]

Be·na·res (bɪ'nɑːrɪz) *or* **Ba·na·ras** *n.* the former name of **Varanasi.**

Ben Bel·la ('bɛn 'bɛlə) *n.* **Ah·med** ('ɑːmɪd). born 1916, Algerian statesman: first prime minister (1962–65) and president (1963–65) of independent Algeria.

bench (bɛntʃ) *n.* **1.** a long seat for more than one person, usually lacking a back or arms. **2.** a plain stout work table. **3. the bench.** (*sometimes cap.*) **a.** a judge or magistrate sitting in court in a judicial capacity. **b.** judges or magistrates collectively. **4.** *Sport.* the seat on which reserve players and officials sit during a game. **5.** *Geology.* a flat narrow platform of land, esp. one marking a former shoreline. **6.** a ledge in a mine or quarry from which work is carried out. **7.** a platform on which dogs or other domestic animals are exhibited at shows. ~*vb.* (*tr.*) **8.** to provide with benches. **9.** to exhibit (a dog, etc.) at a show. [Old English *benc;* related to Old Norse *bekkr,* Old High German *bank,* Danish, Swedish *bänk;* see BANK[3]]

bench·er ('bɛntʃə) *n.* (*often pl.*) *Brit.* **1.** a member of the governing body of one of the Inns of Court, usually a judge or a Queen's Counsel. **2.** See **backbencher.**

bench mark *n.* **1.** a mark on a stone post or other permanent feature, at a point whose exact elevation and position is known: used as a reference point in surveying. Abbrev.: **BM 2.** a criterion by which to measure something; standard; reference point.

bench war·rant *n.* a warrant issued by a judge or court directing that an offender be apprehended.

bend[1] (bɛnd) *vb.* **bends, bend·ing, bent. 1.** to form or cause to form a curve, as by pushing or pulling. **2.** to turn or cause to turn from a particular direction: *the road bends left past the church.* **3.** (*intr.;* often foll. by *down,* etc.) to incline the body; stoop; bow. **4.** to submit or cause to submit: *to bend before superior force.* **5.** (*tr.*) to turn or direct (one's eyes, steps, attention, etc.). **6.** (*tr.*) to concentrate (the mind); apply oneself closely. **7.** (*tr.*) *Nautical.* to attach or fasten, as a sail to a boom or a line to a cleat. **8. bend over backwards.** *Informal.* to make great efforts; exert oneself to a great extent: *he bends over backwards to accommodate his customers.* **9. bend the rules.** *Informal.* to ignore rules or change them to suit one's own convenience. ~*n.* **10.** a curved part, as in a road or river. **11.** *Nautical.* a knot or eye in a line for joining it to another or to an object. **12.** the act or state of bending. **13. round the bend.** *Brit. slang.* mad; crazy; eccentric. [Old English *bendan;* related to Old Norse *benda,* Middle High German *benden;* see BIND, BAND[3]]

bend[2] (bɛnd) *n. Heraldry.* an ordinary consisting of a diagonal line traversing a shield. [Old English *bend* BAND[2]; see BEND[1]]

Ben Day pro·cess *n. Printing.* a method of adding texture, shading, or detail to line drawings by overlaying a transparent sheet of dots or any other pattern during platemaking. [C20: named after *Benjamin Day* (died 1916), American printer]

Ben·del ('bɛndɛl) *n.* a state of S Nigeria, on the Gulf of Guinea: mainly tropical rain forest. Capital: Benin City. Pop.: 3 535 839 (1976 est.). Area: 39 737 sq. km (15 339 sq. miles). Former name (until 1976): **Mid-Western State.**

bend·er ('bɛndə) *n. Informal.* a drinking bout.

Ben·di·go ('bɛndɪ,gəʊ) *n.* a city in SE Australia, in central Victoria: founded in 1851 after the discovery of gold. Pop.: 45 860 (1971).

bends (bɛndz) *pl. n.* **the.** a nontechnical name for **decompression sickness.**

bend sin·is·ter *n. Heraldry.* a diagonal line bisecting a shield from the top right to the bottom left, typically indicating a bastard line.

bend·y[1] ('bɛndɪ) *adj.* **bend·i·er, bend·i·est. 1.** flexible or pliable. **2.** having many bends: *a bendy road.*

bend·y[2] *or* **ben·dee** ('bɛndɪ) *adj.* (*usually postpositive*) *Heraldry.* striped diagonally.

be·neath (bɪ'niːθ) *prep.* **1.** below, esp. if covered, protected, or obscured by. **2.** not as great or good as would be demanded by: *beneath his dignity.* ~*adv.* **3.** below; underneath. [Old English *beneothan,* from BE- + *neothan* low; see NETHER]

ben·e·di·ci·te (,bɛnɪ'daɪsɪtɪ) *n.* **1.** (esp. in Christian religious orders) a blessing or grace. ~*interj.* **2.** *Obsolete.* an expression of surprise. [C13: from Latin, from *benedīcere,* from *bene* well + *dīcere* to speak]

Ben·e·di·ci·te (,bɛnɪ'daɪsɪtɪ) *n. Christianity.* a canticle that originated as part of the *Song of the Three Holy Children* in the secondary addition to the Book of Daniel, beginning *Benedicite omnia opera Domini Domino* in Latin, and *O all ye Works of the Lord* in English.

Ben·e·dict ('bɛnɪ,dɪkt) *n.* **Saint.** ?480–?547 A.D., Italian monk: founded the Benedictine order at Monte Cassino in Italy in about 540 A.D. His *Regula Monachorum* became the basis of the rule of all Western Christian monastic orders. Feast day: March 21.

Ben·e·dict XV *n.* original name *Giacomo della Chiesa.* 1854–1922, pope (1914–22); noted for his repeated attempts to end World War I and for his organization of war relief.

Ben·e·dic·tine *n.* **1.** (,bɛnɪ'dɪktin, -taɪn). **a.** a monk or nun who is a member of a Christian religious community founded by or following the rule of Saint Benedict. **b.** (*as modifier*): *the Benedictine rule.* **2.** (,bɛnɪ'dɪktiːn) a greenish-yellow liqueur made from a secret formula developed at the Benedictine monastery at Fécamp in France in about 1510.

ben·e·dic·tion (,bɛnɪ'dɪkʃən) *n.* **1.** an invocation of divine blessing, esp. at the end of a Christian religious ceremony. **2.** a Roman Catholic service in which the congregation is blessed with the sacrament. **3.** the state of being blessed. [C15: from Latin *benedictio,* from *benedīcere* to bless; see BENEDICITE] —**,ben·e·'dic·to·ry** *adj.*

Ben·e·dic·tus (,bɛnɪ'dɪktəs) *n.* (*sometimes not cap.*) *Christianity.* **1.** a short canticle beginning *Benedictus qui venit in nomine Domini* in Latin and *Blessed is he that cometh in the name of the Lord* in English. **2.** a canticle beginning *Benedictus Dominus Deus Israel* in Latin and *Blessed be the Lord God of Israel* in English.

ben·e·fac·tion (,bɛnɪ'fækʃən) *n.* **1.** the act of doing good, esp. by giving a donation to charity. **2.** the donation or help given. [C17: from Late Latin *benefactiō,* from Latin *bene* well + *facere* to do]

ben·e·fac·tor ('bɛnɪ,fæktə, ,bɛnɪ'fæk-) *n.* a person who supports or helps a person, institution, etc., esp. by giving money; patron. —**'ben·e,fac·tress** *fem. n.*

be·nef·ic (bɪ'nɛfɪk) *adj.* a rare word for **beneficent.**

ben·e·fice ('bɛnɪfɪs) *n.* **1.** *Christianity.* an endowed Church office yielding an income to its holder; a Church living. **2.** the property or revenue attached to such an office. **3.** (in feudal society) a tenement (piece of land) held by a vassal from a landowner on easy terms or free, esp. in return for military support. See also **vassalage.** ~*vb.* **4.** (*tr.*) to provide with a benefice. [C14: from Old French, from Latin *beneficium* benefit, from *beneficus,* from *bene* well + *facere* to do]

be·nef·i·cence (bɪ'nɛfɪsəns) *n.* **1.** the act of doing good; kindness. **2.** a charitable act or gift.

be·nef·i·cent (bɪ'nɛfɪsᵊnt) *adj.* charitable; generous. [C17: from Latin *beneficent-,* from *beneficus;* see BENEFICE] —**be'nef·i·cent·ly** *adv.*

ben·e·fi·cial (,bɛnɪ'fɪʃəl) *adj.* **1.** (sometimes foll. by *to*) causing a good result; advantageous. **2.** *Law.* entitling a person to receive the profits or proceeds of property: *a beneficial interest in land.* [C15: from Late Latin *beneficiālis,* from Latin *beneficium* kindness] —**,ben·e'fi·cial·ly** *adv.*

ben·e·fi·ciar·y (,bɛnɪ'fɪʃərɪ) *n., pl.* **·ciar·ies. 1.** a person who gains or benefits in some way from something. **2.** *Law.* a person entitled to receive funds or other property under a trust, will, or insurance policy. **3.** the holder of an ecclesiastical or other benefice. ~*adj.* **4.** of or relating to a benefice or the holder of a benefice.

ben·e·fit ('bɛnɪfɪt) *n.* **1.** something that improves or promotes. **2.** advantage or sake: *this is for your benefit.* **3.** (*sometimes pl.*) a payment or series of payments made by an institution, such as an insurance company or trade union, to a person who is ill, unemployed, etc. **4.** a theatrical performance, sports event, etc., to raise money for a charity. ~*vb.* **·fits, ·fit·ing, ·fit·ed** *or esp. U.S.* **·fits, ·fit·ting, ·fit·ted. 5.** to do or receive good; profit. [C14: from Anglo-French *benfet,* from Latin *benefactum,* from *bene facere* to do well]

ben·e·fit as·so·ci·a·tion *n.* a U.S. term for **friendly society.**

ben·e·fit of cler·gy *n. Christianity.* **1.** sanction by the church: *marriage without benefit of clergy.* **2.** (in the Middle Ages) a privilege that placed the clergy outside the jurisdiction of secular courts and entitled them to trial in ecclesiastical courts.

Ben·e·lux ('bɛnɪ,lʌks) *n.* **1.** the customs union formed by Belgium, the Netherlands, and Luxembourg in 1948; became an economic union in 1960. **2.** these countries collectively.

be·nempt (bɪ'nɛmpt) *vb. Archaic.* a past participle of **bename.**

Ben·eš (*Czech* 'bɛnɛʃ) *n.* **Ed·u·ard** ('ɛdʊart). 1884–1948, Czech statesman; president of Czechoslovakia (1935–38; 1946–48) and of its government in exile (1939–45).

Ben·ét (bə'neɪ) *n.* **Ste·phen Vin·cent.** 1898–1943, U.S. poet and novelist, best known for his poem on the American Civil War *John Brown's Body* (1928).

Be·ne·ven·to (,bɛnə'vɛntəʊ) *n.* a city in S Italy, in N Campania: at various times under Samnite, Roman, Lombard, Saracen, Norman, and papal rule. Pop.: 59 016 (1971). Ancient name: **Beneventum.**

be·nev·o·lence (bɪ'nɛvələns) *n.* **1.** inclination or tendency to help or do good to others; charity. **2.** an act of kindness. **3.** (in the Middle Ages) a forced loan or contribution exacted by English kings from their nobility and subjects.

be·nev·o·lent (bɪ'nɛvələnt) *adj.* **1.** intending or showing good will; kindly; friendly: *a benevolent smile; a benevolent old man.* **2.** doing good or giving aid to others, rather than making profit; charitable: *a benevolent organization.* [C15: from Latin *benevolēns,* from *bene* well + *velle* to wish] —**be'nev·o·lent·ly** *adv.*

Ben·fleet ('bɛn,fli:t) *n.* a town in SE England, in S Essex on an inlet of the Thames estuary. Pop.: 47 924 (1971).

Beng. *abbrev. for* Bengal(i).

B.Eng. *abbrev. for* Bachelor of Engineering.

Ben·gal (bɛn'gɔ:l, bɛŋ-) *n.* **1.** a former province of NE India, in the great deltas of the Ganges and Brahmaputra Rivers: in 1947 divided into West Bengal (belonging to India) and East Bengal (Bangladesh). **2. Bay of.** a wide arm of the Indian Ocean, between India and Burma. —**Ben·ga·lese** (,bɛngə'li:z, ,bɛŋ-) *adj., n.*

Ben·ga·li (bɛn'gɔ:lɪ, bɛŋ-) *n.* **1.** a member of a people living chiefly in Bangladesh and in West Bengal. The West Bengalis are mainly Hindus; the East Bengalis of Bangladesh are mainly Muslims. **2.** the language of this people: the official language of Bangladesh and the chief language of West Bengal; it belongs to the Indic branch of the Indo-European family. ~*adj.* **3.** of or relating to Bengal, the Bengalis, or their language.

ben·ga·line ('bɛŋgə,li:n, ,bɛŋgə'li:n) *n.* a heavy corded fabric, esp. silk with woollen or cotton cord. [C19: from French; see BENGAL, -INE¹; first produced in Bengal]

Ben·gal light *n.* a firework or flare that burns with a steady bright blue light, formerly used as a signal.

Ben·gha·zi *or* **Ben·ga·si** (bɛn'gɑ:zɪ) *n.* a port in N Libya, on the Gulf of Sidra: centre of Italian colonization (1911–42); scene of much fighting in World War II. Ancient names: **Hesperides, Berenice.**

Ben·guel·a (bɛŋ'gwɛlə) *n.* a port in W Angola: founded in 1617; a terminus (with Lobito) of the railway that runs from Beira in Mozambique through the Copper Belt of Zambia and Rhodesia. Pop.: 40 996 (1970).

Ben-Gur·i·on (bɛn'gʊərɪən) *n.* **Da·vid.** 1886–1973, Israeli socialist statesman, born in Poland; first prime minister of Israel (1948–53, 1955–63).

Be·ni (*Spanish* 'beni) *n.* a river in N Bolivia, rising in the E Cordillera of the Andes and flowing north to the Marmoré River. Length: over 1600 km (1000 miles).

be·night·ed (bɪ'naɪtɪd) *adj.* **1.** lacking cultural, moral, or intellectual enlightenment; ignorant. **2.** *Archaic.* overtaken by night. —**be'night·ed·ly** *adv.* —**be'night·ed·ness** *n.*

be·nign (bɪ'naɪn) *adj.* **1.** showing kindliness; genial. **2.** (of soil, climate, etc.) mild; gentle. **3.** favourable; propitious. **4.** *Pathol.* (of a tumour, etc.) not threatening to life or health; not malignant. [C14: from Old French *benigne,* from Latin *benignus,* from *bene* well + *gignere* to produce] —**be'nign·ly** *adv.*

be·nig·nant (bɪ'nɪgnənt) *adj.* **1.** kind; gracious, as a king to his subjects. **2.** a less common word for **benign** (senses 3, 4). —**be'nig·nan·cy** *n.* —**be'nig·nant·ly** *adv.*

be·nig·ni·ty (bɪ'nɪgnɪtɪ) *n., pl.* **·ties. 1.** the quality of being benign; favourable attitude. **2.** a kind or gracious act.

Be·ni Ha·san ('bɛnɪ hæ'sɑ:n) *n.* a village in central Egypt, on the Nile, with cliff-cut tombs dating from 2000 B.C.

Be·nin (be'ni:n) *n.* **1.** a republic in W Africa, on the **Bight of Benin,** a section of the Gulf of Guinea: in the early 19th century a powerful Negro kingdom, famed for its women warriors; became a French colony in 1893, gaining independence in 1960. It consists chiefly of coastal lagoons and swamps in the south, a fertile plain and marshes in the centre, and the Atakora Mountains in the northwest. Official language: French. Currency: franc. Capital: Porto Novo. Pop.: 2 760 000 (1971 UN est.). Official name: **People's Republic of Benin.** Former name (until 1975): **Dahomey. 2.** a former kingdom of W Africa, powerful from the 14th to the 17th centuries: now a province of S Nigeria.

Be·nin Cit·y *n.* a city in S Nigeria, capital of Bendel state: former capital of the kingdom of Benin. Pop.: 136 000 (1975 est.).

ben·i·son ('bɛnɪzᵊn, -sᵊn) *n. Archaic.* a blessing, esp. a spoken one. [C13: from Old French *beneison,* from Latin *benedictiō* BENEDICTION]

ben·ja·min ('bɛndʒəmɪn) *n.* **1.** another name for **benzoin** (sense 1). **2. benjamin bush.** another name for **spicebush.** [C16: variant of *benzoin;* influenced in form by the name *Benjamin*]

Ben·ja·min ('bɛndʒəmɪn) *n.* **1.** *Old Testament.* **a.** the youngest and best-loved son of Jacob and Rachel (Genesis 35:16–18; 42:4). **b.** the tribe descended from this patriarch. **c.** the territory of this tribe, northwest of the Dead Sea. **2.** *Archaic.* a youngest and favourite son.

Ben Lo·mond ('bɛn 'ləʊmənd) *n.* **1.** a mountain in W central Scotland, on the E side of Loch Lomond. Height: 973 m (3192 ft.). **2.** a mountain in NE Tasmania. Height: 1527 m (5010 ft.). **3.** a mountain in SE Australia, in NE New South Wales. Height: 1520 m (4986 ft.).

ben·ne ('bɛnɪ) *n.* **1.** another name for **sesame. 2. benne oil.** the edible oil obtained from sesame seeds. [from Malay *bene;* compare Bambara *bene*]

ben·net ('bɛnɪt) *n.* short for **herb bennet.**

Ben·nett ('bɛnɪt) *n.* **1. (Enoch) Ar·nold.** 1867–1931, English novelist, noted for *The Old Wives' Tale* (1908), *Clayhanger* (1910), and other works set in the Staffordshire Potteries. **2. Rich·ard Rod·ney.** born 1936, English composer, noted for his operas *The Mines of Sulphur* (1965) and *Victory* (1970). **3.** Sir **Wil·liam Stern·dale.** 1816–75, English composer.

Ben Ne·vis ('bɛn 'nɛvɪs) *n.* a mountain in W Scotland, in the Grampian mountains: highest peak in Great Britain. Height: 1343 m (4406 ft.).

Ben·ning·ton ('bɛnɪŋtən) *n.* a town in SW Vermont: the site of a British defeat (1777) in the War of American Independence. Pop.: 7950 (1970).

ben·ny¹ ('bɛnɪ) *n., pl.* **·nies.** *Slang.* an amphetamine tablet, esp. benzedrine: a stimulant. [C20: shortened from BENZEDRINE]

ben·ny² ('bɛnɪ) *n., pl* **·nies.** *U.S. slang.* a man's overcoat. [C19: from *Benjamin,* perhaps from a tailor's name]

Be·noît de Sainte-Maure (*French* bənwa də sɛ̃t 'mɔ:r) *n.* 12th-century French trouvère: author of the *Roman de Troie,* which contains the episode of Troilus and Cressida.

Be·no·ni (bɪ'nəʊnɪ) *n.* a city in NE South Africa, in S Transvaal: gold mines. Pop.: 149 563 (1970).

bent¹ (bɛnt) *adj.* **1.** not straight; curved. **2.** (foll. by *on*) fixed (on a course of action); resolved (to); determined (to). **3.** *Slang.* **a.** dishonest; corrupt. **b.** (of goods) stolen. **c.** crazy; mad. **d.** sexually deviant, esp. homosexual. ~*n.* **4.** personal inclination, propensity, or aptitude. **5.** capacity of endurance (esp. in the phrase **to the top of one's bent**). 6. *Civil engineering.* a framework placed across a structure to stiffen it.

bent² (bɛnt) *n.* **1.** short for **bent grass. 2.** a stalk of bent grass. **3.** *Archaic.* any stiff grass or sedge. **4.** *Archaic or Scot. and Northern Brit. dialect.* heath or moorland. [Old English *bionot;* related to Old Saxon *binet,* Old High German *binuz* rush]

bent grass *n.* any perennial grass of the genus *Agrostis,* esp. *A. tenuis,* which has a spreading panicle of tiny flowers. Some species are planted for hay or in lawns. Sometimes shortened to **bent.**

Ben·tham ('bɛnθəm) *n.* **Jer·e·my.** 1748–1832, English philosopher and jurist: a founder of utilitarianism. His works include *A Fragment on Government* (1776) and *Introduction to the Principles of Morals and Legislation* (1789). —**'Ben·tham·ism** *n.* —**'Ben·tham·ite** *n., adj.*

ben·thos ('bɛnθɒs) *or* **ben·thon** *n.* **1.** the animals and plants living at the bottom of a sea or lake. **2.** the bottom of a sea or lake. [C19: from Greek: depth; related to *bathus* deep] —**'ben·thic, 'ben·thal,** *or* **ben'thon·ic** *adj.*

Ben·tinck ('bɛntɪŋk) *n.* Lord **Wil·liam Cav·en·dish.** 1774–1839, English statesman, first governor general of India (1828–35).

Bent·ley ('bɛntlɪ) *n.* **1. Ed·mund Cler·i·hew.** 1875–1956, English journalist, noted for his invention of the clerihew. **2. Rich·ard.** 1662–1742, English classical scholar, noted for his imaginative textual emendations.

ben+ton+ite ('bɛntəˌnaɪt) *n.* a valuable clay, formed by the decomposition of volcanic ash, that swells as it absorbs water: used as a filler in the building, paper, and pharmaceutical industries.

bent+wood ('bɛntˌwʊd) *n.* **a.** wood bent in moulds after being heated by steaming, used mainly for furniture. **b.** (*as modifier*): *a bentwood chair.*

Be·nu·e ('bɛnʊˌeɪ) *n.* **1.** a state of SE Nigeria, formed in 1976 from part of Benue-Plateau state. Capital: Makurdi. Pop.: 2 641 496 (1976 est.). Area: 19 200 sq. km (7412 sq. miles). **2.** a river in W Africa, rising in N Cameroon and flowing west across Nigeria: chief tributary of the River Niger. Length: 1400 km (870 miles).

Be·nu·e-Con·go *n.* **1.** a branch of the Niger-Congo family of African languages, consisting of the Bantu languages together with certain other languages of W Africa. ~*adj.* **2.** relating or belonging to this group of languages.

be+numb (bɪ'nʌm) *vb.* (*tr.*) **1.** to make numb or powerless; deaden physical feeling in, as by cold. **2.** (*usually passive*) to make inactive; stupefy (the mind, senses, will, etc.). —**be+'numb+ing+ly** *adv.*

ben+zal+de+hyde (bɛn'zældɪˌhaɪd) *n.* a yellowish fragrant volatile oil used in the manufacture of dyes, perfumes, and flavourings and as a solvent for oils and resins. Formula: C_6H_5CHO.

Ben+ze+drine ('bɛnzɪˌdri:n, -drɪn) *n.* a trademark for **amphetamine.**

ben+zene ('bɛnzi:n, bɛn'zi:n) *n.* a colourless flammable poisonous aromatic liquid used in the manufacture of styrene, phenol, etc., as a solvent for fats, resins, etc., and as an insecticide. Formula: C_6H_6. See also **benzene ring.**

ben+zene hex·a+chlo+ride *n.* See **hexachlorocyclohexane.**

ben+zene ring *n.* the hexagonal ring of bonded carbon atoms in the benzene molecule or its derivatives. Also called: **benzene nucleus.** See also **Kekulé formula.**

ben+zi+dine ('bɛnzɪˌdi:n, -dɪn) *n.* a grey or reddish poisonous crystalline powder used mainly in the manufacture of dyes, esp. Congo red. Formula: $NH_2(C_6H_4)_2NH_2$.

ben+zine ('bɛnzi:n, bɛn'zi:n) *or* **ben+zin** ('bɛnzɪn) *n.* **1.** a volatile mixture of the lighter aliphatic hydrocarbon constituents of petroleum. See **ligroin, petroleum ether. 2.** *Austral.* a rare name for **petrol.**

ben·zo- *or sometimes before a vowel* **benz-** *combining form.* **1.** indicating a benzene ring fused to another ring in a polycyclic compound: *benzofuran.* **2.** indicating derivation from benzene or benzoic acid or the presence of phenyl groups: *benzophenone.* [from BENZOIN]

ben+zo+ate ('bɛnzəʊˌeɪt, -ɪt) *n.* any salt or ester of benzoic acid, containing the group C_6H_5COO- or the ion $C_6H_5COO^-$.

ben+zo+ate of so·da *n.* another name for **sodium benzoate.**

ben+zo+caine ('bɛnzəʊˌkeɪn) *n.* a white crystalline ester used as a local anaesthetic; ethyl *para*-aminobenzoate. Formula: $C_9H_{11}NO_2$.

ben+zo+fu+ran (ˌbɛnzəʊ'fjʊəræn) *n.* a colourless insoluble aromatic liquid obtained from coal tar and used in the manufacture of synthetic resins. Formula: C_8H_6O. Also called: **coumarone, cumarone.**

ben+zo+ic (bɛn'zəʊɪk) *adj.* of, containing, or derived from benzoic acid or benzoin.

ben+zo+ic ac·id *n.* a white crystalline solid occurring in many natural resins, used in the manufacture of benzoates, plasticizers, and dyes and as a food preservative. Formula: C_6H_5COOH.

ben+zo+in ('bɛnzɔɪn, -zəʊɪn; bɛn'zəʊɪn) *n.* **1.** Also called: **benjamin.** a gum resin containing benzoic acid, obtained from various trees of the genus *Styrax*, esp. *S. benzoin* of Java and Sumatra, and used in ointments, perfume, etc. **2.** a white or yellowish crystalline compound with a camphor-like odour used as an antiseptic and flavouring; 2-hydroxy-2-phenylacetophenone. Formula: $C_6H_5CHOHCOC_6H_5$. **3.** any lauraceous aromatic shrub or tree of the genus *Lindera*, esp. *L. benzoin* (spicebush). [C16: from French *benjoin*, from Old Catalan *benjui*, from Arabic *lubān jāwī*, literally: frankincense of Java]

ben+zol *or* **ben+zole** ('bɛnzɒl) *n.* **1.** a crude form of benzene, containing toluene, xylene, and other hydrocarbons, obtained from coal tar or coal gas and used as a fuel. **2.** an obsolete name for **benzene.**

ben+zo+phe+none (ˌbɛnzəʊfɪ'nəʊn) *n.* a white sweet-smelling crystalline solid used mainly in the manufacture of organic compounds and in perfume. Formula: $C_6H_5COC_6H_5$.

ben+zo+qui+none (ˌbɛnzəʊkwɪ'nəʊn, -'kwɪnəʊn) *n.* a yellow crystalline water-soluble unsaturated ketone manufactured from aniline and used in the production of dyestuffs. Formula: $C_6H_4O_2$. Also called: **quinone.**

ben+zo+yl ('bɛnzəʊɪl) *n.* (*modifier*) of, consisting of, or containing the monovalent group C_6H_5CO-: *benzoyl group or radical.*

Ben-Zvi (bɛn'zvi:; *Hebrew* bɛn'tsvi:) *n.* **Itz·hak** ('jɪtsxak). 1884–1963, Israeli statesman; president (1952–63).

ben+zyl ('bɛnzɪl) *n.* (*modifier*) of, consisting of, or containing the monovalent group $C_6H_5CH_2$-: *benzyl alcohol.*

Be·o·grad (bɛ'ɔgrad) *n.* the Serbo-Croatian name for **Belgrade.**

Be·o+wulf ('beɪəˌwʊlf) *n.* an anonymous Old English epic poem in alliterative verse, believed to have been composed in the 8th century A.D.

be+queath (bɪ'kwi:ð, -'kwi:θ) *vb.* (*tr.*) **1.** *Law.* to dispose of (property, esp. personal property) by will. Compare **devise** (sense 2). **2.** to hand down; pass on, as to following generations. [Old English *becwethan*; related to Old Norse *kvetha* to speak, Gothic *qithan*, Old High German *quethan*] —**be+'queath+er** *n.*

be+quest (bɪ'kwɛst) *n.* **1. a.** the act of bequeathing. **b.** something that is bequeathed. **2.** *Law.* a gift of property by will, esp. personal property. Compare **devise** (senses 4, 5). [C14: BE- + Old English -*cwiss* degree; see BEQUEATH]

Bé·ran·ger (*French* berɑ̃'ʒe) *n.* **Pierre Jean de** (pjɛ:r 'ʒɑ̃ də). 1780–1857, French lyric and satirical poet.

Be+rar (bɛ'rɑ:) *n.* a region of W central India: part of Madhya Pradesh state since 1950; important for cotton-growing.

be+rate (bɪ'reɪt) *vb.* (*tr.*) to scold harshly.

Ber+ber ('bɜ:bə) *n.* **1.** a member of a Caucasoid Muslim people of N Africa. **2.** the language of this people, forming a subfamily of the Afro-Asiatic family of languages. There are extensive differences between dialects. ~*adj.* **3.** of or relating to this people or their language.

Ber+ber·a ('bɜ:bərə) *n.* a port in N Somalia, on the Gulf of Aden. Pop.: 25 000 (1972 est.).

ber+ber+i+da+ceous (ˌbɜ:bərɪ'deɪʃəs) *adj.* of, relating to, or belonging to the *Berberidaceae*, a mainly N temperate family of flowering plants (mostly shrubs), including barberry and barrenwort. [C19: from Medieval Latin *berberis*, from Arabic *barbārīs* BARBERRY]

ber+ber+ine ('bɜ:bəˌri:n) *n.* a yellow bitter-tasting alkaloid obtained from barberry and other plants and used medicinally, esp in tonics. Formula: $C_{20}H_{19}NO_5$. [from German *Berberin*, from New Latin *berberis* BARBERRY]

ber+ber+is ('bɜ:bərɪs) *n.* any shrub of the berberidaceous genus *Berberis.* See **barberry.** [C19: from Medieval Latin, of unknown origin]

ber+bice chair ('bɜ:bi:s) *n.* a large armchair with long arms that can be folded inwards to act as leg rests. [C20: named after *Berbice*, a river in Guyana]

ber+ceuse (*French* bɛr'sø:z) *n.* **1.** a cradlesong or lullaby. **2.** an instrumental piece suggestive of this, in six-eight time. [C19: from French: lullaby, from *bercer* to rock]

Berch+tes+ga+den (*German* 'bɛrçtəsˌga:dᵊn) *n.* a town in SE West Germany, in SE Bavaria: site of the fortified mountain retreat of Adolf Hitler. Pop.: 5752 (1958).

Ber+di+chev (*Russian* bɪr'ditʃɪf) *n.* an industrial city in the SW Soviet Union, in the central Ukrainian SSR. Pop.: 71 475 (1970).

Ber·dya·yev (*Russian* bɪr'djajɪf) *n.* **Ni·ko·lai Al·eks·and·ro·vich** (nika'laj alɪk'sandrəvitʃ). 1874–1948, Russian philosopher. Although he was a Marxist, his Christian views led him to criticize Soviet communism and he was forced into exile (1922).

be+reave (bɪ'ri:v) *vb.* (*tr.*) **1.** (usually foll. by *of*) to deprive (of) something or someone valued, esp. through death. **2.** *Obsolete.* to remove by force. ~See also **bereft.** [Old English *bereafian*; see REAVE[1]] —**be+'reave+ment** *n.*

be+reft (bɪ'rɛft) *adj.* (usually foll. by *of*) deprived; parted (from): *bereft of hope.*

Ber·en·son ('bɛrənsən) *n.* **Ber·nard.** 1865–1959, U.S. art historian, born in Lithuania: an authority on art of the Italian Renaissance.

be+ret ('bɛreɪ) *n.* a round close-fitting brimless cap of soft wool material or felt. [C19: from French *béret*, from Old Provençal *berret*, from Medieval Latin *birrettum* cap; see BIRETTA]

Be+re+zi+na (*Russian* bɪrɪzi'na) *n.* a river in the W Soviet Union, in the Byelorussian SSR, rising in the north and flowing south to the River Dnieper: linked with the River Dvina and the Baltic Sea by the **Berezina Canal.** Length: 563 km (350 miles).

Be+rez+ni+ki (*Russian* bɪrɪzni'ki) *n.* a city in the E Soviet Union: chemical industries. Pop.: 167 000 (1975 est.).

berg[1] (bɜ:g) *n.* short for **iceberg.**

berg[2] (bɜ:g) *n.* a South African word for **mountain.**

Berg (bɜ:g; *German* bɛrk) *n.* **Al·ban** ('alba:n). 1885–1935, Austrian composer: a pupil of Schoenberg. His works include the operas *Wozzeck* (1921) and *Lulu* (1935), chamber works, and songs.

Ber+ga+ma (bɛə'gɑ:mə, 'bɜ:gəmə) *n.* a town in W Turkey. Pop.: 26 973 (1970). Ancient name: **Pergamum.**

Ber+ga+mo (*Italian* 'bɛrgamo) *n.* a walled city in N Italy, in Lombardy. Pop.: 129 511 (1975 est.).

ber+ga+mot ('bɜ:gəˌmɒt) *n.* **1.** Also called: **bergamot orange.** a small Asian spiny rutaceous tree, *Citrus bergamia*, having sour pear-shaped fruit. **2. essence of bergamot.** a fragrant essential oil from the fruit rind of this plant, used in perfumery. **3.** a Mediterranean mint, *Mentha citrata*, that yields an oil similar to essence of bergamot. **4. wild bergamot.** a North American plant, *Monarda fistulosa*, with clusters of purple flowers: family *Labiatae* (labiates). **5.** a variety of pear. [C17: from French *bergamote*, from Italian *bergamotta*, of Turkic origin; related to Turkish *bey-armudu* prince's pear; see BEY]

Berg+da+ma (ˌbɜ:g'dɑ:mə) *n.* another name for a **Damara.**

Ber+gen *n.* **1.** (*Norwegian* 'bærgən) a port in SW Norway: chief city in medieval times. Pop.: 214 019 (1974 est.). **2.** ('bɛrxən). the Flemish name for **Mons.**

Ber·ge·rac (*French* bɛrʒə'rak) *n.* See **Cyrano de Bergerac.**

Ber·gius (*German* 'bɛrgjʊs) *n.* **Fried·rich** ('fri:drɪç). 1884–1949, German chemist, who invented a process for producing oil by high-pressure hydrogenation of coal: Nobel prize for chemistry 1931.

Berg·man ('bɜ:gmən) *n.* **1. Ing·mar** ('iŋmar). born 1918, Swedish film director, whose films include *The Seventh Seal* (1956), *Wild Strawberries* (1957), the trilogy *Through a Glass Darkly* (1961), *Winter Light* (1962), and *The Silence* (1963), and *Persona* (1966). **2. Ing·rid.** 1915-82, Swedish film actress, working in Hollywood 1938-48; noted for her leading roles in many films, including *Casablanca* (1942), *For Whom the Bell Tolls* (1943), *Anastasia* (1956), and *The Inn of the Sixth Happiness* (1958).

berg+schrund (*German* 'bɛrkʃrʊnt) *n.* a crevasse at the head of a glacier. [German: mountain crack]

Berg·son ('bɜːgsᵊn; *French* bɛrk'sɔn) *n.* **Hen·ri Louis** (ɑ̃ri 'lwi). 1859-1941, French philosopher, who sought to bridge the gap between metaphysics and science. His main works are *Memory and Matter* (1896, trans. 1911) and *Creative Evolution* (1907, trans. 1911): Nobel prize for literature 1927. **—Berg+son+i·an** (bɜːg'səʊnɪən) *adj., n.*

Berg+son+ism ('bɜːgsəˌnɪzəm) *n.* the philosophy of Bergson, which emphasizes duration as the basic element of experience and asserts the existence of a life-giving force that permeates the entire natural order. Compare **élan vital.**

berg wind *n.* a hot dry wind in South Africa blowing from the plateau down to the coast.

Be·ri·a ('bɛrɪə; *Russian* 'bjerijə) *n.* **La·vren·ti Pa·vlo·vich** (la'vrjentij 'pavləvitʃ). 1899-1953, Soviet chief of secret police; killed by his associates shortly after Stalin's death.

ber·i+ber·i (ˌbɛrɪ'bɛrɪ) *n.* a disease, endemic in E and S Asia, caused by dietary deficiency of thiamine (vitamin B_1). It affects the nerves to the limbs, producing pain, paralysis, and swelling. [C19: from Sinhalese, by reduplication from *beri* weakness]

Ber·ing *or* **Beh·ring** ('bɛrɪŋ, 'bɛər-; *Danish* 'beːreŋ) *n.* **Vi·tus** ('viːtʊs). 1681-1741, Danish navigator, who explored the N Pacific for the Russians and discovered Bering Island and the Bering Strait.

Ber·ing Sea *n.* a part of the N Pacific Ocean, between NE Siberia and Alaska. Area: about 2 275 000 sq. km (878 000 sq. miles).

Ber·ing Strait *n.* a strait between Alaska and the Soviet Union, connecting the Bering Sea and the Arctic Ocean.

Be·rio (*Italian* 'bɛːrjo) *n.* **Lu·cia·no** (lu'tʃaːno). born 1925, Italian composer, noted esp. for works that exploit instrumental and vocal timbre and technique.

Be·ri·o·so·va (bɛrɪ'əʊsəvə) *n.* **Svet·la·na** (svɪt'lanə). born 1932, British ballet dancer, born in Russia.

berk (bɜːk) *n. Brit. slang.* a variant spelling of **burk.**

Berke+le·ian (bɑː'kliːən) *adj.* **1.** denoting or relating to the philosophy of George Berkeley. ~*n.* **2.** a follower of his teachings.

Berke+le·ian+ism (bɑː'kliːəˌnɪzəm) *n.* the philosophical system of George Berkeley, holding that objects exist only when perceived, that God's perception sustains the universe, and that matter is only the substratum in which these perceptions inhere, not an independent thing or quality.

Berke·ley[1] ('bɜːklɪ) *n.* a city in W California, on San Francisco Bay: seat of the University of California. Pop.: 111 637 (1973 est.).

Berke·ley[2] *n.* **1.** ('bɜːklɪ). **Bus·by.** original name *William Berkeley.* 1895-1976, U.S. dance director, noted esp. for his choreography of film musicals. **2.** ('bɑːklɪ). **George.** 1685-1753, Irish philosopher and Anglican bishop, whose system of subjective idealism was expounded in his works *A Treatise concerning the Principles of Human Knowledge* (1710) and *Three Dialogues between Hylas and Philonous* (1713). He also wrote *Essay towards a New Theory of Vision* (1709). **3.** ('bɑːklɪ). Sir **Len·nox** (**Randal Francis**). born 1903, English composer.

ber+ke·li·um (bɜː'kiːlɪəm, 'bɜːklɪəm) *n.* a metallic transuranic element produced by bombardment of americium. Symbol: Bk; atomic no.: 97; half-life of most stable isotope, ^{247}Bk: 1400 years. [C20: named after BERKELEY[1], where it was discovered]

Berks. (bɑːks) *abbrev. for* Berkshire.

Berk+shire ('bɑːkʃɪə, -ʃə) *n.* **1.** a county of S England: the River Thames marks the N boundary and the **Berkshire Downs** occupy central parts. Administrative centre: Reading. Pop.: 659 000 (1976 est.). Area: 1877 sq. km (725 sq. miles). Abbrev.: **Berks. 2.** a breed of pork and bacon pig having a black body and white points.

ber+ley ('bɜːlɪ) *n.* an Austral. name for **ground bait.**

Ber+lich+ing+en (*German* 'bɛrlɪçɪŋən) *n.* **Götz von** (gœts fɔn), called *the Iron Hand.* 1480-1562, German warrior knight, who robbed merchants and kidnapped nobles for ransom.

ber+lin (bə'lɪn, 'bɜːlɪn) *n.* **1.** (*sometimes cap.*) Also called: **berlin wool.** a fine wool yarn used for tapestry work, etc. **2.** a four-wheeled two-seated covered carriage, popular in the 18th century. **3.** a limousine with a glass partition between the front and rear seats. ~Also called (for senses 2, 3): **ber+line** (bə'liːn, 'bɜːliːn).

Ber+lin[1] (bɜː'lɪn; *German* bɛr'liːn) *n.* a city in N Germany, divided since 1945 into the eastern sector, capital of East Germany, and the western sectors, which form an exclave in East German territory closely affiliated politically and economically with West Germany: a wall dividing the sectors was built in 1961 by the East German authorities to stop the flow of refugees from east to west; formerly the capital of Brandenburg, Prussia, and Germany. Pop.: (East Berlin) 1 094 496 (1975 est.); (West Berlin) 2 047 948 (1974 est.). **—Ber+'lin+er** *n.*

Ber·lin[2] (bɜː'lɪn) *n.* **Ir·ving.** original name *Israel Baline,* born 1888, U.S. composer and writer of lyrics, born in Russia. His musical comedies include *Annie Get Your Gun* (1946); his most popular song is *White Christmas.*

Ber·lin·guer (*Italian* berliŋ'gwɛr) *n.* **En·ri·co** (en'riːko). born 1922, Italian politician; leader of the Italian Communist Party since 1972.

Ber·li·oz ('bɛəlɪˌəʊz; *French* bɛr'ljoːz) *n.* **Hec·tor** (ɛk'tɔːr). 1803-69, French composer, regarded as a pioneer of modern orchestration. His works include the cantata *La Damnation de Faust* (1846), the operas *Les Troyens* (1856-59) and *Béatrice et Bénédict* (1860-62), the *Symphonie fantastique* (1830), and the oratorio *L'Enfance du Christ* (1854).

berm *or* **berme** (bɜːm) *n.* **1.** a narrow path or ledge at the edge of a slope, road, or canal. **2.** *Fortifications.* a narrow path or ledge between a moat and a rampart. [C18: from French *berme,* from Dutch *berm,* probably from Old Norse *barmr* BRIM]

Ber+me·jo (*Spanish* ber'mexo) *n.* a river in Argentina, rising in the northwest and flowing southeast to the Paraguay River. Length: about 1600 km (1000 miles).

Ber+mu+da (bə'mjuːdə) *n.* a British colony consisting of a group of over 300 coral islands (**The Bermudas**) in the NW Atlantic: discovered in 1515, first colonized by the British in 1684. Capital: Hamilton. Pop.: 62 330 (1970). Area: 53 sq. km (20 sq. miles). **—Ber+'mu+dan** *or* **Ber+'mu+di·an** *n., adj.*

Ber+mu+da grass *n.* a widely distributed grass, *Cynodon dactylon,* with wiry creeping rootstocks and several purplish spikes of flowers arising from a single point: used for lawns, pasturage, binding sand dunes, etc. Also called: **scutch grass, wire grass.**

Ber+mu+da rig *n.* a fore-and-aft sailing boat rig characterized by a tall mainsail (**Bermudian mainsail**) that tapers to a point. **—Ber·'mu·da-'rigged** *adj.*

Ber+mu+da shorts *pl. n.* close-fitting shorts that come down to the knees. Also called: **Bermudas.**

Bern (bɜːn; *German* bɛrn) *n.* **1.** the capital of Switzerland, in the W part, on the Aar River: entered the Swiss confederation in 1353 and became the capital in 1848. Pop.: 152 800 (1975 est.). **2.** a canton of Switzerland, between the French frontier and the Bernese Alps. Capital: Bern. Pop.: 983 296 (1970). Area: 6884 sq. km (2658 sq. miles). French name: **Berne** (bɛrn).

Ber·na·dette (ˌbɜːnə'dɛt) *n.* **Saint.** original name *Marie Bernarde Soubirous.* 1844-79, French peasant girl born in Lourdes, whose visions of the Virgin Mary led to the establishment of Lourdes as a centre of pilgrimage, esp. for the sick or crippled. Feast day: Feb. 18.

Ber·na·dotte ('bɜːnəˌdɒt; *French* bɛrna'dɔt) *n.* **Jean Bap·tiste Jules** (ʒɑ̃ batist 'ʒyl). 1764-1844, French marshal under Napoleon; king of Norway and Sweden (1818-44) as Charles XIV.

Ber·nard *n.* **1.** (*French* bɛr'naːr). **Claude** (kloːd). 1813-78, French physiologist, noted for his research on the action of secretions of the alimentary canal and the glycogenic function of the liver. **2. Saint** ('bɜːnəd), known as *Bernard of Menthon* and the *Apostle of the Alps.* 923-1008, French monk who founded hospices in the Alpine passes.

Ber+nard+ine ('bɜːnədɪn, -ˌdiːn) *n.* **1.** a monk of one of the reformed and stricter branches of the Cistercian order. ~*adj.* **2. a.** of or relating to this branch of the Cistercians. **b.** of or relating to Saint Bernard of Clairvaux.

Ber·nard of Clair+vaux *n.* **Saint.** ?1090-1153, French abbot and theologian, who founded the stricter branch of the Cistercians in 1115.

Ber+nese Alps *or* **O·ber+land** ('bɜːniːz) *n.* a mountain range in SW Switzerland, the N central part of the Alps. Highest peak: Finsteraarhorn, 4274 m (14 024 ft.).

Bern·hardt ('bɜːnhɑːt; *French* bɛr'naːr) *n.* **Sar·ah.** original name *Rosine Bernard.* 1844-1923, French actress, regarded as one of the greatest tragic actresses of all time.

ber+ni+cle goose ('bɜːnɪkᵊl) *n.* a former name for the **brent** or **barnacle goose.**

Ber+ni+na (bə'niːnə; *Italian* ber'niːna) *n.* **Piz.** a mountain in SE Switzerland, the highest peak of the **Bernina Alps,** in the S Rhaetian Alps. Height: 4049 m (13 284 ft.).

Ber+ni+na Pass *n.* a pass in the Alps between SE Switzerland and N Italy, east of Piz Bernina. Height: 2323 m (7622 ft.).

Ber·ni·ni (*Italian* ber'niːni) *n.* **Gio·van·ni Lo·ren·zo** (dʒo'vanni lo'rɛntso). 1598-1680, Italian painter, architect, and sculptor: the greatest exponent of the Italian baroque.

Ber·noul·li *or* **Ber·nouil·li** (*French* bɛrnu'ji; *German* bɛr'nʊli) *n.* **1. Da·niel** (da'njɛl), son of Jean Bernoulli. 1700-82, Swiss mathematician and physicist, who developed an early form of the kinetic theory of gases and stated the principle of conservation of energy in fluid dynamics. **2. Jacques** (ʒɑːk) *or* **Ja·kob** ('jaːkɔp). 1654-1705, Swiss mathematician, noted for his work on calculus and the theory of probability. **3.** his brother, **Jean** (ʒɑ̃) *or* **Jo·hann** ('joːhan). 1667-1748, Swiss mathematician who developed the calculus of variations.

Ber·noul·li's prin+ci+ple *or* **law** *n. Physics.* the principle that in a liquid flowing through a pipe the sum of the pressure energy, potential energy, and kinetic energy at any point is constant, provided no work is done on or by the liquid.

Bern·stein ('bɜːnstaɪn, -stiːn) *n.* **Leon·ard.** born 1918, U.S. conductor and composer, whose works include *The Age of Anxiety* (1949), the score of the musical *West Side Story* (1957), and *Mass* (1971).

ber+ret+ta (bɪ'rɛtə) *n.* a variant spelling of **biretta.**

ber+ry ('bɛrɪ) *n., pl.* **+ries. 1.** any of various small edible fruits such as the blackberry and strawberry. **2.** *Botany.* an indehiscent fruit with two or more seeds and a fleshy pericarp, such as the grape or gooseberry. **3.** any of various seeds or dried kernels, such as a coffee bean. **4.** the egg of a lobster, crayfish, or similar animal. ~*vb.* **+ries, +ry+ing, +ried.** (*intr.*) **5.** to bear or produce berries. 6. to gather or look for berries. [Old English *berie;* related to Old High German *beri,* Dutch *bezie*]

Ber·ry ('bɛrɪ) *n.* **Chuck.** original name *Charles Edward Berry.* born 1931, U.S. rock-and-roll singer, guitarist, and songwriter. His many songs include *Roll Over Beethoven* (1956), *Johnny B. Goode* (1958), *Sweet Little Sixteen* (1958), and *Memphis Tennessee* (recorded ?1958; released 1964).

ber·sa·glie·re (ˌbɛəsɑːˈljɛərɪ) *n., pl.* **·ri** (-riː). a member of a rifle regiment in the Italian Army. [C19: from Italian, from *bersaglio* target, from Old French *bersail,* from *berser* to fire at]

ber·seem (bəːˈsiːm) *n.* a Mediterranean clover, *Trifolium alexandrinum,* grown as a forage crop and to improve the soil in the southwestern U.S. Also called: **Egyptian clover.** [from Arabic *barsīm,* from Coptic *bersīm*]

ber·serk (bəˈzɜːk, -ˈsɜːk) *adj.* **1.** frenziedly violent or destructive (esp. in the phrase **go berserk**). ~*n.* **2.** Also called: **ber·serk·er.** a member of a class of ancient Norse warriors who worked themselves into a frenzy before battle and fought with insane fury and courage. [C19: Icelandic *berserkr,* from *björn* bear + *serkr* shirt]

berth (bɜːθ) *n.* **1.** a bed or bunk in a vessel or train, usually narrow and fixed to a wall. **2.** *Nautical.* a place assigned to a ship at a mooring. **3.** *Nautical.* sufficient distance from the shore or from other ships or objects for a ship to manoeuvre. **4. give a wide berth to.** to keep clear of; avoid. **5.** *Nautical.* accommodation on a ship. **6.** *Informal.* a job, esp. as a member of a ship's crew. ~*vb.* **7.** (*tr.*) *Nautical.* to assign a berth to (a vessel). **8.** *Nautical.* to dock (a vessel). **9.** (*tr.*) to provide with a sleeping place, as on a vessel or train. **10.** (*intr.*) *Nautical.* to pick up a mooring in an anchorage. [C17: probably from BEAR[1] + -TH[1]]

ber·tha (ˈbɜːθə) *n.* a wide deep capelike collar, often of lace, usually to cover up a low neckline. [C19: from French *berthe,* from *Berthe,* 8th-century Frankish queen, mother of Charlemagne]

Ber·til·lon sys·tem (ˈbɜːtɪˌlɒn; *French* bɛrtiˈjɔ̃) *n.* a system formerly in use for identifying persons, esp. criminals, by means of a detailed record of physical characteristics. [named after Alphonse *Bertillon* (1853–1914), French detective]

Ber·to·luc·ci (*Italian* bertoˈluttʃi) *n.* **Ber·nar·do** (berˈnardo). born 1940, Italian film director: his films include *The Spider's Stratagem* (1969), *The Conformist* (1970), and *1900* (1975).

Ber·wick (ˈbɛrɪk) *n.* **1.** (until 1975) a county of SE Scotland, now part of the Borders region.

Ber·wick-up·on-Tweed (ˈbɛrɪk əpɒn ˈtwiːd) *n.* a town in N England, in N Northumberland at the mouth of the Tweed: much involved in border disputes between England and Scotland between the 12th and 16th centuries; neutral territory 1551–1885. Pop.: 11 644 (1971). Also called: **Berwick.**

ber·yl (ˈbɛrɪl) *n.* a green, blue, yellow, or white hard mineral consisting of beryllium aluminium silicate in hexagonal crystalline form. It occurs principally in coarse granite and is the chief ore of beryllium. Emerald and aquamarine are transparent varieties. Formula: $Be_3Al_2Si_6O_{18}$. [C13: from Old French, from Latin *bēryllus,* from Greek *bērullos,* of Indic origin] —ˈ**ber·yl·ine** *adj.*

be·ryl·li·um (bɛˈrɪlɪəm) *n.* a corrosion-resistant toxic silvery-white metallic element that occurs chiefly in beryl and is used mainly in x-ray windows and in the manufacture of alloys. Symbol: Be; atomic no.: 4; atomic wt.: 9.012; valency: 2; relative density: 1.85; melting pt.: 1278°C; boiling pt.: 2970°C. Former name: **glucinum** or **glucinium.** [C19: from Latin *bēryllus,* from Greek *bērullos*]

Ber·ze·li·us (bəˈziːlɪəs; *Swedish* bærˈseːlius) *n.* Baron **Jöns Ja·kob** (ˈjœns ˈjɑːkɔb). 1779–1848, Swedish chemist, who invented the present system of chemical symbols and formulas, discovered several elements, and determined the atomic and molecular weight of many substances.

Bes (bɛs) *n.* an ancient Egyptian god represented as a grotesque hairy dwarf: the patron of music and pleasure.

Be·san·çon (*French* bəzɑ̃ˈsɔ̃) *n.* a city in E France, on the Doubs River: university (1422). Pop.: 126 187 (1975).

Bes·ant (ˈbɛzᵊnt, bɪˈzænt) *n.* **An·nie,** *née* **Wood.** 1847–1933, British theosophist, writer, and political reformer in England and India.

be·seech (bɪˈsiːtʃ) *vb.* **·seech·es, ·seech·ing, ·sought** *or* **·seeched.** (*tr.*) to ask (someone) earnestly (to do something *or* for something); beg. [C12: see BE-, SEEK; related to Old Frisian *besēka*] —**beˈseech·er** *n.* —**beˈseech·ing** *adj.* —**beˈseech·ing·ly** *adv.*

be·seem (bɪˈsiːm) *vb. Archaic.* to be suitable for; befit.

be·set (bɪˈsɛt) *vb.* **·sets, ·set·ting, ·set.** (*tr.*) **1.** (esp. of dangers, temptations, or difficulties) to trouble or harass constantly. **2.** to surround or attack from all sides. **3.** *Archaic.* to cover with, esp. with jewels. —**beˈset·ter** *n.*

be·set·ting (bɪˈsɛtɪŋ) *adj.* tempting, harassing, or assailing (esp. in the phrase **besetting sin**).

be·shrew (bɪˈʃruː) *vb.* (*tr.*) *Archaic.* to wish evil on; curse (used in mild oaths such as **beshrew me**). [C14: see BE-, SHREW[1]]

be·side (bɪˈsaɪd) *prep.* **1.** next to; at, by, or to the side of. **2.** as compared with. **3.** away from; wide of: *beside the point.* **4.** *Archaic.* besides. **5. beside oneself.** (*postpositive;* often foll. by *with*) overwhelmed; overwrought: *beside oneself with grief.* ~*adv.* **6.** at, by, to, or along the side of something or someone. [Old English *be sīdan;* see BY, SIDE]

be·sides (bɪˈsaɪdz) *prep.* **1.** apart from; even considering: *besides costing too much, the scheme is impractical.* ~ **2.** (*sentence connector*) anyway; moreover. ~*adv.* **3.** as well.

be·siege (bɪˈsiːdʒ) *vb.* (*tr.*) **1.** to surround (a fortified area, esp. a city) with military forces to bring about its surrender. **2.** to crowd round; hem in. **3.** to overwhelm, as with requests or queries. —**beˈsieg·er** *n.*

be·smear (bɪˈsmɪə) *vb.* (*tr.*) **1.** to smear over; daub. **2.** to sully; defile (often in the phrase **besmear (a person's) reputation).**

be·smirch (bɪˈsmɜːtʃ) *vb.* (*tr.*) **1.** to make dirty; soil. **2.** to reduce the brightness or lustre of. **3.** to sully (often in the phrase **besmirch (a person's) name).**

be·som (ˈbiːzəm) *n.* **1.** a broom, esp. one made of a bundle of twigs tied to a handle. **2.** *Curling.* a broom or brush used to sweep the ice in front of the stone to make it slide farther. **3.** *Archaic.* a derogatory term (chiefly northern Brit. dialect) for a **woman.** ~*vb.* (*tr.*) **4.** to sweep with a besom. [Old English *besma;* related to Old High German *besmo* broom]

be·sot·ted (bɪˈsɒtɪd) *adj.* **1.** stupefied with drink; intoxicated. **2.** infatuated; doting. **3.** foolish; muddled.

be·sought (bɪˈsɔːt) *vb.* the past tense or past participle of **beseech.**

be·span·gle (bɪˈspæŋgᵊl) *vb.* (*tr.*) to cover or adorn with or as if with spangles.

be·spat·ter (bɪˈspætə) *vb.* (*tr.*) **1.** to splash all over, as with dirty water. **2.** to defile; slander; besmirch.

be·speak (bɪˈspiːk) *vb.* **·speaks, ·speak·ing, ·spoke; ·spo·ken** *or* **·spoke.** (*tr.*) **1.** to engage, request, or ask for in advance. **2.** to indicate or suggest: *this act bespeaks kindness.* **3.** *Poetic.* to speak to; address. **4.** *Archaic.* to foretell.

be·spec·ta·cled (bɪˈspɛktəkᵊld) *adj.* wearing spectacles.

be·spoke (bɪˈspəʊk) *adj. Chiefly Brit.* **1.** (of a suit, jacket, etc.) made to the customer's specifications. **2.** making or selling such suits, jackets, etc.: *a bespoke tailor.*

be·spread (bɪˈsprɛd) *vb.* **·spreads, ·spread·ing, ·spread.** (*tr.*) to cover (a surface) with something.

be·sprent (bɪˈsprɛnt) *adj. Poetic.* sprinkled over. [C14: past participle of Old English *besprengan* to BESPRINKLE]

be·sprin·kle (bɪˈsprɪŋkᵊl) *vb.* (*tr.*) to sprinkle all over with liquid, powder, etc.

Bes·sa·ra·bi·a (ˌbɛsəˈreɪbɪə) *n.* a region of the SW Soviet Union, mostly in the Moldavian SSR: long disputed by the Turks and Russians; a province of Rumania from 1918 until 1940. Area: about 44 300 sq. km (17 100 sq. miles).

Bes·sel (ˈbɛsᵊl) *n.* **Frie·drich Wil·helm** (ˈfriːdrɪç ˈvɪlhɛlm). 1784–1846, German astronomer and mathematician. He made the first authenticated measurement of a star's distance from the earth (1841) and systematized a series of mathematical functions used in physics.

Bes·se·mer con·vert·er (ˈbɛsɪmə) *n.* a refractory-lined furnace used to convert pig iron into steel by the Bessemer process.

Bes·se·mer pro·cess *n.* **1.** a process for producing steel by blowing air through molten pig iron at about 1250°C in a Bessemer converter: silicon, manganese, and phosphorus impurities are removed and the carbon content is controlled. **2.** a similar process for removing sulphur and iron from copper matte. [C19: named after Sir Henry *Bessemer* (1813–98), English engineer]

best (bɛst) *adj.* **1.** the superlative of **good. 2.** most excellent of a particular group, category, etc. **3.** most suitable, advantageous, desirable, attractive, etc. **4. the best part of.** most of: *the best part of an hour.* **5. put one's best foot forward.** to do one's utmost to make progress. ~*adv.* **6.** the superlative of **well. 7.** in a manner surpassing all others; most excellently, advantageously, attractively, etc. **8.** (*in combination*) in or to the greatest degree or extent; most: *the best-loved hero.* **9. as best one can** *or* **may.** as effectively as possible within one's limitations. **10. had best.** would be wise, sensible, etc., to: *you had best go now.* ~*n.* **11. the best.** the most outstanding or excellent person, thing, or group in a category. **12.** (often preceded by *at*) the most excellent, pleasing, or skilled quality or condition: *journalism at its best.* **13.** the most effective effort of which a person or group is capable: *even their best was inadequate.* **14.** a winning majority: *the best of three games.* **15.** Also: **all the best.** best wishes: *she sent him her best.* **16.** a person's smartest outfit of clothing. **17. at best. a.** in the most favourable interpretation. **b.** under the most favourable conditions. **18. for the best. a.** for an ultimately good outcome. **b.** with good intentions: *he meant it for the best.* **19. get** *or* **have the best of.** to surpass, defeat, or outwit; better. **20. give (someone) the best.** to concede (someone's) superiority. **21. make the best of.** to cope as well as possible in the unfavourable circumstances of (often in the phrases **make the best of a bad job, make the best of it**). **22. six of the best.** *Informal.* six strokes with a cane on the buttocks or hand. ~*vb.* **23.** (*tr.*) to gain the advantage over or defeat. [Old English *betst;* related to Gothic *batista,* Old High German *bezzist*]

Best (bɛst) *n.* **Charles Her·bert.** 1899–1978, Canadian physiologist: associated with Banting and Macleod in their discovery of insulin in 1922.

best-ball *adj. Golf.* of, relating to, or denoting a match in which one player competes against the best individual totals of two or more other players at each hole.

be·stead (bɪˈstɛd) *Archaic.* ~*vb.* **·steads, ·stead·ing, ·stead·ed; ·stead·ed** *or* **·stead. 1.** (*tr.*) to help; avail. ~*adj. also* **be·sted. 2.** placed; situated. [C13: see BE-, STEAD]

best end *n.* the end of the neck of lamb, pork, etc., nearest to the ribs.

best girl *n. Archaic.* one's sweetheart.

bes·ti·al ('bɛstɪəl) *adj.* **1.** brutal or savage. **2.** sexually depraved; carnal. **3.** lacking in refinement; brutish. **4.** of or relating to a beast. [C14: from Late Latin *bestiālis,* from Latin *bestia* BEAST] —'**bes·ti·al·ly** *adv.*

bes·ti·al·i·ty (ˌbɛstɪ'ælɪtɪ) *n., pl.* **-ties. 1.** bestial behaviour, character, or action. **2.** sexual activity between a person and an animal.

bes·ti·al·ize *or* **bes·ti·al·ise** ('bɛstɪəˌlaɪz) *vb.* (*tr.*) to make bestial or brutal.

bes·ti·ar·y ('bɛstɪərɪ) *n., pl.* **-ar·ies.** a moralizing medieval collection of descriptions of real and/or mythical animals.

be·stir (bɪ'stɜː) *vb.* **-stirs, -stir·ring, -stirred.** (*tr.*) to cause (oneself, or, rarely, another person) to become active; rouse.

best man *n.* the (male) attendant of the bridegroom at a wedding.

be·stow (bɪ'stəʊ) *vb.* (*tr.*) **1.** to present (a gift) or confer (an award or honour). **2.** *Archaic.* to apply (energy, resources, etc.). **3.** *Archaic.* to house (a person) or store (goods, etc.). —**be·'stow·al** *or* **be·'stow·ment** *n.* —**be·'stow·er** *n.*

be·strew (bɪ'struː) *vb.* **-strews, -strew·ing, -strewed; -strewn** *or* **-strewed.** (*tr.*) to scatter or be scattered over (a surface).

be·stride (bɪ'straɪd) *vb.* **-strides, -strid·ing, -strode** *or* **-strid; -strid·den** *or* **-strid.** (*tr.*) **1.** to have or put a leg on either side of. **2.** to extend across; span. **3.** to stride over or across.

best sell·er *n.* **1.** a book, gramophone record, or other product that has sold in great numbers, esp. over a short period. **2.** the author of one or more such books, etc.

bet (bɛt) *n.* **1.** an agreement between two parties that a sum of money or other stake will be paid by the loser to the party who correctly predicts the outcome of an event. **2.** the money or stake risked. **3.** the predicted result in such an agreement: *his bet was that the horse would win.* **4.** a person, event, etc., considered as likely to succeed or occur: *it's a good bet that they will succeed.* **5.** a course of action (esp. in the phrase **one's best bet**). **6.** *Informal.* an opinion; view: *my bet is that you've been up to no good.* ~*vb.* **bets, bet·ting, bet** *or* **bet·ted. 7.** (when *intr.* foll. by *on* or *against*) to make or place a bet with (a person or persons). **8.** (*tr.*) to stake (money, etc.) in a bet. **9.** (*tr.; may take a clause as object*) *Informal.* to predict (a certain outcome): *I bet she fails.* **10. you bet.** *Informal.* of course; naturally. [C16: probably short for ABET]

bet. *abbrev. for* between.

be·ta ('biːtə) *n.* **1.** the second letter in the Greek alphabet (Β or β), a consonant, transliterated as *b.* **2.** the second highest grade or mark, as in an examination. **3.** (*modifier*) **a.** involving or relating to electrons: *beta emitter.* **b.** relating to one of two or more allotropes or crystal structures of a solid: *beta iron.* **c.** relating to one of two or more isomeric forms of a chemical compound. [from Greek *bēta,* from Hebrew; see BETH]

Be·ta ('biːtə) *n.* (*foll. by the genitive case of a specified constellation*) the second brightest star in a constellation: *Beta Persei.*

be·ta de·cay *n.* the radioactive transformation of an atomic nucleus accompanying the emission of an electron. It involves unit change of atomic number but none in mass number. Also called: **beta transformation** *or* **process.**

be·ta glob·u·lin *n.* another name for **transferrin.**

be·ta·ine ('biːtəˌiːn, -ɪn, bɪ'teɪiːn, -ɪn) *n.* a sweet-tasting alkaloid that occurs in the sugar beet and other plants and in animals. Formula: $C_5H_{11}NO_2$. [C19: from New Latin *Bēta* beet + -INE[2]]

be·ta i·ron *n.* a nonmagnetic allotrope of pure iron stable between 770°C and 910°C.

be·take (bɪ'teɪk) *vb.* **-takes, -tak·ing, -took, -tak·en.** (*tr.*) **1. betake oneself.** to go; move. **2.** *Archaic.* to apply (oneself) to.

be·ta par·ti·cle *n.* a high-speed electron or positron emitted by a nucleus during radioactive decay or nuclear fission.

be·ta ray *n.* a stream of beta particles.

be·ta rhythm *or* **wave** *n. Physiol.* the normal electrical activity of the cerebral cortex, occurring at a frequency of 13 to 30 hertz and detectable with an electroencephalograph. See also **brain wave.**

be·ta·tron ('biːtəˌtrɒn) *n.* a type of particle accelerator for producing high-energy beams of electrons, having an alternating magnetic field to keep the electrons in a circular orbit of fixed radius and accelerate them by magnetic induction. It produces energies of up to about 300 MeV.

be·tel ('biːtᵊl) *n.* an Asian piperaceous climbing plant, *Piper betle,* the leaves of which are chewed, with the betel nut, by the peoples of SE Asia. [C16: from Portuguese, from Malayalam *vettila*]

Be·tel·geuse *or* **Be·tel·geux** (ˌbiːtᵊl'dʒɜːz, 'biːtᵊlˌdʒɜːz) *n.* a variable red supergiant, Alpha Orionis: the second brightest star in the constellation Orion. Distance: 260 light years; diameter: 330–460 times solar diameter. [from French, from Arabic *bīt al-jauzā',* literally: shoulder of the giant, that is, of Orion]

be·tel nut *n.* the seed of the betel palm, chewed with betel leaves and lime by people in S and SE Asia as a digestive stimulant and narcotic.

be·tel palm *n.* a tropical Asian feather palm, *Areca catechu,* with scarlet or orange fruits. See **betel nut.**

bête noire *French.* (bɛt 'nwaːr) *n., pl.* **bêtes noires** (bɛt 'nwaːr) a person or thing that one particularly dislikes or dreads. [literally: black beast]

beth (bɛt) *n.* the second letter of the Hebrew alphabet (ב) transliterated as *b.* [from Hebrew *bēth-, bayith* house]

Beth·a·ny ('bɛθənɪ) *n.* a village on the west bank of the River Jordan, near Jerusalem at the foot of the Mount of Olives: in the New Testament, the home of Lazarus and the lodging place of Jesus during Holy Week.

Be·the ('beɪtə) *n.* **Hans Al·brecht** (hans 'albrɛçt). born 1906, U.S. physicist, born in Germany, noted for his research on astrophysics and nuclear physics: Nobel prize for physics 1967.

Beth·el ('bɛθəl) *n.* **1.** an ancient town on the west bank of the River Jordan, near Jerusalem: in the Old Testament, the place where the dream of Jacob occurred (Genesis 28:19). **2.** a chapel of any of certain Nonconformist Christian sects. **3.** a seamen's chapel. [C17: from Hebrew *bēth 'Ēl* house of God]

Be·thes·da (bə'θɛzdə) *n.* **1.** *New Testament.* a pool in Jerusalem reputed to have healing powers, where a paralytic was healed by Jesus (John 5:2). **2.** a chapel of any of certain Nonconformist Christian sects.

be·think (bɪ'θɪŋk) *Archaic or dialect.* ~*vb.* **-thinks, -think·ing, -thought. 1.** to cause (oneself) to consider or meditate. **2.** (*tr.; often foll. by of*) to remind (oneself).

Beth·le·hem ('bɛθlɪˌhɛm, -lɪəm) *n.* a town on the west bank of the River Jordan, near Jerusalem: birthplace of Jesus and early home of King David.

Beth·mann Holl·weg (*German* 'beːtman 'hɔlveːk) *n.* **The·o·bald von** ('teːobalt fɔn). 1856–1921, chancellor of Germany (1909–17).

be·thought (bɪ'θɔːt) *vb.* the past tense and past participle of **bethink.**

Beth·sai·da (bɛθ'seɪdə) *n.* a ruined town in N Israel, near the N shore of the Sea of Galilee.

be·tide (bɪ'taɪd) *vb.* to happen or happen to; befall (often in the phrase **woe betide (someone)**). [C13: see BE-, TIDE[2]]

be·times (bɪ'taɪmz) *adv. Archaic.* **1.** in good time; early. **2.** in a short time; soon. [C14 *bitimes;* see BY, TIME]

bê·tise (beˈtiːz) *n. Rare.* folly or lack of perception. [French, from *bête* foolish, from *bête* (n.) stupid person, BEAST]

Bet·je·man ('bɛtʃəmən) *n.* Sir **John.** born 1906, English poet, noted for his nostalgic and humorous verse and essays and for his concern for the preservation of historic buildings, esp. of the Victorian era. Appointed poet laureate 1972.

be·to·ken (bɪ'təʊkən) *vb.* (*tr.*) **1.** to indicate; signify: *black clothes betoken mourning.* **2.** to portend; augur.

bet·o·ny ('bɛtənɪ) *n., pl.* **-nies. 1.** a Eurasian plant, *Betonica* (or *Stachys*) *officinalis,* with a spike of reddish-purple flowers, formerly used in medicine and dyeing: family *Labiatae* (labiates). **2.** any of several related plants of the genus *Stachys.* **3. wood betony.** a North American scrophulariaceous plant, *Pedicularis canadensis.* See also **lousewort.** [C14: from Old French *betoine,* from Latin *betonica,* variant of *vettonica,* probably named after the *Vettones,* an ancient Iberian tribe]

be·took (bɪ'tʊk) *vb.* the past tense of **betake.**

be·tray (bɪ'treɪ) *vb.* (*tr.*) **1.** to aid an enemy of (one's nation, friend, etc.); be a traitor to: *to betray one's country.* **2.** to hand over or expose (one's nation, friend, etc.) treacherously to an enemy. **3.** to disclose (a secret, confidence, etc.) treacherously. **4.** to break (a promise) or be disloyal to (a person's trust). **5.** to disappoint the expectations of; fail: *his tired legs betrayed him.* **6.** to show signs of; indicate: *if one taps china, the sound betrays any faults.* **7.** to reveal unintentionally: *his grin betrayed his satisfaction.* **8. betray oneself.** to reveal one's true character, intentions, etc. **9.** to lead astray; deceive. **10.** *Euphemistic.* to seduce and then forsake (a woman). [C13: from BE- + *trayen,* from Old French *trair,* from Latin *trādere*] —**be·'tray·al** *n.* —**be·'tray·er** *n.*

be·troth (bɪ'trəʊð) *vb.* (*tr.*) *Archaic.* to promise to marry or to give in marriage. [C14 *betreuthen,* from BE- + *treuthe* TROTH, TRUTH]

be·troth·al (bɪ'trəʊðəl) *n.* **1.** engagement to be married. **2.** a mutual promise to marry.

be·trothed (bɪ'trəʊðd) *adj.* **1.** engaged to be married: *he was betrothed to her.* ~*n.* **2.** the person to whom one is engaged; fiancé or fiancée.

bet·ta ('bɛtə) *n.* another name for **fighting fish.** [C19: from New Latin, of unknown origin]

bet·ter[1] ('bɛtə) *adj.* **1.** the comparative of **good. 2.** more excellent than other members of a particular group, category, etc. **3.** more suitable, advantageous, attractive, etc. **4.** improved in health. **5.** fully recovered in health. **6. better off.** in more favourable circumstances, esp. financially. **7. the better part of.** a large part of: *the better part of a day.* ~*adv.* **8.** the comparative of **well. 9.** in a more excellent manner; more advantageously, attractively, etc. **10.** in or to a greater degree or extent; more: *she is better loved than her sister.* **11. go one better.** (*Brit. intr.; U.S. tr.*) to outdo (a person) or improve upon (someone else's effort). **12. had better.** would be wise, sensible, etc. to: *I had better be off.* **13. know better than to.** not to be so stupid as to. **14. think better of. a.** to change one's course of action after reconsideration. **b.** to rate more highly. ~*n.* **15. the better.** something that is the more excellent, useful, etc., of two such things. **16.** (*usually pl.*) a person who is superior, esp. in social standing or ability. **17. all the better for.** improved as a result of. **18. all the better to.** more suitable to. **19. for better for worse.** whatever the subsequent events or changes may be. **20. for the better.** by way of improvement: *a change for the better.* **21. get the better of.** to defeat, outwit, or surpass. ~*vb.* **22.** to make or become better. **23.** (*tr.*) to improve upon; surpass. [Old English *betera;* related to Old Norse *betri,* Gothic *batiza,* Old High German *beziro*]

bet·ter[2] *or esp. U.S.* **bet·tor** ('bɛtə) *n.* a person who bets.

bet·ter half *n. Humorous.* one's spouse.

bet·ter·ment ('bɛtəmənt) *n.* **1.** a change for the better;

improvement. **2.** *Property law.* an improvement effected on real property that enhances the value of the property.

Bet·ti (*Italian* 'betti) *n.* **U·go** ('u:go). 1892–1953, Italian writer, noted esp. for his plays, including *La Padrona* (1927), *Corruzione al palazzo di giustizia* (1949), and *La Regina e gli insorte* (1951).

bet·ting shop *n.* (in Britain) a licensed bookmaker's premises not on a racecourse.

bet·u·la·ceous (ˌbɛtjʊ'leɪʃəs) *adj.* of, relating to, or belonging to the *Betulaceae*, a family of mostly N temperate catkin-bearing trees and shrubs such as birch and alder, some species of which reach the northern limits of tree growth. [C19: from Latin *betula* birch]

be·tween (bɪ'twi:n) *prep.* **1.** at a point or in a region intermediate to two other points in space, times, degrees, etc. **2.** in combination; together: *between them, they saved enough money to buy a car.* **3.** confined or restricted to: *between you and me.* **4.** indicating a reciprocal relation or comparison: *an argument between a man and his wife.* **5.** indicating two or more alternatives: *a choice between going now and staying all night.* ~*adv. also* **in be·tween. 6.** between one specified thing and another: *two houses with a garage between.* [Old English *betwēonum;* related to Gothic *tweihnai* two together; see TWO, TWAIN]

Usage. In careful usage, *between* is restricted to cases where only two objects, possibilities, etc., are concerned. Where three or more are involved, *among* is used. An exception to this rule is made in cases when not more than two of the things covered by *between* need be involved at any one time: *treaties were drawn up between the nations.* Grammatically, *between* is a preposition and for this reason, *between you and I* is incorrect, although the mistake is usually the result of an attempt to be correct. The proper construction is *between you and me. And,* not *or,* is the connector that should be used after *between: she had to choose between staying and* (not *or*) *leaving immediately.*

be·tween·times (bɪ'twi:nˌtaɪmz) *or* **be·tween·whiles** *adv.* between other activities; during intervals.

be·twixt (bɪ'twɪkst) *prep., adv.* **1.** *Archaic.* another word for **between. 2. betwixt and between.** in an intermediate, indecisive, or middle position. [Old English *betwix;* related to Old High German *zwiski* two each]

Beu·lah ('bju:lə) *n. Old Testament.* the land of Israel (Isaiah 62:4). [Hebrew, literally: married woman]

Beu·then ('bɔɪtᵊn) *n.* the German name for **Bytom.**

BeV (in the U.S.) *abbrev. for* gigaelectronvolts (GeV). [C20: from *b(illion) e(lectron) v(olts)*]

Bev·an ('bɛvən) *n.* **A·neu·rin** (ə'naɪᵊrɪn), known as *Nye.* 1897–1960, British Labour statesman, born in Wales: noted for his oratory. As minister of health (1945–51) he introduced the National Health Service (1948).

bev·a·tron ('bɛvəˌtrɒn) *n.* a proton synchrotron at the University of California. [C20: from BEV + -TRON]

bev·el ('bɛvᵊl) *n.* **1. a.** Also called: **cant.** a surface that meets another at an angle other than a right angle. Compare **chamfer** (sense 1). **b.** (*as modifier*): *a bevel edge; bevel square.* ~*vb.* **·els, ·el·ling, ·elled** *or U.S.* **·els, ·el·ing, ·eled. 2.** (*intr.*) to be inclined; slope. **3.** (*tr.*) to cut a bevel on (a piece of timber, etc.). [C16: from Old French *bevel* (unattested), from *baïf,* from *baer* to gape; see BAY[1]]

bev·el gear *n.* a gear having teeth cut into a conical surface. Two such gears mesh together to transmit power between two shafts at an angle to each other.

bev·el square *n.* a woodworker's square with an adjustable arm that can be set to mark out an angle or to check the slope of a surface.

bev·er·age ('bɛvərɪdʒ, 'bɛvrɪdʒ) *n.* any drink, usually other than water. [C13: from Old French *bevrage,* from *beivre* to drink, from Latin *bibere*]

Bev·e·ridge ('bɛvərɪdʒ) *n.* **Wil·liam Hen·ry,** 1st Baron Beveridge. 1879–1963, British economist, whose *Report on Social Insurance and Allied Services* (1942) formed the basis of social-security legislation in Britain.

Bev·er·ly Hills ('bɛvəlɪ) *n.* a city in SW California, near Los Angeles: famous as the home of film stars. Pop.: 33 416 (1970).

Bev·in ('bɛvɪn) *n.* **Er·nest.** 1881–1951, British Labour statesman and trade unionist, who was largely responsible for the creation of the Transport and General Workers' Union (1922): minister of labour (1940–45); foreign secretary (1945–51).

bev·vy ('bɛvɪ) *n., pl.* **·vies.** *Liverpool dialect.* **1.** a drink, esp. an alcoholic one: *we had a few bevvies last night.* **2.** a night of drinking. [probably from Old French *bevee, buvee* drinking]

bev·y ('bɛvɪ) *n., pl.* **bev·ies. 1.** a flock of quails. **2.** a group, esp. of girls. **3.** a group of roedeer. [C15: of uncertain origin]

be·wail (bɪ'weɪl) *vb.* to express great sorrow over (a person or thing); lament. —**be·'wail·er** *n.* —**be·'wail·ing·ly** *adv.*

be·ware (bɪ'wɛə) *vb.* (*usually used in the imperative or infinitive,* often foll. by *of*) to be cautious or wary (of); be on one's guard (against). [C13 *be war,* from BE (imperative) + *war* WARY]

Bew·ick ('bju:ɪk) *n.* **Thom·as.** 1753–1828, English wood engraver; his best-known works are *Chillingham Bull* (1789), a large woodcut, *Aesop's Fables* (1818), and his *History of British Birds* (1797–1804).

be·wil·der (bɪ'wɪldə) *vb.* (*tr.*) **1.** to confuse utterly; puzzle. **2.** *Archaic.* to cause to become lost. [C17: see BE-, WILDER] —**be·'wil·der·ing·ly** *adv.* —**be·'wil·der·ment** *n.*

be·witch (bɪ'wɪtʃ) *vb.* (*tr.*) **1.** to attract and fascinate; enchant. **2.** to cast a spell over. [C13 *bewicchen;* see BE-, WITCH] —**be·'witch·ing·ly** *adv.*

be·wray (bɪ'reɪ) *vb.* (*tr.*) an obsolete word for **betray.** [C13: from BE- + Old English *wrēgan* to accuse; related to Gothic *wrōhjan*] —**be·'wray·er** *n.*

Bex·hill(-on-Sea) (ˌbɛks'hɪl) *n.* a resort in S England, in East Sussex on the English Channel. Pop.: 32 849 (1971).

Bex·ley ('bɛkslɪ) *n.* a borough of Greater London. Pop.: 213 500 (1976 est.).

bey (beɪ) *n.* **1.** (in the Ottoman Empire) a title given to senior officers, provincial governors, certain other officials or nobles, and (sometimes) Europeans. **2.** (in modern Turkey) a title of address, corresponding to *Mr.* ~Also called: **beg.** [C16: Turkish: lord]

Bey·oğ·lu ('beɪɔ:lu:) *n.* a district of Istanbul, north of the Golden Horn: the European quarter. Former name: **Pera.**

be·yond (bɪ'jɒnd) *prep.* **1.** at or to a point on the other side of; at or to the further side of: *beyond those hills there is a river.* **2.** outside the limits or scope of: *beyond this country's jurisdiction.* ~*adv.* **3.** at or to the other or far side of something. **4.** outside the limits of something. ~*n.* **5. the beyond.** the unknown; the world outside the range of man's perception, esp. life after death in certain religious beliefs. [Old English *begeondan;* see BY, YOND]

Bey·routh (beɪ'ru:t, 'beɪru:t) *n.* a variant spelling of **Beirut.**

bez·ant, bez·zant ('bɛzᵊnt, bɪ'zænt), *or* **byz·ant** *n.* **1.** a medieval Byzantine gold coin. **2.** *Architect.* an ornament in the form of a flat disc. **3.** *Heraldry.* a small gold circle. [C13: from Old French *besant,* from Medieval Latin *Bȳzantius* Byzantine (coin)]

bez·el ('bɛzᵊl) *n.* **1.** the sloping face adjacent to the working edge of a cutting tool. **2.** the upper oblique faces of a cut gem. **3.** a grooved ring or part holding a gem, watch crystal, etc. [C17: probably from French *biseau,* perhaps from Latin *bis* twice]

Bé·ziers (*French* be'zje) *n.* a city in S France: scene of a massacre (1209) during the Albigensian Crusade. It is a centre of the wine trade. Pop.: 85 677 (1975).

be·zique (bɪ'zi:k) *n.* **1.** a card game for two or more players with tricks similar to whist but with additional points scored for honours and sequences: played with two packs with nothing below a seven. **2.** (in this game) the queen of spades and jack of diamonds declared together. [C19: from French *bésigue,* of unknown origin]

be·zoar ('bi:zɔ:) *n.* a hard mass, such as a stone or hairball, in the stomach and intestines of animals, esp. ruminants, and man: formerly thought to be an antidote to poisons. [C15: from Old French *bézoard,* from Arabic *bāzahr,* from Persian *bādzahr,* from *bād* against + *zahr* poison]

be·zo·ni·an (bɪ'zəʊnɪən) *n. Archaic.* a knave or rascal. [C16: from Italian *bisogno* ill-equipped raw recruit; literally, need]

Bez·wa·da ('beɪzˌwɑ:də) *n.* the former name of **Vijayawada.**

b.f. *abbrev. for:* **1.** *Brit. informal.* bloody fool. **2.** *Printing.* bold face.

B/F *or* **b/f** *Book-keeping. abbrev. for* brought forward.

BG *international car registration for* Bulgaria.

BH *international car registration for* British Honduras.

Bha·gal·pur ('bɑ:gəlˌpʊə) *n.* a city in NE India, in E Bihar on the River Ganges. Pop.: 172 202 (1971).

Bha·ga·vad-Gi·ta ('bʌgəvəd 'gi:tə) *n.* a sacred Hindu text composed about 200 B.C. and incorporated into the *Mahabharata,* a Sanskrit epic. [from Sanskrit: song of the Blessed One, from *bhaga* blessing + *gītā* a song]

Bhai (baɪ) *n.* a title or form of address prefixed to the names of distinguished Sikhs. [from Hindi *bhāī,* from Sanskrit *bhrātr* BROTHER]

bhak·ti ('bʌktɪ) *n. Hinduism.* loving devotion to God leading to nirvana. [from Sanskrit: portion, from *bhajati* he allocates]

bhang *or* **bang** (bæŋ) *n.* a preparation of the leaves and flower tops of Indian hemp, which has narcotic and intoxicating properties: much used in India. See also **cannabis.** [C16: from Hindi *bhāng*]

bhar·al *or* **bur·hel** ('bʌrəl) *n.* a wild Himalayan sheep, *Pseudois nayaur,* with a bluish-grey coat and round backward-curving horns. [Hindi]

Bha·rat ('bʌrʌt) *n.* transliteration of the Hindi name for **India.**

Bha·ra·ti·ya ('bɑ:rəˌti:jə) *adj.* of or relating to India; Indian.

Bha·rat Nat·yam ('bʌrət 'nɑ:tjəm) *n.* a form of Indian classical ballet. [from Sanskrit *bharatanātya* Bharata's dancing, from *Bharata* the sage supposed to have written of dramatic art and dancing + *nātya* dancing]

Bhat·pa·ra (bɑ:t'pɑ:rə) *n.* a city in NE India, in West Bengal on the Hooghly River: jute and cotton mills. Pop.: 204 750 (1971).

bha·van ('bʌvən) *or* **bha·wan** *n.* (in India) a large house or building.

Bhav·na·gar ('bɑ:vnəgə) *n.* a port in W India, in S Gujarat. Pop.: 225 358 (1971).

bhin·di ('bɪndɪ) *n.* the okra as used in Indian cooking: its green pods are eaten as vegetables. Also called: **lady's finger.** [Hindi]

bhish·ti *or* **bhees·ty** ('bi:stɪ) *n., pl.* **·ties.** (formerly in India) a water-carrier. [C18: from Hindi *bhistī,* from Persian *bihishtī* heavenly one, from *bihisht* paradise]

Bho·pal (bəʊ'pɑ:l) *n.* a city in central India, the capital of Madhya Pradesh state and of the former state of Bhopal. Pop.: 298 022 (1971).

B ho·ri·zon *n.* the layer of a soil profile immediately below the A horizon, containing deposits of leached material.

b.h.p. *abbrev. for* brake horsepower.

Bhu+ba+nes+war (ˌbubəˈneɪʃwə) *n.* an ancient city in E India, the capital of Orissa state: many temples built between the 7th and 16th centuries. Pop.: 105 491 (1971).

Bhu+tan (buːˈtɑːn) *n.* a kingdom in central Asia: disputed by Tibet, China, India, and Britain since the 18th century, the conflict now being chiefly between China and India (which is responsible for Bhutan's external affairs); contains inaccessible stretches of the E Himalayas in the north. Official language: Dzongka; Nepali is also spoken. Religion: mostly Mahayana Buddhist. Currency: rupee. Capital: Thimbu. Pop.: 1 146 000 (1974 UN est.). Area: about 46 600 sq. km (18 000 sq. miles). —ˌ**Bhu+tan+ˈese** *n., adj.*

Bhut·to (ˈbuːtəʊ) *n.* **Zul·fi·kar A·li** (ˈzʊlfɪkɑː ˈɑːlɪ). 1928-79, Pakistani statesman; president (1971-73) and prime minister (1973-77) of Pakistan. Tried and executed for the murder of a political rival.

Bi *the chemical symbol for* bismuth.

bi-[1] *or sometimes before a vowel* **bin-** *combining form.* **1.** two; having two: *bifocal.* **2.** occurring every two; lasting for two: *biennial.* **3.** on both sides, surfaces, directions, etc.: *bilateral.* **4.** occurring twice during: *biweekly.* **5. a.** denoting an organic compound containing two identical cyclic hydrocarbon systems: *biphenyl.* **b.** (rare in technical usage) indicating an acid salt of a dibasic acid: *sodium bicarbonate.* **c.** (not in technical usage) equivalent of **di-**[1] (sense 2). [from Latin, from *bis* TWICE]

bi-[2] *combining form.* a variant of **bio-.**

Bi+a·fra (bɪˈæfrə) *n.* **1.** a region of E Nigeria: seceded as an independent republic (1967–70) during Civil War, but defeated by Nigerian government forces. **2. Bight of.** former name (until 1975) of (the Bight of) **Bonny.** —**Bi+ˈa·fran** *adj., n.*

Bi·ak (biːˈjɑːk) *n.* an island in Indonesia, north of West Irian: the largest of the Schouten Islands. Area: 2455 sq. km (948 sq. miles).

Bia+ły+stok (*Polish* bjaˈwɪstɔk) *n.* a city in E Poland: belonged to Prussia (1795–1807) and to Russia (1807–1919). Pop.: 187 100 (1974 est.).

bi·an+nu·al (baɪˈænjʊəl) *adj.* occurring twice a year. Compare **biennial.** —**bi+ˈan+nu+al+ly** *adv.*

bi+an+nu+late (baɪˈænjʊlɪt, -ˌleɪt) *adj. Zoology.* having two bands, esp. of colour.

Biar+ritz (ˈbɪərɪts, bɪəˈrɪts; *French* bjaˈrits) *n.* a town in SW France, on the Bay of Biscay: famous resort, patronized by Napoleon III and by Queen Victoria and Edward VII of England. Pop.: 27 653 (1975).

bi·as (ˈbaɪəs) *n.* **1.** mental tendency or inclination, esp. an irrational preference or prejudice. **2.** a diagonal line or cut across the weave of a fabric. **3.** *Electronics.* the voltage applied to an electrode of a transistor or valve to establish suitable working conditions. **4.** *Bowls.* **a.** a bulge or weight inside one side of a bowl. **b.** the curved course of such a bowl on the green. **5.** *Statistics.* a latent influence that disturbs an analysis. ~*adj.* **6.** slanting obliquely; diagonal: *a bias fold.* ~*adv.* **7.** obliquely; diagonally. ~*vb.* **+as·es, +as+ing, +ased** or **+as·ses, +as+sing, +assed.** (*tr.*) **8.** (*usually passive*) to cause to have a bias; prejudice; influence. [C16: from Old French *biais,* from Old Provençal, perhaps ultimately from Greek *epikarsios* oblique]

bi·as bind+ing *n.* a strip of material cut on the bias for extra stretch and often doubled, used for binding hems, etc.

bi+ath+lon (baɪˈæθlən, -lɒn) *n. Sport.* a contest in which skiers with rifles shoot at four targets along a 20-kilometre (12.5-mile) cross-country course.

bi+au·ric·u·late (ˌbaɪɔːˈrɪkjʊlɪt, -ˌleɪt) *or* **bi+au·ric·u+lar** *adj.* having two auricles or earlike parts.

bi+ax+i·al (baɪˈæksɪəl) *adj.* (esp. of a crystal) having two axes.

bib (bɪb) *n.* **1.** a piece of cloth or plastic worn, esp. by babies, to protect their clothes while eating. **2.** the upper part of some aprons, dungarees, etc., that covers the upper front part of the body. **3.** Also called: **pout, whiting pout.** a light-brown European marine gadoid food fish, *Gadus* (or *Trisopterus*) *luscus,* with a barbel on its lower jaw. **4. stick one's bib in.** *Austral. informal.* to interfere. ~*vb.* **bibs, bib+bing, bibbed. 5.** *Archaic.* to drink (something); tipple. [C14 *bibben* to drink, probably from Latin *bibere*]

Bib. *abbrev. for:* **1.** Bible. **2.** Biblical.

bib and brace *n.* a work garment consisting of trousers and an upper front part supported by straps over the shoulders.

bib and tuck+er *n. Informal.* an outfit of clothes (esp. in the phrase **best bib and tucker**).

bibb (bɪb) *n.* **1.** *Nautical.* a wooden support on a mast for the trestletrees. **2.** another name for **bibcock.** [C18: variant of BIB]

bib+ber (ˈbɪbə) *n.* a drinker; tippler (esp. in the expression **wine-bibber**).

bib+cock (ˈbɪbˌkɒk) *or* **bibb** *n.* a tap with a nozzle bent downwards.

bi+be·lot (ˈbɪbləʊ; *French* bibˈlo) *n.* **1.** an attractive or curious trinket. **2.** a miniature book. [C19: from French, from Old French *beubelet,* perhaps from a reduplication of *bel* beautiful]

bibl. *abbrev. for:* **1.** bibliographical. **2.** bibliography.

Bibl. *abbrev. for* Biblical.

Bi+ble (ˈbaɪbᵊl) *n.* **1. a. the.** the sacred writings of the Christian religion, comprising the Old and New Testaments and, in the Roman Catholic Church, the Apocrypha. **b.** (*as modifier*): *a Bible reading.* **2.** (*often not cap.*) any book containing the sacred writings of a religion. **3.** (*usually not cap.*) a book regarded as authoritative: *the angler's bible.* [C13: from Old French, from Medieval Latin *biblia* books, from Greek, plural of *biblion* book, diminutive of *biblos* papyrus, from *Bublos* Phoenician port from which Greece obtained Egyptian papyrus]

Bi·ble-bash+er *n. Slang.* an enthusiastic or aggressive exponent of the Bible. —**ˈBi·ble-ˌbash+ing** *n., adj.*

Bi+ble Belt *n.* **the.** certain regions of the U.S., esp. in the South, where Protestant fundamentalism is dominant.

Bi+ble pa+per *n.* **1.** a thin tough opaque paper used for Bibles, prayer books, and reference books. **2.** (not in technical usage) another name for **India paper.**

bib+li+cal (ˈbɪblɪkᵊl) *adj.* **1.** of, occurring in, or referring to the Bible. **2.** resembling the Bible in written style. —**ˈbib+li+cal+ly** *adv.*

Bib+li+cal Ar·a+ma+ic *n.* the form of Aramaic that was the common language of Palestine in New Testament times. It was widespread throughout the Persian Empire from the 5th century and is found in the later books of the Old Testament (esp. Daniel 2:4–7:28).

Bib+li+cal Lat+in *n.* the form of Latin used in versions of the Bible, esp. the form used in the Vulgate. See also **Late Latin.**

Bib+li+cist (ˈbɪblɪsɪst) *or* **Bib+list** *n.* **1.** a biblical scholar. **2.** a person who takes the Bible literally.

bib·li·o- *combining form.* indicating book or books: *bibliography; bibliomania.* [from Greek *biblion* book]

bibliog. *abbrev. for:* **1.** bibliographer. **2.** bibliography.

bib+li+og+ra+phy (ˌbɪblɪˈɒgrəfɪ) *n., pl.* **+phies. 1.** a list of books or other material on a subject. **2.** a list of sources used in the preparation of a book, thesis, etc. **3.** a list of the works of a particular author or publisher. **4. a.** the study of the history, classification, etc., of literary material. **b.** a work on this subject. —ˌ**bib+li+ˈog+ra+pher** *n.* —**bib+li·o+graph+ic** (ˌbɪblɪəʊˈgræfɪk) *or* ˌ**bib+li·o+ˈgraph·i·cal** *adj.* —ˌ**bib+li·o+ˈgraph·i·cal+ly** *adv.*

bib+li+ol·a·try (ˌbɪblɪˈɒlətrɪ) *n.* **1.** excessive devotion to or reliance on the Bible. **2.** extreme fondness for books.

bib+li·o+man+cy (ˈbɪblɪəʊˌmænsɪ) *n.* prediction of the future by interpreting a passage chosen at random from a book, esp. the Bible.

bib+li·o+ma+ni·a (ˌbɪblɪəʊˈmeɪnɪə) *n.* extreme fondness for books. —ˌ**bib+li·o+ˈma+ni+ac** *n., adj.*

bib+li·o+phile (ˈbɪblɪəˌfaɪl) *or* **bib+li·o+phil** (ˈbɪblɪəfɪl) *n.* a person who collects or is fond of books. —**bib+li+oph+ism** (ˌbɪblɪˈɒfɪzəm) *n.* —ˌ**bib+li+ˌoph·i+ˈlis+tic** *adj.*

bib+li·o+pole (ˈbɪblɪəʊˌpəʊl) *or* **bib+li+op·o+list** (ˌbɪblɪˈɒpəlɪst) *n.* a dealer in books, esp. rare or decorative ones. [C18: from Latin *bibliopōla,* from Greek *bibliopōlēs* bookseller, from BIBLIO- + *pōlein* to sell] —ˌ**bib+li+ˈop·o+ly** *n.*

bib+li·o+the+ca (ˌbɪblɪəʊˈθiːkə) *n., pl.* **+cas** *or* **+cae** (-kiː). **1.** a library or collection of books. **2.** a printed catalogue compiled by a bibliographer. [Latin: library, from Greek *bibliothēkē,* from BIBLIO- + *thēkē* receptacle]

bib·u+lous (ˈbɪbjʊləs) *adj.* addicted to alcohol. [C17: from Latin *bibulus,* from *bibere* to drink] —**ˈbib·u+lous+ly** *adv.* —**ˈbib·u+lous+ness** *n.*

bi+cam·er+al (baɪˈkæmərəl) *adj.* (of a legislature) consisting of two chambers [C19: from BI-[1] + Latin *camera* CHAMBER] —**bi+ˈcam+er+al+ism** *n.* —**bi+ˈcam+er+al+ist** *n.*

bi+cap+su+lar (baɪˈkæpsjʊlə) *adj.* (of plants) having two capsules or one capsule with two chambers.

bicarb (ˈbaɪkɑːb) *n.* short for **bicarbonate of soda.** See **sodium bicarbonate.**

bi+car+bo+nate (baɪˈkɑːbənɪt, -ˌneɪt) *n.* **1.** a salt of carbonic acid containing the ion HCO_3^-; an acid carbonate. **2.** (*modifier*) consisting of, containing, or concerned with the ion HCO_3^-: *a bicarbonate compound.* Also called: **hydrogen carbonate. 3.** short for **bicarbonate of soda.**

bi+car+bo+nate of so·da *n.* sodium bicarbonate, esp. when used as a medicine or as a raising agent in baking.

bice (baɪs) *n.* **1.** Also called: **bice blue.** a medium blue colour; azurite. **2.** Also called: **bice green.** a yellowish-green colour; malachite. [C14: from Old French *bis* dark grey, of uncertain origin]

bi+cen+te·nar·y (ˌbaɪsɛnˈtiːnərɪ) *or U.S.* **bi+cen+ten+ni·al** (ˌbaɪsɛnˈtɛnɪəl) *adj.* **1.** marking a 200th anniversary. **2.** occurring every 200 years. **3.** lasting 200 years. ~*n., pl.* **+nar·ies. 4.** a 200th anniversary.

bi+ceph·a+lous (baɪˈsɛfələs) *adj.* **1.** *Biology.* having two heads. **2.** crescent-shaped.

bi+ceps (ˈbaɪsɛps) *n., pl.* **+ceps** *or* **+ceps·es.** *Anatomy.* any muscle having two heads or origins, esp. the muscle that flexes the forearm. [C17: from Latin: having two heads, from BI-[1] + *caput* head]

Biche-la-mar (ˌbiːtʃ lə ˈmɑː) *n.* another name for **Beach-la-Mar.**

bi+chlo+ride (baɪˈklɔːraɪd) *n.* another name for **dichloride.**

bi+chlo+ride of mer+cu+ry *n.* another name for **mercuric chloride.**

bi+chro+mate (baɪˈkrəʊmeɪt, -mɪt) *n.* another name for **dichromate.**

bi+cip+i+tal (baɪˈsɪpɪtᵊl) *adj.* **1.** having two heads. **2.** of or relating to a biceps muscle. [C17: see BICEPS, -AL[1]]

bick+er (ˈbɪkə) *vb.* **1.** (*intr.*) to argue over petty matters; squabble. **2.** (*intr.*) *Poetic.* **a.** (esp. of a stream) to run quickly. **b.** to flicker; glitter. ~*n.* **3.** a petty squabble. [C13: of unknown origin] —**ˈbick+er+er** *n.*

bi+col+lat+er+al (ˌbaɪkɒˈlætərəl) *adj. Botany.* (of a vascular bundle) having two phloem groups to the inside and outside, respectively, of the xylem.

bi+col+our (ˈbaɪˌkʌlə), **bi+col+oured** *or U.S.* **bi+col+or, bi+col+ored** *adj.* two-coloured.

bi+con+cave (baɪˈkɒnkeɪv, ˌbaɪkɒnˈkeɪv) *adj.* (of a lens) having concave faces on both sides; concavo-concave. —**bi+con+cav+i+ty** (ˌbaɪkɒnˈkævɪtɪ) *n.*

bi+con+di+tion+al (ˌbaɪkənˈdɪʃənᵊl) *n.* another name for **equivalence** (senses 2, 3).

bi+con+vex (baɪˈkɒnvɛks, ˌbaɪkɒnˈvɛks) *adj.* (of a lens) having convex faces on both sides; convexo-convex.

bi+corn (ˈbaɪkɔːn), **bi+cor+nate** (baɪˈkɔːnɪt, -neɪt), *or* **bi+cor+nu+ate** (baɪˈkɔːnjʊɪt, -ˌeɪt) *adj.* having two horns or hornlike parts. [C19: from Latin *bicornis,* from BI-[1] + *cornu* horn]

bi+cus+pid (baɪˈkʌspɪd) *or* **bi+cus+pi+date** (baɪˈkʌspɪˌdeɪt) *adj.* **1.** having or terminating in two cusps or points. ~*n.* **2.** a bicuspid tooth; premolar.

bi+cus+pid valve *n.* another name for **mitral valve.**

bi+cy+cle (ˈbaɪsɪkᵊl) *n.* **1.** a vehicle with a tubular metal frame mounted on two spoked wheels, one behind the other. The rider sits on a saddle, propels the vehicle by means of pedals that drive the rear wheels through a chain, and steers with handlebars on the front wheel. Often shortened to **bike** (informal), **cycle.** ~*vb.* **2.** (*intr.*) to ride a bicycle; cycle. —ˈ**bi+cy+clist** *or* ˈ**bi+cy+cler** *n.*

bi+cy+cle clip *n.* one of a pair of clips worn around the ankles by cyclists to keep the trousers tight and out of the chain.

bi+cy+cle pump *n.* a hand pump for pumping air into the tyres of a bicycle.

bi+cy+clic (baɪˈsaɪklɪk, -ˈsɪklɪk) *or* **bi+cy+cli+cal** *adj.* **1.** of, forming, or formed by two circles, cycles, etc. **2.** (of stamens, petals, etc.) arranged in two whorls. **3.** (of a chemical compound) having atoms arranged in two rings fused together with at least two atoms common to each ring: *naphthalene is bicyclic.*

bid (bɪd) *vb.* **bids; bid+ding; bad, bade,** *or* **bid; bid+den** *or* **bid. 1.** (often foll. by *for* or *against*) to offer (an amount) in attempting to buy something, esp. in competition with others as at an auction. **2.** (*tr.*) to say (a greeting, blessing, etc.): *to bid farewell.* **3.** to order; command: *do as you are bid!* **4.** (*intr.;* usually foll. by *for*) to attempt to attain power, etc. **5.** (*tr.*) to invite; ask kindly: *she bade him sit down.* **6.** (*tr.*) to utter; express in words: *to bid defiance.* **7.** *Bridge, etc.* to declare in the auction before play how many tricks one expects to make. **8. bid fair.** to seem probable. ~*n.* **9. a.** an offer of a specified amount, as at an auction. **b.** the price offered. **10. a.** the quoting by a seller of a price. **b.** the price quoted. **11.** an attempt, esp. an attempt to attain power. **12.** *Bridge, etc.* **a.** the number of tricks a player undertakes to make. **b.** a player's turn to make a bid. **13.** short for **bid price.** ~See also **bid in, bid up.** [Old English *biddan;* related to German *bitten*] —ˈ**bid+der** *n.*

b.i.d. (in prescriptions) *abbrev. for* bis in die. [Latin: twice a day]

Bi·da (ˈbaɪdɑː) *or* **El Be·da** (ɛl ˈbeɪdɑː) *n.* the former name of **Doha.**

bi+dar+ka (baɪˈdɑːkə) *or* **bi+dar+kee** (baɪˈdɑːkiː) *n.* a canoe covered in animal skins, esp. sealskin, used by the Eskimos of Alaska. [from Russian *baidarka* diminutive of *baidara*]

bid+da·ble (ˈbɪdəbᵊl) *adj.* **1.** having sufficient value to be bid on, as a hand or suit at bridge. **2.** docile; obedient. —ˈ**bid+da·ble+ness** *n.* —ˈ**bid+da+bly** *adv.*

bid+den (ˈbɪdᵊn) *vb.* the past participle of **bid.**

bid+ding (ˈbɪdɪŋ) *n.* **1.** an order; command (often in the phrases **do** *or* **follow the bidding of, at someone's bidding**). **2.** an invitation; summons. **3.** the act of making bids, as at an auction or in bridge. **4.** *Bridge, etc.* a group of bids considered collectively, esp. those made on a particular deal.

Bid·dle (ˈbɪdᵊl) *n.* **John.** 1615–62, English theologian; founder of Unitarianism in England.

bid+dy[1] (ˈbɪdɪ) *n., pl.* **+dies.** a dialect word for **chicken** or **hen.** [C17: perhaps imitative of calling chickens]

bid+dy[2] (ˈbɪdɪ) *n., pl.* **+dies.** *Informal.* a woman, esp. an old gossipy or interfering one. [from pet form of *Bridget*]

bid·dy-bid·dy *n., pl.* **-bid·dies. 1.** a low-growing rosaceous plant, *Acaena viridior,* of New Zealand, having prickly burs. **2.** the burs of this plant. ~Also called: **bid·dy-bid, bidg·ee-widg·ee** (ˈbɪdʒɪ ˈwɪdʒɪ).

bide (baɪd) *vb.* **bides, bid+ing, bid+ed** *or* **bode, bid+ed. 1.** (*intr.*) *Archaic or dialect.* to continue in a certain place or state; stay. **2.** (*tr.*) *Archaic or dialect.* to tolerate; endure. **3. bide one's time.** to wait patiently for an opportunity. [Old English *bīdan;* related to Old Norse *bītha* to wait, Gothic *beidan,* Old High German *bītan*]

bi+den+tate (baɪˈdɛnteɪt) *adj.* having two teeth or toothlike parts or processes.

bi+det (ˈbiːdeɪ) *n.* a small low basin for washing the genitals and anal area. [C17: from French: small horse, probably from Old French *bider* to trot]

bid in *vb.* (*adv.*) (in an auction) to outbid all previous offers for (one's own property) to retain ownership or increase the final selling price.

bid price *n. Stock Exchange.* the price at which a stockjobber is prepared to purchase a specific security. Compare **offer price.**

bid up *vb.* (*adv.*) to increase the market price of (a commodity) by making artificial bids.

Bie+der+mei+er (ˈbiːdəˌmaɪə) *adj.* **1.** of or relating to a decorative and furnishing style in mid-19th-century Germany, noted for its solidity and conventionality. **2.** boringly conventional in outlook; bourgeois. [C19: after Gottlieb *Biedermeier,* a fictitious character portrayed as a conventional unimaginative bourgeois and the author of poems actually written by several satirical poets]

Biel (biːl) *n.* **1.** a town in NW Switzerland, on Lake Biel. Pop.: 64 333 (1970). French name: **Bienne. 2. Lake.** a lake in NW Switzerland: remains of lake dwellings were discovered here in the 19th century. Area: 39 sq. km (15 sq. miles). German name: **Biel+er+see** (ˈbiːlərˌzeː).

bield (biːld) *n. Northern Brit. dialect.* a shelter; home. [Old English *bieldo, byldo* boldness (hence: refuge); related to Gothic *balthei,* Old English *beald* BOLD]

Bie+le·feld (*German* ˈbiːləˌfɛlt) *n.* a city in West Germany, in NE North Rhine-Westphalia. Pop.: 321 200 (1974 est.).

Biel·sko-Bia·ła (*Polish* ˈbjɛlskɔˈbjawa) *n.* a town in S Poland: created in 1951 by the union of Bielsko and Biała Krakowska; a leading textile centre since the 16th century. Pop.: 116 100 (1974 est.).

Bien Ho·a (ˈbjɛn ˈhəʊə) *n.* a town in S Vietnam: a former capital of Cambodia. Pop.: 177 513 (1971).

Bienne (bjɛn) *n.* the French name for **Biel.**

bi+en+ni·al (baɪˈɛnɪəl) *adj.* **1.** occurring every two years. **2.** lasting two years. Compare **biannual.** ~*n.* **3.** a plant, such as the carrot, that completes its life cycle in two years, developing vegetative storage parts during the first year. Compare **annual** (sense 3), **perennial** (sense 3). **4.** an event that takes place every two years. —**bi+ˈen+ni+al+ly** *adv.*

bier (bɪə) *n.* a platform or stand on which a corpse or a coffin containing a corpse rests before burial. [Old English *bǣr;* related to *beran* to BEAR[1], Old High German *bāra* bier, Sanskrit *bhārá* a burden]

Bierce (bɪəs) *n.* **Am·brose (Gwinett).** 1842–?1914, U.S. journalist and author of humorous sketches, horror stories, and tales of the supernatural: he disappeared during a mission in Mexico (1913).

bier+kel+ler (ˈbɪəˌkɛlə) *n. Brit.* a public house decorated in German style, selling German beers. [C20: German, literally: beer cellar]

biest+ings (ˈbiːstɪŋz) *n.* a variant spelling of **beestings.**

bi+fa+cial (baɪˈfeɪʃəl) *adj.* **1.** having two faces or surfaces. **2.** *Botany.* (of leaves, etc.) having upper and lower surfaces differing from each other. **3.** *Archaeol.* (of flints) flaked by percussion from two sides along the chopping edge.

bi+far·i·ous (baɪˈfɛərɪəs) *adj. Botany.* having parts arranged in two rows on either side of a central axis. [C17: from Latin *bifārius* double] —**bi+ˈfar·i·ous+ly** *adv.*

biff (bɪf) *Slang.* ~*n.* **1.** a blow with the fist. ~*vb.* **2.** (*tr.*) to give (someone) such a blow. [C20: probably of imitative origin]

bif+fin (ˈbɪfɪn) *n. Brit.* a variety of red cooking apple. [C18: from *beefin* ox for slaughter, from BEEF; referring to the apple's colour]

bi+fid (ˈbaɪfɪd) *adj.* divided into two lobes by a median cleft: *bifid leaves.* [C17: from Latin *bifidus* from BI-[1] + *-fidus,* from *findere* to split] —**bi+ˈfid+i+ty** *n.* —ˈ**bi+fid+ly** *adv.*

bi+fi+lar (baɪˈfaɪlə) *adj.* **1.** having two parallel threads, as in the suspension of certain measuring instruments. **2.** of or relating to a resistor in which the wire is wound in a loop around a coil, the two leads being parallel, to reduce the inductance. —**bi+ˈfi+lar+ly** *adv.*

bi+flag+el+late (baɪˈflædʒɪˌleɪt, -lɪt) *adj. Biology.* having two flagella: *biflagellate protozoans.*

bi+fo+cal (baɪˈfəʊkᵊl) *adj.* **1.** *Optics.* having two different focuses. **2.** relating to a compound lens permitting near and distant vision.

bi+fo+cals (baɪˈfəʊkᵊlz) *pl. n.* a pair of spectacles with bifocal lenses.

bi+fo+li+ate (baɪˈfəʊlɪˌeɪt, -ɪt) *adj.* having two leaves or leaflets.

bi+fo+li·o+late (baɪˈfəʊlɪəʊˌleɪt, -lɪt) *adj.* (of compound leaves) consisting of two leaflets.

bi+fo+rate (ˈbaɪfəˌreɪt) *adj. Biology.* having two openings, pores, or perforations. [C19: from New Latin *biforātus,* from BI-[1] + *forāre* to pierce]

bi+form (ˈbaɪˌfɔːm) *or* **bi+formed** *adj.* having or combining the characteristics of two forms, as a centaur.

Bif+rost (ˈbɪvrɒst, ˈbiːfrɒst) *n. Norse myth.* the rainbow bridge of the gods from their realm Asgard to earth.

bi+fur+cate *vb.* (ˈbaɪfəˌkeɪt). **1.** to fork or divide into two parts or branches. ~*adj.* (ˈbaɪfəˌkeɪt, -kɪt). **2.** forked or divided into two sections or branches. [C17: from Medieval Latin *bifurcātus,* from Latin *bifurcus* from BI-[1] + *furca* fork] —ˌ**bi+fur+ˈca+tion** *n.*

big (bɪg) *adj.* **big+ger, big+gest. 1.** of great or considerable size, height, weight, number, power, or capacity. **2.** having great significance; important: *a big decision.* **3.** important through having power, influence, wealth, authority, etc.: *the big four banks.* **4.** (intensifier usually qualifying something undesirable): *a big dope.* **5.** *Informal.* considerable in extent or intensity (esp. in the phrase **in a big way**). **6. a.** elder: *my big brother.* **b.** grown-up: *when you're big, you can stay up later.* **7. a.** generous; magnanimous: *that's very big of you.* **b.** (in combination): *big-hearted.* **8.** (often foll. by *with*) brimming; full: *my heart is big with sadness.* **9.** extravagant; boastful: *he's full of big talk.* **10. too big for one's boots** *or* **breeches.** conceited; unduly self-confident. **11.** in an advanced stage of pregnancy (esp. in the phrase **big with child**). **12. big on.** *Informal.* enthusiastic about: *that company is big on research.* ~*adv. Informal.* **13.** boastfully; pretentiously (esp. in the phrase **talk big**). **14.** in an exceptional way; well: *his talk went over big with the audience.* **15.** on a grand scale (esp. in the phrase **think big**). [C13: perhaps of Scandinavian origin; compare Norwegian dialect *bugge* big man] —ˈ**big+gish** *adj.* —ˈ**big+ness** *n.*

big·a·my ('bɪgəmɪ) *n., pl.* **·mies.** the crime of marrying a person while one is still legally married to someone else. [C13: via French from Medieval Latin *bigamus;* see BI-[1], -GAMY] —**'big·a·mist** *n.* —**'big·a·mous** *adj.* —**'big·a·mous·ly** *adv.*
big·ar·reau ('bɪgəˌrəʊ, ˌbɪgə'rəʊ) *n.* any of several heart-shaped varieties of sweet cherry that have firm flesh. [C17: from French, from *bigarré* mottled]
big band *n.* a large jazz or dance band, popular esp. in the 1930s to the 1950s.
big-bang the·o·ry *n.* a cosmological theory postulating that approximately 10 000 million years ago all the matter of the universe, packed into a small superdense mass, was hurled in all directions by a cataclysmic explosion. As the fragments slowed down, the galaxies and stars evolved but the universe is still expanding. Compare **steady-state theory.**
Big Ben *n.* **1.** the bell in the clock tower of the Houses of Parliament, London. **2.** the clock in this tower. **3.** the tower.
Big Ber·tha *n.* a large German gun of World War I.
Big Board *n. U.S. informal.* **1.** the quotation board in the New York Stock Exchange. **2.** the New York Stock Exchange.
Big Broth·er *n.* a person, organization, etc., that exercises total dictatorial control. [C20: after a character in George Orwell's novel *1984* (1949)]
big busi·ness *n.* large commercial organizations collectively, esp. when considered as exploitative or socially harmful.
big cheese *n. Slang.* an important person.
big Chief *n. Slang.* an important person, boss, or leader. Also called: **big White Chief, big Daddy.**
big deal *interj. Slang.* an exclamation of scorn, derision, etc., used esp. to belittle a claim or offer.
big dip·per *n.* (in amusement parks) a narrow railway with open carriages that run swiftly over a route of sharp curves and steep inclines. Also called: **roller coaster.**
Big Dip·per *n.* the U.S. name for the **Plough** (constellation).
big end *n. Brit.* **1.** the larger end of a connecting rod in an internal-combustion engine. Compare **little end. 2.** the bearing surface between the larger end of a connecting rod and the crankpin of the crankshaft.
bi·gen·er ('baɪdʒɪnə) *n. Biology.* a hybrid between individuals of different genera. [C20: back formation from *bigeneric;* see BI-[1], GENUS] —**bi·ge·ner·ic** (ˌbaɪdʒɪ'nɛrɪk) *adj.*
big·eye ('bɪgˌaɪ) *n., pl.* **·eye** *or* **·eyes.** any tropical or subtropical red marine percoid fish of the family *Priacanthidae,* having very large eyes and rough scales.
Big Five *n.* **the.** the five countries considered to be the major world powers. In the period immediately following World War II, the U.S., Britain, the Soviet Union, China, and France were regarded as the Big Five.
big game *n.* **1.** large animals that are hunted or fished for sport. **2.** *Informal.* the objective of an important or dangerous undertaking.
big·gin *or* **big·gon** ('bɪgɪn) *n.* a plain close-fitting cap, often tying under the chin, worn in the Middle Ages and by children in the 17th century. [C16: from French *béguin;* see BEGUINE]
big gun *n. Slang.* an important person.
big·head ('bɪgˌhɛd) *n.* **1.** *Informal.* a conceited person. **2.** *U.S. informal.* conceit; egotism. **3.** *Vet. science.* **a.** an abnormal bulging or increase in the size of an animal's skull, as from osteomalacia. **b.** any of various diseases of sheep characterized by swelling of the head, esp. any caused by infection with *Clostridium* bacteria. —ˌ**big·'head·ed** *adj.* —ˌ**big·'head·ed·ly** *adv.* —ˌ**big·'head·ed·ness** *n.*
big·horn ('bɪgˌhɔːn) *n., pl.* **·horns** *or* **·horn.** a large wild sheep, *Ovis canadensis,* inhabiting mountainous regions in North America and NE Asia: family *Bovidae,* order *Artiodactyla.* The male has massive curved horns, and the species is well adapted for climbing and leaping.
bight (baɪt) *n.* **1.** a wide indentation of a shoreline, or the body of water bounded by such a curve. **2.** the slack middle part of an extended rope. **3.** a curve or loop in a rope. ~*vb.* **4.** (*tr.*) to fasten or bind with a bight. [Old English *byht;* see BOW[2]]
big·mouth ('bɪgˌmaʊθ) *n. Slang.* a noisy, indiscreet, or boastful person. —**'big-ˌmouthed** *adj.*
big noise *n. Brit. slang.* an important person.
big·no·ni·a (bɪg'nəʊnɪə) *n.* any tropical American bignoniaceous climbing shrub of the genus *Bignonia* (or *Doxantha*), cultivated for their trumpet-shaped yellow or reddish flowers. See also **cross vine.** [C19: from New Latin, named after the Abbé Jean-Paul *Bignon* (1662–1743)]
big·no·ni·a·ceous (bɪgˌnəʊnɪ'eɪʃəs) *adj.* of, relating to, or belonging to the *Bignoniaceae,* a chiefly tropical family of trees, shrubs, and lianas, including jacaranda, bignonia, and catalpa.
big-note *vb. Austral. informal.* to boast about (oneself).
big·ot ('bɪgət) *n.* a person who is intolerant of any ideas other than his own, esp. on religion, politics, or race. [C16: from Old French: name applied contemptuously to the Normans by the French, of obscure origin] —**'big·ot·ed** *adj.*
big·ot·ry ('bɪgətrɪ) *n., pl.* **·ries.** the attitudes, behaviour, or way of thinking of a bigot; prejudice; intolerance.
big screen *n.* an informal name for the **cinema.**
big shot *n. Slang, chiefly U.S.* an important or influential person.
big smoke *n.* **the.** *Informal.* a large city, esp. London.
big stick *n. Informal.* force or the threat of using force.
big time *n. Slang.* **a. the.** the highest or most profitable level of an occupation or profession, esp. the entertainment business. **b.** (*as modifier*): *a big-time comedian.* —**'big-'tim·er** *n.*
big top *n. Informal.* **1.** the main tent of a circus. **2.** the circus itself.
big tree *n.* a giant Californian coniferous tree, *Sequoiadendron giganteum,* with a wide tapering trunk and thick spongy bark: family *Taxodiaceae.* It often reaches a height of 90 metres. Also called: **giant sequoia.** See also **sequoia.**
bi·gua·nide (baɪ'gwɑːnaɪd) *n.* any of a class of compounds some of which are used in the treatment of certain forms of diabetes. See also **phenformin.** [C19: from BI-[1] + GUANIDINE + -IDE]
big wheel *n.* **1.** another name for a **Ferris wheel. 2.** *Slang.* an important person.
big·wig ('bɪgˌwɪg) *n. Slang.* an important person.
Bi·har (bɪ'hɑː) *n.* a state of NE India: hilly in the south, with the Ganges plain in the north; important for rice and mineral resources, esp. coal. Capital: Patna. Pop.: 56 353 369 (1971). Area: 174 038 sq. km (67 875 sq. miles).
Bi·ha·ri (bɪ'hɑːrɪ) *n.* **1.** a member of an Indian people living chiefly in Bihar but also in Bangladesh and Pakistan. **2.** the language of this people, comprising a number of highly differentiated dialects, belonging to the Indic branch of the Indo-European family. ~*adj.* **3.** of or relating to this people, their language, or Bihar.
Biisk (*Russian* bijsk) *n.* a variant spelling of **Biysk.**
Bi·ja·pur (bɪ'dʒɑːpʊə) *n.* an ancient city in W India, in N Mysore: capital of a former kingdom, which fell at the end of the 17th century. Pop.: 103 931 (1971).
bi·jec·tion (baɪ'dʒɛkʃən) *n.* a mathematical function or mapping that is both an injection and a surjection and therefore has an inverse. —**bi·'jec·tive** *adj.*
bi·jou ('biːʒuː) *n., pl.* **·joux** (-ʒuːz). **1.** something small and delicately worked, such as a trinket. **2.** (*modifier*) *Often ironic.* small but elegant and tasteful: *a bijou residence.* [C19: from French, from Breton *bizou* finger ring, from *biz* finger; compare Welsh *bys* finger, Cornish *bis*]
bi·jou·te·rie (biː'ʒuːtərɪ) *n.* **1.** jewellery esteemed for the delicacy of the work rather than the value of the materials. **2.** a collection of such jewellery.
bi·ju·gate ('baɪdʒʊˌgeɪt, baɪ'dʒuːgeɪt) *or* **bi·ju·gous** *adj.* (of compound leaves) having two pairs of leaflets.
Bi·ka·ner ('biːkəˌnɪə) *n.* a walled city in NW India, in Rajasthan: capital of the former state of Bikaner, on the edge of the Thar Desert. Pop.: 188 518 (1971).
bike (baɪk) *n., vb. Informal.* short for **bicycle** or **motorcycle.**
bik·ie ('baɪkɪ) *n. Austral. slang.* a member of a motorcycle gang.
Bi·ki·la (bɪ'kiːlə) *n.* **A·be·be** (ə'beɪbeɪ). 1932–73, Ethiopian long-distance runner: winner of the Marathon at the Olympic Games in Rome (1960) and Tokyo (1964).
bi·ki·ni (bɪ'kiːnɪ) *n.* a woman's very brief two-piece swimming costume. [C20: after Bikini atoll, from a comparison between the devastating effect of the atom-bomb test and the effect caused by women wearing bikinis]
Bi·ki·ni (bɪ'kiːnɪ) *n.* an atoll in the N Pacific; one of the Marshall Islands: site of a U.S. atom-bomb test in 1946.
bi·la·bi·al (baɪ'leɪbɪəl) *adj.* **1.** of, relating to, or denoting a speech sound articulated using both lips: (p) *is a bilabial stop,* (w) *a bilabial semivowel.* ~*n.* **2.** a bilabial speech sound.
bi·la·bi·ate (baɪ'leɪbɪˌeɪt, -ɪt) *adj. Botany.* divided into two lips: *the snapdragon has a bilabiate corolla.*
bil·an·der ('bɪləndə) *n.* a small two-masted cargo ship. [C17: from Dutch, literally: by-lander, because used on canals]
bi·lat·er·al (baɪ'lætərəl) *adj.* **1.** having or involving two sides. **2.** affecting or undertaken by two parties; mutual: *a bilateral treaty.* **3.** denoting or relating to bilateral symmetry. **4.** having identical sides or parts on each side of an axis; symmetrical. **5.** *Sociol.* relating to descent through both maternal and paternal lineage. Compare **unilateral** (sense 5). **6.** *Brit.* relating to an education that combines academic and technical courses. —**bi·'lat·er·al·ly** *adv.*
bi·lat·er·al sym·met·ry *n.* the property of an organism or part of an organism such that, if cut in only one plane, the two cut halves are mirror images of each other. See also **radial symmetry.**
Bil·ba·o (bɪl'bɑːəʊ; *Spanish* bil'βao) *n.* a port in N Spain, on the Bay of Biscay: famous since medieval times for the production of iron and steel goods, esp. swords; still contains the country's largest iron and steel works and exports iron ore. Pop.: 410 490 (1970).
bil·ber·ry ('bɪlbərɪ) *n., pl.* **·ries. 1.** any of several ericaceous shrubs of the genus *Vaccinium,* such as the whortleberry, having edible blue or blackish berries. See also **blueberry. 2. a.** the fruit of any of these plants. **b.** (*as modifier*): *bilberry pie.* [C16: probably of Scandinavian origin; compare Danish *böllebær,* from *bölle* bilberry + *bær* BERRY]
bil·bo ('bɪlbəʊ) *n., pl.* **·bos** *or* **·boes.** (formerly) a sword with a marked temper and elasticity. [C16: from *Bilboa,* variant (in English) of *Bilbao,* Spain, noted for its blades]
bil·boes ('bɪlbəʊz) *pl. n.* a long iron bar with two sliding shackles, formerly used to confine the ankles of a prisoner. [C16: perhaps changed from BILBAO]
Bild·ungs·ro·man *German.* ('bɪldʊŋzroˌmaːn) *n.* a novel concerned with a person's formative years and development.
bile (baɪl) *n.* **1.** a bitter greenish to golden brown alkaline fluid secreted by the liver and stored in the gall bladder. It is discharged during digestion into the duodenum, where it aids the emulsification and absorption of fats. **2.** irritability or peevishness. **3.** *Archaic.* either of two bodily humours, one of which (**black bile**) was thought to cause melancholy and the

other (**yellow bile**) anger. [C17: from French, from Latin *bīlis*, probably of Celtic origin compare Welsh *bustl* bile]
bi+lec+tion (baɪˈlɛkʃən) *n.* another word for **bolection.**
bile+stone (ˈbaɪlˌstəʊn) *n.* another name for **gallstone.**
bilge (bɪldʒ) *n.* **1.** *Nautical.* the parts of a vessel's hull where the vertical sides curve inwards to form the bottom. **2.** (*often pl.*) the parts of a vessel between the lowermost floorboards and the bottom. **3.** Also called: **bilge wa+ter.** the dirty water that collects in a vessel's bilge. **4.** *Informal.* silly rubbish; nonsense. **5.** the widest part of the belly of a barrel or cask. ~*vb.* **6.** (*intr.*) *Nautical.* (of a vessel) to take in water at the bilge. **7.** (*tr.*) *Nautical.* to damage (a vessel) in the bilge, causing it to leak. [C16: probably a variant of BULGE] —**ˈbilg·y** *adj.*
bilge keel *n.* one of two keel-like projections along the bilges of some vessels to improve sideways stability.
bil+har+zi·a (bɪlˈhɑːtsɪə) *n.* **1.** another name for a **schistosome.** **2.** another name for **schistosomiasis.** [C19: New Latin, named after Theodor *Bilharz* (1825–62), German parasitologist who discovered schistosomes]
bil+har+zi·a+sis (ˌbɪlhɑːˈtsaɪəsɪs) *or* **bil+har+zi·o+sis** (bɪlˌhɑːtsɪˈəʊsɪs) *n.* another name for **schistosomiasis.**
bil·i+ar·y (ˈbɪlɪərɪ) *adj.* of or relating to bile, to the ducts that convey bile, or to the gall bladder.
bi+lin+e·ar (baɪˈlɪnɪə) *adj.* **1.** of or referring to two lines. **2.** consisting of two first-degree variables.
bi+lin+gual (baɪˈlɪŋgwəl) *adj.* **1.** able to speak two languages, esp. with fluency. **2.** written or expressed in two languages. ~*n.* **3.** a bilingual person. —**bi+ˈlin+gual+ism** *n.* —**bi+ˈlin+gual+ly** *adv.*
bil·i+ous (ˈbɪlɪəs) *adj.* **1.** of or relating to bile. **2.** affected with or denoting any disorder related to excess secretion of bile. **3.** *Informal.* (esp. of colours) extremely distasteful; nauseating: *a bilious green.* **4.** *Informal.* bad-tempered; irritable. [C16: from Latin *bīliōsus* full of BILE] —**ˈbil+ious+ness** *n.*
bil·i+ru+bin (ˌbɪlɪˈruːbɪn, ˌbaɪ-) *n.* an orange-yellow pigment in the bile formed as a breakdown product of haemoglobin. Excess amounts in the blood produce the yellow appearance associated with jaundice. Formula: $C_{32}H_{36}O_6N_4$. [C19: from BILE + Latin *ruber* red + -IN]
bil·i+ver+din (ˌbɪlɪˈvɜːdɪn) *n.* a dark green pigment in the bile formed by the oxidation of bilirubin. Formula: $C_{33}H_{34}O_6N_4$. [C19: coined in Swedish, from Latin *bīlis* bile + Old French *verd* green + -IN]
bilk (bɪlk) *vb.* (*tr.*) **1.** to balk; thwart. **2.** (often foll. by *of*) to cheat or deceive, esp. to avoid making payment to. **3.** to escape from; elude. **4.** *Cribbage.* to play a card that hinders (one's opponent) from scoring in his crib. ~*n.* **5.** a swindle or cheat. **6.** a person who swindles or cheats. [C17: perhaps variant of BALK] —**ˈbilk+er** *n.*
bill[1] (bɪl) *n.* **1.** money owed for goods or services supplied: *an electricity bill.* **2.** a written or printed account or statement of money owed. **3.** *Chiefly Brit.* such an account for food and drink in a restaurant, hotel, etc. Usual U.S. word: **check.** **4.** any printed or written list of items, events, etc., such as a theatre programme: *who's on the bill tonight?* **5.** **fill the bill.** *Informal.* to be entirely satisfactory. **6.** a statute in draft, before it becomes law. **7.** a printed notice or advertisement; poster. **8.** *U.S.* a piece of paper money; note. **9.** an obsolete name for **promissory note.** **10.** *Law.* See **bill of indictment.** **11.** See **bill of exchange.** **12.** See **bill of fare.** **13.** *Archaic.* any document. ~*vb.* (*tr.*) **14.** to send or present an account for payment to (a person). **15.** to enter (items, goods, etc.) on an account or statement. **16.** to advertise by posters. **17.** to schedule as a future programme: *the play is billed for next week.* [C14: from Anglo-Latin *billa*, alteration of Late Latin *bulla* document, BULL[3]]
bill[2] (bɪl) *n.* **1.** the mouthpart of a bird, consisting of projecting jaws covered with a horny sheath; beak. It varies in shape and size according to the type of food eaten and may also be used as a weapon. **2.** any beaklike mouthpart in other animals. **3.** a narrow promontory: *Portland Bill.* **4.** *Nautical.* the pointed tip of the fluke of an anchor. ~*vb.* (*intr.*) (esp. in the phrase **bill and coo**). **5.** (of birds, esp. doves) to touch bills together. **6.** (of lovers) to kiss and whisper amorously. [Old English *bile*; related to *bill* BILL[3]]
bill[3] (bɪl) *n.* **1.** a hooked weapon with a long handle, such as a halberd. **2.** short for **billhook.** [Old English *bill* sword, related to Old Norse *bīldr* instrument used in blood-letting, Old High German *bil* pickaxe]
bill[4] (bɪl) *n. Ornithol.* another word for **boom**[1] (sense 4). [C18: from dialect *beel* BELL (vb.)]
bil+la+bong (ˈbɪləˌbɒŋ) *n. Austral.* **1.** a stagnant pool in the bed of an intermittent stream. **2.** a branch of a river running to a dead end. [C19: from a native Australian language, from *billa* river + *bong* dead]
bill+board[1] (ˈbɪlˌbɔːd) *n. Chiefly U.S.* another name for **hoarding.** [C19: from BILL[1] + BOARD]
bill+board[2] (ˈbɪlˌbɔːd) *n.* a fitting at the bow of a vessel for securing an anchor. [C19: from BILL[2] + BOARD]
bil+let[1] (ˈbɪlɪt) *n.* **1.** accommodation, esp. for a soldier, in civilian lodgings. **2.** the official requisition for such lodgings. **3.** a space or berth allocated, esp. for slinging a hammock, in a ship. **4.** *Informal.* a job. **5.** *Archaic.* a brief letter or document. ~*vb.* **6.** (*tr.*) to assign a lodging to (a soldier). **7.** (*tr.*) *Informal.* to assign to a post or job. **8.** to lodge or be lodged. [C15: from Old French *billette*, from *bulle* a document; see BULL[3]] —**ˌbil+let·ˈee** *n.* —**ˈbil+let+er** *n.*
bil+let[2] (ˈbɪlɪt) *n.* **1.** a chunk of wood, esp. for fuel. **2.** *Metallurgy.* **a.** a metal bar of square or circular cross section. **b.** an ingot cast into the shape of a prism. **3.** *Architect.* a carved ornament in a moulding, with short cylinders or blocks evenly spaced. [C15: from Old French *billette* a little log, from *bille* log, probably of Celtic origin]
bil·let-doux (ˌbɪlɪˈduː; *French* bijɛˈdu) *n., pl.* **bil·lets-doux** (ˌbɪlɪˈduːz; *French* bijɛˈdu). *Old-fashioned or jocular.* a love letter. [C17: from French, literally: a sweet letter, from *billet* (see BILLET[1]) + *doux* sweet, from Latin *dulcis*]
bill+fish (ˈbɪlˌfɪʃ) *n., pl.* **+fish** *or* **+fish·es.** *U.S.* any of various fishes having elongated jaws, esp. any fish of the family *Istiophoridae*, such as the spearfish and marlin.
bill+fold (ˈbɪlˌfəʊld) *n.* a U.S. word for **wallet.**
bill+hook (ˈbɪlˌhʊk) *n.* a cutting tool with a wooden handle and a curved blade terminating in a hook at its tip, used for pruning, chopping, etc. Also called: **bill.**
bil+liard (ˈbɪljəd) *n.* (*modifier*) of or relating to billiards: *a billiard table; a billiard cue; a billiard ball.*
bil+liards (ˈbɪljədz) *n.* **1.** any of various games in which long cues are used to drive balls made of ivory or composition. It is played on a rectangular table covered with a smooth tight-fitting cloth and having raised cushioned edges. **2.** a version of this, played on a rectangular table having six pockets let into the corners and the two longer sides. Points are scored by striking one of three balls with the cue to contact the other two or one of the two. Compare **pool**[2] (sense 5). [C16: from Old French *billard* curved stick, from Old French *bille* log; see BILLET[2]]
bill+ing (ˈbɪlɪŋ) *n.* **1.** *Theatre.* the relative importance of a performer or act as reflected in the prominence given in programmes, advertisements, etc. **2.** *Chiefly U.S.* public notice or advertising (esp. in the phrase **advance billing).**
bil+lings+gate (ˈbɪlɪŋzˌgeɪt) *n.* obscene or abusive language. [C17: after BILLINGSGATE, which was notorious for such language]
Bil+lings+gate (ˈbɪlɪŋzˌgeɪt) *n.* the largest fish market in London, on the N bank of the River Thames.
bil+lion (ˈbɪljən) *n., pl.* **+lions** *or* **+lion.** **1.** (in Britain) one million million: written as 1 000 000 000 000 or 10^{12}. U.S. word: **trillion.** **2.** (in the U.S.) one thousand million: written as 1 000 000 000 or 10^9. **3.** (*often pl.*) any exceptionally large number. ~*determiner.* **4.** (preceded by *a* or a cardinal number) **a.** amounting to a billion: *it seems like a billion years ago.* **b.** (*as pronoun*): *we have a billion here.* [C17: from French, from BI-[1] + *-llion* as in *million*] —**ˈbil+lionth** *adj., n.*
bil+lion+aire (ˌbɪljəˈnɛə) *n.* a person whose assets are worth over a billion of the monetary units of his country.
Bil+li+ton (ˈbɪlɪtɒn, bɪˈliːtɒn) *n.* an island of Indonesia, in the Java Sea between Borneo and Sumatra. Chief town: Tandjungpandan. Area: 4833 sq. km (1866 sq. miles). Also called: **Belitung.**
bill of ad+ven+ture *n.* a certificate made out by a merchant to show that goods handled by him and his agents are the property of another party at whose risk the dealing is done.
bill of at+tain+der *n.* (formerly) a legislative act finding a person guilty without trial of treason or felony and declaring him attainted. See also **attainder** (sense 1).
bill of ex+change *n.* (now chiefly in foreign transactions) a document, usually negotiable, containing an instruction to a third party to pay a stated sum of money at a designated future date or on demand.
bill of fare *n.* another name for **menu.**
bill of health *n.* **1.** a certificate, issued by a port officer, that attests to the health of a ship's company. **2.** **clean bill of health.** *Informal.* **a.** a good report of one's physical condition. **b.** a favourable account of a person's or a company's financial position.
bill of in+dict+ment *n. Criminal Law.* a formal document accusing a person or persons of crime, formerly presented to a grand jury for certification as a true bill but now signed by a court official.
bill of lad+ing *n.* (in foreign trade) a document containing full particulars of goods shipped or for shipment. Usual U.S. name: **waybill.**
Bill of Rights *n.* **1.** an English statute of 1689 guaranteeing the rights and liberty of the individual subject. **2.** the first ten amendments to the U.S. Constitution, added in 1791, which guarantee the liberty of the individual. **3.** (*usually not caps.*) any charter or summary of basic human rights.
bill of sale *n. Law.* a deed transferring personal property, either outright or as security for a loan or debt.
bil+lon (ˈbɪlən) *n.* **1.** an alloy consisting of gold or silver and a base metal, usually copper, used esp. for coinage. **2.** any coin made of such an alloy. [C18: from Old French: ingot, from *bille* log; see BILLET[2]]
bil+low (ˈbɪləʊ) *n.* **1.** a large sea wave. **2.** a swelling or surging mass, as of smoke or sound. **3.** (*pl.*) *Poetic.* the sea itself. ~*vb.* **4.** to rise up, swell out, or cause to rise up or swell out. [C16: from Old Norse *bylgja*; related to Swedish *bölja*, Danish *bölg*, Middle High German *bulge*; see BELLOW, BELLY]
bil+low·y (ˈbɪləʊɪ) *adj.* full of or forming billows: *a billowy sea.* —**ˈbil+low·i+ness** *n.*
bill+post·er (ˈbɪlˌpəʊstə) *or* **bill+stick·er** *n.* a person who is employed to stick advertising posters to walls, fences, etc. —**ˈbill+ˌpost·ing** *or* **ˈbill+ˌstick·ing** *n.*
bil+ly[1] (ˈbɪlɪ) *n., pl.* **+lies.** *U.S.* a wooden club esp. a policeman's truncheon. [C19: special use of the name *Billy*, pet form of *William*]
bil+ly[2] (ˈbɪlɪ) *or* **bil+ly+can** (ˈbɪlɪˌkæn) *n., pl.* **+lies** *or* **+ly+cans.** a

metal can or pot for boiling water, etc., over a camp fire. [C19: from Scot. English *billypot,* cooking vessel]

bil·ly·cock ('bɪlɪkɒk) *n. Rare, chiefly Brit.* any of several round-crowned brimmed hats of felt, such as the bowler. [C19: named after *William Coke,* Englishman for whom it was first made]

bil·ly goat *n.* a male goat. Compare **nanny goat.**

bill·y·o *or* **bill·y·oh** ('bɪlɪˌəʊ) *n.* **like billyo.** *Informal.* (intensifier): *snowing like billyo.* [C19: of unknown origin]

Bil·ly the Kid *n.* nickname of *William H. Bonney.* 1859–81, U.S. outlaw.

bi·lo·bate (baɪ'ləʊbeɪt) *or* **bi·lobed** ('baɪˌləʊbd) *adj.* divided into or having two lobes: *a bilobate leaf.*

bi·loc·u·lar (baɪ'lɒkjʊlə) *or* **bi·loc·u·late** *adj. Biology.* divided into two chambers or cavities: *some flowering plants have bilocular ovaries.*

bil·tong ('bɪlˌtɒŋ) *n. S. African.* strips of meat dried and cured in the sun. [C19: Afrikaans, from Dutch *bil* buttock + *tong* TONGUE]

Bim (bɪm) *n. Informal.* a native or inhabitant of Barbados. [C19: of unknown origin]

B.I.M. *abbrev. for* British Institute of Management.

bi·mah *or* **bi·ma** ('bi:mə) *n.* variant spellings of **bema.**

bim·a·nous ('bɪmənəs, baɪ'meɪ-) *adj.* (of man and the higher primates) having two hands distinct in form and function from the feet. [C19: from New Latin *bimana* two handed, from BI-[1] + Latin *manus* hand]

bim·bo ('bɪmbəʊ) *n., pl.* **·bos** *or* **·boes.** *Slang, usually derogatory.* **1.** a fellow; person. **2.** a whore. [C20: from Italian: little child]

bi·mes·tri·al (baɪ'mɛstrɪəl) *adj.* **1.** lasting for two months. **2.** a less common word for **bimonthly** (sense 1). [C19: from Latin *bimēstris,* from BI-[1] + *mēnsis* month] **—bi·'mes·tri·al·ly** *adv.*

bi·me·tal·lic (ˌbaɪmɪ'tælɪk) *adj.* **1.** consisting of two metals. **2.** of, relating to, or based on bimetallism.

bi·me·tal·lic strip *n.* a strip consisting of two metals of different coefficients of expansion welded together so that it buckles on heating: used in thermostats, etc.

bi·met·al·lism (baɪ'mɛtəˌlɪzəm) *n.* **1.** the use of two metals, esp. gold and silver, in fixed relative values as the standard of value and currency. **2.** the economic policies or doctrine supporting a bimetallic standard. **—bi·'met·al·list** *n.*

bi·mil·le·nar·y (ˌbaɪmɪ'li:nərɪ, baɪ'mɪlɪnərɪ) *adj.* marking a two-thousandth anniversary. *~n. pl.,* **·nar·ies.** a two-thousandth anniversary.

bi·mo·lec·u·lar (ˌbaɪmə'lɛkjʊlə) *adj.* (of a chemical complex, collision, etc.) having or involving two molecules.

bi·month·ly (baɪ'mʌnθlɪ) *adj., adv.* **1.** every two months. **2.** (often avoided because of confusion with sense 1) twice a month; semimonthly. See **bi-**[1]. *~n., pl.* **·lies. 3.** a periodical published every two months.

bi·morph ('baɪmɔ:f) *or* **bi·morph cell** *n. Electronics.* an assembly of two piezoelectric crystals cemented together so that an applied voltage causes one to expand and the other to contract, converting electrical signals into mechanical energy. Conversely, bending can generate a voltage: used in loudspeakers, gramophone pickups, etc.

bin (bɪn) *n.* **1.** a large container or enclosed space for storing something in bulk, such as coal, grain, or wool. **2.** Also called: **bread bin.** a small container for bread. **3.** Also called: **dustbin, rubbish bin.** a container for litter, rubbish, etc. **4.** *Brit.* **a.** a storage place for bottled wine. **b.** one particular bottling of wine. *~vb.* **bins, bin·ning, binned. 5.** (*tr.*) to store in a bin. [Old English *binne* basket, probably of Celtic origin; related to *bindan* to BIND]

bin- *prefix.* variant, esp. before a vowel, of **bi-**[1]: *binocular.*

bi·nal ('baɪnᵊl) *adj.* twofold; double. [C17: from New Latin *bīnālis;* see BIN-]

bi·na·ry ('baɪnərɪ, -nɛ-) *adj.* **1.** composed of, relating to, or involving two; dual. **2.** *Maths., computer technol.* of, relating to, or expressed in binary notation or binary code. **3.** (of a compound or molecule) containing atoms of two different elements. **4.** *Metallurgy.* (of an alloy) consisting of two components or phases. **5.** (of an educational system) consisting of two parallel forms of education such as the grammar school and the secondary modern in Britain. *~n., pl.* **·ries. 6.** something composed of two parts or things. **7.** Also called: **binary number.** *Maths.* a number expressed in binary notation. **8.** *Astronomy.* See **binary star.** [C16: from Late Latin *bīnārius;* see BIN-]

bi·na·ry code *n. Computer technol.* the representation of each one of a set of numbers, letters, etc., in a unique group of bits, each having one of two possible values.

bi·na·ry-cod·ed dec·i·mal *n.* a number in binary code written in groups of four bits, each group representing one digit of the corresponding decimal number, as *0110, 0011* for the decimal *63.* Abbrev.: **BCD**

bi·na·ry dig·it *n.* either of the two digits 0 or 1, used in binary notation. Abbrev.: **bit.**

bi·na·ry fis·sion *n.* asexual reproduction in unicellular organisms by division into two similar daughter cells.

bi·na·ry form *n. Music.* a structure consisting of two sections, each being played twice.

bi·na·ry no·ta·tion *or* **sys·tem** *n.* a number system having a base of two, numbers being expressed by combinations of the digits 0 and 1: used in computing, as 0 and 1 can be represented electrically as *off* and *on.*

bi·na·ry op·er·a·tion *n.* a mathematical operation applied to two numbers, quantities, expressions, sets, etc.

bi·na·ry star *n.* a double star system containing two associated stars revolving around a common centre of gravity in different orbits. A **visual binary** can be seen through a telescope. A **spectroscopic binary** can only be observed by the spectroscopic Doppler shift as each star moves towards or away from the earth. Sometimes shortened to **binary.** See also **optical double star, eclipsing binary.**

bi·nate ('baɪneɪt) *adj. Botany.* occurring in two parts or in pairs: *binate leaves.* [C19: from New Latin *bīnātus,* probably from Latin *combīnātus* united] **—'bi·nate·ly** *adv.*

bin·au·ral (baɪ'nɔ:rəl, bɪn-) *adj.* **1.** relating to, having, or hearing with both ears. **2.** employing two separate channels for recording or transmitting sound; so creating an impression of depth: *a binaural recording.* **—bin·'au·ral·ly** *adv.*

bind (baɪnd) *vb.* **binds, bind·ing, bound. 1.** to make or become fast or secure with or as if with a tie or band. **2.** (*tr.;* often foll. by *up*) to encircle or enclose with a band: *to bind the hair.* **3.** (*tr.*) to place (someone) under obligation; oblige. **4.** (*tr.*) to impose legal obligations or duties upon (a person or party to an agreement). **5.** (*tr.*) to make (a bargain, agreement, etc.) irrevocable; seal. **6.** (*tr.*) to restrain or confine with or as if with ties, as of responsibility or loyalty. **7.** (*tr.*) to place under certain constraints; govern. **8.** (*tr.;* often foll. by *up*) to bandage or swathe: *to bind a wound.* **9.** to cohere or stick or cause to cohere or stick: *egg binds fat and flour.* **10.** to make or become compact, stiff, or hard: *frost binds the earth.* **11. a.** (*tr.*) to enclose and fasten (the pages of a book) between covers. **b.** (*intr.*) (of a book) to undergo this process. **12.** (*tr.*) to provide (a garment, hem, etc.) with a border or edging, as for decoration or to prevent fraying. **13.** (*tr.;* sometimes foll. by *out* or *over*) to employ as an apprentice; indenture. **14.** (*intr.*) *Slang.* to complain. *~n.* **15.** something that binds. **16.** the act of binding or state of being bound. **17.** *Informal.* a difficult or annoying situation. **18.** another word for **bine. 19.** *Music.* another word for **tie** (sense 17). **20.** *Mining.* clay between layers of coal. **21.** *Fencing.* a pushing movement with the blade made to force one's opponent's sword from one line into another. *~*See also **bind over.** [Old English *bindan;* related to Old Norse *binda,* Old High German *bintan,* Latin *offendix* BAND[2], Sanskrit *badhnāti* he binds]

bind·er ('baɪndə) *n.* **1.** a firm cover or folder with rings or clasps for holding loose sheets of paper together. **2.** a material used to bind separate particles together, give an appropriate consistency, or facilitate adhesion to a surface. **3.** a person who binds books; bookbinder. **4.** something used to fasten or tie, such as rope or twine. **5.** Also called: **reaper binder.** *Obsolete.* a machine for cutting grain and binding it into bundles or sheaves. Compare **combine harvester. 6.** an informal agreement giving insurance coverage pending formal issue of a policy. **7.** a tie, beam, or girder, used to support floor joists. **8.** a stone for binding masonry; bondstone.

bind·er·y ('baɪndərɪ) *n., pl.* **·er·ies.** a place in which books are bound.

bin·di-eye ('bɪndɪˌaɪ) *n. Austral.* any of various small weedy Australian herbaceous plants of the genus *Calotis,* with burlike fruits: family *Compositae* (composites). [C20: perhaps from a native Australian language]

bind·ing ('baɪndɪŋ) *n.* **1.** anything that binds or fastens. **2.** the covering within which the pages of a book are bound. **3.** the material or tape used for binding hems, etc. *~adj.* **4.** imposing an obligation or duty: *a binding promise.* **5.** causing hindrance; restrictive.

bind·ing en·er·gy *n. Physics.* **1.** the energy that must be supplied to a stable nucleus before it can undergo fission. It is equal to the mass defect. **2.** the energy required to remove a particle from a system, esp. an electron from an atom.

bind o·ver *vb.* (*tr., adv.*) to place (a person) under a legal obligation, such as one to keep the peace.

bind·weed ('baɪndˌwi:d) *n.* **1.** any convolvulaceous plant of the genera *Convolvulus* and *Calystegia* that twines around a support. See also *convolvulus.* **2.** any of various other trailing or twining plants, such as black bindweed.

bine (baɪn) *n.* **1.** the climbing or twining stem of any of various plants, such as the woodbine or bindweed. **2.** any plant with such a stem. [C19: variant of BIND]

Bi·net-Si·mon scale ('bi:neɪ'saɪmən) *n. Psychol.* a test comprising questions and tasks, used to determine the mental age of subjects, usually children. Also called: **Binet scale** *or* **test.** See also **Stanford-Binet test.** [C20: named after Alfred *Binet* (1857–1911) + Théodore *Simon* (1873–1961), French psychologists]

binge (bɪndʒ) *n. Informal.* **1.** a bout of excessive eating or drinking. **2.** excessive indulgence in anything: *a shopping binge.* [C19: probably Lincolnshire dialect *binge* to soak]

Bing·en ('bɪŋən) *n.* a town in W West Germany on the Rhine: wine trade and tourist centre. Pop.: 23 700 (1970).

bin·gey *or* **bin·gy** ('bɪndʒɪ) *n., pl.* **bin·geys** *or* **bin·gies.** *Austral. informal.* the stomach; belly. [C19: from a native Australian language]

bin·ghi ('bɪŋgaɪ) *n. Austral. slang, often derogatory.* an Aborigine. [C19: from a native Australian language, literally: brother]

bin·gle ('bɪŋgᵊl) *n. Austral. informal.* a minor crash or upset, as in a car or on a surfboard. [C20: of uncertain origin]

bin·go ('bɪŋgəʊ) *n.* **1.** a gambling game, usually played with several people, in which numbers selected at random are called out and the players cover the numbers on their individual cards. The first to cover a given arrangement of numbers is the winner. Compare **lotto.** *~interj.* **2.** a cry by the winner of a game of bingo. **3.** an expression of surprise at a sudden occurrence or the successful completion of something: *and bingo! the lights went out.* [C19: perhaps from *bing*, imitative of a bell ringing to mark the win]

Binh Dinh *or* **Binh·dinh** ('bɪn'dɪn) *n.* a city in SE Vietnam. Pop.: 147 000 (1968 est.).

Bi·ni *or* **Be·ni** (bə'ni:) *n., pl.* **·ni** *or* **·nis.** another name for **Edo.**

bin·na·cle ('bɪnək³l) *n.* a housing for a ship's compass. [C17: changed from C15 *bitakle*, from Portuguese *bitácula*, from Late Latin *habitāculum* dwelling-place, from Latin *habitāre* to inhabit; spelling influenced by BIN]

bin·oc·u·lar (bɪ'nɒkjʊlə, baɪ-) *adj.* involving, relating to, seeing with or intended for both eyes: *binocular vision.* [C18: from BI-[1] + Latin *oculus* eye]

bin·oc·u·lars (bɪ'nɒkjʊləz, baɪ-) *pl. n.* an optical instrument for use with both eyes, consisting of two small telescopes joined together. Also called: **field glasses.**

bi·no·mi·al (baɪ'nəʊmɪəl) *n.* **1.** a mathematical expression consisting of two terms, such as $3x + 2y$. **2.** a two-part taxonomic name for an animal or plant. See **binomial nomenclature.** ~*adj.* **3.** referring to two names or terms. [C16: from Medieval Latin *binōmius* from BI-[1] + Latin *nōmen* NAME] —**bi'no·mi·al·ly** *adv.*

bi·no·mi·al dis·tri·bu·tion *n.* a statistical distribution giving the probability of obtaining a specified number of successes in a specified number of trials of an experiment, with a constant probability of success in each trial.

bi·no·mi·al *or* **bi·nom·i·nal no·men·cla·ture** *n.* a system for naming plants and animals by means of two Latin names: the first indicating the genus and the second the species to which the organism belongs, as in *Panthera leo* (the lion).

bi·no·mi·al the·o·rem *n.* a mathematical theorem that gives the expansion of any binomial raised to a positive integral power, *n.* It contains $n + 1$ terms: $(x + a)^n = x^n + (n/1!) a.x^{n-1} + [(n-1)/2!]a.x^{n-2} \ldots a^n$.

bi·nom·i·nal (baɪ'nɒmɪn³l) *Biology.* ~*adj.* **1.** of or denoting the binomial nomenclature. ~*n.* **2.** a two-part taxonomic name; binomial.

bint (bɪnt) *n. Slang.* a derogatory term for **girl** or **woman.** [C19: from Arabic, literally: daughter]

bin·tu·rong ('bɪntjʊ,rɒŋ, bɪn'tjʊərɒŋ) *n.* an arboreal SE Asian viverrine mammal, *Arctictis binturong*, closely related to the palm civets but larger and having long shaggy black hair. [from Malay]

bi·nu·cle·ate (baɪ'nju:klɪ,eɪt, -ɪt) *adj. Biology.* having two nuclei: *a binucleate cell.* Also: **bi'nu·cle·ar, bi'nu·cle,at·ed.**

bi·o- *or before a vowel* **bi-** *combining form.* indicating life or living organisms: *biography; biogenesis; biolysis.* [from Greek *bios* life]

bi·o·as·say *n.* (,baɪəʊə'seɪ, -'æseɪ). **1.** a method of determining the concentration, activity, or effect of a drug, hormone, or vitamin by testing its effect on a living organism and comparing this with the activity of an agreed standard. ~*vb.* (,baɪəʊə'seɪ). **2.** (*tr.*) to subject to a bio-assay.

bi·o·as·tro·nau·tics (,baɪəʊ,æstrə'nɔ:tɪks) *n.* (*functioning as sing.*) the study of the effects of space flight on living organisms. See **space medicine.**

Bi·o-Bi·o (*Spanish* 'bio 'bio) *n.* a river in central Chile, rising in the Andes and flowing northwest to the Pacific. Length: about 390 km (240 miles).

bi·o·cat·a·lyst (,baɪəʊ'kætəlɪst) *n.* a chemical, esp. an enzyme, that initiates or modifies the rate of a biochemical reaction. —**bi·o·cat·a·lyt·ic** (,baɪəʊ,kætə'lɪtɪk) *adj.*

bi·oc·el·late (baɪ'ɒsɪ,leɪt, ,baɪəʊ'sɛlɪt) *adj.* (of animals and plants) marked with two eyelike spots or ocelli.

bi·o·ce·nol·o·gy (,baɪəʊsɪ'nɒlədʒɪ) *n.* the branch of ecology concerned with the relationships and interactions between the members of a natural community. [C20: from BIO- + *ceno-*, from Greek *koinos* common + -LOGY]

bi·o·chem·i·cal ox·y·gen de·mand *n.* a measure of the organic pollution of water: the amount of oxygen, in mg per litre of water, absorbed by a sample kept at 20°C for five days. *Abbrev.:* **B.O.D.**

bi·o·chem·is·try (,baɪəʊ'kɛmɪstrɪ) *n.* the study of the chemical compounds, reactions, etc., occurring in living organisms. —**bi·o·chem·i·cal** (,baɪəʊ'kɛmɪk³l) *adj.* —,**bi·o'chem·i·cal·ly** *adv.* —,**bi·o'chem·ist** *n.*

bi·o·cide ('baɪə,saɪd) *n.* a chemical, such as a pesticide, capable of killing living organisms. —,**bi·o'cid·al** *adj.*

bi·o·cli·ma·tol·o·gy (,baɪəʊ,klaɪmə'tɒlədʒɪ) *n.* the study of the effects of climatic conditions on living organisms.

bi·o·cy·cle ('baɪəʊ,saɪk³l) *n. Ecology.* any of the major regions of the biosphere, such as the land or sea, which are capable of supporting life.

bi·o·de·grad·a·ble (,baɪəʊdɪ'greɪdəb³l) *adj.* (of sewage constituents, packaging material, etc.) capable of being decomposed by bacteria or other biological means. —**bi·o·deg·ra·da·tion** (,baɪəʊ,dɛgrə'deɪʃən) *n.*

bi·o·dy·nam·ics (,baɪəʊdaɪ'næmɪks, -dɪ-) *n.* (*functioning as sing.*) the branch of biology that deals with the energy production and activities of organisms. —,**bi·o·dy'nam·ic** *or* ,**bi·o·dy'nam·i·cal** *adj.*

bi·o·e·col·o·gy (,baɪəʊɪ'kɒlədʒɪ) *n.* another word for **ecology** (sense 1). —**bi·o·e·co·log·i·cal** (,baɪəʊ,i:kə'lɒdʒɪk³l) *adj.* —,**bi·o,e·co'log·i·cal·ly** *adv.* —,**bi·o·e'col·o·gist** *n.*

bi·o·en·er·get·ics (,baɪəʊ,ɛnə'dʒɛtɪks) *n.* (*functioning as sing.*) the study of energy relationships in living organisms, esp. in natural communities. —,**bi·o,en·er'get·ic** *adj.*

bi·o·en·gi·neer·ing (,baɪəʊ,ɛndʒɪ'nɪərɪŋ) *n.* **1.** the design and manufacture of aids, such as artificial limbs, to rectify defective body functions. **2.** the design, manufacture, and maintenance of engineering equipment used in biosynthetic processes, such as fermentation. —,**bi·o,en·gi'neer** *n.*

bi·o·feed·back (,baɪəʊ'fi:d,bæk) *n. Physiol., psychol.* a technique for controlling autonomic functions, such as the rate of heartbeat or breathing, by concentrating on the desired effect.

bi·o·fla·vo·noid (,baɪəʊ'fleɪvə,nɔɪd) *n.* another name for **vitamin P.**

biog. *abbrev. for:* **1.** biographical. **2.** biography.

bi·o·gen ('baɪədʒən) *n.* a hypothetical protein assumed to be the basis of the formation and functioning of body cells and tissues.

bi·o·gen·e·sis (,baɪəʊ'dʒɛnɪsɪs) *n.* the principle that a living organism must originate from a parent organism similar to itself. Compare **abiogenesis.** —,**bi·o·ge'net·ic,** ,**bi·o·ge'net·i·cal,** *or* **bi·og·e·nous** (baɪ'ɒdʒənəs) *adj.* —,**bi·o·ge'net·i·cal·ly** *adv.*

bi·o·ge·og·ra·phy (,baɪəʊdʒɪ'ɒgrəfɪ) *n.* the branch of biology concerned with the geographical distribution of plants and animals. —**bi·o·ge·o·graph·i·cal** (,baɪəʊ,dʒɪə'græfɪk³l) *adj.* —,**bi·o,ge·o'graph·i·cal·ly** *adv.*

bi·og·ra·phy (baɪ'ɒgrəfɪ) *n., pl.* **·phies.** **1.** an account of a person's life by another. **2.** such accounts collectively. —**bi'og·raph·er** *n.* —**bi·o·graph·i·cal** (,baɪə'græfɪk³l) *or* (*archaic*) ,**bi·o'graph·ic** *adj.* —,**bi·o'graph·i·cal·ly** *adv.*

bi·o·herm ('baɪəʊ,hɜ:m) *n.* a mass of organic material, esp. a coral reef, surrounded by rocks of different origin. [C20: from BIO- + Greek *herma* submerged rock]

biol. *abbrev. for:* **1.** biological. **2.** biology.

bi·o·log·i·cal (,baɪə'lɒdʒɪk³l) *or* (*archaic*) **bi·o·log·ic** *adj.* **1.** of or relating to biology. ~*n.* **2.** (*usually pl.*) a drug, such as a vaccine, that is derived from a living organism. —,**bi·o'log·i·cal·ly** *adv.*

bi·o·log·i·cal clock *n.* **1.** an inherent periodicity in the physiological processes of living organisms that is not dependent on the periodicity of external factors. **2.** the hypothetical mechanism responsible for this periodicity. ~See also **circadian.**

bi·o·log·i·cal war·fare *n.* the use of living organisms or their toxic products to induce death or incapacity in humans and animals and damage to plant crops, etc.

bi·ol·o·gy (baɪ'ɒlədʒɪ) *n.* **1.** the study of living organisms, including their structure, functioning, evolution, distribution, and interrelationships. **2.** the structure, functioning, etc., of a particular organism or group of organisms. **3.** the animal and plant life of a particular region. —**bi'ol·o·gist** *n.*

bi·o·lu·mi·nes·cence (,baɪəʊ,lu:mɪ'nɛsəns) *n.* the production of light by living organisms as a result of the oxidation of a light-producing substance (luciferin) by the enzyme luciferase: occurs in many marine organisms, insects such as the firefly, etc. —,**bi·o,lu·mi'nes·cent** *adj.*

bi·ol·y·sis (baɪ'ɒlɪsɪs) *n.* **1.** the death and dissolution of a living organism. **2.** the disintegration of organic matter by the action of bacteria etc. —**bi·o·lyt·ic** (,baɪə'lɪtɪk) *adj.*

bi·o·mass ('baɪəʊ,mæs) *n.* the total amount of living organisms in a given area, expressed in terms of living or dry weight per unit area.

bi·ome ('baɪ,əʊm) *n.* a major ecological community, extending over a large area and usually characterized by a dominant vegetation. See **formation** (sense 6). [C20: from BIO- + -OME]

bi·om·e·try (baɪ'ɒmɪtrɪ) *or* **bi·o·met·rics** (,baɪə'mɛtrɪks) *n.* **1.** the study of biological data by means of statistical analysis. **2.** the statistical calculation of the probable duration of human life. —**bi·o·met·ric** (,baɪə'mɛtrɪk) *adj.* —,**bi·o'met·ri·cal·ly** *adv.*

bi·on·ic (baɪ'ɒnɪk) *adj.* **1.** of or relating to bionics. **2.** (in science fiction) having certain physiological functions augmented or replaced by electronic equipment: *the bionic man.*

bi·on·ics (baɪ'ɒnɪks) *n.* (*functioning as sing.*) the study of certain biological functions, esp. those relating to the brain, that are applicable to the development of electronic equipment, such as computer hardware, designed to operate in a similar manner.

bi·o·nom·ics (,baɪə'nɒmɪks) *n.* (*functioning as sing.*) a less common name for **ecology** (senses 1, 2). —,**bi·o'nom·ic** *adj.* —,**bi·o'nom·i·cal·ly** *adv.* —**bi·on·o·mist** (baɪ'ɒnəmɪst) *n.*

bi·o·phys·ics (,baɪəʊ'fɪzɪks) *n.* (*functioning as sing.*) the physics of biological processes and the application of methods used in physics to biology. —,**bi·o'phys·i·cal** *adj.* —,**bi·o'phys·i·cal·ly** *adv.* —**bi·o·phys·i·cist** (,baɪəʊ'fɪzɪsɪst) *n.*

bi·o·plasm ('baɪəʊ,plæzəm) *n.* living matter; protoplasm. —,**bi·o'plas·mic** *adj.*

bi·o·poi·e·sis (,baɪəʊpɔɪ'i:sɪs) *n.* the synthesis of living matter from nonliving matter, esp. considered as an evolutionary process.

bi·op·sy ('baɪɒpsɪ) *n., pl.* **·sies.** examination, esp. under a microscope, of tissue from a living body to determine the cause or extent of a disease. [C20: from BIO- + Greek *opsis* sight] —**bi·op·tic** (baɪ'ɒptɪk) *adj.*

bi·o·scope ('baɪə,skəʊp) *n.* **1.** a kind of early film projector. **2.** a South African word for **cinema.**

bi·os·co·py (baɪ'ɒskəpɪ) *n., pl.* **·pies.** examination of a body to determine whether it is alive.

-bi·o·sis *n. combining form.* indicating a specified mode of life: *symbiosis.* [New Latin, from Greek *biōsis*; see BIO-, -OSIS] —**-bi·ot·ic** *adj. combining form.*

bi·o·sphere ('baɪə,sfɪə) *n.* the part of the earth's surface and atmosphere inhabited by living things.

bi·o·stat·ics (,baɪəʊ'stætɪks) *n.* (*functioning as sing.*) the branch of biology that deals with the structure of organisms in relation to their function. —ˌ**bi·o·'stat·ic** *adj.* —ˌ**bi·o·'stat·i·cal·ly** *adv.*

bi·o+strome ('baɪəˌstrəʊm) *n.* a thin rocky layer consisting of a deposit of organic material, such as fossils. [C20: from BIO- + Greek *strōma*]

bi·o+syn+the+sis (ˌbaɪəʊ'sɪnθɪsɪs) *n.* the formation of complex compounds from simple substances by living organisms. —**bi·o+syn+thet+ic** (ˌbaɪəʊˌsɪn'θɛtɪk) *adj.* —ˌ**bi·o+**ˌ**syn+'thet+i+cal+ly** *adv.*

bi·o+ta (baɪ'əʊtə) *n.* the plant and animal life of a particular region or period. [C20: from New Latin, from Greek *biotē* way of life, from *bios* life]

bi·o+tech+nol+o·gy (ˌbaɪəʊtɛk'nɒlədʒɪ) *n.* the U.S. name for **ergonomics.** —**bi·o+tech+no+log+i+cal** (ˌbaɪəʊˌtɛknə'lɒdʒɪkᵊl) *adj.* —ˌ**bi·o+**ˌ**tech+no+'log+i+cal+ly** *adv.* —ˌ**bi·o+tech+'nol·o+gist** *n.*

bi+ot+ic (baɪ'ɒtɪk) *adj.* of or relating to living organisms. [C17: from Greek *biotikos,* from *bios* life]

bi·o+tin ('baɪətɪn) *n.* a vitamin of the B complex, abundant in egg yolk and liver, deficiency of which causes dermatitis and loss of hair. Formula: $C_{10}H_{16}N_2O_3S$. See also **avidin.** [C20: *biot-* from Greek *biotē* life, way of life + -IN]

bi·o+tite ('baɪəˌtaɪt) *n.* a dark brown to black mica. Formula: $K(Mg,Fe)_3AlSi_3O_{10}(OH)_2$. —**bi·o+tit+ic** (ˌbaɪə'tɪtɪk) *adj.*

bi·o+tope ('baɪəˌtəʊp) *n. Ecology.* a small area, such as the bark of a tree, that supports its own distinctive community. [C20: from BIO- + Greek *topos* place]

bi·o+type ('baɪəˌtaɪp) *n.* a group of plants or animals within a species that resemble, but differ physiologically from, other members of the species. —**bi·o+typ+ic** (ˌbaɪə'tɪpɪk) *adj.*

bi+pa+ri+e·tal (ˌbaɪpə'raɪɪtᵊl) *adj. Anatomy.* relating to or connected to both parietal bones.

bip+ar+ous ('bɪpərəs) *adj.* **1.** *Zoology.* producing offspring in pairs. **2.** *Botany.* (esp. of an inflorescence) producing two branches from one stem.

bi+par+ti+san (ˌbaɪpɑːtɪ'zæn, baɪ'pɑːtɪˌzæn) *adj.* consisting of or supported by two or more political parties. —ˌ**bi+par+ti+'san+ship** *n.*

bi+par+tite (baɪ'pɑːtaɪt) *adj.* **1.** consisting of or having two parts. **2.** affecting or made by two parties; bilateral: *a bipartite agreement.* **3.** *Botany.* (esp. of some leaves) divided into two parts almost to the base. —**bi+'par+tite+ly** *adv.* —**bi+par+ti+tion** (ˌbaɪpɑː'tɪʃən) *n.*

bi+ped ('baɪpɛd) *n.* **1.** any animal with two feet. ~*adj. also* **bi+ped+al** (baɪ'piːdᵊl, -'pɛdᵊl). **2.** having two feet.

bi+pet+al+ous (baɪ'pɛtələs) *adj.* having two petals.

bi+phen+yl (baɪ'fɛnᵊl, -'fiː-) *n.* **1.** a white or colourless crystalline solid used as a heat-transfer agent, as a fungicide, and in the manufacture of dyes, etc. Formula: $C_6H_5C_6H_5$. **2.** any substituted derivative of biphenyl. ~Also called: **diphenyl.**

bi+pin+nate (baɪ'pɪneɪt) *adj.* (of compound leaves) having both the leaflets and the stems bearing them arranged pinnately. —**bi+'pin+nate+ly** *adv.*

bi+plane ('baɪˌpleɪn) *n.* an early type of aeroplane having two sets of wings, one above the other. Compare **monoplane.**

bi+pod ('baɪpɒd) *n.* a two-legged support or stand.

bi+po+lar (baɪ'pəʊlə) *adj.* **1.** having two poles: *a bipolar dynamo; a bipolar neuron.* **2.** relating to or found at the North and South Poles. **3.** having or characterized by two opposed opinions, natures, etc. **4.** (of a transistor) utilizing both majority and minority charge carriers.

bi+pro+pel+lant (ˌbaɪprə'pɛlənt) *n.* a rocket propellant consisting of two substances, usually a fuel and an oxidizer. Also called: **dipropellant.** Compare **monopropellant.**

bi+quad+rate (baɪ'kwɒdreɪt, -rɪt) *n. Maths.* the fourth power.

bi+quad+rat+ic (ˌbaɪkwɒ'drætɪk) *Maths.* ~*adj. also* **quar+tic. 1.** of or relating to the fourth power. ~*n.* **2.** a biquadratic equation, such as $x^4 + x + 6 = 0$.

bi+quar+ter+ly (baɪ'kwɔːtəlɪ) *adj.* occurring twice every three months.

bi+ra+cial (baɪ'reɪʃəl) *adj.* for, representing, or including members of two races, esp. White and Black. —**bi+'ra+cial+ism** *n.* —**bi+'ra+cial+ly** *adv.*

bi+ra+di·al (baɪ'reɪdɪəl) *adj.* showing both bilateral and radial symmetry, as certain sea anemones.

bi+ra+mous ('bɪrəməs) *adj.* divided into two parts, as the appendages of crustaceans.

birch (bɜːtʃ) *n.* **1.** any betulaceous tree or shrub of the genus *Betula,* having thin peeling bark. See also **silver birch. 2.** the hard close-grained wood of any of these trees. **3. the birch.** a bundle of birch twigs or a birch rod used, esp. formerly, for flogging offenders. ~*adj.* **4.** of, relating to, or belonging to the birch. **5.** consisting or made of birch. ~*vb.* **6.** (*tr.*) to flog with a birch. [Old English *bierce;* related to Old High German *birihha,* Sanskrit *bhūrja*] —**'birch+en** *adj.*

Birch+er ('bɜːtʃə), **Birch+ist,** *or* **Birch+ite** *n.* a member or supporter of the John Birch Society. —**'Birch+ism** *n.*

bird (bɜːd) *n.* **1.** any warm-blooded egg-laying vertebrate of the class *Aves,* characterized by a body covering of feathers and forelimbs modified as wings. Birds vary in size between the ostrich and the humming bird. Related adj.: **avian. 2.** *Informal.* a person (usually preceded by a qualifying adjective, as in the phrases **rare bird, odd bird, clever bird**). **3.** *Slang, chiefly Brit.* a girl or young woman, esp. one's girlfriend. **4.** *Slang.* prison or a term in prison (esp. in the phrase **do bird**). **5. a bird in the hand.** something definite or certain. **6. the bird has flown.** *Informal.* the person in question has fled or escaped. **7. birds of a feather.** *Often derogatory.* people with characteristics, ideas, interests, etc., in common. **8. get the bird.** *Informal.* **a.** to be fired or dismissed. **b.** (esp. of a public performer) to be hissed at, booed, or derided. **9. give (someone) the bird.** *Informal.* to tell (someone) rudely to depart; scoff at; hiss. **10. kill two birds with one stone.** to accomplish two things at the same time. **11. like a bird.** without resistance or difficulty. **12. a little bird.** a (supposedly) unknown informant: *a little bird told me it was your birthday.* **13. (strictly) for the birds.** *Informal.* deserving of disdain or contempt; not important. [Old English *bridd,* of unknown origin] —**'bird+like** *adj.*

Bird (bɜːd) *n.* nickname of (Charlie) **Parker.**

bird+bath ('bɜːdˌbɑːθ) *n.* a small basin or trough for birds to bathe in, usually in a garden.

bird-brained *adj. Informal.* dull; stupid.

bird+cage ('bɜːdˌkeɪdʒ) *n.* **1.** a wire or wicker cage in which captive birds are kept. **2.** any object of a similar shape, construction, or purpose.

bird call *n.* **1.** the characteristic call or song of a bird. **2.** an imitation of this. **3.** an instrument imitating the call of a bird, used esp. by hunters or bird-catchers.

bird cher+ry *n.* a small Eurasian rosaceous tree, *Prunus padus,* with clusters of white flowers and small black fruits. See also **cherry** (sense 1).

bird dog *U.S.* ~*n.* **1.** *Hunting.* a dog used or trained to retrieve game birds after they are shot. ~*vb.* **bird-dog, -dogs, -dog·ging, -dogged. 2.** *Informal.* to control closely with unceasing vigilance.

bird+house ('bɜːdˌhaʊs) *n.* **1.** a small shelter or box for birds to nest in. **2.** an enclosure or large cage for captive birds; aviary.

bird+ie ('bɜːdɪ) *n.* **1.** *Golf.* a score of one stroke under par for a hole. **2.** *Informal.* a bird, esp. a small bird.

bird+lime ('bɜːdˌlaɪm) *n.* **1.** a sticky substance, prepared from holly, mistletoe, or other plants, smeared on twigs to catch small birds. ~*vb.* **2.** (*tr.*) to smear (twigs) with birdlime to catch (small birds).

bird+man ('bɜːdˌmæn, -mən) *n., pl.* **+men. 1.** a man concerned with birds, such as a fowler or ornithologist. **2.** a man who attempts to fly using his own muscle power. **3.** an obsolete informal name for **airman.**

bird-nest·ing *or* **birds'-nest·ing** *n.* searching for birds' nests as a hobby, often to steal the eggs.

bird of par+a+dise *n.* **1.** any songbird of the family *Paradisaeidae* of New Guinea and neighbouring regions, the males of which have brilliantly coloured ornate plumage. **2. bird-of-paradise flower.** any of various musaceous plants of the genus *Strelitzia,* esp. *S. reginae,* that are native to tropical southern Africa and South America and have purple bracts and large orange or yellow flowers resembling birds' heads.

bird of pas+sage *n.* **1.** a bird that migrates seasonally. **2.** a transient person or one who roams about.

bird of peace *n.* a figurative name for **dove**[1] (sense 1).

bird of prey *n.* a bird, such as a hawk, eagle, or owl, that hunts and kills other animals, esp. vertebrates, for food. It has strong talons and a sharp hooked bill.

bird pep+per *n.* **1.** a tropical solanaceous plant, *Capsicum frutescens,* thought to be the ancestor of the sweet pepper and many hot peppers. **2.** the narrow podlike hot-tasting fruit of this plant.

bird+seed ('bɜːdˌsiːd) *n.* a mixture of various kinds of seeds for feeding cage birds. Also called: **canary seed.**

bird's-eye *adj.* **1. a.** seen or photographed from high above. **b.** summarizing the main points of a topic; summary (esp. in the phrase **bird's-eye view**). **2.** having markings resembling birds' eyes. ~*n.* **3. bird's-eye primrose.** a Eurasian primrose, *Primula farinosa,* having clusters of purplish flowers with yellow centres. **4. bird's-eye speedwell.** the usual U.S. name for **germander speedwell. 5.** any of several other plants having flowers of two contrasting colours. **6.** a pattern in linen and cotton fabrics, made up of small diamond shapes with a dot in the centre of each. **7.** a linen or cotton fabric with such a pattern.

bird's-foot *or* **bird-foot** *n., pl.* **-foots. 1.** a European papilionaceous plant, *Ornithopus perpusillus,* with red-veined white flowers and curved pods resembling a bird's claws. **2.** any of various other plants whose flowers, leaves, or pods resemble a bird's foot or claw.

bird's-foot tre+foil *n.* a creeping papilionaceous Eurasian plant, *Lotus corniculatus,* with red-tipped yellow flowers and seed pods resembling the claws of a bird. Also called: **bacon-and-eggs.**

bird's-nest *vb.* (*intr.*) to search for the nests of birds in order to collect the eggs.

bird's-nest fun+gus *n.* any fungus of the family *Nidulariaceae,* having a nestlike spore-producing body containing egglike spore-filled structures.

bird's-nest or+chid *n.* a brown parasitic Eurasian orchid, *Neottia nidus-avis,* whose thick fleshy roots resemble a bird's nest and contain a fungus on which the orchid feeds.

bird's-nest soup *n.* a rich spicy Chinese soup made from the outer part of the nests of SE Asian swifts of the genus *Collocalia.*

bird spi+der *n.* any large hairy predatory bird-eating spider of the family *Aviculariidae,* of tropical America.

bird strike *n.* a collision of an aircraft with a bird.

bird ta+ble *n.* a table or platform in the open on which food for birds may be placed.

bird-watch·er *n.* a person who studies wild birds in their natural surroundings. —**bird-watch·ing** *n.*

bi·re·frin·gence (ˌbaɪrɪˈfrɪndʒəns) *n.* another name for **double refraction.** —ˌ**bi·re·ˈfrin·gent** *adj.*

bi·reme (ˈbaɪriːm) *n.* an ancient galley having two banks of oars. [C17: from Latin *birēmus,* from BI-[1] + *-rēmus* oar]

Bi·ren·dra Bir Bik·ram Shah Dev (bɪˈrɛndrɑː bɪə ˈbɪkræm ʃɑː dɛv) *n.* born 1945, king of Nepal since 1972.

bi·ret·ta *or* **ber·ret·ta** (bɪˈrɛtə) *n. R.C. Church.* a stiff clerical cap having either three or four upright pieces projecting outwards from the centre to the edge: coloured black for priests, purple for bishops, red for cardinals, and white for certain members of religious orders. [C16: from Italian *berretta,* from Old Provençal *berret,* from Late Latin *birrus* hooded cape]

Bir·git (ˈbɪəgɪt) *n.* **Saint.** See (Saint) **Bridget.**

bi·ri·a·ni (ˌbɪrɪˈɑːnɪ) *n.* any of a variety of Indian dishes made with rice, highly flavoured and coloured with saffron or turmeric, mixed with meat or fish. [from Urdu]

Bir·ken·head[1] (ˌbɜːkənˈhɛd) *n.* a port in NW England, in Merseyside: shipbuilding centre. Pop.: 137 738 (1971).

Bir·ken·head[2] (ˈbɜːkənˌhɛd) *n.* **Fred·er·ick Ed·win Smith,** 1st Earl of, known as *F. E. Smith.* 1872–1930, English Conservative statesman, lawyer, and orator.

birl[1] (bɜːl) *vb.* **1.** *U.S.* to cause (a floating log) to spin using the feet, esp. as a sport among lumberjacks. ~*n.* **2.** a variant spelling of **burl**[2]. [C18: probably imitative and influenced by WHIRL and HURL]

birl[2] (bɜːl) *vb. Archaic, dialect.* to ply (one's guests, etc.) with drink. [Old English *byrelian;* related to *byrele* cup-bearer]

Bir·ming·ham *n.* **1.** (ˈbɜːmɪŋəm) an industrial city in central England, in West Midlands: the second largest city in Great Britain. Pop.: 1 013 366 (1971). **2.** (ˈbɜːmiŋˌhæm) an industrial city in N central Alabama: rich local deposits of coal, iron ore, and other minerals. Pop.: 295 686 (1973 est.).

Bi·ro (ˈbaɪrəʊ) *n., pl.* **·ros.** *Trademark, Brit.* a kind of ballpoint.

Bi·ro·bi·dzhan (*Russian* birəbiˈdʒan) *n.* **1.** a city in the Soviet Union, in SE Siberia: capital of the Jewish Autonomous Region. Pop.: 55 724 (1970). **2.** another name for the **Jewish Autonomous Region.**

birr[1] (bɜː) *Chiefly U.S. and Scot.* ~*vb.* **1.** to make or cause to make a whirring sound. ~*n.* **2.** a whirring sound. **3.** force, as of wind. **4.** vigour; energy. [Old English *byre* storm, related to Old Norse *byrr* favourable wind]

birr[2] (bɜː) *n.* the standard monetary unit of Ethiopia, divided into 100 cents. [C20: from Amharic]

birth (bɜːθ) *n.* **1.** the process of bearing young; parturition; childbirth. Related adj.: **natal. 2.** the act or fact of being born; nativity. **3.** the coming into existence of something; origin. **4.** ancestry; lineage: *of high birth.* **5.** noble ancestry: *a man of birth.* **6.** natural or inherited talent: *an artist by birth.* **7.** *Archaic.* the offspring or young born at a particular time or of a particular mother. **8. give birth (to). a.** to bear or bring forth (offspring). **b.** to produce or create (an idea, plan, etc.). ~*vb.* (*tr.*) *Rare.* **9.** to bear or bring forth (a child). [C12: from Old Norse *byrth;* related to Gothic *gabaurths,* Old Swedish *byrdh* Old High German *berd* child; see BEAR[1], BAIRN]

birth cer·tif·i·cate *n.* an official form giving details of the time and place of a person's birth, and his name, sex, and parents.

birth con·trol *n.* limitation of childbearing by means of contraception. See also **family planning.**

birth·day (ˈbɜːθˌdeɪ) *n.* **1. a.** an anniversary of the day of one's birth. **b.** (*as modifier*): *birthday present.* **2.** the day on which a person was born. **3.** any anniversary.

Birth·day hon·ours *n.* (in Britain) honorary titles conferred on the official birthday of the sovereign.

birth·day suit *n. Informal, humorous.* a state of total nakedness, as at birth.

birth·mark (ˈbɜːθˌmɑːk) *n.* a blemish or new growth on skin formed before birth, usually brown or dark red; nevus.

birth·place (ˈbɜːθˌpleɪs) *n.* the place where someone was born or where something originated.

birth rate *n.* the ratio of live births in a specified area, group, etc., to the population of that area, etc., usually expressed per 1000 population per year.

birth·right (ˈbɜːθˌraɪt) *n.* **1.** privileges or possessions that a person has or is believed to be entitled to as soon as he is born. **2.** the privileges or possessions of a first-born son. **3.** inheritance; patrimony.

birth·root (ˈbɜːθˌruːt) *n.* any of several North American plants of the genus *Trillium,* esp. *T. erectum,* whose tuber-like roots were formerly used by the American Indians as an aid in childbirth: family *Trilliaceae.*

birth·stone (ˈbɜːθˌstəʊn) *n.* a precious or semiprecious stone associated with a month or sign of the zodiac and thought to bring luck if worn by a person born in that month.

birth·wort (ˈbɜːθˌwɜːt) *n.* any of several climbing plants of the genus *Aristolochia,* esp. *A. clematitis* of Europe, once believed to ease childbirth: family *Aristolochiaceae.*

Birt·whis·tle (ˈbɜːtˌwɪsəl) *n.* **Har·ri·son.** born 1934, English composer, whose works include the opera *Punch and Judy* (1967).

bis (bɪs) *adv.* **1.** twice; for a second time (used in musical scores to indicate a part to be repeated). ~*interj.* **2.** encore! again! [via Italian from Latin, from Old Latin *duis*]

Bi·sa·yas (biˈsajas) *pl.n.* the Spanish name for the **Visayan Islands.**

Bis·cay (ˈbɪskeɪ, -kɪ) *n.* **Bay of.** a large bay of the Atlantic Ocean between W France and N Spain: notorious for storms.

bis·cuit (ˈbɪskɪt) *n.* **1.** *Brit.* a small flat dry sweet or plain cake of many varieties, baked from a dough. U.S. word: **cookie. 2.** *U.S.* a kind of small roll similar to a muffin. **3. a.** a pale brown or yellowish-grey colour. **b.** (*as adj.*): *biscuit gloves.* **4.** Also called: **bisque.** earthenware or porcelain that has been fired but not glazed. **5. take the biscuit.** *Brit.* to be regarded (by the speaker) as the most surprising thing that could have occurred. [C14: from Old French, from (*pain*) *bescuit* twice-cooked (bread), from *bes* BIS + *cuire* to cook, from Latin *coquere*]

bise (biːz) *n.* a cold dry northerly wind in Switzerland and the neighbouring parts of France and Italy, usually in the spring. [C14: from Old French, of Germanic origin; compare Old Swedish *bīsa* whirlwind]

bi·sect (baɪˈsɛkt) *vb.* **1.** (*tr.*) *Maths.* to divide into two equal parts. **2.** to cut or split into two. [C17: BI-[1] + *-sect* from Latin *secāre* to cut] —**bi·sec·tion** (baɪˈsɛkʃən) *n.*

bi·sec·tor (baɪˈsɛktə) *n. Maths.* a straight line or plane that bisects an angle.

bi·sec·trix (baɪˈsɛktrɪks) *n., pl.* **bi·sec·tri·ces** (baɪˈsɛktrɪˌsiːz). **1.** another name for **bisector. 2.** the bisector of the angle between the optic axes of a crystal.

bi·ser·rate (baɪˈsɛreɪt, -ɪt) *adj.* **1.** *Botany.* (of leaf margins, etc.) having serrations that are themselves serrated. **2.** *Zoology.* serrated on both sides, as the antennae of some insects.

bi·sex·u·al (baɪˈsɛksjʊəl) *adj.* **1.** sexually attracted by both men and women. **2.** showing characteristics of both sexes: *a bisexual personality.* **3.** (of some plants and animals) having both male and female reproductive organs. **4.** of or relating to both sexes. ~*n.* **5.** a bisexual organism; a hermaphrodite. **6.** a bisexual person. —**bi·ˈsex·u·al·ism** *or* **bi·sex·u·al·i·ty** (baɪˌsɛksjʊˈælɪtɪ) *n.* —**bi·ˈsex·u·al·ly** *adv.*

bish (bɪʃ) *n. Brit. slang.* a mistake. [C20: of unknown origin]

bish·op (ˈbɪʃəp) *n.* **1.** (in the Roman Catholic, Anglican, and Greek Orthodox Churches) a clergyman having spiritual and administrative powers over a diocese or province of the Church. See also **suffragan.** Related adj.: **episcopal. 2.** (in some Protestant Churches) a spiritual overseer of a local church or a number of churches. **3.** a chess piece, capable of moving diagonally over any number of unoccupied squares of the same colour. **4.** mulled wine, usually port, spiced with oranges, cloves, etc. [Old English *biscop,* from Late Latin *epīscopus,* from Greek *episkopos,* from EPI- + *skopos* watcher]

Bish·op Auck·land *n.* a town in N England, in central Durham: seat of the bishops of Durham since the 12th century. Pop.: 33 292 (1971).

bish·op·bird (ˈbɪʃəpˌbɜːd) *n.* any African weaverbird of the genus *Euplectes* (or *Pyromelana*), the males of which have black plumage marked with red or yellow.

bish·op·ric (ˈbɪʃəprɪk) *n.* the see, diocese, or office of a bishop.

bish·op's-cap *n.* another name for **mitrewort.**

bish·op sleeve *n.* a full sleeve gathered at the wrist.

bish·op's mi·tre *n.* a European heteropterous bug, *Aelia acuminata,* whose larvae are a pest of cereal grasses: family *Pentatomidae.*

bish·op's weed *n.* another name for **goutweed.**

Bi·si·tun (ˌbiːsɪˈtuːn) *n.* another name for **Behistun.**

bisk (bɪsk) *n.* a less common spelling of **bisque**[1].

Bisk (*Russian* bijsk) *n.* a variant spelling of **Biysk.**

Bis·kra (ˈbɪskrɑː) *n.* a town and oasis in NE Algeria, in the Sahara. Pop.: 59 052 (1966).

Bis·marck[1] (ˈbɪzmɑːk) *n.* a city in North Dakota, on the Missouri River: the state capital. Pop.: 34 703 (1970).

Bis·marck[2] (*German* ˈbɪsmark) *n.* Prince **Ot·to (Eduard Leopold) von** (ˈɔto fɔn), called *the Iron Chancellor.* 1815–98, German statesman; prime minister of Prussia (1862–90). Under his leadership Prussia defeated Austria and France, and Germany was united. In 1871 he became the first chancellor of the German Reich.

Bis·marck Ar·chi·pel·a·go *n.* a group of over 200 islands in the SW Pacific, northeast of New Guinea: part of Papua New Guinea. Main islands: New Britain, New Ireland, Lavongai, and the Admiralty Islands. Chief town: Rabaul, on New Britain. Pop.: 218 265 (1966). Area: 49 658 sq. km (19 173 sq. miles).

Bis·marck her·ring *n.* marinaded herring, served cold.

bis·muth (ˈbɪzməθ) *n.* a brittle pinkish-white crystalline metallic element having low thermal and electrical conductivity, which expands on cooling. It is widely used in alloys, esp. low-melting alloys in fire safety devices; its compounds are used in medicines. Symbol: Bi; atomic no.: 83; atomic wt.: 208.98; valency: 3 or 5; relative density: 9.75; melting pt.: 271.3°C; boiling pt.: 1560°C. [C17: from New Latin *bisemūtum,* from German *Wismut,* of unknown origin] —**ˈbis·muth·al** (ˈbɪzməθəl) *adj.*

bis·mu·thic (bɪzˈmjuːθɪk, -ˈmʌθɪk) *adj.* of or containing bismuth in the pentavalent state.

bis·muth·in·ite (bɪzˈmʌθɪˌnaɪt) *or* **bis·muth glance** *n.* a grey mineral consisting of bismuth sulphide in orthorhombic crystalline form. It occurs in veins associated with tin, copper, silver, lead, etc., and is a source of bismuth. Formula: Bi_2S_3.

bis·muth·ous (ˈbɪzməθəs) *adj.* of or containing bismuth in the trivalent state.

bi·son (ˈbaɪsən) *n., pl.* **·son. 1.** Also called: **American bison, buffalo.** a member of the cattle tribe, *Bison bison,* formerly widely distributed over the prairies of W North America but now confined to reserves and parks, with a massive head, shaggy forequarters, and a humped back. **2.** Also called: **wisent, European bison.** a closely related and similar animal, *Bison bonasus,* formerly widespread in Europe. [C14: from

Latin *bisōn*, of Germanic origin; related to Old English *wesand*, Old Norse *vīsundr*]
bisque[1] (bɪsk) *n.* a thick rich soup made from shellfish. [C17: from French]
bisque[2] (bɪsk) *n.* **1. a.** a pink to yellowish tan colour. **b.** (*as adj.*): *a bisque tablecloth.* **2.** *Ceramics.* another name for **biscuit** (sense 4). [C20: shortened from BISCUIT]
bisque[3] (bɪsk) *n. Tennis, golf, croquet.* an extra point, stroke, or turn allowed to an inferior player, usually taken when desired. [from French, of obscure origin]
Bis·sau (bɪˈsaʊ) *or* **Bis·são** (*Portuguese* biˈsɐ̃ʊ) *n.* a port in W Guinea-Bissau, on the Atlantic: until 1974 the capital of Portuguese Guinea. Pop.:71 169 (1970).
bis·sex·tile (bɪˈsɛkstaɪl) *adj.* **1.** (of a month or year) containing the extra day of a leap year. ~*n.* **2.** a rare name for **leap year.** [C16: from Late Latin *bissextilis annus* leap year, from Latin *bissextus*, from BI-[1] + *sextus* sixth; referring to February 24, the 6th day before the Calends of March]
bist (bɪst) *vb. Southwest English dialect.* a form of the second person singular of **be.**
bi·sta·ble (baɪˈsteɪbᵊl) *adj.* having two stable states: *bistable circuit.*
bis·tort (ˈbɪstɔːt) *n.* **1.** Also called: **snakeroot, snakeweed, Easter-ledges.** a Eurasian polygonaceous plant, *Polygonum bistorta,* having leaf stipules fused to form a tube around the stem and a spike of small pink flowers. **2.** Also called: **snakeroot.** a related plant, *Polygonum bistortoides,* of W North America, with oval clusters of pink or white flowers. **3.** any of several other plants of the genus *Polygonum.* [C16: from French *bistorte,* from Latin *bis* twice + *tortus* from *torquēre* to twist]
bis·tou·ry (ˈbɪstərɪ) *n., pl.* **·ries.** a long surgical knife with a narrow blade. [C15: from Old French *bistorie* dagger, of unknown origin]
bis·tre *or U.S.* **bis·ter** (ˈbɪstə) *n.* **1.** a transparent water-soluble brownish-yellow pigment made by boiling the soot of wood, used for pen and wash drawings. **2. a.** a yellowish-brown to dark brown colour. **b.** (*as adj.*): *bistre paint.* [C18: from French, of unknown origin]
bis·tro (ˈbiːstrəʊ) *n., pl.* **·tros.** a small restaurant. [French: of obscure origin]
bi·sul·cate (baɪˈsʌlkeɪt) *adj.* **1.** marked by two grooves. **2.** *Zoology.* **a.** cleft or cloven, as a hoof. **b.** having cloven hoofs.
bi·sul·phate (baɪˈsʌlfeɪt) *n.* **1.** a salt or ester of sulphuric acid containing the monovalent group $-HSO_4$ or the ion HSO_4^-. **2.** (*modifier*) consisting of, containing, or concerned with the group $-HSO_4$ or the ion HSO_4^-: *bisulphate ion.* ~Also called: **hydrogen sulphate.**
bi·sul·phide (baɪˈsʌlfaɪd) *n.* another name for **disulphide.**
bi·sul·phite (baɪˈsʌlfaɪt) *n.* **1.** a salt or ester of sulphurous acid containing the monovalent group $-HSO_3$ or the ion HSO_3^-. **2.** (*modifier*) consisting of or containing the group $-HSO_3$ or the ion HSO_3^-: *bisulphite ion.* ~Also called: **hydrogen sulphite.**
Bi·su·tun (ˌbiːsʊˈtuːn) *n.* another name for **Behistun.**
bi·sym·met·ric (ˌbaɪsɪˈmɛtrɪk) *or* **bi·sym·met·ri·cal** *adj.* **1.** *Botany.* showing symmetry in two planes at right angles to each other. **2.** (of plants and animals) showing bilateral symmetry. —ˌ**bi·sym·ˈmet·ri·cal·ly** *adv.* —**bi·sym·met·ry** (baɪˈsɪmɪtrɪ) *n.*
bit[1] (bɪt) *n.* **1.** a small piece, portion, or quantity. **2.** a short time or distance. **3.** *U.S. informal.* the value of an eighth of a dollar: spoken of only in units of two: *two bits.* **4.** any small coin. **5.** short for **bit part. 6.** *Informal.* way of behaving, esp. one intended to create a particular impression: *she's doing the prima donna bit.* **7. a bit.** rather; somewhat: *a bit dreary.* **8. a bit of. a.** rather: *a bit of a dope.* **b.** a considerable amount: *that must take quite a bit of courage.* **9. a bit of all right, bit of crumpet, bit of skirt, bit of stuff,** *or* **bit of tail.** *Brit. slang.* **a.** an attractive woman. **b.** sexual intercourse. **10. bit by bit.** gradually. **11. do one's bit.** to make one's expected contribution. **12. every bit.** (foll. by *as*) to the same degree: *she was every bit as clever as her brother.* **13. not a bit (of it).** not in the slightest; not at all. **14. to bits.** completely apart: *to fall to bits.* [Old English *bite* action of biting; see BITE]
bit[2] (bɪt) *n.* **1.** a metal mouthpiece, for controlling a horse on a bridle. **2.** anything that restrains or curbs. **3. take the bit in** *or* **between one's teeth. a.** to undertake a task with determination. **b.** to rebel against control. **4.** a cutting or drilling tool, part, or head in a brace, drill, etc. **5.** the blade of a plane. **6.** the part of a pair of pincers designed to grasp an object. **7.** the copper end of a soldering iron. **8.** the part of a key that engages the levers of a lock. ~*vb.* **bits, bit·ting, bit·ted.** (*tr.*) **9.** to put a bit in the mouth of (a horse). **10.** to restrain; curb. [Old English *bita;* related to Old English *bītan* to BITE]
bit[3] (bɪt) *vb.* the past tense of **bite.**
bit[4] (bɪt) *n.* **1.** either of the two digits 0 or 1, used in binary notation. **2.** a unit of information representing the physical state of a system having one of two values, such as *on* or *off.* [C20: from B(INARY + DIG)IT]
bi·tar·trate (baɪˈtɑːtreɪt) *n.* (not in technical usage) a salt or ester of tartaric acid containing the monovalent group $-HC_4H_4O_6$ or the ion $HC_4H_4O_6^-$. Also called: **hydrogen tartrate.**
bitch (bɪtʃ) *n.* **1.** a female dog or other female canine animal, such as a wolf. **2.** *Slang, derogatory.* a malicious, spiteful, or coarse woman. **3.** *Slang.* a complaint. **4.** *Slang.* a difficult situation or problem. ~*vb. Slang.* **5.** (*intr.*) to complain; grumble. **6.** to behave (towards) in a spiteful or malicious manner. **7.** (*tr.,* often foll. by *up*) to botch; bungle. [Old English *bicce*]
bitch·y (ˈbɪtʃɪ) *adj.* **bitch·i·er, bitch·i·est.** *Slang.* characteristic of or behaving like a bitch; malicious; snide.
bite (baɪt) *vb.* **bites, bit·ing, bit, bit·ten. 1.** to grip, cut off, or tear with or as if with the teeth or jaws. **2.** (of animals, insects, etc.) to injure by puncturing or tearing (the skin or flesh) with the teeth, fangs, etc., esp. as a natural characteristic. **3.** (*tr.*) to cut or penetrate, as with a knife. **4.** (of corrosive material such as acid) to eat away or into. **5.** to smart or cause to smart; sting: *mustard bites the tongue.* **6.** (*intr.*) *Angling.* (of a fish) to take or attempt to take the bait or lure. **7.** to take firm hold of or act effectively upon. **8.** to grip or hold (a workpiece) with a tool or chuck. **9.** (of a screw, thread, etc.) to cut into or grip (an object, material, etc.). **10.** (*tr.*) *Slang.* to annoy or worry: *what's biting her?* **11.** (*often passive*) *Slang.* to cheat. **12.** (*tr.;* often foll. by *for*) *Austral. slang.* to ask (for); scrounge from. **13. bite off more than one can chew.** *Informal.* to attempt a task beyond one's capability. **14. bite someone's head off.** *Informal.* to respond harshly and rudely (to). **15. bite the dust.** *Slang.* **a.** to fall down dead. **b.** to be rejected: *another good idea bites the dust.* **16. bite the hand that feeds one.** to repay kindness with injury or ingratitude. **17. once bitten, twice shy.** *Informal.* after an unpleasant experience one is cautious in similar situations. ~*n.* **18.** the act of biting. **19.** a thing or amount bitten off. **20.** a wound, bruise, or sting inflicted by biting. **21.** *Angling.* an attempt by a fish to take the bait or lure. **22.** *Informal.* an incisive or penetrating effect or quality: *that's a question with a bite.* **23.** *Informal.* a light meal; snack. **24.** a cutting, stinging, or smarting sensation. **25.** the depth of cut of a machine tool. **26.** the grip or hold applied by a tool or chuck to a workpiece. **27.** *Dentistry.* the angle or manner of contact between the upper and lower teeth when the mouth is closed naturally. **28.** the surface of a file or rasp with cutting teeth. **29.** the corrosive action of acid, as on a metal etching plate. [Old English *bītan;* related to Latin *findere* to split, Sanskrit *bhedati* he splits] —ˈ**bit·er** *n.*
bite back *vb.* (*tr., adv.*) to restrain (a hurtful, embarrassing, or indiscreet remark); avoid saying.
Bi·thyn·i·a (bɪˈθɪnɪə) *n.* an ancient country on the Black Sea in NW Asia Minor.
bit·ing (ˈbaɪtɪŋ) *adj.* **1.** piercing; keen: *a biting wind.* **2.** sarcastic; incisive: *a biting comment.* —ˈ**bit·ing·ly** *adv.*
bit·ing midge *n.* any small fragile dipterous fly of the family *Ceratopogonidae,* most of which suck the blood of mammals, birds, or other insects.
Bi·tolj (*Serbo-Croatian* ˈbitolj) *n.* a city in S Yugoslavia, in Macedonia: under Turkish rule from 1382 until 1913. Pop.: 65 851 (1971).
bit part *n.* a very small acting role with few lines to speak.
bit·ser (ˈbɪtsə) *n. Austral. informal.* a mongrel dog. [C20: from *bits o'* bits of, as in *his dog is bits o' this and bits o' that*]
bit·stock (ˈbɪtˌstɒk) *n.* the handle or stock of a tool into which a drilling bit is fixed.
bitt (bɪt) *Nautical.* ~*n.* **1.** one of a pair of strong posts on the deck of a ship for securing mooring and other lines. **2.** another word for **bollard** (sense 1). ~*vb.* **3.** (*tr.*) to secure (a line) by means of a bitt. [C14: probably of Scandinavian origin; compare Old Norse *biti* cross beam, Middle High German *bizze* wooden peg]
bit·ten (ˈbɪtᵊn) *vb.* the past participle of **bite.**
bit·ter (ˈbɪtə) *adj.* **1.** having or denoting an unpalatable harsh taste, as the peel of an orange or coffee dregs. Compare **sour** (sense 1). **2.** showing or caused by strong unrelenting hostility or resentment: *he was still bitter about the divorce.* **3.** difficult or unpleasant to accept or admit: *a bitter blow.* **4.** cutting; sarcastic: *bitter words.* **5.** bitingly cold: *a bitter night.* ~*adv.* **6.** very; extremely (esp. in the phrase **bitter cold**). ~*n.* **7.** a thing that is bitter. **8.** *Brit.* draught beer with a high hop content, with a slightly bitter taste. ~*vb.* **9.** to make or become bitter. [Old English *biter;* related to *bītan* to BITE] —ˈ**bit·ter·ly** *adv.* —ˈ**bit·ter·ness** *n.*
bit·ter ap·ple *n.* another name for **colocynth.**
bit·ter end *n.* **1.** *Nautical.* the end of a line, chain, or cable, esp. the end secured in the chain locker of a vessel. **2. to the bitter end. a.** until the finish of a task, job, etc., however unpleasant or difficult. **b.** until final defeat or death. [C19: in both senses perhaps from BITT]
Bit·ter Lakes *pl. n.* two lakes, the **Great Bitter Lake** and **Little Bitter Lake,** in NE Egypt: part of the Suez Canal.
bit·ter·ling (ˈbɪtəlɪŋ) *n.* a small brightly coloured European freshwater cyprinid fish, *Rhodeus sericeus:* a popular aquarium fish.
bit·tern[1] (ˈbɪtən) *n.* any wading bird of the genera *Ixobrychus* and *Botaurus,* related and similar to the herons but with shorter legs and neck, a stouter body, and a booming call: family *Ardeidae,* order *Ciconiiformes.* [C14: from Old French *butor,* perhaps from Latin *būtiō* bittern + *taurus* bull; referring to its cry]
bit·tern[2] (ˈbɪtən) *n.* the bitter liquid remaining after common salt has been crystallized out of sea water: a source of magnesium, bromine, and iodine compounds. [C17: variant of *bittering;* see BITTER]
bit·ter·nut (ˈbɪtəˌnʌt) *n.* **1.** an E North American hickory tree, *Carya cordiformis,* with thin-shelled nuts and bitter kernels. **2.** the nut of this plant.
bit·ter or·ange *n.* another name for **Seville orange.**
bit·ter prin·ci·ple *n.* any of various bitter-tasting substances, such as aloin, usually extracted from plants.
bit·ters (ˈbɪtəz) *pl. n.* **1.** bitter-tasting spirits of varying alcoholic content flavoured with plant extracts. **2.** a similar

liquid containing a bitter-tasting substance, used as a tonic to stimulate the appetite or improve digestion.

bit·ter·sweet ('bɪtəˌswi:t) *n.* **1.** any of several North American woody climbing plants of the genus *Celastrus,* esp. *C. scandens,* having orange capsules that open to expose scarlet-coated seeds: family *Celastraceae.* **2.** another name for **woody nightshade.** ~*adj.* **3.** tasting of or being a mixture of bitterness and sweetness. **4.** pleasant but tinged with sadness.

bit·ter·weed ('bɪtəˌwi:d) *n.* any of various plants that contain a bitter-tasting substance.

bit·ter·wood ('bɪtəˌwʊd) *n.* any of several simaroubaceous trees of the genus *Picrasma* of S and SE Asia and the West Indies, whose bitter bark and wood are used in medicine as a substitute for quassia.

bit·ty ('bɪtɪ) *adj.* **·ti·er, ·ti·est. 1.** lacking unity; disjointed. **2.** containing bits, sediment, etc.

bi·tu·men ('bɪtjʊmɪn) *n.* **1.** any of various viscous or solid impure mixtures of hydrocarbons that occur naturally in asphalt, tar, mineral waxes, etc.: used as a road surfacing and roofing material. **2.** the constituents of coal that can be extracted by an organic solvent. **3. the bitumen.** *Austral. informal.* any road with a bitumen surface, esp. (*cap.*) the road in the Northern Territory between Darwin and Alice Springs. **4.** a transparent brown pigment or glaze made from asphalt. [C15: from Latin *bitūmen,* perhaps of Celtic origin] —**bi·tu·mi·nous** (bɪ'tju:mɪnəs) *adj.*

bi·tu·mi·nize *or* **bi·tu·mi·nise** (bɪ'tju:mɪˌnaɪz) *vb.* (*tr.*) to treat with or convert into bitumen. —**bi·ˌtu·mi·ni·'za·tion** *or* **bi·ˌtu·mi·ni·'sa·tion** *n.*

bi·tu·mi·nous coal *n.* a soft black coal, rich in volatile hydrocarbons, that burns with a smoky yellow flame. Fixed carbon content: 46–86 per cent; calorific value: 1.93×10^7–3.63×10^7 J/kg. Also called: **soft coal.**

bi·va·lent (baɪ'veɪlənt, 'bɪvə-) *adj.* **1.** *Chem.* another word for **divalent. 2.** (of homologous chromosomes) associated together in pairs. ~*n.* **3.** a structure formed during meiosis consisting of two homologous chromosomes associated together. —**bi·'va·len·cy** *n.*

bi·valve ('baɪˌvælv) *n.* **1.** Also called: **lamellibranch, pelecypod.** any marine or freshwater mollusc of the class *Bivalvia* (or *Lamellibranchia, Pelecypoda*), having a laterally compressed body, a shell consisting of two hinged valves, and gills for respiration. The group includes clams, cockles, oysters, and mussels. ~*adj.* **2.** Also: **lamellibranch, pelecypod.** of, relating to, or belonging to the *Bivalvia.* **3.** Also: **bivalvate.** *Biology.* having or consisting of two valves or similar parts: *a bivalve seed capsule.* —**bi·'val·vu·lar** *adj.*

biv·ou·ac ('bɪvʊˌæk, 'bɪvwæk) *n.* **1.** a temporary encampment with few facilities, as used by soldiers, mountaineers, etc. ~*vb.* **·acs, ·ack·ing, ·acked. 2.** (*intr.*) to make such an encampment. [C18: from French *bivuac,* probably from Swiss German *Beiwacht,* literally: BY + WATCH]

biv·vy ('bɪvɪ) *n., pl.* **·vies.** *Slang.* a small tent or shelter. [C20: shortened from BIVOUAC]

bi·week·ly (baɪ'wi:klɪ) *adj., adv.* **1.** every two weeks. **2.** (often avoided because of confusion with sense 1) twice a week; semiweekly. See **bi-**[1]. ~*n., pl.* **·lies. 3.** a periodical published every two weeks.

bi·year·ly (baɪ'jɪəlɪ) *adj., adv.* **1.** every two years; biennial or biennially. **2.** (often avoided because of confusion with sense 1) twice a year; biannual or biannually. See **bi-**[1].

Biysk, Biisk, *or* **Bisk** (*Russian* bijsk) *n.* a city in the SW Soviet Union, at the foot of the Altai Mountains. Pop: 207 000 (1975 est.).

biz (bɪz) *n. Informal.* short for **business.**

bi·zarre (bɪ'zɑ:) *adj.* odd or unusual, esp. in an interesting or amusing way. [C17: from French: from Italian *bizzarro* capricious, of uncertain origin] —**bi·'zarre·ly** *adv.* —**bi·'zarre·ness** *n.*

Bi·zer·te (bɪ'zɜ:tə; *French* bi'zɛrt) *or* **Bi·zer·ta** *n.* a port in N Tunisia, on the Mediterranean at the canalized outlet of **Lake Bizerte.** Pop.: 346 445 (1975 est.).

Bi·zet ('bi:zeɪ; *French* bi'zɛ) *n.* **Georges** (ʒɔrʒ). 1838–75, French composer, whose works include the opera *Carmen* (1875) and incidental music to Daudet's *L'Arlésienne* (1872).

Björ·ne·borg (ˌbjœrnə'bɔrj) *n.* the Swedish name for **Pori.**

Bk *the chemical symbol for* berkelium.

bk. *abbrev. for:* **1.** bank. **2.** book.

bkcy. *abbrev. for* bankruptcy.

bkg. *abbrev. for* banking.

bkpt. *abbrev. for* bankrupt.

bks. *abbrev. for:* **1.** barracks. **2.** books.

bl. *abbrev. for:* **1.** bale. **2.** barrel. **3.** black. **4.** blue.

B.L. *abbrev. for:* **1.** Bachelor of Laws. **2.** Bachelor of Letters. **3.** Barrister-at-Law. **4.** British Library.

B/L, b/l, *or* **b.l.** *pl.* **Bs/L, bs/l,** *or* **bs.l.** *abbrev. for* bill of lading.

blab (blæb) *vb.* **blabs, blab·bing, blabbed. 1.** to divulge (secrets, etc.) indiscreetly. **2.** (*intr.*) to chatter thoughtlessly; prattle. ~*n.* **3.** a less common word for **blabber** (senses 1, 2). [C14: of Germanic origin; compare Old High German *blabbizōn,* Icelandic *blabbra*]

blab·ber ('blæbə) *n.* **1.** a person who blabs. **2.** idle chatter. ~*vb.* **3.** (*intr.*) to talk without thinking; chatter. [C15 *blabberen,* probably of imitative origin]

blab·ber·mouth ('blæbəˌmaʊθ) *n. Informal.* a person who talks too much or indiscreetly.

black (blæk) *adj.* **1.** of the colour of jet or carbon black, having no hue due to the absorption of all or nearly all incident light. Compare **white** (sense 1). **2.** without light; completely dark. **3.** without hope or alleviation; gloomy: *the future looked black.* **4.** very dirty or soiled: *black factory chimneys.* **5.** angry or resentful: *she gave him black looks.* **6.** (of a play or other work) dealing with the unpleasant realities of life, esp. in a pessimistic or macabre manner: *black comedy.* **7.** (of coffee or tea) without milk or cream. **8.** causing, resulting from, or showing great misfortune: *black areas of unemployment.* **9. a.** wicked or harmful: *a black lie.* **b.** (*in combination*): *black-hearted.* **10.** causing or deserving dishonour or censure: *a black crime.* **11.** (of the face) purple, as from suffocation. **12.** *Brit.* (of goods, jobs, works, etc.) being subject to boycott by trade unionists, esp. in support of industrial action elsewhere. ~*n.* **13.** a black colour. **14.** a dye or pigment of or producing this colour. **15.** black clothing, worn esp. as a sign of mourning. **16.** *Chess, draughts.* **a.** a black or dark-coloured piece or square. **b.** the player playing with such pieces. **17.** complete darkness: *the black of the night.* **18.** a black ball in snooker, etc. **19.** (in roulette and other gambling games) one of two colours on which players may place even bets, the other being red. **20. in the black.** in credit or without debt. **21.** *Archery.* a black ring on a target, between the outer and the blue, scoring three points. ~*vb.* **22.** another word for **blacken. 23.** (*tr.*) to polish (shoes, etc.) with blacking. **24.** (*tr.*) to bruise so as to make black: *he blacked her eye.* **25.** (*tr.*) *Brit.* (of trade unionists) to organize a boycott of (specified goods, jobs, work, etc.), esp. in support of industrial action elsewhere. ~See also **blackout.** [Old English *blæc;* related to Old Saxon *blak* ink, Old High German *blakra* to blink] —**'black·ish** *adj.* —**'black·ish·ly** *adv.* —**'black·ly** *adv.* —**'black·ness** *n.*

Black (blæk) *n.* **1.** a member of a dark-skinned race, esp. a Negro or an Australian Aborigine. ~*adj.* **2.** of or relating to a Black or Blacks: *a Black ghetto.*

black·a·moor ('blækəˌmʊə, -ˌmɔ:) *n. Archaic.* a Negro or other person with dark skin. [C16: see BLACK, MOOR]

black-and-blue *adj.* **1.** (of the skin) discoloured, as from a bruise. **2.** feeling pain or soreness, as from a beating.

black and tan *n.* a mixture of stout or porter and ale.

Black and Tan *n.* a member of the armed force sent to Ireland in 1921 by the British Government to combat Sinn Fein: named after the colour of their uniforms.

black-and-tan ter·ri·er *n.* a less common name for **Manchester terrier.**

black-and-white *n.* **1. a.** a photograph, picture, sketch, etc., in black, white, and shades of grey rather than in colour. **b.** (*as modifier*): *black-and-white film.* **2.** the neutral tones of black, white, and intermediate shades of grey. Compare **colour** (sense 2). **3. in black and white. a.** in print or writing. **b.** in extremes: *he always saw things in black and white.*

black art *n.* **the.** another name for **black magic.**

black-backed gull *n.* either of two common black-and-white European coastal gulls, *Larus fuscus* (**lesser black-backed gull**) and *L. marinus* (**great black-backed gull**).

black·ball ('blækˌbɔ:l) *n.* **1.** a negative vote or veto. **2.** a black wooden ball used to indicate disapproval or veto in a vote. ~*vb.* (*tr.*) **3.** to vote against in a ballot. **4.** to exclude (someone) from a group, profession, etc.; ostracize. [C18: see sense 2]

black bass (bæs) *n.* any of several predatory North American percoid freshwater game fishes of the genus *Micropterus:* family *Centrarchidae* (sunfishes, etc.).

black bean *n.* an Australian leguminous tree, *Castanospermum australe,* having thin smooth bark and yellow or reddish flowers: used in furniture manufacture. Also called: **Moreton Bay chestnut.**

black bear *n.* **1. American black bear.** a bear, *Euarctos* (or *Ursus*) *americanus,* inhabiting forests of North America. It is smaller and less ferocious than the brown bear. **2. Asiatic black bear.** a bear, *Selenarctos thibetanus,* of central and E Asia, whose coat is black with a pale V-shaped mark on the chest.

Black·beard ('blækˌbɪəd) *n.* nickname of (Edward) **Teach.**

black bee·tle *n.* another name for the **oriental cockroach** (see **cockroach**).

black belt *n.* **1.** *Judo.* **a.** a black belt worn by an instructor or expert competitor in the dan grades, usually from first to fifth dan. **b.** a person entitled to wear this. **2. the.** a region of the southern U.S. extending from Georgia across central Alabama and Mississippi, in which the population contains a large number of Blacks: also noted for its fertile black soil.

black·ber·ry ('blækbərɪ) *n., pl.* **·ries. 1.** Also called: **bramble.** any of several woody plants of the rosaceous genus *Rubus,* esp. *R. fruticosus,* that have thorny stems and black or purple glossy edible berry-like fruits (drupelets). **2. a.** the fruit of any of these plants. **b.** (*as modifier*): *blackberry jam.* **3. blackberry lily.** an ornamental Chinese iridaceous plant, *Belamcanda chinensis,* that has red-spotted orange flowers and clusters of black seeds that resemble blackberries. ~*vb.* **·ries, ·ry·ing, ·ried. 4.** (*intr.*) to gather blackberries.

black bile *n. Archaic.* one of the four bodily humours; melancholy. See **humour** (sense 8).

black bind·weed *n.* a twining polygonaceous European plant, *Polygonum convolvulus,* with heart-shaped leaves and triangular black seed pods.

black·bird ('blækˌbɜ:d) *n.* **1.** a common European thrush, *Turdus merula,* in which the male has a black plumage and yellow bill and the female is brown. **2.** any of various American orioles having a dark plumage, esp. any of the genus *Agelaius.* **3.** (formerly) a person, esp. a South Sea islander, who was kidnapped and sold as a slave, esp. in Australia. ~*vb.* **4.** (*tr.*) (formerly) to kidnap and sell into slavery.

black+board (ˈblækˌbɔːd) *n.* a sheet of slate, wood, or any of various other materials, used for writing or drawing on with chalk, esp. in teaching and esp. in a more or less upright position so that all students in a class can see it.

black bod·y *n. Physics.* a hypothetical body that would be capable of absorbing all the electromagnetic radiation falling on it. Also called: **full radiator.**

black book *n.* **1.** a book containing the names of people to be punished, blacklisted, etc. **2. in someone's black books.** *Informal.* out of favour with someone.

black bot+tom *n.* a dance of the late 1920s that originated in America, involving a sinuous rotation of the hips.

black box *n.* **1.** a self-contained unit in an electronic or computer system whose circuitry need not be known to understand its function. **2.** an informal name for **flight recorder.**

black+boy (ˈblækˌbɔɪ) *n.* another name for **grass tree** (sense 1).

black bread *n.* a kind of very dark coarse rye bread.

black bry·o·ny *n.* a climbing herbaceous Eurasian plant, *Tamus communis,* having small greenish flowers and poisonous red berries: family *Dioscoreaceae.*

black+buck (ˈblækˌbʌk) *n.* an Indian antelope, *Antilope cervicapra,* the male of which has spiral horns, a dark back, and a white belly.

Black+burn (ˈblækbɜːn) *n.* **1.** a city in NW England, in central Lancashire: textile industries. Pop: 101 672 (1971). **2. Mount.** a mountain in SE Alaska, the highest peak in the Wrangell Mountains. Height: 5037 m (16 523 ft.).

black+butt (ˈblækˌbʌt) *n.* any of various Australian eucalyptus trees having rough fibrous bark and hard wood used as timber.

black+cap (ˈblækˌkæp) *n.* **1.** a brownish-grey Old World warbler, *Sylvia atricapilla,* the male of which has a black crown. **2.** any of various similar birds, such as the black-capped chickadee (*Parus atricapillus*). **3.** *U.S.* a popular name for **raspberry** (sense 3). **4.** *Brit.* (formerly) the cap worn by a judge when passing a death sentence.

black-coat·ed *adj. Brit.* (esp. formerly) (of a worker) clerical or professional, as distinguished from commercial or industrial.

black+cock (ˈblækˌkɒk) *n.* the male of the black grouse. Also called: **heath cock.** Compare **greyhen.**

Black Coun+try *n.* **the.** the heavily industrialized region of the West Midlands of England.

black+cur+rant (ˌblækˈkʌrənt) *n.* **1.** a N temperate shrub, *Ribes nigrum,* having red or white flowers and small edible black berries: family *Grossulariaceae.* **2. a.** the fruit of this shrub. **b.** (*as modifier*): *blackcurrant jelly.*

black+damp (ˈblækˌdæmp) *n.* air that is low in oxygen content and high in carbon dioxide as a result of an explosion in a mine. Also called: **chokedamp.**

Black Death *n.* **the.** a form of bubonic plague pandemic in Europe and Asia during the 14th century, when it killed over 50 million people. See **bubonic plague.**

black di·a+mond *n.* **1.** another name for **carbonado**[2]. **2.** (*usually pl.*) a figurative expression for **coal.**

black earth *n.* another name for **chernozem.**

black+en (ˈblækən) *vb.* **1.** to make or become black or dirty. **2.** (*tr.*) to defame; slander (esp. in the phrase **blacken someone's name**).

Black·ett (ˈblækɪt) *n.* **Pat·rick May·nard Stu·art,** Baron. 1897–1974, English physicist, noted for his work on cosmic radiation and his discovery of the positron. Nobel prize for physics 1948.

black eye *n. Informal.* bruising round the eye.

black-eyed pea *n.* another name for **cowpea** (sense 2).

black-eyed Su+san *n.* **1.** any of several North American plants of the genus *Rudbeckia,* esp. *R. hirta,* having flower heads of orange-yellow rays and brown-black centres: family *Compositae* (composites). **2.** a tropical African climbing plant, *Thunbergia alata,* having yellow flowers with purple centres: family *Thunbergiaceae.*

black+face (ˈblækˌfeɪs) *n.* **1. a.** a performer made up to imitate a Negro. **b.** the make-up used by such a performer, usually consisting of burnt cork. **2.** *Printing.* a less common name for **Gothic** (sense 9).

black+fel·low (ˈblækˌfɛləʊ) *n.* an archaic name for **Aborigine** (sense 1).

black+fish (ˈblækˌfɪʃ) *n., pl.* **·fish** *or* **·fish·es. 1.** a minnow-like Alaskan freshwater fish, *Dallia pectoralis,* related to the pikes and thought to be able to survive prolonged freezing. **2.** a female salmon that has recently spawned. Compare **redfish** (sense 1). **3.** any of various other dark fishes, such as the tautog. **4.** another name for **pilot whale.**

black flag *n.* another name for the **Jolly Roger.**

black+fly (ˈblækˌflaɪ) *n., pl.* **·flies.** a black aphid, *Aphis fabae,* that infests beans, sugar beet, and other plants. Also called: **bean aphid.**

black fly *n.* any small blackish stout-bodied dipterous fly of the family *Simuliidae,* which suck the blood of man, mammals, and birds. See also **buffalo gnat.**

Black+foot (ˈblækˌfʊt) *n.* **1.** (*pl.* **·feet** *or* **·foot**) a member of a warlike group of North American Indian peoples formerly living in the northwestern Plains. **2.** any of the languages of these peoples, belonging to the Algonquian family. [C19: translation of Blackfoot *Siksika*]

Black For+est *n.* **the.** a hilly wooded region of SW West Germany, in Baden-Württemberg: many resorts. German name: **Schwarzwald.**

Black Fri+ar *n.* a Dominican friar.

black frost *n.* a frost without snow or rime that is severe enough to blacken vegetation.

black grouse *n.* **1.** a large N European grouse, *Lyrurus tetrix,* the male of which has a bluish-black plumage and lyre-shaped tail. **2.** a related and similar species, *Lyrurus mlokosiewiczi,* of W Asia.

black+guard (ˈblægɑːd, -gəd) *n.* **1. a.** an unprincipled contemptible person; scoundrel. **b.** (*as modifier*): *blackguard language.* ~*vb.* **2.** (*tr.*) to ridicule or denounce with abusive language. **3.** (*intr.*) to behave like a blackguard. [C16: see BLACK, GUARD] —ˈ**black+guard+ism** *n.* —ˈ**black+guard+ly** *adj.*

black guil+le+mot *n.* a common guillemot, *Cepphus grylle:* its summer plumage is black with white wing patches and its winter plumage white with greyish wings.

Black Hand *n.* **1.** a group of Sicilian blackmailers and terrorists formed in the 1870s and operating in the U.S. in the early 20th century. **2.** (in 19th-century Spain) an organization of anarchists.

black+head (ˈblækˌhɛd) *n.* **1.** a black-tipped plug of fatty matter clogging a pore of the skin, esp. the duct of a sebaceous gland. Technical name: **comedo. 2.** an infectious and often fatal disease of turkeys and some other fowl caused by parasitic protozoa. Technical name: **infectious enterohepatitis. 3.** any of various birds, esp. gulls or ducks, with black plumage on the head.

black+heart (ˈblækˌhɑːt) *n.* **1.** an abnormal darkening of the woody stems of some plants, thought to be caused by extreme cold. **2.** any of various diseases of plants, such as the potato, in which the central tissues are blackened. **3.** a variety of cherry that has large sweet fruit with purplish flesh and an almost black skin.

Black Hills *pl. n.* a group of mountains in W South Dakota and NE Wyoming: famous for the gigantic sculptures of U.S. presidents on the side of Mount Rushmore. Highest peak: Harney Peak, 2208 m (7242 ft.).

black hole *n. Astronomy.* a hypothetical region of space resulting from the gravitational collapse of a star following the exhaustion of its nuclear fuel. The gravitational field around the region would be so high that neither matter nor radiation could escape from it.

Black Hole of Cal+cut+ta *n.* **1.** a small dungeon in which in 1756 the Nawab of Bengal reputedly confined 146 English prisoners, of whom only 23 survived. **2.** *Informal, chiefly Brit.* any uncomfortable or overcrowded place.

black hore+hound *n.* a hairy unpleasant-smelling chiefly Mediterranean plant, *Ballota nigra,* having clusters of purple flowers: family *Labiatae* (labiates).

black ice *n.* a thin transparent layer of new ice on a road or similar surface.

black+ing (ˈblækɪŋ) *n.* any preparation, esp. one containing lampblack, for giving a black finish to shoes, metals, etc.

black+jack[1] (ˈblækˌdʒæk) *Chiefly U.S.* ~*n.* **1.** a truncheon of leather-covered lead with a flexible shaft. ~*vb.* **2.** (*tr.*) to hit with or as if with a blackjack. **3.** (*tr.*) to compel (a person) by threats. [C19: from BLACK + JACK[1] (implement)]

black+jack[2] (ˈblækˌdʒæk) *n. Cards.* **1.** pontoon or any of various similar card games. **2.** the ace of spades. [C20: from BLACK + JACK[1] (the knave)]

black+jack[3] (ˈblækˌdʒæk) *n.* a dark iron-rich variety of the mineral sphalerite. [C18: from BLACK + JACK[1] (originally a miner's name for this useless ore)]

black+jack[4] (ˈblækˌdʒæk) *n.* a small oak tree, *Quercus marilandica,* of the southeastern U.S., with blackish bark and fan-shaped leaves. Also called: **blackjack oak.** [C19: from BLACK + JACK[1] (from the proper name, popularly used in many plant names)]

black+jack[5] (ˈblækˌdʒæk) *n.* a tarred leather tankard or jug. [C16: from BLACK + JACK[3]]

black knot *n.* a fungal disease of plums and cherries caused by *Dibotryon morbosum,* characterized by rough black knotlike swellings on the twigs and branches.

black lead (lɛd) *n.* another name for **graphite.**

black+leg (ˈblækˌlɛg) *n.* **1.** Also called (esp. U.S.): **scab.** *Brit.* **a.** a person who acts against the interests of a trade union, as by continuing to work during a strike or taking over a striker's job. **b.** (*as modifier*): *blackleg labour.* **2.** an acute infectious disease of cattle, sheep, and pigs, characterized by gas-filled swellings, esp. on the legs, caused by *Clostridium* bacteria. **3.** *Plant pathol.* **a.** a fungal disease of cabbages and related plants caused by *Phoma lingam,* characterized by blackening and decay of the lower stems. **b.** a similar disease of potatoes, caused by bacteria. **4.** a person who cheats in gambling, esp. at cards or in racing. ~*vb.* **·legs, ·leg·ging, ·legged. 5.** *Brit.* to act against the interests of a trade union, esp. by refusing to join a strike.

black let+ter *n. Printing.* another name for **Gothic** (sense 9).

black light *n.* the invisible electromagnetic radiation in the ultraviolet and infrared regions of the spectrum.

black+list (ˈblækˌlɪst) *n.* **1.** a list of persons or organizations under suspicion, or considered untrustworthy, disloyal, etc., esp. one compiled by a government or an organization. ~*vb.* **2.** (*tr.*) to put on a blacklist.

black mag+ic *n.* magic used for evil purposes by invoking the power of the devil.

black+mail (ˈblækˌmeɪl) *n.* **1.** the act of attempting to obtain money by intimidation, as by threats to disclose discreditable information. **2.** the exertion of pressure or threats, esp. unfairly, in an attempt to influence someone's actions. ~*vb.* (*tr.*) **3.** to exact or attempt to exact (money or anything of value) from (a person) by threats or intimidation; extort. **4.** to attempt to influence the actions of (a person), esp. by unfair

pressure or threats. [C16: see BLACK, MAIL[3]] —'**black+mail+er** *n.*
Black Ma·ri·a (mə'raɪə) *n.* a police van for transporting prisoners.
black mark *n.* an indication of disapproval, failure, etc.
black mar+ket *n.* **1.** any system in which goods or currencies are sold and bought illegally, esp. in violation of controls or rationing. **2.** the place where such a system operates. ~*vb.* **black-mar·ket. 3.** to sell (goods) on the black market. —**black mar+ke+teer** *n.*
black mass *n.* (*sometimes cap.*) a blasphemous travesty of the Christian Mass, performed by practitioners of black magic.
black mea+sles *pl. n.* (*often functioning as sing.*) a severe form of measles characterized by dark eruptions caused by bleeding under the skin.
black med+ick *n.* a small European papilionaceous plant, *Medicago lupulina,* with trifoliate leaves, small yellow flowers, and black pods. Also called: **nonesuch.**
Black·more ('blækmɔː) *n.* **R(ichard) D(oddridge).** 1825–1900, English novelist; author of *Lorna Doone* (1869).
black mould *n.* another name for **bread mould.**
Black Moun+tains *pl. n.* **1.** a mountain range in S Wales, in E Dyfed and W Powys. Highest peak: Carmarthen Van, 802 m (2632 ft.). **2.** a mountain range in S Wales, in E Gwent. Highest peak: Waun Fach, 811 m (2660 ft.).
Black Mus+lim *n.* (esp. in the U.S.) a political and religious movement of Black people who adapt the religious practices of Islam and seek to establish a new Black nation. Official name: **Nation of Islam.**
black mus+tard *n.* a Eurasian cruciferous plant, *Brassica* (or *Sinapsis*) *nigra,* with clusters of yellow flowers and pungent seeds from which the condiment mustard is made.
black night+shade *n.* a poisonous solanaceous plant, *Solanum nigrum,* a common weed in cultivated land, having small white flowers with backward-curved petals and black berry-like fruits.
black+out ('blækaʊt) *n.* **1.** the extinguishing or hiding of all artificial light, esp. in a city visible to an enemy attack from the air. **2.** a momentary loss of consciousness, vision, or memory. **3.** a temporary electrical power failure or cut. **4.** *Electronics.* a temporary loss of sensitivity in a valve following a short strong pulse. **5.** a temporary loss of radio communications between a spacecraft and earth, esp. on re-entry into the earth's atmosphere. **6.** the suspension of radio or television broadcasting, as by a strike or for political reasons. ~*vb.* **black out.** (*adv.*) **7.** (*tr.*) to obliterate or extinguish (lights). **8.** (*tr.*) to create a blackout in (a city etc.). **9.** (*intr.*) *Informal.* to lose vision, consciousness, or memory temporarily. **10.** (*tr., adv.*) to stop (news, a television programme) from being released or broadcast.
Black Pan+ther *n.* (in the U.S.) a member of a militant Black political party founded in 1965 to end the political dominance of Whites.
black pep+per *n.* a pungent condiment made by grinding the dried unripe berries, together with their black husks, of the pepper plant *Piper nigrum.*
black+poll ('blæk,pəʊl) *n.* a North American warbler, *Dendroica striata,* the male of which has a black-and-white head.
Black+pool ('blæk,puːl) *n.* a town and resort in NW England, in Lancashire on the Irish Sea: famous for its tower, 158 m (520 ft.) high, and its illuminations. Pop.: 151 311 (1971).
black pow+der *n.* a U.S. name for **gunpowder.**
Black Pow+er *n.* a social, economic, and political movement of Black people, esp. in the U.S. and Australia, to obtain equality with Whites.
Black Prince *n.* **the.** See **Edward** (Prince of Wales).
black pud+ding *n.* a kind of black sausage made from minced pork fat, pig's blood, and other ingredients. Also called: **blood pudding.** Usual U.S. name: **blood sausage.**
black rat *n.* a common rat, *Rattus rattus:* a household pest that has spread from its native Asia to all countries.
Black Rod *n.* **1.** (in Britain) an officer of the House of Lords and of the Order of the Garter, whose main duty is summoning the Commons at the opening and proroguing of Parliament. **2.** a similar officer in any of certain other legislatures.
black rot *n.* any of various plant diseases of fruits and vegetables, producing blackening, rotting, and shrivelling and caused by bacteria (including *Xanthomonas campestris*) and fungi (such as *Physalospora malorum*).
black rust *n.* a stage in any of several diseases of cereals and grasses caused by rust fungi in which black masses of spores appear on the stems or leaves.
Black Sash *n.* (in South Africa) an organization of women opposed to apartheid.
Black Sea *n.* an inland sea between SE Europe and Asia: connected to the Aegean Sea by the Bosporus, the Sea of Marmara, and the Dardanelles, and to the Sea of Azov by the Kerch Strait. Area: about 415 000 sq. km (160 000 sq. miles). Also called: **Euxine Sea.** Ancient name: **Pontus Euxinus.**
black sheep *n.* a person who is regarded as a disgrace or failure by his family or peer group.
Black+shirt ('blæk,ʃɜːt) *n.* (in Europe) a member of a fascist organization, esp. a member of the Italian Fascist party before and during World War II.
black+smith ('blæk,smɪθ) *n.* an artisan who works iron with a furnace, anvil, hammer, etc. [C15: see BLACK, SMITH]
black+snake ('blæk,sneɪk) *n.* **1.** any of several Old World black venomous elapid snakes, esp. *Pseudechis porphyriacus* (**Australian blacksnake**). **2.** any of various dark nonvenomous snakes, such as *Coluber constrictor* (black racer). **3.** U.S. a long heavy pliant whip of braided leather or rawhide.
black spot *n.* **1.** a place on a road where accidents frequently occur. **2.** any dangerous or difficult place.
black spruce *n.* a coniferous tree, *Picea mariana,* of the northern regions of North America, growing mostly in cold bogs and having dark green needles. Also called: **spruce pine.**
Black·stone ('blæk,stəʊn, -stən) *n.* Sir **Wil·liam.** 1723–80, English jurist noted particularly for his *Commentaries on the Laws of England* (1865–69), which had a profound influence on jurisprudence in the U.S.
black+strap mo+las+ses ('blæk,stræp) *pl. n.* the molasses remaining after the maximum quantity of sugar has been extracted from the raw material.
black stump *n.* **the.** *Austral.* an imaginary marker of the extent of civilization (esp. in the phrase **beyond the black stump**).
black swan *n.* a large Australian swan, *Cygnus atratus,* that has a black plumage and red bill.
black+tail ('blæk,teɪl) *n.* a variety of mule deer having a black tail.
black tea *n.* tea made from fermented tea leaves.
black+thorn ('blæk,θɔːn) *n.* a thorny Eurasian rosaceous shrub, *Prunus spinosa,* with black twigs, white flowers, and small sour plumlike fruits. Also called: **sloe.**
black tie *n.* **1.** a black bow tie worn with a dinner jacket. **2.** (*modifier*) denoting an occasion when a dinner jacket should be worn. ~Compare **white tie.**
black+top ('blæk,tɒp) *n.* *Chiefly U.S.* a bituminous mixture used for paving.
black track·er *n.* *Austral.* an Aboriginal tracker working for the police.
black trea+cle *n.* *Brit.* another term for **treacle** (sense 1).
black vel+vet *n.* **1.** a mixture of stout and champagne in equal proportions. **2.** *Austral. slang.* Aboriginal women collectively.
Black Vol+ta *n.* a river in W Africa, rising in SW Upper Volta and flowing northeast, then south into Lake Volta: forms part of the border of Ghana with Upper Volta and with the Ivory Coast. Length: about 800 km (500 miles).
black vom+it *n.* **1.** vomit containing blood, often a manifestation of disease, such as yellow fever. **2.** *Informal.* yellow fever.
Black+wall hitch ('blæk,wɔːl) *n.* a knot for hooking tackle to the end of a rope, holding fast when pulled but otherwise loose. [after *Blackwall,* London]
black wal+nut *n.* **1.** a North American walnut tree, *Juglans nigra,* with hard dark wood and edible oily nuts. **2.** the valuable wood of this tree, used for cabinet work. **3.** the nut of this tree. ~Compare **butternut** (senses 1–4).
Black Watch *n.* **the.** the Royal Highland Regiment in the British army.
black+wa·ter fe+ver ('blæk,wɔːtə) *n.* a rare and serious complication of chronic malaria caused by *Plasmodium falciparum,* characterized by massive destruction of red blood cells, producing dark red or blackish urine.
black whale *n.* another name for **pilot whale.**
black wid+ow *n.* an American spider, *Latrodectus mactans,* the female of which is black with red markings, highly venomous, and commonly eats its mate.
black+wood ('blæk,wʊd) *n.* a tall Australian acacia tree, *A. melanoxylon,* having small clusters of flowers and curved pods and yielding highly valued black timber. Also called: **Sally Wattle.**
Black+wood ('blæk,wʊd) *n.* *Bridge.* a conventional bidding sequence of four and five no-trumps, which are requests to the partner to show aces and kings respectively. [C20: named after Easeley F. *Blackwood,* its American inventor]
blad+der ('blædə) *n.* **1.** *Anatomy.* a distensible membranous sac, usually containing liquid or gas, esp. the urinary bladder. Related adj.: **vesical. 2.** an inflatable part of something. **3.** a blister, cyst, vesicle, etc., usually filled with fluid. **4.** a hollow vesicular or saclike part or organ in certain plants, such as the bladderwrack. [Old English *blǣdre*] —'**blad+der·y** *adj.*
blad+der cam+pi+on *n.* a European caryophyllaceous plant, *Silene vulgaris,* having white flowers with an inflated calyx.
blad+der ket+mi·a ('kɛtmɪə) *n.* another name for **flower-of-an-hour.**
blad·der+nose ('blædə,nəʊz) *n.* another name for **hooded seal.**
blad·der+nut ('blædə,nʌt) *n.* **1.** any temperate shrub or small tree of the genus *Staphylea,* esp. *S. pinnata* of S Europe, that has bladder-like seed pods: family *Staphyleaceae.* **2.** the pod of any such tree.
blad+der sen+na *n.* a Eurasian papilionaceous plant, *Colutea arborescens,* with yellow and red flowers and membranous inflated pods.
blad+der worm *n.* an encysted saclike larva of the tapeworm. The main types are cysticercus, hydatid and coenurus.
blad·der+wort ('blædə,wɜːt) *n.* any aquatic plant of the genus *Utricularia,* some of whose leaves are modified as small bladders to trap minute aquatic animals: family *Lentibulariaceae.*
blad·der+wrack ('blædə,ræk) *n.* any of several seaweeds of the genera *Fucus* and *Ascophyllum,* esp. *F. vesiculosus,* that grow in the intertidal regions of rocky shores and have branched brown fronds with air bladders.
blade (bleɪd) *n.* **1.** the part of a sharp weapon, tool, etc., that forms the cutting edge. **2.** (*pl.*) *Austral.* hand shears used for shearing sheep. **3.** the thin flattish part of various tools, implements, etc., as of a propeller. **4.** the flattened expanded

part of a leaf, sepal, or petal. **5.** the long narrow leaf of a grass or related plant. **6.** the striking surface of a bat, club, stick, or oar. **7.** the metal runner on an ice skate. **8.** *Archaeol.* a long thin flake of flint, possibly used as a tool. **9.** the upper part of the tongue lying directly behind the tip. **10.** *Archaic.* a dashing or swaggering young man. **11.** short for **shoulder blade. 12.** a poetic word for a **sword** or **swordsman.** [Old English *blæd;* related to Old Norse *blath* leaf, Old High German *blat,* Latin *folium* leaf] —**'blad+ed** *adj.*

blade grad+er *n.* another name for **grader** (sense 2).

blae+ber·ry ('bleɪbərɪ) *n., pl.* **·ries.** *Brit.* another name for **whortleberry** (senses 1, 2). [C15: from northern dialect *bla* bluish + BERRY]

Bla+go+vesh+chensk (*Russian* bləga'vjeʃtʃɪnsk) *n.* a city and port in the SE Soviet Union, in Siberia on the Amur River. Pop.: 165 000 (1975 est.).

blague (*French* blag) *n.* pretentious but empty talk; nonsense.

blah *or* **blah blah** (blɑː) *Slang.* ~*n.* **1.** worthless or silly talk; claptrap. ~*adj.* **2.** uninteresting; insipid. ~*vb.* **3.** (*intr.*) to talk nonsense or boringly.

blain (bleɪn) *n.* a blister, blotch, or sore on the skin. [Old English *blegen;* related to Middle Low German *bleine*]

Blake (bleɪk) *n.* **1. Rob·ert.** 1599–1657, English admiral, who commanded Cromwell's fleet against the Royalists, the Dutch, and the Spanish. **2. Wil·liam.** 1757–1827, English poet, painter, engraver, and mystic. His literary works include *Songs of Innocence* (1789) and *Songs of Experience* (1794), *The Marriage of Heaven and Hell* (1793), and *Jerusalem* (1820). His chief works in the visual arts include engravings of a visionary nature, such as the illustrations for *The Book of Job* (1826), for Dante's poems, and for his own *Prophetic Books* (1783–1804).

blame (bleɪm) *n.* **1.** responsibility for something that is wrong or deserving censure; culpability. **2.** an expression of condemnation; reproof. **3. be to blame.** to be at fault or culpable. ~*vb.* (*tr.*) **4.** (usually foll. by *for*) to attribute responsibility to; accuse: *I blame him for the failure.* **5.** (usually foll. by *on*) to ascribe responsibility for (something) to: *I blame the failure on him.* **6.** to find fault with. [C12: from Old French *blasmer,* ultimately from Late Latin *blasphēmāre* to BLASPHEME] —**'blam+a·ble** *or* **'blame+a·ble** *adj.* —**'blam+a·bly** *or* **'blame+a·bly** *adv.*

blamed (bleɪmd) *adj., adv. Chiefly U.S.* a euphemistic word for **damned** (senses 2, 3).

blame+ful ('bleɪmfʊl) *adj.* deserving blame; guilty. —**'blame+ful+ly** *adv.* —**'blame+ful+ness** *n.*

blame+less ('bleɪmlɪs) *adj.* free from blame; innocent. —**'blame+less+ly** *adv.* —**'blame+less+ness** *n.*

blame+wor·thy ('bleɪm,wɜːðɪ) *adj.* deserving disapproval or censure. —**'blame+,wor·thi+ness** *n.*

Bla·mey ('bleɪmɪ) *n.* Sir **Thom·as Al·bert.** 1884–1951, Australian soldier; the first Australian field marshal. He served in both World Wars and was commander in chief of the Allied Land Forces in the SW Pacific (1942–45).

Blanc[1] (*French* blɑ̃) *n.* **1. Mont.** See **Mont Blanc. 2. Cape.** a headland in N Tunisia: the northernmost point of Africa. **3. Cape.** Also called: **Cape Blan+co** ('blæŋkəʊ). a peninsula in Mauritania, on the Atlantic coast.

Blanc[2] (*French* blɑ̃) *n.* **(Jean Joseph Charles) Louis** (lwi). 1811–82, French socialist and historian: author of *L'Organisation du travail* (1840), in which he advocated the establishment of cooperative workshops subsidized by the state.

blanc fixe *French.* (blɑ̃ 'fiks) *n.* another name for **barium sulphate.** [literally: fixed white]

blanch (blɑːntʃ) *vb.* (*mainly tr.*) **1.** to remove colour from; whiten: *the sun blanched the carpet.* **2.** (*usually intr.*) to become or cause to become pale, as with sickness or fear. **3.** to plunge tomatoes, nuts, etc., into boiling water to loosen the skin. **4.** to plunge (meat, green vegetables, etc.) in boiling water or bring to the boil in water in order to whiten, preserve the natural colour, or reduce or remove a bitter or salty taste. **5.** to cause (celery, chicory, etc.) to grow free of chlorophyll by the exclusion of sunlight. **6.** *Metallurgy.* to whiten (a metal), usually by treating it with an acid or by coating it with tin. **7.** (*tr.,* usually foll. by *over*) to attempt to conceal something. [C14: from Old French *blanchir* from *blanc* white; see BLANK]

Blanch (blɑːntʃ) *n.* **Stu·art Yar·worth.** born 1918, English churchman; archbishop of York since 1975.

blanc+mange (blə'mɒnʒ) *n.* a jelly-like dessert, stiffened usually with cornflour and set in a mould. [C14: from Old French *blanc manger,* literally: white food]

bland (blænd) *adj.* **1.** devoid of any distinctive or stimulating characteristics; uninteresting; dull: *bland food.* **2.** gentle and agreeable; suave. **3.** (of the weather) mild and soothing. **4.** unemotional or unmoved: *a bland account of atrocities.* [C15: from Latin *blandus* flattering] —**'bland+ly** *adv.* —**'bland+ness** *n.*

blan+dish ('blændɪʃ) *vb.* (*tr.*) to seek to persuade or influence by mild flattery; coax. [C14: from Old French *blandir* from Latin *blandīrī*]

blan+dish+ments ('blændɪʃmənts) *pl. n.* (*rarely sing.*) flattery intended to coax or cajole.

blank (blæŋk) *adj.* **1.** (of a writing surface) bearing no marks; not written on. **2.** (of a form, etc.) with spaces left for details to be filled in. **3.** without ornament or break; unrelieved: *a blank wall.* **4.** not filled in; empty; void: *a blank space.* **5.** exhibiting no interest or expression: *a blank look.* **6.** lacking understanding; confused: *he looked blank even after the explanations.* **7.** absolute; complete: *blank rejection.* **8.** devoid of ideas or inspiration: *his mind went blank in the exam.* **9.** unproductive; barren. ~*n.* **10.** an emptiness; void; blank space. **11.** an empty space for writing in, as on a printed form. **12.** a printed form containing such empty spaces. **13.** something characterized by incomprehension or mental confusion: *my mind went a complete blank.* **14.** a mark, often a dash, in place of a word, esp. a taboo word. **15.** short for **blank cartridge. 16.** a plate or plug used to seal an aperture. **17.** a piece of material prepared for stamping, punching, forging, or some other operation. **18.** *Archery.* the white spot in the centre of a target. **19. draw a blank. a.** to choose a lottery ticket that fails to win. **b.** *Informal.* to get no results from something. ~*vb.* (*tr.*) **20.** (usually foll. by *out*) to cross out, blot, or obscure. **21.** to forge, stamp, punch, or cut (a piece of material) in preparation for forging, die-stamping, or drawing operations. **22.** (often foll. by *off*) to seal (an aperture) with a plate or plug. **23.** *U.S.* to prevent (an opponent) from scoring in a game. [C15: from Old French *blanc* white, of Germanic origin; related to Old English *blanca* a white horse] —**'blank+ly** *adv.* —**'blank+ness** *n.*

blank car+tridge *n.* a gun cartridge containing powder but no bullet: used in battle practice or as a signal.

blank cheque *n.* **1.** a cheque that has been signed but on which the amount payable has not been specified. **2.** complete freedom of action.

blank en+dorse+ment *n.* an endorsement on a bill of exchange, cheque, etc., naming no payee and thus making the endorsed sum payable to the bearer. Also called: **endorsement in blank.**

blan+ket ('blæŋkɪt) *n.* **1.** a large piece of thick cloth for use as a bed covering, animal covering, etc., enabling a person or animal to retain much of his natural body heat. **2.** a concealing cover or layer, as of smoke, leaves, or snow. **3.** a rubber or plastic sheet wrapped round a cylinder, used in offset printing to transfer the image from the plate, stone, or forme to the paper. **4.** *Physics.* a layer of a fertile radioactive substance placed round the core of a nuclear reactor as a reflector and often to breed new fissionable fuel. **5.** (*modifier*) applying to or covering a wide group or variety of people, conditions, situations, etc.: *blanket insurance against loss, injury, and theft.* ~*vb.* (*tr.*) **6.** to cover with or as if with a blanket; overlie. **7.** (usually foll. by *out*) to obscure or suppress: *the storm blanketed out the television picture.* **8.** *Nautical.* to prevent wind from reaching the sails of (another sailing vessel) by passing close to windward of it. [C13: from Old French *blancquete,* from *blanc* see BLANK]

blan+ket stitch *n.* a strong reinforcing stitch for the edges of blankets and other thick material.

blank+e·ty ('blæŋkɪtɪ) *adj., adv.* a euphemism for any taboo word. [C20: from BLANK]

blank verse *n. Prosody.* unrhymed verse, esp. in iambic pentameters.

blan+quette de veau (blæŋ'kɛt də 'vəʊ) *n.* a ragout or stew of veal in a white sauce. [French]

Blan·tyre-Lim·be (blæn'taɪə 'lɪmbeɪ) *n.* a city in S Malawi: largest city in the country; formed in 1956 from the adjoining towns of Blantyre and Limbe. Pop.: 109 461 (1966).

blare (blɛə) *vb.* **1.** to sound loudly and harshly. **2.** to proclaim loudly and sensationally. ~*n.* **3.** a loud and usually harsh or grating noise. [C14: from Middle Dutch *bleren;* of imitative origin]

blar+ney ('blɑːnɪ) *n.* **1.** flattering talk. ~*vb.* **2.** to cajole with flattery; wheedle. [C19: after the BLARNEY STONE]

Blar+ney Stone *n.* a stone in **Blarney Castle,** in the SW Republic of Ireland, said to endow whoever kisses it with skill in flattery.

Blas·co I·bá·ñez (*Spanish* 'blasko i'βaɲeθ) *n.* **Vi·cen·te** (bi'θente). 1867–1928, Spanish novelist, whose books include *Blood and Sand* (1909) and *The Four Horsemen of the Apocalypse* (1916).

bla+sé ('blɑːzeɪ) *adj.* **1.** indifferent to something because of familiarity or surfeit. **2.** lacking enthusiasm; bored. [C19: from French, past participle of *blaser* to cloy]

blas+pheme (blæs'fiːm) *vb.* **1.** (*tr.*) to show contempt or disrespect for (God, a divine being, or sacred things), esp. in speech. **2.** (*intr.*) to utter profanities, curses, or impious expressions. [C14: from Late Latin *blasphēmāre,* from Greek *blasphēmein* from *blasphēmos* BLASPHEMOUS] —**blas+'phem+er** *n.*

blas+phe+mous ('blæsfɪməs) *adj.* expressing or involving impiousness or gross irreverence towards God, a divine being, or something sacred. [C15: via Late Latin, from Greek *blasphēmos* evil-speaking, from *blapsis* evil + *phēmē* speech] —**'blas+phe+mous+ly** *adv.*

blas+phe+my ('blæsfɪmɪ) *n., pl.* **+mies.** blasphemous behaviour or language.

blast (blɑːst) *n.* **1.** an explosion, as of dynamite. **2.** the rapid movement of air resulting from an explosion; shock wave. **3.** the charge of explosive used in a single explosion. **4.** a sudden strong gust of wind or air. **5.** a sudden loud sound, as of a trumpet. **6.** a violent verbal outburst, as of criticism. **7.** a forcible jet or stream of air, esp. one used to intensify the heating effect of a furnace, increase the draught in a steam engine, or break up coal at a coalface. **8.** any of several diseases of plants and animals, esp. one producing withering in plants. **9. (at) full blast.** at maximum speed, volume etc. ~*interj.* **10.** *Slang.* an exclamation of annoyance (esp. in phrases such as **blast it! blast him!**). ~*vb.* **11.** to destroy or blow up with explosives, shells, etc. **12.** to make or cause to make a loud harsh noise. **13.** (*tr.*) to remove, open, etc., by an explosion: *to blast a hole in a wall.* **14.** (*tr.*) to ruin; shatter: *the rain blasted* *our plans for a picnic.* **15.** to wither or cause to wither; blight or be blighted. **16.** to criticize severely. **17.** *Slang.* to shoot or shoot at: *he blasted the hat off her head; he blasted away at the trees.* [Old English *blǣst,* related to Old Norse *blāstr*] —'**blast·er** *n.*

-blast *n. combining form.* (in biology) indicating an embryonic cell or formative layer: *mesoblast.* [from Greek *blastos* bud]

blast·ed ('blɑːstɪd) *adj.* **1.** blighted or withered. ~*adj.* (*prenominal*), *adv.* **2.** *Slang.* (intensifier): *a blasted idiot.*

blas·te·ma (blæ'stiːmə) *n., pl.* **·mas** *or* **·ma·ta** (-mətə). a mass of undifferentiated animal cells that will develop into an organ or tissue: present at the site of regeneration of a lost part. [C19: from New Latin, from Greek: offspring, from *blastos* bud] —**blas·te·mic** (blæ'stiːmɪk, -'stɛm-) *adj.*

blast fur·nace *n.* a vertical cylindrical furnace for smelting iron, copper, lead, and tin ores. The ore, scrap, solid fuel, and slag-forming materials are fed through the top and a blast of preheated air is forced through the charge from the bottom. Metal and slag are run off from the base.

blast·ing ('blɑːstɪŋ) *n. Informal.* a distortion of sound caused by overloading certain components of a radio system.

blas·to- *combining form.* (in biology) indicating an embryo or bud or the process of budding: *blastoderm.* [from Greek *blastos.* See -BLAST]

blas·to·coel *or* **blas·to·coele** ('blæstəʊˌsiːl) *n. Embryol.* the cavity within a blastula. Also called: **segmentation cavity.**

blas·to·cyst ('blæstəʊˌsɪst) *n. Embryol.* **1.** Also called: **blastosphere.** the blastula of mammals: a sphere of cells (trophoblast) enclosing an inner mass of cells and a fluid-filled cavity (blastocoel). **2.** another name for **germinal vesicle.**

blas·to·derm ('blæstəʊˌdɜːm) *or* **blas·to·disc** *n. Embryol.* **1.** a flat disc of cells formed after cleavage in a heavily yolked egg, such as a bird's egg. **2.** a layer of cells on the inside of the blastula surrounding the blastocoel. ~Also called: **germinal disc.** —ˌ**blas·to·'derm·ic** *adj.*

blast·off ('blɑːstˌɒf) *n.* **1.** the launching of a rocket under its own power. **2.** the time at which this occurs. ~*vb.* **blast off. 3.** (*adv.; when tr., usually passive*) (of a rocket, spacemen, etc.) to be launched.

blas·to·gen·e·sis (ˌblæstəʊ'dʒɛnɪsɪs) *n.* **1.** the theory that inherited characteristics are transmitted only by germ plasm. See also **pangenesis. 2.** asexual reproduction, esp. budding. —ˌ**blas·to·'gen·ic** *or* ˌ**blas·to·ge·'net·ic** *adj.*

blas·to·mere ('blæstəʊˌmɪə) *n. Embryol.* any of the cells formed by cleavage of a fertilized egg. —**blas·to·mer·ic** (ˌblæstəʊ'mɛrɪk) *adj.*

blas·to·pore ('blæstəʊˌpɔː) *n. Embryol.* the opening of the archenteron in the gastrula that develops into the anus of some animals. —ˌ**blas·to·'por·ic** *or* ˌ**blas·to·'por·al** *adj.*

blas·to·sphere ('blæstəʊˌsfɪə) *n.* **1.** another name for **blastula. 2.** another name for **blastocyst** (sense 1).

blas·tu·la ('blæstjʊlə) *n., pl.* **·las** *or* **·lae** (-liː). an early form of an animal embryo that develops from a morula, consisting of a sphere of cells with a central cavity. Also called: **blastosphere.** [C19: New Latin; see BLASTO-] —'**blas·tu·lar** *adj.*

blat (blæt) *vb.* **blats, blat·ting, blat·ted.** *U.S.* **1.** (*intr.*) to cry out or bleat like a sheep. **2.** (*tr.*) *Informal.* to utter indiscreetly in a loud voice. [C19: of imitative origin]

bla·tant ('bleɪtᵊnt) *adj.* **1.** glaringly conspicuous or obvious: *a blatant lie.* **2.** offensively noisy. **3.** *Archaic.* (of animals) bleating. [C16: coined by Edmund Spenser; probably influenced by Latin *blatīre* to babble; compare Middle Low German *pladderen*] —'**bla·tan·cy** *n.* —'**bla·tant·ly** *adv.*

blath·er ('blæðə) *vb.* **1.** (*intr.*) to speak foolishly. ~*n.* **2.** foolish talk; nonsense. [C15: from Old Norse *blathra* from *blathr* nonsense]

blath·er·skite ('blæðəˌskaɪt) *n.* **1.** a talkative silly person. **2.** foolish talk; nonsense. [C17: see BLATHER, SKATE³]

blau·bok ('blaʊˌbɒk) *n., pl.* **·bok** *or* **·boks.** a large blue-haired antelope, *Hippotragus leucophaeus,* of southern Africa: extinct since 1800. Also called: **blue buck.** [C18: via Afrikaans from Dutch *blauwbok*]

Blau·e Rei·ter *German.* ('blaʊə 'raɪtər) *n.* **der.** a group of German expressionist painters formed in Munich in 1911, including Kandinsky and Klee, who sought to express the spiritual side of man and nature, which they felt had been neglected by impressionism. [C20: literally: blue rider, name adopted by Kandinsky and Marc because they liked the colour blue, horses, and riders]

Bla·vat·sky (blə'vætskɪ) *n.* **El·e·na Pe·trov·na** (jɪ'ljɛnə pɪ'trɔvnə), called *Madame Blavatsky.* 1831–91, Russian theosophist; author of *Isis Unveiled* (1877).

Blay·don ('bleɪdᵊn) *n.* an industrial town in NE England, in Tyneside. Pop: 32 018 (1971).

blaze¹ (bleɪz) *n.* **1.** a strong fire or flame. **2.** a very bright light or glare. **3.** an outburst (of passion, acclaim, patriotism, etc.). **4.** brilliance; brightness. ~*vb.* (*intr.*) **5.** to burn fiercely. **6.** to shine brightly. **7.** (often foll. by *up*) to become stirred, as with anger or excitement. **8.** (usually foll. by *away*) to shoot continuously. [Old English *blæse*]

blaze² (bleɪz) *n.* **1.** a mark, usually indicating a path, made on a tree, esp. by chipping off the bark. **2.** a light-coloured marking on the face of a domestic animal, esp. a horse. ~*vb.* (*tr.*) **3.** to indicate or mark (a tree, path, etc.) with a blaze. **4. blaze a trail.** to explore new territories, areas of knowledge, etc., in such a way that others can follow. [C17: probably from Middle Low German *bles* white marking; compare BLEMISH]

blaze³ (bleɪz) *vb.* (*tr;* often foll. by *abroad*) to make widely known; proclaim. [C14: from Middle Dutch *blāsen,* from Old High German *blāsan;* related to Old Norse *blāsa*]

blaz·er ('bleɪzə) *n.* a fairly lightweight jacket, often striped or in the colours of a sports club, school, etc.

blaz·es ('bleɪzɪz) *pl. n.* **1.** *Slang.* a euphemistic word for **hell** (esp. in the phrase **go to blazes**). **2.** *Informal.* (intensifier): *to run like blazes; what the blazes are you doing?*

blaz·ing star *n. U.S.* **1.** a North American plant, *Chamaelirium luteum,* with a long spike of small white flowers: family *Compositae* (composites). **2.** any North American plant of the related genus *Liatris,* having clusters of small red or purple flowers.

bla·zon ('bleɪzᵊn) *vb.* (*tr.*) **1.** (often foll. by *abroad*) to proclaim loudly and publicly. **2.** *Heraldry.* to describe (heraldic arms) in proper terms. **3.** to draw and colour (heraldic arms) conventionally. ~*n.* **4.** *Heraldry.* a conventional description or depiction of heraldic arms. **5.** any description or recording, esp. of good qualities. [C13: from Old French *blason* coat of arms] —'**bla·zon·er** *n.*

bla·zon·ry ('bleɪzənrɪ) *n., pl.* **·ries. 1.** the art or process of describing heraldic arms in proper form. **2.** heraldic arms collectively. **3.** colourful or ostentatious display.

bldg. *abbrev. for* building.

bleach (bliːtʃ) *vb.* **1.** to make or become white or colourless, as by exposure to sunlight, by the action of chemical agents, etc. ~*n.* **2.** a bleaching agent. **3.** the degree of whiteness resulting from bleaching. **4.** the act of bleaching. [Old English *blǣcan;* related to Old Norse *bleikja,* Old High German *bleih* pale] —'**bleach·a·ble** *adj.* —'**bleach·er** *n.*

bleach·ers ('bliːtʃəz) *pl. n.* **1.** (*sometimes sing.*) a tier of seats in a sports stadium, etc., that are unroofed and inexpensive. **2.** the people occupying such seats.

bleach·ing pow·der *n.* a white powder with the odour of chlorine, consisting of chlorinated calcium hydroxide with an approximate formula $CaCl(OCl).4H_2O$. It is used in solution as a bleaching agent and disinfectant. Also called: **chloride of lime, chlorinated lime.**

bleak¹ (bliːk) *adj.* **1.** exposed and barren; desolate. **2.** cold and raw. **3.** offering little hope or excitement; dismal: *a bleak future.* [Old English *blāc* bright, pale; related to Old Norse *bleikr* white, Old High German *bleih* pale] —'**bleak·ly** *adv.* —'**bleak·ness** *n.*

bleak² (bliːk) *n.* any slender silvery European cyprinid fish of the genus *Alburnus,* esp. *A. lucidus,* occurring in slow-flowing rivers. [C15: probably from Old Norse *bleikja* white colour; related to Old High German *bleiche* BLEACH]

blear (blɪə) *Archaic.* ~*vb.* **1.** (*tr.*) to make (eyes or sight) dim with or as if with tears; blur. ~*adj.* **2.** a less common word for **bleary.** [C13: *blere* to make dim; related to Middle High German *blerre* blurred vision]

blear·y ('blɪərɪ) *adj.* **blear·i·er, blear·i·est. 1.** (of eyes or vision) dimmed or blurred, as by tears or tiredness. **2.** indistinct or unclear. **3.** exhausted; tired. —'**blear·i·ly** *adv.* —'**blear·i·ness** *n.*

blear·y-eyed *or* **blear-eyed** *adj.* **1.** with eyes blurred, as with old age or after waking. **2.** physically or mentally unperceptive.

bleat (bliːt) *vb.* **1.** (*intr.*) (of a sheep, goat, or calf) to utter its characteristic plaintive cry. **2.** (*intr.*) to speak with any similar sound. **3.** to whine; whimper. ~*n.* **4.** the characteristic cry of sheep, goats, and young calves. **5.** any sound similar to this. **6.** a weak complaint or whine. [Old English *blǣtan;* related to Old High German *blāzen,* Dutch *blaten,* Latin *flēre* to weep; see BLARE] —'**bleat·er** *n.* —'**bleat·ing·ly** *adv.*

bleb (blɛb) *n.* **1.** a fluid-filled blister on the skin. **2.** a small air bubble. [C17: variant of BLOB] —'**bleb·by** *adj.*

bleed (bliːd) *vb.* **bleeds, bleed·ing, bled. 1.** (*intr.*) to lose or emit blood. **2.** (*tr.*) to remove or draw blood from (a person or animal). **3.** (*intr.*) to be injured or die, as for a cause or one's country. **4.** (of plants) to exude (sap or resin), esp. from a cut. **5.** (*tr.*) *Informal.* to obtain relatively large amounts of money, goods, etc., esp. by extortion. **6.** (*tr.*) to draw liquid or gas from (a container or enclosed system): *to bleed the hydraulic brakes.* **7.** (*intr.*) (of dye or paint) to run or become mixed, as when wet. **8.** to print or be printed so that text, illustrations, etc., run off the trimmed page. **9.** (*tr.*) to trim (the edges of a printed sheet) so closely as to cut off some of the printed matter. **10. one's heart bleeds.** used to express sympathetic grief, but often used ironically. ~*n.* **11.** *Printing.* **a.** an illustration or sheet trimmed so that some matter is bled. **b.** (*as modifier*): *a bleed page.* **12.** *Printing.* the trimmings of a sheet that has been bled. [Old English *blēdan;* see BLOOD]

bleed·er ('bliːdə) *n.* **1.** *Slang.* **a.** *Derogatory.* a despicable person: *a rotten bleeder.* **b.** any person; fellow: *where's the bleeder gone?* **2.** *Pathol.* a nontechnical name for a **haemophiliac.**

bleed·er re·sis·tor *n.* a resistor connected across the output terminals of a power supply in order to improve voltage regulation and to discharge filter capacitors.

bleed·er's dis·ease *n.* a nontechnical name for **haemophilia.**

bleed·ing ('bliːdɪŋ) *adj., adv. Brit. slang.* (intensifier): *a bleeding fool; it's bleeding beautiful.*

bleed·ing heart *n.* any of several plants of the genus *Dicentra,* esp. the widely cultivated Japanese species *D. spectabilis,* which has finely divided leaves and heart-shaped nodding pink flowers: family *Fumariaceae.*

bleed valve *n.* a valve for running off a liquid from a tank, tube, etc., or for allowing accumulations of gas in a liquid to blow off. Also called: **bleed nipple.**

bleep (bli:p) *n.* **1.** a single short high-pitched signal made by an electronic apparatus; beep. **2.** Also called: **bleeper.** *Informal.* a small portable radio receiver, worn esp. by doctors, that sounds a coded bleeping signal to call the wearer. ~*vb.* **3.** (*intr.*) to make such a noise. **4.** (*tr.*) *Informal.* to call (someone) by triggering the bleep he is wearing. [C20: of imitative origin]

blem+ish ('blɛmɪʃ) *n.* **1.** a defect; flaw; stain. ~*vb.* **2.** (*tr.*) to flaw the perfection of; spoil; tarnish. [C14: from Old French *blemir* to make pale, probably of Germanic origin] —**'blem+ish+er** *n.*

blench[1] (blɛntʃ) *vb.* (*intr.*) to shy away, as in fear; quail. [Old English *blencan* to deceive] —**'blench+er** *n.*

blench[2] (blɛntʃ) *vb.* to make or become pale or white. [C19: variant of BLANCH]

blend (blɛnd) *vb.* **1.** to mix or mingle (components) together thoroughly. **2.** (*tr.*) to mix (different grades or varieties of tea, whisky, tobacco, etc.) to produce a particular flavour, consistency, etc. **3.** (*intr.*) to look good together; harmonize. **4.** (*intr.*) (esp. of colours) to shade imperceptibly into each other. ~*n.* **5.** a mixture or type produced by blending. **6.** the act of blending. **7.** Also called: **portmanteau word.** a word formed by joining together the beginning and the end of two other words: *"brunch" is a blend of "breakfast" and "lunch."* [Old English *blandan;* related to *blendan* to deceive, Old Norse *blanda,* Old High German *blantan*]

blende (blɛnd) *n.* **1.** another name for **sphalerite. 2.** any of several sulphide ores, such as antimony sulphide. [C17: German *Blende,* from *blenden* to deceive, BLIND; so called because it is easily mistaken for galena]

blend+er ('blɛndə) *n.* **1.** a person or thing that blends. **2.** Also called: **liquidizer.** a kitchen appliance with blades used for puréeing vegetables, blending liquids, etc.

Blen+heim ('blɛnɪm) *n.* a village in SW Germany, site of a victory of Anglo-Austrian forces under the Duke of Marlborough and Prince Eugène of Savoy that saved Vienna from the French and Bavarians (1704) during the War of the Spanish Succession. Modern name: **Blindheim.**

blen+ni+oid ('blɛnɪˌɔɪd) *adj.* **1.** of, relating to, or belonging to the *Blennioidea,* a large suborder of small mainly marine spiny-finned fishes having an elongated body with reduced pelvic fins. The group includes the blennies, butterfish, and gunnel. ~*n.* **2.** any fish belonging to the *Blennioidea.*

blen+ny ('blɛnɪ) *n., pl.* **+nies. 1.** any blennioid fish of the family *Blenniidae* of coastal waters, esp. of the genus *Blennius,* having a tapering scaleless body, a long dorsal fin, and long raylike pelvic fins. **2.** any of various related fishes. [C18: from Latin *blennius,* from Greek *blennos* slime; from the mucus that coats its body]

blent (blɛnt) *vb. Archaic or literary.* a past participle of **blend.**

bleph·a+ri+tis (ˌblɛfə'raɪtɪs) *n.* inflammation of the eyelids. [C19: from Greek *blephar(on)* eyelid + -ITIS] —**bleph·a+rit+ic** (ˌblɛfə'rɪtɪk) *adj.*

Blé·riot (*French* bler'jo) *n.* **Louis** (lwi). 1872–1936, French aviator and aeronautical engineer: made the first flight across the English Channel (1909).

bles+bok *or* **bles+buck** ('blɛsˌbʌk) *n., pl.* **+boks, +bok** *or* **+bucks, +buck.** an antelope, *Damaliscus dorcas* (or *albifrons*), of southern Africa. The coat is a deep reddish-brown with a white blaze between the eyes; the horns are lyre-shaped. [C19: Afrikaans, from Dutch *bles* BLAZE[2] + *bok* goat, BUCK[1]]

bless (blɛs) *vb.* **bless·es, bless+ing, blessed** *or* **blest.** (*tr.*) **1.** to consecrate or render holy, beneficial, or prosperous by means of a religious rite. **2.** to give honour or glory to (a person or thing) as divine or holy. **3.** to call upon God to protect; give a benediction to. **4.** to worship or adore (God); call or hold holy. **5.** (*often passive*) to grant happiness, health, or prosperity to: *they were blessed with perfect peace.* **6.** (*usually passive*) to endow with a talent, beauty, etc.: *she was blessed with an even temper.* **7.** *Rare.* to protect against evil or harm. **8. bless you!** (*interj.*) **a.** a traditional phrase said to a person who has just sneezed or coughed. **b.** an exclamation of well-wishing or surprise. **9. bless me!** *or* **(God) bless my soul!** (*interj.*) an exclamation of surprise. **10. not have a penny to bless oneself with.** to be desperately poor. [Old English *blǣdsian* to sprinkle with sacrificial blood; related to *blōd* BLOOD]

bless+ed ('blɛsɪd, blɛst) *adj.* **1.** made holy by religious ceremony; consecrated. **2.** worthy of deep reverence or respect. **3.** *R.C. Church.* (of a person) beatified by the pope. **4.** characterized by happiness or good fortune: *a blessed time.* **5.** bringing great happiness or good fortune. **6.** a euphemistic word for **damned,** used in mild oaths: *I'm blessed if I know.* ~*n.* **7. the blessed.** *Christianity.* the dead who are already enjoying heavenly bliss. —**'bless+ed+ly** *adv.* —**'bless+ed+ness** *n.*

Bless+ed Sac+ra+ment *n. Chiefly R.C. Church.* the consecrated elements of the Eucharist.

Bless+ed Vir+gin *n. Chiefly R.C. Church.* another name for the **Virgin Mary.**

bless+ing ('blɛsɪŋ) *n.* **1.** the act of invoking divine protection or aid. **2.** the words or ceremony used for this. **3.** a short prayer of thanksgiving before or after a meal; grace. **4.** approval; good wishes: *her father gave his blessing to the marriage.* **5.** the bestowal of a divine gift or favour. **6.** a happy event or state of affairs: *a blessing in disguise.*

blest (blɛst) *vb.* a past participle of **bless.**

blet (blɛt) *n.* a state of softness or decay in certain fruits, such as the medlar, brought about by overripening. [C19: from French *blettir* to become overripe]

bleth+er ('blɛðə) *vb.* a variant spelling of **blather.**

blew (blu:) *vb.* the past tense of **blow.**

blew+its ('blu:ɪts) *n.* (*functioning as sing.*) an edible saprophytic agaricaceous fungus, *Tricholoma saevum,* having a pale brown cap and bluish stalk. [C19: probably based on BLUE]

Bli+da ('bli:də) *n.* a city in N Algeria, on the edge of the Mitidja Plain. Pop: 93 000 (1966 est.).

Bligh (blaɪ) *n.* **Wil·liam.** 1754–1817, British admiral: as a captain, commander of *H.M.S. Bounty* when the crew mutinied in 1789.

blight (blaɪt) *n.* **1.** any plant disease characterized by withering and shrivelling without rotting. **2.** any factor, such as bacterial attack or air pollution, that causes the symptoms of blight in plants. **3.** a person or thing that mars or prevents growth, improvement, or prosperity. **4.** an ugly urban district. **5.** the state or condition of being blighted or spoilt. ~*vb.* **6.** to cause or suffer a blight. **7.** (*tr.*) to frustrate or disappoint. **8.** (*tr.*) to spoil; destroy. [C17: perhaps related to Old English *blǣce* rash; compare BLEACH]

blight+er ('blaɪtə) *n. Brit. informal.* **1.** a fellow: *where's the blighter gone?* **2.** a despicable or irritating person or thing.

Blight·y ('blaɪtɪ) *n.* (*sometimes not cap.*) *Brit. slang.* (used esp. by troops serving abroad) **1.** England; home. **2.** (esp. in World War I) **a.** Also called: **a blighty one.** a slight wound that causes the recipient to be sent home to England. **b.** leave in England. [C20: from Hindi *bilāyatī* foreign land, England, from Arabic *wilāyat* country, from *waliya* he rules]

bli+mey ('blaɪmɪ) *interj. Brit. slang.* an exclamation of surprise or annoyance. [C19: short for *gorblimey* God blind me]

blimp[1] (blɪmp) *n.* **1.** a small nonrigid airship, esp. one used for observation or as a barrage balloon. **2.** *Films.* a soundproof cover fixed over a camera during shooting. [C20: probably from (*type*) *B-limp*]

blimp[2] (blɪmp) *n.* (*often cap.*) *Chiefly Brit.* a person, esp. a military officer, who is stupidly complacent and reactionary. Also called: **Colonel Blimp.** [C20: after a character created by David Low (born 1891), British cartoonist]

blind (blaɪnd) *adj.* **1. a.** unable to see; sightless. **b.** (*as collective n.* preceded by *the*): *the blind.* **2.** (usually foll. by *to*) unable or unwilling to understand or discern. **3.** not based on evidence or determined by reason: *blind hatred.* **4.** acting or performed without control or preparation. **5.** done without being able to see, relying on instruments for information. **6.** hidden from sight: *a blind corner; a blind stitch.* **7.** closed at one end: *a blind alley.* **8.** completely lacking awareness or consciousness: *a blind stupor.* **9.** *Informal.* very drunk. **10.** having no openings or outlets: *a blind wall.* **11.** without having been seen beforehand: *a blind purchase.* **12.** (of cultivated plants) having failed to produce flowers or fruits. **13.** (intensifier): *not a blind bit of notice.* **14. turn a blind eye (to).** to disregard or pretend not to notice (something, esp. a command with which one disagrees or an action of which one disapproves). ~*adv.* **15.** without being able to see ahead or using only instruments: *to drive blind; flying blind.* **16.** without adequate knowledge or information; carelessly: *to buy a house blind.* **17.** (intensifier) (in the phrase **blind drunk**). **18. bake blind.** to bake (the empty crust of a pie, pastry, etc.) by half filling with dried peas, crusts of bread, etc., to keep it in shape. ~*vb.* (*mainly tr.*) **19.** to deprive of sight permanently or temporarily. **20.** to deprive of good sense, reason, or judgment. **21.** to darken; conceal. **22.** (foll. by *with*) to overwhelm by showing detailed knowledge: *to blind somebody with science.* **23.** (*intr.*) *Brit. slang.* to drive very fast. ~*n.* **24.** (*modifier*) for or intended to help the blind: *a blind school.* **25.** a shade for a window, usually on a roller. **26.** any obstruction or hindrance to sight, light, or air. **27.** a person, action, or thing that serves to deceive or conceal the truth. **28.** a person who acts on behalf of someone who does not wish his identity or actions to be known. **29.** *Brit. slang.* a drunken orgy; binge. **30.** *Poker.* a stake put up by a player before he examines his cards. **31.** *Hunting, chiefly U.S.* a screen of brush or undergrowth, in which hunters hide to shoot their quarry. Brit. name: **hide.** [Old English *blind;* related to Old Norse *blindr,* Old High German *blint;* Lettish *blendu* to see dimly; see BLUNDER] —**'blind+ly** *adv.* —**'blind+ness** *n.*

blind+age ('blaɪndɪdʒ) *n. Military.* (esp. formerly) a protective screen or structure, as over a trench.

blind al+ley *n.* **1.** an alley open at one end only; cul-de-sac. **2.** *Informal.* a situation in which no further progress can be made.

blind date *n. Informal.* **1.** a social meeting between a man and a woman who have not met before. **2.** either of the persons involved.

blin+ders ('blaɪndəz) *pl. n.* the usual U.S. word for **blinkers.**

blind+fish ('blaɪndˌfɪʃ) *n., pl.* **+fish** *or* **+fish·es.** any of various small fishes, esp. the cavefish, that have rudimentary or functionless eyes and occur in subterranean streams.

blind+fold ('blaɪndˌfəuld) *vb.* (*tr.*) **1.** to prevent (a person or animal) from seeing by covering (the eyes). **2.** to prevent from perceiving or understanding. ~*n.* **3.** a piece of cloth, bandage, etc., used to cover the eyes. **4.** any interference to sight. ~*adj., adv.* **5.** having the eyes covered with a cloth or bandage. **6.** *Chess.* not seeing the board and pieces. **7.** rash; inconsiderate. [changed (C16) through association with FOLD[1] from Old English *blindfellian* to strike blind; see BLIND, FELL[2]]

Blind Fred·die *n. Austral. informal.* an imaginary person representing the highest degree of incompetence (esp. in the phrase **Blind Freddie could see that!**).

Blind+heim ('blɪntˌhaɪm) *n.* the German name for **Blenheim.**

blind+ing ('blaɪndɪŋ) *n.* **1.** sand or grit spread over a road surface to fill up cracks. **2.** the process of laying blinding. **3.** Also called: **mattress.** a layer of concrete spread over soft ground.

blind man's buff *n.* a game in which a blindfolded person tries

to catch and identify the other players. [C16: *buff,* perhaps from Old French *buffe* a blow; see BUFFET[1]]
blind snake *n.* any burrowing snake of the family *Typhlopidae* and related families of warm and tropical regions, having very small or vestigial eyes.
blind spot *n.* **1.** a small oval-shaped area of the retina in which vision is not experienced. It marks the nonphotosensitive site of entrance into the eyeball of the optic nerve. See **optic disc.** **2.** a place or area, as in an auditorium or part of a road, where vision is completely or partially obscured or hearing is difficult or impossible. **3.** a subject about which a person is ignorant or prejudiced, or an occupation in which he is inefficient. **4.** a location within the normal range of a radio transmitter with weak reception.
blind stag+gers *n. Vet. science.* another name for **staggers.**
blind stamp+ing *n. Bookbinding.* an impression on a book cover without using colour or gold leaf. Also called: **book tooling.**
blind+sto·rey *or* **blind+sto·ry** ('blaɪnd,stɔːrɪ) *n., pl.* **·reys** *or* **·ries.** a storey without windows, such as a gallery in a Gothic church. Compare **clerestory.**
blind+worm ('blaɪnd,wɜːm) *n.* another name for **slowworm.**
blin·i ('blɪnɪ) *or* **blin+is** ('blɪnɪz) *pl. n.* a kind of Russian pancake of buckwheat flour and yeast. [from Russian: plural of *blin,* from Old Russian *mlinŭ*]
blink (blɪŋk) *vb.* **1.** to close and immediately reopen (the eyes or an eye), usually involuntarily. **2.** (*intr.*) to look with the eyes partially closed, as in strong sunlight. **3.** to shine intermittently, as in signalling, or unsteadily. **4.** (*tr.;* foll. by *away, from,* etc.) to clear the eyes of (dust, tears, etc.). **5.** (when *tr.,* usually foll. by *at*) to be surprised or amazed: *he blinked at the splendour of the ceremony.* **6.** (when *intr.,* foll. by *at*) to pretend not to know or see (a fault, injustice, etc.). ~*n.* **7.** the act or an instance of blinking. **8.** a glance; glimpse. **9.** short for **iceblink** (sense 1). **10. on the blink.** *Slang.* not working properly. [C14: variant of BLENCH[1]; related to Middle Dutch *blinken* to glitter, Danish *blinke* to wink, Swedish *blinka*]
blink+er ('blɪŋkə) *n.* **1.** a flashing light for sending messages, as a warning device, etc., such as a direction indicator on a road vehicle. **2.** (*often pl.*) a slang word for **eye.**
blink+ers ('blɪŋkəz) *pl. n.* **1.** (*sometimes sing.*) *Chiefly Brit.* leather sidepieces attached to a horse's bridle to prevent sideways vision. Usual U.S. word: **blinders.** **2.** a slang word for **goggles** (sense 4).
blink+ing ('blɪŋkɪŋ) *adj., adv. Informal.* (intensifier): *a blinking fool; a blinking good film.*
blinks (blɪŋks) *n.* (*functioning as sing.*) a small temperate portulacaceous plant, *Montia fontana* with small white flowers. [C19: from BLINK, because the flowers do not fully open and thus seem to blink at the light]
blintz *or* **blintze** (blɪnts) *n.* a thin pancake folded over a filling usually of apple, cream cheese, or meat. [from Yiddish *blintse,* from Russian *blinyets* little pancakes; see BLINI]
blip (blɪp) *n.* **1.** a repetitive sound, such as that produced by an electronic device, by dripping water, etc. **2.** Also called: **pip.** the spot of light or a sharply peaked pulse on a radar screen indicating the position of an object. —*vb.* **blips, blip+ping, blipped.** **3.** (*intr.*) to produce such a noise. [C20: of imitative origin]
bliss (blɪs) *n.* **1.** perfect happiness; serene joy. **2.** the ecstatic joy of heaven. [Old English *blīths;* related to *blīthe* BLITHE, Old Saxon *blīdsea* bliss] —**'bliss+less** *adj.*
Bliss (blɪs) *n.* Sir **Ar·thur.** 1891–1975, English composer; Master of the Queen's Musick (1953–75). His works include the *Colour Symphony* (1922), film and ballet music, and a cello concerto (1970).
bliss+ful ('blɪsfəl) *adj.* **1.** serenely joyful or glad. **2. blissful ignorance.** unawareness or inexperience of something unpleasant. —**'bliss+ful+ly** *adv.* —**'bliss+ful+ness** *n.*
blis+ter ('blɪstə) *n.* **1.** a small bubble-like elevation of the skin filled with serum, produced as a reaction to a burn, mechanical irritation, etc. **2.** a swelling containing air or liquid, as on a painted surface. **3.** a transparent dome or any bulge on the fuselage of an aircraft, such as one used for observation. **4.** *Slang.* an irritating person. ~*vb.* **5.** to have or cause to have blisters. **6.** (*tr.*) to attack verbally with great scorn or sarcasm. [C13: from Old French *blestre,* probably from Middle Dutch *bluyster* blister; see BLAST] —**'blis+ter+ing+ly** *adv.* —**'blis+ter·y** *adj.*
blis+ter bee+tle *n.* any beetle of the family *Meloidae,* many of which produce a secretion that blisters the skin. See also **Spanish fly.**
blis+ter cop+per *n.* an impure form of copper having a blister-like surface due to the release of gas during cooling.
blis+ter rust *n.* a disease of certain pines caused by rust fungi of the genus *Cronartium,* causing swellings on the bark from which orange masses of spores are released.
blithe (blaɪð) *adj.* **1.** very happy or cheerful; gay. **2.** heedless; casual and indifferent. [Old English *blīthe*] —**'blithe+ly** *adv.* —**'blithe+ness** *n.*
blith+er+ing ('blɪðərɪŋ) *adj.* **1.** talking foolishly; jabbering. **2.** *Informal.* stupid; foolish: *you blithering idiot.* [C19: variant of BLATHER + -ING[2]]
blithe+some ('blaɪðsəm) *adj. Literary.* cheery; merry. —**'blithe+some+ly** *adv.* —**'blithe+some+ness** *n.*
B.Litt. *or* **B.Lit.** *abbrev. for:* **1.** Bachelor of Letters. **2.** Bachelor of Literature. [Latin *Baccalaureus Litterarum*]
blitz (blɪts) *n.* **1.** a violent and sustained attack, esp. with intensive aerial bombardment. **2.** any sudden intensive attack or concerted effort. ~*vb.* **3.** (*tr.*) to attack suddenly and intensively. [C20: shortened from German *Blitzkrieg* lightning war]
Blitz (blɪts) *n.* **the.** the systematic nighttime bombing of the British in 1940–41 by the German Luftwaffe.
blitz+krieg ('blɪts,kriːg) *n.* an intensive military attack designed to defeat the opposition quickly. [C20: from German: lightning war]
bliz+zard ('blɪzəd) *n.* a strong bitterly cold wind accompanied by a widespread heavy snowfall. [C19: of uncertain origin]
blk. *abbrev. for:* **1.** black. **2.** block. **3.** bulk.
bloat (bləʊt) *vb.* **1.** to swell or cause to swell, as with a liquid, air, or wind. **2.** to become or cause to be puffed up, as with conceit. **3.** (*tr.*) to cure (fish, esp. herring) by half-drying in smoke. ~*n.* **4.** *Vet. science.* an abnormal distention of the abdomen in cattle, sheep, etc., caused by accumulation of gas in the stomach. [C17: probably related to Old Norse *blautr* soaked, Old English *blāt* pale]
bloat+er ('bləʊtə) *n.* a herring, or sometimes a mackerel, that has been salted in brine, smoked, and cured.
blob (blɒb) *n.* **1.** a soft mass or drop, as of some viscous liquid. **2.** a spot, dab, or blotch of colour, ink, etc. **3.** an indistinct or shapeless form or object. **4.** *Cricket slang.* a score of nought; a duck. ~*vb.* **blobs, blob+bing, blobbed.** **5.** (*tr.*) to put blobs, as of ink or paint, on. [C15: perhaps of imitative origin; compare BUBBLE]
bloc (blɒk) *n.* a group of people or countries combined by a common interest or aim: *the Soviet bloc.* [from French: BLOCK]
Bloch (blɒk) *n.* **1. Er·nest.** 1880–1959, U.S. composer, born in Switzerland, who found inspiration in Jewish liturgical and folk music: his works include the symphonies *Israel* (1916) and *America* (1926). **2. Fe·lix.** born 1905, U.S. physicist, born in Switzerland: Nobel prize for physics (1952) for his work on the magnetic moments of atomic particles. **3. Kon·rad E·mil.** born 1912, U.S. biochemist, born in Germany: shared the Nobel prize for medicine in 1964 for his work on fatty-acid metabolism.
block (blɒk) *n.* **1.** a large solid piece of wood, stone, or other material with flat rectangular sides, as for use in building. **2.** any large solid piece of wood, stone, etc., usually having at least one face fairly flat. **3.** such a piece on which particular tasks may be done, as chopping, cutting, or beheading. **4.** Also called: **building block.** one of a set of wooden or plastic cubes as a child's toy. **5.** a form on which things are shaped or displayed: *a wig block.* **6.** *Informal.* a person's head (esp. in the phrase **knock someone's block off**). **7. do one's block.** *Austral. slang.* to become angry. **8.** a dull, unemotional, or hard-hearted person. **9.** a large building of offices, flats, etc. **10.** *Chiefly U.S.* **a.** a group of buildings in a city bounded by intersecting streets on each side. **b.** the area or distance between such intersecting streets. **11.** an area of land, esp. one to be divided for building or settling. **12.** See **cylinder block.** **13. a.** a piece of wood, metal, or other material having an engraved, cast, or carved design in relief, used either for printing or for stamping book covers, etc. **b.** *Brit.* a letterpress printing plate, esp. one mounted type-high on wood or metal. **14.** a casing housing one or more freely rotating pulleys. See also **block and tackle.** **15. on the block.** *Chiefly U.S.* up for auction. **16.** the act of obstructing or condition of being obstructed, as in sports. **17.** an obstruction or hindrance. **18.** *Pathol.* **a.** interference in the normal physiological functioning of an organ or part. **b.** See **heart block.** **19.** *Psychol.* a short interruption of perceptual or thought processes. **20.** obstruction of an opponent in a sport. **21. a.** a section or quantity, as of tickets or shares, handled or considered as a single unit. **b.** (*as modifier*): *a block booking; block voting.* **22. a.** a stretch of railway in which only one train may travel at a time. **b.** (*as modifier*): *a block signal.* **23.** an unseparated group of four or more postage stamps. Compare **strip**[2] (sense 3). **24.** a pad of paper. **25.** *Computer technol.* a group of words on magnetic tape treated as a unit of data. **26.** *Athletics.* short for **starting block.** **27.** *Cricket.* a mark made near the popping crease by a batsman to indicate his position in relation to the wicket. **28. a chip off the old block.** *Informal.* a person who resembles one of his or her parents in behaviour. ~*vb.* (*mainly tr.*) **29.** to shape or form (something) into a block. **30.** to fit with or mount on a block. **31.** to shape by use of a block: *to block a hat.* **32.** (*often* foll. by *up*) to obstruct (a passage, channel, etc.) or prevent or impede the motion or flow of (something or someone) by introducing an obstacle: *to block the traffic; to block up a pipe.* **33.** to impede, retard, or prevent (an action, procedure, etc.). **34.** to stamp (a title, design, etc.) on (a book cover, etc.) by means of a block (see sense 13a.), esp. using gold leaf or other foil. **35.** (esp. of a government or central bank) to limit the use or conversion of assets or currency. **36.** (*also intr.*) *Sports.* to obstruct or impede movement by (an opponent). **37.** (*intr.*) to suffer a psychological block. **38.** to interrupt a physiological function, as by use of an anaesthetic. **39.** (*also intr.*) *Cricket.* to play (a ball) defensively. ~See also **block out.** [C14: from Old French *bloc,* from Dutch *blok;* related to Old High German *bloh*] —**'block+er** *n.*
block+ade (blɒ'keɪd) *n.* **1.** *Military.* the interdiction of a nation's sea lines of communications, esp. of an individual port by the use of sea power. **2.** something that prevents access or progress. ~*vb.* (*tr.*) **3.** to impose a blockade on. **4.** to obstruct the way to. [C17: from BLOCK + *-ade,* as in AMBUSCADE] —**block+'ad+er** *n.*
block+age ('blɒkɪdʒ) *n.* **1.** the act of blocking or state of being blocked. **2.** an object causing an obstruction.

B

block and tack+le *n.* a hoisting device in which a rope or chain is passed around a pair of blocks containing one or more pulleys. The upper block is secured overhead and the lower block supports the load, the effort being applied to the free end of the rope or chain.

block+board ('blɒk,bɔ:d) *n.* a type of plywood in which soft wood strips are bonded together and sandwiched between two layers of veneer.

block+bust+er ('blɒk,bʌstə) *n. Informal.* **1.** a large bomb used to demolish extensive areas or strengthened targets. **2.** a very forceful person, thing, etc.

block+bust+ing ('blɒk,bʌstɪŋ) *n. U.S. informal.* the act or practice of inducing the sale of property cheaply by exploiting the owners' fears of lower prices if racial minorities live in the area.

block di·a+gram *n.* **1.** a diagram showing the interconnections between the parts of an industrial process or the components of an electronic or electrical system. **2.** a three-dimensional drawing representing a block of the earth's crust, showing geological structure.

blocked (blɒkt) *adj. Slang.* influenced by a narcotic drug.

blocked shoe *n.* a dancing shoe with a stiffened toe that enables a ballet dancer to dance on the tips of the toes.

block+head ('blɒk,hɛd) *n. Derogatory.* a stupid person. —**'block+,head·ed** *adj.* —**'block+,head·ed+ly** *adv.* —**'block+,head·ed+ness** *n.*

block+house ('blɒk,haʊs) *n.* **1.** (formerly) a wooden fortification with ports or loopholes for defensive fire, observation, etc. **2.** a concrete structure strengthened to give protection against enemy fire, with apertures to allow defensive gunfire. **3.** a building constructed of logs or squared timber. **4.** a reinforced concrete building close to a rocket-launching site for protecting personnel and equipment during launching.

block+ish ('blɒkɪʃ) *adj.* lacking vivacity or imagination; stupid. —**'block+ish+ly** *adv.* —**'block+ish+ness** *n.*

block la·va *n.* volcanic lava occurring as rough-surfaced jagged blocks.

block let+ter *n.* **1.** *Printing.* a less common name for **sans serif. 2.** Also called: **block capital.** a plain capital letter.

block out *vb.* (*tr., adv.*) **1.** to plan or describe (something) in a general fashion. **2.** to prevent the entry or consideration of (something). **3.** *Photography, printing.* to mask part of (a negative), in order that light may not pass through it.

block plane *n.* a carpenter's small plane used to cut across the end grain of wood.

block print+ing *n.* printing from hand engraved or carved blocks of wood or linoleum.

block re+lease *n. Brit.* the release of industrial trainees from work for study at a college for several weeks.

block tin *n.* pure tin, esp. when cast into ingots.

Bloem+fon+tein ('blu:mfɒn,teɪn) *n.* a city in central South Africa: capital of the Orange Free State and judicial capital of the Republic. Pop.: 148 282 (1970).

Blois (*French* blwa) *n.* a city in N central France, on the Loire: 13th-century castle. Pop.: 51 950 (1975).

Blok (blɒk) *n.* **A·le·ksan·dr A·le·ksan·dro·vich** (alɪ'ksandᵊr alɪ'ksandrəvitʃ). 1880–1921, Russian poet whose poems, which include *Verses about the Beautiful Lady* (1901–2) and *Rasput'ya* (1902–4), contain a mixture of symbolism, romanticism, tragedy, and irony.

bloke (bləʊk) *n. Brit.* an informal word for **man.** [C19: from Shelta]

blond (blɒnd) *adj.* **1.** (of hair) of a light colour; fair. **2.** (of people or a race) having fair hair, a light complexion, and, typically, blue or grey eyes. **3.** (of soft furnishings, wood, etc.) light in colour. ~*n.* **4.** a man or boy having light-coloured hair and skin. [C15: from Old French *blond,* probably of Germanic origin; related to Late Latin *blundus* yellow, Italian *biondo,* Spanish *blondo*] —**'blond+ness** *n.*

blonde (blɒnd) *n.* **1.** a woman or girl having light-coloured hair. **2.** Also called: **blonde lace.** a French pillow lace, originally of unbleached cream-coloured Chinese silk, later of bleached or black-dyed silk. ~*adj.* **3.** (of a woman's or girl's hair) of a light colour; fair. **4.** (of a woman or girl) having light-coloured hair and skin. —**'blonde+ness** *n.*

blood (blʌd) *n.* **1.** a reddish fluid in vertebrates that is pumped by the heart through the arteries and veins, supplies tissues with nutrients, oxygen, etc., and removes waste products. It consists of a fluid (see **blood plasma**) containing cells (erythrocytes and leucocytes) and platelets. **2.** a similar fluid in such invertebrates as annelids and arthropods. **3.** bloodshed, esp. when resulting in murder. **4.** the guilt or responsibility for killing or injuring (esp. in the phrase **to have blood on one's hands** *or* **head**). **5.** life itself; lifeblood. **6.** relationship through being of the same family, race, or kind; kinship. **7. flesh and blood. a.** near kindred or kinship, esp. that between a parent and child. **b.** human nature (esp. in the phrase **it's more than flesh and blood can stand**). **8.** ethnic or national descent: *of Spanish blood.* **9. in one's blood.** as a natural or inherited characteristic or talent. **10. the blood.** royal or noble descent: *a prince of the blood.* **11.** temperament; disposition; temper. **12. a.** good or pure breeding; pedigree. **b.** (*as modifier*): *blood horses.* **13.** people viewed as members of a group, esp. as an invigorating force (in the phrases **new blood, young blood**). **14.** *Chiefly Brit., rare.* a dashing young man; dandy; rake. **15.** the sensual or carnal nature of man. **16.** *Obsolete.* one of the four bodily humours. See **humour** (sense 8). **17. bad blood.** hatred; ill feeling. **18. blood is thicker than water.** family duties and loyalty outweigh other ties. **19. have** *or* **get one's blood up.** to be or cause to be angry or inflamed. **20. in cold blood. a.** cruelly and ruthlessly. **b.** deliberately and calmly. **21. make one's blood boil.** to cause to be angry or indignant. **22. make one's blood run cold.** to fill with horror. ~*vb.* (*tr.*) **23.** *Hunting.* to cause (young hounds) to taste the blood of a freshly killed quarry and so become keen to hunt. **24.** *Hunting.* to smear the cheeks or forehead of (a person) with the blood of the kill as an initiation in hunting. **25.** to initiate (a person) to war. [Old English *blōd;* related to Old Norse *blōth,* Old High German *bluot*]

blood-and-thun·der *adj.* denoting or relating to a melodramatic adventure story.

blood bank *n.* a place where whole blood or blood plasma is stored until required in transfusion.

blood bath *n.* indiscriminate slaughter; a massacre.

blood broth+er *n.* **1.** a brother by birth. **2.** a man or boy who has sworn to treat another as his brother, often in a ceremony in which their blood is mingled.

blood count *n.* determination of the number of red and white blood corpuscles in a specific sample of blood. See **haemocytometer.**

blood+cur·dling ('blʌd,kɜ:dlɪŋ) *adj.* terrifying; horrifying. —**'blood+,cur·dling+ly** *adv.*

blood do+nor *n.* a person who gives his blood to be used for transfusion.

blood-drop em+lets ('ɛmlɪts) *n.* (*functioning as sing.*) a Chilean scrophulariaceous plant, *Mimulus luteus,* naturalized in central Europe, having red-spotted yellow flowers. See also **monkey flower, musk** (sense 3).

blood+ed ('blʌdɪd) *adj.* **1.** (of horses, cattle, etc.) of good breeding. **2.** (*in combination*) having blood or temperament as specified: *hot-blooded, cold-blooded, warm-blooded, red-blooded, blue-blooded.*

blood feud *n.* a feud in which the members of hostile families or clans murder each other.

blood+fin ('blʌd,fɪn) *n.* a silvery red-finned South American freshwater fish, *Aphyocharax rubripinnis:* a popular aquarium fish: family *Characidae* (characins).

blood fluke *n.* any parasitic flatworm, such as a schistosome, that lives in the blood vessels of man and other vertebrates: class *Digenea.* See also **trematode.**

blood group *n.* any one of the various groups into which human blood is classified on the basis of its agglutinogens. Also called: **blood type.**

blood guilt *n.* guilt of murder or shedding blood. —**'blood-,guilt·y** *adj.* —**'blood-,guilt·i+ness** *n.*

blood heat *n.* the normal temperature of the human body, 98.6°F. or 37°C.

blood+hound ('blʌd,haʊnd) *n.* **1.** a large breed of hound with loose wrinkled skin on its head, much used in tracking and police work. **2.** *Informal.* a detective.

blood+less ('blʌdlɪs) *adj.* **1.** without blood. **2.** conducted without violence (esp. in the phrase **bloodless revolution**). **3.** anaemic-looking; pale. **4.** lacking vitality; lifeless. **5.** lacking in emotion; cold; unfeeling. —**'blood+less+ly** *adv.* —**'blood+less+ness** *n.*

Blood+less Rev·o+lu+tion *n.* **the.** another name for the **Glorious Revolution.**

blood-let·ting ('blʌd,lɛtɪŋ) *n.* **1.** the therapeutic removal of blood, as in relieving congestive heart failure. See also **phlebotomy. 2.** bloodshed, esp. in a blood feud.

blood+mo·bile ('blʌdmə,bi:l) *n. U.S.* a motor vehicle equipped for collecting blood from donors.

blood mon+ey *n.* **1.** compensation paid to the relatives of a murdered person. **2.** money paid to a hired murderer. **3.** a reward for information about a criminal, esp. a murderer.

blood or+ange *n.* a variety of orange all or part of the pulp of which is dark red when ripe.

blood plas+ma *n.* **1.** the pale yellow fluid portion of the blood; blood from which blood cells and platelets have been removed. **2.** a sterilized preparation of this fluid for use in transfusions.

blood poi+son+ing *n.* a nontechnical term for **septicemia.**

blood pres+sure *n.* the pressure exerted by the blood on the inner walls of the arteries, being relative to the elasticity and diameter of the vessels and the force of the heart beat.

blood pud+ding *n.* another name for **black pudding.**

blood red *n.* **a.** a deep red colour. **b.** (*as adj.*): *blood-red roses.*

blood re+la+tion *or* **rel·a+tive** *n.* a person related to another by birth, as distinct from one related by marriage.

blood+root ('blʌd,ru:t) *n.* **1.** Also called: **red puccoon.** a North American papaveraceous plant, *Sanguinaria canadensis,* having a single whitish flower and a fleshy red root that yields a red dye. **2.** another name for **tormentil.**

blood sau+sage *n.* another term (esp. U.S.) for **black pudding.**

blood se+rum *n.* blood plasma from which the clotting factors have been removed.

blood+shed ('blʌd,ʃɛd) *n.* slaughter; killing.

blood+shot ('blʌd,ʃɒt) *adj.* (of an eye) inflamed.

blood sport *n.* any sport involving the killing of an animal, esp. hunting.

blood+stain ('blʌd,steɪn) *n.* a dark discoloration caused by blood, esp. dried blood. —**'blood+,stained** *adj.*

blood+stock ('blʌd,stɒk) *n.* thoroughbred horses, esp. those bred for racing.

blood+stone ('blʌd,stəʊn) *n.* a dark-green variety of chalcedony with red spots: used as a gemstone. Also called: **heliotrope.**

blood stream *n.* the flow of blood through the vessels of a living body.

blood·suck·er ('blʌdˌsʌkə) *n.* **1.** an animal that sucks blood, esp. a leech or mosquito. **2.** *Informal.* a person or thing that preys upon another person, esp. by extorting money.

blood test *n.* analysis of a blood sample to determine blood group, alcohol level, etc.

blood·thirst·y ('blʌdˌθɜːstɪ) *adj.* **·thirst·i·er, ·thirst·i·est. 1.** murderous; cruel. **2.** taking pleasure in bloodshed or violence. **3.** describing or depicting killing and violence; gruesome: *a bloodthirsty film.* —**'blood·ˌthirst·i·ly** *adv.* —**'blood·ˌthirst·i·ness** *n.*

blood type *n.* another name for **blood group.**

blood ves·sel *n.* an artery, capillary, or vein.

blood·worm ('blʌdˌwɜːm) *n.* **1.** the red wormlike aquatic larva of the midge *Chironomus plumosus,* which lives at the bottom of stagnant pools and ditches. **2.** any similar invertebrate.

blood·y ('blʌdɪ) *adj.* **blood·i·er, blood·i·est. 1.** covered or stained with blood. **2.** resembling or composed of blood. **3.** marked by much killing and bloodshed: *a bloody war.* **4.** cruel or murderous: *a bloody tyrant.* **5.** of a deep red colour; blood-red. ~*adv., adj.* **6.** *Slang, chiefly Brit.* (intensifier): *a bloody fool; bloody fine food.* ~*vb.* **blood·ies, blood·y·ing, blood·ied. 7.** (*tr.*) to stain with blood. —**'blood·i·ly** *adv.* —**'blood·i·ness** *n.*

Blood·y Mar·y *n.* a drink consisting of tomato juice and vodka.

blood·y-mind·ed *adj. Brit. informal.* deliberately obstructive and unhelpful.

bloom[1] (bluːm) *n.* **1.** a blossom on a flowering plant; a flower. **2.** the state, time, or period when flowers open (esp. in the phrases **in bloom, in full bloom**). **3.** open flowers collectively: *a tree covered with bloom.* **4.** a healthy, vigorous, or flourishing condition; prime (esp. in the phrase **the bloom of youth**). **5.** youthful or healthy rosiness in the cheeks or face; glow. **6.** a fine whitish coating on the surface of fruits, leaves, etc., consisting of minute grains of a waxy substance. **7.** any coating similar in appearance, such as that on new coins. **8.** Also called: **chill.** a dull area on the surface of old gloss paint, lacquer, or varnish. ~*vb.* (*intr.*) **9.** (of flowers) to open; come into flower. **10.** to bear flowers; blossom. **11.** to flourish or grow. **12.** to be in a healthy, glowing, or flourishing condition. [C13: of Germanic origin; compare Old Norse *blōm* flower, Old High German *bluomo,* Middle Dutch *bloeme;* see BLOW[3]] —**'bloom·y** *adj.*

bloom[2] (bluːm) *n.* **1.** a rectangular mass of metal obtained by rolling or forging a cast ingot. See also **billet**[2] (sense 2). ~*vb.* **2.** (*tr.*) to convert (an ingot) into a bloom by rolling or forging. [Old English *blōma* lump of metal]

bloomed (bluːmd) *adj. Photog., optics.* (of a lens) coated with a thin film of magnesium fluoride or some other substance to reduce the amount of light lost by reflection. Also: **coated.**

bloom·er[1] ('bluːmə) *n.* **1.** a plant that flowers, esp. in a specified way: *a night bloomer.* **2.** *Brit.* a medium-sized loaf, baked on the sole of the oven, glazed and notched on top.

bloom·er[2] ('bluːmə) *n. Brit. informal.* a stupid mistake; blunder. [C20: from BLOOMING]

bloom·ers ('bluːməz) *pl. n.* **1.** (formerly) women's loose baggy knickers, usually gathered just above the knee. **2.** close-fitting knickers reaching to just above the knee. [from *bloomer,* a similar garment introduced in about 1850 and publicized by Mrs. A. *Bloomer* (1818–94), U.S. social reformer]

bloom·er·y ('bluːmərɪ) *n., pl.* **·er·ies.** a place in which malleable iron is produced directly from iron ore.

Bloom·field ('bluːmˌfiːld) *n.* **Leon·ard.** 1887–1949, U.S. linguist, influential for his strictly scientific and descriptive approach to comparative linguistics; author of *Language* (1933).

bloom·ing ('bluːmɪŋ) *adv., adj. Brit. informal.* (intensifier): *a blooming genius; blooming painful.* [C19: euphemistic for BLOODY]

Bloom·ing·ton ('bluːmɪŋtən) *n.* a city in central Indiana: seat of the University of Indiana (1820). Pop.: 42 890 (1970).

Blooms·bur·y ('bluːmzbərɪ, -brɪ) *n.* **1.** a district of central London in the borough of Camden: contains the British Museum, part of the University of London, and many publishers' offices. ~*adj.* **2.** relating to or characteristic of the Bloomsbury Group.

Blooms·bur·y Group *n.* a group of writers, artists, and intellectuals living and working in and around Bloomsbury in London from about 1907 to 1930. Influenced by the philosophy of G. E. Moore, they included Leonard and Virginia Woolf, Clive and Vanessa Bell, Roger Fry, E. M. Forster, Lytton Strachey, Duncan Grant, and John Maynard Keynes.

bloop·er ('bluːpə) *n. Informal, chiefly U.S.* a blunder; bloomer; stupid mistake. [C20: from *bloop* (imitative of an embarrassing sound) + -ER[1]]

blos·som ('blɒsəm) *n.* **1.** the flower or flowers of a plant, esp. conspicuous flowers producing edible fruit. **2.** the time or period of flowering (esp. in the phrases **in blossom, in full blossom**). ~*vb.* (*intr.*) **3.** (of plants) to come into flower. **4.** to develop or come to a promising stage: *youth had blossomed into maturity.* [Old English *blōstm;* related to Middle Low German *blōsem,* Latin *flōs* flower] —**'blos·som·less** *adj.* —**'blos·som·y** *adj.*

blot[1] (blɒt) *n.* **1.** a stain or spot of ink, paint, dirt, etc. **2.** something that spoils or detracts from the beauty or worth of something. **3.** a blemish or stain on one's character or reputation. ~*vb.* **blots, blot·ting, blot·ted. 4.** (of ink, dye, etc.) to form spots or blobs on (a material) or (of a person) to cause such spots or blobs to form on (a material). **5. blot one's copybook.** *Informal.* to spoil one's reputation by making a mistake, offending against social customs, etc. **6.** (*intr.*) to stain or become stained or spotted. **7.** (*tr.*) to cause a blemish in or on; disgrace. **8.** to soak up (excess ink, etc.) by using blotting paper or some other absorbent material. **9.** (of blotting paper or some other absorbent material) to absorb (excess ink, etc.). **10.** (*tr.;* often foll. by *out*) **a.** to darken or hide completely; obscure; obliterate. **b.** to destroy; annihilate. [C14: probably of Germanic origin; compare Middle Dutch *bluyster* BLISTER]

blot[2] (blɒt) *n.* **1.** *Backgammon.* a man exposed by being placed alone on a point and therefore able to be taken by the other player. **2.** *Archaic.* a weak spot. [C16: perhaps from Middle Dutch *bloot* poor]

blotch (blɒtʃ) *n.* **1.** an irregular spot or discoloration, esp. a dark and relatively large one such as an ink stain. ~*vb.* **2.** to become or cause to become marked by such discoloration. **3.** (*intr.*) (of a pen or ink) to write or flow unevenly in blotches. [C17: probably from BOTCH, influenced by BLOT[1]] —**'blotch·y** *adj.* —**'blotch·i·ly** *adv.* —**'blotch·i·ness** *n.*

blot·ter ('blɒtə) *n.* **1.** something used to absorb excess ink or other liquid, esp. a sheet of blotting paper with a firm backing. **2.** *U.S.* a daily record of events, such as arrests, in a police station (esp. in the phrase **police blotter**).

blot·ting pa·per *n.* a soft absorbent unsized paper, used esp. for soaking up surplus ink.

blot·to ('blɒtəʊ) *adj. Slang.* unconscious, esp. through drunkenness. [C20: from BLOT[1] (vb.); compare *blot out*]

blouse (blaʊz) *n.* **1.** a woman's shirtlike garment made of cotton, nylon, etc. **2.** a loose-fitting smocklike garment, often knee length and belted, worn esp. by E European peasants. **3.** a loose-fitting waist-length jacket worn by soldiers. ~*vb.* **4.** to hang or make so as to hang in full loose folds. [C19: from French, of unknown origin]

blou·son ('bluːzɒn) *n.* a short jacket having the shape of a blouse.

blow[1] (bləʊ) *vb.* **blows, blow·ing, blew, blown. 1.** (of a current of air, the wind, etc.) to be or cause to be in motion. **2.** (*intr.*) to move or be carried by or as if by wind or air: *a feather blew in through the window.* **3.** to expel (air, cigarette smoke, etc.) through the mouth or nose. **4.** to force or cause (air, dust, etc.) to move (into, in, over, etc.) by using an instrument or by expelling breath. **5.** (*intr.*) to breathe hard; pant. **6.** (sometimes foll. by *up*) to inflate with air or the breath. **7.** (*intr.*) (of wind, a storm, etc.) to make a roaring or whistling sound. **8.** to cause (a whistle, siren, etc.) to sound by forcing air into it, as a signal, or (of a whistle, etc.) to sound thus. **9.** (*tr.*) to force air from the lungs through (the nose) to clear out mucus or obstructing matter. **10.** (often foll. by *up, down, in,* etc.) to explode, break, or disintegrate completely: *the bridge blew down in the gale.* **11.** *Electronics.* to burn out (a fuse, valve, etc.) because of excessive current or (of a fuse, valve, etc.) to burn out. **12. blow a fuse.** *Slang.* to lose one's temper. **13.** (*intr.*) (of a whale) to spout water or air from the lungs. **14.** (*tr.*) to wind (a horse) by making it run excessively. **15.** to cause (a wind instrument) to sound by forcing one's breath into the mouthpiece, or (of such an instrument) to sound in this way. **16.** (*intr.*) (of flies) to lay eggs (in). **17.** to shape (glass, ornaments, etc.) by forcing air or gas through the material when molten. **18.** (*intr.*) *Chiefly Austral.* to boast or brag. **19.** (*tr.*) *Slang.* **a.** to spend (money) freely. **b.** *U.S.* to treat or entertain. **20.** (*tr.*) *Slang.* to use (an opportunity) ineffectively. **21.** *Slang.* to go suddenly away (from). **22.** (*tr.*) *Slang* to inhale (a narcotic drug). **23.** (*intr.*) *Slang.* to masturbate. **24.** (past participle: **blowed**). *Informal.* another word for **damn** (esp. in the phrases **I'll be blowed, blow it! blow me!**). **25.** *Draughts.* another word for **huff** (sense 4). **26. blow hot and cold.** *Informal.* to vacillate. **27. blow a kiss** *or* **kisses.** to kiss one's hand, then blow across it as if to carry the kiss through the air to another person. **28. blow one's own trumpet.** to boast of one's own skills or good qualities. **29. blow someone's mind.** *Slang.* **a.** (of a drug, esp. LSD) to cause hallucinatory experiences in a person. **b.** to produce a pleasant or shocking feeling in someone. **30. blow one's top** *or* (esp. U.S.) **lid** *or* **stack.** *Slang.* to lose one's temper. ~*n.* **31.** the act or an instance of blowing. **32.** the sound produced by blowing. **33.** a blast of air or wind. **34.** *Metallurgy.* **a.** a stage in the Bessemer process in which air is blasted upwards through molten pig iron. **b.** the quantity of metal treated in a Bessemer converter. **35.** *Mining.* **a.** a rush of air into a mine. **b.** the collapse of a mine roof. ~See also **blow in, blow into, blow off, blow on, blow out, blow over, blow through, blow up.** [Old English *blāwan,* related to Old Norse *blǣr* gust of wind, Old High German *blāen,* Latin *flāre*]

blow[2] (bləʊ) *n.* **1.** a powerful or heavy stroke with the fist, a weapon, etc. **2. at one** *or* **a blow.** by or with only one action; all at one time. **3.** a sudden setback; unfortunate event: *to come as a blow.* **4. come to blows. a.** to fight. **b.** to result in a fight. **5.** an attacking action: *a blow for freedom.* **6.** *Austral.* a stroke of the shears in sheep-shearing. [C15: probably of Germanic origin; compare Old High German *bliuwan* to beat]

blow[3] (bləʊ) *vb.* **blows, blow·ing, blew, blown. 1.** (*intr.*) (of a plant or flower) to blossom or open out. **2.** (*tr.*) to produce (flowers). ~*n.* **3.** a mass of blossoms. **4.** the state or period of blossoming (esp. in the phrase **in full blow**). [Old English *blōwan;* related to Old Frisian *blōia* to bloom, Old High German *bluoen,* Latin *flōs* flower; see BLOOM[1]]

blow-by-blow *adj.* (*prenominal*) explained in great detail: *a blow-by-blow account of the argument.*

blow·er ('bləʊə) *n.* **1.** a mechanical device, such as a fan, that blows. **2.** a low-pressure compressor, esp. in a furnace or internal-combustion engine. See also **supercharger. 3.** an informal name for **telephone. 4.** an informal name for a **whale. 5.** *Mining.* a discharge of firedamp from a crevice.

blow·fish ('bləʊˌfɪʃ) *n., pl.* **·fish** *or* **·fish·es.** a popular name for **puffer** (sense 2).

blow·fly ('bləʊˌflaɪ) *n., pl.* **·flies.** any of various dipterous flies of the genus *Calliphora* and related genera that lay their eggs in rotting meat, dung, carrion, and open wounds: family *Calliphoridae.* Also called: **bluebottle.**

blow·gun ('bləʊˌgʌn) *n.* the U.S. word for **blowpipe** (sense 1).

blow·hard ('bləʊˌhɑːd) *Informal.* ~*n.* **1.** a boastful person. ~*adj.* **2.** blustering or boastful.

blow·hole ('bləʊˌhəʊl) *n.* **1.** the nostril, paired or single, of whales, situated far back on the skull. **2.** a hole in ice through which whales, seals, etc., breathe. **3.** a vent for air or gas, esp. to release fumes from a tunnel, passage, etc. **4.** a bubble-like defect in an ingot resulting from gas being trapped during solidification.

blow·ie ('bləʊɪ) *n. Austral. informal.* a blowfly.

blow in *vb. (intr., adv.) Informal.* to arrive or enter suddenly.

blow-in *n. Austral. informal.* an unwelcome newcomer or stranger.

blow in·to *vb. (intr., prep.) Informal.* to arrive in or enter (a room, etc.) suddenly.

blow job *n. Taboo.* a slang term for **fellatio.**

blow·lamp ('bləʊˌlæmp) *n.* a small burner that produces a very hot flame, used to remove old paint, melt soft metal, etc. U.S. name: **blowtorch.**

blow mould·ing *n.* a process for moulding single-piece plastic objects in which a thermoplastic is extruded into a split mould and blown against its sides.

blown (bləʊn) *vb.* the past participle of **blow**[1] and **blow**[3].

blow off *vb. (adv.)* **1.** to permit (a gas under pressure, esp. steam) to be released. **2.** *(intr.) Brit. slang.* to emit wind noisily from the anus. **3. blow off steam.** See **let off** (sense 7). ~*n.* **blow-off. 4.** a discharge of a surplus fluid, such as steam, under pressure. **5.** a device through which such a discharge is made.

blow on *vb. (intr., prep.)* to defame or discredit (a person).

blow out *vb. (adv.)* **1.** to extinguish (a flame, candle, etc.) or (of a flame, etc.) to become extinguished. **2.** *(intr.)* (of a tyre) to puncture suddenly, esp. at high speed. **3.** *(intr.)* (of a fuse) to melt suddenly. **4.** *(tr.; often reflexive)* to diminish or use up the energy of: *the storm blew itself out.* **5.** *(intr.)* (of an oil or gas well) to lose oil or gas in an uncontrolled manner. **6. blow one's brains out.** to kill oneself by shooting oneself in the head. ~*n.* **blow·out. 7.** the sudden melting of an electrical fuse. **8.** a sudden burst in a tyre. **9.** the uncontrolled escape of oil and gas from an oil or gas well. **10.** the failure of a jet engine, esp. when in flight. **11.** *Slang.* a large filling meal or lavish entertainment.

blow o·ver *vb. (intr., adv.)* **1.** to cease or be finished: *the storm blew over.*

blow·pipe ('bləʊˌpaɪp) *n.* **1.** a long tube from which pellets, poisoned darts, etc., are shot by blowing. U.S. word: **blowgun. 2.** Also called: **blow tube.** a tube for blowing air or oxygen into a flame to intensify its heat and direct it onto a small area. **3.** a long narrow iron pipe used to gather molten glass and blow it into shape.

blow through *vb. (intr., adv.) Austral. informal.* to leave; make off.

blow·torch ('bləʊˌtɔːtʃ) *n.* the U.S. name for **blowlamp.**

blow up *vb. (adv.)* **1.** to explode or cause to explode. **2.** *(tr.)* to increase the importance of (something): *they blew the whole affair up.* **3.** *(intr.) Informal.* to come into consideration: *we lived well enough before this thing blew up.* **4.** *(intr.)* to come into existence with sudden force: *a storm had blown up.* **5.** *Informal.* to lose one's temper (with a person). **6.** *Informal.* *(tr.)* to enlarge the size or detail of (a photograph). ~*n.* **blow-up. 7.** an explosion. **8.** *Informal.* an enlarged photograph or part of a photograph. **9.** *Informal.* a fit of temper or argument.

blow-wave *vb.* **1.** Also: **blow-dry.** *(tr.)* to set (the hair) in a smooth casual style by combing or brushing sections of it while drying it with a hair dryer. —*n.* **2.** this method or style of setting the hair.

blow·y ('bləʊɪ) *adj.* **blow·i·er, blow·i·est.** another word for **windy** (sense 1).

blowz·y *or* **blows·y** ('blaʊzɪ) *adj.* **blowz·i·er, blowz·i·est** *or* **blows·i·er, blows·i·est. 1.** (esp. of a woman) untidy in appearance; slovenly or sluttish. **2.** (of a woman) ruddy in complexion; red-faced. [C18: from dialect *blowze* beggar girl, of unknown origin] —**'blowz·i·ly** *or* **'blows·i·ly** *adv.* —**'blowz·i·ness** *or* **'blows·i·ness** *n.*

blub (blʌb) *vb.* **blubs, blub·bing, blubbed.** *Brit.* a slang word for **blubber** (senses 1-3).

blub·ber ('blʌbə) *vb.* **1.** to sob without restraint. **2.** to utter while sobbing. **3.** *(tr.).* to make (the face) wet and swollen or disfigured by crying. ~*n.* **4.** a thick insulating layer of fatty tissue below the skin of aquatic mammals such as the whale: used by man as a source of oil. **5.** *Informal.* excessive and flabby body fat. **6.** the act or an instance of weeping without restraint. ~*adj.* **7.** *(often in combination)* swollen or fleshy: *blubber-faced; blubber-lips.* [C12: perhaps from Low German *blubbern* to BUBBLE, of imitative origin] —**'blub·ber·er** *n.* —**'blub·ber·y** *adj.*

blu·cher ('bluːkə, -tʃə) *n. Obsolete.* a high shoe with laces over the tongue. [C19: named after Field Marshal BLÜCHER]

Blü·cher (*German* 'blyçər) *n.* **Geb·hard Le·be·recht von** ('gɛphart 'leːbəˌrɛçt fɔn). 1742–1819, Prussian field marshal, who commanded the Prussian army against Napoleon at Waterloo (1815).

bludge (blʌdʒ) *Austral. informal.* ~*vb.* **1.** (when *intr.*, often foll. by *on*) to scrounge from (someone). **2.** *(intr.)* to skive. ~*n.* **3.** a very easy task; undemanding employment. [C19: back formation from slang *bludger* pimp, from BLUDGEONER] —**'bludg·er** *n.*

bludg·eon ('blʌdʒən) *n.* **1.** a stout heavy club, typically thicker at one end. **2.** a person, line of argument, etc., that is effective but unsubtle. ~*vb. (tr.)* **3.** to hit or knock down with or as with a bludgeon. **4.** (often foll. by *into*) to force; bully; coerce: *they bludgeoned him into accepting the job.* [C18: of uncertain origin] —**'bludg·eon·er** *n.*

blue (bluː) *n.* **1.** any of a group of colours, such as that of a clear unclouded sky, that have wavelengths in the range 490–445 nanometres. Blue is the complementary colour of yellow and with red and green forms a set of primary colours. **2.** a dye or pigment of any of these colours. **3.** blue cloth or clothing: *dressed in blue.* **4.** a sportsman who represents or has represented Oxford or Cambridge University and has the right to wear the university colour (dark blue for Oxford, light blue for Cambridge): *an Oxford blue.* **5.** *Brit.* an informal name for **Tory. 6.** any of numerous small blue-winged butterflies of the genera *Lampides, Polyommatus,* etc.: family *Lycaenidae.* **7.** *Archaic.* short for **bluestocking. 8.** *Slang.* a policeman. **9.** *Archery.* a blue ring on a target, between the red and the black, scoring five points. **10.** a blue ball in snooker, etc. **11.** another name for **blueing. 12.** *Austral. slang.* an argument or fight: *he had a blue with a taxi driver.* **13.** Also: **bluey.** *Austral. informal.* a summons. **14.** *Austral. informal.* a mistake; error. **15. out of the blue.** apparently from nowhere; unexpectedly: *the opportunity came out of the blue.* **16. into the blue.** into the unknown or the far distance. ~*adj.* **blu·er, blu·est. 17.** of the colour blue. **18.** (of the flesh) having a purple tinge, as from cold or contusion. **19.** depressed, moody, or unhappy. **20.** dismal or depressing: *a blue day.* **21.** indecent, titillating, or pornographic: *blue films.* **22.** bluish in colour or having parts or marks that are bluish: *a blue fox; a blue whale.* **23.** *Rare.* aristocratic; noble; patrician: *a blue family.* See **blue blood.** ~*vb.* **blues, blue·ing** *or* **blu·ing, blued. 24.** to make, dye, or become blue. **25.** *(tr.)* to treat (laundry) with blueing. **26.** *(tr.)* *Slang.* to spend extravagantly or wastefully; squander. [C13: from Old French *bleu,* of Germanic origin; compare Old Norse *blǣr,* Old High German *blāo,* Middle Dutch *blā;* related to Latin *flāvus* yellow] —**'blue·ly** *adv.* —**'blue·ness** *n.*

Blue (bluː) *n. Austral. informal.* a person with red hair.

blue ba·by *n.* a baby born with a bluish tinge to the skin because of lack of oxygen in the blood, esp. caused by a congenital defect of the heart.

blue bag *n. Brit.* a fabric bag for a barrister's robes.

Blue·beard ('bluːˌbɪəd) *n.* **1.** a villain in European folk tales who marries several wives and murders them in turn. In many versions the seventh and last wife escapes the fate of the others. **2.** a man who has had several wives.

blue·bell ('bluːˌbɛl) *n.* **1.** Also called: **wild** *or* **wood hyacinth.** a European liliaceous woodland plant, *Endymion* (or *Scilla*) *non-scriptus,* having a one-sided cluster of blue bell-shaped flowers. **2.** a Scot. name for **harebell. 3.** any of various other plants with blue bell-shaped flowers.

blue·ber·ry ('bluːbərɪ, -brɪ) *n., pl.* **·ries. 1.** Also called: **huckleberry.** any of several North American ericaceous shrubs of the genus *Vaccinium,* such as *V. pennsylvanicum,* that have blue-black edible berries with tiny seeds. See also **bilberry. 2. a.** the fruit of any of these plants. **b.** *(as modifier): blueberry pie.*

blue·bill ('bluːˌbɪl) *n. U.S.* another name for **scaup.**

blue·bird ('bluːˌbɜːd) *n.* **1.** any North American songbird of the genus *Sialia,* having a blue or partly blue plumage: subfamily *Turdinae* (thrushes). **2. fairy bluebird.** any songbird of the genus *Irena,* of S and SE Asia, having a blue-and-black plumage: family *Irenidae.* **3.** any of various other birds having a blue plumage.

blue blood *n.* royal or aristocratic descent. [C19: translation of Spanish *sangre azul*] —**'blue-'blood·ed** *adj.*

blue·bon·net ('bluːˌbɒnɪt) *or* **blue·cap** ('bluːˌkæp) *n.* another name for **Balmoral**[1] (sense 3).

blue·book ('bluːˌbʊk) *n.* **1.** (in Britain) a government publication bound in a stiff blue paper cover: usually the report of a royal commission or a committee. **2.** *Informal, chiefly U.S.* a register of well-known people.

blue·bot·tle ('bluːˌbɒtᵊl) *n.* **1.** another name for the **blowfly. 2.** any of various blue-flowered plants, esp. the cornflower. **3.** *Brit.* an informal word for a **policeman. 4.** *Austral.* an informal name for **Portuguese man-of-war.**

blue buck *n.* another name for the **blaubok.**

blue butch·er *n.* a Eurasian orchid, *Orchis mascula,* with purplish-crimson flowers and stems marked with blackish-purple spots. Also called: **early purple orchid.**

blue cheese *n.* cheese containing a blue mould, esp. Stilton, Roquefort, or Danish Blue.

blue chip *n.* **1.** a gambling chip with the highest value. **2.** *Finance.* **a.** a stock considered reliable with respect to both dividend income and capital value. **b.** *(as modifier): a blue-chip stock.*

blue-col·lar *adj.* of, relating to, or designating manual industrial workers. Compare **white-collar.**

blue dev·ils *n.* **1.** a fit of depression or melancholy. **2.** an attack of delirium tremens.

blue-eyed boy *n. Informal, chiefly Brit.* the favourite or darling of a person or group. Usual U.S. equivalent: **fair-haired boy.**

blue-eyed grass *n.* any of various mainly North American iridaceous marsh plants of the genus *Sisyrinchium* that have grasslike leaves and small flat starlike blue flowers.

blue-eyed Mar·y *n.* a blue-flowered boraginaceous plant, *Omphalodes verna,* native to S Europe and cultivated in Britain.
blue-eyed soul *n. Informal.* soul music written and performed by White singers in a style derived from the blues.
blue+fish ('blu:ˌfɪʃ) *n., pl.* **+fish** *or* **+fish·es. 1.** Also called: **snapper.** a bluish marine percoid food and game fish, *Pomatomus saltatrix,* related to the horse mackerel: family *Pomatomidae.* **2.** any of various other bluish fishes.
blue fox *n.* **1.** a variety of the arctic fox that has a pale grey winter coat and is bred for its fur. **2.** the fur of this animal.
blue funk *n. Informal, chiefly Brit.* a state of great terror or loss of nerve.
blue+gill ('blu:ˌgɪl) *n.* a common North American freshwater sunfish, *Lepomis macrochirus:* an important food and game fish.
blue+grass ('blu:ˌgrɑ:s) *n.* **1.** any of several North American bluish-green grasses of the genus *Poa,* esp. *P. pratensis* (**Kentucky bluegrass**), grown for forage. **2.** a type of folk music originating in Kentucky, characterized by a simple harmonized accompaniment.
blue-green al+gae *pl. n.* the algae of the family *Cyanophyceae* (or *Myxophyceae*), including nostoc, which contain a blue pigment in addition to chlorophyll.
blue ground *n. Mineralogy.* another name for **kimberlite.**
blue grouse *n.* a grouse, *Dendragapus obscurus,* of W North America, having a bluish-grey plumage with a black tail.
blue gum *n.* **1.** a tall fast-growing widely cultivated Australian myrtaceous tree, *Eucalyptus globulus,* having aromatic leaves containing a medicinal oil, bark that peels off in shreds, and hard timber. The juvenile leaves are bluish in colour. **2.** any of several other eucalyptus trees. ~See also **red gum** (sense 1).
blue+ing *or* **blu+ing** ('blu:ɪŋ) *n.* **1.** a blue material, such as indigo, used in laundering to counteract yellowing. **2.** a rinse for tinting grey hair a silvery-blue colour. **3.** the formation of a film of blue oxide on a steel surface.
blue+jack·et ('blu:ˌdʒækɪt) *n.* a sailor in the Navy.
blue jay *n.* a common North American jay, *Cyanocitta cristata,* having bright blue plumage with greyish-white underparts.
blue john *n.* a blue or purple fibrous variety of fluorspar occurring only in Derbyshire: used for vases, etc.
blue laws *n. U.S. history.* one of a number of repressive puritanical laws of the colonial period, forbidding any secular activity on Sundays.
Blue Man+tle *n.* one of the four pursuivants of the British College of Arms.
blue moon *n.* **once in a blue moon.** *Informal.* very rarely; almost never.
blue mould *n.* **1.** Also called: **green mould.** any fungus of the genus *Penicillium* that forms a bluish mass on decaying food, leather, etc. **2.** any fungal disease of fruit trees characterized by necrosis and a bluish growth on the affected tissue: mostly caused by *Penicillium* species.
Blue Moun+tains *pl. n.* **1.** a mountain range in NE Oregon and SE Washington. Highest peak: Rock Creek Butte, 2773 m (9097 ft.). **2.** a mountain range in the West Indies, in E Jamaica: Blue Mountain coffee is grown on its slopes. Highest peak: Blue Mountain Peak, 2270 m (7445 ft.). **3.** a plateau in SE Australia, in E New South Wales: part of the Great Dividing Range. Highest part: about 1360 m (4460 ft.).
Blue Nile *n.* a river in E Africa, rising in central Ethiopia as the Abbai and flowing southeast, then northwest to join the White Nile. Length: about 1530 km (950 miles).
blue+nose ('blu:ˌnəʊz) *n.* **1.** *U.S. slang.* a puritanical or prudish person. **2.** *Informal.* a native or inhabitant of Nova Scotia.
blue note *n. Jazz.* a flattened third or seventh, used frequently in the blues.
blue pen+cil *n.* **1.** deletion, alteration, or censorship of the contents of a book or other work. ~*vb.* **blue-pen·cil, ·cils, ·cil+ling, ·cilled** *or U.S.* **·cils, ·cil+ing, ·ciled. 2.** (*tr.*) to alter or delete parts of (a book, film, etc.), esp. to censor.
blue pe+ter *n.* a signal flag of blue with a white square at the centre, displayed by a vessel about to leave port. [from the name *Peter*]
blue point+er *n.* a large shark, *Isuropsis mako,* of Australian coastal waters, having a blue back and pointed snout.
blue+print ('blu:ˌprɪnt) *n.* **1.** Also called: **cyanotype.** a photographic print of plans, technical drawings, etc., consisting of white lines on a blue background. **2.** an original plan or prototype that influences subsequent design or practice: *the Montessori method was the blueprint for education in the 1940s.* ~*vb.* **3.** (*tr.*) to make a blueprint of (a plan, etc.).
blue rac+er *n.* a long slender blackish-blue fast-moving colubrid snake, *Coluber constrictor flaviventris,* of the U.S.
blue rib+band *n.* **1.** (*sometimes caps.*) Also (esp. U.S.): **blue ribbon.** (formerly) the record for the fastest trans-Atlantic passage by a passenger liner, esp. between New York and Southampton. **2.** any event, victory in which is a coveted distinction.
blue rib+bon *n.* **1.** (in Britain) a badge of blue silk worn by members of the Order of the Garter. **2.** a badge awarded as the first prize in a competition. **3.** *U.S.* a badge worn by a member of a temperance society.
blue-rib·bon ju·ry *n.* a U.S. name for a **special jury.**
Blue Ridge Moun+tains *pl. n.* a mountain range in the eastern U.S., extending from West Virginia into Georgia: part of the Appalachian mountains. Highest peak: Mount Mitchell, 2038 m (6684 ft.).
Blue Rod *n. Brit.* officer of the Order of St. Michael and St. George. Full title: **Gentleman Usher of the Blue Rod.**
blues (blu:z) *pl. n.* (*sometimes functioning as sing.*) **the. 1.** a feeling of depression or deep unhappiness. **2.** a type of folk song originating among Black Americans at the beginning of the 20th century, usually employing a basic 12-bar chorus, the tonic, subdominant, and dominant chords, frequent minor intervals, and blue notes.
blue shift *n.* a shift in the spectral lines of a stellar spectrum towards the blue end of the visible region relative to the wavelengths of these lines in the terrestrial spectrum: thought to be a result of the **Doppler effect** caused by stars approaching the solar system. Compare **red shift.**
blue-sky law *n. U.S.* a state law regulating the trading of securities: intended to protect investors from fraud.
blue spruce *n.* a spruce tree, *Picea pungens glauca,* native to the Rocky Mountains of North America, having blue-green needle-like leaves. Also called: **balsam spruce.**
blue+stock·ing ('blu:ˌstɒkɪŋ) *n. Usually disparaging.* a scholarly or intellectual woman. [from the blue worsted stockings worn by members of a C18 literary society]
blue+stone ('blu:ˌstəʊn) *n.* **1.** a blue-grey sandstone containing much clay, used for building and paving. **2.** the blue crystalline form of copper sulphate. **3.** a blue variety of basalt found in Australia and used as a building stone.
bluet ('blu:ɪt) *n.* a North American rubiaceous plant, *Houstonia caerulea,* with small four-petalled blue flowers.
blue+throat ('blu:ˌθrəʊt) *n.* a small brownish European songbird, *Cyanosylvia svecica,* related to the thrushes, the male of which has a blue throat: family *Muscicapidae.*
blue+tit ('blu:ˌtɪt) *n.* a common European tit, *Parus caeruleus,* having a blue crown, wings, and tail, yellow underparts, and a black and grey head.
blue+tongue ('blu:tʌŋ) *n.* an Australian lizard, *Tiliqua scincoides,* having a cobalt-blue tongue.
blue vit+ri+ol *n.* the fully hydrated blue crystalline form of copper sulphate.
blue+weed ('blu:ˌwi:d) *n. U.S.* another name for **viper's bugloss.**
blue whale *n.* the largest mammal: a widely distributed bluish-grey whalebone whale, *Sibbaldus* (or *Balaenoptera*) *musculus,* closely related and similar to the rorquals: family *Balaenopteridae.* Also called: **sulphur-bottom.**
blu+ey ('blu:ɪ) *n. Austral. informal.* **1.** a blanket. **2.** a swagman's bundle. **3. hump (one's) bluey.** to carry one's bundle; tramp. **4.** a variant of **blue** (sense 13). **5.** a cattle dog. [(for senses 1, 2, 4) C19: from BLUE (on account of their colour) + -Y[2]]
Blu+ey ('blu:ɪ) *n.* a variant of **Blue.**
bluff[1] (blʌf) *vb.* **1.** to pretend to be confident about an uncertain issue or to have undisclosed resources, in order to influence or deter (someone). ~*n.* **2.** deliberate deception intended to create the impression of a stronger position or greater resources than one actually has. **3. call someone's bluff.** to challenge someone to give proof of his claims. [C19: originally U.S. poker-playing term, from Dutch *bluffen* to boast] —**'bluff+er** *n.*
bluff[2] (blʌf) *n.* **1.** a steep promontory, bank, or cliff, esp. one formed by river erosion on the outside bend of a meander. **2.** *Canadian.* a clump of trees on the prairie; copse. ~*adj.* **3.** good-naturedly frank and hearty. **4.** (of a bank, cliff, etc.) presenting a steep broad face. [C17 (in the sense: nearly perpendicular): perhaps from Middle Dutch *blaf* broad] —**'bluff+ly** *adv.* —**'bluff+ness** *n.*
blu+ish *or* **blue+ish** ('blu:ɪʃ) *adj.* somewhat blue. —**'blu+ish+ness** *or* **'blue+ish+ness** *n.*
Blum (blu:m) *n.* **Lé·on** (le'ɔ̃). 1872–1950, French socialist statesman; premier of France (1936–37; 1938; 1946–47).
blun+der ('blʌndə) *n.* **1.** a stupid or clumsy mistake. **2.** a foolish tactless remark. ~*vb.* (*mainly intr.*) **3.** to make stupid or clumsy mistakes. **4.** to make foolish tactless remarks. **5.** (often foll. by *about, into,* etc.) to act clumsily; stumble: *he blundered into a situation he knew nothing about.* **6.** (*tr.*) to mismanage; botch. [C14: of Scandinavian origin; compare Old Norse *blunda* to close one's eyes, Norwegian dialect *blundra;* see BLIND] —**'blun+der+er** *n.* —**'blun+der+ing+ly** *adv.*
blun+der+buss ('blʌndəˌbʌs) *n.* **1.** an obsolete short musket with large bore and flared muzzle, used to scatter shot at short range. **2.** *Informal.* a clumsy unsubtle person. [C17: changed (through the influence of BLUNDER) from Dutch *donderbus;* from *donder* THUNDER + obsolete *bus* gun]
blunge (blʌndʒ) *vb.* (*tr.*) to mix (clay or a similar substance) with water in order to form a suspension for use in ceramics. [C19: probably from BLEND + PLUNGE]
blung+er ('blʌndʒə) *n.* a large vat in which the contents, esp. clay and water, are mixed by rotating arms.
blunt (blʌnt) *adj.* **1.** (esp. of a knife or blade) lacking sharpness or keenness; dull. **2.** not having a sharp edge or point: *a blunt instrument.* **3.** (of people, manner of speaking, etc.) lacking refinement or subtlety; straightforward and uncomplicated. **4.** outspoken; direct and to the point: *a blunt Yorkshireman.* ~*vb.* (*tr.*) **5.** to make less sharp. **6.** to diminish the sensitivity or perception of; make dull. [C12: probably of Scandinavian origin; compare Old Norse *blundr* dozing, *blunda* to close one's eyes; see BLUNDER, BLIND] —**'blunt+ly** *adv.* —**'blunt+ness** *n.*
blur (blɜ:) *vb.* **blurs, blur+ring, blurred. 1.** to make or become vague or less distinct: *heat haze blurs the hills; education blurs class distinctions.* **2.** to smear or smudge. **3.** (*tr.*) to make (the judgment, memory, or perception) less clear; dim. ~*n.* **4.** something vague, hazy, or indistinct. **5.** a smear or smudge. [C16: perhaps a variant of BLEAR] —**'blur+red+ly** ('blɜ:rɪdlɪ, 'blɜ:d-) *adv.* —**'blur+red+ness** *n.* —**'blur+ry** *adj.*

blurb (blɜːb) *n.* a promotional description, as found on the jackets of books. [C20: coined by Gelett Burgess (1866–1951), U.S. humorist and illustrator]

blurt (blɜːt) *vb.* (*tr.;* often foll. by *out*) to utter suddenly and involuntarily. [C16: probably of imitative origin]

blush (blʌʃ) *vb.* **1.** (*intr.*) to become suddenly red in the face from embarrassment, shame, modesty, or guilt; redden. **2.** to make or become reddish or rosy. *~n.* **3.** a sudden reddening of the face from embarrassment, shame, modesty, or guilt. **4.** a rosy glow: *the blush of a peach.* **5.** a reddish or pinkish tinge. **6.** **at first blush.** when first seen; as a first impression. [Old English *blȳscan;* related to *blȳsian* to burn, Middle Low German *blüsen* to light a fire] —**'blush+er** *n.* —**'blush+ful** *adj.* —**'blush+ing+ly** *adv.*

blus+ter ('blʌstə) *vb.* **1.** to speak or say loudly or boastfully. **2.** to act in a bullying way. **3.** (*tr.,* foll. by *into*) to force or attempt to force (a person) into doing something by behaving thus. **4.** (*intr.*) (of the wind) to be noisy or gusty. *~n.* **5.** boisterous talk or action; swagger. **6.** empty threats or protests. **7.** a strong wind; gale. [C15: probably from Middle Low German *blüsteren* to storm, blow violently] —**'blus+ter+er** *n.* —**'blus+ter+ing+ly** *or* **'blus+ter+ous+ly** *adv.* —**'blus+ter·y** *or* **'blus+ter+ous** *adj.*

Blvd. *abbrev. for* Boulevard.

Blyth (blaɪð) *n.* a port in N England, in SE Northumberland, on the North Sea. Pop.: 34 617 (1971).

b.m. *abbrev. for:* **1.** board measure. **2.** bowel movement.

B.M. *abbrev. for:* **1.** Bachelor of Medicine. **2.** *Surveying.* bench mark. **3.** British Museum.

B.M.A. *abbrev. for* British Medical Association.

B.M.J. *abbrev. for* British Medical Journal.

BMR *abbrev. for* basal metabolic rate.

B.Mus. *abbrev. for* Bachelor of Music.

Bn. *abbrev. for:* **1.** Baron. **2.** Battalion.

B'nai B'rith (bə'neɪ bə'riːθ, brɪθ) *n.* a Jewish fraternal organization of men founded in New York in 1843, having moral, philanthropic, social, educational, and political aims. [from Hebrew *benē berīth* sons of the covenant]

bo *or* **boh** (bəʊ) *interj.* an exclamation uttered to startle or surprise someone, esp. a child in a game.

b.o. *abbrev. for:* **1.** back order. **2.** branch office. **3.** broker's order. **4.** buyer's option.

B.O. *abbrev. for:* **1.** *Informal.* body odour. **2.** box office.

B/O *abbrev. for:* **1.** *Book-keeping.* brought over. **2.** buyer's option.

bo·a ('bəʊə) *n.* **1.** any large nonvenomous snake of the family *Boidae,* most of which occur in Central and South America and the West Indies. They have vestigial hind limbs and kill their prey by constriction. **2.** a woman's long thin scarf, usually of feathers or fur. [C19: from New Latin, from Latin: a large Italian snake, water snake]

Bo·ab·dil (*Spanish* ˌboaβ'ðil) *n.* original name *Abu-Abdullah,* called *El Chico,* ruled as *Mohammed XI.* died ?1538, last Moorish king of Granada (1482–83; 1486–92).

B.O.A.C. (formerly) *abbrev. for* British Overseas Airways Corporation.

bo·a con+stric·tor *n.* a very large snake, *Constrictor constrictor,* of tropical America and the West Indies, that kills its prey by constriction: family *Boidae* (boas).

Bo·a·di·ce·a (ˌbəʊədɪ'siːə) *n.* died 62 A.D., a queen of the Iceni, who led a revolt against Roman rule in Britain; after being defeated she poisoned herself. Original name: **Boudicca.**

Bo·a·ner·ges (ˌbəʊə'nɜːdʒiːz) *n.* **1.** *New Testament.* a nickname applied by Jesus to James and John in Mark 3:17. **2.** a fiery preacher, esp. one with a powerful voice. [C17: from Hebrew *benē reghesh* sons of thunder]

boar (bɔː) *n.* **1.** an uncastrated male pig. **2.** See **wild boar.** [Old English *bār;* related to Old High German *bēr*]

board (bɔːd) *n.* **1.** a long wide flat relatively thin piece of sawn timber. **2. a.** a smaller flat piece of rigid material for a specific purpose: *ironing board.* **b.** (*in combination*): *breadboard; cheeseboard.* **3.** a person's food or meals, provided regularly for money or sometimes as payment for work done (esp. in the phrases **full board, board and lodging**). **4.** *Archaic.* a table, esp. one used for eating at, and esp. when laden with food. **5. a.** (*sometimes functioning as pl.*) a group of people who officially administer a company, trust, etc.: *a board of directors.* **b.** (*as modifier*): *a board meeting.* **6.** any other committee or council: *a board of interviewers.* **7. the boards.** (*pl.*) the acting profession; the stage. **8.** short for **blackboard, chessboard, notice board, skateboard,** or **springboard. 9.** stiff cardboard or similar material covered with paper, cloth, etc., used for the outside covers of a book. **10.** a flat thin rectangular sheet of composite material, such as plasterboard or chipboard. **11.** *Chiefly U.S.* **a.** a list on which stock-exchange securities and their prices are posted. **b.** *Informal.* the stock exchange itself. **12.** *Nautical.* **a.** the side of a ship. **b.** the leg that a sailing vessel makes on a beat to windward. **13.** *Austral.* the part of the floor of a sheep-shearing shed, esp. a raised part, where the shearers work. **14. a.** any of various portable surfaces specially designed for indoor games such as chess, backgammon, etc. **b.** (*as modifier*): *board games.* **15.** Also called: **deck.** the flat top part of a skateboard, made of any of various substances, such as wood, fibreglass, or plastic. **16.** See **above board. 17. go by the board.** *Informal.* to be in disuse, neglected, or lost: *in these days courtesy goes by the board.* **18. on board.** on or in a ship, boat, aeroplane, or other vehicle. **19. sweep the board.** to win every event or prize in a contest. *~vb.* **20.** to go aboard (a vessel, train, aircraft, or other vehicle). **21.** *Nautical.* to come alongside (a vessel) before attacking or going aboard. **22.** to attack (a ship) by forcing one's way aboard. **23.** (*tr.;* often foll. by *up, in,* etc.) to cover or shut with boards. **24.** (*intr.*) to give or receive meals or meals and lodging in return for money or work. **25.** (sometimes foll. by *out*) to receive or arrange for (someone, esp. a child) to receive food and lodging away from home, usually in return for payment. [Old English *bord;* related to Old Norse *borth* ship's side, table, Old High German *bort* ship's side, Sanskrit *bardhaka* a cutting off; compare BROTHEL] —**'board+a·ble** *adj.*

board-and-shin·gle *n. Caribbean.* a small peasant dwelling with wooden walls and a shingle roof.

board+er ('bɔːdə) *n.* **1.** *Brit.* a pupil who lives at school during term time. **2.** *U.S.* a child who lives away from its parents and is cared for by a person or organization receiving payment. **3.** another word for **lodger. 4.** a person who boards a ship, esp. one who forces his way aboard in an attack: *stand by to repel boarders.*

board foot *n.* a unit of board measure: the cubic content of a piece of wood one foot square and one inch thick.

board+ing ('bɔːdɪŋ) *n.* **1.** a structure of boards, such as a floor or fence. **2.** timber boards collectively. **3. a.** the act of embarking on an aircraft, train, ship, etc. **b.** (*as modifier*): *a boarding pass.* **4.** a process used in tanning to accentuate the natural grain of hides, in which the surface of a softened leather is lightly creased by folding grain to grain and the fold is worked to and fro across the leather.

board+ing house *n.* **1.** a private house in which accommodation and meals are provided for paying guests. **2.** *Austral.* a house (see sense 10) for boarders at a school.

board+ing school *n.* a school providing living accommodation for some or all of its pupils.

board meas+ure *n.* a system of units for measuring wood based on the board foot. 1980 board feet equal one standard.

board of trade *n. U.S.* another name for a **chamber of commerce.**

Board of Trade *n.* (in the United Kingdom) a ministry within the Department of Trade: responsible for the supervision of commerce and the promotion of export trade.

Board of Trade u·nit *n.* a unit of electrical energy equal to 1 kilowatt-hour. Abbrev.: **B.T.U.**

board+room ('bɔːdˌruːm, -ˌrʊm) *n.* **a.** a room where the board of directors of a company meets. **b.** (*as modifier*): *a boardroom power struggle.*

board rule *n.* a measuring device for estimating the number of board feet in a quantity of wood.

board+walk ('bɔːdˌwɔːk) *n. U.S.* a promenade, esp. along a beach, usually made of planks.

boar+fish ('bɔːˌfɪʃ) *n., pl.* **+fish** *or* **+fish·es.** any of various spiny-finned marine teleost fishes of the genera *Capros, Antigonia,* etc., related to the dories, having a deep compressed body, a long snout, and large eyes.

boar+hound ('bɔːˌhaʊnd) *n.* any very large hound, esp. a Great Dane, used for hunting boars.

boar+ish ('bɔːrɪʃ) *adj.* coarse, cruel, or sensual. —**'boar+ish+ly** *adv.* —**'boar+ish+ness** *n.*

boart (bɔːt) *n.* a variant spelling of **bort.**

Bo·as ('bəʊæz; *German* 'boːas) *n.* **Franz** (frants). 1858–1942, U.S. anthropologist, born in Germany. He made major contributions to cultural and linguistic anthropology in studies of North American Indians, including *The Mind of Primitive Man* (1911; 1938).

boast[1] (bəʊst) *vb.* **1.** (*intr.;* sometimes foll. by *of* or *about*) to speak in exaggerated or excessively proud terms of one's possessions, skills, or superior qualities; brag. **2.** (*tr.*) to possess (something to be proud of): *the city boasts a fine cathedral. ~n.* **3.** a bragging statement. **4.** a possession, attribute, attainment, etc., that is or may be bragged about. [C13: of uncertain origin] —**'boast+er** *n.* —**'boast+ing+ly** *adv.*

boast[2] (bəʊst) *vb.* (*tr.*) to shape or dress (stone) roughly with a broad chisel. [C19: of unknown origin]

boast+ful ('bəʊstfʊl) *adj.* tending to boast; characterized by boasting. —**'boast+ful+ly** *adv.* —**'boast+ful+ness** *n.*

boat (bəʊt) *n.* **1.** a small vessel propelled by oars, paddle, sails, or motor for travelling, transporting goods, etc., esp. one that can be carried aboard a larger vessel. **2.** (*not in technical use*) another word for **ship. 3.** a container for gravy, sauce, etc. **4.** a small boat-shaped container for incense, used in some Christian churches. **5. in the same boat.** sharing the same problems. **6. burn one's boats.** See **burn**[1] (sense 16). **7. miss the boat.** *Informal.* to fail to do something at the right time. **8. push the boat out.** *Brit. informal.* to celebrate, esp. lavishly and expensively. **9. rock the boat.** *Informal.* to cause a disturbance in the existing situation. *~vb.* **10.** (*intr.*) to travel or go in a boat, esp. as a form of recreation. **11.** (*tr.*) to transport or carry in a boat. [Old English *bāt;* related to Old Norse *beit* boat]

boat+bill ('bəʊtˌbɪl) *or* **boat-billed her+on** *n.* a nocturnal tropical American wading bird, *Cochlearius cochlearius,* similar to the night herons but with a broad flattened bill: family *Ardeidae,* order *Ciconiiformes.*

boat deck *n.* the deck of a ship on which the lifeboats are kept.

boat drill *n.* practice in launching the lifeboats and taking off the passengers and crew of a ship.

boat+el *or* **bo+tel** (bəʊ'tɛl) *n.* **1.** a waterside hotel catering for boating people. **2.** a ship that functions as a hotel. [C20: from BOAT + (HOT)EL]

boat+er ('bəʊtə) *n.* a stiff straw hat with a straight brim and flat crown.

boat+hook ('bəʊtˌhʊk) *n.* a pole with a hook at one end, used aboard a vessel for fending off other vessels or obstacles or for catching a line or mooring buoy.

boat·house ('bəʊt,haʊs) *n.* a shelter by the edge of a river, lake, etc., for housing boats.

boat·ing ('bəʊtɪŋ) *n.* the practice of rowing, sailing, or cruising in boats as a form of recreation.

boat·load ('bəʊt,ləʊd) *n.* the amount of cargo or number of people held by a boat or ship.

boat·man ('bəʊtmən) *n., pl.* **·men. 1.** a man who works on, hires out, repairs, or operates a boat or boats. **2.** short for **water boatman.**

boat neck *n.* a high slitlike neckline of a garment that extends onto the shoulders. Also called: **bateau neckline.**

boat race *n.* **the.** *Brit.* a rowing event held annually in the spring, in which an eight representing Oxford University rows against one representing Cambridge on the Thames between Putney and Mortlake.

boat·swain, bo's'n, *or* **bo·sun** ('bəʊsᵊn) *n.* a petty officer on a merchant ship or a warrant officer on a warship who is responsible for the maintenance of the ship and its equipment. [Old English *bātswegen;* see BOAT, SWAIN]

boat·swain's chair *n. Nautical.* a seat consisting of a short flat board slung from ropes, used to support a man working on the side of a vessel or in its rigging.

boat train *n.* a train scheduled to take passengers to or from a particular ship.

Bo·a Vis·ta (*Portuguese* 'boa 'vista) *n.* a town in N Brazil, capital of the federal territory of Roraima, on the Rio Branco. Pop.: 37 062 (1970).

Bo·az ('bəʊæz) *n. Old Testament.* a kinsman of Naomi, who married her daughter-in-law Ruth (Ruth 2–4); one of David's ancestors.

bob[1] (bɒb) *vb.* **bobs, bob·bing, bobbed. 1.** to move or cause to move up and down repeatedly, as while floating in water. **2.** to move or cause to move with a short abrupt movement, as of the head. **3.** to make (a bow or curtsy): *the little girl bobbed before the visitor.* **4.** (*intr.;* usually foll. by *up*) to appear or emerge suddenly. **5.** (*intr.;* foll. by *under, below,* etc.) to disappear suddenly, as beneath a surface. **6.** (*intr.;* usually foll. by *for*) to attempt to get hold (of a floating or hanging object, esp. an apple) in the teeth as a game. ~*n.* **7.** a short abrupt movement, as of the head. **8.** a quick curtsy or bow. **9.** *Changeringing.* a particular set of changes. **10.** *Angling.* short for **bobfloat.** [C14: of uncertain origin]

bob[2] (bɒb) *n.* **1.** a hair style for women and children in which the hair is cut short evenly all round the head. **2.** a dangling or hanging object, such as the weight on a pendulum or on a plumb line. **3.** a polishing disc on a rotating spindle. It is usually made of felt, leather, etc., impregnated with an abrasive material. **4.** short for **bob skate** or **bobsleigh. 5.** a runner or pair of runners on a bobsled. **6.** *Angling.* a small knot of worms, maggots, etc., used as bait. **7.** a very short line of verse at the end of a stanza or preceding a rhyming quatrain (the wheel) at the end of a stanza. **8.** a refrain or burden with such a short line or lines. **9.** a docked tail, esp. of a horse. **10.** *Brit. dialect.* a hanging cluster, as of flowers or ribbons. ~*vb.* **bobs, bob·bing, bobbed. 11.** (*tr.*) to cut (the hair) in a bob. **12.** (*tr.*) to cut short (something, esp. the tail of an animal); dock or crop. **13.** (*intr.*) to ride on a bobsled. [C14 *bobbe* bunch of flowers, perhaps of Celtic origin]

bob[3] (bɒb) *vb.* **bobs, bob·bing, bobbed. 1.** to tap or cause to tap or knock lightly (against). ~*n.* **2.** a light knock; tap. [C13 *bobben* to rap, beat; see BOP[2]]

bob[4] (bɒb) *n., pl.* **bob.** *Brit.* an informal word for a **shilling** or 5p. [C19: of unknown origin]

bob·ber·y ('bɒbərɪ) *n., pl.* **·ber·ies. 1.** Also called: **bobbery pack.** a mixed pack of hunting dogs, often not belonging to any of the hound breeds. **2.** *Informal.* a noisy commotion. ~*adj.* **3.** *Informal.* noisy or excitable. [C19: from Hindi *bāp re,* literally: oh father!]

bob·bin ('bɒbɪn) *n.* **1.** a spool or reel on which thread or yarn is wound, being unwound as required; spool; reel. **2.** narrow braid or cord used as binding or for trimming. **3.** a device consisting of a short bar and a length of string, used to control a wooden door latch. **4. a.** a spool on which insulated wire is wound to form the coil of a small electromagnetic device, such as a bell or buzzer. **b.** the coil of such a spool. [C16: from Old French *bobine,* of unknown origin]

bob·bi·net (,bɒbɪ'nɛt) *n.* a netted fabric of hexagonal mesh, made on a lace machine. [C19: see BOBBIN, NET[1]]

bob·bin lace *n.* lace made with bobbins rather than with needle and thread (needlepoint lace); pillow lace.

bob·ble ('bɒbᵊl) *n.* **1.** a short jerky motion, as of a cork floating on disturbed water; bobbing movement. **2.** a tufted ball, usually for ornament, as on a knitted hat. **3.** any small dangling ball or bundle. ~*vb.* **4.** *U.S. informal.* to handle (something) ineptly; muff; bungle: *he bobbled the ball and lost the game.* [C19: from BOB[1] (vb.)]

bob·by ('bɒbɪ) *n., pl.* **·bies.** *Informal.* a British policeman. [C19: from *Bobby,* after *Robert* PEEL, who, as Home Secretary, set up the Metropolitan Police Force in 1828]

bob·by-daz·zler *n. Brit. dialect.* anything outstanding, striking, or showy, esp. an attractive girl. [C19: expanded form of *dazzler* something striking or attractive]

bob·by pin *n. Chiefly U.S.* a metal hair pin bent in order to hold the hair in place.

bob·by socks *pl. n.* ankle-length socks worn by teenage girls, esp. in the U.S. in the 1940s.

bob·by·sox·er ('bɒbɪ,sɒksə) *n. Informal, chiefly U.S.* an adolescent girl wearing bobby socks, esp. in the 1940s.

bob·cat ('bɒb,kæt) *n.* a North American feline mammal, *Lynx rufus,* closely related to but smaller than the lynx, having reddish-brown fur with dark spots or stripes, tufted ears, and a short tail. Also called: **bay lynx.** [C19: from BOB[2] (referring to its short tail) + CAT]

bob·float ('bɒb,fləʊt) *n. Angling.* a small buoyant float, usually consisting of a quill stuck through a piece of cork.

bob·let ('bɒblɪt) *n.* a two-man bobsleigh. [C20: from BOB[2] + -LET]

Bo·bo-Diou·las·so ('bəʊbəʊ dju:'læsəʊ) *n.* a city in W Upper Volta. Pop.: 78 478 (1970 est.).

bo·bol ('bʌbɔ:l) *Eastern Caribbean.* ~*n.* **1.** a fraud carried out by one or more persons with access to public funds in collusion with someone in a position of authority. ~*vb.* **2.** (*intr.*) to commit a bobol. [C20: of uncertain origin]

bob·o·link ('bɒbə,lɪŋk) *n.* an American songbird, *Dolichonyx oryzivorus,* the male of which has a white back and black underparts in the breeding season: family *Icteridae* (American orioles). Also called (U.S.): **reedbird, ricebird.** [C18: of imitative origin]

bo·bo·tie (bʊ'bʊtɪ) *n.* a South African dish consisting of curried mincemeat with a topping of beaten egg baked to a crust. [C19: from Afrikaans, probably from Malay]

bob·owl·er ('bɒb,aʊlə) *n. Midland English dialect.* a large moth. [of uncertain origin]

bob skate *n. Chiefly U.S.* an ice skate with two parallel blades. [C20: from *bob(sled)* + SKATE[1]]

bob·sleigh ('bɒb,sleɪ) *n.* **1.** a racing sledge for two or more people, with a steering mechanism enabling the driver to direct it down a steeply banked ice-covered run. **2.** (esp. formerly) **a.** a sleigh made of two short sledges joined one behind the other. **b.** one of these two short sledges. ~*vb.* **3.** (*intr.*) to ride on a bobsleigh. ~Also called (esp. U.S.): **bob·sled** ('bɒb,slɛd). [C19: BOB[2] + SLEIGH]

bob·stay ('bɒb,steɪ) *n.* a strong stay between a bowsprit and the stem of a vessel for holding down the bowsprit.

bob·sy-die ('bɒbzɪ,daɪ) *n. N.Z. informal.* fuss; confusion; pandemonium (esp. in the phrases **kick up bobsy-die, play bobsy-die**). [from C19 *bob's a-dying*]

bob·tail ('bɒb,teɪl) *n.* **1.** a docked or diminutive tail. **2.** an animal with such a tail. ~*adj. also* **bob·tailed. 3.** having the tail cut short. ~*vb.* (*tr.*) **4.** to dock the tail of. **5.** to cut short; curtail.

bob·white ('bɒb,waɪt) *n.* a brown North American quail, *Colinus virginianus,* the male of which has white markings on the head: a popular game bird. [C19: of imitative origin]

bo·cage (bɒ'kɑ:ʒ) *n.* **1.** the wooded countryside characteristic of northern France, with small irregular-shaped fields and many hedges and copses. **2.** woodland scenery represented in ceramics. [C17: from French, from Old French *bosc;* see BOSCAGE]

Boc·cac·cio (*Italian* bok'kattʃo) *n.* **Gio·van·ni** (dʒo'vanni). 1313–75, Italian poet and writer, noted particularly for his *Decameron* (1353), a collection of 100 short stories. His other works include *Filostrato* (?1338) and *Teseida* (1341).

Boc·che·ri·ni (*Italian* ,bokke'ri:ni) *n.* **Lu·i·gi** (lu'i:dʒi). 1743–1805, Italian composer and cellist.

boc·cie, boc·ci, boc·ce ('bɒtʃi:), *or* **boc·cia** ('bɒtʃə) *n.* an Italian version of bowls played on a lawn shorter and narrower than a bowling green. [from Italian *bocce* bowls, plural of *boccia* ball; see BOSS[2]]

Boc·cio·ni (*Italian* bot'tʃo:ni) *n.* **Um·ber·to** (um'bɛrto). 1882–1916, Italian painter and sculptor: principal theorist of the futurist movement.

Boche (bɒʃ) *n. Derogatory slang.* (esp. in World Wars I and II) **1.** a German, esp. a German soldier. **2. the.** (*usually functioning as pl.*) Germans collectively, esp. German soldiers regarded as the enemy. [C20: from French, probably shortened from *alboche* German, from *allemand* German + *caboche* pate]

Bo·chum (*German* 'bo:xʊm) *n.* an industrial city in West Germany, in W North Rhine-Westphalia, in the Ruhr Valley. Pop.: 338 022 (1974 est.).

bock beer *or* **bock** (bɒk) *n.* **1.** *U.S.* heavy dark strong beer. **2.** (in France) a light beer. [C19: from German *Bock bier,* literally: buck beer, name given through folk etymology to beer brewed in *Einbeck,* near Hanover]

bod (bɒd) *n. Informal.* a fellow; chap: *he's a queer bod.* [C18: short for BODY]

B.O.D. *abbrev. for* biochemical oxygen demand.

bode[1] (bəʊd) *vb.* **1.** to be an omen of (good or ill, esp. of ill); portend; presage. **2.** (*tr.*) *Archaic.* to predict; foretell. [Old English *bodian;* related to Old Norse *botha* to proclaim, Old Frisian *bodia* to invite] —**'bode·ment** *n.*

bode[2] (bəʊd) *vb.* the past tense of **bide** (senses 1–3).

bo·de·ga (bəʊ'di:gə; *Spanish* bo'ðeγa) *n.* a shop selling wine and sometimes groceries, esp. in a Spanish-speaking country. [C19: from Spanish, ultimately from Greek *apothēkē* storehouse, from *apotithenai* to store, put away]

Bo·den·see ('bo:dᵊn,ze:) *n.* the German name for (Lake) **Constance.**

bodge (bɒdʒ) *vb. Informal.* to make a mess of; botch. [C16: changed from BOTCH]

bodg·er ('bɒdʒə) *adj. Austral. informal.* worthless or second-rate. [C20: from BODGE]

bodg·ie ('bɒdʒɪ) *n. Austral.* an unruly or uncouth young man, esp. in the 1950s; teddy boy. [C20: from BODGE]

Bodh Ga·ya ('bɒd gə'jɑː) *n.* a variant spelling of **Buddh Gaya.**

Bo+dhi+satt+va (ˌbəʊdɪ'sætvə, -wə, ˌbɒd-; ˌbəʊdiː'sʌtvə) *n.* (in Mahayana Buddhism) a divine being worthy of nirvana who remains on the human plane to help men to salvation. Compare **Arhat.** [Sanskrit, literally: one whose essence is enlightenment, from *bodhi* enlightenment + *sattva* essence]

bod+ice ('bɒdɪs) *n.* **1.** the upper part of a woman's dress, from the shoulder to the waist. **2.** a tight-fitting corset worn laced over a blouse, as in certain European national costumes, or (formerly) as a woman's undergarment. [C16: originally Scottish *bodies,* plural of BODY]

-bod·ied *adj.* (*in combination*) having a body or bodies as specified: *able-bodied; long-bodied; many-bodied.*

bod·i+less ('bɒdɪlɪs) *adj.* having no body or substance; incorporeal or insubstantial.

bod·i+ly ('bɒdɪlɪ) *adj.* **1.** relating to or being a part of the human body. ~*adv.* **2.** by taking hold of the body: *he threw him bodily from the platform.* **3.** in person; in the flesh.

bod+kin ('bɒdkɪn) *n.* **1.** a blunt large-eyed needle used esp. for drawing tape through openwork. **2.** *Archaic.* a dagger. **3.** *Printing.* a pointed steel tool used for extracting characters when correcting metal type. **4.** *Archaic.* a long ornamental hairpin. [C14: probably of Celtic origin; compare Gaelic *biodag* dagger]

Bod+lei+an (bɒd'liːən, 'bɒdlɪ-) *n.* the principal library of Oxford University: a copyright deposit library. [C17: named after Sir Thomas *Bodley* (1545–1613), English scholar who founded it in 1602]

Bod+min ('bɒdmɪn) *n.* a market town in SW England, administrative centre of Cornwall, near **Bodmin Moor,** a granite upland rising to 420 m (1375 ft.). Pop.: 9204 (1971).

Bo+do+ni (bə'dəʊnɪ) *n.* a style of type designed by the Italian printer Giambattista **Bodoni** (1740–1813).

bod·y ('bɒdɪ) *n., pl.* **bod·ies. 1. a.** the entire physical structure of an animal or human being. Related adj.: **corporeal. b.** (*as modifier*): *body odour.* **2.** the trunk or torso, not including the limbs, head, or tail. **3.** a dead human or animal; corpse. **4.** the largest or main part of anything: *the body of a vehicle; the body of a plant.* **5.** a separate or distinct mass of water or land. **6.** the main part; majority: *the body of public opinion was against the plan.* **7.** the central part of a written work or document: *the body of a thesis as opposed to the footnotes.* **8.** a number of individuals regarded as a single entity; group: *the student body; they marched in a body to London.* **9.** *Physics.* an object or substance that has three dimensions, a mass, and is distinguishable from surrounding objects. **10.** the characteristic full quality of certain wines, determined by the density and the content of alcohol or tannin: *a Burgundy has a heavy body.* **11.** substance or firmness, esp. of cloth. **12.** the sound box of a guitar, violin, or similar stringed instrument. **13.** the part of a dress covering the body from the shoulders to the waist. **14.** another name for **shank** (sense 11). **15. a.** the pigment contained in or added to paint, dye, etc. **b.** the opacity of a paint in covering a surface. **16.** (in water-colour painting) **a.** a white filler mixed with pigments to make them opaque. **b.** (*as modifier*): *body colour.* See also **gouache. 17.** an informal or dialect word for a **person. 18. keep body and soul together.** to manage to keep alive; survive. **19.** (*modifier*) of or relating to the main reading matter of a book as distinct from headings, illustrations, appendices, etc.: *the body text.* ~*vb.* **bod·ies, bod·y+ing, bod+ied.** (*tr.*) **20.** (usually foll. by *forth*) to give a body or shape to. [Old English *bodig;* related to Old Norse *buthkr* box, Old High German *botah* body]

bod·y blow *n.* a severe disappointment or setback: *unavailability of funds was a body blow to the project.*

bod·y build+ing *n.* the practice of performing regular exercises designed to make the muscles of the body conspicuous.

bod·y cav+i·ty *n.* the internal cavity of any multicellular animal that contains the digestive tract, heart, kidneys, etc. In vertebrates it develops from the coelom.

bod·y-cen·tred *adj.* (of a crystal) having a lattice point at the centre of each unit cell as well as at the corners. Compare **face-centred.**

bod·y+check ('bɒdɪˌtʃɛk) *n.* **1.** *Ice hockey.* obstruction of another player. **2.** *Wrestling.* the act of blocking a charging opponent with the body. ~*vb.* **3.** (*tr.*) to deliver a bodycheck to (an opponent).

bod·y cor+po+rate *n. Law.* a group of persons incorporated to carry out a specific enterprise. See **corporation** (sense 1).

bod·y+guard ('bɒdɪˌgɑːd) *n.* a man or group of men who escort and protect someone, esp. a political figure.

bod·y im+age *n. Psychol.* an individual's concept of his own body.

bod·y lan+guage *n.* the nonverbal imparting of information by means of conscious or subconscious bodily gestures, posture, etc.

bod·y-line *adj. Cricket.* denoting or relating to fast bowling aimed at the batsman's body.

Bod·y of Christ *n.* the Christian Church.

bod·y pol·i+tic *n.* **the.** the people of a nation or the nation itself considered as a political entity; the state.

bod·y snatch+er *n.* (formerly) a person who robbed graves and sold the corpses for dissection. **—bod·y snatch+ing** *n.*

bod·y stock+ing *n.* a one-piece undergarment for women, usually of nylon, covering the torso.

bod·y+work ('bɒdɪˌwɜːk) *n.* the external shell of a motor vehicle.

Boehm+ite ('bɜːmaɪt) *n.* a grey, red, or brown mineral that consists of alumina in rhombic crystalline form and occurs in bauxite. Formula: AlO(OH). [C20: from German *Böhmit,* after J. *Böhm,* 20th-century German scientist]

Boe·o+ti·a (bɪ'əʊʃɪə) *n.* **1.** a region of ancient Greece, northwest of Athens. It consisted of ten city-states, which formed the Boeotian League, led by Thebes: at its height in the 4th century B.C. **2.** the ancient name for **Voiotia. —Boe·'o·ti·an** *n.*

Bo·er (buə, 'bəʊə, bɔː) *n.* **1. a.** a descendant of any of the Dutch or Huguenot colonists who settled in South Africa, mainly in Cape Colony, the Orange Free State, and the Transvaal. **b.** (*as modifier*): *a Boer farmer.* [C19: from Dutch *Boer;* see BOOR]

Bo·er War *n.* either of two conflicts between Britain and the South African Boers, the first in 1881 when the Boers sought to regain the independence given up for British aid against the Zulus, the second in 1899, when the Orange Free State and Transvaal declared war on Britain.

Bo·e·thi·us (bəʊ'iːθɪəs) *n.* **A·nic·i·us Man·li·us Sev·e·ri·nus** (ə'nɪsɪəs 'mænlɪəs ˌsɛvə'raɪnəs). ?480–?524 A.D., Roman philosopher and statesman, noted particularly for his work *De Consolatione Philosophiae.* He was accused of treason and executed by Theodoric.

boeuf bour+gui+gnon (*French* bøf burgi'ɲɔ̃) *n.* a casserole of beef, vegetables, herbs, etc., cooked in red wine. Also called: **boeuf à la bourguignonne.** [French: Burgundy beef]

bof+fin ('bɒfɪn) *n. Brit. informal.* a scientist, esp. one carrying out military research. [C20: of uncertain origin]

Bo+fors gun ('bəʊfəz) *n.* an automatic double-barrelled anti-aircraft gun with 40 millimetre bore. [C20: named after *Bofors,* Sweden, where it was first made]

bog (bɒg) *n.* **1.** wet spongy ground consisting of decomposing vegetation, which ultimately forms peat. **2.** an area of such ground. **3.** a place or thing that prevents or slows progress or improvement. **4.** *Brit., Austral.* a slang word for **lavatory** (sense 1). **5.** *Austral. slang.* the act or an instance of defecating. ~See also **bog down, bog in.** [C13: from Gaelic *bogach* swamp, from *bog* soft] **—'bog+gy** *adj.* **—'bog+gi+ness** *n.*

bo+gan ('bəʊgən) *n. Canadian.* (esp. in the Maritime Provinces) a sluggish side stream. Also called: **logan, pokelogan.** [of Algonquian origin]

Bo·garde ('bəʊgɑːd) *n.* **Dirk.** born 1920, British film actor: his films include *The Servant* (1963), *Accident* (1967), and *Death in Venice* (1971).

Bo·gart ('bəʊgɑːt) *n.* **Hum·phrey,** nicknamed *Bogey.* 1899–1957, U.S. film actor: his films include *The Maltese Falcon* (1941), *High Sierra* (1941), *Casablanca* (1942), *The African Queen* (1951), and *The Caine Mutiny* (1954).

bog as+pho+del *n.* either of two liliaceous plants, *Narthecium ossifragum* of Europe or *N. americanum* of North America, that grow in boggy places and have small yellow flowers and grasslike leaves.

Bo+ğaz+köy (*Turkish* bɔː'azkœj) *n.* a village in central Asia Minor: site of the ancient Hittite capital.

bog+bean ('bɒgˌbiːn) *n.* another name for **buckbean.**

bog down *vb.* **bogs, bog+ging, bogged.** (*adv.;* when *tr., often passive*) to impede or be impeded physically or mentally.

bo+gey[1] *or* **bo·gy** ('bəʊgɪ) *n.* **1.** an evil or mischievous spirit. **2.** something that worries or annoys. **3.** *Golf.* **a.** a standard score for a hole or course, regarded as one that a good player should make. **b.** a score of one stroke over par on a hole. Compare **par** (sense 5). **4.** *Slang.* a piece of dried mucus discharged from the nose. **5.** *Military slang.* an unidentified or hostile aircraft. **6.** *Slang.* a detective; policeman. [C19: probably related to BUG[2] and BOGLE; compare BUGABOO]

bo+gey[2] *or* **bo+gie** ('bəʊgɪ) *Austral.* ~*vb.* **1.** to bathe or swim. ~*n.* **2.** a bathe or swim. [C19: perhaps from a native Australian language]

bo+gey hole *n. Austral.* a natural pool used for swimming.

bo·gey+man ('bəʊgɪˌmæn) *n., pl.* **+men.** a person, real or imaginary, used as a threat, esp. to children.

bog+gart ('bɒgət) *n. Northern English dialect.* a ghost or poltergeist. [perhaps from *bog,* variant of BUG[2] + -ARD]

bog+gle ('bɒgᵊl) *vb.* (*intr.;* often foll. by *at*) **1.** to be surprised, confused, or alarmed (esp. in the phrase **the mind boggles**). **2.** to hesitate or be evasive when confronted with a problem. [C16: probably variant of BOGLE]

bo+gie[1] *or* **bo·gy** ('bəʊgɪ) *n.* **1.** an assembly of four or six wheels forming a pivoted support at either end of a railway coach. It provides flexibility on curves. **2.** *Chiefly Brit.* a small railway truck of short wheelbase, used for conveying coal, ores, etc. [C19: of unknown origin]

bo+gie[2] ('bəʊgɪ) *n.* a variant spelling of **bogey**[2].

bog in *vb.* (*intr., adv.*) *Austral. informal.* **1.** to start energetically on a task. **2.** to start eating; tuck in. ~Also (prep.): **bog into.**

bo+gle ('bəʊgᵊl, 'bɒg-) *n.* a dialect or archaic word for **bogey**[1] (sense 1). [C16: from Scottish *bogill,* perhaps from Gaelic; compare Welsh *bygel;* see BUG[2]]

bog moss *n.* another name for **peat moss.**

bog myr+tle *n.* another name for **sweet gale.**

Bog+nor Re+gis ('bɒgnə 'riːdʒɪs) *n.* a resort in S England, in West Sussex on the English Channel. *Regis* was added to the name after King George V's convalescence here in 1929. Pop.: 34 389 (1971).

bog oak *n.* oak or other wood preserved in peat bogs; bogwood.

bo+gong ('bəʊˌgɒŋ) *or* **bu+gong** ('buːˌgɒŋ) *n.* an edible dark-coloured Australian noctuid moth, *Agrotis infusa.*

Bo+gor ('bəʊgɔː) *n.* a city in Indonesia, in W Java: botanical gardens and research institutions. Pop.: 195 882 (1971). Former name: **Buitenzorg.**

bog or+chid *n.* an orchid, *Hammarbya* (or *Malaxis*) *paludosa,* growing in sphagnum bogs in the N hemisphere. It has greenish-yellow flowers and its leaves bear a fringe of tiny bulbils.

Bo·go·tá (ˌbəʊgəˈtɑː; *Spanish* ˌboɣoˈta) *n.* the capital of Colombia, on a central plateau of the E Andes: originally the centre of Chibcha civilization; founded as a city in 1538 by the Spaniards. Pop.: 2 855 065 (1973).

bog·rush (ˈbɒgˌrʌʃ) *n.* a blackish tufted cyperaceous plant, *Schoenus nigricans,* growing on boggy ground.

bog·trot·ter (ˈbɒgˌtrɒtə) *n.* a derogatory term for an Irishman, esp. an Irish peasant.

bo·gus (ˈbəʊgəs) *adj.* spurious or counterfeit; not genuine: *a bogus note.* [C19: from *bogus* apparatus for making counterfeit money; perhaps related to BOGIE[1]] —**ˈbo·gus·ly** *adv.* —**ˈbo·gus·ness** *n.*

bog·wood (ˈbɒgˌwʊd) *n.* another name for **bog oak.**

bo·gy (ˈbəʊgɪ) *n., pl.* **·gies.** a variant spelling of **bogey**[1] or **bogie**[1].

boh (bəʊ) *interj.* a variant spelling of **bo.**

bo·hea (bəʊˈhiː) *n.* a black Chinese tea, once regarded as the choicest, but now as an inferior grade. [C18: from Chinese (Fukien dialect) *bu-i,* from Mandarin Chinese *Wu-i Shan* range of hills on which this tea was grown]

Bo·he·mi·a (bəʊˈhiːmɪə) *n.* **1.** a former kingdom of central Europe, surrounded by mountains: independent from the 9th to the 13th century; belonged to the Hapsburgs from 1526 until 1918. **2.** the Czech-speaking part of W Czechoslovakia, formerly a province (1918–49). From 1939 until 1945 it formed part of the German protectorate of **Bohemia-Moravia.** Czech name: **Čechy.** German name: **Böh·men** (ˈbøːmən). **3.** a district frequented by unconventional people, esp. artists or writers.

Bo·he·mi·an (bəʊˈhiːmɪən) *n.* **1.** a native or inhabitant of Bohemia, esp. of the old kingdom of Bohemia; a Czech. **2.** (*often not cap.*) a person, esp. an artist or writer, who lives an unconventional life. **3.** the Czech language. ~*adj.* **4.** of, relating to, or characteristic of Bohemia, its people, or their language. **5.** unconventional in appearance, behaviour, etc.

Bo·he·mi·an Breth·ren *pl. n.* a Protestant Christian sect formed in the 15th century from various Hussite groups, which rejected oaths and military service and advocated a pure and disciplined spiritual life. It was reorganized in 1722 as the Moravian Church. Also called: **Unitas Fratrem.**

Bo·he·mi·an For·est *n.* a mountain range between SW Czechoslovakia and SE West Germany. Highest peak: Arber, 1457 m (4780 ft.). Czech name: **Čes·ký Les** (ˈtʃɛskiː ˈlɛs). German name: **Böh·mer·wald** (ˈbøːmərˌvalt).

Bo·he·mi·an·ism (bəʊˈhiːmiəˌnɪzəm) *n.* unconventional behaviour or appearance, esp. of an artist.

Böhm (*German* bøːm) *n.* **Karl** (karl). 1894–1981, Austrian orchestral conductor.

Böh·me, Boeh·me (*German* ˈbøːmə), *or* **Böhm** *n.* **Ja·kob** (ˈjaːkɔp). 1575–1624, German mystic.

Böhm flute *n.* a type of flute in which the holes are covered with keys; the standard type of modern flute. [C19: named after Theobald *Böhm* (1793–1881), its inventor]

Bo·hol (bəʊˈhɔːl) *n.* an island of the central Philippines. Chief town: Tagbilaran. Pop.: 683 297 (1970). Area: about 3900 sq. km (1500 sq. miles).

Bohr (bɔː; *Danish* boːr) *n.* **Niels (Henrik David)** (neːls). 1885–1962, Danish physicist, who applied the quantum theory to Rutherford's model of the atom to explain spectral lines: Nobel prize for physics 1922.

Bohr the·o·ry *n.* a theory of atomic structure that explains the spectrum of hydrogen atoms. It assumes that the electron orbiting around the nucleus can exist only in certain energy states, a jump from one state to another being accompanied by the emission or absorption of a quantum of radiation. [C20: after N. BOHR]

bo·hunk (ˈbəʊˌhʌŋk) *n. U.S. derogatory slang.* a labourer from east or central Europe. [C20: blend of *Bo(hemian)* + *Hung(arian),* with alteration of *g* to *k*]

Bo·iar·do (*Italian* boˈjardo) *n.* **Mat·te·o Ma·ri·a** (matˈtɛːo maˈriːa). 1434–94, Italian poet; author of the historical epic *Orlando Innamorato* (1487).

boil[1] (bɔɪl) *vb.* **1.** to change or cause to change from a liquid to a gas, esp. by the application of heat. **2.** to reach or cause to reach boiling point. **3.** to cook or be cooked by the process of boiling. **4.** (*intr.*) to bubble and be agitated like something boiling; seethe: *the ocean was boiling.* **5.** (*intr.*) to be extremely angry or indignant (esp. in the phrase **make one's blood boil**): *she was boiling at his dishonesty.* **6.** (*intr.*) to contain a boiling liquid: *the pot is boiling.* ~*n.* **7.** the state or action of boiling (esp. in the phrases **on the boil, off the boil**). ~See also **boil away, boil down, boil off, boil over, boil up.** [C13: from Old French *boillir,* from Latin *bullīre* to bubble, from *bulla* a bubble] —**ˈboil·a·ble** *adj.* —**ˈboil·ing·ly** *adv.*

boil[2] (bɔɪl) *n.* a red painful swelling with a hard pus-filled core caused by bacterial infection of the skin and subcutaneous tissues, esp. at a hair follicle. Technical name: **furuncle.** [Old English *bȳle;* related to Old Norse *beyla* swelling, Old High German *būlla* bladder, Gothic *ufbauljan* to inflate]

boil a·way *vb.* (*adv.*) to cause (liquid) to evaporate completely by boiling or (of liquid) to evaporate completely.

boil down *vb.* (*adv.*) **1.** to reduce or be reduced in quantity and usually altered in consistency by boiling: *to boil a liquid down to a thick glue.* **2. boil down to. a.** (*intr.*) to be the essential element in something. **b.** (*tr.*) to summarize; reduce to essentials.

Boi·leau (*French* bwaˈlo) *n.* **Ni·co·las** (nikɔˈlɑ). full name *Nicolas Boileau-Despréaux.* 1636–1711, French poet and critic; author of satires, epistles, and *L'Art Poétique* (1674), in which he laid down the basic principles of French classical literature.

boiled shirt *n.* an informal term for **dress shirt.**

boiled sweet *n. Brit.* a hard sticky sweet of boiled sugar with any of various flavourings.

boil·er (ˈbɔɪlə) *n.* **1.** a closed vessel or arrangement of enclosed tubes in which water is heated to supply steam to drive an engine or turbine or provide heat. **2.** a domestic device burning solid fuel, gas, or oil, to provide hot water, esp. for central heating. **3.** a large tub for boiling laundry. **4.** a tough old chicken for cooking by boiling.

boil·er·mak·er (ˈbɔɪləˌmeɪkə) *n.* **1.** a person who works with metal in heavy industry; plater or welder. **2.** a drink of whisky mixed with beer or whisky followed by a beer chaser.

boil·er·plate (ˈbɔɪləˌpleɪt) *n.* a form of mild-steel plate used in the production of boiler shells.

boil·er suit *n. Brit.* a work garment covering the entire body except for the head, hands, and feet.

boil·ing (ˈbɔɪlɪŋ) *adj., adv.* very warm: *a boiling hot day.*

boil·ing point *n.* **1.** the temperature at which a liquid boils at a given pressure, usually atmospheric pressure at sea level; the temperature at which the vapour pressure of a liquid equals the external pressure. **2.** *Informal.* the condition of being angered or highly excited.

boil·ing-wa·ter re·ac·tor *n.* a nuclear reactor using water as coolant and moderator, steam being produced in the reactor itself. Abbrev.: **BWR.**

boil off *vb.* to remove or be removed (from) by boiling: *to boil off impurities.*

boil·o·ver (ˈbɔɪlˌəʊvə) *n. Austral.* a surprising result in a sporting event, esp. in a horse race.

boil o·ver *vb.* (*adv.*) **1.** to overflow or cause to overflow while boiling. **2.** (*intr.*) to burst out in anger or excitement: *she boiled over at the mention of his name.*

boil up *vb.* (*intr., adv.*) *Austral.* to make tea.

bois-brû·lé (ˌbwɑːbruːˈleɪ) *n.* (*sometimes cap.*) *Canadian.* a half-breed of Indian and White (usually French Canadian) ancestry; Métis. Also called: **Brule.** [French, literally: burnt wood]

Bois de Bou·logne (*French* bwa də buˈlɔɲ) *n.* a large park in W Paris, formerly a forest: includes the racecourses of Auteuil and Longchamp.

Boi·se *or* **Boi·se Cit·y** (ˈbɔɪzɪ, -sɪ) *n.* a city in SW Idaho: the state capital. Pop.: 74 990 (1970).

Bois-le-Duc (bwa lə ˈdyk) *n.* the French name for **'s Hertogenbosch.**

bois·ter·ous (ˈbɔɪstərəs, -strəs) *adj.* **1.** noisy and lively; unrestrained or unruly. **2.** (of the wind, sea, etc.) turbulent or stormy. [C13 *boistuous,* of unknown origin] —**ˈbois·ter·ous·ly** *adv.* —**ˈbois·ter·ous·ness** *n.*

Bo·i·to (*Italian* ˈbɔːito) *n.* **Ar·ri·go** (arˈriːgo). 1842–1918, Italian operatic composer and librettist, whose works include the opera *Mefistofele* (1868) and the librettos for Verdi's *Otello* and *Falstaff.*

Bo·kas·sa I (bəˈkæsə) *n.* original name *Jean Bedel Bokassa,* born 1921, emperor of the Central African Empire (1977–79); president for life (1972); deposed 1979.

Bo·kha·ra (bʊˈxɑːrə) *n.* a variant spelling of **Bukhara.**

bok·ma·kie·rie (ˌbɒkməˈkɪərɪ) *n. S. African.* a large yellow shrike, *Telephorus zeylonus,* of southern Africa, known for its melodious song. [C19: from Afrikaans, imitative of its call]

Bok·mål (*Norwegian* ˈbuːkˌmoːl) *n.* one of the two official forms of written Norwegian, closely related to Danish. Also called: **Dano-Norwegian.** Formerly called: **Riksmål.** Compare **Nynorsk.** [Norwegian, literally: book language]

Bol. *abbrev. for* Bolivia(n).

bo·la (ˈbəʊlə) *or* **bo·las** (ˈbəʊləs) *n., pl.* **·las** *or* **·las·es.** a missile used by gauchos and Indians of South America, consisting of two or more heavy balls on a cord. It is hurled at a running quarry, such as an ox or emu, so as to entangle its legs. [Spanish: ball, from Latin *bulla* knob]

Bo·land (ˈbʊəlant) *n.* an area of high altitude in the SW Cape Province of South Africa.

Bo·lan Pass (bəʊˈlɑːn) *n.* a mountain pass in W central Pakistan through the Brahui Range, between Sibi and Quetta, rising to 1800 m (5900 ft.).

bold (bəʊld) *adj.* **1.** courageous, confident, and fearless; ready to take risks. **2.** showing or requiring courage: *a bold plan.* **3.** immodest or impudent: *she gave him a bold look.* **4.** standing out distinctly; conspicuous: *a figure carved in bold relief.* **5.** very steep: *the bold face of the cliff.* **6.** imaginative in thought or expression: *the novel's bold plot.* **7.** *Printing.* set in bold face. ~*n.* **8.** *Printing.* short for **bold face.** [Old English *beald;* related to Old Norse *ballr* dangerous, terrible, *baldinn* defiant, Old High German *bald* bold] —**ˈbold·ly** *adv.* —**ˈbold·ness** *n.*

bold face *n.* **1.** *Printing.* a weight of type characterized by thick heavy lines, as the entry words in this dictionary. Compare **light face.** ~*adj.* **bold·face.** **2.** (of type) having this weight.

bole[1] (bəʊl) *n.* the trunk of a tree. [C14: from Old Norse *bolr;* related to Middle High German *bole* plank]

bole[2] (bəʊl) *or* **bo·lus** *n.* **1.** a reddish soft variety of clay used as a pigment. **2.** a moderate reddish-brown colour. [C13: from Late Latin *bōlus* lump, from Greek *bōlos*]

bo·lec·tion (bəʊˈlɛkʃən) *n. Architect.* a stepped moulding covering and projecting beyond the joint between two members having surfaces at different levels. Also called: **bilection.** [C18: of unknown origin]

bo·le·ro (bəˈlɛərəʊ) *n., pl.* **·ros.** **1.** a Spanish dance, often accompanied by the guitar and castanets, usually in triple time. **2.** a piece of music composed for or in the rhythm of this dance. **3.** (*also* 'bɒlərəʊ) a kind of short jacket not reaching the waist, worn by women. [C18: from Spanish; perhaps related to *bola* ball]

bo·le·tus (bəʊ'li:təs) *n., pl.* **·tus·es** *or* **·ti** (-ˌtaɪ). any saprophytic basidiomycetous fungus of the genus *Boletus*, having a brownish umbrella-shaped cap with spore-bearing tubes in the underside: family *Boletineae*. Many species are edible. [C17: from Latin: variety of mushroom, from Greek *bōlitēs*; perhaps related to Greek *bōlos* lump]

Bo·leyn (bʊ'lɪn, 'bʊlɪn) *n.* **Anne.** 1507–36, second wife of Henry VIII of England; mother of Elizabeth I. She was executed on a charge of adultery.

bo·lide ('bəʊlaɪd, -lɪd) *n.* a large exceptionally bright meteor that often explodes. Also called: **fireball.** [C19: from French, from *bolis* missile; see BALLISTA]

Bol·ing·broke ('bɒlɪŋˌbrʊk) *n.* **1.** the surname of **Henry IV** of England. **2. Hen·ry St. John,** 1st Viscount Bolingbroke. 1678–1751, English politician; fled to France in 1714 and acted as secretary of state to the Old Pretender; returned to England in 1723. His writings include *A Dissertation on Parties* (1733–34) and *Idea of a Patriot King* (1738).

bol·i·var ('bɒlɪˌvɑ:; *Spanish* bo'liβar) *n., pl.* **·vars** *or* **·var·es** (-βares) the standard monetary unit of Venezuela, equal to 100 centimos. [named after Simon BOLIVAR]

Bol·i·var ('bɒlɪˌvɑ:; *Spanish* bo'liβar) *n.* **Si·mon** (si'mon). 1783–1830, South American soldier and liberator. He drove the Spaniards from Venezuela, Colombia, Ecuador, and Peru and hoped to set up a republican confederation, but was prevented by separatist movements in Venezuela and Colombia (1829–30). Upper Peru became a separate state and was called Bolivia in his honour.

Bo·liv·i·a (bə'lɪvɪə) *n.* an inland republic in central S America: original Aymará Indian population conquered by the Incas in the 13th century; colonized by Spain from 1538; became a republic in 1825; consists of low plains in the east, with ranges of the Andes rising to over 6400 m (21 000 ft.) and the Altiplano, a plateau averaging 3900 m (13 000 ft.) in the west; contains some of the world's highest inhabited regions; important producer of tin and other minerals. Official languages: Spanish, Quechua, and Aymara. Religion: Roman Catholic. Currency: peso. Capital: La Paz. Pop.: 5 063 000 (1971 est.). Area: 1 098 580 sq. km (424 260 sq. miles). —**Bo·'liv·i·an** *adj., n.*

bo·li·vi·a·no (bəʊˌlɪvi:'ɑ:nəʊ; *Spanish* ˌboli'βjano) *n., pl.* **·nos.** See **peso.**

boll (bəʊl) *n.* the fruit of such plants as flax and cotton, consisting of a rounded capsule containing the seeds. [C13: from Dutch *bolle*; related to Old English *bolla* BOWL[1]]

Böll (*German* bœl) *n.* **Hein·rich** ('haɪnrɪç). born 1917, German novelist and short-story writer; his novels include *Gruppenbild mit Dame* (1971): Nobel prize for literature (1972).

bol·lard ('bɒlɑ:d, 'bɒləd) *n.* **1.** a strong wooden or metal post mounted on a wharf, quay, etc., used for securing mooring lines. **2.** *Brit.* a small post or marker placed on a kerb or traffic island to make it conspicuous to motorists. **3.** *Mountaineering.* an outcrop of rock or pillar of ice that may be used to belay a rope. [C14: perhaps from BOLE[1] + -ARD]

bol·locks ('bɒləks), **bal·locks,** *or U.S.* **bol·lix** *Taboo slang.* ~*pl. n.* **1.** another word for **testicles.** ~*interj.* **2.** an exclamation of annoyance, disbelief, etc. ~*vb.* (usually foll. by *up*) **3.** to muddle or botch. [Old English *beallucas*, diminutive (pl.) of *beallu* (unattested); see BALL[1]]

boll wee·vil *n.* a greyish weevil, *Anthonomus grandis*, of the southern U.S. and Mexico, whose larvae live in and destroy cotton bolls. See also **weevil** (sense 1).

boll·worm ('bəʊlˌwɜ:m) *n.* any of various moth caterpillars, such as *Pectinophora* (or *Platyedra*) *gossypiella* (**pink bollworm**), that feed on and destroy cotton bolls.

bo·lo ('bəʊləʊ) *n., pl.* **·los.** a large single-edged knife, originating in the Philippines. [Philippine Spanish, probably from a native word]

Bo·lo·gna (bə'ləʊnjə; *Italian* bo'loɲɲa) *n.* a city in N Italy, at the foot of the Apennines: became a free city in the Middle Ages; university (1088). Pop.: 491 330 (1975 est.). Ancient name: **Bononia.** —**Bo·lo·gnese** (ˌbɒlə'ni:z, -'neɪz) *adj., n.*

bo·lo·gna sau·sage *n. Chiefly U.S.* a large smoked sausage made of seasoned mixed meats. Also called: **baloney, boloney, polony.**

bo·lom·e·ter (bəʊ'lɒmɪtə) *n.* a sensitive instrument for measuring radiant energy by the increase in the resistance of an electrical conductor. [C19: from *bol-*, from Greek *bolē* ray of light, stroke, from *ballein* to throw + -METER] —**bo·lo·met·ric** (ˌbəʊlə'mɛtrɪk) *adj.* —ˌ**bo·lo·'met·ri·cal·ly** *adv.* —**bo·'lom·e·try** *n.*

bo·lo·ney (bə'ləʊnɪ) *n.* another name for **bologna sausage.**

Bol·she·vik ('bɒlʃɪvɪk) *n., pl.* **·viks** *or* **·vi·ki** (-'vi:kɪ). **1.** (formerly) a Russian Communist. Compare **Menshevik. 2.** any Communist. **3.** (*often not cap.*) *Informal and derogatory.* any political radical, esp. a revolutionary. [C20: from Russian *Bol'shevik* majority, from *bol'shoi* great; from the fact that this group formed a majority of the Russian Social Democratic Party in 1903] —'**Bol·she·ˌvism** *n.* —'**Bol·she·ˌvist** *adj., n.* —ˌ**Bol·she·'vis·tic** *adj.*

bol·shie *or* **bol·shy** ('bɒlʃɪ) (*sometimes cap.*) *Brit. informal.* ~*adj.* **1.** difficult to manage; rebellious. **2.** politically radical or left-wing. ~*n., pl.* **·shies. 3.** *Derogatory.* any political radical. [C20: shortened from BOLSHEVIK]

bol·son (bəʊl'səʊn) *n. Southwestern U.S.* a desert valley surrounded by mountains, with a shallow lake at the centre. [C19: from American Spanish *bolsón*, from Spanish *bolsa* purse, from Late Latin *bursa* bag; see PURSE]

bol·ster ('bəʊlstə) *vb.* (*tr.*). **1.** (often foll. by *up*) to support or reinforce; strengthen: *to bolster morale.* **2.** to prop up with a pillow or cushion. **3.** to add padding to: *to bolster a dress.* ~*n.* **4.** a long narrow pillow or cushion. **5.** any pad or padded support. **6.** *Architect.* a short horizontal length of timber fixed to the top of a post to increase the bearing area and reduce the span of the supported beam. **7.** a cold chisel having a broad blade splayed towards the cutting edge, used for cutting stone slabs, etc. [Old English *bolster*; related to Old Norse *bolstr*, Old High German *bolstar*, Dutch *bulster*] —'**bol·ster·er** *n.* —'**bol·ster·ing·ly** *adv.*

bolt[1] (bəʊlt) *n.* **1.** a bar that can be slid into a socket to lock a door, gate, etc. **2.** a bar or rod that forms part of a locking mechanism and is moved by a key or a knob. **3.** a metal rod or pin that has a head at one end and a screw thread at the other to take a nut. **4.** a sliding bar in a breech-loading firearm that ejects the empty cartridge, replaces it with a new one, and closes the breech. **5.** a flash of lightning. **6. a bolt from the blue.** a sudden, unexpected, and usually unwelcome event. **7.** a sudden start or movement, esp. in order to escape: *they made a bolt for the door.* **8.** an unexpected or sudden happening. **9.** *U.S.* a sudden desertion, esp. from a political party. **10.** a roll of something, such as cloth, wallpaper, etc. **11.** an arrow, esp. for a crossbow. **12. shoot one's bolt.** to exhaust one's efforts: *the runner had shot his bolt.* ~*vb.* **13.** (*tr.*) to secure or lock with or as with a bolt or bolts: *bolt your doors.* **14.** (*tr.*) to eat hurriedly: *don't bolt your food.* **15.** (*intr.*; usually foll. by *from* or *out*) to move or jump suddenly: *he bolted from the chair.* **16.** (*intr.*) (esp. of a horse) to start hurriedly and run away without warning. **17.** (*tr.*) to roll or make (cloth, wallpaper, etc.) into bolts. **18.** *U.S.* to desert (a political party, etc.). **19.** (*intr.*) (of cultivated plants) to produce flowers and seeds prematurely. ~*adv.* **20.** stiffly, firmly, or rigidly (archaic except in the phrase **bolt upright**). [Old English *bolt* arrow; related to Old High German *bolz* bolt for a crossbow] —'**bolt·er** *n.*

bolt[2] *or* **boult** (bəʊlt) *vb.* (*tr.*) **1.** to pass (flour, a powder, etc.) through a sieve. **2.** to examine and separate. [C13: from Old French *bulter*, probably of Germanic origin; compare Old High German *būtil* bag] —'**bolt·er** *n.*

bolt·er ('bəʊltə) *n. Austral. informal.* **1.** an outsider in a contest or race. **2.** *Archaic.* an escaped convict; bushranger.

bolt hole *n.* a way of escape from danger.

Bol·ton ('bəʊltən) *n.* a city in NW England, in Greater Manchester: centre of the woollen trade since the 14th century; later important for cotton. Pop.: 153 977 (1971).

bol·to·ni·a (bəʊl'təʊnɪə) *n.* any North American plant of the genus *Boltonia*, having daisy-like flowers with white, violet, or pinkish rays: family *Compositae* (composites). [C18: New Latin, named after James *Bolton*, C18 English botanist]

bolt·rope ('bəʊltˌrəʊp) *n. Nautical.* a rope sewn to the foot or luff of a sail to strengthen it.

Boltz·mann (*German* 'bɔltsman) *n.* **Lud·wig** ('lu:tvɪç). 1844–1906, Austrian physicist. He established the principle of the equipartition of energy and developed the kinetic theory of gases with J. C. Maxwell.

Boltz·mann con·stant *n. Physics.* the ratio of the gas constant to the Avogadro constant, equal to $1.380\,622 \times 10^{-23}$ joule per kelvin. Symbol: *k*

bo·lus ('bəʊləs) *n., pl.* **·lus·es. 1.** a small round soft mass, esp. of chewed food. **2.** a large pill or tablet used in veterinary and clinical medicine. **3.** another word for **bole**[2]. [C17: from New Latin, from Greek *bōlos* clod, lump]

Bol·za·no (*Italian* bol'tsa:no) *n.* a city in NE Italy, in Trentino-Alto Adige: belonged to Austria until 1919. Pop.: 107 277 (1975 est.). German name: **Bozen.**

bo·ma ('bɔma) *n.* (in central and E Africa) **1.** an enclosure, esp. a palisade or fence of thorn bush, set up to protect a camp, herd of animals, etc. **2. a.** a police post. **b.** a magistrate's office. [C19: from Swahili]

bomb (bɒm) *n.* **1. a.** a hollow projectile containing explosive, incendiary, or other destructive substance, esp. one carried by aircraft. **b.** (*as modifier*): *bomb disposal; a bomb bay.* **c.** (*in combination*): *a bombload; bombproof.* **2.** any container filled with explosive: *a car bomb; a letter bomb.* **3. the bomb.** a hydrogen or atom bomb considered as the ultimate destructive weapon. **4.** a round or pear-shaped mass of volcanic rock, solidified from molten lava that has been thrown into the air. **5.** *Med.* a container for radioactive material, applied therapeutically to any part of the body: *a cobalt bomb.* **6.** *Brit. slang.* a large sum of money (esp. in the phrase **make a bomb**). **7.** *U.S. slang.* a disastrous failure: *the new play was a total bomb.* **8.** *Austral. slang.* an old or dilapidated motor car. **9. like a bomb.** *Brit. informal.* with great speed or success; very well (esp. in the phrase **go like a bomb**). ~*vb.* **10.** to attack with or as if with a bomb or bombs; drop bombs (on). **11.** (*intr.*; often foll. by *off, along,* etc.) to move or go very quickly. **12.** (*intr.*) *U.S. slang.* to fail disastrously; be a flop: *the new play bombed.* ~See also **bomb out.** [C17: from French *bombe*, from Italian *bomba*, probably from Latin *bombus* a booming sound, from Greek *bombos*, of imitative origin; compare Old Norse *bumba* drum]

bom·ba·ca·ceous (ˌbɒmbə'keɪʃəs) *adj.* of, relating to, or belonging to the *Bombacaceae*, a family of tropical trees, including the kapok tree and baobab, that have very thick stems, often with water-storing tissue. [C19: from New Latin *Bombācāceae*, from Medieval Latin *bombāx* cotton, from Latin *bombyx* silkworm, silk, from Greek *bombux*]

bom·bard *vb.* (bɒm'bɑ:d). (*tr.*) **1.** to attack with concentrated artillery fire or bombs. **2.** to attack with vigour and persistence: *the boxer bombarded his opponent with blows to the body.* **3.** to attack verbally, esp. with questions: *the journalists bombarded her with questions.* **4.** *Physics.* to direct high-energy particles or photons against (atoms, nuclei, etc.), esp. to produce ions or nuclear transformations. ~*n.* ('bɒmbɑːd). **5.** an ancient type of cannon that threw stone balls. [C15: from Old French *bombarder* to pelt, from *bombarde* stone-throwing cannon, probably from Latin *bombus* booming sound; see BOMB] —**bom+'bard+ment** *n.*

bom+bar+dier (ˌbɒmbəˈdɪə) *n.* **1.** the member of a bomber aircrew responsible for aiming and releasing the bombs. **2.** *Brit.* a non-commissioned rank below the rank of sergeant in the Royal Artillery. **3.** Also called: **bombardier beetle.** any of various small carabid beetles of the genus *Brachinus,* esp. *B. crepitans* of Europe, which defend themselves by ejecting a jet of volatile fluid. **4.** *Canadian.* a snow tractor, usually having caterpillar tracks at the rear and skis at the front. [C16: from Old French: one directing a bombard; see BOMBARD]

bom+bar+don ('bɒmbədən, bɒm'bɑːdᵊn) *n.* **1.** a brass instrument of the tuba type, similar to a sousaphone. **2.** a 16-foot bass reed stop on an organ. [C19: from Italian *bombardone;* see BOMBARD]

bom+bast ('bɒmbæst) *n.* **1.** pompous and grandiloquent language. **2.** *Obsolete.* material used for padding. [C16: from Old French *bombace,* from Medieval Latin *bombāx* cotton; see BOMBACACEOUS] —**bom+'bas+tic** *adj.* —**bom+'bas+ti+cal+ly** *adv.*

Bom+bay (bɒm'beɪ) *n.* a port in W India, capital of Maharashtra state, on the Arabian Sea: India's largest city; ceded by Portugal to England in 1661 and of major importance in British India; commercial and industrial centre, esp. for cotton. Pop.: 5 970 575 (1971).

Bom+bay duck *n.* a teleost fish, *Harpodon nehereus,* that resembles and is related to the lizard fishes: family *Harpodontidae.* It is eaten dried with curry dishes as a savoury. Also called: **bummalo.** [C19: changed from *bombil* (see BUMMALO) through association with Bombay, from which it was exported]

bom+ba+zine *or* **bom+ba+sine** (ˌbɒmbəˈziːn, ˈbɒmbəˌziːn) *n.* a twilled fabric, esp. one with a silk warp and worsted weft, formerly worn dyed black for mourning. [C16: from Old French *bombasin,* from Latin *bombȳcinus* silken, from *bombyx* silkworm, silk; see BOMBACACEOUS]

bomb cal·o+rim+e+ter *n. Chem.* a device for determining heats of combustion by igniting a sample in a high pressure of oxygen in a sealed vessel and measuring the resulting rise in temperature: used for measuring the calorific value of foods.

bombe (bɒmb) *n.* **1.** Also called: **bombe glacée.** a dessert of ice cream lined or filled with custard, cake crumbs, etc. **2.** a mould shaped like a bomb in which this dessert is made. [French, literally: BOMB; from its rounded shape]

bom+bé (bɒm'beɪ; *French* bɔ̃'be) *adj.* (of furniture) having a projecting swollen shape. [French, literally: bomb-shaped, from *bombe* BOMB]

bomb+er ('bɒmə) *n.* **1.** a military aircraft designed to carry out bombing missions. **2.** a person who plants bombs. **3.** *Navy slang.* a Polaris submarine.

bomb+ing run *n.* an approach by a bomber to a target.

bom+bor·a (bɒm'bɔːrə) *n. Austral.* **a.** a submerged reef. **b.** a turbulent area of sea over such a reef. [from a native Australian language]

bomb out *vb.* (*adv.; tr., usually passive*) to make homeless by bombing: *24 families in this street have been bombed out.*

bomb+shell ('bɒmˌʃɛl) *n.* **1.** (esp. formerly) a bomb or artillery shell. **2.** a shocking or unwelcome surprise: *the news of his death was a bombshell.* **3.** *Informal.* an attractive girl or woman (esp. in the phrase **blonde bombshell**).

bomb+sight ('bɒmˌsaɪt) *n.* a mechanical or electronic device in an aircraft for aiming bombs.

bomb site *n.* an area where the buildings have been destroyed by bombs.

bom+by+cid ('bɒmbɪsɪd) *n.* **1.** any moth, including the silkworm moth, of the family *Bombycidae,* most of which occur in Africa and SE Asia. ~*adj.* **2.** of, relating to, or belonging to the *Bombycidae.* [C19: from Latin *bombyx* silkworm]

Bo·mu ('bəʊmuː) *or* **Mbo+mu** (ᵊm'bəʊmuː) *n.* a river in central Africa, rising in the SE Central African Empire and flowing west into the Uele River, forming the Ubangi River. Length: about 800 km (500 miles).

Bon[1] (bɔːn) *n.* **1.** Also called: **Feast** (*or* **Festival**) **of Lanterns.** an annual festival celebrated by Japanese Buddhists. **2. a.** the pre-Buddhist priests of Tibet or one such priest. **b.** their religion. [from Japanese *bon* bowl, lantern]

Bon[2] (bɒn) *n.* **Cape.** a peninsula of NE Tunisia.

Bo·na ('bəʊnə) *n.* **Mount.** a mountain in S Alaska, in the Wrangell Mountains. Height: 5005 m (16 420 ft.).

bo·na fi·de ('bəʊnə 'faɪdɪ) *adj.* **1.** real or genuine: *a bona fide manuscript.* **2.** undertaken in good faith: *a bona fide agreement.* [C16: from Latin]

bo·na fi+des ('bəʊnə 'faɪdiːz) *n. Law.* good faith; honest intention. [Latin]

Bon+aire (bɒn'ɛə) *n.* an island in the S West Indies, in the E Netherlands Antilles: one of the Windward Islands. Chief town: Kralendijk. Pop.: 8181 (1972 est.). Area: about 260 sq. km (100 sq. miles).

bo+nan+za (bə'nænzə) *n.* **1.** a source, usually sudden and unexpected, of luck or wealth. **2.** *U.S.* a mine or vein rich in ore. [C19: from Spanish, literally: calm sea, hence, good luck, from Medieval Latin *bonacia,* from Latin *bonus* good + *malacia* dead calm, from Greek *malakia* softness]

Bo·na·parte ('bəʊnəˌpɑːt; *French* bɔna'part) *n.* **1.** See **Napoleon. 2. Jé·rôme** (ʒe'roːm), brother of Napoleon I. 1784–1860, king of Westphalia (1807–13). **3. Jo·seph** (ʒo'zɛf), brother of Napoleon I. 1768–1844, king of Naples (1806–08) and of Spain (1808–13). **4. Louis** (lwi), brother of Napoleon I. 1778–1846, king of Holland (1806–10). **5. Lu·cien** (ly'sjɛ̃), brother of Napoleon I. 1775–1840, prince of Canino.

Bo+na+part+ism ('bəʊnəˌpɑːtɪzəm) *n.* **1.** a political system resembling the rule of Napoleon I: centralized government by a military dictator, who enjoys popular support given expression in plebiscites. **2.** (esp. in France) support for the government or dynasty of Napoleon Bonaparte. —**'Bo+na+ˌpart+ist** *n.*

bo·na va+can+ti·a ('bəʊnə və'kæntɪə) *pl. n. Law.* unclaimed goods.

Bon·a·ven·tu·ra (ˌbɒnəvɛn'tjʊərə) *or* **Bon·a·ven·ture** ('bɒnəˌvɛntʃə) *n.* **Saint,** called *the Seraphic Doctor.* 1221–74, Italian Franciscan monk, mystic, theologian, and philosopher; author of a *Life of St. Francis* and *Journey of the Soul to God.* Feast day: July 14.

bon+bon ('bɒnbɒn) *n.* a sweet. [C19: from French, originally a children's word from *bon* good]

bonce (bɒns) *n. Brit. slang.* the head. [C19 (originally: a type of large playing marble): of unknown origin]

bond (bɒnd) *n.* **1.** something that binds, fastens, or holds together, such as a chain or rope. **2.** (*often pl.*) something that brings or holds people together; tie: *a bond of friendship.* **3.** (*pl.*) something that restrains or imprisons; captivity or imprisonment. **4.** something that governs behaviour; obligation; duty. **5.** a written or spoken agreement, esp. a promise: *marriage bond.* **6.** adhesive quality or strength. **7.** *Finance.* a certificate of debt issued in order to raise funds. It carries a fixed rate of interest and is repayable with or without security at a specified future date. **8.** *Law.* a written acknowledgment of an obligation to pay a sum or to perform a contract. **9.** *Insurance, U.S.* a policy guaranteeing payment of a stated sum to an employer in compensation for financial losses incurred through illegal or unauthorized acts of an employee. **10.** any of various arrangements of bricks or stones in a wall in which they overlap so as to provide strength. **11.** See **chemical bond. 12.** See **bond paper. 13. in bond.** *Commerce.* deposited in a bonded warehouse. ~*vb.* (*mainly tr.*) **14.** (*also intr.*) to hold or be held together, as by a rope or an adhesive; bind; connect. **15.** to put or hold (goods) in bond. **16.** *Law.* to place under bond. **17.** *Finance.* to issue bonds on; mortgage. **18.** to arrange (bricks, etc.) in a bond. [C13: from Old Norse *band;* see BAND[2]]

bond+age ('bɒndɪdʒ) *n.* **1.** slavery or serfdom; servitude. **2.** Also called: **villeinage.** (in medieval Europe) the condition and status of unfree peasants who provided labour and other services for their lord in return for holdings of land.

bond+ed ('bɒndɪd) *adj.* **1.** *Finance.* consisting of, secured by, or operating under a bond or bonds. **2.** *Commerce.* deposited in a bonded warehouse; placed or stored in bond.

bond+ed ware+house *n.* a warehouse in which imported goods are deposited until they are re-exported or duty is paid.

bond+hold·er ('bɒndˌhəʊldə) *n.* an owner of one or more bonds issued by a company or other institution.

bond+maid ('bɒndˌmeɪd) *n.* an unmarried female serf or slave.

bond pa+per *n.* a superior quality of strong white paper, used esp. for writing and typing.

bond+ser·vant ('bɒndˌsɜːvənt) *n.* a serf or slave.

bonds+man ('bɒndzmən) *n., pl.* **+men. 1.** *Law.* a person bound by bond to act as surety for another. **2.** another word for **bondservant.**

bond+stone ('bɒndˌstəʊn) *n.* a long stone or brick laid in a wall as a header. Also called: **bonder.**

bond wash+ing *n.* a series of illegal deals in bonds made with the intention of avoiding taxation.

bone (bəʊn) *n.* **1.** any of the various structures that make up the skeleton in most vertebrates. **2.** the porous rigid tissue of which these parts are made, consisting of a matrix of collagen and inorganic salts, esp. calcium phosphate, interspersed with canals and small holes. **3.** something consisting of bone or a bonelike substance. **4.** (*pl.*) *Informal.* the human skeleton or body: *they laid his bones to rest; come and rest your bones.* **5.** a thin strip of whalebone, light metal, plastic, etc., used to stiffen corsets and brassieres. **6.** (*pl.*) the essentials (esp. in the phrase **the bare bones**): *to explain the bones of a situation.* **7.** (*pl.*) *Informal.* dice. **8.** (*pl.*) an informal nickname for a **doctor. 9. feel in one's bones.** to have an intuition of. **10. have a bone to pick.** to have grounds for a quarrel. **11. make no bones about. a.** to be direct and candid about. **b.** to have no objections to. **12. near** *or* **close to the bone. a.** risqué or indecent: *his jokes are rather near the bone.* **b.** in poverty; destitute. **13. (never) make old bones.** (not) live to a ripe old age. **14. point the bone.** (often foll. by *at*) *Austral.* **a.** to wish bad luck (on) **b.** to threaten to bring about the downfall (of). ~*vb.* (*mainly tr.*) **15.** to remove the bones from (meat for cooking, etc.). **16.** to stiffen (a corset, etc.) by inserting bones. **17.** to fertilize with bone meal. **18.** *Brit.* a slang word for **steal.** ~See also **bone up.** [Old English *bān;* related to Old Norse *bein,* Old Frisian *bēn,* Old High German *bein*] —**'bone+less** *adj.*

Bône (*French* boːn) *n.* a former name of **Annaba.**

bone ash *n.* the residue obtained when bones are burned in air, consisting mainly of calcium phosphate. It is used as a fertilizer and in the manufacture of bone china.

bone+black ('bəʊnˌblæk) *n.* a black residue from the destructive distillation of bones, containing about 10 per cent carbon

and 80 per cent calcium phosphate, used as a decolourizing agent and pigment.
bone chi+na *n.* porcelain containing bone ash.
bone-dry *adj. Informal.* **a.** completely dry: *a bone-dry well.* **b.** (*postpositive*): *the well was bone dry.*
bone+fish ('bəʊn,fɪʃ) *n., pl.* **+fish** *or* **+fish·es. 1.** a silvery marine clupeoid game fish, *Albula vulpes,* occurring in warm shallow waters: family *Albulidae.* **2.** a similar related fish, *Dixonina nemoptera,* of the Pacific Ocean.
bone+head ('bəʊn,hɛd) *n. Slang.* a stupid or obstinate person. —'**bone+,head·ed** *adj.*
bone i·dle *adj.* very idle; extremely lazy.
bone meal *n.* the product of dried and ground animal bones, used as a fertilizer or in stock feeds.
bone of con+ten+tion *n.* the grounds or subject of a dispute.
bone oil *n.* a dark brown pungent oil, containing pyridine and hydrocarbons, obtained by the destructive distillation of bones.
bon+er ('bəʊnə) *n. Slang.* a blunder.
bone+set ('bəʊn,sɛt) *n.* any of various North American plants of the genus *Eupatorium,* esp. *E. perfoliatum,* which has flat clusters of small white flowers: family *Compositae* (composites). Also called: **agueweed, feverwort, thoroughwort.**
bone+set+ter ('bəʊn,sɛtə) *n.* a person who sets broken or dislocated bones, esp. one who has no formal medical qualifications.
bone+shak·er ('bəʊn,ʃeɪkə) *n.* **1.** an early type of bicycle having solid tyres and no springs. **2.** *Slang.* any decrepit or rickety vehicle.
bone up (*adv.;* when *intr.,* usually foll. by *on*) *Informal, chiefly U.S.* to study intensively.
bone+yard ('bəʊn,jɑ:d) *n.* an informal name for a **cemetery.**
bon+fire ('bɒn,faɪə) *n.* a large outdoor fire. [C15: alteration (through influence of French *bon* good) of *bone-fire;* from the use of bones as fuel]
bong (bɒŋ) *n.* **1.** a deep reverberating sound, as of a large bell. ~*vb.* **2.** to make a deep reverberating sound. [C20: of imitative origin]
bon+go[1] ('bɒŋgəʊ) *n., pl.* **+go** *or* **+gos.** a rare spiral-horned antelope, *Boocercus* (or *Taurotragus*) *eurycerus,* inhabiting forests of central Africa. The coat is bright red-brown with narrow vertical stripes. [of African origin]
bon+go[2] ('bɒŋgəʊ) *n., pl.* **+gos** *or* **+goes.** a small bucket-shaped drum, usually one of a pair, played by beating with the fingers. [American Spanish, probably of imitative origin]
bon+go[3] ('bɒŋgəʊ) *Slang.* a head injury. [C20: probably from BONG + -O]
Bon·go ('bɒŋgəʊ) *n.* **Al·bert Ber·nard.** born 1935, Gabonese statesman; president of Gabon since 1967.
Bon·heur (*French* bɔ'nœ:r) *n.* **Ro·sa** (ro'za). 1822–99, French painter of animals.
Bon·hoef·fer (*German* 'bo:nhœfər) *n.* **Die·trich** ('di:trɪç). 1906–45, German Lutheran theologian: executed by the Nazis.
bon+ho+mie ('bɒnə,mɪ; *French* bɔnɔ'mi) *n.* exuberant friendliness. [C18: from French, from *bonhomme* good-humoured fellow, from *bon* good + *homme* man]
Bon·i·face ('bɒnɪ,feɪs) *n.* **Saint.** original name *Wynfrith.* ?680–?755 A.D. Anglo-saxon missionary: archbishop of Mainz (746–755). Feast day: June 5.
Bo+nin Is+lands ('bəʊnɪn) *pl. n.* a group of 27 volcanic islands in the W Pacific: occupied by the U.S. after World War II; returned to Japan in 1968. Largest island: Chichijima. Area: 103 sq. km (40 sq. miles).
bon+ism ('bəʊnɪzəm) *n.* the doctrine that the world is good, although not the best of all possible worlds. [C19: from Latin *bonus* good + -ISM] —'**bon+ist** *n., adj.*
bo+ni+to (bə'ni:təʊ) *n., pl.* **+tos** *or* **+toes. 1.** any of various small tunny-like marine food fishes of the genus *Sarda,* of warm Atlantic and Pacific waters: family *Scombridae* (tunnies and mackerels). **2.** any of various similar or related fishes, such as *Katsuwonus pelamis* (**oceanic bonito**), the flesh of which is dried and flaked and used in Japanese cookery. [C16: from Spanish *bonito,* from Latin *bonus* good]
bonk+ers ('bɒŋkəz) *adj. Slang, chiefly Brit.* mad; crazy. [C20 (originally in the sense: slightly drunk, tipsy): of unknown origin]
bon mot (*French* bɔ̃ 'mo) *n., pl.* **bons mots** (bɔ̃ 'mo). a clever and fitting remark. [French, literally: good word]
Bonn (bɒn; *German* bɔn) *n.* the capital of West Germany, in North Rhine-Westphalia on the Rhine: became the capital in 1949; university (1786). Pop.: 283 260 (1974 est.).
Bon·nard (*French* bɔ'na:r) *n.* **Pierre** (pjɛ:r). 1867–1947, French painter and lithographer, noted for the effects of light and colour in his landscapes and sunlit interiors.
bonne *French.* (bɔn) *n.* a housemaid or female servant. [C18: feminine of *bon* good]
bonne bouche *French.* (bɔn 'buʃ) *n., pl.* ***bonnes bouches*** (bɔn 'buʃ). a tasty titbit or morsel. [literally: good mouth(ful)]
bon+net ('bɒnɪt) *n.* **1.** any of various hats worn, esp. formerly, by women and girls, usually framing the face and tied with ribbons under the chin. **2.** (in Scotland) a flat brimless cap worn by men. **3.** the hinged metal part of a motor vehicle body that provides access to the engine, or to the luggage space in a rear-engined vehicle. **4.** a cowl on a chimney. **5.** *Nautical.* a piece of sail laced to the foot of a foresail to give it greater area in light winds. **6.** *U.S.* a headdress of feathers worn by some tribes of American Indians, esp. formerly as a sign of war. [C14: from Old French *bonet,* from Medieval Latin *abonnis,* of unknown origin]
bon+net mon+key *n.* an Indian macaque, *Macaca radiata,* with a bonnet-like tuft of hair.
bon+net rouge *French.* (bɔnɛ 'ru:ʒ) *n.* **1.** a red cap worn by ardent supporters of the French Revolution. **2.** an extremist or revolutionary. [French, literally: red cap]
bon+ny ('bɒnɪ) *adj.* **+ni+er, +ni+est. 1.** *Scot. and northern Brit. dialect.* beautiful or handsome: *a bonny lass.* **2.** merry or lively: *a bonny family.* **3.** good or fine: *a bonny house.* **4.** (esp. of babies) plump. ~*adv.* **5.** *Informal.* agreeably or well: *to speak bonny.* [C15: from Old French *bon* good, from Latin *bonus*]
Bon+ny ('bɒnɪ) *n.* **Bight of.** a wide bay at the E end of the Gulf of Guinea off the coasts of Nigeria and Cameroon. Former name (until 1975): **Bight of Biafra.**
bon+sai ('bɒnsaɪ) *n., pl.* **+sai. 1.** the art of growing dwarfed ornamental varieties of trees or shrubs in small shallow pots by selective pruning, etc. **2.** a tree or shrub grown by this method. [Japanese: plant grown in a pot, from *bon* basin, bowl + *sai* to plant]
bon+sel·a (bɒn'sɛlə) *n. S. African.* a small gift to a Black African. Also called: **bansela, pasela.** [from a Bantu language]
bon+spiel ('bɒn,spi:l, -spəl) *n.* a curling match. [C16: probably from Low German; compare Flemish *bonespel* children's game; see SPIEL]
bon+te+bok ('bɒntɪ,bʌk) *n., pl.* **+boks** *or* **+bok.** an antelope, *Damaliscus pygargus* (or *dorcas*), of southern Africa, having a deep reddish-brown coat with a white blaze, tail, and rump patch. [C18: Afrikaans, from *bont* pied + *bok* BUCK[1]]
bon ton *French.* (bɔ̃ 'tɔ̃) *n. Literary.* **1.** sophisticated manners or breeding. **2.** fashionable society. [French, literally: good tone]
bo+nus ('bəʊnəs) *n.* **1.** something given, paid, or received above what is due or expected: *a Christmas bonus for all employees.* **2.** *Chiefly Brit.* an extra dividend allotted to shareholders out of profits. **3.** *Insurance, Brit.* a dividend, esp. a percentage of net profits, distributed to policyholders either annually or when the policy matures. **4.** *Brit.* a slang word for a **bribe.** [C18: from Latin *bonus* (adj.) good]
bo+nus is+sue *n. Brit.* an issue of shares made by a company without charge and distributed pro rata among existing shareholders. Also called: **scrip issue.**
bon vi+vant *French.* (bɔ̃ vi'vɑ̃) *n., pl.* ***bons vi+vants*** (bɔ̃ vi'vɑ̃). a person who enjoys luxuries, esp. good food and drink. Also called (but not in French): **bon vi+veur** (,bɒn vi:'vɜ:). [literally: good living (man)]
bon vo+yage (*French* bɔ̃ vwa'ja:ʒ) *interj.* a phrase used to wish a traveller a pleasant journey. [French, literally: good journey]
bon·y ('bəʊnɪ) *adj.* **bon·i+er, bon·i·est. 1.** resembling or consisting of bone or bones. **2.** having many bones. **3.** having prominent bones: *bony cheeks.* **4.** thin or emaciated: *a bony old woman.* **5.** (of fishes) having a skeleton of bone, rather than of cartilage. —'**bon·i·ness** *n.*
bonze (bɒnz) *n.* a Chinese or Japanese Buddhist priest or monk. [C16: from French, from Portuguese *bonzo,* from Japanese *bonsō,* from Chinese *fan sêng,* from *fan* Buddhist (from Sanskrit *brāhmanas* BRAHMAN) + *sêng* MONK]
bon+zer ('bɒnzə) *adj. Austral. slang, archaic.* excellent; very good. [C20: of uncertain origin; perhaps from BONANZA]
boo (bu:) *interj.* **1.** an exclamation uttered to startle or surprise someone, esp. a child. **2.** a shout uttered to express disgust, dissatisfaction, or contempt, esp. at a theatrical production, political meeting, etc. **3. would not say boo to a goose.** is extremely timid or diffident. ~*vb.* **boos, boo+ing, booed. 4.** to shout "boo" at (someone or something), esp. as an expression of disgust, dissatisfaction, or disapproval: *to boo the actors.*
boob (bu:b) *Slang.* ~*n.* **1.** an ignorant or foolish person; booby. **2.** *Brit.* an embarrassing mistake; blunder. **3.** a female breast. ~*vb.* **4.** (*intr.*) *Brit.* to make a blunder. [C20: back formation from BOOBY]
boo+bi+al+la (,bu:bɪ'ælə) *n. Austral.* **1.** another name for **golden wattle** (sense 2). **2.** any of various trees or shrubs of the genus *Myoporum,* esp. *M. insulare.*
boo-boo *n., pl.* **-boos.** an embarrassing mistake; blunder. [C20: perhaps from nursery talk; compare BOOHOO]
boo+book ('bu:bʊk) *n.* a small spotted brown Australian owl, *Ninox boobook.*
boob tube *n. Slang, chiefly U.S.* a television receiver.
boo+by ('bu:bɪ) *n. pl.* **+bies. 1.** an ignorant or foolish person. **2.** *Brit.* the losing player in a game. **3.** any of several tropical marine birds of the genus *Sula:* family *Sulidae,* order *Pelecaniformes* (pelicans, cormorants, etc.). They have a straight stout bill and the plumage is white with darker markings. Compare **gannet.** [C17: from Spanish *bobo,* from Latin *balbus* stammering]
boo+by hatch *n.* **1.** a hoodlike covering for a hatchway on a ship. **2.** *U.S. slang.* a mental hospital.
boo+by prize *n.* a mock prize given to the person having the lowest score or worst performance in a competition.
boo+by trap *n.* **1.** a hidden explosive device primed in such a way as to be set off by an unsuspecting intruder. **2.** a trap for an unsuspecting person, esp. one intended as a practical joke, such as an object balanced above a door to fall on the person who opens it. ~*vb.* **boo·by-trap, -traps, -trap+ping, -trapped. 3.** (*tr.*) to set a booby trap in or on (a building or object) or for (a person).
boo+dle ('bu:dᵊl) *Slang, chiefly U.S.* ~*n.* **1.** money or valuables, esp. when stolen, counterfeit, or used as a bribe. **2.** another word for **caboodle.** ~*vb.* **3.** to give or receive money corruptly or illegally. [C19: from Dutch *boedel* all one's

possessions, from Old Frisian *bōdel* movable goods, inheritance; see CABOODLE]

boo+gie ('bu:gɪ) *vb.* +**gies,** +**gie+ing,** +**gied.** *Slang.* **1.** to dance to pop music. ~*n.* **2.** a session of dancing to pop music.

boo·gie-woo·gie ('bʊgɪ'wʊgɪ, 'bu:gɪ'wu:gɪ) *n.* a style of piano jazz using a dotted bass pattern, usually with eight notes in a bar and the harmonies of the 12-bar blues.

boo+hoo (ˌbu:'hu:) *vb.* +**hoos,** +**hoo+ing,** +**hooed. 1.** to sob or pretend to sob noisily. ~*n., pl.* +**hoos. 2.** (*sometimes pl.*) distressed or pretended sobbing. [C20: nursery talk]

book (bʊk) *n.* **1.** a number of printed or written pages bound together along one edge and usually protected by thick paper or stiff pasteboard covers. See also **hardback, paperback. 2. a.** a written work or composition, such as a novel, technical manual, or dictionary. **b.** (*as modifier*): *the book trade; book reviews.* **c.** (*in combination*): *bookseller; bookshop; bookshelf; bookrack.* **3.** a number of blank or ruled sheets of paper bound together, used to record lessons, keep accounts, etc. **4.** the script of a play or the libretto of an opera, musical, etc. **5.** a major division of a written composition, as of a long novel or of the Bible. **6.** a number of tickets, sheets, stamps, etc., fastened together along one edge. **7.** (in card games) the number of tricks that must be taken by a side or player before any trick has a scoring value: *in bridge, six of the 13 tricks form the book.* **8.** strict or rigid regulations, rules, or standards (esp. in the phrases **according to the book, by the book**). **9.** a source of knowledge or authority: *the book of life.* **10.** a telephone directory (in the phrase **in the book**). **11. an open book.** a person or subject that is thoroughly understood. **12. a closed book.** a person or subject that is unknown or beyond comprehension: *chemistry is a closed book to him.* **13. bring to book.** to reprimand or require (someone) to give an explanation of his conduct. **14. close the books.** *Book-keeping.* to balance accounts in order to prepare a statement or report. **15. cook the books.** *Informal.* to make fraudulent alterations to business or other accounts. **16. in someone's good** (*or* **bad**) **books.** *Informal.* regarded by someone with favour (or disfavour). **17. keep the books.** to keep written records of the finances of a business or other enterprise. **18. on the books. a.** enrolled as a member. **b.** registered or recorded. **19. read (someone) like a book.** to understand (a person, his motives, character, etc.) thoroughly and clearly. **20. suit one's book.** to be pleasing or acceptable to one. **21. throw the book at. a.** to charge with every relevant offence. **b.** to inflict the most severe punishment on. ~*vb.* **22.** to reserve (a place, passage, etc.) or engage the services of (a performer, driver, etc.) in advance: *to book a flight; to book a band.* **23.** (*tr.*) to take the name and address of (a person guilty of a minor offence) with a view to bringing a prosecution: *he was booked for ignoring a traffic signal.* **24.** (*tr.*) (of a football referee) to take the name of (a player) who grossly infringes the rules while playing, three such acts resulting in the player's dismissal from the field. **25.** (*tr.*) *Archaic.* to record in a book. ~See also **book in, book into, book out.** [Old English *bōc;* related to Old Norse *bōk,* Old High German *buoh* book, Gothic *bōka* letter; see BEECH (the bark of which was used as a writing surface)]

book+bind·er ('bʊkˌbaɪndə) *n.* a person whose business or craft is binding books. —**'book+ˌbind+ing** *n.*

book+bind·er·y ('bʊkˌbaɪndərɪ) *n., pl.* **·er·ies.** a place in which books are bound. Often shortened to **bindery.**

book+case ('bʊkˌkeɪs) *n.* a piece of furniture containing shelves for books, often fitted with glass doors.

book club *n.* a club that sells books at low prices to members, esp. on condition that they buy a minimum number.

book end *n.* one of a pair of usually ornamental supports for holding a row of books upright.

book·ie ('bʊkɪ) *n. Informal.* short for **bookmaker.**

book in *vb.* (*adv.*) **1.** to reserve a room for (oneself or someone else) at a hotel. **2.** *Chiefly Brit.* to record something in a book or register, esp. one's arrival at a hotel.

book+ing ('bʊkɪŋ) *n.* **1.** *Chiefly Brit.* **a.** a reservation, as of a table or room in a hotel, seat in a theatre, or seat on a train, aircraft, etc. **b.** (*as modifier*): *the booking office at a railway station.* **2.** *Theatre.* an engagement for the services of an actor or acting company.

book in·to *vb.* (*prep.*) to reserve a room for (oneself or someone else) at (a hotel, etc.).

book+ish ('bʊkɪʃ) *adj.* **1.** fond of reading; studious. **2.** consisting of or forming opinions or attitudes through reading rather than direct personal experience; academic: *a bookish view of life.* **3.** of or relating to books: *a bookish career in publishing.* —**'book+ish+ly** *adv.* —**'book+ish+ness** *n.*

book-keep·ing *n.* the skill or occupation of systematically recording business transactions. —**'book-ˌkeep·er** *n.*

book-learn·ing *n.* **1.** knowledge gained from books rather than from direct personal experience. **2.** formal education.

book+let ('bʊklɪt) *n.* a thin book, esp. one having paper covers; pamphlet.

book+louse ('bʊkˌlaʊs) *n., pl.* +**lice.** any small insect of the order *Psocoptera,* esp. *Trogium pulsatorium* (**common booklouse**), a wingless species that feeds on bookbinding paste, etc.

book+mak·er ('bʊkˌmeɪkə) *n.* a person who as an occupation accepts bets, esp. on horseraces, and pays out to winning betters.

book+mark ('bʊkˌmɑ:k) *or* **book+mark·er** *n.* a strip or band of some material, such as leather or ribbon, put between the pages of a book to mark a place.

book+mo·bile ('bʊkməˌbi:l) *n.* the U.S. word for **mobile library.**

book of ac+count *n.* another name for **journal** (sense 4a.).

Book of Chang·es *n.* another name for the **I Ching.**

Book of Com+mon Prayer *n.* the official book of church services of the Church of England, first published in 1549. The version now in most common use dates from 1662.

Book of Mor+mon *n.* a sacred book of the Mormon Church, believed by Mormons to be a history of certain ancient peoples in America, written on golden tablets (now lost) and revealed by the prophet Mormon to Joseph Smith.

book of o·rig·i+nal en+try *n.* another name for **journal** (sense 4a.).

book out *vb.* (*adv.*) **1.** (*usually intr.*) to leave or cause to leave a hotel. **2.** (*tr.*) to remove (a book or borrowed article) from a library or store and sign for it.

book+plate ('bʊkˌpleɪt) *n.* a label bearing the owner's name and an individual design or coat of arms, pasted into a book.

book scor+pi+on *n.* any of various small arachnids of the order *Pseudoscorpionida* (false scorpions), esp. *Chelifer cancroides,* which are sometimes found in old books, etc.

book+stall ('bʊkˌstɔ:l) *n.* a stall or stand where periodicals, newspapers, or books are sold. U.S. word: **newsstand.**

book to+ken *n. Brit.* a gift token to be exchanged for books.

book val·ue *n.* **1.** the value of an asset of a business according to its books. **2. a.** the net capital value of an enterprise as shown by the excess of book assets over book liabilities. **b.** the value of a share computed by dividing the net capital value of an enterprise by its issued shares. Compare **par value, market value.**

book+worm ('bʊkˌwɜ:m) *n.* **1.** any of various small insects that feed on the binding paste of books, esp. the book louse. **2.** a person excessively devoted to studying.

Boole (bu:l) *n.* **George.** 1815–64, English mathematician. In *Mathematical Analysis of Logic* (1847) and *An Investigation of the Laws of Thought* (1854), he applied mathematical formulae to logic, creating Boolean algebra.

Bool+e·an al+ge+bra ('bu:lɪən) *n.* a system of symbolic logic devised by George Boole to codify nonmathematical logical operations. It is used in computers.

boom[1] (bu:m) *vb.* **1.** to make a deep prolonged resonant sound, as of thunder or artillery fire. **2.** to prosper or cause to prosper vigorously and rapidly: *business boomed.* ~*n.* **3.** a deep prolonged resonant sound: *the boom of the sea.* **4.** the cry of certain animals, esp. the bittern. **5.** a period of high economic growth characterized by rising wages, profits, and prices, full employment, and high levels of investment, trade, and other economic activity. Compare **depression** (sense 6). [C15: perhaps from Dutch *bommen,* of imitative origin]

boom[2] (bu:m) *n.* **1.** *Nautical.* a spar to which a sail is fastened to control its position relative to the wind. **2.** a beam or spar pivoting at the foot of the mast of a derrick, controlling the distance from the mast at which a load is lifted or lowered. **3.** a pole, usually extensible, carrying an overhead microphone and projected over a film or television set. **4. a.** a barrier across a waterway, usually consisting of a chain of connected floating logs, to confine free-floating logs, protect a harbour from attack, etc. **b.** the area so barred off. [C16: from Dutch *boom* tree, BEAM]

boom+er ('bu:mə) *n. Austral.* **1.** a large male kangaroo. **2.** *Informal.* anything exceptionally large.

boom+er+ang ('bu:məˌræŋ) *n.* **1.** a curved flat wooden missile of Australian aborigines, which can be made to return to the thrower. **2.** an action or statement that recoils on its originator. ~*vb.* **3.** (*intr.*) to recoil or return unexpectedly, causing harm to its originator; backfire. [C19: from a native Australian language]

boom+kin ('bu:mkɪn) *n. Nautical.* a short boom projecting from the deck of a ship, used to secure the main-brace blocks or to extend the lower edge of the foresail. [C17: from Dutch *boomken,* from *boom* tree; see BEAM, -KIN]

boom+slang ('bu:mˌslæŋ) *n.* a large greenish venomous arboreal colubrid snake, *Dispholidus typus,* of southern Africa. [C18: from Afrikaans, from *boom* tree + *slang* snake]

boom town *n. Chiefly U.S.* a town that is enjoying sudden prosperity or has grown rapidly.

boon[1] (bu:n) *n.* **1.** something extremely useful, helpful, or beneficial; a blessing or benefit: *the car was a boon to him.* **2.** *Archaic.* a favour; request: *he asked a boon of the king.* [C12: from Old Norse *bōn* request; related to Old English *bēn* prayer]

boon[2] (bu:n) *adj.* **1.** close, special, or intimate (in the phrase **boon companion**). **2.** *Archaic.* jolly or convivial. [C14: from Old French *bon,* from Latin *bonus* good]

boon+docks ('bu:nˌdɒks) *pl. n.* **the.** *U.S. slang.* **1.** wild, desolate, or uninhabitable country. **2.** a remote rural or provincial area. [C20: from Tagalog *bundok* mountain]

boon+dog+gle ('bu:nˌdɒgᵊl) *U.S. slang.* ~*vb.* **1.** (*intr.*) to do futile and unnecessary work. ~*n.* **2.** futile and unnecessary work. [C20: said to have been coined by R. H. Link, American scoutmaster] —**'boon+ˌdog+gler** *n.*

Boone (bu:n) *n.* **Dan+iel.** 1734–1820, American pioneer, explorer, and guide, esp. in Kentucky.

boong (bu:ŋ) *n. Austral. offensive.* a coloured person. [C20: perhaps of native Australian origin]

boor (bʊə) *n.* an ill-mannered, clumsy, or insensitive person. [Old English *gebūr;* related to Old High German *gibūr* farmer, dweller, Albanian *būr* man; see NEIGHBOUR] —**'boor+ish** *adj.* —**'boor+ish+ly** *adv.* —**'boor+ish+ness** *n.*

boost (bu:st) *n.* **1.** encouragement, improvement, or help: *a boost to morale.* **2.** an upward thrust or push: *he gave him a boost over the wall.* **3.** an increase or rise: *a boost in salary.* **4.** the amount by which the induction pressure of a supercharged internal-combustion engine exceeds that of the ambient pressure. ~*vb.* (*tr.*) **5.** to encourage, assist, or improve: *to boost morale.* **6.** to lift by giving a push from below or behind. **7.** to increase or raise: *to boost the voltage in an electrical circuit.* **8.** to cause to rise; increase: *to boost sales.* **9.** to increase the induction pressure of (an internal-combustion engine) above that of the ambient pressure; supercharge. [C19: of unknown origin]

boost·er ('bu:stə) *n.* **1.** a person or thing that supports, assists, or increases power or effectiveness. **2.** Also called: **launching vehicle.** the first stage of a multistage rocket. **3.** *Radio, television.* **a.** a radio-frequency amplifier connected between an aerial and a receiver to amplify weak incoming signals. **b.** a radio-frequency amplifier that amplifies incoming signals, retransmitting them at higher power. **4.** another name for **supercharger. 5.** short for **booster shot.**

boost·er shot *n. Informal.* a supplementary injection of a vaccine given to maintain the immunization provided by an earlier dose.

boot[1] (bu:t) *n.* **1.** a strong outer covering for the foot; shoe that extends above the ankle, often to the knee. See also **chukka boot, top boot, Wellington boot, surgical boot. 2.** *Brit.* an enclosed compartment of a car for holding luggage, etc., usually at the rear. U.S. name: **trunk. 3.** a protective covering over a mechanical device, such as a rubber sheath protecting a coupling joining two shafts. **4.** *U.S.* a rubber patch used to repair a puncture in a tyre. **5.** an instrument of torture used to crush the foot and lower leg. **6.** a protective covering for the lower leg of a horse. **7.** *Informal.* a kick: *he gave the door a boot.* **8.** *Brit. slang.* an ugly person. **9. the boot.** *Slang.* dismissal from employment; the sack. **10. bet one's boots.** to be certain: *you can bet your boots he'll come.* **11. lick the boots of.** to be servile, obsequious, or flattering towards. **12. die with one's boots on. a.** to die while still active. **b.** to die in battle. **13. put the boot in.** *Brit. slang.* **a.** to kick a person, esp. when he is already down. **b.** to harass someone or aggravate a problem. **14. too big for one's boots.** self-important or conceited. **15. the boot is on the other foot** *or* **leg.** the situation is or has now reversed. ~*vb.* (*tr.*) **16.** (esp. in football) to kick. **17.** to equip with boots. **18.** *Informal.* **a.** (often foll. by *out*) to eject forcibly. **b.** to dismiss from employment. [C14 *bote,* from Old French, of uncertain origin]

boot[2] (bu:t) *vb.* (*usually impersonal*) **1.** *Archaic.* to be of advantage or use to (a person): *what boots it to complain?* ~*n.* **2.** *Obsolete.* an advantage. **3.** *Dialect.* something given in addition, esp. to equalize an exchange: *a ten pound boot to settle the bargain.* **4. to boot.** as well; in addition: *it's cold and musty, and damp to boot.* [Old English *bōt* compensation; related to Old Norse *bōt* remedy, Gothic *bōta,* Old High German *buoza* improvement]

boot·black ('bu:tˌblæk) *n.* (esp. formerly) a person who shines boots and shoes.

boot·ed ('bu:tɪd) *adj.* **1.** wearing boots. **2.** *Ornithol.* **a.** (of birds) having an undivided tarsus covered with a horny sheath. **b.** (of poultry) having a feathered tarsus.

boot·ee ('bu:ti:, bu:'ti:) *n.* **1.** a soft shoe for a baby, esp. a knitted one. **2.** a boot for women and children, esp. an ankle-length one.

Bo·ö·tes (bəʊ'əʊti:z) *n., Latin genitive* **Bo·ö·tis** (bəʊ'əʊtɪs). a constellation in the N hemisphere lying near Ursa Major and containing the first magnitude star Arcturus. [C17: via Latin from Greek: ploughman, from *boōtein* to plough, from *bous* ox]

booth (bu:ð, bu:θ) *n., pl.* **booths** (bu:ðz). **1.** a stall for the display or sale of goods, esp. a temporary one at a fair or market. **2.** a small enclosed or partially enclosed room or cubicle, such as one containing a telephone (**telephone booth**) or one in which a person casts his vote at an election (**polling booth**). **3.** *Chiefly U.S.* two long high-backed benches with a long table between, used esp. in bars and inexpensive restaurants. **4.** (formerly) a temporary structure for shelter, dwelling, storage, etc. [C12: of Scandinavian origin; compare Old Norse *buth,* Swedish, Danish *bod* shop, stall; see BOWER]

Booth (bu:ð) *n.* **1. Ed·win Thom·as,** son of Junius Brutus Booth. 1833–93, U.S. actor. **2. John Wilkes,** son of Junius Brutus Booth. 1838–65, U.S. actor; assassin of Abraham Lincoln. **3. Ju·ni·us Bru·tus** ('dʒu:nɪəs 'bru:təs). 1796–1852, U.S. actor, born in England. **4. Wil·liam.** 1829–1912, English religious leader; founder and first general of the Salvation Army (1878).

Boo·thi·a Pen·in·su·la ('bu:θɪə) *n.* a peninsula of N Canada: the northernmost part of the mainland of North America, lying west of the **Gulf of Boothia,** an arm of the Arctic Ocean.

boot·jack ('bu:tˌdʒæk) *n.* a device that grips the heel of a boot to enable the foot to be withdrawn easily.

boot·lace ('bu:tˌleɪs) *n.* a strong lace for fastening a boot.

Boo·tle ('bu:tᵊl) *n.* a port in NW England, on the River Mersey adjoining Liverpool. Pop.: 74 208 (1971).

boot·leg ('bu:tˌlɛg) *vb.* **·legs, ·leg·ging, ·legged. 1.** to make, carry, or sell (illicit goods, esp. alcohol). ~*n.* **2.** something made or sold illicitly, such as alcohol during Prohibition in the U.S. ~*adj.* **3.** produced, distributed, or sold illicitly: *bootleg whisky; a bootleg record.* [C17: see BOOT[1], LEG; from the practice of smugglers of carrying bottles of liquor concealed in their boots] —**'boot·ˌleg·ger** *n.*

boot·less ('bu:tlɪs) *adj.* of little or no use; vain; fruitless: *a bootless search.* [Old English *bōtlēas,* from *bōt* compensation; Old Norse *bótalauss*]

boot·lick ('bu:tˌlɪk) *vb. Informal.* to seek favour by servile or ingratiating behaviour towards (someone, esp. someone in authority); toady. —**'boot·ˌlick·er** *n.*

boot·load·er ('bu:tˌləʊdə) *n. Computer technol.* short for **bootstrap loader.**

boots (bu:ts) *n., pl.* **boots.** *Brit.* (formerly) a bootblack who cleans the guest's shoes in a hotel.

boots and all *Austral. informal.* ~*adv.* **1.** making every effort; with no holds barred. ~*adj.* (**boots-and-all** *when prenominal*) **2.** behaving or conducted in such a manner.

boots and sad·dles *n.* a bugle call formerly used in the U.S. Cavalry to summon soldiers to mount.

boot·strap ('bu:tˌstræp) *n.* **1.** a leather or fabric loop on the back or side of a boot for pulling it on. **2. by one's (own) bootstraps.** by one's own efforts; unaided. **3.** (*modifier*) self-acting or self-sufficient, as an electronic amplifier that uses its output voltage to bias its input or a self-consistent theory of nuclear interactions. **4. a.** a technique for loading the first few program instructions into a computer main store to enable the rest of the program to be introduced from an input device. **b.** (*as modifier*): *a bootstrap loader.*

boot tree *n.* **1.** a shoetree for a boot, often having supports to stretch the leg of the boot. **2.** a last for making boots.

boo·ty ('bu:tɪ) *n., pl.* **·ties.** any valuable article or articles, esp. when obtained as plunder. [C15: from Old French *butin,* from Middle Low German *buite* exchange; related to Old Norse *býta* to exchange, *býti* barter]

booze (bu:z) *Informal.* ~*n.* **1.** alcoholic drink. **2.** a drinking bout or party. ~*vb.* **3.** (*usually intr.*) to drink (alcohol), esp. in excess. [C13: from Middle Dutch *būsen*]

booz·er ('bu:zə) *n. Informal.* **1.** a person who is fond of drinking. **2.** *Chiefly Brit. and Austral.* a bar or pub.

booze-up *n. Brit. and Austral. slang.* a drinking spree.

booz·y ('bu:zɪ) *adj.* **booz·i·er, booz·i·est.** *Informal.* inclined to or involving excessive drinking of alcohol; drunken: *a boozy lecturer; a boozy party.* —**'booz·i·ness** *n.*

bop[1] (bɒp) *n.* **1.** a form of jazz originating in the 1940s, characterized by rhythmic and harmonic complexity and instrumental virtuosity. Originally called: **bebop. 2.** *Informal.* a session of dancing to pop music. ~*vb.* **bops, bop·ping, bopped. 3.** (*intr.*) *Informal.* to dance to pop music, as in a discotheque. [C20: shortened from BEBOP] —**'bop·per** *n.*

bop[2] (bɒp) *Informal.* ~*vb.* **bops, bop·ping, bopped. 1.** (*tr.*) to strike; hit. ~*n.* **2.** a blow. [C19: of imitative origin]

bo-peep (ˌbəʊ'pi:p) *n.* **1.** a game for very young children, in which one hides (esp. hiding one's face in one's hands) and reappears suddenly. **2.** *Austral. informal.* a look (esp. in the phrase **have a bo-peep**).

Bo·phu·that·swa·na (ˌbəʊpu:tɑ:t'swɑ:nə) *n.* a Bantustan in N South Africa: consists of six separate areas, the smallest (in the Orange Free State) being about 201 km (125 miles) from the nearest other area in the Bantustan; became an autonomous state in 1977. Capital: Mmabatho. Pop.: 1 200 000 (1977 est.). Area: 40 330 sq. km (15 571 sq. miles).

bor. *abbrev. for* borough.

bo·ra[1] ('bɔ:rə) *n.* (*sometimes cap.*) a violent cold north wind blowing from the mountains to the E coast of the Adriatic, usually in winter. [C19: from Italian (Venetian dialect), from Latin *boreās* the north wind]

bo·ra[2] ('bɔ:rə) *n.* an initiation ceremony of Australian Aborigines, introducing youths to manhood. [from a native Australian language]

Bo·ra Bo·ra ('bɔ:rə 'bɔ:rə) *n.* an island in the S Pacific, in the Society Islands: one of the Leeward Islands. Area: 39 sq. km (15 sq. miles).

bo·ra·cic (bə'ræsɪk) *adj.* another word for **boric.**

bo·ra·cite ('bɔ:rəˌsaɪt) *n.* a white mineral that forms salt deposits of magnesium borate and chloride in cubic crystalline form. Formula: $Mg_6Cl_2B_{14}O_{26}$.

bor·age ('bɒrɪdʒ, 'bʌrɪdʒ) *n.* **1.** a Mediterranean boraginaceous plant, *Borago officinalis,* with star-shaped blue flowers. The young leaves have a cucumber-like flavour and are sometimes used in salads or as seasoning. **2.** any of several related plants. [C13: from Old French *bourage,* perhaps from Arabic *abū 'āraq* literally: father of sweat, from its use as a diaphoretic]

bo·rag·i·na·ceous (bəˌrædʒɪ'neɪʃəs) *adj.* of, relating to, or belonging to the *Boraginaceae,* a family of temperate and tropical typically hairy-leaved flowering plants that includes forget-me-not, lungwort, borage, comfrey, and heliotrope. [C19: from New Latin *Borāgināceae,* from *Borāgō* genus name; see BORAGE]

bo·rak ('bɔ:rək) *n. Austral. slang.* rubbish; nonsense. [from a native Australian language]

bo·rane ('bɔ:reɪn) *n.* any compound of boron and hydrogen, used in the synthesis of other boron compounds and as high-energy fuels. [C20: from BOR(ON) + -ANE]

Bo·rås (*Swedish* bu'ro:s) *n.* a city in SW Sweden, chiefly producing textiles. Pop.: 105 559 (1974 est.).

bo·rate *n.* ('bɔ:reɪt, -ɪt). **1.** a salt or ester of boric acid. Salts of boric acid consist of BO_3 and BO_4 units linked together. ~*vb.* ('bɔ:reɪt). **2.** (*tr.*) to treat with borax, boric acid, or borate.

bo·rax ('bɔ:ræks) *n., pl.* **·rax·es** *or* **·ra·ces** (-rəˌsi:z). **1.** Also called: **tincal.** a soluble readily fusible white mineral consisting of impure hydrated disodium tetraborate in monoclinic crystalline form, occurring in alkaline soils and salt deposits. Formula: $Na_2B_4O_7.10H_2O$. **2.** pure disodium tetraborate. [C14: from Old French *boras,* from Medieval Latin *borax,* from Arabic *būraq,* from Persian *būrah*]

bo·ra·zon ('bɔ:rəˌzɒn, -zᵊn) *n.* an extremely hard form of boron nitride. [C20: from BOR(ON) + AZO- + -ON]

bor·bo·ryg·mus (ˌbɔ:bə'rɪgməs) *n., pl.* **·mi** (-maɪ). rumbling of the stomach. [C18: from Greek] —ˌbor+bo+'ryg+mal *or* ˌbor+bo+'ryg+mic *adj.*

Bor+deaux (bɔː'dəʊ; *French* bɔr'do) *n.* **1.** a port in SW France, on the River Garonne: a major centre of the wine trade. Pop.: 226 281 (1975). **2.** any of several red, white, or rosé wines produced around Bordeaux.

Bor+deaux mix+ture *n. Horticulture.* a fungicide consisting of a solution of equal quantities of copper sulphate and quicklime. [C19: loose translation of French *bouillie bordelaise,* from *bouillir* to boil + *bordelais* of BORDEAUX]

Bor+de·laise (ˌbɔːdə'leɪz; *French* bɔrdə'lɛz) *adj. Cookery.* denoting a brown sauce flavoured with red wine and sometimes mushrooms. [French: of BORDEAUX]

bor+del+lo (bɔː'dɛləʊ) *n., pl.* **+los.** a brothel. Also called (archaic): **bor+del** ('bɔːdᵊl). [C16: from Italian, from Old French *borde* hut, cabin]

bor+der ('bɔːdə) *n.* **1.** a band or margin around or along the edge of something. **2.** the dividing line or frontier between political or geographic regions. **3. a.** a region straddling such a boundary. **b.** (*as modifier*): *border country.* **4. a.** a design or ornamental strip around the edge or rim of something, such as a printed page or dinner plate. **b.** (*as modifier*): *a border illustration.* **5.** a long narrow strip of ground planted with flowers, shrubs, trees, etc., that skirts a path or wall or surrounds a lawn or other area: *a herbaceous border.* ~*vb.* **6.** (*tr.*) to decorate or provide with a border. **7.** (when *intr.*, foll. by *on* or *upon*) **a.** to be adjacent (to); lie along the boundary (of): *his land borders on mine.* **b.** to be nearly the same (as); verge (on): *his stupidity borders on madness.* [C14: from Old French *bordure,* from *border* to border, from *bort* side of a ship, of Germanic origin; see BOARD]

Bor+der ('bɔːdə) *n.* **the. 1.** (*sometimes pl.*) the area straddling the border between England and Scotland. **2.** the region in the Cape Province of South Africa around East London.

bor+de·reau (ˌbɔːdə'rəʊ; *French* bɔrdə'ro) *n., pl.* **·reaux** (-'rəʊ, -'rəʊz; *French* -'ro). a memorandum or invoice prepared for a company by an underwriter, containing a list of reinsured risks. [C20: from French]

bor+der+er ('bɔːdərə) *n.* a person who lives in a border area, esp. the border between England and Scotland.

bor·der+land ('bɔːdəˌlænd) *n.* **1.** land located on or near a frontier or boundary. **2.** an indeterminate region: *the borderland between intellect and intelligence.*

bor·der+line ('bɔːdəˌlaɪn) *n.* **1.** a border; dividing line; line of demarcation. **2.** an indeterminate position between two conditions or qualities: *the borderline between friendship and love.* ~*adj.* **3.** on the edge of one category and verging on another: *a borderline failure in the exam.*

Bor+ders Re+gion *n.* a local government region in S Scotland, formed in 1975 from Berwick, Peebles, Roxburgh, Selkirk, and part of Midlothian: generally hilly with the Merse (fertile lowlands) in the southeast. Administrative centre: Newton St. Boswells. Pop.: 99 917 (1976 est.). Area: 4700 sq. km (1800 sq. miles).

bor+der ter+ri+er *n.* a small rough-coated breed of terrier.

bor+dure ('bɔːdjʊə) *n. Heraldry.* the outer edge of a shield, esp. when decorated distinctively. [C15: from Old French; see BORDER]

bore[1] (bɔː) *vb.* **1.** to produce (a hole) in (a material) by use of a drill, auger, or rotary cutting tool. **2.** to increase the diameter of (a hole), as by an internal turning operation on a lathe or similar machine. **3.** (*tr.*) to produce (a hole in the ground, tunnel, mine shaft, etc.) by digging, drilling, cutting, etc. **4.** (*intr.*) *Informal.* (of a horse or athlete in a race) to push other competitors, esp. in order to try to get them out of the way. ~*n.* **5.** a hole or tunnel in the ground, esp. one drilled in search of minerals, oil, etc. **6. a.** a circular hole in a material produced by drilling or turning. **b.** the diameter of such a hole. **7. a.** the hollow part of a tube or cylinder, esp. of a gun barrel. **b.** the diameter of such a hollow part; calibre. [Old English *borian;* related to Old Norse *bora,* Old High German *borōn* to bore, Latin *forāre* to pierce, Greek *pharos* ploughing, *phárunx* PHARYNX]

bore[2] (bɔː) *vb.* **1.** (*tr.*) to tire or make weary by being dull, repetitious, or uninteresting. ~*n.* **2.** a dull, repetitious, or uninteresting person, activity, or state. [C18: of unknown origin]

bore[3] (bɔː) *n.* a high steep-fronted wave moving up a narrow estuary, caused by the tide. [C17: from Old Norse *bāra* wave, billow]

bore[4] (bɔː) *vb.* the past tense of **bear**[1].

bo+re·al ('bɔːrɪəl) *adj.* of or relating to the north or the north wind. [C15: from Latin *boreās* the north wind]

Bo+re·al ('bɔːrɪəl) *adj.* **1.** of or denoting the northern coniferous forests. **2.** designating a climatic zone having snowy winters and short summers. **3.** designating a dry climatic period from about 7500 to 5500 B.C., characterized by cold winters, warm summers, and a flora dominated by pines and hazels.

Bo·re·as ('bɔːrɪəs) *n. Greek myth.* the god personifying the north wind. [C14: via Latin from Greek]

bore+cole ('bɔːkəʊl) *n.* another name for **kale.**

bore+dom ('bɔːdəm) *n.* the state of being bored; tedium.

bor·ee ('bɔːriː) *n. Austral.* another name for **myall.** [from a native Australian language]

bor+er ('bɔːrə) *n.* **1.** a machine or hand tool for boring holes. **2.** any of various insects, insect larvae, or molluscs that bore into plant material, esp. wood. See also **woodborer, corn borer.**

Borg (bɔːg; *Swedish* bɔrj) *n.* **Björn** (bjœrn). born 1956, Swedish tennis player: Wimbledon champion 1976–80.

Bor+ger+hout (*Flemish* bɔrxər'hɔʊt) *n.* a city in N Belgium, near Antwerp. Pop.: 49 002 (1970).

Bor·ges (*Spanish* 'borxes) *n.* **Jor·ge Luis** ('xorxe lwis). born 1899, Argentinian poet, short-story writer, and literary scholar. The short stories collected in *Ficciones* (1944) he described as "games with infinity".

Bor·ghe·se (*Italian* bor'geːse) *n.* a noble Italian family whose members were influential in Italian art and politics from the 16th to the 19th century.

Borg+holm (*Swedish* 'bɔrjhɔlm) *n.* a port and resort in SE Sweden, on the W coast of Öland Island, of which it is the chief town. Pop.: 6836 (1970).

Bor·gia (*Italian* 'bɔrdʒa) *n.* **1. Ce·sa·re** ('tʃeːzare), son of Rodrigo Borgia (Pope Alexander VI). 1475–1507, Italian cardinal, politician, and military leader; model for Machiavelli's *The Prince.* **2.** his sister, **Lu·cre·zia** (lu'krɛttsja), daughter of Rodrigo Borgia. 1480–1519, Italian noblewoman. Her first marriage (1493) was annulled; her second husband was murdered (1500); she was also said to have committed incest with her father and brother. Her third marriage (1501), to the Duke of Ferrara, was more normal, and she became a patron of the arts and science. **3. Rod·ri·go** (rod'riːgo). See **Alexander VI.**

Bor·glum ('bɔːgləm) *n.* **Gut·zon** ('gʌtsən). 1867–1941, U.S. sculptor, noted for his monumental busts of U.S. presidents carved in the mountainside of Mount Rushmore.

bo+ric ('bɔːrɪk) *adj.* of or containing boron. Also: **boracic.**

bo+ric ac·id *n.* **1.** Also called: **orthoboric acid.** a white soluble weakly acid crystalline solid used in the manufacture of heat-resistant glass and porcelain enamels, as a fireproofing material, and as a mild antiseptic. Formula: H_3BO_3. **2.** any other acid containing boron.

bo+ride ('bɔːraɪd) *n.* a compound in which boron is the most electronegative element. [C19: from BOR(ON) + -IDE]

bor+ing[1] ('bɔːrɪŋ) *n.* **1. a.** the act or process of making or enlarging a hole. **b.** the hole made in this way. **2.** (*often pl.*) a fragment, particle, chip, etc., produced during boring.

bor+ing[2] ('bɔːrɪŋ) *adj.* dull; repetitious; uninteresting.

born (bɔːn) *vb.* **1.** the past participle (in passive usage) of **bear**[1] (sense 4). **2. was not born yesterday.** is not gullible or foolish. ~*adj.* **3.** possessing or appearing to have possessed certain qualities from birth: *a born musician.* **4. a.** being at birth in a particular social status or other condition as specified: *ignobly born.* **b.** (*in combination*): *lowborn.* **5. in all one's born days.** *Informal.* so far in one's life.

Born (bɔːn) *n.* **Max.** 1882–1970, British nuclear physicist, born in Germany, noted for his fundamental contribution to quantum mechanics: Nobel prize for physics 1954.

borne (bɔːn) *vb.* **1.** the past participle of **bear**[1] (for all active uses of the verb; also for all passive uses except sense 5). **2. be borne in on** *or* **upon.** (of a fact, etc.) to be realized by (someone): *it was borne in on us how close we had been to disaster.*

Bor+ne·o ('bɔːnɪˌəʊ) *n.* an island in the W Pacific, between the Sulu and Java Seas, part of the Malay Archipelago: divided into Kalimantan (**Indonesian Borneo**), the Malaysian states of Sarawak and Sabah, and the British-protected sultanate of Brunei; mountainous and densely forested. Area: about 750 000 sq. km (290 000 sq. miles).

bor+ne·ol ('bɔːnɪˌɒl) *n.* a white solid terpene alcohol extracted from the Malaysian tree *Dryobalanops aromatica,* used in perfume and in the manufacture of organic esters. Formula: $C_{10}H_{17}OH$. [C19: from BORNE(O) + -OL[1]]

Born+holm (*Danish* ˌbɔrn'hɔlm) *n.* an island in the Baltic Sea, south of Sweden: administratively part of Denmark. Chief town: Rønne. Pop.: 47 121 (1971). Area: 588 sq. km (227 sq. miles).

Born+holm dis+ease ('bɔːnˌhɒlm)*n.* an epidemic virus infection characterized by pain round the base of the chest.

born+ite ('bɔːnaɪt) *n.* a mineral consisting of a sulphide of copper and iron that tarnishes to purple or dark red. It occurs in copper deposits. Formula: Cu_5FeS_4. Also called: **peacock ore.** [C19: named after I. von *Born* (1742–91), Austrian mineralogist; see -ITE[1]]

Bor+nu ('bɔːnuː) *n.* a state of NE Nigeria, on Lake Chad: the second largest state, formed in 1976 from part of North-Eastern State. Capital: Maiduguri. Pop.: 2 990 526 (1976 est.). Area: 116 589 sq. km (45 006 sq. miles).

Bo·ro·din ('bɒrədɪn; *Russian* bəra'din) *n.* **A·le·ksan·dr Por·fir·e·vich** (alɪk'sandᵊr pərfi'rjevitʃ). 1834–87, Russian composer, whose works include the unfinished opera *Prince Igor,* symphonies, songs, and chamber music.

Bo+ro+di+no (ˌbɒrə'diːnəʊ; *Russian* bərədi'nɔ) *n.* a village in the W Soviet Union, about 110 km (70 miles) west of Moscow: scene of a battle (1812) in which Napoleon defeated the Russians but irreparably weakened his army.

bo+ron ('bɔːrɒn) *n.* a very hard almost colourless crystalline metalloid element that in impure form exists as a brown amorphous powder. It occurs principally in borax and is used in hardening steel. The naturally occurring isotope **boron-10** is used in nuclear control rods and neutron detection instruments. Symbol: B; atomic no.: 5; atomic wt.: 10.81; valency: 3; relative density: 2.34 (crystalline), 2.37 (amorphous); melting pt.: 2300°C; boiling pt.: 2550°C. [C19: from BOR(AX) + (CARB)ON]

bo+ron car+bide *n.* a black extremely hard inert substance having a high capture cross section for thermal neutrons. It is used as an abrasive and refractory and in control rods in nuclear reactors. Formula: B_4C.

bo+ro+ni·a (bə'rəʊnɪə) *n.* any aromatic rutaceous shrub of the Australian genus *Boronia.*

bo+ron ni+tride *n.* a white inert crystalline solid existing both in a graphite-like form and in an extremely hard diamond-like form (borazon). It is used as a refractory, high temperature lubricant and insulator, and heat shield. Formula BN.

bo+ro+sil+i+cate (ˌbɔːrəʊˈsɪlɪkɪt, -ˌkeɪt) *n.* a salt of boric and silicic acids.

bor+ough (ˈbʌrə) *n.* **1.** a town, esp. (in Britain) one that forms the constituency of an M.P. or that was originally incorporated by royal charter. See also **burgh. 2.** any of the 32 constituent divisions that together with the City of London make up Greater London. **3.** any of the five constituent divisions of New York City. **4.** (in the U.S.) a self-governing incorporated municipality. **5.** (in medieval England) a fortified town or village or a fort. **6.** (in New Zealand) a small municipality with a governing body. [Old English *burg;* related to *beorgan* to shelter, Old Norse *borg* wall, Gothic *baurgs* city, Old High German *burg* fortified castle]

bor·ough-Eng·lish *n. English law.* (until 1925) a custom in certain English boroughs whereby the youngest son inherited land to the exclusion of his older brothers. Compare **primogeniture, gavelkind.** [C14: from Anglo-French *tenure en burgh Engloys* tenure in an English borough; so called because the custom was unknown in France]

bor+row (ˈbɒrəʊ) *vb.* **1.** to obtain or receive (something, such as money) on loan for temporary use, intending to give it, or something equivalent or identical, back to the lender. **2.** to adopt (ideas, words, etc.) from another source; appropriate. **3.** *Not standard.* to lend. **4.** *Golf.* to putt the ball uphill of the direct path to the hole: *make sure you borrow enough.* **5.** (*intr.*) *Golf.* (of a ball) to deviate from a straight path because of the slope of the ground. ~*n.* **6.** *Golf.* a deviation of a ball from a straight path because of the slope of the ground: *a left borrow.* **7. living on borrowed time. a.** living an unexpected extension of life. **b.** close to death. [Old English *borgian;* related to Old High German *borgēn* to take heed, give security] —**ˈbor+row+er** *n.*

Usage. See at **lend.**

Bor·row (ˈbɒrəʊ) *n.* **George.** 1803–81, English traveller and writer. His best-known works are the semiautobiographical novels of Gypsy life and language, *Lavengro* (1851) and its sequel *The Romany Rye* (1857).

Bors (bɔːs) *n.* **Sir.** (in Arthurian legend) **1.** one the knights of the Round Table, nephew of Lancelot. **2.** an illegitimate son of King Arthur.

borsch, borsh (bɔːʃ), **borscht** (bɔːʃt), *or* **borshch** (bɔːʃtʃ) *n.* a Russian and Polish soup based on beetroot. [from Russian *borshch*]

bor+stal (ˈbɔːstəl) *n.* (in England) an establishment in which offenders aged 15 to 21 may be detained for corrective training. [C20: named after *Borstal,* village in Kent where the first institution was founded]

bort, boart (bɔːt), *or* **bortz** (bɔːts) *n.* an inferior grade of diamond used for cutting and drilling or, in powdered form, as an industrial abrasive. [Old English *gebrot* fragment; related to Old Norse *brot* piece, Old High German *broz* bud] —**ˈbort·y** *adj.*

bor+zoi (ˈbɔːzɔɪ) *n., pl.* **+zois.** a tall fast-moving breed of dog with a long coat, originally used in Russia for hunting wolves. Also called: **Russian wolfhound.** [C19: from Russian *borzoi,* literally: swift; related to Old Slavonic *brŭzŭ* swift]

bos+cage *or* **bos+kage** (ˈbɒskɪdʒ) *n. Literary.* a mass of trees and shrubs; thicket. [C14: from Old French *bosc,* probably of Germanic origin; see BUSH[1], -AGE]

Bosch (bɒʃ) *n.* **Hier·on·y·mus** (hɪˈrɒnɪməs), original name probably *Jerome van Aken* (or *Aeken*). ?1450–1516, Dutch painter, noted for his macabre allegorical representations of biblical subjects in brilliant transparent colours, esp. the triptych *The Garden of Earthly Delights.*

bosch+bok (ˈbɒʃˌbʌk) *n., pl.* **+boks** *or* **+bok.** *S. African.* another name for **bushbuck.** [Afrikaans]

Bosch pro+cess *n.* an industrial process for manufacturing hydrogen by the catalytic reduction of steam with carbon monoxide. [C20: named after Carl *Bosch* (1874–1940), German chemist]

bosch+vark (ˈbɒʃˌvɑːk) *n. S. African.* another name for **bushpig.** [Afrikaans]

Bose (bəʊs) *n.* **1.** Sir **Ja·ga·dis Chan·dra** (dʒəgəˈdiːs ˈtʃʌndrə). 1858–1937, Indian physicist and plant physiologist. **2. Sa·tyen·dra Nath** (səˈtjɛndrə ˈnɑːθ). 1894–1974, Indian physicist, who collaborated with Einstein in devising Bose-Einstein statistics.

Bose-Ein·stein sta+tis+tics *pl. n.* (*functioning as sing.*) *Physics.* the branch of quantum statistics applied to systems of particles that do not obey the exclusion principle. Compare **Fermi-Dirac statistics.**

bosh[1] (bɒʃ) *n. Informal.* empty or meaningless talk or opinions; nonsense. [C19: from Turkish *boş* empty]

bosh[2] (bɒʃ) *n.* **1.** the lower tapering portion of a blast furnace, situated immediately above the air-inlet tuyères. **2.** the deposit of siliceous material that occurs on the surfaces of vessels in which copper is refined. **3.** a water tank for cooling glass-making tools, etc. **4.** *South Wales dialect.* a kitchen sink or wash basin. [C17: probably from German; compare *böschen* to slope, *Böschung* slope]

bosk (bɒsk) *n. Literary.* a small wood of bushes and small trees. [C13: variant of *busk* BUSH[1]]

bos+ket *or* **bos+quet** (ˈbɒskɪt) *n.* a clump of small trees or bushes; thicket. [C18: from French *bosquet,* from Italian *boschetto,* from *bosco* wood, forest; see BUSH[1]]

Bos+kop (ˈbɒskɒp) *n.* **a.** a prehistoric race of the late Pleistocene period in sub-Saharan Africa. **b.** (*as modifier*): *Boskop man.* [C20: named after *Boskop,* in the Transvaal, where remains of this race were first discovered]

bosk·y (ˈbɒskɪ) *adj.* **bosk·i+er, bosk·i·est.** *Literary.* containing or consisting of bushes or thickets: *a bosky wood.*

bo's'n (ˈbəʊsᵊn) *n. Nautical.* a variant spelling of **boatswain.**

Bos+ni·a (ˈbɒznɪə) *n.* a region of central Yugoslavia: belonged to Turkey (1463–1878), then to Austria-Hungary (1879–1918); now part of Bosnia and Herzegovina. —**ˈBos+ni·an** *adj.*

Bos+ni·a and Her+ze·go+vi+na *or* **Her+ce·go+vi+na** *n.* a constituent republic of Yugoslavia, in the W central part: mostly barren and mountainous, with forests in the east. Capital: Sarajevo. Pop.: 3 746 111 (1971). Area: about 51 500 sq. km (19 900 sq. miles).

bos+om (ˈbʊzəm) *n.* **1.** the chest or breast of a person, esp. (*pl.*) the female breasts. **2.** the part of a woman's dress, coat, etc., that covers the chest. **3.** a protective centre or part: *the bosom of the family.* **4.** the breast considered as the seat of emotions. **5.** (*modifier*) very dear; intimate: *a bosom friend.* ~*vb.* (*tr.*) **6.** to embrace. **7.** to conceal or carry in the bosom. [Old English *bōsm;* related to Old High German *buosam*]

bos+om·y (ˈbʊzəmɪ) *adj.* (of a woman) having large breasts.

bos+on (ˈbəʊzɒn) *n.* any of a group of elementary particles, such as a photon or pion, that has zero or integral spin and obeys the rules of Bose-Einstein statistics. Compare **fermion.** [C20: named after Satyendra Nath BOSE]

Bos+po+rus (ˈbɒspərəs) *or* **Bos+pho+rus** (ˈbɒsfərəs) *n.* **the.** a strait between European and Asian Turkey, linking the Black Sea and the Sea of Marmara.

bos+quet (ˈbɒskɪt) *n.* a variant spelling of **bosket.**

boss[1] (bɒs) *Informal.* ~*n.* **1.** a person in charge of or employing others. **2.** *Chiefly U.S.* a professional politician who controls a party machine or political organization, often using devious or illegal methods. ~*vb.* **3.** to employ, supervise, or be in charge of. **4.** (usually foll. by *around* or *about*) to be domineering or overbearing towards (others). ~*adj.* **5.** *Slang.* excellent; fine: *a boss hand at carpentry; that's boss!* [C19: from Dutch *baas* master; probably related to Old High German *basa* aunt, Frisian *baes* master]

boss[2] (bɒs) *n.* **1.** a knob, stud, or other circular rounded protuberance, esp. an ornamental one on a vault, a ceiling, or a shield. **2.** *Biology.* any of various protuberances or swellings in plants and animals. **3. a.** an area of increased thickness, usually cylindrical, that strengthens or provides room for a locating device on a shaft, hub of a wheel, etc. **b.** a similar projection around a hole in a casting or fabricated component. **4.** a rounded mass of igneous rock, esp. the uppermost part of an underlying batholith. ~*vb.* (*tr.*) **5.** to ornament with bosses; emboss. [C13: from Old French *boce,* from Vulgar Latin *bottia* (unattested); related to Italian *bozza* metal knob, swelling]

boss[3] (bɒs) *or* **boss·y** *n., pl.* **boss·es** *or* **boss·ies.** *U.S.* a calf or cow. [from dialect *buss* calf, perhaps ultimately from Latin *bōs* cow, ox]

BOSS (bɒs) *n. acronym for* Bureau of State Security; a branch of the South African security police.

bos+sa no·va (ˈbɒsə ˈnəʊvə) *n.* **1.** a dance similar to the samba, originating in Brazil. **2.** a piece of music composed for or in the rhythm of this dance. [Portuguese, literally: new voice]

boss+boy (ˈbɒsˌbɔɪ) *n. S. African.* a Black African foreman of a gang of workers.

boss cock·y *n. Austral. informal.* a boss or person in power, esp. an overbearing one.

boss-eyed *adj. Informal.* having a squint. [C19: from *boss* to miss or bungle a shot at a target (dialect)]

boss+ism (ˈbɒsɪzəm) *n. U.S.* the domination or the system of domination of political organizations by bosses.

Bos·suet (*French* bɔˈsɥɛ) *n.* **Jacques Bé·nigne** (ʒɑːk beˈniɲ). 1627–1704, French bishop: noted for his funeral orations.

boss·y[1] (ˈbɒsɪ) *adj.* **boss·i+er, boss·i+est.** *Informal.* domineering, overbearing, or authoritarian. —**ˈboss·i+ly** *adv.* —**ˈboss·i+ness** *n.*

boss·y[2] (ˈbɒsɪ) *adj.* (of furniture) ornamented with bosses.

bos+ton (ˈbɒstən) *n.* **1.** a card game for four, played with two packs. **2.** *Chiefly U.S.* a slow gliding dance, a variation of the waltz.

Bos+ton (ˈbɒstən) *n.* **1.** a port in E Massachusetts, the state capital. Pop.: 618 275 (1973 est.). **2.** a port in E England, in SE Lincolnshire. Pop.: 25 995 (1971).

Bos+ton crab *n.* a wrestling hold in which a wrestler seizes both or one of his opponent's legs, turns him face downwards, and exerts pressure over his back.

Bos+ton i·vy *n.* the U.S. name for **Virginia creeper** (sense 2).

Bos+ton Tea Par+ty *n. American history.* a raid in 1773 made by citizens of Boston (disguised as Indians) on three British ships in the harbour as a protest against taxes on tea and the monopoly given to the East India Company. The contents of several hundred chests of tea were dumped into the harbour.

Bos+ton ter+ri+er *or* **bull** *n.* a short stocky smooth-haired breed of terrier, originally developed by crossing the French and English bulldogs with the English terrier.

bo+sun (ˈbəʊsᵊn) *n. Nautical.* a variant spelling of **boatswain.**

Bos·well (ˈbɒzwəl) *n.* **James.** 1740–95, Scottish author and lawyer, noted particularly for his *Life of Samuel Johnson* (1791). —**Bos+wel+li·an** (bɒzˈwɛlɪən) *adj.*

Bos+worth Field (ˈbɒzwɜːθ, -wəθ) *n. English history.* the site, two miles south of Market Bosworth in Leicestershire, of the battle that ended the Wars of the Roses. Richard III was killed and Henry Tudor was crowned king as Henry VII.

bot[1] *or* **bott** (bɒt) *n.* **1.** the larva of a botfly, which typically develops inside the body of a horse, sheep, or man. **2.** any similar larva. [C15: probably from Low German; related to Dutch *bot*, of obscure origin]

bot[2] (bɒt) *Austral. informal.* ~*vb.* **1.** to scrounge or borrow. **2.** (*intr.*; often foll. by *on*) to scrounge (from); impose (on). ~*n.* **3.** a scrounger. **4. on the bot (for).** wanting to scrounge: *he's on the bot for a cigarette.* [C20: perhaps from BOTFLY, alluding to the creature's bite; see BITE (sense 12)]

bot. *abbrev. for:* **1.** botanical. **2.** botany. **3.** bottle.

B.o.T. *abbrev. for* Board of Trade.

bo·tan·i·cal (bəˈtænɪkᵊl) *or* **bo·tan·ic** *adj.* **1.** of or relating to botany or plants. ~*n.* **2.** any drug that is made from parts of a plant. [C17: from Medieval Latin *botanicus*, from Greek *botanikos* relating to plants, from *botanē* plant, pasture, from *boskein* to feed; perhaps related to Latin *bōs* ox, cow] —**bo·ˈtan·i·cal·ly** *adv.*

bo·tan·i·cal gar·den *n.* a place in which plants are grown, studied, and exhibited.

bot·a·nize *or* **bot·a·nise** (ˈbɒtəˌnaɪz) *vb.* **1.** (*intr.*) to collect or study plants. **2.** (*tr.*) to explore and study the plants in (an area).

bot·a·ny (ˈbɒtənɪ) *n., pl.* **·nies. 1.** the study of plants, including their classification, structure, physiology, ecology, and economic importance. **2.** the plant life of a particular region or time. **3.** the biological characteristics of a particular group of plants. [C17: from BOTANICAL; compare ASTRONOMY, ASTRONOMICAL] —**ˈbot·a·nist** *n.*

Bot·a·ny Bay *n.* **1.** an inlet of the Tasman Sea, on the SE coast of Australia: surrounded by the suburbs of Sydney. **2.** (in the 19th century) a British penal settlement that was in fact at Port Jackson, New South Wales.

Bot·a·ny wool *n.* a fine wool from the merino sheep.

bo·tar·go (bəˈtɑːgəʊ) *n., pl.* **·goes.** a relish consisting of the roe of mullet or tunny, salted and pressed into rolls. [C15: from obsolete Italian, from Arabic *butarkhah*]

botch (bɒtʃ) *vb.* (*tr.*; often foll. by *up*) **1.** to spoil through clumsiness or ineptitude. **2.** to repair badly or clumsily. ~*n.* **3.** a badly done piece of work or repair (esp. in the phrase **make a botch of (something)**). [C14: of unknown origin] —**ˈbotch·er** *n.*

botch·y (ˈbɒtʃɪ) *adj.* **botch·i·er, botch·i·est.** clumsily done or made. —**ˈbotch·i·ly** *adv.* —**ˈbotch·i·ness** *n.*

bo·tel (bəʊˈtɛl) *n.* variant spelling of **boatel.**

bot·fly (ˈbɒtˌflaɪ) *n., pl.* **·flies.** any of various stout-bodied hairy dipterous flies of the families *Oestridae* and *Gasterophilidae*, the larvae of which are parasites of man, sheep, and horses.

both (bəʊθ) *determiner.* **1. a.** the two; two considered together: *both dogs were dirty.* **b.** (*as pronoun*): *both are to blame.* ~*conj.* **2.** (*coordinating*) used preceding words, phrases, or clauses joined by *and*, used to emphasize that not just one, but also the other of the joined elements is included: *both Ellen and Keith enjoyed the play; both new and exciting.* [C12: from Old Norse *bāthir*; related to Old High German *bēde*, Latin *ambō*, Greek *amphō*]

Usage. *Both* is used to refer to two objects, persons, etc., and should be avoided where a group of three or more is involved, as in *both the preface and the two editions of the book were banned. Both* is redundant when employed together with *as well as, equal, equally, alike,* or *together.* Sentences such as *they are both alike, they are both equal,* however, do occur frequently in informal English.

Bo·tha (ˈbɑːtə) *n.* **1. Lou·is.** 1862-1919, South African statesman and general; first prime minister of the Union of South Africa (1910-19). **2. Pie·ter Wil·lem** (ˈpɪːtər). born 1916, South African politician; defence minister 1965; prime minister 1978.

both·er (ˈbɒðə) *vb.* **1.** (*tr.*) to give annoyance, pain, or trouble to; irritate: *his bad leg is bothering him again.* **2.** (*tr.*) to trouble (a person) by repeatedly disturbing; pester: *stop bothering your father!* **3.** (*intr.*) to take the time or trouble; concern oneself: *don't bother to come with me.* **4.** (*tr.*) to make (a person) alarmed or confused: *the thought of her husband's return clearly bothered her.* ~*n.* **5.** a state of worry, trouble, or confusion. **6.** a person or thing that causes fuss, trouble, or annoyance. **7.** *Informal.* a disturbance or fight; trouble (esp. in the phrase **a spot of bother**). ~*interj.* **8.** *Chiefly Brit.* an exclamation of slight annoyance. [C18: perhaps from Irish Gaelic *bodhar* deaf, vexed; compare Old Irish *buadrim* I vex]

both·er·a·tion (ˌbɒðəˈreɪʃən) *n., interj. Informal.* another word for **bother** (senses 5, 8).

both·er·some (ˈbɒðəsəm) *adj.* causing bother; troublesome.

Both·ni·a (ˈbɒθnɪə) *n.* **Gulf of.** an arm of the Baltic Sea, extending north between Sweden and Finland.

Both·well (ˈbɒθwəl, ˈbɒð-) *n.* **Earl of,** title of *James Hepburn.* 1535–78, Scottish nobleman; third husband of Mary Queen of Scots. He is generally considered to have instigated the murder of Darnley (1567).

both·y (ˈbɒθɪ) *n., pl.* **both·ies.** *Chiefly Scot.* a small roughly built shelter or outhouse, esp. a hut on a mountain pasture. [C18: perhaps related to BOOTH]

bo tree (bəʊ) *n.* another name for the **peepul.** [C19: from Sinhalese, from Pali *bodhitaru* tree of wisdom, from Sanskrit *bodhi* wisdom, awakening; see BODHISATTVA]

bot·ry·oi·dal (ˌbɒtrɪˈɔɪdᵊl) *or* **bot·ry·ose** (ˈbɒtrɪˌəʊs, -ˌəʊz) *adj.* (of minerals, parts of plants, etc.) shaped like a bunch of grapes. [C18: from Greek *botruoeidēs*, from *botrus* cluster of grapes; see -OID]

bots (bɒts) *n.* (*functioning as sing.*) a digestive disease of horses and some other animals caused by the presence of botfly larvae in the stomach.

Bot·swa·na (bʊˈtʃwɑːnə; bʊtˈswɑːnə, bɒt-) *n.* a republic in southern Africa: established as the British protectorate of Bechuanaland in 1885 as a defence against the Boers; became an independent state within the Commonwealth in 1966; consists mostly of a plateau averaging 1000 m (3300 ft.), with the extensive Okavango swamps in the northwest and the Kalahari Desert in the southwest. Languages: English and Tswana. Religion: mostly animist. Currency: pula. Capital: Gaborone. Pop.: 608 656 (1971). Area: about 570 000 sq. km (220 000 sq. miles).

bott (bɒt) *n.* a variant spelling of **bot.**

botte *French.* (bɔt) *n. Fencing.* a thrust or hit.

Bot·ti·cel·li (*Italian* ˌbottiˈtʃɛlli) *n.* **San·dro** (ˈsandro). 1444–1510, Italian (Florentine) painter, illustrator, and engraver, noted for the graceful outlines and delicate details of his mythological and religious paintings.

bot·tle[1] (ˈbɒtᵊl) *n.* **1. a.** a vessel, often of glass and typically cylindrical with a narrow neck that can be closed with a cap or cork, for containing liquids. **b.** (*as modifier*): *a bottle rack.* **2.** Also called: **bottleful.** the amount such a vessel will hold. **3. a.** a container equipped with a teat that holds a baby's milk or other liquid; nursing bottle. **b.** the contents of such a container: *the baby drank his bottle.* **4.** short for **magnetic bottle. 5. the bottle.** *Informal.* drinking of alcohol, esp. to excess. ~*vb.* (*tr.*) **6.** to put or place (wine, beer, jam, etc.) in a bottle or bottles. **7.** to store (gas) in a portable container under pressure. **8.** *Slang.* to injure by thrusting a broken bottle into (a person). ~See also **bottle up.** [C14: from Old French *botaille*, from Medieval Latin *butticula*, literally: a little cask, from Late Latin *buttis* cask, BUTT[4]]

bot·tle[2] (ˈbɒtᵊl) *n. Brit. dialect.* a bundle, esp. of hay. [C14: from Old French *botel*, from *botte* bundle, of Germanic origin]

bot·tle·brush (ˈbɒtᵊlˌbrʌʃ) *n.* **1.** any of various Australian myrtaceous shrubs or trees of the genera *Callistemon* and *Melaleuca*, having dense spikes of large red flowers with protruding brushlike stamens. **2.** any of various similar trees or shrubs. **3.** a cylindrical brush on a thin shaft, used for cleaning bottles.

bot·tle-feed *vb.* **-feeds, -feed·ing, -fed.** to feed (a baby) with milk from a bottle instead of breast-feeding.

bot·tle gourd *n.* **1.** an Old World cucurbitaceous climbing plant, *Lagenaria siceraria*, having large hard-shelled gourds as fruits. **2.** the fruit of this plant. ~Also called: **calabash.**

bot·tle green *n., adj.* **a.** a dark green colour. **b.** (*as adj.*): *a bottle-green car.*

bot·tle·neck (ˈbɒtᵊlˌnɛk) *n.* **1. a.** a narrow stretch of road or a junction at which traffic is or may be held up. **b.** the hold up. **2.** something that holds up progress, esp. of a manufacturing process. **3.** *Music.* **a.** the broken-off neck of a bottle placed over a finger and used to produce a buzzing effect in a style of guitar-playing originally part of the American blues tradition. **b.** the style of guitar playing using a bottleneck. ~*vb.* **4.** (*tr.*) *U.S.* to be or cause an obstruction in.

bot·tle·nose dol·phin (ˈbɒtᵊlˌnəʊz) *n.* any dolphin of the genus *Tursiops*, esp. *T. truncatus*, which has been kept in captivity and trained to perform tricks.

bot·tle-o *or* **bot·tle-oh** *n. Austral. informal.* a dealer in empty bottles.

bot·tle par·ty *n.* a party to which guests bring drink.

bot·tler (ˈbɒtᵊlə) *n. Austral. informal.* an excellent or outstanding person or thing.

bot·tle tree *n.* any of several Australian sterculiaceous trees of the genus *Sterculia* (or *Brachychiton*) that have a bottle-shaped swollen trunk.

bot·tle up *vb.* (*tr., adv.*) **1.** to restrain (powerful emotion). **2.** *Informal.* to keep (an army or other force) contained or trapped: *the French fleet was bottled up in Le Havre.*

bot·tle-wash·er *n. Informal.* a menial or factotum.

bot·tom (ˈbɒtəm) *n.* **1.** the lowest, deepest, or farthest removed part of a thing: *the bottom of a hill.* **2.** the least important or successful position: *the bottom of a class.* **3.** the ground underneath a sea, lake, or river. **4. touch bottom.** to run aground. **5.** the inner depths of a person's true feelings (esp. in the phrase **from the bottom of one's heart**). **6.** the underneath part of a thing. **7.** *Nautical.* the parts of a vessel's hull that are under water. **8.** (in literary or commercial contexts) a boat or ship. **9.** *Billiards, etc.* a strike in the centre of the cue ball. **10.** a dry valley or hollow. **11.** the lowest level worked in a mine. **12.** (esp. of horses) staying power; stamina. **13.** *Informal.* the buttocks. **14. at bottom.** in reality; basically or despite appearances to the contrary: *he's a kind man at bottom.* **15. be at the bottom of.** to be the ultimate cause of. **16. get to the bottom of.** to discover the real truth about. **17. knock the bottom out of. a.** to destroy or eliminate. **b.** to show to be of little or no value. ~*adj.* (*prenominal*) **18.** lowest or last: *the bottom price.* **19. bet (*or* put) one's bottom dollar on.** to be absolutely sure of (one's opinion, a person, project, etc.). **20.** of, relating to, or situated at the bottom or a bottom: *the bottom shelf.* **21.** fundamental; basic. ~*vb.* **22.** (*tr.*) to provide (a chair, etc.) with a bottom or seat. **23.** (*tr.*) to discover the full facts or truth of; fathom. **24.** (usually foll. by *on* or *upon*) to base or be founded (on an idea, etc.). **25.** (*intr.*) *Nautical.* to strike the ground beneath the water with a vessel's bottom. **26.** *Austral.* **a.** to mine (a hole, claim, etc.) deep enough to reach any gold there is. **b.** (*intr.*; foll. by *on*) to reach (gold, mud, etc.) on bottoming. [Old English *botm*; related to Old Norse *botn*, Old High German *bodam*, Latin *fundus*, Greek *puthmēn*]

bot·tom drawer *n. Brit.* a container in which a young woman collects linen, cutlery, etc., in anticipation of marriage. U.S. equivalent: **hope chest.**

bot+tom house *n. Caribbean.* **1.** the open space beneath a house built upon high pillars. **2.** such a space partially enclosed and floored for use as servants' quarters.

bot+tom+less ('bɒtəmlɪs) *adj.* **1.** having no bottom. **2.** unlimited; inexhaustible. **3.** very deep.

bot·tom+most ('bɒtəmˌməʊst) *adj.* lowest or most fundamental.

bot+tom out *vb.* (*intr., adv.*) to reach the lowest point.

bot+tom+ry ('bɒtəmrɪ) *n., pl.* **+ries.** *Maritime law.* a contract whereby the owner of a ship borrows money to enable the vessel to complete the voyage and pledges the ship as security for the loan. [C16: from Dutch *bodemerij,* from *bodem* BOTTOM (hull of a ship) + *-erij* -RY]

bot+toms up! *interj.* an informal drinking toast.

Bot+trop (*German* 'bɔtrɔp) *n.* an industrial city in West Germany, in North Rhine-Westphalia in the Ruhr. Pop.: 103 458 (1974 est.).

bot·u+lin ('bɒtjʊlɪn) *n.* a potent toxin produced by the bacterium *Clostridium botulinum* in imperfectly preserved food, etc., causing botulism. [C19: from BOTULINUS]

bot·u+li+nus (ˌbɒtjʊ'laɪnəs) *n., pl.* **+nus·es.** an anaerobic bacterium, *Clostridium botulinum,* whose toxins (botulins) cause botulism: family *Bacillaceae.* [C19: from New Latin, from Latin *botulus* sausage]

bot·u+lism ('bɒtjʊˌlɪzəm) *n.* poisoning from ingestion of botulin, which affects the central nervous system producing difficulty in swallowing, visual disturbances, and respiratory paralysis. [C19: first formed as German *Botulismus* literally: sausage poisoning, from Latin *botulus* sausage]

Bot·vin·nik ('bɒtvɪnɪk) *n.* **Mi·kha·il Moi·se·iv·ich** (mixa'il məi'sjejɪvitʃ). born 1911, Soviet chess player; world champion (1948–57, 1958–60, 1961–63).

Boua+ké (*French* bwa'ke) *n.* a market town in S central Ivory Coast. Pop.: about 100 000 (1969 est.).

bou+chée (buː'ʃeɪ) *n.* a small pastry case filled with a savoury mixture, served hot with cocktails or as an hors d'oeuvre. [French: mouthful]

Bou·cher (*French* bu'ʃe) *n.* **Fran·çois** (frɑ̃'swa). 1703–70, French rococo artist, noted for his delicate ornamental paintings of pastoral scenes and mythological subjects.

Bouches-du-Rhône (*French* buʃ dy 'roːn) *n.* a department of S central France, in Provence-Côte-d'Azur region. Capital: Marseille. Pop.: 1 646 679 (1975). Area: 5284 sq. km (2047 sq. miles).

Bou·ci·cault ('buːsɪˌkəʊ) *n.* **Di·on** ('daɪɒn). original name *Dionysius Lardner Boursiquot.* 1822–90, Irish dramatist and actor. His plays include *London Assurance* (1841), *The Corsican Brothers* (1852), and *The Poor of New York* (1857).

bou+clé ('buːkleɪ) *n.* **1.** a curled or looped yarn or fabric giving a thick knobbly effect. ~*adj.* **2.** of or designating such a yarn or fabric: *a bouclé wool coat.* [French *bouclé* curly, from *boucle* a curl, BUCKLE]

bou+clée ('buːkleɪ) *n.* a support for a cue in billiards formed by doubling the first finger so that its tip is aligned with the thumb at its second joint, to form a loop through which the cue may slide. [from French, literally: curled]

Bou·dic·ca (bəʊ'dɪkə) *n.* See **Boadicea.**

bou+doir ('buːdwɑː, -dwɔː) *n.* a woman's bedroom or private sitting room. [C18: from French, literally: room for sulking in, from *bouder* to sulk]

bouf+fant ('buːfɔːŋ) *adj.* **1.** (of a hair style) having extra height and width through back-combing; puffed out. **2.** (of sleeves, skirts, etc.) puffed out. ~*n.* **3.** a bouffant hair style. [from French, from *bouffer* to puff up]

bouffe (buːf) *n.* See **opéra bouffe.**

Bou+gain+ville[1] ('buːgənˌvɪl) *n.* the largest of the Solomon Islands; a province of Papua New Guinea. Chief town: Kieta. Pop.: 96 363 (1971). Area: about 10 360 sq. km (4000 sq. miles). Now called: **North Solomon Islands Province.**

Bou·gain·ville[2] (*French* bugɛ̃'vil) *n.* **Louis An·toine de** (lwi ɑ̃'twan də). 1729–1811, French navigator.

bou+gain+vil+le·a *or* **bou+gain+vil+lae·a** (ˌbuːgən'vɪlɪə) *n.* any woody nyctaginaceous widely cultivated American vine of the genus *Bougainvillea,* having inconspicuous flowers surrounded by showy red or purple bracts. [C19: New Latin, named after L. A. de BOUGAINVILLE]

bough (baʊ) *n.* any of the main branches of a tree. [Old English *bōg* arm, twig; related to Old Norse *bōgr* shoulder, ship's bow, Old High German *buog* shoulder, Greek *pēkhus* forearm, Sanskrit *bāhu;* see BOW[3], ELBOW]

bought (bɔːt) *vb.* **1.** the past tense and past participle of **buy.** ~*adj.* **2.** purchased from a shop; not homemade.

bought+en ('bɔːtᵊn) *adj.* a dialect word for **bought** (sense 2).

bou+gie ('buːʒiː, buː'ʒiː) *n. Med.* a long slender semiflexible cylindrical instrument for inserting into body passages such as the rectum or urethra to dilate structures, introduce medication, etc. [C18: from French, originally a wax candle from *Bougie,* (Bujiya), Algeria]

bouil+la+baisse (ˌbuːjə'bɛs) *n.* a rich stew or soup of fish and vegetables flavoured with spices, esp. saffron. [C19: from French, from Provençal *bouiabaisso,* literally: boil down]

bouil+lon ('buːjɒn) *n.* a plain unclarified broth or stock. [C18: from French, from *bouillir* to BOIL[1]]

Bou·lan·ger (*French* bulɑ̃'ʒe) *n.* **1. Georges** (ʒɔrʒ). 1837-91, French general and minister of war (1886-87). Accused of attempting a coup d'état, he fled to Belgium, where he committed suicide. **2. Na·dia** ('nadja). 1887-1979, French teacher of musical composition: her pupils include Elliott Carter, Aaron Copland, Darius Milhaud, and Virgil Thomson. She is noted also for her work in reviving the works of Monteverdi.

boul+der ('bəʊldə) *n.* a smooth rounded mass of rock that has been shaped by erosion and transported by ice or water from its original position. [C13: probably of Scandinavian origin; compare Swedish dialect *bullersten,* from Old Swedish *bulder* rumbling + *sten* STONE]

boul+der clay *n.* an unstratified glacial deposit consisting of fine clay, boulders, and pebbles. See also **till**[4].

Boul+der Dam *n.* the former name (1933–47) of **Hoover Dam.**

boule (buːl) *n.* a pear-shaped imitation ruby, sapphire, etc., made from synthetic corundum. [C19: from French: ball]

boules *French.* (bul) *pl. n.* (*construed as sing.*) a game similar to bowls, popular in France, played mainly with metal bowls on rough surfaces. [plural of *boule* BALL[1] see BOWL[2]]

boule+vard ('buːlvɑː, -vɑːd) *n.* **1. a.** a wide usually tree-lined road in a city, often used as a promenade. **b.** (*cap. as part of a street name*): *Sunset Boulevard.* **2.** *Chiefly Canadian.* **a.** a grass strip between the pavement and road. **b.** the centre strip of a road dividing traffic travelling in different directions. [C18: from French, from Middle Dutch *bolwerc* BULWARK; so called because originally often built on the ruins of an old rampart]

boule+var+di+er (buːl'vɑːdɪˌeɪ) *n.* (originally in Paris) a fashionable man, esp. one who frequents public places.

Bou+lez ('buːlɛz; *French* bu'lɛː) *n.* **Pierre** (pjɛːr). born 1925, French composer and conductor, whose works employ total serialization.

boulle, boule, *or* **buhl** (buːl) *adj.* **1.** denoting or relating to a type of marquetry of patterned inlays of brass and tortoiseshell, occasionally with other metals such as pewter, much used on French furniture from the 17th century. ~*n.* **2.** Also called: **boulle+work.** something ornamented with such marquetry. [C18: named after André Charles *Boulle* (1642–1732), French cabinet-maker]

Bou+logne (bʊ'lɔɪn; *French* bu'lɔɲ) *n.* a port in N France, on the English Channel. Pop.: 49 284 (1975). Official name: **Bou·logne-sur-Mer** (*French* bulɔɲsyr'mɛːr).

Bou·logne-Bil·lan+court (*French* bu'lɔɲ bijɑ̃'kuːr) *n.* an industrial suburb of SW Paris. Pop.: 103 948 (1975). Also called: **Bou·logne-sur-Seine** (*French* bulɔɲsyr'sɛn).

boult (bəʊlt) *vb.* a variant spelling of **bolt**[2].

Boult (bəʊlt) *n.* Sir **A·dri·an (Cedric).** 1889–1983, English conductor.

Bou·mé·di·enne (buːˌmeɪdɪ'ɛn) *n.* **Hou·ar·i** ('haʊərɪ). 1927-78, Algerian statesman and soldier: prime minister of Algeria since overthrowing Ben Bella in a coup (1965).

bounce (baʊns) *vb.* **1.** (*intr.*) (of an elastic object, such as a ball) to rebound from an impact. **2.** (*tr.*) to cause (such an object) to hit a solid surface and spring back. **3.** to rebound or cause to rebound repeatedly. **4.** to move or cause to move suddenly, excitedly, or violently; spring: *she bounced up from her chair.* **5.** (*intr.*) *Slang.* (of a cheque) to be sent back by a bank to a payee unredeemed because of lack of funds in the drawer's account. **6.** (*tr.*) *Slang.* to cause (a cheque) to bounce. **7.** (*tr.*) *Slang.* to force (a person) to leave (a place or job); throw out; eject. **8.** (*tr.*) *Brit.* to hustle (a person) into believing or doing something. ~*n.* **9.** the action of rebounding from an impact. **10.** a leap; jump; bound. **11.** the quality of being able to rebound; springiness. **12.** *Informal.* vitality; vigour; resilience. **13.** *Brit.* swagger or impudence. **14. the bounce.** *Australian Rules.* the start of play at the beginning of each quarter or after a goal. **15. get** *or* **give the bounce.** *U.S. informal.* to dismiss or be dismissed from a job. [C13: probably of imitative origin; compare Low German *bunsen* to beat, Dutch *bonken* to thump]

bounce back *vb.* (*intr., adv.*) to recover one's health, good spirits, confidence, etc., easily after a setback.

bounc+er ('baʊnsə) *n.* **1.** *Slang.* a man employed at a club, restaurant, etc., to throw out drunks or troublemakers and stop fights. **2.** *Slang.* a dishonoured cheque. **3.** *Cricket.* another word for **bumper. 4.** a person or thing that bounces.

bounc+ing ('baʊnsɪŋ) *adj.* (when *postpositive,* foll. by *with*) vigorous and robust (esp. in the phrase **a bouncing baby**).

bounc+ing Bet (bɛt) *n.* another name for **soapwort.**

bounc·y ('baʊnsɪ) *adj.* **bounc·i+er, bounc·i+est. 1.** lively, exuberant, or self-confident. **2.** having the capability or quality of bouncing: *a bouncy ball.* **3.** responsive to bouncing; springy: *a bouncy bed.* —**'bounc·i+ly** *adv.* —**'bounc·i+ness** *n.*

bound[1] (baʊnd) *vb.* **1.** the past tense and past participle of **bind.** ~*adj.* **2.** in bonds or chains; tied with or as if with a rope: *a bound prisoner.* **3.** (*postpositive,* foll. by an infinitive) destined; sure; certain: *it's bound to happen.* **4.** (*postpositive,* foll. by *on*) resolved; determined: *bound on winning.* **5.** (*postpositive,* often foll. by *by*) compelled or obliged to act, behave, or think in a particular way, as by duty, circumstance, or convention. **6.** *Rare.* constipated. **7.** (of a book) secured within a cover or binding: *to deliver bound books.* See also **half-bound. 8.** *Linguistics.* denoting a morpheme, such as the prefix *non-,* that occurs only as part of another word and not as a separate word in itself. Compare **free** (sense 19). **9.** *Logic.* denoting an occurrence of a variable within the scope of a quantifier; constrained. Compare **free** (sense 20). **10. bound up with.** closely or inextricably linked with: *his irritability is bound up with his work.*

bound[2] (baʊnd) *vb.* **1.** to move forwards or make (one's way) by leaps or jumps. **2.** to bounce; spring away from an impact. ~*n.* **3.** a jump upwards or forwards. **4. by leaps and bounds.** with sudden irregular rapidity: *her condition improved by leaps* *and bounds.* **5.** a sudden pronounced sense of excitement: *his heart gave a sudden bound when he saw her.* **6.** a bounce, as of a ball. [C16: from Old French *bond* a leap, from *bondir* to jump, resound, from Vulgar Latin *bombitīre* (unattested) to buzz, hum, from Latin *bombus* booming sound]

bound[3] (baʊnd) *vb.* **1.** (*tr.*) to place restrictions on; limit. **2.** (when *intr.*, foll. by *on*) to form a boundary of (an area of land or sea, political or administrative region, etc.). ~*n.* **3.** *Maths.* a number that is greater than or equal to every member of a set of numbers (**upper bound**), or less than or equal to every member of a set of numbers (**lower bound**). **4.** See **bounds.** [C13: from Old French *bonde,* from Medieval Latin *bodina,* of Gaulish origin]

bound[4] (baʊnd) *adj.* **a.** (*postpositive,* often foll. by *for*) going or intending to go towards; on the way to: *a ship bound for Jamaica; homeward bound.* **b.** (*in combination*): *northbound traffic.* [C13: from Old Norse *buinn,* past participle of *būa* to prepare]

bound·a·ry ('baʊndərɪ, -drɪ) *n., pl.* **·ries. 1.** something that indicates the farthest limit, as of an area; border. **2.** *Cricket.* **a.** the marked limit of the playing area. **b.** a stroke that hits the ball beyond this limit. **c.** the four runs scored with such a stroke, or the six runs if the ball crosses the boundary without touching the ground.

bound·a·ry lay·er *n.* the layer of fluid closest to the surface of a solid past which the fluid flows: it has a lower rate of flow than the bulk of the fluid because of its adhesion to the solid.

bound·a·ry rid·er *n. Austral.* an employee on a sheep or cattle station whose job is to maintain fences in good repair and to prevent stock from straying.

bound·en ('baʊndən) *adj.* morally obligatory (archaic except in the phrase **bounden duty**).

bound·er ('baʊndə) *n.* **1.** *Brit. informal, rare.* a morally reprehensible person; cad. **2.** a person or animal that bounds.

bound·less ('baʊndlɪs) *adj.* unlimited; vast: *boundless energy.* —**'bound·less·ly** *adv.* —**'bound·less·ness** *n.*

bounds (baʊndz) *pl. n.* **1.** (*sometimes sing.*) a limit; boundary (esp. in the phrase **know no bounds**). **2.** something that restrains or confines, esp. the standards of a society: *within the bounds of modesty.* ~See also **out of bounds.**

boun·te·ous ('baʊntɪəs) *adj. Literary.* **1.** giving freely; generous: *the bounteous goodness of God.* **2.** plentiful; abundant. —**'boun·te·ous·ly** *adv.* —**'boun·te·ous·ness** *n.*

boun·ti·ful ('baʊntɪfʊl) *adj.* **1.** plentiful; ample (esp. in the phrase **a bountiful supply**). **2.** giving freely; generous. —**'boun·ti·ful·ly** *adv.* —**'boun·ti·ful·ness** *n.*

boun·ty ('baʊntɪ) *n., pl.* **·ties. 1.** generosity in giving to others; liberality. **2.** a generous gift; something freely provided. **3.** a payment made by a government, as, formerly, to a sailor on enlisting or to a soldier after a campaign. **4.** any reward or premium: *a bounty of 20p for every rat killed.* [C13 (in the sense: goodness): from Old French *bontet,* from Latin *bonitās* goodness, from *bonus* good]

Boun·ty ('baʊntɪ) *n.* a British naval ship commanded by Captain William Bligh, which was on a scientific voyage in 1789 between Tahiti and the West Indies when her crew mutinied.

bou·quet *n.* **1.** (bəʊ'keɪ, buː-). a bunch of flowers, esp. a large carefully arranged one. **2.** (buː'keɪ). the characteristic aroma or fragrance of a wine or liqueur. **3.** a compliment or expression of praise. [C18: from French: thicket, from Old French *bosc* forest, wood, probably of Germanic origin; see BUSH[1]]

bou·quet gar·ni ('buːkeɪ gɑː'niː) *n., pl.* **bou·quets gar·nis** ('buːkeɪz gɑː'niː). a bunch of herbs tied together and used for flavouring soups, stews, etc. [French, literally: garnished bouquet]

bour·bon ('bɜːbᵊn) *n.* a whiskey distilled, chiefly in the U.S., from maize, esp. one containing at least 51 per cent maize (the rest being malt and rye) and aged in charred white-oak barrels. [C19: named after *Bourbon* county, Kentucky, where it was first made]

Bour·bon ('bʊəbᵊn; *French* bur'bɔ̃) *n.* **1. a.** a member of the European royal line that ruled in France from 1589 to 1793 (when Louis XVI was executed by the revolutionaries) and was restored in 1815, continuing to rule in its Orleans branch from 1830 until 1848. Bourbon dynasties also ruled in Spain (1700–1808; 1813–1931) and Naples and Sicily (1734–1806; 1815–1860). **b.** (*as modifier*): *the Bourbon kings.* **2.** *U.S.* an extreme reactionary in political or social matters. —**'Bour·bon·ist** *n.*

Bour·bon bis·cuit *n.* a rich chocolate-flavoured biscuit with a chocolate-cream filling.

Bour·bon·ism ('bʊəbəˌnɪzəm) *n.* **1.** support for Bourbon rule. **2.** *U.S.* extreme political and social conservatism.

bour·don ('bʊədᵊn, 'bɔːdᵊn) *n.* **1.** a 16-foot organ stop of the stopped diapason type. **2.** the drone of a bagpipe. **3.** a drone or pedal point in the bass of a harmonized melody. [C14: from Old French: drone (of a musical instrument), of imitative origin]

Bour·don gauge *n.* a type of pressure gauge consisting of a flattened curved tube attached to a pointer that moves around a dial. As the pressure in the tube increases the tube tends to straighten and the pointer indicates the applied pressure.

bourg (bʊəg; *French* buːr) *n.* a French market town, esp. one beside a castle. [C15: French, from Old French *borc,* from Late Latin *burgus* castle, of Germanic origin; see BOROUGH]

bour·geois[1] ('bʊəʒwɑː, bʊə'ʒwɑː) *Often disparaging.* ~*n., pl.* **·geois. 1.** a member of the middle class, esp. one regarded as being conservative and materialistic or (in Marxist thought) a capitalist exploiting the working class. **2.** a mediocre, unimaginative, or materialistic person. ~*adj.* **3.** characteristic of, relating to, or comprising the middle class. **4.** conservative or materialistic in outlook: *a bourgeois mentality.* **5.** (in Marxist thought) dominated by capitalists or capitalist interests. [C16: from Old French *borjois, burgeis* burgher, citizen, from *bourg* town; see BURGESS] —**bour·geoise** ('bʊəʒwɑːz, bʊə'ʒwɑːz) *fem. n.*

bour·geois[2] (bəː'dʒɔɪs) *n.* (formerly) a size of printer's type approximately equal to 9 point. [C19: perhaps from its size, midway between long primer and brevier]

Bour·geois (*French* bur'ʒwa) *n.* **Lé·on Vic·tor Au·guste** (leɔ̃ viktɔr o'gyst). 1851–1925, French statesman; first chairman of the League of Nations: Nobel peace prize 1920.

bour·geoi·sie (ˌbʊəʒwɑː'ziː) *n.* **the. 1.** the middle classes. **2.** (in Marxist thought) the ruling class of the two basic classes of capitalist society, consisting of capitalists, manufacturers, bankers, and other employers. The bourgeoisie owns the most important of the means of production, through which it exploits the working class.

bour·geon ('bɜːdʒən) *n., vb.* a variant spelling of **burgeon.**

Bourges (*French* burʒ) *n.* a city in central France. Pop.: 80 379 (1975).

Bour·gogne (bur'gɔɲ) *n.* the French name for **Burgundy.**

Bour·gui·ba (bʊə'giːbə) *n.* **Ha·bib ben A·li** (hæ'bɪb bɛn 'ɑːlɪ). born 1903, Tunisian statesman: president of Tunisia since 1957; a moderate and an advocate of gradual social change.

bourn[1] *or* **bourne** (bɔːn) *n. Archaic.* **1.** a destination; goal. **2.** a boundary. [C16: from Old French *borne;* see BOUND[3]]

bourn[2] (bɔːn) *n. Chiefly southern Brit.* a stream, esp. an intermittent one in chalk areas. Compare **burn**[2]. [C16: from Old French *bodne* limit; see BOUND[3]]

Bourne·mouth ('bɔːnməθ) *n.* a resort in S England, in SE Dorset on the English Channel. Pop.: 153 425 (1971).

bour·rée ('bʊəreɪ; *French* bu're) *n.* **1.** a traditional French dance in fast duple time, resembling a gavotte. **2.** a piece of music composed in the rhythm of this dance. [French, literally: bundle of sticks, from *bourrer* to stuff, from Late Latin *burra* shaggy garment]

Bourse (bʊəs) *n.* a stock exchange of continental Europe, esp. Paris. [C19: from French, literally: purse, from Medieval Latin *bursa,* ultimately from Greek: leather]

bouse *or* **bowse** (baʊz) *vb.* (*tr.*) *Nautical.* to raise or haul with a tackle. [C16: of unknown origin]

bou·stro·phe·don (ˌbuːstrə'fiːdᵊn, ˌbaʊ-) *adj.* having alternate lines written from right to left and from left to right. [C17: from Greek, literally: turning as in ploughing with oxen, from *bous* ox + *-strophēdon* from *strephein* to turn; see STROPHE]

bout (baʊt) *n.* **1. a.** a period of time spent doing something, such as drinking. **b.** a period of illness. **2.** a contest or fight, esp. a boxing or wrestling match. [C16: variant of obsolete *bought* turn; related to German *Bucht* BIGHT; see ABOUT]

bou·tique (buː'tiːk) *n.* a shop, esp. a small one selling fashionable clothes and other items. [C18: from French, probably from Old Provençal *botica,* ultimately from Greek *apothēkē* storehouse; see APOTHECARY]

bou·ton·ni·ere (ˌbutɒnɪ'ɛə) *n.* another name for **buttonhole** (sense 2). [French: buttonhole, from *bouton* BUTTON]

bou·zouk·i (buː'zuːkɪ) *n.* a Greek long-necked stringed musical instrument related to the mandolin. [from Modern Greek *mpouzouki,* perhaps from Turkish *büjük* large]

bo·vid ('bəʊvɪd) *adj.* **1.** of, relating to, or belonging to the *Bovidae,* a family of ruminant artiodactyl hollow-horned mammals including sheep, goats, cattle, antelopes, and buffalo. ~*n.* **2.** any bovid animal. [C19: from New Latin *Bovidae,* from Latin *bōs* ox]

bo·vine ('bəʊvaɪn) *adj.* **1.** of, relating to, or belonging to the *Bovini* (cattle), a bovid tribe including domestic cattle. **2.** (of people) dull; sluggish; stolid. ~*n.* **3.** any animal belonging to the *Bovini.* [C19: from Late Latin *bovīnus* concerning oxen or cows, from Latin *bōs* ox, cow] —**'bo·vine·ly** *adv.*

Bov·ril ('bɒvrɪl) *n. Trademark.* a concentrated beef extract, used for flavouring, as a stock, etc.

bov·ver ('bɒvə) *n. Brit. slang.* **a.** rowdiness, esp. caused by gangs of teenage youths. **b.** (*as modifier*): *a bovver boy.* [C20: slang pronunciation of BOTHER]

bov·ver boots *pl. n. Brit. slang.* heavy boots worn by some teenage youths in Britain, used in gang fights.

bow[1] (baʊ) *vb.* **1.** to lower (one's head) or bend (one's knee or body) as a sign of respect, greeting, assent, or shame. **2.** to bend or cause to bend; incline downwards. **3.** (*intr.;* usually foll. by *to* or *before*) to comply or accept: *bow to the inevitable.* **4.** (*tr.;* foll. by *in, out, to,* etc.) to usher (someone) into or out of a place with bows and deference: *the manager bowed us to our car.* **5.** (*tr.;* usually foll. by *down*) to bring (a person, nation, etc.) to a state of submission. **6. bow and scrape.** to behave in an excessively deferential or obsequious way. ~*n.* **7.** a lowering or inclination of the head or body as a mark of respect, greeting, or assent. **8. take a bow.** to acknowledge or receive applause or praise. ~See also **bow out.** [Old English *būgan,* related to Old Norse *bjūgr* bent, Old High German *biogan* to bend, Dutch *buigen*]

bow[2] (bəʊ) *n.* **1.** a weapon for shooting arrows, consisting of an arch of elastic wood bent by a string (**bowstring**) fastened at each end. See also **crossbow. 2. a.** a long slightly curved stick across which are stretched strands of horsehair, used for playing the strings of a violin, viola, cello, or related instrument. **b.** a stroke with such a stick. **3. a.** a decorative interlacing of ribbon or other fabrics, usually having two loops and two loose ends. **b.** the knot forming such an interlacing; bowknot. **4. a.** something that is curved, bent, or arched. **b.** (*in combination*):

rainbow; oxbow; saddlebow. **5.** a person who uses a bow and arrow; archer. **6.** *U.S.* **a.** a frame of a pair of spectacles. **b.** a sidepiece of the frame of a pair of spectacles that curls round behind the ear. **7.** a metal ring forming the handle of a pair of scissors or of a large old-fashioned key. **8.** *Architect.* part of a building curved in the form of a bow. See also **bow window.** ~*vb.* **9.** to form or cause to form a curve or curves. **10.** to make strokes of a bow across (violin strings). [Old English *boga* arch, bow; related to Old Norse *bogi* a bow, Old High German *bogo,* Old Irish *bocc,* and BOW¹]

bow³ (baʊ) *n.* **1.** *Chiefly Nautical.* **a.** (*often pl.*) the forward end or part of a vessel. **b.** (*as modifier*): *the bow mooring line.* **2.** *Rowing.* short for **bowman².** **3. on the port** (*or* **starboard**) **bow.** *Nautical.* within 45 degrees to the port (or starboard) of straight ahead. **4. a shot across someone's bows.** *Informal.* a warning. [C15: probably from Low German *boog;* related to Dutch *boeg,* Danish *bov* ship's bow, shoulder; see BOUGH]

bow col+lec+tor (bəʊ) *n.* a sliding current collector, consisting of a bow-shaped strip mounted on a hinged framework, used on trains, etc., to collect current from an overhead-wire. Compare **skate¹** (sense 4).

bow com+pass (bəʊ) *n. Geom.* a compass in which the legs are joined by a flexible metal bow-shaped spring rather than a hinge, the angle being adjusted by a screw. Also called: **bow-spring compass.**

bowd+ler+ize *or* **bowd+ler+ise** (ˈbaʊdləˌraɪz) *vb.* (*tr.*) to remove passages or words regarded as indecent from (a play, novel, etc.); expurgate. [C19: after Thomas *Bowdler* (1754–1825), English editor who published an expurgated edition of Shakespeare] —ˌ**bowd+ler+i+ˈza+tion** *or* ˌ**bowd+ler+i+ˈsa+tion** *n.* —ˈ**bowd+ler+ism** *n.*

bow+el (ˈbaʊəl) *n.* **1.** an intestine, esp. the large intestine in man. **2.** (*pl.*) innards; entrails. **3.** (*pl.*) the deep or innermost part (esp. in the phrase **the bowels of the earth**). **4.** (*pl.*) *Archaic.* the emotions, esp. of pity or sympathy. [C13: from Old French *bouel,* from Latin *botellus* a little sausage, from *botulus* sausage]

bow+el move+ment *n.* **1.** the discharge of faeces; defecation. **2.** the waste matter discharged; faeces.

bow+er¹ (ˈbaʊə) *n.* **1.** a shady leafy shelter or recess, as in a wood or garden; arbour. **2.** *Literary.* a lady's bedroom or apartments, esp. in a medieval castle; boudoir. **3.** *Literary.* a country cottage, esp. one regarded as charming or picturesque. [Old English *būr* dwelling; related to Old Norse *būr* pantry, Old High German *būr* dwelling]

bow+er² (ˈbaʊə) *n. Nautical.* a vessel's bow anchor. [C18: from BOW³ + -ER¹]

bow+er³ (ˈbaʊə) *n.* a jack in euchre and similar card games. [C19: from German *Bauer* peasant, jack (in cards)]

bow·er+bird (ˈbaʊəˌbɜːd) *n.* **1.** any of various songbirds of the family *Ptilonorhynchidae,* of Australia and New Guinea. The males build bower-like display grounds in the breeding season to attract the females. **2.** *Informal, chiefly Austral.* a collector of unconsidered trifles.

Bow+er·y (ˈbaʊərɪ) *n.* **the.** a street in New York City noted for its cheap hotels and bars, frequented by vagrants and drunks. [C17: from Dutch *bouwerij,* from *bouwen* to farm + *erij* -ERY; see BOOR, BOER]

bow+fin (ˈbəʊˌfɪn) *n.* a primitive North American freshwater bony fish, *Amia calva,* with an elongated body and a very long dorsal fin: family *Amiidae.*

bow+head (ˈbəʊˌhɛd) *n.* a large-mouthed arctic whale, *Balaena mysticetus,* that has become rare through overfishing but is now a protected species.

Bow·ie (ˈbaʊɪ) *n.* **Da·vid.** original name *David Jones.* born 1947, English rock singer and composer. His recordings include *Space Oddity* (1969), *The Rise and Fall of Ziggy Stardust* (1972), *Aladdin Sane* (1973), *Station to Station* (1976), and *Low* (1977).

bow·ie knife (ˈbəʊɪ) *n.* a stout hunting knife with a short hilt and a guard for the hand. [C19: named after Jim *Bowie* (1796–1836), Texan adventurer, who popularized it]

bow+ing (ˈbəʊɪŋ) *n.* the technique of using the bow in playing a violin, viola, cello, or related instrument.

bow+knot (ˈbəʊˌnɒt) *n.* a decorative knot usually having two loops and two loose ends; bow.

bowl¹ (bəʊl) *n.* **1.** a round container open at the top, used for holding liquid, keeping fruit, serving food, etc. **2.** Also: **bowlful.** the amount a bowl will hold. **3.** the rounded or hollow part of an object, esp. of a spoon or tobacco pipe. **4.** any container shaped like a bowl, such as a sink or lavatory. **5.** a bowl-shaped building or other structure, such as a football stadium or amphitheatre. **6.** a bowl-shaped depression of the land surface. See also **dust bowl.** **7.** *Literary.* **a.** a drinking cup. **b.** intoxicating drink. [Old English *bolla;* related to Old Norse *bolli,* Old Saxon *bollo*]

bowl² (bəʊl) *n.* **1.** a wooden ball used in the game of bowls, having flattened sides, one side usually being flatter than the other in order to make it run on a curved course. **2.** a large heavy ball with holes for gripping with the fingers and thumb, used in tenpin bowling. ~*vb.* **3.** to roll smoothly or cause to roll smoothly, esp. by throwing underarm along the ground. **4.** (*intr.;* usually foll. by *along*) to move easily and rapidly, as in a car. **5.** *Cricket.* **a.** to send (a ball) down the pitch from one's hand towards the batsman, keeping the arm straight while doing so. **b.** Also: **bowl out.** to dismiss (a batsman) by delivering a ball that breaks his wicket. **6.** (*intr.*) to play bowls or tenpin bowling. **7.** (*tr.*) (in tenpin bowling, etc.) to score (a specified amount): *he bowled 120.* ~See also **bowl over.** [C15: from French *boule,* ultimately from Latin *bulla* bubble]

bow legs (bəʊ) *pl. n.* a condition in which the legs curve outwards like a bow between the ankle and the thigh. Also called: **bandy legs.** —**bow-leg·ged** (bəʊˈlɛgɪd, bəʊˈlɛgd) *adj.*

bowl+er¹ (ˈbəʊlə) *n.* **1.** one who bowls in cricket. **2.** a player at the game of bowls.

bowl+er² (ˈbəʊlə) *n.* a stiff felt hat with a rounded crown and narrow curved brim. U.S. name: **derby.** [C19: named after John *Bowler,* 19th-century London hatter]

bow+ler³ (ˈbaʊlə) *n. Dublin dialect.* a dog. [perhaps from B(OW-WOW) + (H)OWLER]

bow+line (ˈbəʊlɪn) *n. Nautical.* **1.** a line for controlling the weather leech of a square sail when a vessel is close-hauled. **2. on a bowline.** beating close to the wind. **3.** a knot used for securing a loop that will not slip at the end of a piece of rope. [C14: probably from Middle Low German *bōlīne,* equivalent to BOW³ + LINE¹]

bowl+ing (ˈbəʊlɪŋ) *n.* **1.** any of various games in which a heavy ball is rolled down a special alley, usually made of wood, at a group of wooden pins, esp. the games of tenpin bowling (tenpins) and skittles (ninepins). **2.** the game of bowls. **3.** *Cricket.* the act of delivering the ball to the batsman. **4.** (*modifier*) of or relating to bowls or bowling: *a bowling team.*

bowl+ing al+ley *n.* **1. a.** a long narrow wooden lane down which the ball is rolled in tenpin bowling. **b.** a similar lane or alley, usually with raised sides, for playing skittles (ninepins). **2.** a building having several lanes for tenpin bowling.

bowl+ing crease *n. Cricket.* a line marked at the wicket, over which a bowler must not advance fully before delivering the ball.

bowl+ing green *n.* an area of closely mown turf on which the game of bowls is played.

bowl o·ver *vb.* (*tr., adv.*) **1.** *Informal.* to surprise (a person) greatly, esp. in a pleasant way; astound; amaze: *he was bowled over by our gift.* **2.** to knock (a person or thing) down; cause to fall over.

bowls (bəʊlz) *pl. n.* **1. a.** a game played on a bowling green in which a small bowl (the jack) is pitched from a mark and two opponents or opposing teams take turns to roll biased wooden bowls towards it, the object being to finish as near the jack as possible. **b.** (*as modifier*): *a bowls tournament.* **2.** skittles or tenpin bowling.

bow+man¹ (ˈbəʊmən) *n., pl.* **+men.** *Archaic.* an archer.

bow+man² (ˈbaʊmən) *n., pl.* **+men** *Nautical.* an oarsman at the bow of a boat. Also called: **bow oar.**

bow out (baʊ) *vb.* (*adv.; usually tr.;* often foll. by *of*) to retire or withdraw gracefully.

bow+saw (ˈbəʊˌsɔː) *n.* a saw with a thin blade in a bow-shaped frame, used for cutting curves.

bowse (baʊz) *vb.* a variant spelling of **bouse.**

bow+ser (ˈbaʊzə) *n.* **1.** a tanker containing fuel for aircraft, military vehicles, etc. **2.** *Austral., N.Z.* a petrol pump at a filling station. [originally a U.S. proprietary name]

bow+shot (ˈbəʊˌʃɒt) *n.* the distance an arrow travels from the bow (esp. in the phrases **within bowshot, out of bowshot**).

bow+sprit (ˈbəʊsprɪt) *n. Nautical.* a spar projecting from the bow of a vessel, esp. a sailing vessel, used to carry the headstay as far forward as possible. [C13: from Middle Low German *bōchsprēt,* from *bōch* BOW³ + *sprēt* pole]

Bow Street run+ner (bəʊ) *n. Brit.* (from 1749 to 1829) an officer at Bow Street magistrates' court, London, whose duty was to pursue and arrest criminals.

bow+string (ˈbəʊˌstrɪŋ) *n.* the string of an archer's bow, usually consisting of three strands of hemp.

bow+string hemp *n.* **1.** a hemplike fibre obtained from the sansevieria. **2.** another name for **sansevieria.**

bow tie (bəʊ) *n.* a man's tie tied in a bow, now chiefly in plain black for formal evening wear.

bow weight (bəʊ) *n. Archery.* the poundage required to draw a bow to the full length of the arrow.

bow win+dow (bəʊ) *n.* a bay window in the shape of a curve.

bow-wow (ˈbaʊˌwaʊ, -ˈwaʊ) *n.* **1.** a child's word for **dog.** **2.** an imitation of the bark of a dog. ~*vb.* **3.** (*intr.*) to bark or imitate a dog's bark.

bow+yangs (ˈbəʊjæŋz) *pl. n. Austral., N.Z.* a pair of strings or straps secured round each trouser leg below the knee, worn esp. by sheep-shearers and other labourers. [C19: from English dialect *bowy-yanks* leggings]

bow+yer (ˈbəʊjə) *n.* a person who makes or sells archery bows.

box¹ (bɒks) *n.* **1.** a receptacle or container made of wood, cardboard, etc., usually rectangular and having a removable or hinged lid. **2.** Also called: **boxful.** the contents of such a receptacle or the amount it can contain: *he ate a whole box of chocolates.* **3.** any of various containers for a specific purpose: *a money box; letter box.* **4.** (*often in combination*) any of various small cubicles, kiosks, or shelters: *a telephone box or callbox; a sentry box; a signal box on a railway.* **5.** a separate compartment in a public place for a small group of people, as in a theatre or certain restaurants. **6.** an enclosure within a courtroom. See **jurybox, witness box.** **7.** a compartment for a horse in a stable or a vehicle. See **loose box, horse box.** **8.** *Brit.* a small country house occupied by sportsmen when following a field sport, esp. shooting. **9. a.** a protective housing for machinery or mechanical parts. **b.** the contents of such a box. **c.** (*in combination*): *a gearbox.* **10.** a shaped device of light tough material worn by sportsmen to protect the genitals, esp. in cricket. **11.** a section of printed matter on a page, enclosed by lines, a border, or white space. **12.** a central agency to which mail is addressed and by which it is redistributed: *a post-office box; to reply to a box number in a* newspaper advertisement. **13.** the penalty area of a soccer pitch. **14.** *Baseball.* either of the designated areas for the batter or the pitcher. **15.** the raised seat on which the driver sits in a horse-drawn coach. **16.** *Austral.* an accidental mixing of herds or flocks. **17.** a hole cut into the base of a tree to collect the sap. **18.** *Brit.* (esp. formerly) a present, esp. of money, given at Christmas to tradesmen, etc. **19.** a device for dividing water into two or more ditches in an irrigation system. **20.** an informal name for a **coffin. 21.** *Austral. taboo slang.* the female genitals. **22. the box.** *Brit. informal.* television. **23. out of the box.** *Austral. informal.* outstanding or excellent. ~*vb.* **24.** (*tr.*) to put into a box. **25.** (*tr.;* usually foll. by *in* or *up*) to prevent from moving freely; confine. **26.** (*tr.*) to make a cut in the base of (a tree) in order to collect the sap. **27.** *Austral.* to mix (flocks or herds) or (of flocks) to become mixed accidentally. **28.** *Nautical.* short for **boxhaul. 29. box the compass.** *Nautical.* to name the compass points in order. [Old English *box,* from Latin *buxus, from Greek puxos* BOX³] —**'box+ˌlike** *adj.*

box² (bɒks) *vb.* **1.** (*tr.*) to fight (an opponent) in a boxing match. **2.** (*intr.*) to engage in boxing. **3.** (*tr.*) to hit (a person) with the fist; punch or cuff. ~*n.* **4.** a punch with the fist, esp. on the ear. [C14: of uncertain origin; perhaps related to Dutch *boken* to shunt, push into position]

box³ (bɒks) *n.* **1.** any evergreen tree or shrub of the genus *Buxus,* esp. *B. sempervirens,* which has small shiny leaves and is used for hedges, borders, and garden mazes: family *Buxaceae.* **2.** the wood of this tree. See **boxwood** (sense 1). **3.** any of several trees the timber or foliage of which resembles this tree, esp. species of *Eucalyptus.* [Old English, from Latin *buxus*]

box+ber·ry ('bɒksbərɪ) *n., pl.* **·ries. 1.** the fruit of the partridgeberry or wintergreen. **2.** another name for **partridgeberry** and **wintergreen** (sense 1).

box+board ('bɒksˌbɔːd) *n.* a tough paperboard made from wood and wastepaper pulp: used for making boxes, etc.

box calf *n.* black calfskin leather, tanned with chromium salts, having a pattern of fine creases formed by boarding. [C20: named after Joseph *Box,* London shoemaker]

box cam+er·a *n.* a simple box-shaped camera having an elementary lens, shutter, and viewfinder.

box can+yon *n. Western U.S.* a canyon with vertical or almost vertical walls.

box+car ('bɒksˌkɑː) *n. U.S.* a closed railway van.

box coat *n.* **1.** a plain short coat that hangs loosely from the shoulders. **2.** a heavy overcoat, worn formerly by coachmen.

box el+der *n.* a medium-sized fast-growing widely cultivated North American maple, *Acer negundo,* which has compound leaves with lobed leaflets. Also called: **ash-leaved maple.**

box+er ('bɒksə) *n.* **1.** a man who boxes, either professionally or as a hobby; pugilist. **2.** a large smooth-haired breed of dog with a short nose and a docked tail.

Box+er ('bɒksə) *n.* **a.** a member of a nationalistic Chinese secret society that led an unsuccessful rebellion in 1900 against foreign interests in China. **b.** (*as modifier*)*: the Boxer Rebellion.* [C18: rough translation of Chinese *I Ho Ch'üan,* literally: virtuous harmonious fist, altered from *I Ho T'uan* virtuous harmonious society]

box+fish ('bɒksˌfɪʃ) *n., pl.* **+fish** *or* **+fish·es.** another name for **trunkfish.**

box gird+er *n.* **a.** a girder that is hollow and square or rectangular in shape. **b.** (*as modifier*)*: a box-girder bridge.*

box+haul ('bɒksˌhɔːl) *vb. Nautical.* to bring (a square-rigger) onto a new tack by backwinding the foresails and steering hard round.

box+ing ('bɒksɪŋ) *n.* **a.** the act, art, or profession of fighting with the fists, esp. the modern sport practised under Queensberry rules. **b.** (*as modifier*)*: a boxing enthusiast.*

Box+ing Day *n. Brit.* the first weekday after Christmas, observed as a holiday. [C19: from the custom of giving Christmas boxes to tradesmen and staff on this day]

box+ing glove *n.* one of a pair of thickly padded mittens worn for boxing.

box junc+tion *n.* (in Britain) a road junction having yellow cross-hatching painted on the road surface. Vehicles may only enter the hatched area when their exit is clear.

box kite *n.* a kite with a boxlike frame open at both ends.

box of+fice *n.* **1.** an office at a theatre, cinema, etc., where tickets are sold. **2.** the receipts from a play, film, etc. **3. a.** the public appeal of an actor or production: *the musical was bad box office.* **b.** (*as modifier*)*: a box-office success.*

box pleat *n.* a flat double pleat made by folding under the fabric on either side of it.

box+room ('bɒksˌruːm, -ˌrʊm) *n.* a small room or large cupboard in which boxes, cases, etc., may be stored.

box seat *n.* **1.** a seat in a theatre box. **2. in the box seat.** *Austral. informal.* in the best position.

box span+ner *n.* a spanner consisting of a steel cylinder with a hexagonal end that fits over a nut of the appropriate size and shape.

box spring *n.* a coiled spring contained in a boxlike frame, used as base for mattresses, chairs, etc.

box+thorn ('bɒksˌθɔːn) *n.* another name for **matrimony vine.**

box+wood ('bɒksˌwʊd) *n.* **1.** the hard close-grained yellow wood of the box tree, used to make tool handles, small turned or carved articles, etc. **2.** the box tree.

boy (bɔɪ) *n.* **1.** a male child; lad; youth. **2.** a man regarded as immature or inexperienced: *he's just a boy when it comes to dealing with women.* **3.** See **old boy. 4. the boys.** *Informal.* a group of men, esp. a group of friends. **5.** (esp. in former colonial territories) a native servant. **6.** short for **boyfriend. 7. boys will be boys.** youthful indiscretion or exuberance must be expected and tolerated. **8. jobs for the boys.** *Informal.* appointment of one's supporters to posts, without reference to their qualifications or ability. ~*interj.* **9.** an exclamation of surprise, pleasure, contempt, etc. [C13 (in the sense: male servant; C14: young male): of uncertain origin; perhaps related to Old English *Bōia,* man's name; from Old High German *Buobo,* man's name]

bo+yar ('bəʊjɑː, 'bɔɪə) *n.* a member of an old order of Russian nobility, ranking immediately below the princes: abolished by Peter the Great. [C16: from Old Russian *boyarin,* from Old Slavic *boljarinŭ,* probably from Old Turkic *boila* a title]

Boyce (bɔɪs) *n.* **Wil·liam.** ?1710–79, English composer, noted esp. for his church music and symphonies.

boy+cott ('bɔɪkɒt) *vb.* **1.** (*tr.*) to refuse to have dealings with (a person, organization, etc.) or refuse to buy (a product) as a protest or means of coercion: *to boycott foreign produce.* ~*n.* **2.** an instance or the use of boycotting. [C19: after Captain C. C. *Boycott* (1832–97), Irish land agent for the Earl of Erne, County Mayo, Ireland, who was a victim of such practices for refusing to reduce rents]

Boyd (bɔɪd) *n.* **Ar·thur.** born 1920, Australian painter and sculptor, noted for his large ceramic sculptures and his series of engravings.

Boyd Orr ('bɔɪd 'ɔː) *n.* **John,** 1st Baron Boyd Orr. 1880–1971, Scottish biologist; director general of the United Nations Food and Agriculture Organization: Nobel peace prize 1949.

Boy·er (*French* bwa'je) *n.* **Charles** (ʃarl), known as the *great lover.* 1899–1978, French film actor.

boy+friend ('bɔɪˌfrɛnd) *n.* a male friend with whom a person is romantically or sexually involved; sweetheart or lover.

boy+hood ('bɔɪhʊd) *n.* the state or time of being a boy: *his boyhood was happy.*

boy+ish ('bɔɪɪʃ) *adj.* of or like a boy in looks, behaviour, or character, esp. when regarded as attractive or endearing: *a boyish smile.* —**'boy+ish+ly** *adv.* —**'boy+ish+ness** *n.*

boy+la ('bɔɪlə) *n. Austral.* an Aboriginal witch doctor. [from a native Australian language]

Boyle (bɔɪl) *n.* **Rob·ert.** 1627–91, Irish scientist who helped to dissociate chemistry from alchemy. He established that air has weight and studied the behaviour of gases; author of *The Sceptical Chymist* (1661).

Boyle's law *n.* the principle that the pressure of a gas varies inversely with its volume at constant temperature. [C18: named after Robert BOYLE]

boy-meets-girl *adj.* conventionally or trivially romantic: *a boy-meets-girl story.*

Boyne (bɔɪn) *n.* a river in the E Republic of Ireland, rising in the Bog of Allen and flowing northeast to the Irish Sea: William III of England defeated the deposed James II in a battle (**Battle of the Boyne**) on its banks in 1690, completing the overthrow of the Stuart cause in Ireland. Length: about 112 km (70 miles).

Bo+yo·ma Falls (bɔɪ'əʊmə) *pl. n.* a series of seven cataracts in NE Zaïre, on the upper River Congo: forms an unnavigable stretch of 90 km (56 miles), which falls 60 m (200 ft.). Former name: **Stanley Falls.**

Boys' Bri+gade *n. Brit.* an organization for boys, founded in 1883, with the aim of promoting discipline and self-respect.

boy scout *n.* See **Scout.**

boy·sen+ber·ry ('bɔɪzᵊnbərɪ) *n., pl.* **·ries. 1.** a type of bramble: a hybrid of the loganberry and various blackberries and raspberries. **2.** the large red edible fruit of this plant. [C20: named after Rudolph *Boysen,* American botanist who developed it]

Boz (bɒz) *n.* pen name of (Charles) **Dickens.**

Boz+ca·a·da (ˌbɔzdʒaa'da) *n.* the Turkish name for **Tenedos.**

Bo+zen ('boːtsᵊn) *n.* the German name for **Bolzano.**

bo·zo ('bəʊzəʊ) *n., pl.* **·zos.** *U.S. slang.* a man, esp. a stupid one. [C20: of uncertain origin; perhaps based on BEAU]

bp. *abbrev. for:* **1.** baptized. **2.** birthplace. **3.** bishop.

b.p. *abbrev. for:* **1.** (of alcoholic density) below proof. **2.** boiling point.

B.P. *abbrev. for* British Pharmacopoeia.

B/P *or* **b.p.** *abbrev. for* bills payable.

B.P.C. *abbrev. for* British Pharmaceutical Codex.

B.Pharm *abbrev. for* Bachelor of Pharmacy.

B.Phil. *abbrev. for* Bachelor of Philosophy.

b.p.i. *abbrev. for* bits per inch (used of a computer tape).

b.pt. *abbrev. for* boiling point.

Br *the chemical symbol for* bromine.

B.R. *abbrev. for* British Rail (formerly British Railways).

BR *international car registration for* Brazil.

br. *abbrev. for:* **1.** branch. **2.** bronze. **3.** brother.

Br. *abbrev. for:* **1.** Breton. **2.** Britain. **3.** British. **4.** (in a religious order) Brother.

B/R *or* **b.r.** *abbrev. for* bills receivable.

bra (brɑː) *n.* short for **brassiere.**

braa+ta ('brɑːtə), *or* **braa+tas** *n. Caribbean.* a small portion added to a purchase of food by a market vendor, to encourage the customer to return. Also called: **broughta** or **broughtas.** [perhaps from Spanish *barata* a bargain]

Bra+bant (brə'bænt) *n.* **1.** a former duchy of W Europe: divided when Belgium became independent (1830), the south forming the Belgian provinces of Antwerp and Brabant and the north forming the province of North Brabant in the Netherlands. **2.** a province of central Belgium: densely populated and intensively farmed, with large industrial centres. Capital: Brussels. Pop.: 2 220 088 (1975 est.). Area: 3284 sq. km (1268 sq. miles).

brab+ble ('bræbᵊl) *vb., n.* a rare word for **squabble.** [C16: from Middle Dutch *brabbelen* to jabber] —**'brab+bler** *n.*

brace (breɪs) *n.* **1.** a hand tool for drilling holes, with a socket to hold the drill at one end and a cranked handle by which the tool can be turned. See also **brace and bit. 2.** something that steadies, binds, or holds up another thing. **3.** a structural member, such as a beam or prop, used to stiffen a framework. **4.** a sliding loop, usually of leather, attached to the cords of a drum: used to change its tension. **5.** a pair; two, esp. of game birds: *a brace of partridges.* **6.** either of a pair of characters, {}, used for connecting lines of printing or writing or as a third sign of aggregation in complex mathematical or logical expressions that already contain parentheses and square brackets. **7.** Also called: **accolade.** a line or bracket connecting two or more staves of music. **8.** (*often pl.*) an appliance of metal bands and wires that can be tightened to maintain steady pressure on the teeth for correcting uneven alignment. **9.** *Med.* any of various appliances for supporting the trunk or a limb. **10.** another word for **bracer**[2]. **11.** (in square-rigged sailing ships) a rope that controls the movement of a yard and thus the position of a sail. **12.** See **braces.** ~*vb.* (*mainly tr.*) **13.** to provide, strengthen, or fit with a brace. **14.** to steady or prepare (oneself or something) as before an impact. **15.** (*also intr.*) to stimulate; freshen; invigorate: *sea air is bracing.* **16.** to control the horizontal movement of (the yards of a square-rigged sailing ship). [C14: from Old French: the two arms, from Latin *bracchia* arms]

brace and bit *n.* a hand tool for boring holes, consisting of a cranked handle into which a drilling bit is inserted.

brace+let ('breɪslɪt) *n.* **1.** an ornamental chain worn around the arm or wrist. **2.** an expanding metal band for a wristwatch. [C15: from Old French, from *bracel,* literally: a little arm, from Latin *bracchium* arm; see BRACE]

brace+lets ('breɪslɪts) *pl. n.* a slang name for **handcuffs.**

brac+er[1] ('breɪsə) *n.* **1.** a person or thing that braces. **2.** *Informal.* a tonic, esp. an alcoholic drink taken as a tonic.

brac+er[2] ('breɪsə) *n. Archery, fencing.* a leather guard worn to protect the arm. [C14: from Old French *braciere,* from *braz* arm, from Latin *bracchium* arm]

brac·es ('breɪsɪz) *pl. n. Brit.* a pair of straps worn over the shoulders by men for holding up the trousers. U.S. word: **suspenders.**

brach (brætʃ) *or* **brach+et** ('brætʃɪt) *n. Archaic.* a bitch hound. [C14: back formation from *brachez* hunting dogs, from Old French, plural of *brachet,* of Germanic origin; compare Old High German *braccho* hound]

bra+chi·al ('breɪkɪəl, 'bræk-) *adj.* of or relating to the arm or to an armlike part or structure.

bra+chi+ate *adj.* ('breɪkɪɪt, -ˌeɪt, 'bræk-). **1.** *Botany.* having widely divergent paired branches. ~*vb.* ('breɪkɪˌeɪt, 'bræk-). **2.** (*intr.*) (of some arboreal apes and monkeys) to swing by the arms from one hold to the next. [C19: from Latin *bracchiātus* with armlike branches] —**ˌbra+chi·'a+tion** *n.*

bra·chi·o- *or before a vowel* **bra·chi-** *combining form.* indicating a brachium: *brachiopod.*

bra+chi·o+pod ('breɪkɪəˌpɒd, 'bræk-) *n.* any marine invertebrate animal of the phylum *Brachiopoda,* having a ciliated feeding organ (lophophore) and a shell consisting of dorsal and ventral valves. Also called: **lamp shell.** See also **bryozoan.** [C19: from New Latin *Brachiopoda;* see BRACHIUM, -POD]

bra+chi·o+saur+us (ˌbreɪkɪə'sɔːrəs, ˌbræk-) *n.* a dinosaur of the genus *Brachiosaurus,* up to 30 metres long: the largest land animal ever known. See also **sauropod.**

bra+chi·um ('breɪkɪəm, 'bræk-) *n., pl.* **+chi·a** (-kɪə). **1.** *Anatomy.* the arm, esp. the upper part. **2.** a corresponding part, such as a wing, in an animal. **3.** *Biology.* a branching or armlike part. [C18: New Latin, from Latin *bracchium* arm, from Greek *brakhiōn*]

brach·y- *combining form.* indicating something short: *brachycephalic.* [from Greek *brakhus* short]

brach·y·ce·phal+ic (ˌbrækɪsɪ'fælɪk) *adj. also* **brach·y+ceph·a+lous** (ˌbrækɪ'sɛfələs). **1.** having a head nearly as broad from side to side as from front to back, esp. one with a cephalic index over 80. ~*n.* **2.** an individual with such a head. ~Compare **dolichocephalic, mesocephalic.** —**ˌbrach·y+'ceph·a+ly** *or* **ˌbrach·y+'ceph·a+lism** *n.*

brach·y+dac+tyl+ic (ˌbrækɪdæk'tɪlɪk) *adj.* having abnormally short fingers or toes. —**ˌbrach·y+dac+'tyl·i·a** *or* **ˌbrach·y+'dac+tyl+ism** *n.*

bra+chyl+o·gy (bræ'kɪlədʒɪ) *n., pl.* **·gies. 1.** a concise style in speech or writing. **2.** a colloquial shortened form of expression that is not the result of a regular grammatical process: *the omission of "good" in the expression "Afternoon" is a brachylogy.* —**bra+'chyl·o·gous** *adj.*

bra+chyp+ter+ous (bræ'kɪptərəs) *adj.* having very short or incompletely developed wings: *brachypterous insects.*

brach·y+ur+an (ˌbrækɪ'jʊərən) *n.* **1.** any decapod crustacean of the group (formerly suborder) *Brachyura,* which includes the crabs. ~*adj.* **2.** of, relating to, or belonging to the *Brachyura.* [C19: from New Latin *Brachyura* (literally: short-tailed creatures), from BRACHY- + Greek *oura* tail]

brac+ing ('breɪsɪŋ) *adj.* **1.** refreshing; stimulating; invigorating: *the air here is bracing.* ~*n.* **2.** a system of braces used to strengthen or support: *the bracing supporting the building is perfectly adequate.* —**'brac+ing+ly** *adv.*

brack+en ('brækən) *n.* **1.** Also called: **brake.** any of various large coarse ferns, esp. *Pteridium aquilinum,* having large fronds with spore cases along the undersides and extensive underground stems. **2.** a clump of any of these ferns. [C14: of Scandinavian origin; compare Swedish *bräken,* Danish *bregne*]

brack+et ('brækɪt) *n.* **1.** an L-shaped or other support fixed to a wall to hold a shelf, etc. **2.** one or more wall shelves carried on brackets. **3.** *Architect.* a support projecting from the side of a wall or other structure. See also **corbel, ancon, console**[2]. **4.** Also called: **square bracket.** either of a pair of characters, [ ], used to enclose a section of writing or printing to separate it from the main text. **5.** a general name for **parenthesis, square bracket,** and **brace** (sense 6). **6.** a group or category falling within or between certain defined limits: *the lower income bracket.* **7.** the distance between two preliminary shots of artillery fire in range-finding. **8.** a skating figure consisting of two arcs meeting at a point, tracing the shape {. ~*vb.* (*tr.*) **9.** to fix or support by means of a bracket or brackets. **10.** to put (written or printed matter) in brackets, esp. as being irrelevant, spurious, or bearing a separate relationship of some kind to the rest of the text. **11.** to couple or join (two lines of text, etc.) with a brace. **12.** (often foll. by *with*) to group or class together: *to bracket Marx with the philosophers.* **13.** to adjust (artillery fire) until the target is hit. [C16: from Old French *braguette* codpiece, diminutive of *bragues* breeches, from Old Provençal *braga,* from Latin *brāca* breeches]

brack+et fun+gus *n.* any saprophytic or parasitic fungus of the basidiomycetous family *Polyporaceae,* growing as a shelf-like mass (bracket) from tree trunks and producing spores in vertical tubes in the bracket.

brack+et+ing ('brækɪtɪŋ) *n.* a set of brackets.

brack+ish ('brækɪʃ) *adj.* (of water) slightly briny or salty. [C16: from Middle Dutch *brac* salty; see -ISH] —**'brack+ish+ness** *n.*

Brack+nell ('bræknəl) *n.* a new town in E Berkshire, founded in 1949. Pop.: 33 953 (1971).

bract (brækt) *n.* a specialized leaf with a single flower or inflorescence growing in its axil. [C18: from New Latin *bractea,* Latin: thin metal plate, goldleaf, variant of *brattea,* of obscure origin] —**'bract+e·al** *adj.* —**'bract+less** *adj.*

brac+te+ate ('bræktɪɪt, -ˌeɪt) *adj.* **1.** (of a plant) having bracts. ~*n.* **2.** *Archaeol.* a fine decorated dish or plate of precious metal. [C19: from Latin *bracteātus* gold-plated; see BRACT]

brac+te+ole ('bræktɪˌəʊl) *n.* a secondary or small bract. Also called: **bractlet.** [C19: from New Latin *bracteola,* from *bractea* thin metal plate; see BRACT] —**brac+te·o+late** ('bræktɪəlɪt, -ˌleɪt) *adj.*

brad (bræd) *n.* a small tapered nail having a small head that is either symmetrical or formed on one side only. [Old English *brord* point, prick; related to Old Norse *broddr* spike, sting, Old High German *brort* edge]

brad+awl ('brædˌɔːl) *n.* an awl used to pierce wood, leather, or other materials for the insertion of brads, screws, etc.

Brad+ford ('brædfəd) *n.* an industrial city in N England, in West Yorkshire: a centre of the woollen industry since the 14th century and of the worsted trade since the 18th century. Pop.: 293 756 (1971).

Brad·ley ('brædlɪ) *n.* **1. An·drew Cec·il.** 1851–1935, English critic; author of *Shakespearian Tragedy* (1904). **2. Fran·cis Her·bert.** 1846–1924, English idealist philosopher and metaphysical thinker; author of *Ethical Studies* (1876), *Principles of Logic* (1883), and *Appearance and Reality* (1893). **3. Hen·ry.** 1845–1923, English lexicographer; one of the editors of the *Oxford English Dictionary.* **4. James.** 1693–1762, English astronomer who discovered the aberration of light and the nutation of the earth's axis.

Brad·man ('brædmən) *n.* (Sir) **Don(ald George).** born 1908, Australian cricketer: an outstanding batsman.

Brad·shaw ('brædˌʃɔː) *n.* a British railway timetable, published annually from 1839 to 1961. [C19: named after its original publisher, George *Bradshaw* (1801–53)]

brad·y- *combining form.* indicating slowness: *bradycardia.* [from Greek *bradus* slow]

brad·y+car+di·a (ˌbrædɪ'kɑːdɪə) *n. Pathol.* an abnormally low rate of heartbeat. Compare **tachycardia.** —**brad·y+car+diac** (ˌbrædɪ'kɑːdɪˌæk) *adj.*

brad·y+kin+in (ˌbrædɪ'kaɪnɪn, ˌbreɪdɪ-) *n.* a protein in blood plasma that dilates blood vessels and causes contraction of smooth muscles. Formula: $C_{50}H_{73}N_{15}O_{11}$. [C20: from BRADY- + Greek *kin(ēsis)* motion + -IN]

brae (breɪ) *n. Scot.* a hill or hillside; slope. [Old English *brǣw* BROW, eyelid; related to Old Norse *brā* eyelash, Old High German *brāwa* eyelid, eyebrow]

brag (bræg) *vb.* **brags, brag+ging, bragged. 1.** to speak of (one's own achievements, possessions, etc.) arrogantly and boastfully. ~*n.* **2.** boastful talk or behaviour, or an instance of this. **3.** something boasted of: *his brag was his new car.* **4.** a braggart; boaster. **5.** a card game: an old form of poker. [C13: of unknown origin] —**'brag+ger** *n.* —**'brag+ging+ly** *adv.*

Bra+ga (*Portuguese* 'braɣə) *n.* a city in N Portugal: capital of the Roman province of Lusitania; 12th-century cathedral, seat of the Primate of Portugal. Pop.: 101 877 (1970). Ancient name: **Bracara Augusta.**

Bragg (bræg) *n.* Sir **Wil·liam Hen·ry,** 1862–1942, and his son, Sir **(William) Law·rence,** 1890–1971, English physicists, who shared a Nobel prize for physics (1915) for their study of crystal structures by means of x-rays.

brag+ga+do+ci·o (ˌbrægə'dəʊtʃɪˌəʊ) *n., pl.* **·os. 1.** vain empty boasting. **2.** a person who boasts; braggart. [C16: from *Braggadocchio,* name of a boastful character in Spenser's *Faerie Queen;* probably from BRAGGART + Italian *-occhio* (augmentative suffix)]

brag+gart ('brægət) *n.* **1.** a person who boasts loudly or exaggeratedly; bragger. ~*adj.* **2.** boastful. [C16: see BRAG]
Bragg's law *n.* the principle that when a beam of x-rays of wavelength λ enters a crystal, the maximum intensity of the reflected ray occurs when sin θ = *n*λ/2*d*, where θ is the complement of the angle of incidence, *n* is a whole number, and *d* is the distance between layers of atoms.
Bra·gi ('brɑːgɪ) *or* **Bra·ge** ('brɑːgə) *n. Norse myth.* the god of poetry and music, son of Odin.
Bra·he (brɑː, 'brɑːhɪ; *Danish* 'braːə) *n.* **Ty·cho** ('tygo). 1546–1601, Danish astronomer who designed and constructed instruments that he used to plot accurately the positions of the planets, sun, moon, and stars.
Brah+ma[1] ('brɑːmə) *n.* **1.** a Hindu god: in later Hindu tradition, the Creator who, with Vishnu, the Preserver, and Shiva, the Destroyer, constitutes the triad known as the Trimurti. **2.** another name for **Brahman** (sense 2). [from Sanskrit, from *brahman* praise]
Brah+ma[2] ('brɑːmə, 'breɪ-) *n.* a heavy breed of domestic fowl with profusely feathered legs and feet. [shortened from *Brahmaputra* (river); from its having been imported originally from Lakhimpur, a town on the Brahmaputra]
Brah+man ('brɑːmən) *n., pl.* **+mans. 1.** (*sometimes not cap.*) Also (esp. formerly): **Brahmin.** a member of the highest or priestly caste in the Hindu caste system. **2.** *Hinduism.* the ultimate and impersonal divine reality of the universe, from which all being originates and to which it returns. **3.** another name for **Brahma**[1]. [C14: from Sanskrit *brāhmana,* from *brahman* prayer] **—Brah+man+ic** (brɑː'mænɪk) *or* **Brah+'man·i+cal** *adj.*
Brah+ma+na ('brɑːmənə) *n. Hinduism.* any of a number of sacred treatises added to each of the Vedas.
Brah+ma+ni ('brɑːmənɪ) *n., pl.* **+nis.** (*sometimes not cap.*) a woman of the Brahman caste.
Brah+man+ism ('brɑːməˌnɪzəm) *or* **Brah+min+ism** (*sometimes not cap.*) ~*n.* **1.** the religious and social system of orthodox Hinduism, characterized by diversified pantheism, the caste system, and the sacrifices and family ceremonies of Hindu tradition. **2.** the form of Hinduism prescribed in the Vedas, Brahmanas, and Upanishads. **—'Brah+man+ist** *or* **'Brah+min+ist** *n.*
Brah+ma+pu+tra (ˌbrɑːmə'puːtrə) *n.* a river in S Asia, rising in SW Tibet as the Tsangpo and flowing through the Himalayas and NE India to join the Ganges at its delta in Bangladesh. Length: about 2900 km (1800 miles).
Brah+min ('brɑːmɪn) *n., pl.* **+min** *or* **+mins. 1.** the older spelling of **Brahman** (a Hindu priest). **2.** *U.S.* a highly intelligent or socially exclusive person, esp. a member of one of the older New England families. **3.** an intellectual or social snob. **—Brah+'min+ic** *or* **Brah+'min·i+cal** *adj.*
Brahms (brɑːmz) *n.* **Jo·han·nes** (jo'hanəs). 1833–97, German composer, whose music, though classical in form, exhibits a strong lyrical romanticism. His works include four symphonies, four concertos, chamber music, and *A German Requiem* (1868).
Bra+hu·i (brɑː'huːɪ) *n.* **1.** a language spoken in Pakistan, forming an isolated branch of the Dravidian family. **2.** (*pl.* **+hu·i** *or* **+hu·is**) a member of the people that speaks this language.
braid (breɪd) *vb.* (*tr.*) **1.** to interweave several strands of (hair, thread, etc.); plait. **2.** to make by such weaving: *to braid a rope.* **3.** to dress or bind (the hair) with a ribbon, etc. **4.** to decorate with an ornamental trim or border: *to braid a skirt.* ~*n.* **5.** a length of hair, fabric, etc., that has been braided; plait. **6.** narrow ornamental tape of woven silk, wool, etc. [Old English *bregdan* to move suddenly, weave together; compare Old Norse *bregtha,* Old High German *brettan* to draw a sword] **—'braid+er** *n.*
braid+ed ('breɪdɪd) *adj.* (of a river or stream) flowing in several shallow interconnected channels separated by banks of deposited material.
braid+ing ('breɪdɪŋ) *n.* **1.** braids collectively. **2.** work done in braid. **3.** a piece of braid.
brail (breɪl) *Nautical.* ~*n.* **1.** one of several lines fastened to the leech of a fore-and-aft sail to aid in furling it. ~*vb.* **2.** (*tr.;* sometimes foll. by *up*) to furl (a fore-and-aft sail) using brails. [C15: from Old French *braiel,* from Medieval Latin *brācāle* belt for breeches, from Latin *brāca* breeches]
Bră+i·la (*Rumanian* brə'ila) *n.* a port in E Rumania: belonged to Turkey (1544–1828). Pop.: 165 803 (1974 est.).
Braille[1] (breɪl) *n.* **1.** a system of writing for the blind consisting of raised dots that can be interpreted by touch, each dot or group of dots representing a letter, numeral, or punctuation mark. **2.** any writing produced by this method. ~*vb.* **3.** (*tr.*) to print or write using this method.
Braille[2] (*French* braj) *n.* **Louis** (lwi). 1809–52, French inventor, musician, and teacher of the blind, who himself was blind from the age of three and who devised the Braille system of raised writing.
brain (breɪn) *n.* **1.** the soft convoluted mass of nervous tissue within the skull of vertebrates that is the controlling and coordinating centre of the nervous system and the seat of thought, memory, and emotion. It includes the cerebrum, brain stem, and cerebellum. Technical name: **encephalon.** Related adj.: **cerebral. 2.** the main neural bundle or ganglion of certain invertebrates. **3.** (*often pl.*) *Informal.* intellectual ability: *he's got brains.* **4.** *Informal.* shrewdness or cunning. **5.** *Informal.* an intellectual or intelligent person. **6.** (*usually pl.*) *Informal.* a person who plans and organizes an undertaking or is in overall control of an organization, etc. **7. on the brain.** *Informal.* constantly in mind: *I had that song on the brain.* **8. pick someone's brains.** *Informal.* to obtain information or ideas from someone. ~*vb.* (*tr.*) **9.** to smash the skull of. **10.** *Slang.* to hit hard on the head. [Old English *brægen;* related to Old Frisian *brein,* Middle Low German *bregen,* Greek *brekhmos* forehead]
brain+child ('breɪnˌtʃaɪld) *n., pl.* **+chil·dren.** *Informal.* an idea or plan produced by creative thought; invention.
brain cor+al *n.* a stony coral of the genus *Meandrina,* in which the polyps lie in troughlike thecae resembling the convoluted surface of a human brain.
brain death *n.* irreversible cessation of respiration due to irreparable brain damage, even though the heart may continue beating with the aid of a mechanical ventilator: widely considered as the criterion of death. **—brain dead** *adj.*
brain drain *n. Informal.* the emigration of scientists, technologists, academics, etc., for better pay, equipment, or conditions.
brain fe+ver *n.* inflammation of the brain or its covering membranes.
brain-fe·ver bird *n.* an Indian cuckoo, *Cuculus varius,* that utters a repetitive call.
brain+less ('breɪnlɪs) *adj.* stupid or foolish. **—'brain+less+ly** *adv.* **—'brain+less+ness** *n.*
brain+pan ('breɪnˌpæn) *n. Informal.* the skull.
brain+sick ('breɪnˌsɪk) *adj.* relating to or caused by insanity; crazy; mad. **—'brain+ˌsick+ly** *adv.* **—'brain+ˌsick+ness** *n.*
brain stem *n.* the stalklike part of the brain consisting of the medulla oblongata, the midbrain, and the pons Varolii.
brain+storm ('breɪnˌstɔːm) *n.* **1.** a severe outburst of excitement, often as the result of a transitory disturbance of cerebral activity. **2.** *Brit. informal.* a sudden mental aberration. **3.** *U.S. informal.* another word for **brain wave** (sense 2). **—'brain+ˌstorm+er** *n.*
brain+storm·ing ('breɪnˌstɔːmɪŋ) *n.* intensive discussion to solve problems or generate ideas.
brains trust *n.* **1.** a group of knowledgeable people who discuss topics in public or on radio or television. **2.** Also: **brain trust.** *U.S.* a group of experts who advise the government.
brain-teas·er *or* **brain-twist·er** *n. Informal.* a difficult problem.
brain+wash ('breɪnˌwɒʃ) *vb.* (*tr.*) to effect a radical change in the ideas and beliefs of (a person), esp. by methods based on conditioning. **—'brain+ˌwash+er** *n.* **—'brain+ˌwash+ing** *n.*
brain wave *n.* **1.** any of the fluctuations of electrical potential in the brain as represented on an electroencephalogram. They vary in frequency from 1 to 30 hertz. See also **alpha rhythm, beta rhythm, delta rhythm. 2.** *Informal.* a sudden idea or inspiration.
brain·y ('breɪnɪ) *adj.* **brain·i+er, brain·i+est.** *Informal.* clever; intelligent. **—'brain·i+ness** *n.*
braise (breɪz) *vb.* to cook (meat, vegetables, etc.) by lightly browning in fat and then cooking slowly in a closed pan with a small amount of liquid. [C18: from French *braiser,* from Old French *brese* live coals, probably of Germanic origin; compare Old English *brædan,* Old High German *brātan* to roast]
brake[1] (breɪk) *n.* **1. a.** (*often pl.*) a device for slowing or stopping a vehicle, wheel, shaft, etc., or for keeping it stationary, esp. by means of friction. See also **drum brake, disc brake, hydraulic brake, air brake, handbrake. b.** (*as modifier*): *the brake pedal.* **2.** a machine or tool for crushing or breaking flax or hemp to separate the fibres. **3.** Also called: **brake harrow.** a heavy harrow for breaking up clods. **4.** short for **brake van. 5.** short for **shooting brake. 6.** an obsolete word for **the rack** (an instrument of torture). ~*vb.* **7.** to slow down or cause to slow down, by or as if by using a brake. **8.** (*tr.*) to crush or break up using a brake. [C18: from Middle Dutch *braeke;* related to *breken* to BREAK] **—'brake+less** *adj.*
brake[2] (breɪk) *n.* an area of dense undergrowth, shrubs, brushwood, etc.; thicket. [Old English *bracu;* related to Middle Low German *brake,* Old French *bracon* branch]
brake[3] (breɪk) *n.* another name for **bracken.** See also **rock brake.**
brake[4] (breɪk) *vb. Archaic, chiefly biblical.* a past tense of **break.**
brake band *n.* a strip of fabric, leather, or metal tightened around a pulley or shaft to act as a brake.
brake drum *n.* the cast-iron drum attached to the hub of a wheel of a motor vehicle fitted with drum brakes. See also **brake shoe.**
brake flu+id *n.* an oily liquid used to transmit pressure in a hydraulic brake or clutch system.
brake horse+pow·er *n.* the rate at which an engine does work, expressed in horsepower. It is measured by the resistance of an applied brake. Abbrev.: **b.h.p.**
brake light *n.* a red light attached to the rear of a motor vehicle that lights up when the brakes are applied, serving as a warning to following drivers. Also called: **stoplight.**
brake lin+ing *n.* a curved thin strip of an asbestos composition riveted to a brake shoe to provide it with a renewable surface.
brake+man ('breɪkmən) *n., pl.* **+men.** *U.S.* a crew member of a goods or passenger train. His duties include controlling auxiliary braking power and inspecting the train.
brake par·a+chute *n.* a parachute attached to the rear of an aircraft and opened during landing to assist braking. Also called: **brake chute, parachute brake, parabrake.**
brake shoe *n.* the curved metal casting to which the brake lining is riveted in a drum brake. Sometimes shortened to **shoe.**
brakes+man ('breɪksmən) *n., pl.* **+men.** a pithead winch operator.
brake van *n. Railways, Brit.* the coach or vehicle from which

the guard applies the brakes; guard's van. U.S. equivalent: **caboose.**

Brak+pan ('bræk,pæn) *n.* a city in E South Africa, in S Transvaal: gold-mining centre. Pop.: 72 489 (1970).

Bra·man·te (*Italian* bra'mante) *n.* **Do·na·to** (do'na:to). ?1444–1514, Italian architect and artist of the High Renaissance. He modelled his designs for domed centrally planned churches on classical Roman architecture.

bram+ble ('bræmbᵊl) *n.* **1.** any of various prickly herbaceous plants or shrubs of the rosaceous genus *Rubus*, esp. the blackberry. See also **stone bramble. 2.** any of several similar and related shrubs, such as the dog rose. ~*vb.* **3.** (*intr.*) to gather blackberries. [Old English *brǣmbel;* related to Old Saxon *brāmal,* Old High German *brāmo*] —'**bram+bly** *adj.*

bram+bling ('bræmblɪŋ) *n.* a Eurasian finch, *Fringilla montifringilla,* with a speckled head and back and, in the male, a reddish brown breast and darker wings and tail.

Bram+ley ('bræmlɪ) *or* **Bram·ley's seed+ling** *n.* a variety of cooking apple having juicy firm flesh. [C19: named after Matthew *Bramley,* 19th-century English butcher, said to have first grown it]

bran (bræn) *n.* **1.** husks of cereal grain separated from the flour by sifting. **2.** food prepared from these husks. [C13: from Old French, probably of Gaulish origin]

branch (brɑ:ntʃ) *n.* **1.** a secondary woody stem arising from the trunk or bough of a tree or the main stem of a shrub. **2.** a subdivision of the stem or root of any other plant. **3.** an offshoot or secondary part: *a branch of a deer's antlers.* **4. a.** a subdivision or subsidiary section of something larger or more complex: *branches of learning; branch of the family.* **b.** (*as modifier*): *a branch office.* **5.** *U.S.* any small stream. **6.** *Maths.* a section of a curve separated from the rest of the curve by discontinuities or special points. **7.** Also called: **jump.** *Computer technol.* a departure from the normal sequence of programmed instructions into a subroutine. ~*vb.* **8.** (*intr.*) (of a tree or other plant) to produce or possess branches. **9.** (*intr.;* usually foll. by *from*) (of stems, roots, etc.) to grow and diverge (from another part). **10.** to divide or be divided into subsidiaries or offshoots. **11.** (*intr.;* often foll. by *off*) to diverge from the main way, road, topic, etc. ~See also **branch out.** [C13: from Old French *branche,* from Late Latin *branca* paw, foot] —'**branch+less** *adj.* —'**branch+,like** *adj.* —'**branch·y** *adj.*

-branch *adj. and n. combining form.* (in zoology) indicating gills: *lamellibranch.* [from Latin: BRANCHIA]

branched chain *n. Chem.* an open chain of atoms with one or more side chains attached to it. Compare **straight chain.**

bran+chi·a ('bræŋkɪə) *n., pl.* **+chi·ae** (-kɪ,i:). a gill in aquatic animals. —'**bran+chi·al** *adj.* —'**bran+chi+,ate** *adj.*

branch+ing ('brɑ:ntʃɪŋ) *n. Physics.* the occurrence of several decay processes (**branches**) in the disintegration of a particular nuclide. The **branching fraction** is the proportion of the disintegrating nuclei that follow a particular branch to the total number of disintegrating nuclides.

bran+chi·o+pod ('bræŋkɪə,pɒd) *n.* any crustacean of the mainly freshwater subclass *Branchiopoda,* having flattened limblike appendages for swimming, feeding, and respiration. The group includes the water fleas.

branch line *n. Railways.* a secondary route to a place or places not served by a main line.

branch of+fic+er *n.* (in the British navy since 1949) any officer who holds warrant.

branch out *vb.* (*intr., adv.;* often foll. by *into*) *Informal.* to expand or extend one's interests: *our business has branched out into computers now.*

Bran·cu·si (bræŋ'ku:zɪ; *Rumanian* brɘŋ'kuʃj) *n.* **Con·stan·tin** (konstan'tin). 1876–1957, Rumanian sculptor, noted for his streamlined abstractions of animal forms.

brand (brænd) *n.* **1.** a trade name identifying a manufacturer or a product; trademark. **2.** a particular kind or variety: *he had his own brand of humour.* **3.** an identifying mark made, usually by burning, on the skin of animals or (formerly) slaves or criminals, esp. as a proof of ownership. **4.** an iron heated and used for branding animals, etc. **5.** a mark of disgrace or infamy; stigma: *he bore the brand of a coward.* **6.** a burning or burnt piece of wood, as in a fire. **7.** *Archaic or poetic.* **a.** a flaming torch. **b.** a sword. **8.** a fungal disease of garden plants characterized by brown spots on the leaves, caused by the rust fungus *Puccinia arenariae.* ~*vb.* (*tr.*) **9.** to label, burn, or mark with or as with a brand. **10.** to place indelibly in the memory: *the scene of slaughter was branded in their minds.* **11.** to denounce; stigmatize: *they branded him a traitor.* [Old English *brand-* related to Old Norse *brandr,* Old High German *brant;* see BURN[1]] —'**brand+er** *n.*

Bran+den+burg ('brændən,bɜ:g; *German* 'brandᵊn,burk) *n.* **1.** a former electorate in NE Germany that expanded under the Hohenzollerns to become the kingdom of Prussia (1701). The district east of the Oder River became Polish in 1945, the remainder being part of East Germany. **2.** a city in central East Germany: former capital of the Prussian province of Brandenburg. Pop.: 94 841 (1972 est.).

bran+dish ('brændɪʃ) *vb.* **1.** (*tr.*) to wave or flourish (a weapon, etc.) in a triumphant, threatening, or ostentatious way. ~*n.* **2.** a threatening or defiant flourish. [C14: from Old French *brandir,* from *brand* sword, of Germanic origin; compare Old High German *brant* weapon] —'**bran+dish+er** *n.*

brand+ling ('brændlɪŋ) *n.* a small red earthworm, *Eisenia foetida* (or *Helodrilus foetidus*), found in manure and used as bait by anglers.

brand-new *adj.* absolutely new. [C16: from BRAND (n.) + NEW, likened to newly forged iron]

Bran·do ('brændəʊ) *n.* **Mar·lon.** born 1924, U.S. actor; his films include *A Streetcar named Desire* (1952), *On the Waterfront* (1954), for which he won an Oscar, *The Godfather* (1972), and *Last Tango in Paris* (1973).

Brandt (*German* brant) *n.* **Wil·ly** ('vɪlɪ). born 1913, German statesman; socialist chancellor of West Germany (1969–74). His policy of détente and reconciliation with E Europe brought him international acclaim. Nobel prize for peace 1971.

bran+dy ('brændɪ) *n., pl.* **+dies. 1.** an alcoholic drink consisting of spirit distilled from grape wine. **2.** a distillation of wines made from other fruits: *plum brandy.* [C17: from earlier *brandewine,* from Dutch *brandewijn,* burnt wine, from *bernen* to burn or distil + *wijn* WINE; compare German *Branntwein*]

bran+dy bot+tle *n.* another name for a **yellow water lily.**

bran+dy but+ter *n.* another name for **hard sauce.**

bran+dy snap *n.* a crisp sweet biscuit, rolled into a cylinder after baking and often filled with whipped cream.

branks (bræŋks) *pl. n.* (formerly) an iron bridle used to restrain scolding women. [C16: of unknown origin]

bran+le ('brænᵊl) *n.* an old French country dance performed in a linked circle. [from Old French *branler* to shake, variant of *brandir* to BRANDISH]

brant (brænt) *n., pl.* **brants** *or* **brant.** a variant spelling (esp. U.S.) of **brent** (the goose).

Brant+ford ('bræntfəd) *n.* a city in central Canada, in SW Ontario. Pop.: 64 421 (1971).

bran tub *n. Brit.* a tub containing bran in which small wrapped gifts are hidden, used at parties, fairs, etc.

Braque (*French* brak) *n.* **Georges** (ʒɔrʒ). 1882–1963, French painter who developed cubism with Picasso (1908–14).

brash[1] (bræʃ) *adj.* **1.** tastelessly or offensively loud, showy, or bold. **2.** hasty; rash. **3.** impudent. [C19: perhaps influenced by RASH[1]] —'**brash+ly** *adv.* —'**brash+ness** *n.*

brash[2] (bræʃ) *n.* loose rubbish, such as broken rock, hedge clippings, etc.; debris. [C18: of unknown origin]

brash[3] (bræʃ) *n. Pathol.* another name for **heartburn.** [C16: perhaps of imitative origin]

brash·y ('bræʃɪ) *adj.* **brash·i·er, brash·i·est. 1.** loosely fragmented; rubbishy. **2.** (of timber) brittle. —'**brash·i·ness** *n.*

bra+si+er ('breɪzɪə) *n.* a less common spelling of **brazier.**

Bra+sil (bra'zil) *n.* the Portuguese spelling of **Brazil.**

bra+sil+e·in (brə'zɪlɪɪn) *n.* a variant spelling of **brazilein.**

Bra+síl·ia (brə'zɪljə; *Portuguese* bra'zilja) *n.* the capital of Brazil (since 1960), on the central plateau: the former capital was Rio de Janeiro. Pop.: 272 002 (1970).

bras·i·lin ('bræzɪlɪn) *n.* a variant spelling of **brazilin.**

Bra+şov (*Rumanian* bra'ʃov) *n.* an industrial city in central Rumania: formerly a centre for expatriate Germans; ceded by Hungary to Rumania in 1920. Pop.: 198 753 (1974 est.). Former name (1950–61): **Stalin.** German name: **Kronstadt.** Hungarian name: **Brassó.**

brass (brɑ:s) *n.* **1.** an alloy of copper and zinc containing more than 50 per cent of copper. **Alpha brass** (containing less than 35 per cent of zinc) is used for most engineering materials requiring forging, pressing, etc. **Alpha-beta brass** (35–45 per cent zinc) is used for hot working and extrusion. **Beta brass** (45–50 per cent zinc) is used for castings. Compare **bronze** (sense 1). **2.** an object, ornament, or utensil made of brass. **3. a.** the large family of wind instruments including the trumpet, trombone, French horn, etc., each consisting of a brass tube blown directly by means of a cup- or funnel-shaped mouthpiece. **b.** (*sometimes functioning as pl.*) instruments of this family forming a section in an orchestra. **c.** (*as modifier*): *a brass ensemble.* **4.** a renewable sleeve or bored semicylindrical shell made of brass or bronze, used as a liner for a bearing. **5.** (*functioning as pl.*) *Informal.* important or high-ranking officials, esp. military officers: *the top brass.* See also **brass hat. 6.** *Northern English dialect.* money: *where there's muck, there's brass!* **7.** *Brit.* an engraved brass memorial tablet or plaque, set in the wall or floor of a church. **8.** *Informal.* bold self-confidence; cheek; nerve: *he had the brass to ask for more time.* **9.** (*modifier*) of, consisting of, or relating to brass or brass instruments: *a brass ornament; a brass band.* [Old English *bræs;* related to Old Frisian *bres* copper, Middle Low German *bras* metal]

bras+sard ('bræsɑ:d) *or* **bras+sart** ('bræsət) *n.* **1.** an identifying armband or badge. **2.** a piece of armour for the upper arm. [C19: from French, from *bras* arm, from Latin BRACHIUM]

brass band *n.* See **band**[1] (sense 2).

brass+bound ('brɑ:s,baʊnd) *adj.* inflexibly entrenched: *brass-bound traditions.*

bras+se+rie ('bræsərɪ) *n.* **1.** a bar in which drinks and often food are served. **2.** a small and usually cheap restaurant. [C19: from French, from *brasser* to stir, brew]

brass hat *n. Brit. informal.* a top-ranking official, esp. a military officer. [C20: from the gold leaf decoration on the peaks of caps worn by officers of high rank]

bras+si+ca ('bræsɪkə) *n.* any cruciferous plant of the genus *Brassica,* native to the Mediterranean region and grown widely as vegetables, such as cabbage, rape, swede, turnip, and mustard. [C19: from Latin: cabbage] —**bras+si+ca+ceous** (,bræsɪ'keɪʃəs) *adj.*

brass·ie *or* **brass·y** ('bræsɪ, 'brɑ:-) *n., pl.* **brass·ies.** *Golf.* a club, a No. 2 wood, originally having a brass-plated sole and with a shallower face than a driver to give more loft.

bras+siere ('bræsɪə, 'bræz-) *n.* a woman's undergarment for covering and supporting the breasts. Often shortened to **bra.**

[C20: from C17 French: bodice, from Old French *braciere* a protector for the arm, from *braz* arm]

Bras+só ('brɔʃʃo:) *n.* the Hungarian name for **Braşov.**

brass tacks *pl. n. Informal.* basic realities; hard facts (esp. in the phrase **get down to brass tacks**).

brass·y ('brɑ:sɪ) *adj.* **brass·i+er, brass·i+est.** **1.** *Informal.* insolent; brazen. **2.** flashy; showy. **3.** (of sound) harsh, strident, or resembling the sound of a brass instrument. **4.** like brass, esp. in colour. **5.** decorated with or made of brass. —'**brass·i+ly** *adv.* —'**brass·i+ness** *n.*

brat[1] (bræt) *n.* a child, esp. one who is dirty or unruly: used contemptuously or playfully. [C16: perhaps special use of earlier *brat* rag, from Old English *bratt* cloak, of Celtic origin; related to Old Irish *bratt* cloth, BRAT[2]]

brat[2] (bræt) *n. Northern Brit. dialect.* an apron or overall. [from Old English *bratt* cloak; related to Old Irish *bratt* cloth used to cover the body]

Bra+ti+sla+va (ˌbrætɪ'slɑ:və) *n.* a port in S Czechoslovakia on the River Danube: capital of Slovakia since 1918; capital of Hungary (1541–1784) and seat of the Hungarian parliament until 1848. Pop.: 328 765 (1974 est.). German name: **Pressburg.** Hungarian name: **Pozsony.**

brat+tice ('brætɪs) *n.* **1.** a partition of wood or treated cloth used to control ventilation in a mine. **2.** *Medieval fortifications.* a fixed wooden tower or parapet. ~*vb.* **3.** (*tr.*) *Mining.* to fit with a brattice. [C13: from Old French *bretesche* wooden tower, from Medieval Latin *breteschia,* probably from Latin *Britō* a Briton]

brat+tish+ing ('brætɪʃɪŋ) *n. Architect.* decorative work along the coping or on the cornice of a building. [C16: variant of *bratticing;* see BRATTICE]

brat+wurst ('brɑ:tˌwɜ:st; *German* 'bra:tˌvʊrʃt) *n.* a type of small pork sausage. [German, from Old High German, from *brāto* meat + *wurst* sausage; related to Old Saxon *brādo* ham]

Braun (*German* braʊn) *n.* **1. E·va** ('e:fa). 1910–45, Adolf Hitler's mistress. **2.** See (Wernher) **von Braun.**

braun+ite ('braʊnaɪt) *n.* a brown or black mineral that consists of manganese oxide and silicate and is a source of manganese. Formula: Mn_7SiO_{12}. [C19: named after A. E. *Braun* (1809–56), German official in the treasury at Gotha]

Braun+schweig ('braʊnˌʃvaɪk) *n.* the German name for **Brunswick.**

bra+va+do (brə'vɑ:dəʊ) *n., pl.* **+does** *or* **+dos.** vaunted display of courage or self-confidence; swagger. [C16: from Spanish *bravada* (modern *bravata*), from Old Italian *bravare* to challenge, provoke, from *bravo* wild, BRAVE]

Bra+vais lat+tice ('brævei, brə'veɪ) *n. Crystallog.* any of 14 possible space lattices found in crystals. [named after Auguste *Bravais,* 19th-century French physicist]

brave (breɪv) *adj.* **1. a.** having or displaying courage, resolution, or daring; not cowardly or timid. **b.** (*as collective n.* preceded by *the*): *the brave.* **2.** fine; splendid: *a brave sight; a brave attempt.* **3.** *Archaic.* excellent or admirable. ~*n.* **4.** a warrior of a North American Indian tribe. **5.** an obsolete word for **bully.** ~*vb.* (*tr.*) **6.** to dare or defy: *to brave the odds.* **7.** to confront with resolution or courage: *to brave the storm.* **8.** *Obsolete.* to make splendid, esp. in dress. [C15: from French, from Italian *bravo* courageous, wild, perhaps ultimately from Latin *barbarus* BARBAROUS] —'**brave+ly** *adv.* —'**brave+ness** *n.* —'**brav+er·y** *n.*

bra+vis+si+mo (brɑ:'vɪsɪˌməʊ) *interj.* very well done! excellent! [C18: from Italian, superlative of BRAVO]

bra+vo *interj.* **1.** (brɑ:'vəʊ). well done! ~*n.* **2.** (brɑ:'vəʊ), *pl.* **+vos.** a cry of "bravo." **3.** ('brɑ:vəʊ), *pl.* **+voes** *or* **+vos.** a hired killer or assassin. [C18: from Italian: splendid! see BRAVE]

bra+vu+ra (brə'vjʊərə, -'vʊərə) *n.* **1.** a display of boldness or daring. **2.** *Music.* **a.** a passage or piece requiring great spirit and technical skill by the performer. **b.** (*as modifier*): *a bravura passage.* [C18: from Italian: spirit, courage, from *bravare* to show off, see BRAVADO]

braw (brɔ:, brɑ:) *adj. Chiefly Scot.* fine or excellent, esp. in appearance or dress. [C16: Scottish variant of BRAVE]

brawl[1] (brɔ:l) *n.* **1.** a loud disagreement or fight. **2.** *U.S. slang.* an uproarious party. ~*vb.* (*intr.*) **3.** to quarrel or fight noisily; squabble. **4.** (esp. of water) to flow noisily. [C14: probably related to Dutch *brallen* to boast, behave aggressively] —'**brawl+er** *n.*

brawl[2] (brɔ:l) *n.* a dance: the English version of the branle.

brawn (brɔ:n) *n.* **1.** strong well-developed muscles. **2.** physical strength, esp. as opposed to intelligence. **3.** *Brit.* a seasoned jellied loaf made from the head and sometimes the feet of a pig or calf. [C14: from Old French *braon* slice of meat, of Germanic origin; compare Old High German *brāto,* Old English *brǣd* flesh]

brawn·y ('brɔ:nɪ) *adj.* **brawn·i+er, brawn·i+est.** muscular and strong. —'**brawn·i+ly** *adv.* —'**brawn·i+ness** *n.*

brax·y ('bræksɪ) *n.* an acute and usually fatal bacterial disease of sheep characterized by high fever, coma, and inflammation of the fourth stomach, caused by infection with *Clostridium septicum.* [C18: of unknown origin]

bray[1] (breɪ) *vb.* **1.** (*intr.*) (of a donkey) to utter its characteristic loud harsh sound; heehaw. **2.** (*intr.*) to make a similar sound, as in laughing: *he brayed at the joke.* **3.** (*tr.*) to utter with a loud harsh sound. ~*n.* **4.** the loud harsh sound uttered by a donkey. **5.** a similar loud cry or uproar: *a bray of protest.* [C13: from Old French *braire,* probably of Celtic origin] —'**bray+er** *n.*

bray[2] (breɪ) *vb.* **1.** (*tr.*) to distribute (ink) over printing type or plates. **2.** (*tr.*) to pound into a powder, as in a mortar. **3.** *Northern English dialect.* to hit or beat (someone or something) hard; bang. [C14: from Old French *breier,* of Germanic origin; see BREAK] —'**bray+er** *n.*

Braz. *abbrev. for* Brazil(ian).

braze[1] (breɪz) *vb.* (*tr.*) **1.** to decorate with or make of brass. **2.** to make like brass, as in hardness. [Old English *bræsen,* from *bræs* BRASS]

braze[2] (breɪz) *vb.* (*tr.*) to make a joint between (two metal surfaces) by fusing a layer of brass or high-melting solder between them. [C16: from Old French: to burn, of Germanic origin; see BRAISE] —'**braz+er** *n.*

bra+zen ('breɪzᵊn) *adj.* **1.** shameless and bold. **2.** made of or resembling brass. **3.** having a ringing metallic sound like that of a brass trumpet. ~*vb.* (*tr.*) **4.** (usually foll. by *out* or *through*) to face and overcome boldly or shamelessly: *the witness brazened out the prosecutor's questions.* **5.** to make (oneself, etc.) bold or brash. [Old English *bræsen,* from *bræs* BRASS] —'**bra+zen+ly** *adv.* —'**bra+zen+ness** *n.*

bra·zen-faced *adj.* shameless or impudent.

bra+zi+er[1] *or* **bra+si+er** ('breɪzɪə) *n.* a person engaged in brass-working or brass-founding. [C14: from Old English *bræsian* to work in brass + -ER[1]] —'**bra·zi·er·y** *n.*

bra+zi+er[2] *or* **bra+si+er** ('breɪzɪə) *n.* a portable metal receptacle for burning charcoal or coal, used for cooking, heating, etc. [C17: from French *brasier,* from *braise* live coals; see BRAISE]

bra+zil *or* **bra+sil** (brə'zɪl) *n.* **1.** Also called: **brazil wood.** the red wood obtained from various caesalpiniaceous tropical trees of the genus *Caesalpinia,* such as *C. echinata* of America: used for cabinetwork. **2.** the red or purple dye extracted from any of these woods. See also **brazilin. 3.** short for **brazil nut.** [C14: from Old Spanish *brasil,* from *brasa* glowing coals, of Germanic origin; referring to the redness of the wood; see BRAISE]

Bra+zil (brə'zɪl) *n.* a republic in South America, comprising about half the area and half the population of South America: colonized by the Portuguese from 1500 onwards; became independent in 1822 and a republic in 1889; consists chiefly of the tropical Amazon basin in the north, semiarid scrub in the northeast, and a vast central tableland; an important producer of coffee and minerals, esp. iron ore. Official language: Portuguese. Religion: chiefly Roman Catholic. Currency: cruzeiro. Capital: Brasília. Pop.: 93 215 301 (1970). Area: 8 511 957 sq. km (3 286 470 sq. miles). —**Bra+'zil+i+an** *adj., n.*

bra+zil+e·in *or* **bra+sil+e·in** (brə'zɪlɪɪn) *n.* a red crystalline solid obtained by the oxidation of brazilin and used as a dye. Formula: $C_{16}H_{12}O_5$. [C19: from German *Brasilein,* from BRAZILIN]

braz·i+lin *or* **bras·i+lin** ('bræzɪlɪn) *n.* a pale yellow soluble crystalline solid, turning red in alkaline solution, extracted from brazil wood and sappanwood and used in dyeing and as an indicator. Formula: $C_{16}H_{14}O_5$. [C19: from French *brésiline,* from *brésil* brazil wood]

bra+zil nut *n.* **1.** a tropical South American tree, *Bertholletia excelsa,* producing large globular capsules, each containing several closely packed triangular nuts: family *Lecythidaceae.* **2.** the nut of this tree, having an edible oily kernel and a woody shell. ~Often shortened to **brazil.**

Braz+za+ville (*French* braza'vil) *n.* the capital of the Congo Republic, in the south on the River Congo. Pop.: 250 000 (1972 est.).

B.R.C.S. *abbrev. for* British Red Cross Society.

breach (bri:tʃ) *n.* **1.** a crack, break, or rupture. **2.** a breaking, infringement, or violation of a promise, obligation, etc. **3.** any severance or separation: *there was a breach between the two factions of the party.* **4.** the act of a whale in breaking clear of the water. **5.** the breaking of sea waves on a shore or rock. **6.** an obsolete word for **wound**[1]. ~*vb.* **7.** (*tr.*) to break through or make an opening, hole, or incursion in. **8.** (*tr.*) to break a promise, law, etc. **9.** (*intr.*) (of a whale) to break clear of the water. [Old English *bræc;* influenced by Old French *brèche,* from Old High German *brecha,* from *brechan* to BREAK]

breach of prom+ise *n. Law.* (formerly) failure to carry out one's promise to marry.

breach of the peace *n. Law.* an offence against public order causing an unnecessary disturbance of the peace.

breach of trust *n. Law.* a violation of duty by a trustee or any other person in a fiduciary position.

bread (brɛd) *n.* **1.** a food made from a dough of flour or meal mixed with water or milk, usually raised with yeast or baking powder and then baked. **2.** necessary food; nourishment: *give us our daily bread.* **3.** a slang word for **money. 4.** *Christianity.* a small loaf, piece of bread, or wafer of unleavened bread used in the Eucharist. **5. break bread.** See **break** (sense 44). **6. cast one's bread upon the waters.** to do good without expectation of advantage or return. **7. know which side one's bread is buttered.** *Informal.* to know what to do in order to keep one's advantages or privileges. **8. take the bread out of (someone's) mouth.** to deprive of a livelihood. ~*vb.* **9.** (*tr.*) to cover with bread crumbs before cooking. [Old English *brēad;* related to Old Norse *braud,* Old Frisian *brād,* Old High German *brōt*]

bread and but+ter *Informal.* ~*n.* **1.** a means of support or subsistence; livelihood: *the inheritance was their bread and butter.* ~*modifier.* **2.** (**bread-and-butter**) **a.** providing a basic means of subsistence: *a bread-and-butter job.* **b.** solid, reliable, or practical: *a bread-and-butter player.* **c.** expressing gratitude, as for hospitality (esp. in the phrase **bread-and-butter letter**).

bread+bas+ket ('brɛdˌbɑ:skɪt) *n.* **1.** a basket for carrying bread or rolls. **2.** a slang word for **stomach.**

bread+board ('brɛdˌbɔ:d) *n.* **1.** a wooden board on which dough is kneaded or bread is sliced. **2.** an experimental arrangement of electronic circuits giving access to components so that modifications can be carried out easily.

bread·fruit ('brɛd,fru:t) *n., pl.* **·fruits** *or* **·fruit. 1.** a moraceous tree, *Artocarpus communis* (or *A. altilis*), of the Pacific Islands, having edible round, usually seedless, fruit. **2.** the fruit of this tree, which is eaten baked or roasted and has a texture like bread.

bread·line ('brɛd,laɪn) *n.* **1.** a queue of people waiting for free food given out by a government agency or a charity organization. **2. on the breadline.** *Informal.* impoverished; living at subsistence level.

bread mould *or* **black mould** *n.* a black phycomycete fungus, *Rhizopus nigricans,* occurring on decaying bread and vegetable matter.

bread·nut ('brɛd,nʌt) *n.* **1.** a moraceous tree, *Brosimum alicastrum,* of Central America and the West Indies. **2.** the nutlike fruit of this tree, ground to produce a substitute for wheat flour, esp. in the West Indies.

bread·root ('brɛd,ru:t) *n.* a papilionaceous plant, *Psoralea esculenta,* of central North America, having an edible starchy root. Also called: **prairie turnip.**

bread sauce *n.* a béchamel sauce thickened with breadcrumbs and served with roast poultry, esp. chicken.

breadth (brɛdθ, brɛtθ) *n.* **1.** the linear extent or measurement of something from side to side; width. **2.** a piece of fabric, etc., having a standard or definite width. **3.** distance, extent, size, or dimension. **4.** openness and lack of restriction, esp. of viewpoint or interest; liberality. [C16: from obsolete *brēde* (from Old English *brǣdu,* from *brād* BROAD) + -TH[1]; related to Gothic *braidei,* Old High German *breitī*]

breadth·ways ('brɛdθ,weɪz, 'brɛtθ-) *or esp. U.S.* **breadth·wise** ('brɛdθ,waɪz, 'brɛtθ-) *adv.* from side to side.

bread·win·ner ('brɛd,wɪnə) *n.* a person supporting a family with his or her earnings.

break (breɪk) *vb.* **breaks, break·ing, broke, bro·ken. 1.** to separate or become separated into two or more pieces: *this cup is broken.* **2.** to damage or become damaged so as to be inoperative: *my radio is broken.* **3.** to crack or become cracked without separating. **4.** to burst or cut the surface of (skin, etc.). **5.** to discontinue or become discontinued: *they broke for lunch; to break a journey.* **6.** to disperse or become dispersed: *the clouds broke.* **7.** (*tr.*) to fail to observe (an agreement, promise, law, etc.): *to break one's word.* **8.** (foll. by *with*) to discontinue an association (with). **9.** to disclose or be disclosed: *he broke the news gently.* **10.** (*tr.*) to fracture (a bone) in (a limb, etc.). **11.** (*tr.*) to divide (something complete or perfect): *to break a set of books.* **12.** to bring or come to an end: *the summer weather broke at last.* **13.** (*tr.*) to bring to an end by or as if by force: *to break a strike.* **14.** (when *intr.,* often foll. by *out*) to escape (from): *he broke jail; he broke out of jail.* **15.** to weaken or overwhelm or be weakened or overwhelmed, as in spirit. **16.** (*tr.*) to cut through or penetrate: *a cry broke the silence.* **17.** (*tr.*) to improve on or surpass: *to break a record.* **18.** (*tr.;* often foll. by *in*) to accustom (a horse) to the bridle and saddle, to being ridden, etc. **19.** (*tr.;* often foll. by *of*) to cause (a person) to give up (a habit): *this cure will break you of smoking.* **20.** (*tr.*) to weaken the impact or force of: *this net will break his fall.* **21.** (*tr.*) to decipher: *to break a code.* **22.** (*tr.*) to lose the order of: *to break ranks.* **23.** (*tr.*) to reduce to poverty or the state of bankruptcy. **24.** (when *intr.,* foll. by *into*) to obtain, give, or receive smaller units in exchange for; change: *to break a pound note.* **25.** (*tr.*) *Chiefly military.* to demote to a lower rank. **26.** (*intr.;* often foll. by *from* or *out of*) to proceed suddenly. **27.** (*intr.*) to come into being: *light broke over the mountains.* **28.** (*intr.;* foll. by *into* or *out into*) to burst into song, laughter, etc. **29.** (*tr.*) to open with explosives: *to break a safe.* **30.** (*intr.*) (of waves) **a.** (often foll. by *against*) to strike violently. **b.** to collapse into foam or surf. **31.** (*intr.*) (esp. of fish) to appear above the surface of the water. **32.** (*intr.*) *Informal, chiefly U.S.* to turn out in a specified manner: *things are breaking well.* **33.** (*intr.*) (of prices, esp. stock exchange quotations) to fall sharply. **34.** (*intr.*) to make a sudden effort, as in running, horse racing, etc. **35.** (*intr.*) *Cricket.* (of a ball) to change direction on bouncing. **36.** (*tr.*) *Cricket.* (of a player) to knock down at least one bail from (a wicket). **37.** (*intr.*) *Billiards.* to scatter the balls at the start of a game. **38.** (*intr.*) *Horse racing.* to commence running in a race: *they broke even.* **39.** (*intr.*) *Boxing, wrestling.* (of two fighters) to separate from a clinch. **40.** (*intr.*) *Music.* **a.** (of the male voice) to undergo a change in register, quality, and range at puberty. **b.** (of the voice or some instruments) to undergo a change in tone, quality, etc., when changing registers. **41.** (*intr.*) *Phonetics.* (of a vowel) to turn into a diphthong, esp. as a development in the language. **42.** (*tr.*) to open the breech of (certain firearms) by snapping the barrel away from the butt on its hinge. **43.** (*tr.*) to interrupt the flow of current in (an electrical circuit). Compare **make**[1] (sense 26). **44. break bread. a.** to eat a meal, esp. with others. **b.** *Christianity.* to administer or participate in Holy Communion. **45. break camp.** to pack up equipment and leave a camp. **46. break (new) ground. a.** to begin an activity. **b.** to make one or more discoveries or innovations. **47. break one's back.** to overwork or work very hard. **48. break the back of.** to complete the greatest or hardest part of (a task). **49. break the bank.** to ruin financially or deplete the resources of a bank (as in gambling). **50. break the ice. a.** to relieve shyness or reserve, esp. between strangers. **b.** to be the first of a group to do something. **51. break service.** *Tennis.* to win a game in which an opponent is serving. **52. break wind.** to emit wind from the anus or mouth. ~*n.* **53.** the act or result of breaking; fracture. **54.** a crack formed as the result of breaking. **55.** a brief respite: *a break from one's toil.* **56.** a sudden rush, esp. to escape: *to make a break for freedom.* **57.** a breach in a relationship: *she has made a break from her family.* **58.** any sudden interruption in a continuous action. **59.** *Brit.* a short period between classes at school. U.S. equivalent: **recess. 60.** *Informal.* a fortunate opportunity, esp. to prove oneself. **61.** (esp. in a stock exchange) a sudden and substantial decline in prices. **62.** *Prosody.* a pause in a line of verse; caesura. **63.** *Billiards.* **a.** a series of successful shots during one turn. **b.** the points scored in such a series. **64.** *Billiards.* **a.** the opening shot with the cue ball that scatters the placed balls. **b.** the right to take this first shot. **65.** Also called: **service break, break of serve.** *Tennis.* the act or instance of breaking an opponent's service. **66.** one of the intervals in a sporting contest. **67.** *Horse racing.* the start of a race: *an even break.* **68.** (in tenpin bowling) failure to knock down all the pins after the second attempt. **69.** *Jazz.* a short passage during which a soloist plays unaccompanied: it is usually improvised. **70.** a discontinuity in an electrical circuit. **71.** an open four-wheeled horse-drawn carriage. ~*interj.* **72.** *Boxing, wrestling.* a command by a referee for two opponents to separate. ~See also **breakaway, break down, break even, break in, break into, break off, break out, break through, break up, break with.** [Old English *brecan;* related to Old Frisian *breka,* Gothic *brikan,* Old High German *brehhan,* Latin *frangere,* Sanskrit *bhráj* bursting forth]

break·a·ble ('breɪkəbᵊl) *adj.* **1.** capable of being broken. ~*n.* **2.** (*usually pl.*) a fragile easily broken article.

break·age ('breɪkɪdʒ) *n.* **1.** the act or result of breaking. **2.** the quantity or amount broken: *the total breakage was enormous.* **3.** compensation or allowance for goods damaged while in use, transit, etc.

break·a·way ('breɪkə,weɪ) *n.* **1. a.** loss or withdrawal of a group of members from an association, club, etc. **b.** (*as modifier*): *a breakaway faction.* **2.** *Sport.* **a.** a sudden attack, esp. from a defensive position, in football, hockey, etc. **b.** an attempt to get away from the rest of the field in a race. ~*vb.* **break a·way.** (*intr., adv.*) **3.** (often foll. by *from*) to leave hastily or escape. **4.** to withdraw or secede. **5.** *Sport.* to make a breakaway. **6.** *Horse racing.* to start prematurely.

break·bone fe·ver ('breɪk,bəʊn) *n.* another name for **dengue.**

break down *vb.* (*adv.*) **1.** (*intr.*) to cease to function; become ineffective: *communications had broken down.* **2.** to yield or cause to yield, esp. to strong emotion or tears: *she broke down in anguish.* **3.** (*tr.*) to crush or destroy. **4.** (*intr.*) to have a nervous breakdown. **5.** to analyse or be subjected to analysis. **6. break it down.** *Austral. informal.* **a.** stop it. **b.** don't expect me to believe that; come off it. ~*n.* **break·down. 7.** an act or instance of breaking down; collapse. **8.** short for **nervous breakdown. 9.** an analysis or classification of something into its component parts: *he prepared a breakdown of the report.* **10.** a desired electrical discharge between two electrodes in a gas discharge tube, occurring at and above a particular voltage. **11.** a lively American country dance.

break·down van *or* **truck** *n.* a motor vehicle equipped for towing away wrecked or disabled cars. U.S. names: **wrecker, tow truck.**

break·er[1] ('breɪkə) *n.* **1.** a person or thing that breaks something, such as a person or firm that breaks up old cars, etc. **2.** a large wave with a white crest on the open sea or one that breaks into foam on the shore. **3.** *Electronics.* short for **circuit breaker. 4.** a machine or plant for crushing rocks or coal. **5.** Also called: **breaking plough.** a plough with a long shallow mould board for turning virgin land or sod land. **6.** *Textiles.* a machine for extracting fibre preparatory to carding.

break·er[2] ('breɪkə) *n.* a small water cask for use in a boat. [C19: anglicized variant of Spanish *barrica,* from French (Gascon dialect) *barrique*]

break e·ven *vb.* **1.** (*intr., adv.*) to attain a level of activity, as in commerce, or a point of operation, as in gambling, at which there is neither profit nor loss. ~*n.* **break·e·ven. 2.** *Accounting.* **a.** the level of commercial activity at which the total cost and total revenue of a business enterprise are equal. **b.** (*as modifier*): *breakeven prices.*

break·e·ven chart *n. Accounting.* a graph measuring the value of an enterprise's revenue and costs against some index of its activity, such as percentage capacity. The intersection of the total revenue and total cost curves gives the breakeven point.

break·fast ('brɛkfəst) *n.* **1. a.** the first meal of the day. **b.** (*as modifier*): *breakfast cereal; a breakfast room.* **2.** the food at this meal. ~*vb.* **3.** to eat or supply with breakfast. [C15: from BREAK + FAST[2]] —**'break·fast·er** *n.*

break·front ('breɪk,frʌnt) *adj.* (*prenominal*) (of a bookcase, bureau, etc.) having a slightly projecting central section.

break in *vb.* (*adv.*) **1.** (sometimes foll. by *on*) to interrupt. **2.** (*intr.*) to enter a house, etc., illegally, esp. by force. **3.** (*tr.*) to accustom (a person or animal) to normal duties or practice. **4.** (*tr.*) to use or wear (shoes, new equipment, etc.) until comfortable or running smoothly. ~*n.* **break-in. 5. a.** the illegal entering of a building, esp. by thieves. **b.** (*as modifier*): *the break-in plans.*

break·ing ('breɪkɪŋ) *n. Linguistics.* (in Old English, Old Norse, etc.) the change of a vowel into a diphthong. [C19: translation of German *Brechung*]

break·ing and en·ter·ing *n.* (formerly) the gaining of unauthorized access to a building with intent to commit a crime or, having committed the crime, the breaking out of the building.

break in·to *vb.* (*intr., prep.*) **1.** to enter (a house, etc.) illegally, esp. by force. **2.** to change abruptly from a slower to a faster speed: *the horse broke into a gallop.* **3.** to consume (supplies held in reserve): *at the end of the exercise the soldiers had to break into their iron rations.*

break·neck ('breɪk,nɛk) *adj.* (*prenominal*) (of speed, pace, etc.) excessive and dangerous.

break of day *n.* another term for **dawn** (sense 1).

break off *vb.* **1.** to sever or detach or be severed or detached: *it broke off in my hands; he broke a piece off the bar of chocolate.* **2.** (*adv.*) to end (a relationship, association, etc.) or (of a relationship, etc.) to be ended. **3.** (*intr., adv.*) to stop abruptly; halt: *he broke off in the middle of his speech.* ~*n.* **break·off. 4.** the act or an instance of breaking off or stopping.

break out *vb.* (*intr., adv.*) **1.** to begin or arise suddenly: *panic broke out.* **2.** to make an escape, esp. from prison or confinement. **3.** (foll. by *in*) (of the skin) to erupt (in a rash, pimples, etc.). ~*n.* **break-out. 4.** an escape, esp. from prison or confinement.

break·point ('breɪk,pɔɪnt) *n. Computer technol.* **a.** an instruction inserted by a debug program causing a return to the debug program. **b.** the point in a program at which such an instruction operates.

break through *vb.* **1.** (*intr.*) to penetrate. **2.** (*intr., adv.*) to achieve success, make a discovery, etc., esp. after lengthy efforts. ~*n.* **break·through. 3.** a significant development or discovery, esp. in science. **4.** the penetration of an enemy's defensive position or line in depth and strength.

break up *vb.* (*adv.*) **1.** to separate or cause to separate. **2.** to put an end to (a relationship) or (of a relationship) to come to an end. **3.** to dissolve or cause to dissolve; disrupt or be disrupted: *the meeting broke up at noon.* **4.** *Slang.* to lose or cause to lose control of the emotions: *the news of his death broke her up.* **5.** *Slang.* to be or cause to be overcome with laughter. ~*n.* **break-up. 6.** a separation or disintegration.

break·wa·ter ('breɪk,wɔ:tə) *n.* **1.** Also called: **mole.** a massive wall built out into the sea to protect a shore or harbour from the force of waves. **2.** another name for **groyne.** ~*vb.* **break water. 3.** (of a woman in labour) to rupture the amniotic sac thus releasing amniotic fluid.

break with *vb.* (*intr., prep.*) to end a relationship or association with (someone or an organization or social group).

bream[1] (bri:m; *Austral.* brɪm) *or Austral.* **brim** (brɪm) *n., pl.* **bream** *or* **brim. 1.** any of several Eurasian freshwater cyprinid fishes of the genus *Abramis,* esp. *A. brama,* having a deep compressed body covered with silvery scales. **2. white** *or* **silver bream.** a similar cyprinid, *Blicca bjoerkna.* **3.** short for **sea bream.** [C14: from Old French *bresme,* of Germanic origin; compare Old High German *brahsema;* perhaps related to *brehan* to glitter]

bream[2] (bri:m) *vb. Nautical.* (formerly) to clean debris from (the bottom of a vessel) by heating to soften the pitch. [C15: probably from Middle Dutch *bremme* broom; from using burning broom as a source of heat]

Bream (bri:m) *n.* **Jul·ian.** born 1933, English guitarist and lutenist.

breast (brɛst) *n.* **1.** the front part of the body from the neck to the abdomen; chest. **2.** either of the two soft fleshy milk-secreting glands on the chest in sexually mature human females. **3.** a similar organ in certain other mammals. **4.** anything that resembles a breast in shape or position: *the breast of the hill.* **5.** a source of nourishment: *the city took the victims to its breast.* **6.** the source of human emotions. **7.** the part of a garment that covers the breast. **8.** a projection from the side of a wall, esp. that formed by a chimney. **9.** *Mining.* the face being worked at the end of a tunnel. **10. beat one's breast. a.** to display guilt and remorse publicly or ostentatiously. **b.** to make a show of victory or success. **11. make a clean breast of.** to make a confession of. ~*vb.* (*tr.*) **12.** to confront boldly; face: *breast the storm.* **13.** to oppose with the breast or meet at breast level: *breasting the waves.* **14.** to come alongside of: *breast the ship.* **15.** to reach the summit of: *breasting the mountain top.* **16. keep someone breasted of.** to keep someone informed of. [Old English *brēost;* related to Old Norse *brjóst,* Old High German *brust,* Dutch *borst,* Swedish *bräss,* Old Irish *brū* belly, body]

breast·bone ('brɛst,bəun) *n.* the nontechnical name for **sternum.**

breast-feed *vb.* **-feeds, -feed·ing, -fed. 1.** to feed (a baby) with milk from the breast; suckle. **2.** (*tr.*) *Informal.* to pamper; coddle.

breast·pin ('brɛst,pɪn) *n.* a brooch worn on the breast, esp. to close a garment.

breast·plate ('brɛst,pleɪt) *n.* **1.** a piece of armour covering the chest. **2.** the strap of a harness covering a horse's breast. **3.** *Judaism.* a square vestment ornamented with 12 precious stones, representing the 12 tribes of Israel, worn by the high priest when praying before the holy of holies. **4.** *Zoology.* a nontechnical name for **plastron.**

breast·stroke ('brɛst,strəuk) *n.* a swimming stroke in which the arms are extended in front of the head and swept back on either side while the legs are drawn up beneath the body and thrust back together.

breast·work ('brɛst,wɜ:k) *n. Fortifications.* a temporary defensive work, usually breast-high. Also called: **parapet.**

breath (brɛθ) *n.* **1.** the intake and expulsion of air during respiration. **2.** the air inhaled or exhaled during respiration. **3.** a single respiration or inhalation of air, etc. **4.** the vapour, heat, or odour of exhaled air: *his breath on the window melted the frost.* **5.** a slight gust of air. **6.** a short pause or rest: *take a breath for five minutes.* **7.** a brief time: *it was done in a breath.* **8.** a suggestion or slight evidence; suspicion: *a breath of scandal.* **9.** a whisper or soft sound. **10.** life, energy, or vitality: *the breath of new industry.* **11.** *Phonetics.* the passage of air through the completely open glottis without vibration of the vocal cords, as in exhaling or pronouncing fricatives such as (f) or (h) or stops such as (p) or (k). Compare **voice** (sense 11). **12. catch one's breath.** to rest until breathing is normal, esp. after exertion. **13. in the same breath.** done or said at the same time. **14. out of breath.** gasping for air after exertion. **15. save one's breath.** to refrain from useless talk. **16. take one's breath away.** to overwhelm with surprise, etc. **17. under** *or* **below one's breath.** in a quiet voice or whisper. [Old English *brǣth;* related to *brǣdan* to burn, Old High German *brādam* heat, breath]

breath·a·lyse *or U.S.* **breath·a·lyze** ('brɛθə,laɪz) *vb.* (*tr.*) to apply a Breathalyzer test to (someone).

Breath·a·lyz·er *or* **Breath·a·lys·er** ('brɛθə,laɪzə) *n. Brit., trademark.* a device for estimating the amount of alcohol in the breath: used in testing people suspected of driving under the influence of alcohol. U.S. equivalent: **drunkometer.**

breathe (bri:ð) *vb.* **1.** to take in oxygen from (the surrounding medium, esp. air) and give out carbon dioxide; respire. **2.** (*intr.*) to exist; be alive: *every animal that breathes on earth.* **3.** (*intr.*) to rest to regain breath, composure, etc.: *stop your questions, and give me a chance to breathe.* **4.** (*intr.*) (esp. of air) to blow lightly: *the wind breathed through the trees.* **5.** (*intr.*) *Machinery.* **a.** to take in air, esp. for combustion: *the engine breathes through this air filter.* **b.** to equalize the pressure within a container, chamber, etc., with atmospheric pressure: *the crankcase breathes through this duct.* **6.** (*tr.*) *Phonetics.* to articulate (a speech sound) without vibration of the vocal cords. Compare **voice** (sense 19). **7.** to exhale or emit: *the dragon breathed fire.* **8.** (*tr.*) to impart; instill: *to breathe confidence into the actors.* **9.** (*tr.*) to speak softly; whisper: *to breathe words of love.* **10.** (*tr.*) to permit to rest: *to breathe a horse.* **11. breathe again, freely,** *or* **easily.** to feel relief: *I could breathe again after passing the exam.* **12. breathe down (someone's) neck.** to stay close to (someone), esp. to oversee what they are doing. **13. breathe one's last.** to die or be finished or defeated. [C13: from BREATH]

breathed (brɛθt, bri:ðd) *adj. Phonetics.* relating to or denoting a speech sound for whose articulation the vocal cords are not made to vibrate. Compare **voiced.**

breath·er ('bri:ðə) *n.* **1.** *Informal.* a short pause for rest. **2.** a person who breathes in a specified way: *a deep breather.* **3.** a vent in a container to equalize internal and external pressure, such as the pipe in the crankcase of an internal-combustion engine. **4.** a small opening in a room, container, cover, etc., supplying air for ventilation.

breath·ing ('bri:ðɪŋ) *n.* **1.** the passage of air into and out of the lungs to supply the body with oxygen. **2.** a single breath: *a breathing between words.* **3.** an utterance: *a breathing of hate.* **4.** a soft movement, esp. of air. **5.** a rest or pause. **6.** *Phonetics.* **a.** expulsion of breath (**rough breathing**) or absence of such expulsion (**smooth breathing**) preceding the pronunciation of an initial vowel or rho in ancient Greek. **b.** either of two symbols indicating this.

breath·ing space *n.* **1.** enough area to permit for freedom of movement: *the country gives us some breathing space.* **2.** a pause for rest, etc.: *a coffee break was their only breathing space.*

breath·less ('brɛθlɪs) *adj.* **1.** out of breath; gasping, etc. **2.** holding one's breath or having it taken away by excitement, etc.: *a breathless confrontation.* **3.** (esp. of the atmosphere) motionless and stifling. **4.** *Rare.* lifeless; dead. —**'breath·less·ly** *adv.* —**'breath·less·ness** *n.*

breath·tak·ing ('brɛθ,teɪkɪŋ) *adj.* causing awe or excitement: *a breathtaking view.* —**'breath·,tak·ing·ly** *adv.*

breath test *n. Brit.* a chemical test of a driver's breath to determine the amount of alcohol he has consumed.

breath·y ('brɛθɪ) *adj.* **breath·i·er, breath·i·est. 1.** (of the speaking voice) accompanied by an audible emission of breath. **2.** (of the singing voice) lacking resonance. —**'breath·i·ly** *adv.* —**'breath·i·ness** *n.*

brec·ci·a ('brɛtʃɪə) *n.* a rock consisting of angular fragments embedded in a finer matrix, formed by erosion, volcanic activity, etc. [C18: from Italian, from Old High German *brecha* a fragment; see BREACH] —**'brec·ci·,at·ed** *adj.*

Brecht (*German* brɛçt) *n.* **Ber·tolt** ('bɛrtɔlt). 1898–1956, German dramatist, theatrical producer, and poet, who developed a new style of "epic" theatre and a new theory of theatrical alienation, notable also for his wit and compassion. His early works include *The Threepenny Opera* (1928) and *Rise and Fall of the City of Mahagonny* (1930) (both with music by Kurt Weill). His later plays are concerned with moral and political dilemmas and include *Mother Courage and her Children* (1941), *The Good Woman of Setzuan* (1943), and *The Caucasian Chalk Circle* (1955).

Brec·on ('brɛkən) *or* **Breck·nock** ('brɛknɒk) *n.* **1.** a town in SE Wales: textile and leather industries. Pop.: 6283 (1971). **2.** short for **Breconshire.**

Brec·on·shire ('brɛkən,ʃɪə, -ʃə) *or* **Breck·nock·shire** ('brɛknɒk,ʃɪə, -ʃə) *n.* (until 1974) a county of SE Wales, now part of Powys: over half its area forms the **Brecon Beacons National Park.**

bred (brɛd) *vb.* the past tense or past participle of **breed.**

Bre·da ('bri:də; *Dutch* bre'da:) *n.* a city in the S Netherlands, in North Brabant province: residence of Charles II of England during his exile. Pop.: 118 594 (1974 est.).

brede (bri:d) *n., vb.* an archaic spelling of **braid.**

bree *or* **brie** (bri:) *n. Scot. literary.* a thin soup or broth. [Old English *brīg,* variant of *brīw* pottage; related to Old High German *brīo* soup, Old English *brīwan* to cook, Middle Irish *brēo* flame]

breech *n.* (bri:tʃ). **1.** the lower dorsal part of the human trunk; buttocks; rump. **2.** the lower part or bottom of something: *the breech of the bridge.* **3.** the lower portion of a pulley block, esp. the part to which the rope or chain is secured. **4.** the part of a firearm behind the barrel or bore. **5.** *Obstetrics.* short for **breech delivery.** ~*vb.* (bri:tʃ, brɪtʃ). (*tr.*) **6.** to fit (a gun) with a breech. **7.** *Archaic.* to clothe in breeches or any other clothing. [Old English *brēc,* plural of *brōc* leg covering; related to Old Norse *brōk,* Old High German *bruoh*]

breech+block ('bri:tʃ,blɒk) *n.* a metal block in breech-loading firearms that is withdrawn to insert the cartridge and replaced to close the breech before firing.

breech+cloth ('bri:tʃ,klɒθ) *or* **breech+clout** ('bri:tʃ,klaʊt) *n.* other names for **loincloth.**

breech de+liv+er·y *n.* birth of a baby with the feet or buttocks appearing first.

breech·es ('brɪtʃɪz, 'bri:-) *pl. n.* **1.** trousers extending to the knee or just below, worn for riding. **2.** *Informal or dialect.* any trousers or pants, esp. extending to the knee.

breech·es buoy *n.* a ring-shaped life buoy with a support in the form of a pair of short breeches, in which a person is suspended for safe transfer from a ship.

breech+ing ('brɪtʃɪŋ, 'bri:-) *n.* **1.** the strap of a harness that passes behind a horse's haunches. **2.** *Naval.* (formerly) the rope used to check the recoil run of a ship's guns or to secure them against rough weather. **3.** the parts comprising the breech of a gun.

breech+load·er ('bri:tʃ,ləʊdə) *n.* a firearm that is loaded at the breech. —**'breech-,load·ing** *adj.*

breed (bri:d) *vb.* **breeds, breed+ing, bred. 1.** to bear (offspring). **2.** (*tr.*) to bring up; raise. **3.** to produce or cause to produce by mating; propagate. **4.** to produce and maintain new or improved strains of (domestic animals and plants). **5.** to produce or be produced; generate: *to breed trouble; violence breeds in densely populated areas.* ~*n.* **6.** a group of organisms within a species, esp. a group of domestic animals, originated and maintained by man and having a clearly defined set of characteristics. **7.** a lineage or race: *a breed of Europeans.* **8.** a kind, sort, or group: *a special breed of hatred.* [Old English *brēdan,* of Germanic origin; related to BROOD]

breed+er ('bri:də) *n.* **1.** a person who breeds plants or animals. **2.** something that reproduces, esp. to excess: *rabbits are persistent breeders.* **3.** an animal kept for breeding purposes. **4.** a source or cause: *a breeder of discontent.* **5.** short for **breeder reactor.**

breed+er re+ac+tor *n.* a type of nuclear reactor that produces more fissionable material than it consumes. Compare **converter reactor.** See also **fast- breeder reactor.**

breed+ing ('bri:dɪŋ) *n.* **1.** the process of bearing offspring; reproduction. **2.** the process of producing plants or animals by hybridization, inbreeding, or other methods of reproduction. **3.** the result of good training, esp. the knowledge of correct social behaviour; refinement: *a man of breeding.* **4.** a person's line of descent: *his breeding was suspect.* **5.** *Physics.* a process occurring in a nuclear reactor as a result of which more fissionable material is produced than is used up.

Breed's Hill (bri:dz) *n.* a hill in E Massachusetts, adjoining Bunker Hill: site of the Battle of Bunker Hill (1775).

breeks (bri:ks) *pl. n.* a Scot. name for **breeches.**

breeng+er ('bri:ndʒə) *n. West central Scot. dialect.* an impetuous person. [from Scots *breenge* a dash, of uncertain origin]

breeze[1] (bri:z) *n.* **1.** a gentle or light wind. **2.** *Meteorol.* a wind of force two to six inclusive on the Beaufort scale. **3.** *U.S. informal.* an easy task or state of ease: *being happy here is a breeze.* **4.** *Informal, chiefly Brit.* a disturbance, esp. a lively quarrel. ~*vb.* (*intr.*) **5.** to move quickly or casually: *he breezed into the room.* **6.** (of wind) to blow: *the south wind breezed over the fields.* [C16: probably from Old Spanish *briza* northeast wind]

breeze[2] (bri:z) *n.* an archaic or dialect name for the **gadfly.** [Old English *briosa,* of unknown origin]

breeze[3] (bri:z) *n.* ashes of coal, coke, or charcoal used to make breeze blocks. [C18: from French *braise* live coals; see BRAISE]

breeze block *n.* a light building brick made from the ashes of coal, coke, etc., bonded together by cement and used esp. for walls that bear relatively small loads. Usual U.S. names: **cinder block, clinker block.**

breeze+way ('bri:z,weɪ) *n.* a roofed passageway connecting two buildings, sometimes with the sides enclosed.

breez·y ('bri:zɪ) *adj.* **breez·i·er, breez·i·est. 1.** fresh; windy: *a breezy afternoon.* **2.** casual or carefree; lively; light-hearted: *her breezy nature.* **3.** *Informal.* lacking substance; light: *a breezy conversation.* —**'breez·i+ly** *adv.* —**'breez·i·ness** *n.*

Bre+genz (*German* 'bre:gɛnts) *n.* a resort in W Austria, the capital of Vorarlberg province. Pop.: 22 839 (1971).

breg+ma ('brɛgmə) *n., pl.* **+ma+ta** (-mətə). the point on the top of the skull where the coronal and sagittal sutures meet: in infants this corresponds to the anterior fontanelle. [C16: New Latin from Greek: front part of the head]

brei (breɪ) *vb.* **breis, brei+ing, breid.** (*intr.*) *S. African informal.* to speak with a uvular *r,* esp. in Afrikaans. Also: **brey.** Compare **burr**[2]. [C20: from Afrikaans; compare BRAY[1]]

brek+ky ('brɛkɪ) *n. Chiefly Austral.* a slang word for breakfast.

Bre+men ('breɪmən) *n.* **1.** a state of N West Germany, centred on the city of Bremen and its outport Bremerhaven. Pop.: 722 732 (1970). Area: 404 sq. km (156 sq. miles). **2.** an industrial city and port in N West Germany, on the Weser estuary. Pop.: 584 265 (1974 est.).

Brem+er+ha+ven (*German* ,bre:mər'ha:fən) *n.* a port in N West Germany: an outport for Bremen. Pop.: 144 578 (1974 est.). Former name (until 1947): **Wesermünde.**

brems+strah+lung ('brɛm,ʃtrɑ:ləŋ) *n.* the x-radiation produced when an electrically charged particle, such as an electron, is slowed down by the electric field of an atomic nucleus. [German: braking radiation]

Bren·del (*German* 'brɛndᵊl) *n.* **Al·fred.** born 1931, Austrian pianist.

Bren gun (brɛn) *n.* an air-cooled gas-operated submachine gun taking .303 calibre ammunition: used by the British in World War II. [C20: after *Br(no),* Czechoslovakia, where it was first made and *En(field),* England, where manufacture was continued]

Bren+ner Pass ('brɛnə) *n.* a pass over the E Alps, between Austria and Italy. Highest point: 1372 m (4501 ft.).

brent (brɛnt) *or esp. U.S.* **brant** *n., pl.* **brents, brants** *or* **brent, brant.** a small goose, *Branta bernicla,* that has a dark grey plumage and short neck and occurs in most northern coastal regions. Also called: **brent goose.** [C16: perhaps of Scandinavian origin; compare Old Norse *brandgās* sheldrake]

Brent (brɛnt) *n.* a borough of Greater London, in the northwestern part. Pop.: 256 500 (1976 est.).

Bren·ta·no (*German* brɛn'ta:no) *n.* **Cle·mens (Maria)** ('kle:-məns). 1778–1842, German romantic poet and compiler of fairy stories and folk songs esp. (with Achim von Arnim) the collection *Des Knaben Wunderhorn* (1805–08).

Brent+wood ('brɛnt,wʊd) *n.* a residential town in SE England, in SW Essex near London. Pop.: 57 976 (1971).

br'er (brɜ:, brɛə) *n. Southern U.S. Negro dialect.* brother: usually prefixed to a name: *Br'er Jones.*

Bre+scia (*Italian* 'breʃʃa) *n.* a city in N Italy, in Lombardy: at its height in the 16th century. Pop.: 215 654 (1975 est.). Ancient name: **Brixia.**

Bres+lau ('brɛslaʊ) *n.* the German name for **Wrocław.**

Bres·son (*French* brɛ'sɔ̃) *n.* **Ro·bert** (rɔ'bɛ:r). born 1901, French film director: his films include *Le Journal d'un curé de campagne* (1951) and *Une Femme douce* (1970).

Brest (brɛst) *n.* **1.** a port in NW France, in Brittany: chief naval station of the country, planned by Richelieu in 1631 and fortified by Vauban. Pop.: 172 176 (1975). **2.** a city in the W Soviet Union, in SW Byelorussia: Polish until 1795 and from 1921 to 1945. Pop.: 122 000 (1970). Former name (until 1921): **Brest Li+tovsk** (brɛst lji'tɔfsk). Polish name: **Brześć nad Bu+giem** ('bʒɛʃtʃ nad 'bugjɛm).

Bre+tagne (brə'taɲ) *n.* the French name for **Brittany.**

breth+ren ('brɛðrɪn) *pl. n. Archaic except in religious contexts.* a plural of **brother.**

Bret+on[1] ('brɛtᵊn; *French* brə'tɔ̃) *adj.* **1.** of, relating to, or characteristic of Brittany, its people, or their language. ~*n.* **2.** a native or inhabitant of Brittany, esp. one who speaks the Breton language.

Bre·ton[2] (*French* brə'tɔ̃) *n.* **An·dré** (ã'dre). 1896–1966, French poet and art critic: founder and chief theorist of surrealism, publishing the first surrealist manifesto in 1924.

Bret+ton Woods Con+fer+ence ('brɛtᵊn) *n.* an international monetary conference held in 1944 at Bretton Woods in New Hampshire, which resulted in the establishment of the World Bank and the International Monetary Fund.

Breu·er ('brɔɪə) *n.* **1. Jo·sef** ('jo:zɛf). 1842–1925, Austrian physician: treated the mentally ill by hypnosis. **2. Mar·cel La·jos** (ma:r'sɛl 'lɔjoʃ). 1902-81, U.S. architect and furniture designer, born in Hungary. He developed bent plywood and tubular metal furniture and designed the UNESCO building in Paris (1953-58).

Breu·ghel ('brɔɪgᵊl) *n.* a variant spelling of **Brueghel.**

breve (bri:v) *n.* **1.** an accent, ˘, placed over a vowel to indicate that it is of short duration or is pronounced in a specified way. **2.** *Music.* a note, now rarely used, equivalent in time value to two semibreves. **3.** *R.C. Church.* a less common word for **brief** (papal letter). [C13: from Medieval Latin *breve,* from Latin *brevis* short; see BRIEF]

bre+vet ('brɛvɪt) *n.* **1.** a document entitling a commissioned officer to hold temporarily a higher military rank without the appropriate pay and allowances. ~*vb.* **+vets, +vet+ting, +vet+ted** *or* **+vets, +vet+ing, +vet+ed. 2.** (*tr.*) to promote by brevet. [C14: from Old French *brievet* a little letter, from *brief* letter; see BRIEF] —**'brev+et+cy** *n.*

brev·ia+ry ('brɛvjərɪ, 'bri:-) *n., pl.* **+ries. 1.** *R.C. Church.* a book of psalms, hymns, prayers, etc., to be recited daily by clerics in major orders and certain members of religious orders as part of the divine office. **2.** a similar book in the Orthodox Church. [C16: from Latin *breviārium* an abridged version, from *breviāre* to shorten, from *brevis* short]

bre+vier (brə'vɪə) *n.* (formerly) a size of printer's type approximately equal to 8 point. [C16: probably from Dutch, literally: BREVIARY; so called because this type size was used for breviaries]

brev+i·ty ('brɛvɪtɪ) *n., pl.* **·ties. 1.** conciseness of expression; lack of verbosity. **2.** a short duration; brief time. [C16: from Latin *brevitās* shortness, from *brevis* BRIEF]

brew (bru:) *vb.* **1.** to make (beer, ale, etc.) from malt and other ingredients by steeping, boiling, and fermentation. **2.** to prepare (a drink, such as tea) by boiling or infusing. **3.** (*tr.*) to devise or plan: *to brew a plot.* **4.** (*intr.*) to be in the process of being brewed: *the tea was brewing in the pot.* **5.** (*intr.*) to be impending or forming: *there's a storm brewing.* ~*n.* **6.** a beverage produced by brewing: *a strong brew.* **7.** an instance or time of brewing: *last year's brew.* [Old English *brēowan* related to Old Norse *brugga,* Old Saxon *breuwan,* Old High German *briuwan*] —**'brew+er** *n.*

brew+age ('bru:ɪdʒ) *n.* **1.** a product of brewing; brew. **2.** the process of brewing.

brew+er's yeast *n.* **1.** a yeast, *Saccharomyces cerevisiae,* used in brewing. See **yeast** (sense 2). **2.** yeast obtained as a by-product of brewing.

brew+er·y ('brʊərɪ) *n., pl.* **+er·ies.** a place where beer, ale, etc., is brewed.

brew+ing ('bru:ɪŋ) *n.* a quantity of a beverage brewed at one time.

brew+is ('bru:ɪs) *or* **brev+is** ('brɛvɪs) *n. Dialect, chiefly northern Brit. or U.S.* **1.** bread soaked in broth, gravy, etc. **2.** thickened broth. [C16: from Old French *broez,* from *broet,* diminutive of *breu* BROTH]

Brew·ster ('bru:stə) *n.* Sir **Da·vid.** 1781–1868, Scottish physicist, noted for his studies of the polarization of light.

brey (breɪ) *vb.* (*intr.*) *S. African informal.* a variant spelling of **brei.**

Brezh·nev ('brɛʒnɛf; *Russian* 'brjɛʒnɪf) *n.* **Le·o·nid I·lyich** (lɪa-'nit 'iljitʃ). 1906–82, Soviet statesman; president of the Soviet Union from 1977; general secretary of the Soviet Communist Party from 1964.

BRG *international car registration for* Guyana (formerly British Guiana).

Bri·an ('braɪən) *n.* **Ha·ver·gal** ('hævəgəl). 1876–1972, English composer, who wrote 32 symphonies, including the large-scale *Gothic Symphony* (1919–27).

Bri·an Bo·ru ('braɪən bə'ru:) *n.* ?941–1014, king of Ireland (1002–14): killed during the defeat of the Danes at the battle of Clontarf.

Bri·and (*French* bri'ã) *n.* **A·ri·stide** (ari'stid). 1862–1932, French socialist statesman: prime minister of France 11 times. He was responsible for the separation of Church and State (1905) and he advocated a United States of Europe. Nobel peace prize 1926.

bri+ar[1] *or* **bri+er** ('braɪə) *n.* **1.** Also called: **tree heath.** an ericaceous shrub, *Erica arborea,* of S Europe, having a hard woody root (briarroot). **2.** a tobacco pipe made from the root of this plant. [C19: from French *bruyère* heath, from Late Latin *brūcus,* of Gaulish origin] —**'bri+ar·y** *or* **'bri+er·y** *adj.*

bri+ar[2] ('braɪə) *n.* a variant spelling of **brier**[1].

Bri·ar·e·us (braɪ'ɛərɪəs) *n. Greek myth.* a giant with a hundred arms and fifty heads who aided Zeus and the Olympians against the Titans. —**Bri+'ar+e·an** *adj.*

bri·ar+root *or* **bri·er+root** ('braɪəˌru:t) *n.* **1.** the hard woody root of the briar, used for making tobacco pipes. **2.** any of several other woods used to make tobacco pipes. ~Also called: **briarwood, brierwood.**

bribe (braɪb) *vb.* **1.** to promise, offer, or give something, esp. money, to (a person) to procure services or gain influence. ~*n.* **2.** a reward, such as money or favour, given or offered for this purpose. **3.** any persuasion or lure. **4.** a length of flawed or damaged cloth removed from the main piece. [C14: from Old French *briber* to beg, of obscure origin] —**'brib·a·ble** *or* **'bribe+a·ble** *adj.* —**'brib+er** *n.*

brib+er·y ('braɪbərɪ) *n., pl.* **+er·ies.** the process of giving or taking bribes.

bric-a-brac ('brɪkəˌbræk) *n.* miscellaneous small objects, esp. furniture and curios, kept because they are ornamental or rare. [C19: from French; phrase based on *bric* piece]

brick (brɪk) *n.* **1. a.** a rectangular block of clay mixed with sand and fired in a kiln or baked by the sun, used in building construction. **b.** (*as modifier*): *a brick house.* **2.** the material used to make such blocks. **3.** any rectangular block: *a brick of ice.* **4.** bricks collectively. **5.** *Informal.* a reliable, trustworthy, or helpful person. **6.** *Brit.* a child's building block. **7.** short for **brick red. 8. drop a brick.** *Brit. informal.* to make a tactless or indiscreet remark. **9. like a ton of bricks.** *Informal.* with great force; heavily: *the book landed like a ton of bricks.* ~*vb.* **10.** (*tr.; usually foll. by in, up, or over*) to construct, line, pave, fill, or wall up with bricks: *to brick up a window; brick over a patio.* [C15: from Old French *brique,* from Middle Dutch *bricke;* related to Middle Low German *brike,* Old English *brecan* to BREAK] —**'brick·y** *adj.*

brick+bat ('brɪkˌbæt) *n.* **1.** a piece of brick or similar material, esp. one used as a weapon. **2.** *Informal.* blunt criticism: *the critic threw several brickbats at the singer.*

brick+lay·er ('brɪkˌleɪə) *n.* a person trained or skilled in laying bricks.

brick+lay·ing ('brɪkˌleɪɪŋ) *n.* the technique or practice of laying bricks.

brick+le ('brɪkᵊl) *adj. Northern Brit. dialect.* brittle; fragile; breakable. [Old English *brycel;* related to *brecan* to BREAK, Middle Low German *brökel* fragile] —**'brick+le+ness** *n.*

brick red *n., adj.* **a.** a reddish-brown colour. **b.** (*as adj.*): *a brick-red carpet.*

brick+work ('brɪkˌwɜ:k) *n.* **1.** a structure, such as a wall, built of bricks. **2.** construction using bricks.

brick+yard ('brɪkˌjɑ:d) *n.* a place in which bricks are made, stored, or sold.

bri+cole (brɪ'kəʊl, 'brɪkᵊl) *n.* **1.** *Billiards.* a shot in which the cue ball touches a cushion after striking the object ball and before touching another ball. **2.** (in ancient and medieval times) a military catapult for throwing stones, etc. **3.** (esp. formerly) a harness worn by soldiers for dragging guns. **4.** an indirect or unexpected stroke or action. [C16: from Old French: catapult, from Medieval Latin *bricola,* of uncertain origin]

brid+al ('braɪdᵊl) *adj.* **1.** of or relating to a bride or a wedding; nuptial. ~*n.* **2.** *Obsolete.* a wedding or wedding feast. [Old English *brȳdealu,* literally: "bride ale", that is, wedding feast]

brid+al wreath *n.* any of several N temperate rosaceous shrubs of the genus *Spiraea,* esp. *S. prunifolia,* cultivated for their sprays of small white flowers.

bride[1] (braɪd) *n.* a woman who has just been or is about to be married. [Old English *brȳd;* related to Old Norse *brūthr,* Gothic *brūths* daughter-in-law, Old High German *brūt*]

bride[2] (braɪd) *n. Lacemaking, needlework.* a thread or loop that joins parts of a pattern. Also called: **bar.** [C19: from French, literally: BRIDLE, probably of Germanic origin]

Bride (braɪd) *n.* See (Saint) **Bridget.**

bride+groom ('braɪdˌgru:m, -ˌgrʊm) *n.* a man who has just been or is about to be married. [C14: changed (through influence of GROOM) from Old English *brȳdguma,* from *brȳd* BRIDE[1] + *guma* man; related to Old Norse *brūthgumi,* Old High German *brūtigomo*]

bride price *or* **wealth** *n.* (in some societies) money, property, or services given by a bridegroom to the kinsmen of his bride in order to establish his rights over the woman.

brides+maid ('braɪdzˌmeɪd) *n.* a girl or young unmarried woman who attends a bride at her wedding. Compare **matron of honour, maid of honour.**

bride+well ('braɪdˌwɛl, -wəl) *n.* a house of correction; jail, esp. for minor offences. [C16: after *Bridewell* (originally, *St. Bride's Well*), a house of correction in London]

bridge[1] (brɪdʒ) *n.* **1.** a structure that spans and provides a passage over a road, railway, river, or some other obstacle. **2.** something that resembles this in shape or function: *his letters provided a bridge across the centuries.* **3. a.** the hard ridge at the upper part of the nose, formed by the underlying nasal bones. **b.** any anatomical ridge or connecting structure. Compare **pons. 4.** the part of a pair of glasses that rests on the nose. **5.** Also called: **bridgework.** a dental plate containing one or more artificial teeth that is secured to the surrounding natural teeth. **6.** a platform athwartships and above the rail, from which a ship is piloted and navigated. **7.** a piece of wood, usually fixed, supporting the strings of a violin, guitar, etc., and transmitting their vibrations to the sounding board. **8.** Also called: **bridge passage.** a passage in a musical, literary, or dramatic work linking two or more important sections. **9.** Also called: **bridge circuit.** *Electronics.* any of several networks, such as a Wheatstone bridge, consisting of two branches across which a measuring device is connected. The resistance, capacitance, etc., of one component can be determined from the known values of the others when the voltage in each branch is balanced. **10.** *Billiards.* **a.** a support for a cue made by placing the fingers on the table and raising the thumb. **b.** a cue rest with a notched end for shots beyond normal reach. **11.** *Theatre.* **a.** a platform of adjustable height above or beside the stage for the use of stagehands, light operators, etc. **b.** *Chiefly Brit.* a part of the stage floor that can be raised or lowered. **12.** a partition in a furnace or boiler to keep the fuel in place. **13. burn one's bridges.** See **burn**[1] (def. 16). **14. cross a bridge when (one) comes to it.** to deal with a problem only when it arises. ~*vb.* (*tr.*) **15.** to build or provide a bridge over something; span: *to bridge a river.* **16.** to connect or reduce the distance between: *let us bridge our differences.* [Old English *brycg;* related to Old Norse *bryggja* gangway, Old Frisian *bregge,* Old High German *brucka,* Danish, Swedish *bro*] —**'bridge+a·ble** *adj.* —**'bridge+less** *adj.*

bridge[2] (brɪdʒ) *n.* a card game for four players, based on whist, in which one hand (the dummy) is exposed and the trump suit decided by bidding between the players. See also **contract bridge, duplicate bridge, auction bridge.** [C19: of uncertain origin, but compare Turkish *bir-üç* (unattested phrase) one-three (said perhaps to refer to the one exposed hand and the three players' hands]

Bridge (brɪdʒ) *n.* **Frank.** 1879–1941, English composer, esp. of chamber music. He taught Benjamin Britten.

bridge+board ('brɪdʒˌbɔ:d) *n.* a board on both sides of a staircase that is cut to support the treads and risers. Also called: **cut string.**

bridge+head ('brɪdʒˌhɛd) *n. Military.* **1.** an area of ground secured or to be taken on the enemy's side of an obstacle. **2.** a fortified or defensive position at the end of a bridge nearest to the enemy.

Bridge of Sighs *n.* a covered 16th-century bridge in Venice, between the Doge's Palace and the prisons, through which prisoners were formerly led to trial or execution.

Bridge+port ('brɪdʒˌpɔ:t) *n.* a port in SW Connecticut, on Long Island Sound. Pop.: 148 337 (1973 est.).

Bridg·es ('brɪdʒɪz) *n.* **Rob·ert (Seymour).** 1844–1930, English poet laureate (1913–30).

Brid·get ('brɪdʒɪt) *n.* **Saint. 1.** Also called: **Bride, Brigid.** 453–523 A.D., Irish abbess; a patron saint of Ireland. Feast day: Feb. 1. **2.** Also called: **Birgit.** ?1303–73, Swedish nun and visionary; patron saint of Sweden. Feast day: Oct. 8.

Bridge+town ('brɪdʒˌtaʊn) *n.* the capital of Barbados, a port on the SW coast. Pop.: 8789 (1970).

bridge+work ('brɪdʒˌwɜ:k) *n.* **1. a.** a partial denture attached to the surrounding teeth. See **bridge**[1] (sense 5). **b.** the technique of making such appliances. **2.** the process or occupation of constructing bridges.

bridg+ing ('brɪdʒɪŋ) *n.* one or more timber struts fixed between floor or roof joists to stiffen the construction and distribute the loads.

Bridg·man (ˈbrɪdʒmən) *n.* **Per·cy Wil·liams.** 1882–1961, U.S. physicist: Nobel prize for physics (1946) for his work on high-pressure physics and thermodynamics.

Bridg+wa·ter (ˈbrɪdʒˌwɔːtə) *n.* a town in SW England, in central Somerset. Pop.: 26 598 (1971).

bri+die (ˈbraɪdɪ) *n. Scot. dialect.* a semicircular pie containing meat and onions. [of unknown origin]

bri+dle (ˈbraɪdᵊl) *n.* **1.** a headgear for a horse, etc., consisting of a series of buckled straps and a metal mouthpiece (bit) by which the animal is controlled through the reins. **2.** something that curbs or restrains; check. **3.** a Y-shaped cable, rope, or chain, used for holding, towing, etc. **4.** *Machinery.* a device by which the motion of a component is limited, often in the form of a linkage or flange. ~*vb.* **5.** (*tr.*) to put a bridle on (a horse, mule, etc.). **6.** (*intr.*) (of a horse) to respond correctly to the pull of the reins. **7.** (*tr.*) to restrain; curb: *he bridled his rage.* **8.** (*intr.*; often foll. by *at*) to show anger, scorn, or indignation. [Old English *brigdels;* related to *bregdan* to BRAID, Old High German *brittil,* Middle Low German *breidel*] —**ˈbri+dler** *n.*

bri+dle path *n.* a path suitable for riding or leading horses.

bri·dle+wise (ˈbraɪdᵊlˌwaɪz) *adj. U.S.* (of a horse) obedient to the pressure of the reins on the neck rather than to the bit.

bri+doon (brɪˈduːn) *n.* a horse's bit: a small snaffle used in double bridles. [C18: from French *bridon,* from *bride* bridle; compare Middle English *bride*]

brie (briː) *n.* a variant spelling of **bree.**

Brie (briː) *n.* a soft creamy white cheese, similar to Camembert but milder. [French, named after *Brie,* region in N France where it originated]

brief (briːf) *adj.* **1.** short in duration: *a brief holiday.* **2.** short in length or extent; scanty: *a brief bikini.* **3.** abrupt in manner; brusque: *the professor was brief with me this morning.* **4.** terse or concise; containing few words: *he made a brief statement.* ~*n.* **5.** a condensed or short statement or written synopsis; abstract. **6.** *Law.* a document containing all the facts and points of law of a case by which a solicitor instructs a barrister to represent a client. **7.** *R.C. Church.* a letter issuing from the Roman court written in modern characters, as contrasted with a papal bull; papal brief. **8.** short for **briefing. 9.** a paper outlining the arguments and information on one side of a debate. **10. hold a brief for.** to argue for; champion. **11. in brief.** in short; to sum up. ~*vb.* (*tr.*) **12.** to prepare or instruct by giving a summary of relevant facts. **13.** to make a summary or synopsis of. **14.** *English law.* **a.** to instruct (a barrister) by brief. **b.** to retain (a barrister) as counsel. [C14: from Old French *bref,* from Latin *brevis;* related to Greek *brakhus*] —**ˈbrief+ly** *adv.* —**ˈbrief+ness** *n.*

brief+case (ˈbriːfˌkeɪs) *n.* a flat portable case, often of leather, for carrying papers, books, etc.

brief+ing (ˈbriːfɪŋ) *n.* **1.** a meeting at which detailed information or instructions are given, as for military operations, etc. **2.** the facts presented during such a meeting.

brief+less (ˈbriːflɪs) *adj.* (said of a barrister) without clients.

briefs (briːfs) *pl. n.* men's underpants or women's pants without legs.

bri+er[1] *or* **bri+ar** (ˈbraɪə) *n.* any of various thorny shrubs or other plants, such as the sweetbrier and greenbrier. [Old English *brēr, brǣr,* of obscure origin] —**ˈbri+er·y** *or* **ˈbri+ar·y** *adj.*

bri+er[2] (ˈbraɪə) *n.* a variant spelling of **briar**[1].

bri·er+root (ˈbraɪəˌruːt) *n.* a variant spelling of **briarroot.** Also called: **bri·er+wood.**

brig[1] (brɪg) *n.* **1.** *Nautical.* a two-masted square-rigger. **2.** *Chiefly U.S.* a prison, esp. in a navy ship. [C18: shortened from BRIGANTINE]

brig[2] (brɪg) *n.* a northern Brit. word for a **bridge.**

Brig. *abbrev. for:* **1.** Brigade. **2.** Brigadier.

bri+gade (brɪˈgeɪd) *n.* **1.** a formation of fighting units, together with support arms and services, smaller than a division and usually commanded by a brigadier. **2.** a group of people organized for a certain task: *a rescue brigade.* ~*vb.* (*tr.*) **3.** to organize into a brigade. **4.** to put or group together. [C17: from Old French, from Old Italian, from *brigare* to fight, perhaps of Celtic origin; see BRIGAND]

brig·a+dier (ˌbrɪgəˈdɪə) *n.* **1.** an officer of the British Army or Royal Marines who holds a rank junior to a major general but senior to a colonel, usually commanding a brigade. **2.** an equivalent rank in other armed forces. **3.** *U.S. Army.* short for **brigadier general. 4.** *History.* a noncommissioned rank in the armies of Napoleon I. [C17: from French, from BRIGADE]

brig·a+dier gen+er+al *n., pl.* **brig·a+dier gen+er+als. 1.** an officer of the U.S. Army, Air Force, or Marine Corps who holds a rank junior to a major general but senior to a colonel, usually commanding a brigade. **2.** the former name for a **brigadier** (sense 1).

brig·a+low (ˈbrɪgələʊ) *n. Austral.* **a.** any of various acacia trees. **b.** (*as modifier*): *brigalow country.* [C19: from a native Australian language]

brig+and (ˈbrɪgənd) *n.* a bandit or plunderer, esp. a member of a gang operating in mountainous areas. [C14: from Old French, from Old Italian *brigante* fighter, from *brigare* to fight, from *briga* strife, of Celtic origin] —**ˈbrig+and+age** *or* **ˈbrig+and+ry** *n.*

brig+an+dine (ˈbrɪgənˌdiːn, -ˌdaɪn) *n.* a coat of mail, invented in the Middle Ages to increase mobility, consisting of metal rings or sheets sewn on to cloth or leather. [C15: from Old French, from BRIGAND + -INE[1]]

brig+an+tine (ˈbrɪgənˌtiːn, -ˌtaɪn) *n.* a two-masted sailing ship, rigged square on the foremast and fore-and-aft with square topsails on the mainmast. [C16: from Old Italian *brigantino* pirate ship, from *brigante* BRIGAND]

Brig. Gen. *abbrev. for* brigadier general.

Briggs (brɪgz) *n.* **Hen·ry.** 1561–1631, English mathematician: introduced common logarithms.

Brig+house (ˈbrɪgˌhaʊs) *n.* a town in N England, in West Yorkshire. Pop.: 34 111 (1971).

bright (braɪt) *adj.* **1.** emitting or reflecting much light; shining. **2.** (of colours) intense or vivid. **3.** full of promise: *a bright future.* **4.** full of animation; cheerful: *a bright face.* **5.** *Informal.* quick witted or clever: *a bright child.* **6.** magnificent; glorious: *a bright victory.* **7.** polished; glistening: *a bright finish.* **8.** (of the voice) distinct and clear. **9.** (of a liquid) translucent and clear: *a circle of bright water.* **10. bright and early.** very early in the morning. ~*n.* **11.** a thin flat paintbrush with a straight sharp edge used for highlighting in oil painting. **12.** *Poetic.* brightness or splendour: *the bright of his armour.* ~*adv.* **13.** brightly: *the fire was burning bright.* [Old English *beorht;* related to Old Norse *bjartr,* Gothic *bairhts* clear, Old High German *beraht,* Norwegian *bjerk,* Swedish *brokig* pied] —**ˈbright+ly** *adv.*

Bright (braɪt) *n.* **John.** 1811–89, British liberal statesman, economist, and advocate of free trade: with Richard Cobden he led the Anti-Corn-Law League (1838–46).

bright+en (ˈbraɪtᵊn) *vb.* **1.** to make or become bright or brighter. **2.** to make or become cheerful. —**ˈbright+en+er** *n.*

bright lights *pl. n.* **the.** *Informal.* places of entertainment in a city.

bright+ness (ˈbraɪtnɪs) *n.* **1.** the condition of being bright. **2.** *Physics.* a former name for **luminosity** (sense 4).

Bright+on (ˈbraɪtᵊn) *n.* **1.** a resort in S England, in East Sussex: patronized by the Prince Regent, who had the Royal Pavilion built (1782); seat of the University of Sussex. Pop.: 166 081 (1971). **2.** a port and resort in SE Australia, in S Victoria. Pop.: 39 109 (1971).

brights (braɪts) *pl. n. U.S. slang.* the high beam of the headlights of a motor vehicle.

Bright's dis+ease *n.* chronic inflammation of the kidneys; chronic nephritis. [C19: named after Richard *Bright* (1789–1858), British physician]

bright+work (ˈbraɪtˌwɜːk) *n.* **1.** shiny metal trimmings or fittings on ships, cars, etc. **2.** varnished or plain woodwork on a vessel.

Brig·id (ˈbrɪdʒɪd) *n.* See (Saint) **Bridget.**

brill (brɪl) *n., pl.* **brill** *or* **brills.** a European food fish, *Scophthalmus rhombus,* a flatfish similar to the turbot but lacking tubercles on the body: family *Bothidae.* [C15: probably from Cornish *brȳthel* mackerel, from Old Cornish *brȳth* speckled; related to Welsh *brith* spotted]

Bril·lat-Sa·va·rin (*French* briˈja savaˈrɛ̃) *n.* **An·thelme** (ɑ̃ˈtɛlm). 1755–1826, French politician and gourmet; author of *Physiologie du Goût* (1825).

bril+liance (ˈbrɪljəns) *or* **bril+lian+cy** *n.* **1.** great brightness; radiance. **2.** excellence or distinction in physical or mental ability; exceptional talent. **3.** splendour; magnificence: *the brilliance of the royal court.* **4.** *Physics.* a former term for **luminance.**

bril+liant (ˈbrɪljənt) *adj.* **1.** shining with light; sparkling. **2.** (of a colour) having a high saturation and reflecting a considerable amount of light; vivid. **3.** outstanding; exceptional: *a brilliant success.* **4.** splendid; magnificent: *a brilliant show.* **5.** of outstanding intelligence or intellect: *a brilliant mind; a brilliant idea.* **6.** *Music.* **a.** (of the tone of an instrument) having a large proportion of high harmonics above the fundamental. **b.** Also: **bril+liant** (*French* briˈjɑ̃), **bril+liante** (*French* briˈjɑ̃ːt). with spirit; lively. ~*n.* **7.** Also called: **brilliant cut. a.** a popular circular cut for diamonds and other gemstones in the form of two many-faceted pyramids (the top one truncated) joined at their bases. **b.** a diamond of this cut. **8.** (formerly) a size of a printer's type approximately equal to 4 point. [C17: from French *brillant* shining, from *briller* to shine, from Italian *brillare,* from *brillo* BERYL] —**ˈbril+liant+ly** *adv.*

bril+lian+tine (ˈbrɪljənˌtiːn) *n.* **1.** a perfumed oil used to make the hair smooth and shiny. **2.** *Chiefly U.S.* a glossy fabric made of mohair and cotton. [C19: from French, from *brillant* shining]

brim (brɪm) *n.* **1.** the upper rim of a vessel: *the brim of a cup.* **2.** a projecting rim or edge: *the brim of a hat.* **3.** the brink or edge of something. ~*vb.* **brims, brim+ming, brimmed. 4.** to fill or be full to the brim: *eyes brimming with tears.* [C13: from Middle High German *brem,* probably from Old Norse *barmr;* see BERM] —**ˈbrim+less** *adj.*

brim+ful *or* **brim+full** (ˌbrɪmˈfʊl) *adj.* (*postpositive,* foll. by *of*) filled up to the brim (with).

brim+mer (ˈbrɪmə) *n.* a vessel, such as a glass or bowl, filled to the brim.

brim+stone (ˈbrɪmˌstəʊn) *n.* **1.** an obsolete name for **sulphur. 2.** a common yellow butterfly, *Gonepteryx rhamni,* of N temperate regions of the Old World: family *Pieridae.* **3.** *Archaic.* a scolding nagging woman; virago. [Old English *brynstān;* related to Old Norse *brennistein;* see BURN[1], STONE]

Brin+di+si (*Italian* ˈbrindizi) *n.* a port in SE Italy, in SE Apulia: important naval base in Roman times and a centre of the Crusades in the Middle Ages. Pop.: 79 784 (1971). Ancient name: **Brundisium.**

brin+dle (ˈbrɪndᵊl) *n.* **1.** a brindled animal. **2.** a brindled colouring. [C17: back formation from BRINDLED]

brin+dled ('brɪndᵊld) *adj.* brown or grey streaked or patched with a darker colour: *a brindled dog.* [C17: changed from C15 *brended,* literally: branded, probably of Scandinavian origin; compare Old Norse *bröndottr;* see BRAND]

brine (braɪn) *n.* **1.** a strong solution of salt and water, used for salting and pickling meats, etc. **2.** the sea or its water. **3.** *Chem.* any solution of a salt in water: *a potassium chloride brine.* ~*vb.* **4.** (*tr.*) to soak in or treat with brine. [Old English *brīne;* related to Middle Dutch *brīne,* Old Slavonic *bridŭ* bitter, Sanskrit *bibhrāya* burnt] —**'brin+ish** *adj.*

Bri+nell num+ber (brɪ'nɛl) *n.* a measure of the hardness of a material obtained by pressing a hard steel ball into its surface; it is expressed as the ratio of the load on the ball in kilograms to the area of the depression made by the ball in square millimetres. [C19: named after Johann A. *Brinell* (1849–1925), Swedish engineer]

bring (brɪŋ) *vb.* **brings, bring+ing, brought.** (*tr.*) **1.** to carry, convey, or take (something or someone) to a designated place or person: *bring that book to me; will you bring Jessica to Tom's party?* **2.** to cause to happen or occur to (oneself or another): *to bring disrespect on oneself.* **3.** to cause to happen as a consequence: *responsibility brings maturity.* **4.** to cause to come to mind: *it brought back memories.* **5.** to cause to be in a certain state, position, etc.: *the punch brought him to his knees.* **6.** to force, persuade, or make (oneself): *I couldn't bring myself to do it.* **7.** to sell for; fetch: *the painting brought 20 pounds.* **8.** *Law.* **a.** to institute (proceedings, charges, etc.). **b.** to put (evidence, etc.) before a tribunal. **9. bring forth.** to give birth to. **10. bring home to.** to convince of: *his account brought home to us the gravity of the situation.* **11. bring to bear.** See **bear**[1]. ~See also **bring about, bring down, bring forward, bring in, bring off, bring on, bring out, bring round, bring to, bring up.** [Old English *bringan;* related to Gothic *briggan,* Old High German *bringan*] —**'bring+er** *n.*

bring a·bout *vb.* (*tr., adv.*) **1.** to cause to happen: *to bring about a change in the law.* **2.** to turn (a ship) around.

bring-and-buy sale *n. Brit.* an informal sale, often conducted for charity, to which people bring items for sale and buy those that others have brought.

bring down *vb.* (*tr., adv.*) **1.** to cause to fall: *the fighter aircraft brought the enemy down; the ministers agreed to bring down the price of oil.* **2.** (*usually passive*) *Slang.* to cause to be elated and then suddenly depressed, as from using drugs.

bring for+ward *vb.* (*tr., adv.*) **1.** to present or introduce (a subject) for discussion. **2.** *Book-keeping.* to transfer (a figure representing the sum of the figures on a page or in a column) to the top of the next page or column.

bring in *vb.* (*tr., adv.*) **1.** to yield (income, profit, or cash): *his investments brought him in £100.* **2.** to produce or return (a verdict). **3.** to put forward or introduce (a legislative bill, etc.).

bring·ing-up *n.* another term for **upbringing.**

bring off *vb.* (*tr., adv.*) **1.** to succeed in achieving (something), esp. with difficulty or contrary to expectations: *he managed to bring off the deal.* **2.** *Taboo.* to cause to have an orgasm.

bring on *vb.* (*tr., adv.*) **1.** to induce or cause: *these pills will bring on labour.* **2.** *Taboo.* to cause sexual excitement in; stimulate.

bring out *vb.* (*tr., adv.*) **1.** to produce or publish or have published: *when are you bringing out a new dictionary?* **2.** to expose, reveal, or cause to be seen: *she brought out the best in me.* **3.** to encourage (a shy person) to be less reserved (often in the phrase **bring (someone) out of himself** *or* **herself**). **4.** *Brit.* (of a trade union, provocative action by management, misunderstanding, etc.) to cause (workers) to strike. **5.** (foll. by *in*) to cause (a person) to become covered (with spots, a rash, etc.). **6.** *Brit.* to introduce (a girl) formally into society as a debutante.

bring o·ver *vb.* (*tr., adv.*) to cause (a person) to change allegiances.

bring round *or* **a·round** *vb.* (*tr., adv.*) **1.** to restore (a person) to consciousness, esp. after a faint. **2.** *Informal.* to convince (another person, usually an opponent) of an opinion or point of view.

bring to *vb.* (*tr.*) **1.** (*adv.*) to restore (a person) to consciousness. **2.** (*adv.*) to cause (a ship) to turn into the wind and reduce her headway. **3.** (*prep.*) to make (something) equal to (an amount of money): *that brings your bill to £17.*

bring up *vb.* (*tr., adv.*) **1.** to care for and train (a child); rear: *we had been brought up to go to church.* **2.** to raise (a subject) for discussion; mention. **3.** to vomit (food). **4.** (foll. by *against*) to cause (a person) to face or confront. **5.** (foll. by *to*) to cause (something) to be of a required standard.

brin+jal ('brɪndʒəl) *n.* (in India and Africa) another name for the **aubergine.** [C17: from Portuguese *berinjela,* from Arabic; see AUBERGINE]

brink (brɪŋk) *n.* **1.** the edge, border, or verge of a steep place: *the brink of the precipice.* **2.** the highest point; top: *the sun fell below the brink of the hill.* **3.** the land at the edge of a body of water. **4.** the verge of an event or state: *the brink of disaster.* [C13: from Middle Dutch *brinc,* of Germanic origin; compare Old Norse *brekka* slope, Middle Low German *brink* edge of a field]

brink+man+ship ('brɪŋkmən,ʃɪp) *n.* the art or practice of pressing a dangerous situation, esp. in international affairs, to the limit of safety and peace in order to win an advantage from a threatening or tenacious foe.

brin+ny ('brɪnɪ) *n. Austral. children's slang.* a stone, esp. when thrown.

brin·y ('braɪnɪ) *adj.* **brin·i·er, brin·i·est. 1.** of or resembling brine; salty. ~*n.* **2.** (preceded by *the*) an informal name for the **sea.** —**'brin·i+ness** *n.*

bri·o ('bri:əʊ) *n.* liveliness or vigour; spirit. See also **con brio.** [C19: from Italian, of Celtic origin]

bri+oche ('bri:əʊʃ, -ɒʃ; *French* bri'ɔʃ) *n.* a soft roll or loaf made from a very light yeast dough, sometimes mixed with currants. [Norman dialect, from *brier* to knead, of Germanic origin; compare French *broyer* to pound, BREAK]

bri·o+lette (,bri:əʊ'lɛt) *n.* a pear-shaped gem cut with long triangular facets. [C19: from French, alteration of *brillolette,* from *brignolette* little dried plum, after *Brignoles,* France, where these plums are produced]

bri·o+ny ('braɪənɪ) *n., pl.* **+nies.** a variant spelling of **bryony.**

bri+quette *or* **bri+quet** (brɪ'kɛt) *n.* **1.** a small brick made of compressed coal dust, saw dust, charcoal, etc., used for fuel. **2.** a small brick of any substance: *an ice-cream briquette.* ~*vb.* **3.** (*tr.*) to make into the form of a brick or bricks: *to briquette clay.* [C19: from French: a little brick, from *brique* BRICK]

bri+sance ('bri:zəns; *French* bri'zɑ̃:s) *n.* the shattering effect or power of an explosion or explosive. [C20: from French, from *briser* to break, ultimately of Celtic origin; compare Old Irish *brissim* I break]

Bris+bane ('brɪzbən) *n.* a port in E Australia, the capital of Queensland: founded in 1824 as a penal settlement; vast agricultural hinterland. Pop.: 958 800 (1975 est.).

brise-so·leil (,bri:zsəʊ'leɪ) *n.* a structure used in hot climates to protect a window from the sun, usually consisting of horizontal or vertical strips of wood, concrete, etc. [French: break-sun, from *briser* to break + *soleil* sun]

brisk (brɪsk) *adj.* **1.** lively and quick; vigorous: *a brisk walk; trade was brisk.* **2.** invigorating or sharp: *brisk weather.* [C16: probably variant of BRUSQUE] —**'brisk+ly** *adv.* —**'brisk+ness** *n.*

bris+ket ('brɪskɪt) *n.* **1.** the breast of a four-legged animal. **2.** the meat from this part, esp. of beef. [C14: probably of Scandinavian origin; related to Old Norse *brjōsk* gristle, Norwegian and Danish *brusk*]

bris+ling ('brɪslɪŋ) *n.* another name for a **sprat,** esp. a Norwegian sprat seasoned, smoked, and canned in oil. [C20: from Norwegian; related to obsolete Danish *bretling,* German *Breitling*]

bris+tle ('brɪsᵊl) *n.* **1.** any short stiff hair of an animal or plant, such as any of the hairs on a pig's back. **2.** something resembling these hairs: *toothbrush bristle.* ~*vb.* **3.** (when *intr.,* often foll. by *up*) to stand up or cause to stand up like bristles: *the angry cat's fur bristled.* **4.** (*intr.;* sometimes foll. by *up*) show anger, indignation, etc.: *she bristled at the suggestion.* **5.** (*intr.*) to be thickly covered or set: *the target bristled with arrows.* **6.** (*intr.*) to be in a state of agitation or movement: *the office was bristling with activity.* **7.** (*tr.*) to provide with a bristle or bristles. [C13 *bristil, brustel,* from earlier *brust,* from Old English *byrst;* related to Old Norse *burst,* Old High German *borst*] —**'bris+tly** *adj.*

bris·tle-grass *n.* any of various grasses of the genus *Setaria,* such as *S. viridis,* having a bristly inflorescence.

bris·tle+tail ('brɪsᵊl,teɪl) *n.* any primitive wingless insect of the orders *Thysanura* and *Diplura,* such as the silverfish and firebrat, having a flattened body and long tail appendages.

bris+tle worm *n.* a popular name for a **polychaete.**

Bris+tol ('brɪstᵊl) *n.* a port and industrial city in SW England, administrative centre of the county of Avon, on the River Avon seven miles from its mouth on the Bristol Channel: a major port, trading with America, in the 17th and 18th centuries; the modern port consists chiefly of docks at Avonmouth and Portishead; noted for the **Clifton Suspension Bridge** (designed by I. K. Brunel, 1834) over the Avon gorge; university (1909). Pop.: 425 203 (1971).

Bris+tol board *n.* a heavy smooth cardboard of fine quality, used for printing and drawing.

Bris+tol Chan+nel *n.* an inlet of the Atlantic, between S Wales and SW England, merging into the Severn estuary. Length: about 137 km (85 miles).

Bris+tol fash+ion *adv., adj.* (*postpositive*) **1.** *Nautical.* clean and neat, with newly painted and scrubbed surfaces, brass polished, etc. **2. shipshape and Bristol fashion.** in good order; efficiently arranged.

bris+tols ('brɪstᵊlz) *pl. n. Brit. slang.* a woman's breasts. [C20: short for *Bristol Cities,* rhyming slang for *titties*]

brit (brɪt) *n.* (*functioning as sing. or pl.*) **1.** the young of a herring, sprat, or similar fish. **2.** minute marine crustaceans, esp. copepods, forming food for many fishes and whales. [C17: perhaps from Cornish *brȳthel* mackerel; see BRILL]

Brit (brɪt) *n. Informal.* a British person.

Brit. *abbrev. for:* **1.** Britain. **2.** British.

Brit+ain ('brɪtᵊn) *n.* another name for **Great Britain.**

Bri+tan+ni·a (brɪ'tænɪə) *n.* **1.** a female warrior carrying a trident and wearing a helmet, personifying Great Britain or the British Empire. **2.** (in the ancient Roman Empire) the S part of Great Britain.

Bri+tan+ni·a met+al *n.* an alloy of low melting point consisting of tin with 5–10 per cent antimony, 1–3 per cent copper, and sometimes small quantities of zinc, lead, or bismuth: used for decorative purposes and for bearings.

Bri+tan+nic (brɪ'tænɪk) *adj.* of Britain; British (esp. in the phrases **His** *or* **Her Britannic Majesty**).

britch·es ('brɪtʃɪz) *pl. n.* **1.** a variant spelling of **breeches. 2. too big for one's britches.** *Informal.* over-confident; arrogant.

Brit·i·cism ('brɪtɪˌsɪzəm) *n.* a custom, linguistic usage, or other feature peculiar to Britain or its people.

Brit·ish ('brɪtɪʃ) *adj.* **1.** relating to, denoting, or characteristic of Britain or its inhabitants. **2.** relating to or denoting the English language as spoken and written in Britain, esp. the S dialect generally regarded as standard. See also **Southern British English, Received Pronunciation. 3.** relating to or denoting the ancient Britons. **4.** of or relating to the Commonwealth: *British subjects.* ~*n.* **5.** (preceded by *the; functioning as pl.*) the natives or inhabitants of Britain. **6.** the extinct Celtic language of the ancient Britons. See also **Brythonic.** —**'Brit·ish·ness** *n.*

Brit·ish Ant·arc·tic Ter·ri·to·ry *n.* a British colony in the S Atlantic: created in 1962 and consisting of the South Shetland Islands, the South Orkney Islands, and Graham Land; formerly part of the Falkland Islands Dependencies.

Brit·ish Cam·e·roons *n.* a former British trust territory of West Africa. See **Cameroon.**

Brit·ish Co·lum·bi·a *n.* a province of W Canada, on the Pacific coast: largely mountainous with extensive forests, rich mineral resources, and important fisheries. Capital: Victoria. Pop.: 2 466 608 (1976). Area: 930 532 sq. km (359 279 sq. miles).

Brit·ish Com·mon·wealth of Na·tions *n.* the former name of the **Commonwealth.**

Brit·ish East Af·ri·ca *n.* the former British possessions of Uganda, Kenya, Tanganyika, and Zanzibar, before their independence in the 1960s.

Brit·ish Em·pire *n.* (formerly) the United Kingdom and the territories under its control, which reached its greatest extent at the end of World War I when it embraced over a quarter of the world's population and more than a quarter of the world's land surface.

Brit·ish·er ('brɪtɪʃə) *n.* (*not used by the British*) **1.** a native or inhabitant of Great Britain, esp. of England. **2.** any British subject.

Brit·ish Gui·an·a *n.* the former name (until 1966) of **Guyana.**

Brit·ish Hon·du·ras *n.* the former name of **Belize.**

Brit·ish In·di·a *n.* the 17 provinces of India formerly governed by the British under the British sovereign: ceased to exist in 1947 when the independent states of India and Pakistan were created.

Bri·tish In·di·an O·cean Ter·ri·to·ry *n.* a colony in the Indian Ocean: consists of the Chagos Archipelago (formerly a dependency of Mauritius) and (until 1976) Aldabra, Farquhar, and Des Roches, now administratively part of the Seychelles.

Brit·ish Isles *n.* a group of islands in W Europe, consisting of Great Britain, Ireland, the Isle of Man, Orkney, the Shetland Islands, the Channel Islands belonging to Great Britain, and the islands adjacent to these.

Brit·ish·ism ('brɪtɪˌʃɪzəm) *n.* a variant of **Briticism.**

Brit·ish Is·ra·el·ite *n.* a member of a religious movement claiming that the British people are descended from the lost tribes of Israel.

Brit·ish Le·gion *n. Brit.* an organization founded in 1921 to provide services and assistance for former members of the armed forces.

Brit·ish Mu·se·um *n.* a museum in London, founded in 1753: contains one of the world's richest collections of antiquities and the British national library.

Brit·ish North A·mer·i·ca *n.* Canada or its constituent regions or provinces that formed part of the British Empire.

Brit·ish So·ma·li·land *n.* a former British protectorate (1884–1960) in E Africa, on the Gulf of Aden: united with Italian Somaliland in 1960 to form the Somali Republic.

Brit·ish Stand·ards In·sti·tu·tion *n.* an association, founded in London in 1901, that establishes and maintains standards for units of measurements, clothes sizes, technical terminology, etc., as used in Britain. Abbrev.: **BSI** Compare **National Bureau of Standards, International Standards Organization.**

Brit·ish Stand·ard Time *n.* the standard time used in Britain all the year round from 1968 to 1971, set one hour ahead of Greenwich Mean Time and equalling Central European Time.

Brit·ish Sum·mer Time *n.* time set one hour ahead of Greenwich Mean Time: used in Britain from the end of March to the end of October, providing an extra hour of daylight in the evening. Abbrev.: **B.S.T.** Compare **daylight-saving time.**

Brit·ish ther·mal u·nit *n.* a unit of heat in the fps system equal to the quantity of heat required to raise the temperature of 1 pound of water by 1°F. 1 British thermal unit is equivalent to 1055.06 joules or 251.997 calories. Abbrevs.: **btu, B.Th.U.**

Brit·ish Un·ion of Fas·cists *n.* the British fascist party founded by Sir Oswald Mosley (1932), which advocated a strong corporate state and promoted anti-Semitism.

Brit·ish Vir·gin Is·lands *n.* a British colony in the West Indies, consisting of 36 islands in the E Virgin Islands: formerly part of the Federation of the Leeward Islands (1871–1956). Capital: Road Town, on Tortola. Pop.: 9672 (1970). Area: 153 sq. km (59 sq. miles).

Brit·ish West Af·ri·ca *n.* the former British possessions of Nigeria, Gambia, Sierra Leone, and the Gold Coast, and the former trust territories of Togoland and Cameroons.

Brit·ish West In·dies *n.* the states in the Caribbean that are members of the Commonwealth: the Bahamas, Barbados, Jamaica, Trinidad and Tobago, the Leeward Islands, and the Windward Islands.

Brit·on ('brɪtᵊn) *n.* **1.** a native or inhabitant of Britain. **2.** a citizen of the United Kingdom. **3.** *History.* any of the early Celtic inhabitants of S Britain who were largely dispossessed by the Anglo-Saxon invaders after the fifth century A.D. [C13: from Old French *Breton,* from Latin *Britto,* of Celtic origin]

Brit·ta·ny ('brɪtənɪ) *n.* a region of NW France, the peninsula between the English Channel and the Bay of Biscay: settled by Celtic refugees from Wales and Cornwall during the Anglo-Saxon invasions; disputed between England and France until 1364. Breton name: **Breiz** (braɪz). French name: **Bretagne.**

Brit·ten ('brɪtᵊn) *n.* **(Edward) Ben·ja·min,** Baron Britten. 1913–76, English composer, pianist, and conductor. His works include the operas *Peter Grimes* (1945) and *Billy Budd* (1951), the choral works *Hymn to St. Cecilia* (1942) and *A War Requiem* (1962), and numerous orchestral pieces.

brit·tle ('brɪtᵊl) *adj.* **1.** easily cracked, snapped, or broken; fragile. **2.** curt or irritable: *a brittle reply.* **3.** hard or sharp in quality. ~*n.* **4.** a crunchy sweet made with treacle and nuts: *peanut brittle.* [C14: from Old English *brytel* (unattested); related to *brytsen* fragment, *brēotan* to break] —**'brit·tle·ness** *n.*

brit·tle-star *n.* any echinoderm of the class *Ophiuroidea,* occurring on the sea bottom and having five long slender arms radiating from a small central disc. See also **basket-star.**

Brit·ton·ic (brɪ'tɒnɪk) *n., adj.* another word for **Brythonic.**

britz·ka *or* **brits·ka** ('brɪtskə) *n.* a long horse-drawn carriage with a folding top over the rear seat and a rear-facing front seat. [C19: from German, variant of *Britschka,* from Polish *bryczka* a little cart, from *bryka* cart]

Brix scale (brɪks) *n.* a scale for calibrating hydrometers used for measuring the concentration and density of sugar solutions at a given temperature. [C19: named after A. F. W. *Brix,* 19th-century German inventor]

BRN *international car registration for* Bahrain.

Br·no ('bɜːnəʊ; *Czech* 'brnɔ) *n.* a city in central Czechoslovakia, capital of Moravia: the country's second largest city. Pop.: 343 860 (1974 est.). German name: **Brünn.**

bro. (brəʊ) *abbrev. for* brother.

broach (brəʊtʃ) *vb.* **1.** (*tr.*) to initiate (a topic) for discussion: *to broach a dangerous subject.* **2.** (*tr.*) to tap or pierce (a container) to draw off (a liquid): *to broach a cask; to broach wine.* **3.** (*tr.*) to open in order to begin to use: *to broach a shipment.* **4.** (*intr.*) to break the surface of the water: *the trout broached after being hooked.* **5.** (*intr.*) *Nautical.* (of a sailing vessel) to swerve sharply and dangerously in a following sea so as to be broadside to the waves. **6.** (*tr.*) *Machinery.* to enlarge and finish (a hole) by reaming. ~*n.* **7.** a long tapered toothed cutting tool for enlarging holes. **8.** a spit for roasting meat, etc. **9.** a roof covering the corner triangle on the top of a square tower having an octagonal spire. **10.** a pin, forming part of some types of lock, that registers in the hollow bore of a key. **11.** a tool used for tapping casks. **12.** a less common spelling of **brooch.** [C14: from Old French *broche,* from Vulgar Latin *brocca* (unattested), from Latin *brochus* projecting] —**'broach·er** *n.*

broad (brɔːd) *adj.* **1.** having relatively great breadth or width. **2.** of vast extent; spacious: *a broad plain.* **3.** (*postpositive*) from one side to the other: *four miles broad.* **4.** of great scope or potential: *that invention had broad applications.* **5.** not detailed; general: *broad plans.* **6.** clear and open; full (esp. in the phrase **broad daylight**). **7.** obvious or plain: *broad hints.* **8.** liberal; tolerant: *a broad political stance.* **9.** widely spread; extensive: *broad support.* **10.** outspoken or bold: *a broad manner.* **11.** vulgar; coarse; indecent: *a broad joke.* **12.** unrestrained; free: *broad laughter.* **13.** (of a dialect or pronunciation) consisting of a large number of speech sounds characteristic of a particular geographical area: *a broad Yorkshire accent.* **14.** *Phonetics.* **a.** of or relating to a type of pronunciation transcription in which symbols correspond approximately to phonemes without taking account of allophonic variations. **b. broad a.** the long vowel in English words such as *father, half,* as represented in the received pronunciation of Southern British English. **15. as broad as it is long.** *Informal.* amounting to the same thing; without advantage either way. ~*n.* **16.** the broad part of something. **17.** *Slang, chiefly U.S.* a girl or woman. **18.** *Brit. dialect.* a river spreading over a lowland. See also **Broads. 19.** *East Anglia dialect.* a shallow lake. ~*adv.* **20.** widely or fully: *broad awake.* [Old English *brād;* related to Old Norse *breithr,* Old Frisian *brēd,* Old High German *breit,* Gothic *braiths*] —**'broad·ly** *adv.*

broad ar·row *n.* **1.** a mark shaped like a broad arrowhead designating British government property and formerly used on prison clothing. **2.** an arrow with a broad head.

broad bean *n.* **1.** an erect annual Eurasian bean plant, *Vicia faba,* cultivated for its large edible flattened seeds, used as a vegetable, and for its pods, used as animal fodder. **2.** the seed of this plant. ~Also called: **horse bean.**

broad·bill ('brɔːdˌbɪl) *n.* **1.** any passerine bird of the family *Eurylaimidae,* of tropical Africa and Asia, having bright plumage and a short wide bill. **2.** *U.S.* any of various wide-billed birds, such as the scaup and shoveler. **3.** *U.S.* another name for **sword-fish.**

broad·brim ('brɔːdˌbrɪm) *n.* a broad-brimmed hat, esp. one worn by the Quakers in the 17th century.

broad·cast ('brɔːdˌkɑːst) *vb.* **·casts, ·cast·ing, ·cast** *or* **·cast·ed. 1.** to transmit (announcements or programmes) on radio or television. **2.** (*intr.*) to take part in a radio or television programme. **3.** (*tr.*) to make widely known throughout an area: *to broadcast news.* **4.** (*tr.*) to scatter (seed, etc.) over an area, esp. by hand. ~*n.* **5. a.** a transmission or programme on radio or television. **b.** (*as modifier*): *a broadcast signal.* **6. a.** the act of scattering seeds. **b.** (*as modifier*): *the broadcast method of sowing.* ~*adj.* **7.** dispersed over a wide area:

broadcast seeds. ~*adv.* **8.** far and wide: *seeds to be sown broadcast.* —**'broad+,cast+er** *n.*

Broad Church *n.* **1.** a party within the Church of England which favours a broad and liberal interpretation of Anglican formularies and rubrics and objects to positive definition in theology. Compare **High Church, Low Church.** ~*adj.* **Broad-Church. 2.** of or relating to this party.

broad+cloth ('brɔːdˌklɒθ) *n.* **1.** fabric woven on a wide loom. **2.** a closely woven fabric of wool, worsted, cotton, or rayon with lustrous finish, used for clothing.

broad+en ('brɔːdᵊn) *vb.* to make or become broad or broader; widen.

broad gauge *n.* **1.** a railway track with a greater distance between the lines than the standard gauge of 56½ inches used now by most mainline railway systems. ~*adj.* **broad-gauge. 2.** of, relating to, or denoting a railway having this track.

broad jump *n.* the usual U.S. term for **long jump.**

broad+leaf ('brɔːdˌliːf) *n., pl.* **+leaves.** any tobacco plant having broad leaves, used esp. in making cigars.

broad-leaved *adj.* denoting trees other than conifers; having broad rather than needleshaped leaves.

broad+loom ('brɔːdˌluːm) *n.* (*modifier*) of or designating carpets or carpeting woven on a wide loom to obviate the need for seams.

broad-mind·ed *adj.* **1.** tolerant of opposing viewpoints; not prejudiced; liberal. **2.** not easily shocked by permissive sexual habits, pornography, etc. —**ˌbroad-'mind·ed·ly** *adv.* —**ˌbroad-'mind·ed·ness** *n.*

Broad+moor ('brɔːdˌmɔː) *n.* an institution in Berkshire, England, for housing and treating mentally ill criminals.

Broads (brɔːdz) *pl. n.* **the. 1.** a group of shallow navigable lakes, connected by a network of rivers, in E England, in Norfolk and Suffolk. **2.** the region around these lakes: a tourist centre; several bird sanctuaries.

broad seal *n.* the official seal of a nation and its government.

broad+sheet ('brɔːdˌʃiːt) *n.* **1.** a newspaper having a large format, approximately 15 by 24 inches (38 by 61 centimetres). Compare **tabloid. 2.** another word for **broadside** (sense 4).

broad+side ('brɔːdˌsaɪd) *n.* **1.** *Nautical.* the entire side of a vessel, from stem to stern and from waterline to rail. **2.** *Naval.* **a.** all the armament fired from one side of a warship. **b.** the simultaneous discharge of such armament. **3.** a strong or abusive verbal or written attack. **4.** Also called: **broadside ballad.** a ballad or popular song printed on one side of a sheet of paper and sold by hawkers, esp. in 16th-century England. **5.** any standard size of paper before cutting or folding: *demy broadside.* **6.** another name for **broadsheet** (sense 1). **7.** a large flat surface: *the broadside of the barn.* ~*adv.* **8.** with a broader side facing an object; sideways: *the train hit the lorry broadside.*

broad-spec·trum *n.* (*modifier*) *Pharmacol.* effective against a wide variety of diseases or microorganisms: *a broad-spectrum antibiotic.*

broad+sword ('brɔːdˌsɔːd) *n.* a broad-bladed sword used for cutting rather than stabbing. Also called: **backsword.**

broad+tail ('brɔːdˌteɪl) *n.* **1.** the highly valued black wavy fur obtained from the skins of newly born karakul lambs; caracul. **2.** another name for **karakul.**

Broad+way ('brɔːdˌweɪ) *n.* **1.** a thoroughfare in New York City, famous for its theatres: the centre of the commercial theatre in the U.S. ~*adj.* **2.** of or relating to or suitable for the commercial theatre, esp. on Broadway.

Bro·ca (*French* brɔ'ka) *n.* **Paul** (pɔl). 1824–80, French surgeon and anthropologist who discovered the motor speech centre of the brain and did pioneering work in brain surgery.

bro+cade (brəʊ'keɪd) *n.* **1. a.** a rich fabric woven with a raised design, often using gold or silver threads. **b.** (*as modifier*): *brocade curtains.* ~*vb.* **2.** (*tr.*) to weave with such a design. [C17: from Spanish *brocado,* from Italian *broccato* embossed fabric, from *brocco* spike, from Latin *brochus* projecting; see BROACH]

broc·a+telle *or U.S.* **broc·a+tel** (ˌbrɒkə'tɛl) *n.* **1.** a heavy brocade with the design in deep relief, used chiefly in upholstery. **2.** a type of variegated marble from France and Italy. [C17: from French, from Italian *broccatello,* diminutive of *broccato* BROCADE]

broc+co+li ('brɒkəlɪ) *n.* **1.** a cultivated variety of cabbage, *Brassica oleracea italica,* having branched greenish flower heads. **2.** the flower head of this plant, eaten as a vegetable before the buds have opened. **3.** a variety of this plant that does not form a head, whose stalks are eaten as a vegetable. [C17: from Italian, plural of *broccolo* a little sprout, from *brocco* sprout, spike; see BROCADE]

broch (brɒk, brɒx) *n.* (in Scotland) a circular dry-stone tower large enough to serve as a fortified home: characteristic of late sixth-century building. [C17: variant of Middle English (Scottish) *brugh* BOROUGH]

bro+ché (brəʊ'ʃeɪ; *French* brɔ'ʃe) *adj.* woven with a raised design, as brocade. [C19: from French *brocher* to brocade, stitch; see BROACH]

bro+chette (brɒ'ʃɛt; *French* brɔ'ʃɛt) *n.* a skewer or small spit, used for holding pieces of meat, etc., while roasting or grilling. [C19: from Old French *brochete* small pointed tool; see BROACH]

bro+chure ('brəʊʃjʊə, -ʃə) *n.* a pamphlet or stitched booklet, esp. one containing summarized or introductory information or advertising. [C18: from French, from *brocher* to stitch (a book)]

brock (brɒk) *n.* a Brit. name for **badger** (sense 1): used esp. as a form of address in stories, etc. [Old English *broc,* of Celtic origin; compare Welsh *broch*]

Brock+en (*German* 'brɔkᵊn) *n.* a mountain in East Germany: the highest peak of the Harz Mountains; important in German folklore. Height: 1142 m (3747 ft.). The **Brocken Bow** or **Brocken Spectre** is an atmospheric phenomenon in which an observer, when the sun is low, may see his enlarged shadow against the clouds, often surrounded by coloured lights.

brock+et ('brɒkɪt) *n.* any small deer of the genus *Mazama,* of tropical America, having small unbranched antlers. [C15: from Anglo-French *broquet,* from *broque* horn, from Vulgar Latin *brocca* (unattested); see BROACH]

brod+dle ('brɒdᵊl) *vb.* (*tr.*) *Yorkshire dialect.* to poke or pierce (something). [perhaps from BRADAWL]

bro+de+rie an+glaise (ˌbrəʊdəriː ɑːŋ'glɛz) *n.* open embroidery on white cotton, fine linen, etc. [French: English embroidery]

Broed·er+bond ('brʊdəˌbɔːnt, 'bruːdəˌbɒnt) *n.* (in South Africa) a secret society of Afrikaner Nationalists committed to securing and maintaining Afrikaner control over important areas of government. [Afrikaans: band of brothers]

bro+gan ('brəʊgən) *n.* a heavy laced usually ankle-high work boot. [C19: from Gaelic *brōgan* a little shoe, from *brōg* shoe; see BROGUE²]

Brog·lie (brɔːj) *n.* **1.** Prince **Louis Vic·tor de** (lwi vik'tɔːr də). born 1892, French physicist, noted for his research in quantum mechanics and his development of wave mechanics: Nobel prize for physics 1929. **2.** his brother, **Mau·rice** (mɔris), Duc de Broglie. 1875–1960, French physicist, noted for his research into x-ray spectra.

brogue¹ (brəʊg) *n.* a broad gentle-sounding dialectal accent, esp. that used by the Irish in speaking English. [C18: probably from BROGUE², alluding to the footwear of the peasantry]

brogue² (brəʊg) *n.* **1.** a sturdy walking shoe, often with ornamental perforations. **2.** an untanned shoe worn formerly in Ireland and Scotland. [C16: from Old Irish *brōc* shoe, probably from Old Norse *brōk* leg covering]

broi+der ('brɔɪdə) *vb.* (*tr.*) an archaic word for **embroider.** [C15: from Old French *brosder,* of Germanic origin; see EMBROIDER]

broil¹ (brɔɪl) *vb.* **1.** the usual U.S. word for **grill¹** (sense 1). **2.** to become or cause to become extremely hot. **3.** (*intr.*) to be furious. ~*n.* **4.** the process of broiling. **5.** something broiled. [C14: from Old French *bruillir* to burn, of uncertain origin]

broil² (brɔɪl) *n.* **1.** a loud quarrel or disturbance; brawl. ~*vb.* **2.** (*intr.*) to brawl; quarrel. [C16: from Old French *brouiller* to mix, from Old French *breu* broth; see BREWIS, BROSE]

broil+er ('brɔɪlə) *n.* **1.** a young tender chicken suitable for roasting. **2.** a pan, grate, etc. for broiling food.

broil+er house *n.* a building in which broiler chickens are reared in confined conditions.

broke (brəʊk) *vb.* **1.** the past tense of **break.** ~*adj. Informal.* **2.** having no money; bankrupt. **3. go for broke.** to risk everything in a gambling or other venture.

bro+ken ('brəʊkən) *vb.* **1.** the past participle of **break.** ~*adj.* **2.** fractured, smashed, or splintered: *a broken vase.* **3.** imperfect or incomplete; fragmentary: *a broken set of books.* **4.** interrupted; disturbed; disconnected: *a broken telephone call; broken sleep.* **5.** intermittent or discontinuous: *broken sunshine.* **6.** varying in direction or intensity, as of pitch: *a broken note; a broken run.* **7.** not functioning: *a broken radio.* **8.** spoilt or ruined by divorce (esp. in the phrases **broken home, broken marriage**). **9.** (of a trust, promise, contract, etc.) violated; infringed. **10.** overcome with grief or disappointment: *a broken heart.* **11.** (of the speech of a foreigner) imperfect in grammar, vocabulary, and pronunciation: *broken English.* **12.** Also: **broken-in.** made tame or disciplined by training: *a broken horse; a broken recruit.* **13.** exhausted or weakened. as through ill-health or misfortune. **14.** confused or disorganized: *broken ranks of soldiers.* **15.** breached or opened: *broken defensive lines.* **16.** irregular or rough; uneven: *broken ground.* **17.** bankrupt or out of money: *a broken industry.* —**'bro+ken+ly** *adv.*

bro·ken-down *adj.* **1.** worn out, as by age or long use; dilapidated: *a broken-down fence.* **2.** not in working order: *a broken-down tractor.* **3.** physically or mentally ill.

bro·ken+heart·ed (ˌbrəʊkən'hɑːtɪd) *adj.* overwhelmed by grief or disappointment. —**ˌbro·ken+'heart·ed·ly** *adv.* —**ˌbro·ken+'heart·ed·ness** *n.*

Bro+ken Hill *n.* a city in SE Australia, in W New South Wales: mining centre for lead, silver, and zinc. Pop.: 28 160 (1975 est.).

bro+ken wind (wɪnd) *n. Vet. science.* another name for **heaves** (sense 1).

bro+ker ('brəʊkə) *n.* **1.** an agent who, acting on behalf of a principal, buys or sells goods, securities, etc., in return for a commission: *insurance broker.* **2.** short for **stockbroker.** [C14: from Anglo-French *brocour* broacher (of casks, hence, one who sells, agent), from Old Northern French *broquier* to tap a cask, from *broque* tap of a cask; see BROACH]

bro+ker+age ('brəʊkərɪdʒ) *n.* **1.** commission charged by a broker to his clients. **2.** a broker's business or office.

brol+ga ('brɒlgə) *n.* a large grey Australian crane, *Grus rubicunda,* having a red-and-green head and a trumpeting call. Also called: **Australian crane, native companion.** [C19: from a native Australian language]

brol+ly ('brɒlɪ) *n., pl.* **+lies.** an informal Brit. name for **umbrella** (sense 1).

bro+mal ('brəʊməl) *n.* a yellowish oily synthetic liquid used medicinally as a sedative and hypnotic; tribromoacetaldehyde. Formula: Br_3CCHO. [C19: from BROM(INE) + AL(COHOL)]

bro+mate ('brəʊmeɪt) *n.* **1.** any salt or ester of bromic acid, containing the monovalent group $-BrO_3$ or ion BrO_3^-. ~*vb.* **2.** another word for **brominate.** [C19: probably from German *Bromat;* see BROMO-, -ATE[1]]

Brom+berg ('brɒmbɛrk) *n.* the German name for **Bydgoszcz.**

brome grass *or* **brome** (brəʊm) *n.* any of various grasses of the genus *Bromus,* having small flower spikes in loose drooping clusters. Some species are used for hay. [C18: via Latin from Greek *bromos* oats, of obscure origin]

bro+me·li+ad (brəʊ'mi:lɪ,æd) *n.* any plant of the tropical American family *Bromeliaceae,* typically epiphytes with a rosette of fleshy leaves. The family includes the pineapple and Spanish moss. [C19: from New Latin *Bromelia* type genus, after Olaf *Bromelius* (1639–1705), Swedish botanist] **—bro+,me·li·'a+ceous** *adj.*

brom+e·o+sin (brəʊ'mi:əsɪn) *n. Chem.* another name for **eosin.** [C20: from BROMO- + EOSIN]

bro+mic ('brəʊmɪk) *adj.* of or containing bromine in the trivalent or pentavalent state.

bro+mic ac·id *n.* a colourless unstable water-soluble liquid used as an oxidizing agent in the manufacture of dyes and pharmaceuticals. Formula: $HBrO_3$.

bro+mide ('brəʊmaɪd) *n.* **1.** any salt of hydrobromic acid, containing the monovalent ion Br^- (**bromide ion**). **2.** any compound containing a bromine atom, such as methyl bromide. **3.** a dose of sodium or potassium bromide given as a sedative. **4.** *Informal.* **a.** a trite saying; platitude. **b.** a dull or boring person.

bro+mide pa+per *n.* a type of photographic paper coated with an emulsion of silver bromide usually containing a small quantity of silver iodide.

bro+mid+ic (brəʊ'mɪdɪk) *adj. Informal.* ordinary; dull.

bro+min+ate ('brəʊmɪ,neɪt) *vb.* to treat or react with bromine. Also: **bromate.** **—,bro+min·'a+tion** *n.*

bro+mine ('brəʊmi:n, -mɪn) *n.* a pungent dark red volatile liquid element of the halogen series that occurs in brine and is used in the production of chemicals, esp. ethylene dibromide. Symbol: Br; atomic no.: 35; atomic wt.: 79.91; valency: 1,3,5, or 7; relative density 3.12; density (gas): 7.59 kg/m^3; melting pt.: -7.2°C; boiling pt.: 58.78°C. [C19: from French *brome* bromine, from Greek *brōmos* bad smell, of uncertain origin]

bro+mism ('brəʊmɪzəm) *or* **bro+min+ism** *n.* poisoning caused by the excessive intake of bromine or compounds containing bromine.

Brom+ley ('brɒmlɪ) *n.* a SE borough of Greater London. Pop.: 299 100 (1976 est.).

bro·mo- *or before a vowel* **brom-** *combining form.* indicating the presence of bromine: *bromoform.*

bro+mo+form ('brəʊmə,fɔ:m) *n.* a heavy colourless liquid substance with a sweetish taste and an odour resembling that of chloroform; tribromomethane. Formula: $CHBr_3$.

Broms+grove ('brɒmz,grəʊv) *n.* a town in W central England, in NE Hereford and Worcester. Pop.: 40 669 (1971).

bron+chi ('brɒŋkaɪ) *n.* the plural of **bronchus.**

bron+chi·a ('brɒŋkɪə) *pl. n.* another name for **bronchial tubes.** [C17: from Late Latin, from Greek *bronkhia,* plural of *bronkhion,* diminutive of *bronkhus* windpipe, throat]

bron+chi·al ('brɒŋkɪəl) *adj.* of or relating to the bronchi or the bronchial tubes. **—'bron+chi+al+ly** *adv.*

bron+chi·al tubes *pl. n.* the bronchi or their smaller divisions.

bron+chi+ec+ta+sis (,brɒŋkɪ'ɛktəsɪs) *n.* chronic dilation of the bronchi or bronchial tubes, which often become infected. [C19: from BRONCHO- + Greek *ektasis* a stretching]

bron+chi+ole ('brɒŋkɪ,əʊl) *n.* any of the smallest bronchial tubes, usually ending in alveoli. [C19: from New Latin *bronchiolum,* diminutive of Late Latin *bronchium,* singular of BRONCHIA] **—bron+chi·o+lar** (,brɒŋkɪ'əʊlə) *adj.*

bron+chi+tis (brɒŋ'kaɪtɪs) *n.* inflammation of the bronchial tubes, characterized by coughing, difficulty in breathing, etc., caused by infection or irritation of the respiratory tract. **—bron+chit+ic** (brɒŋ'kɪtɪk) *adj., n.*

bron·cho- *or before a vowel* **bronch-** *combining form.* indicating or relating to the bronchi: *bronchitis.* [from Greek: BRONCHUS]

bron+cho+pneu+mo+ni·a (,brɒŋkəʊnju:'məʊnɪə) *n.* inflammation of the lungs, originating in the bronchioles.

bron+cho+scope ('brɒŋkə,skəʊp) *n.* an instrument for examining and providing access to the interior of the bronchial tubes. **—bron+cho+scop+ic** (,brɒŋkə'skɒpɪk) *adj.* **—bron+chos+co+pist** (brɒŋ'kɒskəpɪst) *n.* **—bron+'chos+co+py** *n.*

bron+chus ('brɒŋkəs) *n., pl.* **+chi** (-kaɪ). either of the two main branches of the trachea, which contain cartilage within their walls. [C18: from New Latin, from Greek *bronkhos* windpipe]

bron+co *or* **bron+cho** ('brɒŋkəʊ) *n., pl.* **+cos** *or* **+chos.** *U.S.* a wild or partially tamed pony or mustang of the western plains. [C19: from Mexican Spanish, short for Spanish *potro bronco* unbroken colt, probably from Latin *broccus* projecting (as knots on wood), hence, rough, wild]

bron·co+bust·er ('brɒŋkəʊ,bʌstə) *n. Western U.S.* a cowboy who breaks in broncos or wild horses.

Bron·të ('brɒntɪ) *n.* **1. Anne,** pen name *Acton Bell.* 1820–49, English novelist; author of *The Tenant of Wildfell Hall* (1847). **2.** her sister, **Char·lotte,** pen name *Currer Bell.* 1816–55, English novelist, author of *Jane Eyre* (1847), *Villette* (1853), and *The Professor* (1857). **3.** her sister, **Em·i·ly (Jane),** pen name *Ellis Bell.* 1818–48, English novelist and poet; author of *Wuthering Heights* (1847).

bron+to+sau+rus (,brɒntə'sɔ:rəs) *or* **bron+to+saur** ('brɒntə,sɔ:) *n.* any very large herbivorous quadrupedal dinosaur of the genus *Apatosaurus,* common in the U.S. in late Jurassic times, having a long neck and long tail: suborder *Sauropoda* (sauropods). [C19: from New Latin, from Greek *brontē* thunder + *sauros* lizard]

Bronx (brɒŋks) *n.* **the.** a borough of New York City, on the mainland, separated from Manhattan by the Harlem River. Pop.: 1 471 701 (1970).

bronze (brɒnz) *n.* **1. a.** any hard water-resistant alloy consisting of copper and smaller proportions of tin and sometimes zinc and lead. **b.** any similar copper alloy containing other elements in place of tin, such as aluminium bronze, beryllium bronze, etc. See also **phosphor bronze, gunmetal.** Compare **brass** (sense 1). **2.** a yellowish-brown colour or pigment. **3.** a statue, medal, or other object made of bronze. ~*adj.* **4.** made of or resembling bronze. **5.** of a yellowish-brown colour: *a bronze skin.* ~*vb.* **6.** (esp. of the skin) to make or become brown; tan. **7.** (*tr.*) to give the appearance of bronze to. [C18: from French, from Italian *bronzo,* perhaps ultimately from Latin *Brundisium* Brindisi, famed for its bronze] **—'bronz·y** *adj.*

bronze age *n. Classical myth.* a period of man's existence marked by war and violence, following the golden and silver ages and preceding the iron age.

Bronze Age *n. Archaeol.* **a.** a technological stage between the Stone and Iron Ages, beginning in the Middle East about 4500 B.C. and lasting in Britain from about 2000 to 500 B.C., during which weapons and tools were made of bronze and there was intensive trading. **b.** (*as modifier*): *a Bronze-Age tool.*

bronze med+al *n.* a medal of bronze, awarded to a competitor who comes third in a contest or race. Compare **gold medal, silver medal.**

brooch (brəʊtʃ) *n.* an ornament with a hinged pin and catch, worn fastened to clothing. [C13: from Old French *broche;* see BROACH]

brood (bru:d) *n.* **1.** a number of young animals, esp. birds, produced at one hatching. **2.** all the offspring in one family: often used jokingly or contemptuously. **3.** a group of a particular kind; breed. **4.** (*as modifier*) kept for breeding: *a brood mare.* ~*vb.* **5.** (of a bird) **a.** to sit on or hatch (eggs). **b.** (*tr.*) to cover (young birds) protectively with the wings. **6.** (when *intr.,* often foll. by *on, over,* or *upon*) to ponder morbidly or persistently. [Old English *brōd;* related to Middle High German *bruot,* Dutch *broed;* see BREED]

brood+er ('bru:də) *n.* **1.** an enclosure or other structure, usually heated, used for rearing young chickens or other fowl. **2.** a person or thing that broods.

brood pouch *n.* **1.** a pouch or cavity in certain animals, such as frogs and fishes, in which their eggs develop and hatch. **2.** another name for **marsupium.**

brood·y ('bru:dɪ) *adj.* **brood·i+er, brood·i+est. 1.** moody; meditative; introspective. **2.** (of poultry) wishing to sit on or hatch eggs. **3.** *Informal.* (of a woman) wishing to have a baby of her own. **—'brood·i+ness** *n.*

brook[1] (brʊk) *n.* a natural freshwater stream smaller than a river. [Old English *brōc;* related to Old High German *bruoh* swamp, Dutch *broek*]

brook[2] (brʊk) *vb.* (*tr.*) (*usually used with a negative*) to bear; tolerate. [Old English *brūcan;* related to Gothic *brūkjan* to use, Old High German *brūhhan,* Latin *fruī* to enjoy] **—'brook+a·ble** *adj.*

Brook (brʊk) *n.* **Pe·ter (Paul Stephen).** born 1925, British stage and film director, noted esp. for his experimental work in the theatre.

Brooke (brʊk) *n.* **1. Al·an Fran·cis.** See (1st Viscount) **Alanbrooke. 2.** Sir **James.** 1803–68, English soldier; first rajah of Sarawak (1841–63). **3. Ru·pert.** 1887–1915, English lyric poet, noted for his charm and his early death.

Brook Farm *n.* an experimental communist community established by writers and scholars in West Roxbury, Massachusetts, from 1841 to 1847.

brook+ite ('brʊkaɪt) *n.* a reddish-brown to black mineral consisting of titanium oxide in orthorhombic crystalline form: occurs in silica veins. Formula: TiO_2. [C19: named after Henry J. *Brooke* (died 1857), English mineralogist]

brook+let ('brʊklɪt) *n.* a small brook.

brook+lime ('brʊk,laɪm) *n.* either of two blue-flowered scrophulariaceous trailing plants, *Veronica americana* of North America or *V. beccabunga* of Europe and Asia, growing in moist places. See also **speedwell.** [C16: variant of C15 *brokelemk* speedwell, from BROOK[1] + *-lemk,* from Old English *hleomoce;* influenced by LIME]

Brook+lyn ('brʊklɪn) *n.* a borough of New York City, on the SW end of Long Island. Pop.: 2 602 012 (1970).

Brooks Range *n.* a mountain range in N Alaska. Highest peak: Mount Isto, 2761 m (9058 ft.).

brook trout *n.* a North American freshwater trout, *Salvelinus fontinalis,* introduced in Europe and valued as a food and game fish. Also called: **speckled trout.**

brook+weed ('brʊk,wi:d) *n.* either of two white-flowered primulaceous plants, *Samolus valerandi* of Europe or *S. floribundus* of North America, growing in moist places. Also called: **water pimpernel.** See also **pimpernel.**

broom (bru:m, brʊm) *n.* **1.** an implement for sweeping consisting of a brush of straw, bristles, or twigs, bound together and attached to a long handle. **2.** any of various yellow-flowered Eurasian papilionaceous shrubs of the genera *Cytisus* and *Sarothamnus,* esp. *S. scoparius.* **3.** any of various similar Eurasian plants of the related genera *Genista* and *Spartium.* **4.**

new broom. a newly appointed official, etc., eager to make radical changes. ~*vb.* **5.** (*tr.*) to sweep with a broom. [Old English *brōm;* related to Old High German *brāmo,* Middle Dutch *bremme*]

broom+corn (ˈbruːmˌkɔːn, ˈbrʊm-) *n.* a variety of sorghum, *Sorghum vulgare technicum,* the long stiff flower stalks of which have been used for making brooms.

Broome (bruːm) *n.* **Da·vid.** born 1940, English show-jumping rider.

broom+rape (ˈbruːmˌreɪp, ˈbrʊm-) *n.* any orobanchaceous plant of the genus *Orobanche:* brownish small-flowered leafless parasites on the roots of other plants, esp. on broom. [C16: adaptation and partial translation of Medieval Latin *rāpum genistae* tuber (hence: root nodule) of Genista (a type of broom plant); compare PLANTAGENET]

broom+stick (ˈbruːmˌstɪk, ˈbrʊm-) *n.* the long handle of a broom.

Broon·zy (ˈbruːnzɪ) *n.* **Wil·liam Lee Con·ley,** called *Big Bill.* 1893–1958, U.S. blues singer and guitarist.

bros. *or* **Bros.** *abbrev. for* brothers.

brose (brəʊz) *n. Scot.* a porridge made by adding a boiling liquid to meal, esp. oatmeal. [C13 *broys,* from Old French *broez,* from *breu* broth, of Germanic origin]

broth (brɒθ) *n.* **1.** a soup made by boiling meat, fish, vegetables, etc., in water. **2.** another name for **stock** (sense 19). [Old English *broth;* related to Old Norse *broth,* Old High German *brod,* German *brodeln* to boil; see BREW]

broth+el (ˈbrɒθəl) *n.* **1.** a house or other place where men pay to have sexual intercourse with prostitutes. **2.** *Austral. informal.* any untidy or messy place. [C16: short for *brothel-house,* from C14 *brothel* useless person, from Old English *brēothan* to deteriorate; related to *briethel* worthless]

broth+er (ˈbrʌðə) *n.* **1.** a male person having the same parents as another person. **2.** short for **half-brother** or **stepbrother. 3. a.** a male person belonging to the same group, profession, nationality, trade union, etc., as another or others; fellow member. **b.** (*as modifier*): *brother workers.* **4.** *Informal.* comrade; friend: used as a form of address. **5.** *Christianity.* **a.** a member of a male religious order who undertakes work for the order without actually being in holy orders. **b.** a lay member of a male religious order. ~Related adj.: **fraternal.** ~*interj.* **6.** *Slang.* an exclamation of amazement, disgust, surprise, disappointment, etc. [Old English *brōthor;* related to Old Norse *brōthir,* Old High German *bruoder,* Latin *frāter,* Greek *phratēr,* Sanskrit *bhrātar*]

broth·er+hood (ˈbrʌðəˌhʊd) *n.* **1.** the state of being related as a brother or brothers. **2.** an association or fellowship, such as a trade union. **3.** all persons engaged in a particular profession, trade, etc. **4.** the belief, feeling, or hope that all men should regard and treat one another as brothers.

broth·er-in-law *n., pl.* **broth·ers-in-law. 1.** the brother of one's wife or husband. **2.** the husband of one's sister. **3.** the husband of the sister of one's husband or wife.

Broth+er Jon·a+than *n. Archaic.* the government or people of the United States. [C19: perhaps originally applied to a New Englander (perhaps alluding to the many Old Testament names among New England settlers)]

broth+er+ly (ˈbrʌðəlɪ) *adj.* **1.** of, resembling, or suitable to a brother, esp. in showing loyalty and affection; fraternal. ~*adv.* **2.** in a brotherly way; fraternally. —**ˈbroth+er+li+ness** *n.*

brough+am (ˈbruːəm, bruːm) *n.* **1.** a four-wheeled horse-drawn closed carriage having a raised open driver's seat in front. **2.** *Obsolete.* a large car with an open compartment at the front for the driver. **3.** *Obsolete.* an early electric car. [C19: named after Henry Peter, Lord *Brougham* (1778–1868)]

brought (brɔːt) *vb.* the past tense or past participle of **bring.**

brough+ta (ˈbrɔːtə) *or* **brough+tas** (ˈbrɔːtəs) *n.* variants of **braata.**

brou+ha+ha (bruːˈhɑːhɑː) *n.* a loud confused noise; commotion; uproar. [French, of imitative origin]

brow (braʊ) *n.* **1.** the part of the face from the eyes to the hairline; forehead. **2.** short for **eyebrow. 3.** the expression of the face; countenance: *a troubled brow.* **4.** the top of a mine shaft; pithead. **5.** the jutting top of a hill, etc. **6.** *Northern English dialect.* a steep slope on a road. [Old English *brū;* related to Old Norse *brūn* eyebrow, Lithuanian *bruvis,* Greek *ophrus,* Sanskrit *bhrūs*]

brow+band (ˈbraʊˌbænd) *n.* the strap of a horse's bridle that goes across the forehead.

brow+beat (ˈbraʊˌbiːt) *vb.* **+beats, +beat+ing, +beat, +beat+en.** (*tr.*) to discourage or frighten with threats or a domineering manner; intimidate. —**ˈbrow+ˌbeat+er** *n.*

brown (braʊn) *n.* **1.** any of various colours, such as those of wood or earth, that consist of approximately equal proportions of red and green and a small proportion of blue. **2.** a dye or pigment producing these colours. **3.** brown cloth or clothing: *dressed in brown.* **4.** any of numerous reddish-brown butterflies of the genera *Maniola, Lasiommata,* etc., such as *M. jurtina* (**meadow brown**): family *Satyridae.* ~*adj.* **5.** of the colour brown. **6.** (of bread) made from a dark flour, such as wheatmeal or wholemeal flour. **7.** deeply tanned or sunburnt. ~*vb.* **8.** to make (esp. food as a result of cooking) brown or (esp. of food) to become brown. [Old English *brūn;* related to Old Norse *brūnn,* Old High German *brūn,* Greek *phrunos* toad, Sanskrit *babhru* reddish-brown] —**ˈbrown+ish** *or* **ˈbrown·y** *adj.* —**ˈbrown+ness** *n.*

Brown (braʊn) *n.* **1.** Sir **Ar·thur Whit·ten** (ˈwɪtᵊn). 1886–1948, English aviator who with J. W. Alcock made the first flight across the Atlantic (1919). **2. George (Alfred),** Lord George-Brown. born 1914, British Labour leader; vice-chairman and deputy leader of the Labour party (1960–70); foreign secretary 1966–68. **3. John.** 1800–59, U.S. abolitionist leader, hanged after leading an unsuccessful rebellion of slaves at Harper's Ferry, Virginia. **4. Lan·ce·lot,** called *Capability Brown.* 1716–83, English landscape gardener. **5. Rob·ert.** 1773–1858, Scottish botanist who was the first to observe the Brownian movement in fluids.

brown al+gae *pl. n.* any algae of the family *Phaeophyceae,* such as the wracks and kelps, which contain a brown pigment in addition to chlorophyll.

brown bear *n.* **1.** a large ferocious brownish bear, *Ursus arctos,* inhabiting temperate forests of North America, Europe, and Asia. See also **grizzly bear, Kodiak bear. 2.** a brown variety of the American black bear *Euarctos americanus.*

brown coal *n.* another name for **lignite.**

Browne (braʊn) *n.* Sir **Thom·as.** 1605–82, English physician and author, noted for his magniloquent prose style. His works include *Religio Medici* (1642) and *Hydriotaphia or Urn Burial* (1658).

browned-off *adj. Informal, chiefly Brit.* thoroughly discouraged or disheartened; fed-up.

Brown+i·an move+ment (ˈbraʊnɪən) *n.* random movement of microscopic particles suspended in a fluid, caused by bombardment of the particles by molecules of the fluid. First observed in 1827, it provided strong evidence in support of the kinetic theory of molecules. [C19: named after Robert BROWN]

brown·ie (ˈbraʊnɪ) *n.* **1.** *Chiefly U.S.* a flat nutty chocolate cake. **2.** (in folklore) an elf said to do helpful work at night, esp. household chores. **3.** *Austral.* a bread made with currants. [C16: diminutive of BROWN (that is, a small brown man)]

Brown·ie Guide *or* **Brown·ie** (ˈbraʊnɪ) *n.* a member of the junior branch of the Guides.

brown+ing (ˈbraʊnɪŋ) *n. Brit.* a substance used to darken soups, gravies, etc.

Brow·ning[1] (ˈbraʊnɪŋ) *n.* **1. E·liz·a·beth Bar·rett.** 1806–61, English poet and critic; author of the *Sonnets from the Portuguese* (1850). **2.** her husband, **Rob·ert.** 1812–89, English poet, noted for his dramatic monologues and *The Ring and the Book* (1868–69).

Brown·ing[2] (ˈbraʊnɪŋ) *n.* **1.** Also called: **Browning automatic rifle.** a portable gas-operated air-cooled automatic rifle using .30 calibre ammunition and capable of firing between 200 and 350 rounds per minute. Abbrev.: **BAR. 2.** Also called: **Browning machine gun.** a water-cooled automatic machine gun using .30 or .50 calibre ammunition and capable of firing over 500 rounds per minute. [C20: named after John M. *Browning* (1855–1926), American designer of firearms]

brown+out (ˈbraʊnˌaʊt) *n. Chiefly U.S.* **1.** a dimming or reduction in the use of electric lights in a city, esp. to conserve electric power or as a defensive precaution in wartime. **2.** a temporary reduction in electrical power. Compare **blackout** (sense 3).

brown rat *n.* a common brownish rat, *Rattus norvegicus:* a serious pest in all parts of the world. Also called: **Norway rat.**

brown rice *n.* unpolished rice, in which the grains retain the outer yellowish-brown layer (bran).

brown rot *n.* a disease of apples, peaches, etc., caused by fungi of the genus *Sclerotinia* and characterized by yellowish-brown masses of spores on the plant surface.

Brown Shirt *n.* **1.** (in Nazi Germany) a storm trooper. **2.** a member of any fascist party or group.

brown snake *n. Austral.* any of various common venomous snakes of the genus *Pseudonaja.*

brown-state *adj.* (of linen and lace fabrics) undyed.

brown+stone (ˈbraʊnˌstəʊn) *n. U.S.* a reddish-brown iron-rich sandstone used for building.

brown stud·y *n.* a mood of deep absorption or thoughtfulness; reverie.

brown sug+ar *n.* sugar that is unrefined or only partially refined.

brown-tail moth *n.* a small brown-and-white European moth, *Euproctis phaeorrhoea,* naturalized in the eastern U.S. where it causes damage to shade trees: family *Lymantriidae* (or *Liparidae*). See also **tussock moth.**

brown trout *n.* a common brownish variety of the trout *Salmo trutta* that occurs in the rivers of N Europe and has been successfully introduced in North America. Compare **sea trout** (sense 1).

browse (braʊz) *vb.* **1.** to look through (a book, articles for sale in a shop, etc.) in a casual leisurely manner. **2.** (of deer, goats, etc.) to feed upon (vegetation) by continual nibbling. ~*n.* **3.** the act or an instance of browsing. **4.** the young twigs, shoots, leaves, etc., on which certain animals feed. [C15: from French *broust, brost* (modern French *brout*) bud, of Germanic origin; compare Old Saxon *brustian* to bud] —**ˈbrows+er** *n.*

Broz (*Serbo-Croatian* brɔːz) *n.* **Jo·sip** (ˈjɔsip). original name of (Marshal) **Tito.**

BRS *abbrev. for* British Road Services.

Bru·beck (ˈbruːbɛk) *n.* **Dave.** born 1920, U.S. modern jazz pianist and composer. He studied composition with Darius Milhaud and Arnold Schoenberg; formed his own quartet in 1951.

Bruce (bruːs) *n.* **1. Len·ny.** 1925–66, U.S. comedian, whose satirical sketches, esp. of the sexual attitudes of his contemporaries, brought him prosecutions for obscenity, but are now regarded as full of insight as well as wit. **2. Rob·ert the.** See **Robert I. 3. Stan·ley Mel·bourne,** 1st Viscount Bruce of

Melbourne. 1883–1967, Australian statesman; prime minister, in coalition with Sir Earle Page's Country Party, of Australia (1923–29).

bru+cel+lo+sis (ˌbruːsɪˈləʊsɪs) *n.* an infectious disease of cattle, goats, and pigs, caused by bacteria of the genus *Brucella* and transmittable to man (e.g. by drinking contaminated milk): symptoms include fever, chills, and severe headache. Also called: **undulant fever.** [C20: from New Latin *Brucella*, named after Sir David *Bruce* (1855–1931), Australian bacteriologist and physician]

Bruch (*German* brʊx) *n.* **Max** (maks). 1838–1920, German composer, noted chiefly for his three violin concertos.

bruc+ine (ˈbruːsiːn, -sɪn) *n.* a bitter poisonous alkaloid resembling strychnine and obtained from the tree *Strychnos nux-vomica:* used mainly in the denaturation of alcohol. Formula: $C_{23}H_{26}N_2O_4$. [C19: named after James *Bruce* (1730–94), Scottish explorer of Africa]

Brück·e (*German* ˈbrykə) *n.* **die** (diː). a group of German Expressionist painters (1905–13), including Karl Schmidt-Rottluff, Fritz Bleyl, Erich Heckel, and Ernst Ludwig Kirchner. In 1912 they exhibited with *der Blaue Reiter.* [German: literally, the bridge]

Bruck·ner (*German* ˈbrʊknər) *n.* **An·ton** (ˈantoːn). 1824–96, Austrian composer and organist in the Romantic tradition. His works include nine symphonies, four masses, and a Te Deum.

Brue·ghel, Brue·gel, *or* **Breu·ghel** (ˈbrɔɪgəl; *Flemish* ˈbrøːxəl) *n.* **1. Jan** (jɑn). 1568–1625, Flemish painter, noted for his detailed still lifes and landscapes. **2.** his father, **Pie·ter** (ˈpiːtər), called *the Elder.* ?1525–69, Flemish painter, noted for his landscapes, his satirical paintings of peasant life, and his allegorical biblical scenes. **3.** his son, **Pie·ter,** called *the Younger.* ?1564–1637, Flemish painter, noted for his gruesome pictures of hell.

Bruges (bruːʒ; *French* bryːʒ) *n.* a city in NW Belgium, capital of West Flanders province: centre of the medieval European wool and cloth trade. Pop.: 118 023 (1971 est.). Flemish name: **Brug+ge** (ˈbryxə).

bru+in (ˈbruːɪn) *n.* a name for a bear, used in children's tales, fables, etc. [C17: from Dutch *bruin* brown, the name of the bear in the epic *Reynard the Fox*]

bruise (bruːz) *vb.* (*mainly tr.*) **1.** (*also intr.*) to injure (tissues) without breaking the skin, usually with discoloration, or (of tissues) to be injured in this way. **2.** to offend or injure (someone's feelings) by an insult, unkindness, etc. **3.** to damage the surface of (something), as by a blow. **4.** to crush (food, etc.) by pounding or pressing. ~*n.* **5.** a bodily injury without a break in the skin, usually with discoloration; contusion. [Old English *brȳsan*, of Celtic origin; compare Irish *brūigim* I bruise]

bruis+er (ˈbruːzə) *n. Informal.* a strong tough person, esp. a boxer or a bully.

bruit (bruːt) *vb.* **1.** *Archaic or U.S.* (*tr.; often passive;* usually foll. by *about*) to report; rumour: *it was bruited about that the king was dead.* ~*n.* **2.** *Med.* an abnormal sound heard within the body during auscultation, esp. a heart murmur. **3.** *Archaic.* **a.** a rumour. **b.** a loud outcry; clamour. [C15: via French from Medieval Latin *brūgītus*, probably from Vulgar Latin *bragere* (unattested) to yell + Latin *rugīre* to roar]

Bru+le *or* **Brû+lé** (bruːˈleɪ) *n.* (*sometimes not cap.*) short for **bois-brûlé.**

Bru+maire *French.* (bryˈmɛːr) *n.* the month of mist: the second month of the French revolutionary calendar, extending from Oct. 23 to Nov. 21. [C19: from *brume* mist, from Latin *brūma* winter; see BRUME]

bru+mal (ˈbruːməl) *adj.* of, characteristic of, or relating to winter; wintry.

brum+by (ˈbrʌmbɪ) *n., pl.* **+bies.** *Austral.* a wild horse, esp. one descended from runaway stock. [C19: of unknown origin]

brume (bruːm) *n. Rare.* heavy mist or fog. [C19: from French: mist, winter, from Latin *brūma*, contracted from *brevissima diēs* the shortest day] —ˈ**bru+mous** *adj.*

Brum+ma+gem (ˈbrʌmədʒəm) *n.* **1.** an informal name for **Birmingham.** Often shortened to **Brum. 2.** (*sometimes not cap.*) something that is cheap and flashy, esp. imitation jewellery. ~*adj.* **3.** (*sometimes not cap.*) cheap and gaudy; tawdry. [C17: from earlier *Bromecham*, local variant of BIRMINGHAM]

Brum·mell (ˈbrʌməl) *n.* **George Bry·an,** called *Beau Brummell.* 1778–1840, English dandy: leader of fashion in the Regency period.

Brum+mie (ˈbrʌmɪ) *n. Informal.* a native or inhabitant of Birmingham. [C20: from BRUMMAGEM]

brunch (brʌntʃ) *n. Chiefly U.S.* a meal eaten late in the morning, combining breakfast with lunch. [C20: from BR(EAKFAST) + (L)UNCH]

Brun+dis+i·um (brʌnˈdɪzɪəm) *n.* the ancient name for **Brindisi.**

Bru+nei (bruːˈnaɪ, ˈbruːnaɪ) *n.* **1.** a sultanate in NW Borneo, consisting of two separate areas on the South China Sea, otherwise bounded by Sarawak: controlled all of Borneo and parts of the Philippines and the Sulu Islands in the 16th century; under British protection since 1888; internally self-governing since 1971. The economy depends chiefly on oil and natural gas. Official language: Malay; English is also widely spoken. Religion: Muslim. Currency: Brunei dollar. Capital: Bandar Seri Begawan. Pop.: 136 256 (1971). Area: 5767 sq. km (2226 sq. miles). **2.** the former name of **Bandar Seri Begawan.**

Bru+nel (bruːˈnɛl) *n.* **1. Is·am·bard King·dom** (ˈɪzəmˌbɑːd). 1806–59, English engineer: designer of the Clifton Suspension Bridge (1828), many railway lines, tunnels, bridges, etc., and the steamships *Great Western* (1838), *Great Britain* (1845), and *Great Eastern* (1858). **2.** his father, Sir **Marc Is·am·bard.** 1769–1849, French engineer in England.

Bru·nel·les·chi (*Italian* ˌbrunelˈleski) *n.* **Fi·lip·po** (fiˈlippo). 1377–1446, Italian architect, whose works in Florence include the dome of the cathedral, the Pazzi chapel of Santa Croce, and the church of San Lorenzo.

bru+nette (bruːˈnɛt) *n.* **1.** a girl or woman with dark brown hair. ~*adj. also* **bru+net. 2.** dark brown: *brunette hair.* [C17: from French, feminine of *brunet* dark, brownish, from *brun* brown, of Germanic origin; see BROWN]

Brun·hild (ˈbrʊnhɪld, -hɪlt) *or* **Brünn·hil·de** (*German* ˌbrynˈhɪldə) *n.* (in the *Nibelungenlied*) a legendary queen won for King Gunther by the magic of Siegfried: corresponds to Brynhild in Norse mythology.

Brün·ing (*German* ˈbryːnɪŋ) *n.* **Hein·rich** (ˈhaɪnrɪç). 1885–1970, German statesman; chancellor (1930–32). He was forced to resign in 1932, making way for the Nazis.

Brünn (bryn) *n.* the German name for **Brno.**

Bru·no (*Italian* ˈbruːno) *n.* **Gior·da·no** (dʒorˈdaːno). 1548–1600, Italian philosopher, who developed a pantheistic monistic philosophy: he was burnt at the stake for heresy.

Bruns+wick (ˈbrʌnzwɪk) *n.* **1.** a former duchy (1635–1918) and state (1918–46) of central Germany: now part of Lower Saxony in West Germany. **2.** a city in E West Germany: formerly capital of the duchy and state of Brunswick. Pop.: 218 939 (1974 est.). German name: **Braunschweig.**

brunt (brʌnt) *n.* **1.** the main force or shock of a blow, attack, etc. (esp. in the phrase **bear the brunt of**). **2.** *Archaic.* a violent blow or attack. [C14: of unknown origin]

Bru+sa (*Turkish* ˈbruːsɑː) *n.* the former name of **Bursa.**

brush[1] (brʌʃ) *n.* **1.** a device made of bristles, hairs, wires, etc., set into a firm back or handle: used to apply paint, clean or polish surfaces, groom the hair, etc. **2.** the act or an instance of brushing. **3.** a light stroke made in passing; graze. **4.** a brief encounter or contact, esp. an unfriendly one; skirmish. **5.** the bushy tail of a fox, often kept as a trophy after a hunt. **6.** an electric conductor, esp. one made of carbon, that conveys current between stationary and rotating parts of a generator, motor, etc. **7.** a dark brush-shaped region observed when a biaxial crystal is viewed through a microscope, caused by interference between beams of polarized light. **8.** *Austral. slang.* **a.** a woman. **b.** Also: **the brush.** women collectively. ~*vb.* **9.** (*tr.*) to clean, polish, scrub, paint, etc., with a brush. **10.** (*tr.*) to apply or remove with a brush or brushing movement: *brush the crumbs off the table.* **11.** (*tr.*) to touch lightly and briefly. **12.** (*intr.*) to move so as to graze or touch something lightly. ~See also **brush aside, brush off, brush up.** [C14: from Old French *broisse*, perhaps from *broce* BRUSH[2]] —ˈ**brush+er** *n.* —ˈ**brush+ˌlike** *or* ˈ**brush·y** *adj.*

brush[2] (brʌʃ) *n.* **1.** a thick growth of shrubs and small trees; scrub. **2.** land covered with scrub. **3.** broken or cut branches or twigs; brushwood. **4.** wooded sparsely populated country; backwoods. [C16 (dense undergrowth), C14 (cuttings of trees): from Old French *broce*, from Vulgar Latin *bruscia* (unattested) brushwood] —ˈ**brush·y** *adj.*

brush a·side *or* **a·way** *vb.* (*tr., adv.*) to dismiss without consideration; disregard.

brush dis+charge *n.* a slightly luminous electrical discharge between points of high charge density when the charge density is insufficient to cause a spark or around sharp points on a highly charged conductor because of ionization of air molecules in their vicinity.

brushed (brʌʃt) *adj. Textiles.* treated with a brushing process to raise the nap and give a softer finish: *brushed nylon.*

brush off *Slang.* ~*vb.* (*tr., adv.*) **1.** to dismiss and ignore (a person), esp. curtly. ~*n.* **brush+off** (ˈbrʌʃɒf). **2.** an abrupt dismissal or rejection.

brush tur+key *n.* any of several gallinaceous birds, esp. *Alectura lathami*, of New Guinea and Australia, having a black plumage: family *Megapodidae* (megapodes).

brush up *vb.* (*adv.*) *Informal.* **1.** (*tr.;* often foll. by *on*) to refresh one's knowledge, skill, or memory of (a subject). **2.** to make (a person or oneself) tidy, clean, or neat as after a journey. ~*n.* **brush-up. 3.** *Brit.* the act or an instance of tidying one's appearance (esp. in the phrase **wash and brush-up**).

brush+wood (ˈbrʌʃˌwʊd) *n.* **1.** cut or broken-off tree branches, twigs, etc. **2.** another word for **brush**[2] (sense 1).

brush+work (ˈbrʌʃˌwɜːk) *n.* **1.** a characteristic manner of applying paint with a brush: *that is not Rembrandt's brushwork.* **2.** work done with a brush.

brusque (bruːsk, brʊsk) *adj.* blunt or curt in manner or speech. [C17: from French, from Italian *brusco* sour, rough, from Medieval Latin *bruscus* butcher's broom] —ˈ**brusque+ly** *adv.* —ˈ**brusque+ness** *n.*

Brus+sels (ˈbrʌsəlz) *n.* the capital of Belgium, in the central part: became capital of Belgium in 1830; seat of the Common Market Commission. Pop.: 1 073 111 (1970). Flemish name: **Brus+sel** (ˈbrysəl). French name: **Bruxelles.**

Brus+sels car+pet *n.* a worsted carpet with a heavy pile formed by uncut loops of wool on a linen warp.

Brus+sels lace *n.* a fine lace with a raised or appliqué design.

Brus+sels sprout *n.* **1.** a variety of cabbage, *Brassica oleracea gemmifera*, having a stout stem studded with budlike heads of tightly folded leaves, resembling tiny cabbages. **2.** the head of this plant, eaten as a vegetable.

brut (bruːt; *French* bryt) *adj.* (of champagne) not sweet; dry. [from French raw, rough, from Latin *brūtus* heavy; see BRUTE]

bru+tal ('bru:tᵊl) *adj.* **1.** cruel; vicious; savage. **2.** extremely honest or coarse in speech or manner. **3.** harsh; severe; extreme: *brutal cold.* —**bru+'tal+i+ty** *n.* —**'bru+tal+ly** *adv.*

bru+tal+ize *or* **bru+tal+ise** ('bru:tə,laɪz) *vb.* **1.** to make or become brutal. **2.** (*tr.*) to treat brutally. —**,bru+tal+i+'za+tion** *or* **,bru+tal+i+'sa+tion** *n.*

brute (bru:t) *n.* **1. a.** any animal except man; beast; lower animal. **b.** (*as modifier*): *brute nature.* **2.** a brutal person. ~*adj.* (*prenominal*) **3.** wholly instinctive or physical (esp. in the phrases **brute strength, brute force**). **4.** without reason or intelligence. **5.** coarse and grossly sensual. [C15: from Latin *brūtus* heavy, irrational; related to *gravis* heavy]

bru+ti+fy ('bru:tɪ,faɪ) *vb.* **+fies, +fy+ing, +fied.** a less common word for **brutalize** (sense 1).

brut+ish ('bru:tɪʃ) *adj.* **1.** of, relating to, or resembling a brute or brutes; animal. **2.** coarse; cruel; stupid. —**'brut+ish+ly** *adv.* —**'brut+ish+ness** *n.*

Bru·tus ('bru:təs) *n.* **1. Lu·ci·us Ju·ni·us** ('lu:ʃəs 'dʒu:nɪəs). late 6th century B.C., Roman statesman who ousted the tyrant Tarquin (509) and helped found the Roman republic. **2. Mar·cus Ju·ni·us** ('mɑ:kəs 'dʒu:nɪəs) ?85–42 B.C., Roman statesman who, with Cassius, led the conspiracy to assassinate Caesar (44): committed suicide after being defeated by Antony and Octavian (Augustus) at Philippi (42).

Brux+elles (bry'sɛl) *n.* the French name for **Brussels.**

Bry+ansk (brɪ'ænsk; *Russian* brjansk) *n.* a city in the W Soviet Union. Pop.: 366 000 (1975 est.).

Bryn·hild ('brɪnhɪld) *n. Norse myth.* a Valkyrie won as the wife of Gunnar by Sigurd who wakes her from an enchanted sleep: corresponds to Brunhild in the *Nibelungenlied.*

bry+ol+o·gy (braɪ'ɒlədʒɪ) *n.* the branch of botany concerned with the study of bryophytes. —**bry·o+log·i+cal** (,braɪə'lɒdʒɪkᵊl) *adj.* —**bry+'ol·o+gist** *n.*

bry·o+ny *or* **bri·o+ny** ('braɪənɪ) *n., pl.* **+nies.** any of several herbaceous climbing plants of the cucurbitaceous genus *Bryonia,* of Europe and N Africa. See also **black bryony, white bryony.** [Old English *bryōnia,* from Latin, from Greek *bruōnia*]

bry·o+phyte ('braɪə,faɪt) *n.* any plant of the division *Bryophyta,* having stems and leaves but lacking true vascular tissue and roots and reproducing by spores: includes the mosses and liverworts. —**bry·o+phyt+ic** (,braɪə'fɪtɪk) *adj.*

bry·o+zo·an (,braɪə'zəʊən) *n.* **1.** any aquatic invertebrate animal of the phylum *Bryozoa,* forming colonies of polyps each having a ciliated feeding organ (lophophore). Popular name: **sea mat.** ~*adj.* **2.** of, relating to, or belonging to the *Bryozoa.* ~Also: **polyzoan, ectoproct.**

Bryth+on ('brɪθən) *n.* a Celt who speaks a Brythonic language. Compare **Goidel.** [C19: from Welsh; see BRITON]

Bry+thon+ic (brɪ'θɒnɪk) *n.* **1.** the S group of Celtic languages, consisting of Welsh, Cornish, and Breton. ~*adj.* **2.** of, relating to, or characteristic of this group of languages. ~Also called: **Brittonic.**

Brześć nad Bu+giem ('bʒɛʃtʃ nad 'bugjɛm) *n.* the Polish name for **Brest** (sense 2).

BS **1.** (indicating the catalogue or publication number of the British Standards Institution) *abbrev. for* British Standard(s). **2.** *international car registration for* Bahamas.

b.s. *abbrev. for:* **1.** balance sheet. **2.** bill of sale.

B.S. *abbrev. for* Bachelor of Surgery.

B/S *or* **b/s** *abbrev. for:* **1.** bags. **2.** bales. **3.** bill of sale.

B.Sc. *abbrev. for* Bachelor of Science.

BSI *abbrev. for* British Standards Institution.

Bs/L *abbrev. for* bills of lading.

B Spe+cial *n.* a member of a part-time largely Protestant police force formerly functioning in Northern Ireland.

B.S.S. *abbrev. for* British Standards Specification.

B.S.Sc. *or* **B.Soc.Sc.** *abbrev. for* Bachelor of Social Science.

B.S.T. *abbrev. for* British Summer Time.

Bt. *abbrev. for* Baronet.

btl. *abbrev. for* bottle.

btry. *Military. abbrev. for* battery.

btu *or* **B.Th.U.** *abbrev. for* British thermal unit. U.S. abbrev.: **BTU**

B.T.U. *abbrev. for* Board of Trade Unit.

bu. *abbrev. for* bushel.

bub (bʌb) *n.* **1.** *U.S. informal.* fellow; youngster: used as a form of address. **2.** *Austral. slang.* **a.** a baby. **b. bubs grade.** the first grade of schooling; nursery school. [C20: perhaps from German *Bube* boy]

bu+bal ('bju:bᵊl) *or* **bu+ba+lis** ('bju:bəlɪs) *n.* any of various antelopes, esp. an extinct N African variety of hartebeest. [C15: from Latin *būbalus* African gazelle, from Greek *boubalos,* from Greek *bous* ox]

bu+ba+line ('bju:bə,laɪn, -lɪn) *adj.* **1.** (of antelopes) related to or resembling the bubal. **2.** resembling or relating to the buffalo.

bub+ble ('bʌbᵊl) *n.* **1.** a thin film of liquid forming a hollow globule around air or a gas: *a soap bubble.* **2.** a small globule of air or a gas in a liquid or a solid, as in carbonated drinks, glass, etc. **3.** the sound made by a bubbling liquid. **4.** something lacking substance, stability, or seriousness. **5.** a dome, esp. a transparent glass or plastic one. ~*vb.* **6.** to form or cause to form bubbles. **7.** (*intr.*) to move or flow with a gurgling sound. **8.** (*intr.; often foll. by over*) to overflow (with excitement, anger, etc.). [C14: probably of Scandinavian origin; compare Swedish *bubbla,* Danish *boble,* Dutch *bobbel,* all of imitative origin]

bub+ble and squeak *n. Brit.* a dish of leftover boiled cabbage, potatoes, and sometimes cooked meat fried together.

bub+ble bath *n.* **1.** a powder, liquid, or crystals used to scent, soften, and foam in bath water. **2.** a bath to which such a substance has been added.

bub+ble car *n. Brit.* a small car, often having three wheels, with a transparent bubble-shaped top.

bub+ble cham+ber *n.* a device that enables the tracks of ionizing particles to be photographed as a row of bubbles in a superheated liquid. Immediately before the particles enter the chamber the pressure is reduced so that the ionized particles act as centres for small vapour bubbles.

bub+ble gum *n.* a type of chewing gum that can be blown into large bubbles.

bub+bler ('bʌblə) *n.* **1.** a drinking fountain in which the water is forced in a stream from a small vertical nozzle. **2.** *Chem.* any device for bubbling gas through a liquid.

bub+bly ('bʌblɪ) *adj.* **+bli+er, +bli+est.** **1.** full of or resembling bubbles. **2.** lively; animated; excited: *a bubbly personality.* ~*n.* **3.** an informal name for **champagne.**

Bu·ber ('bu:bə) *n.* **Mar·tin.** 1878–1965, Jewish theologian, existentialist philosopher, and scholar of Hasidism, born in Austria, whose works include *I and Thou* (1923), *Between Man and Man* (1946), and *Eclipse of God* (1952).

bu·bo ('bju:bəʊ) *n., pl.* **·boes.** *Pathol.* inflammation and swelling of a lymph node, often with the formation of pus, esp. in the region of the armpit or groin. [C14: from Medieval Latin *bubō* swelling, from Greek *boubōn* groin, glandular swelling] —**bu+bon+ic** (bju:'bɒnɪk) *adj.*

bu+bon+ic plague *n.* an acute infectious febrile disease characterized by chills, prostration, delirium, and formation of buboes: caused by the bite of a rat flea infected with the bacterium *Pasteurella pestis.* See also **plague.**

bu+bon·o+cele (bju:'bɒnə,si:l) *n.* an incomplete hernia in the groin; partial inguinal hernia. [C17: from Greek *boubōn* groin + *kēlē* tumour]

Bu+ca+ra+man+ga (*Spanish* bu,kara'maŋga) *n.* a city in N central Colombia, in the Cordillera Oriental: centre of a district growing coffee, tobacco, and cotton. Pop.: 291 661 (1973).

buc+cal ('bʌkᵊl) *adj.* **1.** of or relating to the cheek. **2.** of or relating to the mouth; oral: *buccal lesion.* [C19: from Latin *bucca* cheek]

buc+ca+neer (,bʌkə'nɪə) *n.* **1.** a pirate, esp. one who preyed on the Spanish colonies and shipping in America and the Caribbean in the 17th and 18th centuries. ~*vb.* (*intr.*) **2.** to be or act like a buccaneer. [C17: from French *boucanier,* from *boucaner* to smoke meat, from Old French *boucan* frame for smoking meat, of Tupian origin]

buc+ci+na+tor ('bʌksɪ,neɪtə) *n.* a thin muscle that compresses the cheeks and holds them against the teeth during chewing, etc. [C17: from Latin, from *buccināre* to sound the trumpet, from *buccina* trumpet]

bu+cen+taur (bju:'sɛntɔ:) *n.* the state barge of Venice from which the doge and other officials dropped a ring into the sea on Ascension Day to symbolize the ceremonial marriage of the state with the Adriatic. [C17: from Italian *bucentoro,* of uncertain origin]

Bu+ceph·a+lus (bju:'sɛfələs) *n.* the favourite horse of Alexander the Great. [C17: from Latin, from Greek *Boukephalos,* from *bous* ox + *kephalē* head]

Buch·an ('bʌkən) *n.* **John,** 1st Baron Tweedsmuir. 1875–1940, Scottish statesman, historian, and writer of adventure stories, esp. *The Thirty-Nine Steps* (1915) and *Greenmantle* (1916); governor general of Canada (1935–40).

Bu+chan+an[1] (bju:'kænən) *n.* a port in Liberia with an artificial harbour constructed esp. for loading iron ore. Pop.: 11 909 (1962).

Bu·chan·an[2] (bju:'kænən) *n.* **James.** 1791–1868, 15th president of the U.S. (1857–61).

Bu+cha+rest (,bu:kə'rɛst, ,bju:-) *n.* the capital of Rumania, in the southeast. Pop.: 1 565 872 (1974 est.). Rumanian name: **Bucureşti.**

Buch+en+wald (*German* 'bu:xᵊn,valt) *n.* a village in SW East Germany, near Weimar: site of a Nazi concentration camp (1937–45).

Buch+man+ism ('bʊkmə,nɪzəm) *n.* another name for **Moral Rearmament.** [C20: named after Frank *Buchman* (1878–1961), U.S. evangelist who founded it] —**'Buch+man+ite** *n.*

Buch·ner (*German* 'bu:xnər) *n.* **E·du·ard** ('e:duart). 1860–1917, German chemist who demonstrated that alcoholic fermentation is due to the action of enzymes in the yeast: Nobel prize for chemistry 1907.

Büch·ner (*German* 'by:çnər) *n.* **Ge·org** ('ge:ɔrk). 1813–37, German dramatist regarded as a forerunner of the Expressionists: author of *Danton's Death* (1835) and *Woyzeck* (1837).

Buch·ner fun+nel ('bʌknə) *n.* a laboratory filter funnel used under reduced pressure. It consists of a shallow porcelain cylinder with a flat base perforated with small holes. [named after its inventor, E. BUCHNER]

bu+chu ('bu:ku:) *n.* any of several S. African rutaceous shrubs of the genus *Barosma,* esp. *B. betulina,* whose leaves are used as an antiseptic and diuretic. [C18: from a South African Bantu name]

buck[1] (bʌk) *n.* **1. a.** the male of various animals including the goat, hare, kangaroo, rabbit, and reindeer. **b.** (*as modifier*): *a buck antelope.* **2.** *Informal.* a robust spirited young man. **3.** *U.S. slang, derogatory.* a young male Indian or Negro. **4.** *S. African.* an antelope or deer of either sex. **5.** *Archaic.* a dandy; fop. **6.** the act of bucking. ~*vb.* **7.** (*intr.*) (of a horse or other animal) to jump vertically, with legs stiff and back arched. **8.** (*tr.*) (of a horse, etc.) to throw (its rider) by bucking. **9.** (when *intr., often foll. by against) Informal, chiefly U.S.* to resist or oppose obstinately: *to buck against change; to buck change.* **10.** (*tr.; usually passive*) *Informal.* to cheer or encourage: *I was very bucked at passing the exam.* **11.** *U.S. informal.* (esp. of a car) to move forward jerkily; jolt. **12.** *U.S.* to charge against (something) with the head down; butt. ~See also **buck up.** [Old English *bucca* he-goat; related to Old Norse *bukkr,* Old High German *bock,* Old Irish *bocc*] —**'buck·er** *n.*

buck[2] (bʌk) *n. U.S. and Austral. slang.* a dollar. [C19: of obscure origin]

buck[3] (bʌk) *n.* **1.** *Gymnastics.* a type of vaulting horse. **2.** a U.S. word for **sawhorse.** [C19: short for SAWBUCK]

buck[4] (bʌk) *n.* **1.** *Poker.* a marker in the jackpot to remind the winner of some obligation when his turn comes to deal. **2. pass the buck.** *Informal.* to shift blame or responsibility onto another. [C19: probably from *buckhorn knife,* placed before a player in poker to indicate that he was the next dealer]

Buck (bʌk) *n.* **Pearl S(ydenstricker).** 1892–1973, U.S. novelist, noted particularly for her novel of Chinese life *The Good Earth* (1931): Nobel prize for literature 1938.

buck and wing *n. U.S.* a boisterous tap dance, derived from Negro and Irish clog dances.

buck·a·roo ('bʌkəˌru:, ˌbʌkə'ru:) *n. Southwestern U.S.* a cowboy. [C19: variant of Spanish *vaquero,* from *vaca* cow, from Latin *vacca*]

buck·bean ('bʌkˌbi:n) *n.* a marsh plant, *Menyanthes trifoliata,* with white or pink flowers: family *Menyanthaceae.* Also called: **bogbean.**

buck·board ('bʌkˌbɔ:d) *n. U.S.* an open four-wheeled horse-drawn carriage with the seat attached to a flexible board between the front and rear axles.

buck·een (bʌ'ki:n) *n.* (in Ireland) a poor young man who aspires to the habits and dress of the wealthy. [C18: from BUCK[1] + *-een,* from Irish *-īn,* diminutive suffix]

buck·et ('bʌkɪt) *n.* **1.** an open-topped roughly cylindrical container; pail. **2.** Also called: **bucketful.** the amount a bucket will hold. **3.** any of various bucket-like parts of a machine, such as the scoop on a mechanical shovel. **4.** a cupped blade or bucket-like compartment on the outer circumference of a water wheel, paddle wheel, etc. **5.** *Computer technol.* a unit of storage on a direct-access device from which data can be retrieved. **6. kick the bucket.** *Informal.* to die. ~*vb.* **7.** (*tr.*) to carry in or put into a bucket. **8.** (*intr.;* (often foll. by *along*) *Informal, chiefly Brit.* to travel or drive fast. **9.** (*tr.*) *Chiefly Brit.* to ride (a horse) hard without consideration. [C13: from Anglo-French *buket,* from Old English *būc;* compare Old High German *būh* belly, German *Bauch* belly]

buck·et a·bout *vb.* (*intr.*) *Brit.* (esp. of a boat in a storm) to toss or shake violently.

buck·et down *vb.* (*intr.*) (of rain) to fall very heavily.

buck·et lad·der *n.* **a.** a series of buckets that move in a continuous chain, used to dredge riverbeds, etc., or to excavate land. **b.** (*as modifier*): *a bucket-ladder dredger.*

buck·et out *vb.* (*tr.*) to empty out with or as if with a bucket.

buck·et seat *n.* a seat in a car, aircraft, etc., having curved sides that partially enclose and support the body.

buck·et shop *n. Slang.* **1.** an unregistered firm of stockbrokers that engages in fraudulent speculation with the funds of its clients. **2.** *Chiefly Brit.* any small business that cannot be relied upon to fulfil its obligations.

buck·eye ('bʌkˌaɪ) *n.* any of several North American trees of the genus *Aesculus,* esp. *A. glabra* (Ohio buckeye), having erect clusters of white or red flowers and prickly fruits: family *Hippocastanaceae.* See also **horse chestnut.**

buck fe·ver *n.* nervous excitement felt by inexperienced hunters at the approach of game.

buck·horn ('bʌkˌhɔ:n) *n.* **1.** horn from a buck, used for knife handles, etc. **2.** Also called: **buck's horn plantain.** a small Eurasian plant, *Plantago coronopus,* having narrow leaves resembling a buck's horn: family *Plantaginaceae.*

buck·hound ('bʌkˌhaʊnd) *n.* a hound, smaller than a staghound, used for hunting the smaller breeds of deer, esp. fallow deer.

Buck·ing·ham[1] ('bʌkɪŋəm) *n.* a town in S central England, in Buckinghamshire. Pop.: 5075 (1971).

Buck·ing·ham[2] ('bʌkɪŋəm) *n.* **1. George Vil·li·ers, 1st Duke of.** 1592–1628, English courtier and statesman; favourite of James I and Charles I: his arrogance, military incompetence, and greed increased the tensions between the King and Parliament that eventually led to the Civil War. **2.** his son, **George Vil·li·ers, 2nd Duke of.** 1628–87, English courtier and writer; chief minister of Charles II and member of the Cabal (1667–73).

Buck·ing·ham Pal·ace *n.* the London residence of the British sovereign: built in 1703, rebuilt by John Nash in 1821–36 and partially redesigned in the early 20th century.

Buck·ing·ham·shire ('bʌkɪŋəmˌʃɪə, -ʃə) *n.* a county in SE central England, containing the Vale of Aylesbury and parts of the Chiltern Hills. Administrative centre: Aylesbury. Pop.: 512 000 (1976 est.). Area: 1883 sq. km (727 sq. miles). Abbrev.: **Bucks.**

buck·ish ('bʌkɪʃ) *adj. Archaic.* foppish; being a dandy. —**'buck·ish·ly** *adv.* —**'buck·ish·ness** *n.*

buck·jump·er ('bʌkˌdʒʌmpə) *n. Austral.* an untamed horse.

buck·le ('bʌkᵊl) *n.* **1.** a clasp for fastening together two loose ends, esp. of a belt or strap, usually consisting of a frame with an attached movable prong. **2.** an ornamental representation of a buckle, as on a shoe. **3.** a kink, bulge, or other distortion: *a buckle in a railway track.* ~*vb.* **4.** to fasten or be fastened with a buckle. **5.** to bend or cause to bend out of shape, esp. as a result of pressure or heat. [C14: from Old French *bocle,* from Latin *buccula* a little cheek, hence, cheek strap of a helmet, from *bucca* cheek]

buck·le down *vb.* (*intr., adv.*) *Informal.* to apply oneself with determination: *to buckle down to a job.*

buck·ler ('bʌklə) *n.* **1.** a small round shield worn on the forearm or held by a short handle. **2.** a means of protection; defence. ~*vb.* **3.** (*tr.*) *Archaic.* to defend. [C13: from Old French *bocler,* from *bocle* shield boss; see BUCKLE, BOSS[2]]

buck·ler-fern *n.* any of various ferns of the genus *Dryopteris,* such as *D. dilatata* (broad buckler-fern): family *Polypodiaceae.*

Buck·ley's chance ('bʌklɪz) *n. Austral. slang.* no chance at all. Often shortened to **Buckley's.** [C19: of obscure origin]

buck·ling ('bʌklɪŋ) *n.* another name for a **bloater.** [C20: from German *Bückling*]

buck·o ('bʌkəʊ) *n., pl.* **·oes.** *Irish.* a young fellow: often a term of address.

buck·ra ('bʌkrə) *n.* (used contemptuously by Negroes, esp. in the southeastern U.S.) a white man. [C18: probably from Efik *mba-ka-ra* master]

buck rab·bit *or* **rare·bit** *n. Brit.* Welsh rabbit with either an egg or a piece of toast on top.

buck·ram ('bʌkrəm) *n.* **1. a.** cotton or linen cloth stiffened with size, etc., used in lining or clothes, bookbinding, etc. **b.** (*as modifier*): *a buckram cover.* **2.** *Archaic.* stiffness of manner. ~*vb.* **·rams, ·ram·ing, ·ramed. 3.** (*tr.*) to stiffen with buckram. [C14: from Old French *boquerant,* from Old Provençal *bocaran,* ultimately from BUKHARA, once an important source of textiles]

Bucks. (bʌks) *abbrev. for* Buckinghamshire.

buck·saw ('bʌkˌsɔ:) *n.* a woodcutting saw having its blade set in a frame and tensioned by a turnbuckle across the back of the frame.

buck·shee (ˌbʌk'ʃi:) *adj. Brit. slang.* without charge; free. [C20: from BAKSHEESH]

buck·shot ('bʌkˌʃɒt) *n.* lead shot of large size used in shotgun shells, esp. for hunting game. [C15 (original sense: the distance at which a buck can be shot)]

buck·skin ('bʌkˌskɪn) *n.* **1.** the skin of a male deer. **2. a.** a strong greyish-yellow suede leather, originally made from deerskin but now usually made from sheepskin. **b.** (*as modifier*): *buckskin boots.* **3.** *U.S.* (*sometimes cap.*) a person wearing buckskin clothes, esp. an American soldier of the Civil War. **4.** a stiffly starched cotton cloth. **5.** a strong and heavy satin-woven woollen fabric. ~*adj.* **6.** greyish-yellow.

buck·skins ('bʌkˌskɪnz) *pl. n.* (in the U.S.) breeches, shoes, or a suit of buckskin.

buck's turn *n.* the Australian name for a **stag party.**

buck·thorn ('bʌkˌθɔ:n) *n.* **1.** any of several thorny small-flowered shrubs of the genus *Rhamnus,* esp. the Eurasian species *R. cathartica,* whose berries were formerly used as a purgative: family *Rhamnaceae.* **2. sea buckthorn.** a thorny Eurasian shrub, *Hippophaë rhamnoides,* growing on sea coasts and having silvery leaves and orange fruits: family *Elaeagnaceae.* [C16: from BUCK[1] (from the spiny branches, imagined as resembling antlers) + THORN]

buck·tooth ('bʌkˌtu:θ) *n., pl.* **·teeth.** *Derogatory.* a projecting upper front tooth. [C18: from BUCK[1] (deer) + TOOTH]

buck up *vb.* (*adv.*) *Informal.* **1.** to make or cause to make haste. **2.** to make or become more cheerful, confident, etc.

buck·wheat ('bʌkˌwi:t) *n.* **1.** any of several polygonaceous plants of the genus *Fagopyrum,* esp. *F. esculentum,* which has fragrant white flowers and is cultivated, esp. in the U.S., for its seeds. **2.** the edible seeds of this plant, ground into flour or used as animal fodder. **3.** the flour obtained from these seeds. [C16: from Middle Dutch *boecweite,* from *boeke* BEECH + *weite* WHEAT, from the resemblance of their seeds to beech nuts]

bu·col·ic (bju:'kɒlɪk) *adj.* also **bu·col·i·cal. 1.** of or characteristic of the countryside or country life; rustic. **2.** of or relating to shepherds; pastoral. ~*n.* **3.** (*sometimes pl.*) a pastoral poem, often in the form of a dialogue. **4.** a rustic; farmer or shepherd. [C16: from Latin *būcolicus,* from Greek *boukolikos,* from *boukolos* cowherd, from *bous* ox] —**bu·'col·i·cal·ly** *adv.*

Bu·co·vi·na (ˌbu:kə'vi:nə) *n.* a variant spelling of **Bukovina.**

Bu·cu·reşti (buku'reʃtj) *n.* the Rumanian name for **Bucharest.**

bud[1] (bʌd) *n.* **1.** a swelling on a plant stem consisting of overlapping immature leaves or petals. **2. a.** a partially opened flower. **b.** (*in combination*): *rosebud.* **3.** any small budlike outgrowth: *taste buds.* **4.** something small or immature. **5.** an asexually produced outgrowth in simple organisms such as yeasts and the hydra that develops into a new individual. **6. in bud.** at the stage of producing buds. **7. nip in the bud.** to put an end to (an idea, movement, etc.) in its initial stages. ~*vb.* **buds, bud·ding, bud·ded. 8.** (*intr.*) (of plants and some animals) to produce buds. **9.** (*intr.*) to begin to develop or grow: *the project is budding.* **10.** (*tr.*) *Horticulture.* to graft (a bud) from one plant onto another, usually by insertion under the bark. [C14 *budde,* of Germanic origin; compare Icelandic *budda* purse, Dutch *buidel*]

bud[2] (bʌd) *n. Informal, chiefly U.S.* short for **buddy:** used as a term of address.

Bu·da·pest (ˌbju:də'pɛst; *Hungarian* 'budɔpɛʃt) *n.* the capital of Hungary, in the central part, on the River Danube: formed in 1873 from the towns of Buda and Pest. Traditionally Buda, the old Magyar capital, was the administrative and Pest the trade centre: suffered severely in the Russian siege of 1945 and in the unsuccessful revolt against the Communist regime (1956). Pop.: 2 051 354 (1974 est.).

bud·dha ('bʊdə) *n.* **1.** *Buddhism.* (*often cap.*) a person who has achieved a state of perfect enlightenment. **2.** an image or picture of the Buddha. [C17: from Sanskrit: awakened, from *bōdhati* he awakes]

Bud·dha ('budə) *n.* **the.** ?563–483 B.C., a title applied to Gautama Siddhartha, a nobleman and religious teacher of N India, regarded by his followers as the most recent rediscoverer of the path to enlightenment: the founder of Buddhism.

Buddh Ga·ya ('bud gə'jɑː), **Bud·dha Ga·ya,** *or* **Bodh Ga·ya** *n.* a village in NE India, in central Bihar: site of the sacred bo tree under which Gautama Siddhartha attained enlightenment and became the Buddha; pilgrimage centre. Pop.: 6299 (1961).

Bud·dhism ('budɪzəm) *n.* a religious teaching propagated by the Buddha and his followers, which declares that by destroying greed, hatred, and delusion, which are the causes of all suffering, man can attain perfect enlightenment. See **nirvana.** —'**Bud·dhist** *n., adj.*

bud·dle ('bʌdᵊl) *n.* **1.** a sloping trough in which ore is washed. ~*vb.* **2.** (*tr.*) to wash (ore) in a buddle. [C16: of unknown origin]

bud·dle·ia ('bʌdlɪə) *n.* any ornamental shrub of the genus *Buddleia,* esp. *B. davidii,* which has long spikes of mauve flowers and is frequently visited by butterflies: family *Buddleiaceae.* Also called: **butterfly bush.** [C19: named after A. *Buddle* (died 1715), British botanist]

bud·dy ('bʌdɪ) *n., pl.* **·dies.** *Chiefly U.S.* an informal word for **friend.** Also (as a term of address): **bud.** [C19: probably a baby-talk variant (U.S.) of BROTHER]

budge[1] (bʌdʒ) *vb.* (*usually used with a negative*) **1.** to move, however slightly: *the car won't budge.* **2.** to change or cause to change opinions, etc. [C16: from Old French *bouger,* from Vulgar Latin *bullicāre* (unattested) to bubble, from Latin *bullīre* to boil, from *bulla* bubble]

budge[2] (bʌdʒ) *n.* a lambskin dressed for the fur to be worn on the outer side. [C14: from Anglo-French *bogee,* of obscure origin]

Budge (bʌdʒ) *n.* **Don(ald).** born 1915, U.S. tennis player, the first man to win the singles championships of Australia, France, and the U.S. in one year (1938).

budg·er·i·gar ('bʌdʒərɪˌgɑː) *n.* a small green Australian parrot, *Melopsittacus undulatus:* a popular cage bird that is bred in many different coloured varieties. Often shortened (informal) to **budgie.** [C19: from a native Australian language, from *budgeri* good + *gar* cockatoo]

budg·et ('bʌdʒɪt) *n.* **1.** a summary of probable financial outlays and incomes over a specified period. **2.** the total amount of money allocated for a specific purpose during a specified period. **3.** a stock, quantity, or supply. ~*vb.* **4.** (*tr.*) to enter or provide for in a budget. **5.** to plan the expenditure of (money, time, etc.). **6.** (*intr.*) to make a budget. [C15 (meaning: leather pouch, wallet): from Old French *bougette,* diminutive of *bouge,* from Latin *bulga,* of Gaulish origin; compare Old English *bælg* bag]

Budg·et ('bʌdʒɪt) *n.* **the.** an estimate of British government expenditures and revenues for the ensuing fiscal year presented annually to the House of Commons by the Chancellor of the Exchequer.

bud·get ac·count *n.* **1.** an account with a department store, etc., enabling a customer to make monthly payments to cover his past and future purchases. **2.** a bank account for paying household bills, being credited with regular or equal monthly payments from the customer's current account.

budg·ie ('bʌdʒɪ) *n. Informal.* short for **budgerigar.**

bud scale *n.* one of the hard protective sometimes hairy or resinous specialized leaves surrounding the buds of certain plants, such as the rhododendron.

Bud·weis ('butvaɪs) *n.* the German name for **České Budějovice.**

Bue·na·ven·tu·ra (*Spanish* ˌbwenaβen'tura) *n.* a major port in W Colombia, on the Pacific coast. Pop.: 115 770 (1973).

Bue·na Vis·ta (*Spanish* 'bwena 'vista) *n.* a village in NE Mexico, near Saltillo: site of the defeat of the Mexicans by U.S. forces (1847).

Bue·no (*Portuguese* 'bwenu) *n.* **Ma·ri·a.** (ma'ria). born 1939, Brazilian tennis player.

Bue·nos Ai·res ('bweɪnɒs 'aɪrɪz; *Spanish* 'bwenos 'aires) *n.* the capital of Argentina, a major port and industrial city on the Río de la Plata estuary: became capital in 1880; university (1821). Pop.: 2 976 000 (1974 est.).

B.U.F. *abbrev. for* British Union of Fascists.

buff[1] (bʌf) *n.* **1. a.** a soft thick flexible undyed leather made chiefly from the skins of buffalo, oxen, and elk. **b.** (*as modifier*): *a buff coat.* **2. a.** a dull yellow or yellowish-brown colour. **b.** (*as adj.*): *buff paint.* **3.** Also called: **buffer. a.** a cloth or pad of material used for polishing an object. **b.** a flexible disc or wheel impregnated with a fine abrasive for polishing metals, etc., with a power tool. **4.** *Informal.* one's bare skin (esp. in the phrase **in the buff**). ~*vb.* **5.** to clean or polish (a metal, floor, shoes, etc.) with a buff. **6.** to remove the grain surface of (a leather). [C16: from Old French *buffle,* from Old Italian *bufalo,* from Late Latin *būfalus* BUFFALO]

buff[2] (bʌf) *vb.* **1.** (*tr.*) to deaden the force of. ~*n.* **2.** *Archaic.* a blow or buffet (now only in the phrase **blind man's buff**). [C15: back formation from BUFFET[2]]

buff[3] (bʌf) *n. U.S. informal.* an expert on or devotee of a given subject: *a cheese buff.* [C20: originally: an enthusiastic fire-watcher, from the buff-coloured uniforms worn by volunteer firemen in New York City]

buf·fa·lo ('bʌfəˌləʊ) *n., pl.* **·loes, ·los,** *or* **·lo. 1.** Also called: **Cape buffalo.** a member of the cattle tribe, *Synercus caffer,* mostly found in game reserves in southern and eastern Africa and having upward-curving horns. **2.** short for **water buffalo. 3.** a U.S. name for **bison** (sense 1). ~*vb.* (*tr.*) *U.S. informal.* **4.** (*often passive*) to confuse. **5.** to intimidate or overawe. [C16: from Italian *bufalo,* from Late Latin *būfalus,* alteration of Latin *būbalus;* see BUBAL]

Buf·fa·lo ('bʌfəˌləʊ) *n.* a port in W New York State, at the E end of Lake Erie. Pop.: 425 101 (1973 est.).

Buf·fa·lo Bill *n.* nickname of *William Frederick Cody.* 1846–1917, U.S. showman who toured Europe and the U.S. with his famous *Wild West Show.*

buf·fa·lo fish *n.* any of several freshwater North American hump-backed cyprinoid fishes of the genus *Ictiobus:* family *Catostomidae* (suckers).

buf·fa·lo gnat *n.* any of various small North American blood-sucking dipterous insects of the genus *Simulium* and related genera: family *Simuliidae.* Also called: **black fly.**

buf·fa·lo grass *n.* **1.** a short grass, *Buchloë dactyloides,* growing on the dry plains of the central U.S. **2.** *Austral.* a grass, *Stenotaphrum americanum,* introduced from North America.

buff·er[1] ('bʌfə) *n.* **1.** one of a pair of spring-loaded steel pads attached at both ends of railway vehicles and at the end of a railway track to reduce shock due to contact. **2.** a person or thing that lessens shock or protects from damaging impact, circumstances, etc. **3.** *Chem.* **a.** an ionic compound, usually a salt of a weak acid or base, added to a solution to resist changes in its acidity or alkalinity and thus stabilize its pH. **b.** Also called: **buffer solution.** a solution containing such a compound. **4.** *Computer technol.* a memory device for temporarily storing data. **5.** *Electronics.* an isolating circuit used to minimize the reaction between a driving and a driven circuit. **6.** short for **buffer state.** ~*vb.* **7.** (*tr.*) *Chem.* to add a buffer to (a solution). [C19: from BUFF[2]]

buff·er[2] ('bʌfə) *n.* **1.** any device used to shine, polish, etc.; buff. **2.** a person who uses such a device.

buff·er[3] ('bʌfə) *n. Brit. informal.* a stupid or bumbling man (esp. in the phrase **old buffer**). [C18: perhaps from Middle English *buffer* stammerer]

buff·er state *n.* a small and usually neutral state between two rival powers.

buf·fet[1] *n.* **1.** ('bufeɪ). a counter where light refreshments are served. **2.** ('bufeɪ). **a.** a meal at which guests help themselves from a number of dishes and often eat standing up. **b.** (*as modifier*): *a buffet lunch.* **3.** ('bʌfɪt, 'bufeɪ). a sideboard, esp. of the 16th or 17th century. **4.** ('bʌfɪ). *Northern Brit. dialect.* a kind of low stool, pouffe, or hassock. [C18: from French, of unknown origin]

buf·fet[2] ('bʌfɪt) *vb.* **·fets, ·fet·ing, ·fet·ed. 1.** (*tr.*) to knock against or about; batter: *the wind buffeted the boat.* **2.** (*tr.*) to hit, esp. with the fist; cuff. **3.** to force (one's way), as through a crowd. **4.** (*intr.*) to struggle; battle. ~*n.* **5.** a blow, esp. with a fist or hand. [C13: from Old French *buffeter,* from *buffet* a light blow, from *buffe,* of imitative origin] —'**buf·fet·er** *n.*

Buf·fet (*French* by'fɛ) *n.* **Ber·nard** (bɛr'naːr). born 1928, French painter and engraver. His works are characterized by sombre tones and thin angular forms.

buf·fet car *n. Brit.* a railway coach where light refreshments are served.

buff·ing wheel *n.* a wheel covered with a soft material, such as lamb's wool or leather, used for shining and polishing. Also called: **buff wheel.**

buf·fle·head ('bʌfᵊlˌhɛd) *n.* a small North American diving duck, *Bucephala* (or *Glaucionetta*) *albeola:* the male has black-and-white plumage and a fluffy head. Also called: **butterball.** [C17 *buffle* from obsolete *buffle* wild ox (see BUFF[1]), referring to the duck's head]

buf·fo ('bufəʊ; *Italian* 'buffo) *n.* **1.** (in Italian opera of the 18th century) a comic part, esp. one for a bass. **2.** Also called: **buffo bass, bas·so buf·fo** (*Italian* 'basso 'buffo). a bass singer who performs such a part. [C18: from Italian (adj.): comic, from *buffo* (n.) BUFFOON]

Buf·fon (*French* by'fõ) *n.* **Georges Louis Le·clerc** (ʒɔrʒ lwi lə'klɛːr), **Comte de.** 1707–88, French encyclopedist of natural history; principal author of *Histoire Naturelle* (36 vols., 1749–89), containing the *Époques de la Nature* (1777), which foreshadowed later theories of evolution.

buf·foon (bə'fuːn) *n.* **1.** a person who amuses others by ridiculous or odd behaviour, jokes, etc. **2.** a foolish person. [C16: from French *bouffon,* from Italian *buffone,* from Medieval Latin *būfō,* from Latin: toad]

bug[1] (bʌg) *n.* **1.** any insect of the order *Hemiptera,* esp. any of the suborder *Heteroptera,* having piercing and sucking mouth-parts specialized as a beak (rostrum). See also **assassin bug, bedbug, chinch bug. 2.** *Chiefly U.S.* any insect, such as the June bug or the Croton bug. **3.** *Informal.* **a.** a microorganism, esp. a bacterium, that produces disease. **b.** a disease, esp. a stomach infection, caused by a microorganism. **4.** *Informal.* an obsessive idea, hobby, etc.; craze. **5.** (*often pl.*) *Informal.* an error or fault, as in a machine or system. **6.** *Informal.* a concealed microphone used for recording conversations, as in spying. **7.** *U.S.* (in poker) a joker used as an ace or wild card to complete a straight or flush. ~*vb.* **bugs, bug·ging, bugged.** *Informal.* **8.** (*tr.*) to irritate; bother. **9.** (*tr.*) to conceal a microphone in (a room, etc.). **10.** (*intr.*) *U.S.* (of eyes) to protrude. [C16: of uncertain origin; perhaps related to Old English *budda* beetle]

bug[2] (bʌg) *n. Obsolete.* an evil spirit or spectre; hobgoblin. [C14 *bugge,* perhaps from Middle Welsh *bwg* ghost. See also BUGBEAR, BUGABOO]

Bug (*Russian* buk) *n.* **1.** Also called: **Southern Bug.** a river in the SW Soviet Union, rising in the W Ukraine and flowing southeast to the Dnieper estuary and the Black Sea. Length: 853 km (530 miles). **2.** Also called: **Western Bug.** a river in E central Europe, rising in the Soviet Union in the SW Ukraine and flowing northwest to the River Vistula in Poland, forming part of the border between Poland and the Soviet Union. Length: 724 km (450 miles).

bug·a·boo ('bʌgə,bu:) *n., pl.* **·boos.** an imaginary source of fear; bugbear; bogey. [C18: probably of Celtic origin; compare Cornish *buccaboo* the devil]

Bu·gan·da (bu'gændə) *n.* a federated state of Uganda: a powerful Bantu kingdom from the 17th century. Capital: Kampala. Pop.: 2 667 332 (1969). Area: about 66 304 sq. km (25 600 sq. miles).

bug·bane ('bʌg,beɪn) *n.* any of several ranunculaceous plants of the genus *Cimicifuga,* esp. *C. foetida* of Europe, whose flowers are reputed to repel insects.

bug·bear ('bʌg,bɛə) *n.* **1.** a thing that causes obsessive fear or anxiety. **2.** (in English folklore) a goblin said to eat naughty children and thought to be in the form of a bear. [C16: from BUG[2] + BEAR[2]; compare BUGABOO]

bug·ger ('bʌgə) *n.* **1.** a person who practises buggery. **2.** *Taboo slang.* a person or thing considered to be contemptible, unpleasant, or difficult. **3.** *Slang.* a humorous or affectionate term for a man or child: *a silly old bugger; a friendly little bugger.* **4. bugger all.** *Slang.* nothing. ~*vb.* **5.** to practise buggery (with). **6.** (*tr.*) *Slang, chiefly Brit.* to ruin, complicate, or frustrate. **7.** *Slang.* to tire; weary: *he was absolutely buggered.* ~*interj.* **8.** *Taboo slang.* an exclamation of annoyance or disappointment. [C16: from Old French *bougre,* from Medieval Latin *Bulgarus* Bulgarian; from the condemnation of the Eastern Orthodox Bulgarians as heretics]

bug·ger a·bout *or* **a·round** *vb.* (*adv.*) *Brit. slang.* **1.** (*intr.*) to fool about and waste time. **2.** (*tr.*) to create difficulties or complications for (a person).

bug·ger off *vb. Brit. taboo slang.* (*intr., adv.*) to go away; depart.

bug·ger·y ('bʌgərɪ) *n.* anal intercourse between a man and another man, a woman, or an animal. Compare **sodomy.**

bug·gy[1] ('bʌgɪ) *n., pl.* **·gies. 1.** a light horse-drawn carriage having either four wheels (esp. in the U.S.) or two wheels (esp. in Britain and India). **2.** short for **beach buggy. 3.** short for **baby buggy.** [C18: of unknown origin]

bug·gy[2] ('bʌgɪ) *adj.* **·gi·er, ·gi·est. 1.** infested with bugs. **2.** *U.S. slang.* insane. —**'bug·gi·ness** *n.*

bug·house ('bʌg,haʊs) *Offensive slang, chiefly U.S.* ~*n.* **1.** a mental hospital or asylum. ~*adj.* **2.** insane; crazy. [C20: from BUG[1] + (MAD)HOUSE]

bu·gle[1] ('bju:gᵊl) *n.* **1.** *Music.* a brass instrument similar to the cornet but usually without valves: used for military fanfares, signal calls, etc. ~*vb.* **2.** (*intr.*) to play or sound (on) a bugle. [C14: short for *bugle horn* ox horn (musical instrument), from Old French *bugle,* from Latin *būculus* young bullock, from *bōs* ox] —**'bu·gler** *n.*

bu·gle[2] ('bju:gᵊl) *n.* any of several Eurasian plants of the genus *Ajuga,* esp. *A. reptans,* having small blue or white flowers: family *Labiatae* (labiates). Also called: **bugleweed.** See also **ground pine.** [C13: from Late Latin *bugula,* of uncertain origin]

bu·gle[3] ('bju:gᵊl) *n.* a tubular glass or plastic bead sewn onto clothes for decoration. [C16: of unknown origin]

bu·gle·weed ('bju:gᵊl,wi:d) *n.* **1.** Also called: **water horehound.** *U.S.* any aromatic plant of the genus *Lycopus,* having small whitish or pale blue flowers: family *Labiatae* (labiates). See also **gipsywort. 2.** another name for **bugle**[2].

bu·gloss ('bju:glɒs) *n.* any of various hairy Eurasian boraginaceous plants of the genera *Anchusa, Lycopsis,* and *Echium,* esp. *L. arvensis,* having clusters of blue flowers. See also **viper's bugloss.** [C15: from Latin *būglōssa,* from Greek *bouglōssos* ox-tongued, from *bōs* ox + *glōssa* tongue]

bu·gong ('bu:gɒŋ) *n.* another name for **bogong.**

buhl (bu:l) *adj., n.* the usual U.S. spelling of **boulle.**

buhr·stone, bur·stone, *or* **burr·stone** ('bɜ:,stəʊn) *n.* **1.** a hard tough rock containing silica, fossils, and cavities, formerly used as a grindstone. **2.** a grindstone or millstone made of this rock. [C18 *burr,* perhaps identical to BURR[1] (alluding to roughness)]

bu·i·bu·i ('bʊɪ'bʊɪ) *n.* a piece of black cloth worn as a shawl by Muslim women, esp. on the E African coast. [from Swahili]

build (bɪld) *vb.* **builds, build·ing, built. 1.** to make, construct, or form by joining parts or materials: *to build a house.* **2.** (*intr.*) to be a builder by profession. **3.** (*tr.*) to order the building of: *the government builds most of our hospitals.* **4.** (foll. by *on* or *upon*) to base; found: *his theory was not built on facts.* **5.** (*tr.*) to establish and develop: *it took ten years to build a business.* **6.** (*tr.*) to make in a particular way or for a particular purpose: *the car was not built for speed.* **7.** (*intr.;* often foll. by *up*) to increase in intensity: *the wind was building.* **8.** *Card games.* **a.** to add cards to each other to form (a sequence or set). **b.** (*intr.*) to add to the layout of cards on the table from one's hand. ~*n.* **9.** physical form, figure, or proportions: *a man with an athletic build.* ~See also **build in, build into, build up.** [Old English *byldan;* related to *bylda* farmer, *bold* building, Old Norse *bōl* farm, dwelling; see BOWER[1]]

build·er ('bɪldə) *n.* **1.** a person who builds, esp. one who contracts for and supervises the construction or repair of buildings. **2.** a substance added to a soap or detergent as a filler or abrasive.

build in *vb.* (*tr., adv.*) to incorporate or construct as an integral part: *to build in safety features.*

build·ing ('bɪldɪŋ) *n.* **1.** something built with a roof and walls, such as a house or factory. **2.** the act, business, occupation, or art of building houses, boats, etc.

build·ing and loan as·so·ci·a·tion *n.* a U.S. name for **building society.**

build·ing line *n.* the boundary line along a street beyond which buildings must not project.

build·ing so·ci·e·ty *n.* a cooperative banking enterprise financed by deposits on which interest is paid and from which mortgage loans are advanced on homes and real estate. U.S. equivalents: **savings and loan association, building and loan association, cooperative bank.**

build in·to *vb.* (*tr., prep.*) to make (something) a definite part of (a contract, agreement, etc.).

build up *vb.* (*adv.*) **1.** (*tr.*) to construct gradually, systematically, and in stages. **2.** to increase or strengthen, esp. by degrees: *the murmur built up to a roar.* **3.** (*tr.*) to improve the health or physique of (a person). **4.** (*tr., usually passive*) to cover (an area) with buildings. **5.** (*tr.*) to cause (a person, enterprise, etc.) to become better known; publicize: *they built several actresses up into stars.* ~*n.* **build-up. 6.** progressive increase in number, size, etc.: *the build-up of industry.* **7.** extravagant publicity or praise, esp. in the form of a campaign. **8.** *Military.* the process of attaining the required strength of forces and equipment, esp. prior to an operation.

built (bɪlt) *vb.* the past tense or past participle of **build.**

built-in *adj.* **1.** made or incorporated as an integral part: *a built-in cupboard; a built-in escape clause.* **2.** essential; inherent. ~*n.* **3.** *Austral.* a built-in cupboard.

built-up *adj.* **1.** having many buildings (esp. in the phrase **built-up area**). **2.** increased by the addition of parts: *built-up heels.*

Bui·ten·zorg (*Dutch* 'bœjtən,zɔrx) *n.* the former name of **Bogor.**

Bu·jum·bu·ra (,bu:dʒəm'bʊərə) *n.* the capital of Burundi, a port at the NE end of Lake Tanganyika. Pop.: 78 810 (1970 est.). Former name: **Usumbura.**

Bu·ka·vu (bu:'kɑ:vu:) *n.* a port in E Zaïre, on Lake Kivu: commercial and industrial centre. Pop.: 181 774 (1974 est.). Former name (until 1966): **Costermansville.**

Bu·kha·ra *or* **Bo·kha·ra** (bʊ'xɑ:rə) *n.* **1.** a city in the SW Soviet Union, in W Uzbekistan: capital of the former emirate of Bukhara. Pop.: 139 000 (1975 est.). **2.** a former emirate of central Asia: a powerful kingdom and centre of Islam; became a territory of the Soviet Union (1920) and was divided between the Uzbek, Tadzhik, and Turkmen SSRs.

Bu·kha·ra rug *or* **Bo·kha·ra rug** *n.* a kind of rug, typically having a black-and-white geometrical pattern on a reddish ground.

Bu·kha·rin (*Russian* bu'xarin) *n.* **Ni·ko·lai I·va·no·vich** (nika'laj i'vanəvitʃ). 1888–1938, Soviet Bolshevik leader: executed in one of Stalin's purges.

Bu·ko·vi·na *or* **Bu·co·vi·na** (,bu:kə'vi:nə) *n.* a region of E central Europe, part of the NE Carpathians: the north was seized by the Soviet Union (1940) and later became part of the Ukrainian SSR; the south remained Rumanian.

Bul (bu:l) *n.* the eighth month of the Old Hebrew calendar, corresponding to Heshvan of the Babylonian or post-exilic Jewish calendar: a period from mid-October to mid-November. [from Hebrew *būl,* of Canaanite origin]

bul. *abbrev. for* bulletin.

Bu·la·wa·yo (,bʊlə'weɪəʊ) *n.* a city in SW Rhodesia founded (1893) on the site of the kraal of Lobengula, the last Matabele king; the country's main industrial centre. Pop.: 307 000 (1973 est.).

bulb (bʌlb) *n.* **1.** a rounded organ of vegetative reproduction in plants such as the tulip and onion: a flattened stem bearing a central shoot surrounded by fleshy nutritive inner leaves and thin brown outer leaves. Compare **corm. 2.** a plant, such as a hyacinth or daffodil, that grows from a bulb. **3.** See **light bulb. 4.** a rounded part of an instrument such as a syringe or thermometer. **5.** *Anatomy.* a rounded expansion of a cylindrical organ or part, such as the medulla oblongata. **6.** Also called: **bulbous bow.** a bulbous protuberance at the forefoot of a ship to reduce turbulence. [C16: from Latin *bulbus,* from Greek *bolbos* onion]

bulb·ar ('bʌlbə) *adj. Chiefly anatomy.* of or relating to a bulb, esp. the medulla oblongata.

bulb·if·er·ous (bʌl'bɪfərəs) *adj.* (of plants) producing bulbs.

bul·bil ('bʌlbɪl) *or* **bul·bel** *n.* **1.** a small bulblike organ of vegetative reproduction growing in leaf axils or on flower stalks of plants such as the onion and tiger lily. **2.** any small bulb of a plant. [C19: from New Latin *bulbillus,* from Latin *bulbus* BULB]

bulb·ous ('bʌlbəs) *or* **bul·ba·ceous** (bʌl'beɪʃəs) *adj.* **1.** shaped like a bulb; swollen; bulging. **2.** growing from or bearing bulbs. —**'bulb·ous·ly** *or* **bul·'ba·ceous·ly** *adv.*

bul·bul ('bʊlbʊl) *n.* **1.** any songbird of the family *Pycnonotidae* of tropical Africa and Asia, having brown plumage and, in many species, a distinct crest. **2.** a songbird, taken to be the nightingale, often mentioned in Persian poetry. [C18: via Persian from Arabic]

Bulg. *abbrev. for* Bulgaria(n).

Bul·ga·nin (*Russian* bul'ganin) *n.* **Ni·ko·lai A·le·ksan·dro·vich** (nika'laj alɪ'ksandrəvitʃ). 1895–1975, Soviet statesman and military leader; chairman of the council of ministers (1955–58).

Bul·gar ('bʌlgɑ:, 'bʊl-) *n.* **1.** a member of a group of non-Indo-European peoples that settled in SE Europe in the late seventh century A.D. and adopted the language and culture of their Slavonic subjects. **2.** a rare name for a **Bulgarian.**

Bul·gar·i·a (bʌlˈgɛərɪə, bʊl-) *n.* a republic in SE Europe, on the Balkan Peninsula on the Black Sea: under Turkish rule from 1395 until 1878; became an independent kingdom in 1908 and a republic in 1946; consists chiefly of the Danube valley in the north, the Balkan Mountains in the central part, separated from the Rhodope Mountains of the south by the valley of the Maritsa River. Language: Bulgarian. Currency: lev. Capital: Sofia. Pop.: 8 678 000 (1974 est.). Area: 110 911 sq. km (42 823 sq. miles).

Bul·gar·i·an (bʌlˈgɛərɪən, bʊl-) *adj.* **1.** of, relating to, or characteristic of Bulgaria, its people, or their language. ~*n.* **2.** the official language of Bulgaria, belonging to the S Slavonic branch of the Indo-European family. **3.** a native, inhabitant, or citizen of Bulgaria.

bulge (bʌldʒ) *n.* **1.** a swelling or an outward curve. **2.** a sudden increase in number or volume, esp. of population. **3.** *Brit.* the projecting part of an army's front line; salient. ~*vb.* **4.** to swell outwards. [C13: from Old French *bouge,* from Latin *bulga* bag, probably of Gaulish origin] —**ˈbulg·ing·ly** *adv.* —**ˈbulg·y** *adj.* —**ˈbulg·i·ness** *n.*

Bulge (bʌldʒ) *n.* **Battle of the.** (in World War II) the final major German counteroffensive in 1944 when the Allied forces were pushed back into NE Belgium: the Germans were repulsed by Jan. 1945.

bu·lim·i·a (bjuːˈlɪmɪə) *n.* pathologically insatiable hunger, esp. when caused by a brain lesion. [C17: from New Latin, from Greek *boulimia,* from *bous* ox + *limos* hunger]

bulk (bʌlk) *n.* **1.** volume, size, or magnitude, esp. when great. **2.** the main part: *the bulk of the work is repetitious.* **3.** a large body, esp. of a person: *he eased his bulk out of the chair.* **4.** unpackaged cargo or goods. **5.** a ship's cargo or hold. **6.** *Printing.* **a.** the thickness of a number of sheets of paper or cardboard. **b.** the thickness of a book excluding its covers. **7. in bulk. a.** in large quantities. **b.** (of a cargo, etc.) unpackaged. ~*vb.* **8.** to cohere or cause to cohere in a mass. **9.** to place, hold, or transport (several cargoes of goods) in bulk. **10. bulk large.** to be or seem important or prominent: *the problem bulked large in his mind.* [C15: from Old Norse *bulki* cargo]

bulk·head (ˈbʌlkˌhɛd) *n.* *Nautical.* any upright wall-like partition in a vessel.

bulk mod·u·lus *n.* a coefficient of elasticity of a substance equal to the ratio of the applied stress (p) to the resulting fractional change in volume (dV/V) in a specified reference state (dV/V is the **bulk strain**). Symbol: K

bulk up *vb.* (*adv.*) to increase or cause to increase in size or importance.

bulk·y (ˈbʌlkɪ) *adj.* **bulk·i·er, bulk·i·est.** very large and massive, esp. so as to be unwieldy. —**ˈbulk·i·ly** *adv.* —**ˈbulk·i·ness** *n.*

bull[1] (bʊl) *n.* **1.** any male bovine animal, esp. one that is sexually mature. Related adj.: **taurine. 2.** the uncastrated adult male of any breed of domestic cattle. **3.** the male of various other animals including the elephant and whale. **4.** a very large, strong, or aggressive person. **5.** *Stock Exchange.* **a.** a speculator who buys in anticipation of rising prices in order to make a profit on resale. **b.** (*as modifier*): *a bull market.* Compare **bear**[2] (sense 5). **6.** *Chiefly Brit.* short for **bull's-eye** (senses 1, 2). **7.** *Slang.* short for **bullshit. 8.** short for **bulldog, bull terrier. 9. a bull in a china shop.** a clumsy person. **10. shoot the bull.** *U.S. slang.* **a.** to pass time talking lightly. **b.** to boast or exaggerate. **11. take the bull by the horns.** to face and tackle a difficulty without shirking. ~*adj.* **12.** male; masculine: *a bull elephant.* **13.** large; strong. ~*vb.* **14.** (*tr.*) to raise or attempt to raise the price or prices of (a stock market or a security) by speculative buying. **15.** (*intr.*) *U.S. slang.* to talk lightly or foolishly. [Old English *bula,* from Old Norse *boli;* related to Middle Low German *bulle,* Middle Dutch *bolle*]

bull[2] (bʊl) *n.* a ludicrously self-contradictory or inconsistent statement. Also called: **Irish bull.** [C17: of uncertain origin]

bull[3] (bʊl) *n.* a formal document issued by the pope, written in antiquated characters and often sealed with a leaden bulla. [C13: from Medieval Latin *bulla* seal attached to a bull, from Latin: round object]

Bull[1] (bʊl) *n.* **the.** the constellation Taurus, the second sign of the zodiac.

Bull[2] (bʊl) *n.* **1. John.** 1563–1628, English composer and organist. **2.** See **John Bull.**

bull. *abbrev. for* bulletin.

bul·la (ˈbʊlə, ˈbʌlə) *n., pl.* **·lae** (-liː). **1.** a leaden seal affixed to a papal bull, having a representation of Saints Peter and Paul on one side and the name of the reigning pope on the other. **2.** an ancient Roman rounded metal or leather box containing an amulet, worn around the neck. **3.** *Pathol.* another word for **blister** (sense 1). [C19: from Latin: round object, bubble]

bul·lace (ˈbʊlɪs) *n.* a small Eurasian rosaceous tree, *Prunus domestica insititia* (or *P. insititia*), of which the damson is the cultivated form. See also **plum**[1] (sense 1). [C14: from Old French *beloce,* from Medieval Latin *bolluca,* perhaps of Gaulish origin]

bul·late (ˈbʌleɪt, -ɪt, ˈbʊl-) *adj.* *Botany, anatomy, etc.* puckered or blistered in appearance: *the bullate leaves of the primrose.* [C19: from Medieval Latin *bullātus* inflated, from Latin *bulla* bubble]

bull·bat (ˈbʊlˌbæt) *n.* another name for **nighthawk** (sense 1).

bull·dog (ˈbʊlˌdɒg) *n.* **1.** a sturdy thickset breed of dog with an undershot jaw, broad head, and a muscular body. **2.** (at Oxford University) an official who accompanies the proctors on ceremonial occasions.

bull·dog ant *n.* any large Australian ant of the genus *Myrmecia,* having a powerful sting: subfamily *Ponerinae.*

bull·dog clip *n.* a clip for holding papers together, consisting of two T-shaped metal clamps held in place by a cylindrical spring.

bull·doze (ˈbʊlˌdəʊz) *vb.* (*tr.*) **1.** to move, demolish, flatten, etc., with a bulldozer. **2.** *Informal.* to force; push: *he bulldozed his way through the crowd.* **3.** *Informal.* to intimidate or coerce. [C19: probably from BULL[1] + DOSE]

bull·doz·er (ˈbʊlˌdəʊzə) *n.* **1.** a powerful tractor fitted with caterpillar tracks and a blade at the front, used for moving earth, rocks, etc. **2.** *Informal.* a person who bulldozes.

bull dust *n.* *Austral.* **1.** fine dust. **2.** *Slang.* nonsense.

bul·let (ˈbʊlɪt) *n.* **1. a.** a small metallic missile enclosed in a cartridge, used as the projectile of a gun, rifle, etc. **b.** the entire cartridge. **2.** something resembling a bullet, esp. in shape or effect. **3.** *Skateboarding slang.* a position for racing downhill, having the body crouched, feet in the centre of the board, and often arms stretched out in front. **4.** a capsule containing a drug. [C16: from French *boulette,* diminutive of *boule* ball; see BOWL[2]] —**ˈbul·let-ˌlike** *adj.*

bul·le·tin (ˈbʊlɪtɪn) *n.* **1.** an official statement on a matter of public interest, such as the illness of a public figure. **2.** a broadcast summary of the news. **3.** a periodical publication of an association, etc. ~*vb.* **4.** (*tr.*) to make known by bulletin. [C17: from French, from Italian *bullettino,* from *bulletta,* diminutive of *bulla* papal edict, BULL[3]]

bul·le·tin board *n.* the U.S. name for **notice board.**

bul·let·proof (ˈbʊlɪtˌpruːf) *adj.* **1.** not penetrable by bullets: *bulletproof glass.* ~*vb.* **2.** (*tr.*) to make bulletproof.

bull·fight (ˈbʊlˌfaɪt) *n.* a traditional Spanish, Portuguese, and Latin American spectacle in which a matador, assisted by banderilleros and mounted picadors, baits and usually kills a bull in an arena. —**ˈbull·ˌfight·er** *n.* —**ˈbull·ˌfight·ing** *n.*

bull·finch[1] (ˈbʊlˌfɪntʃ) *n.* **1.** a common European finch, *Pyrrhula pyrrhula:* the male has a bright red throat and breast, black crown, wings, and tail, and a grey-and-white back. **2.** any of various similar finches. [C14: see BULL[1], FINCH; probably so called from its stocky shape and thick neck]

bull·finch[2] (ˈbʊlˌfɪntʃ) *n.* *Brit.* a high thick hedge too difficult for a horse and rider to jump. [C19: perhaps changed from the phrase *bull fence*]

bull·frog (ˈbʊlˌfrɒg) *n.* any of various large frogs, such as *Rana catesbeiana* (**American bullfrog**), having a loud deep croak.

bull·head (ˈbʊlˌhɛd) *n.* **1.** any of various small northern mainly marine scorpaenoid fishes of the family *Cottidae* that have a large head covered with bony plates and spines. **2.** any freshwater North American catfish of the genus *Ameiurus* (or *Ictalurus*), having a large head bearing several long barbels. **3.** a scorpion fish, *Scorpaena guttata,* of North American Pacific coastal waters. **4.** *Informal.* a stupidly stubborn or unintelligent person.

bull-head·ed *adj.* blindly obstinate; stubborn, headstrong, or stupid. —**ˌbull-ˈhead·ed·ly** *adv.* —**ˌbull-ˈhead·ed·ness** *n.*

bull·horn (ˈbʊlˌhɔːn) *n.* the U.S. name for **loud-hailer.**

bul·lion (ˈbʊljən) *n.* **1.** gold or silver in mass. **2.** gold or silver in the form of bars and ingots, suitable for further processing. **3.** Also called: **bullion fringe.** a thick gold or silver wire or fringed cord used as a trimming, as on military uniforms. [C14 (in the sense: melted gold or silver): from Anglo-French: mint, probably from Old French *bouillir* to boil, from Latin *bullīre*]

bull·ish (ˈbʊlɪʃ) *adj.* **1.** like a bull. **2.** *Stock Exchange.* causing, expecting, or characterized by a rise in prices: *a bullish market.*

bull mas·tiff *n.* a large powerful breed of dog with a short usually tan coat, developed by crossing the bulldog with the mastiff.

bull-necked *adj.* having a short thick neck.

bull nose *n.* **1.** a disease of pigs caused by infection with the bacterium *Actinomyces necrophorus,* characterized by swelling of the snout. **2.** a rounded edge of a brick, step, etc. **3.** a rounded exterior angle, as where two walls meet.

bull-nosed *adj.* having a rounded end.

bull·ock (ˈbʊlək) *n.* **1.** a gelded bull; steer. **2.** *Archaic.* a bull calf. ~*vb.* **3.** (*intr.*) *Austral. informal.* to work hard and long. [Old English *bulluc;* see BULL[1], -OCK]

bull·ock's heart *n.* another name for **custard apple** (senses 1, 2).

bull·ock·y (ˈbʊləkɪ) *n.* *Austral. informal.* the driver of a team of bullocks.

bull·pen (ˈbʊlˌpɛn) *n.* *U.S. informal.* a large cell where prisoners are confined together temporarily.

bull·ring (ˈbʊlˌrɪŋ) *n.* an arena for bullfighting.

bull·roar·er (ˈbʊlˌrɔːrə) *n.* a wooden slat attached to a thong that makes a roaring sound when the thong is whirled: used esp. by Australian aborigines in religious rites.

Bull Run *n.* the site of two battles during the American Civil War (July, 1861 and August, 1862), in both of which the Federal army was routed by the Confederates.

bull ses·sion *n.* *U.S. informal.* an informal discussion among men.

bull's-eye *n.* **1.** the small central disc of a target, usually the highest valued area. **2.** a shot hitting this. **3.** *Informal.* something that exactly achieves its aim. **4.** a small circular or oval window or opening. **5.** a thick disc of glass set into a ship's deck, etc., to admit light. **6.** the glass boss at the centre of a sheet of blown glass. **7. a.** a small thick plano-convex lens used as a condenser. **b.** a lamp or lantern containing such a lens. **8.** a peppermint-flavoured, usually striped, boiled sweet. **9.** *Nautical.* a circular or oval wooden block with a groove around it for the strop of a shroud and a hole at its centre for a line. Compare **deadeye.** **10.** *Meteorol.* the eye or centre of a cyclone.

bull·shit ('bʊlʃɪt) *Taboo slang.* ~*n.* **1.** exaggerated or foolish talk; nonsense. **2.** (in the British Army) exaggerated zeal, esp. for ceremonial drill, cleaning, polishing, etc. Usually shortened to **bull.** ~*vb.* **·shits, ·shit·ting, ·shit·ted. 3.** (*intr.*) to talk in an exaggerated or foolish manner. —**'bull·shit·ter** *n.*

bull snake *n.* any burrowing North American nonvenomous colubrid snake of the genus *Pituophis,* typically having yellow and brown markings. Also called: **gopher snake.**

bull ter·ri·er *n.* a breed of terrier having a short smooth coat, developed by crossing a bulldog with the original English terrier.

bull tongue *Chiefly U.S.* ~*n.* **1.** a heavy plough used in growing cotton, having an almost vertical mouldboard. **2.** a plough or cultivator with a single shovel.

bull trout *n.* any large trout, esp. the salmon trout.

bull·whip ('bʊl,wɪp) *n.* **1.** a long tapering heavy whip, esp. one of plaited rawhide. ~*vb.* **·whips, ·whip·ping, ·whipped. 2.** (*tr.*) to whip with a bullwhip.

bul·ly ('bʊlɪ) *n., pl.* **·lies. 1.** a person who hurts, persecutes, or intimidates weaker people. **2.** *Archaic.* a hired ruffian. **3.** *Obsolete.* a procurer; pimp. **4.** *Obsolete.* a fine fellow or friend. **5.** *Obsolete.* a sweetheart; darling. ~*vb.* **·lies, ·ly·ing, ·lied. 6.** (when *tr.,* often foll. by *into*) to hurt, intimidate, or persecute (a weaker or smaller person), esp. to make him do something. ~*adj.* **7.** dashing; jolly: *my bully boy.* **8.** *Informal.* very good; fine. ~*interj.* **9.** Also: **bully for you, him,** etc. *Informal.* well done! bravo! [C16 (in the sense: sweetheart, hence fine fellow, hence swaggering coward): probably from Middle Dutch *boele* lover, from Middle High German *buole,* perhaps childish variant of *bruoder* BROTHER]

bul·ly beef *n.* canned corned beef. Often shortened to **bully.** [C19 *bully,* anglicized version of French *bouilli,* from *boeuf bouilli* boiled beef]

bul·ly-off *Hockey.* ~*n.* **1.** the method by which a game is started. Two opposing players stand with the ball between them and alternately strike their sticks together and against the ground three times before trying to hit the ball. ~*vb.* **bul·ly off. 2.** (*intr., adv.*) to start play with a bully-off. ~Often shortened to **bully.** Compare **face-off.**

bul·ly·rag ('bʊlɪ,ræg) *vb.* **·rags, ·rag·ging, ·ragged.** (*tr.*) to bully, esp. by means of cruel practical jokes. Also: **ballyrag.**

buln·buln ('bʊln'bʊln) *n. Austral.* another name for **lyrebird.** [C19: from a native Australian language]

Bü·low (*German* 'by:lo) *n.* Prince **Bern·hard von** ('bɛrnhart fɔn). 1849–1929, chancellor of Germany (1900–09).

bul·rush ('bʊl,rʌʃ) *n.* **1.** Also called: **reed mace, cat's-tail.** any tall reedlike marsh plant of the genus *Typha,* having thick straplike leaves and flowers in long dense brown cylindrical spikes: family *Typhaceae.* **2.** a grasslike cyperaceous marsh plant, *Scirpus lacustris,* used for making mats, chair seats, etc. **3.** a biblical word for **papyrus** (the plant). [C15 *bulrish, bul-* perhaps from BULL[1] + *rish* RUSH[2], referring to the largeness of the plant]

bul·wark ('bʊlwək) *n.* **1.** a wall or similar structure used as a fortification; rampart. **2.** a person or thing acting as a defence against injury, annoyance, etc. **3.** (*often pl.*) *Nautical.* a solid vertical fencelike structure along the outward sides of a deck. **4.** a breakwater or mole. ~*vb.* **5.** (*tr.*) to defend or fortify with or as if with a bulwark. [C15: via Dutch from Middle High German *bolwerk,* from *bol* plank, BOLE[1] + *werk* WORK]

Bul·wer-Lyt·ton ('bʊlwə'lɪtᵊn) *n.* See (1st Baron) **Lytton.**

bum[1] (bʌm) *n. Brit. slang.* the buttocks or anus. [C14: of uncertain origin]

bum[2] (bʌm) *Informal, chiefly U.S.* ~*n.* **1.** a disreputable loafer or idler. **2.** a tramp; hobo. **3.** an irresponsible, unpleasant, or mean person. **4.** a person who spends a great deal of time on a specified sport: *baseball bum.* **5. on the bum. a.** living as a loafer or vagrant. **b.** out of repair; broken. ~*vb.* **bums, bum·ming, bummed. 6.** (*tr.*) to get by begging; cadge: *to bum a lift.* **7.** (*intr.;* often foll. by *around*) to live by begging or as a vagrant or loafer. **8.** (*intr.;* usually foll. by *around*) to spend time to no good purpose; loaf; idle. ~*adj.* **9.** (*prenominal*) of poor quality; useless. [C19: probably shortened from earlier *bummer* a loafer, probably from German *bummeln* to loaf]

bum·bail·iff (,bʌm'beɪlɪf) *n. Brit. derogatory.* (formerly) an officer employed to collect debts and arrest debtors for nonpayment. [C17: from BUM[1] + BAILIFF, so called because he follows hard behind debtors]

bum·ble[1] ('bʌmbᵊl) *vb.* **1.** to speak or do in a clumsy, muddled, or inefficient way: *he bumbled his way through his speech.* **2.** (*intr.*) to proceed unsteadily; stumble. ~*n.* **3.** a blunder or botch. [C16: perhaps a blend of BUNGLE + STUMBLE] —**'bum·bler** *n.*

bum·ble[2] ('bʌmbᵊl) *vb.* (*intr.*) to make a humming sound. [C14 *bomblen* to buzz, boom, of imitative origin]

bum·ble·bee ('bʌmbᵊl,bi:) *or* **hum·ble·bee** *n.* any large hairy social bee of the genus *Bombus* and related genera, of temperate regions: family *Apidae.* [C16: from BUMBLE[2] + BEE]

bum·ble·dom ('bʌmbəldəm) *n.* self-importance in a minor office. [C19: after *Bumble,* name of the beadle in Dickens' *Oliver Twist* (1837–38)]

bum·ble-pup·py *n.* **1.** a game in which a ball, attached by string to a post, is hit so that the string winds round the post. **2.** (*modifier*) (of whist or bridge) played unskilfully.

bum·boat ('bʌm,bəʊt) *n.* any small boat used for ferrying supplies or goods for sale to a ship at anchor or at a mooring. [C17 (in the sense: scavenger's boat): *bum,* from Dutch *boomschip* canoe (from *bom* tree) + BOAT]

bumf (bʌmf) *n.* a variant spelling of **bumph.**

bum·kin ('bʌmkɪn) *n.* a variant spelling of **boomkin.**

bum·ma·lo ('bʌməˌləʊ) *n., pl.* **·lo.** another name for **Bombay duck.** [C17: from Marathi *bombīla*]

bum·ma·ree (,bʌmə'ri:) *n. Brit.* (formerly) **1.** a dealer at Billingsgate fish market. **2.** a porter at Smithfield meat market. [C18: of unknown origin]

bum·mer ('bʌmə) *n. Slang.* **1.** a vagrant or idler. **2.** person or thing considered inferior. **3.** an adverse reaction to a drug, characterized by panic or fear.

bump (bʌmp) *vb.* **1.** (when *intr.,* usually foll. by *against* or *into*) to knock or strike with a jolt. **2.** (*intr.;* often foll. by *along*) to travel or proceed in jerks and jolts. **3.** (*tr.*) to hurt by knocking: *he bumped his head on the ceiling.* **4.** (*tr.*) to knock out of place; dislodge: *the crash bumped him from his chair.* **5.** (*tr.*) *Brit.* to throw (a child) into the air, one other child holding each limb, and let him down again to touch the ground. **6.** (in rowing races, esp. at Oxford and Cambridge) to catch up with and touch (another boat that started a fixed distance ahead). **7.** *Cricket.* to bowl (a ball) so that it bounces high on pitching or (of a ball) to bounce high when bowled. **8.** (*intr.*) *Chiefly U.S.* to dance erotically by thrusting the pelvis forward (esp. in the phrase **bump and grind**). **9.** (*tr.*) *Poker.* to raise (someone). ~*n.* **10.** an impact; knock; jolt; collision. **11.** a dull thud or other noise from an impact or collision. **12.** the shock of a blow or collision. **13.** a lump on the body caused by a blow. **14.** a protuberance, as on a road surface. **15.** any of the natural protuberances of the human skull, said by phrenologists to indicate underlying faculties and character. **16.** a rising current of air that gives an aircraft a severe upward jolt. **17.** (*pl.*) the act of bumping a child. See sense 5. **18.** *Rowing.* the act of bumping. See **bumping race. 19. bump ball.** *Cricket.* a ball that bounces into the air after being hit directly into the ground by the batsman. ~See also **bump into, bump off, bump up.** [C16: probably of imitative origin]

bump·er[1] ('bʌmpə) *n.* **1.** a horizontal metal bar attached to the front or rear end of a car, lorry, etc., to protect against damage from impact. **2.** a person or machine that bumps. **3.** *Cricket.* a ball bowled so that it bounces high on pitching; bouncer.

bump·er[2] ('bʌmpə) *n.* **1.** a glass, tankard, etc., filled to the brim, esp. as a toast. **2.** an unusually large or fine example of something. ~*adj.* **3.** unusually large, fine, or abundant: *a bumper crop.* ~*vb.* **4.** (*tr.*) to toast with a bumper. **5.** (*tr.*) to fill to the brim. **6.** (*intr.*) to drink bumpers. [C17 (in the sense: a brimming glass): probably from *bump* (obsolete vb.) to bulge; see BUMP]

bump·er[3] ('bʌmpə) *n. Austral. informal.* a cigarette end. [C19: perhaps from a blend of BUTT[1] and STUMP]

bump·er car *n.* a low-powered electrically propelled vehicle driven and bumped against similar cars in a special rink at a funfair. Also called: **Dodgem.**

bumph *or* **bumf** (bʌmf) *n. Brit.* **1.** *Informal, derogatory.* offical documents, forms, etc. **2.** *Slang.* toilet paper. [C19: short for earlier *bumfodder;* see BUM[1]]

bump·ing race *n.* (esp. at Oxford and Cambridge) a race in which rowing eights start an equal distance one behind the other and each tries to bump the boat in front.

bump in·to *vb.* (*intr., prep.*) to meet by chance; encounter unexpectedly.

bump·kin[1] ('bʌmpkɪn) *n.* an awkward simple rustic person (esp. in the phrase **country bumpkin**). [C16 (perhaps originally applied to Dutchmen): perhaps from Dutch *boomken* small tree, or from Middle Dutch *boomekijn* small barrel, alluding to a short or squat person]

bump·kin[2] ('bʌmpkɪn) *or* **bum·kin** *n.* variant spellings of **boomkin.**

bump off *vb.* (*tr., adv.*) *Slang.* to murder; kill.

bump start *Brit.* ~*n.* **1.** a method of starting a motor vehicle by engaging a low gear with the clutch depressed and pushing it or allowing it to run down a hill until sufficient momentum has been acquired to turn the engine by releasing the clutch. ~*vb.* **bump-start. 2.** (*tr.*) to start (a motor vehicle) using this method.

bump·tious ('bʌmpʃəs) *adj.* offensively self-assertive or conceited. [C19: perhaps a blend of BUMP + FRACTIOUS] —**'bump·tious·ly** *adv.* —**'bump·tious·ness** *n.*

bump up *vb.* (*tr., adv.*) *Informal.* to raise or increase: *prices are being bumped up daily.*

bump·y ('bʌmpɪ) *adj.* **bump·i·er, bump·i·est. 1.** having an uneven surface: *a bumpy road.* **2.** full of jolts; rough: *a bumpy flight.* —**'bump·i·ly** *adv.* —**'bump·i·ness** *n.*

bum's rush *n. U.S. slang.* **1.** forcible ejection, as from a gathering. **2.** rapid dismissal, as of an idea.

bum steer *n. Slang, chiefly U.S.* false or misleading information or advice.

bum·suck·ing ('bʌm,sʌkɪŋ) *n. Brit. taboo slang.* obsequious behaviour; toadying. —**'bum,suck·er** *n.*

bun (bʌn) *n.* **1.** a small roll, similar to bread but usually containing sweetening, currants, spices, etc. **2.** a hair style in which long hair is gathered into a bun shape at the back of the head. [C14: of unknown origin]

Bu·na ('bu:nə, 'bju:-) *n. Trademark.* a synthetic rubber formed by polymerizing butadiene or by copolymerizing it with such compounds as acrylonitride or styrene.

bunch (bʌntʃ) *n.* **1.** a number of things growing, fastened, or grouped together: *a bunch of grapes; a bunch of keys.* **2.** a collection; group: *a bunch of queries.* **3.** *Informal.* a group or company: *a bunch of boys.* **4.** *Archaic.* a protuberance. ~*vb.* **5.** (sometimes foll. by *up*) to group or be grouped into a bunch. [C14: of obscure origin]

Bunche (bʌntʃ) *n.* **Ralph John·son.** 1904–71, U.S. diplomat and United Nations official: awarded the Nobel peace prize in 1950 for his work as UN mediator in Palestine (1948–49); UN under-secretary (1954–71).

bunch·es ('bʌntʃɪz) *pl. n. Brit.* a hair style in which hair is tied into two sections on either side of the head at the back.

bunch·y ('bʌntʃɪ) *adj.* **bunch·i·er, bunch·i·est. 1.** composed of or resembling bunches. **2.** bulging. —**'bunch·i·ness** *n.*

bun+co *or* **bun+ko** ('bʊŋkəʊ) *U.S. informal.* ~*n., pl.* **+cos** *or* **+kos. 1.** a swindle, esp. one by confidence tricksters. ~*vb.* **+cos, +co+ing, +coed** *or* **+kos, +ko+ing, +koed. 2.** (*tr.*) to swindle; cheat. [C19: perhaps from Spanish *banca* bank (in gambling), from Italian *banca* BANK[1]]

bun+combe ('bʌŋkəm) *n.* a variant spelling (esp. U.S.) of **bunkum.**

bund (bʌnd) *n.* (in India and the Far East) **1.** an embankment; dyke. **2.** an embanked road or quay. [from Hindi *band,* from Persian; related to Sanskrit *bandha* BAND[1]]

Bund (bʊnd; *German* bʊnt) *n., pl.* **Bunds** *or* **Bün+de** (*German* 'byndə). **1.** (*sometimes not cap.*) a federation or league. **2.** short for **German American Bund,** an organization of U.S. Nazis and Nazi sympathizers in the 1930s and 1940s. **3.** an organization of socialist Jewish workers in Russia founded in 1897. **4.** the confederation of N German states, which existed from 1867-71.

Bun+da+berg ('bʌndəˌbɜːg) *n.* a city in E Australia, near the E coast of Queensland: centre of a sugar-growing area, with a nearby deep-water port. Pop.: 29 100 (1975 est.).

Bun+del+khand (ˌbʌnd^{ə}l'kʌnd, -'xʌnd) *n.* a region of central India: formerly native states, now mainly part of Madhya Pradesh.

Bun+des+rat ('bʊndəsˌrɑːt) *n.* **1.** (in West Germany) the council of state ministers with certain legislative and administrative powers, representing the state governments at federal level. **2.** (in Austria) an assembly with some legislative power that represents state interests at the federal level. **3.** (in Switzerland) the executive council of the confederation. **4.** (in the German empire from 1871–1918) the council representing the governments of the constituent states, with administrative, judicial, and legislative powers. [German, from *Bund* federation + *Rat* council]

Bun+des+tag ('bʊndəsˌtɑːg) *n.* (in West Germany) the legislative assembly, which is elected by universal adult suffrage and elects the federal chancellor. [German, from *Bund* federation + *-tag,* from *tagen* to meet]

bundh (bʌnd) *n.* a variant spelling of **bandh.**

bun+dle ('bʌnd^{ə}l) *n.* **1.** a number of things or a quantity of material gathered or loosely bound together: *a bundle of sticks.* Related adj.: **fascicular. 2.** something wrapped or tied for carrying; package. **3.** *Slang.* a large sum of money. **4. go a bundle on.** *Slang.* to be extremely fond of. **5.** *Biology.* a collection of strands of specialized tissue such as nerve fibres. **6.** *Botany.* short for **vascular bundle. 7.** *Textiles.* a measure of yarn or cloth; 60 000 yards of linen yarn; 5 or 10 pounds of cotton hanks. **8. drop one's bundle.** *Austral. slang.* to panic or give up hope. ~*vb.* **9.** (*tr.*; often foll. by *up*) to make into a bundle. **10.** (foll. by *out, off, into,* etc.) to go or cause to go, esp. roughly or unceremoniously: *we bundled him out of the house.* **11.** (*tr.*; usually foll. by *into*) to push or throw, esp. quickly and untidily: *to bundle shirts into a drawer.* **12.** (*intr.*) to sleep or lie in one's clothes on the same bed as one's betrothed: formerly a custom in New England, Wales, and elsewhere. [C14: probably from Middle Dutch *bundel;* related to Old English *bindele* bandage; see BIND, BOND] —**'bun+dler** *n.*

bun+dle up *vb.* (*adv.*) **1.** to dress (somebody) warmly and snugly. **2.** (*tr.*) to make (something) into a bundle or bundles, esp. by tying.

bun+do+bust ('bʌndəbʌst) *n.* a variant spelling of **bandobust.**

bun+du ('bʊndʊ) *n. S. African and Rhodesian slang.* **a.** a largely uninhabited wild region far from towns. **b.** (*as modifier*): *a bundu hat.* [C20: from a Bantu language]

bun+du bash+ing *n. Rhodesian slang.* living temporarily or travelling in the bundu.

bun fight *n. Brit. slang.* a tea party.

bung[1] (bʌŋ) *n.* **1.** a stopper, esp. of cork or rubber, for a cask, piece of laboratory glassware, etc. **2.** short for **bunghole.** ~*vb.* (*tr.*) **3.** (often foll. by *up*) *Informal.* to close or seal with or as with a bung: *the car's exhaust was bunged up with mud.* **4.** *Brit. slang.* to throw; sling. [C15: from Middle Dutch *bonghe,* from Late Latin *puncta* PUNCTURE]

bung[2] (bʌŋ) *Midland English dialect.* ~*n.* **1.** a gratuity; tip. ~*vb.* **2.** (*tr.*) to give (someone a tip). [C16 (originally in the sense: a purse): perhaps from Old English *pung,* changed through the influence of BUNG[1]]

bung[3] (bʌŋ) *adj. Austral. slang.* **1.** dead. **2.** destroyed. **3.** useless. **4. go bung. a.** to die. **b.** to fail or collapse. [C19: from a native Australian language]

bun+ga+low ('bʌŋgəˌləʊ) *n.* **1.** a one-storey house, sometimes with an attic. **2.** (in India) a one-storey house, usually surrounded by a veranda. [C17: from Hindi *banglā* (house) of the Bengal type]

bung+er ('bʌŋə) *n. Austral. slang.* a firework.

bung+hole ('bʌŋˌhəʊl) *n.* a hole in a cask, barrel, etc., through which liquid can be poured or drained.

bun+gle ('bʌŋg^{ə}l) *vb.* **1.** (*tr.*) to spoil (an operation) through clumsiness, incompetence, etc.; botch. ~*n.* **2.** a clumsy or unsuccessful performance or piece of work; mistake; botch. [C16: perhaps of Scandinavian origin; compare dialect Swedish *bangla* to work without results] —**'bun+gler** *n.* —**'bun+gling** *adj., n.*

Bu+nin (*Russian* 'bunin) *n.* **I·van A·le·kse·ye·vich** (i'van alɪ'ksjejɪvitʃ). 1870–1953, Russian novelist and poet; author of *The Gentleman from San Francisco* (1922).

bun+ion ('bʌnjən) *n.* swelling of the first joint of the big toe, which is displaced to one side. An inflamed bursa forms over the joint. [C18: perhaps from obsolete *bunny* a swelling, of uncertain origin]

bunk[1] (bʌŋk) *n.* **1.** a narrow shelflike bed fixed along a wall. **2.** short for **bunk bed. 3.** *Informal.* any place where one sleeps. ~*vb.* **4.** (*intr.*; often foll. by *down*) to prepare to sleep: *he bunked down on the floor.* **5.** (*intr.*) to occupy a bunk or bed. **6.** (*tr.*) to provide with a bunk or bed. [C19: probably short for BUNKER]

bunk[2] (bʌŋk) *n. Informal.* short for **bunkum** (sense 1).

bunk[3] (bʌŋk) *Brit. slang.* ~*n.* **1.** a hurried departure, usually under suspicious circumstances (esp. in the phrase **do a bunk**). ~*vb.* **2.** (*intr.*) to run away; scram. [C19: perhaps from BUNK[1] (in the sense: to occupy a bunk, hence a hurried departure, as on a ship)]

bunk bed *n.* one of a pair of beds constructed one above the other to save space.

bun+ker ('bʌŋkə) *n.* **1.** a large storage container or tank, as for coal. **2.** Also called (esp. U.S.): **sand trap.** an obstacle on a golf course, usually a sand-filled hollow bordered by a ridge. **3.** an underground shelter with a bank and embrasures for guns above ground. ~*vb.* **4.** (*tr.*) *Golf.* **a.** to drive (the ball) into a bunker. **b.** (*passive*) to have one's ball trapped in a bunker. **5.** (*tr.*) *Nautical.* **a.** to fuel (a ship). **b.** to transfer (cargo) from a ship to a storehouse. [C16 (in the sense: chest, box): from Scottish *bonkar,* of unknown origin]

Bun+ker Hill *n.* the first major battle of the War of American Independence at which American colonial forces were defeated by British forces on June 17, 1775.

bunk+house ('bʌŋkˌhaʊs) *n. U.S.* a building containing the sleeping quarters of workers on a ranch, etc.

bun+ko ('bʌŋkəʊ) *n., pl.* **+kos,** *vb.* **+kos, +ko+ing, +koed.** a variant spelling of **bunco.**

bun+kum *or* **bun+combe** ('bʌŋkəm) *n.* **1.** empty talk; nonsense. **2.** *Chiefly U.S.* empty or insincere speechmaking by a politician to please voters or gain publicity. [C19: after *Buncombe,* a county in North Carolina, alluded to in an inane speech by its Congressional representative Felix Walker (about 1820)]

bun+ny ('bʌnɪ) *n., pl.* **+nies. 1.** Also: **bunny rabbit.** a child's word for **rabbit** (sense 1). **2.** Also: **bunny girl.** a night-club hostess whose costume includes rabbit-like tail and ears. **3.** *Austral. slang.* a mug; dupe. [C17: from Scottish Gaelic *bun* scut of a rabbit]

bun+ny hug *n.* **1.** a ballroom dance with syncopated rhythm, popular in America in the early 20th century. **2.** a piece of music in the rhythm of this dance.

bun+rak·u (bʊn'rɑːkuː) *n.* a Japanese form of puppet theatre in which each puppet is manipulated by three puppeteers.

Bun·sen ('bʌns^{ə}n; *German* 'bʊnz^{ə}n) *n.* **Ro·bert Wil·helm** ('roːbɛrt 'vɪlhɛlm). 1811–99, German chemist who with Kirchhoff developed spectrum analysis and discovered the elements caesium and rubidium. He invented the Bunsen burner and the ice calorimeter.

Bun+sen burn+er *n.* a gas burner, widely used in scientific laboratories, consisting of a metal tube with an adjustable air valve at the base. [C19: named after R. W. BUNSEN]

bunt[1] (bʌnt) *vb.* **1.** (of an animal) to butt (something) with the head or horns. **2.** to cause (an aircraft) to fly in part of an inverted loop or (of an aircraft) to fly in such a loop. **3.** *U.S.* (in baseball) to hit (a pitched ball) very gently. ~*n.* **4.** the act or an instance of bunting. [C19: perhaps nasalized variant of BUTT[3]]

bunt[2] (bʌnt) *n. Nautical.* the baggy centre of a fishing net or other piece of fabric, such as a square sail. [C16: perhaps from Middle Low German *bunt* BUNDLE]

bunt[3] (bʌnt) *n.* a disease of cereal plants caused by smut fungi (genus *Tilletia*). [C17: of unknown origin]

bunt+al· ('bʌnt^{ə}l) *n.* straw obtained from leaves of the talipot palm. [C20: from Tagalog]

bunt+ing[1] ('bʌntɪŋ) *n.* **1.** a coarse, loosely woven cotton fabric used for flags, etc. **2.** decorative flags, pennants, and streamers. **3.** flags collectively, esp. those of a boat. [C18: of unknown origin]

bunt+ing[2] ('bʌntɪŋ) *n.* any of numerous seed-eating songbirds of the families *Fringillidae* (finches, etc.) or *Emberizidae,* esp. those of the genera *Emberiza* of the Old World and *Passerina* of North America. They all have short stout bills. [C13: of unknown origin]

bunt+line ('bʌntlɪn, -ˌlaɪn) *n. Nautical.* one of several lines fastened to the foot of a square sail for hauling it up to the yard when furling.

Buñ+uel (*Spanish* bu'ɲwel) *n.* **Luis** (lwis). born 1900, Spanish film director. He collaborated with Salvador Dali on the first surrealist films, *Un Chien andalou* (1929) and *L'Age d'or* (1930). His later films include *Viridiana* (1961), *Belle de jour* (1966), *The Discreet Charm of the Bourgeoisie* (1972), and *That Obscure Object of Desire* (1977).

bun·ya-bun·ya ('bʌnjə'bʌnjə) *n.* a tall dome-shaped Australian coniferous tree, *Araucaria bidwillii,* having edible seeds and

thickish flattened needles. [from a native Australian language]
Bun·yan ('bʌnjən) *n.* **John.** 1628–88, English preacher and writer, noted particularly for his allegory *The Pilgrim's Progress* (1678).
bun+yip ('bʌnjɪp) *n. Austral.* a legendary monster said to inhabit swamps and lagoons of the Australian interior. [C19: from a native Australian language]
Buo·na·par·te (ˌbwona'parte) *n.* the Italian spelling of **Bonaparte.**
Buo·nar·ro·ti (*Italian* ˌbwonar'rɔ:ti) *n.* See **Michelangelo.**
buoy (bɔɪ; *U.S.* 'bu:ɪ) *n.* **1.** a distinctively shaped and coloured float, anchored to the bottom, for designating moorings, navigable channels, or obstructions in a body of water. See also **life buoy.** ~*vb.* **2.** (*tr.;* usually foll. by *up*) to prevent from sinking: *the life belt buoyed him up.* **3.** (*tr.;* usually foll. by *up*) to raise the spirits of; hearten. **4.** (*tr.*) *Nautical.* to mark (a channel or obstruction) with a buoy or buoys. **5.** (*intr.*) to rise to the surface; float. [C13: probably of Germanic origin; compare Middle Dutch *boeie, boeye;* see BEACON]
buoy+age ('bɔɪɪdʒ) *n.* **1.** a system of buoys. **2.** the buoys used in such a system. **3.** the providing of buoys.
buoy+an+cy ('bɔɪənsɪ) *n.* **1.** the ability to float in a liquid or to rise in liquid, air, or other gas. **2.** the tendency of a fluid to exert a lifting effect on a body that is wholly or partly submerged in it. **3.** the ability to recover quickly after setbacks; resilience. **4.** cheerfulness.
buoy+ant ('bɔɪənt) *adj.* **1.** able to float in or rise to the surface of a liquid. **2.** (of a liquid or gas) able to keep a body afloat or cause it to rise. **3.** cheerful or resilient. [C16: probably from Spanish *boyante,* from *boyar* to float, from *boya* buoy, ultimately of Germanic origin]
bu+pres·tid (bju:'prɛstɪd) *n.* **1.** any beetle of the mainly tropical family *Buprestidae,* the adults of which are brilliantly coloured and the larvae of which bore into and cause damage to trees, roots, etc. ~*adj.* **2.** of, relating to, or belonging to the family *Buprestidae.* [C19: from Latin *buprestis* poisonous beetle, causing the cattle who eat it to swell up, from Greek, from *bous* ox + *prēthein* to swell up]
bur (bɜ:) *n.* **1.** a seed vessel or flower head, as of burdock, having hooks or prickles. **2.** any plant that produces burs. **3.** a person or thing that clings like a bur. **4.** a small surgical or dental drill. **5.** a variant spelling of **burr**[3], **burr**[4]. ~*vb.* **burs, bur+ring, burred. 6.** (*tr.*) to remove burs from. ~Also (for senses 1–4, 6): **burr.** [C14: probably of Scandinavian origin; compare Danish *burre* bur, Swedish *kardborre* burdock]
BUR *international car registration for* Burma.
Bur. *abbrev. for* Burma.
bu+ran (bu:'rɑ:n) *or* **bu·ra** (bu:'rɑ:) *n.* (in central Asia) **1.** a blizzard, with the wind blowing from the north and reaching gale force. **2.** a summer wind from the north, causing dust storms. [from Russian, of Turkic origin; related to Kazan Tatar *buran*]
Bu+ray+dah *or* **Bu+rai+da** (bʊ'raɪdə) *n.* a town and oasis in central Saudi Arabia. Pop.: 50 000 (1961 est.).
Bur·bage ('bɜ:bɪdʒ) *n.* **Rich·ard.** ?1567–1619, English actor, closely associated with Shakespeare.
Bur+ber+ry ('bɜ:bərɪ) *n., pl.* **+ries.** *Trademark.* a light good-quality raincoat, esp. of gabardine.
bur+ble ('bɜ:bᵊl) *vb.* **1.** to make or utter with a bubbling sound; gurgle. **2.** (*intr.;* often foll. by *away* or *on*) to talk quickly and excitedly. **3.** (*intr.*) (of the airflow around a body) to become turbulent. ~*n.* **4.** a bubbling or gurgling sound. **5.** a flow of excited speech. **6.** turbulence in the airflow around a body. [C14: probably of imitative origin; compare Spanish *borbollar* to bubble, gush, Italian *borbugliare*] —**'bur+bler** *n.*
bur+bot ('bɜ:bət) *n., pl.* **+bots** *or* **+bot.** a freshwater gadoid food fish, *Lota lota,* that has barbels around its mouth and occurs in Europe, Asia, and North America. [C14: from Old French *bourbotte,* from *bourbeter* to wallow in mud, from *bourbe* mud, probably of Celtic origin]
bur+den[1] ('bɜ:dᵊn) *n.* **1.** something that is carried; load. **2.** something that is exacting, oppressive, or difficult to bear: *the burden of responsibility.* Related adj.: **onerous. 3.** *Nautical.* **a.** the cargo capacity of a ship. **b.** the weight of a ship's cargo. ~*vb.* (*tr.*) **4.** (sometimes foll. by *up*) to put or impose a burden on; load. **5.** to weigh down; oppress: *the old woman was burdened with cares.* [Old English *byrthen;* related to *beran* to BEAR, Old Frisian *berthene* burden, Old High German *burdin*]
bur+den[2] ('bɜ:dᵊn) *n.* **1.** a line of words recurring at the end of each verse of a ballad or similar song; chorus or refrain. **2.** the principal or recurrent theme of a speech, book, etc. **3.** another word for **bourdon.** [C16: from Old French *bourdon* bass horn, droning sound, of imitative origin]
bur+den of proof *n. Law.* the obligation, in criminal cases resting initially on the prosecution, to provide evidence that will convince the court or jury of the truth of one's contention.
bur+den+some ('bɜ:dᵊnsəm) *adj.* hard to bear; onerous.
bur+dock ('bɜ:ˌdɒk) *n.* a coarse weedy Eurasian plant of the genus *Arctium,* having large heart-shaped leaves, tiny purple flowers surrounded by hooked bristles, and burlike fruits: family *Compositae* (composites). [C16: from BUR + DOCK[4]]
bu+reau ('bjʊərəʊ) *n., pl.* **+reaus** *or* **+reaux** (-rəʊz). **1.** *Chiefly Brit.* a writing desk with pigeonholes, drawers, etc., against which the writing surface can be closed when not in use. **2.** *U.S.* a chest of drawers. **3.** an office or agency, esp. one providing services for the public. **4. a.** a government department. **b.** a branch of a government department. [C17: from French: desk, office, originally: type of cloth used for covering desks and tables, from Old French *burel,* from Late Latin *burra* shaggy cloth]
bu+reau+cra+cy (bjʊə'rɒkrəsɪ) *n., pl.* **+cies. 1.** a system of administration based upon organization into bureaus, division of labour, a hierarchy of authority, etc.: designed to dispose of a large body of work in a routine manner. **2.** government by such a system. **3.** government or other officials collectively. **4.** any administration in which action is impeded by unnecessary official procedures and red tape.
bu+reau+crat ('bjʊərəˌkræt) *n.* **1.** an official in a bureaucracy. **2.** an official who adheres to bureaucracy, esp. rigidly. —ˌ**bu+reau+'crat+ic** *adj.* —ˌ**bu+reau+'crat·i+cal+ly** *adv.* —**bu+reau+crat+ism** (bjʊə'rɒkrəˌtɪzəm) *n.*
bu+reau+cra+tize *or* **bu+reau+cra+tise** (bjʊə'rɒkrəˌtaɪz) *vb.* (*tr.*) to administer by or transform into a bureaucracy. —**bu+ˌreau+crat·i+'za+tion** *or* **bu+ˌreau+crat·i+'sa+tion** *n.*
bu+rette *or* **bu+ret** (bjʊ'rɛt) *n.* a graduated glass tube with a stopcock on one end for dispensing and transferring known volumes of fluids, esp. liquids. [C15: from French: cruet, oil can, from Old French *buire* ewer, of Germanic origin; compare Old English *būc* pitcher, belly]
burg (bɜ:g) *n.* **1.** *History.* a fortified town. **2.** *U.S. informal.* a town or city. [C18 (in the sense: fortress): from Old High German *burg* fortified town; see BOROUGH]
burg+age ('bɜ:gɪdʒ) *n. History.* **1.** (in England) tenure of land or tenement in a town or city, which originally involved a fixed money rent. **2.** (in Scotland) the tenure of land direct from the crown in Scottish royal burghs in return for watching and warding. [C14: from Medieval Latin *burgāgium,* from *burgus,* from Old English *burg;* see BOROUGH]
Bur+gas (*Bulgarian* bur'gas) *n.* a port in SE Bulgaria on an inlet of the Black Sea. Pop.: 106 115 (1965).
bur+gee ('bɜ:dʒi:) *n. Nautical.* a triangular or swallow-tailed flag flown from the mast of a merchant ship for identification and from the mast of a yacht to indicate its owner's membership of a particular yacht club. [C18: perhaps from French (Jersey dialect) *bourgeais* shipowner, from Old French *borgeis;* see BOURGEOIS, BURGESS]
Bur+gen+land (*German* 'bʊrgᵊnˌlant) *n.* a province of E Austria. Capital: Eisenstadt. Pop.: 272 119 (1971). Area: 3965 sq. km (1531 sq. miles).
bur+geon *or* **bour+geon** ('bɜ:dʒən) *vb.* **1.** (often foll. by *forth* or *out*) (of a plant) to sprout (buds). **2.** (*intr.;* often foll. by *forth* or *out*) to develop or grow rapidly; flourish. ~*n.* **3.** a bud of a plant. [C13: from Old French *burjon,* perhaps ultimately from Late Latin *burra* shaggy cloth; from the downiness of certain buds]
burg+er ('bɜ:gə) *n.* **1.** *Informal, chiefly U.S.* **a.** short for **hamburger. b.** (*in combination*): *a cheeseburger.* **2.** *Slang.* a graze.
Bür·ger (*German* 'byrgər) *n.* **Gott·fried Au·gust** ('gɔtfri:t 'aʊgʊst). 1747–94, German lyric poet, noted particularly for his ballad *Lenore* (1773).
bur+gess ('bɜ:dʒɪs) *n.* **1.** (in England) **a.** a citizen or freeman of a borough. **b.** any inhabitant of a borough. **2.** *English history.* a Member of Parliament from a borough, corporate town, or university. **3.** a member of the colonial assembly of Maryland or Virginia. [C13: from Old French *burgeis,* from *borc* town, from Late Latin *burgus,* of Germanic origin; see BOROUGH]
Bur·gess ('bɜ:dʒɪs) *n.* **1. An·tho·ny.** born 1917, English novelist and critic: author of satirical novels, such as *A Clockwork Orange* (1962), *Tremor of Intent* (1966), and *Beard's Roman Women* (1977). **2. Guy.** 1911–63, British spy, who fled to the Soviet Union (with Donald Maclean) in 1951.
burgh ('bʌrə) *n.* **1.** (in Scotland) a town that enjoys a degree of self-government: incorporated by charter. See also **small burgh. 2.** an archaic form of **borough** (sense 1). [C14: Scottish form of BOROUGH] —**burgh+al** ('bɜ:gᵊl) *adj.*
burgh+er ('bɜ:gə) *n.* **1.** a member of the trading or mercantile class of a medieval city. **2.** a respectable citizen; bourgeois. **3.** *Archaic.* a citizen or inhabitant of a corporate town, esp. on the Continent. [C16: from German *Bürger,* or Dutch *burger* freeman of a BOROUGH]
Burgh·ley *or* **Bur·leigh** ('bɜ:lɪ) *n.* **Wil·liam Cec·il,** 1st Baron Burghley. 1520–98, English statesman: chief adviser to Elizabeth I; secretary of state (1558–72) and Lord High Treasurer (1572–98).
bur+glar ('bɜ:glə) *n.* a person who commits burglary; housebreaker. [C15: from Anglo-French *burgler,* from Medieval Latin *burglātor,* probably from *burgāre* to thieve, from Latin *burgus* castle, fortress, of Germanic origin]
bur+glar+ize *or* **bur+glar+ise** ('bɜ:gləˌraɪz) *vb.* (*tr.*) *U.S.* to break into (a place) and steal from (someone); burgle.
bur+gla+ry ('bɜ:glərɪ) *n., pl.* **+ries.** *English criminal law.* the crime of either entering a building as a trespasser with the intention of committing theft, rape, grievous bodily harm, or damage, or, having entered as a trespasser, of committing one or more of these offences. —**bur+glar·i+ous** (bɜ:'glɛərɪəs) *adj.*
bur+gle ('bɜ:gᵊl) *vb.* to commit burglary upon (a house, etc.).
bur+go+mas+ter ('bɜ:gəˌmɑ:stə) *n.* **1.** the chief magistrate of a town in Austria, Belgium, Germany, or the Netherlands; mayor. **2.** a popular name for the **glaucous gull.** [C16: partial translation of Dutch *burgemeester;* see BOROUGH, MASTER]
bur+go+net ('bɜ:gəˌnɛt) *n.* a light 16th-century helmet, usually made of steel, with hinged cheekpieces. [C16: from French *bourguignotte,* from *bourguignot* of Burgundy, from *Bourgogne* Burgundy]
bur+goo ('bɜ:gu:, bɜ:'gu:) *n., pl.* **+goos. 1.** *Nautical slang.* porridge. **2.** *Southern U.S.* **a.** a thick highly seasoned soup or stew of meat and vegetables. **b.** a picnic or gathering at which

such soup is served. [C18: perhaps from Arabic *burghul* crushed grain]

Bur·goyne (bɜːˈgɔɪn) *n.* **John.** 1722–92, British general in the War of American Independence who was forced to surrender at Saratoga (1777).

bur·grave (ˈbɜːgreɪv) *n.* **1.** the military governor of a German town or castle, esp. in the 12th and 13th centuries. **2.** a nobleman ruling a German town or castle by hereditary right. [C16: from German *Burggraf,* from Old High German *burg* BOROUGH + *grāve* count]

Bur·gun·dy (ˈbɜːgəndɪ) *n., pl.* **·dies. 1.** a region of E France famous for its wines, lying west of the Saône: formerly a semi-independent duchy; annexed to France in 1482. French name: **Bourgogne. 2. Free County of.** another name for **Franche-Comté. 3.** a monarchy (1384–1477) of medieval Europe, at its height including the Low Countries, the duchy of Burgundy, and Franche-Comté. **4. Kingdom of.** a kingdom in E France, established in the early 6th century A.D., eventually including the later duchy of Burgundy, Franche-Comté, and the Kingdom of Provence: known as the Kingdom of Arles from the 13th century. **5. a.** any red or white wine produced in the region of Burgundy, around Dijon. **b.** any heavy red table wine. **6.** (*often not cap.*) a blackish-purple to purplish-red colour. —**Bur·gun·di·an** (bɜːˈgʌndɪən) *adj., n.*

bur·hel (ˈbʌrəl) *n.* a variant spelling of **bharal.**

bur·i·al (ˈbɛrɪəl) *n.* the act of burying, esp. the interment of a dead body. [Old English *byrgels* burial place, tomb; see BURY, -AL[2]]

bur·i·al ground *n.* a graveyard or cemetery.

bur·i·er (ˈbɛrɪə) *n.* a person or thing that buries.

bu·rin (ˈbjʊərɪn) *n.* **1.** a chisel of tempered steel with a sharp lozenge-shaped point, used for engraving furrows in metal, wood, or marble. **2.** an engraver's individual style. **3.** *Archaeol.* a prehistoric flint tool with a very small transverse edge. [C17: from French, perhaps from Italian *burino,* of Germanic origin: compare Old High German *boro* auger; see BORE[1]]

burk *or* **berk** (bɜːk) *n. Brit. slang.* a stupid person; fool. [C20: shortened from *Berkeley* or *Berkshire Hunt,* rhyming slang for *cunt*]

bur·ka (ˈbɜːkə) *n.* a long enveloping garment worn by Muslim women in public. [C19: from Arabic]

burke (bɜːk) *vb.* (*tr.*) **1.** to murder in such a way as to leave no marks on the body, usually by suffocation. **2.** to get rid of, silence, or suppress. [C19: named after W. *Burke* (1792–1829), Irishman executed in Edinburgh for a murder of this type]

Burke (bɜːk) *n.* **1. Ed·mund.** 1729–97, British Whig statesman, conservative political theorist, and orator: defended parliamentary government and campaigned for a more liberal treatment of the American colonies. **2. Rob·ert O'Ha·ra.** 1820-61, Irish explorer, who led the first expedition (1860-61) across Australia from South to North. He was accompanied by W. J. Wills, George Grey, and John King; King alone survived the return journey.

burl[1] (bɜːl) *n.* **1.** a small knot or lump in wool. **2.** a roundish warty outgrowth from the trunk, roots, or branches of certain trees. ~*vb.* **3.** (*tr.*) to remove the burls from (cloth). [C15: from Old French *burle* tuft of wool, probably ultimately from Late Latin *burra* shaggy cloth] —**ˈburl·er** *n.*

burl[2] *or* **birl** (bɜːl) *n. Austral. informal.* an attempt; try (esp. in the phrase **give it a burl**). [C20: perhaps from BIRL in northern English dialect sense: a twist or turn]

bur·lap (ˈbɜːlæp) *n.* a coarse fabric woven from jute, hemp, or the like. [C17: from *borel* coarse cloth, from Old French *burel* (see BUREAU) + LAP[1]]

Bur·leigh (ˈbɜːlɪ) *n.* a variant spelling of **Burghley.**

bur·lesque *or* **bur·lesk** (bɜːˈlɛsk) *n.* **1.** an artistic work, esp. literary or dramatic, satirizing a subject by caricaturing it. **2.** a ludicrous imitation or caricature. **3.** a play of the 17th–19th centuries that parodied some contemporary dramatic fashion or event. **4.** *U.S. theatre.* a bawdy comedy show of the late 19th and early 20th centuries: the striptease eventually became one of its chief elements. Slang name: **burleycue.** ~*adj.* **5.** of, relating to, or characteristic of a burlesque. ~*vb.* **·lesques, ·lesqu·ing, ·lesqued** *or* **·lesks, ·lesk·ing, ·lesked. 6.** to represent or imitate (a person or thing) in a ludicrous way; caricature. [C17: from French, from Italian *burlesco,* from *burla* a jest, piece of nonsense] —**bur·ˈles·quer** *or* **bur·ˈlesk·er** *n.*

bur·ley (ˈbɜːlɪ) *n.* a light thin-leaved tobacco, grown esp. in Kentucky. [C19: probably from the name *Burley*]

Bur·ling·ton (ˈbɜːlɪŋtən) *n.* **1.** a city in S Canada on Lake Ontario, northeast of Hamilton. Pop.: 87 023 (1971). **2.** a city in NW Vermont on Lake Champlain: largest city in the state; University of Vermont (1791). Pop.: 38 633 (1970).

bur·ly (ˈbɜːlɪ) *adj.,* **·li·er, ·li·est.** large and thick of build; sturdy; stout. [C13: of Germanic origin; compare Old High German *burlīh* lofty] —**ˈbur·li·ness** *n.*

Bur·ma (ˈbɜːmə) *n.* a republic in SE Asia, on the Bay of Bengal and the Andaman Sea: unified from small states in 1752; annexed by Britain (1823–85) and made a province of India in 1886; became independent in 1948. It is generally mountainous, with the basins of the Chindwin and Irrawaddy Rivers in the central part and the Irrawaddy delta in the south. Language: Burmese. Religion: chiefly Buddhist. Currency: kyat. Capital: Rangoon. Pop.: 28 885 867 (1972). Area: 678 000 sq. km (261 789 sq. miles). Official name: **Socialist Republic of the Union of Burma.**

bur mar·i·gold *n.* any plant of the genus *Bidens* that has yellow flowers and pointed fruits that cling to fur and clothing: family *Compositae* (composites). Also called: **beggar-ticks, sticktight.**

Bur·ma Road *n.* the route extending from Lashio in Burma to Chungking in China, which was used by the Allies during World War II to supply military equipment to Chiang Kai-shek's forces in China.

Bur·mese (bɜːˈmiːz) *adj. also* **Bur·man. 1.** of, relating to, or characteristic of Burma, its people, or their language. ~*n., pl.* **·mese. 2.** a native or inhabitant of Burma. **3.** the official language of Burma, belonging to the Sino-Tibetan family.

Bur·mese cat *n.* a breed of cat similar in shape to the Siamese but having a dark brown or blue-grey coat.

burn[1] (bɜːn) *vb.* **burns, burn·ing, burnt** *or* **burned. 1.** to undergo or cause to undergo combustion. **2.** to destroy or be destroyed by fire. **3.** (*tr.*) to damage, injure, or mark by heat: *he burnt his hand; she was burnt by the sun.* **4.** to die or put to death by fire: *to burn at the stake.* **5.** (*intr.*) to be or feel hot: *my forehead burns.* **6.** to smart or cause to smart: *brandy burns one's throat.* **7.** (*intr.*) to feel strong emotion, esp. anger or passion. **8.** (*tr.*) to use for the purposes of light, heat, or power: *to burn coal.* **9.** (*tr.*) to form by or as if by fire: *to burn a hole.* **10.** to char or become charred: *the potatoes are burning in the saucepan.* **11.** (*tr.*) to brand or cauterize. **12.** to produce by or subject to heat as part of a process: *to burn charcoal.* **13.** *Card games, chiefly Brit.* to discard or exchange (one or more useless cards). **14.** (*tr.; usually passive*) *Informal.* to cheat, esp. financially. **15.** *Slang, chiefly U.S.* to electrocute or be electrocuted. **16. burn one's boats** *or* **bridges.** *Informal.* to proceed in such a way as to eliminate all alternative courses of action. **17. burn the candle at both ends.** *Informal.* to overwork or take on too much. **18. burn one's fingers.** *Informal.* to suffer from having meddled or interfered. ~*n.* **19.** an injury caused by exposure to heat, electrical, chemical, or radioactive agents. Burns are classified according to the depth of tissue affected: **first-degree burn:** skin surface painful and red; **second-degree burn:** blisters appear on the skin; **third-degree burn:** destruction of both epidermis and dermis. **20.** a mark, e.g. on wood, caused by burning. **21.** a controlled use of rocket propellant, esp. for a course correction. **22.** *Slang.* tobacco or a cigarette. ~See also **burn in, burn off, burn out.** [Old English *beornan* (intr.), *bærnan* (tr.); related to Old Norse *brenna* (tr. or intr.), Gothic *brinnan* (intr.), Latin *fervēre* to boil, seethe]

burn[2] (bɜːn) *n. Northern Brit.* a small stream; brook. [Old English *burna;* related to Old Norse *brunnr* spring, Old High German *brunno,* Lithuanian *briáutis* to burst forth]

burned (bɜːnd) *adj. Slang.* **1.** having been cheated in a sale of drugs. **2. a.** revealed as a drug-peddler by a police informer. **b.** revealed to drug-users as a police informer.

burned out *adj. Slang.* recovered from dependence on drugs.

Burne-Jones (ˈbɜːn ˈdʒəʊnz) *n.* Sir **Ed·ward.** 1833–98, English Pre-Raphaelite painter and designer of stained-glass windows and tapestries.

burn·er (ˈbɜːnə) *n.* **1.** the part of a stove, lamp, etc., that produces flame or heat. **2.** an apparatus for burning something, as fuel or refuse: *an oil burner.*

bur·net (ˈbɜːnɪt) *n.* **1.** a plant of the rosaceous genus *Sanguisorba* (or *Poterium*), such as *S. minor* (or *P. sanguisorba*) **(salad burnet),** which has purple-tinged green flowers and leaves that are sometimes used for salads. **2. burnet rose.** Also called: **Scotch rose.** a very prickly Eurasian rose, *Rosa pimpinellifolia,* with white flowers and purplish-black fruits. **3. burnet saxifrage.** a Eurasian umbelliferous plant of the genus *Pimpinella,* having umbrella-like clusters of white or pink flowers. **4.** a moth of the genus *Zygaena,* having red-spotted dark green wings and antennae with enlarged tips: family *Zygaenidae.* [C14: from Old French *burnete,* variant of *brunete* dark brown (see BRUNETTE); so-called from the colour of the flowers of some of the plants]

Bur·net (bəˈnɛt, ˈbɜːnɪt) *n.* Sir **Mac·far·lane** (məkˈfɑːlən). born 1899, Australian physician and virologist, who shared a Nobel prize for medicine and physiology in 1960 with P. B. Medawar for their work in immunology.

Bur·nett (bɜːˈnɛt) *n.* **Fran·ces Hodg·son** (ˈhɒdʒsən). 1849–1924, U.S. novelist, born in England; author of *Little Lord Fauntleroy* (1886).

Bur·ney (ˈbɜːnɪ) *n.* **1. Charles.** 1726–1814, English composer and music historian, whose books include *A General History of Music* (1776–89). **2. Fran·ces.** called *Fanny;* married name *Madame D'Arblay.* 1752–1840, English novelist and diarist: author of *Evelina* (1778). Her *Diaries and Letters* (1768–1840) are of historical interest.

Burn·ham scale (ˈbɜːnəm) *n.* the salary scale for teachers in English state schools, which is revised periodically. [C20: named after Lord *Burnham* (1862–1933), chairman of the committee that originally set it up]

burn in *vb.* (*tr., adv.*) to darken (areas on a photographic print) by exposing them to light while masking other regions.

burn·ing (ˈbɜːnɪŋ) *adj.* **1.** intense; passionate. **2.** urgent; crucial: *a burning problem.* ~*n.* **3.** a form of heat treatment used to harden and finish ceramic materials or to prepare certain ores for further treatment by calcination. **4.** overheating of an alloy during heat treatment in which local fusion or excessive oxide formation and penetration occur, weakening the alloy. —**ˈburn·ing·ly** *adv.*

burn·ing bush *n.* **1.** any of several shrubs or trees, esp. the wahoo, that have bright red fruits or seeds. **2.** another name for **gas plant. 3.** any of several plants, esp. the summer cypress, with a bright red autumn foliage. **4.** *Old Testament.* the bush that burned without being consumed, from which God spoke to Moses (Exodus 3:2–4).

burn·ing glass *n.* a convex lens for concentrating the sun's rays into a small area to produce heat or fire.

bur·nish ('bɜːnɪʃ) *vb.* **1.** to make or become shiny or smooth by friction; polish. ~*n.* **2.** a shiny finish; lustre. [C14 *burnischen*, from Old French *brunir* to make brown, from *brun* BROWN] —'**burn·ish·a·ble** *adj.* —'**burn·ish·er** *n.*

Burn·ley ('bɜːnlɪ) *n.* an industrial town in NW England, in E Lancashire. Pop.: 76 483 (1971).

burn off *vb.* (*tr., adv.*) **1.** to clear (land) of vegetation by burning. ~*n.* **burn-off. 2.** an act or the process of burning land off.

bur·noose, bur·nous, *or* **bur·nouse** (bɜː'nuːs, -'nuːz) *n.* a long circular cloak with a hood attached, worn esp. by Arabs. [C20: via French *burnous* from Arabic *burnus,* from Greek *birros* cloak] —**bur·'noosed** *or* **bur·'noused** *adj.*

burn out *vb.* (*adv.*) **1.** to become or cause to become worn out or inoperative as a result of heat or friction: *the clutch burnt out.* **2.** (*intr.*) (of a rocket, jet engine, etc.) to cease functioning as a result of exhaustion of the fuel supply. **3.** (*tr.; usually passive*) to destroy by fire. **4.** to become or cause to become exhausted through overwork or dissipation. ~*n.* **burn·out. 5.** the failure of a mechanical device from excessive heating.

Burns (bɜːnz) *n.* **Rob·ert.** 1759–96, Scottish lyric poet. His verse, written mostly in dialect, includes love songs, nature poetry, and satires, of which *Auld Lang Syne* and *Tam o' Shanter* are among the best known.

burn·sides ('bɜːnˌsaɪdz) *pl. n. U.S.* thick side whiskers worn with a moustache and clean-shaven chin. [C19: named after General A. E. *Burnside* (1824–81), Union general in the U.S. Civil War]

burnt (bɜːnt) *vb.* **1.** a past tense or past participle of **burn**[1]. ~*adj.* **2.** affected by or as if by burning; charred. **3.** (of various pigments, such as ochre and orange) calcined, with a resultant darkening of colour.

burnt al·mond *n.* a sweet consisting of an almond enclosed in burnt sugar.

burnt of·fer·ing *n.* a sacrificial offering burnt, usually on an altar, to honour, propitiate, or supplicate a deity.

burnt si·en·na *n.* **1.** a reddish-brown dye or pigment obtained by roasting raw sienna in a furnace. **2.** a dark reddish-orange to reddish-brown colour.

burnt um·ber *n.* **1.** a brown pigment obtained by heating umber. **2.** a dark brown colour.

burn-up *n. Slang.* a period of fast driving.

bur oak *n.* an E North American oak, *Quercus macrocarpa,* having fringed acorn cups and durable timber.

bu·roo (bəˈruː) *n., pl.* **·roos.** *Scot. and Irish dialect.* **1.** the government office from which unemployment benefit is distributed. **2.** the unemployment benefit itself (esp. in the phrase **on the buroo**). [C20: from BUREAU]

burp (bɜːp) *n.* **1.** *Informal.* a belch. ~*vb.* **2.** (*intr.*) *Informal.* to belch. **3.** (*tr.*) to cause (a baby) to burp to relieve flatulence after feeding. [C20: of imitative origin]

burp gun *n. U.S. slang.* an automatic pistol or submachine gun.

burr[1] (bɜː) *n.* **1.** a small power-driven hand-operated rotary file, esp. for removing burrs or for machining recesses. **2.** a rough edge left on a workpiece after cutting, drilling, etc. **3.** a rough or irregular protuberance, such as a burl on a tree. **4.** *Brit.* **a.** a burl on the trunk or root of a tree, sliced across for use as decorative veneer. **b.** (*as modifier*): *burr walnut.* ~*n., vb.* **5.** a variant spelling of **bur.** ~*vb.* (*tr.*) **6.** to form a rough edge on (a workpiece). **7.** to remove burrs from (a workpiece); deburr. [C14: variant of BUR]

burr[2] (bɜː) *n.* **1.** *Phonetics.* an articulation of (r) characteristic of certain English dialects, esp. the uvular fricative trill of Northumberland or the retroflex *r* of the West of England. **2.** a whirring sound. ~*vb.* **3.** to pronounce (words) with a burr. **4.** to make a whirring sound. [C18: either special use of BUR (in the sense: rough sound) or of imitative origin]

burr[3] *or* **bur** (bɜː) *n.* **1.** a washer fitting around the end of a rivet. **2.** a blank punched out of sheet metal. [C16 (in the sense: broad ring on a spear): variant of *burrow* (in obsolete sense: BOROUGH)]

burr[4], **buhr,** *or* **bur** (bɜː) *n.* **1.** short for **buhrstone. 2.** a mass of hard siliceous rock surrounded by softer rock. [C18: probably from BUR, from its qualities of roughness]

bur·ra·wang ('bʌrəwæŋ) *n.* any of several Australian cycads of the genus *Macrozamia,* having an edible nut. [C19: from Mount *Budawang,* New South Wales]

bur reed *n.* a marsh plant of the genus *Sparganium,* having narrow leaves, round clusters of small green flowers, and round prickly fruit: family *Sparganiaceae.*

bur·ro ('bʊrəʊ) *n., pl.* **·ros.** a donkey, esp. one used as a pack animal. [Spanish, from Portuguese, from *burrico* donkey, ultimately from Latin *burrīcus* small horse]

Bur·roughs ('bʌrəʊz) *n.* **1. Ed·gar Rice.** 1875–1950, U.S. novelist, author of the *Tarzan* stories. **2. Wil·liam.** born 1914, U.S. novelist, noted for his works portraying the life of drug addicts, esp. *The Naked Lunch* (1959), and his science fiction, including *The Ticket that Exploded* (1962) and *Nova Express* (1964).

bur·row ('bʌrəʊ) *n.* **1.** a hole or tunnel dug in the ground by a rabbit, fox, or other small animal, for habitation or shelter. **2.** a small snug place affording shelter or retreat. ~*vb.* **3.** to dig (a burrow) in, through, or under (ground). **4.** (*intr.; often foll. by through*) to move through by or as by digging: *to burrow through the forest.* **5.** (*intr.*) to hide or live in a burrow. **6.** (*intr.*) to delve deeply: *he burrowed into his pockets.* **7.** to hide (oneself). [C13: probably a variant of BOROUGH] —'**bur·row·er** *n.*

burr·stone ('bɜːˌstəʊn) *n.* a variant spelling of **buhrstone.**

bur·ry ('bɜːrɪ) *adj.* **·ri·er, ·ri·est. 1.** full of or covered in burs. **2.** resembling burs; prickly.

bur·sa ('bɜːsə) *n., pl.* **·sae** (-siː) *or* **·sas.** a small fluid-filled sac that reduces friction between movable parts of the body, esp. at joints. [C19: from Medieval Latin: bag, pouch, from Greek: skin, hide; see PURSE] —'**bur·sal** *adj.*

Bur·sa ('bɜːsə) *n.* a city in NW Turkey: founded in the 2nd century B.C.; seat of Bithynian kings. Pop.: 346 103 (1975). Former name: **Brusa.**

bur·sar ('bɜːsə) *n.* **1.** an official in charge of the financial management of a school, college, or university. **2.** *Scot.* a student holding a bursary. [C13: from Medieval Latin *bursārius* keeper of the purse, from *bursa* purse]

bur·sar·i·al (bɜː'sɛərɪəl) *adj.* of, relating to, or paid by a bursar or bursary.

bur·sa·ry ('bɜːsərɪ) *n., pl.* **·ries. 1.** Also called: '**bur·sar·ˌship.** a scholarship or grant awarded in Scottish schools and universities. **2.** *Brit.* the treasury of a college, etc. **3.** *Brit.* the bursar's room in a college.

Bur·schen·schaft *German.* ('bʊrʃənˌʃaft) *n.* a students' fraternity, originally one concerned with Christian ideals, patriotism, etc. [literally: youth association]

burse (bɜːs) *n.* **1.** *Chiefly R.C. Church.* a flat case used at Mass as a container for the corporal. **2.** *Scot.* **a.** a fund providing allowances for students. **b.** the allowance provided. [C19: from Medieval Latin *bursa* purse]

bur·ser·a·ceous (ˌbɜːsə'reɪʃəs) *adj.* of, relating to, or belonging to the *Burseraceae,* a tropical family of trees and shrubs having compound leaves and resin or balsam in their stems. The family includes bdellium and some balsams. [C19: from New Latin *Bursera* type genus, named after J. *Burser* (1593–1649), German botanist]

bur·si·form ('bɜːsɪˌfɔːm) *adj.* shaped like a pouch or sac. [C19: from Latin *bursa* bag + -FORM]

bur·si·tis (bɜː'saɪtɪs) *n.* inflammation of a bursa, esp. one in the shoulder joint.

burst (bɜːst) *vb.* **bursts, burst·ing, burst. 1.** to break or cause to break open or apart suddenly and noisily, esp. from internal pressure; explode. **2.** (*intr.*) to come, go, etc., suddenly and forcibly: *he burst into the room.* **3.** (*intr.*) to be full to the point of breaking open. **4.** (*intr.*) to give vent (to) suddenly or loudly: *to burst into song.* **5.** to cause or suffer the rupture of: *to burst a blood vessel.* ~*n.* **6.** a sudden breaking open or apart; explosion. **7.** a break; breach; rupture. **8.** a sudden display or increase of effort or action; spurt: *a burst of speed.* **9.** a sudden and violent emission, occurrence, or outbreak: *a burst of heavy rain; a burst of applause.* **10.** a volley of fire from a weapon or weapons. [Old English *berstan;* related to Old Norse *bresta,* Old Frisian *bersta,* Old High German *brestan;* compare BREAK] —'**burst·er** *n.*

bur·stone ('bɜːˌstəʊn) *n.* a variant spelling of **buhrstone.**

bur·then ('bɜːðən) *n., vb.* an archaic word for **burden**[1]. —'**bur·then·some** *adj.*

bur·ton ('bɜːtᵊn) *n.* **1.** *Nautical.* a kind of light hoisting tackle. **2. go for a burton.** *Brit. slang.* **a.** to be broken, useless, or lost. **b.** to die. [C15: of uncertain origin]

Bur·ton ('bɜːtᵊn) *n.* **1.** Sir **Rich·ard Fran·cis.** 1821–90, English explorer, Orientalist, and writer who discovered Lake Tanganyika with John Speke (1858); produced the first unabridged translation of *The Thousand Nights and a Night* (1885–88). **2. Rich·ard (Jenkins).** born 1925, British stage and film actor: films include *Becket* (1964), *Who's Afraid of Virginia Woolf?* (1966), and *Equus* (1977). **3. Rob·ert,** pen name *Democritus Junior.* 1577–1640, English clergyman, scholar, and writer, noted for his *Anatomy of Melancholy* (1621).

Bur·ton-up·on-Trent *n.* a town in W central England, in E Staffordshire: famous for brewing. Pop.: 50 175 (1971).

Bu·run·di (bə'rʊndɪ) *n.* a republic in E central Africa: inhabited chiefly by the Bahutu, Watutsi, and Batwa; made part of German East Africa in 1899; part of the Belgian territory of Ruanda-Urundi from 1923 until it became independent in 1962; consists mainly of high plateaus along the main Nile-Congo dividing range, dropping rapidly to the Great Rift Valley in the west. Languages: Kirundi and French. Currency: Burundi franc. Capital: Bujumbura. Pop.: 3 350 000 (1971). Area: 27 731 sq. km (10 707 sq. miles). Former name (until 1962): **Urundi.**

bur·weed ('bɜːˌwiːd) *n.* any of various plants that bear burs, such as the burdock.

bur·y ('bɛrɪ) *vb.* **bur·ies, bur·y·ing, bur·ied.** (*tr.*) **1.** to place (a corpse) in a grave, usually with funeral rites; inter. **2.** to place in the earth and cover with soil. **3.** to lose through death. **4.** to cover from sight; hide. **5.** to embed; sink: *to bury a nail in plaster.* **6.** to occupy (oneself) with deep concentration; engross: *to be buried in a book.* **7.** to dismiss from the mind; abandon: *to bury old hatreds.* **8. bury the hatchet.** to cease hostilities and become reconciled. **9. bury one's head in the sand.** to refuse to face a problem. [Old English *byrgan* to bury, hide; related to Old Norse *bjarga* to save, preserve, Old English *beorgan* to defend] —'**bur·i·er** *n.*

Bur·y ('bɛrɪ) *n.* a town in NW England, part of Greater Manchester: an early textile centre. Pop.: 67 776 (1971).

Bur·yat *or* **Bur·iat** (bʊə'jɑːt, bʊərɪ'ɑːt) *n.* **1.** a member of a Mongoloid people living chiefly in the Buryat ASSR. **2.** the language of this people, belonging to the Mongolic branch of the Altaic family.

Bur+yat Au·ton·o+mous So+vi+et So·cial+ist Re+pub+lic *n.* an administrative division of the SE central Soviet Union, in the RSFSR, on Lake Baikal: mountainous, with forests covering over half the total area. Capital: Ulan-Ude. Pop.: 812 251 (1970). Area: 350 300 sq. km (135 650 sq. miles).

bur·y+ing bee+tle *n.* a beetle of the genus *Necrophorous,* which buries the dead bodies of small animals by excavating beneath them, using the corpses as food for themselves and their larvae: family *Silphidae.* Also called: **sexton.**

Bur·y St. Ed+munds ('bɛrɪ sənt 'ɛdməndz) *n.* a market town in E England, in Suffolk. Pop.: 25 629 (1971).

bus (bʌs) *n., pl.* **bus·es** *or* **bus+ses. 1.** a large motor vehicle designed to carry passengers between stopping places along a regular route. More formal name: **omnibus.** Sometimes called: **motorbus. 2.** short for **trolley bus. 3.** (*modifier*) of or relating to a bus or buses: *a bus driver; a bus station.* **4.** *Informal.* a car or aircraft, esp. one that is old and shaky. **5.** *Electronics, computer technol.* short for **busbar. 6. miss the bus.** to miss an opportunity; be too late. ~*vb.* **bus·es, bus+ing, bused** *or* **bus·ses, bus+sing, bussed. 7.** to travel or transport by bus. **8.** *Chiefly U.S.* to transport (children) by bus from one area to a school in another in order to create racially integrated classes.

bus. *abbrev. for* business.

bus+bar ('bʌz,bɑː) *n.* **1.** an electrical conductor, maintained at a specific voltage and capable of carrying a high current, usually used to make a common connection between several circuits in a system. **2.** a group of such electrical conductors maintained at a low voltage, used for carrying data in binary form between the various parts of a computer or its peripherals. ~Sometimes shortened to **bus.**

bus boy *n. U.S.* a waiter's assistant.

bus+by ('bʌzbɪ) *n., pl.* **+bies. 1.** a tall fur helmet with a bag hanging from the top to the right side, worn by certain soldiers, usually hussars, as in the British Army. **2.** another name for **bearskin** (the hat). [C18 (in the sense: large bushy wig): perhaps from a proper name]

bu+se·ra (bʊ'sɛrə) *n.* **1.** an alcoholic drink of Uganda made from millet: sometimes mixed with honey. **2.** a porridge made out of millet. [from Rukiga, a language of SW Uganda]

bush[1] (bʊʃ) *n.* **1.** a dense woody plant, smaller than a tree, with many branches arising from the lower part of the stem; shrub. **2.** a dense cluster of such shrubs; thicket. **3.** something resembling a bush, esp. in density: *a bush of hair.* **4. a.** (often preceded by *the*) an uncultivated or sparsely settled area, esp. in Africa, Australia, New Zealand, or Canada: usually covered with trees or shrubs. **b.** (*as modifier*): *a bush fire.* **5.** a forested area; woodland. **6.** (often preceded by *the*) *Informal.* the countryside, as opposed to the city: *out in the bush.* **7.** a fox's tail; brush. **8.** *Obsolete.* **a.** a bunch of ivy hung as a vintner's sign in front of a tavern. **b.** any tavern sign. **9. beat about the bush.** to avoid the point at issue; prevaricate. ~*adj.* **10.** *West African informal.* ignorant or stupid, esp. as considered typical of unwesternized rustic life. **11. go bush.** *Informal, chiefly Austral.* **a.** to go off into the bush. **b.** to run wild. ~*vb.* **12.** (*intr.*) to grow thick and bushy. **13.** (*tr.*) to cover, decorate, support, etc., with bushes. [C13: of Germanic origin; compare Old Norse *buski,* Old High German *busc,* Middle Dutch *bosch;* related to Old French *bosc* wood, Italian *bosco*]

bush[2] (bʊʃ) *n.* **1.** Also called (esp. U.S.): **bushing.** a thin metal sleeve or tubular lining serving as a bearing or guide. ~*vb.* **2.** to fit a bush to (a casing, bearing, etc.). [C15: from Middle Dutch *busse* box, bush; related to German *Büchse* tin, Swedish *hjulbössa* wheel-box, Late Latin *buxis* BOX[1]]

Bush (bʊʃ) *n.* **George.** born 1924, U.S. Republican politician; vice president of the U.S. from 1981.

bush+ba·by ('bʊʃ,beɪbɪ) *n., pl.* **+ba·bies.** any agile nocturnal arboreal prosimian primate of the genera *Galago* and *Euoticus,* occurring in Africa south of the Sahara: family *Lorisidae* (lorises). They have large eyes and ears and a long tail. Also called: **galago.**

bush+buck ('bʊʃ,bʌk) *or* **bosch+bok** *n., pl.* **+bucks, +buck** *or* **+boks, +bok.** a small nocturnal spiral-horned antelope, *Tragelaphus scriptus,* of the bush and tropical forest of Africa. Its coat is reddish-brown with a few white markings.

bush+craft ('bʊʃ,krɑːft) *n. Chiefly Austral.* ability and experience in matters concerned with living in the bush.

bushed (bʊʃt) *adj. Informal.* **1.** (*postpositive*) *U.S. and Canadian.* extremely tired; exhausted. **2.** *Canadian.* mentally disturbed from living in isolation, esp. in the north. **3.** *Austral.* lost or bewildered, as in the bush.

bush+el[1] ('bʊʃəl) *n.* **1.** a Brit. unit of dry or liquid measure equal to 8 Imperial gallons. 1 Imperial bushel is equivalent to 0.036 37 cubic metres. **2.** a U.S. unit of dry measure equal to 64 U.S. pints. 1 U.S. bushel is equivalent to 0.035 24 cubic metres. **3.** a container with a capacity equal to either of these quantities. **4.** *Informal.* a large amount; great deal. **5. hide one's light under a bushel.** to conceal one's abilities or good qualities. [C14: from Old French *boissel,* from *boisse* one sixth of a bushel, of Gaulish origin]

bush+el[2] ('bʊʃəl) *vb.* **+els, +el+ling, +elled** *or U.S.* **+els, +el+ing, +eled.** (*tr.*) *U.S.* to alter or mend (a garment). [C19: probably from German *bosseln* to do inferior work, patch, from Middle High German *bōzeln* to beat, from Old High German *bōzan*] —**'bush+el+ler** *or* **'bush+el+man** *n.*

bush+ham·mer ('bʊʃ,hæmə) *n.* a hammer with small pyramids projecting from its working face, used for dressing stone. [C19: from German *Bosshammer,* from *bossen* to beat + HAMMER]

bush house *n. Chiefly Austral.* a shed or hut in the bush or a garden.

Bu+shi+do (,buːʃɪ'dəʊ) *n.* (*sometimes not cap.*) the feudal code of the Japanese samurai, stressing self-discipline, courage and loyalty. [C19: from Japanese *bushi* warrior (from Chinese *wushih*) + *dō* way (from Chinese *tao*)]

bush·ie ('bʊʃɪ) *n.* a variant spelling of **bushy**[2].

bush+ing ('bʊʃɪŋ) *n.* **1.** another word for **bush**[2] (sense 1). **2.** an adapter having ends of unequal diameters, often with internal screw threads, used to connect pipes of different sizes. **3.** a layer of electrical insulation enabling a live conductor to pass through an earthed wall, etc.

Bu+shire (bjuː'ʃaɪə) *n.* a port in SW Iran, on the Persian Gulf. Pop.: 23 547 (1966). Persian name: **Bu+shehr** (buː'ʃɛr).

bush jack+et *or* **shirt** *n.* a casual jacket or shirt having four patch pockets and a belt.

bush law+yer *n. Austral. informal.* a person who gives legal opinions but is not qualified to do so.

bush+man ('bʊʃmən) *n., pl.* **+men.** *Austral.* a person who lives or travels in the bush, esp. one versed in bush lore.

Bush+man ('bʊʃmən) *n., pl.* **+man** *or* **+men. 1.** a member of a hunting and gathering people of southern Africa, esp. the Kalahari region, typically having leathery yellowish skin, short stature, and prominent buttocks. **2.** any language of this people, belonging to the Khoisan family. [C18: from Afrikaans *boschjesman*]

bush+mas·ter ('bʊʃ,mɑːstə) *n.* a large greyish-brown highly venomous snake, *Lachesis muta,* inhabiting wooded regions of tropical America: family *Crotalidae* (pit vipers).

bush oys+ter *n. Austral., euphemistic.* a bull's testicle when cooked and eaten.

bush+pig ('bʊʃ,pɪg) *n.* a wild pig, *Potamochoerus porcus,* inhabiting forests in tropical Africa and Madagascar. It is brown or black, with pale markings on the face. Also called: **boschvark.**

bush+rang·er ('bʊʃ,reɪndʒə) *n.* **1.** *Austral.* an escaped convict or robber living in the bush. **2.** *U.S.* a person who lives away from civilization; backwoodsman.

bush shrike *n.* **1.** any shrike of the African subfamily *Malaconotinae,* such as *Chlorophoneus nigrifrons* (**black-fronted bush shrike**). **2.** another name for **ant bird.**

bush tea *n.* **1.** a leguminous shrub of the genus *Cyclopia,* of southern Africa. **2.** a beverage prepared from the dried leaves of any of these plants.

bush tel·e+graph *n.* **1.** a means of communication between primitive peoples over large areas, as by drum beats. **2.** *Informal.* a means of spreading rumour, gossip, etc.

bush+tit ('bʊʃ,tɪt) *n.* any small grey active North American songbird of the genus *Psaltriparus,* such as *P. minimus* (**common bushtit**): family *Paridae* (titmice).

Bush+veld ('bʊʃ,fɛlt, -,vɛlt) *n.* **the.** an area of low altitude in the NE Transvaal, South Africa, having scrub vegetation. Also called: **Lowveld.**

bush+walk+ing *n. Austral.* an expedition on foot in the bush.

bush+whack ('bʊʃ,wæk) *vb. U.S.* **1.** (*tr.*) to ambush. **2.** (*intr.*) to cut or beat one's way through thick woods. **3.** (*intr.*) *Also Austral.* to range or move around in woods or the bush. **4.** (*intr.*) to fight as a guerrilla in wild or uncivilized regions.

bush+whack·er ('bʊʃ,wækə) *n.* **1.** *U.S., Austral.* a person who travels around or lives in thinly populated woodlands. **2.** *Austral. slang.* an unsophisticated person; boor. **3.** a Confederate guerrilla during the American Civil War. **4.** *U.S.* any guerrilla.

bush wren *n.* a wren, *Xenicus longipes,* occurring in New Zealand: family *Xenicidae.* See also **rifleman** (sense 2).

bush·y[1] ('bʊʃɪ) *adj.* **bush·i·er, bush·i·est. 1.** covered or overgrown with bushes. **2.** thick and shaggy: *bushy eyebrows.* —**'bush·i·ly** *adv.* —**'bush·i·ness** *n.*

bush·y[2] *or* **bush·ie** ('bʊʃɪ) *n., pl.* **bush·ies.** *Austral. informal.* **1.** a person who lives in the bush. **2.** an unsophisticated uncouth person.

bus·i+ly ('bɪzɪlɪ) *adv.* in a busy manner; industriously.

busi+ness ('bɪznɪs) *n.* **1.** trade or profession. **2.** industrial, commercial, or professional operation; purchase and sale of goods and services: *the tailoring business.* **3.** a commercial or industrial establishment, such as a firm or factory. **4.** volume or quantity of commercial activity: *business is poor today.* **5.** commercial policy or procedure: *overcharging is bad business.* **6.** proper or rightful concern or responsibility (often in the phrase **mind one's own business**). **7.** a special task; assignment. **8.** an affair; matter. **9.** serious work or activity: *get down to business.* **10.** *Informal.* a vaguely defined collection or area: *jets, fast cars, and all that business.* **11.** Also called: **stage business.** *Theatre.* an incidental action, such as lighting a pipe, performed by an actor for dramatic effect. **12. mean business.** to be in earnest. **13.** a euphemistic word for **defecation** (esp. in the phrase **do one's business**). **14.** a slang word for **prostitution** (sense 1). [Old English *bisignis* solicitude, attentiveness, from *bisig* BUSY + *-nis* -NESS]

busi+ness col+lege *n.* a college providing courses in secretarial studies, business management, accounting, commerce, etc.

busi+ness cy+cle *n.* another name (esp. U.S.) for **trade cycle.**

busi+ness end *n. Informal.* the part of a tool or weapon that does the work, as contrasted with the handle.

busi·ness+like ('bɪznɪs,laɪk) *adj.* **1.** efficient and methodical. **2.** earnest or severe.

busi·ness+man ('bɪznɪs,mæn, -mən) *or* (*fem.*) **busi·ness+wom·an** *n., pl.* **+men** *or* **+wom·en.** a person engaged in commercial or industrial business, esp. as an owner or executive.

busk[1] (bʌsk) *n.* **1.** a strip of whalebone, wood, steel, etc., inserted into the front of a corset to stiffen it. **2.** *Archaic or dialect.* the corset itself. [C16: from Old French *busc*, probably from Old Italian *busco* splinter, stick, of Germanic origin]

busk[2] (bʌsk) *vb.* (*intr.*) *Brit.* to make money by singing, dancing, acting, etc., in public places, as in front of theatre queues. [C20: of unknown origin] —**'busk·er** *n.*

busk[3] (bʌsk) *vb.* (*tr.*) *Archaic.* **1.** to make ready; prepare. **2.** to dress or adorn. [C14: from Old Norse *būask*, from *būa* to make ready, dwell; see BOWER]

bus·kin ('bʌskɪn) *n.* **1.** (formerly) a sandal-like covering for the foot and leg, reaching the calf and usually laced. **2.** Also called: **cothurnus.** a thick-soled laced half boot resembling this, worn esp. by actors of ancient Greece. **3.** (usually preceded by *the*) *Chiefly literary.* tragic drama. [C16: perhaps from Spanish *borzegui;* related to Old French *bouzequin,* Italian *borzacchino,* of obscure origin]

bus·man's hol·i·day ('bʌsmənz) *n. Informal.* a holiday spent doing the same sort of thing as one does at work. [C20: alluding to a bus driver having a driving holiday]

Bu·so·ni (*Italian* bu'zo:ni) *n.* **Fer·ru·ccio Ben·ve·nu·to** (fer'ruttʃo benve'nu:to). 1866–1924, Italian pianist and composer, esp. of works for piano.

Bus·ra *or* **Bus·rah** ('bʌsrə) *n.* variant spellings of **Basra.**

buss (bʌs) *n., vb.* an archaic or dialect word for **kiss.** [C16: probably of imitative origin; compare French *baiser,* German dialect *Bussi* little kiss]

bus shel·ter *n.* a covered structure at a bus stop providing protection against the weather for people waiting for a bus.

bus stop *n.* a place on a bus route, usually marked by a sign, at which buses stop for passengers to alight and board.

bust[1] (bʌst) *n.* **1.** the chest of a human being, esp. a woman's bosom. **2.** a sculpture of the head, shoulders, and upper chest of a person. [C17: from French *buste,* from Italian *busto* a sculpture, of unknown origin]

bust[2] (bʌst) *Informal.* ~*vb.* **busts, bust·ing, bust·ed** *or* **bust. 1.** to burst or break. **2.** to make or become bankrupt. **3.** (*tr.*) (of the police) to raid, search, or arrest: *the girl was busted for drugs.* **4.** (*tr.*) *U.S.* to demote, esp. in military rank. **5.** (*tr.*) *U.S.* to break or tame (a horse, etc.). **6.** (*tr.*) *Chiefly U.S.* to punch; hit. ~*n.* **7.** a raid, search, or arrest by the police. **8.** *Chiefly U.S.* a punch; hit. **9.** *U.S.* a failure, esp. a financial one; bankruptcy. **10.** a drunken party. ~ *adj.* **11.** broken. **12.** bankrupt. **13. go bust.** to become bankrupt.

bus·tard ('bʌstəd) *n.* any terrestrial bird of the family *Otididae,* inhabiting open regions of the Old World: order *Gruiformes* (cranes, rails, etc.). They have long strong legs, a heavy body, a long neck, and speckled plumage. [C15: from Old French *bistarde,* influenced by Old French *oustarde,* both from Latin *avis tarda* slow bird]

bus·tee *or* **bus·ti** ('bʌsti:) *n.* variant spellings of **basti.**

bust·er ('bʌstə) *n. Slang.* **1.** (in combination) a person or thing destroying something as specified: *dambuster.* **2.** *U.S.* a term of address for a boy or man. **3.** *U.S.* a person who breaks horses. **4.** *U.S.* a spree, esp. a drinking bout. **5.** *Austral.* short for **southerly buster.**

bus·tle[1] ('bʌsᵊl) *vb.* **1.** (when *intr.,* often foll. by *about*) to hurry or cause to hurry with a great show of energy or activity. ~*n.* **2.** energetic and noisy activity. [C16: probably from obsolete *buskle* to make energetic preparation, from dialect *busk,* from Old Norse *būask* to prepare] —**'bus·tler** *n.*

bus·tle[2] ('bʌsᵊl) *n.* a cushion or a metal or whalebone framework worn by women in the late 19th century at the back below the waist in order to expand the skirt. [C18: of unknown origin]

bust-up *Informal.* *n.* **1.** a quarrel, esp. a serious one ending a friendship, etc. **2.** *Brit.* a disturbance or brawl. ~*vb.* **bust up** (*adv.*). **3.** (*intr.*) to quarrel and part. **4.** (*tr.*) to disrupt (a meeting), esp. violently.

bust·y ('bʌstɪ) *adj.* **bust·i·er, bust·i·est.** (of a woman) having a prominent bust.

bu·suu·ti (bu:'su:tɪ) *n.* a long garment with short sleeves and a square neckline, worn by Ugandan women, esp. in S Uganda. [C20: from Luganda]

bus·y ('bɪzɪ) *adj.* **bus·i·er, bus·i·est. 1.** actively or fully engaged; occupied. **2.** crowded with or characterized by activity: *a busy day.* **3.** *Chiefly U.S.* (of a room, telephone line, etc.) in use; engaged. **4.** overcrowded with detail: *a busy painting.* **5.** meddlesome; inquisitive; prying. ~*vb.* **bus·ies, bus·y·ing, bus·ied. 6.** (*tr.*) to make or keep (someone, esp. oneself) busy; occupy. [Old English *bisig;* related to Middle Dutch *besich,* perhaps to Latin *festīnāre* to hurry] —**'bus·i·ly** *adv.* —**'bus·y·ness** *n.*

bus·y·bod·y ('bɪzɪ,bɒdɪ) *n., pl.* **·bod·ies.** a meddlesome, prying, or officious person.

bus·y Liz·zie ('lɪzɪ) *n.* a balsaminaceous plant, *Impatiens balsamina,* that has fast-growing drooping stems and is often grown as a pot plant.

bus·y sig·nal *n.* U.S. equivalent of **engaged tone.**

but[1] (bʌt; *unstressed* bət) *conj.* (*coordinating*) **1.** contrary to expectation: *he cut his knee but didn't cry.* **2.** in contrast; on the contrary: *I like opera but my husband doesn't.* **3.** (*usually used after a negative*) other than: *we can't do anything but wait.* **4.** only: *I can but try.* ~*conj.* (*subordinating*). **5.** (*usually used after a negative*) without it happening or being the case that: *we never go out but it rains.* **6.** (foll. by *that*) except that: *nothing is impossible but that we live forever.* **7.** *Archaic.* if not; unless. ~ *sentence connector.* **8.** *Informal.* used to introduce an exclamation: *my, but you're nice.* ~*prep.* **9.** except; save: *they saved all but one of the pigs.* **10. but for.** were it not for: *but for you, we couldn't have managed.* ~*adv.* **11.** just; merely: *he was but a child.* **12.** *Austral.* though; however: *it's a rainy day; warm, but.* **13. all but.** almost; practically: *he was all but dead when we found him.* ~*n.* **14.** an objection (esp. in the phrase **ifs and buts**). [Old English *būtan* without, outside, except, from *be* BY + *ūtan* OUT; related to Old Saxon *biūtan,* Old High German *biūzan*]

but[2] (bʌt) *n. Scot.* the outer room of a two-roomed cottage: usually the kitchen. Compare **ben**[1] (sense 1). [C18 from *but* (adv.) outside, hence, outer room; see BUT[1]]

bu·ta·di·ene (,bju:tə'daɪi:n) *n.* a colourless easily liquefiable flammable gas that polymerizes readily and is used mainly in the manufacture of synthetic rubbers. Formula: CH_2:CHCH:CH_2. [C20: from BUTA(NE) + DI-[1] + -ENE]

bu·tane ('bju:teɪn, bju:'teɪn) *n.* a colourless flammable gaseous alkane that exists in two isomeric forms, both of which occur in natural gas. The stable isomer, *n*-butane, is used mainly in the manufacture of rubber and fuels (such as Calor Gas). Formula: C_4H_{10}. [C20: from BUT(YL) + -ANE]

bu·ta·nol ('bju:tə,nɒl) *n.* a colourless substance existing in four isomeric forms. The three liquid isomers are used as solvents for resins, lacquers, etc., and in the manufacture of organic compounds. Formula: C_4H_9OH. Also called: **butyl alcohol.**

bu·ta·none ('bju:tə,nəʊn) *n.* a colourless soluble flammable liquid used mainly as a solvent for resins, as a paint remover, and in lacquers, cements, and adhesives. Formula: $CH_3COC_2H_5$. Also called: **methyl ethyl ketone.**

bu·tat (bu'tʊt) *n.* a Gambian monetary unit worth one hundredth of a dalasi.

butch (bʊtʃ) *Slang.* ~*adj.* **1.** (of a woman or man) markedly or aggressively masculine. ~*n.* **2.** a lesbian who is noticeably masculine. **3.** a strong rugged man. [C18: back formation from BUTCHER]

butch·er ('bʊtʃə) *n.* **1.** a retailer of meat. **2.** a person who slaughters or dresses meat for market. **3.** an indiscriminate or brutal murderer. **4.** a person who destroys, ruins, or bungles something. ~*vb.* (*tr.*) **5.** to slaughter or dress (animals) for meat. **6.** to kill indiscriminately or brutally. **7.** to make a mess of; botch; ruin. [C16: from Old French *bouchier,* from *bouc* he-goat, probably of Celtic origin; see BUCK[1]; compare Welsh *bwch* he-goat]

butch·er·bird ('bʊtʃə,bɜ:d) *n.* **1.** a shrike, esp. one of the genus *Lanius.* **2.** any of several Australian magpies of the genus *Cracticus* that impale their prey on thorns.

butch·er's ('bʊtʃəz) *or* **butch·er's hook** *n. Brit. slang.* a look. [C19: rhyming slang]

butch·er's-broom *n.* a liliaceous evergreen shrub, *Ruscus aculeatus,* that has stiff prickle-tipped flattened green stems, which resemble and function as true leaves. The plant was formerly used for making brooms.

butch·er·y ('bʊtʃərɪ) *n., pl.* **·er·ies. 1.** the business or work of a butcher. **2.** wanton and indiscriminate slaughter; carnage. **3.** a less common word for **slaughterhouse.**

Bute[1] (bju:t) *n.* **1.** (until 1975) a county of SW Scotland, now part of Strathclyde region, consisting of islands in the Firth of Clyde and Kilbrannan Sound. **2.** an island off the coast of SW Scotland, in the Firth of Clyde, separated from the Cowal peninsula by the **Kyles of Bute.** Chief town: Rothesay. Pop.: 8455 (1971). Area: 121 sq. km (47 sq. miles).

Bute[2] (bju:t) *n.* **John Stu·art,** 3rd Earl of Bute. 1713–92, British Tory statesman; prime minister (1762–63).

bu·tene ('bju:ti:n) *n.* a pungent colourless gas existing in four isomeric forms, all of which are used in the manufacture of organic compounds. Formula: C_4H_8. Also called: **butylene.** [C20: from BUTYL + -ENE]

bu·tene·di·o·ic ac·id (,bju:ti:ndaɪ'əʊɪk) *n.* either of two geometrical isomers with the formula HOOCCH:CHCOOH. See **fumaric acid, maleic acid.**

but·ler ('bʌtlə) *n.* the male servant of a household in charge of the wines, table, etc.: usually the head servant. [C13: from Old French *bouteillier,* from *bouteille* BOTTLE]

But·ler ('bʌtlə) *n.* **1. Jo·seph.** 1692–1752, English theologian and author. **2. Sam·u·el.** 1612–80, English poet and satirist; author of *Hudibras* (1663–78). **3. Sam·u·el.** 1835–1902, English novelist, noted for his satirical work *Erewhon* (1872) and his autobiographical novel *The Way of All Flesh* (1903).

but·ler·y ('bʌtlərɪ) *n., pl.* **·ler·ies. 1.** a butler's room. **2.** another name for **buttery**[2] (sense 1).

butt[1] (bʌt) *n.* **1.** the thicker or blunt end of something, such as the end of the stock of a rifle. **2.** the unused end of something, esp. of a cigarette; stub. **3.** *Tanning.* the portion of a hide covering the lower backside of the animal. **4.** *U.S. informal.* the buttocks. **5.** *U.S.* a slang word for **cigarette. 6.** *Building.* short for **butt joint** or **butt hinge.** [C15 (in the sense: thick end of something, buttock): related to Old English *buttuc* end, ridge, Middle Dutch *bot* stumpy]

butt[2] (bʌt) *n.* **1.** a person or thing that is the target of ridicule, wit, etc. **2.** *Shooting, archery.* **a.** a mound of earth behind the target on a target range that stops bullets or wide shots. **b.** the target itself. **c.** (*pl.*) the target range. **3.** a low barrier, usually of sods or peat, behind which sportsmen shoot game birds, esp. grouse. **4.** *Archaic.* goal; aim. ~*vb.* **5.** (usually foll. by *on* or *against*) to lie or be placed end on to; abut: *to butt a beam against a wall.* [C14 (in the sense: mark for archery practice): from Old French *but;* related to French *butte* knoll, target]

butt[3] (bʌt) *vb.* **1.** to strike or push (something) with the head or horns. **2.** (*intr.*) to project; jut. **3.** (*intr.;* foll. by *in* or *into*) to intrude, esp. into a conversation; interfere; meddle. ~*n.* **4.** a blow with the head or horns. [C12: from Old French *boter,* of Germanic origin; compare Middle Dutch *botten* to strike; see BEAT, BUTTON] —**'butt·er** *n.*

butt[4] (bʌt) *n.* **1.** a large cask, esp. one with a capacity of two hogsheads, for storing wine or beer. **2.** a U.S. unit of liquid measure equal to 126 U.S. gallons. [C14: from Old French *botte,* from Old Provençal *bota,* from Late Latin *buttis* cask, perhaps from Greek *butinē* chamber pot]

Butt (bʌt) *n.* Dame **Cla·ra.** 1872–1936, English contralto.

butte (bjuːt) *n. Western U.S. and Canadian.* an isolated steep-sided flat-topped hill. [C19: from French, from Old French *bute* mound behind a target, from *but* target; see BUTT[2]]

but·ter (ˈbʌtə) *n.* **1. a.** an edible fatty whitish-yellow solid made from cream by churning, for cooking and table use. **b.** (*as modifier*): *butter icing.* **2.** any substance with a butter-like consistency, such as peanut butter or vegetable butter. **3. look as if butter wouldn't melt in one's mouth.** to look innocent, although probably not so. ~*vb.* (*tr.*) **4.** to put butter on or in. **5.** to flatter. ~See also **butter up.** [Old English *butere,* from Latin *būtyrum,* from Greek *bouturon,* from *bous* cow + *turos* cheese]

but·ter-and-eggs *n.* (*functioning as sing.*) any of various plants, such as toadflax, the flowers of which are of two shades of yellow.

but·ter·ball (ˈbʌtəˌbɔːl) *n.* **1.** another name for **bufflehead. 2.** *Informal.* a chubby or fat person.

but·ter bean *n.* a variety of lima bean that has large pale flat edible seeds and is grown in the southern U.S.

but·ter·bur (ˈbʌtəˌbɜː) *n.* a plant of the Eurasian genus *Petasites* with fragrant whitish or purple flowers, woolly stems, and leaves formerly used to wrap butter: family *Compositae* (composites).

but·ter·cup (ˈbʌtəˌkʌp) *n.* any of various yellow-flowered ranunculaceous plants of the genus *Ranunculus,* such as *R. acris* (meadow buttercup), which is native to Europe but common throughout North America. See also **crowfoot, goldilocks** (sense 2), **spearwort, lesser celandine.**

but·ter·fat (ˈbʌtəˌfæt) *n.* the fatty substance of milk from which butter is made, consisting of a mixture of glycerides, mainly butyrin, olein, and palmitin.

but·ter·fin·gers (ˈbʌtəˌfɪŋgəz) *n. Informal.* a person who drops things inadvertently or fails to catch things. —**ˈbut·ter·ˌfin·gered** *adj.*

but·ter·fish (ˈbʌtəˌfɪʃ) *n., pl.* **·fish** *or* **·fish·es.** an eel-like blennioid food fish, *Pholis gunnellus,* occurring in North Atlantic coastal regions: family *Pholidae* (gunnels). It has a slippery scaleless golden brown skin with a row of black spots along the base of the long dorsal fin.

but·ter·flies (ˈbʌtəˌflaɪz) *pl. n. Informal.* tremors in the stomach region due to nervousness.

but·ter·fly (ˈbʌtəˌflaɪ) *n., pl.* **·flies. 1.** any diurnal insect of the order *Lepidoptera* that has a slender body with clubbed antennae and typically rests with the wings (which are often brightly coloured) closed over the back. Compare **moth. 2.** a person who never settles with one group, interest, or occupation for long. **3.** a swimming stroke in which the arms are plunged forward together in large circular movements. [Old English *buttorflēoge;* the name perhaps is based on a belief that butterflies stole milk and butter]

but·ter·fly bush *n.* another name for **buddleia.**

but·ter·fly fish *n.* any small tropical marine percoid fish of the genera *Chaetodon, Chelmon,* etc., that has a deep flattened brightly coloured body and brush-like teeth: family *Chaetodontidae.* See also **angelfish** (sense 1).

but·ter·fly nut *n.* another name for **wing nut.**

but·ter·fly valve *n.* **1.** a disc that acts as a valve by turning about a diameter, esp. one used as the throttle valve in a carburettor. **2.** a non-return valve consisting of two semicircular plates hinged about a common central spindle.

but·ter·fly weed *n.* a North American asclepiadaceous plant, *Asclepias tuberosa* (or *A. decumbens*), having flat-topped clusters of bright orange flowers. Also called: **orange milkweed, pleurisy root.**

but·ter·ine (ˈbʌtəˌriːn, -rɪn) *n.* an artificial butter made partly from milk.

But·ter·mere (ˈbʌtəˌmɪə) *n.* a lake in NW England, in Cumbria, in the Lake District, southwest of Keswick. Length: 2 km (1.25 miles).

but·ter·milk (ˈbʌtəˌmɪlk) *n.* the sourish liquid remaining after the butter has been separated from milk, often used for making scones and soda bread.

but·ter mus·lin *n.* a fine loosely woven cotton material originally used for wrapping butter.

but·ter·nut (ˈbʌtəˌnʌt) *n.* **1.** a walnut tree, *Juglans cinerea* of E North America. Compare **black walnut. 2.** the oily edible egg-shaped nut of this tree. **3.** the hard brownish-grey wood of this tree. **4.** the bark of this tree or an extract from it, formerly used as a laxative. **5.** a brownish colour or dye. ~Also called: **white walnut.**

but·ter·scotch (ˈbʌtəˌskɒtʃ) *n.* **1.** a kind of hard brittle toffee made with butter, brown sugar, etc. **2. a.** a flavouring made from these ingredients. **b.** (*as modifier*): *butterscotch icing.* [C19: perhaps first made in Scotland]

but·ter up *vb.* (*tr., adv.*) to flatter.

but·ter·wort (ˈbʌtəˌwɜːt) *n.* a plant of the genus *Pinguicula,* esp. *P. vulgaris,* that grows in wet places and has violet-blue spurred flowers and fleshy greasy glandular leaves on which insects are trapped and digested: family *Lentibulariaceae.*

but·ter·y[1] (ˈbʌtərɪ) *adj.* **1.** containing, like, or coated with butter. **2.** *Informal.* grossly or insincerely flattering; obsequious. —**ˈbut·ter·i·ness** *n.*

but·ter·y[2] (ˈbʌtərɪ) *n., pl.* **·ter·ies. 1.** a room for storing foods or wines. **2.** *Brit.* (in some universities) a room in which food is supplied or sold to students. [C14: from Anglo-French *boterie,* from Anglo-Latin *buteria,* probably from *butta* cask, BUTT[4]]

butt hinge *n.* a hinge made of two matching leaves, one recessed into a door and the other into the jamb so that they are in contact when the door is shut. Sometimes shortened to **butt.**

butt joint *n.* a joint between two plates, planks, bars, sections, etc., when they are fastened end to end without overlapping. Sometimes shortened to **butt.**

but·tock (ˈbʌtək) *n.* **1.** either of the two large fleshy masses of thick muscular tissue that form the human rump. See also **gluteus.** Related adj.: **gluteal. 2.** the analogous part in some mammals. [C13: perhaps from Old English *buttuc* round slope, diminutive of *butt* (unattested) strip of land; see BUTT[1], -OCK]

but·ton (ˈbʌtᵊn) *n.* **1.** a disc or knob of plastic, wood, etc., attached to a garment, etc., usually for fastening two surfaces together by passing it through a buttonhole or loop. **2.** a small round object, such as any of various sweets, decorations, or badges. **3.** a small disc that completes an electric circuit when pushed, as one that operates a doorbell or machine. **4.** *Biology.* any rounded knoblike part or organ, such as an unripe mushroom. **5.** *Fencing.* the protective knob fixed to the point of a foil. **6.** a small amount of metal, usually lead, with which gold or silver is fused, thus concentrating it during assaying. **7.** the piece of a weld that pulls out during the destructive testing of spot welds. **8.** *Rowing.* a projection around the loom of an oar that prevents it slipping through the rowlock. **9.** *Brit.* an object of no value (esp. in the phrase **not worth a button). 10.** *Slang.* intellect; mental capacity (in such phrases as **a button short, to have all one's buttons on,** etc.). ~*vb.* **11.** to fasten with a button or buttons. **12.** (*tr.*) to provide with buttons. **13.** (*tr.*) *Fencing.* to hit (an opponent) with the button of one's foil. ~See also **buttons, button up.** [C14: from Old French *boton,* from *boter* to thrust, butt, of Germanic origin; see BUTT[3]] —**ˈbut·ton·er** *n.* —**ˈbut·ton·less** *adj.* —**ˈbut·ton·y** *adj.*

but·ton·ball (ˈbʌtᵊnˌbɔːl) *n. U.S.* an American plane tree, *Platanus occidentalis.* See **plane tree.**

but·ton day *n. Austral.* the usual name for **flag day.**

but·ton·hole (ˈbʌtᵊnˌhəʊl) *n.* **1.** a slit in a garment, etc., through which a button is passed to fasten two surfaces together. **2.** a flower or small bunch of flowers worn pinned to the lapel or in the buttonhole, esp. at weddings, formal dances, etc. U.S. name: **boutonniere.** ~*vb.* (*tr.*) **3.** to detain (a person) in conversation. **4.** to make buttonholes in. **5.** to sew with buttonhole stitch.

but·ton·hole stitch *n.* a reinforcing looped stitch for the edge of material, such as around a buttonhole.

but·ton·hook (ˈbʌtᵊnˌhʊk) *n.* a thin tapering hooked instrument formerly used for pulling buttons through the buttonholes of gloves, shoes, etc.

but·ton·mould (ˈbʌtᵊnˌməʊld) *n.* the small core of plastic, wood, or metal that is the base for buttons covered with fabric, leather, etc.

but·ton quail *n.* any small quail-like terrestrial bird of the genus *Turnix,* such as *T. sylvatica* (striped button quail), occurring in tropical and subtropical regions of the Old World: family *Turnicidae,* order *Gruiformes* (cranes, rails, etc.). Also called: **hemipode.**

but·tons (ˈbʌtᵊnz) *n. Brit. informal.* a page boy.

but·ton tree *or* **but·ton·wood** *n.* a small West Indian tree, *Conocarpus erectus,* with button-like fruits and heavy hard compact wood: family *Combretaceae.*

but·ton up *vb.* (*tr., adv.*) **1.** to fasten (a garment) with a button or buttons. **2.** *Informal.* to conclude (business) satisfactorily. **3. button up one's lip** *or* **mouth.** *Slang.* to be silent.

but·ton·wood (ˈbʌtᵊnˌwʊd) *or* **but·ton tree** *n.* an American plane tree, *Platanus occidentalis.* See **plane tree.**

butt plate *n.* a plate made usually of metal and attached to the butt end of a gunstock.

but·tress (ˈbʌtrɪs) *n.* **1.** Also called: **pier.** a construction, usually of brick or stone, built to support a wall. See also **flying buttress. 2.** any support or prop. **3.** something shaped like a buttress, such as a projection from a mountainside. **4.** either of the two pointed rear parts of a horse's hoof. ~*vb.* (*tr.*) **5.** to support (a wall) with a buttress. **6.** to support or sustain. [C13: from Old French *bouterez,* short for *ars bouterez* thrusting arch, from *bouter* to thrust, BUTT[3]]

but·tress root *n.* a root that supports the trunk of a tree, usually growing from the stem, as in the mangrove.

butt shaft *n.* a blunt-headed unbarbed arrow.

butt weld *n.* a butt joint that is welded.

but·ty[1] (ˈbʌtɪ) *n., pl.* **·ties.** *Chiefly northern English dialect.* a sandwich: *a jam butty.* [C19: from *buttered bread*]

but·ty[2] (ˈbʌtɪ) *n., pl.* **·ties.** *English dialect.* (esp. in mining parlance) a friend or workmate. [C19: perhaps from obsolete *booty* sharing, from BOOT[2], later applied to a middleman in a mine]

Bu·tung (ˈbuːtʊŋ) *n.* an island of Indonesia, southeast of Celebes: hilly and forested. Chief town: Baubau. Area: 4555 sq. km (1759 sq. miles).

bu·tyl (ˈbjuːˌtaɪl, -tɪl) *n.* (*modifier*) of, consisting of, or containing any of four isomeric forms of the group C_4H_9-: *butyl rubber.* [C19: from BUT(YRIC ACID) + -YL]

bu·tyl al·co·hol *n.* another name for **butanol.**

bu·tyl·ene (ˈbjuːtɪˌliːn) *n.* another name for **butene.**

bu·tyr·a·ceous (ˌbjuːtɪˈreɪʃəs) *adj.* of, containing, or resembling butter. [C17: *butyr-*, from Latin *būtyrum* BUTTER + -ACEOUS]

bu+tyr+al+de+hyde (ˌbju:tɪˈrældɪˌhaɪd) *n.* a colourless flammable pungent liquid used in the manufacture of resins. Formula: $CH_3(CH_2)_2CHO$. [C20: from BUTYR(IC ACID) + ALDEHYDE]

bu+tyr+ate (ˈbju:tɪˌreɪt) *n.* any salt or ester of butyric acid, containing the monovalent group C_3H_7COO- or ion $C_3H_7COO^-$.

bu+tyr+ic ac·id (bju:ˈtɪrɪk) *n.* a carboxylic acid existing in two isomeric forms, one of which produces the smell in rancid butter. Its esters are used in flavouring. Formula: $CH_3(CH_2)_2COOH$. [C19 *butyric*, from Latin *būtyrum* BUTTER]

bu+tyr+in (ˈbju:tɪrɪn) *n.* a colourless liquid ester or oil found in butter. It is formed from butyric acid and glycerin. [C20: from BUTYR(IC + GLYCER)IN]

bux+om (ˈbʌksəm) *adj.* **1.** (esp. of a woman) healthily plump, attractive, and vigorous. **2.** (of a woman) full-bosomed. [C12: *buhsum* compliant, pliant, from Old English *būgan* to bend, BOW[1]; related to Middle Dutch *būchsam* pliant, German *biegsam*] —ˈ**bux+om+ly** *adv.* —ˈ**bux+om+ness** *n.*

Bux·te·hu·de (*German* ˌbʊkstəˈhu:də) *n.* **Die·trich** (ˈdi:trɪç). 1637–1707, Danish composer and organist, resident in Germany from 1668, who influenced Bach and Handel.

Bux+ton (ˈbʌkstən) *n.* a town in N England, in NW Derbyshire in the Peak District: thermal springs.

buy (baɪ) *vb.* **buys, buy+ing, bought.** (*mainly tr.*) **1.** to acquire by paying or promising to pay a sum of money or the equivalent; purchase. **2.** to be capable of purchasing: *money can't buy love.* **3.** to acquire by any exchange or sacrifice: *to buy time by equivocation.* **4.** (*intr.*) to act as a buyer. **5.** to bribe or corrupt; hire by or as by bribery. **6.** *Informal, chiefly U.S.* to accept as true, practical, etc. **7.** (*intr.*; foll. by *into*) to purchase shares of (a company): *we bought into General Motors.* **8.** (*tr.*) *Theol.* (esp. of Christ) to ransom or redeem (a Christian or the soul of a Christian). **9. have bought it.** *Slang.* to be killed. ~*n.* **10.** *Informal.* a purchase (often in the phrases **good** or **bad buy**). ~See also **buy in, buy into, buy off, buy out, buy up.** [Old English *bycgan;* related to Old Norse *byggja* to let out, lend, Gothic *bugjan* to buy]

buy+er (ˈbaɪə) *n.* **1.** a person who buys; purchaser; customer. **2.** a person employed to buy merchandise, materials, etc., as for a shop or factory.

buy+ers' mar+ket *n.* a market in which supply exceeds demand and buyers can influence prices.

buy in *vb.* (*adv.*) **1.** (*tr.*) to buy back for the owner (an item in an auction) at or below the reserve price. **2.** (*intr.*) to purchase shares in a company. **3.** (*intr.*) to buy goods or securities on the open market against a defaulting seller, charging this seller with any market differences. **4.** (*tr.*) Also: **buy into.** *Informal.* to pay money to secure a position or place for (someone, esp. oneself) in some organization, esp. a business or club. **5.** to purchase (goods, etc.) in large quantities: *to buy in for the winter.*

buy in·to *vb.* (*intr., prep.*) *Austral.* to get involved in (an argument, fight, etc.).

buy off *vb.* (*tr., adv.*) to pay (a person or group) to drop a charge, end opposition, relinquish a claim, etc.

buy out *vb.* (*tr., adv.*) **1.** to purchase the ownership, controlling interest, shares, etc., of (a company, etc.). **2.** to gain the release of (a person) from the armed forces by payment of money.

Buys Bal+lot's Law (ˈbaɪs bəˈlɒts, ˈbɔɪs) *n.* a law stating that if an observer stands with his back to the wind in the N hemisphere, atmospheric pressure is lower on his left, and vice versa in the S hemisphere. [named after C. H. D. *Buys Ballot,* 19th-century Dutch meteorologist]

buy up *vb.* (*tr., adv.*) **1.** to purchase all, or all that is available, of (something). **2.** *Commerce.* to purchase a controlling interest in (a company, etc.), as by the acquisition of shares.

buzz (bʌz) *n.* **1.** a rapidly vibrating humming sound, as that of a prolonged *z* or of a bee in flight. **2.** a low sound, as of many voices in conversation. **3.** a rumour; report; gossip. **4.** *Informal.* a telephone call: *I'll give you a buzz.* **5.** *U.S. slang.* a pleasant sensation, as from a drug such as cannabis. ~*vb.* **6.** (*intr.*) to make a vibrating sound like that of a prolonged *z.* **7.** (*intr.*) to talk or gossip with an air of excitement or urgency: *the town buzzed with the news.* **8.** (*tr.*) to utter or spread (a rumour). **9.** (*intr.*; often foll. by *about*) to move around quickly and busily; bustle. **10.** (*tr.*) to signal or summon with a buzzer. **11.** (*tr.*) *Informal.* to call by telephone. **12.** (*tr.*) *Informal.* **a.** to fly an aircraft very low over (an object): *to buzz a ship.* **b.** to fly an aircraft very close to or across the path of (another aircraft), esp. to warn or intimidate. **13.** (*tr.*) (esp. of insects) to make a buzzing sound with (wings, etc.). [C16: of imitative origin]

buz+zard (ˈbʌzəd) *n.* **1.** any diurnal bird of prey of the genus *Buteo,* typically having broad wings and tail and a soaring flight: family *Accipitridae* (hawks, etc.). Compare **turkey buzzard. 2. honey buzzard.** any of various similar related birds, esp. the Eurasian *Pernis apivorus,* which feeds on grubs and honey from bees' nests. **3.** a mean or cantankerous person. [C13: from Old French *buisard,* variant of *buison* buzzard, from Latin *būteō* hawk, falcon]

buzz bomb *n.* another name for the **V-1.**

buzz+er (ˈbʌzə) *n.* **1.** a person or thing that buzzes. **2.** a device that produces a buzzing sound, esp. one similar to an electric bell without a hammer or gong.

buzz off *vb.* (*intr., adv.; often imperative*) *Informal, chiefly Brit.* to go away; leave; depart.

buzz saw *n. U.S.* a power-operated circular saw.

B.V. *abbrev. for:* **1.** Beata Virgo. [Latin: Blessed Virgin] **2.** bene vale. [Latin: farewell]

B.V.M. *abbrev. for* Beata Virgo Maria. [Latin: Blessed Virgin Mary]

B/W *Photog. abbrev. for* black and white.

bwa+na (ˈbwɑ:nə) *n.* (in E Africa) a master, often used as a respectful form of address corresponding to *sir.* [Swahili, from Arabic *abūna* our father]

B.W.G. *abbrev. for* Birmingham Wire Gauge: a notation for the diameters of metal rods, ranging from 0 (0.340 inch) to 36 (0.004 inch).

BWR *abbrev. for* boiling-water reactor.

BWV (*preceding a number*) *Music. abbrev. for* Bach Werke-Verzeichnis: indicating the serial number in the catalogue of the works of J. S. Bach made by Wolfgang Schmieder (born 1901), published in 1950.

bx. *abbrev. for* box.

by (baɪ) *prep.* **1.** used to indicate the agent after a passive verb: *seeds eaten by the birds.* **2.** used to indicate the person responsible for a creative work: *this song is by Schubert.* **3.** via; through: *enter by the back door.* **4.** foll. by a gerund to indicate a means used: *he frightened her by hiding behind the door.* **5.** beside; next to; near: *a tree by the house.* **6.** passing the position of; past: *he drove by the old cottage.* **7.** not later than; before: *return the books by Tuesday.* **8.** used to indicate extent, after a comparative: *it is hotter by five degrees than it was yesterday.* **9.** (esp. in oaths) invoking the name of: *I swear by all the gods.* **10.** multiplied or divided by: *four by three equals twelve.* **11.** (*in habitual sentences*) during the passing of (esp. in the phrases **by day, by night). 12.** placed between measurements of the various dimensions of something: *a plank fourteen inches by seven.* ~*adv.* **13.** near: *the house is close by.* **14.** away; aside: *he put some money by each week for savings.* **15.** passing a point near something; past: *he drove by.* ~*n., pl.* **byes. 16.** a variant spelling of **bye.** [Old English *bī;* related to Gothic *bi,* Old High German *bī,* Sanskrit *abhi* to, towards]

by- *or* **bye-** *prefix.* **1.** near: *bystander.* **2.** secondary or incidental: *by-effect; by-election; by-path; by-product.* [from BY]

by and by *adv.* **1.** presently or eventually. ~*n.* **by-and-by. 2.** *U.S.* a future time or occasion.

by and large *adv.* in general; on the whole. [C17: originally nautical (meaning: to the wind and off it)]

by-bid·der *n.* a bidder at an auction who bids up the price of an item for the benefit of a seller.

by-blow *n.* **1.** a passing or incidental blow. **2.** an archaic word for a **bastard.**

Byd+goszcz (*Polish* ˈbɪdgɔʃtʃ) *n.* an industrial city and port in N Poland: under Prussian rule from 1772 to 1919. Pop.: 310 600 (1974 est.). German name: **Bromberg.**

bye (baɪ) *n.* **1.** *Sport.* the situation in which a player or team in an eliminatory contest wins a preliminary round by virtue of having no opponent. **2.** *Golf.* one or more holes of a stipulated course that are left unplayed after the match has been decided. **3.** *Cricket.* a run scored off a ball not struck by the batsman: allotted to the team as an extra and not to the individual batsman. See also **leg bye. 4.** something incidental or secondary. **5. by the bye.** incidentally; by the way: used as a sentence connector. [C16: variant of BY]

bye-bye *interj. Brit informal.* goodbye.

bye-byes *n.* an informal word for **sleep,** used esp. in addressing children (as in the phrase **go to bye-byes).**

by-e·lec·tion *or* **bye-e·lec·tion** *n.* **1.** (in Great Britain and other countries of the Commonwealth) an election held during the life of a parliament to fill a vacant seat in the lower chamber. **2.** (in the U.S.) a special election to fill a vacant elective position with an unexpired term.

Byel·go·rod-Dnes·trov·ski *or* **Bel·go·rod-Dnes·trov+ski** (*Russian* ˈbjɛlgərət dnjɪˈstrɔfskij) *n.* a port in the SW Soviet Union, in the SW Ukrainian SSR, on the Dniester estuary: belonged to Rumania from 1918 until 1940; ceded to the Soviet Union in 1944. Rumanian name: **Cetatea Alba.** Former name (until 1946): **Akkerman.**

Bye+lo+rus+sian *or* **Be+lo+rus+sian** (ˌbjɛləʊˈrʌʃən, ˌbɛl-) *adj.* **1.** of, relating to, or characteristic of Byelorussia, its people, or their language. ~*n.* **2.** the official language of the Byelorussian SSR: an East Slavonic language closely related to Russian. **3.** a native or inhabitant of Byelorussia. ~Also called: **White Russian.**

Bye+lo+rus+sian So+vi+et So+cial+ist Re+pub+lic *n.* an administrative division of the W Soviet Union: mainly low-lying and forested. Capital: Minsk. Pop.: 9 002 338 (1970). Area: 207 600 sq. km (80 134 sq. miles). Also: **Be+lo+rus+sian So+vi+et So+cial+ist Re+pub+lic,** or **Bye+lo+rus+sia, Be+lo+rus+sia** (ˌbjɛləʊˈrʌʃə, ˌbɛl-). Also called: **White Russia.**

Bye+lo+stok (bjɪlaˈstɔk) *n.* a Russian name for **Białystok.**

Bye+lo+vo *or* **Be+lo+vo** (*Russian* ˈbjɛləvə) *n.* a city in the S Soviet Union, in the southwestern RSFSR. Pop.: 108 209 (1970).

by+gone (ˈbaɪˌgɒn) *adj.* **1.** (*usually prenominal*) past; former. ~*n.* **2.** (*often pl.*) a past occurrence. **3. let bygones be bygones.** to agree to forget past quarrels.

by+law *or* **bye-law** (ˈbaɪˌlɔ:) *n.* **1.** a rule made by a local authority for the regulation of its affairs or management of the area it governs. **2.** a regulation of a company, society, etc. **3.** a subsidiary law. [C13: probably of Scandinavian origin; compare Old Norse *býr* dwelling, town; see BOWER[1], LAW]

by-line *n.* **1.** *Journalism.* a line under the title of a newspaper or magazine article giving the author's name. **2.** *Soccer.* another word for **touchline.**

Byng (bɪŋ) *n.* **1. John.** 1704–57, English admiral: executed after failing to relieve Minorca. **2. Ju·li·an Hed·worth George,** 1st Viscount Byng of Vimy. 1862–1935, British general in World War I; governor general of Canada (1921–26).

B.Y.O. *n. Austral.* an unlicensed restaurant at which diners may drink their own wine, etc. [C20: from the phrase *bring your own*]

by+pass ('baɪˌpɑːs) *n.* **1.** a main road built to avoid a city or other congested area. **2.** a means of redirecting the flow of a substance around an appliance through which it would otherwise pass. **3.** *Electronics.* **a.** an electrical circuit, esp. one containing a capacitor, connected in parallel around one or more components, providing an alternative path for certain frequencies. **b.** (*as modifier*): *a bypass capacitor.* ~*vb.* **+pass·es, +pass+ing, +passed** *or* **+past.** (*tr.*) **4.** to go around or avoid (a city, obstruction, problem, etc.). **5.** to cause (traffic, fluid, etc.) to go through a bypass. **6.** to proceed without reference to (regulations, a superior, etc.); get round; avoid.

by+pass en+gine *n.* a gas turbine in which a part of the compressor delivery bypasses the combustion zone, flowing directly into or around the main exhaust gas flow to provide additional thrust. Compare **turbofan.**

by+pass ra+ti·o *n. Aeronautics.* the ratio of the amount of air that bypasses the combustion chambers of an aircraft gas turbine to that passing through them.

by+path ('baɪˌpɑːθ) *n.* a little-used path or track.

by-play *n. Chiefly U.S.* secondary action or talking carried on apart while the main action proceeds, esp. in a play.

by-prod·uct *n.* **1.** a secondary or incidental product of a manufacturing process. **2.** a side effect.

Byrd (bɜːd) *n.* **1. Rich·ard Eve·lyn.** 1888–1957, U.S. rear admiral, aviator, and polar explorer. **2. Wil·liam.** 1543–1623, English composer and organist, noted for his madrigals, masses, and music for virginals.

Byrd Land *n.* a part of Antarctica, east of the Ross Ice Shelf and the Ross Sea: claimed for the U.S. by Richard E. Byrd in 1929. Former name: **Marie Byrd Land.**

byre (baɪə) *n. Brit.* a shelter for cows. [Old English *bȳre;* related to *būr* hut, cottage; see BOWER[1]]

byr+nie ('bɜːnɪ) *n.* an archaic word for **coat of mail.** [Old English *byrne;* related to Old Norse *brynja,* Gothic *brunjō,* Old High German *brunnia* coat of mail, Old Irish *bruinne* breast]

by+road ('baɪˌrəʊd) *or* **by+lane** *n.* a secondary or side road.

By·ron ('baɪərən) *n.* **George Gor·don,** 6th Baron. 1788–1824, English Romantic poet, noted also for his passionate and disastrous love affairs. His major works include *Childe Harold's Pilgrimage* (1812–18), and *Don Juan* (1819–24). He spent much of his life abroad and died while fighting for Greek independence. **—By+ron+ic** (baɪ'rɒnɪk) *adj.* **—By+'ron·i+cal+ly** *adv.* **—'By+ron+ism** *n.*

bys+si+no+sis (ˌbɪsɪ'nəʊsɪs) *n.* a lung disease caused by prolonged inhalation of fibre dust in textile factories. [C19: from New Latin, from Greek *bussinos* of linen (see BYSSUS) + -OSIS]

bys+sus ('bɪsəs) *n., pl.* **bys+sus·es** *or* **bys+si** ('bɪsaɪ). a mass of strong threads secreted by a sea mussel or similar mollusc that attaches the animal to a hard fixed surface. [C17: from Latin, from Greek *bussos* linen, flax, ultimately of Egyptian origin]

by+stand·er ('baɪˌstændə) *n.* a person present but not involved; onlooker; spectator.

by+street ('baɪˌstriːt) *n.* an obscure or secondary street.

byte (baɪt) *n. Computer technol.* **1.** a sequence of bits, usually six or eight, processed as a single unit of information. **2.** the storage space in a memory or other storage device that is allocated to one character. **3.** a subdivision of a word. [C20: probably a blend of BIT[4] + BITE]

By+tom (*Polish* 'bɪtəm) *n.* an industrial city in SW Poland, in Upper Silesia: under Prussian and German rule from 1742 to 1945. Pop.: 193 400 (1974 est.). German name: **Beuthen.**

by+way ('baɪˌweɪ) *n.* **1.** a secondary or side road, esp. in the country. **2.** an area, field of study, etc., that is very obscure or of secondary importance.

by+word ('baɪˌwɜːd) *n.* **1.** a person, place, or thing regarded as a perfect or proverbial example of something: *their name is a byword for good service.* **2.** an object of scorn or derision. **3.** a common saying; proverb. [Old English *bīwyrde;* see BY, WORD; compare Old High German *pīwurti,* from Latin *prōverbium* proverb]

by-your-leave *n.* a request for permission (esp. in the phrase **without so much as a by-your-leave).**

Byz. *abbrev. for* Byzantine.

Byz+an+tine (bɪ'zænˌtaɪn, -ˌtiːn, baɪ-; 'bɪzənˌtiːn, -ˌtaɪn) *adj.* **1.** of, characteristic of, or relating to Byzantium or the Byzantine Empire. **2.** of, relating to, or characterizing the Orthodox Church or its rites and liturgy. **3.** of or relating to the highly coloured stylized form of religious art developed in the Byzantine Empire. **4.** of or relating to the style of architecture developed in the Byzantine Empire, characterized by massive domes with square bases, rounded arches, spires and minarets, and the extensive use of mosaics. **5.** denoting the Medieval Greek spoken in the Byzantine Empire. **6.** (of attitudes, etc.) inflexible or complicated. ~*n.* **7.** an inhabitant of Byzantium. **—Byz+an+tin+ism** (bɪ'zæntaɪˌnɪzəm, -tiː-, baɪ-; 'bɪzəntiːˌnɪzəm, -taɪ-) *n.*

Byz+an+tine Church *n.* another name for the **Orthodox Church.**

Byz+an+tine Em+pire *n.* the continuation of the Roman Empire in the East, esp. after the deposition of the last emperor in Rome (476 A.D.). It was finally extinguished by the fall of Constantinople, its capital, in 1453. See also **Eastern Roman Empire.**

By+zan+ti+um (bɪ'zæntɪəm, baɪ-) *n.* an ancient Greek city on the Bosphorus: founded about 660 B.C.; rebuilt by Constantine I in 330 A.D. and called Constantinople; present-day Istanbul.

bz. *or* **bz** *abbrev. for* benzene.

C

c *or* **C** (si:) *n., pl.* **c's, C's,** *or* **Cs. 1.** the third letter and second consonant of the modern English alphabet. **2.** a speech sound represented by this letter, in English usually either a voiceless alveolar fricative, as in *cigar,* or a voiceless velar stop, as in *case.* **3.** the third in a series, esp. the third highest grade in an examination. **4. a.** something shaped like a C. **b.** (*in combination*): *a C-spring.*

c *symbol for:* **1.** centi-. **2.** cubic. **3.** cycle. **4.** *Maths.* constant. **5.** specific heat capacity. **6.** the velocity of electromagnetic radiation.

C *symbol for:* **1.** *Music.* **a.** a note having a frequency of 261.63 hertz (**middle C**) or this value multiplied or divided by any power of 2; the first degree of a major scale containing no sharps or flats (**C major**). **b.** a key, string, or pipe producing this note. **c.** the major or minor key having this note as its tonic. **d.** a time signature denoting four crotchet beats to the bar. See also **alla breve** (sense 2), **common time. 2.** *Chem.* carbon. **3.** capacitance. **4.** heat capacity. **5.** cold (water). **6.** *Physics.* compliance. **7.** Celsius. **8.** centigrade. **9.** century: *C20.* ~ **10.** *the Roman numeral for* 100. See **Roman numerals.** ~ **11.** *international car registration for* Cuba.

c. *abbrev. for:* **1.** carat. **2.** carbon (paper). **3.** *Cricket.* caught. **4.** cent(s). **5.** century or centuries. **6.** (*pl.* **cc.**) chapter. **7.** (used esp. preceding a date) circa: *c. 1800.* [Latin: about]. **8.** colt. **9.** contralto. **10.** copyright. **11.** coulomb.

C. *abbrev. for:* **1.** (on maps as part of name) Cape. **2.** Catholic. **3.** Celtic. **4.** Conservative. **5.** Corps.

c/- *Austral., N.Z.* (in addresses) *abbrev. for* care of.

C- (of U.S. military aircraft) *abbrev. for* cargo transport: *C-5.*

© *symbol for* copyright.

C3 *or* **C-3** ('si:'θri:) *adj.* **1.** in poor health or having a poor physique. **2.** *Informal.* inferior; worthless. Compare **A1.**

Ca *the chemical symbol for* calcium.

ca. *abbrev. for* circa. [Latin: about]

C.A. *abbrev. for:* **1.** Central America. **2.** chartered accountant. **3.** chief accountant. **4.** consular agent. **5.** (in Britain) Consumers' Association.

C/A *abbrev. for:* **1.** capital account. **2.** credit account. **3.** current account.

C.A.A. (in Britain) *abbrev. for* Civil Aviation Authority.

Caa+ba ('kɑ:bə) *n.* a variant spelling of **Kaaba.**

cab[1] (kæb) *n.* **1. a.** a taxi. **b.** (*as modifier*): *a cab rank.* **2.** the enclosed compartment of a lorry, locomotive, crane, etc., from which it is driven or operated. **3.** (formerly) a light horse-drawn vehicle used for public hire. **4. first cab off the rank.** *Austral. informal.* the first person, etc., to do or take advantage of something. [C19: shortened from *taximeter cab*]

cab[2] *or* **kab** (kæb) *n.* an ancient Hebrew measure equal to about 2.3 litres (4 pints). [C16: from Hebrew *qabh* container, something hollowed out]

C.A.B. *abbrev. for:* **1.** (in Britain) Citizens' Advice Bureau. **2.** (in the U.S.) Civil Aeronautics Board.

ca+bal (kə'bæl) *n.* **1.** a small group of intriguers, esp. one formed for political purposes. **2.** a secret plot, esp. a political one; conspiracy; intrigue. **3.** a secret or exclusive set of people; clique. ~*vb.* **+bals, +bal+ling, +balled. 4.** (*intr.*) to form a cabal; conspire; plot. [C17: from French *cabale,* from Medieval Latin *cabala;* see CABBALA]

Ca+bal (kə'bæl) *n.* **the.** *English history.* a group of ministers of Charles II that governed from 1667–73: consisting of Clifford, Ashley, Buckingham, Arlington, and Lauderdale. [see CABBALA; by a coincidence, the initials of Charles II's ministers can be arranged to form this word]

ca+ba+la (kə'bɑ:lə) *n.* a variant spelling of **cabbala.** **—cab·a+lism** ('kæbə,lɪzəm) *n.* **—'cab·a+list** *n.* **—,cab·a+'lis+tic** *adj.*

Ca·ba·llé (*Spanish* ,kaβa'ʎe) *n.* **Mont·ser·rat** (,monser'rat). born 1933, Spanish operatic soprano.

ca+bal+le+ro (,kæbə'ljɛərəʊ; *Spanish* ,kaβa'ʎero) *n., pl.* **+ros** (-rəʊz; *Spanish* -ros). **1.** a Spanish gentleman. **2.** a southwestern U.S. word for **horseman.** [C19: from Spanish: gentleman, horseman, from Late Latin *caballārius* rider, groom, from *caballus* horse; compare CAVALIER]

ca+ba+na (kə'bɑ:nə) *n. Chiefly U.S.* a tent used as a dressing room by the sea. [from Spanish *cabaña:* CABIN]

Ca+ba+na+tuan (,kɑ:bənə'twɑ:n) *n.* a city in the Philippines, in S central Luzon. Pop.: 117 995 (1975 est.).

cab·a+ret ('kæbə,reɪ) *n.* **1.** a floor show of dancing, singing, or other light entertainment at a nightclub or restaurant. **2.** *Chiefly U.S.* a nightclub or restaurant providing such entertainment. [C17: from Norman French: tavern, probably from Late Latin *camera* an arched roof, CHAMBER]

cab+bage[1] ('kæbɪdʒ) *n.* **1.** Also called: **cole.** any of various cultivated varieties of the cruciferous plant *Brassica oleracea capitata,* typically having a short thick stalk and a large head of green or reddish edible leaves. See also **brassica, savoy.** Compare **skunk cabbage, Chinese cabbage. 2. wild cabbage.** a Mediterranean cruciferous plant, *Brassica oleracea,* with broad leaves and a long spike of yellow flowers: the plant from which the cabbages, cauliflower, broccoli, and Brussels sprout have been bred. **3. a.** the head of a cabbage. **b.** the edible leaf bud of the cabbage palm. **4.** *Informal.* a dull or unimaginative person. **5.** *Informal.* a person who has no mental faculties and is dependent on others for his subsistence. [C14: from Norman French *caboche* head; perhaps related to Old French *boce* hump, bump, Latin *caput* head]

cab+bage[2] ('kæbɪdʒ) *Brit. archaic.* ~*n.* **1.** snippets of cloth appropriated by a tailor from a customer's material. ~*vb.* **2.** to steal; pilfer. [C17: of uncertain origin; perhaps related to Old French *cabas* theft]

cab+bage bug *n.* another name for the **harlequin bug.**

cab+bage let+tuce *n.* any of several varieties of lettuce that have roundish flattened heads resembling cabbages.

cab+bage palm *or* **tree** *n.* **1.** a West Indian palm, *Roystonea* (or *Oreodoxa*) *oleracea,* whose leaf buds are eaten like cabbage. **2.** a similar Brazilian palm, *Euterpe oleracea.* **3.** an Australian palm tree, *Livistona australis.*

cab+bage pal+met+to *n.* a tropical American fan palm, *Sabal palmetto,* with edible leaf buds and leaves used in thatching.

cab+bage root fly *n.* a dipterous fly, *Erioischia brassicae,* whose larvae feed on the roots and stems of cabbages and other brassicas: family *Muscidae* (houseflies, etc.).

cab·bage+town ('kæbɪdʒ,taʊn) *n. Canadian.* a city slum.

cab+bage white *n.* any large white butterfly of the genus *Pieris,* esp. the Eurasian species *P. brassicae* and *P. rapae,* the larvae of which feed on the leaves of cabbages and related vegetables: family *Pieridae.*

cab·bage+worm ('kæbɪdʒ,wɜ:m) *n. U.S.* any caterpillar that feeds on cabbages, esp. that of the cabbage white.

cab+ba+la, ca+ba+la, kab+ba+la, *or* **ka+ba+la** (kə'bɑ:lə) *n.* **1.** an ancient Jewish mystical tradition based on an esoteric interpretation of the Old Testament. **2.** any secret or occult doctrine or science. [C16: from Medieval Latin, from Hebrew *qabbālāh* tradition, what is received, from *qābal* to receive] **—cab+ba+lism, cab·a+lism, kab+ba+lism,** *or* **kab·a+lism** ('kæbə,lɪzəm) *n.* **—'cab+ba+list, 'cab·a+list, 'kab+ba+list,** *or* **'kab·a+list** *n.* **—,cab+ba+'lis+tic, ,cab·a+'lis+tic, ,kab+ba+'lis+tic,** *or* **,kab·a+'lis+tic** *adj.*

cab+by *or* **cab+bie** ('kæbɪ) *n., pl.* **+bies.** *Informal.* a cab driver.

ca+ber ('keɪbə) *n. Scot.* a heavy wooden pole or beam, esp. one thrown in the air as a trial of strength in the Highland sport of **tossing the caber.** [C16: from Gaelic *cabar* pole]

cab+e·zon ('kæbɪzɒn) *or* **cab+e·zone** ('kæbɪ,zəʊn) *n.* a large food fish, *Scorpaenichthys marmoratus,* of North American Pacific coastal waters, having greenish flesh: family *Cottidae* (bullheads and sea scorpions). [Spanish, from *cabeza* head, ultimately from Latin *caput*]

Ca+bi+mas (*Spanish* ka'bimas) *n.* a town in NW Venezuela, on the NE shore of Lake Maracaibo. Pop.: 122 239 (1971).

cab+in ('kæbɪn) *n.* **1.** a small simple dwelling; hut. **2.** a simple house providing accommodation for travellers or holiday-makers at a motel or holiday camp. **3.** a room used as an office or living quarters in a ship. **4.** a covered compartment used for shelter or living quarters in a small boat. **5.** (in a warship) the compartment or room reserved for the commanding officer. **6.** *Brit.* another name for **signal box. 7. a.** the enclosed part of a light aircraft in which the pilot and passengers sit. **b.** the part of an airliner in which the passengers are carried. **c.** the section of an aircraft used for cargo. ~*vb.* **8.** to confine in a small space. [C14: from Old French *cabane,* from Old Provençal *cabana,* from Late Latin *capanna* hut]

cab+in boy *n.* a boy who waits on the officers and passengers of a ship.

cab+in class *n.* a class of accommodation on a passenger ship between first class and tourist class.

cab+in cruis+er *n.* a power boat fitted with a cabin and comforts for pleasure cruising or racing.

Ca+bin+da (kə'bi:ndə) *n.* an exclave of Angola, separated from the rest of the country by part of Zaïre. Pop.: 58 547 (1960). Area: 7270 sq. km (2807 sq. miles).

cab·i+net ('kæbɪnɪt) *n.* **1. a.** a piece of furniture containing shelves, cupboards, or drawers for storage or display. **b.** (*as modifier*): *cabinet teak.* **2.** the outer case of a television, radio, etc. **3. a.** (*often cap.*) the executive and policy-making body of a country, consisting of all government ministers or just the senior ministers. **b.** (*sometimes cap.*) an advisory council to a president, sovereign, governor, etc. **c.** (*as modifier*): *a cabinet reshuffle; a cabinet minister.* **4 a.** a standard size of paper, 6 × 4 inches (15 × 10 cm) or 6½ × 4¼ inches (16.5 × 10.5 cm), for mounted photographs. **b.** (*as modifier*): *a cabinet photograph.* **5.** *Printing.* an enclosed rack for holding cases of type, etc. **6.** *Archaic.* a private room. **7.** (*modifier*) suitable in size, value, decoration, etc., for a display cabinet: *a cabinet edition of Shakespeare.* **8.** (*modifier*) (of a drawing or projection of a three-dimensional object) constructed with true horizontal and vertical representation of scale but with oblique distances reduced to about half scale to avoid the appearance of distortion. **9.** (*modifier*) (of a wine) specially selected and usually rare. [C16: from Old French, diminutive of *cabine,* of uncertain origin]

cab·i·net-mak·er *n.* a craftsman specializing in the making of fine furniture. —**'cab·i·net-,mak·ing** *n.*

cab·i·net pud·ding *n.* a steamed suet pudding enriched with dried fruit.

cab·i·net·work ('kæbɪnɪt,wɜːk) *n.* **1.** the making of furniture, esp. of fine quality. **2.** an article made by a cabinet-maker.

ca·ble ('keɪbᵊl) *n.* **1.** a strong thick rope, usually of twisted hemp or steel wire. **2.** *Nautical.* an anchor chain or rope. **3.** Also called: **cable length, cable's length.** a unit of length in nautical use that has various values. It is most commonly taken as 120 fathoms (720 feet) in the U.S. and one tenth of a nautical mile (608 feet) in Britain. It is also sometimes taken as 100 fathoms (600 feet). **4.** a wire or bundle of wires that conducts electricity: *a submarine cable.* See also **coaxial cable. 5.** Also called: **overseas telegram, cablegram.** a telegram sent abroad by submarine cable, radio, communications satellite, or by telephone line. **6.** See **cable stitch.** ~*vb.* **7.** to send (a message) to (someone) by cable. **8.** (*tr.*) to fasten or provide with a cable or cables. [C13: from Old Norman French, from Late Latin *capulum* halter]

ca·ble car *n.* the passenger car on a cable railway.

ca·ble·gram ('keɪbᵊl,græm) *n.* a more formal name for **cable** (sense 5).

ca·ble-laid *adj.* (of a rope) made of three plain-laid ropes twisted together in a left-handed direction.

ca·ble rail·way *n.* a railway on which individual cars are drawn along by a strong cable or metal chain operated by a stationary motor.

ca·ble re·lease *n.* a short length of flexible cable, used to operate the shutter of a camera without shaking it.

ca·ble stitch *n.* **a.** a pattern or series of knitting stitches producing a design like a twisted rope. **b.** (*as modifier*): *a cable-stitch sweater.* Sometimes shortened to **cable.**

ca·blet ('keɪblɪt) *n.* a small cable, esp. a cable-laid rope that has a circumference of less than 25 centimetres (ten inches).

ca·ble·way ('keɪbᵊl,weɪ) *n.* a system for moving bulk materials in which suspended cars, buckets, etc., run on cables that extend between terminal towers.

cab·man ('kæbmən) *n., pl.* **·men.** the driver of a cab.

ca·bob (kə'bɒb) *n.* a variant spelling of **kebab.**

cab·o·chon ('kæbə,ʃɒn; *French* kabɔ'ʃɔ̃) *n.* a smooth domed gem, polished but unfaceted. [C16: from Old French, from Old Norman French *caboche* head; see CABBAGE[1]]

ca·boo·dle (kə'buːdᵊl) *n. Informal.* a lot, bunch, or group (esp. in the phrases **the whole caboodle, the whole kit and caboodle**). [C19: probably contraction of KIT and BOODLE]

ca·boose (kə'buːs) *n.* **1.** *U.S. informal.* short for **calaboose. 2.** *Railways. U.S.* a guard's van, esp. one with sleeping and eating facilities for the train crew. **3.** *Nautical.* **a.** a deckhouse for a galley aboard ship. **b.** *Chiefly Brit.* the galley itself. **4.** *Canadian.* **a.** a mobile bunkhouse used by lumbermen, etc. **b.** an insulated cabin on runners, equipped with a stove. [C18: from Dutch *cabūse,* of unknown origin]

Ca·bo·ra Bas·sa (kə'bɔːrə 'bæsə) *n.* the site on the Zambezi River in N Mozambique of the largest dam in southern Africa.

Cab·ot ('kæbət) *n.* **1. John,** Italian name *Giovanni Caboto.* 1450–98, Italian explorer, who landed in North America in 1497, under patent from Henry VII of England, and explored the coast from Nova Scotia to Newfoundland. **2.** his son, **Se·bas·ti·an.** ?1476–1557, English navigator and cartographer who explored the La Plata region of Brazil (1526–30).

cab·o·tage ('kæbə,tɑːʒ) *n.* **1.** *Nautical.* coastal navigation or shipping, esp. within the borders of one country. **2.** reservation to a country's carriers of its internal traffic, esp. air traffic. [C19: from French, from *caboter* to sail near the coast, apparently from Spanish *cabo* CAPE[2]]

Ca·bral (*Portuguese* kə'bral) *n.* **Pe·dro Ál·va·rez** ('pedru 'alvərəʃ). ?1460–?1526, Portuguese navigator: discovered and took possession of Brazil for Portugal in 1500.

ca·bret·ta (kə'brɛtə) *n. Chiefly U.S.* a soft leather obtained from the skins of certain South American or African sheep. [from Spanish *cabra* she-goat]

ca·bril·la (kə'brɪlə) *n.* any of various serranid food fishes, esp. *Epinephelus analogus,* occurring in warm seas around Florida and the West Indies. [Spanish, literally: little goat]

cab·ri·ole ('kæbrɪ,əʊl) *n.* **1.** Also called: **cabriole leg.** a type of furniture leg, popular in the first half of the 18th century, in which an upper convex curve descends tapering to a concave curve. **2.** *Ballet.* a leap in the air with one leg outstretched and the other beating against it. [C18: from French, from *cabrioler* to caper; from its being based on the leg of a capering animal; see CABRIOLET]

cab·ri·o·let (,kæbrɪəʊ'leɪ) *n.* **1.** a small two-wheeled horse-drawn carriage with two seats and a folding hood. **2.** a former name for a **drophead coupé.** [C18: from French, literally: a little skip, from *cabriole,* from Latin *capreolus* wild goat, from *caper* goat; referring to the lightness of movement]

ca'can·ny (kə'kænɪ) *n. Scot.* **1.** moderation or wariness. **2. a.** a policy of restricting the output of work; a go-slow. **b.** (*as modifier*): *a ca'canny policy.* [C19: literally, *call canny* to drive gently]

ca·ca·o (kə'kɑːəʊ, -'keɪəʊ) *n.* **1.** a small tropical American evergreen tree, *Theobroma cacao,* having yellowish flowers and reddish-brown seed pods from which cocoa and chocolate are prepared: family *Sterculiaceae.* **2. cacao bean.** another name for **cocoa bean. 3. cacao butter.** another name for **cocoa butter.** [C16: from Spanish, from Nahuatl *cacauatl* cacao beans]

cac·cia·to·re (,kɑːtʃə'tɔːrɪ, ,kætʃ-) *or* **cac·cia·to·ra** *adj.* (*immediately postpositive*) prepared with tomatoes, mushrooms, herbs, and other seasonings. [Italian, literally: hunter]

Cá·ce·res (*Spanish* 'kaθeres) *n.* a city in W Spain: held by the Moors (1142–1229). Pop.: 56 064 (1970).

cach·a·lot ('kæʃə,lɒt) *n.* another name for **sperm whale.** [C18: from French, from Portuguese, *cachalote,* of unknown origin]

cache (kæʃ) *n.* **1.** a hidden store of provisions, weapons, treasure, etc. **2.** the place where such a store is hidden. ~*vb.* **3.** (*tr.*) to store in a cache. [C19: from French, from *cacher* to hide]

cache·pot ('kæʃ,pɒt, kæʃ'pəʊ) *n.* an ornamental container for a flowerpot. [French: pot-hider]

ca·chet ('kæʃeɪ) *n.* **1.** an official seal on a document, letter, etc. **2.** a distinguishing mark; stamp. **3.** prestige; distinction. **4.** *Philately.* **a.** a mark stamped by hand on mail for commemorative purposes. **b.** a small mark made by dealers and experts on the back of postage stamps. Compare **overprint** (sense 3), **surcharge** (sense 5). **5.** a hollow wafer, formerly used for enclosing an unpleasant-tasting medicine. [C17: from Old French, from *cacher* to hide]

ca·chex·i·a (kə'kɛksɪə) *or* **ca·chex·y** *n.* a generally weakened condition of body or mind resulting from any debilitating chronic disease. [C16: from Late Latin from Greek *kakhexia,* from *kakos* bad + *hexis* condition, habit] —**ca·chec·tic** (kə'kɛktɪk) *adj.*

cach·in·nate ('kækɪ,neɪt) *vb.* (*intr.*) to laugh loudly. [C19: from Latin *cacchināre,* probably of imitative origin] —**,cach·in·'na·tion** *n.* —**,cach·in·'na·to·ry** *adj.*

ca·chou ('kæʃuː, kæ'ʃuː) *n.* **1.** a lozenge eaten to sweeten the breath. **2.** another name for **catechu.** [C18: via French from Portuguese, from Malay *kāchu*]

ca·chu·cha (kə'tʃuːtʃə) *n.* **1.** a graceful Spanish solo dance in triple time. **2.** music composed for this dance. [C19: from Spanish]

ca·cique (kə'siːk) *or* **ca·zique** (kə'ziːk) *n.* **1.** an American Indian chief in a Spanish-speaking region. **2.** (esp. in Spanish America) a local political boss. **3.** any of various tropical American songbirds of the genus *Cacicus* and related genera: family *Icteridae* (American orioles). [C16: from Spanish, of Arawak origin; compare Taino *cacique* chief]

ca·ciqu·ism (kə'siːkɪzəm) *n.* (esp. in Spanish America) government by local political bosses.

cack-hand·ed (,kæk'hændɪd) *adj. Informal.* **1.** left-handed. **2.** clumsy. [from *cack* excrement, from the fact that clumsy people usually make a mess]

cack·le ('kækᵊl) *vb.* **1.** (*intr.*) (esp. of a hen that has just laid an egg) to squawk with shrill broken notes. **2.** (*intr.*) to laugh or chatter raucously and noisily. **3.** (*tr.*) to utter in a cackling manner. ~*n.* **4.** the noise or act of cackling. **5.** noisy chatter. **6. cut the cackle.** *Informal.* to stop chattering or giggling; be quiet. [C13: probably from Middle Low German *kākelen,* of imitative origin] —**'cack·ler** *n.*

cac·o- *combining form.* bad, unpleasant, or incorrect: *cacophony.* [from Greek *kakos* bad]

cac·o·de·mon *or* **cac·o·dae·mon** (,kækə'diːmən) *n.* an evil spirit or devil. [C16: from Greek *kakodaimōn* evil genius]

cac·o·dyl ('kækədaɪl) *n.* another name for **tetramethyldiarsine.** [C19: from Greek *kakōdēs* evil-smelling (from *kakos* CACO- + *ozein* to smell) + -YL] —**cac·o·dyl·ic** (,kækə'dɪlɪk) *adj.*

cac·o·ep·y (kə'kəʊɪpɪ) *n.* bad or mistaken pronunciation. [C19: from Greek *kakoepeia*] —**cac·o·e·pis·tic** (kə,kəʊɪ'pɪstɪk) *adj.*

cac·o·e·thes (,kækəʊ'iːθiːz) *n.* an uncontrollable urge or desire, esp. for something harmful; mania: *a cacoethes for smoking.* [C16: from Latin *cacoēthes* malignant disease, from Greek *kakoēthēs* of an evil disposition, from *kakos* CACO- + *ēthos* character] —**cac·o·eth·ic** (,kækəʊ'ɛθɪk) *adj.*

cac·o·gen·ics (,kækəʊ'dʒɛnɪks) *n.* another name for **dysgenics.** [C20: from CACO- + EUGENICS] —**,cac·o·'gen·ic** *adj.*

ca·cog·ra·phy (kæ'kɒgrəfɪ) *n.* **1.** bad handwriting. Compare **calligraphy. 2.** incorrect spelling. Compare **orthography.** —**ca·'cog·ra·pher** *n.* —**cac·o·graph·ic** (,kækə'græfɪk) *or* **,cac·o·'graph·i·cal** *adj.*

ca·col·o·gy (kə'kɒlədʒɪ) *n.* a bad choice of words; faulty speech. [C17 (in the sense: ill report): from Greek *kakologia*]

cac·o·mis·tle ('kækə,mɪsᵊl) *or* **cac·o·mix·le** ('kækə,mɪksəl) *n.* **1.** a catlike omnivorous mammal, *Bassariscus astutus,* of S North America, related to but smaller than the raccoons: family *Procyonidae,* order *Carnivora* (carnivores). It has yellowish-grey fur and a long bushy tail banded in black and white. **2.** a related smaller animal, *Jentinkia* (or *Bassariscus*) *sumichrasti,* of Central America. [C19: from Mexican Spanish, from Nahuatl *tlacomiztli,* from *tlaco* half + *miztli* cougar]

ca·coph·o·nous (kə'kɒfənəs) *or* **cac·o·phon·ic** (,kækə'fɒnɪk) *adj.* jarring in sound; discordant; harsh. —**ca·'coph·o·nous·ly** *or* **,cac·o·'phon·i·cal·ly** *adv.*

ca·coph·o·ny (kə'kɒfənɪ) *n., pl.* **·nies. 1.** harsh discordant sound; dissonance. **2.** the use of unharmonious or dissonant speech sounds in language. Compare **euphony.**

cac·tus ('kæktəs) *n., pl.* **·tus·es** *or* **·ti** (-taɪ). **1.** any spiny succulent plant of the family *Cactaceae* of the arid regions of America. Cactuses have swollen tough stems, leaves reduced to spines or scales, and large brightly coloured flowers. **2. cactus dahlia.** a double-flowered variety of dahlia. [C17: from Latin: prickly plant, from Greek *kaktos* cardoon] —**cac·ta·ceous** (kæk'teɪʃəs) *adj.*

ca·cu·mi·nal (kæ'kjuːmɪnᵊl) *Phonetics.* ~*adj.* **1.** Also called: **cerebral.** relating to or denoting a consonant articulated with the tip of the tongue turned back towards the hard palate.

~*n.* **2.** a consonant articulated in this manner. [C19: from Latin *cacūmen* point, top]

cad (kæd) *n. Brit. informal; old-fashioned.* a man who does not behave in a gentlemanly manner towards others. [C18: shortened from CADDIE] —**'cad·dish** *adj.*

ca·das·ter *or* **ca·das·tre** (kə'dæstə) *n.* an official register showing details of ownership, boundaries, and value of real property in a district, made for taxation purposes. [C19: from French, from Provençal *cadastro,* from Italian *catastro,* from Late Greek *katastikhon* register, from *kata stikhon* line by line, from *kata* (see CATA-) + *stikhos* line, STICH] —**ca·'das·tral** *adj.*

ca·dav·er (kə'deɪvə, -'dɑːv-) *n. Med.* a corpse. [C16: from Latin, from *cadere* to fall] —**ca·'dav·er·ic** *adj.*

ca·dav·er·ine (kə'dævəˌriːn) *n.* a toxic diamine with an unpleasant smell, produced by protein hydrolysis during putrefaction of animal tissue. Formula: $NH_2(CH_2)_5NH_2$.

ca·dav·er·ous (kə'dævərəs) *adj.* **1.** of or like a corpse, esp. in being deathly pale; ghastly. **2.** thin and haggard; gaunt. —**ca·'dav·er·ous·ly** *adv.* —**ca·'dav·er·ous·ness** *n.*

cad·die *or* **cad·dy** ('kædɪ) *n., pl.* **·dies.** **1.** *Golf.* an attendant who carries clubs, etc., for a player. ~*vb.* **·dies, ·dy·ing, ·died.** **2.** (*intr.*) to act as a caddie. [C17 (originally: a gentleman learning the military profession by serving in the army without a commission, hence C18 (Scottish): a person looking for employment, an errand-boy): from French CADET]

cad·die car *or* **cad·die cart** *n. Golf.* a small light two-wheeled trolley for carrying clubs.

cad·dis *or* **cad·dice** ('kædɪs) *n.* a type of coarse woollen yarn, braid, or fabric.

cad·dis fly *n.* any small mothlike insect of the order *Trichoptera,* having two pairs of hairy wings and aquatic larvae (caddis worms). [C17: of unknown origin]

cad·dis worm *or* **cad·dis** ('kædɪs) *n.* the aquatic larva of a caddis fly, which constructs a protective case around itself made of silk, sand, stones, etc. Also called: **caseworm, strawworm.**

Cad·do·an ('kædəʊən) *n.* a family of North American Indian languages, including Pawnee, formerly spoken in a wide area of the Middle West.

cad·dy[1] ('kædɪ) *n., pl.* **·dies.** *Chiefly Brit.* a small container, esp. for tea. [C18: from Malay *kati;* see CATTY[2]]

cad·dy[2] ('kædɪ) *n., pl.* **·dies,** *vb.* **·dies, ·dy·ing, ·died.** a variant spelling of **caddie.**

cade[1] (keɪd) *n.* a juniper tree, *Juniperus oxycedrus* of the Mediterranean region, the wood of which yields an oily brown liquid (**oil of cade**) used to treat skin ailments. [C16: via Old French from Old Provençal, from Medieval Latin *catanus*]

cade[2] (keɪd) *adj.* (of a young animal) left by its mother and reared by humans, usually as a pet. [C15: of unknown origin]

Cade (keɪd) *n.* **Jack.** died 1450, English leader of the Kentish rebellion against the misgovernment of Henry VI (1450).

-cade *n. combining form.* indicating a procession of a specified kind: *motorcade.* [abstracted from CAVALCADE]

ca·delle (kə'dɛl) *n.* a widely distributed beetle, *Tenebroides mauritanicus,* that feeds on flour, grain, and other stored foods: family *Trogositidae.* [French, from Provençal *cadello,* from Latin *catellus* a little dog]

ca·dence ('keɪdᵊns) *or* **ca·den·cy** *n., pl.* **·denc·es** *or* **·den·cies.** **1.** the beat or measure of something rhythmic. **2.** a fall in the pitch of the voice, as at the end of a sentence. **3.** modulation of the voice; intonation. **4.** a rhythm or rhythmical construction in verse or prose; measure. **5.** the close of a musical phrase or section. [C14: from Old French, from Old Italian *cadenza,* literally: a falling, from *cadere* to fall, from Latin]

ca·den·cy ('keɪdᵊnsɪ) *n., pl.* **·cies.** **1.** *Heraldry.* the line of descent from a younger member of a family. **2.** another word for **cadence.**

ca·dent ('keɪdᵊnt) *adj.* **1.** having cadence; rhythmic. **2.** *Archaic.* falling; descending. [C16: from Latin *cadēns* falling, from *cadere* to fall]

ca·den·za (kə'dɛnzə) *n.* a virtuoso solo passage occurring near the end of a piece of music, formerly improvised by the soloist but now usually specially composed. [C19: from Italian; see CADENCE]

ca·det (kə'dɛt) *n.* **1.** a young person undergoing preliminary training, usually before full entry to the uniformed services, police, etc., esp. for officer status. **2.** (in England and in France before 1789) a gentleman, usually a younger son, who entered the army to prepare for a commission. **3.** a younger son or brother. **4.** **cadet branch.** the family or family branch of a younger son. **5.** (in New Zealand) a person learning sheep farming on a sheep station. [C17: from French, from dialect (Gascon) *capdet* captain, ultimately from Latin *caput* head] —**ca·'det·ship** *n.*

cadge (kædʒ) *vb.* **1.** to get (food, money, etc.) by sponging or begging. ~*n.* **2.** *Brit.* a person who cadges. **3.** **on the cadge.** *Brit. informal.* engaged in cadging. [C17: of unknown origin] —**'cadg·er** *n.*

ca·di *or* **ka·di** ('kɑːdɪ, 'keɪdɪ) *n., pl.* **·dis.** a judge in a Muslim community. [C16: from Arabic *qādī* judge]

Cá·diz (kə'dɪz; *Spanish* 'kaðiθ) *n.* **1.** a port in SW Spain, on a narrow peninsula that forms the **Bay of Cádiz** at the E end of the **Gulf of Cádiz:** founded about 1100 B.C. as a Phoenician trading colony; centre of trade with America from the 16th to 18th centuries. Pop.: 135 743 (1970).

Cad·me·an vic·to·ry *n.* another name for **Pyrrhic victory.**

cad·mi·um ('kædmɪəm) *n.* a malleable ductile toxic bluish-white metallic element that occurs in association with zinc ores. It is used in electroplating, alloys, and as a neutron absorber in the control of nuclear fission. Symbol: Cd; atomic no.: 48; atomic wt.: 112.4; valency: 2; relative density: 8.65; melting pt.: 320.9°C; boiling pt.: 765°C. [C19: from New Latin, from Latin *cadmīa* zinc ore, CALAMINE, referring to the fact that both calamine and cadmium are found in the ore]

cad·mi·um cell *n.* **1.** a photocell with a cadmium electrode that is especially sensitive to ultraviolet radiation. **2.** a former name for **Weston standard cell.**

cad·mi·um sul·phide *n.* an orange or yellow insoluble solid used as a pigment in paints, etc. (**cadmium yellow**). Formula: CdS.

Cad·mus ('kædməs) *n. Greek myth.* a Phoenician prince who killed a dragon and planted its teeth, from which sprang a multitude of warriors who fought among themselves until only five remained, who joined Cadmus to found Thebes. —**'Cad·me·an** *adj.*

ca·dre ('kɑːdə) *n.* **1.** the nucleus of trained professional servicemen forming the basis for the training of new units or other military expansion. **2.** a basic unit or structure, esp. of personnel; nucleus; core. **3.** a member of a cadre. [C19: from French, from Italian *quadro,* from Latin *quadrum* square]

ca·du·ce·us (kə'djuːsɪəs) *n., pl.* **·ce·i** (-sɪˌaɪ). **1.** *Classical myth.* a staff entwined with two serpents and bearing a pair of wings at the top, carried by Hermes (Mercury) as messenger of the gods. **2.** an insignia resembling this staff used as an emblem of the medical profession. Compare **staff of Aesculapius.** [C16: from Latin, from Doric Greek *karukeion,* from *karux* herald]

ca·du·ci·ty (kə'djuːsɪtɪ) *n.* **1.** perishableness. **2.** senility. [C18: from French, from Latin *cadūcus* CADUCOUS]

ca·du·cous (kə'djuːkəs) *adj. Biology.* (of parts of a plant or animal) shed during the life of the organism. [C17: from Latin *cadūcus* falling, from *cadere* to fall]

cae·cil·i·an (siː'sɪlɪən) *n.* any tropical limbless cylindrical amphibian of the order *Apoda* (or *Gymnophiona*), resembling earthworms and inhabiting moist soil. [C19: from Latin *caecilia* a kind of lizard, from *caecus* blind]

cae·cum *or U.S.* **ce·cum** ('siːkəm) *n., pl.* **·ca** (-kə). *Anatomy.* any structure or part that ends in a blind sac or pouch, esp. the pouch that marks the beginning of the large intestine. [C18: short for Latin *intestinum caecum* blind intestine, translation of Greek *tuphlon enteron*] —**'cae·cal** *or U.S.* **'ce·cal** *adj.*

Cæd·mon ('kædmən) *n.* 7th-century A.D. Anglo-Saxon poet and monk, the earliest English poet whose name survives.

Cae·li·an ('siːlɪən) *n.* the southeasternmost of the Seven Hills of Rome.

Cae·lum ('siːləm) *n., Latin genitive* **Cae·li** ('siːlaɪ). a small faint constellation in the S hemisphere close to Eridanus. [Latin: the sky, heaven]

Caen (kɒŋ; *French* kã) *n.* an industrial city in NW France. Pop.: 122 794 (1975).

cae·no·gen·e·sis (ˌsiːnəʊ'dʒɛnɪsɪs), **cai·no·gen·e·sis, kai·no·gen·e·sis** *or U.S.* **ce·no·gen·e·sis, ke·no·gen·e·sis** *n.* the development of structures and organs in an embryo or larva that are adaptations to its way of life and are not retained in the adult form. Compare **recapitulation** (sense 2). —**cae·no·ge·net·ic** (ˌsiːnəʊdʒə'nɛtɪk), **ˌcai·no·ge·'net·ic, ˌkai·no·ge·'net·ic** *or U.S.* **ˌce·no·ge·'net·ic, ˌke·no·ge·'net·ic** *adj.* —**ˌcae·no·ge·'net·i·cal·ly, ˌcai·no·ge·'net·i·cal·ly, ˌkai·no·ge·'net·i·cal·ly** *or U.S.* **ˌce·no·ge·'net·i·cal·ly, ˌke·no·ge·'net·i·cal·ly** *adv.*

Cae·no·zo·ic (ˌsiːnə'zəʊɪk) *adj.* a variant spelling of **Cenozoic.**

cae·o·ma (siː'əʊmə) *n.* an aecium in some rust fungi that has no surrounding membrane. [New Latin, from Greek *kaiein* to burn; referring to its glowing colour]

Caer·le·on (kɑː'lɪən) *n.* a town in SE Wales, in Gwent on the River Usk: traditionally the seat of King Arthur's court. Pop.: 6235 (1971).

Caer·nar·fon *or* **Caer·nar·von** (kɑː'nɑːvᵊn) *n.* a port and resort in NW Wales, in Gwynedd on the Menai Strait: 13th-century castle. Pop.: 9253 (1971).

Caer·nar·von·shire (kɑː'nɑːvᵊnˌʃɪə, -ʃə) *n.* (until 1974) a county of NW Wales, now part of Gwynedd.

Caer·phil·ly (kɛə'fɪlɪ) *n.* **1.** a market town in SE Wales, in SE Mid Glamorgan: site of the largest castle in Wales (13th–14th centuries). Pop.: 40 689 (1971). **2.** a creamy white mild-flavoured cheese.

caes·al·pin·i·a·ceous (ˌsɛzælˌpɪnɪ'eɪʃəs) *adj.* of, relating to, or belonging to the *Caesalpiniaceae,* a mainly tropical family of leguminous plants that have irregular flowers: includes carob, senna, brazil, cassia, and poinciana. [from New Latin *Caesalpinia* type genus, named after Andreas *Caesalpino* (1519–1603), Italian botanist]

Cae·sar ('siːzə) *n.* **1.** **Gai·us Ju·li·us** ('gaɪəs 'dʒuːlɪəs). 100–44 B.C., Roman general, statesman, and historian. He formed the first triumvirate with Pompey and Crassus (60), conquered Gaul (58–50), invaded Britain (55–54), mastered Italy (49), and defeated Pompey (46). As dictator of the Roman Empire (49–44) he destroyed the power of the corrupt Roman nobility. He also introduced the Julian calendar and planned further reforms, but fear of his sovereign power led to his assassination (44) by conspirators led by Marcus Brutus and Cassius Longinus. **2.** any Roman emperor. **3.** (*sometimes not cap.*) any emperor, autocrat, dictator, or other powerful ruler. **4.** a title of the Roman emperors from Augustus to Hadrian. **5.** (in the Roman Empire) **a.** a title borne by the imperial heir from the reign of Hadrian. **b.** the heir, deputy, and subordinate ruler to either of the two emperors under Diocletian's system of government.

Cae+sar+au·gus+ta (ˌsiːzərɔːˈgʌstə) *n.* the Latin name for **Zaragoza.**

Caes·a+re·a (ˌsiːzəˈrɪə) *n.* an ancient port in NW Israel, capital of Roman Palestine: founded by Herod the Great.

Caes·a+re·a Maz·a·ca (ˈmæzəkə) *n.* the ancient name of **Kayseri.**

Cae+sar+e·an, Cae+sar+i·an, *or U.S.* **Ce+sar+e·an, Ce+sar+i·an** (sɪˈzɛərɪən) *adj.* **1.** of or relating to any of the Caesars, esp. Julius Caesar. ~*n.* **2.** (*sometimes not cap.*) *Surgery.* **a.** short for **Caesarean section. b.** (*as modifier*): *Caesarean birth; Caesarean operation.*

Cae+sar+e·an sec+tion *n.* surgical incision through the abdominal and uterine walls in order to deliver a baby. [C17: from the belief that Julius Caesar was so delivered, the name allegedly being derived from *caesus,* past participle of *caedere* to cut]

Cae+sar+ism (ˈsiːzəˌrɪzəm) *n.* an autocratic system of government. See also **Bonapartism.** —**ˈCae+sar+ist** *n.* —**ˌCae+sar+ˈis+tic** *adj.*

cae+si·um *or U.S.* **ce+si·um** (ˈsiːzɪəm) *n.* a ductile silvery-white element of the alkali metal group that is the most electropositive metal. It occurs in pollucite and lepidolite and is used in photocells. The radioisotope **caesium-137,** with a half-life of 30.2 years, is used in radiotherapy. Symbol: Cs; atomic no.: 55; atomic wt.: 132.905; valency: 1; relative density: 1.87; melting pt.: 28.5°C; boiling pt.: 690°C.

cae+si·um clock *n.* a type of atomic clock that uses the frequency of radiation absorbed in changing the spin of electrons in caesium atoms. See also **second.**

caes+pi+tose *or U.S.* **ces+pi+tose** (ˈsɛspɪˌtəʊs) *adj. Botany.* growing in dense tufts. —**ˈcaes+pi+ˌtose+ly** *or U.S.* **ˈces+pi+ˌtose+ly** *adv.*

cae+su+ra (sɪˈzjʊərə) *n., pl.* **+ras** *or* **+rae** (-riː). **1.** (in modern prosody) a pause, esp. for sense, usually near the middle of a verse line. Usual symbol: ‖ **2.** (in classical prosody) a break between words within a metrical foot, usually in the third or fourth foot of the line. [C16: from Latin, literally: a cutting, from *caedere* to cut] —**cae+ˈsu+ral** *adj.*

Cae·ta·no (kaɪˈtɑːnəʊ; *Portuguese* ˌkajˈtɐnu) *n.* **Mar·cel·lo** (marˈselu). 1906-80, prime minister of Portugal from 1968 until he was replaced by an army coup in 1974.

C.A.F. *abbrev. for* cost and freight.

ca+fard (*French* kaˈfaːr) *n.* a feeling of severe depression. [C20: from French, literally: cockroach, hypocrite]

ca·fé (ˈkæfeɪ, ˈkæfɪ) *n.* a small or inexpensive restaurant or coffee bar, serving light meals and refreshments. [C19: from French: COFFEE]

ca·fé au lait *French.* (kafe o ˈlɛ) *n.* **1.** coffee with milk. **2.** a light brown colour.

ca·fé noir *French.* (kafe ˈnwaːr) *n.* black coffee.

caf+e·te·ri·a (ˌkæfɪˈtɪərɪə) *n.* a self-service restaurant. [C20: from American Spanish: coffee shop]

caff (kæf) *n.* a slang word for **café.**

caf+feine *or* **caf+fein** (ˈkæfiːn, ˈkæfɪˌiːn) *n.* a white crystalline bitter alkaloid responsible for the stimulant action of tea, coffee, and cocoa: a constituent of many tonics and analgesics. Formula: $C_8H_{10}N_4O_2$. See also **xanthine** (sense 2). [C19: from German *Kaffein,* from *Kaffee* COFFEE]

caf+tan (ˈkæfˌtæn, -ˌtɑːn) *n.* a variant spelling of **kaftan.**

cage (keɪdʒ) *n.* **1. a.** an enclosure, usually made with bars or wire, for keeping birds, monkeys, mice, etc. **b.** (*as modifier*): *cagebird.* **2.** a thing or place that confines or imprisons. **3.** something resembling a cage in function or structure: *the rib cage.* **4.** the enclosed platform of a lift, esp. as used in a mine. **5.** *Informal.* the basket used in basketball. **6.** *Informal.* the goal in ice hockey. **7.** *U.S.* a steel framework on which guns are supported. ~*vb.* **8.** (*tr.*) to confine in or as in a cage. [C13: from Old French, from Latin *cavea* enclosure, from *cavus* hollow]

Cage (keɪdʒ) *n.* **John.** born 1912, U.S. composer of experimental music for a variety of conventional, modified, or invented instruments. He evolved a type of music apparently undetermined by the composer, such as in *Imaginary Landscape* (1951) for 12 radio sets.

cage+ling (ˈkeɪdʒlɪŋ) *n.* a bird kept in a cage.

cag+ey *or* **cag·y** (ˈkeɪdʒɪ) *adj.* **·i+er, ·i+est.** *Informal.* not open or frank; cautious; wary. [C20: of unknown origin] —**ˈcag·i+ly** *adv.* —**ˈcag·i+ness** *n.*

cag-hand·ed (ˌkægˈhændɪd) *adj. Brit. dialect.* a variant of **cack-handed.**

Ca+glia+ri[1] (kælˈjɑːrɪ; *Italian* ˈkaʎʎari) *n.* a port in and the capital of Sardinia, on the S coast. Pop.: 236 931 (1975 est.).

Ca·glia·ri[2] (*Italian* ˈkaʎʎari) *n.* **Pa·o·lo** (ˈpaːolo), original name of (Paolo) **Veronese.**

Ca·glio·stro (*Italian* kaʎˈʎɔstro) *n.* Count **A·les·san·dro di** (ˌalesˈsandro diː), original name *Giuseppe Balsamo.* 1743–95, Italian adventurer and magician, who was imprisoned for life by the Inquisition for his association with freemasonry.

cag+mag (ˈkægˌmæg) *Midland English dialect.* ~*adj.* **1.** done shoddily; left incomplete. ~*vb.* **2.** to chat idly; gossip. [C18: of uncertain origin]

Cag·ney (ˈkægnɪ) *n.* **James.** born 1899, U.S. film actor, esp. of gangster roles; his films include *Public Enemy* (1931), *G-Men* (1935), *Angels with Dirty Faces* (1938), and *Yankee Doodle Dandy* (1942).

ca+goule (kəˈguːl) *n.* a lightweight usually knee-length type of anorak. [C20: from French]

ca+hier *French.* (kaˈje) *n.* **1.** a notebook. **2.** a written or printed report, esp. of the proceedings of a meeting.

Ca+ho+ki·a Mounds (kəˈhəʊkɪə) *pl. n.* the largest group of prehistoric Indian earthworks in the U.S., located northeast of East St. Louis.

ca+hoots (kəˈhuːts) *pl. n.* (*sometimes sing.*) *Informal.* **1.** *U.S.* partnership; league (esp. in the phrases **go in cahoots with, go cahoot**). **2. in cahoots.** in collusion. [C19: of uncertain origin]

Cai·a·phas (ˈkaɪəˌfæs) *n. New Testament.* the high priest at the beginning of John the Baptist's preaching and during the trial of Jesus (Luke 3:2; Matthew 26).

Cai+cos Is+lands (ˈkeɪkəs) *pl. n.* a group of islands in the West Indies: part of the British colony of the **Turks and Caicos Islands.**

cai+man (ˈkeɪmən) *n., pl.* **+mans.** a variant spelling of **cayman.**

cain *or* **kain** (keɪn) *n. History.* (in Scotland and Ireland) payment in kind, usually farm produce paid as rent. [C12: from Scottish Gaelic *cāin* rent, perhaps ultimately from Late Latin *canōn* tribute (see CANON); compare Middle Irish *cāin* law]

Cain (keɪn) *n.* **1.** the first son of Adam and Eve, who killed his brother Abel (Genesis 4:1–16). **2. raise Cain.** *Slang.* to cause a commotion; cause trouble.

cai+no+gen+e·sis (ˌkaɪnəʊˈdʒɛnɪsɪs) *n.* a variant spelling of **caenogenesis.** —**cai+no+ge·net+ic** (ˌkaɪnəʊdʒəˈnɛtɪk) *adj.* —**ˌcai+no+ge·ˈnet+i+cal+ly** *adv.*

Cai+no+zo+ic (ˌkaɪnəʊˈzəʊɪk, ˌkeɪ-) *adj.* a variant spelling of **Cenozoic.**

ca·ïque (kaɪˈiːk) *n.* **1.** a long narrow light rowing skiff used on the Bosporus. **2.** a sailing vessel of the E Mediterranean with a sprit mainsail, square topsail, and two or more jibs or other sails. [C17: from French, from Italian *caicco,* from Turkish *kayik*]

caird (kɛəd) *n. Scot. obsolete.* a travelling tinker; vagrant. [C17: from Scottish Gaelic; related to Welsh *cerdd* craft]

Caird Coast (kɛəd) *n.* a region of Antarctica: a part of Coats Land on the SE coast of the Weddell Sea; now included in the British Antarctic Territory.

cairn (kɛən) *n.* **1.** a mound of stones erected as a memorial or marker. **2.** Also called: **cairn terrier.** a small rough-haired breed of terrier originally from Scotland. [C15: from Gaelic *karn*]

cairn+gorm (ˈkɛənˌgɔːm) *n.* a smoky yellow, grey, or brown variety of quartz, used as a gemstone. Also called: **smoky quartz.** [C18: from *Cairn Gorm* (literally: blue cairn), mountain in Scotland where it is found]

Cairn+gorm Moun+tains *pl. n.* a mountain range of NE Scotland: part of the Grampians. Highest peak: Ben Macdhui, 1309 m (4296 ft.). Also called: **The Cairngorms.**

Cairns (kɛənz) *n.* a port in NE Australia, in Queensland. Pop.: 35 200 (1975 est.).

Cai+ro (ˈkaɪrəʊ) *n.* the capital of Egypt, on the Nile: the largest city in Africa and in the Middle East; industrial centre; site of the university and mosque of Al Azhar (founded in 972). Pop.: 4 219 853 (1966). Arabic name: **El Qa+hi+ra** (ɛl ˈkahiːrɑ).

cais+son (kəˈsuːn, ˈkeɪsᵊn) *n.* **1.** a watertight chamber open at the bottom and containing air under pressure, used to carry out construction work under water. **2.** a watertight float filled with air, used to raise sunken ships. See also **camel** (sense 2). **3.** a watertight structure placed across the entrance of a basin, dry dock, etc., to exclude water from it. **4. a.** a box containing explosives formerly used as a mine. **b.** an ammunition chest. **c.** a two-wheeled vehicle carrying an ammunition chest. **5.** another name for **coffer** (sense 3). [C18: from French, assimilated to *caisse* CASE[2]]

cais+son dis+ease *n.* another name for **decompression sickness.**

Caith+ness (keɪθˈnɛs) *n.* (until 1975) a county of NE Scotland, now part of the Highland region.

cai+tiff (ˈkeɪtɪf) *Archaic or poetic.* ~*n.* **1.** a cowardly or base person. ~*adj.* **2.** cowardly; base. [C13: from Old French *caitif* prisoner, from Latin *captīvus* CAPTIVE]

Cai·us (ˈkaɪəs) *n.* a variant of **Gaius.**

caj+e·put (ˈkædʒəˌpʊt) *n.* a variant spelling of **cajuput.**

ca+jole (kəˈdʒəʊl) *vb.* to persuade (someone) by flattery or pleasing talk to do what one wants; wheedle; coax. [C17: from French *cajoler* to coax, of uncertain origin] —**ca+ˈjole+ment** *n.* —**ca+ˈjol+er** *n.* —**ca+ˈjol+er·y** *n.* —**ca+ˈjol+ing+ly** *adv.*

Ca+jun (ˈkeɪdʒən) *n.* **1.** a native of Louisiana descended from 18th-century Acadian immigrants. **2.** the dialect of French spoken by such people. ~*adj.* **3.** denoting or relating to such people or their language. [C19: alteration of ACADIAN; compare *Injun* for *Indian*]

caj·u·put *or* **caj+e·put** (ˈkædʒəˌpʊt) *n.* **1.** a small Australian myrtaceous tree or shrub, *Melaleuca leucadendron,* with whitish flowers and leaves. **2.** a green aromatic oil derived from this tree, used to treat skin diseases. **3.** a lauraceous tree, *Umbellularia californica,* whose aromatic leaves are used in medicine. [C18: from Malay *kayu puteh,* from *kayu* tree + *puteh* white]

cake (keɪk) *n.* **1.** a baked food, usually in loaf or layer form, typically made from a mixture of flour, sugar, and eggs. **2.** a flat thin mass of bread, esp. unleavened bread. **3.** a shaped mass of dough or other food of similar consistency: *a fish cake.* **4.** a mass, slab, or crust of a solidified or compressed substance, as of soap or ice. **5. have one's cake and eat it.** to enjoy both of two desirable but incompatible alternatives. **6. go** *or* **sell like hot cakes.** *Informal.* to be sold very quickly or in large quantities. **7. piece of cake.** *Informal.* something that is easily achieved or obtained. **8. take the cake.** *Informal.* to surpass all others, esp. in stupidity, folly, etc. **9.** *Informal.* the whole or total of something that is to be shared or divided: *the miners are demanding a larger slice of the cake; that is a fair method of sharing the cake.* ~*vb.* **10.** (*tr.*) to cover with a hard layer; encrust: *the hull was caked with salt.* **11.** to form or be formed into a hardened mass. [C13: from Old Norse *kaka;* related to Danish *kage,* German *Kuchen*]

cake+walk ('keɪk,wɔːk) *n.* **1.** a dance based on a march with intricate steps, originally performed by American Negroes with the prize of a cake for the best performers. **2.** a piece of music composed for this dance. ~*vb.* **3.** (*intr.*) to perform the cakewalk. —**'cake+,walk·er** *n.*

cal. *abbrev. for:* **1.** calibre. **2.** calorie (small).

Cal. *abbrev. for:* **1.** Calorie (large). **2.** California.

Cal·a+bar ('kælə,bɑː) *n.* a port in SE Nigeria, capital of Cross River state. Pop.: 103 000 (1975 est.).

Cal·a+bar bean (,kælə'bɑː, 'kælə,bɑː) *n.* the dark brown very poisonous seed of a leguminous woody climbing plant, *Physostigma venenosum* of tropical Africa, used as a source of the drug physostigmine.

cal·a+bash ('kælə,bæʃ) *n.* **1.** Also called: **calabash tree.** a tropical American evergreen tree, *Crescentia cujete,* that produces large round gourds: family *Bignoniaceae.* **2.** another name for the **bottle gourd. 3.** the gourd of either of these plants. **4.** the dried hollow shell of a gourd used as the bowl of a tobacco pipe, a bottle, rattle, etc. **5. calabash nutmeg.** a tropical African shrub, *Monodora myristica,* whose oily aromatic seeds can be used as nutmegs: family *Annonaceae.* [C17: from obsolete French *calabasse, from Spanish calabaza, perhaps from Arabic qar'ah yābisah* dry gourd, from *qar'ah* gourd + *yābisah* dry]

cal·a+boose ('kælə,buːs) *n. U.S. informal.* a prison; jail. [C18: from Creole French, from Spanish *calabozo* dungeon, of unknown origin]

Ca+lab+ri·a (kə'læbrɪə) *n.* **1.** a region of SW Italy: mostly mountainous and subject to earthquakes. Chief town: Reggio di Calabria. Pop.: 1 962 899 (1971). Area: 15 080 sq. km. (5822 sq. miles). **2.** an ancient region of extreme SE Italy (3rd century B.C. to about 668 A.D.); now part of Apulia.

ca+la+di·um (kə'leɪdɪəm) *n.* any of various tropical plants of the aroid genus *Caladium,* which are widely cultivated as potted plants for their colourful variegated foliage. [C19: from New Latin, from Malay *kĕladi* araceous plant]

Cal+ais ('kæleɪ, 'kælɪ; *French* ka'lɛ) *n.* a port in N France, on the Strait of Dover: the nearest French port to England; belonged to England 1347–1558. Pop.: 79 369 (1975).

cal·a+lu *or* **cal·a+loo** ('kælǝluː) *n. Caribbean.* the edible leaves of various plants, used as greens or in making thick soups. [probably of African origin]

cal·a+man+co (,kælə'mæŋkəʊ) *n.* a glossy woollen fabric woven with a checked design that shows on one side only. [C16: of unknown origin]

cal·a+man+der ('kælə,mændə) *n.* the hard black-and-brown striped wood of several trees of the genus *Diospyros,* esp. *D. quaesita* of India and Ceylon, used in making furniture: family *Ebenaceae.* See also **ebony** (sense 2). [C19: metathetic variant of COROMANDEL COAST]

cal·a+mine ('kælə,maɪn) *n.* **1.** a pink powder consisting of zinc oxide and ferric oxide, used medicinally in the form of soothing lotions or ointments. **2.** the former Brit. name for **smithsonite. 3.** the former U.S. name for **hemimorphite.** [C17: from Old French, from Medieval Latin *calamīna,* from Latin *cadmīa;* see CADMIUM]

cal·a+mint ('kæləmɪnt) *n.* any aromatic Eurasian plant of the genus *Satureja* (or *Calamintha*), having clusters of purple or pink flowers: family *Labiatae* (labiates). [C14: from Old French *calament* (but influenced by English MINT[1]), from Medieval Latin *calamentum,* from Greek *kalaminthē*]

cal·a+mite ('kælə,maɪt) *n.* any extinct treelike pteridophyte plant of the genus *Calamites,* of Carboniferous times, related to the horsetails. [C19: from New Latin *Calamītes* type genus, from Greek *kalamitēs* reedlike, from *kalamos* reed]

ca+lam·i+tous (kə'læmɪtəs) *adj.* causing, involving, or resulting in a calamity; disastrous. —**ca+'lam·i+tous+ly** *adv.* —**ca+'lam·i+tous+ness** *n.*

ca+lam+i·ty (kə'læmɪtɪ) *n., pl.* **·ties. 1.** a disaster or misfortune, esp. one causing extreme havoc, distress, or misery. **2.** a state or feeling of deep distress or misery. [C15: from French *calamité,* from Latin *calamitās;* related to Latin *incolumis* uninjured]

cal·a+mon+din ('kælə,mʌndɪn) *or* **cal·a+mon+din or+ange** *n.* **1.** a small citrus tree, *Citrus mitis,* of the Philippines. **2.** the acid-tasting fruit of this tree, resembling a small orange. [from Tagalog *kalamunding*]

cal·a+mus ('kæləməs) *n., pl.* **+mi** (-,maɪ). **1.** any tropical Asian palm of the genus *Calamus,* some species of which are a source of rattan and canes. **2.** another name for **sweet flag. 3.** the aromatic root of the sweet flag. **4.** *Ornithol.* the basal hollow shaft of a feather; quill. [C14: from Latin, from Greek *kalamos* reed, cane, stem]

cal+an+dri·a (kə'lændrɪə) *n.* a cylindrical vessel through which vertical tubes pass, esp. one forming part of an evaporator, heat exchanger, or nuclear reactor. [C20: arbitrarily named, from Spanish, literally: lark]

ca+lash (kə'læʃ) *or* **ca+lèche** *n.* **1.** a horse-drawn carriage with low wheels and a folding top. **2.** the folding top of such a carriage. **3.** a woman's folding hooped hood worn in the 18th century. [C17: from French *calèche,* from German *Kalesche,* from Czech *kolesa* wheels]

cal·a+thus ('kæləθəs) *n., pl.* **+thi** (-,θaɪ). a vase-shaped basket represented in ancient Greek art, used as a symbol of fruitfulness. [C18: from Latin, from Greek *kalathos*]

ca+lav+er+ite (kə'lævə,raɪt) *n.* a metallic pale yellow mineral consisting of a telluride of gold in the form of elongated striated crystals. It is a source of gold in Australia and North America. Formula: $AuTe_2$. [C19: named after *Calaveras,* county in California where it was discovered]

calc- *combining form.* variant of **calci-** before a vowel.

cal+ca+ne·us (kæl'keɪnɪəs) *or* **cal+ca+ne·um** *n., pl.* **+ne·i** (-nɪ,aɪ) **1.** the largest tarsal bone, forming the heel in man. Nontechnical name: **heel bone. 2.** the corresponding bone in other vertebrates. [C19: from Late Latin: heel, from Latin *calx* heel] —**cal+'ca+ne·al** *or* **cal+'ca+ne·an** *adj.*

cal+car ('kæl,kɑː). *n., pl.* **cal+car·i·a** (kæl'kɛərɪə). a spur or spurlike process, as on the leg of a bird or the corolla of a flower. [C19: from Latin, from *calx* heel]

cal+car+e·ous (kæl'kɛərɪəs) *adj.* of, containing, or resembling calcium carbonate; chalky. [C17: from Latin *calcārius,* from *calx* lime]

cal+ca+rif+er+ous (,kælkə'rɪfərəs) *adj. Biology.* having a spur or spurs.

cal+ce·i+form ('kælsɪɪ,fɔːm, kæl'siː-) *or* **cal+ce·o+late** ('kælsɪə,leɪt) *adj. Botany.* shaped like a shoe or slipper. [C19: from Latin *calceus* shoe]

cal+ce·o+lar+i·a (,kælsɪə'lɛərɪə) *n.* any tropical American scrophulariaceous plant of the genus *Calceolaria:* cultivated for their speckled slipper-shaped flowers. Also called: **slipperwort.** [C18: from Latin *calceolus* small shoe, from *calceus*]

cal+ces ('kælsiːz) *n.* a plural of **calx.**

Cal·chas ('kælkæs) *n. Greek myth.* a soothsayer who assisted the Greeks in the Trojan War.

cal·ci- *or before a vowel* **calc-** *combining form.* indicating lime or calcium: *calcify.* [from Latin *calx, calc-* limestone]

cal+cic ('kælsɪk) *adj.* of, containing, or concerned with lime or calcium. [C19: from Latin *calx* lime]

cal+ci+cole ('kælsɪ,kəʊl) *n.* any plant that thrives in lime-rich soils. [C20: from CALCI- + *-cole,* from Latin *colere* to dwell] —**cal+cic·o·lous** (kæl'sɪkələs) *adj.*

cal+cif+er+ol (kæl'sɪfərɒl) *n.* a fat-soluble steroid, found esp. in fish-liver oils, produced by the action of ultraviolet radiation on ergosterol. It increases the absorption of calcium from the intestine and is used in the treatment of rickets. Formula: $C_{28}H_{43}OH$. Also called: **vitamin D_2.** [C20: from CALCIF(EROUS + ERGOST)EROL]

cal+cif+er+ous (kæl'sɪfərəs) *adj.* forming or producing salts of calcium, esp. calcium carbonate.

cal+cif+ic (kæl'sɪfɪk) *adj.* forming or causing to form lime or chalk.

cal+ci+fi+ca+tion (,kælsɪfɪ'keɪʃən) *n.* **1.** the process of calcifying or becoming calcified. **2.** *Pathol.* a tissue hardened by deposition of lime salts. **3.** any calcified object or formation.

cal+ci+fuge ('kælsɪ,fjuːdʒ) *n.* any plant that thrives in acid soils. —**cal+ci+fu+gal** (,kælsɪ'fjuːgᵊl) *adj.* —**cal+cif·u+gous** (kæl'sɪfjəgəs) *adj.*

cal+ci+fy ('kælsɪ,faɪ) *vb.* **+fies, +fy+ing, +fied. 1.** to convert or be converted into lime. **2.** to harden or become hardened by impregnation with calcium salts.

cal+ci+mine ('kælsɪ,maɪn, -mɪn) *or* **kal+so+mine** *n.* **1.** a white or pale tinted wash for walls. ~*vb.* **2.** (*tr.*) to cover with calcimine. [C19: changed from *Kalsomine,* a trademark]

cal+cine ('kælsaɪn, -sɪn) *vb.* **1.** (*tr.*) to heat (a substance) so that it is oxidized, reduced, or loses water. **2.** (*intr.*) to oxidize as a result of heating. [C14: from Medieval Latin *calcināre* to heat, from Latin *calx* lime] —**cal+ci+na+tion** (,kælsɪ'neɪʃən) *n.*

cal+cite ('kælsaɪt) *n.* a common colourless or white mineral consisting of calcium carbonate in rhombohedral crystalline form: the transparent variety is Iceland spar. Formula: $CaCO_3$. —**cal+cit+ic** (kæl'sɪtɪk) *adj.*

cal+ci+ton+in (,kælsɪ'təʊnɪn) *n.* a hormone secreted by the thyroid that inhibits the release of calcium from the skeleton and prevents a build-up of calcium in the blood. Also called: **thyrocalcitonin.** Compare **parathyroid hormone.** [C20: from CALCI- + TONIC + -IN]

cal+ci·um ('kælsɪəm) *n.* a malleable silvery-white metallic element of the alkaline earth group; the fifth most abundant element in the earth's crust (3.6 per cent), occurring esp. as forms of calcium carbonate. It is an essential constituent of bones and teeth and is used as a deoxidizer in steel. Symbol: Ca; atomic no.: 20; atomic wt.: 40.08; valency: 2; relative density: 1.55; melting pt.: 842–8°C; boiling pt.: 1487°C. [C19: from New Latin, from Latin *calx* lime]

cal+ci·um car+bide *n.* a grey salt of calcium used in the production of acetylene (by its reaction with water) and calcium cyanamide. Formula: CaC_2. Sometimes shortened to **carbide.**

cal+ci·um car+bon+ate *n.* a white crystalline salt occurring in limestone, chalk, marble, calcite, coral, and pearl: used in the production of lime and cement. Formula: $CaCO_3$.

cal+ci·um chlo+ride *n.* a white deliquescent salt occurring naturally in seawater and used in the de-icing of roads and as a drying agent. Formula: $CaCl_2$.

cal+ci·um cy+an·a+mide *n.* a white crystalline compound formed by heating calcium carbide with nitrogen. It is important in the fixation of nitrogen and can be hydrolysed to ammonia or used as a fertilizer. Formula: $CaCN_2$.

cal+ci·um hy+drox+ide *n.* a white crystalline slightly soluble alkali with many uses, esp. in cement, water softening, and the neutralization of acid soils. Formula: $Ca(OH)_2$. Also called: **lime, slaked lime, hydrated lime, calcium hydrate, caustic lime, lime hydrate.**

cal·ci·um light *n.* another name for **limelight.**

cal·ci·um ox·ide *n.* a white crystalline base used in the production of calcium hydroxide and bleaching powder and in the manufacture of glass, paper, and steel. Formula: CaO. Also called: **lime, quicklime, calx, burnt lime, calcined lime, fluxing lime.**

cal·ci·um phos·phate *n.* **1.** the insoluble nonacid calcium salt of orthophosphoric acid: occurs in bones and is the main constituent of bone ash. Formula: $Ca_3(PO_4)_2$. **2.** any calcium salt of a phosphoric acid. Calcium phosphates are found in many rocks and used esp. in fertilizers.

calc·sin·ter ('kælkˌsɪntə) *n.* another name for **travertine.** [C19: from German *Kalksinter,* from *Kalk* lime + *sinter* dross; see CHALK, SINTER]

calc·spar ('kælkˌspɑː) *n.* another name for **calcite.** [C19: partial translation of Swedish *kalkspat,* from *kalk* lime (ultimately from Latin *calx*) + spat SPAR³]

calc·tu·fa ('kælkˌtuːfə) *or* **calc·tuff** ('kælkˌtʌf) *n.* another name for **tufa.**

cal·cu·la·ble ('kælkjʊləbᵊl) *adj.* **1.** that may be computed or estimated. **2.** predictable; dependable. —ˌ**cal·cu·la·'bil·i·ty** *n.* —'**cal·cu·la·bly** *adv.*

cal·cu·late ('kælkjʊˌleɪt) *vb.* **1.** to solve (one or more problems) by a mathematical procedure; compute. **2.** (*tr.; may take a clause as object*) to determine beforehand by judgment, reasoning, etc.; estimate. **3.** (*tr.; usually passive*) to design specifically; aim: *the car was calculated to appeal to women.* **4.** (*intr.;* foll. by *on* or *upon*) to depend; rely. **5.** (*tr.; may take a clause as object*) *U.S. dialect.* **a.** to suppose; think. **b.** to intend (to do something). [C16: from Late Latin *calculāre,* from *calculus* pebble used as a counter; see CALCULUS] —**cal·cu·la·tive** ('kælkjʊlətɪv) *adj.*

cal·cu·lat·ed ('kælkjʊˌleɪtɪd) *adj.* (*usually prenominal*) **1.** undertaken after considering the likelihood of success or failure: *a calculated risk.* **2.** deliberately planned; premeditated: *a calculated insult.*

cal·cu·lat·ing ('kælkjʊˌleɪtɪŋ) *adj.* **1.** selfishly scheming. **2.** shrewd; cautious. —'**cal·cu·ˌlat·ing·ly** *adv.*

cal·cu·lat·ing ma·chine *n.* an electronic or mechanical device for performing arithmetical operations. Also called: **calculator.** Compare **adding machine.**

cal·cu·la·tion (ˌkælkjʊ'leɪʃən) *n.* **1.** the act, process, or result of calculating. **2.** an estimation of probability; forecast. **3.** careful planning or forethought, esp. for selfish motives.

cal·cu·la·tor ('kælkjʊˌleɪtə) *n.* **1.** another name for **calculating machine. 2.** a person or thing that calculates. **3.** a set of tables used as an aid to calculations.

cal·cu·lous ('kælkjʊləs) *adj. Pathol.* of or suffering from a calculus.

cal·cu·lus ('kælkjʊləs) *n., pl.* **·lus·es. 1.** a branch of mathematics, developed independently by Newton and Leibnitz. Both **differential calculus** and **integral calculus** are concerned with the effect on a function of an infinitesimal change in the independent variable as it tends to zero. **2.** *pl.* **·li** (-ˌlaɪ). *Pathol.* a stonelike concretion of minerals and salts found in ducts or hollow organs of the body. **3.** any mathematical system of calculation involving the use of symbols. [C17: from Latin: pebble, stone used in reckoning, from *calx* small stone, counter]

cal·cu·lus of var·i·a·tions *n.* a branch of calculus concerned with maxima and minima of definite integrals.

Cal·cut·ta (kæl'kʌtə) *n.* a port in E India, capital of West Bengal state, on the Hooghly River: former capital of the country (1833–1912); major commercial and industrial centre; two universities. Pop.: 3 148 746 (1971).

cal·dar·i·um (kæl'dɛərɪəm) *n., pl.* **·dar·i·a** (-'dɛərɪə). (in ancient Rome) a room for taking hot baths. [C18: from Latin, from *calidus* warm, from *calēre* to be warm]

Cal·der ('kɔːldə) *n.* **Al·ex·an·der.** born 1898, U.S. sculptor, who originated mobiles and stabiles (moving or static abstract sculptures, generally suspended from wire).

cal·de·ra (kæl'dɛərə, 'kɔːldərə) *n.* any enlarged volcanic crater formed by the explosion or collapse of the cone. [C19: from Spanish *Caldera* (literally: CAULDRON), name of a crater in the Canary Islands]

Cal·de·rón de la Bar·ca (*Spanish* ˌkalde'ron ðe la 'barka) *n.* **Pe·dro** ('peðro). 1600–81, Spanish dramatist, whose best-known work is *La Vida es Sueño.* He also wrote *autos sacramentales,* outdoor plays for the feast of Corpus Christi, 76 of which survive.

cal·dron ('kɔːldrən) *n.* a variant spelling of **cauldron.**

Cald·well ('kɔːldwɛl, -wəl) *n.* **Er·skine** ('ɜːskɪn). born 1903, U.S. novelist whose works include *Tobacco Road* (1932).

ca·lèche (*French* ka'lɛʃ) *n.* a variant spelling of **calash.**

Cal·e·do·ni·a (ˌkælɪ'dəʊnɪə) *n.* the Roman name for **Scotland.**

Cal·e·do·ni·an (ˌkælɪ'dəʊnɪən) *adj.* **1.** of or relating to Scotland. **2.** of or denoting a period of mountain building in NW Europe in the Palaeozoic era. ~*n.* **3.** *Literary.* a native or inhabitant of Scotland.

Cal·e·do·ni·an Ca·nal *n.* a canal in N Scotland, linking the Atlantic with the North Sea through the Great Glen: built 1803–47; now little used.

cal·e·fa·cient (ˌkælɪ'feɪʃənt) *adj.* **1.** causing warmth. ~*n.* **2.** *Med.* an agent that warms, such as a mustard plaster. [C17: from Latin *calefaciēns,* from *calefacere* to heat] —**cal·e·fac·tion** (ˌkælɪ'fækʃən) *n.*

cal·e·fac·to·ry (ˌkælɪ'fæktərɪ) *adj.* **1.** giving warmth. ~*n., pl.* **·ries. 2.** a heated room in a monastery. [C16: from Latin *calefactōrius,* from *calefactus* made warm; see CALEFACIENT]

cal·en·dar ('kælɪndə) *n.* **1.** a system for determining the beginning, length, and order of years and their divisions. See also **Gregorian calendar, Jewish calendar, Julian calendar, Revolutionary calendar, Roman calendar. 2.** a table showing any such arrangement, esp. as applied to one or more successive years. **3.** a list, register, or schedule of social events, pending court cases, appointments, etc. ~*vb.* **4.** (*tr.*) to enter in a calendar; schedule; register. [C13: via Norman French from Medieval Latin *kalendārium* account book, from *Kalendae* the CALENDS, when interest on debts became due] —**ca·len·dri·cal** (kæ'lɛndrɪkᵊl) *or* **ca·'len·dric** *adj.*

cal·en·dar day *n.* See **day** (sense 1).

cal·en·dar month *n.* See **month** (sense 1).

cal·en·dar year *n.* See **year** (sense 1).

cal·en·der¹ ('kælɪndə) *n.* **1.** a machine in which paper or cloth is glazed or smoothed by passing between rollers. ~*vb.* **2.** (*tr.*) to subject (material) to such a process. [C17: from French *calandre,* of unknown origin]

cal·en·der² ('kælɪndə) *n.* a member of a mendicant order of dervishes in Turkey, Iran, and India. [from Persian *kalandar*]

cal·ends *or* **kal·ends** ('kælɪndz) *pl. n.* the first day of each month in the ancient Roman calendar. [C14 from Latin *kalendae;* related to Latin *calāre* to proclaim]

ca·len·du·la (kæ'lɛndjʊlə) *n.* **1.** any Eurasian plant of the genus *Calendula,* esp. the pot marigold, having orange-and-yellow rayed flowers: family *Compositae* (composites). **2.** the dried flowers of the pot marigold, formerly used medicinally and for seasoning. [C19: from Medieval Latin, from Latin *kalendae* CALENDS; perhaps from its supposed efficacy in curing menstrual disorders]

cal·en·ture ('kælənˌtjʊə) *n.* a mild fever of tropical climates, similar in its symptoms to sunstroke. [C16: from Spanish *calentura* fever, ultimately from Latin *calēre* to be warm]

calf¹ (kɑːf) *n., pl.* **calves. 1.** the young of cattle, esp. domestic cattle. **2.** the young of certain other mammals, such as the buffalo, elephant, giraffe, and whale. **3.** a large piece of ice detached from an iceberg, etc. **4. kill the fatted calf.** to celebrate lavishly, esp. as a welcome. **5.** another name for **calfskin.** [Old English *cealf;* related to Old Norse *kālfr,* Gothic *kalbō,* Old High German *kalba*]

calf² (kɑːf) *n., pl.* **calves.** the thick fleshy part of the back of the leg between the ankle and the knee. [C14: from Old Norse *kalfi*]

calf love *n.* temporary infatuation or love of an adolescent for a member of the opposite sex. Also called: **puppy love.**

calf's-foot jel·ly *n.* a jelly made from the stock of boiled calves' feet and flavourings, formerly often served to invalids.

calf·skin ('kɑːfˌskɪn) *n.* **1.** the skin or hide of a calf. **2.** Also called: **calf. a.** fine leather made from this skin. **b.** (*as modifier*): **calfskin boots.**

Cal·ga·ry ('kælgərɪ) *n.* a city in Canada, in S Alberta: centre of a large agricultural region; oilfields. Pop.: 403 319 (1971).

Ca·li (*Spanish* 'kali) *n.* a city in SW Colombia: commercial centre in a rich agricultural region. Pop.: 898 253 (1973).

Cal·i·ban ('kælɪˌbæn) *n.* a brutish or brutalized man. [C19: after a character in Shakespeare's *The Tempest* (1610)]

cal·i·brate ('kælɪˌbreɪt) *vb.* (*tr.*) **1.** to measure the calibre of (a gun, mortar, etc.). **2.** to mark (the scale of a measuring instrument) so that readings can be made in appropriate units. **3.** to determine the accuracy of (a measuring instrument, etc.). **4.** (*tr.*) to determine or check the range of (a piece of artillery). —ˌ**cal·i·'bra·tion** *n.* —'**cal·i·ˌbra·tor** *or* '**cal·i·ˌbrat·er** *n.*

cal·i·bre *or U.S.* **cal·i·ber** ('kælɪbə) *n.* **1.** the diameter of a cylindrical body, esp. the internal diameter of a tube or the bore of a firearm. **2.** the diameter of a shell or bullet. **3.** ability; distinction: *a musician of high calibre.* **4.** personal character: *a man of high calibre.* [C16: from Old French, from Italian *calibro,* from Arabic *qālib* shoemaker's last, mould] —'**cal·i·bred** *or U.S.* '**cal·i·bered** *adj.*

cal·i·ces ('kælɪˌsiːz) *n.* the plural of **calix.**

ca·li·che (kæ'liːtʃɪ) *n.* **1.** a bed of sand or clay in arid regions that contains Chile saltpetre, sodium chloride, and other soluble minerals. **2.** a surface layer of soil encrusted with calcium carbonate, occurring in arid regions. [C20: from American Spanish, from Latin *calx* lime]

cal·i·cle ('kælɪkᵊl) *n.* a variant spelling of **calycle.** —**ca·lic·u·lar** (kə'lɪkjʊlə) *adj.*

cal·i·co ('kælɪˌkəʊ) *n., pl.* **·coes** *or* **·cos. 1.** a white or unbleached cotton fabric with no printed design. **2.** *Chiefly U.S.* a coarse printed cotton fabric. **3.** (*modifier*) made of calico. [C16: based on *Calicut,* town in India]

cal·i·co bush *n.* another name for **mountain laurel.**

Cal·i·cut ('kælɪˌkʌt) *n.* the former name for **Kozhikode.**

ca·lif ('keɪlɪf, 'kæl-) *n.* a variant spelling of **caliph.**

Calif. *abbrev. for* California.

cal·if·ate ('kælɪˌfeɪt, -fɪt) *n.* a variant spelling of **caliphate.**

Cal·i·for·ni·a (ˌkælɪ'fɔːnɪə) *n.* **1.** a state on the W coast of the U.S.: the third largest state in area and the largest in population; consists of a narrow, warm coastal plain rising to the Coast Range, deserts in the south, the fertile central valleys of the Sacramento and San Joaquin Rivers, and the mountains of the Sierra Nevada in the east; major industries include the growing of citrus fruits and grapes, fishing, oil production, and films. Capital: Sacramento. Pop.: 19 953 134 (1970). Area: 411 015 sq. km (158 693 sq. miles). Abbrevs.: **Cal., Calif.** or (with zip code) **CA 2. Gulf of.** an arm of the Pacific Ocean, between Sonora and Lower California.

Cal·i·for·ni·a pop·py *n.* a papaveraceous plant, *Eschscholtzia* *californica,* of the Pacific coast of North America, having yellow or orange flowers and finely divided bluish-green leaves.

cal·i·for·ni·um (ˌkælɪˈfɔːnɪəm) *n.* a metallic transuranic element artificially produced from curium. Symbol: Cf; atomic no.: 98; half-life of most stable isotope, ^{251}Cf: 800 years (approx.). [C20: New Latin; discovered at the University of *California*]

ca·lig·i·nous (kəˈlɪdʒɪnəs) *adj. Archaic.* dark; dim. [C16: from Latin *cālīginōsus* from *cālīgō* darkness] —**ca·lig·i·nos·i·ty** (kəˌlɪdʒɪˈnɒsɪtɪ) *n.*

Ca·lig·u·la (kəˈlɪgjʊlə) *n.* original name *Gaius Caesar,* son of Germanicus. 12–41 A.D., Roman emperor (37–41), noted for his cruelty and tyranny; assassinated.

Cal·i·mere (ˈkælɪmɪə) *n.* **Point.** a cape on the SE coast of India, on the Palk Strait.

cal·i·pash *or* **cal·li·pash** (ˈkælɪˌpæʃ) *n.* the greenish glutinous edible part of the turtle found next to the upper shell, considered a delicacy. [C17: perhaps changed from Spanish *carapacho* CARAPACE]

cal·i·pee (ˈkælɪˌpiː) *n.* the yellow glutinous edible part of the turtle found next to the lower shell, considered a delicacy. [C17: perhaps a variant of CALIPASH]

cal·i·per (ˈkælɪpə) *n.* the usual U.S. spelling of **calliper.**

ca·liph, ca·lif, ka·lif, *or* **kha·lif** (ˈkeɪlɪf, ˈkæl-) *n. Islam.* the title of the successors of Mohammed as rulers of the Islamic world, later assumed by the Sultans of Turkey. [C14: from Old French, from Arabic *khalīfa* successor]

ca·li·phate, ca·li·fate, *or* **ka·li·fate** (ˈkeɪlɪˌfeɪt, -fɪt, ˈkæl-) *n.* the office, jurisdiction, or reign of a caliph.

cal·i·sa·ya (ˌkælɪˈseɪə) *n.* the bark of any of several tropical trees of the rubiaceous genus *Cinchona,* esp. *C. calisaya,* from which quinine is extracted. Also called: **calisaya bark, yellow-bark, cinchona.** [C19: from Spanish, from the name of a Bolivian Indian who taught the uses of quinine to the Spanish]

cal·is·then·ics (ˌkælɪsˈθɛnɪks) *n.* a variant spelling (esp. U.S.) of **callisthenics.** —ˌ**cal·is·ˈthen·ic** *adj.*

ca·lix (ˈkeɪlɪks, ˈkæ-) *n., pl.* **cal·i·ces** (ˈkælɪˌsiːz). a cup; chalice. [C18: from Latin: CHALICE]

calk[1] (kɔːk) *vb.* a variant spelling of **caulk.**

calk[2] (kɔːk) *or* **cal·kin** (ˈkɔːkɪn, ˈkæl-) *n.* **1.** a metal projection on a horse's shoe to prevent slipping. **2.** *Chiefly U.S.* a spiked plate attached to the sole of a shoe to prevent slipping. ~*vb.* (*tr.*) **3.** to provide with calks. **4.** to wound with a calk. [C17: from Latin *calx* heel]

calk[3] (kɔːk) *vb.* (*tr.*) to transfer (a design) by tracing it with a blunt point from one sheet backed with loosely fixed colouring matter onto another placed underneath. [C17: from French *calquer* to trace; see CALQUE]

call (kɔːl) *vb.* **1.** (often foll. by *out*) to speak or utter (words, sounds, etc.) loudly so as to attract attention: *he called out her name.* **2.** (*tr.*) to ask or order to come: *to call a policeman.* **3.** (*intr.*; sometimes foll. by *on*) to make a visit (to): *she called on him.* **4.** (often foll. by *up*) to telephone (a person): *he called back at nine.* **5.** (*tr.*) to summon to a specific office, profession, etc.: *they called out the army.* **6.** (of animals or birds) to utter (a characteristic sound or cry). **7.** (*tr.*) to summon (a bird or animal) by imitating its cry. **8.** (*tr.*) to name or style: *they called the dog Rover.* **9.** (*tr.*) to designate: *they called him a coward.* **10.** (*tr.*) *Brit. dialect.* to speak ill of or scold. **11.** (*tr.*) to regard in a specific way: *I call it a foolish waste of time.* **12.** (*tr.*) to attract (attention). **13.** (*tr.*) to read (a list, register, etc.) aloud to check for omissions or absentees. **14.** (when *tr.,* usually foll. by *for*) to give an order (for): *to call a strike.* **15.** (*intr.*) to try to predict the result of tossing a coin. **16.** (*tr.*) to awaken: *I was called early this morning.* **17.** (*tr.*) to cause to assemble: *to call a meeting.* **18.** (*tr.*) *Sport.* (of an umpire, referee, etc.) to pass judgment upon (a shot, player, etc.) with a call. **19.** *Austral.* to broadcast a commentary on a race, esp. a horse race. **20.** (*tr.*) to demand repayment of (a loan, redeemable bond, security, etc.). **21.** (*tr.*; often foll. by *up*) *Company accounting.* to demand payment of (a portion of a share issue not yet paid by subscribers). **22.** *Brit.* to award (a student at an Inn of Court) the degree of barrister (esp. in the phrase **call to the bar**). **23.** (*tr.*) *Poker.* to demand that (a player) expose his hand, after equalling his bet. **24.** (*intr.*) *Bridge.* to make a bid. **25.** (*tr.*) to expose (a person's misleading statements, boasts, etc.): *I called his bluff.* **26.** (in square dancing) to call out (instructions) to the dancers. **27.** *Billiards.* to ask (a player) to say what kind of shot he will play or (of a player) to name his shot. **28.** (*intr.*; foll by *for*) **a.** to require: *this problem calls for study.* **b.** to come or go (for) in order to fetch: *I will call for my book later.* **29.** (*intr.*; foll. by *on* or *upon*) to make an appeal or request (to): *they called upon him to reply.* **30. call into being.** to create. **31. call into play.** to begin to operate. **32. call into question.** See **question** (sense 12). **33. call it a day.** to bring an activity to an end. **34. call to mind.** to cause to be remembered. ~*n.* **35.** a cry or shout. **36.** the characteristic cry of a bird or animal. **37.** a device, such as a whistle, intended to imitate the cry of a bird or animal. **38.** a summons or invitation. **39.** a summons or signal sounded on a horn, bugle, etc. **40.** *Hunting.* any of several notes or patterns of notes, blown on a hunting horn as a signal **41.** *Hunting.* **a.** an imitation of the characteristic cry of a wild animal or bird to lure it to the hunter. **b.** an instrument for producing such an imitation. **42.** a short visit: *the doctor made six calls this morning.* **43.** an inner urge to some task or profession; vocation. **44.** allure or fascination, esp. of a place: *the call of the forest.* **45.** *Brit.* the summons to the bar of a student member of an Inn of Court. **46.** need, demand, or occasion: *there is no call to shout; we don't get much call for stockings these days.* **47.** demand a notice or claim (esp. in the phrase **the call of duty**). **48.** *Theatre.* a notice to actors informing them of times of rehearsals. **49.** (in square dancing) an instruction to execute new figures. **50.** a conversation or a request for a connection by telephone. **51.** *Commerce.* **a.** a demand for repayment of a loan. **b.** (*as modifier*): *call money.* **52.** *Finance.* **a.** a demand for redeemable bonds or shares to be presented for repayment. **b.** a demand for an instalment payment on the issue price of bonds or shares. **53.** *Billiards.* a demand to an opponent to say what kind of shot he will play. **54.** *Poker.* a demand for a hand or hands to be exposed. **55.** *Bridge.* a bid, or a player's turn to bid. **56.** *Sport.* a decision of an umpire or referee regarding a shot, pitch, etc. **57.** *Austral.* a broadcast commentary on a race, esp. a horse race. **58.** Also called: **call option.** *Stock Exchange.* an option to buy a stated amount of securities at a specified price during a specified period. Compare **put** (sense 20). **59.** See **roll call. 60. call for margin.** *Stock Exchange.* a demand made by a stockbroker for partial payment of a client's debt due to decreasing value of the collateral. **61. call of nature.** See **nature** (sense 15). **62. on call. a.** (of a loan, etc.) repayable on demand. **b.** (of a doctor, etc.) available when summoned; on duty. **63. within call.** within range; accessible. ~See also **call down, call forth, call in, call off, call out, call up.** [Old English *ceallian;* related to Old Norse *kalla,* Old High German *kallōn,* Old Slavonic *glasŭ* voice]

cal·la (ˈkælə) *n.* **1.** Also called: **calla lily, arum lily.** any southern African plant of the aroid genus *Zantedeschia,* esp. *Z. aethiopica,* which has a white funnel-shaped spathe enclosing a yellow spadix. **2.** an aroid plant, *Calla palustris,* that grows in wet places and has a white spathe enclosing a greenish spadix, and red berries. [C19: from New Latin, probably from Greek *kalleia* wattles on a cock, probably from *kallos* beauty]

call·a·ble (ˈkɔːləbᵊl) *adj.* **1.** (of a security) subject to redemption before maturity. **2.** (of money loaned) repayable on demand.

Cal·la·ghan (ˈkæləˌhæn) *n.* **(Leonard) James.** born 1912, English Labour statesman; prime minister of Great Britain and Northern Ireland 1976-1979.

cal·lais (ˈkæleɪ) *n.* a green stone found as beads and ornaments in the late Neolithic and early Bronze Age of W Europe. [C19: from Greek *kallais*]

cal·lant (ˈkɑːlənt) *or* **cal·lan** (ˈkɑːlən) *n.* a youth; lad. [C16: from Flemish *kalant* customer, fellow]

Ca·lla·o (*Spanish* kaˈʎao) *n.* a port in W Peru, near Lima, on **Callao Bay:** chief import centre of Peru. Pop.: 296 721 (1972).

Cal·las (ˈkæləs) *n.* **Ma·ri·a.** 1923–77, Greek operatic soprano, born in the U.S.

call box *n.* a soundproof enclosure for a public telephone. Also called: **telephone box, telephone kiosk.**

call·boy (ˈkɔːlˌbɔɪ) *n.* a person who notifies actors when it is time to go on stage.

call down *vb.* (*tr., adv.*) to request or invoke: *to call down God's anger.*

call·er[1] (ˈkɔːlə) *n.* a person or thing that calls, esp. a person who makes a brief visit.

cal·ler[2] (ˈkælə) *adj. Scot.* **1.** (of food, esp. fish) fresh. **2.** cool: *a caller breeze.* [C14: Scottish variant of *calver,* probably from Old English *calwer* curds]

call forth *vb.* (*tr., adv.*) to cause (something) to come into action or existence: *she called forth all her courage.*

call girl *n.* a prostitute with whom appointments are made by telephone.

cal·li- *combining form.* beautiful: *calligraphy.* [from Greek *kalli-,* from *kallos* beauty]

Cal·lic·ra·tes (kəˈlɪkrəˌtiːz) *n.* 5th century B.C., Greek architect: with Ictinus, designed the Parthenon.

cal·lig·ra·phy (kəˈlɪgrəfɪ) *n.* handwriting, esp. beautiful handwriting considered as an art. Also called: **chirography.** —**cal·ˈlig·ra·pher** *or* **cal·ˈlig·ra·phist** *n.* —**cal·li·graph·ic** (ˌkælɪˈgræfɪk) *adj.* —ˌ**cal·li·ˈgraph·i·cal·ly** *adv.*

Cal·lim·a·chus (kəˈlɪməkəs) *n.* ?305–?240 B.C., Greek poet of the Alexandrian School; author of hymns and epigrams.

call in *vb.* (*adv.*) **1.** (*intr.*; often foll. by *on*) to pay a visit, esp. a brief or informal one: *call in if you are in the neighbourhood.* **2.** (*tr.*) to demand payment of: *to call in a loan.* **3.** (*tr.*) to take (something) out of circulation, because it is defective or no longer useful.

call·ing (ˈkɔːlɪŋ) *n.* **1.** a strong inner urge to follow an occupation, etc.; vocation. **2.** an occupation, profession, or trade.

call·ing card *n.* the usual U.S. term for **visiting card.**

cal·li·o·pe (kəˈlaɪəpɪ) *n.* the U.S. name for **steam organ.** [C19: after CALLIOPE (literally: beautiful-voiced)]

Cal·li·o·pe (kəˈlaɪəpɪ) *n. Greek myth.* the Muse of epic poetry.

cal·li·op·sis (ˌkælɪˈɒpsɪs) *n.* another name for **coreopsis.**

cal·li·pash (ˈkælɪˌpæʃ) *n.* a variant spelling of **calipash.**

cal·li·per *or U.S.* **cal·i·per** (ˈkælɪpə) *n.* **1.** (*often pl.*) Also called: **calliper compasses.** an instrument for measuring internal or external dimensions, consisting of two steel legs hinged together. **2.** Also called: **calliper splint.** *Med.* a splint consisting of two metal rods with straps attached, for supporting or exerting tension on the leg. ~*vb.* **3.** (*tr.*) to measure the dimensions of (an object) with callipers.

cal·li·per rule *n.* a measuring instrument having two parallel jaws, one fixed at right angles to the end of a calibrated scale and the other sliding along it.

cal·li·pyg·i·an (ˌkælɪˈpɪdʒɪən) *or* **cal·li·py·gous** (ˌkælɪˈpaɪgəs) *adj.* having beautifully shaped buttocks. [C19: from Greek *kallipugos,* epithet of a statue of Aphrodite, from CALLI- + *pugē* buttocks]

cal·lis·then·ics *or* **cal·is·then·ics** (ˌkælɪsˈθɛnɪks) *n.* **1.** (*functioning as pl.*) light exercises designed to promote general fitness, develop muscle tone, etc. **2.** (*functioning as sing.*) the practice of callisthenic exercises. [C19: from CALLI- + Greek *sthenos* strength] —ˌ**cal·lis·ˈthen·ic** *or* ˌ**cal·is·ˈthen·ic** *adj.*

Cal·lis·to[1] (kəˈlɪstəʊ) *n.* the second largest of the 12 satellites of Jupiter and the fifth nearest to the planet. Approximate diameter: 4500 km.

Cal·lis·to[2] (kəˈlɪstəʊ) *n. Greek myth.* a nymph who attracted the love of Zeus and was changed into a bear by Hera. Zeus then set her in the sky as the constellation Ursa Major.

call let·ters *n. Chiefly U.S. and Canadian.* another name for **call sign.**

call loan *n.* a loan that is repayable on demand. Also called: **demand loan.** Compare **time loan.**

call mon·ey *n.* money loaned by banks and recallable on demand.

call num·ber *n.* the number given to a book in a library, indicating its shelf location. Also called: **call mark.**

call off *vb.* (*tr., adv.*) **1.** to cancel or abandon: *the game was called off because of rain.* **2.** to order (an animal or person) to desist or summon away: *the man called off his dog.* **3.** to stop (something) or give the order to stop.

cal·los·i·ty (kəˈlɒsɪtɪ) *n., pl.* **·ties. 1.** hard-heartedness. **2.** another name for **callus** (sense 1).

cal·lous (ˈkæləs) *adj.* **1.** unfeeling; insensitive. **2.** (of skin) hardened and thickened. ~*vb.* **3.** *Pathol.* to make or become callous. [C16: from Latin *callōsus;* see CALLUS] —ˈ**cal·lous·ly** *adv.* —ˈ**cal·lous·ness** *n.*

call out *vb.* (*adv.*) **1.** to utter aloud, esp. loudly. **2.** (*tr.*) to summon. **3.** (*tr.*) to order (workers) to strike.

cal·low (ˈkæləʊ) *adj.* **1.** lacking experience of life; immature. **2.** *Rare.* (of a young bird) unfledged and usually lacking feathers. [Old English *calu;* related to Old High German *kalo,* Old Slavonic *golú* bare, naked, Lithuanian *galva* head, Latin *calvus* bald] —ˈ**cal·low·ness** *n.*

call rate *n.* the interest rate on call loans.

call sign *or* **sig·nal** *n.* a group of letters and numbers identifying a radio transmitting station. Also called: **call letters.**

call slip *n.* a form for requesting a library book by title and call number. Also called: **call card, requisition form.**

call up *vb.* (*adv.*) **1.** to summon to report for active military service, as in time of war. **2.** (*tr.*) to recall (something); evoke: *his words called up old memories.* **3.** (*tr.*) to bring or summon (people, etc.) into action: *to call up reinforcements.* ~*n.* **call-up. 4. a.** a general order to report for military service. **b.** the number of men so summoned.

cal·lus (ˈkæləs) *n., pl.* **·lus·es. 1.** Also called: **callosity.** an area of skin that is hard or thick, esp. on the palm of the hand or sole of the foot, as from continual friction or pressure. **2.** an area of bony tissue formed during the healing of a fractured bone. **3.** *Botany.* a mass of hard protective tissue produced in woody plants at the site of an injury. ~*vb.* **4.** to produce or cause to produce a callus. [C16: from Latin, variant of *callum* hardened skin]

calm (kɑːm) *adj.* **1.** almost without motion; still: *a calm sea.* **2.** *Meteorol.* of force 0 on the Beaufort scale; without wind. **3.** not disturbed, agitated, or excited; under control: *he stayed calm throughout the confusion.* **4.** tranquil; serene: *a calm voice.* ~*n.* **5.** an absence of disturbance or rough motion; stillness. **6.** absence of wind. **7.** tranquillity. ~*vb.* **8.** (often foll. by *down*) to make or become calm. [C14: from Old French *calme,* from Old Italian *calma,* from Late Latin *cauma* heat, hence a rest during the heat of the day, from Greek *kauma* heat, from *kaiein* to burn] —ˈ**calm·ly** *adv.* —ˈ**calm·ness** *n.*

cal·ma·tive (ˈkælmətɪv, ˈkɑːmə-) *adj.* **1.** (of a remedy or agent) sedative. ~*n.* **2.** a sedative remedy or drug.

cal·o·mel (ˈkæləˌmɛl, -məl) *n.* a colourless tasteless powder consisting chiefly of mercurous chloride, used medicinally, esp. as a cathartic. Formula: Hg_2Cl_2. [C17: perhaps from New Latin *calomelas* (unattested), literally: beautiful black (perhaps so named because it was originally sublimed from a black mixture of mercury and mercuric chloride), from Greek *kalos* beautiful + *melas* black]

Cal·or Gas (ˈkælə) *n. Trademark.* butane gas liquefied under pressure in portable containers for domestic use.

ca·lor·ic (kəˈlɒrɪk, ˈkælərɪk) *adj.* **1.** of or concerned with heat or calories. ~*n.* **2.** *Obsolete.* a hypothetical elastic fluid formerly postulated as the embodiment of heat. —**cal·o·ric·i·ty** (ˌkæləˈrɪsɪtɪ) *n.*

cal·o·rie *or* **cal·o·ry** (ˈkælərɪ) *n., pl.* **·ries.** a unit of heat, equal to 4.1868 joules (**International Table calorie**): formerly defined as the quantity of heat required to raise the temperature of 1 gram of water by 1°C under standard conditions. It has now largely been replaced by the joule for scientific purposes. Abbrev.: **cal.** Also called: **gram calorie, small calorie.** Compare **Calorie.** [C19: from French, from Latin *calor* heat]

Cal·o·rie (ˈkælərɪ) *n.* **1.** Also called: **kilogram calorie, kilocalorie, large calorie.** a unit of heat, equal to one thousand calories, often used to express the heat output of an organism or the energy value of food. Abbrev.: **Cal. 2.** the amount of a specific food capable of producing one thousand calories of energy.

cal·o·rif·ic (ˌkæləˈrɪfɪk) *adj.* of, concerning, or generating heat. —ˌ**cal·o·ˈrif·i·cal·ly** *adv.*

cal·o·rif·ic val·ue *n.* the quantity of heat produced by the complete combustion of a given mass of a fuel, usually expressed in joules per kilogram.

cal·o·rim·e·ter (ˌkæləˈrɪmɪtə) *n.* an apparatus for measuring amounts of heat, esp. to find specific heat capacities, calorific values, etc. —**cal·o·ri·met·ric** (ˌkælərɪˈmɛtrɪk) *or* ˌ**cal·o·ri·ˈmet·ri·cal** *adj.* —ˌ**cal·o·ri·ˈmet·ri·cal·ly** *adv.* —ˌ**cal·o·ˈrim·e·try** *n.*

ca·lotte (kəˈlɒt) *n.* **1.** a skullcap worn by Roman Catholic clergy. **2.** *Architect.* a concavity in the form of a niche or cup, serving to reduce the apparent height of an alcove or chapel. [C17: from French, from Provençal *calota,* perhaps from Greek *kaluptra* hood]

cal·o·yer (ˈkælɔɪə) *n.* a monk of the Greek Orthodox Church, esp. of the Basilian Order. [C17: from French, from Medieval Greek *kalogēros* venerable, from Greek *kalos* beautiful + *gēras* old age]

cal·pac, cal·pack, *or* **kal·pak** (ˈkælpæk) *n.* a large black brimless hat made of sheepskin or felt, worn by men in parts of the Near East. [C16: from Turkish *kalpāk*]

Cal·pe (ˈkælpɪ) *n.* the ancient name for the (Rock of) **Gibraltar.**

calque (kælk) *n.* **1.** another word for **loan translation.** ~*vb.* **calques, calqu·ing, calqued. 2.** (*tr.*) another word for **calk**[3]. [C20: from French: a tracing, from *calquer,* from Latin *calcāre* to tread]

Cal·ta·nis·set·ta (*Italian* ˌkaltanisˈsetta) *n.* a city in central Sicily: sulphur mines. Pop.: 60 072 (1971).

Cal·tech (ˈkælˈtɛk) *n.* the California Institute of Technology.

cal·trop, cal·trap (ˈkæltrəp), *or* **cal·throp** (ˈkælθrəp) *n.* **1.** any tropical or subtropical plant of the zygophyllaceous genera *Tribulus* and *Kallstroemia* that have spiny burs or bracts. **2. water caltrop.** another name for **water chestnut** (sense 1). **3.** another name for the **star thistle. 4.** *Military.* a metal ball with protruding spikes laid upon the ground as a device to lame cavalry horses, puncture tyres, etc. [Old English *calcatrippe* (the plant), from Medieval Latin *calcatrippa,* probably from Latin *calx* heel + *trippa* TRAP[1]]

cal·u·met (ˈkæljʊˌmɛt) *n.* a less common name for **peace pipe.** [C18: from Canadian French, from French (Normandy dialect): straw, from Late Latin *calamellus* a little reed, from Latin: CALAMUS]

ca·lum·ni·ate (kəˈlʌmnɪˌeɪt) *vb.* (*tr.*) to slander. —**ca·ˈlum·ni·a·ble** *adj.* —**ca**ˌ**lum·ni·ˈa·tion** *n.* —**ca·ˈlum·ni**ˌ**a·tor** *n.*

ca·lum·ni·ous (kəˈlʌmnɪəs) *or* **ca·lum·ni·a·to·ry** (kəˈlʌmnɪətərɪ, -trɪ) *adj.* **1.** of or using calumny. **2.** (of a person) given to calumny.

cal·um·ny (ˈkæləmnɪ) *n., pl.* **·nies. 1.** the malicious utterance of false charges or misrepresentation; slander; defamation. **2.** such a false charge or misrepresentation. [C15: from Latin *calumnia* deception, slander]

cal·u·tron (ˈkæljʊˌtrɒn) *n.* a large mass spectrometer used for the separation of isotopes. [C20: from Cal(ifornia) U(niversity) + -TRON]

Cal·va·dos (ˈkælvəˌdɒs) *n.* **1.** a department of N France in the Basse-Normandie region. Capital: Caen. Pop.: 572 421 (1975). Area: 5693 sq. km (2198 sq. miles). **2.** an apple brandy distilled from cider in this region.

cal·var·i·a (kælˈvɛərɪə) *n.* the top part of the skull of vertebrates. Nontechnical name: **skullcap.** [C14: from Late Latin: (human) skull, from Latin *calvus* bald]

cal·va·ry (ˈkælvərɪ) *n., pl.* **·ries. 1.** (*often cap.*) a representation of Christ's crucifixion, usually sculptured and in the open air. **2.** any experience involving great suffering.

Cal·va·ry (ˈkælvərɪ) *n.* the place just outside the walls of Jerusalem where Jesus was crucified. Also called: **Golgotha.** [from Late Latin *Calvāria,* translation of Greek *kranion* skull, translation of Aramaic *gulgulta* Golgotha]

Cal·va·ry cross *n.* a Latin cross with a representation of three steps beneath it.

calve (kɑːv) *vb.* **1.** to give birth to (a calf). **2.** (of a glacier or iceberg) to release (masses of ice) in breaking up.

Cal·vert (ˈkælvət) *n.* **1.** Sir **George,** 1st Baron Baltimore. ?1580–1632, English statesman; founder of the colony of Maryland. **2.** his son, **Leon·ard.** 1606–47, English statesman; first colonial governor of Maryland (1634–47).

calves (kɑːvz) *n.* the plural of **calf.**

Cal·vin (ˈkælvɪn) *n.* **1. John,** original name *Jean Cauvin, Caulvin* or *Chauvin.* 1509–64, French theologian: a leader of the Protestant Reformation in France and Switzerland, establishing the first presbyterian government in Geneva. His theological system is described in his *Institutes of the Christian Religion* (1536). **2. Mel·vin.** born 1911, U.S. chemist, noted particularly for his research on photosynthesis: Nobel prize for chemistry 1961.

Cal·vin·ism (ˈkælvɪˌnɪzəm) *n.* **1.** the theological system of Calvin and his followers, characterized by emphasis on the doctrines of predestination, the irresistibility of grace, and justification by faith. —ˈ**Cal·vin·ist** *n., adj.* —ˌ**Cal·vin·ˈis·tic** *or* ˌ**Cal·vin·ˈis·tic·al** *adj.*

cal·vi·ti·es (kælˈvɪʃɪˌiːz) *n.* baldness. [C17: from Late Latin, from Latin *calvus* bald]

calx (kælks) *n., pl.* **calx·es** *or* **cal·ces** (ˈkælsiːz). **1.** the powdery metallic oxide formed when an ore or mineral is roasted. **2.** another name for **calcium oxide.** [C15: from Latin: lime, from Greek *khalix* pebble]

cal·y·ces (ˈkælɪˌsiːz, ˈkeɪlɪ-) *n.* plural of **calyx.**

cal·y·cine (ˈkælɪˌsaɪn) *or* **ca·lyc·i·nal** (kəˈlɪsɪnᵊl) *adj.* relating to, belonging to, or resembling a calyx.

cal·y·cle (ˈkælɪkᵊl) *or* **ca·lyc·u·lus** (kəˈlɪkjʊləs) *n.* **1.** *Zoology.* a cup-shaped structure, as in the coral skeleton. **2.** *Botany.* another name for **epicalyx.** [C18: from Latin, diminutive of CALYX] —**ca·lyc·u·lar** (kəˈlɪkjʊlə) *adj.*

Cal·y·do·ni·an boar (ˌkælɪˈdəʊnɪən) *n. Greek myth.* a savage boar sent by Artemis to destroy Calydon, a city in Aetolia, because its king had neglected to sacrifice to her. It was killed by Meleager, the king's son.

ca+lyp+so[1] (kəˈlɪpsəʊ) *n., pl.* +**sos.** **1.** a popular type of satirical, usually topical, West Indian ballad, esp. from Trinidad, usually extemporized to a percussive syncopated accompaniment. **2.** a dance done to the rhythm of this song. [C20: probably from CALYPSO]

ca+lyp+so[2] (kəˈlɪpsəʊ) *n., pl.* +**sos.** a rare N temperate orchid, *Calypso* (or *Cytherea*) *bulbosa*, whose flower is pink or white with purple and yellow markings. [C19: named after CALYPSO]

Ca·lyp·so (kəˈlɪpsəʊ) *n. Greek myth.* (in Homer's *Odyssey*) a sea nymph who detained Odysseus on the island of Ogygia for seven years.

ca+lyp+tra (kəˈlɪptrə) *n. Botany.* **1.** a membranous hood covering the spore-bearing capsule of mosses and liverworts. **2.** any hoodlike structure, such as a root cap. [C18: from New Latin, from Greek *kaluptra* hood, from *kaluptein* to cover] —**ca+lyp+trate** (kəˈlɪptreɪt) *adj.*

ca+lyp+tro+gen (kəˈlɪptrədʒən) *n.* a layer of rapidly dividing cells at the tip of a plant root, from which the root cap is formed. It occurs in grasses and many other plants. [C19: from CALYPTRA + -GEN]

ca+lyx (ˈkeɪlɪks, ˈkælɪks) *n., pl.* **ca+lyx·es** *or* **cal·y+ces** (ˈkælɪˌsiːz, ˈkeɪlɪ-). **1.** the sepals of a flower collectively, forming the outer floral envelope that protects the developing flower bud. Compare **corolla. 2.** any cup-shaped cavity or structure, esp. any of the divisions of the human kidney (**renal calyx**) that form the renal pelvis. [C17: from Latin, from Greek *kalux* shell, from *kaluptein* to cover, hide] —**cal·y+cate** (ˈkælɪˌkeɪt) *adj.*

cam (kæm) *n.* a rotating cylinder with an irregular profile, attached to a revolving shaft to give a reciprocating motion to a part in contact with it.

Cam (kæm) *n.* a river in E England, in Cambridgeshire, flowing through Cambridge to the River Ouse. Length: about 64 km (40 miles).

Ca+ma+güey (ˈkæməˌgweɪ; *Spanish* ˌkamaˈɣwɛj) *n.* a city in E central Cuba. Pop.: 197 720 (1970).

ca+mail (ˈkæmeɪl) *n. Armour.* a head, cheek, chin, and neck covering of mail worn with and laced to the basinet.

ca+ma+ra+de·rie (ˌkæməˈrɑːdərɪ) *n.* a spirit of familiarity and trust existing between friends. [C19: from French, from *camarade* COMRADE]

cam·a+ril+la (ˌkæməˈrɪlə; *Spanish* ˌkamaˈriʎa) *n.* a group of confidential advisers, esp. formerly, to the Spanish kings; cabal. [C19: from Spanish: literally: a little room]

cam+ass *or* **cam+as** (ˈkæmæs) *n.* **1.** Also called: **quamash.** any of several North American plants of the liliaceous genus *Camassia*, esp. *C. quamash*, which has a cluster of blue or white flowers and a sweet edible bulb. **2. death camass.** any liliaceous plant of the genus *Zygadenus* (or *Zigadenus*), of the western U.S., that is poisonous to livestock, esp. sheep. [C19: from Chinook Jargon *kamass*, from Nootka *chamas* sweet]

Camb. *abbrev. for* Cambridge.

Cam+bay (kæmˈbeɪ) *n.* **Gulf of.** an inlet of the Arabian Sea on the W coast of India, southeast of the Kathiawar Peninsula.

cam+ber (ˈkæmbə) *n.* **1.** a slight upward curve to the centre of the surface of a road, ship's deck, etc. **2.** another name for **bank**[2] (sense 7). **3.** an outward inclination of the front wheels of a road vehicle so that they are slightly closer together at the bottom than at the top. **4.** Also called: **hog.** a small arching curve of a beam or girder provided to lessen deflection and improve appearance. **5.** the curvature of an aerofoil section from the leading edge to the trailing edge. ~*vb.* **6.** to form or be formed with a surface that curves upwards to its centre. [C17: from Old French (northern dialect) *cambre* curved, from Latin *camurus;* related to *camera* CHAMBER]

Cam+ber+well beau+ty (ˈkæmbəˌwɛl, -wəl) *n.* a nymphalid butterfly, *Nymphalis antiopa*, of temperate regions, having dark purple wings with cream-yellow borders. U.S. name: **mourning cloak.**

cam+bist (ˈkæmbɪst) *n. Finance.* **1.** a dealer or expert in foreign exchange. **2.** a manual of currency exchange rates and similar equivalents of weights and measures. [C19: from French *cambiste*, from Italian *cambista*, from *cambio* (money) exchange] —ˈ**cam+bist+ry** *n.*

cam+bi·um (ˈkæmbɪəm) *n., pl.* +**bi·ums** *or* +**bi·a** (-bɪə). *Botany.* a meristem that increases the girth of stems and roots by producing additional xylem and phloem. See also **cork cambium.** [C17: from Medieval Latin: exchange, from Late Latin *cambiāre* to exchange, barter] —ˈ**cam+bi·al** *adj.*

Cam+bo+di·a (kæmˈbəʊdɪə) *n.* a state in SE Asia: became part of French Indochina in 1887; declared independence in 1949; became a republic in 1970 with civil war continuing between the Khmer Rouge and Vietnamese-backed forces; contains the central plains of the Mekong River, with the Cardamom Mountains in the southwest. Language: Khmer. Currency: riel. Capital: Phnom Penh. Pop.: 8 110 000 (1975 UN est.). Area: 181 035 sq. km (69 898 sq. miles). Offical name (since 1976): **Kampuchea.** —**Cam**+ˈ**bo+di·an** *adj., n.*

cam+bo+gi·a (kæmˈbəʊdʒɪə) *n.* another name for **gamboge** (senses 1, 2).

cam+boose (kæmˈbuːs) *n.* (formerly in Canada) a cabin used by lumbermen.

Cam·borne-Red·ruth (ˈkæmbɔːn ˈrɛdˌruːθ) *n.* a town in SW England, in Cornwall: formed in 1934 by the amalgamation of neighbouring towns. Pop.: 42 029 (1971).

Cam+brai (*French* kɑ̃ˈbrɛ) *n.* a town in NE France: textile industry. Pop.: 41 109 (1975).

cam+brel (ˈkæmbrəl) *n.* a variant of **gambrel.**

Cam+bri·a (ˈkæmbrɪə) *n.* the Medieval Latin name for **Wales.**

Cam+bri·an (ˈkæmbrɪən) *adj.* **1.** of, denoting, or formed in the first 100 million years of the Palaeozoic era, during which marine invertebrates, esp. trilobites, flourished. **2.** of or relating to Wales. ~*n.* **3. the.** the Cambrian period or rock system. **4.** a Welshman.

Cam+bri·an Moun+tains *pl. n.* a mountain range in Wales, extending from S Dyfed to Clwyd. Highest peak: Aran Fawddwy 891 m (2970 ft.).

cam+bric (ˈkeɪmbrɪk) *n.* a fine white linen or cotton fabric. [C16: from Flemish *Kamerijk*, CAMBRAI]

Cam+bridge (ˈkeɪmbrɪdʒ) *n.* **1.** a city in E England, administrative centre of Cambridgeshire, on the River Cam: centred around the university, founded in the 12th century. Pop.: 98 519 (1971). Medieval Latin name: **Cantabrigia. 2.** short for **Cambridgeshire. 3.** a city in E Massachusetts: educational centre, with Harvard University (1636) and the Massachusetts Institute of Technology. Pop.: 100 361 (1970).

Cam+bridge blue *n.* **1. a.** a lightish blue colour. **b.** (*as adj.*): *a Cambridge-blue scarf.* **2.** a person who has been awarded a blue from Cambridge University.

Cam+bridge+shire (ˈkeɪmbrɪdʒˌʃɪə, -ʃə) *n.* a county of E England, in East Anglia: includes the former counties of the Isle of Ely and Huntingdon and lies largely in the Fens. Administrative centre: Cambridge. Pop.: 563 000 (1976 est.). Area: 3496 sq. km (1350 sq. miles).

Cambs. *abbrev. for* Cambridgeshire.

Cam·by·ses (kæmˈbaɪsiːz) *n.* died ?522 B.C., king of Persia (529–522 B.C.), who conquered Egypt (525); son of Cyrus the Great.

Cam+den[1] (ˈkæmdən) *n.* **1.** a borough of N Greater London. Pop.: 185 800 (1976 est.). **2.** a city in SW New Jersey, on the Delaware River opposite Philadelphia. Pop.: 100 171 (1973 est.).

Cam·den[2] (ˈkæmdən) *n.* **Wil·liam.** 1551–1623, English antiquary and historian; author of *Britannia* (1586).

came[1] (keɪm) *vb.* the past tense of **come.**

came[2] (keɪm) *n.* a grooved strip of lead used to join pieces of glass in a stained-glass window or a leaded light. [C17: of unknown origin]

cam+el (ˈkæməl) *n.* **1.** either of two cud-chewing artiodactyl mammals of the genus *Camelus* (see **Arabian camel, Bactrian camel**): family *Camelidae.* They are adapted for surviving long periods without food or water in desert regions, esp. by using humps on the back for storing fat. **2.** a float attached to a vessel to increase its buoyancy. See also **caisson** (sense 2). **3.** a raft or float used as a fender between a vessel and a wharf. **4. a.** a fawn colour. **b.** (*as adj.*): *a camel dress.* [Old English, from Latin *camēlus*, from Greek *kamēlos*, of Semitic origin; related to Arabic *jamal*]

cam+el+eer (ˌkæmɪˈlɪə) *n.* a camel-driver.

ca+mel+li·a (kəˈmiːlɪə) *n.* any ornamental shrub of the Asian genus *Camellia*, esp. *C. japonica*, having glossy evergreen leaves and showy roselike flowers, usually white, pink or red in colour: family *Theaceae.* Also called: **japonica.** [C18: New Latin, named after Georg Josef *Kamel* (1661–1706), Moravian Jesuit missionary, who introduced it to Europe]

ca+mel·o+pard (ˈkæmɪləˌpɑːd, kəˈmɛl-) *n.* an obsolete word for **giraffe.** [C14: from Medieval Latin *camēlopardus*, from Greek *kamēlopardalis*, from *kamēlos* CAMEL + *pardalis* LEOPARD, because the giraffe was thought to have a head like a camel's and spots like a leopard's]

Ca+mel·o+par+dus (kəˌmɛləˈpɑːdəs) *or* **Ca+mel·o+par+da+lis** (kəˌmɛləˈpɑːdəlɪs) *n., Latin genitive* **Ca+mel·o+par+di** (kəˌmɛləˈpɑːdaɪ) or **Ca+mel·o+par+da+lis** (kəˌmɛləˈpɑːdəlɪs). a faint extensive constellation in the N hemisphere close to Ursa Major and Cassiopeia.

Cam+e·lot (ˈkæmɪˌlɒt) *n.* (in Arthurian legend) the English town where King Arthur's palace and court were situated.

cam+el's hair *or* **cam·el+hair** *n.* **1.** the hair of a camel, used in rugs, etc., or woven into cloth. **2. a.** soft cloth made of this hair or a mixture containing it, usually tan in colour. **b.** (*as modifier*): *a camelhair coat.* **3.** (*modifier*) (of a painter's brush) made from the tail hairs of squirrels.

Cam+em+bert (ˈkæməmˌbɛə; *French* kamɑ̃ˈbɛːr) *n.* a rich soft creamy cheese. [French, from *Camembert*, a village in Normandy where it originated]

Ca+me·nae (kəˈmiːniː) *pl. n. Roman myth.* a group of nymphs originally associated with a sacred spring in Rome, later identified with the Greek Muses.

cam·e·o (ˈkæmɪˌəʊ) *n., pl.* **cam·e·os. 1. a.** a medallion, as on a brooch or ring, with a profile head carved in relief. **b.** (*as modifier*): *a cameo necklace.* **2.** an engraving upon a gem or other stone of at least two differently coloured layers, such as sardonyx, so carved that the background is of a different colour from the raised design. **3.** a stone with such an engraving. **4. a.** a single and often brief dramatic scene played by a well-known actor or actress in a film or television play. **b.** (*as modifier*): *a cameo performance.* **5. a.** a short literary work or dramatic sketch. **b.** (*as modifier*): *a cameo sketch.* [C15: from Italian *cammeo*, of uncertain origin]

cam·e·o ware *n.* jasper ware with applied decoration of classical motifs, resembling a cameo.

cam·er·a (ˈkæmərə, ˈkæmrə) *n.* **1.** an optical device consisting of a lens system set in a light-proof construction inside which a light-sensitive film or plate can be positioned. See also **cine**

camera. 2. *Television.* the equipment used to convert the optical image of a scene being televised into the corresponding electrical signals. 3. See **camera obscura.** 4. *pl.* +**er·ae** (-əˌriː). a judge's private room. 5. **in camera. a.** *Law.* relating to a hearing from which members of the public are excluded. **b.** in private. 6. **on camera.** (esp. of an actor) being filmed. [C18: from Latin: vault, from Greek *kamara*]

cam+er+al (ˈkæmərəl) *adj.* of or relating to a judicial or legislative chamber. [C18: from Medieval Latin *camerālis;* see CAMERA]

cam+er·a lu+ci+da (ˈluːsɪdə) *n.* an instrument attached to a microscope, etc. to enable an observer to view simultaneously the image and a drawing surface to facilitate the sketching of the image. [New Latin: light chamber]

cam·er·a+man (ˈkæmərəˌmæn, ˈkæmrə-) *n., pl.* +**men.** a person who operates a film or television camera.

cam+er·a ob+scu+ra (ɒbˈskjʊərə) *n.* a darkened chamber or small building in which images of outside objects are projected onto a flat surface by a convex lens in an aperture. Sometimes shortened to **camera.** [New Latin: dark chamber]

cam·er·a-read·y cop·y *n. Printing.* type matter ready to be photographed for plate-making without further alteration. Also called (in the U.S.): **mechanical.**

cam·er·a-shy *adj.* having an aversion to being photographed or filmed.

ca+mé+ra sty+lo (*French* kamera stiˈlo) *n. Films.* the use of the camera as a means of personal expression, especially as practised by some directors of the New Wave. [French, literally: camera stylograph]

cam+er·a tube *n.* the part of a television camera that converts an optical image into electrical signals of video frequency. See also **image orthicon, vidicon, plumbicon, iconoscope.**

cam+er+len+go (ˌkæməˈlɛŋgəʊ) *or* **cam+er+lin+go** (ˌkæməˈlɪŋgəʊ) *n., pl.* +**gos.** *R.C. Church.* a cardinal who acts as the pope's financial secretary and the papal treasurer. [C17: from Italian *camerlingo,* of Germanic origin; compare CHAMBERLAIN]

Cam+e·roon (ˌkæməˈruːn, ˈkæməˌruːn) *n.* 1. a republic in West Africa, on the Gulf of Guinea: became a German colony in 1884; divided in 1919 into the **Cameroons** (administered by Britain) and **Cameroun** (administered by France); Cameroun and the S part of the Cameroons formed a republic in 1961 (the N part joined Nigeria). Official languages: French and English. Religions: Christian, Muslim, and animist. Currency: franc. Capital: Yaoundé. Pop.: 6 398 000 (1975 UN est.). Area: 475 500 sq. km (183 591 sq. miles). French name: **Cameroun.** 2. an active volcano in W Cameroon: the highest peak on the West African coast. Height: 4070 m (13 352 ft.).

Came+roun (kamˈrun) *n.* the French name for **Cameroon.**

cam·i+knick+ers (ˈkæmɪˌnɪkəz) *pl. n.* (formerly) women's knickers attached to a camisole top. Short form: **camiknicks.**

cam·i+on (ˈkæmɪən; *French* kaˈmjɔ̃) *n.* a lorry, or, esp. formerly, a large dray. [C19: from French, of obscure origin]

cam·i+sa+do (ˌkæmɪˈsɑːdəʊ) *or* **cam·i+sade** (ˌkæmɪˈseɪd) *n., pl.* +**sa+dos** *or* +**sades.** (formerly) an attack made under cover of darkness. [C16: from obsolete Spanish *camisada,* literally: an attack in one's shirt (worn over the armour as identification), from *camisa* shirt]

ca+mise (kəˈmiːz) *n.* a loose light shirt, smock, or tunic originally worn in the Middle Ages. [C19: from Arabic *qamīs,* from Late Latin *camīsia*]

cam·i+sole (ˈkæmɪˌsəʊl) *n.* 1. a woman's underbodice with shoulder straps, originally designed as a cover for a corset. 2. a woman's dressing jacket or short negligée. 3. (*modifier*) resembling a camisole (the underbodice), as in fitting snugly around the bust and having a straight neckline: *a camisole slip; a camisole top.* [C19: from French, from Provençal *camisola,* from *camisa* shirt, from Late Latin *camīsia*]

cam+let (ˈkæmlɪt) *n.* 1. a tough waterproof cloth. 2. a garment or garments made from such cloth. 3. a soft woollen fabric used in medieval Asia. [C14: from Old French *camelot,* perhaps from Arabic *hamlat* plush fabric]

Cam·o·ëns (ˈkæməʊˌɛns) *or* **Ca·mões** (*Portuguese* kaˈmõjʃ) *n.* **Luis Vaz de** (lwiʃ vaʃ də), 1524–80, Portuguese epic poet; author of *The Lusiads* (1572).

cam·o+mile *or* **cham·o+mile** (ˈkæməˌmaɪl) *n.* 1. any aromatic plant of the Eurasian genus *Anthemis,* esp. *A. nobilis,* whose finely dissected leaves and daisy-like flowers are used medicinally: family *Compositae* (composites). 2. any plant of the related genus *Matricaria,* esp. *M. chamomilla* (**German** or **wild camomile**). 3. **camomile tea.** a medicinal beverage made from the fragrant leaves and flowers of any of these plants. [C14: from Old French *camomille,* from Medieval Latin *chamomilla,* from Greek *khamaimēlon,* literally, earth-apple (referring to the apple-like scent of the flowers)]

ca+moo+di (kæˈmuːdɪ) *n.* a Caribbean name for **anaconda.** [C19: from an American Indian language of Guyana]

Ca+mor+ra (kəˈmɒrə) *n.* 1. a secret society organized in about 1820 in Naples, which thrived on blackmail and extortion. 2. any similar clandestine group. [C19: from Italian, probably from Spanish: quarrel]

cam·ou+flage (ˈkæməˌflɑːʒ) *n.* 1. the exploitation of natural surroundings or artificial aids to conceal or disguise the presence of military units, equipment, etc. 2. the means by which animals escape the notice of predators, usually because of a resemblance to their surroundings: includes cryptic and apatetic coloration. 3. a device or expedient designed to conceal or deceive. ~*vb.* 4. (*tr.*) to conceal by camouflage. [C20: from French, from *camoufler,* from Italian *camuffare* to disguise, deceive, of uncertain origin]

camp[1] (kæmp) *n.* 1. **a.** a place where tents, cabins, or other temporary structures are erected for the use of military troops, for training soldiers, etc. **b.** (*as modifier*): *a camp fire.* 2. the military life. 3. tents, cabins, etc., used as temporary lodgings by a group of travellers, holidaymakers, Scouts, gipsies, etc. 4. the group of people living in such lodgings. 5. a group supporting a given doctrine or theory: *the socialist camp.* 6. (*modifier*) suitable for use in temporary quarters, on holiday, etc., esp. by being portable and easy to set up: *a camp bed; a camp chair.* ~*vb.* 7. (*intr.;* often foll. by *down*) to establish or set up a camp. 8. (*intr.;* often foll. by *out*) to live temporarily in or as if in a tent. 9. (*tr.*) to put in a camp. [C16: from Old French, ultimately from Latin *campus* field] —**ˈcamp+ing** *n.*

camp[2] (kæmp) *Informal.* ~*adj.* 1. effeminate; affected in mannerisms, dress, etc. 2. homosexual. 3. consciously artificial, exaggerated, vulgar, or mannered; self-parodying, esp. when in dubious taste. ~*vb.* 4. (*tr.*) to perform or invest with a camp quality. 5. **camp it up. a.** to seek to focus attention on oneself by making an ostentatious display, overacting, etc. **b.** to flaunt one's homosexuality. ~*n.* 6. a camp quality, style, etc. [C20: of uncertain origin]

cam+pa+gna (kæmˈpɑːnjə) *n.* another word for **champaign** (sense 1).

Cam+pa+gna (kæmˈpɑːnjə) *n.* a low-lying plain surrounding Rome, Italy: once fertile, it deteriorated to malarial marshes; recently reclaimed. Area: about 2000 sq. km (800 sq. miles). Also called: **Cam+pa+gna di Ro·ma.**

cam+paign (kæmˈpeɪn) *n.* 1. a series of coordinated activities, such as public speaking and demonstrating, designed to achieve a social, political, or commercial goal: *a presidential campaign; an advertising campaign.* 2. *Military.* a number of complementary operations aimed at achieving a single objective, usually constrained by time or geographic area. ~*vb.* 3. (*intr.;* often foll. by *for*) to conduct, serve in, or go on a campaign. [C17: from French *campagne* open country, from Italian *campagna,* from Late Latin *campānia,* from Latin *campus* field] —**cam+ˈpaign+er** *n.*

Cam+pa+ni·a (kæmˈpeɪnɪə; *Italian* kamˈpaɲɲa) *n.* a region of SW Italy: includes the islands of Capri and Ischia. Chief town: Naples. Pop.: 5 054 822 (1971). Area: 13 595 sq. km (5248 sq. miles).

cam+pa+ni+le (ˌkæmpəˈniːlɪ) *n.* (esp. in Italy) a bell tower, not usually attached to another building. Compare **belfry.** [C17: from Italian, from *campana* bell]

cam+pa+nol+o·gy (ˌkæmpəˈnɒlədʒɪ) *n.* the art or skill of ringing bells musically. [C19: from New Latin *campānologia,* from Late Latin *campāna* bell] —**cam+pa+no+log·i·cal** (ˌkæmpənəˈlɒdʒɪkəl) *adj.* —**ˌcam+pa+ˈnol+o+gist** *or* **ˌcam+pa+ˈnol+o+ger** *n.*

cam+pan·u+la (kæmˈpænjʊlə) *n.* any N temperate plant of the campanulaceous genus *Campanula,* typically having blue or white bell-shaped flowers. Also called: **bellflower. See also Canterbury bell, harebell.** [C17: from New Latin: a little bell, from Late Latin *campāna* bell; see CAMPANILE]

cam+pan·u·la+ceous (kəmˌpænjʊˈleɪʃəs) *adj.* of, relating to, or belonging to the *Campanulaceae,* a family of temperate and subtropical plants, including the campanulas, having bell-shaped nodding flowers.

cam+pan·u·late (kæmˈpænjʊlɪt, -ˌleɪt) *adj.* (esp. of flower corollas) shaped like a bell. [C17: from New Latin *campanulātus;* see CAMPANULA]

Camp·bell (ˈkæmbəl) *n.* 1. Sir **Col·in,** Baron Clyde. 1792–1863, British field marshal, who led the relief of Lucknow (1857) and suppressed the Indian Mutiny (1857–58). 2. **Don·ald.** 1921–67, English water speed record-holder. 3. his father, Sir **Mal·colm.** 1885–1948, English racing driver and land speed record-holder. 4. Mrs. **Pat·rick.** original name *Beatrice Stella Tanner.* 1865–1940, English actress. 5. **Roy.** 1901–57, South African poet. His poetry is often satirical and includes *The Flaming Terrapin* (1924). 6. **Thom·as.** 1777–1844, Scottish poet and critic, noted particularly for his war poems *Hohenlinden* and *Ye Mariners of England.*

Camp·bell-Ban·ner·man (ˈkæmbəl ˈbænəmən) *n.* Sir **Hen·ry.** 1836–1908, British statesman and leader of the Liberal Party (1899–1908); prime minister (1905–8), who granted self-government to the Transvaal and the Orange River Colony.

Camp·bell-Stokes re+cord+er *n.* an instrument for recording hours of sunshine per day, consisting of a solid glass sphere that focuses rays of sunlight onto a light-sensitive card on which a line is traced.

Cam+pe·che (*Spanish* kamˈpetʃe) *n.* 1. a state of SE Mexico, on the SW of the Yucatán peninsula: forestry and fishing. Capital: Campeche. Pop.: 251 556 (1970). Area: 56 114 sq. km (21 666 sq. miles). 2. a port in SE Mexico, capital of Campeche state. Pop.: 81 147 (1970). 3. **Bay of.** the SW part of the Gulf of Mexico. Also called: **Gulf of Cam+pe·che.**

camp+er (ˈkæmpə) *n.* 1. a person who lives or temporarily stays in a tent, cabin, etc. 2. *U.S.* a vehicle equipped for camping out.

cam+pes+tral (kæmˈpɛstrəl) *adj.* of or relating to open fields or country. [C18: from Latin *campester,* from *campus* field]

camp fol+low+er *n.* 1. any civilian, esp. a prostitute, who unofficially provides services to military personnel. 2. a nonmember who is sympathetic to a particular group, theory, etc.

cam+phene (ˈkæmfiːn) *n.* a colourless crystalline insoluble optically active terpene derived from pinene and present in many essential oils. Formula: $C_{10}H_{16}$. [C19: from CAMPHOR + -ENE]

cam+phire (ˈkæmfaɪə) *n.* an archaic name for **henna** (senses 1, 2).

cam+phor ('kæmfə) *n.* a whitish crystalline aromatic terpene ketone obtained from the wood of the camphor tree or made from pinene: used in the manufacture of celluloid and in medicine as a liniment and treatment for colds. Formula: $C_{10}H_{16}O$. [C15: from Old French *camphre,* from Medieval Latin *camphora,* from Arabic *kāfūr,* from Malay *kāpūr* chalk; related to Khmer *kāpōr* camphor] —**cam+phor+ic** (kæm'fɒrɪk) *adj.*
cam+pho+rate ('kæmfəˌreɪt) *vb.* (*tr.*) to apply, treat with, or impregnate with camphor.
cam+pho+rat+ed oil *n.* a liniment consisting of camphor and peanut oil, used as a counterirritant.
cam+phor ball *n.* another name for **mothball** (sense 1).
cam+phor ice *n.* an ointment consisting of camphor, white wax, spermaceti, and castor oil, used to treat skin ailments, esp. chapped skin.
cam+phor tree *n.* **1.** a lauraceous evergreen E Asian tree, *Cinnamomum camphora,* whose aromatic wood yields camphor. **2.** any similar tree, such as the dipterocarpaceous tree *Dryobalanops aromatica* of Borneo.
Cam+pi+na Gran+de (*Portuguese* kəm'pina 'grəndi) *n.* a city in NE Brazil, in E Paraíba state. Pop.: 163 206 (1970).
Cam+pi+nas (kæm'pi:nəs; *Portuguese* kəm'pinas) *n.* a city in SE Brazil, in São Paulo state: centre of a rich agricultural region, producing esp. coffee. Pop.: 328 629 (1970).
camp+ing ground *n.* another word for **camp site.**
cam+pi+on ('kæmpɪən) *n.* any of various caryophyllaceous plants of the genera *Silene* and *Lychnis,* having red, pink, or white flowers. See also **bladder campion.** [C16: probably from *campion,* obsolete variant of CHAMPION, perhaps so called because originally applied to *Lychnis coronaria,* the leaves of which were used to crown athletic champions]
Cam·pi·on ('kæmpɪən) *n.* **1. Ed·mund.** 1540–81, English Jesuit martyr. He joined the Jesuits in 1573 and returned to England (1580) as a missionary. He was charged with treason and hanged. **2. Thom·as.** 1567–1620, English poet and musician, noted particularly for his songs for the lute.
camp meet+ing *n. Chiefly U.S.* a religious meeting held in a large tent or outdoors, often lasting several days.
cam+po ('kæmpəʊ) *n., pl.* **+pos.** (*often pl.*) level or undulating savanna country, esp. in the uplands of Brazil. [American Spanish, from Latin *campus*]
Cam+po+bel+lo (ˌkæmpə'bɛləʊ) *n.* an island in the Bay of Fundy, off the coast of SE Canada: part of New Brunswick province. Area: about 52 sq. km (20 sq. miles). Pop.: 1971 (1971).
Cam+po For+mio (*Italian* 'kampo 'fɔrmjo) *n.* a village in NE Italy, in Friuli-Venezia Giulia: scene of the signing of a treaty in 1797 that ended the war between revolutionary France and Austria. Modern name: **Cam+po+for+mi+do** (ˌkampo'fɔrmido).
Cam+po Gran+de (*Portuguese* 'kəmpu 'grəndi) *n.* a city in SW Brazil, capital of Mato Grosso do Sul state on the São Paulo–Corumbá railway: market town. Pop.: 130 792 (1970).
camp·o+ree (ˌkæmpə'ri:) *n.* a local meeting or assembly of Scouts. [C20: from CAMP[1] + JAMBOREE]
Cam+pos (*Portuguese* 'kəmpuʃ) *n.* a city in E Brazil, in E Rio de Janeiro state on the Paraíba River. Pop.: 153 310 (1970).
camp site *n.* an area on which holiday-makers may pitch a tent, etc. Also called: **camping site.**
cam+pus ('kæmpəs) *n., pl.* **+pus·es. 1.** the grounds and buildings of a university. **2.** *Chiefly U.S.* the outside area of a college, university, etc. [C18: from Latin: field]
cam+pus u·ni·ver·si·ty *n. Brit.* a university in which the buildings, often including shops and cafés, are all on one site. Compare **redbrick.**
Cam Ranh ('kæm 'ræn) *n.* a port in SE Vietnam: large natural harbour, in recent years used as a naval base by French, Japanese, and U.S. forces successively. Pop.: 104 666 (1971).
cam+shaft ('kæmˌʃɑ:ft) *n.* a shaft having one or more cams attached to it, esp. one used to operate the valves of an internal-combustion engine.
Ca·mus (*French* ka'my) *n.* **Al·bert** (al'bɛ:r). 1913–60, French novelist, dramatist, and essayist, noted for his pessimistic portrayal of man's condition of isolation in an absurd world: author of the novels *L'Étranger* (1942) and *La Peste* (1947), the plays *Le Malentendu* (1945) and *Caligula* (1946), and the essays *Le Mythe de Sisyphe* (1942) and *L'Homme revolté* (1951): Nobel prize for literature 1957.
cam+wood ('kæmˌwʊd) *n.* **1.** a W African leguminous tree, *Baphia nitida,* whose hard wood was formerly used in making a red dye. **2.** the wood of this tree. [C20: perhaps from Temne]
can[1] (kæn; *unstressed* kən) *vb. past* **could.** (takes an infinitive without *to* or an implied infinitive) used as an auxiliary: **1.** to indicate ability, skill, or fitness to perform a task: *I can run a mile in under four minutes.* **2.** to indicate permission or the right to something: *can I have a drink?* **3.** to indicate knowledge of how to do something: *he can speak three languages fluently.* **4.** to indicate the possibility, opportunity, or likelihood: *my trainer says I can win the race if I really work hard.* [Old English *cunnan;* related to Old Norse *kunna,* Old High German *kunnan,* Latin *cognōscere* to know, Sanskrit *jānāti* he knows; see KEN, UNCOUTH]
Usage. See at **may.**
can[2] (kæn) *n.* **1.** a container, esp. for liquids, usually of thin sheet metal: *a petrol can; milk can.* **2.** another name (esp. U.S.) for **tin** (metal container). **3.** Also **canful.** the contents of a can or the amount a can will hold. **4.** a slang word for **prison. 5.** *U.S.* a slang word for **toilet** or **buttocks. 6.** *U.S. Navy.* a slang word for **destroyer. 7.** *Naval slang.* a depth charge. **8.** a shallow cylindrical metal container of varying size used for storing and handling film. **9. can of worms.** *Informal.* a complicated problem. **10. in the can. a.** (of a film, piece of music, etc.) having been recorded, processed, edited, etc. **b.** *Informal.* arranged or agreed: *the contract is almost in the can.* **11. carry the can.** See **carry** (sense 36). ~*vb.* **cans, can+ning, canned. 12.** to put (food, etc.) into a can or cans; preserve in a can. **13.** (*tr.*) *U.S. slang.* to dismiss from a job. **14.** (*tr.*) *U.S. informal.* to stop (doing something annoying or making an annoying noise) (esp. in the phrase **can it!**). [Old English *canne;* related to Old Norse, Old High German *kanna,* Irish *gann,* Swedish *kana* sled]
can. *abbrev. for:* **1.** *Music.* canon. **2.** canto.
Can. *abbrev. for:* **1.** Canada. **2.** Canadian.
Ca·na ('keɪnə) *n. New Testament.* the town in Galilee, north of Nazareth, where Jesus performed his first miracle by changing water into wine (John 2:1, 11).
Ca+naan ('keɪnən) *n.* an ancient region between the River Jordan and the Mediterranean, corresponding roughly to Palestine: the Promised Land of the Israelites.
Ca+naan+ite ('keɪnəˌnaɪt) *n.* **1.** a member of an ancient Semitic people who occupied the land of Canaan before the Israelite conquest. **2.** the extinct language of this people, belonging to the Canaanitic branch of the Semitic subfamily of the Afro-Asiatic family. **3.** (in later books of the Old Testament) a merchant or trader (Job 40:30; Proverbs 31:24).
Ca+naan+it+ic (ˌkeɪnə'nɪtɪk) *n.* **1.** a group of ancient languages belonging to the Semitic subfamily of the Afro-Asiatic family and including Canaanite, Phoenician, Ugaritic, and Hebrew. ~*adj.* **2.** denoting, relating to, or belonging to this group of languages.
Canad. *abbrev. for* Canadian.
Can+a+da ('kænədə) *n.* a country in North America: the second largest country in the world; first permanent settlement made by the French at Quebec; ceded to Britain in 1763 after a series of colonial wars; established as the Dominion of Canada in 1867; member of the Commonwealth. It consists generally of sparsely inhabited tundra regions, rich in natural resources, in the north, the Rocky Mountains in the west, the Canadian Shield in the east, and vast central prairies; the bulk of the population is concentrated along the U.S. border and the Great Lakes in the south. Languages: English and French. Currency: Canadian dollar. Capital: Ottawa. Pop.: 22 992 604 (1976). Area: 9 976 185 sq. km (3 851 809 sq. miles).
Can·a·da bal+sam *n.* **1.** a yellow transparent resin obtained from the balsam fir. Because its refractive index is similar to that of glass, it is used as an adhesive in optical devices and as a mounting medium for microscope specimens. **2.** another name for **balsam fir.**
Can·a·da goose *n.* a large common greyish-brown North American goose, *Branta canadensis,* with a black neck and head and a white throat patch.
Can·a·da lil·y *n.* a lily, *Lilium canadense,* of NE North America, with small orange funnel-shaped nodding flowers. Also called: **meadow lily.**
Can·a·da this+tle *n.* the U.S. name for **creeping thistle.**
Ca+na+di·an (kə'neɪdɪən) *adj.* **1.** of or relating to Canada or its people. ~*n.* **2.** a native, citizen, or inhabitant of Canada.
Ca+na+di·an foot+ball *n.* a game resembling American football, played on a grass pitch between two teams of 12 players.
Ca+na+di·an French *n.* **1.** the French language as spoken in Canada, esp. in Quebec. ~*adj.* **2.** denoting this language or a French-speaking Canadian.
Ca+na+di·an+ism (kə'neɪdɪəˌnɪzəm) *n.* **1.** the Canadian national character or spirit. **2.** loyalty to Canada, its political independence, culture, etc. **3.** a linguistic usage, custom, or other feature peculiar to or characteristic of Canada, its people, or their culture.
Ca+na+di·an pond+weed *n.* a North American aquatic plant, *Elodea* (or *Anacharis*) *canadensis,* naturalized in Europe, having crowded dark green leaves: family *Hydrocharitaceae.* It is used in aquariums.
Ca+na+di·an Riv+er *n.* a river in the southern U.S., rising in NE New Mexico and flowing east to the Arkansas River in E Oklahoma. Length: 1458 km (906 miles).
Ca+na+di·an Shield *n.* (in Canada) the wide area of Precambrian rock extending west from the Labrador coast to the basin of the Mackenzie and north from the Great Lakes to Hudson Bay and the Arctic: rich in minerals. Also called: **Laurentian Shield, Laurentian Plateau.** See **shield** (sense 7).
ca+nai+gre (kə'naɪgə) *n.* a dock, *Rumex hymenosepalus,* of the southern U.S., the root of which yields a substance used in tanning. [C19: from Mexican Spanish]
ca+naille *French.* (ka'nɑ:j) *n.* the masses; mob; rabble. [C17: from French, from Italian *canaglia* pack of dogs]
can·a+kin ('kænɪkɪn) *n.* a variant spelling of **cannikin.**
ca+nal (kə'næl) *n.* **1.** an artificial waterway constructed for navigation, irrigation, water power, etc. **2.** any of various tubular passages or ducts: *the alimentary canal.* **3.** any of various elongated intercellular spaces in plants. **4.** *Astronomy.* any of the indistinct surface features of Mars originally thought to be a network of channels but not seen on close-range photographs. They are caused by an optical illusion in which faint geological features appear to have a geometric structure. ~*vb.* **+nals, +nal+ling, +nalled** *or U.S.* **+nals, +nal+ing, +naled.** (*tr.*) **5.** to dig a canal through. **6.** to provide with a canal or canals. [C15 (in the sense: pipe, tube): from Latin *canālis* channel, waterpipe, from *canna* reed, CANE]
ca+nal boat *n.* a long narrow boat used on canals, esp. for carrying freight.
Can·a·let·to (*Italian* ˌkana'letto) *n.* original name *Giovanni*

Antonio Canale. 1697–1768, Italian painter and etcher, noted particularly for his highly detailed paintings of cities, esp. Venice, which are marked by strong contrasts of light and shade.

can·a·lic·u·lus (ˌkænəˈlɪkjʊləs) *n., pl.* **·li** (-ˌlaɪ). a small channel, furrow, or groove, as in some bones and parts of plants. [C16: from Latin: a little channel, from *canālis* CANAL] —ˌ**can·a·ˈlic·u·lar, can·a·lic·u·late** (ˌkænəˈlɪkjʊlɪt, -ˌleɪt), *or* ˌ**can·a·ˈlic·u·ˌlat·ed** *adj.*

can·a·lize *or* **can·a·lise** (ˈkænəˌlaɪz) *vb.* (*tr.*) **1.** to provide with or convert into a canal or canals. **2.** to give a particular direction to or provide an outlet for; channel. —ˌ**can·a·li·ˈza·tion** *or* ˌ**can·a·li·ˈsa·tion** *n.*

ca·nal ray *n. Physics.* a stream of positive ions produced in a discharge tube by boring small holes in the cathode.

Ca·nal Zone *n.* an administrative region of the U.S., on the Isthmus of Panama around the Panama Canal: bordered on each side by the Republic of Panama which, under an agreement with the U.S. (1977), expects to gain full control of the Canal Zone by the year 2000. Area: 963 sq. km (372 sq. miles). Pop.: 44 198 (1970). Also called: **Panama Canal Zone.**

can·a·pé (ˈkænəpɪ, -ˌpeɪ; *French* kanaˈpe) *n.* **1.** a small piece of bread, toast, etc., spread with a savoury topping. **2.** (in French cabinetwork) a sofa. [C19: from French: sofa]

Ca·na·ra (kəˈnɑːrə) *n.* a variant spelling of **Kanara.**

ca·nard (kæˈnɑːd; *French* kaˈnaːr) *n.* **1.** a false report; rumour or hoax. **2.** an aircraft in which the tailplane is mounted in front of the wing. [C19: from French: a duck, hoax, from Old French *caner* to quack, of imitative origin]

Ca·na·rese (ˌkænəˈriːz) *n., pl.* **·rese,** *adj.* a variant spelling of **Kanarese.**

ca·nar·y (kəˈnɛərɪ) *n., pl.* **·nar·ies. 1.** a small finch, *Serinus canaria,* of the Canary Islands and Azores: a popular cage bird noted for its singing. Wild canaries are streaked yellow and brown, but most domestic breeds are pure yellow. **2.** See **canary yellow.** [C16: from Old Spanish *canario* of or from the Canary Islands]

ca·nar·y creep·er *n.* a climbing plant, *Tropaeolum peregrinum,* similar to the nasturtium but with smaller yellow flowers and lobed leaves.

ca·nar·y grass *n.* **1.** any of various grasses of the genus *Phalaris,* esp. *P. canariensis,* that is native to Europe and N Africa and has straw-coloured seeds used as birdseed. **2. reed canary grass.** a related plant, *Phalaris arundinacea,* used as fodder throughout the N hemisphere.

Ca·nar·y Is·lands *or* **Ca·nar·ies** *pl. n.* a group of mountainous islands in the Atlantic off the NW coast of Africa, forming the Spanish provinces of Las Palmas and Santa Cruz de Tenerife. Pop.: 1 170 224 (1970).

ca·nar·y seed *n.* another name for **birdseed.**

ca·nar·y yel·low *n.* **a.** a moderate yellow colour, sometimes with a greenish tinge. **b.** (*as adj.*): *a canary-yellow car.* Sometimes shortened to **canary.**

ca·nas·ta (kəˈnæstə) *n.* **1.** a card game for two to six players who seek to amass points by declaring sets of cards. **2.** Also called: **meld.** a declared set in this game, containing seven or more like cards, worth 500 points if the canasta is pure or 300 if wild (containing up to three jokers). [C20: from Spanish: basket (because two packs, or a basketful, of cards are required), variant of *canastro,* from Latin *canistrum;* see CANISTER]

can·as·ter (ˈkænəstə) *n.* coarsely broken dried tobacco leaves. [C19: (meaning: rush basket in which tobacco was packed): from Spanish *canastro;* see CANISTER]

Ca·nav·er·al (kəˈnævərəl) *n.* **Cape.** a cape on the E coast of Florida: site of the U.S. Air Force Missile Test Centre, from which the majority of U.S. space missions have been launched. Former name (1963–73): Cape **Kennedy.**

Can·ber·ra (ˈkænbərə, -brə) *n.* the capital of Australia, in Australian Capital Territory: founded in 1913 as a planned capital. Pop.: 189 400 (1975 est.).

can buoy *n.* a cylindrical unlighted buoy, painted black. Compare **nun buoy.**

canc. *abbrev. for:* **1.** cancelled. **2.** cancellation.

can·can (ˈkænˌkæn) *n.* a high-kicking dance performed by a female chorus, originating in the music halls of 19th-century Paris. [C19: from French, of uncertain origin]

can·cel (ˈkænsᵊl) *vb.* **·cels, ·cel·ling, ·celled** *or U.S.* **·cels, ·cel·ing, ·celed.** (*mainly tr.*) **1.** to order (something already arranged, such as a meeting or event) to be postponed indefinitely; call off. **2.** to revoke or annul: *the order for the new television set was cancelled.* **3.** to delete (writing, numbers, etc.); cross out: *he cancelled his name and substituted hers.* **4.** to mark (a cheque, postage stamp, ticket, etc.) with an official stamp or by a perforation to prevent further use. **5.** (*also intr.;* usually foll. by *out*) to counterbalance; make up for (a deficiency, etc.): *his generosity cancelled out his past unkindness.* **6. a.** to close (an account) by discharging any outstanding debts. **b.** (sometimes foll. by *out*) *Accounting.* to eliminate (a debit or credit) by making an offsetting entry on the opposite side of the account. **7.** *Maths.* **a.** to eliminate (numbers, quantities, or terms) as common factors from both the numerator and denominator of a fraction or as equal terms from opposite sides of an equation. **b.** (*intr.*) to be able to be eliminated in this way. ~*n.* **8.** a new leaf or section of a book replacing a defective one, one containing errors, or one that has been omitted. **9.** a less common word for **cancellation. 10.** *Music.* a U.S. word for **natural** (sense 19a.). [C14: from Old French *canceller,* from Medieval Latin *cancellāre,* from Late Latin: to strike out, make like a lattice, from Latin *cancellī* lattice, grating] —ˈ**can·cel·ler** *or U.S.* ˈ**can·cel·er** *n.*

can·cel·late (ˈkænsɪˌleɪt), **can·cel·lous** (ˈkænsɪləs), *or* **can·cel·lat·ed** *adj.* **1.** *Anatomy.* having a spongy or porous internal structure: *cancellate bones.* **2.** *Botany.* forming a network; reticulate: *a cancellate venation.* [C17: from Latin *cancellāre* to make like a lattice; see CANCEL]

can·cel·la·tion (ˌkænsɪˈleɪʃən) *n.* **1.** the fact or an instance of cancelling. **2.** something that has been cancelled, such as a theatre ticket, esp. when it is available for another person to take: *we have a cancellation in the balcony.* **3.** the marks or perforation made by cancelling.

can·cer (ˈkænsə) *n.* **1.** any type of malignant growth or tumour, caused by abnormal and uncontrolled cell division: may spread through the lymphatic system or blood stream to other parts of the body. **2.** the condition resulting from this. **3.** an evil influence that spreads dangerously. [C14: from Latin: crab, a creeping tumour; related to Greek *karkinos* crab, Sanskrit *karkata*] —ˈ**can·cer·ous** *adj.* —ˈ**can·cer·ous·ly** *adv.*

Can·cer (ˈkænsə) *n. Latin genitive* **Can·cri** (ˈkæŋkriː). **1.** *Astronomy.* a small faint zodiacal constellation in the N hemisphere, lying between Leo and Gemini on the ecliptic and containing the star cluster Praesepe. **2.** *Astrology.* **a.** Also called: the **Crab.** the fourth sign of the zodiac, symbol ♋, having a cardinal water classification and ruled by the moon. The sun is in this sign between about June 21 and July 22. **b.** a person born during a period when the sun is in this sign. **3.** See **tropic of Cancer.** See **tropic** (sense 1). ~*adj.* **4.** *Astrology.* born under or characteristic of Cancer. ~ **5.** Also (for senses 2b., 4): **Can·cer·i·an** (kænˈsɪərɪən).

can·cer stick *n.* a slang name for **cigarette.**

can·croid (ˈkæŋkrɔɪd) *adj.* **1.** resembling a cancerous growth. **2.** resembling a crab. ~*n.* **3.** a skin cancer, esp. one of only moderate malignancy.

c & b *Cricket. abbrev. for* caught and bowled (by).

can·de·la (kænˈdiːlə, -ˈdeɪlə) *n.* the basic SI unit of luminous intensity; the intensity, in a perpendicular direction, of a surface of 1/600 000 square metre of a black body at the temperature of freezing platinum under a pressure of 101 325 newtons per square metre. Symbol: cd Also called: **candle, standard candle.** [C20: from Latin: CANDLE]

can·de·la·brum (ˌkændɪˈlɑːbrəm) *or* **can·de·la·bra** *n., pl.* **·bra** (-brə), **·brums,** *or* **·bras.** a large, branched table candle holder. [C19: from Latin, from *candēla* CANDLE]

can·dent (ˈkændənt) *adj.* an archaic word for **incandescent.** [C16: from Latin *candēre* to shine]

can·des·cent (kænˈdɛsᵊnt) *adj. Rare.* glowing or starting to glow with heat. [C19: from Latin *candescere,* from *candēre* to be white, shine] —**can·ˈdes·cence** *n.* —**can·ˈdes·cent·ly** *adv.*

C & G *abbrev. for* City and Guilds.

Can·dia (ˈkandja) *n.* the Italian name for **Iráklion.**

can·did (ˈkændɪd) *adj.* **1.** frank and outspoken: *he was candid about his dislike of our friends.* **2.** without partiality; unbiased. **3.** unposed or informal: *a candid photograph.* **4.** *Obsolete.* **a.** white. **b.** clear or pure. [C17: from Latin *candidus* white, from *candēre* to be white] —ˈ**can·did·ly** *adv.* —ˈ**can·did·ness** *n.*

can·di·date (ˈkændɪˌdeɪt, -dɪt) *n.* **1.** a person seeking or nominated for election to a position of authority or honour or selection for a job, promotion, etc. **2.** a person taking an examination or test. **3.** a person or thing regarded as suitable or likely for a particular fate or position: *this wine is a candidate for his cellar.* [C17: from Latin *candidātus* clothed in white (because the candidate wore a white toga), from *candidus* white] —**can·di·da·cy** (ˈkændɪdəsɪ) *or* **can·di·da·ture** (ˈkændɪdətʃə) *n.*

can·did cam·er·a *n.* a small camera that may be used to take informal photographs of people, usually without their knowledge.

can·died (ˈkændɪd) *adj.* **1.** impregnated or encrusted with or as if with sugar or syrup: *candied peel.* **2.** (of sugar, honey, etc.) crystallized.

Can·di·ot (ˈkændɪˌɒt) *or* **Can·di·ote** (ˈkændɪˌəʊt) *adj.* **1.** of or relating to Candia (Iráklion) or Crete; Cretan. ~*n.* **2.** a native or inhabitant of Crete; a Cretan.

can·dle (ˈkændᵊl) *n.* **1.** a cylindrical piece of wax, tallow, or other fatty substance surrounding a wick, which is burned to produce light. **2.** *Physics.* **a.** see **international candle. b.** another name for **candela. 3. burn the candle at both ends.** *Informal.* to exhaust oneself, esp. by being up late enjoying oneself and getting up early to work. **4. not hold a candle to.** *Informal.* to be inferior or contemptible in comparison with: *your dog doesn't hold a candle to mine.* **5. not worth the candle.** *Informal.* not worth the price or trouble entailed (esp. in the phrase **the game's not worth the candle**). ~*vb.* **6.** (*tr.*) to examine (eggs) for freshness or the likelihood of being hatched by viewing them against a bright light. [Old English *candel,* from Latin *candēla,* from *candēre* to be white, glitter] —ˈ**can·dler** *n.*

can·dle·ber·ry (ˈkændᵊlbərɪ) *n., pl.* **·ries.** another name for **wax myrtle.**

can·dle·fish (ˈkændᵊlˌfɪʃ) *n., pl.* **·fish** *or* **·fish·es.** a salmonoid food fish, *Thaleichthys pacificus,* that occurs in the N Pacific and has oily flesh. Also called: **eulachon.**

can·dle·light (ˈkændᵊlˌlaɪt) *n.* **1. a.** the light from a candle or candles: *they ate by candlelight.* **b.** (*as modifier*): *a candlelight dinner.* **2.** dusk; evening.

Can·dle·mas (ˈkændᵊlməs) *n. Christianity.* Feb. 2, the Feast of the Purification of the Virgin Mary and the presentation of Christ in the Temple: the day on which the church candles are blessed. In Scotland it is one of the four quarter days.

can·dle·nut (ˈkændᵊlˌnʌt) *n.* **1.** a euphorbiaceous tree, *Aleurites mollucana,* of tropical Asia and Polynesia. **2.** the nut of this tree, which yields an oil used in paints and varnishes. In their native regions the nuts are strung together and burned as candles.

can·dle·pin (ˈkændᵊlˌpɪn) *n.* a bowling pin, as used in skittles, tenpin bowling, candlepins, etc.

can·dle·pins (ˈkændᵊlˌpɪnz) *n.* (*functioning as sing.*) a type of bowling game, employing a smaller ball than tenpins, in which three balls are allowed to a frame and fallen pins are not removed from the alley.

can·dle·pow·er (ˈkændᵊlˌpaʊə) *n.* the luminous intensity of a source of light in a given direction: now expressed in candelas but formerly in terms of the international candle.

can·dle·stick (ˈkændᵊlˌstɪk) *or* **can·dle·hold·er** (ˈkændᵊlˌhəʊldə) *n.* a holder, usually ornamental, with a spike or socket for a candle.

can·dle-tree *n.* another name for **wax myrtle.**

can·dle·wick (ˈkændᵊlˌwɪk) *n.* **1.** unbleached cotton or muslin into which loops of yarn are hooked and then cut to give a tufted pattern. It is used for bedspreads, dressing gowns, etc. **2.** the wick of a candle. **3.** (*modifier*) being or made of candlewick fabric.

can·dle·wood (ˈkændᵊlˌwʊd) *n.* **1.** the resinous wood of any of several trees, used for torches and candle substitutes. **2.** any tree or shrub, such as ocotillo, that produces this wood.

can·dour *or U.S.* **can·dor** (ˈkændə) *n.* **1.** the quality of being open and honest; frankness. **2.** fairness; impartiality. **3.** *Obsolete.* purity or brightness. [C17: from Latin *candor* from *candēre* to be white, shine]

C &W *abbrev. for* country and western.

can·dy (ˈkændɪ) *n., pl.* **·dies. 1.** *Chiefly U.S.* confectionery in general; sweets, chocolate, etc. ~*vb.* **·dies, ·dy·ing, ·died. 2.** to cause (sugar, etc.) to become crystalline, esp. by boiling or (of sugar) to become crystalline through boiling. **3.** to preserve (fruit peel, ginger, etc.) by boiling in sugar. **4.** to cover with any crystalline substance, such as ice or sugar. [C18: from Old French *sucre candi* candied sugar, from Arabic *qandi* candied, from *qand* cane sugar, of Dravidian origin]

can·dy·floss (ˈkændɪˌflɒs) *n. Brit.* a very light fluffy confection made from coloured spun sugar, usually held on a stick. U.S. name: **cotton candy.**

can·dy store *n.* a U.S. term for **sweet shop.**

can·dy-striped *adj.* (esp. of clothing fabric) having narrow coloured stripes on a white background. —**can·dy stripe** *n.*

can·dy·tuft (ˈkændɪˌtʌft) *n.* any of various widely cultivated Mediterranean cruciferous plants of the genus *Iberis,* having clusters of white, red, or purplish flowers. [C17: *Candy,* obsolete variant of CANDIA (Crete) + TUFT]

cane (keɪn) *n.* **1. a.** the long jointed pithy or hollow flexible stem of the bamboo, rattan, or any similar plant. **b.** any plant having such a stem. **2. a.** strips of such stems, woven or interlaced to make wickerwork, the seats and backs of chairs, etc. **b.** (*as modifier*): *a cane chair.* **3.** the woody stem of a reed, young grapevine, blackberry, raspberry, or loganberry. **4.** any of several grasses with long stiff stems, esp. *Arundinaria gigantea* of the southeastern U.S. **5.** a flexible rod with which to administer a beating as a punishment, as to schoolboys. **6.** a slender rod, usually wooden and often ornamental, used for support when walking; walking-stick. **7.** see **sugar cane. 8.** a slender rod or cylinder, as of glass. ~*vb.* (*tr.*) **9.** to whip or beat with or as if with a cane. **10.** to make or repair with cane. [C14: from Old French, from Latin *canna,* from Greek *kanna,* of Semitic origin; related to Arabic *qanāh* reed] —ˈ**can·er** *n.*

Ca·ne·a (kæˈnɪə) *n.* the capital and chief port of Crete, on the NW coast. Pop.: 40 564 (1971). Greek name: **Khaniá.**

cane·brake (ˈkeɪnˌbreɪk) *n. U.S.* a thicket of canes.

cane grass *n. Austral.* any of several tall perennial hard-stemmed grasses, esp. *Eragrostis australasica,* of inland swamps.

ca·nel·la (kəˈnɛlə) *n.* the fragrant cinnamon-like inner bark of a West Indian tree, *Canella winterana* (family *Canellaceae*) used as a spice and in medicine. [C17: from Medieval Latin: cinnamon, from Latin *canna* cane, reed]

cane piece *n.* (in the Caribbean) a field of sugar cane, esp. a peasant's isolated field.

cane rat *n.* **1.** Also called (in W Africa): **cutting grass.** a tropical African cavy-like hystricomorph rodent, *Thryonomys swinderianus,* that lives in swampy regions: family *Thryonomyidae.* **2.** a similar but smaller species, *T. gregorianus.*

ca·nes·cent (kəˈnɛsᵊnt) *adj.* **1.** *Biology.* white or greyish due to the presence of numerous short white hairs. **2.** becoming hoary, white, or greyish. [C19: from Latin *cānescere* to grow white, become hoary, from *cānēre* to be white] —**caˈnes·cence** *n.*

cane sug·ar *n.* **1.** the sucrose obtained from sugar cane, which is identical to that obtained from sugar beet. See also **beet sugar. 2.** another name for **sucrose.**

Ca·nes Ve·nat·i·ci (ˈkɑːniːz vɪˈnætɪˌsaɪ) *n., Latin genitive* **Ca·num Ve·nat·i·co·rum** (ˈkɑːnəm vɪˌnætɪˈkɔːrəm). a small faint constellation in the N hemisphere near Ursa Major that contains the globular cluster M3 and the spiral galaxy M51. [Latin: hunting dogs]

can·field (ˈkænˌfiːld) *n. Cards.* a gambling game adapted from a type of patience.

cangue *or* **cang** (kæŋ) *n.* (formerly in China) a large wooden collar worn by petty criminals as a punishment. [C18: from French, from Portuguese *canga* yoke]

Ca·nic·u·la (kəˈnɪkjʊlə) *n.* another name for **Sirius.** [Latin, literally: little dog, from *canis* dog]

ca·nic·u·lar (kəˈnɪkjʊlə) *adj.* of or relating to the star Sirius or its rising.

can·i·kin (ˈkænɪkɪn) *n.* a variant spelling of **cannikin.**

ca·nine (ˈkeɪnaɪn, ˈkæn-) *adj.* **1.** of or resembling a dog; doglike. **2.** of, relating to, or belonging to the *Canidae,* a family of mammals, including dogs, jackals, wolves, and foxes, typically having a bushy tail, erect ears, and a long muzzle: order *Carnivora* (carnivores). **3.** of or relating to any of the four teeth, two in each jaw, situated between the incisors and the premolars. ~*n.* **4.** any animal of the family *Canidae.* **5.** a canine tooth. [C17: from Latin *canīnus,* from *canis* dog]

Ca·nis Ma·jor (ˈkeɪnɪs) *n., Latin genitive* **Ca·nis Ma·jo·ris** (məˈdʒɔːrɪs). a constellation in the S hemisphere close to Orion, containing Sirius, the brightest star in the sky. Also called: the **Great Dog.** [Latin: the greater dog]

Ca·nis Mi·nor *n., Latin genitive* **Ca·nis Mi·no·ris** (maɪˈnɔːrɪs). a small constellation in the N hemisphere close to Orion, containing the first magnitude star Procyon. Also called: the **Little Dog.** [Latin: the lesser dog]

can·is·ter (ˈkænɪstə) *n.* **1.** a container, usually made of metal, in which dry food, such as tea or coffee, is stored. **2.** (formerly) **a.** a type of shrapnel shell for firing from a cannon. **b.** Also called: **canister shot, case shot.** the shot or shrapnel packed inside this. [C17: from Latin *canistrum* basket woven from reeds, from Greek *kanastron,* from *kanna* reed, CANE]

can·ker (ˈkæŋkə) *n.* **1.** an ulceration, esp. of the lips or lining of the oral cavity. **2.** *Vet. science.* **a.** a disease of horses in which the horn of the hoofs becomes soft and spongy. **b.** an ulcerative disease of the lining of the external ear, esp. in dogs and cats. **3.** an open wound in the stem of a tree or shrub, caused by injury or parasites. **4.** something evil that spreads and corrupts. ~*vb.* **5.** to infect or become infected with or as if with canker. [Old English *cancer,* from Latin *cancer* crab, cancerous sore]

can·ker·ous (ˈkæŋkərəs) *adj.* **1.** having cankers. **2.** infectious; corrupting.

can·ker·worm (ˈkæŋkəˌwɜːm) *n.* the larva of either of two geometrid moths, *Paleacrita vernata* or *Alsophila pometaria,* which feed on and destroy fruit and shade trees in North America.

can·na (ˈkænə) *n.* any of various tropical plants constituting the genus *Canna,* having broad leaves and red or yellow showy flowers for which they are cultivated: family *Cannaceae.* [C17: from New Latin CANE]

can·na·bin (ˈkænəbɪn) *n.* a greenish-black poisonous resin obtained from the hemp plant and thought to be the active narcotic principle. Also called: **cannabis resin.**

can·na·bis (ˈkænəbɪs) *n.* **1.** another name for **hemp** (the plant), esp. Indian hemp (*Cannabis indica*). **2.** the dried tops of the female flowers of the hemp plant, which are chewed or smoked for their euphoric effect. See also **cannabin, hashish, marijuana, bhang.** [C18: from Latin, from Greek *kannabis;* see HEMP] —ˈ**can·na·bic** *adj.*

Can·nae (ˈkæniː) *n.* an ancient city in SE Italy: scene of a victory by Hannibal over the Romans (216 B.C.).

canned (kænd) *adj.* **1.** preserved and stored in airtight cans or tins: *canned meat.* **2.** *Informal.* prepared or recorded in advance; artificial; not spontaneous: *canned music.* **3.** a slang word for **drunk** (sense 1).

can·nel coal *or* **can·nel** (ˈkænᵊl) *n.* a dull coal having a high volatile content and burning with a smoky luminous flame. [C16: from northern English dialect *cannel* candle: so called from its bright flame]

can·nel·lo·ni *or* **can·ne·lo·ni** (ˌkænɪˈləʊnɪ) *pl. n.* tubular pieces of pasta filled with meat or cheese. [Italian, plural of *cannellone,* from *cannello* stalk, from *canna* CANE]

can·ne·lure (ˈkænəˌlʊə) *n.* a groove or fluting, esp. one around the cylindrical part of a bullet. [C18: from French, ultimately from Latin *canālis* CANAL]

can·ner (ˈkænə) *n.* a person or organization whose job is to can foods.

can·ner·y (ˈkænərɪ) *n., pl.* **·ner·ies.** a place where foods are canned.

Cannes (kæn, kænz; *French* kan) *n.* a port and resort in SE France: developed in the 19th century from a fishing village; annual film festival. Pop.: 71 080 (1975).

can·ni·bal (ˈkænɪbᵊl) *n.* **1. a.** a person who eats the flesh of other human beings. **b.** (*as modifier*): *cannibal tribes.* **2.** an animal that feeds on the flesh of others of its kind. [C16: from Spanish *Canibales,* name used by Columbus to designate the Caribs of Cuba and Haiti, from Arawak *caniba,* variant of CARIB]

can·ni·bal·ism (ˈkænɪbəˌlɪzəm) *n.* **1.** the act of eating human flesh or the flesh of one's own kind. **2.** savage and inhuman cruelty. —ˌ**can·ni·bal·ˈis·tic** *adj.* —ˌ**can·ni·bal·ˈis·ti·cal·ly** *adv.*

can·ni·bal·ize *or* **can·ni·bal·ise** (ˈkænɪbəˌlaɪz) *vb.* (*tr.*) to use (serviceable parts from one machine or vehicle) to repair another, esp. as an alternative to using new parts. —ˌ**can·ni·bal·i·ˈza·tion** *or* ˌ**can·ni·bal·i·ˈsa·tion** *n.*

can·ni·kin, can·a·kin, *or* **can·i·kin** (ˈkænɪkɪn) *n.* a small can, esp. one used as a drinking vessel. [C16: from Middle Dutch *kanneken;* see CAN², -KIN]

can+ning ('kænɪŋ) *n.* the process or business of sealing food in cans or tins to preserve it.

Can+ning ('kænɪŋ) *n.* **1. Charles John,** 1st Earl Canning. 1812–62, British statesman; governor general of India (1856–58) and first viceroy (1858–62). **2.** his father, **George.** 1770–1827, British Tory statesman; foreign secretary (1822–27) and prime minister (1827).

Can+ning Ba+sin *n.* an arid basin in NW Western Australia, largely unexplored. Area: about 400 000 sq. km (150 000 sq. miles).

Can+nock ('kænək) *n.* a town in W central England, in S Staffordshire: **Cannock Chase** (a public area of heathland, once a royal preserve) is just to the E. Pop.: 55 873 (1971).

can+non ('kænən) *n., pl.* **+nons** *or* **+non. 1.** a heavy artillery piece consisting of a metal tube mounted on a carriage. **2.** an automatic aircraft gun of large calibre. **3.** a heavy tube or drum, esp. one that can rotate freely on the shaft by which it is supported. **4.** the metal loop at the top of a bell, from which it is suspended. **5.** See **cannon bone. 6.** *Billiards.* **a.** a shot in which the cue ball is caused to contact one object ball after another. **b.** the points scored by this. Usual U.S. word: **carom. 7.** a rebound or bouncing back, as of a ball off a wall. **8.** either of the two parts of a vambrace. *~vb.* **9.** short for **cannonade. 10.** (*intr.*) *Billiards.* to make a cannon. [C16: from Old French *canon,* from Italian *cannone* cannon, large tube, from *canna* tube, CANE]

can+non+ade (ˌkænə'neɪd) *n.* **1.** an intense and continuous gunnery bombardment. *~vb.* **2.** to attack (a target) with cannon.

can·non+ball ('kænənˌbɔːl) *n.* **1.** a projectile fired from a cannon: usually a solid round metal shot. **2.** *Tennis.* **a.** a very fast low serve. **b.** (*as modifier*): *a cannonball serve.* **3.** a jump into water by a person who has his arms tucked into the body to form a ball. *~vb.* (*intr.*) **4.** (often foll. by *along,* etc.) to rush along, like a cannonball. **5.** to execute a cannonball jump. *~adj.* **6.** very fast or powerful.

can+non bone *n.* a bone in the legs of horses and other hoofed animals consisting of greatly elongated fused metatarsals or metacarpals.

can+non+eer (ˌkænə'nɪə) *n.* (formerly) a soldier who served and fired a cannon; artilleryman.

can+non fod+der *n.* men regarded as expendable because they are part of a huge army.

can+non+ry ('kænənrɪ) *n., pl.* **+ries. 1.** a volley of artillery fire. **2.** artillery in general.

can+not ('kænɒt, kæ'nɒt) *vb.* an auxiliary verb expressing incapacity, inability, withholding permission, etc.; can not.

can+nu+la *or* **can+u+la** ('kænjʊlə) *n., pl.* **+las** *or* **+lae** (-ˌliː). *Surgery.* a small tube for insertion into a bodily cavity, as for draining off fluid, introducing medication, etc. [C17: from Latin: a small reed, from *canna*]

can+nu+late *or* **can+u+late** *vb.* ('kænjʊˌleɪt). **1.** to insert a cannula into. *~adj.* ('kænjʊˌleɪt, -ˌlɪt), *also* **can+nu+lar** *or* **can+u+lar. 2.** shaped like a cannula. —ˌ**can+nu+'la+tion** *or* ˌ**can+u+'la+tion** *n.*

can+ny ('kænɪ) *adj.* **+ni+er, +ni+est. 1.** shrewd, esp. in business; astute or wary; knowing. **2.** *Scot. and northeast English dialect.* good or nice: used as a general term of approval. **3.** *Scot.* lucky or fortunate. *~adv.* **4.** *Scot. and northeast English dialect.* quite; rather: *a canny long while.* [C16: from CAN[1] (in the sense: to know how) + -Y[1]] —'**can+ni+ly** *adv.* —'**can+ni+ness** *n.*

ca+noe (kə'nuː) *n.* **1.** a light narrow open boat, propelled by one or more paddles. *~vb.* **+noes, +noe+ing, +noed. 2.** to go in or transport by canoe. [C16: from Spanish *canoa,* of Carib origin] —**ca+'noe+ist** *n.*

ca·noe+wood (kə'nuːˌwʊd) *n.* another name for the **tulip tree.**

can+on[1] ('kænən) *n.* **1.** *Christianity.* a Church decree enacted to regulate morals or religious practices. **2.** (*often pl.*) a general rule or standard, as of judgment, morals, etc. **3.** (*often pl.*) a principle or accepted criterion applied in a branch of learning or art. **4.** *R.C. Church.* the complete list of the canonized saints. **5.** *R.C. Church.* the prayer in the Mass in which the Host is consecrated. **6.** *Ecclesiast.* a list of sacred books, etc., officially recognized as genuine. **7.** a piece of music in which an extended melody in one part is imitated successively in one or more other parts. See also **round** (sense 30), **catch** (sense 32). **8.** a list of the works of an author that are accepted as authentic. **9.** (formerly) a size of printer's type equal to 48 point. [Old English, from Latin, from Greek *kanōn* rule, rod for measuring, standard; related to *kanna* reed, CANE]

can+on[2] ('kænən) *n.* **1.** a priest who is a member of a cathedral chapter. **2.** *R.C. Church.* a member of any of several religious orders (**canons regular**). [C13: from Anglo-French *canunie,* from Late Latin *canonicus* one living under a rule, from CANON[1]]

can+on+ess ('kænənɪs) *n. R.C. Church.* a woman belonging to any one of several religious orders and living under a rule but not under a vow.

ca+non·i·cal (kə'nɒnɪkᵊl) *or* **ca+non+ic** *adj.* **1.** belonging to or included in the canon of Scripture. **2.** belonging to or in conformity with canon law. **3.** according to recognized law; accepted. **4.** *Music.* in the form of a canon. **5.** of or relating to a cathedral chapter. —**ca+'non·i·cal+ly** *adv.*

ca+non·i·cal hour *n.* **1.** *R.C. Church.* **a.** one of the seven prayer times appointed for each day by canon law. **b.** the services prescribed for these times, namely matins, prime, terce, sext, nones, vespers, and compline. **2.** *Church of England.* any time between 8:00 a.m. and 6:00 p.m. at which marriages may lawfully be celebrated.

ca+non·i+cals (kə'nɒnɪkᵊlz) *pl. n.* the vestments worn by clergy when officiating.

ca+non·i+cate (kə'nɒnɪˌkeɪt, -kɪt) *n.* the office or rank of a canon; canonry.

can+on+ic·i·ty (ˌkænə'nɪsɪtɪ) *n.* the fact or quality of being canonical.

can+on+ist ('kænənɪst) *n.* a specialist in canon law.

can+on+ize *or* **can+on+ise** ('kænəˌnaɪz) *vb.* (*tr.*) **1.** *R.C. Church.* to declare (a person) to be a saint and thus admit to the canon of saints. **2.** to regard as holy or as a saint. **3.** to sanction by canon law; pronounce valid. —ˌ**can+on·i+'za+tion** *or* ˌ**can+on·i+'sa+tion** *n.*

can+on law *n.* the codified body of laws enacted by the supreme authorities of a Christian Church, esp. those based on papal and conciliar decisions, governing the affairs of a Christian Church.

can+on+ry ('kænənrɪ) *n., pl.* **+ries. 1.** the office, benefice, or status of a canon. **2.** canons collectively. [C15: from CANON[2] + -RY]

ca+noo+dle (kə'nuːdᵊl) *vb.* (*intr.;* often foll. by *with*) *Slang.* to kiss and cuddle; pet; fondle. [C19: of unknown origin] —**ca+'noo+dler** *n.*

can-o·pen·er *n.* another name for **tin-opener.**

Ca+no+pic jar, urn, *or* **vase** (kə'nəʊpɪk) *n.* (in ancient Egypt) one of four containers with tops in the form of animal heads of the gods, for holding the entrails of a mummy.

Ca+no+pus[1] (kə'nəʊpəs) *n.* the brightest star in the constellation Carina and the second brightest star in the sky. Visual magnitude: -0.7; spectral type: F0; distance: 110 light years.

Ca+no+pus[2] (kə'nəʊpəs) *n.* a port in ancient Egypt east of Alexandria where granite monuments have been found inscribed with the name of Rameses II and written in languages similar to those of the Rosetta stone. —**Ca+'no+pic** *adj.*

can·o·py ('kænəpɪ) *n., pl.* **+pies. 1.** an ornamental awning above a throne or bed or held over a person of importance on ceremonial occasions. **2.** a rooflike covering over an altar, niche, etc. **3.** a roofed structure serving as a sheltered passageway or area. **4.** a large or wide covering, esp. one high above: *the sky was a grey canopy.* **5.** the nylon or silk hemisphere that forms the supporting surface of a parachute. **6.** the transparent cover of an aircraft cockpit. *~vb.* **+pies, +py+ing, +pied. 7.** (*tr.*) to cover with or as if with a canopy. [C14: from Medieval Latin *canōpeum* mosquito net, from Latin *cōnōpeum* gauze net, from Greek *kōnōpeion* bed with protective net, from *kōnōps* mosquito]

ca+no+rous (kə'nɔːrəs) *adj. Rare.* tuneful; melodious. [C17: from Latin *canōrus,* from *canere* to sing] —**ca+'no+rous+ly** *adv.* —**ca+'no+rous+ness** *n.*

Ca+nos+sa (kə'nɒsə; *Italian* ka'nɔssa) *n.* a ruined castle in N Italy, in Emilia near Reggio nell'Emilia: scene of the penance done by the Holy Roman Emperor Henry IV before Pope Gregory VII.

Ca·no·va (*Italian* ka'nɔːva) *n.* **An·to·nio** (an'tɔːnjo). 1757–1822, Italian neoclassical sculptor.

cans (kænz) *pl. n.* an informal name for **headphones.**

Can+so ('kænsəʊ) *n.* **1. Cape.** a cape in Canada, at the NE tip of Nova Scotia. **2. Strait of.** Also called: **Gut of Canso.** a channel in Canada, between the Nova Scotia mainland and S Cape Breton Island.

canst (kænst) *vb. Archaic.* the form of **can**[1] used with the pronoun *thou* or its relative form.

can't (kɑːnt) *vb. a contraction of* cannot.

cant[1] (kænt) *n.* **1.** insincere talk, esp. concerning religion or morals; pious platitudes. **2.** stock phrases that have become meaningless through repetition. **3.** specialized vocabulary of a particular group, such as thieves, journalists, or lawyers; jargon. **4.** singsong whining speech, as used by beggars. *~vb.* **5.** (*intr.*) to speak in or use cant. [C16: probably via Norman French *canter* to sing, from Latin *cantāre;* used disparagingly, from the 12th century, of chanting in religious services] —'**cant+er** *n.* —'**cant+ing+ly** *adv.*

cant[2] (kænt) *n.* **1.** inclination from a vertical or horizontal plane; slope; slant. **2.** a sudden movement that tilts or turns something. **3.** the angle or tilt thus caused. **4.** a corner or outer angle, esp. of a building. **5.** an oblique or slanting surface, edge, or line. *~vb.* (*tr.*) **6.** to tip, tilt, or overturn, esp. with a sudden jerk. **7.** to set in an oblique position. **8.** another word for **bevel** (sense 1). *~adj.* **9.** oblique; slanting. **10.** having flat surfaces and without curves. [C14 (in the sense: edge, corner): perhaps from Latin *canthus* iron hoop round a wheel, of obscure origin] —'**cant+ic** *adj.*

cant[3] (kɑːnt) *adj. Northern Brit. dialect.* lusty; merry; hearty. [C14: related to Low German *kant* bold, merry]

Cant. *abbrev. for:* **1.** Canterbury. **2.** Canticles.

Cantab. (kæn'tæb) *abbrev. for* Cantabrigiensis. [Latin: of Cambridge]

can+ta+bi+le (kæn'tɑːbɪlɪ) *Music.* *~adj., adv.* **1.** singing; as if sung. *~n.* **2.** a piece or passage performed in this way. [Italian, from Late Latin *cantābilis,* from Latin *cantāre* to sing]

Can+ta+bri·an Moun+tains (kæn'teɪbrɪən) *pl. n.* a mountain chain along the N coast of Spain, consisting of a series of high ridges that rise over 2400m (8000 ft.): rich in minerals (esp. coal and iron).

Can+ta+brig+i·an (ˌkæntə'brɪdʒɪən) *adj.* **1.** of, relating to, or characteristic of Cambridge or Cambridge University, or of Cambridge, Massachusetts, or Harvard University. *~n.* **2.** a member or graduate of Cambridge University or Harvard University. **3.** an inhabitant or native of Cambridge. [C17: from Medieval Latin *Cantabrigia*]

Can·tal (*French* kã'tal) *n.* **1.** a department of S central France, in the Auvergne region. Capital: Aurillac. Pop.: 173 578 (1975). Area: 5779 sq. km (2254 sq. miles). **2.** a hard strong cheese made in this area.

can·ta·la (kæn'tɑːlə) *n.* **1.** a tropical American plant, *Agave cantala,* similar to the century plant: family *Agavaceae* (agaves). **2.** the coarse tough fibre of this plant, used in making twine. [of unknown origin]

can·ta·loupe *or* **can·ta·loup** ('kæntəˌluːp) *n.* **1.** a cultivated variety of muskmelon, *Cucumis melo cantalupensis,* with ribbed warty rind and orange flesh. **2.** any of several other muskmelons. [C18: from French, from *Cantaluppi,* former papal villa near Rome, where it was first cultivated in Europe]

can·tan·ker·ous (kæn'tæŋkərəs) *adj.* quarrelsome; irascible. [C18: perhaps from C14 (obsolete) *conteckour* a contentious person, from *conteck* strife, from Anglo-French *contek,* of obscure origin] —**can·'tan·ker·ous·ly** *adv.* —**can·'tan·ker·ous·ness** *n.*

can·ta·ta (kæn'tɑːtə) *n.* a musical setting of a text, esp. a religious text, consisting of arias, duets, and choruses interspersed with recitatives. [C18: from Italian, from *cantare* to sing, from Latin]

can·ta·trice (*French* kãta'tris) *n.* a female singer, esp. a professional soloist.

can·teen (kæn'tiːn) *n.* **1.** a restaurant attached to a factory, school, etc., providing meals for large numbers of people. **2. a.** a small shop that provides a limited range of items, such as toilet requisites, to a military unit. **b.** a recreation centre for military personnel. **3.** a soldier's eating and drinking utensils. **4.** a temporary or mobile stand at which food is provided. **5. a.** a box in which a set of cutlery is laid out. **b.** the cutlery itself. **6.** a flask or canister for carrying water or other liquids, as used by soldiers or travellers. [C18: from French *cantine,* from Italian *cantina* wine cellar, from *canto* corner, from Latin *canthus* iron hoop encircling chariot wheel; see CANT²]

can·ter ('kæntə) *n.* **1.** an easy three-beat gait of horses, etc., between a trot and a gallop in speed. **2. at a canter.** easily; without effort: *he won at a canter.* ~*vb.* **3.** to move or cause to move at a canter. [C18: short for *Canterbury trot,* the supposed pace at which pilgrims rode to Canterbury]

Can·ter·bur·y ('kæntəbərɪ, -brɪ) *n.* **1.** a city in SE England, in E Kent: St. Augustine's starting point for the conversion of England (597 A.D.) to Christianity; cathedral where St. Thomas à Becket was martyred (1170); seat of the archbishop and primate of England; seat of the University of Kent. Pop.: 33 157 (1971). Latin name: **Durovernum. 2.** a provincial district of New Zealand, on E central South Island on **Canterbury Bight:** mountainous with coastal lowlands; agricultural. Chief town: Christchurch. Pop.: 182 825 (1971). Area: 36 440 sq. km (14 070 sq. miles). **3.** a city in SE Australia, in E New South Wales: a suburb of Sydney. Pop.: 113 334 (1971).

Can·ter·bur·y bell *n.* a campanulaceous biennial European plant, *Campanula medium,* widely cultivated for its blue, violet, or white flowers.

can·thar·i·des (kæn'θærɪˌdiːz) *pl. n., sing.* **can·tha·ris** ('kænθərɪs). a diuretic and urogenital stimulant or irritant prepared from the dried bodies of Spanish fly, once thought to be an aphrodisiac. Also called: **Spanish fly.** [C15: from Latin, plural of *cantharis,* from Greek *kantharis* Spanish fly]

Can Tho ('kʌn 'təʊ, 'kæn) *n.* a town in S Vietnam, on the River Mekong. Pop.: 153 769 (1971).

cant hook *or* **dog** *n. Forestry.* a wooden pole with an adjustable hook at one end, used for handling logs.

can·thus ('kænθəs) *n., pl.* **·thi** (-ˌθaɪ). the inner or outer corner or angle of the eye, formed by the natural junction of the eyelids. [C17: from New Latin, from Latin: iron tyre] —**'can·thal** *adj.*

can·ti·cle ('kæntɪkᵊl) *n.* **1.** a nonmetrical hymn, derived from the Bible and used in the liturgy of certain Christian churches. **2.** a song, poem, or hymn, esp. one that is religious in character. [C13: from Latin *canticulum,* diminutive of *canticus* a song, from *canere* to sing]

Can·ti·cle of Can·ti·cles *n.* another name for the **Song of Solomon,** used in the Douay Bible.

can·ti·le·na (ˌkæntɪ'leɪnə) *n.* a smooth flowing style in the writing of vocal music.

can·ti·le·ver ('kæntɪˌliːvə) *n.* **1. a.** a beam, girder, or structural framework that is fixed at one end only. **b.** (*as modifier*): *a cantilever wing.* **2.** a wing or tailplane of an aircraft that has no external bracing or support. **3.** a part of a beam or a structure projecting outwards beyond its support. ~*vb.* **4.** (*tr.*) to construct (a building member, beam, etc.) so that it is fixed at one end only. **5.** (*intr.*) to project like a cantilever. [C17: perhaps from CANT² + LEVER]

can·ti·le·ver bridge *n.* a bridge having spans that are constructed as cantilevers.

can·til·late ('kæntɪˌleɪt) *vb.* **1.** to chant (passages from Scripture) according to the traditional Jewish musical notations provided in the Hebrew Bible. **2.** to intone or chant. [C19: from Late Latin *cantillāre* to sing softly, from Latin *cantāre* to sing] —**ˌcan·til·'la·tion** *n.*

can·ti·na (kæn'tiːnə) *n.* a bar or wine shop, esp. in a Spanish-speaking country. [from Spanish]

cant·ing arms *pl. n. Heraldry.* a coat of arms making visual reference to the surname of its owner.

can·tle ('kæntᵊl) *n.* **1.** the back part of a saddle that slopes upwards. **2.** a slice; a broken-off piece. [C14: from Old Northern French *cantel,* from *cant* corner; see CANT²]

can·to ('kæntəʊ) *n., pl.* **·tos. 1.** *Music.* **a.** *Archaic.* a melody or song. **b.** another word for **cantus** (sense 2). **2.** a main division of a long poem. [C16: from Italian: song, from Latin *cantus,* from *canere* to sing]

can·ton ('kæntɒn, kæn'tɒn) *n.* **1.** any of the 22 political divisions of Switzerland. **2.** a subdivision of a French arrondissement. **3.** ('kæntən). *Heraldry.* a small square or oblong charge on a shield, usually in the top left corner. ~*vb.* **4.** (kæn'tɒn). (*tr.*) to divide into cantons. **5.** (kən'tuːn). (esp. formerly) to allocate accommodation to (military personnel, etc.). [C16: from Old French: corner, division, from Italian *cantone,* from *canto* corner, from Latin *canthus* iron rim; see CANT²] —**'can·ton·al** *adj.*

Can·ton *n.* **1.** (kæn'tɒn). a port in SE China, capital of Kwangtung province, on the Pearl River: the first Chinese port open to European trade. Pop.: 3 000 000 (1965 Western est.). Chinese name: **Kwangchow. 2.** ('kæntən). a city in NE Ohio. Pop.: 106 897 (1973 est.).

Can·ton crepe ('kæntɒn, -tən) *n.* a fine crinkled silk or rayon crepe fabric, slightly heavier than crepe de Chine. [C19: named after *Canton,* China, where it was originally made]

Can·ton·ese (ˌkæntə'niːz) *n.* **1.** the Chinese language spoken in Canton, Kwangtung and Kwangsi provinces, Hong Kong, and elsewhere outside China. **2.** (*pl.* **·ese**) a native or inhabitant of Canton or Kwangtung province. ~*adj.* **3.** of or relating to Canton, Kwangtung province, or the Chinese language spoken there.

Can·ton flan·nel ('kæntɒn, -tən) *n.* another name for **cotton flannel.** [C19: named after *Canton,* China]

can·ton·ment (kən'tuːnmənt) *n. Military.* (esp. formerly) **1.** a large training camp. **2.** living accommodation, esp. the winter quarters of a campaigning army.

Can·ton Ri·ver (kæn'tɒn) *n.* another name for the **Chu Chiang.**

can·tor ('kæntɔː) *n.* **1.** *Judaism.* the leading singer in the synagogue liturgy. **2.** *Christianity.* the leader of the singing in a church choir. [C16: from Latin: singer, from *canere* to sing]

can·to·ri·al (kæn'tɔːrɪəl) *adj.* **1.** of or relating to a precentor. **2.** (of part of a choir) on the same side of a cathedral, etc., as the precentor; on the N side of the choir. Compare **decanal.**

can·tor·is (kæn'tɔːrɪs) *adj.* (in antiphonal music) to be sung by the cantorial side of a choir. Compare **decani.** [Latin: genitive of *cantor* precentor]

can·trip ('kæntrɪp) *n. Scot.* **1.** a magic spell. **2.** a mischievous trick. [C18: Scottish, of unknown origin]

Cantuar. ('kæntjʊˌɑː) *abbrev. for* Cantuarensis. [Latin: (Archbishop) of Canterbury]

can·tus ('kæntəs) *n., pl.* **·tus. 1.** a medieval form of church singing; chant. **2.** Also called: **canto.** the highest part in a piece of choral music. **3.** (in 15th- or 16th-century music) a piece of choral music, usually secular, in polyphonic style. [Latin: song, from *canere* to sing]

can·tus fir·mus ('fɜːməs) *n., pl.* **can·tus fir·mi** ('fɜːmiː). a melody used as the basis of and usually forming an independent part in a polyphonic composition. Also called: **can·to fer·mo** ('kæntəʊ 'fɜːməʊ). [Medieval Latin, literally: fixed song]

cant·y ('kæntɪ, 'kɑːn-) *adj.* **cant·i·er, cant·i·est.** *Northern Brit. dialect.* lively; brisk. [C18: see CANT³] —**'cant·i·ly** *adv.* —**'cant·i·ness** *n.*

Ca·nuck (kə'nʌk) *n. Slang, chiefly U.S.* a Canadian, esp. a French Canadian. [C19: from *Canadian* + *-uck,* of uncertain origin]

ca·nu·la ('kænjʊlə) *n., pl.* **·las** *or* **·lae** (-ˌliː). *Surgery.* a variant spelling of **cannula.**

Ca·nute, Cnut, *or* **Knut** (kə'njuːt) *n.* d. 1035, Danish king of England (1016–35), Denmark (1018–35), and Norway (1028–35). He defeated Edmund II of England (1016), but divided the kingdom with him until Edmund's death. An able ruler, he invaded Scotland (1027) and drove Olaf II from Norway (1028).

can·vas ('kænvəs) *n.* **1. a.** a heavy durable cloth made of cotton, hemp, or jute, used for sails, tents, etc. **b.** (*as modifier*): *a canvas bag.* **2. a.** a piece of canvas or a similar material on which a painting is done, usually in oils. **b.** a painting on this material, esp. in oils. **3.** a tent or tents collectively. **4.** *Nautical.* any cloth of which sails are made. **5.** *Nautical.* the sails of a vessel collectively. **6.** any coarse loosely woven cloth on which embroidery, tapestry, etc., is done. **7.** (preceded by *the*) the floor of a boxing or wrestling ring. **8.** *Rowing.* the tapering covered part at either end of a racing boat, sometimes referred to as a unit of length: *to win by a canvas.* **9. under canvas. a.** in tents. **b.** *Nautical.* with sails unfurled. [C14: from Norman French *canevas,* ultimately from Latin *cannabis* hemp]

can·vas·back ('kænvəsˌbæk) *n., pl.* **·backs** *or* **·back.** a North American diving duck, *Aythyra valisineria,* the male of which has a white body and reddish-brown head.

can·vass ('kænvəs) *vb.* **1.** to solicit votes, orders, advertising, etc., from. **2.** to determine the feelings and opinions of (voters before an election, etc.), esp. by conducting a survey. **3.** to investigate (something) thoroughly, esp. by discussion or debate. **4.** *Chiefly U.S.* to inspect (votes) officially to determine their validity. ~*n.* **5.** a solicitation of opinions, votes, sales orders, etc. **6.** close inspection; scrutiny. [C16: probably from obsolete sense of CANVAS (to toss someone in a canvas sheet, hence, to harass, criticize); the development of current senses is unexplained] —**'can·vass·er** *n.*

can·yon *or* **ca·ñon** ('kænjən) *n.* a gorge or ravine, esp. in North America, usually formed by the down-cutting of a river in a dry area where there is insufficient rainfall to erode the sides of the valley. [C19: from Spanish *cañon,* from *caña* tube, from Latin *canna* cane]

can·zo·na (kænˈzəʊnə) *n.* a type of 16th- or 17th-century contrapuntal music, usually for keyboard, lute, or instrumental ensemble. [C19: from Italian, from Latin *cantiō* song, from *canere* to sing]

can·zo·ne (kænˈzəʊnɪ) *n., pl.* **·ni** (-nɪ). **1.** a Provençal or Italian lyric, often in praise of love or beauty. **2. a.** a song, usually of a lyrical nature. **b.** (in 16th-century choral music) a polyphonic song from which the madrigal developed. [C16: from Italian: song, from Latin *cantiō*, from *canere* to sing]

can·zo·net (ˌkænzəˈnɛt) *or* **can·zo·net·ta** (ˌkænzəˈnɛtə) *n.* a short cheerful or lively song of the 16th to 18th centuries. [C16: Italian *canzonetta*, diminutive of CANZONE]

caou·tchouc (ˈkaʊtʃuːk, -tʃʊk; kaʊˈtʃuːk, -ˈtʃʊk) *n.* another name for **rubber**[1] (sense 1). [C18: from French, from obsolete Spanish *cauchuc*, from Quechua]

cap (kæp) *n.* **1.** a covering for the head, esp. a small close-fitting one made of cloth or knitted. **2.** such a covering serving to identify the wearer's rank, occupation, etc.: *a nurse's cap.* **3.** something that protects or covers, esp. a small lid or cover: *lens cap.* **4.** an uppermost surface or part: *the cap of a wave.* **5. a.** See **percussion cap. b.** a small amount of explosive enclosed in paper and used in a toy gun. **6.** *Sport, chiefly Brit.* **a.** an emblematic hat or beret given to someone chosen for a representative team: *he has won three England caps.* **b.** a player chosen for such a team. **7.** the upper part of a pedestal in a classical order. **8.** the roof of a windmill, sometimes in the form of a dome. **9.** *Botany.* the pileus of a mushroom or toadstool. **10.** *Hunting.* **a.** money contributed to the funds of a hunt by a follower who is neither a subscriber nor a farmer, in return for a day's hunting. **b.** a collection taken at a meet of hounds, esp. for a charity. **11.** *Anatomy.* **a.** the natural enamel covering a tooth. **b.** an artificial protective covering for a tooth. **12.** See **Dutch cap** (sense 2). **13.** a mortarboard when worn with a gown at an academic ceremony (esp. in the phrase **cap and gown**). **14. set one's cap for** *or* **at.** (of a woman) to be determined to win as a husband or lover. **15. cap in hand.** humbly, as when asking a favour. ~*vb.* **caps, cap·ping, capped.** (*tr.*) **16.** to cover, as with a cap: *snow capped the mountain tops.* **17.** *Informal.* to outdo; excel: *your story caps them all; to cap an anecdote.* **18. cap it all.** to provide the finishing touch: *we had sun, surf, cheap wine, and to cap it all a free car.* **19.** *Sport, Brit.* to select (a player) for a representative team: *he was capped 30 times by Scotland.* **20.** *Hunting.* to ask (hunt followers) for a cap. **21.** *Chiefly Scot.* to award a degree to. [Old English *cæppe*, from Late Latin *cappa* hood, perhaps from Latin *caput* head] —ˈ**cap·per** *n.*

cap. *abbrev. for:* **1.** capacity. **2.** capital. **3.** capitalize. **4.** capital letter. **5.** caput. [Latin: chapter]

ca·pa·bil·i·ty (ˌkeɪpəˈbɪlɪtɪ) *n., pl.* **·ties. 1.** the quality of being capable; ability. **2.** the quality of being susceptible to the use or treatment indicated: *the capability of a metal to be fused.* **3.** (*usually pl.*) a characteristic that may be developed; potential aptitude.

Ca·pa·blan·ca (*Spanish* ˌkapaˈblaŋka) *n.* **Jo·sé Ra·úl** (xoˈse raˈul), called *Capa* or *the Chess Machine.* 1888–1942, Cuban chess player; world champion 1921–27.

ca·pa·ble (ˈkeɪpəbᵊl) *adj.* **1.** having ability, esp. in many different fields; competent. **2.** (*postpositive;* foll. by *of*) able or having the skill (to do something): *she is capable of hard work.* **3.** (*postpositive;* foll. by *of*) having the temperament or inclination (to do something): *he seemed capable of murder.* [C16: from French, from Late Latin *capābilis* able to take in, from Latin *capere* to take] —ˈ**ca·pa·ble·ness** *n.* —ˈ**ca·pa·bly** *adv.*

ca·pa·cious (kəˈpeɪʃəs) *adj.* capable of holding much; roomy; spacious. [C17: from Latin *capāx*, from Latin *capere* to take] —**ca**ˈ**pa·cious·ly** *adv.* —**ca**ˈ**pa·cious·ness** *n.*

ca·pac·i·tance (kəˈpæsɪtəns) *n.* **1.** the property of a system that enables it to store electric charge. **2.** a measure of this, equal to the charge that must be added to such a system to raise its electrical potential by one unit. Symbol: *C* Former name: **capacity.** [C20: from CAPACITY + -ANCE] —**ca**ˈ**pac·i·tive** *adj.* —**ca**ˈ**pac·i·tive·ly** *adv.*

ca·pac·i·tate (kəˈpæsɪˌteɪt) *vb.* (*tr.*) **1.** to make legally competent. **2.** *Rare.* to make capable. —**ca**ˌ**pac·i**ˈ**ta·tion** *n.*

ca·pac·i·tor (kəˈpæsɪtə) *n.* a device for accumulating electric charge, usually consisting of two conducting surfaces separated by a dielectric. Former name: **condenser.**

ca·pac·i·ty (kəˈpæsɪtɪ) *n., pl.* **·ties. 1.** the ability or power to contain, absorb, or hold. **2.** the amount that can be contained; volume: *a capacity of six gallons.* **3. a.** the maximum amount something can contain or absorb (esp. in the phrase **filled to capacity**). **b.** (*as modifier*): *a capacity crowd.* **4.** the ability to understand or learn; aptitude; capability: *he has a great capacity for Greek.* **5.** the ability to do or produce (often in the phrase **at capacity**): *the factory's output was not at capacity.* **6.** a specified position or function: *he was employed in the capacity of manager.* **7.** a measure of the electrical output of a piece of apparatus such as a motor, generator, or accumulator. **8.** *Electronics.* a former name for **capacitance. 9.** *Computer technol.* **a.** the number of words or characters that can be stored in a particular storage device. **b.** the range of numbers that can be processed in a register. **10.** legal competence: *the capacity to make a will.* [C15: from Old French *capacite*, from Latin *capācitās*, from *capāx* spacious, from *capere* to take]

cap and bells *n.* the traditional garb of a court jester, including a cap with bells attached to it.

cap-a-pie (ˌkæpəˈpiː) *adv.* (dressed, armed, etc.) from head to foot. [C16: from Old French]

ca·par·i·son (kəˈpærɪsᵊn) *n.* **1.** a decorated covering for a horse or other animal, esp. (formerly) for a warhorse. **2.** rich or elaborate clothing and ornaments. ~*vb.* **3.** (*tr.*) to put a caparison on. [C16: via obsolete French from Old Spanish *caparazón* saddle cloth, probably from *capa* CAPE[1]]

cape[1] (keɪp) *n.* **1.** a sleeveless garment like a cloak but usually shorter. **2.** a strip of material attached to a coat or other garment so as to fall freely, usually from the shoulders. [C16: from French, from Provençal *capa*, from Late Latin *cappa;* see CAP]

cape[2] (keɪp) *n.* a headland or promontory. [C14: from Old French *cap*, from Old Provençal, from Latin *caput* head]

Cape (keɪp) *n.* **the. 1.** the SW region of the Cape Province of South Africa. **2.** See **Cape of Good Hope.**

Cape Bret·on Is·land *n.* an island off SE Canada, in NE Nova Scotia, separated from the mainland by the Strait of Canso: its easternmost point is **Cape Breton.** Pop.: 170 007 (1971). Area: 10 280 sq. km (3970 sq. miles).

Cape buf·fa·lo *n.* another name for **buffalo** (sense 1).

Cape Cod *n.* **1.** a long sandy peninsula in SE Massachusetts, between **Cape Cod Bay** and the Atlantic. **2.** a one-storey cottage of timber construction with a simple gable roof and a large central chimney: originated on Cape Cod in the 18th century. Also called: **Cape Cod cottage.**

Cape Col·o·ny *n.* the former name (until 1910) of the **Cape Province** of South Africa.

Cape Col·oured *n.* (in South Africa) another name for a **Coloured** (sense 2).

Cape doc·tor *n. S. African informal.* a strong fresh SE wind blowing in the vicinity of Cape Town, esp. in the summer.

Cape Dutch *n.* an obsolete name for **Afrikaans.**

Cape Flats *pl. n.* the strip of low-lying land in South Africa joining the Cape Peninsula proper to the African mainland.

cape goose·ber·ry *n.* another name for **strawberry tomato.**

Cape Horn *n.* a rocky headland on an island at the extreme S tip of South America, belonging to Chile. It is notorious for gales and heavy seas; until the building of the Panama Canal it lay on the only sea route between the Atlantic and the Pacific. Also called: **the Horn.**

Cape jas·mine *n.* a widely cultivated gardenia shrub, *Gardenia jasminoides.* See **gardenia.**

Ča·pek (*Czech* ˈtʃapɛk) *n.* **Ka·rel** (ˈkarɛl). 1890–1938, Czech dramatist and novelist; author of *R.U.R.* (1921), which introduced the word "robot", and (with his brother **Josef**) *The Insect Play* (1921).

cap·e·lin (ˈkæpəlɪn) *or* **cap·lin** (ˈkæplɪn) *n.* a small marine food fish, *Mallotus villosus*, occurring in northern and Arctic seas: family *Osmeridae* (smelts). [C17: from French *capelan*, from Old Provençal, literally: CHAPLAIN]

Ca·pel·la (kəˈpɛlə) *n.* the brightest star in the constellation Auriga; it is a yellow giant and a spectroscopic binary. Visual magnitude: 0.1; spectral type: G8; distance: 46 light years. [C17: New Latin, from Latin, diminutive of *capra* she-goat, from *caper* goat]

Cape of Good Hope *n.* a cape in SW South Africa south of Cape Town.

Cape Pen·in·su·la *n.* (in South Africa) the peninsula and the part of the mainland on which Cape Town and most of its suburbs are located.

Cape Prov·ince *n.* a province occupying the southern tip of South Africa: mainly a high plateau, rising over 2700 m (9000 ft.). Capital: Cape Town. Pop.: 4 224 150 (1970). Area: 720 000 sq. km (278 380 sq. miles). Former name (until 1910): **Cape Colony.**

ca·per[1] (ˈkeɪpə) *n.* **1.** a playful skip or leap. **2.** a high-spirited escapade. **3. cut a caper.** to leap or dance about. **4.** *U.S. slang.* a crime, esp. an organized robbery. ~*vb.* **5.** (*intr.*) to leap or dance about in a light-hearted manner. [C16: probably from CAPRIOLE] —ˈ**ca·per·er** *n.* —ˈ**ca·per·ing·ly** *adv.*

ca·per[2] (ˈkeɪpə) *n.* **1.** a spiny trailing Mediterranean capparidaceous shrub, *Capparis spinosa*, with edible flower buds. **2.** any of various similar plants or their edible parts. See also **bean caper.** [C15: from earlier *capers, capres* (assumed to be plural), from Latin *capparis*, from Greek *kapparis*]

cap·er·cail·lie (ˌkæpəˈkeɪljɪ) *or* **cap·er·cail·zie** (ˌkæpəˈkeɪljɪ, -ˈkeɪlzɪ) *n.* a large European woodland grouse, *Tetrao urogallus*, having a black plumage and fan-shaped tail in the male. [C16: from Scottish Gaelic *capull coille* horse of the woods]

Ca·per·na·um (kəˈpɜːnɪəm) *n.* a ruined town in N Israel, on the NW shore of the Sea of Galilee: closely associated with Jesus Christ during his ministry.

ca·pers (ˈkeɪpəz) *pl. n.* the flower buds of the caper plant, which are pickled and used as a condiment.

cape·skin (ˈkeɪpˌskɪn) *n.* **1.** a soft leather obtained from the skins of a type of lamb or sheep having hairlike wool. ~*adj.* **2.** made of this leather. [C19: named after the *Cape of Good Hope*]

Cape spar·row *n.* a sparrow, *Passer melanurus*, very common in southern Africa: family *Ploceidae.* Also called (esp. in South Africa): **mossie.**

Ca·pet (ˈkæpɪt, kæˈpɛt; *French* kaˈpɛ) *n.* **Hugh** *or* **Hugues** (yg). ?938–996 A.D., king of France (987–96); founder of the Capetian dynasty.

Ca·pe·tian (kəˈpiːʃən) *n.* **1.** a member of the dynasty founded by Hugh Capet, which ruled France from 987–1328 A.D. ~*adj.* **2.** of or relating to the Capetian kings or their rule.

Cape Town *n.* the legislative capital of South Africa and capital of Cape Province, situated in the southwest on Table

Bay: founded in 1652, the first White settlement in southern Africa; important port. Pop.: 691 296 (1970).

Cape Verde Is·lands (vɜːd) *pl. n.* a group of volcanic islands in the Atlantic, west of Cape Verde, Senegal: an overseas territory of Portugal until 1975, when the islands became independent; eventual union with Guinea-Bissau is planned. Capital: Praia. Pop.: 272 071 (1970). Area: 4033 sq. km (1557 sq. miles).

Cape Wrath (rɒθ) *n.* a promontory at the NW extremity of the Scottish mainland.

Cape York *n.* the northernmost point of the Australian mainland, in N Queensland on the Torres Strait at the tip of **Cape York Peninsula** (a peninsula between the Coral Sea and the Gulf of Carpentaria).

Cap-Ha·i·tien (*French* kapai'sjɛ̃, -'tjɛ̃) *n.* a port in N Haiti: capital during the French colonial period. Pop.: 30 000 (1971 est.). Also called: **Le Cap** (lə 'kap).

ca·pi·as ('keɪpɪˌæs, 'kæp-) *n. Law.* a writ directing a sheriff or other officer to arrest a named person. [C15: from Latin, literally: you must take, from *capere*]

cap·il·la·ceous (ˌkæpɪ'leɪʃəs) *adj.* **1.** having numerous filaments resembling hairs or threads. **2.** resembling a hair; capillary. [C18: from Latin *capillāceus* hairy, from *capillus* hair]

cap·il·lar·i·ty (ˌkæpɪ'lærɪtɪ) *n.* a phenomenon caused by surface tension and resulting in the distortion, elevation, or depression of the surface of a liquid in contact with a solid. Also called: **capillary action.**

ca·pil·lar·y (kə'pɪlərɪ) *adj.* **1.** resembling a hair; slender. **2.** (of tubes) having a fine bore. **3.** *Anatomy.* of or relating to any of the delicate thin-walled blood vessels that form an interconnecting network between the arterioles and the venules. **4.** *Physics.* of or relating to capillarity. *~n., pl.* **-lar·ies. 5.** *Anatomy.* any of the capillary blood vessels. **6.** a fine hole or narrow passage in any substance. [C17: from Latin *capillāris,* from *capillus* hair]

ca·pil·lar·y tube *n.* a glass tube with a fine bore and thick walls, used in thermometers, etc.

cap·i·ta ('kæpɪtə) *n.* **1.** See **per capita. 2.** *Anatomy.* the plural of **caput.**

cap·i·tal[1] ('kæpɪtᵊl) *n.* **1. a.** the seat of government of a country or other political unit. **b.** (*as modifier*): *a capital city.* **2.** material wealth owned by an individual or business enterprise. **3.** wealth available for or capable of use in the production of further wealth, as by industrial investment. **4. make capital (out) of.** to get advantage from. **5.** (*sometimes cap.*) the capitalist class or their interests: *capital versus labour.* **6.** *Accounting.* **a.** the ownership interests of a business as represented by the excess of assets over liabilities. **b.** the nominal value of the authorized or issued shares. **c.** (*as modifier*): *capital issues.* **7.** any assets or resources, esp. when used to gain profit or advantage. **8. a.** a capital letter. Abbrev.: **cap** or **cap. b.** (*as modifier*): *capital B.* **9. with a capital A, B, etc.** (used to give emphasis to a statement): *he is mean with a capital M.* *~adj.* **10.** (*prenominal*) *Law.* involving or punishable by death: *a capital offence.* **11.** very serious; fatal: *a capital error.* **12.** primary, chief, or principal: *our capital concern is that everyone be fed.* **13.** of, relating to, or designating the large modern majuscule letter used chiefly as the initial letter in personal names and place names and other uniquely specificatory nouns, and often for abbreviations and acronyms. Compare **small** (sense 8). See also **upper case. 14.** *Chiefly Brit.* excellent; first-rate: *a capital idea.* [C13: from Latin *capitālis* (adj.) concerning the head, chief, from *caput* head; compare Medieval Latin *capitāle* (n.) wealth, from *capitālis* (adj.)]

cap·i·tal[2] ('kæpɪtᵊl) *n.* the upper part of a column or pier that supports the entablature. Also called: **chapiter, cap.** [C14: from Old French *capitel,* from Late Latin *capitellum,* diminutive of *caput* head]

cap·i·tal ac·count *n.* **1.** *Economics.* that portion of the balance of payments composed of capital movements and international loans and grants. Compare **current account** (sense 2). **2.** *Accounting.* a statement of the net value of a business at a specified date. It is defined as total assets minus total liabilities and represents ownership interests. **3.** *U.S.* an account of fixed assets.

cap·i·tal as·sets *pl. n.* another name for **fixed assets.**

cap·i·tal ex·pen·di·ture *n.* expenditure on acquisitions of or improvements to fixed assets.

cap·i·tal gain *n.* the amount by which the selling price of a financial asset exceeds its cost.

cap·i·tal gains tax *n.* a tax on the profit made from sale of an asset.

cap·i·tal goods *pl. n. Economics.* goods that are themselves utilized in the production of other goods rather than being sold to consumers. Also called: **producer goods.** Compare **consumer goods.**

cap·i·tal·ism ('kæpɪtəˌlɪzəm) *n.* an economic system based on the private ownership of the means of production, distribution, and exchange, characterized by the freedom of capitalists to operate or manage their property for profit in competitive conditions. Also called: **free enterprise, private enterprise.** Compare **socialism** (sense 1).

cap·i·tal·ist ('kæpɪtəlɪst) *n.* **1.** a person who owns capital, esp. capital invested in a business. **2.** *Politics.* a supporter of capitalism. **3.** *Informal, usually derogatory.* a rich person. *~adj.* **4.** of or relating to capital, capitalists, or capitalism. **—ˌcap·i·tal·'ist·ic** *adj.*

cap·i·tal·i·za·tion or **cap·i·tal·i·sa·tion** (ˌkæpɪtəlaɪ'zeɪʃən) *n.* **1. a.** the act of capitalizing. **b.** the sum so derived. **2.** *Accounting.* the par value of the total share capital issued by a company, including the loan capital and sometimes reserves. **3.** the act of estimating the present value of future payments, earnings, etc. **4.** the act of writing or printing in capital letters.

cap·i·tal·i·za·tion is·sue *n.* another name for **rights issue.**

cap·i·tal·ize or **cap·i·tal·ise** ('kæpɪtəˌlaɪz) *vb.* (*mainly tr.*) **1.** (*intr.;* foll. by *on*) to take advantage (of); profit (by). **2.** to write or print (text) in capital letters or with the first letter of (a word or words) in capital letters. **3.** to convert (debt or retained earnings) into capital stock. **4.** to authorize (a business enterprise) to issue a specified amount of capital stock. **5.** *Accounting.* to treat (expenditures) as assets. **6. a.** to estimate the present value of (a periodical income). **b.** to compute the present value of (a business) from actual or potential earnings.

cap·i·tal lev·y *n.* a tax on capital or property as contrasted with a tax on income.

cap·i·tal·ly ('kæpɪtəlɪ) *adv. Chiefly Brit.* in an excellent manner; admirably.

cap·i·tal mar·ket *n.* the financial institutions collectively that deal with medium-term and long-term capital and loans. Compare **money market.**

cap·i·tal pun·ish·ment *n.* the punishment of death for a crime; death penalty.

cap·i·tal ship *n.* one of the largest and most heavily armed ships in a naval fleet.

cap·i·tal stock *n.* **1.** the par value of the total share capital that a company is authorized to issue. **2.** the total physical capital existing in an economy at any moment of time.

cap·i·tal sur·plus *n.* another name (esp. U.S.) for **share premium.**

cap·i·tal trans·fer tax *n.* (in Britain) a tax payable at progressive rates on the cumulative total of gifts of money or property made during the donor's lifetime or after his death. Also called: **gift tax.**

cap·i·tate ('kæpɪˌteɪt) *adj.* **1.** *Botany.* shaped like a head, as certain flowers or inflorescences. **2.** *Zoology.* having an enlarged headlike end: *a capitate bone.* [C17: from Latin *capitātus* having a (large) head, from *caput* head]

cap·i·ta·tion (ˌkæpɪ'teɪʃən) *n.* **1.** a tax levied on the basis of a fixed amount per head. **2. capitation grant.** a grant of money given to every person who qualifies under certain conditions. **3.** the process of assessing or numbering by counting heads. [C17: from Late Latin *capitātiō,* from Latin *caput* head] **—'cap·i·ta·tive** *adj.*

Cap·i·tol ('kæpɪtᵊl) *n.* **1. a.** another name for the **Capitoline. b.** the temple on the Capitoline. **2. the.** the main building of the U.S. Congress. **3.** (*sometimes not cap.*) Also called: **statehouse.** (in the U.S.) the building housing any state legislature. [C14: from Latin *Capitōlium,* from *caput* head]

Cap·i·to·line ('kæpɪtᵊˌlaɪn, kə'pɪtəʊ-) *n.* **1. the.** the most important of the Seven Hills of Rome. The temple of Jupiter was on the southern summit and the ancient citadel on the northern summit. *~adj.* **2.** of or relating to the Capitoline or the temple of Jupiter.

ca·pit·u·lar (kə'pɪtjʊlə) *adj.* **1.** of or associated with a cathedral chapter. **2.** of or relating to a capitulum. [C17: from Medieval Latin *capitulāris,* from *capitulum* CHAPTER] **—ca·'pit·u·lar·ly** *adv.*

ca·pit·u·lar·y (kə'pɪtjʊlərɪ) *n., pl.* **-lar·ies.** any of the collections of ordinances promulgated by the Frankish kings (8th–10th centuries A.D.). [C17: from Medieval Latin *capitulāris;* see CAPITULAR]

ca·pit·u·late (kə'pɪtjʊˌleɪt) *vb.* (*intr.*) to surrender, esp. under agreed conditions. [C16 (meaning: to arrange under heads, draw up in order; hence, to make terms of surrender): from Medieval Latin *capitulare* to draw up under heads, from *capitulum* CHAPTER] **—ca·'pit·u·ˌla·tor** *n.*

ca·pit·u·la·tion (kəˌpɪtjʊ'leɪʃən) *n.* **1.** the act of capitulating. **2.** a document containing terms of surrender. **3.** a statement summarizing the main divisions of a subject. **—ca·'pit·u·la·to·ry** *adj.*

ca·pit·u·lum (kə'pɪtjʊləm) *n., pl.* **-la** (-lə). **1.** a racemose inflorescence in the form of a disc of sessile flowers, the youngest at the centre. It occurs in the daisy and related plants. **2.** *Anatomy, zoology.* a headlike part, esp. the enlarged knoblike terminal part of a long bone, antenna, etc. [C18: from Latin, literally: a little head, from *caput* head]

cap·lin ('kæplɪn) *n.* a variant spelling of **capelin.**

ca·po[1] ('keɪpəʊ, 'kæpəʊ) *n., pl.* **·pos.** a device fitted across all the strings of a guitar, lute, etc., so as to raise the pitch of each string simultaneously. Compare **barré.** Also called: **ca·po tas·to** ('kæpəʊ 'tæstəʊ). [from Italian *capo tasto* head stop]

ca·po[2] ('kæpəʊ; *Italian* 'kapo) *n., pl.* **·pos.** the presumed title of a leader in the Mafia. [Italian: head]

cap of main·te·nance *n.* a ceremonial cap or hat worn or carried as a symbol of office, rank, etc.

ca·pon ('keɪpən) *n.* a castrated cock fowl fattened for eating. [Old English *capun,* from Latin *cāpō* capon; related to Greek *koptein* to cut off]

Ca·pone (kə'pəʊn) *n.* **Al·phonse,** called *Al.* 1899–1947, U.S. gangster in Chicago during Prohibition.

ca·pon·ize or **ca·pon·ise** ('keɪpəˌnaɪz) *vb.* (*tr.*) to make (a cock) into a capon.

cap·o·ral (ˌkæpə'rɑːl) *n.* a strong coarse dark tobacco. [C19: from French *tabac du caporal* corporal's tobacco, denoting its superiority to *tabac du soldat* soldier's tobacco]

Cap·o·ret·to (ˌkapo'retto) *n.* the Italian name for **Kobarid.**

ca·pote (kə'pəʊt; *French* ka'pɔt) *n.* a long cloak or soldier's coat, usually with a hood. [C19: from French: cloak, from *cape*; see CAPE[1]]

Cap·pa·do·ci·a (ˌkæpəˈdəʊsɪə) *n.* an ancient region of E Asia Minor famous for its horses. —ˌ**Cap·pa·ˈdo·ci·an** *adj., n.*

cap·pa·ri·da·ceous (ˌkæpərɪˈdeɪʃəs) *adj.* of, relating to, or belonging to the *Capparidaceae*, a family of plants, mostly shrubs including the caper, of warm and tropical regions. [C19: from New Latin *Capparidaceae*, from Latin *capparis* caper]

cap·pie (ˈkæpɪ) *n. Central Scot. dialect.* an ice-cream cone. [C19: diminutive of C18 *cap* wooden drinking vessel, from Old English *copp* or Old Norse *koppr*]

cap·puc·ci·no (ˌkæpʊˈtʃiːnəʊ) *n., pl.* **·nos.** coffee with steamed milk, sometimes served with whipped cream. [Italian: CAPUCHIN]

cap·re·o·late (ˈkæprɪəˌleɪt, kəˈpriː-) *adj. Biology.* possessing or resembling tendrils. [C18: from Latin *capreolus* tendril]

Ca·pri (kəˈpriː; *Italian* ˈkaːpri) *n.* an island off W Italy, in the Bay of Naples: resort since Roman times. Pop.: 7723 (1971). Area: about 13 sq. km (5 sq. miles).

cap·ric ac·id (ˈkæprɪk) *n.* another name for **decanoic acid.** [C19: from Latin *caper* goat, so named from its smell]

ca·pric·ci·o (kəˈprɪtʃɪˌəʊ) *or* **ca·price** *n., pl.* **·pric·ci·os, ·pric·ci** (-ˈpriːtʃɪ), *or* **·pric·es.** *Music.* a lively piece composed freely and without adhering to the rules for any specific musical form. [C17: from Italian: CAPRICE]

ca·pric·ci·o·so (kəˌprɪtʃɪˈəʊzəʊ) *adv. Music.* to be played in a free and lively style. [Italian: from *capriccio* CAPRICE]

ca·price (kəˈpriːs) *n.* **1.** a sudden or unpredictable change of attitude, behaviour, etc.; whim. **2.** a tendency to such changes. **3.** another word for **capriccio.** [C17: from French, from Italian *capriccio* a shiver, caprice, from *capo* head + *riccio* hedgehog, suggesting a convulsive shudder in which the hair stood on end like a hedgehog's spines; meaning also influenced by Italian *capra* goat, by folk etymology]

ca·pri·cious (kəˈprɪʃəs) *adj.* characterized by or liable to sudden unpredictable changes in attitude or behaviour; impulsive; fickle. —**ca·ˈpri·cious·ly** *adv.* —**ca·ˈpri·cious·ness** *n.*

Cap·ri·corn (ˈkæprɪˌkɔːn) *n.* **1.** *Astrology.* **a.** Also called: the **Goat, Capricornus.** the tenth sign of the zodiac, symbol ♑, having a cardinal earth classification and ruled by the planet Saturn. The sun is in this sign between about Dec. 22 and Jan. 19. **b.** a person born during the period when the sun is in this sign. **2.** *Astronomy.* another name for **Capricornus. 3.** See **tropic of Capricorn.** See **tropic** (sense 1). ~*adj.* **4.** *Astrology.* born under or characteristic of Capricorn. ~Also (for senses 1b., 4): **Cap·ri·cor·ne·an** (ˌkæprɪˈkɔːnɪən). [C14: from Latin *Capricornus* (translating Greek *aigokerōs* goat-horned) from *caper* goat + *cornū* horn]

Cap·ri·cor·nus (ˌkæprɪˈkɔːnəs) *n., Latin genitive* **·ni** (-naɪ). a faint zodiacal constellation in the S hemisphere, lying between Sagittarius and Aquarius.

cap·ri·fi·ca·tion (ˌkæprɪfɪˈkeɪʃən) *n.* a method of pollinating the edible fig by hanging branches of caprifig flowers in edible fig trees. Parasitic wasps in the caprifig flowers transfer pollen to the edible fig flowers. [C17: from Latin *caprificātiō*, from *caprificāre* to pollinate figs by this method, from *caprificus* CAPRIFIG]

cap·ri·fig (ˈkæprɪˌfɪg) *n.* a wild variety of fig, *Ficus carica sylvestris*, of S Europe and SW Asia, used in the caprification of the edible fig. [C15: from Latin *caprificus* literally: goat fig, from *caper* goat + *ficus* FIG[1]]

cap·ri·fo·li·a·ceous (ˌkæprɪˌfəʊlɪˈeɪʃəs) *adj.* of, relating to, or belonging to the *Caprifoliaceae*, a family of N temperate shrubs or small trees including honeysuckle, elder, and guelder-rose. [C19: from New Latin *caprifoliāceae*, from *caprifolium* type genus, from Medieval Latin: honeysuckle, from Latin *caper* goat + *folium* leaf]

cap·rine (ˈkæpraɪn) *adj.* of or resembling a goat. [C17: from Latin *caprīnus*, from *caper* goat]

cap·ri·ole (ˈkæprɪˌəʊl) *n.* **1.** *Dressage.* a high upward but not forward leap made by a horse with all four feet off the ground. **2.** *Dancing.* a leap from bent knees. ~*vb.* **3.** (*intr.*) to perform a capriole. [C16: from French, from Old Italian *capriola*, from *capriolo* roebuck, from Latin *capreolus*, *caper* goat]

Ca·pri pants *or* **Ca·pris** *pl. n.* women's tight-fitting trousers.

cap rock *n.* **1.** a layer of rock that overlies a salt dome and consists of limestone, gypsum, etc. **2.** a layer of relatively impervious rock overlying an oil- or gas-bearing rock.

ca·pro·ic ac·id (kəˈprəʊɪk) *n.* another name for **hexanoic acid.** [C19: *caproic*, from Latin *caper* goat, alluding to its smell]

caps. *abbrev. for:* **1.** capital letters. **2.** capsule.

cap·sa·i·cin (kæpˈseɪɪsɪn) *n.* a colourless crystalline bitter alkaloid found in capsicums and used as a flavouring in vinegar and pickles. Formula: $C_{18}H_{27}O_3N$. [C19 *capsicine*, from CAPSICUM + -INE[2]; modern form refashioned from Latin *capsa* box, case + -IN]

cap screw *n.* a screwed bolt with a cylindrical head having a hexagonal recess. The bolt is turned using a wrench of hexagonal cross section.

Cap·si·an (ˈkæpsɪən) *n.* **1.** a late Palaeolithic culture, dating from about 12 000 B.C., found mainly around the salt lakes of Tunisia. The culture is characterized by the presence of microliths, backed blades, and engraved limestone slabs. ~*adj.* **2.** of or relating to this culture. [C20: from French *capsien*, from *Capsa*, Latinized form of *Gafsa*, Tunisia]

cap·si·cum (ˈkæpsɪkəm) *n.* **1.** any tropical American plant of the solanaceous genus *Capsicum*, such as *C. frutescens*, having mild or pungent seeds enclosed in a pod-shaped or bell-shaped fruit. **2.** the fruit of any of these plants, used as a vegetable or ground to produce a condiment. ~See also **pepper** (sense 4). [C18: from New Latin, from Latin *capsa* box, CASE[2]]

cap·sid[1] (ˈkæpsɪd) *n.* any heteropterous bug of the family *Miridae* (formerly *Capsidae*), most of which feed on plant tissues, causing damage to crops. [C19: from New Latin *Capsus* (genus)]

cap·sid[2] (ˈkæpsɪd) *n.* the outer protein coat of a mature virus. [C20: from French *capside*, from Latin *capsa* box]

cap·size (kæpˈsaɪz) *vb.* to overturn accidentally; upset. [C18: of uncertain origin] —**cap·ˈsiz·al** *n.*

cap·stan (ˈkæpstən) *n.* **1.** a windlass with a vertical drum turned by a lever or motor and equipped with a ratchet, used on ships for hauling in ropes, etc. **2.** any similar device, such as the rotating shaft in a tape recorder that pulls the tape past the head. [C14: from Old Provençal *cabestan*, from Latin *capistrum* a halter, from *capere* to seize]

cap·stan bar *n.* a lever, often wooden, for turning a capstan.

cap·stan lathe *n.* a lathe for repetitive work, having a rotatable turret resembling a capstan to hold tools for successive operations. Also called: **turret lathe.**

cap·stone (ˈkæpˌstəʊn) *or* **cope·stone** (ˈkəʊpˌstəʊn) *n.* one of a set of slabs on the top of a wall, building, etc.

cap·su·late (ˈkæpsjʊˌleɪt, -lɪt) *or* **cap·su·lat·ed** *adj.* within or formed into a capsule. —ˌ**cap·su·ˈla·tion** *n.*

cap·sule (ˈkæpsjuːl) *n.* **1.** a soluble case of gelatin enclosing a dose of medicine. **2.** a thin metal cap, seal, or cover, such as the foil covering the cork of a wine bottle. **3.** *Botany.* **a.** a dry fruit that liberates its seeds by splitting, as in the violet, or through pores, as in the poppy. **b.** the spore-producing organ of mosses and liverworts. **4.** *Bacteriol.* a gelatinous layer of polysaccharide or protein surrounding the cell wall of some bacteria: thought to be responsible for the virulence in pathogens. **5.** *Anatomy.* **a.** a cartilaginous, fibrous, or membranous envelope surrounding any of certain organs or parts. **b.** a broad band of white fibres (**internal capsule**) near the thalamus in each cerebral hemisphere. **6.** See **space capsule. 7.** an aeroplane cockpit that can be ejected in a flight emergency, complete with crew, instruments, etc. **8.** (*modifier*) in a highly concise form: *a capsule summary.* [C17: from French, from Latin *capsula*, diminutive of *capsa* box]

cap·sul·ize *or* **cap·sul·ise** (ˈkæpsjʊˌlaɪz) *vb.* (*tr.*) **1.** to state (information, etc.) in a highly condensed form. **2.** to enclose in a capsule.

Capt. *abbrev. for* Captain.

cap·tain (ˈkæptɪn) *n.* **1.** the person in charge of and responsible for a vessel. **2.** an officer of the navy who holds a rank junior to a rear admiral but senior to a commander. **3.** an officer of the army, certain air forces, and the marine corps who holds a rank junior to a major but senior to a lieutenant. **4.** the officer in command of a civil aircraft, usually the senior pilot. **5.** the leader of a team in games. **6.** a person in command over a group, organization, etc.; leader: *a captain of industry.* **7.** *U.S.* a policeman in charge of a precinct. **8.** *U.S.* a head waiter. **9.** *U.S.* a supervisor of bell boys in a hotel. ~*vb.* **10.** (*tr.*) to be captain of. [C14: from Old French *capitaine*, from Late Latin *capitāneus* chief, from Latin *caput* head] —**ˈcap·tain·cy** *or* **ˈcap·tain·ˌship** *n.*

cap·tain's bis·cuit *n.* a type of hard fancy biscuit.

cap·tion (ˈkæpʃən) *n.* **1.** a title, brief explanation, or comment accompanying an illustration; legend. **2.** a heading, title, or headline of a chapter, article, etc. **3.** graphic material, usually containing lettering, used in television presentation. **4.** another name for **subtitle** (sense 2). **5.** the formal heading of a legal document stating when, where, and on what authority it was taken or made. ~*vb.* **6.** to provide with a caption or captions. [C14 (meaning: seizure, an arrest; later, heading of a legal document): from Latin *captiō* a seizing, from *capere* to take]

cap·tious (ˈkæpʃəs) *adj.* apt to make trivial criticisms; fault-finding; carping. [C14 (meaning: catching in error): from Latin *captiōsus*, from *captiō* a seizing; see CAPTION] —**ˈcap·tious·ly** *adv.* —**ˈcap·tious·ness** *n.*

cap·ti·vate (ˈkæptɪˌveɪt) *vb.* (*tr.*) **1.** to hold the attention of by fascinating; enchant. **2.** an obsolete word for **capture.** [C16: from Late Latin *captivāre*, from *captīvus* CAPTIVE] —**ˈcap·ti·vat·ing·ly** *adv.* —ˌ**cap·ti·ˈva·tion** *n.* —**ˈcap·ti·ˌva·tor** *n.*

cap·tive (ˈkæptɪv) *n.* **1.** a person or animal that is confined or restrained, esp. a prisoner of war. **2.** a person whose behaviour is dominated by some emotion: *a captive of love.* ~*adj.* **3.** held as prisoner. **4.** held under restriction or control; confined: *captive water held behind a dam.* **5.** captivated; enraptured. **6.** unable by circumstances to avoid speeches, advertisements, etc. (esp. in the phrase **captive audience**). [C14: from Latin *captīvus*, from *capere* to take]

cap·tiv·i·ty (kæpˈtɪvɪtɪ) *n., pl.* **·ties. 1.** the condition of being captive; imprisonment. **2.** the period of imprisonment.

cap·tor (ˈkæptə) *n.* a person or animal that holds another captive. [C17: from Latin, from *capere* to take]

cap·ture (ˈkæptʃə) *vb.* (*tr.*) **1.** to take prisoner or gain control over: *to capture an enemy; to capture a town.* **2.** (in a game or contest) to win control or possession of: *to capture a pawn in chess.* **3.** to succeed in representing or describing (something elusive): *the artist captured her likeness.* **4.** *Physics.* (of an atom, molecule, ion, or nucleus) to acquire (an additional particle). ~*n.* **5.** the act of taking by force; seizure. **6.** the person or thing captured; booty. **7.** *Physics.* a process by which an atom, molecule, ion, or nucleus acquires an additional particle. **8.** Also called: **piracy.** *Geography.* the process by which the headwaters of one river are diverted into another through erosion caused by the second river's tributaries. [C16: from Latin *captūra* a catching, that which is caught, from *capere* to take] —**'cap+tur+er** *n.*

Cap·u·a ('kæpjʊə; *Italian* 'ka:pua) *n.* a town in S Italy, in NW Campania: strategically important in ancient times, situated on the Appian Way. Pop.: 17 582 (1971).

ca+puche *or* **ca+pouch** (kə'pu:ʃ) *n.* a large hood or cowl, esp. that worn by Capuchin friars. [C17: from French, from Italian *cappuccio,* hood, from Late Latin *cappa* cloak]

cap·u+chin ('kæpjʊtʃɪn, -ʃɪn) *n.* **1.** any agile intelligent New World monkey of the genus *Cebus,* inhabiting forests in South America, typically having a cowl of thick hair on the top of the head. **2.** a woman's hooded cloak. **3.** (*sometimes cap.*) a rare variety of domestic fancy pigeon. [C16: from French, from Italian *cappuccino,* from *cappuccio* hood; see CAPUCHE]

Cap·u·chin ('kæpjʊtʃɪn, -ʃɪn) *n.* a friar belonging to a strict and autonomous branch of the Franciscan Order founded in 1528. [C16: from French; see CAPUCHE]

ca+put ('keɪpət, 'kæp-) *n., pl.* **cap·i·ta** ('kæpɪtə). **1.** *Anatomy.* a technical name for the **head. 2.** the main or most prominent part of an organ or structure. [C18: from Latin]

cap·y+ba+ra (ˌkæpɪ'bɑ:rə) *n.* the largest rodent: a pig-sized amphibious hystricomorph, *Hydrochoerus hydrochaeris,* resembling a guinea pig and inhabiting river banks in Central and South America: family *Hydrochoeridae.* [C18: from Portuguese *capibara,* from Tupi]

Ca+que+tá (*Spanish* kake'ta) *n.* the Japurá River from its source in Colombia to the border with Brazil.

car (kɑ:) *n.* **1. a.** Also called: **motorcar, automobile.** a self-propelled road vehicle designed to carry passengers, esp. one with four wheels that is powered by an internal-combustion engine. **b.** (*as modifier*): *car coat.* **2.** a conveyance for passengers, freight, etc., such as a cable car or the carrier of an airship or balloon. **3.** *Brit.* a railway vehicle for passengers only, such as a sleeping car or buffet car. **4.** *Chiefly U.S.* a railway carriage or van. **5.** a poetic word for **chariot.** [C14: from Anglo-French *carre,* ultimately related to Latin *carra, carrum* two-wheeled wagon, probably of Celtic origin; compare Old Irish *carr*]

car·a+ba·o (ˌkærə'beɪəʊ) *n., pl.* **·os.** another name for **water buffalo.** [from Visayan *karabáw;* compare Malay *karbaw*]

car·a+bid ('kærəbɪd) *n.* **1.** any typically dark-coloured beetle of the family *Carabidae,* including the bombardier and other ground beetles. ~*adj.* **2.** of, relating to, or belonging to the *Carabidae.* [C19: from New Latin, from Latin *cārabus* a kind of crab (name applied to these beetles)]

car·a+bin ('kærəbɪn) *or* **car·a+bine** ('kærəˌbaɪn) *n.* variants of **carbine** (sense 2).

car·a+bi+neer *or* **car·a+bi+nier** (ˌkærəbɪ'nɪə) *n.* variants of **carbineer.**

ca+ra+bi+nie+re *Italian.* (ˌkarabi'njɛ:re) *n., pl.* **+ri** (-ri). an Italian national policeman.

car·a+cal ('kærəˌkæl) *n.* **1.** Also called: **desert lynx.** a lynxlike feline mammal, *Lynx caracal,* inhabiting deserts of N Africa and S Asia, having long legs, a smooth coat of reddish fur, and black-tufted ears. **2.** the fur of this animal. [C18: from French, from Turkish *kara kŭlāk,* literally: black ear]

Car·a·cal·la (ˌkærə'kælə) *n.* real name *Marcus Aurelius Antoninus,* original name *Bassianus.* 188–217 A.D., Roman emperor (211–17): ruled with cruelty and extravagance; assassinated.

ca+ra+ca+ra (ˌkɑ:rə'kɑ:rə) *n.* any of various large carrion-eating diurnal birds of prey of the genera *Caracara, Polyborus,* etc., of S North, Central, and South America, having long legs and naked faces: family *Falconidae* (falcons). [C19: from Spanish or Portuguese, from Tupi; of imitative origin]

Ca+ra+cas (kə'rækəs, -'rɑ:-; *Spanish* ka'rakas) *n.* the capital of Venezuela, in the north: founded in 1567; major industrial and commercial centre, notably for oil companies. Pop.: 1 662 627 (1971).

car·a+cole ('kærəˌkəʊl) *or* **car·a+col** ('kærəˌkɒl) *n.* **1.** *Dressage.* a half turn to the right or left. **2.** a spiral staircase. ~*vb.* (*intr.*) **3.** *Dressage.* to execute a half turn to the right or left. [C17: from French, from Spanish *caracol* snail, spiral staircase, turn]

car·a+cul ('kærəˌkʌl) *n.* **1.** Also called: **Persian lamb.** the black loosely curled fur obtained from the skins of newly born lambs of the karakul sheep. **2.** a variant spelling of **karakul.**

ca+rafe (kə'ræf, -'rɑ:f) *n.* **a.** a glass bottle for table use, for water or wine. **b.** (*as modifier*): *a carafe wine.* [C18: from French, from Italian *caraffa,* from Spanish *garrafa,* from Arabic *gharrāfah* vessel]

car·a+geen ('kærəˌgi:n) *n.* a variant spelling of **carrageen.**

ca+ram+ba (kə'ræmbə) *or* **ca+ram+bo+la** (ˌkærəm'bəʊlə) *n.* **1.** a cultivated tree, *Averrhoa carambola,* of SE Asia: family *Averrhoaceae.* **2.** the smooth-skinned yellow edible fruit of this tree, which is borne on the older stems.

car·a+mel ('kærəməl, -ˌmɛl) *n.* **1.** burnt sugar, used for colouring and flavouring food. **2.** a chewy sweet made from sugar, butter, milk, etc. ~See also **crème caramel.** [C18: from French, from Spanish *caramelo,* of uncertain origin]

car·a+mel+ize *or* **car·a+mel+ise** ('kærəməˌlaɪz) *vb.* to convert or be converted into caramel.

ca+ran+gid (kə'rændʒɪd, -'ræŋgɪd) *or* **ca+ran+goid** (kə'ræŋgɔɪd) *n.* **1.** any marine percoid fish of the family *Carangidae,* having a compressed body and deeply forked tail. The group includes the jacks, horse mackerel, pompano, and pilot fish. ~*adj.* **2.** of, relating to, or belonging to the *Carangidae.* [C19: from New Latin *Carangidae,* from *Caranx* type genus, from French *carangue* shad, from Spanish *caranga,* of obscure origin]

car·a+pace ('kærəˌpeɪs) *n.* the thick hard shield, made of chitin or bone, that covers part of the body of crabs, lobsters, tortoises, etc. [C19: from French, from Spanish *carapacho,* of unknown origin]

car+at ('kærət) *n.* **1.** a measure of the weight of precious stones, esp. diamonds. It was formerly defined as 3.17 grains, but the international carat is now standardized as 0.20 grams. **2.** Usual U.S. spelling: **karat.** a measure of the proportion of gold in an alloy, expressed as the number of parts of gold in 24 parts of the alloy. [C16: from Old French, from Medieval Latin *carratus,* from Arabic *qīrāt* weight of four grains, carat, from Greek *keration* a little horn, from *keras* horn]

Ca·rat·a·cus (kə'rætəkəs), **Ca·rac·ta·cus,** or **Ca·rad·oc** (kə'rædək) *n.* died ?54 A.D., British chieftain: led an unsuccessful resistance against the Romans (43–50).

Ca·ra·vag·gio (*Italian* ˌkara'vaddʒo) *n.* **Mi·chel·an·ge·lo Me·ri·si da** (ˌmike'landʒelo me'ri:zi da). 1573–1610, Italian painter, noted for his realistic depiction of religious subjects and for his dramatic use of chiaroscuro.

car·a+van ('kærəˌvæn) *n.* **1. a.** a large enclosed vehicle capable of being pulled by a car or lorry and equipped to be lived in. U.S. name: **trailer. b.** (*as modifier*): *a caravan site.* **2.** (esp. in some parts of Asia and Africa) a company of traders or other travellers journeying together, often with a train of camels, through the desert. **3.** a group of wagons, pack mules, camels, etc., esp. travelling in single file. **4.** a large covered vehicle, esp. a gaily coloured one used by Gypsies, circuses, etc. ~*vb.* **+vans, +van+ning, +vanned. 5.** (*intr.*) *Brit.* to travel or have a holiday in a caravan. [C16: from Italian *caravana,* from Persian *kārwān*]

car·a+van+se+rai (ˌkærə'vænsəˌraɪ, -ˌreɪ) *or* **car·a+van+sa+ry** (ˌkærə'vænsərɪ) *n., pl.* **+rais** *or* **+ries.** (in some Eastern countries, esp. formerly) a large inn enclosing a courtyard, providing accommodation for caravans. [C16: from Persian *kārwānsarāī* caravan inn]

car·a+vel ('kærəˌvɛl) *or* **car+vel** *n.* a two- or three-masted sailing ship, esp. one with a broad beam, high poopdeck, and lateen rig that was used by the Spanish and Portuguese in the 15th and 16th centuries. [C16: from Portuguese *caravela,* diminutive of *caravo* ship, ultimately from Greek *karabos* crab, horned beetle]

car·a+way ('kærəˌweɪ) *n.* **1.** an umbelliferous Eurasian plant, *Carum carvi,* having finely divided leaves and clusters of small whitish flowers. **2. caraway seed.** the pungent aromatic one-seeded fruit of this plant, used in cooking and in medicine. [C14: probably from Medieval Latin *carvi,* from Arabic *karawyā,* from Greek *karon*]

car+ba+mate ('kɑ:bəˌmeɪt) *n.* a salt or ester of carbamic acid. The salts contain the monovalent ion NH_2COO^-, and the esters contain the group NH_2COO-.

car+bam+ic ac·id (kɑ:'bæmɪk) *n.* a hypothetical compound known only in the form of carbamate salts and esters. Formula: NH_2COOH.

car+bam·i+dine (kɑ:'bæmɪˌdaɪn) *n.* another name for **guanidine.**

car+ban+i·on (kɑ:'bænaɪən) *n. Chem.* a negatively charged organic ion, such as H_3C^-, derived from a free radical by addition of one electron. Compare **carbonium ion.**

car+ba+zole ('kɑ:bəˌzəʊl) *n.* a colourless insoluble solid obtained from coal tar and used in the production of some dyes. Formula: $C_{12}H_9N$. Also called: **diphenylenimine.**

car+bene ('kɑ:bi:n) *n. Chem.* a neutral divalent free radical, such as methylene, $:CH_2$.

car+bide ('kɑ:baɪd) *n.* **1.** an inorganic compound of carbon with a more electropositive element. See also **acetylide. 2.** See **calcium carbide.**

car+bine ('kɑ:baɪn) *n.* **1.** a light automatic or semiautomatic rifle of limited range. **2.** Also called: **carabin, carabine.** a light short-barrelled shoulder rifle formerly used by cavalry. [C17: from French *carabine,* from Old French *carabin* carabineer, perhaps variant of *escarrabin* one who prepares corpses for burial, from *scarabée,* from Latin *scarabaeus* SCARAB]

car+bi+neer (ˌkɑ:bɪ'nɪə), **car·a+bi+neer,** *or* **car·a+bi·nier** (ˌkærəbɪ'nɪə) *n.* (formerly) a soldier equipped with a carbine.

car·bo- *or before a vowel* **carb-** *combining form.* carbon: *carbohydrate; carbonate.*

car+bo+hy+drate (ˌkɑ:bəʊ'haɪdreɪt) *n.* any of a large group of organic compounds, including sugars, such as sucrose, and polysaccharides, such as cellulose, glycogen, and starch, that contain carbon, hydrogen, and oxygen, with the general formula $C_m(H_2O)_n$: an important source of food and energy for animals.

car+bo+lat+ed ('kɑ:bəˌleɪtɪd) *adj.* containing carbolic acid.

car+bol+ic ac·id (kɑ:'bɒlɪk) *n.* another name for **phenol,** esp. when it is used as an antiseptic or disinfectant. [C19: *carbolic,* from CARBO- + -OL[1] + -IC]

car+bo+lize *or* **car+bo+lise** ('kɑ:bəˌlaɪz) *vb.* (*tr.*) another word for **phenolate.**

car+bon ('kɑ:bᵊn) *n.* **1. a.** a nonmetallic element existing in the three allotropic forms: amorphous carbon, graphite, and diamond: occurring in carbon dioxide, coal, oil, and all organic compounds. The isotope **carbon-12** has been adopted as the standard for atomic wt.; **carbon-14,** a radioisotope with a half-life of 5700 years, is used in radiocarbon dating and as a tracer. Symbol: C; atomic no.: 6; atomic wt.: 12.011 15; valency: 2, 3, or 4; relative density: 1.8–2.1 (amorphous), 1.9–2.3 (graphite), 3.1–3.5 (diamond); sublimes above 3500°C; boiling pt.: 4827°C. **b.** (*as modifier*): *a carbon compound.* **2.** short for **carbon paper** or **carbon copy. 3.** a carbon electrode used in a carbon-arc light or in carbon-arc welding. **4.** a rod or plate, made of carbon, used in some types of battery. [C18: from

French *carbone,* from Latin *carbō* charcoal, dead or glowing coal] —'**car·bon·ous** *adj.*
car·bo·na·ceous (ˌkɑːbəˈneɪʃəs) *adj.* of, resembling, or containing carbon.
car·bo·nade (ˌkɑːbəˈneɪd, -ˈnɑːd) *n.* a stew of beef and onions cooked in beer. [C20: from French]
car·bo·na·do[1] (ˌkɑːbəˈneɪdəʊ, -ˈnɑːdəʊ) *n., pl.* **·does** *or* **·dos. 1.** a piece of meat, fish, etc., scored and grilled. ~*vb.* **·dos, ·do·ing, ·doed.** (*tr.*) **2.** to score and grill (meat, fish, etc.). **3.** *Archaic.* to hack or slash. [C16: from Spanish *carbonada,* from *carbón* charcoal; see CARBON]
car·bo·na·do[2] (ˌkɑːbəˈneɪdəʊ, -ˈnɑːdəʊ) *n., pl.* **·dos** *or* **·does.** an inferior dark massive variety of diamond used in industry for polishing and drilling. Also called: **black diamond.** [Portuguese, literally: carbonated]
car·bon arc *n.* **1. a.** an electric arc produced between two carbon electrodes, formerly used as a light source. **b.** (*as modifier*): *carbon-arc light.* **2. a.** an electric arc produced between a carbon electrode and material to be welded. **b.** (*as modifier*): *carbon-arc welding.*
Car·bo·na·ri (ˌkɑːbəˈnɑːrɪ) *pl. n., sing.* **·na·ro** (-ˈnɑːrəʊ). members of a secret political society with liberal republican aims, originating in S Italy about 1811 and particularly engaged in the struggle for Italian unification. [C19: from Italian, plural of *carbonaro* seller or burner of charcoal, name adopted by the society]
car·bon·ate *n.* (ˈkɑːbəˌneɪt, -nɪt). **1.** a salt or ester of carbonic acid. Carbonate salts contain the divalent ion CO_3^{2-}. ~*vb.* (ˈkɑːbəˌneɪt). **2.** to form or turn into a carbonate. **3.** (*tr.*) to treat with carbon dioxide or carbonic acid, as in the manufacture of soft drinks. [C18: from French, from *carbone* CARBON]
car·bon·a·tion (ˌkɑːbəˈneɪʃən) *n.* **1.** absorption of or reaction with carbon dioxide. **2.** another word for **carbonization.**
car·bon bi·sul·phide *n.* (not in technical usage) another name for **carbon disulphide.**
car·bon black *n.* a black finely divided form of amorphous carbon produced by incomplete combustion of natural gas or petroleum: used to reinforce rubber and in the manufacture of pigments and ink.
car·bon cop·y *n.* **1.** a duplicate copy of writing, typewriting, or drawing obtained by using carbon paper. Often shortened to **carbon. 2.** *Informal.* a person or thing that is identical or very similar to another.
car·bon cy·cle *n.* **1.** the circulation of carbon between living organisms and their surroundings. Carbon dioxide from the atmosphere is synthesized by plants into plant tissue, which is ingested and metabolized by animals and reduced to carbon dioxide again during respiration and decay. **2.** four thermonuclear reactions believed to be the source of energy in many stars. Carbon nuclei function as catalysts in the fusion of protons to form helium nuclei.
car·bon dat·ing *n.* short for **radiocarbon dating.**
car·bon di·ox·ide *n.* a colourless odourless incombustible gas present in the atmosphere and formed during respiration, the decomposition and combustion of organic compounds, and in the reaction of acids with carbonates: used in carbonated drinks, fire extinguishers, and as dry ice for refrigeration. Formula: CO_2. Also called: **carbonic-acid gas.**
car·bon di·ox·ide snow *n.* solid carbon dioxide, used as a refrigerant.
car·bon di·sul·phide *n.* a colourless slightly soluble volatile flammable poisonous liquid commonly having a disagreeable odour due to the presence of impurities: used as an organic solvent and in the manufacture of rayon and carbon tetrachloride. Formula: CS_2. Also called (not in technical usage): **carbon bisulphide.**
car·bon fi·bre *n.* a black silky thread of pure carbon made by heating and stretching textile fibres and used because of its lightness and strength at high temperatures for reinforcing resins, ceramics, and metals, esp. in turbine blades.
car·bon-14 dat·ing *n.* another name for **radiocarbon dating.**
car·bon·ic (kɑːˈbɒnɪk) *adj.* (of a compound) containing carbon, esp. tetravalent carbon.
car·bon·ic ac·id *n.* a weak acid formed when carbon dioxide combines with water: obtained only in aqueous solutions, never in the pure state. Formula: H_2CO_3.
car·bon·ic-ac·id gas *n.* another name for **carbon dioxide.**
car·bon·if·er·ous (ˌkɑːbəˈnɪfərəs) *adj.* yielding coal or carbon.
Car·bon·if·er·ous (ˌkɑːbəˈnɪfərəs) *adj.* **1.** of, denoting, or formed in the fifth period of the Palaeozoic era, between the Devonian and Permian periods, lasting for 80 million years during which coal measures were formed. ~*n.* **2. the.** the Carboniferous period or rock system.
car·bon·i·um i·on (kɑːˈbəʊnɪəm) *n. Chem.* a positively charged organic ion, such as H_3C^+, derived from a free radical by removal of one electron. Compare **carbanion.**
car·bon·ize *or* **car·bon·ise** (ˈkɑːbəˌnaɪz) *vb.* **1.** to turn into carbon as a result of heating. **2.** (*tr.*) to enrich or coat (a substance) with carbon. **3.** (*intr.*) to react or unite with carbon. ~Also (for senses 2, 3): **carburize.** —ˌ**car·bon·i·ˈza·tion** *or* ˌ**car·bon·i·ˈsa·tion** *n.* —ˈ**car·bon·ˌiz·er** *or* ˈ**car·bon·ˌis·er** *n.*
car·bon mi·cro·phone *n.* a microphone in which a diaphragm, vibrated by sound waves, applies a varying pressure to a container packed with carbon granules, altering the resistance of the carbon. A current flowing through the carbon is thus modulated at the frequency of the sound waves.
car·bon mon·ox·ide *n.* a colourless odourless poisonous flammable gas formed when carbon compounds burn in insufficient air and produced by the action of steam on hot carbon: used as a reducing agent in metallurgy and as a fuel. Formula: CO.
car·bon pa·per *n.* **1.** a thin sheet of paper coated on one side with a dark waxy pigment, often containing carbon, that is transferred by the pressure of writing or of typewriter keys onto the copying surface below. Often shortened to **carbon. 2.** another name for **carbon tissue.**
car·bon pro·cess *or* **print·ing** *n.* a photographic process for producing positive prints by exposing sensitized carbon tissue to light passing through a negative. Washing removes the unexposed gelatin leaving the pigmented image in the exposed insoluble gelatin.
car·bon steel *n.* steel whose characteristics are determined by the amount of carbon it contains.
car·bon tet·ra·chlo·ride *n.* a colourless volatile nonflammable sparingly soluble liquid made from chlorine and carbon disulphide; tetrachloromethane. It is used as a solvent, cleaning fluid, and insecticide. Formula: CCl_4.
car·bon tis·sue *n.* a sheet of paper coated with pigmented gelatin, used in the carbon process. Also called: **carbon paper.**
car·bon·yl (ˈkɑːbəˌnaɪl, -nɪl) *n. Chem.* **1.** (*modifier*) of, consisting of, or containing the divalent group =CO: *a carbonyl group or radical.* **2.** any one of a class of inorganic complexes in which carbonyl groups are bound directly to metal atoms. —**car·bon·yl·ic** (ˌkɑːbəˈnɪlɪk) *adj.*
car·bon·yl chlo·ride *n.* (not in technical usage) another name for **phosgene.**
Car·bo·run·dum (ˌkɑːbəˈrʌndəm) *n. Trademark.* **a.** any of various abrasive materials, esp. one consisting of silicon carbide. **b.** (*as modifier*): *a Carborundum wheel.*
car·box·yl·ase (kɑːˈbɒksɪˌleɪz) *n.* any enzyme that catalyses the release of carbon dioxide from certain acids.
car·box·yl·ate (kɑːˈbɒksɪˌleɪt) *n.* any salt or ester of a carboxylic acid having a formula of the type $M(RCOO)_x$, where M is a metal and R an organic group, or R_1COOR_2, where R_1 and R_2 are organic groups.
car·box·yl group *or* **rad·i·cal** (kɑːˈbɒksaɪl, -sɪl) *n.* the monovalent group -COOH, consisting of a carbonyl group bound to a hydroxyl group: the functional group in organic acids. [C19 *carboxyl,* from CARBO- + OXY- + -YL]
car·box·yl·ic ac·id (ˌkɑːbɒkˈsɪlɪk) *n.* any of a class of organic acids containing the carboxyl group. See also **fatty acid.**
car·boy (ˈkɑːˌbɔɪ) *n.* a large glass or plastic bottle, usually protected by a basket or box, used for containing corrosive liquids such as acids. [C18: from Persian *qarāba*]
car·bun·cle (ˈkɑːˌbʌŋkᵊl) *n.* **1.** an extensive skin eruption, similar to but larger than a boil, with several openings: caused by staphylococcal infection. **2.** a rounded gemstone, esp. a garnet cut without facets. **3.** a dark reddish-greyish-brown colour. [C13: from Latin *carbunculus* diminutive of *carbō* coal] —ˈ**car·ˌbun·cled** *adj.* —**car·bun·cu·lar** (kɑːˈbʌŋkjʊlə) *adj.*
car·bu·ra·tion (ˌkɑːbjʊˈreɪʃən) *n.* the process of mixing a hydrocarbon fuel with a correct amount of air to make an explosive mixture for an internal-combustion engine.
car·bu·ret (ˈkɑːbjʊˌrɛt, ˌkɑːbjʊˈrɛt, -bə-) *vb.* **·rets, ·ret·ting, ·ret·ted** *or U.S.* **·rets, ·ret·ing, ·ret·ed.** (*tr.*) to combine or mix (a gas, etc.) with carbon or carbon compounds. [C18: from CARB(ON) + -URET]
car·bu·ret·tor, car·bu·ret·ter (ˌkɑːbjʊˈrɛtə, ˈkɑːbjʊˌrɛtə, -bə-) *or U.S.* **car·bu·re·tor** (ˈkɑːbjʊˌreɪtə, -bə-) *n.* a device used in petrol engines for atomizing the petrol, controlling its mixture with air, and regulating the intake of the air-petrol mixture into the engine. Compare **fuel injection.**
car·bu·rize *or* **car·bu·rise** (ˈkɑːbjʊˌraɪz, -bə-) *vb.* another word for **carbonize.** —ˌ**car·bu·ri·ˈza·tion** *or* ˌ**car·bu·ri·ˈsa·tion** *n.*
car·by (ˈkɑːbɪ) *n., pl.* **·bies.** *Austral. informal.* short for **carburettor.**
car·byl·a·mine (ˌkɑːbɪləˈmiːn, -ˈæmɪn) *n.* another name for **isocyanide.**
car·ca·jou (ˈkɑːkəˌdʒuː, -ˌʒuː) *n.* a North American name for **wolverine.** [C18: from Canadian French, from Algonquian *karkajou*]
car·ca·net (ˈkɑːkəˌnɛt, -nɪt) *n. Archaic.* a jewelled collar or necklace. [C16: from French *carcan,* of Germanic origin; compare Old Norse *kverkband* chin-strap]
car·cass *or* **car·case** (ˈkɑːkəs) *n.* **1.** the dead body of an animal, esp. one that has been slaughtered for food, with the head, limbs, and entrails removed. **2.** *Informal, usually facetious or derogatory.* a person's body. **3.** the skeleton or framework of a structure: *the carcass of an old tyre.* **4.** the remains of anything when its life or vitality is gone; shell. [C14: from Old French *carcasse,* of obscure origin]
Car·cas·sonne (*French* karkaˈsɔn) *n.* a city in SW France: extensive remains of medieval fortifications. Pop.: 44 623 (1975).
Car·chem·ish (ˈkɑːkəmɪʃ, kɑːˈkiː-) *n.* an ancient city in Syria on the Euphrates, lying on major trade routes; site of a victory of the Babylonians over the Egyptians (605 B.C.).
car·cin·o·gen (kɑːˈsɪnədʒən, ˈkɑːsɪnəˌdʒɛn) *n. Pathol.* any substance that produces cancer. [C20: from Greek *karkinos* CANCER + -GEN] —ˌ**car·cin·o·ˈgen·ic** *adj.*
car·ci·no·ma (ˌkɑːsɪˈnəʊmə) *n., pl.* **·mas** *or* **·ma·ta** (-mətə). *Pathol.* **1.** any malignant tumour derived from epithelial tissue. **2.** another name for **cancer** (sense 1). [C18: from Latin, from Greek *karkinōma,* from *karkinos* CANCER] —ˌ**car·ci·ˈno·ma·ˌtoid** *or* ˌ**car·ci·ˈno·ma·tous** *adj.*

car·ci·no·ma·to·sis (ˌkɑːsɪˌnəʊmə'təʊsɪs) *n. Pathol.* a condition characterized by widespread dissemination of carcinomas or by a carcinoma that affects a large area.

card[1] (kɑːd) *n.* **1.** a piece of stiff paper or thin cardboard, usually rectangular, with varied uses, as for filing information in an index, bearing a written notice for display, entering scores in a game, etc. **2.** such a card used for identification, reference, proof of membership, etc.: *library card; identity card; visiting card.* **3.** such a card used for sending greetings, messages, or invitations, often bearing an illustration, printed greetings, etc.: *Christmas card; birthday card.* **4.** one of a set of small pieces of cardboard, variously marked with significant figures, symbols, etc., used for playing games or for fortune-telling. **5. a.** short for **playing card. b.** (*as modifier*): *a card game.* **c.** (*in combination*): *cardsharp.* **6.** *Informal.* a witty, entertaining, or eccentric person. **7.** See **compass card. 8.** Also called: **race card.** *Horse racing.* a daily programme of all the races at a meeting, listing the runners, riders, weights to be carried, distances to be run, and conditions of each race. **9.** a thing or action used in order to gain an advantage, esp. one that is concealed and kept in reserve until needed (esp. in the phrase **a card up one's sleeve**). **10.** *Computer technol.* See **punched card.** ~See also: **cards.** [C15: from Old French *carte,* from Latin *charta* leaf of papyrus, from Greek *khartēs,* probably of Egyptian origin]

card[2] (kɑːd) *n.* **1.** Also called: **carding machine.** a machine for combing fibres of cotton, wool, etc., to remove small unwanted fibres before spinning. **2.** a comblike tool for raising the nap on cloth. ~*vb.* **3.** (*tr.*) to process with such a machine or tool. [C15: from Old French *carde* card, teasel, from Latin *carduus* thistle] —**'card·er** *n.*

Card. *abbrev. for* Cardinal.

car·da·mom, car·da·mum ('kɑːdəməm), *or* **car·da·mon** *n.* **1.** a tropical Asian zingiberaceous plant, *Elettaria cardamomum,* that has large hairy leaves. **2.** the seeds of this plant, used esp. as a spice or condiment. **3.** a related East Indian plant, *Amomum cardamomum,* whose seeds are used as a substitute for cardamom seeds. [C15: from Latin *cardamōmum,* from Greek *kardamōmon,* from *kardamon* cress + *amōmon* an Indian spice]

card·board ('kɑːdˌbɔːd) *n.* **1. a.** a thin stiff board made from paper pulp and used esp. for making cartons. **b.** (*as modifier*): *cardboard boxes.* ~*adj.* (*prenominal*) **2.** without substance: *a cardboard smile; a cardboard general.*

card-car·ry·ing *adj.* being an official member of a specified organization or set: *a card-carrying union member; a card-carrying Communist.*

card cat·a·logue *n.* a catalogue of books, papers, etc., filed on cards.

Cár·de·nas[1] (*Spanish* 'karðeˌnas) *n.* a port in NW Cuba. Pop.: 55 200 (1970).

Cár·de·nas[2] (*Spanish* 'karðeˌnas) *n.* **Lá·za·ro** ('laθaro). (1895–1970), Mexican statesman and general; president of Mexico (1934–40).

card file *n.* another term for **card index.**

car·di·ac ('kɑːdɪˌæk) *adj.* **1.** of or relating to the heart. **2.** of or relating to the portion of the stomach connected to the oesophagus. ~*n.* **3.** a person with a heart disorder. **4.** a drug that stimulates the heart muscle. [C17: from Latin *cardiacus,* from Greek, from *kardia* heart]

car·di·al·gi·a (ˌkɑːdɪ'ældʒɪə, -dʒə) *n.* **1.** pain in or near the heart. **2.** a technical name for **heartburn.** —ˌ**car·di·'al·gic** *adj.*

Car·diff ('kɑːdɪf) *n.* the capital of Wales, situated in the southeast: administrative centre of Glamorgan: an important port. Pop.: 278 221 (1971).

car·di·gan ('kɑːdɪgən) *n.* a knitted jacket or sweater with buttons up the front. [C19: named after J.T. Brudenell (1797–1868), 7th Earl of *Cardigan*]

Car·di·gan ('kɑːdɪgən) *n.* the larger variety of corgi, having a long tail.

Car·di·gan Bay *n.* an inlet of St. George's Channel, on the W coast of Wales.

Car·di·gan·shire ('kɑːdɪgənˌʃɪə, -ʃə) *n.* (until 1974) a county of W Wales, now part of Dyfed.

Car·din (*French* kar'dɛ̃) *n.* **Pierre** (pjɛːr). born 1922, French couturier, noted esp. for his collections for men.

car·di·nal ('kɑːdɪnᵊl) *n.* **1.** *R.C. Church.* any of the members of the Sacred College, ranking next after the pope, who elect the pope and act as his chief counsellors. **2.** Also called: **cardinal red.** a deep vivid red colour. **3.** See **cardinal number. 4.** Also called: **cardinal grosbeak,** (U.S.) **redbird.** a crested North American bunting, *Richmondena* (or *Pyrrhuloxia*) *cardinalis,* the male of which has a bright red plumage and the female a brown one. **5.** a woman's hooded shoulder cape worn in the 17th and 18th centuries. ~*adj.* **6.** (*usually prenominal*) fundamentally important; principal. **7.** of a deep vivid red colour. **8.** *Astrology.* of or relating to the signs Aries, Cancer, Libra, and Capricorn. Compare **mutable** (sense 2), **fixed** (sense 10). [C13: from Latin *cardinālis,* literally: relating to a hinge, hence, that on which something depends, principal, from *cardō* hinge] —**'car·di·nal·ly** *adv.*

car·di·nal·ate ('kɑːdɪnᵊˌleɪt) *or* **car·di·nal·ship** *n.* **1.** the rank, office, or term of office of a cardinal. **2.** the cardinals collectively.

car·di·nal bee·tle *n.* any of various large N temperate beetles of the family *Pyrochroidae,* such as *Pyrochroa serraticornis,* typically scarlet or partly scarlet in colour.

car·di·nal flow·er *n.* a campanulaceous plant, *Lobelia cardinalis* of E North America, that has brilliant scarlet, pink, or white flowers.

car·di·nal num·ber *or* **nu·mer·al** *n.* **1.** a number denoting quantity but not order in a group. Sometimes shortened to **cardinal. 2.** the number of elements in a mathematical set. ~Compare **ordinal number.**

car·di·nal points *pl. n.* the four main points of the compass: north, south, east, and west.

car·di·nal vir·tues *pl. n.* the most important moral qualities, traditionally justice, prudence, temperance, and fortitude.

card in·dex *or* **file** *n.* **1.** an index in which each item is separately listed on systematically arranged cards. ~*vb.* **card-index.** (*tr.*) **2.** to make such an index of (a book, etc.).

card·ing ('kardɪŋ) *n.* the process of preparing the fibres of cotton, wool, etc., for spinning.

car·di·o- *or before a vowel* **car·di-** *combining form.* heart: *cardiogram.* [from Greek *kardia* heart]

car·di·o·gram ('kɑːdɪəʊˌgræm) *n.* short for **electrocardiogram.**

car·di·o·graph ('kɑːdɪəʊˌgrɑːf, -ˌgræf) *n.* **1.** an instrument for recording the mechanical force and form of heart movements. **2.** short for **electrocardiograph.** —**car·di·og·ra·pher** (ˌkɑːdɪ'ɒgrəfə) *n.* —**car·di·o·graph·ic** (ˌkɑːdɪəʊ'græfɪk) *or* ˌ**car·di·o·'graph·i·cal** *adj.* —ˌ**car·di·o·'graph·i·cal·ly** *adv.* —ˌ**car·di·'og·ra·phy** *n.*

car·di·oid ('kɑːdɪˌɔɪd) *n.* a heart-shaped curve generated by a fixed point on a circle as it rolls around another fixed circle of equal radius, *a.* Equation: $r = a(1 - \cos \phi)$, where r is the radius vector and ϕ is the polar angle.

car·di·ol·o·gy (ˌkɑːdɪ'ɒlədʒɪ) *n.* the branch of medical science concerned with the heart and its diseases. —**car·di·o·log·i·cal** (ˌkɑːdɪə'lɒdʒɪkᵊl) *adj.* —ˌ**car·di·'ol·o·gist** *n.*

car·di·o·meg·a·ly (ˌkɑːdɪəʊ'mɛgəlɪ) *n. Pathol.* another name for **megalocardia.**

car·di·o·vas·cu·lar (ˌkɑːdɪəʊ'væskjʊlə) *adj.* of or relating to the heart and the blood vessels.

car·di·tis (kɑː'daɪtɪs) *n.* inflammation of the heart.

car·doon (kɑː'duːn) *n.* a S European plant, *Cynara cardunculus,* closely related to the artichoke, with spiny leaves, purple flowers, and a leafstalk that is blanched and eaten as celery: family *Compositae* (composites). [C17: from French *cardon,* ultimately from Latin *carduus* thistle, artichoke]

card punch *n.* **1.** a device, controlled by a computer, for transferring information from the central processing unit onto punched cards. Compare **card reader. 2.** another name for **key punch.**

card read·er *n.* a device for reading information on a punched card and transferring it to a computer or storage device. Compare **card punch.**

cards (kɑːdz) *n.* **1.** (*usually functioning as sing.*) **a.** any game or games played with cards, esp. playing cards. **b.** the playing of such a game. **2.** an employee's national insurance and other documents held by the employer. **3. ask for** *or* **get one's cards.** to ask or be told to terminate one's employment. **4. on the cards.** possible or likely. U.S. equivalent: **in the cards. 5. play one's cards.** to carry out one's plans (esp. in the phrase **play one's cards right**). **6. put** *or* **lay one's cards on the table.** Also: **show one's cards.** to declare one's intentions, resources, etc.

card·sharp ('kɑːdˌʃɑːp) *or* **card·sharp·er** *n.* a professional card player who cheats. —**'card·ˌsharp·ing** *n.*

car·du·a·ceous (ˌkɑːdjʊ'eɪʃəs) *adj.* of, relating to, or belonging to the *Carduaceae,* a subfamily of composite plants that includes the thistle. [C19: from New Latin *Carduācеae,* from *Carduus* type genus, from Latin: thistle]

Car·duc·ci (*Italian* kar'duttʃi) *n.* **Gio·su·è** (ˌdʒozu'ɛ). 1835–1907, Italian poet: Nobel prize for literature 1906.

card vote *n. Brit.* a vote by delegates, esp. at a trade-union conference, in which each delegate's vote counts as a vote by all his constituents.

care (kɛə) *vb.* **1.** (when *tr., may take a clause as object*) to be troubled or concerned; be affected emotionally: *he is dying, and she doesn't care.* **2.** (*intr.;* foll. by *for* or *about*) to have regard, affection, or consideration (for): *he cares more for his hobby than his job.* **3.** (*intr.;* foll. by *for*) to have a desire or taste (for): *would you care for some tea?* **4.** (*intr.;* foll. by *for*) to provide physical needs, help, or comfort (for): *the nurse cared for her patients.* **5.** (*tr.*) to agree or like (to do something): *would you care to sit down, please?* **6. for all I care** *or* **I couldn't care less.** I am completely indifferent. ~*n.* **7.** careful or serious attention: *under her care the plant flourished; he does his work with care.* **8.** protective or supervisory control: *in the care of a doctor.* **9.** (*often pl.*) trouble; anxiety; worry. **10.** an object of or cause for concern: *the baby's illness was her only care.* **11.** caution: *handle with care.* **12. care of.** at the address of: written on envelopes. Usual abbrev.: **c/o.** [Old English *cearu* (n.), *cearian* (vb.), of Germanic origin; compare Old High German *chara* lament, Latin *garrīre* to gossip]

CARE (kɛə) *n. acronym for* Cooperative for American Relief Everywhere, Inc.: a federation of U.S. charities, giving financial and technical assistance to many regions of the world.

ca·reen (kə'riːn) *vb.* **1.** to sway or cause to sway dangerously over to one side. **2.** (*tr.*) *Nautical.* to cause (a vessel) to keel over to one side, esp. in order to clean or repair its bottom. **3.** (*intr.*) *Nautical.* (of a vessel) to keel over to one side. [C17: from French *carène* keel, from Italian *carena,* from Latin *carīna* keel] —**ca·'reen·age** *n.* —**ca·'reen·er** *n.*

ca·reer (kə'rɪə) *n.* **1.** a path or progress through life or history. **2.** a profession or occupation chosen as one's life's work. **3.** (*modifier*) having or following a career as specified: *a career diplomat.* **4.** a course or path, esp. a swift or headlong one. ~*vb.* **5.** (*intr.*) to move swiftly along; rush in an uncontrolled way. [C16: from French *carrière,* from Late Latin *carrāria* carriage road, from Latin *carrus* two-wheeled wagon, CAR]

ca+reer girl *or* **wom+an** *n.* a girl or woman, often unmarried, who follows a career or profession.

ca+reer+ist (kəˈrɪərɪst) *n.* a person who values success in his career above all else and seeks to advance it by any possible means. —**ca+ˈreer+ism** *n.*

ca+reers mas+ter *or* (*fem.*) **ca+reers mis+tress** *n.* a teacher who gives advice and information about careers to his pupils.

Ca+reers Of+fic+er *n.* a person trained in giving vocational advice, esp. to school leavers.

care+free (ˈkɛəˌfriː) *adj.* without worry or responsibility. —**ˈcare+ˌfree+ness** *n.*

care+ful (ˈkɛəfʊl) *adj.* **1.** cautious in attitude or action; prudent; wary. **2.** painstaking in one's work; exact and thorough: *he wrote very careful script.* **3.** (*usually postpositive;* foll. by *of, in,* or *about*) solicitous; protective: *careful of one's reputation.* **4.** *Archaic.* full of care; anxious. **5.** *Brit.* mean or miserly. —**ˈcare+ful+ly** *adv.* —**ˈcare+ful+ness** *n.*

care+less (ˈkɛəlɪs) *adj.* **1.** done with or acting with insufficient attention; negligent. **2.** (often foll. by *in, of,* or *about*) unconcerned in attitude or action; heedless; indifferent (to): *she's very careless about her clothes.* **3.** (*usually prenominal*) carefree. **4.** (*usually prenominal*) unstudied; artless: *an impression of careless elegance.* —**ˈcare+less+ly** *adv.* —**ˈcare+less+ness** *n.*

ca+ress (kəˈrɛs) *n.* **1.** a gentle touch or embrace, esp. one given to show affection. ~*vb.* **2.** (*tr.*) to touch or stroke gently with affection or as with affection: *the wind caressed her face.* [C17: from French *caresse,* from Italian *carezza,* from Latin *cārus* dear] —**ca+ˈress+er** *n.* —**ca+ˈress+ing+ly** *adv.*

car+et (ˈkærɪt) *n.* a symbol (‸) used to indicate the place in written or printed matter at which something is to be inserted. [C17: from Latin, literally: there is missing, from *carēre* to lack]

care+tak·er (ˈkɛəˌteɪkə) *n.* **1.** a person who is in charge of a place or thing, esp. in the owner's absence: *the caretaker of a school.* **2.** (*modifier*) holding office temporarily; interim: *a caretaker government.* —**ˈcare+ˌtak·ing** *n.*

Ca·rew (kəˈruː) *n.* **Thom·as.** ?1595–?1639, English Cavalier poet.

care+worn (ˈkɛəˌwɔːn) *adj.* showing signs of care, stress, worry, etc.: *a careworn face.*

Car·ey (ˈkɛərɪ) *n.* **Wil·liam.** 1761–1834, English orientalist and pioneer Baptist missionary in India.

Car+ey Street *n.* **1.** (formerly) the street in which the London bankruptcy court was situated. **2.** the state of bankruptcy.

car+fare (ˈkɑːˌfɛə) *n. U.S.* the fare that a passenger is charged for a ride on a bus, etc.

car+fax (ˈkɑːfæks) *n.* a place where principal roads or streets intersect, esp. a place in a town where four roads meet. [C14: from Anglo-French *carfuks,* from Old French *carrefures,* from Latin *quadrifurcus* four-forked]

car+fuf+fle (kəˈfʌfᵊl) *n. Informal, chiefly Brit.* a variant spelling of **kerfuffle.** [C20: of unknown origin]

car+go (ˈkɑːgəʊ) *n., pl.* **+goes** *or* **+gos. 1. a.** goods carried by a ship, aircraft, or other vehicle; freight. **b.** (*as modifier*): *a cargo vessel.* **2.** any load: *the train pulled in with its cargo of new arrivals.* [C17: from Spanish: from *cargar* to load, from Late Latin *carricāre* to load a vehicle, from *carrus* CAR]

car+go cult *n.* a religious movement of the SW Pacific, characterized by expectation of the return of spirits in ships or aircraft carrying goods that will provide for the needs of the followers.

car+hop (ˈkɑːˌhɒp) *n. U.S. informal.* a waiter or waitress at a drive-in restaurant.

Car·i·a (ˈkɛərɪə) *n.* an ancient region of SW Asia Minor, on the Aegean Sea: chief cities were Halicarnassus and Cnidus: corresponds to the present-day Turkish districts of S Aydin and W Muğla.

Car+ib (ˈkærɪb) *n.* **1.** (*pl.* **+ibs** *or* **+ib**) a member of a group of American Indian peoples of NE South America and the Lesser Antilles. **2.** the family of languages spoken by these peoples. [C16: from Spanish *Caribe,* from Arawak]

Car+ib+be·an (ˌkærɪˈbɪən) *adj.* **1.** of or relating to the Caribbean Sea and its islands. **2.** of or relating to the Carib or any of their languages. ~*n.* **3. the.** short for the **Caribbean Sea. 4.** a member of any of the peoples inhabiting the islands of the Caribbean Sea, such as a West Indian or a Carib.

Car+ib+be·an Sea *n.* an almost landlocked sea, part of the Atlantic Ocean, bounded by the West Indies, Central America, and the N coast of South America. Area: 2 718 200 sq. km (1 049 500 sq. miles).

Car+ib+bee bark (ˈkærɪˌbiː) *n.* the bark of any of various tropical American and West Indian rubiaceous trees of the genus *Exostema,* used as a substitute for cinchona bark.

Car+ib+bees (ˈkærɪˌbiːz) *pl. n.* **the.** another name for the **Lesser Antilles.**

Car·i·boo Moun+tains (ˈkærɪˌbuː) *pl. n.* a mountain range in SW Canada, in SE British Columbia. Highest peak: Mount Sir Wilfrid Laurier, 3582 m (11 750 ft.).

car·i·bou (ˈkærɪˌbuː) *n., pl.* **+bous** *or* **+bou.** a large deer, *Rangifer tarandus,* of Arctic regions of North America, having large branched antlers in the male and female: also occurs in Europe and Asia, where it is called a reindeer. [C18: from Canadian French, of Algonquian origin; compare Micmac *khalibu* literally: scratcher]

Car·i·bou Es+ki+mo *n.* a member of any of the Eskimo peoples who inhabit the Barren Lands of N Canada.

car·i+ca+ture (ˈkærɪkəˌtjʊə) *n.* **1.** a pictorial, written, or acted representation of a person, which exaggerates his characteristic traits for comic effect. **2.** a ludicrously inadequate or inaccurate imitation: *he is a caricature of a statesman.* ~*vb.* **3.** (*tr.*) to represent in or produce a caricature of. [C18: from Italian *caricatura* a distortion, exaggeration, from *caricare* to load, exaggerate; see CARGO] —**ˈcar·i+ca+ˌtur+al** *adj.* —**ˈcar·i+ca+ˌtur+ist** *n.*

car·i+es (ˈkɛərɪiːz) *n., pl.* **·i+es.** progressive decay of a bone or a tooth. [C17: from Latin: decay; related to Greek *kēr* death]

CARIFTA (kæˈrɪftə) *n. acronym for* Caribbean Free Trade Area.

ca+ril+lon (kəˈrɪljən) *n. Music.* **1.** a set of bells usually hung in a tower and played either from a set of keys and pedals or mechanically. **2.** a tune played on such bells. **3.** a mixture stop on an organ giving the effect of a bell. **4.** a form of celesta or keyboard glockenspiel. ~*vb.* **+lons, +lon+ning, +lonned. 5.** (*intr.*) to play a carillon. [C18: from French: set of bells, from Old French *quarregnon,* ultimately from Latin *quattuor* four]

ca+ril+lon+neur (kəˌrɪljəˈnɜː) *n.* a person who plays a carillon.

ca+ri+na (kəˈriːnə, -ˈraɪ-) *n., pl.* **+nae** (-niː) *or* **+nas.** a keel-like part or ridge, as in the breastbone of birds. [C18: from Latin: keel]

Ca+ri+na (kəˈriːnə, -ˈraɪ-) *n., Latin genitive* **Ca+ri+nae** (kəˈriːniː, -ˈraɪ-). a large conspicuous constellation in the S hemisphere close to the Southern Cross that contains Canopus, the second brightest star in the sky. It was originally considered part of the more extensive constellation of Argo.

car·i+nate (ˈkærɪˌneɪt) *or* **car·i+nat+ed** *adj. Biology.* having a keel or ridge; shaped like a keel. [C17: from Latin *carīnāre* to furnish with a keel or shell, from *carīna* keel]

Ca+rin+thi·a (kəˈrɪnθɪə) *n.* a province of S Austria: an independent duchy from 976 to 1276; mainly mountainous, with many lakes and resorts. Capital: Klagenfurt. Pop.: 525 728 (1971). Area: 9533 sq. km (3681 sq. miles). German name: **Kärnten.**

car·i·o+ca (ˌkærɪˈəʊkə) *n.* **1.** a Brazilian dance similar to the samba. **2.** a piece of music composed for this dance. [C19: from Brazilian Portuguese]

Car·i·o+can (ˌkærɪˈəʊkən) *or* **Car·i·o+ca** *n.* a native of Rio de Janeiro, Brazil.

car·i·o+gen+ic (ˌkɛərɪəʊˈdʒɛnɪk) *adj.* (of a substance) producing caries, esp. in the teeth.

car·i·ole *or* **car+ri+ole** (ˈkærɪˌəʊl) *n.* **1.** a small open two-wheeled horse-drawn vehicle. **2.** a covered cart. [C19: from French *carriole,* ultimately from Latin *carrus;* see CAR]

car·i·ous (ˈkɛərɪəs) *adj.* (of teeth or bone) affected with caries; decayed. —**car·i+os+i·ty** (ˌkærɪˈɒsɪtɪ, ˌkɛərɪ-) *or* **ˈcar·i·ous+ness** *n.*

cark (kɑːk) *n., vb.* an archaic word for **worry** (senses 1, 2, 11, 13). [C13 *carken* to burden, from Old Northern French *carquier,* from Late Latin *carricāre* to load]

carl *or* **carle** (kɑːl) *n. Archaic or Scot.* another word for **churl.** [Old English, from Old Norse *karl*]

Carl XVI Gus·taf (*Swedish* kaːrl ˈgʊstav) *n.* born 1946, king of Sweden since 1973.

car+line[1] (ˈkɑːlɪn) *n.* a Eurasian thistle-like plant, *Carlina vulgaris,* having spiny leaves and flower heads surrounded by raylike whitish bracts: family *Compositae* (composites). Also called: **carline thistle.** [C16: from French, probably from Latin *cardō* thistle]

car+line[2] *or* **car+lin** (ˈkɑːlɪn) *n.* **1.** *Chiefly Scot.* an old woman, hag, or witch. **2.** variant spellings of **carling.** [C14: from Old Norse *kerling* old woman, diminutive of *karl* man, CHURL]

car+ling (ˈkɑːlɪŋ) *or* **car+line** *n.* a fore-and-aft beam in a vessel, used for supporting the deck, esp. around a hatchway or other opening. [C14: from Old Norse *kerling* old woman, CARLINE[2]]

Car+lisle (kɑːˈlaɪl) *n.* a city in NW England, administrative centre of Cumbria: railway and industrial centre. Pop.: 71 497 (1971). Latin name: **Luguvallum.**

Car+list (ˈkɑːlɪst) *n.* **1.** (in Spain) a supporter of Don Carlos or his descendants as the rightful kings of Spain. **2.** (in France) a supporter of Charles X or his descendants. —**ˈCar+lism** *n.*

Car·los (ˈkɑːlɒs) *n.* **Don.** full name *Carlos María Isidro de Borbón.* 1788–1855, second son of Charles IV: pretender to the Spanish throne and leader of the Carlists.

Car·lo·ta (*Spanish* karˈlota) *n.* original name *Marie Charlotte Amélie Augustine Victoire Clémentine Léopoldine.* 1840–1927, wife of Maximilian; empress of Mexico (1864–67).

Car+lo+vin+gi·an (ˌkɑːləʊˈvɪndʒɪən) *adj., n. History.* a variant of **Carolingian.**

Car+low (ˈkɑːləʊ) *n.* **1.** a county of SE Ireland, in Leinster: mostly flat, with barren mountains in the southeast. County town: Carlow. Pop.: 34 237 (1971). Area: 896 sq. km (346 sq. miles). **2.** a town in SE Ireland, county town of Co. Carlow. Pop.: 10 399 (1971).

Carls+bad (*German* ˈkarlsˌbaːt) *n.* a variant spelling of **Karlsbad.**

Carl+ton (ˈkɑːltən) *n.* a town in N central England, in S Nottinghamshire. Pop.: 45 211 (1971).

Car·lyle (kɑːˈlaɪl) *n.* **Thom·as.** 1795–1881, Scottish essayist and historian. His works include *Sartor Resartus* (1833–34), a spiritual autobiography, *The French Revolution* (1837), and lectures *On Heroes, Hero-Worship, and the Heroic in History* (1841).

car+ma+gnole (ˌkɑːmənˈjəʊl; *French* karmaˈɲɔl) *n.* **1.** a dance and song popular during the French Revolution. **2.** the costume worn by many French Revolutionaries, consisting of a short jacket with wide lapels, black trousers, a red liberty cap, and a tricoloured sash. [C18: from French, probably named after *Carmagnola*, Italy, taken by French Revolutionaries in 1792]

car·man ('kɑːmən) *n., pl.* **·men.** **1.** a man who drives a car or cart; carter. **2.** a man whose business is the transport of goods; haulier. **3.** *U.S.* a tram driver.

Car·mar·then (kɑː'mɑːðən) *n.* **1.** a market town in S Wales, in S Dyfed: Norman castle. Pop.: 13 072 (1971).

Car·mar·then·shire (kɑː'mɑːðən,ʃɪə, -ʃə) *n.* (until 1974) a county of S Wales, now part of Dyfed.

Car·mel ('kɑːməl) *n.* **Mount.** a mountain ridge in NW Israel, extending from the Samarian Hills to the Mediterranean. Highest point: about 540 m (1800 ft.).

Car·mel·ite ('kɑːmə,laɪt) *n. R.C. Church.* **1.** a member of an order of mendicant friars founded about 1154; a White Friar. **2.** a member of a corresponding order of nuns founded in 1452, noted for its austere rule. [C14: from French; named after Mount Carmel, where the order was founded]

car·min·a·tive ('kɑːmɪnətɪv) *adj.* **1.** able to relieve flatulence. ~*n.* **2.** a carminative drug. [C15: from French *carminatif*, from Latin *carmināre* to card wool, remove impurities, from *cārere* to card]

car·mine ('kɑːmaɪn) *n.* **1. a.** a vivid red colour, sometimes with a purplish tinge. **b.** (*as adj.*): *carmine paint.* **2.** a pigment of this colour obtained from cochineal. [C18: from Medieval Latin *carmīnus*, from Arabic *qirmiz* KERMES]

car·nage ('kɑːnɪdʒ) *n.* extensive slaughter, esp. of human beings in battle. [C16: from French, from Italian *carnaggio*, from Medieval Latin *carnāticum*, from Latin *carō* flesh]

car·nal ('kɑːnᵊl) *adj.* relating to the appetites and passions of the body; sensual; fleshly. [C15: from Late Latin: relating to flesh, from Latin *carō* flesh] —'**car·nal·ist** *n.* —**car·'nal·i·ty** *n.* —'**car·nal·ly** *adv.*

car·nal knowl·edge *n. Chiefly law.* **1.** sexual intercourse. **2.** **have carnal knowledge of.** to have sexual intercourse with.

car·nall·ite ('kɑːnə,laɪt) *n.* a white or sometimes coloured mineral consisting of a hydrated chloride of potassium and magnesium in rhombic crystalline form: a source of potassium and also used as a fertilizer. Formula: $KCl.MgCl_2.6H_2O$. [C19: named after Rudolf von *Carnall* (1804–74), German mining engineer; see -ITE[1]]

Car·nar·von (kə'nɑːvᵊn) *n.* a variant spelling of **Caernarfon.**

car·nas·si·al (kɑː'næsɪəl) *adj.* **1.** *Zoology.* of, relating to, or designating the last upper premolar and first lower molar teeth of carnivores, which have sharp edges for tearing flesh. ~*n.* **2.** a carnassial tooth. [C19: from French *carnassier* meat-eating, from Provençal, from *carnasso* abundance of meat, from *carn* meat, flesh, from Latin *carō*]

Car·nat·ic (kɑː'nætɪk) *n.* a region of S India, between the Eastern Ghats and the Coromandel Coast: originally the country of the Kanarese; historically important as a rich and powerful trading centre; now part of Madras state.

car·na·tion (kɑː'neɪʃən) *n.* **1.** Also called: **clove pink.** a Eurasian caryophyllaceous plant, *Dianthus caryophyllus*, cultivated in many varieties for its white, pink, or red flowers, which have a fragrant scent of cloves. **2.** the flower of this plant. **3. a.** a pink or reddish-pink colour. **b.** (*as adj.*): *a carnation dress.* **4.** (*often pl.*) a flesh tint in painting. [C16: from French: flesh colour, from Late Latin *carnātiō* fleshiness, from Latin *carō* flesh]

car·nau·ba (kɑː'naʊbə) *n.* **1.** Also called: **wax palm.** a Brazilian fan palm, *Copernicia cerifera.* **2.** Also called: **carnauba wax.** the wax obtained from the young leaves of this tree, used esp. as a polish. [from Brazilian Portuguese, probably of Tupi origin]

Car·ne·gie ('kɑːnəgiː, kɑː'neɪ-) *n.* **An·drew.** 1835–1919, U.S. steel manufacturer and philanthropist, born in Scotland: endowed public libraries, education, and research trusts.

car·nel·ian (kɑː'niːljən) *n.* a red or reddish-yellow translucent variety of chalcedony, used as a gemstone. [C17: variant of *cornelian*, from Old French *corneline*, of uncertain origin; *car-* spelling influenced by Latin *carneus* flesh-coloured]

car·net ('kɑːneɪ) *n.* **1. a.** a customs licence authorizing the temporary importation of a motor vehicle. **b.** an official document permitting motorists to cross certain frontiers. **2.** a book of tickets, travel coupons, etc. [French: notebook, from Old French *quernet*, ultimately from Latin *quaternī* four at a time; see QUIRE[1]]

car·ni·fy ('kɑːnɪ,faɪ) *vb.* **·fies, ·fy·ing, ·fied.** (*intr.*) *Pathol.* (esp. of lung tissue, as the result of pneumonia) to be altered so as to resemble skeletal muscle. [C17: from Latin *carō* flesh + *facere* to make] —**car·ni·fi·ca·tion** (,kɑːnɪfɪ'keɪʃən) *n.*

Car·ni·o·la (,kɑːnɪ'əʊlə) *n.* a region of NW Yugoslavia: a former duchy and crownland of Austria (1335–1919); divided between Yugoslavia and Italy in 1919; became part of Yugoslavia in 1947. German name: **Krain** (kraɪn). Slovene name: **Kranj.**

car·ni·val ('kɑːnɪvᵊl) *n.* **1. a.** a festive occasion or period marked by merrymaking, processions, etc.: esp. in some Roman Catholic countries, the period just before Lent. **b.** (*as modifier*): *a carnival atmosphere.* **2.** a travelling fair having side shows, merry-go-rounds, etc. **3.** a show or display arranged as an amusement. **4.** *Austral.* a sports meeting. [C16: from Italian *carnevale*, from Old Italian *carnelevare* a removing of meat (referring to the Lenten fast)]

car·ni·vore ('kɑːnɪ,vɔː) *n.* **1.** any placental mammal of the order *Carnivora*, typically having large pointed canine teeth and sharp molars and premolars, specialized for eating flesh. The order includes cats, dogs, bears, raccoons, hyenas, civets, and weasels. **2.** any other animal or any plant that feeds on animals. [C19: probably back formation from CARNIVOROUS]

car·niv·o·rous (kɑː'nɪvərəs) *adj.* **1.** (esp. of animals) feeding on flesh. **2.** (of plants such as the pitcher plant and sundew) able to trap and digest insects and other small animals. **3.** of or relating to the *Carnivora.* [C17: from Latin *carnivorus*, from *carō* flesh + *vorāre* to consume] —**car·'niv·o·rous·ly** *adv.* —**car·'niv·o·rous·ness** *n.*

Car·not ('kɑːnəʊ; *French* kar'no) *n.* **Ni·co·las Lé·o·nard Sa·di** (nikɔla leɔnar sa'di). 1796–1832, French physicist, whose work on a cycle for an ideal heat engine formed the basis for the second law of thermodynamics, enunciated in 1850; author of *Réflexions sur la puissance motrice du feu* (1824).

Car·not cy·cle *n.* an idealized reversible heat-engine cycle giving maximum efficiency and consisting of an isothermal expansion, an adiabatic expansion, an isothermal compression, and an adiabatic compression back to the initial state.

car·no·tite ('kɑːnə,taɪt) *n.* a radioactive yellow mineral consisting of hydrated uranium potassium vanadate: occurs in sedimentary rocks and is a source of uranium, radium, and vanadium. Formula: $K_2(UO_2)_2(V_2O_4)_2.3H_2O$. [C20: named after A. *Carnot* (died 1920), French inspector general of mines]

Car·not prin·ci·ple *n.* the principle that the efficiency of a reversible heat engine depends on the maximum and minimum temperatures of the working fluid during the operating cycle and not on the properties of the fluid.

car·ny *or* **car·ney** ('kɑːnɪ) *vb.* **·nies, ·ny·ing, ·nied** *or* **·neys, ·ney·ing, ·neyed.** *Brit. Informal.* to coax or cajole or act in a wheedling manner. [C19: of unknown origin]

car·ob ('kærəb) *n.* **1.** Also called: **algarroba.** an evergreen caesalpiniaceous Mediterranean tree, *Ceratonia siliqua*, with compound leaves and edible pods. **2.** Also called: **algarroba, Saint John's bread.** the long blackish sugary pod of this tree, used for animal fodder and sometimes for human food. [C16: from Old French *carobe*, from Medieval Latin *carrūbium*, from Arabic *al kharrūbah*]

ca·roche (kə'rɒʃ) *n.* a stately ceremonial carriage used in the 16th and 17th centuries. [C16: from French, ultimately from Latin *carrus* CAR]

car·ol ('kærəl) *n.* **1.** a joyful hymn or religious song, esp. one (a **Christmas carol**) celebrating the birth of Christ. **2.** *Archaic.* an old English circular dance. ~*vb.* **·ols, ·ol·ling, ·olled** *or U.S.* **·ols, ·ol·ing, ·oled. 3.** (*intr.*) to sing carols at Christmas. **4.** to sing (something) in a joyful manner. [C13: from Old French, of uncertain origin] —'**car·ol·er** *n.*

Car·ol II ('kærəl) *n.* 1893–1953, king of Rumania (1930–40), who was deposed by the Iron Guard.

Car·o·li·na (,kærə'laɪnə) *n.* a former English colony on the E coast of North America, first established in 1663: divided in 1729 into North and South Carolina, which are often referred to as **the Carolinas.**

Car·o·line ('kærə,laɪn) *or* **Car·o·le·an** (,kærə'liːən) *adj.* **1.** Also called: **Carolinian.** characteristic of or relating to Charles I or Charles II of England, the society over which they ruled, or their government. **2.** of or relating to any other king called Charles.

Car·o·line Is·lands *pl. n.* an archipelago of over 500 islands and islets in Micronesia, in the W Pacific Ocean east of the Philippines: part of the U.S. Trust Territory of the Pacific Islands; centre of a typhoon zone. Pop.: 70 815 (1971). Area: (land) 1183 sq. km (457 sq. miles).

Car·o·lin·gi·an (,kærə'lɪndʒɪən) *adj.* **1.** of or relating to the Frankish dynasty founded by Pepin the Short, son of Charles Martel, which ruled in France from 751–987 A.D. and in Germany until 911 A.D. ~*n.* **2.** a member of the dynasty of the Carolingian Franks. ~Also: **Carlovingian, Carolinian.**

Car·o·lin·i·an[1] (,kærə'lɪnɪən) *adj.* a variant of **Caroline** or **Carolingian.**

Car·o·lin·i·an[2] (,kærə'lɪnɪən) *adj.* **1.** of or relating to North or South Carolina. ~*n.* **2.** a native or inhabitant of North or South Carolina.

car·o·lus ('kærələs) *n., pl.* **·lus·es** *or* **·li** (-,laɪ). any of several coins struck in the reign of a king called Charles, esp. an English gold coin from the reign of Charles I.

car·om ('kærəm) *n. Billiards.* another word (esp. U.S.) for **cannon** (sense 6). [C18: from earlier *carambole* (taken as *carom ball*), from Spanish *carambola* a sour greenish fruit, from Portuguese, from Marathi *karambal*]

Car·o's ac·id ('kærəʊz, 'kɑː-) *n.* another name for peroxysulphuric acid. [C19: named after Heinrich *Caro* (died 1910), German chemist]

car·o·tene ('kærə,tiːn) *or* **car·o·tin** ('kærətɪn) *n.* any of four orange-red isomers of an unsaturated hydrocarbon present in many plants (β-carotene is the orange pigment of carrots) and converted to vitamin A in the liver. Formula: $C_{40}H_{56}$. [C19: *carotin*, from Latin *carōta* CARROT; see -ENE]

ca·rot·e·noid *or* **ca·rot·i·noid** (kə'rɒtɪ,nɔɪd) *n.* **1.** any of a group of red or yellow pigments, including carotenes, found in plants and certain animal tissues. ~*adj.* **2.** of or resembling carotene or a carotenoid.

ca·rot·id (kə'rɒtɪd) *n.* **1.** either one of the two principal arteries that supply blood to the head and neck. ~*adj.* **2.** of or relating to either of these arteries. [C17: from French, from Greek *karōtides*, from *karoun* to stupefy; so named by Galen, because pressure on them produced unconsciousness] —**ca·'rot·id·al** *adj.*

ca·rous·al (kə'raʊzᵊl) *n.* a merry drinking party.

ca·rouse (kə'raʊz) *vb.* **1.** (*intr.*) to have a merry drinking spree; drink freely. ~*n.* **2.** another word for **carousal.** [C16: via French *carrousser* from German (*trinken*) *gar aus* (to drink) right out] —**ca·'rous·er** *n.*

car·ou·sel (ˌkærəˈsɛl, -ˈzɛl) *n.* **1.** *U.S.* another name for **merry-go-round.** **2.** *History.* a tournament in which horsemen took part in races and various manoeuvres in formation. [C17: from French *carrousel,* from Italian *carosello,* of uncertain origin]

carp[1] (kɑːp) *n., pl.* **carp** *or* **carps. 1.** a freshwater teleost food fish, *Cyprinus carpio,* having a body covered with cycloid scales, a naked head, one long dorsal fin, and two barbels on each side of the mouth: family *Cyprinidae.* **2.** any other fish of the family *Cyprinidae;* a cyprinid. [C14: from Old French *carpe,* of Germanic origin; compare Old High German *karpfo,* Old Norse *karfi*]

carp[2] (kɑːp) *vb.* (*intr.*) to complain or find fault; nag pettily. [C13: from Old Norse *karpa* to boast; related to Latin *carpere* to pluck] —**ˈcarp·er** *n.* —**ˈcarp·ing·ly** *adv.*

-carp *n. combining form.* (in botany) fruit or a reproductive structure that develops into a particular part of the fruit: *epicarp.* [from New Latin *-carpium,* from Greek *-karpion,* from *karpos* fruit]

car·pal (ˈkɑːpᵊl) *n.* **a.** any bone of the wrist. **b.** (*as modifier*): *carpal bones.* Also: **car·pa·le** (kɑːˈpeɪlɪ). [C18: from New Latin *carpālis,* from Greek *karpos* wrist]

car park *n.* an area or building reserved for parking cars. Usual U.S. term: **parking lot.**

Car·pa·thi·an Moun·tains (kɑːˈpeɪθɪən) *or* **Car·pa·thi·ans** *pl. n.* a mountain system of central and E Europe, extending from N Czechoslovakia to central Rumania: mainly forested, with rich iron ore resources. Highest peak: Gerlachovka, 2663 m (8788 ft.).

Car·pa·tho-U·kraine (kɑːˈpeɪθəʊ juːˈkreɪn) *n.* another name for **Ruthenia.**

car·pe di·em *Latin* (ˈkɑːpɪ ˈdiːɛm) *interj.* enjoy the pleasures of the moment, without concern for the future. [literally: seize the day!]

car·pel (ˈkɑːpᵊl) *n.* the female reproductive organ of flowering plants, consisting of an ovary, style, and stigma. The carpels are separate or fused to form a single pistil. [C19: from New Latin *carpellum,* from Greek *karpos* fruit] —**ˈcar·pel·lar·y** *adj.* —**car·pel·late** (ˈkɑːpɪˌleɪt) *adj.*

Car·pen·ta·ri·a (ˌkɑːpənˈtɛərɪə) *n.* **Gulf of.** a shallow inlet of the Arafura Sea, in N Australia between Arnhem Land and Cape York Peninsula.

car·pen·ter (ˈkɑːpɪntə) *n.* **1.** a person skilled in woodwork, esp. in buildings, ships, etc. ~*vb.* **2.** (*intr.*) to do the work of a carpenter. **3.** (*tr.*) to make or fit together by or as if by carpentry. [C14: from Anglo-French, from Latin *carpentārius* wagon-maker, from *carpentum* wagon; of Celtic origin]

Car·pen·ter (ˈkɑːpɪntə) *n.* **John Al·den.** 1876–1951, U.S. composer, who used jazz rhythms in orchestral music: his works include the ballet *Skyscrapers* (1926) and the orchestral suite *Adventures in a Perambulator* (1915).

car·pen·ter bee *n.* any large solitary bee of the genus *Xylocopa* and related genera that lays its eggs in tunnels bored into wood or in plant stems: family *Apidae.*

car·pen·ter moth *n.* any of various large moths of the family *Cossidae,* the larvae of which bore beneath and cause damage to tree bark.

Car·pen·tier (*French* karpɑ̃ˈtje) *n.* **Georges** (ʒɔrʒ), known as *Gorgeous Georges.* 1894–1975, French boxer: world light-heavyweight champion (1920–22).

car·pen·try (ˈkɑːpɪntrɪ) *n.* **1.** the art or technique of working wood. **2.** the work produced by a carpenter; woodwork.

car·pet (ˈkɑːpɪt) *n.* **1. a.** a heavy fabric for covering floors. **b.** (*as modifier*): *a carpet sale.* **2.** a covering like a carpet: *a carpet of leaves.* **3. on the carpet.** *Informal.* **a.** before authority to be reproved for misconduct or error. **b.** under consideration. ~*vb.* (*tr.*) **4.** to cover with or as if with a carpet. **5.** *Informal.* to reprimand. [C14: from Old French *carpite,* from Old Italian *carpita,* from Late Latin *carpeta,* literally: (wool) that has been carded, from Latin *carpere* to pluck, card]

car·pet·bag (ˈkɑːpɪtˌbæg) *n.* a travelling bag originally made of carpeting.

car·pet·bag·ger (ˈkɑːpɪtˌbægə) *n. U.S.* **1.** a politician who seeks public office in a locality where he has no real connections. **2.** a Northern White who went to the South after the Civil War to profit from Reconstruction.

car·pet bee·tle *or U.S.* **car·pet bug** *n.* any of various beetles of the genus *Anthrenus,* the larvae of which feed on carpets, furnishing fabrics, etc.: family *Dermestidae.*

car·pet·ing (ˈkɑːpɪtɪŋ) *n.* carpet material or carpets in general.

car·pet knight *n. Disparaging.* a soldier who spends his life away from battle; idler.

car·pet shark *n.* any of various sharks of the family *Orectolobidae,* having two dorsal fins and a patterned back, typically marked with white and brown.

car·pet slip·per *n.* one of a pair of slippers, originally one made with woollen uppers resembling carpeting.

car·pet snake *or* **py·thon** *n.* a large nonvenomous Australian snake, *Morelia variegata,* having a carpetlike pattern on its back.

car·pet-sweep·er *n.* a household device with a revolving brush for sweeping carpets.

car·pi (ˈkɑːpaɪ) *n.* the plural of **carpus.**

-car·pic *adj. combining form.* variant of **-carpous.**

car·po-[1] *combining form.* (in botany) indicating fruit or a reproductive structure that develops into part of the fruit: *carpophore; carpogonium.* [from Greek *karpos* fruit]

car·po-[2] *combining form.* carpus or carpal bones: *carpometacarpus.*

car·po·go·ni·um (ˌkɑːpəˈgəʊnɪəm) *n., pl.* **-ni·a** (-nɪə). the female sex organ of red algae, consisting of a swollen base containing the ovum and a long neck down which the male gametes pass. —**ˌcar·po·ˈgo·ni·al** *adj.*

car·pol·o·gy (kɑːˈpɒlədʒɪ) *n.* the branch of botany concerned with the study of fruits and seeds. —**car·po·log·i·cal** (ˌkɑːpəˈlɒdʒɪkᵊl) *adj.* —**carˈpol·o·gist** *n.*

car·po·met·a·car·pus (ˌkɑːpəʊˌmɛtəˈkɑːpəs) *n.* a bone in the wing of a bird that consists of the metacarpal bones and some of the carpal bones fused together.

car·poph·a·gous (kɑːˈpɒfəgəs) *adj. Zoology.* feeding on fruit: *carpophagous bats.*

car·po·phore (ˈkɑːpəˌfɔː) *n.* **1.** an elongated part of the receptacle in flowers such as the geranium that bears the carpels and stamens. **2.** a spore-bearing structure in some of the higher fungi.

car·port (ˈkɑːˌpɔːt) *n.* a shelter for a car usually consisting of a roof built out from the side of a building and supported by posts.

car·po·spore (ˈkɑːpəʊˌspɔː) *n.* a sexual spore produced by red algae after fertilization of the carpogonium.

-car·pous *or* **-car·pic** *adj. combining form.* (in botany) indicating a certain kind or number of fruit: *apocarpous.* [from New Latin *-carpus,* from Greek *karpos* fruit]

car·pus (ˈkɑːpəs) *n., pl.* **-pi** (-paɪ). **1.** the technical name for **wrist. 2.** the eight small bones of the human wrist that form the joint between the arm and the hand. **3.** the corresponding joint in other tetrapod vertebrates. [C17: New Latin, from Greek *karpos*]

car·rack (ˈkærək) *n.* a galleon sailed in the Mediterranean as a merchantman in the 15th and 16th centuries. [C14: from Old French *caraque,* from Old Spanish *carraca,* from Arabic *qarāqīr* merchant ships]

car·ra·geen, car·ra·gheen, *or* **car·a·geen** (ˈkærəˌgiːn) *n.* **1.** an edible red seaweed, *Chondrus crispus,* of rocky shores of North America and N Europe, used to make a beverage, medicine, and jelly. **2.** any product of this seaweed. ~Also called: **Irish moss.** [C19: from *Carragheen,* near Waterford, Ireland, where it is very plentiful]

Car·ra·ra (kəˈrɑːrə; *Italian* karˈraːra) *n.* a town in NW Italy, in NW Tuscany: famous for its marble. Pop.: 67 758 (1971).

car·re·four (ˈkærəˌfʊə) *n.* **1.** a rare word for **crossroads. 2.** a public square, esp. one at the intersection of several roads. [C15: from Old French *quarrefour,* ultimately from Latin *quadrifurcus* having four forks]

car·rel *or* **car·rell** (ˈkærəl) *n.* a small individual study room, often in a library, in which a student or researcher can work undisturbed.

Car·rel (kəˈrɛl, ˈkærəl; *French* kaˈrɛl) *n.* **A·lex·is** (əˈlɛksɪs; *French* alɛkˈsi). 1873–1944, French surgeon and biologist, active in the U.S. (1905–39): developed a method of suturing blood vessels, making the transplantation of arteries and organs possible: Nobel prize for physiology or medicine 1912.

car·riage (ˈkærɪdʒ) *n.* **1.** *Brit.* a railway coach for passengers. **2.** the manner in which a person holds and moves his head and body; bearing. **3.** a four-wheeled horse-drawn vehicle for persons. **4.** the moving part of a machine that bears another part: *a typewriter carriage; a lathe carriage.* **5.** (ˈkærɪdʒ, ˈkærɪɪdʒ). **a.** the act of conveying; carrying. **b.** the charge made for conveying (esp. in the phrases **carriage forward,** when the charge is to be paid by the receiver, and **carriage paid**). [C14: from Old Northern French *cariage,* from *carier* to CARRY]

car·riage dog *n.* a former name for **dalmatian.**

car·riage trade *n.* wealthy patrons, as of a theatre, shop, restaurant, etc.

car·riage·way (ˈkærɪdʒˌweɪ) *n. Brit.* the part of a road along which traffic passes in a single line moving in one direction only: *a dual carriageway.*

car·rick bend (ˈkærɪk) *n.* a knot used for joining two ropes or cables together. [C19: perhaps variant of CARRACK]

car·rick bitt *n. Nautical.* either of a pair of strong posts used for supporting a windlass.

car·ri·er (ˈkærɪə) *n.* **1.** a person, thing, or organization employed to carry goods, passengers, etc. **2.** a mechanism by which something is carried or moved, such as a device for transmitting rotation from the faceplate of a lathe to the workpiece. **3.** *Pathol.* another name for **vector** (sense 2). **4.** *Pathol.* a person or animal that, without having any symptoms of a disease, is capable of transmitting it to others. **5.** Also called: **charge carrier.** *Physics.* an electron or hole that carries the charge in a conductor or semiconductor. **6.** Also called: **carrier wave.** *Radio.* a wave of fixed amplitude and frequency that is modulated in amplitude, frequency, or phase in order to carry a signal in radio transmission, etc. **7.** *Chem.* **a.** the inert solid on which a dyestuff is adsorbed in forming a lake. **b.** a substance, such as kieselguhr or asbestos, used to support a catalyst. **c.** an inactive substance containing a radioisotope used in radioactive tracing. **d.** an inert gas used to transport the sample through a gas chromatography column. **e.** a catalyst that effects the transfer of an atom or group from one molecule to another. **8.** See **aircraft carrier. 9.** a breed of domestic fancy pigeon having a large walnut-shaped wattle over the beak; a distinct variety of pigeon from the homing or carrier pigeon. See also **carrier pigeon. 10.** a U.S. name for **roof rack.**

car·ri·er bag *n. Brit.* a large paper or plastic bag for carrying shopping, etc.

car·ri·er pig·eon *n.* any homing pigeon, esp. one used for carrying messages.

car·ri·ole (ˈkærɪˌəʊl) *n.* a variant spelling of **cariole.**

car·ri·on ('kærɪən) *n.* **1.** dead and rotting flesh. **2.** (*modifier*) eating carrion: *carrion beetles.* **3.** something rotten or repulsive. [C13: from Anglo-French *caroine,* ultimately from Latin *carō* flesh]

car·ri·on crow *n.* a common predatory and scavenging European crow, *Corvus corone,* similar to the rook but having a pure black bill. See also **hooded crow.**

car·ri·on flow·er *n.* **1.** a liliaceous climbing plant, *Smilax herbacea* of E North America, whose small green flowers smell like decaying flesh. **2.** any of several other plants, esp. any of the genus *Stapelia,* whose flowers have an unpleasant odour.

Car·roll ('kærəl) *n.* **Lew·is.** pen name of *the Reverend Charles Lutwidge Dodgson.* 1832–98, English writer; an Oxford mathematics don who wrote *Alice's Adventures in Wonderland* (1865) and *Through the Looking-Glass* (1872) and the nonsense poem *The Hunting of the Snark* (1876).

car·ron·ade (ˌkærə'neɪd) *n.* an obsolete light cannon of short barrel and large bore. [C18: named after *Carron,* Scotland, where it was first cast; see -ADE]

car·ron oil ('kærən) *n.* an ointment of limewater and linseed oil, formerly used to treat burns. [C19: named after *Carron,* Scotland, where it was used among the ironworkers]

car·rot ('kærət) *n.* **1.** an umbelliferous plant, *Daucus carota sativa,* with finely divided leaves and flat clusters of small white flowers. See also **wild carrot. 2.** the long tapering orange root of this plant, eaten as a vegetable. **3.** something offered as a lure or incentive. [C16: from Old French *carotte,* from Late Latin *carōta,* from Greek *karōton;* perhaps related to Greek *karē* head]

car·rot·y ('kærətɪ) *adj.* **1.** of a reddish or yellowish-orange colour. **2.** having red hair.

car·rou·sel (ˌkærə'sɛl, -'zɛl) *n.* a variant spelling of **carousel.**

car·ry ('kærɪ) *vb.* **·ries, ·ry·ing, ·ried.** (*mainly tr.*) **1.** (*also intr.*) to take or bear (something) from one place to another: *to carry a baby in one's arms.* **2.** to transfer for consideration; take: *he carried his complaints to her superior.* **3.** to have on one's person: *he always carries a watch.* **4.** (*also intr.*) to be transmitted or serve as a medium for transmitting: *sound carries best over water.* **5.** to contain or be capable of containing: *the jug carries water.* **6.** to bear or be able to bear the weight, pressure, or responsibility of: *her efforts carry the whole production.* **7.** to have as an attribute or result: *this crime carries a heavy penalty.* **8.** to bring or communicate: *to carry news.* **9.** (*also intr.*) to be pregnant with (young): *she is carrying her third child.* **10.** to bear (the head, body, etc.) in a specified manner: *she carried her head high.* **11.** to conduct or bear (oneself) in a specified manner: *she carried herself well in a difficult situation.* **12.** to continue or extend: *the war was carried into enemy territory.* **13.** to cause to move or go: *desire for riches carried him to the city.* **14.** to influence, esp. by emotional appeal: *his words carried the crowd.* **15.** to secure the passage of (a bill, motion, etc.). **16.** to win (an election). **17.** to obtain victory for (a candidate or measure) in an election. **18.** *Chiefly U.S.* to win a plurality or majority of votes in (a district, legislative body, etc.): *the candidate carried 40 states.* **19.** to capture: *our troops carried the town.* **20.** (of communications media) to include as the content: *this newspaper carries no book reviews.* **21.** Also (esp. U.S.): **carry over.** *Book-keeping.* to transfer (an item) to another account, esp. to transfer to the following year's account instead of writing off against profit and loss: *to carry a loss.* **22.** *Maths.* to transfer (a number) from one column of figures to the next, as from units to tens in multiplication and addition. **23.** (of a shop, trader, etc.) to keep in stock: *to carry confectionery.* **24.** to support (a musical part or melody) against the other parts. **25.** to sustain (livestock): *this land will carry twelve ewes to the acre.* **26.** to maintain (livestock) in good health but without increasing their weight or obtaining any products from them. **27.** (*intr.*) (of a ball, projectile, etc.) to travel through the air or reach a specified point: *his first drive carried to the green.* **28.** *Sport, esp. golf.* (of a ball, etc.) to travel beyond: *the drive carried the trees.* **29.** (*intr.*) (of a gun) to have a range as specified: *this rifle carries for 1200 yards.* **30.** to retain contact with and pursue (a line of scent). **31.** (*intr.*) (of ground) to be in such a condition that scent lies well upon it. **32.** *Ice hockey.* to dribble. **33.** *Informal.* to imbibe (alcoholic drink) without showing ill effects. **34. carry all before (one).** to win unanimous support or approval for (oneself). **35. carry a tune.** to be able to sing in tune. **36. carry the can.** *Informal.* to take the responsibility for some misdemeanour, etc. **37. carry the day.** to win a contest or competition; succeed. ~*n., pl.* **·ries. 38.** the act of carrying. **39.** *U.S.* a portion of land over which a boat must be portaged. **40.** the range of a firearm or its projectile. **41.** the distance travelled by a ball, etc., esp. (in golf) the distance from where the ball is struck to where it first touches the ground. [C14 *carien,* from Old Northern French *carier* to move by vehicle, from *car,* from Latin *carrum* transport wagon; see CAR]

car·ry·all[1] ('kærɪˌɔːl) *n.* a light four-wheeled horse-drawn carriage usually designed to carry four passengers.

car·ry·all[2] ('kærɪˌɔːl) *n.* the usual U.S. name for a **holdall.**

car·ry a·way *vb.* (*tr., adv.*) **1.** to remove forcefully. **2.** (usually passive) to cause (a person) to lose self control. **3.** (usually passive) to delight or enrapture: *he was carried away by the music.*

car·ry back *Tax accounting.* ~*vb.* **1.** (*tr., adv.*) to apply (a legally permitted credit, esp. an operating loss) to the taxable income of previous years in order to ease the overall tax burden. ~*n.* **car·ry-back. 2.** an amount carried back.

car·ry·cot ('kærɪˌkɒt) *n.* a light cot with handles, similar to but smaller than the body of a pram and often attachable to an unsprung wheeled frame.

car·ry for·ward *vb.* (*tr., adv.*) **1.** *Book-keeping.* to transfer (a balance) to the next page, column, etc. **2.** *Tax accounting.* to apply (a legally permitted credit, esp. an operating loss) to the taxable income of following years to ease the overall tax burden. ~Also: **carry over.** ~*n.* **car·ry-for·ward. 3.** Also called: **carry-over.** *Tax accounting.* an amount carried forward.

car·ry·ing charge *n.* the opportunity cost of unproductive assets, such as goods stored in a warehouse.

car·ry·ing-on *n., pl.* **car·ry·ings-on.** *Informal.* **1.** unconventional or questionable behaviour. **2.** excited or flirtatious behaviour, esp. when regarded as foolish.

car·ry·ing place *n. Canadian.* another name for **portage.**

car·ry off *vb.* (*tr., adv.*) **1.** to remove forcefully. **2.** to win: *he carried off all the prizes.* **3.** to manage or handle (a situation) successfully: *he carried off the introductions well.* **4.** to cause to die: *he was carried off by pneumonia.*

car·ry on *vb.* (*adv.*) **1.** (*intr.*) to continue or persevere: *we must carry on in spite of our difficulties.* **2.** (*tr.*) to manage or conduct: *to carry on a business.* **3.** (*intr.;* often foll. by *with*) *Informal.* to have an affair. **4.** (*intr.*) *Informal.* to cause a fuss or commotion. ~*n.* **car·ry-on. 5.** *Informal, chiefly Brit.* a fuss or commotion.

car·ry out *vb.* (*tr., adv.*) **1.** to perform or cause to be implemented: *I wish he could afford to carry out his plan.* **2.** to bring to completion; accomplish.

car·ry o·ver *vb.* (*tr., adv.*) **1.** to postpone or defer. **2.** *Book-keeping, tax accounting.* another term for **carry forward. 3.** (on the London Stock Exchange) to postpone (payment or settlement) until the next account day. ~*n.* **car·ry-o·ver. 4.** something left over for future use, esp. goods to be sold. **5.** *Book-keeping.* a sum or balance carried forward. **6.** another name for **contango. 7.** *Tax accounting.* another name for **carry-forward.**

car·ry through *vb.* (*tr., adv.*) **1.** to bring to completion. **2.** to enable to endure (hardship, trouble, etc.); support.

carse (kɑːs) *n. Scot.* an area of low-lying land beside a river. [C14: of uncertain origin]

car·sick ('kɑːˌsɪk) *adj.* nauseated from riding in a car or other vehicle. —**'car·ˌsick·ness** *n.*

Car·son ('kɑːsᵊn) *n.* **1. Chris·to·pher,** called *Kit Carson.* 1809–68, U.S. frontiersman, trapper, scout, and Indian agent. **2. Ra·chel (Louise).** 1907–64, U.S. marine biologist and science writer; author of *Silent Spring* (1962).

Car·son Cit·y *n.* a city in W Nevada, capital of the state. Pop.: 15 468 (1970).

Car·stensz ('kɑːstənz) *n.* **Mount.** a former name of (Mount) **Djaja.**

cart (kɑːt) *n.* **1.** a heavy open vehicle, usually having two wheels and drawn by horses, used in farming and to transport goods. **2.** a light open horse-drawn vehicle having two wheels and springs, for business or pleasure. **3.** any small vehicle drawn or pushed by hand, such as a trolley. **4. in the cart. a.** in an unpleasant or awkward situation. **b.** in the lurch. **5. put the cart before the horse.** to reverse the usual or natural order of things. ~*vb.* **6.** (*usually tr.*) to use or draw a cart to convey (goods, etc.): *to cart groceries.* **7.** (*tr.*) to carry with effort; haul: *to cart wood home.* [C13: from Old Norse *kartr;* related to Old English *cræt* carriage, Old French *carete;* see CAR] —**'cart·a·ble** *adj.* —**'cart·er** *n.*

cart·age ('kɑːtɪdʒ) *n.* the process or cost of carting.

Car·ta·ge·na (ˌkɑːtə'dʒiːnə; *Spanish* ˌkarta'xena) *n.* **1.** a port in NW Colombia, on the Caribbean: centre for the Inquisition and the slave trade in the 16th century; chief oil port of Colombia. Pop.: 292 512 (1973). **2.** a port in SE Spain, on the Mediterranean: important since Carthaginian and Roman times for its minerals. Pop.: 146 904 (1970).

carte (kɑːt) *n.* a variant spelling of **quarte** (in fencing).

Carte (kɑːt) *n.* See (Richard) **D'Oyly Carte.**

carte blanche ('kɑːt 'blɑːntʃ; *French* kartə 'blɑ̃ːʃ) *n., pl.* **cartes blanches** ('kɑːts 'blɑːntʃ; *French* kartə 'blɑ̃ːʃ). **1.** complete discretion or authority: *the government gave their negotiator carte blanche.* **2.** *Cards.* a piquet hand containing no court cards: scoring ten points. [C18: from French: blank paper]

carte du jour ('kɑːt də 'ʒʊə, duː; *French* kart dy 'ʒuːr) *n., pl.* **cartes du jour** ('kɑːts də 'ʒʊə, duː; *French* kart dy 'ʒuːr). a menu listing dishes available on a particular day. [French, literally: card of the day]

car·tel (kɑː'tɛl) *n.* **1.** Also called: **trust.** a collusive international association of independent enterprises formed to monopolize production and distribution of a product or service, control prices, etc. **2.** *Politics.* an alliance of parties or interests to further common aims. [C20: from German *Kartell,* from French, from Italian *cartello* a written challenge, public notice, diminutive of *carta* CARD[1]]

car·tel·ize ('kɑːtəlaɪz) *vb.* to form or be formed into a cartel. —ˌ**car·tel·i·'za·tion** *n.*

Car·ter ('kɑːtə) *n.* **1. El·li·ot (Cook).** born 1908, U.S. composer. His works include the *Piano Sonata* (1945–46), three string quartets, and orchestral pieces: Pulitzer Prize 1960. **2. How·ard.** 1873–1939, English Egyptologist: discovered and excavated the tomb of the Pharaoh Tutankhamen. **3. James Earl,** known as *Jimmy.* born 1924, U.S. Democratic statesman; 39th president of the U.S. (1977–81).

Car·te·ret ('kɑːtərɪt) *n.* **John,** 1st Earl Granville. 1690–1763, British statesman, diplomat, and orator who led the opposition to Walpole (1730–42), after whose fall he became a leading minister as secretary of state (1742–44).

Car·te·si·an (kɑːˈtiːzɪən) *adj.* **1.** of or relating to the works of Descartes. **2.** of, relating to, or used in Descartes' mathematical system: *Cartesian coordinates.* ~*n.* **3.** a follower of the teachings and methods of Descartes. —**Car·ˈte·si·an·ism** *n.*
Car·te·si·an co·or·di·nates *pl. n.* a system of coordinates that defines the location of a point in space in terms of its perpendicular distance from each of a set of mutually perpendicular axes. Written (*x,y,z*) with reference to three axes.
cart·ful (ˈkɑːtˌfʊl) *n.* the amount a cart can hold.
Car·thage (ˈkɑːθɪdʒ) *n.* an ancient city state, on the N African coast near present-day Tunis. Founded about 800 B.C. by Phoenician traders, it grew into an empire dominating N Africa and the Mediterranean. Destroyed and then rebuilt by Rome, it was finally razed by the Arabs in 697 A.D. See also **Punic Wars.** —**Car·tha·gin·i·an** (ˌkɑːθəˈdʒɪnɪən) *adj., n.*
cart·horse (ˈkɑːtˌhɔːs) *n.* a large heavily built horse kept for pulling carts or carriages.
Car·thu·si·an (kɑːˈθjuːzɪən) *n. R.C. Church.* a member of an austere monastic order founded by Saint Bruno in 1084 near Grenoble, France. [C14: from Medieval Latin *Carthusianus,* from Latin *Carthusia* Chartreuse, near Grenoble]
Car·tier (*French* karˈtje) *n.* **Jacques** (ʒɑːk). 1491–1557, French navigator and explorer in Canada, who discovered the St. Lawrence River (1535).
Car·tier-Bres·son (*French* kartjebrɛˈsɔ̃) *n.* **Hen·ri** (ɑ̃ˈri). born 1908, French photographer.
car·ti·lage (ˈkɑːtɪlɪdʒ, ˈkɑːtlɪdʒ) *n.* a tough elastic tissue composing most of the embryonic skeleton of vertebrates. In the adults of higher vertebrates it is mostly converted into bone, remaining only on the articulating ends of bones, in the thorax, trachea, nose, and ears. Nontechnical name: **gristle.** [C16: from Latin *cartilāgō*] —**car·ti·lag·i·nous** (ˌkɑːtɪˈlædʒɪnəs) *adj.*
car·ti·lage bone *n.* any bone that develops within cartilage rather than in a fibrous tissue membrane. Compare **membrane bone.**
car·ti·lag·i·nous fish *n.* any fish of the class *Chondrichthyes,* including the sharks, skates, and rays, having a skeleton composed entirely of cartilage.
cart·load (ˈkɑːtˌləʊd) *n.* **1.** the amount a cart can hold. **2.** a quantity of rubble, ballast, etc., of between one quarter and one half of a cubic yard.
cart off, a·way, *or* **out** *vb.* (*tr., adv.*) *Slang.* to carry or remove brusquely or by force.
car·to·gram (ˈkɑːtəˌɡræm) *n.* a map showing statistical information in diagrammatic form. [C20: from French *cartogramme,* from *carte* map, CHART; see -GRAM]
car·tog·ra·phy *or* **char·tog·ra·phy** (kɑːˈtɒɡrəfɪ) *n.* the art, technique, or practice of compiling or drawing maps or charts. [C19: from French *cartographie,* from *carte* map, CHART] —**car·ˈtog·ra·pher** *or* **char·ˈtog·ra·pher** *n.* —**car·to·graph·ic** (ˌkɑːtəˈɡræfɪk), **ˌcar·to·ˈgraph·i·cal** *or* **ˌchar·to·ˈgraph·ic, ˌchar·to·ˈgraph·i·cal** *adj.* —**ˌcar·to·ˈgraph·i·cal·ly** *or* **ˌchar·to·ˈgraph·i·cal·ly** *adv.*
car·to·man·cy (ˈkɑːtəˌmænsɪ) *n.* the telling of fortunes with playing cards. [C19: from French *carte* card + -MANCY]
car·ton (ˈkɑːtᵊn) *n.* **1.** a cardboard box for containing goods. **2.** a container of waxed paper or plastic in which liquids, such as milk, are sold. **3.** *Shooting.* **a.** a white disc at the centre of a target. **b.** a shot that hits this disc. [C19: from French, from Italian *cartone* pasteboard, from *carta* CARD[1]]
car·toon (kɑːˈtuːn) *n.* **1.** a humorous or satirical drawing, esp. one in a newspaper or magazine, concerning a topical event. **2.** a sequence of drawings in a newspaper, magazine, etc., relating a comic or adventurous situation. U.S. name: **comic strip. 3.** See **animated cartoon. 4.** a full-size preparatory sketch for a fresco, tapestry, mosaic, etc., from which the final work is traced or copied. [C17: from Italian *cartone* pasteboard, sketch on stiff paper; see CARTON] —**car·ˈtoon·ist** *n.*
car·touche *or* **car·touch** (kɑːˈtuːʃ) *n.* **1.** a carved or cast ornamental tablet or panel in the form of a scroll, sometimes having an inscription. **2.** an oblong figure enclosing characters expressing royal or divine names in Egyptian hieroglyphics. **3.** the paper case holding combustible materials in certain fireworks. **4.** *Now rare.* a cartridge or a box for cartridges. [C17: from French: scroll, cartridge, from Italian *cartoccio,* from *carta* paper; see CARD[1]]
car·tridge (ˈkɑːtrɪdʒ) *n.* **1.** a cylindrical, usually metal casing containing an explosive charge and often a bullet, for a rifle or other small arms. **2.** a case for an explosive, such as a blasting charge. **3.** an electromechanical transducer in the pickup of a gramophone, usually either containing a piezoelectric crystal (**crystal cartridge**) or an electromagnet (**magnetic cartridge**). **4.** a container for magnetic tape that is inserted into a tape deck. It is about four times the size of a cassette. **5.** *Photog.* a light-tight film container that enables a camera to be loaded and unloaded in normal light. Also called: **cassette, magazine.** [C16: from earlier *cartage,* variant of CARTOUCHE (cartridge)]
car·tridge belt *n.* a belt with pockets for cartridge clips or loops for cartridges.
car·tridge clip *n.* a metallic container holding cartridges for an automatic firearm.
car·tridge pa·per *n.* **1.** an uncoated type of drawing or printing paper, usually made from bleached sulphate wood pulp with an addition of esparto grass. **2.** a heavy paper used in making cartridges or as drawing or printing paper.
car·tridge pen *n.* a pen having a removable ink reservoir that is replaced when empty.
cart track *n.* a rough track or road in a rural area. Also called: **cart road.**
car·tu·lar·y (ˈkɑːtjʊlərɪ) *or* **char·tu·lar·y** (ˈtʃɑːtjʊlərɪ) *n., pl.* **·lar·ies.** *Law.* **a.** a collection of charters or records, esp. relating to the title to an estate or monastery. **b.** any place where records are kept. [C16: from Medieval Latin *cartulārium,* from Latin *chartula* a little paper, from *charta* paper; see CARD[1]]
cart·wheel (ˈkɑːtˌwiːl) *n.* **1.** the wheel of a cart, usually having wooden spokes and metal tyres. **2.** an acrobatic movement in which the body makes a sideways revolution supported on the hands with arms and legs outstretched. **3.** *U.S. slang.* a large coin, esp. the silver dollar.
cart·wright (ˈkɑːtˌraɪt) *n.* a person who makes carts.
Cart·wright (ˈkɑːtˌraɪt) *n.* **Ed·mund.** 1743–1823, English clergyman, who invented the power loom.
car·un·cle (ˈkærəŋkᵊl, kəˈrʌŋ-) *n.* **1.** a fleshy outgrowth on the heads of certain birds, such as a cock's comb. **2.** an outgrowth near the hilum on the seeds of some plants. **3.** any small fleshy mass in or on the body, either natural or abnormal. [C17: from obsolete French *caruncule,* from Latin *caruncula* a small piece of flesh, from *carō* flesh] —**ca·run·cu·lar** (kəˈrʌŋkjʊlə) *or* **ca·ˈrun·cu·lous** *adj.* —**ca·run·cu·late** (kəˈrʌŋkjʊlɪt, -ˌleɪt) *or* **ca·ˈrun·cu·ˌlat·ed** *adj.*
Ca·ru·so (*Italian* kaˈruːzo) *n.* **En·ri·co** (enˈriːko). 1873–1921, an outstanding Italian operatic tenor; one of the first to make gramophone records.
carve (kɑːv) *vb.* **1.** (*tr.*) to cut or chip in order to form something: *to carve wood.* **2.** to decorate or form (something) by cutting or chipping: *to carve statues.* **3.** to slice (meat) into pieces: *to carve a turkey.* [Old English *ceorfan;* related to Old Frisian *kerva,* Middle High German *kerben* to notch] —**ˈcarv·er** *n.*
car·vel (ˈkɑːvᵊl) *n.* another word for **caravel.**
car·vel-built *adj.* (of a vessel) having a hull with planks made flush at the seams. Compare **clinker-built.**
carv·en (ˈkɑːvᵊn) *vb.* an archaic or literary past participle of **carve.**
carve out *vb.* (*tr., adv.*) *Informal.* to make or create (a career): *he carved out his own future.*
Car·ver (ˈkɑːvə) *n.* **George Wash·ing·ton.** ?1864–1943, U.S. agricultural chemist and botanist.
carve up *vb.* (*tr., adv.*) **1.** to cut (something) into pieces. **2.** to divide or dismember (a country, land, etc.). ~*n.* **carve-up. 3.** *Slang.* the distribution of something, as of booty.
carv·ing (ˈkɑːvɪŋ) *n.* a figure or design produced by carving stone, wood, etc.
carv·ing knife *n.* a long-bladed knife for carving cooked meat for serving.
Car·y (ˈkɛərɪ, ˈkærɪ) *n.* **(Arthur) Joyce (Lunel).** 1888–1957, English novelist; author of *Mister Johnson* (1939), *A House of Children* (1941), and *The Horse's Mouth* (1944).
car·y·at·id (ˌkærɪˈætɪd) *n., pl.* **·ids** *or* **·i·des** (-ɪˌdiːz). a column, used to support an entablature, in the form of a draped female figure. Compare **telamon.** [C16: from Latin *Caryātides,* from Greek *Karuatides* priestesses of Artemis at *Karuai* (Caryae), village in Laconia] —**ˌcar·y·ˈat·i·dal, ˌcar·y·ˌat·i·ˈde·an, ˌcar·y·ˈat·ic,** *or* **car·y·a·tid·ic** (ˌkærɪəˈtɪdɪk) *adj.*
car·y·o- *combining form.* variant of **karyo-.**
car·y·o·phyl·la·ceous (ˌkærɪəʊfɪˈleɪʃəs) *adj.* of, relating to, or belonging to the *Caryophyllaceae,* a family of flowering plants including the pink, carnation, sweet william, and chickweed. [C19: from New Latin *Caryophyllāceae,* from *Caryophyllus* former type genus, from Greek *karuophullon* clove tree, from *karuon* nut + *phullon* leaf]
car·y·op·sis (ˌkærɪˈɒpsɪs) *n., pl.* **·ses** (-siːz) *or* **·si·des** (-sɪˌdiːz). a dry seedlike fruit having the pericarp fused to the seed coat of the single seed: produced by the grasses. [C19: New Latin; see KARYO-, -OPSIS]
car·zey *or* **car·sey** (ˈkɑːzɪ) *n. Cockney slang.* a lavatory; toilet. [C19: from *casa, case* a brothel, from Italian *casa* a house]
ca·sa·ba *or* **cas·sa·ba** (kəˈsɑːbə) *n.* a kind of winter muskmelon having a yellow rind and sweet juicy flesh. [from *Kassaba,* former name of Turgutlu, Turkey]
Cas·a·blan·ca (ˌkæsəˈblæŋkə) *n.* a port in NW Morocco, on the Atlantic: largest city in the country; industrial centre. Pop.: 1 506 373 (1971).
Ca·sals (*Spanish* kaˈsals) *n.* **Pab·lo** (ˈpaβlo). 1876–1973, Spanish cellist and composer, noted for his interpretation of J. S. Bach's cello suites.
Cas·a·no·va (ˌkæsəˈnəʊvə) *n.* **1. Gio·van·ni Ja·co·po** (dʒoˈvanni ˈjaːkopo). 1725–98, Italian adventurer noted for his *Mémoires,* a vivid account of his sexual adventures and of contemporary society. **2.** any man noted for his amorous adventures; a rake.
Ca·sau·bon (kəˈsɔːbᵊn; *French* kazoˈbɔ̃) *n.* **I·sa·ac** (izaˈak). 1559–1614, French Protestant theologian and classical scholar.
cas·bah (ˈkæzbɑː) *n.* (*sometimes cap.*) a variant spelling of **kasbah.**
cas·ca·bel (ˈkæskəˌbɛl) *n.* **1.** a knoblike protrusion on the rear part of the breech of an obsolete muzzle-loading cannon. **2.** the rear part itself. [C17: from Spanish: small bell, rattle, of uncertain origin]
cas·cade (kæsˈkeɪd) *n.* **1.** a waterfall or series of waterfalls over rocks. **2.** something resembling this, such as folds of lace. **3. a.** a consecutive sequence of chemical or physical processes. **b.** (*as modifier*): *cascade liquefaction.* **4. a.** a set of electrical components connected in series. **b.** (*as modifier*): *a cascade amplifier.* **5.** the cumulative process responsible for

the formation of an electrical discharge, cosmic-ray shower, or Geiger counter avalanche in a gas. ~*vb.* **6.** (*intr.*) to flow or fall in or like a cascade. [C17: from French, from Italian *cascata,* from *cascare* to fall, ultimately from Latin *cadere* to fall]

Cas+cade Range *n.* a chain of mountains in the U.S.: a continuation of the Sierra Nevada range from N California through Oregon and Washington to British Columbia. Highest peak: Mount Rainier, 4392 m (14 408 ft.).

cas+ca+ra (kæs'kɑːrə) *n.* **1.** See **cascara sagrada. 2.** Also called: **cascara buckthorn, bearwood.** a shrub or small tree, *Rhamnus purshiana* of NW North America, whose bark is a source of cascara sagrada: family *Rhamnaceae.* [C19: from Spanish: bark, from *cascar* to break, from Vulgar Latin *quassicāre* (unattested) to shake violently, shatter, from Latin *quassāre* to dash to pieces]

cas+ca+ra sa+gra+da (sə'grɑːdə) *n.* the dried bark of the cascara buckthorn, used as a laxative and stimulant. Often shortened to **cascara.** [Spanish, literally: sacred bark]

cas+ca+ril+la (ˌkæskə'rɪlə) *n.* **1.** a West Indian euphorbiaceous shrub, *Croton eluteria,* whose bitter aromatic bark is used as a tonic. **2.** the bark of this shrub. [C17: from Spanish, diminutive of *cáscara* bark; see CASCARA]

case[1] (keɪs) *n.* **1.** a single instance, occurrence, or example of something. **2.** an instance of disease, injury, hardship, etc. **3.** a question or matter for discussion: *the case before the committee.* **4.** a specific condition or state of affairs; situation. **5.** a set of arguments supporting a particular action, cause, etc. **6. a.** a person attended or served by a doctor, social worker, solicitor, etc.; patient or client. **b.** (*as modifier*)*: a case study.* **7. a.** an action or suit at law or something that forms sufficient grounds for bringing an action: *he has a good case.* **b.** the evidence offered in court to support a claim. **8.** *Grammar.* **a.** a set of grammatical categories of nouns, pronouns, and adjectives, marked by inflection in some languages, indicating the relation of the noun, adjective, or pronoun to other words in the sentence. **b.** any one of these categories: *the nominative case.* **9.** *Informal.* an odd person; eccentric. **10.** *U.S. informal.* love or infatuation. **11. as the case may be.** according to the circumstances. **12. in any case.** (*adv.*) no matter what; anyhow: *we will go in any case.* **13. in case.** (*adv.*) **a.** in order to allow for eventualities. **b.** (*as conj.*) in order to allow for the possibility that: *take your coat in case it rains.* **14. in case of.** (*prep.*) in the event of. **15. in no case.** (*adv.*) under no circumstances: *in no case should you fight back.* [Old English *casus* (grammatical) case, associated also with Old French *cas* a happening; both from Latin *cāsus,* a befalling, occurrence, from *cadere* to fall]

case[2] (keɪs) *n.* **1. a.** a container, such as a box or chest. **b.** (*in combination*)*: suitcase; briefcase.* **2.** an outer cover or sheath, esp. for a watch. **3.** a receptacle and its contents: *a case of ammunition.* **4.** a pair or brace, esp. of pistols. **5.** *Architect.* another word for **casing** (sense 3). **6.** a completed cover ready to be fastened to a book to form its binding. **7.** *Printing.* a tray divided into many compartments in which a compositor keeps individual metal types of a particular size and style. Cases were originally used in pairs, one (the **upper case**) for capitals, the other (the **lower case**) for small letters. **8.** *Metallurgy.* the surface of a piece of steel that has been case-hardened. ~*vb.* (*tr.*) **9.** to put into or cover with a case: *to case the machinery.* **10.** *U.S. slang.* to inspect carefully (esp. a place to be robbed). [C13: from Old French *casse,* from Latin *capsa,* from *capere* to take, hold]

ca+se·ase ('keɪsɪˌeɪz) *n.* a proteolytic enzyme formed by certain bacteria that activates the solution of albumin and casein in milk and cheese. [C20: from CASE(IN) + -ASE]

ca+se·ate ('keɪsɪˌeɪt) *vb.* (*intr.*) *Pathol.* to undergo caseation. [C19: from Latin *cāseus* CHEESE]

ca+se·a·tion (ˌkeɪsɪ'eɪʃən) *n.* **1.** the formation of cheese from casein during the coagulation of milk. **2.** *Pathol.* the degeneration of dead tissue into a soft cheeselike mass.

case+bound ('keɪsˌbaʊnd) *adj.* another word for **hardback.**

ca+se·fy ('keɪsɪˌfaɪ) *vb.* **-fies, -fy+ing, -fied.** to make or become similar to cheese. [C20: from Latin *cāseus* CHEESE + -FY]

case-hard·en *vb.* (*tr.*) **1.** *Metallurgy.* to form a hard surface layer of high carbon content on (a steel component) by heating in a carburizing environment with subsequent quenching or heat treatment. **2.** to harden the spirit or disposition of; make callous: *experience had case-hardened the judge.*

case his+to+ry *n.* a record of a person's background, medical history, etc., esp. one used for determining medical treatment.

ca+sein ('keɪsɪɪn, -siːn) *n.* a phosphoprotein, precipitated from milk by the action of rennin, forming the basis of cheese: used in the manufacture of plastics and adhesives. Also called (U.S.): **paracasein.** [C19: from Latin *cāseus* cheese + -IN]

ca+se·in·o+gen (ˌkeɪsɪ'ɪnədʒən, keɪ'siːnə-) *n.* the principal protein of milk, converted to casein by rennin. Sometimes called (U.S.): **casein.**

case knife *n.* another name for **sheath knife.**

case law *n.* law established by following judicial decisions given in earlier cases. Compare **statute law.** See also **precedent** (sense 1).

case+mate ('keɪsˌmeɪt) *n.* an armoured compartment in a ship or fortification in which guns are mounted. [C16: from French, from Italian *casamatta,* perhaps from Greek *khasmata* apertures, plural of *khasma* CHASM] —**'case+ˌmat+ed** *adj.*

case+ment ('keɪsmənt) *n.* **1.** a window frame that is hinged on one side. **2.** a window containing frames hinged at the side or at the top or bottom. **3.** a poetic word for **window.** [C15: probably from Old Northern French *encassement* frame, from *encasser* to frame, encase, from *casse* framework, crate, CASE[2]]

Case·ment ('keɪsmənt) *n.* Sir **Rog·er (David).** 1864–1916, British diplomat and Irish nationalist: hanged by the British for treason in attempting to gain German support for Irish independence.

ca+se·ose ('keɪsɪˌəʊz, -ˌəʊs) *n.* a peptide produced by the peptic digestion of casein. [C20: from Latin *cāseus* cheese + -OSE[2]]

ca+se·ous ('keɪsɪəs) *adj.* of or like cheese. [C17: from Latin *cāseus* CHEESE]

ca+sern *or* **ca+serne** (kə'zɜːn) *n.* (formerly) a billet or accommodation for soldiers in a town. [C17: from French *caserne,* from Old Provençal *cazerna* group of four men, ultimately from Latin *quattuor* four]

Ca+ser+ta (*Italian* ka'sɛrta) *n.* a town in S Italy, in Campania: centre of Garibaldi's campaigns for the unification of Italy (1860); Allied headquarters in World War II. Pop.: 62 928 (1971).

case shot *n.* another name for **canister** (sense 2).

case+work ('keɪsˌwɜːk) *n.* social work based on close study of the personal histories and circumstances of individuals and families. —**'case+ˌwork·er** *n.*

case+worm ('keɪsˌwɜːm) *n.* another name for a **caddis worm.**

cash[1] (kæʃ) *n.* **1.** bank notes and coins, esp. in hand or readily available; money or ready money. **2.** immediate payment, in full or part, for goods or services (esp. in the phrase **cash down**). **3.** (*modifier*) of, for, or paid by cash: *a cash transaction.* ~*vb.* **4.** (*tr.*) to obtain or pay ready money for: *to cash a cheque.* ~See also **cash in, cash up.** [C16: from Old Italian *cassa* money box, from Latin *capsa* CASE[2]] —**'cash+a·ble** *adj.*

cash[2] (kæʃ) *n., pl.* **cash.** any of various Chinese, Indonesian, or Indian coins of low value. [C16: from Portuguese *caixa,* from Tamil *kāsu,* from Sanskrit *karsa* weight of gold or silver]

Cash (kæʃ) *n.* **John·ny.** born 1932, U.S. country-and-western singer, guitarist, and songwriter. His hits include *I walk the Line* (1956), *Folsom Prison Blues* (1957), and *A Boy named Sue* (1969).

cash-and-car·ry *adj., adv.* sold or operated on a basis of cash payment for merchandise that is not delivered but removed by the purchaser.

cash-book *n. Book-keeping.* a journal in which all cash or cheque receipts and disbursements are recorded.

cash crop *n.* a crop grown for sale rather than for subsistence.

cash desk *n.* a counter or till in a shop where purchases are paid for.

cash dis+count *n.* a discount granted to a purchaser who pays before a stipulated date.

cashed up *adj. Austral. informal.* having plenty of money.

cash+ew ('kæʃuː, kæ'ʃuː) *n.* **1.** a tropical American anacardiaceous evergreen tree, *Anacardium occidentale,* bearing kidney-shaped nuts that protrude from a fleshy receptacle. **2.** Also called: **cashew nut.** the nut of this tree, edible only when roasted. [C18: from Portuguese *cajú,* from Tupi *acajú*]

cash flow *n.* **1.** the movement of money into and out of a business. **2.** a prediction of such movement over a given period.

cash+ier[1] (kæ'ʃɪə) *n.* **1.** a person responsible for receiving payments for goods, services, etc., as in a shop. **2.** an employee of a bank responsible for receiving deposits, cashing cheques, and other financial transactions; bank clerk. **3.** any person responsible for handling cash or maintaining records of its receipt and disbursement. [C16: from Dutch *cassier* or French *caissier,* from *casse* money chest; see CASE[2]]

cash+ier[2] (kæ'ʃɪə) *vb.* (*tr.*) **1.** to dismiss with dishonour, esp. from the armed forces. **2.** *Rare.* to put away or discard; reject. [C16: from Middle Dutch *kasseren,* from Old French *casser,* from Latin *quassāre* to QUASH]

cash in *vb.* (*adv.*) **1.** (*tr.*) to give (something) in exchange, esp. for money. **2.** (*intr.;* often foll. by *on*) *Slang.* **a.** to profit (from). **b.** to take advantage (of). **3.** (*intr.*) *U.S.* a slang expression for **die**[1].

cash+mere ('kæʃmɪə) *n.* **1. a.** a fine soft wool from goats of the Kashmir area. **b.** cloth or knitted material made from this or similar wool. **c.** (*as modifier*)*: a cashmere sweater.* **2.** a variant spelling of **kashmir.**

Cash+mere (kæʃ'mɪə) *n.* a variant spelling of **Kashmir.**

cash on de+liv+er·y *n.* a service entailing cash payment to the carrier on delivery of merchandise.

cash ra+ti·o *n.* the ratio of cash on hand to total deposits that by law or custom commercial banks must maintain.

cash reg+is+ter *n.* a till with a keyboard that operates a mechanism for displaying and adding the amounts of cash received in individual sales.

cash up *vb.* (*intr., adv.*) *Brit.* (of cashiers, shopkeepers, etc.) to add up the money taken, esp. at the end of a working day.

cas·i·mere ('kæsɪˌmɪə) *n.* a variant spelling of **cassimere.**

cas+ing ('keɪsɪŋ) *n.* **1.** a protective case or cover. **2.** material for a case or cover. **3.** Also called: **case.** a frame containing a door, window, or staircase. **4.** the intestines of cattle, pigs, etc., or a synthetic substitute, used as a container for sausage meat. **5.** the outer cover of a pneumatic tyre. **6.** a pipe or tube used to line a hole or shaft.

ca+si+no (kə'siːnəʊ) *n., pl.* **+nos. 1.** a public building or room in which gaming takes place, esp. roulette and card games such as baccarat and chemin de fer. **2.** a variant spelling of **cassino.** [C18: from Italian, diminutive of *casa* house, from Latin]

cask (kɑːsk) *n.* **1.** a strong wooden barrel used mainly to hold alcoholic drink: *a wine cask.* **2.** any barrel. **3.** the quantity contained in a cask. [C15: from Spanish *casco* helmet, perhaps from *cascar* to break]

cas+ket ('kɑːskɪt) *n.* **1.** a small box or chest for valuables, esp.

jewels. **2.** a U.S. name for **coffin** (sense 1). [C15: probably from Old French *cassette* little box; see CASE[2]]

Cas+lon ('kæzlən) *n.* a style of type designed by William Caslon, English type-founder (1692–1766).

Cas+par ('kæspə, 'kæspɑː) *n.* (in Christian tradition) one of the Magi, the other two being Melchior and Balthazar.

Cas+par+i·an strip (kæ'spɛərɪən) *n. Botany.* a band of suberized material around the radial walls of endodermal cells: impervious to gases and liquids. [C20: named after Robert *Caspary,* 19th-century German botanist]

Cas+pi·an Sea ('kæspɪən) *n.* a salt lake between SE Europe and Asia: the largest inland sea in the world; fed mainly by the River Volga. Area: 394 299 sq. km (152 239 sq. miles).

casque (kæsk) *n. Zoology.* a helmet or a helmet-like process or structure, as on the bill of most hornbills. [C17: from French, from Spanish *casco;* see CASK] **—casqued** *adj.*

cas+sa+ba (kə'sɑːbə) *n.* a variant spelling of **casaba.**

Cas·san·dra (kə'sændrə) *n.* **1.** *Greek myth.* a daughter of Priam and Hecuba, endowed with the gift of prophecy but fated never to be believed. **2.** anyone whose prophecies of doom are unheeded.

cas+sa+reep ('kæsəˌriːp) *n.* the juice of the bitter cassava root, boiled down to a syrup and used as a flavouring, esp. in West Indian cookery. [C19: of Carib origin]

cas+sa+ta (kə'sɑːtə) *n.* an ice cream, originating in Italy, usually containing nuts and candied fruit. [from Italian]

cas+sa+tion (kæ'seɪʃən) *n. Chiefly law.* (esp. in France) annulment, as of a judicial decision by a higher court. [C15: from Old French, from Medieval Latin *cassātiō,* from Late Latin *cassāre* to cancel, from Latin *quassāre* to QUASH]

Cas·satt (kə'sæt) *n.* **Mar·y.** 1845–1926, U.S. impressionist painter.

cas+sa+va (kə'sɑːvə) *n.* **1.** Also called: **manioc.** any tropical euphorbiaceous plant of the genus *Manihot,* esp. the widely cultivated American species *M. esculenta* (or *utilissima*) (**bitter cassava**) and *M. dulcis* (**sweet cassava**). **2.** a starch derived from the root of this plant: an important food in the tropics and a source of tapioca. [C16: from Spanish *cazabe* cassava bread, from Taino *caçábi*]

Cas+se+grain+i·an tel+e·scope (ˌkæsɪ'greɪnɪən) *n.* an astronomical reflecting telescope in which incident light is reflected from a large concave mirror onto a smaller convex mirror and then back through a hole in the concave mirror to form the image. [C19: named after N. *Cassegrain,* 17th-century French scientist who invented it]

Cas+sel (*German* 'kasᵊl) *n.* a variant spelling of **Kassel.**

cas+se+role ('kæsəˌrəʊl) *n.* **1.** a covered dish of earthenware, glass, etc., in which food is cooked and served. **2.** any food cooked and served in such a dish: *chicken casserole.* ~*vb.* **3.** to cook or be cooked in a casserole. [C18: from French, from Old French *casse* ladle, pan for dripping, from Old Provençal *cassa,* from Late Latin *cattia* dipper, from Greek *kuathion,* diminutive of *kuathos* cup]

cas+sette (kæ'sɛt) *n.* **1. a.** a plastic container for magnetic tape, inserted into a tape deck to be played or used. **b.** (*as modifier*): *a cassette recorder.* **2.** *Photog.* another term for **cartridge** (sense 5). **3.** *Films.* a container for film used to facilitate the loading of a camera or projector, esp. when the film is used in the form of a loop. [C18: from French: little box; see CASE[2]]

cas+si·a ('kæsɪə) *n.* **1.** any plant of the mainly tropical caesalpiniaceous genus *Cassia,* esp. *C. fistula,* whose pods yield **cassia pulp,** a mild laxative. See also **senna. 2.** a lauraceous tree, *Cinnamomum cassia,* of tropical Asia. **3. cassia bark.** the cinnamon-like bark of this tree, used as a spice. [Old English, from Latin *casia,* from Greek *kasia,* of Semitic origin; related to Hebrew *qesīʻāh* cassia]

cas+si+mere *or* **cas·i·mere** ('kæsɪˌmɪə) *n.* a woollen suiting cloth of plain or twill weave. [C18: variant of *cashmere,* from KASHMIR]

cas+si+no *or* **ca+si+no** (kə'siːnəʊ) *n.* a card game for two to four players in which players pair cards from their hands with others exposed on the table.

Cas+si+no (*Italian* kas'siːno) *n.* a town in central Italy, in Latium at the foot of Monte Cassino: an ancient Volscian (and later Roman) town and citadel. Pop.: 24 796 (1971). Latin name: **Casinum.**

Cas·si·o·do·rus (ˌkæsɪəʊ'dɔːrəs) *n.* **Fla·vi·us Mag·nus Au·re·li·us** ('fleɪvɪəs 'mægnəs ɔː'riːlɪəs). ?490–?585 A.D., Roman statesman, writer, and monk; author of *Variae,* a collection of official documents written for the Ostrogoths.

Cas·si·o·pe·ia[1] (ˌkæsɪə'piːə) *n. Greek myth.* the wife of Cepheus and mother of Andromeda.

Cas+si·o+pe·ia[2] (ˌkæsɪə'piːə) *n. Latin genitive* **Cas+si·o+pe·iae** (ˌkæsɪə'piːiː). a very conspicuous W-shaped constellation near the Pole star. **Cassiopeia A** is a very strong radio and x-ray source, identified as faint nebulous filaments that are the remains of the supernova observed in 1572. **—ˌCas+si·o+'pe·ian** *adj.*

Cas·si·rer (*German* ka'siːrər) *n.* **Ernst** (ɛrnst). 1874–1945, German neo-Kantian philosopher. *The Philosophy of Symbolic Forms* (1923–29) analyses the symbols that underlie all manifestations, including myths and language, of human culture.

cas+sis (kɑː'siːs) *n.* a blackcurrant cordial. [C19: from French]

cas+sit+er+ite (kə'sɪtəˌraɪt) *n.* a hard heavy brownish-black mineral consisting of a tin oxide in tetragonal crystalline form. It occurs in veins and alluvial deposits, esp. in Malaysia, and is the chief ore of tin. Formula: SnO_2. Also called: **tinstone.** [C19: from Greek *kassiteros* tin]

Cas·si·us Lon·gi·nus ('kæsɪəs lɒn'dʒaɪnəs) *n.* **Gai·us** ('gaɪəs). died 42 B.C., Roman general: led the conspiracy against Julius Caesar (44); defeated at Philippi by Anthony (42).

cas+sock ('kæsək) *n. Ecclesiast.* an ankle-length garment, usually black, worn by priests and choristers. [C16: from Old French *casaque,* from Italian *casacca* a long coat, of uncertain origin] **—'cas+socked** *adj.*

cas+sou+let (ˌkæsə'leɪ) *n.* a stew originating from France, made from haricot beans and goose, duck, pork, etc. [French, related to *casse* saucepan, bowl]

cas+so+war·y ('kæsəˌwɛərɪ) *n., pl.* **+war·ies.** any large flightless bird of the genus *Casuarius,* inhabiting forests in NE Australia, New Guinea, and adjacent islands, having a horny head crest, black plumage, and brightly coloured neck and wattles: order *Casuariiformes* (see **ratite**). [C17: from Malay *kĕsuari*]

cast (kɑːst) *vb.* **casts, cast+ing, cast.** (*mainly tr.*) **1.** to throw or expel with violence or force. **2.** to throw off or away: *she cast her clothes to the ground.* **3.** to reject or dismiss: *he cast the idea from his mind.* **4.** to shed or drop: *the snake cast its skin; the horse cast a shoe; the ship cast anchor.* **5.** to cause to appear: *to cast a shadow.* **6.** to express (doubts, suspicions, etc.) or cause (them) to be felt. **7.** to direct (a glance, attention, etc.): *cast your eye over this.* **8.** to place, esp. in a violent manner: *he was cast into prison.* **9.** (*also intr.*) *Angling.* to throw (a baited line) into the water. **10.** to draw or choose (lots). **11.** to give or deposit (a vote). **12.** to select (actors) to play parts in (a play, film, etc.). **13. a.** to shape (molten metal, glass, etc.) by pouring or pressing it into a mould. **b.** to make (an object) by such a process. **14.** (*also intr.;* often foll. by *up*) to compute (figures or a total). **15.** to predict: *the old woman cast my fortune.* **16.** *Astrology.* to draw on (a horoscope) details concerning the positions of the planets in the signs of the zodiac at a particular time for interpretation in terms of human characteristics, behaviour, etc. **17.** to contrive (esp. in the phrase **cast a spell**). **18.** to formulate: *he cast his work in the form of a chart.* **19.** (*also intr.*) to twist or cause to twist. **20.** (*also intr.*) *Nautical.* to turn the head of (a sailing vessel) or (of a sailing vessel) to be turned away from the wind in getting under way. **21.** *Hunting.* to direct (a pack of hounds) over (ground) where their quarry may recently have passed. **22.** (*intr.*) (of birds of prey) to eject from the crop and bill a pellet consisting of the indigestible parts of birds or animals previously eaten. **23.** *Falconry.* to hold the body of a hawk between the hands so as to perform some operation upon it. **24.** *Printing.* to stereotype or electrotype. **25. cast in one's lot with.** to share in the activities or fortunes of (someone else). ~*n.* **26.** the act of casting or throwing. **27. a.** Also called: **casting.** something that is shed, dropped, or egested, such as the coil of earth left by an earthworm. **b.** another name for **pellet** (sense 4). **28.** an object that is thrown. **29.** the distance an object is or may be thrown. **30. a.** a throw at dice. **b.** the resulting number shown. **31.** *Angling.* **a.** the act or an instance of casting a line. **b.** another name for **trace**[2] (sense 2). **32. a.** the actors in a play collectively. **b.** (*as modifier*): *a cast list.* **33. a.** an object made of metal, glass, etc., that has been shaped in a molten state by being poured or pressed into a mould. **b.** the mould used to shape such an object. **34.** form or appearance. **35.** sort, kind, or style. **36.** a fixed twist or defect, esp. in the eye. **37.** a distortion of shape. **38.** *Surgery.* a rigid encircling casing, often made of plaster of Paris, for immobilizing broken bones while they heal. **39.** *Pathol.* a mass of fatty, waxy, cellular, or other material formed in a diseased body cavity, passage, etc. **40.** the act of casting a pack of hounds. **41.** *Falconry.* a pair of falcons working in combination to pursue the same quarry. **42.** *Archery.* the speed imparted to an arrow by a particular bow. **43.** a slight tinge or trace, as of colour. **44.** a computation or calculation. **45.** a forecast or conjecture. **46.** fortune or stroke of fate. **47.** *Palaeontol.* a mineral representation of an organic object, esp. a lump of mineral that indicates the shape and internal structure of a shell. ~See also **cast about, castaway, cast back, cast down, cast-off, cast on.** [C13: from Old Norse *kasta*]

cast a·bout *vb.* (*intr., adv.*) to make a mental or visual search: *to cast about for an idea for a book.*

Cas+ta+li·a (kæ'steɪlɪə) *n.* a spring on Mount Parnassus: in ancient Greece sacred to Apollo and the Muses and believed to be a source of inspiration. **—Cas+'ta+li·an** *adj.*

cas+ta+nets (ˌkæstə'nɛts) *pl. n.* curved pieces of hollow wood, usually held between the fingers and thumb and made to click together: used esp. by Spanish dancers. [C17 *castanet,* from Spanish *castañeta,* diminutive of *castaña* CHESTNUT]

cast+a·way ('kɑːstəˌweɪ) *n.* **1.** a person who has been shipwrecked. **2.** something thrown off or away; castoff. ~*adj.* (*prenominal*) **3.** shipwrecked or put adrift. **4.** thrown away or rejected. ~*vb.* **cast a·way. 5.** (*tr., adv.; often passive*) to cause (a ship, person, etc.) to be shipwrecked or abandoned.

cast back *vb.* (*adv.*) to turn (the mind) to the past.

cast down *vb.* (*tr., adv.*) to make (a person) discouraged or dejected.

caste (kɑːst) *n.* **1. a.** any of the four major hereditary classes, namely the **Brahman, Kshatriya, Vaisya,** and **Sudra,** into which Hindu society is divided. **b.** Also called: **caste system.** the system or basis of such classes. **c.** the social position or rank conferred by this system. **2.** any social class or system based on such distinctions as heredity, rank, wealth, profession, etc. **3.** the position conferred by such a system. **4. lose caste.** *Informal.* to lose one's social position. **5.** *Entomol.* any of various types of specialized individual, such as the worker, in social insects (hive bees, ants, etc.). [C16: from Portuguese *casta* race, breed, ancestry, from *casto* pure, chaste, from Latin *castus*]

Cas·tel·lam·ma·re di Sta·bia (*Italian* ˌkastellamˈmaːre diː ˈstabja) *n.* a port and resort in SW Italy, in Campania on the Bay of Naples: site of the Roman resort of Stabiae, which was destroyed by the eruption of Vesuvius in 79 A.D. Pop.: 68 629 (1971).

cas·tel·lan (ˈkæstɪlən) *n. Rare.* a keeper or governor of a castle. Also called: **chatelain.** [C14: from Latin *castellānus*, from *castellum* CASTLE]

cas·tel·la·ny (ˈkæstɪˌleɪnɪ) *n., pl.* **·nies.** *Rare.* **1.** the office, rank, or jurisdiction of a castellan. **2.** land belonging to a castle.

cas·tel·lat·ed (ˈkæstɪˌleɪtɪd) *adj.* **1.** having turrets and battlements, like a castle. **2.** having indentations similar to battlements: *a castellated nut; a castellated filament.* [C17: from Medieval Latin *castellātus*, from *castellāre* to fortify as a CASTLE] —ˌ**cas·tel·ˈla·tion** *n.*

Cas·tel·lón de la Pla·na (*Spanish* ˌkasteˈʎon ðe la ˈplana) *n.* a port in E Spain. Pop.: 93 968 (1970).

cast·er (ˈkɑːstə) *n.* **1.** a person or thing that casts. **2.** a bottle with a perforated top for sprinkling sugar, etc., or a stand containing such bottles. **3.** a small swivelling wheel attached to each leg of a piece of furniture to facilitate movement. Also called (for senses 2, 3): **castor.**

cas·ter sug·ar (ˈkɑːstə) *n.* finely ground white sugar.

cas·ti·gate (ˈkæstɪˌgeɪt) *vb.* (*tr.*) to rebuke or criticize in a severe manner; chastise. [C17: from Latin *castīgāre* to correct, punish, from *castum* pure + *agere* to compel (to be)] —ˌ**cas·ti·ˈga·tion** *n.* —ˈ**cas·ti·ˌga·tor** *n.* —ˌ**cas·ti·ˈga·to·ry** *adj.*

Cas·ti·glio·ne (ˌkæstɪlˈjəʊnɪ) *n.* Count **Bal·das·sa·re** (ˌbaldasˈsaːre). 1478–1529, Italian diplomat and writer, noted particularly for his dialogue on ideal courtly life, *Il Libro del Cortegiano* (The Courtier) (1528).

Cas·tile (kæˈstiːl) *or* **Cas·ti·lla** (*Spanish* kasˈtiʎa) *n.* a former kingdom comprising most of modern Spain: originally part of León, it became an independent kingdom in the 10th century and united with Aragon (1469), the first step in the formation of the Spanish state.

Cas·tile soap *n.* a hard soap made from olive oil and sodium hydroxide.

Cas·til·ian (kæˈstɪljən) *n.* **1.** the Spanish dialect of Castile; the standard form of European Spanish. **2.** a native or inhabitant of Castile. ~*adj.* **3.** denoting, relating to, or characteristic of Castile, its inhabitants, or the standard form of European Spanish.

Cas·ti·lla la Vie·ja (kasˈtiʎa la ˈbjexa) *n.* the Spanish name for **Old Castile.**

cast·ing (ˈkɑːstɪŋ) *n.* **1.** an object or figure that has been cast, esp. in metal from a mould. **2.** the process of transferring molten steel to a mould. **3.** the choosing of actors for a production. **4.** *Hunting.* the act of directing a pack of hounds over ground where their quarry may recently have passed so that they can quest for, discover, or recapture its scent. **5.** *Zoology.* another word for **cast** (sense 27) or **pellet** (sense 4).

cast·ing vote *n.* the deciding vote used by the presiding officer of an assembly when votes cast on both sides are equal in number.

cast i·ron *n.* **1.** iron containing so much carbon (1.7 to 4.5 per cent) that it cannot be wrought and must be cast into shape. ~*adj.* **cast-i·ron. 2.** made of cast iron. **3.** rigid, strong, or unyielding: *a cast-iron decision.*

cas·tle (ˈkɑːsᵊl) *n.* **1.** a fortified building or set of buildings, usually permanently garrisoned, as in medieval Europe. **2.** any fortified place or structure. **3.** a large magnificent house, esp. when the present or former home of a nobleman or prince. **4.** the citadel and strongest part of the fortifications of a medieval town. **5.** *Chess.* another name for **rook**[2]. ~*vb.* **6.** *Chess.* to move (the king) two squares laterally on the first rank and place the nearest rook on the square passed over by the king. [C11: from Latin *castellum*, diminutive of *castrum* fort]

cas·tled (ˈkɑːsᵊld) *adj.* **1.** like a castle in construction; castellated: *a castled mansion.* **2.** (of an area) having many castles.

Cas·tle·ford (ˈkɑːsᵊlfəd) *n.* a town in N England, in West Yorkshire on the River Aire. Pop.: 38 220 (1971).

cas·tle in the air *or* **in Spain** *n.* a hope or desire unlikely to be realized; daydream.

cas·tle nut *n.* a hexagonal nut with six slots in the head, two of which take a locking pin to hold it firmly in position.

Cas·tle·reagh (ˈkɑːsᵊlˌreɪ) *n.* **Vis·count.** title of *Robert Stewart,* Marquis of Londonderry. 1769–1822, British statesman: as foreign secretary (1812–22) led the Grand Alliance against Napoleon and attended the Congress of Vienna (1815).

cast-off *adj.* **1.** (*prenominal*) thrown away; abandoned: *cast-off shoes.* ~*n.* **cast·off. 2.** a person or thing that has been discarded or abandoned. **3.** *Printing.* an estimate of the amount of space that a piece of copy will occupy when printed in a particular size and style of type. ~*vb.* **cast off.** (*adv.*) **4.** to remove (mooring lines) that hold (a vessel) to a dock. **5.** to knot (a row of stitches, esp. the final row) in finishing off knitted or woven material. **6.** *Printing.* to estimate the amount of space that will be taken up by (a book, piece of copy, etc.) when it is printed in a particular size and style of type.

cast on *vb.* (*adv.*) to form (the first row of stitches) in knitting and weaving.

cas·tor[1] (ˈkɑːstə) *n.* **1.** the brownish aromatic secretion of the anal glands of a beaver, used in perfumery and medicine. **2.** the fur of the beaver. **3.** a hat made of beaver or similar fur. **4.** a less common name for **beaver**[1] (sense 1). [C14: from Latin, from Greek *kastōr* beaver]

cas·tor[2] (ˈkɑːstə) *n.* **1.** a variant spelling of **caster** (senses 2, 3). ~*adj.* **2.** *Austral. slang.* good; fine.

Cas·tor (ˈkɑːstə) *n.* **1.** the second brightest star, Alpha Geminorum, in the constellation Gemini: a multiple star consisting of six components lying close to the star Pollux. Distance: 46 light years. **2.** *Classical myth.* See **Castor and Pollux.**

Cas·tor and Pol·lux *n. Classical myth.* the twin sons of Leda: Pollux was fathered by Zeus, Castor by the mortal Tyndareus. After Castor's death, Pollux spent half his days with his half-brother in Hades and half with the gods in Olympus.

cas·tor bean *n. U.S.* **1.** another name for **castor-oil plant. 2.** the seed of this plant.

cas·tor oil *n.* a colourless or yellow glutinous oil obtained from the seeds of the castor-oil plant and used as a fine lubricant and as a cathartic.

cas·tor-oil plant *n.* a tall euphorbiaceous Indian plant, *Ricinus communis*, cultivated in tropical regions for ornament and for its poisonous seeds, from which castor oil is extracted. Also called (U.S.): **castor bean.**

cas·trate (kæˈstreɪt) *vb.* (*tr.*) **1.** to remove the testicles of; emasculate; geld. **2.** to deprive of vigour, masculinity, etc. **3.** to remove the ovaries of; spay. **4.** to expurgate or censor a book, play, etc. [C17: from Latin *castrāre* to emasculate, geld] —**cas·ˈtra·tion** *n.* —**cas·ˈtra·tor** *n.*

cas·tra·tion com·plex *n. Psychoanal.* an unconscious fear of having one's genitals removed. It is an integral part of the Oedipus complex.

cas·tra·to (kæˈstrɑːtəʊ) *n., pl.* **·ti** (-tɪ) *or* **·tos.** (in 17th- and 18th-century opera, etc.) a male singer whose testicles were removed before puberty, allowing the retention of a soprano or alto voice. [C18: from Italian, from Latin *castrātus* castrated]

Cas·tries (kæsˈtriːs) *n.* a port in the West Indies, in the Windward Islands: capital of the British Associated State of St. Lucia. Pop.: 45 000 (1970).

Cas·tro (ˈkæstrəʊ) *n.* **Fi·del** (fiˈdel). full name *Fidel Castro Ruz.* born 1927, Cuban statesman: prime minister since 1959, when he led the Communist overthrow of Batista. —ˈ**Cas·tro·ism** *n.* —ˈ**Cas·tro·ist** *adj., n.*

Ca·strop-Rau·xel *or* **Ka·strop-Rau·xel** (*German* ˈkastrɔp ˈraʊksᵊl) *n.* an industrial city in W West Germany, in North Rhine-Westphalia. Pop.: 83 900 (1970).

cast steel *n.* steel containing varying amounts of carbon, manganese, phosphorus, silicon, and sulphur that is cast into shape rather than wrought.

cas·u·al (ˈkæʒjʊəl) *adj.* **1.** happening by accident or chance: *a casual meeting.* **2.** offhand; not premeditated: *a casual remark.* **3.** shallow or superficial: *a casual affair.* **4.** being or seeming unconcerned or apathetic: *he assumed a casual attitude.* **5.** (esp. of dress) for informal wear: *a casual coat.* **6.** occasional or irregular; part-time: *casual visits; a casual labourer.* ~*n.* **7.** (*usually pl.*) an informal article of clothing or footwear. **8.** a part-time or occasional worker. [C14: from Late Latin *cāsuālis* happening by chance, from Latin *cāsus* event, from *cadere* to fall; see CASE[1]] —ˈ**cas·u·al·ly** *adv.* —ˈ**cas·u·al·ness** *n.*

cas·u·al·ty (ˈkæʒjʊəltɪ) *n., pl.* **·ties. 1.** a serviceman who is killed, wounded, captured, or missing as a result of enemy action. **2.** a person who is injured or killed in an accident. **3.** anything that is lost, damaged, or destroyed as the result of an accident, etc.

cas·u·a·ri·na (ˌkæsjʊəˈraɪnə) *n.* any tree of the genus *Casuarina*, of Australia and the East Indies, having jointed leafless branches: family *Casuarinaceae.* See also **beefwood, she-oak.** [C19: from New Latin, from Malay *kĕsuari* CASSOWARY, referring to the resemblance of the branches to the feathers of the cassowary]

cas·u·ist (ˈkæzjʊɪst) *n.* **1.** a person, esp. a theologian, who attempts to resolve moral dilemmas by the application of general rules. **2.** a person who is oversubtle in his analysis of fine distinctions; sophist. [C17: from French *casuiste*, from Spanish *casuista*, from Latin *cāsus* CASE[1]] —ˌ**cas·u·ˈis·tic** *or* ˌ**cas·u·ˈis·ti·cal** *adj.* —ˌ**cas·u·ˈis·ti·cal·ly** *adv.*

cas·u·ist·ry (ˈkæzjʊɪstrɪ) *n., pl.* **·ries. 1.** *Philosophy.* the application of general ethical principles to particular moral problems, esp. where conflicting obligations arise. **2.** reasoning that is specious, misleading, or oversubtle.

ca·sus bel·li *Latin.* (ˈkɑːsʊs ˈbɛliː) *n., pl.* ***ca·sus bel·li*** (ˈkɑːsʊs ˈbɛliː). **1.** an event or act used to justify a war. **2.** the immediate cause of a quarrel. [literally: occasion of war]

cat[1] (kæt) *n.* **1.** Also called: **domestic cat.** a small domesticated feline mammal, *Felis catus* (or *domesticus*), having thick soft fur and occurring in many breeds in which the colour of the fur varies greatly: kept as a pet or to catch rats and mice. **2.** Also called: **big cat.** any of the larger felines, such as a lion or tiger. 3. any wild feline mammal of the genus *Felis*, such as the lynx or serval, resembling the domestic cat. **4.** *Informal.* a woman who gossips maliciously. **5.** *Slang.* a man; guy. **6.** *Nautical.* a heavy tackle for hoisting an anchor to the cathead. **7.** a short sharp-ended piece of wood used in the game of tipcat. **8.** short for **catboat. 9.** *Informal.* short for **caterpillar** (the vehicle). **10.** short for **cat-o'-nine-tails. 11. fight like Kilkenny cats.** to fight until both parties are destroyed. **12. let the cat out of the bag.** to disclose a secret, often by mistake. **13. like a cat on a hot tin roof** *or* **on hot bricks.** in an uneasy or agitated state. **14. like cat and dog.** quarrelling savagely. **15. look like something the cat brought in.** to appear dishevelled or bedraggled. **16. not a cat in hell's chance.** no chance at all. **17.**

not have room to swing a cat. to have very little space. **18. put, set, etc., the cat among the pigeons.** to introduce some violently disturbing new element. **19. play cat and mouse.** to play with a person or animal in a cruel or teasing way, esp. before a final act of cruelty or unkindness. **20. rain cats and dogs.** to rain very heavily. ~*vb.* **cats, cat+ting, cat+ted. 21.** (*tr.*) to flog with a cat-o'-nine-tails. **22.** (*tr.*) *Nautical.* to hoist (an anchor) to the cathead. **23.** (*intr.*) a slang word for **vomit.** [Old English *catte,* from Latin *cattus;* related to Old Norse *köttr,* Old High German *kazza,* Old French *chat,* Russian *kot*] —**'cat+ˌlike** *adj.* —**'cat+tish** *adj.*

cat² (kæt) *n. Informal.* short for **catamaran** (sense 1).

C.A.T. (in Britain) *abbrev. for* College of Advanced Technology.

cat. *abbrev. for:* **1.** catalogue. **2.** catamaran. **3.** *Ecclesiast.* catechism.

cat·a-, kat·a-, *before an aspirate* **cath-,** *or before a vowel* **cat-** *prefix.* **1.** down; downwards; lower in position: *catadromous; cataphyll.* **2.** indicating reversal, opposition, degeneration, etc.: *cataplasia; catatonia.* [from Greek *kata-,* from *kata.* In compound words borrowed from Greek, *kata-* means: down (*catabolism*), away, off (*catalectic*), against (*category*), according to (*catholic*), and thoroughly (*catalogue*)]

ca+tab·a+sis (kə'tæbəsɪs) *n., pl.* **+ses** (-ˌsi:z). **1.** a descent or downward movement. **2.** the decline of a disease. —**cat·a+bat+ic** (ˌkætɪ'bætɪk) *adj.*

ca+tab·o+lism *or* **ka+tab·o+lism** (kə'tæbəˌlɪzəm) *n.* a metabolic process in which complex molecules are broken down into simple ones with the release of energy; destructive metabolism. Compare **anabolism.** [C19 *katabolism,* from Greek *katabolē* a throwing down, from *kataballein,* from *kata-* down + *ballein* to throw] —**cat·a+bol+ic** *or* **kat·a+bol+ic** (ˌkætə'bɒlɪk) *adj.* —**ˌcat·a+'bol·i+cal+ly** *or* **ˌkat·a+'bol·i+cal+ly** *adv.*

ca+tab·o+lite (kə'tæbəˌlaɪt) *n.* a substance produced as a result of catabolism.

cat·a+caus+tic (ˌkætə'kɔ:stɪk, -'kɒs-) *Physics.* ~*adj.* **1.** (of a caustic curve or surface) formed by reflected light rays. Compare **diacaustic.** ~*n.* **2.** a catacaustic curve or surface.

cat·a+chre+sis (ˌkætə'kri:sɪs) *n.* the incorrect use of words, as *luxuriant* for *luxurious.* [C16: from Latin, from Greek *katakhrēsis* a misusing, from *katakhrēsthai,* from *khrēsthai* to use] —**cat·a+chres+tic** (ˌkætə'krɛstɪk) *or* **ˌcat·a+'chres+ti+cal** *adj.* —**ˌcat·a+'chres+ti+cal+ly** *adv.*

cat·a+cla+sis (ˌkætə'kleɪsɪs) *n., pl.* **+ses** (-si:z). *n. Geology.* the deformation of rocks by crushing and shearing. [C19: New Latin, from Greek, from CATA + *klasis* a breaking] —**cat·a+clas+tic** (ˌkætə'klæstɪk) *adj.*

cat·a+cli+nal (ˌkætə'klaɪnᵊl) *adj.* (of streams, valleys, etc.) running in the direction of the dip of the surrounding rock strata.

cat·a+clysm ('kætəˌklɪzəm) *n.* **1.** a violent upheaval, esp. of a political, military, or social nature. **2.** a disastrous flood; deluge. **3.** *Geology.* another name for **catastrophe** (sense 4). [C17: via French from Latin, from Greek *kataklusmos* deluge, from *katakluzein* to flood, from *kluzein* to wash] —**ˌcat·a+'clys+mic** *or* **ˌcat·a+'clys+mal** *adj.* —**ˌcat·a+'clys+mi+cal+ly** *adv.*

cat·a+comb ('kætəˌkəʊm, -ˌku:m) *n.* **1.** (*usually pl.*) an underground burial place, esp. the galleries at Rome, consisting of tunnels with vaults or niches leading off them for tombs. **2.** a series of underground tunnels or caves. [Old English *catacumbe,* from Late Latin *catacumbas* (singular), name of the cemetery under the Basilica of St. Sebastian, near Rome; origin unknown]

ca+tad+ro+mous (kə'tædrəməs) *adj.* (of fishes such as the eel) migrating down rivers to the sea in order to breed. Compare **anadromous.** [C19: from Greek *katadromos,* from *kata-* down + *dromos,* from *dremein* to run]

cat·a+falque ('kætəˌfælk) *n.* a temporary raised platform on which a body lies in state before or during a funeral. [C17: from French, from Italian *catafalco,* of uncertain origin; compare SCAFFOLD]

Cat·a+lan ('kætəˌlæn, -lən) *n.* **1.** a language of Catalonia, quite closely related to Spanish and Provençal, belonging to the Romance group of the Indo-European family. **2.** a native or inhabitant of Catalonia. ~*adj.* **3.** denoting, relating to, or characteristic of Catalonia, its inhabitants, or their language.

cat·a+lase ('kætəˌleɪz) *n.* an iron-containing enzyme that catalyses the decomposition of peroxides, esp. hydrogen peroxide, to oxygen and water. [C20: from CATALYSIS + -ASE]

cat·a+lec+tic (ˌkætə'lɛktɪk) *adj. Prosody.* (of a line of verse) having an incomplete final foot. [C16: via Late Latin from Greek *katalēktikos* incomplete, from *katalēgein,* from *kata-* off + *lēgein* to stop]

cat·a+lep+sy ('kætəˌlɛpsɪ) *n.* a disturbance of consciousness, occurring esp. in schizophrenia, characterized by prolonged maintenance of rigid postures. [C16: from Medieval Latin *catalēpsia,* variant of Late Latin *catalēpsis,* from Greek *katalēpsis,* literally: a seizing, from *katalambanein* to hold down, from *kata-* down + *lambanein* to grasp] —**ˌcat·a+'lep+tic** *adj.*

Cat·a+li+na Is+land (ˌkætə'li:nə) *n.* another name for **Santa Catalina.**

cat·a+lo ('kætəˌləʊ) *n., pl.* **+loes** *or* **+los.** a variant spelling of **cattalo.**

cat·a+logue *or U.S.* **cat·a+log** ('kætəˌlɒg) *n.* **1.** a complete, usually alphabetical list of items, often with notes giving details. **2.** a list of all the books or resources of a library. **3.** *U.S.* a list of courses offered by a university, etc. ~*vb.* **4.** to compile a catalogue of (a library, etc.). **5.** to add (books, items, etc.) to an existing catalogue. [C15: from Late Latin *catalogus,* from Greek *katalogos,* from *katalegein* to list, from *kata-* completely + *legein* to collect] —**'cat·a+ˌlogu+er** *or* **'cat·a+ˌlogu+ist** *n.*

cat·a+logue rai+son·né (*French* katalɔg rɛzɔ'ne) *n.* a descriptive catalogue, esp. one covering works of art in an exhibition or collection.

Cat·a+lo+ni·a (ˌkætə'ləʊnɪə) *n.* a region of NE Spain, with a strong separatist tradition: an important agricultural and industrial region, with many resorts. Pop.: 5 122 567 (1970). Area: 31 929 sq. km (12 328 sq. miles). Catalan name: **Ca+ta+lu+ny·a** (ˌkatə'lu:nɪə). Spanish name: **Ca+ta+lu+ña** (ˌkata'luɲa).

ca+tal+pa (kə'tælpə) *n.* any bignoniaceous tree of the genus *Catalpa* of North America and Asia, having large leaves, bell-shaped whitish flowers, and long slender pods. [C18: New Latin, from Carolina Creek *kutuhlpa,* literally: winged head, referring to the appearance of the flowers]

cat·a+lyse *or U.S.* **cat·a+lyze** ('kætəˌlaɪz) *vb.* (*tr.*) to influence (a chemical reaction) by catalysis. —**'cat·a+ˌlys+er** *or U.S.* **'cat·a+ˌlyz+er** *n.*

ca+tal·y+sis (kə'tælɪsɪs) *n., pl.* **+ses** (-ˌsi:z). acceleration of a chemical reaction by the action of a catalyst. [C17: from New Latin, from Greek *katalusis,* from *kataluein* to dissolve] —**cat·a+lyt+ic** (ˌkætə'lɪtɪk) *adj.* —**ˌcat·a+'lyt·i+cal+ly** *adv.*

cat·a+lyst ('kætəˌlɪst) *n.* **1.** a substance that increases the rate of a chemical reaction without itself suffering any permanent chemical change. Compare **inhibitor** (sense 1). **2.** a person or thing that causes a change.

cat·a+lyt+ic crack+er *n.* a unit in an oil refinery in which mineral oils with high boiling points are converted to fuels with lower boiling points by a catalytic process. Often shortened to **cat cracker.**

cat·a+ma+ran (ˌkætəmə'ræn) *n.* **1.** a sailing vessel with twin hulls held parallel by a rigid framework. **2.** a primitive raft made of logs lashed together. **3.** *Informal.* a quarrelsome woman. [C17: from Tamil *kattumaram* tied timber]

cat·a+me·ni·a (ˌkætə'mi:nɪə) *pl. n. Physiol.* another word for **menses.** [C18: from New Latin, from Greek *katamēnia* menses] —**ˌcat·a+'me·ni·al** *adj.*

cat·a+mite ('kætəˌmaɪt) *n.* a boy kept for homosexual purposes. [C16: from Latin *Catamītus,* variant of *Ganymēdēs* GANYMEDE]

cat·a+mount ('kætəˌmaʊnt) *or* **cat·a+moun+tain** *n.* any of various medium-sized felines, such as the puma or lynx. [C17: short for *cat of the mountain*]

Ca+ta+nia (*Italian* ka'ta:nja) *n.* a port in E Sicily, near Mount Etna. Pop.: 398 642 (1975 est.).

Ca+tan+za+ro (*Italian* ˌkatan'dza:ro) *n.* a city in S Italy, in Calabria. Pop.: 85 316 (1971).

cat·a+pho+re·sis (ˌkætəfə'ri:sɪs) *n.* another name for **electrophoresis.** —**cat·a+pho+ret+ic** (ˌkætəfə'rɛtɪk) *adj.* —**ˌcat·a+pho+'ret·i+cal+ly** *adv.*

cat·a+phyll ('kætəˌfɪl) *n.* a simplified form of plant leaf, such as a scale leaf or cotyledon.

cat·a+pla+si·a (ˌkætə'pleɪzɪə) *n.* the degeneration of cells and tissues to a less highly developed form. —**cat·a+plas+tic** (ˌkætə'plæstɪk) *adj.*

cat·a+plasm ('kætəˌplæzəm) *n. Med.* another name for **poultice.** [C16: from Latin *cataplasma,* from Greek, from *kataplassein* to cover with a plaster, from *plassein* to shape]

cat·a+plex·y ('kætəˌplɛksɪ) *n.* **1.** sudden temporary paralysis, brought on by intense emotion, etc. **2.** a state of complete absence of movement assumed by animals while shamming death. [C19: from Greek *kataplēxis* amazement, from *kataplēssein* to strike down (with amazement), confound, from *kata-* down + *plēssein* to strike] **'cat·a+ˌplec+tic** *adj.*

cat·a+pult ('kætəˌpʌlt) *n.* **1.** a Y-shaped implement with a loop of elastic fastened to the ends of the two prongs, used mainly by children for shooting small stones, etc. U.S. name: **slingshot. 2.** a heavy war engine used formerly for hurling stones, etc. **3.** a device installed in warships to launch aircraft. ~*vb.* **4.** (*tr.*) to shoot forth from or as if from a catapult. **5.** (foll. by *over, into,* etc.) to move precipitately: *she was catapulted to stardom overnight.* [C16: from Latin *catapulta,* from Greek *katapeltēs,* from *kata-* down + *pallein* to hurl]

cat·a+ract ('kætəˌrækt) *n.* **1.** a large waterfall or rapids. **2.** a deluge; downpour. **3.** *Pathol.* **a.** partial or total opacity of the crystalline lens of the eye. **b.** the opaque area. [C15: from Latin *catarracta,* from Greek *katarrhaktēs,* from *katarassein* to dash down, from *arassein* to strike]

ca+tarrh (kə'tɑ:) *n.* inflammation of a mucous membrane with increased production of mucus, esp. affecting the nose and throat in the common cold. [C16: via French from Late Latin *catarrhus,* from Greek *katarrous,* from *katarrhein* to flow down, from *kata-* down + *rhein* to flow] —**ca+'tarrh+al** *or* **ca+'tarrh+ous** *adj.*

cat+arrh+ine ('kætəˌraɪn) *adj.* **1.** (of apes and Old World monkeys) having the nostrils set close together and opening to the front of the face. **2.** Also: **leptorrhine.** (of humans) having a thin or narrow nose. ~*n.* **3.** an animal or person with this characteristic. ~Compare **platyrrhine.** [C19: from New Latin *Catarrhina* (for sense 1), all ultimately from Greek *katarrhin* having a hooked nose, from *kata-* down + *rhis* nose]

ca+tas+tro+phe (kə'tæstrəfɪ) *n.* **1.** a sudden, extensive, or notable disaster or misfortune. **2.** the dénouement of a play, esp. a classical tragedy. **3.** a final decisive event, usually causing a disastrous end. **4.** any sudden and violent change in the earth's surface caused by flooding, earthquake, or some other process. Also called: **cataclysm.** [C16: from Greek *katastrophē*, from *katastrephein* to overturn, from *strephein* to turn] —**cat·a·stroph·ic** (ˌkætəˈstrɒfɪk) *adj.* —ˌ**cat·a·ˈstroph·i·cal·ly** *adv.*

ca·tas·tro·phism (kəˈtæstrəˌfɪzəm) *n.* the doctrine that explains major changes in fossils, rock strata, etc., in terms of sudden violent catastrophes rather than gradual evolutionary processes. —**ca·ˈtas·tro·phist** *n.*

cat·a·to·ni·a (ˌkætəˈtəʊnɪə) *n.* a form of schizophrenia characterized by muscular rigidity and stupor, with outbreaks of excitement. [C20: New Latin, from German *Katatonie*, from CATA- + Greek *tonos* tension] —**cat·a·ton·ic** (ˌkætəˈtɒnɪk) *adj., n.*

Ca·taw·ba (kəˈtɔːbə) *n.* **1.** (*pl.* **·ba** *or* **·bas**) a member of a North American Indian People, formerly of South Carolina, now almost extinct. **2.** their language, belonging to the Siouan family. **3.** a cultivated variety of red North American grape, widely grown in the eastern U.S. **4.** the wine made from these

cat·bird (ˈkætˌbɜːd) *n.* **1.** any of several North American songbirds of the family *Mimidae* (mockingbirds), esp. *Dumetella carolinensis*, whose call resembles the mewing of a cat. **2.** any of several Australian bowerbirds of the genera *Ailuroedus* and *Scenopoeetes*, having a catlike call.

cat·boat (ˈkætˌbəʊt) *n.* a sailing vessel with a single mast, set well forward and often unstayed, and a large sail, usually rigged with a gaff. Shortened form: **cat.**

cat bri·er *n.* another name for **greenbrier.**

cat bur·glar *n.* a burglar who enters buildings by climbing through upper windows, skylights, etc.

cat·call (ˈkætˌkɔːl) *n.* **1.** a shrill whistle or cry expressing disapproval, as at a public meeting, etc. ~*vb.* **2.** to utter such a call (at); deride with catcalls. —ˈ**cat·call·er** *n.*

catch (kætʃ) *vb.* **catch·es, catch·ing, caught. 1.** (*tr.*) to take hold of so as to retain or restrain: *he caught the ball.* **2.** (*tr.*) to take, seize, or capture, esp. after pursuit. **3.** (*tr.*) to ensnare or deceive, as by trickery. **4.** (*tr.*) to surprise or detect in an act: *he caught the dog rifling the larder.* **5.** (*tr.*) to reach with a blow: *the stone caught him on the side of the head.* **6.** (*tr.*) to overtake or reach in time to board: *if we hurry we should catch the next bus.* **7.** (*tr.*) to see or hear; attend: *I didn't catch the Ibsen play.* **8.** (*tr.*) to be infected with: *to catch a cold.* **9.** to hook or entangle or become hooked or entangled: *her dress caught on a nail.* **10.** to fasten or be fastened with or as if with a latch or other device. **11.** (*tr.*) to attract or arrest: *she tried to catch his eye.* **12.** (*tr.*) to comprehend: *I didn't catch his meaning.* **13.** (*tr.*) to hear accurately: *I didn't catch what you said.* **14.** (*tr.*) to captivate or charm. **15.** (*tr.*) to perceive and reproduce accurately: *the painter managed to catch his model's beauty.* **16.** (*tr.*) to hold back or restrain: *he caught his breath in surprise.* **17.** (*intr.*) to become alight: *the fire won't catch.* **18.** (*tr.*) *Cricket.* to dismiss (a batsman) by intercepting and holding a ball struck by him before it touches the ground. **19.** (*intr.*; often foll. by *at*) **a.** to grasp or attempt to grasp. **b.** to take advantage (of), esp. eagerly: *he caught at the chance.* **20.** (*intr.; used passively*) *Informal.* to make pregnant. **21. catch it.** *Informal.* to be scolded or reprimanded. ~*n.* **22.** the act of catching or grasping. **23.** a device that catches and fastens, such as a latch. **24.** anything that is caught, esp. something worth catching. **25.** the amount or number caught. **26.** *Informal.* a person regarded as an eligible matrimonial prospect. **27.** a check or break in the voice. **28.** a break in a mechanism. **29.** *Informal.* **a.** a concealed, unexpected, or unforeseen drawback or handicap. **b.** (*as modifier*): *a catch question.* **30.** a game in which a ball is thrown from one player to another. **31.** *Cricket.* the catching of a ball struck by a batsman before it touches the ground, resulting in him being out. **32.** *Music.* a type of round popular in the 17th, 18th, and 19th centuries, having a humorous text that is often indecent or bawdy and hard to articulate. See **round** (sense 30), **canon**[1] (sense 7). **33.** *Austral.* another name for **bell sheep. 34.** *Rare.* a fragment. ~See also **catch on, catch out, catch up.** [C13 *cacchen* to pursue, from Old Northern French *cachier*, from Latin *captāre* to snatch, from *capere* to seize] —ˈ**catch·a·ble** *adj.*

catch-all *n. Chiefly U.S.* **a.** something designed to cover a variety of situations or possibilities. **b.** (*as modifier*): *a catchall clause.*

catch-as-catch-can *n.* **1.** a style of wrestling in which trips, holds below the waist, etc., are allowed. ~*adj., adv.* **2.** *Chiefly U.S.* using any method or opportunity that comes to hand.

catch ba·sin *n.* the U.S. name for **catch pit.**

catch crop *n.* a quick-growing crop planted between two regular crops grown in consecutive seasons, or between two rows of regular crops in the same season.

catch·er (ˈkætʃə) *n.* **1.** a person or thing that catches, esp. in a game or sport. **2.** *Baseball.* a fielder who stands behind home plate and catches pitched balls not hit by the batter.

catch·fly (ˈkætʃˌflaɪ) *n., pl.* **·flies.** any of several caryophyllaceous plants of the genus *Silene* that have sticky calyxes and stems on which insects are sometimes trapped.

catch·ing (ˈkætʃɪŋ) *adj.* **1.** infectious. **2.** attractive; captivating.

catch·ment (ˈkætʃmənt) *n.* **1.** the act of catching or collecting water. **2.** a structure in which water is collected. **3.** the water so collected. **4.** *Brit.* the intake of a school from one catchment area.

catch·ment ar·e·a *n.* **1.** the area of land bounded by watersheds draining into a river, basin, or reservoir. Also called: **catchment basin, drainage area, drainage basin. 2.** the area from which people are allocated to a particular school, hospital, etc.

catch on *vb.* (*intr., adv.*) *Informal.* **1.** to become popular or fashionable. **2.** to grasp mentally; understand.

catch out *vb.* (*tr., adv.*) *Informal, chiefly Brit.* to trap (a person), esp. in an error or doing something reprehensible.

catch·pen·ny (ˈkætʃˌpɛnɪ) *adj.* **1.** (*prenominal*) designed to have instant appeal, esp. in order to sell quickly and easily without regard for quality: *catchpenny ornaments.* ~*n., pl.* **·nies. 2.** an item or commodity that is cheap and showy.

catch phrase *n.* a well-known frequently used phrase, esp. one associated with a particular group, etc.

catch pit *n.* a pit in a drainage system in which matter is collected that might otherwise block a sewer. U.S. name: **catch basin.**

catch points *pl. n.* railway points designed to derail a train in order to prevent its running onto a main line accidentally.

catch·pole *or* **catch·poll** (ˈkætʃˌpəʊl) *n.* (in medieval England) a sheriff's officer who arrested debtors. [Old English *cæcepol*, from Medieval Latin *cacepollus* tax-gatherer, literally: chicken-chaser, from *cace-* CATCH + *pollus* (from Latin *pullus* chick)]

catch-22 *n.* a situation characterized by obstacles that defeat all attempts of the victim to escape from it. [C20: from the title of a novel (1961) by J. Heller]

catch up *vb.* (*adv.*) **1.** (*tr.*) to seize and take up (something) quickly. **2.** (when *intr.*, often foll. by *with*) to reach or pass (someone or something), after following: *he soon caught him up.* **3.** (*intr.*; usually foll. by *on* or *with*) to make up for lost ground or deal with a backlog (in some specified task or activity). **4.** (*tr.*; *often passive*) to absorb or involve: *she was caught up in her reading.* **5.** (*tr.*) to raise by or as if by fastening: *the hem of her dress was caught up with ribbons.*

catch·up (ˈkætʃəp, ˈkɛtʃ-) *n.* a variant spelling (esp. U.S.) of **ketchup.**

catch·weight (ˈkætʃˌweɪt) *adj. Wrestling.* of or relating to a contest in which normal weight categories have been waived by agreement.

catch·word (ˈkætʃˌwɜːd) *n.* **1.** a word or phrase made temporarily popular, esp. by a political campaign; slogan. **2.** a word printed as a running head in a reference book. **3.** *Theatre.* an actor's cue to speak or enter. **4.** the first word of a printed or typewritten page repeated at the bottom of the page preceding.

catch·y (ˈkætʃɪ) *adj.* **catch·i·er, catch·i·est. 1.** (of a tune, etc.) pleasant and easily remembered or imitated. **2.** tricky or deceptive: *a catchy question.* **3.** irregular: *a catchy breeze.* —ˈ**catch·i·ness** *n.*

cat crack·er *n.* an informal name for **catalytic cracker.**

cat·e·chet·i·cal (ˌkætɪˈkɛtɪkəl) *or* **cat·e·chet·ic** *adj.* of or relating to teaching by question and answer. —ˌ**cat·e·ˈchet·i·cal·ly** *adv.*

cat·e·chin (ˈkætəkɪn) *n.* a soluble yellow solid substance found in catechu and mahogany wood and used in tanning and dyeing. Formula: $C_{15}H_{14}O_6$. [C19: from CATECHU + -IN]

cat·e·chism (ˈkætɪˌkɪzəm) *n.* **1.** instruction by a series of questions and answers, esp. a book containing such instruction on the religious doctrine of a Christian Church. **2.** rigorous and persistent questioning, as in a test or interview. [C16: from Late Latin *catēchismus*, ultimately from Greek *katēkhizein* to CATECHIZE] —ˌ**cat·e·ˈchis·mal** *adj.*

cat·e·chize *or* **cat·e·chise** (ˈkætɪˌkaɪz) *vb.* (*tr.*) **1.** to teach or examine by means of questions and answers. **2.** *Ecclesiast.* to give oral instruction in Christianity, esp. by using a catechism. **3.** to put questions to (someone). [C15: from Late Latin *catēchizāre*, from Greek *katēkhizein*, from *katēkhein* to instruct orally, literally: to shout down, from *kata-* down + *ēkhein* to sound] —ˈ**cat·e·chist, ˈcat·e·ˌchiz·er** *or* **ˈcat·e·ˌchis·er** *n.* —ˌ**cat·e·ˈchis·tic** *or* ˌ**cat·e·ˈchis·ti·cal** *adj.* —ˌ**cat·e·ˈchis·ti·cal·ly** *adv.* —ˌ**cat·e·chi·ˈza·tion** *or* ˌ**cat·e·chi·ˈsa·tion** *n.*

cat·e·chol (ˈkætɪˌtʃɒl, -ˌkɒl) *n.* a colourless crystalline phenol found in resins and lignins; 1, 2-dihydroxybenzene. It is used as a photographic developer. Formula: $C_6H_4(OH)_2$. Also called: **pyrocatechol.** [C20: from CATECHU + -OL[1]]

cat·e·chol·a·mine (ˌkætəˈkɒləˌmiːn) *n.* any of a group of catechol derivatives, esp. adrenaline and noradrenaline. [C20: from CATECHU + -OL[1] + AMINE]

cat·e·chu (ˈkætɪˌtʃuː), **ca·chou,** *or* **cutch** *n.* a water-soluble astringent resinous substance obtained from any of certain tropical plants, esp. the leguminous tree *Acacia catechu* of S Asia, and used in medicine, tanning, and dyeing. See also **gambier.** [C17: probably from Malay *kachu*, of Dravidian origin]

cat·e·chu·men (ˌkætɪˈkjuːmɛn) *n. Christianity.* a person, esp. in the early Church, undergoing instruction prior to baptism. [C15: via Old French, from Late Latin, from Greek *katēkhoumenos* one being instructed verbally, from *katēkhein*; see CATECHIZE] —ˌ**cat·e·ˈchu·me·nal** *or* **cat·e·chu·men·i·cal** (ˌkætəkjʊˈmɛnɪkəl) *adj.* —ˌ**cat·e·ˈchu·men·ism** *n.*

cat·e·gor·i·cal (ˌkætɪˈgɒrɪkəl) *or* **cat·e·gor·ic** *adj.* **1.** unqualified; positive; unconditional: *a categorical statement.* **2.** relating to or included in a category. **3.** (of a statement in logic) consisting of a subject (X in the following examples) and an attribute (Y) linked by a copula and having one of the following forms: *all* X *are* Y (universal affirmative); *no* X *are* Y (universal negative); *some* X *are* Y (particular affirmative); *some* X *are not* Y (particular negative). —ˌ**cat·e·ˈgor·i·cal·ly** *adv.* —ˌ**cat·e·ˈgor·i·cal·ness** *n.*

cat·e·gor·i·cal im·per·a·tive *n.* (in the ethics of Kant) the unconditional moral principle prescribing that one's behaviour should be governed by duty, not the prospect of reward. Compare **hypothetical imperative.**

cat·e·go·rize *or* **cat·e·go·rise** (ˈkætɪgəˌraɪz) *vb.* (*tr.*) to place in a category; classify. —ˌcat·e·go·ri·'za·tion or ˌcat·e·go·ri·'sa·tion *n.*

cat·e·go·ry ('kætɪgərɪ) *n., pl.* **·ries.** **1.** a class or group of things, people, etc., possessing some quality or qualities in common; a division in a system of classification. **2.** *Metaphysics.* the most basic class into which objects and concepts can be analysed. **3. a.** (in the philosophy of Aristotle) one of ten fundamental modes of being, such as quantity, quality, and substance. **b.** (in the philosophy of Kant) one of twelve concepts required by human beings to interpret the empirical world. [C15: from Late Latin *catēgoria*, from Greek *katēgoria*, from *kategorein* to accuse, assert] —**cat·e·go·ri·al** (ˌkætɪ'gɔːrɪəl) *adj.*

ca·te·na (kə'tiːnə) *n., pl.* **·nae** (-niː). a connected series, esp. of patristic comments on the Bible. [C17: from Latin: chain]

cat·e·nane ('kætɪˌneɪn) *n.* a type of chemical compound in which the molecules have two or more rings that are interlocked like the links of a chain. [C20: from Latin *catena* chain + -ANE]

ca·te·na·ry (kə'tiːnərɪ) *n., pl.* **·ries.** **1.** the curve assumed by a heavy uniform flexible cord hanging freely from two points. When symmetrical about the y-axis and intersecting it at $y = a$, the equation is $y = a \cosh x/a$. **2.** the hanging cable between pylons along a railway track, from which the trolley wire is suspended. ~*adj. also* **cat·e·nar·i·an** (ˌkætɪ'nɛərɪən). **3.** of, resembling, relating to, or constructed using a catenary or suspended chain. [C18: from Latin *catēnārius* relating to a chain]

cat·e·nate ('kætɪˌneɪt) *vb.* **1.** *Biology.* to arrange or be arranged in a series of chains or rings. ~*adj.* **2.** another word for **catenulate.** [C17: from Latin *catēnāre* to bind with chains] —ˌ**cat·e·'na·tion** *n.*

cat·e·noid ('kætəˌnɔɪd) *n.* the geometrical surface generated by rotating a catenary about its axis.

ca·ten·u·late (kə'tɛnjʊˌleɪt, -lɪt) *adj.* (of certain spores, etc.) formed in a row or chain. [C19: from Latin *catēnula*, diminutive of *catēna* chain]

ca·ter ('keɪtə) *vb.* **1.** (*intr.*; foll. by *for* or *to*) to provide what is required or desired (for): *to cater for a need; cater to your tastes.* **2.** (when *intr.*, foll. by *for*) to provide food, services, etc. (for): *we cater for parties; to cater a banquet.* [C16: from earlier *catour* purchaser, variant of *acatour*, from Anglo-Norman *acater* to buy, ultimately related to Latin *acceptāre* to ACCEPT]

cat·er·an ('kætərən) *n.* (formerly) a member of a band of brigands and marauders in the Scottish highlands. [C14: probably from Scottish Gaelic *ceathairneach* robber, plunderer]

cat·er·cor·nered ('kætəˌkɔːnəd) *adj., adv. U.S. informal.* diagonally placed; diagonal. Also: **cat·ty·cor·nered.** [C16: *cater*, from dialect *cater* (adv.) diagonally, from obsolete *cater* (n.) four-spot of dice, from Old French *quatre* four, from Latin *quattuor*]

ca·ter·cous·in ('keɪtəˌkʌzᵊn) *n. Archaic.* a close friend. [C16: perhaps from obsolete *cater* caterer; for sense, compare FOSTER, as in *foster brother*, etc.]

ca·ter·er ('keɪtərə) *n.* a person who caters, esp. one who as a profession provides food for large social events, etc.

ca·ter·ing ('keɪtərɪŋ) *n.* **1.** the trade of a professional caterer. **2.** the food, etc., provided at a function by a caterer.

cat·er·pil·lar ('kætəˌpɪlə) *n.* **1.** the wormlike larva of butterflies and moths, having numerous pairs of legs and powerful biting jaws. It may be brightly coloured, hairy, or spiny. **2.** an endless track, driven by sprockets or wheels, used to propel a heavy vehicle and enable it to cross soft or uneven ground. **3.** a vehicle, such as a tractor, tank, bulldozer, etc., driven by such tracks. [C15 *catyrpel*, probably from Old Northern French *catepelose*, literally: hairy cat]

cat·er·pil·lar hun·ter *n.* any of various carabid beetles of the genus *Calosoma*, of Europe and North America, which prey on the larvae of moths and butterflies.

cat·er·waul ('kætəˌwɔːl) *vb.* (*intr.*) **1.** to make a yowling noise, as a cat on heat. ~*n.* **2.** a shriek or yell made by or sounding like a cat on heat. [C14: of imitative origin] —**'cat·er·ˌwaul·er** *n.*

cates (keɪts) *pl. n.* (*sometimes sing.*) *Archaic.* choice dainty food; delicacies. [C15: variant of *acates* purchases, from Old Northern French *acater* to buy, from Vulgar Latin *accaptāre* (unattested); ultimately related to Latin *acceptāre* to ACCEPT]

cat·fall ('kætˌfɔːl) *n. Nautical.* the line used in a cat.

cat·fish ('kætˌfɪʃ) *n., pl.* **·fish** *or* **·fish·es.** **1.** any of numerous mainly freshwater teleost fishes having whisker-like barbels around the mouth, esp. the silurids of Europe and Asia and the horned pouts of North America. **2.** another name for **wolffish.**

cat·gut ('kætˌgʌt) *n.* a strong cord made from the dried intestines of sheep and other animals that is used for stringing certain musical instruments and sports rackets, and, when sterilized, as surgical ligatures. Often shortened to **gut.**

Cath. *abbrev. for* **1.** Cathedral. **2.** Catholic.

cath- *prefix.* variant of **cata-** before an aspirate: *cathode.*

Cath·ar ('kæθə) *or* **Cath·ar·ist** ('kæθəˌrɪst) *n., pl.* **·ars, ·ar·i** (-ərɪ) *or* **·ar·ists.** a member of a Christian sect in Provence in the 12th and 13th centuries who believed the material world was evil and only the spiritual was good. [from Medieval Latin *Cathari*, from Greek *katharoi* the pure] —**'Cath·ar·ˌism** *n.*

ca·thar·sis *or* **ka·thar·sis** (kə'θɑːsɪs) *n.* **1.** (in Aristotelian literary criticism) the purging or purification of the emotions through the evocation of pity and fear, as in tragedy. **2.** *Psychoanal.* a method of bringing repressed ideas or experiences to consciousness, by means of free association, etc., so that underlying tensions may be relieved. See also **abreaction. 3.** purgation, esp. of the bowels. [C19: New Latin, from Greek *katharsis*, from *kathairein* to purge, purify]

ca·thar·tic (kə'θɑːtɪk) *adj.* **1.** purgative. **2.** effecting catharsis. ~*n.* **3.** a purgative drug or agent. —**ca·'thar·ti·cal·ly** *adv.*

Ca·thay (kæ'θeɪ) *n.* a literary or archaic name for **China.** [C14: from Medieval Latin *Cataya*, of Turkic origin]

cat·head ('kætˌhɛd) *n.* a fitting at the bow of a vessel for securing the anchor when raised.

ca·thec·tic (kə'θɛktɪk) *adj.* of or relating to cathexis.

ca·the·dral (kə'θiːdrəl) *n.* **a.** the principal church of a diocese, containing the bishop's official throne. **b.** (*as modifier*): *cathedral city; cathedral clergy.* [C13: from Late Latin (*ecclesia*) *cathedrālis* cathedral (church), from *cathedra* bishop's throne, from Greek *kathedra* seat]

ca·thep·sin (kə'θɛpsɪn) *n.* a proteolytic enzyme responsible for the autolysis of cells after death. [C20: from Greek *kathepsein* to boil down, soften]

Cath·e·rine ('kæθrɪn) *n.* **Saint.** died 307 A.D., legendary Christian martyr of Alexandria, who was tortured on a spiked wheel and beheaded. Feast day: Nov. 25.

Cath·e·rine I *n.* ?1684–1727, second wife of Peter the Great, whom she succeeded as empress of Russia (1725–27).

Cath·e·rine II *n.* called *the Great.* 1729–96, empress of Russia (1762–96), during whose reign Russia extended her boundaries at the expense of Turkey, Sweden, and Poland: she was a patron of literature and the arts.

Cath·e·rine de' Med·i·ci *or* **de Mé·di·cis** *n.* 1519–89, queen of Henry II of France; mother of Francis II, Charles IX, and Henry III of France; regent of France (1560–74). She was largely responsible for the massacre of Protestants on Saint Bartholomew's Day (1572).

Cath·e·rine of Ar·a·gon *n.* 1485–1536, first wife of Henry VIII of England and mother of Mary I. Henry's divorce from her (1533) against papal authority marked an initial stage in the English Reformation.

Cath·e·rine of Si·en·a *n.* **Saint.** 1347–80, Italian mystic and ascetic; patron saint of the Dominican order. Feast day: April 30.

cath·e·rine wheel *n.* **1.** a type of firework consisting of a powder-filled spiral tube, mounted with a pin through its centre. When lit it rotates quickly, producing a display of sparks and coloured flame. Also called: **pinwheel. 2.** a circular window having ribs radiating from the centre. [C16: named after St. CATHERINE of Alexandria]

cath·e·ter ('kæθɪtə) *n. Med.* a long slender flexible tube for inserting into a natural bodily cavity or passage for introducing or withdrawing fluid. [C17: from Late Latin, from Greek *kathetēr*, from *kathienai* to send down, insert]

cath·e·ter·ize *or* **cath·e·ter·ise** ('kæθɪtəˌraɪz) *vb.* (*tr.*) to insert a catheter into. —ˌ**cath·e·ter·i·'za·tion** *or* ˌ**cath·e·ter·i·'sa·tion** *n.*

ca·thex·is (kə'θɛksɪs) *n., pl.* **·thex·es** (-'θɛksiːz). *Psychoanal.* concentration of psychic energy on a specific object, person, or idea. [C20: from New Latin, from Greek *kathexis*, from *katekhein* to hold fast, intended to render German *Besetzung* a taking possession of]

cath·ode ('kæθəʊd) *n.* **1.** the negative electrode in an electrolytic cell; the electrode by which electrons enter a device from an external circuit. **2.** the negatively charged electron source in an electronic valve. **3.** the positive terminal of a primary cell. ~Compare **anode.** [C19: from Greek *kathodos* a descent, from *kata-* down + *hodos* way] —**ca·thod·al** (kæ'θəʊdᵊl), **ca·thod·ic** (kæ'θɒdɪk, -'θəʊ-), *or* **ca·'thod·i·cal** *adj.*

cath·ode rays *pl. n.* a stream of electrons emitted from the surface of a cathode in a vacuum tube.

cath·ode-ray tube *n.* a vacuum tube in which a beam of high-energy electrons is focused onto a fluorescent screen to give a visible spot of light. The device, with appropriate deflection equipment, is used in television tubes, oscilloscopes, etc.

ca·thod·ic pro·tec·tion *n. Metallurgy.* a technique for protecting metal structures, such as steel ships and pipelines, from electrolytic corrosion by making the structure the cathode in a cell, either by applying an electromotive force directly or by putting it into contact with a more electropositive metal. See also **sacrificial anode.**

cat hole *n.* one of a pair of holes in the after part of a ship through which hawsers are passed for steadying the ship or heaving astern.

cath·o·lic ('kæθəlɪk, 'kæθlɪk) *adj.* **1.** universal; relating to all men; all-inclusive. **2.** comprehensive in interests, tastes, etc.; broad-minded; liberal. [C14: from Latin *catholicus*, from Greek *katholikos* universal, from *katholou* in general, from *kata-* according to + *holos* whole] —**ca·thol·i·cal·ly** *or* **ca·thol·ic·ly** (kə'θɒlɪklɪ) *adv.*

Cath·o·lic ('kæθəlɪk, 'kæθlɪk) *adj. Christianity.* **1.** denoting or relating to the entire body of Christians, esp. to the Church before separation into the Greek or Eastern and Latin or Western Churches. **2.** denoting or relating to the Latin or Western Church after this separation. **3.** denoting or relating to the Roman Catholic Church. **4.** denoting or relating to any church, belief, etc., that claims continuity with or originates in the ancient undivided Church. ~*n.* **5.** a member of any of the Churches regarded as Catholic, esp. the Roman Catholic Church.

Cath·o·lic Church *n.* **1.** short for **Roman Catholic Church. 2.** any of several Churches claiming to have maintained continuity with the ancient and undivided Church.

Cath·o·lic E·pis·tles *pl. n. New Testament.* the epistles of James, I and II Peter, I John, and Jude, which were addressed to the universal Church rather than to an individual or a particular church.
Ca·thol·i·cism (kəˈθɒlɪˌsɪzəm) *n.* **1.** short for **Roman Catholicism. 2.** the beliefs, practices, etc., of any Catholic Church.
cath·o·lic·i·ty (ˌkæθəˈlɪsɪtɪ) *n.* **1.** a wide range of interests, tastes, etc.; liberality. **2.** universality; comprehensiveness.
Cath·o·lic·i·ty (ˌkæθəˈlɪsɪtɪ) *n.* the beliefs, etc., of the Catholic Church.
ca·thol·i·cize *or* **ca·thol·i·cise** (kəˈθɒlɪˌsaɪz) *vb.* **1.** to make or become catholic. **2.** (*often cap.*) to convert to or become converted to Catholicism. —**ca·ˌthol·i·ci·ˈza·tion** *or* **ca·ˌthol·i·ci·ˈsa·tion** *n.*
ca·thol·i·con (kəˈθɒlɪkən) *n.* a remedy for all ills; panacea. [C15: from Medieval Latin; see CATHOLIC]
cat·house (ˈkætˌhaus) *n. U.S.* a slang word for **brothel.**
Cat·i·line (ˈkætɪˌlaɪn) *n.* Latin name *Lucius Sergius Catilina.* ?108–62 B.C., Roman politician: organized an unsuccessful conspiracy against Cicero (63–62). —**Cat·i·li·nar·i·an** (ˌkætɪlɪˈnɛərɪən) *adj.*
cat·i·on (ˈkætaɪən) *n.* a positively charged ion; an ion that is attracted to the cathode during electrolysis. Compare **anion.** [C19: from CATA- + ION] —**cat·i·on·ic** (ˌkætaɪˈɒnɪk) *adj.*
cat·kin (ˈkætkɪn) *n.* an inflorescence consisting of a hanging spike of much reduced flowers of either sex: occurs in birch, hazel, etc. Also called: **ament.** [C16: from obsolete Dutch *katteken* kitten, identical in meaning with French *chaton,* German *Kätzchen*]
cat·ling (ˈkætlɪŋ) *n.* **1.** a long double-edged surgical knife for amputations. **2.** *Rare.* catgut or a string made from it. **3.** an archaic word for **kitten.** [C17: from CAT + -LING]
cat·mint (ˈkætˌmɪnt) *n.* a Eurasian plant, *Nepeta cataria,* having spikes of purple-spotted white flowers and scented leaves of which cats are fond: family *Labiatae* (labiates). Also called: **catnip.**
cat·nap (ˈkætˌnæp) *n.* **1.** a short sleep or doze. ~*vb.* **·naps, ·nap·ping, ·napped. 2.** (*intr.*) to sleep or doze for a short time or intermittently.
cat·nip (ˈkætˌnɪp) *n.* another name for **catmint.**
Ca·to (ˈkeɪtəu) *n.* **1. Mar·cus Por·ci·us** (ˈmɑːkəs ˈpɔːʃɪəs), called *the Elder* or *the Censor.* 234–149 B.C., Roman statesman and writer, noted for his relentless opposition to Carthage. **2.** his great-grandson, **Mar·cus Por·ci·us,** called *the Younger* or *Uticensis.* 95–46 B.C., Roman statesman, general, and Stoic philosopher; opponent of Catiline and Caesar.
cat-o'-moun·tain *n.* another name for **catamount.**
cat-o'-nine-tails *n., pl.* **-tails.** a rope whip consisting of nine knotted thongs, used formerly to flog prisoners. Often shortened to **cat.**
ca·top·trics (kəˈtɒptrɪks) *n.* (*functioning as sing.*) the branch of optics concerned with reflection, esp. the formation of images by mirrors. [C18: from Greek *katoptrikos,* from *katoptron* mirror] —**ca·ˈtop·tric** *or* **ca·ˈtop·tri·cal** *adj.*
cat rig *n.* the rig of a catboat. —**ˈcat·ˌrigged** *adj.*
cat's cra·dle *n.* a game played by making intricate patterns with a loop of string between the fingers.
cat's-ear *n.* any of various European plants of the genus *Hypochoeris,* esp. *H. radicata,* having dandelion-like heads of yellow flowers: family *Compositae* (composites).
cat's-eye *n.* **1.** *Brit.* a glass reflector set into a small fixture, placed at intervals along roads to indicate traffic lanes at night. **2.** any of a group of gemstones, esp. a greenish-yellow variety of chrysoberyl, that reflect a streak of light when cut in a rounded unfaceted shape.
cat's-foot *n., pl.* **-feet.** a European plant, *Antennaria dioica,* with whitish woolly leaves and heads of typically white flowers: family *Compositae* (composites).
Cats·kill Moun·tains (ˈkætskɪl) *pl. n.* a mountain range in SE New York State: resort. Highest peak: Slide Mountain, 1261 m (4204 ft.). Also called: **Catskills.**
cat's-paw *n.* **1.** a person used by another as a tool; dupe. **2.** *Nautical.* a hitch in the form of two loops, or eyes, in the bight of a line, used for attaching it to a hook. **3.** a pattern of ripples on the surface of water caused by a light wind. [(sense 1) C18: so called from the tale of the monkey who used a cat's paw to draw chestnuts out of a fire]
cat's-tail *n.* **1.** another name for **reed mace** (sense 1). **2.** another name for **catkin.**
cat suit *n.* a one-piece usually close-fitting trouser suit.
cat·sup (ˈkætsəp) *n.* a variant spelling (esp. U.S.) of **ketchup.**
cat's whisk·er *n.* **1.** a pointed wire formerly used to make contact with the crystal in a crystal radio receiver. **2.** any wire used to make contact with a semiconductor.
cat's whisk·ers *or* **cat's py·ja·mas** *n.* **the.** *Slang.* a person or thing that is excellent or superior.
cat·ta·lo *or* **cat·a·lo** (ˈkætəˌləu) *n., pl.* **·loes** *or* **·los.** a hardy breed of cattle developed by crossing the American bison with domestic cattle. [C20: from CATT(LE + BUFF)ALO]
Cat·te·gat (ˈkætɪˌgæt) *n.* a variant spelling of **Kattegat.**
cat·ter·y (ˈkætərɪ) *n., pl.* **·ter·ies.** a place where cats are bred or looked after.
cat·tle (ˈkætᵊl) *n.* (*functioning as pl.*) **1.** bovid mammals of the tribe *Bovini* (bovines), esp. those of the genus *Bos.* **2.** Also called: **domestic cattle.** any domesticated bovine mammals, esp. those of the species *Bos taurus* (domestic ox). [C13: from Old Northern French *catel,* Old French *chatel* CHATTEL]
cat·tle-grid *n.* a ditch in a roadway covered by a grid, intended to prevent the passage of livestock while allowing vehicles, etc., to pass unhindered.
cat·tle·man (ˈkætᵊlmən) *n., pl.* **·men. 1.** a person who breeds, rears, or tends cattle. **2.** *Chiefly U.S.* a person who owns or rears cattle on a large scale, usually for beef, esp. the owner of a cattle ranch.
cat·tle plague *n.* another name for **rinderpest.**
cat·tle truck *n.* a railway wagon designed for carrying livestock. U.S. equivalent: **stock car.**
catt·le·ya (ˈkætlɪə) *n.* any tropical American orchid of the genus *Cattleya,* cultivated for their purplish-pink or white showy flowers. [C19: New Latin, named after William *Cattley* (died 1832), English botanist]
cat-train *or* **cat-swing** *n. Canadian.* a train of sleds, cabooses, etc., pulled by a caterpillar tractor, used chiefly in the north during winter to transport freight.
cat·ty[1] (ˈkætɪ) *or* **cat·tish** *adj.* **·ti·er, ·ti·est. 1.** *Informal.* spiteful: *a catty remark.* **2.** of or resembling a cat. —**ˈcat·ti·ly** *or* **ˈcat·tish·ly** *adv.* —**ˈcat·ti·ness** *or* **ˈcat·tish·ness** *n.*
cat·ty[2] *or* **cat·tie** (ˈkætɪ) *n., pl.* **·ties.** a unit of weight, used esp. in China, equal to about one and a half pounds or about 0.67 kilogram. [C16: from Malay *kati*]
cat·ty-cor·nered *adj.* a variant of **cater-cornered.**
Ca·tul·lus (kəˈtʌləs) *n.* **Ga·ius Va·le·ri·us** (ˈgaɪəs vəˈlɪərɪəs). ?84–?54 B.C., Roman lyric poet, noted particularly for his love poems. —**Ca·tul·lan** (kəˈtʌlən) *adj.*
cat·walk (ˈkætˌwɔːk) *n.* a narrow pathway over the stage of a theatre, along a bridge, etc.
Cau·ca (*Spanish* ˈkauka) *n.* a river in W Colombia, rising in the northwest and flowing north to the Magdalena River. Length: about 1350 km (840 miles).
Cau·ca·si·a (kɔːˈkeɪzɪə, -ʒə) *n.* a region of the SW Soviet Union, between the Caspian Sea and the Black Sea: contains the Caucasus Mountains, dividing it into Ciscaucasia in the north and Transcaucasia in the south; one of the most complex ethnic areas in the world, with over 50 different peoples. Also called: the **Caucasus.**
Cau·ca·si·an (kɔːˈkeɪzɪən, -ʒən) *or* **Cau·ca·sic** (kɔːˈkeɪzɪk) *adj.* **1.** another word for **Caucasoid. 2.** of or relating to the Caucasus. ~*n.* **3.** a member of the Caucasoid race; a white man. **4.** a native or inhabitant of Caucasia. **5.** either of two distinct families of languages spoken in the area between the Black Sea and the Caspian: **North Caucasian,** including Circassian and Abkhaz, and **South Caucasian,** including Georgian.
Cau·ca·soid (ˈkɔːkəˌzɔɪd) *adj.* **1.** denoting, relating to, or belonging to the light-complexioned racial group of mankind, which includes the peoples indigenous to Europe, N Africa, SW Asia, and the Indian subcontinent and their descendants in other parts of the world. ~*n.* **2.** a member of this racial group.
Cau·ca·sus (ˈkɔːkəsəs) *n.* **1. the.** a mountain range in the SW Soviet Union, in Caucasia between the Black Sea and the Caspian Sea: mostly over 2700 m (9000 ft.). Highest peak: Mount Elbrus, 5633 m (18 588 ft.). Also called: **Caucasus Mountains. 2.** another name for **Caucasia.**
Cau·chy (ˈkauʃɪ; *French* koˈʃi) *n.* **Au·gus·tin Louis** (ogystɛ̃ ˈlwi), Baron Cauchy. 1789–1857, French mathematician, noted for his work on the theory of functions and the wave theory of light.
cau·cus (ˈkɔːkəs) *n., pl.* **·cus·es. 1.** *Chiefly U.S.* **a.** a closed meeting of the members of one party in a legislative chamber, etc., to coordinate policy, choose candidates, etc. **b.** such a bloc of politicians: *the Democratic caucus in Congress.* **2.** *Chiefly U.S.* **a.** a group of leading politicians of one party. **b.** a meeting of such a group. **3.** *Chiefly U.S.* a local meeting of party members. **4.** *Brit.* a party organization, esp. on a local level. ~*vb.* **5.** (*intr.*) to hold a caucus. [C18: probably of Algonquian origin; related to *caucauasu* adviser]
cau·dad (ˈkɔːdæd) *adv. Anatomy.* towards the tail or posterior part. Compare **cephalad.** [C19: from Latin *cauda* tail + -AD]
cau·dal (ˈkɔːdᵊl) *adj.* **1.** *Anatomy.* of or towards the posterior part of the body. **2.** *Zoology.* relating to, resembling, or in the position of the tail. [C17: from New Latin *caudālis,* from Latin *cauda* tail] —**ˈcau·dal·ly** *adv.*
cau·dal fin *n.* the tail fin of fishes and some other aquatic vertebrates, used for propulsion during locomotion.
cau·date (ˈkɔːdeɪt) *or* **cau·dat·ed** *adj.* having a tail or a tail-like appendage. [C17: from New Latin *caudātus,* from Latin *cauda* tail] —**cau·ˈda·tion** *n.*
cau·dex (ˈkɔːdɛks) *n., pl.* **·di·ces** (-dɪˌsiːz) *or* **·dex·es. 1.** the thickened persistent stem base of some herbaceous perennial plants. **2.** the woody stem of palms and tree ferns. [C19: from Latin]
cau·dil·lo (kɔːˈdiːljəu; *Spanish* kauˈðiʎo) *n., pl.* **·los** (-jəuz; *Spanish* -ʎos). (in Spanish-speaking countries) a military or political leader. [Spanish, from Late Latin *capitellum,* diminutive of Latin *caput* head]
Cau·dine Forks (ˈkɔːdaɪn) *n.* a narrow pass in the Apennines, in S Italy, between Capua and Benevento: scene of the defeat of the Romans by the Samnites (321 B.C.).
cau·dle (ˈkɔːdᵊl) *n.* a hot spiced wine drink made with gruel, formerly used medicinally. [C13: from Old Northern French *caudel,* from Medieval Latin *caldellum,* from Latin *calidus* warm]
caught (kɔːt) *vb.* the past tense and past participle of **catch.**
caul (kɔːl) *n. Anatomy.* **1.** a portion of the amniotic sac sometimes covering a child's head at birth. **2.** a large fold of peritoneum hanging from the stomach across the intestines;

the large omentum. [C13: from Old French *cale,* back formation from *calotte* close-fitting cap, of Germanic origin]

caul+dron *or* **cal+dron** ('kɔːldrən) *n.* a large pot used for boiling, esp. one with handles. [C13: from earlier *cauderon,* from Anglo-French, from Latin *caldārium* hot bath, from *calidus* warm]

cau+les+cent (kɔː'lɛsənt) *adj.* having a stem clearly visible above the ground. [C18: from Latin *caulis* stalk]

cau+li+cle ('kɔːlɪkəl) *n. Botany.* a small stalk or stem. [C17: from Latin *cauliculus,* from *caulis* stem]

cau+li+flow+er ('kɒlɪˌflaʊə) *n.* **1.** a variety of cabbage, *Brassica oleracea botrytis,* having a large edible head of crowded white flowers on a very short thick stem. **2.** the flower head of this plant, used as a vegetable. [C16: from Italian *caoli fiori,* literally: cabbage flowers, from *cavolo* cabbage (from Latin *caulis*) + *fiore* flower (from Latin *flōs*)]

cau+li+flow+er cheese *n.* a dish of cauliflower with a cheese sauce, eaten hot.

cau+li+flow+er ear *n.* permanent swelling and distortion of the external ear as the result of ruptures of the blood vessels: usually caused by blows received in boxing. Also called: **boxer's ear.** Technical name: **aural haematoma.**

cau+line ('kɔːlɪn, -laɪn) *adj.* relating to or growing from a plant stem. [C18: from New Latin *caulīnus,* from Latin *caulis* stem]

cau+lis ('kɔːlɪs) *n., pl.* **+les** (-liːz). *Rare.* the main stem of a plant. [C16: from Latin]

caulk *or* **calk** (kɔːk) *vb.* **1.** to stop up (cracks, crevices, etc.) with a filler. **2.** *Nautical.* to pack (the seams) between the planks of the bottom of (a vessel) with waterproof material to prevent leakage. [C15: from Old Northern French *cauquer* to press down, from Latin *calcāre* to trample, from *calx* heel] —**'caulk+er** *or* **'calk+er** *n.*

caus. *abbrev. for* causative.

caus+al ('kɔːzəl) *adj.* **1.** acting as or being a cause. **2.** stating, involving, or implying a cause: *the causal part of the argument.* **3.** *Grammar.* (of a word, phrase, or clause) indicating cause or reason: "*because*" *is a causal conjunction and the clauses it introduces are causal clauses.* —**'caus+al+ly** *adv.*

cau+sal+gi+a (kɔː'zældʒɪə) *n. Pathol.* a burning sensation along the course of a peripheral nerve together with local changes in the appearance of the skin. [C19: from New Latin, from Greek *kausos* fever + -ALGIA]

cau+sal+i+ty (kɔː'zælɪtɪ) *n., pl.* **·ties. 1. a.** the relationship of cause and effect. **b.** the principle that nothing can happen without being caused. **2.** causal agency or quality.

cau+sa+tion (kɔː'zeɪʃən) *n.* **1.** the act or fact of causing; the production of an effect by a cause. **2.** the relationship of cause and effect. —**cau+'sa+tion+al** *adj.*

caus·a+tive ('kɔːzətɪv) *adj.* **1.** *Grammar.* relating to a form or class of verbs that express causation. **2.** (*often postpositive* and foll. by *of*) producing an effect. ~*n.* **3.** the causative form or class of verbs. —**'caus·a+tive+ly** *adv.* —**'caus·a+tive+ness** *n.*

cause (kɔːz) *n.* **1.** a person, thing, event, state, or action that produces an effect. **2.** a basis or the grounds for action; motive; reason: *her rudeness was a cause for complaint.* **3.** justification; reason: *she had good cause to shout like that.* **4.** the ideals, etc., of a group or movement: *the Communist cause.* **5.** the welfare or interests of a person or group in a dispute: *they fought for the miners' cause.* **6.** a matter of widespread concern or importance: *the cause of public health.* **7. a.** a ground for legal action; matter giving rise to a lawsuit. **b.** the lawsuit itself. **8.** (in the philosophy of Aristotle) any of four requirements for a thing's coming to be, namely material (material cause), its nature (formal cause), an agent (efficient cause), and a purpose (final cause). **9.** *Archaic.* a subject of debate or discussion. **10. make common cause with.** to join with (a person, group, etc.) for a common objective. ~*vb.* **11.** (*tr.*) to be the cause of; bring about; precipitate; be the reason for. [C13: from Latin *causa* cause, reason, motive] —**'caus+a·ble** *adj.* —**ˌcaus+a·'bil+i·ty** *n.* —**'cause+less** *adj.* —**'caus+er** *n.*

cause cé+lè+bre ('kɔːz sə'lɛbrə, -'lɛb; *French* koːz se'lɛbr) *n., pl.* **caus·es cé+lè+bres** ('kɔːz sə'lɛbrəz, -'lɛb; 'kɔːzɪz sə'lɛbrə, -'lɛbz; *French* koːz se'lɛbr). a famous lawsuit, trial, or controversy. [C19: from French: famous case]

cause list *n. Brit.* a list of cases awaiting trial.

cau+se+rie ('kəʊzərɪ; *French* koz'ri) *n.* an informal talk or conversational piece of writing. [C19: from French, from *causer* to chat]

cause+way ('kɔːzˌweɪ) *n.* **1.** a raised path or road crossing water, marshland, sand, etc. **2.** a paved footpath. ~Archaic or dialect word: **cau+sey** ('kɔːzɪ). [C15 *cauciwey* (from *cauci* + WAY); *cauci* paved road, from Medieval Latin (*via*) *calciāta, calciātus* paved with limestone, from Latin *calx* limestone]

caus+tic ('kɔːstɪk) *adj.* **1.** capable of burning or corroding by chemical action: *caustic soda.* **2.** sarcastic; cutting: *a caustic reply.* **3.** of, relating to, or denoting light that is reflected or refracted by a curved surface. ~*n.* **4.** Also called: **caustic surface.** a surface that envelopes the light rays reflected or refracted by a curved surface. **5.** Also called: **caustic curve.** a curve formed by the intersection of a caustic surface with a plane. **6.** *Chem.* a caustic substance, esp. an alkali. [C14: from Latin *causticus,* from Greek *kaustikos,* from *kaiein* to burn] —**'caus+ti+cal** *adj.* —**'caus+ti+cal+ly** *adv.* —**'caus+tic+ness** *or* **caus+tic+i·ty** (kɔː'stɪsɪtɪ) *n.*

caus+tic pot+ash *n.* another name for **potassium hydroxide.**

caus+tic so·da *n.* another name for **sodium hydroxide.**

cau+ter+ant ('kɔːtərənt) *adj.* **1.** caustic; cauterizing. ~*n.* **2.** another name for **cautery** (sense 2).

cau+ter+ize *or* **cau+ter+ise** ('kɔːtəˌraɪz) *vb.* (*tr.*) (esp. in the treatment of a wound) to burn or sear (body tissue) with a hot iron or caustic agent. [C14: from Old French *cauteriser,* from Late Latin *cautērizāre,* from *cautērium* branding iron, from Greek *kautērion,* from *kaiein* to burn] —**ˌcau+ter·i+'za+tion** *or* **ˌcau+ter·i+'sa+tion** *n.*

cau+ter·y ('kɔːtərɪ) *n., pl.* **+ter·ies. 1.** the coagulation of blood or destruction of body tissue by cauterizing. **2.** Also called: **cauterant.** an instrument or chemical agent for cauterizing. [C14: from Old French *cautère,* from Latin *cautērium;* see CAUTERIZE]

cau+tion ('kɔːʃən) *n.* **1.** care, forethought, or prudence, esp. in the face of danger; wariness. **2.** something intended or serving as a warning; admonition. **3.** *Law, chiefly Brit.* a formal warning given to a person suspected or accused of an offence that his words will be taken down and may be used in evidence. **4.** *Informal.* an amusing or surprising person or thing: *she's a real caution.* ~*vb.* **5.** (*tr.*) to urge or warn (a person) to be careful. **6.** (*tr.*) *Law, chiefly Brit.* to give a caution to (a person). **7.** (*intr.*) to warn, urge, or advise: *he cautioned against optimism.* [C13: from Old French, from Latin *cautiō,* from *cavēre* to beware] —**'cau+tion+er** *n.*

cau+tion+ar·y ('kɔːʃənərɪ) *adj.* serving as a warning; intended to warn: *a cautionary tale.*

cau+tion mon+ey *n. Chiefly Brit.* a sum of money deposited as security for good conduct, against possible debts, etc.

cau+tious ('kɔːʃəs) *adj.* showing or having caution; wary; prudent. —**'cau+tious+ly** *adv.* —**'cau+tious+ness** *n.*

Cau+ver·y *or* **Ka+ver·i** ('kɔːvərɪ) *n.* a river in S India, rising in the Western Ghats and flowing southeast to the Bay of Bengal. Length: 765 km (475 miles).

Cav. *or* **cav.** *abbrev. for* cavalry.

Ca·va·fy (kə'vɑːfɪ) *n.* **Con·stan·tine.** Greek name *Kavafis.* 1863–1933, Greek poet of Alexandria in Egypt.

cav+al+cade (ˌkævəl'keɪd) *n.* **1.** a procession of people on horseback, in cars, etc. **2.** any procession: *a cavalcade of guests.* [C16: from French, from Italian *cavalcata,* from *cavalcare* to ride on horseback, from Late Latin *caballicāre,* from *caballus* horse]

cav·a+lier (ˌkævə'lɪə) *adj.* **1.** showing haughty disregard; offhand. ~*n.* **2.** a gallant or courtly gentleman, esp. one acting as a lady's escort. **3.** *Archaic.* a horseman, esp. one who is armed. [C16: from Italian *cavaliere,* from Old Provençal *cavalier,* from Late Latin *caballārius* rider, from *caballus* horse, of obscure origin] —**ˌcav·a+'lier+ly** *adv.*

Cav·a+lier (ˌkævə'lɪə) *n.* a supporter of Charles I during the English Civil War. Compare **Roundhead.**

Cav·a+lier po·ets *pl. n.* a group of mid-17th century English lyric poets, mostly courtiers of Charles I. Chief among them were Robert Herrick, Thomas Carew, Sir John Suckling, and Richard Lovelace.

ca+val+la (kə'vælə) *or* **ca+val+ly** *n., pl.* **+la, +las,** *or* **+lies.** any of various tropical carangid fishes, such as *Gnathanodon speciosus* (golden cavalla). [C19: from Spanish *caballa,* from Late Latin, feminine of *caballus* horse]

cav+al+ry ('kævəlrɪ) *n., pl.* **+ries. 1.** (esp. formerly) the part of an army composed of mounted troops. **2.** the motorized armoured element of a modern army. **3.** (*as modifier*): *a cavalry unit; a cavalry charge.* [C16: from French *cavallerie,* from Italian *cavalleria,* from *cavaliere* horseman; see CAVALIER] —**'cav+al+ry+man** *n.*

cav+al+ry twill *n.* a strong woollen twill fabric used for trousers, etc.

Cav+an ('kævən) *n.* **1.** a county of N Ireland: hilly, with many small lakes and bogs. County town: Cavan. Pop.: 52 618 (1971). Area: 1890 sq. km (730 sq. miles). **2.** a market town in N Ireland, county town of Co. Cavan. Pop.: 3273 (1971).

cav·a+ti+na (ˌkævə'tiːnə) *n., pl.* **+ne** (-nɪ) **1.** a solo song resembling a simple aria. **2.** an instrumental composition reminiscent of this. [C19: from Italian]

cave[1] (keɪv) *n.* **1.** an underground hollow with access from the ground surface or from the sea, often found in limestone areas and on rocky coastlines. **2.** *British history.* a secession or a group seceding from a political party on some issue. **3.** (*modifier*) living in caves. ~*vb.* **4.** (*tr.*) to hollow out. ~See also **caving.** [C13: from Old French, from Latin *cava,* plural of *cavum* cavity, from *cavus* hollow]

ca·ve[2] ('keɪvɪ) *Brit. school slang.* ~*n.* **1.** guard or lookout (esp. in the phrase **keep cave**). ~*interj.* **2.** watch out! [from Latin *cavē* beware!]

ca+ve·at ('keɪvɪˌæt, 'kæv-) *n.* **1.** *Law.* a formal notice requesting the court or officer to refrain from taking some specified action without giving prior notice to the person lodging the caveat. **2.** a warning; caution. [C16: from Latin, literally: let him beware]

ca+ve·at emp+tor ('ɛmptɔː) *n.* the principle that the buyer must bear the risk for the quality of goods purchased unless they are covered by the seller's warranty. [Latin: let the buyer beware]

ca+ve·a+tor ('keɪvɪˌeɪtə, 'kæv-) *n. Law.* a person who enters a caveat.

cave+fish ('keɪvˌfɪʃ) *n., pl.* **+fish** *or* **+fish·es.** any of various small freshwater cyprinodont fishes of the genera *Amblyopsis, Chologaster,* etc., living in subterranean and other waters in S North America. See also **blindfish.**

cave in *vb.* (*intr., adv.*) **1.** to collapse; subside. **2.** *Informal.* to yield completely, esp. under pressure. ~*n.* **cave-in. 3.** the sudden collapse of a roof, piece of ground, etc., into a hollow beneath it; subsidence. **4.** the site of such a collapse, as at a mine or tunnel.

Cav·ell ('kævəl) *n.* **E·dith Lou·i·sa.** 1865–1915, English nurse:

executed by the Germans in World War I for helping Allied prisoners to escape.

cave+man ('keɪvˌmæn) *n., pl.* **+men. 1.** a man of the Palaeolithic age; cave dweller. **2.** *Informal and facetious.* a man who is primitive or brutal in behaviour, etc.

cav+en+dish ('kævəndɪʃ) *n.* tobacco that has been sweetened and pressed into moulds to form bars. [C19: perhaps from the name of the first maker]

Cav·en·dish ('kævəndɪʃ) *n.* **Hen·ry.** 1731–1810, English physicist and chemist: recognized hydrogen, determined the composition of water, and calculated the density of the earth by an experiment named after him.

cav+ern ('kævᵊn) *n.* **1.** a cave, esp. when large and formed by underground water, or a large chamber in a cave. *~vb. (tr.)* **2.** to shut in or as if in a cavern. **3.** to hollow out. [C14: from Old French *caverne,* from Latin *caverna,* from *cavus* hollow; see CAVE[1]]

cav+ern+ous ('kævənəs) *adj.* **1.** suggestive of a cavern in vastness, darkness, etc.: *cavernous hungry eyes.* **2.** filled with small cavities; porous. **3.** (of rocks) containing caverns or cavities. —**'cav+ern+ous+ly** *adv.*

cav+es+son ('kævɪsən) *n.* a kind of hard noseband, used (esp. formerly) in breaking a horse in. [C16: via French from Italian *cavezzone,* from *cavezza* halter, ultimately related to Latin *caput* head]

ca+vet+to (kə'vɛtəʊ; *Italian* ka'vetto) *n., pl.* **+ti** (-tɪ; *Italian* -ti:). *Architect.* a concave moulding, shaped to a quarter circle in cross section. [C17: from Italian, from *cavo* hollow, from Latin *cavus*]

cav·i+ar *or* **cav·i+are** ('kævɪˌɑ:, ˌkævɪ'ɑ:) *n.* **1.** the salted roe of sturgeon, esp. the beluga, usually served as an hors d'oeuvre. **2. caviar to the general.** something too good to appeal to popular taste. [C16: from earlier *cavery,* from Old Italian *caviari,* plural of *caviaro* caviar, from Turkish *havyār*]

cav·i+corn ('kævɪˌkɔ:n) *adj.* (of sheep, goats, etc.) having hollow horns as distinct from the solid antlers of deer. [C19: from Latin *cavus* hollow + *cornū* horn]

ca+vie ('keɪvɪ) *n. Scot.* a hen coop. [C18: via Dutch or Flemish *kavie,* from Latin *cavea* cavity]

cav+il ('kævɪl) *vb.* **+ils, +il+ling, +illed** *or U.S.* **+ils, +il+ing, +iled. 1.** (*intr.;* foll. by *at* or *about*) to raise annoying petty objections; quibble; carp. *~n.* **2.** a captious trifling objection. [C16: from Old French *caviller,* from Latin *cavillārī* to jeer, from *cavilla* raillery] —**'cav+il+ler** *n.* —**'cav+il+ling+ly** *adv.*

cav+ing ('keɪvɪŋ) *n.* the sport of climbing in and exploring caves. —**'cav+er** *n.*

cav·i·ta+tion (ˌkævɪ'teɪʃən) *n.* the formation and collapse of regions of low pressure in a flowing liquid.

Ca+vi·te (kə'vi:tɪ, -teɪ) *n.* a port in the N Philippines, in S Luzon on Manila Bay: U.S. naval base. Pop.: 75 739 (1970).

cav+i·ty ('kævɪtɪ) *n., pl.* **·ties. 1.** a hollow space; hole. **2.** *Dentistry.* a soft decayed area on a tooth. See **caries. 3.** any empty or hollow space within the body: *the oral cavity.* **4.** *Electronics.* See **cavity resonator.** [C16: from French *cavité,* from Late Latin *cavitās, from Latin cavus* hollow]

cav+i·ty block *n.* a precast concrete block that contains a cavity or cavities.

cav+i·ty res·o+na+tor *n. Electronics.* a conducting surface enclosing a space in which an oscillating electromagnetic field can be maintained, the dimensions of the cavity determining the resonant frequency of the oscillations. It is used in microwave devices, such as the klystron, for frequencies exceeding 300 megahertz. Also called: **resonant cavity, rhumbatron.**

cav+i·ty wall *n.* a wall that consists of two separate walls, joined by wall-ties, with an air-space between them.

ca·vo-re·lie·vo *or* **ca·vo-ri·lie·vo** (ˌkɑ:vəʊrɪ'li:vəʊ, ˌkeɪ-) *n., pl.* **·vos** *or* **·vi** (-vɪ). a relief sculpture in which the highest point in the carving is below the level of the original surface. [Italian, literally: hollow relief]

ca+vort (kə'vɔ:t) *vb.* (*intr.*) to prance; caper. [C19: perhaps from CURVET] —**ca+'vort+er** *n.*

Ca·vour (*Italian* ka'vur) *n.* Conte **Ca·mil·lo Ben·so di** (ka'millo 'bɛnzo di:). 1810–61, Italian statesman and premier of Piedmont-Sardinia (1852–59; 1860–61): a leader of the movement for the unification of Italy.

ca·vy ('keɪvɪ) *n., pl.* **·vies.** any small South American hystricomorph rodent of the family *Caviidae,* esp. any of the genus *Cavia,* having a thickset body and very small tail. See also **guinea pig.** [C18: from New Latin *Cavia,* from Galibi *cabiai*]

caw (kɔ:) *n.* **1.** the cry of a crow, rook, or raven. *~vb.* **2.** (*intr.*) to make this cry.

Caw·drey ('kɔ:drɪ) *n.* **Rob·ert.** 16th–17th-century English schoolmaster and lexicographer: compiled the first English dictionary (*A Table Alphabeticall*) in 1604.

Caw·ley ('kɔ:lɪ) *n.* **E·vonne** (née *Goolagong*). born 1951, Australian tennis player: Wimbledon champion 1971; Australian champion 1974–76.

Cawn+pore (ˌkɔ:n'pɔ:) *or* **Cawn+pur** (ˌkɔ:n'pʊə) *n.* the former name of **Kanpur.**

Cax+ton[1] ('kækstən) *n.* **1.** a book printed by William Caxton. **2.** a style of type, imitating the Gothic, that Caxton used in his books.

Cax·ton[2] ('kækstən) *n.* **Wil·liam.** ?1422–91, English printer and translator: published, in Bruges, the first book printed in English (1475) and established the first printing press in England (1477).

cay (keɪ, ki:) *n.* a small low island or bank composed of sand and coral fragments, esp. in the Caribbean area. Also called: **key.** [C18: from Spanish *cayo,* probably from Old French *quai* QUAY]

Cay+enne (keɪ'ɛn) *n.* the capital of French Guiana, on an island at the mouth of the Cayenne River: French penal settlement from 1854 to 1938. Pop.: 24 581 (1971 est.).

cay+enne pep+per (keɪ'ɛn) *n.* a very hot condiment, bright red in colour, made from the dried seeds and pods of various capsicums. Often shortened to **cayenne.** Also called: **red pepper.** [C18: ultimately from Tupi *quiynha*]

Cayes (keɪ; *French* kaj) *n.* short for **Les Cayes.**

cay+man *or* **cai+man** ('keɪmən) *n., pl.* **+mans.** any tropical American crocodilian of the genus *Caiman* and related genera, similar to alligators but with a more heavily armoured belly: family *Alligatoridae* (alligators, etc.). [C16: from Spanish *caimán,* from Carib *cayman,* probably of African origin]

Cay+man Is+lands ('keɪmən) *pl. n.* three coral islands in the Caribbean Sea northwest of Jamaica: a dependency of Jamaica until 1962, now a British colony. Capital: Georgetown. Pop.: 10 249 (1970). Area: about 260 sq. km (100 sq. miles).

Ca+yu+ga (keɪ'ju:gə, kaɪ-) *n.* **1.** (*pl.* **+gas** *or* **+ga**) a member of a North American Indian people (one of the Iroquois peoples) formerly living around Cayuga Lake. **2.** the language of this people, belonging to the Iroquoian family.

cay+use ('kaɪu:s) *n. Western U.S.* a small American Indian pony used by cowboys. [C19: from a Chinookan language]

Cb *the chemical symbol for* columbium.

CB *abbrev. for* Citizens' Band.

c.b. *abbrev. for* centre of buoyancy (of a boat, etc.).

C.B. *abbrev. for:* **1.** Companion of the (Order of the) Bath (a Brit. title). **2.** County Borough.

C bat+ter·y *n. U.S.* a battery for supplying a voltage to the grid of a thermionic valve. Also called: **grid-bias battery.** Compare **A battery, B battery.**

CBC *abbrev. for* Canadian Broadcasting Corporation.

C.B.D. *or* **c.b.d.** *abbrev. for:* **1.** cash before delivery. **2.** central business district.

C.B.E. *abbrev. for* Commander of the (Order of the) British Empire.

C.B.I. *abbrev. for* Confederation of British Industry.

CBS *abbrev. for* Columbia Broadcasting System.

cc *or* **c.c.** *abbrev. for:* **1.** carbon copy *or* copies. **2.** cubic centimetre(s).

cc. *abbrev. for* chapters.

C.C. *abbrev. for:* **1.** City Council. **2.** County Council. **3.** Cricket Club.

C.C.F. (in Britain) Combined Cadet Force.

C clef *n. Music.* a symbol (𝄡), now rarely used, placed at the beginning of the staff, establishing middle C as being on its centre line. See **alto clef, soprano clef, tenor clef.**

cd *abbrev. for* candela.

Cd *the chemical symbol for* cadmium.

Cd. (in Britain) *abbrev. for* command (paper).

c.d. *abbrev. for* cash discount.

C.D. *abbrev. for:* **1.** Civil Defence (Corps). **2.** Corps Diplomatique (Diplomatic Corps).

c/d *Book-keeping. abbrev. for* carried down.

CDN *international car registration for* Canada.

Cdn. *abbrev. for* Canadian.

Cdr. *Military. abbrev. for* Commander.

Cdre. *abbrev. for* Commodore.

CDT *U.S. abbrev. for* Central Daylight Time.

Ce *the chemical symbol for* cerium.

C.E. *abbrev. for:* **1.** chief engineer. **2.** Church of England. **3.** civil engineer. **4.** Common Entrance. **5.** Common Era.

ce·a+no+thus (ˌsi:ə'nəʊθəs) *n.* any shrub of the North American rhamnaceous genus *Ceanothus:* grown for their ornamental, often blue, flower clusters. [C19: New Latin, from Greek *keanōthos* a kind of thistle]

Cea+rá (*Portuguese* ˌsja'ra) *n.* **1.** a state of NE Brazil: sandy coastal plain, rising to a high plateau. Capital: Fortaleza. Pop.: 4 361 603 (1970). Area: 150 630 sq. km (58 746 sq. miles). **2.** another name for **Fortaleza.**

cease (si:s) *vb.* **1.** (when *tr.,* may take a gerund or an infinitive as object) to bring or come to an end; desist from; stop. *~n.* **2. without cease.** without stopping; incessantly. [C14: from Old French *cesser,* from Latin *cessāre,* frequentative of *cēdere* to yield, CEDE]

cease-fire *Chiefly military.* *~n.* **1.** a period of truce, esp. one that is temporary and a preliminary step to establishing a more permanent peace on agreed terms. *~interj., n.* **2.** the order to stop firing.

cease+less ('si:slɪs) *adj.* without stop or pause; incessant. —**'cease+less+ly** *adv.*

Ceau·şes·cu (tʃaʊ'ʃɛsku:) *n.* **Nic·o·lae** (ˌnɪkɒ'laɪ). born 1918, Rumanian statesman; chairman of the state council since 1967 and president of Rumania since 1974.

Ce·bú (sɪ'bu:) *n.* **1.** an island in the central Philippines. Pop.: 1 634 182 (1970). Area: 5086 sq. km (1964 sq. miles). **2.** a port in the Philippines, on E Cebú island. Pop.: 418 517 (1975 est.).

Čech·y ('tʃɛxi) *n.* the Czech name for **Bohemia.**

Cec·il ('sɛsᵊl, 'sɪs-) *n.* **1.** Lord **Da·vid.** born 1902, English literary critic and biographer. **2. Wil·liam.** See (William Cecil) **Burghley. 3. Rob·ert.** See (3rd Marquess of) **Salisbury.**

Ce+cil·ia (sɪ'si:ljə) *n.* **Saint.** died ?230 A.D., Roman martyr; patron saint of music. Feast day: Nov. 22.

ce+ci+ty ('si:sɪtɪ) *n.* a rare word for **blindness.** [C16: from Latin *caecitās, from caecus* blind]

ce+cro+pi·a moth (sɪ'krəʊpɪə) *n.* a large North American saturniid moth, *Hyalophora* (or *Samia*) *cecropia,* with brightly coloured wings and feathery antennae. [C19: New Latin, from Latin *Cecropius* belonging to CECROPS]

Ce·crops ('si:krɒps) *n.* (in ancient Greek tradition) the first king of Attica, represented as half-human, half-dragon.

ce+cum ('si:kəm) *n., pl.* **+ca** (-kə). *U.S.* a variant spelling of **caecum.** —'**ce·cal** *adj.*

ce+dar ('si:də) *n.* **1.** any Old World coniferous tree of the genus *Cedrus,* having spreading branches, needle-like evergreen leaves, and erect barrel-shaped cones: family *Pinaceae.* See also **cedar of Lebanon, deodar. 2.** any of various other conifers, such as the red cedars and white cedars. **3.** the wood of any of these trees. **4.** any of certain other plants, such as the Spanish cedar. *~adj.* **5.** made of the wood of a cedar tree. [C13: from Old French *cedre,* from Latin *cedrus,* from Greek *kedros*]

ce+dar of Leb+a+non *n.* a cedar, *Cedrus libani,* of SW Asia with level spreading branches and fragrant wood.

Ce+dar Rap+ids *n.* a city in E Iowa. Pop.: 109 897 (1973 est.).

cede (si:d) *vb.* **1.** (when *intr.,* often foll. by *to*) to transfer, make over, or surrender (something, esp. territory or legal rights): *the lands were ceded by treaty.* **2.** (*tr.*) to allow or concede (a point in an argument, etc.). [C17: from Latin *cēdere* to yield, give way] —'**ced+er** *n.*

ce·di ('seɪdɪ) *n., pl.* **·di.** the standard monetary unit of Ghana, divided into 100 pesewa.

ce+dil+la (sɪ'dɪlə) *n.* a character (̧) placed underneath a *c* before *a, o,* or *u,* esp. in French, Spanish, or Portuguese, denoting that it is to be pronounced (s), not (k). The same character is used in the scripts of other languages, as in Turkish under *s.* [C16: from Spanish: little *z,* from *ceda* zed, from Late Latin *zeta;* a small *z* was originally written after *c* in Spanish, to indicate a sibilant]

C.E.G.B. *Brit. abbrev. for* Central Electricity Generating Board.

cei+ba ('seɪbə) *n.* **1.** any bombacaceous tropical tree of the genus *Ceiba,* such as the silk-cotton tree. **2.** silk cotton; kapok. [C19: from New Latin, from Spanish, of Arawak origin]

ceil (si:l) *vb.* **1.** (*tr.*) to line (a ceiling) with plaster, boarding, etc. **2.** (*tr.*) to provide with a ceiling. [C15 *celen,* perhaps back formation from CEILING]

cei+lidh ('keɪlɪ) *n.* (esp. in Scotland and Ireland) an informal social gathering with folk music, singing, dancing, and story-telling. [C19: from Gaelic]

ceil+ing ('si:lɪŋ) *n.* **1.** the inner upper surface of a room. **2.** an upper limit, such as one set by regulation on prices or wages. **3.** the upper altitude to which an aircraft can climb measured under specified conditions. See also **service ceiling, absolute ceiling. 4.** *Meteorol.* the highest level in the atmosphere from which the earth's surface is visible at a particular time, usually the base of a cloud layer. **5.** a wooden or metal surface fixed to the interior frames of a vessel for rigidity. [C14: of uncertain origin]

ceil+om+e+ter (si:'lɒmɪtə) *n.* a device for determining the cloud ceiling, esp. by means of a reflected light beam. [C20: from CEILING + -METER]

cel·a·don ('sɛlə,dɒn) *n.* **1.** a type of Chinese porcelain having a greyish-green glaze. **2.** a pale greyish-green colour, sometimes somewhat yellow. [C18: from French, from the name of the shepherd hero of *L'Astrée* (1610), a romance by Honoré d'Urfé]

Ce·lae·no (se'li:nəʊ) *n. Greek myth.* one of the Pleiades.

cel+an+dine ('sɛlən,daɪn) *n.* either of two unrelated plants, *Chelidonium majus* (see **greater celandine**) or *Ranunculus ficaria* (see **lesser celandine**). [C13: earlier *celydon,* from Latin *chelīdonia* (the plant), from *chelīdonius* of the swallow, from Greek *khelidōn* swallow; the plant's season was believed to parallel the migration of swallows]

Ce+la+ya (*Spanish* se'laja) *n.* a city in central Mexico, in Guanajuato state: market town, famous for its sweetmeats; textile-manufacturing. Pop.: 143 703 (1970).

-cele *n. combining form.* tumour or hernia: *hydrocele.* [from Greek *kēlē* tumour]

Cel+e·bes ('sɛlɪbi:z, se'li:bɪz) *n.* an island in E Indonesia: mountainous and forested, with volcanoes and hot springs. Pop.: 8 535 164 (1971). Area: (including adjacent islands) 189 033 sq. km (72 986 sq. miles). Indonesian name: **Sulawesi.**

Cel+e·bes Sea *n.* the part of the Pacific Ocean between Celebes, Borneo, and Mindanao.

cel+e·brant ('sɛlɪbrənt) *n.* **1.** a person participating in a religious ceremony. **2.** *Christianity.* an officiating priest, esp. at the Eucharist.

cel+e·brate ('sɛlɪ,breɪt) *vb.* **1.** to rejoice in or have special festivities to mark (a happy day, event, etc.). **2.** (*tr.*) to observe (a birthday, anniversary, etc.): *she celebrates her ninetieth birthday next month.* **3.** (*tr.*) to perform (a solemn or religious ceremony), esp. to officiate at (Mass). **4.** (*tr.*) to praise publicly; proclaim. [C15: from Latin *celebrāre,* from *celeber* numerous, thronged, renowned] —,**cel+e·'bra+tion** *n.* —'**cel+e·bra+tive** *adj.* —'**cel+e·,bra+tor** *n.* —'**cel+e·,bra+to·ry** *adj.*

cel+e·brat+ed ('sɛlɪ,breɪtɪd) *adj.* (*usually prenominal*) famous: *a celebrated pianist; a celebrated trial.*

ce+leb+ri·ty (sɪ'lɛbrɪtɪ) *n., pl.* **·ties. 1.** a famous person: *a show-business celebrity.* **2.** fame or notoriety.

ce+ler+i+ac (sɪ'lɛrɪ,æk) *n.* a variety of celery, *Apium graveolens rapaceum,* with a large turnip-like root, used as a vegetable. [C18: from CELERY + *-ac,* of unexplained origin]

ce+ler+i·ty (sɪ'lɛrɪtɪ) *n.* rapidity; swiftness; speed. [C15: from Old French *celerite,* from Latin *celeritās,* from *celer* swift]

cel+er·y ('sɛlərɪ) *n.* **1.** an umbelliferous Eurasian plant, *Apium graveolens dulce,* whose blanched leafstalks are used in salads or cooked as a vegetable. See also **celeriac. 2. wild celery. a** related and similar plant, *Apium graveolens.* [C17: from French *céleri,* from Italian (Lombardy) dialect *selleri* (plural), from Greek *selinon* parsley]

cel+er·y pine *n.* a New Zealand gymnosperm tree, *Phyllocladus trichomanoides,* with celerylike shoots and useful wood: family *Phyllocladaceae.*

ce+les+ta (sɪ'lɛstə) *or* **ce+leste** (sɪ'lɛst) *n. Music.* a keyboard percussion instrument consisting of a set of steel plates of graduated length that are struck with key-operated hammers. The tone is an ethereal tinkling sound. Range: four octaves upwards from middle C. [C19: from French, Latinized variant of *céleste* heavenly]

ce+les+ti·al (sɪ'lɛstɪəl) *adj.* **1.** heavenly; divine; spiritual: *celestial peace.* **2.** of or relating to the sky: *celestial bodies.* [C14: from Medieval Latin *cēlestiālis,* from Latin *caelestis,* from *caelum* heaven] —**ce+'les+ti+al+ly** *adv.*

Ce+les+ti·al Em+pire *n.* an archaic or literary name for the **Chinese Empire.**

ce+les+ti·al e·qua+tor *n.* the great circle lying on the celestial sphere the plane of which is perpendicular to the line joining the north and south celestial poles. Also called: **equinoctial, equinoctial circle.**

ce+les+ti·al globe *n.* a spherical model of the celestial sphere showing the relative positions of stars, constellations, etc.

ce+les+ti·al guid+ance *n.* the guidance of a spacecraft or missile by reference to the positions of one or more celestial bodies.

ce+les+ti·al ho+ri+zon *n.* See **horizon** (sense 2b).

ce+les+ti·al lat·i·tude *n.* the angular distance of a celestial body north or south from the ecliptic. Sometimes shortened to **latitude.**

ce+les+ti·al lon+gi+tude *n.* the angular distance measured eastwards from the vernal equinox to the intersection of the ecliptic with the great circle passing through a celestial body and the poles of the ecliptic. Sometimes shortened to **longitude.**

ce+les+ti·al nav·i+ga+tion *n.* navigation by observation of the positions of the stars. Also called: **astronavigation.**

ce+les+ti·al pole *n.* either of the two points at which the earth's axis, extended to infinity, would intersect the celestial sphere. Sometimes shortened to **pole.**

ce+les+ti·al sphere *n.* an imaginary sphere of infinitely large radius enclosing the universe so that all celestial bodies appear to be projected onto its surface.

cel+es+tite ('sɛlɪ,staɪt) *or* **cel+es+tine** ('sɛlɪstɪn, -,staɪn) *n.* a white, red, or blue mineral consisting of strontium sulphate in orthorhombic crystalline form: a source of strontium compounds. Formula: $SrSO_4$. [C19: from German *Zölestin,* from Latin *caelestis* CELESTIAL (referring to the blue colour) + -ITE[1]]

ce+li+ac ('si:lɪ,æk) *adj. Anatomy.* the usual U.S. spelling of **coeliac.**

cel·i+bate ('sɛlɪbɪt) *n.* **1.** a person who is unmarried, esp. one who has taken a religious vow of chastity. *~adj.* **2.** unmarried, esp. by vow. [C17: from Latin *caelibātus,* from *caelebs* unmarried, of obscure origin] —'**cel·i+ba+cy** *n.*

cell (sɛl) *n.* **1.** a small simple room, as in a prison, convent, monastery, or asylum; cubicle. **2.** any small compartment: *the cells of a honeycomb.* **3.** *Biology.* the smallest unit of an organism that is able to function independently. It consists of a nucleus, containing the genetic material, surrounded by the cytoplasm in which are mitochondria, lysosomes, ribosomes, and other organelles. All cells are bounded by a cell membrane; plant cells have an outer cell wall in addition. **4.** *Biology.* any small cavity or area, such as the cavity containing pollen in an anther. **5.** a device for converting chemical energy into electrical energy, usually consisting of a container with two electrodes immersed in an electrolyte. See also **primary cell, secondary cell, dry cell, wet cell, fuel cell. 6.** short for **electrolytic cell. 7.** a small religious house dependent upon a larger one. **8.** a small group of persons operating as a nucleus of a larger political, religious, or other organization: *Communist cell.* [C12: from Medieval Latin *cella* monk's cell, from Latin: room, storeroom; related to Latin *cēlāre* to hide] —'**cell-,like** *adj.*

cel+la ('sɛlə) *n., pl.* **+lae** (-li:). the inner room of a classical temple, esp. the room housing the statue of a deity. Also called: **naos.** [C17: from Latin: room, shrine; see CELL]

cel+lar ('sɛlə) *n.* **1.** an underground room, rooms, or storey of a building, usually used for storage. Compare **basement. 2.** a place where wine is stored. **3.** a stock of bottled wines. *~vb.* **4.** (*tr.*) to store in a cellar. [C13: from Anglo-French, from Latin *cellārium* foodstore, from *cella* CELLA]

cel+lar+age ('sɛlərɪdʒ) *n.* **1.** an area of a cellar. **2.** a charge for storing goods in a cellar, etc.

cel+lar+er ('sɛlərə) *n.* a monastic official responsible for food, drink, etc.

cel+lar+et (,sɛlə'rɛt) *n.* a case, cabinet, or sideboard with compartments for holding wine bottles.

cell di+vi+sion *n. Cytology.* the division of a cell into two new cells during growth or reproduction. See **amitosis, meiosis, mitosis.**

Cel+le (*German* 'tsɛlə) *n.* a city in NE West Germany, on the Aller River in Lower Saxony: from 1378 to 1705 the residence of the Dukes of Brunswick-Lüneburg. Pop.: 57 100 (1970).

Cel·li·ni (tʃɪ'li:nɪ) *n.* **Ben·ve·nu·to** (,benve'nu:to). 1500–71, Italian sculptor, goldsmith, and engraver, noted also for his autobiography.

cell mem+brane *n.* a very thin membrane, composed of lipids and protein, that surrounds the cytoplasm of a cell and controls the passage of substances into and out of the cell. Also called: **plasma membrane.**

cel+lo ('tʃɛləʊ) *n., pl.* +**los.** *Music.* a bowed stringed instrument of the violin family. Range: more than four octaves upwards from C below the bass staff. It has four strings, is held between the knees, and has an extendible metal spike at the lower end, which acts as a support. Full name: **violoncello.** —'**cel+list** *n.*

cel+lo+bi+ose (ˌsɛləʊ'baɪəʊz) *or* **cel+lose** ('sɛləʊz) *n.* a disaccharide obtained by the hydrolysis of cellulose by cellulase. Formula: $C_{12}H_{22}O_{11}$. [C20: from CELLULOSE + BI-[1] + -OSE[2]]

cel+loi+din (sə'lɔɪdɪn) *n.* a nitrocellulose compound derived from pyroxylin, used in a solution of alcohol and ether for embedding specimens before cutting sections for microscopy. [C20: from CELLULOSE + -OID + -IN]

cel+lo+phane ('sɛləˌfeɪn) *n.* a flexible thin transparent sheeting made from wood pulp and used as a moisture-proof wrapping. [C20: originally a trademark, from CELLULOSE + -PHANE]

cel+lu+lar ('sɛljʊlə) *adj.* **1.** of, relating to, or resembling a cell. **2.** consisting of or having cells or small cavities; porous. **3.** *Textiles.* woven with an open texture: *a cellular blanket.* —**cel+lu+lar+i+ty** (ˌsɛljʊ'lærɪtɪ) *n.*

cel+lu+lase ('sɛljʊˌleɪz) *n.* any enzyme that converts cellulose to the disaccharide cellobiose. [C20: from CELLULOSE + -ASE]

cel+lule ('sɛljuːl) *n.* a very small cell. [C17: from Latin *cellula,* diminutive of *cella* CELL]

cel+lu+li+tis (ˌsɛljʊ'laɪtɪs) *n.* inflammation of any of the tissues of the body, characterized by fever, pain, swelling, and redness of the affected area. [C19: from *cellula* CELLULE + -ITIS]

Cel+lu+loid ('sɛljʊˌlɔɪd) *n.* **1.** *Trademark.* a flammable thermoplastic material consisting of cellulose nitrate mixed with a plasticizer, usually camphor: used in sheets, rods, and tubes for making a wide range of articles. **2.** (*usually not cap.*) **a.** a cellulose derivative used for coating film. **b.** one of the transparent sheets on which the constituent drawings of an animated film are prepared. **c.** cinema film.

cel+lu+lose ('sɛljʊˌləʊz, -ˌləʊs) *n.* a polysaccharide consisting of long unbranched chains of linked glucose units: the main constituent of plant cell walls and used in making paper, rayon, and film. [C18: from French *cellule* cell (see CELLULE) + -OSE[2]] —ˌ**cel+lu+'lo+sic** *adj., n.*

cel+lu+lose ac+e+tate *n.* nonflammable material made by acetylating cellulose: used in the manufacture of film, dopes, lacquers, and artificial fibres.

cel+lu+lose ni+trate *n.* a compound made by treating cellulose with nitric and sulphuric acids, used in plastics, lacquers, and explosives: a nitrogen-containing ester of cellulose. Also called (not in chemical usage): **nitrocellulose.** See also **guncotton.**

cel+lu+lous ('sɛljʊləs) *adj. Rare.* consisting of cells; cellular.

cell wall *n.* the outer layer of a cell, esp. the structure in plant cells that consists of cellulose, lignin, etc., and gives mechanical support to the cell.

ce+lom ('siːləm) *n.* a less frequent U.S. spelling of **coelom.**

Cel·si·us ('sɛlsɪəs) *adj.* denoting a measurement on the Celsius scale. Symbol: C [C18: named after Anders *Celsius* (1701–44), Swedish astronomer who invented it]

Cel·si·us scale *n.* a scale of temperature in which 0° represents the melting point of ice and 100° represents the boiling point of water. Also called: **centigrade scale.** Compare **Fahrenheit scale.**

celt (sɛlt) *n. Archaeol.* a stone or metal axelike instrument with a bevelled edge. [C18: from Late Latin *celtes* chisel, of obscure origin]

Celt (kɛlt, sɛlt) *or* **Kelt** *n.* **1.** a person who speaks a Celtic language. **2.** a member of an Indo-European people who in pre-Roman times inhabited Britain, Gaul, Spain, and other parts of W and central Europe.

Celt. *abbrev. for* Celtic.

Celt·i·be·ri·an (ˌkɛltɪ'bɪərɪən, -taɪ-, ˌsɛl-) *n.* **1.** a member of a Celtic people (**Celtiberi**) who inhabited the Iberian peninsula during classical times. **2.** the extinct language of this people, belonging to the Celtic branch of the Indo-European family, recorded in a number of inscriptions.

Celt+ic ('kɛltɪk, 'sɛl-) *or* **Kelt+ic** *n.* **1.** a branch of the Indo-European family of languages that includes Gaelic, Welsh, and Breton, still spoken in parts of Scotland, Ireland, Wales, and Brittany. Modern Celtic is divided into the Brythonic (southern) and Goidelic (northern) groups. ~*adj.* **2.** of, relating to, or characteristic of the Celts or the Celtic languages. —'**Cel+ti+cal+ly** *or* '**Kel+ti+cal+ly** *adv.* —**Celt·i·cism** ('kɛltɪˌsɪzəm, 'sɛl-) *or* '**Kelt·i·cism** *n.* —'**Celt·i·cist,** '**Celt+ist** *or* '**Kelt·i·cist,** '**Kelt+ist** *n.*

Celt+ic cross *n.* a Latin cross with a broad ring surrounding the point of intersection.

cem+ba+lo ('tʃɛmbələʊ) *n., pl.* +**li** (-ˌliː) *or* +**los.** another word for **harpsichord.** [C19: shortened from CLAVICEMBALO] —'**cem+ba+list** *n.*

ce+ment (sɪ'mɛnt) *n.* **1.** a fine grey powder made of a mixture of calcined limestone and clay, used with water and sand to make mortar, or with water, sand, and aggregate, to make concrete. **2.** a binder, glue, or adhesive. **3.** something that unites or joins; bond. **4.** *Dentistry.* any of various materials used in filling teeth. **5.** mineral matter, such as silica and calcite, that binds together particles of rock, bones, etc., to form a solid mass of sedimentary rock. **6.** another word for **cementum.** ~*vb.* (*tr.*) **7.** to join, bind, or glue together with or as if with cement. **8.** to coat or cover with cement. [C13: from Old French *ciment,* from Latin *caementum* stone from the quarry, from *caedere* to hew] —**ce+'ment+er** *n.*

ce+men+ta+tion (ˌsiːmɛn'teɪʃən) *n.* **1.** the process of heating a solid with a powdered material to modify the properties of the solid, esp. the heating of wrought iron, surrounded with charcoal, to 750–900°C to produce steel. **2.** the process of cementing or being cemented.

ce+ment+ite (sɪ'mɛntaɪt) *n.* the hard brittle compound of iron and carbon that forms in carbon steels and some cast irons. Formula: Fe_3C.

ce+men+tum (sɪ'mɛntəm) *n.* a thin bonelike tissue that covers the dentine in the root of a tooth. [C19: New Latin, from Latin: CEMENT]

cem+e+ter+y ('sɛmɪtrɪ) *n., pl.* ·**ter·ies.** a place where the dead are buried, esp. one not attached to a church. [C14: from Late Latin *coemētērium,* from Greek *koimētērion* room for sleeping, from *koiman* to put to sleep]

cen. *abbrev. for* central.

cen·a·cle *or* **coen·a·cle** ('sɛnək°l) *n.* **1.** a supper room, esp. one on an upper floor. **2.** (*cap.*) the room in which the Last Supper took place. [C14: from Old French, from Late Latin *cēnāculum,* from *cēna* supper]

-cene *n. and adj. combining form.* denoting a recent geological period: *Miocene.* [from Greek *kainos* new]

ce+nes+the+si·a (ˌsiːnɪs'θiːzɪə) *n. Psychol.* a variant spelling (esp. U.S.) of **coenaesthesia.**

C. Eng. *abbrev. for* chartered engineer.

Ce+nis (*French* sə'ni) *n.* **Mont.** a pass over the Graian Alps in SE France, between Lanslebourg (France) and Susa (Italy): nearby tunnel, opened in 1871. Highest point: 2049 m (6831 ft.). Italian name: **Mon+te Ce+ni+sio** ('monte tʃe'niːzjo).

ce+no+bite ('siːnəʊˌbaɪt) *n.* a variant spelling of **coenobite.**

ce+no+gen+e·sis (ˌsiːnəʊ'dʒɛnɪsɪs) *n.* a U.S. spelling of **caenogenesis.**

ce+no+spe+cies ('siːnəˌspiːʃiːz) *n., pl.* +**spe+cies.** a species related to another by the ability to interbreed: *dogs and wolves are cenospecies.* [C20: from Greek *koinos* common + SPECIES]

cen·o·taph ('sɛnəˌtɑːf) *n.* a monument honouring a dead person or persons buried elsewhere. [C17: from Latin *cenotaphium,* from Greek *kenotaphion,* from *kenos* empty + *taphos* tomb] —ˌ**cen·o·'taph+ic** *adj.*

ce+no+te (sɪ'nəʊteɪ) *n.* (esp. in the Yucatan peninsula) a natural well formed by the collapse of an overlying limestone crust: often used as a sacrificial site by the Mayas. [C19: via Mexican Spanish from Maya *conot*]

Ce+no+zo+ic (ˌsiːnəʊ'zəʊɪk) *or* **Cai+no+zo+ic** *adj.* **1.** of, denoting, or relating to the most recent geological era, which began 70 000 000 years ago: characterized by the development and increase of the mammals. ~*n.* **2.** **the.** the Cenozoic era. [C19: from Greek *kainos* new, recent + *zōikos,* from *zōion* animal]

cense (sɛns) *vb.* (*tr.*) to burn incense near or before (an altar, shrine, etc.). [C14: from Old French *encenser;* see INCENSE[1]]

cen+ser ('sɛnsə) *n.* a container for burning incense, esp. one swung at religious ceremonies. Also called: **thurible.**

cen+sor ('sɛnsə) *n.* **1.** a person authorized to examine publications, theatrical presentations, films, letters, etc., in order to suppress in whole or part those considered obscene, politically unacceptable, etc. **2.** any person who controls or suppresses the behaviour of others, usually on moral grounds. **3.** (in republican Rome) either of two senior magistrates elected to keep the list of citizens up to date, control aspects of public finance, and supervise public morals. **4.** *Psychoanal.* the postulated factor responsible for regulating the translation of ideas and desires from the unconscious to the conscious mind. See also **superego.** ~*vb.* (*tr.*) **5.** to ban or cut portions of (a publication, film, letter, etc.). **6.** to act as a censor of (behaviour, etc.). [C16: from Latin, from *cēnsēre* to consider, assess] —'**cen+sor+a·ble** *adj.* —**cen+so+ri+al** (sɛn'sɔːrɪəl) *adj.*

cen+so+ri+ous (sɛn'sɔːrɪəs) *adj.* harshly critical; fault-finding. —**cen+'so+ri+ous+ly** *adv.* —**cen+'so+ri+ous+ness** *n.*

cen+sor+ship ('sɛnsəˌʃɪp) *n.* **1.** a policy or programme of censoring. **2.** the act or system of censoring. **3.** *Psychoanal.* the activity of the mind in regulating impulses, etc., from the unconscious so that they are modified before reaching the conscious mind.

cen+sur+a·ble ('sɛnʃərəb°l) *adj.* deserving censure, condemnation, or blame. —'**cen+sur+a·ble+ness** *or* ˌ**cen+sur+a·'bil+i·ty** *n.* —'**cen+sur+a·bly** *adv.*

cen+sure ('sɛnʃə) *n.* **1.** severe disapproval; harsh criticism. ~*vb.* **2.** to criticize (someone or something) severely; condemn. —'**cen+sur+er** *n.*

cen+sus ('sɛnsəs) *n., pl.* +**sus+es.** **1.** an official periodic count of a population including such information as sex, age, occupation, etc. **2.** (in ancient Rome) a registration of the population and a property evaluation for purposes of taxation. [C17: from Latin, from *cēnsēre* to assess] —'**cen·su·al** *adj.*

cent (sɛnt) *n.* **1.** a monetary unit of Australia, Barbados, Botswana, Canada, Sri Lanka, Ethiopia, Guyana, Hong Kong, Kenya, Lesotho, Liberia, Malaysia, Mauritius, the Netherlands, New Zealand, the Republic of China, Sierra Leone, Singapore, the Somali Republic, South Africa, South Vietnam, Swaziland, Tanzania, Trinidad and Tobago, Uganda, the United States, and Western Samoa. It is worth one hundredth of their respective standard units. **2.** an interval of pitch between two frequencies f_2 and f_1 equal to 3986.31 log (f_2/f_1); one twelve-hundredth of the interval between two frequencies having the ratio 1:2 (an octave). [C16: from Latin *centēsimus* hundredth, from *centum* hundred]

cent. *abbrev. for:* **1.** centigrade. **2.** central. **3.** century.

cen+tal ('sɛnt°l) *n.* a unit of weight equal to 100 pounds (45.3 kilograms). [C19: from Latin *centum* hundred]

cen+taur ('sɛntɔː) *n. Greek myth.* one of a race of creatures with the head, arms, and torso of a man, and the lower body and legs of a horse. [C14: from Latin, from Greek *kentauros*, of unknown origin]

Cen+tau+rus (sɛn'tɔ:rəs) *n., Latin genitive* **Cen+tau+ri** (sɛn'tɔ:raɪ). a conspicuous extensive constellation in the S hemisphere, close to the Southern Cross, that contains two first magnitude stars, Alpha Centauri and Beta Centauri, and the globular cluster Omega Centauri. Also called: **The Centaur.**

cen+tau+ry ('sɛntɔ:rɪ) *n., pl.* **+ries. 1.** any Eurasian plant of the genus *Centaurium*, esp. *C. erythraea*, having purplish-pink flowers and formerly believed to have medicinal properties: family *Gentianaceae*. **2.** any plant of the genus *Centaurea*, which includes the cornflower and knapweed: family *Compositae* (composites). [C14: ultimately from Greek *Kentauros* the Centaur; from the legend that Chiron the Centaur was responsible for divulging its healing properties]

cen+ta+vo (sɛn'tɑ:vəʊ) *n., pl.* **+vos.** a monetary unit of Argentina, Bolivia, Brazil, Colombia, Cuba, the Dominican Republic, Ecuador, El Salvador, Guatemala, Honduras, Mexico, Nicaragua, Peru, the Philippines, and Portugal. It is worth one hundredth of their respective standard units. [Spanish: one hundredth part]

cen+te+nar+i+an (ˌsɛntɪ'nɛərɪən) *n.* **1.** a person who is at least 100 years old. *~adj.* **2.** being at least 100 years old. **3.** of or relating to a centenarian.

cen+te+nar·y (sɛn'ti:nərɪ) *adj.* **1.** of or relating to a period of 100 years. **2.** occurring once every 100 years: *centenary celebrations.* *~n., pl.* **+nar·ies. 3.** a 100th anniversary or its celebration. [C17: from Latin *centēnārius* of a hundred, from *centēnī* a hundred each, from *centum* hundred]

cen+ten+ni·al (sɛn'tɛnɪəl) *adj.* **1.** relating to, lasting for, or completing a period of 100 years. **2.** occurring every 100 years. *~n.* **3.** *U.S.* another name for **centenary.** [C18: from Latin *centum* hundred, on the model of BIENNIAL] **—cen+'ten+ni+al+ly** *adv.*

cen+ter ('sɛntə) *n., vb.* the U.S. spelling of **centre.**

cen+ter+ing ('sɛntərɪŋ) *n.* a U.S. spelling of **centring.**

cen+tes·i+mal (sɛn'tɛsɪməl) *n.* **1.** hundredth. *~adj.* **2.** relating to division into hundredths. [C17: from Latin *centēsimus*, from *centum* hundred] **—cen+'tes·i+mal+ly** *adv.*

cen+tes·i+mo (sɛn'tɛsɪˌməʊ) *n., pl.* **+mos.** a fractional monetary unit of Chile, Italy, Panama, and Uruguay. It is worth one hundredth of their respective standard units. [C19: from Spanish and Italian, from Latin *centēsimus* hundredth, from *centum* hundred]

cen·ti- *or before a vowel* **cent-** *prefix.* **1.** denoting one hundredth: *centimetre.* Symbol: c **2.** *Rare.* denoting a hundred: *centipede.* [from French, from Latin *centum* hundred]

cen+ti+are ('sɛntɪˌɛə; *French* sɑ̃'tja:r) *or* **cen+tare** ('sɛntɛə; *French* sɑ̃'ta:r) *n.* a unit of area equal to one square metre. [French, from CENTI- + *are* from Latin *ārea*; see ARE[2], AREA]

cen+ti+grade ('sɛntɪˌgreɪd) *adj.* **1.** another name for **Celsius.** *~n.* **2.** a unit of angle equal to one hundredth of a grade.

Usage. Although still used in meteorology, *centigrade*, when indicating the Celsius scale of temperature, is now usually avoided in other scientific contexts because of its possible confusion with the hundredth part of a grade.

cen+ti+gram *or* **cen+ti+gramme** ('sɛntɪˌgræm) *n.* one hundredth of a gram.

cen+ti+li+tre *or U.S.* **cen+ti+li+ter** ('sɛntɪˌli:tə) *n.* one hundredth of a litre.

cen+til+lion (sɛn'tɪljən) *n., pl.* **+lions** *or* **+lion. 1.** (in Britain and Germany) the number represented as one followed by 600 zeros (10^{600}). **2.** (in the U.S. and France) the number represented as one followed by 303 zeros (10^{303}).

cen+time ('sɒnˌti:m; *French* sɑ̃'tim) *n.* a monetary unit of Algeria, Belgium, Burundi, Cameroun, the Central African Republic, Chad, the Congo Republic, Dahomey, France, Gabon, Guinea, Haiti, the Ivory Coast, Liechtenstein, Luxembourg, the Malagasy Republic, Mali, Mauritania, Niger, Rwanda, Senegal, Switzerland, Tahiti, Togo, and Upper Volta. It is worth one hundredth of their respective standard units. [C18: from French, from Old French *centiesme* from Latin *centēsimus* hundredth, from *centum* hundred]

cen+ti+me+tre *or U.S.* **cen+ti+me+ter** ('sɛntɪˌmi:tə) *n.* one hundredth of a metre.

cen·ti·me·tre-gram-sec·ond *n.* See **cgs units.**

cén+ti+mo ('sɛntɪˌməʊ) *n., pl.* **+mos.** a monetary unit of Costa Rica, Paraguay, Spain, and Venezuela. It is worth one hundredth of their respective standard currency units. [from Spanish; see CENTIME]

cen+ti+pede ('sɛntɪˌpi:d) *n.* any carnivorous arthropod of the genera *Lithobius, Scutigera*, etc., having a body of between 15 and 190 segments, each bearing one pair of legs: class *Chilopoda.* See also **myriapod.**

cen+ti+poise ('sɛntɪˌpɔɪz) *n.* one hundredth of a poise. 1 centipoise is equal to 0.001 newton second per square metre.

cent+ner ('sɛntnə) *n.* **1.** Also called (esp. U.S.): **short hundredweight.** a unit of weight equivalent to 100 pounds (45.3 kilograms). **2.** (in some European countries) a unit of weight equivalent to 50 kilograms (110.23 pounds). **3.** a unit of weight equivalent to 100 kilograms. [C17: from German *Zentner*, ultimately from Latin *centēnārius* of a hundred; see CENTENARY]

cen+to ('sɛntəʊ) *n., pl.* **+tos.** a piece of writing, esp. a poem, composed of quotations from other authors. [C17: from Latin, literally: patchwork garment]

CENTO ('sɛntəʊ) *n. acronym for* Central Treaty Organization; an organization for military and economic cooperation formed in 1959 by the U.K., Iran, Pakistan, and Turkey as a successor to the Baghdad Pact.

cen+tra ('sɛntrə) *n.* the plural of **centrum.**

cen+tral ('sɛntrəl) *adj.* **1.** in, at, of, from, containing, or forming the centre of something: *the central street in a city; the central material of a golf ball.* **2.** main, principal, or chief; most important: *the central cause of a problem.* **3. a.** of or relating to the central nervous system. **b.** of or relating to the centrum of a vertebra. **4.** of, relating to, or denoting a vowel articulated with the tongue held in an intermediate position halfway between the positions for back and front vowels, as for the *a* of English *soda.* **5.** (of a force) directed from or towards a point.

Cen+tral Af+ri+can Fed+er·a+tion *n.* another name for the **Federation of Rhodesia and Nyasaland** or the **Rhodesia and Nyasaland Federation.**

Cen+tral Af+ri+can Re+pub+lic *n.* a landlocked country of central Africa: joined with Chad as a territory of French Equatorial Africa in 1910; became an independent republic in 1960; a parliamentary monarchy (1976-1979); consists of a huge plateau, mostly savanna, with dense forests in the south; drained chiefly by the Shari and Ubangi Rivers. Languages: French and Sangho. Religion: chiefly animist. Currency: franc. Capital: Bangui. Pop.: 1 637 000 (1971 est.). Area: 622 577 sq. km (240 376 sq. miles). Former names: (until 1958) **Ubangi-Shari;** (1976-79) **Central African Empire.** French name: **République Centrafricaine.**

Cen+tral A·mer·i+ca *n.* an isthmus joining the continents of North and South America, extending from the S border of Mexico to the NW border of Colombia and consisting of Belize, Guatemala, Honduras, El Salvador, Nicaragua, Costa Rica, Panama, and the Canal Zone. Area: about 518 000 sq. km (200 000 sq. miles). **—Cen+tral A·mer·i·can** *adj.*

cen+tral an+gle *n.* an angle whose vertex is at the centre of a circle.

cen+tral bank *n.* a national bank that does business mainly with a government and with other banks: it regulates the volume and cost of credit.

Cen+tral Com+mit+tee *n.* (in Communist parties) the body responsible for party policy between meetings of the party congress: in practice, it is in charge of day-to-day operations of the party bureaucracy.

Cen+tral Eur·o+pe·an Time *n.* the standard time adopted by Western European countries one hour ahead of Greenwich Mean Time, corresponding to British Summer Time. Abbrev.: **C.E.T.**

cen+tral heat+ing *n.* a system for heating the rooms of a building by means of radiators or air vents connected by pipes or ducts to a central source of heat.

Cen+tra+li·a (sɛn'treɪlɪə) *n.* an archaic name for **Centre** (sense 1).

Cen+tral In+di·a A·gen+cy *n.* a former group of 89 states in India, under the supervision of a British political agent until 1947: most important were Indore, Bhopal, and Rewa.

Cen+tral In+tel+li+gence A·gen+cy *n.* See **C.I.A.**

cen+tral+ism ('sɛntrəˌlɪzəm) *n.* the principle or act of bringing something under central control; centralization. **—'cen+tral+ist** *n., adj.* **—ˌcen+tral+'is+tic** *adj.*

cen+tral+i·ty (sɛn'trælɪtɪ) *n., pl.* **·ties.** the state or condition of being central.

cen+tral+ize *or* **cen+tral+ise** ('sɛntrəˌlaɪz) *vb.* **1.** to draw or move (something) to or towards a centre. **2.** to bring or come under central control, esp. governmental control. **—ˌcen+tral·i+'za+tion** *or* **ˌcen+tral·i+'sa+tion** *n.* **—'cen+tral+ˌiz+er** *or* **'cen+tral+ˌis+er** *n.*

cen+tral lim+it the·o+rem *n. Statistics.* a theorem stating that under certain general conditions the sum of a group of independent random variables tends to a normal distribution as the number of variables increases.

cen+tral nerv+ous sys+tem *n.* the mass of nerve tissue that controls and coordinates the activities of an animal. In vertebrates it consists of the brain and spinal cord. Abbrev.: **CNS.** Compare **autonomic nervous system.**

Cen+tral Pow+ers *pl. n. European history* **a.** (before World War I) Germany, Italy, and Austria-Hungary after they were linked by the Triple Alliance in 1882. **b.** (during World War I) Germany and Austria-Hungary, together with their allies Turkey and Bulgaria.

cen+tral pro+ces+sing u·nit *n.* the part of a computer that performs logical and arithmetical operations on the data as specified in the instructions. Abbrev.: **CPU**

Cen+tral Prov+inc·es and Be+rar (bɛ'rɑ:) *n.* a former province of central India: reorganized and renamed Madhya Pradesh in 1950.

Cen+tral Re+gion *n.* a local government region in central Scotland, formed in 1975 from Clackmannan, most of Stirling, and parts of Perth, West Lothian, Fife, and Kinross. Administrative centre: Stirling. Pop.: 270 056 (1976 est.). Area: 2590 sq. km (1000 sq. miles).

cen+tral re+serve *or* **res+er·va+tion** *n. Brit.* the strip, often covered with grass, that separates the two sides of a motorway or dual carriageway. U.S. name: **median strip.**

Cen+tral Stand+ard Time *n.* one of the standard times used in North America, based on the local time of the 90° meridian, six hours behind Greenwich Mean Time. Abbrev.: **C.S.T.**

cen+tral sul+cus *n.* a deep cleft in each hemisphere of the brain separating the frontal lobe from the parietal lobe.

cen+tral ten+den+cy *n. Statistics.* the tendency of the values of a random variable to cluster around the mean median and mode.

cen+tre or *U.S.* **cen+ter** ('sɛntə) *n.* **1.** *Geom.* **a.** the midpoint of any line or figure, esp. the point within a circle or sphere that is equidistant from any point on the circumference or surface. **b.** the point within a body through which a specified force may be considered to act, such as the centre of gravity. **2.** the point, axis, or pivot about which a body rotates. **3.** a point, area, or part that is approximately in the middle of a larger area or volume. **4.** a place at which some specified activity is concentrated: *a shopping centre.* **5.** a person or thing that is a focus of interest. **6.** a place of activity or influence: *a centre of power.* **7.** a person, group, policy, or thing in the middle. **8.** (*usually cap.*) *Politics.* **a.** a political party or group favouring moderation, esp. the moderate members of a legislative assembly. **b.** (*as modifier*): *a Centre-Left alliance.* **9.** *Physiol.* any part of the central nervous system that regulates a specific function: *respiratory centre.* **10.** a bar with a conical point upon which a workpiece or part may be turned or ground. **11.** a punch mark or small conical hole in a part to be drilled, which enables the point of the drill to be located accurately. **12.** *Football, hockey, etc.* **a.** a player who plays in the middle of the forward line. **b.** the act or an instance of passing the ball from a wing to the middle of the field, court, etc. **13.** *Basketball.* **a.** the position of a player who jumps for the ball at the start of play. **b.** the player in this position. **14.** *Archery.* **a.** the ring around the bull's eye. **b.** a shot that hits this ring. ~*vb.* **15.** to move towards, mark, put, or be at a centre. **16.** (*tr.*) to focus or bring together: *to centre one's thoughts.* **17.** (*intr.*; often foll. by *on*) to have as a main point of view or theme: *the novel centred on crime.* **18.** (*tr.*) to adjust or locate (a workpiece or part) using a centre. **19.** (*intr.*; foll. by *on* or *round*) to have as a centre. **20.** (*tr.*) *Football, hockey, etc.* to pass (the ball) into the middle of the field or court. [C14: from Latin *centrum* the stationary point of a compass, from Greek *kentron* needle, from *kentein* to prick]
Usage. *To centre round* is considered illogical by many writers and speakers, who prefer the more precise phrase *to centre on.*

Cen+tre *n.* **1.** ('sɛntə) **the.** Also called (archaic): **Centralia.** the sparsely inhabited central region of Australia. **2.** (*French* 'sɑ̃:tr) a region of central France: generally low-lying; drained chiefly by the Rivers Loire, Loir, and Cher.

cen+tre bit *n.* a drilling bit with a central projecting point and two side cutters.

cen·tre+board ('sɛntə,bɔ:d) *n.* a supplementary keel for a sailing vessel, which may be adjusted by raising and lowering. Compare **daggerboard.**

cen+tred dot *n. Printing.* **1.** Also called (esp. U.S.): **bullet.** a heavy dot (·) used to draw attention to a particular paragraph. **2.** a dot placed at a central level in a line of type or writing.

cen·tre-fire *adj.* **1.** (of a cartridge) having the primer in the centre of the base. **2.** (of a firearm) adapted for such cartridges. ~Compare **rim-fire.**

cen·tre+fold or *U.S.* **cen·ter+fold** ('sɛntə,fəʊld) *n.* a large coloured illustration folded so that it forms the central spread of a magazine.

cen+tre for+ward *n. Soccer, hockey, etc.* the central forward in the attack.

cen+tre half *n. Soccer.* a defender who plays in the middle of the defence.

cen+tre of cur+va+ture *n.* the centre of a circle whose radius, the **radius of curvature,** is normal to the concave side of a curve at a given point.

cen+tre of grav+i·ty *n.* the point through which the resultant of the gravitational forces on a body always acts.

cen+tre of mass *n.* the point at which the mass of a system could be concentrated without affecting the behaviour of the system under the action of external forces.

cen+tre of pres+sure *n.* **1.** *Physics.* the point in a body at which the resultant pressure acts when the body is immersed in a fluid. **2.** *Aeronautics.* the point at which the resultant aerodynamic forces intersect the chord line of the aerofoil.

cen·tre+piece ('sɛntə,pi:s) *n.* an object used as the centre of something, esp. for decoration.

cen+tre punch *n.* a small steel tool with a conical tip used to punch a small indentation at the location of the centre of a hole to be drilled.

cen+tre spread *n.* the pair of two facing pages in the middle of a magazine, newspaper, etc., often illustrated.

cen+tre three-quar·ter *n. Rugby.* either of two middle players on the three-quarter line.

cen·tri- *combining form.* variant of **centro-.**

cen+tric ('sɛntrɪk) or **cen+tri+cal** *adj.* **1.** being central or having a centre. **2.** relating to or originating at a nerve centre. —'**cen+tri+cal+ly** *adv.* —**cen+tric+i·ty** (sɛn'trɪsɪtɪ) *n.*

-cen·tric *suffix forming adjectives.* having a centre as specified: *heliocentric.* [abstracted from ECCENTRIC, CONCENTRIC, etc.]

cen+trif·u+gal (sɛn'trɪfjʊgᵊl, 'sɛntrɪ,fju:gᵊl) *adj.* **1.** acting, moving, or tending to move away from a centre. Compare **centripetal. 2.** of, concerned with, or operated by centrifugal force: *centrifugal pump.* **3.** *Botany.* (esp. of certain inflorescences) developing outwards from a centre. **4.** *Physiol.* another word for **efferent.** ~*n.* **5.** any device that uses centrifugal force for its action. **6.** the rotating perforated drum in a centrifuge. [C18: from New Latin *centrifugus,* from CENTRI- + Latin *fugere* to flee] —**cen+'trif·u+gal+ly** *adv.*

cen+trif·u+gal force *n.* a force that acts outwards on any body that rotates or moves along a curved path and is directed away from the axis of rotation or the centre of curvature of the path. Compare **centripetal force.**

cen+tri+fuge ('sɛntrɪ,fju:dʒ) *n.* **1.** any of various rotating machines that separate liquids from solids or dispersions of one liquid in another, by the action of centrifugal force. **2.** any of various rotating devices for subjecting human beings or animals to varying accelerations for experimental purposes. ~*vb.* **3.** (*tr.*) to subject to the action of a centrifuge. —**cen+trif·u+ga+tion** (,sɛntrɪfjʊ'geɪʃən) *n.*

cen+tring ('sɛntrɪŋ) or *U.S.* **cen+ter+ing** ('sɛntərɪŋ) *n.* **1.** a temporary structure, esp. one made of timber, used to support an arch during construction. **2.** the process of coming to or putting into a centre: *centring a target.*

cen+tri+ole ('sɛntrɪ,əʊl) *n.* either of two rodlike bodies in most animal cells that form the poles of the spindle during mitosis. [C19: from New Latin *centriolum,* diminutive of Latin *centrum* CENTRE]

cen+trip+e·tal (sɛn'trɪpɪtᵊl, 'sɛntrɪ,pi:tᵊl) *adj.* **1.** acting, moving, or tending to move towards a centre. Compare **centrifugal. 2.** of, concerned with, or operated by centripetal force. **3.** *Botany.* (esp. of certain inflorescences) developing from the outside towards the centre. **4.** *Physiol.* another word for **afferent.** [C17: from New Latin *centripetus* seeking the centre; see CENTRI-, -PETAL] —**cen+'trip+e·tal+ly** *adv.*

cen+trip+e·tal force *n.* a force that acts inwards on any body that rotates or moves along a curved path and is directed towards the centre of curvature of the path or the axis of rotation. Compare **centrifugal force.**

cen+trist ('sɛntrɪst) *n.* a person holding moderate political views. —'**cen+trism** *n.*

cen·tro-, cen·tri-, or *before a vowel* **centr-** *combining form.* denoting a centre: *centroclinal; centromere; centrosome; centrosphere; centrist.* [from Greek *kentron* CENTRE]

cen+tro+bar+ic (,sɛntrəʊ'bærɪk) *adj.* of or concerned with a centre of gravity. [C18: from Late Greek *kentrobarikos,* from Greek *kentron bareos* centre of gravity]

cen+tro+cli+nal (,sɛntrəʊ'klaɪnᵊl) *adj. Geology.* of, relating to, or designating a rock formation in which the strata slope down and in towards a central point or area.

cen+troid ('sɛntrɔɪd) *n.* **a.** the centre of mass of an object of uniform density, esp. of a geometric figure. **b.** the point in a set whose coordinates are the mean values of the coordinates of the other points in the set.

cen+tro+mere ('sɛntrə,mɪə) *n.* the dense nonstaining region of a chromosome that attaches it to the spindle during mitosis. —**cen+tro+mer+ic** (,sɛntrə'mɛrɪk, -'mɪərɪk) *adj.*

cen+tro+some ('sɛntrə,səʊm) *n.* a small protoplasmic body that surrounds the centrides. Also called: **centrosphere, astrosphere.** —**cen+tro+som+ic** (,sɛntrə'sɒmɪk) *adj.*

cen+tro+sphere ('sɛntrə,sfɪə) *n.* **1.** the central part of the earth, below the crust. **2.** another name for **centrosome.**

cen+trum ('sɛntrəm) *n., pl.* **+trums** or **+tra** (-trə). the main part or body of a vertebra. [C19: from Latin: CENTRE]

cen+tum ('sɛntəm) *adj.* denoting or belonging to the Indo-European languages in which original velar stops (*k*) were not palatalized, namely languages of the Hellenic, Italic, Celtic, Germanic, Anatolian, and Tocharian branches. Compare **satem.** [Latin: HUNDRED, chosen because the *c* represents the Indo-European *k*]

cen+tu+pli+cate *vb.* (sɛn'tju:plɪ,keɪt). **1.** (*tr.*) to increase 100 times. ~*adj.* (sɛn'tju:plɪkɪt, -,keɪt). **2.** increased a hundredfold. ~*n.* (sɛn'tju:plɪkɪt, -,keɪt). **3.** one hundredfold. ~Also **cen+tu+ple** ('sɛntjʊpᵊl). [C17: from Late Latin *centuplicāre,* from *centuplex* hundredfold, from Latin *centum* hundred + *-plex* -fold] —**cen+,tu+pli+'ca+tion** *n.*

cen+tu+ri·al (sɛn'tjʊərɪəl) *adj.* **1.** of or relating to a Roman century. **2.** *Rare.* involving a period of 100 years.

cen+tu+ri+on (sɛn'tjʊərɪən) *n.* the officer commanding a Roman century. [C14: from Latin *centuriō,* from *centuria* CENTURY]

cen+tu+ry ('sɛntʃərɪ) *n., pl.* **+ries. 1.** a period of 100 years. **2.** one of the successive periods of 100 years dated before or after an epoch or event, esp. the birth of Christ. **3. a.** a score or grouping of 100: *to score a century in cricket.* **b.** *Chiefly U.S.* (*as modifier*): *the basketball team passed the century mark in their last game.* **4.** (in ancient Rome) a unit of foot soldiers, originally consisting of 100 men. See also **maniple. 5.** (in ancient Rome) a division of the people for purposes of voting. **6.** (*often cap.*) a style of type. [C16: from Latin *centuria,* from *centum* hundred]

cen+tu+ry plant *n.* a tropical American agave, *Agave americana,* having large greyish leaves and greenish flowers on a tall fleshy stalk. It blooms only once in 10 to 30 years and was formerly thought to flower once in a century. Also called: **American aloe.**

ceorl (tʃeəl) *n.* a freeman of the lowest class in Anglo-Saxon England. [Old English; see CHURL] —'**ceorl+ish** *adj.*

cep (sɛp) *n.* an edible saprophytic basidiomycetous woodland fungus, *Boletus edulis,* with a brown shining cap covering white spore-bearing tubes and having a rich nutty flavour: family *Boletineae.* [C19: from French *cèpe,* from Gascon dialect *cep,* from Latin *cippus* stake]

ceph·a+lad ('sɛfə,læd) *adv. Anatomy.* towards the head or anterior part. Compare **caudad.**

ceph·a+lal+gi·a (,sɛfə'lældʒɪə, -dʒə) *n.* a technical name for **headache.**

ce+phal+ic (sɪ'fælɪk) *adj.* **1.** of or relating to the head. **2.** situated in, on, or near the head.

-ce·phal·ic or **-ceph·a·lous** *adj. combining form.* indicating skull or head; -headed: *brachycephalic.* [from Greek *-kephalos;* see -CEPHALUS] —**-ceph·a·ly** or **-ceph·a·lism** *n. combining form.*

ce+phal+ic in+dex *n.* the ratio of the greatest width of the human head to its greatest length, multiplied by 100.

ceph·a+lin ('sɛfəlɪn, 'kɛf-) *or* **keph·a+lin** ('kɛfəlɪn) *n.* a phosphatide, similar to lecithin, that occurs in the nerve tissue and brain.

ceph·a+li+za+tion *or* **ceph·a+li+sa+tion** (ˌsɛfəlaɪ'zeɪʃən) *n.* (in the evolution of animals) development of a head by the concentration of feeding and sensory organs and nervous tissue at the anterior end.

ceph·a·lo- *or before a vowel* **ceph·al-** *combining form.* indicating the head: *cephalopod.* [via Latin from Greek *kephalo-*, from *kephate* head]

ceph·a+lo+chor+date (ˌsɛfələʊ'kɔːdeɪt) *n.* **1.** any chordate animal of the subphylum *Cephalochordata*, having a fishlike body and no vertebral column; a lancelet. ~*adj.* **2.** of, relating to, or belonging to the *Cephalochordata*.

ceph·a+lom+e·ter (ˌsɛfə'lɒmɪtə) *n.* an instrument for measuring the dimensions of the human head. —**ceph·a+lo+met+ric** (ˌsɛfələʊ'mɛtrɪk) *adj.* —ˌ**ceph·a+'lom+e·try** *n.*

Ceph·a+lo+ni·a (ˌsɛfə'ləʊnɪə) *n.* a mountainous island in the Ionian Sea, the largest of the Ionian Islands, off the W coast of Greece. Pop.: 36 742 (1971). Area: 935 sq. km (365 sq. miles). Modern Greek name: **Kephallinía.**

ceph·a+lo+pod ('sɛfələˌpɒd) *n.* **1.** any marine mollusc of the class *Cephalopoda*, characterized by well-developed head and eyes and a ring of sucker-bearing tentacles. The group includes the octopuses, squids, cuttlefish, and pearly nautilus. ~*adj. also* **ceph·a+lo+pod+ic** *or* **ceph·a+lop·o·dous** (ˌsɛfə'lɒpədəs). **2.** of, relating to, or belonging to the *Cephalopoda*. —ˌ**ceph·a+'lop·o+dan** *adj., n.*

ceph·a+lo+tho+rax (ˌsɛfələʊ'θɔːræks) *n., pl.* **+rax·es** *or* **+ra·ces** (-rəˌsiːz). the anterior part of many crustaceans and some other arthropods consisting of a united head and thorax. —**ceph·a+lo+tho+rac+ic** (ˌsɛfələʊθə'ræsɪk) *adj.*

-ceph·a·lus *n. combining form.* denoting a cephalic abnormality: *hydrocephalus.* [New Latin *-cephalus;* see -CEPHALIC]

Ce+phe·id var·i·a·ble ('siːfɪɪd) *n. Astronomy.* any of a class of variable stars with regular cycles of variations in luminosity (ranging from a few hours up to several years). There is a relationship between the periods of variation and the absolute magnitudes, which is used for measuring the distance of such stars.

Ce+pheus[1] ('siːfjuːs) *n., Latin genitive* **Ce+phe·i** ('siːfɪˌaɪ). a faint constellation in the N hemisphere near Cassiopeia and the Pole Star. See also **Cepheid variable.** [from Latin *Cēpheus* named after the mythical king]

Ce·pheus[2] ('siːfjuːs) *n. Greek myth.* a king of Ethiopia, father of Andromeda and husband of Cassiopeia.

ce+ra+ceous (sɪ'reɪʃəs) *adj.* waxlike or waxy. [C18: from Latin *cēra* wax]

Ce+ram (sɪ'ræm) *n.* an island in Indonesia, in the Moluccas, separated from New Guinea by the **Ceram Sea**: mountainous and densely forested. Area: 17 150 sq. km (6622 sq. miles). Also called: **Seram, Serang.**

ce+ram+al (sə'reɪməl) *n.* another name for **cermet.** [C20: from CERAM(IC) + AL(LOY)]

ce+ram+ic (sɪ'ræmɪk) *n.* **1.** a hard brittle material made by firing clay and similar substances. **2.** an object made from such a material. ~*adj.* **3.** of, relating to, or made from a ceramic: *this vase is ceramic.* **4.** of or relating to ceramics: *ceramic arts and crafts.* [C19: from Greek *keramikos*, from *keramos* potter's clay, pottery]

ce+ram+ics (sɪ'ræmɪks) *n.* (*functioning as sing.*) the art and techniques of producing articles of clay, porcelain, etc. —**cer·a+mist** ('sɛrəmɪst) *or* **ce+'ram+i·cist** *n.*

ce+rar+gy+rite (sɪ'rɑːdʒɪˌraɪt) *n.* a greyish-yellow or colourless soft secondary mineral consisting of silver chloride in cubic crystalline form: a source of silver. Formula: AgCl. Also called: **horn silver.** [C19: from Greek *keras* horn + *arguros* silver + -ITE[1]]

ce+ras+tes (sə'ræstiːz) *n., pl.* **+tes.** any venomous snake of the genus *Cerastes*, esp. the horned viper. [C16: from Latin: horned serpent, from Greek *kerastēs* horned, from *keras* horn]

ce+rate ('sɪərɪt, -reɪt) *n.* a hard ointment or medicated paste consisting of lard or oil mixed with wax or resin. [C16: from Latin *cērātum*, from *cēra* wax]

ce+rat+ed ('sɪəreɪtɪd) *adj.* **1.** (of certain birds, such as the falcon) having a cere. **2.** *Rare.* covered with wax.

cer·a·to- *or before a vowel* **cer·at-** *combining form.* **1.** denoting horn or a hornlike part: *ceratodus.* **2.** *Anatomy.* denoting the cornea. ~Also: **kerato-.** [from Greek *kerat-*, *keras* horn]

ce+rat·o·dus (sɪ'rætədəs, ˌsɛrə'təʊdəs) *n., pl.* **+dus·es.** any of various extinct lungfish constituting the genus *Ceratodus*, common in Cretaceous and Triassic times. Compare **barramunda.** [C19: New Latin, from CERATO- + Greek *odous* tooth]

cer·a+toid ('sɛrəˌtɔɪd) *adj.* having the shape or texture of animal horn.

Cer·ber·us ('sɜːbərəs) *n. Greek myth.* a dog, usually represented as having three heads, that guarded the entrance to Hades. —**Cer+be·re·an** (sə'bɪərɪən) *adj.*

cer+car·i·a (sə'kɛərɪə) *n., pl.* **·i·ae** (-ɪˌiː). one of the larval forms of trematode worms. It has a short forked tail and resembles an immature adult. [C19: New Latin, literally: tailed creature, from Greek *kerkos* tail] —**cer+'car+i·al** *adj.* —**cer+'car+i·an** *adj., n.*

cer+cis ('sɜːsɪs) *n.* any tree or shrub of the leguminous genus *Cercis*, which includes the redbud and Judas tree. [C19: New Latin, from Greek *kerkis* weaver's shuttle, Judas tree]

cer+co+pi+the·coid (ˌsɜːkəʊpɪ'θiːkɔɪd) *adj.* **1.** of, relating to, or belonging to the primate superfamily *Cercopithecoidea* (Old World monkeys). ~*n. also* **cer+co+pi+the·cid** (ˌsɜːkəʊpɪ'θiːsɪd) **2.** an Old World monkey. [C19: from Latin *cercopithēcus* monkey with a tail (from Greek *kerkopithēkos*, from *kerkos* tail + *pithēkos* ape) + -OID]

cer+cus ('sɜːkəs) *n., pl.* **+ci** (-siː). one of a pair of sensory appendages at the tip of the abdomen of some insects and other arthropods. [C19: from New Latin, from Greek *kerkos* tail] —**'cer+cal** *adj.*

cere[1] (sɪə) *n.* a soft waxy swelling, containing the nostrils, at the base of the upper beak in such birds as the parrot. [C15: from Old French *cire* wax, from Latin *cēra*]

cere[2] (sɪə) *vb.* (*tr.*) to wrap (a corpse, etc.) in a cerecloth. [C15: from Latin *cērāre*, from *cēra* wax]

ce+re·al ('sɪərɪəl) *n.* **1.** any grass that produces an edible grain, such as oat, rye, wheat, rice, maize, sorghum, and millet. **2.** the grain produced by such a plant. **3.** any food made from this grain, esp. breakfast food. **4.** (*modifier*) of or relating to any of these plants or their products: *cereal farming.* [C19: from Latin *cereālis* concerning agriculture, of CERES[1]]

cer+e·bel+lum (ˌsɛrɪ'bɛləm) *n., pl.* **+lums** *or* **+la** (-lə). one of the major divisions of the vertebrate brain, situated in man above the medulla oblongata and beneath the cerebrum, whose function is coordination of voluntary movements and maintenance of bodily equilibrium. [C16: from Latin, diminutive of CEREBRUM] —ˌ**cer+e·'bel+lar** *adj.*

cer+e·bral ('sɛrɪbrəl; *U.S. also* sə'riːbrəl) *adj.* **1.** of or relating to the cerebrum or to the entire brain. **2.** involving intelligence rather than emotions or instinct. **3.** *Phonetics.* another word for **cacuminal.** ~*n.* **4.** *Phonetics.* a consonant articulated in the manner of a cacuminal consonant. —**'cer+e·bral+ly** *adv.*

cer+e·bral dom·i·nance *n.* the normal tendency for one half of the brain, usually the left cerebral hemisphere in right-handed people, to be more highly developed in certain functions than the other half.

cer+e·bral hem·i·sphere *n.* either half of the cerebrum.

cer+e·bral pal+sy *n.* a nonprogressive impairment of muscular function and weakness of the limbs, caused by damage to the brain before or during birth.

cer+e·brate ('sɛrɪˌbreɪt) *vb.* (*intr.*) *Usually facetious.* to use the mind; think; ponder; consider.

cer+e·bra+tion (ˌsɛrɪ'breɪʃən) *n.* the act of thinking; consideration; thought. [C19: from Latin *cerebrum* brain]

ce·re·bro- *or before a vowel* **ce·rebr-** *combining form.* indicating the brain: *cerebrospinal.* [from CEREBRUM]

cer+e·bro+side (ˌsɛrɪ'brəʊsaɪd) *n.* any of a group of lipids occurring in large amounts in the myelin sheath of nerves and containing fatty acids, sphingosine, and galactose. [C20: from CEREBRO- + -OSE[2] + -IDE]

cer+e·bro+spi+nal (ˌsɛrɪbrəʊ'spaɪnᵊl) *adj.* of or relating to the brain and spinal cord.

cer+e·bro+spi+nal flu+id *n.* the clear colourless fluid in the spaces inside and around the spinal cord and brain.

cer+e·bro+spi+nal men+in+gi·tis *or* **fe+ver** *n.* an acute infectious form of meningitis caused by the bacterium *Neisseria meningitidis*, characterized by high fever, skin rash, delirium, stupor, and sometimes coma. Also called: **epidemic meningitis.**

cer+e·bro+vas+cu+lar (ˌsɛrɪbrəʊ'væskjʊlə) *adj.* of or relating to the blood vessels and the blood supply of the brain.

cer+e·bro+vas+cu+lar ac+ci+dent *or* **cer+e·bral vas+cu+lar ac+ci+dent** *n.* a sudden interruption of the blood supply to the brain caused by rupture of an artery in the brain (**cerebral haemorrhage**) or the blocking of a blood vessel, as by a clot of blood (**cerebral occlusion**). See **apoplexy, stroke** (sense 4).

cer+e·brum ('sɛrɪbrəm) *n., pl.* **·brums** *or* **·bra** (-brə). **1.** the anterior portion of the brain of vertebrates, consisting of two lateral hemispheres joined by a thick band of fibres: the dominant part of the brain in man, associated with intellectual function, emotion, and personality. See **telencephalon. 2.** the brain considered as a whole. **3.** the main neural bundle or ganglion of certain invertebrates. [C17: from Latin: the brain] —**'cer+e·ˌbroid** *adj.* —**cer+e·bric** ('sɛrɪbrɪk) *adj.*

cere+cloth ('sɪəˌklɒθ) *n.* waxed waterproof cloth of a kind formerly used as a shroud. [C15: from earlier *cered cloth*, from Latin *cērāre* to wax; see CERE[2]]

cere+ment ('sɪəmənt) *n.* **1.** another name for **cerecloth. 2.** any burial clothes. [C17: from French *cirement*, from *cirer* to wax; see CERE[2]]

cer+e·mo·ni·al (ˌsɛrɪ'məʊnɪəl) *adj.* **1.** involving or relating to ceremony or ritual. ~*n.* **2.** the observance of formality, esp. in etiquette. **3.** a plan for formal observances on a particular occasion; ritual. **4.** *Christianity.* **a.** the prescribed order of rites and ceremonies. **b.** a book containing this. —ˌ**cer+e·'mo+ni+al+ism** *n.* —ˌ**cer+e·'mo+ni+al+ist** *n.* —ˌ**cer+e·'mo+ni+al+ly** *adv.*

cer+e·mo+ni+ous (ˌsɛrɪ'məʊnɪəs) *adj.* **1.** especially or excessively polite or formal. **2.** observing ceremony; involving formalities. —ˌ**cer+e·'mo+ni+ous+ly** *adv.* —ˌ**cer+e·'mo+ni+ous+ness** *n.*

cer+e·mo+ny ('sɛrɪmənɪ) *n., pl.* **+nies. 1.** a formal act or ritual, often set by custom or tradition, performed in observation of an event or anniversary: *a ceremony commemorating Shakespeare's birth.* **2.** a religious rite or series of rites. **3.** a courteous gesture or act: *the ceremony of toasting the Queen.* **4.** ceremonial observances or gestures collectively: *the ceremony of a monarchy.* **5. stand on ceremony.** to insist on or act with excessive formality. **6. without ceremony.** in a casual or informal manner. [C14: from Medieval Latin *cērēmōnia*, from Latin *caerimōnia* what is sacred, a religious rite]

Ce·ren·kov (*Russian* tʃɪ'rjɛnkəf) *n.* See (Pavel Alekseyevich) **Cherenkov.**

Ce·res[1] ('sɪəri:z) *n.* the Roman goddess of agriculture. Greek counterpart: **Demeter.**

Ce·res[2] ('sɪəri:z) *n.* the largest asteroid and the first to be discovered. It has a diameter of 670 kilometres.

cer·e·sin ('sɛrɪsɪn) *n.* a white wax extracted from ozocerite. [C19: irregularly from Latin *cēra* wax]

ce·re·us ('sɪərɪəs) *n.* **1.** any tropical American cactus of the genus *Cereus*, esp. *C. jamacaru* of N Brazil, which grows to a height of 13 metres (40 feet). **2.** any of several similar and related cacti, such as the night-blooming cereus. [C18: from New Latin, from Latin *cēreus* a wax taper, from *cēra* wax]

ce·ri·a ('sɪərɪə) *n.* another name (not in technical usage) for **ceric oxide.** [New Latin, from CERIUM]

ce·ric ('sɪərɪk) *adj.* of or containing cerium in the tetravalent state.

ce·ric ox·ide *n.* a white or yellow solid used in ceramics, enamels, and radiation shields. Formula: CeO_2. Also called: **cerium dioxide, ceria.**

ce·rise (sə'ri:z, -'ri:s) *n.* **a.** a moderate to dark red colour. **b.** (*as adj.*): *a cerise scarf.* [C19: from French: CHERRY]

ce·ri·um ('sɪərɪəm) *n.* a malleable ductile steel-grey element of the lanthanide series of metals, used in lighter flints and as a reducing agent in metallurgy. Symbol: Ce; atomic no.: 58; atomic wt.: 140.12; valency: 3 or 4; relative density: 6.77; melting pt.: 795°C; boiling pt.: 3468°C. [C19: New Latin, from CERES (the asteroid) + -IUM]

ce·ri·um met·als *pl. n.* the metals lanthanum, cerium, praseodymium, neodymium, promethium, and samarium, forming a sub-group of the lanthanides.

cer·met ('sɜ:mɪt) *n.* any of several materials consisting of a metal matrix with ceramic particles disseminated through it. They are hard and resistant to high temperatures. Also called: **ceramal.** [C20: from CER(AMIC) + MET(AL)]

CERN (sɜ:n) *n. acronym for* Conseil Européen pour la Recherche Nucléaire; an organization of European states with a centre in Geneva for research in high-energy particle physics.

Cer·nă·uţi (tʃernə'utsj) *n.* the Rumanian name for **Chernovtsy.**

cer·nu·ous ('sɜ:njʊəs) *adj. Botany.* (of some flowers or buds) drooping. [C17: from Latin *cernuus* leaning forwards, of obscure origin]

ce·ro ('sɪərəʊ, 'sɪrəʊ) *n., pl.* **·ro** *or* **·ros. 1.** a large spiny-finned food fish, *Scomberomorus regalis*, of warm American coastal regions of the Atlantic: family *Scombridae* (mackerels, tunnies, etc.). **2.** any similar or related fish. [C19: from Spanish: saw, sawfish, altered spelling of SIERRA]

ce·rog·ra·phy (sɪə'rɒgrəfɪ) *n.* the art of engraving on a waxed plate on which a printing surface is created by electrotyping. —**ce·ro·graph·ic** (ˌsɪərəʊ'græfɪk) *or* ˌ**ce·ro·'graph·i·cal** *adj.* —**ce·'rog·ra·phist** *n.*

ce·ro·plas·tic (ˌsɪərəʊ'plæstɪk) *adj.* **1.** relating to wax modelling. **2.** modelled in wax.

ce·ro·plas·tics (ˌsɪərəʊ'plæstɪks) *n.* the art of wax modelling.

ce·rot·ic ac·id (sɪ'rɒtɪk) *n.* another name (not in technical usage) for **hexacosanoic acid.**

ce·ro·type ('sɪərəˌtaɪp) *n.* a process for preparing a printing plate by engraving a wax-coated copper plate and then using this as a mould for an electrotype.

ce·rous ('sɪərəs) *adj.* of or containing cerium in the trivalent state. [C19: from CERIUM + -OUS]

Cer·ro de Pas·co (*Spanish* 'serro de 'pasko) *n.* a town in central Peru, in the Andes: one of the highest towns in the world, 4400 m (14 436 ft.) above sea level; mining centre. Pop.: 47 000 (1973 est.).

Cer·ro Gor·do (*Spanish* 'serro 'gordo) *n.* a mountain pass in E Mexico, between Veracruz and Jalapa: site of a battle in the Mexican War (1847) in which American forces under General Scott decisively defeated the Mexicans.

cert (sɜ:t) *n. Informal.* something that is a certainty, esp. a horse that is certain to win a race (esp. in the phrase **a dead cert**).

cert. *abbrev. for:* **1.** certificate. **2.** certification. **3.** certified.

cer·tain ('sɜ:tᵊn) *adj.* **1.** (*postpositive*) positive and confident about the truth of something; convinced: *I am certain that he wrote a book.* **2.** (*usually postpositive*) definitely known: *it is certain that they were on the bus.* **3.** (*usually postpositive*) sure; bound; destined: *he was certain to fail.* **4.** decided or settled upon; fixed: *the date is already certain for the invasion.* **5.** unfailing; reliable: *his judgment is certain.* **6.** moderate or minimum: *to a certain extent.* **7. make certain of.** to ensure (that one will get something); confirm. ~*adv.* **8. for certain.** definitely; without a doubt: *he will win for certain.* ~*determiner.* **9. a.** known but not specified or named: *certain people may doubt this.* **b.** (*as pronoun; functioning as pl.*): *certain of the members have not paid their subscriptions.* **10.** named but not known: *he had written to a certain Mrs. Smith.* [C13: from Old French, from Latin *certus* sure, fixed, from *cernere* to discern, decide]

cer·tain·ly ('sɜ:tᵊnlɪ) *adv.* **1.** with certainty; without doubt: *he certainly rides very well.* ~ **2.** *sentence substitute.* by all means; definitely: used in answer to questions.

cer·tain·ty ('sɜ:tᵊntɪ) *n., pl.* **·ties. 1.** the condition of being certain. **2.** something established as certain or inevitable. **3. for a certainty.** without doubt.

Cert. Ed. (in Britain) *abbrev. for* Certificate in Education.

cer·tes ('sɜ:tɪz) *adv. Archaic.* with certainty; truly. [C13: from Old French, ultimately from Latin *certus* CERTAIN]

cer·ti·fi·a·ble ('sɜ:tɪˌfaɪəbᵊl) *adj.* **1.** capable of being certified. **2.** fit to be certified as insane.

cer·tif·i·cate *n.* (sə'tɪfɪkɪt). **1.** an official document attesting the truth of the facts stated, as of birth, marital status, death, health, completion of an academic course, ability to practise a profession, etc. **2.** short for **share certificate.** ~*vb.* (sə'tɪfɪˌkeɪt). **3.** (*tr.*) to authorize by or present with an official document. [C15: from Old French *certificat*, from *certifier* CERTIFY] —**cer·ˌtif·i·'ca·to·ry** *adj.*

cer·tif·i·cate of in·cor·po·ra·tion *n. Company law.* a signed statement that a company is duly incorporated.

cer·tif·i·cate of or·i·gin *n.* a document stating the name of the country that produced a specified shipment of goods: often required before importation of goods.

cer·ti·fi·ca·tion (ˌsɜ:tɪfɪ'keɪʃən) *n.* **1.** the act of certifying or state of being certified. **2.** *Law.* a document attesting the truth of a fact or statement.

cer·ti·fied ('sɜ:tɪˌfaɪd) *adj.* **1.** holding or guaranteed by a certificate. **2.** endorsed or guaranteed: *a certified cheque.* **3.** (of a person) declared legally insane.

cer·ti·fied pub·lic ac·count·ant *n. U.S.* a public accountant certified to have met state legal requirements.

cer·ti·fy ('sɜ:tɪˌfaɪ) *vb.* **·fies, ·fy·ing, ·fied. 1.** to confirm or attest (to), usually in writing: *the letter certified her age.* **2.** (*tr.*) to endorse or guarantee that certain required standards have been met. **3.** to give reliable information or assurances: *he certified that it was Walter's handwriting.* **4.** (*tr.*) to declare legally insane. **5.** (*tr.*) *U.S.* (of a bank) to state in writing on (a cheque) that payment is guaranteed. [C14: from Old French *certifier*, from Medieval Latin *certificāre* to make certain, from Latin *certus* CERTAIN + *facere* to make] —**'cer·ti·ˌfi·a·bly** *adv.* —**'cer·ti·ˌfi·er** *n.*

cer·ti·o·ra·ri (ˌsɜ:tɪɔ:'rɛəraɪ) *n. Law.* a writ from a superior court directing that a record of proceedings in a lower court be sent up for review. See also **mandamus, prohibition.** [C15: from legal Latin: to be informed]

cer·ti·tude ('sɜ:tɪˌtju:d) *n.* confidence; certainty. [C15: from Church Latin *certitūdō*, from Latin *certus* CERTAIN]

ce·ru·le·an (sɪ'ru:lɪən) *n.* **a.** a deep blue colour; azure. **b.** (*as adj.*): *a cerulean sea.* [C17: from Latin *caeruleus*, probably from *caelum* sky]

ce·ru·men (sɪ'ru:mɛn) *n.* the soft brownish-yellow wax secreted by glands in the auditory canal of the external ear. Nontechnical name: **earwax.** [C18: from New Latin, from Latin *cēra* wax + ALBUMEN] —**ce·'ru·mi·nous** *adj.*

ce·ruse (sə'ru:s) *n.* another name for **white lead** (sense 1). [C14: from Old French *céruse*, from Latin *cērussa*, perhaps ultimately from Greek *kēros* wax]

ce·rus·site *or* **ce·ru·site** ('sɪərəˌsaɪt) *n.* a colourless white or grey secondary mineral consisting of lead carbonate in orthorhombic crystalline form: a source of lead. Formula: $PbCO_3$. Also called: **white lead ore.** [C19: from Latin *cērussa* (see CERUSE) + -ITE[1]]

Cer·van·tes (sə'vænti:z; *Spanish* θer'βantes) *n.* **Mi·guel de** (mi'γel ðe), full surname *Cervantes Saavedra.* 1547–1616, Spanish dramatist, poet, and prose writer, most famous for *Don Quixote* (1605), which satirizes the chivalric romances and greatly influenced the development of the novel.

cer·ve·lat ('sɜ:vəˌlæt, -ˌlɑ:) *n.* a smoked sausage made from pork and beef. [C17: via obsolete French from Italian *cervellata*]

cer·vi·cal ('sɜ:vɪkᵊl, sə'vaɪ-) *adj.* of or relating to the neck or cervix. [C17: from New Latin *cervīcālis*, from Latin *cervīx* neck]

cer·vi·cal smear *n. Med.* a smear of secretions and cellular material taken from the neck (cervix) of the uterus for detection of cancer. See also **Pap test.**

cer·vi·ci·tis (ˌsɜ:vɪ'saɪtɪs) *n.* inflammation of the neck of the uterus.

cer·vid ('sɜ:vɪd) *n.* **1.** any ruminant mammal of the family *Cervidae*, including the deer, characterized by the presence of antlers. ~*adj.* **2.** of, relating to, or belonging to the *Cervidae.* [C19: from New Latin *Cervidae*, from Latin *cervus* deer]

Cer·vin (sɛr'vɛ̃) *n.* **Mont.** the French name for the **Matterhorn.**

cer·vine ('sɜ:vaɪn) *adj.* **1.** resembling or relating to a deer. **2.** of a dark yellowish-brown colour. [C19: from Latin *cervīnus*, from *cervus* a deer]

cer·vix ('sɜ:vɪks) *n., pl.* **cer·vix·es** *or* **cer·vi·ces** (sə'vaɪsi:z) **1.** the technical name for **neck. 2.** any necklike part of an organ, esp. the lower part of the uterus that extends into the vagina. [C18: from Latin]

Ce·sar·e·an *or* **Ce·sar·i·an** (sɪ'zɛərɪən) *adj. U.S.* variant spellings of **Caesarean.**

Ce·se·na (*Italian* tʃe'zɛ:na) *n.* a city in N Italy, in Emilia-Romagna. Pop.: 86 584 (1971).

ce·si·um ('si:zɪəm) *n.* the usual U.S. spelling of **caesium.**

Čes·ké Bu·dě·jo·vi·ce (*Czech* 'tʃɛskɛ: 'budɛjɔvitsɛ) *n.* a city in SW Czechoslovakia, on the Vltava (Moldau) River. Pop.: 76 945 (1968 est.). German name: **Budweis.**

Čes·ko·slo·ven·sko ('tʃɛskɔˌslɔvɛnskɔ) *n.* the Czech name for **Czechoslovakia.**

ces·pi·tose ('sɛspɪˌtəʊs) *adj.* a variant spelling (esp. U.S.) of **caespitose.** —**'ces·pi·ˌtose·ly** *adv.*

cess[1] (sɛs) *n.* **1.** *Brit.* any of several special taxes, such as a land tax in Scotland. **2.** (formerly in Ireland) **a.** the obligation to provide the soldiers and household of the lord deputy with supplies at fixed prices. **b.** any military exaction. ~*vb.* **3.** (*tr.*) *Brit.* to tax or assess for taxation. **4.** (*tr.*) (formerly in

Ireland) to impose (soldiers) upon a population, to be supported by them. [C16: short for ASSESSMENT]

cess[2] (sɛs) *n.* an Irish slang word for **luck** (esp. in the phrase **bad cess to you!**) [C19: probably short for SUCCESS]

cess[3] (sɛs) *n.* short for **cesspool.**

ces·sa·tion (sɛˈseɪʃən) *n.* a ceasing or stopping; discontinuance; pause: *temporary cessation of hostilities.* [C14: from Latin *cessātiō* a delaying, inactivity, from *cessāre* to be idle, desist from, from *cēdere* to yield, CEDE]

ces·ser (ˈsɛsə) *n. Law.* the coming to an end of a term interest or annuity.

ces·sion (ˈsɛʃən) *n.* **1.** the act of ceding, esp. of ceding rights, property, or territory. **2.** something that is ceded, esp. land or territory. [C14: from Latin *cessiō,* from *cēdere* to yield]

ces·sion·ar·y (ˈsɛʃənərɪ) *n., pl.* **·ar·ies.** *Law.* a person to whom something is transferred; assignee; grantee.

cess·pool (ˈsɛsˌpuːl) *n.* **1.** Also called: **cesspit, sink, sump.** a covered cistern, etc., for collecting and storing sewage or waste water. **2.** a filthy or corrupt place: *a cesspool of iniquity.* [C17: changed (through influence of POOL) from earlier *cesperalle,* from Old French *souspirail* vent, air, from *soupirer* to sigh; see SUSPIRE]

c'est la vie *French.* (sɛ la ˈvi) that's life.

ces·tode (ˈsɛstəʊd) *n.* any parasitic flatworm of the class *Cestoda,* which includes the tapeworms. [C19: from New Latin *Cestoidea* ribbon-shaped creatures, from Latin *cestus* belt, girdle; see CESTUS[1]]

ces·toid (ˈsɛstɔɪd) *adj.* (esp. of tapeworms and similar animals) ribbon-like in form.

ces·tus[1] (ˈsɛstəs) *or* **ces·tos** (ˈsɛstɒs) *n. Classical myth.* the girdle of Aphrodite (Venus) decorated to cause amorousness. [C16: from Latin, from Greek *kestos* belt, from *kentein* to stitch]

ces·tus[2] *or* **caes·tus** (ˈsɛstəs) *n., pl.* **·tus** *or* **·tus·es.** (in classical Roman boxing) a pugilist's gauntlet of bull's hide loaded or studded with metal. [C18: from Latin *caestus,* probably from *caedere* to strike, slay]

ce·su·ra (sɪˈzjʊərə) *n., pl.* **·ras** *or* **·rae** (-riː). *Prosody.* a variant spelling of **caesura.** —**ceˈsu·ral** *adj.*

C.E.T. *abbrev. for* Central European Time.

ce·ta·cean (sɪˈteɪʃən) *adj. also* **ce·ta·ceous. 1.** of, relating to, or belonging to the *Cetacea,* an order of aquatic placental mammals having no hind limbs and a blowhole for breathing: includes toothed whales (dolphins, porpoises, etc.) and whalebone whales (rorquals, right whales, etc.). ~*n.* **2.** a whale. [C19: from New Latin *Cētācea,* ultimately from Latin *cētus* whale, from Greek *kētos*]

ce·tane (ˈsiːteɪn) *n.* a colourless insoluble liquid alkane hydrocarbon used in the determination of the cetane number of diesel fuel. Formula: $C_{16}H_{34}$. Also called: **hexadecane.** [C19: from Latin *cētus* whale + -ANE, so called because related compounds are found in sperm whale oil]

ce·tane num·ber *n.* a measure of the quality of a diesel fuel expressed as the percentage of cetane in a mixture of cetane and 1-methylnapthalene of the same quality as the given fuel. Also called: **cetane rating.** Compare **octane number.**

Ce·ta·tea Al·bă (tʃeˈtatja ˈalbə) *n.* the Rumanian name for **Byelgorod-Dnestrovski.**

cete (siːt) *n.* a group of badgers. [C15: perhaps from Latin *coetus* assembly, from *coīre* to come together]

ce·te·ris pa·ri·bus (ˈkɛtərɪs ˈpɑːrɪbʊs) other things being equal. [C17: Latin]

Ce·ti·nje (*Serbo-Croatian* ˈtsɛtinjɛ) *n.* a city in S Yugoslavia, in SW Montenegro: former capital of Montenegro (until 1945); palace and fortified monastery, residences of Montenegrin prince-bishops. Pop.: 11 800 (1971 est.).

ce·tol·o·gy (siːˈtɒlədʒɪ) *n.* the branch of zoology concerned with the study of whales (cetaceans). [C19: from Latin *cētus* whale] —**ce·to·log·i·cal** (ˌsiːtəˈlɒdʒɪkᵊl) *adj.* —**ceˈtol·o·gist** *n.*

Ce·tus (ˈsiːtəs) *n., Latin genitive* **Ce·ti** (ˈsiːtaɪ). a large constellation on the celestial equator near Pisces and Aquarius. It contains the variable star Mira Ceti. [Latin: whale]

Ce·u·ta (*Spanish* ˈθeuta) *n.* an enclave in Morocco on the Strait of Gibraltar, consisting of a port and military station: held by Spain since 1580. Pop.: 73 182 (1970).

Cé·vennes (*French* seˈvɛn) *n.* a mountain range in S central France, on the SE edge of the Massif Central. Highest peak: 1754 m (5755 ft.).

Cey·lon (sɪˈlɒn) *n.* **1.** the former name (until 1972) of **Sri Lanka. 2.** an island in the Indian Ocean, off the SE coast of India: consists politically of the republic of Sri Lanka. Area: 64 644 sq. km (24 959 sq. miles). —**Cey·lo·nese** (ˌsɛləˈniːz, ˌsiːlə-) *adj.*

Cey·lon moss *n.* a red East Indian seaweed, *Gracilaria lichenoides,* from which agar is made.

Ce·yx (ˈsiːɪks) *n. Greek myth.* a king of Trachis in Thessaly and the husband of Alcyone. He died in a shipwreck and his wife drowned herself in grief. Compare **Alcyone**[1] (sense 1).

Cé·zanne (*French* seˈzan) *n.* **Paul** (pɔl). 1839–1906, French postimpressionist painter, who was a major influence on modern art, esp. cubism, in stressing the structural elements latent in nature, such as the sphere and the cone.

Cf *the chemical symbol for* californium.

cf. *abbrev. for:* **1.** (in bookbinding, etc.) calfskin. **2.** confer. [Latin: compare]

c.f. *or* **C.F.** *abbrev. for* cost and freight. Also: **c & f.**

C.F. *Chiefly Brit. abbrev. for* Chaplain to the Forces.

c/f *Book-keeping. abbrev. for* carried forward.

C.F.E. *abbrev. for* College of Further Education.

c.f.i. *or* **C.F.I.** *abbrev. for* cost, freight, and insurance (included in the price quoted). Also: **c.i.f.**

cg *abbrev. for* centigram.

c.g. *abbrev. for* centre of gravity.

C.G. *abbrev. for:* **1.** captain general. **2.** coastguard. **3.** Coldstream Guards. **4.** consul general.

C.G.M. *Chiefly Brit. abbrev. for* Conspicuous Gallantry Medal.

C.G.S. *abbrev. for* (in Britain) Chief of General Staff.

cgs u·nits *pl. n.* a metric system of units based on the centimetre, gram, and second. For scientific and technical purposes these units have been replaced by SI units.

CH *international car registration for* Switzerland. [from French *Confédération Helvétique*]

ch. *abbrev. for:* **1.** chain (unit of measure). **2.** chapter. **3.** *Chess.* check. **4.** chief. **5.** church.

c.h. *abbrev. for* custom house.

C.H. *abbrev. for* Companion of Honour (a Brit. title).

chab·a·zite (ˈkæbəˌzaɪt) *n.* a pink, white, or colourless zeolite mineral consisting of a hydrated silicate of calcium, sodium, potassium, and aluminium in hexagonal crystalline form. Formula: $(Ca,Na,K)Al_2Si_4O_{12}.6H_2O$. [C19: from French *chabazie* from Late Greek *khabazios,* erroneous for *khalazios* stone similar to a hailstone, from Greek *khalazios* of hail, from *khalaza* hailstone + -ITE[1]]

chab·lis (ˈʃæblɪ; *French* ʃaˈbli) *n.* (*sometimes cap.*) a dry white burgundy wine made around Chablis, France.

Cha·brol (*French* ʃaˈbrɔl) *n.* **Claude** (kloːd). born 1930, French film director, whose films, such as *Les Biches* (1968), show a penchant for the bizarre.

cha-cha-cha (ˌtʃɑːtʃɑːˈtʃɑː) *or* **cha-cha** *n.* **1.** a modern ballroom dance from Latin America with small steps and swaying hip movements. **2.** a piece of music composed for this dance. ~*vb.* (*intr.*) **3.** to perform this dance. [C20: from American (Cuban) Spanish]

chac·ma (ˈtʃækmə) *n.* a baboon, *Papio* (or *Chaeropithecus*) *ursinus,* having coarse greyish hair and occurring in southern and eastern Africa. [C19: from Hottentot]

Cha·co (*Spanish* ˈtʃako) *n.* See **Gran Chaco.**

cha·conne (ʃəˈkɒn; *French* ʃaˈkɔn) *n.* **1.** a musical form consisting of a set of continuous variations upon a ground bass. See also **passacaglia. 2.** *Archaic.* a dance in slow triple time probably originating in Spain. [C17: from French, from Spanish *chacona,* probably imitative of the castanet accompaniment]

cha·cun à son goût *French.* (ʃakœ̃ na sɔ̃ ˈgu) each to his own taste.

chad (tʃæd) *n.* the small pieces of cardboard or paper removed during the punching of holes in computer cards or paper tape. [C20: perhaps based on CHAFF]

Chad (tʃæd) *n.* **1.** a republic in N central Africa: made a territory of French Equatorial Africa in 1910; became independent in 1960; contains much desert and the Tibesti Mountains, with Lake Chad in the west; produces chiefly cotton and livestock. Official language: French. Religion: chiefly Muslim, also animist. Currency: franc. Capital: Ndjamena. Pop.: 3 800 000 (1971 UN est.). Area: 1 284 000 sq. km (495 750 sq. miles). French name: **Tchad. 2. Lake.** a lake in N central Africa: fed chiefly by the Shari River, it has no apparent outlet. Area: 10 000 to 26 000 sq. km (4000 to 10 000 sq. miles), varying seasonally.

Chad·der·ton (ˈtʃædətᵊn) *n.* a town in NW England, in Greater Manchester. Pop.: 32 406 (1971).

Chad·ic (ˈtʃædɪk) *n.* **1.** a subfamily of the Afro-Asiatic family of languages, spoken in an area west and south of Lake Chad, the chief member of which is Hausa. ~*adj.* **2.** denoting, relating to, or belonging to this group of languages.

Chad·wick (ˈtʃædwɪk) *n.* Sir **James.** 1891–1974, English physicist: discovered the neutron (1932): Nobel prize for physics 1935.

Chaer·o·ne·a (ˌkɛrəˈniːə) *n.* an ancient Greek town in W Boeotia: site of the victory of Philip of Macedon over the Athenians and Thebans (338 B.C.) and of Sulla over Mithridates (86 B.C.).

chae·ta (ˈkiːtə) *n., pl.* **·tae** (-tiː). any of the chitinous bristles on the body of such annelids as the earthworm and the lugworm: used in locomotion; a seta. [C19: New Latin, from Greek *khaitē* long hair]

chae·tog·nath (ˈkiːtɒgˌnæθ) *n.* any small wormlike marine invertebrate of the phylum *Chaetognatha,* including the arrowworms, having a coelom and a ring of bristles around the mouth. [C19: New Latin *Chaetognatha,* literally: hair-jaw, from CHAETA + Greek *gnathos* jaw]

chae·to·pod (ˈkiːtəˌpɒd) *n.* any annelid worm of the classes *Oligochaeta* or *Polychaeta.* See **oligochaete, polychaete.** [C19: from New Latin *Chaetopoda;* see CHAETA, -POD]

chafe (tʃeɪf) *vb.* **1.** to make or become sore or worn by rubbing. **2.** (*tr.*) to warm (the hands, etc.) by rubbing. **3.** to irritate or be irritated or impatient: *he was chafed because he was not allowed out.* **4.** (*intr.;* often foll. by *on, against,* etc.) to cause friction; rub. **5. chafe at the bit.** See **champ**[1] (sense 3). ~*n.* **6.** a soreness or irritation caused by friction. [C14: from Old French *chaufer* to warm, ultimately from Latin *calefacere,* from *calēre* to be warm + *facere* to make]

chaf·er (ˈtʃeɪfə) *n.* any of various scarabaeid beetles, such as the cockchafer and rose chafer. [Old English *ceafor;* related to Old Saxon *kevera,* Old High German *chevar*]

chaff[1] (tʃɑːf) *n.* **1.** the mass of husks, etc., separated from the seeds during threshing. **2.** finely cut straw and hay used to feed cattle. **3.** something of little worth; rubbish (esp. in the phrase

separate the wheat from the chaff). **4.** the dry membranous bracts enclosing the flowers of certain composite plants. **5.** thin strips of metallic foil released into the earth's atmosphere to deflect radar signals and prevent detection. [Old English *ceaf;* related to Old High German *keva* husk] —**'chaff·y** *adj.*

chaff[2] (tʃɑːf) *n.* **1.** light-hearted teasing or joking; banter. ~*vb.* **2.** to tease good-naturedly; banter. [C19: probably a slang variant of CHAFE, perhaps influenced by CHAFF[1]] —**'chaff+er** *n.*

chaf+fer ('tʃæfə) *vb.* **1.** (*intr.*) to haggle or bargain. **2.** to chatter, talk, or say idly; bandy (words). **3.** (*tr.*) *Obsolete.* to deal in; barter. ~*n.* **4.** haggling or bargaining. [C13 *chaffare,* from *chep* bargain + *fare* journey; see CHEAP, FARE] —**'chaf+fer+er** *n.*

chaf+finch ('tʃæfɪntʃ) *n.* a common European finch, *Fringilla coelebs,* with black and white wings and, in the male, a reddish body and blue-grey head.

chaf+ing dish ('tʃeɪfɪŋ) *n.* a vessel with a heating apparatus beneath it, for cooking or keeping food warm at the table.

Cha·gall (*French* ʃa'gal) *n.* **Marc** (mark). born 1887, French painter and illustrator, born in Russia, noted for his richly coloured pictures of men, animals, and objects in fantastic combinations and often suspended in space: his work includes 12 stained glass windows for a synagogue in Jerusalem (1961) and the decorations for the ceiling of the Paris Opera House (1964).

Cha+gas' dis+ease ('ʃɑːgəs) *n.* a form of trypanosomiasis found in South America, caused by the protozoan *Trypanosoma cruzi,* characterized by fever and, often, inflammation of the heart muscles. Also called: **(South) American trypanosomiasis.** Compare **sleeping sickness.** [C20: named after Carlos *Chagas* (1879–1934), Brazilian physician who first described it]

Cha+gres (*Spanish* 'tʃaɣres) *n.* a river in Panama and the Canal Zone, flowing southwest through Gatún Lake, then northwest to the Caribbean Sea.

cha+grin ('ʃægrɪn) *n.* **1.** a feeling of annoyance or mortification. ~*vb.* **2.** to embarrass and annoy; mortify. [C17: from French *chagrin, chagriner,* of unknown origin]

chain (tʃeɪn) *n.* **1.** a flexible length of metal links, used for confining, connecting, pulling, etc., or in jewellery. **2.** (*usually pl.*) anything that confines, fetters, or restrains: *the chains of poverty.* **3.** (*usually pl.*) Also called: **snow chains.** a set of metal links that fit over the tyre of a motor vehicle to increase traction and reduce skidding on an icy surface. **4.** a series of related or connected facts, events, etc. **5. a.** a number of establishments such as hotels, shops, etc., having the same owner or management. **b.** (*as modifier*)*: a chain store.* **6.** Also called: **Gunter's chain.** a unit of length equal to 22 yards. **7.** Also called: **engineer's chain.** a unit of length equal to 100 feet. **8.** Also called: **nautical chain.** a unit of length equal to 15 feet. **9.** *Chem.* two or more atoms or groups bonded together so that the configuration of the resulting molecule, ion, or radical resembles a chain. See also **open chain, ring**[1] (sense 18). **10.** *Geography.* a series of natural features, esp. approximately parallel mountain ranges. ~*vb.* **11.** *Surveying.* to measure with a chain or tape. **12.** (*tr.;* often foll. by *up*) to confine, tie, or make fast with or as if with a chain. **13.** short for **chain-stitch.** [C13: from Old French *chaine,* ultimately from Latin; see CATENA]

Chain (tʃeɪn) *n.* **Ernst Bor·is.** born 1906, English biochemist, born in Germany: purified and adapted penicillin for clinical use; with Fleming and Florey shared the Nobel prize for medicine (1945).

chain gang *n. U.S.* a group of convicted prisoners chained together, usually while doing hard labour.

chain grate *n.* a type of mechanical stoker for a furnace, in which the grate consists of an endless chain that draws the solid fuel into the furnace as it rotates.

chain let+ter *n.* a letter, often with a request for and promise of money, that is sent to many people who add to or recopy it and send it on to others: illegal in many countries.

chain light+ning *n.* another name for **forked lightning.**

chain mail *n.* another term for **mail**[2] (sense 1).

chain+man ('tʃeɪnmən) *n., pl.* **+men.** *Surveying.* a person who does the chaining in a survey.

chain+plate ('tʃeɪnˌpleɪt) *n.* a metal plate on the side of a vessel, to which the shrouds are attached.

chain print+er *n.* a line printer in which the type is on a continuous chain, used to print computer output.

chain-re·act *vb.* (*intr.*) to undergo a chain reaction.

chain re+ac+tion *n.* **1.** a process in which a neutron colliding with an atomic nucleus causes fission and the ejection of one or more other neutrons, which induce other nuclei to split. **2.** a chemical reaction in which the product of one step is a reactant in the following step. **3.** a series of rapidly occurring events, each of which precipitates the next.

chain rule *n. Maths.* a theorem that may be used in the differentiation of the function of a function. It states that $du/dx = (du/dy)(dy/dx)$, where y is a function of x and u a function of y.

chain saw *n.* a motor-driven saw, usually portable, in which the cutting teeth form links in a continuous chain.

chain shot *n.* cannon shot comprising two balls or half balls joined by a chain, much used formerly, esp. in naval warfare.

chain-smoke *vb.* to smoke (cigarettes, etc.) continually, esp. lighting one from the preceding one. —**chain smok+er** *n.*

chain stitch *n.* **1.** an ornamental looped embroidery stitch resembling the links of a chain. ~*vb.* **chain-stitch. 2.** to sew (something) with this stitch.

chair (tʃɛə) *n.* **1.** a seat with a back on which one person sits, typically having four legs and often having arms. **2.** an official position of authority: *a chair on the board of directors.* **3.** a person holding an office of authority, esp. the chairman of a debate or meeting: *all questions are to be addressed to the chair.* **4.** a professorship: *the chair of German.* **5.** *Railways.* an iron or steel socket with a deep groove designed to take the rail and secure it to the sleeper. **6.** short for **sedan chair. 7. in the chair.** chairing a debate or meeting. **8. take the chair.** to preside as chairman for a meeting, etc. **9. the chair.** an informal name for **electric chair.** ~*vb.* (*tr.*) **10.** to preside over (a meeting). **11.** *Brit.* to carry aloft in a sitting position after a triumph or great achievement. **12.** to provide with a chair of office. **13.** to install in a chair. [C13: from Old French *chaiere,* from Latin *cathedra,* from Greek *kathedra,* from *kata-* down + *hedra* seat; compare CATHEDRAL]

chair+borne ('tʃɛəˌbɔːn) *adj. Informal.* having an administrative or desk job rather than a more active one.

chair lift *n.* a series of chairs suspended from a power-driven cable for conveying people, esp. skiers, up a mountain.

chair+man ('tʃɛəmən) *n., pl.* **+men. 1.** Also: (*fem.*) **chair+wom·an, chair+la·dy,** *or* (esp. among supporters of women's lib.) **chair+per·son.** a person who presides over a company's board of directors, a committee, a debate, an administrative department, etc. **2.** someone who wheels or carries people in a chair. —**'chair+man+ˌship** *n.*

chaise (ʃeɪz) *n.* **1.** a light open horse-drawn carriage, esp. one with two wheels designed for two passengers. **2.** short for **post chaise** and **chaise longue. 3.** a gold coin first issued in France in the 14th century, depicting the king seated on a throne. [C18: from French, variant of Old French *chaiere* CHAIR]

chaise longue ('ʃeɪz 'lɒŋ; *French* ʃɛz 'lɔ̃g) *n., pl.* **chaise longues** *or* **chaises longues** ('ʃeɪz 'lɒŋ; *French* ʃɛz 'lɔ̃g). a long low chair for reclining, with a back and single armrest. [C19: from French: long chair]

cha+la+za (kə'leɪzə) *n., pl.* **+zas** *or* **+zae** (-ziː). **1.** one of a pair of spiral threads of albumen holding the yolk of a bird's egg in position. **2.** the basal part of a plant ovule, where the integuments and nucellus are joined. [C18: New Latin, from Greek: hailstone] —**cha+'la+zal** *adj.*

chal+can+thite (kæl'kænθaɪt) *n.* a blue secondary mineral consisting of hydrated copper sulphate in triclinic crystalline form. Formula: $CuSO_4.5H_2O$. [C19: via German from Latin *chalcanthum* copper sulphate solution, from Greek *khalkanthon,* from *khalkos* copper + *anthos* flower; see -ITE[1]]

chal+ced·o+ny (kæl'sɛdənɪ) *n., pl.* **+nies.** a microcrystalline often greyish form of quartz with crystals arranged in parallel fibres: a gemstone. Formula: SiO_2. [C15: from Late Latin *chalcēdōnius,* from Greek *khalkēdōn* a precious stone (Revelation 21:19), perhaps named after *Khalkēdōn* Chalcedon, town in Asia Minor] —**chal+ce·don+ic** (ˌkælsɪ'dɒnɪk) *adj.*

chal+cid *or* **chal+cid fly** ('kælsɪd) *n.* any tiny hymenopterous insect of the family *Chalcididae* and related families, whose larvae are parasites of other insects. [C19: from New Latin *Chalcis* type genus, from Greek *khalkos* copper, referring to its metallic sheen]

Chal+cid·i·ce (kæl'sɪdɪsɪ) *n.* a peninsula of N central Greece, in Macedonia, ending in the three promontories of Kassandra, Sithonia, and Akti. Area: 2945 sq. km (1149 sq. miles). Modern Greek name: **Khalkidhikí.**

Chal+cis ('kælsɪs) *n.* a city in SE Greece, at the narrowest point of the Euripus strait: important since the 7th century B.C., founding many colonies in ancient times. Pop.: 36 300 (1971). Modern Greek name: **Khalkís.** Medieval English name: **Negropont.**

chal·co- *or before a vowel* **chalc-** *combining form.* indicating copper or a copper alloy: *chalcopyrite; chalcolithic.* [from Greek *khalkos* copper]

chal+co+cite ('kælkəˌsaɪt) *n.* a heavy grey mineral consisting of cuprous sulphide in orthorhombic crystalline form: an ore of copper. Formula: Cu_2S. [C19: changed from earlier *chalcosine,* from Greek *khalkos* copper + -ITE[1]]

chal+cog+ra+phy (kæl'kɒgrəfɪ) *n.* the art of engraving on copper or brass. —**chal+'cog+ra+pher** *or* **chal+'cog+ra+phist** *n.* —**chal+co+graph+ic** (ˌkælkə'græfɪk) *or* **ˌchal+co+'graph·i+cal** *adj.*

chal+co+lith+ic (ˌkælkə'lɪθɪk) *adj. Archaeol.* of or relating to a period characterized by the use of both stone and bronze implements.

chal+co+py+rite (ˌkælkə'paɪraɪt, -'paɪə-) *n.* a widely distributed yellow mineral consisting of a sulphide of copper and iron in tetragonal crystalline form: the principal ore of copper. Formula: $CuFeS_2$. Also called: **copper pyrites.**

Chal+de·a *or* **Chal+dae·a** (kæl'diːə) *n.* **1.** an ancient region of Babylonia; the land lying between the Euphrates delta, the Persian Gulf, and the Arabian desert. **2.** another name for **Babylonia.**

Chal+de·an *or* **Chal+dae·an** (kæl'diːən) *n.* **1.** a member of an ancient Semitic people who controlled S Babylonia from the late 8th to the late 7th century B.C. **2.** the dialect of Babylonian spoken by this people. **3.** *Rare.* an astrologer or soothsayer. ~*adj.* **4.** of or relating to the ancient Chaldeans or their language.

Chal+dee (kæl'diː) *n.* **1.** a nontechnical term for **Biblical Aramaic,** once believed to be the language of the ancient Chaldeans. **2.** the actual language of the ancient Chaldeans. See also **Chaldean** (sense 2). **3.** an inhabitant of ancient Chaldea; a Chaldean. ~Also (for senses 1, 2): **Chal+da+ic** (kæl'deɪɪk).

chal+dron ('tʃɔːldrən) *n.* a unit of capacity equal to 36 bushels.

Formerly used in the U.S. for the measurement of solids, being equivalent to 1.268 cubic metres. Used in Britain for both solids and liquids, it is equivalent to 1.309 cubic metres. [C17: from Old French *chauderon* CAULDRON]

cha+let ('ʃæleɪ; *French* ʃa'lɛ) *n.* **1.** a type of wooden house of Swiss origin, typically low, with wide projecting eaves. **2.** a similar house used esp. as a ski lodge, garden house, etc. [C19: from French (Swiss dialect)]

Cha·li·a·pin (*Russian* ʃa'ljapin) *n.* **Fyo·dor I·va·no·vich** ('fjɔdər i'vanəvitʃ). 1873–1938, Russian operatic bass singer.

chal+ice ('tʃælɪs) *n.* **1.** *Poetic.* a drinking cup; goblet. **2.** *Christianity.* a gold or silver cup containing the wine at Mass. **3.** a cup-shaped flower. [C13: from Old French, from Latin *calix* cup; related to Greek *kalux* calyx]

chal+iced ('tʃælɪst) *adj.* (of plants) having cup-shaped flowers.

chal·i+co+there ('kælɪkəʊ,θɪə) *n.* any of various very large extinct Tertiary horselike perissodactyl mammals that had clawed feet but otherwise resembled titanotheres. [C19: from New Latin *Chalicotherium* type genus, from Greek *khalix* gravel + Greek *thērion* a little beast, from *thēr* wild animal]

chalk (tʃɔ:k) *n.* **1.** a soft fine-grained white sedimentary rock consisting of nearly pure calcium carbonate, containing minute fossil fragments of marine organisms, usually without a cementing material. **2.** a line, mark, etc. made with chalk. **3.** *Billiards.* a small cube of prepared chalk or similar substance for rubbing the tip of a cue. **4.** *Brit.* a score, tally, or record. **5.** **as alike** (*or* **different**) **as chalk and cheese.** *Informal.* totally different in essentials. **6. by a long chalk.** *Brit. informal.* by far. **7. can't tell** (*or* **doesn't know**) **chalk from cheese.** to be unable to judge or appreciate important differences. **8. not by a long chalk.** *Brit. informal.* by no means; not possibly. **9.** (*modifier*) made of chalk. ~*vb.* **10.** to draw or mark (something) with chalk. **11.** (*tr.*) to mark, rub, or whiten with or as if with chalk. **12.** (*intr.*) (of paint) to become chalky; powder. **13.** (*tr.*) to spread chalk on (land) as a fertilizer. [Old English *cealc*, from Latin *calx* limestone, from Greek *khalix* pebble] —'**chalk+,like** *adj.* —'**chalk·y** *adj.* —'**chalk·i·ness** *n.*

chalk and talk *n. Sometimes derogatory.* a formal method of teaching, in which the focal points are the blackboard and the teacher's voice, as contrasted with more informal child-centred activities.

chalk+board ('tʃɔ:k,bɔ:d) *n.* a U.S. word for **blackboard.**

chalk out *vb.* (*tr., adv.*) to outline (a plan, scheme, etc.); sketch.

chalk+pit ('tʃɔ:k,pɪt) *n.* a quarry for chalk.

chalk+stone ('tʃɔ:k,stəʊn) *n. Pathol.* another name for **tophus.**

chalk talk *n. U.S.* an informal lecture with pertinent points, explanatory diagrams, etc., shown on a blackboard.

chalk up *vb.* (*tr., adv.*) *Informal.* **1.** to score or register (something): *we chalked up 100 in the game.* **2.** to credit (money) to an account etc. (esp. in the phrase **chalk it up**).

chal+lah *or* **hal+lah** ('hɑ:lə; *Hebrew* xa'la) *n., pl.* **+lahs** *or* **+loth** (*Hebrew* -'lɔt). bread, usually in the form of a plaited loaf, traditionally eaten by Jews to celebrate the Sabbath. [from Hebrew *hallāh*]

chal+lenge ('tʃælɪndʒ) *vb.* (*mainly tr.*) **1.** to invite or summon (someone to do something, esp. to take part in a contest). **2.** (*also intr.*) to call (something) into question; dispute. **3.** to make demands on; stimulate: *the job challenges his ingenuity.* **4.** to order (a person) to halt and be identified or to give a password. **5.** *Law.* to make formal objection to (a juror or jury). **6.** to lay claim to (attention, etc.). **7.** (*intr.*) *Hunting.* (of a hound) to cry out on first encountering the scent of a quarry. **8.** to inject (an experimental animal immunized with a test substance) with disease microorganisms to test for immunity to the disease. ~*n.* **9.** a call to engage in a fight, argument, or contest. **10.** a questioning of a statement or fact; a demand for justification or explanation. **11.** a demanding or stimulating situation, career, object, etc. **12.** a demand by a sentry, watchman, etc., for identification or a password. **13.** *U.S.* an assertion that a person is not entitled to vote or that a vote is invalid. **14.** *Law.* a formal objection to a person selected to serve on a jury (**challenge to the polls**) or to the whole body of jurors (**challenge to the array**). [C13: from Old French *chalenge*, from Latin *calumnia* CALUMNY] —'**chal+lenge+a·ble** *adj.* —'**chal+leng+er** *n.*

chal+lis ('ʃælɪ, -lɪs) *or* **chal+lie** ('ʃælɪ) *n.* a lightweight plain-weave fabric of wool, cotton, etc., usually with a printed design. [C19: probably from a surname]

chal+one ('kæləʊn) *n.* any internal secretion that inhibits a physiological process or function. [C20: from Greek *khalōn*, from *khalan* to slacken]

Châ·lons-sur-Marne (*French* ʃalɔ̃ syr 'marn) *n.* a city in NE France, on the River Marne: scene of Attila's defeat by the Romans (451 A.D.). Pop.: 55 709 (1975). Shortened form: **Châlons.**

Cha·lon-sur-Saône (*French* ʃalɔ̃ syr 'so:n) *n.* an industrial city in E central France, on the Saône River. Pop.: 60 451 (1975). Shortened form: **Chalon.**

cha+lutz *Hebrew.* (xa'lu:ts; *English* hɑ:'lʊts) *n., pl.* ***+lu+tzim*** (-lu:'tsi:m; *English* -'lu:tsɪm). a variant spelling of **halutz.**

cha+lyb+e+ate (kə'lɪbɪɪt) *adj.* **1.** containing or impregnated with iron salts. ~*n.* **2.** any drug, etc., containing or tasting of iron. [C17: from New Latin *chalybēātus*, ultimately from *khalups* iron]

chal·y+bite ('kælɪ,baɪt) *n.* another name for **siderite** (sense 1).

cham (kæm) *n.* an archaic word for **khan**[1] (sense 1). [C16: from French, from Persian *khān*; see KHAN]

Cham (tʃæm) *n.* **1.** (*pl.* **Cham** *or* **Chams**) a member of a people of Indonesian stock living in Cambodia and central Vietnam. **2.** the language of this people, belonging to the Malayo-Polynesian family.

cha+made (ʃə'mɑ:d) *n. Military.* (formerly) a signal by drum or trumpet inviting an enemy to a parley. [C17: from French, from Portuguese *chamada*, from *chamar* to call, from Latin *clamāre*]

Cha+mae+le+on (kə'mi:lɪən) *n., Latin genitive* **Cha+mae+le+on+tis** (kə,mi:lɪ'ɒntɪs). a faint constellation lying between Volans and the South celestial pole.

cham·ae+phyte ('kæmə,faɪt) *n.* a plant whose buds are close to the ground. [C20: from Greek *khamai* on the ground + -PHYTE]

cham+ber ('tʃeɪmbə) *n.* **1.** a meeting hall, esp. one used for a legislative or judicial assembly. **2.** a reception room or audience room in an official residence, palace, etc. **3.** *Archaic or poetic.* a room in a private house, esp. a bedroom. **4. a.** a legislative, deliberative, judicial, or administrative assembly. **b.** any of the houses of a legislature. **5.** an enclosed space; compartment; cavity: *the smallest chamber in the caves.* **6.** the space between two gates of the locks of a canal, dry dock, etc. **7.** an enclosure for a cartridge in the cylinder of a revolver or for a shell in the breech of a cannon. **8.** *Obsolete.* a place where the money of a government, corporation, etc., was stored; treasury. **9.** short for **chamber pot.** **10.** (*modifier*) of, relating to, or suitable for chamber music: *a chamber concert.* ~*vb.* **11.** (*tr.*) to put in or provide with a chamber. [C13: from Old French *chambre*, from Late Latin *camera* room, Latin: vault, from Greek *kamara*]

cham+ber coun+sel *or* **coun+sel+lor** *n.* a counsel who advises in private and does not plead in court.

cham+bered nau+ti+lus *n.* another name for the **pearly nautilus.**

cham+ber+lain ('tʃeɪmbəlɪn) *n.* **1.** an officer who manages the household of a king. **2.** the steward of a nobleman or land owner. **3.** the treasurer of a municipal corporation. [C13: from Old French *chamberlayn*, of Frankish origin; related to Old High German *chamarling* chamberlain, Latin *camera* CHAMBER] —'**cham+ber+lain+,ship** *n.*

Cham·ber·lain ('tʃeɪmbəlɪn) *n.* **1.** (**Arthur**) **Nev·ille.** 1869–1940, British statesman; Conservative prime minister (1937–40): pursued a policy of appeasement towards Germany. **2.** his father, **Jo·seph.** 1836–1914, British statesman; originally a Liberal, he resigned in 1886 over Home Rule for Ireland and became leader of the Liberal Unionists; a leading advocate of preferential trading agreements with members of the British Empire. **3.** his son, Sir **Jo·seph Aus·ten.** 1863–1937, British Conservative statesman; foreign secretary (1924–29); awarded a Nobel peace prize for his negotiation of the Locarno Pact (1925).

cham·ber+maid ('tʃeɪmbə,meɪd) *n.* a woman or girl employed to clean and tidy bedrooms, now chiefly in hotels.

cham+ber mu+sic *n.* music for performance by a small group of instrumentalists.

cham+ber of com+merce *n.* (*sometimes cap.*) an organization composed mainly of local businessmen to promote, regulate, and protect their interests.

cham+ber or+ches+tra *n.* a small orchestra of about 25 players, used for the authentic performance of baroque and early classical music as well as modern music written specifically for a small orchestra.

cham+ber or+gan *n. Music.* a small compact organ used esp. for the authentic performance of pre-classical music.

cham+ber pot *n.* a vessel for urine, used in bedrooms.

cham+bers ('tʃeɪmbəz) *pl. n.* **1.** a judge's room for hearing private cases not taken in open court. **2.** (in England) the set of rooms occupied by barristers where clients are interviewed (in London, mostly in the Inns of Court). **3.** *Brit. archaic.* a suite of rooms; apartments. **4.** (in the U.S.) the private office of a judge.

Cham+ber+tin (*French* ʃɑ̃bɛr'tɛ̃) *n.* a dry red burgundy wine produced in Gevrey-Chambertin in E France.

Cham+bé+ry (*French* ʃɑ̃be'ri) *n.* a city in SE France, in the Alps: skiing centre; former capital of the duchy of Savoy. Pop.: 56 788 (1975).

Cham+bord (*French* ʃɑ̃'bɔ:r) *n.* a village in N central France: site of a famous Renaissance château.

cham+bray ('ʃæmbreɪ) *n.* a smooth light fabric of cotton, linen, etc., with white weft and a coloured warp. [C19: after *Cambrai*; see CAMBRIC]

cha+me+le+on (kə'mi:lɪən) *n.* **1.** any lizard of the family *Chamaeleontidae* of Africa and Madagascar, having long slender legs, a prehensile tail and tongue, and the ability to change colour. **2.** a changeable or fickle person. [C14: from Latin *chamaeleon*, from Greek *khamaileōn*, from *khamai* on the ground + *leōn* LION] —**cha+me·le·on+ic** (kə,mi:lɪ'ɒnɪk) *adj.* —**cha+'me·le·on-,like** *adj.*

cham+fer ('tʃæmfə) *n.* **1.** a narrow flat surface at the corner of a beam, post, etc., esp. one at an angle of 45°. Compare **bevel** (sense 1). ~*vb.* (*tr.*) **2.** to cut such a surface on (a beam, etc.). **3.** another word for **chase**[2] (sense 4). [C16: back formation from *chamfering*, from Old French *chamfrein*, from *chant* edge (see CANT[2]) + *fraindre* to break, from Latin *frangere*] —'**cham+fer+er** *n.*

cham+fron, cham+frain ('tʃæmfrən), *or* **chan+fron** *n.* a piece of armour for a horse's head. [C14: from Old French *chanfrein*, from *chafresner* to harness, from *chief* head + *frener* to bridle]

cham+ois ('ʃæmɪ; *French* ʃa'mwa) *n., pl.* **+ois. 1.** ('ʃæmwɑ:). a sure-footed goat antelope, *Rupicapra rupicapra*, inhabiting mountains of Europe and SW Asia, having vertical horns with backward-pointing tips. **2.** a soft suede leather formerly made from the hide of this animal, now obtained from the skins of sheep and goats. **3.** Also called: **chamois leather, shammy (leather), chammy (leather).** a piece of such leather or similar material used for polishing, etc. **4.** ('ʃæmwɑː). a yellow to greyish-yellow colour. ~*vb.* (*tr.*) **5.** to dress (leather or skin) like chamois. **6.** to polish with a chamois. [C16: from Old French, from Late Latin *camox* of uncertain origin]

cham·o·mile ('kæməˌmaɪl) *n.* a variant spelling of **camomile.**

Cha·mo·nix ('ʃæmənɪ; *French* ʃamɔ'ni) *n.* a town in SE France, in the Alps at the foot of Mont Blanc: skiing and tourist centre. Pop.: 8403 (1968).

champ[1] (tʃæmp) *vb.* **1.** to munch (food) noisily like a horse. **2.** (when *intr.*, often foll. by *on, at,* etc.) to bite (something) nervously or impatiently; gnaw. **3. champ** (*or* **chafe**) **at the bit.** *Informal.* to be impatient to start work, a journey, etc. ~*n.* **4.** the act or noise of champing. **5.** *Ulster dialect.* a dish of mashed potatoes and spring onions or leeks. [C16: probably of imitative origin] —**'champ·er** *n.*

champ[2] (tʃæmp) *n. Informal.* short for **champion** (sense 1).

cham·pac *or* **cham·pak** ('tʃæmpæk, 'tʃʌmpʌk) *n.* a magnoliaceous tree, *Michelia champaca,* of India and the East Indies. Its fragrant yellow flowers yield an oil used in perfumes and its wood is used for furniture. [C18: from Hindi *campak,* from Sanskrit *campaka,* of Dravidian origin]

cham·pagne (ʃæm'peɪn) *n.* **1.** (*sometimes cap.*) a white sparkling wine produced around Reims and Epernay, France. **2.** any effervescent white wine. **3. a.** a colour varying from a pale orange-yellow to a greyish-yellow. **b.** (*as adj.*): *a champagne carpet.*

Cham·pagne-Ar·denne (ʃæm'peɪn ɑː'dɛn; *French* ʃɑ̃paɲ ar'dɛn) *n.* a region of NE France: a countship and commercial centre in medieval times; it consists of a great plain, with sheep and dairy farms and many vineyards.

cham·paign (ʃæm'peɪn) *n.* **1.** Also called: **campagna.** an expanse of open level or gently undulating country. **2.** an obsolete word for **battlefield.** [C14: from Old French *champaigne,* from Late Latin *campānia;* see CAMPAIGN]

cham·pers ('ʃæmpəz) *n.* a slang name for **champagne.**

cham·per·ty ('tʃæmpətɪ) *n., pl.* **·ties.** *Law.* an illegal bargain between a party to litigation and an outsider whereby the latter agrees to pay for the action and thereby share in any proceeds recovered. See also **maintenance.** [C14: from Anglo-French *champartie,* from Old French *champart* share of produce, from *champ* field + *part* share (a feudal lord's)] —**'cham·per·tous** *adj.*

cham·pi·gnon (tʃæm'pɪnjən) *n.* any of various agaricaceous edible mushrooms, esp. *Marasmius oreades* **(fairy ring champignon)** and the meadow mushroom. [C16: from French, perhaps from Vulgar Latin *campīnus* (unattested) of the field, from Latin *campus* plain, field]

Cham·pi·gny-sur-Marne (*French* ʃɑ̃piɲi syr 'marn) *n.* a suburb of Paris, on the River Marne. Pop.: 80 482 (1975).

cham·pi·on ('tʃæmpɪən) *n.* **1. a.** a person who has defeated all others in a competition: *a chess champion.* **b.** (*as modifier*): *a champion team.* **2. a.** a plant or animal that wins first place in a show, etc. **b.** (*as modifier*): *a champion marrow.* **3.** a person who defends a person or cause: *champion of the underprivileged.* **4.** (formerly) a warrior or knight who did battle for another, esp. a king or queen, to defend their rights or honour. ~*adj.* **5.** *Northern Brit. dialect.* first rate; excellent. ~*adv.* **6.** *Northern Brit. dialect.* very well; excellently. ~*vb.* (*tr.*) **7.** to support; defend: *we champion the cause of liberty.* [C13: from Old French, from Late Latin *campiō,* from Latin *campus* field, battlefield]

cham·pi·on·ship ('tʃæmpɪənˌʃɪp) *n.* **1.** (*sometimes pl.*) any of various contests held to determine a champion. **2.** the title or status of being a champion. **3.** support for or defence of a cause, person, etc.

Cham·plain[1] (ʃæm'pleɪn) *n.* **Lake.** a lake in the northeastern U.S., between the Green Mountains and the Adirondack Mountains: linked by the **Champlain Canal** to the Hudson River and by the Richelieu River to the St. Lawrence; a major communications route in colonial times.

Cham·plain[2] (ʃæm'pleɪn; *French* ʃɑ̃'plɛ̃) *n.* **Sam·u·el de** (sa'mɥɛl də). ?1567–1635, French explorer; founder of Quebec (1608) and governor of New France (1633–35).

champ·le·vé *French.* (ʃɑ̃lə've; *English* ˌʃæmplə'veɪ) *adj.* **1.** of or relating to a process of enamelling by which grooves are cut into a metal base and filled with enamel colours. ~*n.* **2.** an object enamelled by this process. [C19: from *champ* field (level surface) + *levé* raised]

Cham·pol·lion (*French* ʃɑ̃pɔ'ljɔ̃) *n.* **Jean Fran·çois** (ʒɑ̃ frɑ̃'swa). 1790–1832, French Egyptologist, who deciphered the hieroglyphics on the Rosetta stone.

Champs É·ly·sées (*French* ʃɑ̃ zeli'ze) *n.* a major boulevard in Paris, leading from the Arc de Triomphe: site of the Élysées Palace and government offices.

Chanc. *abbrev. for:* **1.** chancellor. **2.** chancery.

chance (tʃɑːns) *n.* **1. a.** the unknown and unpredictable element that causes an event to result in a certain way rather than another, spoken of as a real force. **b.** (*as modifier*): *a chance meeting.* Related adj.: **fortuitous. 2.** fortune; luck; fate. **3.** an opportunity or occasion. **4.** a risk; gamble: *you take a chance with his driving.* **5.** the extent to which an event is likely to occur; probability. **6.** an unpredicted event, esp. a fortunate one: *that was quite a chance, finding him here.* **7.** *Archaic.* an unlucky event; mishap. **8. by chance. a.** accidentally: *he slipped by chance.* **b.** perhaps: *do you by chance have a room?* **9. on the chance.** acting on the possibility; in case. **10. the main chance.** the opportunity for personal gain (esp. in the phrase **an eye to the main chance**). ~*vb.* **11.** (*tr.*) to risk; hazard: *I'll chance the worst happening.* **12.** to happen by chance; be the case by chance: *I chanced to catch sight of her as she passed.* **13. chance on** (*or* **upon**). to come upon by accident: *he chanced on the solution to his problem.* **14. chance one's arm.** to attempt to do something although the chance of success may be slight. [C13: from Old French *cheance,* from *cheoir* to fall, occur, from Latin *cadere*] —**'chance·ful** *adj.* —**'chance·less** *adj.*

chan·cel ('tʃɑːnsəl) *n.* the part of a church containing the altar, sanctuary, and choir, usually separated from the nave and transepts by a screen. [C14: from Old French, from Latin *cancellī* (plural) lattice]

chan·cel·ler·y *or* **chan·cel·lo·ry** ('tʃɑːnsələrɪ, -slərɪ) *n., pl.* **·ler·ies** *or* **·lo·ries. 1.** the building or room occupied by a chancellor's office. **2.** the position, rank, or office of a chancellor. **3.** *U.S.* **a.** the residence or office of an embassy or legation. **b.** the office of a consulate. **4.** *Brit.* another name for a diplomatic **chancery.** [C14: from Anglo-French *chancellerie,* from Old French *chancelier* CHANCELLOR]

chan·cel·lor ('tʃɑːnsələ, -slə) *n.* **1.** the head of the government in several European countries. **2.** *U.S.* the president of a university or, in some colleges, the chief administrative officer. **3.** *Brit.* the honorary head of a university. Compare **vice chancellor** (sense 1). **4.** *U.S.* (in some states) the presiding judge of a court of chancery or equity. **5.** *Brit.* the chief secretary of an embassy. **6.** *Christianity.* a clergyman acting as the law officer of a bishop. **7.** *Archaic.* the chief secretary of a prince, nobleman, etc. [C11: from Anglo-French *chanceler,* from Late Latin *cancellārius* porter, secretary, from Latin *cancellī* lattice; see CHANCEL] —**'chan·cel·lor·ˌship** *n.*

Chan·cel·lor of the Duch·y of Lan·cas·ter *n. Brit.* a minister of the crown, nominally appointed as representative of the Queen as Duchess of Lancaster, but in practice chiefly employed on parliamentary work determined by the prime minister.

Chan·cel·lor of the Ex·cheq·uer *n. Brit.* the cabinet minister responsible for finance.

chance-med·ley *n. Law.* a sudden quarrel in which one party kills another; unintentional but not blameless killing. [C15: from Anglo-French *chance medlee* mixed chance]

chan·cer·y ('tʃɑːnsərɪ) *n., pl.* **·cer·ies. 1.** Also called: **Chancery Division.** (in England) the Lord Chancellor's court, now a division of the High Court of Justice. **2.** Also called: **court of chancery.** (in the U.S.) a court of equity. **3.** *Brit.* the political section or offices of an embassy or legation. **4.** another name for **chancellery. 5.** a court of public records; archives. **6.** *Christianity.* a diocesan office under the supervision of a bishop's chancellor, having custody of archives, issuing official enactments, etc. **7. in chancery. a.** *Law.* (of a suit) pending in a court of equity. **b.** *Wrestling.* (of a competitor's head) locked under an opponent's arm. **c.** in an awkward or helpless situation. [C14: shortened from CHANCELLERY]

chan·cre ('ʃæŋkə) *n. Pathol.* a small hard nodular growth, which is the first diagnostic sign of acquired syphilis. [C16: from French, from Latin: CANCER] —**'chan·crous** *adj.*

chan·croid ('ʃæŋkrɔɪd) *n.* **1.** a soft venereal ulcer, esp. of the male genitals, caused by infection with the bacillus *Haemophilus ducreyi.* ~*adj.* **2.** relating to or resembling a chancroid or chancre. —**chan·'croi·dal** *adj.*

chanc·y *or* **chanc·ey** ('tʃɑːnsɪ) *adj.* **chanc·i·er, chanc·i·est.** *Informal.* of uncertain outcome or temperament; risky. —**'chanc·i·ly** *adv.* —**'chanc·i·ness** *n.*

chan·de·lier (ˌʃændɪ'lɪə) *n.* an ornamental hanging light with branches and holders for several candles or bulbs. [C17: from French: candleholder, from Latin CANDELABRUM]

chan·delle (ʃæn'dɛl; *French* ʃɑ̃'dɛl) *n.* **1.** *Aeronautics.* an abrupt climbing turn almost to the point of stalling, in which an aircraft's momentum is used to increase its rate of climb. ~*vb.* **2.** (*intr.*) to carry out a chandelle. [French, literally: CANDLE]

Chan·der·na·gore (ˌtʃʌndənə'gɔː) *n.* a port in E India, in S West Bengal on the Hooghly River: a former French settlement (1686–1950). Pop.: 67 105 (1961).

Chan·di·garh (ˌtʃʌndɪ'gɑː) *n.* a city and Union Territory of N India, joint capital of the Punjab and Haryana: modern city planned in the 1950s by Le Corbusier. Pop.: 218 743 (1971).

chan·dler ('tʃɑːndlə) *n.* **1.** a dealer in a specified trade or merchandise: *corn chandler; ship's chandler.* **2.** a person who makes or sells candles. **3.** *Brit. obsolete.* a retailer of grocery provisions; shopkeeper. [C14: from Old French *chandelier* one who makes or deals in candles, from *chandelle* CANDLE]

Chan·dler ('tʃɑːndlə) *n.* **Ray·mond.** 1888–1959, U.S. thriller writer: created Philip Marlowe, one of the first detective heroes in fiction.

chan·dler·y ('tʃɑːndlərɪ) *n., pl.* **·dler·ies. 1.** the business, warehouse, or merchandise of a chandler. **2.** a place where candles are kept.

Chan·dra·gup·ta (ˌtʃʌndrə'gʊptə) *n.* Greek name *Sandracottos.* died ?297 B.C., ruler of N India, who founded the Maurya dynasty (325) and defeated Seleucus (?305).

Cha·nel (*French* ʃa'nɛl) *n.* **Gab·ri·elle** (gabrɪ'ɛl), known as *Coco.* 1883–1970, French couturier, who created the little black dress and the perfume Chanel No. 5.

Chang (tʃæŋ) *n.* another name for the **Yangtze.**

Chang·an ('tʃæŋ'ɑːn) *n.* a former name of **Sian.**

Chang·chia·kow *or* **Chang·chia·k'ou** ('tʃæŋ'tʃjɑː'kəʊ) *n.* a city in NE China, in NW Hopei province: a military centre, controlling the route to Mongolia, under the Ming and Manchu dynasties. Pop.: 480 000 (1958 est.). Former names: **Wanchüan, Kalgan.**

Chang+chow *or* **Ch'ang-chou** ('tʃæŋ'tʃaʊ) *n.* **1.** a city in E China, in S Kiangsu province, on the Grand Canal: also known as **Wutsin** until 1949, when the 7th-century name was officially readopted. Pop.: 300 000 (1958 est.). **2.** the former name of **Lungki.**

Chang+chun *or* **Ch'ang Ch'un** ('tʃæŋ'tʃʊn) *n.* a city in NE China, capital of Kirin province: as **Hsinking,** capital of the Japanese state of Manchukuo (1932–45). Pop.: 1 800 000 (1965 Western est.).

change (tʃeɪndʒ) *vb.* **1.** to make or become different; alter. **2.** (*tr.*) to replace with or exchange for another: *to change one's name.* **3.** (sometimes foll. by *to* or *into*) to transform or convert or be transformed or converted. **4.** to give and receive (something) in return; interchange: *to change places with someone.* **5.** (*tr.*) to give or receive (money) in exchange for the equivalent sum in a smaller denomination or different currency. **6.** (*tr.*) to remove or replace the coverings of: *to change a baby.* **7.** (when *intr.*, may be foll. by *into* or *out of*) to put on other clothes. **8.** (*intr.*) (of the moon) to pass from one phase to the following one. **9.** to operate (the gear lever of a motor vehicle) in order to change the gear ratio: *to change gear.* **10.** to alight from (one bus, train, etc.) and board another. **11. change face.** to rotate the telescope of a surveying instrument through 180° horizontally and vertically, taking a second sighting of the same object in order to reduce error. **12. change feet.** *Informal.* to put on different shoes, boots, etc. **13. change front. a.** (of a military force) to turn in another direction. **b.** to alter one's attitude, opinion, etc. **14. change hands.** to pass from one owner to another. **15. change one's mind.** to alter one's decision or opinion. **16. change one's tune.** to alter one's attitude or tone of speech. ~*n.* **17.** the act or fact of changing or being changed. **18.** a variation, deviation, or modification. **19.** the substitution of one thing for another; exchange. **20.** anything that is or may be substituted for something else. **21.** variety or novelty (esp. in the phrase **for a change**): *I want to go to France for a change.* **22.** a different or fresh set, esp. of clothes. **23.** money given or received in return for its equivalent in a larger denomination or in a different currency. **24.** the balance of money given or received when the amount tendered is larger than the amount due. **25.** coins of a small denomination regarded collectively. **26.** (*often cap.*) *Archaic.* a place where merchants meet to transact business; an exchange. **27.** the act of passing from one state or phase to another. **28.** the transition from one phase of the moon to the next. **29.** the order in which a peal of bells may be rung. **30.** *Sport.* short for **changeover** (sense 3). **31.** *Slang.* desirable or useful information. **32.** *Obsolete.* fickleness or caprice. **33. change of heart.** a profound change of outlook, opinion, etc. **34. get no change out of (someone).** *Slang.* not to be successful in attempts to exploit or extract information from (someone). **35. ring the changes.** to vary the manner or performance of an action that is often repeated. ~See also **change down, changeover, change round, change up.** [C13: from Old French *changier,* from Latin *cambīre* to exchange, barter] —'**change+less** *adj.* —'**change+less+ly** *adv.* —'**change+less+ness** *n.* —'**chang+er** *n.*

change+a·ble ('tʃeɪndʒəbᵊl) *adj.* **1.** able to change or be changed; fickle: *changeable weather.* **2.** varying in colour when viewed from different angles or in different lights. —ˌ**change+a·'bil+i·ty** *or* '**change+a·ble+ness** *n.* —'**change+a·bly** *adv.*

change down *vb.* (*intr., adv.*) to select a lower gear when driving.

change+ful ('tʃeɪndʒfʊl) *adj.* often changing; inconstant; variable. —'**change+ful+ly** *adv.* —'**change+ful+ness** *n.*

change+ling ('tʃeɪndʒlɪŋ) *n.* **1.** a child believed to have been exchanged by fairies for the parents' true child. **2.** *Archaic.* **a.** an idiot. **b.** a fickle or changeable person.

change of life *n.* a nontechnical name for **menopause.**

change of ven·ue *n. Law.* the removal of a trial out of one jurisdiction into another.

change+o·ver ('tʃeɪndʒˌəʊvə) *n.* **1.** an alteration or complete reversal from one method, system, or product to another: *a changeover to decimal currency.* **2.** a reversal of a situation, attitude, etc. **3.** *Sport.* **a.** the act of transferring to or being relieved by a teammate in a relay race, as by handing over a baton, etc. **b.** Also called: **change, takeover.** the point in a relay race at which the transfer is made. **4.** *Sport, chiefly Brit.* the exchange of ends by two teams, esp. at half time. ~*vb.* **change o·ver.** (*adv.*) **5.** to adopt (a completely different position or attitude): *the driver and navigator changed over after four hours.* **6.** (*intr.*) *Sport, chiefly Brit.* (of two teams) to exchange ends of a playing field, etc., as after half time.

change point *n. Surveying.* a point to which a foresight and backsight are taken in levelling; turning point.

change-ring·ing *n.* **1.** the art of bell-ringing in which a set of bells is rung in an established order which is then changed. **2.** variations on a topic or theme.

change round *vb.* (*adv.*) **1.** to place in or adopt a different or opposite position. ~*n.* **change+round. 2.** the act of changing to a different position.

change up *vb.* (*intr., adv.*) to select a higher gear when driving.

Chang+sha *or* **Ch'ang-sha** ('tʃæŋ'ʃɑː) *n.* a port in SE China, capital of Hunan province, on the Hsiang River. Pop.: 825 000 (1970 est.).

Chang+teh *or* **Ch'ang-te** ('tʃæŋ'teɪ) *n.* a port in SE central China, in N Hunan province, near the mouth of the Yuan River: severely damaged by the Japanese in World War II. Pop.: 94 800 (1953).

chan+nel[1] ('tʃænᵊl) *n.* **1.** a broad strait connecting two areas of sea. **2.** the bed or course of a river, stream, or canal. **3.** a navigable course through a body of water. **4.** (*often pl.*) a means or agency of access, communication, etc.: *to go through official channels.* **5.** a course into which something can be directed or moved: *a new channel of thought.* **6.** *Electronics.* **a.** a band of radio frequencies assigned for a particular purpose, esp. the broadcasting of a television signal. **b.** a path for an electrical signal: *a stereo set has two channels.* **c.** a thin semiconductor layer between the source and drain of a field-effect transistor, the conductance of which is controlled by the gate voltage. **7.** a tubular or trough-shaped passage for fluids. **8.** a groove or flute, as in the shaft of a column. **9.** *Computer technol.* **a.** a path along which data can be transmitted between a central processing unit and one or more peripheral devices. **b.** one of the lines along the length of a paper tape on which information can be stored in the form of punched holes. **10.** short for **channel iron.** ~*vb.* **+nels, +nel+ling, +nelled** *or U.S.* **+nels, +nel+ing, +neled. 11.** to provide or be provided with a channel or channels; make or cut channels in (something). **12.** (*tr.*) to guide into or convey through a channel or channels: *information was channelled through to them.* **13.** (*tr.*) to form a groove or flute in (a column, etc.). [C13: from Old French *chanel,* from Latin *canālis* pipe, groove, conduit; see CANAL] —'**chan+nel+ler** *n.*

chan+nel[2] ('tʃænᵊl) *n. Nautical.* a flat timber or metal ledge projecting from the hull of a vessel above the chainplates to increase the angle of the shrouds. [C18: variant of earlier *chainwale;* see CHAIN, WALE[1] (planking)]

Chan+nel ('tʃænᵊl) *n.* **the.** short for **English Channel.**

Chan+nel Count+ry *n.* **the.** an area of E central Australia, in SW Queensland: crossed by intermittent rivers and subject to both flooding and long periods of drought.

chan+nel i·ron *or* **bar** *n.* a rolled-steel bar with a U-shaped cross section. Sometimes shortened to **channel.**

Chan+nel Is+lands *pl. n.* a group of islands in the English Channel, off the NW coast of France, consisting of Jersey, Guernsey, Alderney, Brechou, Great Sark, Little Sark, Herm, Jethou, and Lihou (British crown dependencies), and the Roches Douvres and the Îles Chausey (which belong to France): the only part of the duchy of Normandy remaining to Britain. Pop.: 128 000 (1975 UN est.). Area: 194 sq. km (75 sq. miles).

chan+nel+ize *or* **chan+nel+ise** ('tʃænəlaɪz) *vb.* (*tr.*) to guide through or as if through a channel; provide a channel for.

chan+son de geste *French.* (ʃɑ̃sɔ̃ də 'ʒɛst) *n.* one of a genre of Old French epic poems celebrating heroic deeds, the most famous of which is the *Chanson de Roland.* [literally: song of exploits]

chant (tʃɑːnt) *n.* **1.** a simple song or melody. **2.** a short simple melody in which several words or syllables are assigned to one note, as in the recitation of psalms. **3.** a psalm or canticle performed by using such a melody. **4.** a rhythmic or repetitious slogan, usually spoken or sung, as by sports supporters, etc. **5.** monotonous or singsong intonation in speech. ~*vb.* **6.** to sing or recite (a psalm, prayer, etc.) as a chant. **7.** to intone (a slogan) rhythmically or repetitiously. **8.** to speak or say monotonously as if intoning a chant. [C14: from Old French *chanter* to sing, from Latin *cantāre,* frequentative of *canere* to sing] —'**chant+ing+ly** *adv.*

chant+er ('tʃɑːntə) *n.* **1.** a person who chants. **2.** the pipe on a set of bagpipes that is provided with finger holes and on which the melody is played.

chan+te+relle (ˌtʃæntə'rɛl) *n.* any saprophytic basidiomycetous fungus of the genus *Cantharellus,* esp. *C. cibarius,* having an edible yellow funnel-shaped mushroom: family *Cantharellaceae.* [C18: from French, from New Latin *cantharella,* diminutive of Latin *cantharus* drinking vessel, from Greek *kantharos*]

chan+teuse (*French* ʃɑ̃'tøːz) *n.* a female singer, esp. in a nightclub or cabaret. [French: singer]

chan+tey ('ʃæntɪ, 'tʃæn-) *n., pl.* **+teys.** the usual U.S. spelling of **shanty**[2].

chan+ti+cleer (ˌtʃæntɪ'klɪə) *or* **chan+te+cler** (ˌtʃæntɪ'klɛə) *n.* a name for a cock, used esp. in fables. [C13: from Old French *Chantecler,* from *chanter cler* to sing clearly]

Chan+til+ly (ʃæn'tɪlɪ; *French* ʃɑ̃ti'ji) *n.* **1.** a town in N France, near the **Forest of Chantilly:** formerly famous for lace and porcelain. Pop.: 10 684 (1975). ~*adj.* **2.** (of cream) lightly sweetened and whipped.

Chan+til+ly lace *n.* (*sometimes not cap.*) a delicate ornamental lace.

chan+try ('tʃɑːntrɪ) *n., pl.* **+tries.** *Christianity.* **1.** an endowment for the singing of Masses for the soul of the founder or others designated by him. **2.** a chapel or altar so endowed. **3.** (*as modifier*): *a chantry priest.* [C14: from Old French *chanterie,* from *chanter* to sing; see CHANT]

chan+ty ('ʃæntɪ, 'tʃæn-) *n., pl.* **+ties.** a variant spelling of **shanty**[2].

Cha+nu+kah *or* **Cha+nuk+kah** ('hɑːnəkə, -nʊˌkɑː; *Hebrew* xanuː'ka) *n.* a variant spelling of **Hanukkah.**

Chao+an ('tʃaʊ'ɑːn) *n.* a city in SE China, in E Kwantung province, on the Han River: river port. Pop.: 101 300 (1953 est.). Former name: **Chaochow.**

Chao+chow ('tʃaʊ'tʃəʊ) *n.* the former name of **Chaoan.**

Chao Phra+ya ('tʃaʊ prə'jɑː) *n.* a river in N Thailand, rising in the N highlands and flowing south to the Gulf of Siam. Length:

(including the headstreams Nan and Ping) 1200 km (750 miles). Also called: **Menam.**

cha·os ('keɪɒs) *n.* **1.** (*usually cap.*) the disordered formless matter supposed to have existed before the ordered universe. **2.** complete disorder; utter confusion. **3.** an obsolete word for **abyss.** [C15: from Latin, from Greek *khaos;* compare CHASM, YAWN] —**cha·ot·ic** (keɪ'ɒtɪk) *adj.* —**cha·'ot·i·cal·ly** *adv.*

chap[1] (tʃæp) *vb.* **chaps, chap·ping, chapped. 1.** (of the skin) to make or become raw and cracked, esp. by exposure to cold. ~*n.* **2.** (*usually pl.*) a cracked or sore patch on the skin caused by chapping. [C14: probably of Germanic origin; compare Middle Dutch, German *kappen* to chop off]

chap[2] (tʃæp) *n. Informal.* a man or boy; fellow. [C16 (in the sense: buyer): shortened from CHAPMAN]

chap[3] (tʃɒp, tʃæp) *n.* a less common word for **chop**[3].

chap. *abbrev. for:* **1.** chaplain. **2.** chapter.

chap·a·re·jos (ˌʃæpə'reɪəʊs; *Spanish* ˌtʃapa'rexos) *or* **chap·a·ra·jos** (ˌʃæpə'reɪəʊs; *Spanish* ˌtʃapa'raxos) *pl. n.* another name for **chaps.** [from Mexican Spanish]

chap·ar·ral (ˌtʃæpə'ræl, ˌʃæp-) *n.* (in the southwestern U.S.) a dense growth of shrubs and trees, esp. evergreen oaks. [C19: from Spanish, from *chaparra* evergreen oak]

chap·ar·ral cock *n.* another name for **roadrunner.**

chap·ar·ral pea *n.* a thorny leguminous Californian shrub, *Pickeringia montana,* with reddish-purple showy flowers.

cha·pat·ti *or* **cha·pa·ti** (tʃə'pætɪ, -'pʌtɪ, -'pɑːtɪ) *n., pl.* **-ti, -tis,** *or* **-ties.** (in Indian cookery) a flat coarse unleavened bread resembling a pancake. [from Hindi]

chap·book ('tʃæpˌbʊk) *n.* a book of popular ballads, stories, etc., formerly sold by chapmen or pedlars.

chape (tʃeɪp) *n.* **1.** a metal tip or trimming for a scabbard. **2.** the metal tongue of a buckle. [C14: from Old French: hood, metal cover, from Late Latin *cappa* CAP] —**'chape·less** *adj.*

cha·peau ('ʃæpəʊ; *French* ʃa'po) *n., pl.* **-peaux** (-pəʊ, -pəʊz; *French* -'po) *or* **-peaus.** a hat. [C16: from French, from Late Latin *cappellus* hood, from *cappa* CAP]

chap·el ('tʃæpᵊl) *n.* **1.** a place of Christian worship in a larger building, esp. a place set apart, with a separate altar, in a church or cathedral. **2.** a similar place of worship in or attached to a large house or institution, such as a college, hospital or prison. **3.** a church subordinate to a parish church. **4.** (in Britain) **a.** a Nonconformist place of worship. **b.** Nonconformist religious practices or doctrine. **c.** (*as adj.*): *he is chapel, but his wife is church.* Compare **church** (sense 5). **5. a.** the members of a trade union in a particular newspaper office, printing house, etc. **b.** a meeting of these members. **6.** a printing office. [C13: from Old French *chapele,* from Late Latin *cappella,* diminutive of *cappa* cloak (see CAP); originally denoting the sanctuary where the cloak of St. Martin of Tours was kept as a relic]

chap·el of ease *n.* a church built to accommodate those living at a distance from the parish church.

chap·er·on *or* **chap·er·one** ('ʃæpəˌrəʊn) *n.* **1.** (esp. formerly) an older or married woman who accompanies or supervises a young unmarried woman on social occasions. **2.** someone who accompanies and supervises a group, esp. of young people, usually when in public places. ~*vb.* **3.** to act as a chaperon to. [C14: from Old French, from *chape* hood, protective covering; see CAP] —**chap·er·on·age** ('ʃæpərənɪdʒ) *n.*

chap·fall·en ('tʃæpˌfɔːlən) *or* **chop·fall·en** *adj.* dejected; downhearted; crestfallen. [C16: from CHOPS + FALLEN]

chap·i·ter ('tʃæpɪtə) *n. Architect.* another name for **capital**[2]. [C15: from Old French *chapitre,* from Latin *capitellum* CAPITAL[2]]

chap·lain ('tʃæplɪn) *n.* a Christian clergyman attached to a private chapel of a prominent person or institution or ministering to a military body, professional group, etc: *a military chaplain; a prison chaplain.* [C12: from Old French *chapelain,* from Late Latin *cappellānus,* from *cappella* CHAPEL] —**'chap·lain·cy, 'chap·lain·ˌship,** *or* **'chap·lain·ry** *n.*

chap·let ('tʃæplɪt) *n.* **1.** an ornamental wreath of flowers, beads, etc., worn on the head. **2.** a string of beads or something similar. **3.** *R.C. Church.* **a.** a string of prayer beads constituting one third of the rosary. **b.** the prayers counted on this string. **4.** a narrow convex moulding in the form of a string of beads; astragal. **5.** a metal support for the core in a casting mould, esp. for the core of a cylindrical pipe. [C14: from Old French *chapelet* garland of roses, from *chapel* hat; see CHAPEAU] —**'chap·let·ed** *adj.*

Chap·lin ('tʃæplɪn) *n.* Sir **Charles Spen·cer,** known as *Charlie Chaplin.* 1889–1977, English comedian, film actor and director. He is renowned for his portrayal of a downtrodden little man with baggy trousers, bowler hat, and cane. His films include *The Gold Rush* (1925), *Modern Times* (1936), and *The Great Dictator* (1940).

chap·man ('tʃæpmən) *n., pl.* **-men.** *Archaic.* a trader, esp. an itinerant pedlar. [Old English *cēapman,* from *cēap* buying and selling (see CHEAP)] —**'chap·man·ˌship** *n.*

Chap·man ('tʃæpmən) *n.* **George.** 1559–1634, English dramatist and poet, noted for his translation of Homer.

chap·pal ('tʃʌpᵊl) *n.* one of a pair of sandals, usually of leather, worn in India. [from Hindi]

chap·pie ('tʃæpɪ) *n. Informal.* another word for **chap**[2].

chaps (tʃæps, ʃæps) *pl. n.* leather overalls without a seat, worn by cowboys. Also called: **chaparajos, chaparejos.** [C19: shortened from CHAPAREJOS]

chap·stick ('tʃæpˌstɪk) *n. Chiefly U.S.* a cylinder of a substance for preventing or soothing chapped lips. [C20: from a trademark]

chap·ter ('tʃæptə) *n.* **1.** a division of a written work, esp. a narrative, usually titled or numbered. **2.** a sequence of events having a common attribute: *a chapter of disasters.* **3.** an episode or period in a life, history, etc. **4.** a numbered reference to that part of a Parliamentary session which relates to a specified Act of Parliament. **5.** a branch of some societies, clubs, etc., esp. of a secret society. **6.** the collective body or a meeting of the canons of a cathedral or collegiate church or of the members of a monastic or knightly order. **7.** a general assembly of some organization. **8. chapter and verse.** exact authority for an action or statement. ~*vb.* **9.** (*tr.*) to divide into chapters. [C13: from Old French *chapitre,* from Latin *capitulum,* literally: little head, hence, section of writing, from *caput* head; in Medieval Latin: chapter of scripture or of a religious rule, a gathering for the reading of this, hence, assemblage of clergy]

chap·ter·house ('tʃæptəˌhaʊs) *n.* **1.** the building attached to a cathedral, collegiate church, or religious house in which the chapter meets. **2.** the meeting place of a society, club, etc.

char[1] (tʃɑː) *vb.* **chars, char·ring, charred. 1.** to burn or be burned partially, esp. so as to blacken the surface; scorch. **2.** (*tr.*) to reduce (wood) to charcoal by partial combustion. [C17: short for CHARCOAL]

char[2] *or* **charr** (tʃɑː) *n., pl.* **char, chars** *or* **charr, charrs.** any of various troutlike fishes of the genus *Salvelinus,* esp. *S. alpinus,* occurring in cold lakes and northern seas: family *Salmonidae* (salmon). [C17: of unknown origin]

char[3] (tʃɑː) *n.* **1.** *Informal.* short for **charwoman.** ~*vb.* **chars, char·ring, charred. 2.** *Brit. informal.* to do housework, cleaning, etc., as a job.

char[4] (tʃɑː) *n. Brit.* a slang word for **tea.** [from Chinese *ch'a*]

char·a·banc ('ʃærəˌbæŋ; *French* ʃara'bã) *n. Brit.* a motor coach, esp. one used for sightseeing tours. [C19: from French *char-à-bancs,* wagon with seats]

char·a·cin ('kærəsɪn) *or* **char·a·cid** *n.* any small carnivorous freshwater cyprinoid fish of the family *Characidae,* of Central and South America and Africa. They are similar to the carps but more brightly coloured. [C19: from New Latin *Characinidae,* from *characinus,* from Greek *kharax* a fish, probably the sea bream]

char·ac·ter ('kærɪktə) *n.* **1.** the combination of traits and qualities distinguishing the individual nature of a person or thing. **2.** one such distinguishing quality; characteristic. **3.** moral force; integrity: *a man of character.* **4. a.** reputation, esp. a good reputation. **b.** (*as modifier*): *character assassination.* **5.** a summary or account of a person's qualities and achievements; testimonial: *my last employer gave me a good character.* **6.** capacity, position, or status: *he spoke in the character of a friend rather than a father.* **7.** a person represented in a play, film, story, etc.; role. **8.** an outstanding person: *one of the great characters of the century.* **9.** *Informal.* an odd, eccentric, or unusual person: *he's quite a character.* **10.** an informal word for **person:** *a shady character.* **11.** a symbol used in a writing system, such as a letter of the alphabet. **12.** Also called: **sort.** *Printing.* any single letter, numeral, punctuation mark, or symbol cast as a type. **13.** *Computer technol.* any such letter, numeral, etc., each of which is a unit of information and can be represented uniquely by binary code. **14.** a style of writing or printing. **15.** *Genetics.* any structure, function, attribute, etc., in an organism that is determined by a gene or group of genes. **16.** a short prose sketch of a distinctive type of person, usually representing a vice or virtue. **17. in** (*or* **out of**) **character.** typical (or not typical) of the apparent character of a person or thing. ~*vb.* (*tr.*) **18.** to write, print, inscribe, or engrave. **19.** *Rare.* to portray or represent. [C14: from Latin: distinguishing mark, from Greek *kharaktēr* engraver's tool, from *kharassein* to engrave, stamp] —**'char·ac·ter·ful** *adj.* —**'char·ac·ter·less** *adj.*

char·ac·ter ac·tor *n.* an actor who specializes in playing odd or eccentric characters.

char·ac·ter·is·tic (ˌkærɪktə'rɪstɪk) *n.* **1.** a distinguishing quality, attribute, or trait. **2.** *Maths.* **a.** the integral part of a common logarithm, indicating the order of magnitude of the associated number: *the characteristic of 2.4771 is 2.* Compare **mantissa. b.** another name for **exponent** (sense 4), esp. in number representation in computing. ~*adj.* **3.** indicative of a distinctive quality, etc.; typical. —ˌ**char·ac·ter·'is·ti·cal·ly** *adv.*

char·ac·ter·is·tic curve *n. Photog.* a graph of the density of a particular photographic material plotted against the logarithm of the exposure producing this density.

char·ac·ter·i·za·tion *or* **char·ac·ter·i·sa·tion** (ˌkærɪktəraɪ'zeɪʃən) *n.* **1.** description of character, traits, etc. **2.** the act of characterizing.

char·ac·ter·ize *or* **char·ac·ter·ise** ('kærɪktəˌraɪz) *vb.* (*tr.*) **1.** to be a characteristic of: *loneliness characterized the place.* **2.** to distinguish or mark as a characteristic. **3.** to describe or portray the character of. —**'char·ac·ter·ˌiz·a·ble** *or* **'char·ac·ter·ˌis·a·ble** *adj.* —**'char·ac·ter·ˌiz·er** *or* **'char·ac·ter·ˌis·er** *n.*

char·ac·ter sketch *n.* a brief description or portrayal of a person's character, qualities, etc.

char·ac·ter type *n. Psychol.* a cluster of personality traits commonly occurring together in an individual.

char·ac·ter·y ('kærɪktərɪ, -trɪ) *n., pl.* **-ter·ies.** *Archaic.* **1.** the use of symbols to express thoughts. **2.** the group of symbols so used.

cha·rade (ʃə'rɑːd) *n.* **1.** an episode or act in the game of charades. **2.** *Chiefly Brit.* an absurd act; travesty.

cha·rades (ʃə'rɑːdz) *n.* a parlour game in which one team acts out each syllable of a word, the other team having to guess the word. [C18: from French *charade* entertainment, from Provençal *charrado* chat, from *charra* chatter, of imitative origin]

char·as ('tʃɑːrəs) *n.* another name for **hashish.** [C19: from Hindi]

char·coal ('tʃɑːˌkəʊl) *n.* **1.** a black amorphous form of carbon made by heating wood or other organic matter in the absence of air: used as a fuel, in smelting metal ores, in explosives, and as an absorbent. See **activated carbon. 2.** a stick or pencil of this for drawing. **3.** a drawing done in charcoal. ~*vb.* **4.** (*tr.*) to write, draw, or blacken with charcoal. [C14: from *char* (origin obscure) + COAL]

char·coal-burn·er *n.* a person who makes charcoal.

char·coal grey *n.* **a.** a very dark grey colour. **b.** (*as adj.*): *charcoal-grey trousers.*

Char·cot (*French* ʃar'ko) *n.* **Jean Mar·tin** (ʒã mar'tɛ̃). 1825–93, French neurologist, noted for his attempt using hypnotism to find an organic cause for hysteria, which influenced Freud.

chard (tʃɑːd) *n.* a variety of beet, *Beta vulgaris cicla,* with large succulent leaves and thick stalks, used as a vegetable. Also called: **Swiss chard, leaf beet, seakale beet.** [C17: probably from French *carde* edible leafstalk of the artichoke, but associated also with French *chardon* thistle, both ultimately from Latin *carduus* thistle; see CARDOON]

Char·din (*French* ʃar'dɛ̃) *n.* **Jean-Bap·tiste Si·mé·on** (ʒã batist sime'ɔ̃). 1699–1779, French still-life and genre painter, noted for his subtle use of scumbled colour.

Cha·rente (*French* ʃa'rɑ̃ːt) *n.* **1.** a department of W central France, in Poitou-Charentes region. Capital: Angoulême. Pop.: 345 445 (1975). Area: 5972 sq. km (2329 sq. miles). **2.** a river in W France, flowing west to the Bay of Biscay. Length: 362 km (225 miles).

Cha·rente-Ma·ri·time (*French* ʃarɑ̃t mari'tim) *n.* a department of W France, in Poitou-Charentes region. Capital: La Rochelle. Pop.: 513 478 (1975). Area: 7232 sq. km (2820 sq. miles).

charge (tʃɑːdʒ) *vb.* **1.** to set or demand (a price): *he charges too much for his services.* **2.** (*tr.*) to hold financially liable; enter a debit against. **3.** (*tr.*) to enter or record as an obligation against a person or his account. **4.** (*tr.*) to accuse or impute a fault to (a person, etc.), as formally in a court of law. **5.** (*tr.*) to command; place a burden upon or assign responsibility to: *I was charged to take the message to headquarters.* **6.** to make a rush at or sudden attack upon (a person or thing). **7.** (*tr.*) to fill (a receptacle) with the proper or appropriate quantity. **8.** (often foll. by *up*) to cause (an accumulator, capacitor, etc.) to take or store electricity or (of an accumulator) to have electricity fed into it. **9.** to fill or suffuse or to be filled or suffused with matter by dispersion, solution, or absorption: *to charge water with carbon dioxide.* **10.** (*tr.*) to fill or suffuse with feeling, emotion, etc.: *the atmosphere was charged with excitement.* **11.** (*tr.*) *Law.* (of a judge) to address (a jury) authoritatively. **12.** (*tr.*) to load (a firearm). **13.** (*tr.*) to aim (a weapon) in position ready for use. **14.** (*tr.*) *Heraldry.* to paint (a shield, banner, etc.) with a charge. **15.** (*intr.*) (of hunting dogs) to lie down at command. ~*n.* **16.** a price charged for some article or service; cost. **17.** a financial liability, such as a tax. **18.** a debt or a book entry recording it. **19.** an accusation or allegation, such as a formal accusation of a crime in law. **20. a.** an onrush, attack, or assault. **b.** the call to such an attack in battle. **21.** custody or guardianship. **22.** a person or thing committed to someone's care. **23. a.** a cartridge or shell. **b.** the explosive required to discharge a firearm or other weapon. **c.** an amount of explosive material to be detonated at any one time. **24.** the quantity of anything that a receptacle is intended to hold. **25.** *Physics.* **a.** the attribute of matter responsible for all electrical phenomena, existing in two forms to which the signs negative and positive are arbitrarily assigned. **b.** a similar property of a body or system determined by the extent to which it contains an excess or deficiency of electrons. **c.** a quantity of electricity determined by the product of an electric current and the time for which it flows, measured in coulombs. **d.** the total amount of electricity stored in a capacitor, equal to the charge on the positive plate. **e.** the total amount of electricity held in an accumulator, usually measured in ampere-hours. Symbol: *q* or *Q.* **26.** a load or burden. **27.** a duty or responsibility; control. **28.** a command, injunction, or order. **29.** *Slang.* a thrill. **30.** *Law.* the address made by a judge to the jury at the conclusion of the evidence. **31.** *Heraldry.* a design, device, or image depicted on heraldic arms: *a charge of three lions.* **32.** the solid propellant used in rockets, sometimes including the inhibitor. **33. in charge.** in command. **34. in charge of. a.** having responsibility for. **b.** *U.S.* under the care of. [C13: from Old French *chargier* to load, from Late Latin *carricāre;* see CARRY]

charge·a·ble ('tʃɑːdʒəbᵊl) *adj.* **1.** charged or liable to be charged. **2.** liable to result in a legal charge. —**'charge·a·ble·ness** *or* ˌ**charge·a·'bil·i·ty** *n.* —**'charge·a·bly** *adv.*

charge ac·count *n.* another term for **credit account.**

char·gé d'af·faires ('ʃɑːʒeɪ dæ'fɛə; *French* ʃarʒe da'fɛːr) *n., pl.* **char·gés d'af·faires** ('ʃɑːʒeɪ, -ʒeɪz; *French* ʃarʒe). **1.** the temporary head of a diplomatic mission in the absence of the ambassador or minister. **2.** the head of a diplomatic mission of the lowest level. [C18: from French: (one) charged with affairs]

charge den·si·ty *n.* the electric charge per unit volume of a medium or body or per unit area of a surface.

charge hand *n. Brit.* a workman whose grade of responsibility is just below that of a foreman.

charge nurse *n. Brit.* a nurse in charge of a ward in a hospital, esp. when a man. Fem. equivalent: **sister.**

charge of quar·ters *n. U.S.* a member of the armed forces who handles administration in his unit, esp. after duty hours.

charg·er[1] ('tʃɑːdʒə) *n.* **1.** a person or thing that charges. **2.** a large strong horse formerly ridden into battle. **3.** a device for charging or recharging an accumulator.

charg·er[2] ('tʃɑːdʒə) *n. Antiques.* a large dish for serving at table or for display. [C14 *chargeour* something to bear a load, from *chargen* to CHARGE]

charge sheet *n. Brit.* a document on which a police officer enters details of the charge against a prisoner and the court in which he will appear.

Cha·ri ('tʃɑːrɪ) *or* **Sha·ri** *n.* a river in N central Africa, rising in the N Central African Empire and flowing north to Lake Chad. Length: about 2250 km (1400 miles).

char·i·ly ('tʃɛərɪlɪ) *adv.* **1.** cautiously; carefully. **2.** sparingly.

char·i·ness ('tʃɛərɪnɪs) *n.* the state of being chary.

Char·ing Cross ('tʃærɪŋ) *n.* a district of London, in the city of Westminster: the modern cross (1863) in front of Charing Cross railway station replaces the one erected by Edward I (1290), the last of twelve marking the route of the funeral procession of his queen, Eleanor.

Cha·ri-Nile ('tʃɑːrɪ 'naɪl) *n.* **1.** a group of languages of E Africa, now generally regarded as a branch of the Nilo-Saharan family, spoken in parts of the Sudan, Zaïre, Uganda, Kenya, Tanzania, and adjacent countries. ~*adj.* **2.** relating to or belonging to this group of languages.

char·i·ot ('tʃærɪət) *n.* **1.** a two-wheeled horse-drawn vehicle used in ancient Egypt, Greece, Rome, etc., in war, races, and processions. **2.** a light four-wheeled horse-drawn ceremonial carriage. **3.** *Poetic.* any stately vehicle. [C14: from Old French, augmentative of *char* CAR]

char·i·ot·eer (ˌtʃærɪə'tɪə) *n.* the driver of a chariot.

cha·ris·ma (kə'rɪzmə) *or* **char·ism** ('kærɪzəm) *n.* **1.** a special personal quality or power of an individual making him capable of influencing or inspiring large numbers of people. **2.** *Theol.* a divinely bestowed power or talent. [C17: from Church Latin, from Greek *kharisma,* from *kharis* grace, favour] —**char·is·mat·ic** (ˌkærɪz'mætɪk) *adj.*

char·i·ta·ble ('tʃærɪtəbᵊl) *adj.* **1.** generous in giving to the needy. **2.** kind or lenient in one's attitude towards others. **3.** concerned with or involving charity. —**'char·i·ta·ble·ness** *n.* —**'char·i·ta·bly** *adv.*

char·i·ty ('tʃærɪtɪ) *n., pl.* **·ties. 1. a.** the giving of help, money, food, etc., to those in need. **b.** (*as modifier*): *a charity show.* **2. a.** an institution or organization set up to provide help, money, etc., to those in need. **b.** (*as modifier*): *charity funds.* **3.** the help, money, etc., given to the needy; alms. **4.** a kindly and lenient attitude towards people. **5.** love of one's fellow men. [C13: from Old French *charite,* from Latin *cāritās* affection, love, from *cārus* dear]

Char·i·ty Com·mis·sion·ers *pl. n.* (in Britian) members of a commission constituted to keep a register of charities and control charitable trusts.

cha·ri·va·ri (ˌʃɑːrɪ'vɑːrɪ), **shiv·a·ree,** *or esp. U.S.* **chiv·a·ree** *n.* **1.** a discordant mock serenade to newlyweds, made with pans, kettles, etc. **2.** a confused noise; din. [C17: from French, from Late Latin *caribaria* headache, from Greek *karēbaria,* from *karē* head + *barus* heavy]

char·kha *or* **char·ka** ('tʃɑːkə) *n.* (in India, etc.) a spinning wheel, esp. for cotton. [from Hindi]

char·la·dy ('tʃɑːˌleɪdɪ) *n., pl.* **·dies.** another name for **charwoman.**

char·la·tan ('ʃɑːlətᵊn) *n.* someone who professes knowledge or expertise, esp. in medicine, that he does not have; quack. [C17: from French, from Italian *ciarlatano,* from *ciarlare* to chatter] —**'char·la·tan·ism** *or* **'char·la·tan·ry** *n.* —ˌ**char·la·tan·'is·tic** *adj.*

Char·le·magne ('ʃɑːləˌmeɪn) *n.* ?742–814 A.D., king of the Franks (768–814) and, as Charles I, Holy Roman Emperor (800–814). He conquered the Lombards (774), the Saxons (772–804), and the Avars (791–799). He instituted many judicial and ecclesiastical reforms, and promoted commerce and agriculture throughout his empire, which extended from the Ebro to the Elbe. Under Alcuin his court at Aachen became the centre of a revival of learning.

Char·le·roi (*French* ʃarlə'rwa) *n.* a town in SW Belgium, in Hainaut province: centre of an industrial region. Pop.: 23 296 (1971 est.).

Charles (tʃɑːlz) *n.* **1.** *Prince of Wales.* born 1948, son of Elizabeth II; heir apparent to the throne of Great Britain and Northern Ireland. He married (1981) Lady Diana Spencer, and their son, Prince William of Wales, was born in 1982. **2. Ray.** born 1930, U.S. rock singer, pianist, and songwriter.

Charles I *n.* **1.** title as Holy Roman Emperor of **Charlemagne. 2.** title as king of France of **Charles II** (Holy Roman Emperor). **3.** title as king of Spain of **Charles V** (Holy Roman Emperor). **4.** title of **Charles Stuart.** 1600–49, king of England, Scotland, and Ireland (1625–49); son of James I. He ruled for 11 years (1629–40) without parliament, advised by his minister Strafford, until rebellion broke out in Scotland. Conflict with the Long Parliament led to the Civil War and after his defeat at Naseby (1645) he sought refuge with the Scots (1646). He was handed over to the English army under Cromwell (1647) and executed. **5.** 1887–1922, emperor of Austria, and, as Charles IV, king of Hungary (1916–18). The last ruler of the Austro-Hungarian monarchy, he was forced to abdicate at the end of World War I.

Charles II *n.* **1.** called *the Bald.* 823–877 A.D., Holy Roman Emperor (875–877) and, as Charles I, king of France (843–877). **2.** 1630–85, king of England, Scotland, and Ireland (1660–85) following the Restoration (1660); son of Charles I. He did much to promote commerce, science, and the Navy, but his Roman Catholic sympathies caused widespread distrust.

Charles IV *n.* title as king of Hungary of **Charles I** (sense 5).

Charles V *n.* 1500–58, Holy Roman Emperor (1519–56), king of Burgundy and the Netherlands (1506–55), and, as Charles I, king of Spain (1516–56): his reign saw the empire threatened by Francis I of France, the Turks, and the spread of Protestantism; abdicated.

Charles VI *n.* called *the Mad* or *the Well-Beloved.* 1368–1422, king of France (1380–1422): defeated by Henry V of England at Agincourt (1415), he was forced by the Treaty of Troyes (1420) to recognize Henry as his successor.

Charles VII *n.* 1403–61, king of France (1422–61), son of Charles VI. He was excluded from the French throne by the Treaty of Troyes, but following Joan of Arc's victory over the English at Orléans (1429), was crowned.

Charles IX *n.* 1550–74, king of France (1560–74), son of Catherine de' Medici and Henry II: his reign was marked by war between Huguenots and Catholics.

Charles X *n.* 1757–1836, king of France (1824–30): his attempt to restore absolutism led to his enforced exile.

Charles XIV *n.* the title as king of Sweden and Norway of (Jean Baptiste Jules) **Bernadotte.**

Charles Ed·ward Stu·art *n.* See (Charles Edward) **Stuart.**

Charles' law *n.* the principle that if a gas is held at constant pressure its volume is directly proportional to its absolute temperature. At constant volume the pressure of a gas also is directly proportional to its absolute temperature. Also called: **Gay-Lussac's law.** [C18: named after Jacques A. C. *Charles* (1746–1823), French physicist who first formulated it]

Charles Mar·tel (mɑː'tɛl) *n.* grandfather of Charlemagne. ?688–741 A.D., Frankish ruler of Austrasia (715–41), who checked the Moslem invasion of Europe by defeating the Moors at Poitiers (732).

Charles's Wain (weɪn) *n.* another name for the **Plough.** [Old English *Carles wægn*, from *Carl* CHARLEMAGNE + *wægn* WAIN]

Charles the Great *n.* another name for **Charlemagne.**

charles+ton ('tʃɑːlstən) *n.* a fast rhythmic dance of the 1920s, characterized by kicking and by twisting of the legs from the knee down.

Charles+ton ('tʃɑːlstən) *n.* **1.** a city in central West Virginia: the state capital. Pop.: 71 505 (1970). **2.** a port in SE South Carolina, on the Atlantic: scene of the first action in the Civil War. Pop.: 66 945 (1970).

Charle·ville-Mé·zières (*French* ʃarlvil me'zjɛːr) *n.* twin towns on opposite sides of the River Meuse in NE France. Pop.: 63 347 (1975). See **Mézières.**

char+ley horse ('tʃɑːlɪ) *n. U.S. informal.* muscle stiffness or cramp following strenuous athletic exercise. [C19: of uncertain origin]

char+lie ('tʃɑːlɪ) *n. Informal.* **1.** *Brit.* a silly person; fool. **2.** *Austral.* a girl.

char+lock ('tʃɑːlɒk) *n.* **1.** Also called: **wild mustard.** a weedy cruciferous Eurasian plant, *Sinapsis arvensis* (or *Brassica kaber*), with hairy stems and foliage and yellow flowers. **2. white charlock.** Also called: **wild radish, runch.** a cruciferous plant, *Raphanus raphanistrum*, with yellow, mauve, or white flowers and podlike fruits. [Old English *cerlic*, of obscure origin]

char+lotte ('ʃɑːlət) *n.* **1.** a baked dessert served hot or cold, commonly made with fruit and layers or a casing of bread or cake crumbs, sponge cake, etc.: *apple charlotte.* **2.** short for **charlotte russe.** [C19: from French, from the name *Charlotte*]

Char+lotte ('ʃɑːlət) *n.* a city in S North Carolina: the largest city in the state. Pop.: 284 738 (1973 est.).

Char+lotte A·ma+li·e ('ʃɑːlət ə'mɑːlɪə) *n.* the capital of the Virgin Islands of the United States, a port on St. Thomas Island. Pop.: 12 220 (1970). Former name (1921–37): **Saint Thomas.**

Char+lot+ten+burg (*German* ʃar'lɔtənˌbʊrk) *n.* a district of West Berlin, formerly an independent city.

char+lotte russe (ruːs) *n.* a cold dessert made in a mould with sponge fingers enclosing a mixture of whipped cream, custard, etc. [French, Russian charlotte]

Char+lotte+town ('ʃɑːlətˌtaʊn) *n.* a port in SE Canada, capital of the province of Prince Edward Island. Pop.: 19 133 (1971).

Charl·ton ('tʃɑːltən) *n.* **Bob·by.** born 1937, English footballer, played for England over 100 times.

charm[1] (tʃɑːm) *n.* **1.** the quality of pleasing, fascinating, or attracting people. **2.** a pleasing or attractive feature. **3.** a small object worn or kept for supposed magical powers of protection; amulet; talisman. **4.** a trinket worn on a bracelet. **5.** a magic spell; enchantment. **6.** a formula or action used in casting such a spell. **7.** *Physics.* a property of certain elementary particles, used to explain some scattering experiments. **8. like a charm.** perfectly; successfully. ~*vb.* **9.** to attract or fascinate; delight greatly. **10.** to cast a magic spell on. **11.** to protect, influence, or heal, supposedly by magic. **12.** (*tr.*) to influence or obtain by personal charm: *he charmed them into believing him.* [C13: from Old French *charme*, from Latin *carmen* song, incantation, from *canere* to sing] —**charm+ed+ly** ('tʃɑːmɪdlɪ) *adv.*

charm[2] (tʃɑːm) *n. Southwest Brit. dialect.* a loud noise, as of a number of people chattering or of birds singing. [C16: variant of CHIRM]

charm+er ('tʃɑːmə) *n.* **1.** an attractive person. **2.** a person claiming or seeming to have magical powers.

Char+meuse (ʃɑː'muːz; *French* ʃar'møːz) *n. Trademark.* a lightweight fabric with a satin-like finish.

Char+mi+nar (ˌtʃɑːmɪ'nɑː) *n.* a 16th-century monument with four minarets at Hyderabad, India.

charm+ing ('tʃɑːmɪŋ) *adj.* delightful; pleasant; attractive. —**'charm+ing+ly** *adv.*

char+nel ('tʃɑːnəl) *n.* **1.** short for **charnel house.** ~*adj.* **2.** ghastly; sepulchral; deathly. [C14: from Old French: burial place, from Latin *carnālis* fleshly, CARNAL]

char+nel house *n.* (esp. formerly) a building or vault where corpses or bones are deposited.

Char+ol+lais *or* **Char+o+lais** ('ʃærəˌleɪ) *n.* a breed of large white beef cattle. [C19: from French: named after Monts du *Charollais*, E France]

Char·on ('kɛərən) *n. Greek myth.* the ferryman who brought the dead across the rivers Styx or Acheron to Hades.

Char·pen·tier (*French* ʃarpã'tje) *n.* **Gus·tave** (gy'stav). 1860–1956, French composer, whose best-known work is the opera *Louise* (1900).

char+poy ('tʃɑːpɔɪ) *or* **char+pai** ('tʃɑːpaɪ) *n.* a bedstead of woven webbing or hemp stretched on a wooden frame on four legs, common in India. [C19: from Urdu *cārpāī*]

char+qui ('tʃɑːkɪ) *n.* meat, esp. beef, cut into strips and dried. [C18: from Spanish, from Quechuan] —**char+quid** ('tʃɑːkɪd) *adj.*

charr (tʃɑː) *n., pl.* **charr** *or* **charrs.** a variant spelling of **char** (the fish).

chart (tʃɑːt) *n.* **1.** a map designed to aid navigation by sea or air. **2.** an outline map, esp. one on which weather information is plotted. **3.** a sheet giving graphical, tabular, or diagrammatical information. **4.** another name for **graph** (sense 1). **5.** *Astrology.* another word for **horoscope** (sense 3). **6. the charts.** *Informal.* the lists produced weekly from various sources of the best-selling pop singles and albums. ~*vb.* (*tr.*) **7.** to make a chart of. **8.** to make a detailed plan of. **9.** to plot or outline the course of. [C16: from Latin, from Greek *khartēs* papyrus, literally: something on which to make marks; related to Greek *kharattein* to engrave] —**'chart+a·ble** *adj.*

char+ter ('tʃɑːtə) *n.* **1.** a formal document from the sovereign or state incorporating a city, bank, college, etc., and specifying its purposes and rights. **2.** (*sometimes cap.*) a formal document granting or demanding from the sovereign power of a state certain rights or liberties. **3.** a document issued by a society or organization authorizing the establishment of a local branch or chapter. **4.** a special privilege or exemption. **5.** (*often cap.*) the fundamental principles of an organization; constitution: *the Charter of the United Nations.* **6. a.** the hire or lease of transportation. **b.** the agreement or contract regulating this. **c.** (*as modifier*): *a charter flight.* **7.** *Maritime law.* another word for **charter party.** ~*vb.* (*tr.*) **8.** to lease or hire by charter party. **9.** to hire (a vehicle, etc.). **10.** to grant a charter of incorporation or liberties to (a group or person). [C13: from Old French *chartre*, from Latin *chartula* a little paper, from *charta* leaf of papyrus; see CHART] —**'char+ter+er** *n.*

char+ter+age ('tʃɑːtərɪdʒ) *n. Rare.* **1.** the act or practice of chartering, esp. ships. **2.** a shipbroker's fee.

char+ter col·o·ny *n. American history.* a colony, such as Virginia or Massachusetts, created by royal charter under the control of an individual, trading company, etc., and exempt from interference by the Crown.

char+tered ac+count+ant *n. Brit.* an accountant who has passed the professional examinations of the Institute of Chartered Accountants.

Char+ter+house ('tʃɑːtəˌhaʊs) *n.* a Carthusian monastery. [C16: changed by folk etymology from Anglo-French *chartrouse*, after *Chartosse* (now Saint-Pierre-de-Chartreuse), village near Grenoble, France, the original home of the Carthusian order]

char+ter mem+ber *n.* an original or founder member of a society or organization.

char+ter par+ty *n.* **1.** *Maritime law.* an agreement for the hire of all or part of a ship for a specified voyage or period of time. **2.** an individual or group that charters a ship, etc.

Chart+ism ('tʃɑːtɪzəm) *n. English history.* the principles of the reform movement in England from 1838 to 1848, which included manhood suffrage, payment of Members of Parliament, equal electoral districts, annual parliaments, voting by ballot, and the abolition of property qualifications for MPs. —**'Chart+ist** *n., adj.*

chart+ist ('tʃɑːtɪst) *n. U.S.* a stock market specialist who analyses and predicts market trends from graphs of recent price and volume movements of selected securities.

chart+less ('tʃɑːtlɪs) *adj.* not mapped; uncharted.

char+tog+ra+phy (kɑː'tɒgrəfɪ) *n.* a rare word for **cartography.** —**char+'tog+ra+pher** *n.* —**char+to+graph+ic** (ˌkɑːtə'græfɪk) *or* ˌ**char+to+'graph+i+cal** *adj.* —ˌ**char+to+'graph+i+cal+ly** *adv.*

Char+tres ('ʃɑːtrə, ʃɑːt; *French* 'ʃartr) *n.* a city in NW France: Gothic cathedral; market town. Pop.: 41 251 (1975).

char+treuse (ʃɑː'trɜːz; *French* ʃar'trøːz) *n.* **1.** either of two liqueurs, green or yellow, made from herbs and flowers. **2. a.** a colour varying from a clear yellowish-green to a strong greenish-yellow. **b.** (*as adj.*): *a chartreuse dress.* [C19: from French, after *La Grande Chartreuse*, monastery near Grenoble, where the liqueur is produced]

char+tu+lar·y ('tʃɑːtjʊlərɪ) *n., pl.* **+lar·ies.** a variant of **cartulary.**

char+wom·an ('tʃɑːˌwʊmən) *n., pl.* **+wom·en.** *Brit.* a woman who is hired to clean, tidy, etc., in a house or office.

char·y ('tʃɛərɪ) *adj.* **char·i·er, char·i·est. 1.** wary; careful. **2.** choosy; finicky. **3.** shy. **4.** sparing; mean. [Old English *cearig;* related to *caru* CARE, Old High German *charag* sorrowful]

Cha·ryb·dis (kə'rɪbdɪs) *n.* a ship-devouring monster in classical mythology, identified with a whirlpool off the north coast of Sicily, lying opposite Scylla on the Italian coast. Compare **Scylla.** —**Cha·'ryb·di·an** *adj.*

chase[1] (tʃeɪs) *vb.* **1.** to follow or run after (a person, animal, or goal) persistently or quickly. **2.** (*tr.;* often foll. by *out, away,* or *off*) to force to run (away); drive (out). **3.** (*tr.*) *Informal.* to court (a member of the opposite sex) in an unsubtle manner. **4.** (*tr.;* often foll. by *up*) *Informal.* to pursue persistently and energetically in order to obtain results, information, etc.: *chase up the builders and get a delivery date.* **5.** (*intr.*) *Informal.* to hurry; rush. ~*n.* **6.** the act of chasing; pursuit. **7.** any quarry that is pursued. **8.** *Brit.* an unenclosed area of land where wild animals are preserved to be hunted. **9.** *Brit.* the right to hunt a particular quarry over the land of others. **10. the chase.** the act or sport of hunting. **11.** short for **steeplechase. 12.** *Real tennis.* a ball that bounces twice, requiring the point to be played again. **13. give chase.** to pursue (a person, animal, or thing) actively. [C13: from Old French *chacier,* from Vulgar Latin *captiāre* (unattested), from Latin *captāre* to pursue eagerly, from *capere* to take; see CATCH] —**'chase·a·ble** *adj.*

chase[2] (tʃeɪs) *n.* **1.** *Letterpress printing.* a rectangular steel or cast-iron frame into which metal type and blocks making up a page are locked for printing or plate-making. **2.** the part of a cannon or mounted gun enclosing the bore. **3.** a groove or channel, esp. one that is cut in a wall to take a pipe, cable, etc. ~*vb.* (*tr.*) **4.** Also: **chamfer.** to cut a groove, furrow, or flute in (a surface, column, etc.). [C17 (in the sense: frame for letterpress matter): probably from French *châsse* frame (in the sense: bore of a cannon, etc.): from Old French *chas* enclosure, from Late Latin *capsus* pen for animals; both from Latin *capsa* CASE[2]]

chase[3] (tʃeɪs) *vb.* (*tr.*) **1.** Also: **enchase.** to ornament (metal) by engraving or embossing. **2.** to form or finish (a screw thread) with a chaser. [C14: from Old French *enchasser* ENCHASE]

chas·er[1] ('tʃeɪsə) *n.* **1.** a person or thing that chases. **2.** a drink drunk after another of a different kind, as beer after spirits. **3.** a cannon on a vessel situated either at the bow (**bow chaser**) or the stern (**stern chaser**) and used during pursuit by or of another vessel.

chas·er[2] ('tʃeɪsə) *n.* **1.** a person who engraves. **2.** a lathe cutting tool for accurately finishing a screw thread, having a cutting edge consisting of several repetitions of the thread form.

Chas·i·dim *or* **Chas·si·dim** ('hæsɪˌdiːm, -dɪm; *Hebrew* xasiː'diːm) *pl. n., sing.* **Chas·id** *or* **Chas·sid** ('hæsɪd; *Hebrew* xa'siːd). variant spellings of **Hasidim.** —**Cha·sid·ic** *or* **Chas·sid·ic** (hə'sɪdɪk) *adj.* —**'Chas·id·ism** *or* **'Chas·sid·ism** *n.*

chasm ('kæzəm) *n.* **1.** a deep cleft in the ground; abyss. **2.** a break in continuity; gap. **3.** a wide difference in interests, feelings, etc. [C17: from Latin *chasma,* from Greek *khasma;* related to Greek *khainein* to gape] —**chas·mal** ('kæzməl) *or* **'chas·mic** *adj.*

chas·sé ('ʃæseɪ) *n.* **1.** one of a series of gliding steps in ballet in which the same foot always leads. **2.** three consecutive dance steps, two fast and one slow, to four beats of music. ~*vb.* **·sés, ·sé·ing, ·séd. 3.** (*intr.*) to perform either of these steps. [C19: from French: a chasing]

chasse·pot ('ʃæspəʊ; *French* ʃas'po) *n.* a breechloading bolt-action rifle formerly used by the French Army. [C19: named after A. A. *Chassepot* (1833–1905), French gunsmith who invented it]

chas·seur (ʃæ'sɜː; *French* ʃa'sœːr) *n.* **1.** *French Army.* a member of a unit specially trained and equipped for swift deployment. **2.** (in some parts of Europe, esp. formerly) a uniformed attendant, esp. one in the livery of a huntsman. ~*adj.* **3.** (*often postpositive*) designating or cooked in a sauce consisting of white wine and mushrooms. [C18: from French: huntsman]

chas·sis ('ʃæsɪ) *n., pl.* **·sis** (-sɪz). **1.** the steel frame, wheels, engine, and mechanical parts of a motor vehicle, to which the body is attached. **2.** *Electronics.* a mounting for the circuit components of an electrical or electronic device, such as a radio or television. **3.** the landing gear of an aircraft. **4.** *Obsolete.* a wooden framework for a window, screen, etc. **5.** the frame on which a cannon carriage moves backwards and forwards. **6.** *Slang.* the body of a person, esp. a woman. [C17 (meaning: windowframe): from French *châssis* frame, from Vulgar Latin *capsicum* (unattested), ultimately from Latin *capsa* CASE[2]]

chaste (tʃeɪst) *adj.* **1.** not having experienced sexual intercourse; virginal. **2.** abstaining from unlawful or immoral sexual intercourse. **3.** (of conduct, speech, etc.) pure; decent; modest. **4.** (of style or taste) free from embellishment; simple; restrained. [C13: from Old French, from Latin *castus* pure; compare CASTE] —**'chaste·ly** *adv.* —**'chaste·ness** *n.*

chas·ten ('tʃeɪsᵊn) *vb.* (*tr.*) **1.** to bring to a state of submission; subdue; tame. **2.** to discipline or correct by punishment. **3.** to moderate; restrain; temper. [C16: from Old French *chastier,* from Latin *castigāre;* see CASTIGATE] —**'chas·ten·er** *n.* —**'chas·ten·ing·ly** *adv.*

chaste tree *n.* a small ornamental verbenaceous tree, *Vitex agnus-castus,* of S Europe and SW Asia, with spikes of pale blue flowers.

chas·tise (tʃæs'taɪz) *vb.* (*tr.*) **1.** to discipline or punish, esp. by beating. **2.** to scold severely. [C14 *chastisen,* irregularly from *chastien* to CHASTEN] —**chas·'tis·a·ble** *adj.* —**chas·tise·ment** (tʃæs'taɪzmənt, 'tʃæstɪz-) *n.* —**chas·'tis·er** *n.*

chas·ti·ty ('tʃæstɪtɪ) *n.* **1.** the state of being chaste; purity. **2.** abstention from sexual intercourse; virginity or celibacy: *a vow of chastity.* [C13: from Old French *chasteté,* from Latin *castitās,* from *castus* CHASTE]

chas·ti·ty belt *n.* a locking beltlike device with a loop designed to go between a woman's legs in order to prevent her from having sexual intercourse.

chas·u·ble ('tʃæzjʊbᵊl) *n. Christianity.* a long sleeveless outer vestment worn by a priest when celebrating Mass. [C13: from French, from Late Latin *casubla* garment with a hood, apparently from *casula* cloak, literally: little house, from Latin *casa* cottage]

chat[1] (tʃæt) *n.* **1.** informal conversation or talk conducted in an easy familiar manner. **2.** any Old World songbird of the subfamily *Turdinae* (thrushes, etc.) having a harsh chattering cry. See also **stonechat, whinchat. 3.** any of various North American warblers, such as *Icteria virens* (**yellow-breasted chat**). **4.** any of various Australian wrens (family *Muscicapidae*) of the genus *Ephthianura* and other genera. ~*vb.* **chats, chat·ting, chat·ted. 5.** (*intr.*) to talk in an easy familiar way. ~See also **chat up.** [C16: short for CHATTER]

chat[2] (tʃæt) *n.* **1.** the catkin of the willow. **2.** the flower of the plantain. [C15: from French *chat* cat, referring to the furry appearance]

cha·teau *or* **châ·teau** ('ʃætəʊ; *French* ʃɑ'to) *n., pl.* **·teaux** (-təʊ, -təʊz; *French* -'to) *or* **·teaus. 1.** a country house, castle, or manor house, esp. in France. **2.** (in Quebec) the residence of a seigneur or (formerly) a governor. **3.** (in the name of a wine) estate or vineyard. **4. château bottled.** (of wine) bottled on the estate where it was made. [C18: from French, from Old French *chastel,* from Latin *castellum* fortress, CASTLE]

Cha·teau·bri·and (*French* ʃatobri'ɑ̃) *n.* **1. Fran·çois Re·né** (frɑ̃swa rə'ne), Vicomte de Chateaubriand. 1768–1848, French writer and statesman: a precursor of the romantic movement in France; his works include *Le Génie du Christianisme* (1802) and *Mémoires d'outre-tombe* (1849–50). **2.** a thick steak cut from the fillet of beef.

Châ·teau·roux (*French* ʃɑto'ru) *n.* a city in central France: tenth-century castle (**Château-Raoul**). Pop.: 55 629 (1975).

Châ·teau-Thier·ry ('ʃætəʊ 'tɪərɪ; *French* ʃɑto tjɛ'ri) *n.* a town in N central France, on the River Marne. Pop.: 13 856 (1975).

cha·teau wine *n.* a wine produced from any of certain vineyards in the Bordeaux region of France.

chat·e·lain ('ʃætᵊˌleɪn; *French* ʃat'lɛ̃) *n.* the keeper or governor of a castle. [C16: from French, from Latin *castellānus* occupant of a CASTLE]

chat·e·laine ('ʃætəˌleɪn; *French* ʃat'lɛn) *n.* **1.** (esp. formerly) the mistress of a castle or fashionable household. **2.** a chain or clasp worn at the waist by women in the 16th to the 19th centuries, with handkerchief, keys, etc., attached. **3.** a decorative pendant worn on the lapel.

Chat·ham[1] ('tʃætəm) *n.* **1.** a town in SE England, in N Kent on the River Medway: royal naval dockyard. Pop.: 56 921 (1971). **2.** a city in SE Canada, in SE Ontario on the Thames River. Pop.: 32 098 (1966).

Chat·ham[2] ('tʃætəm) *n.* **1st Earl of.** title of the elder (William) **Pitt.**

Chat·ham Is·land *n.* another name for **San Cristóbal** (sense 1).

Chat·ham Is·lands *pl. n.* a group of islands in the S Pacific Ocean, forming a county of South Island, New Zealand: consists of the main islands of Chatham, Pitt, and several rocky islets. Chief settlement: Waitangi. Pop.: 716 (1971). Area: 963 sq. km (372 sq. miles).

cha·toy·ant (ʃə'tɔɪənt) *adj.* **1.** having changeable lustre; twinkling. **2.** (of a gem, esp. a cabochon) displaying a band of light reflected off inclusions of other minerals. ~*n.* **3.** a gemstone with a changeable lustre, such as a **cat's eye.** [C18: from French, from *chatoyer* to gleam like a cat's eyes, from *chat* CAT] —**cha·'toy·an·cy** *n.*

chat show *n. Brit.* television or radio show in which guests are interviewed informally. Also called: **talk show.**

Chat·ta·noo·ga (ˌtʃætᵊ'nuːgə) *n.* a city in SE Tennessee, on the Tennessee River: scene of several battles during the Civil War. Pop.: 137 957 (1973 est.).

chat·tel ('tʃætᵊl) *n.* **1.** (*often pl.*) *Property law.* **a. chattel personal.** an item of movable personal property, such as furniture, domestic animals, etc. **b. chattel real.** an interest in land less than a freehold, such as a lease. **2. goods and chattels.** personal property. [C13: from Old French *chatel* personal property, from Medieval Latin *capitāle* wealth; see CAPITAL[1]]

chat·tel house *n.* (esp. in Barbados) a movable wooden dwelling, usually set on a foundation of loose stones on rented land.

chat·tel mort·gage *n. U.S.* a mortgage on movable personal property.

chat·ter ('tʃætə) *vb.* **1.** to speak (about unimportant matters) rapidly and incessantly; prattle. **2.** (*intr.*) (of birds, monkeys, etc.) to make rapid repetitive high-pitched noises resembling human speech. **3.** (*intr.*) (of the teeth) to click together rapidly through cold or fear. **4.** (*intr.*) to make rapid intermittent contact with a component, as in machining, causing irregular cutting. ~*n.* **5.** idle or foolish talk; gossip. **6.** the high-pitched repetitive noise made by a bird, monkey, etc. **7.** the rattling of objects, such as parts of a machine. **8.** the undulating pattern of marks in a machined surface from the vibration of the tool or workpiece. [C13: of imitative origin] —**'chat·ter·y** *adj.*

chat·ter+box ('tʃætəˌbɒks) *n. Informal.* a person who talks constantly, esp. about trivial matters.
chat+ter+er ('tʃætərə) *n.* **1.** someone or something that chatters. **2.** another name for **cotinga.**
chat+ter mark *n.* **1.** any of a series of grooves, pits, and scratches on the surface of a rock, usually made by the movement of a glacier. **2.** a mark or series of marks on a workpiece.
Chat·ter·ton ('tʃætətən) *n.* **Thom·as.** 1752–70, English poet; author of spurious medieval verse and prose: he committed suicide at the age of 17.
chat+ty ('tʃætɪ) *adj.* **+ti+er, +ti+est. 1.** full of trivial conversation; talkative. **2.** informal and friendly; gossipy: *a chatty letter.* —**'chat+ti+ly** *adv.* —**'chat+ti+ness** *n.*
chat up *vb. (tr., adv.) Brit. informal.* **1.** to talk persuasively to (a person), esp. with an ulterior motive. **2.** to talk flirtatiously to (a person of the opposite sex), esp. with the intention of seducing him or her.
Chau·cer ('tʃɔ:sə) *n.* **Geof·frey.** ?1340–1400, English poet, noted for his narrative skill, humour, and insight, particularly in his most famous work, *The Canterbury Tales.* He used the continental tradition of rhyming verse. His other works include *Troilus and Criseyde, The Legende of Good Women,* and *The Parlement of Foules.*
Chau·ce·ri·an (tʃɔ:'sɪərɪən) *adj.* **1.** of, relating to, or characteristic of the writings of Chaucer. ~*n.* **2.** an imitator of Chaucer, esp. one of a group of 15th-century Scottish writers who took him as a model. **3. a.** an admirer of Chaucer's works. **b.** a specialist in the study or teaching of Chaucer.
chaud+froid *French.* (ʃo'frwa) *n.* a sweet or savoury jellied sauce used to coat cold meat, chicken, etc. [literally: hot-cold (because prepared as hot dish, but served cold)]
chauf+fer *or* **chau+fer** ('tʃɔ:fə) *n.* a small portable heater or stove. [C19: from French *chauffoir,* from *chauffer* to heat]
chauf+feur ('ʃəʊfə, ʃəʊ'fɜ:) *n.* **1.** a person employed to drive a car. ~*vb.* **2.** to act as driver for (a person, etc.): *he chauffeured me to the stadium; he chauffeurs for the Duke.* [C20: from French, literally: stoker, from *chauffer* to heat] —**chauf+feuse** (ʃəʊ'fɜ:z) *fem. n.*
chaul+moo+gra (tʃɔ:l'mu:grə) *n.* **1.** a tropical Asian tree, *Taraktogenos* (or *Hydnocarpus*) *kurzii:* family *Flacourtiaceae.* **2.** oil from the seed of this tree, used in treating leprosy. **3.** any of several similar or related trees. [from Bengali *cāulmugrā,* from *cāul* rice + *mugrā* hemp]
chaunt (tʃɔ:nt) *n.* a less common spelling of **chant.** —**'chaunt+er** *n.*
chausses (ʃəʊs) *pl. n.* (*functioning as sing.*) a tight-fitting medieval garment covering the feet and legs, usually made of chain mail. [C15: from Old French *chauces,* plural of *chauce* leg-covering, from Medieval Latin *calcea,* from Latin *calceus* shoe, from *calx* heel]
chau+tau+qua (ʃə'tɔ:kwə) *n. U.S.* a summer school or educational meeting held in the summer. [C19: named after *Chautauqua,* a lake in New York near which such schools were first held]
chau+vin+ism ('ʃəʊvɪˌnɪzəm) *n.* **1.** aggressive or fanatical patriotism; jingoism. **2.** enthusiastic devotion to a cause. **3.** smug irrational belief in the superiority of one's own race, party, sex, etc.: *male chauvinism.* [C19: from French *chauvinisme,* after Nicolas *Chauvin,* legendary French soldier under Napoleon, noted for his vociferous and unthinking patriotism] —**'chau+vin+ist** *n.* —**ˌchau+vin+'is+tic** *adj.* —**ˌchau+vin+'is+ti+cal+ly** *adv.*
Cha·vannes (*French* ʃa'van) *n.* **Pu·vis de.** See (Pierre Cécile) **Puvis de Chavannes.**
chaw (tʃɔ:) *Dialect.* ~*vb.* **1.** to chew (tobacco), esp. without swallowing it. ~*n.* **2.** something chewed, esp. a plug of tobacco. —**'chaw+er** *n.*
cha+yo+te (tʃɑ:'jəʊteɪ, tʃaɪ'əʊtɪ) *n.* **1.** a tropical American cucurbitaceous climbing plant, *Sechium edule,* that has edible pear-shaped fruit enclosing a single enormous seed. **2.** the fruit of this plant, which is cooked and eaten as a vegetable. [from Spanish, from Nahuatl *chayotli*]
cha+zan *Hebrew.* (xa'zan; *English* 'hɑ:zᵊn) *n., pl.* ***+za+nim*** (-za'ni:m). a variant spelling of **hazan.**
Ch.B. *or* **ChB** *abbrev. for* Bachelor of Surgery. [Latin: *Chirurgiae Baccalaureus*]
Ch.E. *abbrev. for* Chemical Engineer.
cheap (tʃi:p) *adj.* **1.** costing relatively little; inexpensive; good value. **2.** charging low prices: *a cheap hairdresser.* **3.** of poor quality; shoddy: *cheap furniture; cheap and nasty.* **4.** worth relatively little: *promises are cheap.* **5.** not worthy of respect; vulgar. **6.** ashamed; embarrassed: *to feel cheap.* **7.** stingy; miserly. **8.** *Informal.* mean; despicable: *a cheap liar.* **9. dirt cheap.** *Informal.* extremely inexpensive. ~*n.* **10. on the cheap.** *Brit. informal.* at a low cost. ~*adv.* **11.** at very little cost. [Old English *ceap* barter, bargain, price, property; related to Old Norse *kaup* bargain, Old High German *kouf* trade, Latin *caupō* innkeeper] —**'cheap+ish** *adj.* —**'cheap+ly** *adv.* —**'cheap+ness** *n.*
cheap+en ('tʃi:pᵊn) *vb.* **1.** to make or become lower in reputation, quality, etc.; degrade or be degraded. **2.** to make or become cheap or cheaper. —**'cheap+en+er** *n.*
cheap-jack *Informal.* ~*n.* **1.** a person who sells cheap and shoddy goods. ~*adj.* **2.** shoddy or inferior. [C19: from CHEAP + *Jack* (name used to typify a person)]
cheap+skate ('tʃi:pˌskeɪt) *n. Informal.* a miserly person.
cheat (tʃi:t) *vb.* **1.** to deceive or practise deceit, esp. for one's own gain; trick or swindle (someone). **2.** (*intr.*) to obtain unfair advantage by trickery, as in a game of cards. **3.** (*tr.*) to escape or avoid (something unpleasant) by luck or cunning: *to cheat death.* **4.** (when *intr.,* usually foll. by on) *Informal.* to be sexually unfaithful to (one's wife, husband, or lover). ~*n.* **5.** a person who cheats. **6.** a deliberately dishonest transaction, esp. for gain; fraud. **7.** *Informal.* sham. **8.** *Law.* the obtaining of another's property by fraudulent means. **9.** the usual U.S. name for **rye-brome.** [C14: short for ESCHEAT] —**'cheat+a·ble** *adj.* —**'cheat+er** *n.* —**'cheat+ing+ly** *adv.*
Cheb (*Czech* xɛp) *n.* a town in W Czechoslovakia, in W Bohemia on the Ohře River: 12th-century castle where Wallenstein was murdered (1634); a centre of the Sudeten-German movement after World War I. Pop.: 26 098 (1968 est.). German name: **Eger.**
Che+bo+ksa+ry (*Russian* tʃɪba'ksarɪ) *n.* a port in the central Soviet Union on the River Volga: capital of the Chuvash ASSR. Pop.: 264 000 (1975 est.).
Che+chen (tʃɪ'tʃɛn) *n., pl.* **+chens** *or* **+chen.** a member of a people of the Soviet Union, speaking a Circassian language and chiefly inhabiting the Checheno-Ingush ASSR.
Che·che·no·In·gush Au·ton·o·mous So+vi+et So·cial+ist Re+pub+lic (tʃɪ'tʃɛnəʊɪŋˌgu:ʃ) *n.* an administrative division of the S Soviet Union, in the RSFSR on the N slopes of the Caucasus Mountains: major oil and natural gas resources. Capital: Grozny. Pop.: 1 064 471 (1970). Area: 19 300 sq. km (7350 sq. miles).
check (tʃɛk) *vb.* **1.** to pause or cause to pause, esp. abruptly. **2.** (*tr.*) to restrain or control: *to check one's tears.* **3.** (*tr.*) to slow the growth or progress of; retard. **4.** (*tr.*) to rebuke or rebuff. **5.** (when *intr.,* often foll. by *on* or *up on*) to examine, investigate, or make an inquiry into (facts, a product, etc.) for accuracy, quality, or progress, esp. rapidly or informally. **6.** (*tr.*) *Chiefly U.S.* to mark off so as to indicate approval, correctness, or preference. Usual Brit. word: **tick. 7.** (*intr.;* often foll. by *with*) *Chiefly U.S.* to correspond or agree: *this report checks with the other.* **8.** (*tr.*) *Chiefly U.S.* to leave in or accept for temporary custody. **9.** *Chess.* to place (an opponent's king) in check. **10.** (*tr.*) to mark with a pattern of squares or crossed lines. **11.** to crack or cause to crack. **12.** *Agriculture.* short for **checkrow. 13.** (*tr.*) *Ice hockey.* to impede (an opponent). **14.** (*intr.*) *Hunting.* (of hounds) to pause in the pursuit of quarry while relocating a lost scent. **15.** (*intr.;* foll. by *at*) *Falconry.* to change from one quarry to another while in flight. **16.** (*intr.*) to decline the option of opening the betting in a round of poker. **17. check the helm.** *Nautical.* to swing back the helm of a vessel to prevent it from turning too quickly or too far. ~*n.* **18.** a break in progress; stoppage. **19.** a restraint or rebuff. **20. a.** a person or thing that restrains, halts, etc. **b.** (*as modifier*): *a check line.* **21. a.** a control, esp. a rapid or informal one, designed to ensure accuracy, progress, etc. **b.** (*as modifier*): *a check list.* **22.** a means or standard to ensure against fraud or error. **23.** the U.S. word for **tick. 24.** the U.S. spelling of **cheque. 25.** *U.S.* the bill in a restaurant. **26.** *Chiefly U.S.* a ticket or tag used to identify clothing or property deposited for custody. **27.** a pattern of squares or crossed lines. **28.** a single square in such a pattern. **29. a.** fabric with a pattern of squares or crossed lines. **b.** (*as modifier*): *a check suit.* **30.** *Chess.* the state or position of a king under direct attack, from which it must be moved or protected by another piece. **31.** a small crack, as one in veneer or one that occurs in timber during seasoning. **32.** part of the action of a piano that arrests the backward motion of a hammer after it has struck a string and holds it until the key is released. **33.** a chip or counter used in some card and gambling games. **34.** *Hunting.* a pause by the hounds in the pursuit of their quarry owing to loss of its scent. **35.** *Angling.* a ratchet fitted to a fishing reel to check the free running of the line. **36.** *Ice hockey.* the act of impeding an opponent with one's body or stick. **37. in check.** under control or restraint. ~*interj.* **38.** *Chess.* a call made to an opponent indicating that his king is in check. **39.** *Chiefly U.S.* an expression of agreement. ~See also **check in, check out, check up.** [C14: from Old French *eschec* a check at chess, hence, a pause (to verify something), via Arabic from Persian *shāh* the king! (in chess)] —**'check+a·ble** *adj.*
checked (tʃɛkt) *adj.* **1.** having a pattern of small squares. **2.** *Phonetics.* (of a syllable) ending in a consonant.
check+er[1] ('tʃɛkə) *n., vb.* **1.** the usual U.S. spelling of **chequer.** ~*n.* **2.** *Textiles.* a variant spelling of **chequer** (sense 2). **3.** the U.S. name for **draughtsman** (sense 3).
check+er[2] ('tʃɛkə) *n. Chiefly U.S.* **1.** a cashier, esp. in a supermarket. **2.** an attendant in a cloakroom, left-luggage office, etc.
check·er·ber·ry ('tʃɛkəbərɪ, -brɪ) *n., pl.* **·ries. 1.** the fruit of any of various plants, esp. the wintergreen (*Gaultheria procumbens*). **2.** any plant bearing this fruit.
check·er+bloom ('tʃɛkəˌblu:m) *n.* a Californian malvaceous plant, *Sidalcea malvaeflora,* with pink or purple flowers.
check·er+board ('tʃɛkəˌbɔ:d) *n.* the U.S. name for a **draughtboard.**
check+ers ('tʃɛkəz) *n.* (*functioning as sing.*) the U.S. name for **draughts.**
check in *vb.* (*adv.*) **1.** (*intr.*) to record one's arrival, as at a hotel or for work; sign in or report. **2.** (*tr.*) to register the arrival of (passengers, etc.). ~*n.* **check-in. 3. a.** the formal registration of arrival, as at an airport or hotel. **b.** (*as modifier*): *check-in time.* **4.** the place where one registers arrival at an airport, etc.
check+ing ac+count *n.* the U.S. name for **current account.**
check list *n.* a list of items, facts, names, etc., to be checked or referred to for comparison, identification, or verification.
check+mate ('tʃɛkˌmeɪt) *n.* **1.** *Chess.* **a.** the winning position in

which an opponent's king is under attack and unable to escape. **b.** the move by which this position is achieved. **2.** utter defeat. ~*vb.* (*tr.*) **3.** *Chess.* to place (an opponent's king) in checkmate. **4.** to thwart or render powerless. ~*interj.* **5.** *Chess.* a call made when placing an opponent's king in checkmate. [C14: from Old French *eschec mat,* from Arabic *shāh māt,* the king is dead; see CHECK]

check out *vb.* (*adv.*) **1.** (*intr.*) to pay the bill and depart, esp. from a hotel. **2.** (*intr.*) to depart from a place; record one's departure from work. **3.** to investigate or prove to be in order after investigation: *the police checked out all the statements; their credentials checked out.* ~*n.* **check+out. 4. a.** the latest time for vacating a room in a hotel, etc. **b.** (*as modifier*): *checkout time.* **5.** a counter, esp. in a supermarket, where customers pay.

check+point ('tʃɛkˌpɔɪnt) *n.* a place, as at a frontier or in a motor rally, where vehicles or travellers are stopped for official identification, inspection, etc.

check+rail ('tʃɛkˌreɪl) *n. Brit.* another word for **guardrail** (sense 2).

check+rein *n.* the usual U.S. word for **bearing rein.**

check+room ('tʃɛkˌruːm, -ˌrʊm) *n.* the U.S. name for **left-luggage office.**

check+row ('tʃɛkˌrəʊ) *U.S. agriculture.* ~*n.* **1.** a row of plants, esp. corn, in which the spaces between adjacent plants are equal to those between adjacent rows to facilitate cultivation. ~*vb.* **2.** (*tr.*) to plant in checkrows.

checks and bal+anc·es *pl. n. Government, chiefly U.S.* competition and mutual restraint among the various branches of government.

check+up ('tʃɛkˌʌp) *n.* **1.** an examination to see if something is in order. **2.** *Med.* a medical examination, esp. one taken at regular intervals to verify a normal state of health or discover a disease in its early stages. ~*vb.* **check up. 3.** (*intr., adv.* sometimes foll. by *on*) to investigate or make an inquiry into (a person's character, evidence, etc.), esp. when suspicions have been aroused.

check valve *n.* a nonreturn valve that closes by fluid pressure to prevent return flow.

check·y ('tʃɛkɪ) *adj.* (*usually postpositive*) *Heraldry.* having squares of alternating tinctures or furs; checked.

Ched+dar ('tʃɛdə) *n.* **1.** (*sometimes not cap.*) any of several types of smooth hard yellow or whitish cheese. **2.** a village in SW England, in N Somerset: situated near **Cheddar Gorge,** a pass through the Mendip Hills renowned for its stalactitic caverns and rare limestone flora.

chedd+ite ('tʃɛdaɪt, 'ʃɛd-) *n.* an explosive made by mixing a powdered chlorate or perchlorate with a fatty substance, such as castor oil. [C20: from *Chedde* town in Savoy, France, where it was first made]

che+der *Hebrew.* ('xɛdɛr; *English* 'heɪdə) *n., pl.* **+da+rim** (-da'riːm). a variant spelling of **heder.**

cheek (tʃiːk) *n.* **1. a.** either side of the face, esp. that part below the eye. **b.** either side of the oral cavity; side of the mouth. **2.** *Informal.* impudence; effrontery. **3.** (*often pl.*) *Informal.* either side of the buttocks. **4.** (*often pl.*) a side of a door jamb. **5.** *Nautical.* one of the two fore-and-aft supports for the trestletrees on a mast of a sailing vessel, forming part of the hounds. **6.** one of the jaws of a vice. **7. cheek by jowl.** close together; intimately linked. **8. turn the other cheek.** to be submissive and refuse to retaliate even when provoked or treated badly. **9. with one's tongue in one's cheek.** See **tongue** (sense 19). ~*vb.* **10.** (*tr.*) *Informal.* to speak or behave disrespectfully to; act impudently towards. [Old English *ceace;* related to Middle Low German *kāke,* Dutch *kaak*] —**'cheek+less** *adj.*

cheek+bone ('tʃiːkˌbəʊn) *n.* the nontechnical name for **zygomatic bone.**

cheek+piece ('tʃiːkˌpiːs) *n.* either of the two straps of a bridle that join the bit to the crownpiece.

cheek pouch *n.* a membranous pouch inside the mouth of many rodents and some other mammals: used for holding food.

cheek·y ('tʃiːkɪ) *adj.* **cheek·i+er, cheek·i+est.** disrespectful in speech or behaviour; impudent: *a cheeky child.* —**'cheek·i+ly** *adv.* —**'cheek·i+ness** *n.*

cheep (tʃiːp) *n.* **1.** the short weak high-pitched cry of a young bird; chirp. ~*vb.* **2.** (*intr.*) (of young birds) to utter characteristic shrill sounds. —**'cheep+er** *n.*

cheer (tʃɪə) *vb.* **1.** (usually foll. by *up*) to make or become happy or hopeful; comfort or be comforted. **2.** to applaud with shouts. **3.** (when *tr.*, sometimes foll. by *on*) to encourage (a team, person, etc.) with shouts, esp. in contests. ~*n.* **4.** a shout or cry of approval, encouragement, etc., often using such words as **hurrah!** or **rah! rah! rah! 5.** happiness; good spirits. **6.** state of mind; spirits (archaic, except in the phrases **be of good cheer, with good cheer**). **7.** *Archaic.* provisions for a feast; fare. [C13 (in the sense: face, welcoming aspect): from Old French *chere,* from Late Latin *cara* face, from Greek *kara* head] —**'cheer+er** *n.* —**'cheer+ing+ly** *adv.*

cheer+ful ('tʃɪəfʊl) *adj.* **1.** having a happy disposition; in good spirits. **2.** pleasantly bright; gladdening: *a cheerful room.* **3.** hearty; ungrudging; enthusiastic: *cheerful help.* —**'cheer+ful+ly** *adv.* —**'cheer+ful+ness** *n.*

cheer·i·o (ˌtʃɪərɪ'əʊ) *interj. Informal, chiefly Brit.* **1.** a farewell greeting. **2.** a drinking toast.

cheer+lead·er ('tʃɪəˌliːdə) *n. U.S.* a person who leads a crowd in formal cheers, esp. at sports events.

cheer+less ('tʃɪəlɪs) *adj.* dreary, gloomy, or pessimistic. —**'cheer+less+ly** *adv.* —**'cheer+less+ness** *n.*

cheer+ly ('tʃɪəlɪ) *adj., adv. Archaic or nautical.* cheerful or cheerfully.

cheers (tʃɪəz) *interj. Informal, chiefly Brit.* **1.** a drinking toast. **2.** goodbye! cheerio! **3.** thanks! **4. three cheers.** three shouts of hurrah given in unison by a group to honour someone or celebrate something.

cheer·y ('tʃɪərɪ) *adj.* **cheer·i·er, cheer·i+est.** showing or inspiring cheerfulness; gay. —**'cheer·i·ly** *adv.* —**'cheer·i+ness** *n.*

cheese[1] (tʃiːz) *n.* **1.** the curd of milk separated from the whey and variously prepared as a food. **2.** a mass or complete cake of this substance. **3.** any of various substances of similar consistency, etc.: *lemon cheese.* **4.** *Slang.* an important person (esp. in the phrase **big cheese**). **5.** *Brit.* **as alike** (*or* **different**) **as chalk and cheese.** See **chalk** (sense 5). [Old English *cēse,* from Latin *cāseus* cheese; related to Old Saxon *kāsi*]

cheese[2] (tʃiːz) *vb. Slang.* **1.** (*tr.*) to stop; desist. **2. cheese it. a.** get away quick. **b.** be quiet! stop what you're doing! **3.** (*intr.*) *Prison slang.* to act in a grovelling manner. [C19: of unknown origin]

cheese+board ('tʃiːzˌbɔːd) *n.* a board from which cheese is served at a meal.

cheese+burg+er ('tʃiːzˌbɜːgə) *n.* a hamburger cooked with a slice of cheese on top of it.

cheese+cake ('tʃiːzˌkeɪk) *n.* **1.** a rich tart with a biscuit base, filled with a mixture of cream cheese, cream, sugar, and often sultanas, sometimes having a fruit topping. **2.** *Slang.* women displayed for their sex appeal, as in photographs in magazines, newspapers, or films. Compare **beefcake.**

cheese+cloth ('tʃiːzˌklɒθ) *n.* a loosely woven cotton cloth formerly used only for wrapping cheese.

cheese cut+ter *n.* **1.** a board with a wire attached for cutting cheese. **2.** *Nautical.* a keel that may be drawn up into the boat when not in use. **3.** a nautical peaked cap worn without a badge.

cheesed off *adj.* (*usually postpositive*) *Brit. slang.* bored, disgusted, or angry. [C20: from CHEESE[2]]

cheese-head *adj.* denoting or relating to a screw or bolt with a cylindrical slotted head.

cheese mite *n.* a white soft-bodied free-living mite, *Tyrophagus* (or *Tyroglyphus*) *longior,* sometimes found in decaying cheese.

cheese+mon+ger ('tʃiːzˌmʌŋgə) *n.* a person dealing in cheese, butter, etc.

cheese+par·ing ('tʃiːzˌpɛərɪŋ) *adj.* **1.** penny-pinching; stingy. ~*n.* **2. a.** a paring of cheese rind. **b.** anything similarly worthless. **3.** stinginess.

cheese skip+per *n.* a dipterous fly, *Piophila casei,* whose larvae feed on cheese and move by jumping: family *Piophilidae.*

cheese straw *n.* a long thin cheese-flavoured strip of pastry.

cheese+wood ('tʃiːzˌwʊd) *n. Austral.* the tough yellowish wood of Australian trees of the genus *Pittosporum:* family *Pittosporaceae.*

chees·y ('tʃiːzɪ) *adj.* **chees·i+er, chees·i+est.** like cheese in flavour, smell, or consistency. —**'chees·i·ness** *n.*

chee+tah *or* **che+tah** ('tʃiːtə) *n.* a large feline mammal, *Acinonyx jubatus,* of Africa and SW Asia: the swiftest mammal, having very long legs, nonretractile claws, and a black-spotted light-brown coat. [C18: from Hindi *cītā,* from Sanskrit *citrakāya* tiger, from *citra* bright, speckled + *kāya* body]

chef (ʃɛf) *n.* a cook, esp. the principal cook in a restaurant. [C19: from French, from Old French *chief* head, CHIEF]

chef-d'œuvre *French.* (ʃɛ'dœːvr) *n., pl.* ***chefs-d'œuvre*** (ʃɛ'dœːvr). a masterpiece.

Che+foo ('tʃiː'fuː) *n.* another name for **Yentai.**

Che Gue+va+ra (tʃeɪ gə'vɑːrə; *Spanish* tʃe ge'βara) *n.* See **Guevara.**

chei·ro- *combining form.* variant of **chiro-.**

Chei·ron ('kaɪrɒn, -rən) *n.* a variant spelling of **Chiron.**

Che+ju ('tʃɛ'dʒuː) *n.* a volcanic island in the N East China Sea, southwest of Korea: constitutes a province of South Korea. Capital: Cheju. Pop.: 336 694 (1966). Area: 1792 sq. km (692 sq. miles). Also called: **Quelpart.**

Che+ka *Russian.* ('tʃɛkə) *n. Russian history.* the secret police set up in 1917 by the Bolshevik government: reorganized in the Soviet Union in Dec. 1922 as the G.P.U. [C20: from Russian, acronym of *Chrezvychainaya Komissiya* Extraordinary Commission (to combat Counter-Revolution)]

Che·khov *or* **Che·kov** ('tʃɛkɒf; *Russian* 'tʃɛxəf) *n.* **An·ton Pav·lo·vich** (an'tɔn 'pavləvitʃ). 1860–1904, Russian dramatist and short-story writer. His plays include *The Seagull* (1896), *Uncle Vanya* (1900), *The Three Sisters* (1901), and *The Cherry Orchard* (1904). —**Che+khov+i·an** *or* **Che+kov+i·an** (tʃɛ'kəʊvɪən) *adj.*

Che+kiang ('tʃɛ'kjæŋ, -kaɪ'æŋ) *n.* a province of E China: mountainous and densely populated. Capital: Hangchow. Pop.: 31 000 000 (1967–71 est.). Area: 102 000 sq. km (39 780 sq. miles).

che+la[1] ('kiːlə) *n., pl.* **+lae** (-liː). a large pincer-like claw of such arthropods as the crab and scorpion. [C17: New Latin, from Greek *khēlē* claw] —**che+lif+er+ous** (kɪ'lɪfərəs) *adj.*

che+la[2] ('tʃeɪlə) *n. Hinduism.* a disciple of a religious teacher. [C19: from Hindi *celā,* from Sanskrit *ceta* servant, slave] —**'che+la+ship** *n.*

che+late ('kiːleɪt) *n.* **1.** *Chem.* a chemical compound whose molecules contain a closed ring of atoms of which one is a metal atom. ~*adj.* **2.** *Zoology.* of or possessing chelae. **3.** *Chem.* of or denoting a chelate. ~*vb.* **4.** (*intr.*) *Chem.* to form a chelate. [C20: from CHELA[1]] —**che+'la+tion** *n.*

che+lic+er+a (kɪˈlɪsərə) *n., pl.* **+er+ae** (-əˌriː). one of a pair of appendages on the head of spiders and other arachnids: often modified as food-catching claws. [C19: from New Latin, from French *chélicère*, from *chél-* (see CHELA[1]) + *-cère* from Greek *keras* horn] **—che+ˈlic+er+al** *adj.*

che+lic+er+ate (kɪˈlɪsəˌreɪt) *adj.* **1.** of, relating to, or belonging to the *Chelicerata*, a subphylum of arthropods, including arachnids and the horseshoe crab, in which the first pair of limbs are modified as chelicerae. *~n.* **2.** any arthropod belonging to the *Chelicerata*.

che+li+form (ˈkiːlɪˌfɔːm) *adj.* shaped like a chela; pincer-like.

Chel+le·an (ˈʃɛlɪən) *n., adj. Archaeol.* (*no longer in technical usage*) another word for **Abbevillian.** [C19: from French *chelléen*, from *Chelles*, France, where various items were found]

Chelms+ford (ˈtʃɛlmzfəd) *n.* a city in SE England, administrative centre of Essex: market town. Pop.: 58 125 (1971).

che+loid (ˈkiːlɔɪd) *n. Pathol.* a variant spelling of **keloid.** **—che+ˈloi+dal** *adj.*

che+lo+ni·an (kɪˈləʊnɪən) *n.* **1.** any reptile of the order *Chelonia*, including the tortoises and turtles, in which most of the body is enclosed in a protective bony capsule. *~adj.* **2.** of, relating to, or belonging to the *Chelonia*. [C19: from New Latin *Chelōnia*, from Greek *khelōnē* tortoise]

chelp (tʃɛlp) *vb.* (*intr.*) *Northern and Midland English dialect.* **1.** (esp. of women or children) to chatter or speak out of turn: *she's always chelping at the teacher.* **2.** (of birds, etc.) to squeak or chirp. [C19: perhaps from *ch*(*irp*) + (*y*)*elp*]

Chel+sea (ˈtʃɛlsɪ) *n.* a residential district of SW London, in the Royal Borough of Kensington and Chelsea: site of the Chelsea Royal Hospital for old and invalid soldiers (**Chelsea Pensioners**).

Chel+sea bun *n.* a rolled yeast currant bun decorated with sugar.

Chel+ten+ham (ˈtʃɛltᵊnəm) *n.* **1.** a town in W England, in central Gloucestershire: famous for its schools, racecourse, and saline springs (discovered in 1716). Pop.: 69 734 (1971). **2.** a style of type.

Chel+ya+binsk (*Russian* tʃɪljaˈbinsk) *n.* an industrial city in the W central Soviet Union, in the southern RSFSR. Pop.: 969 000 (1975 est.).

Che+lyus+kin (*Russian* tʃɪˈljuskin) *n.* **Cape.** a cape in the NW Soviet Union, in N Siberia at the end of the Taimyr Peninsula: the northernmost point of Asia.

chem. *abbrev. for:* **1.** chemical. **2.** chemist. **3.** chemistry.

chem- *combining form.* variant of **chemo-** before a vowel.

chem·i+cal (ˈkɛmɪkᵊl) *n.* **1.** any substance used in or resulting from a reaction involving changes to atoms or molecules. *~adj.* **2.** of or used in chemistry: *chemical balance.* **3.** of, made from, or using chemicals: *chemical fertilizer.* **—ˈchem·i+cal+ly** *adv.*

chem·i+cal bond *n.* a mutual attraction between two atoms resulting from a redistribution of their outer electrons. See also **covalent bond, electrovalent bond, coordinate bond.**

chem·i+cal en+gi+neer+ing *n.* the branch of engineering concerned with the design, operation, maintenance, and manufacture of the plant and machinery used in industrial chemical processes. **—chem·i+cal en+gi+neer** *n.*

chem·i+cal e·qua+tion *n.* a representation of a chemical reaction using symbols of the elements to indicate the amount of substance, usually in moles, of each reactant and product.

chem·i+cal po+ten+tial *n.* a thermodynamic function of a substance in a system that is the partial differential of the Gibbs function of the system with respect to the number of moles of the substance. Symbol: μ

chem·i+cal re+ac+tion *n.* a process that involves changes in the structure and energy content of atoms, molecules, or ions but not their nuclei. Compare **nuclear reaction.**

chem·i+cal war+fare *n.* warfare in which chemicals other than explosives are used as weapons, esp. warfare using asphyxiating gases, poisons, defoliants, incendiaries, etc.

chem·i·co- *combining form.* chemical: *chemicophysical.*

chem·i+lu+mi+nes+cence (ˌkɛmɪˌluːmɪˈnɛsəns) *n.* the phenomenon in which a chemical reaction leads to the emission of light without incandescence. **—ˌchem·i+ˌlu+mi+ˈnes+cent** *adj.*

che+min de fer (ʃəˈmæn də ˈfɛə; *French* ʃəmɛ̃ də ˈfɛːr) *n.* a gambling game, a variation of baccarat. [French: railway, referring to the fast tempo of the game]

che+mise (ʃəˈmiːz) *n.* **1.** Also called: **shift. a.** an unwaisted loose-fitting dress hanging straight from the shoulders. **b.** a loose shirtlike undergarment. [C14: from Old French: shirt, from Late Latin *camisa*, perhaps of Celtic origin]

chem·i+sette (ˌʃɛmɪˈzɛt) *n.* an underbodice of lawn, lace, etc., worn to fill in a low-cut dress. [C19: from French, diminutive of CHEMISE]

chem+ism (ˈkɛmɪzəm) *n. Obsolete.* chemical action.

chem·i+sorb (ˌkɛmɪˈsɔːb) *or* **chem·o+sorb** *vb.* (*tr.*) to take up (a substance) by chemisorption.

chem·i+sorp+tion (ˌkɛmɪˈsɔːpʃən) *n.* an adsorption process in which an adsorbate is held on the surface of an adsorbent by chemical bonds.

chem+ist (ˈkɛmɪst) *n.* **1.** *Brit.* a shop selling medicines, cosmetics, etc. **2.** *Brit.* a qualified dispenser of prescribed medicines. **3.** a person studying, trained in, or engaged in chemistry. **4.** an obsolete word for **alchemist.** [C16: from earlier *chimist*, from New Latin *chimista*, shortened from Medieval Latin *alchimista* ALCHEMIST]

chem+is+try (ˈkɛmɪstrɪ) *n., pl.* **+tries. 1.** the branch of physical science concerned with the composition, properties, and reactions of substances. See also **inorganic chemistry, organic chemistry, physical chemistry. 2.** the composition, properties, and reactions of a particular substance. **3.** the nature and effects of any complex phenomenon: *the chemistry of humour.* **4.** *Informal.* a reaction, taken to be instinctual, between two persons (usually qualified by *good, bad,* etc.). [C17: from earlier *chimistrie*, from *chimist* CHEMIST]

chem+my (ˈʃɛmɪ) *n. Cards.* short for **chemin de fer.**

Chem+nitz (*German* ˈkɛmnɪts) *n.* the former name (until 1953) of **Karl-Marx-Stadt.**

chem·o-, chem·i-, *or before a vowel* **chem-** *combining form.* indicating that chemicals or chemical reactions are involved: *chemotherapy.* [New Latin, from Late Greek *khēmeia*; see ALCHEMY]

chem·o+pro+phy+lax+is (ˌkɛməʊˌprəʊfəˈlæksɪs, -ˌprɒfə-) *n.* the prevention of disease using chemical drugs. **—ˌchem·o+ˌpro+phy+ˈlac+tic** *adj.*

chem·o+re·cep+tor (ˌkɛməʊrɪˈsɛptə) *or* **chem·o·cep+tor** *n. Anatomy.* an end organ, such as a taste bud, able to respond to a chemical stimulus.

chem+os+mo+sis (ˌkɛmɒzˈməʊsɪs) *n.* a chemical reaction between two compounds after osmosis through an intervening semipermeable membrane. **—chem+os+mot+ic** (ˌkɛmɒzˈmɒtɪk) *adj.*

chem·o+sphere (ˈkɛməˌsfɪə) *n. Meteorol.* another name for **thermosphere. —chem·o+spher+ic** (ˌkɛməˈsfɛrɪk) *adj.*

che+mo+stat (ˈkiːməʊˌstæt, ˈkɛm-) *n.* an apparatus for growing bacterial cultures at a constant rate by controlling the supply of nutrient medium.

chem·o+syn+the·sis (ˌkɛməʊˈsɪnθɪsɪs) *n.* the formation of organic material by certain bacteria using energy derived from simple chemical reactions. **—chem·o+syn+thet+ic** (ˌkɛməʊsɪnˈθɛtɪk) *adj.* **—ˌchem·o+syn+ˈthet·i+cal+ly** *adv.*

chem·o+tax+is (ˌkɛməʊˈtæksɪs) *n.* the movement of a microorganism or cell in response to a chemical stimulus. **—ˌchem·o+ˈtac+tic** *adj.* **—ˌchem·o+ˈtac+ti+cal+ly** *adv.*

chem·o+ther·a+py (ˌkɛməʊˈθɛrəpɪ) *n.* treatment of disease by means of chemical agents. **—ˌchem·o+ˈther·a+pist** *n.*

chem·o+tro+pism (ˌkɛməʊˈtrəʊpɪzəm) *n.* the growth response of an organism, esp. a plant, to a chemical stimulus. **—chem·o+trop+ic** (ˌkɛməˈtrɒpɪk) *adj.* **—ˌchem·o+ˈtrop·i+cal+ly** *adv.*

chem+pa+duk (ˈtʃɛmpəˌdʌk) *n.* **1.** an evergreen moraceous tree, *Artocarpus champeden* (or *A. integer*), of Malaysia, similar to the jackfruit. **2.** the fruit of this tree, edible when cooked, having yellow starchy flesh and a leathery rind. [from Malay]

Che+mul+po (ˌtʃɛmʊlˈpəʊ) *n.* a former name of **Inchon.**

chem+ur+gy (ˈkɛmɜːdʒɪ) *n.* the branch of chemistry concerned with the industrial use of organic raw materials, esp. materials of agricultural origin. **—chem+ˈur+gic** *or* **chem+ˈur+gi+cal** *adj.*

Che+nab (tʃɪˈnæb) *n.* a river rising in the Himalayas and flowing southwest to the Sutlej River in Pakistan. Length: 1087 km (675 miles).

Cheng+chow *or* **Cheng-chou** (ˈtʃɛŋˈtʃaʊ) *n.* a city in E central China, capital of Honan province. Pop.: 1 050 000 (1970 est.).

Cheng+teh *or* **Ch'eng-te** (ˈtʃɛŋˈteɪ) *n.* a city in NE China, in Hopeh on the Luan River: summer residence of the Manchu emperors. Pop.: 92 900 (1953).

Cheng+tu *or* **Ch'eng-tu** (ˈtʃɛŋˈtuː) *n.* a city in S central China, capital of Szechwan province. Pop.: 1 250 000 (1970 est.).

Ché·nier (*French* ʃeˈnje) *n.* **An·dré** (**Marie de**) (ɑ̃ˈdre). 1762–94, French poet; his work was influenced by the ancient Greek elegiac poets. He was guillotined during the French Revolution.

che+nille (ʃəˈniːl) *n.* **1.** a thick soft tufty silk or worsted velvet cord or yarn used in embroidery and for trimmings, etc. **2.** a fabric of such yarn. **3.** a rich and hard-wearing carpet of such fabric. [C18: from French, literally: hairy caterpillar, from Latin *canicula*, diminutive of *canis* dog]

che+no+pod (ˈkiːnəˌpɒd, ˈkɛn-) *n.* any flowering plant of the family *Chenopodiaceae*, which includes the beet, mangel-wurzel, spinach, and goosefoot. [C16: from Greek *khēn* goose + *pous* foot] **—che+no+po+di·a+ceous** (ˌkiːnəˌpəʊdɪˈeɪʃəs, ˌkɛn-) *adj.*

cheong+sam (ˈtʃɔːŋˈsæm) *n.* a straight dress, usually of silk or cotton, with a stand-up collar and a slit in one side of the skirt, worn by Chinese women. [from Chinese (Cantonese), variant of Mandarin *ch'ang shan* long jacket]

Che·ops (ˈkiːɒps) *n.* original name *Khufu.* Egyptian king of the fourth dynasty (?2613–?2494 B.C.), who built the largest pyramid at Giza.

cheque *or U.S.* **check** (tʃɛk) *n.* **1.** a bill of exchange drawn on a bank by the holder of a current account; payable on demand, if uncrossed, or into a bank account, if crossed. **2.** *Austral.* the total sum of money received for contract work or a crop.

cheque+book *or U.S.* **check+book** (ˈtʃɛkˌbʊk) *n.* a book containing detachable blank cheques and issued by a bank to holders of current accounts.

cheque card *n.* another name for **banker's card.**

cheq+uer *or U.S.* **check+er** (ˈtʃɛkə) *n.* **1.** any of the marbles, pegs, or other pieces used in the game of Chinese chequers. **2. a.** a pattern consisting of squares of different colours, textures, or materials. **b.** one of the squares in such a pattern. *~vb.* (*tr.*) **3.** to make irregular in colour or character; variegate. **4.** to mark off with alternating squares of colour. [C13: chessboard, from Anglo-French *escheker*, from *eschec* CHECK]

cheq·uer+board (ˈtʃɛkəˌbɔːd) *n.* another name for a **draughtboard.**

cheq+uered *or esp. U.S.* **check+ered** (ˈtʃɛkəd) *adj.* marked by fluctuations of fortune (esp. in the phrase **a chequered career**).

cheq+uered flag *n.* the black-and-white checked flag traditionally shown to the winner and all finishers at the end of a motor race by a senior race official.
cheq+uers ('tʃɛkəz) *n.* another name for **draughts.**
Cheq+uers ('tʃɛkəz) *n.* an estate and country house in S England, in central Buckinghamshire: the official country residence of the Prime Minister.
Cher (*French* ʃɛ:r) *n.* **1.** a department of central France, in E Centre region. Capital: Bourges. Pop.: 322 924 (1975). Area: 7304 sq. km (2849 sq. miles). **2.** a river in central France, rising in the Massif Central and flowing northwest to the Loire. Length: 354 km (220 miles).
Cher+bourg ('ʃɛəbʊəg; *French* ʃɛr'bu:r) *n.* a port in NW France, on the English Channel. Pop.: 34 637 (1975).
Cher+e•miss *or* **Cher+e•mis** (ˌtʃɛərə'mɪs, -'mi:s; 'tʃɛərəˌmɪs, -ˌmi:s) *n.* **1.** (*pl.* **•miss** *or* **•mis**) a member of an Ugrian people of the Volga region, esp. of the Mari ASSR. **2.** the language of this people, belonging to the Finno-Ugric family.
Che+rem+kho+vo (*Russian* tʃɪrɪm'xɔvə) *n.* an industrial city in the S Soviet Union, in the southeastern RSFSR on the Trans-Siberian railway. Pop.: 104 000 (1969 est.).
Che•ren•kov (tʃɪ'rɛŋkɒf; *Russian* tʃɪ'rjenkəf) *n.* **Pa•vel A•le•k•se•ye•vich** ('pavɪl alɪk'sjejɪvitʃ). born 1904, Soviet physicist: noted for work on the effects produced by high-energy particles: shared Nobel Prize for physics 1958.
Che+ren+kov ra+di•a•tion *n.* the electromagnetic radiation produced when a charged particle moves through a medium at a greater velocity than the velocity of light in that medium. [C20: named after P. A. CHERENKOV]
Che+ri+bon ('tʃɪərəˌbɒn) *n.* a variant spelling of **Tjirebon.**
cher+ish ('tʃɛrɪʃ) *vb.* (*tr.*) **1.** to feel or show great tenderness or care for; treasure. **2.** to cling fondly to (a hope, idea, etc.); nurse: *to cherish ambitions.* [C14: from Old French *cherir,* from *cher* dear, from Latin *cārus*] —**'cher+ish+a•ble** *adj.* —**'cher+ish+er** *n.* —**'cher+ish+ing+ly** *adv.*
Cher+nov+tsy (*Russian* tʃɪrnaf'tsi) *n.* a city in the SW Soviet Union, in the W Ukrainian SSR on the Prut River: formerly under Polish, Austro-Hungarian, and Rumanian rule; ceded to the Soviet Union in 1947. Pop.: 203 000 (1975 est.). German name: **Czernowitz.** Rumanian name: **Cernăuţi.**
cher+no+zem *or* **tscher+no+sem** ('tʃɜ:nəʊˌzɛm) *n.* a black soil, rich in humus and carbonates, in cool or temperate semiarid regions, as the grasslands of Russia. [from Russian, contraction of *chernaya zemlya* black earth]
Cher•o+kee ('tʃɛrəˌki:, ˌtʃɛrə'ki:) *n.* **1.** (*pl.* **+kees** *or* **+kee**) a member of a North American Indian people formerly living in and around the Appalachian Mountains, now chiefly in Oklahoma; one of the Iroquois peoples. **2.** the language of this people, belonging to the Iroquoian family.
Cher•o+kee rose *n.* an evergreen climbing Chinese rose, *Rosa laevigata,* that now grows wild in the southern U.S., having large white fragrant flowers.
che+root (ʃə'ru:t) *n.* a cigar with both ends cut off squarely. [C17: from Tamil *curuttu* curl, roll]
cher+ry ('tʃɛrɪ) *n., pl.* **+ries. 1.** any of several trees of the rosaceous genus *Prunus,* such as *P. avium* (**sweet cherry**), having a small fleshy rounded fruit containing a hard stone. See also **bird cherry. 2.** the fruit or wood of any of these trees. **3.** any of various unrelated plants, such as the ground cherry and Jerusalem cherry. **4. a.** a bright red colour; cerise. **b.** (*as adj.*): *a cherry coat.* **5.** *Taboo slang.* virginity or the hymen as its symbol. **6.** (*modifier*) of or relating to the cherry fruit or wood: *cherry tart.* [C14: back formation from Old English *ciris* (mistakenly thought to be plural), ultimately from Late Latin *ceresia,* perhaps from Latin *cerasus* cherry tree, from Greek *kerasios*] —**'cher•ry-ˌlike** *adj.*
cher+ry bran+dy *n.* a red liqueur made of brandy flavoured with cherries.
cher+ry lau+rel *n.* a Eurasian rosaceous evergreen shrub, *Prunus laurocerasus,* having glossy aromatic leaves, white flowers, and purplish-black fruits.
cher+ry pick+er *n.* a hydraulic crane, esp. one mounted on a lorry, that has an elbow joint or telescopic arm supporting a basket-like platform enabling a person to service high power lines or to carry out similar operations above the ground.
cher•ry-pie *n.* a widely planted garden heliotrope, *Heliotropium peruvianum.*
cher+ry plum *n.* a small widely planted Asian rosaceous tree, *Prunus cerasifera,* with white flowers and red or yellow cherry-like fruit. Also called: **myrobalan.**
cher+so+nese ('kɜ:səˌni:s) *n.* **a.** a poetic or rhetorical word for **peninsula. b.** (*cap. when part of a name*): *Thracian Chersonese.* [C17: from Latin, from Greek *khersonēsos,* from *khersos* dry (land) + *nēsos* island]
chert (tʃɜ:t) *n.* an impure black or grey microcrystalline variety of quartz that resembles flint. Formula: SiO_2. Also called: **hornstone.** [C17: of obscure origin] —**'chert•y** *adj.*
Chert+sey ('tʃɜ:tsɪ) *n.* a town in S England, in N Surrey on the River Thames. Pop.: 44 886 (1971).
cher+ub ('tʃɛrəb) *n., pl.* **cher+ubs** *or* **cher•u•bim** ('tʃɛrəbɪm, -ʊbɪm). **1.** *Theol.* a member of the second order of angels, whose distinctive gift is knowledge, often represented as a winged child or winged head of a child. **2.** an innocent or sweet child. [Old English, from Hebrew *kĕrūbh*] —**che+ru+bic** (tʃə'ru:bɪk) *or* **che'ru+bi+cal** *adj.* —**che+'ru+bi•cal+ly** *adv.*
Che•ru•bi•ni (ˌkɛrʊ'bi:nɪ) *n.* **(Maria) Lu•i•gi (Carlo Zenobio Salvatore)** (lu'i:dʒi). 1760–1842, Italian composer, noted particularly for his church music and his operas.
cher+vil ('tʃɜ:vɪl) *n.* **1.** an aromatic umbelliferous Eurasian plant, *Anthriscus cerefolium,* with small white flowers and aniseed-flavoured leaves used as herbs in soups and salads. **2. bur chervil.** a similar and related plant, *Anthriscus caucalis.* **3.** a related plant, *Chaerophyllum temulentum,* having a hairy purple-spotted stem. [Old English *cerfelle,* from Latin *caerephylla,* plural of *caerephyllum* chervil, from Greek *khairephullon,* from *khairein* to enjoy + *phullon* leaf]
cher+vo+nets (tʃə'vɔ:nɛts) *n.* (formerly) a Soviet monetary unit and gold coin worth ten roubles. [from Old Russian *červonyi,* from Old Polish *czerwony* golden, purple]
Ches. *abbrev. for* Cheshire.
Ches•a•peake Bay ('tʃɛsəˌpi:k) *n.* the largest inlet of the Atlantic in the coast of the U.S.: bordered by Maryland and Virginia.
Chesh+ire ('tʃɛʃə, 'tʃɛʃɪə) *n.* a county of NW England: low-lying and undulating, bordering on the Pennines in the east; mainly agricultural. County town: Chester. Pop.: 916 400 (1976 est.). Area: 1262 sq. km (917 sq. miles). Abbrev.: **Ches.**
Chesh+ire cheese *n.* a mild-flavoured cheese with a crumbly texture, originally made in Cheshire.
Chesh+unt ('tʃɛʃənt) *n.* a town in SE England, in SE Hertfordshire: a dormitory town of London. Pop.: 44 947 (1971).
Chesh+van *Hebrew.* (xɛʃ'van) *n. Judaism.* a variant spelling of **Heshvan.**
chess[1] (tʃɛs) *n.* a game of skill for two players using a chessboard on which chessmen are moved. Initially each player has one king, one queen, two rooks, two bishops, two knights, and eight pawns, which have different types of moves according to kind. The object is to checkmate the opponent's king. [C13: from Old French *esches,* plural of *eschec* check (at chess); see CHECK]
chess[2] (tʃɛs) *n. U.S.* a less common name for **rye-brome.** [C18: of unknown origin]
chess[3] (tʃɛs) *n., pl.* **chess** *or* **chess•es.** a floorboard of the deck of a pontoon bridge. [C15 (in the sense: layer, tier): from Old French *chasse* frame, from Latin *capsa* box]
chess+board ('tʃɛsˌbɔ:d) *n.* a square board divided into 64 squares of two alternating colours, used for playing chess or draughts.
ches+sel ('tʃɛsᵊl) *n.* a mould used in cheese-making. [C18: probably from CHEESE[1] + WELL[2]]
chess+man ('tʃɛsˌmæn, -mən) *or* **chess piece** *n., pl.* **+men** *or* **piec•es.** any of the eight major pieces and eight pawns used by each player in a game of chess.
chest (tʃɛst) *n.* **1. a.** the front part of the trunk from the neck to the belly. Related adj.: **pectoral. b.** (*as modifier*): *a chest cold.* **2. get (something) off one's chest.** *Informal.* to unburden oneself of troubles, worries, etc., by talking about them. **3.** a box, usually large and sturdy, used for storage or shipping: *a tea chest.* **4.** Also: **chestful.** the quantity a chest holds. **5.** *Rare.* **a.** the place in which a public or charitable institution deposits its funds. **b.** the funds so deposited. **6.** a sealed container or reservoir for a gas: *a wind chest; a steam chest.* [Old English *cest,* from Latin *cista* wooden box, basket, from Greek *kistē* box] —**'chest+ed** *adj.*
Ches+ter ('tʃɛstə) *n.* a city in NW England, administrative centre of Cheshire, on the River Dee: intact surrounding walls; 16th- and 17th-century double tier shops. Pop.: 62 696 (1971). Latin name: **Deva.**
ches+ter+field ('tʃɛstəˌfi:ld) *n.* **1.** a man's knee-length overcoat, usually with a fly front to conceal the buttons and having a velvet collar. **2.** a large tightly stuffed sofa, often upholstered in leather, with straight upholstered arms of the same height as the back. [C19: named after a 19th-century Earl of *Chesterfield*]
Ches+ter+field[1] ('tʃɛstəˌfi:ld) *n.* an industrial town in N central England, in Derbyshire: famous 14th-century church with twisted spire. Pop.: 70 153 (1971).
Ches•ter•field[2] ('tʃɛstəˌfi:ld) *n. Philip Dormer Stanhope,* 4th Earl of Chesterfield. 1694–1773, English statesman and writer, noted for his elegance, suavity, and wit; author of *Letters to His Son* (1774).
Ches+ter+field+i•an (ˌtʃɛstə'fi:ldɪən) *adj.* of or like Lord Chesterfield; suave; elegant; polished.
Ches•ter•ton ('tʃɛstətᵊn) *n.* **G(ilbert) K(eith).** 1874–1936, English essayist, novelist, poet, and critic.
chest+nut ('tʃɛsˌnʌt) *n.* **1.** any N temperate fagaceous tree of the genus *Castanea,* such as *C. sativa* (**sweet** or **Spanish chestnut**), which produce flowers in long catkins and nuts in a prickly bur. Compare **horse chestnut, water chestnut, dwarf chestnut. 2.** the edible nut of any of these trees. **3.** the hard wood of any of these trees, used in making furniture, etc. **4. a.** a reddish-brown to brown colour. **b.** (*as adj.*): *chestnut hair.* **5.** a horse of a yellow-brown or golden-brown colour. **6.** a small horny callus on the inner surface of a horse's leg. **7.** *Informal.* an old or stale joke. [C16: from earlier *chesten nut: chesten,* from Old French *chastaigne,* from Latin *castanea,* from Greek *kastanea*]
chest of drawers *n.* a piece of furniture consisting of a frame, often on short legs, containing a set of drawers.
chest of vi•ols *n.* a set of viols of different sizes, usually six in number, used in consorts.
chest-on-chest *n.* another term for **tallboy.**
chest voice *or* **reg+is+ter** *n.* a voice of the lowest speaking or singing register. Compare **head voice.**
chest•y ('tʃɛstɪ) *adj.* **chest•i•er, chest•i•est.** *Informal.* **1.** *Brit.* suffering from or symptomatic of chest disease: *a chesty cough.* **2.** having a large well-developed chest or bosom. —**'chest•i+ness** *n.*

che·tah ('tʃi:tə) *n.* a variant spelling of **cheetah.**

Chet·nik ('tʃɛtnɪk, tʃɛt'ni:k) *n.* a Serbian nationalist belonging to a group that fought against the Turks before World War I and engaged in guerrilla warfare during both World Wars. [from Serbian *četnik,* from *četa* troop]

che·val-de-frise (ʃə,vældə'fri:z) *n., pl.* **che·vaux-de-frise** (ʃə,vəʊdə'fri:z). **1.** a portable barrier of spikes, etc., used to obstruct the passage of cavalry. **2.** a row of spikes or broken glass set as an obstacle on top of a wall. [C17: from French, literally: horse from Friesland (where it was first used)]

che·val glass (ʃə'væl) *n.* a full-length mirror that swivels within a frame. [C19: from French *cheval* (literally: horse)]

chev·a·lier (,ʃɛvə'lɪə) *n.* **1.** a member of certain orders of merit, such as the French Legion of Honour. **2.** *French history.* **a.** a mounted soldier or knight, esp. a military cadet. **b.** the lowest title of rank in the old French nobility. **3.** an archaic word for **knight. 4.** a chivalrous man; gallant. [C14: from Old French, from Medieval Latin *caballārius* horseman, CAVALIER]

Che·va·lier (*French* ʃəva'lje) *n.* **Mau·rice** (mɔ'ris). 1888–1972, French singer and film actor.

che·vet (ʃə'veɪ) *n.* a semicircular or polygonal east end of a church, esp. a French Gothic church, often with a number of attached apses. [C19: from French: pillow, from Latin *capitium,* from *caput* head]

Che·vi·ot ('tʃi:vɪət, 'tʃɛv-) *n.* **1.** a large British breed of sheep reared for its wool. **2.** (*often not cap.*) a rough twill-weave woollen suiting fabric.

Che·vi·ot Hills *pl. n.* a range of hills on the border between England and Scotland, mainly in Northumberland.

chev·rette (ʃə'vrɛt) *n.* **1.** the skin of a young goat. **2.** the leather made from this skin. [C18: from French: kid, from *chèvre* goat, from Latin *capra*]

chev·ron ('ʃɛvrən) *n.* **1.** *Military.* a badge or insignia consisting of one or more V-shaped stripes to indicate a noncommissioned rank or length of service. **2.** *Heraldry.* an inverted V-shaped charge on a shield, one of the earliest ordinaries found in English arms. **3.** any V-shaped pattern or device. **4.** Also called: **dancette.** an ornamental moulding having a zigzag pattern. [C14: from Old French, ultimately from Latin *caper* goat; compare Latin *capreoli* two pieces of wood forming rafters (literally: little goats)]

chev·ro·tain ('ʃɛvrə,teɪn, -tɪn) *n.* any small timid ruminant artiodactyl mammal of the genera *Tragulus* and *Hyemoschus,* of S and SE Asia: family *Tragulidae.* They resemble rodents, and the males have long tusklike upper canines. Also called: **mouse deer.** [C18: from French, from Old French *chevrot* kid, from *chèvre* goat, from Latin *capra,* feminine of *caper* goat]

chev·y ('tʃɛvɪ) *n., vb.* a variant spelling of **chivy.**

chew (tʃu:) *vb.* **1.** to work the jaws and teeth in order to grind (food); masticate. **2.** to bite repeatedly: *she chewed her nails anxiously.* **3.** (*intr.*) to use chewing tobacco. **4. chew the fat** *or* **rag.** *Slang.* **a.** to argue over a point. **b.** to talk idly; gossip. ~*n.* **5.** the act of chewing. **6.** something chewed: *a chew of tobacco.* [Old English *ceowan;* related to Old High German *kiuwan,* Latin *gingīva* a gum] —'**chew·a·ble** *adj.* —'**chew·er** *n.*

Che·wa ('tʃeɪwə) *n.* **1.** (*pl.* **·was** *or* **·wa**) a member of a Negro people of Malawi, E Zambia, and N Rhodesia, related to the Bemba. **2.** their language. See **Chichewa.**

chew·ie ('tʃu:ɪ) *n. Austral. informal.* chewing gum.

chew·ing gum *n.* a preparation for chewing, usually made of flavoured and sweetened chicle.

chew out *vb.* (*tr., adv.*) *U.S. informal.* to reprimand.

chew o·ver *vb.* (*tr., adv.*) to consider carefully; ruminate on.

chew up *vb.* (*tr., adv.*) **1.** to damage or destroy (something) by or as by chewing or grinding. **2.** (*usually passive*) *Slang.* to cause (a person) to be nervous or worried: *he was all chewed up about the interview.*

chew·y ('tʃu:ɪ) *adj.* **chew·i·er, chew·i·est.** of a consistency requiring chewing; somewhat firm and sticky.

Chey·enne[1] (ʃaɪ'æn) *n.* **1.** (*pl.* **·enne** *or* **·ennes**) a member of a North American Indian people of the western Plains, now living chiefly in Montana and Oklahoma. **2.** the language of this people, belonging to the Algonquian family. [via Canadian French from Dakota *Shaiyena,* from *shaia* to speak incoherently, from *sha* red + *ya* to speak]

Chey·enne[2] (ʃaɪ'æn, -'ɛn) *n.* a city in SE Wyoming, capital of the state. Pop.: 40 914 (1970).

Cheyne-Stokes breath·ing ('tʃeɪn'stəʊks) *n. Pathol.* alternating shallow and deep breathing, as in comatose patients. [C19: named after John *Cheyne* (1777–1836), Scottish physician, and William *Stokes* (1804–78), Irish physician]

chez *French.* (ʃe) *prep.* **1.** at the home of. **2.** with, among, or in the manner of.

chg. *Commerce, finance, etc. abbrev. for* charge.

chi (kaɪ) *n.* the 22nd letter of the Greek alphabet (χ, X), a consonant, transliterated as *ch* or rarely *kh.*

chi·ack *or* **chy·ack** ('tʃaɪæk) *vb.* (*tr.*) *Austral. informal.* to tease or banter. [C19: from *chi-hike,* a shout or greeting]

Chi·an ('kaɪən) *adj.* **1.** of or relating to Chios. ~*n.* **2.** a native or inhabitant of Chios.

Chiang Ch'ing ('tʃæŋ 'tʃɪŋ) *n.* born 1913, Chinese Communist actress and politician; widow of Mao Tse-tung. She was a leading member of the Gang of Four.

Chiang Ching-kuo ('tʃæŋ tʃɪŋ'kwəʊ) *n.* born 1910, Chinese statesman; the son of Chiang Kai-shek. He was prime minister of Taiwan (1971–78); president since 1978.

Chiang Kai-shek ('tʃæŋ kaɪ'ʃɛk) *n.* original name *Chiang Chung-cheng,* 1897–1975, Chinese general: president of China (1928–31; 1943–49) and of the Republic of China (Taiwan) (1950–75). As chairman of the Kuomintang, he allied with the Communists against the Japanese (1937–45), but in the Civil War that followed was forced to withdraw to Taiwan after his defeat by the Communists (1949).

chi·an·ti (kɪ'æntɪ) *n.* (*sometimes cap.*) a dry red or white wine produced in the Chianti region of Italy.

Chi·an·ti (*Italian* 'kjanti) *pl. n.* a mountain range in central Italy, in Tuscany, rising over 870 m (2900 ft.): part of the Apennines.

Chia·pas (*Spanish* 'tʃaapas) *n.* a state of S Mexico: mountainous and forested; Maya ruins in the northeast; rich mineral resources. Capital: Tuxtla Gutiérrez. Pop.: 1 569 053 (1970). Area: 73 887 sq. km (28 816 sq. miles).

chi·a·ro·scu·ro (kɪ,ɑ:rə'skʊərəʊ) *n., pl.* **·ros. 1.** the artistic distribution of light and dark masses in a picture. **2.** monochrome painting using light and dark only, as in grisaille. [C17: from Italian, from *chiaro* CLEAR + *oscuro* OBSCURE] —**chi·,a·ro·'scu·rist** *n.* —**chi·,a·ro·'scur·ism** *n.*

chi·as·ma (kaɪ'æzmə) *or* **chi·asm** ('kaɪæzəm) *n., pl.* **·mas, ·ma·ta** (-mətə), *or* **·asms. 1.** *Anatomy.* the crossing over of two parts or structures, such as the fibres of the optic nerves in the brain. **2.** *Cytology.* the connection between pairing homologous chromosomes in meiosis, produced by crossing over. [C19: from Greek *khiasma* crosspiece, from *khiazein* to mark with an X, from *khi* CHI] —**chi·'as·mal** *or* **chi·'as·mic** *adj.*

chi·as·mus (kaɪ'æzməs) *n., pl.* **·mi** (-maɪ). *Rhetoric.* reversal of the order of words in the second of two parallel phrases: *he went out and in came she.* [C19: from New Latin, from Greek *khiasmos* crisscross arrangement; see CHIASMA] —**chi·as·tic** (kaɪ'æstɪk) *adj.*

chi·as·to·lite (kaɪ'æstə,laɪt) *n.* a variety of andalusite containing carbon impurities. Also called: **macle.** [C19: from German *Chiastolith,* from Greek *khiastos* crossed, marked with a chi + *lithos* stone]

Chi·ba ('tʃi:ba) *n.* an industrial city in central Japan, in SE Honshu on Tokyo Bay. Pop.: 613 787 (1974 est.).

Chib·chan ('tʃɪbtʃən) *n.* **1.** a family of Indian languages found in Colombia and elsewhere in South America. ~*adj.* **2.** belonging or relating to this family of languages.

chi·bouk *or* **chi·bouque** (tʃɪ'bu:k) *n.* a Turkish tobacco pipe with an extremely long stem. [C19: from French *chibouque,* from *çubuk* pipe]

chic (ʃi:k, ʃɪk) *adj.* **1.** (esp. of fashionable clothes, women, etc.) stylish or elegant. ~*n.* **2.** stylishness, esp. in dress; modishness; fashionable good taste.[C19: from French, of uncertain origin] —'**chic·ly** *adv.*

Chi·ca·go (ʃɪ'kɑ:gəʊ) *n.* a port in NE Illinois, on Lake Michigan: the second largest city in the U.S.; the largest railway and air traffic centre in the world. Pop.: 3 172 929 (1973 est.).

chi·ca·lo·te (,tʃi:kɑ:'ləʊteɪ) *n.* a poppy, *Argemone platyceras,* of the southwestern U.S. and Mexico with prickly leaves and white or yellow flowers. [Spanish, from Nahuatl *chicalotl*]

chi·cane (ʃɪ'keɪn) *n.* **1.** a bridge or whist hand without trumps. **2.** *Motor racing.* a movable barrier sometimes placed before a dangerous corner to reduce speeds by allowing drivers through in single file only. **3.** a less common word for **chicanery.** ~*vb.* **4.** (*tr.*) to deceive or trick by chicanery. **5.** (*tr.*) to quibble about; cavil over. **6.** (*intr.*) to use tricks or chicanery. [C17: from French *chicaner* to quibble, of obscure origin] —**chi·'can·er** *n.*

chi·can·er·y (ʃɪ'keɪnərɪ) *n., pl.* **·er·ies. 1.** verbal deception or trickery, esp. in legal quibbling; dishonest or sharp practice. **2.** a trick, deception, or quibble.

chi·ca·no (tʃɪ'kɑ:nəʊ) *n., pl.* **·nos.** *U.S.* an American citizen of Mexican origin. [C20: from Spanish *mejicano* Mexican]

chic·co·ry ('tʃɪkərɪ) *n., pl.* **·ries.** a variant spelling of **chicory.**

Chich·a·gof Is·land ('tʃɪtʃə,gɔ:f) *n.* an island of Alaska, in the Alexander Archipelago. Area: 5439 sq. km (2100 sq. miles).

Chi·chen It·zá (*Spanish* tʃi'tʃen it'sa) *n.* a village in Yucatán state in Mexico: site of important Mayan ruins.

Chich·es·ter[1] ('tʃɪtʃɪstə) *n.* a town in S England, administrative centre of West Sussex: Roman ruins; 11th-century cathedral. Pop.: 20 547 (1971).

Chich·es·ter[2] ('tʃɪtʃɪstə) *n.* Sir **Fran·cis.** 1901–72, English yachtsman, who sailed alone round the world in *Gipsy Moth IV* (1966–67).

Chi·che·wa (tʃɪ'tʃeɪwə) *n.* the language of the Chewa people of central Africa, widely used as a lingua franca in Malawi. It belongs to the Bantu group of the Niger-Congo family.

chi·chi ('ʃi:,ʃi:) *adj.* **1.** affectedly pretty or stylish. ~*n.* **2.** the quality of being affectedly pretty. [C20: from French]

Chi·chi·haerh *or* **Ch'i-ch'i-haerh** ('tʃi:,tʃi:'hɑ:) *n.* a city in NE China, in Heilungkiang province on the Nonni River. Pop.: 760 000 (1970 est.).

chick (tʃɪk) *n.* **1.** the young of a bird, esp. of a domestic fowl. **2.** *Slang.* a girl or young woman, esp. an attractive one. **3.** a young child: used as a term of endearment. [C14: short for CHICKEN]

chick·a·bid·dy ('tʃɪkə,bɪdɪ) *n., pl.* **·dies.** a term of endearment, esp. for a child. [C18: from CHICK + BIDDY[1]]

chick·a·dee ('tʃɪkə,di:) *n.* any of various small North American songbirds of the genus *Parus,* such as *P. atricapillus* (**black-capped chickadee**), typically having grey-and-black plumage: family *Paridae* (titmice). [C19: imitative of its note]

chick·a·ree ('tʃɪkə,ri:) *n.* another name for **American red squirrel** (see **squirrel** (sense 1)).

Chick·a·saw ('tʃɪkə,sɔ:) *n.* **1.** (*pl.* **·saws** *or* **·saw**) a member of a North American Indian people of N Mississippi. **2.** the language of this people, belonging to the Muskhogean family.

chick+en ('tʃɪkɪn) *n.* **1.** a domestic fowl bred for its flesh or eggs. **2.** the flesh of such a bird used for food. **3.** any of various similar birds, such as a prairie chicken. **4.** *Slang.* a cowardly person. **5.** *Slang.* a young inexperienced person. **6. count one's chickens before they are hatched.** to be over-optimistic in acting on expectations which are not yet fulfilled. ~*adj.* **7.** *Slang.* easily scared; cowardly; timid. [Old English *ciecen;* related to Old Norse *kjūklingr* gosling, Middle Low German *küken* chicken]

chick+en breast *n. Pathol.* another name for **pigeon breast.** —ˌ**chick·en-'breast·ed** *adj.*

chick+en feed *n. Slang.* a trifling amount of money.

chick·en-heart·ed *or* **chick·en-liv·ered** *adj.* easily frightened; cowardly. —ˌ**chick·en-'heart·ed+ly** *adv.* —ˌ**chick·en-'heart·ed+ness** *n.*

chick+en louse *n.* a louse, *Menopon pallidum* (or *gallinae*); a parasite of poultry: order *Mallophaga* (bird lice).

chick+en out *vb.* (*intr., adv.*) *Informal.* to fail to do something through fear or lack of conviction.

chick·en+pox ('tʃɪkɪnˌpɒks) *n.* a highly communicable viral disease most commonly affecting children, characterized by slight fever and the eruption of a rash.

chick+en wire *n.* wire netting with a hexagonal mesh.

chick+pea ('tʃɪkˌpiː) *n.* **1.** a bushy leguminous plant, *Cicer arietinum,* cultivated for its edible pealike seeds in the Mediterranean region, central Asia, and Africa. **2.** the seed of this plant. ~Also called: **garbanzo.** [C16 *ciche peasen,* from *ciche* (from French *chiche,* from Latin *cicer* chickpea) + *peasen;* see PEA]

chick+weed ('tʃɪkˌwiːd) *n.* **1.** any of various caryophyllaceous plants of the genus *Stellaria,* esp. *S. media,* a common garden weed with small white flowers. **2. mouse-ear chickweed.** any of various similar and related plants of the genus *Cerastium.*

Chi+cla+yo (*Spanish* tʃi'klajo) *n.* a city in NW Peru. Pop.: 187 809 (1972).

chic+le ('tʃɪkᵊl) *n.* a gumlike substance obtained from the sapodilla; the main ingredient of chewing gum. Also called: **chicle gum.** [from Spanish, from Nahuatl *chictli*]

chi+co ('tʃiːkəʊ) *n., pl.* **+cos.** another name for **greasewood** (sense 1).

chic·o+ry ('tʃɪkərɪ) *n., pl.* **+ries. 1.** Also called: **succory.** a blue-flowered plant, *Cichorium intybus,* cultivated for its leaves, which are used in salads, and for its roots: family *Compositae* (composites). **2.** the root of this plant, roasted, dried, and used as a coffee substitute. ~Compare **endive.** [C15: from Old French *chicorée,* from Latin *cichorium,* from Greek *kikhōrion*]

chide (tʃaɪd) *vb.* **chides, chid+ing, chid+ed** *or* **chid; chid+ed, chid** *or* **chid+den. 1.** to rebuke or scold. **2.** (*tr.*) to goad into action. [Old English *cīdan*] —**'chid+er** *n.* —**'chid+ing+ly** *adv.*

chief (tʃiːf) *n.* **1.** the head, leader, or most important individual in a group or body of people. **2.** another word for **chieftain** (sense 1). **3.** *Heraldry.* the upper third of a shield. ~*adj.* **4.** (*prenominal*) **a.** most important; principal. **b.** highest in rank or authority. ~*adv.* **5. in chief.** primarily; especially. **6.** *Archaic.* principally. [C13: from Old French, from Latin *caput* head]

Chief Ed·u·ca+tion Of+fic+er *n.* the official name for **director** (sense 3).

chief jus+tice *n.* **1.** (in any of several Commonwealth countries) the judge presiding over a supreme court. **2.** (in the U.S.) the presiding judge of a court composed of a number of members. ~See also **Lord Chief Justice.** —**chief jus+tice+ship** *n.*

chief+ly ('tʃiːflɪ) *adv.* **1.** especially or essentially; above all. **2.** in general; mainly; mostly. ~*adj.* **3.** of or relating to a chief or chieftain.

Chief of Staff *n.* **1.** the senior staff officer under the commander of a major military formation or organization. **2.** the senior officer of each service of the armed forces.

chief pet+ty of+fic+er *n.* the senior naval rank for personnel without commissioned or warrant rank.

Chief Rab+bi *n.* the chief religious minister of a national Jewish community.

chief+tain ('tʃiːftən, -tɪn) *n.* **1.** the head or leader of a tribe or clan. **2.** the chief of a group of people. [C14: from Old French *chevetaine,* from Late Latin *capitāneus* commander; see CAPTAIN] —**'chief+tain+cy** *or* **'chief+tain+ˌship** *n.*

chiff+chaff ('tʃɪfˌtʃæf) *n.* a common European warbler, *Phylloscopus collybita,* with a yellowish-brown plumage.

chif+fon (ʃɪ'fɒn, 'ʃɪfɒn) *n.* **1.** a fine transparent or almost transparent plain-weave fabric of silk, nylon, etc. **2.** (*often pl.*) *Now rare.* feminine finery. ~*adj.* **3.** made of chiffon. **4.** (of soufflés, pies, cakes, etc.) having a very light fluffy texture. [C18: from French, from *chiffe* rag; probably related to CHIP]

chif+fo+nier *or* **chif+fon+nier** (ˌʃɪfə'nɪə) *n.* **1.** a tall, elegant chest of drawers, originally intended for holding needlework. **2.** a wide low open-fronted cabinet, sometimes fitted with two grille doors and shelves. [C19: from French, from *chiffon* rag; see CHIFFON]

Chif·ley ('tʃɪflɪ) *n.* **Jo·seph Ben·e·dict.** 1885–1951, Australian statesman; prime minister of Australia (1945–49).

chig+e·tai (ˌtʃɪgɪ'taɪ) *n.* a variety of the Asiatic wild ass, *Equus hemionus,* of Mongolia. Also spelled: **dziggetai.** [from Mongolian *tchikhitei* long-eared, from *tchikhi* ear]

chig+ger ('tʃɪgə) *n.* **1.** Also called: **chigoe, redbug.** *U.S.* the parasitic larva of any of various free-living mites of the family *Trombidiidae,* which causes intense itching of human skin. **2.** another name for the **chigoe** (sense 1).

chi+gnon ('ʃiːnjɒn; *French* ʃi'ɲɔ̃) *n.* an arrangement of long hair in a roll or knot at the back of the head. [C18: from French, from Old French *chaignon* link, from *chaine* CHAIN; influenced also by Old French *tignon* coil of hair, from *tigne,* moth, from Latin *tinea* moth] —**'chi+gnoned** *adj.*

chig·oe ('tʃɪgəʊ) *n.* **1.** Also called: **chigger, jigger, sand flea.** a tropical flea, *Tunga penetrans,* the female of which lives on or burrows into the skin of its host, which includes man. **2.** another name for **chigger** (sense 1). [C17: from Carib *chigo*]

Chig+well ('tʃɪgwəl) *n.* a town in S England, in W Essex. Pop.: 53 620 (1971).

Chih+li ('tʃiːliː) *n.* **Gulf of.** another name for the **Po Hai.**

Chi+hua+hua (tʃɪ'wɑːwɑː, -wə) *n.* **1.** a state of N Mexico: mostly high plateau; important mineral resources, with many silver mines. Capital: Chihuahua. Pop.: 1 612 525 (1970). Area: 247 087 sq. km (153 194 sq. miles). **2.** a city in N Mexico, capital of Chihuahua state. Pop.: 346 003 (1975 est.). **3.** a breed of tiny dog originally from Mexico, having short hair and protruding eyes.

chil+blain ('tʃɪlˌbleɪn) *n. Pathol.* (*usually pl.*) an inflammation of the fingers, toes, or ears, caused by prolonged exposure to moisture and cold. [C16: from CHILL (n.) + BLAIN] —**'chil+ˌblained** *adj.*

child (tʃaɪld) *n., pl.* **chil+dren. 1. a.** a boy or girl between birth and puberty. **b.** (*as modifier*): *child labour.* **2.** a baby or infant. **3.** an unborn baby. **4. with child.** another term for **pregnant. 5.** a human offspring; a son or daughter. Related adj.: **filial. 6.** a childish or immature person. **7.** a member of a family or tribe; descendant: *a child of Israel.* **8.** a person or thing regarded as the product of an influence or environment: *a child of nature.* **9.** *Midland and western Brit. dialect.* a female infant. [Old English *cild;* related to Gothic *kilthei* womb, Sanskrit *jathara* belly, *jartu* womb] —**'child+less** *adj.* —**'child+less+ness** *n.* —**'child+ly** *adj.*

child-bear·ing *n.* **a.** the act or process of carrying and giving birth to a child. **b.** (*as modifier*): *of childbearing age.*

child+bed ('tʃaɪldˌbɛd) *n.* **a.** (often preceded by *in*) the condition of giving birth to a child. **b.** (*as modifier*): *childbed fever.*

child ben+e·fit *n.* (in Britain) a regular government payment to the parents of children up to a certain age. Austral. equivalent: **child endowment.**

child+birth ('tʃaɪldˌbɜːθ) *n.* the act of giving birth to a child.

child care *n. Brit.* care provided for children without homes (or with a seriously disturbed home life) by a local authority.

childe (tʃaɪld) *n. Archaic.* a young man of noble birth. [C13: variant of CHILD]

chil+der+mas ('tʃɪldəˌmæs) *n. Archaic.* Holy Innocents Day, Dec. 28. [Old English *cylda-mæsse,* from *cidra,* genitive plural of CHILD, + *mæsse* MASS]

child guid+ance *n.* the counselling of emotionally disturbed children.

child+hood ('tʃaɪldhʊd) *n.* the condition of being a child; the period of life before puberty.

child+ish ('tʃaɪldɪʃ) *adj.* **1.** in the manner of, belonging to, or suitable to a child. **2.** foolish or petty; puerile: *childish fears.* —**'child+ish+ly** *adv.* —**'child+ish+ness** *n.*

child la+bour *n.* the full-time employment of children below a minimum age laid down by statute.

child+like ('tʃaɪldˌlaɪk) *adj.* like or befitting a child, as in being innocent, trustful, etc. Compare **childish** (sense 2).

child mind+er *n.* a person who looks after children, esp. those whose parents are working.

chil+dren ('tʃɪldrən) *n.* the plural of **child.**

child's play *n. Informal.* something that is easy to do.

chil·e ('tʃɪlɪ) *n.* a variant spelling of **chilli.**

Chil·e ('tʃɪlɪ) *n.* a republic in South America, on the Pacific, with a total length of about 4090 km (2650 miles) and an average width of only 177 km (110 miles): gained independence from Spain in 1818; the government of President Allende (elected 1970) attempted the implementation of Marxist policies within a democratic system until overthrown by a military coup (1973). Chile consists chiefly of the Andes in the east, the Atacama Desert in the north, a central fertile region, and a huge S region of almost uninhabitable mountains, glaciers, fjords, and islands; an important producer of copper, iron ore, nitrates, etc. Language: Spanish. Religion: Roman Catholic. Currency: peso. Capital: Santiago. Pop.: 10 076 000 (1974 est.). Area: 756 945 sq. km (292 256 sq. miles). —**'Chil+e·an** *adj., n.*

Chil·e pine *n.* another name for the **monkey puzzle.**

Chil·e salt+pe+tre *or* **ni+tre** *n.* a naturally occurring form of sodium nitrate: a soluble white or colourless mineral occurring in arid regions, esp. in Chile and Peru. Also called: **soda nitre.**

chil·i+ad ('kɪlɪˌæd) *n.* **1.** a group of one thousand. **2.** one thousand years. [C16: from Greek *khilias,* from *khilioi* a thousand] —ˌ**chil·i+'ad+al** *or* ˌ**chil·i+'ad+ic** *adj.*

chil·i+asm ('kɪlɪˌæzəm) *n. Christian theol.* another term for **millenarianism** or the **millennium.** [C17: from Greek *khiliasmos,* from *khilioi* a thousand] —**'chil·i+ˌast** *n.* —ˌ**chil·i+'as+tic** *adj.*

Chil+koot Pass ('tʃɪlkuːt) *n.* a mountain pass in North America between SE Alaska and NW British Columbia, over the Coast Range.

chill (tʃɪl) *n.* **1.** a moderate coldness. **2.** a sensation of coldness resulting from a cold or damp environment, or from a sudden emotional reaction. **3.** a feverish cold. **4.** a check on enthusiasm or joy. **5.** a metal plate placed in a sand mould to accelerate cooling and control local grain growth. **6.** another name for **bloom** (sense 8). ~*adj.* **7.** another word for **chilly.** ~*vb.* **8.** (*tr.*) to make or become cold. **9.** (*tr.*) to cool or freeze (food, drinks, etc.). **10.** (*tr.*) **a.** to depress (enthusiasm, etc.). **b.** to discourage. **11.** (*tr.*) to cool (a casting or metal object) rapidly in order to prevent the formation of large grains in the metal. [Old English *ciele;* related to *calan* to COOL, Latin *gelidus* icy] —'**chill·er** *n.* —'**chill·ing·ly** *adv.* —'**chill·ness** *n.*

Chi·llán (*Spanish* tʃi'jan) *n.* a city in central Chile. Pop.: 102 210 (1975 est.).

chil·li ('tʃɪlɪ) *n., pl.* **chil·lies.** the small red hot-tasting pod of a type of capsicum used for flavouring sauces, pickles, etc. [C17: from Spanish *chile,* from Nahuatl *chilli*]

chil·li con car·ne ('tʃɪlɪ kɒn 'kɑːnɪ) *n.* a highly seasoned Mexican dish of meat, onions, beans, and chilli powder. [from Spanish *chile con carne* chilli with meat]

chil·li pow·der *n.* ground chilli blended with other spices.

chil·li sauce *n.* a highly seasoned sauce made of tomatoes cooked with chilli and other spices and seasonings.

Chil·lon (ʃɪ'lɒn; *French* ʃi'jɔ̃) *n.* a castle in W Switzerland, in Vaud at the E end of Lake Geneva.

chil·lum ('tʃɪləm) *n.* a short pipe, usually of clay, used esp. for smoking cannabis. [C18: from Hindi *cilam,* from Persian *chilam*]

chil·ly ('tʃɪlɪ) *adj.* **·li·er, ·li·est. 1.** causing or feeling cool or moderately cold. **2.** without warmth; unfriendly. **3.** (of people) sensitive to cold. —'**chil·li·ness** *n.*

chi·lo·pod ('kaɪləˌpɒd) *n.* any arthropod of the class *Chilopoda,* which includes the centipedes. See also **myriapod.** [C19: from New Latin *Chilopoda,* from Greek *kheilos* lip + *pous* foot; referring to the modification of the first pair of legs into jawlike claws] —**chi·lop·o·dan** (kaɪ'lɒpədᵊn) *n., adj.* —**chi·'lop·o·dous** *adj.*

Chil·pan·cin·go (*Spanish* ˌtʃilpan'siŋgo) *n.* a town in S Mexico, capital of Guerrero state, in the Sierra Madre del Sur. Pop.: 56 904 (1970).

Chil·tern Hills ('tʃɪltən) *pl. n.* a range of low chalk hills in SE England extending northwards from the Thames valley. Highest point: 255 m (852 ft.).

Chil·tern Hun·dreds *n. Brit.* short for **Stewardship of the Chiltern Hundreds;** a nominal office that an MP applies for in order to resign his seat.

Chi·lung *or* **Chi-lung** ('tʃiː'lʊŋ) *n.* a port in N Taiwan: fishing and industrial centre. Pop.: 317 780 (1969 est.). Also called: **Keelung, Kilung.**

chi·mae·ra (kaɪ'mɪərə, kɪ-) *n.* **1.** any tapering smooth-skinned cartilaginous deep-sea fish of the subclass *Holocephali* (or *Bradyodonti*), esp. any of the genus *Chimaera.* They have a skull in which the upper jaw is fused to the cranium. See also **rabbitfish** (sense 1). **2.** *Greek myth.* a variant spelling of **chimera** (sense 1).

chimb (tʃaɪm) *n.* a variant spelling of **chime²**.

Chim·bo·ra·zo (ˌtʃɪmbə'rɑːzəʊ, -'reɪ-; *Spanish* ˌtʃimbo'raθo) *n.* an extinct volcano in central Ecuador, in the Andes: the highest peak in Ecuador. Height: 6267 m (20 681 ft.).

Chim·bo·te (*Spanish* tʃim'bote) *n.* a port in N central Peru: contains Peru's first steelworks (1958), using hydroelectric power from the Santa River. Pop.: 159 045 (1972).

chime¹ (tʃaɪm) *n.* **1.** an individual bell or the sound it makes when struck. **2.** (*often pl.*) the machinery employed to sound a bell in this way. **3.** Also called: **bell.** a percussion instrument consisting of a set of vertical metal tubes of graduated length, suspended in a frame and struck with a hammer. **4.** a harmonious or ringing sound: *the chimes of children's laughter.* **5.** agreement; concord. ~*vb.* **6. a.** to sound (a bell) or (of a bell) to be sounded by a clapper or hammer. **b.** to produce (music or sounds) by chiming. **7.** (*tr.*) to indicate or show (time or the hours) by chiming. **8.** (*tr.*) to summon, announce, or welcome by ringing bells. **9.** (*intr.; foll. by with*) to agree or harmonize. **10.** to speak or recite in a musical or rhythmic manner. [C13: probably shortened from earlier *chymbe bell,* ultimately from Latin *cymbalum* CYMBAL] —'**chim·er** *n.*

chime², chimb (tʃaɪm), *or* **chine** *n.* the projecting edge or rim of a cask or barrel. [Old English *cimb-;* related to Middle Low German *kimme* outer edge, Swedish *kimb*]

chime in *vb.* (*intr., adv.*) *Informal.* **1.** to join in or interrupt (a conversation), esp. repeatedly and unwelcomely. **2.** to voice agreement.

chi·me·ra *or* **chi·mae·ra** (kaɪ'mɪərə, kɪ-) *n.* **1.** (*often cap.*) *Greek myth.* a fire-breathing monster with the head of a lion, body of a goat, and tail of a serpent. **2.** a fabulous beast made up of parts taken from various animals. **3.** a grotesque product of the imagination. **4.** *Biology.* an organism, esp. a cultivated plant, consisting of at least two genetically different kinds of tissue as a result of mutation, grafting, etc. [C16: from Latin *chimaera,* from Greek *khimaira* she-goat, from *khimaros* he-goat]

chi·mere (tʃɪ'mɪə, ʃɪ-), **chim·er,** *or* **chim·ar** ('tʃɪmə, 'ʃɪm-) *n. Anglican Church.* a sleeveless red or black gown, part of a bishop's formal dress though not a vestment. [C14: perhaps from Medieval Latin *chimēra* (see CHIMERA) and related to Spanish *zamarra* sheepskin coat]

chi·mer·i·cal (kaɪ'mɛrɪkᵊl, kɪ-) *or* **chi·mer·ic** *adj.* **1.** wildly fanciful; imaginary. **2.** given to or indulging in fantasies. —**chi·'mer·i·cal·ly** *adv.* —**chi·'mer·i·cal·ness** *n.*

Chim·kent (tʃɪm'kɛnt) *n.* a city in the SW Soviet Union, in the S Kazakh SSR. Pop.: 288 000 (1975 est.).

chim·ney ('tʃɪmnɪ) *n.* **1.** a vertical structure of brick, masonry, or steel that carries smoke or steam away from a fire, engine, etc. **2.** another name for **flue¹** (sense 1). **3.** short for **chimney stack. 4.** an open-ended glass tube fitting around the flame of an oil or gas lamp in order to exclude draughts. **5.** *Brit.* a fireplace, esp. an old and large one. **6.** *Geology.* **a.** the part of a mineral deposit that consists of the most valuable ore. **b.** the vent of a volcano. **7.** *Mountaineering.* a fissure large enough for a person's body to enter. **8.** anything resembling a chimney in shape or function. [C14: from Old French *cheminée,* from Late Latin *camīnāta,* from Latin *camīnus* furnace, from Greek *kaminos* fireplace, oven]

chim·ney breast *n.* the wall or walls that surround the base of a chimney or fireplace.

chim·ney cor·ner *n.* a recess that contains a seat in a large open fireplace; inglenook.

chim·ney·piece ('tʃɪmnɪˌpiːs) *n.* another name (esp. Brit.) for **mantelpiece** (sense 1).

chim·ney·pot ('tʃɪmnɪˌpɒt) *n.* a short pipe on the top of a chimney, which increases the draught and directs the smoke upwards.

chim·ney stack *n.* the part of a chimney that rises above the roof of a building.

chim·ney swal·low *n.* **1.** another name for **common swallow** (see **swallow²**). **2.** a less common name for **chimney swift.**

chim·ney sweep *or* **sweep·er** *n.* a person whose job is the cleaning out of soot from chimneys.

chim·ney swift *n.* a North American swift, *Chaetura pelagica,* that nests in chimneys and similar hollows.

chimp (tʃɪmp) *n. Informal.* short for **chimpanzee.**

chim·pan·zee (ˌtʃɪmpæn'ziː) *n.* a gregarious and intelligent anthropoid ape, *Pan troglodytes,* inhabiting forests in central W Africa. [C18: from Kongo dialect]

chin (tʃɪn) *n.* **1.** the protruding part of the lower jaw. **2.** the front part of the face below the lips. **3. keep one's chin up.** *Informal.* to keep cheerful under difficult circumstances. Sometimes shortened to **chin up! 4. take it on the chin.** *Informal.* to face squarely up to a defeat, adversity, etc. ~*vb.* **chins, chin·ning, chinned. 5.** *Gymnastics.* to raise one's chin to (a horizontal bar, etc.) when hanging by the arms. [Old English *cinn;* related to Old Norse *kinn,* Old High German *kinni,* Latin *gena* cheek, Old Irish *gin* mouth, Sanskrit *hanu*]

Chin. *abbrev. for:* **1.** China. **2.** Chinese.

chi·na¹ ('tʃaɪnə) *n.* **1.** ceramic ware of a type originally from China. **2.** any porcelain or similar ware. **3.** cups, saucers, etc., collectively. **4.** (*modifier*) made of china. [C16 *chiny,* from Persian *chīnī*]

chi·na² ('tʃaɪnə) *n. Brit. slang.* mate; pal (esp. in the phrase **my old china**). [C19: originally Cockney rhyming slang: *china plate, mate*]

Chi·na ('tʃaɪnə) *n.* **1. Peo·ple's Re·pub·lic of.** Also called: **Communist China, Red China.** a republic in E Asia: the third largest and the most populous country in the world; the oldest continuing civilization (beginning over 2000 years B.C.); republic established in 1911 after the overthrow of the Manchu dynasty by Sun Yat-sen; People's Republic formed in 1949; contains vast deserts, steppes, great mountain ranges (Himalayas, Kunlun, Tien Shan, and Nan Shan), a central rugged plateau, and intensively cultivated E plains. Language: Chinese in various dialects, the chief of which is Mandarin. Currency: yuan. Capital: Peking. Pop.: 824 961 000 (1974 UN est.). Area: 9 560 990 sq. km (3 691 502 sq. miles). **2. Re·pub·lic of.** Also called: **Nationalist China, Taiwan.** a republic in E Asia occupying the island of Taiwan, 13 nearby islands, and 64 islands of the Penghu (Pescadores) group: established in 1949 by the Nationalist government of China under Chiang Kai-shek after its expulsion by the Communists from the mainland; under U.S. protection 1954-79. Language: Mandarin Chinese. Religion: predominantly Buddhist and Taoist. Currency: New Taiwan dollar. Capital: Taipei. Pop.: 14 035 000 (1970 UN est.). Area: 35 981 sq. km (13 892 sq. miles). Former name: **Formosa.** ~Related adj.: **Sinitic.**

Chi·na as·ter *n.* a Chinese plant, *Callistephus chinensis,* widely cultivated for its aster-like flowers: family *Compositae* (composites).

chi·na bark *n.* another name for **cinchona** (sense 2).

chi·na·ber·ry ('tʃaɪnəbərɪ) *n., pl.* **·ries. 1.** Also called: **China tree, azedarach.** a spreading Asian meliaceous tree, *Melia azedarach,* widely grown in the U.S. for its ornamental white or purple flowers and beadlike yellow fruits. **2.** another name for **soapberry. 3.** the fruit of any of these trees.

chi·na clay *or* **stone** *n.* another name for **kaolin.**

Chi·na·graph ('tʃaɪnəˌgrɑːf, -ˌgræf) *n. Trademark.* **a.** a coloured pencil used for writing on china, glass, etc. **b.** (*as modifier*): *a Chinagraph pencil.*

Chi·na·man ('tʃaɪnəmən) *n., pl.* **·men. 1.** a native or inhabitant of China. **2.** *Cricket.* a ball bowled by a left-handed bowler to a right-handed batsman that spins from off to leg.

Chi·nan ('tʃiː'næn) *n.* a variant spelling of **Tsinan.**

Chi·na rose *n.* **1.** a rosaceous shrub, *Rosa chinensis* (or *R. indica*), with red, pink, or white fragrant flowers: the ancestor of many cultivated roses. **2.** a related dwarf plant, *Rosa semperflorens,* having crimson flowers. **3.** another name for **hibiscus.**

Chi·na Sea *n.* part of the Pacific Ocean off the coast of China: divided by Taiwan into the East China Sea in the north and the South China Sea in the south.

Chi·na·town ('tʃaɪnəˌtaʊn) *n.* a quarter of any city or town outside China with a predominantly Chinese population.

Chi·na tree *n.* another name for **chinaberry** (sense 1).

chi·na·ware ('tʃaɪnəˌwɛə) *n.* **1.** articles made of china, esp. those made for domestic use. **2.** (*modifier*) made of china.

chin·ca·pin ('tʃɪŋkəpɪn) *n.* a variant spelling of **chinquapin.**

chinch (tʃɪntʃ) *n. Southern U.S.* another name for a **bedbug.** [C17: from Spanish *chinche,* from Latin *cīmex* bug]

chinch bug *n.* **1.** a black-and-white tropical American heteropterous insect, *Blissus leucopterus,* that is very destructive to grasses and cereals in the U.S.: family *Lygaeidae.* **2.** a related and similar European insect, *Ischnodemus sabuleti.*

chin+che+rin+chee (ˌtʃɪntʃərɪn'tʃiː, -'rɪntʃɪ) *n.* a bulbous South African liliaceous plant, *Ornithogalum thyrsoides,* having long spikes of white or yellow long-lasting flowers. [of unknown origin]

chin+chil+la (tʃɪn'tʃɪlə) *n.* **1.** a small gregarious hystricomorph rodent, *Chinchilla laniger,* inhabiting mountainous regions of South America: family *Chinchillidae.* It has a stocky body and is bred in captivity for its soft silvery grey fur. **2.** the highly valued fur of this animal. **3. mountain chinchilla.** Also called: **mountain viscacha.** any of several long-tailed rodents of the genus *Lagidium,* having coarse poor quality fur. **4.** a thick napped woollen cloth used for coats. [C17: from Spanish, perhaps from Aymara]

chin-chin *interj. Informal.* a greeting, farewell, or toast. [C18: from Chinese (Peking) *ch'ing-ch'ing,* please-please]

Chin-Chou *or* **Chin+chow** ('tʃɪn'tʃaʊ) *n.* a city in NE China, in SW Liaoning province. Pop.: 352 200 (1953). Former name (1913–47): **Chin-hsien.**

chin cough *n.* another name for **whooping cough.** [C16: changed (through influence from CHINE and CHIN) from earlier *chink-cough,* from CHINK² + COUGH]

Chin+dit ('tʃɪndɪt) *n.* a member of the Allied forces fighting against the Japanese in Burma (1943–45). [C20: from Burmese *chinthé* a fabulous lion; adoption of title perhaps influenced by CHINDWIN]

Chin+dwin ('tʃɪn'dwɪn) *n.* a river in N Burma, rising in the Kumôn Range and flowing northwest then south to the Irrawaddy, of which it is the main tributary. Length: about 966 km (600 miles).

chine¹ (tʃaɪn) *n.* **1.** the backbone. **2.** the backbone of an animal with adjoining meat, cut for cooking. **3.** a ridge or crest of land. **4.** (in some boats) a corner-like intersection where the bottom meets the side. ~*vb.* **5.** (*tr.*) to cut (meat) along or across the backbone. [C14: from Old French *eschine,* of Germanic origin; compare Old High German *scina* needle, shinbone; see SHIN]

chine² (tʃaɪn) *n.* another word for **chime².**

chine³ (tʃaɪn) *n. Southern Brit. dialect.* a deep fissure in the wall of a cliff. [Old English *cīnan* to crack]

chi+né ('ʃiːneɪ) *adj. Textiles.* having a mottled pattern. [C19: from French *chiner* to make in the Chinese fashion, from *Chine* China]

Chi+nee (tʃaɪ'niː) *n. Informal.* a Chinaman.

Chi+nese (tʃaɪ'niːz) *adj.* **1.** of, relating to, or characteristic of China, its people, or their languages. ~*n.* **2.** (*pl.* **+nese**) a native or inhabitant of China or a descendant of one. **3.** any of the languages of China belonging to the Sino-Tibetan family, sometimes regarded as dialects of one language. They share a single writing system that is not phonetic but ideographic. A phonetic system using the Roman alphabet was officially adopted by the Chinese government in 1966. See also **Mandarin Chinese, Pekingese, Cantonese.**

Chi+nese block *n.* a percussion instrument consisting of a hollow wooden block played with a drumstick.

Chi+nese cab+bage *n.* **1.** Also called: **pe-tsai cabbage.** a Chinese plant, *Brassica pekinensis,* that is related to the cabbage and has crisp edible leaves growing in a loose cylindrical head. **2.** Also called: **pak-choi cabbage.** a similar and related plant, *Brassica chinensis.*

Chi+nese cheq+uers *n.* a board game played with marbles or pegs.

Chi+nese Chip+pen+dale *n.* **a.** a branch of Chippendale style in which Chinese styles and motifs are used. **b.** (*as modifier*): *a Chinese Chippendale cabinet.*

Chi+nese cop·y *n.* an exact copy of an original.

Chi+nese ed·do *n.* another name for **taro.**

Chi+nese Em+pire *n.* China as ruled by the emperors until the establishment of the republic in 1911–12.

Chi+nese lan+tern *n.* **1.** a collapsible lantern made of thin coloured paper. **2.** an Asian solanaceous plant, *Physalis franchetii,* cultivated for its attractive orange-red inflated calyx. See also **winter cherry.**

Chi+nese puz+zle *n.* **1.** an intricate puzzle, esp. one consisting of boxes within boxes. **2.** a complicated problem.

Chi+nese red *n., adj.* (**Chinese-red** *when prenominal*). **a.** a bright red colour. **b.** (*as adj.*): *a Chinese-red bag.*

Chi+nese Rev·o+lu+tion *n.* **1.** the overthrow of the last Manchu emperor and the establishment of a republic in China (1911–1912). **2.** the transformation of China (esp. in the 1940s and 1950s) under the Chinese Communist Party.

Chi+nese sa+cred lil·y *n.* a Chinese amaryllidaceous plant, *Narcissus tazetta orientalis,* widely grown as a house plant for its fragrant yellow and white flowers. See also **polyanthus** (sense 2).

Chi+nese Tur+ke·stan *n.* the E part of the central Asian region of Turkestan: corresponds generally to the present-day Sinkiang-Uighur Autonomous Region of China.

Chi+nese wall *n.* an insurmountable obstacle.

Chi+nese wa+ter tor+ture *n.* a form of torture in which water is made to drip onto a victim's forehead to drive him insane.

Chi+nese wax *or* **tree+wax** *n.* a yellowish wax secreted by an oriental scale insect, *Ceroplastes ceriferus,* and used commercially.

Chi+nese white *n.* white zinc oxide, formerly used in paints. Also called: **zinc white.**

Chi+nese wind+lass *n.* another name for **differential windlass.**

Chi+nese wood oil *n.* another name for **tung oil.**

Ching *or* **Ch'ing** (tʃɪŋ) *adj.* of, relating to, or designating the Manchu dynasty (1644–1912) of China.

Ching+hai *or* **Ch'ing-hai** ('tʃɪŋ'haɪ) *n.* variant spellings of **Tsinghai.**

Ching+tao *or* **Ch'ing-tao** ('tʃɪŋ'taʊ) *n.* variant spellings of **Tsingtao.**

Ch'ing-yü·an ('tʃɪŋ'juːɑːn) *n.* a variant spelling of **Tsingyuan.**

Chin Hills (tʃɪn) *pl. n.* a mountainous region of W Burma: part of the Arakan Yoma system. Highest peak: Mount Victoria, 3053 m (10 075 ft.).

Chin-Hsien ('tʃɪn'ʃjɛn) *n.* the former name (1913–47) of **Chin-Chou.**

chink¹ (tʃɪŋk) *n.* **1.** a small narrow opening, such as a fissure or crack. **2. chink in one's armour.** a small but fatal weakness. ~*vb.* **3.** (*tr.*) *Chiefly U.S.* to fill up or make cracks in. [C16: perhaps variant of earlier *chine,* from Old English *cine* crack; related to Middle Dutch *kene,* Danish *kin*] —**'chink·y** *adj.*

chink² (tʃɪŋk) *vb.* **1.** to make or cause to make a light ringing sound, as by the striking of glasses or coins. ~*n.* **2.** such a sound. [C16: of imitative origin]

Chink (tʃɪŋk) *n., adj.* a derogatory term for **Chinese.** [C20: probably from *Chinese,* influenced by CHINK¹ (referring to the characteristic shape of the Chinese eye)]

chin+ka+pin ('tʃɪŋkəpɪn) *n.* a variant spelling of **chinquapin.**

Chin+kiang ('tʃɪn'kjæŋ, -kaɪ'æŋ) *or* **Cheng-chiang** ('tʃɛŋ'tʃæŋ) *n.* a port in E China, in S Kiangsu at the confluence of the Yangtze River and the Grand Canal. Pop.: 201 400 (1953).

chin+less ('tʃɪnlɪs) *adj.* weak or ineffectual.

chin+less won+der *n. Brit. informal.* a person, esp. an upper-class one, lacking strength of character.

chi+no ('tʃiːnəʊ) *n., pl.* **+nos.** *U.S.* a durable cotton twill cloth. [C20: from American Spanish, of obscure origin]

Chi·no- *combining form.* of or relating to China. See also **Sino-.**

chi+noi+se·rie (ʃiːnˌwɑːzə'riː, -'wɑːzərɪ) *n.* **1.** a style of decorative or fine art based on imitations of Chinese motifs. **2.** an object or objects in this style. [French, from *chinois* CHINESE; see -ERY]

chi+nook (tʃɪ'nuːk, -'nʊk) *n.* **1.** Also called: **snow eater.** a warm dry southwesterly wind blowing down the eastern slopes of the Rocky Mountains. **2.** Also called: **wet chinook.** a warm moist wind blowing onto the Washington and Oregon coasts from the sea. [C19: from Salish *c'inuk*]

Chi+nook (tʃɪ'nuːk, -'nʊk) *n.* **1.** (*pl.* **+nook** *or* **+nooks**) a North American Indian people of the Pacific coast near the Columbia River. **2.** the Chinookan language of this people.

Chi+nook+an (tʃɪ'nuːkən, -'nʊk-) *n.* a family of North American Indian languages of the northwestern U.S.

Chi+nook Jar+gon *n.* a pidgin language containing elements of North American Indian languages, English, and French: formerly used among fur traders and Indians on the NW coast of North America.

Chi+nook sal+mon *n.* a Pacific salmon, *Oncorhynchus tschawytscha,* valued as a food fish. Also called: **quinnat salmon, king salmon.**

chin+qua+pin, chin+ca+pin, *or* **chin+ka+pin** ('tʃɪŋkəpɪn) *n.* **1.** a dwarf chestnut tree, *Castanea pumila,* of the eastern U.S., yielding edible nuts. **2.** Also called: **giant chinquapin.** a large evergreen fagaceous tree, *Castanopsis chrysophylla,* of W North America. **3.** the nut of either of these trees. ~Compare **water chinquapin.** [C17: of Algonquian origin; compare Algonquian *chechinkamin* chestnut]

chintz (tʃɪnts) *n.* **1.** a printed, patterned cotton fabric, with glazed finish. **2.** a painted or stained Indian calico. [C17: from Hindi *chīnt,* from Sanskrit *citra* gaily-coloured]

chintz·y ('tʃɪntsɪ) *adj.* **chintz·i·er, chintz·i·est. 1.** of, resembling, or covered with chintz. **2.** *Brit. informal.* typical of the decor associated with the use of chintz soft furnishings, as in a country cottage.

chin+wag ('tʃɪnˌwæg) *n. Brit. informal.* a chat or gossipy conversation.

chi+on·o·dox·a (kaɪˌɒnə'dɒksə) *n.* any plant of the liliaceous genus *Chionodoxa,* of S Europe and W Asia. See **glory-of-the-snow.** [C19: New Latin, from Greek *khiōn* snow + *doxa* glory]

Chi·os ('kaɪɒs, -əʊs, 'kiː-) *n.* **1.** an island in the Aegean Sea, off the coast of Turkey: belongs to Greece. Capital: Chios. Pop.: 53 948 (1971). Area: 904 sq. km (353 sq. miles). **2.** a port on the island of Chios: in ancient times, one of the 12 Ionian city states. Pop.: 24 084 (1971). Modern Greek name: **Khíos.**

chip (tʃɪp) *n.* **1.** a small piece removed by chopping, cutting, or breaking. **2.** a mark left after a small piece has been chopped, cut, or broken off something. **3.** (in some games) a counter used to represent money. **4.** a thin strip of potato fried in deep fat. **5.** the U.S. name for **crisp** (sense 10). **6.** a small piece or thin slice of food. **7.** *Sport.* a shot, kick, etc., lofted into the air, esp. over an obstacle or an opposing player's head, and travelling only a short distance. **8.** *Electronics.* a tiny wafer of semiconductor material, such as silicon, processed to form a type of integrated circuit or component such as a transistor. **9.** a thin strip of wood or straw used for making woven hats, baskets, etc. **10. chip off the old block.** *Informal.* a person who resembles one of his or her parents in behaviour. **11. have a chip on one's shoulder.** *Informal.* to be aggressively sensitive about a particular thing or bear a grudge. **12. have had one's**

chips. *Brit. informal.* to be defeated, condemned to die, killed, etc. **13. when the chips are down.** *Informal.* at a time of crisis or testing. ~*vb.* **chips, chip+ping, chipped. 14.** to break small pieces from or become broken off in small pieces: *will the paint chip?* **15.** (*tr.*) to break or cut into small pieces: *to chip ice.* **16.** (*tr.*) to shape by chipping. **17.** *Sport.* to strike or kick (a ball) in a high arc. [Old English *cipp* (n.), *cippian* (vb.), of obscure origin] —**'chip+per** *n.*

chip bas+ket *n.* **1.** a wire basket for holding potato chips, etc., while frying in deep fat. **2.** a basket made of thin strips of wood, used esp. for packing fruit.

chip+board ('tʃɪpˌbɔ:d) *n.* a thin rigid sheet made of compressed wood particles bound with a synthetic resin.

chip in *vb.* (*adv.*) *Informal.* **1.** to contribute (money, time, etc.) to a cause or fund. **2.** (*intr.*) interpose a remark or interrupt with a remark.

chip log *n. Nautical.* a log for determining a vessel's speed, consisting of a wooden chip tossed overboard at the end of a line that is marked off in lengths of 47 feet 3 inches; the speed is calculated by counting the number of such intervals that pass overboard in a 28-second interval.

chip+munk ('tʃɪpˌmʌŋk) *n.* any burrowing sciurine rodent of the genera *Tamias* of E North America and *Eutamias* of W North America and Asia, typically having black-striped yellowish fur and cheek pouches for storing food. [C19: of Algonquian origin; compare Ojibwa *atchitamon* squirrel, literally: head first, referring to its method of descent from trees]

chip·o+la+ta (ˌtʃɪpə'lɑ:tə) *n. Chiefly Brit.* a small sausage in a narrow casing. [via French from Italian *cipollata* an onion-flavoured dish, from *cipolla* onion]

chip pan *n.* a deep pan for frying potato chips, etc.

Chip·pen·dale ('tʃɪpᵊnˌdeɪl) *n.* **1. Thom·as.** ?1718–79, English cabinet-maker and furniture designer. ~*adj.* **2.** (of furniture) designed, made by, or in the style of Thomas Chippendale, characterized by the use of Chinese and Gothic motifs, cabriole legs, and massive carving.

chip+per ('tʃɪpə) *adj. Informal, chiefly U.S.* **1.** cheerful; lively. **2.** smartly dressed.

Chip+pe+wa ('tʃɪpɪˌwɑ:) *or* **Chip+pe+way** *n., pl.* **+was, +wa** *or* **+ways, +way.** another name for **Ojibwa.**

chip+ping ('tʃɪpɪŋ) *n.* another name for **chip** (sense 1).

chip+ping spar+row *n.* a common North American sparrow, *Spizella passerina,* having brown-and-grey plumage and a white eye stripe.

chip+py[1] ('tʃɪpɪ) *n., pl.* **+pies.** *Brit.* **1.** a slang word for **carpenter. 2.** *Informal.* a fish-and-chip shop. [C19: from CHIP (n.)]

chip+py[2] *or* **chip+pie** ('tʃɪpɪ) *n., pl.* **+pies.** an informal name for **chipmunk** or **chipping sparrow.**

chip+py[3] *or* **chip+pie** ('tʃɪpɪ) *n., pl.* **+pies.** *Informal, chiefly U.S.* a promiscuous woman. [C19: perhaps from CHIP (n.)]

chip+py[4] ('tʃɪpɪ) *adj.* **+pi+er, +pi+est.** *Canadian.* belligerent or touchy. [C19: from CHIP (n.), sense probably developing from: as dry as a chip of wood, hence irritable, touchy]

chip shot *n. Golf.* a short approach shot to the green, esp. one that is lofted.

Chi·rac (*French* ʃi'rak) *n.* **Jacques (René)** (ʒa:k). born 1932, French Gaullist politician: prime minister of France (1974–76); mayor of Paris since 1977.

Chi·rau (tʃɪ'raʊ) *n.* Chief **Je·re·mi·ah.** born ?1926, Rhodesian politician; leader of the Zimbabwe United People's Organization. He was one of the negotiators of the internal settlement (1978) to pave the way for black majority rule in Rhodesia.

Chi·ri·co (*Italian* 'ki:riko) *n.* **Gior·gio de** ('dʒordʒo de). 1888–1978, Italian artist born in Greece: profoundly influenced the surrealist movement.

chirm (tʃɜ:m) *n.* **1.** the chirping of birds. ~*vb.* **2.** (*intr.*) (esp. of a bird) to chirp. [Old English *cierm* noise; related to Old Saxon *karm*]

chi·ro- *or* **chei·ro-** *combining form.* indicating the hand; of or by means of the hand: *chiromancy; chiropractic.* [via Latin from Greek *kheir* hand]

chi+rog+ra+phy (kaɪ'rɒgrəfɪ) *n.* another name for **calligraphy.** —**chi+'rog+ra+pher** *n.* —**chi+ro+graph+ic** (ˌkaɪrə'græfɪk) *or* **ˌchi+ro+'graph·i·cal** *adj.*

chi+ro+man+cy ('kaɪrəˌmænsɪ) *n.* another word for **palmistry.** —**'chi+ro+ˌman+cer** *n.*

Chi·ron *or* **Chei·ron** ('kaɪrɒn, -rən) *n.* **1.** *Greek myth.* a wise and kind centaur who taught many great heroes in their youth, including Achilles, Actaeon, and Jason. **2.** a minor planet, discovered by Charles Kowal in 1977, revolving round the sun between the orbits of Saturn and Uranus.

chi+rop·o+dy (kɪ'rɒpədɪ) *n.* the treatment of the feet, esp. the treatment of corns, verrucas, etc. —**chi+'rop·o·dist** *n.*

chi+ro+prac+tic (ˌkaɪrə'præktɪk) *n.* a system of treating bodily disorders by manipulation of the spine and other parts, based on the belief that the cause is the abnormal functioning of a nerve. [C20: from CHIRO- + *-practic,* from Greek *praktikos* effective, PRACTICAL] —**'chi+ro+ˌprac+tor** *n.*

chi+rop+ter+an (kaɪ'rɒptərən) *adj.* **1.** of, relating to, or belonging to the *Chiroptera,* an order of placental mammals comprising the bats. ~*n.* **2.** Also called: **chi+rop+ter** (kaɪ'rɒptə) a bat.

chirp (tʃɜ:p) *vb.* **1.** (*intr.*) (esp. of some birds and insects) to make a short high-pitched sound. **2.** to speak in a lively fashion. ~*n.* **3.** a chirping sound, esp. that made by a bird. [C15 (as *chirpinge,* gerund): of imitative origin] —**'chirp+er** *n.* —**'chirp·y** *adj.* —**'chirp·i+ly** *adv.* —**'chirp·i+ness** *n.*

chirr, chirre, *or* **churr** (tʃɜ:) *vb.* **1.** (*intr.*) (esp. of certain insects, such as crickets) to make a shrill trilled sound. ~*n.* **2.** the sound of chirring. [C17: of imitative origin]

chir+rup ('tʃɪrəp) *vb.* **1.** (*intr.*) (esp. of some birds) to chirp repeatedly. **2.** to make clucking sounds with the lips. ~*n.* **3.** such a sound. [C16: variant of CHIRP] —**'chir+rup+er** *n.* —**'chir+rup·y** *adj.*

chi+rur+geon (kaɪ'rɜ:dʒən) *n.* an archaic word for **surgeon.** [C13: from Old French *cirurgeon*] —**chi+'rur+ger·y** *n.*

chis+el ('tʃɪzᵊl) *n.* **1. a.** a hand tool for working wood, consisting of a flat steel blade with a cutting edge attached to a handle of wood, plastic, etc. It is either struck with a mallet or used by hand. **b.** a similar tool without a handle for working stone or metal. ~*vb.* **+els, +el+ling, +elled** *or U.S.* **+els, +el+ing, +eled. 2.** to carve (wood, stone, metal, etc.) or form (an engraving, statue, etc.) with or as with a chisel. **3.** *Slang.* to cheat or obtain by cheating. [C14: via Old French, from Vulgar Latin *cīsellus* (unattested), from Latin *caesus* cut, from *caedere* to cut] —**'chis+el+ler** *n.*

chis+elled *or U.S.* **chis+eled** ('tʃɪzəld) *adj.* **1.** carved or formed with or as if with a chisel. **2.** clear-cut: *finely chiselled features.*

Chi+shi+ma (ˌtʃi:ʃi:'ma) *n.* the Japanese name for the **Kuril Islands.**

Chi+si+ma·io (ˌki:zɪ'mɑ:jəʊ) *n.* a port in S Somalia, on the Indian Ocean. Pop.: 30 000 (1972 est.). Also called: **Kismayu.**

Chi+şi+nău (kiʃi'nəʊ) *n.* the Rumanian name for **Kishinev.**

chi-square dis+tri+bu+tion ('kaɪˌskwɛə) *n. Statistics.* a continuous single-parameter distribution derived as a special case of the gamma distribution and used esp. to measure goodness of fit and to test hypotheses and obtain confidence intervals for the variance of a normally distributed variable.

chi-square test *n. Statistics.* a test derived from the chi-square distribution to compare the goodness of fit of theoretical and observed frequency distributions.

chit[1] (tʃɪt) *n.* **1.** a voucher for a sum of money owed, esp. for food or drink. **2.** Also called: **chitty.** *Chiefly Brit.* **a.** a note or memorandum. **b.** a requisition or receipt. [C18: from earlier *chitty,* from Hindi *cittha* note, from Sanskrit *citra* brightly-coloured]

chit[2] (tʃɪt) *n. Facetious or derogatory.* a pert, impudent, or self-confident girl or child. [C14 (in the sense: young of an animal, kitten): of obscure origin]

Chi+ta (*Russian* tʃi'ta) *n.* an industrial city in the SE central Soviet Union, on the Trans-Siberian railway. Pop.: 242 000 (1971).

chi+tal ('tʃi:tᵊl) *n.* another name for **axis**[2] (the deer). [from Hindi]

chi+tar+ro+ne (ˌkɪtɑ:'rəʊnɪ, ˌtʃɪt-) *n., pl.* **+ni** (-nɪ). a large lute with a double neck in common use during the baroque period, esp. in Italy. [Italian, from *chitarra,* from Greek *kithara* lyre]

chit+chat ('tʃɪtˌtʃæt) *n.* **1.** talk of a gossipy nature. ~*vb.* **+chats, +chat+ting, +chat+ted. 2.** (*intr.*) to gossip.

chi+tin ('kaɪtɪn) *n.* a polysaccharide that is the principal component of the exoskeletons of arthropods and of the bodies of fungi. [C19: from French *chitine,* from Greek *khitōn* CHITON + -IN] —**'chi+tin+ous** *adj.* —**'chi+tin+ˌoid** *adj.*

chi+ton ('kaɪtᵊn, -tɒn) *n.* **1.** (in ancient Greece and Rome) a loose woollen tunic worn knee length by men and full length by women. **2.** Also called: **coat-of-mail shell.** any small primitive marine mollusc of the genus *Chiton* and related genera, having an elongated body covered with eight overlapping shell plates: class *Amphineura.* [C19: from Greek *khitōn* coat of mail, of Semitic origin; related to Hebrew *kethōnet*]

Chit+ta+gong ('tʃɪtəˌgɒŋ) *n.* a port in E Bangladesh, on the Bay of Bengal: industrial centre. Pop.: 889 760 (1974).

chit+ter ('tʃɪtə) *vb.* (*intr.*) **1.** *Chiefly U.S.* to twitter or chirp. **2.** a dialect word for **shiver** or (of the teeth) **chatter.** [C14: of imitative origin]

chit+ter+lings ('tʃɪtəlɪŋz), **chit+lins** ('tʃɪtlɪnz), *or* **chit+lings** ('tʃɪtlɪŋz) *pl. n.* (*sometimes sing.*) the intestines of a pig or other animal prepared as a dish. [C13: of uncertain origin; perhaps related to Middle High German *kutel*]

chiv (tʃɪv) *n. Slang.* **1.** a knife. ~*vb.* **chivs, chiv+ving, chivved. 2.** to stab (someone). [C17: of unknown origin]

chiv+al+rous ('ʃɪvəlrəs) *adj.* **1.** gallant; courteous. **2.** involving chivalry. [C14: from Old French *chevalerous,* from CHEVALIER] —**'chiv+al+rous+ly** *adv.* —**'chiv+al+rous+ness** *n.*

chiv+al+ry ('ʃɪvəlrɪ) *n., pl.* **+ries. 1.** the combination of qualities expected of an ideal knight, esp. courage, honour, justice, and a readiness to help the weak. **2.** courteous behaviour, esp. towards women. **3.** the medieval system and principles of knighthood. **4.** knights, noblemen, etc., collectively. [C13: from Old French *chevalerie,* from CHEVALIER] —**'chiv+al+ric** *adj.*

chiv·a+ree (ˌʃɪvə'ri:, 'ʃɪvəˌri:) *n.* a U.S. spelling of **charivari.**

chive (tʃaɪv) *n.* a small Eurasian purple-flowered alliaceous plant, *Allium schoenoprasum,* whose long slender hollow leaves are used in cooking to flavour soups, stews, etc. Also called: **chives.** [C14: from Old French *cive,* ultimately from Latin *caepa* onion]

chiv·y, chiv+vy ('tʃɪvɪ), *or* **chev·y** *vb.* **chiv·ies, chiv·y+ing, chiv+ied, chiv+vies, chiv+vy+ing, chiv+vied,** *or* **chev·ies, chev·y+ing, chev+ied.** *Brit.* **1.** (*tr.*) to harass or nag. **2.** (*tr.*) to hunt. **3.** (*intr.*) to run about. ~*n., pl.* **chiv·ies, chiv+vies,** *or* **chev·ies. 4.** *Brit.* a hunt. **5.** *Brit. obsolete.* a hunting cry. [C19: variant of *chevy,* probably from *Chevy Chase,* title of a Scottish border ballad]

Chka+lov (*Russian* 'tʃkaləf) *n.* the former name (1938–58) of **Orenburg.**

chlam·y+date ('klæmɪˌdeɪt) *adj.* (of some molluscs) possessing a mantle. [C19: from Latin *chlamydātus* wearing a mantle, from Greek *khlamus* mantle]

chla+myd+e·ous (klə'mɪdɪəs) *adj.* (of plants) relating to or possessing sepals and petals.

chla+myd·o+spore (klæ'mɪdə,spɔ:) *n.* a thick-walled asexual spore of many fungi: capable of surviving adverse conditions.

Chlod·wig ('klo:tvɪç) *n.* the German name for **Clovis I.**

Chlo·e ('kləʊɪ) *n.* See **Daphnis and Chloe.**

chlor- *combining form.* variant of **chloro-** before a vowel.

chlor+ac·ne (klɔ:'ræknɪ) *n.* a disfiguring skin disease that results from contact with or ingestion or inhalation of certain chlorinated aromatic hydrocarbons. [C20: from CHLORO- + ACNE]

chlo+ral ('klɔ:rəl) *n.* **1.** a colourless oily liquid with a pungent odour, made from chlorine and acetaldehyde and used in preparing chloral hydrate and DDT; trichloroacetaldehyde. **2.** short for **chloral hydrate.**

chlo+ral hy+drate *n.* a colourless crystalline soluble solid produced by the reaction of chloral with water and used as a sedative and hypnotic; 2,2,2-trichloro-1,1-ethanediol. Formula: $CCl_3CH(OH)_2$.

chlo+ram+bu+cil (klɔ:'ræmbjʊsɪl) *n.* a drug derived from nitrogen mustard, administered orally in the treatment of leukaemia and other malignant diseases. Formula: $C_{14}H_{19}Cl_2NO_2$.

chlo+ra+mine ('klɔ:rə,mi:n) *n.* **1.** an unstable colourless liquid with a pungent odour, made by the reaction of sodium hypochlorite and ammonia. Formula: NH_2Cl. **2.** any compound produced by replacing hydrogen atoms in an azo or amine group with chlorine atoms.

chlo+ram+phen·i+col (,klɔ:ræm'fɛnɪ,kɒl) *n.* a broad-spectrum antibiotic used esp. in treating typhoid fever and rickettsial infections: obtained from the bacterium *Streptomyces venezuelae* or synthesized. Formula: $C_{11}H_{12}N_2O_5Cl_2$. [C20: from CHLORO- + AM(IDO)- + PHE(NO)- + NI(TRO)- + (GLY)-COL]

chlo+rate ('klɔ:reɪt, -rɪt) *n.* any salt of chloric acid, containing the monovalent ion ClO_3^-.

chlor+dane ('klɔ:deɪn) *or* **chlor+dan** *n.* a white insoluble toxic solid existing in several isomeric forms and usually used, as an insecticide, in the form of a brown impure liquid. Formula: $C_{10}H_6Cl_8$. [C20: from CHLORO- + (IN)D(ENE) + -ANE]

chlo+rel+la (klɔ:'rɛlə, klə-) *n.* any microscopic unicellular green alga of the genus *Chlorella:* some species are used in the preparation of human food. [C19: from New Latin, from CHLORO- + Latin *-ella* diminutive suffix]

chlo+ren+chy+ma (klə'rɛŋkɪmə) *n.* plant tissue consisting of parenchyma cells that contain chlorophyll. [C19: from CHLOR(OPHYLL) + -ENCHYMA]

chlo+ric ('klɔ:rɪk) *adj.* of or containing chlorine in the pentavalent state.

chlo+ric ac·id *n.* a strong acid with a pungent smell, known only in solution and in the form of chlorate salts. Formula: $HClO_3$.

chlo+ride ('klɔ:raɪd) *n.* **1.** any salt of hydrochloric acid, containing the chloride ion Cl^-. **2.** any compound containing a chlorine atom, such as methyl chloride, CH_3Cl. —**chlo+rid+ic** (klə'rɪdɪk) *adj.*

chlo+ride of lime *or* **chlo+rin+at+ed lime** *n.* another name for **bleaching powder.**

chlo+rin+ate ('klɔ:rɪ,neɪt) *vb.* (*tr.*) **1.** to combine or treat (a substance) with chlorine. **2.** to disinfect (water) with chlorine. —,**chlo+rin·'a+tion** *n.* —'**chlo+rin·,a+tor** *n.*

chlo+rine ('klɔ:ri:n) *or* **chlo+rin** ('klɔ:rɪn) *n.* a toxic pungent greenish-yellow gas of the halogen group; the 15th most abundant element in the earth's crust, occurring only in the combined state, mainly in common salt: used in the manufacture of many organic chemicals, in water purification, and as a disinfectant and bleaching agent. Symbol: Cl; atomic no.: 17; atomic wt.: 35.453; valency: 1, 3, 5, or 7; density: 3.214 kg/m^3; melting pt.: –100.98°C; boiling pt.: –34.6°C. [C19 (coined by Sir Humphrey Davy): from CHLORO- + -INE[2], referring to its colour]

chlo+rite[1] ('klɔ:raɪt) *n.* any of a group of green soft secondary minerals consisting of the hydrated silicates of aluminium, iron, and magnesium in monoclinic crystalline form: common in metamorphic rocks. [C18: from Latin *chlōrītis* precious stone of a green colour, from Greek *khlōritis,* from *khlōros* greenish yellow] —**chlo+'rit+ic** (klɔ:'rɪtɪk) *adj.*

chlo+rite[2] ('klɔ:raɪt) *n.* any salt of chlorous acid, containing the monovalent ion ClO_2^-.

chlo·ro- *or before a vowel* **chlor-** *combining form.* **1.** indicating the colour green: *chlorophyll.* **2.** chlorine: *chloroform.*

chlo+ro·a+ce·tic ac·id (,klɔ:rəʊə'si:tɪk) *or* **chlor·a+ce·tic ac·id** (,klɔ:rə'si:tɪk) *n.* **1.** a colourless crystalline soluble strong acid prepared by chlorinating acetic acid and used as an intermediate in the manufacture of many chemicals; monochloracetic acid. Formula: $CH_2ClCOOH$. **2.** either of two related compounds: **dichloracetic acid,** $CHCl_2COOH$, or **trichloracetic acid,** CCl_3COOH.

chlo+ro+ben+zene ('klɔ:rəʊ'bɛnzi:n) *n.* a colourless volatile flammable insoluble liquid with an almond-like odour, made from chlorine and benzene and used as a solvent and in the preparation of many organic compounds, esp. phenol and DDT. Formula: C_6H_5Cl.

chlo+ro+form ('klɔ:rə,fɔ:m) *n.* a heavy volatile liquid with a sweet taste and odour, used as a solvent and cleansing agent and in refrigerants: formerly used as an inhalation anaesthetic. Formula: $CHCl_3$. [C19: from CHLORO- + FORM(YL) (in an obsolete sense that applied to a CH radical)]

chlo+ro+hy+drin (,klɔ:rəʊ'haɪdrɪn) *n.* **1.** any of a class of organic compounds containing a hydroxyl group and a chlorine atom. **2.** a colourless unstable hygroscopic liquid that is used mainly as a solvent; 3-chloropropane-1,2-diol. Formula: $CH_2OHCHOHCH_2Cl$. [C20: from CHLORO- + HYDRO- + -IN]

Chlo+ro+my+ce+tin (,klɔ:rəʊmaɪ'si:tɪn) *n. Trademark.* a brand of **chloramphenicol.**

chlo+ro+phyll *or U.S.* **chlo+ro+phyl** ('klɔ:rəfɪl) *n.* the green pigment of plants, occurring in chloroplasts, that traps the energy of sunlight for photosynthesis and exists in several forms, the most abundant being **chlorophyll a** ($C_{55}H_{72}O_5N_4Mg$): used as a colouring agent. —'**chlo+ro+,phyl+loid** *adj.* —**chlo+ro+phyl+lous** (,klɔ:rəʊ'fɪləs) *adj.*

chlo+ro+pic+rin (,klɔ:rəʊ'pɪkrɪn) *or* **chlor+pic+rin** *n.* a colourless insoluble toxic lachrymatory liquid used as a pesticide and a tear gas; nitrotrichloromethane. Formula: CCl_3NO_2. [C20: from CHLORO- + PICRO- + -IN]

chlo+ro+plast ('klɔ:rəʊ,plæst) *n.* a plastid containing chlorophyll and other pigments, occurring in plants that carry out photosynthesis. —,**chlo+ro+'plast+ic** *adj.*

chlo+ro+prene ('klɔ:rəʊ,pri:n) *n.* a colourless liquid derivative of butadiene that is used in making neoprene rubbers; 2-chloro-1,2-butadiene. Formula: $CH_2:CHCCl:CH_2$. [C20: from CHLORO- + (ISO)PRENE]

chlo+ro+quine ('klɔ:rəʊ,kwi:n) *n.* a synthetic drug administered orally to treat malaria. Formula: $C_{18}H_{26}ClN_3$. [C20: from CHLORO- + QUIN(OLINE)]

chlo+ro+sis (klɔ:'rəʊsɪs) *n.* a disorder, formerly common in adolescent girls, characterized by pale greenish-yellow skin, weakness, and palpitation and caused by insufficient iron in the body. Also called: **greensickness.** [C17: from CHLORO- + -OSIS] —**chlo+rot+ic** (klɔ:'rɒtɪk) *adj.*

chlo+ro+thi·a+zide (,klɔ:rə'θaɪə,zaɪd) *n.* a diuretic drug administered orally in the treatment of chronic heart and kidney disease and hypertension. Formula: $C_7H_6ClN_3O_4S_2$. [C20: from CHLORO- + THI(O)- + (DI)AZ(INE + DIOX)IDE]

chlo+rous ('klɔ:rəs) *adj.* **1.** of or containing chlorine in the trivalent state. **2.** of or containing chlorous acid.

chlor+prom·a+zine (klɔ:'prɒmə,zi:n) *n.* a drug derived from phenothiazine, used as a sedative and tranquillizer, esp. in psychotic disorders. Formula: $C_{17}H_{19}ClN_2S$. [C20: from CHLORO- + PRO(PYL + A)M(INE) + AZINE]

chlor+pro+pa+mide (klɔ:'prəʊpə,maɪd) *n.* a drug that reduces blood glucose and is administered orally in the treatment of diabetes. Formula: $C_{10}H_{13}ClN_2O_3S$.

chlor+tet+ra+cy+cline (klɔ:,tetrə'saɪkli:n) *n.* an antibiotic used in treating many bacterial and rickettsial infections and some viral infections: obtained from the bacterium *Streptomyces aureofaciens.* Formula: $C_{22}H_{23}ClN_2O_8$.

chm. *abbrev. for:* **1.** Also: **chmn.** chairman. **2.** checkmate.

Ch.M. *or* **ChM** *abbrev. for* Master of Surgery. [Latin: *Chirurgiae Magister*]

cho+an·o+cyte ('kəʊənə,saɪt) *n.* any of the flagellated cells in sponges that maintain a flow of water through the body. A collar of protoplasm surrounds the base of the flagellum. Also called: **collar cell.** [C19: from Greek *khoanē* funnel (from *khein* to pour) + -CYTE]

cho+cho ('tʃəʊ,tʃəʊ) *n., pl.* **+chos.** the cucumber-like fruit of a tropical American cucurbitaceous vine, *Sechium edule:* eaten in the West Indies, Australia, and New Zealand. [C18: from a Brazilian Indian name]

choc-ice ('tʃɒk,aɪs) *n.* an ice-cream covered with a thin layer of chocolate.

chock (tʃɒk) *n.* **1.** a block or wedge of wood used to prevent the sliding or rolling of a heavy object. **2.** *Nautical.* **a.** a fairlead consisting of a ringlike device with an opening at the top through which a rope is placed. **b.** a cradle-like support for a boat, barrel, etc. ~*vb.* (*tr.*) **3.** (usually foll. by *up*) *Brit.* to cram full: *chocked up with newspapers.* **4.** to fit with or secure by a chock. **5.** to support (a boat, barrel, etc.) on chocks. ~*adv.* **6.** as closely or tightly as possible: *chock against the wall.* [C17: of uncertain origin; perhaps related to Old French *coche* log; compare Provençal *soca* tree stump]

chock-a-block *adj., adv.* **1.** filled to capacity; in a crammed state. **2.** *Nautical.* with the blocks brought close together, as when a tackle is pulled as tight as possible.

chock+er ('tʃɒkə) *adj.* **1.** *Austral. informal.* full up; packed. **2.** *Brit. slang.* irritated; fed up. [C20: from CHOCK-A-BLOCK]

chock-full, choke-full, *or* **chuck-full** *adj.* (*postpositive*) completely full. [C17 *choke-full;* see CHOKE, FULL]

choc·o ('tʃɒkəʊ) *n., pl.* **·os.** *Slang.* **1.** *Brit., derogatory.* a coloured person. **2.** *Austral.* (in World War II) **a.** a member of the citizen army; militiaman. **b.** a conscript. [C20: shortened from *chocolate soldier*]

choc·o+late ('tʃɒkəlɪt, 'tʃɒklɪt, -lət) *n.* **1.** a food preparation made from roasted ground cacao seeds, usually sweetened and flavoured. **2.** a drink or sweet-meat made from this. **3. a.** a moderate to deep brown colour. **b.** (*as adj.*): *a chocolate carpet.* [C17: from Spanish, from Aztec *xocolatl,* from *xococ* sour, bitter + *atl* water] —'**choc·o+lat·y** *adj.*

choc·o·late-box *n.* (*modifier*) *Informal.* sentimentally pretty or appealing.

choc+taw ('tʃɒktɔ:) *n. Ice skating.* a turn from the inside edge of one skate to the outside edge of the other or vice versa. [C19: after CHOCTAW]

Choc+taw ('tʃɒktɔ:) *n.* **1.** (*pl.* **+taws** *or* **+taw**) a member of a North American Indian people of Alabama. **2.** the language of this people, belonging to the Muskhogean family. [C18: from Choctaw *Chahta*]

Chog·yal ('tʃɒgjɑ:l) *n.* the title of the ruler of Sikkim.
choice (tʃɔɪs) *n.* **1.** the act or an instance of choosing or selecting. **2.** the opportunity or power of choosing. **3.** a person or thing chosen or that may be chosen: *he was a possible choice.* **4.** an alternative action or possibility: *what choice did I have?* **5.** a supply from which to select: *a poor choice of shoes.* ~*adj.* **6.** of superior quality; excellent: *choice wine.* [C13: from Old French *chois,* from *choisir* to CHOOSE] —'**choice·ly** *adv.* —'**choice·ness** *n.*
choir (kwaɪə) *n.* **1.** an organized group of singers, esp. for singing in church services. **2. a.** the part of a cathedral, abbey, or church in front of the altar, lined on both sides with benches, and used by the choir and clergy. Compare **chancel. b.** (*as modifier*): *choir stalls.* **3.** a number of instruments of the same family playing together: *a brass choir.* **4.** Also called: **choir organ.** one of the manuals on an organ controlling a set of soft sweet-toned pipes. Compare **great** (sense 20), **swell** (sense 16). **5.** any of the nine orders of angels in medieval angelology. Archaic spelling: **quire.** [C13 *quer,* from Old French *cuer,* from Latin CHORUS] —'**choir·,like** *adj.*
choir·boy ('kwaɪə,bɔɪ) *n.* one of a number of young boys who sing the treble part in a church choir.
choir loft *n.* a gallery in a cathedral, abbey, or church used by the choir.
choir·mas·ter ('kwaɪə,mɑ:stə) *n.* a person who trains, leads, or conducts a choir.
choir school *n. Brit.* a school, esp. a preparatory school attached to a cathedral, college, etc., offering general education to boys whose singing ability is good.
Choi·seul (*French* ʃwa'zœl) *n.* an island in the SW Pacific Ocean, in the Solomon Islands: hilly and densely forested. Area: 3885 sq. km (1500 sq. miles).
choke (tʃəʊk) *vb.* **1.** (*tr.*) to hinder or stop the breathing of (a person or animal), esp. by constricting the windpipe or by asphyxiation. **2.** (*intr.*) to have trouble or fail in breathing, swallowing, or speaking. **3.** (*tr.*) to block or clog up (a passage, pipe, street, etc.). **4.** (*tr.*) to retard the growth or action of: *the weeds are choking my plants.* **5.** (*tr.*) to suppress emotion: *she choked her anger.* **6.** (*intr.*) *Slang.* to die. **7.** (*tr.*) to enrich the petrol-air mixture by reducing the air supply to (a carburettor, petrol engine, etc.) ~*n.* **8.** the act or sound of choking. **9.** a device in the carburettor of a petrol engine that enriches the petrol-air mixture by reducing the air supply. **10.** any constriction or mechanism for reducing the flow of a fluid in a pipe, tube, etc. **11.** Also called: **choke coil.** *Electronics.* an inductor having a relatively high impedance, used to prevent the passage of high frequencies or to smooth the output of a rectifier. **12.** the inedible centre of the head of an artichoke. [Old English *ācēocian,* of Germanic origin; related to CHEEK] —'**choke·a·ble** *adj.* —'**chok·y** *or* '**chok·ey** *adj.*
choke back *or* **down** *vb.* (*tr., adv.*) to suppress (anger, tears, etc.).
choke·ber·ry ('tʃəʊkbərɪ, -brɪ) *n., pl.* **·ries. 1.** any of various North American rosaceous shrubs of the genus *Aronia.* **2.** the red or purple bitter fruit of any of these shrubs.
choke·bore ('tʃəʊk,bɔ:) *n.* **1.** a shotgun bore that becomes narrower towards the muzzle so that the shot is not scattered. **2.** a shotgun having such a bore.
choke·cher·ry ('tʃəʊk,tʃɛrɪ) *n., pl.* **·ries. 1.** any of several North American species of cherry, esp. *Prunus virginiana,* having very astringent dark red or black fruit. **2.** the fruit of any of these trees.
choke coil *n.* another name for **choke** (sense 11).
choke·damp ('tʃəʊk,dæmp) *n.* another word for **blackdamp.**
choke-full *adj.* a less common spelling of **chock-full.**
chok·er ('tʃəʊkə) *n.* **1.** a woman's high collar, popular esp. in the late 19th century. **2.** any neckband or necklace worn tightly around the throat. **3.** a high clerical collar; stock. **4.** a person or thing that chokes or strangles someone or something.
choke up *vb.* (*tr., adv.*) **1.** to block (a drain, pipe, etc.) completely. **2.** *Informal.* (*usually passive*) to overcome (a person) with emotion, esp. without due cause.
cho·ko ('tʃəʊkəʊ) *n., pl.* **·kos.** *Austral., N.Z.* a variant of **chocho.**
cho·le- *or before a vowel* **chol-** *combining form.* indicating bile or gall: *cholesterol.* [from Greek *kholē*]
cho·le·cal·cif·er·ol (,kəʊlɪkæl'sɪfə,rɒl) *n.* a compound occurring naturally in fish-liver oils, used to treat rickets. Formula: $C_{27}H_{44}O$. Also called: **vitamin D_3.** See also **calciferol.**
chol·e·cyst ('kɒlɪsɪst) *n. Rare.* another name for **gall bladder.**
chol·e·cys·tec·to·my (,kɒlɪsɪ'stɛktəmɪ) *n., pl.* **·mies.** surgical removal of the gall bladder.
chol·er ('kɒlə) *n.* **1.** anger or ill humour. **2.** *Archaic.* one of the four bodily humours; yellow bile. See **humour** (sense 8). **3.** *Obsolete.* biliousness. [C14: from Old French *colère,* from Medieval Latin *cholera,* from Latin: jaundice, CHOLERA]
chol·er·a ('kɒlərə) *n.* an acute intestinal infection characterized by severe diarrhoea, cramp, etc.: caused by ingestion of water or food contaminated with the bacterium *Vibrio comma.* Also called: **Asiatic cholera, epidemic cholera, Indian cholera.** [C14: from Latin, from Greek *kholera* jaundice, from *kholē* bile] —'**chol·e,roid** *adj.*
chol·er·ic ('kɒlərɪk) *adj.* **1.** bad-tempered. **2.** bilious or causing biliousness. —'**chol·er·i·cal·ly** *or* '**chol·er·ic·ly** *adv.*
cho·les·ter·ol (kə'lɛstə,rɒl) *or* **cho·les·ter·in** (kə'lɛstərɪn) *n.* a white or pale yellow almost insoluble sterol found in all animal tissues, blood, bile, and animal fats: a precursor of other body steroids. Evidence exists to implicate a high blood level of cholesterol with certain forms of arterial and heart disease. Formula: $C_{27}H_{45}OH$. [C19: from CHOLE- + Greek *stereos* hard, solid, so called because first observed in gallstones]
cho·li ('kəʊlɪ) *n.* a short-sleeved bodice, as worn by Indian women. [from Hindi]
cho·lic ac·id ('kəʊlɪk) *n.* a crystalline insoluble acid present in bile: used as an emulsifying agent and an intermediate in the synthesis of organic compounds. Formula: $C_{24}H_{40}O_5$. [C19: from Greek *kholikos;* see CHOLE-]
cho·line ('kəʊli:n, -ɪn, 'kɒl-) *n.* a colourless viscous soluble alkaline substance present in animal tissues, esp. as a constituent of lecithin: used as a supplement to the diet of poultry and in medicine for preventing the accumulation of fat in the liver. Formula: $[(CH_3)_3NCH_2CH_2OH]^+OH^-$. [C19: from CHOLE- + -INE[2], so called because of its action in the liver]
cho·lin·er·gic (,kəʊlɪ'nɜ:dʒɪk) *adj.* **1.** denoting nerve fibres that release acetylcholine when stimulated. **2.** of or relating to the type of chemical activity associated with acetylcholine and similar substances. [C20: from (ACETYL)CHOLIN(E) + Greek *ergon* work]
cho·lin·es·ter·ase (,kəʊlɪ'nɛstə,reɪs, ,kɒl-) *n.* an enzyme that hydrolyses acetylcholine to choline and acetic acid.
chol·la ('tʃəʊljɑ:; *Spanish* 'tʃoja) *n.* any of several spiny cacti of the genus *Opuntia* that grow in the southwestern U.S. and Mexico and have cylindrical stem segments. See also **prickly pear.** [Mexican Spanish, from Spanish: head, perhaps from Old French (dialect) *cholle* ball, of Germanic origin]
chol·lers ('tʃɒləz) *pl. n. Northeast English dialect.* the jowls or cheeks. [C18: perhaps from Old English *ceolur* throat. See JOWL[2]]
Cho·lon (tʃə'lʌn; *French* ʃɔ'lɔ̃) *n.* a city in S Vietnam: a suburb of Ho Chi Minh City.
Cho·lu·la (*Spanish* tʃo'lula) *n.* a town in S Mexico, in Puebla state: ancient ruins, notably a pyramid, 53 m (177 ft.) high. Pop.: 12 820 (1969 est.).
chomp (tʃɒmp) *or* **chump** *vb.* **1.** to chew (food) noisily; champ. ~*n.* **2.** the act or sound of chewing in this manner.
Chom·sky ('tʃɒmskɪ) *n.* **No·am.** born 1928, U.S. linguist and political critic. His theory of language structure, based on generative grammar, supersedes the behaviourist view of Bloomfield. —'**Chom·sky·an** *or* '**Chom·sky·,ite** *n., adj.*
chon (tʃəʊn) *n., pl.* **chon.** a Korean monetary unit worth one hundredth of a won.
chon·dri·fy ('kɒndrɪ,faɪ) *vb.* **·fies, ·fy·ing, ·fied.** to become or convert into cartilage. —,**chon·dri·fi·'ca·tion** *n.*
chon·dri·o·some ('kɒndrɪə,səʊm) *n.* another name for **mitochondrion.** —,**chon·dri·o·'so·mal** *adj.*
chon·drite ('kɒndraɪt) *n.* a stony meteorite consisting mainly of silicate minerals in the form of chondrules. Compare **achondrite.** —**chon·drit·ic** (kɒn'drɪtɪk) *adj.*
chon·dro-, chon·dri-, *or before a vowel* **chondr-** *combining form.* **1.** indicating cartilage: *chondroma.* **2.** grain or granular: *chondrule.* [from Greek *khondros* grain, cartilage]
chon·dro·ma (kɒn'drəʊmə) *n., pl.* **·mas** *or* **·ma·ta** (-mətə). *Pathol.* a benign cartilaginous growth or neoplasm. —**chon·'dro·ma·tous** *adj.*
chon·drule ('kɒndru:l) *n.* one of the small spherical masses of mainly silicate minerals present in chondrites.
Chŏng·jin *or* **Chung·jin** ('tʃʌŋ'dʒɪn) *n.* a port in W North Korea, on the Sea of Japan. Pop.: 200 000 (1970).
Chŏn·ju ('tʃʌn'dʒu:) *n.* a city in SW South Korea: centre of large rice-growing region. Pop.: 262 816 (1970).
choo-choo ('tʃu:,tʃu:) *n. Brit.* a child's name for a railway train.
choof off (tʃuf) *vb.* (*intr., adv.*) *Austral. slang.* to go away; make off.
chook (tʃʊk) *vb.* **1.** See **jook.** ~*n.* **2.** Also called: **chookie.** *Informal, chiefly Austral.* a hen or chicken.
choom (tʃʊm) *n.* (*often cap.*) *Austral. slang.* an Englishman.
choose (tʃu:z) *vb.* **choos·es, choos·ing, chose, cho·sen. 1.** to select (a person, thing, course of action, etc.) from a number of alternatives. **2.** (*tr.; takes a clause as object or an infinitive*) to consider it desirable or proper: *I don't choose to read that book.* **3.** (*intr.*) to like; please: *you may stand if you choose.* **4. cannot choose but.** to be obliged to: *we cannot choose but vote for him.* **5. nothing** *or* **little to choose between.** (of two people or objects) almost equal. [Old English *ceosan;* related to Old Norse *kjōsa,* Old High German *kiosan*] —'**choos·er** *n.*
choos·y ('tʃu:zɪ) *adj.* **choos·i·er, choos·i·est.** *Informal.* particular in making a choice; difficult to please.
chop[1] (tʃɒp) *vb.* **chops, chop·ping, chopped. 1.** (often foll. by *down* or *off*) to cut (something) with a blow from an axe or other sharp tool. **2.** (*tr.*) to produce or make in this manner: *to chop firewood.* **3.** (*tr.;* often foll. by *up*) to cut into pieces. **4.** (*tr.*) *Brit. informal.* to dispense with or reduce. **5.** (*intr.*) to move quickly or violently. **6.** *Tennis, cricket, etc.* to hit (a ball) sharply downwards. **7.** *Boxing, karate, etc.* to punch or strike (an opponent) with a short sharp blow. **8.** *West African.* an informal word for **eat.** ~*n.* **9.** a cutting blow. **10.** the act or an instance of chopping. **11.** a piece chopped off. **12.** a slice of mutton, lamb, or pork, generally including a rib. **13.** *Austral. slang.* a share (esp. in the phrase **get** *or* **hop in for one's chop**). **14.** *West African.* an informal word for **food. 15.** *Sport.* a sharp downward blow or stroke. **16. not much chop.** *Austral. informal.* not much good; poor. **17. the chop.** *Slang, chiefly Brit.* dismissal from employment. [C16: variant of CHAP[1]]
chop[2] (tʃɒp) *vb.* **chops, chop·ping, chopped. 1.** (*intr.*) to change direction suddenly; vacillate (esp. in the phrase **chop and change**). **2.** *Obsolete.* to barter. **3. chop logic.** to argue over small points. [Old English *ceapian* to barter; see CHEAP, CHAPMAN]

chop[3] (tʃɒp) *n.* a design stamped on goods as a trademark, esp. in the Far East. [C17: from Hindi *chhāp*]

chop chop *adv.* pidgin English for **quickly.** [C19: from Chinese dialect; related to Cantonese *kap kap*]

chop+fall·en ('tʃɒp,fɔ:lən) *adj.* a variant spelling of **chapfallen.**

chop+house[1] ('tʃɒp,haʊs) *n.* a restaurant specializing in steaks, grills, chops, etc.

chop+house[2] ('tʃɒp,haʊs) *n.* (formerly) a customs house in China.

Cho·pin ('ʃɒpæn; *French* ʃɔ'pɛ̃) *n.* **Fré·dé·ric Fran·çois** (frederik frɑ̃'swa). 1810–49, Polish composer and pianist active in France, who wrote chiefly for the piano: noted for his harmonic imagination and his lyrical and melancholy qualities.

cho+pine (tʃɒ'pi:n) *or* **chop+in** ('tʃɒpɪn) *n.* a sandal-like shoe on tall wooden or cork bases popular in the 18th century. [C16: from Old Spanish *chapín,* probably imitative of the sound made by the shoe when walking]

chop+log·ic ('tʃɒp,lɒdʒɪk) *n.* **a.** fallacious reasoning. **b.** (*as modifier*): *a choplogic speech.* [C16: from CHOP[2] + LOGIC]

chop+per ('tʃɒpə) *n.* **1.** *Chiefly Brit.* a small hand axe. **2.** a butcher's cleaver. **3.** a person or thing that cuts or chops. **4.** an informal name for a **helicopter. 5.** *Chiefly Brit.* a slang name for **penis. 6.** a device for periodically interrupting an electric current or beam of radiation to produce a pulsed current or beam. See also **vibrator** (sense 3). **7.** a type of bicycle or motorcycle with very high handlebars and an elongated saddle. **8.** *Slang, chiefly U.S.* a sub-machine-gun.

chop+pers ('tʃɒpəz) *pl. n. Slang.* teeth, esp. false ones.

chop+per tool *n.* a core tool of flint or stone, with a transverse cutting edge, characteristic of cultures in Asia and parts of the Middle East and Europe.

chop+py ('tʃɒpɪ) *adj.* **+pi+er, +pi+est.** (of the sea, weather, etc.) fairly rough. **—'chop+pi+ly** *adv.* **—'chop+pi+ness** *n.*

chops (tʃɒps) *pl. n.* **1.** the jaws or cheeks; jowls. **2.** the mouth. **3. lick one's chops.** *Informal.* to anticipate with pleasure. [C16: of uncertain origin]

chop+sticks ('tʃɒpstɪks) *pl. n.* a pair of thin sticks, of ivory, wood, etc., used as eating utensils by the Chinese, Japanese, etc. [C17: from pidgin English, from *chop* quick, of Chinese dialect origin + STICK[1]]

chop su·ey ('su:ɪ) *n.* a Chinese-style dish originating in the U.S., consisting of meat or chicken, bean sprouts, etc., stewed and served with rice. [C19: from Chinese (Cantonese) *tsap sui* odds and ends]

cho+ra+gus (kɔ:'reɪgəs) *n., pl.* **+gi** (-dʒaɪ) *or* **+gus·es. 1.** (in ancient Greek drama) **a.** the leader of a chorus. **b.** a sponsor of a chorus. **2.** a conductor of a festival. [C17: from Latin, from Greek *khoragos,* from *khoros* CHORUS + *agein* to lead] **—cho+rag+ic** (kɔ:'rædʒɪk, -'reɪ-) *adj.*

cho+ral ('kɔ:rəl) *adj.* **1.** relating to, sung by, or designed for a chorus or choir. *~n.* (kɒ'rɑ:l) **2.** a variant spelling of **chorale.**

cho+rale *or* **cho+ral** (kɒ'rɑ:l) *n.* **1.** a slow stately hymn tune, esp. of the Lutheran Church. **2.** *Chiefly U.S.* a choir or chorus. [C19: from German *Choralgesang,* translation of Latin *cantus chorālis* choral song]

cho+rale prel+ude *n.* a composition for organ using a chorale as a cantus firmus or as the basis for variations.

chord[1] (kɔ:d) *n.* **1.** an emotional response, esp. one of sympathy: *the story struck the right chord.* **2.** *Maths.* **a.** a straight line connecting two points on a curve or curved surface. **b.** the line segment lying between two points of intersection of a straight line and a curve or curved surface. **3.** *Engineering.* one of the principal members of a truss, esp. one that lies along the top or the bottom. **4.** *Anatomy.* a variant spelling of **cord. 5.** an imaginary straight line joining the leading edge and the trailing edge of an aerofoil. **6.** *Archaic.* the string of a musical instrument. [C16: from Latin *chorda,* from Greek *khordē* gut, string; see CORD] **—'chord+ed** *adj.*

chord[2] (kɔ:d) *n.* **1.** the simultaneous sounding of a group of musical notes, usually three or more in number. See **concord** (sense 4), **discord** (sense 3). *~vb.* **2.** (*tr.*) to provide (a melodic line) with chords. [C15: short for ACCORD; spelling influenced by CHORD[1]] **—'chord+al** *adj.*

chor+date ('kɔ:deɪt) *n.* **1.** any animal of the phylum *Chordata,* including the vertebrates and protochordates, characterized by a notochord, dorsal tubular nerve cord, and pharyngeal gill slits. *~adj.* **2.** of, relating to, or belonging to the *Chordata.*

chord+ing ('kɔ:dɪŋ) *n. Music.* **1.** the distribution of chords throughout a piece of harmony. **2.** the intonation of a group of instruments or voices.

chord·o+phone ('kɔ:də,fəʊn) *n.* any musical instrument producing sounds through the vibration of strings, such as the piano, harp, violin, or guitar.

chord sym+bol *n. Music.* any of a series of letters and numerals, used as a shorthand indication of chords, esp. in jazz, folk, or pop music: *B7 indicates the dominant seventh chord in the key of E.*

chore (tʃɔ:) *n.* **1.** a small routine task, esp. a domestic one. **2.** an unpleasant task. [C19: Middle English *chare,* from Old English *cierr* a job]

-chore *n. combining form.* (in botany) indicating a plant that is distributed by a certain means or agency: *anemochore.* [from Greek *khōrein* to move] **—-cho·rous** *or* **-cho·ric** *adj. combining form.*

cho+re·a (kɒ'rɪə) *n.* a disorder of the central nervous system characterized by uncontrollable irregular brief jerky movements. Nontechnical name: **Saint Vitus's dance.** [C19: from New Latin, from Latin: dance, from Greek *khoreia,* from *khoros* dance; see CHORUS] **—cho+'re·al** *or* **cho+'re·ic** *adj.*

cho·re·o- *combining form.* indicating the art of dancing or ballet: *choreodrama; choreography.* [from Greek *khoreios,* from *khoros* dance]

cho+re·o+dra+ma (,kɔ:rɪəʊ'drɑ:mə) *n. Dancing.* dance drama performed by a group.

cho+re·o+graph ('kɒrɪə,græf) *vb.* (*tr.*) to compose the steps and dances for a piece of music or ballet.

cho+re·og+ra+phy (,kɒrɪ'ɒgrəfɪ) *or* **cho+reg+ra+phy** (kɒ'rɛgrəfɪ) *n.* **1.** the composition of dance steps and sequences for ballet and stage dancing. **2.** the steps and sequences of a ballet or dance. **3.** the notation representing such steps. **4.** the art of dancing. [C18: from Greek *khoreia* dance + -GRAPHY] **—,cho+re·'og+ra+pher** *or* **cho+'reg+ra+pher** *n.* **—cho+re·o+graph+ic** (,kɒrɪə'græfɪk) *or* **cho+re·graph+ic** (,kɒrə'græfɪk) *adj.* **—,cho+re·o+'graph·i·cal+ly** *or* **,cho+re·'graph·i·cal+ly** *adv.*

cho+ri+amb ('kɒrɪ,æmb) *or* **cho+ri+am+bus** (,kɒrɪ'æmbəs) *n., pl.* **+ambs** *or* **+am+bi** (-'æmbaɪ). *Prosody.* a metrical foot used in classical verse consisting of four syllables, two short ones between two long ones (¯˘˘¯). [C19: from Late Latin *choriambus,* from Greek *khoriambos,* from *khoreios* trochee, of a chorus, from *khoros* CHORUS] **—,cho+ri+'am+bic** *adj.*

cho+ric ('kɒrɪk) *adj.* of, like, for, or in the manner of a chorus, esp. of singing, dancing, or the speaking of verse.

cho+ri+on ('kɔ:rɪən) *n.* the outer of two membranes (see also **amnion**) that form a sac around the embryonic reptile, bird, or mammal: contributes to the placenta in mammals. [C16: from Greek *khorion* afterbirth] **—,cho+ri+'on+ic** *or* **'cho+ri·al** *adj.*

chor+is+ter ('kɒrɪstə) *n.* a singer in a choir, esp. a choirboy. [C14: from Medieval Latin *chorista*]

chor·i+zo (tʃɔ:'ri:zəʊ) *n., pl.* **+zos.** a kind of highly seasoned pork sausage of Spain or Mexico. [C19: Spanish]

C ho+ri+zon *n.* the layer of a soil profile immediately below the B horizon and above the bedrock, composed of weathered rock little affected by soil-forming processes.

Chor+ley ('tʃɔ:lɪ) *n.* a town in NW England, in S Lancashire: cotton textiles. Pop.: 31 609 (1971).

cho+rog+ra+phy (kɒ'rɒgrəfɪ) *n. Geography.* **1.** the technique of mapping regions. **2.** a description or map of a region, as opposed to a small area. [C16: via Latin from Greek *khōrographia,* from *khōros* place, country + -GRAPHY] **—cho+'rog+ra+pher** *n.* **—cho+ro+graph+ic** (,kɒrə'græfɪk) *or* **,cho+ro+'graph·i+cal** *adj.* **—,cho+ro+'graph·i·cal+ly** *adv.*

cho+roid ('kɔ:rɔɪd) *or* **cho+ri+oid** ('kɔ:rɪ,ɔɪd) *adj.* **1.** resembling the chorion, esp. in being vascular. *~n.* **2.** the brownish vascular membrane of the eyeball between the sclera and the retina. [C18: from Greek *khoroeidēs,* erroneously for *khorioeidēs,* from CHORION]

cho+roid plex+us *n.* a multilobed vascular membrane, projecting into the cerebral ventricles, that secretes cerebrospinal fluid.

cho+rol+o·gy (kə'rɒlədʒɪ) *n.* **1.** the study of the causal relations between geographical phenomena occurring within a particular region. **2.** the study of the spatial distribution of organisms. [C20: from German *Chorologie,* from Greek *choros* place + -LOGY]

chor+tle ('tʃɔ:tᵊl) *vb.* **1.** (*intr.*) *Informal.* to chuckle gleefully. *~n.* **2.** *Informal.* a gleeful chuckle. [C19: coined (1871) by Lewis Carroll in "Through the Looking-glass"; probably a blend of CHUCKLE + SNORT] **—'chor+tler** *n.*

cho+rus ('kɔ:rəs) *n., pl.* **+rus·es. 1.** a large choir of singers or a piece of music composed for such a choir. **2.** a body of singers or dancers who perform together, in contrast to principals or soloists. **3.** a section of a song in which a soloist is joined by a group of singers, esp. in a recurring refrain. **4.** an intermediate section of a pop song, blues, etc., as distinct from the verse. **5.** *Jazz.* any of a series of variations on a theme. **6.** (in ancient Greece) **a.** a lyric poem sung by a group of dancers, originally as a religious rite. **b.** an ode or series of odes sung by a group of actors. **7. a.** (in classical Greek drama) the actors who sang the chorus and commented on the action of the play. **b.** actors playing a similar role in any drama. **8. a.** (esp. in Elizabethan drama) the actor who spoke the prologue, etc. **b.** the part of the play spoken by this actor. **9.** a group of people or animals producing words or sounds simultaneously. **10.** any speech, song, or other form of utterance produced by a group of people or animals simultaneously: *a chorus of sighs; the dawn chorus.* **11. in chorus.** in unison. *~vb.* **12.** to speak, sing, or utter (words, sounds, etc.) in unison. [C16: from Latin, from Greek *khoros*]

cho+rus girl *n.* a girl who dances or sings in the chorus of a musical comedy, revue, etc.

cho·rus+mas·ter ('kɔ:rəs,mɑ:stə) *n.* the conductor of a choir.

Chor+zów (*Polish* 'xɔʒuf) *n.* an industrial city in SW Poland: under German administration from 1794 to 1921. Pop.: 154 500 (1974 est.). German name: **Königshütte.**

chose[1] (tʃəʊz) *vb.* the past tense of **choose.**

chose[2] (ʃəʊz) *n. Law.* an article of personal property. [C17: from French: thing, from Latin *causa* cause, case, reason]

cho+sen ('tʃəʊzᵊn) *vb.* **1.** the past participle of **choose.** *~adj.* **2.** selected or picked out, esp. for some special quality.

Cho+sen ('tʃəʊ'sɛn) *n.* the official name for **Korea** as a Japanese province (1910–45).

cho+sen peo+ple *pl. n.* any of various peoples believing themselves to be chosen by God, esp. the Jews.

Cho+sŏn ('tʃəʊ'sɒn) *n.* the Korean name for **Korea.**

Cho+ta Nag+pur ('tʃəʊtə 'nɑ:gpʊə) *n.* a plateau in E India, in Bihar state: forested, with rich mineral resources and much heavy industry; produces chiefly lac (world's leading supplier), coal (half India's total output), and mica.

chott (ʃɒt) *n.* a variant spelling of **shott.**

chou (ʃuː) *n., pl.* **choux** (ʃuː). **1.** a type of cabbage. **2.** a rosette. **3.** a round cream bun. [C18 (a bun): from French, from Latin *caulis* cabbage]

Chou (tʃəʊ) *n.* the imperial dynasty of China from about 1126 to 255 B.C.

Chou En-lai (ˈtʃəʊ ɛnˈlaɪ) *n.* 1898–1976, Chinese Communist statesman; foreign minister of the People's Republic of China (1949–58) and premier (1949–76).

chough (tʃʌf) *n.* **1.** a large black passerine bird, *Pyrrhocorax pyrrhocorax,* of parts of Europe, Asia, and Africa, with a long downward-curving red bill: family *Corvidae* (crows). **2. alpine chough.** a smaller related bird, *Pyrrhocorax graculus,* with a shorter yellow bill. [C14: of uncertain origin; probably related to Old French *cauwe,* Old English *cēo*]

choux pas+try (ʃuː) *n.* a very light pastry made with eggs, used for eclairs, etc. [partial translation of French *pâte choux* cabbage dough (from its round shape)]

chow (tʃaʊ) *n.* **1.** *Informal.* food. **2.** short for **chow-chow** (sense 1). **3.** *Chiefly Austral.* a derogatory term for **Chinese.**

chow-chow *n.* **1.** a thick-coated breed of dog with a curled tail, originally from China. Often shortened to **chow. 2.** a Chinese preserve of ginger, orange peel, etc. in syrup. **3.** a mixed vegetable pickle. [C19: from pidgin English, probably based on Mandarin Chinese *cha* miscellaneous]

chow+der (ˈtʃaʊdə) *n. Chiefly U.S.* a thick soup or stew containing clams or fish. [C18: from French *chaudière* kettle, from Late Latin *caldāria;* see CAULDRON]

chow mein (meɪn) *n.* a Chinese-American dish, consisting of mushrooms, meat, shrimps, etc., served with fried noodles. [from Chinese (Cantonese), variant of Mandarin *ch'ao mien* fried noodles]

Chr. *abbrev. for:* **1.** Christ. **2.** Christian.

chre+ma+tis+tic (ˌkriːməˈtɪstɪk) *adj.* of, denoting, or relating to money-making. [C18: from Greek, from *khrēmatizein* to make money, from *khrēma* money] —**ˌchre+ma+ˈtis+tics** *n.*

chres+ard (ˈkrɛsəd) *n.* the amount of water present in the soil that is available to plants. [C20: from Greek *khrēsis* use (from *khrēsthai* to use) + *ardein* to water]

chres+tom+a+thy (krɛsˈtɒməθɪ) *n., pl.* **+thies.** *Rare.* a collection of literary passages, used in the study of language. [C19: from Greek *khrēstomatheia,* from *khrēstos* useful + *mathein* to learn] —**chres+to+math+ic** (ˌkrɛstəʊˈmæθɪk) *adj.*

Chré·tien de Troyes (*French* kretjɛ̃ də ˈtrwa) *n.* 12th-century French poet, who wrote the five Arthurian romances *Erec; Cligès; Lancelot, le chavalier de la charette; Yvain, le chevalier au lion;* and *Perceval, le conte del Graal* (?1155–?1190), the first courtly romances.

chrism *or* **chris+om** (ˈkrɪzəm) *n.* a mixture of olive oil and balsam used for sacramental anointing in the Greek Orthodox and Roman Catholic Churches. [Old English *crisma,* from Medieval Latin, from Greek *khrisma* unction, from *khriein* to anoint] —**chris+mal** (ˈkrɪzməl) *adj.*

chris+ma+to·ry (ˈkrɪzmətərɪ, -trɪ) *n., pl.* **·ries.** *R.C. Church.* a small receptacle containing the three kinds of consecrated oil used in the sacraments.

chris+om (ˈkrɪzəm) *n.* **1.** *Christianity.* a white robe put on an infant at baptism and formerly used as a burial shroud if the infant died soon afterwards. **2.** *Archaic.* an infant wearing such a robe. **3.** a variant spelling of **chrism.**

Chris+sie (ˈkrɪsɪ) *n. Chiefly Austral.* a slang name for **Christmas.**

Christ (kraɪst) *n.* **1.** Jesus of Nazareth (Jesus Christ), regarded by Christians as fulfilling Old Testament prophecies of the Messiah. **2.** the Messiah or anointed one of God as the subject of Old Testament prophecies. **3.** an image or picture of Christ. ~*interj.* **4.** *Taboo slang.* an oath expressing annoyance, surprise, etc. ~See also **Jesus.** [Old English *Crīst,* from Latin *Chrīstus,* from Greek *khristos* anointed one (from *khriein* to anoint), translating Hebrew *māshīah* MESSIAH] —**ˈChrist+ly** *adj.*

Chris+ta+del+phi+an (ˌkrɪstəˈdɛlfɪən) *n.* **1.** a member of a Christian millenarian sect founded in the U.S. about 1848, holding that only the just will enter eternal life, that the wicked will be annihilated, and that the ignorant, the unconverted, and infants will not be raised from the dead. ~*adj.* **2.** of or relating to this body or its beliefs and practices.

Christ+church (ˈkraɪstˌtʃɜːtʃ) *n.* **1.** the second largest city in New Zealand, on E South Island: manufacturing centre of a rich agricultural region. Pop.: 170 600 (1974 est.). **2.** a town and resort in S England, in SW Hampshire. Pop.: 31 373 (1971).

christ+cross (ˈkrɪsˌkrɒs) *n.* **1.** *Archaic.* **a.** the mark of a cross formerly placed in front of the alphabet in hornbooks. **b.** the alphabet itself. **2.** *Archaic.* a cross used in place of a signature by someone unable to sign his name.

chris+ten (ˈkrɪsᵊn) *vb. (tr.)* **1.** to give a Christian name to in baptism as a sign of incorporation into a Christian Church. **2.** another word for **baptize. 3.** to give a name to anything, esp. with some ceremony. **4.** *Informal.* to use for the first time. [Old English *cristnian,* from *Crīst* CHRIST] —**ˈchris+ten+er** *n.*

Chris+ten+dom (ˈkrɪsᵊndəm) *n.* **1.** the collective body of Christians throughout the world or throughout history. **2.** an obsolete word for **Christianity.**

chris+ten+ing (ˈkrɪsᵊnɪŋ) *n.* the Christian sacrament of baptism or the ceremony in which this is conferred.

Christ+hood (ˈkraɪsthʊd) *n.* the state of being the Christ, the anointed one of God.

Chris+tian[1] (ˈkrɪstʃən) *n.* **1. a.** a person who believes in and follows Jesus Christ. **b.** a member of a Christian Church or denomination. **2.** *Informal.* a person who possesses Christian virtues, esp. practical ones. ~*adj.* **3.** of, relating to, or derived from Jesus Christ, his teachings, example, or his followers. **4.** (*sometimes not cap.*) exhibiting kindness or goodness. —**ˈchris+tian+ly** *adj., adv.*

Chris·tian[2] (ˈkrɪstʃən) *n.* **Char·lie.** 1919–1942, U.S. modern-jazz guitarist.

Chris·tian X (ˈkrɪstʃən; *Danish* ˈkresdjan) *n.* 1890–1947, king of Denmark (1912–47) and Iceland (1918–44).

Chris+tian Ac+tion *n.* an inter-Church movement formed in 1946 to promote Christian ideals in society at large.

Chris+tian Broth+ers *pl. n. R.C. Church.* a religious congregation of laymen founded in France in 1684 for the education of the poor. Also called: **Brothers of the Christian Schools.**

Chris+tian E·ra *n.* the period beginning with the year of Christ's birth. Dates in this era are labelled A.D., those previous to it B.C. Also called: **Common Era.**

Chris+ti·a+ni·a (ˌkrɪstɪˈɑːnɪə) *n.* **1.** a former name (1624–1877) of **Oslo. 2. a.** Also called: **Christy, Christie.** *Skiing.* a turn in which the body is swung sharply round with the skis parallel, originating in Norway and used for stopping, slowing down, or changing direction quickly. **b.** *Skateboarding.* a manoeuvre in which the rider crouches down, puts one leg out at right angles, and puts his arms out on either side.

Chris+ti+an+i+ty (ˌkrɪstɪˈænɪtɪ) *n.* **1.** the Christian religion. **2.** Christian beliefs, practices or attitudes. **3.** a less common word for **Christendom.**

Chris+tian+ize *or* **Chris+tian+ise** (ˈkrɪstʃəˌnaɪz) *vb.* **1.** *(tr.)* to make Christian or convert to Christianity. **2.** *(tr.)* to imbue with Christian principles, spirit, or outlook. **3.** *(intr.) Rare.* to become Christian. —**ˌChris+tian·i+ˈza+tion** *or* **ˌChris+tian·i+ˈsa+tion** *n.* —**ˈChris+tian+ˌiz+er** *or* **ˈChris+tian+ˈis+er** *n.*

Chris+tian name *n. Brit.* a personal or given name. It is formally given to Christians at christening. Compare **surname.**

Chris+tian+sand (ˈkrɪstʃənˌsænd; *Norwegian* ˌkristjanˈsan) *n.* a variant spelling of **Kristiansand.**

Chris+tian Sci+ence *n.* the religious system and teaching of the Church of Christ, Scientist. It was founded by Mary Baker Eddy (1866) and emphasizes spiritual healing and the unreality of matter. —**ˈChris+tian ˈSci+en+tist** *n.*

Chris·tie (ˈkrɪstɪ) *n.* **1. Ag·a·tha (Mary Clarissa).** 1891–1976, English author of detective stories, many featuring Hercule Poirot: also several plays, including *The Mousetrap* (1952). **2. John Reg·i·nald Hal·li·day.** 1898–1953, English murderer. His trial influenced legislation regarding the death penalty after he was found guilty of a murder for which Timothy Evans had been hanged.

Chris·ti·na (krɪˈstiːnə) *n.* 1626–89, queen of Sweden (1632–54), daughter of Gustavus Adolphus, noted particularly for her patronage of literature.

Christ+like (ˈkraɪstˌlaɪk) *adj.* resembling or showing the spirit of Jesus Christ. —**ˈChrist+ˌlike·ness** *n.*

Christ+mas (ˈkrɪsməs) *n.* **1. a.** the annual commemoration by Christians of the birth of Jesus Christ on Dec. 25. **b.** Also called: **Christmas Day.** Dec. 25, observed as a day of secular celebrations when gifts and greetings are exchanged. **c.** (*as modifier*): *Christmas celebrations.* **2.** Also called: **Christmas Day.** (in England, Wales and Ireland) Dec. 25, one of the four quarter days. Compare **Lady Day, Midsummer Day, Michaelmas. 3.** Also called: **Christ·mas+tide.** the period of celebrations extending from Dec. 24 to the feast of the Epiphany on Jan. 6. [Old English *Crīstes mæsse* MASS of CHRIST]

Christ+mas bee+tle *n.* any of various greenish-gold Australian scarab beetles of the genus *Anoplognathus,* which are common in summer.

Christ+mas box *n.* a tip or present given at Christmas, esp. to postmen, tradesmen, etc.

Christ+mas cac+tus *n.* a Brazilian cactus, *Zygocactus truncatus,* widely cultivated as an ornamental for its showy red flowers. Also called: **crab cactus.**

Christ+mas card *n.* a greeting card sent at Christmas.

Christ+mas Eve *n.* the evening or the whole day before Christmas Day.

Christ+mas Is+land *n.* **1.** an island in the central Pacific, in the Line Islands: the largest atoll in the world. Pop.: 367 (1968). Area: 359 sq. km (139 sq. miles). **2.** an island in the Indian Ocean, south of Java: administered by Singapore (1900–58), now by Australia; phosphate-mining. Pop.: 2691 (1971). Area: 135 sq. km (52 sq. miles).

Christ+mas pud+ding *n. Brit.* a rich steamed pudding containing suet, dried fruit, spices, brandy, etc., served at Christmas. Also called: **plum pudding.**

Christ+mas rose *n.* an evergreen ranunculaceous plant, *Helleborus niger,* of S Europe and W Asia, with white or pinkish winter-blooming flowers. Also called: **hellebore, winter rose.**

Christ+mas stock+ing *n.* a stocking hung up by children on Christmas Eve for Santa Claus to fill with presents.

Christ·mas+tide (ˈkrɪsməsˌtaɪd) *n.* the season of Christmas, extending from Dec. 24 (Christmas Eve) to Jan. 6 (the festival of the Epiphany or Twelfth Night).

Christ+mas tree *n.* **1.** an evergreen tree or an imitation of one, decorated as part of Christmas celebrations. **2.** Also called (Austral.): **Christmas bush.** any of various trees or shrubs flowering at Christmas and used for decoration.

Christ·o- *combining form.* indicating or relating to Christ: *Christology.*

Chris·toff (ˈkrɪstɒf) *n.* **Bo·ris.** born 1919, Bulgarian bass-baritone, noted esp. for his performance in the title role of Mussorgsky's *Boris Godunov.*

Chris·tol·o·gy (krɪˈstɒlədʒɪ, kraɪ-) *n.* the branch of theology concerned with the person, attributes, and deeds of Christ. —**Chris·to·log·i·cal** (ˌkrɪstəˈlɒdʒɪkᵊl) *adj.* —**Chris·ˈtol·o·gist** *n.*
Chris·tophe (*French* krisˈtɔf) *n.* **Hen·ri** (ãˈri). 1767–1820, Haitian revolutionary leader; king of Haiti (1811–20).
Chris·to·pher (ˈkrɪstəfə) *n.* **Saint.** 3rd century A.D., Christian martyr; patron saint of travellers. Feast day: July 25.
Christ's-thorn *n.* any of several plants of SW Asia, such as *Paliurus spina-christi* and the jujube, that have thorny stems and are popularly believed to have been used for Christ's Crown of Thorns.
Chris·ty (ˈkrɪstɪ) *n., pl.* **·ties.** short for **Christiania** (sense 2).
chro·ma (ˈkrəʊmə) *n.* the attribute of a colour that enables an observer to judge how much chromatic colour it contains irrespective of achromatic colour present. See also **saturation** (sense 4). [C19: from Greek *khrōma* colour]
chro·mate (ˈkrəʊmeɪt) *n.* any salt or ester of chromic acid. Simple chromate salts contain the divalent ion, CrO_4^{2-}, and are orange.
chro·mat·ic (krəˈmætɪk) *adj.* **1.** of, relating to, or characterized by a colour or colours. **2.** *Music.* **a.** involving the sharpening or flattening of notes or the use of such notes in chords and harmonic progressions. **b.** of or relating to the chromatic scale or an instrument capable of producing it: *a chromatic harmonica.* **c.** of or relating to chromaticism. Compare **diatonic.** [C17: from Greek *khrōmatikos,* from *khrōma* colour] —**chro·ˈmat·i·cal·ly** *adv.* —**chro·ˈmat·i·cism** *n.*
chro·mat·ic ab·er·ra·tion *n.* a defect in a lens system characterized by the formation of images with coloured fringes and caused by the variation of the refractive index with the wavelength of light.
chro·mat·ic col·our *n. Physics.* a more formal term for **colour** (sense 2).
chro·ma·tic·i·ty (ˌkrəʊməˈtɪsɪtɪ) *n.* the quality of a colour or light with reference to its purity and its dominant wavelength.
chro·ma·tic·i·ty co·or·di·nates *pl. n. Physics.* three numbers used to specify a colour, each of which is equal to one of the three tristimulus values divided by the sum of these values. Symbols: *x, y, z*
chro·ma·tic·i·ty di·a·gram *n. Physics.* a diagram in which values of two chromaticity coordinates are marked on a pair of rectangular axes, a point in the plane of these axes representing the chromaticity of any colour.
chro·mat·ic·ness (krəʊˈmætɪknɪs) *n. Physics.* the attribute of colour that involves both hue and saturation.
chro·mat·ics (krəʊˈmætɪks) *or* **chro·ma·tol·o·gy** (ˌkrəʊməˈtɒlədʒɪ) *n.* (*functioning as sing.*) the science of colour. —**chro·ma·tist** (ˈkrəʊmətɪst) *or* ˌ**chro·ma·ˈtol·o·gist** *n.*
chro·mat·ic scale *n.* a twelve-note scale including all the semitones of the octave.
chro·ma·tid (ˈkrəʊmətɪd) *n.* either of the two strands into which a chromosome divides during mitosis. They separate to form daughter chromosomes at anaphase.
chro·ma·tin (ˈkrəʊmətɪn) *n. Cytology.* the part of the nucleus that consists of DNA, RNA, and proteins, forms the chromosomes, and stains with basic dyes. See also **euchromatin, heterochromatin.** —ˌ**chro·ma·ˈtin·ic** *adj.* —ˈ**chro·ma·ˌtoid** *adj.*
chro·ma·to- *or before a vowel* **chro·mat-** *combining form.* **1.** indicating colour or coloured: *chromatophore.* **2.** indicating chromatin: *chromatolysis.* [from Greek *khrōma, khrōmat-* colour]
chro·ma·to·gram (ˈkrəʊmətəˌgræm, krəʊˈmæt-) *n.* **1.** a column or strip of material containing constituents of a mixture separated by chromatography. **2.** a graph showing the quantity of a substance leaving a chromatography column as a function of time.
chro·ma·tog·ra·phy (ˌkrəʊməˈtɒgrəfɪ) *n.* the technique of separating and analysing the components of a mixture of liquids or gases by selective adsorption in a column of powder (**column chromatography**) or on a strip of paper (**paper chromatography**). See also **gas chromatography.** —ˌ**chro·ma·ˈtog·ra·pher** *n.* —**chro·ma·to·graph·ic** (ˌkrəʊmətəˈgræfɪk) *adj.* —ˌ**chro·ma·to·ˈgraph·i·cal·ly** *adv.*
chro·ma·tol·o·gy (ˌkrəʊməˈtɒlədʒɪ) *n.* another name for **chromatics.**
chro·ma·tol·y·sis (ˌkrəʊməˈtɒlɪsɪs) *n. Cytology.* the dissolution of chromatin in injured cells.
chro·ma·to·phore (ˈkrəʊmətəˌfɔː) *n.* **1.** a cell in the skin of frogs, chameleons, etc., in which pigment is concentrated or dispersed, causing the animal to change colour. **2.** another name for **chromoplast.** —ˌ**chro·ma·to·ˈphor·ic** *or* **chro·ma·toph·or·ous** (ˌkrəʊməˈtɒfərəs) *adj.*
chrome (krəʊm) *n.* **1. a.** another word for **chromium,** esp. when present in a pigment or dye. **b.** (*as modifier*): *a chrome dye.* **2.** anything plated with chromium, such as fittings on a car body. **3.** a pigment or dye that contains chromium. ~*vb.* **4.** to plate or be plated with chromium, usually by electroplating. **5.** to treat or be treated with a chromium compound, as in dyeing or tanning. [C19: via French from Greek *khrōma* colour]
-chrome *n. and adj. combining form.* colour, coloured, or pigment: *monochrome.* [from Greek *khrōma* colour]
chrome al·um *n.* a violet-red crystalline substance, used as a mordant in dyeing. Formula: $KCr(SO_4)_2.12H_2O$.
chrome green *n.* **1.** any green pigment made by mixing lead chromate with Prussian blue. **2.** any green pigment containing chromic oxide.
chrome red *n.* any red pigment used in paints, consisting of a mixture of lead chromate and lead oxide; basic lead chromate.
chrome steel *n.* any of various hard rust-resistant steels containing chromium. Also called: **chromium steel.**
chrome yel·low *n.* any yellow pigment consisting of lead chromate mixed with lead sulphate.
chro·mic (ˈkrəʊmɪk) *adj.* **1.** of or containing chromium in the trivalent state. **2.** of or derived from chromic acid.
chro·mic ac·id *n.* an unstable dibasic oxidizing acid known only in solution and in the form of chromate salts. Formula: H_2CrO_4.
chro·mi·nance (ˈkrəʊmɪnəns) *n.* the quality of light that causes the sensation of colour. It is determined by comparison with a reference source of the same brightness and of known chromaticity. [C20: from CHROMO- + LUMINANCE]
chro·mite (ˈkrəʊmaɪt) *n.* **1.** a brownish-black mineral consisting of a ferrous chromic oxide in cubic crystalline form, occurring principally in basic igneous rocks: the only commercial source of chromium and its compounds. Formula: $FeCr_2O_4$. **2.** a salt of chromous acid.
chro·mi·um (ˈkrəʊmɪəm) *n.* a hard grey metallic element that takes a high polish, occurring principally in chromite: used in steel alloys and electroplating to increase hardness and corrosion-resistance. Symbol: Cr; atomic no.: 24; atomic wt.: 51.996; valency: 2, 3, or 6; relative density: 7.19; melting pt.: 1890°C; boiling pt.: 2482°C. [C19: from New Latin, from French: CHROME]
chro·mi·um steel *n.* another name for **chrome steel.**
chro·mo (ˈkrəʊməʊ) *n., pl.* **·mos.** short for **chromolithograph.**
chro·mo- *or before a vowel* **chrom-** *combining form.* **1.** indicating colour, coloured, or pigment: *chromogen.* **2.** indicating chromium: *chromyl.* [from Greek *khrōma* colour]
chro·mo·gen (ˈkrəʊmədʒən) *n.* **1.** a compound that forms coloured compounds on oxidation. **2.** a substance that can be converted to a dye. **3.** a bacterium that produces a pigment.
chro·mo·gen·ic (ˌkrəʊməˈdʒɛnɪk) *adj.* **1.** producing colour. **2.** of or relating to a chromogen.
chro·mo·lith·o·graph (ˌkrəʊməʊˈlɪθəˌgrɑːf) *n.* a picture produced by chromolithography.
chro·mo·li·thog·ra·phy (ˌkrəʊməʊlɪˈθɒgrəfɪ) *n.* the process of making coloured prints by lithography. —ˌ**chro·mo·li·ˈthog·ra·pher** *n.* —**chro·mo·lith·o·graph·ic** (ˌkrəʊməʊˌlɪθəˈgræfɪk) *adj.*
chro·mo·mere (ˈkrəʊməˌmɪə) *n. Cytology.* any of the dense areas of chromatin along the length of a chromosome during the early stages of cell division.
chro·mo·ne·ma (ˌkrəʊməˈniːmə) *n., pl.* **·ma·ta** (-mətə). *Cytology.* **1.** the coiled mass of threads within a nucleus at cell division. **2.** a coiled chromatin thread within a single chromosome. [C20: from CHROMO- + Greek *nēma* thread, yarn] —ˌ**chro·mo·ˈne·mal, chro·mo·ne·mat·ic** (ˌkrəʊməʊnɪˈmætɪk), *or* ˌ**chro·mo·ˈne·mic** *adj.*
chro·mo·phore (ˈkrəʊməˌfɔː) *n.* a group of atoms in a chemical compound that are responsible for the colour of the compound. —ˌ**chro·mo·ˈphor·ic** *or* ˌ**chro·mo·ˈphor·ous** *adj.*
chro·mo·plast (ˈkrəʊməˌplæst) *n.* a coloured plastid in a plant cell, esp. one containing carotenoids.
chro·mo·pro·tein (ˌkrəʊməʊˈprəʊtiːn) *n.* any of a group of conjugated proteins, such as haemoglobin, in which the protein is joined to a coloured group, usually a metallic porphyrin.
chro·mo·some (ˈkrəʊməˌsəʊm) *n.* any of the microscopic rod-shaped structures that appear in a cell nucleus during cell division, consisting of nucleoprotein arranged into units (genes) that are responsible for the transmission of hereditary characteristics. See also **homologous chromosomes.** —ˌ**chro·mo·ˈso·mal** *adj.* —ˌ**chro·mo·ˈso·mal·ly** *adv.*
chro·mo·some num·ber *n.* the number of chromosomes present in each somatic cell, which is constant for any one species of plant or animal. In the reproductive cells this number is halved. See also **diploid** (sense 1), **haploid.**
chro·mo·sphere (ˈkrəʊməˌsfɪə) *n.* a gaseous layer of the sun's atmosphere extending from the photosphere to the corona and visible during a total eclipse of the sun. —**chro·mo·spher·ic** (ˌkrəʊməˈsfɛrɪk) *adj.*
chro·mous (ˈkrəʊməs) *adj.* of or containing chromium in the divalent state.
chro·myl (ˈkrəʊməl) *n.* (*modifier*) of, consisting of, or containing the divalent radical CrO_2.
chron. *or* **chronol.** *abbrev. for:* **1.** chronological. **2.** chronology.
Chron. *Bible. abbrev. for* Chronicles.
chro·nax·ie *or* **chro·nax·y** (ˈkrəʊnæksɪ) *n. Physiol.* the minimum time required for excitation of a nerve or muscle when the stimulus is double the minimum (threshold) necessary to elicit a basic response. Compare **rheobase.** [C20: from French, from CHRONO- + Greek *axia* worth, from *axios* worthy, of equal weight]
chron·ic (ˈkrɒnɪk) *adj.* **1.** continuing for a long time; constantly recurring. **2.** (of a disease) developing slowly, or of long duration. Compare **acute** (sense 7). **3.** inveterate; habitual: *a chronic smoker.* **4.** *Informal.* **a.** very bad: *the play was chronic.* **b.** very serious: *he left her in a chronic condition.* [C15: from Latin *chronicus* relating to time, from Greek *khronikos,* from *khronos* time] —ˈ**chron·i·cal·ly** *adv.* —**chro·nic·i·ty** (krɒˈnɪsɪtɪ) *n.*
chron·i·cle (ˈkrɒnɪkᵊl) *n.* **1.** a record or register of events in chronological order. ~*vb.* **2.** (*tr.*) to record in or as if in a chronicle. [C14: from Anglo-French *cronicle,* via Latin

chronica (pl.), from Greek *khronika* annals, from *khronikos* relating to time; see CHRONIC] —ˈ**chron·i·cler** *n.*

chron·i·cle play *n.* a drama based on a historical subject.

Chron·i·cles (ˈkrɒnɪkᵊlz) *n.* either of two historical books (**I** and **II Chronicles**) of the Old Testament.

chron·o- *or before a vowel* **chron-** *combining form.* indicating time: *chronology; chronometer.* [from Greek *khronos* time]

chron·o·bi·ol·o·gy (ˌkrɒnəbaɪˈɒlədʒɪ, ˌkrəʊnə-) *n.* the branch of biology concerned with the periodicity occurring in living organisms. See also **biological clock, circadian.**

chron·o·gram (ˈkrɒnəˌgræm, ˈkrəʊnə-) *n.* **1.** a phrase or inscription in which letters such as M, C, X, L and V can be read as Roman numerals giving a date. **2.** a record kept by a chronograph. —**chron·o·gram·mat·ic** (ˌkrɒnəʊgrəˈmætɪk) *or* ˌ**chron·o·gram·ˈmat·i·cal** *adj.* —ˌ**chron·o·gram·ˈmat·i·cal·ly** *adv.*

chron·o·graph (ˈkrɒnəˌgrɑːf, -ˌgræf, ˈkrəʊnə-) *n.* an accurate instrument for recording small intervals of time. —**chro·nog·ra·pher** (krəˈnɒgrəfə) *n.* —**chron·o·graph·ic** (ˌkrɒnəˈgræfɪk) *adj.* —ˌ**chron·o·ˈgraph·i·cal·ly** *adv.*

chron·o·log·i·cal (ˌkrɒnəˈlɒdʒɪkᵊl, ˌkrəʊ-) *or* **chron·o·log·ic** *adj.* **1.** (esp. of a sequence of events) arranged in order of occurrence. **2.** relating to or in accordance with chronology. —ˌ**chron·o·ˈlog·i·cal·ly** *adv.*

chro·nol·o·gy (krəˈnɒlədʒɪ) *n., pl.* **·gies. 1.** the determination of the proper sequence of past events. **2.** the arrangement of dates, events, etc., in order of occurrence. **3.** a table or list of events arranged in order of occurrence. —**chro·ˈnol·o·gist** *n.*

chro·nom·e·ter (krəˈnɒmɪtə) *n.* a timepiece designed to be accurate in all conditions of temperature, pressure, etc., used esp. at sea. —**chron·o·met·ric** (ˌkrɒnəˈmɛtrɪk) *or* ˌ**chron·o·ˈmet·ri·cal** *adj.* —ˌ**chron·o·ˈmet·ri·cal·ly** *adv.*

chro·nom·e·try (krəˈnɒmɪtrɪ) *n.* the science or technique of measuring time with extreme accuracy.

chro·non (ˈkrəʊnɒn) *n.* a unit of time equal to the time that a photon would take to traverse the diameter of an electron: about 10^{-24} seconds.

chron·o·scope (ˈkrɒnəˌskəʊp, ˈkrəʊnə-) *n.* an instrument that registers small intervals of time on a dial, cathode-ray tube, etc. —**chron·o·scop·ic** (ˌkrɒnəˈskɒpɪk, ˌkrəʊnə-) *adj.* —ˌ**chron·o·ˈscop·i·cal·ly** *adv.*

-chro·ous *or* **-chro·ic** *adj. combining form.* coloured in a specified way: *isochroous.* [from Greek *khrōs* skin, complexion, colour]

chrys·a·lid (ˈkrɪsəlɪd) *n.* **1.** another name for **chrysalis.** ~*adj. also* **chry·sal·i·dal** (krɪˈsælɪdᵊl). **2.** of or relating to a chrysalis.

chrys·a·lis (ˈkrɪsəlɪs) *n., pl.* **chrys·a·lis·es** *or* **chry·sal·i·des** (krɪˈsælɪˌdiːz). **1.** the obtect pupa of a moth or butterfly. **2.** anything in the process of developing. [C17: from Latin *chrȳsallis,* from Greek *khrusallis,* from *khrusos* gold, of Semitic origin; compare Hebrew *harūz* gold]

chry·san·the·mum (krɪˈsænθəməm) *n.* **1.** any widely cultivated plant of the genus *Chrysanthemum,* esp. *C. morifolium* of China, having brightly coloured showy flower heads: family *Compositae* (composites). **2.** any other plant of the genus *Chrysanthemum,* such as oxeye daisy. [C16: from Latin: marigold, from Greek *khrusanthemon,* from *khrusos* gold + *anthemon* flower]

chrys·a·ro·bin (ˌkrɪsəˈrəʊbɪn) *n.* a tasteless odourless powder containing anthraquinone derivatives of araroba, formerly used medicinally to treat chronic skin conditions. [C20: from CHRYSO- (referring to its golden colour) + ARAROBA + -IN]

chrys·el·e·phan·tine (ˌkrɪsɛlɪˈfæntɪn) *adj.* (of ancient Greek statues, etc.) made or overlaid with gold and ivory. [C19: from Greek *khruselephantinos,* from *khrusos* gold + *elephas* ivory; see ELEPHANT]

chry·so- *or before a vowel* **chrys-** *combining form.* indicating gold or the colour of gold: *chryselephantine; chrysolite.* [from Greek *khrusos* gold]

chrys·o·ber·yl (ˈkrɪsəˌbɛrɪl) *n.* a rare very hard greenish-yellow mineral consisting of beryllium aluminate in orthorhombic crystalline form and occurring in coarse granite: used as a gemstone in the form of cat's eye and alexandrite. Formula: $BeAl_2O_4$.

chrys·o·lite (ˈkrɪsəˌlaɪt) *n.* a brown or yellowish-green olivine consisting of magnesium iron silicate: used as a gemstone (see **peridot**). Formula: $(Mg,Fe)_2SiO_4$. —**chrys·o·lit·ic** (ˌkrɪsəˈlɪtɪk) *adj.*

chrys·o·prase (ˈkrɪsəˌpreɪz) *n.* an apple-green variety of chalcedony: a gemstone. [C13 *crisopace,* from Old French, from Latin *chrȳsoprasus,* from Greek *khrusoprasos,* from CHRYSO- + *prason* leek]

Chrys·os·tom (ˈkrɪsəstəm) *n.* Saint **John.** ?345–407 A.D., Greek patriarch; archbishop of Constantinople (398–404). Feast day: Jan. 27.

chrys·o·tile (ˈkrɪsətɪl) *n.* a green, grey, or white fibrous mineral, a variety of serpentine, that is an important source of commercial asbestos. Formula: $Mg_3Si_2O_5(OH)_4$. [C20: from CHRYSO- + Greek *tilos* something plucked, shred, thread, from *tillein* to pluck]

chs. *abbrev. for* chapters.

chtho·ni·an (ˈθəʊnɪən) *or* **chtho·nic** (ˈθɒnɪk) *adj.* of or relating to the underworld. [C19: from Greek *khthonios* in or under the earth, from *khthōn* earth]

chub (tʃʌb) *n., pl.* **chub** *or* **chubs. 1.** a common European freshwater cyprinid game fish, *Leuciscus* (or *Squalius*) *cephalus,* having a cylindrical dark-greenish body. **2.** any of various North American fishes, esp. certain whitefishes and minnows. [C15: of unknown origin]

Chubb (tʃʌb) *n. Trademark.* a type of patent lock containing a device that sets the bolt immovably if the lock is picked.

chub·by (ˈtʃʌbɪ) *adj.* **·bi·er, ·bi·est.** (esp. of the human form) plump and round. [C17: perhaps from CHUB, with reference to the plump shape of the fish] —ˈ**chub·bi·ness** *n.*

Chu Chiang *or* **Chu Kiang** (ˈtʃuː ˈkjæŋ, kaɪˈæŋ) *n.* a river in SE China, in S Kwantung, flowing southeast from Kwangchow to the South China Sea. Length: about 177 km (110 miles). Also called: **Canton River, Pearl River.**

chuck[1] (tʃʌk) *vb.* (*mainly tr.*) **1.** *Informal.* to throw. **2.** to pat affectionately, esp. under the chin. **3.** *Informal.* (sometimes foll. by *in* or *up*) to give up; reject: *he chucked up his job; she chucked her boyfriend.* **4.** (*intr.*) *Slang, chiefly U.S.* (usually foll. by *up*) to vomit. ~*n.* **5.** a throw or toss. **6.** a playful pat under the chin. **7. the chuck.** *Informal.* dismissal. ~See also **chuck in, chuck out.** [C16: of unknown origin]

chuck[2] (tʃʌk) *n.* **1.** Also called: **chuck steak.** a cut of beef extending from the neck to the shoulder blade. **2.** a device that holds a workpiece in a lathe or tool in a drill, having a number of adjustable jaws geared to move in unison to centralize the workpiece or tool. [C17: variant of CHOCK]

chuck[3] (tʃʌk) *vb.* **1.** (*intr.*) a less common word for **cluck** (sense 2). ~*n.* **2.** a clucking sound. **3.** *Archaic.* a term of endearment. [C14 *chukken* to cluck, of imitative origin]

chuck[4] (tʃʌk) *n. Canadian W coast.* **1.** a large body of water. **2.** short for **saltchuck** (the sea). [C19: from Chinook Jargon, from Nootka *chauk*]

chuck-full *adj.* a less common spelling of **chock-full.**

chuck in *Austral. informal.* ~*vb.* (*intr., adv.*) **1.** to contribute to the cost of something. ~*n.* **2.** such a contribution.

chuck·le (ˈtʃʌkᵊl) *vb.* (*intr.*) **1.** to laugh softly or to oneself. **2.** (of animals, esp. hens) to make a clucking sound. ~*n.* **3.** a partly suppressed laugh. [C16: probably from CHUCK[3]] —ˈ**chuck·ler** *n.* —ˈ**chuck·ling·ly** *adv.*

chuck·le·head (ˈtʃʌkᵊlˌhɛd) *n. Informal.* a stupid person; blockhead; dolt. —ˈ**chuck·le·ˌhead·ed** *adj.* —ˈ**chuck·le·ˌhead·ed·ness** *n.*

chuck out *vb.* (*tr., adv.;* often foll. by *of*) *Informal.* to eject forcibly (from); throw out (of): *he was chucked out of the lobby.*

chuck wag·on *n.* a wagon carrying provisions and cooking utensils for men, such as cowboys, who work in the open. [C19: perhaps from CHUCK[2] (beef, food)]

chuck·wal·la (ˈtʃʌkˌwɒlə) *n.* a lizard, *Sauromalus obesus,* that has an inflatable body and inhabits desert regions of the southwestern U.S.: family *Iguanidae* (iguanas). [from Mexican Spanish *chacahuala,* from Shoshonean *tcaxxwal*]

chuck-will's-wid·ow *n.* a large North American nightjar, *Caprimulgus carolinensis,* similar to the whippoorwill.

chud·dar, chud·der (ˈtʃʌdə), *or* **chud·dah** *n.* a large Indian shawl. [from Hindi *caddar,* from Persian *chaddar*]

Chud·sko·ye O·ze·ro (*Russian* ˈtʃutskəjɪ ˈɔzɪrə) *n.* the Russian name for Lake **Peipus.**

chu·fa (ˈtʃuːfə) *n.* a sedge, *Cyperus esculentus,* of warm regions of the Old World, with nutlike edible tubers. [C19: from Old Spanish: a morsel, joke, from *chufar* to joke, from *chuflar* to deride, ultimately from Latin *sībilāre* to whistle]

chuff[1] (tʃʌf) *n.* **1.** a puffing sound of or as if of a steam engine. ~*vb.* **2.** (*intr.*) to move while emitting such sounds: *the train chuffed on its way.* [C15: of unknown origin]

chuff[2] (tʃʌf) *n. Brit. dialect.* a boor; churl; sullen fellow. [C17: from obsolete *chuff* (n.) fat cheek, of obscure origin]

chuff[3] (tʃʌf) *vb.* (*tr.; usually passive*) *Brit. slang.* to please or delight: *he was chuffed by his pay rise.* [probably from *chuff* (adj.) pleased, happy (earlier: chubby), from C16 *chuff* (obsolete n.) a fat cheek, of unknown origin]

chuf·fy *or* **chuf·fie** (ˈtʃʌfɪ) *adj.* **·fi·er, ·fi·est. 1.** *Scot. or Brit. dialect.* plump or chubby. **2.** *Brit. dialect.* surly.

chug (tʃʌg) *n.* **1.** a short dull sound, esp. one that is rapidly repeated, such as that made by an engine. ~*vb.* **chugs, chug·ging, chugged. 2.** (*intr.*) (of an engine, etc.) to operate while making such sounds. [C19: of imitative origin]

chu·kar (tʃʌˈkɑː) *n.* a common partridge, *Alectoris chukar* (or *graeca*), having red legs and bill and a black-barred sandy plumage. [from Hindi *cakor,* from Sanskrit *cakora,* probably of imitative origin]

Chuk·chi Pen·in·su·la (ˈtʃʊktʃɪ) *n.* a peninsula in the extreme NE Soviet Union, in NE Siberia: mainly tundra. Also called: **Chu·kots Peninsula** (ˈtʃʊkɒts).

Chuk·chi Sea (ˈtʃʊktʃɪ) *n.* part of the Arctic Ocean, north of the Bering Strait between Asia and North America. Russian name: **Chu·kot·sko·ye Mo·re** (tʃuˈkɔtskəji ˈmɔrji). Also called: **Chu·kots Sea** (ˈtʃʊkɒts).

Chu Kiang (ˈtʃuː ˈkjæŋ, kaɪˈæŋ) *n.* a variant spelling of **Chu Chiang.**

chuk·ka boot (ˈtʃʌkə) *or* **chuk·ka** *n.* an ankle-high boot made of suede or rubber and worn for playing polo. [C19: from CHUKKER]

chuk·ker *or* **chuk·ka** (ˈtʃʌkə) *n. Polo.* a period of continuous play, generally lasting 7½ minutes. [C20: from Hindi *cakkar,* from Sanskrit *cakra* wheel, circle]

chum[1] (tʃʌm) *n.* **1.** *Informal.* a close friend. ~*vb.* **chums, chum·ming, chummed. 2.** (*intr.;* usually foll. by *up with*) to be or become an intimate friend (of). **3.** (*tr.*) *Edinburgh dialect.* to accompany: *I'll chum you home.* [C17 (meaning: a person sharing rooms with another): probably shortened from *chamber fellow,* originally student slang (Oxford); compare CRONY]

chum[2] (tʃʌm) *n. Angling, chiefly U.S.* chopped fish, meal, etc., used as groundbait. [C19: origin uncertain]

chum³ (tʃʊm) *n.* a Pacific salmon, *Oncorhynchus keta.* [from Chinook Jargon *tsum* spots, marks, from Chinook]
chum·my ('tʃʌmɪ) *adj.* **·mi·er, ·mi·est.** *Informal.* friendly. —'**chum·mi·ly** *adv.* —'**chum·mi·ness** *n.*
chump¹ (tʃʌmp) *n.* **1.** *Informal.* a stupid person. **2.** a thick heavy block of wood. **3. a.** the thick blunt end of anything, esp. of a piece of meat. **b.** (*as modifier*): *a chump chop.* **4.** *Brit. slang.* the head (esp. in the phrase **off one's chump**). [C18: perhaps a blend of CHUNK and LUMP]
chump² (tʃʌmp) *vb.* a less common word for **chomp.**
chump·ing ('tʃʌmpɪŋ) *n. Yorkshire dialect.* collecting wood for bonfires on Guy Fawkes Day. [from CHUMP¹ (sense 2)]
chun·der ('tʃʌndə) *Slang, chiefly Austral.* ~*vb.* (*intr.*) **1.** to vomit. ~*n.* **2.** vomit. [C20: of uncertain origin]
chun·der·ous ('tʃʌndərəs) *adj. Austral. slang.* nauseating.
Chung·king ('tʃʊŋ'kɪŋ, 'tʃʌŋ-) *or* **Ch'ung-ch'ing** ('tʃʊŋ'tʃɪŋ, 'tʃʌŋ-) *n.* a port in SW China, in Szechwan province at the confluence of the Yangtze and Chialing rivers: site of a city since the 3rd millennium B.C.; wartime capital of China (1938–45); major trade centre for W China. Pop.: 2 400 000 (1970 est.). Also called: **Pahsien.**
chunk (tʃʌŋk) *n.* **1.** a thick solid piece, as of meat, wood, etc. **2.** a considerable amount. [C17: variant of CHUCK²]
chunk·y ('tʃʌŋkɪ) *adj.* **chunk·i·er, chunk·i·est. 1.** thick and short. **2.** consisting of or containing thick pieces: *chunky dog food.* **3.** *Chiefly Brit.* (of clothes, esp. knitwear) made of thick bulky material. —'**chunk·i·ly** *adv.* —'**chunk·i·ness** *n.*
Chun·nel ('tʃʌnᵊl) *n. Informal.* a proposed tunnel to be built under the English Channel, linking England and France. [C20: from CH(ANNEL) + (T)UNNEL]
chun·ter ('tʃʌntə) *vb.* (*intr.*) *Brit. informal.* to mutter or grumble. [C16: probably of imitative origin]
chu·pat·i *or* **chu·patt·y** (tʃə'pætɪ, -'pʌtɪ, -'pɑːtɪ) *n.* variant spellings of **chapatti.**
chup·pah ('xʊpə) *n.* a variant spelling of **huppah.**
Chur (*German* kuːr) *n.* a city in E Switzerland, capital of Grisons canton. Pop.: 31 193 (1970). Ancient name: **Curia Rhaetorum.** French name: **Coire.**
church (tʃɜːtʃ) *n.* **1.** a building designed for public forms of worship, esp. Christian worship. **2.** an occasion of public worship. **3.** the clergy as distinguished from the laity. **4.** (*usually cap.*) institutionalized forms of religion as a political or social force: *conflict between Church and State.* **5.** (*usually cap.*) the collective body of all Christians. **6.** (*often cap.*) a particular Christian denomination or group of Christian believers. **7.** (*often cap.*) the Christian religion. **8.** (in Britain) the practices or doctrines of the Church of England and similar denominations. Compare **chapel** (sense 4b). Related adj.: **ecclesiastical.** ~*vb.* (*tr.*) **9.** *Church of England.* to bring (someone, esp. a woman after childbirth) to church for special ceremonies. **10.** *U.S.* to impose church discipline upon. [Old English *cirice,* from Late Greek *kurikon,* from Greek *kuriakon* (*dōma*) the Lord's (house), from *kuriakos* of the master, from *kurios* master, from *kuros* power]
Church Ar·my *n.* a voluntary Anglican organization founded in 1882 to assist the parish clergy.
Church Com·mis·sion·ers *pl. n. Brit.* a group of representatives of Church and State that administers the endowments and property of the Church of England.
church·go·er ('tʃɜːtʃ,gəʊə) *n.* **1.** a person who attends church regularly. **2.** an adherent of an established Church in contrast to a Nonconformist. —'**church·,go·ing** *n.*
Church·ill¹ ('tʃɜːtʃɪl) *n.* **1.** a river in E Canada, rising in SE Labrador and flowing north and southeast over Churchill Falls, then east to the Atlantic. Length: about 1000 km (600 miles). Former name: **Hamilton River. 2.** a river in central Canada, rising in NW Saskatchewan and flowing east through several lakes to Hudson Bay at the town of Churchill. Length: about 1600 km (1000 miles). **3.** a town in Canada, in N Manitoba on Hudson Bay: an important port for shipping grain from the Prairies. Pop.: 1604 (1971).
Church·ill² ('tʃɜːtʃɪl) *n.* **1. John.** See (1st Duke of) **Marlborough. 2.** Lord **Ran·dolph.** 1849–95, British Conservative politician: secretary of state for India (1885–86) and chancellor of the Exchequer and leader of the House of Commons (1886). **3.** his son, Sir **Win·ston (Leonard Spencer).** 1874–1965, British Conservative statesman, orator, and writer, noted for his leadership during World War II. He held various posts under both Conservative and Liberal governments, including 1st Lord of the Admiralty (1911–15), before becoming prime minister (1940–45; 1951–55). His writings include *The World Crisis* (1923–29), *Marlborough* (1933–38), *The Second World War* (1948–54), and *History of the English-Speaking Peoples* (1956–58): Nobel prize for literature 1953.
Church·ill Falls *pl. n.* a waterfall in E Canada, in SW Labrador on the Churchill River: site of one of the largest hydroelectric power projects in the world. Height: 73 m (245 ft.). Former name: **Grand Falls.**
church key *n. U.S.* a device with a triangular point at one end for making holes in the tops of cans.
church·ly ('tʃɜːtʃlɪ) *adj.* appropriate to, associated with, or suggestive of church life and customs. —'**church·li·ness** *n.*
church·man ('tʃɜːtʃmən) *n., pl.* **·men. 1.** a clergyman. **2.** a male practising member of a church. —'**church·man·ly** *adj.* —'**church·man·,ship** *n.*
Church of Christ, Sci·en·tist *n.* the official name for the **Christian Scientists.**
Church of Eng·land *n.* the reformed established state Church in England, Catholic in order and basic doctrine, with the Sovereign as its temporal head.
Church of Je·sus Christ of Lat·ter-Day Saints *n.* the official name for the **Mormon Church.**
Church of Rome *n.* another name for the **Roman Catholic Church.**
Church of Scot·land *n.* the established church in Scotland, Calvinist in doctrine and Presbyterian in constitution.
Church Sla·von·ic *or* **Slav·ic** *n.* Old Church Slavonic, esp. as preserved in the liturgical use of the Orthodox church.
church text *n.* a heavy typeface in Gothic style.
church·ward·en (,tʃɜːtʃ'wɔːdᵊn) *n.* **1.** *Church of England, Episcopal Church.* one of two assistants of a parish priest who administer the secular affairs of the church. **2.** a long-stemmed tobacco pipe made of clay.
church·wom·an ('tʃɜːtʃ,wʊmən) *n., pl.* **·wom·en.** a female practising member of a church.
church·y ('tʃɜːtʃɪ) *adj.* **church·i·er, church·i·est. 1.** like a church, church service, etc. **2.** excessively religious.
church·yard ('tʃɜːtʃ,jɑːd) *n.* the grounds surrounding a church, usually used as a graveyard.
chu·ri·dars ('tʃuːrɪ,dɑːz) *pl. n.* long tight-fitting trousers, worn by Indian men and women. Also called: **churidar pyjamas.** [from Hindi]
chu·rin·ga (tʃə'rɪŋgə) *n., pl.* **·ga** *or* **·gas.** a sacred amulet of the Australian Aborigines. [from a native Australian language]
churl (tʃɜːl) *n.* **1.** a surly ill-bred person. **2.** a farm labourer. **3.** a variant spelling of **ceorl. 4.** a miserly person. [Old English *ceorl;* related to Old Norse *karl,* Middle Low German *kerle,* Greek *gerōn* old man]
churl·ish ('tʃɜːlɪʃ) *adj.* **1.** rude or surly. **2.** of or relating to peasants. **3.** miserly. **4.** *Rare.* difficult to work or manage. —'**churl·ish·ly** *adv.* —'**churl·ish·ness** *n.*
churn (tʃɜːn) *n.* **1.** *Brit.* a large container for milk. **2.** a vessel or machine in which cream or whole milk is vigorously agitated to produce butter. **3.** any similar device. ~*vb.* **4. a.** to stir or agitate (milk or cream) in order to make butter. **b.** to make (butter) by this process. **5.** (sometimes foll. by *up*) to move or cause to move with agitation: *ideas churned in his head.* [Old English *ciern;* related to Old Norse *kjarni,* Middle Low German *kerne* churn, German dialect *Kern* cream] —'**churn·er** *n.*
churn·ing ('tʃɜːnɪŋ) *n.* **1.** the quantity of butter churned at any one time. **2. a.** the act, process, or effect of someone or something that churns. **b.** (*as modifier*): *a churning stomach.*
churn out *vb.* (*tr., adv.*) *Informal.* **1.** to produce (something) at a rapid rate: *to churn out ideas.* **2.** to perform (something) mechanically: *to churn out a song.*
churr (tʃɜː) *vb., n.* a variant spelling of **chirr.**
chur·ri·gue·resque (,tʃʊərɪgə'rɛsk) *or* **chur·ri·gue·res·co** *adj.* of or relating to a style of baroque architecture of Spain in the late 17th and early 18th centuries. [C19: from Spanish *churrigueresco* in the style of José *Churriguera* (1650–1725), Spanish architect and sculptor]
chute¹ (ʃuːt) *n.* **1.** an inclined channel or vertical passage down which water, parcels, coal, etc., may be dropped. **2.** a steep slope, used as a slide as for toboggans. **3.** a slide into a swimming pool. **4.** a narrow passageway through which animals file for branding, spraying, etc. **5.** a rapid or waterfall. [C19: from Old French *cheoite,* feminine past participle of *cheoir* to fall, from Latin *cadere;* in some senses, a variant spelling of SHOOT]
chute² (ʃuːt) *n., vb. Informal.* short for **parachute.** —'**chut·ist** *n.*
Chu Teh ('tʃuː 'teɪ) *n.* 1886–1976, Chinese military leader and politician; he became commander in chief of the Red Army (1931) and was chairman of the Standing Committee of the National People's Congress of the People's Republic of China (1959–76).
chut·ney ('tʃʌtnɪ) *n.* a pickle of Indian origin, made from fruit, vinegar, spices, sugar, etc.: *mango chutney.* [C19: from Hindi *catni,* of uncertain origin]
chut·tie *or* **chut·ty** ('tʃʌtɪ) *n., pl.* **·ties.** *Austral. informal.* chewing gum. [C20: perhaps from the phrase *chew it*]
chutz·pah *or* **hutz·pah** ('xʊtspə) *n. U.S. informal.* shameless audacity; impudence. [C20: from Yiddish]
Chu·vash (tʃʊ'vɑːʃ) *n.* **1.** (*pl.* **·vash** *or* **·vash·es**) a member of a Mongoloid people of the Soviet Union, living chiefly in the middle Volga region. **2.** the language of this people, belonging to the Turkic branch of the Altaic family.
Chu·vash Au·ton·o·mous So·vi·et So·cial·ist Re·pub·lic *n.* an administrative division of the W central Soviet Union, in the middle Volga valley: generally low and undulating, with large areas of forest. Capital: Cheboksary. Pop.: 1 223 675 (1970). Area: 18 300 sq. km (7064 sq. miles).
chy·ack ('tʃaɪæk) *vb.* a variant spelling of **chiack.**
chyle (kaɪl) *n.* a milky fluid composed of lymph and emulsified fat globules, formed in the small intestine during digestion. [C17: from Late Latin *chȳlus,* from Greek *khulos* juice pressed from a plant; related to Greek *khein* to pour] —**chy·la·ceous** (kaɪ'leɪʃəs) *or* '**chy·lous** *adj.*
chyme (kaɪm) *n.* the thick fluid mass of partially digested food that leaves the stomach. [C17: from Late Latin *chȳmus,* from Greek *khumos* juice; compare CHYLE] —'**chy·mous** *adj.*
chy·mo·sin ('kaɪməsɪn) *n.* another name for **rennin.** [C20: from CHYME + -OSE² + -IN]
chy·mo·tryp·sin (,kaɪməʊ'trɪpsɪn) *n.* a powerful proteolytic enzyme secreted from the pancreas in the form of chymotrypsinogen, being converted to the active form by trypsin. [C20: from CHYME + TRYPSIN]
chy·mo·tryp·sin·o·gen (,kaɪməʊtrɪp'sɪnədʒɪn) *n.* the inactive

precursor of chymotrypsin. [C20: from CHYMOTRYPSIN + -GEN]

chypre *French.* ('ʃipr) *n.* a perfume made from sandalwood. [literally: Cyprus, where it perhaps originated]

Ci *abbrev. for* curie.

CI *international car registration for* Ivory Coast.

C.I. *abbrev. for* Channel Islands.

C.I.A. *abbrev. for* Central Intelligence Agency; a federal U.S. bureau created in 1947 to coordinate and conduct espionage and intelligence activities.

ciao *Italian.* (tʃaʊ) *interj.* an informal word for **hello** or **goodbye.**

Cib·ber ('sɪbə) *n.* **Col·ley** ('kɒlɪ). 1671–1757, English actor and dramatist; poet laureate (1730–57).

ci+bo+ri·um (sɪ'bɔ:rɪəm) *n., pl.* **+ri·a** (-rɪə). *Christianity.* **1.** a goblet-shaped lidded vessel used to hold consecrated wafers in Holy Communion. **2.** a freestanding canopy fixed over an altar and supported by four pillars. [C17: from Medieval Latin, from Latin: drinking cup, from Greek *kibōrion* cup-shaped seed vessel of the Egyptian lotus, hence, a cup]

ci+ca+da (sɪ'kɑ:də) *or* **ci+ca+la** *n., pl.* **+das, +dae** (-di:) *or* **+las, +le** (-lɛ). any large broad insect of the homopterous family *Cicadidae,* most common in warm regions. Cicadas have membranous wings and the males produce a high-pitched drone by vibration of a pair of drumlike abdominal organs. [C19: from Latin]

ci+ca+la (sɪ'kɑ:lə; *Italian* tʃi'ka:la) *n., pl.* **+las** *or* **+le** (-lɛ). another name for **cicada.** [C19: from Italian, from Latin: CICADA]

cic·a+tric+le ('sɪkə,trɪkᵊl) *n.* **1.** *Zoology.* the blastoderm in the egg of a bird. **2.** *Biology.* any small scar or mark. [C17: from Latin *cicātrīcula* a little scar, from CICATRIX]

cic·a+trix ('sɪkətrɪks) *n., pl.* **cic·a+tri+ces** (,sɪkə'traɪsi:z). **1.** the tissue that forms in a wound during healing; scar. **2.** a scar on a plant indicating the former point of attachment of a part, esp. a leaf. [C17: from Latin: scar, of obscure origin] **—cic·a+tri+cial** (,sɪkə'trɪʃəl) *adj.* **—ci+cat+ri+cose** (sɪ'kætrɪ,kəʊs, 'sɪkə-) *adj.*

cic·a+trize *or* **cic·a+trise** ('sɪkə,traɪz) *vb.* (of a wound or defect in tissue) to be closed by scar formation; heal. **—,cic·a+'tri+zant** *or* **,cic·a+'tri+sant** *adj.* **—,cic·a+tri+'za+tion** *or* **,cic·a+tri+'sa+tion** *n.* **—'cic·a+,triz+er** *or* **'cic·a+,tris+er** *n.*

cic+e·ly ('sɪsəlɪ) *n., pl.* **·lies.** short for **sweet cicely.** [C16: from Latin *seselis,* from Greek, of obscure origin; influenced in spelling by the English proper name *Cicely*]

cic+e·ro ('sɪsə,rəʊ) *n., pl.* **·ros.** a measure for type that is somewhat larger than the pica. [C19: from its first being used in a 15th-century edition of CICERO]

Cic·e·ro ('sɪsə,rəʊ) *n.* **Mar·cus Tul·li·us** ('mɑ:kəs 'tʌlɪəs). 106–43 B.C., Roman consul, orator, and writer. He foiled Catiline's conspiracy (63) and was killed by Mark Antony's agents after he denounced Antony in the *Philippics.* His writings are regarded as a model of Latin prose. Formerly known in English as **Tully.**

cic+e+ro+ne (,sɪsə'rəʊnɪ, ,tʃɪtʃ-) *n., pl.* **+nes** *or* **+ni** (-nɪ). a person who conducts and informs sightseers. [C18: from Italian: antiquarian scholar, guide, after CICERO, alluding to the eloquence and erudition of these men]

Cic+e+ro+ni·an (,sɪsə'rəʊnɪən) *adj.* **1.** of or resembling Cicero or his rhetorical style; eloquent. **2.** (of literary style) characterized by the use of antithesis and long periods.

cich+lid ('sɪklɪd) *n.* **1.** any tropical freshwater percoid fish of the family *Cichlidae,* which includes the mouthbrooders. Cichlids are popular aquarium fishes. *~adj.* **2.** of, relating to, or belonging to the *Cichlidae.* [C19: from New Latin *Cichlidae,* ultimately from Greek *kikhlē* a sea fish] **—'cich+loid** *adj.*

ci+cis+be·o *Italian.* (,tʃitʃiz'bɛ:o) *n., pl.* **+be·i** (-'bɛ:i). the escort or lover of a married woman, esp. in 18th-century Italy.

Cid (sɪd; *Spanish* θið) *n.* **El** *or* **the.** original name *Rodrigo Diaz de Vivar.* ?1043–99, Spanish soldier and hero of the wars against the Moors.

C.I.D. *n.* (in Britain) *abbrev. for* Criminal Investigation Department; the detective division of a police force.

-cide *n. combining form.* **1.** indicating a person or thing that kills: *insecticide.* **2.** indicating a killing; murder: *homicide.* [from Latin *-cīda* (agent), *-cīdium* (act), from *caedere* to kill] **—-ci·dal** *adj. combining form.*

ci+der *or* **cy+der** ('saɪdə) *n.* **1.** Also called (U.S.): **hard cider.** an alcoholic drink made from the fermented juice of apples. **2.** Also called: **sweet cider.** *U.S.* an unfermented drink made from apple juice. [C14: from Old French *cisdre,* via Medieval Latin, from Late Greek *sikera* strong drink, from Hebrew *shēkhār*]

ci-de·vant *French.* (sidə'vã) *adj.* (esp. of an officeholder) former; recent. [literally: heretofore]

C.I.E. (formerly) *abbrev. for* Companion of the Indian Empire.

Cien+fue+gos (*Spanish* sjen'fweɣos) *n.* a port in S Cuba, on **Cienfuegos Bay.** Pop.: 85 200 (1970).

c.i.f. *or* **C.I.F.** *abbrev. for* cost, insurance, and freight (included in the price quoted).

cig (sɪg) *or* **cig+gy** ('sɪgɪ) *n., pl.* **cigs** *or* **cig+gies.** *Informal.* a cigarette.

ci+gar (sɪ'gɑ:) *n.* a cylindrical roll of cured tobacco leaves, for smoking. [C18: from Spanish *cigarro,* perhaps from Mayan *sicar* to smoke]

cig·a+rette *or U.S. (sometimes)* **cig·a+ret** (,sɪgə'rɛt) *n.* a short tightly rolled cylinder of tobacco, wrapped in thin paper and often having a filter tip, for smoking. Shortened forms: **cig, ciggy.** [C19: from French, literally: a little CIGAR]

cig·a+rette card *n.* a small picture card, formerly given away with cigarettes, now collected as a hobby.

cig·a+rette end *n.* the part of a cigarette that is held in the mouth and that remains unsmoked after it is finished.

cig·a+rette hold+er *n.* a mouthpiece of wood, ivory, etc., used for holding a cigarette while it is smoked.

cig·a+rette light+er *n.* See **lighter**¹.

cig·a+rette pa+per *n.* a piece of thin paper rolled around tobacco to form a cigarette.

cig·a+ril+lo (,sɪgə'rɪləʊ) *n., pl.* **+los.** a small cigar, often only slightly larger than a cigarette.

C.I.G.S. (in Britain, formerly) *abbrev. for* Chief of the Imperial General Staff.

cil·i·a ('sɪlɪə) *n.* the plural of **cilium.**

cil·i·ar·y ('sɪlɪərɪ) *adj.* **1.** of or relating to cilia. **2.** of or relating to the ciliary body.

cil·i·ar·y bod·y *n.* the part of the vascular tunic of the eye that connects the choroid with the iris.

cil·i·ate ('sɪlɪɪt, -eɪt) *adj.* **1.** Also: **cil·i·at+ed.** possessing or relating to cilia: *a ciliate epithelium.* **2.** of or relating to protozoans of the subclass *Ciliata,* which have an outer layer of cilia. *~n.* **3.** a protozoan of the subclass *Ciliata.* **—,cil·i+'a·tion** *n.*

cil+ice ('sɪlɪs) *n.* a haircloth fabric or garment. [Old English *cilic,* from Latin *cilicium* shirt made of Cilician goats' hair, from Greek *kilikion,* from *Kilikia* CILICIA]

Ci+li+ci·a (sɪ'lɪʃɪə) *n.* an ancient region and former kingdom of SE Asia Minor, between the Taurus Mountains and the Mediterranean: corresponds to the region around present-day Adana. **—Ci+'li+ci·an** *adj., n.*

Ci+li+ci·an Gates *pl. n.* a pass in S Turkey, over the Taurus Mountains. Turkish name: **Gülek Bogaz.**

cil·i·o+late ('sɪlɪəlɪt, -,leɪt) *adj.* covered with minute hairs, as some plants. [C19: from New Latin *ciliolum,* diminutive of CILIUM]

cil+i·um ('sɪlɪəm) *n., pl.* **cil·i·a** ('sɪlɪə). **1.** any of the short threads projecting from the surface of a cell, organism, etc., whose rhythmic beating causes movement of the organism or of the surrounding fluid. **2.** the technical name for **eyelash.** [C18: New Latin, from Latin: (lower) eyelid, eyelash]

Ci·ma·bu·e (*Italian* ,tʃima'bu:e) *n.* **Gio·van·ni** (dʒo'vanni). ?1240–?1302, Italian painter of the Florentine school, who anticipated the movement, led by Giotto, away from the Byzantine tradition in art towards a greater naturalism.

cim+ba+lom *or* **cym+ba+lom** ('tsɪmbələm) *n.* a type of dulcimer, esp. of Hungary. See **dulcimer** (sense 1). [C19: Hungarian, from Italian *cembalo;* see CEMBALO]

Cim+bri ('sɪmbri:, 'kɪm-) *pl. n.* a Germanic people from N Jutland who migrated southwards in the 2nd century B.C.: annihilated by Marius in the Po valley (101 B.C.). **—Cim+bri·an** ('sɪmbrɪən) *n., adj.* **—'Cim+bric** *adj.*

ci+mex ('saɪmɛks) *n., pl.* **cim·i·ces** ('sɪmɪ,si:z). any of the heteropterous insects of the genus *Cimex,* esp. the bedbug. [C16: from Latin: bug]

Cim+me+ri·an (sɪ'mɪərɪən) *adj.* **1.** (*sometimes not cap.*) very dark; gloomy. *~n.* **2.** *Greek myth.* one of a people who lived in a land of darkness at the edge of the world.

Ci·mon ('saɪmən) *n.* died 449 B.C., Athenian military and naval commander: defeated the Persians at Eurymedon (?466).

C in C *or* **C.-in-C.** *Military. abbrev. for* Commander in Chief.

cinch¹ (sɪntʃ) *n.* **1.** *Slang.* an easy task. **2.** *Slang.* a certainty. **3.** a U.S. name for **girth** (sense 3). **4.** *U.S. informal.* a firm grip. *~vb.* **5.** (often foll. by *up*) *U.S.* to fasten a girth around (a horse). **6.** (*tr.*) *Informal.* to make sure of. **7.** (*tr.*) *Informal, chiefly U.S.* to get a firm grip on. [C19: from Spanish *cincha* saddle girth, from Latin *cingula* girdle, from *cingere* to encircle]

cinch² (sɪntʃ) *n.* a card game in which the five of trumps ranks highest. [C19: probably from CINCH¹]

cin+cho+na (sɪŋ'kəʊnə) *n.* **1.** any tree or shrub of the South American rubiaceous genus *Cinchona,* esp. *C. calisaya,* having medicinal bark. **2.** Also called: **cinchona bark, Peruvian bark, calisaya, china bark.** the dried bark of any of these trees, which yields quinine and other medicinal alkaloids. **3.** any of the drugs derived from cinchona bark. [C18: New Latin, named after the Countess of *Chinchón* (1576–1639), vicereine of Peru] **—cin+chon+ic** (sɪŋ'kɒnɪk) *adj.*

cin+chon·i·dine (sɪŋ'kɒnɪ,di:n) *n.* an alkaloid that is a stereoisomer of cinchonine, with similar properties and uses.

cin+cho+nine ('sɪŋkə,ni:n) *n.* an insoluble crystalline alkaloid isolated from cinchona bark and used as a substitute for quinine. Formula: $C_{19}H_{22}N_2O$.

cin+chon+ism ('sɪŋkə,nɪzəm) *n.* a condition resulting from an excessive dose of cinchona bark or its alkaloids, characterized chiefly by headache, ringing in the ears, and vomiting.

cin+cho+nize *or* **cin+cho+nise** ('sɪŋkə,naɪz) *vb.* (*tr.*) to treat (a patient) with cinchona or one of its alkaloids, esp. quinine. **—,cin+cho+ni+'za+tion** *or* **,cin+cho+ni+'sa+tion** *n.*

Cin+cin+nat·i (,sɪnsɪ'nætɪ) *n.* a city in SW Ohio, on the Ohio River. Pop.: 426 245 (1973 est.).

Cin·cin·na·tus (,sɪnsɪ'nɑ:təs) *n.* **Lu·ci·us Quinc·ti·us** ('lu:sɪəs 'kwɪŋktɪəs). ?519–438 B.C., Roman general and statesman, regarded as a model of simple virtue; dictator of Rome during two crises (458; 439), retiring to his farm after each one.

cinc+ture ('sɪŋktʃə) *n.* something that encircles or surrounds, esp. a belt, girdle, or border. [C16: from Latin *cinctūra,* from *cingere* to gird]

cin+der ('sɪndə) *n.* **1.** a piece of incombustible material left after the combustion of coal, coke, etc.; clinker. **2.** a piece of charred material that burns without flames; ember. **3.** Also called: **sinter.** any solid waste from smelting or refining. **4.** (*pl.*) fragments of volcanic lava; scoriae. *~vb.* **5.** (*tr.*) *Rare.* to burn to cinders. [Old English *sinder;* related to Old Norse

sindr, Old High German *sintar*, Old Slavonic *sedra* stalactite] —'**cin·der·y** *adj.*
cin+der block *n.* the usual U.S. name for **breeze block.**
Cin·der·el·la (ˌsɪndəˈrɛlə) *n.* **1.** a girl who achieves fame after being obscure. **2.** a poor, neglected, or unsuccessful person or thing. **3.** (*modifier*) *Chiefly U.S.* relating to dramatic success: *a Cinderella story.* [C19: after *Cinderella*, the heroine of a fairy tale who is aided by a fairy godmother]
cin+der track *n.* a race track covered with fine cinders.
cin·e- *combining form.* indicating motion picture or cinema: *cinecamera; cinephotography.*
cin+e·aste (ˈsɪnɪˌæst) *n.* an enthusiast for films. [C20: French, from CINEMA + *-aste*, as *-ast* in *enthusiast*]
cin·e cam+er·a (ˈsɪnɪ) *n. Brit.* a camera in which a strip of film moves past the lens, usually to give 16 or 25 exposures per second, thus enabling moving pictures to be taken. U.S. term: **movie camera.**
cin·e film *n. Brit.* photographic film, wound on a spool, usually 8 or 16 millimetres wide, up to several hundred metres long, and having one or two lines of sprocket holes along its length enabling it to be used in a cine camera. U.S. term: **movie film.**
cin+e·ma (ˈsɪnɪmə) *n.* **1.** *Chiefly Brit.* **a.** a place designed for the exhibition of films. **b.** (*as modifier*): *a cinema seat.* **2. the cinema. a.** the art or business of making films. **b.** films collectively. [C19 (earlier spelling: *kinema*): shortened from CINEMATOGRAPH] —**cin+e·mat+ic** (ˌsɪnɪˈmætɪk) *adj.* —ˌ**cin+e·'mat·i·cal+ly** *adv.*
Cin+e·ma+scope (ˈsɪnɪməˌskəʊp) *n. Trademark.* an anamorphic process of wide-screen film projection in which an image of approximately twice the usual width is squeezed into a 35mm frame and then screened by a projector having complementary lenses.
cin+e·ma+theque (ˌsɪnɪməˈtɛk) *n.* a small intimate cinema. [C20: from French *cinémathèque* film library, from CINEMA + (*biblio*)*thèque* library]
cin+e·mat·o+graph (ˌsɪnɪˈmætəˌgrɑːf, -ˌgræf) *Chiefly Brit.* ~*n.* **1.** a combined camera, printer, and projector. ~*vb.* **2.** to take (pictures) with a film camera. [C19 (earlier spelling: *kinematograph*): from Greek *kinēmat-*, *kinēma* motion + -GRAPH] —**cin+e·ma+tog+ra+pher** (ˌsɪnɪməˈtɒgrəfə) *n.* —**cin+e·mat·o·graph+ic** (ˌsɪnɪˌmætəˈgræfɪk) *adj.* —ˌ**cin+e·ˌmat·o+'graph·i·cal+ly** *adv.* —ˌ**cin+e·ma+'tog+ra+phy** *n.*
ci+né·ma vé·ri·té (*French* sinema veriˈte) *n.* films characterized by subjects, actions, etc., that have the appearance of real life. [French, literally: cinema truth]
cin+e·ol (ˈsɪnɪˌɒl) *or* **cin+e·ole** (ˈsɪnɪˌəʊl) *n.* another name for **eucalyptol.** [C19: changed from New Latin *oleum cinae*, literally: oil of wormseed]
Cin+e·ra+ma (ˌsɪnəˈrɑːmə) *n. Trademark.* wide-screen presentation of films using either three separate 35mm projectors or one 70mm projector to produce an image on a large deeply curved screen.
cin+e·rar·i·a (ˌsɪnəˈrɛərɪə) *n.* a plant, *Senecio cruentus*, of the Canary Islands, widely cultivated for its blue, purple, red, or variegated daisy-like flowers: family *Compositae* (composites). [C16: from New Latin, from Latin *cinerārius* of ashes, from *cinis* ashes; from its downy leaves]
cin+e·rar+i·um (ˌsɪnəˈrɛərɪəm) *n., pl.* **+rar·i·a** (-ˈrɛərɪə). a place for keeping the ashes of the dead after cremation. [C19: from Latin, from *cinerārius* relating to ashes; see CINERARIA] —**cin+e·rar·y** (ˈsɪnərərɪ) *adj.*
cin+er·a·tor (ˈsɪnəˌreɪtə) *n.* another name (esp. U.S.) for **cremator** (sense 1). —ˌ**cin+e·'ra+tion** *n.*
ci+ner+e·ous (sɪˈnɪərɪəs) *or* **cin+er·i·tious** (ˌsɪnəˈrɪʃəs) *adj.* **1.** of a greyish colour. **2.** resembling or consisting of ashes. [C17: from Latin *cinereus*, from *cinis* ashes]
cin+e·rin (ˈsɪnərɪn) *n.* either of two similar organic compounds found in pyrethrum and used as insecticides. Formulas: $C_{20}H_{28}O_3$ (**cinerin I**), $C_{21}H_{28}O_5$ (**cinerin II**). [C20: from Latin *ciner-*, *cinis* ashes + -IN]
cin+gu+lum (ˈsɪŋgjʊləm) *n., pl.* **+la** (-lə). *Anatomy.* a girdle-like part, such as the ridge round the base of a tooth or the band of fibres connecting parts of the cerebrum. [C19: from Latin: belt, from *cingere* to gird] —**cin+gu+late** (ˈsɪŋgjʊlɪt, -ˌleɪt) *or* **'cin+gu+ˌlat+ed** *adj.*
Cin·na (ˈsɪnə) *n.* **Lu·ci·us Cor·ne·li·us** (ˈluːsɪəs kɔːˈniːlɪəs). died 84 B.C., Roman patrician; an opponent of Sulla.
cin+na+bar (ˈsɪnəˌbɑː) *n.* **1.** a heavy red mineral consisting of mercuric sulphide in hexagonal crystalline form: the chief ore of mercury. Formula: HgS. **2.** the red form of mercuric sulphide, esp. when used as a pigment. **3.** a bright red to reddish-orange; vermilion. **4.** a large red-and-black European moth, *Callimorpha jacobaeae:* family *Arctiidae* (tiger moths, etc.). [C15: from Old French *cenobre*, from Latin *cinnābaris*, from Greek *kinnabari*, of Oriental origin]
cin+nam+ic ac·id (sɪˈnæmɪk) *n.* a white crystalline water-insoluble weak organic acid existing in two isomeric forms; 3-phenylpropenoic acid. The *trans-* form occurs naturally and its esters are used in perfumery. Formula: $C_6H_5CH{:}CHCOOH$. [C19: from CINNAM(ON) + -IC; from its being found in cinnamon oil]
cin+na+mon (ˈsɪnəmən) *n.* **1.** a tropical Asian lauraceous tree, *Cinnamomum zeylanicum*, having aromatic yellowish-brown bark. **2.** the spice obtained from the bark of this tree, used for flavouring food and drink. **3. Saigon cinnamon.** an E Asian lauraceous tree, *Cinnamomum loureirii*, the bark of which is used as a cordial and to relieve flatulence. **4.** any of several similar or related trees or their bark. See **cassia** (sense 2). **5.** a light yellowish-brown. [C15: from Old French *cinnamome*, via Latin and Greek, from Hebrew *qinnamown*] —**cin+'nam+ic** *or* **cin+na+mon+ic** (ˌsɪnəˈmɒnɪk) *adj.*
cin+na+mon bear *n.* a reddish-brown variety of the American black bear. See **black bear** (sense 1).
cin+na+mon stone *n.* another name for **hessonite.**
cin+quain (sɪŋˈkeɪn, ˈsɪŋkeɪn) *n.* a stanza of five lines. [C18 (in the sense: a military company of five): from French *cinq* five, from Latin *quinque*; compare QUATRAIN]
cinque (sɪŋk) *n.* the number five in cards, dice, etc. [C14: from Old French *cinq* five]
cin+que·cen+to (ˌtʃɪŋkwɪˈtʃɛntəʊ) *n.* the 16th century in Italian art, architecture, or literature. [C18: Italian, shortened from *milcinquecento* 1500] —ˌ**cin+que·'cen+tist** *n.*
cinque+foil (ˈsɪŋkˌfɔɪl) *n.* **1.** any plant of the N temperate rosaceous genus *Potentilla*, typically having five-lobed compound leaves. **2.** an ornamental carving in the form of five arcs arranged in a circle and separated by cusps. **3.** *Heraldry.* a charge representing a five-petalled flower. [C13 *sink foil*, from Old French *cincfoille*, from Latin *quinquefolium* plant with five leaves, translating Greek *pentaphullon* from *pente* five + *phullon* leaf]
Cinque Ports (sɪŋk) *pl. n.* an association of ports on the SE coast of England, originally consisting of Hastings, Romney, Hythe, Dover, and Sandwich, which from late Anglo-Saxon times provided ships for the king's service in return for the profits of justice in their courts. The Cinque Ports declined with the growth of other ports and surrendered their charters in 1685.
Cin+za+no (tʃɪnˈzɑːnəʊ) *n. Trademark.* an Italian vermouth.
C.I.O. *U.S. abbrev. for* Congress of Industrial Organizations.
Ci+pan+go (sɪˈpæŋgəʊ) *n.* (in medieval legend) an island E of Asia: called Zipangu by Marco Polo and sought by Columbus; identified with Japan.
ci+pher *or* **cy+pher** (ˈsaɪfə) *n.* **1.** a method of secret writing using substitution or transposition of letters according to a key. **2.** a secret message. **3.** the key to a secret message. **4.** an obsolete name for **zero** (sense 1). **5.** any of the Arabic numerals (0, 1, 2, 3, etc., to 9) or the Arabic system of numbering as a whole. **6.** a person or thing of no importance; nonentity. **7.** a design consisting of interwoven letters; monogram. **8.** *Music.* a defect in an organ resulting in the continuous sounding of a pipe, the key of which has not been depressed. ~*vb.* **9.** to put (a message) into secret writing. **10.** (*intr.*) (of an organ pipe) to sound without having the appropriate key depressed. **11.** *Rare.* to perform (a calculation) arithmetically. [C14: from Old French *cifre* zero, from Medieval Latin *cifra*, from Arabic *sifr* zero, empty]
cip·o+lin (ˈsɪpəlɪn) *n.* an Italian marble with alternating white and green streaks. [C18: from French, from Italian *cipollino* a little onion, from *cipolla* onion, from Late Latin *cēpulla*, diminutive of Latin *cēpa* onion; from its likeness to the layers of an onion]
cir. *or* **circ.** *abbrev. for:* **1.** (preceding a date) circa. **2.** circular. **3.** circulation. **4.** circumference.
cir+ca (ˈsɜːkə) *prep.* (used with a date) at the approximate time of: *circa 1182* B.C. Abbrev: *c* [Latin: about; related to Latin *circus* circle, CIRCUS]
cir+ca+di+an (sɜːˈkeɪdɪən) *adj.* of or relating to biological processes that occur regularly at 24-hour intervals, even in the absence of periodicity in the environment. See also **biological clock.** [C20: from Latin *circa* about + *diēs* day]
Cir+cas+si·a (sɜːˈkæsɪə) *n.* a region of the S Soviet Union, on the Black Sea north of the Caucasus Mountains.
Cir+cas+si·an (sɜːˈkæsɪən) *n.* **1.** a native of Circassia. **2.** Also called: **Adygei.** a language spoken in Circassia, belonging to the North Caucasian family. ~*adj. also* **Cir+cas+sic. 3.** relating to Circassia, its people, or language.
Cir·ce (ˈsɜːsɪ) *n. Greek myth.* an enchantress who detained Odysseus on her island and turned his men into swine. —**Cir+'ce·an** *adj.*
cir+ci+nate (ˈsɜːsɪˌneɪt) *adj.* (of part of a plant, such as a young fern) coiled so that the tip is at the centre. [C19: from Latin *circināre* to make round, from *circinus* pair of compasses, from *circus*, see CIRCUS] —**'cir+ci+ˌnate+ly** *adv.*
Cir+ci+nus (ˈsɜːsɪnəs) *n., Latin genitive* **Cir+ci+ni** (ˈsɜːsɪˌnaɪ). a small faint constellation in the S hemisphere close to Centaurus and the Southern Cross. [C19: from Latin, a pair of compasses]
cir+cle (ˈsɜːkᵊl) *n.* **1.** a closed plane curve every point of which is equidistant from a given fixed point, the centre. Equation: $(x-h)^2 + (y-k)^2 = r^2$ where r is the radius and (h, k) are the coordinates of the centre; area: πr^2; circumference: $2\pi r$. **2.** the figure enclosed by such a curve. **3.** *Theatre.* the section of seats above the main level of the auditorium, usually comprising the dress circle and the upper circle. **4.** something formed or arranged in the shape of a circle. **5.** a group of people sharing an interest, activity, upbringing, etc.; set: *golf circles; a family circle.* **6.** a domain or area of activity, interest, or influence. **7.** a circuit. **8.** a process or chain of events or parts that forms a connected whole; cycle. **9.** a parallel of latitude. See also **great circle, small circle. 10.** the ring of a circus. **11.** one of a number of Neolithic or Bronze Age rings of standing stones, such as Stonehenge, found in Europe and thought to be associated with some form of ritual or astronomical measurement. **12.** *Hockey.* See **striking circle. 13. go** *or* **run round in circles.** to engage in energetic but fruitless activity. **14. come full circle.** to arrive back at one's starting point. See also **vicious circle.** ~*vb.* **15.** to move in a circle (around): *we circled the city by car.* **16.** to enclose in a circle; encircle. [C14: from Latin *circulus* a circular figure, from *circus* ring, circle] —**'cir+cler** *n.*

cir+clet ('sɜːklɪt) *n.* a small circle or ring, esp. a circular ornament worn on the head. [C15: from Old French *cerclet* a little CIRCLE]

Cir+clo+ra+ma (ˌsɜːklə'rɑːmə) *n. Trademark.* a system of film projection in which a number of projectors and screens are employed to produce a picture that surrounds the viewer.

cir+cuit ('sɜːkɪt) *n.* **1. a.** a complete route or course, esp. one that is curved or circular or that lies around an object. **b.** the area enclosed within such a route. **2.** the act of following such a route: *we made three circuits of the course.* **3. a.** a complete path through which an electric current can flow. **b.** (*as modifier*): *a circuit diagram.* **4. a.** a periodical journey around an area, as made by judges, salesmen, etc. **b.** the route traversed or places visited on such a journey. **c.** the persons making such a journey. **5.** *English law.* one of six areas into which England is divided for the administration of justice. **6.** a number of theatres, cinemas, etc., under one management or in which the same film is shown or in which a company of performers plays in turn. **7.** *Sport.* **a.** a series of tournaments in which the same players regularly take part: *the international tennis circuit.* **b.** (usually preceded by *the*) the contestants who take part in such a series. **8.** *Chiefly Brit.* a motor racing track, usually of irregular shape. ~*vb.* **9.** to make or travel in a circuit around (something). [C14: from Latin *circuitus* a going around, from *circumīre,* from *circum* around + *īre* to go] —'**cir+cuit+al** *adj.*

cir+cuit bind+ing *n.* a style of limp-leather binding, used esp. for Bibles and prayer books, in which the edges of the cover bend over to protect the edges of the pages.

cir+cuit break+er *n.* a device that under abnormal conditions, such as a short circuit, stops the flow of current in an electrical circuit. Sometimes shortened to **breaker.** Compare **fuse**[2] (sense 6).

cir+cuit judge *n. Brit.* a judge presiding over a county court or crown court.

cir+cu+i+tous (sə'kjuːɪtəs) *adj.* indirect and lengthy; roundabout: *a circuitous route.* —**cir+'cu+i+tous+ly** *adv.* —**cir+'cu+i+tous+ness** *n.*

cir+cuit rid+er *n. U.S.* (formerly) a minister of religion who preached from place to place along an established circuit.

cir+cuit+ry ('sɜːkɪtrɪ) *n.* **1.** the design of an electrical circuit. **2.** the system of circuits used in an electronic device.

cir+cuit train+ing *n.* a form of athletic training in which a number of exercises are performed in turn.

cir+cu+i·ty (sə'kjuːɪtɪ) *n., pl.* **·ties.** (of speech, reasoning, etc.) a roundabout or devious quality.

cir+cu+lar ('sɜːkjʊlə) *adj.* **1.** of, involving, resembling, or shaped like a circle. **2.** circuitous. **3.** (of arguments, etc.) futile because of an inevitable return to the starting point. **4.** travelling or occurring in a cycle. **5.** (of letters, announcements, etc.) intended for general distribution. ~*n.* **6.** a printed or duplicated advertisement or notice for mass distribution. —**cir+cu+lar+i·ty** (ˌsɜːkjʊ'lærɪtɪ) *or* '**cir+cu+lar+ness** *n.* —'**cir+cu+lar+ly** *adv.*

cir+cu+lar func+tion *n.* another name for **trigonometric function** (sense 1).

cir+cu+lar+ize *or* **cir+cu+lar+ise** ('sɜːkjʊləˌraɪz) *vb.* (*tr.*) **1.** to distribute circulars to. **2.** to canvass or petition (people), as for support, votes, etc., by distributing letters, etc. **3.** to make circular. —ˌ**cir+cu+lar·i+'za+tion** *or* ˌ**cir+cu+lar·i+'sa+tion** *n.* —'**cir+cu+lar+ˌiz+er** *or* '**cir+cu+lar+ˌis+er** *n.*

cir+cu+lar meas+ure *n.* the measurement of an angle in radians.

cir+cu+lar mil *n.* a unit of area of cross section of wire, equal to the area of a circle whose diameter is one thousandth of an inch. 1 circular mil is equal to 0.785×10^{-6} square inch or 0.2×10^{-9} square metre.

cir+cu+lar po+lar+i+za+tion *n.* a transformation of electromagnetic radiation (esp. light) to a form in which the vector representing the instantaneous intensity of the electric field describes a circle about the direction of propagation at any point in the path of the radiation.

cir+cu+lar saw *n.* a power-driven saw in which a circular disc with a toothed edge is rotated at high speed.

cir+cu+lar tri+an+gle *n.* a triangle in which each side is the arc of a circle.

cir+cu+late ('sɜːkjʊˌleɪt) *vb.* **1.** to send, go, or pass from place to place or person to person: *don't circulate the news.* **2.** to distribute or be distributed over a wide area. **3.** to move or cause to move through a circuit, system, etc., returning to the starting point: *blood circulates through the body.* **4.** to move in a circle: *the earth circulates around the sun.* [C15: from Latin *circulārī* to assemble in a circle, from *circulus* CIRCLE] —'**cir+cu+ˌla+tive** *adj.* —'**cir+cu+ˌla+tor** *n.* —'**cir+cu+la+to·ry** *adj.*

cir+cu+lat+ing dec·i·mal *n.* another name for **recurring decimal.**

cir+cu+lat+ing li+brar·y *n.* **1.** another word (esp. U.S.) for **lending library. 2.** a small library circulated in turn to a group of schools or other institutions. **3.** a rare word for **subscription library.**

cir+cu+lat+ing me+di·um *n. Finance.* currency serving as a medium of exchange.

cir+cu+la+tion (ˌsɜːkjʊ'leɪʃən) *n.* **1.** the transport of oxygenated blood through the arteries to the capillaries, where it nourishes the tissues, and the return of oxygen-depleted blood through the veins to the heart, where the cycle is renewed. **2.** the flow of sap through a plant. **3.** any movement through a closed circuit. **4.** the spreading or transmission of something to a wider group of people or area. **5.** (of air and water) free movement within an area or volume. **6. a.** the distribution of newspapers, magazines, etc. **b.** the number of copies of an issue of such a publication that are distributed. **7.** *Library science.* **a.** a book loan, as from a library lending department. **b.** each loan transaction of a particular book. **c.** the total issue of library books over a specified period. **8.** a rare term for **circulating medium. 9. in circulation. a.** (of currency) serving as a medium of exchange. **b.** (of people) active in a social or business context.

cir·cum- *prefix.* around; surrounding; on all sides: *circumlocution; circumrotate.* [from Latin *circum* around, from *circus* circle]

cir+cum+am+bi+ent (ˌsɜːkəm'æmbɪənt) *adj.* surrounding. [C17: from Late Latin *circumambīre,* from CIRCUM- + *ambīre* to go round] —ˌ**cir+cum+'am+bi+ence** *or* ˌ**cir+cum+'am+bi+en+cy** *n.*

cir+cum+am+bu+late (ˌsɜːkəm'æmbjʊˌleɪt) *vb.* **1.** to walk around (something). **2.** (*intr.*) to avoid the point. [C17: from Late Latin CIRCUM- + *ambulāre* to walk] —ˌ**cir+cum+ˌam+bu+'la+tion** *n.* —ˌ**cir+cum+'am+bu+ˌla+tor** *n.* —ˌ**cir+cum+'am+bu+la+to·ry** *adj.*

cir+cum+ben+di+bus (ˌsɜːkəm'bɛndɪbəs) *n. Humorous.* a circumlocution. [C17: coined from CIRCUM- + BEND, with a pseudo-Latin ending]

cir+cum+cise ('sɜːkəmˌsaɪz) *vb.* (*tr.*) **1.** to remove the foreskin of (a male). **2.** to incise surgically the skin over the clitoris of (a female). **3.** to perform the religious rite of circumcision on (someone). [C13: from Latin *circumcīdere,* from CIRCUM- + *caedere* to cut] —'**cir+cum+ˌcis+er** *n.*

cir+cum+ci+sion (ˌsɜːkəm'sɪʒən) *n.* **1. a.** surgical removal of the foreskin of males. **b.** *Rare.* surgical incision into the skin covering the clitoris in females. **2.** the act of circumcision, performed as a religious rite by Jews and Muslims. **3.** *R.C. Church.* the festival celebrated on Jan. 1 in commemoration of the circumcision of Jesus.

cir+cum+fer+ence (sə'kʌmfərəns) *n.* **1.** the boundary of a specific area or geometric figure, esp. of a circle. **2.** the length of a closed geometric curve, esp. of a circle. The circumference of a circle is equal to the diameter multiplied by π. [C14: from Old French *circonference,* from Latin *circumferre* to carry around, from CIRCUM- + *ferre* to bear] —**cir+cum+fer+en+tial** (səˌkʌmfə'rɛnʃəl) *adj.* —**cir+ˌcum+fer+'en+tial+ly** *adv.*

cir+cum+flex ('sɜːkəmˌflɛks) *n.* **1.** a mark (ˆ) placed over a vowel to show that it is pronounced with rising and falling pitch, as in ancient Greek, as a long vowel rather than a short one, as in French, or with some other different quality. ~*adj.* **2.** (of certain nerves, arteries, or veins) bending or curving around. [C16: from Latin *circumflexus,* from *circumflectere* to bend around, from CIRCUM- + *flectere* to bend] —ˌ**cir+cum+'flex+ion** *n.*

cir+cum+flu+ous (sə'kʌmfluəs) *adj.* **1.** Also: **cir+cum+flu+ent** (sə'kʌmfluənt). flowing all around. **2.** surrounded by or as if by water. [C17: from Latin *circumfluere* to flow around, from CIRCUM- + *fluere* to flow] —**cir+'cum+flu+ence** *n.*

cir+cum+fuse (ˌsɜːkəm'fjuːz) *vb.* (*tr.*) **1.** to pour or spread (a liquid, powder, etc.) around. **2.** to surround with a substance, such as a liquid. [C16: from Latin *circumfūsus,* from *circumfundere* to pour around, from CIRCUM- + *fundere* to pour] —**cir+cum+fu+sion** (ˌsɜːkəm'fjuːʒən) *n.*

cir+cum+lo+cu+tion (ˌsɜːkəmlə'kjuːʃən) *n.* **1.** an indirect way of expressing something. **2.** an indirect expression. —**cir+cum+loc·u·to·ry** (ˌsɜːkəm'lɒkjətərɪ, -trɪ) *adj.*

cir+cum+lu+nar (ˌsɜːkəm'luːnə) *adj.* around or revolving around the moon: *a circumlunar orbit.*

cir+cum+nav·i·gate (ˌsɜːkəm'nævɪˌgeɪt) *vb.* (*tr.*) to sail or fly completely around. —ˌ**cir+cum+'nav·i·ga·ble** *adj.* —ˌ**cir+cum+ˌnav·i+'ga+tion** *n.* —ˌ**cir+cum+'nav·i+ˌga+tor** *n.*

cir+cum+nu+tate (ˌsɜːkəm'njuːteɪt) *vb.* (*intr.*) (of the tip of a plant stem) to grow in an irregular curve, ellipse, or spiral. [C19: from CIRCUM- + *-nutate,* from Latin *nūtāre* to nod repeatedly, sway] —ˌ**cir+cum+nu+'ta+tion** *n.*

cir+cum+po+lar (ˌsɜːkəm'pəʊlə) *adj.* **1.** (of a star or constellation) visible above the horizon at all times at a specified locality on the earth's surface. **2.** surrounding or located at or near either of the earth's poles.

cir+cum+scis+sile (ˌsɜːkəm'sɪsaɪl) *adj.* (of the dry dehiscent fruits of certain plants) opening completely by a transverse split. [C19: from CIRCUM- + Latin *scissilis* capable of splitting, from *scindere* to split]

cir+cum+scribe (ˌsɜːkəm'skraɪb, 'sɜːkəmˌskraɪb) *vb.* (*tr.*) **1.** to restrict within limits. **2.** to mark or set the bounds of. **3.** to draw a geometric construction around (another construction) so that the two are in contact but do not intersect. Compare **inscribe** (sense 4). **4.** to draw a line round. [C15: from Latin *circumscrībere,* from CIRCUM- + *scrībere* to write] —ˌ**cir+cum+'scrib+a·ble** *adj.* —ˌ**cir+cum+'scrib+er** *n.*

cir+cum+scrip+tion (ˌsɜːkəm'skrɪpʃən) *n.* **1.** the act of circumscribing or the state of being circumscribed. **2.** something that limits or encloses. **3.** a circumscribed space. **4.** an inscription around a coin or medal. —ˌ**cir+cum+'scrip+tive** *adj.* —ˌ**cir+cum+'scrip+tive+ly** *adv.*

cir+cum+so+lar (ˌsɜːkəm'səʊlə) *adj.* surrounding or rotating around the sun.

cir+cum+spect ('sɜːkəmˌspɛkt) *adj.* cautious, prudent, or discreet. [C15: from Latin *circumspectus,* from CIRCUM- + *specere* to look] —ˌ**cir+cum+'spec+tion** *n.* —ˌ**cir+cum+'spec+tive** *adj.* —'**cir+cum+ˌspect+ly** *adv.*

cir+cum+stance ('sɜːkəmstəns) *n.* **1.** (usually *pl.*) a condition of time, place, etc., that accompanies or influences an event or condition. **2.** an incident or occurrence, esp. a chance one. **3.** accessory information or detail. **4.** formal display or ceremony (archaic except in the phrase **pomp and circumstance**). **5. under** *or* **in no circumstances.** in no case; never. **6. under the**

circumstances. because of conditions; this being the case. **7. in good** (*or* **bad**) **circumstances.** (of a person) in a good (or bad) financial situation. ~*vb.* (*tr.*) **8.** to place in a particular condition or situation. **9.** *Obsolete.* to give in detail. [C13: from Old French *circonstance,* from Latin *circumstantia,* from *circumstāre* to stand around, from CIRCUM- + *stāre* to stand]

cir+cum+stan+tial (ˌsɜːkəmˈstænʃəl) *adj.* **1.** of or dependent on circumstances. **2.** fully detailed. **3.** incidental. —**cir+cum+stan+ti+al+i·ty** (ˌsɜːkəmˌstænʃɪˈælɪtɪ) *n.* —ˌ**cir+cum+ˈstan+tial+ly** *adv.*

cir+cum+stan+tial ev·i+dence *n.* indirect evidence that tends to establish a conclusion by inference. Compare **direct evidence.**

cir+cum+stan+ti+ate (ˌsɜːkəmˈstænʃɪˌeɪt) *vb.* (*tr.*) to support by giving particulars. —ˌ**cir+cum+ˌstan+ti·ˈa+tion** *n.*

cir+cum+val+late (ˌsɜːkəmˈvæleɪt) *vb.* (*tr.*) to surround with a defensive fortification. [C19: from Latin *circumvallāre,* from CIRCUM- + *vallum* rampart] —ˌ**cir+cum+val+ˈla+tion** *n.*

cir+cum+vent (ˌsɜːkəmˈvɛnt) *vb.* (*tr.*) **1.** to evade or go around. **2.** to outwit. **3.** to encircle (an enemy) so as to intercept or capture. [C15: from Latin *circumvenīre,* from CIRCUM- + *venīre* to come] —ˌ**cir+cum+ˈvent+er** *or* ˌ**cir+cum+ˈven+tor** *n.* —ˌ**cir+cum+ˈven+tion** *n.* —ˌ**cir+cum+ˈven+tive** *adj.*

cir+cum+vo+lu+tion (ˌsɜːkəmvəˈluːʃən) *n.* **1.** the act of turning, winding, or folding around a central axis. **2.** a single complete turn, cycle, or fold. **3.** anything winding or sinuous. **4.** a roundabout course or procedure. [C15: from Medieval Latin *circumvolūtiō,* from Latin *circumvolvere,* from CIRCUM- + *volvere* to roll] —ˌ**cir+cum+vo+ˈlu+to·ry** *adj.*

cir+cus (ˈsɜːkəs) *n., pl.* **+cus·es. 1.** a travelling company of entertainers such as acrobats, clowns, trapeze artists, and trained animals. **2.** a public performance given by such a company. **3.** an oval or circular arena, usually tented and surrounded by tiers of seats, in which such a performance is held. **4.** (in ancient Rome) **a.** an open-air stadium, usually oval or oblong, for chariot races or public games. **b.** the games themselves. **5.** *Brit.* **a.** an open place, usually circular, in a town, where several streets converge. **b.** (*cap. when part of a name*): *Piccadilly Circus.* **6.** *Informal.* noisy or rowdy behaviour. **7.** *Informal.* a person or group of people whose behaviour is wild, disorganized, or (esp. unintentionally) comic. [C16: from Latin, from Greek *kirkos* ring]

Cir+cus Max·i+mus (ˈmæksɪməs) *n.* an amphitheatre in Rome, used in ancient times for chariot races, public games, etc.

ci·ré (ˈsɪəreɪ) *adj.* **1.** (of fabric) treated with a heat or wax process to make it smooth. ~*n.* **2.** such a surface on a fabric. **3.** a fabric having such a surface. [C20: French, from *cirer* to wax, from *cire,* from Latin *cēra* wax]

Cir+e+na·i+ca (ˌsaɪrəˈneɪɪkə, ˌsɪrə-) *n.* a variant spelling of **Cyrenaica.**

Ci+ren+ces+ter (ˈsaɪrənˌsɛstə) *n.* a market town in S England, in Gloucestershire: Roman amphitheatre. Pop.: 13 022 (1971). Latin name: **Corinium.**

cire per+due *French.* (sir pɛrˈdy) *n.* a method of casting bronze, in which a mould is formed around a wax pattern, which is subsequently melted and drained away. [literally: lost wax]

cirque (sɜːk) *n.* **1.** Also called: **corrie, cwm.** a steep-sided semicircular depression found in mountainous regions, often containing a lake. **2.** *Archaeol.* an obsolete term for **circle** (sense 11). **3.** *Poetic.* a circle, circlet, or ring. [C17: from French, from Latin *circus* ring, circle, CIRCUS]

cir+rate (ˈsɪreɪt), **cir+rose,** *or* **cir+rous** *adj. Biology.* bearing or resembling cirri. [C19: from Latin *cirrātus* curled, from CIRRUS]

cir+rho+sis (sɪˈrəʊsɪs) *n.* any of various chronic progressive diseases of the liver, characterized by death of liver cells, irreversible fibrosis, etc.: caused by inadequate diet, excessive alcohol, chronic infection, etc. Also called: **cirrhosis of the liver.** [C19: New Latin, from Greek *kirrhos* orange-coloured + -OSIS; referring to the appearance of the diseased liver] —**cir+ˈrhosed** *adj.* —**cir+rhot+ic** (sɪˈrɒtɪk) *adj.*

cir+ri (ˈsɪraɪ) *n.* the plural of **cirrus.**

cir+ri+ped (ˈsɪrɪˌpiːd) *or* **cir+ri+ped** (ˈsɪrɪˌpɛd) *n.* **1.** any marine crustacean of the subclass *Cirripedia,* including the barnacles, the adults of which are sessile or parasitic. ~*adj.* **2.** of, relating to, or belonging to the *Cirripedia.*

cir·ro- *or* **cir·ri-** *combining form.* indicating cirrus or cirri: *cirrocumulus; cirriped.*

cir+ro+cu+mu+lus (ˌsɪrəʊˈkjuːmjʊləs) *n., pl.* **+li** (-ˌlaɪ). *Meteorol.* a high cloud of ice crystals grouped into small separate globular masses, usually occurring above 6000 metres (20 000 feet). See also **mackerel sky.**

cir+rose (ˈsɪrəʊs, sɪˈrəʊs) *or* **cir+rous** (ˈsɪrəs) *adj.* **1.** *Biology.* another word for **cirrate. 2.** characteristic of cirrus clouds.

cir+ro+stra+tus (ˌsɪrəʊˈstrɑːtəs) *n., pl.* **+ti** (-taɪ). a uniform layer of cloud above about 6000 metres (20 000 feet). —ˌ**cir+ro+ˈstra+tive** *adj.*

cir+rus (ˈsɪrəs) *n., pl.* **+ri** (-raɪ). **1.** *Meteorol.* a thin wispy fibrous cloud at high altitudes, composed of ice particles. **2.** a plant tendril or similar part. **3.** a slender tentacle or filament in barnacles and other marine invertebrates. [C18: from Latin: curl, tuft, fringe]

cir+soid (ˈsɜːsɔɪd) *adj. Pathol.* resembling a varix. Also: **varicoid.** [C19: from Greek *kirsoeidēs,* from *kirsos* swollen vein + -OID]

cis- *prefix.* **1.** on this or the near side of: *cisalpine.* **2.** (often in italics) indicating that two groups of atoms in an unsaturated compound lie on the same side of a double bond: *cis*-butadiene. Compare **trans-** (sense 5). [from Latin]

cis+al+pine (sɪsˈælpaɪn) *adj.* **1.** on this (the southern) side of the Alps, as viewed from Rome. **2.** relating to a movement in the Roman Catholic Church to minimize the authority of the pope and to emphasize the independence of branches of the Church. Compare **ultramontane** (sense 2).

Cis+al+pine Gaul *n.* (in the ancient world) that part of Gaul between the Alps and the Apennines.

Cis+cau+ca+si·a (ˌsɪskɔːˈkeɪzɪə, -ʒə) *n.* the part of Caucasia north of the Caucasus Mountains.

cis+co (ˈsɪskəʊ) *n., pl.* **+coes** *or* **+cos.** any of various whitefish, esp. *Coregonus artedi* (also called **lake herring**), of cold deep lakes of North America. [C19: short for Canadian French *ciscoette,* from Ojibwa *pemitewiskawet* fish with oily flesh]

Cis+kei (ˈsɪskaɪ) *n.* a Bantu state in South Africa for Xhosa-speaking peoples, consisting of 17 closely grouped areas of the E Cape Province. Pop.: 527 159 (1970).

cis+lu+nar (sɪsˈluːnə) *adj.* of or relating to the space between the earth and the moon. Compare **translunar.**

cis+mon+tane (sɪsˈmɒnteɪn) *adj.* on this (the writer's or speaker's) side of the mountains, esp. the Alps. Compare **ultramontane** (sense 1). [C18: from Latin CIS- + *montānus* of the mountains, from *mōns* mountain]

cis+pa+dane (ˈsɪspəˌdeɪn, sɪsˈpeɪdeɪn) *adj.* on this (the southern) side of the River Po, as viewed from Rome. Compare **transpadane.** [from Latin CIS- + *Padānus* of the Po]

cis+soid (ˈsɪsɔɪd) *n.* **1.** a geometric curve whose two branches meet in a cusp at the origin and are asymptotic to a line parallel to the *y*-axis. Its equation is $y^2(2a - x) = x^3$ where 2a is the distance between the *y*-axis and this line. ~*adj.* **2.** contained between the concave sides of two intersecting curves. Compare **sistroid.** [C17: from Greek *kissoeidēs,* literally: ivy-shaped, from *kissos* ivy]

cist[1] (sɪst) *n.* a wooden box for holding ritual objects used in ancient Rome and Greece. [C19: from Latin *cista* box, chest, basket, from Greek *kistē*]

cist[2] (sɪst) *or* **kist** *n. Archaeol.* a box-shaped burial chamber made from stone slabs or a hollowed tree-trunk. [C19: from Welsh: chest, from Latin *cista* box; see CIST[1]]

cis+ta+ceous (sɪˈsteɪʃəs) *adj.* of, relating to, or belonging to the *Cistaceae,* a family of shrubby or herbaceous plants that includes the rockroses. [C19: from New Latin *Cistaceae,* from Greek *kistos* rockrose]

Cis+ter+cian (sɪˈstɜːʃən) *n.* a member of a Christian order of monks and nuns founded in 1098, which follows an especially strict form of the Benedictine rule. Also called: **White Monk.** [C17: from French *Cistercien,* from Medieval Latin *Cisterciānus,* from *Cistercium* (modern *Cîteaux*), original home of the order]

cis+tern (ˈsɪstən) *n.* **1.** a tank for the storage of water, esp. on or within the roof of a house or connected to a W.C. **2.** an underground reservoir for the storage of a liquid, esp. rainwater. **3.** *Anatomy.* another name for **cisterna.** [C13: from Old French *cisterne,* from Latin *cisterna* underground tank, from *cista* box] —**cis+ter+nal** (sɪˈstɜːnəl) *adj.*

cis+ter+na (sɪˈstɜːnə) *n., pl.* **+nae** (-niː). a sac or partially closed space containing body fluid, esp. lymph or cerebrospinal fluid. [New Latin, from Latin; see CISTERN]

cis-trans test (ˈsɪsˈtrɑːnz) *n. Genetics.* a test to define the unit of genetic function, based on whether two mutations of the same character occur in a single chromosome (the cis position) or in different cistrons in each chromosome of a homologous pair (the trans position). [C20: see CIS-, TRANS-]

cis+tron (ˈsɪstrən) *n. Genetics.* the section of a chromosome that controls a single function; a functional gene. [C20: from *cis-trans;* see CIS-TRANS TEST]

cis+tus (ˈsɪstəs) *n.* any plant of the genus *Cistus.* See **rockrose.** [C16: New Latin, from Greek *kistos*]

cit. *abbrev. for:* **1.** citation. **2.** cited. **3.** citizen.

cit·a+del (ˈsɪtədəl, -ˌdɛl) *n.* **1.** a stronghold within or close to a city. **2.** any strongly fortified building or place of safety; refuge. **3.** a specially strengthened part of the hull of a warship. [C16: from Old French *citadelle,* from Old Italian *cittadella,* a little city, from *cittade* city, from Latin *cīvitās*]

ci+ta+tion (saɪˈteɪʃən) *n.* **1.** the quoting of a book or author in support of a fact. **2.** a passage or source cited for this purpose. **3.** a listing or recounting, as of facts. **4.** an official commendation or award, esp. for bravery or outstanding service, work, etc., usually in the form of a formal statement made in public. **5.** *Law.* **a.** an official summons to appear in court. **b.** the document containing such a summons. **6.** *Law.* the quoting of decided cases to serve as guidance to a court. —**ci+ta+to·ry** (ˈsaɪtətərɪ, -trɪ) *adj.*

cite (saɪt) *vb.* (*tr.*) **1.** to quote or refer to (a passage, book, or author) in substantiation as an authority, proof, or example. **2.** to mention or commend (a soldier, etc.) for outstanding bravery or meritorious action. **3.** to summon to appear before a court of law. **4.** to enumerate: *he cited the king's virtues.* **5.** *Archaic.* to excite. [C15: from Old French *citer* to summon, from Latin *citāre* to rouse, from *citus* quick, from *ciēre* to excite] —ˈ**cit+a·ble** *or* ˈ**cite+a·ble** *adj.* —ˈ**cit+er** *n.*

cith·a+ra (ˈsɪθərə) *or* **kith·a+ra** *n.* a stringed musical instrument of ancient Greece and elsewhere, similar to the lyre and played with a plectrum. [C18: from Greek *kithara*]

cith+er (ˈsɪθə) *or* **cith+ern** (ˈsɪθən) *n.* a variant spelling of **cittern.** [C17: from Latin *cithara,* from Greek *kithara* lyre]

cit·i+fied *or* **cit·y+fied** (ˈsɪtɪˌfaɪd) *adj. Often derogatory.* having the customs, manners, or dress of city people.

cit·i+fy *or* **cit·y+fy** (ˈsɪtɪˌfaɪ) *vb.* **+fies, +fy+ing, +fied.** (*tr.*) **1.** to cause to conform to or adopt the customs, habits, or dress of city people. **2.** to make urban. —ˌ**cit·i·fi·'ca·tion** *or* ˌ**cit·y·fi·'ca·tion** *n.*

cit·i·zen ('sɪtɪzᵊn) *n.* **1.** a native or naturalized member of a state, nation, or other political community. Compare **alien. 2.** an inhabitant of a city or town. **3.** a native or inhabitant of any place. **4.** a civilian, as opposed to a soldier, public official, etc. [C14: from Anglo-French *citesein,* from Old French *citeien,* from *cité* CITY] —**cit·i·zen·ess** ('sɪtɪzənɪs, -ˌnɛs) *fem. n.* —'**cit·i·zen·ly** *adj.*

cit·i·zen·ry ('sɪtɪzənrɪ) *n., pl.* **·ries.** citizens collectively.

Cit·i·zens' Band *n. Chiefly U.S.* a range of radio frequencies assigned officially for use by the public for private communication.

cit·i·zen·ship ('sɪtɪzənˌʃɪp) *n.* **1.** the condition or status of a citizen, with its rights and duties. **2.** a person's conduct as a citizen: *an award for good citizenship.*

Ci·tlal·té·petl (ˌsi:tlɑ:l'teɪpɛtᵊl) *n.* a volcano in SE Mexico, in central Veracruz state: the highest peak in the country. Height: 5699 m (18 692 ft.). Spanish name: **Pico de Orizaba.**

cit·ole ('sɪtəʊl, sɪ'təʊl) *n.* a rare word for **cittern.** [C14: from Old French, probably from Latin *cithara* CITHER]

cit·ral ('sɪtrəl) *n.* a yellow volatile liquid with a lemon-like odour, found in oils of lemon grass, orange, and lemon and used in perfumery: a terpene aldehyde consisting of the *cis*-isomer (**citral-a** or **geranial**) and the *trans-* isomer (**citral-b** or **neral**). Formula: $(CH_3)_2C{:}CH(CH_2)_2C(CH_3){:}CHCHO$. [C19: from CITR(US) + -AL[3]]

cit·rate ('sɪtreɪt, -rɪt; 'saɪtreɪt) *n.* any salt or ester of citric acid. Salts of citric acid are used in beverages and pharmaceuticals. [C18: from CITR(US) + -ATE[1]]

cit·re·ous ('sɪtrɪəs) *adj.* of a greenish-yellow colour; citron.

cit·ric ('sɪtrɪk) *adj.* of or derived from citrus fruits or citric acid.

cit·ric ac·id *n.* a water-soluble weak tribasic acid found in many fruits, esp. citrus fruits, and used in pharmaceuticals and as a flavouring. It is extracted from citrus fruits or made by fermenting molasses and is an intermediate in carbohydrate metabolism. Formula: $CH_2(COOH)C(OH)(COOH)CH_2COOH$.

cit·ric ac·id cy·cle *n.* another name for **Krebs cycle.**

cit·ri·cul·ture ('sɪtrɪˌkʌltʃə) *n.* the cultivation of citrus fruits. —ˌ**cit·ri·'cul·tur·ist** *n.*

cit·rin ('sɪtrɪn) *n.* another name for **vitamin P.**

cit·rine ('sɪtrɪn) *n.* **1.** a brownish-yellow variety of quartz: a gemstone; false topaz. **2.** the yellow colour of a lemon.

cit·ron ('sɪtrən) *n.* **1.** a small Asian rutaceous tree, *Citrus medica,* having lemon-like fruit with a thick aromatic rind. See also **citron wood. 2.** the fruit of this tree. **3.** Also called: **citron melon.** a variety of watermelon, *Citrullus vulgaris citroides,* that has an inedible fruit with a hard rind. **4.** the rind of either of these fruits, candied and used for decoration and flavouring of foods. **5.** a greenish-yellow colour. [C16: from Old French, from Old Provençal, from Latin *citrus* citrus tree]

cit·ron·el·la (ˌsɪtrə'nɛlə) *n.* **1.** Also called: **citronella grass.** a tropical Asian grass, *Cymbopogon* (or *Andropogon*) *nardus,* with bluish-green lemon-scented leaves. **2.** Also called: **citronella oil.** the yellow aromatic oil obtained from this grass, used in insect repellents, soaps, perfumes, etc. [C19: New Latin, from French *citronnelle* lemon balm, from *citron* lemon]

cit·ron·el·lal (ˌsɪtrə'nɛlæl) *n.* a colourless slightly water-soluble liquid with a lemon-like odour, a terpene aldehyde found esp. in citronella and certain eucalyptus oils: used as a flavouring and in soaps and perfumes. Formula: $(CH_3)_2C{:}CH(CH_2)_2CH(CH_3)CH_2CHO$. Also called: **rhodinal.**

cit·ron wood *n.* **1.** the wood of the citron tree. **2.** the wood of the sandarac.

cit·rul·line ('sɪtrəˌli:n) *n.* an amino acid that occurs in watermelons and is an intermediate in the formation of urea. Formula: $NH_2CONH(CH_2)_3CHNH_2COOH$. [C20: from Medieval Latin *citrullus* a kind of watermelon, from Latin *citron,* referring to its colour]

cit·rus ('sɪtrəs) *n., pl.* **·rus·es. 1.** any tree or shrub of the tropical and subtropical rutaceous genus *Citrus,* which includes the orange, lemon, lime, grapefruit, citron, and calamondin. ~*adj. also* **cit·rous. 2.** of, relating to, or belonging to the genus *Citrus* or to the fruits of plants of this genus. [C19: from Latin: citrus tree, sandarac tree; related to Greek *kedros* cedar]

Cit·tà del Va·ti·ca·no (tʃit'ta del vati'ka:no) *n.* the Italian name for **Vatican City.**

cit·tern ('sɪtɜ:n), **cith·er,** *or* **cith·ern** *n.* a medieval stringed instrument resembling a lute but having wire strings and a flat back. Compare **gittern.** [C16: perhaps a blend of CITHER + GITTERN]

cit·y ('sɪtɪ) *n., pl.* **cit·ies. 1.** any large town or populous place. **2.** (in Britain) a large town that has received this title from the Crown: usually the seat of a bishop. **3.** (in the U.S.) an incorporated urban centre with its own government and administration established by state charter. **4.** an ancient Greek city-state; polis. **5.** the people of a city collectively. **6.** (*modifier*) in or characteristic of a city: *a city girl; city habits.* ~Related adjs.: **civic, urban, municipal.** [C13: from Old French *cité,* from Latin *cīvitās* citizenship, state, from *cīvis* citizen]

Cit·y ('sɪtɪ) *n.* **the. 1.** short for **City of London:** the original settlement of London on the N bank of the Thames; a municipality governed by the Lord Mayor and Corporation. Resident pop.: 4234 (1971). **2.** the area in central London in which the United Kingdom's major financial business is transacted. **3.** the various financial institutions located in this area.

Cit·y and Guilds In·sti·tute *n. Brit.* an examining body for technical and craft skills, many of the examinations being at a lower standard than for a degree.

cit·y blues *n. Jazz.* another name for **urban blues.**

Cit·y Com·pa·ny *n. Brit.* a corporation that represents one of the historic trade guilds of London.

cit·y desk *n.* **1.** *Brit.* the department of a newspaper office dealing with financial and commercial news. **2.** *U.S.* the department of a newspaper office dealing with local news.

cit·y ed·i·tor *n.* (on a newspaper) **1.** *Brit.* the editor in charge of financial and commercial news. **2.** *U.S.* the editor in charge of local news.

cit·y fa·ther *n.* a person who is active or prominent in the public affairs of a city, such as an alderman.

cit·y hall *n.* **1.** the building housing the administrative offices of a city or municipal government. **2.** *Chiefly U.S.* **a.** municipal government. **b.** the officials of a municipality collectively. **3.** *U.S. informal.* bureaucracy.

cit·y man·a·ger *n.* (in the U.S.) an administrator hired by a municipal council to manage its affairs. See also **council-manager plan.**

Cit·y of God *n.* **1.** *Christianity.* heaven conceived of as the New Jerusalem. **2.** the Church in contrast to the world, as described by St. Augustine.

cit·y plan·ning *n.* the U.S. term for **town planning.** —**cit·y plan·ner** *n.*

cit·y·scape ('sɪtɪskeɪp) *n.* an urban landscape; view of a city.

cit·y slick·er *n. Informal.* **1.** a person with the sophistication often attributed to city people. **2.** a smooth tricky untrustworthy person.

cit·y-state *n.* a state consisting of a sovereign city and its dependencies. Among the most famous are the great independent cities of the ancient world, such as Athens, Sparta, Carthage, and Rome.

Ciu·dad Bo·lí·var (*Spanish* sju'ðað bo'livar) *n.* a port in E Venezuela, on the Orinoco River: accessible to ocean-going vessels. Pop.: 103 728 (1971). Former name (1764–1846): **Angostura.**

Ciu·dad Juá·rez (*Spanish* sju'ðað 'xwares) *n.* a city in N Mexico, in Chihuahua state on the Río Grande, opposite El Paso, Texas. Pop.: 520 539 (1975 est.). Former name (until 1888): **El Pa·so del Nor·te** (el 'paso del 'norte).

Ciu·dad Re·al (*Spanish* θju'ðað re'al) *n.* a market town in S central Spain. Pop.: 41 708 (1970).

Ciu·dad Tru·jil·lo (*Spanish* sju'ðað tru'xijo) *n.* the former name (1936–61) of **Santo Domingo.**

Ciu·dad Vic·to·ria (*Spanish* sju'ðað vik'torja) *n.* a city in E central Mexico, capital of Tamaulipas state. Pop.: 95 000 (1970).

civ. *abbrev. for:* **1.** civil. **2.** civilian.

civ·et ('sɪvɪt) *n.* **1.** any catlike viverrine mammal of the genus *Viverra* and related genera, of Africa and S Asia, typically having blotched or spotted fur and secreting a powerfully smelling fluid from anal glands. **2.** the yellowish fatty secretion of such an animal, used as a fixative in the manufacture of perfumes. **3.** the fur of such an animal. **4.** short for **palm civet.** [C16: from Old French *civette,* from Italian *zibetto,* from Arabic *zabād* civet perfume]

civ·ic ('sɪvɪk) *adj.* of or relating to a city, citizens, or citizenship: *civic duties.* [C16: from Latin *cīvicus,* from *cīvis* citizen] —'**civ·i·cal·ly** *adv.*

civ·ic cen·tre *n. Brit.* the public buildings of a town, including recreational facilities and offices of local administration.

civ·ics ('sɪvɪks) *n.* (*functioning as sing.*) **1.** the study of the rights and responsibilities of citizenship. **2.** *U.S.* the study of government and its workings.

civ·ies ('sɪvɪz) *pl. n. Informal.* a variant spelling of **civvies.**

civ·il ('sɪvᵊl) *adj.* **1.** of the ordinary life of citizens as distinguished from military, legal, or ecclesiastical affairs. **2.** of or relating to the citizen as an individual: *civil rights.* **3.** of or occurring within the state or between citizens: *civil strife.* **4.** polite or courteous: *a civil manner.* **5.** a less common word for **civic. 6.** of or in accordance with Roman law. **7.** relating to the private rights of citizens. [C14: from Old French, from Latin *cīvīlis,* from *cīvis* citizen] —'**civ·il·ly** *adv.* —'**civ·il·ness** *n.*

civ·il day *n.* another name for **calendar day.** See **day** (sense 1).

civ·il death *n. Law.* (formerly) the loss of all civil rights because of a serious conviction. See also **attainder.**

civ·il de·fence *n.* the organizing of civilians to deal with enemy attacks.

civ·il dis·o·be·di·ence *n.* a refusal to obey laws, pay taxes, etc.: a nonviolent means of protesting or of attempting to achieve political goals.

civ·il en·gi·neer *n.* a person qualified to design, construct, and maintain public works, such as roads, bridges, harbours, etc. —**civ·il en·gi·neer·ing** *n.*

ci·vil·ian (sɪ'vɪljən) *n.* **a.** a person whose primary occupation is civil or nonmilitary. **b.** (*as modifier*): *civilian life.* [C14 (originally: a practitioner of civil law): from *civile* (from the Latin phrase *jūs cīvīle* civil law) + -IAN]

ci·vil·i·ty (sɪ'vɪlɪtɪ) *n., pl.* **·ties. 1.** politeness or courtesy, esp. when formal. **2.** (*often pl.*) an act of politeness.

civ·i·li·za·tion *or* **civ·i·li·sa·tion** (ˌsɪvɪlaɪ'zeɪʃən) *n.* **1.** a human society that has highly developed material and spiritual resources and a complex cultural, political, and legal organization; an advanced state in social development. **2.** the peoples or nations collectively who have achieved such a state. **3.** the total culture and way of life of a particular people, nation, region, or period: *classical civilization.* **4.** the process of bringing or achieving civilization. **5.** intellectual, cultural, and moral refinement. **6.** cities or populated areas, as contrasted with sparsely inhabited areas, deserts, etc.

civ·i·lize *or* **civ·i·lise** ('sɪvɪˌlaɪz) *vb.* (*tr.*) **1.** to bring out of savagery or barbarism into a state characteristic of civilization. **2.** to refine, educate, or enlighten. —'**civ·i·ˌliz·a·ble** *or* '**civ·i·ˌlis·a·ble** *adj.* —'**civ·i·ˌliz·er** *or* '**civ·i·ˌlis·er** *n.*

civ·i·lized *or* **civ·i·lised** ('sɪvɪˌlaɪzd) *adj.* **1.** having a high state of culture and social development. **2.** cultured; polite.

civ·il law *n.* **1.** the law of a state relating to private and civilian affairs. **2.** the body of law in force in ancient Rome, esp. the law applicable to private citizens. **3.** any system of law based on the Roman system as distinguished from the common law and canon law. **4.** the law of a state as distinguished from international law.

civ·il lib·er·ty *n.* the right of an individual to certain freedoms of speech and action.

civ·il list *n.* (in Britain) the annuities voted by Parliament for the support of the royal household and the royal family.

civ·il mar·riage *n. Law.* a marriage performed by some official other than a clergyman.

civ·il rights *pl. n.* **1.** the personal rights of the individual citizen, in most countries upheld by law, as in the U.S. **2.** (*modifier*) of, relating to, or promoting equality in social, economic, and political rights.

civ·il serv·ant *n.* a member of the civil service.

civ·il serv·ice *n.* **1.** the service responsible for the public administration of the government of a country. It excludes the legislative, judicial, and military branches. Members of the civil service have no official political allegiance and are not generally affected by changes of governments. **2.** the members of the civil service collectively.

civ·il war *n.* war between parties, factions, or inhabitants of different regions within the same nation.

Civ·il War *n.* **1.** *English history.* the conflict between Charles I and the Parliamentarians resulting from disputes over their respective prerogatives. Parliament gained decisive victories at Marston Moor in 1644 and Naseby in 1645, and Charles was executed in 1649. **2.** *U.S. history.* the war fought from 1861 to 1865 between the North and the South, sparked off by Lincoln's election as president but with deep-rooted political and economic causes, exacerbated by the slavery issue. The advantages of the North in terms of population, finance, and communications brought about the South's eventual surrender at Appomattox.

civ·il year *n.* another name for **calendar year.** See **year** (sense 1).

civ·ism ('sɪvɪzəm) *n. Rare.* good citizenship. [C18: from French *civisme,* from Latin *cīvis* citizen]

civ·vy ('sɪvɪ) *n., pl.* **civ·vies** *or* **civ·ies.** *Slang.* **1.** a civilian. **2.** (*pl.*) civilian dress as opposed to uniform. **3. civvy street.** civilian life.

C.J. *abbrev. for* Chief Justice.

Cl *the chemical symbol for* chlorine.

CL *international car registration for* Ceylon.

cl. *abbrev. for:* **1.** class. **2.** classification. **3.** clerk. **4.** cloth. **5.** clergyman. **6.** centilitre.

cla·chan (*Gaelic* 'klaxən, 'klæ-) *n. Scot. and Irish dialect.* a small village; hamlet. [C15: from Scottish Gaelic: probably from *clach* stone]

clack (klæk) *vb.* **1.** to make or cause to make a sound like that of two pieces of wood hitting each other. **2.** to jabber. **3.** a less common word for **cluck.** ~*n.* **4.** a short sharp sound. **5.** a person or thing that produces this sound. **6.** chatter. **7.** Also called: **clack valve.** a simple nonreturn valve using either a hinged flap or a ball. [C13: probably from Old Norse *klaka* to twitter, of imitative origin] —'**clack·er** *n.*

Clack·man·nan (klæk'mænən) *n.* (until 1975) a county of central Scotland, now part of the Central region.

Clac·ton *or* **Clac·ton-on-Sea** ('klæktən) *n.* a town and resort in SE England, in E Essex. Pop.: 37 942 (1971).

Clac·to·ni·an (klæk'təʊnɪən) *n.* **1.** one of the Lower Palaeolithic cultures found in England, characterized by the use of chopper tools. ~*adj.* **2.** of, designating, or relating to this culture. [after *Clacton-on-Sea,* Essex, where the tools of this culture were first found]

clad[1] (klæd) *vb.* a past participle of **clothe.** [Old English *clāthode* clothed, from *clāthian* to CLOTHE]

clad[2] (klæd) *vb.* **clads, clad·ding, clad.** (*tr.*) to bond a metal to (another metal), esp. to form a protective coating. [C14 (in the obsolete sense: to clothe): special use of CLAD[1]]

clad·ding ('klædɪŋ) *n.* **1.** the process of protecting one metal by bonding a second metal to its surface. **2.** the protective coating so bonded to metal. **3.** the material used for the outside facing of a building, etc.

cla·doc·er·an (klə'dɒsərən) *n.* **1.** any minute freshwater crustacean of the order *Cladocera,* which includes the water fleas. ~*adj.* **2.** of, relating to, or belonging to the *Cladocera.* [C19: from New Latin *Cladocera,* from Greek *klados* shoot + *keras* horn]

clad·ode ('klædəʊd) *n. Botany.* a flattened stem resembling and functioning as a leaf, as in butcher's broom. Also called: **cladophyll, phylloclade.** [C19: from New Latin *cladōdium,* from Late Greek *kladōdēs* having many shoots]

clad·o·phyll ('klædəfɪl) *n.* another name for **cladode.** [C19: from Greek *klados* branch + *phullon* leaf]

claim (kleɪm) *vb.* (*mainly tr.*) **1.** to demand as being due or as one's property; assert one's title or right to: *he claimed the record.* **2.** (*takes a clause as object or an infinitive*) to assert as a fact; maintain against denial: *he claimed to be telling the truth.* **3.** to call for or need; deserve: *this problem claims our attention.* **4.** to take: *the accident claimed four lives.* ~*n.* **5.** an assertion of a right; a demand for something as due. **6.** an assertion of something as true, real, or factual: *he made claims for his innocence.* **7.** a right or just title to something; basis for demand: *a claim to fame.* **8. lay claim to** *or* **stake a claim to.** to assert one's possession of or right to. **9.** anything that is claimed, esp. in a formal or legal manner, such as a piece of land staked out by a miner. **10. a.** a demand for payment in connection with an insurance policy, etc. **b.** the sum of money demanded. [C13: from Old French *claimer* to call, appeal, from Latin *clāmāre* to shout] —'**claim·a·ble** *adj.* —'**claim·ant** *or* '**claim·er** *n.*

claim·ing race *n. U.S. horse racing.* a race in which each owner declares beforehand the price at which his horse will be offered for sale after the race.

clair·au·di·ence (ˌklɛər'ɔːdɪəns) *n. Psychol.* the postulated ability to hear sounds beyond the range of normal hearing. Compare **clairvoyance.** [C19: from French *clair* clear + AUDIENCE, after CLAIRVOYANCE]

clair-ob·scure (ˌklɛərəb'skjʊə) *n.* another word for **chiaroscuro.** [C18: from French, literally: clear-obscure]

clair·voy·ance (klɛə'vɔɪəns) *n.* **1.** the alleged power of perceiving things beyond the natural range of the senses. See also **extrasensory perception. 2.** keen intuitive understanding. [C19: from French: clear-seeing, from *clair* clear, from Latin *clārus* + *voyance,* from *voir* to see, from Latin *vidēre*]

clair·voy·ant (klɛə'vɔɪənt) *adj.* **1.** of, possessing, or relating to clairvoyance. **2.** having great insight or second sight. ~*n.* **3.** a person claiming to have the power to foretell future events. —**clair·'voy·ant·ly** *adv.*

clam[1] (klæm) *n.* **1.** any of various burrowing bivalve molluscs of the genera *Mya, Venus,* etc. Many species, such as the quahog and soft-shell clam, are edible and *Tridacna gigas* is the largest known bivalve, nearly 1.5 metres long. **2.** the edible flesh of such a mollusc. **3.** *Informal.* a reticent person. ~*vb.* **clams, clam·ming, clammed. 4.** (*intr.*) *Chiefly U.S.* to gather clams. ~See also **clam up.** [C16: from earlier *clamshell,* that is, shell that clamps; related to Old English *clamm* fetter, Old High German *klamma* constriction; see CLAMP[1]]

clam[2] (klæm) *vb.* **clams, clam·ming, clammed.** a variant spelling of **clem.**

cla·mant ('kleɪmənt) *adj.* **1.** noisy. **2.** calling urgently. [C17: from Latin *clāmāns,* from *clāmāre* to shout]

clam·a·to·ri·al (ˌklæmə'tɔːrɪəl) *adj.* of or relating to the American flycatchers (family *Tyrannidae*). See **flycatcher** (sense 2). [C19: from New Latin *clāmātōres,* plural of Latin *clāmātor* one who shouts; see CLAMANT]

clam·bake ('klæmˌbeɪk) *n. U.S.* **1.** a picnic, often by the sea, at which clams, etc., are baked. **2.** an informal party.

clam·ber ('klæmbə) *vb.* **1.** (usually foll. by *up, over,* etc.) to climb (something) awkwardly, esp. by using both hands and feet. ~*n.* **2.** a climb performed in this manner. [C15: probably a variant of CLIMB] —'**clam·ber·er** *n.*

clam·my ('klæmɪ) *adj.* **·mi·er, ·mi·est. 1.** unpleasantly sticky; moist: *clammy hands.* **2.** (of the weather, atmosphere, etc.) close; humid. [C14: from Old English *clǣman* to smear; related to Old Norse *kleima,* Old High German *kleimen*] —'**clam·mi·ly** *adv.* —'**clam·mi·ness** *n.*

clam·our *or U.S.* **clam·or** ('klæmə) *n.* **1.** a loud persistent outcry, as from a large number of people. **2.** a vehement expression of collective feeling or outrage: *a clamour against higher prices.* **3.** a loud and persistent noise: *the clamour of traffic.* ~*vb.* **4.** (*intr.;* often foll. by *for* or *against*) to make a loud noise or outcry; make a public demand. **5.** (*tr.*) to move, influence, or force by outcry: *the people clamoured him out of office.* [C14: from Old French *clamour,* from Latin *clāmor,* from *clāmāre* to cry out] —'**clam·our·er** *or U.S.* '**clam·or·er** *n.* —'**clam·or·ous** *adj.* —'**clam·or·ous·ly** *adv.* —'**clam·or·ous·ness** *n.*

clamp[1] (klæmp) *n.* **1.** a mechanical device with movable jaws with which an object can be secured to a bench or with which two objects may be secured together. **2.** a means by which a fixed joint may be strengthened. **3.** *Nautical.* a horizontal beam fastened to the ribs for supporting the deck beams in a wooden vessel. ~*vb.* (*tr.*) **4.** to fix or fasten with or as if with a clamp. **5.** to inflict or impose forcefully: *they clamped a curfew on the town.* [C14: from Dutch or Low German *klamp;* related to Old English *clamm* bond, fetter, Old Norse *kleppr* lump]

clamp[2] (klæmp) *Brit. agriculture.* ~*n.* **1.** a mound formed out of a harvested root crop, covered with straw and earth to protect it from winter weather. **2.** a pile of bricks ready for processing in a furnace. ~*vb.* **3.** (*tr.*) to enclose (a harvested root crop) in a mound. [C16: from Middle Dutch *klamp* heap; related to CLUMP]

clamp down *vb.* (*intr., adv.;* often foll. by *on*) **1.** to behave repressively; attempt to suppress something regarded as undesirable. ~*n.* **clamp·down. 2.** a sudden restrictive measure.

clamp·er ('klæmpə) *n.* a spiked metal frame fastened to the sole of a shoe to prevent slipping on ice.

clam·shell ('klæmˌʃɛl) *n.* **1.** *U.S.* a dredging bucket that is hinged like the shell of a clam. **2.** *Aeronautics.* another name for **eyelid** (sense 2).

clam up *vb.* (*intr., adv.*) *Informal.* to keep or become silent or withhold information.

clam·worm ('klæmˌwɜːm) *n.* the U.S. name for the **ragworm.**

clan (klæn) *n.* **1.** a group of people interrelated by ancestry or marriage. **2.** a group of families with a common surname and a common ancestor, acknowledging the same leader, esp. among the Scots and the Irish. **3.** a group of people united by common characteristics, aims, or interests. [C14: from Scottish Gaelic *clann* family, descendants, from Latin *planta* sprout, PLANT]

clan+des+tine (klæn'dɛstɪn) *adj.* secret and concealed, often for illicit reasons; furtive. [C16: from Latin *clandestīnus,* from *clam* secretly; related to Latin *celāre* to hide] **—clan+'des+tine+ly** *adv.* **—clan+'des+tine+ness** *n.*

clang (klæŋ) *vb.* **1.** to make or cause to make a loud resounding noise, as metal when struck. **2.** (*intr.*) to move or operate making such a sound: *the engine clanged on its way.* ~*n.* **3.** a resounding metallic noise. **4.** the harsh cry of certain birds. [C16: from Latin *clangere*]

clang+er ('klæŋə) *n.* **1.** *Informal.* a conspicuous mistake (esp. in the phrase **drop a clanger**). **2.** something that clangs or causes a clang. [C20: from CLANG, referring to a mistake whose effects seem to clang]

clang+or *or* **clang+our** ('klæŋgə, 'klæŋə) *n.* **1.** a loud resonant often-repeated noise. **2.** an uproar. ~*vb.* **3.** (*intr.*) to make or produce a loud resonant noise. **—'clang+or+ous** *or* **'clang+our+ous** *adj.* **—'clang+or+ous+ly** *or* **'clang+our+ous+ly** *adv.*

clank (klæŋk) *n.* **1.** an abrupt harsh metallic sound. ~*vb.* **2.** to make or cause to make such a sound. **3.** (*intr.*) to move or operate making such a sound. [C17: of imitative origin] **—'clank+ing+ly** *adv.*

clan+nish ('klænɪʃ) *adj.* **1.** of or characteristic of a clan. **2.** tending to associate closely within a limited group to the exclusion of outsiders; cliquish. **—'clan+nish+ly** *adv.* **—'clan+nish+ness** *n.*

clans+man ('klænzmən) *or* (*fem.*) **clans+wom·an** *n., pl.* **+men** *or* **+wom·en.** a person belonging to a clan.

clap[1] (klæp) *vb.* **claps, clap+ping, clapped. 1.** to make or cause to make a sharp abrupt sound, as of two nonmetallic objects struck together. **2.** to applaud (someone or something) by striking the palms of the hands together sharply. **3.** (*tr.*) to strike (a person) lightly with an open hand, in greeting, encouragement, etc. **4.** (*tr.*) to place or put quickly or forcibly: *they clapped him into jail.* **5.** (of certain birds) to flap (the wings) noisily. **6.** (*intr.;* foll. by *up* or *together*) to contrive or put together hastily: *they soon clapped up a shed.* **7. clap eyes on.** *Informal.* to catch sight of. **8. clap hold of.** *Informal.* to grasp suddenly or forcibly. ~*n.* **9.** the sharp abrupt sound produced by striking the hands together. **10.** the act of clapping, esp. in applause: *he deserves a good clap.* **11.** a sudden sharp sound, esp. of thunder. **12.** a light blow. **13.** *Archaic.* a sudden action or mishap. [Old English *clæppan;* related to Old High German *klepfen,* Middle Dutch *klape* rattle, Dutch *klepel* clapper; all of imitative origin]

clap[2] (klæp) *n.* (usually preceded by *the*) a slang word for **gonorrhoea.** [C16: from Old French *clapoir* venereal sore, from *clapier* brothel, from Old Provençal, from *clap* heap of stones, of obscure origin]

clap+board ('klæp,bɔ:d, 'klæbəd) *n.* **1. a.** a long thin timber board with one edge thicker than the other, used esp. in the U.S. in wood-frame construction by lapping each board over the one below. **b.** (*as modifier*): *a clapboard house.* ~*vb.* **2.** (*tr.*) to cover with such boards. [C16: partial translation of Low German *klappholt,* from *klappen* to crack + *holt* wood; related to Dutch *claphout;* see BOARD]

Clap+ham Sect ('klæpəm) *n.* an informal group of early 19th-century Church-of-England evangelicals advocating personal piety, missionary zeal, the abolition of slavery, etc. [C19: named after *Clapham,* a district of London]

clap-net *n.* a net, used esp. by entomologists, that can be closed instantly by pulling a string.

clap on *vb.* (*tr.*) to don hastily: *they clapped on their armour.*

clapped out *adj.* (**clapped-out** *when prenominal*). *Brit. informal.* (esp. of machinery) worn out; dilapidated.

clap+per ('klæpə) *n.* **1.** a person or thing that claps. **2.** a contrivance for producing a sound of clapping, as for scaring birds. **3.** Also called: **tongue.** a small piece of metal suspended within a bell that causes it to sound when made to strike against its side. **4.** a slang word for **tongue** (sense 1). ~*vb.* **5. go (run, move) like the clappers.** *Brit. informal.* to move extremely fast.

clap·per+board ('klæpə,bɔ:d) *n.* a pair of hinged boards clapped together during film shooting in order to aid in synchronizing sound and picture prints.

clap+per bridge *n.* a primitive type of bridge in which planks or slabs of stone rest on piles of stones.

clap·per+claw ('klæpə,klɔ:) *vb.* (*tr.*) *Archaic.* **1.** to claw or scratch with the hands and nails. **2.** to revile; abuse. [C16: perhaps from CLAPPER + CLAW] **—'clap·per+,claw·er** *n.*

Clap·ton ('klæptən) *n.* **Er·ic.** born 1945, English rock guitarist; a member of the groups Cream (1966–68), Blind Faith (1968), and Derek and the Dominos (1970 onwards). His albums include *Layla* (1970).

clap+trap ('klæp,træp) *n. Informal.* **1.** contrived but foolish talk. **2.** insincere and pretentious talk: *politicians' claptrap.* [C18 (in the sense: something contrived to elicit applause): from CLAP[1] + TRAP]

claque (klæk) *n.* **1.** a group of people hired to applaud. **2.** a group of fawning admirers. [C19: from French, from *claquer* to clap, of imitative origin]

clar·a+bel+la *or* **clar·i+bel+la** (,klærə'bɛlə) *n.* an eight-foot flute stop on an organ. [C19: from Latin *clāra,* feminine of *clārus* clear + *bella,* feminine of *bellus* beautiful]

Clare[1] (klɛə) *n.* a county of W Ireland, in Munster between Galway Bay and the Shannon estuary. County town: Ennis. Pop.: 75 008 (1971). Area: 3188 sq. km (1231 sq. miles).

Clare[2] (klɛə) *n.* **John.** 1793–1864, English poet, noted for his descriptions of country life, particularly in *The Shepherd's Calendar* (1827) and *The Rural Muse* (1835). He was confined in a lunatic asylum from 1837.

clar+ence ('klærəns) *n.* a closed four-wheeled horse-drawn carriage, having a glass front. [C19: named after the Duke of *Clarence* (1765–1837)]

Clar+en+ceux ('klærənsu:) *n. Heraldry.* the second King-of-Arms in England.

clar+en+don ('klærəndən) *n. Printing.* a style of boldface roman type. [C20: named after the Clarendon Press at Oxford University]

Clar+en+don[1] ('klærəndən) *n.* a village near Salisbury in S England: site of a council held by Henry II in 1164 that produced a code of laws (the **Constitutions of Clarendon**) defining relations between church and state.

Clar·en·don[2] ('klærəndən) *n.* **1st Earl of,** title of *Edward Hyde.* 1609–74, English statesman and historian; chief adviser to Charles II (1660–67); author of *History of the Rebellion and Civil Wars in England* (1704–07).

Clar+en+don Code *n. English history.* four acts passed by the Cavalier Parliament between 1661 and 1665 to deal with the religious problems of the Restoration. [C17: named after Edward Hyde, first Earl of CLARENDON, who was not, however, a supporter of the code]

Clare of As+si+si *n.* **Saint.** 1194–1253, Italian nun; founder of the Franciscan Order of Poor Clares. Feast day: Aug. 12.

clar+et ('klærət) *n.* **1.** *Chiefly Brit.* a red wine, esp. one from the Bordeaux district of France. **2. a.** a purplish-red colour. **b.** (*as adj.*): *a claret carpet.* [C14: from Old French (*vin*) *claret* clear (wine), from Medieval Latin *clārātum,* from *clārāre* to make clear, from Latin *clārus* CLEAR]

clar+et cup *n.* an iced drink made of claret, brandy, lemon, sugar, and sometimes sherry, curaçao, etc.

clar·i+fy ('klærɪ,faɪ) *vb.* **+fies, +fy+ing, +fied. 1.** to make or become clear or easy to understand. **2.** to make or become free of impurities. **3.** to make (fat, butter, etc.) clear by heating, etc., or (of fat, etc.) to become clear as a result of such a process. [C14: from Old French *clarifier,* from Late Latin *clārificāre,* from Latin *clārus* clear + *facere* to make] **—,clar·i+fi+'ca+tion** *n.* **—'clar·i+,fi+er** *n.*

clar·i+net (,klærɪ'nɛt) *n. Music.* **1.** a keyed woodwind instrument with a cylindrical bore and a single reed. It is a transposing instrument, most commonly pitched in A or B flat. Obsolete spelling: **clar·i·o+net** (,klærɪə'nɛt). **2.** an orchestral musician who plays the clarinet. [C18: from French *clarinette,* probably from Italian *clarinetto,* from *clarino* trumpet] **—,clar·i+'net+ist** *or* **,clar·i+'net+tist** *n.*

cla+rin·o (klæ'ri:nəʊ) *Music.* ~*adj.* **1.** of or relating to a high passage for the trumpet in 18th-century music. ~*n., pl.* **+nos** *or* **+ni** (-nɪ). **2.** the high register of the trumpet. **3.** an organ stop similar to the high register of the trumpet. **4.** a trumpet or clarion.

clar·i+on ('klærɪən) *n.* **1.** a four-foot reed stop of trumpet quality on an organ. **2.** an obsolete, high-pitched, small-bore trumpet. **3.** the sound of such an instrument or any similar sound. ~*adj.* **4.** (*prenominal*) clear and ringing; inspiring: *a clarion call to action.* ~*vb.* **5.** to proclaim loudly. [C14: from Medieval Latin *clāriō* trumpet, from Latin *clārus* clear]

clar+i·ty ('klærɪtɪ) *n.* **1.** clearness, as of expression. **2.** clearness, as of water. [C16: from Latin *clāritās,* from *clārus* CLEAR]

Clark (klɑ:k) *n.* **1. (Charles) Joseph,** called *Joe.* born 1939, Canadian politician; prime minister 1979–80. **2. James,** called *Jim.* 1936–68, Scottish racing driver; World Champion (1963, 1965). **3.** Lord **Ken·neth.** 1903–83, English art historian: his books include *Civilization* (1969), which he first presented as a television series.

Clark cell *n. Physics.* a cell having a mercury anode surrounded by a paste of mercuric sulphate and a zinc cathode in a saturated solution of zinc sulphate. Formerly used as a standard, its emf is 1.4345 volts. [C19: named after Hosiah *Clark* (died 1898), English scientist]

clark·i·a ('klɑ:kɪə) *n.* any North American onagraceous plant of the genus *Clarkia:* cultivated for their red, purple, or pink flowers. [C19: New Latin, named after William *Clark* (1770–1838), American explorer who discovered it]

clarts (klɑ:ts) *pl. n. Northern English dialect.* lumps of mud, esp. on shoes. [of unknown origin] **—'clart·y** *adj.*

clar·y ('klɛərɪ) *n., pl.* **clar·ies.** any of several European plants of the genus *Salvia,* having aromatic leaves and blue flowers: family *Labiatae* (labiates). [C14: from earlier *sclarreye,* from Medieval Latin *sclareia,* of obscure origin]

-clase *n. combining form.* (in mineralogy) indicating a particular type of cleavage: *plagioclase.* [via French from Greek *klasis* a breaking, from *klan* to break]

clash (klæʃ) *vb.* **1.** to make or cause to make a loud harsh sound, esp. by striking together. **2.** (*intr.*) to be incompatible; conflict. **3.** (*intr.*) to engage together in conflict or contest. **4.** (*intr.*) (of dates or events) to coincide. **5.** (of colours) to look ugly or inharmonious together. ~*n.* **6.** a loud harsh noise. **7.** a collision or conflict. **8.** *Scot.* gossip; tattle. [C16: of imitative origin] **—'clash+er** *n.* **—'clash+ing+ly** *adv.*

clasp (klɑ:sp) *n.* **1.** a fastening, such as a catch or hook, used for holding things together. **2.** a firm grasp, hold, or embrace. **3.** *Military.* a bar or insignia on a medal ribbon, to indicate either a second award or the battle, campaign, or reason for its award. ~*vb.* (*tr.*) **4.** to hold in a firm grasp. **5.** to grasp firmly with the hand. **6.** to fasten together with or as if with a clasp. [C14: of uncertain origin; compare Old English *clyppan* to embrace] —**'clasp·er** *n.*

clasp knife *n.* a large knife with one or more blades or other devices folding into the handle.

class (klɑ:s) *n.* **1.** a collection or division of people or things sharing a common characteristic, attribute, quality, or property. **2.** a group of persons sharing a similar social position and certain economic, political, and cultural characteristics. **3.** (in Marxist theory) a group of persons sharing the same relationship to the means of production. **4. a.** the pattern of divisions that exist within a society on the basis of rank, economic status, etc. **b.** (*as modifier*): *the class struggle; class distinctions.* **5. a.** a group of pupils or students who are taught and study together. **b.** a meeting of a group of students for tuition. **6.** *U.S.* a group of students who graduated in a specified year: *the class of '53.* **7.** (*in combination and as modifier*) *Brit.* a grade of attainment in a university honours degree: *second-class honours.* **8.** one of several standards of accommodation in public transport. See also **first class, second class, third class. 9.** *Informal.* excellence or elegance, esp. in dress, design, or behaviour: *that girl's got class.* **10. a.** outstanding speed and stamina in a racehorse. **b.** (*as modifier*): *the class horse in the race.* **11.** *Biology.* any of the taxonomic groups into which a phylum is divided and which contains one or more orders. *Amphibia, Reptilia,* and *Mammalia* are three classes of phylum *Chordata.* **12.** *Maths.* another name for **set**[2] (sense 3). **13. in a class by oneself** *or* **in a class of its own.** unequalled; unparalleled. ~*vb.* **14.** to have or assign a place within a group, grade, or class. [C17: from Latin *classis* class, rank, fleet; related to Latin *calāre* to summon] —**'class·a·ble** *adj.* —**'class·er** *n.*

class. *abbrev. for:* **1.** classic(al). **2.** classification. **3.** classified.

class-con·scious *adj.* aware of belonging to a particular social rank or grade, esp. in being hostile or proud because of class distinctions. —**'class-'con·scious·ness** *n.*

clas·sic ('klæsɪk) *adj.* **1.** of the highest class, esp. in art or literature. **2.** serving as a standard or model of its kind; definitive. **3.** adhering to an established set of rules or principles in the arts or sciences: *a classic proof.* **4.** characterized by simplicity, balance, regularity, and purity of form; classical. **5.** of lasting interest or significance. **6.** continuously in fashion because of its simple and basic style: *a classic day dress.* ~*n.* **7.** an author, artist, or work of art of the highest excellence. **8.** a creation or work considered as definitive. **9.** *Horse racing.* **a.** any of the five principal races for three-year-old horses in Britain, namely the One Thousand Guineas, Two Thousand Guineas, Derby, Oaks, and Saint Leger. **b.** a race equivalent to any of these in other countries. [C17: from Latin *classicus* of the first rank, from *classis* division, rank, CLASS]
Usage. The adjectives *classic* and *classical* can often be treated as synonyms, but there are two contexts in which they should be carefully distinguished. *Classic* is applied to that which is of the first rank, esp. in art and literature, as in: *Lewis Carroll's classic works for children. Classical* is used to refer to Greek and Roman culture.

clas·si·cal ('klæsɪkᵊl) *adj.* **1.** of, relating to, or characteristic of the ancient Greeks and Romans or their civilization, esp. in the period of their ascendancy. **2.** designating, following, or influenced by the art or culture of ancient Greece or Rome: *classical architecture.* **3.** *Music.* **a.** of, relating to, or denoting any music or its period of composition marked by stability of form, intellectualism, and restraint. Compare **romantic** (sense 5). **b.** accepted as a standard: *the classical suite.* **c.** denoting serious art music in general. Compare **pop**[2]. **4.** *Music.* of or relating to a style of music composed, esp. at Vienna, during the late 18th and early 19th centuries. This period is marked by the establishment, esp. by Haydn and Mozart, of sonata form. **5.** denoting or relating to a style in any of the arts characterized by emotional restraint and conservatism: *a classical style of painting.* See **classicism** (sense 1). **6.** well versed in the art and literature of ancient Greece and Rome. **7.** (of an education) based on the humanities and the study of Latin and Greek. **8.** *Physics.* **a.** not involving the quantum theory or the theory of relativity: *classical mechanics.* **b.** obeying the laws of Newtonian mechanics or 19th-century physics: *a classical gas.* **9.** another word for **classic** (sense 4). —**ˌclas·si·'cal·i·ty** *or* **'clas·si·cal·ness** *n.* —**'clas·si·cal·ly** *adv.*
Usage. See at **classic.**

clas·si·cal col·lege *n.* (in Quebec) a college offering a programme that emphasizes the classics and leads to university entrance.

clas·si·cal con·di·tion·ing *n. Psychol.* the process of altering behaviour by pairing two stimuli so that the second stimulus alone eventually will elicit a response that could originally be produced only by the first stimulus.

clas·sic blues *n.* (*functioning as sing. or pl.*) *Jazz.* a type of city blues performed by a female singer accompanied by a small group.

clas·si·cism ('klæsɪˌsɪzəm) *or* **clas·si·cal·ism** ('klæsɪkəˌlɪzəm) *n.* **1.** a style based on the study of Greek and Roman models, characterized by emotional restraint and regularity of form, associated esp. with the 18th century in Europe; the antithesis of romanticism. Compare **neoclassicism. 2.** knowledge or study of the culture of ancient Greece and Rome. **3. a.** a Greek or Latin form or expression. **b.** an expression in a modern language, such as English, that is modelled on a Greek or Latin form.

clas·si·cist ('klæsɪsɪst) *or* **clas·si·cal·ist** ('klæsɪkəlɪst) *n.* **1. a.** a student of ancient Latin and Greek. **b.** a person who advocates the study of ancient Latin and Greek. **2.** an adherent of classicism in literature or art. —**ˌclas·si·'cis·tic** *adj.*

clas·si·cize *or* **clas·si·cise** ('klæsɪˌsaɪz) *vb.* **1.** (*tr.*) to make classic. **2.** (*intr.*) to imitate classical style.

clas·sics ('klæsɪks) *n.* **the. 1.** a body of literature regarded as great or lasting, esp. that of ancient Greece or Rome. **2.** the ancient Greek and Latin languages.

clas·si·fi·ca·tion (ˌklæsɪfɪ'keɪʃən) *n.* **1.** systematic placement in categories. **2.** one of the divisions in a system of classifying. **3.** *Biology.* **a.** the placing of animals and plants in a series of increasingly specialized groups because of similarities in structure, origin, etc., that indicate a common relationship. The major groups are kingdom, phylum (in animals) or division (in plants), class, order, family, genus, and species. **b.** the study of the principles and practice of this process; taxonomy. **4.** *Government.* the designation of an item of information as being secret and not available to people outside a restricted group. [C18: from French; see CLASS, -IFY, -ATION] —**ˌclas·si·fi·'ca·tion·al** *adj.* —**ˌclas·si·fi·'ca·to·ry** *adj.*

clas·si·fi·ca·tion sched·ule *n. Library science.* the printed scheme of a system of classification.

clas·si·fied ('klæsɪˌfaɪd) *adj.* **1.** arranged according to some system of classification. **2.** *Government.* (of information) not available to people outside a restricted group, esp. for reasons of national security. **3.** *U.S. informal.* (of information) closely concealed or secret. **4.** (of advertisements in newspapers, etc.) arranged according to type. **5.** *Brit.* (of newspapers) containing sports results, esp. football results. **6.** (of British roads) having a number in the national road system. If the number is preceded by an M the road is a motorway, if by an A it is a first-class road, and if by a B it is a secondary road.

clas·si·fy ('klæsɪˌfaɪ) *vb.* **·fies, ·fy·ing, ·fied.** (*tr.*) **1.** to arrange or order by classes; categorize. **2.** *Government.* to declare (information, documents, etc.) of possible aid to an enemy and therefore not available to people outside a restricted group. [C18: back formation from CLASSIFICATION] —**'clas·si·ˌfi·a·ble** *adj.* —**'clas·si·ˌfi·er** *n.*

clas·sis ('klæsɪs) *n., pl.* **clas·ses** ('klæsi:z). (in some Reformed Churches) **1.** a governing body of elders or pastors. **2.** the district or group of local churches directed by such a body. [C16: from Latin; see CLASS]

class·less ('klɑ:slɪs) *adj.* **1.** not belonging to or forming a class. **2.** characterized by the absence of economic and social distinctions. —**'class·less·ness** *n.*

class list *n. Brit.* a list categorizing students according to the class of honours they have obtained in their degree examination.

class mark *n.* **1.** *Statistics.* a value within a frequency class interval for the purposes of quantitative analysis and computational convenience. **2.** Also called: **class number.** *Library science.* a symbol on a book or other publication indicating its subject field, shelf position, etc.

class·mate ('klɑ:sˌmeɪt) *n.* a friend or contemporary of the same class in a school, college, etc.

class·room ('klɑ:sˌru:m, -ˌrʊm) *n.* a room in which classes are conducted, esp. in a school or college.

class strug·gle *n.* **the.** *Marxism.* the continual conflict between the capitalist and working classes for economic and political power. Also called: **class war.**

class·y ('klɑ:sɪ) *adj.* **class·i·er, class·i·est.** *Slang.* elegant; stylish. —**'class·i·ly** *adv.* —**'class·i·ness** *n.*

clas·tic ('klæstɪk) *adj.* **1.** (of sediments, rocks, etc.) composed of fragments of pre-existing rocks. **2.** *Biology.* dividing into parts: *a clastic cell.* **3.** able to be dismantled for study or observation: *a clastic model of the brain.* [C19: from Greek *klastos* shattered, from *klan* to break]

clath·rate ('klæθreɪt) *adj.* **1.** *Botany.* resembling a net or lattice. ~*n.* **2.** *Chem.* a solid compound in which molecules of one substance are physically trapped in the crystal lattice of another. [C17: from Latin *clāthrāre* to provide with a lattice, from Greek *klēthra,* from *klaithron* a bar]

clat·ter ('klætə) *vb.* **1.** to make or cause to make a rattling noise, esp. as a result of movement. **2.** (*intr.*) to chatter. **3.** (*tr.*) *Northern English dialect.* to box the ears of. ~*n.* **4.** a rattling sound or noise. **5.** a noisy commotion, such as one caused by loud chatter. [Old English *clatrung* clattering (gerund); related to Dutch *klateren* to rattle, German *klatschen* to smack, Norwegian *klattra* to knock] —**'clat·ter·er** *n.* —**'clat·ter·ing·ly** *adv.* —**'clat·ter·y** *adj.*

Clau·del (*French* klo'dɛl) *n.* **Paul (Louis Charles)** (pɔl). 1868–1955, French dramatist, poet, and diplomat, whose works testify to his commitment to the Roman Catholic faith. His plays include *L'Annonce faite à Marie* (1912) and *Le Soulier de satin* (1919–24).

Claude Lor·rain (*French* klod lɔ'rɛ̃) *n.* pseudonym of *Claude Gelée.* 1600–82, French painter, esp. of idealized landscapes, noted for his subtle depiction of light.

clau·di·ca·tion (ˌklɔ:dɪ'keɪʃən) *n.* **1.** limping; lameness. **2.** *Pathol.* short for **intermittent claudication.** [C18: from Latin *claudicātiō,* from *claudicāre,* from *claudus* lame]

Clau·di·us ('klɔ:dɪəs) *n.* full name *Tiberius Claudius Drusus Nero Germanicus.* 10 B.C.–54 A.D., Roman emperor (41–54); invaded Britain (43); poisoned by his fourth wife, Agrippina.

Clau·di·us II *n.* full name *Marcus Aurelius Claudius,* called *Gothicus.* 214–270 A.D., Roman emperor (268–270).

clause (klɔ:z) *n.* **1.** *Grammar.* a group of words, consisting of a subject and a predicate including a finite verb, that does not necessarily constitute a sentence. See also **main clause, subordinate clause, coordinate clause. 2.** a section of a legal document such as a contract, will, or statute. [C13: from Old French, from Medieval Latin *clausa* a closing (of a rhetorical period), back formation from Latin *clausula*, from *claudere* to close] —'**claus+al** *adj.*

Clau·se·witz (*German* 'klaʊzəˌvɪts) *n.* **Karl von** ('karl fɔn). 1780–1831, Prussian general, noted for his works on military strategy, esp. *Vom Kriege* (1833).

Clau·si·us (*German* 'klaʊziʊs) *n.* **Ru·dolf Ju·li·us** ('ruːdɔlf 'juːliʊs). 1822–88, German physicist and mathematician. He enunciated the second law of thermodynamics (1850) and developed the kinetic theory of gases.

claus+tral ('klɔːstrəl) *adj.* a less common spelling of **cloistral.**

claus+tro+pho+bi·a (ˌklɔːstrə'fəʊbɪə, ˌklɒs-) *n.* an abnormal fear of being closed in or of being in a confined space. —'**claus+tro+ˌphobe** *n.* —ˌ**claus+tro+'pho+bic** *adj.*

cla+vate ('kleɪveɪt, -vɪt) *or* **clav·i+form** *adj.* shaped like a club with the thicker end uppermost. [C19: from Latin *clāva* club] —'**cla+vate+ly** *adv.*

clave[1] (kleɪv, klɑːv) *n. Music.* one of a pair of hardwood sticks struck together to make a hollow sound. [C20: from American Spanish, from Latin *clavis* key]

clave[2] (kleɪv) *vb. Archaic.* a past tense of **cleave.**

clav+er ('kleɪvə) *vb.* (*intr.*) *Scot.* to talk idly; gossip. [C13: of uncertain origin]

clav·i+cem+ba+lo (ˌklævɪ'tʃɛmbələʊ) *n., pl.* **+los.** another name for **harpsichord.** [C18: from Italian, from Medieval Latin *clāvis* key + *cymbalum* CYMBAL]

clav·i+chord ('klævɪˌkɔːd) *n.* a keyboard instrument consisting of a number of thin wire strings struck from below by brass tangents. The instrument is noted for its delicate tones, since the tangents do not rebound from the string until the key is released. [C15: from Medieval Latin *clāvichordium*, from Latin *clāvis* key + *chorda* string, CHORD[2]] —'**clav·i+ˌchord+ist** *n.*

clav·i+cle ('klævɪkᵊl) *n.* **1.** either of the two bones connecting the shoulder blades with the upper part of the breastbone. Nontechnical name: **collarbone. 2.** the corresponding structure in other vertebrates. [C17: from Medieval Latin *clāvicula*, from Latin *clāvis* key] —**cla+vic·u+lar** (klə'vɪkjʊlə) *adj.* —**cla+vic·u+late** (klə'vɪkjʊˌleɪt) *adj.*

clav·i+corn ('klævɪˌkɔːn) *n.* **1.** any beetle of the group *Clavicornia*, including the ladybirds, characterized by club-shaped antennae. ~*adj.* **2.** of, relating to, or belonging to the *Clavicornia.* [C19: from New Latin *Clavicornia*, from Latin *clāva* club + *cornū* horn]

cla+vier (klə'vɪə, 'klævɪə) *n.* **a.** any keyboard instrument. **b.** the keyboard itself. [C18: from French: keyboard, from Old French (in the sense: key bearer), from Latin *clāvis* key]

clav·i+form ('klævɪˌfɔːm) *adj.* another word for **clavate.** [C19: from Latin *clāva* club]

Cla+vi+us ('kleɪvɪəs) *n.* one of the largest of the craters on the moon, about 230 kilometres (145 miles) in diameter, whose walls have peaks up to 5700 metres (19 000 feet) above the floor. It lies in the SE quadrant.

claw (klɔː) *n.* **1.** a curved pointed horny process on the end of each digit in birds, some reptiles, and certain mammals. **2.** a corresponding structure in some invertebrates, such as the pincer of a crab. **3.** a part or member like a claw in function or appearance. **4.** *Botany.* the narrow basal part of certain petals and sepals. ~*vb.* **5.** to scrape, tear, or dig (something or someone) with claws, etc. **6.** (*tr.*) to create by scratching as with claws: *to claw an opening.* [Old English *clawu;* related to Old High German *kluwi*, Sanskrit *glau-* ball, sphere] —'**claw+er** *n.* —'**claw+less** *adj.*

claw back *vb.* (*tr., adv.*) **1.** to get back (something) with difficulty. **2.** to recover (a part of a tax, duty, etc.) in the form of an allowance. ~*n.* **claw+back. 3.** the recovery of part of a tax, etc., in the form of an allowance. **4.** the sum so recovered.

claw ham+mer *n.* a hammer with a cleft at one end of the head for extracting nails. Also called: **carpenter's hammer.**

claw hatch+et *n.* a hatchet with a claw at one end of its head for extracting nails.

claw off *vb.* (*adv., usually tr.*) *Nautical.* to avoid the dangers of (a lee shore or other hazard) by beating.

claw set+ting *n. Brit.* a jewellery setting with clawlike prongs. U.S. equivalent: **Tiffany setting.**

clay (kleɪ) *n.* **1.** a very fine-grained material that consists of hydrated aluminium silicate, quartz, and organic fragments and occurs as sedimentary rocks, soils, and other deposits. It becomes plastic when moist but hardens on heating and is used in the manufacture of bricks, cement, ceramics, etc. **2.** earth or mud in general. **3.** *Poetic.* the material of the human body. ~*vb.* **4.** (*tr.*) to cover or mix with clay. [Old English *clǣg;* related to Old High German *klīa*, Norwegian *kli*, Latin *glūs* glue, Greek *gloios* sticky oil] —'**clay+ey,** '**clay+ish,** *or* '**clay+ˌlike** *adj.*

Clay (kleɪ) *n.* **1.** See **Muhammad Ali. 2. Hen·ry.** 1777–1852, U.S. statesman and orator; secretary of state (1825–29).

clay+bank ('kleɪˌbæŋk) *n. U.S.* **a.** a dull brownish-orange colour. **b.** (*as adj.*): *a claybank horse.*

clay min+er+al *n.* any of a group of minerals consisting of hydrated aluminium silicates: the major constituents of clays.

clay+more ('kleɪˌmɔː) *n.* a large two-edged broadsword used formerly by Scottish Highlanders. [C18: from Gaelic *claidheamh mōr* great sword]

clay+pan ('kleɪˌpæn) *n.* a layer of stiff impervious clay situated just below the surface of the ground, which holds water after heavy rain.

clay pig+eon *n.* **1.** a disc of baked clay hurled into the air from a machine as a target to be shot at. **2.** *U.S. slang.* a person in a defenceless position; sitting duck.

clay+stone ('kleɪˌstəʊn) *n.* a compact very fine-grained rock consisting of consolidated clay particles.

clay+to+ni·a (kleɪ'təʊnɪə) *n.* any low-growing North American succulent portulacaceous plant of the genus *Claytonia.* [C18: named after John *Clayton* (1693–1773), American botanist]

-cle *suffix forming nouns.* indicating smallness: *cubicle; particle.* [via Old French from Latin *-culus.* See -CULE]

clean (kliːn) *adj.* **1.** without dirt or other impurities; unsoiled. **2.** without anything in it or on it: *a clean page.* **3.** without extraneous or foreign materials. **4.** without defect, difficulties, or problems: *a clean test flight.* **5. a.** (of a nuclear weapon) producing little or no radioactive fall-out or contamination. **b.** uncontaminated. Compare **dirty** (sense 11). **6.** (of a wound, etc.) having no pus or other sign of infection. **7.** pure; morally sound. **8.** without objectionable language or obscenity: *a clean joke.* **9.** (of printer's proofs, etc.) relatively free from errors; easily readable: *clean copy.* **10.** thorough or complete: *a clean break.* **11.** dexterous or adroit: *a clean throw.* **12.** *Sport.* played fairly and without fouls. **13.** simple in design: *a ship's clean lines.* **14.** *Aeronautics.* causing little turbulence; streamlined. **15.** (of an aircraft) having no projections, such as rockets, flaps, etc., into the airstream. **16.** honourable or respectable. **17.** habitually neat. **18.** (esp. of a driving licence) showing or having no record of offences. **19.** *Slang.* **a.** innocent; not guilty. **b.** not carrying illegal drugs, weapons, etc. **20.** *Nautical.* (of a vessel) **a.** having its bottom clean. **b.** having a satisfactory bill of health. **21.** *Old Testament.* **a.** (of persons) free from ceremonial defilement. **b.** (of animals, birds, and fish) lawful to eat. **22.** *New Testament.* morally and spiritually pure. ~*vb.* **23.** to make or become free of dirt, filth, etc.: *the stove cleans easily.* **24.** to remove in making clean: *to clean marks off the wall.* **25.** (*tr.*) to prepare (fish, poultry, etc.) for cooking: *to clean a chicken.* ~*adv.* **26.** in a clean way; cleanly. **27.** *Not standard.* (intensifier): *clean forgotten; clean dead.* **28. clean bowled.** *Cricket.* bowled by a ball that breaks the wicket without hitting the batsman or his bat. **29. come clean.** *Informal.* to make a revelation or confession. ~*n.* **30.** the act or an instance of cleaning: *he gave his shoes a clean.* [Old English *clǣne;* related to Old Frisian *klēne* small, neat, Old High German *kleini*] —'**clean+a·ble** *adj.* —'**clean+ness** *n.*

clean-cut *adj.* **1.** clearly outlined; neat: *clean-cut lines of a ship.* **2.** definite: *a clean-cut decision in boxing.*

clean+er ('kliːnə) *n.* **1.** a person, device, chemical agent, etc., that removes dirt, as from clothes or carpets. **2.** (*usually pl.*) a shop, etc. that provides a dry-cleaning service.

clean-limbed *adj.* having well-proportioned limbs.

clean+ly *adv.* ('kliːnlɪ). **1.** in a fair manner. **2.** easily or smoothly: *the screw went into the wood cleanly.* ~*adj.* ('klɛnlɪ), **+li+er, +li+est. 3.** habitually clean or neat. —**clean+li+ly** ('klɛnlɪlɪ) *adv.* —**clean+li+ness** ('klɛnlɪnɪs) *n.*

clean out *vb.* (*tr., adv.*) **1.** (foll. by *of* or *from*) *Slang.* to remove (something) (from or away from). **2.** *Slang.* to leave (someone) with no money: *gambling had cleaned him out.* **3.** *Slang.* to exhaust (stocks, goods, etc.) completely.

cleanse (klɛnz) *vb.* (*tr.*) **1.** to remove dirt, filth, etc., from. **2.** to remove guilt from. **3.** *Archaic.* to cure. [Old English *clǣnsian;* related to Middle Low German *klēnsen;* see CLEAN] —'**cleans+a·ble** *adj.*

cleans+er ('klɛnzə) *n.* a cleansing agent, such as a detergent.

clean-shav·en *adj.* (of men) having the facial hair shaved off.

clean+skin ('kliːnˌskɪn) *n. Austral.* **1.** an unbranded animal. **2.** *Slang.* a person without a criminal record.

Cle·an·thes (klɪ'ænθiːz) *n.* ?300–?232 B.C., Greek philosopher: succeeded Zeno as head of the Stoic school.

clean up *vb.* (*adv.*) **1.** to rid (something) of dirt, filth, or other impurities. **2.** to make (someone or something) orderly or presentable. **3.** (*tr.*) to rid (a place) of undesirable people or conditions: *the campaign against vice had cleaned up the city.* **4.** *Informal, chiefly U.S.* to make (a great profit). ~*n.* **clean+up. 5. a.** the process of cleaning up or eliminating something. **b.** (*as modifier*): *a cleanup campaign.* **6.** *Informal, chiefly U.S.* a great profit.

clear (klɪə) *adj.* **1.** free from darkness or obscurity; bright. **2.** (of weather) free from dullness or clouds. **3.** transparent: *clear water.* **4.** even and pure in tone or colour: *clear blue.* **5.** without discoloration, blemish, or defect: *a clear skin.* **6.** easy to see or hear; distinct. **7.** free from doubt or confusion: *his instructions are not clear.* **8.** (*postpositive*) certain in the mind; sure: *are you clear?* **9.** evident or obvious: *it is clear that he won't come now.* **10.** (of sounds or the voice) not harsh or hoarse. **11.** serene; calm. **12.** without qualification or limitation; complete: *a clear victory.* **13.** free of suspicion, guilt, or blame: *a clear conscience.* **14.** free of obstruction; open: *a clear passage.* **15.** free from debt or obligation. **16.** (of money, profits, etc.) without deduction; net. **17.** emptied of freight or cargo. **18.** (of timber) having a smooth, unblemished surface. **19.** (of a message, etc.) not in code. **20.** Also: **light.** *Phonetics.* denoting an (l) in whose articulation the main part of the tongue is brought forward giving the sound of a front-vowel timbre. **21.** *Showjumping.* (of a round) ridden without any fences being knocked down or any points being lost. ~*adv.* **22.** in a clear or distinct manner. **23.** completely or utterly. **24.** (*postpositive;* often foll. by *of*) not in contact (with); free: *stand clear of the gates.* ~*n.* **25.** a clear space. **26.** another word for **clearance. 27. in the clear. a.** free of suspicion, guilt, or blame. **b.** *Sport.* able to receive a pass without being tackled. ~*vb.* **28.** to make or become free from darkness, obscurity, etc. **29.** (*intr.*) **a.** (of the weather) to become free from dullness, fog, rain, etc. **b.** (of mist, fog, etc.) to disappear. **30.** (*tr.*) to free from impurity or blemish. **31.** (*tr.*) to free from doubt or confusion: *to clear one's mind.* **32.** (*tr.*) to rid of objects, obstructions, etc. **33.** (*tr.*) to make or form (a path, way, etc.) by removing obstructions. **34.** (*tr.*) to free or remove (a person or thing) from something, as of suspicion, blame, or guilt. **35.** (*tr.*) to move or pass by or over without contact or involvement: *he cleared the wall easily.* **36.** (*tr.*) to rid (the throat) of phlegm or obstruction. **37.** (*tr.*) to make or gain (money) as profit. **38.** (*tr.;* often foll. by *off*) to discharge or settle (a debt). **39.** (*tr.*) to free (a debtor) from obligation. **40.** (*intr.*) (of a cheque) to pass through one's bank and be charged against one's account. **41.** *Banking.* to settle accounts by exchanging (commercial documents) in a clearing house. **42.** to permit (ships, aircraft, cargo, passengers, etc.) to unload, disembark, depart, etc., after fulfilling the customs and other requirements, or (of ships, etc.) to be permitted to unload, etc. **43.** to obtain or give (clearance). **44.** (*tr.*) to obtain clearance from. **45.** (*tr.*) to make microscope specimens transparent by immersion in a fluid such as xylene. **46.** (*tr.*) to permit (a person, company, etc.) to see or handle classified information. **47.** (*tr.*) *Military, etc.* **a.** to achieve transmission of (a signalled message) and acknowledgment of its receipt at its destination. **b.** to decode (a message, etc.). **48.** (*tr.*) *Sport.* to hit, kick, carry, or throw (the ball) out of the defence area. **49.** (*tr.*) *Computer technol.* to remove data from a storage device and replace it with particular characters that usually indicate zero. **50. clear the air.** to dispel tension, confusion, etc. **51. clear the decks.** to make ready so as to take action, fight, etc. ~See also **clear away, clear off, clear out, clear up.** [C13: *clere,* from Old French *cler,* from Latin *clārus* clear, bright, brilliant, illustrious] —**'clear·a·ble** *adj.* —**'clear·er** *n.* —**'clear·ly** *adv.* —**'clear·ness** *n.*

clear·ance ('klɪərəns) *n.* **1. a.** the process or an instance of clearing: *slum clearance.* **b.** (*as modifier*): *a clearance order.* **2.** space between two parts in motion or in relative motion. **3.** permission for an aircraft, ship, passengers, etc., to proceed. **4.** *Banking.* the exchange of commercial documents drawn on the members of a clearing house. **5. a.** the disposal of merchandise at reduced prices. **b.** (*as modifier*): *a clearance sale.* **6.** *Sport.* **a.** the act of hitting or kicking a ball out of the defensive area, as in football. **b.** an instance of this. **7.** a less common word for **clearing.**

clear a·way *vb.* (*adv.*) to remove (objects) from (the table) after a meal.

clear·cole ('klɪəkəʊl) *n.* **1.** a type of size containing whiting. ~*vb.* **2.** (*tr.*) to paint (a wall, etc.) with this size. [C19: from French *claire colle* clear size]

clear-cut *adj.* (**clear cut** *when postpositive*). **1.** definite; not vague: *a clear-cut proposal.* **2.** clearly outlined.

clear-eyed *adj.* **1.** discerning; perceptive. **2.** having clear eyes or sharp vision.

clear-head·ed *adj.* mentally alert; sensible; judicious. —**ˌclear-'head·ed·ly** *adv.* —**ˌclear-'head·ed·ness** *n.*

clear·ing ('klɪərɪŋ) *n.* an area with few or no trees or shrubs in wooded or overgrown land.

clear·ing bank *n. Brit.* any bank that makes use of the central clearing house in London for the transfer of credits and cheques between banks.

clear·ing house *n.* **1.** *Banking.* an institution where cheques and other commercial papers drawn on member banks are cancelled against each other so that only net balances are payable. **2.** a central agency for the collection and distribution of information or materials.

clear off *vb.* (*intr., adv.*) *Informal.* to go away: often used imperatively.

clear out *vb.* (*adv.*) **1.** (*intr.*) *Informal.* to go away: often used imperatively. **2.** (*tr.*) to remove and sort the contents of (a room, container, etc.). **3.** (*tr.*) *Slang.* to leave (someone) with no money. **4.** (*tr.*) *Slang.* to exhaust (stocks, goods, etc.) completely.

clear-sight·ed *adj.* **1.** involving accurate perception or judgment: *a clear-sighted compromise.* **2.** having clear vision. —**ˌclear-'sight·ed·ly** *adv.* —**ˌclear-'sight·ed·ness** *n.*

clear·sto·ry ('klɪəˌstɔːrɪ) *n.* a variant spelling of **clerestory.** —**'clear·ˌsto·ried** *adj.*

clear up *vb.* (*adv.*) **1.** (*tr.*) to explain or solve (a mystery, misunderstanding, etc.). **2.** to put (a place or thing that is disordered) in order. **3.** (*intr.*) (of the weather) to become brighter.

clear·way ('klɪəˌweɪ) *n. Brit.* a stretch of road on which motorists may stop only in an emergency.

clear·wing *or* **clear·wing moth** ('klɪəˌwɪŋ) *n.* any moth of the family *Sesiidae* (or *Aegeriidae*), characterized by the absence of scales from the greater part of the wings.

cleat (kliːt) *n.* **1.** a wedge-shaped block, usually of wood, attached to a structure to act as a support. **2.** a device consisting of two hornlike prongs projecting horizontally in opposite directions from a central base, used for securing lines on vessels, wharves, etc. **3.** a short length of angle iron used as a bracket. **4.** a piece of metal, leather, etc., attached to the sole of a shoe to prevent wear or slipping. **5.** a small triangular-shaped nail used in glazing. **6.** any of the main cleavage planes in a coal seam. ~*vb.* (*tr.*) **7.** to supply or support with a cleat or cleats. **8.** to secure (a line) on a cleat. [C14: of Germanic origin, compare Old High German *chlōz* clod, lump, Dutch *kloot* ball]

cleav·age ('kliːvɪdʒ) *n.* **1.** *Informal.* the separation between a woman's breasts, esp. as revealed by a low-cut dress. **2.** a division or split. **3.** (of crystals) the act of splitting or the tendency to split along definite planes so as to yield smooth surfaces. **4.** Also called: **segmentation.** *Embryol.* (in animals) the repeated division of a fertilized ovum into a solid ball of cells (a morula), which later becomes hollow (a blastula). **5.** the breaking of a chemical bond in a molecule to give smaller molecules or radicals.

cleave[1] (kliːv) *vb.* **cleaves, cleav·ing; cleft, cleaved,** *or* **clove; cleft, cleaved,** *or* **clo·ven. 1.** to split or cause to split, esp. along a natural weakness. **2.** (*tr.*) to make by or as if by cutting: *to cleave a path.* **3.** (when *intr.,* foll. by *through*) to penetrate or traverse. [Old English *clēofan;* related to Old Norse *kljūfa,* Old High German *klioban,* Latin *glūbere* to peel] —**'cleav·a·ble** *adj.* —**ˌcleav·a·'bil·i·ty** *n.*

cleave[2] (kliːv) *vb.* (*intr.;* foll. by *to*) to cling or adhere. [Old English *cleofian;* related to Old High German *klebēn* to stick]

cleav·er ('kliːvə) *n.* a heavy knife or long-bladed hatchet, esp. one used by butchers.

cleav·ers ('kliːvəz) *n.* (*functioning as sing.*) a Eurasian rubiaceous plant, *Galium aparine,* having small white flowers and prickly stems and fruits. Also called: **goosegrass, hairif.** [Old English *clīfe;* related to *clīfan* to CLEAVE[2]]

cleck[1] (klɛk) *vb.* (*tr.*) *Scot.* **1.** (of birds) to hatch. **2.** to lay or hatch (a plot or scheme). [C15: from Old Norse *klekja*]

cleck[2] (klɛk) *South Wales dialect.* ~*vb.* **1.** (*intr.;* often foll. by *on*) to gossip (about); tell (on). ~*n.* **2.** (*often pl.*) a piece of gossip. [from Welsh, from *clecan* to gossip, and *clec* gossip] —**'cleck·y** *adj.*

cleek (kliːk) *n.* **1.** *Golf.* a club, a long-shafted iron (No. 1) used for long low shots. **2.** *Chiefly Scot.* a large hook, such as one used to land fish. [C15: of uncertain origin]

Clee·thorpes ('kliːθɔːps) *n.* a resort in E England, in SE Humberside. Pop.: 35 785 (1971).

clef (klɛf) *n.* one of several symbols placed on the left-hand side beginning of each stave indicating the pitch of the music written after it. See also **alto clef, C clef, soprano clef, tenor clef, bass clef.** [C16: from French: key, clef, from Latin *clāvis;* related to Latin *claudere* to close]

cleft (klɛft) *vb.* **1.** the past tense or a past participle of **cleave.** ~*n.* **2.** a fissure or crevice. **3.** an indentation or split in something, such as the chin, palate, etc. ~*adj.* **4.** split; divided. **5.** (of leaves) having one or more incisions reaching nearly to the midrib. [Old English *geclyft* (n.); related to Old High German *kluft* tongs, German *Kluft* gap, fissure; see CLEAVE[1]]

cleft pal·ate *n.* a congenital crack or fissure in the midline of the hard palate, often associated with a harelip.

cleg (klɛg) *n.* another name for a **horsefly,** esp. one of the genus *Haematopota.*

clei·do·ic egg (klaɪ'dəʊɪk) *n.* the egg of birds and insects, which is enclosed in a protective shell limiting the exchange of water, gases, etc. [C20: from Greek *kleidoun* to lock up, from *kleid-, kleis* key]

Cleis·the·nes ('klaɪsθəˌniːz) *n.* 6th century B.C., Athenian statesman: democratized the political structure of Athens.

cleis·tog·a·my (klaɪ'stɒgəmɪ) *n.* self-pollination and fertilization of an unopened flower, as in the violet. —**cleis·'tog·a·mous** *or* **cleis·to·gam·ic** (ˌklaɪstə'gæmɪk) *adj.*

clem (klɛm) *or* **clam** *vb.* **clems, clem·ming, clemmed** *or* **clams, clam·ming, clammed.** *English dialect.* (when *tr., usually passive*) to be hungry or cause to be hungry. [C16: of Germanic origin; related to Dutch, German *klemmen* to pinch, cramp; compare Old English *beclemman* to shut in]

clem·a·tis ('klɛmətɪs) *n.* any N temperate ranunculaceous climbing plant or erect shrub of the genus *Clematis,* having plumelike fruits. Many species are cultivated for their large colourful flowers. See also **traveller's joy.** [C16: from Latin, from Greek *klēmatis* climbing plant, brushwood, from *klēma* twig]

Cle·men·ceau (*French* klemɑ̃'so) *n.* **Georges Eu·gène Ben·ja·min** (ʒɔrʒ œʒɛn bɛ̃ʒa'mɛ̃). 1841–1929, French statesman; prime minister of France (1906–09; 1917–20); negotiated the Treaty of Versailles (1919).

clem·en·cy ('klɛmənsɪ) *n., pl.* **·cies. 1.** mercy or leniency. **2.** mildness, esp. of the weather. [C15: from Latin *clēmentia,* from *clēmēns* gentle]

Clem·ens ('klɛmənz) *n.* **Sam·u·el Lang·horne** ('læŋˌhɔːn). See (Mark) **Twain.**

clem·ent ('klɛmənt) *adj.* **1.** merciful. **2.** (of the weather) mild. [C15: from Latin *clēmēns* mild; probably related to Greek *klinein* to lean] —**'clem·ent·ly** *adv.*

Clem·ent I ('klɛmənt) *n.* **Saint,** called *Clement of Rome.* pope (?88–?97 A.D.). Feast day: Nov. 23.

Clem·ent V *n.* original name *Bertrand de Got.* ?1264–1314, pope (1305–14): removed the papal seat from Rome to Avignon in France (1309).

Clem·ent VII *n.* original name *Giulio de' Medici.* 1478–1534, pope (1523–34): refused to sanction the divorce of Henry VIII of England from Catherine of Aragon (1533).

clem·en·tine ('klɛmənˌtiːn, -ˌtaɪn) *n.* a citrus fruit thought to be either a variety of tangerine or a hybrid between a tangerine and sweet orange. [C20: from French *clémentine,* perhaps from the female Christian name]

Clem·ent of Al·ex·an·dri·a *n.* original name *Titus Flavius Clemens.* ?150–?215 A.D., Greek Christian theologian: head of the catechetical school at Alexandria; teacher of Origen.

clench (klɛntʃ) *vb.* (*tr.*) **1.** to close or squeeze together (the teeth, a fist, etc.) tightly. **2.** to grasp or grip firmly. ~*n.* **3.** a firm grasp or grip. **4.** a device that grasps or grips, such as a clamp. ~*n., vb.* **5.** another word for **clinch.** [Old English *beclencan,* related to Old High German *klenken* to tie, Middle High German *klank* noose, Dutch *klinken* rivet]

cle·o·me (klɪ'əʊmɪ) *n.* any herbaceous or shrubby plant of the mostly tropical capparidaceous genus *Cleome,* esp. *C. spinosa,* cultivated for their clusters of white or purplish flowers with long stamens. [C19: New Latin, of obscure origin]

Cle·on ('kli:ɒn) *n.* died 422 B.C., Athenian demagogue and military leader.

Cle·o·pat·ra (ˌkli:ə'pætrə, -'pɑ:-) *n.* ?69–30 B.C., queen of Egypt (51–30), renowned for her beauty: the mistress of Julius Caesar and later of Mark Antony. She killed herself with an asp to avoid capture by Octavian (Augustus).

Cle·o·pat·ra's Nee·dle *n.* either of two Egyptian obelisks, originally set up at Heliopolis about 1500 B.C.: one was moved to the Thames Embankment, London, in 1878, the other to Central Park, New York, in 1880.

clepe (kli:p) *vb.* **clepes, clep·ing; cleped** (kli:pt, klɛpt), **clept, y·cleped,** *or* **y·clept.** (*tr.*) *Archaic.* to call by the name of. [Old English *cleopian;* related to Middle Low German *kleperen* to rattle]

clep·sy·dra ('klɛpsɪdrə) *n., pl.* **·dras** *or* **·drae** (-ˌdri:). an ancient device for measuring time by the flow of water or mercury through a small aperture. Also called: **water clock.** [C17: from Latin, from Greek *klepsudra,* from *kleptein* to steal + *hudōr* water]

clep·to·ma·ni·a (ˌklɛptəʊ'meɪnɪə, -'meɪnjə) *n.* a variant spelling of **kleptomania.** —ˌ**clep·to·'ma·ni·ˌac** *n.*

clere·sto·ry *or* **clear·sto·ry** ('klɪəˌstɔ:rɪ) *n., pl.* **·ries. 1.** a row of windows in the upper part of the wall of a church that divides the nave from the aisle, set above the aisle roof. **2.** the part of the wall in which these windows are set. Compare **blindstorey.** [C15: from CLEAR + STOREY] —'**clere·ˌsto·ried** *or* '**clear·ˌsto·ried** *adj.*

cler·gy ('klɜ:dʒɪ) *n., pl.* **·gies.** the collective body of men and women ordained as ministers of the Christian Church. [C13: from Old French *clergie,* from *clerc* ecclesiastic, CLERK]

cler·gy·man ('klɜ:dʒɪmən) *n., pl.* **·men.** a member of the clergy.

cler·ic ('klɛrɪk) *n.* a member of the clergy. [C17: from Church Latin *clēricus* priest, CLERK]

cler·i·cal ('klɛrɪkᵊl) *adj.* **1.** relating to or associated with the clergy: *clerical dress.* **2.** of or relating to office clerks or their work: *a clerical error.* **3.** supporting or advocating clericalism. —'**cler·i·cal·ly** *adv.*

cler·i·cal col·lar *n.* a stiff white collar with no opening at the front that buttons at the back of the neck; the distinctive mark of the clergy in certain Churches. Informal name: **dog collar.**

cler·i·cal·ism ('klɛrɪkᵊˌlɪzəm) *n.* **1.** a policy of upholding the power of the clergy. **2.** the power of the clergy esp. when excessively strong. —'**cler·i·cal·ist** *n.*

cler·i·cals ('klɛrɪkᵊlz) *pl. n.* the distinctive dress of a clergyman.

cler·i·hew ('klɛrɪˌhju:) *n.* a form of comic or satiric verse, consisting of two couplets of metrically irregular lines, containing the name of a well-known person. [C20: named after Edmund *Clerihew* Bentley (1875–1956), English writer who invented it]

clerk (klɑ:k; *U.S.* klɜ:rk) *n.* **1.** a worker, esp. in an office, who keeps records, files, etc. **2. clerk to the justices.** (in England) a legally qualified person who sits in court with lay justices to advise them on points of law. **3.** an employee of a court, legislature, board, corporation, etc., who keeps records and accounts, etc.: *a town clerk.* **4.** Also called: **clerk of the House.** *Brit.* a senior official of the House of Commons. **5.** Also called: **clerk in holy orders.** a cleric. **6.** *U.S.* short for **salesclerk. 7.** Also called: **desk clerk.** *U.S.* a hotel receptionist. **8.** *Archaic.* a scholar. ~*vb.* **9.** (*intr.*) to serve as a clerk. [Old English *clerc,* from Church Latin *clēricus,* from Greek *klērikos* cleric, relating to the heritage (alluding to the Biblical Levites, whose inheritance was the Lord), from *klēros* heritage] —'**clerk·dom** *n.* —'**clerk·ish** *adj.* —'**clerk·ship** *n.*

clerk·ess (klɑ:'kɛs) *n. Chiefly Scot.* a female office clerk.

clerk·ly ('klɑ:klɪ) *adj.* **·li·er, ·li·est. 1.** of or like a clerk. **2.** *Obsolete.* learned. ~*adv.* **3.** *Obsolete.* in the manner of a clerk. —'**clerk·li·ness** *n.*

clerk of the works *n.* an employee who supervises building work in progress or the upkeep of existing buildings.

Cler·mont-Fer·rand (*French* klɛrmɔ̃ fɛ'rɑ̃) *n.* a city in S central France: capital of Puy-de-Dôme department; industrial centre. Pop.: 161 203 (1975).

cle·ru·chy ('klɛəˌru:kɪ) *n., pl.* **·chies.** (in the ancient world) a special type of Athenian colony, in which settlers (**cleruchs**) retained their Athenian citizenship and the community remained a political dependency of Athens. —**cle·ru·chi·al** (klɪ'ru:kɪəl) *adj.*

cleve·ite ('kli:vaɪt) *n.* a crystalline variety of the mineral uranitite. [C19: named after P. T. *Cleve* (1840–1905), Swedish chemist and geologist; see -ITE[1]]

Cleve·land[1] ('kli:vlənd) *n.* **1.** a county of NE England formed in 1974 from parts of E Durham and N Yorkshire. Administrative centre: Middlesbrough. Pop.: 567 900 (1976 est.). Area: 595 sq. km (230 sq. miles). **2.** a port in NE Ohio, on Lake Erie: major heavy industries. Pop.: 678 615 (1973 est.). **3.** a hilly region of NE England, extending from the **Cleveland Hills** to the River Tees.

Cleve·land[2] ('kli:vlənd) *n.* **Ste·phen Gro·ver.** 1837–1908, U.S. Democratic politician; the 22nd and 24th president of the U.S. (1885–89; 1893–97).

clev·er ('klɛvə) *adj.* **1.** displaying sharp intelligence or mental alertness. **2.** adroit or dexterous, esp. with the hands. **3.** smart in a superficial way. **4.** *Brit. informal.* sly; cunning. **5.** (*predicative; used with a negative*) *Brit. dialect.* healthy; fit. [C13 *cliver* (in the sense: quick to seize, adroit), of uncertain origin] —'**clev·er·ish** *adj.* —'**clev·er·ly** *adv.* —'**clev·er·ness** *n.*

clev·er-clev·er *adj. Informal.* clever in a showy manner; artful; over-clever.

clev·er Dick *or* **clev·er·dick** ('klɛvəˌdɪk) *n. Informal.* a person considered to have an unwarrantably high opinion of his own ability or knowledge.

clev·is ('klɛvɪs) *n.* a coupling device for attaching a drawbar to a plough or similar implement. [C16: related to CLEAVE[1]]

clew (klu:) *n.* **1.** a ball of thread, yarn, or twine. **2.** *Nautical.* either of the lower corners of a square sail or the after lower corner of a fore-and-aft sail. **3.** (*usually pl.*) the rigging of a hammock. **4.** a rare variant of **clue.** ~*vb.* **5.** (*tr.*) to coil or roll into a ball. [Old English *cliewen* (vb.); related to Old High German *kliu* ball]

clew line *n. Nautical.* any of several lines fastened to the clews of a square sail and used for furling it.

clew up *vb.* (*adv.*) *Nautical.* to furl (a square sail) by gathering its clews up to the yard by means of clew lines.

cli·an·thus (klɪ'ænθəs) *n.* any Australian plant of the leguminous genus *Clianthus,* with ornamental clusters of slender scarlet flowers. [C19: New Latin, probably from Greek *klei-, kleos* glory + *anthos* flower]

cli·ché ('kli:ʃeɪ) *n.* **1.** a word or expression that has lost much of its force through overexposure, as for example the phrase: *it's got to get worse before it gets better.* **2.** an idea, action, or habit that has become trite from overuse. **3.** *Printing, chiefly Brit.* a stereotype or electrotype plate. [C19: from French, from *clicher* to stereotype; imitative of the sound made by the matrix when it is dropped into molten metal] —'**cli·ché'd** *or* '**cli·chéd** *adj.*

Cli·chy (kli:'ʃi:) *n.* an industrial suburb of NW Paris: residence of the Merovingian kings (7th century). Pop.: 47 956 (1975). Official name: **Cli·chy-la-Ga·renne** (*French* kliʃi la ga'rɛn).

click (klɪk) *n.* **1.** a short light often metallic sound. **2. a.** the locking member of a rachet mechanism, such as a pawl or detent. **b.** the movement of such a mechanism between successive locking positions. **3.** *Phonetics.* any of various stop consonants, found in Khoisan and as borrowings in southern Bantu languages, that are produced by the suction of air into the mouth. ~*vb.* **4.** to make or cause to make a clicking sound: *to click one's heels.* **5.** (*intr.*) *Slang.* to be a great success: *that idea really clicked.* **6.** (*intr.*) *Informal.* to become suddenly clear: *it finally clicked when her name was mentioned.* **7.** (*intr.*) *Slang.* to go or fit together with ease: *they clicked from their first meeting.* [C17: of imitative origin] —'**click·er** *n.*

click bee·tle *n.* any beetles of the family *Elateridae,* having the ability to right themselves with a snapping movement when placed on their backs. Also called: **snapping beetle, skipjack.** See also **wireworm.**

click·er ('klɪkə) *n.* **1.** a person or thing that clicks. **2.** *Informal.* a foreman in a shoe factory or printing works.

cli·ent ('klaɪənt) *n.* **1.** a person, company, etc., that seeks the advice of a professional man or woman. **2.** a customer. **3.** (in the U.S.) a person who is receiving aid from a welfare agency. **4.** a person depending on another's patronage. [C14: from Latin *cliēns* retainer, dependent; related to Latin *clīnāre* to lean] —**cli·en·tal** (klaɪ'ɛntᵊl) *adj.*

cli·en·tele (ˌkli:ɒn'tɛl) *or* **cli·en·tage** ('klaɪəntɪdʒ) *n.* customers or clients collectively. [C16: from Latin *clientēla,* from *cliēns* CLIENT]

cliff (klɪf) *n.* a steep high rock face, esp. one that runs along the seashore and has the strata exposed. [Old English *clif;* related to Old Norse *kleif,* Middle Low German *klēf,* Dutch *klif;* see CLEAVE[2]] —'**cliff·y** *adj.*

cliff·hang·er ('klɪfˌhæŋə) *n.* **1. a.** a situation of imminent disaster usually occurring at the end of each episode of a serialized film. **b.** the serialized film itself. **2.** a situation that is dramatic or uncertain. —'**cliff·ˌhang·ing** *adj.*

cliff swal·low *n.* an American swallow, *Petrochelidon pyrrhonota,* that has a square-tipped tail and builds nests of mud on cliffs, walls, etc.

cli·mac·ter·ic (klaɪ'mæktərɪk, ˌklaɪmæk'tɛrɪk) *n.* **1.** a critical event or period. **2.** another name for **menopause. 3.** the period in the life of a man corresponding to the menopause, chiefly characterized by diminished sexual activity. ~*adj. also* **cli·mac·ter·i·cal** (ˌklaɪmæk'tɛrɪkᵊl). **4.** involving a crucial event or period. [C16: from Latin *clīmactēricus,* from Greek *klimaktērikos,* from *klimakter,* rung of a ladder from *klimax* ladder; see CLIMAX] —ˌ**cli·mac·'ter·i·cal·ly** *adv.*

cli·mac·tic (klaɪ'mæktɪk) *or* **cli·mac·ti·cal** *adj.* consisting of, involving, or causing a climax. —**cli·'mac·ti·cal·ly** *adv.*

cli·mate ('klaɪmɪt) *n.* **1.** the long-term prevalent weather conditions of an area, determined by latitude, position relative to oceans or continents, altitude, etc. **2.** an area having a particular kind of climate. **3.** a prevailing trend or current of feeling: *the political climate.* [C14: from Late Latin *clima,* from Greek *klima* inclination, region; related to Greek *klinein* to lean] —**cli·mat·ic** (klaɪ'mætɪk), **cli·'mat·i·cal,** *or* '**cli·mat·al** *adj.* —**cli·'mat·i·cal·ly** *adv.*

cli·ma·tol·o·gy (ˌklaɪmə'tɒlədʒɪ) *n.* the study of climates. —**cli·ma·to·log·ic** (ˌklaɪmətə'lɒdʒɪk) *or* ˌ**cli·ma·to·'log·i·cal** *adj.* —ˌ**cli·ma·to·'log·i·cal·ly** *adv.* —ˌ**cli·ma·'tol·o·gist** *n.*

cli·max ('klaɪmæks) *n.* **1.** the most intense or highest point of an experience or of a series of events: *the party was the climax of the week.* **2.** a decisive moment in a dramatic or other work. **3.** a rhetorical device by which a series of sentences,

clauses, or phrases are arranged in order of increasing intensity. **4.** *Ecology.* the stage in the development of a community during which it remains stable under the prevailing environmental conditions. **5.** Also called: **sexual climax.** (esp. in referring to women) another word for **orgasm.** ~*vb.* **6.** to reach or bring to a climax. [C16: from Late Latin, from Greek *klimax* ladder]
Usage. In formal English careful writers avoid the use of *climax* as a verb. The phrase *reach a climax* is preferred.

climb (klaɪm) *vb.* (*mainly intr.*) **1.** (*also tr.;* often foll. by *up*) to go up or ascend (stairs, a mountain, etc.). **2.** (often foll. by *along*) to progress with difficulty: *to climb along a ledge.* **3.** to rise to a higher point or intensity: *the temperature climbed.* **4.** to incline or slope upwards: *the road began to climb.* **5.** to ascend in social position. **6.** (of plants) to grow upwards by twining, using tendrils or suckers, etc. **7.** *Informal.* (foll. by *into*) to put (on) or get (into). **8.** to be a climber or mountaineer. ~*n.* **9.** the act of climbing. **10.** a place or thing to be climbed, esp. a route in mountaineering. [Old English *climban;* related to Old Norse *klembra* to squeeze, Old High German *climban* to clamber] —**'climb·a·ble** *adj.*

climb down *vb.* (*intr., adv.*) **1.** to descend. **2.** (often foll. by *from*) to retreat (from an opinion, position, etc.). ~*n.* **climb-down. 3.** a retreat from an opinion, etc.

climb·er ('klaɪmə) *n.* **1.** a person or thing that climbs. **2.** a plant that lacks rigidity and grows upwards by twining, scrambling, or clinging with tendrils and suckers. **3.** *Chiefly Brit.* short for **social climber.**

climb·ing fish *or* **perch** *n.* an Asian labyrinth fish, *Anabas testudineus,* that resembles a perch and can travel over land on its spiny gill covers and pectoral fins.

climb·ing frame *n.* a structure of wood or metal tubing used by children for climbing.

climb·ing i·rons *pl. n.* spiked steel frames worn on the feet to assist in climbing trees, ice-slopes, etc.

clime (klaɪm) *n. Poetic.* a region or its climate. [C16: from Late Latin *clima;* see CLIMATE]

cli·nan·dri·um (klɪ'nændrɪəm) *n., pl.* **·dri·a** (-drɪə). *Botany.* a cavity in the upper part of the column of an orchid flower that contains the anthers. Also called: **androclinium.** [C19: from New Latin, literally: bed for stamen, from Greek *klīnē* couch + *anēr* man + -IUM]

clinch (klɪntʃ) *vb.* **1.** (*tr.*) to secure a driven nail, by bending the protruding point over. **2.** (*tr.*) to hold together in such a manner: *to clinch the corners of the frame.* **3.** (*tr.*) to settle something, such as an argument, bargain, etc., in a definite way. **4.** (*tr.*) *Nautical.* to fasten by means of a clinch. **5.** (*intr.*) to engage in a clinch, as in boxing or wrestling. ~*n.* **6.** the act of clinching. **7. a.** a nail with its point bent over. **b.** the part of such a nail, etc., that has been bent over. **8.** *Boxing, wrestling, etc.* an act or an instance in which one or both competitors hold on to the other to avoid punches, regain wind, etc. **9.** *Slang.* a lovers' embrace. **10.** *Nautical.* a loop or eye formed in a line by seizing the end to the standing part. ~Also (for senses 1, 2, 4, 7, 8, 10): **clench.** [C16: variant of CLENCH]

clinch·er ('klɪntʃə) *n.* **1.** *Informal.* something decisive, such as fact, score, etc. **2.** a person or thing that clinches.

cline (klaɪn) *n.* a continuous variation in form between members of a species having a wide variable geographical or ecological range. [C20: from Greek *klinein* to lean] —**'clin·al** *adj.* —**'clin·al·ly** *adv.*

-cline *n. combining form.* indicating a slope: *anticline.* [back formation from INCLINE] —**-cli·nal** *combining form of adjectives.*

cling (klɪŋ) *vb.* **clings, cling·ing, clung.** (*intr.*) **1.** (often foll. by *to*) to hold fast or adhere closely (to something), as by gripping or sticking. **2.** (foll. by *together*) to remain in contact (with each other). **3.** to be or remain physically or emotionally close: *to cling to outmoded beliefs.* ~*n.* **4.** *Agriculture, chiefly U.S.* the tendency of cotton fibres in a sample to stick to each other. **5.** *Agriculture.* diarrhoea or scouring in animals. **6.** short for **clingstone.** [Old English *clingan;* related to CLENCH] —**'cling·er** *n.* —**'cling·ing·ly** *adv.* —**'cling·y** *adj.* —**'cling·i·ness** *or* **'cling·ing·ness** *n.*

cling·fish ('klɪŋ,fɪʃ) *n., pl.* **·fish** *or* **·fish·es.** any small marine teleost fish of the family *Gobiesocidae,* having a flattened elongated body with a sucking disc beneath the head for clinging to rocks, etc.

cling·ing vine *n. U.S. informal.* a woman who displays excessive emotional dependence on a man.

cling·stone ('klɪŋ,stəʊn) *n.* **a.** a fruit, such as certain peaches, in which the flesh tends to adhere to the stone. **b.** (*as modifier*): *a clingstone peach.* Compare **freestone** (sense 2).

clin·ic ('klɪnɪk) *n.* **1.** a place in which outpatients are given medical treatment or advice, often connected to a hospital. **2.** a similar place staffed by physicians or surgeons specializing in one or more specific areas: *eye clinic.* **3.** *Brit.* a private hospital or nursing home. **4.** the teaching of medicine to students at the bedside. **5.** *U.S.* a place where medical lectures are given. **6.** *U.S.* a clinical lecture. **7.** *Chiefly U.S.* a group or centre that offers advice or instruction: *a vocational clinic.* [C17: from Latin *clīnicus* one on a sickbed, from Greek, from *klīnē* bed]

clin·i·cal ('klɪnɪkᵊl) *adj.* **1.** of or relating to a clinic. **2.** of or relating to the bedside of a patient, the course of his disease, or the observation and treatment of patients directly: *a clinical lecture; clinical medicine.* **3.** scientifically detached; strictly objective: *a clinical attitude to life.* **4.** plain, simple, and usually unattractive: *clinical furniture.* —**'clin·i·cal·ly** *adv.* —**'clin·i·cal·ness** *n.*

clin·i·cal ther·mom·e·ter *n.* a finely calibrated thermometer for determining the temperature of the body, usually placed under the tongue or in the rectum.

cli·ni·cian (klɪ'nɪʃən) *n.* a physician, psychiatrist, etc., who specializes in clinical work as opposed to one engaged in laboratory or experimental studies.

clink[1] (klɪŋk) *vb.* **1.** to make or cause to make a light and sharply ringing sound. **2.** (*intr.*) *Rare.* to rhyme. ~*n.* **3.** a light and sharply ringing sound. **4.** *Rare.* a rhyme. **5.** *Brit.* a pointed steel tool used for breaking up the surface of a road before it is repaired. [C14: perhaps from Middle Dutch *klinken;* related to Old Low German *chlanch,* German *Klang* sound]

clink[2] (klɪŋk) *n.* a slang word for **prison.** [C16: after *Clink,* name of a prison in Southwark, London]

clink·er ('klɪŋkə) *n.* **1.** the ash and partially fused residues from a coal-fired furnace or fire. **2.** Also called: **clinker brick.** a hard brick used as a paving stone. **3.** a partially vitrified brick or mass of brick. **4.** *U.S. slang.* a mistake or fault, esp. a wrong note in music. ~*vb.* **5.** (*intr.*) to form clinker during burning. [C17: from Dutch *klinker* a type of brick, from obsolete *klinckaerd,* literally: something that clinks (referring to the sound produced when one was struck), from *klinken* to CLINK[1]]

clink·er-built *or* **clinch·er-built** *adj.* (of a boat or ship) having a hull constructed with each plank overlapping that below. Also called: **lapstrake.** Compare **carvel-built.** [C18 *clinker* a nailing together, probably from CLINCH]

clink·stone ('klɪŋk,stəʊn) *n.* a variety of phonolite that makes a metallic sound when struck.

cli·no- *or before a vowel* **clin-** *combining form.* indicating a slope or inclination: *clinometer.* [from New Latin, from Greek *klinein* to slant, lean]

cli·nom·e·ter (klaɪ'nɒmɪtə) *n.* an instrument used in surveying for measuring an angle of inclination. —**cli·no·met·ric** (,klaɪnə'mɛtrɪk) *or* **,cli·no·'met·ri·cal** *adj.* —**cli·'nom·e·try** *n.*

cli·no·stat ('klaɪnəʊ,stæt) *n.* an apparatus for studying tropisms in plants, usually a rotating disc to which the plant is attached so that it receives an equal stimulus on all sides.

clin·quant ('klɪŋkənt) *adj.* **1.** glittering, esp. with tinsel. ~*n.* **2.** tinsel or imitation gold leaf. [C16: from French, from *clinquer* to clink, from Dutch *klinken,* of imitative origin]

clin·to·ni·a (klɪn'təʊnɪə) *n.* any temperate liliaceous plant of the genus *Clintonia,* having white, greenish-yellow, or purplish flowers, broad ribbed leaves, and blue berries. [C19: named after De Witt *Clinton*]

Cli·o ('klaɪəʊ) *n. Greek myth.* the Muse of history. [C19: from Latin, from Greek *Kleiō,* from *kleein* to celebrate]

clip[1] (klɪp) *vb.* **clips, clip·ping, clipped.** (*mainly tr.*) **1.** (*also intr.*) to cut, snip, or trim with or as if with scissors or shears, esp. in order to shorten or remove a part. **2.** *Brit.* to punch (a hole) in something, esp. a ticket. **3.** to curtail or cut short. **4.** to move a short section from (a film, etc.). **5.** to shorten (a word). **6.** (*intr.*) to trot or move rapidly, esp. over a long distance: *a horse clipping along the road.* **7.** *Informal.* to strike with a sharp, often slanting, blow. **8.** *Slang.* to defraud or swindle, esp. by overcharging. **9. clip (someone's) wings.** to restrict (someone's) freedom. ~*n.* **10.** the act or process of clipping. **11.** something clipped off. **12.** a short extract from a film, newspaper, etc. **13.** *Informal.* a sharp, often slanting, blow. **14.** *Informal.* speed: *a rapid clip.* **15.** *Austral.* the total quantity of wool shorn, as in one place, season, etc. **16.** another word for **clipped form.** [C12: from Old Norse *klippa* to cut; related to Low German *klippen*] —**'clip·pa·ble** *adj.*

clip[2] (klɪp) *n.* **1.** any of various small implements used to hold loose articles together or to attach one article to another. **2.** an article of jewellery that can be clipped onto a dress, hat, etc. **3.** short for **paperclip** or **cartridge clip. 4.** the pointed flange on a horseshoe that secures it to the front part of the hoof. **5.** *Archaic or dialect.* an embrace or hug. ~*vb.* **clips, clip·ping, clipped.** (*tr.*) **6.** to hold together tightly, as with a clip. **7.** *Archaic or dialect.* to embrace. [Old English *clyppan* to embrace; related to Old Frisian *kleppa,* Lithuanian *glebiu*]

clip·board ('klɪp,bɔ:d) *n.* a portable writing board with a spring clip at the top for holding paper.

clip-clop *n.* the sound made by a horse's hooves.

clip-fed *adj.* (of an automatic firearm) loaded from a cartridge clip.

clip joint *n. Slang.* a place, such as a nightclub or restaurant, in which customers are overcharged.

clipped form *n.* a shortened form of a word, as for example *doc* for *doctor.*

clip·per ('klɪpə) *n.* **1.** any fast sailing ship. **2.** a person or thing that cuts or clips. **3.** something, such as a horse or sled, that moves quickly. **4.** *Electronics.* another word for **limiter.**

clip·pers ('klɪpəz) *or* **clips** *pl. n.* **1.** a hand tool with two cutting blades for clipping fingernails, veneers, etc. **2.** a hairdresser's tool, operated either by hand or electrically, with one fixed and one reciprocating set of teeth for cutting short hair.

clip·pie ('klɪpɪ) *n. Brit. informal.* a bus conductress.

clip·ping ('klɪpɪŋ) *n.* **1.** something cut out or trimmed off, esp. an article from a newspaper; cutting. ~*adj.* **2.** (*prenominal*) *Informal.* fast: *a clipping pace.*

clique (kli:k, klɪk) *n.* a small, exclusive group of friends or associates. [C18: from French, perhaps from Old French: latch, from *cliquer* to click; suggestive of the necessity to exclude nonmembers] —**'cli·quey** *or* **'cli·quy** *adj.* —**'cli·quish** *adj.* —**'cli·quish·ly** *adv.* —**'cli·quish·ness** *n.*

clish·ma·clav·er (,klɪʃmə'kleɪvə) *n. Scot.* idle talk; gossip. [C16: from *clish-clash,* reduplication of CLASH + CLAVER]

Clis·the·nes ('klaɪsθə,ni:z) *n.* a variant spelling of **Cleisthenes.**

cli+tel+lum (klɪ'tɛləm) *n., pl.* +**la** (-lə). a thickened saddle-like region of epidermis in earthworms and leeches whose secretions bind copulating worms together and later form a cocoon around the eggs. [C19: from New Latin, from Latin *clītellae* (plural) pack-saddle]

clit+ic ('klɪtɪk) *adj.* **1.** (of a word) incapable of being stressed, usually pronounced as if part of the word that follows or precedes it: for example, in French, *me, te,* and *le* are clitic pronouns. See also **proclitic, enclitic.** ~*n.* **2.** a clitic word. [C20: back formation from ENCLITIC and PROCLITIC]

clit·o+ris ('klɪtərɪs, 'klaɪ-) *n.* a part of the female genitalia consisting of a small elongated highly sensitive erectile organ at the front of the vulva: homologous with the penis. [C17: from New Latin, from Greek *kleitoris;* related to Greek *kleiein* to close] —'**clit·o+ral** *adj.*

Clive (klaɪv) *n.* **Rob·ert,** Baron Clive of Plassey. 1725–74, British general and statesman, whose victory at Plassey (1757) strengthened British control in India.

Cllr. *abbrev. for* Councillor.

clo·a+ca (kləʊ'eɪkə) *n., pl.* +**cae** (-ki:). **1.** a cavity in the pelvic region of most vertebrates, except higher mammals, and certain invertebrates, into which the alimentary canal and the genital and urinary ducts open. **2.** a sewer. [C18: from Latin: sewer; related to Greek *kluzein* to wash out] —**clo·'a+cal** *adj.*

cloak (kləʊk) *n.* **1.** a wraplike outer garment fastened at the throat and falling straight from the shoulders. **2.** something that covers or conceals. ~*vb. (tr.)* **3.** to cover with or as if with a cloak. **4.** to hide or disguise. [C13: from Old French *cloque,* from Medieval Latin *clocca* cloak, bell; referring to the bell-like shape]

cloak-and-dag·ger *n. (modifier)* characteristic of or concerned with intrigue and espionage.

cloak+room ('kləʊk,ru:m, -,rʊm) *n.* **1.** a room in which hats, coats, luggage, etc., may be temporarily deposited. **2.** *Brit.* a euphemistic word for **lavatory.**

clob+ber[1] ('klɒbə) *vb. (tr.) Slang.* **1.** to beat or batter. **2.** to defeat utterly. **3.** to criticize severely. [C20: of unknown origin]

clob+ber[2] ('klɒbə) *n. Brit. slang.* personal belongings, such as clothes and accessories. [C19: of unknown origin]

clob+ber[3] ('klɒbə) *vb. (tr.)* to paint over existing decoration on (pottery, etc.). [C19 (originally in the sense: to patch up): of uncertain origin; perhaps related to CLOBBER[2]]

cloche (klɒʃ) *n.* **1.** a bell-shaped cover used to protect young plants. **2.** a woman's almost brimless close-fitting hat, typical of the 1920s and 1930s. [C19: from French bell, from Medieval Latin *clocca*]

clock[1] (klɒk) *n.* **1.** a timepiece, usually free-standing, hanging, or built into a tower, having mechanically or electrically driven pointers that move constantly over a dial showing the numbers of the hours. Compare **digital clock, watch** (sense 7). **2.** any clocklike device for recording or measuring, such as a taximeter or pressure gauge. **3.** the downy head of a dandelion that has gone to seed. **4.** an electrical circuit which generates pulses at a predetermined rate and interval. **5.** short for **time clock. 6. around** *or* **round the clock.** all day and all night. **7.** (usually preceded by *the*) an informal word for **speedometer** or **mileometer. 8.** *Brit.* a slang word for **face. 9. against the clock. a.** under pressure, as to meet a deadline. **b.** (in certain sports, such as show jumping) timed by a stop clock: *the last round will be against the clock.* **10. put the clock back.** to regress. ~*vb.* **11.** *(tr.) Brit. and Austral. slang.* to strike, esp. on the face or head. **12.** *(tr.)* to record time as with a stopwatch, esp. in the calculation of speed. ~See also **atomic clock, biological clock.** [C14: from Middle Dutch *clocke* clock, from Medieval Latin *clocca* bell, ultimately of Celtic origin] —'**clock+er** *n.* —'**clock+,like** *adj.*

clock[2] (klɒk) *n.* an ornamental design either woven in or embroidered on the side of a stocking. [C16: from Middle Dutch *clocke,* from Medieval Latin *clocca* bell]

clock golf *n.* a putting game played on a circular area on a lawn.

clock+mak·er ('klɒk,meɪkə) *n.* a person who makes or mends clocks, watches, etc.

clock off *or* **out** *vb. (intr., adv.)* to depart from work, esp. when it involves registering the time of departure on a card.

clock on *or* **in** *vb. (intr., adv.)* to arrive at work, esp. when it involves registering the time of arrival on a card.

clock up *vb. (tr., adv.)* to record or register: *this car has clocked up 80 000 miles.*

clock-watch·er *n.* an employee who checks the time in anticipation of a break or of the end of the working day.

clock+wise ('klɒk,waɪz) *adv., adj.* in the direction that the hands of a clock rotate; from top to bottom towards the right when seen from the front.

clock+work ('klɒk,wɜ:k) *n.* **1.** the mechanism of a clock. **2.** any similar mechanism, as in a wind-up toy. **3. like clockwork.** with complete regularity and precision.

clod (klɒd) *n.* **1.** a lump of earth or clay. **2.** earth, esp. when heavy or in hard lumps. **3.** Also called: **clodpole, clod poll, clodpate.** a dull or stupid person. **4.** a cut of beef taken from the shoulder. [Old English *clod-* (occurring in compound words) lump; related to CLOUD] —'**clod+dy** *adj.* —'**clod+dish** *adj.* —'**clod+dish+ly** *adv.* —'**clod+dish+ness** *n.*

clod+hop+per ('klɒd,hɒpə) *n. Informal.* **1.** a clumsy person; lout. **2.** *(usually pl.)* a large heavy shoe or boot. —'**clod+,hop+ping** *adj.*

clog (klɒg) *vb.* **clogs, clog+ging, clogged. 1.** to obstruct or become obstructed with thick or sticky matter. **2.** *(tr.)* to encumber; hinder; impede. **3.** *(tr.)* to fasten a clog or impediment to (an animal, such as a horse). **4.** *(intr.)* to adhere or stick in a mass. **5.** *Slang.* (in soccer) to foul (an opponent). ~*n.* **6. a.** any of various wooden or wooden-soled shoes. **b.** *(as modifier): clog dance.* **7.** a heavy block, esp. of wood, fastened to the leg of a person or animal to impede motion. **8.** something that impedes motion or action; hindrance. [C14 (in the sense: block of wood): of unknown origin] —'**clog+gy** *adj.* —'**clog+gi+ness** *n.*

cloi+son+né (klwɑ:'zɒneɪ; *French* klwazɔ'ne) *n.* **1. a.** a design made by filling in with coloured enamel an outline of flattened wire put on edge. **b.** the method of doing this. ~*adj.* **2.** of, relating to, or made by cloisonné. [C19: from French, from *cloisonner* to divide into compartments, from *cloison* partition, ultimately from Latin *claudere* to CLOSE]

clois+ter ('klɔɪstə) *n.* **1.** a covered walk, usually around a quadrangle in a religious institution, having an open arcade or colonnade on the inside and a wall on the outside. **2.** *(sometimes pl.)* a place of religious seclusion, such as a monastery. **3.** life in a monastery or convent. ~*vb.* **4.** *(tr.)* to confine or seclude in or as if in a monastery. [C13: from Old French *cloistre,* from Medieval Latin *claustrum* monastic cell, from Latin: bolt, barrier, from *claudere* to close; influenced in form by Old French *cloison* partition] —'**clois·ter-,like** *adj.*

clois+tered ('klɔɪstəd) *adj.* **1.** secluded or shut up from the world. **2.** living in a monastery or nunnery. **3.** (of a building, courtyard, etc.) having or provided with a cloister.

clois+tral ('klɔɪstrəl) *or* **claus+tral** *adj.* of, like, or characteristic of a cloister.

clomb (kləʊm) *vb. Archaic.* a past tense or past participle of **climb.**

clomp (klɒmp) *n., vb.* a less common word for **clump** (senses 2, 7).

clone (kləʊn) *n. also* **clon** (klɒn, kləʊn). **1.** a group of organisms or cells of the same genetic constitution that are descended from a common ancestor by asexual reproduction, as by cuttings, grafting, etc., in plants. ~*vb.* **2.** to produce or cause to produce a clone. [C20: from Greek *klōn* twig, shoot; related to *klan* to break] —'**clon+al** *adj.* —'**clon+al+ly** *adv.*

clonk (klɒŋk) *vb. (intr.)* **1.** to make a loud dull thud. **2.** *(tr.) Informal.* to hit. ~*n.* **3.** a loud thudding sound.

clo+nus ('kləʊnəs) *n.* a type of convulsion characterized by rapid contraction and relaxation of a muscle. [C19: from New Latin, from Greek *klonos* turmoil] —**clon+ic** ('klɒnɪk) *adj.* —**clo+nic+i·ty** (klɒ'nɪsɪtɪ) *n.*

clop (klɒp) *vb.* **clops, clop+ping, clopped. 1.** *(intr.)* to make or move along with a sound as of a horse's hooves striking the ground. ~*n.* **2.** a sound of this nature. [C20: of imitative origin]

close *vb.* (kləʊz). **1.** to put or be put in such a position as to cover an opening; shut: *the door closed behind him.* **2.** *(tr.)* to bar, obstruct, or fill up (an entrance, a hole, etc.): *to close a road.* **3.** to bring the parts or edges of (a wound, etc.) together or (of a wound, etc.) to be brought together: *to close ranks.* **4.** *(intr.;* foll. by *on, over,* etc.) to take hold: *his hand closed over the money.* **5.** to bring or be brought to an end; terminate. **6.** (of agreements, deals, etc.) to complete or be completed successfully. **7.** to cease or cause to cease to render service: *the shop closed at six.* **8.** *(intr.) Stock exchange.* to have a value at the end of a day's trading, as specified: *steels closed two points down.* **9.** to complete an electrical circuit. **10.** *(tr.) Nautical.* to pass near. **11.** *(tr.) Archaic.* to enclose or shut in. **12. close one's eyes. a.** *Euphemistic.* to die. **b.** (often foll. by *to*) to ignore. ~*adj.* (kləʊs). **13.** near in space or time; in proximity. **14.** having the parts near together; dense: *a close formation.* **15.** down or near to the surface; short: *a close haircut.* **16.** near in relationship: *a close relative.* **17.** intimate or confidential: *a close friend.* **18.** almost equal or even: *a close contest.* **19.** not deviating or varying greatly from a model or standard: *a close resemblance; a close translation.* **20.** careful, strict, or searching: *a close study.* **21.** (of a style of play in football, hockey, etc.) characterized by short passes. **22.** confined or enclosed. **23.** shut or shut tight. **24.** oppressive, heavy, or airless: *a close atmosphere.* **25.** strictly guarded: *a close prisoner.* **26.** neat or tight in fit: *a close cap.* **27.** secretive or reticent. **28.** miserly; not generous, esp. with money. **29.** (of money or credit) hard to obtain; scarce. **30.** restricted as to public admission or membership. **31.** hidden or secluded. **32.** Also: **closed.** restricted or prohibited as to the type of game or fish able to be taken. **33.** Also: **closed.** *Phonetics.* denoting a vowel pronounced with the lips relatively close together. ~*adv.* (kləʊs). **34. close to the wind.** *Nautical.* sailing as nearly as possible towards the direction from which the wind is blowing. **35.** closely; tightly. **36.** near or in proximity. ~*n.* (kləʊz). **37.** the act of closing. **38.** the end or conclusion: *the close of the day.* **39.** a place of joining or meeting. **40.** (kləʊs). *Law.* private property, usually enclosed by a fence, hedge, or wall. **41.** (kləʊs). *Brit.* a courtyard or quadrangle enclosed by buildings or an entry leading to such a courtyard. **42.** (kləʊs). *Brit. (cap. when part of a street name)* a small quiet residential road: *Hillside Close.* **43.** *Brit.* a field. **44.** (kləʊs). the precincts of a cathedral or similar building. **45.** (kləʊz). *Music.* another word for **cadence.** A perfect cadence is called a **full close,** an imperfect one a **half close. 46.** (kləʊz). *Archaic or rare.* an encounter in battle; grapple. ~See also **close down, close in, close out, close-up, close with.** [C13: from Old French *clos* close, enclosed, from Latin *clausus* shut up, from *claudere* to close] —**close+ly** ('kləʊslɪ) *adv.* —**close+ness** ('kləʊsnɪs) *n.* —**clos+er** ('kləʊzə) *n.*

close call (kləʊs) *n. U.S.* another expression for **close shave.**

close com+pa+ny (kləus) *n. Brit.* a company under the control of its directors or less than five independent participants. Also: **closed company.**

closed (kləuzd) *adj.* **1.** blocked against entry; shut. **2.** restricted; exclusive. **3.** not open to question or debate. **4.** (of a hunting season, etc.) close. **5.** *Maths.* **a.** (of a curve or surface) completely enclosing an area or volume. **b.** (of a set) having members that can be produced by a specific operation on other members of the same set: *the integers are a closed set under multiplication.* **6.** Also: **checked.** *Phonetics.* **a.** denoting a syllable that ends in a consonant. **b.** another word for **close** (sense 33). **7.** not open to public entry or membership: *a closed society.*

closed book *n. Informal.* **1.** something deemed unknown or incapable of being understood. **2.** a matter that has been finally concluded and admits of no further consideration.

closed chain *n. Chem.* another name for **ring**[1] (sense 18).

closed cir+cuit *n.* a complete electrical circuit through which current can flow when a voltage is applied. Compare **open circuit.**

closed-cir·cuit tel·e+vi+sion *n.* a television system in which signals are transmitted from the television camera to the receivers by cables or telephone links forming a closed circuit, as used in shops, hospitals, etc.

closed cor+por·a+tion *n. U.S.* a corporation the stock of which is owned by a small number of persons and is rarely traded on the open market. Also: **close corporation.**

closed game *n. Chess.* a relatively complex game involving closed ranks and files and permitting only nontactical positional manoeuvring. Compare **open game.**

close down (kləuz) *vb. (adv.)* **1.** to cease or cause to cease operations: *the shop closed down.* ~*n.* **close-down** ('kləuz,daun). **2.** a closure or stoppage of operations, esp. in a factory. **3.** *Brit. radio, television.* the end of a period of broadcasting, esp. late at night.

closed pri+ma+ry *n. U.S. government.* a primary in which only members of a particular party may vote. Compare **open primary.**

closed schol+ar+ship *n.* a scholarship for which only certain people, such as those from a particular school or with a particular surname, are eligible.

closed sen+tence *n. Logic.* a formula that contains no free occurrence of any variable. Compare **open sentence.**

closed shop *n.* an industrial establishment in which there exists a contract between a trade union and the employer permitting the employment of the union's members only. Compare **open shop** (sense 1), **union shop.**

close-fist·ed (,kləus'fɪstɪd) *adj.* very careful with money; mean. —**,close-'fist·ed+ness** *n.*

close-grained (,kləus'greɪnd) *adj.* (of wood) dense or compact in texture.

close har+mo+ny (kləus) *n.* a type of singing in which all the parts except the bass lie close together and are confined to the compass of a tenth.

close-hauled (,kləus'hɔ:ld) *adj. Nautical.* with the sails flat, so as to sail as close to the wind as possible.

close in (kləuz) *vb. (intr., adv.)* **1.** (of days) to become shorter with the approach of winter. **2.** (foll. by *on* or *upon*) to advance (on) so as to encircle or surround.

close-knit (,kləus'nɪt) *adj.* closely united, esp. by social ties.

close-lipped (,kləus'lɪpt) *or* **close-mouthed** (,kləus'mauðd, -'mauθt) *adj.* not talking or revealing much.

close out (kləuz) *vb. (adv.)* to terminate (a client's or other account) on which the margin is inadequate or exhausted, usually by sale of securities to realize cash.

close quar+ters (kləus) *pl. n.* **1.** a narrow cramped space or position. **2. at close quarters. a.** engaged in hand-to-hand combat. **b.** in close proximity; very near together.

close sea+son (kləus) *or* **closed sea+son** *n.* the period of the year when it is prohibited to kill certain game or fish.

close shave (kləus) *n. Informal.* a narrow escape.

close-stool ('kləus ,stu:l) *n.* a wooden stool containing a covered chamber pot.

clos+et ('klɒzɪt) *n.* **1.** a small cupboard or recess. **2.** a small private room. **3.** short for **water closet. 4.** *(modifier) U.S.* private or secret. **5.** *(modifier) U.S.* suited or appropriate for use in private: *closet meditations.* **6.** *(modifier) U.S.* based on or devoted to theory; speculative: *a closet strategist.* ~*vb.* **7.** *(tr.)* to shut up or confine in a small private room, esp. for conference or meditation. [C14: from Old French, from *clos* enclosure; see CLOSE]

clos+et dra+ma *n. Chiefly U.S.* **a.** drama suitable for reading rather than performing. **b.** a play of this kind.

clos+et queen *n. Informal.* a man who is homosexual but does not admit the fact.

close-up ('kləus,ʌp) *n.* **1.** a photograph taken at close range. **2.** a detailed or intimate view or examination: *a close-up of modern society.* ~*vb.* **close up** (kləuz). *(adv.)* **3.** to shut entirely. **4.** *(intr.)* to draw together: *the ranks closed up.* **5.** *(intr.)* (of wounds) to heal completely. **6.** *(intr.)* (in filming) to move close to the subject of the action.

close with (kləuz) *vb. (intr., prep.)* to engage in battle with (an enemy).

clos+ing time ('kləuzɪŋ) *n.* the time at which pubs must legally stop selling alcoholic drinks.

clos+trid+i·um (klɒ'strɪdɪəm) *n., pl.* **+i·ums** *or* **·i·a** (-ɪə). any anaerobic typically rod-shaped bacterium of the genus *Clostridium,* occurring in soil and the intestines of man and animals: family *Bacillaceae.* The genus includes the species causing botulism and tetanus. [C20: from New Latin, literally: small spindle, from Greek *klōstēr* spindle, from *klōthein* to spin; see -IUM] —**clos+'trid+i+al** *or* **clos+'trid+i·an** *adj.*

clo+sure ('kləuʒə) *n.* **1.** the act of closing or the state of being closed. **2.** an end or conclusion. **3.** something that closes or shuts, such as a cap or seal for a container. **4.** (in a deliberative body) a procedure by which debate may be halted and an immediate vote taken. See also **cloture, guillotine, gag rule. 5.** *Geology.* the vertical distance between the crest of an anticline and the lowest contour that surrounds it. **6.** *Phonetics.* the obstruction of the breath stream at some point along the vocal tract, such as the complete occlusion preliminary to the articulation of a stop. ~*vb.* **7.** *(tr.)* (in a deliberative body) to end (debate) by closure. [C14: from Old French, from Late Latin *clausūra* bar, from Latin *claudere* to close]

clot (klɒt) *n.* **1.** a soft thick lump or mass: *a clot of blood.* **2.** *Brit. slang.* a stupid person; fool. ~*vb.* **clots, clot+ting, clot+ted. 3.** to form or cause to form into a soft thick lump or lumps. [Old English *clott,* of Germanic origin; compare Middle Dutch *klotte* block, lump]

cloth (klɒθ) *n., pl.* **cloths** (klɒθs, klɒðz). **1. a.** a fabric formed by weaving, felting or knitting wool, cotton, etc. **b.** *(as modifier): a cloth bag.* **2.** a piece of such fabric used for a particular purpose, as for a dishcloth. **3.** (usually preceded by *the*) **a.** the clothes worn by a clergyman. **b.** the clergy. **4.** *Obsolete.* clothing. **5.** *Nautical.* any of the panels of a sail. **6.** *Chiefly Brit.* a piece of coloured fabric, used on the stage as scenery. **7.** *West African.* a garment in a traditional non-European style. [Old English *clāth;* related to Old Frisian *klēth,* Middle High German *kleit* cloth, clothing]

cloth+bound ('klɒθ,baund) *adj.* (of a book) bound in stiff boards covered in cloth.

cloth cap *n. Brit.* **1.** Also called: **flat cap.** a flat woollen cap with a stiff peak. **2.** *Informal.* **a.** a symbol of working-class ethos or origin. **b.** *(as modifier): cloth-cap attitudes.*

clothe (kləuð) *vb.* **clothes, cloth+ing, clothed** *or* **clad.** *(tr.)* **1.** to dress or attire (a person). **2.** to provide with clothing or covering. **3.** to conceal or disguise. **4.** to endow or invest. [Old English *clāthian,* from *clāth* CLOTH; related to Old Norse *klæða*]

cloth-eared *adj. Informal.* deaf or insensitive.

clothes (kləuðz) *pl. n.* **1. a.** articles of dress. **b.** *(as modifier): clothes brush.* **2.** *Chiefly Brit.* short for **bedclothes.** [Old English *clāthas,* plural of *clāth* CLOTH]

clothes+horse ('kləuðz,hɔ:s) *n.* **1.** a frame on which to hang laundry for drying or airing. **2.** *Informal.* a dandy.

clothes+line ('kləuðz,laɪn) *n.* a piece of rope, cord, or wire on which clean washing is hung to dry or air.

clothes moth *n.* any of various tineid moths, esp. *Tineola bisselliella,* the larvae of which feed on wool or fur.

clothes peg *n.* a small wooden or plastic clip for attaching washing to a clothesline.

clothes-press *n.* a piece of furniture for storing clothes, usually containing wide drawers and a cabinet.

clo+thi+er ('kləuðɪə) *n.* a person who makes, sells, or deals in clothes or cloth.

cloth+ing ('kləuðɪŋ) *n.* **1.** garments collectively. **2.** something that covers or clothes.

Clo·tho ('kləuθəu) *n. Greek myth.* one of the three Fates, spinner of the thread of life. [Latin, from Greek *Klōtho,* one who spins, from *klōthein* to spin]

cloth of gold *n.* cloth woven from silk threads interspersed with gold.

clot+ted cream *n. Brit.* a thick cream made from scalded milk, esp. in SW England. Also called: **Devonshire cream.**

clo+ture ('kləutʃə) *n.* **1.** closure in the U.S. Senate. ~*vb.* **2.** *(tr.)* to end (debate) in the U.S. Senate by cloture. [C19: from French *clôture,* from Old French CLOSURE]

cloud (klaud) *n.* **1.** a mass of water or ice particles visible in the sky, usually white or grey, from which rain or snow falls when the particles coagulate. See also **cirrus, cumulonimbus, cumulus, stratus. 2.** any collection of particles visible in the air, esp. of smoke or dust. **3.** a large number of insects or other small animals in flight. **4.** something that darkens, threatens, or carries gloom. **5.** *Jewellery.* a cloudlike blemish in a transparent stone. **6. in the clouds.** not in contact with reality. **7. under a cloud. a.** under reproach or suspicion. **b.** in a state of gloom or bad temper. **8. on cloud nine.** *Informal.* elated; very happy. ~*vb.* **9.** (when *intr.,* often foll. by *over* or *up*) to make or become cloudy, overcast, or indistinct. **10.** *(tr.)* to make obscure; darken. **11.** to make or become gloomy or depressed. **12.** *(tr.)* to place under or render liable to suspicion or disgrace. **13.** to render (liquids) milky or dull or (of liquids) to become milky or dull. **14.** to become or render mottled or variegated. [C13 (in the sense: a mass of vapour): from Old English *clūd* rock, hill; probably related to CLOD] —**'cloud+less** *adj.* —**'cloud+less+ly** *adv.* —**'cloud+less+ness** *n.* —**'cloud+,like** *adj.*

cloud+ber·ry ('klaudbərɪ, -brɪ) *n., pl.* **·ries.** a creeping Eurasian herbaceous rosaceous plant, *Rubus chamaemorus,* with white flowers and orange berry-like fruits (drupelets).

cloud+burst ('klaud,bɜ:st) *n.* a heavy downpour.

cloud cham+ber *n. Physics.* an apparatus for detecting high-energy particles by observing their tracks through a chamber containing a supersaturated vapour. Each particle ionizes molecules along its path and small droplets condense on them to produce a visible track. Also called: **Wilson cloud chamber.**

cloud-cuck·oo-land *or* **cloud+land** ('klaud,lænd) *n.* a realm of fantasy, dreams, or impractical notions.

cloud+let ('klaʊdlɪt) *n.* a small cloud.
cloud rack *n.* a group of moving clouds.
cloud+scape ('klaʊdskeɪp) *n.* **1.** a picturesque formation of clouds. **2.** a picture or photograph of such a formation.
cloud·y ('klaʊdɪ) *adj.* **cloud·i+er, cloud·i+est. 1.** covered with cloud or clouds. **2.** of or like a cloud or clouds. **3.** streaked or mottled like a cloud. **4.** opaque or muddy. **5.** obscure or unclear. **6.** troubled by gloom or depression: *his face had a cloudy expression.* —**'cloud·i+ly** *adv.* —**'cloud·i+ness** *n.*
Clou·et (*French* klu'ɛ) *n.* **Fran·çois** (frã'swa), ?1515–72, and his father, **Jean** (ʒã), ?1485–?1540, French portrait painters.
clough (klʌf) *n. Brit. dialect.* a gorge or narrow ravine.
Clough (klʌf) *n.* **Ar·thur Hugh.** 1819–61, English poet.
clout (klaʊt) *n.* **1.** *Informal.* a blow with the hand or a hard object. **2.** *Archery.* **a.** the target used in long-distance shooting. **b.** the centre of this target. **c.** a shot that hits the centre. **3.** Also called: **clout nail.** a short, flat-headed nail used esp. for attaching sheet metal to wood. **4.** *Brit. dialect.* **a.** a piece of cloth: *a dish clout.* **b.** a garment. ~*vb.* (*tr.*) **5.** *Informal.* to give a hard blow to, esp. with the hand. **6.** to patch with a piece of cloth or leather. [Old English *clūt* piece of metal or cloth, *clūtian* to patch (C14: to strike with the hand); related to Dutch *kluit* a lump, and to CLOD] —**'clout+er** *n.*
clove[1] (kləʊv) *n.* **1.** a tropical evergreen myrtaceous tree, *Eugenia aromatica,* native to the East Indies but cultivated elsewhere, esp. Zanzibar. **2.** the dried unopened flower buds of this tree, used as a pungent fragrant spice. [C14: from Old French *clou de girofle,* literally: nail of clove, *clou* from Latin *clāvus* nail + *girofle* clove tree]
clove[2] (kləʊv) *n.* any of the small bulbs that arise from the axils of the scales of a large bulb. [Old English *clufu* bulb; related to Old High German *klovolouh* garlic; see CLEAVE[1]]
clove[3] (kləʊv) *vb.* a past tense of **cleave**[1].
clove hitch *n.* a knot or hitch used for securing a rope to a spar, post, or larger rope.
clo+ven ('kləʊvᵊn) *vb.* **1.** a past participle of **cleave**[1]. ~*adj.* **2.** split; cleft; divided.
clo+ven hoof *or* **foot** *n.* **1.** the divided hoof of a pig, goat, cow, deer, or related animal, which consists of the two middle digits of the foot. **2.** the mark or symbol of Satan. —**ˌclo·ven-'hoofed** *or* **ˌclo·ven-'foot·ed** *adj.*
clove pink *n.* another name for **carnation** (sense 1).
clo+ver ('kləʊvə) *n.* **1.** any plant of the papilionaceous genus *Trifolium,* having trifoliate leaves and dense flower heads. Many species, such as red clover, white clover, and alsike, are grown as forage plants. **2.** any of various similar or related plants. **3. sweet clover.** another name for **melilot. 4. pin clover.** another name for **alfilaria. 5. in clover.** *Informal.* in a state of ease or luxury. [Old English *clāfre;* related to Old High German *klēo,* Middle Low German *klēver,* Dutch *klāver*]
clo·ver+leaf ('kləʊvəˌli:f) *n., pl.* **+leaves. 1.** an arrangement of connecting roads, resembling a four-leaf clover in form, that joins two intersecting main roads. **2.** (*modifier*) in the shape or pattern of a leaf of clover.
clo·ver+leaf aer+i·al *n.* a type of aerial, having three or four similar coplanar loops arranged symmetrically around an axis, to which in-phase signals are fed.
Clo·vis I ('kləʊvɪs) *n.* German name *Chlodwig.* ?466–511 A.D., king of the Franks (481–511), who extended the Merovingian kingdom to include most of Gaul and SW Germany.
clo+vis point ('kləʊvɪs) *n.* a concave-based flint projectile dating from the 10th millennium B.C., found throughout most of Central and North America.
clown (klaʊn) *n.* **1.** a comic entertainer, usually grotesquely costumed and made up, appearing in the circus. **2.** any performer who elicits an amused response. **3.** someone who plays jokes or tricks. **4.** a person who acts in a comic or buffoon-like manner. **5.** a coarse clumsy rude person; boor. **6.** *Archaic.* a countryman or rustic. ~*vb.* (*intr.*) **7.** to perform as a clown. **8.** to play jokes or tricks. **9.** to act foolishly. [C16: perhaps of Low German origin; compare Frisian *klönne,* Icelandic *klunni* clumsy fellow] —**'clown+er·y** *n.* —**'clown+ish** *adj.* —**'clown+ish+ly** *adv.* —**'clown+ish+ness** *n.*
cloy (klɔɪ) *vb.* to make weary or cause weariness through an excess of something initially pleasurable or sweet. [C14 (originally: to nail, hence, to obstruct): from earlier *acloyen,* from Old French *encloer,* from Medieval Latin *inclavāre,* from Latin *clāvāre* to nail, from *clāvus* a nail] —**cloy+ed+ness** ('klɔɪɪdnɪs) *n.* —**'cloy+ing+ly** *adv.* —**'cloy+ing+ness** *n.*
club (klʌb) *n.* **1.** a stout stick, usually with one end thicker than the other, esp. one used as a weapon. **2.** a stick or bat used to strike the ball in various sports, esp. golf. See **golf club. 3.** short for **Indian club. 4.** a group or association of people with common aims or interests: *a wine club.* **5. a.** the room, building, or facilities used by such a group. **b.** (*in combination*): *clubhouse.* **6.** a building in which elected, fee-paying members go to meet, dine, read, etc. **7.** a commercial establishment providing drinks, food, etc. See also **nightclub. 8.** *Chiefly Brit.* an organization, esp. in a shop, set up as a means of saving. **9.** *Brit.* an informal word for **friendly society. 10. a.** the black trefoil symbol on a playing card. **b.** a card with one or more of these symbols or (*when pl.*) the suit of cards so marked. **11.** *Nautical.* **a.** a spar used for extending the clew of a gaff topsail beyond the peak of the gaff. **b.** short for **club foot** (sense 3). **12. in the club.** *Brit. slang.* pregnant. **13. on the club.** *Brit. slang.* away from work due to sickness, esp. when receiving sickness benefit. ~*vb.* **clubs, club+bing, clubbed. 14.** (*tr.*) to beat with or as if with a club. **15.** (often foll. by *together*) to gather or become gathered into a group. **16.** (often foll. by *together*) to unite or combine (resources, efforts, etc.) for a common purpose. **17.** (*tr.*) to use (a rifle or similar firearm) as a weapon by holding the barrel and hitting with the butt. **18.** (*intr.*) *Nautical.* to drift in a current, reducing speed by dragging anchor. [C13: from Old Norse *klubba,* related to Middle High German *klumpe* group of trees, CLUMP, Old English *clympre* lump of metal] —**'club+ber** *n.*
club+ba·ble *or* **club+a·ble** ('klʌbəbᵊl) *adj. Rare.* suitable to be a member of a club; sociable. —**ˌclub+ba·'bil+i·ty** *or* **ˌclub+a·'bil+i·ty** *n.*
club+by ('klʌbɪ) *adj.* **+bi+er, +bi+est. 1.** sociable, esp. effusively so. **2.** exclusive or cliquish. —**'club+bi+ly** *adv.*
club foot *n.* **1.** a congenital deformity of the foot, esp. one in which the foot is twisted so that most of the weight rests on the heel. Technical name: **talipes. 2.** a foot so deformed. **3.** *Nautical.* a boom attached to the foot of a jib. —**ˌclub-'foot·ed** *adj.*
club hand *n.* **1.** a deformity of the hand, analogous to club foot. **2.** a hand so deformed. —**ˌclub-'hand·ed** *adj.*
club+haul ('klʌbˌhɔ:l) *vb. Nautical.* to force (a sailing vessel) onto a new tack, esp. in an emergency, by fastening a lee anchor to the lee quarter, dropping the anchor as the vessel comes about, and hauling in the anchor cable to swing the stern to windward.
club+house ('klʌbˌhaʊs) *n.* the premises of a sports or other club, esp. a golf club.
club+land ('klʊblənd) *n. Brit.* the area of London around St. James's, which contains most of the famous London clubs.
club+man ('klʌbmən) *or* (*fem.*) **club+wom·an** *n., pl.* **+men** *or* **+wom·en.** a person who is an enthusiastic member of a club or clubs.
club moss *n.* any mosslike pteridophyte plant of the order *Lycopodiales,* having erect or creeping stems covered with tiny overlapping leaves.
club root *n.* a disease of cabbages and related plants, caused by the fungus *Plasmodiophora brassicae,* in which the roots become thickened and distorted.
club sand+wich *n. Chiefly U.S.* a sandwich consisting of three or more slices of toast or bread with a filling.
cluck (klʌk) *n.* **1.** the low clicking sound made by a hen or any similar sound. ~*vb.* **2.** (*intr.*) (of a hen) to make a clicking sound. **3.** (*tr.*) to call or express (a feeling) by making a similar sound. [C17: of imitative origin]
cluck·y ('klʌkɪ) *adj. Austral. slang.* pregnant.
clue (klu:) *n.* **1.** something that helps to solve a problem or unravel a mystery. **2. not to have a clue. a.** to be completely baffled. **b.** to be completely ignorant or incompetent. ~*vb.* **clues, clu+ing, clued. 3.** (*tr.;* usually foll. by *in* or *up*) to provide with helpful information. ~*n., vb.* **4.** a variant spelling of **clew.** [C15: variant of CLEW]
clue+less ('klu:lɪs) *adj. Slang.* helpless; stupid.
Cluj (klʊʃ, klu:ʒ) *n.* an industrial city in NW Rumania, on the Someşul-Mic River: former capital of Transylvania. Pop.: 218 703 (1974 est.). German name: **Klausenburg.** Hungarian name: **Kolozsvár.**
clum+ber span+iel ('klʌmbə) *n.* a type of thickset spaniel with longish silky hair. Often shortened to **clumber.** [C19: named after *Clumber,* stately home of the Dukes of Newcastle]
clump (klʌmp) *n.* **1.** a cluster, as of trees or plants. **2.** a dull heavy tread or any similar sound. **3.** an irregular mass: *a clump of hair or earth.* **4.** an inactive mass of microorganisms, esp. a mass of bacteria produced as a result of agglutination. **5.** an extra sole on a shoe. **6.** *Slang.* a blow. ~*vb.* **7.** (*intr.*) to walk or tread heavily. **8.** to gather or be gathered into clumps, clusters, clots, etc. **9.** to cause (bacteria, blood cells, etc.) to collect together or (of bacteria, etc.) to collect together. See also **agglutination** (sense 3). **10.** (*tr.*) *Slang.* to punch (someone). [Old English *clympe;* related to Middle Dutch *klampe* heap of hay, Middle Low German *klampe* CLAMP, Swedish *klimp* small lump] —**'clump·y, 'clump+ish,** *or* **'clump+like** *adj.*
clum+sy ('klʌmzɪ) *adj.* **+si+er, +si+est. 1.** lacking in skill or physical coordination. **2.** awkwardly constructed or contrived. [C16 (in obsolete sense: benumbed with cold; hence, awkward): perhaps from C13 dialect *clumse* to benumb, probably from Scandinavian; compare Swedish dialect *klumsig* numb] —**'clum+si+ly** *adv.* —**'clum+si+ness** *n.*
clung (klʌŋ) *vb.* the past tense or past participle of **cling.**
clunk (klʌŋk) *n.* **1.** a blow or the sound of a blow. **2.** a dull metallic sound. **3.** a dull or stupid person. **4.** *Chiefly Scot.* **a.** the gurgling sound of a liquid. **b.** the sound of a cork being removed from a bottle. ~*vb.* **5.** to make or cause to make such a sound. [C19: of imitative origin]
Clu+ny ('klu:nɪ; *French* kly'ni) *n.* a town in E central France: reformed Benedictine order founded here in 910; important religious and cultural centre in the Middle Ages. Pop.: 4268 (1968). —**'Clu+ni+ac** *adj.*
Clu+ny lace *n.* a strong heavy silk and cotton bobbin lace made at Cluny or elsewhere.
clu+pe·id ('klu:pɪɪd) *n.* **1.** any widely distributed soft-finned teleost fish of the family *Clupeidae,* typically having oily flesh, and including the herrings, sardines, shad, etc. ~*adj.* **2.** of, relating to, or belonging to the family *Clupeidae.* [C19: from New Latin *Clupeidae,* from Latin *clupea* small river fish]
clu+pe·oid ('klu:pɪˌɔɪd) *adj.* **1.** of, relating to, or belonging to the *Isospondyli* (or *Clupeiformes*), a large order of soft-finned fishes, including the herrings, salmon, and tarpon. ~*n.* **2.** any fish belonging to the order *Isospondyli.* [C19: from Latin *clupea* small fish + -OID]
clus+ter ('klʌstə) *n.* **1.** a number of things growing, fastened, or occurring close together. **2.** a number of persons or things

grouped together. **3.** *Military.* a metal insignia worn on a medal ribbon to indicate a second award or a higher class of a decoration or order. **4.** *Military.* **a.** a group of bombs dropped in one stick, esp. fragmentation and incendiary bombs. **b.** the basic unit of mines used in laying a minefield. **5.** *Astronomy.* an aggregation of stars or galaxies moving together through space. ~*vb.* **6.** to gather or be gathered in clusters. [Old English *clyster;* related to Low German *Kluster;* see CLOD, CLOT] —**'clus·tered** *adj.* —**'clus·ter·ing·ly** *adv.* —**'clus·ter·y** *adj.*

clus·ter fly *n.* a dipterous fly, *Pollenia rudis,* that tends to gather in large numbers in attics in the autumn: family *Calliphoridae.* The larvae are parasitic in earthworms.

clutch[1] (klʌtʃ) *vb.* **1.** (*tr.*) to seize with or as if with hands or claws. **2.** (*tr.*) to grasp or hold firmly. **3.** (*intr.;* usually foll. by *at*) to attempt to get hold or possession (of). ~*n.* **4.** a device that enables two revolving shafts to be joined or disconnected as required, esp. one that transmits the drive from the engine to the gearbox in a vehicle. **5.** a device for holding fast. **6.** a firm grasp. **7.** a hand, claw, or talon in the act of clutching: *in the clutches of a bear.* **8.** (*often pl.*) power or control: *in the clutches of the Mafia.* **9.** Also called: **clutch bag.** a handbag without handles. [Old English *clyccan;* related to Old Frisian *kletsie* spear, Swedish *klyka* clasp, fork]

clutch[2] (klʌtʃ) *n.* **1.** a hatch of eggs laid by a particular bird or laid in a single nest. **2.** a brood of chickens. **3.** *Informal.* a group, bunch, or cluster. ~*vb.* **4.** (*tr.*) to hatch (chickens). [C17 (Northern English dialect) *cletch,* from Old Norse *klekja* to hatch]

clut·ter ('klʌtə) *vb.* **1.** (*usually tr.;* often foll. by *up*) to strew or amass (objects) in a disorderly manner. **2.** (*intr.*) to move about in a bustling manner. **3.** (*intr.*) to chatter or babble. ~*n.* **4.** a disordered heap or mass of objects. **5.** a state of disorder. **6.** unwanted echoes that confuse the observation of signals on a radar screen. [C15 *clotter,* from *clotteren* to CLOT]

Clw·yd ('klu:ɪd) *n.* a county in NE Wales, formed in 1974 from Flintshire, most of Denbighshire, and part of Merionethshire: generally hilly or mountainous. Administrative centre: Mold. Pop.: 376 000 (1976 est.). Area: 2425 sq. km (936 sq. miles).

Clyde (klaɪd) *n.* **1. Firth of.** an inlet of the Atlantic in SW Scotland. Length: 103 km (64 miles). **2.** a river in S Scotland, rising in SE Strathclyde and flowing northwest to the Firth of Clyde: extensive shipyards. Length: 170 km (106 miles).

Clyde·bank ('klaɪd,bæŋk) *n.* a town in SW Scotland, in Strathclyde region on the River Clyde: shipyards. Pop.: 48 296 (1971).

Clydes·dale ('klaɪdz,deɪl) *n.* a heavy powerful breed of carthorse, originally from Scotland.

clype (klaɪp) *vb.* (*intr.*) *Scot.* to tell tales; be an informer. [C15: from Old English *clipian, cleopian;* see CLEPE]

clyp·e·us ('klɪpɪəs) *n., pl.* **clyp·e·i** ('klɪpɪ,aɪ). a cuticular plate on the head of some insects between the labrum and the frons. [C19: from New Latin, from Latin *clipeus* round shield] —**'clyp·e·al** *adj.* —**clyp·e·ate** ('klɪpɪ,eɪt) *adj.*

clys·ter ('klɪstə) *n. Med.* a former name for **enema.** [C14: from Greek *klustēr,* from *kluzein* to rinse]

Cly·tem·nes·tra *or* **Cly·taem·nes·tra** (,klaɪtɪm'nɛstrə) *n. Greek myth.* the wife of Agamemnon, whom she killed on his return from the Trojan War.

cm *or* **cm.** *abbrev. for* centimetre.

Cm *the chemical symbol for* curium.

c.m. *abbrev. for* court-martial.

Cmdr. *Military. abbrev. for* Commander.

C.M.F. *Austral. abbrev. for* Citizen Military Forces.

C.M.G. *abbrev. for* Companion of St. Michael and St. George (a Brit. title).

cml. *abbrev. for* commercial.

C/N, c/n, *or* **c.n.** *Commerce. abbrev. for* credit note.

CNAA *abbrev. for* the Council for National Academic Awards: a degree-awarding body separate from the universities.

C.N.D. (in Britain) *abbrev. for* Campaign for Nuclear Disarmament.

cni·dar·i·an (naɪ'dɛərɪən, knaɪ-) *n.* **1.** any coelenterate of the subphylum *Cnidaria,* which includes all coelenterates except the ctenophores. ~*adj.* **2.** of, relating to, or belonging to the *Cnidaria.* [C20: from New Latin *Cnidaria,* from Greek *knidē* nettle]

cnid·o·blast ('naɪdəʊ,blɑ:st, 'knaɪ-) *n. Zoology.* any of the cells of a coelenterate that contain nematocysts. [C19: from New Latin *cnida,* from Greek *knidē* nettle + -BLAST]

Cni·dus ('naɪdəs, 'knaɪ-) *n.* an ancient Greek city in SW Asia Minor: famous for its school of medicine.

Cnos·sus ('nɒsəs, 'knɒs-) *n.* a variant spelling of **Knossos.**

CNS *or* **C.N.S.** *abbrev. for* central nervous system.

Cnut (kə'nju:t) *n.* a variant of **Canute.**

Co *the chemical symbol for* cobalt.

CO *international car registration for* Colombia.

Co. *or* **co.** *abbrev. for:* **1.** (*esp. in names of business organizations*) Company. **2. and co.** (kəʊ) *Informal.* and the rest of them: *Harold and co.*

Co. *abbrev. for* County.

C.O. *abbrev. for:* **1.** Commanding Officer. **2.** conscientious objector.

co- *prefix.* **1.** together; joint or jointly; mutual or mutually: *coproduction.* **2.** indicating partnership or equality: *costar; copilot.* **3.** to the same or a similar degree: *coextend.* **4.** (in mathematics and astronomy) of the complement of an angle: *cosecant; codeclination.* [from Latin, reduced form of COM-]

c/o *abbrev. for:* **1.** care of. **2.** *Book-keeping.* carried over.

co·ac·er·vate (kəʊ'æsəvɪt, -,veɪt) *n.* either of two liquid phases that may separate from a hydrophilic sol, each containing a different concentration of a dispersed solid. [C17: from Latin *coacervāre* to heap up, from *acervus* a heap] —**co·,ac·er·'va·tion** *n.*

coach (kəʊtʃ) *n.* **1.** a vehicle for several passengers, used for transport over long distances, sightseeing, etc. **2.** a large four-wheeled enclosed carriage, usually horse-drawn. **3.** a railway carriage carrying passengers. **4.** a trainer or instructor: *a drama coach.* **5.** a tutor who prepares students for examinations. **6.** *Austral.* a tame bullock used as a decoy to attract wild cattle. ~*vb.* **7.** to give tuition or instruction to (a pupil). **8.** (*tr.*) to transport in a bus or coach. [C16: from French *coche,* from Hungarian *kocsi szekér* wagon of Kocs, village in Hungary where coaches were first made; in the sense: to teach, probably from the idea that the instructor carried his pupils] —**'coach·er** *n.*

coach box *n.* the seat of a coachman on a horse-drawn carriage.

coach-built *adj.* (of a vehicle) having specially built bodywork. —**'coach-,build·er** *n.*

coach dog *n.* a former name for **dalmatian.**

coach house *n.* **1.** a building in which a coach is kept. **2.** Also called: **coaching house, coaching inn.** *History.* an inn along a coaching route at which horses were changed.

coach·man ('kəʊtʃmən) *n., pl.* **·men. 1.** the driver of a coach or carriage. **2.** a fishing fly with white wings and a brown hackle.

coach screw *n.* a large screw with a square head used in timber work in buildings, etc.

coach·wood ('kəʊtʃ,wʊd) *n.* an Australian tree, *Ceratopetalum apetalum,* yielding light aromatic wood used for furniture, turnery, etc.

coach·work ('kəʊtʃ,wɜ:k) *n.* **1.** the design and manufacture of car bodies. **2.** the body of a car.

co·ac·tion[1] (kəʊ'ækʃən) *n.* **1.** any relationship between organisms within a community. **2.** joint action. [C17: CO- + ACTION] —**co·'ac·tive** *adj.* —**co·'ac·tive·ly** *adv.* —**,co·ac·'tiv·i·ty** *n.*

co·ac·tion[2] (kəʊ'ækʃən) *n. Obsolete.* a force or compulsion, either to compel or restrain. [C14: from Late Latin *coāctiō,* from Latin *cōgere* to constrain, compel]

co·ad·ju·tant (kəʊ'ædʒətənt) *adj.* **1.** cooperating. ~*n.* **2.** a helper.

co·ad·ju·tor (kəʊ'ædʒʊtə) *n.* **1.** a bishop appointed as assistant to a diocesan bishop. **2.** *Rare.* an assistant. [C15: via Old French from Latin *co-* together + *adjūtor* helper, from *adjūtāre* to assist, from *juvāre* to help] —**co·'ad·ju·tress** *or* **co·'ad·ju·trix** *fem. n.*

co·ad·u·nate (kəʊ'ædjʊnɪt, -,neɪt) *adj. Biology.* another word for **connate** (sense 3). [C19: from Late Latin *coadūnāre* to join together, from Latin *adūnāre* to join to, from *ūnus* one] —**co·,ad·u·'na·tion** *n.* —**co·'ad·u·,na·tive** *adj.*

co·ag·u·lant (kəʊ'ægjʊlənt) *or* **co·ag·u·la·tor** (kəʊ'ægjʊ,leɪtə) *n.* a substance that aids or produces coagulation.

co·ag·u·lase (kəʊ'ægjʊ,leɪz) *n.* any enzyme that causes coagulation of blood.

co·ag·u·late *vb.* (kəʊ'ægjʊ,leɪt). **1.** to cause (a fluid, such as blood) to change into a soft semisolid mass or (of such a fluid) to change into such a mass; clot; curdle. **2.** *Chem.* to separate or cause to separate into distinct constituent phases. ~*n.* (kəʊ'ægjʊlɪt, -,leɪt). **3.** the solid or semisolid substance produced by coagulation. [C16: from Latin *coāgulāre* to make (a liquid) curdle, from *coāgulum* rennet, from *cōgere* to drive together] —**co·'ag·u·la·ble** *adj.* —**co·,ag·u·la·'bil·i·ty** *n.* —**co·,ag·u·'la·tion** *n.* —**co·ag·u·la·tive** (kəʊ'ægjʊlətɪv) *adj.*

co·ag·u·lum (kəʊ'ægjʊləm) *n., pl.* **·la** (-lə). any coagulated mass; clot; curd. [C17: from Latin: curdling agent; see COAGULATE]

Co·a·hui·la (*Spanish* ,koa'wila) *n.* a state of N Mexico: mainly plateau, crossed by several mountain ranges that contain rich mineral resources. Capital: Saltillo. Pop.: 1 114 956 (1970). Area: 151 571 sq. km (59 112 sq. miles).

coal (kəʊl) *n.* **1. a.** a compact black or dark-brown carbonaceous rock consisting of layers of partially decomposed vegetation deposited in the Carboniferous period: a fuel and a source of coke, coal gas, and coal tar. See also **anthracite, bituminous coal, lignite, peat. b.** (*as modifier*): *coal cellar; coal merchant; coal mine; coal dust.* **2.** one or more lumps of coal. **3.** short for **charcoal. 4. coals to Newcastle.** something supplied where it already exists. ~*vb.* **5.** to take in, provide with, or turn into coal. [Old English *col;* related to Old Norse *kol,* Old High German *kolo,* Old Irish *gūal*] —**'coal·y** *adj.*

coal·er ('kəʊlə) *n.* **1.** a ship, train, etc., used to carry or supply coal. **2.** a person who sells or supplies coal.

co·a·lesce (,kəʊə'lɛs) *vb.* (*intr.*) to unite or come together in one body or mass; merge; fuse; blend. [C16: from Latin *coalēscere* from CO- + *alēscere* to increase, from *alere* to nourish] —**,co·a·'les·cence** *n.* —**,co·a·'les·cent** *adj.*

coal·face ('kəʊl,feɪs) *n.* the exposed seam of coal in a mine.

coal·field ('kəʊl,fi:ld) *n.* an area rich in deposits of coal.

coal·fish ('kəʊl,fɪʃ) *n., pl.* **·fish** *or* **·fish·es.** a dark-coloured gadoid food fish, *Pollachius virens,* occurring in northern seas. Also called (Brit.): **saithe, coley.**

coal gas *n.* a mixture of gases produced by the distillation of bituminous coal and used for heating and lighting: consists mainly of hydrogen, methane, and carbon monoxide.

coal heav·er *n.* a workman who moves coal.

coal hole *n. Brit. informal.* a small coal cellar.

co·a·li·tion (,kəʊə'lɪʃən) *n.* **1. a.** an alliance or union between groups, factions, or parties, esp. for some temporary and specific reason. **b.** (*as modifier*): *a coalition government.* **2.** a fusion or merging into one body or mass. [C17: from Medieval Latin *coalitiō*, from Latin *coalēscere* to COALESCE] —ˌ**co·a**+'**li**+**tion**+**al** *adj.* —ˌ**co·a**+'**li**+**tion**+**ist** *or* ˌ**co·a**+'**li**+**tion**+**er** *n.*

Coal Meas+ures *pl. n.* **the.** a series of coal-bearing rocks formed in the upper Carboniferous period; the uppermost series of the Carboniferous system.

coal oil *n.* **1.** *U.S.* petroleum or a refined product from petroleum, esp. kerosene. **2.** a crude oil produced, together with coal gas, during the distillation of bituminous coal.

Coal+port ('kəʊlˌpɔːt) *n. Antiques.* a white translucent bone china having richly coloured moulded patterns, made in the 19th century at Coalport near Shrewsbury.

coal pot *n.* a cooking device using charcoal, consisting of a raised iron bowl and a central grid.

Coal Sack *n.* a dark nebula in the Milky Way close to the Southern Cross.

coal scut+tle *n.* a domestic metal container for coal.

coal tar *n.* a black tar, produced by the distillation of bituminous coal, that can be further distilled to yield benzene, toluene, xylene, anthracene, phenol, etc.

coal-tar pitch *n.* a residue left by the distillation of coal tar: a mixture of hydrocarbons and finely divided carbon used as a binder for fuel briquettes, road surfaces, and carbon electrodes.

coal tit *n.* a small European songbird, *Parus ater,* having a black head with a white patch on the nape: family *Paridae* (tits).

coam+ing ('kəʊmɪŋ) *n.* a raised frame around the cockpit or hatchway of a vessel for keeping out water. [C17: of unknown origin]

co+ap+ta+tion (ˌkəʊæp'teɪʃən) *n.* the joining or reuniting of two surfaces, esp. the ends of a broken bone or the edges of a wound. [C16: from Late Latin *coaptātiō* a meticulous joining together, from Latin *co-* together + *aptāre* to fit]

co+arc+tate (kəʊ'ɑːkteɪt) *adj.* **1.** (of a pupa) enclosed in a hard barrel-shaped case (puparium), as in the housefly. **2.** crowded or pressed together; constricted. [C15: from Latin *coarctāre,* to press together, from *artus* tight] —ˌ**co+arc+'ta+tion** *n.*

coarse (kɔːs) *adj.* **1.** rough in texture, structure, etc.; not fine: *coarse sand.* **2.** lacking refinement or taste; indelicate; vulgar: *coarse jokes.* **3.** of inferior quality; not pure or choice. **4.** (of a metal) not refined. **5.** (of a screw) having widely spaced threads. [C14: of unknown origin] —'**coarse+ly** *adv.* —'**coarse+ness** *n.*

coarse fish *n.* a freshwater fish that is not a member of the salmon family. Compare **game fish.** —**coarse fish+ing** *n.*

coars+en ('kɔːsᵊn) *vb.* to make or become coarse.

coast (kəʊst) *n.* **1. a.** the line or zone where the land meets the sea or some other large expanse of water. **b.** (*in combination*): *coastland.* Related adj.: **littoral. 2.** *Brit.* the seaside. **3.** *U.S.* **a.** a slope down which a sledge may slide. **b.** the act or an instance of sliding down a slope. **4.** *Obsolete.* borderland or frontier. **5. the coast is clear.** *Informal.* the obstacles or dangers are gone. ~*vb.* **6.** to move or cause to move by momentum or force of gravity. **7.** (*intr.*) to proceed without great effort: *to coast to victory.* **8.** to sail along (a coast). [C13: from Old French *coste* coast, slope, from Latin *costa* side, rib] —'**coast+al** *adj.* —'**coast+al+ly** *adv.*

coast+er ('kəʊstə) *n.* **1.** *Brit.* a vessel or trader engaged in coastal commerce. **2.** a small tray, sometimes on wheels, for holding a decanter, wine bottle, etc. **3.** a person or thing that coasts. **4.** *Chiefly U.S.* a protective disc or mat for glasses or bottles. **5.** *U.S.* short for **roller coaster. 6.** *West African.* a European resident on the coast.

coast+guard ('kəʊstˌgɑːd) *n.* **1.** a maritime force which aids shipping, saves lives at sea, prevents smuggling, etc. **2.** Also called: **coast+guards+man.** a member of such a force.

coast+line ('kəʊstˌlaɪn) *n.* the outline of a coast, esp. when seen from the sea, or the land adjacent to it.

Coast Moun+tains *pl. n.* a mountain range in Canada, on the Pacific coast of British Columbia. Highest peak: Mount Waddington, 3978 m (13 260 ft.).

coat (kəʊt) *n.* **1.** an outdoor garment with sleeves, covering the body from the shoulders to waist, knee, or foot. **2.** any similar garment, esp. one forming the top to a suit. **3.** a layer that covers or conceals a surface: *a coat of dust.* **4.** the hair, wool, or fur of an animal. **5.** *Rare.* the garb worn by members of a profession or group. **6.** short for **coat of arms.** ~*vb.* **7.** (*tr.;* often foll. by *with*) to cover (with) a layer or covering. **8.** (*tr.*) to provide with a coat. [C16: from Old French *cote* of Germanic origin; compare Old Saxon *kotta,* Old High German *kozzo*]

coat ar+mour *n. Heraldry.* **1.** coat of arms. **2.** an emblazoned surcoat.

Coat+bridge ('kəʊtˌbrɪdʒ) *n.* an industrial town in central Scotland, in Strathclyde region. Pop.: 52 131 (1971).

coat+ed ('kəʊtɪd) *adj.* **1.** covered with an outer layer, film, etc. **2.** (of paper) having a coating of a mineral, esp. china clay, to provide a very smooth surface. **3.** (of textiles) having been given a plastic or other surface. **4.** *Photog., optics.* another word for **bloomed.**

coat·ee (kəʊ'tiː, 'kəʊtiː) *n. Chiefly Brit.* a short coat, esp. for a baby.

Coates (kəʊts) *n.* **Jo·seph Gor·don.** 1878–1943, New Zealand statesman; prime minister of New Zealand (1925–28).

coat hang+er *n.* a curved piece of wood, wire, plastic, etc., fitted with a hook and used to hang up clothes.

co·a+ti (kəʊ'ɑːtɪ), **co·a·ti-mon·di,** *or* **co·a·ti-mun·di** (kəʊˌɑːtɪ'mʌndɪ) *n., pl.* +**tis** *or* ·**dis.** any omnivorous mammal of the genera *Nasua* and *Nasuella,* of Central and South America: family *Procyonidae,* order *Carnivora* (carnivores). They are related to but larger than the raccoons, having a long flexible snout and a brindled coat. [C17: from Portuguese *coatí,* from Tupi, literally: belt-nosed, from *cua* belt + *tim* nose]

coat+ing ('kəʊtɪŋ) *n.* **1.** a layer or film spread over a surface for protection or decoration. **2.** a heavy fabric suitable for coats.

coat of arms *n.* **1.** the heraldic bearings of a person or family. **2.** a surcoat decorated with family or personal bearings.

coat of mail *n.* a protective garment made of linked metal rings (mail) or of overlapping metal plates; hauberk.

coat-of-mail shell *n.* another name for **chiton** (sense 2).

coat-tail *n.* the long tapering tails at the back of a man's tailed coat.

co+au·thor (kəʊ'ɔːθə) *n.* **1.** a person who shares the writing of a book, article, etc., with another. ~*vb.* **2.** (*tr.*) to be the joint author of (a book, article, etc.).

coax[1] (kəʊks) *vb.* **1.** to seek to manipulate or persuade (someone) by tenderness, flattery, pleading, etc. **2.** (*tr.*) to obtain by persistent coaxing. **3.** (*tr.*) *Obsolete.* to caress. **4.** (*tr.*) *Obsolete.* to deceive. [C16: verb formed from obsolete noun *cokes* fool, of unknown origin] —'**coax+er** *n.* —'**coax+ing+ly** *adv.*

co·ax[2] ('kəʊæks) *n.* short for **coaxial cable.**

co+ax+i·al (kəʊ'æksɪəl) *or* **co+ax+al** (kəʊ'æksᵊl) *adj.* **1.** having or mounted on a common axis. **2.** *Geom.* (of a set of circles) having the same radical axis. **3.** *Electronics.* formed from, using, or connected to a coaxial cable.

co+ax+i·al ca+ble *n.* a cable consisting of an inner insulated core of stranded or solid wire surrounded by an outer insulated flexible wire braid, used esp. as a transmission line for radio-frequency signals. Often shortened to **coax.**

cob[1] (kɒb) *n.* **1.** a male swan. **2.** a thickset type of riding and draught horse. **3.** short for **corncob, corncob pipe,** or **cobnut. 4.** *Brit.* another name for **hazel** (sense 1). **5.** a small rounded lump or heap of coal, ore, etc. **6.** *Brit.* a building material consisting of a mixture of clay and chopped straw. **7.** Also called: **cob loaf.** *Brit.* a round loaf of bread. ~*vb.* **cobs, cob+bing, cobbed. 8.** (*tr.*) *Brit. informal.* to beat, esp. on the buttocks. [C15: of uncertain origin; probably related to Icelandic *kobbi* seal; see CUB]

cob[2] *or* **cobb** (kɒb) *n.* an archaic or dialect name for a **gull** esp. the greater black-backed gull (*Larus marinus*). [C16: of Germanic origin; related to Dutch *kob, kobbe*]

co+balt ('kəʊbɔːlt) *n.* a brittle hard silvery-white element that is a ferromagnetic metal: occurs principally in cobaltite and smaltite and is widely used in alloys. The radioisotope **cobalt-60,** with a half-life of 5.3 years, is used in radiotherapy and as a tracer. Symbol: Co; atomic no.: 27; atomic wt.: 58.933; valency: 2 or 3; relative density: 8.9; melting pt.: 1495°C; boiling pt.: 2870°C. [C17: German *Kobalt,* from Middle High German *kobolt* goblin; from the miners' belief that malicious goblins placed it in the silver ore]

co+balt bloom *n.* another name for **erythrite** (sense 1).

co+balt blue *n., adj.* (**cobalt-blue** *when prenominal*). **1.** Also called: **Thénard's blue.** any greenish-blue pigment containing cobalt aluminate, usually made by heating cobaltous sulphate, aluminium oxide, and phosphoric acid together. **2. a.** a deep blue to greenish-blue colour. **b.** (*as adj.*): *a cobalt-blue car.*

co+balt bomb *n.* a nuclear weapon consisting of a hydrogen bomb encased in cobalt, which releases large quantities of radioactive cobalt-60 into the atmosphere.

co+bal·tic (kəʊ'bɔːltɪk) *adj.* of or containing cobalt, esp. in the trivalent state.

co+bal·tite (kəʊ'bɔːltaɪt, 'kəʊbɔːlˌtaɪt) *or* **co+bal+tine** ('kəʊbɔːlˌtiːn, -tɪn) *n.* a rare silvery-white mineral consisting of cobalt arsenic sulphide in cubic crystalline form: a major ore of cobalt, used in ceramics. Formula: CoAsS.

co+bal·tous (kəʊ'bɔːltəs) *adj.* of or containing cobalt in the divalent state.

cob+ber ('kɒbə) *n. Austral., archaic.* a friend; mate: used as a term of address to males. [C19: from dialect *cob* to take a liking to someone]

Cob·bett ('kɒbɪt) *n.* **Wil·liam.** 1763–1835, English journalist and social reformer; founded *The Political Register* (1802); author of *Rural Rides* (1830).

cob+ble[1] ('kɒbᵊl) *n.* **1.** short for **cobblestone.** ~*vb.* **2.** (*tr.*) to pave (a road, etc.) with cobblestones. [C15 (in *cobblestone*): from COB[1]]

cob+ble[2] ('kɒbᵊl) *vb.* (*tr.*) **1.** to make or mend shoes. **2.** to put together clumsily. [C15: back formation from COBBLER[1]]

cob+bler[1] ('kɒblə) *n.* **1.** a person who makes or mends shoes. **2.** *Austral. slang.* the last sheep to be shorn. [C13 (as surname): of unknown origin]

cob+bler[2] ('kɒblə) *n.* **1.** a sweetened iced drink, usually made from fruit and wine or liqueur. **2.** *Chiefly U.S.* a hot dessert made of fruit covered with a rich cakelike crust. [C19: (for sense 1) perhaps shortened from *cobbler's punch;* (for both senses) compare *cobble* (vb.)]

cob+blers ('kɒbləz) *Brit. taboo slang.* ~*pl. n.* **1.** another word for **testicles.** ~*interj.* **2.** rubbish; nonsense.

cob+bler's wax *n.* a resin used for waxing thread.

cob+bles ('kɒbᵊlz) *pl. n.* **1.** coal in small rounded lumps. **2.** cobblestones.

cob·ble+stone ('kɒbᵊlˌstəʊn) *n.* a rounded stone used for paving. Sometimes shortened to **cobble.** Compare **sett.**

Cob·den ('kɒbdən) *n.* **Rich·ard.** 1804–65, English economist and statesman: a leader of the successful campaign to abolish the Corn Laws (1846).

co·bel·lig·er·ent (ˌkəʊbɪˈlɪdʒərənt) *n.* a country fighting in a war on the side of another country.

Cóbh (kəʊv) *n.* a port in S Ireland, in SE Co. Cork: port of call for Atlantic liners. Pop.: 7141 (1971). Former name (1849–1922): **Queenstown.**

Cob·ham (ˈkɒbəm) *n.* **Lord,** title of (Sir John) **Oldcastle.**

co·bi·a (ˈkəʊbɪə) *n.* a large dark-striped percoid game fish, *Rachycentron canadum,* of tropical and subtropical seas: family *Rachycentridae.* [of unknown origin]

co·ble (ˈkəʊbᵊl, ˈkɒbᵊl) *n. Northern Brit.* a small single-masted flat-bottomed fishing boat. [C13: probably of Celtic origin; compare Welsh *ceubal* skiff]

Co·blenz (*German* ˈkoːblɛnts) *n.* a variant spelling of **Koblenz.**

cob mon·ey *n.* crude silver coins issued in the Spanish colonies of the New World from about 1600 until 1820.

cob·nut (ˈkɒbˌnʌt) *or* **cob** *n.* other names for a **hazelnut.** [C16: from earlier *cobylle nut;* see COBBLE[1], NUT]

COBOL (ˈkəʊˌbɒl) *n.* a high-level computer programming language designed for general commercial use. [C20: *co(mmon) b(usiness) o(riented) l(anguage)*]

co·bra (ˈkəʊbrə) *n.* **1.** any highly venomous elapid snake of the genus *Naja,* such as *N. naja* (**Indian cobra**), of tropical Africa and Asia. When alarmed they spread the skin of the neck region into a hood. **2.** any related snake, such as the king cobra. [C19: from Portuguese *cobra (de capello)* snake (with a hood), from Latin *colubra* snake]

co·bra de ca·pel·lo (diː kəˈpɛləʊ) *n., pl.* **co·bras de ca·pel·lo.** a cobra, *Naja tripudians,* that has ringlike markings on the body and exists in many varieties in S and SE Asia.

co·burg (ˈkəʊˌbɜːg) *n.* (*sometimes cap.*) a rounded loaf with a cross cut on the top. Also called: **coburg loaf.** [C19: apparently named in honour of Prince Albert (of SAXE-COBURG-GOTHA)]

Co·burg (ˈkəʊbɜːg; *German* ˈkoːbʊrk) *n.* a city in E West Germany, in N Bavaria. Pop.: 42 200 (1970).

cob·web (ˈkɒbˌwɛb) *n.* **1.** a web spun by certain spiders, esp. those of the family *Theridiidae,* often found in the corners of disused rooms. **2.** a single thread of such a web. **3.** something like a cobweb, as in its flimsiness or ability to trap. [C14: *cob,* from *coppe,* from Old English *(ātor)coppe* spider; related to Middle Dutch *koppe* spider, Swedish (dialect) *etterkoppa*] —ˈ**cob·ˌwebbed** *adj.* —ˈ**cob·ˌweb·by** *adj.*

cob·webs (ˈkɒbˌwɛbz) *pl. n.* **1.** mustiness, confusion, or obscurity. **2.** *Informal.* stickiness of the eyelids experienced upon first awakening.

co·ca (ˈkəʊkə) *n.* **1.** either of two shrubs, *Erythroxylon coca* or *E. truxiuense,* native to the Andes: family *Erythroxylaceae.* **2.** the dried leaves of these shrubs and related plants, which contain cocaine and are chewed by the peoples of the Andes for their stimulating effects. [C17: from Spanish, from Quechuan *kúka*]

Co·ca-Co·la (ˌkəʊkəˈkəʊlə) *n. Trademark.* a carbonated soft drink flavoured with coca leaves, cola nuts, caramel, etc.

co·caine *or* **co·cain** (kəˈkeɪn) *n.* an addictive narcotic drug derived from coca leaves or synthesized, used medicinally as a topical anaesthetic. Formula: $C_{17}H_{21}NO_4$. [C19: from COCA + -INE[1]]

co·cain·ism (kəʊˈkeɪˌnɪzəm, ˈkəʊkə-) *n.* habitual or excessive use of cocaine, resulting in impaired physical or mental abilities.

co·cain·ize *or* **co·cain·ise** (kəʊˈkeɪˌnaɪz, ˈkəʊkəˌnaɪz) *vb.* (*tr.*) to anaesthetize with cocaine. —ˌ**co·cain·i·ˈza·tion** *or* **co·ˌcain·i·ˈsa·tion** *n.*

coc·ci (ˈkɒksaɪ) *n.* the plural of **coccus.**

coc·cid (ˈkɒksɪd) *n.* any homopterous insect of the superfamily *Coccoidea,* esp. any of the family *Coccidae,* which includes the scale insects. [C19: from New Latin *Coccidae;* see COCCUS]

coc·cid·i·oi·do·my·co·sis (kɒkˌsɪdɪˌɔɪdəʊmaɪˈkəʊsɪs) *n.* a disease of the skin or viscera, esp. the lungs, caused by infection with the fungus *Coccidioides immitis.* [C20: from New Latin *Coccidioides* + -O- + MYCOSIS]

coc·cid·i·o·sis (kɒkˌsɪdɪˈəʊsɪs) *n.* any disease of domestic and other animals caused by parasitic protozoa of the order *Coccidia.* One species, *Isospora hominis,* occasionally infects humans. [C19: from New Latin; see COCCUS, -OSIS]

coc·cif·er·ous (kɒkˈsɪfərəs) *adj.* (of plants) **1.** supporting the cochineal insect. **2.** *Obsolete.* bearing berries.

coc·co·lith (ˈkɒkəlɪθ) *n.* any of the round calcareous plates in chalk formations: formed the outer layer of extinct unicellular plankton. [C19: New Latin, from Greek *kokkos* berry + *lithos* stone]

coc·cus (ˈkɒkəs) *n., pl.* **·ci** (-saɪ). **1.** any spherical or nearly spherical bacterium, such as a staphylococcus. Compare **bacillus** (sense 1), **spirillum** (sense 1). **2.** the part of a fruit that contains one seed and separates from the whole fruit at maturity. **3.** any of the scale insects of the genus *Coccus.* [C18: from New Latin, from Greek *kokkos* berry, grain] —ˈ**coc·coid,** ˈ**coc·cal,** *or* **coc·cic** (ˈkɒksɪk) *adj.* —ˈ**coc·cous** *adj.*

coc·cyx (ˈkɒksɪks) *n., pl.* **coc·cy·ges** (kɒkˈsaɪdʒiːz). a small triangular bone at the end of the spinal column in man and some apes, representing a vestigial tail. [C17: from New Latin, from Greek *kokkux* cuckoo, of imitative origin; from the likeness of the bone to a cuckoo's beak] —**coc·cyg·e·al** (kɒkˈsɪdʒɪəl) *adj.*

Co·cha·bam·ba (*Spanish* ˌkotʃaˈβamba) *n.* a city in central Bolivia. Pop.: 184 340 (1975 est.).

Co·chin (ˈkəʊtʃɪn, ˈkɒtʃ-) *n.* **1.** a region and former state of SW India: part of Kerala state since 1956. **2.** a port in SW India, on the Malabar Coast: the first European settlement in India, founded by Vasco da Gama in 1502. Pop.: 438 420 (1971). **3.** a large breed of domestic fowl with dense plumage and feathered legs.

Co·chin Chi·na *n.* a former French colony of Indochina (1862–1948): now the part of Vietnam that lies south of Phan Thiet.

coch·i·neal (ˌkɒtʃɪˈniːl, ˈkɒtʃɪˌniːl) *n.* **1.** Also called: **cochineal insect.** a Mexican homopterous insect, *Dactylopius coccus,* that feeds on cacti. **2.** a crimson substance obtained from the crushed bodies of these insects, used for colouring food and for dyeing. **3. a.** the colour of this dye. **b.** (*as adj.*): *cochineal shoes.* [C16: from Old Spanish *cochinilla,* from Latin *coccineus* scarlet-coloured, from *coccum* cochineal kermes, from Greek *kokkos* kermes berry]

Co·chise (kəʊˈtʃiːs, -ˈtʃiːz) *n.* died 1874, Apache Indian chief.

coch·le·a (ˈkɒklɪə) *n., pl.* **·le·ae** (-lɪˌiː). the spiral tube, shaped like a snail's shell, that forms part of the internal ear, converting sound vibrations into nerve impulses. [C16: from Latin: snail, spiral, from Greek *kokhlias;* probably related to Greek *konkhē* CONCH] —ˈ**coch·le·ar** *adj.*

coch·le·ate (ˈkɒklɪˌeɪt, -lɪɪt) *or* **coch·le·at·ed** *adj. Biology.* shaped like a snail's shell; spirally twisted.

cock[1] (kɒk) *n.* **1.** the male of the domestic fowl. **2. a.** any other male bird. **b.** the male of certain other animals, such as the lobster. **c.** (*as modifier*): *a cock sparrow.* **3.** short for **stopcock** or **weathercock. 4.** a taboo slang word for **penis. 5. a.** the hammer of a firearm. **b.** its position when the firearm is ready to be discharged. **6.** *Brit. informal.* a friend, mate, or fellow. **7.** a jaunty or significant tilting or turning upwards: *a cock of the head.* **8.** *Brit. informal.* nonsense. ~*vb.* **9.** (*tr.*) to set or pull the hammer of (a firearm) into firing position. **10.** (*tr.; sometimes foll. by up*) to raise in an alert or jaunty manner. **11.** (*intr.*) to stick or stand up conspicuously. ~See also **cockup.** [Old English *cocc* (referring to the male fowl; the development of C15 sense spout, tap, and other transferred senses is not clear), ultimately of imitative origin; related to Old Norse *kokkr,* French *coq,* Late Latin *coccus*]

cock[2] (kɒk) *n.* **1.** a small, cone-shaped heap of hay, straw, etc. ~*vb.* **2.** (*tr.*) to stack (hay, etc.) in such heaps. [C14 (in Old English, *cocc* is attested in place names): perhaps of Scandinavian origin; compare Norwegian *kok,* Danish dialect *kok*]

cock·ade (kɒˈkeɪd) *n.* a feather or ribbon worn on military headwear. [C18: changed from earlier *cockard,* from French *cocarde,* feminine of *cocard* arrogant, strutting, from *coq* COCK[1]] —**cock·ˈad·ed** *adj.*

cock-a-doo·dle-doo (ˌkɒkəˌduːdᵊlˈduː) *interj.* an imitation or representation of a cock crowing.

cock-a-hoop *adj.* (*usually postpositive*) **1.** in very high spirits. **2.** boastful. **3.** askew; confused. [C16: perhaps from the phrase *to set the cock a hoop* to live prodigally, literally: to put a cock on a *hoop,* a full measure of grain]

Cock·aigne *or* **Cock·ayne** (kɒˈkeɪn) *n. Medieval legend.* an imaginary land of luxury and idleness. [C14: from Old French *cocaigne,* from Middle Low German *kōkenje* small CAKE (of which the houses in the imaginary land are built); related to Spanish *cucaña,* Italian *cuccagna*]

cock-a-leek·ie *or* **cock·y-leek·y** (ˌkɒkəˈliːkɪ) *n.* a soup made from a fowl boiled with leeks, etc.

cock·a·lo·rum (ˌkɒkəˈlɔːrəm) *n.* **1.** a self-important little man. **2.** bragging talk; crowing. [C18: from COCK[1] + *-alorum,* variant of Latin genitive plural ending *-orum;* perhaps intended to suggest: the cock of all cocks]

cock-and-bull sto·ry *n. Informal.* an obviously improbable story, esp. a boastful one or one used as an excuse.

cock·a·tiel *or* **cock·a·teel** (ˌkɒkəˈtiːl) *n.* a crested Australian parrot, *Leptolophus hollandicus,* having a greyish-brown and yellow plumage. [C19: from Dutch *kaketielje,* from Portuguese *cacatilha* a little cockatoo, from *cacatua* COCKATOO]

cock·a·too (ˌkɒkəˈtuː, ˈkɒkəˌtuː) *n., pl.* **·toos. 1.** any of various parrots of the genus *Kakatoe* and related genera, such as *K. galerita* (**sulphur-crested cockatoo**), of Australia and New Guinea. They have an erectile crest and most of them are light-coloured. **2.** *Austral.* a small farmer or settler. **3.** *Austral. informal.* a lookout during some illegal activity. [C17: from Dutch *kaketoe,* from Malay *kakatua*]

cock·a·trice (ˈkɒkətrɪs, -ˌtraɪs) *n.* **1.** a legendary monster, part snake and part cock, that could kill with a glance. **2.** another name for **basilisk.** [C14: from Old French *cocatris,* from Medieval Latin *cocatrix,* from Late Latin *calcātrix* trampler, tracker (translating Greek *ikhneumon* ICHNEUMON), from Latin *calcāre* to tread, from *calx* heel]

Cock·ayne (kɒˈkeɪn) *n.* a variant spelling of **Cockaigne.**

cock·boat (ˈkɒkˌbəʊt) *or* **cock·le·boat** *n.* any small boat. [C15 *cokbote,* perhaps ultimately from Late Latin *caudica* dug-out canoe, from Latin *caudex* tree trunk]

cock·chaf·er (ˈkɒkˌtʃeɪfə) *n.* any of various Old World scarabaeid beetles, esp. *Melolontha melolontha* of Europe, whose larvae feed on crops and grasses. Also called: **May beetle, May bug.** [C18: from COCK[1] + CHAFER]

Cock·croft (ˈkɒkˌkrɒft) *n.* Sir **John Doug·las.** 1897–1967, English nuclear physicist. With E. T. S. Walton, he produced the first artificial transmutation of an atomic nucleus (1932) and shared the Nobel prize for physics 1951.

cock·crow (ˈkɒkˌkrəʊ) *or* **cock·crow·ing** *n.* daybreak.

cocked hat *n.* **1.** a hat with opposing brims turned up and caught together in order to give two points (bicorn) or three points (tricorn). **2. knock into a cocked hat.** *Slang.* to outdo or defeat someone.

cock·er[1] ('kɒkə) *n.* **1.** a devotee of cockfighting. **2.** short for **cocker spaniel.**

cock·er[2] ('kɒkə) *vb.* **1.** (*tr.*) *Rare.* to pamper or spoil by indulgence. ~*n.* **2.** *Brit. informal.* a mate (esp. in the phrase **old cocker**). [C15: perhaps from COCK[1] with the sense: to make a cock (i.e. pet) of]

cock·er·el ('kɒkərəl, 'kɒkrəl) *n.* a young domestic cock, usually less than a year old. [C15: diminutive of COCK[1]]

cock·er span·iel *n.* a breed of spaniel having wavy silky hair with white and brown or yellow patches. [C19 *cocker,* from *cocking* hunting woodcocks]

cock·eye ('kɒk,aɪ) *n. Informal.* an eye affected with strabismus or one that squints.

cock·eye bob *or* **cock·eyed bob** *n. Austral. slang.* a sudden storm or cyclone.

cock·eyed ('kɒk,aɪd) *adj. Informal.* **1.** afflicted with crosseye, squint, or any other visible abnormality of the eyes. **2.** appearing to be physically or logically abnormal, absurd, etc.; askew: *cockeyed ideas.* **3.** drunk.

cock feath·er *n. Archery.* the odd-coloured feather set on the shaft of an arrow at right angles to the nock. Compare **shaft feather.**

cock·fight ('kɒk,faɪt) *n.* a fight between two gamecocks fitted with sharp metal spurs. —**'cock·,fight·ing** *n.*

cock·horse (,kɒk'hɔːs) *n.* another name for **rocking horse** or **hobbyhorse.**

cock·i·ness ('kɒkɪnɪs) *n.* conceited self-assurance.

cock·le[1] ('kɒkᵊl) *n.* **1.** any sand-burrowing bivalve mollusc of the family *Cardiidae,* esp. *Cardium edule* (**edible cockle**) of Europe, typically having a rounded shell with radiating ribs. **2.** any of certain similar or related molluscs. **3.** short for **cockleshell** (sense 1). **4.** a wrinkle or puckering, as in cloth or paper. **5.** a small furnace or stove. **6. cockles of one's heart.** one's deepest feelings (esp. in the phrase **warm the cockles of one's heart**). ~*vb.* **7.** to contract or cause to contract into wrinkles. [C14: from Old French *coquille* shell, from Latin *conchȳlium* shellfish, from Greek *konkhulion,* diminutive of *konkhule* mussel; see CONCH]

cock·le[2] ('kɒkᵊl) *n.* any of several plants, esp. the corn cockle, that grow as weeds in cornfields.

cock·le·boat ('kɒkᵊl,bəʊt) *n.* another word for **cockboat.**

cock·le·bur ('kɒkᵊl,bɜː) *n.* **1.** any coarse weed of the genus *Xanthium,* having spiny burs: family *Compositae* (composites). **2.** the bur of any of these plants.

cock·le·shell ('kɒkᵊl,ʃɛl) *n.* **1.** the shell of the cockle. **2.** any of the valves of the shells of certain other bivalve molluscs, such as the scallop. **3.** any small light boat. **4.** a badge worn by pilgrims.

cock·loft ('kɒk,lɒft) *n.* a small loft, garret, or attic.

cock·ney ('kɒknɪ) *n.* **1.** (*often cap.*) a native of London, esp. of the working class born in the East End, speaking a characteristic dialect of English. Traditionally defined as someone born within the sound of the bells of St. Mary-le-Bow church. **2.** the urban dialect of London or its East End. **3.** *Austral.* a young snapper fish. ~*adj.* **4.** characteristic of cockneys or their dialect of English. [C14: from *cokeney,* literally: cock's egg, later applied contemptuously to townsmen, from *cokene,* genitive plural of *cok* COCK[1] + *ey* EGG] —**'cock·ney·ish** *adj.*

cock·ney·fy *or* **cock·ni·fy** ('kɒknɪ,faɪ) *vb.* **·fies, ·fy·ing, ·fied.** (*tr.*) to cause (one's speech, manners, etc.) to fit the stereotyped idea of a cockney. —**,cock·ney·fi·'ca·tion** *or* **,cock·ni·fi·'ca·tion** *n.*

cock·ney·ism ('kɒknɪ,ɪzəm) *n.* a characteristic of speech or custom peculiar to cockneys.

cock-of-the-rock *n.* either of two tropical South American birds, *Rupicola rupicola* or *R. peruviana,* having an erectile crest and (in the male) a brilliant red or orange plumage: family *Cotingidae* (cotingas).

cock of the walk *n. Informal.* a person who asserts himself in a strutting pompous way.

cock·pit ('kɒk,pɪt) *n.* **1.** the compartment in a small aircraft in which the pilot, crew, and sometimes the passengers sit. Compare **flight deck** (sense 1). **2.** the driver's compartment in a racing car. **3.** *Nautical.* **a.** an enclosed area towards the stern of a small vessel containing the wheel and tiller. **b.** (formerly) an apartment in a warship used as quarters for junior officers and as a first-aid station during combat. **4.** the site of numerous battles or campaigns. **5.** an enclosure used for cockfights.

cock·roach ('kɒk,rəʊtʃ) *n.* any insect of the suborder *Blattodea* (or *Blattaria*), such as *Blatta orientalis* (**oriental cockroach** or **black beetle**): order *Dictyoptera.* They have an oval flattened body with long antennae and biting mouthparts and are common household pests. See also **German cockroach, mantis.** [C17: from Spanish *cucaracha,* of obscure origin]

cocks·comb *or* **cox·comb** ('kɒks,kəʊm) *n.* **1.** the comb of a domestic cock. **2.** an amaranthaceous garden plant, *Celosia cristata,* with yellow, crimson, or purple flowers in a broad spike resembling the comb of a cock. **3.** any similar species of *Celosia.* **4.** *Informal.* a conceited dandy.

cocks·foot ('kɒks,fʊt) *n., pl.* **·foots.** a perennial Eurasian grass, *Dactylis glomerata,* cultivated as a pasture grass in North America and South Africa.

cock·shy ('kɒk,ʃaɪ) *n., pl.* **·shies.** *Brit.* **1.** a target aimed at in throwing games. **2.** the throw itself. ~Often shortened to **shy.** [C18: from shying (throwing objects at) a cock, which was given as a prize to the person who hit it]

cock·spur ('kɒk,spɜː) *n.* **1.** a spur on the leg of a cock. **2.** an annual grass, *Echinochloa crus-galli,* widely distributed in tropical and warm temperate regions. **3.** a small thorny North American hawthorn tree, *Crataegus crus-galli.*

cock·sure (,kɒk'ʃʊə, -'ʃɔː) *adj.* over-confident; arrogant. [C16: of uncertain origin] —**,cock·'sure·ly** *adv.* —**,cock·'sure·ness** *n.*

cock·swain ('kɒksən, -,sweɪn) *n.* a variant spelling of **coxswain.**

cock·tail[1] ('kɒk,teɪl) *n.* **1. a.** any mixed drink with a spirit base, usually drunk before meals. **b.** (*as modifier*): *the cocktail hour.* **2.** an appetizer of seafood, mixed fruits, etc. **3.** (*modifier*) appropriate for formal occasions: *a cocktail dress.* [C19: of unknown origin]

cock·tail[2] ('kɒk,teɪl) *n.* **1.** a horse with a docked tail. **2.** an animal of unknown or mixed breeding. **3.** *Archaic.* a person of little breeding pretending to be a gentleman. [C19: originally *cocktailed* (adj.) having a tail like a cock's]

cock·tail lounge *n.* a room in a hotel, restaurant, etc., where cocktails or other alcoholic drinks are served.

cock·tail stick *n.* a small pointed stick used for holding cherries, olives, etc., in cocktails, and for serving snacks, such as small sausages.

cock·up ('kɒk,ʌp) *n.* **1.** *Brit. slang.* something done badly. **2.** *Printing.* a letter rising above other letters in the line, esp. one of a large type size. ~*vb.* **cock up.** (*tr., adv.*). **3.** (of an animal) to raise (a leg, ears, etc.), esp. in an alert manner. **4.** (*tr.*) *Brit. slang.* to botch.

cock·y[1] ('kɒkɪ) *adj.* **cock·i·er, cock·i·est.** excessively proud of oneself. —**'cock·i·ly** *adv.* —**'cock·i·ness** *n.*

cock·y[2] ('kɒkɪ) *n. Austral. informal.* short for **cockatoo** (sense 2).

co·co ('kəʊkəʊ) *n., pl.* **·cos.** short for **coconut** or **coconut palm.** [C16: from Portuguese *coco* grimace; from the likeness of the three holes of the nut to a face]

co·coa ('kəʊkəʊ) *or* **ca·ca·o** *n.* **1.** a powder made from cocoa beans after they have been roasted, ground, and freed from most of their fatty oil. **2.** a hot or cold drink made from cocoa and milk or water. **3. a.** a light to moderate brown colour. **b.** (*as adj.*): *cocoa paint.*

co·coa bean *n.* the seed of the cacao.

co·coa but·ter *n.* a yellowish-white waxy solid that is obtained from cocoa beans and used for confectionery, soap, etc.

co·co de mer (də 'mɛə) *n.* **1.** a palm tree, *Lodoicea maldivica,* of the Seychelles, producing a large fruit containing a two-lobed edible nut. **2.** the nut of this palm. ~Also called: **double coconut.** [French: coconut of the sea]

co·co·nut *or* **co·coa·nut** ('kəʊkə,nʌt) *n.* **1.** the fruit of the coconut palm, consisting of a thick fibrous oval husk inside which is a thin hard shell enclosing edible white meat. The hollow centre is filled with a milky fluid (**coconut milk**). **2.** the meat of the coconut, often shredded and used in cakes, curries, etc. ~*adj.* **3.** *Brit.* made of the outer fibres of coconut husks: *coconut matting.* [C18: see COCO]

co·co·nut but·ter *n.* a solid form of coconut oil.

co·co·nut ice *n.* a sweetmeat made from dessicated coconut and sugar.

co·co·nut mat·ting *n.* a form of coarse matting made from the fibrous husk of the coconut.

co·co·nut milk *n.* **1.** See **coconut** (sense 1). **2.** (in Malaysia) the liquid pressed from the white meat of the coconut.

co·co·nut oil *n.* the fatty oil obtained from the meat of the coconut and used for making soap, cosmetics, etc.

co·co·nut palm *n.* a tall palm tree, *Cocos nucifera,* widely planted throughout the tropics, having coconuts as fruits. Also called: **coco palm, coconut tree.**

co·co·nut shy *n.* a fairground stall in which balls are thrown to knock coconuts off stands.

co·coon (kə'kuːn) *n.* **1. a.** a silky protective envelope secreted by silkworms and certain other insect larvae, in which the pupae develop. **b.** a similar covering for the eggs of the spider, earthworm, etc. **2.** a protective spray covering used as a seal on machinery. **3.** a cosy warm covering. ~*vb.* **4.** (*tr.*) to wrap in a cocoon. [C17: from French *cocon,* from Provençal *coucoun* eggshell, from *coco* shell, from Latin *coccum* kermes berry, from Greek *kokkos* grain, seed, berry; compare COCCUS]

co·co·pan ('kəʊkəʊ,pæn) *n.* (in South Africa) a small wagon running on narrow-gauge railway lines used in mines. Also called: **hopper.** [C20: from Zulu *'ngkumbana* short truck]

Co·cos Is·lands ('kəʊkɒs, 'kəʊkəs) *pl. n.* a group of 27 coral islands in the Indian Ocean, southwest of Java: a Territory of Australia since 1955. Pop.: 611 (1970). Area: 13 sq. km (5 sq. miles). Also called: **Keeling Islands.**

co·cotte (kəʊ'kɒt, kə-; *French* kɔ'kɔt) *n.* a prostitute or promiscuous woman. [C19: from French, from nursery word for a hen, feminine of *coq* COCK[1]]

co·co·yam ('kəʊkəʊ,jæm) *n.* **1.** either of two food plants of West Africa, the taro or the yantia, both of which have edible underground stems. **2.** the underground stem of either of these plants. [C20: from COCOA + YAM]

Coc·teau (*French* kɔk'to) *n.* **Jean** (ʒɑ̃). 1889–1963, French dramatist, novelist, poet, critic, designer, and film director. His works include the novel *Les Enfants terribles* (1929) and the play *La Machine infernale* (1934).

cod[1] (kɒd) *n., pl.* **cod** *or* **cods. 1.** any of the gadoid food fishes of the genus *Gadus,* esp. *G. morhua* (or *G. callarias*), which occurs in the North Atlantic and has a long body with three rounded dorsal fins: family *Gadidae.* They are also a source of cod-liver oil. **2.** any other fish of the family *Gadidae* (see **gadid**). [C13: probably of Germanic origin; compare Old High German *cutte*]

cod² (kɒd) *n.* **1.** *Brit. and U.S. dialect.* a pod or husk. **2.** *Taboo.* an obsolete word for **scrotum. 3.** *Obsolete.* a bag or envelope. [Old English *codd* husk, bag; related to Old Norse *koddi,* Danish *kodde*]

cod³ (kɒd) *Brit. slang.* ~*vb.* **cods, cod·ding, cod·ded.** (*tr.*) **1.** to make fun of; tease. **2.** to play a trick on; befool. ~*n.* **3.** a hoax or trick. [C19: perhaps from earlier *cod* a fool, perhaps shortened from CODGER]

cod⁴ (kɒd) *n. Northern Brit. dialect.* a fellow; chap: *he's a nice old cod.* [of unknown origin]

Cod *n.* **Cape.** See **Cape Cod.**

Cod. *or* **cod.** *abbrev. for* codex.

C.O.D. *abbrev. for:* **1.** cash on delivery. **2.** (in the U.S.) collect on delivery.

co·da (ˈkəʊdə) *n. Music.* the final, sometimes inessential, part of a musical structure. [C18: from Italian tail, from Latin *cauda*]

cod·der¹ (ˈkɒdə) *n.* a cod fisherman or his boat.

cod·der² (ˈkɒdə) *n. Yorkshire dialect.* the leader of a team of workers on a press at a steelworks. [perhaps from COD⁴]

cod·dle (ˈkɒdᵊl) *vb.* (*tr.*) **1.** to treat with indulgence. **2.** to cook (something, esp. eggs) in water just below the boiling point. ~*n.* **3.** *Irish dialect.* stew made from ham and bacon scraps. [C16: of obscure origin; perhaps related to CAUDLE] —ˈ**cod·dler** *n.*

code (kəʊd) *n.* **1.** a system of letters or symbols, and rules for their association by means of which information can be represented or communicated for reasons of secrecy, brevity, etc.: *binary code; Morse code.* See also **genetic code. 2.** a message in code. **3.** a symbol used in a code. **4.** a conventionalized set of principles, rules, or expectations: *a code of behaviour.* **5.** a system of letters or digits used for identification or selection purposes. ~*vb.* (*tr.*) **6.** to translate, transmit, or arrange into a code. [C14: from French, from Latin *cōdex* book, CODEX] —ˈ**cod·er** *n.*

co·dec·li·na·tion (ˌkəʊdɛklɪˈneɪʃən) *n.* another name for **polar distance.**

co·deine (ˈkəʊdiːn) *n.* a white crystalline alkaloid prepared mainly from morphine and having a similar but milder action. It is used as an analgesic, a sedative, and to relieve coughing. Formula: $C_{18}H_{21}NO_3$. [C19: from Greek *kōdeia* head of a poppy, from *kōos* hollow place + -INE²]

Code Na·po·lé·on *French.* (kɔd napɔleˈɔ̃) *n.* the civil code of France, promulgated between 1804 and 1810, comprising the main body of French civil law. English name: **Napoleonic Code.**

co·dex (ˈkəʊdɛks) *n., pl.* **co·di·ces** (ˈkəʊdɪˌsiːz, ˈkɒdɪ-). **1.** a volume of manuscripts of an ancient text. **2.** *Obsolete.* a legal code. [C16: from Latin: tree trunk, wooden block, book]

Co·dex Ju·ris Ca·non·i·ci (ˈkəʊdɛks ˈdʒʊərɪs kəˈnɒnɪˌsaɪ) *n.* the official code of canon law in force in the Roman Catholic Church. [Latin: book of canon law]

cod·fish (ˈkɒdˌfɪʃ) *n., pl.* **·fish** *or* **fish·es.** a cod, esp. *Gadus morhua.*

codg·er (ˈkɒdʒə) *n. Informal.* a man, esp. an old or eccentric one: a term of affection or mild derision (often in the phrase **old codger**). [C18: probably variant of CADGER]

co·di·ces (ˈkəʊdɪˌsiːz, ˈkɒdɪ-) *n.* the plural of **codex.**

cod·i·cil (ˈkɒdɪsɪl) *n.* **1.** *Law.* a supplement modifying a will or revoking some provision of it. **2.** an additional provision; appendix. [C15: from Late Latin *cōdicillus,* literally: a little book, diminutive of CODEX] —**cod·i·cil·la·ry** (ˌkɒdɪˈsɪlərɪ) *adj.*

co·di·col·o·gy (ˌkəʊdɪˈkɒlədʒɪ) *n.* the study of manuscripts. [C20: via French from Latin *codic-,* CODEX + -LOGY] —**co·di·co·log·i·cal** (ˌkəʊdɪkəˈlɒdʒɪkᵊl) *adj.*

cod·i·fi·ca·tion (ˌkəʊdɪfɪˈkeɪʃən, ˌkɒ-) *n.* **1.** systematic organization of methods, rules, etc. **2.** *Law.* the collection into one body of the principles of a system of law.

cod·i·fy (ˈkəʊdɪˌfaɪ, ˈkɒ-) *vb.* **·fies, ·fy·ing, ·fied.** (*tr.*) to organize or collect together (laws, rules, procedures, etc.) into a system or code. —ˈ**cod·i·ˌfi·er** *n.*

cod·ling¹ (ˈkɒdlɪŋ) *or* **cod·lin** (ˈkɒdlɪn) *n.* **1.** any of several varieties of long tapering apples used for cooking. **2.** any unripe apple. [C15 *querdlyng,* of uncertain origin]

cod·ling² (ˈkɒdlɪŋ) *n.* a codfish, esp. a young one.

cod·ling moth *or* **cod·lin moth** *n.* a tortricid moth, *Carpocapsa pomonella,* the larvae of which are a pest of apples.

cod·lins-and-cream *n.* an onagraceous plant, *Epilobium hirsutum,* native to Europe and Asia and introduced into North America, having purplish-red flowers and hairy stems and leaves. Also called: **hairy willowherb.**

cod-liv·er oil *n.* an oil extracted from the livers of cod and related fish, rich in vitamins A and D and used to treat deficiency of these vitamins.

co·do·main (ˌkəʊdəʊˈmeɪn) *n. Maths.* another name for **range** (sense 7).

co·don (ˈkəʊdɒn) *n. Genetics, biochem.* a unit that consists of three adjacent bases on a DNA molecule and that determines the position of a specific amino acid in a protein molecule during protein synthesis. [C20: from CODE + -ON]

cod·piece (ˈkɒdˌpiːs) *n.* a bag covering the male genitals, attached to hose or breeches by laces, etc., worn in the 15th and 16th centuries. [C15: from COD² + PIECE]

co-driv·er (ˈkəʊˌdraɪvə) *n.* one of two drivers who take turns to drive a car, esp. in a rally.

cods·wal·lop (ˈkɒdzˌwɒləp) *n. Brit. slang.* nonsense. [C20: of unknown origin]

cod war *n.* any of three disputes that occurred in 1958, 1972–73, and 1975–76 between Britain and Iceland, concerning Iceland's unilateral extension of her fishing limits.

Co·dy (ˈkəʊdɪ) *n.* **Wil·liam Fred·er·ick.** the original name of **Buffalo Bill.**

co-ed (ˌkəʊˈɛd) *adj.* **1.** coeducational. ~*n.* **2.** *U.S.* a female student in a coeducational college or university. **3.** *Brit.* a school or college providing coeducation.

co·ed·it (kəʊˈɛdɪt) *vb.* (*tr.*) to edit (a book, newspaper, etc.) jointly. —**coˈed·i·tor** *n.*

co·ed·u·ca·tion (ˌkəʊɛdjʊˈkeɪʃən) *n.* instruction in schools, colleges, etc., attended by both sexes. —ˌ**co·ed·u·ˈca·tion·al** *adj.* —ˌ**co·ed·u·ˈca·tion·al·ly** *adv.*

co·ef·fi·cient (ˌkəʊɪˈfɪʃənt) *n.* **1.** *Maths.* **a.** a numerical or constant factor in an algebraic term: *the coefficient of the term 3xyz is 3.* **b.** the product of all the factors of a term excluding one or more specified variables: *the coefficient of x in 3axyz is 3ayz.* **2.** *Physics.* a number that is the value of a given substance under specified conditions. [C17: from New Latin *coefficiēns,* from Latin *co-* together + *efficere* to EFFECT]

coel- *prefix.* indicating a cavity within a body or a hollow organ or part: *coelacanth; coelenterate; coelenteron.* [New Latin, from Greek *koilos* hollow]

coe·la·canth (ˈsiːləˌkænθ) *n.* a primitive marine bony fish of the genus *Latimeria* (subclass *Crossopterygii*), having fleshy limblike pectoral fins and occurring off the coast of E Africa: thought to be extinct until a living specimen was discovered in 1938. [C19: from New Latin *coelacanthus,* literally: hollow spine, from COEL- + Greek *akanthos* spine]

coe·len·ter·ate (sɪˈlɛntəˌreɪt, -rɪt) *n.* **1.** any invertebrates of the phylum *Coelenterata,* having a saclike body with a single opening (mouth), which occurs in polyp and medusa forms. The group includes the hydra, jellyfishes, sea anemones, and corals. ~*adj.* **2.** of, relating to, or belonging to the *Coelenterata.* [C19: from New Latin *Coelenterata,* hollow-intestined (creatures); see COEL-, ENTERON] —**coe·len·ter·ic** (ˌsiːlɛnˈtɛrɪk) *adj.*

coe·len·ter·on (sɪˈlɛntəˌrɒn) *n., pl.* **·ter·a** (-tərə). the simple saclike body cavity of a coelenterate.

coe·li·ac *or U.S.* **ce·li·ac** (ˈsiːlɪˌæk) *adj.* of or relating to the abdomen. [C17: from Latin *coeliacus,* from Greek *koiliakos,* from *koilia* belly]

coe·li·ac dis·ease *n.* a chronic intestinal disorder of young children, characterized by distention of the abdomen and frothy and pale foul-smelling stools as the result of inadequate absorption of fat.

coe·lom *or esp. U.S.* **ce·lom** (ˈsiːləum, -ləm) *n.* the body cavity of many multicellular animals, situated in the mesoderm and containing the digestive tract and other visceral organs. [C19: from Greek *koilōma* cavity, from *koilos* hollow; see COEL-]

coe·lo·stat (ˈsiːləˌstæt) *n.* an astronomical instrument consisting of a plane mirror mounted parallel to the earth's axis and rotated about this axis once every two days so that light from a celestial body, esp. the sun, is reflected onto a second mirror, which reflects the beam into a telescope. Compare **siderostat.** [C19: *coelo-,* from Latin *caelum* heaven, sky + -STAT]

coen·a·cle (ˈsɛnəkᵊl) *n.* a variant spelling of **cenacle.**

coe·nes·the·si·a, ce·nes·the·si·a (ˌsiːnɪsˈθiːzɪə) *or* **coe·nes·the·sis, ce·nes·the·sis** (ˌsiːnɪsˈθiːsɪs) *n. Psychol.* general awareness of one's own body. —**coe·nes·thet·ic** *or* **ce·nes·thet·ic** (ˌsiːnɪsˈθɛtɪk) *adj.*

coe·no- *or* (*before a vowel*) **coen-** *combining form.* common: *coenocyte.* [New Latin, from Greek *koinos* common]

coe·no·bite *or* **ce·no·bite** (ˈsiːnəʊˌbaɪt) *n.* a member of a religious order following a communal rule of life. Compare **eremite.** [C17: from Old French or ecclesiastical Latin, from Greek *koinobion* convent, from *koinos* common + *bios* life] —**coe·no·bit·ic** (ˌsiːnəʊˈbɪtɪk), ˌ**coe·no·ˈbit·i·cal** *or* ˌ**ce·no·ˈbit·ic,** ˌ**ce·no·ˈbit·i·cal** *adj.*

coe·no·cyte (ˈsiːnəʊˌsaɪt) *n. Botany.* a mass of protoplasm containing many nuclei and enclosed by a cell wall: occurs in many fungi and some algae. —**coe·no·cyt·ic** (ˌsiːnəˈsɪtɪk) *adj.*

coe·no·sarc (ˈsiːnəʊˌsɑːk) *n.* a system of protoplasmic branches connecting the polyps of colonial organisms such as corals. [C19: from COENO- + Greek *sarx* flesh]

coe·nu·rus (siːˈnjʊərəs) *n., pl.* **·ri** (-raɪ). an encysted larval form of the tapeworm *Multiceps,* containing many encapsulated heads. In sheep it can cause the gid, and when eaten by dogs it develops into several adult forms. [C19: from New Latin, from COENO- + Greek *oura* tail, literally: common tail, referring to the single body with its many heads]

co·en·zyme (kəʊˈɛnzaɪm) *n. Biochem.* a nonprotein organic molecule that forms a complex with certain enzymes and is essential for their activity. See also **apoenzyme.**

co·e·qual (kəʊˈiːkwəl) *adj.* **1.** of the same size, rank, etc. ~*n.* **2.** a person or thing equal with another. —**co·e·qual·i·ty** (ˌkəʊɪˈkwɒlɪtɪ) *or* **coˈe·qual·ness** *n.* —**coˈe·qual·ly** *adv.*

co·erce (kəʊˈɜːs) *vb.* (*tr.*) to compel or restrain by force or authority without regard to individual wishes or desires. [C17: from Latin *coercēre* to confine, restrain, from *co-* together + *arcēre* to enclose] —**coˈerc·er** *n.* —**coˈer·ci·ble** *adj.*

co·er·cion (kəʊˈɜːʃən) *n.* **1.** the act or power of coercing. **2.** government by force. —**coˈer·cion·ist** *n.* —**co·er·cive** (kəʊˈɜːsɪv) *adj.* —**coˈer·cive·ly** *adv.* —**coˈer·cive·ness** *n.*

co·er·cive force *n.* a measure of the magnetization of a ferromagnetic material as expressed by the external magnetic field strength necessary to demagnetize it. Measured in amperes per metre. Compare **coercivity.**

co·er·civ·i·ty (ˌkəʊɜːˈsɪvɪtɪ) *n.* the magnetic-field strength necessary to demagnetize a ferromagnetic material that is magnetized to saturation. It is measured in amperes per metre. Compare **coercive force.**

co·es·sen·tial (ˌkəʊɪˈsɛnʃəl) *adj. Theol.* being one in essence or nature: a term applied to the three persons of the Trinity. —**co·es·sen·ti·al·i·ty** (ˌkəʊɪˌsɛnʃɪˈælɪtɪ) *or* ˌ**co·es·ˈsen·tial·ness** *n.* —ˌ**co·es·ˈsen·tial·ly** *adv.*

co·e·ta·ne·ous (ˌkəʊɪˈteɪnɪəs) *adj. Rare.* of the same age or period. [C17: from Latin *coaetāneus,* from *co-* same + *aetās* age] —ˌ**co·e·ˈta·ne·ous·ly** *adv.* —ˌ**co·e·ˈta·ne·ous·ness** *n.*

co·e·ter·nal (ˌkəʊɪˈtɜːnəl) *adj.* existing together eternally. —ˌ**co·e·ˈter·nal·ly** *adv.*

co·e·ter·ni·ty (ˌkəʊɪˈtɜːnɪtɪ) *n.* existence for, from, or in eternity with another being.

Coeur de Lion (ˈkɜː də ˈliːən; *French* kœr dəˈljɔ̃) *n.* Lion Heart: an epithet applied to Richard I of England.

co·e·val (kəʊˈiːvəl) *adj.* **1.** of or belonging to the same age or generation. ~*n.* **2.** a contemporary. [C17: from Late Latin *coaevus* from Latin *co-* + *aevum* age] —**co·e·val·i·ty** (ˌkəʊɪˈvælɪtɪ) *n.* —**coˈe·val·ly** *adv.*

co·ex·ec·u·tor (ˌkəʊɪgˈzɛkjʊtə) *n. Law.* a person acting jointly with another or others as executor. —ˌ**co·ex·ˈec·u·trix** *fem. n.*

co·ex·ist (ˌkəʊɪgˈzɪst) *vb.* (*intr.*) **1.** to exist together at the same time or in the same place. **2.** to exist together in peace. —ˌ**co·ex·ˈist·ence** *n.* —ˌ**co·ex·ˈist·ent** *adj.*

co·ex·tend (ˌkəʊɪkˈstɛnd) *vb.* to extend or cause to extend equally in space or time. —ˌ**co·ex·ˈten·sion** *n.*

co·ex·ten·sive (ˌkəʊɪkˈstɛnsɪv) *adj.* of the same limits or extent. —ˌ**co·ex·ˈten·sive·ly** *adv.*

C. of C. *abbrev. for* Chamber of Commerce.

C. of E. *abbrev. for* Church of England.

coff (kɒf) *vb.* **coffs, coff·fing, coffed** *or* **coft.** *Scot.* to buy; purchase. [C15: from the past participle of obsolete *copen* to buy, of Low German origin; compare German *kaufen* to buy]

cof·fee (ˈkɒfɪ) *n.* **1. a.** a drink consisting of an infusion of the roasted and ground or crushed seeds of the coffee tree. **b.** (*as modifier*): *coffee grounds.* **2.** Also called: **coffee beans.** the beanlike seeds of the coffee tree, used to make this beverage. **3.** short for **coffee tree. 4. a.** a medium to dark-brown colour. **b.** (*as adj.*): *a coffee carpet.* [C16: from Italian *caffè,* from Turkish *kahve,* from Arabic *qahwah* coffee, wine]

cof·fee bag *n.* a small bag containing ground coffee beans, infused to make coffee.

cof·fee bar *n.* a café; snack bar.

cof·fee cup *n.* a cup from which coffee may be drunk, usually smaller than a teacup.

cof·fee house *n.* a place where coffee is served, esp. one that was a fashionable meeting place in 18th-century London.

cof·fee mill *n.* a machine for grinding roasted coffee beans.

cof·fee morn·ing *n.* a social event (often held in order to raise money) at which coffee is served.

cof·fee nut *n.* **1.** the fruit of the Kentucky coffee tree. **2.** another name for **Kentucky coffee tree.**

cof·fee·pot (ˈkɒfɪˌpɒt) *n.* a pot in which coffee is brewed or served.

cof·fee shop *n.* a shop where coffee is sold or drunk.

cof·fee ta·ble *n.* a low table, on which newspapers, etc., may be placed and coffee served.

cof·fee-ta·ble book *n.* a book designed to be looked at rather than read.

cof·fee tree *n.* **1.** any of several rubiaceous trees of the genus *Coffea,* esp. *C. arabica,* the seeds of which are used in the preparation of the beverage coffee. **2.** short for **Kentucky coffee tree.**

cof·fer (ˈkɒfə) *n.* **1.** a chest, esp. for storing valuables. **2.** (*usually pl.*) a store of money. **3.** Also called: **caisson, lacuna.** an ornamental sunken panel in a ceiling, dome, etc. **4.** a watertight box or chamber. **5.** short for **cofferdam.** ~*vb.* (*tr.*) **6.** to store, as in a coffer. **7.** to decorate (a ceiling, dome, etc.) with coffers. [C13: from Old French *coffre,* from Latin *cophinus* basket, from Greek *kophinos*]

cof·fer·dam (ˈkɒfəˌdæm) *n.* a watertight structure that encloses an area under water, pumped dry to enable construction work to be carried out. Often shortened to **coffer.**

cof·fin (ˈkɒfɪn) *n.* **1.** a box in which a corpse is buried or cremated. **2.** the part of a horse's foot that contains the coffin bone. **3.** Also called: **coffin block.** a frame for holding electrotype or stereotype printing plates. ~*vb.* **4.** (*tr.*) to place in or as in a coffin. [C14: from Old French *cofin,* from Latin *cophinus* basket; see COFFER]

cof·fin bone *n.* the terminal phalangeal bone inside the hoof of the horse and similar animals.

cof·fin nail *n. Chiefly U.S.* a slang word for **cigarette.**

cof·fle (ˈkɒfəl) *n.* (esp. formerly) a line of slaves, beasts, etc., fastened together. [C18: from Arabic *qāfilah* caravan]

C. of S. *abbrev. for* Church of Scotland.

cog[1] (kɒg) *n.* **1.** any of the teeth or projections on the rim of a gearwheel. **2.** a gearwheel, esp. a small one. **3.** a person or thing playing a small part in a large organization or process. ~*vb.* **cogs, cog·ging, cogged. 4.** (*tr.*) *Metallurgy.* to roll (cast steel ingots) to convert them into blooms. [C13: of Scandinavian origin; compare Danish *kogge,* Swedish *kugge,* Norwegian *kug*]

cog[2] (kɒg) *vb.* **cogs, cog·ging, cogged.** *Slang.* to cheat in (a game, esp. dice), as by loading a dice. [C16: originally a dice-playing term, of unknown origin]

cog[3] (kɒg) *n.* **1.** a tenon that projects from the end of a timber beam for fitting into a mortise. ~*vb.* **cogs, cog·ging, cogged. 2.** (*tr.*) to join (pieces of wood) with cogs. [C19: of uncertain origin]

cog. *abbrev. for* cognate.

co·gent (ˈkəʊdʒənt) *adj.* compelling belief or assent; forcefully convincing. [C17: from Latin *cōgent-, cōgēns,* driving together, from *cōgere,* from *co-* together + *agere* to drive] —ˈ**co·gen·cy** *n.* —ˈ**co·gent·ly** *adv.*

Cog·gan (ˈkɒgən) *n.* **Fred·er·ick Don·ald.** born 1909, Archbishop of York (1961–74); Archbishop of Canterbury from 1974.

cog·i·ta·ble (ˈkɒdʒɪtəbəl) *adj. Rare.* conceivable.

cog·i·tate (ˈkɒdʒɪˌteɪt) *vb.* to think deeply about (a problem, possibility, etc.); ponder. [C16: from Latin *cōgitāre,* from *co-* (intensive) + *agitāre* to turn over, AGITATE] —ˈ**cog·i·ˌtat·ing·ly** *adv.* —ˌ**cog·i·ˈta·tion** *n.* —ˈ**cog·i·ˌta·tor** *n.*

cog·i·ta·tive (ˈkɒdʒɪtətɪv) *adj.* **1.** capable of thinking. **2.** thoughtful. —ˈ**cog·i·ta·tive·ly** *adv.* —ˈ**cog·i·ta·tive·ness** *n.*

co·gi·to, er·go sum *Latin.* (ˈkɒgɪˌtəʊ ˈɜːgəʊ ˈsʊm) I think, therefore I am; the basis of Descartes' philosophy.

Cog·nac (ˈkɒnjæk; *French* kɔˈɲak) *n.* **1.** a town in SW France: centre of the district famed for its brandy. Pop.: 22 612 (1975). **2.** (*sometimes not cap.*) a high-quality grape brandy.

cog·nate (ˈkɒgneɪt) *adj.* **1.** akin; related: *cognate languages.* **2.** related by blood or descended from a common maternal ancestor. Compare **agnate. 3. cognate object.** *Grammar.* a noun functioning as the object of a verb to which it is etymologically related, as in *think a thought* or *sing a song.* ~*n.* **4.** something that is cognate with something else. [C17: from Latin *cognātus,* from *co-* same + *gnātus* born, variant of *nātus,* past participle of *nāscī* to be born] —ˈ**cog·nate·ly** *adv.* —ˈ**cog·nate·ness** *n.* —**cog·ˈna·tion** *n.*

cog·ni·tion (kɒgˈnɪʃən) *n.* **1.** the mental act or process by which knowledge is acquired, including perception, intuition, and reasoning. **2.** the knowledge that results from such an act or process. [C15: from Latin *cognitiō,* from *cognōscere* from *co-* (intensive) + *nōscere* to learn; see KNOW] —**cog·ˈni·tion·al** *adj.* —**cog·ni·tive** (ˈkɒgnɪtɪv) *adj.*

cog·ni·tive dis·so·nance *n. Psychol.* an uncomfortable state resulting from conflicting cognitions of an object.

cog·ni·za·ble *or* **cog·ni·sa·ble** (ˈkɒgnɪzəbəl, ˈkɒnɪ-) *adj.* **1.** perceptible. **2.** *Law.* susceptible to the jurisdiction of a court. —ˈ**cog·ni·za·bly** *or* ˈ**cog·ni·sa·bly** *adv.*

cog·ni·zance *or* **cog·ni·sance** (ˈkɒgnɪzəns, ˈkɒnɪ-) *n.* **1.** knowledge; acknowledgment. **2. take cognizance of.** to take notice of; acknowledge, esp. officially. **3.** the range or scope of knowledge or perception. **4.** *Law.* **a.** the right of a court to hear and determine a cause or matter. **b.** knowledge of certain facts upon which the court must act without requiring proof. **d.** *Chiefly U.S.* confession. **5.** *Heraldry.* a distinguishing badge or bearing. [C14: from Old French *conoissance,* from *conoistre* to know, from Latin *cognōscere* to learn; see COGNITION]

cog·ni·zant *or* **cog·ni·sant** (ˈkɒgnɪzənt, ˈkɒnɪ-) *adj.* (usually foll. by *of*) aware; having knowledge.

cog·nize *or* **cog·nise** (ˈkɒgnaɪz, kɒgˈnaɪz) *vb.* (*tr.*) to perceive, become aware of, or know.

cog·no·men (kɒgˈnəʊmɛn) *n., pl.* **·no·mens** *or* **·nom·i·na** (-ˈnɒmɪnə, -ˈnəʊ-). (originally) an ancient Roman's third name or nickname, which later became his family name. See also **agnomen, nomen, praenomen.** [C19: from Latin: additional name, from *co-* together + *nōmen* name; influenced in form by *cognōscere* to learn] —**cog·nom·i·nal** (kɒgˈnɒmɪnəl, -ˈnəʊ-) *adj.* —**cog·ˈnom·i·nal·ly** *adv.*

co·gno·scen·ti (ˌkɒnjəʊˈʃɛntɪ, ˌkɒgnə-) *or* **con·o·scen·ti** *pl. n., sing.* **·te** (-tiː). (*sometimes sing.*) people with informed appreciation of a particular field, esp. in the fine arts; connoisseurs. [C18: from obsolete Italian (modern *conoscente*), from Latin *cognōscere* to know, learn about]

co·gon (ˈkəʊgəʊn) *n.* any of the coarse tropical grasses of the genus *Imperata,* esp. *I. cylindrica* and *I. exaltata* of the Philippines, which are used for thatching. [from Spanish *cogón,* from Tagalog *kugon*]

cog rail·way *or* **cog·way** (ˈkɒgˌweɪ) *n. Chiefly U.S.* other terms for **rack railway.**

cog·wheel (ˈkɒgˌwiːl) *n.* another name for **gearwheel.**

co·hab·it (kəʊˈhæbɪt) *vb.* (*intr.*) to live together as husband and wife, esp. without being married. [C16: via Late Latin, from Latin *co-* together + *habitāre* to live] —**co·ˈhab·it·ant** *or* **co·ˈhab·it·er** *n.* —**co·ˌhab·i·ˈta·tion** *n.*

co·heir (kəʊˈɛə) *n.* a person who inherits jointly with others. —**co·ˈheir·ess** *fem. n.*

co·here (kəʊˈhɪə) *vb.* (*intr.*) **1.** to hold or stick firmly together. **2.** to connect or be connected logically; be consistent. **3.** *Physics.* to be held together by the action of molecular forces. [C16: from Latin *cohaerēre* from *co-* together + *haerēre* to cling, adhere]

co·her·ence (kəʊˈhɪərəns) *or* **co·her·en·cy** *n.* **1.** logical or natural connection or consistency. **2.** another word for **cohesion** (sense 1).

co·her·ent (kəʊˈhɪərənt) *adj.* **1.** capable of logical and consistent speech, thought, etc. **2.** logical; consistent and orderly. **3.** cohering or sticking together. **4.** *Physics.* (of two or more waves) having the same frequency and the same phase or a fixed phase difference: *coherent light.* **5.** (of a system of units) consisting only of units the quotient or product of any two of which yield the unit of the resultant quantity. —**co·ˈher·ent·ly** *adv.*

co·he·sion (kəʊˈhiːʒən) *n.* **1.** the act or state of cohering; tendency to unite. **2.** *Physics.* the force that holds together the atoms or molecules in a solid or liquid, as distinguished from adhesion. **3.** *Botany.* the fusion in some plants of flower parts, such as petals, that are usually separate. [C17: from Latin *cohaesus* stuck together, past participle of *cohaerēre* to COHERE]

co+he+sive (kəʊ'hi:sɪv) *adj.* **1.** characterized by or causing cohesion. **2.** tending to cohere or stick together. —**co+'he+sive+ly** *adv.* —**co+'he+sive+ness** *n.*

co+ho ('kəʊhəʊ) *n., pl.* **·ho** *or* **·hos.** a Pacific salmon, *Oncorhynchus kisutch.* Also called: **silver salmon.** [origin unknown; probably from an American Indian language]

co+ho+bate ('kəʊhəʊˌbeɪt) *vb.* (*tr.*) *Pharmacol.* to redistil (a distillate), esp. by allowing it to mingle with the remaining matter. [C17: from New Latin *cohobāre,* perhaps from Arabic *ka'aba* to repeat an action]

co+hort ('kəʊhɔ:t) *n.* **1.** one of the ten units of between 300 and 600 men in an ancient Roman Legion. **2.** any band of warriors or associates: *the cohorts of Satan.* **3.** *Biology.* a taxonomic group that is a subdivision of a subclass (usually of mammals) or subfamily (of plants). [C15: from Latin *cohors* yard, company of soldiers; related to *hortus* garden]

co+hosh ('kəʊhɒʃ, kəʊ'hɒʃ) *n.* any of several North American plants, such as the **blue cohosh** (*Caulophyllum thalictroides:* family *Leonticaceae*) and **black cohosh** (*Cimicifuga racemosa:* family *Ranunculaceae*). [C18: probably of Algonquian origin]

co+hune (kəʊ'hu:n) *n.* a tropical American feather palm, *Attalea* (or *Orbignya*) *cohune,* whose large oily nuts yield an oil similar to coconut oil. Also called: **cohune palm.** See also **coquilla nut.** [C19: from American Spanish, from South American Indian *ókhún*]

C.O.I. (in Britain) *abbrev. for* Central Office of Information.

coif (kɔɪf) *n.* **1.** a close-fitting cap worn under a veil, worn in the Middle Ages by many women but now only by nuns. **2.** any similar cap, such as a leather cap worn under a chainmail hood. **3.** *Brit.* (formerly) the white cap worn by a sergeant at law. **4.** a base for the elaborate women's headdresses of the 16th century. **5.** (kwɑ:f). a less common word for **coiffure** (sense 1). ~*vb.* **coifs, coif+fing, coiffed.** (*tr.*) **6.** to cover with or as if with a coif. **7.** (kwɑ:f). to arrange (the hair). [C14: from Old French *coiffe,* from Late Latin *cofea* helmet, cap, of obscure origin]

coif+feur (kwɑ:'fɜ:; *French* kwa'fœ:r) *n.* a hairdresser. —**coif+feuse** (kwɑ:'fɜ:z; *French* kwa'fø:z) *fem. n.*

coif+fure (kwɑ:'fjʊə; *French* kwa'fy:r) *n.* **1.** a hairstyle. **2.** an obsolete word for **headdress.** ~*vb.* **3.** (*tr.*) to dress or arrange (the hair).

coign *or* **coigne** (kɔɪn) *n.* variant spellings of **quoin.**

coign of van+tage *n.* an advantageous position or stance for observation or action.

coil[1] (kɔɪl) *vb.* **1.** to wind or gather (ropes, hair, etc.) into loops or (of rope, hair, etc.) to be formed in such loops. **2.** (*intr.*) to move in a winding course. ~*n.* **3.** something wound in a connected series of loops. **4.** a single loop of such a series. **5.** an arrangement of pipes in a spiral or loop, as in a condenser. **6.** an electrical conductor wound into the form of a spiral, sometimes with a soft iron core, to provide inductance or a magnetic field. See also **induction coil. 7.** an intrauterine contraceptive device in the shape of a coil. **8.** the transformer in a petrol engine that supplies the high voltage to the sparking plugs. [C16: from Old French *coillir* to collect together; see CULL] —**'coil+er** *n.*

coil[2] (kɔɪl) *n.* the troubles and activities of the world (in the Shakespearian phrase **this mortal coil**). [C16: of unknown origin]

coil spring *n.* a helical spring formed from wire.

Co+im+ba+tore (ˌkɔ:ɪmbə'tɔ:) *n.* an industrial city in SW India, in W Tamil Nadu. Pop.: 356 368 (1971).

Coim+bra (*Portuguese* 'kwimbrə) *n.* a city in central Portugal: capital of Portugal from 1190 to 1260; seat of the country's oldest university. Pop.: 108 046 (1970).

coin (kɔɪn) *n.* **1.** a metal disc or piece used as money. **2.** metal currency, as opposed to securities, paper currency, etc. **3.** *Architect.* a variant spelling of **quoin. 4. pay (a person) back in (his) own coin.** to treat (a person) in the way that he has treated others. ~*vb.* **5.** (*tr.*) to make or stamp (coins). **6.** (*tr.*) to make into a coin. **7.** (*tr.*) to fabricate or invent (words, etc.). **8.** (*tr.*) *Informal.* to make (money) rapidly (esp. in the phrase **coin it in**). **9. to coin a phrase.** said ironically after one uses a cliché. **10. the other side of the coin.** the opposite view of a matter. [C14: from Old French: stamping die, from Latin *cuneus* wedge] —**'coin+a·ble** *adj.* —**'coin+er** *n.*

coin+age ('kɔɪnɪdʒ) *n.* **1.** coins collectively. **2.** the act of striking coins. **3.** the currency of a country. **4.** the act of inventing something, esp. a word or phrase. **5.** a newly invented word, phrase, usage, etc.

coin box *n.* the part of a coin-operated machine into which coins are placed.

co+in+cide (ˌkəʊɪn'saɪd) *vb.* (*intr.*) **1.** to occur or exist simultaneously. **2.** to be identical in nature, character, etc. **3.** to agree. [C18: from Medieval Latin *coincidere,* from Latin *co-* together + *incidere* to occur, befall, from *cadere* to fall]

co+in+ci+dence (kəʊ'ɪnsɪdəns) *n.* **1.** a chance occurrence of events remarkable either for being simultaneous or for apparently being connected. **2.** the fact, condition, or state of coinciding. **3.** (*modifier*) *Electronics.* of or relating to a circuit that produces an output pulse only when both its input terminals receive pulses within a specified interval: *coincidence gate.* Compare **anticoincidence.**

co+in+ci+dent (kəʊ'ɪnsɪdənt) *adj.* **1.** having the same position in space or time. **2.** (usually *postpositive* and foll. by *with*) in exact agreement; consonant. —**co+ˌin+ci+'dent+al** *adj.* —**co+ˌin+ci+'dent+al+ly** *adv.*

coin-op ('kɔɪnˌɒp) *n.* a launderette or other service installation in which the machines are operated by insertion of a coin.

co+in+sur+ance (ˌkəʊɪn'ʃʊərəns, -'ʃɔ:-) *n.* **1.** a method of insurance by which property is insured for a certain percentage of its value by a commercial insurance policy while the owner assumes liability for the remainder. **2.** joint insurance held by two or more persons.

co+in+sure (ˌkəʊɪn'ʃʊə, -'ʃɔ:) *vb.* **1.** to take out coinsurance. **2.** to insure (property) jointly with another. —ˌ**co+in+'sur+er** *n.*

Coin+treau ('kwɑ:ntrəʊ) *n. Trademark.* a colourless liqueur with orange flavouring.

coir ('kɔɪə) *n.* the fibre prepared from the husk of the coconut, used in making rope and matting. [C16: from Malayalam *kāyar* rope, from *kāyaru* to be twisted]

Coire (kwa:r) *n.* the French name for **Chur.**

coit (kɔɪt) *n. Austral. slang.* buttocks; backside. Also called: **quoit.** [C20: perhaps a variant and special use of QUOIT, referring to roundness]

co·i+tus ('kəʊɪtəs) *or* **co·i+tion** (kəʊ'ɪʃən) *n.* a technical term for **sexual intercourse.** [C18 *coitus:* from Latin: a uniting, from *coīre* to meet, from *īre* to go] —**'co·i+tal** *adj.*

co·i+tus in·ter+rup+tus (ˌɪntə'rʌptəs) *n.* the deliberate withdrawal of the penis from the vagina before ejaculation.

co·i+tus res+er+va+tus (ˌrɛzə'vɑ:təs) *n.* the deliberate delaying or avoidance of orgasm during intercourse.

co+jo+nes *Spanish.* (ko'xones) **1.** testicles. **2.** manly courage.

coke[1] (kəʊk) *n.* **1.** a solid-fuel product containing about 80 per cent of carbon produced by distillation of coal to drive off its volatile constituents: used as a fuel and in metallurgy as a reducing agent for converting metal oxides into metals. **2.** any similar material, such as the layer formed in the cylinders of a car engine by incomplete combustion of the fuel. ~*vb.* **3.** to become or convert into coke. [C17: probably a variant of C14 northern English dialect *colk* core, of obscure origin]

coke[2] (kəʊk) *n. Slang.* short for **cocaine.**

Coke[1] (kəʊk) *n. Trademark.* short for **Coca-Cola.**

Coke[2] (kʊk, kəʊk) *n.* Sir **Ed·ward.** 1552–1634, English jurist, noted for his defence of the common law against encroachment from the Crown: the Petition of Right (1628) was largely his work.

cok·u+lo+ris (ˌkɒkə'lɔ:rɪs) *n. Films.* a palette with irregular holes, placed between lighting and camera to prevent glare. [C20: of unknown origin]

col (kɒl; *French* kɔl) *n.* **1.** a strip of land or a ridge connecting two outlying features, such as mountain peaks. **2.** *Meteorol.* a pressure region between two anticyclones and two depressions, associated with variable weather. [C19: from French: neck, col, from Latin *collum* neck]

col. *abbrev. for:* **1.** colour(ed). **2.** column.

Col. *abbrev. for:* **1.** Colombia(n). **2.** Colonel. **3.** *Bible.* Colossians.

col-[1] *prefix.* variant of **com-** before *l: collateral.*

col-[2] *prefix.* variant of **colo-** before a vowel: *colectomy.*

co·la[1] *or* **ko·la** ('kəʊlə) *n.* **1.** either of two tropical sterculiaceous trees, *Cola nitida* or *C. acuminata,* widely cultivated in tropical regions for their seeds (see **cola nut**). **2.** a sweet carbonated drink flavoured with cola nuts. [C18: from *kola,* probably variant of Mandingo *kolo* nut]

co·la[2] ('kəʊlə) *n.* the plural of **colon**[1] (sense 3) or **colon**[2].

col+an+der ('kɒləndə, 'kʌl-) *or* **cul+len+der** *n.* a pan with a perforated bottom for straining or rinsing foods. [C14 *colyndore,* probably from Old Provençal *colador,* via Medieval Latin, from Late Latin *cōlāre* to filter, from Latin *cōlum* sieve]

co·la nut *n.* any of the seeds of the cola tree, which contain caffeine and theobromine and are used medicinally and in the manufacture of soft drinks.

co+lat·i·tude (kəʊ'lætɪˌtju:d) *n. Astronomy, navigation.* the complement of the celestial latitude.

Col·bert (*French* kɔl'bɛ:r) *n.* **1. Clau·dette** (klo'dɛt). original name *Claudette Cauchoin,* born 1905, U.S. film actress, born in France. Her films include *It happened one Night* (1934), *Cleopatra* (1934), *The Palm Beach Story* (1942), *The Egg and I* (1947), and *Three came Home* (1950). **2. Jean Bap·tiste** (ʒã ba'tist). 1619–83, French statesman; chief minister to Louis XIV: reformed the taille and pursued a mercantalist policy, creating a powerful navy and merchant fleet and building roads and canals.

col+can+non (kəl'kænən, 'kɒlˌkænən) *n.* a dish, originating in Ireland, of potatoes and cabbage or other greens boiled and mashed together. [C18: from Irish Gaelic *cāl ceannan,* literally: white-headed cabbage]

Col+ches+ter ('kəʊltʃɪstə) *n.* a town in E England, in NE Essex. Pop.: 76 145 (1971). Latin name: **Camulodunum.**

col+chi+cine ('kɒltʃɪˌsi:n, -sɪn, 'kɒlkɪ-) *n.* a pale-yellow crystalline alkaloid extracted from seeds or corms of the autumn crocus and used in the treatment of gout. Formula: $C_{22}H_{25}NO_6$. [C19: from COLCHICUM + -INE[2]]

col+chi+cum ('kɒltʃɪkəm, 'kɒlkɪ-) *n.* **1.** any Eurasian liliaceous plant of the genus *Colchicum,* such as the autumn crocus. **2.** the dried seeds or corms of the autumn crocus: a source of colchicine. [C16: from Latin, from Greek *kolkhikon,* from *kolkhikos* of COLCHIS]

Col+chis ('kɒlkɪs) *n.* an ancient country on the Black Sea south of the Caucasus; the land of Medea and the Golden Fleece in Greek mythology.

col+co+thar ('kɒlkəˌθɑ:) *n.* a finely powdered form of ferric oxide produced by heating ferric sulphate and used as a pigment and as jewellers' rouge. Also called: **crocus.** [C17: from

French *colcotar*, from Spanish *colcótar*, from Arabic dialect *qulqutār*]

cold (kəʊld) *adj.* **1.** having relatively little warmth; of a rather low temperature: *cold weather; cold hands.* **2.** without sufficient or proper warmth: *this meal is cold.* **3.** lacking in affection, enthusiasm, or warmth of feeling: *a cold manner.* **4.** not affected by emotion; objective: *cold logic.* **5.** dead. **6.** sexually unresponsive or frigid. **7.** lacking in freshness: *a cold scent; cold news.* **8.** chilling to the spirit; depressing. **9.** (of a colour) having violet, blue, or green predominating; giving no sensation of warmth. **10.** *Metallurgy.* denoting or relating to a process in which work-hardening occurs as a result of the plastic deformation of a metal at too low a temperature for annealing to take place. **11.** *Informal.* (of a seeker) far from the object of a search. **12. cold comfort.** little or no comfort. **13. cold steel.** the use of bayonets, knives, etc., in combat. **14. in cold blood.** without feeling pity or remorse; ruthlessly. **15. leave (someone) cold.** *Informal.* to fail to excite: *the performance left me cold.* **16. throw cold water on.** *Informal.* to be unenthusiastic about or discourage. ~*n.* **17.** the absence of heat regarded as a positive force: *the cold took away our breath.* **18.** the sensation caused by loss or lack of heat. **19. (out) in the cold.** *Informal.* neglected; ignored. **20.** an acute viral infection of the upper respiratory passages characterized by discharge of watery mucus from the nose, sneezing, etc. ~*adv.* **21.** *Informal.* without preparation: *he played his part cold.* **22.** *Informal, chiefly U.S.* thoroughly: *he learnt his lesson cold.* [Old English *ceald;* related to Old Norse *kaldr,* Gothic *kalds,* Old High German *kalt;* see COOL] —**'cold·ish** *adj.* —**'cold·ly** *adv.* —**'cold·ness** *n.*

cold-blood·ed *adj.* **1.** having or showing a lack of feeling or pity: *a cold-blooded killing.* **2.** *Informal.* particularly sensitive to cold. **3.** (of all animals except birds and mammals) having a body temperature that varies with that of the surroundings. Technical term: **poikilothermic.** —**,cold-'blood·ed·ly** *adv.* —**,cold-'blood·ed·ness** *n.*

cold cath·ode *n. Electronics.* a cathode from which electrons are emitted at an ambient temperature, due to a high potential gradient at the surface.

cold chis·el *n.* a toughened steel chisel.

cold cream *n.* an emulsion of water and fat used cosmetically for softening and cleansing the skin.

cold cuts *pl. n.* cooked meats sliced and served cold.

cold-drawn *adj.* (of metal wire, bars, etc.) having been drawn unheated through a die to reduce dimensions, toughen, and improve surface finish.

cold duck *n.* an alcoholic beverage made from equal parts of burgundy and champagne.

cold feet *n. Informal.* loss or lack of courage or confidence.

cold frame *n.* an unheated wooden frame with a glass top, used to protect young plants from the cold.

cold front *n. Meteorology.* **1.** the boundary line between a warm air mass and the cold air pushing it from beneath and behind as it moves. **2.** the line on the earth's surface where the cold front meets it. ~Compare **warm front.**

cold-heart·ed *adj.* lacking in feeling or warmth; unkind. —**,cold-'heart·ed·ly** *adv.* —**,cold-'heart·ed·ness** *n.*

cold light *n.* light emitted at low temperatures from a source that is not incandescent, as in fluorescence, phosphorescence, bioluminescence, or triboluminescence.

cold pack *n.* **1. a.** a method of lowering the body temperature by wrapping a person in a sheet soaked in cold water. **b.** the sheet so used. **2.** a tinning process in which raw food is packed in cans or jars and then heated.

cold rub·ber *n.* synthetic rubber made at low temperatures (about 5°C). It is stronger than that made at higher temperatures and is used for car tyres.

cold shoul·der *n. Informal.* **1.** (often preceded by *the*) a show of indifference; a slight. ~*vb.* **cold-shoul·der.** (*tr.*) **2.** to treat with indifference.

cold snap *n.* a sudden short spell of cold weather.

cold sore *n.* a cluster of blisters at the margin of the lips that sometimes accompanies the common cold, caused by a viral infection. Technical name: **herpes labialis.**

cold stor·age *n.* **1.** the storage of things in an artificially cooled place for preservation. **2.** *Informal.* a state of temporary suspension: *to put an idea into cold storage.*

cold sweat *n. Informal.* a bodily reaction to fear or nervousness, characterized by chill and moist skin.

cold tur·key *n. U.S. slang.* a method of curing drug addiction by abrupt withdrawal of all doses.

cold war *n.* a state of political hostility and military tension between two countries or power blocs, involving propaganda, subversion, threats, etc., esp. that between the American and Soviet blocs after World War II (the **Cold War**).

cold war·ri·or *n.* a person who engages in or promotes a cold war.

cold wave *n.* **1.** *Meteorol.* a sudden spell of low temperatures over a wide area, often following the passage of a cold front. **2.** *Hairdressing.* a permanent wave made by chemical agents applied at normal temperatures.

cold-weld *vb.* (*tr.*) to join (two metal surfaces) without heat by forcing them together so that the oxide films are broken and adhesion occurs. —**cold weld·ing** *n.*

cold work *n.* **1.** the craft of shaping metal without heat. ~*vb.* **cold-work.** (*tr.*) **2.** to shape metal in this way.

cole (kəʊl) *n.* any of various plants of the genus *Brassica,* such as the cabbage and rape. Also called: **colewort.** [Old English *cāl,* from Latin *caulis* plant stalk, cabbage]

co·lec·to·my (kə'lɛktəmɪ) *n., pl.* **·mies.** surgical removal of part or all of the colon.

cole·man·ite ('kəʊlmə,naɪt) *n.* a colourless or white glassy mineral consisting of hydrated calcium borate in monoclinic crystalline form. It occurs with and is a source of borax. Formula: $Ca_2B_6O_{11}.5H_2O$. [C19: named after William T. *Coleman* (1824–93), American pioneer, owner of the mine in which it was discovered]

col·e·op·ter·an (,kɒlɪ'ɒptərən) *n. also* **col·e·op·ter·on. 1.** any of the insects of the cosmopolitan order *Coleoptera,* in which the forewings are modified to form shell-like protective elytra. The order includes the beetles and weevils. ~*adj. also* **col·e·op·ter·ous. 2.** of, relating to, or belonging to the order *Coleoptera.* [C18: from New Latin *Coleoptera,* from Greek *koleoptera,* from *koleopteros* sheath-winged, from *koleon* sheath + *pteron* wing]

col·e·op·tile (,kɒlɪ'ɒptaɪl) *n.* a protective sheath around the plumule in grasses. [C19: from New Latin *coleoptilum,* from Greek *koleon* sheath + *ptilon* down, soft plumage]

col·e·o·rhi·za (,kɒlɪə'raɪzə) *n., pl.* **·zae** (-zi:). a protective sheath around the radicle in grasses. [C19: from New Latin, from Greek *koleon* sheath + *rhiza* root]

Co·le·ridge ('kəʊlərɪdʒ) *n.* **Sam·u·el Tay·lor.** 1772–1834, English Romantic poet and critic, noted for poems such as *The Rime of the Ancient Mariner* (1798), *Kubla Khan* (1816), and *Christabel* (1816), and for his critical work *Biographia Literaria* (1817).

cole·slaw ('kəʊl,slɔ:) *n.* a salad of shredded cabbage, mayonnaise, carrots, onions, etc. [C19: from Dutch *koolsla,* from *koolsalade,* literally: cabbage salad]

Col·et ('kɒlɪt) *n.* **John.** ?1467–1519, English humanist and theologian; founder of St. Paul's School, London (1509).

Co·lette (kɒ'lɛt) *n.* pen name of *Sidonie Gabrielle Claudine Colette.* 1873–1954, French novelist; her works include *Chéri* (1920), *Gigi* (1944), and the series of *Claudine* books.

co·le·us ('kəʊlɪəs) *n., pl.* **·us·es.** any plant of the Old World genus *Coleus:* cultivated for their variegated leaves, typically marked with red, yellow, or white: family *Labiatae* (labiates). [C19: from New Latin, from Greek *koleos,* variant of *koleon* sheath; from the way in which the stamens are joined]

cole·wort ('kəʊl,wɜ:t) *n.* another name for **cole.**

col·ey ('kəʊlɪ, 'kɒlɪ) *n. Brit.* any of various edible fishes, esp. the coalfish.

col·ic ('kɒlɪk) *n.* a condition characterized by acute spasmodic abdominal pain, esp. that caused by inflammation, distention, etc., of the gastrointestinal tract. [C15: from Old French *colique,* from Late Latin *cōlicus* ill with colic, from Greek *kōlon,* variant of *kolon* COLON[2]] —**'col·ick·y** *adj.*

col·ic·root ('kɒlɪk,ru:t) *n.* **1.** either of two North American liliaceous plants, *Aletris farinosa* or *A. aurea,* having tubular white or yellow flowers and a bitter root formerly used to relieve colic. **2.** any of various other plants formerly used to relieve colic.

col·ic·weed ('kɒlɪk,wi:d) *n.* any of several plants of the genera *Dicentra* or *Corydalis,* such as the squirrel corn and Dutchman's-breeches: family *Fumariaceae.*

col·i·form bac·te·ri·a ('kɒlɪfɔ:m) *n.* a large group of bacteria that inhabit the intestinal tract of man and animals and may cause disease.

Co·lig·ny *or* **Co·lig·ni** (*French* kɔli'ɲi) *n.* **Gas·pard de** (gas'pa:r də). 1519–72, French Huguenot leader.

Co·li·ma (*Spanish* ko'lima) *n.* **1.** a state of SW Mexico, on the Pacific coast: mainly a coastal plain, rising to the foothills of the Sierra Madre, with important mineral resources. Capital: Colima. Pop.: 241 153 (1970). Area: 5455 sq. km (2106 sq. miles). **2.** a city in SW Mexico, capital of Colima state, on the Colima River. Pop.: 72 074 (1970). **3. Ne·va·do de.** a volcano in SW Mexico, in Jalisco state. Height: 4339 m (14 235 ft.).

col·i·se·um (,kɒlɪ'sɪəm) *or* **col·os·se·um** (,kɒlə'sɪəm) *n.* a large building, such as a stadium or theatre, used for entertainments, sports, etc. [C18: from Medieval Latin *Colisseum,* variant of COLOSSEUM]

co·li·tis (kɒ'laɪtɪs, kə-) *or* **col·o·ni·tis** (,kɒlə'naɪtɪs) *n.* inflammation of the colon. —**co·lit·ic** (kɒ'lɪtɪk) *adj.*

coll. *abbrev. for:* **1.** colleague. **2.** collection. **3.** collector. **4.** college. **5.** collegiate. **6.** colloquial.

col·lab·o·rate (kə'læbə,reɪt) *vb.* (*intr.*) **1.** (often foll. by *on, with,* etc.) to work with another or others on a joint project. **2.** to cooperate as a traitor, esp. with an enemy occupying one's own country. [C19: from Late Latin *collabōrāre,* from Latin *com-* together + *labōrāre* to work] —**col·,lab·o·'ra·tion** *n.* —**col·'lab·o·ra·tive** *adj.* —**col·'lab·o·,ra·tor** *or* **col·,lab·o·'ra·tion·ist** *n.*

col·lage (kə'lɑ:ʒ, kɒ-; *French* kɔ'la:ʒ) *n.* **1.** an art form in which compositions are made out of pieces of paper, cloth, photographs, and other miscellaneous objects, juxtaposed and pasted on a dry ground. **2.** a composition made in this way. **3.** any collection of unrelated things. [C20: French, from *coller* to stick, from *colle* glue, from Greek *kolla*] —**col·'lag·ist** *n.*

col·la·gen ('kɒlədʒən) *n.* a fibrous scleroprotein of connective tissue and bones that is rich in glycine and proline and yields gelatin on boiling. [C19: from Greek *kolla* glue + -GEN] —**col·la·gen·ic** (,kɒlə'dʒɛnɪk) *or* **col·la·gen·ous** (kə'lædʒənəs) *adj.*

col·lap·sar (kɒ'læpsɑ:) *n. Astronomy.* another name for **black hole.**

col·lapse (kə'læps) *vb.* **1.** (*intr.*) to fall down or cave in suddenly: *the whole building collapsed.* **2.** (*intr.*) to fail completely: *his story collapsed on investigation.* **3.** (*intr.*) to break down or fall down from lack of strength. **4.** to fold (furniture, etc.) compactly or (of furniture, etc.) to be designed to fold compactly. ~*n.* **5.** the act or instance of suddenly falling down, caving in, or crumbling. **6.** a sudden failure or breakdown. [C18: from Latin *collāpsus,* from *collābī* to fall in ruins, from *lābī* to fall] —**col+'laps+i·ble** *or* **col+'laps+a·ble** *adj.* —**col+,laps+i·'bil+i·ty** *n.*

col+lar ('kɒlə) *n.* **1.** the part of a garment around the neck and shoulders, often detachable or folded over. **2.** any band, necklace, garland, etc., encircling the neck: *a collar of flowers.* **3.** a band or chain of leather, rope, or metal placed around an animal's neck to restrain, harness, or identify it. **4.** *Biology.* a marking or structure resembling a collar, such as that found around the necks of some birds or at the junction of a stem and a root. **5.** a section of a shaft or rod having a locally increased diameter to provide a bearing seat or a locating ring. **6.** a cut of meat, esp. bacon, taken from around the neck of an animal. **7. hot under the collar.** *Informal.* angry; excited. ~*vb.* (*tr.*) **8.** to put a collar on; furnish with a collar. **9.** to seize by the collar. **10.** *Informal.* to seize; arrest; detain. [C13: from Latin *collāre* neckband, neck chain, collar, from *collum* neck]

col·lar+bone ('kɒlə,bəʊn) *n.* the nontechnical name for **clavicle.**

col+lar cell *n.* another name for **choanocyte.**

col+lard ('kɒləd) *n.* **1.** a variety of the cabbage, *Brassica oleracea acephala,* having a crown of edible leaves. See also **kale. 2.** the leaves of this plant, eaten as a vegetable. [C18: variant of COLEWORT]

col+lared dove *n.* a European dove, *Streptopelia decaocto,* having a brownish-grey plumage with a black band on the back of the neck.

col+lar+ette (,kɒlə'rɛt) *n.* a woman's fur or lace collar.

collat. *abbrev. for* collateral.

col+late (kɒ'leɪt, kə-) *vb.* (*tr.*) **1.** to examine and compare (texts, statements, etc.) in order to note points of agreement and disagreement. **2.** (in library work) to check the number and order of (the pages of a book). **3.** *Bookbinding.* **a.** to check the sequence of (the sections of a book) after gathering. **b.** a nontechnical word for **gather** (sense 9). **4.** (often foll. by *to*) *Christianity.* to appoint (an incumbent) to a benefice. [C16: from Latin *collātus* brought together (past participle of *conferre* to gather) from *com-* together + *lātus,* past participle of *ferre* to bring]

col+lat+er+al (kɒ'lætərəl, kə-) *n.* **1. a.** security pledged for the repayment of a loan. **b.** (*as modifier*): *a collateral loan.* **2.** a person, animal, or plant descended from the same ancestor as another but through a different line. ~*adj.* **3.** situated or running side by side. **4.** descended from a common ancestor but through different lines. **5.** serving to support or corroborate. **6.** aside from the main issue. **7.** uniting in tendency. [C14: from Medieval Latin *collaterālis,* from Latin *com-* together + *laterālis* of the side, from *latus* side] —**col+'lat+er+al+ly** *adv.*

col+la+tion (kɒ'leɪʃən, kə-) *n.* **1.** the act or process of collating. **2.** a description of the technical features of a book. **3.** *R.C. Church.* a light meal permitted on fast days. **4.** any light informal meal. **5.** the appointment of a clergyman to a benefice.

col+la+tive (kɒ'leɪtɪv, 'kɒlə-) *adj.* **1.** involving collation. **2.** (of benefices) presented or held by collation.

col+la+tor (kɒ'leɪtə, kəʊ-; 'kɒleɪtə, 'kəʊ-) *n.* **1.** a person or machine that collates texts or manuscripts. **2.** *Computer technol.* a device for matching or checking punched cards in separate files and for merging two or more files sorted into the same ordered sequence.

col+league ('kɒli:g) *n.* a fellow worker or member of a staff, department, etc. [C16: from French *collègue,* from Latin *collēga* one selected at the same time as another, from *com-* together + *lēgāre* to choose]

col+lect[1] (kə'lɛkt) *vb.* **1.** to gather together or be gathered together. **2.** to accumulate (stamps, books, etc.) as a hobby or for study. **3.** (*tr.*) to call for or receive payment of (taxes, dues, etc.). **4.** (*tr.*) to regain control of (oneself, one's emotions, etc.) as after a shock or surprise: *he collected his wits.* **5.** (*tr.*) to fetch: *collect your own post.* **6.** (*intr.;* sometimes foll. by *on*) *Slang.* to receive large sums of money, as from an investment, etc.: *he really collected when the will was read.* **7.** *Austral. informal.* to collide with; be hit by. **8. collect on delivery.** the U.S. term for **cash on delivery.** ~*adv., adj.* **9.** *U.S.* (of telephone calls, etc.) on a transferred-charge basis. ~*n. Austral. informal.* a winning bet. [C16: from Latin *collēctus* collected, from *colligere* to gather together, from *com-* together + *legere* to gather] —**col+'lect+a·ble** *or* **col+'lect+i·ble** *adj.*

col+lect[2] ('kɒlɛkt) *n. Christianity.* a short Church prayer generally preceding the lesson or epistle in Communion and other services. [C13: from Medieval Latin *collecta* (from the phrase *ōrātiō ad collēctam* prayer at the (people's) assembly), from Latin *colligere* to COLLECT[1]]

col+lec+ta+ne·a (,kɒlɛk'teɪnɪə) *pl. n.* a collection of excerpts from one or more authors; miscellany; anthology. [C18: from Latin, from *collectāneus* assembled, from *colligere* to COLLECT[1]]

col+lect+ed (kə'lɛktɪd) *adj.* **1.** in full control of one's faculties; composed. **2.** assembled in totality or brought together into one volume or a set of volumes: *the collected works of Dickens.* **3.** (of a horse or a horse's pace) controlled so that movement is in short restricted steps: *a collected canter.* —**col+'lect+ed+ly** *adv.* —**col+'lect+ed+ness** *n.*

col+lec+tion (kə'lɛkʃən) *n.* **1.** the act or process of collecting. **2.** a number of things collected or assembled together. **3.** something gathered into a mass or pile; accumulation: *a collection of rubbish.* **4.** a sum of money collected or solicited, as in church. **5.** removal, esp. regular removal of letters from a postbox. **6.** (*often pl.*) (at Oxford University) a college examination or an oral report by a tutor.

col+lec+tive (kə'lɛktɪv) *adj.* **1.** formed or assembled by collection. **2.** forming a whole or aggregate. **3.** of, done by, or characteristic of individuals acting in cooperation. ~*n.* **4. a.** a cooperative enterprise or unit, such as a collective farm. **b.** the members of such a cooperative. **5.** short for **collective noun.** —**col+'lec+tive+ly** *adv.* —**col+'lec+tive+ness** *n.*

col+lec+tive bar+gain+ing *n.* negotiation between a trade union and an employer or an employers' organization on the incomes and working conditions of the employees.

col+lec+tive farm *n.* (chiefly in Communist countries) a farm or group of farms managed and owned, through the state, by the community. Russian name: **kolkhoz.**

col+lec+tive fruit *n.* another name for **multiple fruit.**

col+lec+tive noun *n.* a noun that is singular in form but that refers to a group of people or things.

Usage. Collective nouns are usually used with singular verbs: *the family is on holiday; General Motors is mounting a big sales campaign.* In British usage, however, plural verbs are sometimes employed in this context, esp. where reference is being made to a collection of individual objects or persons rather than to the group as a unit: *the family are all on holiday.* Care should be taken that the same collective noun is not treated as both singular and plural in the same sentence: *the family is well and sends its best wishes* or *the family are all well and send their best wishes,* but not *the family is well and send their best wishes.*

col+lec+tive own+er+ship *n.* ownership by a group for the benefit of members of that group.

col+lec+tive pitch lev+er *n.* a lever in a helicopter to change the angle of attack of all the rotor blades simultaneously, causing it to rise or descend. Compare **cyclic pitch lever.**

col+lec+tive se+cu+ri·ty *n.* a system of maintaining world peace and security by concerted action on the part of the nations of the world.

col+lec+tive un+con+scious *n. Psychol.* (in Jungian psychological theory) a part of the unconscious mind incorporating patterns of memories, instincts, and experiences common to all mankind. These patterns are inherited, may be arranged into archetypes, and are observable through their effects on dreams, behaviour, etc.

col+lec+tiv+ism (kə'lɛktɪ,vɪzəm) *n.* **1.** the principle of ownership of the means of production, by the state or the people. **2.** a social system based upon such a principle. —**col+'lec+tiv+ist** *n.* —**col+,lec+tiv+'is+tic** *adj.*

col+lec+tiv+i·ty (,kɒlɛk'tɪvɪtɪ) *n., pl.* **·ties. 1.** the quality or state of being collective. **2.** a collective whole or aggregate. **3.** people regarded as a whole.

col+lec+ti+vize *or* **col+lec+ti+vise** (kə'lɛktɪ,vaɪz) *vb.* (*tr.*) to organize according to the principles of collectivism. —**col+,lec+tiv·i+'za+tion** *or* **col+,lec+tiv·i+'sa+tion** *n.*

col+lec+tor (kə'lɛktə) *n.* **1.** a person or thing that collects. **2.** a person employed to collect debts, rents, etc. **3.** the head of a district administration in India. **4.** a person who collects or amasses objects as a hobby. **5.** *Electronics.* the region in a transistor into which charge carriers flow from the base. —**col+'lec+tor+,ship** *n.*

col+lec+to+rate (kə'lɛktərɪt) *n.* the office of a collector in India.

col+leen ('kɒli:n, kɒ'li:n) *n.* **1.** an Irish word for **girl. 2.** an Irish girl. [C19: from Irish *cailín* a little girl, from *caile* girl]

col+lege ('kɒlɪdʒ) *n.* **1.** an institution of higher education; part of a university. **2.** a school or an institution providing specialized courses or teaching: *a college of music.* **3.** the building or buildings in which a college is housed. **4.** the staff and students of a college. **5.** an organized body of persons with specific rights and duties: *an electoral college.* See also **Sacred College. 6.** a body of clerics living in community and supported by endowment. **7.** *Chiefly Brit.* an obsolete slang word for **prison.** [C14: from Latin *collēgium* company, society, band of associates, from *collēga;* see COLLEAGUE]

col+lege of ad+vanced tech+nol+o·gy *n. Brit.* a college offering degree or equivalent courses in technology, with research facilities. Abbrev.: **CAT**

col+lege of arms *n.* any of several institutions in Great Britain having a royal charter to deal with matters of heraldry, grant armorial bearings, record and trace genealogies, etc. Also called: **herald's college.**

Col+lege of Car+di+nals *n. R.C. Church.* the collective body of cardinals having the function of electing and advising the pope.

col+lege of ed·u+ca+tion *n. Brit.* a professional training college for teachers.

Col+lege of Jus+tice *n.* the official name for the Scottish Court of Session; the supreme court of Scotland.

col+lege pud+ding *n. Brit.* a baked or steamed suet pudding containing dried fruit and spice.

col+le·gi·an (kə'li:dʒɪən) *n.* a current member of a college; student.

col+le·gi+ate (kə'li:dʒɪɪt) *adj.* **1.** Also: **col+le·gi·al·** (kə'li:dʒɪəl). of or relating to a college or college students. **2.** (of a university) composed of various colleges of equal standing. ~*n.* **3.** (in various Canadian provinces) a high school offering a purely academic education.

col+le·gi+ate church *n.* **1.** *R.C. Church, Church of England.* a church that has an endowed chapter of canons and prebendaries attached to it but that is not a cathedral. **2.** *U.S. Protestant.* one of a group of churches presided over by a body of pastors. **3.** *Scot. Protestant.* a church served by two or more ministers. **4.** a large church endowed in the Middle Ages to become a school. **5.** a chapel either endowed by or connected with a college.

col+le·gi+ate in+sti+tute *n. Canadian.* a high school concentrating on an academic education.

col+le·gi·um (kəˈliːdʒɪəm) *n., pl.* **·gi·ums** *or* **·gi·a** (-dʒɪə). **1.** (in the Soviet Union) a board in charge of a department, etc. **2.** another term for **College of Cardinals** or **Sacred College.** [Latin: COLLEGE]

col+lem+bo+lan (kəˈlɛmbələn) *n.* **1.** any small primitive wingless insect of the order *Collembola,* which comprises the springtails. ~*adj.* **2.** of, relating to, or belonging to the *Collembola.* [C19: from New Latin *Collembola,* from Greek *kolla* glue + *embolon* peg, wedge]

col+len+chy+ma (kəˈlɛŋkɪmə) *n.* a strengthening and supporting tissue in plants, consisting of elongated living cells whose walls are thickened with cellulose and pectins. [C19: New Latin, from Greek *kolla* glue + *enkhuma* infusion] —**col+len+chym·a+tous** (ˌkɒlənˈkɪmətəs) *adj.*

Col·les' frac+ture (ˈkɒlɪs) *n.* a fracture of the radius just above the wrist, resulting in the hand being displaced backwards and outwards. [C19: named after Abraham *Colles* (died 1843), Irish surgeon]

col+let (ˈkɒlɪt) *n.* **1.** (in a jewellery setting) a band or coronet-shaped claw that holds an individual stone. **2.** *Mechanical engineering.* an externally tapered sleeve made in two or more segments and used to grip a shaft passed through its centre when the sleeve is compressed by being inserted in a similarly tapered hole. **3.** *Horology.* a small metal collar that supports the inner end of the hairspring. ~*vb.* **4.** (*tr.*) *Jewellery.* to mount in a collet. [C16: from Old French: a little collar, from *col* neckband, neck, from Latin *collum* neck]

col+lide (kəˈlaɪd) *vb.* (*intr.*) **1.** to crash together with a violent impact. **2.** to conflict in attitude, opinion, or desire; clash; disagree. [C17: from Latin *collīdere* to clash together, from *com-* together + *laedere* to strike, wound]

col+lie (ˈkɒlɪ) *n.* a silky-coated breed of sheepdog with a long ruff and a long narrow head. [C17: Scottish, probably from earlier *colie* black with coal dust, from *cole* COAL]

col+li+er (ˈkɒlɪə) *n. Chiefly Brit.* **1.** a coal miner. **2. a.** a ship designed to transport coal. **b.** a member of its crew. [C14: from COAL + -IER]

col+lier·y (ˈkɒljərɪ) *n., pl.* **+lier·ies.** *Chiefly Brit.* a coal mine.

col+li+gate (ˈkɒlɪˌgeɪt) *vb.* (*tr.*) **1.** to connect or link together; tie; join. **2.** to relate (isolated facts, observations, etc.) by a general hypothesis. [C16: from Latin *colligāre* to fasten together, from *com-* together + *ligāre* to bind] —ˌ**col+li+ˈga+tion** *n.*

col+li+ga+tive (kəˈlɪgətɪv) *adj.* (of a physical property of a substance) depending on the concentrations of atoms, ions, and molecules that are present rather than on their nature.

col+li+mate (ˈkɒlɪˌmeɪt) *vb.* (*tr.*) **1.** to adjust the line of sight of (an optical instrument). **2.** to use a collimator on (a beam of radiation or particles). **3.** to make parallel or bring into line. [C17: from New Latin *collimāre,* erroneously for Latin *collīneāre* to aim, from *com-* (intensive) + *līneāre,* from *līnea* line] —ˌ**col+li+ˈma+tion** *n.*

col+li+ma+tor (ˈkɒlɪˌmeɪtə) *n.* **1.** a small telescope attached to a larger optical instrument as an aid in fixing its line of sight. **2.** an optical system of lenses and slits producing a nondivergent beam of light, usually for use in spectroscopes. **3.** any device for limiting the size and angle of spread of a beam of radiation or particles.

col+lin+e·ar (kɒˈlɪnɪə) *adj.* **1.** lying on the same straight line. **2.** having a common line. —**col+ˈlin+e·ar+ly** *adv.*

col+lins (ˈkɒlɪnz) *n.* a tall fizzy iced drink made with gin, vodka, rum, etc., mixed with fruit juice, soda water, and sugar. [C20: probably after the proper name *Collins*]

Col+lins (ˈkɒlɪnz) *n.* **1. Mi·chael.** 1890–1922, Irish nationalist: a leader of Sinn Fein; negotiated the treaty with Great Britain (1921) that established the Irish Free State. **2. Wil·liam.** 1721–59, English poet, a precursor of romanticism, noted for his odes. **3. (William) Wil·kie.** 1824–89, English author, noted particularly for his crime novel *The Moonstone* (1868).

col+lin+si·a (kəˈlɪnsɪə, -zɪə) *n.* a North American plant of the scrophulariaceous genus *Collinsia,* having blue, white, or purple flowers. [C19: New Latin, named after Zaccheus *Collins* (1764–1831), American botanist]

Col+lins Street Farm+er *n. Austral. slang.* a businessman who invests in farms, land, etc. Also called: **Pitt Street Farmer.** [C20: after a principal business street in Melbourne]

col+li+sion (kəˈlɪʒən) *n.* **1.** a violent impact of moving objects; crash. **2.** the conflict of opposed ideas, wishes, attitudes, etc.: *a collision of interests.* **3.** *Physics.* an event in which two or more bodies or particles come together with a resulting exchange of energy and change of direction. [C15: from Late Latin *collīsiō* from Latin *collīdere* COLLIDE]

col+lo+cate (ˈkɒləˌkeɪt) *vb.* (*tr.*) to group or place together in some system or order. [C16: from Latin *collocāre,* from *com-* together + *locāre* to place, from *locus* place]

col+lo+ca+tion (ˌkɒləˈkeɪʃən) *n.* a grouping together of things in a certain order, as of the words in a sentence.

col+lo+cu+tor (ˈkɒləˌkjuːtə) *n.* a person who talks or engages in conversation with another.

col+lo+di+on (kəˈləʊdɪən) *or* **col+lo+di·um** (kəˈləʊdɪəm) *n.* a colourless or yellow syrupy liquid that consists of a solution of pyroxylin in ether and alcohol: used in medicine and in the manufacture of photographic plates, lacquers, etc. [C19: from New Latin *collōdium,* from Greek *kollōdēs* glutinous, from *kolla* glue]

col+logue (kɒˈləʊg) *vb.* **col+logues, col+lo+guing, col+logued.** (*intr.*; usually foll. by *with*) to confer confidentially; intrigue or conspire. [C16: perhaps from obsolete *colleague* (vb.) to be or act as a colleague, conspire, influenced by Latin *colloquī* to talk with; see COLLEAGUE]

col+loid (ˈkɒlɔɪd) *n.* **1.** Also called: **colloidal solution** *or* **suspension.** a mixture having particles of one component, with diameters between 10^{-7} and 10^{-9} metre, suspended in a continuous phase of another component. The mixture has properties between those of a solution and a fine suspension. **2.** the solid suspended phase in such a mixture. **3.** *Obsolete.* a substance that in solution does not penetrate a semipermeable membrane. Compare **crystalloid** (sense 2). **4.** *Physiol.* a gelatinous substance of the thyroid follicles that holds the hormonal secretions of the thyroid gland. ~*adj.* **5.** *Pathol.* of or relating to the gluelike translucent material found in certain degenerating tissues. **6.** of, denoting, or having the character of a colloid. [C19: from Greek *kolla* glue + -OID] —**col+ˈloi+dal** *adj.* —**col+loi+dal+i·ty** (ˌkɒlɔɪˈdælɪtɪ) *n.*

col+lop (ˈkɒləp) *n. Dialect, chiefly northern Brit.* **1.** a slice of meat. **2.** a small piece of anything. [C14: of Scandinavian origin; compare Swedish *kalops* meat stew]

colloq. *abbrev. for* colloquial(ly).

col+lo+qui·al (kəˈləʊkwɪəl) *adj.* **1.** of or relating to conversation. **2.** denoting or characterized by informal or conversational idiom or vocabulary. Compare **informal.** —**col+ˈlo+qui+al+ly** *adv.* —**col+ˈlo+qui+al+ness** *n.*

col+lo+qui+al+ism (kəˈləʊkwɪəˌlɪzəm) *n.* **1.** a word or phrase appropriate to conversation and other informal situations. **2.** the use of colloquial words and phrases.

col+lo+qui·um (kəˈləʊkwɪəm) *n., pl.* **+qui·ums** *or* **+qui·a** (-kwɪə). **1.** an informal gathering for discussion. **2.** an academic seminar. [C17: from Latin: conversation, conference, COLLOQUY]

col+lo+quy (ˈkɒləkwɪ) *n., pl.* **+quies. 1.** a formal conversation or conference. **2.** a literary work in dialogue form. **3.** an informal conference on religious or theological matters. [C16: from Latin *colloquium* from *colloquī* to talk with, from *com-* together + *loquī* to speak] —**ˈcol+lo+quist** *n.*

col+lo+type (ˈkɒləʊˌtaɪp) *n.* **1.** Also called: **photogelatin process.** a method of printing from a flat surface of hardened gelatin: used mainly for fine-detail reproduction in monochrome or colour. **2.** a print made using this process. [C19: from Greek *kolla* glue + -TYPE] —**col+lo+typ+ic** (ˌkɒləˈtɪpɪk) *adj.*

col+lude (kəˈluːd) *vb.* (*intr.*) to conspire together, esp. in planning a fraud; connive. [C16: from Latin *collūdere,* literally: to play together, hence, conspire together, from *com-* together + *lūdere* to play] —**col+ˈlud+er** *n.*

col+lu+sion (kəˈluːʒən) *n.* **1.** secret agreement for a fraudulent purpose; connivance; conspiracy. **2.** a secret agreement between opponents at law in order to obtain a judicial decision for some wrongful or improper purpose. [C14: from Latin *collūsiō,* from *collūdere* to COLLUDE] —**col+ˈlu+sive** *adj.*

col+lu+vi·um (kəˈluːvɪəm) *n., pl.* **+vi·a** (-vɪə) *or* **+vi·ums.** a mixture of rock fragments from the bases of cliffs. [Latin: collection of filth, from *colluere* to wash thoroughly, from *com-* (intensive) + *luere* to wash] —**col+ˈlu+vi·al** *adj.*

col+ly (ˈkɒlɪ) *Archaic or dialect.* ~*n., pl.* **+lies. 1.** soot or grime, such as coal dust. ~*adj.* **+li+er, +li+est. 2.** dirty; sooty. ~*vb.* **col+lies, col+ly+ing, col+lied. 3.** (*tr.*) to begrime; besmirch. [C16: ultimately from Old English *col* COAL]

col+lyr+i·um (kɒˈlɪrɪəm) *n., pl.* **+lyr·i·a** (-ˈlɪrɪə) *or* **+lyr+i·ums.** a technical name for **eyewash** (sense 1). [C16: from Latin, from Greek *kollurion* poultice, eye salve]

col+ly+wob+bles (ˈkɒlɪˌwɒbᵊlz) *pl. n.* (usually preceded by *the*) *Slang.* **1.** an upset stomach. **2.** acute diarrhoea. **3.** an intense feeling of nervousness. [C19: probably from New Latin *cholera morbus* the disease cholera, influenced through folk etymology by COLIC and WOBBLE]

Col+mar (*French* kɔlˈmaːr) *n.* a city in NE France: annexed to Germany 1871–1919 and 1940–45; textile industry. Pop.: 62 410 (1975). German name: **Kolmar.**

Colo. *abbrev. for* Colorado.

co·lo- *or before a vowel* **col-** *combining form.* indicating the colon: *colostomy; colotomy.*

col·o+bus (ˈkɒləbəs) *n.* any leaf-eating arboreal Old World monkey of the genus *Colobus,* of W and central Africa, having a slender body, long silky fur, long tail, and reduced or absent thumbs. [C19: New Latin, from Greek *kolobos* cut short; referring to its thumb]

col·o+cynth (ˈkɒləsɪnθ) *n.* **1.** a cucurbitaceous climbing plant, *Citrullus colocynthis,* of the Mediterranean region and Asia, having bitter-tasting fruit. **2.** the dried fruit pulp of this plant, used as a strong purgative. ~Also called: **bitter apple.** [C17: from Latin *colocynthis,* from Greek *kolokunthis,* from *kolokunthē* gourd, of obscure origin]

co+log·a+rithm (kəʊˈlɒgəˌrɪðəm) *n.* the logarithm of the reciprocal of a number; the negative value of the logarithm: *the cologarithm of 4 is log* $\frac{1}{4}$. Abbrev.: **colog**

co+logne (kəˈləʊn) *n.* a perfumed liquid or solid made of fragrant essential oils and alcohol. Also called: **Cologne water, eau de cologne.** [C18 *Cologne water,* from COLOGNE, where it was first manufactured (1709)]

Co+logne (kəˈləʊn) *n.* an industrial city and river port in West Germany, in North Rhine-Westphalia on the Rhine: important commercially since ancient times; university (1388). Pop.: 832 396 (1974 est.). German name: **Köln.**

Co·lomb-Bé·char (*French* kɔlɔ̃ beˈʃaːr) *n.* the former name of **Béchar.**

Co+lombes (*French* kɔ'lɔ̃:b) *n.* an industrial and residential suburb of NW Paris. Pop.: 83 518 (1975).

Co+lom+bi·a (kə'lɒmbɪə) *n.* a republic in NW South America: inhabited by Chibchas and other Indians before Spanish colonization in the 16th century; independence won by Bolívar in 1819; became the Republic of Colombia in 1886. It consists chiefly of a hot swampy coastal plain, separated by ranges of the Andes from the pampas and the equatorial forests of the Amazon basin in the east. Language: Spanish. Religion: Roman Catholic. Currency: peso. Capital: Bogotá. Pop.: 21 070 115 (1973). Area: 1 138 908 sq. km (439 735 sq. miles). —**Co+'lom+bi·an** *adj., n.*

Co+lom+bo (kə'lʌmbəʊ) *n.* the capital and chief port of Sri Lanka, on the W coast, with one of the largest artificial harbours in the word. Pop.: 562 000 (1971).

co+lon[1] ('kəʊlən) *n.* **1.** (*pl.* **+lons**) the punctuation mark **:**, usually preceding an explanation or an example of what has gone before, a list, or an extended quotation. **2.** (*pl.* **+lons**) this mark used for certain other purposes, such as expressions of time, as in *2:45 p.m.*, or when a ratio is given in figures, as in *5:3*. **3.** (*pl.* **+la** (-lə)) (in classical prosody) a part of a rhythmical period with two to six feet and one principal accent or ictus. [C16: from Latin, from Greek *kōlon* limb, hence part of a strophe, clause of a sentence]

co+lon[2] ('kəʊlən) *n., pl.* **+lons** *or* **+la** (-lə). the part of the large intestine between the caecum and the rectum. [C16: from Latin: large intestine, from Greek *kolon*]

co+lon[3] (kəʊ'ləʊn; *Spanish* ko'lon) *n., pl.* **+lons** *or* **+lo+nes** (*Spanish* -'lones). **1.** the standard monetary unit of Costa Rica, divided into 100 centimos. **2.** the standard monetary unit of El Salvador, divided into 100 centavos. [C19: American Spanish, from Spanish, after Cristóbal *Colón* Christopher Columbus]

co+lon[4] (kə'lɒn; *French* kɔ'lɔ̃) *n.* a colonial farmer or plantation owner, esp. in a French colony. [French: colonist, from Latin *colōnus*, from *colere* to till, inhabit]

Co+lón (kɒ'lɒn; *Spanish* ko'lon) *n.* **1.** a port in Panama, at the Caribbean entrance to the Panama Canal. Chief Caribbean port. Pop.: 1 340 286 (1970). Former name: **Aspinwall. 2. Ar+chi+pié+la+go de** (ˌartʃi'pjelaɣo ðe). the official name of the **Galápagos Islands.**

colo+nel ('kɜːnᵊl) *n.* an officer of land or air forces junior to a brigadier but senior to a lieutenant colonel. [C16: via Old French, from Old Italian *colonnello* column of soldiers, from *colonna* COLUMN] —**'colo+nel+cy** *or* **'colo+nel+ˌship** *n.*

Colo+nel Blimp *n.* See **blimp**[2].

co+lo+ni·al (kə'ləʊnɪəl) *adj.* **1.** of, characteristic of, relating to, possessing, or inhabiting a colony or colonies. **2.** (*often cap.*) characteristic of or relating to the 13 British colonies that became the United States of America (1776). **3.** (*often cap.*) of or relating to the colonies of the British Empire. **4.** denoting, relating to, or having the style of Neoclassical architecture used in the British colonies in America in the 17th and 18th centuries. **5.** (of organisms such as corals and bryozoans) existing as a colony of polyps. **6.** (of animals and plants) having become established in a community in a new environment. ~*n.* **7.** a native of a colony. —**co+'lo+ni+al+ly** *adv.*

co+lo+ni·al ex+pe+ri+ence *n. Austral.* experience of farming, etc., gained by a young Englishman in colonial Australia. —**co+'lo+ni·al ex+'pe+ri+enc+er** *n.*

co+lo+ni+al+ism (kə'ləʊnɪəˌlɪzəm) *n.* the policy and practice of a power in extending control over weaker peoples or areas. Also called: **imperialism.** —**co+'lo+ni+al+ist** *n., adj.*

co+lon+ic (kə'lɒnɪk) *adj.* **1.** *Anatomy.* **a.** of or relating to the colon. **b.** *Med.* relating to irrigation of the colon for cleansing purposes. ~*n.* **2.** *Med.* irrigation of the colon by injecting large amounts of fluid high into the colon: *a high colonic.*

Col·o+nies ('kɒlənɪz) *pl. n.* **the. 1.** *Brit.* the subject territories formerly in the British Empire. **2.** *U.S. history.* the 13 states forming the original United States of America when they declared their independence (1776). These were Connecticut, North and South Carolina, Delaware, Georgia, New Hampshire, New York, Maryland, Massachusetts, Pennsylvania, Rhode Island, Virginia, and New Jersey.

col·o+nist ('kɒlənɪst) *n.* **1.** a person who settles or colonizes an area. **2.** an inhabitant or member of a colony.

col·o+ni+tis (ˌkɒlə'naɪtɪs) *n. Pathol.* another word for **colitis.**

col·o+nize *or* **col·o+nise** ('kɒləˌnaɪz) *vb.* **1.** to send colonists to or establish a colony in (an area). **2.** to settle in (an area) as colonists. **3.** (*tr.*) to transform (a community, etc.) into a colony. **4.** (of plants and animals) to become established in (a new environment). —**'col·o+ˌniz+a·ble** *or* **'col·o+ˌnis+a·ble** *adj.* —**ˌcol·o+ni+'za+tion** *or* **ˌcol·o+ni+'sa+tion** *n.* —**'col·o+ˌniz+er** *or* **'col·o+ˌnis+er** *n.*

col+on+nade (ˌkɒlə'neɪd) *n.* **1.** a set of evenly-spaced columns. **2.** a row of regularly spaced trees. [C18: from French, from *colonne* COLUMN; on the model of Italian *colonnato*, from *colonna* column] —**ˌcol+on+'nad+ed** *adj.*

Col+on+say ('kɒlənseɪ, -zeɪ) *n.* an island in W Scotland, in the Inner Hebrides. Area: about 41 sq. km (16 sq. miles).

col·o+ny ('kɒlənɪ) *n., pl.* **+nies. 1.** a body of people who settle in a country distant from their homeland but maintain ties with it. **2.** the community formed by such settlers. **3.** a subject territory occupied by a settlement from the ruling state. **4. a.** a community of people who form a national, racial, or cultural minority: *an artist's colony; the American colony in London.* **b.** the area itself. **5.** *Zoology.* **a.** a group of the same type of animal or plant living or growing together. **b.** an interconnected group of polyps of a colonial organism. **6.** *Bacteriol.* a group of bacteria, fungi, etc., derived from one or a few spores, esp. when grown on a culture medium. [C16: from Latin *colōnia*, from *colere* to cultivate, inhabit]

col·o+phon ('kɒləˌfɒn, -fən) *n.* **1.** a publisher's emblem on a book. **2.** (formerly) an inscription at the end of a book showing the title, printer, date, etc. [C17: via Late Latin, from Greek *kolophōn* a finishing stroke]

co+loph·o+ny (kɒ'lɒfənɪ) *n.* another name for **rosin** (sense 1). [C14: from Latin *Colophōnia rēsina* resin from Colophon]

col·o+quin+ti+da (ˌkɒlə'kwɪntɪdə) *n.* another name for **colocynth.** [C14: from Medieval Latin, from *colocynthid-* COLOCYNTH]

col+or ('kʌlə) *n.* the U.S. spelling of **colour.** —**'col+or+a·ble** *adj.* —**'col+or+er** *n.* —**'col+or+ful** *adj.* —**'col+or+ing** *n.* —**'col+or+ist** *n.* —**'col+or+less** *adj.*

Col·o+ra+do (ˌkɒlə'rɑːdəʊ) *n.* **1.** a state of the central U.S.: consists of the Great Plains in the east and the Rockies in the west; drained chiefly by the Colorado, Arkansas, South Platte, and Rio Grande Rivers. Capital: Denver. Pop.: 2 209 528 (1970). Area: 269 998 sq. km (104 247sq. miles). Abbrevs.: **Colo.** or (with zip code) **CO 2.** a river in SW North America, rising in the Rocky Mountains and flowing southwest to the Gulf of California: famous for the 1600 km (1000 miles) of canyons along its course. Length: about 2320 km (1440 miles). **3.** a river in central Texas, flowing southeast to the Gulf of Mexico. Length: about 1450 km (900 miles). **4.** a river in central Argentina, flowing southeast to the Atlantic. Length: about 850 km (530 miles). [Spanish, literally: red, from Latin *colōrātus* coloured, tinted red; see COLOUR]

Col·o+ra+do bee+tle *n.* a black-and-yellow beetle, *Leptinotarsa decemlineata,* that is a serious pest of potatoes, feeding on the leaves: family *Chrysomelidae.* Also called: **potato beetle.**

Col·o+ra+do Des+ert *n.* an arid region of SE California and NW Mexico, West of the Colorado River. Area: over 5000 sq. km (2000 sq. miles).

Col·o+ra+do Springs *n.* a city and resort in central Colorado. Pop.: 175 745 (1973 est.).

col+or+ant ('kʌlərənt) *n.* any substance that imparts colour, such as a pigment, dye, or ink; colouring matter.

col+or·a+tion (ˌkʌlə'reɪʃən) *n.* **1.** arrangement of colour and tones; colouring. **2.** the colouring or markings of insects, birds, etc. See also **apatetic, aposematic, cryptic.**

col·o+ra+tu+ra (ˌkɒlərə'tʊərə) *or* **col+or·a+ture** ('kɒlərəˌtjʊə) *n. Music.* **1. a.** (in 18th- and 19th-century arias) a florid virtuoso passage. **b.** (*as modifier*): *a coloratura aria.* **2.** Also called: **coloratura soprano.** a lyric soprano who specializes in such music. [C19: from obsolete Italian, literally: colouring, from Latin *colōrāre* to COLOUR]

col+or+if+ic (ˌkʌlə'rɪfɪk) *adj.* producing, imparting, or relating to colour.

col+or+im+e+ter (ˌkʌlə'rɪmɪtə) *n.* **1.** Also called: **tintometer.** an apparatus for determining the concentration of a solution of a coloured substance by comparing the intensity of its colour with that of a standard solution or with standard colour slides. **2.** any apparatus for measuring the quality of a colour by comparison with standard colours or combinations of colours. —**col+or+i+met+ric** (ˌkʌlərɪ'metrɪk) *or* **ˌcol+or+i+'met+ri+cal** *adj.* —**ˌcol+or+i+'met+ri+cal+ly** *adv.* —**ˌcol+or+'im+e+try** *n.*

Co+los+sae (kə'lɒsiː) *n.* an ancient city in SW Phrygia in Asia Minor: seat of an early Christian Church.

co+los+sal (kə'lɒsᵊl) *adj.* **1.** of immense size; huge; gigantic. **2.** (in figure sculpture) approximately twice life-size. Compare **heroic** (sense 7). **3.** Also: **giant.** *Architect.* of or relating to the order of columns and pilasters that extend more than one storey in a facade. —**co+'los+sal+ly** *adv.*

col+os+se·um (ˌkɒlə'sɪəm) *n.* a variant spelling of **coliseum.**

Col+os+se·um (ˌkɒlə'sɪəm) *n.* an amphitheatre in Rome built about 75–80 A.D.

Co+los+sian (kə'lɒʃən) *n.* **1.** a native or inhabitant of Colossae. **2.** *New Testament.* any of the Christians of Colossae to whom St. Paul's Epistle was addressed.

Co+los+sians (kə'lɒʃənz) *n.* (*functioning as sing.*) a book of the New Testament (in full **The Epistle of Paul the Apostle to the Colossians**).

co+los+sus (kə'lɒsəs) *n., pl.* **+si** (-saɪ) *or* **+sus·es.** something very large, esp. a statue. [C14: from Latin, from Greek *kolossos*]

Co+los+sus of Rhodes *n.* a giant bronze statue of Apollo built on Rhodes in about 292–280 B.C.; destroyed by an earthquake in 225 B.C.; one of the Seven Wonders of the World.

co+los+to+my (kə'lɒstəmɪ) *n., pl.* **+mies.** the surgical formation of an opening from the colon onto the surface of the body, which functions as an anus.

co+los+trum (kə'lɒstrəm) *n.* the thin milky secretion from the nipples that precedes and follows true lactation. It consists largely of serum and white blood cells. [C16: from Latin, of obscure origin] —**co+'los+tral** *adj.*

co+lot·o+my (kə'lɒtəmɪ) *n., pl.* **+mies.** a colonic incision.

col+our *or U.S.* **col+or** ('kʌlə) *n.* **1. a.** an attribute of things that results from the light they reflect, transmit, or emit in so far as this light causes a visual sensation that depends on its wavelengths. **b.** the aspect of visual perception by which an observer recognizes this attribute. **c.** the quality of the light producing this aspect of visual perception. **d.** (*as modifier*): *colour vision.* **2.** Also called: **chromatic colour. a.** a colour, such as red or green, that possesses hue, as opposed to achromatic colours such as white or black. **b.** (*as modifier*): *a colour television; a colour film.* Compare **black-and-white** (sense 2). **3.** a substance, such as a dye, pigment, or paint, that imparts colour to something. **4. a.** the skin complexion of a person, esp. as determined by his race. **b.** (*as modifier*): *colour prejudice; colour problem.* **5.** the use of all the hues in painting as distinct from composition, form, and light and shade. **6.** the quantity and quality of ink used in a printing process. **7.** the distinctive tone of a musical sound; timbre. **8.** vividness, authenticity, or individuality: *period colour.* **9.** semblance or pretext (esp. in the phrases **take on a different colour, under colour of**). **10.** *U.S.* a precious mineral particle, esp. gold, found in auriferous gravel. **11. off colour. a.** not well; ill. **b.** in bad taste. ~*vb.* **12.** to give or apply colour to (something). **13.** (*tr.*) to give a convincing or plausible appearance to (something, esp. to that which is spoken or recounted): *to colour an alibi.* **14.** (*tr.*) to influence or distort (something, esp. a report or opinion): *anger coloured her judgment.* **15.** (*intr.*; often foll. by *up*) to become red in the face, esp. when embarrassed or annoyed. **16.** (*intr.*) (esp. of ripening fruit) to change hue. ~See also **colours.** [C13 from Old French *colour* from Latin *color* tint, hue]

col·our·a·ble ('kʌlərəbᵊl) *adj.* **1.** capable of being coloured. **2.** appearing to be true; plausible: *a colourable excuse.* **3.** pretended; feigned: *colourable affection.* —ˌ**col·our·a·'bil·i·ty** *or* **'col·our·a·ble·ness** *n.* —**'col·our·a·bly** *adv.*

col·our bar *n.* discrimination against people of a different race, esp. as practised by Whites against Blacks.

col·our-blind *adj.* of or relating to any defect in the normal ability to distinguish certain colours. See **deuteranopia, protanopia, tritanopia.** —**col·our blind·ness** *n.*

col·our code *n.* a system of easily distinguishable colours, as for the identification of electrical wires or resistors.

col·oured ('kʌləd) *adj.* **1.** possessing colour. **2.** having a strong element of fiction or fantasy; distorted (esp. in the phrase **highly coloured**).

Col·oured ('kʌləd) *n., pl.* **Col·oureds** *or* **Col·oured. 1.** an individual who is not a White, esp. a Negro. **2.** Also called: **Cape Coloured.** (in South Africa) a person of racially mixed parentage or descent. ~*adj.* **3.** designating or relating to a Coloured or Coloureds: *a Coloured gentleman.*

col·our·fast ('kʌləˌfɑ:st) *adj.* (of a fabric) having a colour that does not run or change when washed or worn. —**'col·our·ˌfast·ness** *n.*

col·our fil·ter *n. Photog.* a thin layer of coloured gelatin, glass, etc., that transmits light of its own colour but considerably reduces the transmission of other colours.

col·our·ful ('kʌləfʊl) *adj.* **1.** having intense colour or richly varied colours. **2.** vivid, rich, or distinctive in character. —**'col·our·ful·ly** *adv.* —**'col·our·ful·ness** *n.*

col·our guard *n.* a military guard in a parade, ceremony, etc., that carries and escorts the flag or regimental colours.

col·our in·dex *n.* **1.** *Astronomy.* the difference between the photographic magnitude and the visual magnitude of a star, indicating its colour and temperature. **2.** *Geology.* the sum of the dark or coloured minerals of a rock, expressed as a percentage of the total minerals.

col·our·ing ('kʌlərɪŋ) *n.* **1.** the process or art of applying colour. **2.** anything used to give colour, such as dye, paint, etc. **3.** appearance with regard to shade and colour. **4.** arrangements of colours and tones, as in the markings of birds and animals. **5.** the colour of a person's features or complexion. **6.** a false or misleading appearance.

col·our·ist ('kʌlərɪst) *n.* **1.** a person who uses colour, esp. an artist. **2.** a person who colours photographs, esp. black-and-white ones. —ˌ**col·our·'is·tic** *adj.*

col·our·less ('kʌləlɪs) *adj.* **1.** without colour. **2.** lacking in interest: *a colourless individual.* **3.** grey or pallid in tone or hue. **4.** without prejudice; neutral. —**'col·our·less·ly** *adv.* —**'col·our·less·ness** *n.*

col·our line *n.* the social separation of racial groups within a community (esp. in the phrase **to cross the colour line**).

col·our·man ('kʌləmən) *n., pl.* **·men.** a person who deals in paints.

col·our phase *n.* **1.** a seasonal change in the coloration of some animals. **2.** an abnormal variation in the coloration shown by a group of animals within a species.

col·ours ('kʌləz) *pl. n.* **1. a.** the flag that indicates nationality. **b.** *Military.* the ceremony of hoisting or lowering the colours. **2.** true nature or character (esp. in the phrase **show one's colours**). **3.** a distinguishing badge or flag, as of an academic institution. **4.** *Sport., Brit.* a badge or other symbol denoting membership of a team, esp. at a school or college. **5. nail one's colours to the mast.** to refuse to admit defeat. **6. with flying colours.** with great credit; very successfully.

col·our scheme *n.* a planned combination or juxtaposition of colours, as in interior decorating.

col·our ser·geant *n.* a sergeant who carries the regimental, battalion, or national colours, as in a colour guard.

col·our sup·ple·ment *n. Brit.* an illustrated magazine accompanying a newspaper, esp. a Sunday newspaper.

col·our·y *or* **col·or·y** ('kʌlərɪ) *adj.* possessing colour.

-co·lous *adj. combining form.* inhabiting or living on: *arenicolous.* [from Latin *-cola* inhabitant + -OUS; related to *colere* to inhabit]

col·pi·tis (kɒl'paɪtɪs) *n. Pathol.* another name for **vaginitis.** [C19: from Greek *kolpos* bosom, womb, vagina + -ITIS]

col·po- *or before a vowel* **colp-** *combining form.* indicating the vagina: *colpitis; colpotomy.* [from Greek *kolpos* womb]

col·por·teur ('kɒlˌpɔ:tə; *French* kɔlpɔr'tœ:r) *n.* a hawker of books, esp. bibles. [C18: from French, from *colporter,* probably from Old French *comporter* to carry (see COMPORT); influenced through folk etymology by *porter à col* to carry on one's neck] —**'col·ˌpor·tage** *n.*

colt (kəʊlt) *n.* **1.** a male horse or pony under the age of four. **2.** an awkward or inexperienced young person. **3.** *Sport.* **a.** a young and inexperienced player. **b.** a member of a junior team. [Old English *colt* young ass, of obscure origin; compare Swedish dialect *kult* young animal, boy]

Colt (kəʊlt) *n. Trademark.* a type of revolver. [C19: named after Samuel *Colt* (1814–62), American inventor]

col·ter ('kəʊltə) *n.* a variant spelling (esp. U.S.) of **coulter.** [Old English *culter,* from Latin: ploughshare, knife]

colt·ish ('kəʊltɪʃ) *adj.* **1.** inexperienced; unruly. **2.** playful and lively. —**'colt·ish·ly** *adv.* —**'colt·ish·ness** *n.*

Col·trane (kɒl'treɪn) *n.* **John.** 1926–1967, U.S. jazz tenor and soprano saxophonist.

colts·foot ('kəʊlts,fʊt) *n., pl.* **·foots.** a European plant, *Tussilago farfara,* with yellow daisy-like flowers and heart-shaped leaves: a common weed: family *Compositae* (composites).

col·u·brid ('kɒljʊbrɪd) *n.* **1.** any snake of the family *Colubridae,* including many harmless snakes, such as the grass snake and whip snakes, and some venomous types. ~*adj.* **2.** of, relating to, or belonging to the *Colubridae.* [C19: from New Latin *Colubridae,* from Latin *coluber* snake]

col·u·brine ('kɒljʊˌbraɪn, -brɪn) *adj.* **1.** of or resembling a snake. **2.** of, relating to, or belonging to the *Colubrinae,* a subfamily of harmless colubrid snakes. [C16: from Latin *colubrīnus,* from *coluber* snake]

co·lu·go (kə'lu:gəʊ) *n., pl.* **·gos.** another name for **flying lemur.** [from a native word in Malaya]

Col·um ('kɒləm) *n.* **Pa·draic** ('pɑ:drɪk). 1881–1972, Irish lyric poet, resident in the U.S. (1914–72).

Co·lum·ba[1] (kə'lʌmbə) *n., Latin genitive* **Co·lum·bae** (kə'lʌmbi:), as in *Alpha Columbae.* a small constellation in the S hemisphere south of Orion. [Latin, literally: dove]

Co·lum·ba[2] (kə'lʌmbə) *n.* **Saint.** ?521–597 A.D., Irish missionary: founded the monastery at Iona (563) from which the Picts were converted to Christianity. Feast day: June 9.

col·um·bar·i·um (ˌkɒləm'bɛərɪəm) *n., pl.* **·i·a** (-ɪə). **1.** another name for a **dovecote. 2.** a vault having niches for funeral urns. **3.** a hole in a wall into which a beam is inserted. [C18: from Latin, from *columba* dove]

Co·lum·bi·a (kə'lʌmbɪə) *n.* **1.** a river in NW North America, rising in the Rocky Mountains and flowing through British Columbia, then west to the Pacific. Length: about 1930 km (1200 miles). **2.** a city in central South Carolina, on the Congaree River: the state capital. Pop.: 112 164 (1973 est.).

Co·lum·bi·an (kə'lʌmbɪən) *adj.* **1.** of or relating to the United States. **2.** relating to Christopher Columbus. ~*n.* **3.** a size of printers type, approximately equal to 16 point; two-line Brevier.

co·lum·bic (kə'lʌmbɪk) *adj.* another word for **niobic.**

Col·um·bine ('kɒləmˌbaɪn) *n.* **1.** (originally) the character of a servant girl in commedia dell'arte. **2.** (later) the sweetheart of Harlequin in English pantomime.

col·um·bine[1] ('kɒləmˌbaɪn) *n.* any plant of the ranunculaceous genus *Aquilegia,* having purple, blue, yellow, or red flowers with five spurred petals. Also called: **aquilegia.** [C13: from Medieval Latin *columbīna herba* dovelike plant, from Latin *columbīnus* dovelike, from the resemblance of the flower to a group of doves]

col·um·bine[2] ('kɒləmˌbaɪn) *adj.* of, relating to, or resembling a dove. [C14: from Old French *colombin,* from Latin *columbīnus* dovelike, from *columba* dove]

co·lum·bite (kə'lʌmbaɪt) *n.* a black mineral consisting of a mixed niobium and tantalum oxide of iron and manganese in orthorhombic crystalline form: occurs in coarse granite, often with tantalite, and is an ore of niobium and tantalum. Formula: $(Fe, Mn)(Nb,Ta)_2O_6$. Also called: **niobite.** [C19: from COLUMBIUM + -ITE[1]]

co·lum·bi·um (kə'lʌmbɪəm) *n.* former name of **niobium.** [C19: from New Latin, from *Columbia,* the United States of America]

co·lum·bous (kə'lʌmbəs) *adj.* another word for **niobous.**

Co·lum·bus[1] (kə'lʌmbəs) *n.* **1.** a city in central Ohio: the state capital. Pop.: 540 933 (1973 est.). **2.** a city in W Georgia, on the Chattahoochee River. Pop.: 161 209 (1973 est.).

Co·lum·bus[2] (kə'lʌmbəs) *n.* **Chris·to·pher.** Spanish name *Cristóbal Colón,* Italian name *Cristoforo Colombo.* 1451–1506, Italian navigator and explorer in the service of Spain, who discovered the New World (1492).

Co·lum·bus Day *n.* Oct. 12, a legal holiday in most states of the U.S.: the date of Columbus' landing in the West Indies in 1492.

col·u·mel·la (ˌkɒljʊ'mɛlə) *n., pl.* **·lae** (-li:). **1.** the central part of plant or animal organs, as of the spore-producing body of some fungi and mosses. **2.** Also called: **columella auris.** a small rodlike bone in the middle ear of frogs, reptiles, and birds that transmits sound to the inner ear: homologous to the mammalian stapes. [C16: from Latin: diminutive of *columna* COLUMN] —ˌ**col·u·'mel·lar** *adj.*

col·umn ('kɒləm) *n.* **1.** an upright post or pillar usually having a cylindrical shaft, a base, and a capital. **2. a.** a form or structure in the shape of a column: *a column of air.* **b.** a monument. **3.** a row, line, or file, as of people in a queue. **4.** *Military.* a formation in which individual units follow one behind the other. **5.** *Journalism.* **a.** a single row of type on a newspaper. **b.** a regular article or feature in a paper: *the fashion column.* **6.** a vertical array of numbers or mathematical terms. **7.** *Botany.* a long structure in the flower of an orchid, consisting of the united stamens and style. [C15: from

Latin *columna,* from *columen* top, peak; related to Latin *collis* hill] —**co·lum·nar** (kəˈlʌmnə) *n.* —ˈ**col·umned** *or* **col·um·nat·ed** (ˈkɒləmˌneɪtɪd) *adj.*
co·lum·ni·a·tion (kəˌlʌmnɪˈeɪʃən) *n.* the arrangement of architectural columns.
col·umn inch *n.* a unit of measurement for advertising space, one inch deep and one column wide.
col·umn·ist (ˈkɒləmɪst, -əmnɪst) *n.* a journalist who writes a regular feature in a newspaper: *a gossip columnist.*
co·lure (kəˈlʊə, ˈkəʊlʊə) *n.* either of the two great circles on the celestial sphere, one of which passes through the celestial poles and the equinoxes and the other through the poles and the solstices. [C16: from Late Latin *colūrī* (plural), from Greek *kolourai* cut short, dock-tailed, from *kolos* docked + *oura* tail; so called because the view of the lower part is curtailed]
Col·wyn Bay (ˈkɒlwɪn) *n.* a town and resort in N Wales, in NW Clwyd. Pop.: 25 535 (1971).
co·ly (ˈkəʊlɪ) *n., pl.* **·lies.** any of the arboreal birds of the genus *Colius,* family *Coliidae,* and order *Coliiformes,* of southern Africa. They have a soft hairlike plumage, crested head, and very long tail. Also called: **mousebird.** [C19: from New Latin *colius,* probably from Greek *kolios* woodpecker]
col·za (ˈkɒlzə) *n.* another name for **rape**[2]. [C18: via French (Walloon) *kolzat* from Dutch *koolzaad,* from *kool* cabbage, COLE + *zaad* SEED]
col·za oil *n.* the oil obtained from the seeds of the rape plant and used in making lubricants and synthetic rubber.
COM (kɒm) *n.* **a.** computer output on microfilm; a process in which a computer output is converted direct to microfiche or film, esp. 35 or 16 millimetre film. **b.** (*as modifier*): *a COM machine.*
com. *abbrev. for:* **1.** comedy. **2.** comic. **3.** commerce. **4.** commercial. **5.** committee.
Com. *abbrev. for:* **1.** Commander. **2.** committee. **3.** Commodore. **4.** Communist.
com- *or* **con-** *prefix.* together; with; jointly: *commingle.* [from Latin *com-;* related to *cum* with. In compound words of Latin origin, *com-* becomes *col-* and *cor-* before *l* and *r, co-* before *gn, h,* and most vowels, and *con-* before consonants other than *b, p,* and *m.* Although its sense in compounds of Latin derivation is often obscured, it means: together, with, etc. (*combine, compile*); similar (*conform*); extremely, completely (*consecrate*)]
co·ma[1] (ˈkəʊmə) *n., pl.* **·mas.** a state of unconsciousness from which a person cannot be aroused, caused by injury to the head, rupture of cerebral blood vessels, narcotics, poisons, etc. [C17: from medical Latin, from Greek *kōma* heavy sleep; related to Greek *koitē* bed, perhaps to Middle Irish *cuma* grief]
co·ma[2] (ˈkəʊmə) *n., pl.* **·mae** (-miː). **1.** *Astronomy.* the luminous cloud surrounding the frozen solid nucleus in the head of a comet, formed by vaporization of part of the nucleus when the comet is close to the sun. **2.** *Botany.* **a.** a tuft of hairs attached to the seed coat of some seeds. **b.** the terminal crown of leaves of palms and moss stems. **3.** *Optics.* a type of lens defect characterized by the formation of a diffuse pear-shaped image from a point object. [C17: from Latin: hair of the head, from Greek *komē*] —ˈ**co·mal** *adj.*
Co·ma Ber·e·ni·ces (ˈkəʊmə ˌberɪˈnaɪsiːz) *n., Latin genitive* **Co·mae Ber·e·ni·ces** (ˈkəʊmiː). a faint constellation in the N hemisphere between Ursa Major and Boötes containing the **Coma Cluster,** a cluster of approximately 10 000 galaxies, at a mean distance of 220 million light years. [from Latin, literally: Berenice's hair, named after *Berenice* (died 221 B.C.), consort of Ptolemy III]
Co·man·che (kəˈmæntʃɪ) *n.* **1.** (*pl.* **·ches** *or* **·che**) a member of a North American Indian people, formerly ranging from the River Platte to the Mexican border, now living in Oklahoma. **2.** the language of this people, belonging to the Shoshonean subfamily of the Uto-Aztecan family.
Co·man·che·an (kəˈmæntʃɪən) (in North America) ~*adj.* **1.** of or relating to the early part of the Cretaceous system and period. ~*n.* **2.** the strata and time corresponding to the early Cretaceous.
Co·man·eci (*Rumanian* ˈkomənetʃ) *n.* **Na·dia** (ˈnadja). born 1961, Rumanian gymnast. She became world champion at the 1976 Olympic Games.
co·mate (ˈkəʊmeɪt) *adj. Botany.* **1.** having tufts of hair; hairy. **2.** having or relating to a coma. [C17: from Latin *comātus,* from *coma* hair]
co·ma·tose (ˈkəʊməˌtəʊs, -ˌtəʊz) *adj.* **1.** in a state of coma. **2.** torpid; lethargic. —ˈ**co·ma·tose·ly** *adv.*
co·mat·u·lid (kəˈmætjʊlɪd) *or* **co·mat·u·la** *n., pl.* **·lids** *or* **·lae** (-liː). any of a group of crinoid echinoderms, including the feather stars, in which the adults are free-swimming. [C19: from New Latin *Comatulidae,* from *Comatula* type genus, from Latin *comātus* hairy]
comb (kəʊm) *n.* **1.** a toothed device of metal, plastic, wood, etc., used for disentangling or arranging hair. **2.** a tool or machine that separates, cleans, and straightens wool, cotton, etc. **3.** *Austral.* the fixed cutter on a sheep-shearing machine. **4.** anything resembling a toothed comb in form or function. **5.** the fleshy deeply serrated outgrowth on the top of the heads of certain birds, esp. the domestic fowl. **6.** anything resembling the comb of a bird. **7.** a currycomb. **8.** a honeycomb. **9. go over with a fine-tooth comb.** to search for or revise thoroughly. ~*vb.* **10.** to use a comb on. **11.** (when *tr.,* often foll. by *through*) to search or inspect with great care: *the police combed the woods.* See also **comb out.** [Old English *camb;* related to Old Norse *kambr,* Old High German *camb*]
comb. *abbrev. for* combining.
com·bat *n.* (ˈkɒmbæt, -bət, ˈkʌm-). **1.** a fight, conflict, or struggle. **2. a.** an action fought between two military forces. **b.** (*as modifier*): *a combat jacket.* **3. single combat.** a fight between two individuals; duel. **4. close** *or* **hand-to-hand combat.** fighting at close quarters. ~*vb.* (kəmˈbæt; ˈkɒmbæt, ˈkʌm-). **5.** (*tr.*) to fight or defy. **6.** (*intr.;* often foll. by *with* or *against*) to struggle or strive (against); be in conflict (with): *to combat against disease.* [C16: from French, from Old French *combattre,* from Vulgar Latin *combattere* (unattested), from Latin *com-* with + *battuere* to beat, hit] —**com·ˈbat·a·ble** *adj.* —**com·ˈbat·er** *n.*
com·bat·ant (ˈkɒmbətᵊnt, ˈkʌm-) *n.* **1.** a person or group engaged in or prepared for a fight, struggle, or dispute. ~*adj.* **2.** engaged in or ready for combat.
com·bat fa·tigue *n.* another term for **battle fatigue.**
com·bat·ive (ˈkɒmbətɪv, ˈkʌm-) *adj.* eager or ready to fight, argue, etc.; aggressive. —ˈ**com·bat·ive·ly** *adv.*
combe *or* **comb** (kuːm) *n.* variant spellings of **coomb.**
comb·er (ˈkəʊmə) *n.* **1.** a person, tool, or machine that combs wool, flax, etc. **2.** a long curling wave; roller.
com·bi·na·tion (ˌkɒmbɪˈneɪʃən) *n.* **1.** the act of combining or state of being combined. **2.** a union of separate parts, qualities, etc. **3.** an alliance of people or parties; group having a common purpose. **4. a.** the set of numbers that opens a combination lock. **b.** the mechanism of this type of lock. **5.** *Brit.* a motorcycle with a sidecar attached. **6.** *Maths.* **a.** an arrangement of the numbers, terms, etc., of a set into specified groups without regard to order in the group: *the combinations of a, b, and c, taken two at a time, are ab, bc, ac.* **b.** a group formed in this way. The number of combinations of *n* objects taken *r* at a time is $n!/[(n-r)!r!]$. Symbol: $_nC_r$. Compare **permutation** (sense 1). **7.** the chemical reaction of two or more compounds, usually to form one other compound. **8.** a coordinated sequence of chess moves. —ˌ**com·bi·ˈna·tion·al** *adj.*
com·bi·na·tion lock *n.* a type of lock that can only be opened when a set of dials releasing the tumblers of the lock are turned to show a specific sequence of numbers.
com·bi·na·tion room *n. Brit.* (at Cambridge University) a common room.
com·bi·na·tions (ˌkɒmbɪˈneɪʃənz) *pl. n. Brit.* a one-piece woollen undergarment with long sleeves and legs. Often shortened to **combs.** U.S. term: **union suit.**
com·bi·na·tion tone *n.* a musical sound produced when two loud notes are sounded together.
com·bi·na·tive (ˈkɒmbɪˌneɪtɪv, -nətɪv), **com·bi·na·to·ri·al,** *or* **com·bi·na·to·ry** *adj.* **1.** resulting from being, tending to be, or able to be joined or mixed together. **2.** *Linguistics.* (of a sound change) occurring only in specific contexts or as a result of some other factor, such as change of stress within a word. Compare **isolative** (sense 1).
com·bi·na·to·ri·al a·nal·y·sis *n.* the branch of mathematics concerned with combinations and permutations.
com·bine *vb.* (kəmˈbaɪn). **1.** to integrate or cause to be integrated; join together. **2.** to unite or cause to unite to form a chemical compound. **3.** *Agriculture.* to harvest (crops) with a combine. ~*n.* (ˈkɒmbaɪn). **4.** *Agriculture.* short for **combine harvester. 5.** an association of enterprises, esp. in order to gain a monopoly of a market. **6.** *U.S. informal.* an association for the promotion of commercial or other interests, esp. by doubtful means. [C15: from Late Latin *combīnāre,* from Latin *com-* together + *bīnī* two by two] —**com·ˈbin·a·ble** *adj.* —**com·ˌbin·a·ˈbil·i·ty** *n.* —**com·ˈbin·er** *n.*
com·bine har·ves·ter (ˈkɒmbaɪn) *n.* a machine that simultaneously cuts, threshes, and cleans a standing crop of grain.
comb·ings (ˈkəʊmɪŋz) *pl. n.* **1.** the loose hair, wool, etc., removed by combing, esp. that of animals. **2.** the unwanted loose short fibres removed in combing cotton, etc.
com·bin·ing form *n.* a linguistic element that occurs only as part of a compound word, such as *anthropo-* in *anthropology* and *anthropomorph.*
comb jel·ly *n.* another name for a **ctenophore.**
com·bo (ˈkɒmbəʊ) *n., pl.* **·bos. 1.** a small group of musicians, esp. of jazz musicians. **2.** *Informal.* any combination. **3.** *Austral. slang.* a white man who lives with an Aboriginal woman.
comb out *vb.* (*tr., adv.*) **1.** to remove (tangles or knots) from (the hair) with a comb. **2.** to isolate and remove for a purpose. **3.** to survey carefully; examine systematically. ~*n.* **comb-out. 4.** an act of combing out.
com·bust (kəmˈbʌst) *adj.* **1.** *Astrology.* (of a star or planet) invisible for a period between 24 and 30 days each year due to its proximity to the sun. ~*vb.* **2.** *Chem.* to burn.
com·bus·ti·ble (kəmˈbʌstəbᵊl) *adj.* **1.** capable of igniting and burning. **2.** easily annoyed; excitable. ~*n.* **3.** a combustible substance. —**com·ˌbus·ti·ˈbil·i·ty** *or* **com·ˈbus·ti·ble·ness** *n.* —**com·ˈbus·ti·bly** *adv.*
com·bus·tion (kəmˈbʌstʃən) *n.* **1.** the process of burning. **2.** any process in which a substance reacts with oxygen to produce a significant rise in temperature and the emission of light. **3.** a chemical process in which two compounds, such as sodium and chlorine, react together to produce heat and light. **4.** a process in which a compound reacts slowly with oxygen to produce little heat and no light. [C15: from Old French, from Latin *combūrere* to burn up, from *com-* (intensive) + *ūrere* to burn] —**com·ˈbus·tive** *n., adj.*
com·bus·tion cham·ber *n.* an enclosed space in which combustion takes place, such as the space above the piston in the cylinder head of an internal-combustion engine or the

chambers in a gas turbine or rocket engine in which fuel and oxidant burn.

com·bus·tor (kəm'bʌstə) *n.* the combustion system of a jet engine or ramjet, comprising the combustion chamber, the fuel injection apparatus, and the igniter.

comdg. *Military. abbrev. for* commanding.

Comdr. *Military. abbrev. for* Commander.

Comdt. *Military. abbrev. for* Commandant.

come (kʌm) *vb.* **comes, com·ing, came, come.** (*mainly intr.*) **1.** to move towards a specified person or place: *come to my desk.* **2.** to arrive by movement or by making progress. **3.** to become perceptible: *light came into the sky.* **4.** to occur in the course of time: *Christmas comes but once a year.* **5.** to exist or occur at a specific point in a series: *your turn comes next.* **6.** to happen as a result: *no good will come of this.* **7.** to originate or be derived: *good may come of evil.* **8.** to occur to the mind: *the truth suddenly came to me.* **9.** to extend or reach: *she comes up to my shoulder.* **10.** to be produced or offered: *that dress comes in red only.* **11.** to arrive at or be brought into a particular state or condition: *you will soon come to grief; the new timetable comes into effect on Monday.* **12.** (foll. by *from*) to be or have been a resident or native (of): *I come from London.* **13.** to become: *your wishes will come true.* **14.** (*tr.; takes an infinitive*) to be given awareness: *I came to realize its enormous value.* **15.** (of grain) to germinate. **16.** *Taboo slang.* to have an orgasm. **17.** (*tr.*) *Brit. informal.* to play the part of: *don't come the fine gentleman with me.* **18.** (*tr.*) *Brit. informal.* to cause or produce: *don't come that nonsense again.* **19. as...as they come.** the most characteristic example of a class or type. **20. come again?** *Informal.* what did you say? **21. come and.** (*imperative or dependent imperative*) to move towards a particular person or thing or accompany a person with some specified purpose: *come and see what I've found.* **22. come clean.** *Informal.* to make a revelation or confession. **23. come good.** *Austral. informal.* to recover after a setback; succeed. **24. come to light.** to be revealed. **25. come to light with.** *Austral. informal.* to find or produce. **26. come to pass.** to take place. **27. how come?** *Informal.* how did that happen? ~*interj.* **28.** an exclamation expressing annoyance, irritation, etc.: *come now! come come!* ~See also **come about, come across, come along, come at, come away, comeback, come between, come by, comedown, come forward, come in, come into, come of, come off, come-on, come out, come over, come round, come through, come to, come up, come upon.** [Old English *cuman;* related to Old Norse *koma,* Gothic *qiman,* Old High German *queman* to come, Sanskrit *gámati* he goes]

come a·bout *vb.* (*intr., adv.*) **1.** to take place; happen. **2.** *Nautical.* to change tacks.

come a·cross *vb.* (*intr.*) **1.** (*prep.*) to meet or find by accident. **2.** (*adv.*) (of a person or his words) to communicate the intended meaning or impression. **3.** (often foll. by *with*) to provide what is expected.

come a·long *vb.* **1.** (*intr., adv.*) to progress: *how's your French coming along?* **2. come along!** **a.** hurry up! **b.** make an effort!

come at *vb.* (*intr., prep.*) **1.** to discover or reach (facts, the truth, etc.). **2.** to attack (a person): *he came at me with an axe.* **3.** (*usually used with a negative*) *Austral. slang.* to agree to do (something).

come-at-a·ble *adj.* an informal expression for **accessible.**

come a·way *vb.* (*intr., adv.*) **1.** to become detached. **2.** (foll. by *with*) to leave (with).

come·back ('kʌm,bæk) *n. Informal.* **1.** a return to a former position, status, etc. **2.** a return or response, esp. recriminatory. **3.** a quick reply; retort. ~*vb.* **come back.** (*intr., adv.*) **4.** to return, esp. to the memory. **5.** to become fashionable again. **6.** *U.S.* to argue back; retort.

come be·tween *vb.* (*intr., prep.*) to cause the estrangement or separation of (two people): *nothing could come between the two lovers.*

come by *vb.* (*intr., prep.*) to find or obtain (a thing) esp. accidentally: *do you ever come by any old books?*

Com·e·con ('kɒmɪ,kɒn) *n.* an association of Soviet-oriented Communist nations, founded in 1949 to coordinate economic development, etc. [C20: *Co(uncil for) M(utual) Econ(omic Aid)*]

co·me·di·an (kə'mi:dɪən) *n.* **1.** an entertainer who specializes in jokes, comic skits, etc. **2.** an actor in comedy.

co·me·dic (kə'mi:dɪk) *adj.* of or relating to comedy.

Co·mé·die Fran·çaise *French.* (kɔmedi frɑ̃'sɛ:z) *n.* the French national theatre, founded in Paris in 1680.

co·me·di·enne (kə,mi:dɪ'ɛn) *n.* a female comedian.

com·e·do ('kɒmɪ,dəʊ) *n., pl.* **com·e·dos** *or* **com·e·do·nes** (,kɒmɪ'dəuni:z). *Pathol.* the technical name for **blackhead.** [C19: from New Latin, from Latin: glutton, from *comedere* to eat up, from *com-* (intensive) + *edere* to eat]

come·down ('kʌm,daʊn) *n.* **1.** a decline in position, status, or prosperity. **2.** *Informal.* a disappointment. **3.** *Slang.* a depressed or unexcited state. ~*vb.* **come down.** (*intr., adv.*) **4.** to come to a place regarded as lower. **5.** to lose status, wealth, etc. (esp. in the phrase **to come down in the world**). **6.** to reach a decision: *the report came down in favour of a pay increase.* **7.** (often foll. by *to*) to be handed down or acquired by tradition or inheritance. **8.** *Brit.* to leave college or university. **9.** (foll. by *with*) to succumb (to illness or disease). **10.** (foll. by *on*) to rebuke or criticize harshly. **11.** (foll. by *to*) to amount in essence (to): *it comes down to two choices.* **12.** *Slang.* to lose the effects of a drug and return to a normal or more normal state.

com·e·dy ('kɒmɪdɪ) *n., pl.* **·dies. 1.** a dramatic or other work of light and amusing character. **2.** the genre of drama represented by works of this type. **3.** (in classical literature) a play in which the main characters and motive triumph over adversity. **4.** the humorous aspect of life or of events. **5.** an amusing event or sequence of events. **6.** humour or comic style: *the comedy of Chaplin.* [C14: from Old French *comédie,* from Latin *cōmoedia,* from Greek *kōmōidia,* from *kōmos* village festival + *aeidein* to sing]

com·e·dy of man·ners *n.* **1.** a comedy dealing with the way of life and foibles of a social group. **2.** the genre represented by works of this type.

come for·ward *vb.* (*intr., adv.*) **1.** to offer one's services; volunteer. **2.** to present oneself.

come-hith·er *adj.* (*usually prenominal*) *Informal.* alluring; seductive: *a come-hither look.*

come in *vb.* (*intr., mainly adv.*) **1.** to enter, used in the imperative when admitting a person. **2.** to prove to be: *it came in useful.* **3.** to become fashionable or seasonable. **4.** *Cricket.* to begin an innings. **5.** *Athletics, horse racing, etc.* to finish a race (in a certain position). **6.** (of a politician or political party) to win an election. **7.** *Radio, television.* to be received: *news is coming in of a big fire in Glasgow.* **8.** (of money) to be received as income. **9.** to play a role; advance one's interests: *where do I come in?* **10.** (foll. by *for*) to be the object of: *the Chancellor came in for a lot of criticism in the Commons.* **11. this is where we came in.** we are at the same point now as when we began.

come in·to *vb.* (*intr., prep.*) **1.** to enter. **2.** to inherit. **3. come into one's own.** to become fulfilled: *she really came into her own when she got divorced.*

come·ly ('kʌmlɪ) *adj.* **·li·er, ·li·est. 1.** good-looking; attractive. **2.** *Archaic.* suitable; fitting. [Old English *cȳmlīc* beautiful; related to Old High German *cūmi* frail, Middle High German *komlīche* suitably] —**'come·li·ness** *n.*

Co·me·ni·us (kə'meɪnɪəs) *n.* **John A·mos,** Czech name *Jan Amos Komensky.* 1592–1670, Czech educational reformer.

come of *vb.* (*intr., prep.*) **1.** to be descended from. **2.** to result from: *nothing came of his experiments.*

come off *vb.* (*intr., mainly adv.*) **1.** (*also prep.*) to fall (from), losing one's balance. **2.** to become detached or be capable of being detached. **3.** (*prep.*) to be removed from (a price, tax, etc.): *will anything come off income tax in the budget?* **4.** (*copula*) to emerge from or as if from a trial or contest: *he came off the winner.* **5.** *Informal.* to take place or happen. **6.** *Informal.* to have the intended effect; succeed: *his jokes did not come off.* **7.** *Taboo slang.* to have an orgasm. **8. come off it!** *Informal.* stop trying to fool me!

come-on *n. Informal.* **1.** anything that serves as a lure or enticement. ~*vb.* **come on** (*intr., mainly adv.*) **2.** (of power, a water supply, etc.) to become available; start running or functioning. **3.** to make or show progress; develop: *my plants are coming on nicely.* **4.** to advance, esp. in battle. **5.** to begin: *she felt a cold coming on; a new bowler has come on.* **6.** *Theatre.* to make an entrance on stage. **7.** to be considered, esp. in a court of law. **8.** (*prep.*) See **come upon. 9. come on! a.** hurry up! **b.** cheer up! pull yourself together! **c.** make an effort! **10. come on strong.** to make a forceful or exaggerated impression.

come out *vb.* (*intr., adv.*) **1.** to be made public or revealed: *the news of her death came out last week.* **2.** to make a debut in society or on stage. **3.** to declare openly that one is a homosexual. **4.** *Chiefly Brit.* to go on strike. **5.** to declare oneself: *the government came out in favour of scrapping the project.* **6.** to be shown visibly or clearly: *you came out very well in the photos.* **7.** to yield a satisfactory solution: *these sums just won't come out.* **8.** to be published: *the paper comes out on Fridays.* **9.** (foll. by *in*) to become covered with: *you're coming out in spots.* **10.** (foll. by *with*) to speak or declare openly: *you can rely on him to come out with the facts.*

come o·ver *vb.* (*intr.*) **1.** (*adv.*) (of a person or his words) to communicate the intended meaning or impression: *he came over very well.* **2.** (*adv.*) to change allegiances: *some people came over to our side in the war.* **3.** *Informal.* to undergo or feel a particular sensation: *I came over funny.*

com·er ('kʌmə) *n.* **1.** (*in combination*) a person who comes: *all-comers; newcomers.* **2.** *Informal.* a potential success.

come round *or* **a·round** *vb.* (*intr., adv.*) **1.** to be restored to life or consciousness. **2.** to change or modify one's mind or opinion.

co·mes·ti·ble (kə'mɛstɪbᵊl) *n.* **1.** (*usually pl.*) food. ~*adj.* **2.** a rare word for **edible.** [C15: from Late Latin *comestibilis,* from *comedere* to eat up; see COMEDO]

com·et ('kɒmɪt) *n.* a celestial body that travels around the sun, usually in a highly elliptical orbit: thought to consist of a solid frozen nucleus part of which vaporizes on approaching the sun to form a gaseous luminous coma and a long luminous tail. [C13: from Old French *comète,* from Latin *comēta,* from Greek *komētēs* long-haired, from *komē* hair] —**'com·e·tar·y** *or* **co·met·ic** (kɒ'mɛtɪk) *adj.*

come through *vb.* (*intr.*) **1.** (*adv.*) to emerge successfully. **2.** (*prep.*) to survive (an illness, setback, etc.).

come to *vb.* (*intr.*) **1.** (when *prep., used reflexively*) to regain consciousness or return to one's normal state. **2.** (*adv.*) *Nautical.* to slow a vessel or bring her to a stop. **3.** (*prep.*) to amount to (a sum of money): *your bill comes to four pounds.* **4.** (*prep.*) to arrive at (a certain state): *what is the world coming to?*

come up *vb.* (*intr., adv.*) **1.** to come to a place regarded as higher. **2.** (of the sun) to rise. **3.** to begin: *a wind came up.* **4.** to be regurgitated or vomited. **5.** to present itself or be discussed: *that question will come up again.* **6.** *Brit.* to begin a term, esp. one's first term, at a college or university. **7.** to appear from out of the ground: *my beans have come up early* *this year.* **8.** *Informal.* to win: *have your premium bonds ever come up?* **9. come up against.** to be faced with; come into conflict or competition with. **10. come up to.** to equal or meet a standard: *that just doesn't come up to scratch.* **11. come up with.** to produce or find: *she always comes up with the right answer.*

come up·on *vb. (intr., prep.)* to meet or encounter unexpectedly: *I came upon an old friend in the street today.*

come+up+pance (ˌkʌm'ʌpəns) *n. Slang.* just retribution.

com+fit ('kʌmfɪt, 'kɒm-) *n.* a sugar-coated sweet containing a nut or seed. [C15: from Old French, from Latin *confectum* something prepared, from *conficere* to produce; see CONFECT]

com+fort ('kʌmfət) *n.* **1.** a state of ease or well-being. **2.** relief from affliction, grief, etc. **3.** a person, thing, or event that brings solace or ease. **4.** *Obsolete.* support. **5.** *(usually pl.)* something that affords physical ease and relaxation. ~*vb. (tr.)* **6.** to ease the pain of; soothe; cheer. **7.** to bring physical ease to. [C13: from Old French *confort,* from Late Latin *confortāre* to strengthen very much, from Latin *con-* (intensive) + *fortis* strong] —**'com+fort+ing** *adj.* —**'com+fort+ing+ly** *adv.* —**'com+fort+less** *adj.* —**'com+fort+less+ly** *adv.* —**'com+fort+less+ness** *n.*

com+fort+a·ble ('kʌmftəbᵊl, 'kʌmfətəbᵊl) *adj.* **1.** giving comfort or physical relief. **2.** at ease. **3.** free from affliction or pain. **4.** (of a person or situation) relaxing. **5.** *Informal.* having adequate income. **6.** *Informal.* (of income, etc.) adequate to provide comfort. —**'com+fort+a·ble+ness** *n.* —**'com+fort+a·bly** *adv.*

com+fort+er ('kʌmfətə) *n.* **1.** a person or thing that comforts. **2.** *Chiefly Brit.* a woollen scarf. **3.** a baby's dummy.

Com+fort+er ('kʌmfətə) *n. Christianity.* an epithet of the Holy Spirit. [C14: translation of Latin *consolātor,* representing Greek *paraklētos;* see PARACLETE]

com+fort sta+tion *n. U.S.* a public lavatory and rest room.

com+frey ('kʌmfrɪ) *n.* any hairy Eurasian boraginaceous plant of the genus *Symphytum,* having blue, purplish-pink, or white flowers. [C15: from Old French *cunfirie,* from Latin *conferva* water plant; see CONFERVA]

com+fy ('kʌmfɪ) *adj.* **+fi+er, +fi+est.** *Informal.* short for **comfortable.**

com+ic ('kɒmɪk) *adj.* **1.** of, relating to, characterized by, or characteristic of comedy. **2.** *(prenominal)* acting in, writing, or composing comedy: *a comic writer.* **3.** humorous; funny. ~*n.* **4.** a person who is comic, esp. a comic actor; comedian. **5.** a book or magazine containing comic strips. **6.** *(usually pl.) Chiefly U.S.* comic strips in newspapers, etc. [C16: from Latin *cōmicus,* from Greek *kōmikos* relating to COMEDY]

com·i·cal ('kɒmɪkᵊl) *adj.* **1.** causing laughter. **2.** ludicrous; laughable. —**'com·i·cal+ly** *adv.* —**'com·i·cal+ness** *n.*

com+ic op·er·a *n.* a play largely set to music, employing comic effects or situations. See also **opéra bouffe, opera buffa.**

com+ic strip *n.* a sequence of drawings in a newspaper, magazine, etc., relating a comic or adventurous situation.

Co·mines *or* **Com·mines** (*French* kɔ'min) *n.* **Phi·lippe de** (fi'lip də). ?1447–?1511, French diplomat and historian, noted for his *Mémoires* (1489–98).

Com+in+form ('kɒmɪnˌfɔːm) *n.* short for **Communist Information Bureau:** established 1947 to exchange information among nine European Communist parties and coordinate their activities; dissolved in 1956.

com+ing ('kʌmɪŋ) *adj.* **1.** *(prenominal)* (of time, events, etc.) approaching or next: *this coming Thursday.* **2.** promising (esp. in the phrase **up and coming**). **3. coming up!** *Informal.* an expression used to announce that a meal is about to be served. **4. have it coming to one.** *Informal.* to deserve what one is about to suffer. **5. not know whether one is coming or going.** to be totally confused. ~*n.* **6.** arrival or approach. **7.** *(often cap.)* the return of Christ in glory. See also **Second Coming.**

Com+in+tern *or* **Kom+in+tern** ('kɒmɪnˌtɜːn) *n.* short for **Communist International;** an international Communist organization founded by Lenin in Moscow in 1919 and dissolved in 1943; it degenerated under Stalin into an instrument of Soviet politics. Also called: **Third International.**

co+mi+ti·a (kə'mɪʃɪə) *n.* an ancient Roman assembly that elected officials and exercised judicial and legislative authority. [C17: from Latin *comitium* assembly, from *com-* together + *īre* to go] —**co+mi+tial** (kə'mɪʃəl) *adj.*

com+i·ty ('kɒmɪtɪ) *n., pl.* **·ties.** **1.** mutual civility; courtesy. **2.** short for **comity of nations.** **3.** the policy whereby one religious denomination refrains from proselytizing the members of another. [C16: from Latin *cōmitās,* from *cōmis* affable, obliging, of uncertain origin]

com+i·ty of na+tions *n.* the friendly recognition accorded by one nation to the laws and usages of another.

comm. *abbrev. for:* **1.** commerce. **2.** commercial. **3.** committee. **4.** commonwealth.

com+ma ('kɒmə) *n.* **1.** the punctuation mark , indicating a slight pause in the spoken sentence and used where there is a listing of items or to separate a nonrestrictive clause or phrase from a main clause. **2.** *Music.* a minute interval. [C16: from Latin, from Greek *komma* clause, from *koptein* to cut]

com+ma ba+cil+lus *n.* a comma-shaped bacterium, *Vibrio comma,* that causes cholera in man: family *Spirillaceae.*

com+ma but·ter+fly *n.* an orange-brown European nymphalid butterfly, *Polygonia c-album,* with a white comma-shaped mark on the underside of each hind wing.

com+mand (kə'mɑːnd) *vb.* **1.** (when *tr., may take a clause as object or an infinitive*) to order, require, or compel. **2.** to have or be in control or authority over (a person, situation, etc.). **3.** *(tr.)* to have knowledge or use of: *he commands the language.* **4.** *(tr.)* to receive as due or because of merit: *his nature commands respect.* **5.** to dominate (a view, etc.) as from a height. ~*n.* **6.** an order; mandate. **7.** the act of commanding. **8.** the power or right to command. **9.** the exercise of the power to command. **10.** ability or knowledge; control: *a command of French.* **11.** *Chiefly military.* the jurisdiction of a commander. **12.** a military unit or units commanding a specific area or function, as in the R.A.F. **13.** *Brit.* **a.** an invitation from the monarch. **b.** *(as modifier): a command performance.* **14.** *Computer technol.* another name for **instruction** (sense 3). [C13: from Old French *commander,* from Latin *com-* (intensive) + *mandāre* to entrust, enjoin, command] —**com+'mand+ing+ly** *adv.*

com+man+dant ('kɒmənˌdænt, -ˌdɑːnt) *n.* an officer commanding a place, group, or establishment.

com+man+deer (ˌkɒmən'dɪə) *vb. (tr.)* **1.** to seize for public or military use. **2.** to seize arbitrarily. [C19: from Afrikaans *kommandeer,* from French *commander* to COMMAND]

com+mand+er (kə'mɑːndə) *n.* **1.** an officer in command of a military formation or operation. **2.** a naval commissioned rank junior to captain but senior to lieutenant commander. **3.** the second in command of larger British warships. **4.** someone who holds authority. **5.** a high-ranking member of some knightly or fraternal orders. **6.** an officer responsible for a district of the Metropolitan Police in London. **7.** *History.* the administrator of a commandery of a medieval religious order. —**com+'mand+er+ˌship** *n.*

com+mand+er in chief *n., pl.* **com+mand+ers in chief.** **1.** the officer holding supreme command of the forces in an area or operation. **2.** the officer holding command of a major subdivision of one military service.

com+mand guid+ance *n.* a method of controlling a missile during flight by transmitting information to it.

com+mand+ing (kə'mɑːndɪŋ) *adj.* *(usually prenominal)* **1.** being in command. **2.** having the air of authority: *a commanding voice.* **3.** (of a position, situation, etc.) exerting control. **4.** (of a height, viewpoint, etc.) overlooking; advantageous. —**com+'mand+ing+ly** *adv.*

com+mand+ing of+fic+er *n.* an officer in command of a military unit.

com+mand+ment (kə'mɑːndmənt) *n.* **1.** a divine command, esp. one of the Ten Commandments of the Old Testament. **2.** *Literary.* any command.

com+mand mod+ule *n.* the cone-shaped module used as the living quarters in an Apollo spacecraft and functioning as the splashdown vehicle.

com+man+do (kə'mɑːndəʊ) *n., pl.* **+dos** *or* **+does.** **1. a.** an amphibious military unit trained for raiding. **b.** a member of such a unit. **2.** the basic unit of the Royal Marine Corps. **3.** (originally) an armed force raised by Boers during the Boer War. **4.** *(modifier)* denoting or relating to a commando or force of commandos: *a commando raid; a commando unit.* [C19: from Afrikaans *kommando,* from Dutch *commando* command, from French *commander* to COMMAND]

com+mand pa+per *n.* (in Britain) a government document that is presented to Parliament, in theory by royal command. See also **green paper, white paper.**

com+mand per+form+ance *n.* a performance of a play, opera, etc., at the request of a ruler or of royalty.

com+mand post *n. Military.* the position from which a unit commander and his staff exercise command.

com+mea+sure (kə'mɛʒə) *vb. (tr.)* to coincide with in degree, extent, quality, etc. —**com+'meas+ur+a·ble** *adj.*

com+me·di·a dell'ar+te (*Italian* kɔm'mɛdja del'larte) *n.* a form of popular comedy developed in Italy during the 16th to 18th centuries, with stock characters such as Punchinello, Harlequin, and Columbine, in situations improvised from a plot outline. [Italian, literally: comedy of art]

comme il faut *French.* (kɔ mil 'fo) as it should be; correctly.

com+mem·o+rate (kə'mɛməˌreɪt) *vb. (tr.)* to honour or keep alive the memory of. [C16: from Latin *commemorāre* be mindful of, from *com-* (intensive) + *memorāre* to remind, from *memor* mindful] —**com+'mem·o+ra+tive** *or* **com+'mem·o+ra+to+ry** *adj.* —**com+'mem·o+ra+tive+ly** *adv.* —**com+'mem·o+ˌra+tor** *n.*

com+mem·o+ra+tion (kəˌmɛmə'reɪʃən) *n.* **1.** the act or an instance of commemorating. **2.** a ceremony or service in memory of a person or event. —**com+ˌmem·o+'ra+tion+al** *adj.*

com+mence (kə'mɛns) *vb.* to start or begin; come or cause to come into being, operation, etc. [C14: from Old French *comencer,* from Vulgar Latin *cominitiāre* (unattested), from Latin *com-* (intensive) + *initiāre* to begin, from *initium* a beginning] —**com+'menc+er** *n.*

com+mence+ment (kə'mɛnsmənt) *n.* **1.** the beginning; start. **2.** *U.S.* a ceremony for the conferment of academic degrees.

com+mend (kə'mɛnd) *vb.* **1.** to present or represent as being worthy of regard, confidence, kindness, etc.; recommend. **2.** to give in charge; entrust. **3.** to express a good opinion of; praise. **4.** to give the regards of: *commend me to your aunt.* [C14: from Latin *commendāre* to commit to someone's care, from *com-* (intensive) + *mandāre* to entrust] —**com+'mend+a·ble** *adj.* —**com+'mend+a·ble+ness** *n.* —**com+'mend+a·bly** *adv.* —**com+'mend·a+to·ry** *adj.*

com+men+dam (kə'mɛndæm) *n.* **1.** the temporary holding of an ecclesiastical benefice. **2.** a benefice so held. [C16: from Medieval Latin phrase *dare in commendam* to give in trust, from *commenda* trust, back formation from Latin *commendāre* to entrust, COMMEND]

com+men+da+tion (ˌkɒmɛn'deɪʃən) *n.* **1.** the act or an instance of commending; praise. **2.** *U.S.* an award. **3.** (*often pl.*) *Archaic.* a greeting.

com·men·sal (kəˈmɛnsəl) *adj.* **1.** (of two different species of plant or animal) living in close association without being interdependent. **2.** *Rare.* of or relating to eating together, esp. at the same table: *commensal pleasures.* ~*n.* **3.** a commensal plant or animal. **4.** *Rare.* a companion at table. [C14: from Medieval Latin *commensālis*, from Latin *com-* together + *mensa* table] —**comˈmen·sal·ism** *n.* —**com·men·sal·i·ty** (ˌkɒmɛnˈsælɪtɪ) *n.* —**comˈmen·sal·ly** *adv.*

com·men·su·ra·ble (kəˈmɛnsərəbəl, -ʃə-) *adj.* **1.** *Maths.* **a.** having a common factor. **b.** having units of the same dimensions and being related by whole numbers: *hours and minutes are commensurable.* **2.** well-proportioned; proportionate. —**comˌmen·su·ra·ˈbil·i·ty** *n.* —**comˈmen·su·ra·bly** *adv.*

com·men·su·rate (kəˈmɛnsərɪt, -ʃə-) *adj.* **1.** having the same extent or duration. **2.** corresponding in degree, amount, or size; proportionate. **3.** able to be measured by a common standard; commensurable. [C17: from Late Latin *commēnsūrātus*, from Latin *com-* same + *mēnsūrāre* to MEASURE] —**comˈmen·su·rate·ly** *adv.* —**comˈmen·su·rate·ness** *n.* —**com·men·su·ra·tion** (kəˌmɛnsəˈreɪʃən, -ʃə-) *n.*

com·ment (ˈkɒmɛnt) *n.* **1.** a remark, criticism, or observation. **2.** talk or gossip. **3.** a note explaining or criticizing a passage in a text. **4.** explanatory or critical matter added to a text. ~*vb.* **5.** (when *intr.*, often foll. by *on;* when *tr.*, takes a clause as object) to remark or express an opinion. **6.** (*intr.*) to write notes explaining or criticizing a text. [C15: from Latin *commentum* invention, from *comminiscī* to contrive, related to *mens* mind] —**ˈcom·ment·er** *n.*

com·men·tar·y (ˈkɒməntərɪ, -trɪ) *n., pl.* **-tar·ies.** **1.** an explanatory series of notes or comments. **2.** a spoken accompaniment to a broadcast, film, etc., esp. of a sporting event. **3.** an explanatory essay or treatise on a text. **4.** (*usually pl.*) a personal record of events or facts: *the commentaries of Caesar.* —**com·men·tar·i·al** (ˌkɒmənˈtɛərɪəl) *adj.*

com·men·tate (ˈkɒmənˌteɪt) *vb.* **1.** to serve as a commentator. **2.** (*tr.*) to make a commentary on (a text, event, etc.).

Usage. The verb *commentate,* derived from *commentator,* is sometimes used as a synonym for *comment on* or *provide a commentary for.* It is not yet fully accepted as standard, though widespread in sports reporting and journalism.

com·men·ta·tor (ˈkɒmənˌteɪtə) *n.* **1.** a person who provides a spoken commentary for a broadcast, film, etc., esp. of a sporting event. **2.** a person who writes notes on a text, etc.

com·merce (ˈkɒmɜːs) *n.* **1.** the activity embracing all forms of the purchase and sale of goods and services. **2.** social relations and exchange, esp. of opinions, attitudes, etc. **3.** *Archaic.* sexual intercourse. [C16: from Latin *commercium* trade, from *commercārī*, from *mercārī* to trade, from *merx* merchandise]

com·mer·cial (kəˈmɜːʃəl) *adj.* **1.** of, connected with, or engaged in commerce; mercantile. **2.** sponsored or paid for by an advertiser: *commercial television.* **3.** having profit as the main aim: *commercial music.* **4.** (of goods, chemicals, etc.) of unrefined quality or presentation and produced in bulk for use in industry. ~*n.* **5.** a commercially sponsored advertisement on radio or television. —**com·mer·ci·al·i·ty** (kəˌmɜːʃɪˈælɪtɪ) *n.* —**comˈmer·cial·ly** *adv.*

com·mer·cial art *n.* graphic art for commercial uses such as advertising, packaging, etc. —**com·mer·cial art·ist** *n.*

com·mer·cial bank *n.* a bank primarily engaged in making short-term loans from funds deposited in current accounts.

com·mer·cial col·lege *n.* a college providing tuition in commercial skills, such as shorthand and book-keeping.

com·mer·cial·ism (kəˈmɜːʃəˌlɪzəm) *n.* **1.** the spirit, principles, or procedure of commerce. **2.** exclusive or inappropriate emphasis on profit. —**comˈmer·cial·ist** *n.* —**comˌmer·cial·ˈis·tic** *adj.*

com·mer·cial·ize *or* **com·mer·cial·ise** (kəˈmɜːʃəˌlaɪz) *vb.* (*tr.*) **1.** to make commercial in aim, methods, or character. **2.** to exploit for profit, esp. at the expense of quality. —**comˌmer·cial·i·ˈza·tion** *or* **comˌmer·cial·i·ˈsa·tion** *n.*

com·mer·cial pa·per *n.* *Chiefly U.S.* a short-term negotiable document, such as a bill of exchange, promissory note, etc., calling for the transference of a specified sum of money at a designated date.

com·mer·cial trav·el·ler *n.* another name for a **travelling salesman.**

com·mer·cial ve·hi·cle *n.* a vehicle for carrying goods or (less commonly) passengers.

com·mère (ˈkɒmɛə; *French* kɔˈmɛːr) *n.* a female compere. [French: literally, godmother, from COM- + *mère* mother; see COMPERE]

com·mie *or* **com·my** (ˈkɒmɪ) *n., pl.* **-mies.** *adj. Informal and derogatory, chiefly U.S.* short for **communist.**

com·mi·na·tion (ˌkɒmɪˈneɪʃən) *n.* **1.** the act or an instance of threatening punishment or vengeance. **2.** *Church of England.* a recital of prayers, including a list of God's judgments against sinners, in the office for Ash Wednesday. [C15: from Latin *comminātiō*, from *comminārī* to menace, from *com-* (intensive) + *minārī* to threaten] —**com·min·a·to·ry** (ˈkɒmɪnətərɪ, -trɪ) *adj.*

Com·mines (*French* kɔˈmin) *n.* a variant spelling of (Philippe de) **Comines.**

com·min·gle (kɒˈmɪŋgᵊl) *vb.* to mix or be mixed; blend.

com·mi·nute (ˈkɒmɪˌnjuːt) *vb.* **1.** to break (a bone) into several small fragments. **2.** to divide property into small lots. **3.** to pulverize. [C17: from Latin *comminuere*, from *com-* (intensive) + *minuere* to reduce; related to MINOR] —**ˌcom·miˈnu·tion** *n.*

com·mi·nut·ed frac·ture *n.* a fracture in which the bone is splintered or fragmented.

com·mis (ˈkɒmɪs, ˈkɒmɪ) *n., pl.* **-mis.** **1.** an agent or deputy. **2.** an apprentice waiter or chef. [C16 (meaning: deputy): from French, from *commettre* to employ, COMMIT]

com·mis·er·ate (kəˈmɪzəˌreɪt) *vb.* (when *intr.*, usually foll. by *with*) to feel or express sympathy or compassion (for). [C17: from Latin *commiserārī*, from *com-* together + *miserārī* to bewail, pity, from *miser* wretched] —**comˈmis·er·a·ble** *adj.* —**comˌmis·er·ˈa·tion** *n.* —**comˈmis·er·a·tive** *adj.* —**comˈmis·er·a·tive·ly** *adv.* —**comˈmis·er·ˌa·tor** *n.*

com·mis·sar (ˈkɒmɪˌsɑː, ˌkɒmɪˈsɑː) *n.* (in the Soviet Union) **1.** Also called: **political commissar.** an official of the Communist Party responsible for political education, esp. in a military unit. **2.** Also called: **People's Commissar.** (before 1946) the head of a government department. Now called: **minister.** [C20: from Russian *kommissar*, from German, from Medieval Latin *commissārius* COMMISSARY]

com·mis·sar·i·at (ˌkɒmɪˈsɛərɪət) *n.* **1.** (in the Soviet Union) a government department before 1946. Now called: **ministry. 2. a.** a military department in charge of food supplies, etc. **b.** the offices of such a department. **3.** food supplies. [C17: from New Latin *commissāriātus*, from Medieval Latin *commissārius* COMMISSARY]

com·mis·sar·y (ˈkɒmɪsərɪ) *n., pl.* **-sar·ies.** **1.** *U.S.* a shop supplying food or equipment, as in a military camp. **2.** *U.S. army.* an officer responsible for supplies and food. **3.** *U.S.* a snack bar or restaurant in a film studio. **4.** a representative or deputy, esp. an official representative of a bishop. [C14: from Medieval Latin *commissārius* official in charge, from Latin *committere* to entrust, COMMIT] —**com·mis·sar·i·al** (ˌkɒmɪˈsɛərɪəl) *adj.* —**ˈcom·mis·sar·yˌship** *n.*

com·mis·sion (kəˈmɪʃən) *n.* **1.** a duty or task committed to a person or group to perform. **2.** authority to undertake or perform certain duties or functions. **3.** a document granting such authority. **4.** *Military.* **a.** a document conferring a rank on an officer. **b.** the rank or authority thereby granted. **5.** a group of people charged with certain duties: *a commission of inquiry.* **6.** a government agency or board empowered to exercise administrative, judicial, or legislative authority. See also **Royal Commission. 7. a.** the authority given to a person or organization to act as an agent to a principal in commercial transactions. **b.** the fee allotted to an agent for services rendered. **8.** the state of being charged with specific duties or responsibilities. **9.** the act of committing a sin, crime, etc. **10.** something, esp. a sin, crime, etc., that is committed. **11.** good working condition or (esp. of a ship) active service (esp. in the phrases **in** *or* **into commission, out of commission**). **12.** *U.S.* the head of a department of municipal government. ~*vb.* (*tr.*) **13.** to grant authority to; charge with a duty or task. **14.** *Military.* to confer a rank or authorize an action. **15.** to equip and test (a ship) for active service. **16.** to place an order for (something): *to commission a portrait.* [C14: from Old French, from Latin *commissiō* a bringing together, from *committere* to COMMIT] —**comˈmis·sion·al** *or* **comˈmis·sion·ar·y** *adj.*

com·mis·sion·aire (kəˌmɪʃəˈnɛə) *n.* *Chiefly Brit.* a uniformed doorman at a hotel, theatre, etc. [C18: from French, from COMMISSION]

com·mis·sioned of·fic·er *n.* a military officer holding a commission, such as Second Lieutenant in the British Army, Acting Sub-Lieutenant in the Royal Navy, Pilot Officer in the Royal Air Force, and officers of all ranks senior to these.

com·mis·sion·er (kəˈmɪʃənə) *n.* **1.** a person authorized to perform certain tasks or endowed with certain powers. **2.** *Government.* any of several types of civil servant. See also **Parliamentary Commissioner. 3.** a member of a commission. —**comˈmis·sion·erˌship** *n.*

com·mis·sion·er for oaths *n.* a solicitor authorized to authenticate oaths on sworn statements.

com·mis·sion plan *n.* (in the U.S.) a system of municipal government that combines legislative and executive authority in a commission of five or six elected members.

com·mis·sure (ˈkɒmɪˌsjʊə) *n.* **1.** a band of tissue linking two parts or organs, such as the nervous tissue connecting the right and left sides of the brain in vertebrates. **2.** any of various joints between parts, as between the carpels, leaf lobes, etc., of a plant. [C15: from Latin *commissūra* a joining together, from *committere* COMMIT] —**com·mis·su·ral** (kəˈmɪsjʊrəl, ˌkɒmɪˈsjʊərəl) *adj.*

com·mit (kəˈmɪt) *vb.* **-mits, -mit·ting, -mit·ted.** (*tr.*) **1.** to hand over, as for safekeeping; charge; entrust: *to commit a child to the care of its aunt.* **2. commit to memory.** to learn by heart; memorize. **3.** to confine officially or take into custody: *to commit someone to prison.* **4.** (*usually passive*) to pledge or align (oneself), as to a particular cause, action, or attitude: *a committed radical.* **5.** to order (forces) into action. **6.** to perform (a crime, error, etc.); do; perpetrate. **7.** to surrender, esp. for destruction: *she committed the letter to the fire.* **8.** to refer (a bill, etc.) to a committee of a legislature. [C14: from Latin *committere* to join, from *com-* together + *mittere* to put, send] —**comˈmit·ta·ble** *adj.* —**comˈmit·ter** *n.*

com·mit·ment (kəˈmɪtmənt) *n.* **1.** the act of committing or pledging. **2.** the state of being committed or pledged. **3.** the referral of a bill to a committee or legislature. **4.** Also called (esp. formerly): **mittimus.** *Law.* a written order of a court directing that a person be imprisoned. **5.** the official consignment of a person to a mental hospital or prison. **6.** commission or perpetration, esp. of a crime. **7.** a future financial obligation or contingent liability. ~Also called (esp. for senses 4 and 5): **com·mit·tal** (kəˈmɪtᵊl).

com·mit·tee *n.* **1.** (kəˈmɪtɪ). a group of people chosen or appointed to perform a specified service or function. **2.** (ˌkɒmɪˈtiː). (formerly) a person to whom the care of a mentally incompetent person or his property was entrusted by a court. See also **receiver** (sense 2). [C15: from *committen* to entrust + -EE]

com·mit·tee·man (kəˈmɪtɪmən, -ˌmæn) *n., pl.* **·men.** *Chiefly U.S.* a member of one or more committees. —**com·ˈmit·tee·ˌwom·an** *fem. n.*

Com·mit·tee of the Whole House *n. Brit.* an informal sitting of the House of Commons to discuss and amend a bill.

com·mix (kɒˈmɪks) *vb.* a rare word for **mix.** [C15: back formation from *commixt* mixed together; see MIX] —**com·ˈmix·ture** *n.*

com·mo (ˈkɒməʊ) *n., pl.* **·mos.** *adj. Austral. slang.* short for **communist.**

com·mode (kəˈməʊd) *n.* **1.** a piece of furniture, usually highly ornamented, containing drawers or shelves. **2.** a bedside table with a cabinet below for a chamber pot or washbasin. **3.** (formerly) a movable piece of furniture, sometimes in the form of a chair, with a hinged flap concealing a chamber pot. **4.** a woman's high-tiered headdress of lace, worn in the late 17th century. [C17: from French, from Latin *commodus* COMMODIOUS]

com·mo·di·ous (kəˈməʊdɪəs) *adj.* **1.** (of buildings, rooms, etc.) large and roomy; spacious. **2.** *Archaic.* suitable; convenient. [C15: from Medieval Latin *commodiōsus,* from Latin *commodus* convenient, from *com-* with + *modus* measure] —**com·ˈmo·di·ous·ly** *adv.* —**com·ˈmo·di·ous·ness** *n.*

com·mod·i·ty (kəˈmɒdɪtɪ) *n., pl.* **·ties. 1.** an article of commerce. **2.** something of use, advantage, or profit. **3.** *Economics.* an exchangeable unit of economic wealth, such as a consumers' article, producers' article, primary product, or service. **4.** *Obsolete.* **a.** a quantity of goods. **b.** convenience or expediency. [C14: from Old French *commodité,* from Latin *commoditās* suitability, benefit; see COMMODIOUS]

com·mo·dore (ˈkɒməˌdɔː) *n.* **1.** *Brit.* a naval rank junior to rear admiral and senior to captain. **2.** the senior captain of a shipping line. **3.** the officer in command of a convoy of merchant ships. **4.** the titular head of a yacht or boat club. [C17: probably from Dutch *commandeur,* from French, from Old French *commander* to COMMAND]

Com·mo·dus (kəˈməʊdəs, ˈkɒmədəs) *n.* **Lu·ci·us Ae·li·us Au·re·li·us** (ˈluːsɪəs ˈiːlɪəs ɔːˈriːlɪəs), son of Marcus Aurelius. 161–192 A.D., Roman emperor (180–192), noted for his tyrannical reign.

com·mon (ˈkɒmən) *adj.* **1.** belonging to or shared by two or more people: *common property.* **2.** belonging to or shared by members of one or more nations or communities; public: *a common culture.* **3.** of ordinary standard; average: *common decency.* **4.** prevailing; widespread: *common opinion.* **5.** widely known or frequently encountered; ordinary: *a common brand of soap.* **6.** widely known and notorious: *a common nuisance.* **7.** *Derogatory.* considered by the speaker to be low-class, vulgar, or coarse: *a common accent.* **8.** (*prenominal*) having no special distinction, rank, or status: *the common man.* **9.** *Maths.* **a.** having a specified relationship with a group of numbers or quantities: *common denominator.* **b.** (of a tangent) tangential to two or more circles. **10.** *Prosody.* (of a syllable) able to be long or short, or (in nonquantitative verse) stressed or unstressed. **11.** *Grammar.* (in certain languages) denoting or belonging to a gender of nouns, esp. one that includes both masculine and feminine referents: *Latin* sacerdos *is common.* **12.** *Anatomy.* **a.** having branches: *the common carotid artery.* **b.** serving more than one function: *the common bile duct.* **13.** *Christianity.* of or relating to the common of the Mass or divine office. **14. common or garden.** *Informal.* ordinary; unexceptional. ~*n.* **15.** (*sometimes pl.*) a tract of open public land, esp. one now used as a recreation area. **16.** *Law.* the right to go onto someone else's property and remove natural products, as by pasturing cattle or fishing (esp. in the phrase **right of common**). **17.** *Christianity.* **a.** a form of the proper of the Mass used on festivals that have no special proper of their own. **b.** the ordinary of the Mass. **18.** *Archaic.* the ordinary people; the public, esp. those undistinguished by rank or title. **19. in common.** mutually held or used with another or others. [C13: from Old French *commun,* from Latin *commūnis* general, universal] —**ˈcom·mon·ness** *n.*

com·mon·a·ble (ˈkɒmənəbᵊl) *adj.* **1.** (of land) held in common. **2.** *English history.* (esp. of sheep and cattle) entitled to be pastured on common land.

com·mon·age (ˈkɒmənɪdʒ) *n.* **1.** *Chiefly law.* **a.** the use of something, esp. a pasture, in common with others. **b.** the right to such use. **2.** the state of being held in common. **3.** something held in common, such as land. **4.** another word for **commonalty** (sense 1).

com·mon·al·i·ty (ˌkɒməˈnælɪtɪ) *n., pl.* **·ties. 1.** the fact of being common to more than one individual; commonness. **2.** another word for **commonalty** (sense 1).

com·mon·al·ty (ˈkɒmənəltɪ) *n., pl.* **·ties. 1.** the ordinary people as distinct from those with authority, rank, or title, esp. when considered as a political and social unit or estate of the realm. Compare **third estate. 2.** the members of an incorporated society. [C13: from Old French *comunalte,* from *comunal* communal]

com·mon car·ri·er *n.* a person or firm engaged in the business of transporting goods or passengers.

com·mon chord *n. Music.* a major or minor triad, based on the keynote, in which the fifth is perfect: *the notes G, B, and D form the common chord of G major.*

com·mon cold *n.* a mild viral infection of the upper respiratory tract, characterized by sneezing, coughing, watery eyes, nasal congestion, etc.

com·mon de·nom·i·na·tor *n.* **1.** an integer exactly divisible by each denominator of a group of fractions: *1/3, 1/4, and 1/6 have a common denominator of 12.* **2.** a belief, attribute, etc., held in common by members of a class or group.

com·mon di·vi·sor *n.* another name for **common factor.**

Com·mon En·trance *n. Brit.* an entrance examination for a public school, usually taken at the age of 13.

com·mon·er (ˈkɒmənə) *n.* **1.** a person who does not belong to the nobility. **2.** a person who has a right in or over common land jointly with another or others. **3.** *Brit.* a student at a university or other institution who is not on a scholarship.

Com·mon E·ra *n.* another name for **Christian Era.**

com·mon fac·tor *n.* a number or quantity that is a factor of each member of a group of numbers or quantities: *5 is a common factor of 15 and 20.* Also called: **common divisor.**

com·mon fee *n.* (in Australia) the agreed usual charge for any medical service, which determines the amount of reimbursement under the federal health scheme.

com·mon frac·tion *n.* another name for **simple fraction.**

com·mon good *n.* the part of the property of a Scottish burgh, in the form of land or funds, that is at the disposal of the community.

com·mon ground *n.* an agreed basis, accepted by both or all parties, for identifying issues in an argument.

com·mon know·ledge *n.* something widely or generally known.

com·mon law *n.* **1.** the body of law based on judicial decisions and custom, as distinct from statute law. **2.** the law of a state that is of general application, as distinct from regional customs.

com·mon-law mar·riage *n.* a state of marriage deemed to exist between a man and a woman after a number of years of cohabitation as man and wife.

com·mon log·a·rithm *n.* a logarithm to the base ten. Usually written $\log_{10}$ or log Compare **natural logarithm.** See also **base**[1] (sense 16).

com·mon·ly (ˈkɒmənlɪ) *adv.* **1.** usually; ordinarily: *he was commonly known as Joe.* **2.** *Derogatory.* in a coarse or vulgar way: *she dresses commonly.*

Com·mon Mar·ket *n.* **the.** a Western European economic association, originally composed by the Treaty of Rome (1958) of Belgium, France, West Germany, Italy, Luxembourg, and the Netherlands, joined in 1973 by the United Kingdom, the Irish Republic, and Denmark, and in 1981 by Greece. Officially called: **European Economic Community.**

com·mon meas·ure *n.* **1.** another term for **common time. 2.** the usual stanza form of a ballad, consisting of four iambic lines rhyming a b c b or a b a b.

com·mon me·tre *n.* a stanza form, used esp. for hymns, consisting of four lines, two of eight syllables alternating with two of six.

com·mon mul·ti·ple *n.* an integer or polynomial that is a multiple of each integer or polynomial in a group: *20 is a common multiple of 2, 4, 5, 10.*

com·mon noun *n. Grammar.* a noun that refers to each member of a whole class sharing the features connoted by the noun, as for example *planet, orange,* and *drum.* Compare **proper noun.**

com·mon·place (ˈkɒmənˌpleɪs) *adj.* **1.** ordinary; everyday: *commonplace duties.* **2.** dull and obvious; trite: *commonplace prose.* ~*n.* **3.** something dull and trite, esp. a remark; platitude; truism. **4.** a passage in a book marked for inclusion in a commonplace book, etc. **5.** an ordinary or common thing. [C16: translation of Latin *locus commūnis* argument of wide application, translation of Greek *koinos topos*] —**ˈcom·mon·ˌplace·ness** *n.*

com·mon·place book *n.* a notebook in which quotations, poems, remarks, etc., that catch the owner's attention are entered.

com·mon pleas *n.* short for **Court of Common Pleas.**

com·mon prayer *n.* the liturgy of public services of the Church of England, esp. Morning and Evening Prayer.

com·mon room *n. Chiefly Brit.* a sitting room in schools, colleges, etc., for the relaxation of students or staff.

com·mons (ˈkɒmənz) *n.* **1.** (*functioning as pl.*) people not of noble birth viewed as forming a political order. **2.** (*functioning as pl.*) the lower classes as contrasted to the ruling classes of society; the commonalty. **3.** (*functioning as sing.*) *Brit.* a building or hall for dining, recreational purposes, etc., usually attached to a college, etc. **4.** (*usually functioning as pl.*) *Brit.* food or rations (esp. in the phrase **short commons).**

Com·mons (ˈkɒmənz) *n.* **the.** See **House of Commons.**

com·mon seal *n.* the official seal of a corporate body.

com·mon sense *n.* **1.** plain ordinary good judgment; sound practical sense. ~*adj.* **com·mon-sense;** *also* **com·mon-sen·si·cal. 2.** inspired by or displaying sound practical sense.

com·mon stock *n.* the U.S. name for **ordinary shares.**

com·mon time *n. Music.* a time signature indicating four crotchet beats to the bar; four-four time. Symbol: **C**

com·mon·weal (ˈkɒmənˌwiːl) *n. Archaic.* **1.** the good of the community. **2.** another name for **commonwealth.**

com·mon·wealth (ˈkɒmənˌwɛlθ) *n.* **1.** the people of a state or nation viewed politically; body politic. **2.** a state or nation in which the people possess sovereignty; republic. **3.** the body politic organized for the general good. **4.** a group of persons united by some common interest. **5.** *Obsolete.* the general good; public welfare.

Com·mon·wealth ('kɒmən,wɛlθ) *n.* **the. 1.** Official name: **the Commonwealth of Nations.** an association of sovereign states that are or at some time have been ruled by Britain. All member states recognize the reigning British sovereign as **Head of the Commonwealth. 2. a.** the republic that existed in Britain from 1649 to 1660. **b.** the part of this period up to 1653, when Cromwell became Protector. **3.** the official designation of Australia, four states of the U.S. (Kentucky, Massachusetts, Pennsylvania, and Virginia), and Puerto Rico.

Com·mon·wealth Day *n.* the anniversary of Queen Victoria's birth, May 24, celebrated as a holiday in many parts of the Commonwealth. Former name: **Empire Day.**

com·mo·tion (kə'məʊʃən) *n.* **1.** violent and turbulent disturbance; upheaval. **2.** political insurrection; disorder. **3.** a confused noise; din. [C15: from Latin *commōtiō*, from *commovēre* to throw into disorder, from *com-* (intensive) + *movēre* to MOVE] —**com·'mo·tion·al** *adj.*

com·move (kə'mu:v) *vb. (tr.) Rare.* **1.** to disturb; stir up. **2.** to agitate or excite emotionally.

com·mu·nal ('kɒmjʊnᵊl) *adj.* **1.** belonging or relating to a community as a whole. **2.** relating to different groups within a society: *communal strife.* **3.** of or relating to a commune or a religious community. —**com·mu·nal·i·ty** (,kɒmjʊ'nælɪtɪ) *n.* —**'com·mu·nal·ly** *adv.*

com·mu·nal·ism ('kɒmjʊnə,lɪzəm) *n.* **1.** a system or theory of government in which the state is seen as a loose federation of self-governing communities. **2.** an electoral system in which ethnic groups vote separately for their own representatives. **3.** loyalty to the interests of one's own ethnic group rather than to society as a whole. **4.** the practice or advocacy of communal living or ownership. —**'com·mu·nal·ist** *n.* —**,com·mu·nal·'is·tic** *adj.*

com·mu·nal·ize *or* **com·mu·nal·ise** ('kɒmjʊnə,laɪz) *vb. (tr.)* to render (something) the property of a commune or community. —**,com·mu·nal·i·'za·tion** *or* **,com·mu·nal·i·'sa·tion** *n.* —**'com·mu·nal·,iz·er** *or* **'com·mu·nal·,is·er** *n.*

com·mu·nard ('kɒmjʊ,nɑ:d) *n.* a member of a commune.

Com·mu·nard ('kɒmjʊ,nɑ:d) *n.* any person who participated in or supported the Paris Commune formed after the Franco-Prussian War in 1871. [C19: from French]

com·mune[1] *vb.* (kə'mju:n). *(intr.;* usually foll. by *with)* **1.** to talk or converse intimately. **2.** to experience strong emotion or spiritual feelings (for): *to commune with nature.* ~*n.* ('kɒmju:n). **3.** intimate conversation; exchange of thoughts; communion. [C13: from Old French *comuner* to hold in common, from *comun* COMMON]

com·mune[2] (kə'mju:n) *vb. (intr.) Christianity, chiefly U.S.* to partake of Communion. [C16: back formation from COMMUNION]

com·mune[3] ('kɒmju:n) *n.* **1.** a group of families or individuals living together and sharing possessions and responsibilities. **2.** any small group of people having common interests or responsibilities. **3.** the smallest administrative unit in Belgium, France, Italy, and Switzerland, governed by a mayor and council. **4.** the government or inhabitants of a commune. **5.** a medieval town enjoying a large degree of autonomy. [C18: from French, from Medieval Latin *commūnia*, from Latin: things held in common, from *commūnis* COMMON]

Com·mune ('kɒmju:n) *n. French history.* **1.** See **Paris Commune. 2.** a committee that governed Paris during the French Revolution and played a leading role in the Reign of Terror: suppressed 1794.

com·mu·ni·ca·ble (kə'mju:nɪkəbᵊl) *adj.* **1.** capable of being communicated. **2.** (of a disease or its causative agent) capable of being passed on readily. —**com·,mu·ni·ca·'bil·i·ty** *or* **com·'mu·ni·ca·ble·ness** *n.* —**com·'mu·ni·ca·bly** *adv.*

com·mu·ni·cant (kə'mju:nɪkənt) *n.* **1.** *Christianity.* a person who receives Communion. **2.** a person who communicates or informs. ~*adj.* **3.** communicating.

com·mu·ni·cate (kə'mju:nɪ,keɪt) *vb.* **1.** to impart (knowledge) or exchange (thoughts, feelings, or ideas) by speech, writing, gestures, etc. **2.** *(tr.;* usually foll. by *to)* to allow (a feeling, emotion, etc.) to be sensed (by), willingly or unwillingly; transmit (to): *the dog communicated his fear to the other animals.* **3.** *(intr.)* to have a sympathetic mutual understanding. **4.** *(intr.;* usually foll. by *with)* to make or have a connecting passage or route; connect: *the kitchen communicates with the dining room.* **5.** *(tr.)* to transmit (a disease); infect. **6.** *Christianity.* to receive or administer Communion. [C16: from Latin *commūnicāre* to share, from *commūnis* COMMON] —**com·'mu·ni·,ca·tor** *n.* —**com·'mu·ni·ca·to·ry** *adj.*

com·mu·ni·ca·tion (kə,mju:nɪ'keɪʃən) *n.* **1.** the act or an instance of communicating; the imparting or exchange of information, ideas, or feelings. **2.** something communicated, such as a message, letter, or telephone call. **3. a.** *(usually pl.; sometimes functioning as sing.)* the study of ways in which human beings communicate, including speech, gesture, telecommunication systems, publishing and broadcasting media, etc. **b.** *(as modifier): communication theory.* **4.** a connecting route, passage, or link. **5.** *(pl.) Military.* the system by which forces, supplies, etc., are moved up to or within an area of operations.

com·mu·ni·ca·tion cord *n. Brit.* a cord or chain in a train which may be pulled by a passenger to stop the train in an emergency.

com·mu·ni·ca·tions sat·el·lite *n.* an artificial satellite used to relay radio, television, and telephone signals around the earth's surface. A **passive satellite** merely reflects transmissions from its surface. An **active satellite** receives and retransmits signals. See also **syncom.**

com·mu·ni·ca·tive (kə'mju:nɪkətɪv) *adj.* **1.** inclined or able to communicate readily; talkative. **2.** of or relating to communication. —**com·'mu·ni·ca·tive·ly** *adv.* —**com·'mu·ni·ca·tive·ness** *n.*

com·mun·ion (kə'mju:njən) *n.* **1.** an exchange of thoughts, emotions, etc. **2.** possession or sharing in common; participation. **3.** (foll. by *with*) strong emotional or spiritual feelings (for): *communion with nature.* **4.** a religious group or denomination having a common body of beliefs, doctrines, and practices. **5.** the spiritual union held by Christians to exist between individual Christians and Christ, their Church, or their fellow Christians. [C14: from Latin *commūniō* general participation, from *commūnis* COMMON] —**com·'mun·ion·al** *adj.* —**com·'mun·ion·al·ly** *adv.*

Com·mun·ion (kə'mju:njən) *n. Christianity.* **1.** the act of participating in the Eucharist. **2.** the celebration of the Eucharist, esp. the part of the service during which the consecrated elements are received. **3. a.** the consecrated elements of the Eucharist. **b.** *(as modifier): Communion cup.* ~Also called: **Holy Communion.**

com·mun·ion of saints *n. Christianity.* the spiritual fellowship of all true Christians, living and dead.

com·mu·ni·qué (kə'mju:nɪ,keɪ) *n.* an official communication or announcement, esp. to the press or public. [C19: from French, from *communiquer* to COMMUNICATE]

com·mun·ism ('kɒmjʊ,nɪzəm) *n.* **1.** advocacy of a classless society in which private ownership has been abolished and the means of production and subsistence belong to the community. **2.** any social, economic, or political movement or doctrine aimed at achieving such a society. **3.** *(usually cap.)* a political movement based upon the writings of Marx that considers history in terms of class conflict and revolutionary struggle, resulting eventually in the victory of the proletariat and the establishment of a socialist order based on public ownership of the means of production. See also **Marxism, Marxism-Leninism, socialism. 4.** *(usually cap.)* a social order or system of government established by a ruling Communist Party, esp. in the Soviet Union. **5.** *(often cap.) Chiefly U.S.* any leftist political activity or thought, esp. when considered to be subversive. **6.** communal living; communalism. [C19: from French *communisme*, from *commun* COMMON]

com·mun·ist ('kɒmjʊnɪst) *n.* **1.** a supporter of any form of communism. **2.** *(often cap.)* a supporter of Communism or a Communist movement or state. **3.** *(often cap.)* a member of a Communist party. **4.** a person who practises communal living; communalist. **5.** another name for **Communard.** ~*adj.* **6.** of, characterized by, favouring, or relating to communism; communistic.

Com·mu·nist Chi·na *n.* another name for (the People's Republic of) **China.**

com·mu·nis·tic (,kɒmjʊ'nɪstɪk) *adj.* of, characteristic of, or relating to communism. —**,com·mu·'nis·ti·cal·ly** *adv.*

Com·mun·ist Man·i·fes·to *n.* a political pamphlet written by Marx and Engels in 1848: a fundamental statement of Marxist principles.

Com·mun·ist Par·ty *n.* **1.** (in non-Communist countries) a political party advocating Communism. **2.** (in Communist countries) the single official party of the state, composed of those who officially espouse Communism.

com·mu·ni·tar·i·an (kə,mju:nɪ'tɛərɪən) *n.* **1.** a member of a communist community. **2.** an advocate of communalism.

com·mu·ni·ty (kə'mju:nɪtɪ) *n., pl.* **-ties. 1. a.** the people living in one locality. **b.** the locality in which they live. **c.** *(as modifier): community spirit.* **2.** a group of people having cultural, religious, ethnic, or other characteristics in common: *the Protestant community.* **3.** a group of nations having certain interests in common. **4.** the public in general; society. **5.** common ownership or participation. **6.** similarity or agreement: *community of interests.* **7.** (in Wales since 1974 and Scotland since 1975) the smallest unit of local government; a subdivision of a district. **8.** *Ecology.* a group of interdependent plants and animals inhabiting the same region and interacting with each other through food and other relationships. [C14: from Latin *commūnitās*, from *commūnis* COMMON]

com·mu·ni·ty cen·tre *n.* a building used by members of a community for social gatherings, etc.

com·mu·ni·ty chest *n. U.S.* a fund raised by voluntary contribution for local welfare activities.

com·mu·ni·ty col·lege *n.* **1.** *Brit.* another term for **village college. 2.** *Chiefly U.S.* a nonresidential college offering two-year courses of study.

com·mu·ni·ty home *n.* (in Britain) a boarding school for the instruction and rehabilitation of young offenders.

com·mu·ni·ty school *n. Brit.* a school offering some nonacademic activities related to life in a particular community and often serving as a community centre.

com·mu·ni·ty sing·ing *n.* singing, esp. of hymns, by a large gathering of people.

com·mu·nize *or* **com·mu·nise** ('kɒmjʊ,naɪz) *vb. (tr.) (sometimes cap.)* **1.** to make (property) public; nationalize. **2.** to make (a person or country) communist. —**,com·mu·ni·'za·tion** *or* **,com·mu·ni·'sa·tion** *n.*

com·mut·a·ble (kə'mju:təbᵊl) *adj.* **1.** *Law.* (of a punishment, etc.) capable of being reduced in severity. **2.** able to be exchanged. —**com·,mut·a·'bil·i·ty** *or* **com·'mut·a·ble·ness** *n.*

com·mu·tate ('kɒmjʊ,teɪt) *vb. (tr.)* **1.** to reverse the direction of (an electric current). **2.** to convert (an alternating current) into a direct current.

com+mu+ta+tion (ˌkɒmjʊ'teɪʃən) *n.* **1.** a substitution or exchange. **2. a.** the replacement of one method of payment by another. **b.** the payment substituted. **3.** the reduction in severity of a penalty imposed by law. **4.** the process of commutating an electric current. **5.** *U.S.* the travelling done by a commuter.

com+mu+ta+tion tick+et *n.* a U.S. name for **season ticket.**

com+mu+ta+tive (kə'mju:tətɪv, 'kɒmjʊˌteɪtɪv) *adj.* relating to or involving substitution. —**com+'mu+ta+tive+ly** *adv.*

com+mu+ta+tive law *n.* a law of mathematics and logic that states that certain operations, such as addition, multiplication, conjunction, and alternation, are independent of the order in which the numbers, symbols, or statements are considered, as in $5 + 7 = 7 + 5$.

com+mu+ta+tor ('kɒmjʊˌteɪtə) *n.* **1.** a device used to reverse the direction of flow of an electric current. **2.** the segmented metal cylinder or disc mounted on the armature shaft of an electric motor, generator, etc., used to make electrical contact with the rotating coils.

com+mute (kə'mju:t) *vb.* **1.** (*intr.*) to travel some distance regularly between one's home and one's place of work. **2.** (*tr.*) to substitute; exchange. **3.** (*tr.*) *Law.* to reduce (a sentence) to one less severe. **4.** to pay (an annuity, etc.) at one time, esp. with a discount, instead of in instalments. **5.** (*tr.*) to transform; change: *to commute base metal into gold.* **6.** (*intr.*) to act as or be a substitute. **7.** (*intr.*) to make a substitution; change. [C17: from Latin *commūtāre* to replace, from *com-* mutually + *mūtāre* to change] —**com+'mut+a+ble** *adj.* —**com+'mut+a+ble+ness** *or* **com+ˌmut+a+'bil+i+ty** *n.*

com+mut+er (kə'mju:tə) *n.* **a.** a person who travels to work over an appreciable distance, usually from the suburbs to the centre of a city. **b.** (*as modifier*): *the commuter belt.*

Com+ne+nus (kɒm'ni:nəs) *n.* an important Byzantine family from which the imperial dynasties of Constantinople (1057–59; 1081–1185) and Trebizond (1204–1461) derived.

Co+mo ('kəʊməʊ; *Italian* 'kɔ:mo) *n.* **1.** a city in N Italy, in Lombardy at the SW end of **Lake Como**: tourist centre. Pop.: 97 395 (1971). Latin name: **Comum.**

Com+o+rin ('kɒmərɪn) *n.* **Cape.** a headland at the southernmost point of India, in Tamil Nadu state.

Com+o+ro Is+lands ('kɒməˌrəʊ) *pl. n.* a group of volcanic islands in the Indian Ocean, off the NW coast of Madagascar: a French territory from 1947 until 1976, when the islands became an independent republic (except for Mayotte which chose to remain French). Pop.: 290 000 (1973 est.). Area: 2170 sq. km (838 sq. miles). Official name: **Federal and Islamic Republic of the Comoros.**

co+mose ('kəʊməʊs, kəʊ'məʊs) *adj. Botany.* another word for **comate.** [C18: from Latin *comōsus* hairy, from *coma* long hair; see COMA[2]]

comp (kɒmp) *Informal.* ~*n.* **1.** a compositor. **2.** an accompanist. **3.** an accompaniment. **4.** a competition. ~*vb.* **5.** (*intr.*) to work as a compositor in the printing industry. **6.** to play an accompaniment (to).

comp. *abbrev. for:* **1.** companion. **2.** comparative. **3.** compare. **4.** compiled. **5.** compiler. **6.** complete. **7.** composer. **8.** composition. **9.** compositor. **10.** compound. **11.** comprising.

com+pact[1] *adj.* (kəm'pækt). **1.** closely packed together; dense. **2.** neatly fitted into a restricted space. **3.** concise; brief. **4.** well constructed; solid; firm. **5.** (foll. by *of*) composed or made up (of). **6.** *U.S.* (of a car) small and economical. ~*vb.* (kəm'pækt). (*tr.*) **7.** to pack or join closely together; compress; condense. **8.** (foll. by *of*) to create or form by pressing together: *sediment compacted of three types of clay.* **9.** *Metallurgy.* to compress (a metal powder) to form a stable product suitable for sintering. ~*n.* ('kɒmpækt). **10.** a small flat case containing a mirror, face powder, etc., designed to be carried in a woman's handbag. **11.** *U.S.* a small and economical car. **12.** *Metallurgy.* a mass of metal prepared for sintering by cold-pressing a metal powder. [C16: from Latin *compactus,* from *compingere* to put together, from *com-* together + *pangere* to fasten] —**com+'pact+er** *n.* —**com+'pact+ly** *adv.* —**com+'pact+ness** *n.*

com+pact[2] ('kɒmpækt) *n.* an official contract or agreement. [C16: from Latin *compactum,* from *compacīscī* to agree, from *com-* together + *pacīscī* to contract; see PACT]

com+pa+dre (kɒm'pɑ:dreɪ, kəm-) *n. Southwestern U.S.* a masculine friend. [from Spanish: godfather, from Medieval Latin *compater,* from Latin *com-* with + *pater* father]

com+pan+der (kəm'pændə) *n.* a system for improving the signal-to-noise ratio of a signal at a transmitter or recorder by first compressing the volume range of the signal and then restoring it to its original amplitude level at the receiving or reproducing apparatus. [C20: from COM(PRESSOR) + (EX)PANDER]

com+pan+ion[1] (kəm'pænjən) *n.* **1.** a person who is an associate of another or others; comrade. **2.** (esp. formerly) an employee, usually a woman, who provides company for an employer, esp. an elderly woman. **3. a.** one of a pair; match. **b.** (*as modifier*): *a companion volume.* **4.** a guidebook or handbook. **5.** a member of the lowest rank of any of certain orders of knighthood. **6.** *Astronomy.* the fainter of the two components of a double star. ~*vb.* **7.** (*tr.*) to accompany or be a companion to. [C13: from Late Latin *compāniō,* literally: one who eats bread with another, from Latin *com-* with + *pānis* bread] —**com+'pan+ion+less** *adj.*

com+pan+ion[2] (kəm'pænjən) *n. Nautical.* **a.** a raised frame on an upper deck with windows to give light to the deck below. **b.** (*as modifier*): *a companion ladder.* [C18: from Dutch *kompanje* quarterdeck, from Old French *compagne,* from Old Italian *compagna* pantry, perhaps ultimately from Latin *pānis* bread]

com+pan+ion+a+ble (kəm'pænjənəbᵊl) *adj.* suited to be a companion; sociable. —**com+'pan+ion+a+ble+ness** *or* **com+ˌpan+ion+a+'bil+i+ty** *n.* —**com+'pan+ion+a+bly** *adv.*

com+pan+ion+ate (kəm'pænjənɪt) *adj.* **1.** resembling, appropriate to, or acting as a companion. **2.** harmoniously suited.

com+pan+ion set *n.* a set of fire irons on a stand.

com+pan+ion+ship (kəm'pænjənˌʃɪp) *n.* the relationship of friends or companions; fellowship.

com+pan+ion+way (kəm'pænjənˌweɪ) *n.* a stairway or ladder leading from one deck to another in a boat or ship.

com+pa+ny ('kʌmpənɪ) *n., pl.* **+nies. 1.** a number of people gathered together; assembly. **2.** the fact of being with someone; companionship: *I enjoy her company.* **3.** a social visitor or visitors; guest or guests. **4.** a business enterprise. **5.** the members of an enterprise not specifically mentioned in the enterprise's title. Abbrev.: **Co., co. 6.** a group of actors, usually including business and technical personnel. **7.** a small unit of troops, usually comprising two or more platoons. **8.** the officers and crew of a ship. **9.** *English history.* a medieval guild. **10. keep** *or* **bear company. a.** to accompany (someone). **b.** (esp. of lovers) to associate with each other; spend time together. **11. part company. a.** to end a friendship, esp. as a result of a quarrel. **b.** to separate. ~*vb.* **+nies, +ny+ing, +nied. 12.** *Archaic.* to keep company or associate (with someone). [C13: from Old French *compaignie,* from *compain* companion, fellow, from Late Latin *compāniō*; see COMPANION]

com+pa+ny sec+re+tar+y *n. Brit.* an officer of an incorporated company who has certain legal obligations.

com+pa+ny ser+geant-ma+jor *n. Military.* the senior noncommissioned officer in a company.

com+pa+ny un+ion *n. Chiefly U.S.* an unaffiliated union of workers in a single business enterprise.

compar. *abbrev. for* comparative.

com+pa+ra+ble ('kɒmpərəbᵊl) *adj.* **1.** worthy of comparison. **2.** able to be compared (with). —**ˌcom+pa+ra+'bil+i+ty** *or* **'com+pa+ra+ble+ness** *n.* —**'com+pa+ra+bly** *adv.*

com+par+a+tive (kəm'pærətɪv) *adj.* **1.** denoting or involving comparison: *comparative literature.* **2.** judged by comparison; relative: *a comparative loss of prestige.* **3.** *Grammar.* denoting the form of an adjective that indicates that the quality denoted is possessed to a greater extent. In English the comparative form of an adjective is usually marked by the suffix *-er* or the word *more.* Compare **positive** (sense 10), **superlative** (sense 2). ~*n.* **4.** the comparative form of an adjective. —**com+'par+a+tive+ly** *adv.* —**com+'par+a+tive+ness** *n.*

com+par+a+tor (kəm'pærətə) *n.* **1.** any instrument used to measure a property of a system by comparing it with a standard system. **2.** an electric circuit that compares two signals and gives an indication of the extent of their similarity.

com+pare (kəm'pɛə) *vb.* **1.** (*tr.;* foll. by *to*) to regard or represent as analogous or similar; liken: *the general has been compared to Napoleon.* **2.** (*tr.*) to examine in order to observe resemblances or differences: *to compare rum and gin.* **3.** (*intr.;* usually foll. by *with*) to be of the same or similar quality or value: *gin compares with rum in alcoholic content.* **4.** (*intr.*) to bear a specified relation of quality or value when examined: *this car compares badly with the other.* **5.** (*tr.*) *Grammar.* to give the positive, comparative, and superlative forms of (an adjective). **6.** (*intr.*) *Archaic.* to compete or vie. **7. compare notes.** to exchange opinions. ~*n.* **8.** comparison or analogy (esp. in the phrase **beyond compare**). [C15: from Old French *comparer,* from Latin *comparāre* to couple together, match, from *compar* equal to one another, from *com-* together + *par* equal; see PAR] —**com+'par+er** *n.*

com+par+i+son (kəm'pærɪsᵊn) *n.* **1.** the act or process of comparing. **2.** the state of being compared. **3.** comparable quality or qualities; likeness: *there was no comparison between them.* **4.** a rhetorical device involving comparison, such as a simile. **5.** Also called: **degrees of comparison.** *Grammar.* the listing of the positive, comparative, and superlative forms of an adjective or adverb. **6. bear** *or* **stand comparison (with).** to be sufficiently similar in class or range to be compared with (something else), esp. favourably.

com+part+ment (kəm'pɑ:tmənt) *n.* **1.** one of the sections into which an area, esp. an enclosed space, is divided or partitioned. **2.** any separate part or section: *a compartment of the mind.* **3.** a small storage space; locker. [C16: from French *compartiment,* ultimately from Late Latin *compartīrī* to share, from Latin *com-* with + *partīrī* to apportion, from *pars* PART] —**com+part+men+tal** (ˌkɒmpɑ:t'mɛntᵊl) *adj.* —**ˌcom+part+'men+tal+ly** *adv.*

com+part+men+tal+ize *or* **com+part+men+tal+ise** (ˌkɒmpɑ:t'mɛntᵊˌlaɪz) *vb.* (*usually tr.*) to put or divide into (compartments, categories, etc.), esp. to an excessive degree. —**ˌcom+part+ˌmen+tal+i+'za+tion** *or* **ˌcom+part+ˌmen+tal+i+'sa+tion** *n.*

com+pass ('kʌmpəs) *n.* **1.** an instrument for finding direction, usually having a magnetized needle swinging freely on a pivot, which points to magnetic north. **2.** (*often pl.*) Also called: **pair of compasses.** an instrument used for drawing circles, measuring distances, etc., that consists of two arms, joined at one end, one arm of which serves as a pivot or stationary reference point, while the other is extended or describes a circle. **3.** limits or range: *within the compass of education.* **4.** *Music.* the interval between the lowest and highest note attainable by a voice or musical instrument. **5.** *Archaic.* a circular course. ~*vb.* (*tr.*) **6.** to encircle or surround; hem in. **7.** to comprehend or grasp mentally. **8.** to achieve; attain; accomplish. **9.** *Obsolete.* to plot. [C13: from Old French *compas,* from *compasser* to measure, from Vulgar Latin *compassāre* (unattested) to pace out, ultimately from Latin *passus* step] —'**com·pass·a·ble** *adj.*

com·pass card *n.* a compass in the form of a card that rotates so that "0°" or "North" points to magnetic north.

com·pas·sion (kəm'pæʃən) *n.* a feeling of distress and pity for the suffering or misfortune of another, often including the desire to alleviate it. [C14: from Old French, from Late Latin *compassiō* fellow-feeling, from *compatī* to suffer with, from Latin *com-* with + *patī* to bear, suffer]

com·pas·sion·ate (kəm'pæʃənət) *adj.* **1.** showing or having compassion. **2. compassionate leave.** leave granted, esp. to a serviceman, on the grounds of bereavement, family illness, etc. —**com·'pas·sion·ate·ly** *adv.* —**com·'pas·sion·ate·ness** *n.*

com·pass plant *n.* **1.** Also called: **rosinweed.** a tall plant, *Silphium laciniatum,* of central North America, that has yellow flowers and lower leaves that tend to align themselves at right angles to the strongest light, esp. in a north-south plane: family *Compositae* (composites). **2.** any of several similar plants.

com·pass rose *n.* a circle or decorative device printed on a map or chart showing the points of the compass measured from true north and usually magnetic north.

com·pass saw *n.* a hand saw with a narrow tapered blade for making a curved cut.

com·pass win·dow *n. Architect.* a bay window having a semicircular shape.

com·pat·i·ble (kəm'pætəbᵊl) *adj.* **1.** (usually foll. by *with*) able to exist together harmoniously. **2.** (usually foll. by *with*) consistent or congruous: *her deeds were not compatible with her ideology.* **3.** (of plants) **a.** capable of forming successful grafts. **b.** capable of self-fertilization. **4.** (of pieces of machinery, computer equipment, etc.) capable of being used together without special modification or adaptation. [C15: from Medieval Latin *compatibilis,* from Late Latin *compatī* to be in sympathy with; see COMPASSION] —**com·,pat·i·'bil·i·ty** *or* **com·'pat·i·ble·ness** *n.* —**com·'pat·i·bly** *adv.*

com·pat·ri·ot (kəm'pætrɪət) *n.* a fellow countryman. [C17: from French *compatriote,* from Late Latin *compatriōta;* see PATRIOT] —**com·,pat·ri·'ot·ic** *adj.* —**com·'pat·ri·ot·ism** *n.*

com·peer ('kɒmpɪə) *n.* **1.** a person of equal rank, status, or ability; peer. **2.** a companion or comrade. [C13: from Old French *comper,* from Medieval Latin *compater* godfather; see COMPADRE]

com·pel (kəm'pɛl) *vb.* **·pels, ·pel·ling, ·pelled.** (*tr.*) **1.** to cause (someone) by force (to be or do something). **2.** to obtain by force; exact: *to compel obedience.* **3.** to overpower or subdue. **4.** *Archaic.* to herd or drive together. [C14: from Latin *compellere* to drive together, from *com-* together + *pellere* to drive] —**com·'pel·la·ble** *adj.* —**com·'pel·la·bly** *adv.* —**com·'pel·ler** *n.*

com·pel·la·tion (,kɒmpɛ'leɪʃən) *n.* a rare word for **appellation.** [C17: from Latin *compellātiō,* from *compellāre* to accost, from *appellāre* to call]

com·pel·ling (kəm'pɛlɪŋ) *n.* arousing or denoting strong interest, esp. admiring interest.

com·pen·di·ous (kəm'pɛndɪəs) *adj.* containing or stating the essentials of a subject in a concise form; succinct. —**com·'pen·di·ous·ly** *adv.* —**com·'pen·di·ous·ness** *n.*

com·pen·di·um (kəm'pɛndɪəm) *n., pl.* **·di·ums** *or* **·di·a** (-dɪə). **1.** *Brit.* a book containing a collection of useful hints. **2.** *Brit.* a selection, esp. of different games or other objects in one container. **3.** a concise but comprehensive summary of a larger work. [C16: from Latin: a saving, literally: something weighed, from *pendere* to weigh]

com·pen·sa·ble (kəm'pɛnsəbᵊl) *adj. Chiefly U.S.* entitled to compensation or capable of being compensated.

com·pen·sate ('kɒmpɛn,seɪt) *vb.* **1.** to make amends to (someone), esp. for loss or injury. **2.** (*tr.*) to serve as compensation or damages for (injury, loss, etc.). **3.** to offset or counterbalance the effects of (a force, weight, movement, etc.) so as to nullify the effects of an undesirable influence and produce equilibrium. **4.** (*intr.*) to attempt to conceal or offset one's shortcomings by the exaggerated exhibition of qualities regarded as desirable. [C17: from Latin *compēnsāre,* from *pensāre,* from *pendere* to weigh] —**com·pen·sa·tive** ('kɒmpən,seɪtɪv, kəm'pɛnsə-) *or* **com·pen·sa·to·ry** ('kɒmpɛn,seɪtərɪ; kəm'pɛnsətərɪ, -trɪ) *adj.* —'**com·pen·,sa·tor** *n.*

com·pen·sa·tion (,kɒmpɛn'seɪʃən) *n.* **1.** the act or process of making amends for something. **2.** something given as reparation for loss, injury, etc.; indemnity. **3.** the automatic movements made by the body to maintain balance. **4.** the attempt to conceal or offset one's shortcomings by the exaggerated exhibition of qualities regarded as desirable. **5.** *Biology.* abnormal growth and increase in size in one organ in response to the removal or inactivation of another. —,**com·pen·'sa·tion·al** *adj.*

com·pen·sa·to·ry spend·ing *n.* another name for **deficit spending.**

com·pere ('kɒmpɛə) *Brit.* ~*n.* **1.** a master of ceremonies who introduces cabaret, television acts, etc. ~*vb.* **2.** to act as a compere (for). [C20: from French, literally: godfather; see COMPEER, COMPADRE]

com·pete (kəm'pi:t) *vb.* (*intr.;* often foll. by *with*) to contend (against) for profit, an award, athletic supremacy, etc.; engage in a contest (with). [C17: from Late Latin *competere* to strive together, from Latin: to meet, come together, agree, from *com-* together + *petere* to seek]

com·pe·tence ('kɒmpɪtəns) *n.* **1.** the condition of being capable; ability. **2.** a sufficient income to live on. **3.** the state of being legally competent or qualified. **4.** *Embryol.* the ability of embryonic tissues to react to external conditions in a way that influences subsequent development.

com·pe·ten·cy ('kɒmpɪtənsɪ) *n., pl.* **·cies.** **1.** *Law.* capacity to testify in a court of law; eligibility to be sworn. **2.** a less common word for **competence** (senses 1, 2).

com·pe·tent ('kɒmpɪtənt) *adj.* **1.** having sufficient skill, knowledge, etc.; capable. **2.** suitable or sufficient for the purpose: *a competent answer.* **3.** *Law.* (of a witness, etc.) having legal capacity; qualified to testify, etc. **4.** (*postpositive;* foll. by *to*) belonging as a right; appropriate. [C14: from Latin *competēns,* from *competere* to be competent; see COMPETE] —'**com·pe·tent·ly** *adv.* —'**com·pe·tent·ness** *n.*

com·pe·ti·tion (,kɒmpɪ'tɪʃən) *n.* **1.** the act of competing; rivalry. **2.** a contest in which a winner is selected from among two or more entrants. **3.** a series of games, sports events, etc. **4.** the opposition offered by a competitor or competitors. **5.** a competitor or competitors offering opposition. **6.** *Ecology.* the struggle between individuals of the same or different species for food, space, light, etc., when these are inadequate to supply the needs of all.

com·pet·i·tive (kəm'pɛtɪtɪv) *or* **com·pet·i·to·ry** *adj.* **1.** involving or determined by rivalry: *competitive sports.* **2.** sufficiently low in price or high in quality to be successful against commercial rivals. **3.** relating to or characterized by an urge to compete: *a competitive personality.* —**com·'pet·i·tive·ly** *adv.* —**com·'pet·i·tive·ness** *n.*

com·pet·i·tor (kəm'pɛtɪtə) *n.* a person, group, team, firm, etc., that vies or competes; rival.

Com·piègne (*French* kɔ̃'pjɛn) *n.* a city in N France, on the Oise River: scene of the armistices of both World Wars. Pop.: 40 720 (1975).

com·pi·la·tion (,kɒmpɪ'leɪʃən) *n.* **1.** something collected or compiled, such as a list, report, etc. **2.** the act or process of collecting or compiling.

com·pi·la·tion film *n.* film from an archive used in a film or documentary to give a feeling of the relevant period.

com·pile (kəm'paɪl) *vb.* (*tr.*) **1.** to make or compose from other materials or sources: *to compile a list of names.* **2.** to collect or gather for a book, hobby, etc. **3.** *Computer technol.* to create (a set of machine instructions) from a high-level programming language, using a compiler. [C14: from Latin *compīlāre* to pile together, plunder, from *com-* together + *pīlāre* to thrust down, pack]

com·pil·er (kəm'paɪlə) *n.* **1.** a person who collects or compiles something. **2.** a computer program by which a high-level programming language, such as COBOL or FORTRAN, is converted into machine language that can be acted upon by a computer. Compare **assembler.**

com·pla·cen·cy (kəm'pleɪsənsɪ) *or* **com·pla·cence** *n., pl.* **·cen·cies** *or* **·cenc·es.** **1.** a feeling of satisfaction, esp. extreme self-satisfaction; smugness. **2.** an obsolete word for **complaisance.**

com·pla·cent (kəm'pleɪsᵊnt) *adj.* **1.** pleased or satisfied, esp. extremely self-satisfied. **2.** an obsolete word for **complaisant.** [C17: from Latin *complacēns* very pleasing, from *complacēre* to be most agreeable to, from *com-* (intensive) + *placēre* to please] —**com·'pla·cent·ly** *adv.*

com·plain (kəm'pleɪn) *vb.* (*intr.*) **1.** to express resentment, displeasure, etc., esp. habitually; grumble. **2.** (foll. by *of*) to state the presence of pain, illness, etc., esp. in the hope of sympathy: *she complained of a headache.* [C14: from Old French *complaindre,* from Vulgar Latin *complangere* (unattested), from Latin *com-* (intensive) + *plangere* to bewail] —**com·'plain·er** *n.* —**com·'plain·ing·ly** *adv.*

com·plain·ant (kəm'pleɪnənt) *n. Law.* a person who makes a complaint, usually before justices; plaintiff.

com·plaint (kəm'pleɪnt) *n.* **1.** the act of complaining; an expression of grievance. **2.** a cause for complaining; grievance. **3.** a mild ailment. **4.** *English law.* a statement by which a civil proceeding in a magistrates' court is commenced.

com·plai·sance (kəm'pleɪzəns) *n.* **1.** deference to the wishes of others; willing compliance. **2.** an act of willing compliance.

com·plai·sant (kəm'pleɪzᵊnt) *adj.* showing a desire to comply or oblige; polite. [C17: from French *complaire,* from Latin *complacēre* to please greatly; compare COMPLACENT] —**com·'plai·sant·ly** *adv.*

com·plect (kəm'plɛkt) *vb.* (*tr.*) *Archaic.* to interweave or entwine. [C16: from Latin *complectī;* see COMPLEX]

com·plect·ed (kəm'plɛktɪd) *adj.* (*in combination*) a U.S. dialect word for **complexioned.**

com·ple·ment *n.* ('kɒmplɪmənt). **1.** a person or thing that completes something. **2.** one of two parts that make up a whole or complete each other. **3.** a complete amount, number, etc. (often in the phrase **full complement**). **4.** the officers and crew needed to man a ship. **5.** *Grammar.* **a.** a noun phrase that follows a copula or similar verb, as for example *an idiot* in the sentence *He is an idiot.* **b.** a clause that serves as the subject or direct object of a verb or the direct object of a preposition, as for example *that he would be early* in the sentence *I hoped that he would be early.* **6.** *Maths.* the angle that when added to a specified angle produces a right angle. **7.** *Logic.* the class of all the things that are not members of a given class. **8.** *Music.* the inverted form of an interval that, when added to the interval, completes the octave: *the sixth is the complement of the third.* **9.** *Immunol.* a heat-sensitive component of blood serum that destroys pathogenic substances, esp. bacteria. ~*vb.* ('kɒmplɪ,mɛnt). **10.** (*tr.*) to add to, make complete, or form a complement to. [C14: from Latin *complēmentum*, from *complēre* to fill up, from *com-* (intensive) + *plēre* to fill]

com+ple+men+ta·ry (ˌkɒmplɪˈmɛntərɪ, -trɪ) *or* **com+ple+men+tal** *adj.* **1.** acting as or forming a complement; completing. **2.** forming a satisfactory or balanced whole. **3.** forming a mathematical complement: *sine and cosine are complementary functions.* **4.** (of genes) producing an effect in association with other genes. —**ˌcom+ple+ˈmen+ta+ri+ly** *or* **ˌcom+ple+ˈmen+tal+ly** *adv.* —**ˌcom+ple+ˈmen+ta+ri+ness** *n.* —**com+ple+men+ta+ri·ty** (ˌkɒmplɪmɛnˈtærɪtɪ) *n.*

com+ple+men+ta·ry an+gle *n.* either of two angles whose sum is 90°.

com+ple+men+ta·ry col+our *n.* one of any pair of colours, such as yellow and blue, that give white or grey when mixed in the correct proportions.

com+ple+men+ta·ry wave+length *n. Physics.* the wavelength of monochromatic light that could be mixed in suitable proportions with a given coloured light so as to produce some specified achromatic light.

com+ple+ment fix·a+tion test *n. Med.* a serological test for detecting the presence of a specific antibody or antigen, used in the diagnosis of syphilis, etc.

com+ple+men+tiz+er (ˈkɒmplɪmənˌtaɪzə) *n. Generative grammar.* a word or morpheme that serves to introduce a complement clause or a reduced form of such a clause, as *that* in *I wish that he would leave.*

com+plete (kəmˈpliːt) *adj.* **1.** having every necessary part or element; entire. **2.** ended; finished. **3.** (*prenominal*) thorough; absolute: *he is a complete rogue.* **4.** perfect in quality or kind: *he is a complete scholar.* **5.** (of a logical system) constituted such that a contradiction arises on the addition of any proposition that cannot be deduced from the axioms of the system. Compare **consistent** (sense 4). **6.** (of flowers) having sepals, petals, stamens, and carpels. **7.** *Archaic.* expert or skilled; accomplished. ~*vb.* (*tr.*) **8.** to make whole or perfect. **9.** to end; finish. [C14: from Latin *complētus*, past participle of *complēre* to fill up; see COMPLEMENT] —**com+ˈplete+ly** *adv.* —**com+ˈplete+ness** *n.* —**com+ˈplet+er** *n.* —**com+ˈple+tion** *n.* —**com+ˈple+tive** *adj.*

com+plex (ˈkɒmplɛks) *adj.* **1.** made up of various interconnected parts; composite. **2.** (of thoughts, writing, etc.) intricate or involved. **3.** *Grammar.* **a.** (of a word) containing at least one bound form. **b.** (of a noun phrase) containing both a lexical noun and an embedded clause, as for example the italicized parts of the following sentence: I didn't know *the man who served me.* **4.** *Maths.* **a.** of or involving one or more complex numbers. **b.** consisting of a real and an imaginary part, either of which can be zero. ~*n.* **5.** a whole made up of interconnected or related parts: *a building complex.* **6.** *Psychoanal.* a group of emotional ideas or impulses that have been banished from the conscious mind but that continue to influence a person's behaviour. **7.** *Informal.* an obsession or excessive fear: *he's got a complex about cats.* **8.** Also called: **coordination compound.** a chemical compound in which molecules, groups, or ions are attached to a central metal atom, esp. a transition metal atom, by coordinate bonds. **9.** any chemical compound in which one molecule is linked to another by a coordinate bond. [C17: from Latin *complexus*, from *complectī* to entwine, from *com-* together + *plectere* to braid] —**ˈcom+plex+ly** *adv.* —**ˈcom+plex+ness** *n.*

com+plex con+ju+gate *n. Maths.* the complex number whose imaginary part is the negation of that of a given complex number, the real parts of both numbers being equal: *$a - ib$ is the complex conjugate of $a + ib$.*

com+plex frac+tion *n. Maths.* a fraction in which the numerator or denominator or both contain fractions. Also called: **compound fraction.**

com+plex+ion (kəmˈplɛkʃən) *n.* **1.** the colour and general appearance of a person's skin, esp. of the face. **2.** aspect, character, or nature: *the general complexion of a nation's finances.* **3.** *Obsolete.* **a.** the temperament of a person. **b.** the temperature and general appearance of the body. [C14: from medical Latin *complexiō* one's bodily characteristics, from Latin: a combination, from *complectī* to embrace; see COMPLEX] —**com+ˈplex+ion+al** *adj.*

com+plex+ioned (kəmˈplɛkʃənd) *adj.* (*in combination*) of a specified complexion: *light-complexioned.*

com+plex+i·ty (kəmˈplɛksɪtɪ) *n., pl.* **·ties. 1.** the state or quality of being intricate or complex. **2.** something intricate or complex; complication.

com+plex num+ber *n.* any number of the form $a + bi$, where a and b are real numbers and $i = \sqrt{-1}$. Complex numbers include real and imaginary numbers.

com+plex salt *n.* a salt that contains one or more complex ions. Compare **double salt.**

com+plex sen+tence *n. Grammar.* a sentence containing at least one main clause and one subordinate clause.

com+pli+ance (kəmˈplaɪəns) *or* **com+pli+an+cy** *n.* **1.** the act of complying; acquiescence. **2.** a disposition to yield to or comply with others. **3.** a measure of the ability of a mechanical system to respond to an applied vibrating force, expressed as the reciprocal of the system's stiffness. Symbol: *C.*

com+pli+ant (kəmˈplaɪənt) *or* **com+pli+a·ble** *adj.* complying, obliging, or yielding. —**com+ˈpli+ant+ly** *or* **com+ˈpli+a·bly** *adv.* —**com+ˈpli+ant+ness** *or* **com+ˈpli+a·ble+ness** *n.*

com+pli+ca+cy (ˈkɒmplɪkəsɪ) *n., pl.* **+cies.** a less common word for **complexity.**

com+pli+cate *vb.* (ˈkɒmplɪˌkeɪt). **1.** to make or become complex, etc. ~*adj.* (ˈkɒmplɪkɪt). **2.** *Biology.* folded on itself: *a complicate leaf.* **3.** a less common word for **complicated.** [C17: from Latin *complicāre* to fold together, from *plicāre* to fold]

com+pli+cat+ed (ˈkɒmplɪˌkeɪtɪd) *adj.* made up of intricate parts or aspects that are difficult to understand or analyse. —**ˈcom+pli+ˌcat+ed+ly** *adv.* —**ˈcom+pli+ˌcat+ed+ness** *n.*

com+pli+ca+tion (ˌkɒmplɪˈkeɪʃən) *n.* **1.** a condition, event, etc., that is complex or confused. **2.** the act or process of complicating. **3.** a situation, event, or condition that complicates or frustrates: *her coming was a serious complication.* **4.** a disease or disorder arising as a consequence of another disease.

com+plice (ˈkɒmplɪs, ˈkʌm-) *n. Obsolete.* an associate or accomplice. [C15: from Old French, from Late Latin *complex* partner, associate, from Latin *complicāre* to fold together; see COMPLICATE]

com+plic+i·ty (kəmˈplɪsɪtɪ) *n., pl.* **·ties. 1.** the fact or condition of being an accomplice, esp. in a criminal act. **2.** a less common word for **complexity.**

com+pli+ment *n.* (ˈkɒmplɪmənt). **1.** a remark or act expressing respect, admiration, etc. **2.** (*usually pl.*) a greeting of respect or regard. **3.** *Archaic.* a gift or gratuity; tip. ~*vb.* (ˈkɒmplɪˌmɛnt). (*tr.*) **4.** to express admiration of; congratulate or commend. **5.** to express or show respect or regard for, esp. by a gift. ~Compare **complement.** [C17: from French, from Italian *complimento*, from Spanish *cumplimiento*, from *cumplir* to complete, do what is fitting, be polite]

com+pli+men+ta·ry (ˌkɒmplɪˈmɛntərɪ, -trɪ) *adj.* **1.** conveying, containing, or resembling a compliment. **2.** expressing praise; flattering. **3.** given free, esp. as a courtesy or for publicity purposes. —**ˌcom+pli+ˈmen+ta+ri+ly** *adv.*

com+pline (ˈkɒmplɪn, -plaɪn) *or* **com+plin** (ˈkɒmplɪn) *n. R.C. Church.* the last of the seven canonical hours of the divine office. [C13: from Old French *complie*, from Medieval Latin *hōra complēta*, literally: the completed hour, from Latin *complēre* to fill up, COMPLETE]

com+plot *Archaic.* ~*n.* (ˈkɒmplɒt). **1.** a plot or conspiracy. ~*vb.* (kəmˈplɒt), **+plots, +plot+ting, +plot+ted. 2.** to plot together; conspire. [C16: from Old French, of unknown origin] —**com+ˈplot+ter** *n.*

com+ply (kəmˈplaɪ) *vb.* **+plies, +ply+ing, +plied.** (*intr.*) **1.** (usually foll. by *with*) to act in accordance with rules, wishes, etc.; be obedient (to). **2.** *Obsolete.* to be obedient or complaisant. [C17: from Italian *complire*, from Spanish *cumplir* to complete; see COMPLIMENT] —**com+ˈpli+er** *n.*

com+po (ˈkɒmpəʊ) *n., pl.* **+pos. 1.** a mixture of materials, such as mortar, plaster, etc. **2.** *Austral. informal.* compensation, esp. for injury or loss of work. ~*adj.* **3.** intended to last for several days: *compo rations; a compo pack.*

com+po+nent (kəmˈpəʊnənt) *n.* **1.** a constituent part or aspect of something more complex: *a component of a car.* **2.** Also called: **element.** any electrical device, such as a resistor, that has distinct electrical characteristics and that may be connected to other electrical devices to form a circuit. **3.** *Maths.* **a.** one of a set of two or more vectors whose resultant is a given vector. **b.** the projection of this given vector onto a specified line. **4.** one of the minimum number of chemically distinct constituents necessary to describe fully the composition of each phase in a system. See **phase rule.** ~*adj.* **5.** forming or functioning as a part or aspect; constituent. [C17: from Latin *compōnere* to put together, from *pōnere* to place, put] —**com+po+nen+tial** (ˌkɒmpəˈnɛnʃəl) *adj.*

com+po+ny (kəmˈpəʊnɪ) *or* **com+po+né** (kəmˈpəʊneɪ) *adj.* (*usually postpositive*) *Heraldry.* made up of alternating metal and colour, colour and fur, or fur and metal. [C16: from Old French *componé*, from *copon* piece, COUPON]

com+port (kəmˈpɔːt) *vb.* **1.** (*tr.*) to conduct or bear (oneself) in a specified way. **2.** (*intr.*; foll. by *with*) to agree (with); correspond (to). [C16: from Latin *comportāre* to bear, collect, from *com-* together + *portāre* to carry]

com+port+ment (kəmˈpɔːtmənt) *n.* conduct; bearing.

com+pose (kəmˈpəʊz) *vb.* (*mainly tr.*) **1.** to put together or make up by combining; put in proper order. **2.** to be the component elements of. **3.** to produce or create (a musical or literary work). **4.** (*intr.*) to write music. **5.** to calm (someone, esp. oneself); make quiet. **6.** to adjust or settle (a quarrel, etc.). **7.** to order the elements of (a painting, sculpture, etc.); design. **8.** *Printing.* to set up (type). [C15: from Old French *composer*, from Latin *compōnere* to put in place; see COMPONENT]

com+posed (kəmˈpəʊzd) *adj.* (of people) calm; tranquil; serene. —**com+pos+ed+ly** (kəmˈpəʊzɪdlɪ) *adv.* —**com+ˈpos+ed+ness** *n.*

com+pos+er (kəmˈpəʊzə) *n.* **1.** a person who composes music. **2.** a person or machine that composes anything, esp. type for printing.

com+pos+ing room *n.* the room in a printing establishment in which type is set.

com+po+site (ˈkɒmpəzɪt) *adj.* **1.** composed of separate parts; compound. **2.** of, relating to, or belonging to the plant family *Compositae.* **3.** *Maths.* capable of being factorized: *a composite function.* **4.** (*sometimes cap.*) denoting or relating to one of the five classical orders of architecture: characterized by a combination of the Ionic and Corinthian styles. See also **Doric, Tuscan.** ~*n.* **5.** something composed of separate parts; compound. **6.** any plant of the family *Compositae*, typically having flower heads composed of ray flowers (e.g. dandelion), disc flowers (e.g. thistle), or both (e.g. daisy). **7.** a material, such as reinforced concrete, made of two or more distinct materials. [C16: from Latin *compositus* well arranged, from *compōnere* to collect, arrange; see COMPONENT] —**ˈcom+pos+ite+ly** *adv.* —**ˈcom+pos+ite+ness** *n.*

com+po+site num+ber *n.* an integer that can be factorized into two or more other integers. Compare **prime number.**

com+po+site pho·to+graph *n.* a photograph formed by superimposing two or more separate photographs.

com+po+site school *n. Canadian.* a secondary school offering both academic and nonacademic courses.

com+po+si+tion (ˌkɒmpəˈzɪʃən) *n.* **1.** the act of putting together or making up by combining parts or ingredients. **2.** something formed in this manner or the resulting state or quality; a mixture. **3.** the parts of which something is composed or made up; constitution. **4.** a work of music, art, or literature. **5.** the harmonious arrangement of the parts of a work of art in relation to each other and to the whole. **6.** a piece of writing undertaken as an academic exercise in grammatically acceptable writing; an essay. **7.** *Printing.* the act or technique of setting up type. **8.** *Linguistics.* the formation of compound words. **9. a.** a settlement by mutual consent, esp. a legal agreement whereby the creditors agree to accept partial payment of a debt in full settlement. **b.** the sum so agreed. [C14: from Old French, from Latin *compositus;* see COMPOSITE, -ION] —ˌ**com+po+ˈsi+tion+al** *adj.*

com+po+si+tion of forc·es *n.* the combination of two or more forces into a single equivalent force (the resultant).

com+pos·i+tor (kəmˈpɒzɪtə) *n. Printing.* a person who sets and corrects type and generally assembles plating and other matter. Sometimes shortened to **comp.** —**com+pos·i+to+ri·al** (kəmˌpɒzɪˈtɔːrɪəl) *adj.*

com+pos men+tis *Latin.* (ˈkɒmpəs ˈmɛntɪs) *adj.* (*postpositive*) of sound mind; sane.

com+pos+si·ble (kɒmˈpɒsɪbᵊl) *adj. Rare.* possible in coexistence with something else.

com+post (ˈkɒmpɒst) *n.* **1.** a mixture of organic residues such as decomposed vegetation, manure, etc., used as a fertilizer. **2.** *Rare.* a compound or mixture. ~*vb.* (*tr.*) **3.** to make (vegetable matter) into compost. **4.** to fertilize with compost. [C14: from Old French *compost,* from Latin *compositus* put together; see COMPOSITE]

Com+po+ste+la (*Spanish* ˌkomposˈtela) *n.* See **Santiago de Compostela.**

com+po+sure (kəmˈpəʊʒə) *n.* calmness, esp. of the mind; tranquillity; serenity.

com+po+ta+tion (ˌkɒmpəˈteɪʃən) *n. Rare.* the act of drinking together in a company. [C16: from Latin *compōtātiō,* translation of Greek SYMPOSIUM] —ˈ**com+po+ˌta+tor** *n.*

com+pote (ˈkɒmpəʊt; *French* kõˈpɔt) *n.* a dish of fruit stewed with sugar or in a syrup and served hot or cold. [C17: from French *composte,* from Latin *composita,* feminine of *compositus* put in place; see COMPOSITE]

com+pound[1] *n.* (ˈkɒmpaʊnd). **1.** a substance that contains atoms of two or more chemical elements held together by chemical bonds. **2.** any combination of two or more parts, aspects, etc. **3.** a word formed from two existing words or combining forms. ~*vb.* (kəmˈpaʊnd). (*mainly tr.*) **4.** to mix or combine so as to create a compound or other product. **5.** to make by combining parts, elements, aspects, etc.: *to compound a new plastic.* **6.** to intensify by an added element: *his anxiety was compounded by her crying.* **7.** *Finance.* to calculate or pay (interest) on both the principal and its accrued interest. **8.** (*also intr.*) to come to an agreement in (a quarrel, dispute, etc.). **9.** (*also intr.*) to settle (a debt, promise, etc.) for less than what is owed; compromise. **10.** *Law.* to agree not to prosecute in return for a consideration: *to compound a crime.* **11.** *Electrical engineering.* to place duplex windings on the field coil of (a motor or generator), one acting as a shunt, the other being in series with the main circuit, thus making the machine self-regulating. ~*adj.* (ˈkɒmpaʊnd). **12.** composed of or created by the combination of two or more parts, elements, etc. **13.** (of a word) consisting of elements that are also words or productive combining forms. **14.** (of a verb or the tense, mood, etc., of a verb) formed by using an auxiliary verb in addition to the main verb: *the future in English is a compound tense involving the use of such auxiliary verbs as "shall" and "will."* **15.** *Music.* **a.** denoting a time in which the number of beats per bar is a multiple of three: *six-four is an example of compound time.* **b.** (of an interval) greater than an octave. **16.** *Zoology.* another word for **colonial** (sense 6). **17.** (of a steam engine, turbine, etc.) having multiple stages in which the steam or working fluid from one stage is used in a subsequent stage. **18.** (of a piston engine) having a supercharger powered by a turbine in the exhaust stream. [C14: from earlier *compounen,* from Old French *compondre* to collect, set in order, from Latin *compōnere*] —**com+ˈpound+a·ble** *adj.* —**com+ˈpound+er** *n.*

com+pound[2] (ˈkɒmpaʊnd) *n.* **1.** (esp. in South Africa) an enclosure in which native workers are housed. **2.** any similar enclosure, such as a camp for prisoners of war. **3.** another name for **kampong.** [C17: by folk etymology (influenced by COMPOUND[1]) from Malay *kampong* village]

com+pound en+gine *n.* **1.** a steam engine in which the steam is expanded in more than one stage, first in a high-pressure cylinder and then in one or more low-pressure cylinders. **2.** a reciprocating engine in which the exhaust gases are expanded in a turbine to drive a supercharger.

com+pound eye *n.* the convex eye of insects and some crustaceans, consisting of numerous separate light-sensitive units (ommatidia).

com+pound flow+er *n.* a flower head made up of many small flowers appearing as a single bloom, as in the daisy.

com+pound frac+tion *n.* another name for **complex fraction.**

com+pound frac+ture *n.* a fracture in which the broken bone either pierces the skin or communicates with an open wound.

com+pound in+ter+est *n.* interest calculated on both the principal and its accrued interest. Compare **simple interest.**

com+pound leaf *n.* a leaf consisting of two or more leaflets borne on the same leafstalk.

com+pound lens *n.* another term for **lens** (sense 2).

com+pound mi·cro+scope *n.* an instrument for magnifying small objects, consisting of a lens of short focal length for forming an image that is further magnified by a second lens of longer focal length. Compare **simple microscope.**

com+pound num+ber *n.* a quantity expressed in two or more different but related units: *3 hours 10 seconds is a compound number.*

com+pound sen+tence *n.* a sentence containing at least two coordinate clauses.

com+pra+dor *or* **com+pra+dore** (ˌkɒmprəˈdɔː) *n.* (formerly in China and some other Asian countries) a native agent of a foreign enterprise. [C17: from Portuguese: buyer, from Late Latin *comparātor,* from Latin *comparāre* to purchase, from *parāre* to prepare]

com+pre+hend (ˌkɒmprɪˈhɛnd) *vb.* **1.** to perceive or understand. **2.** (*tr.*) to comprise or embrace; include. [C14: from Latin *comprehendere,* from *prehendere* to seize]

com+pre+hen+si·ble (ˌkɒmprɪˈhɛnsəbᵊl) *adj.* capable of being comprehended. —ˌ**com+pre+ˌhen+si·ˈbil+i·ty** *or* ˌ**com+pre+ˈhen+si·ble+ness** *n.* —ˌ**com+pre+ˈhen+si·bly** *adv.*

com+pre+hen+sion (ˌkɒmprɪˈhɛnʃən) *n.* **1.** the act or capacity of understanding. **2.** the state of including or comprising something; comprehensiveness. **3.** *Logic.* the attributes implied by a given concept or term; connotation.

com+pre+hen+sive (ˌkɒmprɪˈhɛnsɪv) *adj.* **1.** of broad scope or content; including all or much. **2.** (of a car insurance policy) providing protection against most risks, including third-party liability, fire, theft, and damage. **3.** having the ability to understand. **4.** of, relating to, or being a comprehensive school. ~*n.* **5.** short for **comprehensive school.** —ˌ**com+pre+ˈhen+sive+ly** *adv.* —ˌ**com+pre+ˈhen+sive+ness** *n.*

com+pre+hen+sive school *n.* **1.** *Chiefly Brit.* a large secondary school for children of all abilities from the same district. **2.** *Canadian.* another name for **composite school.**

com+press *vb.* (kəmˈprɛs). **1.** (*tr.*) to squeeze together or compact into less space; condense. ~*n.* (ˈkɒmprɛs). **2.** a wet or dry cloth or gauze pad with or without medication, applied firmly to some part of the body to relieve discomfort, reduce fever, drain a wound, etc. **3.** a machine for packing material, esp. cotton, under pressure. [C14: from Late Latin *compressāre,* from Latin *comprimere,* from *premere* to press] —**com+ˈpress+i·ble** *adj.* —**com+ˌpress+i·ˈbil+i·ty** *or* **com+ˈpress·i+ble+ness** *n.* —**com+ˈpress+i·bly** *adv.*

com+pressed (kəmˈprɛst) *adj.* **1.** squeezed together or condensed. **2.** (of the form of flatfishes, certain plant parts, etc.) flattened laterally along the whole length.

com+pressed air *n.* air at a higher pressure than atmospheric pressure: used esp. as a source of power for machines.

com+pres+sion (kəmˈprɛʃən) *n.* **1.** Also called: **com+pres+sure** (kəmˈprɛʃə). the act of compressing or the condition of being compressed. **2.** an increase in pressure of the charge in an engine or compressor obtained by reducing its volume.

com+pres+sion ra+ti·o *n.* the ratio of the volume enclosed by the cylinder of an internal-combustion engine at the beginning of the compression stroke to the volume enclosed at the end of it.

com+pres+sive (kəmˈprɛsɪv) *adj.* compressing or having the power or capacity to compress. —**com+ˈpres+sive+ly** *adv.*

com+pres+sor (kəmˈprɛsə) *n.* **1.** any reciprocating or rotating device that compresses a gas. **2.** the part of a gas turbine that compresses the air before it enters the combustion chambers. **3.** any muscle that causes compression of any part or structure. **4.** a medical instrument for holding down a part of the body. **5.** an electronic device for reducing the variation in signal amplitude in a transmission system. Compare **expander, compander.**

com+prise (kəmˈpraɪz) *vb.* (*tr.*) **1.** to include; contain. **2.** to constitute the whole of; consist of: *her singing comprised the entertainment.* [C15: from French *compris* included, understood, from *comprendre* to COMPREHEND] —**com+ˈpris+a·ble** *adj.* —**com+ˈpris+al** *n.*

com+pro+mise (ˈkɒmprəˌmaɪz) *n.* **1.** settlement of a dispute by concessions on both or all sides. **2.** the terms of such a settlement. **3.** something midway between two or more different things. **4.** an exposure of one's good name, reputation, etc., to injury. ~*vb.* **5.** to settle (a dispute) by making concessions. **6.** (*tr.*) to expose (a person or persons) to disrepute. **7.** (*tr.*) to prejudice unfavourably; weaken: *his behaviour compromised his chances.* **8.** (*tr.*) *Obsolete.* to pledge mutually. [C15: from Old French *compromis,* from Latin *comprōmissum* mutual agreement to accept the decision of an arbiter, from *comprōmittere,* from *prōmittere* to promise] —ˈ**com+pro+ˌmis+er** *n.* —ˈ**com+pro +ˌmis+ing+ly** *adv.*

compte ren+du *French.* (kõt rãˈdy) *n., pl.* ***comptes ren+dus*** (kõt rãˈdy). **1.** a short review or notice, esp. of a book. **2.** a statement of account. [literally: account rendered]

Comp+tom+e·ter (kɒmpˈtɒmɪtə) *n. Trademark.* a high-speed calculating machine.

Comp·ton (ˈkɒmptən) *n.* **Ar·thur Hol·ly.** 1892–1962, U.S. physicist, noted for his research on x-rays, gamma rays, and nuclear energy: Nobel prize for physics 1927.

Comp·ton-Bur·nett (ˈkɒmptən bɜːˈnɛt, ˈbɜːnɪt) *n.* **I·vy.** 1892–1969, English novelist. Her novels include *Men and Wives* (1931) and *Mother and Son* (1955).

Comp·ton ef·fect *n.* a phenomenon in which a collision between a photon and a particle results in an increase in the kinetic energy of the particle and a corresponding increase in the wavelength of the photon. [C20: named after A. H. COMPTON]

comp·trol·ler (kən'trəʊlə) *n.* a variant spelling of **controller** (sense 2), esp. as a title of any of various financial executives. —**comp·'trol·ler·ˌship** *n.*

com·pul·sion (kəm'pʌlʃən) *n.* **1.** the act of compelling or the state of being compelled. **2.** something that compels. **3.** *Psychiatry.* an inner drive that causes a person to perform actions, often of a trivial and repetitive nature, against his will. See also **obsession.** [C15: from Old French, from Latin *compellere* to COMPEL]

com·pul·sive (kəm'pʌlsɪv) *adj.* **1.** relating to or involving compulsion. ~*n.* **2.** *Psychiatry.* an individual who is subject to a psychological compulsion. —**com·'pul·sive·ly** *adv.* —**com·'pul·sive·ness** *n.*

com·pul·so·ry (kəm'pʌlsərɪ) *adj.* **1.** required by regulations or laws; obligatory: *compulsory education.* **2.** involving or employing compulsion; compelling; necessary; essential. —**com·'pul·so·ri·ly** *adv.* —**com·'pul·so·ri·ness** *n.*

com·pul·so·ry pur·chase *n.* purchase of a house or other property by a local authority or government department for public use or to make way for development, regardless of whether or not the owner wishes to sell.

com·punc·tion (kəm'pʌŋkʃən) *n.* a feeling of remorse, guilt, or regret. [C14: from Church Latin *compunctiō,* from Latin *compungere* to sting, from *com-* (intensive) + *pungere* to puncture; see POINT] —**com·'punc·tious** *adj.* —**com·'punc·tious·ly** *adv.*

com·pur·ga·tion (ˌkɒmpɜː'geɪʃən) *n.* *Law.* (formerly) a method of trial whereby a defendant might be acquitted if a sufficient number of persons swore to his innocence. [C17: from Medieval Latin *compurgātiō,* from Latin *compurgāre* to purify entirely, from *com-* (intensive) + *purgāre* to PURGE] —**'com·pur·ˌga·tor** *n.* —**com·'pur·ga·to·ry** *or* **com·ˌpur·ga·'to·ri·al** *adj.*

com·pu·ta·tion (ˌkɒmpjʊ'teɪʃən) *n.* a calculation involving numbers or quantities. —**ˌcom·pu·'ta·tion·al** *adj.*

com·pute (kəm'pjuːt) *vb.* **1.** to calculate (an answer, result, etc.), often with the aid of a computer. ~*n.* **2.** calculation; computation (esp. in the phrase **beyond compute**). [C17: from Latin *computāre,* from *putāre* to think] —**com·'put·a·ble** *adj.* —**com·ˌput·a·'bil·i·ty** *n.*

com·put·er (kəm'pjuːtə) *n.* **1. a.** a device, usually electronic, that processes data according to a set of instructions. The **digital computer** stores data in discrete units and performs arithmetical and logical operations at very high speed. The **analog computer** has no memory and is slower than the digital computer but has a continuous rather than a discrete input. The **hybrid computer** combines some of the advantages of digital and analog computers. **b.** (*as modifier*): *computer technology.* **2.** a person who computes or calculates.

com·put·er·ize *or* **com·put·er·ise** (kəm'pjuːtəˌraɪz) *vb.* **1.** (*tr.*) to cause (certain operations) to be performed by a computer, esp. as a replacement for human labour. **2.** (*intr.*) to install a computer. **3.** (*tr.*) to control or perform (operations within a system) by means of a computer. **4.** (*tr.*) to process or store (information) by means of or in a computer. —**com·ˌput·er·i·'za·tion** *or* **com·ˌput·er·i·'sa·tion** *n.*

com·put·er type·set·ting *n.* a system for the high-speed composition of type by a device driven by punched paper tape or magnetic tape that has been processed by a computer. Also called: **automatic typesetting.**

Comr. *abbrev. for* Commissioner.

com·rade ('kɒmreɪd, -rɪd) *n.* **1.** an associate or companion. **2.** a fellow member of a political party, esp. a fellow Communist or socialist. [C16: from French *camarade,* from Spanish *camarada* group of soldiers sharing a billet, from *cámara* room, from Latin; see CAMERA, CHAMBER] —**'com·rade·ly** *adj.* —**'com·rade·ˌship** *n.*

com·sat ('kɒmsæt) *n.* short for **communications satellite.**

com·stock·er·y ('kʌmˌstɒkərɪ, 'kɒm-) *n.* *U.S.* immoderate censorship on grounds of immorality. [C20: coined by G. B. Shaw (1905) after *Anthony Comstock* (1844–1915), U.S. moral crusader, who founded the Society for the Suppression of Vice]

Com·stock Lode ('kʌmˌstɒk, 'kɒm-) *n.* an extensive gold and silver vein in W Nevada, near Virginia City. [C19: named after T. P. *Comstock* (1820–1870), American prospector]

Comte (*French* kɔ̃ːt) *n.* **(Isidore) Au·guste (Marie François)** (o'gyst). 1798–1857, French mathematician and philosopher; the founder of positivism. —**Comt·ism** ('kɔːnˌtɪzəm) *n.* —**'Comt·ist** *or* **'Comt·i·an** *adj., n.*

Co·mus ('kəʊməs) *n.* (in late Roman mythology) a god of revelry. [C17: from Latin, from Greek *kōmos* a revel]

Com. Ver. *abbrev. for* Common Version (of the Bible).

con[1] (kɒn) *Slang.* ~*n.* **1. a.** short for **confidence trick. b.** (*as modifier*): *con man.* ~*vb.* **cons, con·ning, conned. 2.** (*tr.*) to swindle or defraud. [C19: from CONFIDENCE]

con[2] (kɒn) *n.* (*usually pl.*) **1.** an argument or vote against a proposal, motion, etc. **2.** a person who argues or votes against a proposal, motion, etc. ~Compare **pro**[1]. See also **pros and cons.** [from Latin *contrā* against, opposed to]

con[3] (kɒn) *n. Slang.* short for **convict.**

con[4] *or* (*esp. U.S.*) **conn** (kɒn) *Nautical.* ~*vb.* **cons** *or* **conns, con·ning, conned. 1.** (*tr.*) to direct the steering of (a vessel). ~*n.* **2.** the place where a person who cons a vessel is stationed. [C17 *cun,* from earlier *condien* to guide, from Old French *conduire,* from Latin *condūcere;* see CONDUCT]

con[5] (kɒn) *vb.* **cons, con·ning, conned.** (*tr.*) *Archaic.* to study attentively or learn (esp. in the phrase **con by rote**). [C15: variant of CAN[1] in the sense: to come to know]

con. *abbrev. for:* **1.** concerto. **2.** conclusion. **3.** connection. **4.** consolidated. **5.** continued. **6.** contra. [Latin: against]

Con. *abbrev. for:* **1.** Conformist. **2.** Consul.

con- *prefix.* variant of **com-.**

Co·na·kry *or* **Ko·na·kri** (*French* kɔna'kri) *n.* the capital of Guinea, a port on the island of Tombo. Pop.: 197 267 (1967 est.).

con a·mo·re (kɒn æ'mɔːrɪ) *adj., adv. Music.* lovingly. [C19: from Italian: with love]

Co·nan Doyle ('kəʊnən 'dɔɪl, 'kɒnən) *n.* Sir **Ar·thur.** 1859–1930, British author of detective stories and historical romances and the creator of *Sherlock Holmes.*

co·na·tion (kəʊ'neɪʃən) *n.* the element in psychological processes that tends towards activity or change and appears as desire, volition, and striving. [C19: from Latin *cōnātiō* an attempting, from *cōnārī* to try] —**co·'na·tion·al** *adj.*

con·a·tive ('kɒnətɪv, 'kəʊ-) *adj.* **1.** *Grammar.* denoting an aspect of verbs in some languages used to indicate the effort of the agent in performing the activity described by the verb. **2.** of or relating to conation.

co·na·tus (kəʊ'neɪtəs) *n., pl.* **·tus. 1.** an effort or striving of natural impulse. **2.** (esp. in the philosophy of Spinoza) the tendency of all things to persist in their own being. [C17: from Latin: effort, from *cōnārī* to try]

con bri·o (kɒn 'briːəʊ) *adj., adv. Music.* with liveliness or spirit, as in the phrase **allegro con brio.** [Italian: with energy]

conc. *abbrev. for:* **1.** concentrate. **2.** concentrated. **3.** concentration. **4.** concerning. **5.** concerto.

con·cat·e·nate (kɒn'kætɪˌneɪt) *vb.* **1.** (*tr.*) to link or join together, esp. in a chain or series. ~*adj.* **2.** linked or joined together. [C16: from Late Latin *concatēnāre* from Latin *com-* together + *catēna* CHAIN]

con·cat·e·na·tion (kɒnˌkætɪ'neɪʃən) *n.* **1.** a series of interconnected events, concepts, etc. **2.** the act of linking together or the state of being joined.

con·cave ('kɒnkeɪv, kɒn'keɪv) *adj.* **1.** curving inwards. **2.** *Physics.* having one or two surfaces curved or ground in the shape of a section of the interior of a sphere, paraboloid, etc.: *a concave lens.* **3.** *Maths.* (of a polygon) containing an interior angle greater than 180°. **4.** an obsolete word for **hollow.** ~*vb.* **5.** (*tr.*) to make concave. ~Compare **convex.** [C15: from Latin *concavus* arched, from *cavus* hollow] —**'con·cave·ly** *adv.* —**'con·cave·ness** *n.*

con·cav·i·ty (kɒn'kævɪtɪ) *n., pl.* **·ties. 1.** the state or quality of being concave. **2.** a concave surface or thing; cavity.

con·cav·o-con·cave (kɒnˌkeɪvəʊkɒn'keɪv) *adj.* (esp. of a lens) having both sides concave; biconcave.

con·cav·o-con·vex *adj.* **1.** having one side concave and the other side convex. **2.** (of a lens) having a concave face with greater curvature than the convex face. Compare **convexo-concave** (sense 2).

con·ceal (kən'siːl) *vb.* (*tr.*) **1.** to keep from discovery; hide. **2.** to keep secret. [C14: from Old French *conceler,* from Latin *concēlāre,* from *com-* (intensive) + *cēlāre* to hide] —**con·'ceal·a·ble** *adj.* —**con·'ceal·er** *n.* —**con·'ceal·ment** *n.*

con·cede (kən'siːd) *vb.* **1.** (when *tr., may take a clause as object*) to admit or acknowledge (something) as true or correct. **2.** to yield or allow (something, such as a right). **3.** (*tr.*) to admit as certain in outcome: *to concede an election.* [C17: from Latin *concēdere,* from *cēdere* to give way, CEDE] —**con·'ced·ed·ly** *adv.* —**con·'ced·er** *n.*

con·ceit (kən'siːt) *n.* **1.** a high, often exaggerated, opinion of oneself or one's accomplishments; vanity. **2.** *Literary.* an elaborate image or far-fetched comparison, esp. as used by the English Metaphysical poets. **3.** *Archaic.* **a.** a witty expression. **b.** fancy; imagination. **c.** an idea. **4.** *Obsolete.* a small ornament. ~*vb.* (*tr.*) **5.** *Northern Brit. dialect.* to like or be able to bear (something, such as food or drink). **6.** *Obsolete.* to think or imagine. [C14: from CONCEIVE]

con·ceit·ed (kən'siːtɪd) *adj.* **1.** having a high or exaggerated opinion of oneself or one's accomplishments. **2.** *Archaic.* fanciful. **3.** *Obsolete.* witty or intelligent. —**con·'ceit·ed·ly** *adv.* —**con·'ceit·ed·ness** *n.*

con·ceiv·a·ble (kən'siːvəb[ə]l) *adj.* capable of being understood, believed, or imagined; possible. —**con·ˌceiv·a·'bil·i·ty** *or* **con·'ceiv·a·ble·ness** *n.* —**con·'ceiv·a·bly** *adv.*

con·ceive (kən'siːv) *vb.* **1.** (when *intr.,* foll. by *of;* when *tr., often takes a clause as object*) to have an idea (of); imagine; think. **2.** (*tr.; takes a clause as object or an infinitive*) to hold as an opinion; believe. **3.** (*tr.*) to develop or form, esp. in the mind: *she conceived a passion for music.* **4.** to become pregnant with (a child). **5.** (*tr.*) *Rare.* to express in words. [C13: from Old French *conceivre,* from Latin *concipere* to take in, from *capere* to take] —**con·'ceiv·er** *n.*

con·cel·e·brate (kən'sɛlɪˌbreɪt) *vb. Christianity.* to celebrate (the Eucharist or Mass) jointly with one or more other priests. [C16: from Latin *concelebrāre*] —**con·ˌcel·e·'bra·tion** *n.*

con·cent (kən'sɛnt) *n. Archaic.* a concord, as of sounds, voices, etc. [C16: from Latin *concentus* harmonious sounds, from *concinere* to sing together, from *canere* to sing]

con·cen·trate ('kɒnsənˌtreɪt) *vb.* **1.** (*tr.*) to come or cause to come to a single purpose or aim: *to concentrate one's hopes on winning.* **2.** to make or become denser or purer by the removal of certain elements, esp. the solvent of a solution. **3.** (*tr.*) to remove rock or sand from (an ore) to make it purer. **4.** (*intr.; often foll. by on*) to bring one's faculties to bear (on); think intensely (about). *~n.* **5.** a concentrated material or solution: *tomato concentrate.* [C17: back formation from CONCENTRATION, ultimately from Latin *com-* same + *centrum* CENTRE] —**'con+cen+ˌtra+tor** *n.*

con+cen+tra+tion (ˌkɒnsən'treɪʃən) *n.* **1.** intense mental application; complete attention. **2.** the act or process of concentrating. **3.** something that is concentrated. **4.** the strength of a solution, esp. the amount of dissolved substance in a given volume of solvent, usually expressed in moles per cubic metre or cubic decimetre (litre). Symbol: *c* **5.** the process of increasing the concentration of a solution. **6.** *Military.* **a.** the act of bringing together military forces. **b.** the application of fire from a number of weapons against a target. **7.** another name (esp. U.S.) for **Pelmanism.**

con+cen+tra+tion camp *n.* a guarded prison camp in which prisoners are held, esp. one in Nazi Germany.

con+cen+tra+tive ('kɒnsənˌtreɪtɪv) *adj.* tending to concentrate; characterized by concentration. —**'con+cen+ˌtra+tive+ly** *adv.* —**'con+cen+ˌtra+tive+ness** *n.*

con+cen+tre (kɒn'sɛntə) *vb.* to converge or cause to converge on a common centre; concentrate. [C16: from French *concentrer;* see CONCENTRATE]

con+cen+tric (kən'sɛntrɪk) *adj.* having a common centre: *concentric circles.* Compare **eccentric** (sense 3). [C14: from Medieval Latin *concentricus,* from Latin *com-* same + *centrum* CENTRE] —**con+'cen+tri+cal+ly** *adv.* —**con+cen+tric+i+ty** (ˌkɒnsən'trɪsɪtɪ) *n.*

Con+cep+ción (*Spanish* ˌkonsep'sjon) *n.* an industrial city in S central Chile. Pop.: 169 570 (1975 est.).

con+cept ('kɒnsɛpt) *n.* **1.** something formed in the mind; abstract idea; thought. **2.** *Philosophy.* **a.** a general idea of something formed by mentally combining all specific parts and characteristic features. **b.** an abstract notion, theoretical construct, or directly intuited object of thought. [C16: from Latin *conceptum* something received or conceived, from *concipere* to take in, CONCEIVE]

con+cep+ta+cle (kən'sɛptək^əl) *n.* a flask-shaped cavity containing the reproductive organs in some algae and fungi. [C17: from Latin *conceptāculum* receptacle, from *concipere* to receive, CONCEIVE]

con+cep+tion (kən'sɛpʃən) *n.* **1.** something conceived; notion, idea, design, or plan. **2.** the state or condition of an ovum being fertilized by a sperm in the womb. **3.** the product of such fertilization: an embryo or fetus. **4.** origin or beginning: *from its conception the plan was a failure.* **5.** the act or power of forming notions; invention. [C13: from Latin *conceptiō,* from *concipere* to CONCEIVE] —**con+'cep+tion+al** *or* **con+'cep+tive** *adj.*

con+cep+tu·al (kən'sɛptjʊəl) *adj.* of or characterized by concepts or the forming of concepts. —**con+'cep+tu+al+ly** *adv.*

con+cep+tu+al+ism (kən'sɛptjʊəˌlɪzəm) *n.* the philosophical theory that the application of general words to a variety of objects reflects the existence of some mental entity through which the application is mediated. Compare **nominalism, realism, Platonism.** —**con+'cep+tu+al+ist** *n.* —**con+ˌcep+tu+al+'is+tic** *adj.*

con+cep+tu+al+ize *or* **con+cep+tu+al+ise** (kən'sɛptjʊəˌlaɪz) *vb.* to form (a concept or concepts) out of observations, experience, data, etc.; think in concepts (about). —**con+ˌcep+tu+al·i+'za+tion** *or* **conˌcep+tu+al·i+'sa+tion** *n.*

con+cern (kən'sɜːn) *vb.* (*tr.*) **1.** to relate to; be of importance or interest to; affect. **2.** (usually foll. by *with* or *in*) to involve or interest (oneself): *he concerns himself with other people's affairs.* *~n.* **3.** something that affects or is of importance to a person; affair; business. **4.** regard for or interest in a person or a thing: *he felt a strong concern for her.* **5.** anxiety, worry, or solicitude. **6.** important bearing or relation: *his news has great concern for us.* **7.** a commercial company or enterprise. **8.** *Informal.* a material thing, esp. one of which one has a low opinion. [C15: from Late Latin *concernere* to mingle together, from Latin *com-* together + *cernere* to sift, distinguish]

con+cerned (kən'sɜːnd) *adj.* **1.** (*postpositive*) interested, guilty, involved, or appropriate: *I shall find the boy concerned and punish him.* **2.** worried, troubled, or solicitous. —**con+cern+ed+ly** (kən'sɜːnɪdlɪ) *adv.* —**con+'cern+ed+ness** *n.*

con+cern+ing (kən'sɜːnɪŋ) *prep.* **1.** about; regarding; on the subject of. *~adj.* **2.** worrying or troublesome.

con+cern+ment (kən'sɜːnmənt) *n.* **1.** *Rare.* affair or business; concern. **2.** *Archaic.* a matter of importance.

con+cert *n.* ('kɒnsɜːt, -sət). **1. a.** a performance of music by players or singers that does not involve theatrical staging. Compare **recital** (sense 1). **b.** (*as modifier*): *a concert version of an opera.* **2.** agreement in design, plan, or action. **3. in concert. a.** acting in a co-ordinated fashion with a common purpose. **b.** (of musicians, etc., esp. rock musicians) performing live. *~vb.* (kən'sɜːt). **4.** to arrange or contrive (a plan) by mutual agreement. [C16: from French *concerter* to bring into agreement, from Italian *concertare,* from Late Latin *concertāre* to work together, from Latin: to dispute, debate, from *certāre* to contend]

con+cer+tan+te (ˌkɒntʃə'tæntɪ) *Music.* *~adj.* **1.** characterized by contrastive passages or phrases between a soloist and the rest of the instrumental or vocal forces involved. *~n., pl.* **+ti** (-tɪ). **2.** a composition characterized by such contrasts. [C18: from Italian, from *concertare* to perform a concert, from *concerto* CONCERT]

con+cert+ed (kən'sɜːtɪd) *adj.* **1.** mutually contrived, planned, or arranged; combined (esp. in the phrases **concerted action, concerted effort**). **2.** *Music.* arranged in parts for a group of singers or players. —**con+'cert+ed+ly** *adv.*

con+cert+go+er ('kɒnsɜːtˌgəʊə) *n.* a person who attends concerts of music.

con+cert grand *n.* a grand piano of the largest size.

con+cer+ti+na (ˌkɒnsə'tiːnə) *n.* **1.** a hexagonal musical instrument of the reed-organ family similar to the accordion. Notes are produced by pressing buttons. *~vb.* **+nas, +na+ing, +naed.** **2.** (*intr.*) to collapse or fold up like a concertina. [C19: CONCERT + *-ina*] —**ˌcon+cer+'ti+nist** *n.*

con+cer+ti+no (ˌkɒntʃə'tiːnəʊ) *n., pl.* **+ni** (-nɪ). **1.** the small group of soloists in a concerto grosso. Compare **ripieno. 2.** a short concerto. [C19: from Italian: a little CONCERTO]

con+cer+tize *or* **con+cer+tise** ('kɒnsəˌtaɪz) *vb.* (*intr.*) (esp. of a soloist or conductor) to give concerts.

con·cert+mas·ter ('kɒnsətˌmɑːstə) *n.* a U.S. word for **leader** (of an orchestra).

con+cer+to (kən'tʃɛətəʊ) *n., pl.* **+tos** *or* **+ti** (-tɪ). **1.** a composition for an orchestra and one or more soloists. The classical concerto usually consisted of three movements. See also **sonata** (sense 1), **symphony** (sense 1). **2.** another word for **ripieno.** [C18: from Italian: CONCERT]

con+cer+to gros+so ('grɒsəʊ) *n., pl.* **con+cer+ti gros+si** ('grɒsɪ) *or* **con+cer+to gros+sos.** a composition for an orchestra and a group of soloists, chiefly of the baroque period. [Italian, literally: big concerto]

con+cert o·ver+ture *n.* See **overture** (sense 1c.).

con+cert pitch *n.* **1.** the frequency of 440 hertz assigned to the A above middle C. See **pitch**[1] (sense 26b.), **international pitch. 2.** *Informal.* a state of extreme readiness.

con+ces+sion (kən'sɛʃən) *n.* **1.** the act of yielding or conceding, as to a demand or argument. **2.** something conceded. **3.** any grant of rights, land, or property by a government, local authority, corporation, or individual. **4.** the right, esp. an exclusive right, to market a particular product in a given area. **5.** *U.S.* **a.** the right to maintain a subsidiary business on a lessor's premises. **b.** the premises so granted or the business so maintained. **c.** a free rental period for such premises. **6.** *Canadian.* (chiefly in Ontario and Quebec) **a.** a land subdivision in a township survey. **b.** another name for a **concession road.** [C16: from Latin *concēssiō* an allowing, from *concēdere* to CONCEDE] —**con+'ces+si·ble** *adj.*

con+ces+sion+aire (kənˌsɛʃə'nɛə), **con+ces+sion+er** (kən'sɛʃənə), or **con+ces+sion+ar·y** *n.* someone who holds or operates a concession.

con+ces+sion+ar·y (kən'sɛʃənərɪ) *adj.* **1.** of, granted, or obtained by a concession. *~n., pl.* **+ar·ies. 2.** another word for **concessionaire.**

con+ces+sion road *n. Canadian.* (esp. in Ontario) any of a number of roughly parallel roads forming a grid pattern along township survey lines.

con+ces+sive (kən'sɛsɪv) *adj.* **1.** implying or involving concession; tending to concede. **2.** *Grammar.* a conjunction, preposition, phrase, or clause describing a state of affairs that might have been expected to rule out what is described in the main clause but in fact does not: *"Although" in the sentence "Although they had been warned, they refused to take care" is a concessive conjunction.* [C18: from Late Latin *concēssīvus,* from Latin *concēdere* to CONCEDE]

conch (kɒŋk, kɒntʃ) *n., pl.* **conchs** (kɒŋks) *or* **conch·es** ('kɒntʃɪz). **1.** any of various tropical marine gastropod molluscs of the genus *Strombus* and related genera, esp. *S. gigas* (giant conch), characterized by a large brightly coloured spiral shell. **2.** the shell of such a mollusc, used as a trumpet. **3.** *Architect.* another name for **concha** (sense 2). [C16: from Latin *concha,* from Greek *konkhē* shellfish]

con+cha ('kɒŋkə) *n., pl.* **+chae** (-kiː). **1.** any bodily organ or part resembling a shell in shape, such as the external ear. **2.** Also called: **conch.** *Architect.* the half dome of an apse. —**'con+chal** *adj.*

con+chie or **con+chy** ('kɒntʃɪ) *n., pl.* **+chies.** *Informal.* short for **conscientious objector.**

con+chif+er+ous (kɒŋ'kɪfərəs) *adj.* **1.** (esp. of molluscs) having or producing a shell. **2.** (of rocks) containing shells.

con+chi·o+lin (kɒŋ'kaɪəlɪn) *n.* a fibrous insoluble protein that forms the basic structure of the shells of molluscs. Formula: $C_{30}H_{48}O_{11}N_9$. [C19: from CONCH; see -IN]

Con·cho·bar ('kɒŋkəʊwə, 'kɒnʊə) *n.* (in Irish legend) a king of Ulster at about the beginning of the Christian era. See also **Deirdre.**

con+choid ('kɒŋkɔɪd) *n. Geom.* a plane curve consisting of two branches situated about a line to which they are asymptotic, so that a line from a fixed point (the pole) intersecting both branches is of constant length between asymptote and either branch. Equation: $(x - a)^2(x^2 + y^2) = b^2x^2$ where *a* is the distance between the pole and a vertical asymptote and *b* is the length of the constant segment.

con+choi+dal (kɒŋ'kɔɪd^əl) *adj.* **1.** (of the fracture of minerals and rocks) having smooth shell-shaped convex and concave surfaces. **2.** (of minerals and rocks, such as flint) having such a fracture. —**con+'choi+dal+ly** *adv.*

con+chol+o·gy (kɒŋ'kɒlədʒɪ) *n.* the study and collection of mollusc shells. —**con+cho+log·i+cal** (ˌkɒŋkə'lɒdʒɪk^əl) *adj.* —**con+'chol·o+gist** *n.*

con+ci+erge (ˌkɒnsɪ'ɛəʒ; *French* kɔ̃'sjɛrʒ) *n.* (esp. in France) a caretaker of a block of flats, hotel, etc., esp. one who lives on the premises. [C17: from French, ultimately from Latin *conservus,* from *servus* slave]

con·cil·i·ar (kən'sɪlɪə) *adj.* of, from, or by means of a council, esp. an ecclesiastical one. —**con·'cil·i·ar·ly** *adv.*

con·cil·i·ate (kən'sɪlɪˌeɪt) *vb.* (*tr.*) **1.** to overcome the hostility of; placate; win over. **2.** to win or gain (favour, regard, etc.), esp. by making friendly overtures. **3.** *Archaic.* to make compatible; reconcile. [C16: from Latin *conciliāre* to bring together, from *concilium* COUNCIL] —**con·'cil·i·a·ble** *adj.* —**con·ˌcil·i·'a·tion** *n.* —**con·'cil·i·ˌa·tor** *n.*

con·cil·ia·to·ry (kən'sɪljətərɪ, -trɪ) *or* **con·cil·ia·tive** (kən'sɪljətɪv) *adj.* intended to placate or reconcile. —**con·'cil·ia·to·ri·ly** *adv.* —**con·'cil·ia·to·ri·ness** *n.*

con·cin·ni·ty (kən'sɪnɪtɪ) *n., pl.* **·ties.** a harmonious arrangement of parts, esp. in literary works, speeches, etc. [C16: from Latin *concinnitās* a skilful combining of various things, from *concinnāre* to adjust, of obscure origin] —**con·'cin·nous** *adj.*

con·cise (kən'saɪs) *adj.* expressing much in few words; brief and to the point. [C16: from Latin *concīsus* cut up, cut short, from *concīdere* to cut to pieces, from *caedere* to cut, strike down] —**con·'cise·ly** *adv.* —**con·'cise·ness** *n.*

con·ci·sion (kən'sɪʒən) *n.* **1.** the quality of being concise; brevity; terseness. **2.** *Archaic.* a cutting apart or off; severing; division.

con·clave ('kɒnkleɪv, 'kɒŋ-) *n.* **1.** a confidential or secret meeting. **2.** *R.C. Church.* **a.** the closed apartments where the college of cardinals elects a new pope. **b.** a meeting of the college of cardinals for this purpose. [C14: from Medieval Latin *conclāve*, from Latin: cage, place that may be locked, from *clāvis* key] —**'con·clav·ist** *n.*

con·clude (kən'klu:d) *vb.* (*mainly tr.*) **1.** (*also intr.*) to come or cause to come to an end or conclusion. **2.** (*takes a clause as object*) to decide by reasoning; deduce: *the judge concluded that the witness had told the truth.* **3.** to arrange finally; settle: *to conclude a treaty; it was concluded that he should go.* **4.** *Obsolete.* to confine. [C14: from Latin *conclūdere* to enclose, end, from *claudere* to close] —**con·'clud·er** *n.*

con·clu·sion (kən'klu:ʒən) *n.* **1.** end or termination. **2.** the last main division of a speech, lecture, essay, etc. **3.** the outcome or result of an act, process, event, etc. (esp. in the phrase **a foregone conclusion**). **4.** an intuitive rather than well reasoned deduction: *you jump too readily to conclusions.* **5.** a final decision or judgment; resolution (esp. in the phrase **come to a conclusion**). **6.** *Logic.* a proposition inferred from a set of premisses that can be shown, on logical grounds, to be true if the premisses are true. **7.** *Law.* **a.** an admission or statement binding on the party making it; estoppel. **b.** the close of a pleading or of a conveyance. **8. in conclusion.** lastly; to sum up. **9. try conclusions with.** *Archaic.* to engage in competition with (someone). [C14: via Old French from Latin; see CONCLUDE, -ION]

con·clu·sive (kən'klu:sɪv) *adj.* **1.** putting an end to doubt; decisive; final. **2.** approaching or involving an end or conclusion. —**con·'clu·sive·ly** *adv.* —**con·'clu·sive·ness** *n.*

con·coct (kən'kɒkt) *vb.* (*tr.*) **1.** to make by combining different ingredients. **2.** to invent; make up; contrive. [C16: from Latin *concoctus* cooked together, from *concoquere,* from *coquere* to cook] —**con·'coct·er** *or* **con·'coc·tor** *n.* —**con·'coc·tive** *adj.*

con·coc·tion (kən'kɒkʃən) *n.* **1.** the act or process of concocting. **2.** something concocted. **3.** an untruth; lie.

con·com·i·tance (kən'kɒmɪtəns) *n.* **1.** existence or occurrence together or in connection with another. **2.** a thing that exists in connection with another. **3.** *Theol.* the doctrine that the body and blood of Christ are present in the Eucharist.

con·com·i·tant (kən'kɒmɪtənt) *adj.* **1.** existing or occurring together; associative. ~*n.* **2.** a concomitant act, person, etc. [C17: from Late Latin *concomitārī* to accompany, from *com-* with + *comes* companion, fellow] —**con·'com·i·tant·ly** *adv.*

con·cord ('kɒnkɔ:d, 'kɒŋ-) *n.* **1.** agreement or harmony between people or nations; amity. **2.** a treaty establishing peaceful relations between nations. **3.** agreement or harmony between things, ideas, etc. **4.** *Music.* a combination of musical notes, esp. one containing a series of consonant intervals. Compare **discord** (sense 3). **5.** *Grammar.* another word for **agreement** (sense 6). [C13: from Old French *concorde,* from Latin *concordia,* from *concors* of the same mind, harmonious, from *com-* same + *cors* heart]

Con·cord ('kɒŋkəd) *n.* **1.** a town in NE Massachusetts: scene of one of the opening military actions (1775) of the War of American Independence. Pop.: 16 148 (1970). **2.** a city in SE Australia, in E New South Wales: a W suburb of Sydney. Pop.: 25 903 (1971).

con·cord·ance (kən'kɔ:dᵊns) *n.* **1.** a state or condition of agreement or harmony. **2.** a book that indexes the principal words in a literary work, often with the immediate context and an account of the meaning. **3.** an index produced by computer or machine, alphabetically listing every word in a text. **4.** an alphabetical list of subjects or topics.

con·cord·ant (kən'kɔ:dᵊnt) *adj.* being in agreement: harmonious. —**con·'cord·ant·ly** *adv.*

con·cor·dat (kɒn'kɔ:dæt) *n.* a pact or treaty, esp. one between the Vatican and another state concerning the interests of religion in that state. [C17: via French, from Medieval Latin *concordātum,* from Latin: something agreed, from *concordāre* to be of one mind; see CONCORD]

Con·corde ('kɒnkɔ:d, 'kɒŋ-) *n.* the first commercial supersonic airliner. Of Anglo-French construction, it is capable of over 2160 km per hr (1200 mph).

Con·cord grape ('kɒŋkəd, 'kɒnkɔ:d) *n.* a variety of grape with purple-black fruit covered with a bluish bloom. [C19: discovered at CONCORD, Mass.]

con·cours d'é·lé·gance *French.* (kõkur dele'gã:s) *n.* a parade of cars or other vehicles, prizes being awarded to the most elegant, best designed, or best turned-out.

con·course ('kɒnkɔ:s, 'kɒŋ-) *n.* **1.** a crowd; throng. **2.** a coming together; confluence: *a concourse of events.* **3.** a large open space for the gathering of people in a public place. **4.** *Chiefly U.S.* a ground for sports, racing, athletics, etc. [C14: from Old French *concours,* ultimately from Latin *concurrere* to run together, from *currere* to run]

con·cres·cence (kən'krɛsəns) *n. Biology.* a growing together of initially separate parts or organs. [C17: from Latin *concrēscentia,* from *concrēscere* to grow together, from *crēscere* to grow; see CRESCENT]

con·crete ('kɒnkri:t) *n.* **1. a.** a building material made of a mixture of cement, sand, aggregate, and water that hardens as it dries. **b.** (*as modifier*): *a concrete slab.* **2.** *Physics.* a mass formed by the coalescence of separate particles. ~*adj.* **3.** relating to a particular instance or object; specific as opposed to general: *a concrete example.* **4. a.** relating to or characteristic of things capable of being perceived by the senses, as opposed to abstractions. **b.** (*as n.*): *the concrete.* **5.** formed by the coalescence of particles; condensed; solid. ~*vb.* **6.** (*tr.*) to construct in or cover with concrete. **7.** (kən'kri:t). to become or cause to become solid; coalesce. [C14: from Latin *concrētus* grown together, hardened, from *concrēscere;* see CONCRESCENCE] —**'con·crete·ly** *adv.* —**'con·crete·ness** *n.* —**con·'cre·tive** *adj.* —**con·'cre·tive·ly** *adv.*

con·crete mu·sic *n.* music consisting of an electronically modified montage of tape-recorded sounds.

con·crete noun *n.* a noun that refers to a material object. Compare **abstract noun.**

con·crete num·ber *n.* a number referring to a particular object or objects, as in *three dogs, ten men.*

con·crete po·e·try *n.* poetry in which the visual form of the poem is used to convey meaning.

con·cre·tion (kən'kri:ʃən) *n.* **1.** the act or process of coming or growing together; coalescence. **2.** a solid or solidified mass. **3.** something made real, tangible, or specific. **4.** any of various rounded or irregular mineral masses that are different in composition from the sedimentary rock that surrounds them. **5.** *Pathol.* another word for **calculus.** —**con·'cre·tion·ar·y** *adj.*

con·cre·tize *or* **con·cre·tise** ('kɒnkrɪˌtaɪz, 'kɒŋ-) *vb.* (*tr.*) to render concrete; make real or specific; give tangible form to. —**ˌcon·cret·i·'za·tion** *or* **ˌcon·cret·i·'sa·tion** *n.*

con·cu·bi·nage (kɒn'kju:bɪnɪdʒ) *n.* **1.** cohabitation without legal marriage. **2.** the state of living as a concubine.

con·cu·bine ('kɒŋkjʊˌbaɪn, 'kɒn-) *n.* **1.** (in polygamous societies) a secondary wife, usually of lower social rank. **2.** a woman who cohabits with a man. [C13: from Old French, from Latin *concubīna,* from *concumbere* to lie together, from *cubere* to lie] —**con·'cu·bi·nar·y** *n., adj.*

con·cu·pis·cence (kən'kju:pɪsəns) *n.* strong desire, esp. sexual desire. [C14: from Church Latin *concupiscentia,* from Latin *concupiscere* to covet ardently, from *cupere* to wish, desire] —**con·'cu·pis·cent** *adj.*

con·cur (kən'kɜ:) *vb.* **·curs, ·cur·ring, ·curred.** (*intr.*) **1.** to agree; be of the same mind; be in accord. **2.** to combine, act together, or cooperate. **3.** to occur simultaneously; coincide. **4.** *Rare.* to converge. [C15: from Latin *concurrere* to run together, from *currere* to run] —**con·'cur·ring·ly** *adv.*

con·cur·rence (kən'kʌrəns) *n.* **1.** the act of concurring. **2.** agreement in opinion; accord; assent. **3.** cooperation or combination. **4.** simultaneous occurrence; coincidence. **5.** *Geom.* a point at which three or more lines intersect. **6.** *Rare.* rivalry or competition. ~Also (for senses 1–4): **con·cur·ren·cy.**

con·cur·rent (kən'kʌrənt) *adj.* **1.** taking place at the same time or in the same location. **2.** cooperating. **3.** meeting at, approaching, or having a common point: *concurrent lines.* **4.** having equal authority or jurisdiction. **5.** in accordance or agreement; harmonious. ~*n.* **6.** something joint or contributory; a concurrent circumstance or cause. **7.** *Archaic.* a competitor or rival. —**con·'cur·rent·ly** *adv.*

con·cuss (kən'kʌs) *vb.* (*tr.*) **1.** to injure (the brain) by a violent blow, fall, etc. **2.** to shake violently; agitate; disturb. [C16: from Latin *concussus* violently shaken, from *concutere* to disturb greatly, from *quatere* to shake]

con·cus·sion (kən'kʌʃən) *n.* **1.** a jarring of the brain, caused by a blow or a fall, usually resulting in loss of consciousness. **2.** any violent shaking; jarring. —**con·'cus·sive** *adj.*

Con·dé (*French* kõ'de) *n.* **Prince de** (prẽs də), title of *Louis II de Bourbon, Duc d'Enghien,* called *the Great Condé.* 1621–86, French general, who led Louis XIV's armies against the Fronde (1649) but joined the Fronde in a new revolt (1650–52). He later fought for both France and Spain.

con·demn (kən'dɛm) *vb.* (*tr.*) **1.** to express strong disapproval of; censure. **2.** to pronounce judicial sentence on. **3.** to demonstrate the guilt of: *his secretive behaviour condemned him.* **4.** to judge or pronounce unfit for use: *that food has been condemned.* **5.** to compel or force into a particular state or activity: *his disposition condemned him to boredom.* [C13: from Old French *condempner,* from Latin *condemnāre,* from *damnāre* to condemn; see DAMN] —**con·demn·a·ble** (kən'dɛməbᵊl) *adj.* —**con·'demn·a·bly** *adv.* —**ˌcon·dem·'na·tion** *n.* —**con·dem·na·to·ry** (ˌkɒndɛm'neɪtərɪ, kən'dɛmnətərɪ, -trɪ) *adj.* —**con·'demn·er** *n.* —**con·'demn·ing·ly** *adv.*

con·demned cell *n.* a prison cell in which a person condemned to death awaits execution.

con·den·sate (kən'dɛnseɪt) *n.* a substance formed by condensation, such as a liquid from a vapour.

con·den·sa·tion (ˌkɒndɛn'seɪʃən) *n.* **1.** the act or process of condensing, or the state of being condensed. **2.** anything that has condensed from a vapour on a window. **3.** *Chem.* a type of reaction in which two organic molecules combine to form a larger molecule as well as a simple molecule such as water, methanol, etc. **4.** anything that has been shortened, esp. an abridged version of a book. **5.** *Psychoanal.* **a.** the fusion of two or more ideas, etc., into one symbol, occurring esp. in dreams. **b.** the reduction of many experiences into one word or action, as in a phobia. —ˌ**con+den+'sa+tion+al** *adj.*

con+den+sa+tion trail *n.* another name for **vapour trail.**

con+dense (kənˈdɛns) *vb.* **1.** (*tr.*) to increase the density of; compress. **2.** to reduce or be reduced in volume or size; make or become more compact. **3.** to change or cause to change from a gaseous to a liquid or solid state. **4.** *Chem.* to undergo or cause to undergo condensation. [C15: from Latin *condēnsāre,* from *dēnsāre* to make thick, from *dēnsus* DENSE] —**con+'den+sa·ble** *or* **con+'den+si·ble** *adj.* —**con+ˌden+sa·'bil+i·ty** *or* **con+ˌden+si·'bil+i·ty** *n.*

con+densed (kənˈdɛnst) *adj.* **1.** (of printers' type) narrower than usual for a particular height. Compare **expanded** (sense 1). **2.** *Botany.* designating an inflorescence in which the flowers are crowded together and are almost or completely sessile.

con+densed milk *n.* milk reduced by evaporation to a thick concentration, with sugar added. Compare **evaporated milk.**

con+dens+er (kənˈdɛnsə) *n.* **1. a.** an apparatus for reducing gases to their liquid or solid form by the abstraction of heat. **b.** a device for abstracting heat, as in a refrigeration unit. **2.** a lens that concentrates light into a small area. **3.** another name for **capacitor. 4.** a person or device that condenses.

con+de+scend (ˌkɒndɪˈsɛnd) *vb.* (*intr.*) **1.** to act graciously towards another or others regarded as being on a lower level; behave patronizingly. **2.** to do something that one regards as below one's dignity. [C14: from Church Latin *condēscendere* to stoop, condescend, from Latin *dēscendere* to DESCEND]

con+de+scend+ence (ˌkɒndɪˈsɛndəns) *n.* **1.** *Scot. law.* a statement of facts presented by the plaintiff in a cause. **2.** a less common word for **condescension.**

con+de+scend+ing (ˌkɒndɪˈsɛndɪŋ) *adj.* showing or implying condescension by stooping to the level of one's inferiors, esp. in a patronizing way. —ˌ**con+de+'scend+ing+ly** *adv.*

con+de+scen+sion (ˌkɒndɪˈsɛnʃən) *n.* the act or an instance of behaving in a patronizing way.

con+dign (kənˈdaɪn) *adj.* (esp. of a punishment) fitting; deserved. [C15: from Old French *condigne,* from Latin *condignus,* from *dignus* worthy] —**con+'dign+ly** *adv.*

Con·dil·lac (*French* kɔ̃diˈjak) *n.* **É·tienne Bon·not de** (etjɛn bɔˈno də). 1715–80, French philosopher. He developed Locke's view that all knowledge derives from the senses in his *Traité des sensations* (1754).

con+di+ment (ˈkɒndɪmənt) *n.* any spice or sauce such as salt, pepper, mustard, etc. [C15: from Latin *condīmentum* seasoning, from *condīre* to pickle]

con+di+tion (kənˈdɪʃən) *n.* **1.** a particular state of being or existence; situation with respect to circumstances: *the human condition.* **2.** something that limits or restricts something else; a qualification: *you may enter only under certain conditions.* **3.** (*pl.*) external or existing circumstances: *conditions were right for a takeover.* **4.** an assumption in logical or inductive reasoning that should or must be fulfilled. See **sufficient** (sense 2), **necessary** (sense 3c.). **5.** something required as part of an agreement or pact; terms: *the conditions of the lease are set out.* **6.** *Law.* **a.** a declaration or provision in a will, contract, etc., that makes some right or liability contingent upon the happening of some event. **b.** the event itself. **7.** something indispensable to the existence of something else: *your happiness is a condition of mine.* **8.** state of health or physical fitness, esp. good health (esp. in the phrases **in condition, out of condition**). **9.** an ailment or physical disability: *a heart condition.* **10.** rank, status, or position in life. **11. on** (or **upon**) **condition that.** (*conj.*) provided that. ~*vb.* (*mainly tr.*) **12.** *Psychol.* **a.** to alter the response of (a person or animal) to a particular stimulus or situation. **b.** to establish a conditioned response in (a person or animal). **13.** to put into a fit condition or state. **14.** to accustom or inure. **15.** to subject to a condition. **16.** (*intr.*) *Archaic.* to make conditions. [C14: from Latin *conditiō,* from *condīcere* to discuss, agree together, from *con-* together + *dīcere* to say]

con+di+tion+al (kənˈdɪʃənᵊl) *adj.* **1.** depending on other factors; not certain. **2.** *Grammar.* (of a clause, conjunction, form of a verb, or whole sentence) expressing a condition on which something else is contingent: "*If he comes*" *is a conditional clause in the sentence* "*If he comes I shall go*". **3. a.** (of an equation or inequality) true for only certain values of the variable: $x^2 - 1 = x + 1$ is a conditional equation, only true for $x = 2$ or -1. **b.** (of an infinite series) convergent, but becoming divergent when the absolute values of the terms are considered. **4.** Also: **hypothetical.** *Logic.* (of a proposition) consisting of two component propositions associated by the words *if...then* so that the proposition is false only when the antecedent is true and the consequent false. Usually written: $p \rightarrow q$ or $p \supset q$, where *p* is the antecedent, *q* the consequent, and $\rightarrow$ or $\supset$ symbolizes *implies.* ~*n.* **5.** *Grammar.* **a.** a conditional form of a verb. **b.** a conditional clause or sentence. **6.** *Logic.* a conditional proposition. —**con+ˌdi+tion+'al+i·ty** *n.* —**con+'di+tion+al+ly** *adv.*

con+di+tioned (kənˈdɪʃənd) *adj.* **1.** *Psychol.* of or denoting a response that has been learned. Compare **unconditioned. 2.** (foll. by *to*) accustomed; inured; prepared by training.

con+di+tioned re+sponse *n. Psychol.* a response, elicited as an unconditioned response to one stimulus, that becomes attached to a second stimulus through repeated association of the second stimulus with the first. A classic example is salivation by a dog when it hears a bell ring, because food has always been presented when the bell has been rung previously. Also called (esp. formerly): **conditioned reflex.** See also **unconditioned response.**

con+di+tion+er (kənˈdɪʃənə) *n.* **1.** a person or thing that conditions. **2.** a substance, esp. a cosmetic, applied to something to improve its condition: *hair conditioner.*

con+di+tion+ing (kənˈdɪʃənɪŋ) *n. Psychol.* the process by which the behaviour of an organism becomes dependent on an event occurring in its environment. See also **classical conditioning, instrumental conditioning.**

con+dole (kənˈdəʊl) *vb.* (*intr.;* foll. by *with*) to express sympathy with someone in grief, pain, etc. [C16: from Church Latin *condolēre* to suffer pain (with another), from Latin *com-* together + *dolēre* to grieve, feel pain] —**con+'do+la+to+ry** *adj.* —**con+'dol+er** *n.* —**con+'dol+ing+ly** *adv.*

con+do+lence (kənˈdəʊləns) *or* **con+dole+ment** *n.* (*often pl.*) an expression of sympathy with someone in grief, etc.

con do+lo+re (kɒn dɒˈlɔːrɪ) *adj., adv. Music.* in a sad manner. [Italian: with sorrow]

con+dom (ˈkɒndəm) *n.* an elastic sheath worn on the penis during sexual intercourse to prevent conception or infection. [C18: of unknown origin]

con+do+min+i+um (ˌkɒndəˈmɪnɪəm) *n., pl.* **·ums. 1.** joint rule or sovereignty. **2.** a country ruled by two or more foreign powers. **3.** *U.S.* **a.** an apartment building in which each apartment is individually wholly owned and the common areas are jointly owned. **b.** the title under which an apartment in such a building is owned. Compare **cooperative** (sense 5). [C18: from New Latin, from Latin *com-* together + *dominium* ownership; see DOMINION]

con+done (kənˈdəʊn) *vb.* (*tr.*) **1.** to overlook or forgive an offence, etc. **2.** *Law.* (esp. of a spouse) to pardon or overlook (an offence, usually adultery). [C19: from Latin *condōnāre* to remit a debt, from *com-* (intensive) + *dōnāre* to DONATE] —**con+'don+a·ble** *adj.* —**con+do+na+tion** (ˌkɒndəʊˈneɪʃən) *n.* —**con+'don+er** *n.*

con+dor (ˈkɒndɔː) *n.* either of two very large rare New World vultures, *Vultur gryphus* (**Andean condor**), which has black plumage with white around the neck, and *Gymnogyps californianus* (**California condor**), which is similar but nearly extinct. [C17: from Spanish *cóndor,* from Quechuan *kuntur*]

con+dot+tie+re (ˌkɒndɒˈtjɛərɪ) *n., pl.* **·ri** (-riː). a commander or soldier in a professional mercenary company in Europe from the 13th to the 16th centuries. [C18: from Italian, from *condotto* leadership, from *condurre* to lead, from Latin *condūcere;* see CONDUCT]

con+duce (kənˈdjuːs) *vb.* (*intr.;* foll. by *to*) to lead or contribute (to a result). [C15: from Latin *condūcere* to lead together, from *com-* together + *dūcere* to lead] —**con+'duc+er** *n.* —**con+'duc+i·ble** *adj.* —**con+'duc+ing+ly** *adv.*

con+du+cive (kənˈdjuːsɪv) *adj.* (when *postpositive,* foll. by *to*) contributing, leading, or tending. —**con+'du+cive+ness** *n.*

con+duct *n.* (ˈkɒndʌkt). **1.** the manner in which a person behaves; behaviour. **2.** the way of managing a business, affair, etc.; handling. **3.** *Rare.* the act of guiding or leading. **4.** *Rare.* a guide or leader. ~*vb.* (kənˈdʌkt). **5.** (*tr.*) to accompany and guide (people, a party, etc.) (esp. in the phrase **conducted tour**). **6.** (*tr.*) to lead or direct (affairs, business, etc.); control. **7.** (*tr.*) to behave or manage (oneself): *the child conducted himself well.* **8.** Also (esp. U.S.): **direct.** to control or guide (an orchestra, choir, etc.) by the movements of the hands or a baton. **9.** to transmit (heat, electricity, etc.): *metals conduct heat.* [C15: from Medieval Latin *conductus* escorted, from Latin: drawn together, from *condūcere* to CONDUCE] —**con+'duct+i·ble** *adj.* —**con+ˌduct+i·'bil+i·ty** *n.*

con+duct+ance (kənˈdʌktəns) *n.* the ability of a system to conduct electricity, measured by the ratio of the current flowing through the system to the potential difference across it; the reciprocal of resistance. It is measured in reciprocal ohms, mhos, or siemens. Symbol: *G*

con+duc+tion (kənˈdʌkʃən) *n.* **1.** the transfer of heat or electricity through a medium. **2.** the transmission of an electrical or chemical impulse along a nerve fibre. **3.** the act of conveying or conducting, as through a pipe. **4.** *Physics.* another name for **conductivity** (sense 1). —**con+'duc+tion+al** *adj.*

con+duc+tive (kənˈdʌktɪv) *adj.* of, denoting, or having the property of conduction. —**con+'duc+tive+ly** *adv.*

con+duc+tiv+i+ty (ˌkɒndʌkˈtɪvɪtɪ) *n., pl.* **·ties. 1.** Also called: **conduction.** the property of transmitting heat, electricity, or sound. **2.** a measure of the ability of a substance to conduct electricity, as determined by the current flowing between opposite faces of a unit cube of the substance when there is unit potential difference between them; the reciprocal of resistivity. Symbol: κ. Formerly called: **specific conductance. 3.** See **thermal conductivity.**

con+duc+tor (kənˈdʌktə) *n.* **1.** an official on a bus who collects fares, checks tickets, etc. **2.** Also called: (esp. U.S.): **director.** a person who conducts an orchestra, choir, etc. **3.** a person who leads or guides. **4.** *U.S.* a railway official in charge of a train. **5.** a substance, body, or system that conducts electricity, heat, etc. **6.** See **lightning conductor.** —**con+'duc+tor+ˌship** *n.* —**con+duc+tress** (kənˈdʌktrɪs) *fem. n.*

con+duit (ˈkɒndɪt, -djʊɪt) *n.* **1.** a pipe or channel for carrying a fluid. **2.** a rigid tube or duct for carrying and protecting electrical wires or cables. **3.** a rare word for **fountain.** [C14: from Old French, from Medieval Latin *conductus* channel, aqueduct, from Latin *condūcere* to lead, CONDUCE]

con·du·pli·cate (kɒn'dju:plɪkɪt) *adj. Botany.* folded lengthways on itself: *conduplicate leaves in the bud.* [C18: from Latin *conduplicāre* to double; see DUPLICATE] —**con·ˌdu·pli·'ca·tion** *n.*

con·dyle ('kɒndɪl) *n.* the rounded projection on the articulating end of a bone, such as the ball portion of a ball-and-socket joint. [C17: from Latin *condylus* knuckle, joint, from Greek *kondulos*] —**'con·dy·lar** *adj.*

con·dy·loid ('kɒndɪˌlɔɪd) *adj.* of or resembling a condyle.

con·dy·lo·ma (ˌkɒndɪ'ləʊmə) *n., pl.* **·mas** *or* **·ma·ta** (-mətə). a wartlike tumour of the skin near the anus or genital organs, esp. as a result of syphilis. [C17: from New Latin, from Greek *kondulōma,* from *kondulos* CONDYLE + -OMA] —**con·dy·lom·a·tous** (ˌkɒndɪ'lɒmətəs, -'ləʊ-) *adj.*

cone (kəʊn) *n.* **1. a.** a geometric solid consisting of a plane base bounded by a closed curve, usually a circle or an ellipse, every point of which is joined to a fixed point, the vertex, lying outside the plane of the base. A **right circular cone** has a vertex perpendicularly above or below the centre of a circular base. Volume of a cone: $\frac{1}{3}\pi r^2 h$, where r is the radius of the base and h is the height of the cone. **b.** a geometric surface formed by a line rotating about the vertex and connecting the peripheries of two closed plane bases, usually circular or elliptical, above and below the vertex. See also **conic section. 2.** anything that tapers from a circular section to a point, such as a wafer shell used to contain ice cream. **3. a.** the reproductive body of conifers and related plants, made up of overlapping scales, esp. the mature **female cone,** whose scales each bear a seed. **b.** a similar structure in horsetails, club mosses, etc. Technical name: **strobilus. 4.** Also called: **retinal cone.** any one of the cone-shaped cells in the retina of the eye, sensitive to colour and bright light. ~*vb.* **5.** (*tr.*) to shape like a cone or part of a cone. [C16: from Latin *cōnus,* from Greek *kōnus* pine cone, geometrical cone]

cone·flow·er ('kəʊnˌflaʊə) *n.* any North American plant of the genera *Rudbeckia, Ratibida,* and *Echinacea,* which have rayed flowers with a conelike centre: family *Compositae* (composites). See also **black-eyed Susan.**

cone off *vb.* (*tr., adv.*) to restrict or divert the movement of traffic by placing cone-shaped bollards around (an area).

cone shell *n.* any of various tropical marine gastropod molluscs of the genus *Conus* and related genera, having a smooth conical shell. Sometimes shortened to **cone.**

con es·pres·sio·ne (*Italian* kon ˌespre'sjo:ne) *adj., adv. Music.* with feeling; expressively. [Italian, literally: with expression]

Con·es·to·ga wag·on (ˌkɒnɪ'stəʊgə) *n. U.S.* a large heavy horse-drawn covered wagon used in the 19th century. [C19: after *Conestoga,* Pennsylvania, where it was first made]

co·ney ('kəʊnɪ) *n.* a variant spelling of **cony.**

Co·ney Is·land ('kəʊnɪ) *n.* an island off the S shore of Long Island, New York: site of a large amusement park.

conf. *abbrev. for* conference.

con·fab ('kɒnfæb) *Informal.* ~*n.* **1.** a conversation or chat. ~*vb.* **·fabs, ·fab·bing, ·fabbed. 2.** (*intr.*) to converse.

con·fab·u·late (kən'fæbjʊˌleɪt) *vb.* (*intr.*) **1.** to talk together; converse; chat. **2.** *Psychiatry.* to replace the gaps left by a disorder of the memory with imaginary remembered experiences consistently believed to be true. See also **paramnesia.** [C17: from Latin *confābulārī,* from *fābulārī* to talk, from *fābula* a story; see FABLE] —**con·ˌfab·u·'la·tion** *n.* —**con·'fab·u·ˌla·tor** *n.* —**con·'fab·u·la·to·ry** *adj.*

con·fect (kən'fɛkt) *vb.* (*tr.*) **1.** to prepare by combining ingredients. **2.** to make; construct. [C16: from Latin *confectus* prepared, from *conficere* to accomplish, from *com-* (intensive) + *facere* to make]

con·fec·tion (kən'fɛkʃən) *n.* **1.** the act or process of compounding or mixing. **2.** any sweet preparation of fruit, nuts, etc., such as a preserve or a sweet. **3.** *Old-fashioned.* an elaborate article of clothing, esp. for women. **4.** *Informal.* anything regarded as overelaborate or frivolous: *the play was merely an ingenious confection.* **5.** a medicinal drug sweetened with sugar, honey, etc. [C14: from Old French, from Latin *confectiō* a preparing, from *conficere* to produce; see CONFECT]

con·fec·tion·ar·y (kən'fɛkʃənərɪ) *n., pl.* **·ar·ies. 1.** a place where confections are kept or made. **2.** a rare word for **confection.** ~*adj.* **3.** of or characteristic of confections.

con·fec·tion·er (kən'fɛkʃənə) *n.* a person who makes or sells sweets or confections.

con·fec·tion·ers' sug·ar *n.* the U.S. term for **icing sugar.**

con·fec·tion·er·y (kən'fɛkʃənərɪ) *n., pl.* **·er·ies. 1.** sweets and other confections collectively. **2.** the art or business of a confectioner.

con·fed·er·a·cy (kən'fɛdərəsɪ, -'fɛdrəsɪ) *n., pl.* **·cies. 1.** a union or combination of peoples, states, etc.; alliance; league. **2.** a combination of groups or individuals for unlawful purposes. [C14: from Anglo-French *confederacie,* from Late Latin *confoederātiō* agreement, CONFEDERATION]

Con·fed·er·a·cy (kən'fɛdərəsɪ, -'fɛdrəsɪ) *n.* **the.** another name for the **Confederate States of America.**

con·fed·er·ate *n.* (kən'fɛdərɪt, -'fɛdrɪt). **1.** a nation, state, or individual that is part of a confederacy. **2.** someone who is part of a conspiracy; accomplice. ~*adj.* (kən'fɛdərɪt, -'fɛdrɪt). **3.** united in a confederacy; allied. ~*vb.* (kən'fɛdəˌreɪt). **4.** to form into or become part of a confederacy. [C14: from Late Latin *confoederātus,* from *confoederāre* to unite by a league, from Latin *com-* together + *foedus* treaty]

Con·fed·er·ate (kən'fɛdərɪt, -'fɛdrɪt) *adj.* **1.** of, supporting, or relating to the Confederate States of America. ~*n.* **2.** a supporter of the Confederate States of America.

Con·fed·er·ate States of A·mer·i·ca *n. U.S. history.* the 11 Southern states (Alabama, Arkansas, Florida, Georgia, North Carolina, South Carolina, Texas, Virginia, Tennessee, Louisiana, and Mississippi) that seceded from the Union in 1861, precipitating a civil war with the North. The Confederacy was defeated in 1865 and the South reincorporated into the U.S.

con·fed·er·a·tion (kənˌfɛdə'reɪʃən) *n.* **1.** the act or process of confederating or the state of being confederated. **2.** a loose alliance of political units. The union of the Swiss cantons is the oldest surviving confederation. Compare **federation. 3.** (esp. in Canada) another name for a **federation.** —**con·ˌfed·er·'a·tion·ˌism** *n.* —**con·ˌfed·er·'a·tion·ist** *n.* —**con·'fed·er·a·tive** *adj.*

Con·fed·er·a·tion (kənˌfɛdə'reɪʃən) *n.* **the. 1.** *U.S. history.* the original 13 states of the United States of America constituted under the Articles of Confederation and superseded by the more formal union established in 1789. **2.** the federation of Canada, formed by federating three British colonies in 1867.

con·fer (kən'fɜ:) *vb.* **·fers, ·fer·ring, ·ferred. 1.** (*tr.;* foll. by *on* or *upon*) to grant or bestow (an honour, gift, etc.). **2.** (*intr.*) to hold or take part in a conference or consult together. **3.** (*tr.*) an obsolete word for **compare.** [C16: from Latin *conferre* to gather together, compare, from *com-* together + *ferre* to bring] —**con·'fer·ment** *or* **con·'fer·ral** *n.* —**con·'fer·ra·ble** *adj.* —**con·'fer·rer** *n.*

con·fer·ee *or* **con·fer·ree** (ˌkɒnfɜ:'ri:) *n.* **1.** a person who takes part in a conference. **2.** a person on whom an honour or gift is conferred.

con·fer·ence ('kɒnfərəns, -frəns) *n.* **1.** a meeting for consultation, exchange of information, or discussion, esp. one with a formal agenda. **2.** a formal meeting of two or more states, political groups, etc., esp. to discuss differences or formulate common policy. **3.** an assembly of the clergy or of clergy and laity of any of certain Protestant Christian Churches acting as representatives of their denomination: *the Methodist conference.* **4.** *Sport, U.S.* a league of clubs or teams. **5.** *Rare.* an act of bestowal. [C16: from Medieval Latin *conferentia,* from Latin *conferre* to bring together; see CONFER] —**con·fer·en·tial** (ˌkɒnfə'rɛnʃəl) *adj.*

con·fer·va (kɒn'fɜ:və) *n., pl.* **·vae** (-vi:) *or* **·vas.** any of various threadlike green algae, esp. any of the genus *Tribonema,* typically occurring in fresh water. [C18: from Latin: a water plant, from *confervēre* to grow together, heal, literally: to seethe, from *fervēre* to boil; named with reference to its reputed healing properties] —**con·'fer·val** *adj.* —**con·'fer·void** *n., adj.*

con·fess (kən'fɛs) *vb.* (when *tr., may take a clause as object*) **1.** (when *intr.,* often foll. by *to*) to make an acknowledgment or admission (of faults, misdeeds, crimes, etc.). **2.** (*tr.*) to admit or grant to be true; concede. **3.** *Christianity, chiefly R.C. Church.* to declare (one's sins) to God or to a priest as his representative, so as to obtain pardon and absolution. **4.** (*tr.*) *Archaic.* to acknowledge one's belief or faith in; declare allegiance to. [C14: from Old French *confesser,* from Late Latin *confessāre,* from Latin *confessus* confessed, from *confitērī* to admit, from *fatērī* to acknowledge; related to Latin *fārī* to speak] —**con·'fess·a·ble** *adj.*

con·fess·ant (kən'fɛsᵊnt) *n. Christianity, chiefly R.C. Church.* a person who makes a confession.

con·fess·ed·ly (kən'fɛsɪdlɪ) *adv.* (*sentence modifier*) by admission or confession; avowedly.

con·fes·sion (kən'fɛʃən) *n.* **1.** the act of confessing. **2.** something confessed. **3.** an acknowledgment or declaration, esp. of one's faults, misdeeds, or crimes. **4.** *Christianity, chiefly R.C. Church.* the act of a penitent accusing himself of his sins. **5. confession of faith.** a formal public avowal of religious beliefs. **6.** a religious denomination or sect united by a common system of beliefs. —**con·'fes·sion·ar·y** *adj.*

con·fes·sion·al (kən'fɛʃənᵊl) *adj.* **1.** of, like, or suited to a confession. ~*n.* **2.** *Christianity, chiefly R.C. Church.* a small stall, usually enclosed and divided by a screen or curtain, where a priest hears confessions. **3.** a book of penitential prayers.

con·fes·sor (kən'fɛsə) *n.* **1.** *Christianity, chiefly R.C. Church.* a priest who hears confessions and sometimes acts as a spiritual counsellor. **2.** *History.* a person who bears witness to his Christian religious faith by the holiness of his life, esp. in resisting threats or danger, but does not suffer martyrdom. **3.** a person who makes a confession.

con·fet·ti (kən'fɛtɪ) *n.* small pieces of coloured paper thrown on festive occasions, esp. at the bride and groom at weddings. [C19: from Italian, plural of *confetto,* originally, a bonbon; see COMFIT]

con·fi·dant *or* (*fem.*) **con·fi·dante** (ˌkɒnfɪ'dænt, 'kɒnfɪˌdænt) *n.* a person to whom private matters are confided. [C17: from French *confident,* from Italian *confidente,* n. use of adj.: trustworthy, from Latin *confīdens* CONFIDENT]

con·fide (kən'faɪd) *vb.* **1.** (usually foll. by *in;* when *tr., may take a clause as object*) to disclose (secret or personal matters) in confidence (to); reveal in private (to). **2.** (*intr.;* foll. by *in*) to have complete trust. **3.** (*tr.*) to entrust into another's keeping. [C15: from Latin *confīdere,* from *fīdere* to trust; related to Latin *foedus* treaty] —**con·'fid·er** *n.*

con·fi·dence ('kɒnfɪdəns) *n.* **1.** a feeling of trust in a person or thing: *I have confidence in his abilities.* **2.** belief in one's own abilities; self-assurance. **3.** trust or a trustful relationship: *take me into your confidence.* **4.** something confided or entrusted; secret. **5. in confidence.** as a secret.

con·fi·dence in·ter·val *n. Statistics.* an interval of values bounded by **confidence limits** within which the true value of a population parameter is stated to lie with a specified probability.

con+fi+dence man *or* **trick+ster** *n.* another name for **con man.**

con+fi+dence trick *or U.S.* **con+fi+dence game** *n.* a swindle involving money, goods, etc., in which the victim's trust is won by the swindler. Informal shortened form: **con trick.**

con+fi+dent ('kɒnfɪdənt) *adj.* **1.** (*postpositive;* foll. by *of*) having or showing confidence or certainty; sure: *confident of success.* **2.** sure of oneself; bold. **3.** presumptuous; excessively bold. [C16: from Latin *confīdens* trusting, having self-confidence, from *confīdere* to have complete trust in; see CONFIDE] —'**con+fi+dent+ly** *adv.*

con+fi+den+tial (ˌkɒnfɪ'dɛnʃəl) *adj.* **1.** spoken, written, or given in confidence; secret; private. **2.** entrusted with another's confidence or secret affairs: *a confidential secretary.* **3.** suggestive of or denoting intimacy: *a confidential approach.* —ˌ**con+fi+ˌden+ti+'al+i+ty** *or* ˌ**con+fi+'den+tial+ness** *n.* —ˌ**con+fi+'den+tial+ly** *adv.*

con+fid+ing (kən'faɪdɪŋ) *adj.* unsuspicious; trustful. —**con+'fid+ing+ly** *adv.* —**con+'fid+ing+ness** *n.*

con+fig+u+ra+tion (kənˌfɪgjʊ'reɪʃən) *n.* **1.** the arrangement of the parts of something. **2.** the external form or outline achieved by such an arrangement. **3.** *Physics, chem.* **a.** Also called: **conformation.** the shape of a molecule as determined by the arrangement of its atoms. **b.** the structure of an atom or molecule as determined by the arrangement of its electrons and nucleons. **4.** *Psychol.* the unit or pattern in perception studied by Gestalt psychologists. [C16: from Late Latin *configūrātiō* a similar formation, from *configūrāre* to model on something, from *figūrāre* to shape, fashion] —**con+ˌfig+u+'ra+tion+al** *or* **con+'fig+u+ra+tive** *adj.* —**con+ˌfig+u+'ra+tion+al+ly** *adv.*

con+fig+u+ra+tion+ism (kənˌfɪgjʊ'reɪʃəˌnɪzəm) *n.* another term for **Gestalt psychology.** —**con+ˌfig+u+'ra+tion+ist** *n.*

con+fine *vb.* (kən'faɪn). (*tr.*) **1.** to keep or close within bounds; limit; restrict. **2.** to keep shut in; restrict the free movement of: *arthritis confined him to bed.* ~*n.* ('kɒnfaɪn). **3.** (*often pl.*) a limit; boundary. [C16: from Medieval Latin *confīnāre* from Latin *confīnis* adjacent, from *fīnis* end, boundary] —**con+'fin+a+ble** *or* **con+'fine+a+ble** *adj.* —'**con+fine+less** *adj.* —**con+'fin+er** *n.*

con+fined (kən'faɪnd) *adj.* **1.** enclosed or restricted; limited. **2.** in childbed; undergoing childbirth. —**con+fin+ed+ly** (kən'faɪnɪdlɪ) *adv.* —**con+'fin+ed+ness** *n.*

con+fine+ment (kən'faɪnmənt) *n.* **1.** the act of confining or the state of being confined. **2.** the period from the onset of labour to the birth of a child. **3.** *Physics.* another name for **containment** (sense 3).

con+firm (kən'fɜːm) *vb.* (*tr.*) **1.** (*may take a clause as object*) to prove to be true or valid; corroborate; verify. **2.** (*may take a clause as object*) to assert for a second or further time, so as to make more definite: *he confirmed that he would appear in court.* **3.** to strengthen or make more firm: *his story confirmed my doubts.* **4.** to make valid by a formal act or agreement; ratify. **5.** to administer the rite of confirmation to. [C13: from Old French *confermer,* from Latin *confirmāre,* from *firmus* FIRM[1]] —**con+'firm+a+ble** *adj.* —**con+'firm+a+to+ry** *or* **con+'firm+a+tive** *adj.* —**con+'firm+er** *n.*

con+firm+and ('kɒnfəˌmænd) *n.* a candidate for confirmation.

con+fir+ma+tion (ˌkɒnfə'meɪʃən) *n.* **1.** the act of confirming. **2.** something that confirms; verification. **3.** a rite in several Christian churches that confirms a baptized person in his faith and admits him to full participation in the church.

con+firmed (kən'fɜːmd) *adj.* **1.** (*prenominal*) long-established in a habit, way of life, etc. **2.** having received the rite of confirmation. **3.** (of a disease) another word for **chronic.** —**con+firm+ed+ly** (kən'fɜːmɪdlɪ) *adv.* —**con+firm+ed+ness** (kən'fɜːmɪdnɪs, -'fɜːmd-) *n.*

con+fis+ca+ble (kən'fɪskəbəl) *adj.* subject or liable to confiscation or seizure.

con+fis+cate ('kɒnfɪˌskeɪt) *vb.* (*tr.*) **1.** to seize (property), esp. for public use and esp. by way of a penalty. ~*adj.* **2.** seized or confiscated; forfeit. **3.** having lost or been deprived of property through confiscation. [C16: from Latin *confiscāre* to seize for the public treasury, from *fiscus* basket, treasury] —ˌ**con+fis+'ca+tion** *n.* —'**con+fis+ˌca+tor** *n.* —**con+fis+ca+to+ry** (kən'fɪskətərɪ, -trɪ) *adj.*

Con+fit+e+or (kən'fɪtɪˌɔː) *n. R.C. Church.* a prayer consisting of a general confession of sinfulness and an entreaty for forgiveness. [C13: from Latin: I confess; from the beginning of the Latin prayer of confession]

con+fi+ture ('kɒnfɪˌtjʊə) *n.* a confection, preserve of fruit, etc. [C19: from French, from Old French *confire* to prepare, from Latin *conficere* to produce; see CONFECT]

con+fla+grant (kən'fleɪgrənt) *adj. Rare.* burning fiercely.

con+fla+gra+tion (ˌkɒnflə'greɪʃən) *n.* a large destructive fire. [C16: from Latin *conflagrātiō,* from *conflagrāre* to be burnt up, from *com-* (intensive) + *flagrāre* to burn; related to Latin *fulgur* lightning] —'**con+fla+ˌgra+tive** *adj.*

con+flate (kən'fleɪt) *vb.* (*tr.*) to combine or blend (two things, esp. two versions of a text) so as to form a whole. [C16: from Latin *conflāre* to blow together, from *flāre* to blow] —**con+'fla+tion** *n.*

con+flict *n.* ('kɒnflɪkt). **1.** a struggle or clash between opposing forces; battle. **2.** a state of opposition between ideas, interests, etc.; disagreement or controversy. **3.** a clash, as between two appointments made for the same time. **4.** *Psychol.* opposition between two simultaneous but incompatible wishes or impulses, sometimes leading to a state of emotional tension and thought to be responsible for neuroses. ~*vb.* (kən'flɪkt). (*intr.*) **5.** to come into opposition; clash. **6.** to fight. [C15: from Latin *conflictus,* from *confligere* to combat, from *fligere* to strike] —**con+'flict+ing+ly** *adv.* —**con+'flic+tion** *n.* —**con+'flic+tive** *or* **con+'flic+to+ry** *adj.*

con+flu+ence ('kɒnfluəns) *or* **con+flux** ('kɒnflʌks) *n.* **1.** a merging or flowing together, esp. of rivers. **2.** a gathering together, esp. of people.

con+flu+ent ('kɒnfluənt) *adj.* **1.** flowing together or merging. ~*n.* **2.** a stream that flows into another, usually of approximately equal size. [C17: from Latin *confluēns,* from *confluere* to flow together, from *fluere* to flow]

con+fo+cal (kɒn'fəʊkəl) *adj.* having a common focus or common foci: *confocal ellipses.*

con+form (kən'fɔːm) *vb.* **1.** (*intr.;* usually foll. by *to*) to comply in actions, behaviour, etc., with accepted standards or norms. **2.** (*intr.;* usually foll. by *with*) to be in accordance; fit in: *he conforms with my idea of a teacher.* **3.** to make or become similar in character or form. **4.** (*intr.*) to comply with the practices of an established church, esp. the Church of England. **5.** (*tr.*) to bring (oneself, ideas, etc.) into harmony or agreement. [C14: from Old French *conformer,* from Latin *confirmāre* to establish, strengthen, from *firmāre* to make firm, from *firmus* FIRM[1]] —**con+'form+er** *n.* —**con+'form+ing+ly** *adv.*

con+form+a+ble (kən'fɔːməbəl) *adj.* **1.** corresponding in character; similar. **2.** obedient; submissive. **3.** (foll. by *to*) in agreement or harmony (with); consistent (with). **4.** (of rock strata) lying in a parallel arrangement so that their original relative positions have remained undisturbed. **5.** *Maths.* (of two matrices) related so that the number of columns in one is equal to the number of rows in the other. —**con+ˌform+a+'bil+i+ty** *or* **con+'form+a+ble+ness** *n.* —**con+'form+a+bly** *adv.*

con+for+mal (kən'fɔːməl) *adj.* **1.** *Maths.* **a.** (of a transformation) preserving the angles of the depicted surface. **b.** (of a parameter) relating to such a transformation. **2.** Also called: **orthomorphic.** (of a map projection) maintaining true shape over a small area and scale in every direction. [C17: from Late Latin *conformālis* having the same shape, from Latin *com-* same + *forma* shape]

con+for+ma+tion (ˌkɒnfɔː'meɪʃən) *n.* **1.** the general shape or outline of an object; configuration. **2.** the arrangement of the parts of an object. **3.** the act or state of conforming. **4.** *Chem.* **a.** another name for **configuration** (sense 3a.). **b.** one of the configurations of a molecule that can easily change its shape and can consequently exist in equilibrium with molecules of different configuration.

con+form+ist (kən'fɔːmɪst) *n.* **1.** a person who conforms to standards of behaviour, dress, etc., esp. to an excessive degree. **2.** a person who complies with the practices of an established church, esp. the Church of England. ~*adj.* **3.** of a conforming nature or character.

con+form+i+ty (kən'fɔːmɪtɪ) *or* **con+form+ance** *n., pl.* **+i+ties** *or* **+anc+es. 1.** compliance in actions, behaviour, etc., with certain accepted standards or norms. **2.** correspondence or likeness in form or appearance; congruity; agreement. **3.** compliance with the practices of an established church.

con+found (kən'faʊnd) *vb.* (*tr.*) **1.** to astound or perplex; bewilder. **2.** to mix up; confuse. **3.** to treat mistakenly as similar to or identical with (one or more other things). **4.** (kɒn'faʊnd) to curse or damn (usually as an expletive in the phrase **confound it!**). **5.** to contradict or refute (an argument, etc.). **6.** to rout or defeat (an enemy). **7.** *Archaic.* to put to shame; abash. **8.** *Obsolete.* to waste. [C13: from Old French *confondre,* from Latin *confundere* to mingle, pour together, from *fundere* to pour] —**con+'found+a+ble** *adj.* —**con+'found+er** *n.*

con+found+ed (kən'faʊndɪd) *adj.* **1.** bewildered; confused. **2.** (*prenominal*) *Informal.* execrable; damned. —**con+'found+ed+ly** *adv.* —**con+'found+ed+ness** *n.*

con+fra+ter+ni+ty (ˌkɒnfrə'tɜːnɪtɪ) *n., pl.* **+ties.** a group of men united for some particular purpose, esp. Christian laymen organized for religious or charitable service; brotherhood. [C15: from Medieval Latin *confrāternitās;* see CONFRÈRE, FRATERNITY] —ˌ**con+fra+'ter+nal** *adj.*

con+frère ('kɒnfrɛə) *n.* a fellow member of a profession, etc. [C15: from Old French, from Medieval Latin *confrāter* fellow member, from Latin *frāter* brother]

con+front (kən'frʌnt) *vb.* (*tr.*) **1.** (usually foll. by *with*) to present or face (with something), esp. in order to accuse or criticize. **2.** to face boldly; oppose in hostility. **3.** to be face to face with; be in front of. **4.** to bring together for comparison. [C16: from Medieval Latin *confrontārī* to stand face to face with, from *frons* forehead] —**con+fron+ta+tion** (ˌkɒnfrʌn'teɪʃən) *or* **con+'front+ment** *n.* —**con+'front+er** *n.*

Con+fu+cian (kən'fjuːʃən) *adj.* **1.** of or relating to the doctrines of Confucius. ~*n.* **2.** a follower of Confucius.

Con+fu+cian+ism (kən'fjuːʃəˌnɪzəm) *n.* the ethical system of Confucius, emphasizing devotion to family (including ancestral spirits), peace, justice, and treating others as one would want to be treated. —**Con+'fu+cian+ist** *n.*

Con+fu+cius (kən'fjuːʃəs) *n.* Chinese name *K'ung Fu-tse.* 551–479 B.C., Chinese philosopher and teacher of ethics (see **Confucianism**). His doctrines were compiled after his death under the title *The Analects of Confucius.*

con fu+o+co (kɒn fuː'əʊkəʊ) *adj., adv. Music.* in a fiery manner. [Italian: with fire]

con+fuse (kən'fjuːz) *vb.* (*tr.*) **1.** to bewilder; perplex. **2.** to mix up (things, ideas, etc.); jumble. **3.** to make unclear: *he confused his talk with irrelevant details.* **4.** to fail to recognize the difference between; mistake (one thing) for another. **5.** to disconcert; embarrass. **6.** to cause to become disordered: *the enemy ranks were confused by gas.* [C18: back formation from *confused,* from Latin *confūsus* mingled together, from *confundere* to pour together; see CONFOUND] —**con·'fus·a·ble** *adj.* —**con·,fus·a·'bil·i·ty** *n.* —**con·'fus·a·bly** *adv.* —**con·fus·ed·ly** (kən'fjuːzɪdlɪ, -'fjuːzd-) *adv.* —**con·'fus·ed·ness** *n.* —**con·'fus·ing·ly** *adv.*

con·fu·sion (kən'fjuːʒən) *n.* **1.** the act of confusing or the state of being confused. **2.** disorder; jumble. **3.** bewilderment; perplexity. **4.** lack of clarity; indistinctness. **5.** embarrassment; abashment. —**con·'fu·sion·al** *adj.*

con·fute (kən'fjuːt) *vb.* (*tr.*) **1.** to prove (a person or thing) wrong, invalid, or mistaken; disprove. **2.** *Obsolete.* to put an end to. [C16: from Latin *confūtāre* to check, silence] —**con·'fut·a·ble** *adj.* —**con·fu·ta·tion** (,kɒnfjʊ'teɪʃən) *n.* —**con·'fu·ta·tive** *adj.* —**con·'fut·er** *n.*

cong. *abbrev. for:* **1.** *Pharmacol.* congius. [Latin: gallon] **2.** congregation.

Cong. *abbrev. for* Congregational.

con·ga ('kɒŋgə) *n.* **1.** a Latin American dance of three steps and a kick to each bar, usually performed by a number of people in single file. **2.** Also called: **conga drum.** a large tubular bass drum, used chiefly in Afro-American jazz and usually played with the hands. ~*vb.* **·gas, ·ga·ing, ·gaed. 3.** (*intr.*) to perform this dance. [C20: from American Spanish, feminine of *congo* belonging to the CONGO]

con·gé ('kɒnʒeɪ) *n.* **1** permission to depart or dismissal, esp. when formal. **2.** a farewell. **3.** *Architect.* a concave moulding. See also **cavetto.** [C16: from Old French *congié,* from Latin *commeātus* leave of absence, from *meātus* movement, from *meāre* to go, pass]

con·geal (kən'dʒiːl) *vb.* **1.** to change or cause to change from a soft or fluid state to a firm or solid state. **2.** to form or cause to form into a coagulated mass; curdle; jell. **3.** (*intr.*) (of ideas, etc.) to take shape or become fixed in form. [C14: from Old French *congeler,* from Latin *congelāre,* from *com-* together + *gelāre* to freeze] —**con·'geal·a·ble** *adj.* —**con·'geal·er** *n.* —**con·'geal·ment** *n.*

con·ge·la·tion (,kɒndʒɪ'leɪʃən) *n.* **1.** the process of congealing. **2.** something formed by this process.

con·ge·ner (kən'dʒiːnə, 'kɒndʒɪnə) *n.* a member of a class, group, or other category, esp. any animal of a specified genus. [C18: from Latin, from *com-* same + *genus* kind]

con·ge·ner·ic (,kɒndʒɪ'nɛrɪk) *or* **con·gen·er·ous** (kɒn'dʒɛnərəs) *adj.* belonging to the same group, esp. (of animals or plants) belonging to the same genus.

con·gen·ial (kən'dʒiːnjəl, -nɪəl) *adj.* **1.** friendly, pleasant, or agreeable: *a congenial atmosphere to work in.* **2.** having a similar disposition, tastes, etc.; compatible; sympathetic. [C17: from CON- (same) + GENIAL] —**con·ge·ni·al·i·ty** (kən,dʒiːnɪ'ælɪtɪ) *or* **con·'gen·ial·ness** *n.* —**con·'gen·ial·ly** *adv.*

con·gen·i·tal (kən'dʒɛnɪtᵊl) *adj.* **1.** denoting or relating to any nonhereditary condition, esp. an abnormal condition, existing at birth: *congenital blindness.* **2.** *Informal.* complete, as if from birth: *a congenital idiot.* [C18: from Latin *congenitus* born together with, from *genitus* born, from *gignere* to bear, beget] —**con·'gen·i·tal·ly** *adv.* —**con·'gen·i·tal·ness** *n.*

con·ger ('kɒŋgə) *n.* any large marine eel of the family *Congridae,* esp. *Conger conger,* occurring in temperate and tropical coastal waters. [C14: from Old French *congre,* from Latin *conger,* from Greek *gongros* sea eel]

con·ge·ries (kɒn'dʒɪəriːz) *n.* (functioning as *sing.* or *pl.*) a collection of objects or ideas; mass; heap. [C17: from Latin, from *congerere* to pile up, from *gerere* to carry]

con·gest (kən'dʒɛst) *vb.* **1.** to crowd or become crowded to excess; overfill. **2.** to overload or clog (an organ or part) with blood or (of an organ or part) to become overloaded or clogged with blood. **3.** (*tr.; usually passive*) to block (the nose) with mucus. [C16: from Latin *congestus* pressed together, from *congerere* to assemble; see CONGERIES] —**con·'gest·i·ble** *adj.* —**con·'ges·tion** *n.* —**con·'ges·tive** *adj.*

con·gi·us ('kɒndʒɪəs) *n., pl.* **·gi·i** (-dʒɪ,aɪ). **1.** *Pharmacol.* a unit of liquid measure equal to 1 Imperial gallon. **2.** an ancient Roman unit of liquid measure equal to about 0.7 Imperial gallon or 0.84 U.S. gallon. [C14: from Latin, probably from Greek *konkhos* liquid measure, CONCH]

con·glo·bate ('kɒŋgləʊ,beɪt) *vb.* **1.** to form into a globe or ball. ~*adj.* **2.** a rare word for **globular.** [C17: from Latin *conglobāre* to gather into a ball, from *globāre* to make round, from *globus* a sphere] —,**con·glo·'ba·tion** *n.*

con·glom·er·ate *n.* (kən'glɒmərɪt). **1.** a thing composed of heterogeneous elements; mass. **2.** any coarse-grained sedimentary rock consisting of rounded fragments of rock embedded in a finer matrix. Compare **agglomerate** (sense 3). **3.** a large corporation consisting of a group of companies dealing in widely diversified goods, services, etc. ~*vb.* (kən'glɒmə,reɪt). **4.** to form into a cluster or mass. ~*adj.* (kən'glɒmərɪt). **5.** made up of heterogeneous elements; massed. **6.** (of sedimentary rocks) consisting of rounded fragments within a finer matrix. [C16: from Latin *conglomerāre* to roll up, from *glomerāre* to wind into a ball, from *glomus* ball of thread]

con·glom·er·a·tion (kən,glɒmə'reɪʃən) *n.* **1.** a conglomerate mass. **2.** a mass of miscellaneous things. **3.** the act of conglomerating or the state of being conglomerated.

con·glu·ti·nant (kən'gluːtɪnənt) *adj.* (of the edges of a wound or fracture) promoting union; adhesive.

con·glu·ti·nate (kən'gluːtɪ,neɪt) *vb.* **1.** to cause (the edges of a wound or fracture) to join during the process of healing or (of the edges of a wound or fracture) to join during this process. **2.** to stick or become stuck together. [C16: from Latin *conglūtināre* to glue together, from *glūtināre* to glue, from *glūten* GLUE] —**con·,glu·ti·'na·tion** *n.* —**con·'glu·ti·na·tive** *adj.*

Con·go ('kɒŋgəʊ) *n.* **1. Re·pub·lic of the.** a republic in W Central Africa: formerly the French colony of Middle Congo, part of French Equatorial Africa, it became independent in 1960; consists mostly of equatorial forest, with savanna and extensive swamps; drained chiefly by the Rivers Congo and Ubangi. Official language: French. Religion: animist and Christian. Currency: franc. Capital: Brazzaville. Pop.: 1 300 106 (1974). Area: 349 000 sq. km (134 749 sq. miles). Former names: **Middle Congo** (until 1958), **Congo-Brazzaville. 2. Dem·o·crat·ic Re·pub·lic of the.** a former name (1960–71) of **Zaïre. 3.** the second longest river in Africa, rising as the Lualaba on the Katanga plateau in Zaïre and flowing in a wide northerly curve to the Atlantic: forms the border between the Congo Republic and Zaïre. Length: about 4800 km (3000 miles). Area of basin: about 3 000 000 sq. km (1 425 000 sq. miles). Zaïrese name (since 1971): **Zaïre. 4.** a variant spelling of **Kongo** (the people and language). —**Con·go·lese** (,kɒŋgə'liːz) *adj., n.*

con·go eel *or* **snake** *n.* an aquatic salamander, *Amphiuma means,* having an eel-like body with gill slits and rudimentary limbs and inhabiting still muddy waters in the southern U.S.: family *Amphiumidae.*

Con·go Free State *n.* a former name (1885–1908) of **Zaïre.**

Con·go red *n.* a brownish-red soluble powder, used as a dye, a diagnostic indicator, a biological stain, and a chemical indicator. Formula: $C_{32}H_{22}N_6O_6S_2Na_2$.

con·gou ('kɒŋguː) *or* **con·go** ('kɒŋgəʊ) *n.* a kind of black tea from China. [C18: from Chinese (Amoy) *kong hu tē* tea prepared with care]

con·grats (kən'græts) *or* (*Chiefly Brit.*) **con·grat·ters** (kən'grætəz) *pl. n., interj.* informal shortened forms of **congratulations.**

con·grat·u·late (kən'grætjʊ,leɪt) *vb.* (*tr.*) **1.** (usually foll. by *on*) to communicate pleasure, approval, or praise to (a person or persons); compliment. **2.** (often foll. by *on*) to consider (oneself) clever or fortunate (as a result of): *she congratulated herself on her tact.* **3.** *Obsolete.* to greet; salute. [C16: from Latin *congrātulārī,* from *grātulārī* to rejoice, from *grātus* pleasing] —**con·,grat·u·'la·tion** *n.* —**con·'grat·u·,la·tor** *n.* —**con·'grat·u·la·to·ry** *or* **con·'grat·u·la·tive** *adj.*

con·grat·u·la·tions (kən,grætjʊ'leɪʃənz) *pl. n., interj.* expressions of pleasure or joy; felicitations.

con·gre·gant ('kɒŋgrɪgənt) *n.* a member of a congregation, esp. a Jewish congregation.

con·gre·gate *vb.* ('kɒŋgrɪ,geɪt). **1.** to collect together in a body or crowd; assemble. ~*adj.* ('kɒŋgrɪgɪt, -,geɪt). **2.** collected together; assembled. **3.** relating to collecting; collective. [C15: from Latin *congregāre* to collect into a flock, from *grex* flock] —**'con·gre·,ga·tive** *adj.* —**'con·gre·,ga·tive·ness** *n.* —**'con·gre·,ga·tor** *n.*

con·gre·ga·tion (,kɒŋgrɪ'geɪʃən) *n.* **1.** a group of persons gathered for worship, prayer, etc., esp. in a church or chapel. **2.** the act of congregating or collecting together. **3.** a group of people, objects, etc., collected together; assemblage. **4.** the group of persons habitually attending a given church, chapel, etc. **5.** *R.C. Church.* **a.** a society of persons who follow a common rule of life but who are bound only by simple vows. **b.** an administrative subdivision of the papal curia. **c.** an administrative committee of bishops for arranging the business of a general council. **6.** *Chiefly Brit.* an assembly of senior members of a university.

con·gre·ga·tion·al (,kɒŋgrɪ'geɪʃənᵊl) *adj.* **1.** of or relating to a congregation. **2.** (*usually cap.*) of, relating to, or denoting the Congregational Church, its members, or its beliefs. —,**con·gre·'ga·tion·al·ly** *adv.*

Con·gre·ga·tion·al Church *n.* any member church of an association of evangelical Protestant Christian churches that are governed according to the principles of Congregationalism. In 1972 the Congregational Church in England and Wales became part of the United Reformed Church.

Con·gre·ga·tion·al·ism (,kɒŋgrɪ'geɪʃənə,lɪzəm) *n.* a system of Christian doctrines and ecclesiastical government in which each congregation is self-governing and maintains bonds of faith with other similar local congregations. —,**Con·gre·'ga·tion·al·ist** *adj., n.*

con·gress ('kɒŋgrɛs) *n.* **1.** a meeting or conference, esp. of representatives of a number of sovereign states. **2.** a national legislative assembly. **3.** a society or association. **4.** sexual intercourse. [C16: from Latin *congressus* from *congredī* to meet with, from *com-* together + *gradī* to walk, step]

Con·gress ('kɒŋgrɛs) *n.* **1.** the bicameral federal legislature of the U.S., consisting of the House of Representatives and the Senate. **2.** this body during any two-year term. **3.** Also called: **Congress Party.** (in India) a major political party, which controlled the Union government from 1947 to 1977. Official name: **Indian National Congress.** —**Con·'gres·sion·al** *adj.*

con·gres·sion·al (kən'grɛʃənᵊl) *adj.* of or relating to a congress. —**con·'gres·sion·al·ist** *n.* —**con·'gres·sion·al·ly** *adv.*

Con·gres·sion·al dis·trict *n.* (in the U.S.) an electoral division of a state, entitled to send one member to the U.S. House of Representatives.

Con·gres·sion·al Med·al of Hon·or *n.* the highest U.S. military decoration, awarded for conspicuous bravery in action.

Con·gres·sion·al Rec·ord *n.* (in the U.S.) the government journal that publishes all proceedings of Congress.

Con·gress·man ('kɒŋgrɛsmən) *or* (*fem.*) **Con·gress·wom·an**

n., pl. **-men** *or* **-wom·en.** (in the U.S.) a member of Congress, esp. of the House of Representatives.

Con·gress of In·dus·tri·al Or·gan·i·za·tions *n.* (in the U.S.) a federation of industrial unions formed in 1935. It united with the AFL in 1955 to form the AFL-CIO. Abbrev.: **CIO.**

Con·gress of Vi·en·na *n.* the European conference held at Vienna from 1814–15 to settle the territorial problems left by the Napoleonic Wars.

Con·greve ('kɒŋgri:v) *n.* **Wil·liam,** 1670–1729, English dramatist, a major exponent of Restoration comedy; author of *Love for Love* (1695) and *The Way of the World* (1700).

con·gru·ence ('kɒŋgruəns) *or* **con·gru·en·cy** *n.* **1.** the quality or state of corresponding, agreeing, or being congruent. **2.** the relationship between two integers, *x* and *y*, such that their difference, with respect to another integer called the modulus, *n*, is a multiple of the modulus. Usually written $x \equiv y$ (mod *n*), as in *25 ≡ 11 (mod 7)*.

con·gru·ent ('kɒŋgruənt) *adj.* **1.** agreeing; corresponding; congruous. **2.** having identical shapes so that all parts correspond: *congruent triangles.* Compare **similar** (sense 2). **3.** of or concerning two integers related by a congruence. [C15: from Latin *congruere* to meet together, agree] —'**con·gru·ent·ly** *adv.*

con·gru·ous ('kɒŋgruəs) *adj.* **1.** corresponding or agreeing. **2.** suitable; appropriate. [C16: from Latin *congruus* suitable, harmonious; see CONGRUENT] —**con·gru·i·ty** (kən'gru:ɪtɪ) *or* '**con·gru·ous·ness** *n.* —'**con·gru·ous·ly** *adv.*

con·ic ('kɒnɪk) *adj. also* **con·i·cal. 1. a.** having the shape of a cone. **b.** of or relating to a cone. ~*n.* **2.** another name for **conic section.** —'**con·i·cal·ly** *adv.*

con·ic pro·jec·tion *or* **con·i·cal pro·jec·tion** *n.* a map projection on which the earth is shown as projected onto a cone with its apex over one of the poles and with parallels of latitude radiating from this apex.

con·ics ('kɒnɪks) *n.* (*functioning as sing.*) the branch of geometry concerned with the parabola, ellipse, and hyperbola.

con·ic sec·tion *n.* one of a group of curves formed by the intersection of a plane and a right circular cone. It is either a circle, ellipse, parabola, or hyperbola, depending on the eccentricity, *e*, which is constant for a particular curve: $e = 0$ for a circle; $e > 1$ for an ellipse; $e = 1$ for a parabola; $e < 1$ for a hyperbola. Often shortened to **conic.**

co·nid·i·o·phore (kəʊ'nɪdɪə,fɔ:) *n.* a simple or branched hypha that bears spores (conidia) in such fungi as *Penicillium.* [C19: from CONIDIUM + -PHORE] —**co·nid·i·oph·o·rous** (kəʊ,nɪdɪ'ɒfərəs, kə-) *adj.*

co·nid·i·um (kəʊ'nɪdɪəm) *n., pl.* **-nid·i·a** (-'nɪdɪə). an asexual spore formed at the tip of a specialized hypha (conidiophore) in fungi such as *Penicillium.* [C19: from New Latin, from Greek *konis* dust + -IUM] —**co'nid·i·al** *or* **co'nid·i·an** *adj.*

co·ni·fer ('kəʊnɪfə, 'kɒn-) *n.* any gymnosperm tree or shrub of the group *Coniferae,* typically bearing cones and evergreen leaves. The group includes the pines, spruces, firs, larches, yews, junipers, cedars, cypresses, and sequoias. [C19: from Latin, from *cōnus* CONE + *ferre* to bear]

co·nif·er·ous (kə'nɪfərəs, kɒ-) *adj.* of, relating to, or belonging to the plant group *Coniferae.* See **conifer.**

co·ni·ine ('kəʊnɪ,i:n, -nɪɪn, -ni:n), **co·nin** ('kəʊnɪn), *or* **co·nine** ('kəʊni:n, -nɪn) *n.* a colourless poisonous soluble liquid alkaloid found in hemlock; 2-propylpiperidine. Formula: $C_5H_{10}NC_3H_7$. Also called: **cicutine, conicine.** [C19: from CONIUM + -INE[2]]

co·ni·ol·o·gy (,kəʊnɪ'ɒlədʒɪ) *n.* a variant spelling of **koniology.**

Con·is·ton Wa·ter ('kɒnɪstən) *n.* a lake in NW England, in Cumbria: scene of the establishment of world water speed records by Sir Malcolm Campbell (1939) and his son Donald Campbell (1959). Length: 8 km (5 miles).

co·ni·um ('kəʊnɪəm) *n.* **1.** either of the two N temperate plants of the umbelliferous genus *Conium,* esp. hemlock. **2.** an extract of either of these plants, used to treat spasmodic disorders. [C19: from Late Latin: hemlock, from Greek *kōneion;* perhaps related to Greek *kōnos* CONE]

conj. *abbrev. for:* **1.** *Grammar.* conjugation, conjunction, *or* conjunctive. **2.** *Astronomy.* conjunction.

con·jec·tur·al (kən'dʒɛktʃərəl) *adj.* involving or inclined to conjecture. —**con'jec·tur·al·ly** *adv.*

con·jec·ture (kən'dʒɛktʃə) *n.* **1.** the formation of conclusions from incomplete evidence; guess. **2.** the inference or conclusion so formed. **3.** *Obsolete.* interpretation of occult signs. ~*vb.* **4.** to infer or arrive at (an opinion, conclusion, etc.) from incomplete evidence. [C14: from Latin *conjectūra* an assembling of facts, from *conjicere* to throw together, from *jacere* to throw] —**con'jec·tur·a·ble** *adj.* —**con'jec·tur·a·bly** *adv.* —**con'jec·tur·er** *n.*

con·join (kən'dʒɔɪn) *vb.* to join or become joined. [C14: from Old French *conjoindre,* from Latin *conjungere,* from *jungere* to JOIN] —**con'join·er** *n.*

con·joint (kən'dʒɔɪnt) *adj.* united, joint, or associated. —**con'joint·ly** *adv.*

con·ju·gal ('kɒndʒʊgəl) *adj.* of or relating to marriage or the relationship between husband and wife: *conjugal rights.* [C16: from Latin *conjugālis,* from *conjunx* wife or husband, from *conjungere* to unite; see CONJOIN] —**con·ju·gal·i·ty** (,kɒndʒʊ'gælɪtɪ) *n.* —'**con·ju·gal·ly** *adv.*

con·ju·gant ('kɒndʒʊgənt) *n.* either of a pair of organisms or gametes undergoing conjugation.

con·ju·gate *vb.* ('kɒndʒʊ,geɪt). **1.** (*tr.*) *Grammar.* to inflect (a verb) systematically; state or set out the conjugation of (a verb). **2.** (*intr.*) (of a verb) to undergo inflection according to a specific set of rules. **3.** (*tr.*) to join (two or more substances) together, esp. in such a way that the resulting substance may easily be turned back into its original components. **4.** (*intr.*) *Biology.* to undergo conjugation. **5.** (*tr.*) *Obsolete.* to join together, esp. in marriage. **6.** (*intr.*) *Rare.* to have sexual intercourse. ~*adj.* ('kɒndʒʊgɪt, -,geɪt). **7.** joined together in pairs; coupled. **8.** *Maths.* **a.** (of two angles) having a sum of 360°. **b.** (of two complex numbers) differing only in the sign of the imaginary part as $4 + 3i$ and $4 - 3i$. **c.** (of two algebraic numbers) being roots of the same irreducible algebraic equation with rational coefficients: *$3 \pm 2\sqrt{2}$ are conjugate algebraic numbers, being roots of $x^2 - 6x + 1$.* **d.** (of two elements of a determinant) interchanged when the rows and columns are interchanged. **9.** *Chem.* of, denoting, or concerning the state of equilibrium in which two liquids can exist as two separate phases that are both solutions. The liquid that is the solute in one phase is the solvent in the other. **10.** another word for **conjugated. 11.** *Chem.* (of acids and bases) related by loss or gain of a proton: *Cl^- is the conjugate base of HCl; HCl is the conjugate acid of Cl^-.* **12.** *Physics.* (of points connected with a lens) having the property that an object placed at one point will produce an image at the other point. **13.** (of a compound leaf) having one pair of leaflets. **14.** (of words) cognate; related in origin. ~*n.* ('kɒndʒʊgɪt). **15.** one of a pair or set of conjugate substances, values, quantities, words, etc. [C15: from Latin *conjugāre* to join together, from *com-* together + *jugāre* to marry, connect, from *jugum* a yoke] —'**con·ju·ga·ble** *adj.* —'**con·ju·gate·ly** *adv.* —'**con·ju·gate·ness** *n.* —'**con·ju,ga·tive** *adj.* —'**con·ju,ga·tor** *n.*

con·ju·gat·ed ('kɒndʒʊ,geɪtɪd) *adj.* **1.** *Chem.* **a.** (of a molecule, compound, or substance) containing two or more double bonds alternating with single bonds. **b.** (of a double bond) separated from another double bond by one single bond. **2.** *Chem.* formed by the union of two compounds: *a conjugated protein.* ~Also called: **conjugate.**

con·ju·gat·ed pro·tein *n.* a biochemical compound consisting of a sequence of amino acids making up a simple protein to which another nonprotein group (a prosthetic group), such as a carbohydrate or lipid group, is attached.

con·ju·ga·tion (,kɒndʒʊ'geɪʃən) *n.* **1.** *Grammar.* **a.** inflection of a verb for person, number, tense, voice, mood, etc. **b.** the complete set of the inflections of a given verb. **2.** a joining, union, or conjunction. **3.** a type of sexual reproduction in ciliate protozoans involving the temporary union of two individuals and the subsequent migration and fusion of the gametic nuclei. **4.** the union of gametes, esp. isogametes, as in some algae and fungi. **5.** the pairing of chromosomes in the early phase of a meiotic division. —,**con·ju'ga·tion·al** *adj.* —,**con·ju'ga·tion·al·ly** *adv.*

con·junct (kən'dʒʌŋkt, 'kɒndʒʌŋkt) *adj.* **1.** joined; united. **2.** *Music.* relating to or denoting two adjacent degrees of a scale. ~*n.* **3.** *Logic.* one of the propositions or formulas in a conjunction. [C15: from Latin *conjunctus,* from *conjugere* to unite; see CONJOIN] —**con'junct·ly** *adv.*

con·junc·tion (kən'dʒʌŋkʃən) *n.* **1.** the act of joining together; combination; union. **2.** simultaneous occurrence of events; coincidence. **3.** any word or group of words, other than a relative pronoun, that connects words, phrases, or clauses; for example *and* and *while.* Abbrev.: **conj.** See also **coordinating conjunction, subordinating conjunction. 4.** *Astronomy.* **a.** the position of a planet or the moon when it is in line with the sun as seen from the earth. The inner planets are in **inferior conjunction** when the planet is between the earth and the sun and in **superior conjunction** when the sun lies between the earth and the planet. Compare **opposition** (sense 8a.). **b.** the apparent proximity or coincidence of two celestial bodies on the celestial sphere. **5.** *Astrology.* an exact aspect of 0° between two planets, etc., an orb of 8° being allowed. Compare **opposition** (sense 9) and **square** (sense 8). **6.** *Logic.* **a.** a compound proposition in which the component propositions are joined by *and,* which is true only if the component propositions are true. Usually written: $p \wedge q$, $p \cdot q$, pq, where p and q are component propositions and ∧,·, symbolize *and.* **b.** the relation between the terms of such a proposition. —**con'junc·tion·al** *adj.* —**con'junc·tion·al·ly** *adv.*

con·junc·tion-re·duc·tion *n. Transformational grammar.* a rule that reduces coordinate sentences, applied, for example, to convert *John lives in Ireland and Brian lives in Ireland* into *John and Brian live in Ireland.*

con·junc·ti·va (,kɒndʒʌŋk'taɪvə) *n., pl.* **-vas** *or* **-vae** (-vi:). the delicate mucous membrane that covers the eyeball and the under surface of the eyelid. [C16: from New Latin *membrāna conjunctīva* the conjunctive membrane, from Late Latin *conjunctīvus* CONJUNCTIVE] —,**con·junc'ti·val** *adj.*

con·junc·tive (kən'dʒʌŋktɪv) *adj.* **1.** joining; connective. **2.** joined. **3.** of or relating to conjunctions or their use. **4.** *Logic.* characterizing, containing, or included in a conjunction. ~*n.* **5.** a less common word for **conjunction** (sense 3). [C15: from Late Latin *conjunctīvus,* from Latin *conjungere* to CONJOIN] —**con'junc·tive·ly** *adv.*

con·junc·ti·vi·tis (kən,dʒʌŋktɪ'vaɪtɪs) *n.* inflammation of the conjunctiva.

con·junc·ture (kən'dʒʌŋktʃə) *n.* **1.** a combination of events, esp. a critical one. **2.** *Rare.* a union; conjunction. —**con'junc·tur·al** *adj.*

con·jur·a·tion (,kɒndʒʊ'reɪʃən) *n.* **1.** a magic spell; incantation. **2.** a less common word for **conjuring. 3.** *Archaic.* supplication; entreaty.

con·jure ('kʌndʒə) *vb.* **1.** (*intr.*) to practise conjuring or be a conjurer. **2.** (*intr.*) to call upon supposed supernatural forces by spells and incantations. **3.** (*tr.*) (kən'dʒʊə). to appeal earnestly or strongly to: *I conjure you to help me.* **4. a name to conjure with. a.** a person thought to have great power or influence. **b.** any name that excites the imagination. ~See also **conjure up.** [C13: from Old French *conjurer* to plot, from Latin *conjūrāre* to swear together, form a conspiracy, from *jūrāre* to swear]

con+jur+er *or* **con+jur+or** (ˈkʌndʒərə) *n.* **1.** a person who practises conjuring, esp. for people's entertainment. **2.** a person who practises magic; sorcerer.

con+jure up *vb. (tr., adv.)* **1.** to present to the mind; evoke or imagine: *he conjured up a picture of his childhood.* **2.** to call up or command (a spirit or devil) by an incantation.

con+jur+ing (ˈkʌndʒərɪŋ) *n.* **1.** the performance of tricks that appear to defy natural laws. ~*adj.* **2.** denoting or relating to such tricks or entertainment.

conk (kɒŋk) *Slang.* ~*vb.* **1.** to strike (someone) a blow, esp. on the head or nose. ~*n.* **2.** a punch or blow, esp. on the head or nose. **3.** the head or (esp. Brit.) the nose. [C19: probably changed from CONCH]

conk+er (ˈkɒŋkə) *n.* an informal name for the **horse chestnut.**

conk+ers (ˈkɒŋkəz) *n.* (*functioning as sing.*) *Brit.* a game in which a player swings a horse chestnut (conker), threaded onto a string, against that of another player to try to break it.

conk out *vb. (intr.) Informal.* **1.** (of machines, cars, etc.) to fail suddenly. **2.** to tire suddenly or collapse, as from exhaustion.

con man *n. Informal.* **1.** a person who swindles another by means of a confidence trick. **2.** a plausible character. More formal term: **confidence man.**

con mo·to (kɒn ˈməʊtəʊ) *adj., adv. Music.* in a brisk or lively manner. [Italian, literally: with movement]

conn (kɒn) *vb., n.* a variant spelling (esp. U.S.) of **con**[4].

Conn. *abbrev. for* Connecticut.

Con+nacht (ˈkɒnət) *n.* a province and ancient kingdom of NW Ireland: consists of the counties of Galway, Leitrim, Mayo, Roscommon, and Sligo. Pop.: 390 702 (1971). Area: 17 122 sq. km (6611 sq. miles). Former name: **Connaught.**

con+nate (ˈkɒneɪt) *adj.* **1.** existing in a person or thing from birth; congenital or innate. **2.** allied or associated in nature or origin; cognate: *connate qualities.* **3.** Also called: **coadunate.** *Biology.* (of similar parts or organs) closely joined or united together by growth. **4.** *Geology.* (of fluids) produced or originating at the same time as the rocks surrounding them: *connate water.* [C17: from Late Latin *connātus* born at the same time, from Latin *nātus,* from *nāscī* to be born] —**ˈcon+nate+ly** *adv.* —**ˈcon+nate+ness** *n.*

con+nat·u+ral (kəˈnætʃərəl) *adj.* **1.** having a similar nature or origin. **2.** congenital or innate; connate. —**con+ˈnat·u+ral+ly** *adv.*

Con+naught (ˈkɒnɔːt) *n.* the former name of **Connacht.**

con+nect (kəˈnɛkt) *vb.* **1.** to link or be linked together; join; fasten. **2.** (*tr.*) to relate or associate: *I connect him with my childhood.* **3.** (*tr.*) to establish telephone communications with or between. **4.** (*intr.*) (of two public vehicles, such as trains or buses) to have the arrival of one timed to occur just before the departure of the other, for the convenient transfer of passengers. **5.** (*intr.*) *Informal.* to hit, punch, kick, etc., solidly. **6.** (*intr.*) *U.S. informal.* to be successful. **7.** (*intr.*) *Slang.* to find a source of drugs, esp. illegal drugs. [C17: from Latin *connectere* to bind together, from *nectere* to bind, tie] —**con+ˈnect+i+ble** *or* **con+ˈnect+a+ble** *adj.* —**con+ˈnect+or** *or* **con+ˈnect+er** *n.*

con+nect+ed (kəˈnɛktɪd) *adj.* **1.** joined or linked together. **2.** (of speech) coherent and intelligible. —**con+ˈnect+ed+ly** *adv.*

Con+nect·i·cut (kəˈnɛtɪkət) *n.* **1.** a state of the northeastern U.S., in New England. Capital: Hartford. Pop.: 3 032 217 (1970). Area: 12 973 sq. km (5009 sq. miles). Abbrevs.: **Conn.** or (with zip code) **CT** **2.** a river in the northeastern U.S., rising in N New Hampshire and flowing south to Long Island Sound. Length: 651 km (407 miles).

con+nect+ing rod *n.* **1.** a rod or bar for transmitting motion, esp. one that connects a rotating part to a reciprocating part. **2.** such a rod that connects the piston to the crankshaft in an internal-combustion engine or reciprocating pump. See also **big end, little end. 3.** a similar rod that connects the crosshead of a steam engine to the crank.

con+nec+tion *or* **con+nex+ion** (kəˈnɛkʃən) *n.* **1.** the act or state of connecting; union. **2.** something that connects, joins, or relates; link or bond. **3.** a relationship or association. **4.** logical sequence in thought or expression; coherence. **5.** the relation of a word or phrase to its context: *in this connection the word has no political significance.* **6.** (*often pl.*) an acquaintance, esp. one who is influential or has prestige. **7.** a relative, esp. if distant and related by marriage. **8. a.** an opportunity to transfer from one train, bus, aircraft, ship, etc., to another. **b.** the vehicle, aircraft, etc., scheduled to provide such an opportunity. **9.** a link, usually a wire or metallic strip, between two components in an electric circuit. **10.** a communications link between two points, esp. by telephone. **11.** *Slang.* a supplier of illegal drugs, such as heroin. **12.** *Rare.* sexual intercourse. **13.** *Rare.* a small sect or religious group united by a body of distinct beliefs or practices. —**con+ˈnec+tion+al** *or* **con+ˈnex+ion+al** *adj.*

con+nec+tive (kəˈnɛktɪv) *adj.* **1.** serving to connect or capable of connecting. ~*n.* **2.** a thing that connects. **3.** *Grammar.* **a.** a less common word for **conjunction** (sense 3). **b.** any word that connects phrases, clauses, or individual words. **4.** *Botany.* the tissue of a stamen that connects the two lobes of the anther. **5.** *Logic.* a symbol used in a formal language in the construction of compound sentences from simpler sentences, corresponding to terms such as *or, and, not,* etc., in ordinary speech. —**con+ˈnec+tive+ly** *adv.* —**con+nec+tiv+i·ty** (ˌkɒnɛkˈtɪvɪtɪ) *n.*

con+nec+tive tis+sue *n.* an animal tissue developed from the embryonic mesoderm that consists of collagen or elastic fibres, fibroblasts, fatty cells, etc., within a jelly-like matrix. It supports organs, fills the spaces between them, and forms tendons and ligaments.

Con+ne+ma+ra (ˌkɒnɪˈmɑːrə) *n.* a barren coastal region of W Ireland, in Co. Galway: consists of quartzite mountains, peat bogs, and many lakes.

con+ning tow+er (ˈkɒnɪŋ) *n.* **1.** a superstructure of a submarine, used as the bridge when the vessel is on the surface. **2.** the armoured pilot house of a warship. [C19: see CON[4]]

con+nip+tion (kəˈnɪpʃən) *n.* (*often pl.*) *U.S. slang.* a fit of rage or tantrums. [C19: arbitrary pseudo-Latin coinage]

con+niv+ance (kəˈnaɪvəns) *n.* **1.** the act or fact of conniving. **2.** *Law.* the tacit encouragement of or assent to another's wrongdoing, esp. (formerly) of the petitioner in a divorce suit to the respondent's adultery.

con+nive (kəˈnaɪv) *vb. (intr.)* **1.** to plot together, esp. secretly; conspire. **2.** *Law.* (foll. by *at*) to give assent or encouragement (to the commission of a wrong). [C17: from French *conniver,* from Latin *connīvēre* to blink, hence, leave uncensured; *-nīvēre* related to *nictāre* to wink] —**con+ˈniv+er** *n.* —**con+ˈniv+ing+ly** *adv.*

con+niv+ent (kəˈnaɪvənt) *adj.* (of parts of plants and animals) touching without being fused, as some petals, insect wings, etc. [C17: from Latin *connīvēns,* from *connīvēre* to shut the eyes, CONNIVE] —**con+ˈniv+ent+ly** *adv.*

con+nois+seur (ˌkɒnɪˈsɜː) *n.* a person with special knowledge or appreciation of a field, esp. in the arts. [C18: from French, from Old French *conoiseor,* from *connoistre* to know, from Latin *cognōscere*] —**ˌcon+nois+ˈseur+ship** *n.*

Con+nors (ˈkɒnəz) *n.* **Jim·my.** born 1952, U.S. tennis player: Wimbledon champion 1974 and 1982; U.S. champion 1974, 1976, 1978, and 1982.

con+no+ta+tion (ˌkɒnəˈteɪʃən) *n.* **1.** an association or idea suggested by a word or phrase; implication. **2.** the act or fact of connoting. **3.** *Logic.* another name for **intension** (sense 1). —**con+no+ta+tive** (ˈkɒnəˌteɪtɪv, kəˈnəʊtə-) *or* **con+ˈno+tive** *adj.*

con+note (kɒˈnəʊt) *vb.* (*tr.; often takes a clause as object*) **1.** (of a word, phrase, etc.) to imply or suggest (associations or ideas) other than the literal meaning: *the word "maiden" connotes modesty.* **2.** to involve as a consequence or condition. [C17: from Medieval Latin *connotāre,* from *notāre* to mark, make a note, from *nota* mark, sign, note]

con+nu+bi·al (kəˈnjuːbɪəl) *adj.* of or relating to marriage; conjugal: *connubial bliss.* [C17: from Latin *cōnūbiālis* from *cōnūbium* marriage, from *com-* together + *nūbere* to marry] —**con+ˌnu+bi+ˈal+i·ty** *n.* —**con+ˈnu+bi+al+ly** *adv.*

co+no+dont (ˈkəʊnədɒnt, ˈkɒn-) *n.* any of various small Palaeozoic toothlike fossils derived from an extinct unknown animal. [C19: from Greek *kōnos* CONE + -ODONT]

co+noid (ˈkəʊnɔɪd) *n.* **1.** a geometric surface formed by rotating a parabola, ellipse, or hyperbola about one axis. ~*adj. also* **co+noi+dal** (kəʊˈnɔɪdᵊl). **2.** conical: cone-shaped. [C17: from Greek *kōnoeidēs,* from *kōnos* CONE] —**co+ˈnoi+dal+ly** *adv.*

con·o·scen+ti (ˌkɒnəʊˈʃɛntɪ) *pl. n., sing.* **+te** (-tiː). a variant spelling of **cognoscenti.**

con+quer (ˈkɒŋkə) *vb.* **1.** to overcome (an enemy, army, etc.); defeat. **2.** to overcome (an obstacle, feeling, desire, etc.); surmount. **3.** (*tr.*) to gain possession or control of by or as if by force or war; win. **4.** (*tr.*) to gain the love, sympathy, etc., of (someone) by seduction or force of personality. [C13: from Old French *conquerre,* from Vulgar Latin *conquērere* (unattested) to obtain, from Latin *conquīrere* to search for, collect, from *quaerere* to seek] —**ˈcon+quer+a·ble** *adj.* —**ˈcon+quer+a·ble+ness** *n.* —**ˈcon+quer+ing+ly** *adv.* —**ˈcon+quer+or** *n.*

Con+quer+or (ˈkɒŋkərə) *n.* **Wil·liam the.** See **William I.**

con+quest (ˈkɒnkwɛst, ˈkɒŋ-) *n.* **1.** the act or an instance of conquering or the state of having been conquered; victory. **2.** a person, thing, etc., that has been conquered or won. **3.** the act or art of gaining a person's compliance, love, etc., by seduction or force of personality. **4.** a person, whose compliance, love, etc., has been won over by seduction or force of personality. [C13: from Old French *conqueste,* from Vulgar Latin *conquēsta* (unattested), from Latin *conquīsīta,* feminine past participle of *conquīrere* to seek out, procure; see CONQUER]

Con+quest (ˈkɒnkwɛst, ˈkɒŋ-) *n.* **the.** See **Norman Conquest.**

con+qui·an (ˈkɒŋkɪən) *n.* another word for **cooncan.**

con+quis+ta+dor (kɒnˈkwɪstəˌdɔː; *Spanish* koŋˌkistaˈðor) *n., pl.* **+dors** *or* **+do+res** (*Spanish* -ˈðores). an adventurer or conqueror, esp. one of the Spanish conquerors of the New World in the 16th century. [C19: from Spanish, from *conquistar* to conquer; see CONQUEST]

Con+rad (ˈkɒnræd) *n.* **Jo·seph.** original name *Teodor Josef Konrad Korzeniowski.* 1857–1924, English novelist born in Poland, noted for sea stories such as *The Nigger of the Narcissus* (1897) and *Lord Jim* (1900) and novels of politics and revolution such as *Nostromo* (1904) and *Under Western Eyes* (1911).

cons. *abbrev. for:* **1.** consecrated. **2.** consigned. **3.** consignment. **4.** consolidated. **5.** consonant. **6.** constitutional. **7.** construction. **8.** consulting.

Cons. *or* **cons.** *abbrev. for:* **1.** Constitution. **2.** Consul. **3.** Conservative.

con+san+guin+i·ty (ˌkɒnsænˈgwɪnɪtɪ) *n.* **1.** relationship by blood; kinship. **2.** close affinity or connection. [C14: see CON-, SANGUINE] —**ˌcon+san+ˈguin+e·ous** *or* **con+ˈsan+guine** *adj.* —**ˌcon+san+ˈguin+e·ous+ly** *adv.*

con·science (ˈkɒnʃəns) *n.* **1. a.** the sense of right and wrong that governs a person's thoughts and actions. **b.** conformity to this sense. **2.** conscientiousness; diligence. **3.** a feeling of guilt or anxiety: *he has a conscience about his unkind action.* **4.** *Obsolete.* consciousness. **5. in (all) conscience. a.** with regard to truth and justice. **b.** certainly. **6. on one's conscience.** causing feelings of guilt or remorse. [C13: from Old French, from Latin *conscientia* knowledge, consciousness, from *conscīre* to know; see CONSCIOUS] —ˈ**con·science·less** *adj.*

con·science clause *n.* a clause in a law or contract exempting persons with moral scruples.

con·science mon·ey *n.* money paid voluntarily to compensate for dishonesty, esp. money paid voluntarily for taxes formerly evaded.

con·science-strick·en *adj.* feeling anxious or guilty. Also: **con·science-smit·ten.**

con·sci·en·tious (ˌkɒnʃɪˈɛnʃəs) *adj.* **1.** involving or taking great care; painstaking; diligent. **2.** governed by or done according to conscience. —ˌ**con·sci·ˈen·tious·ly** *adv.* —ˌ**con·sci·ˈen·tious·ness** *n.*

con·sci·en·tious ob·jec·tor *n.* a person who refuses to serve in the armed forces on the grounds of conscience.

con·scion·a·ble (ˈkɒnʃənəbᵊl) *adj. Obsolete.* acceptable to one's conscience. [C16: from *conscions*, obsolete form of CONSCIENCE] —ˈ**con·scion·a·ble·ness** *n.* —ˈ**con·scion·a·bly** *adv.*

con·scious (ˈkɒnʃəs) *adj.* **1. a.** denoting or relating to a part of the human mind that is aware of a person's self, environment, and mental activity and that to a certain extent determines his choices of action. **b.** (*as n.*): *the conscious is only a small part of the mind.* **2.** alert and awake; not sleeping or comatose. **3. a.** aware of a particular fact or phenomenon: *I am conscious of your great kindness to me.* **b.** (*in combination*): *clothes-conscious.* ~Compare **unconscious.** [C17: from Latin *conscius* sharing knowledge, from *com-* with + *scīre* to know] —ˈ**con·scious·ly** *adv.* —ˈ**con·scious·ness** *n.*

con·script *n.* (ˈkɒnskrɪpt). **1. a.** a person who is enrolled for compulsory military service. **b.** (*as modifier*): *a conscript army.* ~*vb.* (kənˈskrɪpt). **2.** (*tr.*) to enrol (youths, civilians, etc.) for compulsory military service. [C15: from Latin *conscrīptus*, past participle of *conscrībere* to write together in a list, enrol, from *scrībere* to write]

con·script fa·thers *pl. n. Literary.* august legislators, esp. Roman senators.

con·scrip·tion (kənˈskrɪpʃən) *n.* compulsory military service.

con·se·crate (ˈkɒnsɪˌkreɪt) *vb.* (*tr.*) **1.** to make or declare sacred or holy; sanctify. **2.** to dedicate (one's life, time, etc.) to a specific purpose. **3.** to ordain (a bishop). **4.** to cause to be respected or revered; venerate: *time has consecrated this custom.* ~*adj.* **5.** *Archaic.* consecrated. [C15: from Latin *consecrāre*, from *com-* (intensive) + *sacrāre* to devote, from *sacer* sacred] —ˌ**con·se·ˈcra·tion** *n.* —ˈ**con·se·ˌcra·tor** *n.* —**con·se·cra·to·ry** (ˌkɒnsɪˈkreɪtərɪ) *or* ˈ**con·se·ˌcra·tive** *adj.*

con·se·cu·tion (ˌkɒnsɪˈkjuːʃən) *n.* **1.** a sequence or succession of events or things. **2.** a logical sequence of deductions; inference. [C16: from Latin *consecūtiō*, from *consequī* to follow up, pursue]

con·sec·u·tive (kənˈsɛkjʊtɪv) *adj.* **1.** (of a narrative, account, etc.) following chronological sequence. **2.** following one another without interruption; successive. **3.** characterized by logical sequence. **4.** *Music.* another word for **parallel** (sense 3). [C17: from French *consécutif*, from Latin *consecūtus* having followed, from *consequī* to pursue] —**con·ˈsec·u·tive·ly** *adv.* —**con·ˈsec·u·tive·ness** *n.*

con·sen·su·al (kənˈsɛnsjʊəl) *adj.* **1.** *Law.* (of a contract, agreement, etc.) existing by consent. **2.** (of certain reflex actions of a part of the body) responding to stimulation of another part. —**con·ˈsen·su·al·ly** *adv.*

con·sen·sus (kənˈsɛnsəs) *n.* general or widespread agreement (esp. in the phrase **consensus of opinion**). [C19: from Latin from *consentīre* to feel together, agree; see CONSENT]
Usage. Since *consensus* refers to a collective opinion, the words *of opinion* in the phrase *consensus of opinion* are redundant and are therefore avoided in careful usage.

con·sent (kənˈsɛnt) *vb.* **1.** to give assent or permission (to do something); agree; accede. **2.** (*intr.*) *Obsolete.* to be in accord; agree in opinion, feelings, etc. ~*n.* **3.** acquiescence to or acceptance of something done or planned by another; permission. **4.** accordance or harmony in opinion; agreement (esp. in the phrase **with one consent**). **5. age of consent.** the lowest age at which the law recognizes the right of a person, esp. a girl, to consent to sexual intercourse. [C13: from Old French *consentir*, from Latin *consentīre* to feel together, agree, from *sentīre* to feel] —**con·ˈsent·er** *n.* —**con·ˈsent·ing·ly** *adv.*

con·sen·ta·ne·ous (ˌkɒnsɛnˈteɪnɪəs) *adj. Rare.* **1.** (foll. by *to*) accordant or consistent (with). **2.** done by general consent. [C17: from Latin *consentāneus*, from *consentīre* to CONSENT] —ˌ**con·sen·ˈta·ne·ous·ly** *adv.* —**con·sen·ta·ne·i·ty** (kənˌsɛntəˈniːɪtɪ) *or* ˌ**con·sen·ˈta·ne·ous·ness** *n.*

con·sen·tient (kənˈsɛnʃənt) *adj.* being in agreement; united in opinion. —**con·ˈsen·tience** *n.*

con·sent·ing ad·ult *n. Brit.* a male person over the age of twenty-one, who may legally engage in homosexual behaviour in private.

con·se·quence (ˈkɒnsɪkwəns) *n.* **1.** a result or effect of some previous occurrence. **2.** an unpleasant result (esp. in the phrase **take the consequences**). **3.** an inference reached by reasoning; logical conclusion. **4.** *Logic.* the relationship between an effect and its cause. **5.** significance or importance (esp. in the phrase **man of consequence**). **6. in consequence.** as a result.

con·se·quenc·es (ˈkɒnsɪkwənsɪz) *pl. n.* (*functioning as sing.*) *Brit.* a game in which each player writes down a part of a story, folds over the paper, and passes it on to another player who continues the story. After several stages, the resulting (nonsensical) stories are read out.

con·se·quent (ˈkɒnsɪkwənt) *adj.* **1.** following as an effect or result. **2.** following as a logical conclusion or by rational argument. **3.** (of a river) flowing in the direction of the original slope of the land or dip of the strata. ~*n.* **4.** something that follows something else, esp. as a result. **5.** *Logic.* the second or resultant proposition in a conditional, such as *he is British* in *if Ian was born in Scotland then he is British.* **6.** an obsolete term for **denominator** (sense 1). [C15: from Latin *consequēns* following closely, from *consequī* to pursue]
Usage. See at **consequential.**

con·se·quen·tial (ˌkɒnsɪˈkwɛnʃəl) *adj.* **1.** important or significant. **2.** self-important; conceited. **3.** following as a consequence; resultant, esp. indirectly: *consequential loss.* —ˌ**con·se·ˌquen·ti·ˈal·i·ty** *or* ˌ**con·se·ˈquen·tial·ness** *n.* —ˌ**con·se·ˈquen·tial·ly** *adv.*
Usage. Although both *consequential* and *consequent* can refer to that which follows as a result, *consequent* is more frequently used in this sense in modern English: *the new measures were put into effect, and the consequent protest led to the dismissal of those responsible.*

con·se·quent·ly (ˈkɒnsɪkwəntlɪ) *adv., sentence connector.* as a result or effect; therefore; hence.

con·serv·an·cy (kənˈsɜːvənsɪ) *n., pl.* **·cies. 1.** (in Britain) a court or commission with jurisdiction over a river, port, area of countryside, etc. **2.** another word for **conservation** (sense 2).

con·ser·va·tion (ˌkɒnsəˈveɪʃən) *n.* **1.** the act or an instance of conserving or keeping from change, loss, injury, etc. **2. a.** protection, preservation, and careful management of natural resources and of the environment. **b.** (*as modifier*): *a conservation area.* —ˌ**con·ser·ˈva·tion·al** *adj.*

con·ser·va·tion·ist (ˌkɒnsəˈveɪʃənɪst) *n.* a person who advocates or strongly promotes preservation and careful management of natural resources and of the environment.

con·ser·va·tion of charge *n.* the principle that the total charge of any isolated system is constant and independent of changes that take place within the system.

con·ser·va·tion of en·er·gy *n.* the principle that the total energy of any isolated system is constant and independent of any changes occurring within the system. Compare **conservation of mass and energy.**

con·ser·va·tion of mass *n.* the principle that the total mass of any isolated system is constant and is independent of any chemical and physical changes taking place within the system. Compare **conservation of mass and energy.**

con·ser·va·tion of mass and en·er·gy *n.* the principle that the sum of the mass and energy in an isolated system is constant. Compare **conservation of mass** and **conservation of energy.**

con·ser·va·tion of mo·men·tum *n.* the principle that the total linear or angular momentum in any isolated system is constant, provided that no external force is applied.

con·ser·va·tion of par·i·ty *n.* the principle that the parity of the total wave function describing a system of elementary particles is conserved. In fact it is not conserved in weak interactions.

con·serv·a·tism (kənˈsɜːvəˌtɪzəm) *n.* **1.** opposition to change and innovation. **2.** a political philosophy advocating the preservation of the best of the established order in society and opposing radical change.

Con·serv·a·tism (kənˈsɜːvəˌtɪzəm) *n.* (in Britain, Canada, etc.) **1.** the form of conservatism advocated by the Conservative Party. **2.** the policies, doctrines, or practices of the Conservative Party.

con·serv·a·tive (kənˈsɜːvətɪv) *adj.* **1.** favouring the preservation of established customs, values, etc., and opposing innovation. **2.** of, characteristic of, or relating to conservatism. **3.** tending to be moderate or cautious: *a conservative estimate.* **4.** conventional in style or type: *a conservative suit.* **5.** *Physics.* (of a field of force, system, etc.) doing work by moving an object or particle but being independent of the path along which the object or particle is displaced: *electrostatic fields of force are conservative.* ~*n.* **6.** a person who is reluctant to change or consider new ideas; conformist. **7.** a supporter or advocate of conservatism. ~*adj., n.* **8.** a less common word for **preservative.** —**con·ˈserv·a·tive·ly** *adv.* —**con·ˈserv·a·tive·ness** *n.*

Con·serv·a·tive (kənˈsɜːvətɪv) (in Britain, Canada, and elsewhere) ~*adj.* **1.** of, supporting, or relating to a Conservative Party. **2.** of, relating to, or characterizing Conservative Judaism. ~*n.* **3.** a supporter or member of a Conservative Party.

Con·serv·a·tive Ju·da·ism *n.* a movement opposed to extreme change, favouring certain moderate adaptations or relaxations of Jewish law and tradition.

Con·serv·a·tive Par·ty *n.* **1.** (in Britain) the major right-wing party, which developed from the Tories in the 1830s. It advocates a mixed economy, encourages property owning, and in this century has been responsible for some important social legislation. **2.** (in Canada) short for **Progressive Conservative Party. 3.** (in other countries) any of various political parties generally opposing change.

con·serv·a·toire (kənˈsɜːvəˌtwɑː) *n.* an institution or school for instruction in music. Also called: **conservatory.** [C18: from French: CONSERVATORY]

con·ser·va·tor (ˈkɒnsəˌveɪtə, kənˈsɜːvə-) *n.* a person who conserves or keeps safe; custodian, guardian, or protector.
con·serv·a·to·ri·um (kənˌsɜːvəˈtɔːrɪəm) *n. Austral.* the usual term for **conservatoire.**
con·serv·a·tory (kənˈsɜːvətrɪ) *n., pl.* **·tories. 1.** a greenhouse, esp. one attached to a house. **2.** another word for **conservatoire.** ~*adj.* **3.** preservative.
con·serve *vb.* (kənˈsɜːv). (*tr.*) **1.** to keep or protect from harm, decay, loss, etc. **2.** to preserve (a foodstuff, esp. fruit) with sugar. ~*n.* (ˈkɒnsɜːv, kənˈsɜːv). **3.** a preparation of fruit in sugar, similar to jam but containing whole pieces of fruit. [(vb.) C14: from Latin *conservāre* to keep safe, from *servāre* to save, protect; (n.) C14: from Medieval Latin *conserva,* from Latin *conservāre*] —**conˈserv·a·ble** *adj.* —**conˈserv·er** *n.*
Con·sett (ˈkɒnsɪt) *n.* a town in N England, in N Durham: iron works. Pop.: 35 391 (1971).
con·sid·er (kənˈsɪdə) *vb.* (*mainly tr.*) **1.** (*also intr.*) to think carefully about or ponder on (a problem, decision, etc.); contemplate. **2.** (*may take a clause as object*) to judge, deem, or have as an opinion: *I consider him a fool.* **3.** to have regard for; respect: *consider your mother's feelings.* **4.** to look at; regard: *he considered her face.* **5.** (*may take a clause as object*) to bear in mind as possible or acceptable: *when buying a car consider this make.* **6.** to describe or discuss: *in this programme we consider the traffic problem.* **7.** (*may take a clause as object*) to keep in mind and make allowances (for): *consider his childhood.* [C14: from Latin *consīderāre* to inspect closely, literally: to observe the stars, from *sīdus* star] —**conˈsid·er·er** *n.*
con·sid·er·a·ble (kənˈsɪdərəbᵊl) *adj.* **1.** large enough to reckon with: *a considerable quantity.* **2.** a lot of; much: *he had considerable courage.* **3.** worthy of respect: *a considerable man in the scientific world.* —**conˈsid·er·a·bly** *adv.*
con·sid·er·ate (kənˈsɪdərɪt) *adj.* **1.** thoughtful towards other people; kind. **2.** *Rare.* carefully thought out; considered. —**conˈsid·er·ate·ly** *adv.* —**conˈsid·er·ate·ness** *n.*
con·sid·er·a·tion (kənˌsɪdəˈreɪʃən) *n.* **1.** the act or an instance of considering; deliberation; contemplation. **2. take into consideration.** to bear in mind; consider. **3. under consideration.** being currently discussed or deliberated. **4.** a fact or circumstance to be taken into account when making a judgment or decision. **5. on no consideration.** for no reason whatsoever; never. **6.** thoughtfulness for other people; kindness. **7.** payment for a service; recompense; fee. **8.** thought resulting from deliberation; opinion. **9.** *Law.* the promise, object, etc., given by one party to persuade another to enter into a contract. **10.** estimation; esteem. **11. in consideration of. a.** because of. **b.** in return for.
con·sid·ered (kənˈsɪdəd) *adj.* **1.** presented or thought out with care: *a considered opinion.* **2.** (*qualified by a preceding adverb*) esteemed: *highly considered.*
con·sid·er·ing (kənˈsɪdərɪŋ) *prep.* **1.** in view of. ~*adv.* **2.** *Informal.* all in all; taking into account the circumstances: *it's not bad considering.* ~*conj.* **3.** (*subordinating*) in view of the fact that.
con·sign (kənˈsaɪn) *vb.* (*mainly tr.*) **1.** to hand over or give into the care or charge of another; entrust. **2.** to commit irrevocably: *he consigned the papers to the flames.* **3.** to commit for admittance: *to consign someone to jail.* **4.** to address or deliver (goods) for sale, disposal, etc.: *it was consigned to his London address.* **5.** (*intr.*) *Obsolete.* to assent; agree. [C15: from Old French *consigner,* from Latin *consignāre* to put one's seal to, sign, from *signum* mark, SIGN] —**conˈsign·a·ble** *adj.* —**ˌcon·sign·ˈa·tion** *n.*
con·sign·ee (ˌkɒnsaɪˈniː) *n.* a person, agent, organization, etc., to which merchandise is consigned.
con·sign·ment (kənˈsaɪnmənt) *n.* **1.** the act of consigning; commitment. **2.** a shipment of goods consigned. **3. on consignment.** for payment by the consignee after sale: *he made the last shipment on consignment.*
con·sign·or (kənˈsaɪnə, ˌkɒnsaɪˈnɔː) *or* **con·sign·er** (kənˈsaɪnə) *n.* a person, enterprise, etc., that consigns goods.
con·sist (kənˈsɪst) *vb.* (*intr.*) **1.** (foll. by *of* or *in*) to be composed (of); be formed (of): *syrup consists of sugar and water.* **2.** (foll. by *in* or *of*) to have its existence (in); lie (in); be expressed (by): *his religion consists only in going to church.* **3.** to be compatible or consistent; accord. [C16: from Latin *consistere* to halt, stand firm, from *sistere* to stand, cause to stand; related to *stāre* to STAND]
con·sist·en·cy (kənˈsɪstənsɪ) *or* **con·sist·ence** *n., pl.* **·en·cies** *or* **·enc·es. 1.** agreement or accordance with facts, form, or characteristics previously shown or stated. **2.** agreement or harmony between parts of something complex; compatibility. **3.** degree of viscosity or firmness. **4.** the state or quality of holding or sticking together and retaining shape.
con·sist·ent (kənˈsɪstənt) *adj.* **1.** showing consistency; not self-contradictory. **2.** in agreement or harmony; accordant. **3.** *Maths.* (of two or more equations) satisfied by at least one common set of values of the variables: $x + y = 4$ *and* $x - y = 2$ *are consistent.* **4.** *Logic.* (of a logical system) constituted so that the propositions deduced from different axioms of the system do not contradict each other. Compare **complete** (sense 5). **5.** *Obsolete.* stuck together; cohering. —**conˈsist·ent·ly** *adv.*
con·sis·to·ry (kənˈsɪstərɪ) *n., pl.* **·ries. 1.** *Church of England.* **a.** the court of a diocese (other than Canterbury) administering ecclesiastical law. **b.** the area in a church where the consistory meets. **2.** *R.C. Church.* an assembly of the cardinals and the pope. **3.** (in certain Reformed Churches) the governing body of a local congregation or church. **4.** *Archaic.* a council or assembly. [C14: from Old French *consistorie,* from Medieval Latin *consistōrium* ecclesiastical tribunal, ultimately from Latin *consistere* to stand still] —**con·sis·to·ri·al** (ˌkɒnsɪˈstɔːrɪəl) *or* **ˌcon·sisˈto·ri·an** *adj.*
con·so·ci·ate *vb.* (kənˈsəʊʃɪˌeɪt). **1.** to enter into or bring into friendly association. ~*adj.* (kənˈsəʊʃɪɪt, -ˌeɪt). **2.** associated or united. ~*n.* (kənˈsəʊʃɪɪt, -ˌeɪt). **3.** an associate or partner. [C16: from Latin *consociāre,* from *socius* partner] —**conˌso·ci·ˈa·tion** *n.*
con·so·cies (kənˈsəʊʃiːz) *n., pl.* **·cies.** *Ecology.* a natural community with a single dominant species. [C20: from CONSOCIATE + SPECIES]
con·so·la·tion (ˌkɒnsəˈleɪʃən) *n.* **1.** the act of consoling or state of being consoled; solace. **2.** a person or thing that is a source of comfort in a time of suffering, grief, disappointment, etc. —**con·sol·a·to·ry** (kənˈsɒlətərɪ, -trɪ) *adj.*
con·so·la·tion prize *n.* a prize given to console a loser of a game.
con·sole[1] (kənˈsəʊl) *vb.* to serve as a source of comfort to (someone) in disappointment, loss, sadness, etc. [C17: from Latin *consōlārī,* from *sōlārī* to comfort; see SOLACE] —**conˈsol·a·ble** *adj.* —**conˈsol·er** *n.* —**conˈsol·ing·ly** *adv.*
con·sole[2] (ˈkɒnsəʊl) *n.* **1.** an ornamental bracket, esp. one used to support a wall fixture, bust, etc. **2.** the part of an organ comprising the manuals, pedals, stops, etc. **3.** a desk or table on which the controls of an electronic system are mounted. **4.** a cabinet for a television, gramophone, etc., designed to stand on the floor. **5.** See **console table.** [C18: from French, shortened from Old French *consolateur* one that provides support, hence, supporting bracket, from Latin *consōlātor* a comforter; see CONSOLE[1]]
con·sole ta·ble (ˈkɒnsəʊl) *n.* a table with one or more curved legs of bracket-like construction, designed to stand against a wall.
con·sol·i·date (kənˈsɒlɪˌdeɪt) *vb.* **1.** to form or cause to form into a solid mass or whole; unite or be united. **2.** to make or become stronger or more stable. **3.** *Military.* to strengthen or improve one's control over (a situation, force, newly captured area, etc.). [C16: from Latin *consolidare* to make firm, from *solidus* strong, SOLID] —**conˈsol·i·ˌda·tor** *n.*
con·sol·i·dat·ed fund *n. Brit.* a fund into which tax revenue is paid in order to meet standing charges, esp. interest payments on the national debt.
con·sol·i·da·tion (kənˌsɒlɪˈdeɪʃən) *n.* **1.** the act of consolidating or state of being consolidated. **2.** something that is consolidated or integrated. **3.** *Law.* **a.** the combining of two or more actions at law. **b.** the combination of a number of Acts of Parliament into one codifying statute. **4.** *Geology.* the process, including compression and cementation, by which a loose deposit is transformed into a hard rock. —**conˈsol·i·ˌda·tive** *adj.*
con·sols (ˈkɒnsɒlz, kənˈsɒlz) *pl. n.* irredeemable British government securities carrying annual interest of two and a half per cent. Also called: **bank annuities.** [short for *consolidated stock*]
con·so·lute (ˈkɒnsəˌluːt) *adj.* **1.** (of two or more liquids) mutually soluble in all proportions. **2.** (of a substance) soluble in each of two conjugate liquids. **3.** of or concerned with the particular state in which two partially miscible liquids become totally miscible. [C20: from Late Latin *consolūtus,* from Latin *con-* together + *solvere* to dissolve]
con·som·mé (kənˈsɒmeɪ, ˈkɒnsɒˌmeɪ; *French* kɔ̃sɔˈme) *n.* a clear soup made from meat or chicken stock. [C19: from French, from *consommer* to finish, use up, from Latin *consummāre;* so called because all the goodness of the meat goes into the liquid]
con·so·nance (ˈkɒnsənəns) *or* **con·so·nan·cy** *n., pl.* **·nanc·es** *or* **·nan·cies. 1.** agreement, harmony, or accord. **2.** *Prosody.* similarity between consonants, but not between vowels, as between the *s* and *t* sounds in *sweet silent thought.* Compare **assonance** (sense 1). **3.** *Music.* **a.** an aesthetically pleasing sensation or perception associated with the interval of the octave, the perfect fourth and fifth, the major and minor third and sixth, and chords based on these intervals. Compare **dissonance** (sense 3). **b.** an interval or chord producing this sensation.
con·so·nant (ˈkɒnsənənt) *n.* **1.** a speech sound or letter of the alphabet other than a vowel; a stop, fricative, or continuant. ~*adj.* **2.** (*postpositive;* foll. by *with* or *to*) consistent; in agreement. **3.** harmonious in tone or sound. **4.** *Music.* characterized by the presence of a consonance. **5.** being or relating to a consonant. [C14: from Latin *consonāns,* from *consonāre* to sound at the same time, be in harmony, from *sonāre* to sound] —**ˈcon·so·nant·ly** *adv.*
con·so·nan·tal (ˌkɒnsəˈnæntᵊl) *adj.* **1.** relating to, functioning as, or constituting a consonant, such as the semivowel *w* in English *work.* **2.** consisting of or characterized by consonants: *a consonantal cluster.* —**ˌcon·soˈnan·tal·ly** *adv.*
con·sort *vb.* (kənˈsɔːt). **1.** (*intr.;* usually foll. by *with*) to keep company (with undesirable people); associate. **2.** (*intr.*) to agree or harmonize. **3.** (*tr.*) *Rare.* to combine or unite. ~*n.* (ˈkɒnsɔːt). **4.** (esp. formerly) **a.** a small group of instruments, either of the same type, such as viols, (a **whole consort**) or of different types (a **broken consort**). **b.** (*as modifier*): *consort music.* **5.** the husband or wife of a reigning monarch. **6.** a partner or companion, esp. a husband or wife. **7.** a ship that escorts another. **8.** *Obsolete.* **a.** companionship or association. **b.** agreement or accord. [C15: from Old French, from Latin *consors* sharer, partner, from *sors* lot, fate, portion] —**conˈsort·a·ble** *adj.* —**conˈsort·er** *n.*

con·sor·ti·um (kənˈsɔːtɪəm) *n., pl.* **·ti·a** (-tɪə). **1.** an association of financiers, companies, etc., esp. one formed for a particular purpose. **2.** *Law.* the right of husband or wife to the company, assistance, and affection of the other. [C19: from Latin: community of goods, partnership; see CONSORT] —**conˈsor·ti·al** *adj.*

con·spe·cif·ic (ˌkɒnspɪˈsɪfɪk) *adj.* (of animals or plants) belonging to the same species.

con·spec·tus (kənˈspɛktəs) *n.* **1.** an overall view; survey. **2.** a summary; resumé. [C19: from Latin: a viewing, from *conspicere* to observe, from *specere* to look]

con·spic·u·ous (kənˈspɪkjʊəs) *adj.* **1.** clearly visible; obvious or showy. **2.** attracting attention because of a striking quality or feature: *conspicuous stupidity.* [C16: from Latin *conspicuus,* from *conspicere* to perceive; see CONSPECTUS] —**conˈspic·u·ous·ly** *adv.* —**conˈspic·u·ous·ness** *n.*

con·spir·a·cy (kənˈspɪrəsɪ) *n., pl.* **·cies. 1.** a secret plan or agreement to carry out an illegal or harmful act, esp. with political motivation; plot. **2.** the act of making such plans in secret. —**conˈspir·a·tor** *n.* —**con·spir·a·to·ri·al** (kənˌspɪrəˈtɔːrɪəl) *or* **conˈspir·a·to·ry** *adj.* —**conˌspir·aˈto·ri·al·ly** *adv.*

con·spire (kənˈspaɪə) *vb.* (when *intr.,* sometimes foll. by *against*) **1.** to plan or agree on (a crime or harmful act) together in secret. **2.** (*intr.*) to act together towards some end as if by design: *the elements conspired to spoil our picnic.* [C14: from Old French *conspirer,* from Latin *conspīrāre* to plot together, literally: to breathe together, from *spīrāre* to breathe] —**conˈspir·er** *n.* —**conˈspir·ing·ly** *adv.*

con spi·ri·to (kɒn ˈspɪrɪtəʊ) *adj., adv. Music.* in a spirited or lively manner (also in the phrases **allegro con spirito, presto con spirito**). [Italian: with spirit]

const. *abbrev. for* constitution.

con·sta·ble (ˈkʌnstəbᵊl, ˈkɒn-) *n.* **1.** (in Britain, Australia, Canada, etc.) a police officer of the lowest rank. **2.** any of various officers of the peace, esp. one who arrests offenders, serves writs, etc. **3.** the keeper or governor of a royal castle or fortress. **4.** (in medieval Europe) the chief military officer and functionary of a royal household, esp. in France and England. **5.** an officer of a hundred in medieval England, originally responsible for raising the military levy but later assigned other administrative duties. [C13: from Old French, from Late Latin *comes stabulī* officer in charge of the stable, from Latin *comes* comrade + *stabulum* dwelling, stable; see also COUNT²] —**ˈcon·sta·ble·ˌship** *n.*

Con·sta·ble (ˈkʌnstəbᵊl) *n.* **John.** 1776–1837, English landscape painter, noted particularly for his skill in rendering atmospheric effects of changing light.

con·stab·u·lar·y (kənˈstæbjʊlərɪ) *Chiefly Brit.* ~*n., pl.* **·lar·ies. 1.** the police force of a town or district. ~*adj.* **2.** of or relating to constables, constabularies, or their duties.

Con·stance (ˈkɒnstəns) *n.* **1.** a city in S West Germany, in Baden-Württemberg at the outlet of the Rhine from Lake Constance: tourist centre. Pop.: 61 600 (1970). German name: **Konstanz. 2. Lake.** a lake in W Europe, bounded by West Germany, W Austria, and N Switzerland, through which the Rhine flows. Area: 536 sq. km. (207 sq. miles). German name: **Bodensee.**

con·stan·cy (ˈkɒnstənsɪ) *n.* **1.** the quality of having a resolute mind, purpose, or affection; steadfastness. **2.** freedom from change or variation; stability. **3.** *Psychol.* the perceptual phenomenon in which attributes of an object appear to remain the same in a variety of different presentations.

con·stant (ˈkɒnstənt) *adj.* **1.** fixed and invariable; unchanging. **2.** continual or continuous; incessant: *constant interruptions.* **3.** resolute in mind, purpose, or affection; loyal. ~*n.* **4.** something that is permanent or unchanging. **5.** a specific quantity that is always invariable: *the velocity of light is a constant.* **6. a.** *Maths.* a symbol representing an unspecified number that remains invariable throughout a particular series of operations. **b.** *Physics.* a theoretical or experimental quantity or property that is considered invariable throughout a particular series of calculations or experiments. [C14: from Old French, from Latin *constāns* standing firm, from *constāre* to be steadfast, from *stāre* to stand] —**ˈcon·stant·ly** *adv.*

Con·stant (*French* kɔ̃ˈstɑ̃) *n.* **Ben·ja·min** (bɛ̃ʒaˈmɛ̃). original name *Henri Benjamin Constant de Rebecque.* 1767–1830, French writer and politician: author of the psychological novel *Adolphe* (1816).

Con·stan·ţa (*Rumanian* konˈstantsa) *n.* a port and resort in SE Rumania, on the Black Sea: founded by the Greeks in the 6th century B.C. and rebuilt by Constantine the Great (4th century); exports petroleum. Pop.: 193 720 (1974 est.).

con·stant·an (ˈkɒnstənˌtæn) *n.* an alloy of copper (60 per cent) and nickel (40 per cent) used as an electrical resistance since it has a high volume resistivity and a low coefficient of expansion. [C20: formed from CONSTANT]

Con·stan·tine (ˈkɒnstənˌtaɪn; *French* kɔ̃stɑ̃ˈtiːn) *n.* a walled city in NE Algeria: built on an isolated rock; military and trading centre. Pop.: 243 558 (1966).

Con·stan·tine I (ˈkɒnstənˌtaɪn, -ˌtiːn) *n.* **1.** called *the Great.* Latin name *Flavius Valerius Aurelius Constantinus.* ?280–337 A.D., first Christian Roman emperor (306–337): moved his capital to Byzantium, which he renamed Constantinople (330). **2.** 1868–1923, king of Greece (1913–17; 1920–22): deposed (1917), recalled by a plebiscite (1920), but forced to abdicate again (1922) after defeat by the Turks.

Con·stan·tine II *n.* official title *Constantine XIII.* born 1940, king of Greece (1964–67): went into exile when the army seized power in 1967.

Con·stan·tine XI *n.* 1404–53, last Byzantine emperor (1448–53): killed when Constantinople was captured by the Turks.

Con·stan·ti·no·ple (ˌkɒnstæntɪˈnəʊpᵊl) *n.* the former name (330–1930) of **Istanbul.**

con·sta·ta·tion (ˌkɒnstəˈteɪʃən) *n.* **1.** the process of verification. **2.** a statement or assertion. [C20: from French, from *constater* to verify, from Latin *constat* it is certain; see CONSTANT]

con·stel·late (ˈkɒnstɪˌleɪt) *vb.* to form into clusters in or as if in constellations.

con·stel·la·tion (ˌkɒnstɪˈleɪʃən) *n.* **1. a.** any of the 88 groups of stars as seen from the earth and the solar system, many of which were named by the ancient Greeks after animals, objects, or mythological persons. **b.** an area on the celestial sphere containing such a group. **2.** a gathering of brilliant or famous people or things. **3.** *Psychoanal.* a group of ideas felt to be related. [C14: from Late Latin *constellātiō,* from Latin *com-* together + *stella* star] —**ˌcon·stelˈla·tion·al** *adj.* —**con·stel·la·to·ry** (kənˈstɛlətərɪ, -trɪ) *adj.*

con·ster·nate (ˈkɒnstəˌneɪt) *vb.* (*tr.; usually passive*) to fill with anxiety, dismay, dread, or confusion. [C17: from Latin *consternāre,* from *sternere* to lay low, spread out]

con·ster·na·tion (ˌkɒnstəˈneɪʃən) *n.* a feeling of anxiety, dismay, dread, or confusion.

con·sti·pate (ˈkɒnstɪˌpeɪt) *vb.* (*tr.*) to cause constipation in. [C16: from Latin *constīpāre* to press closely together, from *stīpāre* to crowd together] —**ˈcon·stiˌpat·ed** *adj.*

con·sti·pa·tion (ˌkɒnstɪˈpeɪʃən) *n.* infrequent or difficult evacuation of the bowels, with hard faeces, caused by functional or organic disorders or improper diet.

con·stit·u·en·cy (kənˈstɪtjʊənsɪ) *n., pl.* **·cies. 1.** the whole body of voters who elect one representative to a legislature or all the residents represented by one deputy. **2. a.** a district that sends one representative to a legislature. **b.** (*as modifier*): *constituency organization.*

con·stit·u·ent (kənˈstɪtjʊənt) *adj.* (*prenominal*) **1.** forming part of a whole; component. **2.** having the power to frame a constitution or to constitute a government (esp. in the phrases **constituent assembly, constituent power**). **3.** *Becoming rare.* electing or having the power to elect. ~*n.* **4.** a component part; ingredient. **5.** a resident of a constituency, esp. one entitled to vote. **6.** *Chiefly law.* a person who appoints another to act for him, as by power of attorney. **7.** *Linguistics.* a word, phrase, or clause forming a part of a larger construction. Compare **immediate constituent, ultimate constituent.** [C17: from Latin *constituēns* setting up, from *constituere* to establish, CONSTITUTE] —**conˈstit·u·ent·ly** *adv.*

con·sti·tute (ˈkɒnstɪˌtjuːt) *vb.* (*tr.*) **1.** to make up; form; compose: *the people who constitute a jury.* **2.** to appoint to an office or function: *a legally constituted officer.* **3.** to set up (a school or other institution) formally; found. **4.** *Law.* to give legal form to (a court, assembly, etc.). **5.** *Law, obsolete.* to set up or enact (a law, etc.). [C15: from Latin *constituere,* from *com-* (intensive) + *statuere* to place] —**ˈcon·stiˌtut·er** *or* **ˈcon·stiˌtu·tor** *n.*

con·sti·tu·tion (ˌkɒnstɪˈtjuːʃən) *n.* **1.** the act of constituting or state of being constituted. **2.** the way in which a thing is composed; physical make-up; structure. **3.** the fundamental political principles on which a state is governed, esp. when considered as embodying the rights of the subjects of that state. **4.** (*often cap.*) (in certain countries, esp. the U.S.) a statute embodying such principles. **5.** a person's state of health. **6.** a person's disposition of mind; temperament.

con·sti·tu·tion·al (ˌkɒnstɪˈtjuːʃənᵊl) *adj.* **1.** denoting, characteristic of, or relating to a constitution. **2.** authorized by or subject to a constitution. **3.** of or inherent in the physical make-up or basic nature of a person or thing: *a constitutional weakness.* **4.** beneficial to one's general physical well-being. ~*n.* **5.** a regular walk taken for the benefit of one's health. —**ˌcon·stiˈtu·tion·al·ly** *adv.*

con·sti·tu·tion·al·ism (ˌkɒnstɪˈtjuːʃənəˌlɪzəm) *n.* **1.** the principles, spirit, or system of government in accord with a constitution, esp. a written constitution. **2.** adherence to or advocacy of such a system or such principles. —**ˌcon·stiˈtu·tion·al·ist** *n.*

con·sti·tu·tion·al·i·ty (ˌkɒnstɪˌtjuːʃəˈnælɪtɪ) *n.* the quality or state of being in accord with a constitution.

con·sti·tu·tion·al mon·ar·chy *n.* a monarchy governed according to a constitution that limits and defines the powers of the sovereign. Also called: **limited monarchy.**

con·sti·tu·tion·al psy·chol·o·gy *n.* a school of thought postulating that the personality of an individual is dependent on the type of his physique (somatotype).

con·sti·tu·tive (ˈkɒnstɪˌtjuːtɪv) *adj.* **1.** having power to enact, appoint, or establish. **2.** *Chem.* (of a physical property) determined by the arrangement of atoms in a molecule rather than by their nature. **3.** another word for **constituent** (sense 1). —**ˈcon·stiˌtu·tive·ly** *adv.*

constr. *abbrev. for* construction.

con·strain (kənˈstreɪn) *vb.* (*tr.*) **1.** to compel or force, esp. by persuasion, circumstances, etc.; oblige. **2.** to restrain by or as if by force; confine. [C14: from Old French *constreindre,* from Latin *constringere* to bind together, from *stringere* to bind] —**conˈstrain·er** *n.*

con·strained (kənˈstreɪnd) *adj.* embarrassed, unnatural, or forced: *a constrained smile.* —**con·strain·ed·ly** (kənˈstreɪnɪdlɪ) *adv.*

con·straint (kənˈstreɪnt) *n.* **1.** compulsion, force, or restraint. **2.** repression or control of natural feelings or impulses. **3.** a forced unnatural manner; inhibition. **4.** something that serves to constrain; restrictive condition: *social constraints kept him silent.*

con+strict (kən'strɪkt) *vb.* (*tr.*) **1.** to make smaller or narrower, esp. by contracting at one place. **2.** to hold in or inhibit; limit. [C18: from Latin *constrictus* compressed, from *constringere* to tie up together; see CONSTRAIN]

con+stric+tion (kən'strɪkʃən) *n.* **1.** a feeling of tightness in some part of the body, such as the chest. **2.** the act of constricting or condition of being constricted. **3.** something that is constricted. —**con+'stric+tive** *adj.* —**con+'stric+tive+ly** *adv.* —**con+'stric+tive+ness** *n.*

con+stric+tor (kən'strɪktə) *n.* **1.** any of various very large nonvenomous snakes, such as the pythons, boas, and anaconda, that coil around and squeeze their prey to kill it. **2.** any muscle that constricts or narrows a canal or passage; sphincter. **3.** a person or thing that constricts.

con+stringe (kən'strɪndʒ) *vb.* (*tr.*) *Rare.* to shrink or contract. [C17: from Latin *constringere* to bind together; see CONSTRAIN] —**con+'strin+gen+cy** *n.* —**con+'strin+gent** *adj.*

con+struct *vb.* (kən'strʌkt) (*tr.*) **1.** to put together substances or parts, esp. systematically, in order to make or build (a building, bridge, etc.); assemble. **2.** to compose or frame mentally (an argument, sentence, etc.). **3.** *Geom.* to draw (a line, angle, or figure) so that certain requirements are satisfied. ~*n.* ('kɒnstrʌkt) **4.** something formulated or built systematically. **5.** a complex idea resulting from a synthesis of simpler ideas. **6.** *Psychol.* a model devised on the basis of observation, designed to relate what is observed to some theoretical framework. [C17: from Latin *constructus* piled up, from *construere* to heap together, build, from *struere* to arrange, erect] —**con+'struct+i+ble** *adj.* —**con+'struc+tor** *or* **con+'struct+er** *n.*

con+struc+tion (kən'strʌkʃən) *n.* **1.** the process or act of constructing or manner in which a thing is constructed. **2.** the thing constructed; a structure. **3. a.** the business or work of building dwellings, offices, etc. **b.** (*as modifier*): *a construction site.* **4.** an interpretation or explanation of a law, text, action, etc.: *they put a sympathetic construction on her behaviour.* **5.** *Grammar.* a group of words that together make up one of the constituents into which a sentence may be analysed; a phrase or clause. **6.** *Geom.* a drawing of a line, angle, or figure satisfying certain conditions, used in solving a problem or proving a theorem. **7.** an abstract work of art in three dimensions or relief. See also **constructivism.** —**con+'struc+tion+al** *adj.* —**con+'struc+tion+al+ly** *adv.*

con+struc+tion+ist (kən'strʌkʃənɪst) *n. U.S.* a person who interprets constitutional law in a certain way, esp. strictly.

con+struc+tive (kən'strʌktɪv) *adj.* **1.** serving to build or improve; positive: *constructive criticism.* **2.** *Law.* deduced by inference or construction; not expressed but inferred. **3.** *Law.* having an implied legal effect: *constructive notice.* **4.** another word for **structural.** —**con+'struc+tive+ly** *adv.* —**con+'struc+tive+ness** *n.*

con+struc+tiv+ism (kən'strʌktɪˌvɪzəm) *n.* a movement in abstract art evolved in Russia after World War I, primarily by Naum Gabo, which explored the use of movement and machine-age materials in sculpture and had considerable influence on modern art and architecture. —**con+'struc+tiv+ist** *adj., n.*

con+strue (kən'struː) *vb.* **+strues, +stru+ing, +strued.** (*mainly tr.*) **1.** to interpret the meaning of (something): *you can construe that in different ways.* **2.** (*may take a clause as object*) to discover by inference; deduce. **3.** to analyse the grammatical structure of; parse (esp. a Latin or Greek text as a preliminary to translation). **4.** to combine words syntactically. **5.** (*also intr.*) *Old-fashioned.* to translate literally, esp. aloud as an academic excercise. ~*n.* **6.** *Old-fashioned.* something that is construed, such as a piece of translation. [C14: from Latin *construere* to pile up; see CONSTRUCT] —**con+'stru+a+ble** *adj.* —**con+ˌstru+a·'bil+i+ty** *n.* —**con+'stru+er** *n.*

con+sub+stan+tial (ˌkɒnsəb'stænʃəl) *adj. Christian theol.* (esp. of the three persons of the Trinity) regarded as identical in substance or essence though different in aspect. —**ˌcon+sub+ˌstan+ti+'al+i+ty** *n.* —**ˌcon+sub+'stan+tial+ly** *adv.*

con+sub+stan+ti+ate (ˌkɒnsəb'stænʃɪˌeɪt) *vb.* (*intr.*) *Christian theol.* (of the Eucharistic bread and wine and Christ's body and blood) to undergo consubstantiation.

con+sub+stan+ti+a+tion (ˌkɒnsəbˌstænʃɪ'eɪʃən) *n. Christian theol.* (in the belief of High-Church Anglicans) **1.** the doctrine that after the consecration of the Eucharist the substance of the body and blood of Christ coexists within the substance of the consecrated bread and wine. **2.** the mystical process by which this is believed to take place during consecration. ~Compare **transubstantiation.**

con+sue·tude ('kɒnswɪˌtjuːd) *n.* an established custom or usage, esp. one having legal force. [C14: from Latin *consuētūdō,* from *consuēscere* to accustom, from CON- + *suēscere* to be wont] —**ˌcon+sue·'tu+di+nar·y** *adj.*

con+sul ('kɒnsəl) *n.* **1.** an official appointed by a sovereign state to protect its commercial interests and aid its citizens in a foreign city. **2.** (in ancient Rome) either of two annually elected magistrates who jointly exercised the highest authority in the republic. **3.** (in France from 1799 to 1804) any of the three chief magistrates of the First Republic. [C14: from Latin, from *consulere* to CONSULT] —**con+su+lar** ('kɒnsjʊlə) *adj.* —**'con+sul+ˌship** *n.*

con+su+lar a·gent *n.* a consul of one of the lower grades.

con+su+late ('kɒnsjʊlɪt) *n.* **1.** the business premises or residence of a consul. **2.** government by consuls. **3.** the office or period of office of a consul or consuls. **4.** (*often cap.*) **a.** the government of France by the three consuls from 1799 to 1804. **b.** this period of French history. **5.** (*often cap.*) **a.** the consular government of the Roman republic. **b.** the office or rank of a Roman consul.

con+sul gen+er+al *n., pl.* **con+suls gen+er+al.** a consul of the highest grade, usually stationed in a city of considerable commercial importance.

con+sult (kən'sʌlt) *vb.* **1.** (when *intr.*, often foll. by *with*) to ask advice from (someone); confer with (someone). **2.** (*tr.*) to refer to for information: *to consult a map.* **3.** (*tr.*) to have regard for (a person's feelings, interests, etc.) in making decisions or plans; consider. **4.** (*intr.*) to make oneself available to give professional advice, esp. at scheduled times and for a fee. [C17: from French *consulter,* from Latin *consultāre* to reflect, take counsel, from *consulere* to consult] —**con+'sult+a·ble** *adj.* —**con+'sult+er** *or* **con'+sul+tor** *n.*

con+sult+ant (kən'sʌltənt) *n.* **1. a.** a physician, esp. a specialist, who is asked to confirm a diagnosis. **b.** a physician or surgeon holding the highest appointment in a particular branch of medicine or surgery in a hospital. **2.** a specialist who gives expert advice or information. **3.** a person who asks advice in a consultation. —**con+'sul+tan+cy** *n.*

con+sul+ta+tion (ˌkɒnsəl'teɪʃən) *n.* **1.** the act or procedure of consulting. **2.** a conference for discussion or the seeking of advice, esp. from doctors or lawyers.

con+sul+ta+tive (kən'sʌltətɪv), **con+sul+ta+to·ry** (kən'sʌltətərɪ, -trɪ), *or* **con+sul+tive** *adj.* available for, relating to, or involving consultation; advisory. —**con+'sul+ta+tive+ly** *adv.*

con+sult+ing (kən'sʌltɪŋ) *adj.* (*prenominal*) acting in an advisory capacity on professional matters: *a consulting engineer.*

con+sult+ing room *n.* a room in which a doctor, esp. a general practitioner, sees his patients.

con+sum+a·ble (kən'sjuːməbəl) *adj.* **1.** capable of being consumed. ~*n.* **2.** (*usually pl.*) goods intended to be bought and used; consumer goods.

con+sume (kən'sjuːm) *vb.* **1.** (*tr.*) to eat or drink. **2.** (*tr.; often passive*) to engross or obsess. **3.** (*tr.*) to use up; expend: *my car consumes little oil.* **4.** to destroy or be destroyed by burning, decomposition, etc.: *fire consumed the forest.* **5.** (*tr.*) to waste or squander: *the time consumed on that project was excessive.* **6.** (*intr.; passive*) to waste away. [C14: from Latin *consūmere* to devour, from *com-* (intensive) + *sūmere* to take up, from *emere* to take, purchase] —**con+'sum+ing+ly** *adv.*

con+sum+ed+ly (kən'sjuːmɪdlɪ) *adv. Old-fashioned.* (intensifier): *a consumedly fascinating performance.*

con+sum+er (kən'sjuːmə) *n.* **1.** a person who purchases goods and services for his own personal needs. Compare **producer** (sense 4). **2.** a person or thing that consumes. **3.** (*usually pl.*) *Ecology.* an organism, esp. an animal, within a community that feeds upon plants or other animals. See also **decomposer, producer** (sense 6).

con+sum+er goods *pl. n.* goods that satisfy personal needs rather than those required for the production of other goods or services. Compare **capital goods.**

con+sum+er+ism (kən'sjuːməˌrɪzəm) *n.* **1.** protection of the interests of consumers. **2.** advocacy of a high rate of consumption and spending as a basis for a sound economy. —**con+'sum+er+ist** *n., adj.*

con+sum+mate *vb.* ('kɒnsəˌmeɪt). **1.** (*tr.*) to bring to completion or perfection; fulfil. **2.** (*tr.*) to complete (a marriage) legally by sexual intercourse. ~*adj.* (kən'sʌmɪt, 'kɒnsəmɪt). **3.** accomplished or supremely skilled: *a consummate artist.* **4.** (*prenominal*) (intensifier): *a consummate fool.* [C15: from Latin *consummāre* to complete, from *summus* highest, utmost] —**con+'sum+mate+ly** *adv.* —**ˌcon+sum+'ma+tion** *n.* —**'con+sum+ˌma+tive** *or* **con+'sum+ma+to·ry** *adj.* —**'con+sum+ˌma+tor** *n.*

con+sump+tion (kən'sʌmpʃən) *n.* **1.** the act of consuming or the state of being consumed, esp. by eating, burning, etc. **2.** *Economics.* expenditure on goods and services for final personal use. **3.** the quantity consumed. **4.** *Pathol.* a condition characterized by a wasting away of the tissues of the body, esp. as seen in tuberculosis of the lungs. [C14: from Latin *consumptiō* a wasting, from *consūmere* to CONSUME]

con+sump+tive (kən'sʌmptɪv) *adj.* **1.** causing consumption; wasteful; destructive. **2.** *Pathol.* relating to or affected with consumption, esp. tuberculosis of the lungs. ~*n.* **3.** *Pathol.* a person who suffers from consumption. —**con+'sump+tive+ly** *adv.* —**con+'sump+tive+ness** *n.*

cont. *abbrev. for:* **1.** containing. **2.** contents. **3.** continent(al). **4.** continued.

con+tact *n.* ('kɒntækt). **1.** the act or state of touching physically. **2.** the state or fact of close association or communication (esp. in the phrases **in contact, make contact**). **3. a.** a junction of two or more electrical conductors. **b.** the part of the conductors that make the junction. **c.** the part of an electrical device to which such connections are made. **4.** an acquaintance, esp. one who might be useful in business, as a means of introduction, etc. **5.** any person who has been exposed to a contagious disease. **6.** *Photog.* See **contact print. 7.** (*usually pl.*) an informal name for **contact lens. 8.** (*modifier*) of or relating to irritation or inflammation of the skin caused by touching the causative agent: *contact dermatitis.* **9.** (*modifier*) of or maintaining contact. ~*vb.* ('kɒntækt, kən'tækt). **10.** (when *intr.*, often foll. by *with*) to put, come, or be in association, touch, or communication. ~*interj.* **11.** *Aeron.* (formerly) a call made by the pilot to indicate that an aircraft's ignition is switched on and that the engine is ready for starting by swinging the propeller. [C17: from Latin *contactus,* from *contingere* to touch on all sides, pollute, from *tangere* to touch] —**con·tac·tu·al** (kɒn'tæktjʊəl) *adj.* —**con·'tac·tu·al·ly** *adv.*

con·tact flight *n.* **1.** a flight in which the pilot remains in sight of land or water. **2.** air navigation by observation of prominent landmarks, beacons, etc.

con·tact lens *n.* a thin convex lens, usually of plastic, placed directly on the surface of the eye to correct defects of vision.

con·tact man *n.* an intermediary or go-between.

con·tac·tor (kɒn'tæktə) *n.* a type of switch for repeatedly opening and closing an electric circuit. Its operation can be mechanical, electromagnetic, or pneumatic.

con·tact print *n.* a photographic print made by placing a negative directly onto the printing paper and exposing it to light.

con·ta·gion (kən'teɪdʒən) *n.* **1.** the transmission of disease from one person to another by direct or indirect contact. **2.** a contagious disease. **3.** another name for **contagium. 4.** a corrupting or harmful influence that tends to spread; pollutant. **5.** the spreading of an emotional or mental state among a number of people: *the contagion of mirth.* [C14: from Latin *contāgiō* a touching, infection, from *contingere;* see CONTACT]

con·ta·gious (kən'teɪdʒəs) *adj.* **1.** (of a disease) capable of being passed on by direct contact with a diseased individual or by handling clothing, etc., contaminated with the causative agent. Compare **infectious. 2.** (of an organism) harbouring or spreading the causative agent of a transmissible disease. **3.** causing or likely to cause the same reaction or emotion in several people; catching; infectious: *her laughter was contagious.* —**con·'ta·gious·ly** *adv.* —**con·'ta·gious·ness** *n.*

con·ta·gious a·bor·tion *n.* another name for **brucellosis.**

con·ta·gi·um (kən'teɪdʒɪəm) *n., pl.* **·gi·a** (-dʒɪə). *Pathol.* the specific virus or other direct cause of any infectious disease. [C17: from Latin, variant of *contāgiō* CONTAGION]

con·tain (kən'teɪn) *vb.* (*tr.*) **1.** to hold or be capable of holding or including within a fixed limit or area: *this contains five pints.* **2.** to keep (one's feelings, behaviour, etc.) within bounds; restrain. **3.** to consist of; comprise: *the book contains three different sections.* **4.** *Military.* to prevent (enemy forces) from operating beyond a certain level or area. **5.** to be a multiple of, leaving no remainder: *6 contains 2 and 3.* [C13: from Old French *contenir,* from Latin *continēre,* from *com-* together + *tenēre* to hold] —**con·'tain·a·ble** *adj.*

con·tain·er (kən'teɪnə) *n.* **1.** an object used for or capable of holding, esp. for transport or storage, such as a carton, box, etc. **2. a.** a large cargo-carrying standard-sized container that can be loaded from one mode of transport to another. **b.** (*as modifier*): *a container port; a container ship.*

con·tain·er·ize *or* **con·tain·er·ise** (kən'teɪnə,raɪz) *vb.* (*tr.*) **1.** to convey (cargo) in standard-sized containers. **2.** to adapt (a port or transportation system) to the use of standard-sized containers. —**con·,tain·er·i·'za·tion** *or* **con·,tain·er·i·'sa·tion** *n.*

con·tain·ment (kən'teɪnmənt) *n.* **1.** the act or condition of containing, esp. of restraining the ideological or political power of a hostile country or the operations of a hostile military force. **2.** (from 1947 to the mid-1970s) a principle of U.S. foreign policy that seeks to prevent the expansion of Communist power. **3.** Also called: **confinement.** *Physics.* the process of preventing the plasma in a controlled thermonuclear reaction from reaching the walls of the reaction vessel, usually by confining it within a configuration of magnetic fields. See **magnetic bottle.**

con·tam·i·nate *vb.* (kən'tæmɪ,neɪt). (*tr.*) **1.** to make impure, esp. by touching or mixing; pollute. **2.** to make radioactive by the addition of radioactive material. ~*adj.* (kən'tæmɪnɪt, -,neɪt). **3.** *Archaic.* contaminated. [C15: from Latin *contamināre* to defile; related to Latin *contingere* to touch] —**con·'tam·i·na·ble** *adj.* —**con·'tam·i·nant** *n.* —**con·'tam·i·na·tive** *adj.* —**con·'tam·i·,na·tor** *n.*

con·tam·i·na·tion (kən,tæmɪ'neɪʃən) *n.* **1.** the act or process of contaminating or the state of being contaminated. **2.** something that contaminates. **3.** *Linguistics.* the process by which one word or phrase is altered because of mistaken associations with another word or phrase; for example, the substitution of *irregardless* for *regardless* by association with such words as *irrespective.*

con·tan·go (kən'tæŋgəʊ) *n., pl.* **·gos. 1.** (on the London Stock Exchange) postponement of payment for and delivery of stock from one account day to the next. **2.** the fee paid for such a postponement. ~Also called: **carry-over, continuation.** Compare **backwardation.** ~*vb.* **·goes, ·go·ing, ·goed. 3.** to arrange such a postponement: *my brokers will contango these shares.* [C19: apparently an arbitrary coinage based on CONTINUE]

contd. *abbrev. for* continued.

conte *French* (kɔ̃:t) *n.* a tale or short story, esp. of adventure.

con·té ('kɒnteɪ; *French* kɔ̃'te) *n.* a hard crayon used by artists, etc., made of clay and graphite and often coloured a reddish-brown. Also called: **conté-crayon.** [C19: named after N.J. *Conté,* 18th-century French chemist]

con·temn (kən'tɛm) *vb.* (*tr.*) to treat or regard with contempt; scorn. [C15: from Latin *contemnere,* from *temnere* to slight] —**con·temn·er** (kən'tɛmnə, -'tɛmə) *n.* —**con·tem·ni·ble** (kən'tɛmnɪbᵊl) *adj.* —**con·'tem·ni·bly** *adv.*

contemp. *abbrev. for* contemporary.

con·tem·plate ('kɒntɛm,pleɪt, -təm-) *vb.* (*mainly tr.*) **1.** to think about intently and at length; consider calmly. **2.** (*intr.*) to think intently and at length, esp. for spiritual reasons; meditate. **3.** to look at thoughtfully; observe pensively. **4.** to have in mind as a possibility: *to contemplate changing jobs.* [C16: from Latin *contemplāre* from *templum* TEMPLE] —**'con·tem·,pla·tor** *n.*

con·tem·pla·tion (,kɒntɛm'pleɪʃən, -təm-) *n.* **1.** thoughtful or long consideration or observation. **2.** spiritual meditation esp. (in Christian religious practice) concentration of the mind and soul upon God. Compare **meditation. 3.** purpose or intention.

con·tem·pla·tive ('kɒntɛm,pleɪtɪv, -təm-; kən'tɛmplə-) *adj.* **1.** denoting, concerned with, or inclined to contemplation; meditative. ~*n.* **2.** a person dedicated to religious contemplation or to a way of life conducive to this. —**'con·tem·,pla·tive·ly** *adv.* —**'con·tem·,pla·tive·ness** *n.*

con·tem·po·ra·ne·ous (kən,tɛmpə'reɪnɪəs) *adj.* existing, beginning, or occurring in the same period of time. —**con·tem·po·ra·ne·i·ty** (kən,tɛmpərə'ni:ɪtɪ) *or* **con·,tem·po·'ra·ne·ous·ness** *n.* —**con·,tem·po·'ra·ne·ous·ly** *adv.*

con·tem·po·rar·y (kən'tɛmprərɪ) *adj.* **1.** belonging to the same age; living or occurring in the same period of time. **2.** existing or occurring at the present time. **3.** conforming to modern or current ideas in style, fashion, design, etc. **4.** having approximately the same age as one another. ~*n., pl.* **·rar·ies. 5.** a person living at the same time or of approximately the same age as another. **6.** something that is contemporary. **7.** *Journalism.* a rival newspaper. [C17: from Medieval Latin *contemporārius,* from Latin *com-* together + *temporārius* relating to time, from *tempus* time] —**con·'tem·po·rar·i·ly** *adv.* —**con·'tem·po·rar·i·ness** *n.*

Usage. *Contemporary* is most acceptable when used to mean of the same period, in a sentence like *it is useful to compare Shakespeare's plays with those of contemporary* (that is, other Elizabethan) *playwrights.* The word is, however, often used to mean modern or up-to-date in contexts such as *the furniture was of a contemporary design.* The second use should be avoided where ambiguity is likely to arise, as in *a production of* Othello *in contemporary dress. Modern dress* or *Elizabethan dress* should be used in such contexts to avoid ambiguity.

con·tem·po·rize *or* **con·tem·po·rise** (kən'tɛmpə,raɪz) *vb.* to be or make contemporary; synchronize.

con·tempt (kən'tɛmpt) *n.* **1.** the attitude or feeling of a person towards a person or thing that he considers worthless or despicable; scorn. **2.** the state of being scorned; disgrace (esp. in the phrase **hold in contempt**). **3.** wilful disregard of or disrespect for the authority of a court of law or legislative body: *contempt of court.* [C14: from Latin *contemptus* a despising, from *contemnere* to CONTEMN]

con·tempt·i·ble (kən'tɛmptəbᵊl) *adj.* deserving or worthy of contempt; despicable. —**con·,tempt·i·'bil·i·ty** *or* **con·'tempt·i·ble·ness** *n.* —**con·'tempt·i·bly** *adv.*

con·temp·tu·ous (kən'tɛmptjʊəs) *adj.* (when *predicative,* often foll. by *of*) showing or feeling contempt; disdainful. —**con·'temp·tu·ous·ly** *adv.* —**con·'temp·tu·ous·ness** *n.*

con·tend (kən'tɛnd) *vb.* **1.** (*intr.;* often foll. by *with*) to struggle in rivalry, battle, etc.; vie. **2.** to argue earnestly; debate. **3.** (*tr.; may take a clause as object*) to assert or maintain. [C15: from Latin *contendere* to strive, from *com-* with + *tendere* to stretch, aim] —**con·'tend·er** *n.* —**con·'tend·ing·ly** *adv.*

con·tent[1] ('kɒntɛnt) *n.* **1.** (*often pl.*) everything that is inside a container: *the contents of a box.* **2.** (*usually pl.*) **a.** the chapters or divisions of a book. **b.** a list, printed at the front of a book, of chapters or divisions together with the number of the first page of each. **3.** the meaning or significance of a poem, painting, or other work of art, as distinguished from its style or form. **4.** all that is contained or dealt with in a discussion, piece of writing, etc.; substance. **5.** the capacity or size of a thing. **6.** the proportion of a substance contained in an alloy, mixture, etc.: *the lead content of petrol.* [C15: from Latin *contentus* contained, from *continēre* to CONTAIN]

con·tent[2] (kən'tɛnt) *adj.* (*postpositive*) **1.** mentally or emotionally satisfied with things as they are. **2.** assenting to or willing to accept circumstances, a proposed course of action, etc. ~*vb.* **3.** (*tr.*) to make (oneself or another person) content or satisfied: *to content oneself with property.* ~*n.* **4.** peace of mind; mental or emotional satisfaction. ~*interj.* **5.** *Brit.* (in the House of Lords) a formal expression of assent, as opposed to the expression **not content.** [C14: from Old French, from Latin *contentus* contented, that is, having restrained desires, from *continēre* to restrain] —**con·'tent·ly** *adv.* —**con·'tent·ment** *n.*

con·tent·ed (kən'tɛntɪd) *adj.* accepting one's situation or life with equanimity and satisfaction. —**con·'tent·ed·ly** *adv.* —**con·'tent·ed·ness** *n.*

con·ten·tion (kən'tɛnʃən) *n.* **1.** a struggling between opponents; competition. **2.** dispute in an argument (esp. in the phrase **bone of contention**). **3.** a point asserted in argument. [C14: from Latin *contentiō* exertion, from *contendere* to CONTEND]

con·ten·tious (kən'tɛnʃəs) *adj.* **1.** tending to argue or quarrel. **2.** causing or characterized by dispute; controversial. **3.** *Law.* relating to a cause or legal business that is contested, esp. a probate matter. —**con·'ten·tious·ly** *adv.* —**con·'ten·tious·ness** *n.*

con·tent word ('kɒntɛnt) *n.* a word to which an independent meaning can be given by reference to a world outside any sentence in which the word may occur. Compare **function word, lexical meaning.**

con·ter·mi·nous (kən'tɜ:mɪnəs), **con·ter·mi·nal,** *or* **co·ter·mi·nous** (kəʊ'tɜ:mɪnəs) *adj.* **1.** enclosed within a common boundary. **2.** meeting at the ends; without a break or interruption. [C17: from Latin *conterminus,* from *terminus* end, boundary] —**con+'ter+mi+nous+ly, con+'ter+mi+nal+ly,** *or* **co+'ter+mi+nous+ly** *adv.*

con+test *n.* ('kɒntɛst). **1.** a formal game or match in which two or more people, teams, etc., compete and attempt to win. **2.** a struggle for victory between opposing forces or interests. ~*vb.* (kən'tɛst). **3.** (*tr.*) to try to disprove; call in question. **4.** (when *intr.*, foll. by *with* or *against*) to fight, dispute, or contend (with): *a contested election.* [C16: from Latin *contestārī* to introduce a lawsuit, from *testis* witness] —**con+'test+a+ble** *adj.* —**con+'test+a+ble+ness** *or* **con+ˌtest+a+'bil+i+ty** *n.* —**con+'test+a+bly** *adv.* —**ˌcon+tes+'ta+tion** *n.* —**con+'test+er** *n.* —**con+'test+ing+ly** *adv.*

con+test+ant (kən'tɛstənt) *n.* a person who takes part in a contest; competitor.

con+text ('kɒntɛkst) *n.* **1.** the parts of a piece of writing, speech, etc., that precede and follow a word or passage and contribute to its full meaning: *it is unfair to quote out of context.* **2.** the conditions and circumstances that are relevant to an event, fact, etc. [C15: from Latin *contextus* a putting together, from *contexere* to interweave, from *com-* together + *texere* to weave, braid]

con+tex+tu·al (kən'tɛkstjʊəl) *adj.* relating to, dependent on, or using context: *contextual criticism of a book.* —**con+'tex+tu+al+ly** *adv.*

con+tex+tu+al+ize *or* **con+tex+tu+al+ise** (kən'tɛkstjʊəˌlaɪz) *vb.* (*tr.*) to state the social, grammatical, or other context of; put into context.

con+tex+ture (kən'tɛkstʃə) *n.* **1.** the fact, process, or manner of weaving or of being woven together. **2.** the arrangement of assembled parts; structure. **3.** an interwoven structure; fabric. —**con+'tex+tur+al** *adj.*

con+tig·u·ous (kən'tɪgjʊəs) *adj.* **1.** touching along the side or boundary; in contact. **2.** physically adjacent; neighbouring. **3.** preceding or following in time. [C17: from Latin *contiguus*, from *contingere* to touch; see CONTACT] —**con+ti+gu+i+ty** (ˌkɒntɪ'gju:ɪtɪ) *or* **con+'tig·u+ous+ness** *n.* —**con+'tig·u+ous+ly** *adv.*

con+ti+nent[1] ('kɒntɪnənt) *n.* **1.** one of the earth's large land masses (Asia, Australia, Africa, Europe, North and South America, and Antarctica). **2.** that part of the earth's crust that rises above the oceans and is composed of sialic rocks. Including the continental shelves, the continents occupy 30 per cent of the earth's surface. **3.** *Obsolete.* **a.** mainland as opposed to islands. **b.** a continuous extent of land. [C16: from the Latin phrase *terra continens* continuous land, from *continēre*; see CONTAIN] —**con+ti+nen+tal** (ˌkɒntɪ'nɛntᵊl) *adj.* —**ˌcon+ti+'nen+tal+ly** *adv.*

con+ti+nent[2] ('kɒntɪnənt) *adj.* **1.** able to control urination and defecation. **2.** exercising self-restraint, esp. from sexual activity; chaste. [C14: from Latin *continent-*, present participle of *continēre*; see CONTAIN] —**'con+ti+nence** *or* **'con+ti+nen+cy** *n.* —**'con+ti+nent+ly** *adv.*

Con+ti+nent ('kɒntɪnənt) *n.* **the.** the mainland of Europe as distinguished from the British Isles.

Con+ti+nen+tal (ˌkɒntɪ'nɛntᵊl) *adj.* **1.** of or characteristic of Europe, excluding the British Isles. **2.** of or relating to the 13 original British North American colonies during and immediately after the War of American Independence. ~*n.* **3.** (*sometimes not cap.*) an inhabitant of Europe, excluding the British Isles. **4.** a regular soldier of the rebel army during the War of American Independence. **5.** *U.S. History.* a currency note issued by the Continental Congress. —**ˌCon+ti+'nen+tal+ˌism** *n.* —**ˌCon+ti+'nen+tal+ist** *n.*

con+ti+nen+tal break+fast *n.* a light breakfast of coffee and rolls.

con+ti+nen+tal cli+mate *n.* a climate characterized by hot summers, cold winters, and little rainfall, typical of the interior of a continent.

Con+ti+nen+tal Con+gress *n.* the assembly of delegates from the North American rebel colonies held during and after the War of American Independence. It issued the Declaration of Independence (1776) and framed the Articles of Confederation (1777).

con+ti+nen+tal di+vide *n.* the watershed of a continent, esp. (*often caps.*) the principal watershed of North America, formed by the Rocky Mountains.

con+ti+nen+tal drift *n. Geology.* the theory that the earth's continents move gradually over the surface of the planet on a substratum of magma. The present-day configuration of the continents is thought to be the result of the fragmentation of a single landmass, Pangaea, that existed 200 million years ago. See also **plate tectonics.**

con+ti+nen+tal quilt *n. Brit.* a quilt, stuffed with down and containing pockets of air, used as a bed cover in place of the top sheet and blankets. Also called **duvet.**

con+ti+nen+tal shelf *n.* the sea bed surrounding a continent at depths of up to about 200 metres (100 fathoms), at the edge of which the **continental slope** drops steeply to the ocean floor.

Con+ti+nen+tal Sys+tem *n.* **the.** Napoleon's plan in 1806 to blockade Britain by excluding her ships from ports on the mainland of Europe.

con+tin+gence (kən'tɪndʒəns) *n.* **1.** the state of touching or being in contact. **2.** another word for **contingency.**

con+tin+gen+cy (kən'tɪndʒənsɪ) *n., pl.* **+cies. 1. a.** a possible but not very likely future event or condition; eventuality. **b.** (*as modifier*): *a contingency plan.* **2.** something dependent on a possible future event. **3.** a fact, event, etc., incidental to or dependent on something else. **4.** *Logic.* the state of being contingent. **5.** dependence on chance; uncertainty. **6.** *Statistics.* **a.** the degree of association between theoretical and observed common frequencies of two graded or classified variables. It is measured by the chi-square test. **b.** (*as modifier*): *a contingency table; the contingency coefficient.*

con+tin+gent (kən'tɪndʒənt) *adj.* **1.** (when *postpositive*, often foll. by *on* or *upon*) dependent on events, conditions, etc., not yet known; conditional. **2.** *Logic.* (of a proposition) true under certain conditions, false under others. **3.** happening by chance or without known cause; accidental. **4.** that may or may not happen; uncertain. ~*n.* **5.** a part of a military force, parade, etc. **6.** a representative group distinguished by common origin, interests, etc., that is part of a larger group or gathering. **7.** a possible or chance occurrence. [C14: from Latin *contingere* to touch, fall to one's lot, befall; see also CONTACT] —**con+'tin+gent+ly** *adv.*

con+tin+u+al (kən'tɪnjʊəl) *adj.* **1.** recurring frequently, esp. at regular intervals. **2.** occurring without interruption; continuous in time. [C14: from Old French *continuel*, from Latin *continuus* uninterrupted, from *continēre* to hold together, CONTAIN] —**con+ˌtin·u+'al+i+ty** *or* **con+'tin·u+al+ness** *n.* —**con+'tin·u·al+ly** *adv.*

con+tin·u+ance (kən'tɪnjʊəns) *n.* **1.** the act or state of continuing. **2.** the duration of an action, condition, etc. **3.** *U.S.* the postponement or adjournment of a legal proceeding.

con+tin·u+ant (kən'tɪnjʊənt) *Phonetics.* ~*n.* **1.** a speech sound, such as (l), (r), (f), or (s), in which the closure of the vocal tract is incomplete, allowing the continuous passage of the breath. ~*adj.* **2.** relating to or denoting a continuant.

con+tin·u+a+tion (kənˌtɪnjʊ'eɪʃən) *n.* **1.** a part or thing added, esp. to a book or play, that serves to continue or extend; sequel. **2.** a renewal of an interrupted action, process, etc.; resumption. **3.** the act or fact of continuing without interruption; prolongation. **4.** another word for **contango** (senses 1, 2).

con+tin·u+a·tive (kən'tɪnjʊətɪv) *adj.* **1.** serving or tending to continue. **2.** *Grammar.* **a.** (of any word, phrase, or clause) expressing continuation. **b.** (of verbs) another word for **progressive** (sense 8). ~*n.* **3.** a continuative word, phrase, or clause. —**con+'tin·u·a·tive+ly** *adv.*

con+tin·u+a·tor (kən'tɪnjʊˌeɪtə) *n.* a person who continues something, esp. the work of someone else.

con+tin·ue (kən'tɪnju:) *vb.* **·ues, ·u+ing, ·ued. 1.** (when *tr.*, *may take an infinitive*) to remain or cause to remain in a particular condition, capacity, or place. **2.** (when *tr.*, *may take an infinitive*) to carry on uninterruptedly (a course of action); persist in (something): *he continued running.* **3.** (when *tr.*, *may take an infinitive*) to resume after an interruption: *we'll continue after lunch.* **4.** to draw out or be drawn out; prolong or be prolonged: *continue the chord until it meets the tangent.* **5.** (*tr.*) *Law, chiefly Scot.* to postpone or adjourn (legal proceedings). [C14: from Old French *continuer*, from Latin *continuāre* to join together, from *continuus* CONTINUOUS] —**con+'tin·u·a·ble** *adj.* —**con+'tin·u+er** *n.* —**con+'tin·u·ing+ly** *adv.*

con+tin·ued frac+tion *n.* a number plus a fraction whose denominator contains a number and a fraction whose denominator contains a number and a fraction, and so on.

con+ti+nu+i·ty (ˌkɒntɪ'nju:ɪtɪ) *n., pl.* **·ties. 1.** logical sequence, cohesion, or connection. **2.** a continuous or connected whole. **3.** the comprehensive script or scenario of detail and movement in a film or broadcast. **4.** the continuous projection of a film, using automatic rewind.

con+ti+nu+i·ty girl *or* **man** *n.* a girl or man whose job is to ensure continuity and consistency, esp. in matters of dress, make-up, etc., in successive shots of a film, esp. when these shots are filmed on different days.

con+tin·u·o (kən'tɪnjʊˌəʊ) *n., pl.* **·os. 1.** *Music.* **a.** See **basso continuo** (see **thorough bass**). **b.** (*as modifier*): *a continuo accompaniment.* **2.** the thorough-bass part as played on a keyboard instrument, often supported by a cello, bassoon, etc. [Italian, literally: continuous]

con+tin+u·ous (kən'tɪnjʊəs) *adj.* **1.** prolonged without interruption; unceasing: *a continuous noise.* **2.** in an unbroken series or pattern. **3.** *Maths.* (of a function or curve) changing gradually in value as the variable changes in value. At any value $x = a$ of the continuous function $f(x)$, $\lim_{x\to a} f(x) = f(a)$. Compare **discontinuous** (sense 2). **4.** *Statistics.* **a.** (of a variable) having consecutive values that are infinitesimally close, so that its analysis requires integration rather than summation. **b.** (of a distribution) relating to a continuous variable. Compare **discrete** (sense 3). **5.** *Grammar.* another word for **progressive** (sense 8). [C17: from Latin *continuus*, from *continēre* to hold together, CONTAIN] —**con+'tin·u·ous+ly** *adv.* —**con+'tin·u+ous+ness** *n.*

con+tin·u·ous cre·a·tion *n.* **1.** the theory that matter is being created continuously in the universe. See **steady-state theory. 2.** the theory that animate matter is being continuously created from inanimate matter.

con+tin·u·ous spec+trum *n.* a spectrum that contains or appears to contain all wavelengths over a wide portion of its range. The emission spectrum of incandescent solids is continuous; spectra consisting of a large number of lines may appear continuous.

con+tin·u·ous sta+tion+er·y *n.* stationery in which the sheets are joined together and folded alternately, used esp. for computer printouts.

con+tin·u·ous waves *pl. n.* radio waves generated as a continuous train of oscillations having a constant frequency and amplitude. Abbrev: **CW.**

con+tin+u·um (kən'tɪnjʊəm) *n., pl.* **+tin·u·a** (-'tɪnjʊə) *or* **+tin·u·ums. 1.** a continuous series or whole, no part of which is perceptibly different from the adjacent parts. **2.** *Maths.* a set of elements between any two of which a third element can always be inserted: *a continuum of real numbers.* [C17: from Latin, neuter of *continuus* CONTINUOUS]

con+to (ˈkɒntəʊ; *Portuguese* ˈkontu) *n., pl.* **+tos** (-təʊz; *Portuguese* -tuʃ). **1.** a Portuguese monetary unit worth 1000 escudos. **2.** an unofficial Brazilian monetary unit worth 1000 cruzeiros. [C17: from Portuguese, from Late Latin *computus* calculation, from *computāre* to reckon, COMPUTE; see COUNT[1]]

con+tort (kənˈtɔːt) *vb.* to twist or bend severely out of place or shape, esp. in a strained manner. [C15: from Latin *contortus* intricate, obscure, from *contorquēre* to whirl around, from *torquēre* to twist, wrench] **—con+ˈtor+tive** *adj.*

con+tort+ed (kənˈtɔːtɪd) *adj.* **1.** twisted out of shape. **2.** (esp. of petals and sepals in a bud) twisted so that they overlap on one side. **—con+ˈtort+ed+ly** *adv.* **—con+ˈtort+ed+ness** *n.*

con+tor+tion (kənˈtɔːʃən) *n.* **1.** the act or process of contorting or the state of being contorted. **2.** a twisted shape or position. **3.** something twisted or out of the ordinary in character, meaning, etc: *mental contortions.* **—con+ˈtor+tion+al** *adj.* **—con+ˈtor+tioned** *adj.*

con+tor+tion+ist (kənˈtɔːʃənɪst) *n.* **1.** a performer who contorts his body for the entertainment of others. **2.** a person who twists or warps meaning or thoughts: *a verbal contortionist.* **—con+ˌtor+tion+ˈis+tic** *adj.*

con+tour (ˈkɒntʊə) *n.* **1.** the outline of a mass of land, figure, or body; a defining line. **2. a.** See **contour line. b.** (*as modifier*): *a contour map.* **3.** (*often pl.*) the shape or surface, esp. of a curving form: *the contours of her body were full and round.* **4.** (*modifier*) shaped to fit the form of something: *a contour chair.* ~*vb.* (*tr.*) **5.** to shape so as to form the contour of something. **6.** to mark contour lines on. **7.** to construct (a road, railway, etc.) to follow the outline of the land. [C17: from French, from Italian *contorno,* from *contornare* to sketch, from *tornare* to TURN]

con+tour feath+er *n.* any of the feathers that cover the body of an adult bird, apart from the wings and tail, and determine its shape.

con+tour in+ter+val *n.* the difference in altitude represented by the space between two contour lines on a map.

con+tour line *n.* a line on a map or chart joining points of equal height or depth. Often shortened to **contour.**

con+tour plough+ing *n.* ploughing following the contours of the land, to minimize the effects of erosion.

contr. *abbrev. for:* **1.** contraction. **2.** contralto.

con·tra- *prefix.* **1.** against; contrary; opposing; contrasting: *contraceptive; contradistinction.* **2.** (in music) pitched below: *contrabass.* [from Latin, from *contrā* against]

con·tra+band (ˈkɒntrəˌbænd) *n.* **1. a.** goods that are prohibited by law from being exported or imported. **b.** illegally imported or exported goods. **2.** illegal traffic in such goods; smuggling. **3.** Also called: **contraband of war.** *International law.* goods that a neutral country may not supply to a belligerent. **4.** (during the American Civil War) a Black slave captured by the Union forces or escaped to the Union lines. ~*adj.* **5.** (of goods) **a.** forbidden by law from being imported or exported. **b.** illegally imported or exported. [C16: from Spanish *contrabanda,* from Italian *contrabando* (modern *contrabbando*), from Medieval Latin *contrabannum,* from CONTRA- + *bannum* ban, of Germanic origin] **—ˈcon·tra+ˌband+ist** *n.*

con·tra+bass (ˌkɒntrəˈbeɪs) *n.* **1. a.** a member of any of various families of musical instruments that is lower in pitch than the bass. **2.** another name for **double bass.** ~*adj.* **3.** of or denoting the instrument of a family that is lower than the bass. **—con·tra+bass+ist** (ˌkɒntrəˈbeɪsɪst, -ˈbæs-) *n.*

con·tra+bas+soon (ˌkɒntrəbəˈsuːn) *n.* the largest instrument in the oboe family, pitched an octave below the bassoon; double bassoon. **—ˌcon·tra+bas+ˈsoon+ist** *n.*

con·tra+cep+tion (ˌkɒntrəˈsɛpʃən) *n.* the prevention by artificial means of conception. Methods in common use include preventing the sperm from reaching the ovum (using condoms, diaphragms, etc.), inhibiting ovulation (using oral contraceptive pills), preventing implantation (using intrauterine devices), killing the sperm (using spermicides), and preventing the sperm from entering the seminal fluid (by vasectomy). Compare **birth control, family planning.** [C19: from CONTRA- + CONCEPTION]

con·tra+cep+tive (ˌkɒntrəˈsɛptɪv) *adj.* **1.** relating to or used for contraception; able or tending to prevent impregnation. ~*n.* **2.** any device that prevents or tends to prevent conception.

con+tract *vb.* (kənˈtrækt). **1.** to make or become smaller, narrower, shorter, etc.: *metals contract as the temperature is reduced.* **2.** (ˈkɒntrækt). (when *intr.,* sometimes foll. by *for;* when *tr., may take an infinitive*) to enter into an agreement with (a person, company, etc.) to deliver (goods or services) or to do (something) on mutually agreed and binding terms, often in writing. **3.** to draw or be drawn together; coalesce or cause to coalesce. **4.** (*tr.*) to acquire, incur, or become affected by (a disease, liability, debt, etc.). **5.** (*tr.*) to shorten (a word or phrase) by the omission of letters or syllables, usually indicated in writing by an apostrophe. **6.** *Phonetics.* to unite (two vowels) or (of two vowels) to be united within a word or at a word boundary so that a new long vowel or diphthong is formed. **7.** (*tr.*) (of the brow or a muscle) to wrinkle or be drawn together. **8.** (*tr.*) to arrange (a marriage) for; betroth. ~*n.* (ˈkɒntrækt). **9.** a formal agreement between two or more parties. **10.** a document that states the terms of such an agreement. **11.** the branch of law treating of contracts. **12.** marriage considered as a formal agreement. **13.** See **contract bridge. 14.** *Bridge.* **a.** (in the bidding sequence before play) the highest bid, which determines trumps and the number of tricks one side must try to make. **b.** the number and suit of these tricks. [C16: from Latin *contractus* agreement, something drawn up, from *contrahere* to draw together, from *trahere* to draw] **—con+ˈtract+i·ble** *adj.* **—con+ˈtract+i·bly** *adv.*

con+tract bridge (ˈkɒntrækt) *n.* the most common variety of bridge, in which the declarer receives points counting towards game and rubber only for tricks he bids as well as makes, any overtricks receiving bonus points. Compare **auction bridge.**

con+trac+tile (kənˈtræktaɪl) *adj.* having the power to contract or to cause contraction. **—con+trac+til+i·ty** (ˌkɒntrækˈtɪlɪtɪ) *n.*

con+trac+tion (kənˈtrækʃən) *n.* **1.** an instance of contracting or the state of being contracted. **2.** *Physiol.* any normal shortening or tensing of an organ or part, esp. of a muscle. **3.** *Pathol.* any abnormal tightening or shrinking of an organ or part. **4.** a shortening of a word or group of words, often marked in written English by an apostrophe: *I've come* for *I have come.* **—con+ˈtrac+tive** *adj.* **—con+ˈtrac+tive+ly** *adv.* **—con+ˈtrac+tive+ness** *n.*

con+trac+tor (ˈkɒntræktə, kənˈtræk-) *n.* **1.** a person or firm that contracts to supply materials or labour, esp. for building. **2.** something that contracts, esp. a muscle. **3.** *Law.* a person who is a party to a contract. **4.** the declarer in bridge.

con+tract out *vb.* (*intr., adv.*) *Brit.* to agree not to participate in something, esp. the state pension scheme.

con+trac+tu·al (kənˈtræktjʊəl) *adj.* of the nature of or assured by a contract. **—con+ˈtrac+tu+al+ly** *adv.*

con+trac+ture (kənˈtrækʃə) *n.* a disorder in which a skeletal muscle is permanently tightened (contracted), most often caused by spasm or paralysis of the antagonist muscle that maintains normal muscle tension.

con·tra+dance (ˈkɒntrəˌdɑːns) *n.* a variant spelling of **contredanse.**

con·tra+dict (ˌkɒntrəˈdɪkt) *vb.* **1.** (*tr.*) to affirm the opposite of (a proposition, statement, etc.). **2.** (*tr.*) to declare (a proposition, statement, etc.) to be false or incorrect; deny. **3.** (*intr.*) to be argumentative or contrary. **4.** (*tr.*) to be inconsistent with (a proposition, etc.): *the facts contradicted his theory.* **5.** (*intr.*) (of two or more facts, principles, etc.) to be at variance; be in contradiction. [C16: from Latin *contrādīcere,* from CONTRĀ- + *dīcere* to speak, say] **—ˌcon·tra+ˈdict+a·ble** *adj.* **—ˌcon·tra+ˈdict+er** *or* **ˌcon·tra+ˈdic+tor** *n.* **—ˌcon·tra+ˈdic+tive** *or* **ˌcon·tra+ˈdic+tious** *adj.* **—ˌcon·tra+ˈdic+tive+ly** *or* **ˌcon·tra+ˈdic+tious+ly** *adv.* **—ˌcon·tra+ˈdic+tive+ness** *or* **ˌcon·tra+ˈdic+tious+ness** *n.*

con·tra+dic+tion (ˌkɒntrəˈdɪkʃən) *n.* **1.** the act of going against; opposition; denial. **2.** a declaration of the opposite or contrary. **3.** a statement that is at variance with itself (often in the phrase **a contradiction in terms**). **4.** conflict or inconsistency, as between events, qualities, etc. **5.** a person or thing containing conflicting qualities.

con·tra+dic+to·ry (ˌkɒntrəˈdɪktərɪ) *adj.* **1.** inconsistent; incompatible. **2.** given to argument and contention: *a contradictory person.* **3.** *Logic.* (of a pair of propositions) unable to be both true or both false at once. Compare **contrary** (sense 5), **subcontrary** (sense 1). ~*n., pl.* **·ries. 4.** either of two logical propositions that cannot both be true or both be false. **—ˌcon·tra+ˈdic+to+ri+ly** *adv.* **—ˌcon·tra+ˈdic+to+ri+ness** *n.*

con·tra+dis+tinc+tion (ˌkɒntrədɪˈstɪŋkʃən) *n.* a distinction made by contrasting different qualities. **—ˌcon·tra+dis+ˈtinc+tive** *adj.* **—ˌcon·tra+dis+ˈtinc+tive+ly** *adv.*

con·tra+dis+tin+guish (ˌkɒntrədɪˈstɪŋgwɪʃ) *vb.* (*tr.*) to differentiate by means of contrasting or opposing qualities.

con+trail (ˈkɒntreɪl) *n.* another name for **vapour trail.** [C20: from CON(DENSATION) + TRAIL]

con·tra+in+di·cate (ˌkɒntrəˈɪndɪˌkeɪt) *vb.* (*tr.; usually passive*) *Med.* to advise against or indicate the possible danger of (a drug, treatment, etc.). **—ˌcon·tra+ˈin+di+cant** *n.* **—ˌcon·tra+ˌin+di+ˈca+tion** *n.*

con+tral+to (kənˈtræltəʊ, -ˈtrɑːl-) *n., pl.* **+tos** *or* **+ti** (-tɪ). **1.** the alto voice of a female soloist or operatic singer. **2.** a singer with such a voice. Compare **alto.** ~*adj.* **3.** of or denoting a contralto: *the contralto part.* [C18: from Italian; see CONTRA-, ALTO]

con·tra+po+si+tion (ˌkɒntrəpəˈzɪʃən) *n.* **1.** the act of placing opposite or against, esp. in contrast or antithesis. **2.** *Logic.* the conclusion drawn from a proposition by negating its terms and changing their order: *the contraposition of (A implies B) is (not B implies not A).* **—con·tra+pos+i·tive** (ˌkɒntrəˈpɒzɪtɪv) *adj.*

con+trap+tion (kənˈtræpʃən) *n. Informal, often facetious or derogatory.* a device or contrivance, esp. one considered strange, unnecessarily intricate, or improvised. [C19: perhaps from CON(TRIVANCE) + TRAP + (INVEN)TION]

con·tra+pun+tal (ˌkɒntrəˈpʌntᵊl) *adj. Music.* characterized by counterpoint. [C19: from Italian *contrappunto* COUNTERPOINT + -AL[1]] **—ˌcon·tra+ˈpun+tal+ly** *adv.*

con·tra+pun+tist (ˌkɒntrəˈpʌntɪst) *or* **con·tra+pun+tal+ist** *n. Music.* a composer skilled in counterpoint.

con·tra+ri+e·ty (ˌkɒntrəˈraɪətɪ) *n., pl.* **·ties. 1.** opposition between one thing and another; disagreement. **2.** an instance of such opposition; inconsistency; discrepancy. **3.** *Logic.* the relationship between two contraries.

con+tra+ri+ly *adv.* **1.** (kənˈtrɛərɪlɪ). in a perverse or obstinate manner. **2.** (ˈkɒntrərɪlɪ). on the other hand; from the opposite point of view. **3.** (ˈkɒntrərɪlɪ). in an opposite, adverse, or unexpected way.

con+trar·i·ous (kənˈtrɛərɪəs) *adj. Rare.* **1.** (of people or animals) perverse or obstinate. **2.** (of conditions, etc.) unfavourable. **—con+ˈtrar·i·ous+ly** *adv.* **—con+ˈtrar·i·ous+ness** *n.*

con+tra+ri+wise (ˈkɒntrɛərɪˌwaɪz) *adv.* **1.** from a contrasting point of view; on the other hand. **2.** in the reverse way or direction. **3.** (kən'trɛərɪ,waɪz). in a contrary manner.

con·tra·ry ('kɒntrərɪ) *adj.* **1.** opposed in nature, position, etc.: *contrary ideas.* **2.** (kən'trɛərɪ). perverse; obstinate. **3.** (esp. of wind) adverse; unfavourable. **4.** (of plant parts) situated at right angles to each other. **5.** *Logic.* (of a pair of propositions) related so that they cannot both be true at once, although they may both be false together. Compare **subcontrary** (sense 1), **contradictory** (sense 3). ~*n., pl.* **·ries. 6.** the exact opposite (esp. in the phrase **to the contrary**). **7. on the contrary.** quite the reverse; not at all. **8.** either of two exactly opposite objects, facts, or qualities. **9.** either of two contrary logical propositions. ~*adv.* (usually foll. by *to*) **10.** in an opposite or unexpected way: *contrary to usual belief.* **11.** in conflict (with) or contravention (of): *contrary to nature.* [C14: from Latin *contrārius* opposite, from *contrā* against] —**con·'tra·ri·ness** *n.*

con·trast *vb.* (kən'trɑːst). **1.** (often foll. by *with*) to distinguish or be distinguished by comparison of unlike or opposite qualities. ~*n.* ('kɒntrɑːst). **2.** distinction or emphasis of difference by comparison of opposite or dissimilar things, qualities, etc. (esp. in the phrases **by contrast, in contrast to** *or* **with**). **3.** a person or thing showing notable differences when compared with another. **4.** (in painting) the effect of the juxtaposition of different colours, tones, etc. **5. a.** the range of optical density and tone on a photographic negative or print. **b.** the extent to which adjacent areas of an optical image, esp. on a television screen, differ in brightness. [C16: (n.): via French from Italian, from *contrastare* (vb.), from Latin *contra-* against + *stare* to stand] —**con·'trast·a·ble** *adj.* —**con·'trast·a·bly** *adv.* —**con·'trast·ing·ly** *adv.* —**con·'tras·tive** *adj.* —**con·'tras·tive·ly** *adv.*

con·trast·y (kən'trɑːstɪ) *adj.* (of a photograph or subject) having sharp gradations in tone, esp. between light and dark areas.

con·tra·sug·gest·i·ble (ˌkɒntrəsə'dʒɛstɪbᵊl) *adj. Psychol.* responding or tending to respond to a suggestion by doing or believing the opposite. —ˌ**con·tra·sug·ˌgest·i·'bil·i·ty** *n.* —ˌ**con·tra·sug·'ges·tion** *n.*

con·tra·val·la·tion (ˌkɒntrəvə'leɪʃən) *n.* fortifications built by besiegers around the place besieged. [C17: from CONTRA- + Latin *vallātiō* entrenchment; compare French *contrevallation*]

con·tra·vene (ˌkɒntrə'viːn) *vb.* (*tr.*) **1.** to come into conflict with or infringe (rules, laws, etc.). **2.** to dispute or contradict (a statement, proposition, etc.). [C16: from Late Latin *contrāvenīre,* from Latin CONTRA- + *venīre* to come] —ˌ**con·tra·'ven·er** *n.* —**con·tra·ven·tion** (ˌkɒntrə'vɛnʃən) *n.*

con·tra·yer·va (ˌkɒntrə'jɜːvə) *n.* the root of any of several tropical American moraceous plants of the genus *Dorstenia,* esp. *D. contrayerva,* used as a stimulant and tonic. [C17: from Spanish *contrayerba,* from CONTRA- + *yerba* grass, (poisonous) plant, from Latin *herba;* referring to the belief that it was an antidote to poisons]

con·tre·danse *or* **con·tra·dance** ('kɒntrəˌdɑːns) *n.* **1.** a courtly Continental version of the English country dance, similar to the quadrille. **2.** music written for or in the rhythm of this dance. [C19: from French, changed from English *country dance; country* altered to French *contre* (opposite) by folk etymology (because the dancers face each other)]

con·tre·temps ('kɒntrəˌtɑːn; *French* kɔ̃trə'tɑ̃) *n., pl.* **·temps. 1.** an awkward or difficult situation or mishap. **2.** *Fencing.* a feint made with the purpose of producing a counterthrust from one's opponent. [C17: from French, from *contre* against + *temps* time, from Latin *tempus*]

contrib. *abbrev. for:* **1.** contribution. **2.** contributor.

con·trib·ute (kən'trɪbjuːt) *vb.* (often foll. by *to*) **1.** to give (support, money, etc.) for a common purpose or fund. **2.** to supply (ideas, opinions, etc.) as part of a debate or discussion. **3.** (*intr.*) to be partly instrumental (in) or responsible (for): *drink contributed to the accident.* **4.** to write (articles, etc.) for a publication. [C16: from Latin *contribuere* to collect, from *tribuere* to grant, bestow] —**con·'trib·ut·a·ble** *adj.* —**con·'trib·u·tive** *adj.* —**con·'trib·u·tive·ly** *adv.* —**con·'trib·u·tive·ness** *n.*

con·tri·bu·tion (ˌkɒntrɪ'bjuːʃən) *n.* **1.** the act of contributing. **2.** something contributed, such as money or ideas. **3.** an article, story, etc., contributed to a newspaper or other publication. **4.** *Insurance.* a portion of the total liability incumbent on each of two or more companies for a risk with respect to which all of them have issued policies. **5.** *Archaic.* a levy, esp. towards the cost of a war.

con·trib·u·tor (kən'trɪbjʊtə) *n.* **1.** something that is a factor in or is partly responsible for something: *alcohol was a contributor to his death.* **2.** a person who contributes, esp. one who writes for a newspaper or one who makes a donation to a cause, etc.

con·trib·u·to·ry (kən'trɪbjʊtərɪ, -trɪ) *adj.* **1.** (often foll. by *to*) sharing in or being partly responsible (for the cause of something): *a contributory factor.* **2.** giving or donating to a common purpose or fund. **3.** of, relating to, or designating an insurance or pension scheme in which the premiums are paid partly by the employer and partly by the employees who benefit from it. **4.** liable or subject to a tax or levy. ~*n., pl.* **·ries. 5.** a person or thing that contributes. **6.** *Company law.* a member or former member of a company liable to contribute to the assets on the winding-up of the company.

con·trib·u·to·ry neg·li·gence *n. Law.* failure by an injured person to have taken proper precautions to prevent an accident.

con·trite (kən'traɪt, 'kɒntraɪt) *adj.* **1.** full of guilt or regret; remorseful. **2.** arising from a sense of shame or guilt: *contrite promises.* **3.** *Theol.* remorseful for past sin and resolved to avoid future sin. [C14: from Latin *contrītus* worn out, from *conterere* to bruise, from *terere* to grind] —**con·'trite·ly** *adv.* —**con·'trite·ness** *n.*

con·tri·tion (kən'trɪʃən) *n.* **1.** deeply felt remorse; penitence. **2.** *Christianity.* detestation of past sins and a resolve to make amends, either from love of God (**perfect contrition**) or from hope of heaven (**imperfect contrition**).

con·triv·ance (kən'traɪvəns) *n.* **1.** something contrived, esp. an ingenious device; contraption. **2.** the act or faculty of devising or adapting; inventive skill or ability. **3.** an artificial rather than natural selection or arrangement of details, parts, etc. **4.** an elaborate or deceitful plan or expedient; stratagem.

con·trive (kən'traɪv) *vb.* **1.** (*tr.*) to manage (something or to do something), esp. by means of a trick; engineer: *he contrived to make them meet.* **2.** (*tr.*) to think up or adapt ingeniously or elaborately: *he contrived a new mast for the boat.* **3.** to plot or scheme (treachery, evil, etc.). [C14: from Old French *controver,* from Late Latin *contropāre* to represent by figures of speech, compare, from Latin *com-* together + *tropus* figure of speech, TROPE] —**con·'triv·a·ble** *adj.* —**con·'triv·er** *n.*

con·trived (kən'traɪvd) *adj.* obviously planned, artificial, or lacking in spontaneity; forced; unnatural.

con·trol (kən'trəʊl) *vb.* **·trols, ·trol·ling, ·trolled.** (*tr.*) **1.** to command, direct, or rule: *to control a country.* **2.** to check, limit, curb, or regulate; restrain: *to control one's emotions; to control a fire.* **3.** to regulate or operate (a machine). **4.** to verify (a scientific experiment) by conducting a parallel experiment in which the variable being investigated is held constant or is compared with a standard. **5. a.** to regulate (financial affairs). **b.** to examine and verify (financial accounts). ~*n.* **6.** power to direct or determine: *under control; out of control.* **7.** a means of regulation or restraint; curb; check: *a frontier control.* **8.** (*often pl.*) a device or mechanism for operating a car, aircraft, etc. **9.** a standard of comparison used in a statistical analysis or scientific experiment. **10. a.** a device that regulates the operation of a machine. A **dynamic control** is one that incorporates a governor so that it responds to the output of the machine it regulates. **b.** (*as modifier*): *control panel; control room.* **11.** *Spiritualism.* an agency believed to assist the medium in a séance. **12.** Also called: **control mark.** a letter, or letter and number, printed on a sheet of postage stamps, indicating authenticity, date, and series of issue. **13.** one of a number of checkpoints on a car rally, orienteering course, etc., where competitors check in and their time, performance, etc., is recorded. [C15: from Old French *conteroller* to regulate, from *contrerolle* duplicate register, system of checking, from *contre-* COUNTER- + *rolle* ROLL] —**con·'trol·la·ble** *adj.* —**con·ˌtrol·la·'bil·i·ty** *or* **con·'trol·la·ble·ness** *n.* —**con·'trol·la·bly** *adv.*

con·trol ac·count *n. Accounting.* an account to which are posted the debit and credit totals of other accounts, usually in preparation of financial statements.

con·trol chart *n. Statistics.* a chart on which observed values of a variable are plotted in the order in which they occur so that excessive variations in the quality, quantity, etc., of the variable can be detected.

con·trol col·umn *n.* a lever or pillar, usually fitted with a handwheel, used to control the movements of an aircraft. Also called: **control stick, joy stick.**

con·trol ex·per·i·ment *n.* an experiment designed to check or correct the results of another experiment by removing the variable or variables operating in that other experiment. The comparison obtained is an indication or measurement of the effect of the variables concerned.

con·trol grid *n. Electronics.* another name for **grid** (sense 4), esp. in a tetrode or pentode.

con·trol group *n.* any group used as a control in a statistical experiment, esp. a group of patients who receive either a placebo or a standard drug during an investigation of the effects of another drug on other patients.

con·trol·ler (kən'trəʊlə) *n.* **1.** a person who directs, regulates, or restrains. **2.** Also called: **comptroller.** a business executive or government officer who is responsible for financial planning, control, etc. **3.** the equipment concerned with controlling the operation of an electrical device. —**con·'trol·ler·ˌship** *n.*

con·trol rod *n.* one of a number of rods or tubes containing a neutron absorber, such as boron, that can be inserted into or retracted from the core of a nuclear reactor in order to control its rate of reaction.

con·trol stick *n.* the lever by which a pilot controls the lateral and longitudinal movements of an aircraft. Also called: **control column, joy stick.**

con·trol sur·face *n.* a movable aerofoil, such as a rudder, elevator, aileron, etc., that controls an aircraft or rocket.

con·trol tow·er *n.* a tower at an airport from which air traffic is controlled.

con·tro·ver·sy ('kɒntrəˌvɜːsɪ, kən'trɒv-) *n., pl.* **·sies.** dispute, argument, or debate, esp. one concerning a matter about which there is strong disagreement and esp. one carried on in public or in the press. [C14: from Latin *contrōversia,* from *contrōversus* turned in an opposite direction, from CONTRA- + *vertere* to turn] —**con·tro·ver·sial** (ˌkɒntrə'vɜːʃəl) *adj.* —ˌ**con·tro·'ver·sial·ˌism** *n.* —ˌ**con·tro·'ver·sial·ist** *n.* —ˌ**con·tro·'ver·sial·ly** *adv.*

con·tro·vert ('kɒntrəˌvɜːt, ˌkɒntrə'vɜːt) *vb.* (*tr.*) **1.** to deny, refute, or oppose (some argument or opinion). **2.** to argue or wrangle about. [C17: from Latin *contrōversus;* see CONTROVERSY] —'**con·tro·ˌvert·er** *n.* —ˌ**con·tro·'vert·i·ble** *adj.* —ˌ**con·tro·'vert·i·bly** *adv.*

con·tu·ma·cious (ˌkɒntjʊ'meɪʃəs) *adj.* stubbornly resistant to authority; wilfully obstinate. —ˌcon·tu·'ma·cious·ly *adv.* —ˌcon·tu·'ma·cious·ness *n.*

con·tu·ma·cy ('kɒntjʊməsɪ) *n., pl.* **·cies. 1.** obstinate and wilful rebelliousness or resistance to authority; insubordination; disobedience. **2.** the wilful refusal of a person to appear before a court or to comply with a court order. [C14: from Latin *contumācia,* from *contumāx* obstinate; related to *tumēre* to swell, be proud]

con·tu·me·ly ('kɒntjʊmɪlɪ) *n., pl.* **·lies. 1.** scornful or insulting language or behaviour. **2.** a humiliating or scornful insult. [C14: from Latin *contumēlia* invective, from *tumēre* to swell, as with wrath] —**con·tu·me·li·ous** (ˌkɒntjʊ'mi:lɪəs) *adj.* —ˌ**con·tu·'me·li·ous·ly** *adv.* —ˌ**con·tu·'me·li·ous·ness** *n.*

con·tuse (kən'tju:z) *vb.* (*tr.*) to injure (the body) without breaking the skin; bruise. [C15: from Latin *contūsus* bruised, from *contundere* to grind, from *tundere* to beat, batter] —**con·'tu·sive** *adj.*

con·tu·sion (kən'tju:ʒən) *n.* an injury in which the skin is not broken; bruise. —**con·'tu·sioned** *adj.*

co·nun·drum (kə'nʌndrəm) *n.* **1.** a riddle, esp. one whose answer makes a play on words. **2.** a puzzling question or problem. [C16: of unknown origin]

con·ur·ba·tion (ˌkɒnɜ:'beɪʃən) *n.* a large densely populated urban sprawl formed by the growth and coalescence of individual towns or cities. [C20: from CON- + *-urbation,* from Latin *urbs* city; see URBAN]

con·ure ('kɒnjʊə) *n.* any of various small American parrots of the genus *Aratinga* and related genera. [C19: from New Latin *conurus,* from Greek *kōnos* CONE + *oura* tail]

con·va·lesce (ˌkɒnvə'lɛs) *vb.* (*intr.*) to recover from illness, injury, or the aftereffects of a surgical operation, esp. by resting. [C15: from Latin *convalēscere,* from *com-* (intensive) + *valēscere* to grow strong, from *valēre* to be strong]

con·va·les·cence (ˌkɒnvə'lɛsəns) *n.* **1.** gradual return to health after illness, injury, or an operation, esp. through rest. **2.** the period during which such recovery occurs. —ˌ**con·va·'les·cent** *n., adj.* —ˌ**con·va·'les·cent·ly** *adv.*

con·vec·tion (kən'vɛkʃən) *n.* **1.** the process of heat or mass transfer through a fluid, caused by movement of molecules from cool regions to warmer regions of lower density. **2.** *Meteorol.* the process by which masses of relatively warm air are raised into the atmosphere, often cooling and forming clouds, with compensatory downward movements of cooler air. [C19: from Late Latin *convectiō* a bringing together, from Latin *convehere* to bring together, gather, from *vehere* to bear, carry] —**con·'vec·tion·al** *adj.* —**con·'vec·tive** *adj.* —**con·'vec·tive·ly** *adv.*

con·vec·tor (kən'vɛktə) *n.* a space-heating device from which heat is transferred to the surrounding air by convection.

con·ve·nance *French.* (kɔ̃və'nɑ̃:s) *n.* suitable behaviour; propriety. [from *convenir* to be suitable, from Latin *convenīre;* see CONVENIENT]

con·ve·nances *French.* (kɔ̃və'nɑ̃:s) *pl. n.* the accepted social forms; conventions.

con·vene (kən'vi:n) *vb.* **1.** to gather, call together, or summon, esp. for a formal meeting. **2.** (*tr.*) to order to appear before a court of law, judge, tribunal, etc. [C15: from Latin *convenīre* to assemble, from *venīre* to come] —**con·'ven·a·ble** *adj.* —**con·'ven·a·bly** *adv.*

con·ven·er *or* **con·ven·or** (kən'vi:nə) *n.* a person who convenes or chairs a meeting, committee, etc., esp. one who is specifically elected to do so: *a convener of shop stewards.*

con·ven·i·ence (kən'vi:nɪəns) *n.* **1.** the state or quality of being suitable or opportune: *the convenience of the hour.* **2.** a convenient time or situation. **3. at your convenience.** at a time suitable to you. **4. at your earliest convenience.** *Formal.* as soon as possible. **5.** usefulness, comfort, or facility. **6.** an object that is particularly useful, esp. a labour-saving device. **7.** *Euphemistic, chiefly Brit.* a lavatory, esp. a public one. **8. make a convenience of.** to take advantage of; impose upon.

con·ven·i·ence food *n.* food that needs little preparation and can be used at any time.

con·ven·i·ent (kən'vi:nɪənt) *adj.* **1.** suitable for one's purpose or needs; opportune. **2.** easy to use. **3.** close by or easily accessible; handy. [C14: from Latin *conveniēns* appropriate, fitting, from *convenīre* to come together, be in accord with, from *venīre* to come] —**con·'ven·i·ent·ly** *adv.*

con·vent ('kɒnvənt) *n.* **1.** a building inhabited by a religious community, usually of nuns. **2.** the religious community inhabiting such a building. **3.** Also called: **convent school.** a school in which the teachers are nuns. [C13: from Old French *covent,* from Latin *conventus* meeting, from *convenīre* to come together; see CONVENE]

con·ven·ti·cle (kən'vɛntɪkᵊl) *n.* **1.** a secret or unauthorized assembly for worship. **2.** a small meeting house or chapel for a religious assembly, esp. of Nonconformists or Dissenters. [C14: from Latin *conventiculum* a meeting, from *conventus;* see CONVENT] —**con·'ven·ti·cler** *n.*

con·ven·tion (kən'vɛnʃən) *n.* **1. a.** a large formal assembly of a group with common interests, such as a political party or trade union. **b.** the persons attending such an assembly. **2.** *U.S. politics.* an assembly of delegates of one party to select candidates for office. **3.** *Diplomacy.* an international agreement second only to a treaty in formality: *a telecommunications convention.* **4.** any agreement, compact, or contract. **5.** the most widely accepted or established view of what is thought to be proper behaviour, good taste, etc. **6.** an accepted rule, usage, etc.: *a convention used by printers.* **7.** *Bridge.* Also called: **conventional.** a bid or play not to be taken at its face value, which one's partner can interpret according to a prearranged bidding system. [C15: from Latin *conventiō* an assembling, agreeing]

con·ven·tion·al (kən'vɛnʃənᵊl) *adj.* **1.** following the accepted customs and proprieties, esp. in a way that lacks originality: *conventional habits.* **2.** established by accepted usage or general agreement. **3.** of or relating to a convention or assembly. **4.** *Law.* based upon the agreement or consent of parties. **5.** *Arts.* represented in a simplified or generalized way; conventionalized. **6.** (of weapons, warfare, etc.) not nuclear. ~*n.* **7.** *Bridge.* another word for **convention** (sense 7). —**con·'ven·tion·al·ly** *adv.*

con·ven·tion·al·ism (kən'vɛnʃənəˌlɪzəm) *n.* **1.** advocacy of or conformity to that which is established. **2.** something conventional. **3.** *Philosophy.* the theory that principles become established by general agreement rather than rationally or empirically. —**con·'ven·tion·al·ist** *n.*

con·ven·tion·al·i·ty (kənˌvɛnʃə'nælɪtɪ) *n., pl.* **·ties. 1.** the quality or characteristic of being conventional, esp. in behaviour, thinking, etc. **2.** (*often pl.*) something conventional, esp. a normal or accepted rule of behaviour; propriety.

con·ven·tion·al·ize *or* **con·ven·tion·al·ise** (kən'vɛnʃənəˌlaɪz) *vb.* (*tr.*) **1.** to make conventional. **2.** to simplify or stylize (a design, decorative device, etc.). —**con·ˌven·tion·al·i·'za·tion** *or* **con·ˌven·tion·al·i·'sa·tion** *n.*

con·ven·tu·al (kən'vɛntjʊəl) *adj.* **1.** of, belonging to, or characteristic of a convent. ~*n.* **2.** a member of a convent. —**con·'ven·tu·al·ly** *adv.*

con·verge (kən'vɜ:dʒ) *vb.* **1.** to move or cause to move towards the same point. **2.** to meet or cause to meet; join. **3.** (*intr.*) (of opinions, effects, etc.) to tend towards a common conclusion or result. **4.** (*intr.*) *Maths.* (of an infinite series) to approach a finite limit as the number of terms increases. **5.** (*intr.*) (of animals and plants during evolutionary development) to undergo convergence. [C17: from Late Latin *convergere,* from Latin *com-* together + *vergere* to incline]

con·ver·gence (kən'vɜ:dʒəns) *n.* **1.** Also: **con·ver·gen·cy.** the act, degree, or a point of converging. **2.** concurrence of opinions, results, etc. **3.** *Maths.* the property or manner of approaching a finite limit, esp. of an infinite series: *conditional convergence.* **4.** the turning inwards of the eyes to focus on a close object. **5.** Also called: **convergent evolution.** the evolutionary development of a superficial resemblance between unrelated animals that occupy a similar environment, as in the evolution of wings in birds and bats. **6.** *Meteorol.* accumulation of air in a region that has a greater inflow than outflow of air, often giving rise to vertical air currents. See also **Intertropical Convergence Zone.**

con·ver·gent (kən'vɜ:dʒənt) *adj.* **1.** (of two or more lines, paths, etc.) moving towards or meeting at some common point. **2.** (of forces, ideas, etc.) tending towards the same result; merging. **3.** *Maths.* (of an infinite series) having a finite limit.

con·ver·gent think·ing *n. Psychol.* thinking in which a common attribute is abstracted from many different objects or ideas.

con·vers·a·ble (kən'vɜ:səbᵊl) *adj.* **1.** easy or pleasant to talk to. **2.** able or inclined to talk. —**con·'vers·a·ble·ness** *n.* —**con·'vers·a·bly** *adv.*

con·ver·sant (kən'vɜ:sᵊnt) *adj.* (*usually postpositive* and foll. by *with*) experienced (in), familiar (with), or acquainted (with). —**con·'ver·sance** *or* **con·'ver·san·cy** *n.* —**con·'ver·sant·ly** *adv.*

con·ver·sa·tion (ˌkɒnvə'seɪʃən) *n.* **1.** the interchange through speech of information, ideas, etc.; spoken communication. **2. make conversation.** to talk in an artificial way.

con·ver·sa·tion·al (ˌkɒnvə'seɪʃənᵊl) *adj.* **1.** of, using, or in the manner of conversation. **2.** inclined to or skilled in conversation; conversable. —ˌ**con·ver·'sa·tion·al·ly** *adv.*

con·ver·sa·tion·al·ist (ˌkɒnvə'seɪʃənəˌlɪst) *or* **con·ver·sa·tion·ist** *n.* a person who enjoys or excels in conversation.

con·ver·sa·tion piece *n.* **1.** something, esp. an unusual object, that provokes conversation. **2.** (esp. in 18th-century Britain) a group portrait in a landscape or domestic setting. **3.** a play emphasizing dialogue.

con·ver·sa·zio·ne *Italian.* (ˌkonversa'tsjo:ne; *English* ˌkɒnvəˌsætsɪ'əʊnɪ) *n., pl.* ***·zio·ni*** (*Italian* -'tsjo:ni) *or* **·zi·o·nes** (*English* -tsɪ'əʊni:z). a social gathering for discussion of the arts, literature, etc. [C18: literally: conversation]

con·verse[1] *vb.* (kən'vɜ:s). (*intr.; often foll. by with*) **1.** to engage in conversation (with). **2.** to commune spiritually (with). **3.** *Obsolete.* **a.** to associate; consort. **b.** to have sexual intercourse. ~*n.* ('kɒnvɜ:s). **4.** conversation (often in the phrase **hold converse with**). **5.** *Obsolete.* **a.** fellowship or acquaintance. **b.** sexual intercourse. [C16: from Old French *converser,* from Latin *conversārī* to keep company with, from *conversāre* to turn constantly, from *vertere* to turn] —**con·'vers·er** *n.*

con·verse[2] ('kɒnvɜ:s) *adj.* **1.** (*prenominal*) reversed; opposite; contrary. ~*n.* **2.** something that is opposite or contrary. **3.** *Logic.* a proposition inferred from another proposition by the transposition of the subject and predicate: *"all bad men are bald" is the converse of "all bald men are bad".* [C16: from Latin *conversus* turned around; see CONVERSE[1]] —**con·'verse·ly** *adv.*

con·ver·sion (kən'vɜ:ʃən) *n.* **1. a.** a change or adaptation in form, character, or function. **b.** something changed in one of these respects. **2.** a change to another attitude or belief, as in a change of religion. **3.** *Maths.* a change in the units or form of a number or expression: *the conversion of miles to kilometres involves multiplying by 1.61.* **4.** *Logic.* a form of inference by which one proposition is obtained as the converse of another proposition. **5.** *Law.* **a.** unauthorized dealing with or the assumption of rights of ownership to another's personal property. **b.** the changing of real property into personalty or personalty into realty. **6.** *Rugby.* a score made after a try by kicking the ball over the crossbar from a place kick. **7.** *Physics.* a change of fertile material to fissile material in a reactor. **8. a.** an alteration to a car engine to improve its performance. **b.** (*as modifier*): *a conversion kit.* [C14: from Latin *conversiō* a turning around; see CONVERT] —**con+'ver+sion+al** *or* **con+'ver+sion+ar·y** *adj.*

con+vert *vb.* (kən'vɜ:t). (*mainly tr.*) **1.** to change or adapt the form, character, or function of; transform. **2.** to cause (someone) to change in opinion, belief, etc. **3.** to change (a person or his way of life, etc.) for the better. **4.** (*intr.*) to admit of being changed (into): *the table converts into a tray.* **5.** (*also intr.*) to change or be changed into another chemical compound or physical state: *to convert water into ice.* **6.** *Law.* **a.** to assume unlawful proprietary rights over (personal property). **b.** to change (property) from realty into personalty or vice versa. **7.** (*also intr.*) *Rugby.* to make a conversion after (a try). **8.** *Logic.* to transpose the subject and predicate of (a proposition) by conversion. **9.** to change (a value or measurement) from one system of units to another. **10.** to exchange (a security or bond) for something of equivalent value. ~*n.* ('kɒnvɜ:t). **11.** a person who has been converted to another belief, religion, etc. [C13: from Old French *convertir,* from Latin *convertere* to turn around, alter, transform, from *vertere* to turn] —**con+'ver+tive** *adj.*

con+vert+er *or* **con+ver+tor** (kən'vɜ:tə) *n.* **1.** a person or thing that converts. **2.** *Physics.* **a.** a device for converting alternating current to direct current or vice versa. **b.** a device for converting a signal from one frequency to another. **3.** a vessel in which molten metal is refined, using a blast of air or oxygen. See also **Bessemer converter, L-D converter. 4.** short for **converter reactor.**

con+vert+er re+ac+tor *n.* a nuclear reactor for converting one fuel into another, esp. one that transforms fertile material into fissionable material. Compare **breeder reactor.**

con+vert+i·ble (kən'vɜ:təbᵊl) *adj.* **1.** capable of being converted. **2.** (of a car) having a folding or removable roof. **3.** *Finance.* **a.** (of a currency) freely exchangeable into other currencies. **b.** (of a paper currency) exchangeable on demand for precious metal to an equivalent value. ~*n.* **4.** a car with a folding or removable roof. —**con+ˌvert+i·'bil+i·ty** *or* **con+'vert+i·ble+ness** *n.* —**con+'vert+i·bly** *adv.*

con+vert·i+plane, con+vert·a+plane, *or* **con+vert·o+plane** (kən'vɜ:təˌpleɪn) *n.* an aircraft that can land and take off vertically by temporarily directing its propulsive thrust downwards.

con+ver+tite ('kɒnvəˌtaɪt) *n. Archaic.* a convert, esp. a reformed prostitute.

con+vex ('kɒnvɛks, kɒn'vɛks) *adj.* **1.** curving or bulging outwards. **2.** *Physics.* having one or two surfaces curved or ground in the shape of a section of the exterior of a sphere, paraboloid, ellipsoid, etc.: *a convex lens.* **3.** *Maths.* (of a polygon) containing no interior angle greater than 180°. ~*vb.* **4.** (*tr.*) to make convex. ~Compare **concave.** [C16: from Latin *convexus* vaulted, rounded] —**'con+vex+ly** *adv.*

con+vex+i·ty (kən'vɛksɪtɪ) *n., pl.* **·ties. 1.** the state or quality of being convex. **2.** a convex surface, object, etc.; bulge.

con·vex·o-con·cave (kənˌvɛksəʊkɒn'keɪv) *adj.* **1.** having one side convex and the other side concave. **2.** (of a lens) having a convex face with greater curvature than the concave face. Compare **concavo-convex** (sense 2).

con·vex·o-con·vex *adj.* (esp. of a lens) having both sides convex; biconvex.

con+vey (kən'veɪ) *vb.* (*tr.*) **1.** to take, carry, or transport from one place to another. **2.** to communicate (a message, information, etc.). **3.** (of a channel, path, etc.) to conduct, transmit, or transfer. **4.** *Law.* to transmit or transfer (the title to property). **5.** *Archaic.* to steal. [C13: from Old French *conveier,* from Medieval Latin *conviāre* to escort, from Latin *com-* with + *via* way] —**con+'vey+a·ble** *adj.*

con+vey+ance (kən'veɪəns) *n.* **1.** the act of conveying. **2.** a means of transport. **3.** *Law.* **a.** a transfer of the legal title to property. **b.** the document effecting such a transfer. —**con+'vey+anc+er** *n.* —**con+'vey+anc+ing** *n.*

con+vey+or *or* **con+vey+er** (kən'veɪə) *n.* **1.** a person or thing that conveys. **2.** short for **conveyor belt.**

con+vey+or belt *n.* a flexible endless strip of fabric or linked plates driven by rollers and used to transport objects, esp. in a factory.

con+vict *vb.* (kən'vɪkt). (*tr.*) **1.** to pronounce (someone) guilty of an offence. ~*n.* ('kɒnvɪkt). **2.** a person found guilty of an offence against the law, esp. one who is sentenced to imprisonment. **3.** a person serving a prison sentence. ~*adj.* (kən'vɪkt). **4.** *Obsolete.* convicted. [C14: from Latin *convictus* convicted of crime, from *convincere* to prove guilty, CONVINCE] —**con+'vict+a·ble** *or* **con+'vict+i·ble** *adj.*

con+vic+tion (kən'vɪkʃən) *n.* **1.** the state or appearance of being convinced. **2.** a fixed or firmly held belief, opinion, etc. **3.** the act of convincing. **4.** the act or an instance of convicting or the state of being convicted. **5. carry conviction.** to be convincing. —**con+'vic+tion+al** *adj.*

con+vic+tive (kən'vɪktɪv) *adj.* able or serving to convince or convict. —**con+'vic+tive+ly** *adv.*

con+vince (kən'vɪns) *vb.* (*tr.*) **1.** (*may take a clause as object*) to make (someone) agree, understand, or realize the truth or validity of something; persuade. **2.** *Obsolete.* **a.** to overcome. **b.** to prove guilty. [C16: from Latin *convincere* to demonstrate incontrovertibly, from *com-* (intensive) + *vincere* to overcome, conquer] —**con+'vince+ment** *n.* —**con+'vinc+er** *n.* —**con+'vinc+i·ble** *adj.*

con+vinc+ing (kən'vɪnsɪŋ) *adj.* **1.** credible or plausible. **2.** *Chiefly law.* persuading by evidence or argument. —**con+'vinc+ing+ly** *adv.* —**con+'vinc+ing+ness** *n.*

con+viv+i·al (kən'vɪvɪəl) *adj.* sociable; jovial or festive: *a convivial atmosphere.* [C17: from Late Latin *convīviālis* pertaining to a feast, from Latin *convīvium,* a living together, banquet, from *vīvere* to live] —**con+'viv·i+al+ist** *n.* —**con+ˌviv·i+'al+i·ty** *n.* —**con+'viv·i+al+ly** *adv.*

con+vo+ca+tion (ˌkɒnvə'keɪʃən) *n.* **1.** a large formal assembly, esp. one specifically convened. **2.** the act of convoking or state of being convoked. **3.** *Church of England.* either of the synods of the provinces of Canterbury or York. **4.** *Episcopal Church.* **a.** an assembly of the clergy and part of the laity of a diocese. **b.** a district represented at such an assembly. **5.** (*sometimes cap.*) (in some British universities) a legislative assembly composed mainly of graduates. **6.** (in India) a degree-awarding ceremony. —**ˌcon+vo+'ca+tion+al** *adj.* —**'con+vo+ˌca+tor** *n.*

con+voke (kən'vəʊk) *vb.* (*tr.*) to call (a meeting, assembly, etc.) together; summon. [C16: from Latin *convocāre,* from *vocāre* to call] —**con+voc·a+tive** (kən'vɒkətɪv) *adj.* —**con+'vok+er** *n.*

con+vo+lute ('kɒnvəˌlu:t) *vb.* (*tr.*) **1.** to form into a twisted, coiled, or rolled shape. ~*adj.* **2.** *Botany.* rolled longitudinally upon itself: *a convolute petal.* **3.** another word for **convoluted** (sense 2). [C18: from Latin *convolūtus* rolled up, from *convolvere* to roll together, from *volvere* to turn] —**'con+vo+ˌlute+ly** *adv.*

con+vo+lut+ed ('kɒnvəˌlu:tɪd) *adj.* **1.** (esp. of meaning, style, etc.) difficult to comprehend; involved. **2.** wound together; coiled. —**'con+vo+ˌlut+ed+ly** *adv.* —**'con+vo+ˌlut+ed+ness** *n.*

con+vo+lu+tion (ˌkɒnvə'lu:ʃən) *n.* **1.** a twisting together; a turn, twist, or coil. **2.** an intricate, involved, or confused matter or condition. **3.** Also called: **gyrus.** any of the numerous convex folds or ridges of the surface of the brain. —**ˌcon+vo+'lu+tion+al** *or* **ˌcon+vo+'lu+tion+ar·y** *adj.*

con+volve (kən'vɒlv) *vb.* to wind or roll together; coil; twist. [C16: from Latin *convolvere*; see CONVOLUTE]

con+vol+vu+la+ceous (kənˌvɒlvjʊ'leɪʃəs) *adj.* of, relating to, or belonging to the *Convolvulaceae,* a family of plants having trumpet-shaped flowers and typically a climbing, twining, or prostrate habit: includes bindweed, morning-glory, and sweet potato.

con+vol+vu+lus (kən'vɒlvjʊləs) *n., pl.* **+lus·es** *or* **+li** (-ˌlaɪ). any typically twining herbaceous convolvulaceous plant of the genus *Convolvulus,* having funnel-shaped flowers and triangular leaves. See also **bindweed.** [C16: from Latin: bindweed; see CONVOLUTE]

con+voy ('kɒnvɔɪ) *n.* **1.** a group of merchant ships with an escort of warships. **2.** a group of land vehicles assembled to travel together. **3.** the act of travelling or escorting by convoy (esp. in the phrase **in convoy**). ~*vb.* **4.** (*tr.*) to escort while in transit. [C14: from Old French *convoier* to CONVEY]

con+vul+sant (kən'vʌlsənt) *adj.* **1.** producing convulsions. ~*n.* **2.** a drug that produces convulsions. [C19: from French, from *convulser* to CONVULSE]

con+vulse (kən'vʌls) *vb.* **1.** (*tr.*) to shake or agitate violently. **2.** (*tr.*) to cause (muscles) to undergo violent spasms or contractions. **3.** (*intr.*; often foll. by *with*) *Informal.* to shake or be overcome (with violent emotion, esp. laughter). [C17: from Latin *convulsus,* from *convellere* to tear up, from *vellere* to pluck, pull] —**con+'vul+sive** *adj.* —**con+'vul+sive+ly** *adv.* —**con+'vul+sive+ness** *n.*

con+vul+sion (kən'vʌlʃən) *n.* **1.** a violent involuntary contraction of a muscle or muscles. **2.** a violent upheaval, disturbance, or agitation, esp. a social one. **3.** (*usually pl.*) *Informal.* uncontrollable laughter: *I was in convulsions.* —**con+'vul+sion+ar·y** *adj.*

Con+way ('kɒnweɪ) *n.* **Wil+liam.** 1913–77, Irish Roman Catholic cardinal; archbishop of Armagh and primate of all Ireland (1963–77).

co·ny *or* **co+ney** ('kəʊnɪ) *n., pl.* **·nies** *or* **+neys. 1.** a rabbit or fur made from the skin of a rabbit. **2.** (in the Bible) another name for the **hyrax,** esp. the Syrian rock hyrax. **3.** another name for the **pika. 4.** *Archaic.* a fool or dupe. [C13: back formation from *conies,* from Old French *conis,* plural of *conil,* from Latin *cunīculus* rabbit]

coo (ku:) *vb.* **coos, coo+ing, cooed. 1.** (*intr.*) (of doves, pigeons, etc.) to make a characteristic soft throaty call. **2.** (*tr.*) to speak in a soft murmur. **3.** (*intr.*) to murmur lovingly (esp. in the phrase **bill and coo**). ~*n.* **4.** the sound of cooing. ~*interj.* **5.** *Brit. slang.* an exclamation of surprise, awe, etc. —**'coo+er** *n.* —**'coo+ing+ly** *adv.*

Cooch Be+har *or* **Kuch Bi+har** (ku:tʃ bɪ'hɑ:) *n.* **1.** a former state of NE India: part of West Bengal since 1950. **2.** a city in India, in NE West Bengal: capital of the former state of Cooch Behar. Pop.: 53 684 (1971).

coo·ee *or* **coo+ey** ('ku:i:) *interj.* **1.** a call used to attract attention, esp. (originally) a long loud high-pitched call on two notes used in the Australian bush. **2.** *Austral. informal.* calling distance (esp. in the phrase **within (a) cooee (of)**). ~*vb.* **coo+ees, coo+ee+ing, coo+eed** *or* **coo+eys, coo+ey+ing, coo+eyed. 3.** (*intr.*) to utter this call. [C19: from a native Australian language]

cook (kʊk) *vb.* **1.** to prepare (food) by the action of heat, as by boiling, baking, etc., or (of food) to become ready for eating through such a process. Related adj.: **culinary. 2.** to subject or be subjected to the action of intense heat: *the town cooked in* *the sun.* **3.** (*tr.*) *Slang.* to alter or falsify (something, esp. figures, accounts, etc.): *to cook the books.* **4.** (*tr.*) *Slang.* to spoil or ruin (something). **5.** (*intr.*) *Slang.* to happen (esp. in the phrase **what's cooking?**). **6.** (*tr.*) *Slang.* to prepare (any of several drugs) by heating. **7.** *Slang.* **cook someone's goose. a.** to spoil a person's plans. **b.** to bring about someone's ruin, downfall, etc. ~*n.* **8.** a person who prepares food for eating, esp. as an occupation. ~See also **cook up.** [Old English *cōc* (n.), from Latin *coquus* a cook, from *coquere* to cook] —'**cook·a·ble** *adj.*

Cook[1] (kʊk) *n.* **Mount. 1.** Also called: **Aorangi.** a mountain in New Zealand, in the South Island, in the Southern Alps: the highest peak in New Zealand. Height: 3704 m (12 349 ft.). **2.** a mountain in SE Alaska, in the St. Elias Mountains. Height: 4128 m (13 760 ft.).

Cook[2] (kʊk) *n.* **1.** Captain **James.** 1728–79, English navigator and explorer: claimed the E coast of Australia for Britain, circumnavigated New Zealand, and discovered several Pacific and Atlantic islands (1768–79). **2.** Sir **Jo·seph.** 1860–1947, Australian statesman, born in England: prime minister of Australia (1913–14).

cook·er ('kʊkə) *n.* **1.** an apparatus, usually of metal and heated by gas, electricity, oil, or solid fuel, for cooking food; stove. **2.** *Brit.* any large sour apple used in cooking.

cook·er·y ('kʊkərɪ) *n.* **1.** the art, study, or practice of cooking. **2.** *U.S.* a place for cooking.

cook·er·y book *or* (*esp. U.S.*) **cook·book** ('kʊk,bʊk) *n.* a book containing recipes and instructions for cooking.

cook-gen·er·al *n., pl.* **cooks-gen·er·al.** *Brit.* (formerly, esp. in the 1920s and 30s) a domestic servant who did cooking and housework.

cook·house ('kʊk,haʊs) *n.* a place for cooking, esp. a camp kitchen.

cook·ie *or* **cook·y** ('kʊkɪ) *n., pl.* **·ies. 1.** the U.S. word for **biscuit. 2.** a Scot. word for **bun. 3.** *Informal, chiefly U.S.* a person: *smart cookie.* **4. that's the way the cookie crumbles.** *Informal, chiefly U.S.* matters are inevitably or unalterably so.

Cook In·let *n.* an inlet of the Pacific on the coast of S Alaska: part of the Gulf of Alaska.

Cook Is·lands *pl. n.* a group of islands in the SW Pacific, an overseas territory of New Zealand: consists of the **Lower Cooks** and the **Northern Cooks.** Capital: Raratonga. Pop.: 18 112 (1976). Area: 241 sq. km (93 sq. miles).

cook·out ('kʊk,aʊt) *n. U.S.* a party where a meal is cooked and eaten out of doors.

Cook's tour *n. Informal.* a rapid but extensive tour or survey of anything. [C19: after Thomas *Cook* (1808–92), English travel agent]

Cook Strait *n.* the strait between North and South Islands, New Zealand. Width: 26 km (16 miles).

cook up *vb.* (*tr., adv.*) **1.** *Informal.* to concoct or invent (a story, alibi, etc.). **2.** to prepare (a meal), esp. quickly. **3.** *Slang.* to prepare (a drug) for use by heating, as by dissolving heroin in a spoon. ~*n.* **cook-up. 4.** (in the Caribbean) a dish consisting of mixed meats, rice, shrimps, and sometimes vegetables.

cool (ku:l) *adj.* **1.** moderately cold: *a cool day.* **2.** comfortably free of heat: *a cool room.* **3.** producing a pleasant feeling of coldness: *a cool shirt.* **4.** able to conceal emotion; calm: *a cool head.* **5.** lacking in enthusiasm, affection, cordiality, etc.: *a cool welcome.* **6.** calmly audacious or impudent. **7.** *Informal.* (esp. of numbers, sums of money, etc.) without exaggeration; actual: *a cool ten thousand.* **8.** (of a colour) having violet, blue, or green predominating; cold. **9.** (of jazz) characteristic of the late 1940s and early 1950s, economical and rhythmically relaxed. **10.** *Informal.* sophisticated or elegant, esp. in an unruffled way. **11.** *Informal, chiefly U.S.* excellent; marvellous. ~*adv.* **12.** *Not standard.* in a cool manner; coolly. ~*n.* **13.** coolness: *the cool of the evening.* **14.** *Slang.* calmness; composure (esp. in the phrase **keep one's cool**). **15.** *Slang.* unruffled elegance or sophistication. ~*vb.* **16.** (usually foll. by *down* or *off*) to make or become cooler. **17.** (usually foll. by *down* or *off*) to lessen the intensity of (anger or excitement) or (of anger or excitement) to become less intense; calm down. **18. cool it.** (*usually imperative*) *Slang, chiefly U.S.* to calm down; take it easy. **19. cool one's heels.** to wait or be kept waiting. [Old English *cōl*; related to Old Norse *kōlna,* Old High German *kuoli;* see COLD, CHILL] —'**cool·ing·ly** *adv.* —'**cool·ing·ness** *n.* —'**cool·ish** *adj.* —'**cool·ly** *adv.* —'**cool·ness** *n.*

coo·la·bah *or* **coo·li·bah** ('ku:lə,bɑ:) *n.* an Australian myrtaceous tree, *Eucalyptus microtheca,* that grows along rivers and has smooth bark and long narrow leaves. [from a native Australian language]

cool·ant ('ku:lənt) *n.* **1.** a fluid used to cool a system or to transfer heat from one part of it to another. **2.** a liquid, such as an emulsion of oil, water, and soft soap, used to lubricate and cool the workpiece and cutting tool during machining.

cool bag *or* **box** *n.* an insulated container used to keep food cool on picnics, to carry frozen food, etc.

cool·er ('ku:lə) *n.* **1.** a container, vessel, or apparatus for cooling, such as a heat exchanger. **2.** *Informal.* something that cools, esp. an iced drink. **3.** a slang word for **prison.**

Cool·gar·die safe (ku:l'gɑ:dɪ) *n.* a cupboard with wetted hessian walls for keeping food cool: used esp. in Australia. Sometimes shortened to **Coolgardie.** [named after *Coolgardie,* Western Australia, perhaps because of resemblance to COOL and GUARD]

Coo·lidge ('ku:lɪdʒ) *n.* **(John) Cal·vin,** nickname *Silent Cal.* 1872–1933, 30th president of the U.S. (1923–29).

cool·ie *or* **cool·y** ('ku:lɪ) *n., pl.* **·ies. 1.** a cheaply hired unskilled Oriental labourer. **2.** *Derogatory.* an Indian living in South Africa. [C17: from Hindi *kulī,* probably of Dravidian origin; related to Tamil *kūli* hire, hireling]

cool out *vb.* (*intr., adv.*) *Caribbean.* to relax and cool down.

coom *or* **coomb** (ku:m) *n. Dialect, chiefly northern Brit.* waste material, such as dust from coal, grease from axles, etc. [C16 (meaning: soot): probably a variant of CULM[1]]

coomb, combe, coombe, *or* **comb** (ku:m) *n.* **1.** *Chiefly southeastern Brit.* a short valley or deep hollow, esp. in chalk areas. **2.** *Chiefly northern Brit.* another name for a **cirque.** [Old English *cumb* (in place names), perhaps of Celtic origin; compare Old French *combe* small valley, also probably of Celtic origin]

coon (ku:n) *n.* **1.** *Informal.* short for **raccoon. 2.** *Derogatory slang.* a Negro or Australian Aborigine.

coon·can ('ku:n,kæn) *or* **con·qui·an** *n.* a card game for two players, similar to rummy. [C19: from (Mexican) Spanish *con quién* with whom?, apparently with reference to the forming and declaring of sequences and sets of cards]

coon's age *n. U.S. slang.* a long time.

coon·skin ('ku:n,skɪn) *n.* **1.** the pelt of a raccoon. **2.** a raccoon cap with the tail hanging at the back. **3.** *U.S.* an overcoat made of raccoon.

coon·tie ('ku:ntɪ) *n.* **1.** an evergreen plant, *Zamia floridana* of S Florida, related to the cycads and having large dark green leathery leaves: family *Zamiaceae.* **2.** a starch derived from the underground stems of this plant. [C19: from Seminole *kunti* flour from this plant]

coop[1] (ku:p) *n.* **1.** a cage or small enclosure for poultry or small animals. **2.** a small narrow place of confinement, esp. a prison cell. **3.** a wicker basket for catching fish. ~*vb.* **4.** (*tr.;* often foll. by *up* or *in*) to confine in a restricted area. [C15: probably from Middle Low German *kūpe* basket, tub; related to Latin *cūpa* cask, vat]

co·op[2] *or* **co-op** ('kəʊ,ɒp) *n.* a cooperative, cooperative society, or shop run by a cooperative society.

coop. *or* **co-op.** *abbrev. for* cooperative.

coop·er ('ku:pə) *n.* **1.** Also called: **hooper.** a person skilled in making and repairing barrels, casks, etc. ~*vb.* **2.** (*tr.*) to make or mend (barrels, casks, etc.). **3.** (*intr.*) to work as a cooper. [C13: from Middle Dutch *cūper* or Middle Low German *kūper;* see COOP[1]]

Coo·per ('ku:pə) *n.* **1. An·tho·ny Ash·ley.** See (Earl of) **Shaftesbury. 2. Gar·y,** original name *Frank Cooper.* 1901–61, U.S. film actor; his many films include *A Farewell to Arms* (1933) and *High Noon* (1952). **3. James Fen·i·more.** 1789–1851, U.S. novelist, noted for his stories of American Indians, esp. *The Last of the Mohicans* (1826). **4. Sam·u·el.** 1609–72, English miniaturist.

coop·er·age ('ku:pərɪdʒ) *n.* **1.** Also called: **coopery.** the craft, place of work, or products of a cooper. **2.** the labour fee charged by a cooper.

co·op·er·ate *or* **co-op·er·ate** (kəʊ'ɒpə,reɪt) *vb.* (*intr.*) **1.** to work or act together. **2.** to be of assistance or be willing to assist. **3.** *Economics.* (of firms, workers, consumers, etc.) to engage in economic cooperation. [C17: from Late Latin *cooperārī* to work with, combine, from Latin *operārī* to work] —**co·'op·er,a·tor** *or* **co-'op·er,a·tor** *n.*

co·op·er·a·tion *or* **co-op·er·a·tion** (kəʊ,ɒpə'reɪʃən) *n.* **1.** joint operation or action. **2.** assistance or willingness to assist. **3.** *Economics.* the combination of consumers, workers, farmers, etc., in activities usually embracing production, distribution, or trade. **4.** *Ecology.* beneficial but inessential interaction between two species in a community. —**co,op·er'a·tion·ist** *or* **co-,op·er'a·tion·ist** *n.*

co·op·er·a·tive *or* **co-op·er·a·tive** (kəʊ'ɒpərətɪv, -'ɒprə-) *adj.* **1.** willing to cooperate; helpful. **2.** acting in conjunction with others; cooperating. **3. a.** (of an enterprise, farm, etc.) owned collectively and managed for joint economic benefit. **b.** (of an economy or economic activity) based on collective ownership and cooperative use of the means of production and distribution. ~*n.* **4.** a cooperative organization. **5.** Also called: **cooperative apartment.** *U.S.* a block of flats belonging to a corporation in which shares are owned in proportion to the relative value of the flat occupied. Sometimes shortened to **coop.** Compare **condominium** (sense 3). —**co·'op·er·a·tive·ly** *or* **co-'op·er·a·tive·ly** *adv.* —**co·'op·er·a·tive·ness** *or* **co-'op·er·a·tive·ness** *n.*

co·op·er·a·tive bank *n.* a U.S. name for **building society.**

co·op·er·a·tive farm *n.* **1.** a farm that is run in cooperation with others in the purchasing and using of machinery, stock, etc., and in the marketing of produce through its own institutions (**farmers' cooperatives**). **2.** a farm that is owned by a cooperative society. **3.** a farm run on a communal basis, such as a kibbutz. **4.** another name for **collective farm.**

Co·op·er·a·tive Par·ty *n.* (in Great Britain) a political party supporting the cooperative movement and formerly linked with the Labour Party: founded in 1917.

co·op·er·a·tive so·ci·e·ty *n.* a commercial enterprise owned and managed by and for the benefit of customers or workers. Often shortened to **coop, co-op.**

Coo·per's Creek *n.* an intermittent river in E central Australia, in the Channel Country: rises in central Queensland and flows generally southwest, reaching Lake Eyre only during wet-year floods; scene of the death of the explorers Burke and Wills in 1861; the surrounding basin provides cattle pastures after the floods subside. Total length: 1420 km (880 miles). Also called: **Barcoo River.**

Coo·per's hawk *n.* a small North American hawk, *Accipiter* *cooperii,* having a bluish-grey back and wings and a reddish-brown breast. [C19: named after William *Cooper* (died 1864), American naturalist]

coop·er·y (ˈkuːpərɪ) *n., pl.* **·er·ies.** another word for **cooperage** (sense 1).

co·opt *or* **co-opt** (kəʊˈɒpt) *vb.* (*tr.*) **1.** to add (someone) to a committee, board, etc., by the agreement of the existing members. **2.** to appoint summarily; commandeer. [C17: from Latin *cooptāre* to elect, from *optāre* to choose] —**co·ˈop·tion, co-ˈop·tion** *or* **ˌco·op·ˈta·tion, ˌco-op·ˈta·tion** *n.* —**co·ˈop·ta·tive** *or* **co-ˈop·ta·tive** *adj.*

co·or·di·nal *or* **co-or·di·nal** (kəʊˈɔːdɪnᵊl) *adj.* (of animals or plants) belonging to the same order.

co·or·di·nate *or* **co-or·di·nate** *vb.* (kəʊˈɔːdɪˌneɪt). **1.** (*tr.*) to organize or integrate diverse elements in a harmonious operation. **2.** to place (things) in the same class or order, or (of things) to be placed in the same class, etc. **3.** (*intr.*) to work together, esp. harmoniously. **4.** (*intr.*) to take or be in the form of a harmonious order. **5.** *Chem.* to form or cause to form a coordinate bond. ~*n.* (kəʊˈɔːdɪnɪt, -ˌneɪt) **6.** *Maths.* any of a set of numbers that defines the location of a point in space with reference to a system of axes. See **Cartesian coordinates, polar coordinates. 7.** a person or thing equal in rank, type, etc. ~*adj.* (kəʊˈɔːdɪnɪt, -ˌneɪt). **8.** of, concerned with, or involving coordination. **9.** of the same rank, type, etc. **10.** of or involving the use of coordinates: *coordinate geometry.* —**co·ˈor·di·nate·ly** *or* **co-ˈor·di·nate·ly** *adv.* —**co·ˈor·di·nate·ness** *or* **co-ˈor·di·nate·ness** *n.* —**co·ˈor·di·na·tive** *or* **co-ˈor·di·na·tive** *adj.* —**co·ˈor·di·ˌna·tor** *or* **co-ˈor·di·ˌna·tor** *n.*

co·or·di·nate bond *n.* a type of covalent chemical bond in which both the shared electrons are provided by one of the atoms. Also called: **dative bond.**

co·or·di·nate clause *n.* one of two or more clauses in a sentence having the same status and connected by coordinating conjunctions. Compare **subordinate clause.**

co·or·di·nates (kəʊˈɔːdɪnɪts, -ˌneɪts) *pl. n.* clothes of matching or harmonious colours and design, suitable for wearing together. Compare **separates.**

co·or·di·nat·ing con·junc·tion *n.* a conjunction that introduces coordinate clauses, such as *and, but,* and *or.* Compare **subordinating conjunction.**

co·or·di·na·tion *or* **co-or·di·na·tion** (kəʊˌɔːdɪˈneɪʃən) *n.* balanced and effective interaction of movement, actions, etc. [C17: from Late Latin *coordinātiō,* from Latin *ordinātiō* an arranging; see ORDINATION]

co·or·di·na·tion com·pound *n.* another name for **complex** (sense 8).

Coorg (kʊəg) *n.* a former province of SW India: since 1956 part of Karnataka state.

coot (kuːt) *n.* **1.** any aquatic bird of the genus *Fulica,* esp. *F. atra* of Europe and Asia, having lobed toes, dark plumage, and a white bill with a frontal shield: family *Rallidae* (rails, etc.). **2.** a foolish person, esp. an old man (often in the phrase **old coot**). [C14: probably from Low German; compare Dutch *koet*]

cootch *or* **cwtch** (kʊtʃ) *South Wales dialect.* ~*n.* **1.** a hiding place. **2.** a room, shed, etc., used for storage: *a coal cootch.* ~*vb.* **3.** (*tr.*) to hide. **4.** (often foll. by *up*) to cuddle or be cuddled. **5.** (*tr.*) to clasp (someone or something) to oneself. [from French *couche* COUCH, probably influenced by Welsh *cwt* hut]

coot·ie (ˈkuːtɪ) *n. U.S.* a slang name for the **body louse.** See **louse** (sense 1). [C20: perhaps from Malay *kutu* louse]

cop[1] (kɒp) *Slang.* ~*n.* **1.** another name for **policeman. 2.** *Brit.* an arrest (esp. in the phrase **a fair cop**). ~*vb.* **cops, cop·ping, copped.** (*tr.*) **3.** to seize or catch. **4.** to steal. **5.** to buy (illegal drugs). Compare **score** (sense 25). **6.** to suffer (a punishment, etc.): *you'll cop a clout if you do that!* Also in the phrase **cop it.** ~See also **cop out.** [C18: (vb.) perhaps from obsolete *cap* to arrest, from Old French *caper* to seize; sense 1, back formation from COPPER[2]]

cop[2] (kɒp) *n.* **1.** a conical roll of thread wound on a spindle. **2.** *Now chiefly dialect.* the top or crest, as of a hill. [Old English *cop, copp* top, summit, of uncertain origin; perhaps related to Old English *copp* CUP]

cop[3] (kɒp) *n. Brit. slang.* (*usually used with a negative*) worth or value: *that work is not much cop.* [C19: n. use of COP[1] (in the sense: to catch, hence something caught, something of value)]

co·pa·cet·ic, co·pa·set·ic *or* **co·pe·set·ic, co·pe·set·tic** (ˌkəʊpəˈsɛtɪk, -ˈsiːtɪk) *adj. U.S. slang.* very good; excellent; completely satisfactory. [C20: of unknown origin]

co·pai·ba (kəʊˈpaɪbə) *or* **co·pai·va** *n.* a transparent yellowish viscous oleoresin obtained from certain tropical South American trees of the caesalpiniaceous genus *Copaifera:* used in varnishes and ointments. Also called: **copaiba balsam, copaiba resin.** [C18: via Spanish via Portuguese from Tupi]

co·pal (ˈkəʊpᵊl, -pæl) *n.* a hard aromatic resin, yellow, orange, or red in colour, obtained from various tropical trees and used in making varnishes and lacquers. [C16: from Spanish, from Nahuatl *copalli* resin]

co·palm (ˈkəʊˌpɑːm) *n.* **1.** the aromatic brown resin obtained from the sweet gum tree. **2.** another name for the **sweet gum.** [C19: from Louisiana French, from Mexican Spanish *copalme;* see COPAL, PALMATE]

Co·pán (*Spanish* koˈpan) *n.* a village in W Honduras: site of a ruined Mayan city.

co·par·ce·nar·y (kəʊˈpɑːsənərɪ) *or* **co·par·ce·ny** (kəʊˈpɑːsɪnɪ) *n. Law.* a form of joint ownership of property, esp. joint heirship. Also called: **parcenary.**

co·par·ce·ner (kəʊˈpɑːsɪnə) *n. Law.* a person who inherits an estate as coheir with others. Also called: **parcener.**

co·part·ner (kəʊˈpɑːtnə) *n.* a partner or associate, esp. an equal partner in business. —**co·ˈpart·ner·ˌship** *n.*

cope[1] (kəʊp) *vb.* **1.** (*intr.;* foll. by *with*) to contend (against). **2.** (*intr.*) to deal successfully with or handle a situation; manage: *she coped well with the problem.* **3.** (*tr.*) *Archaic.* **a.** to deal with. **b.** to meet in battle. [C14: from Old French *coper* to strike, cut, from *coup* blow; see COUP]

cope[2] (kəʊp) *n.* **1.** a large ceremonial cloak worn at solemn liturgical functions by priests of certain Christian sects. **2.** any covering shaped like a cope. ~*vb.* **3.** (*tr.*) to dress (someone) in a cope. [Old English *cāp,* from Medieval Latin *cāpa,* from Late Latin *cappa* hooded cloak; see CAP[1]]

cope[3] (kəʊp) *vb.* (*tr.*) **1.** to provide (a wall, etc.) with a coping. **2.** to join (two moulded timber members). ~*n.* **3.** another name for **coping.** [C17: probably from French *couper* to cut; see COPE[1]]

co·peck (ˈkəʊpɛk) *n.* a variant spelling of **kopeck.**

Co·pen·ha·gen (ˌkəʊpənˈheɪgən, -ˈhɑː-; ˈkəʊpənˌheɪ-, -ˌhɑː-) *n.* the capital of Denmark, a port on Zealand and Amager Islands on a site inhabited for some 6000 years: exports chiefly agricultural products; iron and steel works; university (1479). Pop.: 736 951 (1974 est.). Danish name: **København.**

Co·pen·ha·gen blue *n.* **a.** a greyish-blue colour. **b.** (*as adj.*): *Copenhagen-blue markings.*

co·pe·pod (ˈkəʊpɪˌpɒd) *n.* **1.** any minute free-living or parasitic crustacean of the subclass *Copepoda* of marine and fresh waters: an important constituent of plankton. ~*adj.* **2.** of, relating to, or belonging to the *Copepoda.* [C19: from New Latin *Copepoda,* from Greek *kōpē* oar + *pous* foot]

co·per (ˈkəʊpə) *n.* a horse-dealer. [C17 (a dealer, chapman): from dialect *cope* to buy, barter, from Low German; related to Dutch *koopen* to buy]

Co·per·ni·can sys·tem *n.* the theory published in 1543 by Copernicus which stated that the earth and the planets rotated around the sun and which opposed the Ptolemaic system.

Co·per·ni·cus[1] (kəˈpɜːnɪkəs) *n.* **Nic·o·la·us** (ˌnɪkəˈleɪəs). Polish name *Mikolaj Kopernik.* 1473–1543, Polish astronomer, whose theory of the solar system (the **Copernican system**) was published in 1543. —**Co·ˈper·ni·can** *adj.*

Co·per·ni·cus[2] (kəˈpɜːnɪkəs) *n.* a conspicuous crater on the moon, over 4000 metres deep and 90 kilometres in diameter, from which a system of rays emanates.

cope·stone (ˈkəʊpˌstəʊn) *n.* **1.** Also called: **coping stone.** a stone used to form a coping. **2.** Also called: **capstone.** the stone at the top of a building, wall, etc.

cop·i·er (ˈkɒpɪə) *n.* **1.** a person or device that copies. **2.** another word for **copyist.**

co·pi·lot (ˈkəʊˌpaɪlət) *n.* a second or relief pilot of an aircraft.

cop·ing (ˈkəʊpɪŋ) *n.* the sloping top course of a wall, usually made of masonry or brick. Also called: **cope.**

cop·ing saw *n.* a handsaw with a U-shaped frame used for cutting curves in a material too thick for a fret saw.

cop·ing stone *n.* another word for **copestone** (sense 1).

co·pi·ous (ˈkəʊpɪəs) *adj.* **1.** abundant; extensive in quantity. **2.** having or providing an abundant supply. **3.** full of words, ideas, etc.; profuse. [C14: from Latin *cōpiōsus* well supplied, from *cōpia* abundance, from *ops* wealth] —**ˈco·pi·ous·ly** *adv.* —**ˈco·pi·ous·ness** *n.*

co·pi·ta (*Spanish* koˈpita; *English* kəˈpiːtə) *n.* **1.** a tulip-shaped sherry glass. **2.** a glass of sherry. [diminutive of *copa* cup]

co·pla·nar (kəʊˈpleɪnə) *adj.* lying in the same plane: *coplanar lines.* —**ˌco·pla·ˈnar·i·ty** *n.*

Cop·land (ˈkəʊplənd) *n.* **Aa·ron.** born 1900, U.S. composer of orchestral and chamber music, ballets, and film music.

Cop·ley (ˈkɒplɪ) *n.* **John Sin·gle·ton.** 1738–1815, U.S. painter.

co·pol·y·mer (kəʊˈpɒlɪmə) *n.* a chemical compound of high molecular weight formed by uniting the molecules of two or more different compounds (monomers). Compare **polymer.**

co·pol·y·mer·ize *or* **co·pol·y·mer·ise** (kəʊˈpɒlɪməˌraɪz) *vb.* to react (two compounds) together to produce a copolymer. —**co·ˌpol·y·mer·i·ˈza·tion** *or* **co·ˌpol·y·mer·i·ˈsa·tion** *n.*

cop out *U.S. slang.* ~*vb.* **1.** (*intr., adv.*) to fail to assume responsibility or to commit oneself. ~*n.* **cop-out. 2.** a way of avoiding responsibility or commitment. **3.** a person who acts in this way. [C20: probably from COP[1]]

cop·per[1] (ˈkɒpə) *n.* **1. a.** a malleable ductile reddish metallic element occurring as the free metal, copper glance, and copper pyrites: used as an electrical and thermal conductor and in such alloys as brass and bronze. Symbol: Cu; atomic no.: 29; atomic wt.: 63.54; valency: 1 or 2; relative density: 8.96; melting pt.: 1083°C; boiling pt.: 2595°C. Related adjs.: **cupric, cuprous.** Related prefix: **cupro-. b.** (*as modifier*): *a copper coin.* **2. a.** the reddish-brown colour of copper. **b.** (*as adj.*): *copper hair.* **3.** *Informal.* any copper or bronze coin. **4.** *Chiefly Brit.* a large vessel, formerly of copper, used for boiling or washing. **5.** any of various small widely distributed butterflies of the genera *Lycaena, Heodes,* etc., typically having reddish-brown wings: family *Lycaenidae.* ~*vb.* **6.** (*tr.*) to coat or cover with copper. [Old English *coper,* from Latin *Cyprium aes* Cyprian metal, from Greek *Kupris* Cyprus]

cop·per[2] (ˈkɒpə) *n.* a slang word for **policeman.** Often shortened to **cop.** [C19: from COP[1] (vb.) + -ER[1]]

cop·per·as (ˈkɒpərəs) *n.* a less common name for **ferrous sulphate.** [C14: *coperose,* via Old French from Medieval Latin

cuperosa, perhaps originally in the phrase *aqua cuprosa* copper water]
Cop+per Belt *n.* a region of Central Africa, along the Zambia-Zaïre border: rich deposits of copper.
cop·per+head ('kɒpəˌhɛd) *n.* **1.** a venomous reddish-brown snake, *Agkistrodon contortrix*, of the eastern U.S.: family *Crotalidae* (pit vipers). **2.** a venomous reddish-brown Australian elapid snake, *Denisonia superba*. **3.** *U.S. informal.* a Yankee supporter of the South during the Civil War.
cop·per+plate ('kɒpəˌpleɪt) *n.* **1.** a polished copper plate on which a design has been etched or engraved. **2.** a print taken from such a plate. **3.** a fine handwriting based upon that used on copperplate engravings.
cop·per py+ri+tes *n.* another name for **chalcopyrite.**
cop·per+smith ('kɒpəˌsmɪθ) *n.* **1.** a person who works copper or copper alloys. **2.** an Asian barbet (a bird), *Megalaima haemacephala*, the call of which has a ringing metallic note.
cop+per sul+phate *n.* a copper salt found naturally as chalcanthite and made by the action of sulphuric acid on copper oxide. It usually exists as blue crystals of the pentahydrate that form a white anhydrous powder when heated: used as a mordant, in electroplating, and in plant sprays. Formula: $CuSO_4$.
cop+pice ('kɒpɪs) *n.* another word (esp. Brit.) for **copse.** [C14: from Old French *copeiz*, from *couper* to cut] —'**cop+piced** *adj.*
cop+ra ('kɒprə) *n.* the dried, oil-yielding kernel of the coconut. [C16: from Portuguese, from Malayalam *koppara*, probably from Hindi *khoprā* coconut]
cop·ro- *or before a vowel* **copr-** *combining form.* indicating dung or obscenity: *coprology*. [from Greek *kopros* dung]
cop+ro+la+li·a (ˌkɒprə'leɪlɪə) *n.* obsessive use of obscene or foul language.
cop+ro+lite ('kɒprəˌlaɪt) *n.* any of various rounded stony nodules thought to be the fossilized faeces of Mesozoic reptiles. —**cop+ro+lit+ic** (ˌkɒprə'lɪtɪk) *adj.*
cop+rol+o·gy (kɒp'rɒlədʒɪ) *n.* preoccupation with excrement. Also called: **scatology.**
cop+roph·a+gous (kɒ'prɒfəgəs) *adj.* (esp. of certain beetles) feeding on dung. —**cop+'roph·a+gy** *n.*
cop+ro+phil·i·a (ˌkɒprəʊ'fɪlɪə) *n.* an abnormal interest in faeces and their evacuation.
co+proph·i+lous (kə'prɒfɪləs) *adj.* growing in or on dung.
co+pros+ma (kə'prɒzmə) *n.* any shrub of the Australasian rubiaceous genus *Coprosma*: sometimes planted for ornament. [C19: New Latin, from Greek *kopros* excrement + *osmē* smell]
copse (kɒps) *or* **cop+pice** *n.* a thicket or dense growth of small trees or bushes. [C16: by shortening from COPPICE]
Copt (kɒpt) *n.* **1.** a member of the Coptic Church. **2.** an Egyptian descended from the ancient Egyptians. [C17: from Arabic *qubt* Copts, from Coptic *kyptios* Egyptian, from Greek *Aiguptios*, from *Aiguptos* Egypt]
cop+ter ('kɒptə) *n. Informal.* short for **helicopter.**
Cop+tic ('kɒptɪk) *n.* **1.** an Afro-Asiatic language, written in the Greek alphabet but descended from ancient Egyptian. It was extinct as a spoken language by about 1600 A.D. but survives in the Coptic Church. ~*adj.* **2.** of or relating to this language. **3.** of or relating to the Copts.
Cop+tic Church *n.* the ancient Christian Church of Egypt.
cop·u·la ('kɒpjʊlə) *n., pl.* **+las** *or* **+lae** (-ˌliː). **1.** a verb, such as *be, seem*, or *taste*, that is used to identify or link the subject with the complement of a sentence. Copulas may serve to link nouns (or pronouns), as in *he became king*, nouns (or pronouns) and adjectival complements, as in *sugar tastes sweet*, or nouns (or pronouns) and adverbial complements, as in *John is in jail*. **2.** anything that serves as a link. [C17: from Latin: bond, connection, from *co-* together + *apere* to fasten] —'**cop·u+lar** *adj.*
cop·u+late ('kɒpjʊˌleɪt) *vb.* (*intr.*) to perform sexual intercourse. [C17: from Latin *copulāre* to join together; see COPULA] —ˌ**cop·u+'la+tion** *n.* —'**cop·u+la+to·ry** *adj.*
cop·u+la+tive ('kɒpjʊlətɪv) *adj.* **1.** serving to join or unite. **2.** of or characteristic of copulation. **3.** *Grammar.* (of a verb) having the nature of a copula. —'**cop·u+la+tive+ly** *adv.*
cop·y ('kɒpɪ) *n., pl.* **cop·ies. 1.** an imitation or reproduction of an original. **2.** a single specimen of something that occurs in a multiple edition, such as a book, article, etc. **3. a.** matter to be reproduced in print. **b.** written matter or text as distinct from graphic material in books, newspapers, etc. **4.** *Journalism, informal.* suitable material for an article or story: *disasters are always good copy*. **5.** *Archaic.* a model to be copied, esp. an example of penmanship. ~*vb.* **cop·ies, cop·y+ing, cop·ied. 6.** (when *tr.*, often foll. by *out*) to make a copy or reproduction of (an original). **7.** to imitate as a model. **8.** (*intr.*) to imitate unfairly. [C14: from Medieval Latin *cōpia* an imitation, something copied, from Latin: abundance, riches; see COPIOUS]
cop·y+book ('kɒpɪˌbʊk) *n.* **1.** a book of specimens, esp. of penmanship, for imitation. **2.** *Chiefly U.S.* a book for or containing documents. **3. blot one's copybook.** *Informal.* to sully or destroy one's reputation. **4.** (*modifier*) trite or unoriginal: *copybook sentiments.*
cop·y+cat ('kɒpɪˌkæt) *n. Informal.* a person, esp. a child, who imitates or copies another.
cop·y desk *n. Journalism.* a desk where copy is edited.
cop·y-ed·it *vb. Journalism, etc.* to prepare (copy) for printing by styling, correcting, etc. —**cop·y ed·i·tor** *n.*
cop·y+graph ('kɒpɪˌgrɑːf, -ˌgræf) *n.* another name for **hectograph.**
cop·y+hold ('kɒpɪˌhəʊld) *n. Law.* (formerly) **a.** a tenure less than freehold of land in England evidenced by a copy of the Court roll. **b.** land held in this way.
cop·y+hold·er ('kɒpɪˌhəʊldə) *n.* **1.** *Printing.* one who reads aloud from the copy as the proof corrector follows the reading in the proof. **2.** *Printing.* a device that holds copy in place for the compositor. **3.** *Law.* (formerly) a person who held land by copyhold tenure.
cop·y+ist ('kɒpɪɪst) *n.* **1.** a person who makes written copies; transcriber. **2.** a person who imitates or copies.
cop·y+read ('kɒpɪˌriːd) *vb.* **+reads, +read+ing, +read.** *U.S.* to subedit.
cop·y+read·er ('kɒpɪˌriːdə) *n. U.S.* a person who edits and prepares newspaper copy for publication; subeditor.
cop·y+right ('kɒpɪˌraɪt) *n.* **1.** the exclusive right to produce copies and to control an original literary, musical, or artistic work, granted by law for a specified number of years (in Britain, usually 50 years from the death of the author, composer, etc.). Symbol: © ~*adj.* **2.** (of a work, etc.) subject to or controlled by copyright. ~*vb.* **3.** (*tr.*) to take out a copyright on. —'**cop·y+ˌright·a·ble** *adj.* —'**cop·y+ˌright·er** *n.*
cop·y+right de+pos+it li+brar·y *n.* one of six libraries legally entitled to receive a gratis copy of every book published in the United Kingdom: the British Library, Bodleian, Cambridge University, Trinity College in Dublin, Scottish National Library, and National Library of Wales.
cop·y tast+er *n.* a person who selects or approves text for publication, esp. in a periodical.
cop·y typ+ist *n.* a typist whose job is to type from written or typed drafts rather than dictation.
cop·y+writ·er ('kɒpɪˌraɪtə) *n.* a person employed to write advertising copy. —'**cop·y+ˌwrit·ng** *n.*
coq au vin *French.* (kɔk o 'vɛ̃) *n.* chicken stewed with red wine, onions, etc. [literally: cock with wine]
coque+li+cot ('kəʊklɪˌkəʊ) *n.* another name for **corn poppy.** [C18: from French: crow of a cock, from its resemblance to a cock's comb]
co+quet (kəʊ'kɛt, kɒ-) *vb.* **+quets, +quet+ting, +quet+ted.** (*intr.*) **1.** to behave flirtatiously. **2.** to dally or trifle. [C17: from French: a gallant, literally: a little cock, from *coq* cock]
co+quet+ry ('kəʊkɪtrɪ, 'kɒk-) *n., pl.* **+ries.** flirtation.
co+quette (kəʊ'kɛt, kɒ'kɛt) *n.* **1.** a woman who flirts. **2.** any humming bird of the genus *Lophornis*, esp. the crested Brazilian species *L. magnifica*. [C17: from French, feminine of COQUET] —**co+'quet+tish** *adj.* —**co+'quet+tish+ly** *adv.* —**co+'quet+tish+ness** *n.*
co+quil+la nut (kɒ'kiːljə) *n.* the nut of a South American palm tree, *Attalea funifera*, having a hard brown shell used for carving. See also **cohune.** [C19: from Portuguese *coquilho*, diminutive of *côco* coconut; see COCO]
co+quille (*French* kɔ'kij) *n.* **1.** any dish, esp. seafood, served in a scallop shell: *Coquilles St. Jacques*. **2.** a scallop shell, or dish resembling a shell. **3.** *Fencing.* a bell-shaped hand guard on a foil. [French, literally: shell, from Latin *conchȳlium* mussel; see COCKLE[1]]
co+qui+na (kɒ'kiːnə) *n.* a soft limestone containing shells, corals, etc., that occurs in parts of the U.S. [C19: from Spanish: shellfish, probably from *concha* shell, CONCH]
co+qui+to (kɒ'kiːtəʊ) *n., pl.* **+tos.** a Chilean palm tree, *Jubaea spectabilis*, yielding edible nuts and a syrup. [C19: from Spanish: a little coco palm, from *coco* coco palm]
cor. *abbrev. for:* **1.** corner. **2.** cornet. **3.** coroner.
Cor. *Bible. abbrev. for* Corinthians.
cor·a+ci·i+form (ˌkɒrə'saɪɪˌfɔːm) *adj.* of, relating to, or belonging to the *Coraciiformes*, an order of birds including the kingfishers, bee-eaters, hoopoes, and hornbills. [C20: from New Latin *Coracias* name of genus, from Greek *korakias* a chough + -I- + -FORM; related to Greek *korax* raven]
cor·a+cle ('kɒrəkᵊl) *n.* a small roundish boat made of waterproofed hides stretched over a wicker frame. [C16: from Welsh *corwgl*; related to Irish *curach* boat]
cor·a+coid ('kɒrəˌkɔɪd) *n.* a paired ventral bone of the pectoral girdle in vertebrates. In mammals it is reduced to a peg (the **coracoid process**) on the scapula. [C18: from New Latin *coracoīdēs*, from Greek *korakoeidēs* like a raven, curved like a raven's beak, from *korax* raven]
cor+al ('kɒrəl) *n.* **1.** any marine mostly colonial coelenterate of the class *Anthozoa* having a calcareous, horny, or soft skeleton. See also **stony coral, sea fan. 2. a.** the calcareous or horny material forming the skeleton of certain of these animals. **b.** (*as modifier*): *a coral necklace*. See also **red coral. 3. a.** a rocklike aggregation of certain of these animals or their skeletons, forming an island or reef. **b.** (*as modifier*): *a coral island*. **4.** an object made of coral, esp. a piece of jewellery. **5. a.** a deep-pink to yellowish-pink colour. **b.** (*as adj.*): *coral lipstick*. **6.** the roe of a lobster or crab, which becomes pink when cooked. [C14: from Old French, from Latin *corāllium*, from Greek *korallion*, probably of Semitic origin]
cor+al fern *n. Austral.* a scrambling fern of the genus *Gleichenia*, having repeatedly forked fronds.
cor+al+line ('kɒrəˌlaɪn) *adj.* **1.** Also: **cor+al+loid.** of, relating to, or resembling coral. **2.** of the colour of coral. ~*n.* **3.** any of various red algae impregnated with calcium carbonate, esp. any of the genus *Corallina*. **4.** any of various animals that resemble coral, such as certain sponges. [C16: from Late Latin *corallīnus* coral red, from Latin *corāllium* CORAL]
cor+al+lite ('kɒrəlaɪt) *n.* the skeleton of a coral polyp.
cor+al+loid ('kɒrəlɔɪd) *adj.* of or resembling coral.

cor·al reef *n.* a marine ridge or reef consisting of coral and other organic material consolidated into limestone.

cor·al·root ('kɒrəlˌruːt) *n.* any N temperate leafless orchid of the genus *Corallorhiza,* with small yellow-green or purple flowers and branched roots resembling coral.

Cor·al Sea *n.* the SW arm of the Pacific, between Australia, New Guinea, and the New Hebrides.

cor·al snake *n.* **1.** any venomous elapid snake of the genus *Micrurus* and related genera, of tropical and subtropical America, marked with red, black, yellow, and white transverse bands. **2.** any of various other brightly coloured elapid snakes of Africa and SE Asia.

cor·al tree *n. Austral.* any of various thorny trees of the papilionaceous genus *Erythrina,* having bright red flowers and reddish shiny seeds.

cor an·glais ('kɔːr 'ɑːŋgleɪ) *n., pl.* **cors an·glais** ('kɔːz 'ɑːŋgleɪ). *Music.* a woodwind instrument, the alto of the oboe family. It is a transposing instrument in F. Range: two and a half octaves upwards from E on the third space of the bass staff. Also called: **English horn.** [C19: from French: English horn]

Co·ran·tijn ('kɔranˌtɛjn) *n.* the Dutch name of **Courantyne.**

co·ran·to (kɒ'ræntəʊ) *n., pl.* **·tos.** a variant of **courante.**

cor·ban ('kɔːbᵊn; *Hebrew* kɔr'ban) *n.* **1.** *Old Testament.* a gift to God. **2.** *New Testament, Judaism.* the Temple treasury or a consecration or gift to it (Matthew 27:6; Mark 7:11). [C14: from Late Latin, from Greek *korban,* from Hebrew *qorbān* offering, literally: a drawing near]

cor·beil *or* **cor·beille** ('kɔːbᵊl; *French* kɔr'bɛj) *n. Architect.* a carved ornament in the form of a basket of fruit, flowers, etc. [C18: from French *corbeille* basket, from Late Latin *corbicula* a little basket, from Latin *corbis* basket]

cor·bel ('kɔːbᵊl) *Architect.* ~*n.* **1.** Also called: **truss.** a bracket, usually of stone or brick. ~*vb.* **·bels, ·bel·ling, ·belled** *or U.S.* **·bels, ·bel·ing, ·beled. 2.** (*tr.*) to lay (a stone or brick) so that it forms a corbel. [C15: from Old French, literally: a little raven, from Medieval Latin *corvellus,* from Latin *corvus* raven]

cor·bel·ling *or U.S.* **cor·bel·ing** ('kɔːbəlɪŋ) *n.* a set of corbels stepped outwards, one above another.

cor·bel out *or* **off** *vb.* (*tr., adv.*) to support on corbels.

cor·bic·u·la (kɔː'bɪkjʊlə) *n., pl.* **·lae** (-ˌliː). the technical name for **pollen basket.** [C19: from Late Latin, diminutive of Latin *corbis* basket]

cor·bie ('kɔːbɪ) *n.* a Scot. name for **raven** or **crow.** [C15: from Old French *corbin,* from Latin *corvīnus* CORVINE]

cor·bie ga·ble *n. Architect.* a gable having corbie-steps.

cor·bie-step *or* **cor·bel step** *n. Architect.* any of a set of steps on the top of a gable. Also called: **crow step.**

cor bli·mey ('kɔː 'blaɪmɪ) *or* **gor·bli·mey** *interj. Brit. slang.* an exclamation of surprise or annoyance. Often shortened to **cor.** [C20: corruption of *God blind me*]

Cor·bu·sier (*French* kɔrby'zje) *n.* **Le.** See **Le Corbusier.**

Cor·by ('kɔːbɪ) *n.* a town in central England, in N Northamptonshire: designated a new town in 1950; iron and steel industry. Pop.: 47 716 (1971).

Cor·co·va·do *n.* **1.** (*Spanish* ˌkorko'βaðo). a volcano in S Chile, in the Andes. Height: 2300 m (7590 ft.). **2.** (*Portuguese* ˌkorko'vadu). a mountain in SE Brazil, in SW Rio de Janeiro city. Height: 704 m (2310 ft.).

Cor·cy·ra (kɔː'saɪərə) *n.* the ancient name for **Corfu.**

cord (kɔːd) *n.* **1.** string or thin rope made of several twisted strands. **2.** a length of woven or twisted strands of silk, etc., sewn on clothing or used as a belt. **3.** a ribbed fabric, esp. corduroy. **4.** any influence that binds or restrains. **5.** the U.S. name for **flex** (sense 1). **6.** *Anatomy.* any part resembling a string or rope: *the spinal cord.* **7.** a unit of volume for measuring cut wood, equal to 128 cubic feet. ~*vb.* (*tr.*) **8.** to bind or furnish with a cord or cords. **9.** to stack (wood) in cords. [C13: from Old French *corde,* from Latin *chorda* cord, from Greek *khordē;* see CHORD[1]] —**'cord·er** *n.* —**'cord·ˌlike** *adj.*

cord·age ('kɔːdɪdʒ) *n.* **1.** *Nautical.* the lines and rigging of a vessel. **2.** an amount of wood measured in cords.

cor·date ('kɔːdeɪt) *adj.* heart-shaped: *a cordate leaf; cordate shells.* —**'cor·date·ly** *adv.*

Cor·day (*French* kɔr'dɛ) *n.* **Char·lotte** (ʃar'lɔt), full name *Marie Anne Charlotte Corday d'Armont.* 1768–93, French Girondist revolutionary, who assassinated Marat.

cord·ed ('kɔːdɪd) *adj.* **1.** bound or fastened with cord. **2.** (of a fabric) ribbed. **3.** (of muscles) standing out like cords.

Cor·de·lier (ˌkɔːdɪ'lɪə) *n. R.C. Church.* a Franciscan friar of the order of the Friars Minor. [C19: from Old French *cordelle,* literally: a little cord, from the knotted cord girdles that they wear]

Cor·de·liers (ˌkɔːdɪ'lɪəz) *n.* **the.** a political club founded in 1790 and meeting at an old Cordelier convent in Paris.

cor·di·al ('kɔːdɪəl) *adj.* **1.** warm and friendly: *a cordial greeting.* **2.** giving heart; stimulating. ~*n.* **3.** a nonalcoholic drink with a fruit base: *lime cordial.* **4.** another word for **liqueur.** [C14: from Medieval Latin *cordiālis,* from Latin *cor* heart] —**'cor·di·al·ly** *adv.* —**'cor·di·al·ness** *n.*

cor·di·al·i·ty (ˌkɔːdɪ'ælɪtɪ) *n., pl.* **·ties.** warmth of feeling.

cor·di·er·ite ('kɔːdɪəˌraɪt) *n.* a grey or violet-blue dichroic mineral that consists of magnesium aluminium iron silicate in orthorhombic crystalline form and is found in metamorphic rocks. Formula: $(MgFe_2)Al_4Si_5O_{18}$. Also called: **dichroite, iolite.** [C19: named after Pierre L. A. *Cordier* (1777–1861), French geologist who described it]

cor·di·form ('kɔːdɪˌfɔːm) *adj.* heart-shaped. [C19: from Latin *cor* heart]

cor·dil·le·ra (ˌkɔːdɪl'jɛərə) *n.* a series of parallel ranges of mountains, esp. in the northwestern U.S. [C18: from Spanish, from *cordilla,* literally: a little cord, from *cuerda* mountain range, CORD] —ˌ**cor·dil·'le·ran** *adj.*

Cor·dil·le·ras (ˌkɔːdɪl'jɛərəz; *Spanish* ˌkorði'jeras) *pl. n.* **the.** the complex of mountain ranges on the W side of the Americas, extending from Alaska to Cape Horn and including the Andes and the Rocky Mountains.

cord·ite ('kɔːdaɪt) *n.* any of various explosive materials used for propelling bullets, shells, etc., containing cellulose nitrate, sometimes mixed with nitroglycerin, plasticizers, and stabilizers. [C19: from CORD + -ITE[1], referring to its stringy appearance]

cord·less ('kɔːdlɪs) *adj.* (of an electrical device) operated by an internal battery that is charged by the mains supply through a flex when not in use.

cor·do·ba ('kɔːdəbə) *n.* the standard monetary unit of Nicaragua, divided into 100 centavos. [Spanish *córdoba,* named in honour of Francisco Fernández de CÓRDOBA]

Cór·do·ba[1] (*Spanish* 'korðoβa) *n.* **1.** a city in central Argentina: university (1613). Pop.: 798 633 (1970). **2.** a city in S Spain, on the Guadalquivir River: centre of Moorish Spain (711–1236). Pop.: 235 632 (1970). English name: **Cordova.**

Cór·do·ba[2] *or* **Cór·do·va** (*Spanish* 'korðoβa) *n.* **Fran·cis·co Fer·nán·dez de** (fran'θisko fer'nandeθ ðe). died 1518, Spanish soldier and explorer, who discovered Yucatán.

cor·don ('kɔːdᵊn) *n.* **1.** a chain of police, soldiers, ships, etc., stationed around an area. **2.** a ribbon worn as insignia of honour or rank. **3.** a cord or ribbon worn as an ornament or fastening. **4.** Also called: **string course, belt course, table.** *Architect.* an ornamental projecting band or continuous moulding along a wall. **5.** *Horticulture.* a form of fruit tree consisting of a single stem bearing fruiting spurs, produced by cutting back all lateral branches. ~*vb.* **6.** (*tr.;* often foll. by *off*) to put or form a cordon (around); close (off). [C16: from Old French, literally: a little cord, from *corde* string, CORD]

cor·don bleu (*French* kɔrdɔ̃ 'blø) *n.* **1.** *French history.* **a.** the sky-blue ribbon worn by members of the highest order of knighthood under the Bourbon monarchy. **b.** a knight entitled to wear the cordon bleu. **2.** any very high distinction. ~*adj.* **3.** of or denoting food prepared to a very high standard. [French, literally: blue ribbon]

cor·don sa·ni·taire *French.* (kɔrdɔ̃ sani'tɛːr) *n.* **1.** a guarded line serving to cut off an infected area. **2.** a series of buffer states, esp. when protecting a nation from infiltration or attack. [C19: literally: sanitary line]

Cor·do·va ('kɔːdəvə) *n.* the English name for **Córdoba**[1] (sense 2).

cor·do·van ('kɔːdəvᵊn) *n.* a fine leather now made principally from horsehide, isolated from the skin layers above and below it and tanned. [C16: from Spanish *cordobán* (n.), from *cordobán* (adj.) of CÓRDOBA]

Cor·do·van ('kɔːdəvᵊn) *n.* **1.** a native or inhabitant of Córdoba, Spain. ~*adj.* **2.** of or relating to Córdoba, Spain.

cords (kɔːdz) *pl. n.* trousers, esp. jeans, made of corduroy.

cor·du·roy ('kɔːdəˌrɔɪ, ˌkɔːdə'rɔɪ) *n.* **a.** a heavy cotton pile fabric with lengthways ribs. **b.** (*as modifier*)*: a corduroy coat.* [C18: perhaps from the proper name *Corderoy*]

cor·du·roy road *n.* a road across swampy ground, made of logs laid transversely.

cor·du·roys (ˌkɔːdə'rɔɪz, 'kɔːdəˌrɔɪz) *pl. n.* trousers or breeches of corduroy.

cord·wain ('kɔːdˌweɪn) *n.* an archaic name for **cordovan.** [C12 *cordewan,* from Old French *cordoan,* from Old Spanish *cordovan* CORDOVAN]

cord·wain·er ('kɔːdˌweɪnə) *n. Archaic.* a shoemaker or worker in cordovan leather. —**'cord·ˌwain·er·y** *n.*

cord·wood ('kɔːdˌwʊd) *n.* wood that has been cut into lengths of four feet so that it can be stacked in cords.

core (kɔː) *n.* **1.** the central part of certain fleshy fruits, such as the apple or pear, consisting of the seeds and supporting parts. **2.** the central, innermost, or most essential part of something: *the core of the argument.* **3.** a piece of magnetic material, such as soft iron, placed inside the windings of an electromagnet or transformer to intensify and direct the magnetic field. **4.** *Geology.* the central part of the earth, beneath the mantle, consisting mainly of iron and nickel. **5.** a cylindrical sample of rock, soil, etc., obtained by the use of a hollow drill. **6.** a material placed in the inside of a mould to produce a cavity in a casting. **7.** *Physics.* the region of a nuclear reactor in which the reaction takes place. **8.** a layer of wood serving as a backing for a veneer. **9.** *Computer technol.* **a.** a ferrite ring used in a computer memory to store one bit of information. **b.** the whole memory of a computer when made up of a number of such rings. **c.** (*as modifier*)*: core memory.* **10.** *Archaeol.* a lump of stone or flint from which flakes or blades have been removed. ~*vb.* **11.** (*tr.*) to remove the core from (fruit). [C14: of uncertain origin] —**'core·less** *adj.*

CORE (kɔː) *n.* (in the U.S.) *acronym for* Congress of Racial Equality.

co·re·li·gion·ist (ˌkəʊrɪ'lɪdʒənɪst) *n.* an adherent of the same religion as another.

co·rel·la (kə'rɛlə) *n.* any of certain white Australian cockatoos of the genus *Kakatoe.* [C19: probably from native Australian *ca-rall*]

Co·rel·li (*Italian* ko'rɛlli) *n.* **Ar·can·ge·lo** (ar'kandʒelo). 1653–1713, Italian violinist and composer of sonatas and concerti grossi.

co·re·op·sis (ˌkɒrɪ'ɒpsɪs) *n.* any plant of the genus *Coreopsis,* of America and tropical Africa, cultivated for their yellow, brown, or yellow-and-red daisy-like flowers: family *Compositae* (composites). Also called: **calliopsis.** Compare **caryopsis.** [C18: from New Latin, from Greek *koris* bedbug + -OPSIS; so called from the appearance of the seed]

co-re·spond+ent (ˌkəʊrɪˈspɒndənt) *n. Law.* a person cited in divorce proceedings, alleged to have committed adultery with the respondent. —ˌ**co-re·ˈspon+den+cy** *n.*

core store *n. Computer technol.* another name for **memory** (sense 7).

core time *n.* See **flexitime.**

corf (kɔːf) *n., pl.* **corves.** *Brit.* a wagon or basket used formerly in mines. [C14: from Middle Dutch *corf* or Middle Low German *korf,* probably from Latin *corbis* basket]

Cor+fam (ˈkɔːfæm) *n. Trademark.* a synthetic water-repellent material used as a substitute for shoe leather.

Cor+fu (kɔːˈfuː) *n.* **1.** an island in the Ionian Sea, in the Ionian Islands: forms, with neighbouring islands, a department of Greece. Pop.: 92 933 (1971). Area: 641 sq. km (250 sq. miles). **2.** a port on E Corfu island. Pop.: 28 630 (1971). Modern Greek name: **Kérkyra.** ~Ancient name: **Corcyra.**

cor+gi (ˈkɔːgɪ) *n.* either of two long-bodied short-legged sturdy breeds of dog, the Cardigan and the Pembroke. Also called: **Welsh corgi.** [C20: from Welsh, from *cor* dwarf + *ci* dog]

co+ri·a+ceous (ˌkɒrɪˈeɪʃəs) *adj.* of or resembling leather. [C17: from Late Latin *coriāceus* from *corium* leather]

co+ri+an+der (ˌkɒrɪˈændə) *n.* **1.** a European umbelliferous plant, *Coriandrum sativum,* widely cultivated for its aromatic seeds. **2.** the dried ripe seeds of this plant collectively, used in flavouring food, etc. [C14: from Old French *coriandre,* from Latin *coriandrum,* from Greek *koriannon,* of uncertain origin]

Cor+inth (ˈkɒrɪnθ) *n.* **1.** a port in S Greece, in the NE Peloponnese: the modern town is near the site of the ancient city, the largest and richest of the city-states after Athens. Pop.: 20 733 (1971). Modern Greek name: **Kórinthos. 2.** a region of ancient Greece, occupying most of the Isthmus of Corinth and part of the NE Peloponnese. **3. Gulf of.** Also called: Gulf of **Lepanto.** an inlet of the Ionian Sea between the Peloponnese and central Greece. **4. Isthmus of.** a narrow strip of land between the Gulf of Corinth and the Saronic Gulf: crossed by the **Corinth Canal,** making navigation possible between the gulfs.

Co+rin+thi·an (kəˈrɪnθɪən) *adj.* **1.** of, characteristic of, or relating to Corinth. **2.** of, denoting, or relating to one of the five classical orders of architecture: characterized by a bell-shaped capital having carved ornaments based on acanthus leaves. See also **Ionic, Doric, Composite, Tuscan. 3.** given to luxury; dissolute. **4.** ornate and elaborate. ~*n.* **5.** a native or inhabitant of Corinth. **6.** an amateur sportsman. **7.** *Rare.* a man about town, esp. one who is dissolute.

Co+rin+thi·ans (kəˈrɪnθɪənz) *n.* (*functioning as sing.*) either of two books of the New Testament (in full **The First and Second Epistles of Paul the Apostle to the Corinthians**).

Cor·i·o·la·nus (ˌkɒrɪəˈleɪnəs) *n.* **Gai·us Mar·ci·us** (ˈgaɪəs ˈmɑːsɪəs). 5th century B.C., a legendary Roman general, who allegedly led an army against Rome but was dissuaded from conquering it by his mother and wife.

Cor·i·o·lis force (ˌkɒrɪˈəʊlɪs) *n.* a hypothetical force postulated to explain a deflection in the path of a body moving relative to the earth when observed from the earth. The deflection (**Coriolis effect**) is due to the earth's rotation and is to the left in the S hemisphere and to the right in the N hemisphere. [C19: named after Gaspard G. *Coriolis* (1792–1843), French civil engineer]

co+ri·um (ˈkɔːrɪəm) *n., pl.* **+ri·a** (-rɪə). **1.** Also called: **derma, dermis.** the deep inner layer of the skin, beneath the epidermis, containing connective tissue, blood vessels, and fat. **2.** *Entomol.* the leathery basal part of the forewing of hemipterous insects. [C19: from Latin: rind, skin, leather]

cork (kɔːk) *n.* **1.** the thick light porous outer bark of the cork oak, used widely as an insulator and for stoppers for bottles, casks, etc. **2.** a piece of cork or other material used as a stopper. **3.** an angling float. **4.** Also called: **phellem.** *Botany.* a protective layer of dead impermeable cells on the outside of the stems and roots of woody plants, produced by the outer layer of the cork cambium. ~*vb.* (*tr.*) **5.** to stop up (a bottle, etc.) with or as if with a cork; fit with a cork. **6.** (often foll. by *up*) to restrain: *to cork up the emotions.* **7.** to black (the face, hands, etc.) with burnt cork. [C14: probably from Arabic *qurq,* from Latin *cortex* bark, especially of the cork oak] —ˈ**cork+ˌlike** *adj.*

Cork (kɔːk) *n.* **1.** a county of SW Ireland, in Munster province: crossed by ridges of low mountains; scenic coastline. County town: Cork. Pop.: 352 883 (1971). Area: 7459 sq. km (2880 sq. miles). **2.** a port in S Ireland, county town of Co. Cork, at the mouth of the River Lee: seat of the University College of Cork (1849). Pop.: 128 645 (1971).

cork+age (ˈkɔːkɪdʒ) *n.* a charge made at a restaurant for serving wine, etc., bought off the premises.

cork+board (ˈkɔːkˌbɔːd) *n.* a thin slab made of granules of cork, used as a floor or wall finish and as an insulator.

cork cam+bi·um *n.* a layer of meristematic cells in the cortex of the stems and roots of woody plants, the outside of which gives rise to cork cells and the inside to secondary cortical cells (phelloderm). Also called: **phellogen.**

corked (kɔːkt) *adj.* **1.** Also: **corky.** (of a wine) tainted through having a cork containing excess tannin. **2.** (*postpositive*) *Brit.* a slang word for **drunk.**

cork+er (ˈkɔːkə) *n.* **1.** *Slang.* **a.** something or somebody striking or outstanding: *that was a corker of a joke.* **b.** an irrefutable remark that puts an end to discussion. **2.** a person or machine that inserts corks.

cork+ing (ˈkɔːkɪŋ) *adj.* (*prenominal*) *Brit. slang.* excellent.

cork oak *n.* an evergreen Mediterranean oak tree, *Quercus suber,* with a porous outer bark from which cork is obtained. Also called: **cork tree.**

cork+screw (ˈkɔːkˌskruː) *n.* **1.** a device for drawing corks from bottles, typically consisting of a pointed metal spiral attached to a handle or screw mechanism. **2.** *Boxing slang.* a blow that ends with a twist of the fist, esp. one intended to cut the opponent. **3.** (*modifier*) resembling a corkscrew in shape. ~*vb.* **4.** to move or cause to move in a spiral or zigzag course.

cork-tipped (ˈkɔːkˌtɪpt) *adj.* (of a cigarette) having a filter of cork or some material resembling cork.

cork+wood (ˈkɔːkˌwʊd) *n.* **1.** a small tree, *Leitneria floridana,* of the southeastern U.S., having very lightweight porous wood: family *Leitneriaceae.* **2.** any other tree with light porous wood. **3.** the wood of any of these trees.

corm (kɔːm) *n.* an organ of vegetative reproduction in plants such as the crocus, consisting of a globular stem base swollen with food and surrounded by papery scale leaves. Compare **bulb** (sense 1). [C19: from New Latin *cormus,* from Greek *kormos* tree trunk from which the branches have been lopped] —ˈ**cor+mous** *adj.*

cor+mel (ˈkɔːməl) *n.* a new small corm arising from the base of a fully developed one.

cor+mo+phyte (ˈkɔːməˌfaɪt) *n.* any of the *Cormophyta,* a major division (now obsolete) of plants having a stem, root, and leaves: includes the mosses, ferns, and seed plants. [C19: from Greek *kormos* tree trunk + -PHYTE] —**cor+mo+phyt+ic** (ˌkɔːməˈfɪtɪk) *adj.*

cor+mo+rant (ˈkɔːmərənt) *n.* any aquatic bird of the family *Phalacrocoracidae,* of coastal and inland waters, having a dark plumage, a long neck and body, and a slender hooked beak: order *Pelecaniformes* (pelicans, etc.). [C13: from Old French *cormareng,* from *corp* raven, from Latin *corvus* + *-mareng* of the sea, from Latin *mare* sea]

corn[1] (kɔːn) *n.* **1.** *Brit.* **a.** any of various cereal plants, esp. the predominant crop of a region, such as wheat in England and oats in Scotland and Ireland. **b.** the seeds of such plants, esp. after harvesting. **c.** a single seed of such plants; a grain. **2.** the usual U.S. name for **maize.** See also **sweet corn** (sense 1), **popcorn** (sense 1). **3. a.** the plants producing these kinds of grain considered as a growing crop: *spring corn.* **b.** (*in combination*): *a cornfield.* **4.** short for **corn whisky. 5.** *Slang.* an idea, song, etc., regarded as banal or sentimental. **6.** *Archaic or dialect.* any hard particle or grain. ~*vb.* (*tr.*) **7.** to feed (animals) with corn, esp. oats. **8. a.** to preserve in brine. **b.** to salt. **9.** to plant corn on. [Old English *corn;* related to Old Norse, Old High German *corn,* Gothic *kaúrn,* Latin *grānum,* Sanskrit *jīrṇá* fragile]

corn[2] (kɔːn) *n.* **1.** a hardening or thickening of the skin, esp. of the toes, caused by pressure or friction. **2. tread on (someone's) corns.** *Brit. informal.* to hurt someone's feelings. [C15: from Old French *corne* horn, from Latin *cornū*]

cor+na+ceous (kɔːˈneɪʃəs) *adj.* of, relating to, or belonging to the *Cornaceae,* a family of temperate plants, mostly trees and shrubs, including dogwood, cornel, and spotted laurel (see **laurel** (sense 5)). [C19: from New Latin *Cornaceae,* from *Cornus* genus name, from Latin: CORNEL]

corn bor+er *n.* the larva of the pyralid moth *Pyrausta nubilalis,* native to S and Central Europe: in E North America a serious pest of maize.

corn bread *n. Chiefly U.S.* a kind of bread made from maize meal. Also called: **Indian bread.**

corn bun+ting *n.* a heavily built European songbird, *Emberiza calandra,* with a streaked brown plumage: family *Emberizidae* (buntings).

corn+cob (ˈkɔːnˌkɒb) *n.* **1.** the core of an ear of maize, to which kernels are attached. **2.** short for **corncob pipe.**

corn+cob pipe *n.* a pipe made from a dried corncob.

corn+cock·le (ˈkɔːnˌkɒkᵊl) *n.* a European caryophyllaceous plant, *Agrostemma githago,* that has reddish-purple flowers and grows in cornfields and by roadsides.

corn+crake (ˈkɔːnˌkreɪk) *n.* a common Eurasian rail, *Crex crex,* of fields and meadows, with a buff speckled plumage and reddish wings.

corn+crib (ˈkɔːnˌkrɪb) *n. Chiefly U.S.* a ventilated building for the storage of unhusked maize.

cor+ne·a (ˈkɔːnɪə) *n., pl.* **+ne·as** (-nɪəs) *or* **+ne·ae** (-nɪˌiː). the convex transparent membrane that forms the anterior covering of the eyeball and is continuous with the sclera. [C14: from Medieval Latin *cornea tēla* horny web, from Latin *cornū* HORN] —ˈ**cor+ne·al** *adj.*

corn ear+worm *n. U.S.* the larva of the noctuid moth *Heliothis armigera,* which feeds on maize and many other crop plants. See also **bollworm.**

corned (kɔːnd) *adj.* (esp. of beef) cooked and then preserved or pickled in salt or brine, now often canned.

Cor+neille (*French* kɔrˈnɛj) *n.* **Pierre** (pjɛːr). 1606–84, French tragic dramatist often regarded as the founder of French classical drama. His plays include *Médée* (1635), *Le Cid* (1636), *Horace* (1640), and *Polyeucte* (1642).

cor+nel (ˈkɔːnᵊl) *n.* any cornaceous plant of the genus *Cornus,* such as the dogwood and dwarf cornel. [C16: probably from Middle Low German *kornelle,* from Old French *cornelle,* from Vulgar Latin *cornicula* (unattested), from Latin *cornum* cornel cherry, from *cornus* cornel tree]

cor+nel+i·an (kɔːˈniːlɪən) *n.* a variant spelling of **carnelian.**

cor+ne·ous (ˈkɔːnɪəs) *adj.* horny; hornlike. [C17: from Latin *corneus* horny, from *cornū* HORN]

cor+ner ('kɔːnə) *n.* **1.** the place, position, or angle formed by the meeting of two converging lines or surfaces. **2.** a projecting angle of a solid object or figure. **3.** the place where two streets meet. **4.** any small, secluded, secret, or private place. **5.** a dangerous or awkward position, esp. from which escape is difficult: *a tight corner.* **6.** any part, region or place, esp. a remote place. **7.** something used to protect or mark a corner, as of the hard cover of a book. **8.** *Commerce.* a monopoly over the supply of a commodity so that its market price can be controlled. **9.** *Soccer, hockey, etc.* a free kick or shot from the corner of the field, taken against a defending team when the ball goes out of play over their goal line after last touching one of their players. **10.** either of two opposite angles of a boxing ring in which the opponents take their rests. **11. cut corners.** to take short cuts; bypass normal channels. **12. (just) round the corner.** close at hand. **13. turn the corner.** to pass the critical point (in an illness, etc.). **14.** (*modifier*) located on a corner: *a corner shop.* **15.** (*modifier*) suitable or designed for a corner: *a corner table.* ~*vb.* **16.** (*tr.*) to manoeuvre (a person or animal) into a position from which escape is difficult or impossible: *finally they cornered the fox.* **17.** (*tr.*) to furnish or provide with corners. **18.** (*tr.*) to place in or move into a corner. **19.** (*tr.*) **a.** to acquire enough of (a commodity) to attain control of the market. **b.** Also: **engross.** to attain control of (a market) in such a manner. Compare **forestall** (sense 3). **20.** (*intr.*) (of vehicles, etc.) to turn a corner. **21.** (*intr.*) *U.S.* to be situated on a corner. **22.** (*intr.*) (in soccer, etc.) to take a corner. [C13: from Old French *corniere,* from Latin *cornū* point, extremity, HORN]

Cor+ner *n.* **the.** *Informal.* an area in central Australia, at the junction of the borders of Queensland and South Australia.

cor·ner+stone ('kɔːnəˌstəʊn) *n.* **1.** a stone at the corner of a wall, uniting two intersecting walls; quoin. **2.** a stone placed at the corner of a building during a ceremony to mark the start of construction. **3.** a person or thing of prime importance; basis: *the cornerstone of the whole argument.*

cor+net ('kɔːnɪt) *n.* **1.** Also called: **cor+net à pis+tons** ('kɔːnɪt ə 'pɪstənz; *French* kɔrnɛ a pi'stɔ̃). a three-valved brass instrument of the trumpet family. Written range: about two and a half octaves upwards from E below middle C. It is a transposing instrument in B flat or A. **2.** a person who plays the cornet. **3.** a variant spelling of **cornett. 4.** a cone-shaped paper container for sweets, etc. **5.** *Brit.* a cone-shaped wafer container for ice cream. **6.** a starched and wired muslin or lace cap worn by women from the 12th to the 15th centuries. **7.** the large white headdress of some nuns. [C14: from Old French, from *corn,* from Latin *cornū* HORN]

cor+net+cy ('kɔːnɪtsɪ) *n., pl.* **+cies.** *Obsolete.* the commission or rank of a military cornet player.

cor+net+ist *or* **cor+net+tist** (kɔː'nɛtɪst) *n.* a person who plays the cornet.

cor+nett (kɔː'nɛt) *or* **cor+net** *n.* a musical instrument consisting of a straight or curved tube of wood or ivory having finger holes like a recorder and a cup-shaped mouthpiece like a trumpet. [from Old French *cornet* a little horn, from *corn* horn, from Latin *cornū*]

corn ex+change *n.* a building where corn is bought and sold.

corn fac+tor *n.* a person who deals in corn.

corn+field ('kɔːnˌfiːld) *n.* a field planted with cereal crops.

corn+flakes ('kɔːnˌfleɪks) *pl. n.* a breakfast cereal made from toasted maize, eaten with milk, sugar, etc.

corn+flour ('kɔːnˌflaʊə) *n.* a fine starchy maize flour, used esp. for thickening sauces. U.S. name: **cornstarch.**

corn+flow·er ('kɔːnˌflaʊə) *n.* a Eurasian herbaceous plant, *Centaurea cyanus,* with blue, purple, pink, or white flowers, formerly a common weed in cornfields: family *Compositae* (composites). Also called: **bluebottle.** See also **bachelor's buttons.**

corn+husk ('kɔːnˌhʌsk) *n. U.S.* the outer protective covering of an ear of maize; the chaff.

cor+nice ('kɔːnɪs) *n.* **1.** *Architect.* **a.** the top projecting mouldings of an entablature. **b.** a continuous horizontal projecting course or moulding at the top of a wall, building, etc. **2.** an overhanging ledge of snow, esp. on the lee side of a mountain. ~*vb.* **3.** (*tr.*) *Architect.* to furnish or decorate with or as if with a cornice. [C16: from Old French, from Italian, perhaps from Latin *cornix* crow, but influenced also by Latin *corōnis* decorative flourish used by scribes, from Greek *korōnis,* from *korōnē* curved object, CROWN]

cor+niche ('kɔːnɪʃ) *n.* a coastal road, esp. one built into the face of a cliff. [C19: from *corniche road,* originally the coastal road between Nice and Monte Carlo; see CORNICE]

cor+nic·u+late (kɔː'nɪkjʊˌleɪt, -lɪt) *adj.* **1.** having horns or hornlike projections. **2.** relating to or resembling a horn. [C17: from Latin *corniculātus* horned, from *corniculum* a little horn, from *cornū* HORN]

Cor+nish ('kɔːnɪʃ) *adj.* **1.** of, relating to, or characteristic of Cornwall, its inhabitants, their former language, or their present-day dialect of English. ~*n.* **2.** a former language of Cornwall, belonging to the S Celtic branch of the Indo-European family and closely related to Breton: extinct by 1800. **3. the.** (*functioning as pl.*) the natives or inhabitants of Cornwall. —**'Cor+nish+man** *n.*

Cor+nish pas+ty *n. Cookery.* a pastry case with a filling of meat and vegetables.

Cor+nish split *n.* another term for **Devonshire split.**

Corn Laws *pl. n.* the laws introduced in Britain in 1804 to protect domestic farmers against foreign competition by the imposition of a heavy duty on foreign corn: repealed in 1846. See also **Anti-Corn Law League.**

corn lil·y *n.* any of several South African iridaceous plants of the genus *Ixia,* which have coloured lily-like flowers.

corn mar·i+gold *n.* an annual plant, *Chrysanthemum segetum,* with yellow daisy-like flower heads: a common weed of cultivated land: family *Compositae* (composites).

corn meal *n.* meal made from maize. Also called: **Indian meal.**

Cor+no (*Italian* 'korno) *n.* **Mon+te** ('monte). a mountain in central Italy: the highest peak in the Apennines. Height: 2912 m (9554 ft.).

corn oil *n.* an oil prepared from maize, used in cooking and in making soaps, lubricants, etc.

corn on the cob *n.* a cob of maize, boiled and eaten as a vegetable.

corn-pick·er *n. Chiefly U.S.* a machine for removing ears of maize from the standing stalks, often also equipped to separate the corn from the husk and shell.

corn pone *n. Southern U.S.* corn bread, esp. a plain type made with water. Sometimes shortened to **pone.**

corn pop+py *n.* a poppy, *Papaver rhoeas,* that has bright red flowers and grows in cornfields. Since World War I it has been the symbol of fallen soldiers. Also called: **coquelicot, Flanders poppy, field poppy.**

corn rose *n. Brit., archaic.* any of several red-flowered weeds of cornfields, such as the corn poppy.

corn row (rəʊ) *n.* a Caribbean Negro hair style in which the hair is plaited in close parallel rows, resembling furrows in a ploughed field.

corn sal+ad *n.* any valerianaceous plant of the genus *Valerianella,* esp. the European species *V. locusta,* which often grows in cornfields and whose leaves are sometimes used in salads. Also called: **lamb's lettuce.**

corn shock *n.* a stack or bundle of bound or unbound corn piled upright for curing or drying.

corn shuck *n. U.S.* the husk of an ear of maize.

corn silk *n. U.S.* the silky tuft of styles and stigmas at the tip of an ear of maize, formerly used as a diuretic.

corn smut *n.* **1.** an ascomycetous parasitic fungus, *Ustilago zeae,* that causes gall-like deformations on maize grain. **2.** the condition produced by this fungus.

corn snow *n. Skiing, U.S.* granular snow formed by alternate freezing and thawing.

corn+stalk ('kɔːnˌstɔːk) *n.* **1.** a stalk or stem of corn. **2.** *Austral. slang.* **a.** (*often cap.*) a native Australian. **b.** a tall thin man.

corn+starch ('kɔːnˌstɑːtʃ) *n.* the U.S. name for **cornflour.**

corn+stone ('kɔːnˌstəʊn) *n.* a mottled green and red limestone.

corn syr+up *n. U.S.* syrup prepared from maize.

cor+nu ('kɔːnjuː) *n., pl.* **+nu·a** (-njʊə). *Anatomy.* a part or structure resembling a horn or having a hornlike pattern, such as a cross section of the grey matter of the spinal cord. [C17: from Latin: a horn] —**'cor+nu·al** *adj.*

cor+nu+co+pi·a (ˌkɔːnjʊ'kəʊpɪə) *n.* **1.** *Greek myth.* the horn of Amalthea, the goat that suckled Zeus. **2.** a representation of such a horn in painting, sculpture, etc., overflowing with fruit, vegetables, etc.; horn of plenty. **3.** a great abundance; overflowing supply. **4.** a horn-shaped container. [C16: from Late Latin, from Latin *cornū cōpiae* horn of plenty] —**ˌcor+nu+'co+pi·an** *adj.*

cor+nute (kɔː'njuːt) *or* **cor+nut+ed** *adj. Biology.* having or resembling cornua; hornlike: *the cornute process of a bone.* [C17: from Latin *cornūtus* horned, from *cornū* HORN]

Corn+wall ('kɔːnˌwɔːl, -wəl) *n.* a county of SW England, including the Scilly Isles: hilly, with a deeply indented coastline. County town: Truro. Pop.: 407 100 (1976 est.). Area: 3514 sq. km (1357 sq. miles).

Corn·wal·lis (kɔːn'wɒlɪs) *n.* **Charles,** 1st Marquis Cornwallis. 1738–1805, British general in the War of American Independence: commanded forces defeated at Yorktown (1781); governor general of India (1786–93, 1805).

corn whis+ky *n.* whisky made from maize.

corn·y ('kɔːnɪ) *adj.* **corn·i+er, corn·i+est.** *Slang.* **1.** trite or banal. **2.** sentimental or mawkish. **3.** abounding in corn. [C16 (C20 in the sense rustic, banal): from CORN¹ + -Y¹]

cor·o·dy *or* **cor+ro+dy** ('kɒrədɪ) *n., pl.* **+dies.** *History.* **1.** (originally) the right of a lord to receive free quarters from his vassal. **2.** an allowance for maintenance. [C15: from Medieval Latin *corrōdium* something provided, from Old French *corroyer* to provide, of Germanic origin]

corol. *or* **coroll.** *abbrev. for* corollary.

co+rol+la (kə'rɒlə) *n.* the petals of a flower collectively, forming an inner floral envelope. Compare **calyx.**

cor+ol+la+ceous (ˌkɒrə'leɪʃəs) *adj.* of, relating to, resembling, or having a corolla.

cor+ol+lar·y (kə'rɒlərɪ) *n., pl.* **+lar·ies.** **1.** a proposition that follows directly from the proof of another proposition. **2.** an obvious deduction. **3.** a natural consequence or result. ~*adj.* **4.** consequent or resultant. [C14: from Latin *corollārium* money paid for a garland, from Latin *corolla* garland, from *corōna* CROWN]

Cor·o·man+del Coast (ˌkɒrə'mændəl) *n.* the SE coast of India, along the Bay of Bengal, extending from Point Calimere to the mouth of the Krishna River.

co+ro+na (kə'rəʊnə) *n., pl.* **+nas** *or* **+nae** (-niː). **1.** a circle of light around a luminous body, usually the moon. **2.** Also called: **aureole.** the outermost region of the sun's atmosphere, visible as a faint halo during a solar eclipse. **3.** *Architect.* the flat vertical face of a cornice just above the soffit. **4.** something resembling a corona or halo. **5.** a circular chandelier suspended from the roof of a church. **6.** *Botany.* **a.** the trumpet-shaped part of the corolla of daffodils and similar plants; the crown. **b.**

a crown of leafy outgrowths from inside the petals of some flowers. **7.** *Anatomy.* a crownlike structure, such as the top of the head. **8.** a long cigar with blunt ends. **9.** *Physics.* short for **corona discharge.** [C16: from Latin: crown, from Greek *korōne* anything curved; related to Greek *korōnis* wreath, *korax* crow, Latin *curvus* curved]

Co·ro·na Aus·tra·lis (ɒ'streɪlɪs) *n., Latin genitive* **Co·ro·nae Aus·tra·lis** (kə'rəuni:). a small faint constellation in the S hemisphere between Ara and Pavo. [literally: Southern crown]

Co·ro·na Bo·re·al·is (ˌbɔ:rɪ'eɪlɪs) *n., Latin genitive* **Co·ro·nae Bo·re·al·is** (kə'rəuni:). a small compact constellation in the N hemisphere lying between Boötes and Hercules. [literally: Northern crown]

co·ro·nach ('kɒrənək) *n. Scot. or Irish.* a dirge or lamentation for the dead. [C16: from Scottish Gaelic *corranach;* related to Irish *rānadh* a crying]

co·ro·na dis·charge *n.* an electrical discharge appearing on and around the surface of a charged conductor, caused by ionization of the surrounding gas. Also called: **corona.** See also **Saint Elmo's fire.**

co·ro·na·graph *or* **co·ro·no·graph** (kə'rəunəˌgrɑ:f, -ˌgræf) *n.* an optical instrument used to simulate an eclipse of the sun so that the faint solar corona can be studied.

cor·o·nal *n.* ('kɒrən^{ə}l). **1.** *Poetic.* a circlet for the head; crown. **2.** a wreath or garland. **3.** *Anatomy.* short for **coronal suture.** ~*adj.* (kə'rəun^{ə}l). **4.** of or relating to a corona or coronal. **5.** *Phonetics.* a less common word for **retroflex.** [C16: from Late Latin *corōnālis* belonging to a CROWN]

cor·o·nal su·ture *n.* the serrated line across the skull between the frontal bone and the parietal bones.

cor·o·nar·y ('kɒrənərɪ) *adj.* **1.** *Anatomy.* designating blood vessels, nerves, ligaments, etc., that encircle a part or structure. ~*n., pl.* **·nar·ies. 2.** short for **coronary thrombosis.** [C17: from Latin *corōnārius* belonging to a wreath or crown; see CORONA]

cor·o·nar·y ar·ter·y *n.* either of two arteries branching from the aorta and supplying blood to the heart.

cor·o·nar·y in·suf·fi·cien·cy *n.* inadequate circulation of blood through the coronary arteries, characterized by attacks of angina pectoris.

cor·o·nar·y throm·bo·sis *n.* a condition of interrupted blood flow to the heart due to a blood clot in a coronary artery, usually as a consequence of atherosclerosis: characterized by intense pain. Sometimes shortened to: **coronary.** Compare **myocardial infarction.**

cor·o·na·tion (ˌkɒrə'neɪʃən) *n.* the act or ceremony of crowning a monarch. [C14: from Old French, from *coroner* to crown, from Latin *corōnāre*]

cor·o·ner ('kɒrənə) *n.* a public official responsible for the investigation of violent, sudden, or suspicious deaths. The investigation (**coroner's inquest**) is held in the presence of a jury (**coroner's jury**). See also **procurator fiscal.** Compare **medical examiner.** [C14: from Anglo-French *corouner* officer in charge of the pleas of the Crown, from Old French *corone* CROWN] —**'cor·o·ner·ˌship** *n.*

cor·o·net ('kɒrənɪt) *n.* **1.** any small crown, esp. one worn by princes or peers as a mark of rank. **2.** a woman's jewelled circlet for the head. **3.** the margin between the skin of a horse's pastern and the horn of the hoof. **4.** *Heraldry.* a support for a crest shaped like a crown. [C15: from Old French *coronete* a little crown, from *corone* CROWN]

cor·o·net·ed (ˌkɒrə'nɛtɪd) *adj.* **1.** wearing a coronet. **2.** belonging to the peerage.

Co·rot (*French* kɔ'ro) *n.* **Jean Bap·tiste Ca·mille** (ʒɑ̃ batist ka'mij). 1796–1875, French landscape painter.

co·ro·zo (kə'rəuzəu) *n., pl.* **·zos.** a tropical American palm, *Corozo oleifera,* whose seeds yield a useful oil. [C18: via Spanish from an Indian name]

corp. *abbrev. for:* **1.** corporation. **2.** corporal.

cor·po·ra ('kɔ:pərə) *n.* the plural of **corpus.**

cor·po·ral[1] ('kɔ:pərəl, 'kɔ:prəl) *adj.* **1.** of or relating to the body; bodily. **2.** an obsolete word for **corporeal.** [C14: from Latin *corporālis* of the body, from *corpus* body] —**ˌcor·po·'ral·i·ty** *n.* —**'cor·po·ral·ly** *adv.*

cor·po·ral[2] ('kɔ:pərəl, -prəl) *n.* **1.** a noncommissioned officer junior to a sergeant in the army, air force, or marines. **2.** (in the Royal Navy) a petty officer who assists the master-at-arms. [C16: from Old French, via Italian, from Latin *caput* head; perhaps also influenced in Old French by *corps* body (of men)] —**'cor·po·ral·ˌship** *n.*

cor·po·ral[3] ('kɔ:pərəl, -prəl) *or* **cor·po·ra·le** (ˌkɔ:pə'reɪlɪ) *n.* a white linen cloth on which the bread and wine are placed during the Eucharist. [C14: from Medieval Latin *corporāle pallium* eucharistic altar cloth, from Latin *corporālis* belonging to the body, from *corpus* body (of Christ)]

cor·por·al pun·ish·ment *n.* punishment of a physical nature, such as caning, flogging, or beating.

cor·po·rate ('kɔ:pərɪt, -prɪt) *adj.* **1.** forming a corporation; incorporated. **2.** of or belonging to a corporation. **3.** of or belonging to a united group; joint. [C15: from Latin *corporātus* made into a body, from *corporāre,* from *corpus* body] —**'cor·po·rate·ly** *adv.* —**'cor·po·rat·ism** *n.*

cor·po·ra·tion (ˌkɔ:pə'reɪʃən) *n.* **1.** an association of persons having a separate identity, with separate powers, duties, and liabilities. **2.** Also called: **municipal corporation.** the municipal authorities of a city or town. **3.** a group of people acting as one body. **4.** *Brit. informal.* a large paunch or belly.

cor·po·ra·tive ('kɔ:pərətɪv, -prətɪv) *adj.* **1.** of or characteristic of a corporation. **2.** (of a state) organized into and governed by corporations of individuals involved in any given profession, industry, etc.

cor·po·ra·tor ('kɔ:pəˌreɪtə) *n.* a member of a corporation.

cor·po·re·al (kɔ:'pɔ:rɪəl) *adj.* **1.** of the nature of the physical body; not spiritual. **2.** of a material nature; physical. [C17: from Latin *corporeus,* from *corpus* body] —**cor·ˌpo·re·'al·i·ty** *or* **cor·'po·re·al·ness** *n.* —**cor·'po·re·al·ly** *adv.*

cor·po·re·i·ty (ˌkɔ:pə'ri:ɪtɪ) *n.* bodily or material nature or substance; physical existence; corporeality.

cor·po·sant ('kɔ:pəˌzænt) *n.* another name for **Saint Elmo's fire.** [C17: from Portuguese *corpo-santo,* literally: holy body, from Latin *corpus sanctum*]

corps (kɔ:) *n., pl.* **corps** (kɔ:z). **1.** a military formation that comprises two or more divisions and additional support arms. **2.** a body of people associated together: *the diplomatic corps.* [C18: from French, from Latin *corpus* body]

corps de bal·let ('kɔ: də 'bæleɪ; *French* kɔr də ba'lɛ) *n.* the members of a ballet company who dance together in a group.

corps dip·lo·ma·tique (ˌdɪpləumæ'ti:k) *n.* another name for **diplomatic corps.** Abbrev.: **C.D., CD.**

corpse (kɔ:ps) *n.* a dead body, esp. of a human being; cadaver. [C14: from Old French *corps* body, from Latin *corpus* body]

corps·man ('kɔ:mən) *n., pl.* **·men.** *U.S. military.* a medical orderly or stretcher-bearer.

cor·pu·lent ('kɔ:pjulənt) *adj.* physically bulky; fat. [C14: from Latin *corpulentus* fleshy] —**'cor·pu·lence** *or* **'cor·pu·len·cy** *n.* —**'cor·pu·lent·ly** *adv.*

cor·pus ('kɔ:pəs) *n., pl.* **·po·ra** (-pərə). **1.** a collection or body of writings, esp. by a single author or on a specific topic: *the corpus of Dickens' works.* **2.** the main body, section, or substance of something. **3.** *Anatomy.* **a.** any distinct mass or body. **b.** the main part of an organ or structure. **4.** a capital or principal sum, as contrasted with a derived income. **5.** *Obsolete.* a human or animal body, esp. a dead one. [C14: from Latin: body]

cor·pus cal·lo·sum (kə'ləusəm) *n., pl.* **cor·po·ra cal·lo·sa** (kə'ləusə). the band of white fibres that connects the cerebral hemispheres in mammals. [New Latin, literally: callous body]

Cor·pus Chris·ti[1] ('krɪstɪ) *n. Chiefly R.C. Church.* a festival in honour of the Eucharist, observed on the Thursday after Trinity Sunday. [C14: from Latin: body of Christ]

Cor·pus Chris·ti[2] ('krɪstɪ) *n.* a port in S Texas, on **Corpus Christi Bay,** an inlet of the Gulf of Mexico. Pop.: 212 431 (1973 est.).

cor·pus·cle ('kɔ:pʌs^{ə}l) *n.* **1.** any cell or similar minute body that is suspended in a fluid, esp. any of the **red blood corpuscles** (see **erythrocyte**) or **white blood corpuscles** (see **leucocyte**). **2.** *Anatomy.* the encapsulated ending of a sensory nerve. **3.** *Physics.* a discrete particle such as an electron, photon, ion, or atom. **4.** Also: **corpuscule.** any minute particle. [C17: from Latin *corpusculum* a little body, from *corpus* body] —**cor·pus·cu·lar** (kɔ:'pʌskjulə) *adj.*

cor·pus·cu·lar the·o·ry *n.* the theory, originally proposed by Newton, and revived with the development of the quantum theory, that light consists of a stream of particles. See **photon.** ~Compare **wave theory.**

cor·pus de·lic·ti (dɪ'lɪktaɪ) *n. Law.* the body of facts that constitute an offence. [New Latin, literally: the body of the crime]

cor·pus ju·ris ('dʒuərɪs) *n.* a body of law, esp. the laws of a nation or state. [from Late Latin, literally: a body of law]

Cor·pus Ju·ris Ca·no·ni·ci (kə'nɒnɪˌsaɪ) *n. R.C. Church.* the principal compilation of canon law from 1499, superseded by the Codex Juris Canonici in 1918. [Medieval Latin, literally: body of canon law]

Cor·pus Ju·ris Ci·vi·lis (sɪ'vaɪlɪs) *n. Law.* the body of Roman or civil law consolidated by Justinian in the sixth century A.D. [New Latin, literally: body of civil law]

cor·pus lu·te·um ('lu:tɪəm) *n., pl.* **cor·po·ra lu·te·a** ('lu:tɪə). a yellow glandular mass of tissue that forms in a Graafian follicle following release of an ovum. It secretes progesterone, a hormone necessary to maintain pregnancy. [New Latin, literally: yellow body]

cor·pus lu·te·um hor·mone *n.* another name for **progesterone.**

cor·pus stri·a·tum (straɪ'eɪtəm) *n., pl.* **cor·po·ra stri·a·ta** (straɪ'eɪtə). a striped mass of white and grey matter situated in front of the thalamus in each cerebral hemisphere. [New Latin, literally: striated body]

cor·pus vi·le ('kɔ:pəs 'vaɪlɪ) *n., pl.* **cor·po·ra vil·i·a** ('kɔ:pərə 'vɪlɪə) *Latin.* a person or thing fit only to be the object of an experiment. [literally: worthless body]

corr. *abbrev. for:* **1.** correct. **2.** corrected. **3.** correction. **4.** correspondence. **5.** correspondent. **6.** corresponding.

cor·rade (kɒ'reɪd) *vb.* (of rivers, streams, etc.) to erode (land) by the abrasive action of rock particles. [C17: from Latin *corrādere* to scrape together, from *rādere* to scrape]

cor·ral (kɒ'rɑ:l) *n.* **1.** *Chiefly U.S.* an enclosure for confining cattle or horses. **2.** *Chiefly U.S.* (formerly) a defensive enclosure formed by a ring of covered wagons. ~*vb.* **·rals, ·ral·ling, ·ralled.** (*tr.*) *U.S.* **3.** to drive into and confine in or as in a corral. **4.** *Informal.* to capture. [C16: from Spanish, from Vulgar Latin *currāle* (unattested) area for vehicles, from Latin *currus* wagon, from *currere* to run]

cor·ra·sion (kə'reɪʒən) *n.* erosion of a rock surface by rock fragments transported over it by water, wind, or ice. Compare **abrasion** (sense 3), **attrition** (sense 3). —**cor·ra·sive** (kə'reɪsɪv) *adj.*

cor+rect (kəˈrɛkt) *vb.* (*tr.*) **1.** to make free from errors. **2.** to indicate the errors in. **3.** to rebuke or punish in order to set right or improve: *to correct a child; to stand corrected.* **4.** to counteract or rectify (a malfunction, ailment, etc.): *these glasses will correct your sight.* **5.** to adjust or make conform, esp. to a standard. ~*adj.* **6.** free from error; true; accurate: *the correct version.* **7.** in conformity with accepted standards: *correct behaviour.* [C14: from Latin *corrigere* to make straight, put in order, from *com-* (intensive) + *regere* to rule] —**corˈrect·a·ble** *or* **corˈrect·i·ble** *adj.* —**corˈrect·ly** *adv.* —**corˈrect·ness** *n.* —**corˈrec·tor** *n.*

cor+rec+tion (kəˈrɛkʃən) *n.* **1.** the act or process of correcting. **2.** something offered or substituted for an error; an improvement. **3.** the act or process of punishing; reproof. **4.** a number or quantity added to or subtracted from a scientific or mathematical calculation or observation to increase its accuracy. —**corˈrec·tion·al** *adj.*

cor+rect·i+tude (kəˈrɛktɪˌtjuːd) *n.* the quality of correctness, esp. conscious correctness in behaviour.

cor+rec+tive (kəˈrɛktɪv) *adj.* **1.** tending or intended to correct. ~*n.* **2.** something that tends or is intended to correct. —**corˈrec·tive·ly** *adv.*

Cor·reg·gio (*Italian* korˈrɛddʒo) *n.* **An·to·nio Al·le·gri da** (anˈtɔːnjo aˈleːgri da). 1494–1534, Italian painter, noted for his striking use of perspective and foreshortening.

Cor+reg·i+dor (kəˈrɛgɪˌdɔː) *n.* an island at the entrance to Manila Bay, in the Philippines: site of the defeat of American forces by the Japanese (1942) in World War II.

correl. *abbrev. for* correlative.

cor+re+late (ˈkɒrɪˌleɪt) *vb.* **1.** to place or be placed in a mutual, complementary, or reciprocal relationship. **2.** (*tr.*) to establish or show a correlation. ~*adj.* **3.** having a mutual, complementary, or reciprocal relationship. ~*n.* **4.** either of two things mutually or reciprocally related. —ˈ**cor·re·ˌlat·a·ble** *adj.*

cor+re+la+tion (ˌkɒrɪˈleɪʃən) *n.* **1.** a mutual or reciprocal relationship between two or more things. **2.** the act or process of correlating or the state of being correlated. **3.** *Statistics.* the degree of quantitative association between two variables or attributes. Correlation is positive or direct when two variables move in the same direction and negative or inverse when they move in opposite directions. [C16: from Medieval Latin *correlātiō*, from *com-* together + *relātiō*, RELATION] —ˌ**cor·reˈla·tion·al** *adj.*

cor+re+la+tion co+ef+fi+cient *n. Statistics.* a statistic measuring the degree of correlation between two variables and usually obtained by dividing their covariance by the square root of the product of their variances.

cor+rel·a+tive (kɒˈrɛlətɪv) *adj.* **1.** in mutual, complementary, or reciprocal relationship; corresponding. **2.** denoting words, usually conjunctions, occurring together though not adjacently in certain grammatical constructions, as for example *neither* and *nor* in such sentences as *he neither ate nor drank.* ~*n.* **3.** either of two things that are correlative. **4.** a correlative word. —**corˈrel·a·tive·ly** *adv.* —**corˈrel·a·tive·ness** *or* **corˌrel·aˈtiv·i·ty** *n.*

cor+re+spond (ˌkɒrɪˈspɒnd) *vb.* (*intr.*) **1.** (usually foll. by *with* or *to*) to conform, be in agreement, or be consistent or compatible (with); tally (with). **2.** (usually foll. by *to*) to be similar or analogous in character or function. **3.** (usually foll. by *with*) to communicate by letter. [C16: from Medieval Latin *correspondēre*, from Latin *respondēre* to RESPOND] —ˌ**cor·reˈspond·ing·ly** *adv.*
Usage. See at **similar.**

cor+re+spond+ence (ˌkɒrɪˈspɒndəns) *n.* **1.** the act or condition of agreeing or corresponding. **2.** similarity or analogy. **3.** agreement or conformity. **4. a.** communication by the exchange of letters. **b.** the letters so exchanged.

cor+re+spond+ence col+umn *n.* a section of a newspaper or magazine in which are printed readers' letters to the editor.

cor+re+spond+ence school *n.* an educational institution that offers tuition (**correspondence courses**) by post.

cor+re+spond+ent (ˌkɒrɪˈspɒndənt) *n.* **1.** a person who communicates by letter or by letters. **2.** a person employed by a newspaper, etc., to report on a special subject or to send reports from a foreign country. **3.** a person or firm that has regular business relations with another, esp. one in a different part of the country or abroad. **4.** something that corresponds to another. ~*adj.* **5.** similar or analogous. —ˌ**cor·reˈspond·ent·ly** *adv.*

Cor+rèze (*French* kɔˈrɛːz) *n.* a department of central France, in Limousin region. Capital: Tulle. Pop.: 250 559 (1975). Area: 5888 sq. km (2296 sq. miles).

cor+ri+da (koˈrriða) *n.* the Spanish word for **bullfight.** [Spanish, from the phrase *corrida de toros,* literally: a running of bulls, from *correr* to run, from Latin *currere*]

cor+ri+dor (ˈkɒrɪˌdɔː) *n.* **1.** a hallway or passage connecting parts of a building. **2.** a strip of land or air space that affords access, either from a landlocked country to the sea (such as the **Polish corridor,** 1919-39, which divided Germany) or from a state to an exclave (such as the **Berlin corridor,** since 1945, which passes through East Germany). **3.** a passageway connecting the compartments of a railway coach. **4. corridors of power.** the higher echelons of government, the Civil Service, etc., considered as the location of power and influence. [C16: from Old French, from Old Italian *corridore,* literally: place for running, from *correre* to run, from Latin *currere*]

cor+rie (ˈkɒrɪ) *n.* **1.** (in Scotland) a circular hollow on a hillside. **2.** *Geology.* another name for **cirque** (sense 1). [C18: from Gaelic *coire* cauldron, kettle]

Cor+rie+dale (ˈkɒrɪˌdeɪl) *n.* a breed of sheep reared for both wool and meat, originally developed in New Zealand.

Cor+rien+tes (*Spanish* ˌkoˈrrjentes) *n.* a port in NE Argentina, on the Paraná River. Pop.: 131 392 (1970).

cor+ri+gen+dum (ˌkɒrɪˈdʒɛndəm) *n., pl.* **·da** (-də). **1.** an error to be corrected. **2.** (*sometimes pl.*) Also called **erratum.** a slip of paper inserted into a book after printing, listing errors and corrections. [C19: from Latin: that which is to be corrected, from *corrigere* to CORRECT]

cor+ri+gi+ble (ˈkɒrɪdʒɪbᵊl) *adj.* **1.** capable of being corrected. **2.** submissive or submitting to correction. [C15: from Old French, from Medieval Latin *corrigibilis,* from Latin *corrigere* to set right, CORRECT] —ˌ**cor·ri·giˈbil·i·ty** *n.* —ˈ**cor·ri·gi·bly** *adv.*

cor+ri+val (kəˈraɪvᵊl) *n., vb.* a rare word for **rival.** [C16: from Old French, from Late Latin *corrīvālis,* from Latin *com-* together, mutually + *rīvālis* RIVAL] —**corˈri·val·ry** *n.*

cor+rob·o+rant (kəˈrɒbərənt) *Archaic.* ~*adj.* **1.** serving to corroborate. **2.** strengthening. ~*n.* **3.** something that strengthens; tonic.

cor+rob·o+rate *vb.* (kəˈrɒbəˌreɪt). **1.** (*tr.*) to confirm or support (facts, opinions, etc.), esp. by providing fresh evidence: *the witness corroborated the accused's statement.* ~*adj.* (kəˈrɒbərɪt). *Archaic.* **2.** serving to corroborate a fact, etc. **3.** (of a fact) corroborated. [C16: from Latin *corrōborāre* to invigorate, from *rōborāre* to make strong, from *rōbur* strength, literally: oak] —**corˌrob·oˈra·tion** *n.* —**corˈrob·o·ra·tive** (kəˈrɒbərətɪv) *adj.* —**corˈrob·o·ra·tive·ly** *adv.* —**corˈrob·oˌra·tor** *n.*

cor+rob·o+ree (kəˈrɒbərɪ) *n. Austral.* **1.** a native assembly of sacred, festive, or warlike character. **2.** any noisy gathering. [C19: from a native Australian language]

cor+rode (kəˈrəʊd) *vb.* **1.** to eat away or be eaten away, esp. by chemical action as in the oxidation or rusting of a metal. **2.** (*tr.*) to destroy gradually; consume: *his jealousy corroded his happiness.* [C14: from Latin *corrōdere* to gnaw to pieces, from *rōdere* to gnaw; see RODENT, RAT] —**corˈrod·ant** *or* **corˈrod·ent** *n.* —**corˈrod·er** *n.* —**corˈrod·i·ble** *adj.* —**corˌrod·i·ˈbil·i·ty** *n.*

cor+ro+dy (ˈkɒrədɪ) *n., pl.* **·dies.** a variant spelling of **corody.**

cor+ro+sion (kəˈrəʊʒən) *n.* **1.** a process in which a solid, esp. a metal, is eaten away and changed by a chemical action, as in the oxidation of iron in the presence of water by an electrolytic process. **2.** slow deterioration by being eaten or worn away. **3.** the condition produced by or the product of corrosion.

cor+ro+sive (kəˈrəʊsɪv) *adj.* **1.** (esp. of acids or alkalis) capable of destroying solid materials. **2.** tending to eat away or consume. **3.** cutting; sarcastic: *a corrosive remark.* ~*n.* **4.** a corrosive substance, such as a strong acid or alkali. —**corˈro·sive·ly** *adv.* —**corˈro·sive·ness** *n.*

cor+ro+sive sub+li+mate *n.* another name for **mercuric chloride.**

cor+ru+gate *vb.* (ˈkɒrʊˌgeɪt). **1.** (*usually tr.*) to fold or be folded into alternate furrows and ridges. ~*adj.* (ˈkɒrʊgɪt, -ˌgeɪt). **2.** folded into furrows and ridges; wrinkled. [C18: from Latin *corrūgāre,* from *rūga* a wrinkle] —ˌ**cor·ruˈga·tion** *n.*

cor+ru+gat+ed i·ron *n.* a thin structural sheet made of iron or steel, formed with alternating ridges and troughs.

cor+ru+gat+ed pa+per *n.* a packaging material made from layers of heavy paper, the top layer of which is grooved and ridged.

cor+ru+ga+tor (ˈkɒrʊˌgeɪtə) *n.* a muscle whose contraction causes wrinkling of the brow.

cor+rupt (kəˈrʌpt) *adj.* **1.** lacking in integrity; open to or involving bribery or other dishonest practices: *a corrupt official; corrupt practices in an election.* **2.** morally depraved. **3.** putrid or rotten. **4.** contaminated; unclean. **5.** (of a text or manuscript) made meaningless or different in meaning from the original by scribal errors or alterations. ~*vb.* **6.** to become or cause to become dishonest or disloyal. **7.** to debase or become debased morally; deprave. **8.** (*tr.*) to infect or contaminate; taint. **9.** (*tr.*) to cause to become rotten. **10.** (*tr.*) to alter (a text, etc.) from the original. [C14: from Latin *corruptus* spoiled, from *corrumpere* to ruin, literally: break to pieces, from *rumpere* to break] —**corˈrupt·er** *or* **corˈrup·tor** *n.* —**corˈrup·tive** *adj.* —**corˈrup·tive·ly** *adv.* —**corˈrupt·ly** *adv.* —**corˈrupt·ness** *n.*

cor+rup+ti·ble (kəˈrʌptəbᵊl) *adj.* susceptible to corruption; capable of being corrupted. —**corˌrupt·iˈbil·i·ty** *or* **corˈrupt·i·ble·ness** *n.* —**corˈrupt·i·bly** *adv.*

cor+rup+tion (kəˈrʌpʃən) *n.* **1.** the act of corrupting or state of being corrupt. **2.** moral perversion; depravity. **3.** dishonesty, esp. bribery. **4.** putrefaction or decay. **5.** alteration, as of a manuscript. **6.** an altered form of a word. —**corˈrup·tion·ist** *n.*

cor+sac (ˈkɔːsæk) *n.* a fox, *Vulpes corsac,* of central Asia. [C19: from a Turkic language]

cor+sage (kɔːˈsɑːʒ) *n.* **1.** a flower or small bunch of flowers worn pinned to the lapel, bosom, etc., or sometimes carried by women. **2.** the bodice of a dress. [C15: from Old French, from *cors* body, from Latin *corpus*]

cor+sair (ˈkɔːsɛə) *n.* **1.** a pirate. **2.** a privateer, esp. of the Barbary Coast. [C15: from Old French *corsaire* pirate, from Medieval Latin *cursārius,* from Latin *cursus* a running, COURSE]

corse (kɔːs) *n.* an archaic word for **corpse.**

Corse (kɔrs) *n.* the French name for **Corsica.**

corse+let (ˈkɔːslɪt) *n.* **1.** Also spelt: **corslet.** a piece of armour for the top part of the body. **2.** a one-piece foundation garment, usually combining a brassiere and a corset. [C15: from Old

French, from *cors* bodice of a garment, from Latin *corpus* body]

cor·set ('kɔ:sɪt) *n.* **1. a.** a stiffened, elasticated, or laced foundation garment, worn esp. by women, that extends from below the chest to the hips and provides support for the spine and stomach. **b.** a similar garment worn because of injury, weakness, etc., by either sex. **2.** a stiffened outer bodice worn by either sex, esp. in the 16th century. ~*vb.* **3.** (*tr.*) to dress or enclose in, or as in, a corset. [C14: from Old French, literally: a little bodice; see CORSELET]

cor·se·tière (ˌkɔ:sɛtɪ'ɛə, kɔ:ˌsɛt-) *or* (*masc.*) **cor·se·tier** (ˌkɔ:sɪ'tɪə) *n.* a person who makes and fits corsets.

cor·set·ry ('kɔ:sɪtrɪ) *n.* **1.** the making of or dealing in corsets. **2.** corsets considered collectively.

Cor·si·ca ('kɔ:sɪkə) *n.* an island in the Mediterranean, west of N Italy: forms, with 43 islets, a region of France; mountainous; settled by Greeks in about 560 B.C.; sold by Genoa to France in 1768. Capital: Ajaccio. Pop.: 277 856 (1975). Area: 8722 sq. km (3367 sq. miles). French name: **Corse.** —'**Cor·si·can** *adj., n.*

cor·tege *or* **cor·tège** (kɔ:'teɪʒ) *n.* **1.** a formal procession, esp. a funeral procession. **2.** a train of attendants; retinue. [C17: from French, from Italian *corteggio*, from *corteggiare* to attend, from *corte* COURT]

Cor·tes ('kɔ:tɛz; *Spanish* 'kortes) *n.* the national assembly of Spain or Portugal. [C17: from Spanish, literally: courts, plural of *corte* court, from Latin *cohors* COHORT]

Cor·tés ('kɔ:tɛz; *Spanish* kor'tes) *or* **Cor·tez** (kɔ:'tɛz) *n.* **Her·nan·do** (er'nando) *or* **Her·nán** (er'nan). 1485–1547, Spanish conquistador: defeated the Aztecs and conquered Mexico (1523).

cor·tex ('kɔ:tɛks) *n., pl.* **·ti·ces** (-tɪˌsi:z). **1.** *Anatomy.* the outer layer of any organ or part, such as the grey matter in the brain that covers the cerebrum (**cerebral cortex**) or the outer part of the kidney (**renal cortex**). **2.** *Botany.* **a.** the unspecialized tissue in plant stems and roots between the vascular bundles and the epidermis. **b.** the outer layer of a part such as the bark of a stem. [C17: from Latin: bark, outer layer] —**cor·ti·cal** ('kɔ:tɪkəl) *adj.* —'**cor·ti·cal·ly** *adv.*

cor·ti·cate ('kɔ:tɪkɪt, -ˌkeɪt) *or* **cor·ti·cat·ed** *adj.* (of plants, seeds, etc.) having a bark, husk, or rind. [C19: from Latin *corticātus* covered with bark] —ˌ**cor·ti·'ca·tion** *n.*

cor·ti·co- *or before a vowel* **cor·tic-** *combining form.* indicating the cortex: *corticotrophin.*

cor·ti·co·ster·oid (ˌkɔ:tɪkəʊ'stɪərɔɪd) *or* **cor·ti·coid** *n.* **1.** any steroid hormone produced by the adrenal cortex that affects carbohydrate, protein, and electrolyte metabolism, gonad function, and immune response. **2.** any similar synthetic substance, used in treating inflammatory and allergic diseases. ~See **glucocorticoid, mineralocorticoid.**

cor·ti·cos·ter·one (ˌkɔ:tɪ'kɒstəˌrəʊn) *n.* a glucocorticoid hormone secreted by the adrenal cortex. Formula: $C_{21}H_{30}O_4$. See also **corticosteroid.** [C20: from CORTICO- + STER(OL) + -ONE]

cor·ti·co·tro·phin (ˌkɔ:tɪkəʊ'trəʊfɪn) *n.* another name for **adrenocorticotropic hormone.** See **ACTH.**

cor·ti·sol ('kɔ:tɪˌsɒl) *n.* another name for **hydrocortisone.** [C20: from CORTIS(ONE) + -OL[2]]

cor·ti·sone ('kɔ:tɪˌsəʊn, -ˌzəʊn) *n.* a glucocorticoid hormone, the synthetic form of which has been used in treating rheumatoid arthritis, allergic and skin diseases, leukaemia, etc.; 17-hydroxy-11-dehydrocorticosterone. Formula: $C_{21}H_{28}O_5$. [C20: shortened from CORTICOSTERONE]

Cor·tot (*French* kɔr'to) *n.* **Al·fred** (al'frɛd). 1877–1962, French pianist, born in Switzerland.

co·run·dum (kə'rʌndəm) *n.* a very hard, often blue mineral consisting of aluminium oxide in hexagonal crystalline form: used as an abrasive. Precious varieties include ruby and sapphire. Formula: Al_2O_3. [C18: from Tamil *kuruntam;* related to Sanskrit *kuruvinda* ruby]

Co·run·na (kə'rʌnə) *n.* the English name for **La Coruña.**

co·rus·cate ('kɒrəˌskeɪt) *vb.* (*intr.*) to emit flashes of light; sparkle. [C18: from Latin *coruscāre* to flash, vibrate]

cor·us·ca·tion (ˌkɒrə'skeɪʃən) *n.* **1.** a gleam or flash of light. **2.** a sudden or striking display of brilliance, wit, etc.

cor·vée ('kɔ:veɪ) *n.* **1.** *European history.* a day's unpaid labour owed by a feudal vassal to his lord. **2.** the practice or an instance of forced labour. [C14: from Old French, from Late Latin *corrogāta* contribution, from Latin *corrogāre* to collect, from *rogāre* to ask]

corves (kɔ:vz) *n.* the plural of **corf.**

cor·vette (kɔ:'vɛt) *n.* a lightly armed escort warship. [C17: from Old French, perhaps from Middle Dutch *corf* basket, small ship, from Latin *corbis* basket]

cor·vine ('kɔ:vaɪn) *adj.* **1.** of, relating to, or resembling a crow. **2.** of, relating to, or belonging to the passerine bird family *Corvidae,* which includes the crows, raven, rook, jackdaw, magpies, and jays. [C17: from Latin *corvīnus* raven-like, from *corvus* a raven]

Cor·vus ('kɔ:vəs) *n., Latin genitive* **Cor·vi** ('kɔ:vaɪ). a small quadrilateral-shaped constellation in the S hemisphere, lying between Virgo and Hydra. [Latin: raven]

Cor·y·bant ('kɒrɪˌbænt) *n., pl.* **Cor·y·bants** *or* **Cor·y·bant·es** (ˌkɒrɪ'bænti:z). *Classical myth.* a wild attendant of the goddess Cybele. [C14: from Latin *Corybās,* from Greek *Korubas,* probably of Phrygian origin] —ˌ**Cor·y·'ban·tian,** ˌ**Cor·y·'ban·tic** *or* ˌ**Cor·y·'ban·tine** *adj.*

co·ryd·a·lis (kə'rɪdəlɪs) *n.* any erect or climbing plant of the N temperate genus *Corydalis,* having finely-lobed leaves and spurred yellow or pinkish flowers: family *Fumariaceae.* Also called: **fumitory.** [C19: from New Latin, from Greek *korudallis* variant of *korudos* crested lark, from *korus* helmet, crest; alluding to the appearance of the flowers]

Cor·y·don ('kɒrɪdən, -ˌdɒn) *n.* (in pastoral literature) a shepherd or rustic: used as a proper name.

cor·ymb ('kɒrɪmb, -rɪm) *n.* an inflorescence in the form of a flat-topped flower cluster with the oldest flowers at the periphery. This type of raceme occurs in the candytuft. [C18: from Latin *corymbus,* from Greek *korumbos* cluster] —'**cor·ymbed** *adj.* —**co·'rym·bose** *or* **co·'rym·bous** *adj.* —**co·'rym·bose·ly** *adv.*

cor·y·phae·us (ˌkɒrɪ'fi:əs) *n., pl.* **·phae·i** (-'fi:aɪ). **1.** (in ancient Greek drama) the leader of the chorus. **2.** *Archaic or literary.* a leader of a group. [C17: from Latin, from Greek *koruphaios* leader, from *koruphē* summit]

cor·y·phée (ˌkɒrɪ'feɪ) *n.* a leading dancer of a corps de ballet. [C19: from French, from Latin *coryphaeus* CORYPHAEUS]

co·ry·za (kə'raɪzə) *n.* acute inflammation of the mucous membrane of the nose, with discharge of mucus; a head cold. [C17: from Late Latin: catarrh, from Greek *koruza*]

cos[1] *or* **cos let·tuce** (kɒs) *n.* a variety of lettuce with a long slender head and crisp leaves. Compare **cabbage lettuce.** Usual U.S. name: **romaine.** [C17: named after *Kos,* the Aegean island of its origin]

cos[2] (kɒz) *abbrev. for* cosine.

Cos (kɒs) *n.* a variant spelling of **Kos.**

Cos. *or* **cos.** *abbrev. for:* **1.** Companies. **2.** Counties.

c.o.s. *or* **C.O.S.** *abbrev. for* cash on shipment.

Co·sa Nos·tra ('kɒsə 'nɒstrə) *n.* a secret criminal organization active in the U.S., modelled on the Sicilian Mafia. See **Mafia.** [Italian, literally: our thing]

co·sec ('kəʊsɛk) *abbrev. for* cosecant.

co·se·cant (kəʊ'si:kənt) *n.* (of an angle) a trigonometric function that in a right-angled triangle is the ratio of the length of the hypotenuse to that of the opposite side; the reciprocal of sine. Abbrev.: **cosec**

co·sech ('kəʊsɛtʃ, -sɛk) hyperbolic cosecant; a hyperbolic function that is the reciprocal of sinh.

co·seis·mal (kəʊ'saɪzməl) *or* **co·seis·mic** *adj.* **1.** of or designating points at which earthquake waves are felt at the same time. **2.** (of a line on a map) connecting such points. ~*n.* **3.** such a line on a map.

Co·sen·za (*Italian* ko'zɛntsa) *n.* a city in S Italy, in Calabria. Pop.: 102 232 (1975 est.).

co·set ('kəʊˌsɛt) *n. Maths.* a set that when added to another set produces a specified larger set.

Cos·grave ('kɒzgreɪv) *n.* **Li·am** ('li:əm). born 1920, Irish politician; prime minister of the Republic of Ireland (1973–77).

cosh[1] (kɒʃ) *Brit.* ~*n.* **1.** a blunt weapon, often made of hard rubber; bludgeon. **2.** an attack with such a weapon. ~*vb.* **3.** to hit with such a weapon, esp. on the head. [C19: from Romany *kosh,* from *koshter* skewer, stick]

cosh[2] (kɒʃ) hyperbolic cosecant; a hyperbolic function, $\cosh z = \frac{1}{2}(e^z + e^{-z})$, related to cosine by the expression $\cosh iz = \cos z$, where $i = \sqrt{-1}$. [C19: from COS(INE) + H(YPERBOLIC)]

cosh·er ('kɒʃə) *vb. Irish* **1.** (*tr.*) to pamper or coddle. **2.** (*intr.*) to live or be entertained at the expense of another.

co·sig·na·to·ry (kəʊ'sɪgnətərɪ, -trɪ) *n., pl.* **·ries. 1.** a person, country, etc., that signs a document jointly with others. ~*adj.* **2.** signing jointly with another or others.

co·sine ('kəʊˌsaɪn) *n.* (of an angle) **1.** a trigonometric function that in a right-angled triangle is the ratio of the length of the adjacent side to that of the hypotenuse; the sine of the complement. **2.** a function that in a circle centred at the origin of a Cartesian coordinate system is the ratio of the abscissa of a point on the circumference to the radius of the circle. Abbrev.: **cos** [C17: from New Latin *cosinus;* see CO-, SINE]

cos·met·ic (kɒz'mɛtɪk) *n.* **1.** any preparation applied to the body, esp. the face, with the intention of beautifying it. ~*adj.* **2.** serving or designed to beautify or improve the body, esp. the face. **3.** having no other function than to beautify: *cosmetic illustrations in a book.* [C17: from Greek *kosmētikos,* from *kosmein* to arrange, from *kosmos* order] —**co'·met·i·cal·ly** *adv.* —**cos·ˌmet·i·'col·o·gist** *n.* —**cos·ˌmet·i·'col·o·gy** *n.*

cos·me·ti·cian (ˌkɒzmɪ'tɪʃən) *n.* a person who makes, sells, or applies cosmetics.

cos·met·ic sur·ger·y *n.* surgery performed to improve the appearance, rather than for medical reasons.

cos·mic ('kɒzmɪk) *adj.* **1.** of or relating to the whole universe: *cosmic laws.* **2.** occurring or originating in outer space, esp. as opposed to the vicinity of the earth, the solar system, or the local galaxy: *cosmic rays.* **3.** immeasurably extended in space or time; vast. **4.** *Rare.* harmonious. —'**cos·mi·cal·ly** *adv.*

cos·mic dust *n.* fine particles of solid matter occurring throughout interstellar space and often collecting into clouds of extremely low density. See also **nebula** (sense 1).

cos·mic rays *pl. n.* radiation consisting of atomic nuclei, esp. protons, of very high energy that reach the earth from outer space. Also called: **cosmic radiation.**

cos·mine ('kɒzmi:n) *or* **cos·min** *n. Zoology.* a substance resembling dentine, forming the outer layer of cosmoid scales. [C20: from Greek *kosmos* arrangement + -INE[1]]

cos·mo- *or before a vowel* **cosm-** *combining form.* indicating the world or universe: *cosmology; cosmonaut; cosmography.* [from Greek: COSMOS]

cos·mo·drome ('kɒzməˌdrəʊm) *n.* a site, esp. one in the Soviet Union, from which spacecraft are launched.

cos·mog·o·ny (kɒz'mɒgənɪ) *n., pl.* **·nies. 1.** the study of the origin and development of the universe or of a particular system in the universe, such as the solar system. **2.** a theory of such an origin or evolution. [C17: from Greek *kosmogonia,* from COSMO- + *gonos* creation] —**cos·'mog·o·nal** *adj.* —**cos·mo·gon·ic** (ˌkɒzmə'gɒnɪk) *or* ˌ**cos·mo·'gon·i·cal** *adj.* —**cos·'mog·o·nist** *n.*

cos·mog·ra·phy (kɒz'mɒgrəfɪ) *n.* **1.** a representation of the world or the universe. **2.** the science dealing with the whole order of nature. —**cos·'mog·ra·pher** *or* **cos·'mog·ra·phist** *n.* —**cos·mo·graph·ic** (ˌkɒzmə'græfɪk) *or* ˌ**cos·mo·'graph·i·cal** *adj.* —ˌ**cos·mo·'graph·i·cal·ly** *adv.*

cos·moid ('kɒzmɔɪd) *adj.* (of the scales of coelacanths and lungfish) consisting of two inner bony layers and an outer layer of cosmine. [C20: from COSM(INE) + -OID]

cos·mol·o·gy (kɒz'mɒlədʒɪ) *n.* **1.** the philosophical study of the origin and nature of the universe. **2.** the branch of astronomy concerned with the evolution and structure of the universe. —**cos·mo·log·i·cal** (ˌkɒzmə'lɒdʒɪkᵊl) *or* ˌ**cos·mo·'log·ic** *adj.* —ˌ**cos·mo·'log·i·cal·ly** *adv.* —**cos·'mol·o·gist** *n.*

cos·mo·naut ('kɒzməˌnɔːt) *n.* a Soviet astronaut. [C20: from Russian *kosmonavt,* from COSMO- + Greek *nautēs* sailor; compare ARGONAUT]

cos·mop·o·lis (kɒz'mɒpəlɪs) *n.* an international city. [C19: see COSMO-, POLIS]

cos·mo·pol·i·tan (ˌkɒzmə'pɒlɪtᵊn) *n.* **1.** a person who has lived and travelled in many countries, esp. one who is free of national prejudices. ~*adj.* **2.** having interest in or familiar with many parts of the world. **3.** sophisticated or urbane. **4.** composed of people or elements from all parts of the world or from many different spheres. **5.** (of plants or animals) widely distributed. [C17: from French, ultimately from Greek *kosmopolitēs,* from *kosmo-* COSMO- + *politēs* citizen] —ˌ**cos·mo·'pol·i·tan·ism** *n.*

cos·mop·o·lite (kɒz'mɒpəˌlaɪt) *n.* **1.** a less common word for **cosmopolitan** (sense 1). **2.** an animal or plant that occurs in most parts of the world. —**cos·'mop·o·lit·ˌism** *n.*

cos·mos ('kɒzmɒs) *n.* **1.** the world or universe considered as an ordered system. **2.** any ordered system. **3.** harmony; order. **4.** (*pl.* **·mos** *or* **·mos·es.**) any tropical American plant of the genus *Cosmos,* cultivated as garden plants for their brightly coloured flowers: family *Compositae* (composites). [C17: from Greek *kosmos* order, world, universe]

Cos·mo·tron ('kɒzməˌtrɒn) *n.* a large synchrotron for accelerating protons to high energies (of the order of 1 GeV). [C20: from COSM(IC RAY) + -TRON]

COSPAR ('kəʊspɑː) *n. acronym for* Committee on Space Research.

coss (kɒs) *n.* another name for **kos.**

Cos·sack ('kɒsæk) *n.* **1.** (formerly) any of the free warrior-peasants of chiefly East Slavonic descent who lived in communes, esp. in the Ukraine, and served as cavalry under the tsars. ~*adj.* **2.** of, relating to, or characteristic of the Cossacks: *a Cossack dance.* [C16: from Russian *kazak* vagabond, of Turkic origin]

cos·sack hat *n.* a warm brimless hat of fur or sheepskin.

cos·set ('kɒsɪt) *vb.* **1.** (*tr.*) to pamper; coddle; pet. ~*n.* **2.** any pet animal, esp. a lamb. [C16: of unknown origin]

cos·sie ('kɒzɪ) *n. Chiefly Austral.* an informal name for a swimming costume.

cost (kɒst) *n.* **1.** the price paid or required for acquiring, producing, or maintaining something, usually measured in money, time, or energy; expense or expenditure; outlay. **2.** suffering or sacrifice; loss; penalty: *count the cost to your health; I know to my cost.* **3. a.** the amount paid for a commodity by its seller: *to sell at cost.* **b.** (*as modifier*): *the cost price.* **4.** *Economics.* short for **opportunity cost. 5.** (*pl.*) *Law.* the expenses of judicial proceedings. **6. at any cost** *or* **at all costs.** regardless of cost or sacrifice involved. **7. at the cost of.** at the expense of losing. ~*vb.* **costs, cost·ing, cost. 8.** (*tr.*) to be obtained or obtainable in exchange for (money or something equivalent); be priced at: *the ride cost one pound.* **9.** to cause or require the expenditure, loss, or sacrifice (of): *the accident cost him dearly.* **10.** to estimate the cost of (a product, process, etc.) for the purposes of pricing, budgeting, control, etc. [C13: from Old French (n.), from *coster* to cost, from Latin *constāre* to stand at, cost, from *stāre* to stand] —**'cost·less** *adj.*

cos·ta ('kɒstə) *n., pl.* **·tae** (-tiː). **1.** the technical name for **rib**[1] (sense 1). **2.** a riblike part, such as the midrib of a plant leaf. [C19: from Latin: rib, side, wall] —**'cos·tal** *adj.*

Cos·ta Bra·va ('kɒstə 'brɑːvə) *n.* a coastal region of NE Spain along the Mediterranean, extending from Barcelona to the French border: many resorts.

cost ac·count·ing *n.* the recording and controlling of all the expenditures of an enterprise in order to facilitate control of separate activities. Also called: **management accounting.** —**cost ac·count·ant** *n.*

co-star *n.* **1.** an actor who shares star billing with another. ~*vb.* **-stars, -star·ring -starred. 2.** (*intr.;* often foll. by *with*) to share star billing (with another actor). **3.** (*tr.*) to present as sharing top billing: *the film co-starred Mae West and W. C. Fields.*

cos·tard ('kʌstəd) *n.* **1.** an English variety of apple tree. **2.** the large ribbed apple of this tree. **3.** *Archaic, humorous.* a slang word for **head.** [C14: from Anglo-Norman, from Old French *coste* rib]

Cos·ta Ri·ca ('kɒstə 'riːkə) *n.* a republic in Central America: gained independence from Spain in 1821; mostly mountainous and volcanic, with extensive forests. Language: Spanish. Religion: Roman Catholic. Currency: colón. Capital: San José. Pop.: 1 871 780 (1973). Area: 50 900 sq. km (19 652 sq. miles). —**Cos·ta Ri·can** *adj., n.*

cos·tate ('kɒsteɪt) *adj.* **1.** *Anatomy.* having ribs. **2.** (of leaves) having veins or ridges, esp. parallel ones. [C19: from Late Latin *costātus,* from Latin *costa* rib]

cost ben·e·fit a·nal·y·sis *n. Economics.* any of several techniques for relating the cost of an enterprise to its social benefits.

cost-ef·fec·tive *adj.* providing adequate financial return in relation to outlay.

Cos·ter·mans·ville ('kɒstəmənzˌvɪl) *n.* the former name (until 1966) of **Bukavu.**

cos·ter·mon·ger ('kɒstəˌmʌŋgə) *or* **cos·ter** *n. Brit., rare.* a person who sells fruit, vegetables, etc., from a barrow. [C16: *coster-,* from COSTARD + MONGER]

cos·tive ('kɒstɪv) *adj.* **1.** having constipation; constipated. **2.** sluggish. **3.** niggardly. [C14: from Old French *costivé,* from Latin *constipātus;* see CONSTIPATE] —**'cos·tive·ly** *adv.* —**'cos·tive·ness** *n.*

cost·ly ('kɒstlɪ) *adj.* **·li·er, ·li·est. 1.** of great price or value; expensive. **2.** entailing great loss or sacrifice: *a costly victory.* **3.** splendid; lavish. —**'cost·li·ness** *n.*

cost·mar·y ('kɒstˌmɛərɪ) *n., pl.* **·mar·ies.** a herbaceous plant, *Chrysanthemum balsamita,* native to Asia. Its fragrant leaves were used as a seasoning and to flavour ale: family *Compositae* (composites). Also called: **alecost.** [C15 *costmarie,* from *coste* costmary, from Latin *costum* (from Greek *kostos*) + *Marie* (the Virgin) Mary]

cost of liv·ing *n.* **1. a.** the basic cost of the food, clothing, shelter, and fuel necessary to maintain life, esp. at a standard of living regarded as basic or minimal. **b.** (*as modifier*): *the cost-of-living index.* **2.** the average expenditure of a person or family in a given period.

cos·tot·o·my (kɒ'stɒtəmɪ) *n., pl.* **·mies.** surgical incision into a rib.

cost-plus *n.* **a.** a method of establishing a selling price in which an agreed percentage is added to the cost price to cover profit. **b.** (*as modifier*): *cost-plus pricing.*

cost-push in·fla·tion *n.* See **inflation.**

cos·trel ('kɒstrəl) *n. Obsolete.* a flask, usually of earthenware or leather. [C14: from Old French *costerel,* from *coste* side, rib, from Latin *costa*]

cos·tume ('kɒstjuːm) *n.* **1.** a complete style of dressing, including all the clothes, accessories, etc., worn at one time, as in a particular country or period; dress: *national costume.* **2.** *Old-fashioned.* a woman's suit. **3.** a set of clothes, esp. unusual or period clothes, worn in a play by an actor or at a fancy dress ball: *a jester's costume.* **4.** short for **swimming costume.** ~*vb.* (*tr.*) **5.** to furnish the costumes for (a show, film, etc.). **6.** to dress (someone) in a costume. [C18: from French, from Italian: dress, habit, CUSTOM]

cos·tume jew·el·ler·y *n.* jewellery that is decorative but has little intrinsic value.

cos·tume piece *n.* any theatrical production, film, television presentation, etc., in which the performers wear the costumes of a former age. Also called: **costume drama.**

cos·tum·i·er (kɒ'stjuːmɪə) *or* **cos·tum·er** *n.* a person or firm that makes or supplies theatrical or fancy costumes.

co·sy *or U.S.* **co·zy** ('kəʊzɪ) *adj.* **·si·er, ·si·est** *or U.S.* **·zi·er, ·zi·est. 1.** warm and snug. **2.** intimate; friendly. **3.** convenient, esp. for devious purposes: *a cosy deal.* ~*n., pl.* **·sies** *or U.S.* **·zies. 4.** a cover for keeping things warm: *egg cosy.* —**'co·si·ly** *or U.S.* **'co·zi·ly** *adv.* —**'co·si·ness** *or U.S.* **'co·zi·ness** *n.*

co·sy a·long *vb.* (*tr., adv.*) to reassure (someone), esp. with false assurances.

cot[1] (kɒt) *n.* **1.** a child's boxlike bed, usually incorporating vertical bars. **2.** a collapsible or portable bed. **3.** a light bedstead. **4.** *Nautical.* a hammock-like bed with a stiff frame. [C17: from Hindi *khāt* bedstead, from Sanskrit *khátvā,* of Dravidian origin; related to Tamil *kattil* bedstead]

cot[2] (kɒt) *n.* **1.** *Literary or archaic.* a small cottage. **2.** Also called: **cote. a.** a small shelter, esp. one for pigeons, sheep, etc. **b.** (*in combination*): *dovecot.* **3.** another name for **finger-stall.** [Old English *cot;* related to Old Norse *kot* little hut, Middle Low German *cot*]

cot[3] (kɒt) *abbrev. for* cotangent.

co·tan ('kəʊˌtæn) *abbrev. for* cotangent.

co·tan·gent (kəʊ'tændʒənt) *n.* (of an angle) a trigonometric function that in a right-angled triangle is the ratio of the length of the adjacent side to that of the opposite side; the reciprocal of tangent. Abbrev.: **cot, cotan, ctn** —**co·tan·gen·tial** (ˌkəʊtæn'dʒɛnʃəl) *adj.*

cot case *n. Austral., humorous.* a person who is incapacitated by drink.

cot death *n.* the unexplained sudden death of an infant during sleep. Also called (U.S.): **crib death.**

cote[1] (kəʊt) *or* **cot** *n.* **1. a.** a small shelter for pigeons, sheep, etc. **b.** (*in combination*): *dovecote.* **2.** *Dialect, chiefly Brit.* a small cottage. [Old English *cote;* related to Low German *Kote;* see COT[2]]

cote[2] (kəʊt) *vb.* (*tr.*) *Archaic.* to pass by, outstrip, or surpass. [C16: perhaps from Old French *costoier* to run alongside, from *coste* side; see COAST]

Côte d'A·zur (*French* kot da'zyːr) *n.* the Mediterranean coast of France, including the French Riviera: forms an administrative region with Provence.

Côte-d'Or (*French* kot'dɔ:r) *n.* a department of E central France, in NE Burgundy. Capital: Dijon. Pop.: 467 557 (1975). Area: 8787 sq. km (3427 sq. miles).

co+tem+po+rar·y (kəʊ'tɛmpərərɪ) *adj.* a variant spelling of **contemporary.**

co+ten+ant (kəʊ'tɛnənt) *n.* a person who holds property jointly or in common with others. —**co+'ten+an+cy** *n.*

co+te·rie ('kəʊtərɪ) *n.* a small exclusive group of friends or people with common interests; clique. [C18: from French, from Old French: association of tenants, from *cotier* (unattested) cottager, from Medieval Latin *cotārius* COTTER²; see COT²]

co+ter+mi+nous (kəʊ'tɜ:mɪnəs) *or* **con+ter+mi+nous** *adj.* **1.** having a common boundary; bordering; contiguous. **2.** coextensive or coincident in range, time, scope, etc.

Côtes-du-Nord (*French* kot dy 'nɔ:r) *n.* a department of W France, on the N coast of Brittany. Capital: St. Brieuc. Pop.: 547 871 (1975). Area: 7218 sq. km (2815 sq. miles).

coth (kɒθ) hyperbolic cotangent; a hyperbolic function that is the ratio of cosh to sinh, being the reciprocal of tanh. [C20: from COT(ANGENT) + H(YPERBOLIC)]

co+thur+nus (kəʊ'θɜ:nəs) *or* **co+thurn** ('kəʊθɜ:n, kəʊ'θɜ:n) *n., pl.* **+thur+ni** (-'θɜ:naɪ) *or* **+thurns.** the buskin worn in ancient Greek tragedy. [C18: from Latin, from Greek *kothornos*]

co+tid+al (kəʊ'taɪdᵊl) *adj.* (of a line on a tidal chart) joining points at which high tide occurs simultaneously.

co+til+lion *or* **co+til+lon** (kə'tɪljən, kəʊ-) *n.* **1.** a French formation dance of the 18th century. **2.** *U.S.* a quadrille. **3.** *U.S.* a complicated dance with frequent changes of partners. [C18: from French *cotillon* dance, from Old French: petticoat, from *cote* COAT]

co+tin+ga (kə'tɪŋgə) *n.* any tropical American passerine bird of the family *Cotingidae,* such as the umbrella bird and the cock-of-the-rock, having a broad slightly hooked bill. Also called: **chatterer.**

Cot·man ('kɒtmən) *n.* **John Sell.** 1782–1842, English landscape watercolourist and etcher.

co+to+ne·as+ter (kə,təʊnɪ'æstə) *n.* any Old World shrub of the rosaceous genus *Cotoneaster:* cultivated for their small ornamental white or pinkish flowers and red or black berries. [C18: from New Latin, from Latin *cotōneum* QUINCE]

Co+to+nou (,kəʊtə'nu:) *n.* the chief port of Benin, on the Bight of Benin. Pop.: 178 000 (1975 est.).

Cot·o+pax·i (*Spanish* ,koto'paksi) *n.* a volcano in central Ecuador, in the Andes: the world's highest active volcano. Height: 5896 m (19 457 ft.).

cot+quean ('kɒt,kwi:n) *n. Archaic.* **1.** a coarse woman. **2.** a man who does housework. [C16: see COT², QUEAN]

Cots+wold ('kɒts,wəʊld, -wəld) *n.* a breed of sheep with long wool that originated in the Cotswolds.

Cots+wolds *pl. n.* a range of low hills in SW England, mainly in Gloucestershire: formerly a centre of the wool industry.

cot+ta ('kɒtə) *n. R.C. Church.* a short form of surplice. [C19: from Italian: tunic, from Medieval Latin; see COAT]

cot+tage ('kɒtɪdʒ) *n.* **1.** a small simple house, esp. in a rural area. **2.** *U.S.* one of several housing units, as at a hospital, for accommodating people in groups. **3.** *Slang.* a public lavatory. [C14: from COT²]

cot+tage cheese *n.* a mild loose soft white cheese made from skimmed milk curds.

cot+tage hos+pi+tal *n. Brit.* a small, rural hospital.

cot+tage in+dus+try *n.* an industry in which employees work in their own homes, often using their own equipment.

cot+tage loaf *n. Brit.* a loaf consisting of two round pieces, the smaller of which sits on top of the larger.

cot+tage pi+an·o *n.* a small upright piano.

cot+tage pie *n. Brit.* another term for **shepherd's pie.**

cot+tag+er ('kɒtɪdʒə) *n.* **1.** a person who lives in a cottage. **2.** a rural labourer. **3.** *Chiefly Canadian.* a person holidaying in a cottage. **4.** *History.* another name for **cotter².**

Cott+bus (*German* 'kɔtbʊs) *n.* an industrial city in East Germany, on the Spree River. Pop.: 88 034 (1972 est.).

cot+ter¹ ('kɒtə) *Machinery.* ~*n.* **1.** any part, such as a pin, wedge, key, etc., that is used to secure two other parts so that relative motion between them is prevented. **2.** short for **cotter pin.** ~*vb.* **3.** (*tr.*) to secure (two parts) with a cotter. [C14: shortened from *cotterel,* of unknown origin]

cot+ter² ('kɒtə) *n.* **1.** Also called: **cottier.** *English history.* a villein in late Anglo-Saxon and early Norman times occupying a cottage and land in return for labour. **2.** Also called: **cot+tar.** a peasant occupying a cottage and land in the Scottish Highlands under the same tenure as an Irish cottier. ~See also **cottier** (sense 2), **cottager** (sense 1). [C14: from Medieval Latin *cotārius,* from Middle English *cote* COT²]

cot+ter pin *n. Machinery.* **1.** a split pin secured, after passing through holes in the parts to be attached, by spreading the ends. **2.** a tapered pin threaded at the smaller end and secured by a nut after insertion.

Cot+ti·an Alps ('kɒtɪən) *pl. n.* a mountain range in SW Europe, between NW Italy and SE France: part of the Alps. Highest peak: Monte Viso, 3841 m (12 600 ft.).

cot+tier ('kɒtɪə) *n.* **1.** another name for **cotter²** (sense 1). **2.** (in Ireland) a peasant farming a smallholding under **cottier tenure** (the holding of not more than half an acre at a rent of not more than five pounds a year). **3.** another name for **cottager** (sense 1). [C14: from Old French *cotier;* see COTE¹, COTERIE]

cot+ton ('kɒtᵊn) *n.* **1.** any of various herbaceous plants and shrubs of the malvaceous genus *Gossypium,* such as **sea-island cotton,** cultivated in warm climates for the fibre surrounding the seeds and the oil within the seeds. **2.** the soft white downy fibre of these plants: used to manufacture textiles. **3.** cotton plants collectively, as a cultivated crop. **4. a.** a cloth or thread made from cotton fibres. **b.** (*as modifier*): *a cotton dress.* **5.** any substance, such as kapok (**silk cotton**), resembling cotton but obtained from other plants. ~See also **cotton on, cotton to.** [C14: from Old French *coton,* from Arabic dialect *qutun,* from Arabic *qutn*] —**'cot+ton·y** *adj.*

cot+ton+ade (,kɒtᵊ'neɪd) *n.* a coarse fabric of cotton or mixed fibres, used for work clothes, etc. [C19: from French *cotonnade,* from *coton* COTTON + -ADE]

cot+ton belt *n.* a belt of land in the southeastern U.S. that specializes in the production of cotton.

cot+ton bush *n. Austral.* any of various downy chenopodiaceous shrubs, esp. *Kochia aphylla,* which is used to feed livestock.

cot+ton cake *n.* cottonseed meal compressed into nuts or cubes of various sizes for feeding to animals.

cot+ton can+dy *n.* the U.S. name for **candy floss.**

cot+ton flan+nel *n.* a plain-weave or twill-weave fabric with nap on one side only. Also called: **Canton flannel.**

cot+ton grass *n.* any of various N temperate and arctic grasslike bog plants of the cyperaceous genus *Eriophorum,* whose dense spikes of flowers resemble cotton tufts.

cot·ton+mouth ('kɒtᵊn,maʊθ) *n.* another name for the **water moccasin.**

cot+ton on *vb.* (*intr., adv.;* often foll. by *to*) *Informal.* **1.** to perceive the meaning (of). **2.** to make use (of).

cot+ton pick+er *n.* **1.** a machine for harvesting cotton fibre. **2.** a person who picks ripe cotton fibre from the plants.

cot·ton-pick·ing *adj. U.S. slang.* (intensifier qualifying something undesirable): *you cotton-picking layabout!*

cot·ton+seed ('kɒtᵊn,si:d) *n., pl.* **+seeds** *or* **+seed.** the seed of the cotton plant: a source of oil and fodder.

cot·ton+seed meal *n.* the residue of cottonseed kernels from which oil has been extracted, used as fodder or fertilizer.

cot·ton+seed oil *n.* a yellowish or dark red oil with a nutlike smell, extracted or expelled from cottonseed, used in cooking and in the manufacture of paints, soaps, etc.

cot+ton stain+er *n.* any of various heteropterous insects of the genus *Dysdercus:* serious pests of cotton, piercing and staining the cotton bolls: family *Pyrrhocoridae.*

cot·ton+tail ('kɒtᵊn,teɪl) *n.* any of several common rabbits of the genus *Sylvilagus,* such as *S. floridanus* (**eastern cottontail**), of American woodlands.

cot+ton to *vb.* (*intr.*) *U.S. informal.* **1.** to become friendly (with). **2.** to approve (of).

cot+ton waste *n.* refuse cotton yarn, esp. when used as a cleaning material.

cot·ton+weed ('kɒtᵊn,wi:d) *n.* **1.** a downy perennial plant, *Otanthus maritimus,* of European coastal regions, having small yellow flowers surrounded by large hairy bracts: family *Compositae* (composites). **2.** any of various similar plants.

cot·ton+wood ('kɒtᵊn,wʊd) *n.* any of several North American poplars, esp. *Populus deltoides,* whose seeds are covered with cottony hairs.

cot+ton wool *n.* **1.** Also called: **purified cotton.** *Chiefly Brit.* bleached and sterilized cotton from which the gross impurities, such as the seeds and waxy matter, have been removed: used for surgical dressings, tampons, etc. Usual U.S. term: **absorbent cotton. 2.** cotton in the natural state. **3.** *Brit. informal.* **a.** a state of pampered comfort and protection. **b.** (*as modifier*): *a cotton-wool existence.*

cot·ton·y-cush·ion scale *n.* a small scale insect, *Icerya purchasi,* that is a serious pest of citrus trees in California: it is controlled by introducing an Australian ladybird, *Rodolia cardinalis,* into affected areas.

cot·y+le·don (,kɒtɪ'li:dᵊn) *n.* **1.** a simple embryonic leaf in seed-bearing plants, which, in some species, forms the first green leaf after germination. **2.** a tuft of villi on the mammalian placenta. [C16: from Latin: a plant, navelwort, from Greek *kotulēdōn,* from *kotulē* cup, hollow] —**,cot·y+'le·do+nous** *or* **,cot·y+'le·do+,noid** *adj.* —**,cot·y+'le·do+nal** *adj.* —**,cot·y+'le·do+na+ry** *adj.*

cot·y+loid ('kɒtɪ,lɔɪd) *or* **cot·y+loi+dal** *adj.* **1.** *Anatomy.* **a.** shaped like a cup. **b.** of or relating to the acetabulum. ~*n.* **2.** a small bone forming part of the acetabular cavity in some mammals. [C18: from Greek *kotuloeidēs* cup-shaped, from *kotulē* a cup]

cou+cal ('ku:kæl, -kᵊl) *n.* any ground-living bird of the genus *Centropus,* of Africa, S Asia, and Australia, having long strong legs: family *Cuculidae* (cuckoos). [C19: from French, perhaps from *couc(ou)* cuckoo + *al(ouette)* lark]

couch (kaʊtʃ) *n.* **1.** a piece of upholstered furniture, usually having a back and armrests, for seating more than one person. **2.** a bed, esp. one used in the daytime by the patients of a doctor or a psychoanalyst. **3.** a frame upon which barley is malted. **4.** a priming layer of paint or varnish, esp. in a painting. **5.** *Papermaking.* **a.** a board on which sheets of handmade paper are dried by pressing. **b.** a felt blanket onto which sheets of partly dried paper are transferred for further drying. **c.** a roll on a papermaking machine from which the wet web of paper on the wire is transferred to the next section. **6.** *Archaic.* the lair of a wild animal. ~*vb.* **7.** (*tr.*) to express in a particular style of language: *couched in an archaic style.* **8.** (when *tr., usually reflexive or passive*) to lie down or cause to lie down for or as for sleep. **9.** (*intr.*) *Archaic.* to crouch or kneel. **10.**

(*intr.*) *Archaic.* to lie in ambush; lurk. **11.** (*tr.*) to spread barley on a frame for malting. **12.** (*intr.*) (of decomposing leaves) to lie in a heap or bed. **13.** (*tr.*) to embroider or depict by couching. **14.** (*tr.*) to lift sheets of handmade paper onto the board on which they will be dried. **15.** (*tr.*) *Surgery.* to remove (a cataract) by downward displacement of the lens of the eye. **16.** (*tr.*) *Archaic.* to lower (a lance) into a horizontal position. [C14: from Old French *couche* a bed, lair, from *coucher* to lay down, from Latin *collocāre* to arrange, from *locāre* to place; see LOCATE] —**'couch·er** *n.*

cou·chant ('kaʊtʃənt) *adj.* (*usually postpositive*) *Heraldry.* in a lying position: *a lion couchant.* [C15: from French: lying, from Old French *coucher* to lay down; see COUCH]

cou·chette (ku:'ʃɛt) *n.* a bed or berth in a railway carriage, esp. one converted from seats. [C20: from French, diminutive of *couche* bed]

couch grass *n.* a grass, *Agropyron repens,* with a yellowish-white creeping underground stem by which it spreads quickly: a troublesome weed. Sometimes shortened to **couch.** Also called: **scutch grass, twitch grass, quitch grass.**

couch·ing ('kaʊtʃɪŋ) *n.* **a.** a method of embroidery in which the thread is caught down at intervals by another thread passed through the material from beneath. **b.** a pattern or work done by this method.

cou-cou ('ku:ku:, 'kʊku:) *n.* a preparation of boiled corn meal and okras stirred to a stiff consistency with a **cou-cou stick:** eaten in the West Indies. [of uncertain origin]

cou·dé (ku:'deɪ) *adj.* (of a reflecting telescope) having plane mirrors positioned to reflect light from the primary mirror along the axis onto a photographic plate or spectroscope. [French, literally: bent in the shape of an elbow, from *coude* an elbow]

Cou·é (*French* kwe) *n.* **É·mile** (e'mil). 1857–1926, French psychologist and pharmacist: advocated psychotherapy by autosuggestion. —**Cou·é·ism** ('ku:eɪˌɪzəm) *n.*

cou·gar ('ku:gə) *n.* another name for **puma.** [C18: from French *couguar,* from Portuguese *cuguardo,* from Tupi *suasuarana,* literally: deerlike, from *suasú* deer + *rana* similar to]

cough (kɒf) *vb.* **1.** (*intr.*) to expel air abruptly and explosively through the partially closed vocal chords. **2.** (*intr.*) to make a sound similar to this. **3.** (*tr.*) to utter or express with a cough or coughs. ~*n.* **4.** an act, instance, or sound of coughing. [Old English *cohhetten;* related to Middle Dutch *kochen,* Middle High German *kūchen* to wheeze; probably of imitative origin] —**'cough·er** *n.*

cough drop *n.* a lozenge to relieve a cough.

cough mix·ture *n.* any medicine that relieves coughing.

cough up *vb.* (*adv.*) **1.** *Informal.* to surrender (money, information, etc.), esp. reluctantly. **2.** (*tr.*) to bring into the mouth or eject (phlegm, food, etc.) by coughing.

could (kʊd) *vb.* (takes an infinitive without *to* or an implied infinitive) used as an auxiliary: **1.** to make the past tense of **can**[1]. **2.** to make the subjunctive mood of **can**[1], esp. used in polite requests or in conditional sentences: *could I see you tonight? she'd telephone if she could.* **3.** to indicate suggestion of a course of action: *you could take the car tomorrow if it's raining.* **4.** (often foll. by *well*) to indicate a possibility: *he could well be a spy.* [Old English *cūthe;* influenced by WOULD, SHOULD; see CAN[1]]

could·n't ('kʊdᵊnt) *a contraction of* could not.

couldst (kʊdst) *vb. Archaic.* the form of **could** used with the pronoun *thou* or its relative form.

cou·lee ('ku:leɪ, -lɪ) *n.* **1. a.** a flow of molten lava. **b.** such lava when solidified. **2.** *Western U.S.* a steep-sided ravine formed by heavy rain or melting snow. **3.** a small intermittent stream in such a ravine. [C19: from Canadian French *coulée* a flow, from French, from *couler* to flow, from Latin *cōlāre* to sift, purify; see COLANDER]

cou·li·bia·ca (ˌku:lɪ'bjɑ:kə) *n.* a variant spelling of **koulibiaca.**

cou·lisse (ku:'li:s) *n.* **1.** Also called: **cullis.** a timber member grooved to take a sliding panel, such as a sluicegate, portcullis, or stage flat. **2. a.** a flat piece of scenery situated in the wings of a theatre; wing flat. **b.** a space between wing flats. **3.** part of the Paris Bourse where unofficial securities are traded. Compare **parquet** (sense 4). [C19: from French: groove, from Old French *couleïce* PORTCULLIS]

cou·loir ('ku:lwɑ:; *French* ku'lwa:r) *n.* a deep gully on a mountain side, esp. in the French Alps. [C19: from French: corridor, from *couler* to pour; see COULEE]

cou·lomb ('ku:lɒm) *n.* the derived SI unit of electric charge; the quantity of electricity transported in one second by a current of 1 ampere. Symbol: C [C19: named after C.A. de COULOMB]

Cou·lomb ('ku:lɒm; *French* ku'lɔ̃) *n.* **Charles Au·gus·tin de** (ʃarl ogy'stɛ̃ də). 1736–1806, French physicist: made many discoveries in the field of electricity and magnetism.

Cou·lomb field *n.* the electrostatic field around an electrically charged body or particle. The interaction between two such fields produces **Coulomb force.**

Cou·lomb's law *n.* the principle that the force of attraction or repulsion between two point electric charges is directly proportional to the product of the charges and inversely proportional to the square of the distance between them. The law also holds for magnetic poles.

cou·lom·e·ter (ku:'lɒmɪtə) *or* **cou·lomb·me·ter** *n.* an electrolytic cell for measuring the magnitude of an electric charge by determining the total amount of decomposition resulting from the passage of the charge through the cell. Also called: **voltameter.** [C19: from COULOMB + METER] —**cou·lo·met·ric** (ˌku:lə'mɛtrɪk) *adj.* —**cou·'lom·e·try** *n.*

coul·ter ('kəʊltə) *n.* a blade or sharp-edged disc attached to a plough so that it cuts through the soil vertically in advance of the ploughshare. Also (esp. U.S.): **colter.**

cou·ma·rin *or* **cu·ma·rin** ('ku:mərɪn) *n.* a white vanilla-scented crystalline ester, used in perfumes and flavourings and as an anticoagulant. Formula: $C_9H_6O_2$. [C19: from French *coumarine,* from *coumarou* tonka-bean tree, from Spanish *cumarú,* from Tupi] —**'cou·ma·ric** *or* **'cu·ma·ric** *adj.*

cou·ma·rone ('ku:məˌrəʊn) *n.* another name for **benzofuran.** [C19: from COUMAR(IN) + -ONE]

coun·cil ('kaʊnsəl) *n.* **1.** an assembly of people meeting for discussion, consultation, etc.: *an emergency council.* **2.** a body of people elected or appointed to serve in an administrative, legislative, or advisory capacity: *a student council.* **3.** *Brit.* (*sometimes cap.;* often preceded by *the*) the local governing authority of a town, county, etc. **4.** a meeting or the deliberation of a council. **5.** (*modifier*) of, relating to, provided for, or used by a local council: *a council chamber; council offices.* **6.** (*modifier*) *Brit.* provided by a local council, esp. (of housing) at a subsidized rent: *a council house; a council estate.* **7.** *Christianity.* an assembly of bishops, theologians, and other representatives of several churches or dioceses, convened for regulating matters of doctrine or discipline. [C12: from Old French *concile,* from Latin *concilium* assembly, from *com-* together + *calāre* to call; influenced also by Latin *consilium* advice, COUNSEL]

coun·cil·lor *or U.S.* **coun·ci·lor** ('kaʊnsələ) *n.* a member of a council. —**'coun·cil·lor·ˌship** *or U.S.* **'coun·ci·lor·ˌship** *n.*

coun·cil·man ('kaʊnsəlmən) *n., pl.* **·men.** *Chiefly U.S.* a member of a council, esp. of a town or city; councillor.

coun·cil-man·ag·er plan *n.* (in the U.S.) a system of local government with an elected legislative council and an appointed administrative manager. See also **city manager.**

Coun·cil of States *n.* another name for **Rajya Sabha.**

Coun·cil of Trent *n.* the council of the Roman Catholic Church that met between 1545 and 1563 at Trent in S Tyrol. Reacting against the Protestants, it reaffirmed traditional Catholic beliefs and formulated the ideals of the Counter-Reformation.

coun·cil of war *n.* **1.** an assembly of military leaders in wartime. **2.** an emergency meeting to formulate a plan.

coun·ci·lor ('kaʊnsələ) *n.* **1.** a variant U.S. spelling of **councillor.** **2.** an archaic spelling of **counsellor.** —**'coun·cil·or·ˌship** *n.*

coun·cil school *n. Brit.* (esp. formerly) any school maintained by the state.

coun·sel ('kaʊnsəl) *n.* **1.** advice or guidance on conduct, behaviour, etc. **2.** discussion, esp. on future procedure; consultation: *to take counsel with a friend.* **3.** a person whose advice or guidance is or has been sought. **4.** a barrister or group of barristers engaged in conducting cases in court and advising on legal matters: *counsel for the prosecution.* **5.** a policy or plan. **6.** *Christianity.* any of the **counsels of perfection** or **evangelical counsels,** namely poverty, chastity, and obedience. **7. counsel of perfection.** excellent but unrealizable advice. **8.** private opinions or plans (esp. in the phrase **keep one's own counsel**). **9.** *Archaic.* wisdom; prudence. ~*vb.* **·sels, ·sel·ling, ·selled** *or U.S.* **·sels, ·sel·ing, ·seled.** **10.** (*tr.*) to give advice or guidance to. **11.** (*tr.; often takes a clause as object*) to recommend the acceptance of (a plan, idea, etc.); urge. **12.** (*intr.*) *Archaic.* to take counsel; consult. [C13: from Old French *counseil,* from Latin *consilium* deliberating body; related to CONSUL, CONSULT] —**'coun·sel·la·ble** *or U.S.* **'coun·sel·a·ble** *adj.*

coun·sel·lor *or U.S.* **coun·se·lor** ('kaʊnsələ) *n.* **1.** a person who gives counsel; adviser. **2.** Also called: **coun·se·lor-at-law.** *U.S.* a lawyer, esp. one who conducts cases in court; attorney. **3.** a senior British diplomatic officer. **4.** a U.S. diplomatic officer ranking just below an ambassador or minister. **5.** a person who advises students or others on personal problems or academic and occupational choice. —**'coun·sel·lor·ˌship** *or U.S.* **'coun·se·lor·ˌship** *n.*

count[1] (kaʊnt) *vb.* **1.** to add up or check (each unit in a collection) in order to ascertain the sum; enumerate: *count your change.* **2.** (*tr.*) to recite numbers in ascending order up to and including. **3.** (*tr.;* often foll. by *in*) to take into account or include: *we must count him in.* **4. not counting.** excluding. **5.** (*tr.*) to believe to be; consider; think; deem: *count yourself lucky.* **6.** (*intr.*) to recite or list numbers in ascending order either in units or groups: *to count in tens.* **7.** (*intr.*) to have value, importance, or influence: *this picture counts as a rarity.* **8.** (*intr.;* often foll. by *for*) to have a certain specified value or importance: *the job counts for a lot.* **9.** (*intr.*) *Music.* to keep time by counting beats. ~*n.* **10.** the act of counting or reckoning. **11.** the number reached by counting; sum: *a blood count.* **12.** *Law.* a paragraph in an indictment containing a distinct and separate charge. **13. keep count.** to keep a record of items, events, etc. **14. lose count.** to fail to keep an accurate record of items, events, etc. **15.** *Boxing, wrestling.* the act of telling off a number of seconds by the referee, as when a boxer has been knocked down or a wrestler pinned by his opponent. **16. out for the count.** *Boxing.* knocked out and unable to continue after a count of ten by the referee. **17. take the count.** *Boxing.* to be unable to continue after a count of ten. **18.** *Archaic.* notice; regard; account. ~See also **count against, countdown, count on, count out.** [C14: from Anglo-French *counter,* from Old French *conter,* from Latin *computāre* to calculate, COMPUTE] —**'count·a·ble** *adj.*

count[2] (kaʊnt) *n.* **1.** a nobleman in any of various European countries having a rank corresponding to that of a British earl. **2.** any of various officials in the late Roman Empire and under various Germanic kings in the early Middle Ages. [C16: from Old French *conte,* from Late Latin *comes* occupant of a state office, from Latin: overseer, associate, literally: one who goes with, from COM- with + *īre* to go]

count a·gainst *vb. (intr., prep.)* to have influence to the disadvantage of: *your bad time-keeping will count against you.*

count+down ('kaʊnt,daʊn) *n.* **1.** the act of counting backwards to time a critical operation exactly, such as the launching of a rocket or the detonation of explosives. ~*vb.* **count down.** *(intr., adv.)* **2.** to count numbers backwards towards zero, esp. in timing such a critical operation.

coun·te+nance ('kaʊntɪnəns) *n.* **1.** the face, esp. when considered as expressing a person's character or mood: *a pleasant countenance.* **2.** support or encouragement; sanction. **3.** composure; self-control (esp. in the phrases **keep** or **lose one's countenance; out of countenance**). ~*vb. (tr.)* **4.** to support or encourage; sanction. **5.** to tolerate; endure. [C13: from Old French *contenance* mien, behaviour, from Latin *continentia* restraint, control; see CONTAIN] —'**coun+te+,nanc+er** *n.*

count+er[1] ('kaʊntə) *n.* **1.** a horizontal surface, as in a shop or bank, over which business is transacted. **2.** (in some cafeterias) a long table on which food is served to customers. **3. a.** a small flat disc of wood, metal, or plastic, used in various board games. **b.** a similar disc or token used as an imitation coin. **4.** a person or thing that may be used or manipulated. **5.** a skating figure consisting of three circles. **6. under the counter.** (**under-the-counter** when prenominal) (of the sale of goods, esp. goods in short supply) clandestine, surreptitious, or illegal; not in an open manner. **7. over the counter.** (**over-the-counter** when prenominal) (of security transactions) through a broker rather than on a stock exchange. [C14: from Old French *comptouer,* ultimately from Latin *computāre* to COMPUTE]

count+er[2] ('kaʊntə) *n.* **1.** a person who counts. **2.** an apparatus that records the number of occurrences of events. **3.** any instrument for detecting or counting ionizing particles or photons. See **Geiger counter, scintillation counter, crystal counter. 4.** *Electronics.* another name for **scaler** (sense 2). [C14: from Old French *conteor,* from Latin *computātor;* see COUNT[1]]

coun+ter[3] ('kaʊntə) *adv.* **1.** in a contrary direction or manner. **2.** in a wrong or reverse direction. **3. run counter to.** to have a contrary effect or action to. ~*adj.* **4.** opposing; opposite; contrary. ~*n.* **5.** something that is contrary or opposite to some other thing. **6.** an act, effect, or force that opposes another. **7.** a return attack, such as a blow in boxing. **8.** *Fencing.* a parry in which the foils move in a circular fashion. **9.** the portion of the stern of a boat or ship that overhangs the water aft of the rudder. **10.** Also called: **void.** *Printing.* the inside area of a typeface that is not type high, such as the centre of an "o", and therefore does not print. **11.** the part of a horse's breast under the neck and between the shoulders. **12.** a piece of leather forming the back of a shoe. ~*vb.* **13.** to say or do (something) in retaliation or response. **14.** *(tr.)* to move, act, or perform in a manner or direction opposite to (a person or thing). **15.** to return the attack of (an opponent). [C15: from Old French *contre,* from Latin *contrā* against]

coun·ter- *prefix.* **1.** against; opposite; contrary: *counterattack.* **2.** complementary; corresponding: *counterfoil.* **3.** duplicate or substitute: *counterfeit.* [via Norman French from Latin *contrā* against, opposite; see CONTRA-]

coun·ter+act (,kaʊntər'ækt) *vb. (tr.)* to oppose, neutralize, or mitigate the effects of by contrary action; check. —,**coun·ter+'ac+tion** *n.* —,**coun·ter+'ac+tive** *adj.* —,**coun·ter+'ac+tive+ly** *adv.*

coun·ter+at+tack ('kaʊntərə,tæk) *n.* **1.** an attack in response to an attack. ~*vb.* **2.** to make a counterattack (against).

coun·ter+at·trac+tion ('kaʊntərə,trækʃən) *n.* a rival attraction.

coun·ter+bal+ance *n.* ('kaʊntə,bæləns). **1.** a weight or force that balances or offsets another. ~*vb.* (,kaʊntə'bæləns). *(tr.)* **2.** to act as a counterbalance. ~Also: **counterpoise.**

coun·ter+blast ('kaʊntə,blɑ:st) *n.* **1.** an aggressive response to a verbal attack. **2.** a blast that counteracts another.

coun·ter+change (,kaʊntə'tʃeɪndʒ) *vb. (tr.)* **1.** to change parts, qualities, etc. **2.** *Poetic.* to chequer, as with contrasting colours.

coun·ter+charge ('kaʊntə,tʃɑ:dʒ) *n.* **1.** a charge brought by an accused person against the accuser. **2.** *Military.* a retaliatory charge. ~*vb.* **3.** *(tr.)* to make a countercharge against.

coun·ter+check *n.* ('kaʊntə,tʃɛk). **1.** a check or restraint, esp. one that acts in opposition to another. **2.** a restraint that reinforces another restraint. **3.** a double check, as for accuracy. ~*vb.* (,kaʊntə'tʃɛk). *(tr.)* **4.** to oppose by counteraction. **5.** to control or restrain by a second check. **6.** to double-check.

coun·ter+claim ('kaʊntə,kleɪm) *Chiefly law.* ~*n.* **1.** a claim set up in opposition to another, esp. by the defendant in a civil action against the plaintiff. ~*vb.* **2.** to set up (a claim) in opposition to another claim. —,**coun·ter+'claim+ant** *n.*

coun·ter+clock·wise (,kaʊntə'klɒk,waɪz) *adv., adj.* the U.S. equivalent of **anticlockwise.** Also: **contraclockwise.**

coun·ter+cul·ture ('kaʊntə,kʌltʃə) *n.* an alternative culture, deliberately at variance with the social norm.

coun·ter+es+pi·o+nage (,kaʊntə'ɛspɪə,nɑ:ʒ) *n.* activities designed to detect and counteract enemy espionage.

coun·ter+fac+tu·al (,kaʊntə'fækʃʊəl) *Logic.* ~*adj.* **1.** expressing what has not happened but could, would, or might under differing conditions. ~*n.* **2.** a conditional statement in which the first clause is a past tense subjunctive statement expressing something contrary to fact, as in: *if she had hurried she would have caught the bus.*

coun·ter+feit ('kaʊntəfɪt) *adj.* **1.** made in imitation of something genuine with the intent to deceive or defraud; forged. **2.** simulated; sham: *counterfeit affection.* ~*n.* **3.** an imitation designed to deceive or defraud. **4.** *Archaic.* an imposter; cheat. **5.** *Archaic.* a portrait. ~*vb.* **6.** *(tr.)* to make a fraudulent imitation of. **7.** *(intr.)* to make counterfeits. **8.** to feign; simulate. **9.** to imitate; copy. [C13: from Old French *contrefait,* from *contrefaire* to copy, from *contre-* COUNTER- + *faire* to make, from Latin *facere*] —'**coun·ter+,feit+er** *n.*

coun·ter+foil ('kaʊntə,fɔɪl) *n. Brit.* the part of a cheque, postal order, receipt, etc., detached and retained as a record of the transaction. Also called (esp. in the U.S.): **stub.**

coun·ter+glow ('kaʊntə,gləʊ) *n.* another name for **gegenschein.**

coun·ter+in+sur+gen+cy (,kaʊntərɪn'sɜ:dʒənsɪ) *n.* action taken to counter the activities of rebels, guerrillas, etc.

coun·ter+in+tel+li+gence (,kaʊntərɪn'tɛlɪdʒəns) *n.* activities designed to frustrate enemy espionage.

coun·ter+ir+ri+tant (,kaʊntər'ɪrɪtᵊnt) *n.* **1.** an agent that causes a superficial irritation of the skin and thereby relieves inflammation of deep structures. ~*adj.* **2.** producing a counterirritation. —,**coun·ter+,ir+ri+'ta+tion** *n.*

coun·ter jump+er *n. Informal, derogatory, and old-fashioned.* a sales assistant in a shop.

coun·ter+mand *vb.* (,kaʊntə'mɑ:nd). *(tr.)* **1.** to revoke or cancel (a command, order, etc.). **2.** to order (forces, etc.) to return or retreat; recall. ~*n.* ('kaʊntə,mɑ:nd). **3.** a command revoking another. [C15: from Old French *contremander,* from *contre-* COUNTER- + *mander* to command, from Latin *mandāre;* see MANDATE]

coun·ter+march ('kaʊntə,mɑ:tʃ) *vb.* **1.** *Chiefly military.* **a.** to march or cause to march back along the same route. **b.** to change the order of soldiers during a march. ~*n.* **2.** the act or instance of countermarching. **3.** a reversal of method, conduct, etc.

coun·ter+meas+ure ('kaʊntə,mɛʒə) *n.* action taken to oppose, neutralize, or retaliate against some other action.

coun·ter+mine *n.* ('kaʊntə,maɪn). **1.** *Military.* a tunnel dug to defeat similar activities by an enemy. **2.** a plot to frustrate another plot. ~*vb.* (,kaʊntə'maɪn). **3.** to frustrate by countermeasures. **4.** *Military.* to take measures to defeat the underground operations of (an enemy). **5.** *Military.* to destroy enemy mines in (an area) with mines of one's own.

coun·ter+move ('kaʊntə,mu:v) *n.* **1.** an opposing move. ~*vb.* **2.** to make or do (something) as an opposing move. —'**coun·ter+,move+ment** *n.*

coun·ter+of+fen+sive ('kaʊntərə,fɛnsɪv) *n.* a series of attacks by a defending force against an attacking enemy.

coun·ter+pane ('kaʊntə,peɪn) *n.* another word for **bedspread.** [C17: from obsolete *counterpoint* (influenced by *pane* coverlet), changed from Old French *coutepointe* quilt, from Medieval Latin *culcita puncta* quilted mattress]

coun·ter+part ('kaʊntə,pɑ:t) *n.* **1.** a person or thing identical to or closely resembling another. **2.** one of two parts that complement or correspond to each other. **3.** a person acting opposite another in a play. **4.** a duplicate, esp. of a legal document; copy.

coun·ter+plot ('kaʊntə,plɒt) *n.* **1.** a plot designed to frustrate another plot. ~*vb.* **+plots, +plot+ting, +plot+ted. 2.** *(tr.)* to oppose with a counterplot. **3.** *(intr.)* to devise or carry out a counterplot.

coun·ter+point ('kaʊntə,pɔɪnt) *n.* **1.** the technique involving the simultaneous sounding of two or more parts or melodies. **2.** a melody or part combined with another melody or part. See also **descant** (sense 1). **3.** the musical texture resulting from the simultaneous sounding of two or more melodies or parts. **4. strict counterpoint.** the application of the rules of counterpoint as an academic exercise. **5.** a contrasting or interacting element, theme, or item; foil. **6.** *Prosody.* the use of a stress or stresses at variance with the regular metrical stress. ~*vb.* **7.** *(tr.)* to set in contrast. ~Related adj.: **contrapuntal.** [C15: from Old French *contrepoint,* from *contre-* COUNTER- + *point* dot, note in musical notation, that is, an accompaniment set against the notes of a melody]

coun·ter+poise ('kaʊntə,pɔɪz) *n.* **1.** a force, influence, etc., that counterbalances another. **2.** a state of balance; equilibrium. **3.** a weight that balances another. **4.** a radial array of metallic wires, rods, or tubes arranged horizontally around the base of a vertical aerial to increase its transmitting efficiency. ~*vb.* **5.** to oppose with something of equal effect, weight, or force; offset. **6.** to bring into equilibrium. **7.** *Archaic.* to consider (one thing) carefully in relation to another.

coun·ter+pro+duc+tive (,kaʊntəprə'dʌktɪv) *adj.* tending to hinder or act against the achievement of an aim.

coun·ter+proof ('kaʊntə,pru:f) *n. Printing.* a reverse impression of a newly printed proof of an engraving made by laying it while wet upon plain paper and passing it through the press.

coun·ter+pro+pos+al ('kaʊntəprə,pəʊzᵊl) *n.* a proposal offered as an alternative to a previous proposal.

coun·ter+punch ('kaʊntə,pʌntʃ) *Boxing.* ~*vb. (intr.)* **1.** to punch an attacking opponent; return an attack. ~*n.* **2.** a return punch.

Coun·ter-Ref·or·ma+tion (,kaʊntə,rɛfə'meɪʃən) *n.* the reform movement of the Roman Catholic Church in the 16th and early 17th centuries considered as a reaction to the Protestant Reformation.

coun·ter-rev·o·lu+tion (,kaʊntə,rɛvə'lu:ʃən) *n.* a revolution opposed to a previous revolution and aimed at reversing its effects. —,**coun·ter-,rev·o·'lu+tion+ist** *n.*

coun·ter-rev·o+lu+tion+ar·y (,kaʊntə,rɛvə'lu:ʃənrɪ) *n., pl.* **+ar·ies. 1.** a person opposed to revolution. **2.** a person who opposes a specific revolution or revolutionary government.

~*adj.* **3.** characterized by opposition to a revolution or revolutions in general.

coun·ter+scarp ('kaʊntəˌskɑːp) *n. Fortifications.* the outer side of the ditch of a fort. Compare **escarp** (sense 1).

coun·ter+shad+ing (ˌkaʊntə'ʃeɪdɪŋ) *n.* (in the coloration of certain animals) a pattern, serving as camouflage, in which dark colours occur on parts of the body exposed to the light and pale colours on parts in the shade.

coun·ter+shaft ('kaʊntəˌʃɑːft) *n.* an intermediate shaft that is driven by, but rotates in the opposite direction to, a main shaft, esp. in a gear train.

coun·ter+sign *vb.* ('kaʊntəˌsaɪn, ˌkaʊntə'saɪn). **1.** (*tr.*) to sign (a document already signed by another). ~*n.* ('kaʊntəˌsaɪn). **2.** Also called: **countersignature.** the signature so written. **3.** a secret sign given in response to another sign. **4.** *Chiefly military.* a password.

coun·ter+sink ('kaʊntəˌsɪŋk) *vb.* **+sinks, +sink+ing, +sank, +sunk.** (*tr.*) **1.** to enlarge the upper part of (a hole) in timber, metal, etc., so that the head of a bolt or screw can be sunk below the surface. **2.** to drive (a screw) or sink (a bolt) into such an enlarged hole. ~*n.* **3.** Also called: **countersink bit.** a tool for countersinking. **4.** a countersunk depression or hole.

coun·ter+spy ('kaʊntəˌspaɪ) *n., pl.* **+spies.** a spy working against or investigating enemy espionage.

coun·ter+sub+ject ('kaʊntəˌsʌbdʒɪkt) *n. Music.* (in a fugue) the theme in one voice that accompanies the statement of the subject in another.

coun·ter+ten+or (ˌkaʊntə'tɛnə) *n.* **1.** an adult male voice with an alto range. **2.** a singer with such a voice.

coun·ter+type ('kaʊntəˌtaɪp) *n.* **1.** an opposite type. **2.** a corresponding type.

coun·ter+vail (ˌkaʊntə'veɪl, 'kaʊntəˌveɪl) *vb.* **1.** (when *intr.*, usually foll. by *against*) to act or act against with equal power or force. **2.** (*tr.*) to make up for; compensate; offset. [C14: from Old French *contrevaloir*, from Latin *contrā valēre*, from *contrā* against + *valēre* to be strong]

coun·ter+weigh (ˌkaʊntə'weɪ) *vb.* another word for **counterbalance.**

coun·ter+weight ('kaʊntəˌweɪt) *n.* a counterbalancing weight, influence, or force. —**'coun·ter+ˌweight+ed** *adj.*

coun·ter+word ('kaʊntəˌwɜːd) *n.* a word widely used in a sense much looser than its original meaning, such as *tremendous* or *awful.*

coun·ter+work ('kaʊntəˌwɜːk) *n.* **1.** work done in opposition to other work. **2.** defensive fortifications put up against attack. —**'coun·ter+ˌwork+er** *n.*

coun+tess ('kaʊntɪs) *n.* **1.** the wife or widow of a count or earl. **2.** a woman of the rank of count or earl.

count+ing house *n. Rare, chiefly Brit.* a room or building used by the accountants of a business.

count+less ('kaʊntlɪs) *adj.* innumerable; myriad.

count noun *n.* a noun that refers to an object that can exist in the plural without change of meaning. Count nouns, such as *telephone, peach,* or *cup,* can be preceded by *a, an,* or *the,* as opposed to mass nouns, such as *water,* which cannot. Compare **mass noun.**

count on *vb.* (*intr., prep.*) to rely or depend on.

count out *vb.* (*tr., adv.*) **1.** *Informal.* to leave out; exclude: *count me out!* **2.** (of a boxing referee) to judge (a floored boxer) to have failed to recover within the specified time. See **count**[1] (sense 15). **3.** to count (something) aloud.

count pal·a+tine *n., pl.* **counts pal·a+tine.** *History.* **1.** (in the Holy Roman Empire) **a.** originally an official who administered the king's domains or his justice. **b.** later, a count who exercised royal authority in his own domains. **2.** (in England and Ireland) an earl or other lord of a county palatine. **3.** (in the late Roman Empire) a palace official who exercised judicial authority.

coun+tri+fied *or* **coun+try+fied** ('kʌntrɪˌfaɪd) *adj.* in the style, manners, etc., of the country; rural.

coun+try ('kʌntrɪ) *n., pl.* **+tries.** **1.** a territory distinguished by its people, culture, language, geography, etc. **2.** an area of land distinguished by its political autonomy; state. **3.** the people of a territory or state: *the whole country rebelled.* **4. a.** the part of the land that is away from cities or industrial areas; rural districts. **b.** (*as modifier*): *country house.* **c.** (*in combination*): *a countryman.* Related adj.: **pastoral, rural. 5. up country.** away from the coast or the capital. **6.** one's native land or nation of citizenship. **7.** (usually preceded by *the*) *Brit. informal.* the outlying area or area furthest from the finish of a sports ground or racecourse. **8.** (*modifier*) rough; uncouth; rustic: *country manners.* **9. across country.** not keeping to roads, etc. **10. go** *or* **appeal to the country.** *Chiefly Brit.* to dissolve Parliament and hold an election. **11. unknown country.** an unfamiliar topic, place, matter, etc. [C13: from Old French *contrée,* from Medieval Latin *contrāta,* literally: that which lies opposite, from Latin *contrā* opposite]

coun·try-and-west·ern *n.* **a.** a type of urban 20th-century White folk music of the southeastern U.S. **b.** (*as modifier*): *country-and-western music.* Abbrev.: **C & W.**

coun+try club *n.* a club in the country, having sporting and social facilities.

coun+try cous+in *n.* an unsophisticated person from the country, esp. one regarded as an object of amusement.

coun+try dance *n.* a type of folk dance in which couples are arranged in sets and perform a series of movements, esp. facing one another in a line. —**coun+try danc+ing** *n.*

coun+try gen·tle+man *n.* a rich man with an estate in the country.

coun·try+man ('kʌntrɪmən) *n., pl.* **+men.** **1.** a person who lives in the country. **2.** a person from a particular country or from one's own country (esp. in the phrase **fellow countryman**). —**'coun·try+ˌwom·an** *fem. n.*

coun+try rock[1] *n.* the rock surrounding a mineral vein or igneous intrusion.

coun+try rock[2] *n.* a style of rock music influenced by country-and-western.

coun+try seat *n.* a large estate or property in the country.

coun·try+side ('kʌntrɪˌsaɪd) *n.* a rural area or its population.

coun+ty ('kaʊntɪ) *n., pl.* **+ties.** **1. a.** any of the administrative subdivisions of certain states, esp. any of the 52 units into which England and Wales, except for seven major conurbations, have been divided for purposes of local government since April 1, 1974. See also **metropolitan county. b.** (*as modifier*): *county cricket.* **2.** *Obsolete.* the lands under the jurisdiction of a count or earl. ~*adj.* **3.** *Brit. informal.* having the characteristics and habits of the inhabitants of country houses and estates, esp. an upper-class accent and an interest in horses, dogs, etc. [C14: from Old French *conté* land belonging to a count, from Late Latin *comitātus* office of a count, from *comes* COUNT[2]]

coun+ty bor+ough *n.* **1.** (in England and Wales from 1888 to 1974) a borough administered independently of the county around it. **2.** (in the Republic of Ireland) any of the four largest boroughs, governed independently of the administrative county around it by an elected council that constitutes an all-purpose authority.

coun+ty court *n.* (in England) a local court exercising limited jurisdiction in civil matters.

coun+ty pal·a+tine *n., pl.* **coun+ties pal·a+tine.** **1.** the lands of a count palatine. **2.** (in England and Ireland) a county in which the earl exercised many royal powers, esp. judicial authority.

coun+ty seat *n. Chiefly U.S.* another term for **county town.**

coun+ty town *n.* the town in which a county's affairs are administered.

coup[1] (kuː) *n.* **1.** a brilliant and successful stroke or action. **2.** short for **coup d'état.** [C18: from French: blow, from Latin *colaphus* blow with the fist, from Greek *kolaphos*]

coup[2] *or* **cowp** (kaʊp) *vb. Scot.* to turn or fall over. [C15: perhaps identical with obsolete *cope* to strike; see COPE[1]]

coup[3] (kaʊp) *vb. Scot.* to barter; traffic; deal. [C14: from Old Norse *kaupa* to buy]

coup de fou+dre *French.* (ku də 'fuːdr) *n., pl.* ***coups de fou+dre*** (ku də 'fuːdr). a sudden and amazing action or event. [literally: lightning flash]

coup de grâce *French.* (ku də 'grɑs) *n., pl.* ***coups de grâce*** (ku də 'grɑs). **1.** a mortal or finishing blow, esp. one delivered as an act of mercy to a sufferer. **2.** a final or decisive stroke. [literally: blow of mercy]

coup de main *French.* (ku də 'mɛ̃) *n., pl.* ***coups de main*** (ku də 'mɛ̃). *Chiefly military.* an attack that achieves complete surprise. [literally: blow with the hand]

coup d'é·tat ('kuː deɪ'tɑː; *French* ku de'ta) *n., pl.* **coups d'é·tat** ('kuːz deɪ'tɑː; *French* ku de'ta). a sudden violent or illegal seizure of government. [French, literally: stroke of state]

coup de thé·â+tre *French.* (ku də te'ɑːtr) *n., pl.* ***coups de thé·â+tre*** (ku də te'ɑːtr). **1.** a dramatic turn of events, esp. in a play. **2.** a sensational device of stagecraft. **3.** a stage success. [literally: stroke of the theatre]

coup d'oeil *French.* (ku 'døj) *n., pl.* ***coups d'oeil*** (ku 'døj). a quick glance. [literally: stroke of the eye]

coupe (kuːp) *n.* **1.** a dessert of fruit and ice cream, usually served in a glass goblet. **2.** a dish or stemmed glass bowl designed for this dessert. [C19: from French: goblet, CUP]

cou+pé ('kuːpeɪ) *n.* **1.** Also called: **fixed-head coupé.** a four-seater car with a fixed roof, a sloping back, and usually two doors. Compare **drophead coupé. 2.** a four-wheeled horse-drawn carriage with two seats inside and one outside for the driver. **3.** an end compartment in a European railway carriage with seats on one side only. [C19: from French, short for *carosse coupé,* literally: cut-off carriage, from *couper* to cut, from *coup* blow, stroke]

Cou·perin (*French* ku'prɛ̃) *n.* **Fran·çois** (frɑ̃'swa). 1668–1733, French composer, noted for his harpsichord suites and organ music.

cou+ple ('kʌpᵊl) *n.* **1.** two people who regularly associate with each other or live together: *an engaged couple.* **2.** (*functioning as sing. or pl.*) two people considered as a pair, for or as if for dancing, games, etc. **3.** *Chiefly hunting or coursing.* **a.** a pair of collars joined by a leash, used to attach hounds to one another. **b.** two hounds joined in this way. **c.** the unit of reckoning for hounds in a pack: *twenty and a half couple.* **4.** a pair of equal and opposite parallel forces that have a tendency to produce rotation with a turning moment equal to the product of either force and the perpendicular distance between them. **5.** *Physics.* **a.** two dissimilar metals, alloys, or semiconductors in electrical contact, across which a voltage develops. See **thermocouple. b.** Also called: **galvanic couple.** two dissimilar metals or alloys in electrical contact that when immersed in an electrolyte act as the electrodes of an electrolytic cell. **6.** a connector or link between two members, such as a tie connecting a pair of rafters in a roof. **7. a couple of.** (*functioning as sing. or pl.*) **a.** a combination of two; a pair of: *a couple of men.* **b.** *Informal.* a small number of; a few: *a couple of days.* ~*pron.* **8.** (usually preceded by *a; functioning as sing. or pl.*) two; a pair: *give him a couple.* ~*vb.* **9.** (*tr.*) to connect (two things) together or to connect (one thing) to (another): *to couple railway carriages.* **10.** (*tr.*) to do (two things) simultaneously or alternately: *he couples studying with teaching.* **11.** to form or be formed into a pair or pairs. **12.** to associate, put, or connect together: *history is coupled with sociology.* **13.** to link (two circuits) by electromagnetic induction. **14.** (*intr.*) to have sexual intercourse. **15.** to join or be joined in marriage; marry. **16.** (*tr.*) to attach (two hounds to each other). [C13: from Old French: a pair, from Latin *cōpula* a bond; see COPULA]

cou+pler ('kʌplə) *n.* **1.** a link or rod transmitting power between two rotating mechanisms or a rotating part and a reciprocating part. **2.** *Music.* a device on an organ or harpsichord connecting two keys, two manuals, etc., so that both may be played at once. **3.** *Electronics.* a device, such as a transformer, used to couple two or more electrical circuits. **4.** a U.S. word for **coupling** (sense 2).

cou+plet ('kʌplɪt) *n.* two successive lines of verse, usually rhymed and of the same metre. [C16: from French, literally: a little pair; see COUPLE]

cou+pling ('kʌplɪŋ) *n.* **1.** a mechanical device that connects two things. **2.** a device for connecting railway cars or trucks together. **3.** the part of the body of a horse, dog, or other quadruped that lies between the forequarters and the hindquarters. **4.** *Electronics.* the act or process of linking two or more circuits so that power can be transferred between them usually by mutual induction, as in a transformer, or by means of a capacitor or inductor common to both circuits. **5.** *Physics.* an interaction between different properties of a system, such as a group of atoms or nuclei, or between two or more systems.

cou+pon ('ku:pɒn) *n.* **1. a.** a detachable part of a ticket or advertisement entitling the holder to a discount, free gift, etc. **b.** a detachable slip usable as a commercial order form. **c.** a voucher given away with certain goods, a certain number of which are exchangeable for goods offered by the manufacturers. **2.** one of a number of detachable certificates attached to a bond, esp. a bearer bond, the surrender of which entitles the bearer to receive interest payments. **3.** one of several detachable cards used for making hire-purchase payments. **4.** a ticket issued to facilitate rationing. **5.** *Brit.* a detachable entry form for any of certain competitions, esp. football pools. [C19: from French, from Old French *colpon* piece cut off, from *colper* to cut, variant of *couper;* see COPE[1]]

cour+age ('kʌrɪdʒ) *n.* **1.** the power or quality of dealing with or facing danger, fear, pain, etc. **2. the courage of one's convictions.** the confidence to act in accordance with one's beliefs. **3. take one's courage in both hands.** to nerve oneself to perform an action. **4.** *Obsolete.* mind; disposition; spirit. [C13: from Old French *corage,* from *cuer* heart, from Latin *cor*]

cou+ra+geous (kə'reɪdʒəs) *adj.* possessing or expressing courage. —**cou+'ra+geous+ly** *adv.* —**cou+'ra+geous+ness** *n.*

cou+rante (kʊ'rɑ:nt) *n. Music.* **1.** a movement of a classical suite, either in simple triple time or exhibiting rhythmical ambiguity. **2.** an old dance in triple time. ~Also called (esp. for the dance): **coranto.** [C16: from French, literally: running, feminine of *courant,* present participle of *courir* to run, from Latin *currere*]

Cour+an+tyne ('kɜ:rənˌtaɪn) *n.* a river in N South America, rising in S Guyana and flowing north to the Atlantic, forming the boundary between Guyana and Surinam. Length: 765 km (475 miles). Dutch name: **Corantijn.**

Cour·bet (*French* kur'bɛ) *n.* **Gus·tave** (gy'stav). 1819–77, French painter, a leader of the realist movement; noted for his depiction of contemporary life.

Cour+be·voie (*French* kurbə'vwa) *n.* an industrial suburb of Paris, on the Seine. Pop.: 54 578 (1975).

cou+reur de bois (*French* kurœ:r də 'bwa) *n., pl.* **cou+reurs de bois** (kurœ:r də 'bwa). *Canadian history.* a French Canadian woodsman who traded with Indians for furs. [Canadian French: trapper (literally: wood-runner)]

cour+gette (kʊə'ʒɛt) *n.* a small variety of vegetable marrow, cooked and eaten as a vegetable. U.S. name: **zucchini.** [from French, diminutive of *courge* marrow, gourd]

cou+ri+er ('kʊərɪə) *n.* **1.** a special messenger, esp. one carrying diplomatic correspondence. **2.** a person who makes arrangements for or accompanies a group of travellers on a journey or tour. [C16: from Old French *courrier,* from Old Italian *corriere,* from *correre* to run, from Latin *currere*]

cour+lan ('kʊələn) *n.* another name for **limpkin.** [C19: from French, variant of *courliri,* from Galibi *kurliri*]

Cour+land *or* **Kur+land** ('kʊələnd) *n.* a region of the W Soviet Union, between the Gulf of Riga and the Lithuanian border: part of the Latvian SSR. Latvian name: **Kurzeme.**

course (kɔ:s) *n.* **1.** a continuous progression from one point to the next in time or space; onward movement: *the course of his life.* **2.** a route or direction followed: *they kept on a southerly course.* **3. a.** the path or channel along which something moves: *the course of a river.* **b.** (*in combination*): *a watercourse.* **4.** an area or stretch of land or water on which a sport is played or a race is run: *a golf course.* **5.** a period of time; duration: *in the course of the next hour.* **6.** the usual order of and time required for a sequence of events; regular procedure: *the illness ran its course.* **7.** a mode of conduct or action: *if you follow that course, you will fail.* **8.** a connected series of events, actions, etc. **9. a.** a prescribed number of lessons, lectures, etc., in an educational curriculum. **b.** the material covered in such a curriculum. **10.** a prescribed regimen to be followed for a specific period of time: *a course of treatment.* **11.** a part of a meal served at one time: *the fish course.* **12.** a continuous, usually horizontal, layer of building material, such as a row of bricks, tiles, etc. **13.** *Nautical.* any of the sails on the lowest yards of a square-rigged ship. **14.** *Knitting.* the horizontal rows of stitches. Compare **wale**[1] (sense 2b.). **15.** (in medieval Europe) a charge by knights in a tournament. **16. a.** a hunt by hounds relying on sight rather than scent. **b.** a match in which two greyhounds compete in chasing a hare. **17.** the part or function assigned to an individual bell in a set of changes. **18.** *Archaic.* a running race. **19. as a matter of course.** as a natural or normal consequence, mode of action, or event. **20. the course of nature.** the ordinary course of events. **21. in course of.** in the process of: *the ship was in course of construction.* **22. in due course.** at some future time, esp. the natural or appropriate time. **23. of course. a.** (*adv.*) as expected; naturally. **b.** (*sentence substitute*) certainly; definitely. **24. run** (*or* **take**) **its course.** (of something) to complete its development or action. ~*vb.* **25.** (*intr.*) to run, race, or flow, esp. swiftly and without interruption. **26.** to cause (hounds) to hunt by sight rather than scent or (of hounds) to hunt (a quarry) thus. **27.** (*tr.*) to run through or over; traverse. **28.** (*intr.*) to take a direction; proceed on a course. [C13: from Old French *cours,* from Latin *cursus* a running, from *currere* to run]

cours+er[1] ('kɔ:sə) *n.* **1.** a person who courses hounds or dogs, esp. greyhounds. **2.** a hound or dog trained for coursing.

cours+er[2] ('kɔ:sə) *n. Literary.* a swift horse; steed. [C13: from Old French *coursier,* from *cours* COURSE]

cours+er[3] ('kɔ:sə) *n.* a terrestrial plover-like shore bird, such as *Cursorius cursor* (cream-coloured courser), of the subfamily *Cursoriinae* of desert and semidesert regions of the Old World: family *Glareolidae,* order *Charadriiformes.* [C18: from Latin *cursōrius* suited for running, from *cursus* COURSE]

cours·es ('kɔ:sɪz) *pl. n.* (*sometimes sing.*) *Physiol.* another word for **menses.**

cours+ing ('kɔ:sɪŋ) *n.* **1.** (of hounds or dogs) hunting by sight. **2.** a sport in which hounds are matched against one another in pairs for the hunting of hares by sight.

court (kɔ:t) *n.* **1.** an area of ground wholly or partly surrounded by walls or buildings. **2.** *Brit.* (*cap. when part of a name*) **a.** a block of flats: *Selwyn Court.* **b.** a mansion or country house. **c.** a short street, sometimes closed at one end. **3.** a space inside a building, sometimes surrounded with galleries. **4. a.** the residence, retinues, or household of a sovereign or nobleman. **b.** (*as modifier*): *a court ball.* **5.** a sovereign or prince and his retinue, advisers, etc. **6.** any formal assembly, reception, etc., held by a sovereign or nobleman with his courtiers. **7.** homage, flattering attention, or amorous approaches (esp. in the phrase **pay court to someone**). **8.** *Law.* a tribunal having power to adjudicate in civil, criminal, military, or ecclesiastical matters. **9.** *Law.* the regular sitting of such a judicial tribunal. **10. a.** a marked outdoor or enclosed area used for any of various ball games, such as tennis, squash, etc. **b.** a marked section of such an area: *the service court.* **11. a.** the board of directors or council of a corporation, company, etc. **b.** *Chiefly Brit.* the supreme council of some universities. **12.** a branch of any of several friendly societies. **13. go to court.** to take legal action. **14. hold court.** to preside over admirers, attendants, etc. **15. out of court. a.** without a trial or legal case: *the case was settled out of court.* **b.** too unimportant for consideration. **c.** *Brit.* so as to ridicule completely (in the phrase **laugh out of court**). **16. the ball is in your court.** you are obliged to make the next move. ~*vb.* **17.** to attempt to gain the love of; woo. **18.** (*tr.*) to pay attention to (someone) in order to gain favour. **19.** (*tr.*) to try to obtain (fame, honour, etc.). **20.** (*tr.*) to invite, usually foolishly, as by taking risks: *to court disaster.* [C12: from Old French, from Latin *cohors* COHORT]

Court (kɔ:t) *n.* **Mar·ga·ret** (née *Smith*). born 1942, Australian tennis player: Australian champion 1960–66, 1969–71, and 1973; U.S. champion 1962, 1965, 1969–70, and 1973; Wimbledon champion 1963, 1965, and 1970.

court-bouil·lon *n.* a stock made from root vegetables, water, and wine or vinegar, used primarily for poaching fish. [from French, from *court* short, from Latin *curtus* + *bouillon* broth, from *bouillir* to BOIL[1]]

court card *n.* (in a pack of playing cards) a king, queen, or jack of any suit. U.S. equivalent: **face card.**

court cir+cu+lar *n.* (in countries having a monarchy) a daily report of the activities, engagements, etc., of the sovereign, published in a national newspaper.

court dress *n.* the formal clothing worn at court.

Cour+telle (kɔ:'tɛl) *n. Trademark.* a synthetic acrylic fibre resembling wool.

cour+te·ous ('kɜ:tɪəs) *adj.* polite and considerate in manner. [C13 *corteis,* literally: with courtly manners, from Old French; see COURT] —**'cour+te·ous+ly** *adv.* —**'cour+te·ous+ness** *n.*

cour+te·san *or* **cour+te·zan** (ˌkɔ:tɪ'zæn) *n.* (esp. formerly) a prostitute, or the mistress of a man of rank. [C16: from Old French *courtisane,* from Italian *cortigiana* female courtier, from *cortigiano* courtier, from *corte* COURT]

cour+te·sy ('kɜ:tɪsɪ) *n., pl.* **·sies. 1.** politeness; good manners. **2.** a courteous gesture or remark. **3.** favour or consent (esp. in the phrase **by courtesy of**). **4.** common consent as opposed to right (esp. in the phrase **by courtesy**). See also **courtesy title. 5.** ('kɜ:tsɪ). an archaic spelling of **curtsy.** [C13 *curteisie,* from Old French, from *corteis* COURTEOUS]

cour+te·sy light *n.* the interior light in a motor vehicle.

cour+te·sy ti+tle *n.* any of several titles having no legal significance, such as those borne by the children of peers.

court hand *n.* a style of handwriting formerly used in English law courts.

court+house ('kɔ:tˌhaʊs) *n.* a public building in which courts of law are held.

cour+ti+er ('kɔ:tɪə) *n.* **1.** an attendant at a court. **2.** a person who seeks favour in an ingratiating manner. [C13: from

Anglo-French *courteour* (unattested), from Old French *corteier* to attend at court]
court-leet *n.* the full name for **leet** (sense 1).
court·ly ('kɔːtlɪ) *adj.* ·**li·er,** ·**li·est. 1.** of or suitable for a royal court. **2.** refined in manner. **3.** ingratiating. —'**court·li·ness** *n.*
court·ly love *n.* a tradition represented in Western European literature between the 12th and the 14th centuries, idealizing love between a knight and a revered (usually married) lady.
court mar·tial *n., pl.* **court mar·tials** *or* **courts mar·tial. 1.** a military court that tries charges of serious breaches of martial law. ~*vb.* **court-mar·tial, ·tials, ·tial·ling, ·tialled** *or U.S.* **·tials, ·tial·ing, ·tialed. 2.** (*tr.*) to try by court martial.
Court of Ap·peal *n.* a branch of the Supreme Court of Judicature that hears appeals from the High Court in both criminal and civil matters and from the county and crown courts.
Court of Com·mon Pleas *n.* **1.** *English law.* (formerly) a superior court exercising jurisdiction in civil actions between private citizens. **2.** *U.S. law.* (in some states) a court exercising original and general jurisdiction.
Court of Ex·cheq·uer *n.* (formerly) an English civil court where Crown revenue cases were tried. Also called: **Exchequer.**
court of first in·stance *n.* a court in which legal proceedings are begun or first heard.
court of hon·our *n.* a military court that is instituted to investigate matters involving personal honour.
court of in·quir·y *n.* **1.** *Brit.* a group of people appointed to investigate the causes of a disaster, accident, etc. **2.** a military court set up to inquire into a military matter.
Court of Jus·ti·ci·ar·y *n.* the supreme criminal court in Scotland.
Court of Ses·sion *n.* the highest court of civil jurisdiction in Scotland.
Court of St. James's *n.* the official name of the royal court of Britain.
court plas·ter *n.* a plaster, composed of isinglass on silk, formerly used to cover superficial wounds. [C18: so called because formerly used by court ladies for beauty spots]
Cour·trai (*French* kur'trɛ) *n.* a town in W Belgium, in West Flanders on the Lys River: the largest producer of linen in W Europe. Pop.: 44 961 (1970). Flemish name: **Kortrijk.**
court roll *n. History.* the register of land holdings, etc., of a manorial court.
court·room ('kɔːtˌruːm, -ˌrʊm) *n.* a room in which the sittings of a law court are held.
court·ship ('kɔːtʃɪp) *n.* **1.** the act, period, or art of seeking the love of someone with intent to marry. **2.** the seeking or soliciting of favours. **3.** *Obsolete.* courtly behaviour.
court ten·nis *n.* the U.S. term for **real tennis.**
court·yard ('kɔːtˌjɑːd) *n.* an open area of ground surrounded by walls or buildings; court.
cous·cous ('kuːskuːs) *n.* a spicy dish, originating from North Africa, consisting of steamed semolina served with a meat stew. [C17: via French from Arabic *kouskous,* from *kaskasa* to pound until fine]
cous·in ('kʌzᵊn) *n.* **1.** Also called: **first cousin, cousin-german, full cousin.** the child of one of one's aunt or uncle. **2.** a relative who has descended from one of one's common ancestors. A person's **second cousin** is the child of one of his parents' first cousins. A person's **third cousin** is the child of one of his parents' second cousins. A **first cousin once removed** (or loosely **second cousin**) is the child of one's first cousin. **3.** a member of a group related by race, ancestry, interests, etc.: *our Australian cousins.* **4.** a title used by a sovereign when addressing another sovereign or a nobleman. [C13: from Old French *cosin,* from Latin *consōbrīnus* cousin, from *sōbrīnus* cousin on the mother's side; related to *soror* sister] —'**cous·in·ˌhood** *or* '**cous·in·ˌship** *n.* —'**cous·in·ly** *adj., adv.*
Cou·sin (*French* ku'zɛ̃) *n.* **Vic·tor** (vik'tɔːr). 1792–1867, French philosopher and educational reformer.
Cous·teau (*French* ku'sto) *n.* **Jacques Yves** (ʒɑːk 'iv). born 1910, French underwater explorer.
cou·teau (kuː'təʊ) *n., pl.* ·**teaux** (-'təʊz). a large two-edged knife used formerly as a weapon. [C17: from Old French *coutel,* from Latin *cultellus* a little knife, from *culter* knife, ploughshare]
couth (kuːθ) *adj.* **1.** *Facetious.* refined. **2.** *Archaic.* familiar; known. [Old English *cūth* known, past participle of *cunnan* to know; sense 1, back formation from UNCOUTH]
couth·ie *or* **couth·y** ('kuːθɪ) *adj. Scot.* **1.** sociable; friendly. **2.** comfortable; snug. [C13: see COUTH, UNCOUTH]
cou·ture (kuː'tʊə; *French* ku'tyːr) *n.* high fashion designing and dressmaking. [from French: sewing, dressmaking, from Old French *cousture* seam, from Latin *consuere* to stitch together, from *suere* to sew]
cou·tu·ri·er (kuː'tʊərɪˌeɪ; *French* kuty'rje) *n.* a person who designs, makes, and sells fashion clothes for women. [from French: dressmaker; see COUTURE] —**cou·tu·ri·ère** (kuːˌtuːrɪ'ɛə; *French* kuty'rjɛːr) *fem. n.*
cou·vade (kuː'vɑːd; *French* ku'vad) *n.* a custom among certain peoples whereby a man imitates the behaviour, etc., of his pregnant wife and at the time of birth is put to bed as though he were bearing the child. [C19: from French, from *couver* to hatch, from Latin *cubāre* to lie down]
co·va·len·cy (kəʊ'veɪlənsɪ) *or U.S.* **co·va·lence** *n.* **1.** the formation and nature of covalent bonds. **2.** the number of covalent bonds that a particular atom can make with other atoms in forming a molecule. —**co·'va·lent** *adj.* —**co·'va·lent·ly** *adv.*
co·va·lent bond *n.* a type of chemical bond involving the sharing of electrons between atoms in a molecule, esp. the sharing of a pair of electrons by two adjacent atoms.
co·var·i·ance (kəʊ'vɛərɪəns) *n. Statistics.* a measure of the association between two variables obtained by dividing the product of the mean deviations of corresponding observed values of the two variables by the number of pairs of observed values.
cove[1] (kəʊv) *n.* **1.** a small bay or inlet, usually between rocky headlands. **2.** a narrow cavern formed in the sides of cliffs, mountains, etc., usually by erosion. **3.** a sheltered place. **4.** Also called: **coving.** *Architect.* a concave curved surface between the wall and ceiling of a room. ~*vb.* **5.** (*tr.*) to form an architectural cove in. [Old English *cofa;* related to Old Norse *kofi,* Old High German *kubisi* tent]
cove[2] (kəʊv) *n. Slang, Brit. old-fashioned and Austral.* a fellow; chap. [C16: probably from Romany *kova* thing, person]
cov·en ('kʌvᵊn) *n.* **1.** a meeting of witches. **2.** a company of 13 witches. [C16: probably from Old French *covin* group, ultimately from Latin *convenīre* to come together; compare CONVENT]
cov·e·nant ('kʌvənənt) *n.* **1.** a binding agreement; contract. **2.** *Law.* **a.** an agreement in writing under seal, as to pay a stated annual sum to a charity. **b.** a particular clause in such an agreement, esp. in a lease. **3.** (in early English law) an action in which damages were sought for breach of a sealed agreement. **4.** *Bible.* God's promise to the Israelites and their commitment to worship him alone. ~*vb.* **5.** to agree to a covenant (concerning). [C13: from Old French, from *covenir* to agree, from Latin *convenīre* to come together, make an agreement; see CONVENE] —**cov·e·nan·tal** (ˌkʌvə'næntᵊl) *adj.* —ˌ**cov·e·'nan·tal·ly** *adv.*
Cov·e·nant ('kʌvənənt) *n. Scottish history.* any of the bonds entered into by Scottish Presbyterians to defend their religion, esp. one in 1638 (**National Covenant**) and one of 1643 (**Solemn League and Covenant**).
cov·e·nan·tee (ˌkʌvənən'tiː) *n.* the person to whom the promise in a covenant is made.
Cov·e·nant·er ('kʌvənəntə, ˌkʌvə'næntə) *n.* a person upholding the National Covenant of 1638 or the Solemn League and Covenant of 1643 between Scotland and England to establish and defend Presbyterianism.
cov·e·nan·tor *or* **cov·e·nant·er** ('kʌvənəntə) *n.* a party who makes a promise and who is to perform the obligation expressed in a covenant.
Cov·ent Gar·den ('kʌvənt, 'kɒv-) *n.* **1.** a district of central London: famous for its former fruit, vegetable, and flower market. **2.** the Royal Opera House (built 1858) in Covent Garden.
Cov·en·try ('kɒvəntrɪ) *n.* **1.** a city in central England, in West Midlands: devastated in World War II; modern cathedral (1954–62); industrial centre, esp. for motor vehicles. Pop.: 334 839 (1971). **2. send to Coventry.** to ostracize or ignore.
cov·er ('kʌvə) *vb.* (*mainly tr.*) **1.** to place or spread something over so as to protect or conceal. **2.** to provide with a covering; clothe. **3.** to put a garment, esp. a hat, on (the body or head). **4.** to extend over or lie thickly on the surface of; spread: *snow covered the fields.* **5.** to bring upon (oneself); invest (oneself) as if with a covering: *covered with shame.* **6.** (sometimes foll. by *up*) to act as a screen or concealment for; hide from view. **7.** *Military.* to protect (an individual, formation, or place) by taking up a position from which fire may be returned if those being protected are fired upon. **8.** (*also intr.,* sometimes foll. by *for*) to assume responsibility for (a person or thing): *to cover a person's work in his absence.* **9.** (*intr.;* foll. by *for* or *up for*) to provide an alibi (for). **10.** to have as one's territory: *this salesman covers your area.* **11.** to travel over: *to cover three miles a day.* **12.** (*tr.*) to have or place in the aim and within the range of (a firearm). **13.** to include or deal with: *his talk covered all aspects of the subject.* **14.** (of an asset or income) to be sufficient to meet (a liability or expense). **15. a.** to insure against loss, risk, etc. **b.** to provide for (loss, risk, etc.) by insurance. **16.** (*also intr.*) *Finance.* to purchase (securities, etc.) in order to meet contracts, esp. short sales. **17.** to deposit (an equivalent stake) in a bet or wager. **18.** (*also intr.*) to play a card higher in rank than (one played beforehand by another player). **19.** to act as reporter or photographer on (a news event, etc.) for a newspaper or magazine: *to cover sports events.* **20.** *Sport.* to guard or protect (an opponent, teammate, or area). **21.** (of a male animal, esp. a horse) to copulate with (a female animal). **22.** (of a bird) to brood (eggs). ~*n.* **23.** anything that covers, spreads over, protects, or conceals. **24.** woods or bushes providing shelter or a habitat for wild creatures. **25. a.** a blanket used on a bed for warmth. **b.** another word for **bedspread. 26.** *Finance.* liquid assets, reserves, or guaranteed income sufficient to discharge a liability, meet an expenditure, etc. **27.** a pretext, disguise, or false identity: *the thief sold brushes as a cover.* **28.** *Insurance.* another word for **coverage** (sense 3). **29.** an envelope or package for sending through the post: *under plain cover.* **30.** *Philately.* **a.** an entire envelope that has been postmarked. **b. on cover.** (of a postage stamp) kept in this form by collectors. **31. a.** an individual table setting, esp. in a restaurant. **b.** (*as modifier*): *a cover charge.* **32.** *Sport.* the guarding or protection of an opponent, teammate, or area. **33.** Also called: **cover version.** a newly recorded version of a well-known musical item. **34.** *Cricket.* **a.** (*often pl.*) the area more or less at right angles to the pitch on the off side and usually about halfway to the boundary: *to field in the covers.* **b.** (*as modifier*): *a cover drive by a batsman.* **c.** Also called: **cover point.** a fielder in such a position. **35. break**

cover. (esp. of game animals) to come out from a shelter or hiding place. **36. take cover.** to make for a place of safety or shelter. **37. under cover.** protected, concealed, or in secret: *under cover of night.* ~See also **cover-up.** [C13: from Old French *covrir,* from Latin *cooperīre* to cover completely, from *operīre* to cover over] —'**cov·er·a·ble** *adj.* —'**cov·er·er** *n.* —'**cov·er·less** *adj.*

cov·er·age ('kʌvərɪdʒ) *n.* **1.** the amount or extent to which something is covered. **2.** *Journalism.* the amount and quality of reporting or analysis given to a particular subject or event. **3.** the extent of the protection provided by insurance. **4.** *Finance.* **a.** the value of liquid assets reserved to meet liabilities. **b.** the ratio of liquid assets to specific liabilities. **c.** the ratio of total net profit to distributed profit in a company. **5.** the section of the public reached by a medium of communication.

cov·er·all ('kʌvər,ɔ:l) *n.* **1.** a thing that covers something entirely. **2.** (*usually pl.*) protective outer garments for the body.

cov·er crop *n.* a crop planted between main crops to prevent leaching or soil erosion or to provide green manure.

Cov·er·dale ('kʌvə,deɪl) *n.* **Miles.** 1488–1568, the first translator of the complete Bible into English (1535).

cov·ered wag·on *n. U.S.* a large horse-drawn wagon with an arched canvas top, used formerly for prairie travel.

cov·er girl *n.* a girl, esp. a glamorous one, whose picture appears on the cover of a newspaper or magazine.

cov·er·ing let·ter *n.* an accompanying letter sent as an explanation, introduction, or record.

cov·er·let ('kʌvəlɪt) *n.* another word for **bedspread.**

Cov·er·ley ('kʌvəlɪ) *n.* See **Sir Roger de Coverley.**

cov·er note *n. Brit.* a certificate providing temporary insurance until a new insurance policy is issued.

cov·er point *n. Cricket.* **a.** a fielding position in the covers. **b.** a fielder in this position.

co·vers ('kəʊvɜ:s) *abbrev. for* coversed sine.

co·versed sine ('kəʊvɜ:st) *n.* a trigonometric function equal to one minus the sine of the specified angle. Abbrev.: **covers**

cov·er-shoul·der *n.* a type of blouse worn in Ghana.

cov·ert ('kʌvət) *adj.* **1.** concealed or secret: *covert jealousy.* **2.** *Archaic.* sheltered; protected. **3.** *Law.* See **feme covert.** Compare **discovert.** ~*n.* **4.** a shelter or disguise. **5.** a thicket or woodland providing shelter for game. **6.** short for **covert cloth. 7.** *Ornithol.* any of the small feathers on the wings and tail of a bird that surround the bases of the larger feathers. **8.** a flock of coots. [C14: from Old French: covered, from *covrir* to COVER] —'**cov·ert·ly** *adv.* —'**cov·ert·ness** *n.*

cov·ert cloth *n.* a twill-weave cotton or worsted suiting fabric. Sometimes shortened to **covert.**

cov·ert coat *n. Brit.* a short topcoat worn for hunting.

cov·er·ture ('kʌvətʃə) *n.* **1.** *Law.* the condition or status of a married woman considered as being under the protection and influence of her husband. **2.** *Rare.* shelter, concealment, or disguise. [C13: from Old French, from *covert* covered; see COVERT]

cov·er-up *n.* **1.** concealment or attempted concealment of a mistake, crime, etc. ~*vb.* **cov·er up.** (*adv.*). **2.** (*tr.*) to cover completely. **3.** (when *intr.*, often foll. by *for*) to attempt to conceal (a mistake or crime): *she tried to cover up for her friend.* **4.** (*intr.*) *Boxing.* to defend the body and head with the arms.

cove stripe *n. Nautical.* a decorative stripe painted along the sheer strake of a vessel, esp. of a sailing boat.

cov·et ('kʌvɪt) *vb. (tr.)* to wish, long, or crave for (something, esp. the property of another person). [C13: from Old French *coveitier,* from *coveitié* eager desire, ultimately from Latin *cupiditās* CUPIDITY] —'**cov·et·a·ble** *adj.* —'**cov·et·er** *n.*

cov·et·ous ('kʌvɪtəs) *adj.* (*usually postpositive* and foll. by *of*) jealously eager for the possession of something (esp. the property of another person). —'**cov·et·ous·ly** *adv.* —'**cov·et·ous·ness** *n.*

cov·ey ('kʌvɪ) *n.* **1.** a small flock of grouse or partridge. **2.** a small group, as of people. [C14: from Old French *covee,* from *cover* to sit on, hatch; see COUVADE]

cov·in ('kʌvɪn) *n. Law.* a conspiracy between two or more persons to act to the detriment or injury of another. [C14: from Old French; see COVEN, CONVENE]

cow[1] (kaʊ) *n.* **1.** the mature female of any species of cattle, esp. domesticated cattle. **2.** the mature female of various other mammals, such as the elephant, whale, and seal. **3.** (*not in technical use*) any domestic species of cattle. **4.** *Informal.* a disagreeable woman. **5.** *Austral. slang.* something objectionable (esp. in the phrase **a fair cow**). **6. till the cows come home.** *Informal.* for a very long time; effectively for ever. [Old English *cū;* related to Old Norse *kýr,* Old High German *kuo,* Latin *bōs,* Greek *boūs,* Sanskrit *gāūs*]

cow[2] (kaʊ) *vb. (tr.)* to frighten or overawe, as with threats. [C17: from Old Norse *kūga* to oppress, related to Norwegian *kue,* Swedish *kuva*]

cow·age *or* **cow·hage** ('kaʊɪdʒ) *n.* **1.** a tropical climbing leguminous plant, *Stizolobium* (or *Mucuna*) *pruriens,* whose bristly pods cause severe itching and stinging. **2.** the pods of this plant or the stinging hairs covering them. [C17: from Hindi *kavāch,* of obscure origin]

cow·ard ('kaʊəd) *n.* a person who shrinks from or avoids danger, pain, or difficulty. [C13: from Old French *cuard,* from *coue* tail, from Latin *cauda;* perhaps suggestive of a frightened animal with its tail between its legs]

Cow·ard ('kaʊəd) *n.* Sir **No·ël (Pierce).** 1899–1973, English dramatist, actor, and composer, noted for his sophisticated comedies, which include *Private Lives* (1930) and *Blithe Spirit* (1941).

cow·ard·ice ('kaʊədɪs) *n.* lack of courage in facing danger, pain, or difficulty.

cow·ard·ly ('kaʊədlɪ) *adj.* of or characteristic of a coward; lacking courage. —'**cow·ard·li·ness** *n.*

cow·bane ('kaʊ,beɪn) *n.* **1.** Also called: **water hemlock.** any of several N temperate poisonous umbelliferous marsh plants of the genus *Cicuta,* esp. *C. virosa,* having clusters of small white flowers. **2.** a similar and related plant, *Oxypolis rigidior* of the southeastern and central U.S. **3.** any umbelliferous plant reputed to be poisonous to cattle.

cow·bell ('kaʊ,bɛl) *n.* **1.** a bell hung around a cow's neck so that the cow can be easily located. **2.** *U.S.* another name for **bladder campion.**

cow·ber·ry ('kaʊbərɪ, -brɪ) *n., pl.* **·ries. 1.** a creeping ericaceous evergreen shrub, *Vaccinium vitis-idaea,* of N temperate and arctic regions, with pink or red flowers and edible slightly acid berries. **2.** the berry of this plant. ~Also called: **red whortleberry.**

cow·bind ('kaʊ,baɪnd) *n.* any of various bryony plants, esp. the white bryony.

cow·bird ('kaʊ,bɜ:d) *n.* any of various American orioles of the genera *Molothrus, Tangavius,* etc., esp. *M. ater* (common or brown-headed cowbird). They have a dark plumage and short bill.

cow·boy ('kaʊ,bɔɪ) *n.* **1.** Also called: **cow·hand.** a hired man who herds and tends cattle, usually on horseback, esp. in the western U.S. **2.** a conventional character of Wild West folklore, films, etc., esp. one involved in fighting Indians. —'**cow·,girl** *fem. n.*

cow·catch·er ('kaʊ,kætʃə) *n. U.S.* a metal frame on the front of a locomotive to clear the track of obstructions.

cow·er ('kaʊə) *vb. (intr.)* to crouch or cringe, as in fear. [C13: from Middle Low German *kūren* to lie in wait; related to Swedish *kura* to lie in wait, Danish *kure* to squat]

Cowes (kaʊz) *n.* a town in S England, on the Isle of Wight: famous for its annual regatta. Pop.: 18 895 (1971).

cow·fish ('kaʊ,fɪʃ) *n., pl.* **·fish** *or* **·fish·es. 1.** any trunkfish, such as *Lactophrys quadricornis,* having hornlike spines over the eyes. **2.** (loosely) any of various large aquatic animals, such as a sea cow.

cow·herb ('kaʊ,hɜ:b) *n.* a European caryophyllaceous plant, *Saponaria vaccaria,* having clusters of pink flowers: a weed in the U.S. See also **soapwort.**

cow·herd ('kaʊ,hɜ:d) *n.* a person employed to tend cattle.

cow·hide ('kaʊ,haɪd) *n.* **1.** the hide of a cow. **2.** the leather made from such a hide. ~Also called: **cowskin.**

Cow·i·chan sweat·er ('kaʊɪtʃən) *n. Canadian.* a heavy sweater with coloured symbolic designs: knitted originally by Cowichan Indians in British Columbia. Also called: **Indian sweater, siwash, siwash sweater.**

cow·itch ('kaʊ,ɪtʃ) *n.* another name for **cowage.** [C17: alteration of COWAGE by folk etymology]

cowk (kaʊk) *vb. (intr.) Northeast Scot. dialect.* to retch or feel nauseated. [of obscure origin]

cowl (kaʊl) *n.* **1.** a hood, esp. a loose one. **2.** the hooded habit of a monk. **3.** a cover fitted to a chimney to increase ventilation and prevent draughts. **4.** the part of a car body that supports the windscreen and the bonnet. **5.** *Aeronautics.* another word for **cowling.** ~*vb. (tr.)* **6.** to cover or provide with a cowl. **7.** to make a monk of. [Old English *cugele,* from Late Latin *cuculla* cowl, from Latin *cucullus* covering, cap, hood]

Cow·ley ('kaʊlɪ) *n.* **A·bra·ham.** 1618–67, English poet and essayist, influenced by the Metaphysical poets.

cow·lick ('kaʊ,lɪk) *n. U.S.* a tuft of hair over the forehead.

cowl·ing ('kaʊlɪŋ) *n.* a streamlined metal covering, esp. one fitted around an aircraft engine. Also called: **cowl.** Compare **fairing**[1].

cowl neck·line *n.* a neckline of women's clothes loosely folded over and sometimes resembling a folded hood.

cow·man ('kaʊmən) *n., pl.* **·men. 1.** *Brit.* another name for **cowherd. 2.** *U.S.* a man who owns cattle; rancher.

co-work·er *n.* a fellow worker; associate.

cow pars·ley *n.* a common Eurasian umbelliferous hedgerow plant, *Anthriscus sylvestris,* having umbrella-shaped clusters of white flowers. Also called: **keck.**

cow pars·nip *n.* any tall coarse umbelliferous plant of the genus *Heracleum,* such as *H. sphondylium* of Europe and Asia, having thick stems and flattened clusters of white or purple flowers. Also called: **hogweed, keck.**

cow·pat ('kaʊ,pæt) *n.* a single dropping of cow dung.

cow·pea ('kaʊ,pi:) *n.* **1.** a leguminous tropical climbing plant, *Vigna sinensis,* producing long pods containing edible pealike seeds: grown for animal fodder and sometimes as human food. **2.** Also called: **black-eyed pea.** the seed of this plant.

Cow·per ('ku:pə, 'kaʊ-) *n.* **Wil·liam.** 1731–1800, English poet, noted for his nature poetry, such as in *The Task* (1785), and his hymns.

Cow·per's glands *pl. n.* two small yellowish glands near the prostate that secrete a mucous substance into the urethra during sexual stimulation in males. Compare **Bartholin's glands.** [C18: named after William *Cowper* (1666–1709), English anatomist who discovered them]

cow pil·low *n.* (in India) a large cylindrical pillow stuffed with cotton and used for reclining rather than sleeping.

cow po·ny *n.* a horse used by cowboys when herding.

cow·pox ('kaʊ,pɒks) *n.* a contagious viral disease of cows characterized by vesicles on the skin, esp. on the teats and udder. Inoculation of humans with this virus provides temporary immunity to smallpox.

cow+punch·er ('kaʊˌpʌntʃə) *or* **cow+poke** ('kaʊˌpəʊk) *n. U.S.* an informal word for **cowboy.**

cow+ry *or* **cow+rie** ('kaʊrɪ) *n., pl.* **+ries. 1.** any marine gastropod mollusc of the mostly tropical family *Cypraeidae,* having a glossy brightly marked shell with an elongated opening. **2.** the shell of any of these molluscs, esp. the shell of *Cypraea moneta* (**money cowry**), used as money in parts of Africa and S Asia. [C17: from Hindi *kaurī,* from Sanskrit *kaparda,* of Dravidian origin; related to Tamil *kōtu* shell]

cow shark *n.* any large primitive shark, esp. *Hexanchus griseum,* of the family *Hexanchidae* of warm and temperate waters. Also called: **six-gilled shark.**

cow+skin ('kaʊˌskɪn) *n.* another word for **cowhide.**

cow+slip ('kaʊˌslɪp) *n.* **1.** Also called: **paigle.** a primrose, *Primula veris,* native to temperate regions of the Old World, having fragrant yellow flowers. **2.** *U.S.* another name for **marsh marigold.** [Old English *cūslyppe;* see COW[1], SLIP]

cow tree *n.* a South American moraceous tree, *Brosimum galactodendron,* producing latex used as a substitute for milk.

cox (kɒks) *n.* **1.** a coxswain, esp. of a racing eight or four. ~*vb.* **2.** to act as coxswain of (a boat). —**'cox+less** *adj.*

Cox (kɒks) *n.* **Da·vid.** 1783–1859, English landscape painter.

cox·a ('kɒksə) *n., pl.* **cox·ae** ('kɒksiː). **1.** a technical name for the hip bone or hip joint. **2.** the basal segment of the leg of an insect. [C18: from Latin: hip] —**'cox+al** *adj.*

cox+al+gi·a (kɒk'sældʒɪə) *n.* **1.** pain in the hip joint. **2.** disease of the hip joint causing pain. [C19: from COXA + -ALGIA] —**cox+'al+gic** *adj.*

cox+comb ('kɒksˌkəʊm) *n.* **1.** a variant spelling of **cockscomb. 2.** *Archaic.* a foppish man. **3.** *Obsolete.* the cap, resembling a cock's comb, worn by a jester.

cox+comb+ry ('kɒksˌkəʊmrɪ) *n., pl.* **+ries.** conceited arrogance or foppishness.

Cox+sack·ie vi+rus (kʊk'sɑːkɪ) *n.* any of various viruses that occur in the intestinal tract of man and cause diseases, some of which resemble poliomyelitis. [C20: after *Coxsackie,* a town in New York state, where the virus was first found]

Cox's Or+ange Pip+pin ('pɪpɪn) *n.* a variety of eating apple with sweet flesh and a red-tinged green skin. Often shortened to **Cox.** [C19: named after R. *Cox,* its English propagator]

cox+swain ('kɒksən, -ˌsweɪn) *n.* the helmsman of a lifeboat, racing shell, etc. Also called: **cockswain.** [C15: from COCK[1] + SWAIN]

coy (kɔɪ) *adj.* **1.** (usually of a woman) affectedly demure, esp. in a playful or provocative manner. **2.** shy; modest. **3.** evasive, esp. in an annoying way. [C14: from Old French *coi* reserved, from Latin *quiētus* QUIET] —**'coy+ish** *adj.* —**'coy+ly** *adv.* —**'coy+ness** *n.*

Coy. *Military. abbrev. for* company.

coy+ote ('kɔɪəʊt, kɔɪ'əʊt, kɔɪ'əʊtɪ) *n., pl.* **+otes** *or* **+ote. 1.** Also called: **prairie wolf.** a predatory canine mammal, *Canis latrans,* related to but smaller than the wolf, roaming the deserts and prairies of North America. **2.** (in American Indian legends of the West) a trickster and culture hero represented as a man or as an animal. [C19: from Mexican Spanish, from Nahuatl *coyotl*]

co+yo+til+lo (ˌkəʊjəʊ'tiːljəʊ) *n., pl.* **+los.** a thorny poisonous rhamnaceous shrub, *Karwinskia humboldtiana* of Mexico and the southwestern U.S., the berries of which cause paralysis. [Mexican Spanish, literally: a little COYOTE]

coy+pu ('kɔɪpuː) *n., pl.* **+pus** *or* **+pu. 1.** an aquatic South American hystricomorph rodent, *Myocastor coypus,* introduced into Europe: family *Capromyidae.* It resembles a small beaver with a ratlike tail and is bred in captivity for its soft grey underfur. **2.** the fur of this animal. ~Also called: **nutria.** [C18: from American Spanish *coipú,* from Araucanian *kóypu*]

coz (kʌz) *n.* an archaic word for **cousin:** used chiefly as a term of address.

co+zen ('kʌzən) *vb.* to cheat or trick (someone). [C16: cant term perhaps related to COUSIN] —**'coz+en+age** *n.* —**'coz+en+er** *n.*

co·zy ('kəʊzɪ) *adj.* **·zi+er, ·zi+est.** *n.* the usual U.S. spelling of **cosy.** —**'co+zi+ly** *adv.* —**'co+zi+ness** *n.*

cp. *abbrev. for* compare

c.p. *abbrev. for:* **1.** candle power. **2.** chemically pure.

CP *abbrev. for:* **1.** *Military.* Command Post. **2.** Canadian Press.

C.P. *abbrev. for:* **1.** Common Prayer. **2.** Communist Party. **3.** Court of Probate. **4.** (in Australia) Country Party.

cpd. *Zoology, botany, chem. abbrev. for* compound.

Cpl. *abbrev. for* Corporal.

C.P.O. *abbrev. for* Chief Petty Officer.

CPR *abbrev. for* Canadian Pacific Railway.

c.p.s. *Physics. abbrev. for* cycles per second.

C.P.S.U. *abbrev. for* Communist Party of the Soviet Union.

CPU *Computer technol. abbrev. for* central processing unit.

CQ 1. *Telegraphy, telephony.* a symbol transmitted by an amateur radio operator requesting two-way communication with any other amateur radio operator listening. **2.** *Military. abbrev. for* charge of quarters.

Cr *the chemical symbol for* chromium.

Cr. *abbrev. for* Counsellor.

CR *international car registration for* Costa Rica.

cr. *abbrev. for:* **1.** credit. **2.** creditor.

C.R. *abbrev. for:* **1.** Costa Rica. **2.** Community of the Resurrection.

craal (krɑːl) *n.* a variant spelling of **kraal.**

crab[1] (kræb) *n.* **1.** any chiefly marine decapod crustacean of the genus *Cancer* and related genera (section *Brachyura*), having a broad flattened carapace covering the cephalothorax, beneath which is folded the abdomen. The first pair of limbs are modified as pincers. See also **fiddler crab, soft-shell crab, pea crab, oyster crab. 2.** any of various similar or related arthropods, such as the hermit crab and horseshoe crab. **3.** short for **crab louse. 4.** a manoeuvre in which an aircraft flies slightly into the crosswind to compensate for drift. **5.** a mechanical lifting device, esp. the travelling hoist of a gantry crane. **6.** *Wrestling.* See **Boston crab. 7. catch a crab.** *Rowing.* to make a stroke in which the oar either misses or digs too deeply, causing the rower to fall backwards. ~*vb.* **crabs, crab+bing, crabbed. 8.** (*intr.*) to hunt or catch crabs. **9.** (*tr.*) to fly (an aircraft) slightly into a crosswind to compensate for drift. **10.** (*intr.*) *Nautical.* to move forwards with a slight sideways motion, as to overcome an offsetting current. **11.** (*intr.*) to move sideways. [Old English *crabba;* related to Old Norse *krabbi,* Old High German *krebiz* crab, Dutch *krabben* to scratch]

crab[2] (kræb) *Informal.* ~*vb.* **crabs, crab+bing, crabbed. 1.** (*intr.*) to find fault; grumble. **2.** (*tr.*) *U.S.* to spoil (esp. in the phrase **crab one's act**). ~*n.* **3.** an irritable person. **4. draw the crabs.** *Austral. informal.* to attract unwelcome attention. [C16: probably back formation from CRABBED]

crab[3] (kræb) *n.* short for **crab apple.** [C15: perhaps of Scandinavian origin; compare Swedish *skrabbe* crab apple]

Crab (kræb) *n.* **the.** the constellation Cancer, the fourth sign of the zodiac.

crab ap+ple *n.* **1.** any of several rosaceous trees of the genus *Malus* that have white, pink, or red flowers and small sour apple-like fruits. **2.** the fruit of any of these trees, used to make jam.

Crabbe (kræb) *n.* **George.** 1754–1832, English narrative poet, noted for his depiction of impoverished rural life in *The Village* (1783) and *The Borough* (1810).

crab+bed ('kræbɪd) *adj.* **1.** surly; irritable; perverse. **2.** (esp. of handwriting) cramped and hard to decipher. **3.** *Rare.* abstruse. [C13: probably from CRAB[1] (from its wayward gait), influenced by CRAB (APPLE) (from its tartness)] —**'crab+bed+ly** *adv.* —**'crab+bed+ness** *n.*

crab+ber ('kræbə) *n.* **1.** a crab fisherman. **2.** a boat used for crab-fishing.

crab+by ('kræbɪ) *adj.* **+bi+er, +bi+est.** bad-tempered.

crab grass *n.* any of several coarse weedy grasses of the genus *Digitaria,* which grow in warm regions and tend to displace other grasses in lawns.

crab louse *n.* a parasitic louse, *Pthirus* (or *Phthirus*) *pubis,* that infests the pubic region in man.

Crab Neb·u·la *n.* the expanding remnant of the supernova observed in 1054 A.D., lying in the constellation Taurus at an approximate distance of 5000 light years.

crabs (kræbz) *pl. n.* (*sometimes functioning as sing.*) the lowest throw in a game of chance, esp. two aces in dice. [plural of CRAB[1]]

crab+stick ('kræbˌstɪk) *n.* **1.** a stick, cane, or cudgel made of crab-apple wood. **2.** *Informal.* a bad-tempered person.

crab+wise ('kræbˌwaɪz) *adj., adv.* (of motion) sideways; like a crab.

crack (kræk) *vb.* **1.** to break or cause to break without complete separation of the parts: *the vase was cracked but unbroken.* **2.** to break or cause to break with a sudden sharp sound; snap: *to crack a nut.* **3.** to make or cause to make a sudden sharp sound: *to crack a whip.* **4.** to cause (the voice) to change tone or become harsh or (of the voice) to change tone, esp. to a higher register; break. **5.** *Informal.* to fail or cause to fail. **6.** to yield or cause to yield: *to crack under torture.* **7.** (*tr.*) to hit with a forceful or resounding blow. **8.** (*tr.*) to break into or force open: *to crack a safe.* **9.** (*tr.*) to solve or decipher (a code, problem, etc.). **10.** (*tr.*) *Informal.* to tell (a joke, etc.). **11.** to break (a molecule) into smaller molecules or radicals by the action of heat, as in the distillation of petroleum. **12.** (*intr.*) *Scot., northern Brit. dialect.* to chat; gossip. **13.** (*tr.*) *Austral. informal.* **a.** to achieve (esp. in the phrase **crack it**). **b.** to find or catch: *to crack a wave in surfing.* **14. crack a smile.** *Informal.* to break into a smile. **15. crack hardy.** *Austral. informal.* to disguise one's discomfort, etc.; put on a bold front. ~*n.* **16.** a sudden sharp noise. **17.** a break or fracture without complete separation of the two parts: *a crack in the window.* **18.** a narrow opening or fissure. **19.** *Informal.* a resounding blow. **20.** a physical or mental defect; flaw. **21.** a moment or specific instant: *the crack of day.* **22.** a broken or cracked tone of voice, as a boy's during puberty. **23.** (often foll. by *at*) *Informal.* an attempt; opportunity to try: *he had a crack at the problem.* **24.** *Slang.* a gibe; wisecrack; joke. **25.** *Slang.* a person that excels. **26.** *Scot., northern Brit. dialect.* a talk; chat. **27.** *Obsolete slang.* a burglar or burglary. **28. crack of dawn. a.** the very instant that the sun rises. **b.** very early in the morning. **29. a fair crack of the whip.** *Informal.* a fair chance or opportunity. **30. crack of doom.** doomsday; the end of the world; the Day of Judgment. ~*adj.* **31.** (*prenominal*) *Slang.* first-class; excellent: *a crack shot.* ~See also **crack down, crack up.** [Old English *cracian;* related to Old High German *krahhōn,* Dutch *kraken,* Sanskrit *gárjati* he roars]

crack+brain ('krækˌbreɪn) *n.* a person who is insane.

crack+brained ('krækˌbreɪnd) *adj.* insane, idiotic, or crazy.

crack down *vb.* (*intr., adv.;* often foll. by *on*) **1.** to take severe measures (against); become stricter (with). ~*n.* **crack+down. 2.** severe or repressive measures.

cracked (krækt) *adj.* **1.** damaged by cracking. **2.** *Slang.* crazy.

crack+er ('krækə) *n.* **1.** a decorated cardboard tube that emits a bang when pulled apart, releasing a toy, a joke, or a paper hat. **2.** short for **firecracker. 3.** a thin crisp biscuit, usually unsweetened. **4.** a person or thing that cracks. **5.** *U.S.* another word for **poor white. 6.** *Brit. slang.* a person of notable qualities or abilities, esp. an attractive girl. **7. not worth a cracker.** *Austral. informal.* worthless; useless.

crack·er-bar·rel *adj. U.S.* rural; rustic; homespun: *a cracker-barrel philosopher.*

crack·er+jack ('krækə,dʒæk) *Informal.* ~*adj.* **1.** excellent. ~*n.* **2.** a person or thing of exceptional quality or ability. [C20: changed from CRACK (first-class) + JACK (man)]

crack+ers ('krækəz) *adj.* (*postpositive*) *Brit.* a slang word for **insane.**

crack+et ('krækɪt) *n. Brit. dialect.* **1.** a low stool, often one with three legs. **2.** a box for a miner to kneel on when working a low seam. [variant of CRICKET[3]]

crack+ing ('krækɪŋ) *adj.* **1.** (*prenominal*) *Informal.* fast; vigorous (esp. in the phrase **a cracking pace**). **2. get cracking.** *Informal.* to start doing something quickly or do something with increased speed. ~*adv., adj.* **3.** *Brit. informal.* first-class; excellent: *a cracking good match.* ~*n.* **4.** the process in which molecules are cracked, esp. the oil-refining process in which heavy oils are broken down into hydrocarbons of lower molecular weight by heat or catalysis. See also **catalytic cracker.**

crack+jaw ('kræk,dʒɔ:) *Informal.* ~*adj.* **1.** difficult to pronounce. ~*n.* **2.** a word or phrase that is difficult to pronounce.

crack+le ('krækᵊl) *vb.* **1.** to make or cause to make a series of slight sharp noises, as of paper being crushed or of a wood fire burning. **2.** (*tr.*) to decorate (porcelain or pottery) by causing a fine network of cracks to appear in the glaze. **3.** (*intr.*) to abound in vivacity or energy. ~*n.* **4.** the act or sound of crackling. **5.** intentional crazing in the glaze of a piece of porcelain or pottery. **6.** Also called: **crack·le+ware.** porcelain or pottery so decorated.

crack+ling ('kræklɪŋ) *n.* the crisp browned skin of roast pork.

crack+nel ('krækmᵊl) *n.* **1.** a type of hard plain biscuit. **2.** *U.S.* (*often pl.*) crisply fried bits of fat pork. [C15: perhaps from Old French *craquelin*, from Middle Dutch *krākelinc*, from *krāken* to CRACK]

crack+pot ('kræk,pɒt) *Informal.* ~*n.* **1.** an eccentric person; crank. ~*adj.* **2.** (*usually prenominal*) eccentric; crazy.

cracks+man ('kræksmən) *n., pl.* **+men.** *Slang.* a burglar, esp. a safe-breaker.

crack up *vb.* (*adv.*) **1.** (*intr.*) to break into pieces. **2.** (*intr.*) *Informal.* to undergo a physical or mental breakdown. **3.** (*tr.*) *Informal.* to present or report, esp. in glowing terms: *it's not all it's cracked up to be.* ~*n.* **crack+up. 4.** *Informal.* a physical or mental breakdown.

Cra+cow ('krækaʊ, -əʊ, -ɒf) *n.* an industrial city in S Poland, on the River Vistula: former capital of the country (1320–1609); university (1364). Pop.: 662 900 (1974 est.). Polish name: **Kraków.**

-cra·cy *n. combining form.* indicating a type of government or rule: *plutocracy; mobocracy.* See also **-crat.** [from Greek *-kratia*, from *kratos* power]

cra+dle ('kreɪdᵊl) *n.* **1.** a baby's bed with enclosed sides, often with a hood and rockers. **2.** a place where something originates or is nurtured during its early life: *the cradle of civilization.* **3.** the earliest period of life: *they knew each other from the cradle.* **4.** a frame, rest, or trolley made to support or transport a piece of equipment, aircraft, ship, etc. **5.** a platform, cage, or trolley, in which workmen are suspended on the side of a building or ship. **6.** another name for **creeper** (sense 5). **7.** *Agriculture.* **a.** a framework of several wooden fingers attached to a scythe to gather the grain into bunches as it is cut. **b.** a scythe equipped with such a cradle; cradle scythe. **c.** a collar of wooden fingers that prevents a horse or cow from turning its head and biting itself. **8.** Also called: **rocker.** a boxlike apparatus for washing rocks, sand, etc., containing gold or gem stones. **9.** *Engraving.* a tool that produces the pitted surface of a copper mezzotint plate before the design is engraved upon it. **10.** a framework used to prevent the bedclothes from touching a sensitive part of an injured person. **11. from the cradle to the grave.** throughout life. **12. rob the cradle.** *Informal.* to take for a lover, husband, or wife a person much younger than oneself. ~*vb.* **13.** (*tr.*) to rock or place in or as if in a cradle; hold tenderly. **14.** (*tr.*) to nurture in or bring up from infancy. **15.** to reap (grain) with a cradle scythe. **16.** (*tr.*) to wash (soil bearing gold, etc.) in a cradle. **17.** *Lacrosse.* to keep (the ball) in the net of the stick, esp. while running with it. **18.** (*intr.*) *Rare.* to lie in a cradle. [Old English *cradol*; related to Old High German *kratto* basket] —'**cra+dler** *n.*

cra+dle snatch+er *n. Informal.* another name for **baby snatcher** (sense 2).

cra·dle+song ('kreɪdᵊl,sɒŋ) *n.* another word for **lullaby.**

cra+dling ('kreɪdlɪŋ) *n. Architect.* a framework of iron or wood, esp. as used in the construction of a ceiling.

craft (krɑ:ft) *n.* **1.** skill or ability, esp. in handiwork. **2.** skill in deception and trickery; guile; cunning. **3.** an occupation or trade requiring special skill, esp. manual dexterity. **4. a.** the members of such a trade, regarded collectively. **b.** (*as modifier*): *a craft guild.* **5.** a single vessel, aircraft, or spacecraft. **6.** (*functioning as pl.*) ships, boats, aircraft, or spacecraft collectively. ~*vb.* **7.** (*tr.*) to make or fashion with skill, esp. by hand. [Old English *cræft* skill, strength; related to Old Norse *kraptr* power, skill, Old High German *kraft*]

crafts+man ('krɑ:ftsmən) *n., pl.* **+men. 1.** a member of a skilled trade; someone who practises a craft; artisan. **2.** an artist skilled in the techniques of an art or craft. —'**crafts+man+ly** *adj.* —'**crafts+man+,ship** *n.*

craft un+ion *n.* a labour organization membership of which is restricted to workers in a specified trade or craft. Compare **industrial union.**

craft·y ('krɑ:ftɪ) *adj.* **craft·i+er, craft·i+est. 1.** skilled in deception; shrewd; cunning. **2.** *Archaic.* skilful. —'**craft·i+ly** *adv.* —'**craft·i+ness** *n.*

crag (kræg) *n.* a steep rugged rock or peak. [C13: of Celtic origin; related to Old Welsh *creik* rock]

Crag (kræg) *n.* a formation of shelly sandstone in E England, deposited during the Pliocene and Pleistocene epochs.

crag+gy ('krægɪ) *or U.S.* **crag+ged** ('krægɪd) *adj.* **+gi+er, +gi+est. 1.** having many crags. **2.** (of the face) rugged; rocklike. —'**crag+gi+ly** *adv.* —'**crag+gi+ness** *n.*

crags+man ('krægzmən) *n., pl.* **+men.** a rock climber.

Craig (kreɪg) *n.* **Ed·ward Gor·don.** 1872–1966, English theatrical designer, actor, and director. His nonrealistic scenic design greatly influenced theatre in Europe and the U.S.

Crai·gie ('kreɪgɪ) *n.* Sir **Wil·liam A(lexander).** 1867–1957, Scottish lexicographer; joint editor of the *Oxford English Dictionary* (1901–33), and of *A Dictionary of American English on Historical Principles* (1938–44).

Cra+io·va (*Rumanian* kra'jova) *n.* a city in SW Rumania, on the Jiul River. Pop.: 194 235 (1974 est.).

crake (kreɪk) *n. Zoology.* any of several rails that occur in the Old World, such as the corncrake and the spotted crake. [C14: from Old Norse *krāka* crow or *krākr* raven, of imitative origin]

cram (kræm) *vb.* **crams, cram+ming, crammed. 1.** (*tr.*) to force (people, material, etc.) into (a room, container, etc.) with more than it can hold; stuff. **2.** to eat or cause to eat more than necessary. **3.** *Informal.* to study or cause to study (facts, etc.), esp. for an examination, by hastily memorizing. ~*n.* **4.** the act or condition of cramming. **5.** a crush. [Old English *crammian*; related to Old Norse *kremja* to press] —'**cram+mer** *n.*

cram+bo ('kræmbəʊ) *n., pl.* **+boes.** a word game in which one team says a rhyme or rhyming line for a word or line given by the other team. [C17: from earlier *crambe*, probably from Latin *crambē repetīta* cabbage repeated, hence an old story, a rhyming game, from Greek *krambē*]

cram-full *adj.* stuffed full.

cram+mer ('kræmə) *n.* a person or school that prepares pupils for an examination, esp. pupils who have already failed that examination.

cram·oi+sy *or* **cram·oi+sie** ('kræmɔɪzɪ, -əzɪ) *Archaic.* ~*adj.* **1.** of a crimson colour. ~*n.* **2.** crimson cloth. [C15: from Old French *cramoisi*, from Arabic *qirmizī* red obtained from kermes; see CRIMSON, KERMES]

cramp[1] (kræmp) *n.* **1.** a painful involuntary contraction of a muscle, typically caused by overexertion, heat, or chill. **2.** temporary partial paralysis of a muscle group: *writer's cramp.* **3.** (*usually pl. in the U.S.*) severe abdominal pain. ~*vb.* **4.** (*tr.*) to affect with or as if with a cramp. [C14: from Old French *crampe*, of Germanic origin; compare Old High German *krampho*]

cramp[2] (kræmp) *n.* **1.** Also called: **cramp iron.** a strip of metal with its ends bent at right angles, used to bind masonry. **2.** a device for holding pieces of wood while they are glued; clamp. **3.** something that confines or restricts. **4.** a confined state or position. ~*vb.* (*tr.*) **5.** to secure or hold with a cramp. **6.** to confine, hamper, or restrict. **7. cramp (someone's) style.** *Informal.* to prevent (a person) from using his abilities or acting freely and confidently. [C15: from Middle Dutch *crampe* cramp, hook, of Germanic origin; compare Old High German *khramph* bent; see CRAMP[1]]

cramped (kræmpt) *adj.* **1.** closed in; restricted. **2.** (esp. of handwriting) small and irregular; difficult to read.

cramp+er ('kræmpə) *n. Curling.* a spiked metal plate used as a brace for the feet in throwing the stone.

cram+pon ('kræmpən) *or* **cram+poon** (kræm'pu:n) *n.* **1.** one of a pair of pivoted steel levers used to lift heavy objects; grappling iron. **2.** (*often pl.*) a metal spike fitted to boots for climbing, walking on ice, etc. [C15: from French, from Middle Dutch *crampe* hook; see CRAMP[2]]

cran (kræn) *n.* a unit of capacity used for measuring fresh herring, equal to 37.5 gallons. [C18: of uncertain origin]

Cra·nach (*German* 'kra:nax) *n.* **Lu·cas** ('lu:kas). 1472–1553, German painter, etcher, and designer of woodcuts.

cran+age ('kreɪnɪdʒ) *n.* **1.** the use of a crane. **2.** a fee charged for such use.

cran+ber·ry ('krænbərɪ, -brɪ) *n., pl.* **·ries. 1.** any of several trailing ericaceous shrubs of the genus *Vaccinium*, such as the European *V. oxycoccus*, that bear sour edible red berries. **2.** the berry of this plant, used to make sauce or jelly. [C17: from Low German *kraanbere*, from *kraan* CRANE + *bere* BERRY]

cran+ber·ry bush *or* **tree** *n.* a North American caprifoliaceous shrub or small tree, *Viburnum trilobum*, producing acid red fruit.

crane (kreɪn) *n.* **1.** any large long-necked long-legged wading bird of the family *Gruidae*, inhabiting marshes and plains in most parts of the world except South America, New Zealand, and Indonesia: order *Gruiformes.* See also **demoiselle** (sense 1), **whooping crane. 2.** (*not in ornithological use*) any similar bird, such as a heron. **3.** a device for lifting and moving heavy objects, typically consisting of a pivoted boom rotating about a vertical axis with lifting gear suspended from the end of the boom. See also **gantry. 4.** *Films.* a large trolley carrying a boom, on the end of which is mounted a camera. ~*vb.* **5.** (*tr.*)

to lift or move (an object) by or as if by a crane. **6.** to stretch out (esp. the neck), as to see over other people's heads. **7.** (*intr.*) (of a horse) to pull up short before a jump. [Old English *cran*; related to Middle High German *krane*, Latin *grūs*, Greek *géranos*]

Crane (kreɪn) *n.* **1.** **(Harold) Hart.** 1899–1932, U.S. poet; author of *The Bridge* (1930). **2. Ste·phen.** 1871–1900, U.S. novelist and short-story writer, noted particularly for his novel *The Red Badge of Courage* (1895).

crane fly *n.* any dipterous fly of the family *Tipulidae*, having long legs, slender wings, and a narrow body. Also called (Brit.): **daddy-longlegs.**

cranes+bill ('kreɪnzˌbɪl) *n.* any of various plants of the genus *Geranium*, having pink or purple flowers and long slender beaked fruits: family *Geraniaceae*. See also **herb robert, storksbill.**

cra+ni·al ('kreɪnɪəl) *adj.* of or relating to the skull. —**'cra+ni+al+ly** *adv.*

cra+ni·al in+dex *n.* the ratio of the greatest length to the greatest width of the cranium, multiplied by 100: used in comparative anthropology. Compare **cephalic index.**

cra+ni·al nerve *n.* any of the 12 paired nerves that have their origin in the brain and reach the periphery through natural openings in the skull.

cra+ni+ate ('kreɪnɪɪt, -ˌeɪt) *adj.* **1.** having a skull or cranium. ~*adj.*, *n.* **2.** another word for **vertebrate.**

cra·ni·o- *or before a vowel* **cra·ni-** *combining form.* indicating the cranium or cranial: *craniotomy.*

cra+ni+ol+o·gy (ˌkreɪnɪ'ɒlədʒɪ) *n.* the branch of science concerned with the shape and size of the human skull, esp. with reference to variations between different races. —**cra+ni·o+log·i·cal** (ˌkreɪnɪə'lɒdʒɪkᵊl) *adj.* —ˌ**cra+ni·o+'log·i·cal+ly** *adv.* —ˌ**cra+ni+'ol·o+gist** *n.*

cra+ni+om+e·ter (ˌkreɪnɪ'ɒmɪtə) *n.* an instrument for measuring the cranium or skull.

cra+ni+om+e·try (ˌkreɪnɪ'ɒmɪtrɪ) *n.* the study and measurement of skulls. —**cra+ni·o+met+ric** (ˌkreɪnɪə'mɛtrɪk) *or* ˌ**cra+ni·o+'met+ri+cal** *adj.* —ˌ**cra+ni·o+'met+ri+cal+ly** *adv.* —ˌ**cra+ni+'om·e+trist** *n.*

cra+ni+ot·o+my (ˌkreɪnɪ'ɒtəmɪ) *n.*, *pl.* **+mies.** **1.** surgical incision into the skull, esp. to expose the brain for neurosurgery. **2.** surgical crushing of a fetal skull to extract a dead fetus.

cra+ni+um ('kreɪnɪəm) *n.*, *pl.* **+ni+ums** *or* **+ni·a** (-nɪə). **1.** the skull of a vertebrate. **2.** the part of the skull that encloses the brain. Nontechnical name: **brainpan.** [C16: from Medieval Latin *crānium* skull, from Greek *kranion*]

crank[1] (kræŋk) *n.* **1.** a device for communicating motion or for converting reciprocating motion into rotary motion or vice versa, consisting of an arm projecting from a shaft, often with a second member attached to it parallel to the shaft. **2.** Also called: **crank handle, starting handle.** a handle incorporating a crank, used to start an engine or motor. **3.** *Informal.* **a.** an eccentric or odd person, esp. someone who stubbornly maintains unusual views. **b.** *U.S.* a bad-tempered person. **4.** *Rare.* a clever turn of speech (esp. in the phrase **quips and cranks**). **5.** *Archaic.* a bend or turn. ~*vb.* **6.** (*tr.*) to rotate (a shaft) by means of a crank. **7.** (*tr.*) to start (an engine, motor, etc.) by means of a crank handle. **8.** (*tr.*) to bend, twist, or make into the shape of a crank. **9.** (*intr.*) *Obsolete.* to twist or wind. [Old English *cranc*; related to Middle Low German *krunke* wrinkle, Dutch *krinkel* CRINKLE]

crank[2] (kræŋk) *or* **crank·y** *adj.* (of a sailing vessel) easily keeled over by the wind; tender. [C17: of uncertain origin; perhaps related to CRANK[1]]

crank+case ('kræŋkˌkeɪs) *n.* the metal housing that encloses the crankshaft, connecting rods, etc., in an internal-combustion engine, reciprocating pump, etc.

Cran·ko ('kræŋkəʊ) *n.* **John.** 1927–73, British choreographer, born in South Africa: director of the Stuttgart Ballet (1961–73).

crank+pin ('kræŋkˌpɪn) *n.* a short cylindrical bearing surface fitted between two arms of a crank and set parallel to the main shaft of the crankshaft.

crank+shaft ('kræŋkˌʃɑːft) *n.* a shaft having one or more cranks, esp. the main shaft of an internal-combustion engine to which the connecting rods are attached.

crank up *vb.* (*intr.*, *adv.*) *Slang.* to inject a narcotic drug.

crank·y[1] ('kræŋkɪ) *adj.* **crank·i·er, crank·i·est.** **1.** *Informal.* eccentric. **2.** *U.S. informal.* fussy and bad-tempered. **3.** shaky; out of order. **4.** full of bends and turns. **5.** *Brit. dialect.* unwell. —**'crank·i+ly** *adv.* —**'crank·i+ness** *n.*

crank·y[2] ('kræŋkɪ) *adj.* **crank·i·er, crank·i·est.** *Nautical.* another word for **crank**[2].

Cran·mer ('krænmə) *n.* **Thom·as.** 1489–1556, the first Protestant archbishop of Canterbury (1533–56) and principal author of the Book of Common Prayer. He was burnt as a heretic by Mary I.

cran+nog ('krænəg) *or* **cran+noge** ('krænədʒ) *n.* an ancient Celtic lake or bog dwelling dating from the late Bronze Age to the 16th century A.D., often fortified and used as a refuge. [C19: from Middle Irish *crannōc*, from Old Irish *crann* tree]

cran+ny ('krænɪ) *n.*, *pl.* **+nies.** a narrow opening, as in a wall or rock face; chink; crevice (esp. in the phrase **every nook and cranny**). [C15: from Old French *cran* notch, fissure; compare CRENEL] —**'cran+nied** *adj.*

Cran+well ('krænwəl) *n.* a village in E England, in Lincolnshire: Royal Air Force College (1920).

crap[1] (kræp) *n.* **1.** a losing throw in the game of craps. **2.** another name for **craps.** [C20: back formation from CRAPS]

crap[2] (kræp) *n. Slang.* **1.** nonsense. **2.** rubbish. **3.** a taboo word for **faeces.** ~*vb.* **craps, crap+ping, crapped.** **4.** (*intr.*) a taboo word for **defecate.** [C15 *crappe* chaff, from Middle Dutch, probably from *crappen* to break off]

cra+paud ('kræpəʊ, 'krɑː-) *n. Caribbean.* a frog or toad. [from French: toad]

crape (kreɪp) *n.* **1.** a variant spelling of **crepe.** **2.** crepe, esp. when used for mourning clothes. **3.** a band of black crepe worn in mourning. —**'crap·y** *adj.*

crape myr+tle *or* **crepe myr+tle** *n.* an oriental lythraceous shrub, *Lagerstroemia indica*, cultivated in warm climates for its pink, red, or white flowers.

crap out *vb.* (*intr.*, *adv.*) *U.S. slang.* **1.** to make a losing throw in craps. **2.** to fail; withdraw. **3.** to rest.

crap+pie ('kræpɪ) *n.*, *pl.* **+pies.** either of two North American freshwater percoid food and game fishes, *Pomoxis nigromaculatus* (**black crappie**) or *P. annularis* (**white crappie**): family *Centrarchidae* (sunfishes, etc.). [C19: from Canadian French *crapet*]

craps (kræps) *n.* (*usually functioning as sing.*) **1.** a gambling game using two dice, in which a player wins the bet if 7 or 11 is thrown first, and loses if 2, 3, or 12 is thrown. **2. shoot craps.** to play this game. [C19: probably from *crabs* lowest throw at dice, plural of CRAB[1]]

crap+shoot·er ('kræpˌʃuːtə) *n. U.S.* a person who plays the game of craps.

crap·u+lent ('kræpjʊlənt) *or* **crap·u+lous** ('kræpjʊləs) *adj.* **1.** given to or resulting from intemperance. **2.** suffering from intemperance; drunken. [C18: from Late Latin *crāpulentus* drunk, from Latin *crāpula*, from Greek *kraipalē* drunkenness, headache resulting therefrom] —**'crap·u+lence** *n.* —**'crap·u+lent+ly** *or* **'crap·u+lous+ly** *adv.* —**'crap·u+lous+ness** *n.*

cra+que+lure ('krækəlʊə) *n.* a network of fine cracks on old paintings caused by the deterioration of pigment or varnish. [C20: from French, from *craqueler* to crackle, from *craquer* to crack, of imitative origin]

crash[1] (kræʃ) *vb.* **1.** to make or cause to make a loud noise as of solid objects smashing or clattering. **2.** to fall or cause to fall with force, breaking in pieces with a loud noise as of solid objects smashing. **3.** (*intr.*) to break or smash in pieces with a loud noise. **4.** (*intr.*) to collapse or fail suddenly: *this business is sure to crash.* **5.** to cause (an aircraft) to hit land or water violently resulting in severe damage or (of an aircraft) to hit land or water in this way. **6.** to collide (a car, etc.) with another car or other object or (of two or more cars) to be involved in a collision. **7.** to move or cause to move violently or noisily: *to crash through a barrier.* **8.** *Brit. informal.* short for **gate-crash.** ~*n.* **9.** an act or instance of breaking and falling to pieces. **10.** a sudden loud noise: *the crash of thunder.* **11.** a collision, as between vehicles. **12.** a sudden descent of an aircraft as a result of which it hits land or water. **13.** the sudden collapse of a business, stock exchange, etc., esp. one causing further financial failure. **14.** (*modifier*) **a.** requiring or using intensive effort and all possible resources in order to accomplish something quickly: *a crash programme.* **b.** sudden or vigorous: *a crash halt; a crash tackle.* ~See also **crash out.** [C14: probably from *crasen* to smash, shatter + *dasshen* to strike violently, DASH; see CRAZE] —**'crash+er** *n.*

crash[2] (kræʃ) *n.* a coarse cotton or linen cloth used for towelling, curtains, etc. [C19: from Russian *krashenina* coloured linen]

Crash·aw ('kræʃɔː) *n.* **Rich·ard.** 1613–49, English religious poet, noted esp. for the *Steps to the Temple* (1646).

crash bar+ri+er *n.* a barrier erected along the centre of a motorway, around a racetrack, etc., for safety purposes.

crash dive *n.* **1.** a sudden steep dive from the surface by a submarine. ~*vb.* **crash-dive.** **2.** (usually of an aircraft) to descend steeply and rapidly, before hitting the ground. **3.** to perform or cause to perform a crash dive.

crash hel+met *n.* a padded helmet worn for motor-cycling, flying, bobsleighing, etc., to protect the head in a crash.

crash+ing ('kræʃɪŋ) *adj.* (*prenominal*) *Informal.* (intensifier) (esp. in the phrase **a crashing bore**).

crash-land *vb.* to land (an aircraft) in an emergency causing some damage to it or (of an aircraft) to land in this way. —**'crash-ˌland·ing** *n.*

crash out *vb.* (*intr.*, *adv.*) *Slang.* **1.** to become finally unconscious after being in a high state of stimulation from a drug. **2.** to go to sleep.

crash pad *n. Slang.* a place to sleep or live temporarily.

cra+sis ('kreɪsɪs) *n.*, *pl.* **+ses** (-siːz). the fusion or contraction of two adjacent vowels into one. Also called: **syneresis.** [C17: from Greek *krasis* a mingling, from *kerannunai* to mix]

crass (kræs) *adj.* **1.** stupid; gross. **2.** *Rare.* thick or coarse. [C16: from Latin *crassus* thick, dense, gross] —**'crass+ly** *adv.* —**'crass+ness** *or* **'cras+si+ˌtude** *n.*

cras+su+la+ceous (ˌkræsjʊ'leɪʃəs) *adj.* of, relating to, or belonging to the *Crassulaceae*, a family of herbaceous or shrubby flowering plants with fleshy succulent leaves, including the houseleeks and stonecrops. [C19: from New Latin *Crassula* name of genus, from Medieval Latin: stonecrop, from Latin *crassus* thick]

Cras·sus ('kræsəs) *n.* **Mar·cus Li·cin·i·us** ('mɑːkəs lɪ'sɪnɪəs). ?115–53 B.C., Roman general; member of the first triumvirate with Caesar and Pompey.

-crat *n. combining form.* indicating a person who takes part in or is a member of a form of government or class: *democrat; technocrat.* See also **-cracy.** [from Greek *-kratēs*, from *-kratia* -CRACY] —**-crat·ic** *or* **-crat·ic+al** *adj. combining form.*

cratch (krætʃ) *n.* a rack for holding fodder for cattle, etc. [C14: from Old French: CRÈCHE]

crate (kreɪt) *n.* **1.** a fairly large container, usually made of wooden slats or wickerwork, used for packing, storing, or transporting goods. **2.** *Slang.* an old car, aeroplane, etc. ~*vb.* **3.** (*tr.*) to pack or place in a crate. [C16: from Latin *crātis* wickerwork, hurdle] —**'crat+er** *n.* —**'crate+ful** *n.*

cra+ter ('kreɪtə) *n.* **1.** the bowl-shaped opening at the top or side of a volcano or top of a geyser through which lava and gases are emitted. **2.** a similarly shaped depression formed by the impact of a meteorite or exploding bomb. **3.** any of the tens of thousands of roughly circular or polygonal walled formations covering the surface of the moon and some other planets, formed probably either by volcanic action or by the impact of meteorites. They can have a diameter of up to 240 kilometres (150 miles) and a depth of 8900 metres (29 000 feet). **4.** a pit in an otherwise smooth surface. **5.** a large open bowl with two handles, used for mixing wines, esp. in ancient Greece. ~*vb.* **6.** to make or form craters in (a surface, such as the ground). [C17: from Latin: mixing bowl, crater, from Greek *kratēr*, from *kerannunai* to mix] —**'cra+ter+less** *adj.* —**'cra·ter-,like** *adj.* —**'cra+ter+ous** *adj.*

Crat+er ('kreɪtə) *n., Latin genitive* **Cra+ter+is** ('kreɪtərɪs). a small faint constellation in the S hemisphere lying between Virgo and Hydra.

craunch (krɔːntʃ) *vb.* a dialect word for **crunch.** —**'craunch+a·ble** *adj.* —**'craunch·y** *adj.* —**'craunch·i+ness** *n.*

cra+vat (krə'væt) *n.* a scarf of silk or fine wool, worn round the neck, esp. by men. [C17: from French *cravate*, from Serbo-Croatian *Hrvat* Croat; so called because worn by Croats in the French army during the Thirty Years' War]

crave (kreɪv) *vb.* **1.** (when *intr.*, foll. by *for* or *after*) to desire intensely; long (for). **2.** (*tr.*) to need greatly or urgently. **3.** (*tr.*) to beg or plead for. [Old English *crafian*; related to Old Norse *krefja* to demand, *krǣfr* strong; see CRAFT] —**'crav+er** *n.* —**'crav+ing** *n.*

cra+ven ('kreɪvᵊn) *adj.* **1.** cowardly; mean-spirited. ~*n.* **2.** a coward. [C13 *cravant*, probably from Old French *crevant* bursting, from *crever* to burst, die, from Latin *crepāre* to burst, crack] —**'cra+ven+ly** *adv.* —**'cra+ven+ness** *n.*

craw (krɔː) *n.* **1.** a less common word for **crop** (sense 6). **2.** the stomach of an animal. **3. stick in someone's craw.** *Slang.* to be unacceptable or irritating to someone. [C14: related to Middle High German *krage*, Middle Dutch *crāghe* neck, Icelandic *kragi* collar]

craw+fish ('krɔː,fɪʃ) *n., pl.* **+fish** *or* **+fish·es.** a variant spelling (esp. U.S.) of **crayfish** (esp. sense 2).

crawl[1] (krɔːl) *vb.* (*intr.*) **1.** to move slowly, either by dragging the body along the ground or on the hands and knees. **2.** to proceed or move along very slowly or laboriously: *the traffic crawled along the road.* **3.** to act or behave in a servile manner; fawn; cringe. **4.** to be or feel as if overrun by crawling creatures: *the pile of refuse crawled with insects.* **5.** (*intr.*) (of insects, worms, snakes, etc.) to move with the body close to the ground. **6.** (*intr.*) to swim the crawl. ~*n.* **7.** a slow creeping pace or motion. **8.** Also called: **Australian crawl, front crawl.** *Swimming.* a stroke in which the feet are kicked like paddles while the arms reach forward and pull back through the water. [C14: probably from Old Norse *krafla* to creep; compare Swedish *kravla*, Middle Low German *krabbelen* to crawl, Old Norse *krabbi* CRAB[1]] —**'crawl+ing+ly** *adv.*

crawl[2] (krɔːl) *n.* an enclosure in shallow, coastal water for fish, lobsters, etc. [C17: from Dutch *kraal* KRAAL]

crawl+er ('krɔːlə) *n.* **1.** *Slang.* a servile flatterer. **2.** a person or animal that crawls. **3.** *U.S.* an informal name for an **earthworm.** **4.** (*pl.*) a baby's overalls; rompers.

Craw+ley ('krɔːlɪ) *n.* a town in S England, in NE West Sussex: designated a new town in 1956. Pop.: 67 709 (1971).

crawl+ing peg *n.* a method of stabilizing exchange rates, prices, etc., by maintaining a fixed level for a specified period or until the rate or price has persisted at an upper or lower limit for a specified period and then permitting a predetermined incremental rise or fall.

crawl·y ('krɔːlɪ) *adj.* **crawl·i+er, crawl·i+est.** *Informal.* feeling or causing a sensation like creatures crawling on one's skin.

cray (kreɪ) *n. Austral. informal.* a crayfish.

cray+fish ('kreɪ,fɪʃ) *or esp. U.S.* **craw+fish** *n., pl.* **+fish** *or* **+fish·es.** **1.** any freshwater decapod crustacean of the genera *Astacus* and *Cambarus*, resembling a small lobster. **2.** any of various similar crustaceans, esp. the spiny lobster. [C14: *cray*, by folk etymology, from Old French *crevice* crab, from Old High German *krebiz* + FISH]

cray+on ('kreɪən, -ɒn) *n.* **1.** a small stick or pencil of charcoal, wax, clay, or chalk mixed with coloured pigment. **2.** a drawing made with crayons. ~*vb.* **3.** to draw or colour with crayons. [C17: from French, from *craie*, from Latin *crēta* chalk] —**'cray+on+ist** *n.*

craze (kreɪz) *n.* **1.** a short-lived current fashion. **2.** a wild or exaggerated enthusiasm: *a craze for chestnuts.* **3.** mental disturbance; insanity. ~*vb.* **4.** to make or become mad. **5.** *Ceramics, metallurgy.* to develop or cause to develop a fine network of cracks. **6.** (*tr.*) *Brit. dialect or obsolete.* to break. **7.** (*tr.*) *Archaic.* to weaken. [C14 (in the sense: to break, shatter): probably of Scandinavian origin; compare Swedish *krasa* to shatter, ultimately of imitative origin]

crazed (kreɪzd) *adj.* **1.** driven insane. **2.** (of porcelain or pottery) having a fine network of cracks in the glaze.

cra+zy ('kreɪzɪ) *adj.* **+zi+er, +zi+est.** **1.** *Informal.* insane. **2.** fantastic; strange; ridiculous: *a crazy dream.* **3.** (*postpositive*; foll. by *about* or *over*) *Informal.* extremely fond (of). **4.** *Slang.* very good or excellent. **5.** *Archaic.* likely to collapse; rickety. —**'cra+zi+ly** *adv.* —**'cra+zi+ness** *n.*

cra+zy bone *n.* the U.S. name for **funny bone.**

cra+zy pav+ing *n. Brit.* a form of paving, as for a path, made of slabs of stone of irregular shape fitted together.

cra+zy quilt *n.* a patchwork quilt made from assorted pieces of material of irregular shape, size, and colour.

creak (kriːk) *vb.* **1.** to make or cause to make a harsh squeaking sound. **2.** (*intr.*) to make such sounds while moving: *the old car creaked along.* ~*n.* **3.** a harsh squeaking sound. [C14: variant of CROAK, of imitative origin] —**'creak·y** *adj.* —**'creak·i+ly** *adv.* —**'creak·i+ness** *n.* —**'creak+ing+ly** *adv.*

cream (kriːm) *n.* **1. a.** the fatty part of milk, which rises to the top if the milk is allowed to stand. **b.** (*as modifier*): *cream buns.* **2.** anything resembling cream in consistency: *shoe cream; beauty cream.* **3.** the best one or most essential part of something; pick: *the cream of the bunch; the cream of the joke.* **4.** a soup containing cream or milk: *cream of chicken soup.* **5.** any of various dishes, cakes, biscuits, etc., resembling or containing cream. **6.** a confection made of fondant or soft fudge, often covered in chocolate. **7. cream sherry.** a full-bodied sweet sherry. **8. a.** a yellowish-white colour. **b.** (*as adj.*): *cream wallpaper.* ~*vb.* **9.** (*tr.*) to skim or otherwise separate the cream from (milk). **10.** (*tr.*) to beat (foodstuffs, esp. butter and sugar) to a light creamy consistency. **11.** (*intr.*) to form cream. **12.** (*tr.*) to add or apply cream or any creamlike substance to: *to cream one's face; to cream coffee.* **13.** (*tr.*; sometimes foll. by *off*) to take away the best part of. **14.** (*tr.*) to prepare or cook (vegetables, chicken, etc.) with cream or milk. **15.** to allow (milk) to form a layer of cream on its surface or (of milk) to form such a layer. **16.** (*tr.*) *Slang, chiefly U.S.* to beat thoroughly. **17.** (*intr.*) *Taboo slang.* (of men) to ejaculate, as during orgasm. [C14: from Old French *cresme*, from Late Latin *crāmum* cream, of Celtic origin; influenced by Church Latin *chrisma* unction, CHRISM] —**'cream+,like** *adj.*

cream cheese *n.* a smooth soft white cheese made from soured cream or milk.

cream crack+er *n. Brit.* a crisp unsweetened biscuit, usually eaten with cheese.

cream+cups ('kriːm,kʌps) *n.* a Californian papaveraceous plant, *Platystemon californicus*, with small cream-coloured or yellow flowers on long flower stalks.

cream+er ('kriːmə) *n.* **1.** a vessel or device for separating cream from milk. **2.** *Chiefly U.S.* a small jug or pitcher for serving cream.

cream+er·y ('kriːmərɪ) *n., pl.* **+er·ies.** **1.** an establishment where milk and cream are made into butter and cheese. **2.** a place where dairy products are sold. **3.** a place where milk is left to stand until the cream rises to the top.

cream+laid ('kriːm,leɪd) *or* **cream+wove** ('kriːm,wəʊv) *adj.* (of paper) cream-coloured and of a ribbed appearance.

cream of tar+tar *n.* another name for **potassium hydrogen tartrate**, esp. when used in baking powders.

cream puff *n.* **1.** a shell of light pastry with a custard or cream filling. **2.** *Informal.* an effeminate man.

cream sauce *n.* a white sauce made from cream, butter, etc.

cream so·da *n. Chiefly U.S.* a soft drink flavoured with vanilla.

cream tea *n.* afternoon tea including bread or scones served with clotted cream and jam.

cream·y ('kriːmɪ) *adj.* **cream·i+er, cream·i+est.** **1.** resembling cream in colour, taste, or consistency. **2.** containing cream. —**'cream·i+ly** *adv.* —**'cream·i+ness** *n.*

crease[1] (kriːs) *n.* **1.** a line or mark produced by folding, pressing, or wrinkling. **2.** a wrinkle or furrow, esp. on the face. **3.** *Cricket.* any three lines near each wicket marking positions for the bowler or batsman. See also **bowling crease, popping crease, return crease.** **4.** *Ice hockey.* the small rectangular area in front of each goal cage. **5.** Also called: **goal crease.** *Lacrosse.* the circular area surrounding the goal. ~*vb.* **6.** to make or become wrinkled or furrowed. **7.** (*tr.*) to graze with a bullet, causing superficial injury. **8.** (often foll. by *up*) *Slang.* to be or cause to be greatly amused. [C15: from earlier *crēst*; probably related to Old French *cresté* wrinkled] —**'crease+less** *adj.* —**'creas+er** *n.* —**'creas·y** *adj.*

crease[2] (kriːs) *n.* a rare spelling of **kris.**

cre+ate (kriː'eɪt) *vb.* **1.** (*tr.*) to cause to come into existence. **2.** (*tr.*) to invest with a new honour, office, or title; appoint. **3.** (*tr.*) to be the cause of: *these circumstances created the revolution.* **4.** (*tr.*) to act (a role) in the first production of a play. **5.** (*intr.*) to be engaged in creative work. **6.** (*intr.*) *Brit. slang.* to make a fuss or uproar. [C14 *creat* created, from Latin *creātus*, from *creāre* to produce, make] —**cre+'at+a·ble** *adj.*

cre·a+tine ('kriːə,tiːn, -tɪn) *or* **cre·a+tin** ('kriːətɪn) *n.* a weakly basic compound found, as the phosphate, in the muscles of vertebrates: used in muscle contraction. Formula: $HN:C(NH_2)NCH_3CH_2COOH$. [C19: *creat-* from Greek *kreas* flesh + -INE[2]]

cre+at·i+nine (kriː'ætə,niːn) *n.* a white crystalline slightly soluble solid produced by catabolism of creatine and found esp. in urine and muscle. Formula: $C_4H_7N_3O$. [C19: from German *Kreatinin*, from *Kreatin* CREATINE + *-in* -INE[2]]

cre·a+tion (kriː'eɪʃən) *n.* **1.** the act or process of creating. **2.** the fact of being created or produced. **3.** something that has been brought into existence or created, esp. a product of human intelligence or imagination. **4.** the whole universe, including the world and all the things in it. **5.** an unusual or striking garment or hat. —**cre·'a+tion+al** *adj.*

Cre·a+tion (kriː'eɪʃən) *n. Theol.* **1.** (often preceded by *the*) God's act of bringing the universe into being. **2.** the universe as thus brought into being by God.

cre·a+tion+ism (kriː'eɪʃə,nɪzəm) *n. Theol.* **1.** the belief that God brings individual human souls into existence at conception or birth. Compare **traducianism.** **2.** the doctrine that ascribes the origins of all things, to God's acts of creation rather than to evolution. —**cre·'a+tion+ist** *n.* —**cre·,a+tion+'is+tic** *adj.*

cre·a+tive (kriːˈeɪtɪv) *adj.* **1.** having the ability or power to create. **2.** characterized by originality of thought or inventiveness; having or showing imagination: *a creative mind.* **3.** designed to or tending to stimulate the imagination or invention: *creative toys.* —**cre·'a+tive+ly** *adv.* —**cre·'a+tive+ness** *n.* —**,cre·a·'tiv+i·ty** *n.*

cre·a+tor (kriːˈeɪtə) *n.* a person or thing that creates; originator. —**cre·'a+tor+,ship** *n.* —**cre·'a+tress** *or* **cre·'a+trix** *fem. n.*

Cre·a+tor (kriːˈeɪtə) *n.* (usually preceded by *the*) an epithet of God.

crea+ture (ˈkriːtʃə) *n.* **1.** a living being, esp. an animal. **2.** something that has been created, whether animate or inanimate: *a creature of the imagination.* **3.** a human being; person: used as a term of scorn, pity, or endearment. **4.** a person who is dependent upon another; tool or puppet. [C13: from Church Latin *creātūra,* from Latin *creāre* to create] —**'crea+tur+al** *or* **'crea+ture+ly** *adj.* —**'crea+ture+li+ness** *n.*

crea+ture com+forts *pl. n.* material things or luxuries that help to provide for one's bodily comfort.

crèche (krɛʃ, kreɪʃ; *French* krɛʃ) *n.* **1.** *Chiefly Brit.* a day nursery for very young children. **2.** a tableau of Christ's Nativity. **3.** a foundling home or hospital. [C19: from Old French: manger, crib, ultimately of Germanic origin; compare Old High German *kripja* crib]

Cré+cy (ˈkrɛsɪ; *French* kreˈsi) *n.* a village in N France: scene of the first decisive battle of the Hundred Years' War when the English defeated the French (1346). Official name **Cré·cy-en-Pon·thieu** (ã pɔ̃ˈtjø). English **Cressy.**

cre+dence (ˈkriːdᵊns) *n.* **1.** acceptance or belief, esp. with regard to the truth of the evidence of others: *I cannot give credence to his account.* **2.** something supporting a claim to belief; recommendation; credential (esp. in the phrase **letters of credence**). **3.** short for **credence table.** [C14: from Medieval Latin *crēdentia* trust, credit, from Latin *crēdere* to believe]

cre+dence ta+ble *n.* **1.** a small sideboard, originally one at which food was tasted for poison before serving. **2.** *Christianity.* a small table or ledge on which the bread, wine, etc., are placed before being consecrated in the Eucharist.

cre+den+dum (krɪˈdɛndəm) *n., pl.* **+da** (-də). (*often pl.*) *Christianity.* an article of faith. [Latin: a thing to be believed, from *crēdere* to believe]

cre+dent (ˈkriːdᵊnt) *adj. Obsolete.* believing or believable. [C17: from Latin *crēdēns* believing]

cre+den+tial (krɪˈdɛnʃəl) *n.* **1.** something that entitles a person to confidence, authority, etc. **2.** (*pl.*) a letter or certificate giving evidence of the bearer's identity or competence. ~*adj.* **3.** entitling one to confidence, authority, etc. [C16: from Medieval Latin *crēdentia* credit, trust; see CREDENCE] —**cre+'den+tialed** *adj.*

cre+den+za (krɪˈdɛnzə) *n.* another name for **credence table.** [Italian: see CREDENCE]

cred+i·bil+i·ty gap *n.* a disparity between claims or statements made and the evident facts of the situation or circumstances to which they relate.

cred+i·ble (ˈkrɛdɪbᵊl) *adj.* **1.** capable of being believed. **2.** trustworthy. [C14: from Latin *crēdibilis,* from Latin *crēdere* to believe] —**'cred+i·ble+ness** *or* **,cred+i·'bil+i·ty** *n.* —**'cred+i·bly** *adv.*

cred+it (ˈkrɛdɪt) *n.* **1.** commendation or approval, as for an act or quality: *she was given credit for her work.* **2.** a person or thing serving as a source of good influence, repute, ability, etc.: *a credit to the team.* **3.** the quality of being believable or trustworthy: *that statement had credit.* **4.** influence or reputation coming from the approval or good opinion of others: *he acquired credit within the community.* **5.** belief in the truth, reliability, quality, etc., of someone or something: *I would give credit to that philosophy.* **6.** a sum of money or equivalent purchasing power, as at a shop, available for a person's use. **7. a.** the positive balance in a person's bank account. **b.** the sum of money that a bank makes available to a client in excess of any deposit. **8. a.** the practice of permitting a buyer to receive goods or services before payment. **b.** the time permitted for paying for such goods or services. **9.** reputation for solvency and commercial or financial probity, inducing confidence among creditors. **10.** *Accounting.* **a.** acknowledgment of an income, liability, or capital item by entry on the right-hand side of an account. **b.** the right-hand side of an account. **c.** an entry on this side. **d.** the total of such entries. **e.** (*as modifier*): *credit entries.* Compare **debit** (sense 1). **11.** *Education.* **a.** a distinction awarded to an examination candidate obtaining good marks. **b.** a section of an examination syllabus satisfactorily completed, as in higher and professional education. **12. letter of credit.** an order authorizing a named person to draw money from correspondents of the issuer. **13. on credit.** with payment to be made at a future date. ~*vb.* (*tr.*) **14.** (foll. by *with*) to ascribe (to); give credit (for): *they credited him with the discovery.* **15.** to accept as true; believe. **16.** to do credit to. **17.** *Accounting.* **a.** to enter (an item) as a credit in an account. **b.** to acknowledge (a payer) by making such an entry. Compare **debit** (sense 2). **18.** to award a credit to (a student). [C16: from Old French *crédit,* from Italian *credito,* from Latin *crēditum* loan, from *crēdere* to believe] —**'cred+it+less** *adj.*

cred+it+a·ble (ˈkrɛdɪtəbᵊl) *adj.* **1.** deserving credit, honour, etc.; praiseworthy. **2.** *Obsolete.* credible. —**'cred+it+a·ble+ness** *or* **,cred+it+a·'bil+i·ty** *n.* —**'cred+it+a·bly** *adv.*

cred+it ac+count *n. Brit.* a credit system by means of which customers may obtain goods and services before payment. Also called: **charge account.**

cred+it card *n.* a card issued by banks, businesses, etc., enabling the holder to obtain goods and services on credit.

cred+it line *n.* **1.** an acknowledgment of origin or authorship, as in a newspaper or film. **2.** Also: **line of credit.** *U.S.* the maximum credit that a customer is allowed.

cred·i+tor (ˈkrɛdɪtə) *n.* a person or commercial enterprise to whom money is owed. Compare **debtor.**

cred+it rat+ing *n.* an evaluation of the creditworthiness of an individual or business enterprise, based on earning power, previous record of debt repayment, etc.

cred+its (ˈkrɛdɪts) *pl. n.* a list of those responsible for the production of a film.

cred+it squeeze *n.* the control of credit facilities as an instrument of economic policy, associated with restrictions on bank loans and overdrafts, raised interest rates, etc.

cred+it stand+ing *n.* reputation for discharging financial obligations.

cred+it un+ion *n.* a cooperative association whose members can obtain low-interest loans out of their combined savings.

cre+do (ˈkriːdəʊ, ˈkreɪ-) *n., pl.* **+dos.** any formal or authorized statement of beliefs, principles, or opinions.

Cre+do (ˈkriːdəʊ, ˈkreɪ-) *n., pl.* **+dos. 1.** the Apostles' Creed or the Nicene Creed. **2.** a musical setting of the Creed. [C12: from Latin literally: I believe; first word of the Apostles' and Nicene Creeds]

cre+du+li·ty (krɪˈdjuːlɪtɪ) *n.* disposition to believe something on little evidence; gullibility.

cred·u+lous (ˈkrɛdjʊləs) *adj.* **1.** tending to believe something on little evidence. **2.** arising from or characterized by credulity: *credulous beliefs.* [C16: from Latin *crēdulus,* from *crēdere* to believe] —**'cred·u+lous+ly** *adv.* —**'cred·u+lous+ness** *n.*

cree (kriː) *n. South Wales and southwest English dialect.* temporary immunity from the rules of a game: said by children. [of unknown origin]

Cree (kriː) *n.* **1.** (*pl.* **Cree** *or* **Crees**) a member of a North American Indian people living in Ontario, Saskatchewan, and Montana. **2.** the language of this people, belonging to the Algonquian family. **3.** a syllabic writing system of this and certain other languages. [from first syllable of Canadian French *Christianaux,* probably based on *Ojibwa Kenistenoag* (tribal name)]

creed (kriːd) *n.* **1.** a concise, formal statement of the essential articles of Christian belief, such as the Apostles' Creed or the Nicene Creed. **2.** any statement or system of beliefs or principles. [Old English *crēda,* from Latin *crēdo* I believe] —**'creed+al** *or* **'cred+al** *adj.*

creek (kriːk) *n.* **1.** *Chiefly Brit.* a narrow inlet or bay, esp. of the sea. **2.** *Chiefly U.S., Canadian, and Australian.* a small stream or tributary. **3. up the creek.** *Slang.* in trouble; in a difficult position. [C13: from Old Norse *kriki* nook; related to Middle Dutch *krēke* creek, inlet]

Creek (kriːk) *n.* **1.** (*pl.* **Creek** *or* **Creeks**) a member of a confederacy of North American Indian peoples formerly living in Georgia and Alabama, now chiefly in Oklahoma. **2.** any of the languages of these peoples, belonging to the Muskhogean family.

creel (kriːl) *n.* **1.** a wickerwork basket, esp. one used to hold fish. **2.** a wickerwork trap for catching lobsters, etc. **3.** the framework on a spinning machine that holds the bobbins. **4.** *West Yorkshire dialect.* a wooden frame suspended from a ceiling, used for drying clothes. [C15: from Scottish, of obscure origin]

creep (kriːp) *vb.* **creeps, creep+ing, crept.** (*intr.*) **1.** to crawl with the body near to or touching the ground. **2.** to move slowly, quietly, or cautiously. **3.** to act in a servile way; fawn; cringe. **4.** to move or slip out of place, as from pressure or wear. **5.** (of plants) to grow along the ground or over rocks, producing roots, suckers, or tendrils at intervals. **6.** (of a body or substance) to become permanently deformed as a result of an applied stress, often when combined with heating. **7.** to develop gradually: *creeping unrest.* **8.** to have the sensation of something crawling over the skin. **9.** (of metals) to undergo slow plastic deformation. ~*n.* **10.** the act of creeping or a creeping movement. **11.** *Slang.* a person considered to be obnoxious or servile. **12.** the continuous permanent deformation of a body or substance as a result of stress or heat. **13.** *Geology.* the gradual downwards movement of loose rock material, soil, etc., on a slope. **14.** a slow relative movement of two adjacent parts, structural components, etc. **15.** slow plastic deformation of metals. [Old English *crēopan;* related to Old Frisian *kriāpa,* Old Norse *krjūpa,* Middle Low German *krūpen*]

creep+er (ˈkriːpə) *n.* **1.** a person or animal that creeps. **2.** a plant, such as the ivy or periwinkle, that grows by creeping. **3.** the U.S. name for the **tree creeper. 4.** a hooked instrument for dragging deep water. **5.** Also called: **cradle.** a flat board or framework mounted on casters, used to lie on when working under cars. **6.** Also called: **daisycutter.** *Cricket.* a bowled ball that keeps low or travels along the ground. **7.** either of a pair of low iron supports for logs in a hearth. **8.** *Informal.* a shoe with a soft sole.

creep·ie (ˈkriːpɪ, ˈkrɪp-) *n. Chiefly Scot.* a low stool.

creep+ing bent grass *n.* a grass, *Agrostris palustris,* grown as a pasture grass in Europe and North America: roots readily from the stem.

creep+ing Jen+nie *or U.S.* **creep+ing Char+lie** *n.* another name for **moneywort.**

creep+ing this+tle *n.* a weedy Eurasian thistle, *Cirsium* *arvense,* common as a fast-spreading weed in the U.S. U.S. name: **Canada thistle.**

creeps (kri:ps) *pl. n.* (preceded by *the*) *Slang.* a feeling of fear, repulsion, disgust, etc.

creep·y ('kri:pɪ) *adj.* **creep·i·er, creep·i·est. 1.** *Informal.* having or causing a sensation of repulsion, horror, or fear, as of creatures crawling on the skin. **2.** creeping; slow-moving. —'**creep·i·ly** *adv.* —'**creep·i·ness** *n.*

creep·y-crawl·y *Brit. informal.* ~*n., pl.* **-crawl·ies. 1.** a small crawling creature. ~*adj.* **2.** feeling or causing a sensation as of creatures crawling on one's skin.

creese (kri:s) *n.* a rare spelling of **kris.**

cre·mate (krɪ'meɪt) *vb.* (*tr.*) to burn up (something, esp. a corpse) and reduce to ash. [C19: from Latin *cremāre*] —**cre·'ma·tion** *n.* —**cre·'ma·tion·ism** *n.* —**cre·'ma·tion·ist** *n.* —**crem·a·to·ry** ('krɛmətərɪ, -trɪ) *adj.*

cre·ma·tor (krɪ'meɪtə) *n.* **1.** Also called (esp. U.S.): **cinerator.** *Brit.* a furnace for cremating corpses. **2.** a person who operates such a furnace.

crem·a·to·ri·um (ˌkrɛmə'tɔ:rɪəm) *n., pl.* **·ri·ums** *or* **·ri·a** (-rɪə). *Brit.* a building in which corpses are cremated. Also called (esp. U.S.): **crematory.**

crème (krɛm, kri:m, kreɪm; *French* krɛm) *n.* **1.** cream. **2.** any of various sweet liqueurs: *crème de moka.* ~*adj.* **3.** (of a liqueur) rich and sweet.

crème brû·lée *French.* (krɛm bru'le) *n.* a cream or custard dessert covered with caramelized sugar. [literally, burnt cream]

crème car·a·mel *n.* a dessert made of eggs, sugar, milk, etc., topped with caramel. Also called: **caramel cream.**

crème de ca·ca·o ('krɛm də kɑ:'kɑ:əʊ, 'kəʊkəʊ, 'kri:m, 'kreɪm) *n.* a sweet liqueur with a chocolate flavour. [French, literally: cream of cacao]

crème de la crème *French.* (krɛm də la 'krɛm) *n.* the very best. [literally: cream of the cream]

crème de menthe ('krɛm də 'mɛnθ, 'mɪnt, 'kri:m, 'kreɪm) *n.* a liqueur flavoured with peppermint, usually bright green in colour. [French, literally: cream of mint]

Cre·mo·na (*Italian* kre'mo:na) *n.* a city in N Italy, in Lombardy on the River Po: noted for the manufacture of fine violins in the 16th–18th centuries. Pop.: 81 983 (1971).

cre·nate ('kri:neɪt) *or* **cre·nat·ed** *adj.* having a scalloped margin, as certain leaves. [C18: from New Latin *crēnātus,* from Medieval Latin, probably from Late Latin *crēna* a notch] —'**cre·nate·ly** *adv.*

cre·na·tion (krɪ'neɪʃən) *or* **cren·a·ture** ('krɛnəˌtjʊə, 'kri:-) *n.* **1.** any of the rounded teeth or the notches between them on a crenate structure. **2.** a crenate formation or condition.

cren·el ('krɛnᵊl) *or* **cre·nelle** (krɪ'nɛl) *n.* **1.** any of a set of openings formed in the top of a wall or parapet and having slanting sides, as in a battlement. **2.** another name for **crenation.** [C15: from Old French, literally: a little notch, from *cren* notch, from Late Latin *crēna*]

cren·el·late *or U.S.* **cren·el·ate** ('krɛnɪˌleɪt) *vb.* (*tr.*) **1.** to supply with battlements. **2.** to form square indentations in (a moulding, etc.). [C19: from Old French *creneler,* from CRENEL] —'**cren·el·ˌlat·ed** *or U.S.* '**cren·el·ˌat·ed** *adj.* —ˌ**cren·el·'la·tion** *or U.S.* ˌ**cren·el·'a·tion** *n.*

cren·u·late ('krɛnjʊˌleɪt, -lɪt) *or* **cren·u·lat·ed** *adj.* having a margin very finely notched with rounded projections, as certain leaves. [C18: from New Latin *crēnulātus,* from *crēnula,* literally: a little notch; see CRENEL]

cren·u·la·tion (ˌkrɛnjʊ'leɪʃən) *n.* **1.** any of the teeth or notches of a crenulate structure. **2.** a crenulate formation.

cre·o·dont ('kri:əˌdɒnt) *n.* any of a group of extinct Tertiary mammals some of which are thought to have been the ancestors of modern carnivores: order *Carnivora.* [C19: from New Latin *Creodonta,* from Greek *kreas* flesh + *odōn* tooth]

cre·ole ('kri:əʊl) *n.* **1.** a language that has its origin in extended contact between two language communities, one of which is generally European. It incorporates features from each and constitutes the mother tongue of a community. Compare **pidgin.** ~*adj.* **2.** denoting, relating to, or characteristic of creole. **3.** (of a sauce or dish) containing or cooked with tomatoes, green peppers, onions, etc. [C17: via French and Spanish probably from Portuguese *crioulo* slave born in one's household, person of European ancestry born in the colonies, probably from *criar* to bring up, from Latin *creāre* to CREATE]

Cre·ole ('kri:əʊl) *n.* **1.** (*sometimes not cap.*) (in the West Indies and Latin America) **a.** a native-born person of European, esp. Spanish, ancestry. **b.** a native-born person of mixed European and Negro ancestry who speaks a French or Spanish creole. **c.** a native-born Negro as distinguished from one brought from Africa. **2.** (in Louisiana and other Gulf States) a native-born person of French ancestry. **3.** the creolized French spoken in Louisiana, esp. in New Orleans. ~*adj.* **4.** of, relating to, or characteristic of any of these peoples.

cre·o·lized *or* **cre·o·lised** ('kri:əˌlaɪzd) *adj.* (of a language) incorporating a considerable range of features from one or more unrelated languages, as the result of contact between language communities.

Cre·on ('kri:ɒn) *n. Greek myth.* the successor to Oedipus as king of Thebes; the brother of Jocasta. See also **Antigone.**

cre·oph·a·gous (krɪ'ɒfəgəs) *adj.* flesh-eating or carnivorous. [C19: from Greek *kreophagos,* from *kreas* flesh + *phagein* to consume] —**cre·oph·a·gy** (krɪ'ɒfədʒɪ) *n.*

cre·o·sol ('kri:əˌsɒl) *n.* a colourless or pale yellow insoluble oily liquid with a smoky odour and a burning taste; 2-methoxy-4-methylphenol: an active principle of creosote. Formula: $CH_3O(CH_3)C_6H_3OH$. [C19: from CREOS(OTE) + -OL[1]]

cre·o·sote ('krɪəˌsəʊt) *n.* **1.** a colourless or pale yellow liquid mixture with a burning taste and penetrating odour distilled from wood tar, esp. from beechwood, contains creosol and other phenols, and is used as an antiseptic. **2.** Also called: **coal-tar creosote.** a thick dark liquid mixture prepared from coal tar, containing phenols: used as a preservative for wood. ~*vb.* **3.** to treat (wood) with creosote. [C19: from Greek *kreas* flesh + *sōtēr* preserver, from *sōzein* to keep safe] —**cre·o·sot·ic** (ˌkrɪə'sɒtɪk) *adj.*

cre·o·sote bush *n.* a shrub, *Larrea* (or *Covillea*) *tridentata* of the western U.S. and Mexico, that has resinous leaves with an odour resembling creosote: family *Zygophyllaceae.* Also called: **greasewood.**

crepe *or* **crape** (kreɪp) *n.* **1. a.** a light cotton, silk, or other fabric with a fine ridged or crinkled surface. **b.** (*as modifier*): *a crepe dress.* **2.** a black armband originally made of this, worn as a sign of mourning. **3.** a very thin pancake, often rolled or folded around a filling. **4.** short for **crepe paper** or **crepe rubber.** ~*vb.* **5.** (*tr.*) to cover or drape with crepe. [C19: from French *crêpe,* from Latin *crispus* curled, uneven, wrinkled]

crepe de Chine (ˌkreɪp də 'ʃi:n) *n.* **a.** a very thin crepe of silk or a similar light fabric. **b.** (*as modifier*): *a crepe-de-Chine blouse.* [C19: from French: Chinese crepe]

crepe hair *n.* artificial hair, usually plaited and made of wool or vegetable fibre, used in theatrical make-up.

crepe pa·per *n.* thin crinkled coloured paper, resembling crepe and used for decorations.

crepe rub·ber *n.* **1.** a type of crude natural rubber in the form of colourless or pale yellow crinkled sheets, prepared by pressing bleached coagulated latex through corrugated rollers: used for the soles of shoes and in making certain surgical and medical goods. Sometimes shortened to **crepe.** Compare **smoked rubber. 2.** a similar synthetic rubber.

crêpe su·zette ('kreɪp su:'zɛt) *n., pl.* **crêpes su·zettes.** (*sometimes pl.*) an orange-flavoured pancake flambéed in a liqueur or brandy.

crep·i·tate ('krɛpɪˌteɪt) *vb.* (*intr.*) to make a rattling or crackling sound; rattle or crackle. [C17: from Latin *crepitāre*] —'**crep·i·tant** *adj.* —ˌ**crep·i·'ta·tion** *n.*

crep·i·tus ('krɛpɪtəs) *n.* **1.** a crackling chest sound heard in pneumonia and other lung diseases. **2.** the grating sound of two ends of a broken bone rubbing together. [C19: from Latin, from *crepāre* to crack, creak]

crept (krɛpt) *vb.* the past tense or past participle of **creep.**

cre·pus·cu·lar (krɪ'pʌskjʊlə) *adj.* **1.** of or like twilight; dim. **2.** (of certain insects, birds, and other animals) active at twilight or just before dawn. [C17: from Latin *crepusculum* dusk, from *creper* dark]

Cres. *abbrev. for* Crescent.

cre·scen·do (krɪ'ʃɛndəʊ) *n., pl.* **·dos** *or* **·di** (-dɪ). **1.** *Music.* **a.** a gradual increase in loudness or the musical direction or symbol indicating this. Abbrev.: **cresc.** Symbol: $<$ (written over the music affected). **b.** (*as modifier*): *a crescendo passage.* **2.** any similar gradual increase in loudness: *the cheers reached a crescendo.* ~*vb.* **·does, ·do·ing, ·doed. 3.** (*intr.*) to increase in loudness or force. ~*adv.* **4.** with a crescendo. [C18: from Italian, literally: increasing, from *crescere* to grow, from Latin]

cres·cent ('krɛsᵊnt, -zᵊnt) *n.* **1.** the biconcave shape of the moon in its first or last quarters. **2.** any shape or object resembling this. **3.** *Chiefly Brit.* **a.** a crescent-shaped street, often lined with houses of the same style. **b.** (*cap. when part of a name*): *Pelham Crescent.* **4.** *Heraldry.* a crescent moon, used as the cadency mark of a second son. **5.** (*often cap.* and preceded by *the*) **a.** the emblem of Islam or Turkey. **b.** Islamic or Turkish power. ~*adj.* **6.** *Archaic or poetic.* increasing or growing. [C14: from Latin *crescēns* increasing, from *crescere* to grow] —**cres·cen·tic** (krə'sɛntɪk) *adj.*

cre·sol ('kri:sɒl) *n.* an aromatic compound derived from phenol, existing in three isomeric forms: found in coal tar and creosote and used in making synthetic resins and as an antiseptic and disinfectant; hydroxytoluene. Formula: $C_6H_4(CH_3)OH$. Also called: **cresylic acid.**

cress (krɛs) *n.* any of various cruciferous plants of the genera *Lepidum, Cardamine, Arabis,* etc., having pungent-tasting leaves often used in salads and as a garnish. See also **watercress, garden cress.** [Old English *cressa;* related to Old High German *cresso* cress, *kresan* to crawl]

cres·set ('krɛsɪt) *n. History.* a metal basket mounted on a pole in which oil or pitch was burned for illumination. [C14: from Old French *craisset,* from *craisse* GREASE]

Cres·si·da ('krɛsɪdə), **Cri·sey·de,** *or* **Cres·sid** *n.* (in medieval adaptations of the story of Troy) a lady who deserts her Trojan lover Troilus for the Greek Diomedes.

Cres·sy ('krɛsɪ) *n.* the English name for **Crécy.**

crest (krɛst) *n.* **1.** a tuft or growth of feathers, fur, or skin along the top of the heads of some birds, reptiles, and other animals. **2.** something resembling or suggesting this. **3.** the top, highest point, or highest stage of something. **4.** a ridge on the neck of a horse, dog, lion, etc. **5.** the mane or hair growing from this ridge. **6.** an ornamental piece, such as a plume, on top of a helmet. **7.** *Heraldry.* a symbol of a family or office, usually representing a beast or bird, borne in addition to a coat of arms and used in medieval times to decorate the helmet. **8.** a ridge along the top of a roof, wall, etc. **9.** a ridge along the surface of a bone. **10.** Also called: **cresting.** *Archery.* identifying rings painted around an arrow shaft. ~*vb.* **11.** (*intr.*) to come or rise to a high point. **12.** (*tr.*) to lie at the top of; cap. **13.** (*tr.*) to go to or reach the top of (a hill, wave, etc.).

[C14: from Old French *creste,* from Latin *crista*] —'**crest+ed** *adj.* —'**crest+less** *adj.*

crest+ed tit *n.* a small European songbird, *Parus cristatus,* that has a greyish-brown plumage with a prominent speckled black-and-white crest: family *Paridae* (tits).

crest+fall·en ('krɛst,fɔːlən) *adj.* dejected, depressed, or disheartened. —'**crest+,fall·en+ly** *adv.*

crest+ing ('krɛstɪŋ) *n.* **1.** an ornamental ridge along the top of a roof, wall, etc. **2.** *Furniture.* a shaped decorative toprail or horizontal carved ornament surmounting a chair, mirror, etc.

cre+syl+ic (krɪ'sɪlɪk) *adj.* of, concerned with, or containing creosote or cresol. [C19: from CRE(O)S(OTE) + -YL + -IC]

cre+ta+ceous (krɪ'teɪʃəs) *adj.* consisting of or resembling chalk. [C17: from Latin *crētāceus,* from *crēta,* literally: Cretan earth, that is, chalk] —**cre+'ta+ceous+ly** *adv.*

Cre+ta+ceous (krɪ'teɪʃəs) *adj.* **1.** of, denoting, or formed in the last period of the Mesozoic era, between the Jurassic and Tertiary periods, lasting 65 million years during which chalk deposits were formed and flowering plants first appeared. ~*n.* **2. the.** the Cretaceous period or rock system.

Crete (kriːt) *n.* a mountainous island in the E Mediterranean, the largest island of Greece: of archaeological importance for the ruins of Minoan civilization. Capital: Canea (Khania). Pop.: 456 642 (1971). Area: 8331 sq. km (3216 sq. miles). Modern Greek name: **Kriti.** —'**Cre+tan** *adj., n.*

cre+tic ('kriːtɪk) *n. Prosody.* a metrical foot consisting of three syllables, the first long, the second short, and the third long (¯˘¯). Also called: **amphimacer.** Compare **amphibrach.** [C16: from Latin *crēticus* consisting of the amphimacer, literally: Cretan, from Greek *krētikos,* from *Krētē* CRETE]

cret+in ('krɛtɪn) *n.* **1.** a person afflicted with cretinism: a mentally retarded dwarf with wide-set eyes, a broad flat nose, and protruding tongue. **2.** a person considered to be extremely stupid. [C18: from French *crétin,* from Swiss French *crestin,* from Latin *Chrīstiānus* CHRISTIAN, alluding to the humanity of such people, despite their handicaps] —'**cret+in+,oid** *adj.* —'**cret+in+ous** *adj.*

cret+in+ism ('krɛtɪ,nɪzəm) *n.* a condition arising from a deficiency of thyroid hormone, present from birth, characterized by dwarfism and mental retardation. See also **myxoedema.**

cre+tonne (krɛ'tɒn, 'krɛtɒn) *n.* **a.** a heavy cotton or linen fabric with a printed design, used for furnishing. **b.** (*as modifier*): *cretonne chair covers.* [C19: from French, from *Creton* Norman village where it originated]

Creuse (*French* krøːz) *n.* a department of central France, in Limousin region. Capital: Guéret. Pop.: 151 341 (1975). Area: 5606 sq. km (2186 sq. miles).

cre+vasse (krɪ'væs) *n.* **1.** a deep crack or fissure, esp. in the ice of a glacier. **2.** *U.S.* a break in a river embankment. ~*vb.* **3.** (*tr.*) *U.S.* to make a break or fissure in (a dyke, wall, etc.). [C19: from French: CREVICE]

crev+ice ('krɛvɪs) *n.* a narrow fissure or crack; split; cleft. [C14: from Old French *crevace,* from *crever* to burst, from Latin *crepāre* to crack]

crew[1] (kruː) *n.* (*sometimes functioning as pl.*) **1.** the men who man a ship, boat, aircraft, etc. **2.** *Nautical.* a group of people assigned to a particular job or type of work. **3.** *Informal.* a gang, company, or crowd. **4.** *Archaic.* a band of armed men. ~*vb.* **5.** to serve on (a ship) as a member of the crew. [C15 *crue* (military) reinforcement, from Old French *creue* augmentation, from Old French *creistre* to increase, from Latin *crescere*]

crew[2] (kruː) *vb. Archaic.* a past tense of **crow**[2].

crew cut *n.* a closely cropped haircut for men, originating in the U.S. [C20: from the style of haircut worn by the boat crews at Harvard and Yale Universities]

Crewe (kruː) *n.* a town in NW England, in Cheshire: major railway junction. Pop.: 51 302 (1971).

crew+el ('kruːɪl) *n.* a loosely twisted worsted yarn, used in fancy work and embroidery. [C15: of unknown origin] —'**crew+el+ist** *n.* —'**crew·el+,work** *n.*

crew neck *n.* a plain round neckline in sweaters. —'**crew-,neck** *or* '**crew-,necked** *adj.*

crib (krɪb) *n.* **1.** a child's bed with slatted wooden sides; cot. **2.** a cattle stall or pen. **3.** a fodder rack or manger. **4.** a bin or granary for storing grain, etc. **5.** a small crude cottage or room. **6.** any small confined space. **7.** *Informal.* a brothel. **8.** a wicker basket. **9.** a representation of the manger in which the infant Jesus was laid at birth. **10.** *Informal.* a theft, esp. of another's writing or thoughts. **11.** Also called (esp. U.S.): **pony** (sense 5). *Informal, chiefly Brit.* a translation of a foreign text or a list of answers used by students, often illicitly, as an aid in lessons, examinations, etc. **12.** short for **cribbage. 13.** *Cribbage.* the discard pile. **14.** Also called: **cribwork.** a framework of heavy timbers laid in layers at right angles to one another, used in the construction of foundations, mines, etc. **15.** a storage area for floating logs contained by booms. **16.** *Austral., N.Z.* food, esp. a light meal. ~*vb.* **cribs, crib+bing, cribbed. 17.** (*tr.*) to put or enclose in or as if in a crib; furnish with a crib. **18.** (*tr.*) *Informal.* to steal another's writings or thoughts. **19.** (*intr.*) *Informal.* to copy either from a crib or from someone else during a lesson or examination. **20.** (*tr.*) to line (a construction hole) with timber beams, logs, or planks. **21.** *Informal.* to grumble. [Old English *cribb;* related to Old Saxon *kribbia,* Old High German *krippa;* compare Middle High German *krēbe* basket] —'**crib+ber** *n.*

crib+bage ('krɪbɪdʒ) *n.* a game of cards for two to four, in which players try to win a set number of points before their opponents. Often shortened to **crib.** [C17: of uncertain origin]

crib+bage board *n.* a board, with pegs and holes, used for scoring at cribbage.

crib-bit·ing *n.* a harmful habit of horses in which the animal leans on the manger or seizes it with the teeth and swallows a gulp of air. —'**crib-,bit·er** *n.*

cri+bel+lum (krɪ'bɛləm) *n., pl.* **+la** (-lə). a sievelike spinning organ in certain spiders that occurs between the spinnerets. [C19: New Latin, from Late Latin *cribellum,* diminutive of Latin *cribrum* a sieve]

crib+ri+form ('krɪbrɪ,fɔːm) *or* **crib+rous** ('krɪbrəs) *adj. Anatomy.* pierced with holes; sievelike. [C18: from New Latin *crībriformis,* from Latin *crībrum* a sieve + -FORM]

crib+work ('krɪb,wɜːk) *n.* another name for **crib** (sense 14).

Crich·ton ('kraɪtᵊn) *n.* **James,** 1560–82. Scottish scholar and poet, called *the Admirable Crichton* because of his alleged talents.

crick[1] (krɪk) *Informal.* ~*n.* **1.** a painful muscle spasm or cramp, esp. in the neck or back. ~*vb.* **2.** (*tr.*) to cause a crick in (the neck, back, etc.). [C15: of uncertain origin]

crick[2] (krɪk) *n. U.S.* a dialect word for **creek.**

Crick (krɪk) *n.* **Fran·cis Har·ry Comp·ton.** born 1916, English molecular biologist: helped to discover the helical structure of DNA; Nobel prize for medicine shared with James Watson and Maurice Wilkins 1962.

crick+et[1] ('krɪkɪt) *n.* **1.** any insect of the orthopterous family *Gryllidae,* having long antennae and, in the males, the ability to produce a chirping sound (stridulation) by rubbing together the leathery forewings. **2.** any of various related insects, such as the mole cricket. [C14: from Old French *criquet,* from *criquer* to creak, of imitative origin]

crick+et[2] ('krɪkɪt) *n.* **1. a.** a game played by two teams of eleven players on a field with a wicket at either end of a 22-yard pitch, the object being for one side to score runs by hitting a hard leather-covered ball with a bat while the other side tries to dismiss them by bowling, catching, running them out, etc. **b.** (*as modifier*): *a cricket bat.* **2. not cricket.** *Informal.* not fair play. ~*vb.* (*intr.*) **3.** to play cricket. [C16: from Old French *criquet* goal post, wicket, of uncertain origin] —'**crick+et+er** *n.*

crick+et[3] ('krɪkɪt) *n.* a small low stool. [C17: of unknown origin]

cri+coid ('kraɪkɔɪd) *adj.* **1.** of or relating to the ring-shaped lowermost cartilage of the larynx. ~*n.* **2.** this cartilage. [C18: from New Latin *cricoīdes,* from Greek *krikoeidēs* ring-shaped, from *krikos* ring]

cri de coeur *French.* (kri də 'kœːr) *n., pl.* ***cris de coeur.*** a cry from the heart; heartfelt or sincere appeal.

cri+er ('kraɪə) *n.* **1.** a person or animal that cries. **2.** (formerly) an official who made public announcements, esp. in a town or court. **3.** a person who shouts advertisements about the goods he is selling.

cri+key ('kraɪkɪ) *interj. Slang.* an expression of surprise. [C19: euphemistic for *Christ!*]

crim (krɪm) *n., adj. Austral. slang.* short for **criminal.**

crim. *abbrev. for* criminal.

crim. con. *Law. abbrev. for* criminal conversation.

crime (kraɪm) *n.* **1.** an act or omission prohibited and punished by law. **2. a.** unlawful acts in general: *a wave of crime.* **b.** (*as modifier*): *crime wave.* **3.** an evil act. **4.** *Informal.* something to be regretted: *it is a crime that he died young.* [C14: from Old French, from Latin *crīmen* verdict, accusation, crime]

Cri+me·a (kraɪ'mɪə) *n.* a peninsula of the SW Soviet Union, in the S Ukrainian SSR between the Black Sea and the Sea of Azov: a former autonomous republic of the Soviet Union (until 1946). Russian name: **Krym.** —**Cri+'me·an** *adj., n.*

Cri+me·an War *n.* the war fought mainly in the Crimea between Russia on one side and Turkey, France, Sardinia, and Britain on the other (1853-56).

crime pas+sion+nel (*French* krim pasjɔ'nɛl) *n., pl.* **crimes pas+sion+nels.** a crime committed from passion, esp. sexual passion. Also called: **crime of passion.** [from French]

crime sheet *n. Mil.* a record of an individual's offences against regulations.

crim·i+nal ('krɪmɪnᵊl) *n.* **1.** a person charged with and convicted of crime. **2.** a person who commits crimes for a living. ~*adj.* **3.** of, involving, or guilty of crime. **4.** (*prenominal*) of or relating to crime or its punishment: *criminal court; criminal lawyer.* **5.** *Informal.* senseless or deplorable: *a criminal waste of money.* [C15: from Late Latin *crīminālis;* see CRIME, -AL[1]] —'**crim·i·nal+ly** *adv.*

crim·i·nal con+ver+sa+tion *n.* **1.** (formerly) a common law action brought by a husband by which he claimed damages against an adulterer. **2.** another term for **adultery.**

crim·i·nal+i·ty (,krɪmɪ'nælɪtɪ) *n., pl.* **·ties. 1.** the state or quality of being criminal. **2.** (*often pl.*) *Now rare.* a criminal act or practice.

crim·i+nal law *n.* the body of law dealing with the constitution of offences and the punishment of offenders.

crim·i+nate ('krɪmɪ,neɪt) *vb.* (*tr.*) *Rare.* **1.** to charge with a crime; accuse. **2.** to condemn or censure (an action, event, etc.). **3.** short for **incriminate.** [C17: from Latin *crīmināri* to accuse] —**,crim·i+'na+tion** *n.* —'**crim·i+na+tive** *or* **crim·i+na+to·ry** ('krɪmɪnətərɪ, -trɪ) *adj.* —'**crim·i+,na+tor** *n.*

crim·i+nol+o·gy (,krɪmɪ'nɒlədʒɪ) *n.* the scientific study of crime, criminal behaviour, law enforcement, etc. See also **penology.** [C19: from Latin *crimin-* CRIME, -LOGY] —**crim·i·no·log·i·cal** (,krɪmɪnə'lɒdʒɪkᵊl) *or* **,crim·i·no+'log+ic** *adj.* —**,crim·i·no+'log·i·cal+ly** *adv.* —**,crim·i+'nol·o·gist** *n.*

crim+mer ('krɪmə) *n.* a variant spelling of **krimmer.**

crimp[1] (krɪmp) *vb. (tr.)* **1.** to fold or press into ridges. **2.** to fold and pinch together (something, such as the edges of two pieces of metal). **3.** to curl or wave (the hair) tightly, esp. with curling tongs. **4.** to decorate (the edge of pastry) by pinching with the fingers to give a fluted effect. **5.** to gash (fish or meat) with a knife to make the flesh firmer and crisper when cooked. **6.** to bend or mould (leather) into shape, as for shoes. **7.** *Metallurgy.* to bend the edges of (a metal plate) before forming into a cylinder. **8.** *U.S. informal.* to hinder. ~*n.* **9.** the act or result of folding or pressing together or into ridges. **10.** a tight wave or curl in the hair. **11.** a crease or fold in a metal sheet for rigidity or to make a lapped joint. **12.** the natural wave of wool fibres. [Old English *crympan;* related to *crump* bent, Old Norse *kreppa* to contract, Old High German *crumpf,* Old Swedish *crumb* crooked; see CRAMP] —**'crimp+er** *n.* —**'crimp·y** *adj.*

crimp[2] (krɪmp) *n.* **1.** (formerly) a person who swindled or pressganged men into military service. ~*vb.* **2.** to recruit by coercion or under false pretences. [C17: of unknown origin]

crim+ple ('krɪmpᵊl) *vb.* to crumple, wrinkle, or curl.

Crimp+lene ('krɪmpli:n) *n. Trademark.* a synthetic material similar to Terylene, characterized by its crease-resistance.

crim+son ('krɪmzən) *n.* **1. a.** a deep or vivid red colour. **b.** (*as adj.*)*: a crimson rose.* ~*vb.* **2.** to make or become crimson. **3.** (*intr.*) to blush. [C14: from Old Spanish *cremesin,* from Arabic *qirmizi* red of the kermes, from *qirmiz* KERMES] —**'crim+son+ness** *n.*

cringe (krɪndʒ) *vb. (intr.)* **1.** to shrink or flinch, esp. in fear or servility. **2.** to behave in a servile or timid way. ~*n.* **3.** the act of cringing. [Old English *cringan* to yield in battle; related to Old Norse *krangr* weak, Middle High German *krenken* to weaken] —**'cring+er** *n.* —**'cring+ing+ly** *adv.*

crin+gle ('krɪŋgᵊl) *n.* an eye at the edge of a sail, usually formed from a thimble or grommet. [C17: from Low German *Kringel* small RING; see CRANK, CRINKLE]

cri+nite[1] ('kraɪnaɪt) *adj. Biology.* covered with soft hairs or tufts. [C16: from Latin *crīnītus* hairy, from *crīnis* hair]

cri+nite[2] ('kraɪnaɪt, 'krɪn-) *n.* short for **encrinite.** [C19: from Greek *krinon* lily + -ITE[1]]

crin+kle ('krɪŋkᵊl) *vb.* **1.** to form or cause to form wrinkles, twists, or folds. **2.** to make or cause to make a rustling noise. ~*n.* **3.** a wrinkle, twist, or fold. **4.** a rustling noise. [Old English *crincan* to bend, give way; related to Middle Dutch *krinkelen* to crinkle, Middle High German *krank* weak, ill, *krenken* to weaken] —**'crin+kly** *adj.*

crin·kle+root ('krɪŋkᵊl,ru:t) *n.* any of several species of the toothwort *Dentaria,* esp. *D. diphylla* of E North America, which has a fleshy pungent rhizome and clusters of white or pinkish flowers: family *Cruciferae* (crucifers).

crin·kum-cran·kum ('krɪŋkəm'kræŋkəm) *n.* a fanciful name for any object that is full of twists and turns. [C18: coinage based on CRANK[1]]

cri+noid ('kraɪnɔɪd, 'krɪn-) *n.* **1.** any primitive echinoderm of the class *Crinoidea,* having delicate feathery arms radiating from a central disc. The group includes the free-swimming feather stars, the sessile sea lilies, and many stemmed fossil forms. ~*adj.* **2.** of, relating to, or belonging to the *Crinoidea.* **3.** shaped like a lily. [C19: from Greek *krinoeidēs* lily-like] —**cri+'noi+dal** *adj.*

crin·o+line ('krɪnᵊlɪn) *n.* **1.** a stiff fabric, originally of horsehair and linen used in lining garments. **2.** a petticoat stiffened with this, worn to distend skirts, esp. in the mid-19th century. **3.** a framework of steel hoops worn for the same purpose. [C19: from French, from Italian *crinolino,* from *crino* horsehair, from Latin *crīnis* hair + *lino* flax, from Latin *līnum*]

cri+num ('kraɪnəm) *n.* any plant of the mostly tropical amaryllidaceous genus *Crinum,* having straplike leaves and clusters of lily-like flowers. Also called: **crinum lily.** [Latin: lily, from Greek *krinon*]

cri+ol+lo (kri:'əuləu; *Spanish* kri'ojo) *n., pl.* **+los** (-ləuz; *Spanish* -jos). **1.** a native or inhabitant of Latin America of European descent, esp. of Spanish descent. **2. a.** any of various South American breeds of domestic animal. **b.** (*as modifier*)*: a criollo pony.* **3.** a high-quality variety of cocoa. ~*adj.* **4.** of, relating to, or characteristic of a criollo or criollos. [Spanish: native; see CREOLE]

cripes (kraɪps) *interj. Slang.* an expression of surprise. [C20: euphemistic for *Christ!*]

Crip·pen ('krɪpᵊn) *n.* **Haw·ley Har·vey,** called *Doctor Crippen.* 1862–1910, U.S. doctor living in England: executed for poisoning his wife; the first criminal to be apprehended by the use of radio-telegraphy.

crip+ple ('krɪpᵊl) *n.* **1.** a person who is lame. **2.** a person who is or seems disabled or deficient in some way: *a mental cripple.* **3.** *U.S. dialect.* a dense thicket, usually in marshy land. ~*vb.* **4.** (*tr.*) to make a cripple of; disable. [Old English *crypel;* related to *crēopan* to CREEP, Old Frisian *kreppel* a cripple, Middle Low German *kröpel*] —**'crip+pler** *n.*

Crip+ple Creek *n.* a village in central Colorado: gold-mining centre since 1891, once the richest in the world.

crip+pling ('krɪplɪŋ) *adj.* very damaging or injurious. —**'crip+pling+ly** *adv.*

Cripps (krɪps) *n.* Sir **Staf·ford.** 1889–1952, British Labour statesman; chancellor of the exchequer (1947–50).

Cri·sey·de (krɪ'seɪdə) *n.* a variant of **Cressida.**

cri+sis ('kraɪsɪs) *n., pl.* **+ses** (-si:z). **1.** a crucial stage or turning point in the course of something, esp. in a sequence of events or a disease. **2.** an unstable period, esp. one of extreme trouble or danger in politics, economics, etc. **3.** *Pathol.* a sudden change, for better or worse, in the course of a disease. [C15: from Latin: decision, from Greek *krisis,* from *krinein* to decide]

crisp (krɪsp) *adj.* **1.** dry and brittle. **2.** fresh and firm: *crisp lettuce.* **3.** invigorating or bracing: *a crisp breeze.* **4.** clear; sharp: *crisp reasoning.* **5.** lively or stimulating: *crisp conversation.* **6.** clean and orderly; neat: *a crisp appearance.* **7.** concise and pithy; terse: *a crisp reply.* **8.** wrinkled or curly: *crisp hair.* ~*vb.* **9.** to make or become crisp. ~*n.* **10.** *Brit.* a very thin slice of potato fried and eaten cold as a snack. **11.** something that is crisp. [Old English, from Latin *crispus* curled, uneven, wrinkled] —**'crisp+ly** *adv.* —**'crisp+ness** *n.*

cris+pate ('krɪspeɪt, -pɪt) *or* **cris+pat+ed** *adj.* having a curled or waved appearance. [C19: from Latin *crispāre* to curl]

cris+pa+tion (krɪ'speɪʃən) *n.* **1.** the act of curling or state of being curled. **2.** any slight muscular spasm or contraction that gives a creeping sensation. **3.** a slight undulation, such as a ripple on the surface of water.

crisp+bread ('krɪsp,brɛd) *n.* a thin dry biscuit made of wheat or rye.

crisp+er ('krɪspə) *n.* a compartment in a refrigerator for storing salads, vegetables, etc., in order to keep them fresh.

Cris·pi (*Italian* 'krispi) *n.* **Fran·ces·co** (fran'tʃesko). 1819–1901, Italian statesman; premier (1887–91; 1893–96).

Cris·pin ('krɪspɪn) *n.* **Saint,** 3rd century A.D., legendary Roman Christian martyr, with his brother **Cris·pin·i·an** (krɪs'pɪnɪən): they are the patron saints of shoemakers. Feast day: Oct. 25.

crisp·y ('krɪspɪ) *adj.* **crisp·i+er, crisp·i+est. 1.** crisp. **2.** having waves or curls. —**'crisp·i+ly** *adv.* —**'crisp·i+ness** *n.*

criss+cross ('krɪs,krɒs) *vb.* **1.** to move or cause to move in a crosswise pattern. **2.** to mark with or consist of a pattern of crossing lines. ~*adj.* **3.** (esp. of a number of lines) crossing one another in different directions. ~*n.* **4.** a pattern made of crossing lines. **5.** a U.S. term for **noughts and crosses.** ~*adv.* **6.** in a crosswise manner or pattern.

cris+sum ('krɪsəm) *n., pl.* **+sa** (-sə). the area or feathers surrounding the cloaca of a bird. [C19: from New Latin, from Latin *crissāre* to move the haunches] —**'cris+sal** *adj.*

cris+ta ('krɪstə) *n., pl.* **+tae** (-ti:). Biology. a structure resembling a ridge or crest, as on the inner membrane of a mitochondrion. [C20: from Latin: CREST]

cris+tate ('krɪsteɪt) *or* **cris+tat+ed** *adj.* **1.** having a crest. **2.** forming a crest. [C17: from Latin *cristātus,* from *crista* CREST]

cris+to+bal+ite (krɪs'təubə,laɪt) *n.* a white microcrystalline mineral consisting of silica and occurring in volcanic rocks. Formula: SiO_2. [C19: from German, named after Cerro San *Cristóbal,* Mexico, where it was discovered]

crit. *abbrev. for:* **1.** *Med.* critical. **2.** criticism.

cri+te+ri+on (kraɪ'tɪərɪən) *n., pl.* **·ri·a** (-rɪə) *or* **·ri+ons.** a standard by which something can be judged or decided. [C17: from Greek *kritērion* from *kritēs* judge, from *krinein* to decide]

Usage. *Criteria,* the plural of *criterion,* is not acceptable as a singular noun in careful written and spoken English: *this criterion is not valid; these criteria are not valid.*

crit+ic ('krɪtɪk) *n.* **1.** a person who judges something. **2.** a professional judge of art, music, literature, etc. **3.** a person who often finds fault and criticizes. [C16: from Latin *criticus,* from Greek *kritikos* capable of judging, from *kritēs* judge; see CRITERION]

crit·i+cal ('krɪtɪkᵊl) *adj.* **1.** containing or making severe or negative judgments. **2.** containing careful or analytical evaluations: *a critical dissertation.* **3.** of or involving a critic or criticism. **4.** of or forming a crisis; crucial; decisive: *a critical operation.* **5.** urgently needed: *critical medical supplies.* **6.** *Physics.* of, denoting, or concerned with a state in which the properties of a system undergo an abrupt change: *a critical temperature.* **7. go critical.** (of a nuclear power station or reactor) to reach a state in which a nuclear-fission chain reaction becomes self-sustaining. —**,crit·i+'cal·i·ty** *n.* —**'crit·i·cal+ly** *adv.* —**'crit·i·cal+ness** *n.*

crit·i+cal an+gle *n.* **1.** the smallest possible angle of incidence for which light rays are totally reflected at an interface between substances of different refractive index. **2.** another name for **stalling angle.**

crit·i+cal ap+pa+rat+us *n.* the variant readings, footnotes, etc. found in a scholarly work or a critical edition of a text. Also called: **apparatus criticus.**

crit·i+cal con+stants *pl. n.* the physical constants that express the properties of a substance in its critical state. See **critical pressure, critical temperature.**

crit·i+cal mass *n.* the minimum mass of fissionable material that can sustain a nuclear chain reaction.

crit·i+cal path a·nal·y+sis *n.* a technique for planning complex projects by analysing alternative systems with reference to the critical path, which is the sequence of stages requiring the longest time.

crit·i+cal pe+ri+od *n. Psychol.* a period in a lifetime during which a specific stage of development usually occurs. If it fails to do so, it cannot afterwards occur.

crit·i+cal point *n.* **1.** *Physics.* **a.** the point on a phase diagram that represents the critical state of a substance. **b.** another name for **critical state. 2.** *Maths.* the U.S. name for **stationary point.**

crit·i+cal pres+sure *n.* the pressure of a gas or the saturated vapour pressure of a substance in its critical state.

crit·i+cal state *n.* the state of a substance in which two of its phases have the same temperature, pressure, and volume. Also called: **critical point.**

crit·i+cal tem+per·a·ture *n.* the temperature of a substance in its critical state. A gas can only be liquefied by pressure alone at temperatures below its critical temperature.

crit·i+cal vol+ume *n.* the volume occupied by one mole or unit mass of a substance in its critical state.

crit·i+cism ('krɪtɪ,sɪzəm) *n.* **1.** the act or an instance of making an unfavourable or severe judgment, comment, etc. **2.** the analysis or evaluation of a work of art, literature, etc. **3.** the occupation of a critic. **4.** a work that sets out to evaluate or analyse. **5.** Also called: **textual criticism.** the investigation of a particular text, with related material, in order to establish an authentic text.

crit·i+cize *or* **crit·i+cise** ('krɪtɪ,saɪz) *vb.* **1.** to judge (something) with disapproval; censure. **2.** to evaluate or analyse (something). —**'crit·i+,ciz+a·ble** *or* **'crit·i+,cis+a·ble** *adj.* —**'crit·i+,ciz+er** *or* **'crit·i+,cis+er** *n.* —**'crit·i+,ciz+ing+ly** *or* **'crit·i+,cis+ing+ly** *adv.*

cri+tique (krɪ'tiːk) *n.* **1.** a critical essay or commentary, esp. on artistic work. **2.** the act or art of criticizing. [C17: from French, from Greek *kritikē*, from *kritikos* able to discern]

crit+ter ('krɪtə) *n. U.S.* a dialect word for **creature.**

croak (krəʊk) *vb.* **1.** (*intr.*) (of frogs, crows, etc.) to make a low, hoarse cry. **2.** to utter (something) in this manner, esp. when exhausted: *he croaked out the news.* **3.** (*intr.*) to grumble or be pessimistic. **4.** *Slang.* **a.** (*intr.*) to die. **b.** (*tr.*) to kill. ~*n.* **5.** a low hoarse utterance or sound. [Old English *crăcettan;* related to Old Norse *krāka* a crow; see CREAK] —**'croak·y** *adj.* —**'croak·i+ly** *adv.* —**'croak·i+ness** *n.*

croak+er ('krəʊkə) *n.* **1.** an animal, bird, etc., that croaks. **2.** any of various mainly tropical marine sciaenid fishes, such as *Umbrina roncador* (**yellowfin croaker**), that utter croaking noises. **3.** a grumbling person.

Cro+at ('krəʊæt) *n.* **1. a.** a native or inhabitant of Croatia. **b.** (esp. in other parts of Yugoslavia) a speaker of Croatian. ~*n., adj.* **2.** another word for **Croatian.**

Cro·a+tia (krəʊ'eɪʃə) *n.* a constituent republic of NW Yugoslavia: settled by Croats in the 7th century; belonged successively to Hungary, Turkey, and Austria, until the formation of Yugoslavia (1918). Capital: Zagreb. Pop.: 4 426 221 (1971). Area: 56 538 sq. km (22 050 sq. miles). Serbo-Croatian name: **Hrvatska.**

Cro·a+tian (krəʊ'eɪʃən) *adj.* **1.** of, relating to, or characteristic of Croatia, its people, or their dialect of Serbo-Croatian. ~*n.* **2.** the dialect of Serbo-Croatian spoken in Croatia. **3. a.** a native or inhabitant of Croatia. **b.** (esp. in other parts of Yugoslavia) a speaker of the Croatian dialect.

Cro·ce (*Italian* 'kroːtʃe) *n.* **Ben·e·det·to** (,bene'detto). 1866–1952, Italian philosopher, critic, and statesman: an opponent of fascism, he helped re-establish liberalism in post-war Italy.

cro+ce·in ('krəʊsɪɪn) *n.* any one of a group of red or orange acid azo dyes. [C20: from Latin *croceus* yellow + -IN]

cro+chet ('krəʊʃeɪ, -ʃɪ) *vb.* **+chets** (-ʃeɪz, -ʃɪz), **+chet+ing** (-ʃeɪɪŋ, -ʃɪɪŋ), **+cheted** (-ʃeɪd, -ʃɪd). **1.** to make (a piece of needlework, a garment, etc.) by looping and intertwining thread with a hooked needle (**crochet hook**). ~*n.* **2.** work made by crocheting. **3.** *Architect.* another name for **crocket.** [C19: from French *crochet*, diminutive of *croc* hook, probably of Scandinavian origin] —**'cro+chet+er** *n.*

cro+cid·o+lite (krəʊ'sɪdə,laɪt) *n.* a blue fibrous amphibole mineral consisting of sodium iron silicate: a variety of asbestos used in cement products and pressure piping. [C19: from Greek *krokis* nap on woollen cloth + -LITE]

crock[1] (krɒk) *n.* **1.** an earthen pot, jar, etc. **2.** a piece of broken earthenware. [Old English *crocc* pot; related to Old Norse *krukka* jug, Middle Low German *krūke* pot]

crock[2] (krɒk) *n.* **1.** *Slang, chiefly Brit.* a person or thing, such as a car, that is old or decrepit (esp. in the phrase **old crock**). **2.** an old broken-down horse or ewe. ~*vb.* **3.** *Slang, chiefly Brit.* to become or cause to become weak or disabled. [C15: originally Scottish; related to Norwegian *krake* unhealthy animal, Dutch *kraak* decrepit person or animal]

crock[3] (krɒk) *n.* **1.** *Dialect, chiefly Brit.* soot or smut. **2.** colour that rubs off fabric. ~*vb.* **3.** (*tr.*) *Dialect, chiefly Brit.* to soil with or as if with soot. **4.** (*intr.*) (of a dyed fabric) to release colour when rubbed, as a result of imperfect dyeing. [C17: probably from CROCK[1]]

crocked (krɒkt) *adj. Slang.* **1.** *Brit.* injured. **2.** *U.S.* drunk.

crock+er·y ('krɒkərɪ) *n.* china dishes, earthen vessels, etc., collectively.

crock+et ('krɒkɪt) *n.* a carved ornament in the form of a curled leaf or cusp, used in Gothic architecture. Also called: **crochet.** [C17: from Anglo-French *croket* a little hook, from *croc* hook, of Scandinavian origin]

Crock·ett ('krɒkɪt) *n.* **Da·vid,** known as *Davy Crockett.* 1786–1836, U.S. frontiersman, politician, and soldier.

Crock+ford ('krɒkfəd) *n.* short for *Crockford's Clerical Directory,* the standard directory of living Anglican clergy.

croc·o+dile ('krɒkə,daɪl) *n.* **1.** any large tropical reptile, such as *C. niloticus* (**African crocodile**), of the family *Crocodylidae:* order *Crocodilia* (crocodilians). They have a broad head, tapering snout, massive jaws, and a thick outer covering of bony plates. **2.** any other reptile of the order *Crocodilia;* a crocodilian. **3. a.** leather made from the skin of any of these animals. **b.** (*as modifier*): *crocodile shoes.* [C13: via Old French, from Latin *crocodīlus*, from Greek *krokodeilos* lizard, ultimately from *krokē* pebble + *drilos* worm; referring to its fondness for basking on shingle]

croc·o+dile bird *n.* an African courser, *Pluvianus aegyptius,* that lives close to rivers and is thought to feed on insects parasitic on crocodiles.

Croc·o+dile Riv+er *n.* another name for the **Limpopo.**

croc·o+dile tears *pl. n.* an insincere show of grief; false tears. [from the belief that crocodiles wept over their prey to allure further victims]

croc·o+dil+i·an (,krɒkə'dɪlɪən) *n.* **1.** any large predatory reptile of the order *Crocodilia,* which includes the crocodiles, alligators, and caymans. They live in or near water and have a long broad snout, powerful jaws, a four-chambered heart, and socketed teeth. ~*adj.* **2.** of, relating to, or belonging to the *Crocodilia.* **3.** of, relating to, or resembling a crocodile.

cro+co+ite ('krəʊkəʊ,aɪt) *or* **cro+co·i+site** (krəʊ'kəʊɪ,saɪt, 'krəʊkwə,saɪt) *n.* a rare orange secondary mineral consisting of lead chromate in monoclinic crystalline form. Formula: $PbCrO_4$. Also called: **red-lead ore.** [C19: from *krokoeis* saffron-coloured, golden + -ITE[1]]

cro+cus ('krəʊkəs) *n., pl.* **+cus·es. 1.** any plant of the iridaceous genus *Crocus,* widely cultivated in gardens, having white, yellow, or purple flowers. See also **autumn crocus. 2.** another name for **jewellers' rouge.** ~*adj.* **3.** of a saffron yellow colour. [C17: from New Latin, from Latin *crocus,* from Greek *krokos* saffron, of Semitic origin]

Croe·sus ('kriːsəs) *n.* **1.** died ?546 B.C., the last king of Lydia (560–546), noted for his great wealth. **2.** any very rich man.

croft (krɒft) *n. Brit.* **1.** a small enclosed plot of land, adjoining a house, worked by the occupier and his family, esp. in Scotland. **2.** *Lancashire dialect.* a patch of waste land, formerly one used for bleaching fabric in the sun. [Old English *croft;* related to Middle Dutch *krocht* hill, field, Old English *creopan* to CREEP]

croft+er ('krɒftə) *n. Brit.* an owner or tenant of a small farm, esp. in Scotland or northern England.

Crohn's dis+ease (krəʊnz) *n.* inflammation, thickening, and ulceration of any of various parts of the intestine, esp. the ileum. Also called: **regional enteritis.** [C20: named after B. B. *Crohn* (born 1884), U.S. physician]

crois+sant ('krwʌsɒŋ; *French* krwa'sã) *n.* a flaky crescent-shaped bread roll made of a yeast dough similar to puff pastry. [French, literally: crescent]

Croix de Guerre *French.* (krwa də 'gɛːr) *n.* a French military decoration awarded for gallantry in battle. [literally: cross of war]

Cro-Mag·non man ('krəʊ 'mænjɒn) *n.* an early type of modern man, *Homo sapiens,* who lived in Europe during late Palaeolithic times, having tall stature, long head, and a relatively large cranial capacity. [C19: named after the cave (Cro-Magnon), Dordogne, France, where the remains were first found]

crom+bec ('krɒmbɛk) *n.* any African Old World warbler of the genus *Sylvietta,* having colourful plumage. [C19: via French from Dutch *krom* crooked + *bek* BEAK]

crom+lech ('krɒmlɛk) *n.* **1.** a megalithic chamber tomb or dolmen. **2.** a circle of prehistoric standing stones or a single one. [C17: from Welsh, from *crom,* feminine of *crwm* bent, arched + *llech* flat stone]

Cromp·ton ('krɒmptən) *n.* **Sam·u·el.** 1753–1827, English inventor of the spinning mule (1779).

Crom·well ('krɒmwəl, -wɛl) *n.* **1. Ol·i·ver.** 1599–1658, English general and statesman. A convinced Puritan, he was an effective leader of the parliamentary army in the Civil War. After the execution of Charles I he quelled the Royalists in Scotland and Ireland, and became Lord Protector of the Commonwealth (1653–58). **2.** his son, **Rich·ard.** 1626–1712, Lord Protector of the Commonwealth (1658–59). **3. Thom·as,** Earl of Essex. ?1485–1540, English statesman. He was secretary to Cardinal Wolsey (1514), after whose fall he became chief adviser to Henry VIII. He drafted most of the Reformation legislation, securing its passage through parliament, the power of which he thereby greatly enhanced. He was executed after losing Henry's favour. —**Crom+wel+li·an** (krɒm'wɛlɪən) *adj., n.*

Crom+well Cur+rent ('krɒmwɛl, -wəl) *n.* an equatorial Pacific current, flowing eastward from the Hawaiian Islands to the Galápagos Islands. [C20: named after T. *Cromwell* (1922–1958), U.S. oceanographer]

crone (krəʊn) *n.* a witchlike old woman. [C14: from Old Northern French *carogne* carrion, ultimately from Latin *caro* flesh]

cronk (krɒŋk) *adj. Austral.* unfit; unsound. [C19: compare CRANK[2]]

Cro·nus ('krəʊnəs), **Cro·nos,** *or* **Kro·nos** ('krəʊnɒs) *n. Greek myth.* a Titan, son of Uranus (sky) and Gaea (earth), who ruled the world until his son Zeus dethroned him. Roman counterpart: **Saturn.**

cro+ny ('krəʊnɪ) *n., pl.* **+nies.** a friend or companion. [C17: student slang (Cambridge), from Greek *khronios* of long duration, from *khronos* time]

crook (kruk) *n.* **1.** a curved or hooked thing. **2.** a staff with a hooked end, such as a bishop's crosier or shepherd's staff. **3.** a turn or curve; bend. **4.** *Informal.* a dishonest person, esp. a swindler or thief. **5.** the act or an instance of crooking or bending. **6.** Also called: **shank.** a piece of tubing added to a brass instrument in order to obtain a lower harmonic series. ~*vb.* **7.** to bend or curve or cause to bend or curve. ~*adj.* **8.** *Austral. slang.* **a.** ill. **b.** of poor quality. **c.** unpleasant; bad. **9. go (off) crook.** *Austral. slang.* to lose one's temper. **10. go crook at** *or* **on.** *Austral. slang.* to rebuke or upbraid. [C12: from Old Norse *krokr* hook; related to Swedish *krok,* Danish *krog* hook, Old High German *krācho* hooked tool]

crook+back ('kruk,bæk) *n.* a rare word for **hunchback.** —**'crook+,backed** *adj.*

crook+ed ('krʊkɪd) *adj.* **1.** bent, angled or winding. **2.** set at an angle; not straight. **3.** deformed or contorted. **4.** *Informal.* dishonest or illegal. **5. crooked on.** (*also* krʊkt) *Austral. informal.* hostile or averse to. —**'crook+ed+ly** *adv.* —**'crook+ed+ness** *n.*

Crookes (krʊks) *n.* Sir **Wil·liam.** 1832–1919, English chemist and physicist: he investigated the properties of cathode rays and invented a type of radiometer and the lens named after him.

Crookes lens *n.* a type of lens, used in sunglasses, that is made from glass containing cerium. It reduces the transmission of ultraviolet radiation.

Crookes ra+di+om+e·ter *n. Physics.* a type of radiometer consisting of an evacuated glass bulb containing a set of lightweight vanes, each blackened on one side. The vanes are mounted on a vertical axis and revolve when light, or other radiant energy, falls on them.

Crookes space *n.* a dark region that occurs near the cathode in some low-pressure gas-discharge tubes. Also called: **Crookes dark space.**

Crookes tube *n.* a type of cathode-ray tube in which the electrons are produced by a glow discharge in a low-pressure gas.

croon (kruːn) *vb.* **1.** to sing or speak in a soft low tone. **2.** *Northern Brit. dialect.* to lament or wail. ~*n.* **3.** a soft low singing or humming. [C14: via Middle Dutch *crōnen* to groan; compare Old High German *chrōnan* to chatter, Latin *gingrīre* to cackle (of geese)] —**'croon+er** *n.*

crop (krɒp) *n.* **1.** the produce of cultivated plants, esp. cereals, vegetables, and fruit. **2. a.** the amount of such produce in any particular season. **b.** the yield of some other farm produce: *the lamb crop.* **3.** a group of products, thoughts, people, etc., appearing at one time or in one season: *a crop of new publications.* **4.** the stock of a thonged whip. **5.** short for **riding crop. 6. a.** a pouchlike expanded part of the oesophagus of birds, in which food is stored or partially digested before passing on to the gizzard. **b.** a similar structure in insects, earthworms, and other invertebrates. **7.** the entire tanned hide of an animal. **8.** a short cropped hair style. See also **Eton crop. 9.** a notch in or a piece cut out of the ear of an animal. **10.** the act of cropping. ~*vb.* **crops, crop+ping, cropped.** (*mainly tr.*) **11.** to cut (hair, grass, etc.) very short. **12.** to cut and collect (mature produce) from the land or plant on which it has been grown. **13.** to clip part of (the ear or ears) of (an animal), esp. as a means of identification. **14.** (*also intr.*) to cause (land) to bear or (of land) to bear or yield a crop: *the land cropped well.* **15.** (of herbivorous animals) to graze on (grass or similar vegetation). **16.** *Photog.* to cut off or mask unwanted edges or areas of (a negative or print). [Old English *cropp;* related to Old Norse *kroppr* rump, body, Old High German *kropf* goitre, Norwegian *kröypa* to bend]

crop-dust·ing *n.* the spreading of fungicide, etc. on crops in the form of dust, often from an aircraft.

crop-eared *adj.* having the ears or hair cut short.

crop out *vb.* (*intr., adv.*) (of a formation of rock strata) to appear or be exposed at the surface of the ground; outcrop.

crop+per ('krɒpə) *n.* **1.** a person who cultivates or harvests a crop. **2. a.** a cutting machine for removing the heads from castings and ingots. **b.** a guillotine for cutting lengths of bar or strip. **3.** a machine for shearing the nap from cloth. **4.** a plant or breed of plant that will produce a certain kind of crop under specified conditions: *a poor cropper on light land.* **5.** (*often cap.*) a variety of domestic pigeon with a puffed-out crop. **6. come a cropper.** *Informal.* **a.** to fall heavily. **b.** to fail completely.

crop ro+ta+tion *n.* the system of growing a sequence of different crops on the same ground so as to maintain or increase its fertility.

crop up *vb.* (*intr., adv.*) *Informal.* to occur or appear unexpectedly.

cro+quet ('krəʊkeɪ, -kɪ) *n.* **1.** a game for two to four players who hit a wooden ball through iron hoops with mallets in order to hit a peg. **2.** the act of croqueting. ~*vb.* **+quets** (-keɪz, -kɪz), **+quet+ing** (-keɪɪŋ, -kɪɪŋ), **+queted** (-keɪd, -kɪd). **3.** to drive away (another player's ball) by hitting one's own ball when the two are in contact. [C19: perhaps from French dialect, variant of CROCHET (little hook)]

cro+quette (krəʊ'kɛt, krɒ-) *n.* a savoury cake of minced meat, fish, etc., fried in breadcrumbs. [C18: from French, from *croquer* to crunch, of imitative origin]

crore (krɔː) *n.* (in Indian English) ten million. [C17: from Hindi *karōr,* from Prakrit *krodi*]

Cros+by[1] ('krɒzbɪ) *n.* a town in NW England, in Merseyside. Pop.: 57 405 (1971).

Cros·by[2] ('krɒzbɪ) *n.* **Bing,** real name *Harry.* 1904–77, U.S. singer and film star; famous for his style of crooning.

cro+sier *or* **cro+zier** ('krəʊʒə) *n.* **1.** a staff surmounted by a crook or cross, carried by bishops as a symbol of pastoral office. **2.** the tip of a young plant, esp. a fern frond, that is coiled into a hook. [C14: from Old French *crossier* staff bearer, from *crosse* pastoral staff, literally: hooked stick, of Germanic origin]

cross (krɒs) *n.* **1.** a structure or symbol consisting essentially of two intersecting lines or pieces at right angles to one another. **2.** a wooden structure used as a means of execution, consisting of an upright post with a transverse piece to which people were nailed or tied. **3.** a representation of the Cross used as an emblem of Christianity or as a reminder of Christ's death. **4.** any mark or shape consisting of two intersecting lines, esp. such a symbol (×) used as a signature, point of intersection, error mark, etc. **5.** a sign representing the Cross made either by tracing a figure in the air or by touching the forehead, breast, and either shoulder in turn. **6.** any conventional variation of the Christian symbol, used emblematically, decoratively, or heraldically, such as a Maltese, tau, or Greek cross. **7.** *Heraldry.* any of several charges in which one line crosses or joins another at right angles. **8.** a cruciform emblem awarded to indicate membership of an order or as a decoration for distinguished service. **9.** (*sometimes cap.*) Christianity or Christendom, esp. as contrasted with non-Christian religions: *Cross and Crescent.* **10.** the place in a town or village where a cross has been set up. **11.** a pipe fitting, in the form of a cross, for connecting four pipes. **12.** *Biology.* **a.** the process of crossing; hybridization. **b.** an individual produced as a result of this process. **13.** a mixture of two qualities or types: *he's a cross between a dictator and a saint.* **14.** an opposition, hindrance, or misfortune; affliction (esp. in the phrase **bear one's cross**). **15.** *Slang.* a match or game in which the outcome has been rigged. **16.** *Slang.* a fraud or swindle. **17.** *Boxing.* a straight punch delivered from the side, esp. with the right hand. **18. on the cross. a.** diagonally. **b.** *Slang.* dishonestly. ~*vb.* **19.** (sometimes foll. by *over*) to move or go across (something); traverse or intersect: *we crossed the road.* **20. a.** to meet and pass: *the two trains crossed.* **b.** (of each of two letters in the post) to be dispatched before receipt of the other. **21.** (*tr.;* usually foll. by *out, off,* or *through*) to cancel with a cross or with lines; delete. **22.** (*tr.*) to place or put in a form resembling a cross: *to cross one's legs.* **23.** (*tr.*) to mark with a cross or crosses. **24.** (*tr.*) *Brit.* to draw two parallel lines across the face of (a cheque) and so make it payable only into a bank account. **25.** (*tr.*) **a.** to trace the form of the Cross, usually with the thumb or index finger upon (someone or something) in token of blessing. **b.** to make the sign of the Cross upon (oneself). **26.** (*intr.*) (of telephone lines) to interfere with each other so that three or perhaps four callers are connected together at one time. **27.** to cause fertilization between (plants or animals of different breeds, races, varieties, etc.). **28.** (*tr.*) to oppose the wishes or plans of; thwart: *his opponent crosses him at every turn.* **29.** (*tr.*) *Nautical.* to set (the yard of a square sail) athwartships. **30. cross a bridge when one comes to it. a.** to deal with matters, problems, etc., as they arise. **b.** not to anticipate difficulties. **31. cross one's fingers.** to fold one finger across another in the hope of bringing good luck: *keep your fingers crossed.* **32. cross one's heart.** to promise or pledge, esp. by making the sign of a cross over one's heart. **33. cross one's mind.** to occur to one briefly or suddenly. **34. cross someone's palm.** to give someone money. **35. cross the path (of).** to meet or thwart (someone). **36. cross swords.** to enter into an argument or contest. ~*adj.* **37.** angry; ill-humoured; vexed. **38.** lying or placed across; transverse: *a cross timber.* **39.** involving interchange; reciprocal. **40.** contrary or unfavourable. **41.** another word for **crossbred** (sense 1). **42.** a Brit. slang word for **dishonest.** [Old English *cros,* from Old Irish *cross* (unattested), from Latin *crux;* see CRUX] —**'cross+er** *n.* —**'cross+ly** *adv.* —**'cross+ness** *n.*

Cross (krɒs) *n.* **the. 1.** the cross on which Jesus Christ was crucified. **2.** the Crucifixion of Jesus.

cross- *combining form.* **1.** indicating action from one individual, group, etc., to another: *cross-cultural; crossfertilize; cross-refer.* **2.** indicating movement, position, etc., across something (sometimes implying interference, opposition, or contrary action): *crosscurrent; crosstalk.* **3.** indicating a crosslike figure or intersection: *crossbones.* [from CROSS (in various senses)]

cross+bar ('krɒs,bɑː) *n.* **1.** a horizontal bar, line, stripe, etc. **2.** a horizontal beam across a pair of goalposts. **3.** a horizontal bar mounted on vertical posts used in athletics or show-jumping. **4.** the horizontal bar on a man's bicycle that joins the handlebar and saddle supports.

cross+beam ('krɒs,biːm) *n.* a beam that spans from one support to another.

cross bed+ding *n. Geology.* layering within one or more beds in a series of rock strata that does not run parallel to the plane of stratification. Also called: **false bedding.**

cross-bench *n.* (usually pl.) *Brit.* a seat in Parliament occupied by a neutral or independent member. —**'cross-,bench+er** *n.*

cross+bill ('krɒs,bɪl) *n.* any of various widely distributed finches of the genus *Loxia,* such as *L. curvirostra,* that occur in coniferous woods and have a bill with crossed mandible tips for feeding on conifer seeds.

cross+bones ('krɒs,bəʊnz) *pl. n.* See **skull and crossbones.**

cross+bow ('krɒs,bəʊ) *n.* a type of medieval bow fixed transversely on a wooden stock grooved to direct a square-headed arrow (quarrel). —**'cross+,bow·man** *n.*

cross+bred ('krɒs,brɛd) *adj.* **1.** (of plants or animals) produced as a result of crossbreeding. ~*n.* **2.** a crossbred plant or animal, esp. an animal resulting from a cross between two pure breeds. Compare **grade** (sense 9), **purebred** (sense 2).

cross+breed ('krɒs,briːd) *vb.* **+breeds, +breed+ing, +bred. 1.** Also: **interbreed.** to breed (animals or plants) using parents of different races, varieties, breeds, etc. ~*n.* **2.** the offspring produced by such a breeding.

cross-but·tock *n.* a wrestling throw in which the hips are used as a fulcrum to throw an opponent.

cross+check (,krɒs'tʃɛk) *vb.* **1.** to verify (a fact, report, etc.) by considering conflicting opinions or consulting other sources. **2.** (in ice hockey) to check illegally, as by chopping at an opponent's arms or stick. ~*n.* **3.** the act or an instance of crosschecking.

cross-coun·try *adj., adv.* **1.** by way of fields, woods, etc., as opposed to roads. **2.** across a country: *a cross-country railway.* ~*n.* **3.** a long race held over open ground.

cross·cur·rent (ˈkrɒsˌkʌrənt) *n.* **1.** a current in a river or sea flowing across another current. **2.** a conflicting tendency moving counter to the usual trend.

cross·cut (ˈkrɒsˌkʌt) *adj.* **1.** cut at right angles or obliquely to the major axis. ~*n.* **2.** a transverse cut or course. **3.** a less common word for **short cut.** **4.** *Mining.* a tunnel through a vein of ore or from the shaft to a vein. ~*vb.* **·cuts, ·cut·ting, ·cut.** **5.** to cut across. **6.** Also called: **intercut.** *Films.* to link (two sequences or two shots) so that they appear to be taking place at the same time.

cross·cut saw *n.* a saw for cutting timber across the grain.

cross-dat·ing *n.* *Archaeol.* a method of dating objects, remains, etc., by comparison and correlation with other sites and levels.

crosse (krɒs) *n.* a light staff with a triangular frame to which a network is attached, used in playing lacrosse. [French, from Old French *croce* CROSIER]

cross-ex·am·ine *vb.* (*tr.*) **1.** *Law.* to examine (a witness for the opposing side), as in attempting to discredit his testimony. Compare **examine-in-chief.** **2.** to examine closely or relentlessly. —**ˈcross-exˌam·iˈna·tion** *n.* —**ˈcross-exˈam·in·er** *n.*

cross-eye *n.* a turning inwards towards the nose of one or both eyes, caused by abnormal alignment. See also **strabismus.** —**ˈcross-ˌeyed** *adj.*

cross-fade *vb.* *Radio, television.* to fade in one sound source as another is being faded out.

cross-fer·ti·li·za·tion *n.* **1.** fertilization by the fusion of male and female gametes from different individuals of the same species. Compare **self-fertilization.** **2.** (*not in technical use*) cross-pollination. —**ˈcross-ˈfer·tile** *adj.*

cross-fer·ti·lize *vb.* to subject or be subjected to cross-fertilization.

cross·fire (ˈkrɒsˌfaɪə) *n.* **1.** *Military, etc.* converging fire from one or more positions. **2.** a lively exchange of ideas, opinions, etc.

cross-gar·net *n.* a hinge with a long horizontal strap fixed to the face of a door and a short vertical leaf fixed to the door frame.

cross-grained *adj.* **1.** (of timber) having the fibres arranged irregularly or in a direction that deviates from the axis of the piece. **2.** perverse, cantankerous, or stubborn.

cross hairs *pl. n.* another name for **cross wires.**

cross·hatch (ˈkrɒsˌhætʃ) *vb.* *Drawing.* to shade or hatch (forms, figures, etc.) with two or more sets of parallel lines that cross one another. —**ˈcross·ˌhatch·ing** *n.*

cross·head (ˈkrɒsˌhɛd) *n.* **1.** *Printing.* a subsection or paragraph heading printed within the body of the text. **2.** a block or beam, usually restrained by sliding bearings in a reciprocating mechanism, esp. the junction piece between the piston rod and connecting rod of a steam engine. **3.** *Nautical.* a bar fixed across the top of the rudder post to which the tiller is attached. **4.** a block, rod, or beam fixed at the head of any part of a mechanism.

cross-in·dex *n.* **1.** a note or notes referring the reader to other material. ~*vb.* **2.** (*intr.*) (of a note in a book, etc.) to refer to related material. **3.** to provide or be provided with cross-indexes.

cross·ing (ˈkrɒsɪŋ) *n.* **1.** the place where one thing crosses another. **2.** a place, often shown by markings, lights, or poles, where a street, railway, etc., may be crossed. **3.** the intersection of the nave and transept in a church. **4.** the act or process of crossbreeding.

cross·ing o·ver *n.* the interchange of sections between pairing homologous chromosomes during the diplotene stage of meiosis. It results in the separation of genes and produces variation in the inherited characteristics of the offspring. See also **linkage** (sense 4).

cross·jack (ˈkrɒsˌdʒæk; *Nautical* ˈkrɔːdʒɪk, ˈkrɒdʒ-) *n.* *Nautical.* a square sail on a ship's mizzenmast.

cross-leg·ged (ˈkrɒsˈlɛgɪd, -ˈlɛgd) *adj.* standing or sitting with one leg crossed over the other.

cross·let *or* **cross cross·let** (ˈkrɒslɪt) *n.* *Heraldry.* a cross having a smaller cross near the end of each arm. [C16 *croslet* a little CROSS]

cross-link *or* **cross-link·age** *n.* a chemical bond, atom, or group of atoms that connects two adjacent chains of atoms in a large molecule such as a polymer or protein.

cross of Lor·raine *n.* a cross with two horizontal bars above and below the midpoint of the vertical bar, the lower longer than the upper.

cros·sop·te·ryg·i·an (krɒˌsɒptəˈrɪdʒɪən) *n.* **1.** any bony fish of the subclass *Crossopterygii*, having fleshy limblike pectoral fins. The group, now mostly extinct, contains the ancestors of the amphibians. See also **coelacanth.** ~*adj.* **2.** of, relating to, or belonging to the *Crossopterygii.* [C19: from New Latin *Crossopterygii*, from Greek *krossoi* fringe, tassels + *pterugion* a little wing, from *pterux* wing]

cross·o·ver (ˈkrɒsˌəʊvə) *n.* **1.** a place at which a crossing is made. **2.** *Genetics.* **a.** another term for **crossing over. b.** a chromosomal structure or character resulting from crossing over. **3.** *Railways.* a point of transfer between two main lines. **4.** short for **crossover network.**

cross·o·ver net·work *n.* an electronic network in a high-fidelity system that divides the output into two or more frequency bands, the lower frequencies being fed to a woofer, the higher frequencies to a tweeter.

cross·patch (ˈkrɒsˌpætʃ) *n.* *Informal.* a peevish bad-tempered person. [C18: from CROSS + obsolete *patch* fool]

cross·piece (ˈkrɒsˌpiːs) *n.* a transverse beam, joist, etc.

cross-ply *adj.* (of a motor tyre) having the fabric cords in the outer casing running diagonally to stiffen the sidewalls. Compare **radial-ply.**

cross-pol·li·nate *vb.* to subject or be subjected to cross-pollination.

cross-pol·li·na·tion *n.* the transfer of pollen from the anthers of one flower to the stigma of another flower by the action of wind, insects, etc. Compare **self-pollination.**

cross press *n.* a fall in wrestling using the weight of the body to pin an opponent's shoulders to the floor.

cross prod·uct *n.* another name for **vector product.**

cross-pur·pose *n.* **1.** a contrary aim or purpose. **2. at cross-purposes.** conflicting; opposed; disagreeing.

cross-ques·tion *vb.* **1.** to cross-examine. ~*n.* **2.** a question asked in cross-examination. —**ˈcross-ˈques·tion·ing** *n.*

cross-re·fer *vb.* to refer from one part of something, esp. a book, to another.

cross-ref·er·ence *n.* **1.** a reference within a text to another part of the text. ~*vb.* **2.** to cross-refer.

cross re·la·tion *n.* another term (esp. U.S.) for **false relation.**

Cross Riv·er *n.* a state of SE Nigeria, on the Gulf of Guinea. Capital: Calabar. Pop.: 4 626 317 (1976 est.). Area: 35 149 sq. km (13 568 sq. miles). Former name (until 1976): **South-Eastern State.**

cross·road (ˈkrɒsˌrəʊd) *n.* *U.S.* **1.** a road that crosses another road. **2.** Also called: **crossway.** a road that crosses from one main road to another.

cross·roads (ˈkrɒsˌrəʊdz) *n.* (*construed as sing.*) **1.** an area or the point at which two or more roads cross each other. **2.** the point at which an important choice has to be made (esp. in the phrase **at the crossroads**).

cross·ruff (ˈkrɒsˌrʌf) *Bridge, whist.* ~*n.* **1.** the alternate trumping of each other's leads by two partners, or by declarer and dummy. ~*vb.* **2.** (*intr.*) to trump alternately in two hands of a partnership.

cross sec·tion *n.* **1.** *Maths.* a plane surface formed by cutting across a solid, esp. perpendicular to its longest axis. **2.** a section cut off in this way. **3.** the act of cutting anything in this way. **4.** a random selection or sample, esp. one regarded as representative: *a cross section of the public.* **5.** *Surveying.* a vertical section of a line of ground at right angles to a survey line. **6.** *Physics.* a measure of the probability that a collision process will result in a particular reaction. It is expressed by the effective area that one participant presents as a target for the other. —**ˈcross-ˈsec·tion·al** *adj.*

cross-slide *n.* the part of a lathe or planing machine on which the tool post is mounted and across which it slides at right angles to the bed of the lathe.

cross-stitch *n.* **1.** an embroidery stitch made by two stitches forming a cross. **2.** embroidery worked with this stitch. ~*vb.* **3.** to embroider (a piece of needlework) with cross-stitch.

cross·talk (ˈkrɒsˌtɔːk) *n.* **1.** *Radio, telephony.* unwanted sounds heard in one receiving channel due to a transfer of energy from one or more other channels. **2.** *Brit.* rapid or witty talk or conversation.

cross-town *adj.* *U.S.* going across or following a route across a town: *a cross-town bus.*

cross·tree (ˈkrɒsˌtriː) *n.* *Nautical.* either of a pair of wooden or metal braces on the head of a lower mast to support the topmast, etc.

cross vine *n.* a woody bignoniaceous vine, *Bignonia capreolata,* of the southeastern U.S., having large trumpet-shaped reddish flowers.

cross·walk (ˈkrɒsˌwɔːk) *n.* the U.S. name for **pedestrian crossing.**

cross·wind (ˈkrɒsˌwɪnd) *n.* a wind that blows at right angles to the direction of travel of an aircraft or ship.

cross wires *pl. n.* two fine mutually perpendicular lines or wires that cross in the focal plane of a theodolite, gunsight, or other optical instrument and are used to define the line of sight. Also called: **cross hairs.**

cross·wise (ˈkrɒsˌwaɪz) *or* **cross·ways** (ˈkrɒsˌweɪz) *adj., adv.* **1.** across; transversely. **2.** in the shape of a cross.

cross·word puz·zle (ˈkrɒsˌwɜːd) *n.* a puzzle in which the solver guesses words suggested by numbered clues and writes them into corresponding boxes in a grid to form a vertical and horizontal pattern.

cross·wort (ˈkrɒsˌwɜːt) *n.* a herbaceous perennial Eurasian rubiaceous plant, *Galium cruciata,* with pale yellow flowers and whorls of hairy leaves. Also called: **mugwort.**

crotch (krɒtʃ) *n.* **1.** Also called: (Brit.): **crutch. a.** the angle formed by the inner sides of the legs where they join the human trunk. **b.** the human external genitals or the genital area. **c.** the corresponding part of a pair of trousers, pants, etc. **2.** a forked region formed by the junction of two members. **3.** a forked pole or stick. [C16: probably variant of CRUTCH] —**crotched** (krɒtʃt) *adj.*

crotch·et (ˈkrɒtʃɪt) *n.* **1.** *Music.* a note having the time value of a quarter of a semibreve. Usual U.S. name: **quarter note.** **2.** a small hook or hooklike device. **3.** a perverse notion. **4.** *Zoology.* a small notched or hooked process, as in an insect. [C14: from Old French *crochet,* literally: little hook, from *croche* hook; see CROCKET]

crotch·et·y (ˈkrɒtʃɪtɪ) *adj.* **1.** *Informal.* cross; irritable; contrary. **2.** full of crotchets. —**ˈcrotch·et·i·ness** *n.*

cro+ton ('krəʊtᵊn) *n.* **1.** any shrub or tree of the chiefly tropical euphorbiaceous genus *Croton*, esp. *C. tiglium*, the seeds of which yield croton oil. **2.** any of various tropical plants of the related genus *Codiaeum*, esp. *C. variegatum pictum*, a house plant with variegated foliage. [C18: from New Latin, from Greek *krotōn* tick, castor-oil plant (whose berries resemble ticks)]

Cro+ton bug *n. U.S.* another name for the **German cockroach.** [C19: named after the *Croton* river, whose water was piped to New York City in 1842]

Cro+to+ne (*Italian* kro'to:ne) *n.* a town in S Italy, on the coast of Calabria: founded in about 700 B.C. by the Achaeans; chemical works and zinc-smelting. Pop.: 50 970 (1971).

cro+ton+ic ac·id (krəʊ'tɒnɪk) *n.* a colourless crystalline insoluble unsaturated carboxylic acid produced by oxidation of crotonaldehyde and used in organic synthesis; *trans*-2-butenoic acid. Formula: $CH_3CH{:}CHCOOH$.

cro+ton oil *n.* a yellowish-brown oil obtained from the plant *Croton tiglium*, formerly used as a drastic purgative. See also **croton** (sense 1).

crouch (kraʊtʃ) *vb.* **1.** (*intr.*) to bend low with the limbs pulled up close together. **2.** (*intr.*) to cringe, as in humility or fear. **3.** (*tr.*) to bend (parts of the body), as in humility or fear. ~*n.* **4.** the act of stooping or bending. [C14: perhaps from Old French *crochir* to become bent like a hook, from *croche* hook]

croup[1] (kru:p) *n.* a throat condition, occurring usually in children, characterized by a hoarse cough and laboured breathing, resulting from inflammation and partial obstruction of the larynx. [C16 *croup* to cry hoarsely, probably of imitative origin] —**'croup+ous** *or* **'croup·y** *adj.*

croup[2] *or* **croupe** (kru:p) *n.* the hindquarters of a quadruped, esp. a horse. [C13: from Old French *croupe;* related to German *Kruppe*]

croup[3] (kru:p) *vb.* (*intr.*) *Northern Brit. dialect.* to squat on one's haunches; crouch. Also: **'croup·y, 'croup·y down.** [extended verbal use of CROUP[2]]

crou+pi+er ('kru:pɪə; *French* kru'pje) *n.* a person who deals cards, collects bets, etc., at a gaming table. [C18: literally: one who rides behind another, from *croupe* CROUP[2]]

crouse (kru:s) *adj. Scot. and northern Brit. dialect.* lively or saucy. [C14 (Scottish and Northern) English: from Middle Low German *krūs* twisted, curled, confused]

croute (kru:t) *n.* a small round of toasted bread on which a savoury mixture is served. [from French: CRUST]

crou+ton ('kru:tɒn) *n.* a small piece of fried or toasted bread, usually served in soup. [French: diminutive of *croûte* CRUST]

crow[1] (krəʊ) *n.* **1.** any large gregarious songbird of the genus *Corvus*, esp. *C. corone* (**carrion crow**) of Europe and Asia: family *Corvidae*. Other species are the raven, rook, and jackdaw and all have a heavy bill, glossy black plumage, and rounded wings. Related adj.: **corvine. 2.** any of various other corvine birds, such as the jay, magpie, and nutcracker. **3.** any of various similar birds of other families. **4.** *Austral. slang.* an old or ugly woman. **5.** short for **crowbar. 6. as the crow flies.** as directly as possible. **7. eat crow.** *U.S. informal.* to be forced to do something humiliating. **8. stone the crows.** (*interj.*) *Brit. and Austral. slang.* an expression of surprise, horror, etc. [Old English *crāwa;* related to Old Norse *krāka*, Old High German *krāia*, Dutch *kraai*]

crow[2] (krəʊ) *vb.* (*intr.*) **1.** (past tense **crowed** *or* **crew**) to utter a shrill squawking sound, as a cock. **2.** (often foll. by *over*) to boast one's superiority. **3.** (esp. of babies) to utter cries of pleasure. [Old English *crāwan;* related to Old High German *krāen*, Dutch *kraaien*] —**'crow+er** *n.* —**'crow+ing+ly** *adv.*

Crow (krəʊ) *n.* **1.** (*pl.* **Crows** *or* **Crow**) a member of a North American Indian people living in E Montana. **2.** the language of this people, belonging to the Siouan family.

crow+bar ('krəʊ,bɑ:) *n.* a heavy iron lever with one pointed end, and one forged into a wedge shape.

crow+ber·ry ('krəʊbərɪ, -brɪ) *n., pl.* **·ries. 1.** a low-growing N temperate evergreen shrub, *Empetrum nigrum*, with small purplish flowers and black berry-like fruit: family *Empetraceae*. **2.** any of several similar or related plants. **3.** the fruit of any of these plants.

crow-bill *n.* a type of forceps used to extract bullets, etc., from wounds.

crow black+bird *n.* another name for **grackle.**

crow+boot ('krəʊ,bu:t) *n.* a type of Eskimo boot made of fur and leather.

crowd[1] (kraʊd) *n.* **1.** a large number of things or people gathered or considered together. **2.** a particular group of people, esp. considered as a social or business set: *the crowd from the office.* **3. a.** (preceded by *the*) the common people; the masses. **b.** (*as modifier*): *crowd ideas.* ~*vb.* **4.** (*intr.*) to gather together in large numbers; throng. **5.** (*tr.*) to press together into a confined space. **6.** (*tr.*) to fill to excess; fill by pushing into. **7.** (*tr.*) *Slang.* to urge or harass by urging. **8. crowd on sail.** *Nautical.* to hoist as much sail as possible. **9. follow the crowd.** to conform with the majority. [Old English *crūdan;* related to Middle Low German *krūden* to molest, Middle Dutch *crūden* to push, Norwegian *kryda* to swarm] —**'crowd+ed** *adj.* —**'crowd+ed+ly** *adv.* —**'crowd+ed+ness** *n.* —**'crowd+er** *n.*

crowd[2] (kraʊd) *n. Music.* an ancient bowed stringed instrument; crwth. [C13: from Welsh *crwth*]

crowd pull+er *n. Informal.* a person, object, event, etc., that attracts a large audience.

crow+foot ('krəʊ,fʊt) *n., pl.* **+foots. 1.** any of several plants of the genus *Ranunculus*, such as *R. sceleratus* and *R. aquatilis* (**water crowfoot**) that have yellow or white flowers and divided leaves resembling the foot of a crow. See also **buttercup. 2.** any of various other plants that have leaves or other parts resembling a bird's foot. **3.** *pl.* **+feet.** *Nautical.* a bridle-like arrangement of lines rove through a wooden block or attached to a ring for supporting an awning from above. **4.** *pl.* **+feet.** *Military.* another name for **caltrop.**

crown (kraʊn) *n.* **1.** an ornamental headdress denoting sovereignty, usually made of gold embedded with precious stones. **2.** a wreath or garland for the head, awarded as a sign of victory, success, honour, etc. **3.** (*sometimes cap.*) monarchy or kingship. **4.** an award, distinction, or title, given as an honour to reward merit, victory, etc. **5.** anything resembling or symbolizing a crown, such as a sergeant major's badge or a heraldic bearing. **6. a.** a coin worth 25 pence (five shillings). **b.** any of several continental coins, such as the krona or krone, with a name meaning *crown.* **7.** the top or summit of something, esp. of a rounded object: *crown of a hill; crown of the head.* **8.** the centre part of a road, esp. when it is cambered. **9.** *Botany.* **a.** the leaves and upper branches of a tree. **b.** the junction of root and stem, usually at the level of the ground. **c.** another name for **corona** (sense 6). **10.** *Zoology.* **a.** the cup and arms of a crinoid, as distinct from the stem. **b.** the crest of a bird. **11.** the outstanding quality, achievement, state, etc.: *the crown of his achievements.* **12. a.** the enamel-covered part of a tooth above the gum. **b. artificial crown.** a substitute crown, usually of gold, porcelain, or acrylic resin, fitted over a decayed or broken tooth. **13.** the part of a cut gem above the girdle. **14.** *Horology.* a knurled knob for winding a watch. **15.** the part of an anchor where the arms are joined to the shank. **16.** the highest part of an arch or vault. **17.** a standard size of printing paper, 15 by 20 inches. ~*vb.* (*tr.*) **18.** to put a crown on the head of, symbolically vesting with royal title, powers, etc. **19.** to place a crown, wreath, garland, etc., on someone's head. **20.** to place something on or over the head or top of: *he crowned the pie with cream.* **21.** to confer a title, dignity, or reward upon: *he crowned her best cook.* **22.** to form the summit, or topmost part of: *the steeple crowned the tower.* **23.** to occur as the culminating event in a series: *to crown it all it rained, too.* **24.** *Draughts.* to promote (a draught) to a king by placing another draught on top of it, as after reaching the end of the board. **25.** to attach a crown to (a tooth). **26.** *Slang.* to hit over the head. [C12: from Old French *corone*, from Latin *corōna* wreath, crown, from Greek *korōnē* crown, something curved] —**'crown+less** *adj.*

Crown (kraʊn) *n.* (*sometimes not cap;* usually preceded by *the*) **1.** the sovereignty or realm of a monarch. **2. a.** the government of a constitutional monarchy. **b.** (*as modifier*): *Crown property.*

Crown A·gent *n.* a member of a board appointed by the Minister for Overseas Development to provide financial, commercial, and professional services for a number of overseas governments and international bodies.

crown and an+chor *n.* a game played with dice marked with crowns and anchors.

crown cap *n. Brit.* an airtight metal seal crimped on the top of most beers, ciders, mineral waters, etc.

crown col·o+ny *n.* a British colony whose administration and legislature is controlled by the Crown.

crown court *n. English law.* a court of criminal jurisdiction holding sessions in towns throughout England and Wales at which circuit judges hear and determine cases.

Crown Der+by *n.* a type of porcelain manufactured at Derby from 1784–1848, marked with a crown.

crown glass *n.* **1.** another name for **optical crown. 2.** an old form of window glass made by blowing a globe and spinning it until it forms a flat disc.

crown graft *n. Horticulture.* a type of graft in which the scion is inserted at the crown of the stock.

crown green *n.* a type of bowling green in which the sides are lower than the middle.

crown im+pe+ri·al *n.* a liliaceous garden plant, *Fritillaria imperialis*, with a cluster of leaves and orange bell-shaped flowers at the top of the stem.

crown jew+els *pl. n.* the jewellery, including the regalia, used by a sovereign on a state occasion.

crown land *n.* **1.** (in the United Kingdom) land belonging to the Crown. **2.** public land in some dominions of the Commonwealth.

crown+land ('kraʊn,lænd) *n.* a large administrative division of the former empire of Austria-Hungary.

crown lens *n.* a lens made of optical crown, esp. the optical-crown part of a compound achromatic lens.

Crown Of+fice *n.* (in England) an office of the Queen's Bench Division of the High Court that is responsible for administration and where actions are entered for trial.

crown-of-thorns *n.* **1.** a starfish, *Acanthaster planci*, that has a spiny test and feeds on living coral in coral reefs. **2.** Also called: **Christ's thorn.** a thorny euphorbiaceous Madagascan shrub, *Euphorbia splendens*, cultivated as a hedging shrub or pot plant, having flowers with scarlet bracts.

crown+piece ('kraʊn,pi:s) *n.* **1.** the piece forming or fitting the top of something. **2.** the strap of a bridle that goes over a horse's head behind the ears.

crown prince *n.* the male heir to a sovereign throne.

crown prin+cess *n.* **1.** the wife of a crown prince. **2.** the female heir to a sovereign throne.

crown saw *n.* a hollow cylinder with cutting teeth forming a rotary saw for trepanning.

crown vetch *n.* a trailing papilionaceous European plant, *Coronilla varia,* with clusters of white or pink flowers: cultivated in North America as a border plant. Also called (U.S.): **axseed.**

crown wheel *n.* **1.** the larger of the two gears in a bevel gear. **2.** *Horology.* the wheel next to the winding knob that has one set of teeth at right angles to the other.

crown+work ('kraʊn,wɜ:k) *n.* **1. a.** the manufacture of artificial crowns for teeth. **b.** such an artificial crown or crowns. **2.** *Fortifications.* a covering or protective outwork.

crow's-foot *n., pl.* **-feet. 1.** (*often pl.*) a wrinkle at the outer corner of the eye. **2.** an embroidery stitch with three points, used esp. as a finishing at the end of a seam. **3.** a system of diverging short ropes to distribute the pull of a single rope, used esp. in balloon and airship riggings.

crow's-nest *n.* a lookout platform high up on a ship's mast.

crow step *n.* another term for **corbie-step.**

Croy+don ('krɔɪdᵊn) *n.* a Greater London borough (since 1965): formerly important for its airport (1915–59). Pop.: 330 600 (1976 est.).

croze (krəʊz) *n.* **1.** the recess cut at the end of a barrel or cask to receive the head. **2.** a tool for cutting this recess. [C17: probably from Old French *crues* a hollow]

cro+zier ('krəʊʒə) *n.* a variant spelling of **crosier.**

C.R.P. (in India) *abbrev. for* Central Reserve Police.

CRT *abbrev. for* cathode-ray tube.

cru (kru:; *French* kry) *n. Winemaking.* (in France) a vineyard; group of vineyards, or wine-producing region. [from French: production, from *crû,* past participle of *croître* to grow]

cru+ces ('kru:si:z) *n.* a plural of **crux.**

cru+cial ('kru:ʃəl) *adj.* **1.** involving a final or supremely important decision or event; decisive; critical. **2.** *Informal.* very important. [C18: from French, from Latin *crux* CROSS] —'**cru+cial+ly** *adv.*

cru+cian ('kru:ʃən) *n.* a European cyprinid fish, *Carassius carassius,* with a dark-green back, a golden-yellow undersurface, and reddish dorsal and tail fins: an aquarium fish. [C18: from Low German *Karusse*]

cru+ci+ate ('kru:ʃɪɪt, -,eɪt) *adj.* shaped or arranged like a cross: *cruciate petals.* [C17: from New Latin *cruciātus,* from Latin *crux* cross] —'**cru+ci+ate+ly** *adv.*

cru+ci+ble ('kru:sɪbᵊl) *n.* **1.** a vessel in which substances are heated to high temperatures. **2.** the hearth at the bottom of a metallurgical furnace in which the metal collects. **3.** a severe trial or test. [C15 *corusible,* from Medieval Latin *crūcibulum* night lamp, crucible, of uncertain origin]

cru+ci+ble steel *n.* a high-quality steel made by melting wrought iron, charcoal, and other additives in a crucible.

cru+ci+fer ('kru:sɪfə) *n.* **1.** any plant of the family *Cruciferae,* having a corolla of four petals arranged like a cross and a fruit called a siliqua. The family includes the brassicas, mustard, cress, and wallflower. **2.** a person who carries a cross. [C16: from Late Latin, from Latin *crux* cross + *ferre* to carry]

cru+cif+er+ous (kru:'sɪfərəs) *adj.* of, relating to, or belonging to the plant family *Cruciferae.* See **crucifer** (sense 1).

cru+ci+fix ('kru:sɪfɪks) *n.* a cross or image of a cross with a figure of Christ upon it. [C13: from Church Latin *crucifixus* the crucified Christ, from *crucifīgere* to CRUCIFY]

cru+ci+fix+ion (,kru:sɪ'fɪkʃən) *n.* a method of putting to death by nailing or binding to a cross, normally by the hands and feet, which was widespread in the ancient world.

Cru+ci+fix+ion (,kru:sɪ'fɪkʃən) *n.* **1.** (usually preceded by *the*) the crucifying of Christ at Calvary, regarded by Christians as the culminating redemptive act of his ministry. **2.** a picture or representation of this.

cru+ci+form ('kru:sɪ,fɔ:m) *adj.* **1.** shaped like a cross. ~*n.* **2.** a geometric curve, shaped like a cross, that has four similar branches asymptotic to two mutually perpendicular pairs of lines. Equation: $x^2y^2 - a^2x^2 - a^2y^2 = 0$, where $x = y = \pm a$ are the four lines. [C17: from Lat *crux* cross + -FORM] —'**cru+ci+,form+ly** *adv.*

cru+ci+fy ('kru:sɪ,faɪ) *vb.* **+fies, +fy+ing, +fied.** (*tr.*) **1.** to put to death by crucifixion. **2.** *Slang.* to defeat, ridicule, etc., totally: *the critics crucified his performance.* **3.** to treat very cruelly; torment. **4.** to subdue (passion, lust, etc.); mortify. [C13: from Old French *crucifier,* from Late Latin *crucifīgere* to crucify, to fasten to a cross, from Latin *crux* cross + *fīgere* to fasten] —'**cru+ci+,fi+er** *n.*

cruck (krʌk) *n.* one of a pair of curved wooden timbers supporting the end of the roof in certain types of building. [C19: variant of CROOK (*n.*)]

crud (krʌd) *Slang, chiefly U.S.* ~*n.* **1.** a sticky substance, esp. when dirty and encrusted. **2.** a despicable person. **3.** (sometimes preceded by *the*) a disease; rot. ~*interj.* **4.** an expression of disgust, disappointment, etc. [C14: earlier form of CURD] —'**crud+dy** *adj.*

crude (kru:d) *adj.* **1.** lacking taste, tact, or refinement; vulgar: *a crude joke.* **2.** in a natural or unrefined state. **3.** lacking care, knowledge, or skill: *a crude sketch.* **4.** (*prenominal*) stark; blunt: *the crude facts.* **5.** (of statistical data) unclassified or unanalysed. **6.** *Archaic.* unripe. ~*n.* **7.** short for **crude oil.** [C14: from Latin *crūdus* bloody, raw; related to Latin *cruor* blood] —'**crude+ly** *adv.* —'**crud+i+ty** *or* '**crude+ness** *n.*

crude oil *n.* petroleum before it has been refined.

cru+el ('kru:əl) *adj.* **1.** causing or inflicting pain without pity: *a cruel teacher.* **2.** causing pain or suffering: *a cruel accident.* [C13: from Old French, from Latin *crūdēlis,* from *crūdus* raw, bloody] —'**cru+el+ly** *adv.* —'**cru+el+ness** *n.*

cru+el+ty ('kru:əltɪ) *n., pl.* **+ties. 1.** deliberate infliction of pain or suffering. **2.** the quality or characteristic of being cruel. **3.** a cruel action. **4.** *Law.* conduct that causes danger to life or limb or a threat to bodily or mental health, on proof of which a decree of divorce may be granted.

cru+et ('kru:ɪt) *n.* **1.** a small container for holding pepper, salt, vinegar, oil, etc., at table. **2.** a set of such containers, esp. on a stand. **3.** *Christianity.* either of a pair of small containers for the wine and water used in the Eucharist. [C13: from Anglo-French, diminutive of Old French *crue* flask, of Germanic origin; compare Old Saxon *krūka,* Old English *crūce* pot]

Cruik·shank ('krʊk,ʃæŋk) *n.* **George.** 1792–1878, English illustrator and caricaturist.

cruise (kru:z) *vb.* **1.** (*intr.*) to make a trip by sea in a liner for pleasure, usually calling at a number of ports. **2.** to sail or travel over (a body of water) for pleasure in a yacht, cruiser, etc. **3.** to search for enemy vessels in a warship. **4.** (*intr.*) (of a vehicle, aircraft, or vessel) to travel at a moderate and efficient speed. **5.** (*intr.*) *Informal.* to search the streets or other public places for a sexual partner. ~*n.* **6.** an act or instance of cruising, esp. a trip by sea. [C17: from Dutch *kruisen* to cross, from *cruis* CROSS; related to French *croiser* to cross, cruise, Spanish *cruzar, German kreuzen*]

cruise mis+sile *n.* an air-breathing subsonic missile that is continuously powered and guided throughout its flight and carries a warhead.

cruis+er ('kru:zə) *n.* **1.** a high-speed, long-range warship of medium displacement, armed with medium calibre weapons or missiles. **2.** Also called: **cabin cruiser.** a pleasure boat, esp. one that is power-driven and has a cabin. **3.** any person or thing that cruises. **4.** *Boxing.* short for **cruiserweight** (see **light heavyweight**).

cruis·er+weight ('kru:zə,weɪt) *n. Boxing.* another term (esp. Brit.) for **light heavyweight.**

cruise+way ('kru:z,weɪ) *n.* a canal used for recreational purposes.

crul+ler *or* **krul+ler** ('krʌlə) *n. U.S.* a light, sweet, ring-shaped cake, fried in deep fat. [C19: from Dutch *krulle,* from *krullen* to CURL]

crumb (krʌm) *n.* **1.** a small fragment of bread, cake, or other baked foods. **2.** a small piece or bit: *crumbs of information.* **3.** the soft inner part of bread. **4.** *Slang.* a contemptible person. ~*vb.* **5.** (*tr.*) to prepare or cover (food) with breadcrumbs. **6.** to break into small fragments. ~*adj.* **7.** (esp. of pie crusts) made with a mixture of biscuit crumbs, sugar, etc. [Old English *cruma;* related to Middle Dutch *krome,* Middle High German *krūme,* Latin *grūmus* heap of earth] —'**crumb+er** *n.*

crum+ble ('krʌmbᵊl) *vb.* **1.** to break or be broken into crumbs or fragments. **2.** (*intr.*) to fall apart or away: *his resolution crumbled.* ~*n.* **3.** *Brit.* a baked pudding consisting of a crumbly mixture of flour, fat, and sugar over stewed fruit: *apple crumble.* [C16: variant of *crimble,* of Germanic origin; compare Low German *krömeln,* Dutch *kruimelen*]

crum+bly ('krʌmblɪ) *adj.* **+bli+er, +bli+est.** easily crumbled or crumbling. —'**crum+bli+ness** *n.*

crumbs (krʌmz) *interj. Slang.* an expression of dismay or surprise. [C20: euphemistic for *Christ!*]

crumb·y ('krʌmɪ) *adj.* **crumb·i+er, crumb·i+est. 1.** full of or littered with crumbs. **2.** soft, like the inside of bread. **3.** a variant spelling of **crummy.**

crum+horn *or* **krumm+horn** ('krʌm,hɔ:n) *n.* a medieval wood-wind instrument of bass pitch, consisting of an almost cylindrical tube curving upwards and blown through a double reed covered by a pierced cap. [C17 *cromorne, krumhorn,* from German *Krummhorn:* curved horn]

Crum+mock Wa+ter ('krʌmək) *n.* a lake in NW England, in Cumbria in the Lake District. Length: 4 km (2.5 miles).

crum+my[1] ('krʌmɪ) *adj.* **+mi+er, +mi+est.** *Slang.* **1.** of little value; inferior; contemptible. **2.** unwell or depressed: *to feel crummy.* [C19: variant spelling of CRUMBY]

crum+my[2] ('krʌmɪ) *n., pl.* **+mies.** *Canadian.* a lorry that carries loggers to work from their camp. [probably originally meaning: makeshift camp, from CRUMMY[1]]

crump (krʌmp) *vb.* **1.** (*intr.*) to thud or explode with a loud dull sound. **2.** to bombard with heavy shells. ~*n.* **3.** a crunching, thudding, or exploding noise. [C17: of imitative origin]

crum+pet ('krʌmpɪt) *n. Chiefly Brit.* **1.** a light soft yeast cake full of small holes on the top side, eaten toasted and buttered. **2.** *Slang.* women collectively. **3. a piece of crumpet.** a sexually desirable woman. **4. not worth a crumpet.** *Austral. slang.* utterly worthless. [C17: of uncertain origin]

crum+ple ('krʌmpᵊl) *vb.* **1.** (when *intr.,* often foll. by *up*) to collapse or cause to collapse: *his courage crumpled.* **2.** (when *tr.,* often foll. by *up*) to crush or cause to be crushed so as to form wrinkles or creases. **3.** (*intr.*) to shrink; shrivel. ~*n.* **4.** a loose crease or wrinkle. [C16: from obsolete *crump* to bend; related to Old High German *krimpfan* to wrinkle, Old Norse *kreppa* to contract] —'**crum+ply** *adj.*

crunch (krʌntʃ) *vb.* **1.** to bite or chew (crisp foods) with a crushing or crackling sound. **2.** to make or cause to make a crisp or brittle sound: *the snow crunched beneath his feet.* ~*n.* **3.** the sound or act of crunching. **4. the crunch.** *Informal.* the critical moment or situation. ~Also: **craunch.** [C19: changed (through influence of MUNCH) from earlier *craunch,* of imitative origin] —'**crunch+a·ble** *adj.* —'**crunch·y** *adj.* —'**crunch·i+ly** *adv.* —'**crunch·i+ness** *n.*

cru+node ('kru:nəʊd) *n.* a point at which two branches of a curve intersect, each branch having a distinct tangent; node. [C19: *cru-* from Latin *crux* cross + NODE]

crup+per ('krʌpə) *n.* **1.** a strap from the back of a saddle that passes under the horse's tail to prevent the saddle from slipping forwards. **2.** the part of the horse's rump behind the saddle. [C13: from Old French *crupiere*, from *crupe* CROUP[2]]

cru·ra ('krʊərə) *n.* the plural of **crus.**

cru·ral ('krʊərəl) *adj.* of or relating to the leg or thigh. [C16: from Latin *crūrālis, from crūs* leg, shin]

crus (krʌs) *n., pl.* **cru·ra** ('krʊərə). **1.** *Anatomy.* the leg, esp. from the knee to the foot. **2.** (*usually pl.*) leglike parts or structures. [C17: from Latin: leg]

cru·sade (kru:'seɪd) *n.* **1.** (*often cap.*) any of the military expeditions undertaken in the 11th, 12th, and 13th centuries by the Christian powers of Europe to recapture the Holy Land from the Muslims. **2.** (formerly) any holy war undertaken on behalf of a religious cause. **3.** a vigorous and dedicated action or movement in favour of a cause. ~*vb.* (*intr.*) **4.** to campaign vigorously for something. **5.** to go on a crusade. [C16: from earlier *croisade*, from Old French *crois* cross, from Latin *crux;* influenced also by Spanish *cruzada*, from *cruzar* to take up the cross] —**cru'sad·er** *n.*

cru·sa·do (kru:'seɪdəʊ) *or* **cru·za·do** (kru:'zeɪdəʊ; *Portuguese* kru'ʃaðu) *n., pl.* **·does** *or* **·dos** (-dəʊz; *Portuguese* -ðuʃ). a former gold or silver coin of Portugal bearing on its reverse the figure of a cross. [C16: literally, marked with a cross, from *cruzar* to bear a cross; see CRUSADE]

cruse (kru:z) *n.* a small earthenware container used, esp. formerly, for liquids. [Old English *crūse;* related to Middle High German *krūse*, Dutch *kroes* jug]

crush (krʌʃ) *vb.* (*mainly tr.*) **1.** to press, mash, or squeeze so as to injure, break, crease, etc. **2.** to break or grind (rock, ore, etc.) into small particles. **3.** to put down or subdue, esp. by force: *to crush a rebellion.* **4.** to extract (juice, water, etc.) by pressing: *to crush the juice from a lemon.* **5.** to oppress harshly. **6.** to hug or clasp tightly: *he crushed her to him.* **7.** to defeat or humiliate utterly, as in argument or by a cruel remark. **8.** (*intr.*) to crowd; throng. **9.** (*intr.*) to become injured, broken, or distorted by pressure. ~*n.* **10.** a dense crowd, esp. at a social occasion. **11.** the act of crushing; pressure. **12.** a drink or pulp prepared by or as if by crushing fruit: *orange crush.* **13.** *Informal.* **a.** an infatuation: *she had a crush on him.* **b.** the person with whom one is infatuated. [C14: from Old French *croissir*, of Germanic origin; compare Gothic *kriustan* to gnash; see CRUNCH] —**'crush·a·ble** *adj.* —**,crush·a·'bil·i·ty** *n.* —**'crush·er** *n.*

crush bar *n.* a bar at a theatre for serving drinks during the intervals of a play.

crush bar·ri·er *n.* a barrier erected to separate sections of large crowds in order to prevent crushing.

crust (krʌst) *n.* **1. a.** the hard outer part of bread. **b.** a piece of bread consisting mainly of this. **2.** the baked shell of a pie, tart, etc. **3.** any hard or stiff outer covering or surface: *a crust of ice.* **4.** the outer layer of the earth, between 10 and 40 kilometres deep, separated from the inner layer (mantle) by the Mohorovicic discontinuity. See also **sial, sima. 5.** the dry covering of a skin sore or lesion; scab. **6.** a layer of acid potassium tartrate deposited by some wine, esp. port, on the inside of the bottle. **7.** the hard outer layer of such organisms as lichens and crustaceans. **8.** *Slang.* impertinence. **9.** *Austral. slang.* a living (esp. in the phrase **earn a crust**). ~*vb.* **10.** to cover with or acquire a crust. **11.** to form or be formed into a crust. [C14: from Latin *crūsta* hard surface, rind, shell]

crus·ta·cean (krʌ'steɪʃən) *n.* **1.** any arthropod of the mainly aquatic class *Crustacea*, typically having a carapace hardened with lime and including the lobsters, crabs, shrimps, woodlice, barnacles, copepods, and water fleas. ~*adj. also* **crus·ta·ceous. 2.** of, relating to, or belonging to the *Crustacea.* [C19: from New Latin *crūstāceus* hard-shelled, from Latin *crūsta* shell, CRUST]

crus·ta·ceous (krʌ'steɪʃəs) *adj.* **1.** forming, resembling, or possessing a surrounding crust or shell. **2.** *Zoology.* another word for **crustacean** (sense 2).

crus·tal ('krʌstᵊl) *adj.* of or relating to the earth's crust.

crust·y ('krʌstɪ) *adj.* **crust·i·er, crust·i·est. 1.** having or characterized by a crust, esp. having a thick crust. **2.** having a rude or harsh character or exterior; surly; curt: *a crusty remark.* —**'crust·i·ly** *adv.* —**'crust·i·ness** *n.*

crutch (krʌtʃ) *n.* **1.** a long staff of wood or metal having a rest for the armpit, for supporting the weight of the body. **2.** something that supports, helps, or sustains: *a crutch to the economy.* **3.** *Brit.* another word for **crotch** (sense 1). **4.** *Nautical.* **a.** a forked support for a boom or oar, etc. **b.** a brace for reinforcing the frames at the stern of a wooden vessel. ~*vb.* **5.** (*tr.*) to support or sustain (a person or thing) as with a crutch. **6.** *Austral. slang.* to clip (wool) from the hindquarters of a sheep. [Old English *crycc;* related to Old High German *krucka*, Old Norse *krykkja;* see CROSIER, CROOK]

Crutched Fri·ar (krʌtʃt, 'krʌtʃɪd) *n.* a member of a mendicant order, suppressed in 1656. [C16: *crutched*, variant of *crouched*, literally: crossed, referring to the cross worn on their habits]

crux (krʌks) *n., pl.* **crux·es** *or* **cru·ces** ('kru:si:z). **1.** a vital or decisive stage, point, etc. (often in the phrase **the crux of the matter**). **2.** a baffling problem or difficulty. **3.** a rare word for **cross.** [C18: from Latin: cross]

Crux (krʌks) *n., Latin genitive* **Cru·cis** ('kru:sɪs). the more formal name for the **Southern Cross.**

crux an·sa·ta (æn'seɪtə) *n., pl.* **cru·ces an·sa·tae** ('kru:si:z æn'seɪti:). another term for **ankh.** [New Latin, literally: cross with a handle]

Cruyff (krɔɪf; *Dutch* krœjf) *n.* **Jo·han** (jo:'hɑn). born 1947, Dutch footballer: one of the world's leading strikers; played for Ajax of Amsterdam (1965–73) and Barcelona (from 1973); captained the Dutch team in the 1974 World Cup.

cru·za·do (kru:'zeɪdəʊ; *Portuguese* kru'ʃaðu) *n., pl.* **·does** *or* **·dos** (-dəʊz; *Portuguese* -ðuʃ). a variant spelling of **crusado.**

cru·zei·ro (kru:'zɛərəʊ; *Portuguese* kru'zejru) *n., pl.* **·ros** (-rəʊz; *Portuguese* -rus). the standard monetary unit of Brazil, divided into 100 centavos. [Portuguese: from *cruz* CROSS]

crwth (kru:θ) *n.* an ancient stringed instrument of Celtic origin similar to the cithara but bowed in later types. [Welsh; compare Middle Irish *crott* harp]

cry (kraɪ) *vb.* **cries, cry·ing, cried. 1.** (*intr.*) to utter inarticulate sounds, esp. when weeping; sob. **2.** (*intr.*) to shed tears; weep. **3.** (*intr.; usually foll. by out*) to scream or shout in pain, terror, etc. **4.** (*tr.; often foll. by out*) to utter or shout (words of appeal, exclamation, fear, etc.). **5.** (*intr.; often foll. by out*) (of animals, birds, etc.) to utter loud characteristic sounds. **6.** (*tr.*) to hawk or sell by public announcement: *to cry newspapers.* **7.** to announce (something) publicly or in the streets. **8.** (*intr.; foll. by for*) to clamour or beg. **9. cry for the moon.** to desire the unattainable. **10. cry one's eyes** *or* **heart out.** to weep bitterly. **11. cry quits** (*or* **mercy**). to give up a task, fight, etc. ~*n., pl.* **cries. 12.** the act or sound of crying; a shout, exclamation, scream, or wail. **13.** the characteristic utterance of an animal or bird: *the cry of gulls.* **14.** *Archaic.* an oral announcement, esp. one made by town criers. **15.** a fit of weeping. **16.** *Hunting.* the baying of a pack of hounds hunting their quarry by scent. **17.** a pack of hounds. **18. a far cry. a.** a long way. **b.** something very different. **19. in full cry. a.** hotly pursuing. **b.** the baying of a pack of hounds hunting together. ~See also **cry down, cry off, cry out.** [C13: from Old French *crier*, from Latin *quirītāre* to call for help]

cry·ba·by ('kraɪ,beɪbɪ) *n., pl.* **·bies.** a person, esp. a child, given to frequent crying or complaint.

cry down *vb.* (*tr., adv.*) **1.** to belittle; disparage. **2.** to silence by making a greater noise: *to cry down opposition.*

cry·ing ('kraɪɪŋ) *adj.* (*prenominal*) notorious; lamentable (esp. in the phrase **crying shame**).

cry·o- *combining form.* indicating low temperature; frost, cold, or freezing: *cryogenics; cryosurgery.* [from Greek *kruos* icy cold, frost]

cry·o·bi·ol·o·gy (,kraɪəʊbaɪ'ɒlədʒɪ) *n.* the branch of biology concerned with the study of the effects of very low temperatures on organisms. —**,cry·o·bi·'ol·o·gist** *n.*

cry·o·ca·ble (,kraɪəʊ'keɪbᵊl) *n.* a highly conducting electrical cable cooled with a refrigerant such as liquid nitrogen.

cry off *vb.* (*intr.*) *Informal.* to withdraw from or cancel (an agreement or arrangement).

cry·o·gen ('kraɪədʒən) *n.* a substance used to produce low temperatures; a freezing mixture.

cry·o·gen·ics (,kraɪə'dʒɛnɪks) *n.* (*functioning as sing.*) the branch of physics concerned with the production of very low temperatures and the phenomena occurring at these temperatures. —**,cry·o·'gen·ic** *adj.*

cry·o·hy·drate (,kraɪəʊ'haɪdreɪt) *n.* a crystalline substance containing water and a salt in definite proportions: a eutectic crystallizing below the freezing point of water.

cry·o·lite ('kraɪə,laɪt) *n.* a white or colourless mineral consisting of a fluoride of sodium and aluminium in monoclinic crystalline form: used in the production of aluminium, glass, and enamel. Formula: Na_3AlF_6.

cry·om·e·ter (kraɪ'ɒmɪtə) *n.* a thermometer for measuring low temperatures. —**cry·'om·e·try** *n.*

cry·on·ics (kraɪ'ɒnɪks) *n.* (*functioning as sing.*) the practice of freezing a human corpse in the hope of restoring it to life in the future.

cry·o·phil·ic (,kraɪə'fɪlɪk) *adj. Biology.* able to thrive at low temperatures.

cry·o·phyte ('kraɪə,faɪt) *n.* a plant, esp. an alga or moss, that grows on snow or ice.

cry·o·plank·ton (,kraɪəʊ'plæŋktən) *pl. n.* minute organisms, esp. algae, living in ice, snow, or icy water.

cry·o·scope ('kraɪə,skəʊp) *n.* any instrument used to determine the freezing point of a substance.

cry·os·co·py (kraɪ'ɒskəpɪ) *n., pl.* **·pies.** the determination of freezing points, esp. for the determination of molecular weights by measuring the lowering of the freezing point of a solvent when a known quantity of solute is added. —**cry·o·scop·ic** (,kraɪə'skɒpɪk) *adj.*

cry·o·stat ('kraɪə,stæt) *n.* an apparatus for maintaining a constant low temperature or a vessel in which a substance is stored at a low temperature.

cry·o·sur·ger·y (,kraɪəʊ'sɜ:dʒərɪ) *n.* surgery involving the local destruction of tissues by quick freezing for therapeutic benefit.

cry·o·ther·a·py (,kraɪəʊ'θɛrəpɪ) *or* **cry·mo·ther·a·py** *n.* medical treatment in which all or part of the body is subjected to cold temperatures, as by means of ice packs.

cry·o·tron ('kraɪə,trɒn) *n.* a miniature switch working at the temperature of liquid helium and depending for its action on the production and destruction of semiconducting properties in the conductor.

cry out *vb.* (*intr., adv.*) **1.** to scream or shout aloud, esp. in pain, terror, etc. **2.** (often foll. by *for*) *Informal.* to demand in an obvious manner: *our inner cities are crying out for redevelopment.* **3. for crying out loud.** *Informal.* an exclamation of anger, impatience, or dismay.

crypt (krɪpt) *n.* **1.** a cellar, vault, or underground chamber, esp. beneath a church, where it is often used as a chapel, burial place, etc. **2.** *Anatomy.* any pitlike recess or depression. [C18:

from Latin *crypta*, from Greek *kruptē* vault, secret place, from *kruptos* hidden, from *kruptein* to hide] —'**crypt+al** *adj.*
cryp+taes+the·si·a *or U.S.* **cryp+tes+the·si·a** (ˌkrɪptəs'θiːzɪə) *n. Psychol.* another term for **extrasensory perception.**
crypt·a·nal·y·sis (ˌkrɪptə'nælɪsɪs) *n.* the study of codes and ciphers; cryptography. [C20: from CRYPTOGRAPH + ANALYSIS] —**crypt+an·a·lyt+ic** (ˌkrɪptænə'lɪtɪk) *adj.* —**crypt+'an·a+lyst** *n.*
cryp+tic ('krɪptɪk) *or* **cryp+ti+cal** *adj.* **1.** hidden; secret; occult. **2.** (esp. of comments, sayings, etc.) esoteric or obscure in meaning. **3.** (of the coloration of animals) tending to conceal by disguising or camouflaging the shape. [C17: from Late Latin *crypticus*, from Greek *kruptikos*, from *kruptos* concealed; see CRYPT] —'**cryp+ti+cal+ly** *adv.*
cryp·to- *or before a vowel* **crypt-** *combining form.* secret, hidden, or concealed: *cryptography; crypto-fascist.* [New Latin, from Greek *kruptos* hidden, from *kruptein* to hide]
cryp+to+clas+tic (ˌkrɪptəʊ'klæstɪk) *adj.* (of minerals and rocks) composed of microscopic fragments.
cryp+to+crys+tal+line (ˌkrɪptəʊ'krɪstəlaɪn) *adj.* (of rocks) composed of crystals that can be distinguished individually only by the use of a polarizing microscope.
cryp+to+gam ('krɪptəʊˌgæm) *n.* (in former classification schemes) any plant that does not produce seeds, including algae, fungi, mosses, and ferns. Compare **phanerogam.** [C19: from New Latin *Cryptogamia*, from CRYPTO- + Greek *gamos* marriage] —ˌ**cryp+to+'gam+ic** *or* **cryp+tog·a+mous** (krɪp'tɒgəməs) *adj.*
cryp+to+gen+ic (ˌkrɪptəʊ'dʒɛnɪk) *adj.* (esp. of diseases) of unknown or obscure origin.
cryp+to+graph ('krɪptəʊˌgrɑːf) *n.* **1.** something written in code or cipher. **2.** a code using secret symbols (**cryptograms**). **3.** a device for translating text into cipher, or vice versa.
cryp+tog+ra+phy (krɪp'tɒgrəfɪ) *or* **cryp+tol+o·gy** (krɪp'tɒlədʒɪ) *n.* the science or study of analysing and deciphering codes, ciphers, etc. Also called: **cryptanalysis.** —**cryp+'tog+ra+pher, cryp+'tog+ra+phist,** *or* **cryp+'tol·o+gist** *n.* —**cryp+to+graph+ic** (ˌkrɪptə'græfɪk) *or* ˌ**cryp+to+'graph·i+cal** *adj.* —ˌ**cryp+to+'graph·i+cal+ly** *adv.*
cryp+to+mer·i·a (ˌkrɪptəʊ'mɪərɪə) *n.* a coniferous tree, *Cryptomeria japonica*, of China and Japan, with curved needle-like leaves and small round cones: family *Taxodiaceae*.
cryp+to+zo+ic (ˌkrɪptəʊ'zəʊɪk) *adj.* (of animals) living in dark places, such as holes, caves, and beneath stones.
Cryp+to+zo+ic (ˌkrɪptəʊ'zəʊɪk) *adj.* of or relating to Precambrian rock strata, fauna, etc. Compare **Phanerozoic.**
cryp+to+zo+ite (ˌkrɪptəʊ'zəʊaɪt) *n.* a malarial parasite at the stage of development in its host before it enters the red blood cells.
cryst. *abbrev. for:* **1.** crystalline. **2.** Also: **crystall.** crystallography.
crys+tal ('krɪstᵊl) *n.* **1.** a piece of solid substance, such as quartz, with a regular shape in which plane faces intersect at definite angles, due to the regular internal structure of its atoms, ions, or molecules. **2.** a single grain of a crystalline substance. **3.** anything resembling a crystal, such as a piece of cut glass. **4. a.** a highly transparent and brilliant type of glass, often used in cut-glass tableware, ornaments, etc. **b.** (*as modifier*): *a crystal chandelier.* **5.** something made of or resembling crystal. **6.** crystal glass articles collectively. **7.** *Electronics.* **a.** a crystalline element used in certain electronic devices as a detector, oscillator, transducer, etc. **b.** (*as modifier*): *crystal pickup; crystal detector.* **8.** a transparent cover for the face of a watch, usually of glass or plastic. **9.** (*modifier*) of or relating to a crystal or the regular atomic arrangement of crystals: *crystal structure; crystal lattice.* ~*adj.* **10.** resembling crystal; transparent: *crystal water.* [Old English *cristalla*, from Latin *crystallum*, from Greek *krustallos* ice, crystal, from *krustainein* to freeze]
crys+tal ball *n.* the glass globe used in crystal gazing.
crys+tal class *n. Crystallog.* any of 32 possible types of crystals, classified according to their rotational symmetry about axes through a point. Also called: **point group.**
crys+tal count+er *n.* an instrument for detecting and measuring the intensity of high-energy radiation, in which particles collide with a crystal and momentarily increase its conductivity.
crys+tal de+tec+tor *n. Electronics.* a demodulator, used esp. in early radio receivers, consisting of a thin metal wire in point contact with a semiconductor crystal.
crys+tal form *n. Crystallog.* a symmetrical set of planes in space, associated with a crystal, having the same symmetry as the crystal class. Compare **crystal habit.**
crys+tal gaz+ing *n.* **1.** the act of staring into a crystal globe (**crystal ball**) supposedly in order to arouse visual perceptions of the future, etc. **2.** the act of trying to foresee or predict something. —'**crys+tal 'gaz+er** *n.*
crys+tal hab+it *n. Crystallog.* the external shape of a crystal. Compare **crystal form.**
crys+tal lat+tice *n.* the regular array of points about which the atoms, ions, or molecules composing a crystal are centred.
crys+tal+line ('krɪstəˌlaɪn) *adj.* **1.** having the characteristics or structure of crystals. **2.** consisting of or containing crystals. **3.** made of or like crystal; transparent; clear. —**crys+tal+lin+i+ty** (ˌkrɪstə'lɪnɪtɪ) *n.*
crys+tal+line lens *n.* a biconvex transparent elastic structure in the eye situated behind the iris, serving to focus images on the retina.
crys+tal+lite ('krɪstəˌlaɪt) *n.* any of the minute rudimentary or imperfect crystals occurring in many glassy rocks. —**crys+tal+lit+ic** (ˌkrɪstə'lɪtɪk) *adj.*
crys+tal+lize, crys+tal+ize *or* **crys+tal+lise, crys+tal+ise** ('krɪstəˌlaɪz) *vb.* **1.** to form or cause to form crystals; assume or cause to assume a crystalline form or structure. **2.** to coat or become coated with sugar: *crystallized fruit.* **3.** to give a definite form or expression to (an idea, argument, etc.) or (of an idea, argument, etc.) to assume a recognizable or definite form. —'**crys+tal+ˌliz+a·ble, 'crys+tal+ˌiz+a·ble** *or* **'crys+tal+ˌlis+a·ble, 'crys+tal+ˌis+a·ble** *adj.* —ˌ**crys+tal+ˌliz+a·'bil+i·ty,** ˌ**crys+tal+ˌiz+a·'bil+i·ty** *or* ˌ**crys+tal+ˌlis+a·'bil+i·ty,** ˌ**crys+tal+ˌis+a·'bil+i·ty** *n.* —ˌ**crys+tal+li+'za+tion,** ˌ**crys+tal·i+'za+tion** *or* ˌ**crys+tal+li+'sa+tion,** ˌ**crys+tal·i+'sa+tion** *n.* —'**crys+tal+ˌliz+er, 'crys+tal+ˌiz+er** *or* **'crys+tal+ˌlis+er, 'crys+tal+ˌis+er** *n.*
crys·tal·lo- *or before a vowel* **crys·tall-** *combining form.* crystal: *crystallography.*
crys+tal+log+ra+phy (ˌkrɪstə'lɒgrəfɪ) *n.* the science concerned with the formation, properties, and structure of crystals. —ˌ**crys+tal+'log+ra+pher** *n.* —**crys+tal+lo+graph+ic** (ˌkrɪstələʊ'græfɪk) *adj.* —ˌ**crys+tal+lo+'graph·i+cal+ly** *adv.*
crys+tal+loid ('krɪstəˌlɔɪd) *adj.* **1.** resembling or having the appearance or properties of a crystal or crystalloid. ~*n.* **2.** a substance that in solution can pass through a semipermeable membrane. Compare **colloid** (sense 3). **3.** *Botany.* any of numerous crystals of protein occurring in certain seeds and other storage organs. —ˌ**crys+tal+'loi+dal** *adj.*
crys+tal pick+up *n.* a gramophone pickup in which the current is generated by the deformation of a piezoelectric crystal caused by the movements of the stylus.
crys+tal set *n.* an early form of radio receiver having a crystal detector to demodulate the radio signals but no amplifier, therefore requiring earphones.
crys+tal sys+tem *n. Crystallog.* any of six, or sometimes seven, classifications of crystals depending on their symmetry. The classes are cubic, tetragonal, hexagonal, orthorhombic, monoclinic, and triclinic. Sometimes an additional system, trigonal, is distinguished, although this is usually included in the hexagonal system. See also **crystal class.**
crys+tal vi+o+let *n.* another name for **gentian violet.**
Cs *the chemical symbol for* caesium.
CS *international car registration for* Czechoslovakia.
cs. *abbrev. for* case.
C.S. *abbrev. for:* **1.** Also: **c.s.** Capital Stock. **2.** chartered surveyor. **3.** Christian Science. **4.** Christian Scientist. **5.** Civil Service. **6.** Also: **c.s.** Court of Session.
CSB *abbrev. for* chemical stimulation of the brain.
csc *abbrev. for* cosecant.
C.S.C. *abbrev. for* Civil Service Commission.
csch a U.S. form of **cosech.**
CSE *n.* (in Britain) *abbrev. for* Certificate of Secondary Education; a series of examinations the first grade of pass of which is an equivalent to a GCE O level.
CS gas *n.* a gas causing tears, salivation, and painful breathing, used in chemical warfare and civil disturbances; *ortho*-chlorobenzal malononitrile. Formula: $C_6H_4ClCH{:}C(CN)_2$. [C20: from the surname initials of its U.S. inventors, Ben Carson and Roger Staughton]
C.S.I.R.O. (in Australia) *abbrev. for* Commonwealth Scientific and Industrial Research Organization.
C.S.M. (in Britain) *abbrev. for* Company Sergeant-Major.
C.S.T. *abbrev. for* Central Standard Time.
ct. *abbrev. for:* **1.** cent. **2.** certificate. **3.** court.
C.T. *abbrev. for* central time.
cte+nid+i+um (tɪ'nɪdɪəm) *n., pl.* **·i+a** (-ɪə). one of the comblike respiratory gills of molluscs. [C19: New Latin, from Greek *ktenidion*, diminutive of *kteis* comb]
cte+noid ('tiːnɔɪd, 'tɛn-) *adj. Biology.* toothed like a comb, as the scales of perches. [C19: from Greek *ktenoeidēs*, from *kteis* comb + *-oeidēs* -OID]
cten+o+phore ('tɛnəˌfɔː, 'tiːnə-) *n.* any marine invertebrate of the phylum *Ctenophora*, including the sea gooseberry and Venus's-girdle, whose body bears eight rows of fused cilia, for locomotion. Also called: **comb jelly.** [C19: from New Latin *ctenophorus*, from Greek *kteno-*, *kteis* comb + -PHORE] —**cte+noph·o+ran** (tɪ'nɒfərən) *adj., n.*
Ctes+i+phon ('tɛsɪˌfɒn) *n.* an ancient city on the River Tigris about 100 km (60 miles) above Babylon. First mentioned in 221 B.C., it was destroyed in the 7th and 8th centuries A.D.
ctn *abbrev. for* cotangent.
C.T.O. *adj. Philately.* (of postage stamps) cancelled to order; postmarked in sheets for private sale.
ctr. *abbrev. for* centre.
cts. *abbrev. for:* **1.** cents. **2.** certificates.
CTV *abbrev. for* Canadian Television Network Ltd.
cu *or* **cu.** *abbrev. for* cubic.
Cu *the chemical symbol for* copper. [from Late Latin *cuprum*]
cub (kʌb) *n.* **1.** the young of certain animals, such as the lion, bear, etc. **2.** a young or inexperienced person. ~*vb.* **cubs, cub+bing, cubbed. 3.** to give birth to (cubs). [C16: perhaps from Old Norse *kubbi* young seal; see COB] —'**cub+bish** *adj.* —'**cub+bish+ly** *adv.*
Cub (kʌb) *n.* short for **Cub scout.**
Cu·ba ('kjuːbə) *n.* a republic and the largest island in the West Indies, at the entrance to the Gulf of Mexico: became a Spanish colony after its discovery by Columbus in 1492; gained independence after the Spanish-American War of 1898 but remained subject to U.S. influence until declared a people's republic under Castro in 1960; subject of an international crisis in 1962, when the U.S. blockaded the island in order to compel

the Soviet Union to dismantle its nuclear missile base. Sugar comprises about 80 per cent of total exports. Language: Spanish. Currency: peso. Capital: Havana. Pop.: 9 090 000 (1974 est.). Area: 114 524 sq. km (44 218 sq. miles). —**'Cu·ban** *adj., n.*

cub·age ('kju:bɪdʒ) *n.* another word for **cubature** (sense 2).

Cu·ba li·bre ('kju:bə 'li:brə) *n. Chiefly U.S.* a drink of rum, cola, lime juice, and ice. [Spanish, literally: free Cuba, a toast during the Cuban War of Independence]

cub·ane ('kju:beɪn) *n.* **a.** a rare octahedral hydrocarbon formed by eight CH groups, each of which is situated at the corner of a cube. Formula: C_8H_8. **b.** (*as modifier*): *cubane chemistry.* [C20: from CUBE + -ANE]

Cu·ban heel *n.* a moderately high heel for a shoe.

cu·ba·ture ('kju:bətʃə) *n.* **1.** the determination of the cubic contents of something. **2.** Also called: **cubage.** cubic contents. [C17: from CUBE[1] + *-ature,* on the model of *quadrature*]

cub·by·hole ('kʌbɪˌhəʊl) *n.* **1.** a small enclosed space or room. **2.** any small compartment, such as a pigeonhole. ~Often shortened to **cub·by** ('kʌbɪ). [C19: from dialect *cub* cattle pen; see COVE]

cube[1] (kju:b) *n.* **1.** a solid having six plane square faces in which the angle between two adjacent sides is a right angle. **2.** the product of three equal factors: the cube of 2 is $2 \times 2 \times 2$ (usually written 2^3). **3.** something in the form of a cube: *a bath cube.* ~*vb.* **4.** to raise (a number or quantity) to the third power. **5.** (*tr.*) to measure the cubic contents of. **6.** (*tr.*) to make, shape, or cut (something, esp. food) into cubes. [C16: from Latin *cubus* die, cube, from Greek *kubos*] —**'cub·er** *n.*

cu·be[2] ('kju:beɪ) *n.* **1.** any of various tropical American plants, esp. any of the leguminous genus *Lonchocarpus,* the roots of which yield rotenone. **2.** an extract from the roots of these plants: a fish poison and insecticide. [American Spanish *cubé,* of unknown origin]

cu·beb ('kju:bɛb) *n.* **1.** a SE Asian treelike piperaceous woody climbing plant, *Piper cubeba,* with brownish berries. **2.** the unripe spicy fruit of this plant, dried and used as a stimulant and diuretic and sometimes smoked in cigarettes. [C14: from Old French *cubebe,* from Medieval Latin *cubēba,* from Arabic *kubābah*]

cube root *n.* the number or quantity whose cube is a given number or quantity: 2 is the cube root of 8 (usually written $\sqrt[3]{8}$ or $8^{1/3}$).

cu·bic ('kju:bɪk) *adj.* **1.** having the shape of a cube. **2. a.** having three dimensions. **b.** denoting or relating to a linear measure that is raised to the third power: *a cubic metre.* Abbrevs.: **cu., c. 3.** *Maths.* of, relating to, or containing a variable to the third power or a term in which the sum of the exponents of the variables is three. **4.** Also: **isometric, regular.** *Crystallog.* relating to or belonging to the crystal system characterized by three equal perpendicular axes. The unit cell of cubic crystals is a cube with a lattice point at each corner (**simple cubic**) and one in the cube's centre (**body-centred cubic**), or a lattice point at each corner and one at the centre of each face (**face-centred cubic**). ~*n.* **5.** *Maths.* **a.** a cubic equation, such as $x^3 + x + 2 = 0$. **b.** a cubic term or expression.

cu·bi·cal ('kju:bɪkᵊl) *adj.* **1.** of or related to volume: *cubical expansion.* **2.** shaped like a cube. **3.** of or involving the third power. —**'cu·bi·cal·ly** *adv.* —**'cu·bi·cal·ness** *n.*

cu·bi·cle ('kju:bɪkᵊl) *n.* a partially or totally enclosed section of a room, as in a dormitory. [C15: from Latin *cubiculum,* from *cubāre* to lie down, lie asleep]

cu·bic meas·ure *n.* a system of units for the measurement of volumes, based on the cubic inch, the cubic centimetre, etc.

cu·bic·u·lum (kju:'bɪkjʊləm) *n., pl.* **·la** (-lə). an underground burial chamber in Imperial Rome, such as those found in the catacombs. [C19: from Latin: CUBICLE]

cu·bi·form ('kju:bɪˌfɔ:m) *adj.* having the shape of a cube.

cub·ism ('kju:bɪzəm) *n.* (*often cap.*) a French school of painting, collage, relief, and sculpture initiated in 1907 by Picasso and Braque, which amalgamated viewpoints of natural forms into a multifaceted surface of geometrical planes. —**'cub·ist** *adj., n.* —**cu·'bis·tic** *adj.* —**cu·'bis·ti·cal·ly** *adv.*

cu·bit ('kju:bɪt) *n.* an ancient measure of length based on the length of the forearm. [C14: from Latin *cubitum* elbow, cubit]

cu·bi·tal ('kju:bɪtᵊl) *adj.* of or relating to the forearm.

cu·boid ('kju:bɔɪd) *adj. also* **cu·boi·dal** (kju:'bɔɪdᵊl). **1.** shaped like a cube; cubic. **2.** of or denoting the cuboid bone. ~*n.* **3.** the cubelike bone of the foot; the outer distal bone of the tarsus. **4.** *Maths.* a geometric solid whose six faces are rectangles; rectangular parallelepiped.

Cu-bop ('kju:ˌbɒp) *n. Jazz.* music of the 1940s in which Cuban rhythms are combined with bop. Compare **Afro-Cuban.**

cub re·port·er *n.* a trainee reporter on a newspaper.

Cub Scout *or* **Cub** *n.* a member of the junior branch of the Scout Association.

Cu·chul·ain, Cu·chul·ainn, *or* **Cu·chul·lain** (ku:'kʌlɪn) *n. Celtic myth.* a legendary hero of Ulster.

cuck·ing stool ('kʌkɪŋ) *n.* a stool to which suspected witches, scolds, etc., were tied and ducked into water as a punishment. [C13: *cucking stol,* literally: defecating chair, from *cukken* to defecate; compare Old Norse *kúkr* excrement]

cuck·old ('kʌkəld) *n.* **1.** a man whose wife has committed adultery, often regarded as an object of scorn. ~*vb.* **2.** (*tr.*) to make a cuckold of. [C13 *cukeweld,* from Old French *cucuault,* from *cucu* CUCKOO; perhaps an allusion to the parasitic cuckoos that lay their eggs in the nests of other birds] —**'cuck·old·ry** *n.*

cuck·oo ('kʊku:) *n., pl.* **·oos. 1.** any bird of the family *Cuculidae,* having pointed wings, a long tail, and zygodactyl feet: order *Cuculiformes.* Many species, including the **European cuckoo** (*Cuculus canorus*), lay their eggs in the nests of other birds and have a two-note call. **2.** *Informal.* an insane or foolish person. ~*adj.* **3.** *Informal.* insane or foolish. ~*interj.* **4.** an imitation or representation of the call of a cuckoo. ~*vb.* **·oos, ·oo·ing, ·ooed. 5.** (*tr.*) to repeat over and over. **6.** (*intr.*) to make the sound imitated by the word *cuckoo.* [C13: from Old French *cucu,* of imitative origin; related to German *kuckuck,* Latin *cucūlus,* Greek *kokkux*]

cuck·oo clock *n.* a clock in which a mechanical cuckoo pops out with a sound like a cuckoo's call when the clock strikes.

cuck·oo·flow·er ('kʊku:ˌflaʊə) *n.* another name for **lady's-smock** and **ragged robin.**

cuck·oo·pint ('kʊku:ˌpaɪnt) *n.* a European aroid plant, *Arum maculatum,* with arrow-shaped leaves, a spathe marked with purple, a pale purple spadix, and scarlet berries. Also called: **lords-and-ladies.**

cuck·oo shrike *n.* any Old World tropical songbird of the family *Campephagidae,* typically having a strong notched bill, long rounded tail, and pointed wings. See also **minivet.**

cuck·oo spit *n.* a white frothy mass on the stems and leaves of many plants, produced by froghopper larvae (**cuckoo spit insects**) which feed on the plant juices. Also called: **frog spit.**

cu·cu·li·form (kjʊ'kju:lɪˌfɔ:m) *adj.* of, relating to, or belonging to the order *Cuculiformes,* which includes the cuckoos. [from Latin *cucūlus* cuckoo + -FORM]

cu·cul·late ('kju:kəˌleɪt, -lɪt) *adj.* shaped like a hood or having a hoodlike part: *cucullate sepals.* [C18: from Late Latin *cucullātus,* from Latin *cucullus* hood, cap] —**'cu·cul·ˌlate·ly** *adv.*

cu·cum·ber ('kju:ˌkʌmbə) *n.* **1.** a creeping cucurbitaceous plant, *Cucumis sativus,* cultivated in many forms for its edible fruit. Compare **squirting cucumber. 2.** the cylindrical fruit of this plant, which has hard thin green rind and white crisp flesh. **3.** any of various similar or related plants or their fruits. [C14: from Latin *cucumis,* of unknown origin]

cu·cum·ber tree *n.* **1.** any of several American trees or shrubs of the genus *Magnolia,* esp. *M. acuminata,* of E and central North America, having cup-shaped greenish flowers and cucumber-shaped fruits. **2.** an E Asian tree, *Averrhoa bilimbi,* with edible fruits resembling small cucumbers: family *Averrhoaceae.* See also **caramba.**

cu·cur·bit (kju:'kɜ:bɪt) *n.* any creeping flowering plant of the mainly tropical and subtropical family *Cucurbitaceae,* which includes the pumpkin, cucumber, squashes, and gourds. [C14: from Old French, from Latin *cucurbita* gourd, cup] —**cu·ˌcur·bi·'ta·ceous** *adj.*

Cú·cu·ta (*Spanish* 'kukuˌta) *n.* a city in E Colombia: commercial centre of a coffee-producing region. Pop.: 219 772 (1973). Official name: **San Jo·sé de Cú·cu·ta** (san xo'se ðe).

cud (kʌd) *n.* **1.** partially digested food regurgitated from the first stomach of cattle and other ruminants to the mouth for a second chewing. **2. chew the cud.** to reflect or think over something. [Old English *cudu,* from *cwidu* what has been chewed; related to Old Norse *kvātha* resin (for chewing), Old High German *quiti* glue, Sanskrit *jatu* rubber]

cud·bear ('kʌdˌbɛə) *n.* another name for **orchil.** [C18: whimsical alteration of *Cuthbert,* the Christian name of Dr. Gordon, 18th-century Scot who patented the dye. See CUDDY[2]]

cud·dle ('kʌdᵊl) *vb.* **1.** to hold (another person or thing) close or (of two people, etc.) to hold each other close, as for affection, comfort, or warmth; embrace; hug. **2.** (*intr.; foll. by up*) to curl or snuggle up into a comfortable or warm position. ~*n.* **3.** a close embrace, esp. when prolonged. [C18: of uncertain origin] —**'cud·dle·some** *adj.* —**'cud·dly** *adj.*

cud·dy[1] ('kʌdɪ) *n., pl.* **·dies. 1.** a small cabin in a boat. **2.** a small room, cupboard, etc. [C17: perhaps from Dutch *kajute;* compare Old French *cahute*]

cud·dy[2] *or* **cud·die** ('kʌdɪ) *n., pl.* **·dies.** *Dialect, chiefly Scot.* **1.** a donkey. **2.** a stupid fellow; fool. [C18: probably from *Cuddy,* nickname for *Cuthbert*]

cudg·el ('kʌdʒəl) *n.* **1.** a short stout stick used as a weapon. **2. take up the cudgels.** (often foll. by *for* or *on behalf of*) to join in a dispute, esp. to defend oneself or another. ~*vb.* **·els, ·el·ling, ·elled** *or U.S.* **·els, ·el·ing, ·eled. 3.** (*tr.*) to strike with a cudgel or similar weapon. **4. cudgel one's brains.** to think hard about a problem. [Old English *cycgel;* related to Middle Dutch *koghele* stick with knob] —**'cudg·el·ler** *n.*

cudg·er·ie ('kʌdʒərɪ) *n. Austral.* **1.** a large tropical rutaceous tree, *Flindersia schottina,* having light-coloured wood. **2.** Also called: **pink poplar.** an anacardiaceous rain-forest tree, *Euroschinus falcatus.*

cud·weed ('kʌdˌwi:d) *n.* **1.** any of various temperate woolly plants of the genus *Gnaphalium,* having clusters of whitish or yellow button-like flowers: family *Compositae* (composites). **2.** any of several similar and related plants of the genus *Filago,* esp. *F. germanica.*

cue[1] (kju:) *n.* **1. a.** (in the theatre, films, music, etc.) anything spoken or done that serves as a signal to an actor, musician, etc., to follow with specific lines or action. **b. on cue.** at the right moment. **2.** a signal or reminder to do something. **3.** *Psychol.* the part of any sensory pattern that is identified as the signal for a response. **4.** the part, function, or action assigned to or expected of a person. ~*vb.* **cues, cu·ing, cued. 5.** (*tr.*) to give a cue or cues to (an actor). **6.** (usually foll. by *in* or *into*) to signal (to something or somebody) at a specific moment in a musical or dramatic performance: *to cue in a flourish of trumpets.* **7.** (*tr.*) to give information or a reminder to (someone). **8.** (*intr.*) to signal the commencement of filming, as with the word

"Action!" [C16: probably from name of the letter *q*, used in an actor's script to represent Latin *quando* when]

cue[2] (kju:) *n.* **1.** *Billiards, etc.* a long tapered shaft with a leather tip, used to drive the balls. **2.** hair caught at the back forming a tail or braid. **3.** *U.S.* a variant spelling of **queue.** ~*vb.* **cues, cu·ing, cued. 4.** to drive (a ball) with a cue. **5.** (*tr.*) to twist or tie (the hair) into a cue. [C18: variant of QUEUE]

cue ball *n. Billiards, etc.* the ball struck by the cue, as distinguished from the object balls.

cue bid *n. Contract bridge.* a bid in a suit made to show an ace or a void in that suit.

Cuen·ca (*Spanish* 'kweŋka) *n.* **1.** a city in SW Ecuador: university (1868). Pop.: 79 140 (1970 est.). **2.** a town in central Spain: prosperous in the Middle Ages for its silver and textile industries. Pop.: 34 485 (1970).

Cuer·na·va·ca (*Spanish* ˌkwerna'vaka) *n.* a city in S central Mexico, capital of Morelos state: resort with nearby Cacahuamilpa Caverns. Pop.: 273 986 (1975 est.).

cues·ta ('kwɛstə) *n.* a long low ridge with a steep scarp slope and a gentle back slope, formed by the differential erosion of strata of differing hardness. [Spanish: shoulder, from Latin *costa* side, rib]

cuff[1] (kʌf) *n.* **1.** the part of a sleeve nearest the hand, sometimes turned back and decorative. **2.** the part of a gauntlet or glove that extends past the wrist. **3.** the U.S. and Australian name for **turnup** (sense 5). **4. off the cuff.** *Informal.* improvised; extemporary. [C14 *cuffe* glove, of obscure origin]

cuff[2] (kʌf) *vb.* **1.** (*tr.*) to strike with an open hand. ~*n.* **2.** a blow of this kind. [C16: of obscure origin]

cuff link *n.* one of a pair of linked buttons, used to join the buttonholes on the cuffs of a shirt.

cuffs (kʌfs) *pl. n. Informal.* short for **handcuffs.**

Cu·fic ('ku:fɪk, 'kju:-) *n., adj.* a variant spelling of **Kufic.**

Cu·ia·bá *or* **Cu·ya·bá** (*Portuguese* ˌkuja'ba) *n.* **1.** a port in W Brazil, capital of Mato Grosso state, on the Cuiabá River. Pop.: 103 427 (1970). **2.** a river in SW Brazil, rising on the Mato Grosso plateau and flowing southwest into the São Lourenço River. Length: 483 km (300 miles).

cui bo·no *Latin.* (kwi: 'bəunəu) for whose benefit? for what purpose?

cui·rass (kwɪ'ræs) *n.* **1.** a piece of armour, of leather or metal covering the chest and back. **2.** a hard outer protective covering of some animals, consisting of shell, plate, or scales. **3.** any similar protective covering, as on a ship. ~*vb.* **4.** (*tr.*) to equip with a cuirass. [C15: from French *cuirasse*, from Late Latin *coriacea*, from *coriaceus* made of leather, from Latin *corium* leather]

cui·ras·sier (ˌkwɪrə'sɪə) *n.* a mounted soldier, esp. of the 16th century, who wore a cuirass.

cuir-bouil·li (ˌkwɪəbu:'ji:) *n.* a type of leather hardened by soaking in wax, used for armour before the 14th century. [French, literally: boiled leather]

cui·sine (kwɪ'zi:n) *n.* **1.** a style or manner of cooking: *French cuisine.* **2.** the food prepared by a restaurant, household, etc. [C18: from French, literally: kitchen, from Late Latin *coquīna*, from Latin *coquere* to cook]

cuisse (kwɪs) *or* **cuish** (kwɪʃ) *n.* a piece of armour for the thigh. [C15: back formation from *cuisses* (plural), from Old French *cuisseaux* thigh guards, from *cuisse* thigh, from Latin *coxa* hipbone]

Cul·bert·son ('kʌlbətsᵊn) *n.* **E·ly** ('i:laɪ). 1891–1955, U.S. authority on contract bridge.

culch *or* **cultch** (kʌltʃ) *n.* **1.** a mass of broken stones, shells, and gravel that forms the basis of an oyster bed. **2.** the oyster spawn attached to such a structure. **3.** *Dialect.* refuse; rubbish. [C17: perhaps ultimately from Old French *culche* bed, COUCH]

cul-de-sac ('kʌldəˌsæk, 'kʊl-) *n., pl.* **culs-de-sac** *or* **cul-de-sacs. 1.** a road with one end blocked off; dead end. **2.** an inescapable position. **3.** any tube-shaped bodily cavity or pouch closed at one end, such as the caecum. [C18: literally: bottom of the bag]

-cule *suffix forming nouns.* indicating smallness: *animalcule.* [from Latin *-culus*, diminutive suffix; compare -CLE]

Cu·le·bra Cut (ku:'lɛbrə) *n.* the former name of the **Gaillard Cut.**

cu·let ('kju:lɪt) *n.* **1.** *Jewellery.* the flat face at the bottom of a gem. **2.** either of the plates of armour worn at the small of the back. [C17: from obsolete French, diminutive of *cul*, from Latin *cūlus* bottom]

cu·lex ('kju:lɛks) *n., pl.* **·li·ces** (-lɪˌsi:z). any mosquito of the genus *Culex*, such as *C. pipiens*, the common mosquito. [C15: from Latin: midge, gnat; related to Old Irish *cuil* gnat]

Cu·lia·cán (*Spanish* ˌkulja'kan) *n.* a city in NW Mexico, capital of Sinaloa state. Pop.: 244 645 (1975 est.).

cu·lic·id (kju:'lɪsɪd) *n.* **1.** any dipterous insect of the family *Culicidae*, which comprises the mosquitos. ~*adj.* **2.** of, relating to, or belonging to the *Culicidae.* [C19: from New Latin *Culicidae*, from Latin *culex* gnat, CULEX]

cul·i·nar·y ('kʌlɪnərɪ) *adj.* of, relating to, or used in the kitchen or in cookery. [C17: from Latin *culīnārius*, from *culīna* kitchen] —**'cul·i·nar·i·ly** *adv.*

cull (kʌl) *vb.* (*tr.*) **1.** to choose or gather the best or required examples. **2.** to take out (an animal, esp. an inferior one) from a herd. **3.** to gather (flowers, fruit, etc.). ~*n.* **4.** the act or product of culling. **5.** an inferior animal taken from a herd. [C15: from Old French *coillir* to pick, from Latin *colligere;* see COLLECT] —**'cull·er** *n.*

cul·len·der ('kʌlɪndə) *n.* a variant of **colander.**

cul·let ('kʌlɪt) *n.* waste glass for melting down to be reused. [C17: perhaps variant of COLLET, (literally: little neck, referring to the glass neck of newly blown bottles, etc.)]

cul·lis ('kʌlɪs) *n.* **1.** a gutter in or at the eaves of a roof. **2.** another word for **coulisse** (sense 1). [C19: from French *coulisse* channel, groove; see COULISSE]

Cul·lod·en (kə'lɒdᵊn) *n.* a moor near Inverness in N Scotland: site of a battle in 1746 in which English troops annihilated the Jacobites under Prince Charles Edward Stuart.

cul·ly ('kʌlɪ) *n., pl.* **·lies.** *Slang.* pal; mate. [C17: of unknown origin]

culm[1] (kʌlm) *n. Mining.* **1.** coalmine waste. **2.** inferior anthracite. [C14: probably related to COAL]

culm[2] (kʌlm) *n.* the hollow jointed stem of a grass or sedge. [C17: from Latin *culmus* stalk; see HAULM]

Culm *or* **Culm Meas·ures** *n.* a formation consisting mainly of shales and sandstone deposited during the Carboniferous period in parts of Europe. [C19: from CULM[1]]

cul·mif·er·ous (kʌl'mɪfərəs) *adj.* (of grasses) having a hollow jointed stem.

cul·mi·nant ('kʌlmɪnənt) *adj.* highest or culminating.

cul·mi·nate ('kʌlmɪˌneɪt) *vb.* **1.** (when *intr.*, usually foll. by *in*) to end or cause to end, esp. to reach or bring to a final or climactic stage. **2.** (*intr.*) (of a celestial body) to cross the meridian of the observer. [C17: from Late Latin *culmināre* to reach the highest point, from Latin *culmen* top]

cul·mi·na·tion (ˌkʌlmɪ'neɪʃən) *n.* **1.** the final, highest, or decisive point. **2.** the act of culminating.

cu·lottes (kju:'lɒts) *pl. n.* women's flared knee-length or ankle-length trousers cut to look like a skirt. [C20: from French, literally: breeches, from *cul* bottom; see CULET]

cul·pa ('kʊlpɑ:) *n., pl.* **·pae** (-pi:). **1.** *Civil law.* an act of neglect. **2.** a fault; sin; guilt. [Latin: fault]

cul·pa·ble ('kʌlpəbᵊl) *adj.* deserving censure; blameworthy. [C14: from Old French *coupable*, from Latin *culpābilis*, from *culpāre* to blame, from *culpa* fault] —ˌ**cul·pa·'bil·i·ty** *or* **'cul·pa·ble·ness** *n.* —**'cul·pa·bly** *adv.*

cul·prit ('kʌlprɪt) *n.* **1.** *Law.* a person awaiting trial, esp. one who has pleaded not guilty. **2.** the person responsible for a particular offence, misdeed, etc. [C17: from Anglo-French *cul-*, short for *culpable* guilty + *prit* ready, indicating that the prosecution was ready to prove the guilt of the one charged]

cult (kʌlt) *n.* **1.** a specific system of religious worship, esp. with reference to its rites and deity. **2.** a sect devoted to the beliefs of a religious or other cult. **3.** *Sociol.* a group having an exclusive ideology and ritual practices centred on sacred symbols, esp. one characterized by lack of organizational structure. **4.** intense interest in and devotion to a person, idea, or activity: *the cult of yoga.* **5.** the person, idea, etc., arousing such devotion. **6.** any popular fashion; craze. **7.** (*modifier*) of, relating to, or characteristic of a cult or cults: *a cult figure.* [C17: from Latin *cultus* cultivation, refinement, from *colere* to till] —**'cul·tic** *adj.* —**'cult·ism** *n.* —**'cult·ist** *n.*

cultch (kʌltʃ) *n.* a variant spelling of **culch.**

cul·ti·gen ('kʌltɪdʒən) *n.* a species of plant that is known only as a cultivated form and did not originate from a wild type. [C20: from CULTI(VATED) + -GEN]

cul·ti·va·ble ('kʌltɪvəbᵊl) *or* **cul·ti·vat·a·ble** ('kʌltɪˌveɪtəbᵊl) *adj.* (of land) capable of being cultivated. [C17: from French, from Old French *cultiver* to CULTIVATE] —ˌ**cul·ti·va·'bil·i·ty** *n.*

cul·ti·var ('kʌltɪˌvɑ:) *n.* a variety of a plant that was produced from a natural species and is maintained by cultivation. [C20: from CULTI(VATED) + VAR(IETY)]

cul·ti·vate ('kʌltɪˌveɪt) *vb.* (*tr.*) **1.** to till and prepare (land or soil) for the growth of crops. **2.** to plant, tend, harvest, or improve (plants) by labour and skill. **3.** to break up (land or soil) with a cultivator or hoe. **4.** to improve or foster (the mind, body, etc.) as by study, education, or labour. **5.** to give special attention to: *to cultivate a friendship; to cultivate a hobby.* **6.** to give or bring culture to (a person, society, etc.); civilize. [C17: from Medieval Latin *cultivāre* to till, from Old French *cultiver*, from Medieval Latin *cultīvus* cultivable, from Latin *cultus* cultivated, from *colere* to till, toil over]

cul·ti·vat·ed ('kʌltɪˌveɪtɪd) *adj.* **1.** cultured, refined, or educated. **2.** (of land or soil) **a.** subjected to tillage or cultivation. **b.** tilled and broken up. **3.** (of plants) specially bred or improved by cultivation.

cul·ti·va·tion (ˌkʌltɪ'veɪʃən) *n.* **1.** *Agriculture.* **a.** the planting, tending, improving, or harvesting of crops or plants. **b.** the preparation of ground to promote their growth. **2.** development, esp. through education, training, etc. **3.** culture or sophistication, esp. social refinement.

cul·ti·va·tor ('kʌltɪˌveɪtə) *n.* **1.** a farm implement equipped with shovels, blades, etc., used to break up soil and remove weeds. **2.** a person or thing that cultivates. **3.** a person who grows, tends, or improves plants or crops.

cul·trate ('kʌltreɪt) *or* **cul·trat·ed** *adj.* shaped like a knife blade: *cultrate leaves.* [C19: from Latin *cultrātus*, from *culter* knife]

cul·tur·al ('kʌltʃərəl) *adj.* **1.** of or relating to artistic or social pursuits or events considered to be valuable or enlightened. **2.** of or relating to a culture or civilization. **3.** (of certain varieties of plant) obtained by specialized breeding. —**'cul·tur·al·ly** *adv.*

cul·tur·al an·thro·pol·o·gy *n.* the branch of anthropology dealing with cultural as opposed to biological and racial features. —**cul·tur·al an·thro·pol·o·gist** *n.*

cul·tur·al lag *or* **cul·ture lag** *n.* the difference in the rate of change between two parts of a culture.

Cul+tur+al Rev·o+lu+tion *n.* (in China) a mass movement (1965–68), in which the youthful Red Guard played a prominent part. It was initiated by Mao Tse-tung to destroy the power of the bureaucrats and to revolutionize the attitudes and behaviour of the people. Also called: **Great Proletarian Cultural Revolution.**

cul+ture ('kʌltʃə) *n.* **1.** the total of the inherited ideas, beliefs, values, and knowledge, which constitute the shared bases of social action. **2.** the total range of activities and ideas of a group of people with shared traditions, which are transmitted and reinforced by members of the group: *the Mayan culture.* **3.** a particular civilization at a particular period. **4.** the artistic and social pursuits, expression, and tastes valued by a society or class, as in the arts, manners, dress, etc. **5.** the enlightenment or refinement resulting from these pursuits. **6.** the cultivation of plants, esp. by scientific methods designed to improve stock or to produce new ones. **7.** *Stockbreeding.* the rearing and breeding of animals, esp. with a view to improving the strain. **8.** the act or practice of tilling or cultivating the soil. **9.** *Biology.* **a.** the experimental growth of microorganisms, such as bacteria and fungi, in a nutrient substance (see **culture medium**), usually under controlled conditions. **b.** a group of microorganisms grown in this way. ~*vb.* (*tr.*) **10.** to cultivate (plants or animals). **11.** to grow (microorganisms) in a culture medium. [C15: from Old French, from Latin *cultūra* a cultivating, from *colere* to till; see CULT] —**'cul+tur+ist** *n.* —**'cul+ture+less** *adj.*

cul+tured ('kʌltʃəd) *adj.* **1.** showing or having good taste, manners, upbringing, and education. **2.** artificially grown or synthesized: *cultured pearls.*

cul+tured pearl *n.* a pearl induced to grow in the shell of an oyster or clam, by the insertion of a small object around which layers of nacre are deposited.

cul+ture me+di·um *n.* a nutritive substance, such as an agar gel, in which cultures of bacteria and fungi are grown.

cul+ture shock *n. Sociol.* the feelings of isolation, rejection, etc., experienced when one culture is brought into sudden contact with another, as when a primitive tribe is confronted by modern civilization.

cul+ture vul+ture *n. Informal.* a person considered to be excessively eager to acquire culture.

cul+tus ('kʌltəs) *n., pl.* **+tus·es** *or* **+ti** (-taɪ). *Chiefly R.C. Church.* another word for **cult** (sense 1). [C17: from Latin: a toiling over something, refinement, CULT]

cul+ver ('kʌlvə) *n.* an archaic or poetic name for **pigeon** or **dove.** [Old English *culfre,* from Latin *columbula* a little dove, from *columba* dove]

cul+ver+in ('kʌlvərɪn) *n.* **1.** a medium to heavy cannon used during the 16th and 17th centuries. **2.** a medieval musket. [C15: from Old French *coulevrine,* from *couleuvre,* from Latin *coluber* serpent]

Cul·ver's root *or* **phys+ic** ('kʌlvəz) *n.* **1.** a tall North American scrophulariaceous plant, *Veronicastrum virginicum,* having spikes of small white or purple flowers. **2.** the dried roots of this plant, formerly used as a cathartic and emetic. [C19: named after a Dr. *Culver,* 18th-century American physician]

cul+vert ('kʌlvət) *n.* **1.** a drain or covered channel that crosses under a road, railway, etc. **2.** a channel for an electric cable. [C18: of unknown origin]

cum (kʌm) *prep.* used between two nouns to designate an object of a combined nature: *a kitchen-cum-dining room.* [Latin: with, together with, along with]

Cu+mae ('kju:mi:) *n.* the oldest Greek colony in Italy, founded about 750 B.C. near Naples. —**Cu+'mae·an** *adj.*

Cu+ma+ná (*Spanish* ˌkuma'na) *n.* a city in NE Venezuela: founded in 1523; the oldest European settlement in South America. Pop.: 119 751 (1971).

cum+ber ('kʌmbə) *vb.* (*tr.*) **1.** to obstruct or hinder. **2.** *Obsolete.* to inconvenience. ~*n.* **3.** a hindrance or burden. [C13: probably from Old French *combrer* to impede, prevent, from *combre* barrier; see ENCUMBER] —**'cum+ber+er** *n.*

Cum+ber+land[1] ('kʌmbələnd) *n.* (until 1974) a county of NW England, now part of Cumbria.

Cum·ber·land[2] ('kʌmbələnd) *n.* **Wil·liam Au·gus·tus,** Duke of Cumberland, called *Butcher Cumberland.* 1721–65, English soldier, younger son of George II, noted for his defeat of Charles Edward Stuart at Culloden (1746) and his subsequent ruthless destruction of Jacobite rebels.

Cum+ber+nauld (ˌkʌmbə'nɔ:ld) *n.* a town in central Scotland, in E central Strathclyde, northeast of Glasgow: developed as a new town since 1956. Pop.: 31 787 (1971).

cum+ber+some ('kʌmbəsəm) *or* **cum+brous** ('kʌmbrəs) *adj.* **1.** awkward because of size, weight, or shape: *cumbersome baggage.* **2.** difficult because of extent or complexity: *cumbersome accounts.* [C14: *cumber,* short for ENCUMBER + -SOME] —**'cum+ber+some+ly** *or* **'cum+brous+ly** *adv.* —**'cum+ber+some+ness** *or* **'cum+brous+ness** *n.*

cum+brance ('kʌmbrəns) *n.* **1.** a burden, obstacle, or hindrance. **2.** trouble or bother.

Cum+bri·a ('kʌmbrɪə) *n.* (since 1974) a county of NW England comprising the former counties of Westmorland and Cumberland together with N Lancashire: includes the Lake District mountain area and surrounding coastal lowlands with the Pennine uplands in the extreme east. Administrative centre: Carlisle. Pop.: 473 600 (1976 est.). Area: 6806 sq. km (2628 sq. miles). —**'Cum+bri·an** *adj., n.*

Cum+bri·an Moun+tains ('kʌmbrɪən) *pl. n.* a mountain range in NW England, in Cumbria. Highest peak: Scafell Pike, 963 m (3210 ft.).

cum div·i+dend (of shares, etc.) with the right to current dividend. Compare **ex dividend.** [*cum,* from Latin: with]

cum gra+no sa+lis *Latin.* (kum 'grɑ:nəʊ 'sɑ:lɪs) *adv.* with a grain of salt; not too literally.

cum+in *or* **cum+min** ('kʌmɪn) *n.* **1.** an umbelliferous Mediterranean plant, *Cuminum cyminum,* with finely divided leaves and small white or pink flowers. **2.** the aromatic seeds (collectively) of this plant, used as a condiment and a flavouring. [C12: from Old French, from Latin *cumīnum,* from Greek *kuminon,* of Semitic origin; compare Hebrew *kammōn*]

cum lau+de (kʌm 'lɔ:dɪ, kum 'laudeɪ) *Chiefly U.S.* with praise: the lowest of three designations for above-average achievement in examinations. [Latin]

cum+mer+bund *or* **kum+mer+bund** ('kʌmə,bʌnd) *n.* a wide sash, worn with a dinner jacket. [C17: from Hindi *kamarband,* from Persian, from *kamar* loins, waist + *band* band]

Cum·mings ('kʌmɪŋz) *n.* **Ed·ward Est·lin** ('ɛstlɪn) (preferred typographical representation of name *e. e. cummings*) 1894–1962, U.S. poet, and artist.

cum+quat ('kʌmkwɒt) *n.* a variant spelling of **kumquat.**

cum+shaw ('kʌmʃɔ:) *n.* (used, esp. formerly, by beggars in Chinese ports) a present or tip. [C19: from pidgin English, from Chinese (Amoy) *kam siā,* from Mandarin *kan hsieh* grateful thanks]

cu+mu+late *vb.* ('kju:mjʊˌleɪt). **1.** to accumulate. ~*adj.* ('kju:mjʊlɪt, -ˌleɪt). **2.** heaped up. [C16: from Latin *cumulāre* from *cumulus* heap] —**'cu+mu+late+ly** *adv.* —**ˌcu+mu+'la+tion** *n.*

cu+mu+la+tive ('kju:mjʊlətɪv) *adj.* **1.** growing in quantity, strength, or effect by successive additions or gradual steps: *cumulative pollution.* **2.** gained by or resulting from a gradual building up: *cumulative benefits.* **3.** *Finance.* **a.** (of preference shares) entitling the holder to receive any arrears of dividend before any dividend is distributed to ordinary shareholders. **b.** (of dividends or interest) intended to be accumulated if not paid when due. **4.** *Statistics.* **a.** (of a frequency) including all values of a variable either below or above a specified value. **b.** (of error) tending to increase as the sample size is increased. —**'cu+mu+la+tive+ly** *adv.* —**'cu+mu+la+tive+ness** *n.*

cu+mu+la+tive ev·i+dence *n. Law.* additional evidence reinforcing testimony previously given.

cu+mu+la+tive vot+ing *n.* a system of voting in which each elector has as many votes as there are candidates in his constituency. Votes may all be cast for one candidate or distributed among several.

cu+mul+et ('kju:mjʊlɪt) *n.* (*sometimes cap.*) a variety of domestic fancy pigeon, pure white or white with light red markings. [C19: from CUMULUS]

cu+mu+li+form ('kju:mjʊlɪˌfɔ:m) *adj.* resembling a cumulus cloud.

cu+mu+lo+nim+bus (ˌkju:mjʊləʊ'nɪmbəs) *n., pl.* **+bi** (-baɪ) *or* **+bus·es.** *Meteorol.* a cumulus cloud of great vertical extent, the top often forming an anvil shape and the bottom being dark coloured, indicating rain or hail: associated with thunderstorms.

cu+mu+lo+stra+tus (ˌkju:mjʊləʊ'streɪtəs) *n., pl.* **+ti** (-taɪ). *Meteorol.* another name for **stratocumulus.**

cu+mu+lous ('kju:mjʊləs) *adj.* resembling or consisting of cumulus clouds.

cu+mu+lus ('kju:mjʊləs) *n., pl.* **+li** (-ˌlaɪ). a bulbous or billowing white or dark grey cloud associated with rising air currents. Compare **cirrus** (sense 1), **stratus.** [C17: from Latin: mass]

Cu+nax·a (kju:'næksə) *n.* the site near the lower Euphrates where Artaxerxes II defeated Cyrus the Younger in 401 B.C.

cunc+ta+tion (kʌŋk'teɪʃən) *n. Rare.* delay. [C16: from Latin *cunctātiō* a hesitation, from *cunctārī* to delay] —**cunc+ta+tive** ('kʌŋktətɪv) *adj.* —**cunc+'ta+tor** *n.*

cu+ne·al ('kju:nɪəl) *adj.* wedge-shaped; cuneiform. [C16: from New Latin *cuneālis,* from *cuneus* wedge]

cu+ne·ate ('kju:nɪɪt, -ˌeɪt) *adj.* wedge-shaped: cuneate leaves are attached at the narrow end. [C19: from Latin *cuneāre* to make wedge-shaped, from *cuneus* a wedge] —**'cu+ne·ate+ly** *adv.*

cu+nei+form ('kju:nɪˌfɔ:m) *adj.* **1.** Also: **cuneal.** wedge-shaped. **2.** of, relating to, or denoting the wedge-shaped characters employed in the writing of several ancient languages of Mesopotamia and Persia, esp. Sumerian, Babylonian, etc. **3.** of or relating to a tablet in which this script is employed. **4.** of or relating to any of the three tarsal bones. ~*n.* **5.** cuneiform characters or writing. **6.** any one of the three tarsal bones. [C17: probably from Old French *cunéiforme,* from Latin *cuneus* wedge]

Cu+ne·o (*Italian* 'ku:neo) *n.* a city in NW Italy, in Piedmont. Pop.: 54 505 (1971).

cun+je·voi ('kʌndʒɪˌvɔɪ) *n. Austral.* **1.** an aroid plant, *Alocasia macrorrhiza,* of tropical Asia and Australia, cultivated for its edible rhizome. **2.** a sea squirt. [C19: from a native Australian language]

cun+ni+lin+gus (ˌkʌnɪ'lɪŋgəs) *or* **cun+ni+linc+tus** (ˌkʌnɪ'lɪŋktəs) *n.* a sexual activity in which the female genitalia are stimulated by the partner's lips and tongue. Compare **fellatio.** [C19: from New Latin, from Latin *cunnus* vulva + *lingere* to lick]

cun+ning ('kʌnɪŋ) *adj.* **1.** crafty and shrewd, esp. in deception; sly: *cunning as a fox.* **2.** made with or showing skill or cleverness; ingenious. ~*n.* **3.** craftiness, esp. in deceiving; slyness. **4.** cleverness, skill, or ingenuity. [Old English *cunnende;* related to *cunnan* to know (see CAN[1]), *cunnian* to test, experience, Old Norse *kunna* to know] —ˈ**cun+ning+ly** *adv.* —ˈ**cun+ning+ness** *n.*

cunt (kʌnt) *n. Taboo slang.* **1.** the female genitals. **2.** *Offensive.* a woman considered sexually. **3.** *Offensive.* a mean or obnoxious person. [C13: of Germanic origin; related to Old Norse *kunta,* Middle Low German *kunte*]

cup (kʌp) *n.* **1.** a small open container, usually having one handle, used for drinking from. **2.** the contents of such a container: *that cup was too sweet.* **3.** Also called: **teacup; cupful.** a unit of capacity used in cooking equal to approximately half a pint, 8 fluid ounces, or about one quarter of a litre. **4.** something resembling a cup in shape or function, such as the flower base of some plants of the rose family or a cuplike bodily organ. **5.** either of two cup-shaped parts of a brassiere, designed to support the breasts. **6.** a cup-shaped trophy awarded as a prize. **7.** *Brit.* **a.** a sporting contest in which a cup is awarded to the winner. **b.** (*as modifier*): *a cup competition.* **8.** a mixed drink with one ingredient as a base, usually served from a bowl: *claret cup.* **9.** *Golf.* the hole or metal container in the hole on a green. **10.** the chalice or the consecrated wine used in the Eucharist. **11.** one's lot in life. **12. one's cup of tea.** *Informal.* one's chosen or preferred thing, task, company, etc.: *she's not my cup of tea.* **13. in one's cups.** drunk. ~*vb.* **cups, cup+ping, cupped.** (*tr.*) **14.** to form (something, such as the hands) into the shape of a cup. **15.** to put into or as if into a cup. **16.** to draw blood to the surface of the body by using a cupping glass. [Old English *cuppe,* from Late Latin *cuppa* cup, alteration of Latin *cūpa* cask] —ˈ**cup+ˌlike** *adj.*

cup+bear·er (ˈkʌpˌbɛərə) *n.* an attendant who fills and serves wine cups, as in a royal household.

cup+board (ˈkʌbəd) *n.* a piece of furniture or a recessed area of a room, with a door concealing storage space.

cup+board love *n.* a show of love inspired only by some selfish or greedy motive.

cup+cake (ˈkʌpˌkeɪk) *n.* a small cake baked in a cup-shaped foil or paper case.

cu+pel (ˈkju:pᵊl, kjʊˈpɛl) *n.* **1.** a refractory pot in which gold or silver is refined. **2.** a small porous bowl made of bone ash in which gold and silver are recovered from a lead button during assaying. ~*vb.* **+pels, +pel+ling +pelled** *or U.S.* **+pels, +pel+ing, +peled. 3.** (*tr.*) to refine (gold or silver) by means of cupellation. [C17: from French *coupelle,* diminutive of *coupe* CUP] —ˈ**cu+pel+ler** *n.*

cu+pel+la+tion (ˌkju:pɪˈleɪʃən) *n.* **1.** the process of recovering precious metals from lead by melting the alloy in a cupel and oxidizing the lead by means of an air blast. **2.** the manufacture of lead oxide by melting and oxidizing lead.

Cup Fi+nal *n.* **1.** (often preceded by *the*) the annual final of the F.A. Cup soccer competition, played at Wembley. **2.** (*often not cap.*) the final of any cup competition.

Cu+pid (ˈkju:pɪd) *n.* **1.** the Roman god of love, represented as a winged boy with a bow and arrow. Greek counterpart: **Eros. 2.** (*not cap.*) any similar figure, esp. as represented in Baroque art. [C14: from Latin *Cupīdō,* from *cupīdō* desire, from *cupidus* desirous; see CUPIDITY]

cu+pid+i·ty (kju:ˈpɪdɪtɪ) *n.* strong desire, esp. for possessions or money; greed. [C15: from Latin *cupiditās,* from *cupidus* eagerly desiring, from *cupere* to long for]

Cu+pid's bow *n.* a shape of the upper lip considered to resemble Cupid's double-curved bow.

cu+po+la (ˈkju:pələ) *n.* **1.** a roof or ceiling in the form of a dome. **2.** a small structure, usually domed, on the top of a roof or dome. **3.** a protective dome for a gun on a warship. **4.** a vertical cylindrical furnace in which metals, esp. iron, are remelted for casting. [C16: from Italian, from Late Latin *cūpula* a small cask, from Latin *cūpa* tub] —**cu+po+lat+ed** (ˈkju:pəˌleɪtɪd) *adj.*

cup+pa *or* **cup+per** (ˈkʌpə) *n. Brit. informal.* a cup of tea.

cupped (kʌpt) *adj.* hollowed like a cup; concave.

cup+ping (ˈkʌpɪŋ) *n. Med.* the process of applying a cupping glass to the skin.

cup+ping glass *n. Med.* a glass vessel from which air can be removed by suction or heat to create a partial vacuum: formerly used in drawing blood to the surface of the skin for slow bloodletting. Also called: **artificial leech.**

cu+pre+ous (ˈkju:prɪəs) *adj.* **1.** of, consisting of, containing, or resembling copper; coppery. **2.** of the reddish-brown colour of copper. [C17: from Late Latin *cupreus,* from *cuprum* COPPER[1]]

cu+pric (ˈkju:prɪk) *adj.* of or containing copper in the divalent state. [C18: from Late Latin *cuprum* copper]

cu+prif+er+ous (kju:ˈprɪfərəs) *adj.* (of a substance such as an ore) containing or yielding copper.

cu+prite (ˈkju:praɪt) *n.* a red secondary mineral consisting of cuprous oxide in cubic crystalline form: a source of copper. Formula: Cu_2O.

cu·pro-, cu·pri-, *or before a vowel* **cupr-** *combining form.* indicating copper: *cupronickel; cuprite.* [from Latin *cuprum*]

cu+pro+nick+el (ˌkju:prəʊˈnɪkᵊl) *n.* any ductile corrosion-resistant copper alloy containing up to 40 per cent nickel: used in condenser tubes, turbine blades, etc.

cu+prous (ˈkju:prəs) *adj.* of or containing copper in the monovalent state.

cu+prum (ˈkju:prəm) *n.* an obsolete name for **copper.** [Latin: COPPER[1]]

cup tie *n. Sport.* an eliminating match or round between two teams in a cup competition.

cup-tied *adj. Sport.* **1.** (of a team, etc.) unable to play another fixture because of involvement in a cup tie. **2.** (of a player) unable to play in a cup tie because of some disallowance.

cu+pu+late (ˈkju:pjʊˌleɪt) *or* **cu+pu+lar** (ˈkju:pjʊlə) *adj.* **1.** shaped like a small cup. **2.** (of plants or animals) having cupules.

cu+pule (ˈkju:pju:l) *n. Biology.* a cup-shaped part or structure, such as the cup around the base of an acorn. [C19: from Late Latin *cūpula;* see CUPOLA]

cur (kɜ:) *n.* **1.** any vicious dog, esp. a mongrel. **2.** a despicable or cowardly person. [C13: shortened from *kurdogge;* probably related to Old Norse *kurra* to growl]

cur. *abbrev. for* currency.

cur+a·ble (ˈkjʊərəbᵊl) *adj.* capable of being cured. —ˌ**cur+a·ˈbil+i·ty** *or* ˈ**cur+a·ble+ness** *n.* —ˈ**cur+a·bly** *adv.*

Cu+ra+çao (ˌkjʊərəˈsəʊ) *n.* **1.** an island in the Caribbean, the largest in the Netherlands Antilles. Capital: Willemstad. Pop.: 150 008 (1972 est.). Area: 444 sq. km (173 sq. miles). **2.** an orange-flavoured liqueur originally made there.

cu+ra+cy (ˈkjʊərəsɪ) *n., pl.* **+cies.** the office or position of curate.

cur+agh *Gaelic.* (ˈkʌrəx; ˈkʌrə) *n.* a variant spelling of **currach.**

cu+ra+re *or* **cu+ra+ri** (kjʊˈrɑ:rɪ) *n.* **1.** black resin obtained from certain tropical South American trees, acting on the motor nerves to cause muscular paralysis: used medicinally as a muscle relaxant and by South American Indians as an arrow poison. **2.** any of various trees of the genera *Chondrodendron* and *Strychnos* from which this resin is obtained. [C18: from Portuguese and Spanish, from Carib *kurari*]

cu+ra+rine (ˈkjʊərəˌri:n) *n.* an alkaloid extracted from curare, used as a muscle relaxant in surgery. Formula: $C_{19}H_{26}ON_2$.

cu+ra+rize *or* **cu+ra+rise** (ˈkjʊərəˌraɪz) *vb.* (*tr.*) to paralyse or treat with curare. —ˌ**cu+ra+ri+ˈza+tion** *or* ˌ**cu+ra+ri+ˈsa+tion** *n.*

cu+ras+sow (ˈkjʊərəˌsəʊ) *n.* any gallinaceous bird of the family *Cracidae,* of S North, Central, and South America. Curassows have long legs and tails and, typically, a distinctive crest of curled feathers. See also **guan.** [C17: anglicized variant of CURAÇAO (island)]

cu+rate (ˈkjʊərɪt) *n.* **1.** a clergyman appointed to assist a parish priest. **2.** a clergyman who has the charge of a parish (**curate-in-charge**). [C14: from Medieval Latin *cūrātus,* from *cūra* spiritual oversight, CURE]

cu+rate's egg *n.* something that is bad but may be euphemistically described as being only partly so. [C20: simile derived from a cartoon in *Punch* (November, 1895) in which a timid curate, who has been served a bad egg while dining with his bishop, says that parts of the egg are excellent]

cu+ra+tive (ˈkjʊərətɪv) *adj.* **1.** able or tending to cure. ~*n.* **2.** anything able to heal or cure. —ˈ**cur·a+tive+ly** *adv.* —ˈ**cur·a+tive+ness** *n.*

cu+ra+tor (kjʊəˈreɪtə) *n.* **1.** the administrative head of a museum, art gallery, or similar institution. **2.** *Law, chiefly Scot.* a guardian of a minor. [C14: from Latin: one who cares, from *cūrāre* to care for, from *cūra* care] —**cu+ra+to+ri+al** (ˌkjʊərəˈtɔ:rɪəl) *adj.* —**cu+ˈra+tor+ˌship** *n.*

curb (kɜ:b) *n.* **1.** something that restrains or holds back. **2.** any enclosing framework, such as a wall of stones around the top of a well. **3. a.** Also called: **curb bit.** a horse's bit with an attached chain or strap, which checks the horse. **b.** Also called: **curb chain.** the chain or strap itself. **4.** a hard swelling on the hock of a horse. ~*vb.* (*tr.*) **5.** to control with or as if with a curb; restrain. ~See also **kerb.** [C15: from Old French *courbe* curved piece of wood or metal, from Latin *curvus* curved]

curb+ing (ˈkɜ:bɪŋ) *n.* the U.S. spelling of **kerbing.**

curb roof *n.* a roof having two or more slopes on each side of the ridge. See also **mansard** (sense 1), **gambrel roof** (sense 2).

curb+stone (ˈkɜ:bˌstəʊn) *n.* the U.S. spelling of **kerbstone.**

curch (kɜ:tʃ) *n.* a woman's plain cap or kerchief. Also called: **curchef.** [C15: probably back formation from *courcheis* (plural), from Old French *couvrechies,* plural of *couvrechef* KERCHIEF]

cur+cu+li·o (kɜ:ˈkju:lɪˌəʊ) *n., pl.* **+li·os.** any of various American weevils, esp. *Conotrachelus nenuphar* (**plum curculio**), a pest of fruit trees. [C18: from Latin: grain weevil]

cur+cu+ma (ˈkɜ:kjʊmə) *n.* any tropical Asian tuberous plant of the genus *Curcuma,* such as *C. longa,* which is the source of turmeric, and *C. zedoaria,* which is the source of zedoary: family *Zingiberaceae.* [C17: from New Latin, from Arabic *kurkum* turmeric]

curd (kɜ:d) *n.* **1.** (*often pl.*) a substance formed from the coagulation of milk by acid or rennet, used in making cheese or eaten as a food. **2.** something similar in consistency. ~*vb.* **3.** to turn into or become curd. [C15: from earlier *crud,* of unknown origin] —ˈ**curd·y** *adj.* —ˈ**curd·i+ness** *n.*

curd cheese *n.* a mild white cheese made from skimmed milk curds, smoother and fattier than cottage cheese.

cur+dle (ˈkɜ:dᵊl) *vb.* **1.** to turn or cause to turn into curd. **2. curdle someone's blood.** to fill someone with fear. [C16 (*crudled,* past participle): from CURD] —ˈ**cur+dler** *n.*

cure (kjʊə) *vb.* **1.** (*tr.*) to get rid of (an ailment, fault, or problem); heal. **2.** (*tr.*) to restore to health or good condition. **3.** (*intr.*) to bring about a cure. **4.** (*tr.*) to preserve (meat, fish, etc.) by salting, smoking, etc. **5.** (*tr.*) **a.** to treat or finish (a substance) by chemical or physical means. **b.** to vulcanize (rubber). **6.** (*tr.*) to assist the hardening of (concrete, mortar, etc.) by keeping it moist. ~*n.* **7.** a return to health, esp. after specific treatment. **8.** any course of medical therapy, esp. one proved effective in combating a disease. **9.** a means of restoring health or improving a condition, situation, etc. **10.** the spiritual and pastoral charge of a parish: *the cure of souls.* **11.** a process or method of preserving meat, fish, etc., by salting, pickling, or smoking. [(n.) C13: from Old French, from Latin *cūra* care; in ecclesiastical sense, from Medieval Latin *cūra* spiritual charge; (vb.) C14: from Old French *curer,* from Latin *cūrāre* to attend to, heal, from *cūra* care] —**'cure·less** *adj.* —**'cur·er** *n.*

cure-all *n.* something reputed to cure anything.

cu·ret *or* **cu·rette** (kjʊə'rɛt) *n.* **1.** a surgical instrument for removing dead tissue, growths, etc., from the walls of certain body cavities. ~*vb.* **·rets** *or* **·rettes, ·ret·ting, ret·ted. 2.** (*tr.*) to scrape or clean with such an instrument. [C18: from French *curette,* from *curer* to heal, make clean; see CURE]

cu·ret·tage (ˌkjʊərɪ'tɑːʒ, kjʊə'rɛtɪdʒ) *or* **cu·rette·ment** (kjʊə'rɛtmənt) *n.* the process of using a curet. See also **D and C.**

cur·few ('kɜːfjuː) *n.* **1.** an official regulation setting restrictions on movement, esp. after a specific time at night. **2.** the time set as a deadline by such a regulation. **3.** (in medieval Europe) **a.** the ringing of a bell to prompt people to extinguish fires and lights. **b.** the time at which the curfew bell was rung. **c.** the bell itself. [C13: from Old French *cuevrefeu,* literally: cover the fire]

cu·ri·a ('kjʊərɪə) *n., pl.* **·ri·ae** (-rɪˌiː). **1.** (*sometimes cap.*) the papal court and government of the Roman Catholic Church. **2.** (in ancient Rome) **a.** any of the ten subdivisions of the Latin, Sabine, or Etruscan tribes. **b.** a meeting place of such a subdivision. **c.** the senate house of Rome. **d.** the senate of an Italian town under Roman administration. **3.** (in the Middle Ages) a court held in the king's name. See also **Curia Regis.** [C16: from Latin, from Old Latin *coviria* (unattested), from CO- + *vir* man] —**'cu·ri·al** *adj.*

Cu·ri·a Re·gis ('riːdʒɪs) *n., pl.* **Cu·ri·ae Re·gis.** (in Norman England) the king's court, which performed all functions of government. [Latin, literally: council of the king]

cu·rie ('kjʊərɪ, -riː) *n.* a unit of radioactivity equal to 3.7×10^{10} disintegrations per second. Abbrev.: Ci [C20: named after Marie CURIE]

Cu·rie ('kjʊərɪ, -riː; *French* ky'ri) *n.* **1. Ma·rie** (ma'ri). 1867–1934, French physicist and chemist, born in Poland: discovered with her husband Pierre the radioactivity of thorium, and discovered and isolated radium and polonium. She shared a Nobel prize for physics (1903) with her husband and Henri Becquerel, and was awarded a Nobel prize for chemistry (1911). **2.** her husband, **Pierre** (pjɛːr). 1859–1906, French physicist and chemist.

Cu·rie point *or* **tem·per·a·ture** *n.* the temperature above which a ferromagnetic substance loses its ferromagnetism and becomes paramagnetic. [C20: named after Pierre CURIE]

Cu·rie's law *n.* the principle that the magnetic susceptibility of a paramagnetic substance is inversely proportional to its thermodynamic temperature. See also **Curie-Weiss law.**

Cu·rie-Weiss law *n.* the principle that the magnetic susceptibility of a paramagnetic substance is inversely proportional to the difference between its temperature and its Curie point. [C20: named after Pierre CURIE and Pierre-Ernest *Weiss* (died 1940), French physicist]

cu·ri·o ('kjʊərɪˌəʊ) *n., pl.* **·ri·os.** a small article valued as a collector's item, esp. something fascinating or unusual. [C19: shortened from CURIOSITY]

cu·ri·o·sa (ˌkjʊərɪ'əʊsə) *n.* (*functioning as pl.*) **1.** curiosities. **2.** books on strange subjects, esp. erotica. [New Latin: from Latin *cūriōsus* CURIOUS]

cu·ri·os·i·ty (ˌkjʊərɪ'ɒsɪtɪ) *n., pl.* **·ties. 1.** an eager desire to know; inquisitiveness. **2. a.** the quality of being curious; strangeness. **b.** (*as modifier*): *the ring had curiosity value only.* **3.** something strange or fascinating. **4.** *Obsolete.* fastidiousness.

cu·ri·ous ('kjʊərɪəs) *adj.* **1.** eager to learn; inquisitive. **2.** over inquisitive; prying. **3.** interesting because of oddness or novelty; strange; unexpected. **4.** *Rare.* (of workmanship, etc.) highly detailed, intricate, or subtle. **5.** *Obsolete.* fastidious or hard to please. [C14: from Latin *cūriōsus* taking pains over something, from *cūra* care] —**'cu·ri·ous·ly** *adv.* —**'cu·ri·ous·ness** *n.*

Cu·ri·ti·ba (ˌkʊərɪ'tiːbə) *n.* a city in SE Brazil, capital of Paraná state: seat of the University of Paraná (1946). Pop.: 483 038 (1970).

cu·ri·um ('kjʊərɪəm) *n.* a silvery-white metallic transuranic element artificially produced from plutonium. Symbol: Cm; atomic no.: 96; half-life of most stable isotope, ^{247}Cm: 1.6×10^7 years; valency: 3; relative density: 13.51 (calculated); melting pt.: 1340°C (approx.). [C20: New Latin, named after Pierre and Marie CURIE]

curl (kɜːl) *vb.* **1.** (*intr.*) (esp. of hair) to grow into curves or ringlets. **2.** (*tr.;* sometimes foll. by *up*) to twist or roll (something, esp. hair) into coils or ringlets. **3.** (often foll. by *up*) to become or cause to become spiral-shaped or curved; coil: *the heat made the leaves curl up.* **4.** (*intr.*) to move in a curving or twisting manner. **5.** (*intr.*) to play the game of curling. **6.** (*intr.;* often foll. by *up*) *Informal.* to feel horrified or disgusted: *horror films make me curl.* **7.** (*tr.*) **curl one's lip.** to show contempt, as by raising a corner of the lip. ~*n.* **8.** a curve or coil of hair. **9.** a curved or spiral shape or mark, as in wood. **10.** the act of curling or state of being curled. **11.** any of various plant diseases characterized by curling of the leaves. **12.** Also called: **rotation.** *Maths.* a vector quantity associated with a vector field that is the vector product of the operator ∇ and a vector function $\boldsymbol{A}$, where $\nabla = \boldsymbol{i}\partial/\partial x + \boldsymbol{j}\partial/\partial y + \boldsymbol{k}\partial/\partial z$, $\boldsymbol{i}, \boldsymbol{j}$, and $\boldsymbol{k}$ being unit vectors. Usually written curl $\boldsymbol{A}$, rot $\boldsymbol{A}$. Compare **divergence** (sense 4), **gradient** (sense 4). ~See also **curl up.** [C14 probably from Middle Dutch *crullen* to curl; related to Middle High German *krol* curly, *krūs* curly]

curl·er ('kɜːlə) *n.* **1.** any of various pins, clasps, or rollers used to curl or wave hair. **2.** a person or thing that curls. **3.** a person who plays curling.

cur·lew ('kɜːljuː) *n.* any large shore bird of the genus *Numenius,* such as *N. arquata* of Europe and Asia: family *Scolopacidae* (sandpipers, etc.), order *Charadriiformes.* They have a long downward-curving bill and occur in northern and arctic regions. Compare **stone curlew.** [C14: from Old French *corlieu,* perhaps of imitative origin]

cur·lew sand·pip·er *n.* a common Eurasian sandpiper, *Calidris ferruginea,* having a brick-red breeding plumage and a greyish winter plumage.

cur·li·cue *or* **cur·ly·cue** ('kɜːlɪˌkjuː) *n.* an intricate ornamental curl or twist. [C19: from CURLY + CUE[2]]

curl·ing ('kɜːlɪŋ) *n.* a game played on ice, esp. in Scotland, in which heavy stones with handles (**curling stones**) are slid towards a target (**tee**).

curl·ing tongs *pl. n.* a metal scissor-like device that is heated, so that strands of hair may be twined around it in order to form curls. Also called: **curling iron, curling irons, curling pins.**

curl·pa·per ('kɜːlˌpeɪpə) *n.* a strip of paper used to roll up and set a section of hair, usually wetted, into a curl.

curl up *vb.* (*adv.*) **1.** (*intr.*) to adopt a reclining position with the legs close to the body and the back rounded. **2.** to become or cause to become spiral-shaped or curved. **3.** (*intr.*) to retire to a quiet cosy setting: *to curl up with a good novel.* **4.** (*intr.*) *Informal.* to be defeated completely. **5.** *Brit. informal.* to be or cause to be disgusted: *his manner makes me curl up.*

curl·y ('kɜːlɪ) *adj.* **curl·i·er, curl·i·est. 1.** tending to curl; curling. **2.** having curls. **3.** (of timber) having irregular curves or waves in the grain. —**'curl·i·ness** *n.*

cur·mudg·eon (kɜː'mʌdʒən) *n.* a surly or miserly person. [C16: of unknown origin] —**cur·'mudg·eon·ly** *adj.*

cur·rach, cur·agh, *or* ***cur·ragh*** *Gaelic.* ('kʌrəx, 'kʌrə) *n.* a Scot. or Irish name for **coracle.** [C15: from Irish Gaelic *currach;* compare CORACLE]

cur·ra·jong ('kʌrəˌdʒɒŋ) *n.* a variant spelling of **kurrajong.**

cur·rant ('kʌrənt) *n.* **1.** a small dried seedless grape of the Mediterranean region, used in cooking. **2.** any of several mainly N temperate shrubs of the genus *Ribes,* esp. *R. rubrum* (redcurrant) and *R. nigrum* (blackcurrant): family *Grossulariaceae.* See also **gooseberry** (sense 1). **3.** the small acid fruit of any of these plants. [C16: shortened from *rayson of Corannte* raisin of Corinth]

cur·ra·wong ('kʌrəˌwɒŋ) *n.* any Australian crowlike songbird of the genus *Strepera,* having black, grey, and white plumage: family *Cracticidae.* Also called: **bell-magpie.** [from a native Australian name]

cur·ren·cy ('kʌrənsɪ) *n., pl.* **·cies. 1.** a metal or paper medium of exchange that is in current use. **2.** general acceptance or circulation; prevalence: *the currency of ideas.* **3.** the period of time during which something is valid, accepted, or in force. **4.** the act of being passed from person to person. [C17: from Medieval Latin *currentia,* literally: a flowing, from Latin *currere* to run, flow]

cur·rent ('kʌrənt) *adj.* **1.** of the immediate present; in progress: *current events.* **2.** most recent; up-to-date: *the current issue of a magazine.* **3.** commonly known, practised, or accepted; widespread: *a current rumour.* **4.** circulating and valid at present: *current coins.* ~*n.* **5.** (esp. of water or air) a steady usually natural flow. **6.** a mass of air, body of water, etc., that has a steady flow in a particular direction. **7.** the rate of flow of such a mass. **8.** Also called: **electric current.** *Physics.* **a.** a flow of electric charge through a conductor. **b.** the rate of flow of this charge. It is usually measured in amperes. Symbol: *I* **9.** a general trend or drift: *currents of opinion.* [C13: from Old French *corant,* literally: running, from *corre* to run, from Latin *currere*] —**'cur·rent·ly** *adv.* —**'cur·rent·ness** *n.*

cur·rent ac·count *n.* **1.** a bank account that usually carries no interest and against which cheques may be drawn at any time. U.S. name: **checking account. 2.** *Economics.* that part of the balance of payments composed of the balance of trade and the invisible balance. Compare **capital account** (sense 1).

cur·rent as·sets *pl. n.* cash and operating assets that are convertible into cash within a year. Also called: **floating assets.** Compare **fixed assets.**

cur·rent den·si·ty *n.* the ratio of the electric current flowing at a particular point in a conductor to the cross-sectional area of the conductor taken perpendicular to the current flow at that point. It is measured in amperes per square metre. Symbol: **J**

cur·rent ex·pens·es *pl. n.* noncapital and usually recurrent expenditures necessary for the operation of a business.

cur·rent li·a·bil·i·ties *pl. n.* business liabilities maturing within a year.

cur·ri·cle ('kʌrɪkᵊl) *n.* a two-wheeled open carriage drawn by two horses side by side. [C18: from Latin *curriculum* from *currus* chariot, from *currere* to run]

cur·ric·u·lum (kə'rɪkjʊləm) *n., pl.* **·la** (-lə) *or* **·lums. 1.** a course of study in one subject at a school or college. **2.** a list of all the courses of study offered by a school or college. **3.** any programme or plan of activities. [C19: from Latin: course, from *currere* to run] —**cur·'ric·u·lar** *adj.*

cur·ric·u·lum vi·tae (kə'rɪkjʊləm 'viːtaɪ, 'vaɪtiː) *n., pl.* **cur·ric·u·la vi·tae** (kə'rɪkjʊlə). an outline of a person's educational and professional history, usually prepared for job applications. [Latin, literally: the course of one's life]

cur·ri·er ('kʌrɪə) *n.* **1.** *Rare.* a person who grooms horses. **2.** a person who curries leather. [C14: from Old French *corier*, from Latin *coriārius* a tanner, from *corium* leather]

cur·ri·er·y ('kʌrɪərɪ) *n., pl.* **·er·ies.** the trade, work, or place of occupation of a leather currier.

cur·rish ('kɜːrɪʃ) *adj.* of or like a cur; rude or bad-tempered. —'**cur·rish·ly** *adv.* —'**cur·rish·ness** *n.*

cur·ry[1] ('kʌrɪ) *n., pl.* **·ries. 1.** a spicy dish of oriental, esp. Indian, origin that is made in many ways but usually consists of meat or fish prepared in a hot piquant sauce. **2.** curry seasoning or sauce. **3. give someone curry.** *Austral. slang.* to assault (a person) verbally or physically. ~*vb.* **·ries, ·ry·ing, ·ried. 4.** (*tr.*) to prepare (food) with curry powder or sauce. [C16: from Tamil *kari* sauce, relish]

cur·ry[2] ('kʌrɪ) *vb.* **·ries, ·ry·ing, ·ried. 1.** to beat vigorously, as in order to clean. **2.** to dress and finish (leather) after it has been tanned to make it strong, flexible, and waterproof. **3.** *Archaic.* to groom (a horse). **4. curry favour.** to ingratiate oneself, esp. with superiors. [C13: from Old French *correer* to make ready, from Vulgar Latin *conrēdāre* (unattested), from *rēdāre* (unattested) to provide, of Germanic origin]

Cur·ry ('kʌrɪ) *n.* **John.** born 1949, English ice skater: won the figure-skating gold medal in the 1976 Olympic Games.

cur·ry·comb ('kʌrɪˌkəʊm) *n.* a square comb consisting of rows of small teeth, used for grooming horses.

cur·ry pow·der *n.* a mixture of finely ground pungent spices, such as turmeric, cumin, coriander, ginger, etc., used in making curries.

cur·ry puff *n.* (in Malaysia) a type of pie or pasty consisting of a pastry case containing curried meat and vegetables.

curse (kɜːs) *n.* **1.** a profane or obscene expression of anger, disgust, surprise, etc.; oath. **2.** an appeal to a supernatural power for harm to come to a specific person, group, etc. **3.** harm resulting from an appeal to a supernatural power: *to be under a curse.* **4.** something that brings or causes great trouble or harm. **5.** a saying, charm, effigy, etc., used to invoke a curse. **6.** an ecclesiastical censure of excommunication. **7.** (preceded by *the*) *Informal.* menstruation or a menstrual period. ~*vb.* **curs·es, curs·ing, cursed** *or* (*Archaic*) **curst. 8.** (*intr.*) to utter obscenities or oaths. **9.** (*tr.*) to abuse (someone) with obscenities or oaths. **10.** (*tr.*) to invoke supernatural powers to bring harm to (someone or something). **11.** (*tr.*) to bring harm upon. **12.** (*tr.*) another word for **excommunicate.** [Old English *cursian* to curse, from *curs* a curse] —'**curs·er** *n.*

curs·ed ('kɜːsɪd, kɜːst) *or* **curst** *adj.* **1.** under a curse. **2.** deserving to be cursed; detestable; hateful. **3.** *Archaic or dialect.* bad-tempered. —'**curs·ed·ly** *adv.* —'**curs·ed·ness** *n.*

curs·es ('kɜːsɪz) *interj. Often facetious.* an expression of disappointment or dismay.

cur·sive ('kɜːsɪv) *adj.* **1.** of or relating to handwriting in which letters are formed and joined in a rapid flowing style. **2.** *Printing.* of or relating to typefaces that resemble handwriting. ~*n.* **3.** a cursive letter or printing type. **4.** a manuscript written in cursive letters. [C18: from Medieval Latin *cursīvus*, running, ultimately from Latin *currere* to run] —'**cur·sive·ly** *adv.*

cur·sor ('kɜːsə) *n.* **1.** the sliding part of a measuring instrument, esp. a transparent sliding square on a slide rule. **2.** any of various devices, typically a movable point of light, that identify a specific position on a visual display unit.

cur·so·ri·al (kɜː'sɔːrɪəl) *adj. Zoology.* adapted for running: *a cursorial skeleton; cursorial birds.*

cur·so·ry ('kɜːsərɪ) *adj.* hasty and usually superficial; quick: *a cursory check.* [C17: from Late Latin *cursōrius* of running, from Latin *cursus* a course, from *currere* to run] —'**cur·so·ri·ly** *adv.* —'**cur·so·ri·ness** *n.*

curst (kɜːst) *vb.* **1.** *Archaic.* a past tense or past participle of **curse.** ~*adj.* **2.** a variant spelling of **cursed.**

curt (kɜːt) *adj.* **1.** rudely blunt and brief; abrupt: *a curt reply.* **2.** short or concise. [C17: from Latin *curtus* cut short, mutilated] —'**curt·ly** *adv.* —'**curt·ness** *n.*

cur·tail (kɜː'teɪl) *vb.* (*tr.*) to cut short; abridge. [C16: changed (through influence of TAIL[1]) from obsolete *curtal* to dock; see CURTAL] —**cur'·tail·er** *n.* —**cur'·tail·ment** *n.*

cur·tail step ('kɜːteɪl) *n.* the step or steps at the foot of a flight of stairs, widened at one or both ends and terminated with a scroll.

cur·tain ('kɜːtᵊn) *n.* **1.** a piece of material that can be drawn across an opening or window, to shut out light or to provide privacy. **2.** a barrier to vision, access, or communication: *a curtain of secrecy.* **3.** a hanging cloth or similar barrier for concealing all or part of a theatre stage from the audience. **4.** (often preceded by *the*) the end of a scene of a play, opera, etc., marked by the fall or closing of the curtain. **5.** the rise or opening of the curtain at the start of a performance. ~*vb.* **6.** (*tr.*; sometimes foll. by *off*) to shut off or conceal with or as if with a curtain. **7.** (*tr.*) to provide (a window, etc.) with curtains. [C13: from Old French *courtine*, from Late Latin *cortīna* enclosed place, curtain, probably from Latin *cohors* courtyard]

cur·tain call *n.* the appearance of performers at the end of a theatrical performance to acknowledge applause.

cur·tain lec·ture *n.* a scolding or rebuke given in private, esp. by a wife to her husband. [alluding to the curtained beds where such rebukes were once given]

cur·tain-rais·er *n.* **1.** *Theatre.* a short dramatic piece presented before the main play. **2.** any preliminary event: *the debate was a curtain-raiser to the election.*

cur·tains ('kɜːtᵊnz) *n. Informal.* death or ruin; the end: *if the enemy see us it will be curtains for us.*

cur·tain speech *n.* **1.** a talk given in front of the curtain after a stage performance, often by the author or an actor. **2.** the final speech of an act or a play.

cur·tain wall *n.* **1.** a non-load-bearing external wall attached to a framed structure, often one that is prefabricated. **2.** a low wall outside the outer wall of a castle, serving as a first line of defence.

cur·tal ('kɜːtᵊl) *Obsolete.* ~*adj.* **1.** cut short. **2.** (of friars) wearing a short frock. ~*n.* **3.** an animal whose tail has been docked. **4.** something that is cut short. [C16: from Old French *courtault* animal whose tail has been docked, from *court* short, from Latin *curtus*; see CURT]

cur·tal axe *n.* an obsolete term for **cutlass.** [C16: alteration by folk etymology of Old French *coutelas* CUTLASS; see CURTAL]

cur·ta·na (kɜː'tɑːnə) *n.* the unpointed sword carried before an English sovereign at a coronation as an emblem of mercy. [C15: from Anglo-Latin, from Old French *cortain*, the name of Roland's sword, which was broken at the point, ultimately from Latin *curtus* short]

cur·tate ('kɜːteɪt) *adj.* shortened. [C17: from Late Latin *curtāre* to shorten, from Latin *curtus* cut short; see CURT]

cur·ti·lage ('kɜːtɪlɪdʒ) *n.* the enclosed area of land adjacent to a dwelling house. [C14: from Old French *cortillage*, from *cortil* a little yard, from *cort* COURT]

Cur·tin ('kɜːtɪn) *n.* **John Jo·seph.** 1885–1945, Australian statesman; prime minister of Australia (1941–45).

curt·sy *or* **curt·sey** ('kɜːtsɪ) *n., pl.* **·sies** *or* **·seys. 1.** a formal gesture of greeting and respect made by women in which the knees are bent, the head slightly bowed, and the skirt held outwards. ~*vb.* **·sies, ·sy·ing, ·sied** *or* **·seys, ·sey·ing, ·seyed. 2.** (*intr.*) to make a curtsy. [C16: variant of COURTESY]

cu·rule ('kjʊəruːl) *adj.* (in ancient Rome) of the highest rank, esp. one entitled to use a curule chair. [C16: from Latin *curūlis* of a chariot, from *currus* chariot, from *currere* to run]

cu·rule chair *n.* an upholstered folding seat with curved legs used by the highest civil officials of ancient Rome.

cur·va·ceous (kɜː'veɪʃəs) *adj. Informal.* (of a woman) having a well-rounded body. —**cur·'va·ceous·ly** *adv.*

cur·va·ture ('kɜːvətʃə) *n.* **1.** something curved or a curved part of a thing. **2.** any normal or abnormal curving of a bodily part: *curvature of the spine.* **3.** *Geom.* the change in inclination of a tangent to a curve over unit length of arc. For a circle or sphere it is the reciprocal of the radius. See also **radius of curvature, centre of curvature. 4.** the act of curving or the state or degree of being curved or bent.

curve (kɜːv) *n.* **1.** a continuously bending line that has no straight parts. **2.** something that curves or is curved, such as a bend in a road or the contour of a woman's body. **3.** the act or extent of curving; curvature. **4.** *Maths.* **a.** a system of points whose coordinates satisfy a given equation; a locus of points. **b.** the graph of a function with one independent variable. **5.** a line representing data, esp. statistical data, on a graph: *an unemployment curve.* **6.** short for **French curve.** ~*vb.* **7.** to take or cause to take the shape or path of a curve; bend. ~Related adj.: **sinuous.** [C15: from Latin *curvāre* to bend, from *curvus* crooked] —**curv·ed·ly** ('kɜːvɪdlɪ) *adv.* —'**curv·ed·ness** *n.* —'**curv·y** *adj.*

cur·vet (kɜː'vɛt) *n.* **1.** *Dressage.* a low leap with all four feet off the ground. ~*vb.* **·vets, ·vet·ting, ·vet·ted** *or* **·vets, ·vet·ing, ·vet·ed. 2.** *Dressage.* to make or cause to make such a leap. **3.** (*intr.*) to prance or frisk about. [C16: from Old Italian *corvetta*, from Old French *courbette*, from *courber* to bend, from Latin *curvāre*]

cur·vi·lin·e·ar (ˌkɜːvɪ'lɪnɪə) *or* **cur·vi·lin·e·al** *adj.* **1.** consisting of, bounded by, or characterized by a curved line. **2.** along a curved line: *curvilinear motion.* **3.** *Maths.* (of a set of coordinates) determined by or determining a system of three orthogonal surfaces. —ˌ**cur·vi·ˌlin·e·'ar·i·ty** *n.* —ˌ**cur·vi·'lin·e·ar·ly** *adv.*

Cur·zon ('kɜːzᵊn) *n.* **1.** Sir **Clif·ford.** 1907-82, English pianist. **2. George Na·than·iel,** 1st Marquis Curzon of Kedleston. 1859-1925, British Conservative statesman; viceroy of India (1898-1905).

Cus·co (*Spanish* 'kusko) *n.* a variant spelling of **Cuzco.**

cus·cus ('kʌskʌs) *n.* any of several large nocturnal phalangers of the genus *Phalanger*, of N Australia, New Guinea, and adjacent islands, having dense fur, prehensile tails, large eyes, and a yellow nose. [C17: New Latin, probably from a native name in New Guinea]

cu·sec ('kjuːsɛk) *n.* a unit of flow equal to 1 cubic foot per second. 1 cusec is equivalent to 0.028 317 cubic metre per second. [C20: from *cu(bic foot per) sec(ond)*]

Cush *or* **Kush** (kʌʃ, kʊʃ) *n. Old Testament.* **1.** the son of Ham and brother of Canaan (Genesis 10:6). **2.** the country of the supposed descendants of Cush (ancient Ethiopia), comprising approximately Nubia and the modern Sudan, and the territory of southern (or Upper) Egypt.

cush·at ('kʌʃət) *n.* another name for **wood pigeon.** [Old English *cūscote*; perhaps related to *sceōtan* to shoot]

Cush·ing ('kʊʃɪŋ) *n.* **Har·vey Wil·liams.** 1869–1939, U.S. neurosurgeon: identified the disease named after him.

Cush·ing's dis·ease *or* **syn·drome** *n.* a rare condition caused by excess corticosteroid hormones in the body, characterized chiefly by obesity of the trunk and face, high blood pressure, fatigue, and loss of calcium from the bones. [C20: named after H.W. CUSHING]

cush·ion ('kʊʃən) *n.* **1.** a bag made of cloth, leather, plastic, etc., filled with feathers, air, or other yielding substance, used for sitting on, leaning against, etc. **2.** something resembling a cushion in function or appearance, esp. one to support or pad or to absorb shock. **3.** the resilient felt-covered rim of a billiard table. **4.** another name for **pillow** (sense 2). **5.** short for **air cushion. 6.** a capital, used in Byzantine, Romanesque, and Norman architecture, in the form of a bowl with a square top. ~*vb.* (*tr.*) **7.** to place, on or as on a cushion. **8.** to provide with cushions. **9.** to protect, esp. against hardship or change. **10.** to lessen or suppress the effects of. **11. a.** to check (the motion) of (a mechanism) gently, esp. by the compression of trapped fluid in a cylinder. **b.** to provide with a means of absorbing shock. [C14: from Old French *coussin,* from Vulgar Latin *coxīnus* (unattested) hip-pillow, from Latin *coxa* hip] —**'cush·ion·y** *adj.*

Cush·it·ic (kʊ'ʃɪtɪk) *n.* **1.** a group of languages of Somalia, Ethiopia, NE Kenya, and adjacent regions: a subfamily within the Afro-Asiatic family of languages. ~*adj.* **2.** denoting, relating to, or belonging to this group of languages.

cush·y ('kʊʃɪ) *adj. Slang.* easy; comfortable: *a cushy job.* [C20: from Hindi *khush* pleasant, from Persian *khōsh*]

cusk (kʌsk) *n., pl.* **cusks** *or* **cusk.** the usual U.S. name for the **torsk.** [C17: probably alteration of *tusk* of Scandinavian origin; compare Old Norse *thorskr* codfish]

CUSO *or* **C.U.S.O.** ('kju:səʊ) *n.* Canadian University Services Overseas; an organization that sends students to work as volunteers in developing countries.

cusp (kʌsp) *n.* **1.** any of the small elevations on the grinding or chewing surface of a tooth. **2.** any of the triangular flaps of a heart valve. **3.** a point or pointed end. **4.** Also called: **spinode.** *Geom.* a point at which two arcs of a curve intersect and at which the two tangents are coincident. **5.** *Architect.* a carving at the meeting place of two arcs. **6.** *Astronomy.* either of the points of a crescent moon or of a satellite or inferior planet in a similar phase. **7.** *Astrology.* any division between houses or signs of the zodiac. [C16: from Latin *cuspis* point, pointed end]

cus·pate ('kʌspɪt, -peɪt), **cus·pat·ed,** *or* **cusped** (kʌspt) *adj.* **1.** having a cusp or cusps. **2.** shaped like a cusp; cusplike.

cus·pid ('kʌspɪd) *n.* a tooth having one point; canine tooth.

cus·pi·date ('kʌspɪˌdeɪt), **cus·pi·dat·ed,** *or* **cus·pi·dal** ('kʌspɪdᵊl) *adj.* **1.** having a cusp or cusps. **2.** (esp. of leaves) narrowing to a point. [C17: from Latin *cuspidāre* to make pointed, from *cuspis* a point]

cus·pi·da·tion (ˌkʌspɪ'deɪʃən) *n. Architect.* decoration using cusps.

cus·pi·dor ('kʌspɪˌdɔ:) *n.* another word (esp. U.S.) for **spittoon.** [C18: from Portuguese, from *cuspir* to spit, from Latin *conspuere,* from *spuere* to spit]

cuss (kʌs) *Informal.* ~*n.* **1.** a curse; oath. **2.** a person or animal, esp. an annoying one. ~*vb.* **3.** another word for **curse** (senses 8, 9).

cuss·ed ('kʌsɪd) *adj. Informal.* **1.** another word for **cursed. 2.** obstinate. **3.** annoying: *a cussed nuisance.* —**'cuss·ed·ly** *adv.* —**'cuss·ed·ness** *n.*

cus·tard ('kʌstəd) *n.* **1.** a baked sweetened mixture of eggs and milk. **2.** a sauce made of milk and sugar thickened with cornflour. [C15: alteration of Middle English *crustade* kind of pie, probably from Old Provençal *croustado,* from *crosta* CRUST]

cus·tard ap·ple *n.* **1.** a West Indian tree, *Annona reticulata:* family *Annonaceae.* **2.** the large heart-shaped fruit of this tree, which has a fleshy edible pulp. **3.** any of several related trees or fruits, esp. the papaw and sweetsop. ~Also called (for senses 1, 2): **bullock's heart.**

cus·tard pie *n.* **a.** a flat, open pie filled with real or artificial custard, as thrown in slapstick comedy. **b.** (*as modifier*): *custard-pie humour.*

cus·tard pow·der *n.* a powder containing cornflour, sugar, etc., for thickening milk to make a yellow sauce. (See **custard** sense 2.).

Cus·ter ('kʌstə) *n.* **George Arm·strong.** 1839–76, U.S. general: killed in a battle with the Sioux Indians at Little Big Horn.

cus·to·di·an (kʌ'stəʊdɪən) *n.* **1.** a person who has custody, as of a prisoner, ward, etc. **2.** a guardian or keeper, as of an art collection, etc. —**cus·'to·di·an·ˌship** *n.*

cus·to·dy ('kʌstədɪ) *n., pl.* **·dies. 1.** the act of keeping safe or guarding, esp. the right of guardianship of a minor. **2.** the state of being held by the police; arrest (esp. in the phrases **in custody, take into custody**). [C15: from Latin *custōdia,* from *custōs* guard, defender] —**cus·to·di·al** (kʌ'stəʊdɪəl) *adj.*

cus·tom ('kʌstəm) *n.* **1.** a usual or habitual practice; typical mode of behaviour. **2.** the long-established habits or traditions of a society collectively; convention: *custom dictates good manners.* **3. a.** a practice which by long-established usage has come to have the force of law. **b.** such practices collectively (esp. in the phrase **custom and practice**). **4.** habitual patronage, esp. of a shop or business. **5.** the customers of a shop or business collectively. **6.** (in feudal Europe) a tribute paid by a vassal to his lord. ~*adj.* **7.** *Chiefly U.S.* made to the specifications of an individual customer (often in the combinations **custom-built, custom-made**). **8.** *Chiefly U.S.* specializing in goods so made. [C12: from Old French *costume,* from Latin *consuētūdō,* from *consuēscere* to grow accustomed to, from *suēscere* to be used to]

cus·tom·a·ble ('kʌstəməbᵊl) *adj.* subject to customs.

cus·tom·ar·y ('kʌstəmərɪ, -təmrɪ) *adj.* **1.** in accordance with custom or habitual practice; usual; habitual. **2.** *Law.* **a.** founded upon long continued practices and usage rather than law. **b.** (of land, esp. a feudal estate) held by custom. ~*n., pl.* **·ar·ies. 3. a.** a statement in writing of customary laws and practices. **b.** a body of such laws and customs. —**'cus·tom·ar·i·ly** *adv.* —**'cus·tom·ar·i·ness** *n.*

cus·tom-built *adj. Chiefly U.S.* (of cars, houses, etc.) made according to the specifications of an individual buyer.

cus·tom·er ('kʌstəmə) *n.* **1.** a person who buys. **2.** *Informal.* a person with whom one has dealings: *a queer customer.*

cus·tom·ize *or* **cus·tom·ise** ('kʌstəˌmaɪz) *vb.* (*tr.*) to make something according to a customer's individual requirements.

cus·tom-made *adj. Chiefly U.S.* (of suits, dresses, etc.) made according to the specifications of an individual buyer.

cus·toms ('kʌstəmz) *n.* (*functioning as sing. or pl.*) **1.** duty on imports or exports. **2.** the government department responsible for the collection of these duties. **3.** the part of a port, airport, frontier station, etc., where baggage and freight are examined for dutiable goods and contraband. **4.** the procedure for examining baggage and freight, paying duty, etc. **5.** (*as modifier*) *customs officer.*

cus·toms house *n.* a government office, esp. at a port, where customs are collected and ships cleared for entry.

cus·toms un·ion *n.* an association of nations which promotes free trade within the union and establishes common tariffs on trade with nonmember nations.

cus·tos ('kʌstɒs) *n., pl.* **cus·to·des** (kʌ'stəʊdi:z). a superior in the Franciscan religious order. Also called (in England): **guardian.** [C15: from Latin: keeper, guard]

cus·tu·mal ('kʌstjʊməl) *n., adj.* another word for **customary** (senses 2, 3). [C16: from Medieval Latin *custumālis* relating to CUSTOM]

cut (kʌt) *vb.* **cuts, cut·ting, cut. 1.** to open up or incise (a person or thing) with a sharp edge or instrument; gash. **2.** (of a sharp instrument) to penetrate or incise (a person or thing). **3.** to divide or be divided with or as if with a sharp instrument: *cut a slice of bread.* **4.** (*intr.*) to use a sharp-edged instrument or an instrument that cuts. **5.** (*tr.*) to trim or prune by or as if by clipping: *to cut hair.* **6.** (*tr.*) to reap or mow (a crop, grass, etc.). **7.** (*tr.*) to geld or castrate. **8.** (*tr.;* sometimes foll. by *out*) to make, form, or shape by cutting: *to cut a suit.* **9.** (*tr.*) to hollow or dig out; excavate: *to cut a tunnel through the mountain.* **10.** to strike (an object) sharply. **11.** (*tr.*) *Sport.* to hit (a ball) with a downward slicing stroke so as to impart spin or cause it to fall short. **12.** *Cricket.* to hit (the ball) to the off side, usually between cover and third man, with a roughly horizontal bat. **13.** to hurt or wound the feelings of (a person), esp. by malicious speech or action. **14.** (*tr.*) *Informal.* to refuse to recognize; snub. **15.** (*tr.*) *Informal.* to absent oneself from (an activity, location, etc.), esp. without permission or in haste: *to cut a class.* **16.** (*tr.*) to abridge, shorten, or edit by excising a part or parts. **17.** (*tr.;* often foll. by *down*) to lower, reduce, or curtail: *to cut losses.* **18.** (*tr.*) to dilute or weaken: *to cut whisky with water.* **19.** (*tr.*) to dissolve or break up: *to cut fat.* **20.** (when *intr.,* foll. by *across* or *through*) to cross or traverse: *the footpath cuts through the field.* **21.** (*intr.*) to make a sharp or sudden change in direction; veer. **22.** to grow (teeth) through the gums or (of teeth) to appear through the gums. **23.** (*intr.*) *Films.* **a.** to call a halt to a shooting sequence. **b.** (foll. by *to*) to move quickly to another scene. **24.** *Films.* to edit film. **25.** to switch off a light, car engine, etc. **26.** (*tr.*) (of a performer, recording company, etc.) to make (a record or tape of a song, concert, performance, etc.). **27.** *Cards.* **a.** to divide (the pack) at random into two parts after shuffling. **b.** (*intr.*) to pick cards from a spread pack to decide dealer, partners, etc. **28.** (*tr.*) to remove (material) from (an object) by means of a chisel, lathe, etc. **29.** (*tr.*) (of a tool) to bite into (an object). **30.** (*intr.*) (of a horse) to injure the leg just above the hoof by a blow from the opposite foot. **31. cut a caper** *or* **capers. a.** to skip or jump playfully. **b.** to act or behave playfully; frolic. **32. cut both ways. a.** to have both good and bad effects. **b.** to affect both sides of something, as two parties in an argument, etc. **33. cut a dash.** to behave or dress showily. **34. cut (a person) dead.** *Informal.* to ignore (a person) completely. **35. cut a (good, poor, etc.) figure.** to appear or behave in a specified manner. **36. cut and run.** *Informal.* to make a rapid escape, esp. from an unpleasant situation. **37. cut it fine.** *Informal.* to leave little or no margin for error. **38. cut corners.** to take the easiest or shortest way, esp. at the expense of high standards: *we could finish this project early only if we cut corners.* **39. cut loose.** to free or become freed from restraint, custody, anchorage, etc. **40. cut no ice.** *Informal.* to fail to make an impression. **41. cut one's teeth on.** *Informal.* **a.** to use at an early age or stage. **b.** to practise on. ~*adj.* **42.** detached, divided, or separated by cutting. **43.** *Botany.* incised or divided: *cut leaves.* **44.** made, shaped, or fashioned by cutting. **45.** reduced or diminished by or as if by cutting: *cut prices.* **46.** gelded or castrated. **47.** weakened or diluted. **48.** *Brit.* a slang word for **drunk:** *half cut.* **49. cut and dried.** *Informal.* settled or arranged in advance. ~*n.* **50.** the act of cutting. **51.** a stroke or incision made by cutting; gash. **52.** a piece or part cut off, esp. a section of food cut from the whole: *a cut of meat.* **53.** the edge of anything cut or sliced. **54.** a passage, channel, path, etc., cut or hollowed out. **55.** an omission or deletion, esp. in a text, film, or play. **56.** a reduction in price, salary, etc. **57.** short for **power cut. 58.** *Chiefly U.S.* a quantity of timber cut during a specific time or operation. **59.** *Informal.* a portion or share. **60.** *Informal.* a straw, slip of paper, etc., used in drawing lots. **61.** the manner or style in which a thing, esp. a garment, is cut; fashion. **62.** a direct route; short cut. **63.** the U.S. name for **block** (sense 13). **64.** *Sport.* the spin of a cut ball. **65.** *Cricket.* a stroke made with the bat in a roughly horizontal position. **66.** *Films.* an immediate transition from one shot to the next, brought about by splicing the two shots together. **67.**

words or an action that hurt another person's feelings. **68.** a refusal to recognize an acquaintance; snub. **69.** *Informal, chiefly U.S.* an unauthorized absence, esp. from a school class. **70.** *Chem.* a fraction obtained in distillation, as in oil refining. **71.** the depth of metal removed in a single pass of a machine tool. **72.** *Brit.* a stretch of water, esp. a canal. **73. a cut above.** *Informal.* superior to; better than. **74. cold cuts.** cooked meats. ~See also **cut across, cut along, cutback, cut down, cut in, cut off, cut out, cut up.** [C13: probably of Scandinavian origin; compare Norwegian *kutte* to cut, Icelandic *kuti* small knife]

cut a·cross *vb.* (*intr., prep.*) **1.** to be contrary to ordinary procedure or limitations: *opinion on the Common Market still cuts clean across party lines.* **2.** to cross or traverse, making a shorter route: *she cut across the field quickly.*

cut a·long *vb.* (*intr., adv.*) *Brit. informal.* to hurry off.

cut and thrust *n.* **1.** *Fencing.* using both the blade and the point of a sword. **2.** (in argument, debate, etc.) a lively and spirited exchange of ideas or opinions.

cu·ta·ne·ous (kju:'teɪnɪəs) *adj.* of, relating to, or affecting the skin. [C16: from New Latin *cutāneus*, from Latin *cutis* skin; see HIDE[2]] —**cu·'ta·ne·ous·ly** *adv.*

cut·a·way ('kʌtəˌweɪ) *n.* **1.** a man's coat cut diagonally from the front waist to the back of the knees. **2. a.** a drawing or model of a machine, engine, etc., in which part of the casing is omitted to reveal the workings. **b.** (*as modifier*): *a cutaway model.*

cut·back ('kʌtˌbæk) *n.* **1.** a decrease or reduction. **2.** another word (esp. U.S.) for **flashback.** ~*vb.* **cut back** (*adv.*). **3.** (*tr.*) to shorten by cutting off the end; prune. **4.** (when *intr.*, foll. by *on*) to reduce or make a reduction (in). **5.** *Chiefly U.S* (in films) to show an event that took place earlier in the narrative; flash back.

cutch (kʌtʃ) *n.* another name for **catechu.**

Cutch (kʌtʃ) *n.* a variant spelling of **Kutch.**

cut·cher·ry *or* **cut·cher·y** ('kʌtʃərɪ) *n., pl.* **·cher·ries** *or* **·cher·ies.** (formerly in India) government offices and law courts collectively.

cut down *vb.* (*adv.*) **1.** (*tr.*) to fell. **2.** (when *intr.*, often foll. by *on*) to reduce or make a reduction (in): *to cut down on drink.* **3.** (*tr.*) to remake (an old garment) in order to make a smaller one. **4.** (*tr.*) to kill: *he was cut down in battle.* **5. cut (a person) down to size.** to reduce in importance or decrease the conceit of.

cute (kju:t) *adj.* **1.** appealing or attractive, esp. in a pretty way. **2.** *Informal, chiefly U.S.* affecting cleverness or prettiness. **3.** clever; shrewd. [C18 (in the sense: clever): shortened from ACUTE] —**'cute·ly** *adv.* —**'cute·ness** *n.*

cut glass *n.* **1.** glass, esp. bowls, vases, etc., decorated by facet-cutting or grinding. **2.** (*modifier*): *a cut-glass vase.*

Cuth·bert ('kʌθbət) *n.* **Saint.** (?635–87A.D.), English monk; bishop of Lindisfarne. Feast day: March 20.

cu·ti·cle ('kju:tɪkᵊl) *n.* **1.** dead skin, esp. that round the base of a fingernail or toenail. **2.** another name for **epidermis. 3.** any covering layer or membrane. **4.** the protective layer, containing cutin, that covers the epidermis of higher plants. **5.** the hard protective layer covering the epidermis of many invertebrates. [C17: from Latin *cutīcula* diminutive of *cutis* skin] —**cu·tic·u·lar** (kju:'tɪkjʊlə) *adj.*

cu·tic·u·la (kju:'tɪkjʊlə) *n., pl.* **·lae** (-li:). *Anatomy.* cuticle. [C18: from Latin; see CUTICLE]

cut·ie *or* **cut·ey** ('kju:tɪ) *n. Slang, chiefly U.S.* a person regarded as appealing or attractive, esp. a girl or woman.

cut in *vb.* (*adv.*) **1.** (*intr.;* often foll. by *on*) Also: **cut into.** to break in or interrupt. **2.** (*intr.*) to interrupt a dancing couple to dance with one of them. **3.** (*intr.*) (of a driver, motor vehicle, etc.) to draw in front of another vehicle leaving too little space. **4.** (*tr.*) *Informal.* to allow to have a share. **5.** (*intr.*) to take the place of a person in a card-game. ~*n.* **cut-in. 6.** *Films.* a separate shot or scene inserted at a relevant point.

cu·tin ('kju:tɪn) *n.* a waxy waterproof substance, consisting of derivatives of fatty acids, that is the main constituent of the plant cuticle. [C19: from Latin *cutis* skin + -IN]

cu·tin·ize *or* **cu·tin·ise** ('kju:tɪˌnaɪz) *vb.* to become or cause to become covered or impregnated with cutin. —**ˌcu·tin·i·'za·tion** *or* **ˌcu·tin·i·'sa·tion** *n.*

cu·tis ('kju:tɪs) *n., pl.* **·tes** (-ti:z) *or* **·tis·es.** *Anatomy.* a technical name for the **skin.** [C17: from Latin: skin]

cut·lass ('kʌtləs) *n.* a curved, one-edged sword formerly used by sailors. [C16: from French *coutelas*, from *coutel* knife, from Latin *cultellus* a small knife, from *culter* knife; see COULTER]

cut·lass fish *n. U.S.* another name for the **hairtail** (the fish).

cut·ler ('kʌtlə) *n.* a person who makes or sells cutlery. [C14: from French *coutelier*, ultimately from Latin *culter* knife; see CUTLASS]

cut·ler·y ('kʌtlərɪ) *n.* **1.** implements used for eating, such as knives, forks, and spoons. **2.** instruments used for cutting. **3.** the art or business of a cutler.

cut·let ('kʌtlɪt) *n.* **1.** a piece of meat taken esp. from the best end of neck of lamb, pork, etc. **2.** a flat croquette of minced chicken, lobster, etc. [C18: from Old French *costelette*, literally: a little rib, from *coste* rib, from Latin *costa*]

cut off *vb.* (*tr., adv.*) **1.** to remove by cutting. **2.** to intercept or interrupt something, esp. a telephone conversation. **3.** to discontinue the supply of: *to cut off the water.* **4.** to bring to an end. **5.** to deprive of rights; disinherit: *she was cut off without a penny.* **6.** to sever or separate: *she was cut off from her family.* **7.** to occupy a position so as to prevent or obstruct (a retreat or escape). ~*n.* **cut·off. 8. a.** the act of cutting off; limit or termination. **b.** (*as modifier*): *the cutoff point.* **9.** *Chiefly U.S.* a route or way that is shorter than the usual one; short cut. **10.** a device to terminate the flow of a fluid in a pipe or duct. **11.** the remnant of metal, plastic, etc., left after parts have been machined or trimmed. **12.** *Electronics.* **a.** the value of voltage, frequency, etc., below or above which an electronic device cannot function efficiently. **b.** (*as modifier*): *cutoff voltage.* **13.** a channel cutting across the neck of a meander, which leaves an oxbow lake. **14.** another name for **oxbow** (the lake).

cut out *vb.* (*adv.*) **1.** (*tr.*) to delete or remove. **2.** (*tr.*) to shape or form by cutting: *to cut out a dress.* **3.** (*tr.; usually passive*) to suit or equip for: *you're not cut out for this job.* **4.** (*intr.*) (of an engine, etc.) to cease to operate suddenly. **5.** (*tr.*) *Printing.* to remove the background from a photograph or drawing to make the outline of the subject stand out. **6.** (*intr.*) (of an electrical device) to switch off, usually automatically. **7.** (*tr.*) *Informal.* to oust and supplant (a rival). **8.** (*intr.*) (of a person) to be excluded from a card game. **9.** (*tr.*) *Informal.* to cease doing something, esp. something undesirable (esp. in the phrase **cut it out**). **10.** (*tr.*) *Soccer.* to intercept (a pass). **11.** (*tr.*) *Austral.* to separate (cattle) from a herd. **12.** (*intr.*) *Austral.* to end or finish: *the road cuts out at the creek.* **13. have one's work cut out.** to have as much work as one can manage. ~*n.* **cut·out. 14.** something that has been or is intended to be cut out from something else. **15.** a photograph or drawing from which the background has been cut away. **16.** a device that switches off or interrupts an electric circuit, esp. a switch acting as a safety device. **17.** an impressed stamp cut out from an envelope for collecting purposes. **18.** *Austral, slang.* the end of shearing.

cut-price *or esp. U.S.* **cut-rate** *adj.* **1.** available at prices or rates below the standard price or rate. **2.** (*prenominal*) offering goods or services at prices below the standard price: *a cut-price shop.*

cut·purse ('kʌtˌpɜ:s) *n.* an archaic word for **pickpocket.**

CUTS (kʌts) *n. acronym for* Computer Users' Tape System.

cut string *n.* another name for **bridgeboard.**

Cut·tack (kʌ'tæk) *n.* a city in NE India, in E Orissa near the mouth of the Mahanadi River: former state capital until 1948. Pop.: 194 068 (1971).

cut·ter ('kʌtə) *n.* **1.** a person or thing that cuts, esp. a person who cuts cloth for clothing. **2.** a sailing boat with its mast stepped further aft so as to have a larger foretriangle than that of a sloop. **3.** a ship's boat, powered by oars or sail, for carrying passengers or light cargo. **4.** a small lightly armed boat, as used in the enforcement of customs regulations. **5.** a pig weighing between 68 and 82 kg, from which fillets and larger joints are cut.

cut·throat ('kʌtˌθrəʊt) *n.* **1.** a person who cuts throats; murderer. **2.** Also called: **cutthroat razor.** *Brit.* a razor with a long blade that usually folds into the handle. U.S. name: **straight razor.** ~*adj.* **3.** bloodthirsty or murderous; cruel. **4.** fierce or relentless in competition: *cutthroat prices.* **5.** (of some games) played by three people: *cutthroat poker.*

cut·ting ('kʌtɪŋ) *n.* **1.** a piece cut off from the main part of something. **2.** *Horticulture.* **a.** a method of vegetative propagation in which a part of a plant, such as a stem or leaf, is induced to form its own roots. **b.** a part separated for this purpose. **3.** Also called (esp. U.S.): **clipping.** an article, photograph, etc., cut from a newspaper or other publication. **4.** the editing process by which a film is cut and made. **5.** an excavation in a piece of high land for a road, railway, etc., enabling it to remain at approximately the same level. **6.** (*modifier*) designed for or adapted to cutting; edged; sharp: *a cutting tool.* ~*adj.* **7.** keen; piercing: *a cutting wind.* **8.** tending to hurt the feelings: *a cutting remark.* —**'cut·ting·ly** *adv.*

cut·ting grass *n.* a W African name for **cane rat** (sense 1).

cut·tle ('kʌtᵊl) *n.* **1.** short for **cuttlefish** or **cuttlebone. 2. little cuttle.** a small cuttlefish, *Sepiola atlantica*, often found on beaches. [Old English *cudele;* related to Old High German *kiot* bag, Norwegian dialect *kaule* cuttle, Old English *codd* bag]

cut·tle·bone ('kʌtᵊlˌbəʊn) *n.* the internal calcareous shell of the cuttlefish, used as a mineral supplement to the diet of cage birds and as a polishing agent.

cut·tle·fish ('kʌtᵊlˌfɪʃ) *n., pl.* **·fish** *or* **·fish·es.** any cephalopod mollusc of the genus *Sepia* and related genera, which occur near the bottom of inshore waters and have a broad flattened body: order *Decapoda* (decapods). Sometimes shortened to **cuttle.** See also **squid.**

cut·ty ('kʌtɪ) *Northern Brit. dialect.* ~*adj.* **1.** short or cut short. ~*n., pl.* **·ties. 2.** something cut short, such as a spoon or short-stemmed tobacco pipe. **3.** an immoral girl or woman (in Scotland used as a general term of abuse for a woman). **4.** a short thickset girl. [C18 (Scottish and northern English): from CUT (vb.)]

Cut·ty Sark *n.* a three-masted merchant clipper built in 1869 which held the blue riband for many years: now kept at Greenwich, London. [C19: named after the witch in Robert Burns' poem *Tam O'Shanter*, who wore only a *cutty sark* (short shirt)]

cut·ty stool *n.* (formerly in Scotland) the church seat on which an unchaste person sat while being harangued by the minister.

cut up *vb.* (*tr., adv.*) **1.** to cut into pieces. **2.** to inflict injuries on. **3.** (*usually passive*) *Informal.* to affect the feelings of deeply. **4.** *Informal.* to subject to severe criticism. **5. cut up rough.** *Brit. informal.* to become angry or bad-tempered.

cut-up tech·nique *n.* a technique of writing involving cutting up lines or pages of prose and rearranging these fragments, popularized by the novelist William Burroughs.

cut+wa·ter ('kʌtˌwɔːtə) *n.* the forward part of the stem of a vessel, which cuts through the water.

cut+work ('kʌtˌwɜːk) *n.* openwork embroidery in which the pattern is cut away from the background.

cut+worm ('kʌtˌwɜːm) *n.* the caterpillar of various noctuid moths, esp. those of the genus *Argrotis,* which is a pest of young crop plants in North America.

cu+vette (kjuː'vɛt) *n.* a shallow dish or vessel for holding liquid. [C17: from French, diminutive of *cuve* cask, from Latin *cupa*]

Cux+ha+ven ('kʊksˌhɑːvᵊn; *German* kʊks'haːfᵊn) *n.* a port in N West Germany, at the mouth of the River Elbe. Pop.: 47 600 (1970).

Cu+ya+bá (*Portuguese* ˌkuja'ba) *n.* a variant spelling of **Cuiabá.**

Cuyp *or* **Kuyp** (kaɪp; *Dutch* kœjp) *n.* **Ael·bert** ('aːlbɛrt). 1620–91, Dutch painter of landscapes and animals.

Cuz+co *or* **Cus+co** (*Spanish* 'kusko) *n.* a city in S central Peru: former capital of the Inca Empire, with extensive Inca remains; university (1692). Pop.: 121 464 (1972).

CVA *abbrev. for* cerebrovascular accident.

C.V.O. *abbrev. for* Commander of the Royal Victorian Order.

CW **1.** *Radio. abbrev. for* continuous wave. ~*n.* **2. a.** an informal term for **Morse code. b.** (*as modifier*)*: his CW speed is 30 words per minute.*

Cwlth. *abbrev. for* Commonwealth.

cwm (kuːm) *n.* **1.** (in Wales) a valley. **2.** *Geology.* another name for **cirque** (sense 1).

Cwm+bran (ˌkuːm'brɑːn) *n.* a new town in SE Wales, in central Gwent, developed in the 1950s. Pop.: 32 614 (1971).

c.w.o. *or* **C.W.O.** *abbrev. for* cash with order.

cwt. *abbrev. for* hundredweight. [*c,* from the Latin numeral *C* one hundred (*centum*)]

CY *international car registration for* Cyprus.

-cy *suffix.* **1.** (*forming nouns from adjectives ending in -t, -tic, -te, and -nt*) indicating state, quality, or condition: *plutocracy; lunacy; intimacy; infancy.* **2.** (*forming abstract nouns from other nouns*) rank or office: *captaincy.* [via Old French from Latin *-cia, -tia,* Greek *-kia, -tia,* abstract noun suffixes]

cy·an ('saɪæn, 'saɪən) *n.* **1.** a highly saturated green-blue that is the complementary colour of red and forms, with magenta and yellow, a set of primary colours. ~*adj.* **2.** of this colour: *a cyan filter.* [C19: from Greek *kuanos* dark blue]

cy·an- *combining form.* variant of **cyano-** before a vowel: *cyanamide; cyanide.*

cy+an·a+mide (saɪ'ænəˌmaɪd, -mɪd) *or* **cy+an·a+mid** (saɪ'ænəmɪd) *n.* **1.** Also called: **cy·a+no+gen·a·mide** ('saɪənəʊ'dʒɛnəˌmaɪd, -mɪd). a white or colourless crystalline soluble weak dibasic acid, which can be hydrolysed to urea. Formula: H_2NCN. **2.** a salt or ester of cyanamide. **3.** short for **calcium cyanamide.**

cy·a+nate ('saɪəˌneɪt) *n.* any salt or ester of cyanic acid, containing the ion ^{-}OCN or the group -OCN.

cy+an+ic (saɪ'ænɪk) *adj. Rare.* having a blue or bluish colour.

cy+an+ic ac·id *n.* a colourless poisonous volatile liquid acid that hydrolyses readily to ammonia and carbon dioxide. Formula: HOCN. Compare **isocyanic acid, fulminic acid.**

cy·a+nide ('saɪəˌnaɪd) *or* **cy·a+nid** ('saɪənɪd) *n.* **1.** any salt of hydrocyanic acid. Cyanides contain the ion CN^- and are extremely poisonous. **2.** another name (not in technical usage) for **nitrile.** —ˌ**cy·a+ni+'da+tion** *n.*

cy·a+nide pro+cess *n.* a process for recovering gold and silver from ores by treatment with a weak solution of sodium cyanide.

cy·a+nine ('saɪəˌniːn) *or* **cy·a+nin** ('saɪənɪn) *n.* **1.** a blue dye used to extend the sensitivity of photographic emulsions to colours other than blue and ultraviolet. **2.** any of a class of chemically related dyes, used for the same purpose.

cy·a+nite ('saɪəˌnaɪt) *n.* a grey, green, or blue mineral consisting of aluminium silicate in triclinic crystalline form. It occurs in metamorphic rocks and is used as a refractory. Formula: Al_2SiO_5. —**cy·a+nit+ic** (ˌsaɪə'nɪtɪk) *adj.*

cy·an·o- *or before a vowel* **cy·an-** *combining form.* **1.** blue or dark blue: *cyanotype.* **2.** indicating cyanogen: *cyanohydrin.* **3.** indicating cyanide. [from Greek *kuanos* (adj.) dark blue, (n.) dark blue enamel, lapis lazuli]

cy·a+no+co+bal·a+min (ˌsaɪənəʊkəʊ'bæləmɪn) *n.* a complex red crystalline compound, containing cyanide and cobalt and occurring in liver: lack of it in the tissues leads to pernicious anaemia. Formula: $C_{63}H_{88}O_{14}N_{14}PCo$. Also called: **vitamin B$_{12}$.** [C20: from CYANO- + COBAL(T) + (VIT)AMIN]

cy+an·o+gen (saɪ'ænədʒɪn) *n.* an extremely poisonous colourless flammable gas with an almond-like odour: has been used in chemical warfare. Formula: $(CN)_2$. [C19: from French *cyanogène;* see CYANO-, -GEN; so named because it is one of the constituents of Prussian blue]

cy·a+no+hy+drin (ˌsaɪənəʊ'haɪdrɪn) *n.* any of a class of organic compounds containing a cyanide group and a hydroxyl group bound to the same carbon atom.

cy·a+no+sis (ˌsaɪə'nəʊsɪs) *n. Pathol.* a bluish-purple discoloration of skin and mucous membranes usually resulting from a deficiency of oxygen in the blood. —**cy·a+not+ic** (ˌsaɪə'nɒtɪk) *adj.*

cy+an·o+type (saɪ'ænəˌtaɪp) *n.* another name for **blueprint** (sense 1).

Cyb·e·le ('sɪbɪlɪ) *n. Classical myth.* the Phrygian goddess of nature, mother of all living things and consort of Attis; identified with the Greek Rhea or Demeter.

cy+ber+nate ('saɪbəˌneɪt) *vb.* to control (a manufacturing process, etc.) with a servomechanism or (of a process) to be controlled by a servomechanism. [C20: from CYBER(NETICS) + -ATE[1]] —ˌ**cy+ber+'na+tion** *n.*

cy+ber+net+ics (ˌsaɪbə'nɛtɪks) *n.* (*functioning as sing.*) the branch of science concerned with control systems in electronic and mechanical devices and the extent to which useful comparisons can be made between man-made and biological systems. See also **feedback** (sense 1). [C20: from Greek *kubernētēs* steersman, from *kubernan* to steer, control] —ˌ**cy+ber+'net+ic** *adj.* —ˌ**cy+ber+'net·i+cist** *n.*

cy+cad ('saɪkæd) *n.* any tropical or subtropical gymnosperm plant of the order *Cycadales,* having an unbranched stem with fernlike leaves crowded at the top. See also **sago palm** (sense 2). [C19: from New Latin *Cycas* name of genus, from Greek *kukas,* scribe's error for *koïkas,* from *koïx* a kind of palm, probably of Egyptian origin] —ˌ**cyc·a+'da+ceous** *adj.*

Cyc+la+des ('sɪkləˌdiːz) *pl. n.* a group of over 200 islands in the S Aegean Sea, forming a department of Greece. Capital: Hermoupolis (Siros). Pop.: 86 084 (1971). Area: 2572 sq. km (1003 sq. miles). Modern Greek name: **Kikládhes.** —**Cy+clad+ic** (sɪ'klædɪk) *adj.*

cy+cla+mate ('saɪkləˌmeɪt, 'sɪkləmeɪt) *n.* a salt or ester of cyclamic acid. Certain of the salts have a very sweet taste and were formerly used as food additives and sugar substitutes. [C20: *cycl(ohexyl-sulph)amate*]

cyc+la+men ('sɪkləmən, -ˌmɛn) *n.* **1.** any Old World plant of the primulaceous genus *Cyclamen,* having nodding white, pink, or red flowers, with reflexed petals. See also **sowbread.** ~*adj.* **2.** of a dark reddish-purple colour. [C16: from Medieval Latin, from Latin *cyclaminos,* from Greek *kuklaminos,* probably from *kuklos* circle, referring to the bulb-like roots]

cy+cle ('saɪkᵊl) *n.* **1.** a recurring period of time in which certain events or phenomena occur and reach completion or repeat themselves in a regular sequence. **2.** a completed series of events that follows or is followed by another series of similar events occurring in the same sequence. **3.** the time taken or needed for one such series. **4.** a vast period of time; age; aeon. **5.** a group of poems or prose narratives forming a continuous story about a central figure or event: *the Arthurian cycle.* **6.** a series of miracle plays: *the Chester cycle.* **7.** a group or sequence of songs (see **song-cycle**). **8.** short for **bicycle, tricycle, motorcycle,** etc. **9.** *Astronomy.* the orbit of a celestial body. **10.** a recurrent series of events or processes in plants and animals: *a life cycle; a growth cycle.* **11.** *Physics.* a continuous change or a sequence of changes in the state of a system that leads to the restoration of the system to its original state after a finite period of time. **12.** one of a series of repeated changes in the magnitude of a periodically varying quantity, such as current or voltage. **13.** *Computer technol.* **a.** a set of operations that can be both treated and repeated as a unit. **b.** the time required to complete a set of operations. **14.** (in generative grammar) the set of cyclic rules. ~*vb.* **15.** (*tr.*) to process through a cycle or system. **16.** (*intr.*) to move in or pass through cycles. **17.** to travel by or ride a bicycle or tricycle. [C14: from Late Latin *cyclus,* from Greek *kuklos* cycle, circle, ring, wheel; see WHEEL]

cy+cle of e·ro+sion *n.* the hypothetical sequence of modifications to the earth's surface by erosion, from the original uplift of the land to the ultimate low plain, usually divided into the youthful, mature, and old stages.

cy+clic ('saɪklɪk, 'sɪklɪk) *or* **cy+cli+cal** *adj.* **1.** recurring or revolving in cycles. **2.** (of an organic compound) containing a closed saturated or unsaturated ring of atoms. See also **heterocyclic** and **homocyclic. 3.** *Botany.* **a.** arranged in whorls: *cyclic petals.* **b.** having parts arranged in this way: *cyclic flowers.* **4.** *Music.* of or relating to a musical form consisting of several movements sharing thematic material. **5.** *Geom.* (of a polygon) having vertices that lie on a circle. **6.** (in generative grammar) denoting one of a set of transformational rules all of which must apply to a clause before any one of them applies to any clause in which the first clause is embedded. —'**cy+cli+cal+ly** *adv.*

cy+clic pitch lev+er *n.* a lever in a helicopter to change the angle of attack of individual rotor blades, causing the helicopter to move forwards, backwards, or sideways. Compare **collective pitch lever.**

cy+clist ('saɪklɪst) *or U.S.* **cy+cler** *n.* a person who rides or travels by bicycle, motorcycle, etc.

cy·clo- *or before a vowel* **cycl-** *combining form.* **1.** indicating a circle or ring: *cyclotron.* **2.** denoting a cyclic compound: *cyclohexane.* [from Greek *kuklos* CYCLE]

cy+clo+al+kane (ˌsaɪkləʊ'ælkeɪn) *n.* any saturated hydrocarbon similar to an alkane but having a cyclic molecular structure and the general formula C_nH_{2n}. Also called: **cycloparaffin.**

cy·clo-cross *n.* **a.** a form of cycle race held over rough ground. **b.** this sport.

cy+clo+graph ('saɪkləʊˌgrɑːf, -ˌgræf) *n.* another name for **arcograph.**

cy+clo+hex+ane (ˌsaɪkləʊ'hɛkseɪn, ˌsɪk-) *n.* a colourless insoluble flammable liquid cycloalkane with a pungent odour, made by hydrogenation of benzene and used as a paint remover and solvent. Formula: C_6H_{12}.

cy+cloid ('saɪklɔɪd) *adj.* **1.** resembling a circle. **2.** (of fish scales) rounded, thin, and smooth-edged, as those of the salmon. **3.** *Psychiatry.* (of a type of personality) characterized by exaggerated swings of mood between elation and depression. See also **cyclothymia.** ~*n.* **4.** *Geom.* the curve described by a point on the circumference of a circle as the circle rolls along a straight line. Compare **trochoid** (sense 1). **5.** a fish that has cycloid scales. —**cy+'cloi+dal** *adj.* —**cy+'cloi+dal+ly** *adv.*

cy·clom·e·ter (saɪˈklɒmɪtə) *n.* a device that records the number of revolutions made by a wheel and hence the distance travelled. —**cy·ˈclom·e·try** *n.*

cy·clone (ˈsaɪkləʊn) *n.* **1.** another name for **depression** (sense 6). **2.** a violent tropical storm; hurricane. ~*adj.* **3.** *Austral.* (of fencing) made of interlaced wire and metal. [C19: from Greek *kuklōn* a turning around, from *kukloein* to revolve, from *kuklos* wheel] —**cy·clon·ic** (saɪˈklɒnɪk), **cy·ˈclon·i·cal,** *or* **ˈcy·clo·nal** *adj.* —**cy·ˈclon·i·cal·ly** *adv.*

cy·clo·nite (ˈsaɪkləˌnaɪt) *n.* a white crystalline insoluble explosive prepared by the action of nitric acid on hexamethylenetetramine; cyclotrimethylenetrinitramine: used in bombs and shells. Formula: $C_3H_6N_6O_6$. [C20: from CYCLO- + (*trimethylene-tri*)*nit*(*ramin*)*e*]

cy·clo·par·af·fin (ˌsaɪkləʊˈpærəfɪn, ˌsɪk-) *n.* another name for **cycloalkane.**

Cy·clo·pe·an (ˌsaɪkləʊˈpiːən, saɪˈkləʊpɪən) *adj.* **1.** of, relating to, or resembling the Cyclops. **2.** denoting, relating to, or having the kind of masonry used in preclassical Greek architecture, characterized by large dry undressed blocks of stone.

cy·clo·pe·di·a *or* **cy·clo·pae·di·a** (ˌsaɪkləʊˈpiːdɪə) *n.* a less common word for **encyclopedia.** —ˌ**cy·clo·ˈpe·dic** *or* ˌ**cy·clo·ˈpae·dic** *adj.* —ˌ**cy·clo·ˈpe·dist** *or* ˌ**cy·clo·ˈpae·dist** *n.*

cy·clo·pen·tane (ˌsaɪkləʊˈpɛnteɪn, ˌsɪk-) *n.* a colourless insoluble cycloalkane found in petroleum and used mainly as a solvent. Formula: C_5H_{10}.

cy·clo·ple·gi·a (ˌsaɪkləʊˈpliːdʒɪə, ˌsɪk-) *n.* paralysis of the muscles that adjust the shape of the lens of the eye, resulting in loss of ability to focus. —ˌ**cy·clo·ˈple·gic** *adj.*

cy·clo·pro·pane (ˌsaɪkləʊˈprəʊpeɪn, ˌsɪk-) *n.* a colourless flammable gaseous hydrocarbon, used in medicine as an anaesthetic; trimethylene. It is a cycloalkane with molecules containing rings of three carbon atoms. Formula: C_3H_6; boiling pt.: –34°C.

Cy·clops (ˈsaɪklɒps) *n., pl.* **Cy·clo·pes** (saɪˈkləʊpiːz) *or* **Cy·clops·es.** *Classical myth.* one of a race of giants having a single eye in the middle of the forehead, encountered by Odysseus in the *Odyssey.* See also **Polyphemus.** [C15: from Latin *Cyclōps,* from Greek *Kuklōps,* literally: round eye, from *kuklos* circle + *ōps* eye]

cy·clo·ram·a (ˌsaɪkləʊˈrɑːmə) *n.* **1.** Also called: **panorama.** a large picture, such as a battle scene, on the interior wall of a cylindrical room, designed to appear in natural perspective to a spectator in the centre. **2.** *Theatre.* **a.** a curtain or wall curving along the back of a stage, usually painted to represent the sky and serving to enhance certain lighting effects. **b.** any set of curtains that enclose the back and sides of a stage setting. [C19: CYCLO- + Greek *horama* view, sight, on the model of *panorama*] —**cy·clo·ram·ic** (ˌsaɪkləʊˈræmɪk) *adj.*

cy·clo·sis (saɪˈkləʊsɪs) *n., pl.* **·ses** (-siːz). *Biology.* the circulation of cytoplasm or cell organelles, such as food vacuoles in some protozoans. [C19: from Greek *kuklōsis* an encircling, from *kukloun* to surround, from *kuklos* circle]

cy·clo·stome (ˈsaɪkləˌstəʊm, ˈsɪk-) *n.* **1.** any primitive aquatic jawless vertebrate of the class *Cyclostomata,* such as the lamprey and hagfish, having a round sucking mouth and pouchlike gills. ~*adj.* **2.** of, relating to, or belonging to the class *Cyclostomata.* ~Also: **marsipobranch.** —**cy·clos·to·mate** (saɪˈklɒstəmɪt, -ˌmeɪt) *or* **cy·clo·stom·a·tous** (ˌsaɪkləʊˈstɒmətəs, -ˈstəʊmə-, ˌsɪk-) *adj.*

cy·clo·style (ˈsaɪkləˌstaɪl) *n.* **1.** a kind of pen with a small toothed wheel, used for cutting minute holes in a specially prepared stencil. Copies of the design so formed can be printed on a duplicator by forcing ink through the holes. **2.** an office duplicator using a stencil prepared in this way. ~*vb.* **3.** (*tr.*) to print on a duplicator using such a stencil. —**ˈcy·clo·ˌstyled** *adj.*

cy·clo·thy·mi·a (ˌsaɪkləʊˈθaɪmɪə, ˌsɪk-) *n. Psychiatry.* a condition characterized by periodical swings of mood between excitement and depression, activity and inactivity. See also **manic-depressive.** —ˌ**cy·clo·ˈthy·mic** *or* ˌ**cy·clo·ˈthy·mi·ˌac** *adj., n.*

cy·clo·tron (ˈsaɪkləˌtrɒn) *n.* a type of particle accelerator in which the particles spiral inside two D-shaped hollow metal electrodes under the effect of a strong vertical magnetic field, gaining energy by a high-frequency voltage applied between these electrodes.

cy·der (ˈsaɪdə) *n.* a variant spelling (esp. Brit.) of **cider.**

Cyd·nus (ˈsɪdnəs) *n.* the ancient name for the (River) **Tarsus.**

cyg·net (ˈsɪgnɪt) *n.* a young swan. [C15 *sygnett,* from Old French *cygne* swan, from Latin *cygnus,* from Greek *kuknos*]

Cyg·nus (ˈsɪgnəs) *n., Latin genitive* **Cyg·ni** (ˈsɪgnaɪ). a constellation in the N hemisphere lying between Pegasus and Draco in the Milky Way. The constellation contains the expanding supernova remnant, the **Cygnus Loop.** It may also contain a black hole. [Latin: swan; see CYGNET]

cyl. *abbrev. for:* **1.** cylinder. **2.** cylindrical.

cyl·in·der (ˈsɪlɪndə) *n.* **1.** a solid consisting of two parallel planes bounded by identical closed curves, usually circles, that are interconnected at every point by a set of parallel lines, usually perpendicular to the planes. Volume: *base area* × *length.* **2.** a surface formed by a line moving round a closed plane curve at a fixed angle to it. **3.** any object shaped like a cylinder. **4.** the chamber in a reciprocating internal-combustion engine, pump, or compressor within which the piston moves. See also **cylinder block. 5.** the rotating mechanism of a revolver, situated behind the barrel and containing cartridge chambers. **6.** *Printing.* any of the rotating drums on a printing press. **7.** Also called: **cylinder seal.** a cylindrical seal of stone, clay, or precious stone decorated with linear designs, found in the Middle East and Balkans: dating from about 6000 B.C. **8.** Also called: **hot-water cylinder.** *Brit.* a vertical cylindrical tank for storing hot water, esp. an insulated one made of copper used in a domestic hot-water system. ~*vb.* **9.** (*tr.*) to provide (a system) with cylinders. [C16: from Latin *cylindrus,* from Greek *kulindros* a roller, from *kulindein* to roll] —**ˈcyl·in·der·ˌlike** *adj.*

cyl·in·der block *n.* the metal casting containing the cylinders and cooling channels or fins of a reciprocating internal-combustion engine. Sometimes shortened to **block.**

cyl·in·der head *n.* the detachable metal casting that fits onto the top of a cylinder block. In an engine it contains part of the combustion chamber and in an overhead-valve four-stroke engine it houses the valves and their operating mechanisms. Sometimes shortened to **head.**

cyl·in·der press *n. Printing.* another name for **flat-bed press.**

cy·lin·dri·cal (sɪˈlɪndrɪkᵊl) *or* **cy·lin·dric** *adj.* of, shaped like, or characteristic of a cylinder. —**cy·ˌlin·dri·ˈcal·i·ty** *or* **cy·ˈlin·dri·cal·ness** *n.* —**cy·ˈlin·dri·cal·ly** *adv.*

cy·lin·dri·cal co·or·di·nates *pl. n.* three coordinates defining the location of a point in three-dimensional space in terms of its polar coordinates (r, θ) in one plane, usually the (x, y) plane, and its perpendicular distance, z, measured from this plane.

cyl·in·droid (ˈsɪlɪnˌdrɔɪd) *n.* **1.** a cylinder with an elliptical cross section. ~*adj.* **2.** resembling a cylinder.

cy·lix (ˈsaɪlɪks, ˈsɪl-) *n., pl.* **·li·ces** (-lɪˌsiːz). a variant of **kylix.**

cy·ma (ˈsaɪmə) *n., pl.* **·mae** (-miː) *or* **·mas. 1.** either of two mouldings having a double curve, part concave and part convex. **Cyma recta** has the convex part nearer the wall and **cyma reversa** has the concave part nearer the wall. **2.** *Botany.* a variant of **cyme.** [C16: from New Latin, from Greek *kuma* something swollen, from *kuein* to be pregnant]

cy·mar (sɪˈmɑː) *n.* a woman's short fur-trimmed jacket, popular in the 17th and 18th centuries. [C17: variant of *simar,* from French *simarre,* perhaps ultimately from Basque *zamar* sheepskin]

cy·ma·ti·um (sɪˈmeɪtɪəm, -ʃɪəm) *n., pl.* **·ti·a** (-tɪə, -ʃɪə). *Architect.* the top moulding of a classical cornice or entablature. [C16: see CYMA]

cym·bal (ˈsɪmbᵊl) *n.* a percussion instrument of indefinite pitch consisting of a thin circular piece of brass, which vibrates when clashed together with another cymbal or struck with a stick. [Old English *cymbala,* from Medieval Latin, from Latin *cymbalum,* from Greek *kumbalon,* from *kumbē* something hollow] —**ˈcym·bal·er,** ˌ**cym·bal·ˈeer,** *or* **ˈcym·bal·ist** *n.* —**ˈcym·bal-ˌlike** *adj.*

cym·ba·lo (ˈsɪmbəˌləʊ) *n., pl.* **·los.** another name for **dulcimer.** [from Italian; see CYMBAL]

cyme (saɪm) *n.* an inflorescence in which the first flower is the terminal bud of the main stem and subsequent flowers develop as terminal buds of lateral stems. [C18: from Latin *cȳma* cabbage sprout, from Greek *kuma* anything swollen; see CYMA] —**cy·mif·er·ous** (saɪˈmɪfərəs) *adj.*

cy·mene (ˈsaɪmiːn) *n.* a colourless insoluble liquid with an aromatic odour that exists in three isomeric forms; methylpropylbenzene: used as solvents and for making synthetic resins. The *para-* isomer is present in several essential oils. Formula: $CH_3C_6H_4CH(CH_3)_2$. [C19: *cym-* from Greek *kuminon* CUMIN + -ENE]

cy·mo·gene (ˈsaɪməˌdʒiːn) *n. U.S.* a mixture of volatile flammable hydrocarbons, mainly butane, obtained in the distillation of petroleum. [C19: from CYMENE + -GENE]

cy·mo·graph (ˈsaɪməˌgrɑːf, -ˌgræf) *n.* **1.** a variant of **kymograph. 2.** an instrument for tracing the outline of an architectural moulding. —**cy·mo·graph·ic** (ˌsaɪməˈgræfɪk) *adj.*

cy·moid (ˈsaɪmɔɪd) *adj. Architect., botany.* resembling a cyme or cyma.

cy·mo·phane (ˈsaɪməˌfeɪn) *n.* a yellow or green opalescent variety of chrysoberyl. [C19: from Greek *kuma* wave, undulation + -PHANE]

cy·mose (ˈsaɪməʊs, -məʊz, saɪˈməʊs) *adj.* having the characteristics of a cyme. —**ˈcy·mose·ly** *adv.*

Cym·ric *or* **Kym·ric** (ˈkɪmrɪk) *n.* **1.** the Welsh language. **2.** the Brythonic group of Celtic languages. ~*adj.* **3.** of or relating to the Cymry, any of their languages, Wales, or the Welsh.

Cym·ry *or* **Kym·ry** (ˈkɪmrɪ) *n.* **the.** (*functioning as pl.*) **1.** the Brythonic branch of the Celtic people, comprising the present-day Welsh and Bretons. See **Brythonic. 2.** the Welsh people. [Welsh: the Welsh]

Cyn·e·wulf, Kyn·e·wulf (ˈkɪnɪˌwʊlf), *or* **Cyn·wulf** (ˈkɪnˌwʊlf) *n.* ?8th century A.D., Anglo-Saxon poet; author of *Juliana, The Ascension, Elene,* and *The Fates of the Apostles.*

cyn·gha·nedd (kʌŋˈhanɛð) *n.* a complex system of rhyme and alliteration used in Welsh verse. [from Welsh]

cyn·ic (ˈsɪnɪk) *n.* **1.** a person who believes the worst about people or the outcome of events. ~*adj.* **2.** a less common word for **cynical. 3.** *Astronomy.* of or relating to Sirius, the Dog Star. [C16: via Latin from Greek *Kunikos,* from *kuōn* dog]

Cyn·ic (ˈsɪnɪk) *n.* a member of a sect founded by Antisthenes that scorned worldly things and held that self-control was the key to the only good.

cyn·i·cal (ˈsɪnɪkᵊl) *adj.* **1.** distrustful or contemptuous of virtue, esp. selflessness in others; believing the worst of others, esp. that all acts are selfish. **2.** sarcastic; mocking. **3.** showing contempt for accepted standards of behaviour, esp. of honesty or morality: *the politician betrayed his promises in a cynical way.* —**ˈcyn·i·cal·ly** *adv.* —**ˈcyn·i·cal·ness** *n.*

cyn·i·cism ('sɪnɪˌsɪzəm) *n.* **1.** the attitude or beliefs of a cynic. **2.** a cynical action, remark, idea, etc.

Cyn·i·cism ('sɪnɪˌsɪzəm) *n.* the doctrines of the Cynics.

cy·no·sure ('sɪnəˌzjʊə, -ʃʊə) *n.* **1.** a person or thing that attracts notice, esp. because of its brilliance or beauty. **2.** something that serves as a guide. [C16: from Latin *Cynosūra* the constellation of Ursa Minor, from Greek *Kunosoura*, from *kuōn* dog + *oura* tail] —ˌ**cy·no·'sur·al** *adj.*

Cyn·thi·a ('sɪnθɪə) *n.* another name for **Artemis** (Diana).

cy·per·a·ceous (ˌsaɪpə'reɪʃəs) *adj.* of, relating to, or belonging to the *Cyperaceae*, a family of grasslike flowering plants with solid triangular stems, including the sedges, bulrush, cotton grass, and certain rushes. Compare **juncaceous.** [C19: from New Latin *Cypērus* type genus, from Latin *cypēros* a kind of rush, from Greek *kupeiros* marsh plant, probably of Semitic origin]

cy·pher ('saɪfə) *n., vb.* a variant spelling of **cipher.**

cy pres ('si: 'preɪ) *n. Law.* the doctrine that the intention of a donor or testator should be carried out as closely as practicable when literal compliance is impossible. [C15: from Anglo-French, literally: as near (as possible, etc.)]

cy·press[1] ('saɪprəs) *n.* **1.** any coniferous tree of the N temperate genus *Cupressus*, having dark green scalelike leaves and rounded cones: family *Cupressaceae*. **2.** any of several similar and related trees, such as the widely cultivated *Chamaecyparis lawsoniana* (**Lawson's cypress**), of the western U.S. **3.** any of various other coniferous trees, esp. the swamp cypress. **4.** the wood of any of these trees. [Old English *cypresse*, from Latin *cyparissus*, from Greek *kuparissos*; related to Latin *cupressus*]

cy·press[2] *or* **cy·prus** ('saɪprəs) *n.* a fabric, esp. a fine silk, lawn, or crepelike material, often black and worn as mourning. [C14 *cyprus* from the island of CYPRUS]

cy·press pine *n.* any coniferous tree of the Australian genus *Callitrus*, having leaves in whorls and yielding valuable timber: family *Cupressaceae*.

cy·press vine *n.* a tropical American convolvulaceous climbing plant, *Quamoclit pennata*, having finely divided compound leaves and scarlet or white tubular flowers.

Cyp·ri·an[1] ('sɪprɪən) *adj.* **1.** of or relating to Cyprus. **2.** of or resembling the ancient orgiastic worship of Aphrodite on Cyprus. ~*n.* **3.** (*often not cap.*) *Obsolete.* a licentious person, esp. a prostitute or dancer. ~*n., adj.* **4.** another word for **Cypriot.**

Cyp·ri·an[2] ('sɪprɪən) *n.* **Saint.** ?200–258 A.D., bishop of Carthage and martyr. Feast day: Sept. 16.

cy·pri·nid (sɪ'praɪnɪd, 'sɪprɪnɪd) *n.* **1.** any teleost fish of the mainly freshwater family *Cyprinidae*, typically having toothless jaws and cycloid scales and including such food and game fishes as the carp, tench, roach, rudd, and dace. ~*adj.* **2.** of, relating to, or belonging to the *Cyprinidae*. **3.** resembling a carp; cyprinoid. [C19: from New Latin *Cyprīnidae*, from Latin *cyprīnus* carp, from Greek *kuprinos*]

cy·prin·o·dont (sɪ'prɪnəˌdɒnt, sɪ'praɪ-) *n.* **1.** any small tropical or subtropical soft-finned fish of the mostly marine family *Cyprinodontidae*, resembling carp but having toothed jaws. The group includes the guppy, killifish, swordtail, and topminnow. ~*adj.* **2.** of, relating to, or belonging to the *Cyprinodontidae*. [C19: from Latin *cyprīnus* carp (see CYPRINID) + -ODONT]

cy·pri·noid ('sɪprɪˌnɔɪd, sɪ'praɪnɔɪd) *adj.* **1.** of, relating to, or belonging to the *Cyprinoidea*, a large suborder of teleost fishes including the cyprinids, characins, electric eels, and loaches. **2.** of, relating to, or resembling the carp. ~*n.* **3.** any fish belonging to the *Cyprinoidea*. [C19: from Latin *cyprīnus* carp]

Cyp·ri·ot ('sɪprɪət) *or* **Cyp·ri·ote** ('sɪprɪˌəʊt) *n.* **1.** a native, citizen, or inhabitant of Cyprus. **2.** the dialect of Ancient or Modern Greek spoken in Cyprus. ~*adj.* **3.** denoting or relating to Cyprus, its inhabitants, or dialects.

cyp·ri·pe·di·um (ˌsɪprɪ'pi:dɪəm) *n.* **1.** any orchid of the genus *Cypripedium*, having large flowers with an inflated pouchlike lip. See also **lady's-slipper. 2.** any cultivated tropical orchid of the genus *Paphiopedilum*, having yellow, green, or brownish-purple waxy flowers. [C18: from New Latin, from Latin *Cypria* the Cyprian, that is, Venus + *pēs* foot (that is, Venus' slipper)]

Cy·prus ('saɪprəs) *n.* an island in the E Mediterranean: ceded to Britain by Turkey in 1878 and made a colony in 1925; became an independent republic in 1960; invaded by Turkey in 1974 following a Greek-supported military coup, leading to the virtual partition of the island. A UN peacekeeping force is currently stationed in Cyprus. Languages: Greek and Turkish. Religions: Greek Orthodox and Muslim. Currency: pound. Capital: Nicosia. Pop.: 631 778 (1973). Area: 9251 sq. km (3572 sq. miles).

cyp·se·la ('sɪpsɪlə) *n., pl.* **·lae** (-ˌli:). the dry one-seeded fruit of the daisy and related plants, which resembles an achene but is surrounded by a calyx sheath. [C19: from New Latin, from Greek *kupselē* chest, hollow vessel]

Cy·ra·no de Ber·ge·rac (*French* sirano də bɛrʒə'rak) *n.* **Sa·vi·nien** (savi'njɛ̃). 1619–55, French writer and soldier, famous as a duellist and for his large nose.

Cyr·e·na·ic (ˌsaɪrə'neɪɪk, ˌsɪrə-) *adj.* **1.** (in the ancient world) of or relating to the city of Cyrene or the territory of Cyrenaica. **2.** of or relating to the philosophical school founded by Aristippus in Cyrene that held pleasure to be the highest good. ~*n.* **3.** an inhabitant of Cyrene or Cyrenaica. **4.** a follower of the Cyrenaic school of philosophy.

Cyr·e·na·i·ca *or* **Cir·e·na·i·ca** (ˌsaɪrə'neɪɪkə, ˌsɪrə-) *n.* a region and former province (1951–63) of E Libya: largely desert; settled by the Greeks in about 630 B.C.; ruled successively by the Egyptians, Romans, Arabs, Turks, and Italians. Area: 855 370 sq. km (330 258 sq. miles).

Cy·re·ne (saɪ'ri:nɪ) *n.* an ancient Greek city of N Africa, near the coast of Cyrenaica: famous for its medical school.

Cyr·il ('sɪrəl) *n.* **Saint.** ?827–869 A.D., Greek Christian theologian, missionary to the Moravians and inventor of the Cyrillic alphabet; he and his brother Saint Methodius were called *the Apostles of the Slavs.* Feast day: July 7.

Cy·ril·lic (sɪ'rɪlɪk) *adj.* **1.** denoting or relating to the alphabet derived from that of the Greeks, supposedly by Saint Cyril, for the writing of Slavonic languages: now used primarily for Russian, Bulgarian, and the Serbian dialect of Serbo-Croatian. ~*n.* **2.** this alphabet.

Cy·rus ('saɪrəs) *n.* **1.** called *the Great* or *the Elder.* died ?529 B.C., king of Persia and founder of the Persian empire. **2.** called *the Younger.* died 401 B.C., Persian satrap of Lydia: revolted against his brother Artaxerxes II, but was killed at the battle of Cunaxa. See also **anabasis, katabasis.**

cyst (sɪst) *n.* **1.** *Pathol.* any abnormal membranous sac or blisterlike pouch containing fluid or semisolid material. **2.** *Anat.* any normal sac or vesicle in the body. **3.** a thick-walled protective membrane enclosing a cell, larva, or organism. [C18: from New Latin *cystis*, from Greek *kustis* pouch, bag, bladder]

-cyst *n. combining form.* indicating a bladder or sac: *otocyst.* [from Greek *kustis* bladder]

cys·tec·to·my (sɪ'stɛktəmɪ) *n., pl.* **·mies. 1.** surgical removal of the gall bladder or of part of the urinary bladder. **2.** surgical removal of any abnormal cyst.

cys·te·ine ('sɪstɪˌi:n, -ɪn) *n.* a sulphur-containing amino acid, present in proteins, that oxidizes on exposure to air to form cystine. Formula: $HSCH_2CH(NH_2)COOH$. [C19: variant of CYSTINE] —ˌ**cys·te·'in·ic** *adj.*

cyst·ic ('sɪstɪk) *adj.* **1.** of, relating to, or resembling a cyst. **2.** having or enclosed within a cyst; encysted. **3.** relating to the gall bladder or urinary bladder.

cys·ti·cer·coid (ˌsɪstɪ'sɜ:kɔɪd) *n.* the larva of any of certain tapeworms, which resembles a cysticercus but has a smaller bladder.

cys·ti·cer·cus (ˌsɪstɪ'sɜ:kəs) *n., pl.* **·ci** (-saɪ). an encysted larval form of many tapeworms, consisting of a head (scolex) inverted in a fluid-filled bladder. See also **hydatid** (sense 1), **coenurus.** [C19: from New Latin, from Greek *kustis* pouch, bladder + *kerkos* tail]

cyst·ic fi·bro·sis *n.* a congenital disease of the exocrine glands, usually affecting young children, characterized by chronic infection of the respiratory tract and by pancreatic insufficiency.

cys·tine ('sɪsti:n, -tɪn) *n.* a sulphur-containing amino acid present in proteins: yields two molecules of cysteine on reduction. Formula: $HOOCCH(NH_2)CH_2SSCH_2CH(NH_2)COOH$. [C19: see CYSTO- (bladder), -INE[2]; named from its being discovered in a type of urinary calculus]

cys·ti·tis (sɪ'staɪtɪs) *n.* inflammation of the urinary bladder.

cys·to- *or before a vowel* **cyst-** *combining form.* indicating a cyst or bladder: *cystocarp; cystoscope.*

cys·to·carp ('sɪstəˌkɑ:p) *n.* a reproductive body in red algae, developed after fertilization and consisting of filaments bearing carpospores. —ˌ**cys·to·'car·pic** *adj.*

cys·to·cele ('sɪstəˌsi:l) *n. Pathol.* a hernia of the urinary bladder, esp. one protruding into the vagina.

cys·toid ('sɪstɔɪd) *adj.* **1.** resembling a cyst or bladder. ~*n.* **2.** a tissue mass, such as a tumour, that resembles a cyst but lacks an outer membrane.

cys·to·lith ('sɪstəlɪθ) *n.* **1.** a knoblike deposit of calcium carbonate in the epidermal cells of such plants as the stinging nettle. **2.** *Pathol.* a urinary calculus.

cys·to·scope ('sɪstəˌskəʊp) *n.* a slender tubular medical instrument for examining the interior of the urethra and urinary bladder. —**cys·to·scop·ic** (ˌsɪstə'skɒpɪk) *adj.* —**cys·tos·co·py** (sɪs'tɒskəpɪ) *n.*

cys·tot·o·my (sɪ'stɒtəmɪ) *n., pl.* **·mies. 1.** surgical incision into the gall bladder or urinary bladder. **2.** surgical incision into the capsule of the lens of the eye.

cy·tas·ter (saɪ'tæstə, 'saɪtæs-) *n. Cytology.* another word for **aster** (sense 3). [C19: from CYTO- + ASTER]

-cyte *n. combining form.* indicating a cell: *spermatocyte.* [from New Latin *-cyta*, from Greek *kutos* container, body, hollow vessel]

Cyth·er·a (sɪ'θɪərə) *n.* **1.** a Greek island off the SE coast of the Peloponnese: in ancient times a centre of the worship of Aphrodite. Pop.: 4102 (1970). Area: about 285 sq. km (110 sq. miles). **2.** the chief town of this island, on the S coast. Pop.: 682 (1970). ~Modern Greek name: **Kíthera.**

Cyth·er·e·a (ˌsɪθə'ri:ə) *n.* another name for **Aphrodite** (Venus). —ˌ**Cyth·er·'e·an** *adj.*

cyt·i·dine ('sɪtɪˌdaɪn) *n. Biochem.* a nucleoside formed by the condensation of cytosine and ribose. [C20: from CYTO- + -IDE + -INE[2]]

cy·to- *combining form.* indicating a cell: *cytolysis; cytoplasm.* [from Greek *kutos* vessel, container; related to *kuein* to contain]

cy·to·chem·is·try (ˌsaɪtəʊ'kɛmɪstrɪ) *n.* the chemistry of living cells. —ˌ**cy·to·'chem·i·cal** *adj.*

cy·to·chrome ('saɪtəʊˌkrəʊm) *n.* any of a group of naturally occurring compounds, consisting of iron, a protein, and a porphyrin, that are important in cell oxidation-reduction reactions.

cy·to·chrome re·duc·tase *n.* another name for **flavoprotein.**

cy+to+gen+e·sis (ˌsaɪtəʊ'dʒɛnɪsɪs) *or* **cy+tog+e·ny** (saɪ'tɒdʒənɪ) *n.* the origin and development of plant and animal cells.

cy+to+ge·net+ics (ˌsaɪtəʊdʒɪ'nɛtɪks) *n.* (*functioning as sing.*) the branch of genetics that correlates the structure of chromosomes with heredity and variation. —ˌ**cy+to+ge·'net+ic** *adj.* —ˌ**cy+to+ge·'net·i·cal·ly** *adv.*

cy+to+ki+ne·sis (ˌsaɪtəʊkɪ'ni:sɪs, -kaɪ-) *n.* division of the cytoplasm of a cell, occurring at the end of mitosis or meiosis.

cy+tol+o·gy (saɪ'tɒlədʒɪ) *n.* the study of plant and animal cells, including their structure, function, and formation. —**cy+to+log·i·cal** (ˌsaɪtə'lɒdʒɪkᵊl) *adj.* —ˌ**cy+to+'log·i·cal+ly** *adv.* —**cy+'tol·o·gist** *n.*

cy+tol·y+sin (saɪ'tɒlɪsɪn) *n.* a substance that can partially or completely destroy animal cells.

cy+tol·y+sis (saɪ'tɒlɪsɪs) *n. Cytology.* the dissolution of cells, esp. by the destruction of their membranes. —**cy+to+lyt+ic** (ˌsaɪtə'lɪtɪk) *adj.*

cy+ton ('saɪtɒn) *n. Physiol.* the body of a nerve cell as distinct from the processes. [C20: CYTO- + -ON, as in *proton*]

cy+to+plasm ('saɪtəʊˌplæzəm) *n.* the protoplasm of a cell contained within the cell membrane but excluding the nucleus: contains organelles, vesicles, and other inclusions. —ˌ**cy+to+'plas+mic** *adj.*

cy+to+plast ('saɪtəʊˌplɑ:st, -ˌplæst) *n.* the intact cytoplasm of a single cell. —**cy+to+plas+tic** (ˌsaɪtəʊ'plæstɪk) *adj.*

cy+to+sine ('saɪtəsɪn) *n.* a white crystalline pyrimidine occurring in nucleic acids; 6-amino-2-hydroxy pyrimidine. Formula: $C_4H_5N_3O$. See also **DNA, RNA.** [C19: from CYTO- + -OSE² + -INE²]

cy+to+tax+on+o·my (ˌsaɪtəʊtæk'sɒnəmɪ) *n.* classification of organisms based on cell structure, esp. the number, shape, etc., of the chromosomes. —ˌ**cy+to+ˌtax·o·'nom+ic** *adj.* —ˌ**cy+to+tax+'on·o+mist** *n.*

Cyz·i·cus ('sɪzɪkəs) *n.* an ancient Greek colony in NW Asia Minor on the S shore of the Sea of Marmara: site of Alcibiades' naval victory over the Peloponnesians (410 B.C.)

czar (zɑ:) *n.* a variant spelling (esp. U.S.) of **tsar.** —'**czar+dom** *n.*

czar+das ('tʃɑ:dæʃ) *n.* **1.** a Hungarian national dance of alternating slow and fast sections. **2.** a piece of music composed for or in the rhythm of this dance. [from Hungarian *csárdás*]

czar+e·vitch ('zɑ:rɪvɪtʃ) *n.* a variant spelling (esp. U.S.) of **tsarevitch.**

cza+rev+na (zɑ:'rɛvnə) *n.* a variant spelling (esp. U.S.) of **tsarevna.**

cza+ri+na (zɑ:'ri:nə) *or* **cza+ri+tza** *n.* variant spellings (esp. U.S.) of **tsarina** or **tsaritsa.**

czar+ism ('zɑ:rɪzəm) *n.* a variant spelling (esp. U.S.) of **tsarism.**

czar+ist ('zɑ:rɪst) *adj., n.* a variant spelling (esp. U.S.) of **tsarist.**

Czech (tʃɛk) *adj.* **1. a.** of, relating to, or characteristic of Bohemia and Moravia, their people, or their language. **b.** (loosely) of, relating to, or characteristic of Czechoslovakia or its people. ~*n.* **2.** one of the two official languages of Czechoslovakia, belonging to the West Slavonic branch of the Indo-European family. Czech and Slovak are closely related and mutually intelligible. **3. a.** a native or inhabitant of Bohemia or Moravia. **b.** (loosely) a native, inhabitant, or citizen of Czechoslovakia. [C19: from Polish, from Czech *Čech*]

Czech. *abbrev. for:* **1.** Czechoslovak. **2.** Czechoslovakian. **3.** Czechoslovakia.

Czech·o+slo+vak (ˌtʃɛkəʊ'sləʊvæk) *adj.* **1.** of, relating to, or characteristic of Czechoslovakia, its peoples, or their languages. ~*n.* **2.** (loosely) either of the two mutually intelligible languages of Czechoslovakia; Czech or Slovak.

Czech·o+slo+va+ki·a (ˌtʃɛkəʊsləʊ'vækɪə) *n.* a republic in central Europe: formed after the defeat of Austro-Hungary (1918) as a nation of Czechs in Bohemia and Moravia and Slovaks in Slovakia; occupied by Germany from 1939 until its liberation by the Soviet Union in 1945; became a people's republic under the Communists in 1948; invaded by Warsaw Pact troops in 1968, ending Dubček's attempt to liberalize communism. It now consists of two federal republics, the **Czech Socialist Republic** and the **Slovak Socialist Republic.** It is mostly wooded and mountainous, with the Carpathians in the E rising over 2400 m (8000 ft.). Languages: Czech and Slovak. Currency: crown. Capital: Prague. Pop.: 14 686 000 (1974 est.). Area: 127 870 sq. km (49 371 sq. miles). Czech name: **Československo.** —ˌ**Czech·o+slo+'va+ki·an** *adj., n.*

Czer+no+witz ('tʃɛrnovɪts) *n.* the German name for **Chernovtsy.**

Czer·ny (*German* 'tʃɛrni) *n.* **Karl** (karl). 1791–1857, Austrian pianist, composer, and teacher, noted for his studies.

Czę+sto+cho+wa (*Polish* tʃɛ̃stɔ'xɔva) *n.* an industrial city in S Poland, on the River Warta: pilgrimage centre. Pop.: 195 400 (1974 est.).

D

d *or* **D** (diː) *n., pl.* **d's, D's,** *or* **Ds. 1.** the fourth letter and third consonant of the modern English alphabet. **2.** a speech sound represented by this letter, usually a voiced alveolar stop, as in *dagger.* **3.** the semicircle on a billiards table having a radius of 11½ inches and its straight edge in the middle of the baulk line.

d *symbol for:* **1.** *Physics.* density or relative density. **2.** *Maths.* a small increment in a given variable or function: used to indicate a derivative of one variable with respect to another, as in dy/dx.

D *symbol for:* **1.** *Music.* **a.** a note having a frequency of 293·66 hertz (**D above middle C**) or this value multiplied or divided by any power of 2; the second note of the scale of C major. **b.** a key, string, or pipe producing this note. **c.** the major or minor key having this note as its tonic. **2.** *Chem.* deuterium. **3.** *Maths.* the first derivative of a function, as in $D(x^3 + x^2) = 3x^2 + 2x$. ~ **4.** *the Roman numeral for* 500. See **Roman numerals.** ~ **5.** *international car registration for* Germany. [from German *Deutschland*]

d. *abbrev. for:* **1.** date. **2.** (in animal pedigrees) dam. **3.** daughter. **4.** day. **5.** degree. **6.** delete. **7.** *Brit. currency before decimalization.* penny *or* pennies. [Latin *denarius* or *denarii*] **8.** depart(s). **9.** diameter. **10.** died. **11.** dinar(s). **12.** dollar(s). **13.** dose. **14.** drachma(s).

D. *abbrev. for:* **1.** *U.S. politics.* Democrat(ic). **2.** *Government.* Department. **3.** Deus. [Latin: God] **4.** *Optics.* diopter. **5.** Director. **6.** Dominus. [Latin: Lord] **7.** Don (a Spanish title). **8.** Duchess. **9.** Duke. **10.** Dutch.

'd *contraction for* would *or* had: *I'd; you'd.*

D.A. *abbrev. for:* **1.** (in the U.S.) District Attorney. **2.** duck's-arse (hair style).

D/A *or* **d.a.** *abbrev. for:* **1.** deposit account. **2.** documents for acceptance.

dab[1] (dæb) *vb.* **dabs, dab+bing, dabbed. 1.** to touch or pat lightly and quickly: *he dabbed the spilt coffee with the cloth.* **2.** *(tr.)* to daub with short tapping strokes: *to dab the wall with paint.* **3.** *(tr.)* to apply (paint, cream, etc.) with short tapping strokes. ~*n.* **4.** a small amount, esp. of something soft or moist: *a dab of ink.* **5.** a small light stroke or tap, as with the hand. **6.** *(often pl.) Chiefly Brit.* a slang word for **fingerprint.** [C14: of imitative origin]

dab[2] (dæb) *n.* **1.** a small common European brown flatfish, *Limanda limanda,* covered with rough toothed scales: family *Pleuronectidae:* a food fish. **2.** *(often pl.)* any of various other small flatfish, esp. flounders. ~Compare **sand dab.** [C15: from Anglo-French *dabbe,* of uncertain origin]

dab[3] (dæb) *n. Brit. informal.* See **dab hand.** [C17: perhaps from DAB[1] (vb.)]

dab+ber ('dæbə) *n.* a pad used by printers and engravers for applying ink, etc., by hand.

dab+ble ('dæbᵊl) *vb.* **1.** to dip, move, or splash (the fingers, feet, etc.) in a liquid. **2.** *(intr.;* usually foll. by *in, with,* or *at)* to deal (with) or work (at) frivolously or superficially; play (at). **3.** *(tr.)* to daub, mottle, splash, or smear: *his face was dabbled with paint.* [C16: probably from Dutch *dabbelen;* see DAB[1]] —**'dab+bler** *n.*

dab+chick ('dæb,tʃɪk) *n.* any of several small grebes of the genera *Podiceps* and *Podilymbus,* such as *Podiceps ruficollis* of the Old World. [C16: probably from Old English *dop* to dive + CHICK; see DEEP, DIP]

dab hand *n. Brit. informal.* a person who is particularly skilled at something; expert: *a dab hand at chess.*

dab+ster ('dæbstə) *n.* **1.** *Brit.* a dialect word for **dab hand. 2.** *U.S. informal.* an incompetent or amateurish worker; bungler. [C18: from DAB[1] + -STER]

da ca·po (dɑː 'kɑːpəʊ) *adj., adv. Music.* to be repeated (in whole or part) from the beginning. Abbrev.: **D.C.** See also **fine**[3]. [C18: from Italian, literally: from the head]

Dac+ca ('dækə) *n.* the capital of Bangladesh, in the E central part: capital of Bengal (1608–39 and 1660–1704) and of East Pakistan (1949–71); jute and cotton mills; university (1921). Pop.: 1 730 253 (1974).

dace (deɪs) *n., pl.* **dace** *or* **dac·es. 1.** a European freshwater cyprinid fish, *Leuciscus leuciscus,* with a slender bluish-green body. **2.** any of various similar fishes. [C15: from Old French *dars* DART, probably referring to its swiftness]

da+cha *or* **da+tcha** ('dætʃə) *n.* a country house or cottage in Russia. [from Russian: a giving, gift]

Da+chau (*German* 'daxaʊ) *n.* a Nazi concentration camp near Munich.

dachs+hund ('dæks,hʊnd; *German* 'daks,hʊnt) *n.* a long-bodied short-legged breed of dog. [C19: from German, from *Dachs* badger + *Hund* dog, HOUND]

Da+ci·a ('deɪsɪə) *n.* an ancient region bounded by the Carpathians, the Tisza, and the Danube, roughly corresponding to modern Rumania. United under kings from about 60 B.C., it later contained the Roman province of the same name (about 105 to 270 A.D.). —**'Da+ci·an** *adj., n.*

da+coit (də'kɔɪt) *n.* (in India and Burma) a member of a gang of armed robbers. [C19: from Hindi *dakait,* from *dākā* robbery]

da+coit·y (də'kɔɪtɪ) *n., pl.* **+coit·ies.** (in India and Burma) robbery by an armed gang.

Da+cron ('deɪkrɒn, 'dæk-) *n.* the U.S. name (trademark) for **Terylene.**

dac+tyl ('dæktɪl) *n.* **1.** Also called: **dactylic.** *Prosody.* a metrical foot of three syllables, one long followed by two short (¯˘˘). Compare **bacchius. 2.** *Zoology.* any digit of a vertebrate. [C14: via Latin from Greek *daktulos* finger, dactyl, comparing the finger's three joints to the three syllables]

dac+tyl+ic (dæk'tɪlɪk) *adj.* **1.** of, relating to, or having a dactyl: *dactylic verse.* ~*n.* **2.** a variant of **dactyl** (sense 1). —**dac+'tyl+i+cal+ly** *adv.*

dac·tyl·o- *or before a vowel* **dac·tyl-** *combining form.* finger or toe: *dactylogram.* [from Greek *daktulos* finger]

dac+tyl+o+gram (dæk'tɪlə,græm) *n. Chiefly U.S.* a technical term for **fingerprint.**

dac+tyl+og+ra+phy (,dæktə'lɒgrəfɪ) *n. Chiefly U.S.* the scientific study of fingerprints for purposes of identification. —**,dac+ty+'log+ra+pher** *n.* —**dac+tyl+o+graph+ic** (dæk,tɪlə'græfɪk) *adj.*

dac+ty+lol+o·gy (,dæktɪ'lɒlədʒɪ) *n., pl.* **·gies.** the method of using manual sign language, as in communicating with the deaf.

dad (dæd) *n.* an informal word for **father.** [C16: childish word; compare Greek *tata,* Sanskrit *tatas*]

Da·da ('dɑːdɑː) *or* **Da+da+ism** ('dɑːdɑː,ɪzəm) *n.* a nihilistic artistic movement of the early 20th century in W Europe and the U.S., founded on principles of irrationality, incongruity, and irreverence towards accepted aesthetic criteria. [C20: from French, from a children's word for hobbyhorse, the name being arbitrarily chosen] —**'Da+da+ist** *n., adj.* —**,Da+da+'is+tic** *adj.* —**,Da+da+'is+ti+cal+ly** *adv.*

dad+dy ('dædɪ) *n., pl.* **+dies. 1.** an informal word for **father. 2. the daddy.** *Slang, chiefly U.S. and Austral.* the supreme or finest example: *the daddy of them all.*

dad·dy-long·legs *n.* **1.** *Brit.* an informal name for a **crane fly. 2.** *U.S.* an informal name for **harvestman** (sense 2).

da·do ('deɪdəʊ) *n., pl.* **+does** *or* **+dos. 1.** the lower part of an interior wall that is decorated differently from the upper part. **2.** *Architect.* the part of a pedestal between the base and the cornice. ~*vb.* **3.** *(tr.)* to provide with a dado. [C17: from Italian: die, die-shaped pedestal, perhaps from Arabic *dad* game]

Da+dra and Na+gar Ha+ve+li (də'drɑː; 'nʌgə ə'velɪ) *n.* a union territory of W India, on the Gulf of Cambay: until 1961 administratively part of Portuguese Damão. Capital: Silvana. Pop.: 74 170 (1971). Area: 489 sq. km (191 sq. miles).

dae+dal *or* **de+dal** ('diːdᵊl) *adj. Literary.* skilful or intricate. [C16: via Latin from Greek *daidalos;* see DAEDALUS]

Daed·a·lus ('diːdələs) *n. Greek myth.* an Athenian architect and inventor who built the labyrinth for Minos on Crete and fashioned wings for himself and his son Icarus to flee their imprisonment on the island. —**Dae+da+li·an, Dae+da+le·an** (dɪ'deɪlɪən) *or* **Dae+dal+ic** (dɪ'dælɪk) *adj.*

dae+mon ('diːmən) *or* **dai+mon** *n.* **1.** a demigod. **2.** the guardian spirit of a place or person. **3.** a variant spelling of **demon** (sense 3). —**dae+mon+ic** (diː'mɒnɪk) *adj.*

daff[1] (dæf) *n. Informal.* short for **daffodil.**

daff[2] (dɑf) *vb. (intr.) Chiefly Scot.* to frolic; play the fool. [C16: from obsolete *daff* fool, of uncertain origin]

daf+fo+dil ('dæfədɪl) *n.* **1.** Also called: **Lent lily.** a widely cultivated Eurasian amaryllidaceous plant, *Narcissus pseudonarcissus,* having spring-blooming yellow nodding flowers. **2.** any other plant of the genus *Narcissus.* **3. a.** a brilliant yellow colour. **b.** *(as adj.): daffodil paint.* [C14: perhaps from Dutch *de affodil* the asphodel, from Medieval Latin *affodillus,* variant of Latin *asphodelus* ASPHODEL]

daff·y ('dæfɪ) *adj.* **daff·i+er, daff·i+est.** *Informal.* another word for **daft** (senses 1, 2). [C19: from obsolete *daff* fool; see DAFT]

daft (dɑːft) *adj. Chiefly Brit.* **1.** *Informal.* foolish, simple, or stupid. **2.** a slang word for **insane. 3.** *Informal. (postpositive;* foll. by *about)* extremely fond (of). **4.** *Slang.* frivolous; giddy. [Old English *gedæfte* gentle, foolish; related to Middle Low German *ondaft* incapable] —**'daft+ly** *adv.* —**daft+ness** *n.*

dag (dæg) *n.* **1.** short for **daglock. 2.** *Austral. informal.* a character; eccentric. ~*vb.* **dags, dag+ging, dagged. 3.** to cut the daglock away from (a sheep). [C18: of obscure origin] —**'dag+ger** *n.*

Da Ga·ma (də 'gɑːmə) *n.* See (Vasco da) **Gama.**

Da+gan ('dɑːgən) *n.* an earth god of the Babylonians and Assyrians.

Dag+en+ham ('dægənəm) *n.* part of the Greater London borough of Barking: motor-vehicle manufacturing.

Da+ge+stan Au+ton·o·mous So+vi+et So+cial+ist Re+pub+lic (,dɑːgɪ'stɑːn) *n.* an administrative division of the S Soviet Union, on the Caspian Sea: annexed from Persia in 1813; rich mineral resources. Capital: Makhachkala. Pop.: 1 428 540 (1970). Area: 50 278 sq. km (19 416 sq. miles). Also called: **Dagestan** or **Daghestan.**

dag+ga ('daxə, 'dɑːgə) *n.* hemp smoked as a narcotic. [C19: from Afrikaans, from Hottentot *dagab*]

dag+ger ('dægə) *n.* **1.** a short stabbing weapon with a pointed blade. **2.** Also called: **obelisk.** a character (†) used in printing to indicate a cross reference, esp. to a footnote. **3. at daggers drawn.** in a state of open hostility. **4. look daggers.** to glare with hostility; scowl. ~*vb.* (*tr.*) **5.** to mark with a dagger. **6.** *Archaic.* to stab with a dagger. [C14: of uncertain origin]

dag·ger+board ('dægə,bɔːd) *n.* a light bladelike board inserted into the water through a slot in the keel of a boat to reduce keeling and leeway. Compare **centreboard.**

dag+lock ('dæg,lɒk) *n.* a dung-caked lock of wool around the hindquarters of a sheep. [C17: see DAG, LOCK²]

da·go ('deɪgəʊ) *n., pl.* **+gos** *or* **+goes.** *Derogatory.* a member of a Latin race, esp. a Spaniard, Portuguese. [C19: alteration of *Diego,* a common Spanish name]

da+go+ba ('dɑːgəbə) *n.* a dome-shaped shrine containing relics of the Buddha or a Buddhist saint. [C19: from Sinhalese *dāgoba,* from Sanskrit *dhātugarbha* containing relics]

Da+gon ('deɪgɒn) *n. Bible.* a god worshipped by the Philistines, represented as half man and half fish. [C14: via Latin and Greek from Hebrew *Dāgōn,* literally: little fish]

Da·guerre (*French* da'gɛːr) *n.* **Louis Jacques Man·dé** (lwi ʒɑk mɑ̃'de). 1789–1851, French inventor, who devised one of the first practical photographic processes (1838).

da+guerre·o+type (də'gɛrəʊ,taɪp) *n.* **1.** one of the earliest photographic processes, in which the image was produced on iodine-sensitized silver and developed in mercury vapour. **2.** a photograph formed by this process. —**da+'guerre·o+,typ+er** *or* **da+'guerre·o+,typ+ist** *n.* —**da+'guerre·o+,typ·y** *n.*

dah (dɑː) *n.* the long sound used in combination with the short sound *dit,* in the spoken representation of Morse and other telegraphic codes. Compare **dash**¹ (sense 13).

da+ha+be·ah, da+ha+bee+yah, *or* **da+ha+bi+ah** (,dɑːhə'biːə) *n.* a houseboat used on the Nile. [from Arabic *dhahabīyah,* literally: the golden one (that is, gilded barge)]

dahl+ia ('deɪljə) *n.* **1.** any herbaceous perennial plant of the Mexican genus *Dahlia,* having showy flowers and tuberous roots, esp. any horticultural variety derived from *D. pinnata:* family *Compositae* (composites). **2.** the flower or root of any of these plants. [C19: named after Anders *Dahl,* 18th-century Swedish botanist; see -IA]

Dah+na ('dɑːxnɑː) *n.* another name for **Rub' al Khali.**

Da+ho+mey (də'həʊmɪ) *n.* the former name (until 1975) of **Benin.**

Dáil Éi+reann ('dɔɪl 'ɛərən) *or* **Dáil** *n.* (in the Republic of Ireland) the lower chamber of parliament. See also **Oireachtas.** [from Irish *dáil* assembly (from Old Irish *dāl*) + *Éireann* of Eire]

dai+lies ('deɪlɪz) *pl. n. Films.* another word for **rushes.**

dai+ly ('deɪlɪ) *adj.* **1.** of or occurring every day or every weekday: *a daily paper.* ~*n., pl.* **+lies. 2.** a daily publication, esp. a newspaper. **3.** Also called: **daily help.** *Brit.* another name for a **charwoman.** ~*adv.* **4.** every day. **5.** constantly; often. [Old English *dæglīc;* see DAY, -LY]

dai+ly dou+ble *n. Horse racing.* a single bet on the winners of two named races in any one day's racing.

dai+mon ('daɪmɒn) *n.* a variant spelling of **daemon** or **demon** (sense 3). —**dai+'mon+ic** *adj.*

dai+myo *or* **dai+mio** ('daɪmjou) *n., pl.* **+myo, +myos** *or* **+mio, +mios.** (in Japan) one of the territorial magnates who dominated much of the country from about the 10th to the 19th century. [from Japanese, from Ancient Chinese *d'âi miäng* great name]

dain+ty ('deɪntɪ) *adj.* **+ti+er, +ti+est. 1.** delicate or elegant: *a dainty teacup.* **2.** pleasing to the taste; choice; delicious: *a dainty morsel.* **3.** refined, esp. excessively genteel; fastidious. ~*n., pl.* **+ties. 4.** a choice piece of food, esp. a small cake or sweet; delicacy. [C13: from Old French *deintié,* from Latin *dignitās* DIGNITY] —**'dain+ti+ly** *adv.* —**'dain+ti+ness** *n.*

dai+qui+ri ('daɪkɪrɪ, 'dæk-) *n., pl.* **+ris.** *Chiefly U.S.* an iced drink containing rum, lime juice, and syrup or sugar. [C20: named after *Daiquiri,* rum-producing town in Cuba]

Dai+ren (daɪ'rɛn) *n.* a former name of **Lü-ta.**

dair·y ('dɛərɪ) *n., pl.* **dair·ies. 1.** a shop or company that supplies milk and milk products. **2.** a room or building where milk and cream are stored or made into butter and cheese. **3. a.** (*modifier*) of or relating to the production of milk and milk products: *dairy cattle.* **b.** (*in combination*): *a dairymaid; a dairyman.* [C13 *daierie,* from Old English *dǣge* servant girl, one who kneads bread; see DOUGH, LADY]

dair·y+ing ('dɛərɪɪŋ) *n.* the business of producing, processing, and selling dairy products.

dair·y+man ('dɛərɪmən) *n., pl.* **+men.** a male dairy worker.

da·is ('deɪɪs, deɪs) *n.* a raised platform, usually at one end of a hall, used by speakers, etc. [C13: from Old French *deis,* from Latin *discus:* DISCUS]

dai+sy ('deɪzɪ) *n., pl.* **+sies. 1.** a small low-growing European plant, *Bellis perennis,* having a rosette of leaves and flower heads of yellow central disc flowers and pinkish-white outer ray flowers: family *Compositae* (composites). **2.** Also called: **oxeye daisy, marguerite, moon daisy.** a Eurasian composite plant, *Chrysanthemum leucanthemum,* having flower heads with a yellow centre and white outer rays. **3.** any of various other composite plants having conspicuous ray flowers, such as the Michaelmas daisy and Shasta daisy. **4.** *Slang.* an excellent person or thing. **5. pushing up the daisies.** dead and buried. [Old English *dægesēge* day's eye] —**'dai+sied** *adj.*

dai+sy bush *n.* any of various shrubs of the genus *Olearia,* of Australia and New Zealand, with daisy-like flowers: family *Compositae* (composites).

dai+sy chain *n.* a garland made, esp. by children, by threading daisies together.

dai·sy+cut·ter ('deɪzɪ,kʌtə) *n. Cricket.* a ball bowled so that it rolls along the ground towards the batsman.

dak *or* **dawk** (dɑːk) *n.* (in India) the mail; post. [C18: from Hindi *dāk,* from Sanskrit *drāk* quickly]

Dak. *abbrev. for* Dakota.

Da+kar ('dækə) *n.* the capital and chief port of Senegal, on the SE side of Cape Verde peninsula. Pop.: 600 000 (1970 est.).

Da·kin's so+lu+tion ('deɪkɪnz) *n.* a dilute solution containing sodium hypochlorite and boric acid, used as an antiseptic in the treatment of wounds. [C20: named after Henry D. *Dakin* (1880–1952), English chemist]

Da+ko+ta (də'kəʊtə) *n.* a former territory of the U.S.: divided into the states of North Dakota and South Dakota in 1889. —**Da+'ko+tan** *adj., n.*

dal (dɑːl) *n.* **1.** split grain, a common foodstuff in India; pulse. **2.** a variant spelling of **dhal.**

Da·la·dier (*French* dala'dje) *n.* **É·douard** (e'dwaːr). 1884–1970, French radical socialist statesman; premier of France (1933; 1934; 1938–40) and signatory of the Munich Pact (1938).

Da·lai La·ma ('dælaɪ 'lɑːmə) *n.* **1.** (until 1959) the chief lama and ruler of Tibet. **2.** born 1935, the 14th holder of this office (1940), who fled to India (1959). [from Mongolian *dalai* ocean; see LAMA]

da+la+si (də'lɑːsɪ) *n.* the standard monetary unit of Gambia, divided into 100 butats. [from a Gambian native name]

dale (deɪl) *n.* an open valley, usually in an area of low hills. [Old English *dæl;* related to Old Frisian *del,* Old Norse *dalr,* Old High German *tal* valley]

Dale (deɪl) *n.* Sir **Hen·ry Hal·let.** 1875–1968, English physiologist: shared a Nobel prize for medicine in 1936 with Otto Loewi for their work on the chemical transmission of nerve impulses.

d'A·lem·bert (*French* dalɑ̃'bɛːr) *n.* See (Jean le Rond d') **Alembert.**

Dales (deɪlz) *pl. n.* (*sometimes not cap.*) **the.** short for the **Yorkshire Dales.**

dales+man ('deɪlzmən) *n., pl.* **+men.** a person living in a dale, esp. in the dales of N England.

da+leth *or* **da+led** ('dɑːlɪd; *Hebrew* 'dalɛt) *n.* the fourth letter of the Hebrew alphabet (ד), transliterated as *d* or, when final, *dh.* [Hebrew]

Dal·hou·sie (dæl'haʊzɪ) *n.* **1. 9th Earl of,** title of *George Ramsay.* 1770–1838, British general; governor of the British colonies in Canada (1819–28). **2.** his son, **1st Marquis and 10th Earl of,** title of *James Andrew Broun Ramsay.* 1812–60, British statesman: governor general of India (1848–56).

Da·li ('dɑːlɪ) *n.* **Sal·va·dor** ('sælvədɔ). born 1904, Spanish surrealist painter.

Dal·la·pic·co·la (*Italian* ,dalla'pikkola) *n.* **Lu·i·gi** (lʊ'iːdʒi). 1904–75, Italian composer of twelve-tone music. His works include the opera *Il Prigioniero* (1944–48) and the ballet *Marsia* (1948).

Dal+las ('dæləs) *n.* a city in NE Texas, on the Trinity River: scene of the assassination of President John F. Kennedy (1963). Pop.: 815 866 (1973 est.).

dal+li+ance ('dælɪəns) *n.* **1.** waste of time in frivolous action or in dawdling. **2.** an archaic word for **flirtation.**

dal+ly ('dælɪ) *vb.* **+lies, +ly+ing, +lied.** (*intr.*) **1.** to waste time idly; dawdle. **2.** (usually foll. by *with*) to deal frivolously: *to dally with someone's affections.* [C14: from Anglo-French *dalier* to gossip, of uncertain origin] —**'dal+li+er** *n.*

Dal+ma+tia (dæl'meɪʃə) *n.* a region of W Yugoslavia, in Croatia along the Adriatic: mountainous, with many offshore islands.

Dal+ma+tian (dæl'meɪʃən) *n.* **1.** Also called (esp. formerly): **carriage dog, coach dog.** a large breed of dog having a short smooth white coat with black or (in liver-spotted dalmatians) brown spots. **2.** a native or inhabitant of Dalmatia. ~*adj.* **3.** of or relating to Dalmatia or its inhabitants.

dal+mat+ic (dæl'mætɪk) *n.* **1.** a wide-sleeved tunic-like vestment open at the sides, worn by deacons and bishops. **2.** a similar robe worn by a king at his coronation. [C15: from Late Latin *dalmatica* (*vestis*) Dalmatian (robe) (originally made of Dalmatian wool)]

dal seg+no ('dæl 'sɛnjəʊ) *adv. Music.* (of a piece of music) to be repeated from the point marked with a sign to the word *fine.* Abbrev.: **D.S.** See also **fine**³. [Italian, literally: from the sign]

dal+ton ('dɔːltən) *n.* another term for the **atomic mass unit.**

Dal·ton ('dɔːltən) *n.* **John.** 1766–1844, English chemist and physicist, who formulated the modern form of the atomic theory and the law of partial pressures for gases. He also gave the first accurate description of colour blindness, from which he suffered.

dal+ton+ism ('dɔːltə,nɪzəm) *n.* colour blindness, esp. the confusion of red and green. [C19: from French *daltonisme,* after J. DALTON] —**dal+ton+ic** (dɔː'l'tɒnɪk) *adj.*

Dal·ton plan *or* **sys+tem** *n.* a system devised to encourage pupils to learn and develop at their own speed, using libraries and other sources to complete long assignments. [C20: named after *Dalton,* Mass. where the plan was used in schools]

Dal·ton's law *n.* the principle that the pressure exerted by a mixture of gases in a fixed volume is equal to the sum of the pressures that each gas would exert if it occupied the whole volume. Also called: **Dalton's law of partial pressures.** [C19: named after J. DALTON]

dam[1] (dæm) *n.* **1.** a barrier of concrete, earth, etc., built across a river to create a body of water, as for a domestic water supply. **2.** a reservoir of water created by such a barrier. **3.** something that resembles or functions as a dam. ~*vb.* **dams, dam+ming, dammed. 4.** (*tr.*; often foll. by *up*) to obstruct or restrict by or as if by a dam. [C12: probably from Middle Low German; compare Old Icelandic *damma* to block up]

dam[2] (dæm) *n.* the female parent of an animal, esp. of domestic livestock. [C13: variant of DAME]

dam[3] (dæm) *interj., adv., adj.* a variant spelling of **damn** (senses 1–4); often used in combination, as in **damfool, damme, dammit.**

Dam (*Danish* dam) *n.* **(Carl Peter) Hen·rik** ('hɛnrəg). 1895–1976, Danish biochemist who discovered vitamin K (1934): Nobel prize for medicine (1943).

dam+age ('dæmɪdʒ) *n.* **1.** injury or harm impairing the function or condition of a person or thing. **2.** loss of something desirable. **3.** *Informal.* cost; expense (esp. in the phrase **what's the damage?**). ~*vb.* **4.** (*tr.*) to cause damage to. **5.** (*intr.*) to suffer damage. [C14: from Old French, from Latin *damnum* injury, loss, fine] —**'dam+age+a·ble** *adj.* —**ˌdam+age+a·'bil+i·ty** *n.* —**'dam+ag+er** *n.* —**'dam+ag+ing+ly** *adv.*

dam+ag·es ('dæmɪdʒɪz) *pl. n. Law.* money to be paid as compensation to a person for injury, loss, etc.

dam+an ('dæmən) *n.* a rare name for the **hyrax,** esp. the Syrian rock hyrax. See also **cony** (sense 2). [from Arabic *damān Isrā'īl* sheep of Israel]

Da+man (dɑː'mɑːn) *n.* **1.** a region of W India: formerly a district of Portuguese India (1559–1961); part of the Union Territory of Goa, Daman, and Diu since 1961. Pop.: 38 739 (1971). Area: 456 sq. km (176 sq. miles). Portuguese name: **Damão. 2.** the chief town of this region, on the coast. Pop.: 9194 (1960).

Da+man+hûr (ˌdɑːmən'hʊə) *n.* a city in NE Egypt, in the Nile delta. Pop.: 175 900 (1974 est.).

Da+mão (da'mɜ̃ʊo) *n.* the Portuguese name for **Daman.**

da+mar ('dæmə) *n.* a variant spelling of **dammar.**

Da+ma+ra (də'mɑːrə) *n.* **1.** (*pl.* **+ras** *or* **+ra**) Also called: **Bergdama.** a member of a Negroid people of South West Africa. **2.** the language of this people, belonging to the Khoisan family.

Da+ma+ra+land (də'mɑːrəˌlænd) *n.* a plateau region of central South West Africa. Pop.: 64 973 (1970).

dam+a+scene ('dæməˌsiːn, ˌdæmə'siːn) *vb.* **1.** (*tr.*) to ornament (metal, esp. steel) by etching or by inlaying other metals, usually gold or silver. ~*n.* **2.** a design or article produced by this process. ~*adj.* **3.** of or relating to this process. [C14: from Latin *damascēnus* of Damascus]

Dam·a+scene ('dæməˌsiːn, ˌdæmə'siːn) *adj.* **1.** of or relating to Damascus. ~*n.* **2.** a native or inhabitant of Damascus. **3.** a variety of domestic fancy pigeon with silvery plumage.

Da+mas+cus (də'mɑːskəs, -'mæs-) *n.* the capital of Syria, in the southwest: reputedly the oldest city in the world, having been inhabited continuously since before 1000 B.C. Pop.: 836 668 (1970). Arabic names: **Dimashq, Esh Sham.**

Da+mas+cus steel *or* **dam+ask steel** *n.* a hard flexible steel decorated with wavy markings and used for sword blades.

dam+ask ('dæməsk) *n.* **1. a.** a reversible fabric, usually silk or linen, with a pattern woven into it. It is used for table linen, curtains, etc. **b.** table linen made from this. **c.** (*as modifier*): *a damask tablecloth.* **2.** short for **Damascus steel. 3.** the wavy markings on such steel. **4. a.** the greyish-pink colour of the damask rose. **b.** (*as adj.*): *damask wallpaper.* ~*vb.* **5.** (*tr.*) another word for **damascene** (sense 1). [C14: from Medieval Latin *damascus,* from Damascus, where this fabric was originally made]

dam+ask rose *n.* a rose, *Rosa damascena,* native to Asia and cultivated for its pink or red fragrant flowers, which are used to make the perfume attar. [C16: from Medieval Latin *rosa damascēna* rose of Damascus]

dame (deɪm) *n.* **1.** (formerly) a woman of rank or dignity; lady. **2.** a nun who has taken the vows of her order, esp. a Benedictine. **3.** *Archaic, chiefly Brit.* a matronly or elderly woman. **4.** *Slang, chiefly U.S.* a woman. **5.** Also called: **pantomime dame.** *Brit.* the role of a comic old woman in a pantomime, usually played by a man. [C13: from Old French, from Latin *domina* lady, mistress of a household]

Dame (deɪm) *n.* (in Britain) **1.** the title of a woman who has been awarded the Order of the British Empire or any of certain other orders of chivalry. **2.** the legal title of the wife or widow of a knight or baronet, placed before her name: *Dame Judith.* Compare **Lady.**

dame school *n.* (formerly) a small school, often in a village, usually run by an elderly lady teacher for children up to the age of 14.

dame's vi·o+let, dame's rock+et, *or* **dame+wort** ('deɪmˌwɜːt) *n.* a Eurasian cruciferous hairy perennial plant, *Hesperis matronalis,* cultivated in gardens for its mauve or white fragrant flowers.

Da+mien (*French* da'mjɛ̃) *n.* **Jo·seph** (ʒo'zɛf), known as *Father Damien.* 1840–89, Belgian Roman Catholic missionary to the leper colony at Molokai, Hawaii.

Dam+i+et+ta (ˌdæmɪ'ɛtə) *n.* a town in NE Egypt, in the Nile delta: important medieval commercial centre. Pop.: 110 000 (1974 est.). Arabic name: **Dumyat.**

dam+mar, da+mar, *or* **dam+mer** ('dæmə) *n.* any of various resins obtained from SE Asian trees, esp. of the genera *Agathis* (conifers) and *Shorea* (family *Dipterocarpaceae*): used for varnishes, lacquers, bases for oil paints, etc. [C17: from Malay *damar* resin]

damn (dæm) *interj.* **1.** *Slang.* an exclamation of annoyance (often in exclamatory phrases such as **damn it! damn you!** etc.). **2.** *Informal.* an exclamation of surprise or pleasure (esp. in the exclamatory phrase **damn me!**). ~*adj.* **3.** (*prenominal*) *Slang.* deserving damnation; detestable. ~*adv., adj.* (*prenominal*) **4.** *Slang.* (intensifier): *damn fool; a damn good pianist.* ~*adv.* **5. damn all.** *Slang.* absolutely nothing. ~*vb.* (*mainly tr.*) **6.** to condemn as bad, worthless, etc. **7.** to curse. **8.** to condemn to eternal damnation. **9.** (*often passive*) to doom to ruin; cause to fail: *the venture was damned from the start.* **10.** (*also intr.*) to prove (someone) guilty: *damning evidence.* **11.** to swear (at) using the word *damn.* **12. as near as damn it.** *Brit. informal.* as near as possible; very near. **13. damn with faint praise.** to praise so unenthusiastically that the effect is condemnation. ~*n.* **14.** *Slang.* something of negligible value; jot (esp. in the phrase **not worth a damn**). **15. not give a damn.** *Informal.* to be unconcerned; not care. [C13: from Old French *dampner,* from Latin *damnāre* to injure, condemn, from *damnum* loss, injury, penalty]

dam+na·ble ('dæmnəbᵊl) *adj.* **1.** execrable; detestable. **2.** liable to or deserving damnation. —**'dam+na·ble+ness** *or* **ˌdam+na·'bil+i·ty** *n.* —**'dam+na·bly** *adv.*

dam+na+tion (dæm'neɪʃən) *n.* **1.** the act of damning or state of being damned. **2.** a cause or instance of being damned. ~*interj.* **3.** an exclamation of anger, disappointment, etc.

dam+na·to·ry ('dæmnətərɪ, -trɪ) *adj.* threatening or occasioning condemnation.

damned (dæmd) *adj.* **1. a.** condemned to hell. **b.** (*as n.*): *the damned.* ~*adv., adj. Slang.* **2.** (intensifier): *a damned good try; a damned liar; I should damned well think so!* **3.** used to indicate amazement, disavowal, or refusal (in such phrases as **I'll be damned** and **damned if I care**).

damned+est ('dæmdɪst) *n. Informal.* utmost; best (esp. in the phrases **do** or **try one's damnedest**).

dam+ni+fy ('dæmnɪˌfaɪ) *vb.* **+fies, +fy+ing, +fied.** (*tr.*) *Law.* to cause loss or damage to (a person); injure. [C16: from Old French *damnifier,* ultimately from Latin *damnum* harm, + *facere* to make] —**ˌdam+ni+fi+'ca+tion** *n.*

Dam·o·cles ('dæməˌkliːz) *n. Classical legend.* a sycophant forced by Dionysius, tyrant of Syracuse, to sit under a sword suspended by a hair to demonstrate that being a king was not the happy state Damocles had said it was. See also **Sword of Damocles.** —**ˌDam·o+'cle·an** *adj.*

Dam·o+dar ('dæməˌdɑː) *n.* a river in NE India, rising in Bihar and flowing east through West Bengal to the Hooghly River: the **Damodar Valley** is an important centre of heavy industry.

dam·oi+selle, dam·o+sel, *or* **dam·o+zel** (ˌdæmə'zɛl) *n.* archaic spellings of **damsel.**

Da·mon and Pyth·i·as ('deɪmən) *n. Classical legend.* two friends noted for their mutual loyalty. Damon offered himself as a hostage for Pythias, who was to be executed for treason by Dionysius of Syracuse. When Pythias returned to save his friend's life, he was pardoned.

damp (dæmp) *adj.* **1.** slightly wet, as from dew, steam, etc. **2.** *Archaic.* dejected. ~*n.* **3.** slight wetness; moisture; humidity. **4.** rank air or poisonous gas, esp. in a mine. See also **firedamp. 5.** a discouragement; damper. **6.** *Archaic.* dejection. ~*vb.* (*tr.*) **7.** to make slightly wet. **8.** (often foll. by *down*) to stifle or deaden: *to damp one's ardour.* **9.** (often foll. by *down*) to reduce the flow of air to (a fire) to make it burn more slowly or to extinguish it. **10.** *Physics.* to reduce the amplitude of (an oscillation or wave). **11.** *Music.* to muffle (a vibrating string, as of a piano or guitar). [C14: from Middle Low German *damp* steam; related to Old High German *demphen* to cause to steam] —**'damp+ish** *adj.* —**'damp+ly** *adv.* —**'damp+ness** *n.*

damp+course ('dæmpˌkɔːs) *n.* a horizontal layer of impervious material in a brick wall, fairly close to the ground, to stop moisture rising. Also called: **damp-proof course.**

damp+en ('dæmpən) *vb.* **1.** to make or become damp. **2.** (*tr.*) to stifle; deaden. —**'damp+en+er** *n.*

damp+er ('dæmpə) *n.* **1.** a person, event, or circumstance that depresses or discourages. **2.** a movable plate to regulate the draught in a stove or furnace flue. **3.** a device to reduce electronic, mechanical, acoustical, or aerodynamic oscillations in a system. **4.** *Music.* the pad in a piano or harpsichord that deadens the vibration of each string as its key is released. **5.** *Chiefly Austral.* and *N.Z.* any of various unleavened loaves and scones, typically cooked on an open fire.

Dam·pi·er ('dæmpɪə) *n.* **Wil·liam.** 1652–1715, English navigator, pirate, and writer: sailed around the world twice.

damp+ing off *n.* any of various similar diseases of plants, esp. the collapse and death of seedlings caused by the parasitic fungus *Pythium debaryanum* and related fungi in conditions of excessive moisture.

damp off *vb.* (*intr., adv.*) (of plants, seedlings, shoots, etc.) to be affected by damping off.

dam+sel ('dæmzᵊl) *n. Archaic or poetic.* a young unmarried woman; maiden. [C13: from Old French *damoisele,* from Vulgar Latin *domnicella* (unattested) young lady, from Latin *domina* mistress; see DAME]

dam·sel+fish ('dæmzᵊlˌfɪʃ) *n., pl.* **+fish** *or* **+fish·es.** any small tropical percoid fish of the family *Pomacentridae,* having a brightly coloured deep compressed body. See also **anemone fish.**

dam·sel+fly ('dæmzᵊlˌflaɪ) *n., pl.* **+flies.** any insect of the suborder *Zygoptera,* similar to but smaller than dragonflies and usually resting with the wings closed over the back: order *Odonata.*

dam+son ('dæmzən) *n.* **1.** a small rosaceous tree, *Prunus domestica institiia* (or *P. insititia*), cultivated for its blue-black edible plumlike fruit and probably derived from the bullace. See also **plum**[1] (sense 1). **2.** the fruit of this tree. [C14: from Latin *prūnum Damascēnum* Damascus plum]

dam+son cheese *n.* thick damson jam.

dan[1] (dæn) *n.* a small buoy used as a marker at sea. Also called: **dan buoy.** [C17: of unknown origin]

dan[2] (dæn) *n. Judo.* **1.** any one of the 12 black-belt grades of proficiency. **2.** a competitor entitled to dan grading. ~Compare **kyu.** [Japanese]

Dan[1] (dæn) *n.* an archaic title of honour, equivalent to *Master* or *Sir: Dan Chaucer.*

Dan[2] (dæn) *n. Old Testament.* **1. a.** the fourth son of Jacob (Genesis 30:1–6). **b.** the tribe descended from him. **2.** a city in the northern territory of Canaan.

Dan. *abbrev. for:* **1.** *Bible.* Daniel. **2.** Danish.

Dan·a·ë ('dænei,i:) *n. Greek myth.* the mother of Perseus by Zeus, who came to her in prison as a shower of gold.

Da·na·i·des (də'neɪɪ,di:z) *pl. n., sing.* **Da·na·id.** *Greek myth.* the fifty daughters of Danaüs. All but Hypermnestra murdered their bridegrooms and were punished in Hades by having to pour water perpetually into a jar with a hole in the bottom. —**Dan·a·id·e·an** (,dænɪ'ɪdɪən, ,dænɪə'di:ən) *adj.*

Da Nang ('dɑ: 'næŋ) *n.* a port in central Vietnam, on the South China Sea. Pop.: 437 668 (1971). Former name: **Tourane.**

Dan·a·üs ('dænɪəs) *n. Greek myth.* a king of Argos who told his fifty daughters, the Danaides, to kill their bridegrooms on their wedding night.

dance (dɑ:ns) *vb.* **1.** (*intr.*) to move the feet and body rhythmically, esp. in time to music. **2.** (*tr.*) to perform (a particular dance). **3.** (*intr.*) to skip or leap, as in joy, etc. **4.** to move or cause to move in a light rhythmical way. **5. dance attendance (on someone).** to attend (someone) solicitously or obsequiously. ~*n.* **6.** a series of rhythmical steps and movements, usually in time to music. **7.** an act of dancing. **8. a.** a social meeting arranged for dancing; ball. **b.** (*as modifier*): *a dance hall.* **9.** a piece of music in the rhythm of a particular dance form, such as a waltz. **10.** dancelike movements made by some insects and birds, esp. as part of a behaviour pattern. **11. lead (someone) a dance.** *Brit. informal.* to cause (someone) continued worry and exasperation; play up. [C13: from Old French *dancier*] —'**danc+er** *n.*

dance of death *n.* a pictorial, literary, or musical representation, current esp. in the Middle Ages, of a dance in which living people, in order of social precedence, are led off to their graves, by a personification of death. Also called (French): **danse macabre.**

dan+cette (dɑ:n'sɛt) *n.* another name for **chevron** (senses 2, 4).

D and C *n. Med.* dilation and curettage; a therapeutic or diagnostic procedure in obstetrics and gynaecology involving dilation of the cervix and curettage of the cavity of the uterus, as for abortion.

dan+de+li+on ('dændɪ,laɪən) *n.* **1.** a plant, *Taraxacum officinale,* native to Europe and Asia and naturalized as a weed in North America, having yellow rayed flowers and deeply notched basal leaves, which are used for salad or wine: family *Compositae* (composites). **2.** any of several similar related plants. [C15: from Old French *dent de lion,* literally: tooth of a lion, referring to its leaves]

dan+der[1] ('dændə) *n.* **1.** small particles or scales of hair or feathers. **2. get one's** (*or* **someone's**) **dander up.** *Slang, chiefly U.S.* to become or cause to become annoyed or angry. [C19: changed from DANDRUFF]

dan+der[2] ('dændə) *Scot. and northern Brit. dialect.* ~*n.* **1.** a stroll. ~*vb.* **2.** (*intr.*) to stroll. [C19: of unknown origin]

Dan+die Din+mont ('dændɪ 'dɪnmɒnt) *n.* a breed of small terrier with a long wiry coat and drooping ears. Also called: **Dandie Dinmont terrier.** [C19: named after a character who owned two terriers in *Guy Mannering* (1815), a novel by Sir Walter Scott]

dan+di+fy ('dændɪ,faɪ) *vb.* **+fies, +fy+ing, +fied.** (*tr.*) to dress like or cause to resemble a dandy. —,**dan+di+fi+'ca+tion** *n.*

dan+di+prat ('dændɪ,præt) *n.* **1.** a small English coin minted in the 16th century. **2.** *Archaic.* **a.** a small boy. **b.** an insignificant person. [C16: of unknown origin]

dan+dle ('dændᵊl) *vb.* (*tr.*) **1.** to move (a young child, etc.) up and down (on the knee or in the arms). **2.** to pet; fondle. [C16: of uncertain origin] —'**dan+dler** *n.*

dan+druff ('dændrəf) *or* **dan+driff** ('dændrɪf) *n.* loose scales of dry dead skin shed from the scalp. [C16: *dand-* of unknown origin + *-ruff,* probably from Middle English *roufe* scab, from Old Norse *hrūfa*] —'**dan+druff·y** *or* '**dan+driff·y** *adj.*

dan+dy ('dændɪ) *n., pl.* **+dies. 1.** a man greatly concerned with smartness of dress; beau. **2.** a yawl or ketch. ~*adj.* **+di+er, +di+est. 3.** *Informal.* very good or fine. [C18: perhaps short for JACK-A-DANDY] —'**dan+di+ly** *adv.* —'**dan+dy+ish** *adj.* —'**dan+dy+ism** *n.*

dan·dy-brush *n.* a stiff brush used for grooming a horse.

dan+dy roll *or* **roll+er** *n.* a light roller used in the manufacture of certain papers to produce watermarks.

Dane (deɪn) *n.* **1.** a native, citizen, or inhabitant of Denmark. **2.** any of the Vikings who invaded England from the late 8th to the 11th century A.D..

Dane+geld ('deɪn,gɛld) *or* **Dane+gelt** ('deɪn,gɛlt) *n.* the tax first levied in the late 9th century in Anglo-Saxon England to provide protection money for or to finance forces to oppose Viking invaders. [C11: from *Dan* Dane + *geld* tribute; see YIELD]

Dane+law *or* **Dane+lagh** ('deɪn,lɔ:) *n.* the northern, central and eastern parts of Anglo-Saxon England in which Danish law and custom were observed. [Old English *Dena lagu* Danes' law; term revived in the 19th century]

dane+wort ('deɪn,wɜ:t) *n.* a caprifoliaceous shrub, *Sambucus ebulus,* native to Europe and Asia and having serrated leaves and white flowers. See also **elder**[2].

dang (dæŋ) *interj., adv., adj.* a euphemistic word for **damn** (senses 1–4).

dan+ger ('deɪndʒə) *n.* **1.** the state of being vulnerable to injury, loss, or evil; risk. **2.** a person or thing, that may cause injury, pain, etc. **3.** *Obsolete.* power. **4. in danger of.** liable to. **5. on the danger list.** critically ill in hospital. [C13 *daunger* power, hence power to inflict injury, from Old French *dongier* (from Latin *dominium* ownership) blended with Old French *dam* injury, from Latin *damnum*] —'**dan+ger+less** *adj.*

dan+ger mon+ey *n.* extra money paid to compensate for the risks involved in certain dangerous jobs.

dan+ger+ous ('deɪndʒərəs) *adj.* causing danger; perilous. —'**dan+ger+ous+ly** *adv.* —'**dan+ger+ous+ness** *n.*

dan+gle ('dæŋgᵊl) *vb.* **1.** to hang or cause to hang freely: *his legs dangled over the wall.* **2.** (*tr.*) to display as an enticement: *the hope of a legacy was dangled before her.* ~*n.* **3.** the act of dangling or something that dangles. [C16: perhaps from Danish *dangle,* probably of imitative origin] —'**dan+gler** *n.* —'**dan+gling+ly** *adv.*

dan+gling par+ti+ci+ple *n. Grammar.* another name (esp. U.S.) for **misplaced modifier.**

Dan·iel ('dænjəl) *n.* **1.** *Old Testament.* **a.** a youth who was taken into the household of Nebuchadnezzar, received guidance and apocalyptic visions from God, and was given divine protection when thrown into the lions' den. **b.** the book that recounts these experiences and visions, (in full **The Book of the Prophet Daniel**). **2.** (often preceded by *a*) a wise upright person. [sense 2: referring to Daniel in the Apochryphal *Book of Susanna*]

Dan·iell cell ('dænjəl) *n. Physics.* a type of cell having a zinc anode in dilute sulphuric acid separated by a porous barrier from a copper cathode in copper sulphate solution. It has an emf of 1.1 volts. [C19: named after John *Daniell* (1790–1845), English scientist]

dan·i·o ('deɪnɪ,əʊ) *n., pl.* **·os.** any brightly coloured tropical freshwater cyprinid fish of the genus *Danio* and related genera: popular aquarium fishes. [C19: from New Latin, of obscure origin]

Dan+ish ('deɪnɪʃ) *adj.* **1.** of, relating to, or characteristic of Denmark, its people, or their language. ~*n.* **2.** the official language of Denmark, belonging to the North Germanic branch of the Indo-European family. **3. the Danish.** (*functioning as pl.*) the people of Denmark collectively.

Dan+ish blue *n.* a strong-tasting white cheese with blue veins.

Dan+ish loaf *n. Brit.* a large white loaf with a centre split having the top crust dusted with flour, esp. one baked on the sole of the oven.

Dan+ish pas+try *n.* a rich flaky pastry filled with apple, almond paste, icing, etc.

Dan+ish West In+dies *pl. n.* the former possession of Denmark in the W Lesser Antilles, sold to the U.S. in 1917 and since then named the **Virgin Islands of the United States.**

dank (dæŋk) *adj.* (esp. of cellars, caves, etc.) unpleasantly damp and chilly. [C14: of probably of Scandinavian origin; compare Swedish *dank* marshy spot] —'**dank+ly** *adv.* —'**dank+ness** *n.*

Dan+mark ('dan,marg) *n.* the Danish name for **Denmark.**

D'An·nun·zio (*Italian* dan'untsjo) *n.* **Ga·bri·e·le** (,gabri'ɛ:le). 1863–1938, Italian poet, dramatist, novelist, war hero, and leading Fascist. His works include the poems in *Alcione* (1904) and the drama *La Figlia di Iorio* (1904).

dan+ny ('dænɪ) *or* **don+ny** *n., pl.* **+nies.** *Brit. dialect.* the hand (used esp. when addressing children). [probably from *dandy,* childish pronunciation of HAND]

Da·no-Nor·we·gian (,deɪnəʊnɔ:'wi:dʒən) *n.* another name for **Bokmål.**

danse ma+cabre *French.* (dɑ̃s ma'kabr) *n.* another name for **dance of death.**

dan+seur *French.* (dɑ̃'sœ:r) *or* (*fem.*) ***dan+seuse*** (dɑ̃'sœ:z) *n.* a ballet dancer.

Dan·te ('dæntɪ, 'dɑ:nteɪ; *Italian* 'dante) *n.* full name **Dan·te A·li·ghie·ri** (*Italian* ali'gjɛ:ri). 1265–1321, Italian poet famous for *La Divina Commedia* (?1309–?1320), an allegorical account of his journey through Hell, Purgatory, and Paradise, guided by Virgil and his idealized love Beatrice. His other works include *La Vita Nuova* (?1292), in which he celebrates his love for Beatrice. —**Dan+te·an** ('dæntɪən, dæn'ti:ən) *or* **Dan+tesque** (dæn'tɛsk) *adj.*

Dan·ton ('dæntən; *French* dɑ̃'tɔ̃) *n.* **Georges Jacques** (ʒɔrʒ 'ʒɑk). 1759–94, French revolutionary leader: a founder member of the Committee of Public Safety (1793) and minister of justice (1792–94). He was overthrown by Robespierre and guillotined.

Dan+ube ('dænju:b) *n.* a river in central and SE Europe, rising in the Black Forest in West Germany and flowing to the Black Sea. Length: 2859 km (1776 miles). German name: **Donau.** Czech name: **Dunaj.** Hungarian name: **Duna.** Serbo-Croat name: **Dunav.** Rumanian name: **Dunărea.** —**Dan·u+bi·an** (dæn'ju:bɪən) *adj.*

Dan+zig ('dænsɪg; *German* 'dantsɪç) *n.* **1.** the German name for **Gdańsk. 2.** a rare variety of domestic fancy pigeon originating in this area.

dap[1] (dæp) *vb.* **daps, dap+ping, dapped. 1.** *Angling.* to let (bait) float on the water. **2.** (*intr.*) (as of a bird, etc.) to dip lightly into water. **3.** to bounce or cause to bounce. [C17: of imitative origin]

dap[2] (dæp) *n. Southwest Brit. dialect.* another word for **plimsoll.** [C20: probably special use of DAP[1] (in the sense: to bounce, skip)]

daph·ne ('dæfnɪ) *n.* any shrub of the Eurasian thymelaeaceous genus *Daphne,* such as the mezereon and spurge laurel: ornamentals with shiny evergreen leaves and clusters of small bell-shaped flowers. See also **laurel** (sense 4). [via Latin from Greek: laurel]

Daph·ne ('dæfnɪ) *n. Greek myth.* a nymph who was saved from the amorous attentions of Apollo by being changed into a laurel tree.

daph+ni·a ('dæfnɪə) *n.* any water flea of the genus *Daphnia,* having a rounded body enclosed in a transparent shell and bearing branched swimming antennae. [C19: from New Latin, probably from DAPHNE]

Daph·nis ('dæfnɪs) *n. Greek myth.* a Sicilian shepherd, the son of Hermes and a nymph, who was regarded as the inventor of pastoral poetry.

Daph·nis and Chlo·e *n.* two lovers in pastoral literature, esp. in a prose idyll attributed to the Greek writer Longus.

dap+per ('dæpə) *adj.* **1.** neat and spruce in dress and bearing; trim. **2.** small and nimble. [C15: from Middle Dutch: active, nimble] —**'dap+per+ly** *adv.* —**'dap+per+ness** *n.*

dap+ple ('dæpᵊl) *vb.* **1.** to mark or become marked with spots or patches of a different colour; mottle. ~*n.* **2.** mottled or spotted markings. **3.** a dappled horse, etc. ~*adj.* **4.** marked with dapples or spots. [C14: of unknown origin]

dap·ple-grey *n.* a horse with a grey coat having spots of darker colour.

Dap+sang (dʌp'sʌŋ) *n.* another name for **K2.**

dar+af ('dærəf) *n. Physics.* a unit of elastance equal to a reciprocal farad. [C20: reverse spelling of FARAD]

dar+bies ('dɑ:bɪz) *pl. n. Brit.* a slang term for **handcuffs.** [C16: perhaps from the phrase *Father Derby's* or *Father Darby's bonds,* a rigid agreement between a usurer and his client]

d'Ar·blay ('dɑ:bleɪ) *n.* **Mad·ame.** married name of (Fanny) **Burney.**

Dar·by and Joan ('dɑ:bɪ) *n.* **1.** an ideal elderly married couple living in domestic harmony. **2. Darby and Joan Club.** a club for elderly people. [C18: a couple in an 18th-century English ballad]

dard (dɑ:d) *n.* a member of any of the Indo-European peoples speaking a Dardic language.

Dar+dan ('dɑ:dᵊn) *or* **Dar+da+ni·an** (dɑ:'deɪnɪən) *n.* another name for a **Trojan.**

Dar+da+nelles (ˌdɑ:də'nɛlz) *n.* the strait between the Aegean and the Sea of Marmara, separating European from Asian Turkey. Ancient name: **Hellespont.**

Dar+da+nus ('dɑ:dənəs) *n. Classical myth.* the son of Zeus and Electra who founded the royal house of Troy.

Dar+dic ('dɑ:dɪk) *adj.* **1.** belonging or relating to a group of languages spoken in Kashmir, N Pakistan, and E Afghanistan, regarded as a subbranch of the Indic branch of the Indo-European family but showing certain Iranian characteristics. ~*n.* **2.** this group of languages.

dare (dɛə) *vb.* **1.** (*tr.*) to challenge (a person to do something) as proof of courage. **2.** (can take an infinitive with or without *to*) to be courageous enough to try (to do something): *she dares to dress differently from the others; you wouldn't dare!* **3.** (*tr.*) *Rare.* to oppose without fear; defy. **4. I dare say.** Also: **I daresay. a.** (it is) quite possible (that). **b.** probably: used as sentence substitute. ~*n.* **5.** a challenge to do something as proof of courage. **6.** something done in response to such a challenge. [Old English *durran;* related to Old High German *turran* to venture; see DURST] —**'dar+er** *n.*

Usage. When used negatively or interrogatively and not followed by an infinitive with *to, dare* does not add *-s: he dare not; dare she come?*

dare+dev·il ('dɛəˌdɛvᵊl) *n.* **1.** a recklessly bold person. ~*adj.* **2.** reckless; daring; bold. —**'dare+ˌdev·il+ry** *or* **'dare+ˌdev·il+try** *n.*

Dar es Sa+laam ('dɑ:r ɛs sə'lɑ:m) *n.* the capital and chief port of Tanzania, on the Indian Ocean: capital of German East Africa (1891–1916); university (1963). Pop.: 517 000 (1975 est.).

Dar+fur (dɑ:'fʊə) *n.* a province of the W Sudan since 1916; an independent kingdom until conquered by Egypt in 1874. Capital: El Fasher. Pop.: 1 838 707 (1973). Area: 496 373 sq. km (191 650 sq. miles).

darg (dɑ:g) *n.* **1.** *Northern Brit. dialect.* a day's work. **2.** *Austral.* a specified amount of work; job. [C15: formed by syncope from *day-work*]

dar+gah *or* **dur+gah** ('dɜ:gɑ:) *n.* the tomb of a Muslim saint; a Muslim shrine. [Persian]

dar+ic ('dærɪk) *n.* a gold coin of ancient Persia. Compare **siglos.** [C16: from Greek *Dareikos,* probably after Darius I of Persia]

Dar+i+en ('dɛərɪən, 'dæ-) *n.* **1.** the E part of the Isthmus of Panama, between the **Gulf of Darien** on the Caribbean coast and the Gulf of San Miguel on the Pacific coast; chiefly within the republic of Panama but extending also into Colombia. **2. Isthmus of.** the former name of the Isthmus of **Panama.** Spanish name: **Da+rién** (da'rjen).

dar+ing ('dɛərɪŋ) *adj.* **1.** bold or adventurous; reckless. ~*n.* **2.** courage in taking risks; boldness. —**'dar+ing+ly** *adv.*

Da·ri·o (*Spanish* da'rio) *n.* **Ru·bén** (ru'βen), pen name of *Félix Rubén García Sarmiento.* 1867–1916, Nicaraguan poet whose poetry includes *Prosas Profanas* (1896).

dar·i·ole ('dærɪˌəʊl) *n.* a small narrow mould used for making individual sweet or savoury dishes. Also called: **dariole mould.** [C14: from Old French]

Da·ri·us I (də'raɪəs) *n.* called *the Great,* surname *Hystaspis.* ?550–486 B.C., king of Persia (521–486), who extended the Persian empire and crushed the revolt of the Ionian city states (500). He led two expeditions against Greece but was defeated at Marathon (490).

Da·ri·us III *n.* died 330 B.C., last Achaemenid king of Persia (336–330), who was defeated by Alexander the Great.

Dar+jee+ling (dɑ:'dʒi:lɪŋ) *n.* **1.** a town in NE India, in West Bengal in the Himalayas, at an altitude of about 2250 m (7500 ft.). Pop.: 42 873 (1971). **2.** a high-quality black tea grown in the mountains around Darjeeling.

dark (dɑ:k) *adj.* **1.** having little or no light: *a dark street.* **2.** (of a colour) reflecting or transmitting little light: *dark brown.* Compare **light**[1] (sense 27), **medium** (sense 2). **3. a.** (of complexion, hair colour, etc.) not fair or blond; swarthy; brunette. **b.** (*in combination*): *dark-eyed.* **4.** gloomy or dismal. **5.** sinister; evil: *a dark purpose.* **6.** sullen or angry: *a dark scowl.* **7.** ignorant or unenlightened: *a dark period in our history.* **8.** secret or mysterious: *keep it dark.* **9.** *Phonetics.* denoting an (l) pronounced with a velar articulation giving back vowel resonance. In English, *l* is usually dark when final or preconsonantal. Compare **light**[1] (sense 28). ~*n.* **10.** absence of light; darkness. **11.** night or nightfall. **12.** a dark place, patch, or shadow. **13.** a state of ignorance (esp. in the phrase **in the dark**). ~*vb.* **14.** an archaic word for **darken.** [Old English *deorc;* related to Old High German *terchennen* to hide] —**'dark+ish** *adj.* —**'dark+ly** *adv.* —**'dark+ness** *n.*

Dark Ag·es *n. European history.* **1.** the period from about the late 5th century A.D. to about 1000 A.D., once considered an unenlightened period. **2.** (occasionally) the whole medieval period.

Dark Con+ti+nent *n.* **the.** a term for Africa when it was relatively unexplored.

dark+en ('dɑ:kən) *vb.* **1.** to make or become dark or darker. **2.** to make or become gloomy, angry, or sad: *his mood darkened.* **3. darken (someone's) door.** (*usually used with a negative*) to visit someone: *never darken my door again!* —**'dark+en+er** *n.*

dark-field il+lu+mi+na+tion *n.* illumination of the field of a microscope from the side so that the specimen is viewed against a dark background.

dark-field mic·ro+scope *n.* another name for an **ultramicroscope.**

dark glass·es *n.* spectacles with lenses tinted to reduce transmitted light.

dark horse *n.* **1.** a competitor in a race or contest about whom little is known; an unknown. **2.** a person who reveals little about himself or his activities, esp. one who has unexpected talents or abilities. **3.** *U.S. politics.* a candidate who is unexpectedly nominated or elected.

dark lan+tern *n.* a lantern having a sliding shutter or panel to dim or hide the light.

dar+kle ('dɑ:kᵊl) *vb. Archaic or literary.* **1.** to grow dark; darken. **2.** to appear dark or indistinct. [C19: back formation from DARKLING]

dark+ling ('dɑ:klɪŋ) *adv., adj. Poetic.* in the dark or night. [C15: from DARK + -LING[2]]

dark re+ac+tion *n. Botany.* the stage of photosynthesis involving the reduction of carbon dioxide and the dissociation of water, using chemical energy stored in ATP: does not require the presence of light. Compare **light reaction.**

dark+room ('dɑ:kˌru:m, -ˌrʊm) *n.* a room in which photographs are processed in darkness or safe light.

dark+some ('dɑ:ksəm) *adj. Literary.* dark or darkish.

dark star *n.* an invisible star known to exist only from observation of its radio, infrared, or other spectrum or of its gravitational effect, such as an invisible component of a binary or multiple star.

dark·y, dark·ie, *or* **dark+ey** ('dɑ:kɪ) *n., pl.* **dark·ies** *or* **dark+eys.** *Informal.* **1.** an offensive word for a Negro. **2.** *Austral.* an offensive word for an Aborigine.

Dar·lan (*French* dar'lã) *n.* **Jean Louis Xa·vier Fran·çois** (ʒã lwi gzavje frã'swa). 1881–1942, French admiral and member of the Vichy government. He cooperated with the Allies after their invasion of North Africa; assassinated.

dar+ling ('dɑ:lɪŋ) *n.* **1.** a person very much loved: often used as a term of address. **2.** a favourite: *the teacher's darling.* ~*adj.* (*prenominal*) **3.** beloved. **4.** much admired; pleasing: *a darling hat.* [Old English *dēorling;* see DEAR, -LING[1]]

Dar·ling ('dɑ:lɪŋ) *n.* **Grace.** 1815–42, English national heroine, famous for her rescue (1838) of some shipwrecked sailors with her father, a lighthouse keeper.

Dar+ling Downs *n.* a plateau in NE Australia, in SE Queensland: a vast agricultural and stock-raising area.

Dar+ling Range *n.* a ridge in SW Western Australia, parallel to the coast. Highest point: about 573 m (1910 ft.).

Dar+ling Riv+er *n.* a river in SE Australia, rising in the Eastern Highlands and flowing southwest to the Murray River. Length: 2740 km (1702 miles).

Dar+ling+ton ('dɑ:lɪŋtən) *n.* an industrial town in NE England in S Durham: developed mainly with the opening of the Stockton-Darlington railway (1825). Pop.: 85 889 (1971).

Darm+stadt ('dɑ:mstæt; *German* 'darmˌʃtat) *n.* an industrial city in central West Germany, in Hesse: former capital of the grand duchy of Hesse-Darmstadt (1567–1945). Pop.: 140 509 (1974 est.).

darn[1] (dɑːn) *vb.* **1.** to mend (a hole or a garment) with a series of crossing or interwoven stitches. ~*n.* **2.** a patch of darned work on a garment. **3.** the process or act of darning. [C16: probably from French (Channel Islands dialect) *darner;* compare Welsh, Breton *darn* piece] —**'darn+er** *n.*

darn[2] (dɑːn) *interj., adj., adv., n.* a euphemistic word for **damn** (senses 1–4, 12).

darned (dɑːnd) *adv., adj. Slang.* **1.** (intensifier): *this darned car won't start; a darned good shot.* ~*adj.* **2.** another word for **damned** (senses 2, 3).

dar+nel ('dɑːnᵊl) *n.* any of several grasses of the genus *Lolium,* esp. *L. temulentum,* that grow as weeds in grain fields in Europe and Asia. [C14: probably related to French (Walloon dialect) *darnelle,* of obscure origin]

darn+ing egg *or* **mush+room** *n.* a rounded piece of wood used in darning to support the fabric around the hole.

darn+ing nee+dle *n.* **1.** a long needle with a large eye used for darning. **2.** *U.S.* a dialect name for a **dragonfly.**

Darn·ley ('dɑːnlɪ) *n.* **Lord.** title of *Henry Stuart* (or *Stewart*). 1545–67, Scottish nobleman; second husband of Mary Queen of Scots and father of James I of England. After murdering his wife's secretary, Rizzio (1566), he was himself assassinated (1567).

da+ro+gha (dɑː'rəʊgɑː) *n.* (in India and Pakistan) **1.** a manager. **2.** an inspector. [Urdu]

dart (dɑːt) *n.* **1.** a small narrow pointed missile that is thrown or shot, as in the game of darts. **2.** a sudden quick movement. **3.** *Zoology.* a slender pointed structure, as in snails for aiding copulation or in nematodes for penetrating the host's tissues. **4.** a tapered tuck made in dressmaking. ~*vb.* **5.** to move or throw swiftly and suddenly; shoot: *she darted across the room.* [C14: from Old French, of Germanic origin; related to Old English *daroth* spear, Old High German *tart* dart] —**'dart+ing+ly** *adv.*

dart+board ('dɑːtˌbɔːd) *n.* a circular piece of wood, cork, etc., used as the target in the game of darts. It is divided into numbered sectors with central inner and outer bullseyes.

dart+er ('dɑːtə) *n.* **1.** Also called: **anhinga, snakebird.** any aquatic bird of the genus *Anhinga* and family *Anhingidae,* of tropical and subtropical inland waters, having a long slender neck and bill: order *Pelecaniformes* (pelicans, cormorants, etc.). **2.** any small brightly coloured North American fresh-water fish of the genus *Etheostoma* and related genera: family *Percidae* (perches).

Dart+ford ('dɑːtfəd) *n.* a town in SE England, in NW Kent. Pop.: 45 670 (1971).

Dart+moor ('dɑːtˌmʊə) *n.* **1.** a moorland plateau in SW England, in SW Devon: a national park since 1951. Area: 945 sq. km (365 sq. miles). **2.** a prison in SW England, on Dartmoor: England's main prison for long-term convicts. **3.** a small strong breed of pony, originally from Dartmoor. **4.** a hardy coarse-wooled breed of sheep, originally from Dartmoor.

Dart+mouth ('dɑːtməθ) *n.* **1.** a port in SW England, in S Devon: Royal Naval College (1905). Pop.: 5696 (1971). **2.** a city in SE Canada, in S Nova Scotia, on Halifax Harbour: oil refineries and shipyards. Pop.: 64 770 (1971).

darts (dɑːts) *n.* any of various competitive games in which darts are thrown at a dartboard.

Dar+win[1] ('dɑːwɪn) *n.* a port in N Australia, capital of the Northern Territory: destroyed by a cyclone in 1974 but rebuilt on the same site. Pop.: 35 281 (1971). Former name (1869–1911): **Palmerston.**

Dar·win[2] ('dɑːwɪn) *n.* **1. Charles** (**Robert**). 1809–82, English naturalist who formulated the theory of evolution by natural selection, expounded in *On the Origin of Species* (1859) and applied to man in *The Descent of Man* (1871). **2. E·ras·mus,** grandfather of Charles Darwin. 1731–1802, English physician and poet; author of *Zoonomia, or the Laws of Organic Life* (1794–96), anticipating Lamarck's views on evolution. **3. Sir George How·ard,** son of Charles Darwin. 1845–1912, English astronomer and mathematician noted for his work on tidal friction.

Dar+win+i·an (dɑː'wɪnɪən) *adj.* **1.** of or relating to Charles Darwin or his theory of evolution. ~*n.* **2.** a person who accepts, supports, or uses this theory.

Dar+win+ism ('dɑːwɪˌnɪzəm) *or* **Dar+win+i·an the·o+ry** *n.* the theory of the origin of animal and plant species by evolution through a process of natural selection. Compare **Lamarckism.** See also **Neo-Darwinism.** —**'Dar+win+ist** *or* **'Dar+win+ite** *n., adj.* —ˌ**Dar+win+'is+tic** *adj.*

Dar+win's finch·es *pl. n.* the finches of the subfamily *Geospizinae,* of the Galapagos Islands, showing great variation in bill structure and feeding habits: provided Darwin with evidence to support his theory of evolution.

dash[1] (dæʃ) *vb.* (*mainly tr.*) **1.** to hurl; crash: *he dashed the cup to the floor; the waves dashed against the rocks.* **2.** to mix: *white paint dashed with blue.* **3.** (*intr.*) to move hastily or recklessly; rush: *he dashed to her rescue.* **4.** (usually foll. by *off* or *down*) to write (down) or finish (off) hastily. **5.** to destroy; frustrate: *his hopes were dashed.* **6.** to daunt (someone); cast down; discourage: *he was dashed by her refusal.* ~*n.* **7.** a sudden quick movement; dart. **8.** a small admixture: *coffee with a dash of cream.* **9.** a violent stroke or blow. **10.** the sound of splashing or smashing: *the dash of the waves.* **11.** panache; style: *he rides with dash.* **12.** the punctuation mark —, used singly in place of a colon, esp. to indicate a sudden change of subject or grammatical anacoluthon, or in pairs to enclose a parenthetical remark. **13.** the symbol (-) used, in combination with the symbol *dot* (·), in the written representation of Morse and other telegraphic codes. Compare **dah. 14.** *Athletics.* another word (esp. U.S.) for **sprint. 15.** *Informal.* short for **dashboard.**

dash[2] (dæʃ) *interj., adj., adv., vb. Informal.* a euphemistic word for **damn** (senses 1, 3, 4, 12).

dash[3] (dæʃ) *W. African.* ~*n.* **1.** a gift, commission, tip, or bribe. ~*vb.* **2.** to give (a dash) to someone. [C16: perhaps from Fanti]

dash+board ('dæʃˌbɔːd) *n.* **1.** Also called (Brit.): **fascia.** the instrument panel in a car, boat, or aircraft. Sometimes shortened to **dash. 2.** *Obsolete.* a board at the side of a carriage or boat to protect against splashing.

da+sheen (dæ'ʃiːn) *n.* another name for **taro.** [C19: perhaps changed from French *de Chine* of China]

dash+er ('dæʃə) *n.* the plunger in a churn, often with paddles attached.

da+shi+ki (dɑː'ʃiːkɪ) *n.* a large loose-fitting buttonless upper garment worn esp. by Negroes in the U.S., Africa, and the Caribbean. [C20: of W African origin]

dash+ing ('dæʃɪŋ) *adj.* **1.** spirited; lively: *a dashing young man.* **2.** stylish; showy: *a dashing hat.* —**'dash+ing+ly** *adv.*

dash+pot ('dæʃˌpɒt) *n.* a device for damping vibrations; the vibrating part is attached to a piston moving in a liquid-filled cylinder. [C20: from DASH[1] + POT]

Dasht-i-Ka·vir *or* **Dasht-e-Ka·vir** (ˌdæʃtiːkæ'vɪə) *n.* a salt waste on the central plateau of Iran: a treacherous marsh beneath a salt crust. Also called: **Kavir Desert.**

Dasht-i-Lut *or* **Dasht-e-Lut** (ˌdæʃtiː'lʊt) *n.* a desert plateau in central and E central Iran.

das+sie ('dæsɪ) *n.* another name for a **hyrax,** esp. the rock hyrax. [C19: from Afrikaans]

das+tard ('dæstəd) *n. Archaic.* a contemptible sneaking coward. [C15 (in the sense: dullard): probably from Old Norse *dæstr* exhausted, out of breath]

das+tard+ly ('dæstədlɪ) *adj.* mean and cowardly. —**'das+tard+li+ness** *n.*

das·y+ure ('dæsɪˌjʊə) *n.* any small carnivorous marsupial, such as *Dasyurus quoll* (**eastern dasyure**), of the subfamily *Dasyurinae,* of Australia, New Guinea, and adjacent islands. See also **Tasmanian devil.** [C19: from New Latin *Dasyūrus,* from Greek *dasus* shaggy + *oura* tail; see DENSE]

dat. *abbrev. for* dative.

da·ta ('deɪtə, 'dɑːtə) *n.* **1.** a series of observations, measurements, or facts; information. **2.** Also called: **information.** *Computer technol.* the information operated on by a computer program. [C17: from Latin, literally: (things) given, from *dare* to give]

Usage. Although now generally used as a singular noun, *data* is properly a plural.

da·ta bank or **da·ta base** *n.* a store of a large amount of information, esp. in a form that can be handled by a computer.

da·ta cap+ture *n.* any process for converting information into a form that can be handled by a computer.

da·ta pro·ces+sing *n.* **a.** a sequence of operations performed on data, esp. by a computer, in order to extract information, reorder files, etc. **b.** (*as modifier*): *a data-processing centre.* See also **automatic data processing.**

da+ta+ry ('deɪtərɪ) *n., pl.* **+ries.** *R.C. Church.* the head of the **da+tar·i·a** (deɪ'tɛərɪə), the papal office that assesses candidates for benefices reserved to the Holy See. [C16: from Medieval Latin *datārius* (unattested) official who dated papal letters, from Late Latin *data* DATE[1]]

da·ta set *n. Computer technol.* another name for **file**[1] (sense 7).

da+tcha ('dætʃə) *n.* a variant spelling of **dacha.**

date[1] (deɪt) *n.* **1.** a specified day of the month: *today's date is October 27.* **2.** the particular day or year of an event: *the date of the Norman Conquest was 1066.* **3.** an inscription on a coin, letter, etc., stating when it was made or written. **4. a.** an appointment for a particular time, esp. with a person of the opposite sex: *she has a dinner date.* **b.** the person with whom the appointment is made. **5.** the present moment; now (esp. in the phrases **to date, up to date**). ~*vb* **6.** (*tr.*) to mark (a letter, coin, etc.) with the day, month, or year. **7.** (*tr.*) to assign a date of occurrence or creation to. **8.** (*intr.;* foll. by *from* or *back to*) to have originated (at a specified time): *his decline dates from last summer.* **9.** (*tr.*) to reveal the age of: *that dress dates her.* **10.** to become old-fashioned: *some good films hardly date at all.* **11.** *Informal, chiefly U.S.* **a.** to be a boy-friend or girl-friend of (someone of the opposite sex). **b.** to accompany (a member of the opposite sex) on a date. [C14: from Old French, from Latin *dare* to give, as in the phrase *epistula data Romae* letter handed over at Rome] —**'dat+a·ble** *or* **'date+a·ble** *adj.* —**'date+less** *adj.*

Usage. See at **day, decade, year.**

date[2] (deɪt) *n.* **1.** the fruit of the date palm, having sweet edible flesh and a single large woody seed. **2.** short for **date palm.** [C13: from Old French, from Latin, from Greek *daktulos* finger]

dat+ed ('deɪtɪd) *adj.* unfashionable; outmoded.

date line *n.* (*often caps.*) short for **International Date Line.**

date+line ('deɪtˌlaɪn) *n. Journalism.* the date and location of a story, placed at the top of an article.

date palm *n.* a tall feather palm, *Phoenix dactylifera,* native to Syria but grown in other tropical regions for its sweet edible fruit (dates).

dates (deɪts) *pl. n.* the years of a person's birth and death or of the beginning and end of an event.

date stamp *n.* **1.** an adjustable rubber stamp for recording the date. **2.** an inked impression made by this.

da·tive ('deɪtɪv) *Grammar.* ~*adj.* **1.** denoting a case of nouns, pronouns, and adjectives used to express the indirect object, to identify the recipients, and for other purposes. ~*n.* **2. a.** the dative case. **b.** a word or speech element in this case. [C15: from Latin *datīvus,* from *dare* to give; translation of Greek *dotikos*] —**da·ti·val** (deɪ'taɪvᵊl) *adj.* —'**da·tive·ly** *adv.*

da·tive bond *n. Chem.* another name for **coordinate bond.**

da·to ('dɑːtəʊ) *n., pl.* **·tos.** the chief of any of certain Muslim tribes in the Philippine Islands. [C19: from Spanish, ultimately from Malay *dato'* grandfather]

da·to·lite ('deɪtəˌlaɪt) *n.* a colourless mineral consisting of a hydrated silicate of calcium and boron in monoclinic crystalline form, occurring in cavities in igneous rocks. Formula: $CaBSiO_4(OH)$. [C19: *dato-* from Greek *dateisthai* to divide + -LITE]

Da·tuk (dæ'tʊk) *n.* **Hus·sein bin Onn** (huː'seɪn bɪn ɒn). born 1922, Malaysian statesman; prime minister of Malaysia since 1976.

da·tum ('deɪtəm, 'dɑːtəm) *n., pl.* **·ta** (-tə). **1.** a single piece of information; fact. **2.** a fact or proposition, known or assumed, from which inferences can be drawn. See also **sense datum.** [C17: from Latin: something given; see DATA]

da·tum plane, lev·el, *or* **line** *n. Surveying.* the horizontal plane from which heights and depths are calculated.

da·tu·ra (də'tjʊərə) *n.* any of various solanaceous plant of the genus *Datura,* such as the moonflower and thorn apple, having large trumpet-shaped flowers, prickly pods, and narcotic properties. [C16: from New Latin, from Hindi *dhatūra* jimson weed, from Sanskrit *dhattūra*]

daub (dɔːb) *vb.* **1.** (*tr.*) to smear or spread (paint, mud, etc.), esp. carelessly. **2.** (*tr.*) to cover or coat (with paint, plaster, etc.) carelessly. **3.** to paint (a picture) clumsily or badly. ~*n.* **4.** an unskilful or crude painting. **5.** something daubed on, esp. as a wall covering. See also **wattle and daub. 6.** a smear (of paint, mud, etc.) **7.** the act of daubing. [C14: from Old French *dauber* to paint, whitewash, from Latin *dealbāre,* from *albāre* to whiten, from *albus* white] —'**daub·er** *n.* —'**daub·y** *adj.*

daube (dəʊb) *n.* a braised meat stew. [from French]

daub·er·y ('dɔːbərɪ) *or* **daub·ry** ('dɔːbrɪ) *n.* **1.** the act or an instance of daubing. **2.** an unskilful painting, etc.

Dau·bi·gny (*French* dobi'ɲi) *n.* **Charles Fran·çois** (ʃarl frɑ̃'swa). 1817–78, French landscape painter associated with the Barbizon School.

Dau·det (*French* do'dɛ) *n.* **Al·phonse** (al'fɔ̃s). 1840–97, French novelist, short-story writer, and dramatist: noted particularly for his humorous sketches of Provençal life, as in *Lettres de mon moulin* (1866).

Dau·ga·va ('daʊgaˌva) *n.* the Latvian name for the Western **Dvina.**

Dau·gav·pils (*Russian* 'daʊgafˌpils) *n.* a city in the W Soviet Union, in the SE Latvian SSR on the Western Dvina River: founded in 1274 by Teutonic Knights; ruled by Poland (1559–1772) and Russia (1772–1915); retaken by the Russians in 1940. Pop.: 110 000 (1975 est.). German name (until 1893): **Dünaburg.** Former Russian name (1893–1920): **Dvinsk.**

daugh·ter ('dɔːtə) *n.* **1.** a female offspring; a girl or woman in relation to her parents. **2.** a female descendant. **3.** a female from a certain country, etc., or one closely connected with a certain environment, etc.: *a daughter of the church.* **4.** (*often cap.*) *Archaic.* a form of address for a girl or woman. ~(*modifier*) **5.** *Biology.* denoting a cell or unicellular organism produced by the division of one of its own kind. **6.** *Physics.* (of a nuclide) formed from another nuclide by radioactive decay. [Old English *dohtor;* related to Old High German *tohter* daughter, Greek *thugatēr,* Sanskrit *duhitá*] —'**daugh·ter·hood** *n.* —'**daugh·ter·less** *adj.* —'**daugh·ter·ˌlike** *adj.* —'**daugh·ter·li·ness** *n.* —'**daugh·ter·ly** *adj.*

daugh·ter-in-law *n., pl.* **daugh·ters-in-law.** the wife of one's son.

Daugh·ters of the A·mer·i·can Rev·o·lu·tion *n.* **the.** an organization of women descended from patriots of the period of the War of Independence. Abbrev.: **D.A.R.**

Dau·mier (*French* do'mje) *n.* **Ho·no·ré** (ɔnɔ're). 1808–79, French painter and lithographer, noted particularly for his political and social caricatures.

daunt (dɔːnt) *vb.* (*tr.; often passive*) **1.** to intimidate. **2.** to dishearten. [C13: from Old French *danter,* changed from *donter* to conquer, from Latin *domitāre* to tame] —'**daunt·er** *n.* —'**daunt·ing·ly** *adv.*

daunt·less ('dɔːntlɪs) *adj.* bold; fearless; intrepid. —'**daunt·less·ly** *adv.* —'**daunt·less·ness** *n.*

dau·phin ('dɔːfɪn; *French* do'fɛ̃) *n.* (from 1349–1830) the title of the direct heir to the French throne; the eldest son of the king of France. [C15: from Old French: originally a family name; adopted as a title by the Counts of Vienne and later by the French crown princes]

dau·phine ('dɔːfiːn; *French* do'fin) *or* **dau·phin·ess** ('dɔːfɪnɪs) *n. French history.* the wife of a dauphin.

Dau·phi·né (*French* dofi'ne) *n.* a former province of SE France: its rulers, the Counts of Vienne, assumed the title of *dauphin;* annexed to France in 1457.

Da·vao (dɑː'vaʊ) *n.* a port in the S Philippines, in SE Mindanao. Pop.: 515 520 (1975 est.).

dav·en·port ('dævənˌpɔːt) *n.* **1.** *Chiefly Brit.* a small decorative writing desk with drawers. **2.** *U.S.* a large sofa, esp. one convertible into a bed. [C19: supposedly the maker's name]

Da·vid ('deɪvɪd) *n.* **1.** the second king of the Hebrews (about 1000–962 B.C.), who united Israel as a kingdom with Jerusalem as its capital. **2.** (*French* da'vid). **Jacques Louis** (ʒɑk 'lwi). 1748–1825, French neoclassical painter of such works as the *Oath of the Horatii* (1784), *Death of Socrates* (1787), and *The Intervention of the Sabine Women* (1799). He actively supported the French Revolution and became court painter to Napoleon Bonaparte in 1804; banished at the Bourbon restoration. **3. Saint.** 6th-century A.D. Welsh bishop; patron saint of Wales. Feast day: March 1.

Da·vid I *n.* 1084–1153, king of Scotland (1124–53) who supported his niece Matilda's claim to the English throne and unsuccessfully invaded England on her behalf.

Da·vies ('deɪvɪs) *n.* **1. Pe·ter Max·well.** born 1934, English composer. His style owes a considerable debt to medieval music; works include the opera *Taverner* (1970). **2. Wil·liam Hen·ry.** 1871–1940, Welsh poet, noted also for his *Autobiography of a Super-tramp* (1908).

da Vin·ci (də 'vɪntʃɪ) *n.* See **Leonardo da Vinci.**

Da·vis ('deɪvɪs) *n.* **1. Bet·te** ('bɛtɪ). born 1908, U.S. film actress, whose films include *Of Human Bondage* (1934), *Jezebel* (1938), *Whatever Happened to Baby Jane?* (1962), and *The Nanny* (1965). **2.** Sir **Col·in.** born 1927, English conductor, noted for his interpretation of the music of Berlioz. **3. Jef·fer·son.** 1808–89, president of the Confederate States of America during the Civil War (1861–65). **4. Joe.** 1901–78, English billiards and snooker player: world champion from 1927 to 1946. **5. John.** Also called: **John Da·vys.** ?1550–1605, English navigator: discovered the Falkland Islands (1592); searched for a Northwest Passage. **6. Miles.** born 1926, U.S. jazz trumpeter and composer.

Da·vis Cup *n.* **1.** an annual international lawn tennis championship for men's teams. **2.** the trophy awarded for this. [C20: after Dwight F. *Davis* (1879–1945), American civic leader who donated the cup]

Da·vis Strait *n.* a strait between Baffin Island, in Canada, and Greenland. [named after John DAVIS]

dav·it ('dævɪt, 'deɪ-) *n.* a cranelike device, usually one of a pair, fitted with a tackle for suspending or lowering equipment, esp. a lifeboat. [C14: from Anglo-French *daviot,* diminutive of *Davi* David]

Da·vy ('deɪvɪ) *n.* Sir **Hum·phrey.** 1778–1829, English chemist who isolated sodium, magnesium, chlorine, and other elements and suggested the electrical nature of chemical combination. He invented the **Davy lamp.**

Da·vy Jones *n.* **1.** Also called: **Davy Jones's locker.** the ocean's bottom, esp. when regarded as the grave of those lost or buried at sea. **2.** the spirit or devil of the sea. [C18: of unknown origin]

Da·vy lamp *n.* See **safety lamp.** [C19: named after Sir H. DAVY, who invented it]

daw (dɔː) *n.* an archaic, dialect, or poetic name for a **jackdaw.** [C15: related to Old High German *taha*]

daw·dle ('dɔːdᵊl) *vb.* **1.** (*intr.*) to be slow or lag behind. **2.** (when *tr.,* often foll. by *away*) to waste (time); trifle. [C17: of uncertain origin] —'**daw·dler** *n.* —'**daw·dling·ly** *adv.*

Dawes (dɔːz) *n.* **Charles Gates.** 1865–1951, U.S. financier, diplomat, and statesman, who devised the Dawes Plan for German reparations payments after World War I; vice president of the U.S. (1925–29); Nobel peace prize 1925.

dawn (dɔːn) *n.* **1.** daybreak; sunrise. Related adj.: **auroral. 2.** the sky when light first appears in the morning. **3.** the beginning of something. ~*vb.* (*intr.*) **4.** to begin to grow light after the night. **5.** to begin to develop, appear, or expand. **6.** (usually foll. by *on* or *upon*) to begin to become apparent (to). [Old English *dagian* to dawn; see DAY] —'**dawn·ˌlike** *adj.*

dawn cho·rus *n.* the singing of large numbers of birds at dawn.

dawn red·wood *n.* a deciduous conifer, *Metasequoia glyptostroboides,* native to China but planted in other regions as an ornamental tree: family *Taxodiaceae.* Until recently it was thought to be extinct.

Daw·son ('dɔːsᵊn) *n.* a town in NW Canada, in the Yukon on the Yukon River: a boom town during the Klondike gold rush (at its height in 1899). Pop.: 762 (1971).

Daw·son Creek *n.* a town in W Canada, in NE British Columbia: SE terminus of the Alaska Highway. Pop.: 11 885 (1971).

day (deɪ) *n.* **1.** Also called: **civil day.** the period of time, the **calendar day,** of 24 hours duration reckoned from one midnight to the next. **2.** the period of light between sunrise and sunset, as distinguished from the night. **3.** the part of a day occupied with regular activity, esp. work: *he took a day off.* **4.** (*sometimes pl.*) a period or point in time: *he was a good singer in his day; in days gone by; any day now.* **5.** the period of time, the **sidereal day,** during which the earth makes one complete revolution on its axis relative to a particular star. The **mean sidereal day** lasts 23 hours 56 minutes 4.1 seconds. **6.** the period of time, the **solar day,** during which the earth makes one complete revolution on its axis relative to the sun. The **mean solar day** lasts 24 hours 3 minutes 56.5 seconds. **7.** the period of time taken by a specified planet to make one complete rotation on its axis: *the Martian day.* **8.** (*often cap.*) a day designated for a special observance, esp. a holiday: *Christmas Day.* **9. all in a day's work.** part of one's normal activity; no trouble. **10. at the end of the day.** in the final reckoning. **11. day of rest.** the Sabbath; Sunday. **12. end one's days.** to pass the end of one's life. **13. every dog has his day.** one's luck will come. **14. in this day and age.** nowadays. **15. it's early days.** it's too early to tell how things will turn out. **16. late in the day.** very late (in a particular situation). **17. that will be the day. a.** I look forward to that. **b.** that is most unlikely to happen. **18.** a time of success, recognition, power, etc.: *his day will soon come.* **19.** a struggle or issue at hand: *the day is lost.* **20. a.** the ground surface over a mine. **b.** (*as modifier*): *the day level.* **21. from day to day.** without thinking of the future. **22. call it a day.** *Informal.* to stop work or other activity: *we tried for weeks to make him change his mind, but eventually had to call it a day.* **23. day after day.** without respite; relentlessly. **24. day by day.** gradually or progressively; daily: *he weakened day by day.* **25. day in, day out.** every day and all day long. **26. one of these days.** at some future time. **27.** (*modifier*) of, relating to, or occurring in the day: *the day shift.* ~Related adj.: **diurnal.** [Old English *dæg;* related to Old High German *tag,* Old Norse *dagr*]

Day+ak ('daɪæk) *n., pl.* **+aks** *or* **+ak.** a variant spelling of **Dyak.**

Da·yan (dɑːˈjɑːn) *n.* **Mo·she** (ˈmɒʃɛ). 1915-81, Israeli soldier and statesman; minister of defence (1967; 1969-74) and foreign minister 1977-79.

day bed *n.* **1.** an armless couch intended for use as a seat by day and as a bed by night. **2.** a long seat on which to recline during the day.

day blind+ness *n.* a nontechnical name for **hemeralopia.**

day+book ('deɪˌbʊk) *n. Book-keeping.* a book in which the transactions of each day are recorded as they occur.

day+boy ('deɪˌbɔɪ) *n. Brit.* a boy who attends a boarding school daily, but returns home each evening.

day+break ('deɪˌbreɪk) *n.* the time in the morning when light first appears; dawn; sunrise.

day-clean *n. Caribbean and West African informal.* the time after first dawn when the sun begins to shine; clear daybreak.

day+dream ('deɪˌdriːm) *n.* **1.** a pleasant dreamlike fantasy indulged in while awake; idle reverie. **2.** a pleasant scheme or wish that is unlikely to be fulfilled; pipe dream. ~*vb.* **3.** (*intr.*) to have daydreams; indulge in idle fantasy. —**'day+ˌdream+er** *n.* —**'day+ˌdream·y** *adj.*

day+flow·er ('deɪˌflaʊə) *n.* any of various tropical and subtropical plants of the genus *Commelina,* having jointed creeping stems, narrow pointed leaves, and blue or purplish flowers which wilt quickly: family *Commelinaceae.*

day+fly ('deɪˌflaɪ) *n., pl.* **+flies.** another name for a **mayfly.**

Day-Lew·is *or* **Day Lew·is** ('deɪ'luːɪs) *n.* **C(ecil).** 1904-72, English poet, critic, and (under the pen name *Nicholas Blake*) author of detective stories; poet laureate (1968-72).

day+light ('deɪˌlaɪt) *n.* **1. a.** light from the sun. **b.** (*as modifier*): *daylight film.* **2.** the period when it is light; daytime. **3.** daybreak. **4. see daylight. a.** to understand something previously obscure. **b.** to realize that the end of a difficult task is approaching.

day+light rob+ber·y *n. Informal.* blatant overcharging.

day+lights ('deɪˌlaɪts) *pl. n.* consciousness or wits (esp. in the phrases **scare, knock,** or **beat the (living) daylights out of someone).**

day·light-sav·ing time *n.* time set usually one hour ahead of the local standard time, widely adopted in the summer to provide extra daylight in the evening. See also **British Summer Time.**

day lil·y *n.* **1.** any widely cultivated Eurasian liliaceous plant of the genus *Hemerocallis,* having large yellow, orange, or red lily-like flowers, which typically last for only one day and are immediately succeeded by others. **2.** the flower of any of these plants.

day+long ('deɪˌlɒŋ) *adj., adv.* lasting the entire day; all day.

day name *n. West African.* a name indicating a person's day of birth.

day-neu·tral *adj.* (of plants) having an ability to mature and bloom that is not affected by day length.

Day of A·tone+ment *n.* another name for **Yom Kippur.**

Day of Judg+ment *n.* another name for **Judgment Day.**

day re+lease *n. Brit.* a system whereby workers are released for part-time education without loss of pay.

day re+turn *n.* a reduced fare for a journey (by train, etc.) travelling both ways in one day.

day room *n.* a communal living room in a residential institution such as a hospital.

days (deɪz) *adv. Informal.* during the day, esp. regularly: *he works days.*

day school *n.* **1.** a private school taking day students only. Compare **boarding school.** **2.** a school giving instruction during the daytime. Compare **night school.**

days of grace *pl. n.* days permitted by custom for payment of a promissory note, bill of exchange, etc., after it falls due.

day+spring ('deɪˌsprɪŋ) *n.* a poetic word for **dawn.**

day+star ('deɪˌstɑː) *n.* **1.** a poetic word for the **sun. 2.** another word for the **morning star.**

day+time ('deɪˌtaɪm) *n.* the time between dawn and dusk; the day as distinct from evening or night.

day-to-day *adj.* routine; everyday: *day-to-day chores.*

Day+ton ('deɪtᵊn) *n.* an industrial city in SW Ohio: aviation research centre. Pop.: 214 377 (1973 est.).

Day+to+na Beach (deɪ'təʊnə) *n.* a city in NE Florida, on the Atlantic: a resort with a beach of hard white sand, used since 1903 for motor speed trials. Pop.: 45 327 (1970).

day trip *n.* a journey made to and from a place within one day. —**'day-ˌtrip·per** *n.*

daze (deɪz) *vb. (tr.)* **1.** to stun or stupefy, esp. by a blow or shock. **2.** to bewilder, amaze, or dazzle. ~*n.* **3.** a state of stunned confusion or shock (esp. in the phrase **in a daze).** [C14: from Old Norse *dasa-,* as in *dasast* to grow weary] —**daz+ed+ly** ('deɪzɪdlɪ) *adv.*

daz+zle ('dæzᵊl) *vb.* **1.** (*usually tr.*) to blind or be blinded partially and temporarily by sudden excessive light. **2.** (*tr.*) to amaze, as with brilliance: *she was dazzled by his wit.* ~*n.* **3.** bright light that dazzles. **4.** bewilderment caused by glamour, brilliance, etc.: *the dazzle of fame.* [C15: from DAZE]

dB *or* **db** *symbol for* decibel or decibels.

D.B.E. *abbrev. for* Dame Commander of the Order of the British Empire (a Brit. title).

D.b.h. *or* **D.B.H.** *Forestry. abbrev. for* diameter at breast height.

D. Bib. *abbrev. for* Douay Bible.

dbl. *abbrev. for* double.

DC *abbrev. for* direct current. Compare **AC.**

D.C. *abbrev. for:* **1.** *Music.* da capo. **2.** *U.S.* District of Columbia.

D.C.B. *abbrev. for* Dame Commander of the Order of the Bath (a Brit. title).

D.C.L. *abbrev. for* Doctor of Civil Law.

D.C.M. *Brit. military. abbrev. for* Distinguished Conduct Medal.

D.C.M.G. *abbrev. for* Dame Commander of the Order of St. Michael and St. George (a Brit. title).

D.C.V.O. *abbrev. for* Dame Commander of the Royal Victorian Order (a Brit. title).

dd. *abbrev. for* delivered.

D.D. *abbrev. for* Doctor of Divinity.

D-day *n.* the day selected for the start of some operation, esp. of the Allied invasion of Europe on June 6, 1944. [C20: from *D(ay)-day;* compare H-HOUR]

DDR *abbrev. for* Deutsche Demokratische Republik (East Germany; G.D.R.).

D.D.S. *or* **D.D.Sc.** *abbrev. for* Doctor of Dental Surgery *or* Science.

DDT *n.* dichlorodiphenyltrichloroethane; a colourless odourless substance used as an insecticide. It is toxic to animals and is known to accumulate in the tissues.

de, De *or before a vowel* **d', D'** (də) of; from: occurring as part of some personal names and originally indicating place of origin: *Simon de Montfort; D'Arcy; de la Mare.* [from Latin *dē;* see DE-]

de- *prefix forming verbs and verbal derivatives.* **1.** removal of or from something specified: *deforest; dethrone.* **2.** reversal of something: *decode; decompose; desegregate.* **3.** departure from: *decamp.* [from Latin, from *dē* (prep.) from, away from, out of, etc. In compound words of Latin origin, *de-* also means away, away from (*decease*); down (*degrade*); reversal (*detect*); removal (*defoliate*); and is used intensively (*devote*) and pejoratively (*detest*)]

dea+con ('diːkən) *n. Christianity.* **1.** (in the Roman Catholic and other episcopal churches) an ordained minister ranking immediately below a priest. **2.** (in Protestant churches) a lay official appointed or elected to assist the minister, esp. in secular affairs. **3.** *Scot.* the president of an incorporated trade or body of craftsmen in a burgh. [Old English, ultimately from Greek *diakonos* servant] —**'dea+con+ˌship** *n.*

dea+con+ess ('diːkənɪs) *n. Christianity.* (in the early church and in some modern Churches) a female member of the laity with duties similar to those of a deacon.

dea+con+ry ('diːkənrɪ) *n., pl.* **+ries. 1.** the office or status of a deacon. **2.** deacons collectively.

de+ac+tiv+ate (diːˈæktɪˌveɪt) *vb.* **1.** (*tr.*) to make (a bomb, etc.) harmless or inoperative. **2.** to make or become less radioactive. —**de+ˌac+ti+'va+tion** *n.* —**de+'ac+ti+ˌva+tor** *n.*

dead (dɛd) *adj.* **1. a.** no longer alive. **b.** (*as n.*): *the dead.* **2.** not endowed with life; inanimate. **3.** no longer in use, valid, effective, or relevant: *a dead issue; a dead language.* **4.** unresponsive or unaware; insensible: *he is dead to my strongest pleas.* **5.** lacking in freshness, interest, or vitality: *a dead handshake.* **6.** devoid of physical sensation; numb: *his gums were dead from the anaesthetic.* **7.** resembling death; deathlike: *a dead sleep.* **8.** no longer burning or hot: *dead coals.* **9.** (*prenominal*) (intensifier): *a dead stop; a dead loss.* **10.** Also: **dead beat.** *Informal.* very tired. **11.** *Electronics.* **a.** drained of electric charge; discharged: *the battery was dead.* **b.** not connected to a source of potential difference or electric charge. **12.** lacking acoustic resonance: *a dead sound; a dead surface.* **13.** *Sport.* (of a ball, etc.) out of play. **14.** unerring; accurate; precise (esp. in the phrase **a dead shot).** **15.** lacking resilience or bounce: *a dead ball.* **16.** *Printing.* **a.** (of type) set but no longer needed for use. Compare **standing** (sense 7). **b.** (of copy) already composed. **17.** not yielding a return; idle: *dead capital.* **18.** *Informal.* certain to suffer a terrible fate; doomed: *you're dead if your mother catches you at that.* **19.** (of colours) not glossy or bright; lacklustre. **20.** stagnant: *dead air.* **21.** *Military.* shielded from view, as by a geographic feature or environmental condition: *a dead zone; dead space.* **22. dead as a doornail.** *Informal.* completely dead. **23. dead from the neck up.** *Informal.* stupid or unintelligent. **24. dead to the world.** *Informal.* fast asleep. **25. wouldn't be seen dead (in, at, etc.).** *Informal.* to refuse to wear, to go (to), etc. ~*n.* **26.** a period during which coldness, darkness, or some other quality associated with death is at its most intense: *the dead of winter.* ~*adv.* **27.** (intensifier): *dead easy; stop dead; dead level.* **28. dead on.** exactly right. [Old English *dēad;* related to Old High German *tōt,* Old Norse *dauthr;* see DIE[1]] —**'dead+ness** *n.*

dead-and-a·live *adj. Brit.* (of a place, activity, or person) dull; uninteresting.

dead-ball line *n. Rugby.* a line ten yards behind the goal line at each end of the field beyond which the ball is out of play.

dead·beat ('dɛd,bi:t) *n.* **1.** *Informal, chiefly U.S.* a lazy or socially undesirable person. **2.** a high grade escapement used in pendulum clocks. **3.** (*modifier*) (of a clock escapement) having a beat without any recoil. **4.** (*modifier*) *Physics.* **a.** (of a system) returning to an equilibrium position with little or no oscillation. **b.** (of an instrument or indicator) indicating a true reading without oscillation.

dead cen·tre *n.* **1.** the exact top (**top dead centre**) or bottom (**bottom dead centre**) of the piston stroke in a reciprocating engine or pump. **2.** a nonrotating pointed rod mounted in the tailstock or headstock of a lathe to support a workpiece. ~Also called: **dead point.**

dead duck *n. Slang.* a person or thing doomed to death, failure, etc., esp. because of a mistake or misjudgment.

dead·en ('dɛdᵊn) *vb.* **1.** to make or become less sensitive, intense, lively, etc; damp or be damped down; dull. **2.** (*tr.*) to make acoustically less resonant: *he deadened the room with heavy curtains.* —'**dead·en·er** *n.*

dead end *n.* **1.** another name for **cul-de-sac. 2.** a situation in which further progress is impossible. **3.** (*as modifier*): *a dead-end street; a dead-end job.*

dead·eye ('dɛd,aɪ) *n.* **1.** *Nautical.* either of a pair of disclike wooden blocks, supported by straps in grooves around them, between which a line is rove so as to draw them together to tighten a shroud. Compare **bull's-eye** (sense 9). **2.** *Informal, chiefly U.S.* an expert marksman.

dead·fall ('dɛd,fɔ:l) *n.* a type of trap, used esp. for catching large animals, in which a heavy weight falls to crush the prey. Also called: **downfall.**

dead hand *n. Law.* a less common word for **mortmain.**

dead·head ('dɛd,hɛd) *U.S. informal.* ~*n.* **1.** a person who uses a free ticket, as for a train, the theatre, etc. **2.** a train, etc., travelling empty. **3.** a dull unenterprising person. ~*vb.* **4.** (*intr.*) to drive an empty bus, train, etc.

Dead Heart *n.* (usually preceded by *the*) *Austral.* the remote interior of Australia. [C20: from the title *The Dead Heart of Australia* (1906) by J. W. Gregory]

dead heat *n.* **a.** a race or contest in which two or more participants tie for first place. **b.** a tie between two or more contestants in any position.

dead let·ter *n.* a law or ordinance that is no longer enforced but has not been formally repealed.

dead·light ('dɛd,laɪt) *n.* **1.** *Nautical.* **a.** a bull's-eye let into the deck or hull of a vessel to admit light to a cabin. **b.** a shutter of wood or metal for sealing off a porthole or cabin window. **2.** a skylight designed not to be opened.

dead·line ('dɛd,laɪn) *n.* a time limit for any activity.

dead load *n.* the intrinsic invariable weight of a structure, such as a bridge. Also called: **dead weight.** Compare **live load.**

dead·lock ('dɛd,lɒk) *n.* **1.** a state of affairs in which further action between two opposing forces is impossible; stalemate. **2.** a tie between opposite sides in a contest. **3.** a lock having a full unchamfered bolt. ~*vb.* **4.** to bring or come to a deadlock.

dead·ly ('dɛdlɪ) *adj.* **·li·er, ·li·est. 1.** likely to cause death: *deadly poison; deadly combat.* **2.** *Informal.* extremely boring. ~*adv., adj.* **3.** like death in appearance or certainty: *deadly pale; a deadly sleep.* —'**dead·li·ness** *n.*

dead·ly night·shade *n.* a poisonous Eurasian solanaceous plant, *Atropa belladonna,* having dull purple bell-shaped flowers and small very poisonous black berries. Also called: **belladonna, dwale.**

dead·ly sins *pl. n. Theol.* the sins of pride, covetousness, lust, envy, gluttony, anger, and sloth.

dead man's fin·gers *n.* (*functioning as sing.*) a soft coral, *Alcyonium digitatum,* with long finger-like polyps.

dead man's han·dle *or* **ped·al** *n.* a safety-switch on a piece of machinery, such as a train, that allows operation only while depressed by the operator.

dead march *n.* a piece of solemn funeral music played to accompany a procession, esp. at military funerals.

dead-net·tle *n.* any Eurasian plant of the genus *Lamium,* such as *L. alba* (white dead-nettle), having leaves resembling nettles but lacking stinging hairs: family *Labiatae* (labiates).

dead·pan ('dɛd,pæn) *adj., adv.* with a deliberately emotionless face or manner: *deadpan humour.*

dead point *n.* another name for **dead centre.**

dead reck·on·ing *n.* a method of establishing one's position using the distance and direction travelled rather than astronomical observations.

Dead Sea *n.* a lake between Israel and Jordan, 397 m (1302 ft.) below sea level: the lowest lake in the world, with no outlet and very high salinity. Area: 1020 sq. km (394 sq. miles).

Dead Sea Scrolls *pl. n.* a collection of manuscripts in Hebrew and Aramaic discovered in caves near the Dead Sea between 1947 and 1956. They are widely held to have been written between about 100 B.C. and 68 A.D. and provide important biblical evidence.

dead set *adv.* **1.** absolutely: *he is dead set against going to Spain.* ~*n.* **2.** the motionless position of a dog when pointing with its muzzle towards game. ~*adj.* **3.** (of a hunting dog) in this position.

dead stock *n.* farm equipment. Compare **livestock.**

dead time *n. Electronics.* the interval of time immediately following a stimulus, during which an electrical device, component, etc., is insensitive to a further stimulus.

dead weight *n.* **1.** a heavy weight or load. **2.** an oppressive burden; encumbrance. **3.** the difference between the loaded and the unloaded weights of a ship. **4.** another name for **dead load. 5.** (in shipping) freight chargeable by weight rather than by bulk.

dead·wood ('dɛd,wʊd) *n.* **1.** dead trees or branches. **2.** *Informal.* a useless person; encumbrance. **3.** *Nautical.* a filler piece between the keel and the stern of a wooden vessel.

deaf (dɛf) *adj.* **1. a.** partially or totally unable to hear. **b.** (*as n.*): *the deaf.* See also **tone-deaf. 2.** refusing to heed: *deaf to the cries of the hungry.* [Old English *dēaf;* related to Old Norse *daufr*] —'**deaf·ly** *adv.* —'**deaf·ness** *n.*

deaf-and-dumb *adj.* **1.** unable to hear or speak. **2.** for the use of those unable to hear or speak.

deaf·en ('dɛfᵊn) *vb.* (*tr.*) to make deaf, esp. momentarily, as by a loud noise. —'**deaf·en·ing·ly** *adv.*

deaf-mute *n.* **1.** a person who is unable to hear or speak. ~*adj.* **2.** unable to hear or speak. [C19: translation of French *sourd-muet*] —'**deaf-,mute·ness** *or* '**deaf-,mut·ism** *n.*

Dea·kin ('di:kɪn) *n.* **Al·fred.** 1856–1919, Australian statesman. He was a leader of the movement for Australian federation; prime minister of Australia (1903–04; 1905–08; 1909–10).

deal[1] (di:l) *vb.* **deals, deal·ing, dealt.** (*mainly intr.*). **1.** (foll. by *with*) to take action on: *to deal with each problem in turn.* **2.** (foll. by *with* or *in*) to treat (some subject matter): *his manuscript deals with art.* **3.** (foll. by *with*) to conduct oneself (towards others), esp. with regard to fairness. **4. a.** (foll. by *with*) to do business. **b.** (foll. by *in*) to engage in commercially: *to deal in upholstery.* **5.** (often foll. by *out*) to apportion (something, such as cards) to a number of people; distribute. **6.** (*tr.*) to give (a blow, etc.) to (someone); inflict. **7.** *Slang.* to sell narcotics. ~*n.* **8.** *Informal.* a bargain, transaction, or agreement. **9.** a particular type of treatment received, esp. as the result of an agreement: *a fair deal.* **10.** an indefinite amount, extent, or degree (esp. in the phrases **good** or **great deal**). **11.** *Cards.* **a.** the process of distributing the cards. **b.** a player's turn to do this. **c.** a single round in a card game. **12. big deal.** *Informal.* an important person, event, or matter of any sort: often used sarcastically. [Old English *dǣlan,* from *dǣl* a part; compare Old High German *teil* a part, Old Norse *deild* a share]

deal[2] (di:l) *n.* **1.** a plank of softwood timber, such as fir or pine, or such planks collectively. **2.** the sawn wood of various coniferous trees, such as that from the Scots pine (**red deal**) or from the Norway Spruce (**white deal**). ~*adj.* **3.** of fir or pine. [C14: from Middle Low German *dele* plank; see THILL]

de·a·late ('di:eɪ,leɪt, -lɪt) *or* **de·a·lat·ed** ('di:eɪ,leɪtɪd) *adj.* (of ants and other insects) having lost their wings, esp. by biting or rubbing them off after mating. —**,de·a·'la·tion** *n.*

deal·er ('di:lə) *n.* **1.** a person or firm engaged in commercial purchase and sale; trader: *a car dealer.* **2.** *Cards.* the person who distributes the cards. **3.** *Slang.* a person who sells narcotics. —'**deal·er·,ship** *n.*

deal·fish ('di:l,fɪʃ) *n., pl.* **·fish** *or* **·fish·es.** any soft-finned deep-sea teleost fish of the genus *Trachipterus,* esp. *T. arcticus,* related to the ribbonfishes and having a very long tapelike body and a fan-shaped tail fin.

deal·ings ('di:lɪŋz) *pl. n.* (*sometimes sing.*) transactions or business relations.

dealt (dɛlt) *vb.* the past tense or past participle of **deal.**

de·am·i·nate (di:'æmɪ,neɪt) *or* **de·am·in·ize, de·am·in·ise** *vb.* (*tr.*) to remove one or more amino groups from (a molecule). —**de·,am·i·'na·tion, de·,am·i·ni·'za·tion,** *or* **de·,am·i·ni·'sa·tion** *n.*

dean (di:n) *n.* **1.** the chief administrative official of a college or university faculty. **2.** (at Oxford and Cambridge universities) a college fellow with responsibility for undergraduate discipline. **3.** *Chiefly Church of England.* the head of a chapter of canons and administrator of a cathedral or a collegiate church. **4.** *R.C. Church.* the cardinal bishop senior by consecration and head of the college of cardinals. Related adj.: **decanal.** See also: **rural dean.** [C14: from Old French *deien,* from Late Latin *decānus* one set over ten persons, from Latin *decem* ten] —'**dean·,ship** *n.*

dean·er·y ('di:nərɪ) *n., pl.* **·er·ies. 1.** the office or residence of dean. **2.** the group of parishes presided over by a rural dean.

Dean of Fac·ul·ty *n.* the president of the Faculty of Advocates in Scotland.

dean of guild *n.* the titular head of the guild or merchant company in a Scots burgh, who exercises jurisdiction over all building in the burgh.

dear (dɪə) *adj.* **1.** beloved; precious. **2.** used in conventional forms of address preceding a title or name, as in *Dear Sir* or *my dear Mr. Smith.* **3.** (*postpositive;* foll. by *to*) important; close: *a wish dear to her heart.* **4. a.** highly priced. **b.** charging high prices. **5.** appealing or pretty: *what a dear little ring!* **6. for dear life.** as though life were in danger. ~*interj.* **7.** used in exclamations of surprise or dismay, such as *Oh dear!* and *dear me!* ~*n.* **8.** (*often used in direct address*) someone regarded with affection and tenderness; darling. ~*adv.* **9.** dearly: *his errors have cost him dear.* [Old English *dēore;* related to Old Norse *dȳrr*] —'**dear·ness** *n.*

Dear·born ('dɪəbən, -bɔ:n) *n.* a city in SE Michigan, near Detroit: automobile industry. Pop.: 104 199 (1970).

Dear John let·ter *n. Informal.* a letter from a girl breaking off a love affair.

dear·ly ('dɪəlɪ) *adv.* **1.** very much: *I would dearly like you to go.* **2.** affectionately. **3.** at a great cost.

dearth (dɜ:θ) *n.* an inadequate amount, esp. of food; scarcity. [C13 *derthe,* from *dēr* DEAR]

dear·y *or* **dear·ie** ('dɪərɪ) *n.* **1.** (*pl.* **dear·ies**) *Informal.* a term of affection: now often sarcastic or facetious. **2. deary** *or* **dearie me!** an exclamation of surprise or dismay.

death (dɛθ) *n.* **1.** the permanent end of all functions of life in an organism or some of its cellular components. **2.** an instance of this: *his death ended an era.* **3.** a murder or killing: *he had five deaths on his conscience.* **4.** termination or destruction: *the death of colonialism.* **5.** a state of affairs or an experience considered as terrible as death: *your constant nagging will be the death of me.* **6.** a cause or source of death. **7.** (*usually cap.*) a personification of death, usually a skeleton or an old man holding a scythe. **8. to death** *or* **to the death.** until dead: *bleed to death; a fight to the death.* **9. at death's door.** likely to die soon. **10. catch one's death (of cold).** *Informal.* to contract a severe cold. **11. do to death. a.** to kill. **b.** to overuse (a joke, etc.) so that it no longer has any effect. **12. in at the death. a.** present when an animal that is being hunted is caught and killed. **b.** present at the finish or climax. **13. like death warmed up.** *Informal.* very ill. **14. like grim death.** as if afraid of one's life. **15. put to death.** to kill deliberately or execute. ~Related adjs.: **fatal, lethal, mortal.** [Old English *dēath;* related to Old High German *tōd* death, Gothic *dauthus*]

death ad·der *n.* a venomous Australian elapid snake, *Acanthophis antarcticus,* resembling an adder.

death·bed ('dɛθˌbɛd) *n.* **1.** the bed in which a person is about to die. **2. on one's deathbed.** about to die.

death·blow ('dɛθˌbləʊ) *n.* a thing or event that destroys life or hope, esp. suddenly.

death cap *or* **an·gel** *n.* a poisonous woodland saprophytic basidiomycetous fungus, *Amanita phalloides,* differing from the edible mushroom (*Agaricus*) only in its white gills (pinkish-brown in *Agaricus*) and the presence of a volva. See also **amanita.**

death cell *n.* a prison cell for criminals sentenced to death.

death cer·ti·fi·cate *n.* a legal document issued by a qualified medical practitioner certifying the death of a person and stating the cause if known.

death du·ty *n.* a tax on property inheritances.

death grant *n.* (in the British National Insurance scheme) a grant payable to a relative, executor, etc., after the death of a person.

death knell *or* **bell** *n.* **1.** something that heralds death or destruction. **2.** a bell rung to announce a death.

death·less ('dɛθləs) *adj.* immortal, esp. because of greatness; everlasting. —**'death·less·ly** *adv.* —**'death·less·ness** *n.*

death·ly ('dɛθlɪ) *adj.* **1.** deadly. **2.** resembling death: *a deathly quiet.*

death mask *n.* a cast of a person's face taken shortly after death. Compare **life mask.**

death pen·al·ty *n.* (often preceded by *the*) capital punishment.

death rate *n.* the ratio of deaths in a specified area, group, etc., to the population of that area, group, etc. Also called (esp. in the U.S.): **mortality rate.**

death rat·tle *n.* a low-pitched gurgling sound sometimes made by a dying person, caused by air passing through an accumulation of mucus in the trachea.

death ray *n.* an imaginary ray capable of killing.

death row *or* **house** *n. U.S.* the part of a prison where those sentenced to death are confined.

death seat *n. U.S. and Austral. slang.* the seat beside the driver of a vehicle.

death's-head *n.* a human skull or a representation of one.

death's-head moth *n.* a European hawk moth, *Acherontia atropos,* having markings resembling a human skull on its upper thorax.

death·trap ('dɛθˌtræp) *n.* a building, vehicle, etc., that is considered very unsafe.

Death Val·ley *n.* a desert valley in E California and W Nevada: the lowest, hottest, and driest area of the U.S. Lowest point: 86 m (282 ft.) below sea level. Area: about 3885 sq. km (1500 sq. miles).

death war·rant *n.* **1.** the official authorization for carrying out a sentence of death. **2. sign one's (own) death warrant.** to cause one's own destruction.

death·watch ('dɛθˌwɒtʃ) *n.* **1.** a vigil held beside a dying or dead person. **2. deathwatch beetle.** any beetle of the family *Anobiidae,* esp. *Xestobium rufovillosum,* that bores into wood and produces a tapping sound that was popularly thought to presage death.

death wish *n.* (in Freudian psychology) the desire for self-annihilation. See also **Thanatos.**

Deau·ville ('dəʊvi:l; *French* do'vil) *n.* a town and resort in NW France: casino. Pop.: 5370 (1968).

deb (dɛb) *n. Informal.* short for **debutante.**

deb. *abbrev. for* debenture.

de·ba·cle (deɪ'bɑ:kəl, dɪ-) *n.* **1.** a sudden disastrous collapse or defeat, esp. one involving a disorderly retreat; rout. **2.** the breaking up of ice in a river during spring or summer, often causing flooding. **3.** a violent rush of water carrying along debris. [C19: from French *débâcle,* from Old French *desbacler* to unbolt, ultimately from Latin *baculum* rod, staff]

de·bag (di:'bæg) *vb.* **·bags, ·bag·ging, ·bagged.** (*tr.*) *Brit. slang.* to remove the trousers from (someone) by force.

de·bar (dɪ'bɑ:) *vb.* **·bars, ·bar·ring, ·barred.** (*tr.;* usually foll. by *from*) to exclude from a place, a right, etc.; bar. —**de·'bar·ment** *n.*

de·bark (dɪ'bɑ:k) *vb.* a less common word for **disembark.** [C17: from French *débarquer,* from *dé-* DIS-[1] + *barque* BARQUE] —**de·bar·ka·tion** (ˌdi:bɑ:'keɪʃən) *n.*

de·base (dɪ'beɪs) *vb.* (*tr.*) to lower in quality, character, or value, as by adding cheaper metal to coins; adulterate. [C16: see DE-, BASE[2]] —**de·bas·ed·ness** (dɪ'beɪsɪdnɪs) *n.* —**de·'base·ment** *n.* —**de·'bas·er** *n.* —**de·'bas·ing·ly** *adv.*

de·bat·a·ble *or* **de·bate·a·ble** (dɪ'beɪtəbəl) *adj.* **1.** open to question; disputable. **2.** *Law.* in dispute, as land or territory to which two parties lay claim.

de·bate (dɪ'beɪt) *n.* **1.** a formal discussion, as in a legislative body, in which opposing arguments are put forward. **2.** discussion or dispute. **3.** the formal presentation and opposition of a specific motion, followed by a vote. ~*vb.* **4.** to discuss (a motion, etc.), esp. in a formal assembly. **5.** to deliberate upon (something): *he debated with himself whether to go.* [C13: from Old French *debatre* to discuss, argue, from Latin *battuere*] —**de·'bat·er** *n.*

de·bauch (dɪ'bɔ:tʃ) *vb.* **1.** (when *tr., usually passive*) to lead into a life of depraved self-indulgence. **2.** (*tr.*) to seduce (a woman). ~*n.* **3.** an instance or period of extreme dissipation. [C16: from Old French *desbaucher* to corrupt, literally: to shape (timber) roughly, from *bauch* beam, of Germanic origin] —**de·bauch·ed·ly** (dɪ'bɔ:tʃɪdlɪ) *adv.* —**de·'bauch·ed·ness** *n.* —**de·'bauch·er** *n.* —**de·'bauch·er·y** *or* **de·'bauch·ment** *n.*

deb·au·chee (ˌdɛbɔ:'tʃi:, -ɔ:'ʃi:) *n.* a man who leads a life of reckless drinking, promiscuity, and self-indulgence.

de·be ('dɛbɛ) *n. E. African.* a tin. [C20: from Swahili]

de Beau·voir (*French* də bo'vwa:r) *n.* See (Simone de) **Beauvoir.**

de·ben·ture (dɪ'bɛntʃə) *n.* **1.** Also called: **debenture bond.** a long-term bond, bearing fixed interest and usually unsecured, issued by a company or governmental agency. **2.** a certificate acknowledging the debt of a stated sum of money to a specified person. **3.** a customs certificate providing for a refund of excise or import duty. [C15: from Latin phrase *dēbentur mihi* there are owed to me, from *dēbēre* to owe] —**de·'ben·tured** *adj.*

de·bil·i·tate (dɪ'bɪlɪˌteɪt) *vb.* (*tr.*) to make feeble; weaken. [C16: from Latin *dēbilitāre,* from *dēbilis* weak] —**de·ˌbil·i·'ta·tion** *n.* —**de·'bil·i·ta·tive** *adj.*

de·bil·i·ty (dɪ'bɪlɪtɪ) *n., pl.* **·ties.** weakness or infirmity.

deb·it ('dɛbɪt) *Accounting.* ~*n.* **1. a.** acknowledgment of a sum owing by entry on the left side of an account. **b.** the left side of an account. **c.** an entry on this side. **d.** the total of such entries. **e.** (*as modifier*): *a debit balance.* Compare **credit** (sense 10). ~*vb.* **2.** (*tr.*) **a.** to record (an item) as a debit in an account. **b.** to charge (a person or his account) with a debt. Compare **credit** (sense 17). [C15: from Latin *dēbitum* DEBT]

deb·o·nair *or* **deb·on·naire** (ˌdɛbə'nɛə) *adj.* (esp. of a man or his manner) **1.** suave and refined. **2.** carefree; gay. **3.** courteous and cheerful; affable. [C13: from Old French *debonaire,* from *de bon aire* having a good disposition] —**ˌdeb·o·'nair·ly** *adv.* —**ˌdeb·o·'nair·ness** *n.*

Deb·o·rah ('dɛbərə, -brə) *n. Old Testament.* **1.** a prophetess and judge of Israel who fought the Canaanites (Judges 4, 5). **2.** Rebekah's nurse (Genesis 35:8).

de·bouch (dɪ'baʊtʃ) *vb.* **1.** (*intr.*) (esp. of troops) to move into a more open space, as from a narrow or concealed place. **2.** (*intr.*) (of a river, glacier, etc.) to flow from a valley into a larger area or body. ~*n.* **3.** Also called: **dé·bou·ché** (*French* debu'ʃe). *Fortifications.* an outlet or passage, as for the exit of troops. [C18: from French *déboucher,* from *dé-* DIS-[1] + *bouche* mouth, from Latin *bucca* cheek]

de·bouch·ment (dɪ'baʊtʃmənt) *n.* **1.** the act or an instance of debouching. **2.** Also called: **de·bou·chure** (ˌdeɪbu:'ʃʊə). an outlet, mouth, or opening.

De·bre·cen ('dɛbrɛˌtsɛn) *n.* a city in E Hungary: seat of the revolutionary government of 1849. Pop.: 179 755 (1974 est.).

dé·bride·ment (dɪ'bri:dmənt, deɪ-) *n.* the surgical removal of dead tissue or cellular debris from the surface of a wound. [C19: from French, from Old French *desbrider* to unbridle, from *des-* DE- + *bride* BRIDLE]

de·brief (di:'bri:f) *vb.* (of a soldier, astronaut, diplomat, etc.) to make or (of his superiors) to elicit a report after a mission or event. Compare **brief** (sense 12).

de·bris *or* **dé·bris** ('deɪbrɪ, 'dɛbrɪ) *n.* **1.** fragments or remnants of something destroyed or broken; rubble. **2.** a collection of loose material derived from rocks, or an accumulation of animal or vegetable matter. [C18: from French, from obsolete *debrisier* to break into pieces, from *bruisier* to shatter, of Celtic origin]

de Bro·glie (*French* də'brɔj) *n.* See (Louis Victor de) **Broglie.**

de Bro·glie waves (də'brəʊglɪ) *pl. n. Physics.* the set of waves that represent the behaviour of an elementary particle, or some atoms and molecules, under certain conditions. The **de Broglie wavelength,** λ, is given by $\lambda = h/mv$, where h is the Planck constant, m the mass, and v the velocity of the particle. [C20: named after Louis Victor de BROGLIE]

Debs (dɛbz) *n.* **Eu·gene Vic·tor.** 1855–1926, U.S. labour leader; five times Socialist presidential candidate (1900–20).

debt (dɛt) *n.* **1.** something that is owed, such as money, goods, or services. **2. bad debt.** a debt that has little or no prospect of being paid. **3.** an obligation to pay or perform something; liability. **4.** the state of owing something, esp. money, or of being under an obligation (esp. in the phrases **in debt, in (someone's) debt**). [C13; from Old French *dette,* from Latin *dēbitum,* from *dēbēre* to owe, from DE- + *habēre* to have; English spelling influenced by the Latin etymon] —**'debt·less** *adj.*

debt of hon·our *n.* a debt that is morally but not legally binding, such as one contracted in gambling.

debt·or ('dɛtə) *n.* a person or commercial enterprise that owes a financial obligation. Compare **creditor.**

de·bug (diː'bʌg) *Informal.* ~*vb.* **·bugs, ·bug·ging, ·bugged.** (*tr.*) **1.** to locate and remove concealed microphones from (a room, etc.). **2.** to locate and remove defects in (a device, system, plan, etc.). **3.** to remove insects from. ~*n.* **4. a.** something, esp. a computer program, that locates and removes defects in (a device, system, etc.) **b.** (*as modifier*): *a debug program.* [C20: from DE- + BUG[1]]

de·bunk (diː'bʌŋk) *vb.* (*tr.*) *Informal.* to expose the pretensions or falseness of, esp. by ridicule. [C20: from DE- + BUNK[2]] —**de'bunk·er** *n.*

de·bus (diː'bʌs) *vb.* **de·bus·es, de·bus·ing, de·bused** *or* **de·bus·ses, de·bus·sing, de·bussed.** to unload (goods, etc.) or (esp. of troops) to alight from a bus.

De·bus·sy (də'bjuːsɪ, 'deɪbjuːsɪ; *French* dəby'si) *n.* **(Achille) Claude** (klod). 1862–1918, French composer and critic, the creator of impressionism in music and a profound influence on contemporary composition. His works include *Prélude à l'après-midi d'un faune* (1894) and *La Mer* (1905) for orchestra, the opera *Pelléas et Mélisande* (1902), and many piano pieces and song settings.

de·but ('deɪbjuː, 'dɛbjuː) *n.* **1.** the first public appearance of an actor, musician, etc. **2.** the presentation of a debutante. [C18: from French *début,* from Old French *desbuter* to play first (hence: make one's first appearance), from *des-* DE- + *but* goal, target; see BUTT[2]]

deb·u·tante ('dɛbjʊˌtɑːnt, -ˌtænt) *n.* **1.** a young woman of upper-class background who is presented to society, usually at a formal ball. **2.** a girl or young woman regarded as being upper-class, wealthy, and of a frivolous or snobbish social set. [C19: from French, from *débuter* to lead off in a game, make one's first appearance; see DEBUT]

dec. *abbrev. for:* **1.** deceased. **2.** declaration. **3.** declension. **4.** declination. **5.** decrease. **6.** *Music.* decrescendo.

Dec. *abbrev. for* December.

dec·a-, dek·a- *or before a vowel* **dec-, dek-** *prefix.* denoting ten: *decagon.* In conjunction with scientific units the symbol **da** is used. [from Greek *deka*]

dec·ade ('dɛkeɪd, dɪ'keɪd) *n.* **1.** a period of ten consecutive years. **2.** a group or series of ten. [C15: from Old French, from Late Latin *decad-, decas,* from Greek *dekas,* from *deka* ten] —**de'ca·dal** *adj.*

dec·a·dence ('dɛkədəns) *or* **dec·a·den·cy** *n.* **1.** deterioration, esp. of morality or culture; decay; degeneration. **2.** the state reached through such a process. **3.** (*often cap.*) the period or style associated with the 19th-century Decadents. [C16: from French, from Medieval Latin *dēcadentia,* literally: a falling away; see DECAY]

dec·a·dent ('dɛkədənt) *adj.* **1.** characterized by decay or decline, as in being self-indulgent or morally corrupt. **2.** belonging to a period of decline in artistic standards. ~*n.* **3.** a decadent person. —**'dec·a·dent·ly** *adv.*

de·caf·fein·ate (dɪ'kæfɪˌneɪt) *vb.* (*tr.*) to remove all or part of the caffeine from (coffee).

dec·a·gon ('dɛkəˌgɒn) *n.* a polygon having ten sides. —**de·cag·o·nal** (dɪ'kægən°l) *adj.* —**de'cag·o·nal·ly** *adv.*

dec·a·he·dron (ˌdɛkə'hiːdrən) *n.* a solid figure having ten plane faces. See also **polyhedron.** —ˌ**dec·a'he·dral** *adj.*

de·cal (dɪ'kæl, 'diːkæl) *n.* **1.** short for **decalcomania.** ~*vb.* **2.** to transfer (a design, etc.) by decalcomania.

de·cal·ci·fy (diː'kælsɪˌfaɪ) *vb.* **·fies, ·fy·ing, ·fied.** (*tr.*) to remove calcium or lime from (bones, teeth, etc.). —**de·cal·ci·fi·ca·tion** (diːˌkælsɪfɪ'keɪʃən) *n.* —**de'cal·ciˌfi·er** *n.*

de·cal·co·ma·ni·a (dɪˌkælkə'meɪnɪə) *n.* **1.** the art or process of transferring a design from prepared paper onto another surface, such as china, glass or paper. **2.** a design so transferred. [C19: from French *décalcomanie,* from *décalquer* to transfer by tracing, from *dé-* DE- + *calquer* to trace + *-manie* -MANIA]

de·ca·les·cence (ˌdiːkə'lɛs°ns) *n.* the absorption of heat when a metal is heated through a particular temperature range, caused by a change in internal crystal structure. [C19: from Late Latin *dēcalescere* to become warm, from Latin DE- + *calescere,* from *calēre* to be warm] —ˌ**de·ca'les·cent** *adj.*

Dec·a·logue ('dɛkəˌlɒg) *n.* another name for the **Ten Commandments.** [C14: from Church Latin *decalogus,* from Greek, from *deka* ten + *logos* word]

de·camp (dɪ'kæmp) *vb.* (*intr.*) **1.** to leave a camp; break camp. **2.** to depart secretly or suddenly; abscond. —**de'camp·ment** *n.*

de·ca·nal (dɪ'keɪn°l) *adj.* **a.** of or relating to a dean or deanery. **b.** (of part of a choir) on the same side of a cathedral, etc., as the dean; on the S side of the choir. Compare **cantorial.** [C18: from Medieval Latin *decānālis, decānus* DEAN] —**de'ca·nal·ly** *or* **de·can·i·cal·ly** (dɪ'kænɪklɪ) *adv.*

dec·ane ('dɛkeɪn) *n.* a liquid alkane hydrocarbon existing in several isomeric forms. Formula: $C_{10}H_{22}$. [C19: from DECA- + -ANE]

dec·ane·di·o·ic ac·id (ˌdɛkeɪndaɪ'əʊɪk) *n.* a white crystalline carboxylic acid obtained by heating castor oil with sodium hydroxide, used in the manufacture of polyester resins and rubbers and plasticizers. Formula: $HOOC(CH_2)_8COOH$. Also called: **sebacic acid.**

de·ca·ni (dɪ'keɪnaɪ) *adj., adv. Music.* to be sung by the decanal side of a choir. Compare: **cantoris.** [Latin: genitive of *decānus*]

dec·a·no·ic ac·id (ˌdɛkə'nəʊɪk) *n.* a white crystalline insoluble carboxylic acid with an unpleasant odour, used in perfumes and for making fruit flavours. Formula: $C_9H_{19}COOH$. Also called: **capric acid.**

de·cant (dɪ'kænt) *vb.* to pour (a liquid, such as wine) from one container to another, esp. without disturbing any sediment. [C17: from Medieval Latin *dēcanthāre,* from *canthus* spout, rim; see CANTHUS]

de·cant·er (dɪ'kæntə) *n.* a stoppered bottle, usually of glass, into which a drink, such as wine, is poured for serving.

de·cap·i·tate (dɪ'kæpɪˌteɪt) *vb.* (*tr.*) to behead. [C17: from Late Latin *dēcapitāre,* from Latin DE- + *caput* head] —**deˌcap·i'ta·tion** *n.* —**de'cap·iˌta·tor** *n.*

dec·a·pod ('dɛkəˌpɒd) *n.* **1.** any crustacean of the mostly marine order *Decapoda,* having five pairs of walking limbs: includes the crabs, lobsters, shrimps, prawns, and crayfish. **2.** any cephalopod mollusc of the order *Decapoda,* having a ring of eight short tentacles and two longer ones: includes the squids and cuttlefish. ~*adj.* **3.** of, relating to, or belonging to either of these orders. **4.** (of any other animal) having ten limbs. —**de·cap·o·dal** (dɪ'kæpəd°l), **de'cap·o·dan,** *or* **de'cap·o·dous** *adj.*

De·cap·o·lis (dɪ'kæpəlɪs) *n.* a league of ten cities, including Damascus, in the northeast of ancient Palestine: established in 63 B.C. by Pompey and governed by Rome.

de·car·bon·ate (diː'kɑːbəˌneɪt) *vb.* (*tr.*) to remove carbon dioxide from (a solution, substance, etc.). —**deˌcar·bon'a·tion** *n.* —**de'car·bonˌa·tor** *n.*

de·car·bon·ize *or* **de·car·bon·ise** (diː'kɑːbəˌnaɪz) *vb.* (*tr.*) to remove carbon from (the walls of the combustion chamber of an internal-combustion engine, etc.). Also: **decoke, decarburize.** —**deˌcar·bon·i'za·tion** *or* **deˌcar·bon·i'sa·tion** *n.* —**de'car·bonˌiz·er** *or* **de'car·bonˌis·er** *n.*

de·car·box·y·la·tion (ˌdiːkɑːˌbɒksə'leɪʃən) *n.* the removal or loss of a carboxyl group from an organic compound.

de·car·bu·rize *or* **de·car·bu·rise** (diː'kɑːbjʊˌraɪz) *vb.* another word for **decarbonize.** —**deˌcar·bu·ri'za·tion, deˌcar·bu·ri'sa·tion,** *or* **deˌcar·bu'ra·tion** *n.*

dec·are ('dɛkɛə, dɛ'kɛə) *n.* ten ares or 1000 square metres. [C19: from French *décare;* see DECA-, ARE[2]]

dec·a·style ('dɛkəˌstaɪl) *n. Architect.* a portico consisting of ten columns.

dec·a·syl·la·ble ('dɛkəˌsɪləb°l) *n.* a word or line of verse consisting of ten syllables. —**dec·a·syl·lab·ic** (ˌdɛkəsɪ'læbɪk) *adj.*

de·cath·lon (dɪ'kæθlɒn) *n.* an athletic contest for men in which each athlete competes in ten different events. Compare **pentathlon.** [C20: from DECA- + Greek *athlon* contest, prize; see ATHLETE]

de·cay (dɪ'keɪ) *vb.* **1.** to decline or cause to decline gradually in health, prosperity, excellence, etc.; deteriorate; waste away. **2.** to rot or cause to rot as a result of bacterial, fungal, or chemical action; decompose. **3.** (*intr.*) Also: **disintegrate.** *Physics.* **a.** (of an atomic nucleus) to undergo radioactive disintegration. **b.** (of an elementary particle) to transform into two or more different elementary particles. **4.** *Physics.* (of a stored charge, magnetic flux, etc.) to decrease gradually when the source of energy has been removed. ~*n.* **5.** the process of decline, as in health, mentality, beauty, etc. **6.** the state brought about by this process. **7.** decomposition, as of vegetable matter. **8.** rotten or decayed matter: *the dentist drilled out the decay.* **9.** *Physics.* **a.** See **radioactive decay. b.** a spontaneous transformation of an elementary particle into two or more different particles. **10.** *Physics.* a gradual decrease of a stored charge, magnetic flux, current, etc., when the source of energy has been removed. See also **time constant.** [C15: from Old Northern French *decaïr,* from Late Latin *dēcadere,* literally: to fall away, from Latin *cadere* to fall] —**de'cay·a·ble** *adj.*

Dec·can ('dɛkən) *n.* **the. 1.** a plateau in S India, between the Eastern Ghats, the Western Ghats, and the Narmada River. **2.** the whole Indian peninsula south of the Narmada River.

decd. *abbrev. for* deceased.

de·cease (dɪ'siːs) *n.* **1.** a more formal word for **death.** ~*vb.* **2.** (*intr.*) a more formal word for **die[1].** [C14 (*n.*): from Old French *deces,* from Latin *dēcēdere* to depart]

de·ceased (dɪ'siːst) *adj.* **a.** a more formal word for **dead** (sense 1). **b.** (*as n.*): *the deceased.*

de·ce·dent (dɪ'siːd°nt) *n. Law, chiefly U.S.* a deceased person. [C16: from Latin *dēcēdēns* departing; see DECEASE]

de·ceit (dɪ'siːt) *n.* **1.** the act or practice of deceiving. **2.** a statement, act, or device intended to mislead; fraud; trick. **3.** a tendency to deceive. [C13: from Old French *deceite,* from *deceivre* to DECEIVE]

de·ceit·ful (dɪ'siːtfʊl) *adj.* full of deceit. —**de'ceit·ful·ly** *adv.* —**de'ceit·ful·ness** *n.*

de·ceive (dɪ'siːv) *vb.* (*tr.*) **1.** to mislead by deliberate misrepresentation or lies. **2.** to delude (oneself). **3.** *Archaic.* to disappoint: *his hopes were deceived.* [C13: from Old French *deceivre,* from Latin *dēcipere* to ensnare, cheat, from *capere* to take] —**de'ceiv·a·ble** *adj.* —**de'ceiv·a·bly** *adv.* —**de'ceiv·a·ble·ness** *or* **deˌceiv·a'bil·i·ty** *n.* —**de'ceiv·er** *n.* —**de'ceiv·ing·ly** *adv.*

de·cel·er·ate (diː'sɛləˌreɪt) *vb.* to slow down or cause to slow down. [C19: from DE- + ACCELERATE] —**deˌcel·er'a·tion** *n.* —**de'cel·erˌa·tor** *n.*

de·cel·e·rom·e·ter (dɪˌsɛlə'rɒmɪtə) *n.* an instrument for measuring deceleration.

De·cem·ber (dɪ'sɛmbə) *n.* the twelfth and last month of the year, consisting of 31 days. [C13: from Old French *decembre,* from Latin *december* the tenth month (the Roman year began with March), from *decem* ten]

De·cem·brist (dɪˈsɛmbrɪst) *n. Russian history.* a participant in the unsuccessful revolt against Tsar Nicolas I in Dec. 1825. [C19: translation of Russian *dekabrist*]

de·cem·vir (dɪˈsɛmvə) *n., pl.* **·virs** *or* **·vi·ri** (-vɪˌriː). **1.** (in ancient Rome) a member of a board of ten magistrates, esp. either of the two commissions established in 451 and 450 B.C. to revise the laws. **2.** a member of any governing body composed of ten men. [C17: from Latin, from *decem* ten + *virī* men] —**deˈcem·vi·ral** *adj.*

de·cem·vi·rate (dɪˈsɛmvɪrɪt, -ˌreɪt) *n.* **1.** a board of decemvirs. **2.** the rule or rank of decemvirs.

de·cen·a·ry *or* **de·cen·na·ry** (dɪˈsɛnərɪ) *adj. History.* of or relating to a tithing. [C13: from Medieval Latin *decēna* a tithing, from *decem* ten]

de·cen·cies (ˈdiːsᵊnsɪz) *pl. n.* **1. the.** those things that are considered necessary for a decent life. **2.** another word for **proprieties.**

de·cen·cy (ˈdiːsᵊnsɪ) *n., pl.* **·cies. 1.** conformity to the prevailing standards of propriety, morality, modesty, etc. **2.** the quality of being decent.

de·cen·ni·al (dɪˈsɛnɪəl) *adj.* **1.** lasting for ten years. **2.** occurring every ten years. ~*n.* **3.** a tenth anniversary or its celebration. —**deˈcen·ni·al·ly** *adv.*

de·cen·ni·um (dɪˈsɛnɪəm) *or* **de·cen·na·ry** (dɪˈsɛnərɪ) *n., pl.* **·ni·ums, ·ni·a** (-nɪə), *or* **·nar·ies.** a less common word for **decade.** [C17: from Latin, from *decem* ten + *annus* year]

de·cent (ˈdiːsᵊnt) *adj.* **1.** polite or respectable: *a decent family.* **2.** proper and suitable; fitting: *a decent burial.* **3.** conforming to conventions of sexual behaviour; not indecent. **4.** free of oaths, blasphemy, etc.: *decent language.* **5.** good or adequate: *a decent wage.* **6.** *Informal.* kind; generous: *he was pretty decent to me.* **7.** *Informal.* sufficiently clothed to be seen by other people: *are you decent?* [C16: from Latin *decēns* suitable, from *decēre* to be fitting] —**ˈde·cent·ly** *adv.* —**ˈde·cent·ness** *n.*

de·cen·tral·ize *or* **de·cen·tral·ise** (diːˈsɛntrəˌlaɪz) *vb.* **1.** to reorganize (a government, industry, etc.) into smaller more autonomous units. **2.** to disperse (a concentration, as of industry or population). —**deˈcen·tral·ist** *n., adj.* —**deˌcen·tral·iˈza·tion** *or* **deˌcen·tral·iˈsa·tion** *n.*

de·cep·tion (dɪˈsɛpʃən) *n.* **1.** the act of deceiving or the state of being deceived. **2.** something that deceives; trick.

de·cep·tive (dɪˈsɛptɪv) *adj.* **1.** likely or designed to deceive; misleading: *appearances can be deceptive.* **2.** *Music.* (of a cadence) another word for **interrupted** (sense 3). —**deˈcep·tive·ly** *adv.* —**deˈcep·tive·ness** *n.*

de·ce·re·brate *vb.* (diːˈsɛrɪˌbreɪt) **1.** (*tr.*) to remove the brain or a large section of the brain or to cut the spinal cord at the level of the brain stem of (a person or animal). ~*n.* (diːˈsɛrɪbrɪt). **2.** a decerebrated individual. [C19: from DE- + CEREBRO- + -ATE[1]] —**deˌce·reˈbra·tion** *n.*

de·cern (dɪˈsɜːn) *vb.* (*tr.*) **1.** *Scot. law.* to decree or adjudge. **2.** an archaic spelling of **discern.** [C15: from Old French *decerner,* from Latin *dēcernere* to judge, from *cernere* to discern]

dec·i- *prefix.* denoting one tenth; 10^{-1}: *decimetre.* Symbol: d [from French *déci-,* from Latin *decimus* tenth]

dec·i·are (ˈdɛsɪˌɛə) *n.* one tenth of an are or 10 square metres. [C19: from French *déciare;* see DECI-, ARE[2]]

dec·i·bel (ˈdɛsɪˌbɛl) *n.* **1.** a unit for comparing two currents, voltages, or power levels, equal to one tenth of a bel. **2.** a similar unit for measuring the intensity of a sound. It is equal to ten times the logarithm to the base ten of the ratio of the intensity of the sound to be measured to the intensity of some reference sound, usually the lowest audible note of the same frequency. Abbrev.: **dB** See also **perceived noise decibel.**

de·cide (dɪˈsaɪd) *vb.* **1.** (*may take a clause or an infinitive as object;* when *intr.,* sometimes foll. by *on* or *about*) to reach a decision: *decide what you want; he decided to go.* **2.** (*tr.*) to cause (a person) to reach a decision: *the weather decided me against going.* **3.** (*tr.*) to determine or settle (a contest or question): *he decided his future plans.* **4.** (*tr.*) to influence decisively the outcome of (a contest or question): *Borg's stamina decided the match.* **5.** (*intr.;* foll. by *for* or *against*) to pronounce a formal verdict. [C14: from Old French *decider,* from Latin *dēcīdere,* literally: to cut off, from *caedere* to cut] —**deˈcid·a·ble** *adj.* —**deˈcid·er** *n.*

de·cid·ed (dɪˈsaɪdɪd) *adj.* (*prenominal*) **1.** unmistakable: *a decided drop in attendance.* **2.** determined; resolute: *a decided effort.* —**deˈcid·ed·ly** *adv.* —**deˈcid·ed·ness** *n.*

de·cid·u·a (dɪˈsɪdjʊə) *n., pl.* **·cid·u·as** *or* **·cid·u·ae** (-ˈsɪdjʊˌiː). the specialized mucous membrane that lines the uterus of some mammals during pregnancy: is shed, with the placenta, at parturition. [C18: from New Latin, from Latin *dēciduus* falling down; see DECIDUOUS] —**deˈcid·u·al** *or* **deˈcid·u·ate** *adj.*

de·cid·u·ous (dɪˈsɪdjʊəs) *adj.* **1.** (of trees and shrubs) shedding all leaves annually at the end of the growing season. Compare **evergreen** (sense 1). **2.** (of antlers, wings, teeth, etc.) being shed at the end of a period of growth. **3.** *Rare.* impermanent; transitory. Compare **evergreen** (sense 2). [C17: from Latin *dēciduus* falling off, from *dēcidere* to fall down, from *cadere* to fall] —**deˈcid·u·ous·ly** *adv.* —**deˈcid·u·ous·ness** *n.*

dec·ile (ˈdɛsɪl, -aɪl) *n. Statistics.* one of nine actual or notional values of a variable dividing its distribution into ten groups with equal frequencies. [C17: from DECA- + -ILE]

de·cil·lion (dɪˈsɪljən) *n.* **1.** (in Britain and Germany) the number represented as one followed by 60 zeros (10^{60}). **2.** (in the U.S. and France) the number represented as one followed by 33 zeros (10^{33}). [C19: from Latin *decem* ten + *-illion* as in *million*] —**deˈcil·lionth** *adj.*

dec·i·mal (ˈdɛsɪməl) *n.* **1.** Also called: **decimal fraction.** a fraction that has a denominator of a power of ten, the power depending on or deciding the decimal place. It is indicated by a decimal point to the left of the numerator, the denominator being omitted. Zeros are inserted between the point and the numerator, if necessary, to obtain the correct decimal place. **2.** any number used in the decimal system. ~*adj.* **3. a.** relating to or using powers of ten. **b.** of the base ten. **4.** (*prenominal*) expressed as a decimal. [C17: from Medieval Latin *decimālis* of tithes, from Latin *decima* a tenth, from *decem* ten] —**ˈdec·i·mal·ly** *adv.*

dec·i·mal clas·si·fi·ca·tion *n.* another term for **Dewey decimal system.**

dec·i·mal cur·ren·cy *n.* a system of currency in which the monetary units are parts or powers of ten.

dec·i·mal frac·tion *n.* another name for **decimal** (sense 1).

dec·i·mal·ize *or* **dec·i·mal·ise** (ˈdɛsɪməˌlaɪz) *vb.* to change (a system, number, etc.) to the decimal system: *Britain has decimalized her currency.* —**ˌdec·i·mal·iˈza·tion** *or* **ˌdec·i·mal·iˈsa·tion** *n.*

dec·i·mal place *n.* **1.** the position of a digit after the decimal point, each successive position to the right having a denominator of an increased power of ten: *in 0.025, 5 is in the third decimal place.* **2.** the number of digits to the right of the decimal point: *3.142 is a number given to three decimal places.* Compare **significant figures** (sense 2).

dec·i·mal point *n.* a full stop or a raised full stop placed between the integral and fractional parts of a number in the decimal system.

Usage. Conventions relating to the use of the decimal point are confused. The IX General Conference on Weights and Measures resolved in 1948 that the decimal point should be a point on the line or a comma, but not a centre dot. It also resolved that figures could be grouped in threes about the decimal point, but that no point or comma should be used for this purpose. These conventions are adopted in this dictionary. However, the Decimal Currency Board recommended that for sums of money the centre dot should be used as the decimal point and that the comma should be used as the thousand marker. Moreover, in some countries the position is reversed, the comma being used as the decimal point and the dot as the thousand marker.

dec·i·mal sys·tem *n.* **1.** the number system in general use, having a base of ten, in which numbers are expressed by combinations of the ten digits 0 to 9. **2.** a system of measurement, such as the metric system, in which the multiple and submultiple units are related to a basic unit by powers of ten.

dec·i·mate (ˈdɛsɪˌmeɪt) *vb.* (*tr.*) **1.** to destroy or kill a large proportion of: *a plague decimated the population.* **2.** (esp. in the ancient Roman army) to kill every tenth man of (a mutinous section). [C17: from Latin *decimāre,* from *decimus* tenth, from *decem* ten] —**ˌdec·iˈma·tion** *n.* —**ˈdec·iˌma·tor** *n.*

dec·i·me·tre *or U.S.* **dec·i·me·ter** (ˈdɛsɪˌmiːtə) *n.* one tenth of a metre. Symbol: **dm.**

de·ci·pher (dɪˈsaɪfə) *vb.* (*tr.*) **1.** to determine the meaning of (something obscure or illegible). **2.** to convert from code into plain text; decode. —**deˈci·pher·a·ble** *adj.* —**deˌci·pher·a·ˈbil·i·ty** *n.* —**deˈci·pher·er** *n.* —**deˈci·pher·ment** *n.*

de·ci·sion (dɪˈsɪʒən) *n.* **1.** a judgment, conclusion, or resolution reached or given; verdict. **2.** the act of making up one's mind. **3.** firmness of purpose or character; determination. [C15: from Old French, from Latin *dēcīsiō,* literally: a cutting off; see DECIDE] —**deˈci·sion·al** *adj.*

de·ci·sive (dɪˈsaɪsɪv) *adj.* **1.** influential; conclusive: *a decisive argument.* **2.** characterized by the ability to make decisions, esp. quickly; resolute. —**deˈci·sive·ly** *adv.* —**deˈci·sive·ness** *n.*

deck (dɛk) *n.* **1.** *Nautical.* any of various platforms built into a vessel: *a promenade deck; the poop deck.* **2.** a similar floor or platform, as in a bus. **3. a.** the horizontal platform that supports the turntable and pickup of a gramophone. **b.** See **tape deck. 4.** a pack of playing cards. **5.** Also called: **pack.** *Computer technol.* a collection of punched cards relevant to a particular program. **6.** *Slang.* a small packet of a narcotic drug. **7.** Also called: **board.** the flat top part of a skateboard, made of any of various materials, such as wood, fibreglass, or plastic. **8. clear the decks.** *Informal.* to prepare for action, as by removing obstacles from a field of activity or combat. **9. hit the deck.** *Informal.* **a.** to fall to the floor or ground, esp. in order to avoid injury. **b.** to prepare for action. **c.** to get out of bed. ~*vb.* (*tr.*) **10.** (often foll. by *out*) to dress or decorate. **11.** to build a deck on (a vessel). [C15: from Middle Dutch *dec* a covering; related to THATCH] —**ˈdeck·er** *n.*

deck chair *n.* a folding chair for use out of doors, consisting of a wooden frame suspending a length of canvas.

-deck·er *adj.* (*in combination*): having a certain specified number of levels or layers: *a double-decker bus.*

Deck·er (ˈdɛkə) *n.* a variant spelling of (Thomas) **Dekker.**

deck hand *n.* **1.** a seaman assigned various duties, such as mooring and cargo handling, on the deck of a ship. **2.** (in Britain) a seaman over 17 years of age who has seen sea duty for at least one year. **3.** a helper aboard a yacht.

deck·house (ˈdɛkˌhaʊs) *n.* a houselike cabin on the deck of a ship.

deck·le *or* **deck·el** (ˈdɛkᵊl) *n.* **1.** a frame used to support pulp in the making of handmade paper. **2.** Also called: **deckle strap.** a strap on each edge of the moving web of paper on a paper-making machine that fixes the width of the paper. **3.** See **deckle edge.** [C19: from German *Deckel* lid, from *decken* to cover]

deck·le edge *n.* **1.** the rough edge of handmade paper made in a deckle, often left as ornamentation in fine books and writing papers. **2.** a trimmed edge imitating this. —**'deck·le-'edged** *adj.*

deck o·ver *vb.* (*tr.*) to complete the construction of the upper deck between the bulwarks of (a vessel).

deck ten·nis *n.* a game played on board ship in which a quoit is tossed to and fro across a high net on a small court resembling a tennis court.

decl. *Grammar. abbrev. for* declension.

de·claim (dɪ'kleɪm) *vb.* **1.** to make (a speech, statement, etc.) loudly and in a rhetorical manner. **2.** to speak lines from (a play, poem, etc.) with studied eloquence; recite. **3.** (*intr.*; foll. by *against*) to protest (against) loudly and publicly. [C14: from Latin *dēclāmāre*, from *clāmāre* to call out] —**de'claim·er** *n.*

dec·la·ma·tion (ˌdɛklə'meɪʃən) *n.* **1.** a rhetorical or emotional speech, made esp. in order to protest or condemn; tirade. **2.** a speech, verse, etc., that is or can be spoken. **3.** the act or art of declaiming. **4.** *Music.* the artistry or technique involved in singing recitative passages.

de·clam·a·to·ry (dɪ'klæmətərɪ, -trɪ) *adj.* **1.** relating to or having the characteristics of a declamation. **2.** merely rhetorical; empty and bombastic. —**de'clam·a·to·ri·ly** *adv.*

de·clar·ant (dɪ'klɛərənt) *n. Chiefly law.* a person who makes a declaration.

dec·la·ra·tion (ˌdɛklə'reɪʃən) *n.* **1.** an explicit or emphatic statement. **2.** a formal statement or announcement; proclamation. **3.** the act of declaring. **4.** the ruling of a judge or court on a question of law, esp. in the chancery division of the High Court. **5.** *Law.* an unsworn statement of a witness admissible in evidence under certain conditions. See also **statutory declaration.** **6.** *Cricket.* the voluntary closure of an innings before all ten wickets have fallen. **7.** *Contract bridge.* the final contract. **8.** a statement or inventory of goods, etc., submitted for tax assessment: *a customs declaration.* **9.** *Cards.* an announcement of points made after taking a trick, as in bezique.

Dec·la·ra·tion of In·de·pend·ence *n.* **1.** the proclamation made by the second American Continental Congress on July 4, 1776, which asserted the freedom and independence of the 13 Colonies from Great Britain. **2.** the document formally recording this proclamation.

de·clar·a·tive (dɪ'klærətɪv) *adj.* making or having the nature of a declaration. —**de'clar·a·tive·ly** *adv.*

de·clar·a·tor (dɪ'klærətə) *n. Scot. law.* an action seeking to have some right, status, etc., judicially ascertained.

de·clar·a·to·ry (dɪ'klærətərɪ, -trɪ) *adj.* **1.** another word for **declarative.** **2.** *Law.* **a.** (of a statute) stating the existing law on a particular subject; explanatory. **b.** (of a decree or judgment) stating the rights of the parties without specifying the action to be taken. —**deˌclar·a'to·ri·ly** *adv.*

de·clare (dɪ'klɛə) *vb.* (*mainly tr.*) **1.** (*may take a clause as object*) to make clearly known or announce officially: *to declare one's interests; war was declared.* **2.** to state officially that (a person, fact, etc.) is as specified: *he declared him fit.* **3.** (*may take a clause as object*) to state emphatically; assert. **4.** to show, reveal, or manifest: *the heavens declare the glory of God.* **5.** (*intr.*; often foll. by *for* or *against*) to make known one's choice or opinion. **6.** to make a complete statement of (dutiable goods, etc.). **7.** (*also intr.*) *Cards.* **a.** to display (a card or series of cards) on the table so as to add to one's score. **b.** to decide (the trump suit) by making the winning bid. **8.** (*intr.*) *Cricket.* to close an innings voluntarily before all ten wickets have fallen. **9.** to authorize the payment of (a dividend) from corporate net profit. [C14: from Latin *dēclārāre* to make clear, from *clārus* bright, clear] —**de'clar·a·ble** *adj.*

de·clar·er (dɪ'klɛərə) *n.* **1.** a person who declares. **2.** *Bridge.* the player who, as first bidder of the suit of the final contract, plays both hands of the partnership.

de·class (di:'klɑ:s) *vb.* (*tr.*) to lower in social status or position; degrade.

dé·clas·sé (*French* dekla'se) *adj.* having lost social standing or status. [C19: from French *déclasser* to DECLASS] —**dé·clas·'sée** *fem. adj.*

de·clas·si·fy (di:'klæsɪˌfaɪ) *vb.* **·fies, ·fy·ing, ·fied.** (*tr.*) to release (a document or information) from the security list. —**de'clas·si·ˌfi·a·ble** *adj.* —**deˌclas·si·fi·'ca·tion** *n.*

de·clen·sion (dɪ'klɛnʃən) *n.* **1.** *Grammar.* **a.** inflection of nouns, pronouns, or adjectives for case, number, and gender. **b.** the complete set of the inflections of such a word: *"puella" is a first-declension noun in Latin.* **2.** a decline or deviation from a standard, belief, etc. **3.** a downward slope or bend. [C15: from Latin *dēclīnātiō*, literally: a bending aside, hence variation, inflection; see DECLINE] —**de'clen·sion·al** *adj.* —**de'clen·sion·al·ly** *adv.*

dec·li·nate ('dɛklɪˌneɪt, -nɪt) *adj.* (esp. of plant parts) descending from the horizontal in a curve; drooping.

dec·li·na·tion (ˌdɛklɪ'neɪʃən) *n.* **1.** *Astronomy.* the angular distance in degrees of a star, planet, etc., from the celestial equator measured north (positive) or south (negative) along the great circle passing through the celestial poles and the body. Symbol: δ. Compare **right ascension.** **2.** See **magnetic declination.** **3.** a refusal, esp. a courteous or formal one. —**ˌdec·li'na·tion·al** *adj.*

de·cline (dɪ'klaɪn) *vb.* **1.** to refuse to do or accept (something), esp. politely. **2.** (*intr.*) to grow smaller; diminish: *demand has declined over the years.* **3.** to slope or cause to slope downwards. **4.** (*intr.*) to deteriorate gradually, as in quality, health, or character. **5.** *Grammar.* to state or list the inflections of (a noun, adjective, or pronoun), or (of a noun, adjective, or pronoun) to be inflected for number, case, or gender. Compare **conjugate** (sense 1). ~*n.* **6.** gradual deterioration or loss. **7.** a movement downward or towards something smaller; diminution. **8.** a downward slope; declivity. **9.** *Archaic.* any slowly progressive disease, such as tuberculosis. [C14: from Old French *decliner* to inflect, turn away, sink, from Latin *dēclīnāre* to bend away, inflect grammatically] —**de'clin·a·ble** *adj.* —**de'clin·er** *n.*

dec·li·nom·e·ter (ˌdɛklɪ'nɒmɪtə) *n.* an instrument for measuring magnetic declination.

de·cliv·i·ty (dɪ'klɪvɪtɪ) *n., pl.* **·ties.** a downward slope, esp. of the ground. Compare **acclivity.** [C17: from Latin *dēclīvitās*, from DE- + *clīvus* a slope, hill] —**de'cliv·i·tous** *adj.*

de·clutch (dɪ'klʌtʃ) *vb.* (*intr.*) to disengage the clutch of a motor vehicle.

de·coct (dɪ'kɒkt) *vb.* to extract (the essence or active principle) from (a medicinal or similar substance) by boiling. [C15: see DECOCTION]

de·coc·tion (dɪ'kɒkʃən) *n.* **1.** *Pharmacol.* the extraction of the water-soluble substances of a drug or medicinal plants by boiling. **2.** the essence or liquor resulting from this. [C14: from Old French, from Late Latin *dēcoctiō*, from *dēcoquere* to boil down, from *coquere* to COOK]

de·code (di:'kəʊd) *vb.* to convert (a message, text, etc.) from code into ordinary language. —**de'cod·er** *n.*

de·coke (di:'kəʊk) *vb.* (*tr.*) another word for **decarbonize.**

de·col·late (dɪ'kɒleɪt, 'dɛkəˌleɪt, ˌdi:kəʊ'leɪt) *vb.* **1.** to separate (continuous stationery, etc.) into individual forms. **2.** an archaic word for **decapitate.** [C16: from Latin *dēcollāre* to behead, from DE- + *collum* neck] —**ˌde·col'la·tion** *n.* —**'de·colˌla·tor** *n.*

dé·colle·tage (ˌdeɪkɒl'tɑ:ʒ; *French* dekɔl'ta:ʒ) *n.* a low-cut neckline or a woman's garment with a low neck. [C19: from French; see DÉCOLLETÉ]

dé·colle·té (deɪ'kɒlteɪ; *French* dekɔl'te) *adj.* **1.** (of a woman's garment) low-cut. **2.** wearing a low-cut garment. [C19: from *décolleter* to cut out the neck (of a dress), from *collet* collar]

de·col·o·nize *or* **de·col·o·nise** (di:'kɒləˌnaɪz) *vb.* (*tr.*) to grant independence to (a colony). —**deˌcol·o·niz·'a·tion** *or* **deˌcol·o·nis·'a·tion** *n.*

de·col·or·ant (di:'kʌlərənt) *adj.* **1.** able to decolour or bleach. ~*n.* **2.** a substance that decolours.

de·col·our (di:'kʌlə), **de·col·or·ize,** *or* **de·col·or·ise** *vb.* (*tr.*) to deprive of colour, as by bleaching. —**deˌcol·or·'a·tion** *n.* —**deˌcol·or·i·'za·tion** *or* **deˌcol·or·i·'sa·tion** *n.*

de·com·pose (ˌdi:kəm'pəʊz) *vb.* **1.** to break down (organic matter) or (of organic matter) to be broken down into constituent elements by bacterial or fungal action; rot. **2.** *Chem.* to break down or cause to break down into simpler chemical compounds. **3.** to break up or separate into constituent parts. —**ˌde·com'pos·a·ble** *adj.* —**ˌde·comˌpos·a·'bil·i·ty** *n.* —**de·com·po·si·tion** (ˌdi:kɒmpə'zɪʃən) *n.*

de·com·pos·er (ˌdi:kəm'pəʊzə) *n. Ecology.* any organism in a community, such as a bacterium or fungus, that breaks down dead tissue into its constituent parts. See also **consumer** (sense 3), **producer** (sense 6).

de·com·pound (ˌdi:kəm'paʊnd) *adj.* **1.** (of a compound leaf) having leaflets consisting of several distinct parts. **2.** made up of one or more compounds. ~*vb.* **3.** (*tr.*) a less common word for **decompose.** **4.** *Obsolete.* to mix with or form from one or more compounds.

de·com·press (ˌdi:kəm'prɛs) *vb.* **1.** to relieve (a substance) of pressure or (of a substance) to be relieved of pressure. **2.** to return (a diver, caisson worker, etc.) to a condition of normal atmospheric pressure from a condition of increased pressure or (of a diver, etc.) to be returned to such a condition. —**ˌde·com'pres·sion** *n.* —**ˌde·com'pres·sive** *adj.*

de·com·pres·sion cham·ber *n.* a chamber in which the pressure of air can be varied slowly for returning people from abnormal pressures to atmospheric pressure without inducing decompression sickness.

de·com·pres·sion sick·ness *or* **ill·ness** *n.* a disorder characterized by severe pain in muscles and joints, cramp, and difficulty in breathing, caused by subjection to a sudden and substantial change in atmospheric pressure. Also called: **caisson disease, aeroembolism.** Nontechnical name: **the bends.**

de·con·gest·ant (ˌdi:kən'dʒɛstənt) *adj.* **1.** relieving congestion, esp. nasal congestion. ~*n.* **2.** a decongestant drug.

de·con·se·crate (di:'kɒnsɪˌkreɪt) *vb.* (*tr.*) to transfer (a church, etc.) to secular use. —**deˌcon·se'cra·tion** *n.*

de·con·tam·i·nate (ˌdi:kən'tæmɪˌneɪt) *vb.* (*tr.*) to render (an area, building, object, etc.) harmless by the removal, distribution, or neutralization of poisons, radioactivity, etc. —**ˌde·con'tam·i·nant** *n.* —**ˌde·conˌtam·i'na·tion** *n.* —**ˌde·con'tam·iˌna·tive** *adj.* —**ˌde·con'tam·iˌna·tor** *n.*

de·con·trol (ˌdi:kən'trəʊl) *vb.* **·trols, ·trol·ling, ·trolled.** (*tr.*) to free of restraints or controls, esp. government controls: *to decontrol prices.*

dé·cor *or* **de·cor** ('deɪkɔ:) *n.* **1.** a style or scheme of interior decoration, furnishings, etc., as in a room or house. **2.** stage decoration; scenery. [C19: from French, from *décorer* to DECORATE]

dec·o·rate ('dɛkəˌreɪt) *vb.* **1.** (*tr.*) to make more attractive by adding ornament, colour, etc. **2.** to paint or wallpaper (a room, house, etc.). **3.** (*tr.*) to confer a mark of distinction, esp. a military medal, upon. **4.** (*tr.*) to evaporate a metal film onto (a crystal) in order to display dislocations in structure. [C16: from Latin *decorāre*, from *decus* adornment; see DECENT]

Dec·o·rat·ed style *or* **ar·chi·tec·ture** *n.* a 14th-century style of English architecture characterized by the ogee arch, geometrical tracery, and floral decoration.

dec·o·ra·tion (ˌdɛkəˈreɪʃən) *n.* **1.** an addition that renders something more attractive or ornate; adornment. **2.** the act, process, or art of decorating. **3.** a medal, badge, etc., conferred as a mark of honour.

dec·o·ra·tive (ˈdɛkərətɪv, ˈdɛkrətɪv) *adj.* serving to decorate or adorn; ornamental. —**ˈdec·o·ra·tive·ly** *adv.* —**ˈdec·o·ra·tive·ness** *n.*

dec·o·ra·tor (ˈdɛkəˌreɪtə) *n.* **1.** *Brit.* a person whose profession is the painting and wallpapering of buildings. **2.** a person who decorates. **3.** See **interior decorator** (sense 1).

dec·o·rous (ˈdɛkərəs) *adj.* characterized by propriety in manners, conduct, etc. [C17: from Latin *decōrus,* from *decor* elegance] —**ˈdec·o·rous·ly** *adv.* —**ˈdec·o·rous·ness** *n.*

de·cor·ti·cate (diːˈkɔːtɪˌkeɪt) *vb.* **1.** (*tr.*) to remove the bark or some other outer layer from. **2.** *Surgery.* to remove the cortex of (an organ or part). [C17: from Latin *dēcorticāre,* from DE- + *-corticāre,* from *cortex* bark] —**de·ˌcor·ti·ˈca·tion** *n.* —**de·ˈcor·ti·ˌca·tor** *n.*

de·co·rum (dɪˈkɔːrəm) *n.* **1.** propriety, esp. in behaviour or conduct. **2.** a requirement of correct behaviour in polite society. [C16: from Latin: propriety]

de·cou·page (ˌdeɪkuːˈpɑːʒ) *n.* **1.** the art or process of decorating a surface with shapes or illustrations cut from paper, card, etc. **2.** anything produced by this technique. [C20: from French, from *découper* to cut out, from DE- + *couper* to cut]

de·cou·pling (diːˈkʌpᵊlɪŋ) *n. Electronics.* the reduction of undesired distortion or oscillations in a circuit, caused by coupling with another circuit.

de·coy *n.* (ˈdiːkɔɪ, dɪˈkɔɪ). **1.** a person or thing used to beguile or lead someone into danger; lure. **2.** *Military.* something designed to deceive an enemy or divert his attention. **3.** a bird or animal, or an image of one, used to lure game into a trap or within shooting range. **4.** an enclosed space or large trap, often with a wide funnelled entrance, into which game can be lured for capture. ~*vb.* (dɪˈkɔɪ). **5.** to lure or be lured by or as if by means of a decoy. [C17: probably from Dutch *de kooi,* literally: the cage, from Latin *cavea* CAGE] —**de·ˈcoy·er** *n.*

de·crease *vb.* (dɪˈkriːs). **1.** to diminish or cause to diminish in size, number, strength, etc. ~*n.* (ˈdiːkriːs, dɪˈkriːs). **2.** the act or process of diminishing; reduction. **3.** the amount by which something has been diminished. [C14: from Old French *descreistre,* from Latin *dēcrescere* to grow less, from DE- + *crescere* to grow] —**de·ˈcreas·ing·ly** *adv.*

de·cree (dɪˈkriː) *n.* **1.** an edict, law, etc., made by someone in authority. **2.** an order or judgment of a court made after hearing a suit, esp. in matrimonial proceedings. See **decree nisi, decree absolute.** ~*vb.* **de·crees, de·cree·ing, de·creed. 3.** to order, adjudge, or ordain by decree. [C14: from Old French *decre,* from Latin *dēcrētum* ordinance, from *dēcrētus* decided, past participle of *dēcernere* to determine; see DECERN] —**de·ˈcree·a·ble** *adj.* —**de·ˈcre·er** *n.*

de·cree ab·so·lute *n.* the final decree in divorce proceedings, which leaves the parties free to remarry. Compare **decree nisi.**

de·cree ni·si (ˈnaɪsaɪ) *n.* a provisional decree, esp. in divorce proceedings, which will later be made absolute unless cause is shown why it should not. Compare **decree absolute.**

de·creet (dɪˈkriːt) *n. Scot. law.* the final judgment or sentence of a court. [C14 *decret:* from Old French, from Latin *dēcrētum* DECREE]

dec·re·ment (ˈdɛkrɪmənt) *n.* **1.** the act of decreasing; diminution. **2.** *Maths.* a negative increment. **3.** *Physics.* a measure of the damping of an oscillator, expressed by the ratio of the amplitude of a cycle to its amplitude after one period. [C17: from Latin *dēcrēmentum,* from *dēcrescere* to DECREASE]

de·crep·it (dɪˈkrɛpɪt) *adj.* **1.** enfeebled by old age; infirm. **2.** broken down or worn out by hard or long use; dilapidated. [C15: from Latin *dēcrepitus,* from *crepāre* to creak] —**de·ˈcrep·it·ly** *adv.* —**de·ˈcrep·i·ˌtude** *n.*

de·crep·i·tate (dɪˈkrɛpɪˌteɪt) *vb.* **1.** (*tr.*) to heat (a substance, such as a salt) until it emits a crackling sound or until this sound stops. **2.** (*intr.*) (esp. of a salt) to crackle, as while being heated. [C17: from New Latin *dēcrepitāre,* from Latin *crepitāre* to crackle, from *crepāre* to creak] —**de·ˌcrep·i·ˈta·tion** *n.*

decresc. *Music. abbrev. for* decrescendo.

de·cre·scen·do (ˌdiːkrɪˈʃɛndəʊ) *n.* another word for **diminuendo.** [Italian, from *decrescere* to DECREASE]

de·cres·cent (dɪˈkrɛsənt) *adj.* (esp. of the moon) decreasing; waning. [C17: from Latin *dēcrescēns* growing less; see DECREASE] —**de·ˈcres·cence** *n.*

de·cre·tal (dɪˈkriːtᵊl) *n.* **1.** *R.C. Church.* a papal edict on doctrine or church law. ~*adj.* **2.** of or relating to a decretal or a decree. [C15: from Old French, from Late Latin *dēcrētālis;* see DECREE] —**de·ˈcre·tal·ist** *n.*

De·cre·tals (dɪˈkriːtᵊlz) *pl. n. R.C. Church.* an authoritative compilation of decretals, as those of Gregory IX (1234).

de·cry (dɪˈkraɪ) *vb.* **·cries, ·cry·ing, ·cried.** (*tr.*) **1.** to express open disapproval of; disparage. **2.** to depreciate by proclamation: *to decry obsolete coinage.* [C17: from Old French *descrier,* from *des-* DIS-[1] + *crier* to CRY] —**de·ˈcri·al** *n.* —**de·ˈcri·er** *n.*

de·crypt (diːˈkrɪpt) *vb.* (*tr.*) another word for **decode.** [C20: from DE- + *crypt,* as in CRYPTIC]

de·cu·bi·tus ul·cer (dɪˈkjuːbɪtəs) *n.* a chronic ulcer of the skin and underlying tissues caused by prolonged pressure on the body surface of bedridden patients. Nontechnical names: **bedsore, pressure sore.** [C19: Latin *decubitus,* past participle of *decumbere* to lie down]

de·cum·bent (dɪˈkʌmbənt) *adj.* **1.** lying down or lying flat. **2.** *Botany.* (of certain stems) lying flat with the tip growing upwards. [C17: from Latin *dēcumbēns,* present participle of *dēcumbere* to lie down] —**de·ˈcum·bence** *or* **de·ˈcum·ben·cy** *n.* —**de·ˈcum·bent·ly** *adv.*

de·cu·ple (ˈdɛkjʊpᵊl) *vb.* **1.** (*tr.*) to increase by ten times. ~*n.* **2.** an amount ten times as large as a given reference. ~*adj.* **3.** increasing tenfold. [C15: from Old French, from Late Latin *decuplus* tenfold, from Latin *decem* ten]

de·cu·ri·on (dɪˈkjʊərɪən) *n.* (in the Roman Empire) **1.** a local councillor. **2.** the commander of a troop of ten cavalrymen. [C14: from Latin *decuriō,* from *decuria* company of ten, from *decem* ten]

de·cur·rent (dɪˈkʌrənt) *adj. Botany.* extending down the stem, esp. (of a leaf) having the base of the blade extending down the stem as two wings. [C15: from Latin *dēcurrere* to run down, from *currere* to run] —**de·ˈcur·rent·ly** *adv.*

de·curved (diːˈkɜːvd) *adj.* bent or curved downwards: *a decurved bill; decurved petals.*

dec·u·ry (ˈdɛkjʊərɪ) *n., pl.* **·ries.** (in ancient Rome) a body of ten men. [C16: from Latin *decuria;* see DECURION]

de·cus·sate *vb.* (dɪˈkʌseɪt). **1.** to cross or cause to cross in the form of the letter X; intersect. ~*adj.* (dɪˈkʌseɪt, dɪˈkʌsɪt). **2.** in the form of the letter X; crossed; intersected. **3.** *Botany.* (esp. of leaves) arranged in opposite pairs, with each pair at right angles to the one above and below it. [C17: from Latin *decussāre,* from *decussis* the number ten, from *decem* ten] —**de·ˈcus·sate·ly** *adv.* —**ˌde·cus·ˈsa·tion** *n.*

de·dal (ˈdiːdᵊl) *adj.* a variant spelling (esp. U.S.) of **daedal.**

de·dans *French.* (dəˈdɑ̃) *n. Real tennis.* the open gallery at the server's end of the court. [literally: interior]

De·dé·ag·ach (ˈdɛdeɪɑːgˈɑːtʃ) *n.* a former name (until the end of World War I) of **Alexandroúpolis.**

ded·i·cate (ˈdɛdɪˌkeɪt) *vb.* (*tr.*) **1.** (often foll. by *to*) to devote (oneself, one's time, etc.) wholly to a special purpose or cause; commit wholeheartedly or unreservedly. **2.** (foll. by *to*) to address or inscribe (a book, artistic performance, etc.) to (a person, cause, etc.) as a token of affection or respect. **3.** to set apart for a deity or for sacred uses; consecrate. ~*adj.* **4.** an archaic word for **dedicated.** [C15: from Latin *dēdicāre* to announce, from *dicāre* to make known, variant of *dīcere* to say] —**ˌded·i·ca·ˈtee** *n.* —**ˈded·i·ˌca·tor** *n.* —**ded·i·ca·to·ry** (ˈdɛdɪˌkeɪtərɪ, ˈdɛdɪkətərɪ, -trɪ) *or* **ˈded·i·ˌca·tive** *adj.*

ded·i·cat·ed (ˈdɛdɪˌkeɪtɪd) *adj.* **1.** devoted to a particular purpose or cause: *a dedicated man.* **2.** *Computer technol.* designed to fulfil one function: *a dedicated microprocessor.*

ded·i·ca·tion (ˌdɛdɪˈkeɪʃən) *n.* **1.** the act of dedicating or the state of being dedicated. **2.** an inscription or announcement prefixed to a book, piece of music, etc., dedicating it to a person or thing. **3.** complete and wholehearted devotion, esp. to a career, ideal, etc. **4.** a ceremony in which something, such as a church, is dedicated. —**ˌded·i·ˈca·tion·al** *adj.*

de·dif·fer·en·ti·a·tion (diːˌdɪfəˌrɛnʃiːˈeɪʃən) *n.* the reversion of the cells of differentiated tissue to a less specialized form.

de·duce (dɪˈdjuːs) *vb.* (*tr.*) **1.** (*may take a clause as object*) to reach (a conclusion about something) by reasoning; conclude (that); infer. **2.** *Archaic.* to trace the origin, course, or derivation of. [C15: from Latin *dēdūcere* to lead away, derive, from DE- + *dūcere* to lead] —**de·ˈduc·i·ble** *adj.* —**de·ˌduc·i·ˈbil·i·ty** *or* **de·ˈduc·i·ble·ness** *n.*

de·duct (dɪˈdʌkt) *vb.* (*tr.*) to take away or subtract (a number, quantity, part, etc.): *income tax is deducted from one's wages.* [C15: from Latin *dēductus,* past participle of *dēdūcere* to DEDUCE]

de·duct·i·ble (dɪˈdʌktɪbᵊl) *adj.* **1.** capable of being deducted. **2.** *U.S.* short for **tax-deductible.** ~*n.* **3.** *Insurance.* the U.S. name for **excess** (sense 6). —**de·ˌduct·i·ˈbil·i·ty** *n.*

de·duc·tion (dɪˈdʌkʃən) *n.* **1.** the act or process of deducting or subtracting. **2.** something, esp. a sum of money, that is or may be deducted. **3.** *Logic.* **a.** a process of reasoning, used esp. in logic and mathematics, by which a specific conclusion necessarily follows from a set of general premisses. **b.** a conclusion reached by this process of reasoning. Compare **induction** (sense 3).

de·duc·tive (dɪˈdʌktɪv) *adj.* of or relating to deduction: *deductive reasoning.* —**de·ˈduc·tive·ly** *adv.*

Dee (diː) *n.* **1.** a river in N Wales and NW England, rising in S Gwynedd and flowing east and north to the Irish Sea. Length: about 112 km (70 miles). **2.** a river in NE Scotland, rising in the Cairngorms and flowing east to the North Sea. Length: about 140 km (87 miles). **3.** a river in S Scotland, flowing south to the Solway Firth. Length: about 80 km (50 miles).

deed (diːd) *n.* **1.** something that is done or performed; act. **2.** a notable achievement; feat; exploit. **3.** action or performance, as opposed to words. **4.** *Law.* a formal legal document signed, sealed, and delivered to effect a conveyance or transfer of property or to create a legal obligation or contract. ~*vb.* **5.** (*tr.*) *U.S.* to convey or transfer (property) by deed. [Old English *dēd;* related to Old High German *tāt,* Gothic *gadeths;* see DO[1]]

deed poll *n. Law.* a deed made by one party only, esp. one by which a person changes his name.

dee·jay (ˈdiːˌdʒeɪ) *n.* an informal name for **disc jockey.** [C20: from the initials D.J.]

deek (diːk) *vb.* (*tr.; imperative*) *Northumbrian dialect.* to look at: *deek that!* [perhaps of Romany origin]

deem (diːm) *vb.* (*tr.*) to judge or consider: *I do not deem him worthy of this honour.* [Old English *dēman;* related to Old High German *tuomen* to judge, Gothic *domjan;* see DOOM]

de·em·pha·size *or* **de·em·pha·sise** (diːˈɛmfəˌsaɪz) *vb.* (*tr.*) to remove emphasis from.
deem·ster (ˈdiːmstə) *n.* the title of one of the two justices in the Isle of Man. Also called: **dempster.** —**ˈdeem·ster·ˌship** *n.*
deep (diːp) *adj.* **1.** extending or situated relatively far down from a surface: *a deep pool.* **2.** extending or situated relatively far inwards, backwards, or sideways: *a deep border of trees.* **3.** *Cricket.* relatively far from the pitch: *the deep field; deep third man.* **4. a.** (*postpositive*) of a specified dimension downwards, inwards, or backwards: *six feet deep.* **b.** (*in combination*): *a six-foot-deep trench.* **5.** coming from or penetrating to a great depth: *a deep breath.* **6.** difficult to understand or penetrate; abstruse. **7.** learned or intellectually demanding: *a deep discussion.* **8.** of great intensity; extreme: *deep happiness; deep trouble.* **9.** (*postpositive;* foll. by *in*) absorbed or enveloped (by); engrossed or immersed (in): *deep in study; deep in debt.* **10.** very cunning or crafty; devious: *a deep plot.* **11.** mysterious or obscure: *a deep secret.* **12.** (of a colour) having an intense or dark hue. **13.** low in pitch or tone: *a deep voice.* **14. deep down.** *Informal.* in reality, esp. as opposed to appearance: *she is a very kind person deep down.* **15. deep in the past.** long ago. **16. go off the deep end.** *Informal.* **a.** to become hysterical; lose one's temper. **b.** *Chiefly U.S.* to act rashly. **17. in deep water.** *Informal.* in a tricky position or in trouble. ~*n.* **18.** any deep place on land or under water, esp. below 6000 metres (3000 fathoms). **19. the deep. a.** a poetic term for the **ocean. b.** *Cricket.* the area of the field relatively far from the pitch. **20.** the most profound, intense, or central part: *the deep of winter.* **21.** a vast extent, as of space or time. **22.** *Nautical.* one of the intervals on a sounding lead, one fathom apart. ~*adv.* **23.** far on in time; late: *they worked deep into the night.* **24.** profoundly or intensely. [Old English *dēop;* related to Old High German *tiof* deep, Old Norse *djupr*] —**ˈdeep·ly** *adv.* —**ˈdeep·ness** *n.*
deep-dish pie *n. Chiefly U.S.* a pie baked in a deep dish and having only a top crust.
deep-dyed *adj. Usually derogatory.* thorough-going; absolute; complete.
deep·en (ˈdiːpᵊn) *vb.* to make or become deep, deeper, or more intense. —**ˈdeep·en·er** *n.*
deep·freeze (ˌdiːpˈfriːz) *n.* **1.** a type of refrigerator in which food, etc., is stored for long periods at temperatures below freezing. **2.** storage in or as if in a deepfreeze. **3.** *Informal.* a state of suspended activity. ~*vb.* **deep-freeze, -freez·es, -froze** *or* **-freezed, -fro·zen** *or* **-freezed. 4.** (*tr.*) to freeze or keep in or as if in a deepfreeze.
deep-fry *vb.* **-fries, -fry·ing, -fried.** to cook (fish, potatoes, etc.) in sufficient hot fat to cover the food entirely.
deep kiss *n.* another name for **French kiss.**
deep-laid *adj.* (of a plot or plan) carefully worked out and kept secret.
deep-root·ed *or* **deep-seat·ed** *adj.* (of ideas, beliefs, prejudices, etc.) firmly fixed, implanted, or held; ingrained.
deep-sea *n.* (*modifier*) of, found in, or characteristic of the deep parts of the sea: *deep-sea fishing.*
deep-six *vb.* (*tr.*) *U.S. slang.* to dispose of (something, such as documents) completely; destroy. [C20: from *six feet deep,* the traditional depth for a grave]
Deep South *n.* the SE part of the U.S., esp. South Carolina, Georgia, Alabama, Mississippi, and Louisiana.
deep space *n.* any region of outer space beyond the system of the earth and moon.
deep struc·ture *n. Generative grammar.* a representation of the presumed structure of a sentence at a level where logical or grammatical relations are made explicit, before transformational rules have been applied. Compare **surface structure.**
deep ther·a·py *n.* radiotherapy with very penetrating shortwave radiation.
deer (dɪə) *n., pl.* **deer** *or* **deers. 1.** any ruminant artiodactyl mammal of the family *Cervidae,* including reindeer, elk, muntjacs, and roe deer, typically having antlers in the male. Related adj.: **cervine. 2.** (in N Canada) another name for **caribou.** [Old English *dēor* beast; related to Old High German *tior* wild beast, Old Norse *dȳr*]
deer·grass (ˈdɪəˌgrɑːs) *n.* a perennial cyperaceous plant, *Trichophorum caespitosum,* that grows in dense tufts in peat bogs of temperate regions.
deer·hound (ˈdɪəˌhaʊnd) *n.* a very large rough-coated breed of dog of the greyhound type.
deer lick *n.* a naturally or artificially salty area of ground where deer come to lick the salt.
deer mouse *n.* any of various mice of the genus *Peromyscus,* esp. *P. maniculatus,* of North and Central America, having brownish fur with white underparts: family *Cricetidae.* See also **white-footed mouse.**
deer·skin (ˈdɪəˌskɪn) *n.* **a.** the hide of a deer. **b.** (*as modifier*): *a deerskin jacket.*
deer·stalk·er (ˈdɪəˌstɔːkə) *n.* **1.** Also called: **stalker.** a person who stalks deer, esp. in order to shoot them. **2.** a hat, peaked in front and behind, with earflaps usually turned up and tied together on the top. —**ˈdeer·ˌstalk·ing** *adj., n.*
de·es·ca·late (diːˈɛskəˌleɪt) *vb.* to reduce the level or intensity of (a crisis, etc.). —**de·ˌes·ca·ˈla·tion** *n.*
def. *abbrev. for:* **1.** defective. **2.** defence. **3.** defendant. **4.** deferred. **5.** definite. **6.** definition.
de·face (dɪˈfeɪs) *vb.* (*tr.*) to spoil or mar the surface, legibility, or appearance of; disfigure. —**de·ˈface·a·ble** *adj.* —**de·ˈface·ment** *n.* —**de·ˈfac·er** *n.*
de fac·to (deɪ ˈfæktəʊ) *adv.* **1.** in fact. ~*adj.* **2.** existing in fact, whether legally recognized or not: *a de facto regime.* Compare **de jure.** [C17: Latin]
de·fal·cate (ˈdiːfælˌkeɪt) *vb.* (*intr.*) *Law.* to misuse or misappropriate property or funds entrusted to one. [C15: from Medieval Latin *dēfalcāre* to cut off, from Latin DE- + *falx* sickle] —**ˌde·fal·ˈca·tion** *n.* —**ˈde·fal·ˌca·tor** *n.*
def·a·ma·tion (ˌdɛfəˈmeɪʃən) *n.* **1.** *Law.* the injuring of a person's good name or reputation. Compare **libel, slander. 2.** the act of defaming or state of being defamed.
de·fam·a·to·ry (dɪˈfæmətərɪ, -trɪ) *adj.* injurious to someone's name or reputation. —**de·ˈfam·a·to·ri·ly** *adv.*
de·fame (dɪˈfeɪm) *vb.* (*tr.*) **1.** to attack the good name or reputation of; slander; libel. **2.** *Archaic.* to indict or accuse. [C14: from Old French *defamer,* from Latin *dēfāmāre,* from *diffāmāre* to spread by unfavourable report, from *fāma* FAME] —**de·ˈfam·er** *n.*
de·fault (dɪˈfɔːlt) *n.* **1.** a failure to act, esp. a failure to meet a financial obligation or to appear in a court of law at a time specified. **2.** absence: *he lost the chess game by default.* **3. in default of.** through or in the lack or absence of. **4. judgment by default.** *Law.* a judgment in the plaintiff's favour when the defendant fails to plead or to appear. **5.** lack, want, or need. ~*vb.* **6.** (*intr.;* often foll. by *on* or *in*) to fail to make payment when due. **7.** (*intr.*) to fail to fulfil or perform an obligation, engagement, etc: *to default in a sporting contest.* **8.** *Law.* to lose (a case) by failure to appear in court. [C13: from Old French *defaute,* from *defaillir* to fail, from Vulgar Latin *dēfallīre* (unattested) to be lacking]
de·fault·er (dɪˈfɔːltə) *n.* **1.** a person who defaults. **2.** *Chiefly Brit.* a person, esp. a soldier, who has broken the disciplinary code of his service.
de·fea·sance (dɪˈfiːzᵊns) *n. Chiefly law.* **1.** the act or process of rendering null and void; annulment. **2. a.** a condition, the fulfilment of which renders a deed void. **b.** the document containing such a condition. [C14: from Old French, from *desfaire* to DEFEAT]
de·fea·si·ble (dɪˈfiːzəbᵊl) *adj. Law.* (of an estate or interest in land) capable of being defeated or rendered void. —**de·ˈfea·si·ble·ness** *or* **de·ˌfea·si·ˈbil·i·ty** *n.*
de·feat (dɪˈfiːt) *vb.* (*tr.*) **1.** to overcome in a contest or competition; win a victory over. **2.** to thwart or frustrate: *this accident has defeated all his hopes of winning.* **3.** *Law.* to render null and void; annul. ~*n.* **4.** the act of defeating or state of being defeated. **5.** an instance of defeat. **6.** overthrow or destruction. **7.** *Law.* an annulment. [C14: from Old French *desfait,* from *desfaire* to undo, ruin, from *des-* DIS-[1] + *faire* to do, from Latin *facere*] —**de·ˈfeat·er** *n.*
de·feat·ism (dɪˈfiːtɪzəm) *n.* a ready acceptance or expectation of defeat. —**de·ˈfeat·ist** *n., adj.*
def·e·cate (ˈdɛfɪˌkeɪt) *vb.* **1.** (*intr.*) to discharge waste from the body through the anus. **2.** (*tr.*) to clarify or remove impurities from (a solution, esp. of sugar). [C16: from Latin *dēfaecāre* to cleanse from dregs, from DE- + *faex* sediment, dregs] —**ˌdef·e·ˈca·tion** *n.* —**ˈdef·e·ˌca·tor** *n.*
de·fect *n.* (dɪˈfɛkt, ˈdiːfɛkt). **1.** a lack of something necessary for completeness or perfection; shortcoming; deficiency. **2.** an imperfection, failing, or blemish. **3.** *Crystallog.* a local deviation from regularity in the crystal lattice of a solid. See also **point defect, dislocation** (sense 3). ~*vb.* (dɪˈfɛkt). **4.** (*intr.*) to desert one's country, cause, allegiance, etc., esp. in order to join the opposing forces. [C15: from Latin *dēfectus,* from *dēficere* to forsake, fail; see DEFICIENT] —**de·ˈfec·tor** *n.*
de·fec·tion (dɪˈfɛkʃən) *n.* **1.** the act or an instance of defecting. **2.** abandonment of duty, allegiance, principles, etc.; backsliding. **3.** another word for **defect** (senses 1, 2).
de·fec·tive (dɪˈfɛktɪv) *adj.* **1.** having a defect or flaw; imperfect; faulty. **2.** (of a person) below the usual standard or level, esp. in intelligence. **3.** *Grammar.* (of a word) lacking the full range of inflections characteristic of its form class, as for example *must,* which has no past tense. —**de·ˈfec·tive·ly** *adv.* —**de·ˈfec·tive·ness** *n.*
de·fence *or U.S.* **de·fense** (dɪˈfɛns) *n.* **1.** resistance against danger, attack, or harm; protection. **2.** a person or thing that provides such resistance. **3.** a plea, essay, speech, etc., in support of something; vindication; justification. **4. a.** military measures or resources protecting a country against a potential or actual opponent. **b.** (*as modifier*): *defence spending.* **5.** *Law.* a defendant's denial of the truth of the allegations or charge against him. **6.** *Law.* the defendant and his legal advisers collectively. Compare **prosecution. 7.** *Sport.* **a.** the action of protecting oneself, one's goal, or one's allotted part of the playing area against an opponent's attacks. **b.** the method of doing this. **c.** (usually preceded by *the*) the players in a team whose function is to do this. **8.** *Psychoanal.* See **defence mechanism. 9.** (*pl.*) fortifications. [C13: from Old French, from Late Latin *dēfensum,* past participle of *dēfendere* to DEFEND] —**de·ˈfence·less** *or U.S.* **de·ˈfense·less** *adj.* —**de·ˈfence·less·ly** *or U.S.* **de·ˈfense·less·ly** *adv.* —**de·ˈfence·less·ness** *or U.S.* **de·ˈfense·less·ness** *n.*
de·fence mech·an·ism *n.* **1.** *Psychoanal.* a usually unconscious mental process designed to reduce the anxiety, shame, etc., associated with instinctive desires. **2.** *Physiol.* the protective response of the body against disease organisms.
de·fend (dɪˈfɛnd) *vb.* **1.** to protect (a person, place, etc.) from harm or danger; ward off an attack on. **2.** (*tr.*) to support in the face of criticism, esp. by argument or evidence. **3.** to represent (a defendant) in court in a civil or criminal action. **4.** *Sport.* to guard or protect (oneself, one's goal, etc.) against attack. **5.** (*tr.*) to protect (a championship or title) against a challenge. [C13: from Old French *defendre,* from Latin *dēfendere* to ward

off, from DE- + *-fendere* to strike] —**de·'fend·a·ble** *adj.* —**de·'fend·er** *n.*

de·fend·ant (dɪ'fɛndənt) *n.* **1.** a person against whom an action or claim is brought in a court of law. Compare **plaintiff.** ~*adj.* **2.** making a defence; defending.

De·fend·er of the Faith *n.* the title conferred upon Henry VIII by Pope Leo X in 1521 in recognition of the King's pamphlet attacking Luther's doctrines and retained by subsequent monarchs of England. Latin: ***Fidei Defensor.***

de·fen·es·tra·tion (diːˌfɛnɪ'streɪʃən) *n.* the act of throwing someone out of a window. [C17: from New Latin *dēfenestrātiō,* from Latin DE- + *fenestra* window]

de·fen·si·ble (dɪ'fɛnsɪbᵊl) *adj.* capable of being defended, as in war, an argument, etc. —**de·ˌfen·si·'bil·i·ty** *or* **de·'fen·si·ble·ness** *n.* —**de·'fen·si·bly** *adv.*

de·fen·sive (dɪ'fɛnsɪv) *adj.* **1.** intended, suitable, or done for defence, as opposed to offence. **2.** rejecting criticisms of oneself or covering up one's failings. ~*n.* **3.** a position of defence. **4. on the defensive.** in an attitude or position of defence, as in being ready to reject criticism. —**de·'fen·sive·ly** *adv.* —**de·'fen·sive·ness** *n.*

de·fer[1] (dɪ'fɜː) *vb.* **·fers, ·fer·ring, ·ferred.** to delay or cause to be delayed until a future time; postpone. [C14: from Old French *differer* to be different, postpone; see DIFFER] —**de·'fer·ra·ble** *or* **de·'fer·a·ble** *adj.* —**de·'fer·rer** *n.*

de·fer[2] (dɪ'fɜː) *vb.* **·fers, ·fer·ring, ·ferred.** (*intr.;* foll. by *to*) to yield (to) or comply (with) the wishes or judgments of another. [C15: from Latin *dēferre,* literally: to bear down, from DE- + *ferre* to bear]

def·er·ence ('dɛfərəns) *n.* **1.** submission to or compliance with the will, wishes, etc., of another. **2.** courteous regard; respect. [C17: from French *déference;* see DEFER[2]]

def·er·ent[1] ('dɛfərənt) *adj.* another word for **deferential.**

def·er·ent[2] ('dɛfərənt) *adj.* **1.** (esp. of a bodily nerve, vessel, or duct) conveying an impulse, fluid, etc., outwards, down, or away; efferent. ~*n.* **2.** *Astronomy.* (in the Ptolemaic system) a circle centred on the earth around which the centre of the epicycle was thought to move. [C17: from Latin *dēferre; see* DEFER[2]]

def·er·en·tial (ˌdɛfə'rɛnʃəl) *adj.* marked by or showing deference or respect; respectful. —**ˌdef·er·'en·tial·ly** *adv.*

de·fer·ment (dɪ'fɜːmənt) *or* **de·fer·ral** (dɪ'fɜːrəl) *n.* the act of deferring or putting off until another time; postponement.

de·ferred (dɪ'fɜːd) *adj.* **1.** withheld over a certain period; postponed: *a deferred payment.* **2.** (of shares) ranking behind other types of shares for dividend.

de·ferred an·nu·i·ty *n.* an annuity that commences not less than one year after the final purchase premium. Compare **immediate annuity.**

de·ferred sen·tence *n. Law.* a sentence that is postponed for a specific period to allow a court to examine the conduct of the offender during the deferment. Compare **suspended sentence.**

de·fi·ance (dɪ'faɪəns) *n.* **1.** open or bold resistance to or disregard for authority, opposition, or power. **2.** a challenging attitude or behaviour; challenge.

de·fi·ant (dɪ'faɪənt) *adj.* marked by resistance or bold opposition, as to authority; challenging. —**de·'fi·ant·ly** *adv.*

de·fib·ril·la·tor (dɪ'faɪbrɪˌleɪtə, -'fɪb-) *n. Med.* an apparatus for stopping fibrillation of the heart by application of an electric current to the chest wall or directly to the heart.

de·fi·cien·cy (dɪ'fɪʃənsɪ) *n., pl.* **·cies. 1.** the state or quality of being deficient. **2.** a lack or insufficiency; shortage. **3.** another word for **deficit.**

de·fi·cien·cy dis·ease *n.* any condition, such as pellagra, beriberi, or scurvy, produced by a lack of vitamins or other essential substances. Compare **avitaminosis.**

de·fi·cient (dɪ'fɪʃənt) *adj.* **1.** lacking some essential; incomplete; defective. **2.** inadequate in quantity or supply; insufficient. [C16: from Latin *dēficiēns* lacking, from *dēficere* to fall short; see DEFECT] —**de·'fi·cient·ly** *adv.*

def·i·cit ('dɛfɪsɪt, dɪ'fɪsɪt) *n.* **1.** the amount by which an actual sum is lower than that expected or required. **2. a.** an excess of liabilities over assets. **b.** an excess of expenditures over revenues during a certain period. **c.** an excess of payments over receipts on the balance of payments. [C18: from Latin, literally: there is lacking, from *dēficere* to be lacking]

def·i·cit spend·ing *n.* government spending in excess of revenues so that a budget deficit is incurred, which is financed by borrowing (**deficit financing**). It is often undertaken as a remedy for economic depression and unemployment. Also called: **compensatory spending.**

de fi·de *Latin.* (diː 'faɪdɪ) *adj. R.C. Church.* (of a doctrine) belonging to the essentials of the faith, esp. by virtue of a papal ruling. [literally: from faith]

def·i·lade (ˌdɛfɪ'leɪd) *Military fortifications.* ~*n.* **1.** protection provided by obstacles against enemy fire or observation. **2.** the disposition of defensive fortifications to produce this protection. ~*vb.* **3.** to provide protection for by defilade. [C19: see DE-, ENFILADE]

de·file[1] (dɪ'faɪl) *vb.* (*tr.*) **1.** to make foul or dirty; pollute. **2.** to tarnish or sully the brightness of; taint; corrupt. **3.** to damage or sully (someone's good name, reputation, etc.). **4.** to make unfit for ceremonial use; desecrate. **5.** to violate the chastity of. [C14: from earlier *defoilen* (influenced by *filen* to FILE[3]), from Old French *defouler* to trample underfoot, abuse, from DE- + *fouler* to tread upon; see FULL[2]] —**de·'file·ment** *n.* —**de·'fil·er** *n.*

de·file[2] ('diːfaɪl, dɪ'faɪl) *n.* **1.** a narrow pass or gorge, esp. one between two mountains. **2.** a single file of soldiers, etc. ~*vb.* **3.** *Chiefly military.* to march or cause to march in single file. [C17: from French *défilé,* from *défiler* to file off, from *filer* to march in a column, from Old French: to spin, from *fil* thread, from Latin *fīlum*]

de·fine (dɪ'faɪn) *vb.* (*tr.*) **1.** to state precisely the meaning of (words, terms, etc.). **2.** to describe the nature, properties, or essential qualities of. **3.** to determine the boundary or extent of. **4.** (*often passive*) to delineate the form or outline of: *the shape of the tree was clearly defined by the light behind it.* **5.** to fix with precision; specify. [C14: from Old French *definer* to determine, from Latin *dēfīnīre* to set bounds to, from *fīnīre* to FINISH] —**de·'fin·a·ble** *adj.* —**de·ˌfin·a·'bil·i·ty** *n.* —**de·'fin·a·bly** *adv.* —**de·'fin·er** *n.*

de·fin·i·en·dum (dɪˌfɪnɪ'ɛndəm) *n., pl.* **·da** (-də). something to be defined, esp. the term or phrase to be accounted for in a dictionary entry. Compare **definiens.** [Latin]

de·fin·i·ens (dɪ'fɪnɪənz) *n., pl.* **de·fin·i·en·tia** (dɪˌfɪnɪ'ɛntʃə). the word or words used to define or give an account of the meaning of another word, as in a dictionary entry. Compare **definiendum.** [Latin: defining]

def·i·nite ('dɛfɪnɪt) *adj.* **1.** clearly defined; exact; explicit. **2.** having precise limits or boundaries. **3.** known for certain; sure: *it is definite that they have won.* **4.** *Botany.* **a.** denoting a type of growth in which the main stem ends in a flower, as in a cymose inflorescence; determinate. **b.** (esp. of flower parts) limited or fixed in number in a given species. [C15: from Latin *dēfīnītus* limited, distinct; see DEFINE] —**'def·i·nite·ness** *n.* —**de·fin·i·tude** (dɪ'fɪnɪˌtjuːd) *n.*

Usage. *Definite* and *definitive* should be carefully distinguished. *Definite* indicates precision and firmness, as in *a definite decision. Definitive* includes these senses but also indicates conclusiveness. *A definite answer* indicates a clear and firm answer to a particular question; *a definitive answer* implies an authoritative resolution of a complex question.

def·i·nite ar·ti·cle *n. Grammar.* a determiner that expresses specificity of reference, such as *the* in English. Compare **indefinite article.**

def·i·nite in·te·gral *n. Maths.* the limit of the sum of the areas of an infinitely large number of adjoining rectangles of infinitesimal width that are bounded by the curve of a function, f(*x*), the *x*-axis, and the two limits $x = a$ and $x = b$, as the width of each rectangle tends to 0. Written $\int_a^b f(x)dx$, where $b > a$.

def·i·nite·ly ('dɛfɪnɪtlɪ) *adv.* **1.** in a definite manner. **2.** (*sentence modifier*) certainly: *he said he was coming, definitely.* **3.** *sentence substitute.* unquestionably: used to confirm an assumption by a questioner.

def·i·ni·tion (ˌdɛfɪ'nɪʃən) *n.* **1.** a formal and concise statement of the meaning of a word, phrase, etc. **2.** the act of defining a word, phrase, etc. **3.** the act of making clear or definite. **4.** the state or condition of being clearly defined or definite. **5.** a measure of the clarity of an optical, photographic, or television image as characterized by its sharpness and contrast. —**ˌdef·i·'ni·tion·al** *adj.*

de·fin·i·tive (dɪ'fɪnɪtɪv) *adj.* **1.** serving to decide or settle finally; conclusive. **2.** most reliable, complete, or authoritative: *the definitive reading of a text.* **3.** serving to define or outline. **4.** *Zoology.* fully developed; complete: *the definitive form of a parasite.* **5. a.** (of postage stamps) permanently on sale. **b.** (*as n.*) a definitive postage stamp. ~*n.* **6.** *Grammar.* a word indicating specificity of reference, such as the definite article or a demonstrative adjective or pronoun. —**de·'fin·i·tive·ly** *adv.* —**de·'fin·i·tive·ness** *n.*

Usage. See at **definite.**

def·la·grate ('dɛfləˌgreɪt, 'diː-) *vb.* to burn or cause to burn with great heat and light. [C18: from Latin *dēflagrāre,* from DE- + *flagrāre* to burn] —**ˌdef·la·'gra·tion** *n.*

de·flate (dɪː'fleɪt) *vb.* **1.** to collapse or cause to collapse through the release of gas. **2.** (*tr.*) to take away the self-esteem or conceit from. **3.** *Economics.* to cause deflation of (an economy, the money supply, etc.). [C19: from DE- + (IN)FLATE] —**de·'fla·tor** *n.*

de·fla·tion (dɪː'fleɪʃən) *n.* **1.** the act of deflating or state of being deflated. **2.** *Economics.* a reduction in economic activity resulting in lower levels of output, employment, investment, trade, profits, and prices. Compare **disinflation.** **3.** the removal of loose rock material, sand, and dust by the wind. —**de·'fla·tion·ar·y** *adj.* —**de·'fla·tion·ist** *n., adj.*

de·fla·tion·ar·y gap *n. Economics.* the situation, characterized by persistent deflation, in which the aggregate demand associated with full employment is less than aggregate supply.

de·flect (dɪ'flɛkt) *vb.* to turn or cause to turn aside from a course; swerve. [C17: from Latin *dēflectere,* from *flectere* to bend] —**de·'flec·tor** *n.*

de·flec·tion *or* **de·flex·ion** (dɪ'flɛkʃən) *n.* **1.** the act of deflecting or the state of being deflected. **2.** the amount of deviation. **3.** the change in direction of a light beam as it crosses a boundary between two media with different refractive indexes. **4.** a deviation of the indicator of a measuring instrument from its zero position. **5.** the movement of a structure or structural member when subjected to a load. —**de·'flec·tive** *adj.*

de·flexed (dɪ'flɛkst, 'diːˌflɛkst) *adj.* (of leaves, petals, etc.) bent sharply outwards and downwards.

de·floc·cu·late (dɪ'flɒkjʊˌleɪt) *vb.* (*tr.*) **1.** to disperse, forming a colloid or suspension. **2.** to prevent flocculation of (a colloid or suspension). —**de·ˌfloc·cu·'la·tion** *n.*

de·flo·ra·tion (ˌdiːflɔː'reɪʃən) *n.* the act of deflowering. [C15: from Late Latin *dēflōrātiō; see* DE-, FLOWER]

de·flow·er (dɪː'flaʊə) *vb.* (*tr.*) **1.** to deprive of virginity, esp. by rupturing the hymen through sexual intercourse. **2.** to despoil of beauty, innocence, etc.; mar; violate. **3.** to rob or despoil of flowers. —**de+'flow+er+er** *n.*

De·foe (dɪ'fəʊ) *n.* **Dan·iel.** ?1660–1731, English novelist, journalist, and pamphleteer, noted particularly for his novel *Robinson Crusoe* (1719). His other novels include *Moll Flanders* (1722) and *A Journal of the Plague Year* (1722).

de+fo+li+ant (diː'fəʊlɪənt) *n.* a chemical sprayed or dusted onto trees to cause their leaves to fall, esp. to remove cover from an enemy in warfare.

de+fo+li+ate *vb.* (diː'fəʊlɪˌeɪt). **1.** to deprive (a plant) of its leaves, as by the use of a herbicide, or (of a plant) to shed its leaves. ~*adj.* (diː'fəʊlɪɪt). **2.** (of a plant) having shed its leaves. [C18: from Medieval Latin *dēfoliāre,* from Latin DE- + *folium* leaf] —**de+ˌfo+li·'a+tion** *n.* —**de+'fo+li·ˌa+tor** *n.*

de+force (dɪ'fɔːs) *vb.* (*tr.*) *Property law.* **1.** to withhold (property, esp. land) wrongfully or by force from the rightful owner. **2.** to eject or keep forcibly from possession of property. [C13: from Anglo-French, from *deforcer*] —**de+'force+ment** *n.*

de+for+est (diː'fɒrɪst) *vb.* (*tr.*) to clear of trees. Also: **disforest.** —**de+ˌfor+est·'a+tion** *n.* —**de+'for+est+er** *n.*

De For·est (də'fɒrɪst) *n.* **Lee.** 1873–1961, U.S. inventor of telegraphic, telephonic, and radio equipment: patented the first triode valve (1907).

de+form (dɪ'fɔːm) *vb.* **1.** to make or become misshapen or distorted. **2.** (*tr.*) to mar the beauty of; disfigure. **3.** (*tr.*) to subject or be subjected to a stress that causes a change of dimensions. [C15: from Latin *dēfōrmāre,* from DE- + *forma* shape, beauty] —**de+'form+a·ble** *adj.* —**de+ˌform+a·'bil+i·ty** *n.* —**de+'form+er** *n.*

de+for+ma+tion (ˌdiːfɔː'meɪʃən) *n.* **1.** the act of deforming; distortion. **2.** the result of deforming; a change in form, esp. for the worse. **3.** a change in the dimensions of an object resulting from a stress.

de+formed (dɪ'fɔːmd) *adj.* **1.** disfigured or misshapen. **2.** morally perverted; warped. —**de+form+ed+ly** (dɪ'fɔːmɪdlɪ) *adv.* —**de+'form+ed+ness** *n.*

de+form+i+ty (dɪ'fɔːmɪtɪ) *n., pl.* **·ties. 1.** a deformed condition; disfigurement. **2.** *Pathol.* an acquired or congenital distortion of an organ or part. **3.** a deformed person or thing. **4.** a defect, esp. of the mind or morals; depravity.

de+fraud (dɪ'frɔːd) *vb.* (*tr.*) to take away or withhold money, rights, property, etc., from (a person) by fraud; cheat; swindle. —**de+frau+da+tion** (ˌdiːfrɔː'deɪʃən) *or* **de+'fraud+ment** *n.* —**de+'fraud+er** *n.*

de+fray (dɪ'freɪ) *vb.* (*tr.*) to furnish or provide money for (costs, expenses, etc.); pay. [C16: from Old French *deffroier* to pay expenses, from *de-* DIS-[1] + *frai* expenditure, originally: cost incurred through breaking something, from Latin *frangere* to break] —**de+'fray+a·ble** *adj.* —**de+'fray+al** *or* **de+'fray+ment** *n.* —**de+'fray+er** *n.*

de+frock (diː'frɒk) *vb.* (*tr.*) to deprive (a person in holy orders) of ecclesiastical status; unfrock.

de+frost (diː'frɒst) *vb.* **1.** to make or become free of frost or ice. **2.** to thaw, esp. through removal from a refrigerator.

de+frost+er (diː'frɒstə) *n.* a device by which the de-icing process of a refrigerator is accelerated, usually by circulating the refrigerant without the expansion process.

deft (dɛft) *adj.* quick and neat in movement; nimble; dexterous. [C13 (in the sense: gentle): see DAFT] —**'deft+ly** *adv.* —**'deft+ness** *n.*

de+funct (dɪ'fʌŋkt) *adj.* **1.** no longer living; dead or extinct. **2.** no longer operative or valid. [C16: from Latin *dēfungī* to discharge (one's obligations), die; see DE-, FUNCTION] —**de+'func+tive** *adj.* —**de+'funct+ness** *n.*

de+fuse *or U.S. (sometimes)* **de+fuze** (diː'fjuːz) *vb.* (*tr.*) **1.** to remove the triggering device of (a bomb, etc.). **2.** to remove the cause of tension from (a crisis, etc.).

de·fy (dɪ'faɪ) *vb.* **+fies, +fy+ing, +fied.** (*tr.*) **1.** to resist (a powerful person, authority, etc.) openly and boldly. **2.** to elude, esp. in a baffling way: *his actions defy explanation.* **3.** *Formal.* to challenge or provoke (someone to do something judged to be impossible); dare: *I defy you to climb that cliff.* **4.** *Archaic.* to invite to do battle or combat. [C14: from Old French *desfier,* from *des-* DE- + *fier* to trust, from Latin *fīdere*] —**de+'fi+er** *n.*

deg. *abbrev. for* degree (of temperature).

dé+ga+gé *French.* (dega'ʒe) *adj.* **1.** unconstrained in manner; casual; relaxed. **2.** uninvolved; detached.

de+gas (diː'gæs) *vb.* **+gas+ses** *or* **+gas·es, +gas+sing, +gassed. 1.** (*tr.*) to remove gas from (a container, vacuum tube, liquid, adsorbent, etc.). **2.** (*intr.*) to lose adsorbed or absorbed gas by desorption. —**de+'gas+ser** *n.*

De·gas ('deɪgɑː; *French* də'gɑ) *n.* **Hi·laire Ger·main Ed·gar** (ilɛːr ʒɛrmɛ̃ ɛd'gar). 1834–1917, French impressionist painter and sculptor, noted for his brilliant draughtsmanship and ability to convey movement, esp. in his studies of horse racing and ballet dancers.

de Gaulle (*French* də'gol) *n.* **Charles (André Joseph Marie)** (ʃarl). 1890–1970, French general and statesman. During World War II, he refused to accept Pétain's armistice with Germany and founded the Free French movement in England (1940). He was head of the provisional governments (1944–46) and, as first president of the Fifth Republic (1959–69), he restored political and economic stability to France.

de+gauss (diː'gaʊs, -'gɔːs) *vb.* (*tr.*) **1.** to neutralize (the magnetic field of a ship's hull, etc.) by producing an opposing magnetic field. **2.** another word for **demagnetize.**

de+gen+er·a·cy (dɪ'dʒɛnərəsɪ) *n., pl.* **+cies. 1.** the act or state of being degenerate. **2.** the process of becoming degenerate. **3.** *Physics.* the number of degenerate energy levels of a particular orbital, degree of freedom, etc.

de+gen+er+ate *vb.* (dɪ'dʒɛnəˌreɪt). (*intr.*) **1.** to become degenerate. **2.** *Biology.* (of organisms or their parts) to become less specialized or functionally useless. ~*adj.* (dɪ'dʒɛnərɪt). **3.** having declined or deteriorated to a lower mental, moral, or physical level; debased; degraded; corrupt. **4.** *Physics.* **a.** (of the constituents of a system) having the same energy but different wave functions. **b.** (of a semiconductor) containing a similar number of electrons in the conduction band to the number of electrons in the conduction band of metals. **c.** (of a resonant device) having two or more modes of equal frequency. **5.** (of a code) containing symbols that represent more than one letter, figure, etc. **6.** (of a plant or animal) having undergone degeneration. ~*n.* (dɪ'dʒɛnərɪt). **7.** a degenerate person. [C15: from Latin *dēgenerāre,* from *dēgener* departing from its kind, ignoble, from DE- + *genus* origin, race] —**de+'gen+er+ate+ly** *adv.* —**de+'gen+er+ate+ness** *n.* —**de+'gen+er·a+tive** *adj.*

de+gen+er·a+tion (dɪˌdʒɛnə'reɪʃən) *n.* **1.** the process of degenerating. **2.** the state of being degenerate. **3.** *Biology.* the loss of specialization, function, or structure by organisms and their parts, as in the development of vestigial organs. **4. a.** impairment or loss of the function and structure of cells or tissues, as by disease or injury, often leading to death (necrosis) of the involved part. **b.** the resulting condition. **5.** *Electronics.* negative feedback of a signal.

de+gen+er·a+tive joint dis+ease *n.* another name for **osteoarthritis.**

de+glu+ti+nate (diː'gluːtɪˌneɪt) *vb.* (*tr.*) to extract the gluten from (a cereal, esp. wheat). [C17: from Latin *dēglūtināre* to unglue, from DE- + *glūtināre,* from *glūten* GLUE] —**de+ˌglu+ti+'na+tion** *n.*

de+glu+ti+tion (ˌdiːglʊ'tɪʃən) *n.* the act of swallowing. [C17: from French *déglutition,* from Late Latin *dēglūtīre* to swallow down, from DE- + *glutīre* to swallow]

de+gra+da·ble (dɪ'greɪdəbᵊl) *adj.* **1.** (of waste products, packaging materials, etc.) capable of being decomposed chemically or biologically. See also **biodegradable. 2.** capable of being degraded.

deg+ra+da+tion (ˌdɛgrə'deɪʃən) *n.* **1.** the act of degrading or the state of being degraded. **2.** a state of degeneration, squalor, or poverty. **3.** some act, constraint, etc., that is degrading. **4.** the wearing down of the surface of rocks, cliffs, etc., by erosion, weathering, or some other process. **5.** *Chem.* a breakdown of a molecule into atoms or smaller molecules. **6.** *Physics.* an irreversible process in which the energy available to do work is decreased. **7.** *R.C. Church.* the permanent unfrocking of a priest.

de+grade (dɪ'greɪd) *vb.* **1.** (*tr.*) to reduce in worth, character, etc.; disgrace; dishonour. **2.** (diː'greɪd) (*tr.*) to reduce in rank, status, or degree; remove from office; demote. **3.** (*tr.*) to reduce in strength, quality, intensity, etc. **4.** to reduce or be reduced by erosion or down-cutting, as a land surface or bed of a river. Compare **aggrade. 5.** *Chem.* to decompose or be decomposed into atoms or smaller molecules. [C14: from Late Latin *dēgradāre,* from Latin DE- + *gradus* rank, degree] —**de+'grad+er** *n.*

de+grad+ing (dɪ'greɪdɪŋ) *adj.* causing humiliation; debasing. —**de+'grad+ing+ly** *adv.* —**de+'grad+ing+ness** *n.*

de+grease (diː'griːs) *vb.* (*tr.*) to remove grease from.

de+gree (dɪ'griː) *n.* **1.** a stage in a scale of relative amount or intensity: *a high degree of competence.* **2.** an academic award conferred by a university or college on successful completion of a course or as an honorary distinction (**honorary degree**). **3.** any of three categories of seriousness of a burn. See **burn**[1] (sense 19). **4.** (in the U.S.) any of the categories into which a crime is divided according to its seriousness: *first-degree murder.* **5.** *Genealogy.* a step in a line of descent, used as a measure of the closeness of a blood relationship. **6.** *Grammar.* any of the forms of an adjective used to indicate relative amount or intensity: in English they are *positive, comparative,* and *superlative.* **7.** *Music.* any note of a diatonic scale relative to the other notes in that scale: *D is the second degree of the scale of C major.* **8.** a unit of temperature on a specified scale: *the normal body temperature of man is 36·8 degrees centigrade.* Symbol: °. See also **Celsius scale, Fahrenheit scale. 9.** a measure of angle equal to one three-hundred-and-sixtieth of the angle traced by one complete revolution of a line about one of its ends. Symbol: °. See also **minute**[1] (sense 2), **second**[2] (sense 2). Compare **radian. 10. a.** a unit of latitude or longitude, divided into 60 minutes, used to define points on the earth's surface or on the celestial sphere. **b.** a point or line defined by units of latitude and/or longitude. Symbol: °. **11.** a unit on any of several scales of measurement, as for alcohol content or specific gravity. Symbol: °. **12.** *Maths.* **a.** the highest power or the sum of the powers of any term in a polynomial or by itself: *$x^4 + x + 3$ and xyz^2 are of the fourth degree.* **b.** the greatest power of the highest order derivative in a differential equation. **13.** *Obsolete.* a step; rung. **14.** *Archaic.* a stage in social status or rank. **15. by degrees.** little by little; gradually. **16. to a degree.** somewhat; rather. **17. degrees of frost.** See **frost** (sense 3). [C13: from Old French *degre,* from Latin DE- + *gradus* step, GRADE] —**de+'gree+less** *adj.*

de+gree day *n.* a day on which university degrees are conferred.

de·gree-day *n.* a unit used in estimating fuel requirements in heating buildings. It is equal to a fall of temperature of 1 degree below the mean outside temperature (usually taken as 18°C) for one day.

de+gree of free+dom *n.* **1.** *Physics.* one of the minimum number of parameters necessary to describe a state or property of a system. **2.** one of the independent components of motion (translation, vibration, and rotation) of an atom or molecule. **3.** *Chem.* one of a number of intensive properties that can be independently varied without changing the number of phases in a system. See also **phase rule. 4.** *Statistics.* one of the independent unrestricted random variables constituting a statistic.

de+gres+sion (dɪˈɡrɛʃən) *n.* **1.** a decrease by stages. **2.** a gradual decrease in the tax rate on amounts below a specified sum. [C15: from Medieval Latin *dēgressiō* descent, from Latin *dēgredī* to go down, from DE- + *gradī* to take steps, go]

de+gust (dɪˈɡʌst) *or* **de+gus+tate** (dɪˈɡʌsteɪt) *vb. (tr.) Rare.* to taste, esp. with care or relish; savour. [C17: from Latin *dēgustāre,* from *gustāre,* from *gustus* a tasting, taste] **—de+gus+ta+tion** (ˌdiːɡʌˈsteɪʃən) *n.*

de+hisce (dɪˈhɪs) *vb. (intr.)* (of fruits, anthers, etc.) to burst open spontaneously, releasing seeds, pollen, etc. [C17: from Latin *dēhiscere* to split open, from DE- + *hiscere* to yawn, gape]

de+his+cent (dɪˈhɪsənt) *adj.* (of fruits, anthers, etc.) opening spontaneously to release seeds or pollen. **—de+ˈhis+cence** *n.*

de+horn (diːˈhɔːn) *vb. (tr.)* **1.** to remove or prevent the growth of the horns of (cattle, sheep, or goats). **2.** to cut back (the larger limbs of a tree) drastically. **—de+ˈhorn+er** *n.*

Deh+ra Dun (ˈdɛərə ˈduːn) *n.* a city in N India, in NW Uttar Pradhesh. Pop.: 166 073 (1971).

de+hu+man+ize *or* **de+hu+man+ise** (diːˈhjuːməˌnaɪz) *vb. (tr.)* **1.** to deprive of human qualities. **2.** to render mechanical, artificial, or routine. **—de+ˌhu+man+i+ˈza+tion** *or* **de+ˌhu+man+i+ˈsa+tion** *n.*

de+hu+mid·i+fi+er (ˌdiːhjuːˈmɪdɪˌfaɪə) *n.* a device for reducing the moisture content of atmosphere.

de+hu+mid·i+fy (ˌdiːhjuːˈmɪdɪˌfaɪ) *vb.* **+fies, +fy+ing, +fied.** *(tr.)* to remove water from (something, esp. the air). **—ˌde+hu+ˌmid·i+fi+ˈca+tion** *n.*

de+hy+drate (diːˈhaɪdreɪt) *vb.* **1.** to lose or cause to lose water; make or become anhydrous. **2.** to lose or cause to lose hydrogen atoms and oxygen atoms in the proportions in which they occur in water, as in a chemical reaction. **3.** to lose or deprive of water, as the body or tissues. **—ˌde+hy+ˈdra+tion** *n.* **—de+ˈhy+dra+tor** *n.*

de+hy·dro+gen+ase (diːˈhaɪdrədʒəˌneɪz) *n.* an enzyme, such as any of the respiratory enzymes, that activates oxidation-reduction reactions by transferring hydrogen from substrate to acceptor.

de+hy·dro+gen+ate (diːˈhaɪdrədʒəˌneɪt), **de+hy·dro+gen+ize,** *or* **de+hy·dro+gen+ise** (diːˈhaɪdrədʒəˌnaɪz) *vb. (tr.)* to remove hydrogen from. **—de+ˌhy·dro+ge·ˈna+tion, de+ˌhy·dro+gen·i+ˈza+tion,** *or* **de+ˌhy·dro+gen·i+ˈsa+tion** *n.*

de+hy·dro+ret·i+nol (diːˌhaɪdrəʊˈrɛtɪnɒl) *n.* another name for **vitamin A_2.**

de+hyp+no+tize *or* **de+hyp+no+tise** (diːˈhɪpnəˌtaɪz) *vb. (tr.)* to bring out of the hypnotic state. **—de+ˌhyp+no+ti+ˈza+tion** *or* **de+ˌhyp+no+ti+ˈsa+tion** *n.*

De·ia·ni·ra (ˌdiːəˈnaɪərə, ˌdeɪə-) *n. Greek myth.* a sister of Meleager and wife of Hercules. She unintentionally killed Hercules by dipping his tunic in the poisonous blood of the Centaur Nessus, thinking it to be a love charm.

de-ice (diːˈaɪs) *vb.* to free or be freed of ice.

de-ic·er (diːˈaɪsə) *n.* **1.** a mechanical or thermal device designed to melt or stop the formation of ice on an aircraft, usually fitted to the aerofoil surfaces. Compare **anti-icer. 2.** a chemical or other substance used for this purpose, esp. an aerosol that can be sprayed on car windscreens to remove ice or frost.

de·i·cide (ˈdiːɪˌsaɪd) *n.* **1.** the act of killing a god. **2.** a person who kills a god. [C17: from ecclesiastical Latin *deicida,* from Latin *deus* god; see -CIDE] **—ˌde·i·ˈci·dal** *adj.*

deic·tic (ˈdaɪktɪk) *adj.* **1.** *Logic.* proving by direct argument. Compare **elenctic. 2.** *Grammar.* **a.** denoting a word, such as *here* or *I,* whose reference is determined by the context of its utterance. **b.** *(as n.): the word "here" is a deictic.* [C17: from Greek *deiktikos* concerning proof, from *deiknunai* to show] **—ˈdeic+ti+cal+ly** *adv.*

de+if·ic (diːˈɪfɪk, deɪ-) *adj.* **1.** making divine or exalting to the position of a god. **2.** divine or godlike.

de·i·fi·ca·tion (ˌdiːɪfɪˈkeɪʃən, ˌdeɪ-) *n.* **1.** the act or process of exalting to the position of a god. **2.** the state or condition of being deified.

de·i·form (ˈdiːɪˌfɔːm) *adj.* having the form or appearance of a god; sacred or divine.

de·i·fy (ˈdiːɪˌfaɪ, ˈdeɪ-) *vb.* **+fies, +fy+ing, +fied.** *(tr.)* **1.** to exalt to the position of a god or personify as a god. **2.** to accord divine honour or worship to. **3.** to exalt in an extreme way; idealize. [C14: from Old French *deifier,* from Late Latin *deificāre,* from Latin *deus* god + *facere* to make] **—ˈde·i+ˌfi+er** *n.*

deign (deɪn) *vb. (tr.)* **1.** to think it fit or worthy of oneself (to do something); condescend: *he will not deign to speak to us.* **2.** *Archaic.* to vouchsafe: *he deigned no reply.* [C13: from Old French *deignier,* from Latin *dignārī* to consider worthy, from *dignus* worthy]

deil (diːl) *n. Scot.* **1.** a devil. **2.** a mischievous person.

Dei+mos (ˈdeɪmɒs) *n.* the smaller of the two satellites of Mars and the more distant from the planet. Approximate diameter: 13 km. Compare **Phobos.**

deip+nos·o+phist (daɪpˈnɒsəfɪst) *n. Rare.* a person who is a master of dinner-table conversation. [C17: from Greek *deipnosophistai,* title of a Greek work by Athenaeus (3rd century), describing learned discussions at a banquet, from *deipnon* meal + *sophistai* wise men; see SOPHIST]

Deir·dre (ˈdɪədrɪ) *n. Celtic myth.* the beautiful daughter of a court bard, often used to symbolize Ireland.

de+ism (ˈdiːɪzəm, ˈdeɪ-) *n.* belief in the existence of God based solely on natural reason, without reference to revelation. Compare **theism.** [C17: from French *déisme,* from Latin *deus* god] **—ˈde+ist** *n., adj.* **—de+ˈist+ic** *or* **de+ˈis+ti+cal** *adj.* **—de+ˈis+ti+cal+ly** *adv.*

de+i·ty (ˈdiːɪtɪ, ˈdeɪ-) *n., pl.* **·ties. 1.** a god or goddess. **2.** the state of being divine; godhead. **3.** the rank, status, or position of a god. **4.** the nature or character of God. [C14: from Old French, from Late Latin *deitās,* from Latin *deus* god]

De+i·ty (ˈdiːɪtɪ, ˈdeɪ-) *n.* **the.** the Supreme Being; God.

deix+is (ˈdaɪksɪs) *n. Grammar.* the use or reference of a deictic word. [C20: from Greek, from *deiknunai* to show]

dé·jà vu (ˈdeɪʒæ ˈvuː; *French* deʒa ˈvy) *n.* the experience of perceiving a new situation as if it had occurred before. It is sometimes associated with exhaustion or certain types of mental disorder. [literally: already seen]

de+ject (dɪˈdʒɛkt) *vb.* **1.** *(tr.)* to have a depressing effect on; dispirit; dishearten. *~adj.* **2.** *Archaic.* downcast; dejected. [C15: from Latin *dēicere* to cast down, from DE- + *iacere* to throw]

de+jec+ta (dɪˈdʒɛktə) *pl. n.* waste products excreted through the anus; faeces. [C19: New Latin: things cast down; see DEJECT]

de+ject+ed (dɪˈdʒɛktɪd) *adj.* miserable; despondent; downhearted. **—de+ˈject+ed+ly** *adv.* **—de+ˈject+ed+ness** *n.*

de+jec+tion (dɪˈdʒɛkʃən) *n.* **1.** lowness of spirits; depression; melancholy. **2. a.** faecal matter evacuated from the bowels; excrement. **b.** the act of defecating; defecation.

de ju·re (deɪˈdʒʊərɪ) *adj.* according to law; by right; legally. Compare **de facto.** [Latin]

dek·a- *or* **dek-** *combining form.* variants of **deca-.**

Dek·ker *or* **Deck·er** (ˈdɛkə) *n.* **Thom·as.** ?1572–?1632, English dramatist and pamphleteer, noted particularly for his comedy *The Shoemaker's Holiday* (1600) and his satirical pamphlet *The Gull's Hornbook* (1609).

dek+ko (ˈdɛkəʊ) *n., pl.* **+kos.** *Brit. slang.* a look; glance; view. [C19: from Hindi *dekho!* look! from *dekhnā* to see]

de Koo·ning (də ˈkuːnɪŋ) *n.* **Wil·lem.** See (Willem de) **Kooning.**

del. *abbrev. for* delegate.

Del. *abbrev. for* Delaware.

De·la·croix (*French* dəlaˈkrwa) *n.* **(Ferdinand Victor) Eu·gène** (øˈʒɛn). 1798–1863, French romantic painter whose use of colour and free composition influenced impressionism. His paintings of historical and contemporary scenes include *The Massacre at Chios* (1824).

Del·a·go·a Bay (ˌdɛləˈɡəʊə) *n.* an inlet of the Indian Ocean, in S Mozambique. Official name: **Baia de Lourenço Marques.**

de+laine (dəˈleɪn) *n.* a sheer wool or wool and cotton fabric. [C19: from French *mousseline de laine* muslin of wool]

De la Mare (də lɑː ˈmɛə) *n.* **Wal·ter (John).** 1873–1956, English poet and novelist, noted esp. for his evocative verse for children. His works include the volumes of poetry *The Listeners and Other Poems* (1912) and *Peacock Pie* (1913) and the novel *Memoirs of a Midget* (1921).

de+lam·i·nate (diːˈlæmɪˌneɪt) *vb.* to divide or cause to divide into thin layers. **—de+ˌlam·i+ˈna+tion** *n.*

de+late (dɪˈleɪt) *vb. (tr.)* **1.** (formerly) to bring a charge against; denounce; impeach. **2.** *Rare.* to report (an offence, etc.). **3.** *Obsolete.* to make known or public. [C16: from Latin *dēlātus,* from *dēferre* to bring down, report, indict, from DE- + *ferre* to bear] **—de+ˈla+tion** *n.* **—de+ˈla+tor** *n.*

De·lau·nay (*French* dəloˈnɛ) *n.* **Ro·bert** (rɔˈbɛːr). 1885–1941, French painter, whose abstract use of colour characterized Orphism.

Del·a+ware[1] (ˈdɛləˌwɛə) *n., pl.* **+wares** *or* **+ware.** a member of a North American Indian people formerly living near the Delaware River.

Del·a+ware[2] (ˈdɛləˌwɛə) *n.* an American variety of grape that has sweet light red fruit.

Del·a+ware[3] (ˈdɛləˌwɛə) *n.* **1.** a state of the northeastern U.S., on the Delmarva Peninsula: mostly flat and low-lying, with hills in the extreme north and cypress swamps in the extreme south. Capital: Dover. Pop.: 548 104 (1970). Area: 5328 sq. km. (2057 sq. miles). Abbrevs.: **Del.** or (with zip code) **DE 2.** a river in the northeastern U.S., rising in the Catskill Mountains and flowing south into **Delaware Bay,** an inlet of the Atlantic. Length 660 km (410 miles). **—ˌDel·a·ˈwar+e·an** *adj.*

De La Warr (ˈdɛləˌwɛə) *n.* **Bar·on,** title of *Thomas West,* known as *Lord Delaware.* 1577–1618, English administrator in America; first governor of Virginia (1610).

de+lay (dɪˈleɪ) *vb.* **1.** *(tr.)* to put off to a later time; defer. **2.** *(tr.)* to slow up, hinder, or cause to be late; detain. **3.** *(intr.)* to be irresolute or put off doing something; procrastinate. **4.** *(intr.)* to linger; dawdle. *~n.* **5.** the act or an instance of delaying or being delayed. **6.** the interval between one event and another; lull; interlude. [C13: from Old French *delaier,* from *des-* off + *laier,* variant of *laissier* to leave, from Latin *laxāre* to loosen, from *laxus* slack, LAX] **—de+ˈlay+er** *n.*

de+layed ac+tion *or* **de+lay ac+tion** *n.* **1.** a device for operating a mechanism, such as a camera shutter, a short time after setting. **2.** *(as modifier): a delayed-action fuse.*

de+layed drop *n.* a parachute descent with the opening of the parachute delayed, usually for a predetermined period.

de+layed neu+tron *n.* a neutron produced in a nuclear reactor by the breakdown of a fission product and released a short time after neutrons produced in the primary process.

de+lay+ing ac+tion *n.* a measure or measures taken to gain time, as when weaker military forces harass the advance of a superior enemy without coming to a pitched battle.

de+lay line *n.* a device in which a known delay time is introduced in the transmission of a signal. An **acoustic delay line** delays a sound wave by circulating it through a liquid or solid medium.

del cre+de+re a·gent (dɛl 'kreɪdərɪ) *n.* an agent who, in addition to obtaining orders, guarantees that the buyer will pay for the goods. [C18: from Italian: of trust]

de·le ('di:lɪ) *n., pl.* **de·les.** **1.** a sign (₰) indicating that typeset matter is to be deleted. Compare **stet.** ~*vb.* **de+les, de+le·ing, de+led. 2.** (*tr.*) to mark (matter to be deleted) with a dele. [C18: from Latin: delete (imperative), from *dēlēre* to destroy, obliterate; see DELETE]

de+lec+ta·ble (dɪ'lɛktəbᵊl) *adj.* highly enjoyable, esp. pleasing to the taste; delightful. [C14: from Latin *dēlectābilis,* from *dēlectāre* to DELIGHT] **—de+'lec+ta·ble+ness** *or* **de+,lec+ta·'bil+i·ty** *n.* **—de+'lec+ta·bly** *adv.*

de+lec+ta+tion (,di:lɛk'teɪʃən) *n.* pleasure; enjoyment.

De·led·da (*Italian* de'ledda) *n.* **Gra·zia** ('grattsja). 1875–1936, Italian novelist, noted for works, such as *La Madre* (1920), on peasant life in Sardinia: Nobel prize for literature 1926.

del+e·ga+cy ('dɛlɪgəsɪ) *n., pl.* **+cies. 1.** a less common word for **delegation** (senses 1, 2). **2. a.** an elected standing committee at some British universities. **b.** a department or institute of a university: *a delegacy of Education.*

del+e·gate *n.* ('dɛlɪ,geɪt, -gɪt). **1.** a person chosen or elected to act for or represent another or others, esp. at a conference or meeting. **2.** *U.S. government.* a representative of a territory in the U.S. House of Representatives. ~*vb.* ('dɛlɪ,geɪt). **3.** to give or commit (duties, powers, etc.) to another as agent or representative; depute. **4.** (*tr.*) to send, authorize, or elect (a person) as agent or representative. **5.** (*tr.*) *Chiefly U.S.* to assign (a person owing a debt to oneself) to one's creditor in substitution for oneself. [C14: from Latin *dēlēgāre* to send on a mission, from *lēgāre* to send, depute; see LEGATE] **—del+e·ga·ble** ('dɛlɪgəbᵊl) *adj.*

del+e·ga+tion (,dɛlɪ'geɪʃən) *n.* **1.** a person or group chosen to represent another or others. **2.** the act of delegating or state of being delegated. **3.** *U.S. politics.* all the members of Congress from one state.

de Les·seps (*French* də lɛ'sɛps) *n.* **Vi·comte.** title of (Ferdinand Marie) **Lesseps.**

de+lete (dɪ'li:t) *vb.* (*tr.*) to remove (something printed or written); erase; cancel; strike out. [C17: from Latin *dēlēre* to destroy, obliterate]

del+e·te·ri+ous (,dɛlɪ'tɪərɪəs) *adj.* harmful; injurious; hurtful. [C17: from New Latin *dēlētērius,* from Greek *dēlētērios* injurious, destructive, from *dēleisthai* to hurt] **—,del+e·'te·ri+ous+ly** *adv.* **—,del+e·'te·ri+ous+ness** *n.*

de+le·tion (dɪ'li:ʃən) *n.* **1.** the act of deleting or fact of being deleted. **2.** a deleted passage, word, etc., in a piece of text. **3.** the loss or absence of a section of a chromosome.

Delft (dɛlft) *n.* **1.** a town in the SW Netherlands, in South Holland province. Pop.: 87 777 (1973 est.). **2.** Also called: **delftware.** tin-glazed earthenware made in Delft since the 17th century, typically having blue decoration on a white ground. **3.** a similar earthenware made in England.

Del·ga+do (dɛl'gɑ:dəʊ) *n.* **Cape.** a headland on the extreme NE coast of Mozambique.

Del+hi ('dɛlɪ) *n.* **1.** the capital of India, in the N central part, on the Jumna river: consists of **Old Delhi** (a walled city reconstructed in 1639 on the site of former cities of Delhi, which date from the 15th century B.C.) and **New Delhi** to the south, chosen as the capital in 1911, replacing Calcutta; university (1922). Pop.: (total) 3 287 883 (1971); (New Delhi) 301 801 (1971). **2.** a Union Territory of N India. Capital: Delhi. Area: 1418 sq. km (553 sq. miles). Pop.: 4 065 698 (1971).

del·i ('dɛlɪ) *n. U.S. and Austral.* an informal word for **delicatessen.**

De+li·an ('di:lɪən) *n.* **1.** a native or inhabitant of Delos. ~*adj.* **2.** of or relating to Delos. **3.** of or relating to Delius.

De+li·an League *or* **Con+fed+er·a+cy** *n.* an alliance of ancient Greek states formed in 478–77 B.C. to fight Persia.

de+lib+er+ate *adj.* (dɪ'lɪbərɪt). **1.** carefully thought out in advance; planned; studied; intentional: *a deliberate insult.* **2.** careful or unhurried in speech or action: *a deliberate pace.* ~*vb.* (dɪ'lɪbə,reɪt). **3.** to consider (something) deeply; ponder; think over. [C15: from Latin *dēlīberāre* to consider well, from *lībrāre* to weigh, from *lībra* scales] **—de+'lib+er+ate+ly** *adv.* **—de+'lib+er+ate+ness** *n.* **—de+'lib+er·,a+tor** *n.*

de+lib+er·a+tion (dɪ,lɪbə'reɪʃən) *n.* **1.** thoughtful, careful, or lengthy consideration. **2.** (*often pl.*) formal discussion and debate, as of a committee, jury, etc. **3.** care, thoughtfulness, or absence of hurry, esp. in movement or speech.

de+lib+er·a·tive (dɪ'lɪbərətɪv) *adj.* **1.** involved in, organized for, or having the function of deliberating: *a deliberative assembly.* **2.** characterized by or resulting from deliberation: *a deliberative conclusion.* **—de+'lib+er·a+tive+ly** *adv.* **—de+'lib+er·a+tive+ness** *n.*

De·libes (*French* də'lib) *n.* **(Clément Philibert) Lé·o** (le'o). 1836–91, French composer, noted particularly for his ballets *Coppélia* (1870) and *Sylvia* (1876), and the opera *Lakmé* (1883).

del·i+ca+cy ('dɛlɪkəsɪ) *n., pl.* **+cies. 1.** fine or subtle quality, character, construction, etc.: *delicacy of craftsmanship.* **2.** fragile, soft, or graceful beauty. **3.** something that is considered choice to eat, such as caviar. **4.** fragile construction or constitution; frailty. **5.** refinement of feeling, manner, or appreciation: *the delicacy of the orchestra's playing.* **6.** fussy or squeamish refinement, esp. in matters of taste, propriety, etc. **7.** need for tactful or sensitive handling. **8.** accuracy or sensitivity of response or operation, as of an instrument. **9.** *Obsolete.* gratification, luxury, or voluptuousness.

del·i+cate ('dɛlɪkɪt) *adj.* **1.** exquisite, fine, or subtle in quality, character, construction, etc. **2.** having a soft or fragile beauty. **3.** (of colour, tone, taste, etc.) pleasantly subtle, soft, or faint. **4.** easily damaged or injured; lacking robustness, esp. in health; fragile. **5.** precise, skilled, or sensitive in action or operation: *a delicate mechanism.* **6.** requiring tact and diplomacy. **7.** sensitive in feeling or manner; showing regard for the feelings of others. **8.** excessively refined; squeamish. ~*n.* **9.** *Archaic.* a delicacy; dainty. [C14: from Latin *dēlicātus* affording pleasure, from *dēliciae* (pl.) delight, pleasure; see DELICIOUS] **—'del·i+cate+ly** *adv.* **—'del·i+cate+ness** *n.*

del·i+ca+tes+sen (,dɛlɪkə'tɛsᵊn) *n.* **1.** various foods, esp. unusual or imported foods, already cooked or prepared. **2.** a shop selling these foods. [C19: from German *Delikatessen,* literally: delicacies, pl. of *Delikatesse* a delicacy, from French *délicatesse*]

de+li+cious (dɪ'lɪʃəs) *adj.* **1.** very appealing to the senses, esp. to the taste or smell. **2.** extremely enjoyable or entertaining: *a delicious joke.* [C13: from Old French, from Late Latin *dēliciōsus,* from Latin *dēliciae* delights, charms, from *dēlicere* to entice; see DELIGHT] **—de+'li+cious+ly** *adv.* **—de+'li+cious+ness** *n.*

de+lict (dɪ'lɪkt, 'di:lɪkt) *n.* **1.** *Law, chiefly Scot.* a wrongful act for which the person injured has the right to a civil remedy. See also **tort. 2.** *Roman law.* a civil wrong redressable by compensation or punitive damages. [C16: from Latin *dēlictum* a fault, crime, from *dēlinquere* to fail, do wrong; see DELINQUENCY]

de+light (dɪ'laɪt) *vb.* **1.** (*tr.*) to please greatly. **2.** (*intr.;* foll. by *in*) to take great pleasure (in). ~*n.* **3.** extreme pleasure or satisfaction; joy. **4.** something that causes this: *music was always his delight.* [C13: from Old French *delit,* from *deleitier* to please, from Latin *dēlectāre,* from *dēlicere* to allure, from DE- + *lacere* to entice; see DELICIOUS; English spelling influenced by *light*] **—de+'light+ed** *adj.* **—de+'light+ed+ly** *adv.* **—de+'light+ed+ness** *n.* **—de+'light+er** *n.*

de+light+ed (dɪ'laɪtɪd) *adj.* **a.** (often foll. by an infinitive) extremely pleased (to do something): *I'm delighted to hear it!* **b.** (*sentence substitute*) I should be delighted to!

de+light+ful (dɪ'laɪtfʊl) *adj.* giving great delight; very pleasing, beautiful, charming, etc. **—de+'light+ful+ly** *adv.* **—de+'light+ful+ness** *n.*

De·li·lah (dɪ'laɪlə) *n.* **1.** Samson's Philistine mistress, who deprived him of his strength by cutting off his hair (Judges 16:4–22). **2.** a voluptuous and treacherous woman; temptress.

de+lim+it (di:'lɪmɪt) *or* **de+lim·i·tate** *vb.* (*tr.*) to mark or prescribe the limits or boundaries of; demarcate. **—de+,lim·i+'ta+tion** *n.* **—de+'lim·i+ta+tive** *adj.*

de+lin+e·ate (dɪ'lɪnɪ,eɪt) *vb.* (*tr.*) **1.** to trace the shape or outline of; sketch. **2.** to represent pictorially, as by making a chart or diagram; depict. **3.** to portray in words, esp. with detail and precision; describe. [C16: from Latin *dēlīneāre* to sketch out, from *līnea* LINE[1]] **—de+'lin+e·a·ble** *adj.* **—de+,lin+e·'a+tion** *n.* **—de+'lin+e·a+tive** *adj.*

de+lin+e·a+tor (dɪ'lɪnɪ,eɪtə) *n.* a tailor's pattern, adjustable for different sizes.

de+lin+quen+cy (dɪ'lɪŋkwənsɪ) *n., pl.* **+cies. 1.** an offence or misdeed, usually of a minor nature, esp. one committed by a young person. See **juvenile delinquency. 2.** failure or negligence in duty or obligation; dereliction. **3.** a delinquent nature or delinquent behaviour. [C17: from Late Latin *dēlinquentia* a fault, offence, from Latin *dēlinquere* to transgress, from DE- + *linquere* to forsake]

de+lin+quent (dɪ'lɪŋkwənt) *n.* **1.** someone, esp. a young person, guilty of delinquency. See **juvenile delinquent. 2.** *Archaic.* a person who fails in an obligation or duty. ~*adj.* **3.** guilty of an offence or misdeed, esp. one of a minor nature. **4.** failing in or neglectful of duty or obligation. [C17: from Latin *dēlinquēns* offending; see DELINQUENCY] **—de+'lin+quent+ly** *adv.*

del·i+quesce (,dɛlɪ'kwɛs) *vb.* (*intr.*) **1.** (esp. of certain salts) to dissolve gradually in water absorbed from the air. **2.** (of a plant stem) to form many branches. [C18: from Latin *dēliquēscere* to melt away, become liquid, from DE- + *liquēscere* to melt, from *liquēre* to be liquid]

del·i+ques+cence (,dɛlɪ'kwɛsᵊns) *n.* **1.** the process of deliquescing. **2.** a solution formed when a solid or liquid deliquesces. **—'del·i·'ques+cent** *adj.*

de+lir·i+ous (dɪ'lɪrɪəs) *adj.* **1.** affected with delirium. **2.** wildly excited, esp. with joy or enthusiasm. **—de+'lir·i·ous+ly** *adv.* **—de+'lir·i+ous+ness** *n.*

de+lir+i·um (dɪ'lɪrɪəm) *n., pl.* **+lir+i·ums, +lir·i·a** (-'lɪrɪə). **1.** a state of excitement and mental confusion, often accompanied by hallucinations, caused by high fever, poisoning, brain injury, etc. **2.** violent excitement or emotion; frenzy. [C16: from Latin: madness, from *dēlīrāre,* literally: to swerve from a furrow, hence be crazy, from DE- + *līra* ridge, furrow] **—de+'lir·i+ant** *adj.*

de+lir+i·um tre+mens ('trɛmɛnz, 'tri:-) *n.* a severe psychotic condition occurring in some persons with chronic alcoholism, characterized by delirium, tremor, anxiety, and vivid hallucinations. Abbrevs.: **D.T.'s** (informal), **d.t.** [C19: New Latin, literally: trembling delirium]

del·i+tes+cence (,dɛlɪ'tɛsᵊns) *n.* the sudden disappearance of a lesion or of the signs and symptoms of a disease. [C18: from Latin *dēlitēscens,* present participle of *dēlitēscere* to lurk, from *latēscere* to become hidden, from *latēre* to be hidden; see LATENT] —ˌ**del·i·'tes·cent** *adj.*

De·li·us ('diːlɪəs) *n.* **Fred·er·ick.** 1862–1934, English composer, who drew inspiration from folk tunes and the sounds of nature. His works include the opera *A Village Romeo and Juliet* (1901), *A Mass of Life* (1905), and the orchestral variations *Brigg Fair* (1907).

de·liv·er (dɪ'lɪvə) *vb.* (*mainly tr.*) **1.** to carry (goods, etc.) to a destination, esp. to carry and distribute (goods, mail, etc.) to several places: *to deliver letters; our local butcher delivers.* **2.** (often foll. by *over* or *up*) to hand over, transfer, or surrender. **3.** (often foll. by *from*) to release or rescue (from captivity, harm, corruption, etc.). **4.** (*also intr.*) **a.** to aid in the birth of (offspring). **b.** to give birth to (offspring). **c.** (usually foll. by *of*) to aid or assist (a female) in the birth (of offspring). **d.** (*passive;* foll. by *of*) to give birth (to offspring). **5.** to utter or present (a speech, oration, idea, etc.). **6.** to utter (an exclamation, noise, etc.): *to deliver a cry of exultation.* **7.** to discharge or release (something, such as a blow or shot) suddenly. **8.** *Chiefly U.S.* to cause (voters, constituencies, etc.) to support a given candidate, cause, etc.: *can you deliver the Bronx?* **9. deliver oneself of.** to speak with deliberation or at length: *to deliver oneself of a speech.* **10. deliver the goods.** *Informal.* to produce or perform something promised or expected. [C13: from Old French *delivrer,* from Late Latin *dēlīberāre* to set free, from Latin DE- + *līberāre* to free] —**de·'liv·er·a·ble** *adj.* —**de·ˌliv·er·a·'bil·i·ty** *n.* —**de·'liv·er·er** *n.*

de·liv·er·ance (dɪ'lɪvərəns) *n.* **1.** a formal pronouncement or expression of opinion. **2.** rescue from moral corruption or evil; salvation. **3.** another word for **delivery** (senses 3–5).

de·liv·er·y (dɪ'lɪvərɪ) *n., pl.* **·er·ies. 1. a.** the act of delivering or distributing goods, mail, etc. **b.** something that is delivered. **c.** (*as modifier*): *a delivery service.* **2.** the act of giving birth to a child: *she had an easy delivery.* **3.** manner or style of utterance, esp. in public speaking or recitation: *the chairman had a clear delivery.* **4.** the act of giving or transferring or the state of being given or transferred. **5.** the act of rescuing or state of being rescued; liberation. **6.** *Sport.* **a.** the act or manner of bowling or throwing a ball. **b.** the ball so delivered: *a fast delivery.* **7.** an actual or symbolic handing over of property, a deed, etc. **8.** the discharge rate of a compressor or pump.

de·liv·er·y van *n.* a small van used esp. for delivery rounds. U.S. name: **panel truck.**

dell (dɛl) *n.* a small, esp. wooded hollow. [Old English; related to Middle Low German *delle* valley; compare DALE]

del·la Rob·bi·a (*Italian* della 'robbja) *n.* See (Luca della) **Robbia.**

Del·mar·va Pen·in·su·la (dɛl'mɑːvə) *n.* a peninsula of the northeast U.S., between Chesapeake Bay and the Atlantic.

de·lo·cal·ize *or* **de·lo·cal·ise** (diː'ləukəˌlaɪz) *vb.* (*tr.*) **1.** to remove from the usual locality. **2.** to free from local influences. —**de·ˌlo·cal·i·'za·tion** *or* **de·ˌlo·cal·i·'sa·tion** *n.*

De·lorme *or* **de l'Orme** (*French* də'lɔrm) *n.* **Phi·li·bert** (fili'bɛːr). ?1510–70, French Renaissance architect of the Tuileries, Paris.

De·los ('diːlɒs) *n.* a Greek island in the SW Aegean Sea, in the Cyclades: a commercial centre in ancient times; the legendary birthplace of Apollo and Artemis. Area: about 5 sq. km (2 sq. miles). Modern Greek name: **Dhilos.**

de los An·ge·les (*Spanish* de lɔs 'aŋxeles) *n.* **Vic·to·ri·a** (βik'toria). born 1923, Spanish soprano.

de·louse (diː'laus, -'lauz) *vb.* (*tr.*) to rid (a person or animal) of lice as a sanitary measure.

Del·phi ('dɛlfɪ) *n.* an ancient Greek city on the S slopes of Mount Parnassus: site of the most famous oracle of Apollo. —**'Del·phi·an** *n., adj.*

Del·phic ('dɛlfɪk) *or* **Del·phi·an** *adj.* **1.** of or relating to Delphi or its oracle or temple. **2.** obscure or ambiguous.

Del·phic or·a·cle *n.* the oracle of Apollo at Delphi that gave answers held by the ancient Greeks to be of great authority but also noted for their ambiguity.

del·phin·i·um (dɛl'fɪnɪəm) *n., pl.* **·i·ums** *or* **·i·a** (-ɪə). any ranunculaceous plant of the genus *Delphinium:* many varieties are cultivated as garden plants for their spikes of blue, pink, or white spurred flowers. See also **larkspur.** [C17: New Latin, from Greek *delphinion* larkspur, from *delphis* DOLPHIN, referring to the shape of the nectary]

Del·phi·nus (dɛl'faɪnəs) *n., Latin genitive* **Del·phi·ni** (dɛl'faɪnaɪ). a small constellation in the N hemisphere, between Pegasus and Sagitta. [C17: from Latin: DOLPHIN]

Del·sarte sys·tem ('dɛlsɑːt) *n.* a method of teaching drama and dancing based on the exercises of Alexandre Delsarte (1811–71), famous teacher at the Paris Conservatoire.

del Sar·to (*Italian* del 'sarto) *n.* See (Andrea del) **Sarto.**

del·ta ('dɛltə) *n.* **1.** the fourth letter in the Greek alphabet (Δ or δ), a consonant transliterated as *d.* **2.** an object resembling a capital delta in shape. **3.** (*cap. when part of name*) the flat alluvial area at the mouth of some rivers where the mainstream splits up into several distributaries: *the Mississippi Delta.* **4.** *Maths.* a finite increment in a variable. [C16: via Latin from Greek, of Semitic origin; compare Hebrew *dāleth*] —**del·ta·ic** (dɛl'teɪɪk) *or* '**del·tic** *adj.*

Del·ta ('dɛltə) *n.* **1.** (*foll. by the genitive case of a specified constellation*) usually the fourth brightest star in a constellation. **2.** any of a group of U.S. launch vehicles used to put unmanned satellites into orbit.

del·ta con·nec·tion *n.* a connection used in a three-phase electrical system in which three elements in series form a triangle, the supply being input and output at the three junctions. Compare **star connection.**

del·ta i·ron *n.* an allotrope of iron that exists between 1400°C and the melting point of iron and has the same structure as alpha iron.

del·ta ray *n.* a particle, esp. an electron, ejected from matter by ionizing radiation.

del·ta rhythm *or* **wave** *n. Physiol.* the normal electrical activity of the cerebral cortex during deep sleep, occurring at a frequency of 1 to 4 hertz and detectable with an electroencephalograph. See also **brain wave.**

del·ta wing *n.* a triangular swept-back aircraft wing.

del·ti·ol·o·gy (ˌdɛltɪ'ɒlədʒɪ) *n.* the collection and study of picture postcards. [C20: from Greek *deltion,* diminutive of *deltos* a writing tablet + -LOGY] —ˌ**del·ti·'ol·o·gist** *n.*

del·toid ('dɛltɔɪd) *n.* the thick muscle forming the rounded contour of the outer edge of the shoulder and acting to raise the arm. [C18: from Greek *deltoeidēs* triangular, from DELTA]

de·lude (dɪ'luːd) *vb.* (*tr.*) **1.** to deceive the mind or judgment of; mislead; beguile. **2.** *Rare.* to frustrate (hopes, expectations, etc.). [C15: from Latin *dēlūdere* to mock, play false, from DE- + *lūdere* to play] —**de·'lud·a·ble** *adj.* —**de·'lud·er** *n.* —**de·'lud·ing·ly** *adv.* —**de·lu·sive** (dɪ'luːsɪv) *adj.* —**de·'lu·sive·ly** *adv.* —**de·'lu·sive·ness** *n.*

del·uge ('dɛljuːdʒ) *n.* **1.** a great flood of water. **2.** torrential rain; downpour. **3.** an overwhelming rush or number: *a deluge of requests.* ~*vb.* (*tr.*) **4.** to flood, as with water; soak, swamp, or drown. **5.** to overwhelm or overrun; inundate. [C14: from Old French, from Latin *dīluvium* a washing away, flood, from *dīluere* to wash away, drench, from *di-* DIS-[1] + *-luere,* from *lavere* to wash]

Del·uge ('dɛljuːdʒ) *n.* **the.** another name for the **Flood.**

de·lu·sion (dɪ'luːʒən) *n.* **1.** a mistaken or misleading opinion, idea, belief, etc.: *he has delusions of grandeur.* **2.** *Psychiatry.* a belief held in the face of evidence to the contrary, that is resistant to all reason. See also **illusion, hallucination. 3.** the act of deluding or state of being deluded. —**de·'lu·sion·al** *adj.* —**de·'lu·sive** *adj.* —**de'lu·so·ry** (dɪ'luːsərɪ) *adj.*

de luxe (də 'lʌks, 'lʊks) *adj.* **1.** (esp. of products, articles for sale, etc.) rich, elegant, or sumptuous; superior in quality, number of accessories, etc.: *the de luxe model of a car.* ~*adv.* **2.** *Chiefly U.S.* in a luxurious manner. [C19: from French *de luxe,* literally: of luxury]

delve (dɛlv) *vb.* (*mainly intr.;* often foll. by *in* or *into*) **1.** to inquire or research deeply or intensively (for information, etc.): *he delved in the Bible for quotations.* **2.** to search or rummage (in a drawer, the pockets, etc.). **3.** (esp. of an animal) to dig or burrow deeply (into the ground, etc.). **4.** (*also tr.*) *Archaic or Brit. dialect.* to dig or turn up (earth, a garden, etc.), as with a spade. [Old English *delfan;* related to Old High German *telban* to dig, Russian *dolbit* to hollow out with a chisel] —**'delv·er** *n.*

Dem. *U.S. abbrev. for* Democrat(ic).

de·mag·net·ize *or* **de·mag·net·ise** (diː'mægnəˌtaɪz) *vb.* to remove or lose magnetic properties. Also: **degauss.** —**de·ˌmag·net·i·'za·tion** *or* **de·ˌmag·net·i·'sa·tion** *n.* —**de·'mag·net·ˌiz·er** *or* **de·'mag·net·ˌis·er** *n.*

dem·a·gog·ic (ˌdɛmə'gɒgɪk) *or* **dem·a·gog·i·cal** *adj.* of, characteristic of, relating to, or resembling a demagogue. —ˌ**dem·a·'gog·i·cal·ly** *adv.*

dem·a·gogue *or U.S.* (*sometimes*) **dem·a·gog** ('dɛməˌgɒg) *n.* **1.** a political agitator who appeals with crude oratory to the prejudice and passions of the mob. **2.** (esp. in the ancient world) any popular political leader or orator. [C17: from Greek *dēmagōgos* people's leader, from *dēmos* people + *agein* to lead]

dem·a·gogu·er·y (ˌdɛmə'gɒgərɪ) *or* **dem·a·gogu·ism** ('dɛməˌgɒgɪzəm) *n.* the methods, practices, or rhetoric of a demagogue.

dem·a·gog·y ('dɛməˌgɒgɪ) *n., pl.* **·gog·ies. 1.** demagoguery. **2.** rule by a demagogue or by demagogues. **3.** a group of demagogues.

de·mand (dɪ'mɑːnd) *vb.* (*tr.; may take a clause as object or an infinitive*) **1.** to request peremptorily or urgently. **2.** to require or need as just, urgent, etc.: *the situation demands attention.* **3.** to claim as a right; exact: *his parents demanded obedience of him.* **4.** *Law.* to make a formal legal claim to (property, esp. realty). ~*n.* **5.** an urgent or peremptory requirement or request. **6.** something that requires special effort or sacrifice: *a demand on one's time.* **7.** the act of demanding something or the thing demanded: *the kidnappers' demand was a million pounds.* **8.** an insistent question or query. **9.** *Economics.* **a.** willingness and ability to purchase goods and services. **b.** the amount of a commodity that consumers are willing and able to purchase at a specified price. Compare **supply**[1] (sense 9). **10.** *Law.* a formal legal claim, esp. to real property. **11. in demand.** sought after; popular. **12. on demand.** as soon as requested: *a draft payable on demand.* [C13: from Anglo-French *demaunder,* from Medieval Latin *dēmandāre,* from Latin: to commit to, from DE- + *mandāre* to command, entrust; see MANDATE] —**de·'mand·a·ble** *adj.* —**de·'mand·er** *n.*

de·mand·ant (dɪ'mɑːndənt) *n. Law.* (formerly) the plaintiff in an action relating to real property. [C14: from Old French, from *demander* to DEMAND]

de·mand bill, draft, *or* **note** *n.* a bill of exchange that is payable on demand. Also called: **sight bill.**

de·mand de·pos·it *n.* a bank deposit from which withdrawals may be made without notice. Compare **time deposit.**

de·mand·ing (dɪ'mɑːndɪŋ) *adj.* requiring great patience, skill, etc.: *a demanding job.* —**de·'mand·ing·ly** *adv.*

de+mand loan *n.* another name for **call loan.**
de+mand note *n.* a promissory note payable on demand.
de·mand-pull in+fla+tion *n.* See **inflation** (sense 2).
de+man+toid (dɪˈmæntɔɪd) *n.* a bright green variety of andradite garnet. [C19: from German, from obsolete *Demant* diamond, from Old French *diamant* + -OID]
de+mar+cate (ˈdi:mɑ:ˌkeɪt) *vb.* (*tr.*) **1.** to mark, fix, or draw the boundaries, limits, etc., of. **2.** to separate or distinguish between (areas with unclear boundaries). —ˈ**de+mar+ˌca+tor** *n.*
de+mar+ca+tion *or* **de+mar+ka+tion** (ˌdi:mɑ:ˈkeɪʃən) *n.* **1.** the act of establishing limits or boundaries. **2.** a limit or boundary. **3. a.** a strict separation of the kinds of work performed by members of different trade unions. **b.** (*as modifier*): *demarcation dispute.* **4.** separation or distinction (often in the phrase **line of demarcation**). [C18: Latinized version of Spanish *demarcación,* from *demarcar* to appoint the boundaries of, from *marcar* to mark, from Italian *marcare,* of Germanic origin; see MARK[1]]
dé+marche *French.* (deˈmarʃ) *n.* **1.** a move, step, or manoeuvre, esp. in diplomatic affairs. **2.** a representation or statement of views, complaints, etc., to a public authority. [C17: literally: walk, gait, from Old French *demarcher* to tread, trample; see DE-, MARCH[1]]
de+ma+te+ri+al+ize *or* **de+ma+te+ri+al+ise** (dɪməˈtɪərɪəˌlaɪz) *vb.* (*intr.*) **1.** to cease to have material existence, as in science fiction or spiritualism. **2.** to disappear without trace; vanish. —**de+ma+ˌte+ri+al+i+ˈza+tion** *or* **de+ma+ˌte+ri+al+i+ˈsa+tion** *n.*
Dem·a+vend (ˈdɛməvɛnd) *n.* **Mount.** a volcanic peak in N Iran, in the Elburz Mountains. Height: 5599 m (18 370 ft.).
deme (di:m) *n.* **1. a.** (in preclassical Greece) the territory inhabited by a tribe. **b.** (in ancient Attica) a geographical unit of local government. **2.** *Biology.* a group of individuals within a species that possess particular characteristics of cytology, genetics, etc. [C19: from Greek *dēmos* district in local government, the populace]
de+mean[1] (dɪˈmi:n) *vb.* (*tr.*) to lower (oneself) in dignity, status, or character; humble; debase. [C17: see DE-, MEAN[2]; on the model of *debase*]
de+mean[2] (dɪˈmi:n) *vb.* (*tr.*) *Rare.* to behave or conduct (oneself) in a specified way. [C13: from Old French *demener,* from DE- + *mener* to lead, drive, from Latin *mināre* to drive (animals), from *minārī* to use threats]
de+mean+our *or U.S.* **de+mean+or** (dɪˈmi:nə) *n.* **1.** the way a person behaves towards others; conduct. **2.** bearing, appearance, or mien. [C15: see DEMEAN[2]]
de+ment (dɪˈmɛnt) *vb.* (*tr.*) *Rare.* to drive mad; make insane. [C16: from Late Latin *dēmentāre* to drive mad, from Latin DE- + *mēns* mind]
de+ment+ed (dɪˈmɛntɪd) *adj.* mad; insane. —**de+ˈment+ed+ly** *adv.* —**de+ˈment+ed+ness** *n.*
de+men+tia (dɪˈmɛnʃə, -ʃɪə) *n.* a state of serious emotional and mental deterioration, of organic or functional origin. [C19: from Latin: madness; see DEMENT]
de+men+tia prae+cox (ˈpri:kɒks) *n.* schizophrenia. [C19: New Latin, literally: premature dementia]
dem+e+rar·a (ˌdɛməˈrɛərə, -ˈrɑ:rə) *n.* **1.** brown crystallized cane sugar from the West Indies and nearby countries. **2.** a highly flavoured rum used mainly for blending purposes. [C19: named after *Demerara,* Guyana]
Dem·e·rar·a (ˌdɛməˈrɛərə, -ˈrɑ:rə) *n.* **the.** a river in Guyana, rising in the central forest area and flowing north to the Atlantic at Georgetown. Length: 346 km (215 miles).
de+mer+it (di:ˈmɛrɪt, ˈdi:ˌmɛrɪt) *n.* **1.** something, esp. conduct, that deserves censure. **2.** *U.S.* a mark given against a person for failure or misconduct, esp. in schools or the armed forces. **3.** a fault or disadvantage. [C14 (originally: worth, desert, later specialized to mean: something worthy of blame): from Latin *dēmerērī* to deserve] —**de+ˌmer+i+ˈto+ri+ous** *adj.* —**de+ˌmer+i+ˈto+ri+ous+ly** *adv.*
de+mer+sal (dɪˈmɜ:sᵊl) *adj.* living or occurring in deep water or on the bottom of a sea or lake: *demersal fish.* [C19: from Latin *dēmersus* submerged (from *dēmergere* to plunge into, from *mergere* to dip) + -AL[1]]
de+mesne (dɪˈmeɪn, -ˈmi:n) *n.* **1.** land, esp. surrounding a house or manor, retained by the owner for his own use. **2.** *Property law.* the possession and use of one's own property or land. **3.** the territory ruled by a state or a sovereign; realm; domain. **4.** a region or district; domain. [C14: from Old French *demeine;* see DOMAIN]
De·me·ter (dɪˈmi:tə) *n. Greek myth.* the goddess of agricultural fertility and protector of marriage and women. Roman counterpart: **Ceres.**
dem·i- *prefix.* **1.** half: *demirelief.* Compare **hemi-, semi-** (sense 1). **2.** of less than full size, status, or rank: *demigod.* [via French from Medieval Latin *dīmedius,* from Latin *dīmidius* half, from *dis-* apart + *medius* middle]
dem·i+bas+ti+on (ˌdɛmɪˈbæstɪən) *n.* *Fortifications.* half a bastion, having only one flank.
dem·i+can+ton (ˌdɛmɪˈkæntɒn, -kænˈtɒn) *n.* either of the two parts of certain Swiss cantons.
dem·i+god (ˈdɛmɪˌgɒd) *n.* **1. a.** a mythological being who is part mortal, part god. **b.** a lesser deity. **2.** a person with outstanding or godlike attributes. [C16: translation of Latin *sēmideus*] —ˈ**dem·i+ˌgod+dess** *fem. n.*
dem·i+john (ˈdɛmɪˌdʒɒn) *n.* a large bottle with a short narrow neck, often with small handles at the neck and encased in wickerwork. [C18: probably by folk etymology from French *dame-jeanne,* from *dame* lady + *Jeanne* Jane]
de+mil·i+ta+rize *or* **de+mil·i+ta+rise** (di:ˈmɪlɪtəˌraɪz) *vb.* (*tr.*) **1.** to remove and prohibit any military presence or function in (an area): *demilitarized zone.* **2.** to free of military character, purpose, etc.: *11 regiments were demilitarized.* —**de+ˌmil·i+ta+ri+ˈza+tion** *or* **de+ˌmil·i+ta+ri+ˈsa+tion** *n.*
De Mille (də ˈmɪl) *n.* **Cec·il B(lount).** 1881–1959, U.S. motion-picture producer and director.
dem·i+lune (ˈdɛmɪˌlu:n, -ˌlju:n) *n.* **1.** *Fortifications.* an outwork in front of a fort, shaped like a crescent moon. **2.** a crescent-shaped object or formation; half-moon. [C18: from French, literally: half-moon]
dem·i+mon+daine (ˌdɛmɪˈmɒndeɪn; *French* dəmimɔ̃ˈdɛn) *n.* a woman of the demimonde. [C19: from French]
dem·i+monde (ˌdɛmɪˈmɒnd; *French* dəmiˈmɔ̃d) *n.* **1.** (esp. in the 19th century) those women considered to be outside respectable society, esp. on account of sexual promiscuity. **2.** any social group considered to be not wholly respectable. [C19: from French, literally: half-world]
de+min+er+al+ize *or* **de+min+er+al+ise** (di:ˈmɪnərəˌlaɪz) *vb.* (*tr.*) to remove dissolved salts from (a liquid, esp. water). —**de+ˌmin+er+al·i+ˈza+tion** *or* **de+ˌmin+er+al·i+ˈsa+tion** *n.*
de·mi-pen·sion *French.* (dəmipɑ̃ˈsjɔ̃) *n.* another name for **half board.**
De·mi·rel (*Turkish* dɛmɪˈrel) *n.* **Sü·ley·man** (sylɛɪˈman). born 1924, Turkish statesman; prime minister of Turkey (1965–71; 1975–77).
dem·i+re·lief (ˌdɛmɪrɪˈli:f) *n.* a less common term for **mezzo-rilievo.**
dem·i+rep (ˈdɛmɪˌrɛp) *n. Rare.* a woman of bad repute, esp. a prostitute. [C18: from DEMI- + REP(UTATION)]
de+mise (dɪˈmaɪz) *n.* **1.** failure or termination: *the demise of one's hopes.* **2.** a euphemistic or formal word for **death. 3.** *Property law.* **a.** a transfer of an estate by lease. **b.** the passing or transfer of an estate on the death of the owner. **4.** the immediate transfer of sovereignty to a successor upon the death, abdication, etc., of a ruler (esp. in the phrase **demise of the crown**). ~*vb.* **5.** to transfer or be transferred by inheritance, will, or succession. **6.** (*tr.*) *Property law.* to transfer (an estate, etc.) for a limited period; lease. **7.** (*tr.*) to transfer (sovereignty, a title, etc.) by or as if by the death, deposition, etc., of a ruler. [C16: from Old French, feminine of *demis* dismissed, from *demettre* to send away, from Latin *dīmittere;* see DISMISS] —**de+ˈmis+a·ble** *adj.*
dem·i+sem·i+qua+ver (ˈdɛmɪˌsɛmɪˌkweɪvə) *n. Music.* a note having the time value of one thirty-second of a semibreve. Usual U.S. name: **thirty-second note.**
de+mis+sion (dɪˈmɪʃən) *n. Rare.* relinquishment of or abdication from an office, responsibility, etc. [C16: from Anglo-French *dimissioun,* from Latin *dīmissiō* a dismissing; see DISMISS]
de+mist (di:ˈmɪst) *vb.* to free or become free of condensation through evaporation produced by a heater and/or blower. —**de+ˈmist+er** *n.*
de+mit (dɪˈmɪt) *vb.* **+mits, +mit+ting, +mit+ted.** *Archaic, chiefly Scot.* **1.** to resign (an office, position, etc.). **2.** (*tr.*) to dismiss. [C16: from Latin *dīmittere* to send forth, discharge, renounce, from DI-[2] + *mittere* to send]
dem·i+tasse (ˈdɛmɪˌtæs; *French* dəmiˈtas) *n.* **1.** a small cup for serving black coffee, as after dinner. **2.** the coffee itself. [C19: French, literally: half-cup]
dem·i+urge (ˈdɛmɪˌɜ:dʒ, ˈdi:-) *n.* **1. a.** (in the philosophy of Plato) the creator of the universe. **b.** (in Gnostic and some other philosophies) the creator of the universe, supernatural but subordinate to the Supreme Being. **2.** (in ancient Greece) a magistrate with varying powers found in any of several states. [C17: from Church Latin *dēmiūrgus,* from Greek *dēmiourgos* skilled workman, literally: one who works for the people, from *dēmos* people + *ergon* work] —**ˌdem·i+ˈur+geous, ˌdem·i+ˈur+gic,** *or* **ˌdem·i+ˈur+gi+cal** *adj.* —**ˌdem·i+ˈur+gi+cal+ly** *adv.*
dem·i+vierge (ˈdɛmɪˌvjɛəʒ) *n.* a woman who engages in promiscuous sexual activity but retains her virginity. [C20: French, literally: half-virgin]
dem·i+volt *or* **dem·i+volte** (ˈdɛmɪˌvɒlt) *n. Dressage.* a half turn on the hind legs.
dem·o (ˈdɛməʊ) *n., pl.* **·os.** short for **demonstration.**
dem·o- *or before a vowel* **dem-** *combining form.* indicating people or population: *demography.* [from Greek *dēmos*]
de+mob (di:ˈmɒb) *Brit. informal.* ~*vb.* **+mobs, +mob+bing, +mobbed. 1.** See **demobilize.** ~*n.* **2. a.** See **demobilization. b.** (*as modifier*): *a demob suit.* **3.** a soldier who has been demobilized.
de+mo+bi+lize *or* **de+mo+bi+lise** (di:ˈməʊbɪˌlaɪz) *vb.* to disband, as troops, etc. —**de+ˌmo+bi+li+ˈza+tion** *or* **de+ˌmo+bi+li+ˈsa+tion** *n.*
de+moc+ra+cy (dɪˈmɒkrəsɪ) *n., pl.* **+cies. 1.** government by the people or their elected representatives. **2.** control of any organization by its members: *industrial democracy.* **3.** a political or social unit governed ultimately by all its members. **4.** the practice or spirit of social equality. **5.** a social condition of classlessness and equality. **6.** the common people, esp. as a political force. [C16: from French *démocratie,* from Late Latin *dēmocratia,* from Greek *dēmokratia* government by the people; see DEMO-, -CRACY]
dem·o+crat (ˈdɛməˌkræt) *n.* **1.** an advocate of democracy; adherent of democratic principles. **2.** a member or supporter of a democratic party or movement.
Dem·o+crat (ˈdɛməˌkræt) *n. U.S. politics.* a member or supporter of the Democratic Party. —**ˌDem·o+ˈcrat+ic** *adj.*
dem·o+crat+ic (ˌdɛməˈkrætɪk) *adj.* **1.** of, characterized by,

derived from, or relating to the principles of democracy. **2.** upholding or favouring democracy or the interests of the common people. **3.** popular with or for the benefit of all: *democratic sports.* —ˌ**dem·o·'crat·i·cal·ly** *adv.*

Dem·o·crat·ic Par·ty *n. U.S. politics.* the older of the two major political parties, so named since 1840. Compare **Republican Party.**

Dem·o·crat·ic-Re·pub·li·can Par·ty *n. U.S. history.* the antifederalist party originally led by Thomas Jefferson, which developed into the modern Democratic Party.

de·moc·ra·tize *or* **de·moc·ra·tise** (dɪ'mɒkrəˌtaɪz) *vb. (tr.)* to make democratic. —**de·ˌmoc·ra·ti·'za·tion** *or* **de·ˌmoc·ra·ti·'sa·tion** *n.*

De·moc·ri·tus (dɪ'mɒkrɪtəs) *n.* ?460–?370 B.C., Greek philosopher who developed the atomist theory of matter of his teacher, Leucippus. See also **atomism.**

dé·mo·dé *French.* (demɔ'de) *adj.* out of fashion; outmoded. [French, from *dé-* out of + *mode* style, fashion]

de·mod·u·late (diː'mɒdjʊˌleɪt) *vb.* to carry out demodulation on (a wave or signal). —**de·'mod·u·ˌla·tor** *n.*

de·mod·u·la·tion (ˌdiːmɒdjʊ'leɪʃən) *n. Electronics.* the act or process by which an output wave or signal is obtained having the characteristics of the original modulating wave or signal; the reverse of modulation.

De·mo·gor·gon (ˌdiːməʊ'gɔːgən) *n.* a mysterious and awesome god in ancient mythology, often represented as ruling in the underworld. [C16: via Late Latin from Greek]

de·mog·ra·phy (dɪ'mɒgrəfɪ) *n.* the science of population statistics. [C19: from French *démographie,* from Greek *dēmos* the populace; see -GRAPHY] —**de·'mog·ra·pher** *or* **de·'mog·ra·phist** *n.* —**de·mo·graph·ic** (ˌdiːmə'græfɪk, ˌdɛmə-) *or* ˌ**de·mo·'graph·i·cal** *adj.* —ˌ**de·mo·'graph·i·cal·ly** *adv.*

dem·oi·selle (dəmwɑː'zɛl) *n.* **1.** Also called: **demoiselle crane, Numidian crane.** a small crane, *Anthropoides virgo,* of central Asia, N Africa, and SE Europe, having grey plumage with long black breast feathers and white ear tufts. **2.** a less common name for a **damselfly. 3.** another name for **damselfish. 4.** a literary word for **damsel.** [C16: from French: young woman; see DAMSEL]

de·mol·ish (dɪ'mɒlɪʃ) *vb. (tr.)* **1.** to tear down or break up (buildings, etc.). **2.** to destroy; put an end to (an argument, etc.). **3.** *Facetious.* to eat up: *she demolished the whole cake!* [C16: from French *démolir,* from Latin *dēmōlīrī* to throw down, destroy, from DE- + *mōlīrī* to strive, toil, construct, from *mōles* mass, bulk] —**de·'mol·ish·er** *n.* —**de·'mol·ish·ment** *n.*

dem·o·li·tion (ˌdɛmə'lɪʃən, ˌdiː-) *n.* **1.** the act of demolishing or state of being demolished. **2.** *Chiefly military.* **a.** destruction by explosives. **b.** (*as modifier*)*: a demolition charge.* —ˌ**dem·o·'li·tion·ist** *n., adj.*

dem·o·li·tions (ˌdɛmə'lɪʃənz, ˌdiː-) *pl. n. Chiefly military.* **a.** explosives, as when used to blow up bridges, etc. **b.** (*as modifier*)*: a demolitions expert.*

de·mon ('diːmən) *n.* **1.** an evil spirit or devil. **2.** a person, habit, obsession, etc., thought of as evil, cruel, or persistently tormenting. **3.** Also called: **daemon, daimon.** an attendant or ministering spirit; genius: *the demon of inspiration.* **4. a.** a person who is extremely skilful in, energetic at, or devoted to a given activity, esp. a sport: *a demon at cycling.* **b.** (*as modifier*)*: a demon cyclist.* **5.** a variant spelling of **daemon** (sense 1). **6.** *Austral. informal.* a detective or policeman. [C15: from Latin *daemōn* evil spirit, spirit, from Greek *daimōn* spirit, deity, fate; see DAEMON]

de·mon·e·tize *or* **de·mon·e·tise** (diː'mʌnɪˌtaɪz) *vb. (tr.)* **1.** to deprive (a metal) of its capacity as a monetary standard. **2.** to withdraw from use as currency. —**de·ˌmon·e·ti·'za·tion** *or* **de·ˌmon·e·ti·'sa·tion** *n.*

de·mo·ni·ac (dɪ'məʊnɪˌæk) *adj. also* **de·mo·ni·a·cal** (ˌdiːmə'naɪəkᵊl). **1.** of, like, or suggestive of a demon; demonic. **2.** suggesting inner possession or inspiration: *the demoniac fire of genius.* **3.** frantic; frenzied; feverish: *demoniac activity.* ~*n.* **4.** a person possessed by an evil spirit or demon. —ˌ**de·mo·'ni·a·cal·ly** *adv.*

de·mon·ic (dɪ'mɒnɪk) *adj.* **1.** of, relating to, or characteristic of a demon; fiendish. **2.** inspired or possessed by a demon, or seemingly so: *demonic laughter.* —**de·'mon·i·cal·ly** *adv.*

de·mon·ism ('diːməˌnɪzəm) *n.* **1. a.** belief in the existence and power of demons. **b.** worship of demons. **2.** another word for **demonology.** —**'de·mon·ist** *n.*

de·mon·ize *or* **de·mon·ise** ('diːməˌnaɪz) *vb. (tr.)* **1.** to make into or like a demon. **2.** to subject to demonic influence.

de·mon·ol·a·ter (ˌdiːmə'nɒlətə) *n.* a person who worships demons. [C19: back formation from DEMONOLATRY]

de·mon·ol·a·try (ˌdiːmə'nɒlətrɪ) *n.* the worship of demons. [C17: see DEMON, -LATRY]

de·mon·ol·o·gy (ˌdiːmə'nɒlədʒɪ) *n.* the study of demons or demonic beliefs. Also called: **demonism.** —**de·mon·o·log·i·cal** (ˌdiːmənə'lɒdʒɪkᵊl) *adj.* —ˌ**de·mon·'ol·o·gist** *n.*

de·mon·stra·ble (dɪ'mɒnstrəbᵊl, 'dɛmən-) *adj.* able to be demonstrated or proved. —**de·ˌmon·stra·'bil·i·ty** *or* **de·'mon·stra·ble·ness** *n.* —**de·'mon·stra·bly** *adv.*

dem·on·strate ('dɛmənˌstreɪt) *vb.* **1.** (*tr.*) to show, manifest, or prove, esp. by reasoning, evidence, etc. **2.** (*tr.*) to explain or illustrate by experiment, example, etc. **3.** (*tr.*) to display, operate, and explain the workings of (a machine, product, etc.). **4.** (*intr.*) to manifest support, protest, etc., by public parades or rallies. **5.** (*intr.*) to be employed as a demonstrator of machinery, etc. **6.** (*intr.*) *Military.* to make a show of force, esp. in order to deceive one's enemy. [C16: from Latin *dēmonstrāre* to point out, from *monstrāre* to show]

dem·on·stra·tion (ˌdɛmən'streɪʃən) *n.* **1.** the act of demonstrating. **2.** proof or evidence leading to proof. **3. a.** an explanation, display, illustration, or experiment showing how something works. **b.** (*as modifier*)*: a demonstration model.* **4.** a manifestation of grievances, support, or protest by public rallies, parades, etc. **5.** a manifestation of emotion. **6.** a show of military force or preparedness. **7.** *Maths.* a logical presentation of the assumptions and equations used in solving a problem or proving a theorem. —ˌ**de·mon·'stra·tion·al** *adj.* —ˌ**de·mon·'stra·tion·ist** *n.*

de·mon·stra·tive (dɪ'mɒnstrətɪv) *adj.* **1.** tending to manifest or express one's feelings easily or unreservedly. **2.** (*postpositive;* foll. by *of*) serving as proof; indicative. **3.** involving or characterized by demonstration: *a demonstrative lecture.* **4.** conclusive; indubitable: *demonstrative arguments.* **5.** *Grammar.* denoting or belonging to a class of determiners used to point out the individual referent or referents intended, such as *this, that, these,* and *those.* Compare **interrogative, relative.** ~*n.* **6.** *Grammar.* a demonstrative word or construction. —**de·'mon·stra·tive·ly** *adv.* —**de·'mon·stra·tive·ness** *n.*

de·mon·stra·tor ('dɛmənˌstreɪtə) *n.* **1.** a person who demonstrates equipment, machines, products, etc. **2.** a person who takes part in a public demonstration.

de·mor·al·ize *or* **de·mor·al·ise** (dɪ'mɒrəˌlaɪz) *vb. (tr.)* **1.** to undermine the morale of; dishearten: *he was demoralized by his defeat.* **2.** to debase morally; corrupt. **3.** to throw into confusion. —**de·ˌmor·al·i·'za·tion** *or* **de·ˌmor·al·i·'sa·tion** *n.* —**de·'mor·al·ˌiz·er** *or* **de·'mor·al·ˌis·er** *n.*

de·mos ('diːmɒs) *n.* **1.** the people of a nation regarded as a political unit. **2.** *Rare.* the common people; masses. [C19: from Greek: the populace; see DEME]

De·mos·the·nes (dɪ'mɒsθəˌniːz) *n.* 384–322 B.C., Athenian statesman, orator, and lifelong opponent of the power of Macedonia over Greece.

de·mote (dɪ'məʊt) *vb. (tr.)* to lower in rank or position; relegate. [C19: from DE- + (PRO)MOTE] —**de·'mo·tion** *n.*

de·mot·ic (dɪ'mɒtɪk) *adj.* **1.** of or relating to the common people; popular. **2.** of or relating to a simplified form of hieroglyphics used in ancient Egypt by the ordinary literate class outside the priesthood. Compare **hieratic.** ~*n.* **3.** the demotic script of ancient Egypt. [C19: from Greek *dēmotikos* of the people, from *dēmotēs* a man of the people, commoner; see DEMOS] —**de·'mot·ist** *n.*

De·mot·ic (dɪ'mɒtɪk) *n.* **1.** the spoken form of Modern Greek, now increasingly used in literature. Compare **Katharevusa.** ~*adj.* **2.** denoting or relating to this.

de·mount (diː'maʊnt) *vb. (tr.)* to remove (a motor, gun, etc.) from its mounting or setting. —**de·'mount·a·ble** *adj.*

Demp·sey ('dɛmpsɪ) *n.* **Jack.** original name *William Harrison Dempsey.* 1895–1983, U.S. boxer; world heavyweight champion (1919–26).

demp·ster ('dɛmpstə) *n.* a variant spelling of **deemster.**

de·mul·cent (dɪ'mʌlsᵊnt) *adj.* **1.** soothing; mollifying. ~*n.* **2.** a drug or agent that soothes the irritation of inflamed or injured skin surfaces. [C18: from Latin *dēmulcēre* to caress soothingly, from DE- + *mulcēre* to stroke]

de·mul·si·fy (diː'mʌlsɪˌfaɪ) *vb.* **·fies, ·fy·ing, ·fied.** to undergo or cause to undergo a process in which an emulsion is permanently broken down into its constituents. [C20: from DE- + EMULSIFY] —**de·ˌmul·si·fi·'ca·tion** *n.* —**de·'mul·si·ˌfi·er** *n.*

de·mur (dɪ'mɜː) *vb.* **·murs, ·mur·ring, ·murred.** (*intr.*) **1.** to raise objections or show reluctance; object. **2.** *Law.* to raise an objection by entering a demurrer. **3.** *Archaic.* to hesitate; delay. ~*n. also* **de·mur·ral** (dɪ'mʌrəl). **4.** the act of demurring. **5.** an objection raised. **6.** *Archaic.* hesitation. [C13: from Old French *demorer,* from Latin *dēmorārī* to loiter, linger, from *morārī* to delay, from *mora* a delay] —**de·'mur·ra·ble** *adj.*

de·mure (dɪ'mjʊə) *adj.* **1.** sedate; decorous; reserved. **2.** affectedly modest or prim; coy. [C14: perhaps from Old French *demorer* to delay, linger; perhaps influenced by *meur* ripe, MATURE] —**de·'mure·ly** *adv.* —**de·'mure·ness** *n.*

de·mur·rage (dɪ'mʌrɪdʒ) *n.* **1.** the delaying of a ship, railway wagon, etc., caused by the charterer's failure to load, unload, etc., before the time of scheduled departure. **2.** the extra charge required as compensation for such delay. **3.** a fee charged by the Bank of England for changing bullion into notes.

de·mur·rer (dɪ'mʌrə) *n.* **1.** *Law.* a pleading that admits an opponent's point but denies that it is a relevant or valid argument. **2.** any objection raised.

de·my (dɪ'maɪ) *n., pl.* **·mies. 1. a.** a size of printing paper, 17½ by 22½ inches (444.5 × 571.5 mm). **b.** a size of writing paper, 15½ by 20 inches (Brit.) (393.7 × 508 mm) or 16 by 21 inches (U.S.) (406.4 × 533.4 mm). **2.** either one of two book sizes, 8½ by 5½ inches (**demy octavo**) or (chiefly Brit.) 11¼ by 8¾ inches (**demy quarto**). [C16: see DEMI-]

de·mys·ti·fy (diː'mɪstɪˌfaɪ) *vb.* **·fies, ·fy·ing, ·fied.** (*tr.*) to remove the mystery from; make clear. —**de·ˌmys·ti·fi·'ca·tion** *n.*

de·my·thol·o·gize *or* **de·my·thol·o·gise** (ˌdiːmɪ'θɒləˌdʒaɪz) *vb. (tr.)* **1.** to eliminate all mythical elements from (a piece of writing, esp. the Bible) so as to arrive at an essential meaning. **2.** to restate (a message, esp. a religious one) in rational terms. —ˌ**de·my·ˌthol·o·gi·'za·tion** *or* ˌ**de·my·ˌthol·o·gi·'sa·tion** *n.*

den (dɛn) *n.* **1.** the habitat or retreat of a lion or similar wild animal; lair. **2.** a small or secluded room in a home, often used for carrying on a hobby. **3.** a squalid or wretched room or retreat. **4.** a site or haunt: *a den of vice.* **5.** *Scot.* a small wooded valley; dingle. **6.** *Scot. and northern Brit. dialect.* a place of sanctuary in certain catching games; home or base. ~*vb.* **dens, den·ning, denned. 7.** (*intr.*) to live in or as if in a den. [Old English *denn;* related to Old High German *tenni* threshing floor, early Dutch *denne* low ground, den, cave]

Den. *abbrev. for* Denmark.

de·nar·i·us (dɪˈnɛərɪəs) *n., pl.* **·nar·i·i** (-ˈnɛərɪˌaɪ). **1.** a silver coin of ancient Rome, often called a penny in translation. **2.** a gold coin worth 25 silver denarii. [C16: from Latin: coin originally equal to ten asses, from *dēnārius* (adj.) containing ten, from *dēnī* ten each, from *decem* ten]

de·na·ry (ˈdiːnərɪ) *adj.* **1.** calculated by tens; based on ten; decimal. **2.** containing ten parts; tenfold. [C16: from Latin *dēnārius* containing ten; see DENARIUS]

de·na·tion·al·ize *or* **de·na·tion·al·ise** (diːˈnæʃənᵊˌlaɪz) *vb.* **1.** to return or transfer (an industry, etc.) from public to private ownership. **2.** to deprive (an individual, people, institution, etc.) of national character or nationality. —**de·ˌna·tion·al·i·ˈza·tion** *or* **de·ˌna·tion·al·i·ˈsa·tion** *n.*

de·nat·u·ral·ize *or* **de·nat·u·ral·ise** (diːˈnætʃrəˌlaɪz) *vb.* (*tr.*) **1.** to deprive of nationality. **2.** to make unnatural. —**de·ˌnat·u·ral·i·ˈza·tion** *or* **de·ˌnat·u·ral·i·ˈsa·tion** *n.*

de·na·ture (diːˈneɪtʃə) *or* **de·na·tur·ize, de·na·tur·ise** (diːˈneɪtʃəˌraɪz) *vb.* (*tr.*) **1.** to change the nature of. **2.** to change (a protein) by chemical or physical means, such as the action of acid or heat, to cause loss of solubility, biological activity, etc. **3.** to render (ethyl alcohol) unfit for drinking by adding methanol or other nauseous substances. **4.** to render (fissile material) unfit for use in nuclear weapons by addition of an isotope. —**de·ˈna·tur·ant** *n.* —**de·ˌna·tur·ˈa·tion** *n.*

de·na·zi·fy (diːˈnɑːtsɪˌfaɪ) *vb.* **·fies, ·fy·ing, ·fied.** (*tr.*) to free or declare (people, institutions, etc.) freed from Nazi influence or ideology. —**de·ˌna·zi·fi·ˈca·tion** *n.*

Den·bigh·shire (ˈdɛnbɪˌʃɪə, -ʃə) *n.* (until 1974) a county of N Wales, now part of Clwyd.

den·dri·form (ˈdɛndrɪˌfɔːm) *adj.* branching or treelike in appearance.

den·drite (ˈdɛndraɪt) *n.* **1.** any of the short branched threadlike extensions of a nerve cell, which conduct impulses towards the cell body. **2.** a branching mosslike crystalline structure in some rocks and minerals. **3.** a crystal that has branched during growth and has a treelike form. [C18: from Greek *dendritēs* relating to a tree] —**den·drit·ic** (dɛnˈdrɪtɪk) *or* **den·ˈdrit·i·cal** *adj.* —**den·ˈdrit·i·cal·ly** *adv.*

den·dro-, den·dri-, *or before a vowel* **dendr-** *combining form.* tree: *dendrochronology; dendrite.* [New Latin, from Greek, from *dendron* tree]

den·dro·chro·nol·o·gy (ˌdɛndrəʊkrəˈnɒlədʒɪ) *n.* the study of the annual rings of trees, used esp. to date past events. —**den·dro·chron·o·log·i·cal** (ˌdɛndrəʊˌkrɒnᵊˈlɒdʒɪkᵊl) *adj.*

den·droid (ˈdɛndrɔɪd) *or* **den·droi·dal** (dɛnˈdrɔɪdᵊl) *adj.* **1.** freely branching; arborescent; treelike. **2.** (esp. of tree ferns) having a tall trunklike stem. [C19: from Greek *dendroeidēs* like a tree]

den·drol·o·gy (dɛnˈdrɒlədʒɪ) *n.* the branch of botany that is concerned with the natural history of trees and shrubs. —**den·dro·log·i·cal** (ˌdɛndrəˈlɒdʒɪkᵊl), **ˌden·dro·ˈlog·ic,** *or* **den·ˈdrol·o·gous** *adj.* —**den·ˈdrol·o·gist** *n.*

dene[1] *or* **dean** (diːn) *n. Brit.* a valley, esp. one that is narrow and wooded. [Old English *denu* valley; see DEN]

dene[2] *or* **dean** (diːn) *n. Dialect, chiefly southern Brit.* a sandy stretch of land or dune near the sea. [C13: probably related to Old English *dūn* hill; see DOWN[3]]

Den·eb (ˈdɛnɛb) *n.* the brightest star in the constellation Cygnus and one of the brightest but remotest stars in the night sky. Visual magnitude: 1.3; spectral type: A2. [C19: from Arabic *dhanab* a tail]

De·neb·o·la (dɪˈnɛbələ) *n.* the second brightest star in the constellation Leo. Visual magnitude: 2.2; spectral type: A2. [from Arabic *dhanab al-(asad)* tail of the (lion)]

de·ne·ga·tion (ˌdɛnɪˈgeɪʃən) *n.* a denial, contradiction, or refusal. [C17: from Late Latin *dēnegātiō*, from Latin *dēnegāre* to deny, refuse, from *negāre* to deny]

D.Eng. *abbrev. for* Doctor of Engineering.

den·gue (ˈdɛŋgɪ) *or* **dan·dy** (ˈdændɪ) *n.* an acute viral disease transmitted by mosquitoes, characterized by headache, fever, pains in the joints, and skin rash. Also called: **breakbone fever.** [C19: from Spanish, probably of African origin; compare Swahili *kidinga*]

Den Haag (dɛn ˈhaːx) *n.* the Dutch name for (The) **Hague.**

Den Hel·der (*Dutch* dɛn ˈhɛldər) *n.* a port in the W Netherlands, in North Holland province: fortified by Napoleon in 1811; naval station. Pop.: 61 457 (1973 est.).

de·ni·a·ble (dɪˈnaɪəbᵊl) *adj.* able to be denied; questionable. —**de·ˈni·a·bly** *adv.*

de·ni·al (dɪˈnaɪəl) *n.* **1.** a refusal to agree or comply with a statement; contradiction. **2.** the rejection of the truth of a proposition, doctrine, etc.: *a denial of God's existence.* **3.** a negative reply; rejection of a request. **4.** a refusal to acknowledge; renunciation; disavowal: *a denial of one's leader.* **5.** a psychological process in which painful truths are forced out of an individual's consciousness. See also **defence mechanism. 6.** abstinence; self-denial.

den·ier[1] *n.* **1.** (ˈdɛnɪˌeɪ, ˈdɛnjə). a unit of weight used to measure the fineness of silk and man-made fibres, esp. when woven into women's tights, etc. It is equal to 1 gram per 9000 metres. **2.** (dəˈnjeɪ, -ˈnɪə). any of several former European coins of various denominations. [C15: from Old French: coin, from Latin *dēnārius* DENARIUS]

de·ni·er[2] (dɪˈnaɪə) *n.* a person who denies.

den·i·grate (ˈdɛnɪˌgreɪt) *vb.* **1.** to belittle or disparage the character of; defame. **2.** a rare word for **blacken.** [C16: from Latin *dēnigrāre* to make very black, defame, from *nigrāre* to blacken, from *niger* black] —**ˌden·i·ˈgra·tion** *n.* —**ˈden·i·ˌgra·tor** *n.*

den·im (ˈdɛnɪm) *n. Textiles.* **1. a.** a hard-wearing twill-weave cotton fabric used for trousers, work clothes, etc. **b.** (*as modifier*): *a denim jacket.* **2. a.** a similar lighter fabric used in upholstery. **b.** (*as modifier*): *denim cushion covers.* [C17: from French (*serge*) *de Nîmes* (serge) of NÎMES]

den·ims (ˈdɛnɪmz) *pl. n.* jeans or overalls made of denim.

Den·is (ˈdɛnɪs; *French* dəˈni) *n.* **1. Mau·rice** (mɔˈris). 1870–1943, French painter and writer on art. One of the leading Nabis, he defined a picture as "essentially a flat surface covered with colours assembled in a certain order." **2. Saint.** Also: **Denys.** 3rd century A.D., first bishop of Paris; patron saint of France. Feast day: Oct. 9.

de·ni·trate (diːˈnaɪtreɪt) *vb.* to undergo or cause to undergo a process in which a compound loses a nitro or nitrate group, nitrogen dioxide, or nitric acid. —**ˌde·ni·ˈtra·tion** *n.*

de·ni·tri·fy (diːˈnaɪtrɪˌfaɪ) *vb.* **·fies, ·fy·ing, ·fied.** to undergo or cause to undergo loss or removal of nitrogen compounds or nitrogen. —**de·ˌni·tri·fi·ˈca·tion** *n.*

den·i·zen (ˈdɛnɪzən) *n.* **1.** an inhabitant; occupant; resident. **2.** *Brit.* an individual permanently resident in a foreign country where he enjoys certain rights of citizenship. **3.** a plant or animal established in a place to which it is not native. **4.** a naturalized foreign word. ~*vb.* **5.** (*tr.*) to make a denizen. [C15: from Anglo-French *denisein,* from Old French *denzein,* from *denz* within, from Latin *de intus* from within]

Den·mark (ˈdɛnmɑːk) *n.* a kingdom in N Europe, between the Baltic and the North Sea: consists of the mainland of Jutland and about 100 inhabited islands (chiefly Zealand, Lolland, Funen, Falster, Langeland, and Bornholm); extended its territory throughout the Middle Ages, ruling Sweden until 1523 and Norway until 1814, and incorporating Greenland as a province in 1953; joined the Common Market in 1973; an important exporter of dairy produce. Language: Danish. Religion: chiefly Lutheran. Currency: krone. Capital: Copenhagen. Pop.: 5 059 000 (1975 est.). Area: 43 031 sq. km (16 614 sq. miles). Danish name: **Danmark.**

Den·mark Strait *n.* a channel between SE Greenland and Iceland, linking the Arctic Ocean with the Atlantic.

Den·ning (ˈdɛnɪŋ) *n.* Baron **Al·fred Thomp·son.** born 1899, English judge; Master of the Rolls since 1962.

denom. *abbrev. for* (religious) denomination.

de·nom·i·nate *vb.* (dɪˈnɒmɪˌneɪt). **1.** (*tr.*) to give a specific name to; designate. ~*adj.* (dɪˈnɒmɪnɪt, -ˌneɪt). **2.** *Maths.* (of a number) representing a multiple of a unit of measurement: *4 is the denominate number in 4 miles.* —**de·ˈnom·i·na·ble** *adj.*

de·nom·i·na·tion (dɪˌnɒmɪˈneɪʃən) *n.* **1.** a group having a distinctive interpretation of a religious faith and usually its own organization. **2.** a grade or unit in a series of designations of value, weight, measure, etc.: *coins of this denomination are being withdrawn.* **3.** a name given to a class or group; classification. **4.** the act of giving a name. **5.** a name; designation. —**de·ˌnom·i·ˈna·tion·al** *adj.* —**de·ˌnom·i·ˈna·tion·al·ly** *adv.*

de·nom·i·na·tion·al·ism (dɪˌnɒmɪˈneɪʃənᵊˌlɪzəm) *n.* **1.** adherence to particular principles, esp. to the tenets of a religious denomination; sectarianism. **2.** the tendency to divide or cause to divide into sects or denominations. **3.** division into denominations. —**de·ˌnom·i·ˈna·tion·al·ist** *n., adj.*

de·nom·i·na·tive (dɪˈnɒmɪnətɪv) *adj.* **1.** giving or constituting a name; naming. **2.** *Grammar.* **a.** (of a word other than a noun) formed from or having the same form as a noun. **b.** (*as n.*): *the verb "to mushroom" is a denominative.* —**de·ˈnom·i·na·tive·ly** *adv.*

de·nom·i·na·tor (dɪˈnɒmɪˌneɪtə) *n.* **1.** the divisor of a fraction, as 8 in $\frac{7}{8}$. Compare **numerator** (sense 1). **2.** *Archaic.* a person or thing that denominates or designates.

de·no·ta·tion (ˌdiːnəʊˈteɪʃən) *n.* **1.** the act or process of denoting; indication. **2.** a sign, term, symbol, etc., that denotes; name. **3.** a particular meaning given by a sign or symbol; something designated or referred to. **4.** explicit or specific meaning as distinguished from suggestive meaning and associations. Compare **connotation. 5.** *Logic.* another name for **extension** (sense 11).

de·no·ta·tive (dɪˈnəʊtətɪv) *adj.* **1.** able to denote; designative. **2.** explicit; overt. —**de·ˈno·ta·tive·ly** *adv.*

de·note (dɪˈnəʊt) *vb.* (*tr.; may take a clause as object*) **1.** to be a sign, symbol, or symptom of; indicate or designate. **2.** (of words, phrases, expressions, etc.) to have as a literal or obvious meaning. [C16: from Latin *dēnotāre* to mark, from *notāre* to mark, NOTE] —**de·ˈnot·a·ble** *adj.* —**de·ˈnote·ment** *n.*

de·noue·ment (deɪˈnuːmɒn) *or* **dé·noue·ment** (*French* denuˈmã) *n.* **1. a.** the final clarification or resolution of a plot in a play or other work. **b.** the point at which this occurs. **2.** final outcome; solution. [C18: from French, literally: an untying, from *dénouer* to untie, from Old French *desnoer*, from *des-* DE- + *noer* to tie, knot, from Latin *nōdāre*, from *nōdus* a knot; see NODE]

de·nounce (dɪˈnaʊns) *vb.* (*tr.*) **1.** to deplore or condemn openly or vehemently. **2.** to give information against; accuse. **3.** to announce formally the termination of (a treaty, etc.). **4.** *Obsolete.* **a.** to announce (something evil). **b.** to portend. [C13: from Old French *denoncier* to proclaim, from Latin *dēnuntiāre* to make an official proclamation, threaten, from DE- + *nuntiāre* to announce] —**de·'nounce·ment** *n.* —**de·'nounc·er** *n.*

de no·vo *Latin.* (di: 'nəʊvəʊ) *adv.* from the beginning; anew.

dense (dɛns) *adj.* **1.** thickly crowded or closely set: *a dense crowd.* **2.** thick; impenetrable: *a dense fog.* **3.** *Physics.* having a high density. **4.** stupid; dull; obtuse. **5.** (of a photographic negative) having many dark or exposed areas. **6.** (of an optical glass, colour, etc.) transmitting little or no light. [C15: from Latin *densus* thick; related to Greek *dasus* thickly covered with hair or leaves] —**'dense·ly** *adv.* —**'dense·ness** *n.*

den·sim·e·ter (dɛn'sɪmɪtə) *n. Physics.* any instrument for measuring density. —**den·si·met·ric** (ˌdɛnsɪ'mɛtrɪk) *adj.* —**den·'sim·e·try** *n.*

den·si·tom·e·ter (ˌdɛnsɪ'tɒmɪtə) *n.* an instrument for measuring the optical density of a material by directing a beam of light onto the specimen and measuring its transmission or reflection. —**den·si·to·met·ric** (ˌdɛnsɪtə'mɛtrɪk) *adj.* —ˌ**den·si·'tom·e·try** *n.*

den·si·ty ('dɛnsɪtɪ) *n., pl.* **·ties. 1.** the degree to which something is filled, crowded, or occupied: *high density of building in towns.* **2.** obtuseness; stupidity. **3.** a measure of the compactness of a substance, expressed as its mass per unit volume. It is measured in kilograms per cubic metre or pounds per cubic foot. Symbol: ρ See also **relative density. 4.** a measure of a physical quantity per unit of length, area, or volume. See **charge density, current density. 5.** *Physics, photog.* See **transmission density, reflection density. 6.** Also called: **density function.** *Statistics.* a function having a specified range and form from which can be obtained probabilities for any value or interval within the range and formulas for parameters, such as the mean and variance. Compare **distribution function.**

dent[1] (dɛnt) *n.* **1.** a hollow or dip in a surface, as one made by pressure or a blow. **2.** an appreciable effect, esp. of lessening: *a dent in our resources.* ~*vb.* **3.** to impress or be impressed with a dent or dents. [C13 (in the sense: a stroke, blow): variant of DINT]

dent[2] (dɛnt) *n.* **1.** a toothlike protuberance, esp. the tooth of a sprocket or gearwheel. **2.** *Textiles.* the space between two wires in a loom through which a warp thread is drawn. [C16: from French: tooth]

dent. *abbrev. for:* **1.** dental. **2.** dentistry.

den·tal ('dɛntᵊl) *adj.* **1.** of or relating to the teeth. **2.** of or relating to dentistry. **3.** *Phonetics.* **a.** pronounced or articulated with the tip of the tongue touching the backs of the upper teeth, as for *t* in French *tout.* **b.** (esp. in the phonology of some languages, such as English) another word for **alveolar.** ~*n.* **4.** *Phonetics.* a dental consonant. [C16: from Medieval Latin *dentālis,* from Latin *dēns* tooth]

den·tal floss *n.* a soft usually flattened thread for cleaning the teeth and the spaces between them.

den·tal hy·giene *n.* the maintenance of the teeth and gums in healthy condition, esp. by proper brushing, the removal of plaque, etc.

den·tal hy·gien·ist *n.* a dentist's assistant skilled in dental hygiene.

den·ta·li·um (dɛn'teɪlɪəm) *n., pl.* **·li·ums** *or* **·li·a** (-lɪə). any scaphopod mollusc of the genus *Dentalium.* See **tusk shell.** [C19: New Latin, from Medieval Latin *dentālis* DENTAL]

den·tal plaque *n.* a filmy deposit on the surface of a tooth consisting of a mixture of mucus, bacteria, food, etc. Also called: **bacterial plaque.**

den·tal sur·geon *n.* another name for **dentist.**

den·tate ('dɛnteɪt) *adj.* **1.** having teeth or toothlike processes. **2.** (of leaves) having a toothed margin. [C19: from Latin *dentātus*] —**'den·tate·ly** *adv.*

den·ta·tion (dɛn'teɪʃən) *n.* **1.** the state or condition of being dentate. **2.** an angular projection or series of projections, as on the margin of a leaf.

den·tex ('dɛntɛks) *n.* a large active predatory sparid fish, *Dentex dentex,* of Mediterranean and E Atlantic waters, having long sharp teeth and powerful jaws. [C19: from Latin *dentix, dentex* from *dens* tooth]

den·ti- *or before a vowel* **dent-** *combining form.* indicating a tooth: *dentiform; dentine.* [from Latin *dēns, dent-*]

den·ti·cle ('dɛntɪkᵊl) *n.* a small tooth or toothlike part, such as any of the placoid scales of sharks. [C14: from Latin *denticulus*]

den·tic·u·late (dɛn'tɪkjʊlɪt, -ˌleɪt) *adj.* **1.** *Biology.* very finely toothed: *denticulate leaves.* **2.** having denticles. **3.** *Architect.* having dentils. [C17: from Latin *denticulātus* having small teeth] —**den·'tic·u·late·ly** *adv.*

den·tic·u·la·tion (dɛnˌtɪkjʊ'leɪʃən) *n.* **1.** a denticulate structure. **2.** a less common word for **denticle.**

den·ti·form ('dɛntɪˌfɔ:m) *adj.* shaped like a tooth.

den·ti·frice ('dɛntɪfrɪs) *n.* any substance, esp. paste or powder, for use in cleaning the teeth. [C16: from Latin *dentifricium* tooth powder, from *dent-, dens* tooth + *fricāre* to rub]

den·til ('dɛntɪl) *n.* one of a set of small square or rectangular blocks evenly spaced to form an ornamental row, usually under a classical cornice on a building, piece of furniture, etc. [C17: from French, from obsolete *dentille* a little tooth, from *dent* tooth]

den·ti·la·bi·al (ˌdɛntɪ'leɪbɪəl) *adj.* another word for **labiodental.**

den·ti·lin·gual (ˌdɛntɪ'lɪŋgwəl) *adj.* **1.** *Phonetics.* pronounced or articulated with the tongue touching the upper teeth. ~*n.* **2.** a consonant so pronounced.

den·tine ('dɛnti:n) *or* **den·tin** ('dɛntɪn) *n.* the calcified tissue surrounding the pulp cavity of a tooth and comprising the bulk of the tooth. [C19: from DENTI- + -IN] —**'den·tin·al** *adj.*

den·tist ('dɛntɪst) *n.* a person qualified to practise dentistry. [C18: from French *dentiste,* from *dent* tooth]

den·tis·try ('dɛntɪstrɪ) *n.* the branch of medical science concerned with the diagnosis and treatment of diseases and disorders of the teeth and gums.

den·ti·tion (dɛn'tɪʃən) *n.* **1.** the arrangement, type, and number of the teeth in a particular species. Man has a **primary dentition** of deciduous teeth and a **secondary dentition** of permanent teeth. **2.** teething or the time or process of teething. [C17: from Latin *dentītiō* a teething]

den·toid ('dɛntɔɪd) *adj.* resembling a tooth.

Den·ton ('dɛntᵊn) *n.* a town in NW England, in SW Lancashire. Pop.: 38 107 (1971).

D'En·tre·cas·teaux Is·lands (*French* dɑ̃trəka'sto) *pl. n.* a group of volcanic islands in the Pacific, off the SE coast of New Guinea: part of Papua New Guinea. Pop.: 100 056 (1966). Area: 3141 sq. km (1213 sq. miles).

den·ture ('dɛntʃə) *n.* (*usually pl.*) **1.** Also called: **dental plate, false teeth.** a partial or full set of artificial teeth. **2.** *Rare.* a set of natural teeth. [C19: from French, from *dent* tooth + -URE]

de·nu·cle·ar·ize *or* **de·nu·cle·ar·ise** (dɪ'nju:klɪəˌraɪz) *vb.* (*tr.*) to deprive (a country, state, etc.) of nuclear weapons. —**de·ˌnu·cle·ar·i·'za·tion** *or* **de·ˌnu·cle·ar·i·'sa·tion** *n.*

den·u·date ('dɛnjʊˌdeɪt, dɪ'nju:deɪt) *vb.* **1.** a less common word for **denude.** ~*adj.* **2.** denuded; bare.

de·nude (dɪ'nju:d) *vb.* (*tr.*) **1.** to divest of covering; make bare; uncover; strip. **2.** to expose (rock) by the erosion of the layers above. —**den·u·da·tion** (ˌdɛnjʊ'deɪʃən, ˌdi:-) *n.* —**de·'nud·er** *n.*

de·nu·mer·a·ble (dɪ'nju:mərəbᵊl) *adj. Maths.* capable of being put into a one-to-one correspondence with the positive integers; countable. —**de·'nu·mer·a·bly** *adv.*

de·nun·ci·ate (dɪ'nʌnsɪˌeɪt) *vb.* (*tr.*) to condemn; denounce. [C16: from Latin *dēnuntiāre;* see DENOUNCE] —**de·'nun·ci·ˌa·tor** *n.* —**de·'nun·ci·a·to·ry** *adj.*

de·nun·ci·a·tion (dɪˌnʌnsɪ'eɪʃən) *n.* **1.** open condemnation; censure; denouncing. **2.** *Law, obsolete.* a charge or accusation of crime made by an individual before a public prosecutor or tribunal. **3.** a formal announcement of the termination of a treaty. **4.** *Archaic.* an announcement in the form of an impending threat or warning.

Den·ver ('dɛnvə) *n.* a city in central Colorado: the state capital. Pop.: 515 593 (1973 est.).

de·ny (dɪ'naɪ) *vb.* **·nies, ·ny·ing, ·nied.** (*tr.*) **1.** to declare (an assertion, statement, etc.) to be untrue: *he denied that he had killed her.* **2.** to reject as false; refuse to accept or believe. **3.** to withhold; refuse to give. **4.** to refuse to fulfil the requests or expectations of: *it is hard to deny a child.* **5.** to refuse to acknowledge or recognize; disown; disavow: *the baron denied his wicked son.* **6.** to refuse (oneself) things desired. [C13: from Old French *denier,* from Latin *dēnegāre,* from *negāre*]

Den·ys ('dɛnɪs; *French* də'ni) *n.* **Saint.** a variant spelling of (Saint) **Denis.**

de·o·dand ('di:əʊˌdænd) *n. English law.* (formerly) a thing that had caused a person's death and was forfeited to the crown for a charitable purpose: abolished 1862. [C16: from Anglo-French *deodande,* from Medieval Latin *deōdandum,* from Latin *Deō dandum* (something) to be given to God, from *deus* god + *dare* to give]

de·o·dar ('di:əʊˌdɑ:) *n.* **1.** a Himalayan cedar, *Cedrus deodara,* with drooping branches. **2.** the durable fragrant highly valued wood of this tree. [C19: from Hindi *deodār,* from Sanskrit *devadāru,* literally: wood of the gods, from *deva* god + *dāru* wood]

de·o·dor·ant (di:'əʊdərənt) *n.* **1. a.** a substance applied to the body to suppress or mask the odour of perspiration or other body odours. **b.** (*as modifier*): *a deodorant spray.* Compare **antiperspirant. 2.** any substance for destroying or masking odours, such as liquid sprayed into the air.

de·o·dor·ize *or* **de·o·dor·ise** (di:'əʊdəˌraɪz) *vb.* (*tr.*) to remove, disguise, or absorb the odour of, esp. when unpleasant. —**de·ˌo·dor·i·'za·tion** *or* **de·ˌo·dor·i·'sa·tion** *n.* —**de·'o·dor·ˌiz·er** *or* **de·'o·dor·ˌis·er** *n.*

De·o gra·ti·as *Latin.* ('deɪəʊ 'grɑ:tɪəs) thanks be to God. Abbrev: **D.G.**

de·on·tic (di:'ɒntɪk) *adj. Logic.* **a.** of or relating to such ethical concepts as obligation and permissibility. **b.** designating the branch of modal logic that deals with the formalization of these concepts. [C19: from Greek *deon* duty, from impersonal *dei* it behoves, it is binding]

de·on·tol·o·gy (ˌdi:ɒn'tɒlədʒɪ) *n.* the branch of ethics dealing with duty, moral obligation, and moral commitment. [C19: from Greek *deon* duty (see DEONTIC) + -LOGY] —**de·on·to·log·i·cal** (dɪˌɒntə'lɒdʒɪkᵊl) *adj.* —ˌ**de·on·'tol·o·gist** *n.*

De·o vo·len·te *Latin.* ('deɪəʊ vɒ'lɛntɪ) God willing. Abbrev.: **D.V.**

de·ox·i·dize *or* **de·ox·i·dise** (di:'ɒksɪˌdaɪz) *vb.* **1.** (*tr.*) **a.** to remove oxygen atoms from (a compound, molecule, etc.). **b.** another word for **deoxygenate. 2.** another word for **reduce** (sense 11). —**de·ˌox·i·di·'za·tion** *or* **de·ˌox·i·di·'sa·tion** *n.* —**de·'ox·i·ˌdiz·er** *or* **de·'ox·i·ˌdis·er** *n.*

de·ox·y- *or* **des·ox·y-** *combining form.* indicating the presence of less oxygen than in a specified related compound: *deoxyribonucleic acid.*

de·ox·y·cor·ti·co·ster·one (di:ˌɒksɪˌkɔ:tɪkəʊ'stɪərəʊn) *or* **de·ox·y·cor·tone** (di:ˌɒksɪ'kɔ:təʊn) *n.* a corticosteroid hormone important in maintaining sodium and water balance in the body.

de·ox·y·gen·ate (diːˈɒksɪdʒɪˌneɪt) *or* **de·ox·y·gen·ize, de·ox·y·gen·ise** (diːˈɒksɪdʒɪˌnaɪz) *vb.* (*tr.*) to remove oxygen from (water, air, etc.). —**de·ˌox·y·gen·ˈa·tion** *n.*

de·ox·y·ri·bo·nu·cle·ic ac·id (dɪˈɒksɪˌraɪbəʊnjuːˈkleɪɪk) *or* **des·ox·y·ri·bo·nu·cle·ic ac·id** *n.* the full name for **DNA**

de·ox·y·ri·bose (diːˌɒksɪˈraɪbəʊs, -bəʊz) *or* **des·ox·y·ri·bose** (dɛsˌɒksɪˈraɪbəʊs, -bəʊz) *n.* a pentose sugar obtained by the hydrolysis of DNA. Formula: $C_5H_{10}O_4$.

dep. *abbrev. for:* **1.** departs. **2.** departure. **3.** deponent. **4.** deposed. **5.** deposit. **6.** depot. **7.** deputy.

de·part (dɪˈpɑːt) *vb.* (*mainly intr.*) **1.** to go away; leave. **2.** to start out; set forth. **3.** (usually foll. by *from*) to deviate; differ; vary: *to depart from normal procedure.* **4.** (*tr.*) to quit (archaic, except in the phrase **depart this life**). [C13: from Old French *departir,* from DE- + *partir* to go away, divide, from Latin *partīrī* to divide, distribute, from *pars* a part]

de·part·ed (dɪˈpɑːtɪd) *adj. Euphemistic.* **a.** dead; deceased. **b.** (*as collective n.* preceded by *the*): *the departed.*

de·part·ment (dɪˈpɑːtmənt) *n.* **1.** a specialized division of a large concern, such as a business, store, or university: *the geography department.* **2.** a major subdivision or branch of the administration of a government. **3.** a branch or subdivision of learning: *physics is a department of science.* **4.** a territorial and administrative division in several countries, such as France. **5.** *Informal.* a specialized sphere of knowledge, skill, or activity: *wine-making is my wife's department.* [C18: from French *département,* from *départir* to divide; see DEPART] —**de·part·men·tal** (ˌdiːpɑːtˈmɛntᵊl) *adj.* —ˌ**de·part·ˈmen·tal·ly** *adv.*

de·part·men·tal·ism (ˌdiːpɑːtˈmɛntᵊˌlɪzəm) *n.* division into departments, esp. when resulting in impaired efficiency.

de·part·ment·al·ize *or* **de·part·ment·al·ise** (ˈdiːpɑːtˈmɛntᵊˌlaɪz) *vb.* (*tr.*) to organize into departments, esp. excessively. —ˌ**de·part·ˌmen·tal·i·ˈza·tion** *or* ˌ**de·part·ˌmen·tal·i·ˈsa·tion** *n.*

de·part·ment store *n.* a large shop divided into departments selling a great many kinds of goods.

de·par·ture (dɪˈpɑːtʃə) *n.* **1.** the act or an instance of departing. **2.** a deviation or variation from previous custom; divergence. **3.** a project, course of action, venture, etc.: *selling is a new departure for him.* **4.** *Nautical.* **a.** the net distance travelled due east or west by a vessel. **b.** Also called: **point of departure.** the latitude and longitude of the point from which a vessel calculates dead reckoning. **5.** a euphemistic word for **death.**

de·pas·ture (diːˈpɑːstʃə) *vb.* **1.** to graze or denude by grazing (a pasture, esp. a meadow specially grown for the purpose). **2.** (*tr.*) to pasture (cattle or sheep).

de·pend (dɪˈpɛnd) *vb.* (*intr.*) **1.** (foll. by *on* or *upon*) to put trust (in); rely (on); be sure (of). **2.** (usually foll. by *on* or *upon;* often with *it* as subject) to be influenced or determined (by); be resultant (from): *whether you come or not depends on what father says; it all depends on you.* **3.** (foll. by *on* or *upon*) to rely (on) for income, support, etc. **4.** (foll. by *from*) *Rare.* to hang down; be suspended. **5.** to be undecided or pending. [C15: from Old French *dependre,* from Latin *dēpendēre* to hang from, from DE- + *pendēre* to hang]

de·pend·a·ble (dɪˈpɛndəbᵊl) *adj.* able to be depended on; reliable; trustworthy. —**de·ˌpend·a·ˈbil·i·ty** *or* **de·ˈpend·a·ble·ness** *n.* —**de·ˈpend·a·bly** *adv.*

de·pend·ant (dɪˈpɛndənt) *n.* a person who depends on another person, organization, etc., for support, aid, or sustenance, esp. financial support.

de·pend·ence *or U.S.* (*sometimes*) **de·pend·ance** (dɪˈpɛndəns) *n.* **1.** the state or fact of being dependent, esp. for support or help. **2.** reliance; trust; confidence. **3.** *Rare.* an object or person relied upon.

de·pend·en·cy *or U.S.* (*sometimes*) **de·pend·an·cy** (dɪˈpɛndənsɪ) *n., pl.* **·cies. 1.** a territory subject to a state on which it does not border. **2.** a dependent or subordinate person or thing. **3.** another word for **dependence.**

de·pend·ent *or U.S.* (*sometimes*) **de·pend·ant** (dɪˈpɛndənt) *adj.* **1.** depending on a person or thing for aid, support, life, etc. **2.** (*postpositive;* foll. by *on* or *upon*) influenced or conditioned (by); contingent (on). **3.** subordinate; subject: *a dependent prince.* **4.** *Obsolete.* hanging down. **5.** *Maths.* **a.** (of a variable) having a value depending on that assumed by a related independent variable. **b.** (of a linear equation) having every solution as a solution of one or more given linear equations. ~*n.* **6.** a variant spelling (esp. U.S.) of **dependant.** —**de·ˈpend·ent·ly** *adv.*

de·pend·ent clause *n. Grammar.* another term for **subordinate clause.**

de·pend·ent var·i·a·ble *n.* a variable in a mathematical equation or statement whose value depends on that taken on by the independent variable: *in "$y = f(x)$", "y" is the dependent variable.*

de·per·son·al·ize *or* **de·per·son·al·ise** (diːˈpɜːsnᵊˌlaɪz) *vb.* (*tr.*) to deprive (a person, organization, system, etc.) of individual or personal qualities; render impersonal. —**de·ˌper·son·al·i·ˈza·tion** *or* **de·ˌper·son·al·i·ˈsa·tion** *n.*

de·pict (dɪˈpɪkt) *vb.* (*tr.*) **1.** to represent by or as by drawing, sculpture, painting, etc.; delineate; portray. **2.** to represent in words; describe. [C17: from Latin *dēpingere,* from *pingere* to paint] —**de·ˈpict·er** *or* **de·ˈpic·tor** *n.* —**de·ˈpic·tion** *n.* —**de·ˈpic·tive** *adj.*

de·pic·ture (dɪˈpɪktʃə) *vb.* (*tr.*) a less common word for **depict.**

dep·i·late (ˈdɛpɪˌleɪt) *vb.* (*tr.*) to remove the hair from. [C16: from Latin *dēpilāre,* from *pilāre* to make bald, from *pilus* hair] —ˌ**dep·i·ˈla·tion** *n.* —ˈ**dep·i·ˌla·tor** *n.*

de·pil·a·to·ry (dɪˈpɪlətərɪ, -trɪ) *adj.* **1.** able or serving to remove hair. ~*n., pl.* **·ries. 2.** a chemical that is used to remove hair from the body.

de·plane (diːˈpleɪn) *vb.* (*intr.*) *Chiefly U.S.* to disembark from an aeroplane. [C20: from DE- + PLANE[1]]

de·plete (dɪˈpliːt) *vb.* (*tr.*) **1.** to use up (supplies, money, energy, etc.); reduce or exhaust. **2.** to empty entirely or partially. **3.** *Med.* to empty or reduce the fluid contents of (an organ or vessel). [C19: from Latin *dēplēre* to empty out, from DE- + *plēre* to fill] —**de·ˈplet·a·ble** *adj.* —**de·ˈple·tion** *n.* —**de·ˈple·tive** *or* **de·ˈple·to·ry** *adj.*

de·plor·a·ble (dɪˈplɔːrəbᵊl) *adj.* **1.** lamentable: *a deplorable lack of taste.* **2.** worthy of censure or reproach; very bad: *deplorable behaviour.* —**de·ˈplor·a·ble·ness** *or* **de·ˌplor·a·ˈbil·i·ty** *n.* —**de·ˈplor·a·bly** *adv.*

de·plore (dɪˈplɔː) *vb.* (*tr.*) **1.** to express or feel sorrow about; lament; regret. **2.** to express or feel strong disapproval of; censure. [C16: from Old French *deplorer,* from Latin *dēplōrāre* to weep bitterly, from *plōrāre* to weep, lament] —**de·ˈplor·er** *n.* —**de·ˈplor·ing·ly** *adv.*

de·ploy (dɪˈplɔɪ) *vb. Chiefly military.* **1.** to adopt or cause to adopt a battle formation, esp. from a narrow front formation. **2.** (*tr.*) to redistribute (forces) to or within a given area. [C18: from French *déployer,* from Latin *displicāre* to unfold; see DISPLAY] —**de·ˈploy·ment** *n.*

de·plume (diːˈpluːm) *vb.* (*tr.*) **1.** to deprive of feathers; pluck. **2.** to deprive of honour, position, wealth, etc. —ˌ**de·plu·ˈma·tion** *n.*

de·po·lar·ize *or* **de·po·lar·ise** (diːˈpəʊləˌraɪz) *vb.* to undergo or cause to undergo a loss of polarity or polarization. —**de·ˌpo·lar·i·ˈza·tion** *or* **de·ˌpo·lar·i·ˈsa·tion** *n.* —**de·ˈpo·lar·ˌiz·er** *or* **de·ˈpo·lar·ˌis·er** *n.*

de·po·lit·i·cize *or* **de·po·lit·i·cise** (ˌdiːpəˈlɪtɪˌsaɪz) *vb.* (*tr.*) to deprive of a political nature; render apolitical: *two years on the committee totally depoliticized him.*

de·pol·y·mer·ize *or* **de·pol·y·mer·ise** (diːˈpɒlɪməˌraɪz) (*vb.*) to break (a polymer) into constituent monomers or (of a polymer) to decompose in this way. —**de·ˌpol·y·mer·i·ˈza·tion** *or* **de·ˌpol·y·mer·i·ˈsa·tion** *n.*

de·pone (dɪˈpəʊn) *vb. Law, chiefly Scot.* to declare (something) under oath; testify; depose. [C16: from Latin *dēpōnere* to put down, from DE- + *pōnere* to put, place]

de·po·nent (dɪˈpəʊnənt) *adj.* **1.** *Grammar.* (of a verb, esp. in Latin) having the inflectional endings of a passive verb but the meaning of an active verb. ~*n.* **2.** *Grammar.* a deponent verb. **3.** *Law.* **a.** a person who makes an affidavit. **b.** a person, esp. a witness, who makes a deposition. [C16: from Latin *dēpōnēns* putting aside, putting down, from *dēpōnere* to put down, DEPONE]

de·pop·u·late (dɪˈpɒpjʊˌleɪt) *vb.* to be or cause to be reduced in population. —**de·ˌpop·u·ˈla·tion** *n.*

de·port (dɪˈpɔːt) *vb.* (*tr.*) **1.** to remove (an alien) forcibly from a country; expel. **2.** to carry (an inhabitant) forcibly away from his homeland; transport; exile; banish. **3.** to conduct, hold, or behave (oneself) in a specified manner. [C15: from French *déporter,* from Latin *dēportāre* to carry away, banish, from DE- + *portāre* to carry] —**de·ˈport·a·ble** *adj.*

de·por·ta·tion (ˌdiːpɔːˈteɪʃən) *n.* **1.** the act of expelling an alien from a country; expulsion. **2.** the act of transporting someone from his country; banishment.

de·por·tee (ˌdiːpɔːˈtiː) *n.* a person deported or awaiting deportation.

de·port·ment (dɪˈpɔːtmənt) *n.* the manner in which a person behaves, esp. in physical bearing: *military deportment.* [C17: from French *déportement,* from Old French *deporter* to conduct (oneself); see DEPORT]

de·pos·al (dɪˈpəʊzᵊl) *n.* another word for **deposition** (sense 2).

de·pose (dɪˈpəʊz) *vb.* **1.** (*tr.*) to remove from an office or position, esp. one of power or rank. **2.** *Law.* to testify or give (evidence, etc.) on oath, esp. when taken down in writing; make a deposition. [C13: from Old French *deposer* to put away, put down, from Late Latin *dēpōnere* to depose from office, from Latin: to put aside; see DEPONE] —**de·ˈpos·a·ble** *adj.* —**de·ˈpos·er** *n.*

de·pos·it (dɪˈpɒzɪt) *vb.* (*tr.*) **1.** to put or set down, esp. carefully or in a proper place; place. **2.** to entrust for safekeeping; consign. **3.** to place (money) in a bank or similar institution in order to earn interest or for safekeeping. **4.** to give (money) in part payment or as security. **5.** to lay down naturally; cause to settle: *the river deposits silt.* ~*n.* **6. a.** an instance of entrusting money or valuables to a bank or similar institution. **b.** the money or valuables so entrusted. **7.** money given in part payment or as security, as when goods are bought on hire-purchase. See also **down payment. 8.** a consideration, esp. money, given temporarily as security against loss of or damage to something borrowed or hired. **9.** an accumulation of sediments, mineral ores, coal, etc. **10.** any deposited material, such as a sediment or a precipitate that has settled out of solution. **11.** a coating produced on a surface, esp. a layer of metal formed by electrolysis. **12.** a depository or storehouse. **13. on deposit.** payable as the first instalment, as when buying on hire-purchase. [C17: from Medieval Latin *dēpositāre,* from Latin *dēpositus* put down]

de·pos·it ac·count *n. Brit.* a bank account that earns interest and usually requires notice of withdrawal.

de·pos·i·tar·y (dɪˈpɒzɪtərɪ, -trɪ) *n., pl.* **·tar·ies. 1.** a person or group to whom something is entrusted for safety or preservation. **2.** a variant spelling of **depository** (sense 1).

dep·o·si·tion (ˌdɛpəˈzɪʃən, ˌdiːpə-) *n.* **1.** *Law.* **a.** the giving of testimony on oath. **b.** the testimony so given. **c.** the sworn statement of a witness used in court in his absence. **2.** the act or instance of deposing. **3.** the act or an instance of depositing. **4.** something that is deposited; deposit. [C14: from Late Latin *dēpositiō* a laying down, disposal, burying, testimony]

Dep·o·si·tion (ˌdɛpəˈzɪʃən, ˌdiːpə-) *n.* the taking down of Christ's body from the Cross or a representation of this.

de·pos·i·tor (dɪˈpɒzɪtə) *n.* a person who places or has money on deposit in a bank or similar organization.

de·pos·i·to·ry (dɪˈpɒzɪtərɪ, -trɪ) *n., pl.* **·ries. 1.** a store, such as a warehouse, for furniture, valuables, etc.; repository. **2.** a variant spelling of **depositary** (sense 1). [C17 (in the sense: place of a deposit): from Medieval Latin *dēpositōrium;* C18 (in the sense: depositary): see DEPOSIT, -ORY[1]]

de·pot (ˈdɛpəʊ) *n.* **1.** a storehouse or warehouse. **2.** *Military.* **a.** a store for supplies. **b.** a training and holding centre for recruits and replacements. **3.** *Chiefly Brit.* a building used for the storage and servicing of buses or railway engines. **4.** *U.S.* **a.** a railway station. **b.** (*as modifier*): *a depot manager.* [C18: from French *dépôt,* from Latin *dēpositum* a deposit, trust]

de·prave (dɪˈpreɪv) *vb.* (*tr.*) **1.** to make morally bad; corrupt; vitiate. **2.** *Obsolete.* to defame; slander. [C14: from Latin *dēprāvāre* to distort, corrupt, from DE- + *prāvus* crooked] **—dep·ra·va·tion** (ˌdɛprəˈveɪʃən) *n.* **—de·ˈprav·er** *n.*

de·praved (dɪˈpreɪvd) *adj.* morally bad or debased; corrupt; perverted. **—de·praved·ness** (dɪˈpreɪvɪdnɪs) *n.*

de·prav·i·ty (dɪˈprævɪtɪ) *n., pl.* **·ties.** the state or an instance of moral corruption.

dep·re·cate (ˈdɛprɪˌkeɪt) *vb.* (*tr.*) **1.** to express disapproval of; protest against. **2.** to depreciate (a person, someone's character, etc.); belittle. **3.** *Archaic.* to try to ward off by prayer. [C17: from Latin *dēprecārī* to avert, ward off by entreaty, from DE- + *precārī* to PRAY] **—ˈdep·re·ˌcat·ing·ly** *adv.* **—ˌdep·re·ˈca·tion** *n.* **—ˈdep·re·ca·tive** *adj.* **—ˈdep·re·ca·tive·ly** *adv.* **—ˈdep·re·ˌca·tor** *n.*

dep·re·ca·to·ry (ˌdɛprɪˈkeɪtərɪ) *adj.* **1.** expressing disapproval; protesting. **2.** expressing apology; apologetic. **—ˌdep·re·ˈca·to·ri·ly** *adv.*

de·pre·cia·ble (dɪˈpriːʃəbᵊl) *adj.* **1.** *U.S.* able to be depreciated for tax deduction. **2.** liable to depreciation.

de·pre·ci·ate (dɪˈpriːʃɪˌeɪt) *vb.* **1.** to reduce or decline in value or price. **2.** (*tr.*) to lessen the value of by derision, criticism, etc.; disparage. [C15: from Late Latin *dēpretiāre* to lower the price of, from Latin DE- + *pretium* PRICE] **—de·ˈpre·ci·ˌat·ing·ly** *adv.* **—de·ˈpre·ci·ˌa·tor** *n.* **—de·pre·ci·a·to·ry** (dɪˈpriːʃɪətərɪ, -trɪ) *or* **de·ˈpre·ci·a·tive** *adj.*

de·pre·ci·a·tion (dɪˌpriːʃɪˈeɪʃən) *n.* **1.** *Accounting.* **a.** the reduction in value of a fixed asset due to use, obsolescence, etc. **b.** the amount deducted from gross profit to allow for such reduction in value. **2.** *Accounting.* a modified amount permitted for purposes of tax deduction. **3.** the act or an instance of depreciating or belittling; disparagement. **4.** a decrease in the exchange value of currency against gold or other currencies brought about by excess supply of that currency under conditions of fluctuating exchange rates. Compare **devaluation** (sense 1).

dep·re·date (ˈdɛprɪˌdeɪt) *vb.* (*tr.*) *Rare.* to plunder or destroy; pillage. [C17: from Late Latin *dēpraedārī* to ravage, from Latin DE- + *praeda* booty; see PREY] **—ˈdep·re·ˌda·tor** *n.* **—dep·re·da·to·ry** (ˈdɛprɪˌdeɪtərɪ, dɪˈprɛdɪtərɪ, -trɪ) *adj.*

dep·re·da·tion (ˌdɛprɪˈdeɪʃən) *n.* the act or an instance of plundering; robbery; pillage.

de·press (dɪˈprɛs) *vb.* (*tr.*) **1.** to lower in spirits; make gloomy; deject. **2.** to weaken or lower the force, vigour, or energy of. **3.** to lower prices of (securities or a security market). **4.** to press or push down. **5.** to lower the pitch of (a musical sound). **6.** *Obsolete.* to suppress or subjugate. [C14: from Old French *depresser,* from Latin *dēprimere* from DE- + *premere* to PRESS] **—de·ˈpress·i·ble** *adj.* **—de·ˈpress·ing·ly** *adv.*

de·pres·sant (dɪˈprɛsᵊnt) *adj.* **1.** *Med.* able to diminish or reduce nervous or functional activity. **2.** causing gloom or dejection; depressing. ~*n.* **3.** a depressant drug.

de·pressed (dɪˈprɛst) *adj.* **1.** low in spirits; downcast; despondent. **2.** lower than the surrounding surface. **3.** pressed down or flattened. **4.** Also: **distressed.** characterized by relative economic hardship, such as unemployment: *a depressed area.* **5.** lowered in force, intensity, or amount. **6.** (of plant parts) flattened as though pressed from above. **7.** *Zoology.* flattened from top to bottom: *the depressed bill of the spoonbill.*

de·pres·sion (dɪˈprɛʃən) *n.* **1.** the act of depressing or state of being depressed. **2.** a depressed or sunken place or area. **3.** *Psychol.* an emotional state of mind characterized by feelings of gloom and inadequacy, leading to withdrawal. **4.** *Pathol.* an abnormal lowering of the rate of any physiological activity or function, such as respiration. **5.** an economic condition characterized by substantial and protracted unemployment, falling prices and security values, and low levels of investment, trade, etc.; slump. **6.** Also called: **cyclone, low.** *Meteorol.* a body of moving air below normal atmospheric pressure, which often brings rain. **7.** (esp. in surveying and astronomy) the angular distance of an object, celestial body, etc., below the horizontal plane through the point of observation. Compare **elevation** (sense 11).

De·pres·sion (dɪˈprɛʃən) *n.* (usually preceded by *the*) the worldwide economic depression of the early 1930s, when there was mass unemployment. Also called: the **Great Depression,** the **Slump.**

de·pres·sive (dɪˈprɛsɪv) *adj.* **1.** tending to depress; causing depression. **2.** *Psychol.* tending to be subject to periods of depression. See also **manic-depressive. —de·ˈpres·sive·ly** *adv.* **—de·ˈpres·sive·ness** *n.*

de·pres·so·mo·tor (dɪˌprɛsəʊˈməʊtə) *adj.* **1.** *Physiol.* retarding motor activity. ~*n.* **2.** a depressomotor drug.

de·pres·sor (dɪˈprɛsə) *n.* **1.** a person or thing that depresses. **2.** any muscle that draws down a part. **3.** any surgical or medical instrument used to press down or aside an organ or part: *a tongue depressor.* **4.** Also called: **depressor nerve.** any nerve that when stimulated produces a fall in blood pressure by dilating the arteries or lowering the heartbeat.

de·pres·sur·ize *or* **de·pres·sur·ise** (dɪˈprɛʃəˌraɪz) *vb.* (*tr.*) to reduce the pressure of a gas inside (a container or enclosed space), as in an aircraft cabin. **—de·ˌpres·sur·i·ˈza·tion** *or* **de·ˌpres·sur·i·ˈsa·tion** *n.*

de·prive (dɪˈpraɪv) *vb.* (*tr.*) **1.** (foll. by *of*) to prevent from possessing or enjoying; dispossess (of). **2.** *Archaic.* to remove from rank or office; depose; demote. [C14: from Old French *depriver,* from Medieval Latin *dēprīvāre,* from Latin DE- + *prīvāre* to deprive of, rob; see PRIVATE] **—de·ˈpriv·a·ble** *adj.* **—de·ˈpriv·al** *n.* **—dep·ri·va·tion** (ˌdɛprɪˈveɪʃən) *n.* **—de·ˈpriv·er** *n.*

de·prived (dɪˈpraɪvd) *adj.* lacking adequate food, shelter, education, etc.: *deprived inner-city areas.*

de pro·fun·dis *Latin.* (deɪ prɒˈfʊndɪs) *adv.* out of the depths of misery or dejection.

dep·side (ˈdɛpsaɪd, -sɪd) *n.* any ester formed by the condensation of the carboxyl group of one phenolic carboxylic acid with the hydroxyl group of another, found in plant cells. [C20: *deps-,* from Greek *depsein* to knead + -IDE]

dept. *abbrev. for* department.

depth (dɛpθ) *n.* **1.** the extent, measurement, or distance downwards, backwards, or inwards. **2.** the quality of being deep; deepness. **3.** intensity or profundity of emotion or feeling. **4.** profundity of moral character; penetration; sagacity; integrity. **5.** complexity or abstruseness, as of thought or objects of thought. **6.** intensity, as of silence, colour, etc. **7.** lowness of pitch. **8.** (*often pl.*) a deep, far, inner, or remote part, such as an inaccessible region of a country. **9.** (*often pl.*) the deepest, most intense, or most severe part: *the depths of winter.* **10.** (*usually pl.*) a low moral state; demoralization: *how could you sink to such depths?* **11.** (*often pl.*) a vast space or abyss. **12. beyond** *or* **out of one's depth. a.** in water deeper than one is tall. **b.** beyond the range of one's competence or understanding. **13. in depth. a.** thoroughly or comprehensively. **b.** (*as modifier*): *an in-depth study.* [C14: from *dep* DEEP + -TH[1]]

depth charge *or* **bomb** *n.* a bomb used to attack submarines that explodes at a pre-set depth of water.

depth of field *n.* the range of distance in front of and behind an object focused by an optical instrument, such as a camera or microscope, within which other objects will also appear clear and sharply defined in the resulting image. Compare **depth of focus.**

depth of fo·cus *n.* the amount by which the distance between the camera lens and the film can be altered without the resulting image appearing blurred. Compare **depth of field.**

depth psy·chol·o·gy *n. Psychol.* the study of unconscious motives and attitudes.

dep·u·rate (ˈdɛpjʊˌreɪt) *vb.* **1.** to cleanse or purify or to be cleansed or purified. **2.** to promote the elimination of waste products from (the body). [C17: from Medieval Latin *dēpūrāre,* from Latin DE- + *pūrāre* to purify; see PURE] **—ˌdep·u·ˈra·tion** *n.* **—ˈdep·u·ˌra·tor** *n.*

dep·u·ra·tive (ˈdɛpjʊˌreɪtɪv, -rətɪv) *adj.* **1.** used for or capable of depurating; purifying; purgative. ~*n.* **2.** a depurative substance or agent.

dep·u·ta·tion (ˌdɛpjʊˈteɪʃən) *n.* **1.** the act of appointing a person or body of people to represent or act on behalf of others. **2.** a person or, more often, a body of people so appointed; delegation.

de·pute (dɪˈpjuːt) *vb.* (*tr.*) **1.** to appoint as an agent, substitute, or representative. **2.** to assign or transfer (authority, duties, etc.) to a deputy; delegate. [C15: from Old French *deputer,* from Late Latin *dēputāre* to assign, allot, from Latin DE- + *putāre* to think, consider]

dep·u·tize *or* **dep·u·tise** (ˈdɛpjʊˌtaɪz) *vb.* to appoint or act as deputy.

dep·u·ty (ˈdɛpjʊtɪ) *n., pl.* **·ties. 1.** a person appointed to act on behalf of or represent another. **2.** a member of the legislative assembly or of the lower chamber of the legislature in various countries, such as France. **3.** *Brit. mining.* another word for **fireman** (sense 4). **4.** (*as modifier*): *the deputy chairman.* [C16: from Old French *depute,* from *deputer* to appoint; see DEPUTE]

De Quin·cey (də ˈkwɪnsɪ) *n.* **Thom·as.** 1785–1859, English critic and essayist, noted particularly for his *Confessions of an English Opium Eater* (1821).

der. *abbrev. for:* **1.** derivation. **2.** derivative.

de·rac·in·ate (dɪˈræsɪˌneɪt) *vb.* (*tr.*) **1.** to pull up by or as if by the roots; uproot; extirpate. **2.** to remove, as from a natural environment. [C16: from Old French *desraciner,* from *des-* DIS-[1] + *racine* root, from Late Latin *rādīcīna* a little root, from Latin *rādīx* a root] **—de·ˌrac·i·ˈna·tion** *n.*

de·raign *or* **dar·raign** (dəˈreɪn) *vb.* (*tr.*) *Obsolete.* **1.** *Law.* to contest (a claim, suit, etc.). **2.** to arrange (soldiers) for battle. [C13: from Old French *deraisnier* to defend, from Vulgar Latin *ratiōnāre* (unattested) to REASON] **—de·ˈraign·ment** *or* **dar·ˈraign·ment** *n.*

de·rail (dɪˈreɪl) *vb.* **1.** to go or cause to go off the rails, as a train, tram, etc. ~*n.* **2.** Also called: **derailer.** *Chiefly U.S.* a device designed to make rolling stock or locomotives leave the rails to avoid a collision or accident. **—de·ˈrail·ment** *n.*

de+rail+leur (dəˈreɪljə) *n.* a mechanism for changing gear on bicycles, consisting of a device that lifts the driving chain from one sprocket wheel to another of different size. [French *dérailleur* derailer]

De·rain (*French* dəˈrɛ̃) *n.* **An·dré** (ɑ̃ˈdre). 1880–1954, French painter, noted for his Fauvist pictures (1905–08).

de+range (dɪˈreɪndʒ) *vb.* (*tr.*) **1.** to disturb the order or arrangement of; throw into disorder; disarrange. **2.** to disturb the action or operation of. **3.** to make insane; drive mad. [C18: from Old French *desrengier, from des-* DIS-[1] + *reng* row, order]

de+range+ment (dɪˈreɪndʒmənt) *n.* **1.** the act of deranging or state of being deranged. **2.** disorder or confusion. **3.** *Psychiatry.* a mental disorder or serious mental disturbance.

de+ra+tion (diːˈræʃən) *vb.* (*tr.*) to end rationing of (food, petrol, etc.).

Der+bent (*Russian* dɪrˈbjɛnt) *n.* a port in the S Soviet Union, in the Dagestan ASSR on the Caspian Sea: founded by the Persians in the 6th century. Pop.: 57 192 (1970).

der+by (ˈdɜːbɪ) *n., pl.* **+bies.** the U.S. name for **bowler**[2].

Der+by[1] (ˈdɑːbɪ; *U.S.* ˈdɜːbɪ) *n.* **1. the.** an annual horse race run at Epsom Downs, Surrey, since 1780: one of the English flat-racing classics. **2.** any of various other horse races. **3. local Derby.** a football match between two teams from the same area. [C18: named after the twelfth Earl of *Derby* (died 1834), who founded it in 1780]

Der+by[2] (ˈdɑːbɪ) *n.* **1.** a city in central England, in Derbyshire: engineering industries (esp. aircraft engines and railway rolling stock). Pop.: 219 348 (1971). **2.** a firm-textured pale-coloured type of cheese. **3. sage Derby.** a green-and-white Derby cheese flavoured with sage.

Der·by[3] (ˈdɑːbɪ) *n.* **Earl of.** title of *Edward George Geoffrey Smith Stanley.* 1799–1869, British statesman; Conservative prime minister (1852; 1858–59; 1866–68).

Der+by+shire (ˈdɑːbɪˌʃɪə, -ʃə) *n.* a county of N central England: contains the Peak district and several resorts with mineral springs. Administrative centre: Matlock. Pop.: 887 600 (1976 est.). Area: 2641 sq. km (1020 sq. miles).

de+reg+is+ter (diːˈrɛdʒɪstə) *vb.* to remove (oneself, a car, etc.) from a register. —**ˌde+reg+is+ˈtra+tion** *n.*

der+e·lict (ˈdɛrɪlɪkt) *adj.* **1.** deserted or abandoned, as by an owner, occupant, etc. **2.** falling into ruins; neglected; dilapidated. **3.** neglectful of duty or obligation; remiss. ~*n.* **4.** a person abandoned or neglected by society; a social outcast or vagrant. **5.** property deserted or abandoned by an owner, occupant, etc. **6.** a vessel abandoned at sea. **7.** a person who is neglectful of duty or obligation. [C17: from Latin *dērelictus* forsaken, from *dērelinquere* to abandon, from DE- + *relinquere* to leave]

der+e·lic+tion (ˌdɛrɪˈlɪkʃən) *n.* **1.** deliberate, conscious, or wilful neglect (esp. in the phrase **dereliction of duty**). **2.** the act of abandoning or deserting or the state of being abandoned or deserted. **3.** *Law.* **a.** accretion of dry land gained by the gradual receding of the sea or by a river changing its course. **b.** the land thus left.

de+re+strict (ˌdiːrɪˈstrɪkt) *vb.* (*tr.*) to render or leave free from restriction, esp. a road from speed limits. —**ˌde+re+ˈstric+tion** *n.*

de+ride (dɪˈraɪd) *vb.* (*tr.*) to speak of or treat with contempt, mockery, or ridicule; scoff or jeer at. [C16: from Latin *dērīdēre* to laugh to scorn, from DE- + *rīdēre* to laugh, smile] —**de+ˈrid+er** *n.* —**de+ˈrid+ing+ly** *adv.*

de ri+gueur *French.* (də riˈgœːr; *English* də rɪˈgɜː) *adj.* required by etiquette or fashion. [literally: of strictness]

de+ris+i·ble (dɪˈrɪzɪbᵊl) *adj.* subject to or deserving of derision; ridiculous.

de+ri+sion (dɪˈrɪʒən) *n.* **1.** the act of deriding; mockery; scorn. **2.** an object of mockery or scorn. [C15: from Late Latin *dērīsiō*, from Latin *dērīsus;* see DERIDE]

de+ri+sive (dɪˈraɪsɪv) *or* **de+ri+so·ry** (dɪˈraɪsərɪ) *adj.* **1.** showing or characterized by derision; mocking; scornful. **2.** subject to or worthy of derision; ridiculous. —**de+ˈri+sive+ly** *adv.* —**de+ˈri+sive+ness** *n.*

deriv. *abbrev. for:* **1.** derivation. **2.** derivative. **3.** derived.

der·i+va+tion (ˌdɛrɪˈveɪʃən) *n.* **1.** the act of deriving or state of being derived. **2.** the source, origin, or descent of something, such as a word. **3.** something derived; a derivative. **4. a.** the process of deducing a mathematical theorem, formula, etc., as a necessary consequence of a set of accepted statements. **b.** this sequence of statements. **c.** the operation of finding a derivative. —**ˌder·i+ˈva+tion+al** *adj.*

de+riv·a+tive (dɪˈrɪvətɪv) *adj.* **1.** resulting from derivation; derived. **2.** based on or making use of other sources; not original or primary. **3.** copied from others, esp. slavishly; plagiaristic. ~*n.* **4.** a term, idea, etc., that is based on or derived from another in the same class. **5.** a word derived from another word. **6.** *Chem.* a compound that is formed from, or can be regarded as formed from, a structurally related compound: *chloroform is a derivative of methane.* **7.** *Maths.* **a.** Also called: **differential coefficient, first derivative.** the change of a function, $f(x)$, with respect to an infinitesimally small change in the independent variable, x; the limit of $[f(a + \Delta x) - f(a)]/\Delta x$, at $x = a$, as the increment, Δx, tends to 0. Symbol: $df(x)/dx$, $f'(x)$, $Df(x)$: the derivative of x^n is nx^{n-1}. **b.** the rate of change of one quantity with respect to another: *velocity is the derivative of distance with respect to time.* **8.** *Psychoanal.* an activity that represents the expression of hidden impulses and desires by channelling them into socially acceptable forms. —**de+ˈriv·a+tive+ly** *adv.*

de+rive (dɪˈraɪv) *vb.* **1.** (usually foll. by *from*) to draw or be drawn (from) in source or origin; trace or be traced. **2.** (*tr.*) to obtain by reasoning; deduce; infer. **3.** (*tr.*) to trace the source or development of. **4.** (usually foll. by *from*) to produce or be produced (from) by a chemical reaction. **5.** *Maths.* to obtain (a function) by differentiation. [C14: from Old French *deriver* to spring from, from Latin *dērīvāre* draw off, from DE- + *rīvus* a stream] —**de+ˈriv+a·ble** *adj.* —**de+ˈriv+er** *n.*

de+rived u·nit *n.* a unit of measurement obtained by multiplication or division of the base units of a system without the introduction of numerical factors.

-derm *n. combining form.* indicating skin: *endoderm.* [via French from Greek *derma* skin]

der+ma[1] (ˈdɜːmə) *n.* another name for **corium.** Also: **derm** (dɜːm). [C18: New Latin, from Greek: skin, from *derein* to skin]

der+ma[2] (ˈdɜːmə) *n.* beef or fowl intestine used as a casing for certain dishes, esp. kishke. [from Yiddish *derme*, plural of *darm* intestine, from Old High German *daram;* related to Old English *thearm* gut, Old Norse *tharmr*]

der+mal (ˈdɜːməl) *adj.* of or relating to the skin.

der+ma+ti+tis (ˌdɜːməˈtaɪtɪs) *n.* inflammation of the skin.

der·mat·o-, der·ma- *or before a vowel* **der·mat-, derm-** *combining form.* indicating skin: *dermatology; dermatome; dermal; dermatitis.* [from Greek *derma* skin]

der+mat·o+gen (dəˈmætədʒən, ˈdɜːməˌtəʊdʒən) *n. Botany.* a meristem at the apex of stems and roots that gives rise to the epidermis.

derm·a+to+glyph+ics (ˌdɜːmətəʊˈglɪfɪks) *pl. n.* **1.** the lines forming a skin pattern, esp. on the palms of the hands and soles of the feet. **2.** (*functioning as sing.*) the study of such skin patterns. [C20: from DERMATO- + Greek *gluphē* a carving; see GLYPH]

der+ma+toid (ˈdɜːməˌtɔɪd) *adj.* resembling skin.

der+ma+tol+o·gy (ˌdɜːməˈtɒlədʒɪ) *n.* the branch of medicine concerned with the skin and its diseases. —**der+ma+to+log·i+cal** (ˌdɜːmətəˈlɒdʒɪkᵊl) *adj.* —**ˌder+ma+ˈtol·o·gist** *n.*

der+ma+tome (ˈdɜːməˌtəʊm) *n.* **1.** a surgical instrument for cutting thin slices of skin, esp. for grafting. **2.** the area of skin supplied by nerve fibres from a single posterior spinal root. **3.** *Embryol.* the part of a somite in a vertebrate embryo that gives rise to the dermis. —**der+ma+tom+ic** (ˌdɜːməˈtɒmɪk) *adj.*

der+ma+to+phyte (ˈdɜːmətəʊˌfaɪt) *n.* any parasitic fungus that affects the skin. —**der+ma+to+phyt+ic** (ˌdɜːmətəˈfɪtɪk) *adj.*

der+ma+to+phy+to+sis (ˌdɜːməˌtəʊfaɪˈtəʊsɪs) *n.* a fungal infection of the skin, esp. the feet. See **athlete's foot.**

der+ma+to+plas+ty (ˈdɜːmətəʊˌplæstɪ) *n.* any surgical operation on the skin, esp. skin grafting. —**ˌder+ma+to+ˈplas+tic** *adj.*

der+ma+to+sis (ˌdɜːməˈtəʊsɪs) *n., pl.* **+to+ses** (-ˈtəʊsiːz). any skin disease.

der+mis (ˈdɜːmɪs) *n.* another name for **corium.** [C19: New Latin, from EPIDERMIS] —**ˈder+mic** *adj.*

der+moid (ˈdɜːmɔɪd) *adj.* **1.** of or resembling skin. ~*n.* **2.** a congenital cystic tumour whose walls are lined with epithelium.

der+nier cri *French.* (dɛrnje ˈkri) the latest fashion; the last word. [literally: last cry]

de+ro (ˈdɛrəʊ) *n. Austral. slang.* **1.** a tramp or derelict. **2.** *Often humorous.* a person. [C20: shortened from DERELICT]

der·o+gate *vb.* (ˈdɛrəˌgeɪt). **1.** (*intr.;* foll. by *from*) to cause to seem inferior or be in disrepute; detract. **2.** (*intr.;* foll. by *from*) to deviate in standard or quality; degenerate. **3.** (*tr.*) to cause to seem inferior, etc.; disparage. ~*adj.* (ˈdɛrəgɪt, -ˌgeɪt). **4.** *Archaic.* debased or degraded. [C15: from Latin *dērogāre* to repeal some part of a law, modify it, from DE- + *rogāre* to ask, propose a law] —**ˈder·o+ˌgate·ly** *adv.* —**ˌder·o+ˈga·tion** *n.* —**de+rog·a+tive** (dɪˈrɒgətɪv) *adj.* —**de+ˈrog·a·tive+ly** *adv.*

de+rog·a+to·ry (dɪˈrɒgətərɪ, -trɪ) *adj.* tending or intended to detract, disparage, or belittle; intentionally offensive. —**de+ˈrog·a+to+ri+ly** *adv.* —**de+ˈrog·a+to+ri+ness** *n.*

der+rick (ˈdɛrɪk) *n.* **1.** a simple crane having lifting tackle slung from a boom. **2.** the framework erected over an oil well to enable drill tubes to be raised and lowered. ~*vb.* **3.** to raise or lower the jib of (a crane). [C17 (in the sense: gallows): from *Derrick,* name of a celebrated hangman at Tyburn]

der+rière (ˌdɛrɪˈɛə; *French* dɛrˈjɛːr) *n.* a euphemistic word for **buttocks.** [C18: literally: behind (prep.), from Old French *deriere,* from Latin *dē retrō* from the back]

der·ring-do (ˈdɛrɪŋˈduː) *n. Archaic or literary.* a daring spirit or deed; boldness or bold action. [C16 (n.): from Middle English *durring don* daring to do, from *durren* to dare + *don* to do]

der+rin+ger *or* **der+in+ger** (ˈdɛrɪndʒə) *n.* a short-barrelled pocket pistol of large calibre. [C19: named after Henry *Deringer,* American gunsmith who invented it]

der+ris (ˈdɛrɪs) *n.* any East Indian leguminous woody climbing plant of the genus *Derris,* esp. *D. elliptica,* whose roots yield the compound rotenone. [C19: New Latin, from Greek: covering, leather, from *deros* skin, hide, from *derein* to skin]

der+ry[1] (ˈdɛrɪ) *n. Austral., N.Z.* **1.** dislike or prejudice. **2. have a derry on.** to have a prejudice or grudge against. [C19: probably from *derry down,* a refrain in some folk songs, alluding to the phrase, *have a down on;* see DOWN[1]]

der+ry[2] (ˈdɛrɪ) *n. Slang.* a derelict house, esp. one used by tramps, drug addicts, etc. [C20: shortened from DERELICT]

Der+ry (ˈdɛrɪ) *n.* another name for **Londonderry.**

derv (dɜːv) *n.* a Brit. name for **diesel oil** when used for road transport. [C20: from *d(iesel) e(ngine) r(oad) v(ehicle)*]

der+vish (ˈdɜːvɪʃ) *n.* a member of any of various Muslim orders of ascetics, some of which (**whirling dervishes**) are noted for a frenzied, ecstatic, whirling dance. [C16: from Turkish: beggar, from Persian *darvīsh* mendicant monk] —**'der·vish-ˌlike** *adj.*

Der+went ('dɜːwənt) *n.* **1.** a river in S Australia, in S Tasmania, flowing southeast to the Tasman Sea. Length: 172 km (107 miles). **2.** a river in N central England, in N Derbyshire, flowing southeast to the River Trent. Length: 96 km (60 miles). **3.** a river in N England, in Yorkshire, rising on the North York Moors and flowing south to the River Ouse. Length: 92 km (57 miles). **4.** a river in NW England, in Cumbria, rising on the Borrowdale Fells and flowing north and west to the Irish Sea. Length: 54 km (34 miles).

Der·went+wa·ter ('dɜːwəntˌwɔːtə) *n.* a lake in NW England, in Cumbria in the Lake District. Area: about 8 sq. km (3 sq. miles).

D.E.S. (in Britain) *abbrev. for* Department of Education and Science.

De·sai (dɛ'saɪ) *n.* **Mor·ar·ji (Ranchhodji)** (mə'rɑːdʒɪ). born 1896, Indian statesman, noted for his asceticism. He founded the Janata party in opposition to Indira Gandhi, whom he defeated in the 1977 election; prime minister of India 1977–79.

de+sal·i+nate (diː'sælɪˌneɪt) *or* **de+sal·i+nize, de+sal·i+nise** *vb. (tr.)* to remove the salt from (esp. from sea water). Also: **de+salt** (diː'sɔːlt).

de+sal·i+na+tion (diːˌsælɪ'neɪʃən) *or* **de+sal·i+ni+za+tion, de+sal·i+ni+sa+tion** *n.* the process of removing salt, esp. from sea water so that it can be used for drinking or irrigation.

desc. *abbrev. for* descendant.

des+cant *n.* ('dɛskænt, 'dɪs-). **1.** Also called: **discant.** a decorative counterpoint added above a basic melody. **2.** a comment, criticism, or discourse. ~*adj.* ('dɛskænt, 'dɪs-) **3.** Also: **discant.** of or pertaining to the highest member in common use of a family of musical instruments: *a descant recorder.* ~*vb.* (dɛs'kænt, dɪs-). *(intr.)* **4.** Also: **discant.** (often foll. by *on* or *upon*) to compose or perform a descant (for a piece of music). **5.** (often foll. by *on* or *upon*) to discourse at length or make varied comments. **6.** *Archaic.* to sing sweetly or melodiously. [C14: from Old Northern French, from Medieval Latin *discanthus,* from Latin DIS-[1] + *cantus* song; see CHANT] —**des+'cant+er** *n.*

Des·cartes ('deɪˌkɑːt; *French* de'kart) *n.* **Re·né** (rə'ne). 1596–1650, French philosopher and mathematician. He provided a mechanistic basis for the philosophical theory of dualism and is regarded as the founder of modern philosophy. He also founded analytic geometry and contributed greatly to the science of optics. His works include *Discours de la méthode* (1637), *Meditationes de Prima Philosophia* (1641), and *Principia Philosophiae* (1644). Related adj.: **Cartesian.**

de+scend (dɪ'sɛnd) *vb. (mainly intr.)* **1.** *(also tr.)* to move, pass, or go down (a hill, slope, staircase, etc.) **2.** (of a hill, slope, or path) to lead or extend down; slope; incline. **3.** to move to a lower level, pitch, etc.; fall. **4.** (often foll. by *from*) to be connected by a blood relationship (to a dead or extinct individual, race, species, etc.). **5.** to be passed on by parents or ancestors; be inherited. **6.** to sink or come down in morals or behaviour; lower oneself. **7.** (often foll. by *on* or *upon*) to arrive or attack in a sudden or overwhelming way: *their relatives descended upon them last week.* **8.** (of the sun, moon, etc.) to move towards the horizon. [C13: from Old French *descendre,* from Latin *dēscendere,* from DE- + *scandere* to climb; see SCAN] —**des+'cend·a·ble** *adj.*

de+scend+ant (dɪ'sɛndənt) *n.* **1.** a person, animal, or plant when described as descended from an individual, race, species, etc. **2.** something that derives or is descended from an earlier form. ~*adj.* **3.** a variant spelling of **descendent.**

De+scend+ant (dɪ'sɛndənt) *n. Astrology.* the point on the ecliptic lying directly opposite the Ascendant.

de+scend+ent (dɪ'sɛndənt) *adj.* **1.** coming or going downwards; descending. **2.** deriving by descent, as from an ancestor. ~*n.* **3.** a variant spelling of **descendant.**

de+scend+er (dɪ'sɛndə) *n.* **1.** a person or thing that descends. **2.** *Printing.* the portion of a letter, such as j, p, or y, below the level of the base of an x or n.

de+scend+i·ble *or* **de+scend+a·ble** (dɪ'sɛndəbᵊl) *adj. Law.* capable of being inherited.

de+scent (dɪ'sɛnt) *n.* **1.** the act of descending. **2.** a downward slope or inclination. **3.** a passage, path, or way leading downwards. **4.** derivation from an ancestor or ancestral group; lineage. **5.** (in genealogy) a generation in a particular lineage. **6.** a decline or degeneration. **7.** a movement or passage in degree or state from higher to lower. **8.** (often foll. by *on*) a sudden and overwhelming arrival or attack. **9.** *Property law.* (formerly) the transmission of real property to the heir on an intestacy.

Des·champs (*French* de'ʃɑ̃) *n.* **Eu·stache** (ø'staʃ). ?1346–?1406, French poet, noted for his *Miroir de mariage,* a satirical attack on women.

de+school (ˌdiː'skuːl) *vb. (tr.)* to separate education from the institution of school and operate through the pupil's life experience as opposed to a set curriculum.

de+scribe (dɪ'skraɪb) *vb. (tr.)* **1.** to give an account or representation of in words. **2.** to pronounce or label: *he has been described as a genius.* **3.** to draw a line or figure, such as a circle. [C15: from Latin *dēscrībere* to copy off, write out, delineate, from DE- + *scrībere* to write] —**de+'scrib+a·ble** *adj.* —**de+'scrib+er** *n.*

de+scrip+tion (dɪ'skrɪpʃən) *n.* **1.** a statement or account that describes; representation in words. **2.** the act, process, or technique of describing. **3.** sort, kind, or variety: *reptiles of every description.* **4.** *Geom.* the act of drawing a line or figure, such as an arc.

de+scrip+tive (dɪ'skrɪptɪv) *adj.* **1.** characterized by or containing description; serving to describe. **2.** *Grammar.* (of an adjective) serving to describe the referent of the noun modified, as for example the adjective *brown* as contrasted with *my* and *former.* **3.** relating to or based upon description or classification rather than explanation or prescription: *descriptive linguistics.* —**de+'scrip+tive+ly** *adv.* —**de+'scrip+tive+ness** *n.*

de+scrip+tive ge+om+e+try *n.* the study of the projection of three-dimensional figures onto a plane surface.

de+scrip+tive lin+guis+tics *n.* the study of the description of the internal phonological, grammatical, and semantic structures of languages at given points in time without reference to their histories or to one another. Also called: **synchronic linguistics.** Compare **historical linguistics, comparative linguistics.**

de+scrip+ti+vism (dɪ'skrɪptɪˌvɪzəm) *n. Ethics.* the theory that moral utterances have a truth value. Compare **prescriptivism, emotivism.**

de+scry (dɪ'skraɪ) *vb.* **+scries, +scry+ing, +scried.** *(tr.)* **1.** to discern or make out; catch sight of. **2.** to discover by looking carefully; detect. [C14: from Old French *descrier* to proclaim, DECRY] —**de+'scri+er** *n.*

des+e·crate ('dɛsɪˌkreɪt) *vb. (tr.)* **1.** to violate or outrage the sacred character of (an object or place) by destructive, blasphemous, or sacrilegious action. **2.** to remove the consecration from (a person, object, building, etc.); deconsecrate. [C17: from DE- + CONSECRATE] —**'des+e·ˌcra+tor** *or* **'des+e·ˌcrat+er** *n.* —**ˌdes+e·'cra+tion** *n.*

de+seg+re+gate (diː'sɛgrɪˌgeɪt) *vb.* to end racial segregation in (a school or other public institution). —**ˌde+seg+re+'ga+tion** *n.* —**ˌde+seg+re+'ga+tion+ist** *n., adj.*

de+sen+si+tize *or* **de+sen+si+tise** (diː'sɛnsɪˌtaɪz) *vb. (tr.)* to render less sensitive or insensitive: *the patient was desensitized to the allergen; to desensitize photographic film.* —**de+ˌsen+si+ti+'za+tion** *or* **de+ˌsen+si+ti+'sa+tion** *n.* —**de+'sen+si+ˌtiz+er** *or* **de+'sen+si+ˌtis+er** *n.*

des+ert[1] ('dɛzət) *n.* **1.** a region that is devoid or almost devoid of vegetation, esp. because of low rainfall. **2.** an uncultivated uninhabited region. **3.** a place which lacks some desirable feature or quality: *a cultural desert.* **4.** *(modifier)* of, relating to, or like a desert; infertile or desolate. [C13: from Old French, from Church Latin *dēsertum,* from Latin *dēserere* to abandon, literally: to sever one's links with, from DE- + *serere* to bind together]

de+sert[2] (dɪ'zɜːt) *vb.* **1.** *(tr.)* to leave or abandon (a person, place, etc.) without intending to return, esp. in violation of a duty, promise, or obligation. **2.** *Military.* to abscond from (a post or duty) with no intention of returning. **3.** *(tr.)* to fail (someone) in time of need: *his good humour temporarily deserted him.* [C15: from French *déserter,* from Late Latin *dēsertāre,* from Latin *dēserere* to forsake; see DESERT[1]] —**de+'sert+er** *n.*

de+sert[3] (dɪ'zɜːt) *n.* **1.** *(often pl.)* something that is deserved or merited; just reward or punishment. **2.** the state of deserving a reward or punishment. **3.** virtue or merit. [C13: from Old French *deserte,* from *deservir* to DESERVE]

des+ert boots *pl. n.* ankle-high suede boots with laces and soft soles, worn informally by men and women.

des+ert cool+er *n.* (in India) a cooling device in which air is driven by an electric fan through wet grass.

de+ser+tion (dɪ'zɜːʃən) *n.* **1.** the act of deserting or abandoning or the state of being deserted or abandoned. **2.** *Law.* wilful abandonment, esp. of one's spouse or children, without consent and in breach of obligations.

des+ert is+land *n.* a small remote tropical island.

des+ert lynx *n.* another name for **caracal.**

des+ert pea *n.* an Australian trailing leguminous plant, *Clianthus formosus,* with scarlet flowers.

des+ert rat *n.* **1.** a jerboa, *Jaculus orientalis,* inhabiting the deserts of N Africa. **2.** *Brit. informal.* a soldier who served in North Africa with the British 7th Armoured Division in 1941–42.

des+ert soil *n.* a type of soil developed in arid climates, characterized by a lack of leaching and small humus content.

de+serve (dɪ'zɜːv) *vb.* **1.** *(tr.)* to be entitled to or worthy of; merit. **2.** *(intr.;* foll. by *of) Obsolete.* to be worthy. [C13: from Old French *deservir,* from Latin *dēservīre* to serve devotedly, from DE- + *servīre* to SERVE] —**de+serv+ed+ness** (dɪ'zɜːvɪdnɪs) *n.* —**de+'serv+er** *n.*

de+serv+ed+ly (dɪ'zɜːvɪdlɪ) *adv.* according to merit; justly.

de+serv+ing (dɪ'zɜːvɪŋ) *adj.* **1.** (often *postpositive* and foll. by *of*) worthy, esp. of praise or reward. ~*n.* **2.** *Rare.* a merit or demerit; desert. —**de+'serv+ing+ly** *adv.* —**de+'serv+ing+ness** *n.*

de+sex·u·al+ize *or* **de+sex·u·al+ise** (diː'sɛksjʊəˌlaɪz) *vb. (tr.)* to deprive of sexual characteristics by the surgical removal of the testicles or ovaries; castrate or spay. Often shortened to **de+sex** (diː'sɛks). —**de+ˌsex·u·al·i+'za+tion** *or* **de+ˌsex·u·al·i+'sa+tion** *n.*

des+ha+bille (ˌdeɪzæ'biːl) *n.* a variant of **dishabille.**

de Si·ca (*Italian* dɛ 'siːka) *n.* **Vit·to·rio** (vit'tɔːrjo). 1902–74, Italian film actor and director. His films, in the realist tradition, include *Shoeshine* (1946) and *Bicycle Thieves* (1948).

des+ic+cant ('dɛsɪkənt) *adj.* **1.** desiccating or drying. ~*n.* **2.** a substance, such as calcium oxide, that absorbs water and is used to remove moisture; a drying agent. [C17: from Latin *dēsiccāns* drying up; see DESICCATE]

des+ic+cate ('dɛsɪˌkeɪt) *vb. (tr.)* **1.** to remove most of the water from (a substance or material); dehydrate. **2.** to preserve (food) by removing moisture; dry. [C16: from Latin *dēsiccāre* to dry up, from DE- + *siccāre* to dry, from *siccus* dry] —ˌdes+ic+'ca+tion *n.* —'des+ic+ca+tive *adj.*

des+ic+ca+ted ('dɛsɪˌkeɪtɪd) *adj.* **1.** dehydrated and powdered: *desiccated coconut.* **2.** lacking in spirit or animation.

des+ic+ca+tor ('dɛsɪˌkeɪtə) *n.* **1.** any apparatus for drying milk, fruit, etc. **2.** an airtight box or jar containing a desiccant, used to dry chemicals and protect them from the water vapour in the atmosphere.

de+sid+er·a+ta (dɪˌzɪdə'rɑːtə) *pl. n.* the plural of **desideratum.**

de+sid+er+ate (dɪ'zɪdəˌreɪt) *vb.* (*tr.*) to feel the lack of or need for; long for; miss. [C17: from Latin *dēsīderāre,* from DE- + *sīdus* star; see DESIRE] —**de+ˌsid+er·'a+tion** *n.*

de+sid+er·a+tive (dɪ'zɪdərətɪv) *adj.* **1.** feeling or expressing desire. **2.** (in certain languages, of a verb) related in form to another verb and expressing the subject's desire or intention to perform the act denoted by the other verb. ~*n.* **3.** a desiderative verb.

de+sid+er·a+tum (dɪˌzɪdə'rɑːtəm) *n., pl.* **+ta** (-tə). something lacked and wanted. [C17: from Latin; see DESIDERATE]

de+sign (dɪ'zaɪn) *vb.* **1.** to work out the structure or form of (something), as by making a sketch, outline, pattern, or plans. **2.** to plan and make (something) artistically or skilfully. **3.** (*tr.*) to form or conceive in the mind; invent. **4.** (*tr.*) to intend, as for a specific purpose; plan. **5.** (*tr.*) *Obsolete.* to mark out or designate. ~*n.* **6.** a plan, sketch, or preliminary drawing. **7.** the arrangement or pattern of elements or features of an artistic or decorative work: *the design of the desk is Chippendale.* **8.** a finished artistic or decorative creation. **9.** the art of designing. **10.** a plan, scheme, or project. **11.** an end aimed at or planned for; intention; purpose. **12.** (*often pl.; often foll. by on or against*) a plot or hostile scheme, often to gain possession of (something) by illegitimate means. **13.** a coherent or purposeful pattern, as opposed to chaos: *God's design appears in nature.* [C16: from Latin *dēsignāre* to mark out, describe, from DE- + *signāre* to mark, from *signum* a mark, SIGN] —**de+'sign+a·ble** *adj.*

des+ig+nate *vb.* ('dɛzɪgˌneɪt). (*tr.*) **1.** to indicate or specify. **2.** to give a name to; style; entitle. **3.** to select or name for an office or duty; appoint. ~*adj.* ('dɛzɪgnɪt, -ˌneɪt). **4.** (*immediately postpositive*) appointed, but not yet in office: *a minister designate.* [C15: from Latin *dēsignātus* marked out, defined; see DESIGN] —**'des+ig+ˌna+tive** *or* **des+ig+na+to+ry** (ˌdɛzɪg'neɪtərɪ) *adj.* —**'des+ig+ˌna+tor** *n.*

des+ig+na+tion (ˌdɛzɪg'neɪʃən) *n.* **1.** something that designates, such as a name or distinctive mark. **2.** the act of designating or the fact of being designated.

de+sign+ed+ly (dɪ'zaɪnɪdlɪ) *adv.* by intention or design; on purpose.

de+sign+er (dɪ'zaɪnə) *n.* **1.** a person who devises and executes designs, as for works of art, clothes, machines, etc. **2.** a person who devises plots or schemes; intriguer.

de+sign+ing (dɪ'zaɪnɪŋ) *adj.* artful and scheming; conniving; crafty. —**de+'sign+ing+ly** *adv.*

des·i+nence ('dɛsɪnəns) *n. Grammar.* an ending or termination, esp. an inflectional ending of a word. [C16: from French *désinence,* from Latin *dēsinēns* ending, from *dēsinere* to leave off, from DE- + *sinere* to leave, permit] —**'des·i+nent** *or* **des·i+nen+tial** (ˌdɛsɪ'nɛnʃəl) *adj.*

de+sir+a·ble (dɪ'zaɪərəbᵊl) *adj.* **1.** worthy of desire or recommendation: *a desirable residence.* **2.** arousing desire, esp. sexual desire; attractive. ~*n.* **3.** a person or thing that is the object of desire. —**de+ˌsir+a·'bil+i·ty** *or* **de+'sir·a·ble+ness** *n.* —**de+'sir+a·bly** *adv.*

de+sire (dɪ'zaɪə) *vb.* (*tr.*) **1.** to wish or long for; crave; want. **2.** to express a wish or make a request for; ask for. ~*n.* **3.** a wish or longing; craving. **4.** an expressed wish; request. **5.** sexual appetite; lust. **6.** a person or thing that is desired. [C13: from Old French *desirer,* from Latin *dēsīderāre* to desire earnestly; see DESIDERATE] —**de+'sir+er** *n.*

de+sir+ous (dɪ'zaɪərəs) *adj.* (usually *postpositive* and foll. by *of*) having or expressing desire (for); having a wish or longing (for). —**de+'sir+ous+ly** *adv.* —**de+'sir+ous+ness** *n.*

de+sist (dɪ'zɪst) *vb.* (*intr.; often foll. by from*) to cease, as from an action; stop or abstain. [C15: from Old French *desister,* from Latin *dēsistere* to leave off, stand apart, from DE- + *sistere* to stand, halt] —**de+'sist+ance** *or* **de+'sist+ence** *n.*

desk (dɛsk) *n.* **1.** a piece of furniture with a writing surface and usually drawers or other compartments. **2.** a service counter or table in a public building, such as a hotel: *information desk.* **3.** a support, lectern, or book rest for the book from which services are read in a church. **4.** the editorial section of a newspaper, etc., responsible for a particular subject: *the news desk.* **5. a.** a music stand shared by two orchestral players. **b.** these two players. **6.** (*modifier*) **a.** made for use at a desk: *a desk calendar.* **b.** done at a desk: *a desk job.* [C14: from Medieval Latin *desca* table, from Latin *discus* disc, dish]

desk clerk *n. U.S.* a hotel receptionist. Also: **clerk.**

des+man ('dɛsmən) *n., pl.* **+mans.** either of two molelike amphibious mammals, *Desmana moschata* (**Russian desman**) or *Galemys pyrenaicus* (**Pyrenean desman**), having dense fur and webbed feet: family *Talpidae,* order *Insectivora* (insectivores). [C18: from Swedish *desmansråtta,* from *desman* musk (of Germanic origin) + *råtta* rat]

des+mid ('dɛsmɪd) *n.* any freshwater green alga of the mainly unicellular family *Desmidiaceae,* typically constricted into two symmetrical halves. [C19: from New Latin *Desmidium* (genus name), from Greek *desmos* bond, from *dein* to bind] —**des+'mid+i·an** *adj.*

des+moid ('dɛsmɔɪd) *adj.* **1.** *Anatomy.* resembling a tendon or ligament. ~*n.* **2.** *Pathol.* a very firm tumour of connective tissue. [C19: from Greek *desmos* band + -OID; see DESMID]

Des Moines (də 'mɔɪn, 'mɔɪnz) *n.* **1.** a city in S central Iowa: state capital. Pop.: 199 145 (1973 est.). **2.** a river in the N central U.S., rising in SW Minnesota and flowing southeast to join the Mississippi. Length: 861 km (535 miles).

Des·mou·lins (*French* dɛmu'lɛ̃) *n.* (**Lucie Simplice**) **Ca·mille** (**Benoît**) (ka'mij). 1760–94, French revolutionary leader, pamphleteer, and orator.

des·o+late *adj.* ('dɛsəlɪt). **1.** uninhabited; deserted. **2.** made uninhabitable; laid waste; devastated. **3.** without friends, hope, or encouragement; forlorn, wretched, or abandoned. **4.** gloomy or dismal; depressing. ~*vb.* ('dɛsəˌleɪt). (*tr.*) **5.** to deprive of inhabitants; depopulate. **6.** to make barren or lay waste; devastate. **7.** to make wretched or forlorn. **8.** to forsake or abandon. [C14: from Latin *dēsōlāre* to leave alone, from DE- + *sōlāre* to make lonely, lay waste, from *sōlus* alone] —**'des·o+ˌlat+er** *or* **'des·o+ˌla+tor** *n.* —**'des·o+late+ly** *adv.* —**'des·o+late+ness** *n.*

des·o+la+tion (ˌdɛsə'leɪʃən) *n.* **1.** the act of desolating or the state of being desolated; ruin or devastation. **2.** solitary misery; wretchedness. **3.** a desolate region; barren waste.

de+sorb (dɪ'sɔːb, -'zɔːb) *vb. Chem.* to change from an adsorbed state on a surface to a gaseous or liquid state.

de+sorp+tion (dɪ'zɔːpʃən) *n.* the action or process of desorbing.

De So·to (də 'səʊtəʊ; *Spanish* de 'soto) *n.* **Her·nan·do** (er'nando). ?1500–42, Spanish explorer, who discovered the Mississippi river (1541). Also: **Fer·nan·do De So·to** (fer'nando).

des·ox·y- *combining form.* variant of **deoxy-.**

des+pair (dɪ'spɛə) *vb.* **1.** (*intr.; often foll. by of*) to lose or give up hope: *I despair of his coming.* **2.** (*tr.*) *Obsolete.* to give up hope of; lose hope in. ~*n.* **3.** total loss of hope. **4.** a person or thing that causes hopelessness or for which there is no hope. [C14: from Old French *despoir* hopelessness, from *desperer* to despair, from Latin *dēspērāre,* from DE- + *spērāre* to hope]

des+patch (dɪ'spætʃ) *vb.* (*tr.*) a less common spelling of **dispatch.** —**des+'patch+er** *n.*

Des·pen·ser (dɪs'pɛnsə) *n.* **Hugh le,** Earl of Winchester. 1262–1326, English statesman, a favourite of Edward II. Together with his son **Hugh,** *the Younger* (?1290–1326), he was executed by the king's enemies.

des+pe+ra+do (ˌdɛspə'rɑːdəʊ) *n., pl.* **+does** *or* **+dos.** a reckless or desperate person, esp. one ready to commit any violent illegal act. [C17: probably pseudo-Spanish variant of obsolete *desperate* (n.) a reckless character]

des+per+ate ('dɛspərɪt, -prɪt) *adj.* **1.** careless of danger, as from despair; utterly reckless. **2.** (of an act) reckless; risky. **3.** used or undertaken in desperation or as a last resort: *desperate measures.* **4.** critical; very grave: *in desperate need.* **5.** (often *postpositive* and foll. by *for*) in distress and having a great need or desire. **6.** moved by or showing despair or hopelessness; despairing. [C15: from Latin *dēspērāre* to have no hope; see DESPAIR] —**'des+per+ate+ly** *adv.* —**'des+per+ate+ness** *n.*

des+per·a+tion (ˌdɛspə'reɪʃən) *n.* **1.** desperate recklessness. **2.** the act of despairing or the state of being desperate.

des+pic+a·ble ('dɛspɪkəbᵊl, dɪ'spɪk-) *adj.* worthy of being despised; contemptible; mean. [C16: from Late Latin *dēspicābilis,* from *dēspicārī* to disdain; compare DESPISE] —ˌ**des+pi+ca·'bil+i·ty** *or* **'des+pi+ca·ble+ness** *n.* —**des+'pi+ca·bly** *adv.*

des+pise (dɪ'spaɪz) *vb.* (*tr.*) to look down on with contempt; scorn: *he despises flattery.* [C13: from Old French *despire,* from Latin *dēspicere* to look down, from DE- + *specere* to look] —**de+'spis+er** *n.*

de+spite (dɪ'spaɪt) *prep.* **1.** in spite of; undeterred by. ~*n.* **2.** *Archaic.* contempt; insult. **3. in despite of.** (*prep.*) *Rare.* in spite of. ~*vb.* **4.** (*tr.*) an archaic word for **spite.** [C13: from Old French *despit,* from Latin *dēspectus* contempt; see DESPISE]

de+spite+ful (dɪ'spaɪtfʊl) *or* **des+pit+e·ous** (dɛ'spɪtɪəs) *adj.* an archaic word for **spiteful.** —**de+'spite+ful+ly** *adv.* —**de+'spite+ful+ness** *n.*

de+spoil (dɪ'spɔɪl) *vb.* (*tr.*) to strip or deprive by force; plunder; rob; loot. [C13: from Old French *despoillier,* from Latin *dēspoliāre,* from DE- + *spoliāre* to rob (esp. of clothing); see SPOIL] —**de+'spoil+er** *n.* —**de+'spoil+ment** *n.*

de+spo+li·a+tion (dɪˌspəʊlɪ'eɪʃən) *n.* **1.** the act of despoiling; plunder or pillage. **2.** the state of being despoiled.

de+spond *vb.* **1.** (*intr.*) (dɪ'spɒnd). to lose heart or hope; become disheartened; despair. ~*n.* **2.** ('dɛspɒnd, dɪ'spɒnd). an archaic word for **despondency.** [C17: from Latin *dēspondēre* to promise, make over to, yield, lose heart, from DE- + *spondēre* to promise] —**de+'spond+ing+ly** *adv.*

de+spond+ent (dɪ'spɒndənt) *adj.* downcast or disheartened; lacking hope or courage; dejected. —**de+'spond+ence** *n.* —**de+'spond+en+cy** *n.* —**de+'spond+ent+ly** *adv.*

des+pot ('dɛspɒt) *n.* **1.** an absolute or tyrannical ruler; autocrat or tyrant. **2.** any person in power who acts tyrannically. **3.** a title borne by numerous persons of rank in the later Roman, Byzantine, and Ottoman Empires: *the despot of Servia.* [C16: from Medieval Latin *despota,* from Greek *despotēs* lord, master; related to Latin *domus* house] —**des+pot+ic** (dɛs'pɒtɪk) *or* **des+'pot+i·cal** *adj.* —**des+'pot+i·cal+ly** *adv.*

des+pot+ism ('dɛspəˌtɪzəm) *n.* **1.** the rule of a despot; arbitrary, absolute, or tyrannical government. **2.** arbitrary or tyrannical authority or behaviour.

Des Prés *or* **De·prez** (*French* de 'pre) *n.* **Jos·quin** (ʒɔs'kɛ̃). ?1450–1521, Flemish Renaissance composer of masses, motets, and chansons.

des+pu+mate (dɪ'spjuːmeɪt, 'dɛspjʊˌmeɪt) *vb.* **1.** (*tr.*) to clarify or purify (a liquid) by skimming a scum from its surface. **2.**

(*intr.*) (of a liquid) to form a scum or froth. [C17: from Latin *dēspūmāre* to skim off, from DE- + *spūma* foam, froth] —ˌdes+pu+'ma+tion *n.*

des+qua+mate ('dɛskwəˌmeɪt) *vb.* (*intr.*) (esp. of the skin in certain diseases) to peel or come off in scales. [C18: from Latin *dēsquāmāre* to scale off, from DE- + *squāma* a scale] —ˌdes+qua+'ma+tion *n.*

Des·sa·lines (*French* desa'lin) *n.* **Jean Jacques** (ʒã 'ʒɑk). ?1758–1806, emperor of Haiti (1804–06) after driving out the French; assassinated.

Des+sau (*German* 'dɛsaʊ) *n.* an industrial city in central East Germany: capital of Anhalt state from 1340 to 1918. Pop.: 100 663 (1975 est.).

des+sert (dɪ'zɜːt) *n.* **1.** the sweet, usually last course of a meal. **2.** *Chiefly Brit.* (esp. formerly) fruit, dates, nuts, etc., served at the end of a meal. [C17: from French, from *desservir* to clear a table, from *des-* DIS-[1] + *servir* to SERVE]

des·sert+spoon (dɪ'zɜːtˌspuːn) *n.* a spoon intermediate in size between a tablespoon and a teaspoon.

des+sia+tine ('dɛsjəˌtiːn) *n.* a Russian unit of area equal to approximately 2.7 acres or 10 800 square metres. [C18: from Russian *desyatina*, literally: tithe, from *desyat* ten]

de-Sta·lin·i+za+tion *or* **de-Sta·lin·i+sa+tion** (diːˌstɑːlɪnaɪ'zeɪʃən) *n.* the elimination of the influence of Stalin.

De Stijl (də 'staɪl) *n.* a group of artists and architects in the Netherlands in the 1920s, including Mondrian and van Doesburg, devoted to neoplasticism and then dada. [Dutch, literally: the style, title of this group's own magazine]

des+ti+na+tion (ˌdɛstɪ'neɪʃən) *n.* **1.** the predetermined end of a journey or voyage. **2.** the ultimate end or purpose for which something is created or a person is destined. **3.** *Rare.* the act of destining or predetermining.

des+tine ('dɛstɪn) *vb.* (*tr.*) to set apart or appoint (for a certain purpose or person, or to do something); intend; design. [C14: from Old French *destiner*, from Latin *dēstināre* to appoint, from DE- + *-stināre*, from *stāre* to stand]

des+tined ('dɛstɪnd) *adj.* (*postpositive*) **1.** foreordained or certain; meant: *he is destined to be famous.* **2.** (usually foll. by *for*) heading (towards a specific destination); directed: *a letter destined for Europe.*

des+ti+ny ('dɛstɪnɪ) *n., pl.* **+nies.** **1.** the future destined for a person or thing; fate; fortune; lot. **2.** the predetermined or inevitable course of events. **3.** the ultimate power or agency that predetermines the course of events. [C14: from Old French *destinee*, from *destiner* to DESTINE]

Des+ti+ny ('dɛstɪnɪ) *n., pl.* **+nies.** the power that predetermines events, personified as a goddess.

des+ti+tute ('dɛstɪˌtjuːt) *adj.* **1.** lacking the means of subsistence; totally impoverished. **2.** (*postpositive;* foll. by *of*) completely lacking; deprived or bereft (of): *destitute of words.* **3.** *Obsolete.* abandoned or deserted. [C14: from Latin *dēstitūtus* forsaken, from *dēstituere* to leave alone, from *statuere* to place] —'des+ti+ˌtute+ness *n.*

des+ti+tu+tion (ˌdɛstɪ'tjuːʃən) *n.* **1.** the state of being destitute; utter poverty. **2.** *Rare.* lack or deficiency.

des+tri+er ('dɛstrɪə) *n.* an archaic word for **warhorse** (sense 1). [C13: from Old French, from *destre* right hand, from Latin *dextra;* from the fact that a squire led a knight's horse with his right hand]

de+stroy (dɪ'strɔɪ) *vb.* (*mainly tr.*) **1.** to ruin; spoil; render useless. **2.** to tear down or demolish; break up; raze. **3.** to put an end to; do away with; extinguish. **4.** to kill or annihilate. **5.** to crush, subdue, or defeat. **6.** (*intr.*) to be destructive or cause destruction. [C13: from Old French *destruire*, from Latin *dēstruere* to pull down, from DE- + *struere* to pile up, build] —de+'stroy+a·ble *adj.*

de+stroy+er (dɪ'strɔɪə) *n.* **1.** a small fast lightly armoured but heavily armed warship. **2.** a person or thing that destroys.

de+stroy+er es+cort *n.* a warship smaller than a destroyer, designed to escort fleets or convoys.

de+struct (dɪ'strʌkt) *vb.* **1.** to destroy (one's own missile, etc.) for safety. **2.** (*intr.*) (of a missile, etc.) to be destroyed, for safety, by those controlling it; self-destruct. ~*n.* **3.** the act of destructing.

de+struct+i·ble (dɪ'strʌktəbᵊl) *adj.* capable of being or liable to be destroyed. —de+ˌstruc+ti·'bil+i·ty *n.*

de+struc+tion (dɪ'strʌkʃən) *n.* **1.** the act of destroying or state of being destroyed; demolition. **2.** a cause of ruin or means of destroying. [C14: from Latin *dēstructiō* a pulling down; see DESTROY]

de+struc+tion+ist (dɪ'strʌkʃənɪst) *n.* a person who believes in destruction, esp. of social institutions.

de+struc+tive (dɪ'strʌktɪv) *adj.* **1.** (often *postpositive* and foll. by *of* or *to*) causing or tending to cause the destruction (of). **2.** intended to disprove or discredit, esp. without positive suggestions or help; negative: *destructive criticism.* Compare **constructive** (sense 1). —de+'struc+tive+ly *adv.* —de+'struc+tive+ness *or* de+struc+tiv+i·ty (ˌdiːstrʌk'tɪvɪtɪ) *n.*

de+struc+tive dis+til+la+tion *n.* the decomposition of a complex substance, such as wood or coal, by heating it in the absence of air and collecting the volatile products.

de+struc+tor (dɪ'strʌktə) *n.* **1.** a furnace or incinerator for the disposal of refuse, esp. one that uses the resulting heat to generate power. **2.** a device used to blow up a dangerously defective missile or rocket after launching.

des·u·e+tude (dɪ'sjuːɪˌtjuːd, 'dɛswɪtjuːd) *n.* the condition of not being in use or practice; disuse: *those ceremonies had fallen into desuetude.* [C15: from Latin *dēsuētūdō*, from *dēsuescere* to lay aside a habit, from DE- + *suescere* to grow accustomed]

de+sul+phur+ize *or* **de+sul+phur+ise** (diː'sʌlfjʊˌraɪz) *vb.* to free or become free from sulphur. —de+ˌsul+phur·i+'za+tion *or* de+ˌsul+phur·i+'sa+tion *n.* —de+'sul+phur+ˌiz+er *or* de+'sul+phur+ˌis+er *n.*

des+ul+to·ry ('dɛsəltərɪ, -trɪ) *adj.* **1.** passing or jumping from one thing to another, esp. in a fitful way; unmethodical; disconnected. **2.** occurring in a random or incidental way; haphazard: *a desultory thought.* [C16: from Latin *dēsultōrius*, relating to one who vaults or jumps, hence superficial, from *dēsilīre* to jump down, from DE- + *salīre* to jump] —'des+ul+ˌto+ri+ly *adv.* —'des+ul+ˌto+ri+ness *n.*

de+tach (dɪ'tætʃ) *vb.* (*tr.*) **1.** to disengage and separate or remove, as by pulling; unfasten; disconnect. **2.** *Military.* to separate (a small unit) from a larger, esp. for a special assignment. [C17: from Old French *destachier*, from *des-* DIS-[1] + *attachier* to ATTACH] —de+'tach+a·ble *adj.* —de+ˌtach+a·'bil+i·ty *n.* —de+'tach+er *n.*

de+tached (dɪ'tætʃt) *adj.* **1.** disconnected or standing apart; not attached: *a detached house.* **2.** having or showing no bias or emotional involvement; disinterested.

de+tach+ment (dɪ'tætʃmənt) *n.* **1.** indifference to other people or to one's surroundings; aloofness. **2.** freedom from self-interest or bias; disinterest. **3.** the act of disengaging or separating something. **4.** the condition of being disengaged or separated; disconnection. **5.** *Military.* **a.** the separation of a small unit from its main body, esp. of ships or troops. **b.** the unit so detached.

de+tail ('diːteɪl) *n.* **1.** an item or smaller part that is considered separately; particular. **2.** an item or circumstance that is insignificant or unimportant: *passengers' comfort was regarded as a detail.* **3.** treatment of or attention to items or particulars: *this essay includes too much detail.* **4.** items collectively; particulars. **5.** a small or accessory section or element in a painting, building, statue, etc., esp. when considered in isolation. **6.** *Military.* **a.** the act of assigning personnel for a specific duty, esp. a fatigue. **b.** the personnel selected. **c.** the duty or assignment. **7. go into detail.** to include all or most particulars. **8. in detail.** including all or most particulars or items thoroughly. ~*vb.* (*tr.*) **9.** to list or relate fully. **10.** *Military.* to select (personnel) for a specific duty. **11.** to decorate or elaborate (carving, etc.) with fine delicate drawing or designs. [C17: from French *détail*, from Old French *detailler* to cut in pieces, from *de-* DIS-[1] + *tailler* to cut; see TAILOR]

de+tail draw+ing *n.* a separate large-scale drawing of a small part or section of a building, machine, etc.

de+tailed ('diːteɪld) *adj.* having many details or giving careful attention to details.

de+tain (dɪ'teɪn) *vb.* (*tr.*) **1.** to delay; hold back; stop. **2.** to confine or hold in custody; restrain. **3.** *Archaic.* to retain or withhold. [C15: from Old French *detenir*, from Latin *dētinēre* to hold off, keep back, from DE- + *tenēre* to hold] —de+'tain+a·ble *adj.* —de+tain·ee (ˌdiːteɪ'niː) *n.* —de+'tain+ment *n.*

de+tain+er (dɪ'teɪnə) *n. Law.* **1.** the wrongful withholding of the property of another person. **2. a.** the detention of a person in custody. **b.** a writ authorizing the further detention of a person already in custody. [C17: from Anglo-French *detener* (n.), from *detener* to DETAIN]

de+tect (dɪ'tɛkt) *vb.* (*tr.*) **1.** to discover, perceive, or notice: *to detect a note of sarcasm.* **2.** to discover, or reveal (a crime, criminal, etc.). **3.** to extract information from (an electromagnetic wave). [C15: from Latin *dētectus* uncovered, from *dētegere* to uncover, from DE- + *tegere* to cover] —de+'tect+a·ble *or* de+'tect+i·ble *adj.* —de+'tect+er *n.*

de+tec+tion (dɪ'tɛkʃən) *n.* **1.** the act of discovering or the fact of being discovered: *detection of crime.* **2.** the act or process of extracting information, esp. at audio or video frequencies, from an electromagnetic wave. See also **demodulation.**

de+tec+tive (dɪ'tɛktɪv) *n.* **1. a.** a police officer who investigates crimes. **b. private detective.** an individual privately employed to investigate a crime or make other inquiries. **c.** (*as modifier*): *a detective story.* ~*adj.* **2.** used in or serving for detection. **3.** serving to detect.

de+tec+tor (dɪ'tɛktə) *n.* **1.** a person or thing that detects. **2.** any mechanical sensing device. **3.** *Electronics.* a device used in the detection of radio signals. **4.** a device, such as a diode, used to rectify an alternating current.

de+tent (dɪ'tɛnt) *n.* the locking piece of a mechanism, often spring-loaded to check the movement of a wheel in one direction only. See also **pawl.** [C17: from Old French *destente*, a loosening, trigger: see DÉTENTE]

dé+tente (deɪ'tɑːnt; *French* de'tãt) *n.* the relaxing or easing of tension, esp. between nations. [French, literally: a loosening, from Old French *destendre* to release, from *tendre* to stretch]

de+ten+tion (dɪ'tɛnʃən) *n.* **1.** the act of detaining or state of being detained. **2. a.** custody or confinement, esp. of a suspect awaiting trial. **b.** (*as modifier*): *a detention order.* **3.** a form of punishment in which a pupil is detained after school. **4.** the withholding of something belonging to or claimed by another. [C16: from Latin *dētentiō* a keeping back; see DETAIN]

de+ten+tion cen+tre *n.* a place where young persons may be detained for short periods by order of a court.

de+ter (dɪ'tɜː) *vb.* **+ters, +ter+ring, +terred.** (*tr.*) to discourage (from acting) or prevent (from occurring), usually by instilling fear, doubt, or anxiety. [C16: from Latin *dēterrēre*, from DE- + *terrēre* to frighten] —de+'ter+ment *n.*

de+terge (dɪ'tɜːdʒ) *vb.* (*tr.*) to wash or wipe away; cleanse: *to deterge a wound.* [C17: from Latin *dētergēre* to wipe away, from DE- + *tergēre* to wipe]

de+ter+gen+cy (dɪ'tɜːdʒənsɪ) *or* **de+ter+gence** *n.* cleansing power.

de+ter+gent (dɪ'tɜːdʒənt) *n.* **1.** a cleansing agent, esp. a surface-active chemical such as an alkyl sulphonate, widely used in industry, laundering, shampoos, etc. *~adj. also* **de+ter+sive** (dɪ'tɜːsɪv). **2.** having cleansing power. [C17: from Latin *dētergēns* wiping off; see DETERGE]

de+te·ri·o+rate (dɪ'tɪərɪəˌreɪt) *vb.* **1.** to make or become worse or lower in quality, value, character, etc.; depreciate. **2.** (*intr.*) to wear away or disintegrate. [C16: from Late Latin *dēteriōrāre*, from Latin *dēterior* worse] **—de+ˌte·ri·o+'ra+tion** *n.* **—de+'te·ri·o+ra+tive** *adj.*

de+ter+mi+na·ble (dɪ'tɜːmɪnəbᵊl) *adj.* **1.** able to be decided, fixed, or found out. **2.** *Law.* liable to termination under certain conditions; terminable. **—de+'ter+mi+na·bly** *adv.*

de+ter+mi+nant (dɪ'tɜːmɪnənt) *adj.* **1.** serving to determine or affect. *~n.* **2.** a factor, circumstance, etc., that influences or determines. **3.** *Maths.* a square array of elements that represents the sum of certain products of these elements, used to solve simultaneous equations, in vector studies, etc. Compare **matrix** (sense 9).

de+ter+mi+nate (dɪ'tɜːmɪnɪt) *adj.* **1.** definitely limited, defined, or fixed; distinct. **2.** a less common word for **determined. 3. a.** able to be predicted or deduced. **b.** (of an effect) obeying the law of causality. **4.** *Botany.* (of an inflorescence) having the main and branch stems ending in flowers; cymose. **5.** (of a structure, stress, etc.) able to be fully analysed or determined. **—de+'ter+mi+nate+ly** *adv.* **—de+'ter+mi+nate+ness** *n.*

de+ter+mi+na+tion (dɪˌtɜːmɪ'neɪʃən) *n.* **1.** the act or an instance of making a decision. **2.** the condition of being determined; resoluteness. **3.** the act or an instance of ending an argument by the opinion or decision of an authority. **4.** the act or an instance of fixing or settling the quality, limit, position, etc., of something. **5.** a decision or opinion reached, rendered, or settled upon. **6.** a resolute movement towards some object or end. **7.** *Law.* the termination of an estate or interest. **8.** *Law.* the decision reached by a court of justice on a disputed matter. **9.** *Logic.* **a.** the process of qualifying or limiting a proposition or concept. **b.** the qualifications or limitations used in this process. **10.** the condition of embryonic tissues of being able to develop into only one particular tissue or organ in the adult.

de+ter+mi+na+tive (dɪ'tɜːmɪnətɪv) *adj.* **1.** able to or serving to settle or determine; deciding. *~n.* **2.** a factor, circumstance, etc., that settles or determines. **3.** *Grammar.* a less common word for **determiner. 4.** (in a logographic writing system) a logogram that bears a separate meaning, from which compounds and inflected forms are built up. **—de+'ter+mi+na+tive+ly** *adv.* **—de+'ter+mi+na+tive+ness** *n.*

de+ter+mine (dɪ'tɜːmɪn) *vb.* **1.** to settle or decide (an argument, question, etc.) conclusively, as by referring to an authority. **2.** (*tr.*) to ascertain or conclude, esp. after observation or consideration. **3.** (*tr.*) to shape or influence; give direction to: *experience often determines ability.* **4.** (*tr.*) to fix in scope, extent, variety, etc.: *the river determined the edge of the property.* **5.** to make or cause to make a decision: *he determined never to marry.* **6.** (*tr.*) *Logic.* to define or limit (a notion) by adding or requiring certain features or characteristics. **7.** (*tr.*) *Geom.* to fix or specify the position, form, or configuration of: *two points determine a line.* **8.** *Chiefly law.* to come or bring to an end, as an estate or interest in land. **9.** (*tr.*) to decide (a legal action or dispute). [C14: from Old French *determiner*, from Latin *dētermin良āre* to set boundaries to, from DE- + *termināre* to limit; see TERMINATE]

de+ter+mined (dɪ'tɜːmɪnd) *adj.* of unwavering mind; resolute; firm. **—de+'ter+mined+ly** *adv.* **—de+'ter+mined+ness** *n.*

de+ter+min+er (dɪ'tɜːmɪnə) *n.* **1.** a word, such as a number, an article, or *all*, that determines the referent or referents of a noun phrase. **2.** a person or thing that determines.

de+ter+min+ism (dɪ'tɜːmɪˌnɪzəm) *n.* the philosophical doctrine that all acts, choices, and events are the inevitable consequence of antecedent sufficient causes. Compare **free will. —de+'ter+min+ist** *n., adj.* **—de+ˌter+min+'is+tic** *adj.*

de+ter+rent (dɪ'tɛrənt) *n.* **1.** something that deters. **2.** a weapon or combination of weapons, esp. nuclear, held by one state, etc., to deter attack by another. *~adj.* **3.** tending or used to deter; restraining. [C19: from Latin *dēterrēns* hindering; see DETER] **—de+'ter+rence** *n.*

de+test (dɪ'tɛst) *vb.* (*tr.*) to dislike intensely; loathe. [C16: from Latin *dētestārī* to curse (while invoking a god as witness), from DE- + *testārī* to bear witness, from *testis* a witness] **—de+'test+er** *n.*

de+test+a·ble (dɪ'tɛstəbᵊl) *adj.* being or deserving to be abhorred or detested; abominable; odious. **—de+ˌtest+a·'bil+i·ty** *or* **de+'test+a·ble+ness** *n.* **—de+'test+a·bly** *adv.*

de+tes+ta+tion (ˌdiːtɛs'teɪʃən) *n.* **1.** intense hatred; abhorrence. **2.** a person or thing that is detested.

de+throne (dɪ'θrəʊn) *vb.* (*tr.*) to remove from a throne or deprive of any high position or title; depose: *the champion was dethroned by a young boxer.* **—de+'throne+ment** *n.* **—de+'thron+er** *n.*

det·i+nue ('dɛtɪˌnjuː) *n. Law.* an action brought by a plaintiff to recover goods wrongfully detained. [C15: from Old French *detenue*, from *detenir* to DETAIN]

Det+mold ('dɛtməʊld; *German* 'detmɔlt) *n.* a city in NW West Germany, in North Rhine-Westphalia. Pop.: 63 700 (1970).

det·o+nate ('dɛtəˌneɪt) *vb.* to cause (a bomb, mine, etc.) to explode or (of a bomb, mine, etc.) to explode; set off or be set off. [C18: from Latin *dētonāre* to thunder down, from DE- + *tonāre* to THUNDER]

det·o+na+tion (ˌdɛtə'neɪʃən) *n.* **1.** an explosion or the act of exploding. **2.** the spontaneous combustion in an internal-combustion engine of part of the mixture before it has been reached by the flame front. **3.** *Physics.* rapid combustion, esp. that occurring within a shock wave. **—'det·o+ˌna+tive** *adj.*

det·o+na+tor ('dɛtəˌneɪtə) *n.* **1.** a small amount of explosive, as in a percussion cap, used to initiate a larger explosion. **2.** a device, such as an electrical generator, used to set off an explosion from a distance. **3.** a substance or object that explodes or is capable of exploding.

de+tour ('diːtʊə) *n.* **1.** a deviation from a direct, usually shorter route or course of action. *~vb.* **2.** to deviate or cause to deviate from a direct route or course of action. [C18: from French *détour*, from Old French *destorner* to divert, turn away, from *des-* DE- + *torner* to TURN]

de+tox·i+cate (diː'tɒksɪˌkeɪt) *vb.* (*tr.*) **1.** to rid (a patient) of a poison or its effects. **2.** to counteract (a poison). [C19: DE- + *-toxicate*, from Latin *toxicum* poison; see TOXIC] **—de+'tox·i+cant** *adj., n.* **—de+ˌtox·i+'ca+tion** *n.*

de+tox·i+fy (diː'tɒksɪˌfaɪ) *vb.* **+fies, +fy+ing, +fied.** (*tr.*) to remove poison from; detoxicate. **—de+ˌtox·i+fi+'ca+tion** *n.*

de+tract (dɪ'trækt) *vb.* **1.** (when *intr.*, usually foll. by *from*) to take away a part (of); diminish: *her anger detracts from her beauty.* **2.** (*tr.*) to distract or divert. **3.** (*tr.*) *Obsolete.* to belittle or disparage. [C15: from Latin *dētractus* drawn away, from *dētrahere* to pull away, disparage, from DE- + *trahere* to drag] **—de+'tract+ing+ly** *adv.* **—de+'trac+tive** *or* **de+'trac+to·ry** *adj.* **—de+'trac+tive+ly** *adv.* **—de+'trac+tor** *n.*

de+trac+tion (dɪ'trækʃən) *n.* **1.** a person, thing, circumstance, etc., that detracts. **2.** the act of discrediting or detracting from another's reputation, esp. by slander; disparagement.

de+train (diː'treɪn) *vb.* to leave or cause to leave a railway train, as passengers, etc. **—de+'train+ment** *n.*

de+trib+al+ize *or* **de+trib+al+ise** (diː'traɪbəˌlaɪz) *vb.* (*tr.*) **1.** to cause members of a tribe to lose their characteristic customs or social, religious, or other organizational features. **2.** to cause tribal people to adopt urban ways of life. **—de+ˌtrib+al·i+'za+tion** *or* **de+ˌtrib+al·i+'sa+tion** *n.*

det+ri+ment ('dɛtrɪmənt) *n.* **1.** disadvantage or damage; harm; loss. **2.** a cause of disadvantage or damage. [C15: from Latin *dētrīmentum*, a rubbing off, hence damage, from *dēterere* to rub away, from DE- + *terere* to rub]

det+ri+men+tal (ˌdɛtrɪ'mɛntᵊl) *adj.* (when *postpositive*, foll. by *to*) harmful; injurious; prejudicial: *smoking can be detrimental to health.* **—ˌdet+ri+'men+tal+ly** *adv.*

de+tri+tion (dɪ'trɪʃən) *n.* the act of rubbing or wearing away by friction. [C17: from Medieval Latin *dētrītiō*, from Latin *dētrītus* worn away; see DETRIMENT]

de+tri+tus (dɪ'traɪtəs) *n.* **1.** a loose mass of stones, silt, etc., worn away from rocks. **2.** an accumulation of disintegrated material or debris. [C18: from French *détritus*, from Latin *dētrītus* a rubbing away; see DETRIMENT] **—de+'tri+tal** *adj.*

De+troit (dɪ'trɔɪt) *n.* **1.** a city in SE Michigan, on the Detroit River: a major Great Lakes port; largest car-manufacturing centre in the world. Pop.: 1 386 817 (1973 est.). **2.** a river in central North America, flowing along the U.S.-Canadian border from Lake St. Clair to Lake Erie.

de trop *French.* (də 'tro) *adj.* (*postpositive*) not wanted; in the way; superfluous. [literally: of too much]

de+trude (dɪ'truːd) *vb.* (*tr.*) to force down or thrust away or out. [C16: from Latin *dētrūdere* to push away, from DE- + *trūdere* to thrust] **—de+tru+sion** (dɪ'truːʒən) *n.*

de+trun+cate (dɪ'trʌŋkeɪt) *vb.* (*tr.*) another word for **truncate. —ˌde+trun+'ca+tion** *n.*

de+tu+mes+cence (ˌdiːtjʊ'mɛsəns) *n.* the subsidence of a swelling, esp. the return of a swollen organ, such as the penis, to the flaccid state. [C17: from Latin *dētumescere* to cease swelling, from DE- + *tumescere*, from *tumēre* to swell]

Deu·ca·li·on (djuː'keɪlɪən) *n.* the son of Prometheus and, with his wife Pyrrha, the only survivor on earth of a flood sent by Zeus (**Deucalion's flood**). Together, they were allowed to repopulate the world by throwing stones over their shoulders, which became men and women.

deuce[1] (djuːs) *n.* **1. a.** a playing card or dice with two pips or spots; two. **b.** a throw of two in dice. **2.** *Tennis, table tennis, etc.* a tied score (in tennis 40-all) that requires one player to gain two successive points to win the game. [C15: from Old French *deus* two, from Latin *duos*, accusative masculine of *duo* two]

deuce[2] (djuːs) *Informal.* *~interj.* **1.** an expression of annoyance or frustration. *~n.* **2. the deuce.** (intensifier): used in such phrases as **what the deuce, where the deuce,** etc. [C17: probably special use of DEUCE[1] (in the sense: lowest throw at dice)]

deu+ced ('djuːsɪd, djuːst) *Brit. informal.* *~adj.* **1.** (intensifier, usually qualifying something undesirable) damned; confounded: *he's a deuced idiot.* *~adv.* **2.** (intensifier): *deuced good luck.* **—'deu+ced+ly** *adv.*

Deur+ne (*Flemish* 'døːrnə) *n.* a town in N Belgium, a suburb of E Antwerp: site of Antwerp airport. Pop.: 80 766 (1970).

De·us *Latin.* ('deɪʊs) *n.* God. [related to Greek *Zeus*]

de·us ex mach·i+na *Latin.* ('deɪʊs ɛks 'mækɪnə) *n.* **1.** (in ancient Greek and Roman drama) a god introduced into a play to resolve the plot. **2.** any unlikely or artificial device serving this purpose. [literally: god out of a machine, translating Greek *theos ek mēkhanēs*]

Deut. *Bible. abbrev. for* Deuteronomy.

deu+ter+ag·o+nist (ˌdjuːtə'rægənɪst) *n.* (in ancient Greek drama) the character next in importance to the protagonist, esp. the antagonist. [C19: from Greek *deuteragōnistēs*, from DEUTERO- + *agōnistēs* contestant, actor]

deu+ter·a+nope ('dju:tərə,nəʊp) *n.* a person who has deuteranopia.

deu+ter·a+no+pi·a (,dju:tərə'nəʊpɪə) *n.* inability to see the colour green; green blindness. [C20: New Latin, from DEUTERO- (referring to the second primary colour, green) + AN- + Greek *-ops* eye] —**deu+ter+an+op+ic** (,dju:tərə'nɒpɪk) *adj.*

deu+ter+ate ('dju:tə,reɪt) *vb.* to treat or combine with deuterium.

deu+ter+ide ('dju:tə,raɪd) *n.* a compound of deuterium with some other element. It is analogous to a hydride.

deu+ter+i·um (dju:'tɪərɪəm) *n.* a stable isotope of hydrogen, occurring in natural hydrogen (156 parts per million) and in heavy water: used as a tracer in chemistry and biology. Symbol: D or ^{2}H; atomic no.: 1; atomic wt.: 2.014; boiling pt.: −249.7°C. [C20: New Latin; see DEUTERO-, -IUM; from the fact that it is the second heaviest hydrogen isotope]

deu+ter+i·um ox+ide *n.* another name for **heavy water.**

deu·ter·o-, deu·to- *or before a vowel* **deu·ter-, deut-** *combining form.* **1.** second or secondary: *deuterogamy; deuterium.* **2.** (in chemistry) indicating the presence of deuterium. [from Greek *deuteros* second]

deu+ter+og·a+my (,dju:tə'rɒgəmɪ) *n.* another word for **digamy.** —,**deu+ter+'og·a+mist** *n.*

deu+ter+on ('dju:tə,rɒn) *n.* the nucleus of a deuterium atom, consisting of one proton and one neutron.

Deu+ter+on·o+mist (,dju:tə'rɒnəmɪst) *n.* one of the writers of Deuteronomy.

Deu+ter+on·o+my (,dju:tə'rɒnəmɪ) *n.* the fifth book of the Old Testament, containing a second statement of the Mosaic Law. [from Late Latin *Deuteronomium,* from Greek *Deuteronomion;* see DEUTERO-, -NOMY] —**Deu+ter·o+no+mic** (,dju:tərə'nɒmɪk) *adj.*

deu+to+plasm ('dju:tə,plæzəm) *or* **deu+te·ro+plasm** ('dju:tərəʊ,plæzəm) *n.* nutritive material in a cell, esp. the yolk in a developing ovum. —,**deu+to+'plas+mic** *or* ,**deu+to+'plas+tic** *adj.*

Deut+sche Mark ('dɔɪtʃə) *n.* the standard monetary unit of West Germany, divided into 100 pfennigs. Abbrev.: **DM**

Deutsch+land ('dɔɪtʃ,lant) *n.* the German name for **Germany.**

deut+zi·a ('dju:tsɪə) *n.* any saxifragaceous shrub of the genus *Deutzia:* cultivated for their clusters of white or pink spring-blooming flowers. [C19: New Latin, named after Jean *Deutz,* 18th-century Dutch patron of botany]

Deux-Sèvres (*French* dø 'sɛ:vr) *n.* a department of W France, in Poitou-Charentes region. Capital: Niort. Pop.: 342 383 (1975). Area: 6054 sq. km (2361 sq. miles).

de·va ('deɪvə) *n.* (in Hinduism and Buddhism) a divine being or god. [C19: from Sanskrit: god]

de Va·ler·a (dɛ və'lɛərə, -'lɪə-) *n.* **Ea·mon** ('eɪmən). 1882–1975, Irish statesman; president of Sinn Fein (1917) and of the Dáil (1918–22); formed the nationalist Fianna Fail party (1927); prime minister (1937–48; 1951–54; 1957–59) and president (1959–73) of the Irish Republic.

de+val·u·a·tion (di:,vælju:'eɪʃən) *n.* **1.** a decrease in the exchange value of a currency against gold or other currencies, brought about by a government. Compare **depreciation** (sense 4). **2.** a reduction in value, status, importance, etc.

de+val·ue (di:'vælju:) *or* **de+val·u·ate** (di:'vælju:,eɪt) *vb.* **+val·ues, +val·u+ing, +val+ued** *or* **+val·u·ates, +val·u·at+ing, +val·u+at+ed. 1.** to reduce (a currency) or (of a currency) be reduced in exchange value. **2.** (*tr.*) to reduce the value or worth of (something).

De+va+na+ga+ri (,deɪvə'nɑ:gərɪ) *n.* a syllabic script in which Sanskrit, Hindi, and other modern languages of India are written. [C18: from Sanskrit: alphabet of the gods, from *deva* god + *nagari* an Indian alphabet]

dev+as+tate ('dɛvə,steɪt) *vb.* (*tr.*) **1.** to lay waste or make desolate; ravage; destroy. **2.** *Informal.* to confound or overwhelm. [C17: from Latin *dēvastāre,* from DE- + *vastāre* to ravage; related to *vastus* waste, empty] —,**dev+as+'ta+tion** *n.* —**'dev+as+,ta+tive** *adj.* —**'dev+as+,ta+tor** *n.*

de+vel+op (dɪ'vɛləp) *vb.* **1.** to come or bring to a later or more advanced or expanded stage; grow or cause to grow gradually. **2.** (*tr.*) to elaborate or work out in detail. **3.** to disclose or unfold (thoughts, a plot, etc.) gradually or (of thoughts, etc.) to be gradually disclosed or unfolded. **4.** to come or bring into existence; generate or be generated: *he developed a new faith in God.* **5.** (*tr.*) to improve the value or change the use of (land), as by building. **6.** (*tr.*) *Photog.* **a.** to treat (film, plate, or paper previously exposed to light, or the latent image in such material) with chemical solutions in order to produce a visible image. **b.** to process (photographic material) in order to produce negatives and prints. **7.** *Biology.* to progress or cause to progress from simple to complex stages in the growth of an individual or the evolution of a species. **8.** (*tr.*) to elaborate upon (a musical theme) by varying the melody, key, etc. **9.** (*tr.*) *Maths.* to expand (a function or expression) in the form of a series. **10.** (*tr.*) *Geom.* to project or roll out (a surface) onto a plane without stretching or shrinking any element. **11.** *Chess.* to bring (a piece) into play from its initial position on the back rank. **12.** (*tr.*) to contract (a disease or illness). **13.** (*tr.*) *Obsolete.* to disclose or reveal. [C19: from Old French *desveloper* to unwrap, from *des-* DIS-[1] + *veloper* to wrap; see ENVELOP] —**de+'vel+op·a+ble** *adj.*

de+vel+op+er (dɪ'vɛləpə) *n.* **1.** a person or thing that develops something, esp. a person who develops property. **2.** *Photog.* a solution of a chemical reducing agent that converts the latent image recorded in the emulsion of a film or paper into a visible image.

de+vel+op+ment (dɪ'vɛləpmənt) *n.* **1.** the act or process of growing, progressing, or developing. **2.** the product or result of developing. **3.** a fact, event, or happening, esp. one that changes a situation. **4.** an area or tract of land that has been developed. **5.** Also called: **development section.** the section of a movement, usually in sonata form, in which the basic musical themes are developed. **6.** *Chess.* **a.** the process of developing pieces. **b.** the manner in which they are developed. **c.** the position of the pieces in the early part of a game with reference to their attacking potential or defensive efficiency. —**de+,vel+op+'men+tal** *adj.* —**de+,vel+op+'men+tal+ly** *adv.*

De+ven+ter ('deɪvəntə; *Dutch* 'deːvəntər) *n.* an industrial city in the E Netherlands, in Overijssel province, on the River IJssel: medieval intellectual centre; early centre of Dutch printing. Pop.: 63 979 (1973 est.).

Dev·e·reux ('dɛvərə) *n.* **Rob·ert.** See (2nd Earl of) **Essex.**

de+vest (dɪ'vɛst) *vb.* (*tr.*) a rare variant spelling of **divest.**

De·vi ('deɪvi:) *n.* a Hindu goddess and embodiment of the female energy of Siva. [Sanskrit: goddess; see DEVA]

de+vi+ant ('di:vɪənt) *adj.* **1.** deviating, as from what is considered acceptable behaviour. ~*n.* **2.** a person whose behaviour, esp. sexual behaviour, deviates from what is considered to be acceptable. —**'de+vi+ance** *n.*

de+vi+ate ('di:vɪ,eɪt) *vb.* **1.** (*usually intr.*) to differ or diverge or cause to differ or diverge, as in belief or thought. **2.** (*usually intr.*) to turn aside or cause to turn aside; diverge or cause to diverge. **3.** (*intr.*) *Psychol.* to depart from an accepted standard or convention. ~*n., adj.* ('di:vɪɪt). **4.** another word for **deviant** (sense 2). [C17: from Late Latin *dēviāre* to turn aside from the direct road, from DE- + *via* road] —**'de+vi·,a+tor** *n.* —**'de+vi·a+to·ry** *adj.*

de+vi·a·tion (,di:vɪ'eɪʃən) *n.* **1.** an act or result of deviating. **2.** *Statistics.* the difference between an observed value in a series of such values and their arithmetic mean. **3.** the error of a compass due to local magnetic disturbances.

de+vi·a·tion+ism (,di:vɪ'eɪʃə,nɪzəm) *n.* ideological deviation (esp. from orthodox Communism). —,**de+vi·'a+tion+ist** *n., adj.*

de+vice (dɪ'vaɪs) *n.* **1.** a machine or tool used for a specific task; contrivance. **2.** a plan or plot, esp. a clever or evil one; scheme; trick. **3.** any ornamental pattern or picture, as in embroidery. **4.** a written, printed, or painted design or figure, used as a heraldic sign, emblem, trademark, etc. **5.** a particular pattern of words, figures of speech, etc., used in literature to produce an effect on the reader. **6.** *Archaic.* the act or process of planning or devising. **7. leave (someone) to his own devices.** to leave (someone) alone to do as he wishes. [C13: from Old French *devis* purpose, contrivance and *devise* difference, intention, from *deviser* to divide, control; see DEVISE]

dev+il ('dɛvᵊl) *n.* **1.** *Theol.* (*often cap.*) the chief spirit of evil and enemy of God, often represented as the ruler of hell and often depicted as a human figure with horns, cloven hoofs, and tail. **2.** *Theol.* one of the subordinate evil spirits of traditional Jewish and Christian belief. **3.** a person or animal regarded as cruel, wicked, or ill-natured. **4.** a person or animal regarded as unfortunate or wretched: *that poor devil was ill for months.* **5.** a person or animal regarded as clever, daring, mischievous, or energetic. **6.** *Informal.* something difficult or annoying. **7.** *Christian Science.* the opposite of truth; an error, lie, or false belief in sin, sickness, and death. **8.** (in Malaysia) a ghost. **9.** a portable furnace or brazier, esp. one used in road-making or one used by plumbers. Compare **salamander** (sense 7). **10.** any of various mechanical devices, such as a machine for making wooden screws or a rag-tearing machine. **11.** See **printer's devil. 12.** *Law.* (in England) a junior barrister who does work for another in order to gain experience, usually for a half fee. **13. between the devil and the deep blue sea.** between equally undesirable alternatives. **14. devil of a.** *Informal.* (intensifier): *a devil of a fine horse.* **15. give the devil his due.** to acknowledge the talent or the success of an opponent or unpleasant person. **16. go to the devil. a.** to fail or become dissipated. **b.** (*interj.*) used to express annoyance with the person causing it. **17. like the devil.** with great speed, determination, etc. **18. play the devil with.** *Informal.* to make much worse; upset considerably: *the damp plays the devil with my rheumatism.* **19. raise the devil. a.** to cause a commotion. **b.** to make a great protest. **20. talk** (*or* **speak**) **of the devil!** (*interj.*) used when an absent person who has been the subject of conversation appears. **21. the devil!** (intensifier): **a.** used in such phrases as **what the devil, where the devil,** etc. **b.** an exclamation of anger, surprise, disgust, etc. **22. the devil's own.** a very difficult or problematic (thing). **23. (let) the devil take the hindmost.** look after oneself and leave others to their fate. **24. the devil to pay.** problems or trouble to be faced as a consequence of an action. **25. the very devil.** something very difficult or awkward. ~*vb.* **+ils, +il+ling, +illed** *or U.S.* **+ils, +il+ing, +iled. 26.** (*tr.*) *Informal.* to harass, vex, torment, etc. **27.** (*tr.*) to prepare (esp. meat, poultry, or fish) by coating with a highly flavoured spiced paste or mixture of condiments before cooking. **28.** (*tr.*) to tear (rags) with a devil. **29.** (*intr.*) to serve as a printer's devil. **30.** (*intr.*) *Chiefly Brit.* to do hackwork, esp. for a lawyer or author; perform arduous tasks, often without pay or recognition of one's services. [Old English *dēofol,* from Latin *diabolus,* from Greek *diabolos* enemy, accuser, slanderer, from *diaballein,* literally: to throw across, hence, to slander]

dev·il+fish ('dɛvᵊl,fɪʃ) *n., pl.* **+fish** *or* **+fish·es. 1.** Also called: **devil ray.** another name for **manta** (the fish). **2.** another name for **octopus.**

dev+il+ish ('dɛvəlɪʃ, 'dɛvlɪʃ) *adj.* **1.** of, resembling, or befitting a devil; diabolic; fiendish. ~*adv., adj. Informal.* **2.** (intensifier):

devilish good food; this devilish heat. —'**dev+il+ish+ly** *adv.* —'**dev+il+ish+ness** *n.*

de Vil·liers (də 'vɪljəz) *n.* **Daw·ie** ('dɑːwɪ). born 1940, South African Rugby Union footballer: halfback for the Springboks (1962–70).

dev·il-may-care *adj.* careless or reckless; happy-go-lucky: *a devil-may-care attitude.*

dev+il+ment ('dɛvᵊlmənt) *n.* devilish or mischievous conduct.

dev+il+ry ('dɛvᵊlrɪ) *or* **dev+il+try** *n., pl.* **+ries** *or* **+tries. 1.** reckless or malicious fun or mischief. **2.** wickedness or cruelty. **3.** black magic or other forms of diabolism. [C18: from French *diablerie,* from *diable* DEVIL]

dev+il's ad+vo+cate *n.* **1.** a person who advocates an opposing or unpopular view, often for the sake of argument. **2.** *R.C. Church.* the official appointed to put the case against the beatification or canonization of a candidate. Technical name: **pro+mo+tor fi+de+i** (prəʊ'məʊtɔː fɪ'deɪiː). [translation of New Latin *advocātus diabolī*]

dev+il's bit *n.* short for **devil's bit scabious** (see **scabious**²(sense 3)).

dev+il's coach-horse *n.* a large black rove beetle, *Ocypus olens,* with large jaws and ferocious habits.

dev+il's darn+ing nee+dle *n.* a popular name for a **dragonfly.**

dev+il's food cake *n. Chiefly U.S.* a rich chocolate cake.

Dev+il's Is+land *n.* one of the three Safety Islands, off the coast of French Guiana: formerly a leper colony, then a French penal colony from 1895 until 1938. Area: less than 2 sq. km (1 sq. mile). French name: **Île du Diable.**

dev·ils-on-horse·back *n.* a savoury of prunes wrapped in bacon slices and served on toast.

de+vi+ous ('diːvɪəs) *adj.* **1.** not sincere or candid; deceitful; underhand. **2.** (of a route or course of action) rambling; indirect; roundabout. **3.** going astray from a proper or accepted way; erring. [C16: from Latin *dēvius* lying to one side of the road, from DE- + *via* road] —'**de+vi+ous+ly** *adv.* —'**de+vi+ous+ness** *n.*

de+vis+a+ble (dɪ'vaɪzəbᵊl) *adj.* **1.** *Law.* (of property, esp. realty) capable of being transferred by will. **2.** able to be invented, contrived, or devised.

de+vis+al (dɪ'vaɪzᵊl) *n.* the act of inventing, contriving, or devising; contrivance.

de+vise (dɪ'vaɪz) *vb.* **1.** to work out, contrive, or plan (something) in one's mind. **2.** (*tr.*) *Law.* to dispose of (property, esp. real property) by will. **3.** (*tr.*) *Obsolete.* to imagine or guess. ~*n. Law.* **4. a.** a disposition of property by will. **b.** the property so transmitted. Compare **bequeath** (sense 1). **5.** a will or clause in a will disposing of real property. Compare **bequest** (sense 2). [C15: from Old French *deviser* to divide, apportion, intend, from Latin *dīvidere* to DIVIDE] —**de+'vis+er** *n.*

de+vi+see (dɪvaɪ'ziː, ˌdɛvɪ-) *n. Property law.* a person to whom property, esp. realty, is devised by will. Compare **legatee.**

de+vi+sor (dɪ'vaɪzə) *n. Property law.* a person who devises property, esp. realty, by will.

de+vi+tal+ize *or* **de+vi+tal+ise** (diː'vaɪtəˌlaɪz) *vb.* (*tr.*) to lower or destroy the vitality of; make weak or lifeless: *the war devitalized the economy.* —**de+ˌvi+tal+i+'za+tion** *or* **de+ˌvi+tal+i+'sa+tion** *n.*

de+vit+ri+fy (diː'vɪtrɪˌfaɪ) *vb.* **+fies, +fy+ing, +fied. 1.** to change from a vitreous state to a crystalline state. **2.** to lose or cause to lose the properties of a glass and become brittle and opaque. —**de+ˌvit+ri+fi+'ca+tion** *n.*

de+voice (diː'vɔɪs) *or* **de+vo+cal+ize, de+vo+cal+ise** (diː'vəʊkəˌlaɪz) *vb.* (*tr.*) *Phonetics.* to make (a voiced speech sound) voiceless.

de+void (dɪ'vɔɪd) *adj.* (*postpositive;* foll. by *of*) destitute or void (of); free (from).

de+voirs (də'vwɑː; *French* də'vwar) *pl. n.* (*sometimes sing.*) compliments or respects; courteous attentions. [C13: from Old French: duty, from *devoir* to be obliged to, owe, from Latin *dēbēre;* see DEBT]

de+vo+lu+tion (ˌdiːvə'luːʃən) *n.* **1.** the act, fact, or result of devolving. **2.** a passing onwards or downwards from one stage to another. **3.** another word for **degeneration** (sense 3). **4.** a transfer or allocation of authority, esp. from a central government to regional governments or particular interests. [C16: from Medieval Latin *dēvolūtiō* a rolling down, from Latin *dēvolvere* to roll down, sink into; see DEVOLVE] —ˌ**de+vo+'lu+tion+ar+y** *adj.* —ˌ**de+vo+'lu+tion+ist** *n., adj.*

de+volve (dɪ'vɒlv) *vb.* **1.** (foll. by *on, upon, to,* etc.) to pass or cause to pass to a successor or substitute, as duties, power, etc. **2.** (*intr.* foll. by *on* or *upon*) *Law.* (of an estate, etc.) to pass to another by operation of law, esp. on intestacy or bankruptcy. **3.** (*intr.;* foll. by *on* or *upon*) to depend (on): *your argument devolves on how you interpret this clause.* **4.** *Archaic.* to roll down or cause to roll down. [C15: from Latin *dēvolvere* to roll down, fall into, from DE- + *volvere* to roll] —**de+'volve+ment** *n.*

Dev+on ('dɛvᵊn) *n.* **1.** a county of SW England, between the Bristol Channel and the English Channel, including the island of Lundy: hilly, rising to the uplands of Exmoor and Dartmoor, with wooded river valleys and a rugged coastline. Administrative centre: Exeter. Pop.: 942 100 (1976 est.). Area: 6711 sq. km (2591 sq. miles). **2.** a breed of large red cattle originally from Devon.

De+vo+ni·an (də'vəʊnɪən) *adj.* **1.** of, denoting, or formed in the fourth period of the Palaeozoic era, between the Silurian and Carboniferous periods, lasting for 50 million years during which amphibians first appeared. **2.** of or relating to Devon. ~*n.* **3. the.** the Devonian period or rock system.

Dev+on+shire cream *n.* another name for **clotted cream.**

Dev+on+shire split *n.* a kind of yeast bun split open and served with whipped cream or butter and jam. Also called: **Cornish split, split.**

de+vote (dɪ'vəʊt) *vb.* (*tr.*) **1.** to apply or dedicate (oneself, time, money, etc.) to some pursuit, cause, etc. **2.** *Obsolete.* to curse or doom. [C16: from Latin *dēvōtus* devoted, solemnly promised, from *dēvovēre* to vow; see DE-, VOW] —**de+'vote+ment** *n.*

de+vot+ed (dɪ'vəʊtɪd) *adj.* **1.** feeling or demonstrating loyalty or devotion; ardent; devout. **2.** (*postpositive;* foll. by *to*) set apart, dedicated, or consecrated. —**de+'vot+ed+ly** *adv.* —**de+'vot+ed+ness** *n.*

dev·o·tee (ˌdɛvə'tiː) *n.* **1.** a person ardently enthusiastic about or devoted to something, such as a sport or pastime. **2.** a zealous follower of a religion.

de+vo+tion (dɪ'vəʊʃən) *n.* **1.** (often foll. by *to*) strong attachment (to) or affection (for a cause, person, etc.) marked by dedicated loyalty. **2.** religious zeal; piety. **3.** (*often pl.*) religious observance or prayers.

de+vo+tion+al (dɪ'vəʊʃənᵊl) *adj.* **1.** relating to, characterized by, or conducive to devotion. ~*n.* **2.** (*often pl.*) a short religious or prayer service. —**de+ˌvo+tion+'al+i+ty** *or* **de+'vo+tion+al+ness** *n.* —**de+'vo+tion+al+ly** *adv.*

de+vour (dɪ'vaʊə) *vb.* (*tr.*) **1.** to swallow or eat up greedily or voraciously. **2.** to waste or destroy; consume: *the flames devoured the curtains.* **3.** to consume greedily or avidly with the senses or mind: *he devoured the manuscripts.* **4.** to engulf or absorb: *the flood devoured the land.* [C14: from Old French *devourer,* from Latin *dēvorāre* to gulp down, from DE- + *vorāre* to consume greedily; see VORACIOUS] —**de+'vour+er** *n.* —**de+'vour+ing+ly** *adv.*

de+vout (dɪ'vaʊt) *adj.* **1.** deeply religious; reverent. **2.** sincere; earnest; heartfelt: *a devout confession.* [C13: from Old French *devot,* from Late Latin *dēvōtus,* from Latin: faithful; see DEVOTE] —**de+'vout+ly** *adv.* —**de+'vout+ness** *n.*

De Vries (*Dutch* də 'vriːs) *n.* **Hu·go** ('hyːxoː). 1848–1935, Dutch botanist, who rediscovered Mendel's laws and developed the mutation theory of evolution.

dew (djuː) *n.* **1. a.** drops of water condensed on a cool surface, esp. at night, from vapour in the air. **b.** (*in combination*): *dewdrop.* **2.** something like or suggestive of this, esp. in freshness: *the dew of youth.* **3.** small drops of moisture, such as tears. ~*vb.* **4.** (*tr.*) *Poetic.* to moisten with or as with dew. [Old English *dēaw;* related to Old High German *tou* dew, Old Norse *dögg*]

de+wan *or* **di+wan** (dɪ'wɑːn) *n.* (formerly in India) the chief minister or finance minister of a state ruled by an Indian prince. [C17: from Hindi *dīwān,* from Persian *dēvan* register, book of accounts; see DIVAN]

Dew·ar ('djuːə) *n.* Sir **James.** 1842–1923, Scottish chemist and physicist. He worked on the liquefaction of gases and the properties of matter at low temperature, invented the vacuum flask, and (with Sir Frederick Abel) was the first to prepare cordite.

Dew·ar flask *n.* a type of vacuum flask, esp. one used in scientific experiments to keep liquid air, helium, etc.; Thermos. [C20: named after Sir James DEWAR]

dew+ber·ry ('djuːbərɪ, -brɪ) *n., pl.* **·ries. 1.** any trailing bramble, such as *Rubus hispidus* of North America and *R. caesius* of Europe and NW Asia, having blue-black fruits. **2.** the fruit of any such plant.

dew+claw ('djuːˌklɔː) *n.* **1.** a nonfunctional claw in dogs; the rudimentary first digit. **2.** an analogous rudimentary hoof in deer, goats, etc. —'**dew+ˌclawed** *adj.*

dew+drop ('djuːˌdrɒp) *n.* **1.** a drop of dew. **2.** *Brit. euphemistic.* a drop of mucus on the end of one's nose.

Dew·ey ('djuːɪ) *n.* **John.** 1859–1952, U.S. pragmatist philosopher and educator: an exponent of progressivism in education, he formulated an instrumentalist theory of learning through experience. His works include *The School and Society* (1899), *Democracy and Education* (1916), and *Logic: the Theory of Inquiry* (1938).

Dew·ey Dec·i·mal Sys+tem *n.* a frequently used system of library book classification and arrangement with ten main subject classes. Also called: **decimal classification.** Abbrev.: **DDS** [C19: named after Melvil *Dewey* (1851–1931), U.S. educator who invented the system]

de Wint (də 'wɪnt) *n.* **Pe·ter.** 1784–1849, English landscape painter.

dew+lap ('djuːˌlæp) *n.* **1.** a loose fold of skin hanging from beneath the throat in cattle, dogs, etc. **2.** loose skin on an elderly person's throat. [C14 *dewlappe,* from DEW (probably changed by folk etymology from an earlier form of different meaning) + LAP¹ (from Old English *læppa* hanging flap), perhaps of Scandinavian origin; compare Danish *doglæp*] —'**dew+ˌlapped** *adj.*

DEW line (djuː) *n. acronym for* distant early warning line, a network of sensors situated mainly in Arctic regions to give early warning of airborne attack on North America.

dew point *n.* the temperature at which water vapour in the air becomes saturated and dew begins to form.

dew pond *n.* a small natural pond.

Dews+bur·y ('djuːzbərɪ, -brɪ) *n.* a town in N England, in West Yorkshire: woollen industry. Pop.: 51 310 (1971).

dew-worm *n. Canadian informal.* any large earthworm that can be seen at night and is used as fishing bait.

dew·y ('djuːɪ) *adj.* **dew·i+er, dew+i·est. 1.** moist with or as with dew: *a dewy complexion.* **2.** of or resembling dew. **3.** *Poetic.* suggesting, falling, or refreshing like dew: *dewy sleep.* —'**dew·i+ly** *adv.* —'**dew·i+ness** *n.*

dew·y-eyed *adj.* naive, innocent, or trusting, esp. in a romantic or childlike way.

Dex+e·drine ('dɛksɪˌdriːn) *n.* a trademark for **dextroamphetamine.**

dex+ter[1] ('dɛkstə) *adj.* **1.** *Archaic.* of or located on the right side. **2.** (*usually postpositive*) *Heraldry.* of, on, or starting from the right side of a shield from the bearer's point of view and therefore on the spectator's left. **3.** *Archaic.* favourable, auspicious, or propitious. ~Compare **sinister.** [C16: from Latin; compare Greek *dexios* on the right hand]

dex+ter[2] ('dɛkstə) *n.* a small breed of red or black cattle, originally from Ireland. [C19: perhaps from the surname of the original breeder]

dex+ter+i·ty (dɛk'stɛrɪtɪ) *n.* **1.** physical, esp. manual, skill or nimbleness. **2.** mental skill or adroitness; cleverness. **3.** *Rare.* the characteristic of being right-handed. [C16: from Latin *dexteritās* aptness, readiness, prosperity; see DEXTER]

dex+ter+ous *or* **dex+trous** ('dɛkstrəs) *adj.* **1.** possessing or done with dexterity. **2.** a rare word for **right-handed.** —'**dex+ter+ous+ly** *or* '**dex+trous+ly** *adv.* —'**dex+ter+ous+ness** *or* '**dex+trous+ness** *n.*

dex+tral ('dɛkstrəl) *adj.* **1.** of, relating to, or located on the right side, esp. of the body; right-hand. **2.** of or relating to a person who prefers to use his right foot, hand, or eye; right-handed. **3.** (of the shells of certain gastropod molluscs) coiling in an anticlockwise direction from the apex; dextrorse. ~Compare **sinistral.** —**dex+tral+i·ty** (dɛk'strælɪtɪ) *n.* —'**dex+tral+ly** *adv.*

dex+tran ('dɛkstrən) *n. Biochem.* a polysaccharide produced by the action of bacteria on sucrose: used as a substitute for plasma in blood transfusions. [C19: from DEXTRO- + -AN]

dex+trin ('dɛkstrɪn) *or* **dex+trine** ('dɛkstrɪn, -triːn) *n.* any of a group of sticky substances that are intermediate products in the conversion of starch to maltose: used as thickening agents in foods and as gums. [C19: from French *dextrine;* see DEXTRO-, -IN]

dex+tro ('dɛkstrəʊ) *adj.* See **dextrorotatory.**

dex·tro- *or before a vowel* **dextr-** *combining form.* **1.** on or towards the right: *dextrorotation.* **2.** (in chemistry) indicating a dextrorotatory compound: *dextroglucose.* [from Latin, from *dexter* on the right side]

dex·tro+am+phet·a+mine (ˌdɛkstrəʊæm'fɛtəˌmiːn, -mɪn) *n.* a dextrorotatory amphetamine, used in medicine.

dex·tro+glu+cose (ˌdɛkstrəʊ'gluːkəʊz, -kəʊs) *n.* another name for **dextrose.**

dex·tro+gy+rate (ˌdɛkstrəʊ'dʒaɪrɪt, -ˌreɪt) *or* **dex·tro+gyre** ('dɛkstrəʊˌdʒaɪə) *adj.* having dextrorotation.

dex·tro+ro+ta+tion (ˌdɛkstrəʊrəʊ'teɪʃən) *n.* a rotation to the right; clockwise rotation, esp. of the plane of polarization of plane-polarized light passing through a crystal, liquid, or solution, as seen by an observer facing the oncoming light. Compare **laevorotation.** —**dex·tro+ro+ta+to·ry** (ˌdɛkstrəʊˌrəʊ'teɪtərɪ, -trɪ) *or* ˌ**dex·tro+'ro+ta+ry** *adj.*

dex+trorse ('dɛkstrɔːs, dɛk'strɔːs) *or* **dex+tror+sal** (dɛk'strɔːsᵊl) *adj.* (of some climbing plants) growing upwards in a spiral from left to right. Compare **sinistrorse.** [C19: from Latin *dextrorsum* towards the right, from DEXTRO- + *vorsus* turned, variant of *versus,* from *vertere* to turn] —'**dex+trorse+ly** *adv.*

dex+trose ('dɛkstrəʊz, -trəʊs) *n.* a white soluble sweet-tasting crystalline solid that is the dextrorotatory isomer of glucose, occurring widely in fruit, honey, and in the blood and tissue of animals. Formula: $C_6H_{12}O_6$. Also called: **grape sugar, dextroglucose.**

dex+trous ('dɛkstrəs) *adj.* a variant spelling of **dexterous.** —'**dex+trous+ly** *adv.* —'**dex+trous+ness** *n.*

dey (deɪ) *n.* **1.** the title given to commanders or (from 1710) governors of the Janissaries of Algiers (1671–1830). **2.** a title applied by Western writers to various other Ottoman governors, such as the bey of Tunis. [C17: from French, from Turkish *dayi,* literally: maternal uncle, hence title given to an older person]

Dezh+nev (*Russian* dɪʒ'njɔf) *n.* **Cape.** a cape in the NE Soviet Union at the E end of Chukotski Peninsula: the northeasternmost point of Asia. Former name: **East Cape.**

D/F *or* **D.F.** *Telecomm. abbrev. for:* **1.** direction finder. **2.** direction finding.

D.F. *abbrev. for* Defender of the Faith.

D.F.C. *abbrev. for* Distinguished Flying Cross.

D.F.M. *abbrev. for* Distinguished Flying Medal.

dg *or* **dg.** *abbrev. for* decigram.

D.G. *abbrev. for:* **1.** Deo gratias. **2.** director-general.

Dhah+ran (dɑː'rɑːn) *n.* a town in E Saudi Arabia: site of the original discovery of oil in the country (1938).

dhak (dɑːk, dɔːk) *n.* a tropical Asian leguminous tree, *Butea frondosa,* that has bright red flowers and yields a red resin, used as an astringent. [C19: from Hindi]

dhal, dal, *or* **dholl** (dɑːl) *n.* **1.** a tropical African and Asian leguminous shrub, *Cajanus cajan,* cultivated in tropical regions for its nutritious pealike seeds. **2.** the seed of this shrub. ~Also called: **pigeon pea.** [C17: from Hindi *dāl* split pulse, from Sanskrit *dal* to split]

dhar+ma ('dɑːmə) *n.* **1.** *Hinduism.* social custom regarded as a religious and moral duty. **2.** *Hinduism.* **a.** the essential principle of the cosmos; natural law. **b.** conduct that conforms with this. **3.** *Buddhism.* ideal truth as set forth in the teaching of Buddha. [Sanskrit: habit, usage, law, from *dhārayati* he holds]

dhar+na *or* **dhur+na** ('dʌnə, 'dɑː-) *n.* (in India) a form of sit-in. [C18: from Hindi, literally: a placing]

Dhau+la+gi+ri (ˌdaʊlə'gɪərɪ) *n.* a mountain in W central Nepal, in the Himalayas. Height: 8043 m (26 810 ft.).

Dhi+los ('ðilos) *n.* transliteration of the modern Greek name for **Delos.**

dho+bi ('dəʊbɪ) *n.* (in India) a washerman. [C19: from Hindi, from *dhōb* washing; related to Sanskrit *dhāvaka* washerman]

dho+bi itch *n.* a tropical disease of the skin: a type of allergic dermatitis.

Dho+dhe+ká+ni+sos (ðoðe'kanisos) *n.* a transliteration of the modern Greek name for the **Dodecanese.**

dhole (dəʊl) *n.* a fierce canine mammal, *Cuon alpinus,* of the forests of central and SE Asia, having a reddish-brown coat and rounded ears: hunts in packs. [C19: of uncertain origin]

dho+ti ('dəʊtɪ), **dhoo+ti, dhoo+tie,** *or* **dhu+ti** ('duːtɪ) *n.* a long loincloth worn by men in India. [C17: from Hindi]

dhow (daʊ) *n.* a lateen-rigged coastal Arab sailing vessel with one or two masts. [C19: from Arabic *dāwa*]

DHSS (in Britain) *abbrev. for* Department of Health and Social Security.

Di *the chemical symbol for* didymium.

di. *or* **dia.** *abbrev. for* diameter.

di-[1] *prefix.* **1.** twice; two; double: *dicotyledon.* **2. a.** containing two specified atoms or groups of atoms: *dimethyl ether; carbon dioxide.* **b.** a non-technical equivalent of **bi-**[1] (sense 5). [via Latin from Greek, from *dis* twice, double, related to *duo* two. Compare BI-[1]]

di-[2] *combining form.* variant of **dia-** before a vowel: *diopter.*

di·a- *or* **di-** *prefix.* **1.** through, throughout, or during: *diachronic.* **2.** across: *diactinic.* **3.** apart: *diacritic.* **4.** (in botany) at right angles: *diatropism.* **5.** in opposite or different directions: *diamagnetism.* [from Greek *dia* through, between, across, by]

di·a+base ('daɪəˌbeɪs) *n.* **1.** *Brit.* an altered dolerite. **2.** *U.S.* another name for **dolerite.** [C19: from French, from Greek *diabasis* a crossing over, from *diabainein* to cross over, from DIA- + *bainein* to go] —ˌ**di·a+'ba+sic** *adj.*

di·a+be+tes (ˌdaɪə'biːtɪs, -tiːz) *n.* any of various disorders, esp. diabetes mellitus, characterized by excretion of an abnormally large amount of urine. [C16: from Latin: siphon, from Greek, literally: a passing through (referring to the excessive urination), from *diabainein* to pass through, cross over; see DIABASE]

di·a+be+tes in+si+pi+dus (ɪn'sɪpɪdəs) *n.* a disorder of the pituitary gland causing excessive thirst and excretion of large quantities of dilute urine. [C18: New Latin, literally: insipid diabetes]

di·a+be+tes mel+li+tus (mə'laɪtəs) *n.* a disorder of carbohydrate metabolism characterized by excessive thirst and excretion of abnormally large quantities of urine containing an excess of sugar, caused by a deficiency of insulin. [C18: New Latin, literally: honey-sweet diabetes]

di·a+bet+ic (ˌdaɪə'bɛtɪk) *adj.* **1.** of, relating to, or having diabetes. **2.** for the use of diabetics: *diabetic chocolate.* ~*n.* **3.** a person who has diabetes.

di·a+ble+rie (dɪ'ɑːblərɪ; *French* djablə'ri) *n.* **1.** magic or witchcraft connected with devils. **2.** demonic love or esoteric knowledge of devils. **3.** the domain of devils. **4.** devilry; mischief. [C18: from Old French, from *diable* devil, from Latin *diabolus;* see DEVIL]

di·a+bol+ic (ˌdaɪə'bɒlɪk) *adj.* **1.** of, relating to, or proceeding from the devil; satanic. **2.** befitting a devil; extremely cruel or wicked; fiendish. **3.** very difficult or unpleasant. [C14: from Late Latin *diabolicus,* from Greek *diabolikos,* from *diabolos* DEVIL] —ˌ**di·a+'bol·i·cal+ly** *adv.* —ˌ**di·a+'bol·i·cal+ness** *n.*

di·a+bol·i+cal (ˌdaɪə'bɒlɪkᵊl) *adj. Informal.* **1.** excruciatingly bad; outrageous. **2.** (intensifier): *a diabolical liberty.* —ˌ**di·a+'bol·i·cal+ly** *adv.* —ˌ**di·a+'bol·i·cal+ness** *n.*

di·ab·o+lism (daɪ'æbəˌlɪzəm) *n.* **1. a.** activities designed to enlist the aid of devils, esp. in witchcraft or sorcery. **b.** worship of devils or beliefs and teachings concerning them. **c.** the nature of devils. **2.** character or conduct that is devilish or fiendish; devilry. —**di+'ab·o+list** *n.*

di+ab·o+lize *or* **di+ab·o+lise** (daɪ'æbəˌlaɪz) *vb.* (*tr.*) **1. a.** to make (someone or something) diabolical. **b.** to subject to the influence of devils. **2.** to portray as diabolical.

di+ab·o+lo (dɪ'æbəˌləʊ) *n., pl.* **+los. 1.** a game in which one throws and catches a spinning top on a cord fastened to two sticks held in the hands. **2.** the top used in this game.

di·a+caus+tic (ˌdaɪə'kɔːstɪk, -'kɒs-) *adj.* **1.** (of a caustic curve or surface) formed by refracted light rays. ~*n.* **2.** a diacaustic curve or surface. ~Compare **catacaustic.**

di+ac+e·tyl+mor+phine (daɪˌæsətɪl'mɔːfiːn) *n.* another name for **heroin.**

di·a+chron+ic (ˌdaɪə'krɒnɪk) *adj.* of, relating to, or studying the development of a phenomenon through time; historical: *diachronic linguistics.* Compare **synchronic.** [C19: from DIA- + Greek *khronos* time]

di+ac·id (daɪ'æsɪd) *adj.* **1.** another word for **diacidic. 2.** (of a salt or acid) containing two acidic hydrogen atoms: *NaH_2PO_4 is a diacid salt of phosphoric acid.* ~*n.* **3.** an acid or salt that contains two acidic hydrogen atoms.

di·a+cid+ic (ˌdaɪə'sɪdɪk) *adj.* (of a base, such as calcium hydroxide $Ca(OH)_2$) capable of neutralizing two protons with one of its molecules. Also: **diacid.** Compare **dibasic.**

di+ac·o+nal (daɪ'ækənᵊl) *adj.* of or associated with a deacon or the diaconate. [C17: from Late Latin *diāconālis*, from *diāconus* DEACON]

di·ac·o·nate (daɪ'ækənɪt, -ˌneɪt) *n.* the office, sacramental status, or period of office of a deacon. [C17: from Late Latin *diāconātus*; see DEACON]

di·a·crit·ic (ˌdaɪə'krɪtɪk) *n.* **1.** Also called: **diacritical mark.** a sign placed above or below a character or letter to indicate that it has a different phonetic value, is stressed, or for some other reason. ~*adj.* **2.** another word for **diacritical.** [C17: from Greek *diakritikos* serving to distinguish, from *diakrinein*, from DIA- + *krinein* to separate]

di·a·crit·i·cal (ˌdaɪə'krɪtɪkəl) *adj.* **1.** of or relating to a diacritic. **2.** showing up a distinction. —ˌ**di·a·'crit·i·cal·ly** *adv.*

di·ac·tin·ic (ˌdaɪæk'tɪnɪk) *adj. Physics.* able to transmit photochemically active radiation. —**di·'ac·tin·ism** *n.*

di·a·del·phous (ˌdaɪə'dɛlfəs) *adj.* **1.** (of stamens) having united filaments so that they are arranged in two groups. **2.** (of flowers) having diadelphous stamens.

di·a·dem ('daɪəˌdɛm) *n.* **1.** a royal crown, esp. a light jewelled circlet. **2.** royal dignity or power. ~*vb.* **3.** (*tr.*) to adorn or crown with or as with a diadem. [C13: from Latin *diadēma*, from Greek: fillet, royal headdress, from *diadein* to bind around, from DIA- + *dein* to bind]

di·a·dem spi·der *n.* a common Eurasian spider, *Araneus diadematus*, that constructs orb webs: family *Argiopidae*.

di·ad·ro·mous (daɪ'ædrəməs) *adj.* **1.** *Botany.* of or possessing a leaf venation in the shape of a fan. **2.** (of some fishes) migrating between fresh and salt water. See also **anadromous, catadromous.**

di·aer·e·sis (daɪ'ɛrɪsɪs) *n., pl.* **·ses** (-ˌsiːz). a variant spelling of **dieresis.** —**di·ae·ret·ic** (ˌdaɪə'rɛtɪk) *adj.*

diag. *abbrev. for* diagram.

di·a·gen·e·sis (ˌdaɪə'dʒɛnɪsɪs) *n.* **1.** the sum of the physical and chemical changes that take place in sediments before they become consolidated into rocks, excluding all metamorphic changes. **2.** *Chem.* recrystallization of a solid to form large crystal grains from smaller ones.

di·a·ge·ot·ro·pism (ˌdaɪədʒiː'ɒtrəˌpɪzəm) *n.* a diatropic response of plant parts, such as rhizomes, to the stimulus of gravity. —**di·a·ge·o·trop·ic** (ˌdaɪəˌdʒiːə'trɒpɪk) *adj.*

Di·agh·i·lev (*Russian* 'djagɪlif) *n.* **Ser·gei Pa·vlo·vich** (sɪr'gjej 'pavləvitʃ). 1872–1929, Russian ballet impresario. He founded (1909) and directed (1909–29) the *Ballet Russe* in Paris, introducing Russian ballet to the West.

di·ag·nose ('daɪəgˌnəʊz) *vb.* **1.** to determine or distinguish by diagnosis. **2.** (*tr.*) to examine (a person or thing), as for a disease. —ˌ**di·ag·'nos·a·ble** *adj.*

di·ag·no·sis (ˌdaɪəg'nəʊsɪs) *n., pl.* **·ses** (-siːz). **1. a.** the identification of diseases from the examination of symptoms. **b.** an opinion or conclusion so reached. **2. a.** thorough analysis of facts or problems in order to gain understanding and aid future planning. **b.** an opinion or conclusion reached through such analysis. **3.** a detailed description of an organism, esp. a plant, for the purpose of classification. [C17: New Latin, from Greek: a distinguishing, from *diagignōskein* to distinguish, from *gignōskein* to perceive, KNOW]

di·ag·nos·tic (ˌdaɪəg'nɒstɪk) *adj.* **1.** of, relating to, or of value in diagnosis. ~*n.* **2.** *Med.* any symptom that provides evidence for making a specific diagnosis. **3.** a diagnosis. —ˌ**di·ag·'nos·ti·cal·ly** *adv.*

di·ag·nos·ti·cian (ˌdaɪəgnɒs'tɪʃən) *n.* a specialist or expert in making diagnoses.

di·ag·nos·tics (ˌdaɪəg'nɒstɪks) *n.* (*functioning as sing.*) the art or practice of diagnosis, esp. of diseases.

di·ag·o·nal (daɪ'ægənəl) *adj.* **1.** *Maths.* connecting any two vertices that in a polygon are not adjacent and in a polyhedron are not in the same face. **2.** slanting; oblique. **3.** marked with slanting lines or patterns. ~*n.* **4.** *Maths.* a diagonal line or plane. **5.** *Chess.* any oblique row of squares of the same colour. **6.** cloth marked or woven with slanting lines or patterns. **7.** something put, set, or drawn obliquely. **8.** another name for **solidus** (sense 1). **9.** one front leg and the hind leg on the opposite side of a horse, which are on the ground together when the horse is trotting. [C16: from Latin *diagōnālis*, from Greek *diagōnios*, from DIA- + *gōnia* angle] —**di·'ag·o·nal·ly** *adv.*

di·a·gram ('daɪəˌgræm) *n.* **1.** a sketch, outline, or plan demonstrating the form or workings of something. **2.** *Maths.* a pictorial representation of a quantity or of a relationship: *a Venn diagram.* ~*vb.* **·grams, ·gram·ming, ·grammed** *or U.S.* **·grams, ·gram·ing, ·gramed. 3.** to show in or as if in a diagram. [C17: from Latin *diagramma*, from Greek, from *diagraphein*, from *graphein* to write] —**di·a·gram·mat·ic** (ˌdaɪəgrə'mætɪk) *adj.* —ˌ**di·a·gram·'mat·i·cal·ly** *adv.*

di·a·graph ('daɪəˌgrɑːf, -ˌgræf) *n.* **1.** a device for enlarging or reducing maps, plans, etc. **2.** a protractor and scale used in drawing. [C19: from French *diagraphe*, from Greek *diagraphein* to represent with lines; see DIAGRAM]

di·a·ki·ne·sis (ˌdaɪəkɪ'niːsɪs, -kaɪ-) *n.* the final stage of the prophase of meiosis, during which homologous chromosomes start to separate after crossing over.

di·al ('daɪəl, daɪl) *n.* **1.** the face of a watch, clock, chronometer, sundial, etc., marked with divisions representing units of time. **2.** the circular graduated disc of various measuring instruments. **3. a.** the control on a radio or television set used to change the station or channel. **b.** the panel on a radio on which the frequency, wavelength, or station is indicated by means of a pointer. **4.** a numbered disc on a telephone that is rotated a set distance for each digit of a number being called. **5.** a miner's compass for surveying in a mine. **6.** *Brit.* a slang word for **face** (sense 1). ~*vb.* **di·als, di·al·ling, di·alled** *or U.S.* **di·als, di·al·ing, di·aled. 7.** to establish or try to establish a telephone connection with (a subscriber or his number) by operating the dial on a telephone. **8.** (*tr.*) to indicate, measure, or operate with a dial. [C15: from Medieval Latin *diālis* daily, from Latin *diēs* day] —**'di·al·ler** *n.*

dial. *abbrev. for* dialect(al).

di·a·lect ('daɪəˌlɛkt) *n.* **a.** a form of a language spoken in a particular geographical area or by members of a particular social class or occupational group, distinguished by its vocabulary, grammar, and pronunciation. **b.** a form of a language that is considered inferior: *the farmer spoke dialect and was despised by the merchants.* **c.** (*as modifier*): *a dialect word.* [C16: from Latin *dialectus*, from Greek *dialektos* speech, dialect, discourse, from *dialegesthai* to converse, from *legein* to talk, speak] —**'di·a·'lec·tal** *adj.*

di·a·lect at·las *n.* another term for **linguistic atlas.**

di·a·lect ge·og·ra·phy *n.* another term for **linguistic geography.** —**di·a·lect ge·og·ra·pher** *n.*

di·a·lec·tic (ˌdaɪə'lɛktɪk) *n.* **1.** the art or practice of assessing the truth of a theory or opinion by discussion and logical disputation. **2.** logical argumentation. **3.** *Philosophy.* a variant of **dialectics** (sense 1). **4.** See **Hegelian dialectic. 5.** (in the writings of Kant) the attempt to determine objects beyond the limits of experience by use of the principles of understanding. ~*adj.* **6.** of or relating to logical disputation. [C17: from Latin *dialectica*, from Greek *dialektikē* (*tekhnē*) (the art) of argument; see DIALECT]

di·a·lec·ti·cal (ˌdaɪə'lɛktɪkəl) *adj.* of or relating to dialectic or dialectics. —ˌ**di·a·'lec·ti·cal·ly** *adv.*

di·a·lec·ti·cal ma·te·ri·al·ism *n.* the economic, political, and philosophical system of Karl Marx and Friedrich Engels that combines traditional materialism and Hegelian dialectic. —**di·a·lec·ti·cal ma·te·ri·al·ist** *n.*

di·a·lec·tics (ˌdaɪə'lɛktɪks) *n.* **1.** Also: **dialectic.** *Philosophy.* **a.** logic or a branch of logic. **b.** any formal system of reasoning. **2.** the rationale of dialectical materialism.

di·a·lec·tol·o·gy (ˌdaɪəlɛk'tɒlədʒɪ) *n.* the study of dialects and dialectal variations. —**di·a·lec·to·log·i·cal** (ˌdaɪəˌlɛktə'lɒdʒɪkəl) *adj.* —ˌ**di·a·ˌlec·to·'log·i·cal·ly** *adv.* —ˌ**di·a·lec·'tol·o·gist** *n.*

di·al gauge *n.* another name for an **indicator** (sense 4).

di·al·lage ('daɪəlɪdʒ) *n.* a green or brownish-black variety of the mineral augite in the form of layers of platelike crystals. [C19: from Greek *diallagē* interchange]

di·al·ling tone *or U.S.* **di·al tone** *n.* a continuous purring heard over a telephone indicating that a number can be dialled. Compare **ringing tone, engaged tone.**

di·al·o·gism (daɪ'æləˌdʒɪzəm) *n.* **1.** *Logic.* a deduction with one premiss and a disjunctive conclusion. **2.** *Rhetoric.* a discussion in an imaginary dialogue or discourse.

di·al·o·gist (daɪ'ælədʒɪst) *n.* a person who writes or takes part in a dialogue. —ˌ**di·a·lo·'gis·tic** *or* ˌ**di·a·lo·'gis·ti·cal** *adj.*

di·al·o·gize *or* **di·al·o·gise** (daɪ'æləˌdʒaɪz) *vb.* (*intr.*) to carry on a dialogue.

di·a·logue *or U.S.* (*often*) **di·a·log** ('daɪəˌlɒg) *n.* **1.** conversation between two or more people. **2.** an exchange of opinions on a particular subject; discussion. **3.** the lines spoken by characters in drama or fiction. **4.** a particular passage of conversation in a literary or dramatic work. **5.** a literary composition in the form of a dialogue. **6.** a political discussion between representatives of two nations or groups. ~*vb. Rare.* **7.** (*tr.*) to put into the form of a dialogue. **8.** (*intr.*) to take part in a dialogue; converse. [C13: from Old French *dialoge*, from Latin *dialogus*, from Greek *dialogos*, from *dialegesthai* to converse; see DIALECT] —**di·a·log·ic** (ˌdaɪə'lɒdʒɪk) *adj.* —**'di·a·ˌlogu·er** *n.*

di·a·lyse *or U.S.* **di·a·lyze** ('daɪəˌlaɪz) *vb.* (*tr.*) to separate by dialysis. —**'di·a·ˌlys·a·ble** *adj.* —ˌ**di·a·ˌlys·a·'bil·i·ty** *n.* —ˌ**di·a·ly·'sa·tion** *n.*

di·a·lys·er *or U.S.* **di·a·lyz·er** ('daɪəˌlaɪzə) *n.* an apparatus used in dialysis.

di·al·y·sis (daɪ'ælɪsɪs) *n., pl.* **·ses** (-ˌsiːz). **1.** the separation of the crystalloids from a solution containing crystalloids and colloids by osmosis of the crystalloids. **2.** *Med.* See **haemodialysis.** [C16: from Late Latin: a separation, from Greek *dialusis* a dissolution, from *dialuein* to tear apart, dissolve, from *luein* to loosen] —**di·a·lyt·ic** (ˌdaɪə'lɪtɪk) *adj.* —ˌ**di·a·'lyt·i·cal·ly** *adv.*

diam. *abbrev. for* diameter.

di·a·mag·net ('daɪəˌmægnɪt) *n.* a substance exhibiting diamagnetism.

di·a·mag·net·ic (ˌdaɪəmæg'nɛtɪk) *adj.* of, exhibiting, or concerned with diamagnetism. —ˌ**di·a·mag·'net·i·cal·ly** *adv.*

di·a·mag·net·ism (ˌdaɪə'mægnɪˌtɪzəm) *n.* the phenomenon exhibited by substances that have a relative permeability less than unity and a negative susceptibility. It is caused by the orbital motion of electrons in the atoms of the material and is unaffected by temperature. Compare **ferromagnetism, paramagnetism.**

di·a·man·té (ˌdaɪə'mæntɪ, ˌdɪə-) *adj.* **1.** decorated with glittering ornaments, such as artificial jewels or sequins. ~*n.* **2.** a fabric so covered. [C20: from French, from *diamanter* to adorn with diamonds, from *diamant* DIAMOND]

di·a·man·tine (ˌdaɪə'mæntaɪn) *adj.* of or resembling diamonds. [C17: from French *diamantin*, from *diamant* DIAMOND]

di·am·e·ter (daɪ'æmɪtə) *n.* **1. a.** a straight line connecting the centre of a geometric figure, esp. a circle or sphere, with two points on the perimeter or surface. **b.** the length of such a line. **2.** the thickness of something, esp. with circular cross section. [C14: from Medieval Latin *diametrus*, variant of Latin *diametros*, from Greek: diameter, diagonal, from DIA- + *metron* measure]

di·am·e·tral (daɪˈæmɪtrəl) *adj.* **1.** located on or forming a diameter: *diametral plane.* **2.** a less common word for **diametric.** —**di·ˈam·e·tral·ly** *adv.*

di·a·met·ric (ˌdaɪəˈmɛtrɪk) *or* **di·a·met·ri·cal** *adj.* **1.** Also: **diametral.** of, related to, or along a diameter. **2.** completely opposed.

di·a·met·ri·cal·ly (ˌdaɪəˈmɛtrɪklɪ) *adv.* completely; utterly (esp. in the phrase **diametrically opposed**).

di·a·mine (ˈdaɪəˌmiːn, -mɪn; ˌdaɪəˈmiːn) *n.* any chemical compound containing two amino groups in its molecules.

di·a·mond (ˈdaɪəmənd) *n.* **1. a.** a usually colourless exceptionally hard allotropic form of carbon in cubic crystalline form that occurs in alluvial deposits and basic and ultrabasic rocks, esp. in southern Africa. It is used as a precious stone and for industrial cutting or abrading. **b.** (*as modifier*): *a diamond ring.* **2.** *Geom.* **a.** a figure having four sides of equal length forming two acute angles and two obtuse angles; rhombus. **b.** (modifier) rhombic. **3. a.** a red lozenge-shaped symbol on a playing card. **b.** a card with one or more of these symbols or (*when pl.*) the suit of cards so marked. **4.** *Baseball.* **a.** the whole playing field. **b.** the square formed by the four bases. **5.** (formerly) a size of printer's type approximately equal to 4½ point. **6. black diamond.** an informal name for **coal. 7. diamond cut diamond.** an encounter between two equally able people. **8. rough diamond.** a person of fine character who lacks refinement and polish. ~*vb.* **9.** (*tr.*) to decorate with or as with diamonds. [C13: from Old French *diamant*, from Medieval Latin *diamas*, modification of Latin *adamas* the hardest iron or steel, diamond; see ADAMANT] —**ˈdi·a·mond-ˌlike** *adj.*

di·a·mond an·ni·ver·sa·ry *n.* a 60th, or occasionally 75th, anniversary.

di·a·mond·back (ˈdaɪəməndˌbæk) *n.* **1.** Also called: **diamondback terrapin** *or* **turtle.** any edible North American terrapin of the genus *Malaclemys*, esp. *M. terrapin*, occurring in brackish and tidal waters and having diamond-shaped markings on the shell: family *Emydidae.* **2.** a large North American rattlesnake, *Crotalus adamanteus*, having cream-and-grey diamond-shaped markings.

di·a·mond bird *n.* any small insectivorous Australian songbird of the genus *Pardalotus*, having a diamond-patterned plumage. Also called: **pardalote.**

di·a·mond ju·bi·lee *n.* the celebration of a 60th, or occasionally 75th, anniversary.

di·a·mond point *n.* a diamond-tipped engraving tool.

di·a·mond snake *n.* a python, *Morelia argus*, of Australia and New Guinea, with yellow diamond-shaped markings.

di·a·mond wed·ding *n.* the 60th, or occasionally the 75th, anniversary of a marriage.

Di·an·a (daɪˈænə) *n.* the virginal Roman goddess of the hunt and the moon. Greek counterpart: **Artemis.**

di·an·drous (daɪˈændrəs) *adj.* (of some flowers or flowering plants) having two stamens.

di·a·net·ics (ˌdaɪəˈnɛtɪks) *n.* the former name for **scientology.** [C20: from *dianetic*, variant of DIANOETIC]

di·a·no·et·ic (ˌdaɪənəʊˈɛtɪk) *adj.* of or relating to thought, esp. to discursive as opposed to intuitive reasoning. Compare **discursive, intuitive.** [C17: from Greek *dianoētikos*, from *dianoia* the thinking process, an opinion, from DIA- + *noein* to think]

di·a·noi·a (ˌdaɪəˈnɔɪə) *n. Philosophy.* **1.** perception and experience regarded as lower modes of knowledge. Compare **noesis. 2.** the faculty of discursive reasoning. [from Greek; see DIANOETIC]

di·an·thus (daɪˈænθəs) *n., pl.* **-thus·es.** any Eurasian caryophyllaceous plant of the widely cultivated genus *Dianthus*, such as the carnation, pink, and sweet william. [C19: New Latin, from Greek DI-[1] + *anthos* flower]

di·a·pa·son (ˌdaɪəˈpeɪzᵊn, -sᵊn) *n. Music.* **1.** either of two stops (**open** *and* **stopped diapason**) usually found throughout the compass of a pipe organ that give it its characteristic tone colour. **2.** the compass of an instrument or voice. **3.** (chiefly in French usage) **a.** a standard pitch used for tuning, esp. the now largely obsolete one of A above middle C = 435 hertz, known as **di·a·pa·son nor·mal** (*French* djapazõ nɔrˈmal). **b.** a tuning fork or pitch pipe. **4.** (in classical Greece) an octave. [C14: from Latin: the whole octave, from Greek: (*hē*) *dia pasōn* (*khordōn sumphōnia*) (concord) through all (the notes), from *dia* through + *pas* all] —**di·a·ˈpa·son·al** *or* **di·a·pa·son·ic** (ˌdaɪəpeɪˈzɒnɪk, -ˈsɒn-) *adj.*

di·a·pause (ˈdaɪəˌpɔːz) *n.* a period of suspended development and growth accompanied by decreased metabolism in insects and some other animals. It is correlated with seasonal changes. [C19: from Greek *diapausis* pause, from *diapauein* to pause, bring to an end, from DIA- + *pauein* to stop]

di·a·pe·de·sis (ˌdaɪəpəˈdiːsɪs) *n.* the passage of blood cells through the unruptured wall of a blood vessel into the surrounding tissues. [C17: New Latin, from Greek: a leaping through, from *diapēdan* to spring through, from DIA- + *pēdan* to leap] —**di·a·pe·det·ic** (ˌdaɪəpəˈdɛtɪk) *adj.*

di·a·pen·te (ˌdaɪəˈpɛntɪ) *n. Music.* (in classical Greece) the interval of a perfect fifth. [C14: from Latin, from Greek *dia pente khordōn sumphōnia* concord through five notes, from *dia* through + *pente* five]

di·a·per (ˈdaɪəpə) *n.* **1.** the U.S. word for **nappy**[1]. **2. a.** a woven pattern on fabric consisting of a small repeating design, esp. diamonds. **b.** fabric having such a pattern. **c.** such a pattern, used as decoration. ~*vb.* **3.** (*tr.*) to decorate with such a pattern. [C14: from Old French *diaspre*, from Medieval Latin *diasprus* made of diaper, from Medieval Greek *diaspros* pure white, from DIA- + *aspros* white, shining]

di·aph·a·nous (daɪˈæfənəs) *adj.* **1.** (usually of fabrics such as silk) fine and translucent. **2.** indistinct; vague; blurred. [C17: from Medieval Latin *diaphanus*, from Greek *diaphanēs* transparent, from *diaphainein* to show through, from DIA- + *phainein* to show] —**di·ˈaph·a·nous·ly** *adv.* —**di·ˈaph·a·nous·ness** *or* **di·aph·a·ne·i·ty** (daɪəfəˈniːɪtɪ) *n.*

di·a·phone (ˈdaɪəˌfəʊn) *n.* **1. a.** the set of all realizations of a given phoneme in a language. **b.** one of any number of corresponding sounds in different dialects of a language. **2.** a foghorn that emits a two-toned signal. [C20: from DIA(LECT) + PHONE[2]]

di·aph·o·ny (daɪˈæfənɪ) *n. Music.* **1.** a style of two-part polyphonic singing; organum or a freer form resembling it. **2.** (in classical Greece) another word for **dissonance** (sense 3). Compare **symphony** (sense 5a). [C17: from Late Latin *diaphōnia*, from Greek, from *diaphōnos* discordant, from DIA- + *phōnē* sound] —**di·a·phon·ic** (ˌdaɪəˈfɒnɪk) *adj.*

di·a·pho·re·sis (ˌdaɪəfəˈriːsɪs) *n.* **1.** a technical name for **perspiration. 2.** perceptible and excessive perspiration; sweat. [C17: via Late Latin from Greek, from *diaphorein* to disperse by perspiration, from DIA- + *phorein* to carry, variant of *pherein*]

di·a·pho·ret·ic (ˌdaɪəfəˈrɛtɪk) *adj.* **1.** relating to or causing perspiration or sweat. ~*n.* **2.** a diaphoretic drug or agent.

di·a·pho·to·trop·ism (ˌdaɪəˌfəʊtəʊˈtrəʊpɪzəm) *n.* growth of a plant or plant part in a direction transverse to that of the light. [C20: from Greek, from DIA- + PHOTOTROPIC] —**di·a·pho·to·trop·ic** (ˌdaɪəˌfəʊtəʊˈtrɒpɪk) *adj.*

di·a·phragm (ˈdaɪəˌfræm) *n.* **1.** *Anatomy.* any separating membrane, esp. the dome-shaped muscular partition that separates the abdominal and thoracic cavities in mammals. **2.** a circular rubber or plastic contraceptive membrane placed over the mouth of the uterine cervix before copulation to prevent entrance of sperm. **3.** any thin dividing membrane. **4.** Also called: **stop.** a disc with a fixed or adjustable aperture to control the amount of light or other radiation entering an optical instrument, such as a camera. **5.** a thin disc that vibrates when receiving or producing sound waves, used to convert sound signals to electrical signals or vice versa in telephones, etc. **6.** *Chem.* **a.** a porous plate or cylinder dividing an electrolytic cell, used to permit the passage of ions and prevent the mixing of products formed at the electrodes. **b.** a semipermeable membrane used to separate two solutions in osmosis. **7.** *Botany.* a transverse plate of cells that occurs in the stems of certain aquatic plants. [C17: from Late Latin *diaphragma*, from Greek, from DIA- + *phragma* fence] —**di·a·phrag·mat·ic** (ˌdaɪəfrægˈmætɪk) *adj.* —**ˌdi·a·phrag·ˈmat·i·cal·ly** *adv.*

di·aph·y·sis (daɪˈæfɪsɪs) *n., pl.* **-ses** (-ˌsiːz). the shaft of a long bone. Compare **epiphysis.** [C19: New Latin, from Greek *diaphusis*, from *diaphuesthai* to grow between, from DIA- + *phuein* to produce] —**di·a·phys·i·al** (ˌdaɪəˈfɪzɪəl) *adj.*

di·a·pir (ˈdaɪəˌpɪə) *n. Geology.* an anticlinal fold in which the brittle overlying rock has been pierced by material, such as salt, from beneath. [C20: from Greek *diapeirainein* to make holes through, pierce]

di·a·poph·y·sis (ˌdaɪəˈpɒfɪsɪs) *n., pl.* **-ses** (-ˌsiːz). *Anatomy.* the upper or articular surface of a transverse vertebral process. [C19: New Latin, from DI-[2] + APOPHYSIS] —**di·ap·o·phys·i·al** (ˌdaɪæpəˈfɪzɪəl) *adj.*

di·a·pos·i·tive (ˌdaɪəˈpɒzɪtɪv) *n.* a positive transparency; slide.

di·arch (ˈdaɪɑːk) *adj. Botany.* (of a vascular bundle) having two strands of xylem. [C19: from Greek DI- + *archē* beginning, origin]

di·ar·chy *or* **dy·ar·chy** (ˈdaɪɑːkɪ) *n., pl.* **-chies.** government by two states, individuals, etc. —**di·ˈar·chic, di·ˈar·chi·cal, di·ˈar·chal,** *or* **dy·ˈar·chic, dy·ˈar·chi·cal, dy·ˈar·chal** *adj.*

di·a·rist (ˈdaɪərɪst) *n.* a person who keeps or writes a diary, esp. one that is subsequently published.

di·ar·rhoe·a *or esp. U.S.* **di·ar·rhe·a** (ˌdaɪəˈrɪə) *n.* frequent and copious discharge of abnormally liquid faeces. [C16: from Late Latin, from Greek *diarrhoia*, from *diarrhein* to flow through, from DIA- + *rhein* to flow] —**ˌdi·ar·ˈrhoe·al, ˌdi·ar·ˈrhoe·ic** *or esp. U.S.* **ˌdi·ar·ˈrhe·al, ˌdi·ar·ˈrhe·ic** *adj.*

di·ar·thro·sis (ˌdaɪɑːˈθrəʊsɪs) *n., pl.* **-ses** (-siːz). *Anatomy.* any freely movable joint, such as the shoulder and hip joints. [C16: New Latin, from DI-[2] + Greek *arthrōsis*, from *arthroun* to fasten by a joint, from *arthron* joint] —**ˌdi·ar·ˈthro·di·al** *adj.*

di·a·ry (ˈdaɪərɪ) *n., pl.* **-ries. 1.** a personal record of daily events, appointments, observations, etc. **2.** a book for keeping such a record. [C16: from Latin *diārium* daily allocation of food or money, journal, from *diēs* day]

Di·as *or* **Di·az** (ˈdiːəs; *Portuguese* ˈdiəʃ) *n.* **Bar·tho·lo·me·u** (ˌbərtuluˈmeʊ). ?1450–1500, Portuguese navigator who discovered the sea route from Europe to the East via the Cape of Good Hope (1488).

di·a·scope (ˈdaɪəˌskəʊp) *n.* an optical projector used to display transparencies.

Di·as·po·ra (daɪˈæspərə) *n.* **1. a.** the dispersion of the Jews from Palestine after the Babylonian captivity. **b.** the Jewish communities that arose after this dispersion. **c.** the places in which these settlements existed. **2.** (in the New Testament) the body of Christians living outside Palestine. **3.** (*often not cap.*) a dispersion or spreading, as of people originally belonging to one nation or having a common culture. [C19: from Greek: a scattering, from *diaspeirein* to disperse, from DIA- + *speirein* to scatter, sow; see SPORE]

di·a·spore ('daɪəˌspɔː) *n.* **1.** a white, yellowish, or grey mineral consisting of hydrated aluminium oxide in orthorhombic crystalline form, found in bauxite and corundum. Formula: $Al_2O_3.H_2O$. **2.** any propagative part of a plant, esp. one that is easily dispersed, such as a spore. [C19: from Greek *diaspora* a scattering, dispersion; see DIASPORA: so named from its dispersion and crackling when highly heated]

di·a·stal·sis (ˌdaɪə'stælsɪs) *n., pl.* **·ses** (-siːz). *Physiol.* a downward wave of contraction occurring in the intestine during digestion. See also **peristalsis.** [C20: New Latin, from DIA- + (PERI)STALSIS] —ˌ**di·a·'stal·tic** *adj.*

di·a·stase ('daɪəˌsteɪs, -ˌsteɪz) *n.* any of a group of enzymes that hydrolyse starch to maltose. They are present in germinated barley and in the pancreas. See also **amylase.** [C19: from French, from Greek *diastasis* a separation; see DIASTASIS] —ˌ**di·a·'sta·sic** *adj.*

di·a·sta·sis (daɪ'æstəsɪs) *n., pl.* **·ses** (-ˌsiːz). **1.** *Pathol.* **a.** the separation of an epiphysis from the long bone to which it is normally attached without fracture of the bone. **b.** the separation of any two parts normally joined. **2.** *Physiol.* the last part of the diastolic phase of the heartbeat. [C18: New Latin, from Greek: a separation, from *diistanai* to separate, from DIA- + *histanai* to place, make stand] —**di·a·stat·ic** (ˌdaɪə'stætɪk) *adj.*

di·a·ste·ma (ˌdaɪə'stiːmə) *n., pl.* **·ma·ta** (-mətə). **1.** an abnormal space, fissure, or cleft in a bodily organ or part. **2.** a gap between the teeth. [C19: New Latin, from Greek: gap, from *diistanai* to separate; see DIASTASIS]

di·as·ter (daɪ'æstə) *n. Cytology.* the stage in cell division at which the chromosomes are in two groups at the poles of the spindle before forming daughter nuclei. [C19: from DI-[1] + Greek *astēr* star] —**di·'as·tral** *adj.*

di·as·to·le (daɪ'æstəlɪ) *n.* the dilation of the chambers of the heart that follows each contraction, during which they refill with blood. Compare **systole.** [C16: via Late Latin from Greek: an expansion, from *diastellein* to expand, from DIA- + *stellein* to place, bring together, make ready] —**di·as·tol·ic** (ˌdaɪə'stɒlɪk) *adj.*

di·as·tro·phism (daɪ'æstrəˌfɪzəm) *n.* movement of the earth's crust that gives rise to mountains, continents, folding, faulting, etc. [C19: from Greek *diastrophē* a twisting; see DIA-, STROPHE] —**di·a·stroph·ic** (ˌdaɪə'strɒfɪk) *adj.*

di·a·style ('daɪəˌstaɪl) *Architect.* ~*adj.* **1.** having columns about three diameters apart. ~*n.* **2.** a diastyle building. [C16: via Latin from Greek *diastȳlos* having spaced pillars]

di·a·tes·sa·ron (ˌdaɪə'tɛsəˌrɒn) *n.* **1.** *Music.* (in classical Greece) the interval of a perfect fourth. **2.** a conflation of the four Gospels into a single continuous narrative. [C14: from Late Latin, from Greek *dia tessarōn khordōn sumphōnia* concord through four notes, from *dia* through + *tessares* four]

di·a·ther·man·cy (ˌdaɪə'θɜːmənsɪ) *n., pl.* **·cies.** the property of transmitting infrared radiation. [C19: from French *diathermansie,* from DIA- + Greek *thermansis* heating, from *thermainein* to heat, from *thermos* hot] —ˌ**di·a·'ther·man·ous** *adj.*

di·a·ther·mic (ˌdaɪə'θəmɪk) *adj.* **1.** of or relating to diathermy. **2.** able to conduct heat; passing heat freely.

di·a·ther·my ('daɪəˌθɜːmɪ) *or* **di·a·ther·mi·a** (ˌdaɪə'θɜːmɪə) *n.* local heating of the body tissues with an electric current for medical or surgical purposes. [C20: from New Latin *diathermia,* from DIA- + Greek *thermē* heat]

di·ath·e·sis (daɪ'æθɪsɪs) *n., pl.* **·ses** (-ˌsiːz). a hereditary or acquired susceptibility of the body to one or more diseases. [C17: New Latin, from Greek: propensity, from *diatithenai* to dispose, from DIA- + *tithenai* to place] —**di·a·thet·ic** (ˌdaɪə'θɛtɪk) *adj.*

di·a·tom ('daɪətəm, -ˌtɒm) *n.* any microscopic unicellular alga of the class *Bacillariophyceae,* occurring in marine or fresh water singly or in colonies, each cell having a cell wall made of two halves and impregnated with silica. See also **diatomite.** [C19: from New Latin *Diatoma* (genus name), from Greek *diatomos* cut in two, from *diatemnein* to cut through, from DIA- + *temnein* to cut]

di·a·to·ma·ceous (ˌdaɪətə'meɪʃəs) *adj.* of, relating to, consisting of, or containing diatoms or their fossil remains.

di·a·to·ma·ceous earth *n.* an unconsolidated form of **diatomite.** Also called: **kieselguhr.**

di·a·tom·ic (ˌdaɪə'tɒmɪk) *adj.* (of a compound or molecule) **a.** containing two atoms. **b.** containing two characteristic groups or atoms: *ethylene glycol is a diatomic alcohol.* —**di·at·o·mic·i·ty** (ˌdaɪætə'mɪsɪtɪ) *n.*

di·at·o·mite (daɪ'ætəˌmaɪt) *n.* a soft very fine-grained whitish rock consisting of the siliceous remains of diatoms deposited in small ponds or lakes. It is used as an absorbent, filtering medium, insulator, filler, etc. See also **diatomaceous earth.**

di·a·ton·ic (ˌdaɪə'tɒnɪk) *adj.* **1.** of, relating to, or based upon any scale of five tones and two semitones produced by playing the white keys of a keyboard instrument, esp. the natural major or minor scales forming the basis of the key system in Western music. Compare **chromatic** (sense 2). **2.** not involving the sharpening or flattening of the notes of the major or minor scale nor the use of such notes as modified by accidentals. [C16: from Late Latin *diatonicus,* from Greek *diatonikos,* from *diatonos* extending, from *diateinein* to stretch out, from DIA- + *teinein* to stretch] —ˌ**di·a·'ton·i·cal·ly** *adv.* —**di·a·ton·i·cism** (ˌdaɪə'tɒnɪˌsɪzəm) *n.*

di·a·tribe ('daɪəˌtraɪb) *n.* a bitter or violent criticism or attack; denunciation. [C16: from Latin *diatriba* learned debate, from Greek *diatribē* discourse, pastime, from *diatribein* to while away, from DIA- + *tribein* to rub]

di·at·ro·pism (daɪ'ætrəˌpɪzəm) *n.* a response of plants or parts of plants to an external stimulus by growing at right angles to the direction of the stimulus. —**di·a·trop·ic** (ˌdaɪə'trɒpɪk) *adj.*

Di·az *n.* **1.** ('diːəs; *Portuguese* 'diəʃ) **Bar·tho·lo·me·u** (ˌbərtulu'meʊ). a variant spelling of (Bartholomeu) **Dias. 2.** ('diːæs; *Spanish* 'diaθ) (**José de la Cruz**) **Por·fi·rio** (pɔr'firjo). 1830–1915, Mexican general and statesman; president of Mexico (1877–80; 1884–1911).

Di·az de Bi·var (*Spanish* 'diaθ ðe bi'βar) *n.* **Ro·dri·go** (rɔ'ðriɣo). the original name of (El) **Cid.**

di·a·zine ('daɪəˌziːn; daɪ'æziːn, -ɪn) *or* **di·a·zin** ('daɪəzɪn, daɪ'æzɪn) *n.* any organic compound whose molecules contain a hexagonal ring of four carbon atoms and two nitrogen atoms, esp. any of three isomers with the formula $C_4N_2H_4$. See also **pyrimidine.**

di·az·o (daɪ'eɪzəʊ) *adj.* **1.** of, consisting of, or containing the divalent group, =N:N, or the divalent group, -N:N-: *diazo compound.* See also **azo. 2.** Also: **dyeline.** of or relating to the reproduction of documents using the bleaching action of ultraviolet radiation on diazonium salts. ~*n., pl.* **·os** *or* **·oes. 3.** a document produced by this method.

di·a·zole (daɪ'eɪzəʊl) *n.* any organic compound whose molecules contain a pentagonal ring of three carbon atoms and two nitrogen atoms, esp. imidazole (**1,3-diazole**) or pyrazole (**1,1-diazole**).

di·az·o·me·thane (daɪˌeɪzəʊ'miːθeɪn) *n.* a yellow odourless explosive gas, used as a methylating agent. Formula: CH_2:N:N.

di·a·zo·ni·um (ˌdaɪə'zəʊnɪəm) *n.* (modifier) of, consisting of, or containing the group, Ar-N:N-, where Ar is an aryl group: *diazonium group or radical; a diazonium compound.* [C19: DIAZO- + (AMM)ONIUM]

di·a·zo·ni·um salt *n.* any of a class of compounds with the general formula $[ArN:N]^-M^+$, where Ar is an aryl group and M is a metal atom; made by the action of nitrous acid on aromatic amines and used in dyeing.

di·a·zo·tize *or* **di·a·zo·tise** (daɪ'eɪzəˌtaɪz) *vb.* (*tr.*) to cause (an aryl amine) to react with nitrous acid to produce a diazonium salt. —**di·ˌa·zo·ti·'za·tion** *or* **di·ˌa·zo·ti·'sa·tion** *n.*

dib (dɪb) *vb.* **dibs, dib·bing, dibbed.** (*intr.*) to fish by allowing the bait to bob and dip on the surface. [C17: perhaps alteration of DAB[1]]

di·ba·sic (daɪ'beɪsɪk) *adj.* **1.** (of an acid, such as sulphuric acid, H_2SO_4) containing two acidic hydrogen atoms. Compare **diacidic. 2.** (of a salt) derived by replacing two acidic hydrogen atoms: *dibasic sodium phosphate,* Na_2HPO_4. —**di·ba·sic·i·ty** (ˌdaɪbeɪ'sɪsɪtɪ) *n.*

dib·ble[1] ('dɪbᵊl) *n.* **1.** Also called (esp. Brit.): **dib·ber** ('dɪbə). a small hand tool used to make holes in the ground for planting or transplanting bulbs, seeds, or roots. ~*vb.* **2.** to make a hole in (the ground) with a dibble. **3.** to plant (seeds, etc.) with a dibble. [C15: of obscure origin] —**'dib·bler** *n.*

dib·ble[2] ('dɪbᵊl) *vb.* (*intr.*) **1.** a variant of **dib. 2.** a less common word for **dabble.**

dib·buk ('dɪbək; *Hebrew* di'buk) *n., pl.* **·buks** *or* **·buk·kim** (*Hebrew* -bu'kim). a variant spelling of **dybbuk.**

di·bran·chi·ate (daɪ'bræŋkɪɪt, -ˌeɪt) *adj.* **1.** of, relating to, or belonging to the *Dibranchiata,* a group or former order of cephalopod molluscs, including the octopuses, squids, and cuttlefish, having two gills. ~*n.* **2.** any dibranchiate mollusc.

di·bro·mide (daɪ'brəʊmaɪd) *n.* any chemical compound that contains two bromine atoms per molecule.

dibs (dɪbz) *pl. n.* **1.** another word for **jacks. 2.** (foll. by *on*) *Informal.* rights (to) or claims (on): used mainly by children. [C18: shortened from *dibstones* children's game played with knucklebones or pebbles, probably from *dib* to tap, dip, variant of DAB[1]]

di·car·box·yl·ic ac·id (daɪˌkɑːbɒk'sɪlɪk) *n.* any carboxylic acid that contains two carboxyl groups per molecule.

dic·ast ('dɪkæst) *n.* (in ancient Athens) a juror in the popular courts chosen by lot from a list of citizens. [C19: from Greek *dikastēs,* from *dikazein* to judge, from *dikē* right, judgment, order] —**di·'cas·tic** *adj.*

dice (daɪs) *pl. n.* **1.** cubes of wood, plastic, etc., each of whose sides has a different number of spots (1 to 6), used in games of chance and in gambling to give random numbers. **2.** (*functioning as sing.*) Also called: **die.** one of these cubes. **3.** small cubes as of vegetables, chopped meat, etc. **4. no dice.** *Slang, chiefly U.S.* an expression of refusal or rejection. ~*vb.* **5.** to cut (food, etc.) into small cubes. **6.** (*intr.*) to gamble with or play at a game involving dice. **7.** (*intr.*) to take a chance or risk (esp. in the phrase **dice with death**). **8.** (*tr.*) *Austral. informal.* to abandon or reject (someone or something). **9.** (*tr.*) to decorate or mark with dicelike shapes. [C14: plural of DIE[2]] —**'dic·er** *n.*

di·cen·tra (daɪ'sɛntrə) *n.* any Asian or North American plant of the genus *Dicentra,* such as bleeding heart and Dutchman's-breeches, having finely divided leaves and ornamental clusters of drooping flowers: family *Fumariaceae.* [C19: New Latin, from Greek *dikentros* having two sharp points, from DI-[1] + *kentron* sharp point, from *kentein* to prick; see CENTRE]

di·ceph·a·lous (daɪ'sɛfələs) *adj.* having two heads. —**di·'ceph·a·lism** *n.*

dice·y ('daɪsɪ) *adj.* **dic·i·er, dic·i·est.** *Slang, chiefly Brit.* difficult or dangerous; risky; tricky.

di·cha·si·um (daɪ'keɪzɪəm) *n., pl.* **·si·a** (-zɪə). a cymose inflorescence in which each branch bearing a flower gives rise to two other flowering branches, as in the stitchwort. Compare monochasium. [C19: New Latin, from Greek *dikhasis* a dividing, from *dikhazein* to divide in two, from *dikha* in two] —di·'cha·si·al *adj.* —di·'cha·si·al·ly *adv.*

di·chla·myd·e·ous (ˌdaɪklə'mɪdɪəs) *adj.* (of a flower) having a corolla and calyx. [C19: from Greek, from DI- + *khlamus* a cloak + -EOUS]

di·chlo·ride (daɪ'klɔːraɪd) *n.* a compound in which two atoms of chlorine are combined with another atom or group. Also called: **bichloride.**

di·chlo·ro·di·fluo·ro·me·thane (daɪˌklɔːrəʊdaɪˌflʊərəʊ'miː-θeɪn) *n.* a colourless nonflammable gas easily liquefied by pressure: used as a propellant in aerosols and fire extinguishers and as a refrigerant. Formula: CCl_2F_2. See also **Freon.**

di·chlo·ro·di·phe·nyl·tri·chlo·ro·e·thane (daɪˌklɔːrəʊdaɪˌfiː-naɪltraɪˌklɔːrəʊ'iːθeɪn, -nɪl-, -ˌfɛn-) *n.* the full name for **DDT.**

di·cho- *or before a vowel* **dich-** *combining form.* in two parts; in pairs: *dichotomy.* [from Greek *dikho-*, from *dikha* in two]

di·chog·a·my (daɪ'kɒgəmɪ) *n.* the maturation of male and female parts of a flower at different times, preventing self-pollination. Compare **homogamy** (sense 2). —**di·'chog·a·mous** *or* **di·cho·gam·ic** (ˌdaɪkəʊ'gæmɪk) *adj.*

di·chot·o·mize *or* **di·chot·o·mise** (daɪ'kɒtəˌmaɪz) *vb.* to divide or become divided into two parts or classifications. —**di·'chot·o·mist** *n.* —**di·ˌchot·o·mi·'za·tion** *or* **di·ˌchot·o·mi·'sa·tion** *n.*

di·chot·o·my (daɪ'kɒtəmɪ) *n., pl.* **-mies. 1.** division into two parts or classifications, esp. when they are sharply distinguished or opposed: *the dichotomy between eastern and western cultures.* **2.** *Logic.* the division of a class into two mutually exclusive subclasses: *the dichotomy of married and single people.* **3.** *Botany.* a simple method of branching by repeated division into two equal parts. **4.** the phase of the moon, Venus, or Mercury when half of the disc is visible. —**di·'chot·o·mous** *or* **di·cho·tom·ic** (ˌdaɪkəʊ'tɒmɪk) *adj.* —**di·'chot·o·mous·ly** *adv.*

di·chro·ic (daɪ'krəʊɪk) *or* **di·chro·it·ic** (ˌdaɪkrəʊ'ɪtɪk) *adj.* **1.** (of a solution or uniaxial crystal) exhibiting dichroism. **2.** another word for **dichromatic.** [C19: from Greek *dikhroos* having two colours, from DI-[1] + *khrōs* colour]

di·chro·ism ('daɪkrəʊˌɪzəm) *n.* **1.** Also called: **dichromaticism.** a property of a uniaxial crystal, such as tourmaline, of showing a perceptible difference in colour when viewed along two different axes in transmitted white light. See also **pleochroism. 2.** a property of certain solutions as a result of which the wavelength (colour) of the light transmitted depends on the concentration of the solution and the length of the path of the light within the solution.

di·chro·ite ('daɪkrəʊˌaɪt) *n.* another name for **cordierite.** [C19: from Greek *dikhroos* two-coloured + -ITE[1]]

di·chro·mate (daɪ'krəʊmeɪt) *n.* any salt or ester of dichromic acid. Dichromate salts contain the ion $Cr_2O_7^{2-}$. Also called: **bichromate.**

di·chro·mat·ic (ˌdaɪkrəʊ'mætɪk) *adj.* **1.** Also: **dichroic.** having or consisting of only two colours. **2.** (of animal species) having two different colour varieties that are independent of sex and age. **3.** able to perceive only two colours. —**di·chro·ma·tism** (daɪ'krəʊməˌtɪzəm) *n.*

di·chro·mat·i·cism (ˌdaɪkrəʊ'mætɪˌsɪzəm) *n.* another name for **dichroism** (sense 1).

di·chro·mic (daɪ'krəʊmɪk) *adj.* of or involving only two colours; dichromatic.

di·chro·mic ac·id *n.* an unstable dibasic oxidizing acid known only in solution and in the form of dichromate salts. Formula: $H_2Cr_2O_7$.

di·chro·scope ('daɪkrəˌskəʊp) *n.* an instrument for investigating the dichroism of solutions or crystals. Also called: **di·chro·i·scope, di·chro·o·scope.** [C19: from Greek *dikhroos* two-coloured + -SCOPE] —**di·chro·scop·ic** (ˌdaɪkrə'skɒpɪk), **ˌdi·chro·i·'scop·ic,** *or* **ˌdi·chro·o·'scop·ic** *adj.*

dick[1] (dɪk) *n. Chiefly U.S.* a slang word for **detective.** [C20: by shortening and alteration from DETECTIVE; probably influenced by proper name *Dick*]

dick[2] (dɪk) *n. Slang.* **1.** *Brit.* a fellow or person. **2. clever dick.** *Brit.* a person who is obnoxiously opinionated or self-satisfied; know-all. **3.** a taboo word for **penis.** [C16 (meaning: fellow): from the name *Dick,* familiar form of *Richard,* applied generally (like *Jack*) to any fellow, lad, etc.; hence, C19: penis]

dick·ens ('dɪkɪnz) *n. Informal.* a euphemistic word for **devil** (used as intensifier in the interrogative phrase **what the dickens**). [C16: from the name *Dickens*]

Dick·ens ('dɪkɪnz) *n.* **Charles** (**John Huffam**), pen name *Boz.* 1812–70, English novelist, famous for the humour and sympathy of his characterization and his criticism of social injustice. His major works include *The Pickwick Papers* (1837), *Oliver Twist* (1839), *Martin Chuzzlewit* (1844), *David Copperfield* (1850), *Bleak House* (1853), *Little Dorrit* (1857), and *Great Expectations* (1861). —**Dick·en·si·an** (dɪ'kɛnzɪən) *n., adj.*

dick·er ('dɪkə) *Chiefly U.S.* ~*vb.* **1.** to trade (goods) by bargaining; barter. **2.** (*intr.*) to negotiate a political deal. ~*n.* **3. a.** a petty bargain or barter. **b.** the item or items bargained or bartered. **4.** a political deal or bargain. [C12: ultimately from Latin *decuria* DECURY; related to Middle Low German *dēker* lot of ten hides]

Dick·in·son ('dɪkɪnsən) *n.* **Em·i·ly.** 1830–86, U.S. poet, noted for her short mostly unrhymed mystical lyrics.

Dick test *n.* a skin test for determining whether a person is immune or susceptible to scarlet fever. [C20: named after George F. *Dick* (1881–1967), American physician who devised it]

dick·y[1] *or* **dick·ey** ('dɪkɪ) *n., pl.* **dick·ies** *or* **dick·eys. 1.** a woman's false blouse front, worn to fill in the neck of a jacket or low-cut dress. **2.** a man's false shirt front, esp. one worn with full evening dress. **3.** Also called: **dicky bow.** *Brit.* a bow tie. **4.** *Chiefly Brit.* an informal name for **donkey,** esp. a male one. **5.** Also called: **dickybird, dickeybird.** a child's word for a **bird,** esp. a small one. **6.** a folding outside seat at the rear of some early cars. U.S. name: **rumble seat.** [C18 (in the senses: donkey, shirt front): from *Dickey,* diminutive of *Dick* (name); the relationship of the various senses is obscure]

dick·y[2] *or* **dick·ey** ('dɪkɪ) *adj.* **dick·i·er, dick·i·est.** *Brit. slang.* in bad condition; shaky, unsteady, or unreliable: *I feel a bit dicky today.* [C18: perhaps from the name *Dick* in the phrase *as queer as Dick's hatband* feeling ill]

di·cli·nous ('daɪklɪnəs, daɪ'klaɪ-) *adj.* (of flowers and flowering plants) unisexual. Compare **monoclinous.** —**'di·cli·nism** *n.* —**di·cli·ny** ('daɪklɪnɪ, daɪ'klaɪ-) *n.*

di·cot·y·le·don (daɪˌkɒtɪ'liːdən, ˌdaɪkɒt-) *n.* any flowering plant of the group *Dicotyledonae,* having two embryonic seed leaves and leaves with netlike veins. The group includes many herbaceous plants and most families of trees and shrubs. Often shortened to **dicot.** Compare **monocotyledon.** —**ˌdi·cot·y·'le·don·ous** *adj.*

di·crot·ic (daɪ'krɒtɪk) *or* **di·cro·tal** ('daɪkrətəl) *adj. Physiol.* having or relating to a double pulse for each heartbeat. [C19: from Greek *dikrotos* double-beating, from DI-[1] + *krotein* to beat] —**di·cro·tism** ('daɪkrəˌtɪzəm) *n.*

dict. *abbrev. for:* **1.** dictation. **2.** dictator. **3.** dictionary.

dic·ta ('dɪktə) *n.* the plural of **dictum.**

Dic·ta·phone ('dɪktəˌfəʊn) *n. Trademark.* a tape recorder designed esp. for dictation and subsequent typing.

dic·tate *vb.* (dɪk'teɪt). **1.** to say (messages, letters, speeches, etc.) aloud for mechanical recording or verbatim transcription by another person. **2.** (*tr.*) to prescribe (commands, etc.) authoritatively. **3.** (*intr.*) to act in a tyrannical manner; seek to impose one's will on others. ~*n.* ('dɪkteɪt). **4.** an authoritative command. **5.** a guiding principle or rule: *the dictates of reason.* [C17: from Latin *dictāre* to say repeatedly, order, from *dīcere* to say]

dic·ta·tion (dɪk'teɪʃən) *n.* **1.** the act of dictating material to be recorded or taken down in writing. **2.** the material dictated. **3.** authoritative commands or the act of giving them. —**dic·'ta·tion·al** *adj.*

dic·ta·tor (dɪk'teɪtə) *n.* **1. a.** a ruler who is not effectively restricted by a constitution, laws, recognized opposition, etc. **b.** an absolute, esp. tyrannical, ruler. **2.** (in ancient Rome) a person appointed during a crisis to exercise supreme authority. **3.** a person who makes pronouncements, as on conduct, fashion, etc., which are regarded as authoritative. **4.** a person who behaves in an authoritarian or tyrannical manner. —**dic·ta·tress** (dɪk'teɪtrɪs) *or* **dic·ta·trix** ('dɪktətrɪks) *fem. n.*

dic·ta·tor·i·al (ˌdɪktə'tɔːrɪəl) *adj.* **1.** of or characteristic of a dictator. **2.** tending to dictate; tyrannical; overbearing. —**ˌdic·ta·'to·ri·al·ly** *adv.* —**ˌdic·ta·'to·ri·al·ness** *n.*

dic·ta·tor·ship (dɪk'teɪtəˌʃɪp) *n.* **1.** the rank, office, or period of rule of a dictator. **2.** government by a dictator or dictators. **3.** a country ruled by a dictator or dictators. **4.** absolute or supreme power or authority.

dic·tion ('dɪkʃən) *n.* **1.** the choice and use of words in writing or speech. **2.** the manner of uttering or enunciating words and sounds; elocution. [C15: from Latin *dictiō* a saying, mode of expression, from *dīcere* to speak, say]

dic·tion·ar·y ('dɪkʃənərɪ, -ʃənrɪ) *n., pl.* **-ar·ies. 1. a.** a reference book that consists of an alphabetical list of words with their meanings and parts of speech, and often a guide to accepted pronunciation and syllabification, irregular inflections of words, derived words of different parts of speech, and etymologies. **b.** a similar reference book giving equivalent words in two or more languages. Such dictionaries often consist of two or more parts, in each of which the alphabetical list is given in a different language: *a German-English dictionary.* **c.** (*as modifier*): *a dictionary definition.* See also **glossary, lexicon, thesaurus. 2.** a reference book listing words or terms of a particular subject or activity, giving information about their meanings and other attributes: *a dictionary of gardening.* **3.** a collection of information or examples with the entries alphabetically arranged: *a dictionary of quotations.* [C16: from Medieval Latin *dictiōnārium* collection of words, from Late Latin *dictiō* word; see DICTION]

dic·tion·ar·y cat·a·logue *n.* a catalogue of the authors, titles and subjects of books in one alphabetical sequence.

Dic·to·graph ('dɪktəˌgrɑːf, -ˌgræf) *n. Trademark.* a telephonic instrument for secretly monitoring or recording conversations by means of a small, sensitive, and often concealed microphone.

dic·tum ('dɪktəm) *n., pl.* **-tums** *or* **-ta** (-tə). **1.** a formal or authoritative statement or assertion; pronouncement. **2.** a popular saying or maxim. **3.** *Law.* See **obiter dictum.** [C16: from Latin, from *dīcere* to say]

di·cyn·o·dont (daɪ'sɪnəˌdɒnt) *n.* any of various extinct Triassic mammal-like reptiles having a single pair of tusklike teeth. [C19: from Greek, from DI- + *kuōn* dog + -ODONT]

did (dɪd) *vb.* the past tense of **do**[1].

Did·a·che ('dɪdəˌkiː) *n.* a treatise, perhaps of the 1st or early 2nd century A.D., on Christian morality and practices. Also called: the **Teaching of the Twelve Apostles.** [C19: from Greek, literally: a teaching, from *didaskein* to teach]

di·dac·tic (dɪ'dæktɪk) *adj.* **1.** intended to instruct, esp. excessively. **2.** morally instructive; improving. **3.** (of works of art or literature) containing a political or moral message to which aesthetic considerations are subordinated. [C17: from Greek *didaktikos* skilled in teaching, from *didaskein* to teach] —**di·'dac·ti·cal·ly** *adv.* —**di·'dac·ti·cism** *n.*

di·dac·tics (dɪ'dæktɪks) *n.* the art or science of teaching.

did·dle[1] ('dɪdᵊl) *vb. Informal.* **1.** (*tr.*) to cheat or swindle. **2.** (*intr.*) an obsolete word for **dawdle.** [C19: back formation from Jeremy *Diddler,* a scrounger in J. Kenney's farce *Raising the Wind* (1803)] —**'did·dler** *n.*

did·dle[2] ('dɪdᵊl) *vb. Dialect.* to jerk (an object) up and down or back and forth; shake rapidly. [C17: probably variant of *doderen* to tremble, totter; see DODDER[1]]

Di·de·rot ('di:dərəʊ; *French* did'ro) *n.* **De·nis** (də'ni). 1713–84, French philosopher, noted particularly for his direction (1745–72) of the great French *Encyclopédie.*

did·ger·i·doo (ˌdɪdʒərɪ'du:) *n. Music.* a native Australian wind instrument. [C20: imitative of its sound]

did·i·coy, did·di·coy ('dɪdɪˌkɔɪ), *or* **did·a·kai** ('dɪdɪˌkaɪ) *n., pl.* **·coys** *or* **·kais.** (in Britain) one of a group of caravan-dwelling roadside scrap-metal dealers, esp. one who breaks up old cars and sells the parts. Often called Gypsies, these people are not true Romanies. [C19: from Romany]

did·n't ('dɪdᵊnt) *contraction of* did not.

di·do ('daɪdəʊ) *n., pl.* **·dos** *or* **·does.** (*usually pl.*) *Informal.* an antic; prank; trick.

Di·do ('daɪdəʊ) *n. Classical myth.* a princess of Tyre who founded Carthage and became its queen. Virgil tells of her suicide when abandoned by her lover Aeneas.

didst (dɪdst) *vb. Archaic.* (used with the pronoun *thou* or its relative equivalent) a form of the past tense of **do**[1].

di·dym·i·um (daɪ'dɪmɪəm, dɪ-) *n.* **1.** a mixture of the metallic rare earths neodymium and praseodymium, once thought to be an element. **2.** a mixture of rare earths and their oxides used in colouring glass. [C19: from New Latin, from Greek *didumos* twin + -IUM]

did·y·mous ('dɪdɪməs) *adj. Biology.* in pairs or in two parts. [C18: from Greek *didumos* twin, from *duo* two]

di·dyn·a·mous (daɪ'dɪnəməs) *adj.* (of plants) having four stamens arranged in two pairs of unequal length, as in the foxglove. [C18: from New Latin *Didynamia* name of former class, from DI[1]- + Greek *dunamis* power, referring to the greater strength of the two long stamens]

die[1] (daɪ) *vb.* **dies, dy·ing, died.** (*mainly intr.*) **1.** (of an organism or its cells, organs, etc.) to cease all biological activity permanently: *she died of pneumonia.* **2.** (of something inanimate) to cease to exist; come to an end: *the memory of her will never die.* **3.** (often foll. by *away, down,* or *out*) to lose strength, power, or energy, esp. by degrees. **4.** (often foll. by *away* or *down*) to become calm or quiet; subside: *the noise slowly died down.* **5.** to stop functioning: *the engine died.* **6.** to languish or pine, as with love, longing, etc. **7.** (usually foll. by *of*) *Informal.* to be nearly overcome (with laughter, boredom, etc.). **8.** *Theol.* to lack spiritual life within the soul, thus separating it from God and leading to eternal punishment. **9.** (*tr.*) to undergo or suffer (a death of a specified kind) (esp. in phrases such as **die a saintly death**). **10.** (foll. by *to*) to become indifferent or apathetic (to): *to die to the world.* **11. never say die.** *Informal.* never give up. **12. die hard.** to cease to exist after resistance or a struggle: *old habits die hard.* **13. die in harness.** to die while still working or active, prior to retirement. **14. be dying.** (foll. by *for* or an infinitive) to be eager or desperate (for something or to do something): *I'm dying to see the new house.* ~See also **dieback, die down, die out.** [Old English *dīegan,* probably of Scandinavian origin; compare Old Norse *deyja,* Old High German *touwen*]

die[2] (daɪ) *n.* **1. a.** a shaped block of metal or other hard material used to cut or form metal in a drop forge, press, or similar device. **b.** a tool of metal, silicon carbide, or other hard material with a conical hole through which wires, rods, or tubes are drawn to reduce their diameter. **2.** an internally-threaded tool for cutting external threads. Compare **tap**[2] (sense 6). **3.** a casting mould giving accurate dimensions and a good surface to the object cast. See also **die-cast. 4.** *Architect.* the dado of a pedestal, usually cubic. **5.** another name for **dice** (sense 2). **6. the die is cast.** the decision that commits a person irrevocably to an action has been taken. [C13 *dee,* from Old French *de,* perhaps from Vulgar Latin *datum* (unattested) a piece in games, n. use of past participle of Latin *dare* to play]

die·back ('daɪˌbæk) *n.* **1.** a disease of trees and shrubs characterized by death of the young shoots, which spreads to the larger branches: caused by injury to the roots or attack by bacteria or fungi. **2.** any similar condition of herbaceous plants. ~*vb.* **die back. 3.** (*intr., adv.*) (of plants) to suffer from dieback.

die-cast *vb.* **-casts, -cast·ing, -cast.** (*tr.*) to shape or form (a metal or plastic object) by introducing molten metal or plastic into a reusable mould, esp. under pressure, by gravity, or by centrifugal force. —**'die-ˌcast·ing** *n.*

di·e·cious (daɪ'i:ʃəs) *adj.* a variant spelling of **dioecious.** —**di·'e·cious·ly** *adv.*

die down *vb.* (*intr., adv.*) **1.** (of some perennial plants) to wither and die above ground, leaving only the root alive during the winter. **2.** to lose strength or power, esp. by degrees. **3.** to become calm or quiet.

Die·fen·ba·ker ('di:fᵊnˌbeɪkə) *n.* **John George.** 1895-1979, Canadian Conservative statesman; prime minister of Canada (1957-63).

Dié·go-Sua·rez (*French* djego sɥa're) *n.* a port in N Madagascar: former French naval base. Pop.: 38 600 (1970 est.).

die-hard *n.* **1.** a person who resists change or who holds onto an untenable position or outdated attitude. **2.** (*modifier*) obstinately resistant to change. —**'die-ˌhard·ism** *n.*

diel·drin ('di:ldrɪn) *n.* a crystalline insoluble substance, consisting of a chlorinated derivative of naphthalene: a contact insecticide. Formula: $C_{12}H_8OCl_6$. [C20: from DIEL(S-AL)D(E)R (REACTION) + -IN]

di·e·lec·tric (ˌdaɪɪ'lɛktrɪk) *n.* **1.** a substance or medium that can sustain an electric field. **2.** a substance or body of very low electrical conductivity; insulator. ~*adj.* **3.** of, concerned with, or having the properties of a dielectric. —**ˌdi·e·'lec·tri·cal·ly** *adv.*

di·e·lec·tric con·stant *n.* another name for **relative permittivity.**

di·e·lec·tric heat·ing *n.* a technique in which an insulator is heated by the application of a high-frequency electric field.

Diels-Al·der re·ac·tion ('di:lz 'ɔ:ldə) *n. Chem.* a type of chemical reaction in which one organic compound containing conjugated double bonds adds to another containing an ethylenic bond to form a product containing a ring. [C20: named after Otto *Diels* (1876–1954) and Kurt *Alder* (1902–58), German chemists]

Dien Bien Phu ('djɛn 'bjɛn 'fu:) *n.* a village in NE Vietnam: French military post during the Indochina War; scene of a major defeat of French forces by the Vietminh (1954).

di·en·ceph·a·lon (ˌdaɪɛn'sɛfəˌlɒn) *n.* the part of the brain that includes the basal ganglia, thalamus, hypothalamus, and associated areas. —**di·en·ce·phal·ic** (ˌdaɪɛnsɪ'fælɪk) *adj.*

-diene *n. combining form.* denoting an organic compound containing two double bonds between carbon atoms: *butadiene.* [from DI[1]- + -ENE]

die out *or* **off** *vb.* (*intr., adv.*) **1.** (of a family, race, etc.) to die one after another until few or none are left. **2.** to become extinct, esp. after a period of gradual decline.

Di·eppe (dɪ'ɛp; *French* djɛp) *n.* a port and resort in N France, on the English Channel. Pop.: 26 111 (1975).

di·er·e·sis *or* **di·aer·e·sis** (daɪ'ɛrɪsɪs) *n., pl.* **·ses** (-ˌsi:z). **1.** the mark ¨, in writing placed over the second of two adjacent vowels to indicate that it is to be pronounced separately rather than forming a diphthong with the first, as in some spellings of *coöperate, naïve,* etc. **2.** this mark used for any other purpose, such as to indicate that a special pronunciation is appropriate to a particular vowel. Compare **umlaut. 3.** a pause in a line of verse occurring when the end of a foot coincides with the end of a word. [C17: from Latin *diaerēsis,* from Greek *diairesis* a division, from *diairein,* from DIA- + *hairein* to take; compare HERESY] —**di·e·ret·ic** *or* **di·ae·ret·ic** (ˌdaɪə'rɛtɪk) *adj.*

die·sel ('di:zᵊl) *n.* **1.** See **diesel engine. 2.** a ship, locomotive, lorry, etc., driven by a diesel engine. **3.** *Informal.* short for **diesel oil** (*or* **fuel**).

Die·sel ('di:zᵊl) *n.* **Ru·dolf** ('ru:dɔlf). 1858–1913, German engineer, who invented the diesel engine (1892).

die·sel cy·cle *n.* a four-stroke cycle in which combustion takes place at constant pressure and heat is rejected at constant volume. Compare **Otto cycle.**

die·sel-e·lec·tric *n.* **1.** a locomotive fitted with a diesel engine driving an electric generator that feeds electric traction motors. ~*adj.* **2.** of or relating to such a locomotive or system.

die·sel en·gine *or* **mo·tor** *n.* a type of internal-combustion engine in which atomized fuel oil is sprayed into the cylinder and ignited by compression alone.

die·sel-hy·drau·lic *n.* **1.** a locomotive driven by a diesel engine through hydraulic transmission and torque converters. ~*adj.* **2.** of or relating to such a locomotive or system.

die·sel oil *or* **fu·el** *n.* a fuel obtained from petroleum distillation that is used in diesel engines. It has a relatively low ignition temperature (540°C) and is ignited by the heat of compression. Also called: **derv.** See also **cetane number.**

Di·es I·rae *Latin.* ('di:eɪz 'ɪəraɪ) *n.* **1.** *Christianity.* a famous Latin hymn of the 13th century, describing the Last Judgment. It is used in the Mass for the dead. **2.** a musical setting of this hymn, usually part of a setting of the Requiem. [literally: day of wrath]

di·e·sis ('daɪɪsɪs) *n., pl.* **·ses** (-ˌsi:z). **1.** *Printing.* another name for **double dagger. 2.** *Music.* **a.** (in ancient Greek theory) any interval smaller than a whole tone, esp. a semitone in the Pythagorean scale. **b.** (in modern theory) the discrepancy of pitch in just intonation between an octave and either a succession of four ascending minor thirds (**great diesis**), or a succession of three ascending major thirds (**minor diesis**). [C16: via Latin from Greek: a quarter tone, literally: a sending through, from *diienai*; the double dagger was originally used in musical notation]

di·es non ('daɪi:z 'nɒn) *n. Law.* a day on which no legal business may be transacted. Also called: **dies non juridicus.** Compare **juridical days.** [C19: shortened from Latin phrase *diēs nōn jūridicus* literally: day which is not juridical, that is, not reserved for legal affairs]

die·stock ('daɪˌstɒk) *n.* the device holding the dies used to cut an external screw thread.

di·e·strus (daɪ'i:strəs) *n.* the U.S. spelling of **diestrus.**

di·et[1] ('daɪət) *n.* **1. a.** a specific allowance or selection of food, esp. prescribed to control weight or in disorders in which certain foods are contraindicated: *a salt-free diet; a 900 Calorie diet.* **b.** (*as modifier*): *a diet bread.* **2.** the food and drink that a person or animal regularly consumes: *a diet of nuts and water.* **3.** regular activities or occupations. ~*vb.* **4.** (*usually intr.*) to follow or cause to follow a dietary regimen. [C13: from

Old French *diete*, from Latin *diaeta*, from Greek *diaita* mode of living, from *diaitan* to direct one's own life] —**'di·et·er** *n.*

di·et² ('daɪət) *n.* **1.** (*sometimes cap.*) a legislative assembly in various countries, such as Japan. **2.** (*sometimes cap.*) Also called: **Reichstag.** the assembly of the estates of the Holy Roman Empire. **3.** *Scot. law.* **a.** the date fixed by a court for hearing a case. **b.** a single session of a court. [C15: from Medieval Latin *diēta* public meeting, probably from Latin *diaeta* DIET¹ but associated with Latin *diēs* day]

di·e·tar·y ('daɪətərɪ, -trɪ) *adj.* **1.** of or relating to a diet. ~*n.*, *pl.* **·tar·ies. 2.** a regulated diet. **3.** a system of dieting.

di·e·tet·ic (ˌdaɪɪ'tɛtɪk) *or* **di·e·tet·i·cal** *adj.* **1.** denoting or relating to diet or the regulation of food intake. **2.** prepared for special dietary requirements. —ˌ**di·e'tet·i·cal·ly** *adv.*

di·e·tet·ics (ˌdaɪɪ'tɛtɪks) *n.* (*functioning as sing.*) the scientific study and regulation of food intake and preparation.

di·eth·yl e·ther (daɪ'ɛθɪl) *n.* a formal name for **ether** (sense 1).

di·eth·yl·stil·boes·trol (daɪˌɛθɪlstɪl'bɛstrɒl, -ˌiːθaɪl-) *n.* another name for **stilboestrol.**

di·e·ti·tian *or* **di·e·ti·cian** (ˌdaɪɪ'tɪʃən) *n.* a person who specializes in dietetics.

Die·trich (*German* 'diːtrɪç) *n.* **Mar·le·ne** (mar'leːnə), stage name of *Maria Magdalene von Losch.* born 1902, U.S. film actress and cabaret singer, born in Germany.

Dieu et mon droit *French.* (djø e mɔ̃ 'drwa) God and my right: motto of the Royal Arms of Great Britain.

diff. *abbrev. for:* **1.** difference. **2.** different.

dif·fer ('dɪfə) *vb.* (*intr.*) **1.** (often foll. by *from*) to be dissimilar in quality, nature, or degree (to); vary (from). **2.** (often foll. by *from* or *with*) to be at variance (with); disagree (with). **3.** *Dialect.* to quarrel or dispute. **4. agree to differ.** to end an argument amicably while maintaining differences of opinion. [C14: from Latin *differre*, literally: to bear off in different directions, hence scatter, put off, be different, from *dis-* apart + *ferre* to bear]

dif·fer·ence ('dɪfərəns, 'dɪfrəns) *n.* **1.** the state or quality of being unlike. **2.** a specific instance of being unlike.. **3.** a distinguishing mark or feature. **4.** a significant change in a situation: *the difference in her is amazing.* **5.** a disagreement or argument: *he had a difference with his wife.* **6.** a degree of distinctness, as between two people or things. **7. a.** the result of the subtraction of one number, quantity, etc., from another. **b.** the single number that when added to the subtrahend gives the minuend; remainder. **8.** *Logic.* another name for **differentia. 9.** *Heraldry.* an addition to the arms of a family to represent a younger branch. **10. make a difference. a.** to have an effect. **b.** to treat differently. **11. split the difference. a.** to compromise. **b.** to divide a remainder equally. **12. with a difference.** with some peculiarly distinguishing quality, good or bad. ~*vb.* (*tr.*) **13.** *Rare.* to distinguish. **14.** *Heraldry.* to add a charge to (arms) to differentiate a branch of a family.

dif·fer·ent ('dɪfərənt, 'dɪfrənt) *adj.* **1.** partly or completely unlike. **2.** not identical or the same; other: *he wears a different tie every day.* **3.** out of the ordinary; unusual. —**'dif·fer·ent·ly** *adv.* —**'dif·fer·ent·ness** *n.*

dif·fer·en·ti·a (ˌdɪfə'rɛnʃɪə) *n., pl.* **·ti·ae** (-ʃɪˌiː). *Logic.* a feature by which two subclasses of the same class of named objects can be distinguished. Also called: **difference.** [C19: from Latin: diversity, DIFFERENCE]

dif·fer·en·ti·a·ble (ˌdɪfə'rɛnʃɪəbᵊl) *adj.* **1.** capable of being differentiated. **2.** *Maths.* possessing a derivative. —ˌ**dif·fer·ˌen·ti·a·'bil·i·ty** *n.*

dif·fer·en·tial (ˌdɪfə'rɛnʃəl) *adj.* **1.** of, relating to, or using a difference. **2.** constituting a difference; distinguishing. **3.** *Maths.* of, containing, or involving one or more derivatives or differentials. **4.** *Physics, engineering.* relating to, operating on, or based on the difference between two opposing effects, motions, forces, etc.: *differential amplifier.* ~*n.* **5.** a factor that differentiates between two comparable things. **6.** *Maths.* **a.** an increment in a given function, expressed as the product of the derivative of that function and the corresponding increment in the independent variable. **b.** an increment in a given function of two or more variables, f(x_1, x_2, ... x_n), expressed as the sum of the products of each partial derivative and the increment in the corresponding variable. **7.** an epicyclic gear train that permits two shafts to rotate at different speeds while being driven by a third shaft. See also **differential gear. 8.** *Chiefly Brit.* the difference between rates of pay for different types of labour, esp. when forming a pay structure within an industry. **9.** (in commerce) a difference in rates, esp. between comparable labour services or transportation routes. —ˌ**dif·fer·'en·tial·ly** *adv.*

dif·fer·en·tial cal·cu·lus *n.* the branch of calculus concerned with the study, evaluation, and use of derivatives and differentials. Compare **integral calculus.**

dif·fer·en·tial co·ef·fi·cient *n. Maths.* another name for **derivative.**

dif·fer·en·tial e·qua·tion *n.* an equation containing differentials or derivatives of a function of one independent variable. A **partial differential equation** results from a function of more than one variable.

dif·fer·en·tial gear *n.* the epicyclic gear mounted in the driving axle of a road vehicle that permits one driving wheel to rotate faster than the other, as when cornering.

dif·fer·en·tial op·er·a·tor *n.* a mathematical operator, ∇, used in vector analysis, where $\nabla = i\partial/\partial x + j\partial/\partial y + k\partial/\partial z$, ***i, j,*** and ***k*** being unit vectors and $\partial/\partial x$, $\partial/\partial y$, and $\partial/\partial z$ the partial derivatives of a function in *x*, *y*, and *z*.

dif·fer·en·tial wind·lass *n.* a windlass employing the velocity ratio incurred in unwinding from a small drum while winding onto a larger drum rotating at a common speed. Also called: **Chinese windlass.**

dif·fer·en·ti·ate (ˌdɪfə'rɛnʃɪˌeɪt) *vb.* **1.** (*tr.*) to serve to distinguish between. **2.** (when *intr.*, often foll. by *between*) to perceive, show, or make a difference (in or between); discriminate. **3.** (*intr.*) to become dissimilar or distinct. **4.** *Maths.* to perform a differentiation on (a quantity, expression, etc.). **5.** (*intr.*) (of unspecialized cells, etc.) to change during development to more specialized forms. —ˌ**dif·fer·'en·ti·ˌa·tor** *n.*

dif·fer·en·ti·a·tion (ˌdɪfəˌrɛnʃɪ'eɪʃən) *n.* **1.** the act, process, or result of differentiating. **2.** *Maths.* an operation used in calculus in which the derivative of a function or variable is determined; the inverse of **integration** (sense 6).

dif·fi·cult ('dɪfɪkᵊlt) *adj.* **1.** not easy to do; requiring effort: *a difficult job.* **2.** not easy to understand or solve; intricate: *a difficult problem.* **3.** hard to deal with; troublesome: *a difficult child.* **4.** not easily convinced, pleased, or satisfied. **5.** full of hardships or trials: *difficult times ahead.* [C14: back formation from DIFFICULTY] —**'dif·fi·cult·ly** *adv.*

dif·fi·cul·ty ('dɪfɪkᵊltɪ) *n., pl.* **·ties. 1.** the state or quality of being difficult. **2.** a task, problem, etc., that is hard to deal with. **3.** (*often pl.*) a troublesome or embarrassing situation, esp. a financial one. **4.** a dispute or disagreement. **5.** (*often pl.*) an objection or obstacle: *he always makes difficulties.* **6.** a trouble or source of trouble; worry. **7.** lack of ease; awkwardness: *he could run only with difficulty.* [C14: from Latin *difficultās*, from *difficilis* difficult, from *dis-* not + *facilis* easy, FACILE]

dif·fi·dent ('dɪfɪdənt) *adj.* lacking self-confidence; timid; shy. [C15: from Latin *diffidere* to distrust, from *dis-* not + *fīdere* to trust] —**'dif·fi·dence** *n.* —**'dif·fi·dent·ly** *adv.*

dif·fract (dɪ'frækt) *vb.* to undergo or cause to undergo diffraction: *to diffract light; the light diffracts at a slit.* —**dif·'frac·tive** *adj.* —**dif·'frac·tive·ly** *adv.* —**dif·'frac·tive·ness** *n.*

dif·frac·tion (dɪ'frækʃən) *n.* **1.** *Physics.* a deviation in the direction of a wave at the edge of an obstacle in its path. **2.** any phenomenon caused by diffraction and interference of light, such as the formation of light and dark fringes by the passage of light through a small aperture. [C17: from New Latin *diffractiō* a breaking to pieces, from Latin *diffringere* to shatter, from *dis-* apart + *frangere* to break]

dif·frac·tion grat·ing *n.* a glass plate or a mirror with a large number of equidistant parallel lines or grooves on its surface. It causes diffraction of transmitted or reflected light, ultraviolet radiation, or x-rays.

dif·frac·tom·e·ter (dɪfræk'tɒmɪtə) *n. Physics.* an instrument used in studying diffraction, as in the determination of crystal structure by diffraction of x-rays.

dif·fuse *vb.* (dɪ'fjuːz). **1.** to spread or cause to spread in all directions. **2.** to undergo or cause diffusion. **3.** to scatter or cause to scatter; disseminate; disperse. ~*adj.* (dɪ'fjuːs). **4.** spread out over a wide area. **5.** lacking conciseness. **6.** (esp. of some creeping stems) spreading loosely over a large area. **7.** characterized by or exhibiting diffusion: *diffuse light; diffuse reflection.* [C15: from Latin *diffūsus* spread abroad, from *diffundere* to pour forth, from *dis-* away + *fundere* to pour] —**dif·fuse·ly** (dɪ'fjuːslɪ) *adv.* —**dif·'fuse·ness** *n.* —**dif·fus·i·ble** (dɪ'fjuːzəbᵊl) *adj.* —**dif·ˌfus·i·'bil·i·ty** *or* **dif·'fus·i·ble·ness** *n.*

dif·fused junc·tion *n.* a semiconductor junction formed by diffusing acceptor or donor impurity atoms into semiconductor material to form regions of p-type or n-type conductivity. See also **photolithography** (sense 2). Compare **alloyed junction.**

dif·fus·er *or* **dif·fu·sor** (dɪ'fjuːzə) *n.* **1.** a person or thing that diffuses. **2.** a part of a lighting fixture consisting of a translucent or frosted covering or of a rough reflector: used to scatter the light and prevent glare. **3.** a cone, wedge, or baffle placed in front of the diaphragm of a loudspeaker to diffuse the sound waves. **4.** a duct, esp. in a wind tunnel or jet engine, that widens gradually in the direction of flow to reduce the speed and increase the pressure of the air or fluid. **5.** *Photog.* a light-scattering medium, such as a screen of fine fabric, placed in the path of a source of light to reduce the sharpness of shadows and thus soften the lighting. **6.** a perforated plate or similar device for distributing compressed air in the aeration of sewage.

dif·fu·sion (dɪ'fjuːʒən) *n.* **1.** the act or process of diffusing or being diffused; dispersion. **2.** verbosity. **3.** *Physics.* **a.** the random thermal motion of atoms, molecules, clusters of atoms, etc., in gases, liquids, and some solids. **b.** the transfer of atoms or molecules by their random motion from one part of a medium to another. **4.** *Physics.* the transmission or reflection of electromagnetic radiation, esp. light, in which the radiation is scattered in many directions and not directly reflected or refracted; scattering. **5.** Also called: **diffusivity.** *Physics.* the degree to which the directions of propagation of reverberant sound waves differ from point to point in an enclosure. **6.** *Anthropol.* the transmission of social institutions, skills, and myths from one culture to another.

dif·fu·sion co·ef·fi·cient *or* **con·stant** *n.* the rate at which a diffusing substance is transported between opposite faces of a unit cube of a system when there is unit concentration difference between them. Symbol: *D* Also called: **diffusivity.**

dif·fu·sive (dɪ'fjuːsɪv) *adj.* characterized by diffusion. —**dif·'fu·sive·ly** *adv.* —**dif·'fu·sive·ness** *n.*

dif·fu·siv·i·ty (ˌdɪfjuː'sɪvɪtɪ) *n.* **1.** a measure of the ability of a substance to transmit a difference in temperature; expressed as the thermal conductivity divided by the product of specific heat capacity and density. **2.** *Physics.* **a.** the ability of a

DE

substance to permit or undergo diffusion. b. another name for **diffusion coefficient.** 3. another name for **diffusion** (sense 5).

dig (dɪg) *vb.* **digs, dig+ging, dug.** 1. (when *tr.*, often foll. by *up*) to cut into, break up, and turn over or remove (earth, soil, etc.), esp. with a spade. 2. to form or excavate (a hole, tunnel, passage, etc.) by digging, usually with an implement or (of animals) with feet, claws, etc.: *to dig a tunnel.* 3. (often foll. by *through*) to make or force (one's way), esp. by removing obstructions: *he dug his way through the crowd.* 4. (*tr.*; often foll. by *out* or *up*) to obtain by digging: *to dig potatoes; to dig up treasure.* 5. (*tr.*; often foll. by *out* or *up*) to find or discover by effort or searching: *to dig out unexpected facts.* 6. (*tr.*; foll. by *in* or *into*) to thrust or jab (a sharp instrument, weapon, etc.); poke: *he dug his spurs into the horse's side.* 7. (*tr.*; foll. by *in* or *into*) to mix (compost, etc.) with soil by digging. 8. (*intr.*; foll. by *in* or *into*) *Informal.* to begin vigorously to consume or do something: *don't wait, just dig in!* 9. *Informal.* to like, understand, or appreciate. 10. (*intr.*) *U.S. slang.* to work hard, esp. for an examination. 11. (*intr.*) *Brit. informal.* to have lodgings: *I dig in South London.* ~*n.* 12. the act of digging. 13. a thrust or poke, esp. in the ribs. 14. a cutting or sarcastic remark. 15. *Informal.* an archaeological excavation. ~See also **dig in.** [C13: *diggen*, of uncertain origin]

dig. *abbrev. for* digest (book or summary).

di+gam+ma (daɪˈgæmə) *n.* a letter of the Greek alphabet (Ϝ) that became obsolete before the classical period of the language. It represented a semivowel like English *W* and was used as a numeral in later stages of written Greek, and passed into the Roman alphabet as *F.* [C17: via Latin from Greek, from DI-[1] + GAMMA; from its shape, which suggests one gamma upon another]

dig·a+my (ˈdɪgəmɪ) *n., pl.* **+mies.** a second marriage contracted after the termination of the first by death or divorce. Also called: **deuterogamy.** Compare **bigamy.** [C17: from Late Latin *digamia*, from Greek, from DI-[1] + *gamos* marriage] —**ˈdig·a+mist** *n.* —**ˈdig·a+mous** *adj.*

di+gas+tric (daɪˈgæstrɪk) *adj.* 1. (of certain muscles) having two fleshy portions joined by a tendon. ~*n.* 2. a muscle of the mandible that assists in lowering the lower jaw. [C17: from New Latin *digastricus* (with two bellies), from DI-[1] + *gastricus* gastric, from Greek *gastēr* belly]

di+gen+e·sis (daɪˈdʒɛnɪsɪs) *n. Zoology.* another name for **alternation of generations.** —**di+ge·net+ic** (ˌdaɪdʒɪˈnɛtɪk) *adj.*

di+gest *vb.* (dɪˈdʒɛst, daɪ-). 1. to subject (food) to a process of digestion. 2. (*tr.*) to assimilate mentally. 3. *Chem.* to soften or disintegrate or be softened or disintegrated by the action of heat, moisture, or chemicals; decompose. 4. (*tr.*) to arrange in a methodical or systematic order; classify. 5. (*tr.*) to reduce to a summary. 6. (*tr.*) *Archaic.* to tolerate. ~*n.* (ˈdaɪdʒɛst). 7. a comprehensive and systematic compilation of information or material, often condensed. 8. a magazine, periodical, etc., that summarizes news of current events. 9. a compilation of rules of law based on decided cases. [C14: from Late Latin *dīgesta* writings grouped under various heads, from Latin *dīgerere* to divide, from *di-* apart + *gerere* to bear]

Di+gest (ˈdaɪdʒɛst) *n. Roman law.* an arrangement of excerpts from the writings and opinions of eminent lawyers, contained in 50 books compiled by order of Justinian in the sixth century A.D.

di+gest+ant (dɪˈdʒɛstənt, daɪ-) *n.* a substance, such as hydrochloric acid or a bile salt, that promotes or aids digestion, esp. one used therapeutically.

di+gest+er (dɪˈdʒɛstə, daɪ-) *n.* 1. *Chem.* an apparatus or vessel, such as an autoclave, in which digestion is carried out. 2. a less common word for **digestant.** 3. a person or thing that digests.

di+gest+i·ble (dɪˈdʒɛstəbᵊl, daɪ-) *adj.* capable of being digested or easy to digest. —**di+ˌgest+i·ˈbil+i·ty** *or* **di+ˈgest+i·ble+ness** *n.* —**di+ˈgest+i·bly** *adv.*

di+ges+tif *French.* (diʒɛˈstif) *n.* something, esp. a drink, taken as an aid to digestion, either before or after a meal.

di+ges+tion (dɪˈdʒɛstʃən, daɪ-) *n.* 1. the act or process in living organisms of breaking down ingested food material into easily absorbed and assimilated substances by the action of enzymes and other agents. 2. mental assimilation, esp. of ideas. 3. *Bacteriol.* the decomposition of sewage by the action of bacteria. 4. *Chem.* the treatment of material with heat, solvents, chemicals, etc., to cause softening or decomposition. [C14: from Old French, from Latin *digestiō* a dissolving, digestion] —**di+ˈges+tion+al** *adj.*

di+ges+tive (dɪˈdʒɛstɪv, daɪ-) *or* **di+ges+tant** (daɪˈdʒɛstənt) *adj.* 1. relating to, aiding, or subjecting to digestion: *a digestive enzyme.* ~*n.* 2. a less common word for **digestant.** 3. short for **digestive biscuit.** —**di+ˈges+tive+ly** *adv.*

di+ges+tive bis+cuit *n.* a round semisweet biscuit made from wholemeal flour.

digged (dɪgd) *vb. Archaic.* a past tense of **dig.**

dig+ger (ˈdɪgə) *n.* 1. a person, animal, or machine that digs. 2. a miner, esp. one who digs for gold. 3. a tool or part of a machine used for excavation, esp. a mechanical digger fitted with a head for digging trenches.

Dig+ger (ˈdɪgə) *n.* 1. (*sometimes not cap.*) *Slang.* a. an Australian or New Zealander, esp. a soldier: often used as a term of address. b. (*as modifier*): *a Digger accent.* 2. one of a number of tribes of America whose diet was largely composed of roots dug out of the ground.

Dig+gers (ˈdɪgəz) *n.* **the.** a radical English Puritan group, led by Gerrard Winstanley, which advocated communal ownership of land (1649–50).

dig+ger wasp *n.* any solitary wasp of the family *Sphecidae* that digs a nest hole in the ground and stocks it with live insects for the larvae.

dig+gings (ˈdɪgɪŋz) *pl. n.* 1. (*functioning as pl.*) material that has been dug out. 2. (*functioning as sing. or pl.*) a place where mining, esp. gold-mining, has taken place. 3. (*functioning as pl.*) *Brit. informal.* a less common name for **digs.**

dight (daɪt) *vb.* **dights, dight+ing, dight** *or* **dight+ed.** (*tr.*) *Archaic.* to adorn or equip, as for battle. [Old English *dihtan* to compose, from Latin *dictāre* to DICTATE]

dig in *vb.* (*adv.*) 1. *Military.* to provide (a defensive position) by digging foxholes, trenches, etc. 2. *Informal.* to entrench (oneself) firmly. 3. (*intr.*) *Informal.* to defend or maintain a position firmly, as in an argument. 4. **dig one's heels in.** *Informal.* to refuse stubbornly to move or be persuaded.

dig+it (ˈdɪdʒɪt) *n.* 1. a finger or toe. 2. Also called: **figure.** any of the ten Arabic numerals from 0 to 9. 3. another name for **finger** (sense 4). 4. *Astronomy.* one twelfth of the diameter of the sun or moon, used to express the magnitude of an eclipse. [C15: from Latin *digitus* toe, finger]

dig·i+tal (ˈdɪdʒɪtᵊl) *adj.* 1. of, relating to, resembling, or possessing a digit or digits. 2. performed with the fingers. 3. *Computer technol.* operating by the use of discrete signals to represent data in the form of numbers or other characters. 4. displaying information as numbers rather than by a pointer moving over a dial: *a digital voltmeter; digital readout.* 5. *Electronics.* responding to discrete values of input voltage and producing discrete output voltage levels, as in a logic circuit: *digital circuit.* Compare **linear** (sense 8). 6. a less common word for **digitate.** ~*n.* 7. *Music.* one of the keys on the manuals of an organ or on a piano, harpsichord, etc. —**ˈdig·i+tal+ly** *adv.*

dig·i+tal clock *or* **watch** *n.* a clock or watch in which the hours, minutes, and sometimes seconds are indicated by digits, rather than by hands on a dial.

dig·i+tal com+pu+ter *n.* an electronic computer in which the input is discrete rather than continuous, consisting of combinations of numbers, letters, and other characters written in an appropriate programming language and represented internally in binary notation. Compare **analog computer.**

dig·i+tal+in (ˌdɪdʒɪˈteɪlɪn) *n.* a poisonous amorphous white glycoside extracted from digitalis leaves and used in treating heart disease. Formula: $C_{36}H_{56}O_{14}$. [C19: from DIGITAL(IS) + -IN]

dig·i+tal+is (ˌdɪdʒɪˈteɪlɪs) *n.* 1. any Eurasian scrophulariaceous plants of the genus *Digitalis*, such as the foxglove, having bell-shaped flowers and a basal rosette of leaves. 2. a drug prepared from the dried leaves or seeds of the foxglove: a mixture of glycosides used medicinally as a heart stimulant. [C17: from New Latin, from Latin: relating to a finger (referring to the corollas of the flower); based on German *Fingerhut* foxglove, literally: finger-hat]

dig·i+tal+ism (ˈdɪdʒɪtəˌlɪzəm) *n.* a serious condition resulting from digitalis poisoning, characterized by nausea, vomiting, and a disturbance in heart rhythm or rate.

dig·i+tal+ize *or* **dig·i+tal+ise** (ˈdɪdʒɪtəˌlaɪz) *vb.* (*tr.*) to administer digitalis to (a patient) for the treatment of certain heart disorders. —**ˌdig·i+tal·i+ˈza+tion** *or* **ˌdig·i+tal·i+ˈsa+tion** *n.*

dig·i+tate (ˈdɪdʒɪˌteɪt) *or* **dig·i+tat+ed** *adj.* 1. (of compound leaves) having the leaflets in the form of a spread hand. 2. (of animals) having digits or corresponding parts. —**ˈdig·i+ˌtate+ly** *adv.* —**ˌdig·i+ˈta+tion** *n.*

dig·i+ti+form (ˈdɪdʒɪtɪˌfɔːm) *adj.* shaped like a finger.

dig·i+ti+grade (ˈdɪdʒɪtɪˌgreɪd) *adj.* 1. (of dogs, cats, horses, etc.) walking so that only the toes touch the ground. ~*n.* 2. a digitigrade animal.

dig+it+ize *or* **dig+it+ise** (ˈdɪdʒɪˌtaɪz) *vb.* (*tr.*) to transcribe (data) into a digital form so that it can be directly processed by a computer. —**ˌdig+it·i+ˈza+tion** *or* **ˌdig+it·i+ˈsa+tion** *n.*

dig·i+tox+in (ˌdɪdʒɪˈtɒksɪn) *n.* a white toxic bitter-tasting glycoside, extracted from digitalis leaves and used in medicine. Formula: $C_{41}H_{64}O_{13}$. [from DIGI(TALIS) + TOXIN]

dig·i+tron (ˈdɪdʒɪˌtrɒn) *n. Electronics.* a type of tube, for displaying information, having a common anode and several cathodes shaped in the form of characters, which can be lit by a glow discharge. Also called: **Nixie tube.** [C20: from DIGIT + -TRON]

di+glot (ˈdaɪglɒt) *adj.* 1. a less common word for **bilingual.** ~*n.* 2. a bilingual book. [C19: from Greek *diglōttos*, from DI-[1] + *glōtta* tongue] —**di+ˈglot+tic** *adj.*

dig+ni+fied (ˈdɪgnɪˌfaɪd) *adj.* characterized by dignity of manner or appearance; stately; noble. —**ˈdig+ni+ˌfied+ly** *adv.* —**ˈdig+ni+ˌfied+ness** *n.*

dig+ni+fy (ˈdɪgnɪˌfaɪ) *vb.* **+fies, +fy+ing, +fied.** (*tr.*) 1. to invest with honour or dignity; ennoble. 2. to add distinction to: *the meeting was dignified by the minister.* 3. to add a semblance of dignity to, esp. by the use of a pretentious name or title: *she dignifies every plant with its Latin name.* [C15: from Old French *dignifier*, from Late Latin *dignificāre*, from Latin *dignus* worthy + *facere* to make]

dig+ni+tar·y (ˈdɪgnɪtərɪ, -trɪ) *n., pl.* **+tar·ies.** a person of high official position or rank, esp. in government or the church.

dig+ni·ty (ˈdɪgnɪtɪ) *n., pl.* **·ties.** 1. a formal, stately, or grave bearing: *he entered the room with great dignity.* 2. the state or quality of being worthy of honour: *the dignity of manual labour.* 3. relative importance; rank: *he is next in dignity to the mayor.* 4. sense of self-importance (often in the phrases **stand** (or **be**) **on one's dignity, beneath one's dignity**). 5. high rank, esp. in government or the church. 6. a person of high rank or such persons collectively. [C13: from Old French *dignite*, from Latin *dignitās* merit, from *dignus* worthy]

di·graph ('daɪgrɑːf, -græf) *n.* a combination of two letters or characters used to represent a single speech sound such as *gh* in English *tough.* Compare **ligature** (sense 5), **diphthong.** —**di·graph·ic** (daɪ'græfɪk) *adj.*

di·gress (daɪ'grɛs) *vb.* (*intr.*) **1.** to depart from the main subject in speech or writing. **2.** to wander from one's path or main direction. [C16: from Latin *dīgressus* turned aside, from *dīgredī,* from *dis-* apart + *gradī* to go] —**di·'gress·er** *n.*

di·gres·sion (daɪ'grɛʃən) *n.* an act or instance of digressing from a main subject in speech or writing. —**di·'gres·sion·al** *adj.*

di·gres·sive (daɪ'grɛsɪv) *adj.* characterized by digression or tending to digress. —**di·'gres·sive·ly** *adv.* —**di·'gres·sive·ness** *n.*

digs (dɪgz) *pl. n. Brit. informal.* lodgings. [C19: shortened from DIGGINGS, perhaps referring to where one *digs* or works, but see also DIG IN]

di·he·dral (daɪ'hiːdrəl) *adj.* **1.** having or formed by two intersecting planes; two-sided: *a dihedral angle.* ~*n.* **2.** Also called: **dihedron, dihedral angle.** the figure formed by two intersecting planes. **3.** the upward or downward inclination of an aircraft wing in relation to the lateral axis. Compare **anhedral.**

di·he·dron (daɪ'hiːdrən) *n.* another name for **dihedral** (sense 2).

di·hy·brid (daɪ'haɪbrɪd) *n. Genetics.* the offspring of two individuals that differ with respect to two pairs of genes; an individual heterozygous for two pairs of genes. —**di·'hy·brid·ism** *n.*

di·hy·dric (daɪ'haɪdrɪk) *adj.* (of an alcohol) containing two hydroxyl groups per molecule.

Di·jon (*French* di'ʒɔ̃) *n.* a city in E France: capital of the former duchy of Burgundy. Pop.: 156 787 (1975).

dik-dik ('dɪkˌdɪk) *n.* any small antelope of the genus *Madoqua,* inhabiting semiarid regions of Africa, having an elongated muzzle and, in the male, small stout horns. [C19: an East African name, probably of imitative origin]

dike (daɪk) *n., vb.* the usual U.S. spelling of **dyke.**

dik·kop ('dɪkəp) *n.* a South African name for **stone curlew.** [from Afrikaans, from *dik* thick + *kop* head]

dik·tat ('dɪktɑːt) *n.* **1.** decree or settlement imposed, esp. by a ruler or a victorious nation. **2.** a dogmatic statement. [German: dictation, from Latin *dictātum,* from *dictāre* to DICTATE]

di·lap·i·date (dɪ'læpɪˌdeɪt) *vb.* to fall or cause to fall into ruin or decay. [C16: from Latin *dīlapidāre* to scatter, waste, from *dis-* apart + *lapidāre* to stone, throw stones, from *lapis* stone]

di·lap·i·da·ted (dɪ'læpɪˌdeɪtɪd) *adj.* falling to pieces or in a state of disrepair; shabby.

di·lap·i·da·tion (dɪˌlæpɪ'deɪʃən) *n.* **1.** the state of being or becoming dilapidated. **2.** (*often pl.*) *Property law.* **a.** the state of disrepair of premises at the end of a tenancy due to neglect. **b.** the extent of repairs necessary to such premises. —**di·'lap·i·ˌda·tor** *n.*

di·la·tan·cy (daɪ'leɪtənsɪ, dɪ-) *n.* a phenomenon caused by the nature of the stacking or fitting together of particles or granules in a heterogeneous system, such as the solidification of certain sols under pressure, and the thixotropy of certain gels.

di·la·tant (daɪ'leɪtᵊnt, dɪ-) *adj.* **1.** tending to dilate; dilating. **2.** *Physics.* of, concerned with, or exhibiting dilatancy. ~*n.* **3.** something, such as a catheter, that causes dilation.

di·late (daɪ'leɪt, dɪ-) *vb.* **1.** to expand or cause to expand; make or become wider or larger: *the pupil of the eye dilates in the dark.* **2.** (*intr.;* often foll. by *on* or *upon*) to speak or write at length; expand or enlarge. [C14: from Latin *dīlātāre* to spread out, amplify, from *dis-* apart + *lātus* wide] —**di·'lat·a·ble** *adj.* —**di·ˌlat·a·'bil·i·ty** *or* **di·'lat·a·ble·ness** *n.* —**di·'la·tion** *or* **di·la·ta·tion** (ˌdaɪlə'teɪʃən, ˌdɪ-) *n.* —**ˌdi·la·'ta·tion·al** *adj.* —**di·la·tive** (daɪ'leɪtɪv, dɪ-) *adj.*

dil·a·tom·e·ter (ˌdɪlə'tɒmɪtə) *n.* any instrument for measuring changes in dimension: often a glass bulb fitted with a long stopper through which a capillary tube runs, used for measuring volume changes of liquids. —**dil·a·to·met·ric** (ˌdɪlətə'mɛtrɪk) *adj.* —**ˌdil·a·to·'met·ri·cal·ly** *adv.* —**ˌdil·a·'tom·e·try** *n.*

di·la·tor, di·lat·er (daɪ'leɪtə, dɪ-), *or* **di·la·ta·tor** (ˌdaɪlə'teɪtə, ˌdɪ-) *n.* **1.** something that dilates an object, esp. a surgical instrument for dilating a bodily cavity. **2.** a muscle that expands an orifice or dilates an organ.

dil·a·to·ry ('dɪlətərɪ, -trɪ) *adj.* **1.** tending or inclined to delay or waste time. **2.** intended or designed to waste time or defer action. [C15: from Late Latin *dīlātōrius* inclined to delay, from *differre* to postpone; see DIFFER] —**'dil·a·to·ri·ly** *adv.* —**'dil·a·to·ri·ness** *n.*

dil·do *or* **dil·doe** ('dɪldəʊ) *n., pl.* **·dos** *or* **·does.** an object used as a substitute for an erect penis. [C17: of unknown origin]

di·lem·ma (dɪ'lɛmə, daɪ-) *n.* **1.** a situation necessitating a choice between two equal, esp. equally undesirable, alternatives. **2.** a problem that seems incapable of a solution. **3.** *Logic.* a form of argument in which one premiss is a conjunction of two conditionals and the second premiss is a disjunction containing one term (or its negative) from each conditional. A simple example is *if p then q and if r then q; either p or r; therefore q.* **4. on the horns of a dilemma. a.** faced with the choice between two equal alternatives. **b.** in an awkward situation. [C16: via Latin from Greek, from DI-[1] + *lēmma* assumption, proposition, from *lambanein* to take, grasp] —**dil·em·mat·ic** (ˌdɪlɪ'mætɪk, ˌdaɪlɪ-) *or* **dil·'em·mic** *adj.*

dil·et·tante (ˌdɪlɪ'tɑːntɪ) *n., pl.* **·tan·tes** *or* **·tan·ti** (-'tɑːntɪ). **1.** a person whose interest in a subject is superficial rather than professional. **2.** a person who loves the arts. ~*adj.* **3.** of or characteristic of a dilettante. [C18: from Italian, from *dilettare* to delight, from Latin *dēlectāre*] —**ˌdil·et·'tan·tish** *or* **ˌdil·et·'tan·te·ish** *adj.* —**ˌdil·et·'tan·tism** *or* **ˌdil·et·'tan·te·ism** *n.*

Dí·li *or* **Dil·li** ('diːliː) *n.* a port in Indonesia, in N Timor: the former capital (until 1976) of Portuguese Timor. Pop.: 6730 (1970).

dil·i·gence[1] ('dɪlɪdʒəns) *n.* **1.** steady and careful application. **2.** proper attention or care. **3.** *Law.* the degree of care required in a given situation. [C14: from Latin *dīligentia* care, attentiveness]

dil·i·gence[2] ('dɪlɪdʒəns; *French* dili'ʒɑ̃s) *n. History.* a stagecoach. [C18: from French, shortened from *carosse de diligence,* literally: coach of speed]

dil·i·gent ('dɪlɪdʒənt) *adj.* **1.** careful and persevering in carrying out tasks or duties. **2.** carried out with care and perseverance: *diligent work.* [C14: from Old French, from Latin *dīligere* to value, from *dis-* apart + *legere* to read] —**'dil·i·gent·ly** *adv.*

dill (dɪl) *n.* **1.** an umbelliferous aromatic Eurasian plant, *Anethum graveolens,* with finely dissected leaves and umbrella-shaped clusters of yellow flowers. **2.** the leaves or seedlike fruits of this plant, used for flavouring in pickles, soups, etc., and in medicine. **3.** *Slang, chiefly Austral.* a fool; idiot. [Old English *dile;* related to Old High German *tilli*] —**'dil·ly** *adj.*

dill pick·le *n.* a pickled cucumber flavoured with dill.

dil·ly ('dɪlɪ) *n., pl.* **·lies.** *Slang, chiefly U.S.* a person or thing that is remarkable. [C20: perhaps from girl's proper name *Dilly*]

dil·ly bag *n. Austral.* a small bag, esp. one made of plaited grass, etc., often used for carrying food. Sometimes shortened to **dilly.**

dil·ly-dal·ly ('dɪlɪˌdælɪ) *vb.* **·lies, ·ly·ing, ·lied.** (*intr.*) *Informal.* to loiter or vacillate. [C17: by reduplication from DALLY]

dil·u·ent ('dɪljʊənt) *adj.* **1.** causing dilution or serving to dilute. ~*n.* **2.** a substance used for or causing dilution. [C18: from Latin *dīluēns* dissolving; see DILUTE]

di·lute (daɪ'luːt) *vb.* **1.** to make or become less concentrated, esp. by adding water or a thinner. **2.** to make or become weaker in force, effect, etc.: *he diluted his story.* ~*adj.* **3.** *Chem.* **a.** (of a solution, suspension, mixture, etc.) having a low concentration or a concentration that has been reduced by admixture. **b.** (of a substance) present in solution, esp. a weak solution in water: *dilute acetic acid.* [C16: from Latin *dīluere,* from *dis-* apart + *-luere,* from *lavāre* to wash] —**ˌdi·lu·'tee** *n.* —**di·'lut·er** *n.*

di·lu·tion (daɪ'luːʃən) *n.* **1.** the act of diluting or state of being diluted. **2.** a diluted solution.

di·lu·vi·al (daɪ'luːvɪəl, dɪ-) *or* **di·lu·vi·an** *adj.* **1.** of or connected with a deluge, esp. with the great Flood described in Genesis. **2.** of or relating to diluvium. [C17: from Late Latin *dīluviālis;* see DILUVIUM]

di·lu·vi·um (daɪ'luːvɪəm, dɪ-) *n., pl.* **·vi·a** (-vɪə). *Geology.* a former name for **drift** (sense 12). [C19: from Latin: flood, from *dīluere* to wash away; see DILUTE]

dim (dɪm) *adj.* **dim·mer, dim·mest. 1.** badly illuminated: *a dim room.* **2.** not clearly seen; indistinct; faint: *a dim shape.* **3.** having weak or indistinct vision: *eyes dim with tears.* **4.** lacking in understanding; mentally dull. **5.** not clear in the mind; obscure: *a dim memory.* **6.** lacking in brilliance, brightness, or lustre: *a dim colour.* **7.** tending to be unfavourable; gloomy (esp. in the phrase **take a dim view**). ~*vb.* **dims, dim·ming, dimmed. 8.** to become or cause to become dim. **9.** (*tr.*) to cause to seem less bright, as by comparison. **10.** the U.S. word for **dip** (sense 5). [Old English *dimm;* related to Old Norse *dimmr* gloomy, dark] —**'dim·ly** *adv.* —**'dim·ness** *n.*

dim. *abbrev. for:* **1.** dimension. **2.** Also: **dimin.** *Music.* diminuendo. **3.** Also: **dimin.** diminutive.

Di·mashq (diː'mæʃk) *n.* an Arabic name for **Damascus.**

dime (daɪm) *n.* **1.** a coin of the U.S. and Canada, worth one tenth of a dollar or ten cents. **2. a dime a dozen.** very cheap or common. [C14: from Old French *disme,* from Latin *decimus* tenth, from *decem* ten]

di·men·hy·dri·nate (ˌdaɪmɛn'haɪdrɪˌneɪt) *n.* a white slightly soluble bitter-tasting crystalline substance, used as an antihistamine and for the prevention of nausea, esp. in travel sickness. Formula: $C_{24}H_{28}ClN_5O_3$. [from DIME(THYL + AMI)N(E) + HYDR(AM)IN(E) + -ATE[1]]

dime nov·el *n. U.S.* (formerly) a cheap melodramatic novel, usually in paperback. Also (esp. Brit.): **penny-dreadful.**

di·men·sion (dɪ'mɛnʃən) *n.* **1.** (*often pl.*) a measurement of the size of something in a particular direction, such as the length, width, height, or diameter. **2.** (*often pl.*) scope; size; extent: *a problem of enormous dimensions.* **3.** aspect: *a new dimension to politics.* **4.** *Maths.* the number of coordinates required to locate a point in space. **5.** *Physics.* **a.** the product or the quotient of the fundamental physical quantities (such as mass, length, or time) raised to the appropriate power in a derived physical quantity: *the dimensions of velocity are length divided by time.* **b.** the power to which such a fundamental quantity has to be raised in a derived quantity. ~*vb.* **6.** (*tr.*) *Chiefly U.S.* **a.** to shape or cut to specified dimensions. **b.** to mark with specified dimensions. [C14: from Old French, from Latin *dīmensiō* an extent, from *dīmētīrī* to measure out, from *mētīrī*] —**di·'men·sion·al** *adj.* —**di·ˌmen·sion·'al·i·ty** *n.* —**di·'men·sion·al·ly** *adv.* —**di·'men·sion·less** *adj.*

di·mer ('daɪmə) *n. Chem.* **a.** a molecule composed of two identical simpler molecules (monomers). **b.** a compound consisting of dimers.

di·mer·cap·rol (ˌdaɪmə'kæprɒl) *n.* a colourless oily liquid with an offensive smell, used as an antidote to lewisite and similar toxic substances. Formula: $CH_2(SH)CH(SH)CH_2OH$. Also called: **BAL.** [C20: by shortening and altering from *dimercaptopropanol*]

dim+er+ous ('dɪmərəs) *adj.* **1.** consisting of or divided into two segments, as the tarsi of some insects. **2.** (of flowers) having their floral parts arranged in whorls of two. [C19: from New Latin *dimerus*, from Greek *dimerēs*, from DI-[1] + *meros* part] —'**dim+er+ism** *n.*

dim·e·ter ('dɪmɪtə) *n. Prosody.* a line of verse consisting of two metrical feet or a verse written in this metre.

di+me·thyl+sulph+ox+ide (daɪˌmiːθaɪlsʌl'fɒksaɪd, -ˌmɛθəl-) *n.* a colourless odourless liquid substance used as a solvent and in medicine as an agent to improve the penetration of drugs applied to the skin. Formula: $(CH_3)_2SO$. Abbrev.: **DMSO.**

di+met+ric (daɪ'mɛtrɪk) *adj. Crystallog.* another word for **tetragonal.**

di+mid·i+ate *adj.* (dɪ'mɪdɪɪt). **1.** divided in halves. **2.** *Biology.* having one of two sides or parts more developed than the other: *dimidiate antlers.* ~*vb.* (dɪ'mɪdɪˌeɪt). (*tr.*) **3.** *Rare.* to divide in half. **4.** *Heraldry.* to halve (two bearings) so that they can be represented on the same shield. [C17: from Latin *dīmidiāre* to halve, from *dīmidius* half, from *dis-* apart + *medius* middle] —**di+ˌmid·i+'a·tion** *n.*

di+min+ish (dɪ'mɪnɪʃ) *vb.* **1.** to make or become smaller, fewer, or less. **2.** (*tr.*) *Architect.* to cause (a column, etc.) to taper. **3.** *Music.* (*tr.*) to decrease (a minor or perfect interval) by a semitone. **4.** to belittle or be belittled; reduce in authority, status, etc.; depreciate. [C15: blend of *diminuen* to lessen (from Latin *dēminuere* to make smaller, from *minuere* to reduce) + archaic MINISH to lessen] —**di+'min+ish+a·ble** *adj.* —**di+'min+ish+ing+ly** *adv.* —**di+'min+ish+ment** *n.*

di+min+ished (dɪ'mɪnɪʃt) *adj.* **1.** reduced or lessened; made smaller. **2.** *Music.* denoting any minor or perfect interval reduced by a semitone. **3.** *Music.* denoting a triad consisting of the root plus a minor third and a diminished fifth. **4.** *Music.* (*postpositive*) (esp. in jazz or pop music) denoting a diminished seventh chord having as its root the note specified: *B diminished.*

di+min+ished re+spon+si·bil+i·ty *n. Law.* a plea under which proof of mental derangement is submitted as demonstrating lack of premeditation and therefore criminal responsibility.

di+min+ished sev+enth chord *n.* a chord often used in an enharmonic modulation and very common in modern music, esp. jazz and pop music, consisting of a diminished triad with an added diminished seventh above the root. Often shortened to **diminished seventh.**

di+min+ish+ing re+turns *pl. n. Economics.* progressively smaller increases in output resulting from equal increases in production.

di+min·u+en+do (dɪˌmɪnjʊ'ɛndəʊ) *n., pl.* **+dos. 1.** *Music.* **a.** a gradual decrease in loudness or the musical direction indicating this. Abbrev.: **dim.** Symbol: $>$ (written over the music affected). **b.** a musical passage affected by a diminuendo. ~*adj.* **2.** gradually decreasing in loudness. **3.** with a diminuendo. ~Also called: **decrescendo.** [C18: from Italian, from *diminuire* to DIMINISH]

dim·i+nu+tion (ˌdɪmɪ'njuːʃən) *n.* **1.** reduction; decrease. **2.** *Music.* the presentation of the subject of a fugue, etc., in which the note values are reduced in length. Compare **augmentation** (sense 3). [C14: from Latin *dēminūtiō*; see DIMINISH]

di+min·u+tive (dɪ'mɪnjʊtɪv) *adj.* **1.** very small; tiny. **2.** *Grammar.* **a.** denoting an affix added to a word to convey the meaning *small* or *unimportant* or to express affection, as for example, the suffix *-ette* in French. **b.** denoting a word formed by the addition of a diminutive affix. ~*n.* **3.** *Grammar.* a diminutive word or affix. ~Compare (for senses 2, 3) **augmentative. 4.** a tiny person or thing. —**di+min·u+ti+val** (dɪˌmɪnjʊ'taɪvəl) *adj.* —**di+'min·u+tive+ly** *adv.* —**di+'min·u+tive+ness** *n.*

dim+is+so·ry (dɪ'mɪsərɪ) *adj.* **1.** granting permission to be ordained: *a bishop's dimissory letter.* **2.** granting permission to depart.

Di+mi+tro+vo (di'mitrovo) *n.* the former name (1949–62) of **Pernik.**

dim+i·ty ('dɪmɪtɪ) *n., pl.* **·ties. a.** a light strong cotton fabric with woven stripes or squares. **b.** (*as modifier*): *a dimity bonnet.* [C15: from Medieval Latin *dimitum*, from Greek *dimiton*, from DI-[1] + *mitos* thread of the warp]

dim+mer ('dɪmə) *n.* **1.** a device, such as a rheostat, for varying the current through an electric light and thus changing the illumination. **2.** (*often pl.*) *U.S.* **a.** a dipped headlight on a road vehicle. **b.** a parking light on a car.

di+morph ('daɪmɔːf) *n.* either of two forms of a substance that exhibits dimorphism.

di+mor+phism (daɪ'mɔːfɪzəm) *n.* **1.** the occurrence within a plant of two distinct forms of any part, such as the leaves of some aquatic plants. **2.** the occurrence in an animal species of two distinct types of individual. **3.** a property of certain substances that enables them to exist in two distinct crystalline forms.

di+mor+phous (daɪ'mɔːfəs) *or* **di+mor+phic** *adj. Chem.* (of a substance) exhibiting dimorphism.

dim+ple ('dɪmpəl) *n.* **1.** a small natural dent or crease in the flesh, esp. on the cheeks or chin. **2.** any slight depression in a surface. **3.** a bubble or dent in glass. ~*vb.* **4.** to make or become dimpled. **5.** (*intr.*) to produce dimples by smiling. [C13 *dympull*; compare Old English *dyppan* to dip, German *Tümpel* pool] —'**dim+ply** *adj.*

dim+wit ('dɪmˌwɪt) *n. Informal.* a stupid or silly person. —ˌ**dim-'wit·ted** *adj.* —ˌ**dim-'wit·ted+ly** *adv.* —ˌ**dim-'wit·ted+ness** *n.*

din (dɪn) *n.* **1.** a loud discordant confused noise. ~*vb.* **dins, din+ning, dinned. 2.** (*tr.*; usually foll. by *into*) to instil (into a person) by constant repetition. **3.** (*tr.*) to subject to a din. **4.** (*tr.*) to make a din. [Old English *dynn*; compare Old Norse *dynr* din, Old High German *tuni*]

DIN *n.* a logarithmic expression of the speed of a photographic film, plate, etc., given as $-10\log_{10}E$, where E is the exposure of a point 0.1 density units above the fog level; high-speed films have high numbers. Compare **ASA/BS.** [C20: from German *D*(*eutsche*) *I*(*ndustrie*) *N*(*orm*) German Industry Standard]

Din. *abbrev. for* dinar.

Di·nah ('daɪnə) *n.* the daughter of Jacob and Leah (Genesis 30:21; 34).

di+nar ('diːnɑː) *n.* **1.** the standard monetary unit of the following countries. Algeria: divided into 100 centimes. Iraq: divided into 1000 fils. Jordan: divided into 1000 fils. Kuwait: divided into 1000 fils. Libya: divided into 100 piastres. Southern Yemen: divided into 1000 fils. Tunisia: divided into 1000 milliemes. Yugoslavia: divided into 100 paras. Abbrev.: **Din., D., d. 2.** an Iranian monetary unit worth one hundredth of a rial. **3.** a coin, esp. one of gold, formerly used in the Middle East. [C17: from Arabic, from Late Greek *dēnarion*, from Latin *dēnārius* DENARIUS]

Di+nar+ic Alps (dɪ'nærɪk, daɪ-) *pl. n.* a mountain range in W Yugoslavia: connected with the main Alpine system by the Julian Alps. Highest peak: Troglav, 1913m (6277 ft.).

dine (daɪn) *vb.* **1.** (*intr.*) to eat dinner. **2.** (*intr.*; often foll. by *on, off,* or *upon*) to make one's meal (of): *the guests dined upon roast beef.* **3.** (*tr.*) *Informal.* to entertain to dinner; (esp. in the phrase **to wine and dine someone).** [C13: from Old French *disner*, contracted from Vulgar Latin *disjējūnāre* (unattested) to cease fasting, from *dis-* not + Late Latin *jējūnāre* to fast; see JEJUNE]

dine out *vb.* (*intr., adv.*) **1.** to dine away from home, esp. in a restaurant. **2.** (foll. by *on*) to have dinner at the expense of someone else mainly for the sake of one's knowledge or conversation about (a subject or story).

din+er ('daɪnə) *n.* **1.** a person eating a meal, esp. in a restaurant. **2.** *Chiefly U.S.* a small cheap restaurant, often at the roadside. **3.** short for **dining car.**

di+ner+ic (dɪ'nɛrɪk) *adj.* of or concerned with the interface between two immiscible liquids. [C20: from DI- + Late Greek *nēron* water + -IC]

Din·e·sen ('dɪnɪsən) *n.* **I·sak** ('aɪzək), pen name of *Baroness Karen Blixen.* 1885–1962, Danish author of short stories in Danish and English, including *Seven Gothic Tales* (1934) and *Winter's Tales* (1942).

di+nette (daɪ'nɛt) *n.* an alcove or small area for use as a dining room.

ding (dɪŋ) *vb.* **1.** to ring or cause to ring, esp. with tedious repetition. **2.** (*tr.*) another word for **din** (sense 2). ~*n.* **3.** an imitation or representation of the sound of a bell. **4.** *Austral. slang, derogatory.* an Italian or Greek immigrant. **5.** *Austral. slang.* a party (the social event). [C13: probably of imitative origin, but influenced by DIN + RING[2]; compare Old Swedish *diunga* to beat]

Din·gaan ('dɪŋgɑːn) *n.* died 1840, Zulu chief (1828–40), who fought the Boer colonists in Natal.

Ding an sich (dɪŋ æn sɪk; *German* dɪŋ an zɪç) *n. Philosophy.* the thing in itself.

ding+bat ('dɪŋˌbæt) *n. U.S. Slang.* any unnamed object, esp. one used as a missile. [C19: of unknown origin]

ding+bats ('dɪŋˌbæts) *Austral. slang.* ~*pl. n.* **1. the.** delirium tremens. **2. give someone the dingbats.** to make someone nervous. ~*adj.* **3.** crazy or stupid.

ding-dong *n.* **1.** the sound of a bell or bells, esp. two bells tuned a fourth or fifth apart. **2.** an imitation or representation of the sound of a bell. **3. a.** a violent exchange of blows or words. **b.** (*as modifier*): *a ding-dong battle.* ~*adj.* **4.** sounding or ringing repeatedly. [C16: of imitative origin; see DING]

dinge[1] (dɪndʒ) *n.* dinginess. [C19: back formation from DINGY]

dinge[2] (dɪndʒ) *U.S. derogatory slang.* ~*n.* **1.** a Negro. ~*adj.* **2.** of or relating to Negroes.

din+ghy, din+gy, *or* **din+gey** ('dɪŋɪ) *n., pl.* **+ghies, +gies,** *or* **+geys.** any small boat, powered by sail, oars, or outboard motor. [C19: from Hindi or Bengali *dingi* a little boat, from *dingā* boat]

din+gle ('dɪŋgəl) *n.* a small wooded dell. [C13: of uncertain origin]

din+go ('dɪŋgəʊ) *n., pl.* **+goes. 1.** a wild dog, *Canis dingo*, of Australia, having a yellowish-brown coat and resembling a wolf. **2.** *Austral. slang.* a cheat or coward. ~*vb.* (*intr.*) **3.** *Austral slang.* **a.** to act in a cowardly manner. **b.** to drop out of something. **4.** (foll. by *on*) *Austral. slang.* to let (someone) down. [C18: native Australian name]

din+gy ('dɪndʒɪ) *adj.* **+gi+er, +gi+est. 1.** lacking light or brightness; drab. **2.** dirty; discoloured. [C18: perhaps from an earlier dialect word related to Old English *dynge* dung] —'**din+gi+ly** *adv.* —'**din+gi+ness** *n.*

din+ing car *n.* a railway coach in which meals are served at tables. Also called: **restaurant car.**

din+ing room *n.* a room where meals are eaten.

di+ni+tro+ben+zene (daɪˌnaɪtrəʊ'bɛnziːn, -bɛn'ziːn) *n.* a yellow crystalline compound existing in three isomeric forms, obtained by reaction of benzene with nitric and sulphuric acids. The *meta-* form is used in the manufacture of dyes and plastics. Formula: $C_6H_4(NO_2)_2$.

di+ni+tro+gen te+trox+ide (daɪ'naɪtrədʒən) *n.* a colourless gaseous substance that exists in equilibrium with nitrogen dioxide. As the temperature is reduced the proportion of the tetroxide increases. Formula: N_2O_4.

dink (dɪŋk) *adj. Scot. and northern Brit. dialect.* **1.** neat or neatly dressed. ~*vb.* **2.** *Austral., chiefly children's slang.* **a.** (*tr.*) to carry a second person on (a horse, bicycle, etc.). **b.** (*intr.*) (of two people) to travel together on a horse, bicycle, etc. [C16: of unknown origin]

Din+ka ('dɪŋkə) *n.* **1.** (*pl.* **+kas** *or* **+ka**) a member of a Nilotic people of the S Sudan, noted for their height, which often reaches seven feet tall: chiefly herdsmen. **2.** the language of this people, belonging to the Nilotic group of the Nilo-Saharan family. [from Dinka *jieng* people]

din+kum ('dɪŋkəm) *adj. Austral. informal.* **1.** genuine or right (usually preceded by *fair* and used esp. as an interjection): *a fair dinkum offer.* **2. dinkum oil.** the truth. [C19: from English dialect: work, of unknown origin]

dink·y ('dɪŋkɪ) *adj.* **dink·i·er, dink·i+est.** *Informal.* **1.** *Brit.* small and neat; dainty. **2.** *U.S.* inconsequential; insignificant. [C18 (in the sense: dainty): from DINK]

dink·y-di ('dɪŋkɪ'daɪ) *adj. Austral. informal.* typical: *dinky-di Pom idleness.* [C20: variant of DINKUM]

din+ner ('dɪnə) *n.* **1.** a meal taken in the evening. **2.** a meal taken at midday, esp. when it is the main meal of the day; lunch. **3. a.** a formal evening meal, as of a club, society, etc. **b.** a public banquet in honour of someone or something. **4.** a complete meal at a fixed price in a restaurant; table d'hôte. **5.** (*modifier*) of, relating to, or used at dinner: *dinner plate; dinner table; dinner hour.* **6. do like a dinner.** (*usually passive*) *Austral. informal.* to do for, overpower, or outdo. [C13: from Old French *disner;* see DINE]

din·ner-dance *n.* a formal dinner followed by dancing.

din+ner jack+et *n.* **1.** a man's semiformal evening jacket without tails, usually black with a silk facing over the collar and lapels. U.S. name: **tuxedo.**

din+ner serv+ice *n.* a set of matching plates, dishes, etc., suitable for serving a meal to a certain number of people.

di+noc+er+as (daɪ'nɒsərəs) *n.* another name for a **uintathere.** [C19: New Latin, from Greek *deinos* fearful + *keras* horn]

di+no+flag+el+late (ˌdaɪnəʊ'flædʒɪlɪt, -ˌleɪt) *n.* **1.** any of a group of unicellular biflagellate aquatic organisms forming a constituent of plankton: can be regarded as an order of protozoans (*Dinoflagellata*) or a class of algae (*Dinophyceae*). ~*adj.* **2.** of or relating to dinoflagellates. [C19: from New Latin *Dinoflagellata,* from Greek *dinos* whirling + FLAGELLUM + -ATE[1]]

di+no+saur ('daɪnəˌsɔː) *n.* any extinct terrestrial reptile of the orders *Saurischia* and *Ornithischia,* many of which were of gigantic size and abundant in the Mesozoic era. See also **saurischian, ornithischian.** Compare **pterosaur, plesiosaur.** [C19: from New Latin *dinosaurus,* from Greek *deinos* fearful + *sauros* lizard] —ˌ**di+no+'saur+i·an** *adj.*

di+no+there ('daɪnəˌθɪə) *n.* any extinct late Tertiary elephant-like mammal of the genus *Dinotherium* (or *Deinotherium*), having a down-turned jaw with tusks curving downwards and backwards. [C19: from New Latin *dinotherium,* from Greek *deinos* fearful + *thērion,* diminutive of *thēr* beast]

dint (dɪnt) *n.* **1. by dint of.** by means or use of: *by dint of hard work.* **2.** *Archaic.* a blow or a mark made by a blow. ~*vb.* **3.** (*tr.*) to mark with dints. ~*n., vb.* **4.** a variant spelling of **dent**[1]. [Old English *dynt;* related to Old Norse *dyttr* blow] —**'dint+less** *adj.*

D'In·ze·o (*Italian* din'dzɛːo) *n.* **Pie·ro** ('pjɛːro), born 1923, and his brother **Rai·mon·do** (raɪ'mondo), born 1925, Italian show-jumping riders.

dioc. *abbrev. for:* **1.** diocesan. **2.** diocese.

Di·o Cas·si·us ('daɪəʊ 'kæsɪəs) *n.* ?155–?230 A.D., Roman historian. His *History of Rome* covers the period of Rome's transition from Republic to Empire.

di+oc+e·san (daɪ'ɒsɪs[ə]n) *adj.* **1.** of or relating to a diocese. ~*n.* **2.** the bishop of a diocese.

di·o+cese ('daɪəsɪs) *n.* the district under the jurisdiction of a bishop. [C14: from Old French, from Late Latin *diocēsis,* from Greek *dioikēsis* administration, from *dioikein* to manage a household, from *oikos* house]

Di·o·cle·tian (ˌdaɪə'kliːʃən) *n.* full name *Gaius Aurelius Valerius Diocletianus.* 245–313 A.D., Roman emperor (284–305), who divided the empire into four administrative units (293) and instigated the last severe persecution of the Christians (303).

di+ode ('daɪəʊd) *n.* **1.** a semiconductor device containing one p-n junction, used in circuits for converting alternating current to direct current. More formal name: **semiconductor diode. 2.** the earliest and simplest type of electronic valve having two electrodes, an anode and a cathode, between which a current can flow only in one direction. It was formerly widely used as a rectifier and detector but has now been replaced in most electrical circuits by the more efficient and reliable semiconductor diode. [C20: from DI-[1] + -ODE[2]]

Di·o·do·rus Sic·u·lus (ˌdaɪə'dɔːrəs 'sɪkjʊləs) *n.* 1st century B.C., Greek historian, noted for his history of the world in 40 books, of which 15 are extant.

di+oe·cious, di+e·cious (daɪ'iːʃəs), *or* **di+oi·cous** (daɪ'ɔɪkəs) *adj.* (of some plants) having the male and female reproductive organs in separate flowers on separate plants. ~Compare **monoecious.** [C18: from New Latin *Dioecia* name of class, from DI-[1] + Greek *oikia* house, dwelling] —**di+'oe·cious+ly, di+'e·cious+ly,** *or* **di+'oi·cous+ly** *adv.* —**di+'oe·cious+ness, di+'e·cious+ness,** *or* **di+'oi·cous+ness** *n.*

di+oe·strus *or U.S.* **di+e·strus** (daɪ'iːstrəs) *n.* a period of sexual inactivity between periods of oestrus in animals that have several oestrous cycles in one breeding season.

Di·og·e·nes (daɪ'ɒdʒɪˌniːz) *n.* ?412–?323 B.C., Greek Cynic philosopher, who rejected social conventions and advocated self-sufficiency and simplicity of life.

di·ol ('daɪɒl) *n. Chem.* any of a class of alcohols that have two hydroxyl groups in each molecule. Also called: **glycol, dihydric alcohol.** [from DI-[1] + (ALCOH)OL]

Di·o+mede Is+lands ('daɪəˌmiːd) *pl. n.* two small islands in the Bering Strait, separated by the international date line and by the boundary line between the U.S. and the Soviet Union.

Di·o·me·des (ˌdaɪə'miːdiːz), **Di·o·mede,** *or* **Di·o·med** *n. Greek myth.* **1.** a king of Argos, and suitor of Helen, who fought with the Greeks at Troy. **2.** a king of the Bistones in Thrace whose savage horses ate strangers.

Di·o·ne[1] (daɪ'əʊnɪ) *n. Greek myth.* a Titaness; the earliest consort of Zeus and mother of Aphrodite.

Di·o+ne[2] (daɪ'əʊnɪ) *n.* one of the ten satellites of the planet Saturn.

Di·o+ny+si·a (ˌdaɪə'nɪzɪə) *n.* (in ancient Greece) festivals of the god Dionysus: a source of Athenian drama.

Di·o+nys·i+ac (ˌdaɪə'nɪzɪˌæk) *adj.* **1.** of or relating to Dionysus or his worship. **2.** a less common word for **Dionysian.**

Di·o+ny+si·an (ˌdaɪə'nɪzɪən) *adj.* **1.** of or relating to Dionysus. **2.** (*sometimes not cap.*) (in the philosophy of Nietzsche) of or relating to the set of creative qualities that encompasses spontaneity, irrationality, the rejection of discipline, etc. **3.** (*often not cap.*) wild or orgiastic. **4.** of or relating to any of the historical characters named Dionysius. Compare (for senses 2, 3) **Apollonian.**

Di·o·ny·si·us (ˌdaɪə'nɪsɪəs) *n.* called *the Elder.* ?430–367 B.C., tyrant of Syracuse (405–367), noted for his successful campaigns against Carthage and S Italy.

Di·o·ny·si·us Ex·ig·u·us (ɛg'zɪgjʊəs) *n.* died ?556 A.D., Scythian monk and scholar, who is believed to have introduced the current method of reckoning dates on the basis of the Christian era.

Di·o·ny·si·us of Hal·i·car+nas+sus *n.* died ?7 B.C., Greek historian and rhetorician; author of a history of Rome.

Di·o·ny·sus *or* **Di·o·ny·sos** (ˌdaɪə'naɪsəs) *n.* the Greek god of wine, fruitfulness, and vegetation, worshipped in orgiastic rites. He was also known as the bestower of ecstasy and god of the drama, and identified with Bacchus.

Di·o+phan+tine e·qua+tion (ˌdaɪəʊ'fæntaɪn) *n.* (in number theory) an equation in more than one variable and with integral coefficients, for which integral solutions are sought.

Di·o·phan·tus (ˌdaɪəʊ'fæntəs) *n.* 3rd century A.D., Greek mathematician, noted for his treatise on the theory of numbers, *Arithmetica.*

di+op+side (daɪ'ɒpsaɪd, -sɪd) *n.* a colourless or pale-green pyroxene mineral consisting of calcium magnesium silicate in monoclinic crystalline form: used as a gemstone. Formula: $CaMgSi_2O_6$. [C19: from DI-[2] + Greek *opsis* sight, appearance + -IDE]

di+op+tase (daɪ'ɒpteɪs, -teɪz) *n.* a green glassy mineral consisting of hydrated copper silicate in hexagonal crystalline form. Formula: H_2CuSiO_4. [C19: from French, from Greek *dia-* through + *optos* visible]

di+op+tom+e·ter (ˌdaɪɒp'tɒmɪtə) *n.* an instrument for measuring ocular refraction. [from DI-[2] + OPT(IC) + -METER] —ˌ**di+op+'tom+e+try** *n.*

di+op+tre *or U.S.* **di+op+ter** (daɪ'ɒptə) *n.* a unit for measuring the refractive power of a lens: the reciprocal of the focal length of the lens expressed in metres. [C16: from Latin *dioptra* optical instrument, from Greek, from *dia-* through + *opsesthai* to see] —**di+'op+tral** *adj.*

di+op+tric (daɪ'ɒptrɪk) *or* **di+op+tri+cal** *adj.* **1.** of or concerned with dioptrics. **2.** of or denoting refraction or refracted light. —**di+'op+tri+cal+ly** *adv.*

di+op+trics (daɪ'ɒptrɪks) *n.* (*functioning as sing.*) the branch of geometrical optics concerned with the formation of images by lenses. [C20: from DIOPTRE + ICS]

Dior (diːɔː; *French* djɔːr) *n.* **Chris·tian** ('krɪstʃən; *French* kris'tjɑ̃). 1905–57, French couturier, noted for his New Look of narrow shoulders and waist with a full skirt (1947); he also created the waistless sack dress.

di·o+ra+ma (ˌdaɪə'rɑːmə) *n.* **1.** a miniature three-dimensional scene, in which models of figures are seen against a background. **2.** a picture made up of illuminated translucent curtains, viewed through an aperture. **3.** a museum display, as of an animal, of a specimen in its natural setting. **4.** *Films.* a scene produced by the rearrangement of lighting effects. [C19: from French, from Greek *dia-* through + Greek *horama* view, from *horan* to see] —**di·o+ram+ic** (ˌdaɪə'ræmɪk) *adj.*

di·o+rite ('daɪəˌraɪt) *n.* a dark coarse-grained igneous plutonic rock consisting of plagioclase feldspar and ferromagnesian minerals such as hornblende. [C19: from French, from Greek *diorizein* to distinguish (from *dia-* apart + *horizein* to define) + -ITE[1]] —**di·o+rit+ic** (ˌdaɪə'rɪtɪk) *adj.*

Di·os·cu·ri (ˌdaɪɒs'kjʊəri) *pl. n.* the Greek name for **Castor and Pollux,** when considered together.

di+ox+an (daɪ'ɒksən) *or* **di+ox+ane** (daɪ'ɒkseɪn) *n.* a colourless insoluble toxic liquid made by heating ethanediol with sulphuric acid; 1,4-diethylene dioxide: used as a solvent, esp. for waxes and cellulose acetate resins. Formula: $(CH_2)_2O(CH_2)_2O$.

di+ox+ide (daɪ'ɒksaɪd) *n.* **1.** any oxide containing two oxygen atoms per molecule, both of which are bonded to an atom of another element. **2.** another name for a **peroxide** (sense 4).

dip (dɪp) *vb.* **dips, dip+ping, dipped. 1.** to plunge or be plunged quickly or briefly into a liquid, esp. to wet or coat. **2.** (*intr.*) to undergo a slight decline, esp. temporarily: *sales dipped in*

November. **3.** (*intr.*) to slope downwards: *the land dips towards the river.* **4.** to sink or appear to sink quickly: *the sun dipped below the horizon.* **5.** (*tr.*) to switch (car headlights) from the main to the lower beam. U.S. word: **dim.** **6.** (*tr.*) **a.** to immerse (poultry, sheep, etc.) briefly in a liquid chemical to rid them of or prevent infestation by insects, etc. **b.** to immerse (grain, vegetables, or wood) in a preservative liquid. **7.** (*tr.*) to stain or dye by immersing in a liquid. **8.** (*tr.*) to baptize (someone) by immersion. **9.** (*tr.*) to plate or galvanize (a metal, etc.) by immersion in an electrolyte or electrolytic cell. **10.** (*tr.*) to scoop up a liquid or something from a liquid in the hands or in a container. **11.** to lower or be lowered briefly: *she dipped her knee in a curtsy.* **12.** (*tr.*) to make (a candle) by plunging the wick into melted wax. **13.** (*intr.*) to plunge a container, the hands, etc., into something, esp. to obtain or retrieve an object: *he dipped in his pocket for money.* **14.** (*intr.;* foll. by *in* or *into*) to draw (upon): *he dipped into his savings.* **15.** (*intr.;* foll. by *in* or *into*) to dabble (in); play (at): *he dipped into black magic.* **16.** (*intr.;* foll. by *in* or *into*) to select passages to read at random (from a book, newspaper, etc.). **17.** (*intr.*) (of an aircraft) to drop suddenly and then regain height. **18.** (*intr.*) (of a rock stratum or mineral vein) to slope downwards from the horizontal. **19.** (*intr.;* often foll. by *for*) (in children's games) to select (a leader, etc.) by reciting any of various rhymes. ~*n.* **20.** the act of dipping or state of being dipped. **21.** a brief swim in water. **22. a.** any liquid chemical preparation in which poultry, sheep, etc. are dipped. **b.** any liquid preservative into which objects, esp. of wood, are dipped. **23.** a preparation of dyeing agents into which fabric is immersed. **24.** a depression, esp. in a landscape. **25.** something taken up by dipping. **26.** a container used for dipping; dipper. **27.** a momentary sinking down. **28.** the angle of slope of rock strata, fault planes, etc., from the horizontal plane. **29.** Also called: **angle of dip, magnetic dip, inclination.** the angle between the direction of the earth's magnetic field and the plane of the horizon; the angle that a magnetic needle free to swing in a vertical plane makes with the horizontal. **30.** a creamy savoury mixture usually made from cheese, into which potato crisps, sticks of celery, etc., are dipped before being eaten. **31.** *Surveying.* the angular distance of the horizon below the plane of observation. **32.** a candle made by plunging a wick repeatedly into wax. **33.** a momentary loss of altitude when flying. **34.** (in gymnastics) a chinning exercise on the parallel bars. **35.** a slang word for **pickpocket.** [Old English *dyppan;* related to Old High German *tupfen* to wash, German *taufen* to baptize; see DEEP]

dip. *or* **Dip.** *abbrev. for* diploma.

Dip. A. D. (in Britain) *abbrev. for* Diploma in Art and Design.

dip cir·cle *n.* an instrument for measuring dip, consisting of a dip needle with a vertical circular scale of angles. Also called: **inclinometer.**

Dip. Ed. (in Britain) *abbrev. for* Diploma in Education.

di·pep·tide (daɪ'pɛptaɪd) *n.* a compound consisting of two linked amino acids. See **peptide.**

di·pet·al·ous (daɪ'pɛtələs) *adj.* another word for **bipetalous.**

di·phase ('daɪˌfeɪz) *or* **di·phas·ic** (daɪ'feɪzɪk) *adj. Physics.* of, having, or concerned with two phases.

di·phe·nyl (daɪ'fi:naɪl, -nɪl, -'fɛnɪl) *n.* another name for **biphenyl.**

di·phe·nyl·a·mine (daɪˌfi:naɪlə'mi:n, -'æmɪn, -nɪl-, -ˌfɛn-) *n.* a colourless insoluble crystalline derivative of benzene, used in the manufacture of dyes, as a stabilizer in plastics, etc. Formula: $(C_6H_5)_2NH$.

di·phe·nyl·hy·dan·to·in so·di·um (daɪˌfi:naɪlhaɪ'dæntəʊɪn, -nɪl-, -ˌfɛn-) *n.* a white soluble bitter-tasting powder used as an anticonvulsant in the treatment of epilepsy. Formula: $C_{15}H_{11}N_2O_2Na$.

di·phos·gene (daɪ'fɒsdʒi:n) *n.* an oily liquid with an extremely poisonous vapour, made by treating methanol with phosgene and chlorinating the product: has been used in chemical warfare. Formula: $ClCOOCCl_3$.

diph·the·ri·a (dɪp'θɪərɪə, dɪf-) *n.* an acute contagious disease caused by the bacillus *Corynebacterium diphtheriae,* producing fever, severe prostration, and difficulty in breathing and swallowing as the result of swelling of the throat and formation of a false membrane. [C19: New Latin, from French *diphthérie,* from Greek *diphthera* leather; from the nature of the membrane] —**diph·'the·ri·al, diph·the·rit·ic** (ˌdɪpθə'rɪtɪk, dɪf-), *or* **diph·ther·ic** (dɪp'θɛrɪk, dɪf-) *adj.* —**'diph·the·ˌroid** *adj.*

diph·thong ('dɪfθɒŋ, 'dɪp-) *n.* **1.** a vowel sound, occupying a single syllable, during the articulation of which the tongue moves from one position to another, causing a continual change in vowel quality, as in the pronunciation of *a* in English *late,* during which the tongue moves from the position of (e) towards (ɪ). **2.** a digraph or ligature representing a composite vowel such as this, as *ae* in *Caesar.* [C15: from Late Latin *diphthongus,* from Greek *diphthongos,* from DI-[1] + *phthongos* sound] —**diph·'thon·gal** *adj.*

diph·thong·ize *or* **diph·thong·ise** ('dɪfθɒŋˌaɪz, -ˌgaɪz, 'dɪp-) *vb.* (*often passive*) to make (a simple vowel) into a diphthong. —ˌ**diph·thong·i·'za·tion** *or* ˌ**diph·thong·i·'sa·tion** *n.*

di·phy·cer·cal (ˌdɪfɪ'sɜ:kəl) *adj. Ichthyol.* of or possessing a symmetrical or pointed tail with the vertebral column extending to the tip, as in primitive fishes. [C19: from Greek *diphuēs* twofold (from DI-[1] + *phuē* growth) + *kerkos* tail]

di·phy·let·ic (ˌdaɪfaɪ'lɛtɪk) *adj.* relating to or characterized by descent from two ancestral groups of animals or plants.

di·phyl·lous (daɪ'fɪləs) *adj.* (of certain plants) having two leaves.

diph·y·o·dont ('dɪfɪəʊˌdɒnt) *adj.* having two successive sets of teeth, as mammals (including man). Compare **polyphyodont.** [C19: from Greek *diphuēs* double (see DIPHYCERCAL) + -ODONT]

dipl. *abbrev. for:* **1.** diplomat(ic). **2.** Also: **dip.** diploma.

di·ple·gia (daɪ'pli:dʒə) *n.* paralysis of corresponding parts on both sides of the body; bilateral paralysis.

di·plex ('daɪplɛks) *adj.* permitting the transmission or reception of two signals simultaneously in the same direction over a radio or telecommunications channel. Compare **duplex** (sense 4), **simplex** (sense 1). [C19: DI-[1] + Latin *-plex* -FOLD, on the model of *duplex*] —'**di·plex·er** *n.*

dip·lo- *or before a vowel* **dipl-** *combining form.* double: *diplococcus.* [from Greek, from *diploos,* from DI-[1] + *-ploos* -fold]

dip·lo·blas·tic (ˌdɪpləʊ'blæstɪk) *adj.* (of jellyfish, corals, and other coelenterates) having a body developed from only two germ layers (ectoderm and endoderm). Compare **triploblastic.**

dip·lo·car·di·ac (ˌdɪpləʊ'kɑ:dɪˌæk) *adj.* (of birds and mammals) having a four-chambered heart, which enables two separate circulations and prevents mixing of the arterial and venous blood.

dip·lo·coc·cus (ˌdɪpləʊ'kɒkəs) *n., pl.* **·coc·ci** (-'kɒksaɪ). any of various spherical Gram-positive bacteria that occur in pairs, esp. any of the genus *Diplococcus,* such as *D. pneumoniae,* which causes pneumonia: family *Lactobacillaceae.* —ˌ**dip·lo·'coc·cal** *or* **dip·lo·coc·cic** (ˌdɪpləʊ'kɒksɪk, -'kɒkɪk) *adj.*

dip·lo·do·cus (ˌdɪpləʊ'dəʊkəs) *n., pl,* **·cus·es.** any herbivorous quadrupedal late Jurassic dinosaur of the genus *Diplodocus,* characterized by a very long neck and tail and a total body length of 27 metres: suborder *Sauropoda* (sauropods). [C19: from New Latin, from DIPLO- + Greek *dokos* beam]

dip·lo·ë ('dɪpləʊˌi:) *n. Anatomy.* the spongy bone separating the two layers of compact bone of the skull. [C17: via New Latin, from Greek: a fold, from *diploos* double]

dip·loid ('dɪplɔɪd) *adj.* **1.** *Biology.* (of cells or organisms) having paired homologous chromosomes so that twice the haploid number is present. **2.** double or twofold. ~*n.* **3.** a diploid cell or organism. —**dip·'loi·dic** *adj.*

di·plo·ma (dɪ'pləʊmə) *n.* **1.** a document conferring a qualification, recording success in examinations or successful completion of a course of study. **2.** an official document that confers an honour or privilege. [C17: from Latin: official letter or document, literally: letter folded double, from Greek; see DIPLO-]

di·plo·ma·cy (dɪ'pləʊməsɪ) *n., pl.* **·cies. 1.** the conduct of the relations of one state with another by peaceful means. **2.** skill in the management of international relations. **3.** tact, skill, or cunning in dealing with people. [C18: from French *diplomatie,* from *diplomatique* DIPLOMATIC]

dip·lo·mat ('dɪpləˌmæt) *n.* **1.** an official such as an ambassador or first secretary, engaged in diplomacy. **2.** a person who deals with people tactfully or skilfully.

dip·lo·mate ('dɪpləˌmeɪt) *n.* any person who has been granted a diploma, esp. a physician certified as a specialist.

dip·lo·mat·ic (ˌdɪplə'mætɪk) *or* **dip·lo·mat·i·cal** *adj.* **1.** of or relating to diplomacy or diplomats. **2.** skilled in negotiating, esp. between states or people. **3.** tactful in dealing with people. **4.** of or relating to diplomatics. [C18: from French *diplomatique* concerning the documents of diplomacy, from New Latin *diplōmaticus;* see DIPLOMA] —ˌ**dip·lo·'mat·i·cal·ly** *adv.*

dip·lo·mat·ic corps *or* **bod·y** *n.* the entire body of diplomats accredited to a given state.

dip·lo·mat·ic im·mun·i·ty *n.* the immunity from local jurisdiction and exemption from taxation in the country to which they are accredited afforded to diplomats.

dip·lo·mat·ics (ˌdɪplə'mætɪks) *n.* **1.** the critical study of historical documents. **2.** a less common word for **diplomacy.**

Dip·lo·mat·ic Serv·ice *n.* **1.** *Brit.* the division of the Civil Service which provides diplomats to represent the U.K. abroad. **2.** (*not caps.*) the equivalent institution of any other country.

di·plo·ma·tist (dɪ'pləʊmətɪst) *n.* a less common word for **diplomat.**

dip·lont ('dɪplɒnt) *n.* an animal or plant that has the diploid number of chromosomes in its somatic cells. [C20: DIPLO- + Greek *ōn* being, from *einai* to be]

di·plo·pi·a (dɪ'pləʊpɪə) *n.* a visual defect in which a single object is seen in duplicate; double vision. [C19: New Latin, from DIPLO- + Greek *ōps* eye] —**di·plop·ic** (dɪ'plɒpɪk) *adj.*

dip·lo·pod ('dɪpləˌpɒd) *n.* any arthropod of the class *Diplopoda,* which includes the millipedes.

di·plo·sis (dɪ'pləʊsɪs) *n. Biology.* the doubling of the haploid number of chromosomes that occurs during fusion of gametes to form a diploid zygote. [C20: from Greek *diplōsis* doubling, from *diploun* to double, from *diploos* double]

dip·lo·ste·mo·nous (ˌdɪpləʊ'sti:mənəs, -'stɛm-) *adj.* (of plants) having twice as many stamens as petals, esp. with the stamens arranged in two whorls. [C19: from New Latin *diplostemonus* (unattested), from DIPLO- + *-stemonus* relating to a STAMEN]

dip·lo·tene ('dɪpləʊˌti:n) *n.* the fourth stage of the prophase of meiosis, during which the chromosomes of each bivalent separate, usually with the interchange of genetic material. See also **chiasma** (sense 2), **crossing over.**

dip nee·dle *n.* a magnetized needle pivoted through its centre of gravity able to rotate freely in a vertical plane, used to determine the inclination of the earth's magnetic field. See also **dip circle.**

dip·no·an (dɪp'nəʊən) *adj.* **1.** of, relating to, or belonging to the *Dipnoi,* a subclass of bony fishes comprising the lungfishes.

~*n.* **2.** any lungfish. [C19: from New Latin *Dipnoi;* from Greek *dipnoos,* double-breathing, from DI-[1] + *pnoē* breathing, air, from *pnein* to breathe]

dip·o·dy ('dɪpədɪ) *n., pl.* **-dies.** *Prosody.* a metrical unit consisting of two feet. [C19: from Late Latin *dipodia,* from Greek DI-[1] + *pous* foot]

di·pole ('daɪˌpəʊl) *n.* **1.** two electric charges or magnetic poles that have equal magnitudes but opposite signs and are separated by a small distance. **2.** a molecule in which the centre of positive charge does not coincide with the centre of negative charge. **3.** Also called: **dipole aerial.** a radio or television aerial consisting of a single straight metal rod with the connecting wire fixed to its midpoint. —**di'po·lar** *adj.*

dip out *vb.* (*intr., adv.;* often foll. by *on*) *Austral. informal.* to fail to take part (in) or advantage (of).

dip·per ('dɪpə) *n.* **1.** a ladle used for dipping. **2.** Also called: **water ouzel.** any aquatic songbird of the genus *Cinclus* and family *Cinclidae,* esp. *C. cinclus.* They inhabit fast-flowing streams and resemble large wrens. **3.** a person or thing that dips, such as the mechanism for directing car headlights downwards. **4.** a small metal cup clipped onto a painter's palette for holding diluent or medium. **5.** *Archaic.* an Anabaptist. ~See also **big dipper.**

dip·py ('dɪpɪ) *adj.* **-pi·er, -pi·est.** *Slang.* odd, eccentric, or crazy. [C20: of unknown origin]

di·pro·pel·lant (ˌdaɪprə'pɛlənt) *n.* another name for **bipropellant.**

di·pro·to·dont (daɪ'prəʊtəʊˌdɒnt) *n.* any marsupial of the group or suborder *Diprotodontia,* including kangaroos, phalangers, and wombats, having fewer than three upper incisor teeth on each side of the jaw. Compare **polyprotodont.** [C19: from Greek from DI-[1] + PROTO- + -ODONT]

dip·so·ma·ni·a (ˌdɪpsəʊ'meɪnɪə) *n.* a compulsive desire to drink alcoholic beverages. [C19: New Latin, from Greek *dipsa* thirst + -MANIA]

dip·so·ma·ni·ac (ˌdɪpsəʊ'meɪnɪˌæk) *n.* **1.** any person who has an uncontrollable and recurring urge to drink alcohol. Shortened form: **dipso.** ~*adj.* **2.** relating to or affected with dipsomania. —**dip·so·ma·ni·a·cal** (ˌdɪpsəʊmə'naɪəkəl) *adj.*

dip·stick ('dɪpˌstɪk) *n.* a graduated rod or strip dipped into a container to indicate the fluid level.

dip switch *n.* a device for dipping car headlights.

dip·ter·al ('dɪptərəl) *adj. Architect.* having a double row of columns.

dip·ter·an ('dɪptərən) *or* **dip·ter·on** ('dɪptəˌrɒn) *n.* **1.** any dipterous insect. ~*adj.* **2.** another word for **dipterous** (sense 1).

dip·ter·o·car·pa·ceous (ˌdɪptərəʊkɑː'peɪʃəs) *adj.* of, relating to, or belonging to the *Dipterocarpaceae,* a family of trees chiefly native to Malaysia, having two-winged fruits. Many species yield useful timber and resins. [C19: via New Latin from Greek *dipteros* two-winged + *karpos* fruit]

dip·ter·ous ('dɪptərəs) *adj.* **1.** Also: **dipteran.** of, relating to, or belonging to the *Diptera,* a large order of insects having a single pair of wings and sucking or piercing mouthparts. The group includes flies, mosquitoes, craneflies, and midges. **2.** *Botany.* having two winglike parts: *a dipterous seed.*

dip·tych ('dɪptɪk) *n.* **1.** a pair of hinged wooden tablets with waxed surfaces for writing. **2.** a painting or carving on two panels, usually hinged like a book.

dir. *abbrev. for* director.

Di·rac (dɪ'ræk) *n.* **Paul A·dri·en Mau·rice.** born 1902, English physicist, noted for his work on the application of relativity to quantum mechanics and his prediction of electron spin and the positron: shared the Nobel prize for physics 1933.

Di·rac con·stant *n.* a constant used in quantum mechanics equal to the Planck constant divided by 2π. It has a value of $1.0544 \pm 0.0003 \times 10^{-34}$ joule seconds. Symbol: $\hbar$ or $\underline{h}$ Also called: **crossed-h, h-bar.**

dire (daɪə) *adj.* (*usually prenominal*) **1.** Also: **direful.** disastrous; fearful. **2.** desperate; urgent: *a dire need.* [C16: from Latin *dīrus* ominous, fearful; related to Greek *deos* fear] —**'dire·ly** *adv.* —**'dire·ness** *n.*

di·rect (dɪ'rɛkt, daɪ-) *vb.* (*mainly tr.*) **1.** to regulate, conduct, or control the affairs of. **2.** (*also intr.*) to give commands or orders with authority to (a person or group): *he directed them to go away.* **3.** to tell or show (someone) the way to a place. **4.** to aim, point, or cause to move towards a goal. **5.** to address (a letter, parcel, etc.). **6.** to address (remarks, words, etc.): *to direct comments at someone.* **7.** (*also intr.*) to provide guidance to (actors, cameramen, etc.) in the rehearsal of a play or the filming of a motion picture. **8.** (*also intr.*) **a.** to conduct (a piece of music or musicians), usually while performing oneself. **b.** another word (esp. U.S.) for **conduct** (sense 8). ~*adj.* **9.** without delay or evasion; straightforward: *a direct approach.* **10.** without turning aside; uninterrupted; shortest; straight: *a direct route.* **11.** without intervening persons or agencies; immediate: *a direct link.* **12.** honest; frank; candid: *a direct answer.* **13.** (*usually prenominal*) precise; exact: *a direct quotation.* **14.** diametrical: *the direct opposite.* **15.** in an unbroken line of descent, as from father to son over succeeding generations: *a direct descendant.* **16.** (of government, decisions, etc.) by or from the electorate rather than through representatives. **17.** *Maths.* **a.** (of a relationship) containing two variables such that an increase (or decrease) in one results in an increase (or decrease) in the other. Compare **inverse** (sense 2). **b.** (of a proof) accepting and using the hypothesis to be proved to show that it is a true statement. Compare **indirect** (sense 5). **18.** *Astronomy.* moving from west to east on the celestial sphere. Compare **retrograde** (sense 4a.). **19. a.** of or relating to direct current. **b.** (of a secondary induced current) having the same direction as the primary current. **20.** *Music.* **a.** (of motion) in the same direction. See **motion** (sense 9). **b.** (of an interval or chord) in root position; not inverted. ~*adv.* **21.** directly; straight: *he went direct to the office.* [C14: from Latin *dīrectus;* from *dīrigere* to guide, from *dis-* apart + *regere* to rule] —**di'rect·ness** *n.*

di·rect ac·cess *n.* a method of reading data from a computer file without reading through the file from the beginning as on a disk or drum. Also called: **random access.** Compare **sequential access.**

di·rect ac·tion *n.* action such as strikes or civil disobedience, employed by organized labour or other groups to obtain demands from an employer, government, etc.

di·rect cur·rent *n.* a continuous electric current that flows in one direction only, without substantial variation in magnitude. Abbrev.: **D.C.** Compare **alternating current.**

di·rect dis·tance di·al·ing *n.* the U.S. equivalent of **subscriber trunk dialling.**

di·rect dye *n.* any of a number of dyes that can be applied without the use of a mordant. They are usually azo dyes applied to cotton or rayon from a liquid bath containing an electrolyte such as sodium sulphate.

di·rect·ed (dɪ'rɛktɪd, daɪ-) *adj. Maths.* (of a number, line, or angle) having either a positive or negative sign to distinguish measurement in one direction or orientation from that in the opposite direction or orientation.

di·rect ev·i·dence *n. Law.* evidence, usually the testimony of a witness, directly relating to the fact in dispute. Compare **circumstantial evidence.**

di·rect-grant school *n. Brit.* a school financed by endowment, fees, and a state grant conditional upon admittance of a percentage of nonpaying pupils nominated by the local education authority.

di·rec·tion (dɪ'rɛkʃən, daɪ-) *n.* **1.** the act of directing or the state of being directed. **2.** management, control, or guidance. **3.** the work of a stage or film director. **4.** the course or line along which a person or thing moves, points, or lies. **5.** the course along which a ship, aircraft, etc., is travelling, expressed as the angle between true or magnetic north and an imaginary line through the main fore-and-aft axis of the vessel. **6.** the place towards which a person or thing is directed. **7.** a line of action; course. **8.** the name and address on a letter, parcel, etc. **9.** *Music.* the process of conducting an orchestra, choir, etc. **10.** *Music.* an instruction in the form of a word or symbol heading or occurring in the body of a passage, movement, or piece to indicate tempo, dynamics, mood, etc. **11.** (*modifier*) *Maths.* **a.** (of an angle) being any one of the three angles that a line in space makes with the three positive directions of the coordinate axes. Usually given as α, β, and γ with respect to the x-, y-, and z- axes. **b.** (of a cosine) being the cosine of any of the direction angles.

di·rec·tion·al (dɪ'rɛkʃənəl, daɪ-) *adj.* **1.** of or relating to a spatial direction. **2.** *Electronics.* **a.** having or relating to an increased sensitivity to radio waves, sound waves, nuclear particles, etc., coming from a particular direction. **b.** (of an aerial) transmitting or receiving radio waves more effectively in some directions than in others. **3.** *Physics, electronics.* **a.** concentrated in, following, or producing motion in a particular direction. **b.** indicating direction. —**diˌrec·tion'al·i·ty** *n.*

di·rec·tion find·er *n.* a highly directional aerial system that can be used to determine the direction of incoming radio signals, used esp. as a navigation aid. Abbrevs.: **D/F** or **D.F.** —**di·rec·tion find·ing** *n.*

di·rec·tions (dɪ'rɛkʃənz, daɪ-) *pl. n.* (*sometimes sing.*) instructions for doing something or for reaching a place.

di·rec·tive (dɪ'rɛktɪv, daɪ-) *n.* **1.** an instruction; order. ~*adj.* **2.** tending to direct; directing. **3.** indicating direction.

di·rect·ly (dɪ'rɛktlɪ, daɪ-) *adv.* **1.** in a direct manner. **2.** at once; without delay. **3.** (foll. by *before* or *after*) immediately; just. ~*conj.* **4.** (*subordinating*) as soon as: *we left directly the money arrived.*

di·rect mail *n. U.S.* mail sent for the purpose of advertising, soliciting donations, etc.

di·rect meth·od *n.* a method of teaching a foreign language with minimal use of the pupil's native language and of formal grammar.

di·rect ob·ject *n. Grammar.* a noun, pronoun, or noun phrase whose referent receives the direct action of a verb. For example, *the man* is the direct object in the sentence *They shot the man with a rifle.* Compare **indirect object.**

Di·rec·toire *French.* (dirɛk'twar) *n.* **1.** *History.* the French Directory. See **Directory.** ~*adj.* **2.** of, in, or relating to a decorative style of the end of the 18th century in France; a form of neoclassicism. **3.** characteristic of women's dress during the French Directory, typically an almost transparent dress with the waistline under the bust.

di·rec·tor (dɪ'rɛktə, daɪ-) *n.* **1.** a person or thing that directs, controls, or regulates. **2.** a member of the governing board of a business concern who may or may not have an executive function. **3.** a person who directs the affairs of an institution, trust, educational programme, etc. **4.** the person responsible for the staging of a play or the making of a film. **5.** *Music.* another word (esp. U.S.) for **conductor** (sense 2). —**di·rec'to·ri·al** *adj.* —**di·rec'to·ri·al·ly** *adv.* —**di'rec·torˌship** *n.* —**di'rec·tress** *fem. n.*

di·rec·to·rate (dɪ'rɛktərɪt, daɪ-) *n.* **1.** a board of directors. **2.** Also: **di'rec·torˌship.** the position of director.

di·rec·tor-gen·er·al *n., pl.* **di·rec·tors-gen·er·al.** the head of a large organization such as the C.B.I. or B.B.C.

di+rec+to·ry (dɪˈrɛktərɪ, -trɪ, daɪ-) *n., pl.* **·ries. 1.** a book, arranged alphabetically or classified by trade listing names, addresses, telephone numbers, etc., of individuals or firms. **2.** a book or manual giving directions. **3.** a book containing the rules to be observed in the forms of worship used in churches. **4.** a less common word for **directorate.** ~*adj.* **5.** directing.

Di+rec+to·ry (dɪˈrɛktərɪ, -trɪ, daɪ-) *n., pl.* **·ries. the.** *History.* the body of five directors in power in France from 1795 until their overthrow by Napoleon in 1799. Also called: **French Directory.**

di+rect pri+ma+ry *n. U.S. government.* a primary in which voters directly select the candidates who will run for office.

di+rect ques+tion *n.* a question asked in direct speech, such as *Why did you come?* Compare **indirect question.**

di+rect+rix (dɪˈrɛktrɪks, daɪ-) *n.* **1.** *Geom.* a fixed reference line, situated on the convex side of a conic section, that is used when defining or calculating its eccentricity. **2.** a directress. [C17: New Latin, feminine of DIRECTOR]

di+rect speech *or esp. U.S.* **di+rect dis+course** *n.* the reporting of what someone has said or written by quoting his exact words.

di+rect tax *n.* a tax paid by the person or organization on which it is levied. Compare **indirect tax.**

dirge (dɜːdʒ) *n.* **1.** a chant of lamentation for the dead. **2.** the funeral service in its solemn or sung forms. **3.** any mourning song or melody. [C13: changed from Latin *dīrige* direct (imperative), opening word of the Latin antiphon used in the office of the dead] —**ˈdirge+ful** *adj.*

dir+ham (ˈdɪəræm) *n.* **1.** the standard monetary unit of Morocco, divided into 100 francs. **2. a.** a Kuwaiti monetary unit worth one tenth of a dinar and 100 fils. **b.** a Tunisian monetary unit worth one tenth of a dinar and 100 millimes. **c.** a Qatari monetary unit worth one hundredth of a riyal. **3.** any of various silver coins minted in North African countries at different periods. [C18: from Arabic, from Latin: DRACHMA]

Di·ri·chlet (*German* ˌdiriˈkleː) *n.* **Pe·ter Gus·tav Le·jeune** (ˈpeːtər ˈgʊstaf ləˈʒøːn). 1805–59, German mathematician, noted for his work on number theory and calculus.

di+rig+i·ble (dɪˈrɪdʒɪbᵊl) *adj.* **1.** able to be steered or directed. ~*n.* **2.** another name for **airship.** [C16: from Latin *dīrigere* to DIRECT] —ˌ**dir+i·gi·ˈbil+i·ty** *n.*

di+ri+ment (ˈdɪrɪmənt) *adj.* **1.** (of an impediment to marriage in canon law) totally invalidating. **2.** *Rare.* nullifying. [C19: from Latin *dirimēns* separating, from Latin *dirimere* to part, from DIS-[1] + *emere* to obtain]

dirk (dɜːk) *n.* **1.** a dagger esp. as formerly worn by Scottish Highlanders. ~*vb.* **2.** (*tr.*) to stab with a dirk. [C16: from Scottish *durk*, perhaps from German *dolch* dagger]

dirn·dl (ˈdɜːndᵊl) *n.* **1.** a woman's dress with a full gathered skirt and fitted bodice; originating from Tyrolean peasant wear. **2.** a gathered skirt of this kind. [German (Bavarian and Austrian): shortened from *Dirndlkleid*, from *Dirndl* little girl + *Kleid* dress]

dirt (dɜːt) *n.* **1.** any unclean substance, such as mud, dust, excrement, etc.; filth. **2.** loose earth; soil. **3. a.** packed earth, gravel, cinders, etc., used to make a racetrack. **b.** (*as modifier*): *a dirt track.* **4.** *Mining.* the gravel or soil from which minerals are extracted. **5.** a person or thing regarded as worthless. **6.** obscene or indecent speech or writing. **7.** moral corruption. **8. do (someone) dirt.** *Slang.* to do something vicious to (someone). **9. eat dirt.** *Slang.* to accept insult without complaining. **10. treat someone like dirt.** to have no respect for someone. [C13: from Old Norse *drit* excrement; related to Middle Dutch *drēte*]

dirt-cheap *adj., adv. Informal.* at an extremely low price.

dirt wag+on *n.* the U.S. name for **dustcart.**

dirt·y (ˈdɜːtɪ) *adj.* **dirt·i+er, dirt·i+est. 1.** covered or marked with dirt; filthy. **2.** obscene; salacious: *dirty books.* **3.** causing one to become grimy: *a dirty job.* **4.** (of a colour) not clear and bright; impure. **5.** unfair; dishonest; unscrupulous; unsporting. **6.** mean; nasty: *a dirty cheat.* **7.** scandalous; unkind: *a dirty rumour.* **8.** revealing dislike or anger: *a dirty look.* **9.** (of weather) rainy or squally; stormy. **10.** (of an aircraft) having projections into the airstream, such as lowered flaps. **11.** (of a nuclear weapon) producing a large quantity of radioactive fallout or contamination. Compare **clean** (sense 5). **12. dirty dog.** a despicable person. **13. dirty linen.** *Informal.* intimate secrets, esp. those that might give rise to gossip. **14. dirty work.** unpleasant or illicit activity. **15. do the dirty on.** *Brit. informal.* to behave meanly or unkindly towards. ~*vb.* **dirt·ies, dirt·y+ing, dirt+ied. 16.** to make or become dirty; stain; soil. —**ˈdirt·i+ly** *adv.* —**ˈdirt·i+ness** *n.*

Dis (dɪs) *n.* **1.** Also called: **Orcus, Pluto.** the Roman god of the underworld. **2.** the abode of the dead; underworld. ~Greek equivalent: **Hades.**

dis-[1] *prefix.* **1.** indicating reversal: *disconnect; disembark.* **2.** indicating negation, lack, or deprivation: *dissimilar; distrust; disgrace.* **3.** indicating removal or release: *disembowel; disburden.* **4.** expressing intensive force: *dissever.* [from Latin *dis-* apart; in some cases, via Old French *des-*. In compound words of Latin origin, *dis-* becomes *dif-* before *f* and *di-* before some consonants]

dis-[2] *combining form.* variant of **di-**[1] before *s*: *dissyllable.*

dis+a·bil+i·ty (ˌdɪsəˈbɪlɪtɪ) *n., pl.* **·ties. 1.** the condition of being unable to perform a task or function because of a physical or mental impairment. **2.** something that disables; handicap. **3.** lack of necessary intelligence, strength, etc. **4.** an incapacity in the eyes of the law to enter into certain transactions.

dis+a·bil+i·ty clause *n.* (in life assurance policies) a clause enabling a policyholder to cease payment of premiums without loss of coverage and often to receive a pension or indemnity if he becomes permanently disabled.

dis+a·ble (dɪsˈeɪbᵊl) *vb.* (*tr.*) **1.** to make ineffective, unfit, or incapable, as by crippling. **2.** to make or pronounce legally incapable. —**dis+ˈa·ble+ment** *n.*

dis+a·ble+ment ben+e·fit *n.* (in the National Insurance scheme) a weekly payment to a person disabled at work.

dis+a·buse (ˌdɪsəˈbjuːz) *vb.* (*tr.; usually foll. by of*) to rid (oneself, another person, etc.) of a mistaken or misguided idea; set right. —ˌ**dis+a·ˈbus+al** *n.*

di+sac+cha+ride (daɪˈsækəˌraɪd, -rɪd) *or* **di+sac+cha+rid** *n.* any of a class of sugars, such as maltose, lactose, and sucrose, having two linked monosaccharide units per molecule.

dis+ac+cord (ˌdɪsəˈkɔːd) *n.* **1.** lack of agreement or harmony. ~*vb.* **2.** (*intr.*) to be out of agreement; disagree.

dis+ac+cred+it (ˌdɪsəˈkrɛdɪt) *vb.* (*tr.*) to take away the authorization or credentials of.

dis+ac+cus+tom (ˌdɪsəˈkʌstəm) *vb.* (*tr.; usually foll. by to*) to cause to lose a habit.

dis+ad+vant+age (ˌdɪsədˈvɑːntɪdʒ) *n.* **1.** an unfavourable circumstance, state of affairs, thing, person, etc. **2.** injury, loss, or detriment. **3.** an unfavourable condition or situation (esp. in the phrase **at a disadvantage**). ~*vb.* **4.** (*tr.*) to put at a disadvantage; handicap.

dis+ad+van+taged (ˌdɪsədˈvɑːntɪdʒd) *adj.* socially or economically deprived or discriminated against.

dis+ad+van+ta+geous (dɪsˌædvɑːnˈteɪdʒəs, ˌdɪsæd-) *adj.* unfavourable; detrimental. —**dis+ˌad+van+ˈta+geous+ly** *adv.* —**dis+ˌad+van+ˈta+geous+ness** *n.*

dis+af+fect (ˌdɪsəˈfɛkt) *vb.* (*tr.; often passive*) to cause to lose loyalty or affection; alienate. —ˌ**dis+af+ˈfect+ed+ly** *adv.* —ˌ**dis+af+ˈfect+ed+ness** *n.* —ˌ**dis+af+ˈfec+tion** *n.*

dis+af+fil+i·ate (ˌdɪsəˈfɪlɪˌeɪt) *vb.* to sever an affiliation (with); dissociate. —ˌ**dis+af+ˌfil+i+ˈa·tion** *n.*

dis+af+firm (ˌdɪsəˈfɜːm) *vb.* (*tr.*) **1.** to deny or contradict (a statement). **2.** *Law.* **a.** to annul or reverse (a decision). **b.** to repudiate obligations. —ˌ**dis+af+ˈfir+mance** *or* **dis+af+fir+ma+tion** (ˌdɪsæfəˈmeɪʃən) *n.*

dis+af+for+est (ˌdɪsəˈfɒrɪst) *vb.* (*tr.*) **1.** *English law.* to reduce (land) from the status of a forest to the state of ordinary ground. **2.** to remove forests from (land). —ˌ**dis+af+ˌfor+es+ˈta+tion** *or* ˌ**dis+af+ˈfor+est+ment** *n.*

dis+a·gree (ˌdɪsəˈgriː) *vb.* **·grees, ·gree+ing, ·greed.** (*intr.; often foll. by with*) **1.** to dissent in opinion (from another person) or dispute (about an idea, fact, etc.). **2.** to fail to correspond; conflict. **3.** to be unacceptable (to) or unfavourable (for); be incompatible (with): *curry disagrees with me.* **4.** to be opposed (to) in principle.

dis+a·gree+a·ble (ˌdɪsəˈgrɪəbᵊl) *adj.* **1.** not likable; bad-tempered. **2.** unpleasant; offensive. —ˌ**dis+a·ˈgree+a·ble+ness** *or* ˌ**dis+a·ˌgree+a·ˈbil+i·ty** *n.* —ˌ**dis+a·ˈgree+a·bly** *adv.*

dis+a·gree+ment (ˌdɪsəˈgriːmənt) *n.* **1.** refusal or failure to agree. **2.** a failure to correspond. **3.** an argument or dispute.

dis+al+low (ˌdɪsəˈlaʊ) *vb.* (*tr.*) **1.** to reject as untrue or invalid. **2.** to cancel. —ˌ**dis+al+ˈlow+a·ble** *adj.* —ˌ**dis+al+ˈlow+ance** *n.*

dis+am+big·u·ate (ˌdɪsæmˈbɪgjʊˌeɪt) *vb.* (*tr.*) to make (an ambiguous expression) unambiguous.

dis+an+nul (ˌdɪsəˈnʌl) *vb.* **+nuls, +nul+ling, +nulled.** (*tr.*) *Chiefly law.* to cancel; make void. —ˌ**dis+an+ˈnul+ment** *n.*

dis+ap+pear (ˌdɪsəˈpɪə) *vb.* (*intr.*) **1.** to cease to be visible; vanish. **2.** to go away or become lost, esp. secretly or without explanation. **3.** to cease to exist, have effect, or be known; become extinct, or lost: *the pain has disappeared.* —ˌ**dis+ap+ˈpear+ance** *n.*

dis+ap+point (ˌdɪsəˈpɔɪnt) *vb.* (*tr.*) **1.** to fail to meet the expectations, hopes, desires, or standards of; let down. **2.** to prevent the fulfilment of (a plan, intention, etc.); frustrate; thwart. [C15 (originally meaning: to remove from office): from Old French *desapointier*; see DIS-[1], APPOINT] —ˌ**dis+ap+ˈpoint+er** *n.* —ˌ**dis+ap+ˈpoint+ing+ly** *adv.*

dis+ap+point+ed (ˌdɪsəˈpɔɪntɪd) *adj.* saddened by the failure of an expectation, etc. —ˌ**dis+ap+ˈpoint+ed+ly** *adv.*

dis+ap+point+ment (ˌdɪsəˈpɔɪntmənt) *n.* **1.** the act of disappointing or the state of being disappointed. **2.** a person, thing, or state of affairs that disappoints.

dis+ap+pro+ba+tion (ˌdɪsæprəʊˈbeɪʃən) *n.* moral or social disapproval.

dis+ap+prov+al (ˌdɪsəˈpruːvᵊl) *n.* the act or a state or feeling of disapproving; censure; condemnation.

dis+ap+prove (ˌdɪsəˈpruːv) *vb.* **1.** (*intr.; often foll. by of*) to consider wrong, bad, etc. **2.** (*tr.*) to withhold approval from. —ˌ**dis+ap+ˈprov+er** *n.* —ˌ**dis+ap+ˈprov+ing+ly** *adv.*

dis+arm (dɪsˈɑːm) *vb.* **1.** (*tr.*) to remove defensive or offensive capability from (a country, army, etc.). **2.** (*tr.*) to deprive of weapons. **3.** (*tr.*) to win the confidence or affection of. **4.** (*intr.*) (of a nation, etc.) to decrease the size and capability of one's armed forces. **5.** (*intr.*) to lay down weapons. —**dis+ˈarm+er** *n.*

dis+arm+a·ment (dɪsˈɑːməmənt) *n.* **1.** the reduction of offensive or defensive fighting capability, as by a nation. **2.** the act of disarming or state of being disarmed.

dis+arm+ing (dɪsˈɑːmɪŋ) *adj.* tending to neutralize or counteract hostility, suspicion, etc. —**dis+ˈarm+ing+ly** *adv.*

dis+ar+range (ˌdɪsəˈreɪndʒ) *vb.* (*tr.*) to throw into disorder. —ˌ**dis+ar+ˈrange+ment** *n.*

dis+ar+ray (ˌdɪsəˈreɪ) *n.* **1.** confusion, dismay, and lack of discipline. **2.** (esp. of clothing) disorderliness; untidiness. ~*vb.* (*tr.*) **3.** to throw into confusion. **4.** *Archaic.* to undress.

dis+ar+tic+u+late (ˌdɪsɑːˈtɪkjʊˌleɪt) *vb.* to separate or cause to

separate at the joints, esp. those of bones. —ˌ**dis+ar+ˌtic·u+'la+tion** *n.* —ˌ**dis+ar+'tic·u+ˌla+tor** *n.*
dis+as+sem+ble (ˌdɪsə'sɛmbᵊl) *vb.* (*tr.*) to take apart (a piece of machinery, etc.); dismantle. —ˌ**dis+as+'sem+bly** *n.*
dis+as+so+ci+ate (ˌdɪsə'səʊʃɪˌeɪt) *vb.* a less common word for **dissociate.** —ˌ**dis+as+ˌso+ci+'a+tion** *n.*
dis+as+ter (dɪ'zɑːstə) *n.* **1.** an occurrence that causes great distress or destruction. **2.** a thing, project, etc., that fails or has been ruined. [C16 (originally in the sense: malevolent astral influence): from Italian *disastro*, from *dis-* (pejorative) + *astro* star, from Latin *astrum*, from Greek *astron*] —**dis+'as+trous** *adj.*
dis+a·vow (ˌdɪsə'vaʊ) *vb.* (*tr.*) to deny knowledge of, connection with, or responsibility for. —ˌ**dis+a·'vow+al** *n.* —ˌ**dis+a·'vow+ed+ly** *adv.* —ˌ**dis+a·'vow+er** *n.*
dis+band (dɪs'bænd) *vb.* to cease to function or cause to stop functioning, as a unit, group, etc. —**dis+'band+ment** *n.*
dis+bar (dɪs'bɑː) *vb.* **+bars, +bar+ring, +barred.** (*tr.*) *Law.* to deprive of the status of barrister; expel from the Bar. —**dis+'bar+ment** *n.*
dis+be+lief (ˌdɪsbɪ'liːf) *n.* refusal or reluctance to believe.
dis+be+lieve (ˌdɪsbɪ'liːv) *vb.* **1.** (*tr.*) to reject as false or lying; refuse to accept as true or truthful. **2.** (*intr.*; usually foll. by *in*) to have no faith (in): *disbelieve in God.* —ˌ**dis+be+'liev+er** *n.* —ˌ**dis+be+'liev+ing+ly** *adv.*
dis+branch (dɪs'brɑːntʃ) *vb.* (*tr.*) to remove or cut (a branch or branches) from (a tree).
dis+bud (dɪs'bʌd) *vb.* **+buds, +bud+ding, +bud+ded.** to remove superfluous buds, flowers, or shoots from (a plant, esp. a fruit tree).
dis+bur+den (dɪs'bɜːdᵊn) *vb.* **1.** to remove (a load) from (a person or animal). **2.** (*tr.*) to relieve (oneself, one's mind, etc.) of a distressing worry or oppressive thought. —**dis+'bur+den+ment** *n.*
dis+burse (dɪs'bɜːs) *vb.* (*tr.*) to pay out. [C16: from Old French *desborser*, from *des-* DIS-[1] + *borser* to obtain money, from *borse* bag, from Late Latin *bursa*] —**dis+'burs+a·ble** *adj.* —**dis+'burse+ment** *n.* —**dis+'burs+er** *n.*
disc (dɪsk) *n.* **1.** a flat circular plate. **2.** something resembling or appearing to resemble this: *the sun's disc.* **3.** another word for (gramophone) **record. 4.** *Anatomy.* any approximately circular flat structure in the body, esp. an intervertebral disc. **5. a.** the flat receptacle of composite flowers, such as the daisy. **b.** (*as modifier*): *a disc flower.* **6.** the middle part of the lip of an orchid. **7. a.** Also called: **parking disc.** a marker or device for display in a parked vehicle showing the time of arrival or the latest permitted time of departure or both. **b.** (*as modifier*): *a disc zone; disc parking.* **8.** *Computer technol.* a variant spelling of **disk** (sense 2). ~*vb.* **9.** to work (land) with a disc harrow.
disc. *abbrev. for:* **1.** discount. **2.** discovered.
dis+calced (dɪs'kælst) *adj.* barefooted: used to denote friars and nuns who wear sandals. [C17: from Latin *discalceātus*, from DIS-[1] + *calceātus* shod, from *calceāre* to provide with shoes, from *calceus* shoe, from *calx* heel]
dis+cant *n.* ('dɪskænt), *vb.* (dɪs'kænt). a variant spelling of **descant** (senses 1, 3, 4). —**dis+'cant+er** *n.*
dis+card *vb.* (dɪs'kɑːd). **1.** (*tr.*) to get rid of as useless or undesirable. **2.** *Cards.* to throw out (a card or cards) from one's hand. **3.** *Cards.* to play (a card not of the suit led nor a trump) when unable to follow suit. ~*n.* ('dɪskɑːd). **4.** a person or thing that has been cast aside. **5.** *Cards.* a discarded card. **6.** the act of discarding. —**dis+'card+er** *n.*
disc brake *n.* a type of brake in which two calliper-operated pads rub against a flat disc attached to the wheel hub when the brake is applied.
dis+cern (dɪ'sɜːn) *vb.* **1.** (*tr.*) to recognize or perceive clearly. **2.** to recognize or perceive (differences). [C14: from Old French *discerner*, from Latin *discernere* to divide, from DIS-[1] (apart) + *cernere* to separate] —**dis+'cern+er** *n.*
dis+cern+i·ble *or* **dis+cern+a·ble** (dɪ'sɜːnəbᵊl) *adj.* able to be discerned; perceptible. —**dis+'cern+i·ble+ness** *or* **dis+'cern+a·ble+ness** *n.* —**dis+'cern+i·bly** *or* **dis+'cern+a·bly** *adv.*
dis+cern+ing (dɪ'sɜːnɪŋ) *adj.* having or showing good taste or judgment; discriminating. —**dis+'cern+ing+ly** *adv.*
dis+cern+ment (dɪ'sɜːnmənt) *n.* keen perception or judgment.
disc flow+er *or* **flo+ret** *n.* any of the small tubular flowers at the centre of the flower head of certain composite plants, such as the daisy. Compare **ray flower.**
dis+charge *vb.* (dɪs'tʃɑːdʒ). **1.** (*tr.*) to release or allow to go: *the hospital discharged the patient.* **2.** (*tr.*) to dismiss from or relieve of duty, office, employment, etc. **3.** to fire or be fired, as a gun. **4.** to pour forth or cause to pour forth: *the boil discharges pus.* **5.** (*tr.*) to remove (the cargo) from (a boat, etc.); unload. **6.** (*tr.*) to perform the duties of or meet the demands of (an office, obligation, etc.): *he discharged his responsibilities as mayor.* **7.** (*tr.*) to relieve (oneself) of (a responsibility, debt, etc.). **8.** *Physics.* **a.** to lose or remove electric charge. **b.** to form an arc, spark, or corona in a gas. **c.** to take or supply electrical current from a cell or battery. **9.** (*tr.*) *Law.* to release (a prisoner from custody, etc.). **10.** (*tr.*) to remove dye from (a fabric), as by bleaching. **11.** (*intr.*) (of a dye or colour) to blur or run. **12.** (*tr.*) *Architect.* **a.** to spread (weight) evenly over a supporting member. **b.** to relieve a member of (excess weight) by distribution of pressure. ~*n.* ('dɪstʃɑːdʒ, dɪs'tʃɑːdʒ). **13.** a person or thing that is discharged. **14. a.** dismissal or release from an office, job, institution, etc. **b.** the document certifying such release. **15.** the fulfilment of an obligation or release from a responsibility or liability. **16.** the act of removing a load, as of cargo. **17.** a pouring forth of a fluid; emission. **18. a.** the act of firing a projectile. **b.** the volley, bullet, missile, etc., fired. **19.** *Law.* **a.** a release, as of a person held under legal restraint. **b.** an annulment, as of a court order. **20.** *Physics.* **a.** the act or process of removing or losing charge or of equalizing a potential difference. **b.** a transient or continuous conduction of electricity through a gas by the formation and movement of electrons and ions in an applied electric field. —**dis+'charge+a·ble** *adj.* —**dis+'charg+er** *n.*
disc har+row *n.* a harrow with sharp-edged slightly concave discs mounted on horizontal shafts and used to cut clods or debris on the surface of the soil or to cover seed after planting.
dis+ci+ple (dɪ'saɪpᵊl) *n.* **1.** a follower of the doctrines of a teacher or a school of thought. **2.** one of the personal followers of Christ (including his 12 apostles) during his earthly life. [Old English *discipul*, from Latin *discipulus* pupil, from *discere* to learn] —**dis+'ci+ple+ˌship** *n.* —**dis+cip·u+lar** (dɪ'sɪpjʊlə) *adj.*
Dis+ci+ples of Christ *pl. n.* a Christian denomination founded in the U.S. in 1809 by Thomas and Alexander Campbell.
dis+ci+pli+nant ('dɪsɪˌplɪnənt) *n.* (*often cap.*) *R.C. Church.* a person belonging to a former order of flagellants in Spain.
dis+ci+pli+nar+i·an (ˌdɪsɪplɪ'nɛərɪən) *n.* **1.** a person who imposes or advocates discipline. ~*adj.* **2.** a less common word for **disciplinary.**
dis+ci+pli+nar·y ('dɪsɪˌplɪnərɪ) *or* **dis+ci+pli+nar+i·an** *adj.* of, promoting, or used for discipline; corrective.
dis+ci+pline ('dɪsɪplɪn) *n.* **1.** training or conditions imposed for the improvement of physical powers, self-control, etc. **2.** systematic training in obedience to regulations and authority. **3.** the state of improved behaviour, etc., resulting from such training or conditions. **4.** punishment or chastisement. **5.** a system of rules for behaviour, methods of practice, etc. **6.** a branch of learning or instruction. **7.** the laws governing members of a Church. **8.** a scourge of knotted cords. ~*vb.* (*tr.*) **9.** to improve or attempt to improve the behaviour, orderliness, etc., of by training, conditions, or rules. **10.** to punish or correct. [C13: from Latin *disciplīna* teaching, from *discipulus* DISCIPLE] —**'dis+ci+ˌplin+a·ble** *adj.* —**dis+ci+pli+nal** (ˌdɪsɪ'plaɪnᵊl, 'dɪsɪplɪnᵊl) *adj.* —**'dis+ci+ˌplin+er** *n.*
disc jock+ey *n.* a person who announces and plays recorded music, esp. pop music, on a radio programme, etc.
dis+claim (dɪs'kleɪm) *vb.* **1.** (*tr.*) to deny or renounce (any claim, connection, etc.). **2.** (*tr.*) to deny the validity or authority of. **3.** *Law.* to renounce, or repudiate (a legal claim or right). —**dis+cla+ma+tion** (ˌdɪsklə'meɪʃən) *n.*
dis+claim+er (dɪs'kleɪmə) *n.* a repudiation or denial.
dis+cli+max (dɪs'klaɪmæks) *n.* *Ecology.* a climax community resulting from the activities of man or domestic animals in climatic and other conditions that would otherwise support a different type of community.
dis+close (dɪs'kləʊz) *vb.* (*tr.*) **1.** to make (information) known. **2.** to allow to be seen; lay bare. —**dis+'clos+er** *n.*
dis+clo+sure (dɪs'kləʊʒə) *n.* **1.** something that is disclosed. **2.** the act of disclosing; revelation.
dis+co ('dɪskəʊ) *n., pl.* **+cos.** *Informal.* short for **discotheque.**
dis+cob·o+lus *or* **dis+cob·o+los** (dɪs'kɒbələs) *n., pl.* **+li** (-ˌlaɪ). **1.** (in classical Greece) a discus thrower. **2.** a statue of a discus thrower. [C18: from Latin, from Greek *diskobolos*, from *diskos* DISCUS + *-bolos*, from *ballein* to throw]
dis+cog+ra+phy (dɪs'kɒgrəfɪ) *n.* **1.** a classified reference list of gramophone records. **2.** the study of gramophone records. —**dis+'cog+ra+pher** *n.*
dis+coid ('dɪskɔɪd) *adj.* also **dis+coi+dal. 1.** like a disc. **2.** (of a composite flower such as the tansy) consisting of disc flowers only. ~*n.* **3.** a disclike object.
dis+col+our *or U.S.* **dis+col+or** (dɪs'kʌlə) *vb.* to change or cause to change in colour; fade or stain. —**dis+ˌcol+or·'a+tion, dis+'col+our+ment,** *or U.S.* **dis+'col+or+ment** *n.*
dis+com+bob·u+late (ˌdɪskəm'bɒbjʊˌleɪt) *vb.* (*tr.*) *Informal, chiefly U.S.* to throw into confusion. [C20: probably a whimsical alteration of DISCOMPOSE or DISCOMFIT]
dis+com+fit (dɪs'kʌmfɪt) *vb.* (*tr.*) **1.** to make uneasy, confused, or embarrassed. **2.** to frustrate the plans or purpose of. **3.** *Archaic.* to defeat in battle. [C14: from Old French *desconfire* to destroy, from *des-* (indicating reversal) + *confire* to make, from Latin *conficere* to produce; see CONFECT] —**dis+'com+fit+er** *n.* —**dis+'com+fi+ture** *n.*
dis+com+fort (dɪs'kʌmfət) *n.* **1.** an inconvenience, distress, or mild pain. **2.** something that disturbs or deprives of ease. ~*vb.* **3.** (*tr.*) to make uncomfortable or uneasy.
dis+com+fort+a·ble (dɪs'kʌmfətəbᵊl, -'kʌmftə-) *adj.* *Archaic.* tending to deprive of mental or physical ease or comfort.
dis+com+mend (ˌdɪskə'mɛnd) *vb.* (*tr.*) **1.** *Rare.* to express disapproval of. **2.** *Obsolete.* to bring into disfavour. —ˌ**dis+com+'mend+a·ble** *adj.* —**dis+ˌcom+men+'da+tion** *n.*
dis+com+mode (ˌdɪskə'məʊd) *vb.* (*tr.*) to cause inconvenience or annoyance to; disturb. —ˌ**dis+com+'mo+di+ous** *adj.* —ˌ**dis+com+'mo+di+ous+ly** *adv.*
dis+com+mod+i·ty (ˌdɪskə'mɒdɪtɪ) *n., pl.* **·ties. 1.** *Economics.* a commodity without utility. **2.** *Archaic.* the state or a source of inconvenience.
dis+com+mon (dɪs'kɒmən) *vb.* (*tr.*) *Law.* to deprive (land) of the character and status of common, as by enclosure.
dis+com+pose (ˌdɪskəm'pəʊz) *vb.* (*tr.*) **1.** to disturb the composure of; disconcert. **2.** *Now rare.* to disarrange. —ˌ**dis+com+'pos+ed+ly** *adv.* —ˌ**dis+com+'pos+ing+ly** *adv.* —ˌ**dis+com+'po+sure** *n.*
dis+con+cert (ˌdɪskən'sɜːt) *vb.* (*tr.*) **1.** to disturb the composure

of. **2.** to frustrate or upset. —ˌ**dis+con+'cert+ing+ly** *adv.* —ˌ**dis+con+'cer+tion** *or* ˌ**dis+con+'cert+ment** *n.*

dis+con+cert+ed (ˌdɪskənˈsɜːtɪd) *adj.* perturbed, embarrassed, or confused. —ˌ**dis+con+'cert+ed+ly** *adv.* —ˌ**dis+con+'cert+ed+ness** *n.*

dis+con+form+i·ty (ˌdɪskənˈfɔːmɪtɪ) *n., pl.* **·ties. 1.** lack of conformity; discrepancy. **2.** the junction between two parallel series of stratified rocks, representing a considerable period of erosion of the much older underlying rocks before the more recent ones were deposited.

dis+con+nect (ˌdɪskəˈnɛkt) *vb.* (*tr.*) to undo or break the connection of or between (something, such as a plug and a socket). —ˌ**dis+con+'nect+er** *n.* —ˌ**dis+con+'nec+tion** *or* ˌ**dis+con+'nex+ion** *n.* —ˌ**dis+con+'nec+tive** *adj.*

dis+con+nect+ed (ˌdɪskəˈnɛktɪd) *adj.* **1.** not rationally connected; confused or incoherent. **2.** not connected or joined. —ˌ**dis+con+'nect+ed+ly** *adv.* —ˌ**dis+con+'nect+ed+ness** *n.*

dis+con+sid+er (ˌdɪskənˈsɪdə) *vb.* (*tr.*) *Archaic.* to discredit. —ˌ**dis+con+ˌsid+er+'a+tion** *n.*

dis+con+so+late (dɪsˈkɒnsəlɪt) *adj.* **1.** sad beyond comfort; dejected. [C14: from Medieval Latin *disconsōlātus,* from DIS-[1] + *consōlātus* comforted; see CONSOLE[1]] —**dis+'con+so+late+ly** *adv.* —**dis+ˌcon+so+'la+tion** *or* **dis+'con+so+late+ness** *n.*

dis+con+tent (ˌdɪskənˈtɛnt) *n.* **1.** Also called: **discontentment.** lack of contentment, as with one's condition or lot in life. **2.** a discontented person. ~*adj.* **3.** dissatisfied. ~*vb.* **4.** (*tr.*) to make dissatisfied. —ˌ**dis+con+'tent+ed** *adj.* —ˌ**dis+con+'tent+ed+ly** *adv.* —ˌ**dis+con+'tent+ed+ness** *n.*

dis+con+tin·ue (ˌdɪskənˈtɪnjuː) *vb.* **·ues, ·u+ing, ·ued. 1.** to come or bring to an end; interrupt or be interrupted; stop. **2.** (*tr.*) *Law.* to terminate or abandon (an action, suit, etc.). —ˌ**dis+con+'tin·u+ance** *n.* —ˌ**dis+con+ˌtin·u·'a+tion** *n.* —ˌ**dis+con+'tin·u+er** *n.*

dis+con+ti+nu+i·ty (dɪsˌkɒntɪˈnjuːɪtɪ) *n., pl.* **·ties. 1.** lack of rational connection or cohesion. **2.** a break or interruption. **3.** *Maths.* **a.** the property of being discontinuous. **b.** the point or the value of the variable at which a curve or function becomes discontinuous. **4.** *Geology.* **a.** a zone within the earth where a sudden change in physical properties, such as the velocity of earthquake waves, occurs. Such a zone marks the boundary between the different layers of the earth, as between the core and mantle. See also **Mohorovičić discontinuity. b.** a surface separating rocks that are not continuous with each other.

dis+con+tin·u+ous (ˌdɪskənˈtɪnjʊəs) *adj.* **1.** characterized by interruptions or breaks; intermittent. **2.** *Maths.* (of a function or curve) changing suddenly in value for one or more values of the variable or at one or more points. Compare **continuous** (sense 3). —ˌ**dis+con+'tin·u+ous+ly** *adv.* —ˌ**dis+con+'tin·u+ous+ness** *n.*

dis+co+phile (ˈdɪskəˌfaɪl) *or* **dis+co+phil** (ˈdɪskəfɪl) *n.* a collector or connoisseur of gramophone records.

dis+cord *n.* (ˈdɪskɔːd). **1.** lack of agreement or harmony; strife. **2.** harsh confused mingling of sounds. **3.** a combination of musical notes, esp. one containing one or more dissonant intervals. See **dissonance** (sense 3); **concord** (sense 4). ~*vb.* (dɪsˈkɔːd). **4.** (*intr.*) to disagree; clash. [C13: from Old French *descort,* from *descorder* to disagree, from Latin *discordāre,* from *discors* at variance, from DIS-[1] + *cor* heart]

dis+cord+ance (dɪsˈkɔːdᵊns) *or* **dis+cord+an+cy** *n.* **1.** *Geology.* an arrangement of rock strata in which the older underlying ones dip at a different angle from the younger overlying ones; unconformity. **2.** lack of agreement or consonance. **3.** variants of **discord.**

dis+cord+ant (dɪsˈkɔːdᵊnt) *adj.* **1.** at variance; disagreeing. **2.** harsh in sound; inharmonious. —**dis+'cor+dant+ly** *adv.*

dis+co+theque (ˈdɪskəˌtɛk) *n.* **1.** a club or other public place for dancing to recorded pop music. **2.** mobile equipment for providing amplified pop music for dancing. ~Often shortened to **disco.** [C20: from French *discothèque,* from Greek *diskos* disc + -O- + Greek *thēkē* case]

dis+count *vb.* (dɪsˈkaʊnt, ˈdɪskaʊnt). (*mainly tr.*) **1.** to leave out of account as being unreliable, prejudiced, or irrelevant. **2.** to anticipate and make allowance for, often so as to diminish the effect of. **3. a.** to deduct (a specified amount or percentage) from the usual price, cost, etc. **b.** to reduce (the regular price, cost, etc.) by a stated percentage or amount. **4.** to sell or offer for sale at a reduced price. **5.** to buy or sell (a bill of exchange, etc.) before maturity, with a deduction for interest determined by the time to maturity and also by risk. **6.** (*also intr.*) to loan money on (a negotiable instrument that is not immediately payable) with a deduction for interest determined by risk and time to maturity. ~*n.* (ˈdɪskaʊnt). **7.** short for **cash discount** or **trade discount. 8.** Also called: **discount rate. a.** the amount of interest deducted in the purchase or sale of or the loan of money on unmatured negotiable instruments. **b.** the rate of interest deducted. **9. a.** (in the issue of shares) a percentage deducted from the par value to give a reduced amount payable by subscribers. **b.** the amount by which the par value of something, esp. shares, exceeds its market value. Compare **premium** (sense 3). **10.** the act or an instance of discounting a negotiable instrument. **11. at a discount. a.** below the regular price. **b.** (of share values) below par. **c.** in low regard. **12.** (*modifier*) offering or selling at reduced prices: *a discount shop.* —**dis+'count+a·ble** *adj.* —**'dis+count+er** *n.*

dis+coun+te·nance (dɪsˈkaʊntɪnəns) *vb.* (*tr.*) **1.** to make ashamed or confused. **2.** to disapprove of. ~*n.* **3.** disapproval.

dis+count house *n.* **1.** *Chiefly Brit.* a financial organization engaged in discounting bills of exchange, etc. on a large scale primarily by borrowing call money from commercial banks. **2.** *Chiefly U.S.* a shop offering for sale most of its merchandise at prices below the recommended prices.

dis+cour+age (dɪsˈkʌrɪdʒ) *vb.* (*tr.*) **1.** to deprive of the will to persist in something. **2.** to inhibit; prevent: *this solution discourages rust.* **3.** to oppose by expressing disapproval. —**dis+'cour+age+ment** *n.* —**dis+'cour+ag+er** *n.* —**dis+'cour+ag+ing+ly** *adv.*

dis+course *n.* (ˈdɪskɔːs; dɪsˈkɔːs). **1.** verbal communication; talk; conversation. **2.** a formal treatment of a subject in speech or writing, such as a sermon or dissertation. **3.** a unit of text used by linguists for the analysis of linguistic phenomena that range over more than one sentence. **4.** *Archaic.* the ability to reason or the reasoning process. ~*vb.* (dɪsˈkɔːs). **5.** (*intr.;* often foll. by *on* or *upon*) to speak or write (about) formally and extensively. **6.** (*intr.*) to hold a discussion. **7.** (*tr.*) *Archaic.* to give forth (music). [C14: from Medieval Latin *discursus* argument, from Latin: a running to and fro, from *discurrere* to run different ways, from DIS-[1] + *currere* to run] —**dis+'cours+er** *n.*

dis+cour+te·ous (dɪsˈkɜːtɪəs) *adj.* showing bad manners; impolite; rude. —**dis+'cour+te·ous+ly** *adv.* —**dis+'cour+te·ous+ness** *n.*

dis+cour+te·sy (dɪsˈkɜːtɪsɪ) *n., pl.* **·sies. 1.** bad manners; rudeness. **2.** a rude remark or act.

dis+cov+er (dɪˈskʌvə) *vb.* (*tr.; may take a clause as object*) **1.** to be the first to find or find out about: *Cook discovered New Zealand.* **2.** to learn about or encounter for the first time; realize: *she discovered the pleasures of wine.* **3.** to find after study or search: *I discovered a leak in the tank.* **4.** to reveal or make known. —**dis+'cov+er+a·ble** *adj.* —**dis+'cov+er+er** *n.*

dis+cov+ert (dɪsˈkʌvət) *adj. Law.* (of a woman) not under the protection of a husband; being a widow, spinster, or divorcee. [C14: from Old French *descovert,* past participle of *descouvrir* to DISCOVER] —**dis+'cov+er+ture** *n.*

dis+cov+er·y (dɪˈskʌvərɪ) *n., pl.* **+er·ies. 1.** the act, process, or an instance of discovering. **2.** a person, place, or thing that has been discovered. **3.** *Law.* the compulsory disclosure by a party to an action of relevant documents in his possession.

Dis+cov+er·y Bay *n.* an inlet of the Indian Ocean in SE Australia.

dis+cred+it (dɪsˈkrɛdɪt) *vb.* (*tr.*) **1.** to damage the reputation of. **2.** to cause to be disbelieved or distrusted. **3.** to reject as untrue or of questionable accuracy. ~*n.* **4.** a person, thing, or state of affairs that causes disgrace. **5.** damage to a reputation. **6.** lack of belief or confidence.

dis+cred+it+a·ble (dɪsˈkrɛdɪtəbᵊl) *adj.* tending to bring discredit; shameful or unworthy. —**dis+'cred+it+a·bly** *adv.*

dis+creet (dɪˈskriːt) *adj.* careful to avoid social embarrassment or distress, esp. by keeping confidences secret; tactful. [C14: from Old French *discret,* from Medieval Latin *discrētus,* from Latin *discernere* to DISCERN] —**dis+'creet+ly** *adv.* —**dis+'creet+ness** *n.*

dis+crep+an+cy (dɪˈskrɛpənsɪ) *n., pl.* **+cies.** a conflict or variation, as between facts, figures, or claims.

dis+crep+ant (dɪˈskrɛpənt) *adj.* inconsistent; conflicting; at variance. [C15: from Latin *discrepāns,* from *discrepāre* to differ in sound, from DIS-[1] + *crepāre* to be noisy] —**dis+'crep+ant+ly** *adv.*

dis+crete (dɪsˈkriːt) *adj.* **1.** separate or distinct in form or concept. **2.** consisting of distinct or separate parts. **3.** *Statistics.* **a.** (of a variable) having consecutive values that are not infinitesimally close, so that its analysis requires summation rather than integration. **b.** (of a distribution) relating to a discrete variable. Compare **continuous** (sense 4). [C14: from Latin *discrētus* separated, set apart; see DISCREET] —**dis+'crete+ly** *adv.* —**dis+'crete+ness** *n.*

dis+cre+tion (dɪˈskrɛʃən) *n.* **1.** the quality of behaving or speaking in such a way as to avoid social embarrassment or distress. **2.** freedom or authority to make judgments and to act as one sees fit (esp. in the phrases **at one's own discretion, at the discretion of**). **3. age** *or* **years of discretion.** the age at which a person is able to manage his own affairs.

dis+cre+tion+ar·y (dɪˈskrɛʃənərɪ, -ənrɪ) *or* **dis+cre+tion+al** *adj.* having or using the ability to decide at one's own discretion: *discretionary powers.* —**dis+'cre+tion+ˌar+i+ly** *or* **dis+'cre+tion+al+ly** *adv.*

dis+cri+mi+nant (dɪˈskrɪmɪnənt) *n.* an algebraic expression related to the coefficients of a polynomial equation whose value gives information about the roots of the polynomial: *$b^2 - 4ac$ is the discriminant of $ax^2 + bx + c = 0$.*

dis+crim·i+nate *vb.* (dɪˈskrɪmɪˌneɪt). **1.** (*intr.*) to single out a particular person, group, etc., for special favour or disfavour, often because of a characteristic such as race, colour, sex, intelligence, etc. **2.** (when *intr.,* foll. by *between* or *among*) to recognize or understand the difference (between); distinguish: *to discriminate right and wrong; to discriminate between right and wrong.* **3.** (*tr.*) to constitute or mark a difference. **4.** (*intr.*) to be discerning in matters of taste. ~*adj.* (dɪˈskrɪmɪnɪt). **5.** showing or marked by discrimination. [C17: from Latin *discrīmināre* to divide, from *discrīmen* a separation, from *discernere* to DISCERN] —**dis+'crim·i+nate+ly** *adv.* —**dis+'crim·i+ˌna+tor** *n.*

dis+crim·i+nat+ing (dɪˈskrɪmɪˌneɪtɪŋ) *adj.* **1.** able to see fine distinctions and differences. **2.** discerning in matters of taste. **3.** (of a tariff, import duty, etc.) levied at differential rates in order to favour or discourage imports or exports. —**dis+'crim·i+ˌnat+ing+ly** *adv.*

dis+crim·i+na+tion (dɪˌskrɪmɪˈneɪʃən) *n.* **1.** unfair treatment of a person, racial group, minority, etc.; action based on prejudice. **2.** subtle appreciation in matters of taste. **3.** the ability to see fine distinctions and differences. **4.** *Electronics.* the selection of a signal having a particular frequency, amplitude, phase, etc., caused by the elimination of other signals by means of a discriminator. **—dis+ˌcrim·i+ˈna+tion+al** *adj.*

dis+crim·i+na+tion learn+ing *n. Psychol.* a learning process in which an organism learns to react differently to different stimuli. Compare **generalization** (sense 3).

dis+crim·i+na+tor (dɪˈskrɪmɪˌneɪtə) *n.* **1.** an electronic circuit that converts a frequency or phase modulation into an amplitude modulation for subsequent demodulation. **2.** an electronic circuit that has an output voltage only when the amplitude of the input pulses exceeds a predetermined value.

dis+crim·i+na+to·ry (dɪˈskrɪmɪnətərɪ, -trɪ) *or* **dis+crim·i+na+tive** (dɪˈskrɪmɪnətɪv) *adj.* **1.** based on or showing prejudice; biased. **2.** capable of making fine distinctions. **—dis+ˈcrim·i+na+to+ri+ly** *or* **dis+ˈcrim·i+na+tive+ly** *adv.*

dis+cur+sive (dɪˈskɜːsɪv) *adj.* **1.** rambling; digressive. **2.** *Philosophy.* of or relating to knowledge obtained by reason and argument rather than intuition. Compare **dianoetic, intuitive.** [C16: from Medieval Latin *discursīvus,* from Late Latin *discursus* DISCOURSE] **—dis+ˈcur+sive+ly** *adv.* **—dis+ˈcur+sive+ness** *n.*

dis+cus (ˈdɪskəs) *n., pl.* **dis+cus·es** *or* **dis+ci** (ˈdɪsaɪ). **1.** (originally) a circular stone or plate used in throwing competitions by the ancient Greeks. **2.** *Field sports.* **a.** a similar disc-shaped object with a heavy middle thrown by athletes. **b.** (*as modifier*): *a discus thrower.* **3.** (preceded by *the*) the event or sport of throwing the discus. **4.** a South American cichlid fish, *Symphysodon discus,* that has a compressed coloured body and is a popular aquarium fish. [C17: from Latin, from Greek *diskos* from *dikein* to throw]

dis+cuss (dɪˈskʌs) *vb.* (*tr.*) **1.** to have a conversation about; consider by talking over; debate. **2.** to treat (a subject) in speech or writing: *the first three volumes discuss basic principles.* **3.** *Facetious, rare.* to eat or drink with enthusiasm. [C14: from Late Latin *discussus* examined, from *discutere* to investigate, from Latin: to dash to pieces, from DIS-[1] + *quatere* to shake, strike] **—dis+ˈcus+sant** *or* **dis+ˈcuss+er** *n.* **—dis+ˈcuss+i·ble** *or* **dis+ˈcuss+a·ble** *adj.*

dis+cus+sion (dɪˈskʌʃən) *n.* the examination or consideration of a matter in speech or writing. **—dis+ˈcus+sion+al** *adj.*

disc wheel *n.* a road wheel of a motor vehicle that has a round pressed disc in place of spokes. Compare **wire wheel.**

dis+dain (dɪsˈdeɪn) *n.* **1.** a feeling or show of superiority and dislike; contempt; scorn. ~*vb.* **2.** (*tr.; may take an infinitive*) to refuse or reject with disdain. [C13 *dedeyne,* from Old French *desdeign,* from *desdeigner* to reject as unworthy, from Latin *dēdignārī;* see DIS-[1], DEIGN]

dis+dain+ful (dɪsˈdeɪnfʊl) *adj.* showing or feeling disdain. **—dis+ˈdain+ful+ly** *adv.* **—dis+ˈdain+ful+ness** *n.*

dis+ease (dɪˈziːz) *n.* **1.** any impairment of normal physiological function affecting all or part of an organism, esp. a specific pathological change caused by infection, stress, etc., producing characteristic symptoms; illness or sickness in general. **2.** a corresponding condition in plants. **3.** any situation or condition likened to this: *the disease of materialism.* [C14: from Old French *desaise;* see DIS-[1], EASE]

dis+eased (dɪˈziːzd) *adj.* having or affected with disease.

dis+em+bark (ˌdɪsɪmˈbɑːk) *vb.* to land or cause to land from a ship, aircraft, etc.: *several passengers disembarked; we will disembark the passengers.* **—dis+em+bar+ka+tion** (dɪsˌɛmbɑːˈkeɪʃən) *or* **ˌdis+em+ˈbark+ment** *n.*

dis+em+bar+rass (ˌdɪsɪmˈbærəs) *vb.* (*tr.*) **1.** to free from embarrassment, entanglement, etc. **2.** to relieve or rid of something burdensome. **—ˌdis+em+ˈbar+rass+ment** *n.*

dis+em+bod+ied (ˌdɪsɪmˈbɒdɪd) *adj.* **1.** lacking a body or freed from the body; incorporeal. **2.** lacking in substance, solidity, or any firm relation to reality.

dis+em+bod·y (ˌdɪsɪmˈbɒdɪ) *vb.* **+bod·ies, +bod·y+ing, +bod+ied.** (*tr.*) to free from the body or from physical form. **—ˌdis+em+ˈbod·i+ment** *n.*

dis+em+bogue (ˌdɪsɪmˈbəʊg) *vb.* **+bogues, +bogu+ing, +bogued.** **1.** (of a river, stream, etc.) to discharge (water) at the mouth. **2.** (*intr.*) to flow out. [C16: from Spanish *desembocar,* from *des-* DIS-[1] + *embocar* put into the mouth, from *em-* in + *boca* mouth, from Latin *bucca* cheek] **—ˌdis+em+ˈbogue+ment** *n.*

dis+em+bow+el (ˌdɪsɪmˈbaʊəl) *vb.* **+els, +el+ling, +elled** *or U.S.* **+els, +el+ing, +eled.** (*tr.*) to remove the entrails of. **—ˌdis+em+ˈbow+el+ment** *n.*

dis+em+broil (ˌdɪsɪmˈbrɔɪl) *vb.* (*tr.*) to free from entanglement or a confused situation.

dis+en+a·ble (ˌdɪsɪˈneɪbəl) *vb.* (*tr.*) to cause to become incapable; prevent. **—ˌdis+en+ˈa·ble+ment** *n.*

dis+en+chant (ˌdɪsɪnˈtʃɑːnt) *vb.* (*tr.*) to free from or as if from an enchantment; disillusion. **—ˌdis+en+ˈchant+er** *n.* **—ˌdis+en+ˈchant+ing+ly** *adv.* **—ˌdis+en+ˈchant+ment** *n.*

dis+en+cum+ber (ˌdɪsɪnˈkʌmbə) *vb.* (*tr.*) to free from encumbrances. **—ˌdis+en+ˈcum+ber+ment** *n.*

dis+en+dow (ˌdɪsɪnˈdaʊ) *vb.* (*tr.*) to take away an endowment from. **—ˌdis+en+ˈdow+er** *n.* **—ˌdis+en+ˈdow+ment** *n.*

dis+en+fran+chise (ˌdɪsɪnˈfræntʃaɪz) *vb.* another word for **disfranchise.** **—dis+en+fran+chise+ment** (ˌdɪsɪnˈfræntʃɪzmənt) *n.*

dis+en+gage (ˌdɪsɪnˈgeɪdʒ) *vb.* **1.** to release or become released from a connection, obligation, etc.: *press the clutch to disengage the gears.* **2.** *Military.* to withdraw (forces) from close action. **3.** *Fencing.* to move (one's blade) from one side of an opponent's blade to another in a circular motion to bring the blade into an open line of attack.

dis+en+gage+ment (ˌdɪsɪnˈgeɪdʒmənt) *n.* **1.** the act or process of disengaging or state of being disengaged. **2.** leisure; ease. **—ˌdis+en+ˈgaged** *adj.*

dis+en+tail (ˌdɪsɪnˈteɪl) *Property law.* ~*vb.* **1.** to free (an estate) from entail. ~*n.* **2.** the act of disentailing; disentailment. **—ˌdis+en+ˈtail+ment** *n.*

dis+en+tan+gle (ˌdɪsɪnˈtæŋgəl) *vb.* **1.** to release or become free from entanglement or confusion. **2.** (*tr.*) to unravel or work out. **—ˌdis+en+ˈtan+gle+ment** *n.*

dis+en+thral *or* **dis+en+thrall** (ˌdɪsɪnˈθrɔːl) *vb.* **+thrals, +thral+ling, +thralled** *or* **+thralls, +thrall+ing, +thralled.** (*tr.*) to set free. **—ˌdis+en+ˈthral+ment** *or* **ˌdis+en+ˈthrall+ment** *n.*

dis+en+ti+tle (ˌdɪsɪnˈtaɪtəl) *vb.* (*tr.*) to deprive of a title, right, or claim.

dis+en+tomb (ˌdɪsɪnˈtuːm) *vb.* (*tr.*) to disinter; unearth.

dis+en+twine (ˌdɪsɪnˈtwaɪn) *vb.* to become or cause to become untwined; unwind.

di+sep·a+lous (daɪˈsɛpələs) *adj.* (of flowers or plants) having two sepals.

dis+e·qui+lib+ri·um (ˌdɪsiːkwɪˈlɪbrɪəm) *n.* a loss or absence of equilibrium, esp. in an economy.

dis+es+tab+lish (ˌdɪsɪˈstæblɪʃ) *vb.* (*tr.*) to deprive (a church, custom, institution, etc.) of established status. **—ˌdis+es+ˈtab+lish+ment** *n.*

dis+es+teem (ˌdɪsɪˈstiːm) *vb.* **1.** (*tr.*) to think little of. ~*n.* **2.** lack of esteem.

di+seuse (*French* diˈzœːz) *n.* (esp. formerly) an actress who presents dramatic recitals, usually accompanied by music. Male counterpart: **di+seur** (*French* diˈzœr). [C19: from French, feminine of *diseur* speaker, from *dire* to speak, from Latin *dīcere*]

dis+fa+vour *or U.S.* **dis+fa+vor** (dɪsˈfeɪvə) *n.* **1.** disapproval or dislike. **2.** the state of being disapproved of or disliked. **3.** an unkind act. ~*vb.* **4.** (*tr.*) to regard or treat with disapproval or dislike.

dis+fea+ture (dɪsˈfiːtʃə) *vb.* (*tr.*) to mar the features or appearance of; deface. **—dis+ˈfea+ture+ment** *n.*

dis+fig+ure (dɪsˈfɪgə) *vb.* (*tr.*) **1.** to spoil the appearance or shape of; deface. **2.** to mar the effect or quality of. **—dis+ˈfig+ur+er** *n.*

dis+fig+ure+ment (dɪsˈfɪgəmənt) *or* **dis+fig+ur·a+tion** *n.* **1.** something that disfigures. **2.** the act of disfiguring or the state of being disfigured.

dis+for+est (dɪsˈfɒrɪst) *vb.* (*tr.*) **1.** another word for **deforest.** **2.** *English law.* a less common word for **disafforest.** **—dis+ˌfor+es+ˈta+tion** *n.*

dis+fran+chise (dɪsˈfræntʃaɪz) *or* **dis+en+fran+chise** *vb.* (*tr.*) **1.** to deprive (a person) of the right to vote or other rights of citizenship. **2.** to deprive (a place) of the right to send representatives to an elected body. **3.** to deprive (a business concern, etc.) of some privilege or right. **4.** to deprive (a person, place, etc.) of any franchise or right. **—dis+fran+chise+ment** (dɪsˈfræntʃɪzmənt) *or* **ˌdis+en+ˈfran+chise+ment** *n.*

dis+frock (dɪsˈfrɒk) *vb.* another word for **unfrock.**

dis+gorge (dɪsˈgɔːdʒ) *vb.* **1.** to throw out (swallowed food, etc.) from the throat or stomach; vomit. **2.** to discharge or empty of (contents). **3.** (*tr.*) to yield up unwillingly or under pressure. **4.** (*tr.*) *Angling.* to remove (a hook) from the mouth or throat of (a fish). **—dis+ˈgorge+ment** *n.*

dis+gorg+er (dɪsˈgɔːdʒə) *n. Angling.* a thin notched metal implement for removing hooks from a fish.

dis+grace (dɪsˈgreɪs) *n.* **1.** a condition of shame, loss of reputation, or dishonour. **2.** a shameful person, thing, or state of affairs. **3.** exclusion from confidence or trust: *he is in disgrace with his father.* ~*vb.* (*tr.*) **4.** to bring shame upon; be a discredit to. **5.** to treat or cause to be treated with disfavour. **—dis+ˈgrac+er** *n.*

dis+grace+ful (dɪsˈgreɪsfʊl) *adj.* shameful; scandalous. **—dis+ˈgrace+ful+ly** *adv.* **—dis+ˈgrace+ful+ness** *n.*

dis+grun+tle (dɪsˈgrʌntəl) *vb.* (*tr.*) to make sulky or discontented. [C17: DIS-[1] + obsolete *gruntle* to complain; see GRUNT] **—dis+ˈgrun+tle+ment** *n.*

dis+guise (dɪsˈgaɪz) *vb.* **1.** to modify the appearance or manner in order to conceal the identity of (oneself, someone, or something). **2.** (*tr.*) to misrepresent in order to obscure the actual nature or meaning: *to disguise the facts.* ~*n.* **3.** a mask, costume, or manner that disguises. **4.** the act of disguising or the state of being disguised. [C14: from Old French *desguisier,* from *des-* DIS-[1] + *guise* manner; see GUISE] **—dis+ˈguis+a·ble** *adj.* **—dis+guis+ed+ly** (dɪsˈgaɪzɪdlɪ) *adv.* **—dis+ˈguis+er** *n.*

dis+gust (dɪsˈgʌst) *vb.* (*tr.*) **1.** to sicken or fill with loathing. **2.** to offend the moral sense, principles, or taste of. ~*n.* **3.** a great loathing or distaste aroused by someone or something. **4.** **in disgust.** as a result of disgust. [C16: from Old French *desgouster,* from *des-* DIS-[1] + *gouster* to taste, from *goust* taste, from Latin *gustus*] **—dis+ˈgust+ed+ly** *adv.* **—dis+ˈgust+ed+ness** *n.*

dis+gust+ing (dɪsˈgʌstɪŋ) *adj.* loathsome; repugnant. Also (rare): **dis+gust+ful.** **—dis+ˈgust+ing+ly** *adv.*

dish (dɪʃ) *n.* **1.** a container used for holding or serving food, esp. an open shallow container of pottery, glass, etc. **2.** the food that is served or contained in a dish. **3.** a particular article or preparation of food: *a local fish dish.* **4.** Also called: **ˈdish+ful.** the amount contained in a dish. **5.** something resembling a dish, esp. in shape. **6.** a concavity or depression. **7.** an informal name for **parabolic aerial.** **8.** *Slang.* an attractive person. **9.**

Informal. something that one particularly enjoys or excels in. ~*vb.* (*tr.*) **10.** to put into a dish. **11.** to make hollow or concave. **12.** *Brit. slang.* to ruin or spoil: *he dished his chances of getting the job.* ~See also: **dish out, dish up.** [Old English *disc,* from Latin *discus* quoit, see DISC] —'**dish**,**like** *adj.*

dis·ha·bille (ˌdɪsæ'bi:l) *or* **des·ha·bille** *n.* **1.** the state of being partly or carelessly dressed. **2.** *Archaic.* clothes worn in such a state. [C17: from French *déshabillé* undressed, from *dés-* DIS-[1] + *habiller* to dress; see HABILIMENT]

dis·har·mo·ny (dɪs'hɑ:mənɪ) *n., pl.* ·**nies.** **1.** lack of accord or harmony. **2.** a situation, circumstance, etc., that is inharmonious. —**dis·har·mo·ni·ous** (ˌdɪshɑ:'məʊnɪəs) *adj.* —ˌ**dis·har·'mo·ni·ous·ly** *adv.*

dish·cloth ('dɪʃˌklɒθ) *n.* a cloth or rag for washing or drying dishes. Also called (dialect): **dishclout.**

dish·cloth gourd *n.* **1.** any of several tropical climbing plants of the cucurbitaceous genus *Luffa,* esp. *L. cylindrica,* which is cultivated for ornament and for the fibrous interior of its fruits (see **loofah**). **2.** the fruit of any of these plants. ~Also called: **vegetable sponge.**

dis·heart·en (dɪs'hɑ:tᵊn) *vb.* (*tr.*) to weaken or destroy the hope, courage, enthusiasm, etc., of. —**dis·'heart·en·ing·ly** *adv.* —**dis·'heart·en·ment** *n.*

dished (dɪʃt) *adj.* **1.** shaped like a dish; concave. **2.** (of a pair of road wheels) arranged so that they are closer to one another at the bottom than at the top. **3.** *Slang.* exhausted or defeated.

di·shev·el (dɪ'ʃɛvᵊl) *vb.* ·**els,** ·**el·ling,** ·**elled** *or U.S.* ·**els,** ·**el·ing,** ·**eled.** to disarrange (the hair or clothes) of (someone). [C15: back formation from DISHEVELLED] —**di·'shev·el·ment** *n.*

di·shev·elled (dɪ'ʃɛvᵊld) *adj.* **1.** (esp. of hair) hanging loosely. **2.** (of general appearance) unkempt; untidy. [C15 *dischevelee,* from Old French *deschevelé,* from *des-* DIS-[1] + *chevel* hair, from Latin *capillus*]

dis·hon·est (dɪs'ɒnɪst) *adj.* not honest or fair; deceiving or fraudulent. —**dis·'hon·est·ly** *adv.*

dis·hon·es·ty (dɪs'ɒnɪstɪ) *n., pl.* ·**ties.** **1.** lack of honesty or fairness; deceit. **2.** a deceiving act or statement; fraud.

dis·hon·our *or U.S.* **dis·hon·or** (dɪs'ɒnə) *vb.* (*tr.*) **1.** to treat with disrespect. **2.** to fail or refuse to pay (a cheque, bill of exchange, etc.). **3.** to cause the disgrace of (a woman) by seduction or rape. ~*n.* **4.** a lack of honour or respect. **5.** a state of shame or disgrace. **6.** a person or thing that causes a loss of honour: *he was a dishonour to his family.* **7.** an insult; affront: *we did him a dishonour by not including him.* **8.** refusal or failure to accept or pay a commercial paper. —**dis·'hon·our·er** *or U.S.* **dis·'hon·or·er** *n.*

dis·hon·our·a·ble *or U.S.* **dis·hon·or·a·ble** (dɪs'ɒnərəbᵊl, -'ɒnrəbᵊl) *adj.* **1.** characterized by or causing dishonour or discredit. **2.** having little or no integrity; unprincipled. —**dis·'hon·our·a·ble·ness** *or U.S.* **dis·'hon·or·a·ble·ness** *n.* —**dis·'hon·our·a·bly** *or U.S.* **dis·'hon·or·a·bly** *adv.*

dish out *vb. Informal.* **1.** (*tr., adv.*) to distribute. **2.** **dish it out.** to inflict punishment: *he can't take it, but he can sure dish it out.*

dish·pan ('dɪʃˌpæn) *n. Chiefly U.S.* a large pan for washing dishes, pots, etc.

dish·tow·el ('dɪʃˌtaʊəl) *n.* another name (esp. U.S.) for a **tea towel.**

dish up *vb.* (*adv.*) **1.** to serve (a meal, food, etc.). **2.** (*tr.*) *Informal.* to prepare or present, esp. in an attractive manner.

dish·wash·er ('dɪʃˌwɒʃə) *n.* **1.** an electrically operated machine for washing, rinsing, and drying dishes, cutlery, etc. **2.** a person who washes dishes, etc.

dish·wa·ter ('dɪʃˌwɔ:tə) *n.* **1.** water in which dishes and kitchen utensils are or have been washed. **2.** something resembling this: *that was dishwater, not coffee.*

dish·y ('dɪʃɪ) *adj.* **dish·i·er, dish·i·est.** *Slang, chiefly Brit.* good-looking or attractive.

dis·il·lu·sion (ˌdɪsɪ'lu:ʒən) *vb.* **1.** (*tr.*) to destroy the ideals, illusions, or false ideas of. ~*n. also* **dis·il·lu·sion·ment.** **2.** the act of disillusioning or the state of being disillusioned. —**dis·il·lu·sive** (ˌdɪsɪ'lu:sɪv) *adj.*

dis·in·cen·tive (ˌdɪsɪn'sɛntɪv) *n.* **1.** something that acts as a deterrent. ~*adj.* **2.** acting as a deterrent: *a disincentive effect on productivity.*

dis·in·cline (ˌdɪsɪn'klaɪn) *vb.* to make or be unwilling, reluctant, or averse. —**dis·in·cli·na·tion** (ˌdɪsɪnklɪ'neɪʃən) *n.*

dis·in·fect (ˌdɪsɪn'fɛkt) *vb.* (*tr.*) to rid of microorganisms potentially harmful to man, esp. by chemical means. —ˌ**dis·in·'fec·tion** *n.* —ˌ**dis·in·'fec·tor** *n.*

dis·in·fect·ant (ˌdɪsɪn'fɛktənt) *n.* an agent that destroys or inhibits the activity of microorganisms that cause disease.

dis·in·fest (ˌdɪsɪn'fɛst) *vb.* (*tr.*) to rid of vermin. —**dis**ˌ**in·fes·'ta·tion** *n.*

dis·in·fla·tion (ˌdɪsɪn'fleɪʃən) *n. Economics.* a reduction or stabilization of the general price level intended to improve the balance of payments without incurring reductions in output, employment, and investment. Compare **deflation** (sense 2).

dis·in·gen·u·ous (ˌdɪsɪn'dʒɛnjʊəs) *adj.* not sincere; lacking candour. —ˌ**dis·in·'gen·u·ous·ly** *adv.* —ˌ**dis·in·'gen·u·ous·ness** *n.*

dis·in·her·it (ˌdɪsɪn'hɛrɪt) *vb.* (*tr.*) **1.** *Law.* to deprive (an heir or next of kin) of inheritance or right to inherit. **2.** to deprive of a right or heritage. —ˌ**dis·in·'her·i·tance** *n.*

dis·in·te·grate (dɪs'ɪntɪˌgreɪt) *vb.* **1.** to break or be broken into fragments or constituent parts; shatter. **2.** to lose or cause to lose cohesion or unity. **3.** (*intr.*) to lose judgment or control; deteriorate. **4.** *Physics.* **a.** to induce or undergo nuclear fission, as by bombardment with fast particles. **b.** another word for **decay** (sense 3a.). —**dis·'in·te·gra·ble** *adj.* —**dis**ˌ**in·te·'gra·tion** *n.* —**dis·'in·te·gra·tive** *adj.* —**dis·'in·te**ˌ**gra·tor** *n.*

dis·in·ter (ˌdɪsɪn'tɜ:) *vb.* ·**ters,** ·**ter·ring,** ·**terred.** (*tr.*) **1.** to remove or dig up; exhume. **2.** to bring (a secret, hidden facts, etc.) to light; expose. —ˌ**dis·in·'ter·ment** *n.*

dis·in·ter·est (dɪs'ɪntrɪst, -tərɪst) *n.* **1.** freedom from bias or involvement. **2.** lack of interest; indifference. ~*vb.* **3.** (*tr.*) to free from concern for personal interests.

dis·in·ter·est·ed (dɪs'ɪntrɪstɪd, -tərɪs-) *adj.* free from bias or partiality; objective. —**dis·'in·ter·est·ed·ly** *adv.* —**dis·'in·ter·est·ed·ness** *n.*

Usage. In spoken and sometimes written English, *disinterested* (impartial) is used where *uninterested* (showing or feeling lack of interest) is meant. Careful writers and speakers avoid this confusion: *a disinterested judge; he was uninterested in public reaction.*

dis·ject (dɪs'dʒɛkt) *vb.* (*tr.*) to break apart; scatter. [C16: from Latin *disjectus,* from *disjicere* to scatter, from DIS-[1] + *jacere* to throw]

dis·jec·ta mem·bra *Latin.* (dɪs'dʒɛktə 'mɛmbrə) *n.* scattered fragments, esp. parts taken from a writing or writings.

dis·join (dɪs'dʒɔɪn) *vb.* to disconnect or become disconnected; separate. —**dis·'join·a·ble** *adj.*

dis·joint (dɪs'dʒɔɪnt) *vb.* **1.** to take apart or come apart at the joints. **2.** (*tr.*) to disunite or disjoin. **3.** to dislocate or become dislocated. **4.** (*tr.; usually passive*) to end the unity, sequence, or coherence of. ~*adj.* **5.** *Maths.* (of two sets) having no members in common. **6.** *Obsolete.* disjointed.

dis·joint·ed (dɪs'dʒɔɪntɪd) *adj.* **1.** having no coherence; disconnected. **2.** separated at the joint. **3.** dislocated. —**dis·'joint·ed·ly** *adv.* —**dis·'joint·ed·ness** *n.*

dis·junct *adj.* (dɪs'dʒʌŋkt). **1.** not united or joined. **2.** (of certain insects) having deep constrictions between the head, thorax, and abdomen. **3.** *Music.* denoting two notes the interval between which is greater than a second. ~*n.* ('dɪsdʒʌŋkt). **4.** one of the propositions or formulas in a disjunction.

dis·junc·tion (dɪs'dʒʌŋkʃən) *n.* **1.** Also called: **dis·junc·ture.** the act of disconnecting or the state of being disconnected; separation. **2.** *Cytology.* the separation of the chromosomes of each homologous pair during the anaphase of meiosis. **3.** Also called: **alternation.** *Logic.* **a.** a compound proposition in which the component propositions are joined by *or.* It is true if only one component is true (exclusive sense) or if at least one component is true (inclusive sense). Usually written: $p \vee q$, where *p* and *q* are component propositions and $\vee$ is the symbol for *or.* **b.** the relation between these terms.

dis·junc·tive (dɪs'dʒʌŋktɪv) *adj.* **1.** serving to disconnect or separate. **2.** *Grammar.* **a.** denoting a word, esp. a conjunction, that serves to express opposition or contrast: *but* in the sentence *She was poor but she was honest.* **b.** denoting an inflection of pronouns in some languages that is used alone or after a preposition, such as *moi* in French. **3.** Also: **alternative.** *Logic.* characterizing, containing, or included in a disjunction. ~*n.* **4.** *Grammar.* **a.** a disjunctive word, esp. a conjunction. **b.** a disjunctive pronoun. **5.** *Logic.* a disjunctive proposition; disjunction. —**dis·'junc·tive·ly** *adv.*

disk (dɪsk) *n.* **1.** a variant spelling (esp. U.S.) of disc. **2.** Also called: **disk pack, magnetic disk.** *Computer technol.* a direct-access storage device consisting of a stack of plates coated with a magnetic layer, the whole assembly rotating rapidly as a single unit. Each surface has a read-write head that can move radially to read or write data on concentric tracks. Compare **drum**[1] (sense 8).

Dis·ko ('dɪskəʊ) *n.* an island in Davis Strait, off the W coast of Greenland: extensive coal deposits.

disk pack *n. Computer technol.* another name for **disk** (sense 2).

dis·like (dɪs'laɪk) *vb.* **1.** (*tr.*) to consider unpleasant or disagreeable. ~*n.* **2.** a feeling of aversion or antipathy. —**dis·'lik·a·ble** *or* **dis·'like·a·ble** *adj.*

dis·limn (dɪs'lɪm) *vb.* (*tr.*) *Poetic.* to efface.

dis·lo·cate ('dɪsləˌkeɪt) *vb.* (*tr.*) **1.** to disrupt or shift out of place or position. **2.** to displace (an organ or part) from its normal position, esp. a bone from its joint.

dis·lo·ca·tion (ˌdɪslə'keɪʃən) *n.* **1.** the act of displacing or the state of being displaced; disruption. **2.** (esp. of the bones in a joint) the state or condition of being dislocated. **3.** a line, plane, or region in which there is a discontinuity in the regularity of a crystal lattice. **4.** *Geology.* a less common word for **fault** (sense 6).

dis·lodge (dɪs'lɒdʒ) *vb.* to remove from or leave a lodging place, hiding place, or previously fixed position. —**dis·'lodg·ment** *or* **dis·'lodge·ment** *n.*

dis·loy·al (dɪs'lɔɪəl) *adj.* not loyal or faithful; deserting one's allegiance or duty. —**dis·'loy·al·ly** *adv.*

dis·loy·al·ty (dɪs'lɔɪəltɪ) *n., pl.* ·**ties.** the condition or an instance of being unfaithful or disloyal.

dis·mal ('dɪzməl) *adj.* **1.** causing gloom or depression. **2.** causing dismay or terror. **3.** *Rare.* calamitous. [C13: from *dismal* (*n.*) list of 24 unlucky days in the year, from Medieval Latin *diēs malī* bad days, from Latin *diēs* day + *malus* bad] —'**dis·mal·ly** *adv.* —'**dis·mal·ness** *n.*

Dis·mal Swamp *or* **Great Dis·mal Swamp** *n.* a coastal marshland in SE Virginia and NE North Carolina: partly reclaimed. Area: about 1940 sq. km (750 sq. miles). Area before reclamation: 5200 sq. km (2000 sq. miles).

dis·man·tle (dɪs'mæntᵊl) *vb.* (*tr.*) **1.** to take apart. **2.** to demolish or raze. **3.** to strip of covering. [C17: from Old French *desmanteler* to remove a cloak from; see MANTLE] —**dis'man·tle·ment** *n.* —**dis'man·tler** *n.*

dis·mast (dɪsˈmɑːst) *vb.* (*tr.*) to break off the mast or masts of (a sailing vessel). —**dis'mast·ment** *n.*

dis·may (dɪsˈmeɪ) *vb.* (*tr.*) **1.** to fill with apprehension or alarm. **2.** to fill with depression or discouragement. ~*n.* **3.** consternation or agitation. [C13: from Old French *desmaiier* (unattested), from *des-* DIS-[1] + *esmayer* to frighten, ultimately of Germanic origin; see MAY[1]]

dis·mem·ber (dɪsˈmɛmbə) *vb.* (*tr.*) **1.** to remove the limbs or members of. **2.** to cut to pieces. **3.** to divide or partition (something, such as an empire). —**dis'mem·ber·er** *n.* —**dis'mem·ber·ment** *n.*

dis·miss (dɪsˈmɪs) *vb.* (*tr.*) **1.** to remove or discharge from employment or service. **2.** to send away or allow to go or disperse. **3.** to dispel from one's mind; discard; reject. **4.** to cease to consider (a subject): *they dismissed the problem.* **5.** to decline further hearing to (a claim or action): *the judge dismissed the case.* **6.** *Cricket.* to bowl out a side for a particular number of runs. [C15: from Medieval Latin *dismissus* sent away, variant of Latin *dīmissus*, from *dīmittere*, from *dī-* DIS-[1] + *mittere* to send] —**dis'miss·i·ble** *adj.* —**dis'miss·ive** *adj.*

dis·mis·sal (dɪsˈmɪsᵊl) *n.* **1.** an official notice of discharge from employment or service. **2.** the act of dismissing or the condition of being dismissed.

dis·mount (dɪsˈmaʊnt) *vb.* **1.** to get off a horse, bicycle, etc. **2.** (*tr.*) to disassemble or remove from a mounting. ~*n.* **3.** the act of dismounting. —**dis'mount·a·ble** *adj.*

Dis·ney (ˈdɪznɪ) *n.* **Walt(er Elias).** 1901–66, U.S. film director, who pioneered animated cartoons: noted esp. for his creations *Mickey Mouse* and *Donald Duck* and films such as *Fantasia* (1940). —ˌ**Dis·ney'esque** *adj.*

Dis·ney·land (ˈdɪznɪˌlænd) *n.* an amusement park in Anaheim, California, founded by Walt Disney and opened in 1955. **Walt Disney World,** a second amusement park, opened in 1971 near Orlando, Florida.

dis·o·be·di·ence (ˌdɪsəˈbiːdɪəns) *n.* lack of obedience.

dis·o·be·di·ent (ˌdɪsəˈbiːdɪənt) *adj.* not obedient; neglecting or refusing to obey. —ˌ**dis·o'be·di·ent·ly** *adv.*

dis·o·bey (ˌdɪsəˈbeɪ) *vb.* to neglect or refuse to obey (someone, an order, etc.). —ˌ**dis·o'bey·er** *n.*

dis·o·blige (ˌdɪsəˈblaɪdʒ) *vb.* (*tr.*) **1.** to disregard the desires of. **2.** to slight; insult. **3.** *Informal.* to cause trouble or inconvenience to. —ˌ**dis·o'blig·ing** *adj.* —ˌ**dis·o'blig·ing·ly** *adv.* —ˌ**dis·o'blig·ing·ness** *n.*

dis·op·er·a·tion (dɪsˌɒpəˈreɪʃən) *n. Ecology.* a relationship between two organisms in a community that is harmful to both.

dis·or·der (dɪsˈɔːdə) *n.* **1.** a lack of order; disarray; confusion. **2.** a disturbance of public order or peace. **3.** an upset of health; ailment. **4.** a deviation from the normal system or order. ~*vb.* (*tr.*) **5.** to upset the order of; disarrange; muddle. **6.** to disturb the health or mind of.

dis·or·der·ly (dɪsˈɔːdəlɪ) *adj.* **1.** untidy; irregular. **2.** uncontrolled; unruly. **3.** *Law.* violating public peace or order. ~*adv.* **4.** in an irregular or confused manner. —**dis'or·der·li·ness** *n.*

dis·or·der·ly con·duct *n. Law.* any of various minor offences tending to cause a disturbance of the peace.

dis·or·der·ly house *n. Law.* an establishment in which unruly behaviour habitually occurs, esp. a brothel or a gaming house.

dis·or·gan·ize *or* **dis·or·gan·ise** (dɪsˈɔːgəˌnaɪz) *vb.* (*tr.*) to disrupt or destroy the arrangement, system, or unity of. —**dis·ˌor·gan·i'za·tion** *or* **dis·ˌor·gan·i'sa·tion** *n.* —**dis'or·gan·ˌiz·er** *or* **dis'or·gan·ˌis·er** *n.*

dis·o·ri·en·tate (dɪsˈɔːrɪɛnˌteɪt) *or* **dis·o·ri·ent** *vb.* (*tr.*) **1.** to cause (someone) to lose his bearings. **2.** to perplex; confuse.

dis·own (dɪsˈəʊn) *vb.* (*tr.*) to deny any connection with; refuse to acknowledge. —**dis'own·er** *n.* —**dis'own·ment** *n.*

dis·par·age (dɪˈspærɪdʒ) *vb.* (*tr.*) **1.** to speak contemptuously of; belittle. **2.** to damage the reputation of. [C14: from Old French *desparagier*, from *des-* DIS-[1] + *parage* equality, from Latin *par* equal] —**dis'par·age·ment** *n.* —**dis'par·ag·er** *n.* —**dis'par·ag·ing·ly** *adv.*

dis·par·ate (ˈdɪspərɪt) *adj.* **1.** utterly different or distinct in kind. ~*n.* **2.** (*pl.*) unlike things or people. [C16: from Latin *disparāre* to divide, from DIS-[1] + *parāre* to prepare; also influenced by Latin *dispar* unequal] —**'dis·par·ate·ly** *adv.* —**'dis·par·ate·ness** *n.*

dis·par·i·ty (dɪˈspærɪtɪ) *n., pl.* **·ties. 1.** inequality or difference, as in age, rank, wages, etc. **2.** dissimilarity.

dis·pas·sion (dɪsˈpæʃən) *n.* detachment; objectivity.

dis·pas·sion·ate (dɪsˈpæʃənɪt) *adj.* devoid of or uninfluenced by emotion or prejudice; objective; impartial. —**dis'pas·sion·ate·ly** *adv.* —**dis'pas·sion·ate·ness** *n.*

dis·patch *or* **des·patch** (dɪˈspætʃ) *vb.* (*tr.*) **1.** to send off promptly, as to a destination or to perform a task. **2.** to discharge or complete (a task, duty, etc.) promptly. **3.** *Informal.* to eat up quickly. **4.** to murder or execute. ~*n.* **5.** the act of sending off a letter, messenger, etc. **6.** prompt action or speed (often in the phrase **with dispatch**). **7.** an official communication or report, sent in haste. **8.** *Journalism.* a report sent to a newspaper, etc., by a correspondent. **9.** murder or execution. [C16: from Italian *dispacciare*, from Provençal *despachar*, from Old French *despeechier* to set free, from *des-* DIS-[1] + *-peechier*, ultimately from Latin *pedica* a fetter] —ˌ**dis'patch·er** *n.*

dis·patch box *n.* a case or box used to hold valuables, documents, etc.

dis·patch case *n.* a case used for carrying papers, documents, books, etc., usually flat and stiff.

dis·patch rid·er *n.* a horseman or motorcyclist who carries dispatches.

dis·pel (dɪˈspɛl) *vb.* **·pels, ·pel·ling, ·pelled.** (*tr.*) to disperse or drive away. [C17: from Latin *dispellere*, from DIS-[1] + *pellere* to drive] —**dis'pel·ler** *n.*

dis·pend (dɪˈspɛnd) *vb.* (*tr.*) *Obsolete.* to spend. [C14: from Old French *despendre*, from Latin *dispendere* to distribute; see DISPENSE]

dis·pen·sa·ble (dɪˈspɛnsəbᵊl) *adj.* **1.** not essential; expendable. **2.** capable of being distributed. **3.** (of a law, vow, etc.) able to be relaxed. —**dis·ˌpen·sa'bil·i·ty** *or* **dis'pen·sa·ble·ness** *n.*

dis·pen·sa·ry (dɪˈspɛnsərɪ, -srɪ) *n., pl.* **·ries.** a place where medicine and medical supplies are dispensed.

dis·pen·sa·tion (ˌdɪspɛnˈseɪʃən) *n.* **1.** the act of distributing or dispensing. **2.** something distributed or dispensed. **3.** a system or plan of administering or dispensing. **4.** *Chiefly R.C. Church.* **a.** permission to dispense with an obligation of church law. **b.** the document authorizing such permission. **5.** any exemption from a rule or obligation. **6.** *Theol.* **a.** the ordering of life and events by God. **b.** a divine decree affecting an individual or group. **c.** a religious system or code of prescriptions for life and conduct regarded as of divine origin. —ˌ**dis·pen'sa·tion·al** *adj.*

dis·pen·sa·to·ry (dɪˈspɛnsətərɪ, -trɪ) *n., pl.* **·ries. 1.** a book listing the composition, preparation, and application of various drugs. ~*adj.* **2.** of or involving dispensation.

dis·pense (dɪˈspɛns) *vb.* **1.** (*tr.*) to give out or distribute in portions. **2.** (*tr.*) to prepare and distribute (medicine), esp. on prescription. **3.** (*tr.*) to administer (the law, etc.). **4.** (*intr.*; foll. by *with*) to do away (with) or manage (without). **5.** to grant a dispensation to (someone) from (some obligation of church law). **6.** to exempt or excuse from a rule or obligation. [C14: from Medieval Latin *dispensāre* to pardon, from Latin *dispendere* to weigh out, from DIS-[1] + *pendere* to weigh]

dis·pens·er (dɪˈspɛnsə) *n.* **1.** a device, such as a vending machine, that automatically dispenses a single item or a measured quantity. **2.** a person or thing that dispenses.

di·sper·mous (daɪˈspɜːməs) *adj.* (of flowering plants) producing or having two seeds. [C18: from DI-[1] + Greek *sperma* seed]

dis·per·sal (dɪˈspɜːsᵊl) *n.* **1.** another word for **dispersion** (sense 1). **2.** the spread of animals, plants, or seeds to new areas.

dis·per·sal pris·on *n.* a prison organized and equipped to accommodate a proportion of the most dangerous and highest security risk prisoners.

dis·per·sant (dɪsˈpɜːsənt) *n.* a liquid or gas used to disperse small particles or droplets, as in an aerosol.

dis·perse (dɪˈspɜːs) *vb.* **1.** to scatter; distribute over a wide area. **2.** to dissipate or cause to dissipate. **3.** to leave or cause to leave a gathering, often in a random manner. **4.** to separate or be separated by dispersion. **5.** (*tr.*) to diffuse or spread (news, information, etc.). **6.** to separate (particles) throughout a solid, liquid, or gas, as in the formation of a suspension or colloid. ~*adj.* **7.** of or consisting of the particles in a colloid or suspension: *disperse phase.* [C14: from Latin *dispersus* scattered, from *dispergere* to scatter widely, from DI-[2] + *spargere* to strew] —**dis·pers·ed·ly** (dɪˈspɜːsɪdlɪ) *adv.* —**dis'pers·er** *n.*

dis·per·sion (dɪˈspɜːʃən) *n.* **1.** the act of dispersing or the condition of being dispersed. **2.** *Physics.* **a.** the separation of electromagnetic radiation into constituents of different wavelengths. **b.** a measure of the ability of a substance to separate by refraction, expressed by the first differential of the refractive index with respect to wavelength at a given value of wavelength. Symbol: *D* **3.** *Statistics.* the degree to which values of a frequency distribution are scattered around some central point, usually the arithmetic mean or median. **4.** *Chem.* a system containing particles dispersed in a solid, liquid, or gas. **5.** *Military.* the pattern of fire from a weapon system. **6.** the deviation of a rocket from its prescribed path.

Dis·per·sion (dɪˈspɜːʃən) *n.* **the.** another name for the **Diaspora.**

dis·per·sion hard·en·ing *n.* the strengthening of an alloy as a result of the presence of fine particles in the lattice.

dis·per·sive (dɪˈspɜːsɪv) *adj.* tending or serving to disperse. —**dis'per·sive·ly** *adv.* —**dis'per·sive·ness** *n.*

dis·per·soid (dɪˈspɜːsɔɪd) *n. Chem.* a system, such as a colloid or suspension, in which one phase is dispersed in another.

dis·pir·it (dɪˈspɪrɪt) *vb.* (*tr.*) to lower the spirit or enthusiasm of; make downhearted or depressed; discourage. —ˌ**dis'pir·it·ed** *adj.* —**dis'pir·it·ed·ly** *adv.* —**dis'pir·it·ed·ness** *n.* —**dis'pir·it·ing** *adj.* —**dis'pir·it·ing·ly** *adv.*

dis·place (dɪsˈpleɪs) *vb.* (*tr.*) **1.** to move from the usual or correct location. **2.** to remove from office or employment. **3.** to occupy the place of; replace; supplant. **4.** to force (someone) to leave home or country, as during a war. **5.** *Chem.* to replace (an atom or group in a chemical compound) by another atom or group. **6.** *Physics.* to cause a displacement of (a quantity of liquid, usually water of a specified type and density). —**dis'place·a·ble** *adj.* —**dis'plac·er** *n.*

dis·placed per·son *n.* a person forced from his home or country, esp. by war or revolution.

dis·place·ment (dɪsˈpleɪsmənt) *n.* **1.** the act of displacing or the condition of being displaced. **2.** the weight or volume displaced by a floating or submerged body in a fluid. **3.** *Chem.* another name for **substitution. 4.** the volume displaced by the piston of a reciprocating pump or engine. **5.** *Psychoanal.* the transferring of emotional feelings from their original object to one that disguises their real nature. **6.** *Geology.* the distance any point on one side of a fault plane has moved in relation to a corresponding point on the opposite side. **7.** *Astronomy.* an apparent change in position of a body, such as a star.

dis+place+ment ac+tiv+i+ty *n. Psychol.* behaviour that occurs typically in a situation of conflict and is characterized by its irrelevance to that situation.

dis+place+ment ton *n.* the full name for **ton**[1] (sense 6).

dis+plant (dɪsˈplɑːnt) *vb.* (*tr.*) *Obsolete.* **1.** to displace. **2.** to transplant (a plant).

dis+play (dɪˈspleɪ) *vb.* (*tr.*) **1.** to show or make visible. **2.** to disclose or make evident; reveal: *to display anger.* **3.** to flaunt in an ostentatious way: *to display military might.* **4.** to spread or open out; unfurl or unfold. **5.** to give prominence to (headings, captions, etc.) by the use of certain typefaces. ~*n.* **6.** the act of exhibiting or displaying; show: *a display of fear.* **7.** something exhibited or displayed. **8.** an ostentatious or pretentious exhibition: *a display of his accomplishments.* **9. a.** an arrangement of certain typefaces to give prominence to headings, captions, etc. **b.** printed matter that is eye-catching. **10.** *Electronics.* **a.** a device capable of representing information visually, as on a cathode-ray tube screen. **b.** the information so presented. **11.** *Zoology.* a pattern of behaviour in birds, fishes, etc., by which the animal attracts attention while it is courting the female, defending its territory, etc. **12.** (*modifier*) relating to or using typefaces that give prominence to the words they are used to set. [C14: from Anglo-French *despleier* to unfold, from Late Latin *displicāre* to scatter, from DIS-[1] + *plicāre* to fold] **—dis+ˈplay+er** *n.*

dis+please (dɪsˈpliːz) *vb.* to annoy, offend, or cause displeasure to (someone). **—dis+ˈpleas+ing+ly** *adv.*

dis+pleas+ure (dɪsˈplɛʒə) *n.* **1.** the condition of being displeased. **2.** *Archaic.* **a.** pain. **b.** an act or cause of offence. ~*vb.* **3.** (*tr.*) an archaic word for **displease.**

dis+plode (dɪsˈpləʊd) *vb.* an obsolete word for **explode.** [C17: from Latin *displōdere from* DIS-[1] + *plaudere* to clap]

dis+port (dɪˈspɔːt) *vb.* **1.** (*tr.*) to indulge (oneself) in pleasure. **2.** (*intr.*) to frolic or gambol. ~*n.* **3.** *Archaic.* amusement. [C14: from Anglo-French *desporter,* from *des-* DIS-[1] + *porter* to carry]

dis+pos+a+ble (dɪˈspəʊzəbᵊl) *adj.* **1.** designed for disposal after use: *disposable cups.* **2.** available for use if needed: *disposable assets.* ~*n.* **3.** something, such as a baby's nappy, that is designed for disposal. **—dis+ˌpos+a+ˈbil+i+ty** *or* **dis+ˈpos+a+ble+ness** *n.*

dis+pos+al (dɪˈspəʊzᵊl) *n.* **1.** the act or means of getting rid of something. **2.** placement or arrangement in a particular order. **3.** a specific method of tending to matters, as in business. **4.** the act or process of transferring something to or providing something for another. **5.** the power or opportunity to make use of someone or something (esp. in the phrase **at one's disposal**). **6.** a means of destroying waste products, as by grinding into particles. ~Also (for senses 2–5): **disposition.**

dis+pose (dɪˈspəʊz) *vb.* **1.** (*intr.*; foll. by *of*) **a.** to deal with or settle. **b.** to give, sell, or transfer to another. **c.** to throw out or away. **d.** to consume, esp. hurriedly. **2.** to arrange or settle (matters) by placing into correct or final condition: *man proposes, God disposes.* **3.** (*tr.*) to make willing or receptive. **4.** (*tr.*) to adjust or place in a certain order or position. **5.** (*tr.*; often foll. by *to*) to accustom or condition. ~*n.* **6.** an obsolete word for **disposal** or **disposition.** [C14: from Old French *disposer,* from Latin *dispōnere* to set in different places, arrange, from DIS-[1] + *pōnere* to place] **—dis+ˈpos+er** *n.*

dis+posed (dɪˈspəʊzd) *adj.* **a.** having an inclination as specified (towards something). **b.** (*in combination*): *well-disposed.*

dis+po+si+tion (ˌdɪspəˈzɪʃən) *n.* **1.** a person's usual temperament or frame of mind. **2.** a natural or acquired tendency, inclination, or habit in a person or thing. **3.** another word for **disposal** (senses 2–5). **4.** *Archaic.* manner of placing or arranging. **—ˌdis+po+ˈsi+tion+al** *adj.*

dis+pos+sess (ˌdɪspəˈzɛs) *vb.* (*tr.*) to take away possession of something, esp. property; expel. **—ˌdis+pos+ˈses+sion** *n.* **—ˌdis+pos+ˈses+sor** *n.* **—ˌdis+pos+ˈses+so+ry** *adj.*

dis+po+sure (dɪˈspəʊʒə) *n.* a rare word for **disposal** or **disposition.**

dis+praise (dɪsˈpreɪz) *vb.* **1.** (*tr.*) to express disapproval or condemnation of. ~*n.* **2.** the disapproval, etc., expressed. **—dis+ˈprais+er** *n.* **—dis+ˈprais+ing+ly** *adv.*

dis+prize (dɪsˈpraɪz) *vb.* (*tr.*) *Archaic.* to scorn; disdain.

dis+proof (dɪsˈpruːf) *n.* **1.** facts that disprove something. **2.** the act of disproving.

dis+pro+por+tion (ˌdɪsprəˈpɔːʃən) *n.* **1.** lack of proportion or equality. **2.** an instance of disparity or inequality. ~*vb.* **3.** (*tr.*) to cause to become exaggerated or unequal. **—ˌdis+pro+ˈpor+tion+a+ble** *adj.* **—ˌdis+pro+ˈpor+tion+a+ble+ness** *n.* **—ˌdis+pro+ˈpor+tion+a+bly** *adv.*

dis+pro+por+tion+ate *adj.* (ˌdɪsprəˈpɔːʃənɪt). **1.** out of proportion; unequal. ~*vb.* (ˌdɪsprəˈpɔːʃəˌneɪt). **2.** *Chem.* to undergo or cause to undergo disproportionation. **—ˌdis+pro+ˈpor+tion+ate+ly** *adv.* **—ˌdis+pro+ˈpor+tion+ate+ness** *n.*

dis+pro+por+tion+a+tion (ˌdɪsprəˌpɔːʃəˈneɪʃən) *n.* a reaction between two identical molecules in which one is reduced and the other oxidized.

dis+prove (dɪsˈpruːv) *vb.* (*tr.*) to show (an assertion, claim, etc.) to be incorrect. **—dis+ˈprov+a+ble** *adj.* **—dis+ˈprov+al** *n.*

dis+put+a+ble (dɪˈspjuːtəbᵊl, ˈdɪspjʊtə-) *adj.* capable of being argued; debatable. **—dis+ˌput+a+ˈbil+i+ty** *or* **dis+ˈput+a+ble+ness** *n.* **—dis+ˈput+a+bly** *adv.*

dis+pu+tant (dɪˈspjuːtᵊnt, ˈdɪspjʊtənt) *n.* **1.** a person who argues; contestant. ~*adj.* **2.** engaged in argument.

dis+pu+ta+tion (ˌdɪspjʊˈteɪʃən) *n.* **1.** the act or an instance of arguing. **2.** a formal academic debate on a thesis. **3.** an obsolete word for **conversation.**

dis+pu+ta+tious (ˌdɪspjʊˈteɪʃəs) *or* **dis+pu+ta+tive** (dɪˈspjuːtətɪv) *adj.* inclined to argument. **—ˌdis+pu+ˈta+tious+ly** *or* **dis+ˈpu+ta+tive+ly** *adv.* **—ˌdis+pu+ˈta+tious+ness** *or* **dis+ˈpu+ta+tive+ness** *n.*

dis+pute (dɪˈspjuːt) *vb.* **1.** to argue, debate, or quarrel about (something). **2.** (*tr.*; *may take a clause as object*) to doubt the validity, etc., of. **3.** (*tr.*) to seek to win; contest for. **4.** (*tr.*) to struggle against; resist. ~*n.* **5.** an argument or quarrel. **6.** *Rare.* a fight. [C13: from Late Latin *disputāre* to contend verbally, from Latin: to discuss, from DIS-[1] + *putāre* to think] **—dis+ˈput+er** *n.*

dis+qual+i+fy (dɪsˈkwɒlɪˌfaɪ) *vb.* **+fies, +fy+ing, +fied.** (*tr.*) **1.** to make unfit or unqualified. **2.** to make ineligible, as for entry to an examination. **3.** to debar (a player or team) from a sporting contest. **4.** to divest or deprive of rights, powers, or privileges: *disqualified from driving.* **—dis+ˈqual+i+ˌfi+a+ble** *adj.* **—dis+ˌqual+i+fi+ˈca+tion** *n.* **—dis+ˈqual+i+ˌfi+er** *n.*

dis+qui+et (dɪsˈkwaɪət) *n.* **1.** a feeling or condition of anxiety or uneasiness. ~*vb.* **2.** (*tr.*) to make anxious or upset. ~*adj.* **3.** *Archaic.* uneasy or anxious. **—dis+ˈqui+et+ed+ly** *or* **dis+ˈqui+et+ly** *adv.* **—dis+ˈqui+et+ed+ness** *or* **dis+ˈqui+et+ness** *n.* **—dis+ˈqui+et+ing** *adj.* **—dis+ˈqui+et+ing+ly** *adv.*

dis+qui+e+tude (dɪsˈkwaɪɪˌtjuːd) *n.* a feeling or state of anxiety or uneasiness.

dis+qui+si+tion (ˌdɪskwɪˈzɪʃən) *n.* a formal written or oral examination of a subject. [C17: from Latin *disquīsītiō,* from *disquīrere* to make an investigation, from DIS-[1] + *quaerere* to seek] **—ˌdis+qui+ˈsi+tion+al** *adj.*

Dis+rae+li (dɪzˈreɪlɪ) *n.* **Ben+ja+min,** 1st Earl of Beaconsfield. 1804–81, British Tory statesman and novelist; prime minister (1868; 1874–80). He gave coherence to the Tory principles of protectionism, democracy, and imperialism, was responsible for the Reform Bill (1867) and, as prime minister, bought a controlling interest in the Suez Canal. His novels include *Coningsby* (1844) and *Sybil* (1845).

dis+rate (dɪsˈreɪt) *vb.* (*tr.*) *Naval.* to punish (an officer) by lowering him in rank.

dis+re+gard (ˌdɪsrɪˈgɑːd) *vb.* (*tr.*) **1.** to give little or no attention to; ignore. **2.** to treat as unworthy of consideration or respect. ~*n.* **3.** lack of attention or respect. **—ˌdis+re+ˈgard+er** *n.* **—ˌdis+re+ˈgard+ful** *adj.* **—ˌdis+re+ˈgard+ful+ly** *adv.* **—ˌdis+re+ˈgard+ful+ness** *n.*

dis+rel+ish (dɪsˈrɛlɪʃ) *vb.* **1.** (*tr.*) to have a feeling of aversion for; dislike. ~*n.* **2.** such a feeling.

dis+re+mem+ber (ˌdɪsrɪˈmɛmbə) *vb. Informal, chiefly U.S.* to fail to recall (someone or something).

dis+re+pair (ˌdɪsrɪˈpɛə) *n.* the condition of being worn out or in poor working order; a condition requiring repairs.

dis+rep+u+ta+ble (dɪsˈrɛpjʊtəbᵊl) *adj.* **1.** having or causing a lack of repute. **2.** disordered in appearance. **—dis+ˌrep+u+ta+ˈbil+i+ty** *or* **dis+ˈrep+u+ta+ble+ness** *n.* **—dis+ˈrep+u+ta+bly** *adv.*

dis+re+pute (ˌdɪsrɪˈpjuːt) *n.* a loss or lack of credit or repute.

dis+re+spect (ˌdɪsrɪˈspɛkt) *n.* **1.** contempt; rudeness. ~*vb.* **2.** (*tr.*) to show lack of respect for. **—ˌdis+re+ˈspect+ful** *adj.* **—ˌdis+re+ˈspect+ful+ly** *adv.* **—ˌdis+re+ˈspect+ful+ness** *n.*

dis+re+spect+a+ble (ˌdɪsrɪˈspɛktəbᵊl) *adj.* unworthy of respect; not respectable. **—ˌdis+re+ˌspect+a+ˈbil+i+ty** *n.*

dis+robe (dɪsˈrəʊb) *vb.* **1.** to remove the clothing of (a person) or (of a person) to undress. **2.** (*tr.*) to divest of authority, etc. **—dis+ˈrobe+ment** *n.* **—dis+ˈrob+er** *n.*

dis+rupt (dɪsˈrʌpt) *vb.* **1.** (*tr.*) to throw into turmoil or disorder. **2.** (*tr.*) to interrupt the progress of (a movement, meeting, etc.). **3.** to break or split (something) apart. [C17: from Latin *disruptus* burst asunder, from *dīrumpere* to dash to pieces, from DIS-[1] + *rumpere* to burst] **—dis+ˈrupt+er** *or* **dis+ˈrup+tor** *n.* **—dis+ˈrup+tion** *n.*

dis+rup+tive (dɪsˈrʌptɪv) *adj.* involving, causing, or tending to cause disruption. **—dis+ˈrup+tive+ly** *adv.*

dis+rup+tive dis+charge *n.* a sudden large increase in current through an insulating medium resulting from failure of the medium to withstand an applied electric field.

dis+sat+is+fied (dɪsˈsætɪsˌfaɪd) *adj.* having or showing dissatisfaction; discontented. **—dis+ˈsat+is+ˌfied+ly** *adv.*

dis+sat+is+fy (dɪsˈsætɪsˌfaɪ) *vb.* **+fies, +fy+ing, +fied.** (*tr.*) to fail to satisfy; disappoint. **—ˌdis+sat+is+ˈfac+tion** *n.* **—ˌdis+sat+is+ˈfac+to+ry** *adj.*

dis+sect (dɪˈsɛkt, daɪ-) *vb.* **1.** to cut open and examine the structure of (a dead animal or plant). **2.** (*tr.*) to examine critically and minutely. [C17: from Latin *dissecāre,* from DIS-[1] + *secāre* to cut] **—dis+ˈsec+ti+ble** *adj.* **—dis+ˈsec+tion** *n.* **—dis+ˈsec+tor** *n.*

dis+sect+ed (dɪˈsɛktɪd, daɪ-) *adj.* **1.** *Botany.* in the form of narrow lobes or segments: *dissected leaves.* **2.** *Geology.* (of plains) cut by erosion into hills and valleys, esp. following tectonic movements.

dis+seise *or* **dis+seize** (dɪsˈsiːz) *vb.* (*tr.*) *Property law.* to deprive of seisin; wrongfully dispossess of a freehold interest in land. [C14: from Anglo-Norman *desseisir,* from DIS-[1] + SEIZE] **—dis+ˈsei+sor** *or* **dis+ˈsei+zor** *n.*

dis+sei+sin *or* **dis+sei+zin** (dɪsˈsiːzɪn) *n.* the act of disseising or state of being disseised. [C14: from Old French *dessaisine;* see DIS-[1], SEISIN]

dis·sem·ble (dɪˈsɛmbᵊl) *vb.* **1.** to conceal (one's real motives, emotions, etc.) by pretence. **2.** (*tr.*) to pretend; simulate. **3.** *Obsolete.* to ignore. [C15: from earlier *dissimulen,* from Latin *dissimulāre;* probably influenced by obsolete *semble* to resemble] —**disˈsem·blance** *n.* —**disˈsem·bler** *n.* —**disˈsem·bling·ly** *adv.*

dis·sem·i·nate (dɪˈsɛmɪˌneɪt) *vb.* (*tr.*) to distribute or scatter about; diffuse. [C17: from Latin *dissēmināre,* from DIS-[1] + *sēmināre* to sow, from *sēmen* seed] —**disˌsem·iˈna·tion** *n.* —**disˈsem·i·na·tive** *adj.* —**disˈsem·iˌna·tor** *n.*

dis·sem·i·nat·ed scle·ro·sis *n.* another name for **multiple sclerosis.**

dis·sem·i·nule (dɪˈsɛmɪˌnjuːl) *n.* any propagative part of a plant, such as a seed or spore, that helps to spread the species. [C20: from DISSEMINATE + -ULE]

dis·sen·sion (dɪˈsɛnʃən) *n.* disagreement, esp. when leading to a quarrel. [C13: from Latin *dissēnsiō,* from *dissentīre* to dissent]

dis·sent (dɪˈsɛnt) *vb.* (*intr.*) **1.** to have a disagreement or withhold assent. **2.** *Christianity.* to refuse to conform to the doctrines, beliefs, or practices of an established church, and to adhere to a different system of beliefs and practices. ~*n.* **3.** a difference of opinion. **4.** *Christianity.* separation from an established church; Nonconformism. **5.** the voicing of a minority opinion in announcing the decision on a case at law; dissenting judgment. [C16: from Latin *dissentīre* to disagree, from DIS-[1] + *sentīre* to perceive, feel] —**disˈsent·er** *n.* —**disˈsent·ing** *adj.* —**disˈsent·ing·ly** *adv.*

Dis·sent·er (dɪˈsɛntə) *n. Christianity, chiefly Brit.* a Nonconformist or a person who refuses to conform to the established church.

dis·sen·tient (dɪˈsɛnʃənt) *adj.* **1.** dissenting, esp. from the opinion of the majority. ~*n.* **2.** a dissenter. —**disˈsen·tience** *or* **disˈsen·tien·cy** *n.* —**disˈsen·tient·ly** *adv.*

dis·sen·tious (dɪˈsɛnʃəs) *adj.* argumentative.

dis·sep·i·ment (dɪˈsɛpɪmənt) *n. Biology.* a dividing partition or membrane, such as that between the chambers of a syncarpous ovary. [C18: from Late Latin *dissaepīmentum,* from DIS-[1] + *saepīmentum* hedge, from *saepīre* to enclose] —**disˌsep·iˈmen·tal** *adj.*

dis·ser·tate (ˈdɪsəˌteɪt) *vb.* (*intr.*) *Rare.* to give or make a dissertation. [C18: from Latin *dissertāre* to debate, from *disserere* to examine, from DIS-[1] + *serere* to arrange] —**ˈdis·serˌta·tor** *n.*

dis·ser·ta·tion (ˌdɪsəˈteɪʃən) *n.* **1.** a written thesis, often based on original research, usually required for a higher degree. **2.** a formal discourse. —**ˌdis·serˈta·tion·al** *adj.* —**ˌdis·serˈta·tion·ist** *n.*

dis·serve (dɪsˈsɜːv) *vb.* (*tr.*) *Archaic.* to do a disservice to.

dis·ser·vice (dɪsˈsɜːvɪs) *n.* an ill turn; wrong; injury, esp. when trying to help. —**disˈser·vice·a·ble** *adj.*

dis·sev·er (dɪˈsɛvə) *vb.* **1.** to break off or become broken off. **2.** (*tr.*) to divide up into parts. [C13: from Old French *dessevrer,* from Late Latin DIS-[1] + *sēparāre* to SEPARATE] —**disˈsev·er·ance, disˈsev·er·ment,** *or* **disˌsev·erˈa·tion** *n.*

dis·si·dent (ˈdɪsɪdənt) *adj.* **1.** disagreeing; dissenting. ~*n.* **2.** a person who disagrees, esp. one who disagrees with the government. [C16: from Latin *dissidēre* to be remote from, from DIS-[1] + *sedēre* to sit] —**ˈdis·si·dence** *n.* —**ˈdis·si·dent·ly** *adv.*

dis·sim·i·lar (dɪˈsɪmɪlə) *adj.* not alike; not similar; different. —**disˈsim·i·lar·ly** *adv.*

dis·sim·i·lar·i·ty (ˌdɪsɪmɪˈlærɪtɪ) *n., pl.* **·ties. 1.** difference; unlikeness. **2.** a point or instance of difference.

dis·sim·i·late (dɪˈsɪmɪˌleɪt) *vb.* **1.** to make or become dissimilar. **2.** (usually foll. by *to*) *Phonetics.* to change or displace (a consonant) or (of a consonant) to be changed to or displaced by (another consonant) so that its manner of articulation becomes less similar to a speech sound in the same word. Thus (r) in the final syllable of French *marbre* is dissimilated to (l) in its English form *marble.* [C19: from DIS-[1] + ASSIMILATE] —**disˈsim·i·la·tive** *adj.* —**disˈsim·i·la·to·ry** *adj.*

dis·sim·i·la·tion (ˌdɪsɪmɪˈleɪʃən) *n.* **1.** the act or an instance of making dissimilar. **2.** *Phonetics.* the alteration or omission of a consonant as a result of being dissimilated. **3.** *Biology.* a less common word for **catabolism.**

dis·si·mil·i·tude (ˌdɪsɪˈmɪlɪˌtjuːd) *n.* **1.** dissimilarity; difference. **2.** a point of difference.

dis·sim·u·late (dɪˈsɪmjʊˌleɪt) *vb.* to conceal (one's real feelings, etc.) by pretence. —**disˌsim·uˈla·tion** *n.* —**disˈsim·u·la·tive** *adj.* —**disˈsim·uˌla·tor** *n.*

dis·si·pate (ˈdɪsɪˌpeɪt) *vb.* **1.** to exhaust or be exhausted by dispersion. **2.** (*tr.*) to scatter or break up. **3.** (*intr.*) to indulge in the pursuit of pleasure. [C15: from Latin *dissipāre* to disperse, from DIS-[1] + *supāre* to throw] —**ˈdis·siˌpat·er** *or* **ˈdis·siˌpa·tor** *n.* —**ˈdis·siˌpa·tive** *adj.*

dis·si·pat·ed (ˈdɪsɪˌpeɪtɪd) *adj.* **1.** indulging without restraint in the pursuit of pleasure; debauched. **2.** wasted, scattered, or exhausted. —**ˈdis·siˌpat·ed·ly** *adv.* —**ˈdis·siˌpat·ed·ness** *n.*

dis·si·pa·tion (ˌdɪsɪˈpeɪʃən) *n.* **1.** the act of dissipating or condition of being dissipated. **2.** unrestrained indulgence in physical pleasures, esp. alcohol. **3.** excessive expenditure; wastefulness. **4.** amusement; diversion.

dis·so·ci·a·ble (dɪˈsəʊʃɪəbᵊl, -ʃə-) *adj.* **1.** able to be dissociated; distinguishable. **2.** incongruous; irreconcilable. **3.** (dɪˈsəʊʃəbᵊl). Also: **dissocial.** a less common word for **unsociable.** —**disˌso·ci·aˈbil·i·ty** *or* **disˈso·ci·a·ble·ness** *n.* —**disˈso·ci·a·bly** *adv.*

dis·so·ci·ate (dɪˈsəʊʃɪˌeɪt, -sɪ-) *vb.* **1.** to break or cause to break the association between (people, organizations, etc.). **2.** (*tr.*) to regard or treat as separate or unconnected. **3.** to undergo or subject to dissociation. —**disˈso·ci·a·tive** *adj.*

dis·so·ci·a·tion (dɪˌsəʊsɪˈeɪʃən, -ʃɪ-) *n.* **1.** the act of dissociating or the state of being dissociated. **2.** *Chem.* **a.** a reversible chemical change of the molecules of a single compound into two or more other molecules, atoms, ions, or radicals. **b.** any decomposition of the molecules of a single compound into two or more other compounds, atoms, ions, or radicals. **3.** separation of molecules or atoms that occurs when a liquid or solid changes to a gas. **4.** *Psychiatry.* the separation of a group of mental processes or ideas from the rest of the personality, so that they lead an independent existence, as in cases of multiple personality.

dis·sol·u·ble (dɪˈsɒljʊbᵊl) *adj.* a less common word for **soluble.** [C16: from Latin *dissolūbilis,* from *dissolvere* to DISSOLVE] —**disˌsol·uˈbil·i·ty** *or* **disˈsol·u·ble·ness** *n.*

dis·so·lute (ˈdɪsəˌluːt) *adj.* given to dissipation; debauched. [C14: from Latin *dissolūtus* loose, from *dissolvere* to DISSOLVE] —**ˈdis·soˌlute·ly** *adv.* —**ˈdis·soˌlute·ness** *n.*

dis·so·lu·tion (ˌdɪsəˈluːʃən) *n.* **1.** the resolution or separation into component parts; disintegration. **2.** destruction by breaking up and dispersing. **3.** the termination of a meeting or assembly, such as Parliament. **4.** the termination of a formal or legal relationship, such as a business enterprise, marriage, etc. **5.** the state of being dissolute; dissipation. **6.** the act or process of dissolving. —**ˈdis·soˌlu·tive** *adj.*

dis·solve (dɪˈzɒlv) *vb.* **1.** to go or cause to go into solution: *salt dissolves in water; water dissolves sugar.* **2.** to become or cause to become liquid; melt. **3.** to disintegrate or disperse. **4.** to come or bring to an end. **5.** to dismiss (a meeting, parliament, etc.) or (of a meeting, etc.) to be dismissed. **6.** to collapse or cause to collapse emotionally: *to dissolve into tears.* **7.** to lose or cause to lose distinctness or clarity. **8.** (*tr.*) to terminate legally, as a marriage, etc. **9.** (*intr.*) *Films, television.* to fade out one scene and replace with another to make two scenes merge imperceptibly (**fast dissolve**) or slowly overlap (**slow dissolve**) over a period of about three or four seconds. ~*n.* **10.** *Films, television.* a scene filmed or televised by dissolving. [C14: from Latin *dissolvere* to make loose, from DIS-[1] + *solvere* to release] —**disˈsolv·a·ble** *adj.* —**disˌsolv·aˈbil·i·ty** *or* **disˈsolv·a·ble·ness** *n.* —**disˈsolv·er** *n.*

dis·sol·vent (dɪˈzɒlvənt) *n.* **1.** a rare word for **solvent** (sense 3). ~*adj.* **2.** able to dissolve.

dis·so·nance (ˈdɪsənəns) *or* **dis·so·nan·cy** *n.* **1.** a discordant combination of sounds. **2.** lack of agreement or consistency. **3.** *Music.* **a.** a sensation commonly associated with all intervals of the second and seventh, all diminished and augmented intervals, and all chords based on these intervals. Compare **consonance** (sense 3). **b.** an interval or chord of this kind.

dis·so·nant (ˈdɪsənənt) *adj.* **1.** discordant; cacophonous. **2.** incongruous or discrepant. **3.** *Music.* characterized by dissonance. [C15: from Latin *dissonāre* to be discordant, from DIS-[1] + *sonāre* to sound] —**ˈdis·so·nant·ly** *adv.*

dis·suade (dɪˈsweɪd) *vb.* (*tr.*) **1.** (often foll. by *from*) to deter (someone) by persuasion from a course of action, policy, etc. **2.** to advise against (an action, etc.). [C15: from Latin *dissuādēre,* from DIS-[1] + *suādēre* to persuade] —**disˈsuad·a·ble** *adj.* —**disˈsuad·er** *n.* —**disˈsua·sion** *n.* —**disˈsua·sive** *adj.* —**disˈsua·sive·ly** *adv.* —**disˈsua·sive·ness** *n.*

dis·syl·la·ble (dɪˈsɪləbᵊl, ˈdɪsˌsɪl-, ˈdaɪsɪl-) *or* **di·syl·la·ble** (ˈdaɪsɪləbᵊl, dɪˈsɪl-) *n. Grammar.* a word of two syllables. —**dis·syl·lab·ic** (ˌdɪsɪˈlæbɪk, ˌdɪssɪ-, ˌdaɪ-) *or* **di·syl·lab·ic** (ˌdaɪsɪˈlæbɪk, ˌdɪ-) *adj.*

dis·sym·me·try (dɪˈsɪmɪtrɪ, dɪsˈsɪm-) *n., pl.* **·tries. 1.** lack of symmetry. **2.** the relationship between two objects when one is the mirror image of the other. —**dis·sym·met·ric** (ˌdɪsɪˈmɛtrɪk, ˌdɪssɪ-) *or* **ˌdis·symˈmet·ri·cal** *adj.* —**ˌdis·symˈmet·ri·cal·ly** *adv.*

dist. *abbrev. for:* **1.** distant. **2.** distinguish(ed). **3.** district.

dis·taff (ˈdɪstɑːf) *n.* **1.** the rod on which wool, flax, etc., is wound preparatory to spinning. **2.** *Figurative.* women's work. [Old English *distæf,* from *dis-* bunch of flax + *stæf* STAFF[1]; see DIZEN]

dis·taff side *n.* the female side or branch of a family. Compare **spear side.**

dis·tal (ˈdɪstᵊl) *adj. Anatomy.* (of a muscle, bone, limb, etc.) situated farthest from the centre, median line, or point of attachment or origin. Compare **proximal.** [C19: from DISTANT + -AL[1]] —**ˈdis·tal·ly** *adv.*

dis·tance (ˈdɪstəns) *n.* **1.** the intervening space between two points or things. **2.** the length of this gap. **3.** the state of being apart in space; remoteness. **4.** an interval between two points in time. **5.** the extent of progress; advance. **6.** a distant place or time: *he lives at a distance from his work.* **7.** a separation or remoteness in relationship; disparity. **8. keep one's distance.** to maintain a proper or discreet reserve in respect of another person. **9.** *Geom.* **a.** the length of the shortest line segment joining two points. **b.** the length along a straight line or curve. **10.** (preceded by *the*) the most distant or a faraway part of the visible scene or landscape. **11.** *Horse racing.* **a.** *Brit.* a point on a racecourse 240 yards from the winning post. **b.** *Brit.* any interval of more than 20 lengths between any two finishers in a race. **c.** *U.S.* the part of a racecourse that a horse must reach in any heat before the winner passes the finishing line in order to qualify for later heats. **12. go the distance.** to be able to complete an assigned task or responsibility. **13.** the distant parts of a picture, such as a landscape. **14. middle distance. a.** (in a picture) halfway between the foreground and the horizon.

b. (in a natural situation) halfway between the observer and the horizon. **15.** (*modifier*) *Athletics.* relating to or denoting the longer races, usually those longer than a mile: *a distance runner.* ~*vb.* (*tr.*) **16.** to hold or place at a distance. **17.** to separate (oneself) mentally or emotionally from something. **18.** to outdo; outstrip.

dis·tant ('dɪstənt) *adj.* **1.** far away or apart in space or time. **2.** (*postpositive*) separated in space or time by a specified distance. **3.** apart in relevance, association, or relationship: *a distant cousin.* **4.** coming from or going to a faraway place: *a distant journey.* **5.** remote in manner; aloof. **6.** abstracted; absent: *a distant look.* [C14: from Latin *distāre* to be distant, from DIS-[1] + *stāre* to stand] —'**dis·tant·ly** *adv.* —'**dis·tant·ness** *n.*

dis·tant ear·ly warn·ing *n.* a U.S. radar detection system to warn of missile attack.

dis·taste (dɪs'teɪst) *n.* **1.** (often foll. by *for*) an absence of pleasure (in); dislike (of); aversion (to): *to look at someone with distaste.* ~*vb.* **2.** (*tr.*) an archaic word for **dislike.**

dis·taste·ful (dɪs'teɪstfʊl) *adj.* unpleasant or offensive. —**dis·'taste·ful·ly** *adv.* —**dis·'taste·ful·ness** *n.*

dis·tem·per[1] (dɪs'tɛmpə) *n.* **1.** any of various infectious diseases of animals, esp. **canine distemper,** a highly contagious viral disease of young dogs, characterized by high fever and a discharge from the nose and eyes. See also **strangles. 2.** *Archaic.* **a.** a disease or disorder. **b.** disturbance. **c.** discontent. ~*vb.* **3.** (*tr.*) *Archaic.* to disturb. [C14: from Late Latin *distemperāre* to derange the health of, from Latin DIS-[1] + *temperāre* to mix in correct proportions]

dis·tem·per[2] (dɪs'tɛmpə) *n.* **1.** a technique of painting in which the pigments are mixed with water, glue, size, etc., used for poster, mural, and scene painting. **2.** the paint used in this technique or any of various water-based paints, including, in Britain, whitewash. ~*vb.* **3.** (*tr.*) to mix (pigments) with water and size. **4.** to paint (something) with distemper. [C14: from Medieval Latin *distemperāre* to soak, from Latin DIS-[1] + *temperāre* to mingle]

dis·tend (dɪ'stɛnd) *vb.* **1.** to expand or be expanded by or as if by pressure from within; swell; inflate. **2.** (*tr.*) to stretch out or extend. **3.** (*tr.*) to magnify in importance; exaggerate. [C14: from Latin *distendere,* from DIS-[1] + *tendere* to stretch] —**dis·'tend·er** *n.* —**dis·'ten·si·ble** *adj.* —**dis·ˌten·si·'bil·i·ty** *n.* —**dis·'ten·sion** *or* **dis·'ten·tion** *n.*

dis·tich ('dɪstɪk) *n. Prosody.* a unit of two verse lines, usually a couplet. [C16: from Greek *distikhos* having two lines, from DI-[1] + *stikhos* STICH] —'**dis·ti·chal** *adj.*

dis·ti·chous ('dɪstɪkəs) *adj.* (of leaves) arranged in two vertical rows on opposite sides of the stem. —'**dis·ti·chous·ly** *adv.*

dis·til *or U.S.* **dis·till** (dɪs'tɪl) *vb.* **·tils** *or* **·tills, ·til·ling, ·tilled. 1.** to subject to or undergo distillation. See also **rectify** (sense 2). **2.** (sometimes foll. by *out* or *off*) to purify, separate, or concentrate, or be purified, separated, or concentrated by distillation. **3.** to obtain or be obtained by distillation: *to distil whisky.* **4.** to exude or give off (a substance) in drops or small quantities. **5.** (*tr.*) to extract the essence of as if by distillation. [C14: from Latin *dēstillāre* to distil, from DE- + *stillāre* to drip] —**dis·'till·a·ble** *adj.*

dis·til·late ('dɪstɪlɪt, -ˌleɪt) *n.* **1.** Also called: **distillation.** the product of distillation. **2.** a concentrated essence.

dis·til·la·tion (ˌdɪstɪ'leɪʃən) *or* **dis·till·ment** *n.* **1.** the act, process, or product of distilling. **2.** the process of evaporating or boiling a liquid and condensing its vapour. **3.** purification or separation of mixture by using different evaporation rates or boiling points of their components. See also **fractional distillation. 4.** the process of obtaining the essence or an extract of a substance, usually by heating it in a solvent. **5.** another name for **distillate** (sense 1). **6.** a concentrated essence. —**dis·'til·la·to·ry** *adj.*

dis·till·er (dɪ'stɪlə) *n.* a person or organization that distils, esp. a company that makes spirits.

dis·till·er·y (dɪ'stɪlərɪ) *n., pl.* **·er·ies.** a place where alcoholic drinks, etc., are made by distillation.

dis·tinct (dɪ'stɪŋkt) *adj.* **1.** easily sensed or understood; clear; precise. **2.** (when postpositive, foll. by *from*) not the same (as); separate (from); distinguished (from). **3.** not alike; different. **4.** sharp; clear. **5.** recognizable; definite: *a distinct improvement.* **6.** explicit; unequivocal. [C14: from Latin *distinctus, from distinguere* to DISTINGUISH] —**dis·'tinct·ly** *adv.* —**dis·'tinct·ness** *n.*

dis·tinc·tion (dɪ'stɪŋkʃən) *n.* **1.** the act or an instance of distinguishing or differentiating. **2.** a distinguishing feature. **3.** the state of being different or distinguishable. **4.** special honour, recognition, or fame. **5.** excellence of character; distinctive qualities: *a man of distinction.* **6.** distinguished appearance. **7.** a symbol of honour or rank.

dis·tinc·tive (dɪ'stɪŋktɪv) *adj.* **1.** serving or tending to distinguish. **2.** denoting one of a set of minimal features of a phoneme in a given language that serve to distinguish it from other phonemes. The distinctive features of /p/ in English are that it is voiceless, bilabial, non-nasal, and plosive; /b/ is voiced, bilabial, non-nasal, and plosive: the two differ by the distinctive feature of voice. —**dis·'tinc·tive·ly** *adv.* —**dis·'tinc·tive·ness** *n.*

dis·tin·gué *French.* (distɛ̃'ge) *adj.* distinguished or noble.

dis·tin·guish (dɪ'stɪŋgwɪʃ) *vb.* (*mainly tr.*) **1.** (when *intr.,* foll. by *between* or *among*) to make, show, or recognize a difference or differences (between or among); differentiate (between). **2.** to be a distinctive feature of; characterize. **3.** to make out; perceive. **4.** to mark for a special honour or title. **5.** to make (oneself) noteworthy: *he distinguished himself by his cowardice.* **6.** to classify; categorize: *we distinguished three species.* [C16: from Latin *distinguere* to separate, discriminate] —**dis·'tin·guish·a·ble** *adj.* —**dis·'tin·guish·a·bly** *adv.* —**dis·'tin·guish·er** *n.* —**dis·'tin·guish·ing·ly** *adv.*

dis·tin·guished (dɪ'stɪŋgwɪʃt) *adj.* **1.** noble or dignified in appearance or behaviour. **2.** eminent; famous; celebrated.

dis·tort (dɪ'stɔːt) *vb.* (*tr.*) **1.** (*often passive*) to twist or pull out of shape; make bent or misshapen; contort; deform. **2.** to alter or misrepresent (facts, motives, etc.). **3.** *Electronics.* to reproduce or amplify (a signal) inaccurately, changing the shape of the waveform. [C16: from Latin *distortus* misshapen, from *distorquēre* to turn different ways, from DIS-[1] + *torquēre* to twist] —**dis·'tort·ed** *adj.* —**dis·'tort·ed·ly** *adv.* —**dis·'tort·ed·ness** *n.* —**dis·'tort·er** *n.* —**dis·'tor·tive** *adj.*

dis·tor·tion (dɪ'stɔːʃən) *n.* **1.** the act or an instance of distorting or the state of being distorted. **2.** something that is distorted. **3.** an aberration of a lens or optical system in which the magnification varies with the lateral distance from the axis. **4.** *Electronics.* **a.** an undesired change in the shape of an electrical wave or signal. **b.** the result of such a change in waveform, esp. a loss of clarity in radio reception or sound reproduction. **5.** *Psychol.* a change in perception so that it does not correspond to reality. **6.** *Psychoanal.* the alteration of unconscious thoughts to let them appear in consciousness. —**dis·'tor·tion·al** *adj.*

distr. *abbrev. for:* **1.** distribution. **2.** distributor.

dis·tract (dɪ'strækt) *vb.* (*tr.*) **1.** (*often passive*) to draw the attention of (a person) away from something. **2.** to divide or confuse the attention of (a person). **3.** to amuse or entertain. **4.** to trouble greatly. **5.** to make mad. [C14: from Latin *distractus* perplexed, from *distrahere* to pull in different directions, from DIS-[1] + *trahere* to drag] —**dis·'tract·er** *n.* —**dis·'tract·i·ble** *adj.* —**dis·ˌtract·i·'bil·i·ty** *n.* —**dis·'tract·ing** *adj.* —**dis·'tract·ing·ly** *adv.* —**dis·'trac·tive** *adj.* —**dis·'trac·tive·ly** *adv.*

dis·tract·ed (dɪ'stræktɪd) *adj.* **1.** bewildered; confused. **2.** mad. —**dis·'tract·ed·ly** *adv.* —**dis·'tract·ed·ness** *n.*

dis·trac·tion (dɪ'strækʃən) *n.* **1.** the act or an instance of distracting or the state of being distracted. **2.** something that serves as a diversion or entertainment. **3.** an interruption; an obstacle to concentration. **4.** mental turmoil or madness.

dis·train (dɪ'streɪn) *vb. Law.* to seize (personal property) by way of distress. [C13: from Old French *destreindre,* from Latin *distringere* to impede, from DIS-[1] + *stringere* to draw tight] —**dis·'train·a·ble** *adj.* —**dis·'train·ment** *n.* —**dis·'trai·nor** *or* **dis·'train·er** *n.*

dis·train·ee (ˌdɪstreɪ'niː) *n. Law.* a person whose property has been seized by way of distraint.

dis·traint (dɪ'streɪnt) *n. Law.* the act or process of distraining; distress.

dis·trait (dɪ'streɪ; *French* di'strɛ) *adj.* absent-minded; abstracted. [C18: from French, from *distraire* to DISTRACT]

dis·traught (dɪ'strɔːt) *adj.* **1.** distracted or agitated. **2.** *Rare.* mad. [C14: changed from obsolete *distract* through influence of obsolete *straught,* past participle of STRETCH]

dis·tress (dɪ'strɛs) *vb.* (*tr.*) **1.** to cause mental pain to; upset badly. **2.** (*usually passive*) to subject to financial or other trouble. **3.** *Law.* a less common word for **distrain. 4.** *Archaic.* to compel. ~*n.* **5.** mental pain; anguish. **6.** the act of distressing or the state of being distressed. **7.** physical or financial trouble. **8. in distress.** (of a ship, aircraft, etc.) in dire need of help. **9.** *Law* **a.** the seizure and holding of property as security for payment of or in satisfaction of a debt, claim, etc.; distraint. **b.** the property thus seized. **c.** *U.S.* (*as modifier*): *distress merchandise.* [C13: from Old French *destresse* distress, via Vulgar Latin, from Latin *districtus* divided in mind; see DISTRAIN] —**dis·'tress·ful** *adj.* —**dis·'tress·ful·ly** *adv.* —**dis·'tress·ful·ness** *n.* —**dis·'tress·ing** *adj.* —**dis·'tress·ing·ly** *adv.*

dis·tressed (dɪ'strɛst) *adj.* **1.** much troubled; upset; afflicted. **2.** in financial straits; poor. **3.** *Economics.* another word for **depressed** (sense 4).

dis·tress mer·chan·dise *n. U.S.* goods sold at reduced prices in order to pay overdue debts, etc.

dis·trib·u·tar·y (dɪ'strɪbjʊtərɪ, -trɪ) *n., pl.* **·tar·ies.** one of several outlet streams draining a river, esp. on a delta.

dis·trib·ute (dɪ'strɪbjuːt) *vb.* (*tr.*) **1.** to give out in shares; dispense. **2.** to hand out or deliver: *to distribute handbills.* **3.** (*often passive*) to spread throughout a space or area: *gulls are distributed along the west coast.* **4.** (*often passive*) to divide into classes or categories; classify: *these books are distributed in four main categories.* **5.** *Printing.* to return (used type) to the correct positions in the type case. **6.** *Logic.* to use (a term) so that it refers to all members of the class it designates. **7.** *Obsolete.* to dispense (justice). [C15: from Latin *distribuere* from DIS-[1] + *tribuere* to give] —**dis·'trib·ut·a·ble** *adj.*

dis·trib·ut·ed term *n. Logic.* a term referring to every member of the class it designates, as *doctors* in *all doctors are overworked.*

dis·trib·u·tee (dɪˌstrɪbjʊ'tiː) *n. Law, chiefly U.S.* a person entitled to share in the estate of an intestate.

dis·tri·bu·tion (ˌdɪstrɪ'bjuːʃən) *n.* **1.** the act of distributing or the state or manner of being distributed. **2.** a thing or portion distributed. **3.** arrangement or location. **4.** *Commerce.* the transporting, merchandising, and marketing of goods from producer to consumer. **5.** *Economics.* the division of the total income of a community among its members, esp. between labour incomes (wages and salaries) and property incomes (rents, interest, and dividends). **6.** *Statistics.* a set of values with reference to their theoretical or observed frequency: *a* *cumulative distribution.* **7.** *Law.* the apportioning of the estate of a deceased intestate among the persons entitled to share in it. —ˌ**dis+tri+ˈbu+tion+al** *adj.*

dis+tri+bu+tion func+tion *n. Statistics.* a function obtained by summing a discrete density or integrating a continuous density from which can be derived cumulative frequencies for any value within the range of the original density. See also **density** (sense 6).

dis+trib·u+tive (dɪˈstrɪbjʊtɪv) *adj.* **1.** characterized by or relating to distribution. **2.** *Grammar.* referring separately to the individual people or items in a group, as the words *each* and *every.* **3.** *Maths., logic.* (of an operation) leading to the same result whether performed before or after a second specified operation: *multiplication is distributive over addition in a*(*b* + *c*) = *ab* + *ac.* ~*n.* **4.** *Grammar.* a distributive word. —**dis+ˈtrib·u+tive+ly** *adv.* —**dis+ˈtrib·u+tive+ness** *n.*

dis+trib·u+tor *or* **dis+trib·ut+er** (dɪˈstrɪbjʊtə) *n.* **1.** a person or thing that distributes. **2.** a wholesaler or middleman engaged in the distribution of a category of goods, esp. to retailers in a specific area. **3.** the device in a petrol engine that distributes the high-tension voltage to the sparking plugs in the sequence of the firing order.

dis+trict (ˈdɪstrɪkt) *n.* **1. a.** an area of land marked off for administrative or other purposes. **b.** (*as modifier*): *district nurse.* **2.** a locality separated by geographical attributes; region. **3.** any subdivision of any territory, region, etc. **4.** (in England and Wales) any of the subdivisions of the nonmetropolitan counties that elects a council responsible for local planning, housing, rates, etc. See also **metropolitan district.** **5.** (in Scotland until 1975) a landward division of a county. **6.** (in Scotland after 1975) any of the 47 subdivisions of the regions that elect a council responsible for environmental health services, housing, etc. **7.** any of the 26 areas into which Northern Ireland has been divided since 1973. Elected district councils are responsible for environmental health services etc. ~*vb.* **8.** (*tr.*) to divide into districts. [C17: from Medieval Latin *districtus* area of jurisdiction, from Latin *distringere* to stretch out; see DISTRAIN]

dis+trict at+tor+ney *n.* (in the U.S.) the state prosecuting officer in a specified judicial district.

dis+trict court *n.* (in the U.S.) **a.** a federal trial court serving a federal judicial district. **b.** (in some states) a court having general jurisdiction in a state judicial district.

Dis+trict of Co+lum+bi·a *n.* a federal district of the eastern U.S., coextensive with the federal capital, Washington. Pop.: 756 510 (1970). Area: 178 sq. km (69 sq. miles). Abbrevs.: **D.C.** or (with zip code) **DC.**

dis+trin+gas (dɪsˈtrɪŋgæs) *n. Law.* (formerly) a writ directing a sheriff to distrain. [from Latin: you shall distrain (the opening word of the writ)]

Dis+tri+to Fe+de+ral (*Portuguese* disˈtritu fedeˈral) *n.* a district in S central Brazil, containing Brasília: detached from Goiás state in 1960. Pop.: 538 351 (1970). Area: 5814 sq. km (2267 sq. miles).

dis+trust (dɪsˈtrʌst) *vb.* **1.** to regard as untrustworthy or dishonest. ~*n.* **2.** suspicion; doubt. —**dis+ˈtrust+er** *n.* —**dis+ˈtrust+ful** *adj.* —**dis+ˈtrust+ful+ly** *adv.* —**dis+ˈtrust+ful+ness** *n.*

dis+turb (dɪˈstɜːb) *vb.* (*tr.*) **1.** to intrude on; interrupt. **2.** to destroy or interrupt the quietness or peace of. **3.** to disarrange; muddle. **4.** (*often passive*) to upset or agitate; trouble: *I am disturbed at your bad news.* **5.** to inconvenience; put out: *don't disturb yourself on my account.* [C13: from Latin *disturbāre,* from DIS-[1] + *turbāre* to confuse] —**dis+ˈturb+er** *n.* —**dis+ˈturb+ing+ly** *adv.*

dis+turb+ance (dɪˈstɜːbəns) *n.* **1.** the act of disturbing or the state of being disturbed. **2.** an interruption or intrusion. **3.** an unruly outburst or tumult. **4.** *Law.* an interference with another's rights. **5.** *Geology.* a minor movement of the earth causing a small earthquake. **6.** *Meteorol.* a small depression. **7.** *Psychiatry.* a mental or emotional disorder.

dis+turbed (dɪˈstɜːbd) *adj. Psychiatry.* emotionally upset, troubled, or maladjusted.

di+sul+fi+ram (ˌdaɪsʌlˈfɪərəm) *n.* a drug used in the treatment of alcoholism that acts by inducing nausea and vomiting following ingestion of alcohol. [C20: from tetraethylthi*uram disulfide*]

di+sul+phate (daɪˈsʌlfeɪt) *n.* another name for **pyrosulphate.**

di+sul+phide (daɪˈsʌlfaɪd) *n.* any chemical compound containing two sulphur atoms per molecule. Also called (not in technical usage): **bisulphide.**

di+sul+phu+ric ac·id (ˌdaɪsʌlˈfjʊərɪk) *n.* another name for **pyrosulphuric acid.**

dis+u+nite (ˌdɪsjʊˈnaɪt) *vb.* **1.** to separate or become separate; disrupt. **2.** (*tr.*) to set at variance; estrange. —**dis+ˈun+ion** *n.* —ˌ**dis+u+ˈnit+er** *n.*

dis+u·ni·ty (dɪsˈjuːnɪtɪ) *n., pl.* **·ties.** dissension or disagreement.

dis+use (dɪsˈjuːs) *n.* the condition of being unused; neglect (often in the phrases **in** *or* **into disuse**).

dis+used (dɪsˈjuːzd) *adj.* no longer used: *a disused mine.*

di+syl+la+ble (ˈdaɪsɪləbᵊl, dɪˈsɪl-) *n.* a variant spelling of **dissyllable.** —**di+syl+lab+ic** (ˌdaɪsɪˈlæbɪk, ˌdɪ-) *adj.*

dit (dɪt) the short sound used, in combination with the long sound *dah,* in the spoken representation of Morse and other telegraphic codes. Compare **dot**[1] (sense 6).

di·ta (ˈdiːtə) *n.* an apocynaceous shrub, *Alstonia scholaris,* of tropical Africa and Asia, having large shiny whorled leaves and medicinal bark. [C19: from Tagalog]

ditch (dɪtʃ) *n.* **1.** a narrow channel dug in the earth, usually used for drainage, irrigation, or as a boundary marker. **2.** any small, natural waterway. **3.** *Informal.* either of the gutters at the side of a tenpin bowling lane. **4. last ditch.** a last resort or place of last defence. ~*vb.* **5.** to make a ditch or ditches in (a piece of ground). **6.** (*intr.*) to edge with a ditch. **7.** *Slang.* to crash or be crashed, esp. deliberately, as to avoid more unpleasant circumstances: *he had to ditch the car.* **8.** (*tr.*) *Slang.* to abandon or discard: *to ditch a girlfriend.* **9.** *Slang.* to land (an aircraft) on water in an emergency. **10.** (*tr.*) *U.S. slang.* to evade: *to ditch the police.* [Old English *dīc;* related to Old Saxon *dīk,* Old Norse *dīki,* Middle High German *tīch* dyke, pond, Latin *fīgere* to stick, see DYKE] —**ˈditch+er** *n.* —**ˈditch+less** *adj.*

di+the·ism (ˈdaɪθiːˌɪzəm) *n. Theol.* **1.** the belief in two equal gods. **2.** the belief that two equal principles reign over the world, one good and one evil. —**ˈdi+the·ist** *n.* —ˌ**di+the·ˈis+tic** *adj.*

dith+er (ˈdɪðə) *vb.* (*intr.*) **1.** *Chiefly Brit.* to be uncertain or indecisive. **2.** *Chiefly U.S.* to be in an agitated state. **3.** to tremble, as with cold. ~*n.* **4.** *Chiefly Brit.* a state of indecision. **5.** a state of agitation. [C17: variant of C14 (northern English dialect) *didder,* of uncertain origin] —**ˈdith+er+er** *n.*

di+thi·o+nite (daɪˈθaɪəˌnaɪt) *n.* any salt of dithionous acid. Also called: **hyposulphite, hydrosulphite.**

di+thi·o+nous ac·id (daɪˈθaɪənəs) *n.* an unstable dibasic acid known only in solution and in the form of dithionite salts. It is a powerful reducing agent. Formula: $H_2S_2O_4$. Also called: **hyposulphurous acid, hydrosulphurous acid.** [from DI-[1] + *thion-,* from Greek *theion* sulphur + -OUS]

dith·y+ramb (ˈdɪθɪˌræm, -ˌræmb) *n.* **1.** (in ancient Greece) a passionate choral hymn in honour of Dionysus; the forerunner of Greek drama. **2.** any utterance or a piece of writing that resembles this. [C17: from Latin *dīthyrambus,* from Greek *dithurambos;* related to *iambos* IAMBUS]

dith·y+ram+bic (ˌdɪθɪˈræmbɪk) *adj.* **1.** *Prosody.* of or relating to a dithyramb. **2.** passionately eloquent. —ˌ**dith·y+ˈram+bi+cal+ly** *adv.*

dit+tan+der (dɪˈtændə, ˈdɪtᵊn-) *n.* a cruciferous plant, *Lepidium latifolium,* of coastal regions of Europe, N Africa, and SW Asia, with clusters of small white flowers.

dit+ta+ny (ˈdɪtənɪ) *n., pl.* **+nies. 1.** an aromatic Cretan plant, *Origanum dictamnus,* with pink drooping flowers: formerly credited with great medicinal properties: family *Labiatae* (labiates). **2.** Also called: **stone mint.** a North American labiate plant, *Cunila origanoides,* with clusters of purplish flowers. **3.** another name for **gas plant.** [C14: from Old French *ditan,* from Latin *dictamnus,* from Greek *diktamnon,* perhaps from *Diktē,* mountain in Crete]

dit+to (ˈdɪtəʊ) *n., pl.* **+tos. 1.** the aforementioned; the above; the same. Used in accounts, lists, etc., to avoid repetition and symbolized by two small marks („) known as **ditto marks,** placed under the thing repeated. Abbrev.: **do. 2.** *Informal.* **a.** a duplicate. **b.** (*as modifier*): *a ditto copy.* ~*adv.* **3.** in the same way. ~ **4.** *sentence substitute. Informal.* used to avoid repeating or to confirm agreement with an immediately preceding sentence. ~*vb.* **+tos, +to+ing, +toed. 5.** (*tr.*) to copy; repeat. [C17: from Italian (Tuscan dialect), variant of *detto* said, from *dicere* to say, from Latin]

dit+tog+ra+phy (dɪˈtɒgrəfɪ) *n., pl.* **+phies. 1.** the unintentional repetition of letters or words. **2.** a passage of manuscript demonstrating dittography. —**dit+to+graph+ic** (ˌdɪtəˈgræfɪk) *adj.*

dit+ty (ˈdɪtɪ) *n., pl.* **+ties.** a short simple song or poem. [C13: from Old French *ditie* poem, from *ditier* to compose, from Latin *dictāre* DICTATE]

dit+ty bag *n.* a sailor's cloth bag for personal belongings or tools. A box used for these purposes is termed a **ditty box.** [C19: perhaps from obsolete *dutty* calico, from Hindi *dhōtī* loincloth, DHOTI]

Di+u (ˈdiːuː) *n.* a small island off the NW coast of India: together with a mainland area, it formed a district of Portuguese India (1535–1961); became part of the Indian Union Territory of Goa, Daman, and Diu in 1962.

di+u·re·sis (ˌdaɪjʊˈriːsɪs) *n.* excretion of an unusually large quantity of urine. [C17: from New Latin, from Greek *diourein* to urinate]

di+u·ret+ic (ˌdaɪjʊˈrɛtɪk) *adj.* **1.** acting to increase the flow of urine. ~*n.* **2.** a drug or agent that increases the flow of urine. —ˌ**di+u·ˈret·i+cal+ly** *adv.* —ˌ**di+u·ˈret·i·cal+ness** *n.*

di+ur+nal (daɪˈɜːnᵊl) *adj.* **1.** happening during the day or daily. **2.** (of flowers) open during the day and closed at night. **3.** (of animals) active during the day. ~Compare **nocturnal.** ~*n.* **4.** a service book containing all the canonical hours except matins. [C15: from Late Latin *diurnālis,* from Latin *diurnus,* from *diēs* day] —**di+ˈur+nal+ly** *adv.*

di+ur+nal par+al+lax *n.* See **parallax** (sense 2).

div[1] (dɪv) *Maths.* short for **divergence** (sense 4).

div[2] (dɪv) *n. Prison slang.* a stupid or foolish person. [C20: probably shortened and changed from DEVIANT]

div. *abbrev. for:* **1.** divide(d). **2.** dividend. **3.** division. **4.** divorce(d).

di·va (ˈdiːvə) *n., pl.* **·vas** *or* **·ve** (-vɪ). a highly distinguished female singer; prima donna. [C19: via Italian from Latin: a goddess, from *dīvus* DIVINE]

di+va+gate (ˈdaɪvəˌgeɪt) *vb. Rare.* to digress or wander. [C16: from Latin DI-[2] + *vagārī* to wander] —ˌ**di+va+ˈga+tion** *n.*

di+va+lent (daɪˈveɪlənt, ˈdaɪˌveɪ-) *adj. Chem.* **1.** having a valency of two. **2.** having two valencies. ~Also: **bivalent.** —**di+ˈva+lency** *n.*

di+van (dɪˈvæn) *n.* **1. a.** a backless sofa or couch, designed to be set against a wall. **b.** a bed resembling such a couch. **2.** (esp. formerly) a room for smoking and drinking, as in a coffee shop. **3. a.** a Muslim law court, council chamber, or counting house. **b.** a Muslim council of state. **4.** a collection of poems. **5.** (in Muslim law) an account book. ~Also (for senses 2–5): **diwan.** [C16: from Turkish *dīvān*, from Persian *dīwān*]

di+var·i+cate *vb.* (daɪˈværɪˌkeɪt). **1.** (*intr.*) (esp. of branches) to diverge at a wide angle. ~*adj.* (daɪˈværɪkɪt, -ˌkeɪt). **2.** branching widely; forked. [C17: from Latin *dīvāricāre* to stretch apart, from DI-[2] + *vāricāre* to stand astride] —**di+ˈvar·i+cate+ly** *adv.* —**di+ˈvar·i+ˌcat+ing+ly** *adv.* —**di+ˌvar·i+ˈca+tion** *n.*

di+var·i·ca+tor (daɪˈværɪˌkeɪtə) *n. Zoology.* a muscle in brachiopods that controls the opening of the shell.

dive (daɪv) *vb.* **dives, div+ing, dived** *or U.S.* **dove, dived.** (*mainly intr.*) **1.** to plunge headfirst into water. **2.** (of a submarine, swimmer, etc.) to submerge under water. **3.** (*also tr.*) to fly (an aircraft) in a steep nose-down descending path, or (of an aircraft) to fly in such a path. **4.** to rush, go, or reach quickly, as in a headlong plunge: *he dived for the ball.* **5.** (*also tr.*; foll. by *in* or *into*) to dip or put (one's hand) quickly or forcefully (into): *to dive into one's pocket.* **6.** (usually foll. by *in* or *into*) to involve oneself (in something); as in eating food. ~*n.* **7.** a headlong plunge into water, esp. one of several formalized movements executed as a sport. **8.** an act or instance of diving. **9.** a steep nose-down descent of an aircraft. **10.** *Slang.* a disreputable or seedy bar or club. **11.** *Boxing slang.* the act of a boxer pretending to be knocked down or out: *he took a dive in the fourth round.* [Old English *dȳfan*; related to Old Norse *dȳfa* to dip, Frisian *dīvi*; see DEEP, DIP]

dive-bomb *vb.* (*tr.*) to bomb (a target) using or in the manner of a dive bomber.

dive bomb+er *n.* a military aircraft designed to release its bombs on a target during a steep dive.

dive brake *n.* another name for **air brake.**

div+er (ˈdaɪvə) *n.* **1.** a person or thing that dives. **2.** a person who works or explores underwater. **3.** any aquatic bird of the genus *Gavia*, family *Gaviidae*, and order *Gaviiformes* of northern oceans, having a straight pointed bill, small wings, and a long body: noted for swiftness and skill in swimming and diving. U.S. name: **loon. 4.** any of various other diving birds.

di+verge (daɪˈvɜːdʒ) *vb.* **1.** to separate or cause to separate and go in different directions from a point. **2.** (*intr.*) to be at variance; differ: *our opinions diverge.* **3.** (*intr.*) to deviate from a prescribed course. **4.** (*intr.*) *Maths.* (of a series) to have no limit. [C17: from Medieval Latin *dīvergere*, from Latin DI-[2] + *vergere* to turn]

di+ver+gence (daɪˈvɜːdʒəns) *n.* **1.** the act or result of diverging or the amount by which something diverges. **2.** the condition of being divergent. **3.** *Meteorol.* the outflowing of airstreams from a particular area, caused by expanding air. **4.** *Maths.* **a.** the scalar product of the operator, ∇, and a vector function, ***A***, where $\nabla = \mathbf{i}\partial/\partial x + \mathbf{j}\partial/\partial y + \mathbf{k}\partial/\partial z$, and ***i, j,*** and ***k*** are unit vectors. Usually written $\nabla\boldsymbol{A}$, div ***A***. Compare **curl** (sense 12), **gradient** (sense 4). **b.** the property of being divergent. **5.** the spreading of a stream of electrons as a result of their mutual repulsion. ~Also called (for senses 1, 2): **divergency.**

di+ver+gent (daɪˈvɜːdʒənt) *adj.* **1.** diverging or causing divergence. **2.** *Maths.* (of a series) having no limit; not convergent. —**di+ˈver+gent+ly** *adv.*

di+ver+gent think+ing *n. Psychol.* thinking in which many different ideas or solutions are generated from a single idea or problem. Compare **convergent thinking.**

di+vers (ˈdaɪvəz) *determiner. Archaic or literary.* **a.** various; sundry; some. **b.** (*as pronoun; functioning as pl.*): *divers of them.* [C13: from Old French, from Latin *dīversus* turned in different directions; see DIVERT]

di+verse (daɪˈvɜːs, ˈdaɪvɜːs) *adj.* **1.** having variety; assorted. **2.** distinct in kind. [C13: from Latin *dīversus*; see DIVERS] —**di+ˈverse+ly** *adv.* —**di+ˈverse+ness** *n.*

di+ver+si+fi+ca+tion (daɪˌvɜːsɪfɪˈkeɪʃən) *n.* **1.** *Commerce.* the practice of varying products, operations, etc., in order to spread risk, expand, exploit spare capacity, etc. **2.** (in regional planning policies) the attempt to provide regions with an adequate variety of industries. **3.** the act of diversifying.

di+ver+si+form (daɪˈvɜːsɪˌfɔːm) *adj.* having various forms.

di+ver+si+fy (daɪˈvɜːsɪˌfaɪ) *vb.* **+fies, +fy+ing, +fied. 1.** (*tr.*) to create different forms of; variegate; vary. **2.** (of an enterprise) to vary (products, operations, etc.) in order to spread risk, expand, etc. **3.** to distribute (investments) among several securities in order to spread risk. [C15: from Old French *diversifier*, from Medieval Latin *dīversificāre*, from Latin *dīversus* DIVERSE + *facere* to make] —**di+ˈver+si+ˌfi+a+ble** *adj.* —**di+ˌver+si+ˌfi+a·ˈbil+i+ty** *n.* —**di+ˈver+si+ˌfi+er** *n.*

di+ver+sion (daɪˈvɜːʃən) *n.* **1.** the act of diverting from a specified course. **2.** *Chiefly Brit.* an official detour used by traffic when a main route is closed. **3.** something that distracts from business, etc.; amusement. **4.** *Military.* a feint attack designed to draw an enemy away from the main attack. —**di+ˈver+sion+al** *or* **di+ˈver+sion+ar+y** *adj.*

di+ver+si·ty (daɪˈvɜːsɪtɪ) *n.* **1.** the state or quality of being different or varied. **2.** a point of difference.

di+vert (daɪˈvɜːt) *vb.* **1.** to turn (a person or thing) aside from a course; deflect. **2.** (*tr.*) to entertain; amuse. **3.** (*tr.*) to distract the attention of. [C15: from French *divertir*, from Latin *dīvertere* to turn aside, from DI-[2] + *vertere* to turn] —**di+ˈvert+ed+ly** *adj.* —**di+ˈvert+er** *n.* —**di+ˈvert+i+ble** *adj.* —**di+ˈvert+ing+ly** *adv.* —**di+ˈver+tive** *adj.*

di+ver+tic·u+li+tis (ˌdaɪvəˌtɪkjʊˈlaɪtɪs) *n.* inflammation of one or more diverticula, esp. of the colon.

di+ver+tic·u+lo+sis (ˌdaɪvəˌtɪkjʊˈləʊsɪs) *n. Pathol.* the presence of several diverticula, esp. in the intestines. [from New Latin, from DIVERTICULUM + -OSIS]

di+ver+tic·u+lum (ˌdaɪvəˈtɪkjʊləm) *n., pl.* **+la** (-lə). any sac or pouch formed by herniation of the wall of a tubular organ or part, esp. the intestines. [C16: from New Latin, from Latin *dēverticulum* by-path, from *dēvertere* to turn aside, from *vertere* to turn] —**ˌdi+ver+ˈtic·u+lar** *adj.*

di+ver+ti+men+to (dɪˌvɜːtɪˈmɛntəʊ) *n., pl.* **+ti** (-tɪ). **1.** a piece of entertaining music in several movements, often scored for a mixed ensemble and having no fixed form. **2.** an episode in a fugue. ~See also **divertissement.** [C18: from Italian]

di+ver+tisse+ment (dɪˈvɜːtɪsmənt; *French* divɛrtisˈmɑ̃) *n.* **1.** a brief entertainment or diversion, usually between the acts of a play. **2.** *Music.* **a.** a fantasia on popular melodies; potpourri. **b.** a piece or pieces written to be played during the intervals in a play, opera, etc. **c.** another word for **divertimento.** [C18: from French: entertainment]

Di·ves (ˈdaɪviːz) *n.* **1.** a rich man in the parable in Luke 16:19–31. **2.** a very rich man.

di+vest (daɪˈvɛst) *vb.* (*tr.*; usually foll. by *of*) **1.** to strip (of clothes): *to divest oneself of one's coat.* **2.** to deprive or dispossess. **3.** *Property law.* to take away an estate or interest in property vested (in a person). [C17: changed from earlier DEVEST] —**di+ˈvest+i+ble** *adj.* —**di+vest·i+ture** (daɪˈvɛstɪtʃə), **di+ves+ture** (daɪˈvɛstʃə), *or* **di+ˈvest+ment** *n.*

di·vi (ˈdɪvɪ) *n.* an alternative spelling of **divvy.**

di+vide (dɪˈvaɪd) *vb.* **1.** to separate or be separated into parts or groups; split up; part. **2.** to share or be shared out in parts; distribute. **3.** to diverge or cause to diverge in opinion or aim: *the issue divided the management.* **4.** (*tr.*) to keep apart or be a boundary between: *the Rio Grande divides Mexico from the United States.* **5.** (*intr.*) (in Parliament and similar legislatures) to vote by separating into two groups. **6.** to categorize; classify. **7.** to calculate the quotient of (one number or quantity) and (another number or quantity) by division: *to divide 50 by 10; to divide 10 into 50; to divide by 10.* **8.** (*intr.*) to diverge: *the roads divide.* **9.** (*tr.*) to mark increments of (length, angle, etc.) as by use of an engraving machine. ~*n.* **10.** *Chiefly U.S.* an area of relatively high ground separating drainage basins; watershed. See also **continental divide. 11.** a division; split. [C14: from Latin *dīvidere* to force apart, from DI-[2] + *vid-* separate, from the source of *viduus* bereaved, *vidua* WIDOW] —**di+ˈvid+a·ble** *adj.*

di+vid+ed (dɪˈvaɪdɪd) *adj.* **1.** *Botany.* another word for **dissected** (sense 1). **2.** split; not united. —**di+ˈvid+ed+ly** *adv.* —**di+ˈvid+ed+ness** *n.*

di+vid+ed high+way *n.* the U.S. term for **dual carriageway.**

div·i+dend (ˈdɪvɪˌdɛnd) *n.* **1.** *Finance.* **a.** a distribution from the net profits of a company to its shareholders. **b.** a pro-rata portion of this distribution received by a shareholder. **2.** the share of a cooperative society's surplus allocated at the end of a period to members. **3.** *Insurance.* a sum of money distributed from a company's net profits to the holders of certain policies. **4.** something extra; bonus. **5.** a number or quantity to be divided by another number or quantity. Compare **divisor. 6.** *Law.* the proportion of an insolvent estate payable to the creditors. [C15: from Latin *dīvidendum* what is to be divided; see DIVIDE]

di+vid+er (dɪˈvaɪdə) *n.* **1.** Also called: **room divider.** an object placed to divide a room into separate areas. **2.** a person or thing that divides.

di+vid+ers (dɪˈvaɪdəz) *pl. n.* a type of compass with two pointed arms, used for measuring lines or dividing them.

div·i-div·i (ˌdɪvɪˈdɪvɪ) *n., pl.* **-div·is** *or* **-div·i. 1.** a tropical American caesalpiniaceous tree, *Caesalpinia coriaria.* **2.** the pods of this plant, which yield a substance used in tanning leather. [C19: from Spanish, of Cariban origin]

div·i+na+tion (ˌdɪvɪˈneɪʃən) *n.* **1.** the art, practice, or gift of discerning or discovering future events or unknown things, as though by supernatural powers. **2.** a prophecy. **3.** a presentiment or guess. —**di+vin·a+to·ry** (dɪˈvɪnətərɪ, -trɪ) *adj.*

di+vine (dɪˈvaɪn) *adj.* **1.** of, relating to, or characterizing God or a deity. **2.** godlike. **3.** of, relating to, or associated with religion or worship: *the divine liturgy.* **4.** of supreme excellence or worth. **5.** *Informal.* splendid; perfect. ~*n.* **6.** (*often cap.*; preceded by *the*) another term for **God. 7.** a priest, esp. one learned in theology. ~*vb.* **8.** to perceive or understand (something) by intuition or insight. **9.** to conjecture (something); guess. **10.** to discern (a hidden or future reality) as though by supernatural power. **11.** (*tr.*) to search for (underground supplies of water, metal, etc.) using a divining rod. [C14: from Latin *dīvīnus*, from *dīvus* a god; related to *deus* a god] —**di+ˈvin+a·ble** *adj.* —**di+ˈvine+ly** *adv.* —**di+ˈvine+ness** *n.* —**di+ˈvin+er** *n.*

di+vine of+fice *n.* (*sometimes cap.*) the canonical prayers (in the Roman Catholic Church those of the breviary) recited daily by priests, those in religious orders, etc.

di+vine right of kings *n. History.* the concept that the right to rule derives from God and that kings are answerable for their actions to God alone.

di+vine ser+vice *n.* a service of the Christian church, esp. one at which no sacrament is given.

div+ing bee+tle *n.* any of the aquatic predatory beetles of the widely distributed family *Dytiscidae*, characterized by flattened hindlegs adapted for swimming and diving.

div+ing bell *n.* an early diving submersible having an open bottom and being supplied with compressed air.

div+ing board *n.* a platform or springboard from which swimmers may dive.

div+ing duck *n.* any of various ducks, such as the pochard, scaup, redhead, and canvasback, that inhabit bays, estuaries, lakes, etc., and can dive and swim beneath the surface of the water.

div+ing suit *or* **dress** *n.* a waterproof suit used by divers, having a heavy detachable helmet and an air supply.

di+vin+ing rod *n.* a rod, usually a forked hazel twig, said to move or dip when held over ground in which water, metal, etc., is to be found. Also called: **dowsing rod.**

di+vin+i·ty (dɪˈvɪnɪtɪ) *n., pl.* **·ties. 1.** the nature of a deity or the state of being divine. **2.** a god or other divine being. **3.** (*often cap.; preceded by the*) another term for **God. 4.** another word for **theology.**

div·i+nize *or* **div·i+nise** (ˈdɪvɪˌnaɪz) *vb.* (*tr.*) to make divine; deify. **—ˌdiv·i+ni+ˈza+tion** *or* **ˌdiv·i+ni+ˈsa+tion** *n.*

di+vis+i·bil+i·ty (dɪˌvɪzɪˈbɪlɪtɪ) *n.* the capacity of a dividend to be exactly divided by a given number.

di+vi+si·ble (dɪˈvɪzəbᵊl) *adj.* capable of being divided, usually with no remainder. **—di+ˈvis+i·ble+ness** *n.* **—di+ˈvis+i·bly** *adv.*

di+vi+sion (dɪˈvɪʒən) *n.* **1.** the act of dividing or state of being divided. **2.** the act of sharing out; distribution. **3.** something that divides or keeps apart, such as a boundary. **4.** one of the parts, groups, etc., into which something is divided. **5.** a part of a government, business, country, etc., that has been made into a unit for administrative, political, or other reasons. **6.** a formal vote in Parliament or a similar legislative body. **7.** a difference of opinion, esp. one that causes separation. **8.** (in sports) a section, category, or class organized according to age, weight, skill, etc. **9.** a mathematical operation, the inverse of multiplication, in which the quotient of two numbers or quantities is calculated. Usually written: $a \div b$, $\frac{a}{b}$, a/b. **10. a.** *Army.* a major formation, larger than a regiment but smaller than a corps, containing the necessary arms to sustain combat. **b.** *Navy.* a group of ships of similar type or a tactical unit of naval aircraft. **c.** *Air Force.* an organization normally comprising two or more wings with required support units. **11.** *Biology.* a major taxonomic division of the plant kingdom that contains one or more classes and corresponds to a phylum. **12.** *Horticulture.* any type of propagation in plants in which a new plant grows from a separated part of the original. **13.** (esp. in 17th-century English music) the art of breaking up a melody into quick phrases, esp. over a ground bass. [C14: from Latin *dīvīsiō*, from *dīvidere* to DIVIDE] **—di+ˈvi+sion+al** *or* **di+ˈvi+sion+ar·y** *adj.* **—di+ˈvi+sion+al+ly** *adv.*

di+vi+sion+ism (dɪˈvɪʒəˌnɪzəm) *n.* the pointillism of Seurat and his followers. **—di+ˈvi+sion+ist** *n., adj.*

di+vi+sion sign *n.* the symbol ÷, placed between the dividend and the divisor to indicate division, as in $12 \div 6 = 2$.

di+vi+sive (dɪˈvaɪsɪv) *adj.* **1.** causing or tending to cause disagreement or dissension. **2.** *Archaic.* having the quality of distinguishing. **—di+ˈvi+sive+ly** *adv.* **—di+ˈvi+sive+ness** *n.*

di+vi+sor (dɪˈvaɪzə) *n.* **1.** a number or quantity to be divided into another number or quantity (the dividend). **2.** a number that is a factor of another number.

di+vorce (dɪˈvɔːs) *n.* **1.** the dissolution of a marriage by judgment of a court or by accepted custom. **2.** a judicial decree declaring a marriage to be dissolved. **3.** a separation, esp. one that is total or complete. *~vb.* **4.** to separate or be separated by divorce; give or obtain a divorce (to a couple or from one's spouse). **5.** (*tr.*) to remove or separate, esp. completely. [C14: from Old French, from Latin *dīvortium* from *dīvertere* to separate; see DIVERT] **—di+ˈvorce+a·ble** *adj.* **—di+ˈvorc+er** *n.* **—di+ˈvor+cive** *adj.*

di+vor+cée (dɪvɔːˈsiː) *or* (*masc.*) **di+vor+cé** (dɪˈvɔːseɪ) *n.* a person who has been divorced.

di+vorce+ment (dɪˈvɔːsmənt) *n.* a less common word for **divorce.**

div+ot (ˈdɪvət) *n.* a piece of turf dug out of a grass surface, esp. by a golf club or by horses' hooves. [C16: from Scottish, of obscure origin]

di+vul+gate (dɪˈvʌlgeɪt) *vb.* (*tr.*) *Archaic.* to make publicly known. [C16: from Latin *dīvulgāre*; see DIVULGE] **—di+ˈvul+ga+tor** *or* **di+ˈvul+gat+er** *n.* **—ˌdiv+ul+ˈga+tion** *n.*

di+vulge (daɪˈvʌldʒ) *vb.* (*tr.; may take a clause as object*) to make known (something private or secret); disclose. [C15: from Latin *dīvulgāre*, from DI-² + *vulgāre* to spread among the people, from *vulgus* the common people] **—di+ˈvul+gence** *or* **di+ˈvulge+ment** *n.* **—di+ˈvulg+er** *n.*

di+vul+sion (daɪˈvʌlʃən) *n.* a tearing or pulling apart. [C17: from Latin *dīvulsiō*, from *dīvulsus* torn apart, from *dīvellere* to rend, from DI-² + *vellere* to pull] **—di+ˈvul+sive** *adj.*

div+vy (ˈdɪvɪ) *Informal.* *~n. pl.* **+vies. 1.** *Brit.* short for **dividend,** esp. (formerly) one paid by a cooperative society. **2.** *U.S.* a share; portion. *~vb.* **+vies, +vy+ing, +vied. 3.** (*tr.; usually foll. by up*) *U.S.* to divide and share.

di+wan (dɪˈwɑːn) *n.* a variant spelling of **dewan** or **divan** (senses 2–5).

dix·ie (ˈdɪksɪ) *n.* **1.** *Chiefly military.* a large metal pot for cooking, brewing tea, etc. **2.** a mess tin. [C19: from Hindi *degcī*, diminutive of *degcā* pot]

Dix·ie (ˈdɪksɪ) *n.* **1.** Also called: **Dixieland.** the southern states of the U.S.; the states that joined the Confederacy during the Civil War. **2.** a song adopted as a marching tune by the Confederate states during the American Civil War. *~adj.* **3.** of, relating to, or characteristic of the southern states of the U.S. [C19: perhaps from the nickname of New Orleans, from *dixie* a ten-dollar bill printed there, from French *dix* ten]

Dix·ie+land (ˈdɪksɪˌlænd) *n.* **1.** a kind of jazz derived from the New Orleans tradition of harmony and ensemble playing, but with more emphasis on melody regular rhythms, etc. **2.** See **Dixie** (sense 1).

D.I.Y. *or* **d.i.y.** (in Britain) *abbrev. for* do-it-yourself.

Di+yar+ba+kir *or* **Di+yar+be·kir** (diːˈjɑːbɛkɪə) *n.* a city in SE Turkey, on the River Tigris: ancient black basalt walls. Pop.: 169 535 (1975). Ancient name: **Amida.**

di+zen (ˈdaɪzᵊn) *vb.* (*tr.*) another word for **bedizen.** [C16: from Middle Dutch *dīsen* to dress a distaff with flax; see DISTAFF] **—ˈdi+zen+ment** *n.*

diz+zy (ˈdɪzɪ) *adj.* **+zi+er, +zi+est. 1.** affected with a whirling or reeling sensation; giddy. **2.** mentally confused or bewildered. **3.** causing or tending to cause vertigo or bewilderment. **4.** *Informal.* foolish or flighty. *~vb.* **+zies, +zy+ing, +zied. 5.** (*tr.*) to make dizzy. [Old English *dysig* silly; related to Old High German *tusīg* weak, Old Norse *dos* quiet] **—ˈdiz+zi+ly** *adv.* **—ˈdiz+zi+ness** *n.*

D.J. *or* **d.j.** *abbrev. for:* **1.** dinner jacket. **2.** disc jockey.

Djai+lo+lo *or* **Ji+lo+lo** (dʒaɪˈləʊləʊ) *n.* the Dutch name for **Halmahera.**

Dja+ja (ˈdʒɑːdʒə) *n.* **Mount.** a mountain in E Indonesia, in West Irian in the Sudirman Range: the highest mountain in New Guinea. Height: 5029 m (16 503 ft.). Former names: (Mount) **Carstensz, Sukarno Peak.**

Dja+ja+pu+ra (ˌdʒɑːdʒɑːˈpʊərə) *n.* a port in NE Indonesia, capital of West Irian, on the N coast. Former names: **Sukarnapura, Kotabaru, Hollandia.**

Dja+kar+ta *or* **Ja+kar+ta** (dʒəˈkɑːtə) *n.* the capital of Indonesia, in N West Java: founded in 1619 and ruled by the Dutch until 1945; the chief trading centre of the East in the 17th century; University of Indonesia (1947). Pop.: 4 576 009 (1971). Former name (until 1949): **Batavia.**

Djam+bi *or* **Jam+bi** (ˈdʒæmbɪ) *n.* a port in W Indonesia, in SE Sumatra on the Hari River. Pop.: 158 559 (1971). Also called: **Telanaipura.**

djeb+el (ˈdʒɛbᵊl) *n.* a variant spelling of **jebel.**

Djer+ba *or* **Jer+ba** (ˈdʒɜːbə) *n.* an island off the SE coast of Tunisia, in the Gulf of Gabès: traditionally Homer's land of the lotus-eaters. Pop.: 65 533 (1966). Area: 510 sq. km (197 sq. miles). Ancient name: **Meninx.**

Dji+bou+ti *or* **Ji+bou+ti** (dʒɪˈbuːtɪ) *n.* **1.** a republic in E Africa, on the Gulf of Aden: a French overseas territory (1946–77); became independent in 1977; mainly desert. Official language: Arabic. Currency: Djibouti franc. Capital: Djibouti. Pop.: 104 000 (1974 UN est.). Area: 23 000 sq. km (8500 sq. miles). Former name (until 1977): (Territory of the) **Afars and the Issas. 2.** the capital of Djibouti, a port on the Gulf of Aden: an outlet for Ethiopian merchandise. Pop.: 62 000 (1970 est.).

djin+ni *or* **djin+ny** (dʒɪˈniː, ˈdʒɪnɪ) *n., pl.* **djinn** (dʒɪn). variant spellings of **jinni.**

Djok+ja+kar+ta (ˌdʒəʊkjɑːˈkɑːtɑː, ˌdʒɒk-) *n.* a variant spelling of **Jogjakarta.**

DK *international car registration for* Denmark.

dk. *abbrev. for:* **1.** dark. **2.** deck. **3.** dock.

D/L *abbrev. for* demand loan.

D.Litt. *or* **D.Lit.** *abbrev. for:* **1.** Doctor of Letters. **2.** Doctor of Literature. [Latin *Doctor Litterarum*]

D.L.P. (formerly) *abbrev. for* Democratic Labor Party (of Australia).

dlr. *abbrev. for* dealer.

dlvy. *abbrev. for* delivery.

dm *abbrev. for* decimetre.

DM *abbrev. for* Deutsche Mark.

DMA *Computer technol. abbrev. for* direct memory access.

D.M.K. (in India) *abbrev. for* Dravida Munnetra Kazgham: a political party in the state of Tamil Nadu.

D.M.S. (in Britain) *abbrev. for* Diploma in Management Studies.

DMSO *abbrev. for* dimethylsulphoxide.

D.Mus. *or* **DMus** *abbrev. for* Doctor of Music.

DMZ *abbrev. for* demilitarized zone.

DNA *n.* deoxyribonucleic acid; a nucleic acid that is the main constituent of the chromosomes of all organisms (except some viruses). The DNA molecule consists of two polynucleotide chains in the form of a double helix, containing phosphate and the sugar deoxyribose and linked by hydrogen bonds between the complementary bases adenine and thymine or cytosine and guanine. DNA is self-replicating, plays a central role in protein synthesis, and is responsible for the transmission of hereditary characteristics from parents to offspring. See also **genetic code.**

Dne+pro+dzer+zhinsk (*Russian* dnɪprədzɪrˈʒinsk) *n.* an industrial city in the SW Soviet Union, in the E central Ukrainian SSR on the Dnieper River. Pop.: 245 000 (1975 est.).

Dne+pro+pe·trovsk (*Russian* dnɪprəpɪˈtrɔfsk) *n.* a city in the SW Soviet Union, in the E central Ukrainian SSR on the Dnieper River: a major centre of the metallurgical industry. Pop.: 958 000 (1975 est.). Former name (1787–1796, 1802–1926): **Yekaterinoslav.**

Dnie+per (ˈdniːpə) *n.* a river in the W Soviet Union, rising in the Valdai Hills NE of Smolensk and flowing south to the Black Sea: the third longest river in Europe; a major navigable waterway. Length: 2286 km (1420 miles). Russian name: **Dnepr** (dnjɛpr).

Dnie+ster (ˈdniːstə) *n.* a river in the SW Soviet Union, rising in the Carpathian Mountains and flowing generally southeast to the Black Sea. Length: 1411 km (877 miles). Russian name: **Dnestr** (dnjɛstr).

D-no·tice *n. Brit.* an official notice sent to newspapers, etc., prohibiting the publication of certain security information. [C20: from their administrative classification letter]

D.N.S. (in Britain) *abbrev. for* Department for National Savings.

do[1] (du:; *unstressed* dʊ, də) *vb.* **does, do+ing, did, done. 1.** to perform or complete (a deed or action): *to do a portrait; the work is done.* **2.** (often *intr.;* foll. by *for*) to serve the needs of; be suitable for (a person, situation, etc.); suffice: *there isn't much food, but it'll do for the two of us.* **3.** (*tr.*) to arrange or fix: *you should do the garden now.* **4.** (*tr.*) to prepare or provide; serve: *this restaurant doesn't do lunch on Sundays.* **5.** (*tr.*) to make tidy, elegant, ready, etc., as by arranging or adorning: *to do one's hair.* **6.** (*tr.*) to improve (esp. in the phrase **do something to** *or* **for**). **7.** (*tr.*) to find an answer to (a problem or puzzle). **8.** (*tr.*) to translate or adapt the form or language of: *the book was done into a play.* **9.** (*intr.*) to conduct oneself: *do as you please.* **10.** (*intr.*) to fare or manage: *how are you doing these days?* **11.** (*tr.*) to cause or produce: *complaints do nothing to help.* **12.** (*tr.*) to give or render: *your portrait doesn't do you justice; do me a favour.* **13.** (*tr.*) to work at, esp. as a course of study or a profession: *he is doing chemistry; what do you do for a living?* **14.** (*tr.*) to perform (a play, etc.); act: *they are doing "Hamlet" next week.* **15.** (*tr.*) to travel at a specified speed, esp. as a maximum: *this car will do 120 mph.* **16.** (*tr.*) to travel or traverse (a distance): *we did 15 miles on our walk.* **17.** (takes an infinitive without *to*) used as an auxiliary before the subject of an interrogative sentence as a way of forming a question: *do you agree? when did John go out?* **18.** (takes an infinitive without *to*) used as an auxiliary to intensify positive statements and commands: *I do like your new house; do hurry!* **19.** (takes an infinitive without *to*) used as an auxiliary before a negative adverb to form negative statements or commands: *he does not like cheese; do not leave me here alone!* **20.** (takes an infinitive without *to*) used as an auxiliary in inverted constructions: *little did he realize that; only rarely does he come in before ten o'clock.* **21.** used as an auxiliary to replace an earlier verb or verb phrase to avoid repetition: *he likes you as much as I do.* **22.** (*tr.*) *Informal.* to visit or explore as a sightseer or tourist: *to do Westminster Abbey.* **23.** (*tr.*) to wear out; exhaust. **24.** (*intr.*) to happen (esp. in the phrase **nothing doing**). **25.** (*tr.*) *Slang.* to serve (a specified period) as a prison sentence: *he's doing three years for burglary.* **26.** (*tr.*) *Slang.* to cheat or swindle. **27.** (*tr.*) *Slang.* to rob: *they did three shops last night.* **28.** (*tr.*) *Austral. slang.* to lose or spend (money) completely. **29.** (*tr.*) *Slang, chiefly Brit.* to treat violently; assault. **30.** (*tr.*) *Taboo slang.* (of a male) to have sexual intercourse with. **31. do (a).** *Informal.* act like; imitate: *he's a good mimic—he can do all his friends well.* **32. do or die.** to make a final or supreme effort. **33. how do you do?** a conventional formula when being introduced. **34. make do.** to manage with whatever is available. ~*n., pl.* **dos** *or* **do's. 35.** *Slang.* an act or instance of cheating or swindling. **36.** *Informal, chiefly Brit.* a formal or festive gathering; party. **37. do's and don'ts.** *Informal.* those things that should or should not be done; rules. ~See also **do away with, do by, do down, do for, do in, done, do out, do over, do up, do with, do without.** [Old English *dōn;* related to Old Frisian *duān,* Old High German *tuon,* Latin *abdere* to put away, Greek *tithenai* to place; see DEED, DOOM]

do[2] (dəʊ) *n., pl.* **dos.** a variant spelling of **doh.**

do. *abbrev. for* ditto.

D.O. *abbrev. for:* **1.** Doctor of Optometry. **2.** Doctor of Osteopathy.

D/O *or* **d.o.** *Commerce. abbrev. for* delivery order.

D.O.A. *abbrev. for* dead on arrival.

do·ab ('dəʊɑ:b) *n.* the alluvial land between two converging rivers, esp. the area between the Ganges and Jumna in N India. [C20: from Persian *dōāb,* from *dō* two + *āb* water]

do+a·ble ('du:əbᵊl) *adj.* capable of being done; practical.

do away with *vb.* (*intr., adv.* + *prep.*) **1.** to kill or destroy. **2.** to discard or abolish.

dob·ber-in (ˌdɒbə'rɪn) *n. Austral. slang.* an informant or traitor. Sometimes shortened to **dobber.**

dob+bin ('dɒbɪn) *n.* a name for a horse, esp. a workhorse, often used in children's tales, etc. [C16: from *Robin,* pet form of *Robert*]

dob+by ('dɒbɪ) *n., pl.* **+bies.** an attachment to a loom, used in weaving small figures. [C17: perhaps from *Dobby,* pet form of *Robert*]

Do·bell's so+lu+tion ('dəʊbəlz) *n.* a solution of sodium borate, sodium bicarbonate, phenol, and glycerol, used as an astringent or antiseptic wash for the throat and nose. [C19: named after Horace B. *Dobell* (1828–1917), British physician]

Do+ber+man pin+scher ('dəʊbəmən 'pɪnʃə) *n.* a fairly large breed of dog, originally from Germany, with a glossy black-and-tan coat, used as a watchdog. [C19: named after L. *Dobermann,* 19th-century German dog breeder who bred it + *Pinscher,* perhaps after *Pinzgau,* district in Austria]

dob in *vb. Austral. slang.* **1.** (*tr., adv.*) to inform against or report, esp. to the police. **2.** (*adv.*) to contribute to a fund for a specific purpose.

do+bla ('dəʊblɑ:) *n.* a medieval Spanish gold coin, probably worth 20 maravedis. [Spanish, from Latin *dupla,* feminine of *duplus* twofold, DOUBLE]

do+blón (də'bləʊn; *Spanish* do'blon) *n.* a variant spelling of **doubloon.** [Spanish; see DOUBLOON]

Do+bro ('dəʊbrəʊ) *n., pl.* **+bros.** *Trademark.* an acoustic guitar having a metal resonator built into the body.

Do+bru+ja (*Bulgarian* 'dɔbruja) *n.* a region of E Europe, between the River Danube and the Black Sea: the north passed to Rumania and the south to Bulgaria after the Berlin Congress (1878). Rumanian name: **Do+bro+gea** (do'brodʒa).

dob·son+fly ('dɒbsᵊnˌflaɪ) *n., pl.* **+flies.** *U.S.* a large North American neuropterous insect, *Corydalis cornutus:* the male has elongated horn-like mouthparts and the larva (a **hellgrammite** or **dobson**) is used as bait by anglers: suborder *Megaloptera.*

do by *vb.* (*intr., prep.*) to treat in the manner specified: *employers do well by hard working employees.*

doc (dɒk) *n. Informal.* short for **doctor,** esp. a medical doctor: often used as a term of address.

doc. *abbrev. for* document.

do+cent (dəʊ'sɛnt; *German* dɔ'tsɛnt) *n.* (in the U.S.) a lecturer in some colleges or universities. [C19: from German *Dozent,* from Latin *docēns* from *docēre* to teach] —**'do+cent+ˌship** *n.*

Do+ce·tism ('dəʊsɪˌtɪzəm) *n.* (in the early Christian Church) a heresy that the humanity of Christ, his sufferings, and his death were apparent rather than real. [C19: from Medieval Latin *Docētae,* from Greek *Dokētai,* from *dokein* to seem]

doc+ile ('dəʊsaɪl) *adj.* **1.** easy to manage, control, or discipline; submissive. **2.** *Rare.* ready to learn; easy to teach. [C15: from Latin *docilis* easily taught, from *docēre* to teach] —**'doc+ile+ly** *adv.* —**do+cil+i·ty** (dɒʊ'sɪlɪtɪ) *n.*

dock[1] (dɒk) *n.* **1.** a wharf or pier. **2.** a space between two wharves or piers for the mooring of ships. **3.** an area of water that can accommodate a ship and can be closed off to allow regulation of the water level. **4.** short for **dry dock. 5. in** *or* **into dock.** *Brit. informal.* **a.** (of people) in hospital. **b.** (of cars, etc.) in a repair shop. **6.** short for **scene dock. 7.** *Chiefly U.S.* a platform from which lorries, goods trains, etc., are loaded and unloaded. ~*vb.* **8.** to moor (a vessel) at a dock or (of a vessel) to be moored at a dock. **9.** to put (a vessel) into a dry dock for repairs or (of a vessel) to come into a dry dock. **10.** (of two spacecraft) to link together in space or link together (two spacecraft) in space. [C14: from Middle Dutch *docke;* perhaps related to Latin *ducere* to lead]

dock[2] (dɒk) *n.* **1.** the bony part of the tail of an animal, esp. a dog or sheep. **2.** the part of an animal's tail left after the major part of it has been cut off. ~*vb.* (*tr.*) **3.** to remove (the tail or part of the tail) of (an animal) by cutting through the bone: *to dock a tail; to dock a horse.* **4.** to deduct (an amount) from (a person's wages, pension, etc.): *they docked a third of his wages.* [C14: *dok* of uncertain origin]

dock[3] (dɒk) *n.* an enclosed space in a court of law where the accused sits or stands during his trial. [C16: from Flemish *dok* sty]

dock[4] (dɒk) *n.* **1.** any of various temperate weedy plants of the polygonaceous genus *Rumex,* having greenish or reddish flowers and typically broad leaves. **2.** any of several similar or related plants. [Old English *docce;* related to Middle Dutch, Old Danish *docke,* Gaelic *dogha*]

dock+age[1] ('dɒkɪdʒ) *n.* **1.** a charge levied upon a vessel for using a dock. **2.** facilities for docking vessels. **3.** the practice of docking vessels.

dock+age[2] ('dɒkɪdʒ) *n.* **1.** a deduction, as from a price or wages. **2.** *Agriculture.* the seeds of weeds and other waste material in commercial seeds, removable by normal cleaning methods.

dock+er[1] ('dɒkə) *n. Brit.* a man employed in the loading or unloading of ships. U.S. equivalent: **longshoreman.** See also **stevedore.**

dock+er[2] ('dɒkə) *n.* a person or thing that docks something, such as the tail of a horse.

dock+et ('dɒkɪt) *n.* **1.** *Chiefly Brit.* a piece of paper accompanying or referring to a package or other delivery, stating contents, delivery instructions, etc., sometimes serving as a receipt. **2.** *Law.* **a.** an official summary of the proceedings in a court of justice. **b.** a register containing such a summary. **3.** *Brit.* **a.** a customs certificate declaring that duty has been paid. **b.** a certificate giving particulars of a shipment and allowing its holder to obtain a delivery order. **4.** a summary of contents, as in a document. **5.** *U.S.* a list of things to be done. **6.** *U.S. law.* **a.** a list of cases awaiting trial. **b.** the names of the parties to pending litigation. ~*vb.* (*tr.*) **7.** to fix a docket to (a package, etc.). **8.** *Law.* **a.** to make a summary of (a document, judgment, etc.). **b.** to abstract and enter in a book or register. **9.** to endorse (a document, etc.) with a summary. [C15: of unknown origin]

dock+land ('dɒkˌlænd) *n.* the area around the docks.

dock+yard ('dɒkˌjɑ:d) *n.* a naval establishment with docks, workshops, etc., for the building, fitting out, and repair of vessels.

doc+tor ('dɒktə) *n.* **1.** a person licensed to practise medicine. **2.** a person who has been awarded a higher academic degree in any field of knowledge. **3.** *Chiefly U.S.* a person licensed to practise dentistry or veterinary medicine. **4.** (*often cap.*) Also called: **Doctor of the Church.** a title given to any of several of the leading Fathers or theologians in the history of the Christian Church down to the late Middle Ages whose teachings have greatly influenced orthodox Christian thought. **5.** *Angling.* any of various gaudy artificial flies. **6.** *Informal.* a person who mends or repairs things. **7.** *Slang.* a cook on a ship or at a camp. **8.** *Archaic.* a man, esp. a teacher, of learning. **9.** a device used for local repair of electroplated surfaces, consisting of an anode of the plating material embedded in an absorbent material containing the solution. **10. go for the doctor.** *Austral. slang.* to make a great effort or move very fast, esp. in a horse race. **11. what the doctor ordered.** something needed or desired. **12. you're the doctor.** you are to make the decision. ~*vb.* **13.** (*tr.*) **a.** to give medical treatment to. **b.** to prescribe for (a disease or disorder). **14.** (*intr.*) *Informal.* to practise medicine: *he doctored in Easter Island for six years.* **15.** (*tr.*) to repair or mend, esp. in a makeshift manner. **16.** (*tr.*) to make different in order to deceive. **17.** (*tr.*) to adapt for a desired end, effect, etc. **18.** (*tr.*) *Informal.* to castrate (a cat, dog, etc.). [C14: from Latin: teacher, from *docēre* to teach] —**'doc·tor·al** *or* **doc·to·ri·al** (dɒk'tɔːrɪəl) *adj.*

doc·tor·ate ('dɒktərɪt, -trɪt) *n.* the highest academic degree in any field of knowledge. Also called: **doctor's degree.**

Doc·tor of Phi·los·o·phy *n.* a doctorate awarded for original research in any subject except law, medicine, or theology. Abbrevs.: **Ph.D., D.Phil.**

doc·tri·naire (ˌdɒktrɪ'nɛə) *adj.* **1.** stubbornly insistent on the observation of the niceties of a theory, esp. without regard to practicality, suitability, etc. **2.** theoretical; impractical. ~*n.* **3.** a person who stubbornly attempts to apply a theory without regard to practical difficulties. —ˌ**doc·tri·'nair·ism** *or* ˌ**doc·tri·'nar·ism** *n.* —ˌ**doc·tri·'nar·i·an** *n.*

doc·trine ('dɒktrɪn) *n.* **1.** a creed or body of teachings of a religious, political, or philosophical group presented for acceptance or belief; dogma. **2.** a principle or body of principles that is taught or advocated. [C14: from Old French, from Latin *doctrīna* teaching, from *doctor* see DOCTOR] —**doc·tri·nal** (dɒk'traɪnᵊl) *adj.* —**doc·tri·nal·i·ty** (ˌdɒktrɪ'nælɪtɪ) *n.* —**doc·'tri·nal·ly** *adv.* —**'doc·trin·ism** *n.* —**'doc·trin·ist** *n.*

doc·trine of de·scent *n.* the theory that animals and plants arose by descent from previously existing organisms; theory of evolution.

doc·u·ment *n.* ('dɒkjʊmənt). **1.** a piece of paper, booklet, etc., providing information, esp. of an official or legal nature. **2.** *Archaic.* evidence; proof. ~*vb.* ('dɒkjʊˌmɛnt). (*tr.*) **3.** to record or report in detail, as in the press, on television, etc.: *the trial was well documented by the media.* **4.** to support (statements in a book) with citations, references, etc. **5.** to support (a claim, etc.) with evidence or proof. **6.** to furnish (a vessel) with official documents specifying its ownership, registration, weight, dimensions, and function. [C15: from Latin *documentum* a lesson, from *docēre* to teach]

doc·u·men·ta·ry (ˌdɒkjʊ'mɛntərɪ, -trɪ) *adj.* **1.** Also: **documental.** consisting of, derived from, or relating to documents. **2.** presenting factual material with little or no fictional additions: *the book gives a documentary account of the massacre.* ~*n., pl.* **·ries. 3.** a factual film or television programme about an event, person, etc., presenting the facts with little or no fiction. —ˌ**doc·u·'men·ta·ri·ly** *adv.*

doc·u·men·ta·tion (ˌdɒkjʊmɛn'teɪʃən) *n.* **1.** the act of supplying with or using documents or references. **2.** the documents or references supplied. **3.** the furnishing and use of documentary evidence, as in a court of law.

DOD (in the U.S.) *abbrev. for* Department of Defense.

dod·der¹ ('dɒdə) *vb.* (*intr.*) **1.** to move unsteadily; totter. **2.** to shake or tremble, as from age. [C17: variant of earlier *dadder;* related to Norwegian *dudra* to tremble] —**'dod·der·er** *n.* —**'dod·der·y** *adj.*

dod·der² ('dɒdə) *n.* any rootless parasitic plant of the convolvulaceous genus *Cuscuta,* lacking chlorophyll and having slender twining stems with suckers for drawing nourishment from the host plant, scalelike leaves, and whitish flowers. [C13: of Germanic origin; related to Middle Dutch, Middle Low German *dodder,* Middle High German *toter*]

dod·der·ing ('dɒdərɪŋ) *adj.* shaky, feeble, or infirm, esp. from old age.

dod·dle ('dɒdᵊl) *n. Brit. slang.* something easily accomplished.

do·dec·a- *n. combining form.* indicating twelve: *dodecagon; dodecahedron; dodecaphonic.* [from Greek *dōdeka* twelve]

do·dec·a·gon (dəʊ'dɛkəˌgɒn) *n.* a polygon having twelve sides. —**do·de·cag·o·nal** (ˌdəʊdɛ'kægənᵊl) *adj.*

do·dec·a·he·dron (ˌdəʊdɛkə'hiːdrən) *n.* a solid figure having twelve plane faces. A **regular dodecahedron** has regular pentagons as faces. See also **polyhedron.** —ˌ**do·dec·a·'he·dral** *adj.*

Do·dec·a·nese (ˌdəʊdɪkə'niːz) *pl. n.* a group of islands in the SE Aegean Sea, forming a department of Greece: part of the Southern Sporades. Capital: Rhodes. Pop.: 120 258 (1971). Area: 2663 sq. km (1028 sq. miles). Modern Greek name: **Dhodhękánisos.**

do·dec·a·no·ic ac·id (ˌdəʊdɛkə'nəʊɪk) *n.* a crystalline fatty acid found as glycerides in many vegetable oils: used in making soaps, insecticides, and synthetic resins. Formula: $CH_3(CH_2)_{10}COOH$. Also called: **lauric acid.** C20: from *dodecane* (see DODECA-, -ANE)]

do·dec·a·phon·ic (ˌdəʊdɛkə'fɒnɪk) *adj.* of or relating to the twelve-tone system of serial music. —ˌ**do·dec·a·'phon·ism** *n.* —ˌ**do·dec·a·'phon·ist** *n.* —ˌ**do·dec·a·'phon·y** *n.*

do·dec·a·syl·la·ble (ˌdəʊdɛkə'sɪləbᵊl) *n. Prosody.* a line of twelve syllables.

dodge (dɒdʒ) *vb.* **1.** to avoid or attempt to avoid (a blow, discovery, etc.), as by moving suddenly. **2.** to evade (questions, etc.) by cleverness or trickery. **3.** (*intr.*) *Change-ringing.* to make a bell change places with its neighbour when sounding in successive changes. **4.** (*tr.*) *Photog.* to lighten or darken (selected areas on a print) by manipulating the light from an enlarger. ~*n.* **5.** a plan or expedient contrived to deceive. **6.** a sudden evasive or hiding movement. **7.** a clever contrivance. **8.** *Change-ringing.* the act of dodging. [C16: of unknown origin]

dodge ball *n.* a game in which the players form a circle and try to hit opponents in the circle with a large ball.

Dodge Cit·y *n.* a city in SW Kansas, on the Arkansas River: famous as a frontier town on the Santa Fe Trail. Pop.: 14 127 (1970).

Dodg·em ('dɒdʒəm) *n. Trademark.* another name for **bumper car.**

dodg·er ('dɒdʒə) *n.* **1.** a person who evades or shirks. **2.** a shifty dishonest person. **3.** a canvas shelter, mounted on a ship's bridge or over the companionway of a sailing yacht to protect the helmsman from bad weather. **4.** *Dialect.* food, esp. bread.

Dodg·son ('dɒdʒsən) *n.* **Charles Lut·widge** ('lʌtwɪdʒ). the original name of (Lewis) **Carroll.**

dodg·y ('dɒdʒɪ) *adj.* **dodg·i·er, dodg·i·est.** *Brit. informal.* **1.** risky, difficult, or dangerous. **2.** uncertain or unreliable; tricky.

do·do ('dəʊdəʊ) *n., pl.* **do·dos** *or* **do·does. 1.** any flightless bird, esp. *Raphus cucullatus,* of the recently extinct family *Raphidae* of Mauritius and adjacent islands: order *Columbiformes* (pigeons, etc.). They had a hooked bill, short stout legs, and greyish plumage. See also **ratite. 2.** *Informal.* an intensely conservative or reactionary person who is unaware of changing fashions, ideas, etc. **3. (as) dead as a dodo.** (of a person or thing) irretrievably dead or defunct. [C17: from Portuguese *doudo,* from *duodo* stupid] —**'do·do·ism** *n.*

Do·do·ma ('doudəmə) *n.* a town in central Tanzania, the proposed new capital of the country. Pop.: 20 000 (1973 est.).

Do·do·na (dəʊ'dəʊnə) *n.* an ancient Greek town in Epirus: seat of an ancient sanctuary and oracle of Zeus and later the religious centre of Pyrrhus' kingdom. —**Do·do·nae·an** *or* **Do·do·ne·an** (ˌdəʊdəʊ'niːən) *adj.*

do down *vb.* (*tr., adv.*) **1.** to belittle or humiliate. **2.** to deceive or cheat.

doe (dəʊ) *n., pl.* **does** *or* **doe.** the female of the deer, hare, rabbit, and certain other animals. [Old English *dā;* related to Old English *dēon* to suck, Sanskrit *dhēnā* cow]

Doe (dəʊ) *n. Law.* (formerly) the name of the fictitious plaintiff in an action of ejectment.

D.O.E. (in Britain) *abbrev. for* Department of the Environment.

doek (dʊk) *n. S. African informal.* a square of cloth worn mainly by African women to cover the head. [C18: from Afrikaans: cloth]

Doe·nitz (*German* 'døːnɪts) *n.* **Karl** (karl). a variant spelling of (Karl) **Dönitz.**

do·er ('duːə) *n.* **1.** a person or thing that does something or acts in a specified manner: *a doer of good.* **2.** an active or energetic person.

does (dʌz) *vb.* (used with a singular noun or the pronouns *he, she,* or *it*) a form of the present tense (indicative mood) of **do**¹.

doe·skin ('dəʊˌskɪn) *n.* **1.** the skin of a deer, lamb, or sheep. **2.** a very supple leather made from this skin and used esp. for gloves. **3.** a heavy smooth satin-weave or twill-weave cloth. **4.** (*modifier*) made of doeskin.

doff (dɒf) *vb.* (*tr.*) **1.** to take off or lift (one's hat) in salutation. **2.** to remove (clothing). [Old English *dōn of;* see DO¹, OFF; compare DON¹] —**'doff·er** *n.*

do for *vb.* (*prep.*) *Informal.* **1.** (*tr.*) to convict of a crime or offence: *they did him for manslaughter.* **2.** (*intr.*) to cause the ruin, death, or defeat of: *the last punch did for him.* **3.** (*intr.*) to do housework for. **4. do well for oneself.** to thrive or succeed.

dog (dɒg) *n.* **1.** a domesticated canine mammal, *Canis familiaris,* occurring in many breeds that show a great variety in size and form. **2. a.** any other carnivore of the family *Canidae,* such as the dingo and coyote. **b.** (*as modifier*): *the dog family.* **3. a.** the male of animals of the dog family. **b.** (*as modifier*): *a dog fox.* **4.** a mechanical device for gripping or holding, esp. one of the axial slots by which gear wheels or shafts are engaged to transmit torque. **5.** *Informal.* a fellow; chap: *you lucky dog.* **6.** *Informal.* a man or boy regarded as unpleasant, contemptible, or wretched. **7.** *U.S. slang.* an unattractive or boring girl or woman. **8.** *U.S. informal.* something unsatisfactory or inferior. **9.** short for **firedog. 10.** short for **sundog** or **fogdog. 11. a dog's chance.** no chance at all. **12. a dog's life.** a wretched existence. **13. dog eat dog.** ruthless competition or self-interest. **14. like a dog's dinner.** dressed smartly or ostentatiously. **15. put on the dog.** *U.S. informal.* to behave pretentiously or ostentatiously. **16. dog tied up.** *Austral. slang.* an unpaid bill, esp. at a public house. ~*vb.* **dogs, dog·ging, dogged.** (*tr.*) **17.** to pursue or follow after like a dog. **18.** to trouble; plague: *to be dogged by ill health.* **19.** to chase with a dog or dogs. **20.** to grip, hold, or secure by a mechanical device. ~See also **dogs.** [Old English *docga,* of obscure origin] —**'dog·ˌlike** *adj.*

dog·bane ('dɒgˌbeɪn) *n.* any of several North American apocynaceous plants of the genus *Apocynum,* esp. *A. androsaemifolium,* having bell-shaped white or pink flowers: thought to be poisonous to dogs.

dog·ber·ry¹ ('dɒgˌbɛrɪ, -bərɪ, -brɪ) *n., pl.* **·ries. 1.** any of certain plants that have berry-like fruits, such as the European dogwood or the bearberry. **2.** the fruit of any of these plants.

dog·ber·ry² ('dɒgˌbɛrɪ, -bərɪ, -brɪ) *n., pl.* **·ries.** (*sometimes cap.*) a foolish, meddling, and usually old official. [after *Dogberry,* character in Shakespeare's *Much Ado about Nothing* (1598)] —**'dog·ˌber·ry·ism** *n.*

dog bis·cuit *n.* a hard biscuit for dogs.

dog box *n. Austral. informal.* a compartment in a railway carriage with no corridor.

dog·cart ('dɒgˌkɑːt) *n.* a light horse-drawn two-wheeled vehicle.

dog-catch·er *n. Now chiefly U.S.* a local official whose job is to catch and impound stray dogs, cats, etc.

dog col+lar *n.* **1.** a collar for a dog. **2.** an informal name for a **clerical collar.** **3.** *Informal.* a tight-fitting necklace.

dog days *pl. n.* **1.** the hot period of the summer reckoned in ancient times from the heliacal rising of Sirius (the Dog Star). **2.** a period marked by inactivity. [C16: translation of Late Latin *diēs caniculārēs,* translation of Greek *hēmerai kunades*]

doge (dəʊdʒ) *n.* (formerly) the chief magistrate in the republics of Venice (until 1797) and Genoa (until 1805). [C16: via French from Italian (Venetian dialect), from Latin *dux* leader] —**'doge+ship** *n.*

dog-ear *vb.* **1.** (*tr.*) to fold down the corner of (a page). ~*n.* *also* **dog's-ear.** **2.** a folded-down corner of a page.

dog-eared *adj.* **1.** having dog-ears. **2.** shabby or worn.

dog-end *n.* an informal name for **cigarette end.**

dog fen+nel *n.* **1.** another name for **mayweed.** **2.** a weedy plant, *Eupatorium capillifolium,* of the southeastern U.S., having divided leaves and greenish rayless flower heads: family *Compositae* (composites).

dog+fight ('dɒɡˌfaɪt) *n.* **1.** close quarters combat between fighter aircraft. **2.** any rough violent fight.

dog+fish ('dɒɡˌfɪʃ) *n., pl.* **+fish** *or* **+fish·es. 1.** any of several small spotted European sharks, esp. *Scyliorhinus caniculus* (**lesser spotted dogfish**): family *Scyliorhinidae.* **2.** any small shark of the family *Squalidae,* esp. *Squalus acanthias* (**spiny dogfish**), typically having a spine on each dorsal fin. **3.** any small smooth-skinned shark of the family *Triakidae,* esp. *Mustelus canis* (**smooth dogfish** or **smooth hound**). **4.** a less common name for the **bowfin.**

dog+ged ('dɒɡɪd) *adj.* obstinately determined; wilful or tenacious. —**'dog+ged+ly** *adv.* —**'dog+ged+ness** *n.*

dog+ger[1] ('dɒɡə) *n.* a Dutch fishing vessel with two masts. [C14: probably from Middle Dutch *dogge* trawler]

dog+ger[2] ('dɒɡə) *n.* a large concretion of consolidated material occurring in certain sedimentary rocks. [C17: of uncertain origin]

dog+ger[3] ('dɒɡə) *n. Austral.* a hunter of dingoes. [C20: from DOG (see sense 2a.) + ER[1]]

Dog·ger ('dɒɡə) *n. Geology.* a formation of mid-Jurassic rocks in N England.

Dog+ger Bank ('dɒɡə) *n.* an extensive submerged sandbank in the North Sea between N England and Denmark: fishing ground.

dog+ger+el ('dɒɡərəl) *or* **dog+rel** ('dɒɡrəl) *n.* **1. a.** comic verse, usually irregular in measure. **b.** (*as modifier*): *a doggerel rhythm.* **2.** nonsense; drivel. [C14 *dogerel* worthless, perhaps from *dogge* DOG]

dog+ger·y ('dɒɡərɪ) *n., pl.* **+ger·ies. 1.** surly behaviour. **2.** dogs collectively. **3.** a mob.

dog+gish ('dɒɡɪʃ) *adj.* **1.** of or like a dog. **2.** surly; snappish. —**'dog+gish+ly** *adv.* —**'dog+gish+ness** *n.*

dog+go ('dɒɡəʊ) *adv. Brit. informal.* out of sight; in hiding (esp. in the phrase **lie doggo**). [C19: probably from DOG]

dog+gone ('dɒɡɒn) *interj. U.S. informal.* **1.** an exclamation of annoyance, disappointment, etc. ~*adj.* (*prenominal*), *adv.* **2.** Also: **doggoned.** another word for **damn** (senses 1, 2, 3, 4). [C19: euphemism for *God damn*]

dog+gy *or* **dog+gie** ('dɒɡɪ) *n., pl.* **+gies. 1.** a children's word for a dog. ~*adj.* **2.** of, like, or relating to a dog. **3.** fond of dogs.

dog+house ('dɒɡˌhaʊs) *n.* **1.** the U.S. name for **kennel. 2.** *Informal.* disfavour (in the phrase **in the doghouse**).

do+gie, do·gy, *or* **do+gey** ('dəʊɡɪ) *n., pl.* **+gies** *or* **+geys.** *Western U.S.* a motherless calf. [C19: of unknown origin]

dog in the man+ger *n.* **1. a.** a person who prevents others from using something he has no use for. **b.** (*as modifier*): *a dog-in-the-manger attitude.*

dog Lat+in *n.* spurious or incorrect Latin.

dog+leg ('dɒɡˌlɛɡ) *n.* **1. a.** a sharp bend or angle. **b.** something with a sharp bend. ~*vb.* **+legs, +leg+ging, +legged. 2** (*intr.*) to go off at an angle. ~*adj.* **3.** of or with the shape of a dogleg. —**dog+leg+ged** (ˌdɒɡ'lɛɡɪd, 'dɒɡˌlɛɡd) *adj.*

dog+leg fence *n. Austral.* a fence made of sloping poles supported by forked uprights.

dog+ma ('dɒɡmə) *n., pl.* **+mas** *or* **ma+ta** (-mətə). **1.** a religious doctrine or system of doctrines proclaimed by ecclesiastical authority as true. **2.** a belief, principle, or doctrine or a code of beliefs, principles, or doctrines: *Marxist dogma.* [C17: via Latin from Greek: opinion, belief, from *dokein* to seem good]

dog+man (ˌdɒɡmən) *n. Austral.* a person who directs the operation of a crane whilst riding on an object being lifted by it.

dog+mat+ic (dɒɡ'mætɪk) *or* **dog+mat·i+cal** *adj.* **1.** characterized by making authoritative or arrogant assertions, opinions, etc.; opinionated and arbitrary. **2.** of, relating to, or constituting dogma: *dogmatic writings.* **3.** *Philosophy.* based on assumption rather than empirical observation. —**dog+'mat·i+cal+ly** *adv.*

dog+mat+ics (dɒɡ'mætɪks) *n.* (*functioning as sing.*) the study of religious dogmas and doctrines. Also called: **dogmatic** (*or* **doctrinal**) **theology.**

dog+ma+tist ('dɒɡmətɪst) *n.* **1.** a dogmatic person. **2.** a person who formulates dogmas.

dog+ma+tize *or* **dog+ma+tise** ('dɒɡməˌtaɪz) *vb.* to say or state (something) in a dogmatic manner. —**'dog+ma+tism** *n.* —ˌ**dog+ma+ti+'za+tion** *or* ˌ**dog+ma+ti+'sa+tion** *n.* —**'dog+ma+ˌtiz+er** *or* **'dog+ma+ˌtis+er** *n.*

do-good·er *n. Informal, usually disparaging.* a well-intentioned person, esp. a naive or impractical one.

dog pad+dle *n.* **1.** a swimming stroke in which the swimmer lies on his front, paddles his hands in imitation of a swimming dog, and beats his legs up and down. ~*vb.* **dog-pad·dle. 2.** (*intr.*) to swim using the dog paddle.

dog rose *n.* a prickly wild rose, *Rosa canina,* that is native to Europe and has pink or white delicate scentless flowers.

dogs (dɒɡz) *pl. n.* **1. the.** *Brit. informal.* greyhound racing. **2.** *Slang.* the feet. **3. go to the dogs.** *Informal.* to go to ruin physically or morally. **4. let sleeping dogs lie.** to leave things undisturbed.

dogs+bod·y ('dɒɡzˌbɒdɪ) *n., pl.* **+bod·ies.** *Informal.* a person who carries out menial tasks for others; drudge.

dog sled *n. Chiefly U.S. and Canadian.* a sleigh drawn by dogs. Also called: **dog sledge** (Brit.), **dog sleigh.**

dog's-tail *n.* any of several grasses of the genus *Cynosurus,* esp. *C. cristatus* (crested dog's-tail), that are native to Europe and have flowers clustered in a dense narrow spike.

Dog Star *n.* **the.** another name for **Sirius.**

dog's-tongue *n.* another name for **hound's-tongue.**

dog's-tooth check *or* **dog-tooth check** *n.* another name for **hound's-tooth check.**

dog tag *n. U.S. slang.* a military personal-identification disc.

dog-tired *adj.* (*usually postpositive*) *Informal.* exhausted.

dog+tooth ('dɒɡˌtuːθ) *n., pl.* **+teeth. 1.** another name for a **canine** (sense 3). **2.** *Architect.* a carved ornament in the form of four leaflike projections radiating from a raised centre, used in England in the 13th century.

dog+tooth vi·o+let *n.* any plant of the liliaceous genus *Erythronium,* esp. the North American *E. americanum,* with yellow nodding flowers, or the European *E. dens-canis,* with purple flowers. Also called: **adders-tongue, fawn lily.**

dog train *n. Canadian.* a sleigh drawn by a team of dogs.

dog+trot ('dɒɡˌtrɒt) *n.* a gently paced trot.

dog+vane ('dɒɡˌveɪn) *n. Nautical.* a light windvane consisting of a feather or a piece of cloth or yarn mounted on the side of a vessel. Also called: **telltale.**

dog vi·o+let *n.* a violet, *Viola canina,* that grows in Europe and N Asia and has blue yellow-spurred flowers.

dog+watch ('dɒɡˌwɒtʃ) *n.* either of two two-hour watches aboard ship, from four to six p.m. or from six to eight p.m.

dog+wood ('dɒɡˌwʊd) *n.* any of various cornaceous trees or shrubs of the genus *Cornus,* esp. *C. sanguinea,* a European shrub with clusters of small white flowers and black berries.

do·gy ('dəʊɡɪ) *n., pl.* **·gies.** a variant spelling of **dogie.**

doh (dəʊ) *n., pl.* **dohs.** *Music.* (tonic sol-fa) the first degree of any major scale. [C18: from Italian; see GAMUT]

Do·ha ('dəʊhɑː, 'dəʊə) *n.* the capital and chief port of Qatar, on the E coast of the peninsula. Pop.: 100 000 (1971 est.). Former name: **Bida, El Beda.**

Doh·ná·nyi (*Hungarian* 'dohnaːnji) *n.* **Er·nö** ('ɛrnøː) or **Ernst von** ('ɛrnst fɔn). 1877–1960, Hungarian pianist and composer whose works include *Variations on a Nursery Theme* (1913) for piano and orchestra.

doi+ly, doy+ley, *or* **doy+ly** ('dɔɪlɪ) *n., pl.* **+lies** *or* **+leys.** a decorative mat of lace or lacelike paper, etc., laid on or under plates. [C18: named after *Doily,* a London draper]

do in *vb.* (*tr., adv.*) *Slang.* **1.** to murder or kill. **2.** to exhaust.

do+ing ('duːɪŋ) *n.* an action or the performance of an action: *whose doing is this?*

do+ings ('duːɪŋz) *pl. n.* **1.** deeds, actions or events. **2.** *Brit. informal.* anything of which the name is not known, or euphemistically left unsaid, etc.: *have you got the doings for starting the car?*

doit (dɔɪt) *n.* **1.** a former small copper coin of the Netherlands. **2.** a trifle. [C16: from Middle Dutch *duit*]

doi+ted ('dɔɪtɪd, -tɪt) *adj. Scot.* foolish or childish, as from senility. [C15: probably from *doten* to DOTE]

do-it-your·self *n.* **a.** the hobby or process of constructing and repairing things oneself. **b.** (*as modifier*): *a do-it-yourself kit.*

do·jo ('dəʊdʒəʊ) *n., pl.* **+jos.** a room or mat for the practice of judo. [C20: from Japanese]

dol (dɒl) *n.* a unit of pain intensity, as measured by dolorimetry. [C20: by shortening, from Latin *dolor* pain]

dol. *abbrev. for:* **1.** *Music.* dolce. **2.** (*pl.* **dols.**) dollar.

do+lab+ri+form (dəʊ'læbrɪˌfɔːm) *or* **do+lab+rate** (dəʊ'læbreɪt) *adj. Botany.* shaped like a hatchet or axe head. [C18: from Latin *dolābra* pickaxe]

Dol+by ('dɒlbɪ) *n. Trademark.* a system used in tape recorders to improve the signal-to-noise ratio of high-frequency sounds by selective amplification.

dol+ce ('dɒltʃɪ; *Italian* 'doltʃe) *adj., adv. Music.* gently and sweetly. [Italian: sweet]

dol+ce far nien+te *Italian.* ('doltʃe far 'njɛnte) *n.* pleasant idleness. [literally: sweet doing nothing]

dol+ce vi·ta ('dɒltʃɪ 'viːtə; *Italian* 'doltʃe 'vita) *n.* a life of luxury. [Italian, literally: sweet life]

dol+drums ('dɒldrəmz) *n.* **the. 1.** a depressed or bored state of mind. **2.** a state of inactivity or stagnation. **3. a.** a belt of light winds or calms along the equator. **b.** the weather conditions experienced in this belt, formerly a hazard to sailing vessels. [C19: probably from Old English *dol* DULL, influenced by TANTRUM]

dole[1] (dəʊl) *n.* **1.** a small portion or share, as of money or food, given to a poor person. **2.** the act of giving or distributing such portions. **3.** (usually preceded by *the*) *Brit. informal.* money received from the state while out of work. **4. on the dole.** *Brit. informal.* receiving such money. **5.** *Archaic.* fate. ~*vb.* **6.** (*tr.;* usually foll. by *out*) to distribute, esp. in small portions. [Old English *dāl* share; related to Old Saxon *dēl,* Old Norse *deild,* Gothic *dails,* Old High German *teil;* see DEAL[1]]

dole[2] (dəʊl) *n. Archaic.* grief or mourning. [C13: from Old French, from Late Latin *dolus,* from Latin *dolēre* to lament]
dole+ful ('dəʊlfʊl) *adj.* dreary; mournful. Archaic word: **dole+some** ('dəʊlsəm). —'**dole+ful+ly** *adv.* —'**dole+ful+ness** *n.*
dol+er+ite ('dɒlə,raɪt) *n.* **1.** a dark basic igneous rock consisting of plagioclase feldspar and a pyroxene, such as augite; a coarse-grained basalt. **2.** any dark igneous rock whose composition cannot be determined with the naked eye. [C19: from French *dolérite,* from Greek *doleros* deceitful; so called because of the difficulty of determining its composition] —**dol+er+it+ic** (,dɒlə'rɪtɪk) *adj.*
dol·i+cho·ce·phal+ic (,dɒlɪkəʊsɪ'fælɪk) *or* **dol·i+cho+ceph·a+lous** (,dɒlɪkəʊ'sɛfələs) *adj.* **1.** having a head much longer than it is broad, esp. one with a cephalic index under 75. ~*n.* **2.** an individual with such a head. ~Compare **brachycephalic, mesocephalic.** —,**dol·i+cho+'ceph·a+lism** *or* ,**dol·i+cho+'ceph·a+ly** *n.*
dol·i+cho+saur+us (,dɒlɪkəʊ'sɔ:rəs) *n.* any of various extinct Cretaceous aquatic reptiles that had long necks and bodies and well-developed limbs. [C20: from Greek, from *dolikhos* long + -SAUR]
do+li+ne *or* **do+li+na** (də'li:nə) *n.* a shallow usually funnel-shaped depression of the ground surface formed by solution in limestone regions. [C20: from Russian *dolina,* valley, plain; related to DALE]
doll (dɒl) *n.* **1.** a small model or dummy of a human being, used as a toy. **2.** *Slang.* a pretty girl or woman of little intelligence: sometimes used as a term of address. [C16: probably from *Doll,* pet name for *Dorothy*] —'**doll+ish** *adj.* —'**doll+ish+ly** *adv.* —'**doll+ish+ness** *n.*
dol+lar ('dɒlə) *n.* **1.** the standard monetary unit of the U.S. and its dependencies, divided into 100 cents. **2.** the standard monetary unit, comprising 100 cents, of the following countries: Australia, the Bahamas, Barbados (and other E Caribbean islands), Belize, Bermuda, British Honduras, Canada, the Cayman Islands, the Fiji Islands, Guyana, Hong Kong, Jamaica, Liberia, Malaysia, Singapore, Brunei, New Zealand, Rhodesia, Taiwan (**New Taiwan dollar**), and Trinidad and Tobago. **3.** *Brit informal.* (formerly) five shillings or a coin of this value. [C16: from Low German *daler,* from German *Taler, Thaler,* short for *Joachimsthaler* coin made from metal mined in *Joachimsthal* Jachymov, town in Czechoslovakia]
dol·lar+bird ('dɒlə,bɜ:d) *n.* a bird, *Eurystomus orientalis,* of S and SE Asia and Australia, with a round white spot on each wing: family *Coraciidae* (rollers), order *Coraciiformes.*
dol+lar di+plo+ma+cy *n. Chiefly U.S.* **1.** a foreign policy that encourages and protects capital investment and commercial and financial involvement abroad. **2.** use of financial power as a diplomatic weapon.
dol·lar+fish ('dɒlə,fɪʃ) *n., pl.* **+fish** *or* **+fish·es.** any of various fishes that have a rounded compressed silvery body, esp. the moonfishes or the American butterfish.
Doll·fuss (*German* 'dɔlfu:s) *n.* **Eng·el·bert** ('ɛŋəl,bɛrt). 1892–1934, Austrian statesman, chancellor (1932–34), who was assassinated by Austrian Nazis.
dol+lop ('dɒləp) *n. Informal.* **1.** a semi-solid lump. **2.** a measure or serving, esp. of food. ~*vb.* (*tr.;* foll. by *out*) to serve out (food). [C16: of unknown origin]
doll up *vb.* (*tr., adv.*) *Slang.* to adorn or dress (oneself or another, esp. a child) in a stylish or showy manner.
dol+ly ('dɒlɪ) *n., pl.* **+lies.** **1.** a child's word for a **doll.** **2.** *Films, television.* a wheeled support on which a camera may be mounted. **3.** a cup-shaped anvil held against the head of a rivet while the other end is being hammered. **4.** a shaped block of lead used to hammer dents out of sheet metal. **5.** a distance piece placed between the head of a pile and the pile-driver to form an extension to the length of the pile. **6.** *Cricket.* **a.** a simple catch. **b.** See **dolly drop.** **7.** Also called: **dolly bird.** *Slang, chiefly Brit.* an attractive and fashionable girl, esp. one who is considered to be unintelligent. ~*vb.* **+lies, +ly+ing, +lied.** **8.** *Films, television.* to wheel (a camera) backwards or forwards on a dolly.
dol+ly drop *n. Cricket.* a full toss bowled in a slow high arc.
doll·y mix+ture *n.* a mixture of tiny coloured sweets.
Dol·ly Var·den ('vɑ:dᵊn) *n.* **1.** a woman's large-brimmed hat trimmed with flowers. **2.** a red-spotted trout, *Salvelinus malma,* occurring in lakes in W North America. [C19: from the name of a character in Dickens' *Barnaby Rudge* (1841)]
dol+man ('dɒlmən) *n., pl.* **+mans.** **1.** a long Turkish outer robe. **2.** Also called: **dolman jacket.** a hussar's jacket worn slung over the shoulder. **3.** a woman's cloak with voluminous capelike sleeves. [C16: via French from German *Dolman,* from Turkish *dolaman* a winding round, from *dolamak* to wind]
dol+man sleeve *n.* a sleeve that is very wide at the armhole and tapers to a tight wrist.
dol+mas ('dɒlməs, -mɑ:s) *or* **dol+ma** ('dɒlmə, -mɑ:) *n.* a Middle Eastern dish of meat and rice, wrapped in vine leaves. [from Turkish, from *dolaman* a wrapping]
dol+men ('dɒlmɛn) *n.* **1.** (in English archaeology) a Neolithic stone formation, consisting of a horizontal stone supported by several vertical stones, and thought to be a tomb. **2.** (in French archaeology) any megalithic tomb. [C19: from French, probably from Old Breton *tol* table, from Latin *tabula* board + Breton *mēn* stone, of Celtic origin; see TABLE]
Dol·metsch ('dɒlmɛtʃ) *n.* **Ar·nold.** 1858–1940, British musician, born in France. He contributed greatly to the revival of interest in early music and instruments.
do+lo+mite ('dɒlə,maɪt) *n.* **1.** a white, colourless, or sometimes pink mineral consisting of calcium magnesium carbonate in hexagonal crystalline form. Formula: $CaMg(CO_3)_2$. **2.** a sedimentary rock resembling limestone but consisting principally of the mineral dolomite. It is an important source of magnesium and its compounds, and is used as a building material and refractory. [C18: named after Déodat de *Dolomieu* (1750–1801), French mineralogist] —**dol·o+mit+ic** (,dɒlə'mɪtɪk) *adj.*
Do+lo+mites ('dɒlə,maɪts) *pl. n.* a mountain range in NE Italy: part of the Alps; formed of dolomitic limestone. Highest peak: Marmolada, 3342 m (10 965 ft.).
dol+or+im+e·try (,dɒlə'rɪmətrɪ) *n.* a technique for measuring the level of pain perception by applying heat to the skin.
do+lo+ro+so (,dɒlə'rəʊsəʊ) *adj., adv. Music.* in a sorrowful manner. [Italian: dolorous]
dol+or+ous ('dɒlərəs) *adj.* causing or involving pain or sorrow. —'**dol+or+ous+ly** *adv.* —'**dol+or+ous+ness** *n.*
dol+our *or U.S.* **dol+or** ('dɒlə) *n. Poetic.* grief or sorrow. [C14: from Latin, from *dolēre* to grieve]
dol+phin ('dɒlfɪn) *n.* **1.** any of various marine cetacean mammals of the family *Delphinidae,* esp. *Delphinus delphis,* that are typically smaller than whales and larger than porpoises and have a beaklike snout. **2.** **river dolphin.** any freshwater cetacean of the family *Platanistidae,* inhabiting rivers of North and South America and S Asia. They are smaller than marine dolphins and have a longer narrower snout. **3.** either of two large marine percoid fishes, *Coryphaena hippurus* or *C. equisetis,* that resemble the cetacean dolphins and have an iridescent coloration. **4.** *Nautical.* a post or buoy for mooring a vessel. [C13: from Old French *dauphin,* via Latin, from Greek *delphin-, delphis*]
dol+phin strik+er *n. Nautical.* a short vertical strut between the bowsprit and a rope or cable (martingale) from the end of the bowsprit to the stem or bows, used for maintaining tension and preventing upward movement of the bowsprit. Also called: **martingale boom, martingale.**
dolt (dəʊlt) *n.* a slow-witted or stupid person; [C16: probably related to Old English *dol* stupid; see DULL] —'**dolt+ish** *adj.* —'**dolt+ish+ly** *adv.* —'**dolt+ish+ness** *n.*
dom (dɒm) *n.* **1.** (*sometimes cap.*) *R.C. Church.* a title given to Benedictine, Carthusian, and Cistercian monks and to certain of the canons regular. **2.** (formerly in Portugal and Brazil) a title borne by royalty, princes of the Church, and nobles. [C18 (monastic title): from Latin *dominus* lord]
DOM *international car registration for* Dominican Republic.
dom. *abbrev. for:* **1.** domain. **2.** domestic.
Dom. *R.C. Church. abbrev. for* Dominican.
D.O.M. *abbrev. for* Deo Optimo Maximo. [Latin: to God, the best, the greatest]
-dom *suffix forming nouns.* **1.** state or condition: *freedom; martyrdom.* **2.** rank or office: *earldom;* **3.** domain: *kingdom; Christendom.* **4.** a collection of persons: *officialdom.* [Old English *-dōm*]
do+main (də'meɪn) *n.* **1.** land governed by a ruler or government. **2.** land owned by one person or family. **3.** a field or scope of knowledge or activity. **4.** a region having specific characteristics or containing certain types of plants or animals. **5.** *Law.* the absolute ownership and right to dispose of land. See also **demesne, eminent domain.** **6.** *Maths.* **a.** the set of values of the independent variable of a function for which the functional value exists: *the domain of sin x is all real numbers.* Compare **range** (sense 7). **b.** any open set containing at least one point. **7.** *Logic.* another term for **universe of discourse** (esp. in the phrase **domain of quantification**). **8.** Also called: **magnetic domain.** *Physics.* one of the regions in a ferromagnetic solid in which all the atoms have their magnetic moments aligned in the same direction. [C17: from French *domaine,* from Latin *dominium* property, from *dominus* lord]
dome (dəʊm) *n.* **1.** a hemispherical roof or vault or a structure of similar form. **2.** something shaped like this. **3.** *Crystallog.* a crystal form in which two planes intersect along an edge parallel to a lateral axis. **4.** a slang word for the **head.** **5.** *Geology.* another name for **pericline** (sense 2). ~*vb.* (*tr.*) **6.** to cover with or as if with a dome. **7.** to shape like a dome. [C16: from French, from Italian *duomo* cathedral, from Latin *domus* house] —'**dome+,like** *adj.* —'**dom·i·cal** (dəʊmɪkᵊl, dɒm-) *adj.*
Do·me·ni·co Ve·ne·zi·a·no (*Italian* do'me:niko ,venet'tsja:no) *n.* died 1461, Italian painter, noted for the St. Lucy Altarpiece.
domes+day ('du:mz,deɪ) *n.* a variant spelling of **doomsday.**
Domes+day Book *or* **Dooms+day Book** *n. History.* the record of a survey of the land of England carried out by the commissioners of William I in 1086.
do+mes+tic (də'mɛstɪk) *adj.* **1.** of or involving the home or family. **2.** enjoying or accustomed to home or family life. **3.** (of an animal) bred or kept by man as a pet or for purposes such as the supply of food. **4.** of, produced in, or involving one's own country or a specific country: *domestic and foreign affairs.* ~*n.* **5.** a household servant. [C16: from Old French *domestique,* from Latin *domesticus* belonging to the house, from *domus* house] —**do+'mes+ti+cal+ly** *adv.*
do+mes+ti+cate (də'mɛstɪ,keɪt) *or U.S.* (*sometimes*) **do+mes+ti+cize** *vb.* **1.** (*tr.*) to bring or keep (wild animals or plants) under control or cultivation. **2.** (*tr.*) to accustom to home life. **3.** (*tr.*) to adapt to an environment: *to domesticate foreign trees.* —**do+'mes+ti+ca·ble** *adj.* —**do+,mes+ti+'ca+tion** *n.* —**do+'mes+ti+ca+tive** *adj.* —**do+'mes+ti+,ca+tor** *n.*
do+mes+tic fowl *n.* a domesticated gallinaceous bird thought to be descended from the red jungle fowl (*Gallus gallus*) and occurring in many varieties. Often shortened to **fowl.**

do·mes·ti·ci·ty (ˌdəʊmɛˈstɪsɪtɪ) *n., pl.* **·ties.** **1.** home life. **2.** devotion to or familiarity with home life. **3.** (*usually pl.*) a domestic duty, matter, or condition.

do+mes+tic sci+ence *n.* the study of cooking, needlework, and other subjects concerned with household skills.

Dom·ett (ˈdɒmɪt) *n.* **Al·fred.** 1811–87, New Zealand poet, colonial administrator, and statesman, born in England: prime minister of New Zealand (1862–63).

dom·i+cile (ˈdɒmɪˌsaɪl) *or* **dom·i+cil** (ˈdɒmɪsɪl) *n.* **1.** a dwelling place. **2.** a permanent legal residence. **3.** *Commerce, Brit.* the place where a bill of exchange is to be paid. *~vb. also* **dom·i+cil·i+ate** (ˌdɒmɪˈsɪlɪˌeɪt). **4.** to establish or be established in a dwelling place. [C15: from Latin *domicilium,* from *domus* house] **—dom·i+cil·i+ar·y** (ˌdɒmɪˈsɪlɪərɪ) *adj.*

dom·i+nance (ˈdɒmɪnəns) *n.* control; ascendancy.

dom·i+nant (ˈdɒmɪnənt) *adj.* **1.** having primary control, authority, or influence; governing; ruling. **2.** predominant or primary: *the dominant topic of the day.* **3.** occupying a commanding position. **4.** *Genetics.* **a.** (of a gene) producing the same phenotype in the organism whether its allele is identical or dissimilar. **b.** (of a character) controlled by such a gene. Compare **recessive** (sense 2). **5.** *Music.* of or relating to the fifth degree of a scale. **6.** *Ecology.* (of a plant or animal species within a community) more prevalent than any other species and determining the appearance and composition of the community. *~n.* **7.** *Genetics.* **a.** a dominant gene or character. **b.** an organism having such a gene or character. **8.** *Music.* **a.** the fifth degree of a scale and the second in importance after the tonic. **b.** a key or chord based on this. **9.** *Ecology.* a dominant plant or animal in a community. **—ˈdom·i+nant+ly** *adv.*

dom·i+nant sev+enth chord *n.* a chord consisting of the dominant and the major third, perfect fifth, and minor seventh above it. Its most natural resolution is to a chord on the tonic.

dom·i+nant ten+e·ment *n. Property law.* the land or tenement with the benefit of an easement over land belonging to another. Compare **servient tenement.**

dom·i+nant wave+length *n. Physics.* the wavelength of monochromatic light that would give the same visual sensation if combined in a suitable proportion with an achromatic light. See also **complementary wavelength.**

dom·i+nate (ˈdɒmɪˌneɪt) *vb.* **1.** to control, rule, or govern (someone or something). **2.** to tower above (surroundings, etc.); overlook. **3.** (*tr.; usually passive*) to predominate in (something or someone). [C17: from Latin *dominārī* to be lord over, from *dominus* lord] **—ˈdom·i+ˌnat+ing+ly** *adv.* **—ˈdom·i+na+tive** *adj.* **—ˈdom·i+ˌna+tor** *n.*

dom·i+na+tion (ˌdɒmɪˈneɪʃən) *n.* **1.** the act of dominating or state of being dominated. **2.** authority; rule; control.

dom·i+na+tions (ˌdɒmɪˈneɪʃənz) *pl. n.* (*sometimes cap.*) the fourth order of medieval angelology. Also called: **dominions.**

do+mi+nee (ˈduːmɪnɪ, ˈdʊə-) *n.* (in South Africa) a minister in any of the Afrikaner Churches. Also called: **predikant.** [from Afrikaans, from Dutch; compare DOMINIE]

dom·i+neer (ˌdɒmɪˈnɪə) *vb.* (*intr.,* often foll by *over*) to act with arrogance or tyranny; behave imperiously. [C16: from Dutch *domineren,* from French *dominer* to DOMINATE] **—ˌdom·i+ˈneer+ing+ly** *adv.* **—ˌdom·i+ˈneer+ing+ness** *n.*

Do·min·go (doˈmɪŋgo) *n.* **Pla·ci·do** (ˈplaθido). born 1941, Spanish operatic tenor.

Dom·i·nic (ˈdɒmɪnɪk) *n.* **Saint.** original name *Domingo de Guzman.* ?1170–1221, Spanish priest; founder of the Dominican order. Feast day: Aug. 4.

Dom·i+ni+ca (ˌdɒmɪˈniːkə, dəˈmɪnɪkə) *n.* a volcanic island in the E West Indies, one of the Windward Islands: a former British colony; became independent in 1978. Capital: Roseau. Pop.: 70 302 (1970). Area: 728 sq. km (290 sq. miles).

do+min·i+cal (dəˈmɪnɪkᵊl) *adj.* **1.** of, relating to, or emanating from Jesus Christ as Lord. **2.** of or relating to Sunday as the Lord's Day. [C15: from Late Latin *dominicālis,* from Latin *dominus* lord,]

do+min·i+cal let+ter *n. Ecclesiast.* any one of the letters A to G as used to denote Sundays in a given year in order to determine the church calendar.

Do+min·i·can¹ (dəˈmɪnɪkən) *n.* **1. a.** a member of an order of preaching friars founded by Saint Dominic in 1215; a Blackfriar. **b.** a nun of one of the orders founded under the patronage of Saint Dominic. *~adj.* **2.** of or relating to Saint Dominic or the Dominican order.

Do+min·i·can² (dəˈmɪnɪkən) *adj.* **1.** of or relating to the Dominican Republic. *~n.* **2.** a native or inhabitant of the Dominican Republic.

Do+min·i·can Re+pub+lic *n.* a republic in the West Indies, occupying the eastern half of the island of Hispaniola: colonized by the Spanish after its discovery by Columbus in 1492; gained independence from Spain in 1821. It is generally mountainous, dominated by the Cordillera Central, which rises over 3000 m (10 000 ft.), with fertile lowlands. Language: Spanish. Religion: mostly Roman Catholic. Currency: peso. Capital: Santo Domingo. Pop.: 4 006 405 (1970). Area: 48 441 sq. km (18 703 sq. miles). Former name (until 1844): **Santo Domingo.**

dom·i+nie (ˈdɒmɪnɪ) *n.* **1.** a Scot. word for **schoolmaster. 2.** a minister or clergyman, also used as a term of address. [C17: from Latin *dominē,* vocative case of *dominus* lord]

do+min+ion (dəˈmɪnjən) *n.* **1.** rule; authority. **2.** the land governed by one ruler or government. **3.** sphere of influence; area of control. **4.** a name formerly applied to self-governing divisions of the British Empire. **5.** *Law.* a less common word for **dominium.** [C15: from Old French, from Latin *dominium* ownership, from *dominus* master]

Do+min+ion Day *n.* (in Canada) July 1, the anniversary of the day in 1867 when Canada became the first British colony to receive dominion status: a bank holiday.

do+min+ions (dəˈmɪnjənz) *pl. n.* (*often cap.*) another term for **dominations.**

do+min+i·um (dəˈmɪnɪəm) *or* **do+min+ion** *n. Property law.* the ownership or right to possession of property, esp. realty. [C19: from Latin: property, ownership; see DOMINION]

dom·i·no¹ (ˈdɒmɪˌnəʊ) *n., pl.* **+noes.** a small rectangular block used in dominoes, divided on one side into two equal areas, each of which is either blank or marked with from one to six dots. [C19: from French, from Italian, perhaps from *domino!* master, said by the winner]

dom·i·no² (ˈdɒmɪˌnəʊ) *n., pl.* **+noes** *or* **+nos. 1.** a large hooded cloak worn with an eye mask at a masquerade. **2.** the eye mask worn with such a cloak. [C18: from French or Italian, probably from Latin *dominus* lord, master]

Dom·in·o (ˈdɒmɪnəʊ) *n.* **Fats.** original name *Antoine Domino.* born 1928, U.S. rock-and-roll pianist, singer, and songwriter. His singles include *Ain't that a Shame* (1955) and *Blueberry Hill* (1956).

dom·i+noes (ˈdɒmɪˌnəʊz) *n.* (*functioning as sing.*) any of several games in which matching halves of dominoes are laid together.

dom·i+no the·o+ry *n.* the theory that a Communist takeover of one country in a vulnerable region, such as SE Asia, will lead to Communist takeovers in all the neighbouring states. [C20: alluding to a row of dominoes, each standing on end, all of which fall when one is pushed]

Do+mi+nus *Latin.* (ˈdɒmɪnʊs) *n.* God or Christ.

Do·mi·tian (dəˈmɪʃən) *n.* full name *Titus Flavius Domitianus.* 51–96 A.D., Roman emperor (81–96): instigated a reign of terror (93); assassinated.

Dom·ré·my-la-Pu·celle (*French* dɔ̃remi la pyˈsɛl) *or* **Dom+ré·my** *n.* a village in NE France, in the Vosges: birthplace of Joan of Arc.

don¹ (dɒn) *vb.* **dons, don+ning, donned.** (*tr.*) to put on (clothing). [C14: from DO¹ + ON; compare DOFF]

don² (dɒn) *n.* **1.** *Brit.* a member of the teaching staff at a university or college, esp. at Oxford or Cambridge. **2.** a Spanish gentleman or nobleman. **3.** *Archaic.* a person of rank. **4.** *Austral. informal.* an expert: *he's a don at public speaking.* [C17: ultimately from Latin *dominus* lord]

Don¹ (dɒn; *Spanish* don) *n.* a Spanish title equivalent to *Mr.*: placed before a name to indicate respect. [C16: via Spanish, from Latin *dominus* lord; see DON²]

Don² (dɒn) *n.* **1.** a river in the SE Soviet Union, rising southeast of Tula and flowing generally south to the Sea of Azov: linked by canal to the River Volga. Length: 1981 km (1224 miles). **2.** a river in NE Scotland, rising in the Cairngorm Mountains and flowing east to the North Sea. Length: 100 km (62 miles). **3.** a river in N central England, rising in S Yorkshire and flowing northeast to the Humber. Length: about 96 km (60 miles).

Do·na (*Portuguese* ˈdonə) *n.* a Portuguese title of address equivalent to *Mrs.* or *Madam*: placed before a name to indicate respect. [C19: from Latin *domina* lady, feminine of *dominus* master]

Do·ña (ˈdɒnja; *Spanish* ˈdoɲa) *n.* a Spanish title of address equivalent to *Mrs.* or *Madam*: placed before a name to indicate respect. [C17: via Spanish, from Latin *domina*; see DONA]

Do·nar (ˈdəʊnɑː; *German* ˈdoːnar) *n.* the Germanic god of thunder, corresponding to Thor in Norse mythology.

do+nate (dəʊˈneɪt) *vb.* to give (money, time, etc.), esp. to a charity. **—do+ˈna+tor** *n.*

Don·a·tel·lo (*Italian* ˌdonaˈtɛllo) *n.* original name *Donato di Betto Bardi.* 1386–1466, Florentine sculptor, regarded as the greatest sculptor of the quattrocento, who was greatly influenced by classical sculpture and contemporary humanist theories. His marble relief of *St. George Killing the Dragon* (1416–17) shows his innovative use of perspective. Other outstanding works are the classic bronze *David,* and the bronze equestrian monument to Gattemalata, which became the model of subsequent equestrian sculpture.

do+na·tion (dəʊˈneɪʃən) *n.* **1.** the act of giving, esp. to a charity. **2.** a contribution. [C15: from Latin *dōnātiō* a presenting, from *dōnāre* to give, from *dōnum* gift]

Don·a·tist (ˈdəʊnətɪst) *n.* a member of a heretical Christian sect originating in N Africa in 311 A.D. [C15: from Late Latin *Dōnātista* a follower of *Dōnātus,* bishop of Carthage] **—ˈDon·a+tism** *n.*

don·a·tive (ˈdəʊnətɪv) *n.* **1.** a gift or donation. **2.** a benefice capable of being conferred as a gift. *~adj.* **3.** of or like a donation. **4.** being or relating to a benefice. [C15: from Latin *dōnātīvum* donation made to soldiers by a Roman emperor, from *dōnāre* to present]

Do·na·tus (dəʊˈnɑːtəs) *n.* **1. Ae·li·us** (ˈiːlɪəs). 4th century A.D. Latin grammarian, who taught Saint Jerome; his textbook *Ars Grammatica* was used throughout the Middle Ages. **2.** 4th century A.D. bishop of Carthage; leader of the Donatists.

Do+nau (ˈdoːnaʊ) *n.* the German name for the **Danube.**

Don+bass *or* **Don+bas** (dɒnˈbɑːs) *n.* an industrial region of the SW Soviet Union, in the E Ukrainian SSR in the plain of the Rivers Donets and lower Dnieper: the largest coalfield in the Soviet Union. Also called: **Donets Basin.**

Don+cas+ter (ˈdɒŋkəstə) *n.* an industrial town in South Yorkshire, on the River Don. Pop.: 82 505 (1971).

done (dʌn) *vb.* **1.** the past participle of **do**¹. **2. be** *or* **have done with.** to end relations with. **3. have done.** to be completely finished: *have you done?* **4. that's done it. a.** an exclamation of frustration when something is ruined. **b.** an exclamation when something is completed. ~*interj.* **5.** an expression of agreement, as on the settlement of a bargain between two parties. ~*adj.* **6.** completed; finished. **7.** cooked enough: *done to a turn.* **8.** used up: *they had to surrender when the ammunition was done.* **9.** socially proper or acceptable: *that isn't done in higher circles.* **10.** *Informal.* cheated; tricked. **11. done for.** *Informal.* **a.** dead or almost dead. **b.** in serious difficulty. **12. done in** *or* **up.** *Informal.* physically exhausted.

do+nee (dəʊ'ni:) *n. Law.* **1.** a person who receives a gift. **2.** a person to whom a power of appointment is given. [C16: from DON(OR) + -EE]

Don+e·gal ('dɒnɪ,gɔ:l, ,dɒnɪ'gɔ:l) *n.* a county in NW Ireland, on the Atlantic: mountainous, with a rugged coastline and many offshore islands. County town: Lifford. Pop.: 108 000 (1971). Area: 4830 sq. km (1865 sq. miles).

Do+nets (*Russian* da'njɛts) *n.* a river in the SW Soviet Union, rising in the Kursk steppe and flowing southeast to the Don River. Length: about 1078 km (670 miles).

Do+nets Ba+sin (də'nɛts) *n.* another name for the **Donbass.**

Do+netsk (*Russian* da'njetsk) *n.* a city in the SW Soviet Union, in the E Ukrainian SSR: the chief industrial centre of the Donbass; first ironworks founded by a Welshman, John Hughes (1872), after whom the town was named **Yuzovka** (Hughesovka). Pop.: 950 000 (1975 est.). Former names (from after the Revolution until 1961): **Stalin** or **Stalino.**

dong[1] (dɒŋ) *n.* the standard monetary unit of North Vietnam. [from Vietnamese]

dong[2] (dɒŋ) *n. U.S.* a slang word for **penis.** [C20: of unknown origin]

dong[3] (dɒŋ) *Austral. informal.* ~*vb.* (*tr.*) **1.** to hit or strike (a person). ~*n.* **2.** a blow. [C20: of imitative origin]

don+ga[1] ('dɒŋgə) *n. S. African.* a steep-sided gully created by soil erosion. [C19: from Afrikaans, of Zulu origin]

don+ga[2] ('dɒŋgə) *n.* (in Papua New Guinea) a house or shelter.

Don+go+la ('dɒŋgələ) *n.* a small town in the N Sudan, on the Nile: built on the site of Old Dongola, the capital of the Christian Kingdom of Nubia (6th to 14th centuries). Pop.: 5937 (1973).

Dö+nitz *or* **Doe+nitz** (*German* 'dø:nɪts) *n.* **Karl** (karl). 1891-1980, German admiral; commander in chief of the German navy (1943–45); as head of state after Hitler's death he surrendered to the Allies (May 7, 1945).

Don·i·zet·ti (,dɒnɪ'zɛtɪ; *Italian* ,doni'dzetti) *n.* **Ga·e·ta·no** (gae'ta:no). 1797–1848, Italian operatic composer: his works include *Lucia di Lammermoor* (1835), *La Fille du régiment* (1840), and *Don Pasquale* (1843).

don+jon ('dʌndʒən, 'dɒn-) *n.* the heavily fortified central tower or keep of a medieval castle. Also: **dungeon.** [C14: archaic variant of *dungeon*]

Don Juan ('dɒn 'dʒu:ən; *Spanish* 'don 'xwan) *n.* **1.** a legendary Spanish nobleman and philanderer: hero of many poems, plays, and operas, including treatments by de Molina, Molière, Goldoni, Mozart, Byron, and Shaw. **2.** a successful seducer of women.

don+key ('dɒŋkɪ) *n.* **1.** Also called: **ass.** a long-eared domesticated member of the horse family (*Equidae*), descended from the African wild ass (*Equus asinus*). **2.** a person who is considered to be stupid or stubborn. **3.** (*modifier*) auxiliary: *a donkey engine; a donkey boiler.* **4. talk the hind leg(s) off a donkey.** to talk endlessly. [C18: perhaps from *dun* dark + *-key,* as in *monkey*]

don+key der+by *n.* a race in which contestants ride donkeys, esp. at a rural fête.

don+key jack+et *n.* a short thick jacket, often worn by workmen.

don+key's years *n. Informal.* an expression meaning a long time.

don+key vote *n. Austral.* a vote on a preferential ballot on which the voter's order of preference follows the order in which the candidates are listed.

don·key-work *n.* **a.** groundwork. **b.** drudgery.

Don+na ('dɒnə; *Italian* 'dɔnna) *n.* an Italian title of address equivalent to *Madam,* indicating respect. [C17: from Italian, from Latin *domina* lady, feminine of *dominus* lord, master]

Donne (dʌn) *n.* **John.** 1573–1631, English metaphysical poet and preacher. He wrote love and religious poems, sermons, epigrams, and elegies including *The Progress of the Soul* (1612) and the sonnet to Death.

don+née *or* ***don+né*** *French.* (dɔ'ne) *n.* **1.** a subject or theme. **2.** a basic assumption or fact. [literally: (a) given]

don+nert ('dɒnət), **don+nard,** *or* **don+nered** ('dɒnəd) *adj. Scot.* stunned. [C18: from Scottish dialect *donner* to astound, perhaps from Dutch *donderen* to thunder, from Middle Dutch *donder* thunder]

don+nish ('dɒnɪʃ) *adj.* of or resembling a university don. —'**don+nish+ly** *adv.* —'**don+nish+ness** *n.*

don+ny ('dɒnɪ) *n.* a variant of **danny.**

don+ny+brook ('dɒnɪ,brʊk) *n.* a rowdy brawl. [C19: after *Donnybrook Fair,* an annual event until 1855 near Dublin]

do+nor ('dəʊnə) *n.* **1.** a person who makes a donation. **2.** *Med.* any person who voluntarily gives blood, skin, etc., for use in the treatment of another person. **3.** *Law.* **a.** a person who makes a gift of property. **b.** a person who bestows upon another a power of appointment over property. **4.** the atom supplying both electrons in a coordinate bond. **5.** an impurity, such as antimony or arsenic, that is added to a semiconductor material in order to increase its n-type conductivity by contributing free electrons. Compare **acceptor** (sense 2). [C15: from Old French *doneur,* from Latin *dōnātor,* from *dōnāre* to give] —'**do+nor+,ship** *n.*

Don Quix·ote ('dɒn ki:'həʊti:, 'kwɪksət; *Spanish* 'don ki'xote) *n.* an impractical idealist. [after the hero of Cervantes' *Don Quixote de la Mancha*]

don't (dəʊnt) *contraction of* do not.

Usage. The use of *don't* for *doesn't* (*he don't care*) is not generally acceptable either in written or spoken English.

don't know *n.* a person who has not reached a definite opinion on a subject, esp. as a response to a questionnaire.

doo+dah ('du:dɑ:) *or U.S.* **doo+dad** ('du:dæd) *n. Informal.* an unnamed thing, esp. an object the name of which is unknown or forgotten. [C20: of uncertain origin]

doo+dle ('du:dᵊl) *Informal.* ~*vb.* **1.** to scribble or draw aimlessly. **2.** to play or improvise idly. **3.** (*intr.;* often foll. by *away*) *U.S.* to dawdle or waste time. ~*n.* **4.** a shape, picture, etc., drawn aimlessly. [C20: perhaps from C17 *doodle* a foolish person, but influenced in meaning by DAWDLE; compare Low German *dudeltopf* simpleton] —'**doo+dler** *n.*

doo·dle+bug ('du:dᵊl,bʌg) *n.* **1.** another name for the **V-1. 2.** a diviner's rod. **3.** a U.S. name for an **antlion** (the larva). **4.** *U.S.* any of certain insect larvae that resemble the antlion. [C20: probably from DOODLE + BUG[1]]

Doo·lit·tle ('du:lɪtᵊl) *n.* **Hil·da.** usually known as *H.D.* 1886–1961, U.S. imagist poet and novelist, living in Europe.

doom (du:m) *n.* **1.** death or a terrible fate. **2.** a judgment or decision. **3.** (*sometimes cap.*) another term for the **Last Judgment.** ~*vb.* **4.** (*tr.*) to destine or condemn to death or a terrible fate. [Old English *dōm;* related to Old Norse *dōmr* judgment, Gothic *dōms* sentence, Old High German *tuom* condition, Greek *thomos* crowd, Sanskrit *dhāman* custom; see DO[1], DEEM, DEED, -DOM]

doom palm *n.* a variant spelling of **doum palm.**

dooms+day *or* **domes+day** ('du:mz,deɪ) *n.* **1.** (*sometimes cap.*) the day on which the Last Judgment will occur. **2.** any day of reckoning. [Old English *dōmes dæg* Judgment Day; related to Old Norse *domsdagr*]

Dooms+day Book *n.* a variant spelling of **Domesday Book.**

doom+watch·er *n.* a person who is pessimistic about the state of the world, and about the future. Also called: **doomster.**

door (dɔ:) *n.* **1. a.** a hinged or sliding panel for closing the entrance to a room, cupboard, etc. **b.** (*in combination*): *doorbell; doorknob.* **2.** a doorway or entrance to a room or building. **3.** a means of access or escape: *a door to success.* **4. lay at someone's door.** to lay (the blame or responsibility) on someone. **5. out of doors.** in or into the open air. **6. show someone the door.** to order someone to leave. ~See also **next door.** [Old English *duru;* related to Old Frisian *dure,* Old Norse *dyrr,* Old High German *turi,* Latin *forēs,* Greek *thura*]

do-or-die *adj.* (*prenominal*) of or involving a determined and sometimes reckless effort to succeed.

door+frame ('dɔ:,freɪm) *n.* a frame that supports a door. Also called: **doorcase.**

door+jamb ('dɔ:,dʒæm) *n.* one of the two vertical members forming the sides of a doorframe. Also called: **doorpost.**

door+keep·er ('dɔ:,ki:pə) *n.* **1.** a person attending or guarding a door or gateway. **2.** *R.C. Church.* (formerly) the lowest grade of holy orders.

door+man ('dɔ:,mæn, -mən) *n., pl.* **+men.** a man employed to attend the doors of certain buildings.

door+mat ('dɔ:,mæt) *n.* **1.** a mat, placed at the entrance to a building, for wiping dirt from shoes. **2.** *Slang.* a person who offers little resistance to ill-treatment by others.

Doorn (*Dutch* do:rn) *n.* a town in the central Netherlands, in Utrecht province: residence of Kaiser William II of Germany from his abdication (1919) until his death (1941).

door+nail ('dɔ:,neɪl) *n.* **(as) dead as a doornail.** dead beyond any doubt.

Door·nik ('do:rnɪk) *n.* the Flemish name for **Tournai.**

door+post ('dɔ:,pəʊst) *n.* another name for **doorjamb.**

door+sill ('dɔ:,sɪl) *n.* a horizontal member of wood, stone, etc., forming the bottom of a doorframe.

door+step ('dɔ:,stɛp) *n.* **1.** a step in front of a door. **2.** *Slang.* a thick slice of bread.

door+stop ('dɔ:,stɒp) *n.* **1.** a heavy object, wedge or other device which prevents an open door from moving.

door to door *adj.* (**door-to-door** *when prenominal*), *adv.* **1.** (of selling, canvassing, etc.) from one house to the next. **2.** (of journeys, deliveries, etc.) direct.

door+way ('dɔ:,weɪ) *n.* **1.** an opening into a building, room, etc., esp. one that has a door. **2.** a means of access or escape: *a doorway to freedom.*

door+yard ('dɔ:,jɑ:d) *n. U.S.* a yard in front of the front or back door of a house.

do out *vb.* (*tr., adv.*) *Informal.* **1.** to make tidy or clean; redecorate. **2.** (foll. by *of*) to deprive (a person) of by swindling or cheating.

do o·ver *vb.* (*tr., adv.*) **1.** *Informal.* to renovate or redecorate. **2.** *Austral. and Brit. slang.* to attack violently.

do·pa ('dəʊpə) *n.* see **L-Dopa.**

do+pant ('dəʊpənt) *n.* an element or compound used to dope a semiconductor. [C20: see DOPE, -ANT]

dope (dəʊp) *n.* **1.** any of a number of preparations made by dissolving cellulose derivatives in a volatile solvent, applied to fabric in order to improve strength, tautness, etc. **2.** an additive used to improve the properties of something, such as an antiknock compound added to petrol. **3.** a thick liquid, such as a lubricant, applied to a surface. **4.** a combustible absorbent material, such as sawdust or wood pulp, used to hold the nitroglycerine in dynamite. **5.** *Slang.* **a.** any illegal drug, such as cannabis or a narcotic. **b.** (*as modifier*): *a dope addict.* **6.** a drug administered to a racehorse or grey-hound to affect its performance. **7.** *Slang.* a person considered to be stupid or slow-witted. **8.** *Slang.* news or facts, esp. confidential information. **9.** *U.S. informal.* a photographic developing solution. ~*vb.* (*tr.*) **10.** *Electronics.* to add impurities to (a semiconductor) in order to produce or modify its properties. **11.** to apply or add dope to. **12.** *Slang.* to administer a drug to (oneself or another). [C19: from Dutch *doop* sauce, from *doopen* to DIP]

dope out *vb.* (*tr., adv.*) *U.S. slang.* to devise, solve, or contrive: *to dope out a floor plan.*

dope sheet *n. Horse racing slang.* a publication giving information on horses running in races.

dope·ster ('dəupstə) *n. U.S. slang.* a person who makes predictions, esp. in sport or politics.

dope·y *or* **dop·y** ('dəupɪ) *adj.* **dop·i·er, dop·i·est.** *Slang.* **1.** silly. **2.** under the influence of a drug. —'**dop·i·ness** *n.*

Dop·pel·gäng·er ('dɒpəlˌgɛŋə; *German* 'dɔpəlˌgɛŋər) *n. Legend.* a ghostly duplicate of a living person. [from German *Doppelgänger,* literally: double-goer]

Dop·per ('dɒpə) *n.* (in South Africa) a member of the most conservative Afrikaner Church, which practises a strict Calvinism. [C19: from Afrikaans, of unknown origin]

Dop·pler ef·fect ('dɒplə) *n.* a phenomenon, observed for sound waves and electromagnetic radiation, characterized by a change in the apparent frequency of a wave as a result of relative motion between the observer and the source. Also called: **Doppler shift.** [C19: named after C. J. *Doppler* (1803–53), Austrian physicist]

dor (dɔː) *n.* any European dung beetle of the genus *Geotrupes* and related genera, esp. *G. stercorarius,* having a droning flight. [Old English *dora* bumblebee; related to Middle Low German *dorte* DRONE[1]]

Do·ra·do (də'rɑːdəu) *n., Latin genitive* **Do·ra·dus** (də'rɑːdəs). a constellation in the S hemisphere lying between Reticulum and Pictor and containing part of the Large Magellanic cloud. [C17: from Spanish, from *dorar* to gild, from Latin DE- + *-aurāre,* from *aurum* gold]

Dor·cas ('dɔːkəs) *n.* a charitable woman of Joppa (Acts 9:36–42).

Dor·cas so·ci·e·ty *n.* a Christian charitable society for women with the aim of providing clothes for the poor.

Dor·ches·ter ('dɔːtʃɪstə) *n.* a town in S England, administrative centre of Dorset: associated with Thomas Hardy, esp. as the Casterbridge of his novels. Pop.: 13 737 (1971). Latin name: **Durnovaria.**

Dor·dogne (*French* dɔr'dɔɲ) *n.* **1.** a river in SW France, rising in the Auvergne Mountains and flowing southwest and west to join the Garonne river and form the Gironde estuary. Length: 472 km (293 miles). **2.** a department of SW France, in Aquitaine region. Capital: Périgueux. Pop.: 381 797 (1975). Area: 9224 sq. km (3597 sq. miles).

Dor·drecht (*Dutch* 'dɔrdrɛxt) *n.* a port in the SW Netherlands, in South Holland province: chief port of the Netherlands until the 17th century. Pop.: 101 198 (1974 est.). Also called: **Dort.**

Do·ré (*French* dɔ're) *n.* **(Paul) Gus·tave** (gys'tav). 1832–83, French illustrator, whose style tended towards the grotesque. He illustrated the Bible, Dante's *Inferno,* Cervantes' *Don Quixote,* and works by Rabelais.

Do·ri·an ('dɔːrɪən) *n.* **1.** a member of a Hellenic people who invaded Greece around 1100 B.C., overthrew the Mycenaean civilization, and settled chiefly in the Peloponnese. ~*adj.* **2.** of or relating to this people or their dialect of Ancient Greek; Doric. **3.** *Music.* of or relating to a mode represented by the ascending natural diatonic scale from D to D. See also **Hypo-.**

Dor·ic ('dɒrɪk) *adj.* **1.** of or relating to the Dorians, esp. the Spartans, or their dialect of Ancient Greek. **2.** of, denoting, or relating to one of the five classical orders of architecture: characterized by a column having no base, a heavy fluted shaft, and a capital consisting of an ovolo moulding beneath a square abacus. See also **Ionic, Composite, Corinthian, Tuscan. 3.** (*sometimes not cap.*) rustic. ~*n.* **4.** one of four chief dialects of Ancient Greek, spoken chiefly in the Peloponnese. Compare **Aeolic, Arcadic, Ionic.**

Do·ris[1] ('dɒrɪs) *n.* (in ancient Greece) **1.** a small landlocked area north of the Gulf of Corinth. Traditionally regarded as the home of the Dorians, it was perhaps settled by some of them during their southward migration. **2.** the coastal area of Caria in SW Asia Minor, settled by Dorians.

Do·ris[2] ('dɒrɪs) *n. Greek myth.* a sea nymph.

Dor·king ('dɔːkɪŋ) *n.* a heavy breed of domestic fowl. [C19: after *Dorking,* town in Surrey]

dorm (dɔːm) *n. Informal.* short for **dormitory.**

dor·mant ('dɔːmənt) *adj.* **1.** quiet and inactive, as during sleep. **2.** latent or inoperative. **3.** (of a volcano) neither extinct nor erupting. **4.** *Biology.* alive but in a resting torpid condition with suspended growth and reduced metabolism. **5.** (*usually postpositive*) *Heraldry.* (of a beast) in a sleeping position. ~Compare **active, passive.** [C14: from Old French *dormant,* from *dormir* to sleep, from Latin *dormīre*] —'**dor·man·cy** *n.*

dor·mer ('dɔːmə) *n.* a construction with a gable roof and a window at its outer end that projects from a sloping roof. Also called: **dormer window.** [C16: from Old French *dormoir,* from Latin *dormītōrium* DORMITORY]

dor·mie *or* **dor·my** ('dɔːmɪ) *adj. Golf.* (of a player or side) as many holes ahead of an opponent as there are still to play: *dormie three.* [C19: of unknown origin]

dor·mi·to·ry ('dɔːmɪtərɪ, -trɪ) *n., pl.* **·ries. 1.** a large room, esp. at a school or institution, containing several beds. **2.** *U.S.* a building, esp. at a college or camp, providing living and sleeping accommodation. **3.** (*modifier*) *Brit.* denoting or relating to an area from which most of the residents commute to work (esp. in the phrase **dormitory suburb**). ~Often shortened (for senses 1,2) to **dorm.** [C15: from Latin *dormītōrium,* from *dormīre* to sleep]

Dor·mo·bile ('dɔːməuˌbiːl) *n. Trademark.* a vanlike vehicle specially equipped for living in while travelling.

dor·mouse ('dɔːˌmaus) *n., pl.* **·mice.** any small Old World rodent of the family *Gliridae,* esp. the Eurasian *Muscardinus avellanarius,* resembling a mouse with a furry tail. [C15: *dor-,* perhaps from Old French *dormir* to sleep, from Latin *dormīre* + MOUSE]

Dorn·birn (*German* 'dɔrnbɪrn) *n.* a city in W Austria, in Vorarlberg. Pop.: 33 810 (1971).

dor·nick[1] ('dɔːnɪk) *or* **dor·neck** *n.* a heavy damask cloth, formerly used for vestments, curtains, etc. [C15: from *Doornik* Tournai in Belgium where it was first manufactured]

dor·nick[2] ('dɔːnɪk) *n. U.S.* a small stone or pebble. [C15: probably from Irish Gaelic *dornōg,* from *dorn* hand]

do·ron·i·cum (də'rɒnɪkəm) *n.* any plant of the Eurasian and N African genus *Doronicum,* such as leopard's-bane, having yellow daisy-like flower heads: family *Compositae* (composites). [C17: New Latin, from Arabic *dorūnaj*]

dorp (dɔːp) *n. Archaic except in S. Africa.* a small town or village. [C16: from Dutch: village; related to THORP]

Dor·pat ('dɔrpat) *n.* the German name for **Tartu.**

dor·sad ('dɔːsæd) *adj. Anatomy.* towards the back or dorsal aspect. [C19: from Latin *dorsum* back + *ad* to, towards]

dor·sal ('dɔːsəl) *adj.* **1.** *Anatomy, zoology.* relating to the back or spinal part of the body. Compare **ventral** (sense 1). **2.** *Botany.* of, relating to, or situated on the side of an organ that is directed away from the axis. **3.** articulated with the back of the tongue, as the (k) sound in English *coot.* [C15: from Medieval Latin *dorsālis,* from Latin *dorsum* back] —'**dor·sal·ly** *adv.*

dor·sal fin *n.* any unpaired median fin on the backs of fishes and some other aquatic vertebrates: maintains balance during locomotion.

Dor·set ('dɔːsɪt) *n.* a county in SW England, on the English Channel: mainly hilly but low-lying in the east. Administrative centre: Dorchester. Pop.: 575 800 (1976 est.). Area: 266 sq. km (103 sq. miles).

Dor·set Horn *n.* a breed of horned sheep with dense fine-textured wool.

dor·sif·er·ous (dɔː'sɪfərəs) *adj. Botany, zoology. Now rare.* bearing or carrying (young, spores, etc.) on the back or dorsal surface.

dor·si·grade ('dɔːsɪˌgreɪd) *adj.* (of animals such as certain armadillos) walking on the backs of the toes. [C19: from Latin, from *dorsum* back + -GRADE]

dor·si·ven·tral (ˌdɔːsɪ'vɛntrəl) *adj.* **1.** (of leaves and similar flat parts) having distinct upper and lower faces. **2.** a variant spelling of **dorsoventral.** —**dor·si·ven·tral·i·ty** (ˌdɔːsɪvɛn'trælɪtɪ) *n.* —ˌ**dor·si·'ven·tral·ly** *adv.*

dor·so-, dor·si-, *or before a vowel* **dors-** *combining form.* indicating dorsum or dorsal: *dorsoventral.*

dor·so·ven·tral (ˌdɔːsəu'vɛntrəl) *adj.* **1.** relating to both the dorsal and ventral sides; extending from the back to the belly. **2.** *Botany.* a variant spelling of **dorsiventral.** —ˌ**dor·so·'ven·tral·ly** *adv.*

dor·sum ('dɔːsəm) *n., pl.* **·sa** (-sə). *Anatomy.* **1.** a technical name for the **back. 2.** any analogous surface: *the dorsum of the hand.* [C18: from Latin: back]

Dort (*Dutch* dɔrt) *n.* another name for **Dordrecht.**

Dort·mund ('dɔːtmənd; *German* 'dɔrtmʊnt) *n.* an industrial city in W West Germany, in North Rhine-Westphalia at the head of the **Dortmund-Ems Canal.** Pop.: 632 317 (1974 est.).

dort·y ('dɔːtɪ) *adj.* **dort·i·er, dort·i·est.** *Scot.* haughty, or sullen. [C17: from Scottish *dort* peevishness] —'**dort·i·ness** *n.*

do·ry[1] ('dɔːrɪ) *n., pl.* **·ries.** *U.S.* a flat-bottomed boat with a high bow and stern. [C18: from Mosquito (an American Indian language of Honduras and Nicaragua) *dóri* dugout]

do·ry[2] ('dɔːrɪ) *n., pl.* **·ries. 1.** any spiny-finned marine teleost food fish of the family *Zeidae,* esp. the John Dory, having a deep compressed body. **2.** another name for **walleye** (the fish). [C14: from French *dorée* gilded, from *dorer* to gild, from Late Latin *deaurāre,* ultimately from Latin *aurum* gold]

dos-à-dos (ˌdəusɪ'dəu; *French* doza'do) *n.* **1.** a seat on which the users sit back to back. **2.** an alternative spelling of **do-si-do.** [literally: back to back]

dos·age ('dəusɪdʒ) *n.* **1.** the administration of a drug or agent in prescribed amounts. **2.** the optimum therapeutic dose and optimum interval between doses. **3.** another name for **dose** (senses 3,4).

dose (dəus) *n.* **1.** *Med.* a specific quantity of a therapeutic drug or agent taken at any one time or at specified intervals. **2.** *Informal.* something unpleasant to experience: *a dose of influenza.* **3.** Also called: **dosage.** the total energy of ionizing radiation absorbed by unit mass of material, esp. of living tissue; usually measured in rads. **4.** Also called: **dosage.** a small amount of syrup added to wine, esp. sparkling wine, when the sediment is removed and the bottle is corked. **5.** *Slang.* a venereal infection, esp. gonorrhoea. **6. like a dose of salts.** very quickly indeed. ~*vb.* (*tr.*) **7.** to administer a dose or doses to (someone). **8.** *Med.* to prescribe (a therapeutic drug or agent) in appropriate quantities. **9.** (often foll. by *up*) to give (someone, esp. oneself) drugs, medicine, etc., esp. in large quantities. **10.** to add syrup to (wine) during bottling. [C15: from French, from Late Latin *dosis*, from Greek: a giving, from *didonai* to give] —'**dos+er** *n.*

do-si-do ('dəusɪ,dəu) *n.* **1.** a square-dance figure in which dancers pass each other with right shoulders close or touching and circle back to back. ~*interj.* **2.** a call instructing dancers to perform such a figure. ~Also: **dos-à-dos.** [C20: from DOS-À-DOS]

do+sim+e·ter (dəu'sɪmɪtə) *or* **dose+me·ter** ('dəus,mɪtə) *n.* an instrument for measuring the dose of x-rays or other radiation absorbed by matter or the intensity of a source of radiation. —**do+si+met+ric** (,dəusɪ'mɛtrɪk) *adj.* —**do+si+me·tri+cian** (,dəusɪmə'trɪʃən) *or* **do+'sim+e·trist** *n.* —**do+'sim+e·try** *n.*

Dos Pas·sos ('dɒs 'pæsɒs) *n.* **John** (**Roderigo**). 1896–1970, U.S. novelist of the Lost Generation; author of *Three Soldiers* (1921), *Manhattan Transfer* (1925), and the trilogy *U.S.A.* (1930–36).

doss (dɒs) *Brit. slang.* ~*vb.* **1.** (*intr.*; often foll. by *down*) to sleep, esp. in a dosshouse. ~*n.* **2.** a bed, esp. in a dosshouse. **3.** a slang word for **sleep. 4.** short for **dosshouse.** [C18: of uncertain origin]

dos+sal *or* **dos+sel** ('dɒsᵊl) *n.* **1.** an ornamental hanging, placed at the back of an altar or at the sides of a chancel. **2.** Also called: **dosser.** *Archaic.* an ornamental covering for the back of a chair. [C17: from Medieval Latin *dossāle*, neuter of *dossālis*, variant of *dorsālis* DORSAL]

dos+ser¹ ('dɒsə) *n.* **1.** *Rare.* a bag or basket for carrying objects on the back. **2.** another word for **dossal** (sense 2). [C14: from Old French *dossier*, from Medieval Latin *dorsārium*, from Latin *dorsum* back]

doss+er² ('dɒsə) *n.* **1.** *Brit. slang.* a person who sleeps in dosshouses. **2.** *Brit. slang.* another word for **dosshouse. 3.** *Dublin dialect.* a lazy person; idler.

doss+house ('dɒs,haus) *n. Brit. slang.* a cheap lodging house, esp. one used by tramps. U.S. name: **flophouse.**

dos+si+er ('dɒsɪ,eɪ, -sɪə; *French* dɔ'sje) *n.* a collection of papers containing information on a particular subject or person. [C19: from French: a file with a label on the back, from *dos* back, from Latin *dorsum*]

dost (dʌst) *vb. Archaic or dialect.* (used with the pronoun *thou* or its relative equivalent) a singular form of the present tense (indicative mood) of **do**¹.

Dos·to·ev·sky, Dos·to·yev·sky, Dos·to·ev·ski, *or* **Dos·to·yev·ski** (,dɒstɔɪ'ɛfskɪ; *Russian* dəsta'jɛfskij) *n.* **Fyo·dor Mi·khai·lo·vich** ('fjɔdər mi'xajləvitʃ). 1821–81, Russian novelist, the psychological perception of whose works has greatly influenced the subsequent development of the novel. His best-known works are *Crime and Punishment* (1866), *The Idiot* (1868), *The Possessed* (1871), and *The Brothers Karamazov* (1879–80).

dot¹ (dɒt) *n.* **1.** a small round mark made with or as with a pen, etc.; spot; speck; point. **2.** anything resembling a dot; a small amount: *a dot of paint.* **3.** the mark (˙) that appears above the main stem of the letters *i, j.* **4.** *Music.* **a.** the symbol (·) placed after a note or rest to increase its time value by half. **b.** this symbol written above or below a note indicating that it must be played or sung staccato. **5.** *Maths., logic.* **a.** the symbol (.) indicating multiplication or logical conjunction. **b.** a decimal point. **6.** the symbol (·) used, in combination with the symbol for *dash* (—), in the written representation of Morse and other telegraphic codes. Compare **dit. 7. the year dot.** *Informal.* as long ago as can be remembered. **8. on the dot.** at exactly the arranged time. ~*vb.* **dots, dot+ting, dot+ted. 9.** (*tr.*) to mark or form with a dot: *to dot a letter; a dotted crotchet.* **10.** (*tr.*) to scatter or intersperse (with dots or something resembling dots): *bushes dotting the plain.* **11.** (*intr.*) to make a dot or dots. **12. dot one's i's and cross one's t's.** *Informal.* to be meticulous. [Old English *dott* head of a boil; related to Old High German *tutta* nipple, Norwegian *dott*, Dutch *dott* lump] —'**dot+ter** *n.*

dot² (dɒt) *n. Civil law.* a woman's dowry. [C19: from French, from Latin *dōs*; related to *dōtāre* to endow, *dāre* to give] —**do+tal** ('dəutᵊl) *adj.*

dot+age ('dəutɪdʒ) *n.* **1.** feebleness of mind, esp. as a result of old age. **2.** foolish infatuation. [C14: from DOTE + -AGE]

do+tard ('dəutəd) *n.* a person who is weak-minded, esp. through senility. [C14: from DOTE + -ARD] —'**do+tard+ly** *adv.*

do+ta+tion (dəu'teɪʃən) *n. Law.* the act of giving a dowry; endowment. [C14: from Latin *dōtātiō*, from *dōtāre* to endow]

dote *or* **doat** (dəut) *vb.* (*intr.*) **1.** (foll. by *on* or *upon*) to love to an excessive or foolish degree. **2.** to be foolish or weak-minded, esp. as a result of old age. [C13: related to Middle Dutch *doten* to be silly, Norwegian *dudra* to shake] —'**dot+er** *or* '**doat+er** *n.*

doth (dʌθ) *vb. Archaic or dialect.* (used with the pronouns *he, she,* or *it* or with a noun) a singular form of the present tense of **do**¹.

dot prod+uct *n.* another name for **scalar product.**

dot+ted ('dɒtɪd) *adj.* **1.** having dots, esp. having a pattern of dots. **2.** *Music.* **a.** (of a note) increased to one and a half times its original time value. See **dot**¹ (sense 4). **b.** (of a musical rhythm) characterized by dotted notes. Compare **double-dotted.** See also **notes inégales. 3. sign on the dotted line.** to agree formally, esp. by signing one's name on a document.

dot+ter+el *or* **dot+trel** ('dɒtrəl) *n.* **1.** a rare Eurasian plover, *Eudromias morinellus*, with reddish-brown underparts and white bands around the head and neck. **2.** *Austral.* any similar and related bird, esp. of the genus *Charadrius.* **3.** *Brit. dialect.* a person who is foolish or easily duped. [C15 *dotrelle*; see DOTE]

dot+tle *or* **dot+tel** ('dɒtᵊl) *n.* the plug of tobacco left in a pipe after smoking. [C15: diminutive of *dot* lump; see DOT¹]

dot+ty ('dɒtɪ) *adj.* +**ti+er,** +**ti+est. 1.** *Slang, chiefly Brit.* feeble-minded; slightly crazy. **2.** *Brit. slang.* (foll. by *about*) extremely fond (of) **3.** marked with dots. —'**dot+ti+ly** *adv.* —'**dot+ti+ness** *n.*

Dou, Dow, *or* **Douw** (dau; *Dutch* dɔu) *n.* **Ge·rard** ('xe:rɑrt). 1613–75, Dutch portrait and genre painter.

Dou·ai ('du:eɪ; *French* dwɛ) *n.* an industrial city in N France: the political and religious centre of exiled English Roman Catholics in the 16th and 17th centuries. Pop.: 47 570 (1975).

Dou·a+la *or* **Du·a+la** (du'ɑ:lə) *n.* the chief port and largest city in W Cameroon, on the Bight of Biafra: capital of the German colony of Kamerun (1901–16). Pop.: 250 000 (1970 est.).

Dou+ay Bi+ble *or* **Ver+sion** ('du:eɪ) *n.* an English translation of the Bible from the Latin Vulgate text completed by Roman Catholic scholars at Douai in 1610.

dou+ble ('dʌbᵊl) *adj.* (*usually prenominal*) **1.** as much again in size, strength, number, etc.: *a double portion.* **2.** composed of two equal or similar parts; in a pair; twofold: *a double egg cup.* **3.** designed for two users: *a double room.* **4.** folded in two; composed of two layers: *double paper.* **5.** stooping; bent over. **6.** having two aspects or existing in two different ways; ambiguous: *a double meaning.* **7.** false, deceitful, or hypocritical: *a double life.* **8.** (of flowers) having more than the normal number of petals. **9.** *Maths.* **a.** (of a root) being one of two equal roots of a polynomial equation. **b.** (of an integral) having an integrand containing two independent variables requiring two integrations, in each of which one variable is kept constant. **10.** *Music.* **a.** (of an instrument) sounding an octave lower than the pitch indicated by the notation: *a double bass.* **b.** (of time) duple, usually accompanied by the direction *alla breve.* ~*adv.* **11.** twice over; twofold. **12.** two together; two at a time (esp. in the phrase **see double**). ~*n.* **13.** twice the number, amount, size, etc. **14.** *Informal.* a double measure of spirits, such as whisky or brandy. **15.** a duplicate or counterpart, esp. a person who closely resembles another; understudy. **16.** a wraith or ghostly apparition that is the exact counterpart of a living person; Doppelgänger. **17.** a sharp turn, esp. a return on one's own tracks. **18.** an evasive shift or artifice; trick. **19.** an actor who plays two parts in one play. **20.** *Bridge.* a call that increases certain scoring points if the last preceding bid becomes the contract. **21.** *Billiards, etc.* a strike in which the object ball is struck so as to make it rebound against the cushion to an opposite pocket. **22.** a bet on two horses in different races in which any winnings from the horse in the first race are placed on the horse in the later race. **23.** (*often cap.*) *Chiefly R.C. Church.* one of the higher-ranking feasts on which the antiphons are recited both before and after the psalms. **24.** *Music, rare.* an ornamental variation, occurring esp. in the classical suite. **25.** Also called: **double time.** a pace of twice the normal marching speed. **26.** *Tennis.* See **double fault. 27. a.** the narrow outermost ring on a dartboard. **b.** a hit on this ring. **28.** *Printing.* another word for **doublet** (sense 6). **29. at** *or* **on the double. a.** at twice normal marching speed. **b.** quickly or immediately. ~*vb.* **30.** to make or become twice as much. **31.** to bend or fold (material, a bandage, etc.). **32.** (*tr.*; sometimes foll. by *up*) to clench (a fist). **33.** (*tr.*; often foll. by *together* or *up*) to join or couple: *he doubled up the team.* **34.** (*tr.*) to repeat exactly; copy. **35.** (*intr.*) to play two parts or serve two roles. **36.** (*intr.*) to turn sharply; follow a winding course. **37.** *Nautical.* to sail around (a headland or other point). **38.** *Music.* **a.** to duplicate (a voice or instrumental part) either in unison or at the octave above or below it. **b.** (*intr.*; usually foll. by *on*) to be capable of performing (upon an instrument additional to one's normal one): *the third trumpeter doubles on cornet.* **39.** *Bridge.* to make a call that will double certain scoring points if the preceding bid becomes the contract. **40.** *Billiards, etc.* to cause (a ball) to rebound or (of a ball) to rebound. **41.** (*intr.*; foll. by *for*) to act as substitute (for an actor or actress). **42.** (*intr.*) to go or march at twice the normal speed. ~See also **double back, doubles, double up.** [C13: from Old French, from Latin *duplus* twofold, from *duo* two + *-plus* -FOLD] —'**dou+ble+ness** *n.* —'**dou+bler** *n.*

dou·ble-act·ing *adj.* **1.** (of a reciprocating engine or pump) having a piston or pistons that are pressurized alternately on opposite sides. Compare **single-acting. 2.** (of a hinge, door, etc.) having complementary actions in opposed directions.

dou+ble a·gent *n.* a spy employed by two mutually antagonistic countries, companies, etc.

dou+ble back *vb.* (*intr., adv.*) to go back in the opposite direction (esp. in the phrase **to double back on one's tracks**).

dou·ble-bank *vb. Austral. informal.* to carry a second person on (a horse, bicycle, etc.).

dou+ble bar *n. Music.* a symbol, consisting of two ordinary bar lines or a single heavy one, that marks the end of a composition or a section within it.

dou·ble-bar·relled *or U.S.* **dou·ble-bar·reled** *adj.* **1.** (of a gun) having two barrels. **2.** extremely forceful or vehement. **3.** *Brit.* (of surnames) having two or more hyphenated parts. **4.** serving two purposes; ambiguous: *a double-barrelled remark.*

dou+ble bass (beɪs) *n.* **1.** Also called (U.S.): **bass viol.** a stringed instrument, the largest and lowest member of the violin family. Range: almost three octaves upwards from E in the space between the fourth and fifth leger lines below the bass staff. It is normally bowed in classical music, but it is very common in a jazz or dance band, where it is practically always played pizzicato. Informal name: **bass fiddle.** ~*adj.* **dou·ble-bass. 2.** of or relating to an instrument whose pitch lies below that regarded as the bass; contrabass.

dou·ble bas·soon *n. Music.* the lowest and largest instrument in the oboe class; contrabassoon.
dou·ble bill *n.* a programme or event with two main items.
dou·ble bind *n.* a situation of conflict from which there is no escape; unresolvable dilemma.
dou·ble-blind *adj.* of or relating to an experiment to discover reactions to certain commodities, drugs, etc., in which neither the experimenters nor the subjects know the particulars of the test items during the experiments. Compare **single-blind.**
dou·ble boil·er *n.* the U.S. name for **double saucepan.**
dou·ble bond *n.* a type of chemical bond consisting of two covalent bonds linking two atoms in a molecule.
dou·ble-breast·ed *adj.* (of a garment) having overlapping fronts such as to give a double thickness of cloth.
dou·ble bri·dle *n.* a bridle with four reins coming from a bit with two rings on each side.
dou·ble-check *vb.* **1.** to check twice or again; verify. *~n.* **dou·ble check. 2.** a second examination or verification. **3.** *Chess.* a simultaneous check from two pieces brought about by moving one piece to give check and thereby revealing a second check from another piece.
dou·ble chin *n.* a fold of fat under the chin. **—ˌdou·ble-ˈchinned** *adj.*
dou·ble con·cer·to *n.* a concerto for two solo instruments.
dou·ble cream *n.* thick cream with a high fat-content.
dou·ble cross *n.* a technique for producing hybrid stock, esp. seed for cereal crops, by crossing the hybrids between two different pairs of inbred lines.
dou·ble-cross *Informal.* *~vb.* **1.** *(tr.)* to cheat or betray. *~n.* **2.** the act or an instance of double-crossing; betrayal. **—ˈdou·ble-ˈcross·er** *n.*
dou·ble dag·ger *n.* a character (‡) used in printing to indicate a cross reference, esp. to a footnote. Also called: **dieses, double obelisk.**
dou·ble-deal·ing *n.* **a.** action characterized by treachery or deceit. **b.** *(as modifier): double-dealing treachery.* **—ˈdou·ble-ˈdeal·er** *n.*
dou·ble-deck·er *n.* **1.** *Chiefly Brit.* a bus with two passenger decks. **2.** *Informal, chiefly U.S.* **a.** a thing or structure having two decks, layers, etc. **b.** *(as modifier): a double-decker sandwich.*
dou·ble-de·clutch *vb. (intr.) Brit.* to change to a lower gear in a motor vehicle by first placing the gear lever into the neutral position before engaging the desired gear, at the same time releasing the clutch pedal and increasing the engine speed. U.S. term: **double-clutch.**
dou·ble de·com·po·si·tion *n.* a chemical reaction between two compounds that results in the interchange of one part of each to form two different compounds, as in $AgNO_3 + KI \rightarrow AgI + KNO_3$. Also called: **metathesis.**
dou·ble-dot·ted *adj. Music.* **1.** (of a note) increased to one and three quarters of its original time value by the addition of two dots. **2.** (of a rhythm) characterized by pairs of notes in which the first one, lengthened by two dots, makes up seven eighths of the time value of the pair.
dou·ble Dutch *n. Brit. informal.* incomprehensible talk; gibberish.
dou·ble ea·gle *n.* a former U.S. gold coin, having a nominal value of 20 dollars.
dou·ble-edged *adj.* **1.** acting in two ways; having a dual effect: *a double-edged law.* **2.** (of a remark, argument, etc.) having two possible interpretations, esp. applicable both for and against. **3.** (of a sword, knife, etc.) having a cutting edge on either side of the blade.
dou·ble en·ten·dre (ˈdʌbᵊl ɑːnˈtɑːndrə, -ˈtɑːnd; *French* dublɑ̃ˈtɑ̃dr) *n.* **1.** a word, phrase, etc., that can be interpreted in two ways, esp. one having one meaning that is indelicate. **2.** the type of humour that depends upon this type of ambiguity. [C17: from obsolete French: double meaning]
dou·ble en·try *n.* **a.** a book-keeping system in which any commercial transaction is entered as a debit in one account and as a credit in another. Compare **single entry. b.** *(as modifier): double-entry book-keeping.*
dou·ble ex·po·sure *n.* **1.** the act or process of recording two superimposed images on a photographic medium, usually done intentionally to produce a special effect. **2.** the photograph resulting from such an act.
dou·ble-faced *adj.* **1.** (of textiles) having a finished nap on each side; reversible. **2.** insincere or deceitful.
dou·ble fault *Tennis.* *~n.* **1.** the serving of two faults in succession, thereby losing a point. *~vb.* **dou·ble-fault. 2.** *(intr.)* to serve a double fault.
dou·ble fea·ture *n. Films.* a programme showing two full-length films. Informal name (U.S.): **twin bill.**
dou·ble first *n. Brit.* a first-class honours degree in two subjects.
dou·ble flat *n.* **1.** *Music.* **a.** an accidental that lowers the pitch of the following note two semitones. Usual symbol: ♭♭ **b.** a note affected by this accidental. *~adj.* **dou·ble-flat. 2.** *(postpositive)* denoting a note of a given letter name lowered in pitch by two semitones.
dou·ble glaz·ing *n.* **1.** two panes of glass in a window, fitted to reduce the transmission of heat, sound, etc. **2.** the fitting of glass in such a manner.
dou·ble Glouces·ter *n.* a type of smooth orange-red cheese of mild flavour.
dou·ble-head·er *n.* **1.** a train drawn by two locomotives coupled together to provide extra power. **2.** Also called: **twin bill.** *Sport, U.S.* two games played consecutively by the same teams or by two different teams. **3.** *Austral. informal.* a coin with the impression of a head on each side. **4.** *Austral. informal.* a double ice-cream cone.
dou·ble-hel·i·cal gear *n.* another name for **herringbone gear.**
dou·ble he·lix *n. Biochem.* the form of the molecular structure of DNA, consisting of two helical polynucleotide chains linked by hydrogen bonds and coiled around the same axis.
dou·ble-hung *adj.* (of a window) having two vertical sashes, the upper one sliding in grooves outside those of the lower.
dou·ble in·dem·ni·ty *n. U.S.* (in life assurance policies) a clause providing for the payment of double the policy's face value in the event of the policyholder's accidental death.
dou·ble jeop·ar·dy *n. Chiefly U.S.* the act of prosecuting a defendant a second time for an offence for which he has already been tried.
dou·ble-joint·ed *adj.* having unusually flexible joints permitting an abnormal degree of motion of the parts.
dou·ble-mind·ed *adj. Rare.* undecided; vacillating. **—ˌdou·ble-ˈmind·ed·ness** *n.*
dou·ble neg·a·tive *n.* a syntactic construction, often considered ungrammatical in standard Modern English, in which two negatives are used where one is needed, as in *I wouldn't never have believed it.*
Usage. There are two contexts where double negatives are found. An adjective with negative force is often used with a negative in order to express a nuance of meaning somewhere between the positive and the negative: *he was a not infrequent visitor; it is not an uncommon sight.* Two negatives are also found together where they reinforce each other rather than conflict: *he never went back, not even to collect his belongings.* These two uses of what is technically a double negative are acceptable. A third case, illustrated by *I shouldn't wonder if it didn't rain today,* has the force of a weak positive statement (*I expect it to rain today*) and is common in informal English.
dou·ble ob·e·lisk *n.* another name for **double dagger.**
dou·ble or quits *n.* a game, throw, toss, etc., to decide whether the stake due is to be doubled or cancelled.
dou·ble-park *vb.* to park (a car or other vehicle) alongside or directly opposite another already parked by the roadside, thereby causing an obstruction.
dou·ble play *n. Baseball.* a play in which two runners are put out.
dou·ble pneu·mo·ni·a *n.* pneumonia affecting both lungs.
dou·ble-quick *adj.* **1.** very quick; rapid. *~adv.* **2.** in a very quick or rapid manner.
dou·ble-reed *adj.* relating to or denoting a wind instrument in which the sounds are produced by air passing over two reeds that vibrate against each other.
dou·ble re·frac·tion *n.* the splitting of a ray of unpolarized light into two unequally refracted rays polarized in mutually perpendicular planes. Also called: **birefringence.**
dou·bles (ˈdʌbᵊlz) *n.* **a.** a game between two pairs of players, as in tennis, badminton, etc. **b.** *(as modifier): a doubles player.*
dou·ble salt *n.* a solid solution of two simple salts formed by crystallizing a solution of the two salts. Compare **complex salt.**
dou·ble sauce·pan *n. Brit.* a cooking utensil consisting of two saucepans, one fitting inside the other. The bottom saucepan contains water that, while boiling, gently heats food in the upper pan. U.S. name: **double boiler.**
dou·ble scull *n. Rowing.* a racing shell in which two scullers sit one behind the other and pull two oars each. Compare **pair-oar.**
dou·ble sharp *n.* **1.** *Music.* **a.** an accidental that raises the pitch of the following note by two semitones. Usual symbol: 𝄪 **b.** a note affected by this accidental. *~adj.* **2.** *(immediately postpositive)* denoting a note of a given letter name raised in pitch by two semitones.
dou·ble-space *vb.* to type (copy) with a full space between lines.
dou·ble stand·ard *n.* a set of principles that allows greater freedom to one person or group than to another.
dou·ble star *n.* two stars, appearing close together when viewed through a telescope; either physically associated (see **binary star**) or not associated (**optical double star**).
dou·ble-stop *vb.* **-stops, -stop·ping, -stopped.** to play (two notes or parts) simultaneously on a violin or related instrument by drawing the bow over two strings.
dou·ble-sys·tem sound re·cord·ing *n. Films.* a system in which picture and sound are taken simultaneously and the sound is recorded separately on magnetic tape.
dou·blet (ˈdʌblɪt) *n.* **1.** (formerly) a man's close-fitting jacket, with or without sleeves (esp. in the phrase **doublet and hose.**) **2. a.** a pair of similar things, esp. two words deriving ultimately from the same source, for example *reason* and *ratio* or *fragile* and *frail.* **b.** one of such a pair. **3.** *Jewellery.* a false gem made by welding a thin layer of a gemstone onto a coloured glass base or by fusing two small stones together to make a larger one. **4.** *Physics.* **a.** a multiplet that has two members. **b.** a closely spaced pair of related spectral lines. **5.** Also called: **double.** *Printing.* the unintentional repetition of lines, words, or letters when composing. **6.** *(in pl.)* two dice each showing the same number of spots on one throw. [C14: from Old French, from DOUBLE]
dou·ble tack·le *n.* a lifting or pulling tackle in which a rope is passed around the twin pulleys of a pair of pulley blocks in sequence.
dou·ble take *n.* (esp. in comedy) a delayed reaction by a person to a remark, situation, etc.
dou·ble talk *n.* **1.** rapid speech with a mixture of nonsense

syllables and real words; gibberish. **2.** empty, deceptive, or ambiguous talk, esp. by politicians.

dou·ble·think ('dʌbᵊl,θɪŋk) *n.* deliberate, perverse, or unconscious acceptance or promulgation of conflicting facts, principles, etc.

dou·ble time *n.* **1.** a doubled wage rate, paid for working on public holidays, etc. **2.** *Music.* **a.** a time twice as fast as an earlier section. **b.** two beats per bar. **3.** *U.S. Army.* **a.** a fast march of 180 paces to the minute. **b.** a slow running pace, keeping in step. ~*vb.* **dou·ble-time. 4.** to move or cause to move in double time.

dou·ble·ton ('dʌbᵊltən) *n. Bridge, etc.* an original holding of two cards only in a suit.

dou·ble-tongue *vb.* **-tongues, -tongu·ing, -tongued.** *Music.* to play (fast staccato passages) on a wind instrument by rapid obstruction and uncovering of the air passage through the lips with the tongue. Compare **single-tongue, triple-tongue.** —**dou·ble tongu·ing** *n.*

dou·ble-tongued *adj.* deceitful or hypocritical in speech.

dou·ble·tree ('dʌbᵊl,tri:) *n.* a horizontal pivoted bar on a vehicle to the ends of which whiffletrees are attached for harnessing two horses side by side.

dou·ble up *vb.* (*adv.*) **1.** to bend or cause to bend in two: *he doubled up with the pain.* **2.** (*intr.*) to share a room or bed designed for one person, family, etc. **3.** (*intr.*) *Brit.* to use the winnings from one bet as the stake for another. U.S. term: **parlay.**

dou·bloon (dʌ'blu:n) *or* **do·blón** *n.* **1.** a former Spanish gold coin. **2.** (*in pl.*) *Slang.* money. [C17: from Spanish *doblón,* from DOBLA]

dou·blure (də'bluə; *French* du'blyr) *n.* a decorative lining of vellum or leather, etc. on the inside of a book cover. [C19: from French: lining, from Old French *doubler* to make double]

dou·bly ('dʌblɪ) *adv.* **1.** to or in a double degree, quantity, or measure: *doubly careful.* **2.** in two ways: *doubly wrong.*

Doubs (*French* du) *n.* **1.** a department of E France, in Franche-Comté region. Capital: Besançon. Pop.: 484 483 (1975). Area: 5260 sq. km (2051 sq. miles). **2.** a river in E France, rising in the Jura Mountains, becoming part of the border between France and Switzerland and flowing generally southwest to the Saône River. Length: 430 km (267 miles).

doubt (daʊt) *n.* **1.** uncertainty about the truth, fact, or existence of something (esp. in the phrases **in doubt, without doubt, beyond a shadow of doubt,** etc.). **2.** (*often pl.*) lack of belief in or conviction about something: *all his doubts about the project disappeared.* **3.** an unresolved difficulty, point, etc. **4.** *Obsolete.* fear. **5. give (someone) the benefit of the doubt.** to presume (someone suspected of guilt) innocent; judge leniently. **6. no doubt.** almost certainly. ~*vb.* **7.** (*tr.; may take a clause as object*) to be inclined to disbelieve: *I doubt we are late.* **8.** (*tr.*) to distrust or be suspicious of: *he doubted their motives.* **9.** (*intr.*) to feel uncertainty or be undecided. **10.** (*tr.*) *Archaic.* to fear. [C13: from Old French *douter,* from Latin *dubitāre*] —**'doubt·a·ble** *adj.* —**'doubt·a·bly** *adv.* —**'doubt·er** *n.* —**'doubt·ing·ly** *adv.*

Usage. Where a clause follows *doubt* in a positive statement, the conjunction may be *whether, that,* or *if. Whether* (*I doubt whether he is there*) is universally accepted; *that* (*I doubt that he is there*) is less widely accepted and *if* (*I doubt if he is there*) is usually restricted to informal contexts. In negative statements, *doubt* is followed by *that: I do not doubt that he is telling the truth.* In such sentences, *but* (*I do not doubt but that he is telling the truth*) is redundant.

doubt·ful ('daʊtfʊl) *adj.* **1.** unlikely; improbable. **2.** characterized by or causing doubt; uncertain: *a doubtful answer.* **3.** unsettled; unresolved. **4.** of questionable reputation or morality. **5.** having reservations or misgivings. —**'doubt·ful·ly** *adv.* —**'doubt·ful·ness** *n.*

doubt·ing Thom·as *n.* a person who insists on proof before he will believe anything; sceptic. [after THOMAS (the apostle), who did not believe that Jesus had been resurrected until he had proof]

doubt·less ('daʊtlɪs) *adv. also* **doubt·less·ly.** *sentence substitute or sentence modifier.* **1.** certainly. **2.** probably. ~*adj.* **3.** certain; assured. —**'doubt·less·ness** *n.*

douc (du:k) *n.* an Old World monkey, *Pygathrix nemaeus,* of SE Asia, with a bright yellow face surrounded by tufts of reddish-brown fur, a white tail, and white hindquarters: one of the langurs.

douce (du:s) *adj. Scot. and northern Brit. dialect.* quiet; sober; sedate. [C14: from Old French, feminine of *dous,* from Latin *dulcis* sweet] —**'douce·ly** *adv.*

dou·ceur (du:'sɜ:; *French* du'sœ:r) *n.* **1.** a gratuity, tip, or bribe. **2.** sweetness. [C17: from French, from Late Latin *dulcor,* from Latin *dulcis* sweet]

douche (du:ʃ) *n.* **1.** a stream of water or air directed onto the body surface or into a body cavity, for cleansing or medical purposes. **2.** the application of such a stream of water or air. **3.** an instrument, such as a special syringe, for applying a douche. ~*vb.* **4.** to cleanse or treat or be cleansed or treated by means of a douche. [C18: from French, from Italian *doccia,* pipe; related to Latin *ductus* DUCT]

dough (dəʊ) *n.* **1.** a thick mixture of flour or meal and water or milk, used for making bread, pastry, etc. **2.** any similar pasty mass. **3.** *Chiefly U.S.* a slang word for **money.** [Old English *dāg;* related to Old Norse *deig,* Gothic *daigs,* Old High German *teig* dough, Sanskrit *degdhi* he daubs; see DAIRY, DUFF[1], LADY]

dough·boy ('dəʊ,bɔɪ) *n.* **1.** *U.S. informal.* an infantryman, esp. in World War I. **2.** dough that is boiled or steamed as a dumpling.

dough·nut *or* **do·nut** ('dəʊnʌt) *n.* **1.** a small cake of sweetened dough, often ring-shaped or spherical with a jam or cream filling, cooked in hot fat. **2.** anything shaped like a ring, such as the reaction vessel of a thermonuclear reactor.

dough·ty ('daʊtɪ) *adj.* **·ti·er, ·ti·est.** hardy; resolute. [Old English *dohtig;* related to Old High German *toht* worth, Middle Dutch *duchtich* strong, Greek *tukhē* luck] —**'dough·ti·ly** *adv.* —**'dough·ti·ness** *n.*

Dough·ty ('daʊtɪ) *n.* **Charles Mon·ta·gu.** 1843–1926, English writer and traveller; author of *Travels in Arabia Deserta* (1888).

dough·y ('dəʊɪ) *adj.* **dough·i·er, dough·i·est.** resembling dough in consistency, colour, etc.; soft, pallid, or flabby.

Doug·las[1] ('dʌgləs) *n.* a town and resort on the Isle of Man, capital of the island, on the E coast. Pop.: 20 385 (1971).

Doug·las[2] ('dʌgləs) *n.* **1. Clif·ford Hugh.** 1879–1952, English economist, who originated the theory of social credit. **2. Gav·in.** ?1474–1522, Scottish poet, the first British translator of the *Aeneid.* **3. (George) Nor·man.** 1868–1952, English writer, esp. of books on southern Italy such as *South Wind* (1917).

Doug·las fir, spruce, *or* **hem·lock** *n.* a North American pyramidal coniferous tree, *Pseudotsuga menziesii,* widely planted for ornament and for timber, having needle-like leaves and hanging cones: family *Pinaceae.* Also called: **Oregon fir, Oregon pine.** [C19: named after David *Douglas* (1798–1834), Scottish botanist]

Doug·las-Home ('dʌgləs 'hju:m) *n.* Sir **Al·ex·an·der (Alec).** See (Baron Alexander) **Home.**

Doug·las scale *n.* an international scale of sea disturbance and swell ranging from 0 to 9 with one figure for disturbance and one for swell. [C20: named after Sir Henry *Douglas* (1876–1939), former director of the British Naval Meteorological Service]

Dou·kho·bors *or* **Du·kho·bors** ('du:kəʊ,bɔ:z) *pl. n.* a Russian sect of Christians that originated in the 18th century. In the late 19th century a large minority emigrated to W Canada, where most Doukhobors now live.

dou·ma *Russian.* ('dumə) *n.* a variant spelling of **duma.**

doum palm *or* **doom palm** (du:m) *n.* an Egyptian palm tree, *Hyphaene thebaica,* with a divided trunk and edible apple-sized fruits. [C19 *doum,* via French from Arabic *dawm*]

do up *vb.* (*adv.; mainly tr.*) **1.** to wrap and make into a bundle: *to do up a parcel.* **2.** to cause the downfall of (a person). **3.** to beautify or adorn. **4.** (*also intr.*) to fasten or be fastened: *this skirt does up at the back.* **5.** *Informal.* to renovate or redecorate. **6.** *Slang.* to assault.

dour (dʊə) *adj.* **1.** sullen. **2.** hard or obstinate. [C14: probably from Latin *dūrus* hard] —**'dour·ly** *adv.* —**'dour·ness** *n.*

dou·ra ('dʊərə) *n.* a variant spelling of **durra.**

dou·rine ('dʊəri:n) *n.* an infectious disease of horses characterized by swollen glands, inflamed genitals, and paralysis of the hindquarters, caused by the protozoan *Trypanosoma equiperdum* contracted during copulation. [C19: from French, from Arabic *darina* to be dirty, scabby]

Dou·ro ('dʊərəʊ; *Portuguese* 'doru) *n.* a river in SW Europe, rising in N central Spain and flowing west to NE Portugal, then south as part of the border between the two countries and finally west to the Atlantic. Length: 895 km (556 miles). Spanish name: **Duero.**

dou·rou·cou·li (,du:ru:'ku:lɪ) *n.* a nocturnal omnivorous New World monkey, *Aotus trivirgatus,* of Central and South America, with large eyes, thick fur, and a round head with pale and dark markings. [from a native South American name]

douse[1] *or* **dowse** (daʊs) *vb.* **1.** to plunge or be plunged into water or some other liquid; duck. **2.** (*tr.*) to drench with water, esp. in order to wash or clean. **3.** (*tr.*) to put out (a light, candle, etc.). ~*n.* **4.** an immersion. [C16: perhaps related to obsolete *douse* to strike, of obscure origin] —**'dous·er** *or* **'dows·er** *n.*

douse[2] (daʊs) *vb.* (*tr.*) **1.** *Nautical.* to lower (sail) quickly. **2.** *Archaic.* to take off (clothes, esp. a hat). **3.** *Archaic.* to strike or beat. ~*n.* **4.** *Archaic.* a blow. [C16: of uncertain origin; perhaps related to DOUSE[1]]

douze·pers ('du:z,pɛəz) *pl. n. French history.* the 12 great peers of the realm, seen as the symbolic heirs of Charlemagne's 12 chosen peers. [C13: from Old French *douze pers;* see DOZEN, PEER[1]]

DOVAP ('dəʊ,væp) *n.* a tracking system for determining the position and velocity of spacecraft, missiles, etc., based on the Doppler effect. [C20: from *Do(ppler) v(elocity) a(nd) p(osition)*]

dove[1] (dʌv) *n.* **1.** any of various birds of the family *Columbidae,* having a heavy body, small head, short legs, and long pointed wings: order *Columbiformes.* They are typically smaller than pigeons. **2.** a gentle or innocent person: used as a term of endearment. **3.** *Politics.* a person opposed to war. Compare **hawk**[1] (sense 3). **4. a.** a greyish brown colour. **b.** (*as adj.*): *dove walls.* [Old English *dūfe* (unattested except as a feminine proper name); related to Old Saxon *dūbva,* Old High German *tūba*] —**'dove,like** *adj.* —**'dov·ish** *adj.*

dove[2] (dəʊv) *vb. Chiefly U.S.* a past tense of **dive.**

Dove (dʌv) *n. Ecclesiast.* **the.** a manifestation of the Holy Ghost (John 1:32).

dove·cote ('dʌv,kəʊt) *or* **dove·cot** ('dʌv,kɒt) *n.* a structure set on a pole or in a building, for housing pigeons.

dove·kie *or* **dove·key** ('dʌvkɪ) *n.* another name for the **little auk** (see **auk**). [C19: Scottish diminutive of DOVE[1]]

Do·ver ('dəʊvə) *n.* **1.** a port in SE England, in E Kent on the Strait of Dover: the only one of the Cinque Ports that is still important; a stronghold since ancient times and Caesar's first point of attack in the invasion of Britain (55 B.C.). Pop.: 34 322 (1971). **2. Strait of.** a strait between SE England and N France, linking the English Channel with the North Sea. Width: about 32 km (20 miles). French name: **Pas de Calais.**

Do·ver's pow+der *n.* a preparation of opium and ipecac, formerly used to relieve pain, induce sweating, and check spasms. [C19: named after Thomas *Dover* (1660–1742), English physician]

dove+tail ('dʌvˌteɪl) *n.* **1.** a wedge-shaped tenon. **2.** Also called: **dovetail joint.** a joint containing such tenons. *~vb.* **3.** (*tr.*) to join by means of dovetails. **4.** to fit or cause to fit together closely or neatly: *he dovetailed his arguments to the desired conclusion.*

dow (daʊ, dəʊ) *vb.* **dows, dow+ing, dowed** *or* **dought.** (*intr.*) *Scot. and northern Brit. dialect.* **1.** to be able. **2.** to do well. [Old English *dugan* (unattested) to be worthy; see DOUGHTY]

Dow (daʊ; *Dutch* dɔʊ) *n.* See (Gerard) **Dou.**

dow+a·ble ('daʊəbəl) *adj. Law.* **1.** capable of being endowed. **2.** (of a person, esp. a widow) entitled to dower.

dow·a+ger ('daʊədʒə) *n.* **1. a.** a widow possessing property or a title obtained from her husband. **b.** (*as modifier*): *the dowager duchess.* **2.** a wealthy or dignified elderly woman. [C16: from Old French *douagiere,* from *douage* DOWER]

Dow·ding ('daʊdɪŋ) *n.* Baron **Hugh Cas·wall Tre·men·heere,** nicknamed *"Dowdy."* 1882–1970, British air chief marshal. As commander in chief of Fighter Command (1936–40), he contributed greatly to the British victory in the Battle of Britain (1940).

dow+dy ('daʊdɪ) *adj.* **+di+er, +di+est.** **1.** (esp. of a woman or a woman's dress) shabby or old-fashioned. *~n., pl.* **+dies.** **2.** a dowdy woman. [C14: *dowd* slut, of unknown origin] —**'dow+di+ly** *adv.* —**'dow+di+ness** *n.* —**'dow+dy+ish** *adj.*

dow+el ('daʊəl) *n. Carpentry, cabinetmaking.* a wooden or metal peg that fits into two corresponding holes to join two adjacent parts. Also called: **dowel pin.** [C14: from Middle Low German *dövel* plug, from Old High German *tubili;* related to Greek *thuphos* wedge]

dow+er ('daʊə) *n.* **1.** the life interest in a part of her husband's estate allotted to a widow by law. **2.** an archaic word for **dowry** (sense 1). **3.** a natural gift or talent. *~vb.* **4.** (*tr.*) to endow. [C14: from Old French *douaire,* from Medieval Latin *dōtārium,* from Latin *dōs* gift] —**'dow+er+less** *adj.*

dow+er house *n.* a house set apart for the use of a widow, often on her deceased husband's estate.

dow+er·y ('daʊərɪ) *n., pl.* **+er·ies.** a variant spelling of **dowry.**

do+wie, do·wy ('daʊɪ, 'dəʊɪ), *or* **dow+ly** ('daʊlɪ, 'dəʊlɪ) *adj.* **+wi+er, +wi+est.** *Northern Brit. dialect.* dull, melancholy, or dismal. [C16: variant of *dolly,* probably from *dol* DULL]

dow+itch+er ('daʊɪtʃə) *n.* either of two snipelike shore birds, *Limnodromus griseus* or *L. scolopaceus,* of arctic and subarctic North America: family *Scolopacidae* (sandpipers, etc.), order *Charadriiformes.* [C19: of Iroquoian origin]

do with *vb.* **1. could** *or* **can do with.** to find useful; benefit from: *she could do with a good night's sleep.* **2. have to do with.** to be involved in or connected with: *his illness has a lot to do with his failing the exam.* **3. to do with.** concerning; related to. **4. what...do with. a.** to put or place: *what did you do with my coat?* **b.** to handle or treat: *what are we going to do with these hooligans?* **c.** to fill one's time usefully: *she didn't know what to do with herself when the project was finished.*

do with+out *vb.* (*intr.*) **1.** to forgo; manage without: *I can't do without cigarettes.* **2.** (*prep.*) not to require (uncalled-for comments or advice): *we can do without your criticisms thank you.*

Dow-Jones av+er+age *n. U.S.* a daily index of stock-exchange prices based on the average price of a selected number of securities. [C20: named after Charles H. *Dow* (died 1902) and Edward D. *Jones* (died 1920), American financial statisticians]

Dow·land ('daʊlənd) *n.* **John.** ?1563–1626, English lutenist and composer of songs and lute music.

down[1] (daʊn) *prep.* **1.** used to indicate movement from a higher to a lower position: *they went down the mountain.* **2.** at a lower or further level or position on, in, or along: *he ran down the street.* *~adv.* **3.** downwards; at or to a lower level or position: *don't fall down.* **4.** (*particle*) used with many verbs when the result of the verb's action is to lower or destroy its object: *pull down; knock down; bring down.* **5.** (*particle*) used with several verbs to indicate intensity or completion: *calm down.* **6.** immediate: *cash down; a down payment.* **7.** on paper: *write this down.* **8.** arranged; scheduled: *the meeting is down for next week.* **9.** in a helpless position: *they had him down on the ground.* **10. a.** away from a more important place: *down from London.* **b.** away from a more northerly place: *down from Scotland.* **c.** (of a member of some British universities) away from the university; on vacation. **d.** in a particular part of a country: *down south.* **11.** *Nautical.* (of a helm) having the rudder to windward. **12.** reduced to a state of lack or want: *down to the last pound.* **13.** lacking a specified amount: *at the end of the day the cashier was ten pounds down.* **14.** lower in price: *bacon is down.* **15.** including all intermediate terms, grades, people, etc.: *from managing director down to tea-lady.* **16.** from an earlier to a later time: *the heirloom was handed down.* **17.** to a finer or more concentrated state: *to grind down; boil down.* **18.** *Sport.* being a specified number of points, goals, etc. behind another competitor, team, etc.: *six goals down.* **19.** (of a person) being inactive, owing to illness: *down with flu.* **20.** (*functioning as imperative*) (to dogs, etc.): *down Rover!* **21.** (*functioning as imperative*) **down with.** wanting the end of somebody or something: *down with the king!* *~adj.* **22.** (*postpositive*) depressed or miserable. **23.** (*prenominal*) of or relating to a train or trains from a more important place or one regarded as higher: *the down line.* *~vb.* **24.** (*tr.*) to knock, push or pull down. **25.** (*intr.*) to go or come down. **26.** (*tr.*) *Informal.* to drink, esp. quickly: *he downed three gins.* **27.** (*tr.*) to bring (someone) down, esp. by tackling. *~n.* **28.** a descent; downward movement. **29.** a lowering or a poor period (esp. in the phrase **ups and downs**). **30. have a down on.** *Informal.* to bear ill will towards (someone or something). [Old English *dūne,* short for *adūne,* variant of *of dūne,* literally: from the hill, from *of,* OFF + *dūn* hill; see DOWN[3]]

down[2] (daʊn) *n.* **1.** the soft fine feathers with free barbs that cover the body of a bird and prevent loss of heat. In the adult they lie beneath and between the contour feathers. **2.** another name for **eiderdown** (sense 1). **3.** *Botany.* a fine coating of soft hairs, as on certain leaves, fruits, and seeds. **4.** any growth or coating of soft fine hair, such as that on the human face. [C14: of Scandinavian origin; related to Old Norse *dūnn*]

down[3] (daʊn) *n. Archaic.* a hill, esp. a sand dune. *~*See also **downs.** [Old English *dūn;* related to Old Frisian *dūne* Old Saxon *dūna* hill, Old Irish *dūn* fortress, Greek *this* sandbank; see DUNE, TOWN]

Down (daʊn) *n.* a county of SE Northern Ireland, on the Irish Sea: generally hilly, rising to the Mountains of Mourne. County town: Downpatrick. Pop.: 310 617 (1971). Area: 2465 sq. km (952 sq. miles).

down+beat ('daʊnˌbiːt) *n.* **1.** *Music.* the first beat of a bar or the downward gesture of a conductor's baton indicating this. Compare **upbeat.** *~adj.* **2.** *Informal.* depressed; gloomy. **3.** *Informal.* relaxed; unemphatic.

down-bow ('daʊnˌbəʊ) *n.* a downward stroke of the bow from its nut to its tip across a stringed instrument. Compare **up-bow.**

down+cast ('daʊnˌkɑːst) *adj.* **1.** dejected. **2.** (esp. of the eyes) directed downwards. *~n.* **3.** *Mining.* a ventilation shaft. **4.** *Geology.* another word for **downthrow.**

down+come ('daʊnˌkʌm) *n.* **1.** *Archaic.* downfall. **2.** another name for **downcomer.**

down+com+er ('daʊnˌkʌmə) *n.* a pipe that connects a cistern to a W.C., wash basin, etc. Also called: **downcome.**

down+er ('daʊnə) *n. Slang.* **1.** Also called: **down.** a barbiturate or tranquillizer pill which reverses the effect of a stimulant. Compare **upper.** **2.** a depressing experience.

down+fall ('daʊnˌfɔːl) *n.* **1.** a sudden loss of position, health, or reputation. **2.** a fall of rain, snow, etc., esp. a sudden heavy one. **3.** another word for **deadfall.**

down+fall·en ('daʊnˌfɔːlən) *adj.* **1.** (of a building, etc.) decrepit. **2.** *Chiefly U.S.* (of a person) ruined; fallen.

down+grade ('daʊnˌgreɪd) *vb.* (*tr.*) **1.** to reduce in importance, esteem, or value, esp. to demote (a person) to a poorer job. **2.** to speak of disparagingly. *~n.* **3.** *Chiefly U.S.* a downward slope, esp. in a road. **4. on the downgrade.** waning in importance, popularity, health, etc.

down+haul ('daʊnˌhɔːl) *n. Nautical.* a line for hauling down a sail or for increasing the tension at its luff.

down+heart·ed (ˌdaʊn'hɑːtɪd) *adj.* discouraged; dejected. —**ˌdown+'heart·ed+ly** *adv.* —**ˌdown+'heart·ed+ness** *n.*

down+hill ('daʊn'hɪl) *adj.* **1.** going or sloping down. *~adv.* **2.** towards the bottom of a hill; downwards. **3. go downhill.** *Informal.* to decline; deteriorate. *~n.* **4.** the downward slope of a hill; descent. **5.** a competitive event in which skiers are timed in a downhill run.

Down+ing Street ('daʊnɪŋ) *n.* **1.** a street in W central London, in Westminster: official residences of the prime minister of Great Britain and the chancellor of the exchequer. **2.** *Informal.* the prime minister or the British Government. [named after Sir George *Downing* (1623–84), English statesman]

down-mar·ket *adj.* relating to commercial products, services, etc., that are cheap, have little prestige, or are poor in quality.

Down+pat+rick (ˌdaʊn'pætrɪk) *n.* a market town in Northern Ireland, county town of Co. Down: associated with Saint Patrick who is said to have been buried here. Pop.: 3642 (1971).

down pay+ment *n.* the deposit paid on an item purchased on hire-purchase, mortgage, etc.

down+pipe ('daʊnˌpaɪp) *n. Brit.* a pipe for carrying rainwater from a roof gutter to the ground or to a drain. Also called: **rainwater pipe, drainpipe.** Usual U.S. name: **downspout.**

down+pour ('daʊnˌpɔː) *n.* a heavy continuous fall of rain.

down+range ('daʊn'reɪndʒ) *adj., adv.* in the direction of the intended flight path of a rocket or missile.

down+right ('daʊnˌraɪt) *adj.* **1.** frank or straightforward; blunt: *downright speech.* **2.** *Archaic.* directed or pointing straight down. *~adv., adj.* (*prenominal*) **3.** (intensifier): *a downright certainty; downright rude.* —**'down+ˌright+ly** *adv.* —**'down+ˌright+ness** *n.*

downs (daʊnz) *pl. n.* rolling upland, esp. in the chalk areas of S Britain, characterized by lack of trees and used mainly as pasture. Also called: **downland.**

Downs (daʊnz) *n.* **the. 1.** any of various ranges of low chalk hills in S England, esp. the **South Downs** in Sussex. **2.** a roadstead off the SE coast of Kent, protected by the Goodwin Sands.

down+spout ('daʊnˌspaʊt) *n.* a U.S. name for **downpipe.**

Down's syn+drome *n. Pathol.* another term for **mongolism.** [C19: after John *Langdon-Down* (1828–96), English physician]

down+stage ('daʊn'steɪdʒ) *Theatre.* *~adv.* **1.** at or towards the front of the stage. *~adj.* **2.** of or relating to the front of the stage. *~n.* **3.** the front half of the stage.

down·stairs ('daʊn'steəz) *adv.* **1.** down the stairs; to or on a lower floor. ~*n.* **2. a.** a lower or ground floor. **b.** (*as modifier*): *a downstairs room.* **3.** *Brit. informal.* the servants of a household collectively. Compare **upstairs** (sense 6).
down·state ('daʊn,steɪt) *U.S. adj.* **1.** in, or relating to the part of the state away from large cities, esp. the southern part. ~*adv.* towards the southern part of a state. ~*n.* the southern part of a state.
down·stream ('daʊn'stri:m) *adv., adj.* in or towards the lower part of a stream; with the current.
down·swing ('daʊn,swɪŋ) *n.* **1.** Also called: **downturn.** a statistical downward trend in business activity, the death rate, etc. **2.** *Golf.* the downward movement or line of a club when striking the ball.
down·throw ('daʊn,θrəʊ) *n.* **1.** the state of throwing down or being thrown down. **2.** *Geology.* the sinking of rocks on one side of a fault plane.
down-to-earth *adj.* sensible; practical; realistic.
down·town ('daʊn'taʊn) *U.S.* ~*n.* **1.** the central or lower part of a city, esp. the main commercial area. ~*adv.* **2.** towards, to, or into this area. ~*adj.* **3.** of, relating to, or situated in the downtown area: *downtown Manhattan.* —'**down·'town·er** *n.*
down·trod·den ('daʊn,trɒdᵊn) *or* **down·trod** *adj.* **1.** subjugated; oppressed. **2.** trodden down; trampled.
down·turn ('daʊn,tɜ:n) *n.* another term for **downswing** (sense 1).
down un·der *Informal.* ~*n.* **1.** Australia or New Zealand. ~*adv.* **2.** in or to Australia or New Zealand.
down·ward ('daʊnwəd) *adj.* **1.** descending from a higher to a lower level, condition, position, etc. **2.** descending from a beginning. ~*adv.* **3.** a variant of **downwards.** —'**down·ward·ly** *adv.* —'**down·ward·ness** *n.*
down·ward mo·bil·i·ty *n.* the movement of an individual, social group, or class to a lower status. See also **vertical mobility.**
down·wards ('daʊnwədz) *or* **down·ward** *adv.* **1.** from a higher to a lower place, level, etc. **2.** from an earlier time or source to a later: *from the Tudors downwards.*
down·wash ('daʊn,wɒʃ) *n.* the downward deflection of an airflow, esp. one caused by an aerofoil of an aircraft.
down·wind ('daʊn'wɪnd) *adv., adj.* **1.** in the same direction towards which the wind is blowing; with the wind from behind. **2.** towards or on the side away from the wind; leeward.
down·y ('daʊnɪ) *adj.* **down·i·er, down·i·est. 1.** covered with soft fine hair or feathers. **2.** light, soft, and fluffy. **3.** made from or filled with down. **4.** resembling downs; undulating. **5.** *Brit. slang.* sharp. —'**down·i·ness** *n.*
down·y mil·dew *n.* **1.** a serious plant disease, characterized by yellowish patches on the undersurface of the leaves, caused by the parasitic fungi of the family *Peronosporaceae,* such as *Peronospora destructor:* affects onions, cauliflower, lettuce, etc. **2.** any of the fungi causing this disease. ~Compare **powdery mildew.**
dow·ry ('daʊərɪ) *or* **dow·er·y** *n., pl.* **·ries** *or* **·er·ies. 1.** the money or property brought by a woman to her husband at marriage. **2.** (esp. formerly) a gift made by a man to his bride or her parents. **3.** *Ecclesiast.* a sum of money required on entering certain orders of nuns. **4.** a natural talent or gift. **5.** *Obsolete.* a widow's dower. [C14: from Anglo-French *douarie,* from Medieval Latin *dōtārium;* see DOWER]
dow·sa·bel ('du:sə,bɛl, 'daʊs-) *n.* an obsolete word for **sweetheart.** [C16: from Latin *Dulcibella* feminine given name, from *dulcis* sweet + *bellus* beautiful]
dowse[1] (daʊs) *vb., n.* a variant spelling of **douse**[1]. —'**dows·er** *n.*
dowse[2] (daʊz) *vb.* (*intr.*) to search for underground water, minerals, etc., using a divining rod; divine. [C17: of unknown origin] —'**dows·er** *n.*
dows·ing rod ('daʊzɪŋ) *n.* another name for **divining rod.**
Dow·son ('daʊsᵊn) *n.* **Er·nest (Christopher).** 1867–1900, English Decadent poet noted for his lyric *Cynara.*
dox·as·tic (dɒks'æstɪk) *adj. Logic.* of or relating to belief. [C18: from Greek *doxastikos* having an opinion, ultimately from *doxazein* to conjecture]
dox·og·ra·pher (,dɒks'ɒgrəfə) *n. Rare.* a person who collects the opinions and conjectures of ancient Greek philosophers. [C19: from New Latin *doxographus,* from Greek *doxa* opinion, conjecture + *graphos* writer] —,**dox·o·'graph·ic** *adj.* —,**dox·'og·raph·y** *n.*
dox·ol·o·gy (dɒk'sɒlədʒɪ) *n., pl.* **·gies.** a hymn, verse, or form of words in Christian liturgy glorifying God. [C17: from Medieval Latin *doxologia,* from Greek, from *doxologos* uttering praise, from *doxa* praise; see -LOGY] —**dox·o·log·i·cal** (,dɒksə'lɒdʒɪkᵊl) *adj.* —,**dox·o·'log·i·cal·ly** *adv.*
dox·y[1] *or* **dox·ie** ('dɒksɪ) *n., pl.* **dox·ies.** opinion or doctrine, esp. concerning religious matters. [C18: independent use of *-doxy* as in *orthodoxy, heterodoxy*]
dox·y[2] ('dɒksɪ) *n., pl.* **dox·ies.** *Archaic slang.* a prostitute or mistress. [C16: probably from Middle Flemish *docke* doll; compare Middle Dutch *docke* doll]
doy·en ('dɔɪən; *French* dwa'jɛ̃) *n.* the senior member of a group, profession, or society. [C17: from French, from Late Latin *decānus* leader of a group of ten; see DEAN] —**doy·enne** (dɔɪ'ɛn; *French* dwa'jɛn) *fem. n.*
Doyle (dɔɪl) *n.* See (Sir Arthur) **Conan Doyle.**
doy·ley ('dɔɪlɪ) *n.* a variant spelling of **doily.**
D'Oyly Carte ('dɔɪlɪ 'kɑ:t) *n.* **Rich·ard.** 1844–1901, English impresario noted for his productions of the operettas of Gilbert and Sullivan.
doz. *abbrev. for* dozen.
doze (dəʊz) *vb.* (*intr.*) **1.** to sleep lightly or intermittently. **2.** (often foll. by *off*) to fall into a light sleep. ~*n.* **3.** a short sleep. [C17: probably from Old Norse *dūs* lull; related to Danish *döse* to drowse, Swedish dialect *dusa* slumber] —'**doz·er** *n.*
doz·en ('dʌzᵊn) *determiner.* **1.** (preceded by *a* or a numeral) **a.** twelve or a group of twelve: *a dozen eggs; two dozen oranges.* **b.** (*as pronoun; functioning as sing. or pl.*): *give me a dozen; there are at least a dozen who haven't arrived yet.* ~*n., pl.* **doz·ens** *or* **doz·en. 2. daily dozen.** *Brit.* regular physical exercises. **3. by the dozen.** in large quantities. **4. baker's dozen.** thirteen. **5. talk nineteen to the dozen.** to talk without stopping. [C13: from Old French *douzaine,* from *douze* twelve, from Latin *duodecim,* from *duo* two + *decem* ten] —'**doz·enth** *adj.*
doz·er ('dəʊzə) *n. Brit.* short for **bulldozer.**
doz·ens ('dʌzᵊnz) *pl. n.* (usually foll. by *of*) *Informal.* a lot: *I've got dozens of things to do.*
doz·y ('dəʊzɪ) *adj.* **doz·i·er, doz·i·est. 1.** drowsy. **2.** *Brit. informal.* stupid. —'**doz·i·ly** *adv.* —'**doz·i·ness** *n.*
D.P. *abbrev. for* displaced person.
D.P.H. *abbrev. for* Diploma in Public Health.
D.Phil, D.Ph., *or* **DPh** *abbrev. for* Doctor of Philosophy. Also: **Ph.D., PhD**
D.P.M. *abbrev. for* Diploma in Psychological Medicine.
DPN *n. Biochem.* diphosphopyridine nucleotide; the former name for **NAD.**
DPNH *n. Biochem.* the reduced form of DPN; the former name for **NADH.**
DPP *or* **D.P.P.** (in Britain) *abbrev. for* Director of Public Prosecutions.
dpt. *abbrev. for* department.
D.P.W. *abbrev. for* Department of Public Works.
dr *or* **dr.** *abbrev. for* dram.
dr. *abbrev. for:* **1.** debit. **2.** debtor. **3.** drachma. **4.** drawer.
Dr. *abbrev. for:* **1.** Doctor. **2.** (in street names) Drive.
drab[1] (dræb) *adj.* **drab·ber, drab·best. 1.** dull; dingy; shabby. **2.** cheerless; dreary: *a drab evening.* **3.** of the colour drab. ~*n.* **4.** a light olive-brown colour. **5.** a fabric of a dull grey or brown colour. [C16: from Old French *drap* cloth, from Late Latin *drappus,* perhaps of Celtic origin] —'**drab·ly** *adv.* —'**drab·ness** *n.*
drab[2] (dræb) *Archaic.* ~*n.* **1.** a slatternly woman. **2.** a whore. ~*vb.* **drabs, drab·bing, drabbed. 3.** (*intr.*) to consort with prostitutes. [C16: of Celtic origin; compare Scottish Gaelic *drabag*]
drab·bet ('dræbɪt) *n. Brit.* a yellowish-brown fabric of coarse linen. [C19: see DRAB[1]]
drab·ble ('dræbᵊl) *vb.* to make or become wet or dirty. [C14: from Low German *drabbelen* to paddle in mud; related to DRAB[2]]
dra·cae·na (drə'si:nə) *n.* **1.** any tropical liliaceous plant of the genus *Dracaena:* some species are cultivated as house plants for their decorative foliage. See also **dragon tree. 2.** any of several similar plants of the related genus *Cordyline.* [C19: from New Latin, from Latin: she-dragon, from Greek *drakaina,* feminine of *drakōn* DRAGON]
drachm (dræm) *n.* **1.** Also called: **fluid dram.** *Brit.* one eighth of a fluid ounce. **2.** *U.S.* another name for **dram** (sense 2). **3.** another name for **drachma.** [C14: learned variant of DRAM]
drach·ma ('drækmə) *n., pl.* **·mas** *or* **·mae** (-mi:). **1.** the standard monetary unit of Greece, divided into 100 lepta. **2.** *U.S.* another name for **dram** (sense 2). **3.** a silver coin of ancient Greece. **4.** a unit of weight in ancient Greece. [C16: from Latin, from Greek *drakhmē* a handful, from *drassesthai* to seize]
Dra·co[1] ('dreɪkəʊ) *n., Latin genitive* **Dra·co·nis** (dreɪ'kəʊnɪs). a faint extensive constellation twisting around the N celestial pole and lying between Ursa Major and Cepheus. [from Latin, from Greek *drakōn* DRAGON]
Dra·co[2] ('dreɪkəʊ) *n.* 7th century B.C., Athenian statesman and lawmaker, whose code of laws (621) prescribed death for almost every offence.
dra·co liz·ard ('dreɪkəʊ) *n.* another name for **flying lizard.**
dra·cone ('drækəʊn) *n.* a large flexible cylindrical container towed by a ship, used for transporting liquids. [C20: from Latin: DRAGON]
Dra·co·ni·an (dreɪ'kəʊnɪən) *or* **Dra·con·ic** (dreɪ'kɒnɪk) *adj.* (*sometimes not cap.*) **1.** of or relating to Draco or his code of laws. **2.** harsh. —**Dra·'co·ni·an·ism** *n.* —**Dra·'con·i·cal·ly** *adv.*
dra·con·ic (dreɪ'kɒnɪk) *adj.* of, like, or relating to a dragon. [C17: from Latin *dracō* DRAGON] —**dra·'con·i·cal·ly** *adv.*
draff (dræf) *n.* the residue of husks after fermentation of the grain used in brewing, used as a food for cattle. [C13: from Old Norse *draf;* related to Old High German *trebir,* Russian *drob* fragment; see DRIVEL] —'**draff·y** *adj.*
draft (drɑ:ft) *n.* **1.** a plan, sketch, or drawing of something. **2.** a preliminary outline of a book, speech, etc. **3.** another word for **bill of exchange. 4.** a demand or drain on something. **5.** the divergent duct leading from a water turbine to its tailrace. **6.** *U.S.* selection for compulsory military service. **7.** detachment of military personnel from one unit to another. **8.** *Commerce.* an allowance on merchandise sold by weight. **9.** a line or narrow border that is chiselled on the surface of a stone to serve as a guide for levelling it. ~*vb.* (*tr.*) **10.** to draw up an outline or sketch for something: *to draft a speech.* **11.** to

prepare a plan or design of. **12.** to detach (military personnel) from one unit to another. **13.** *U.S.* to select for compulsory military service. **14.** to chisel a draft on (stone, etc.). ~*n., vb.* **15.** the usual U.S. spelling of **draught** (senses 1–8, 11). [C16: variant of DRAUGHT] —**'draft·er** *n.*

draft board *n. U.S.* a tribunal responsible for the selection of personnel liable for compulsory military service.

draft dodg·er *n. U.S.* one who evades compulsory military service.

draft·ee (drɑːf'tiː) *n. U.S.* a conscript.

drafts·man ('drɑːftsmən) *n., pl.* **-men.** the usual U.S. spelling of **draughtsman** (senses 1, 2). —**'drafts·man·ship** *n.*

draft·y ('drɑːftɪ) *adj.* **draft·i·er, draft·i·est.** the usual U.S. spelling of **draughty.** —**'draft·i·ly** *adv.* —**'draft·i·ness** *n.*

drag (dræg) *vb.* **drags, drag·ging, dragged. 1.** to pull or be pulled with force, esp. along the ground or other surface. **2.** (*tr.;* often foll. by *away* or *from*) to persuade to come away (from something attractive or interesting): *he couldn't drag himself away from the shop.* **3.** to trail or cause to trail on the ground. **4.** (*tr.*) to move (oneself, one's feet, etc.) with effort or difficulty: *he drags himself out of bed at dawn.* **5.** to linger behind. **6.** (when *intr.*, usually foll. by *for*) to search (the bed of a river, canal, etc.) with a dragnet or hook: *they dragged the river for the body.* **7.** (often foll. by *on* or *out*) to prolong tediously: *his talk dragged on for hours.* **8.** (*tr.* foll. by *out* or *from*) to crush (clods) or level (a soil surface) by use of a drag. **9.** (of hounds) to follow (a fox or its trail) to the place where it has been lying. **10.** (*intr.*) *Slang.* to draw (on a cigarette, pipe, etc.). **11.** (*tr.*) *U.S. slang.* to bore or annoy. **12. drag anchor.** (of a vessel) to move away from its mooring because the anchor has failed to hold. **13. drag one's feet** *or* **heels.** *Informal.* to act with deliberate slowness. **14. drag (someone's) name in the mud.** to disgrace or defame (someone). ~*n.* **15.** the act of dragging or the state of being dragged. **16.** an implement, such as a dragnet, dredge, etc., used for dragging. **17.** Also called: **drag harrow.** a type of harrow consisting of heavy beams, often with spikes inserted, used to crush clods, level soil, or prepare seedbeds. **18.** a sporting coach with seats inside and out, usually drawn by four horses. **19.** a braking or retarding device, such as a metal piece fitted to the underside of the wheel of a horse-drawn vehicle. **20.** a person or thing that slows up progress. **21.** slow progress or movement. **22.** *Aeronautics.* the resistance to the motion of a body passing through a fluid, esp. through air. **23.** the trail of scent left by a fox or other animal hunted with hounds. **24.** an artificial trail of a strong-smelling substance, sometimes including aniseed, drawn over the ground for hounds to follow. **25.** See **drag hunt. 26.** *Slang.* a person or thing that is very tedious; bore: *exams are a drag.* **27.** *Slang.* a car. **28.** *Slang.* short for **drag race. 29.** *Slang.* **a.** women's clothes worn by a man, usually by a transvestite (esp. in the phrase **in drag**). **b.** (*as modifier*): *a drag club; drag show.* **c.** clothes collectively. **30.** *Informal.* a draw on a cigarette, pipe, etc. **31.** *U.S. slang.* influence or persuasive power. **32.** *Chiefly U.S. slang.* a street or road. ~See also **drag down, drag in, drag out of, drag up.** [Old English *dragan* to DRAW; related to Swedish *dragga*]

drag down *vb.* (*tr., adv.*) to depress or demoralize: *the flu really dragged her down.*

dra·gée (dræ'ʒeɪ) *n.* **1.** a sweet made of fruit, nuts, etc., coated with a hard sugar icing. **2.** a tiny beadlike sweet used for decorating cakes, etc. **3.** a medicinal pill coated with sugar to disguise the taste. [C19: from French; see DREDGE²]

drag·gle ('dræg°l) *vb.* **1.** to make or become wet or dirty by trailing on the ground; bedraggle. **2.** (*intr.*) to lag; dawdle.

drag·gle·tailed ('dræg°lˌteɪld) *adj. Archaic.* (esp. of a woman) bedraggled; besmirched.

drag·gy ('drægɪ) *adj.* **-gi·er, -gi·est.** *Slang.* **1.** slow or boring: *a draggy party.* **2.** dull and listless.

drag·hound ('drægˌhaʊnd) *n.* a hound used to follow an artificial trail of scent in a drag hunt.

drag hunt *n.* **1.** a hunt in which hounds follow an artificial trail of scent. **2.** a club that organizes such hunts. ~*vb.* **drag-hunt. 3.** to follow draghounds, esp. on horseback, or cause (draghounds) to follow an artificial trail of scent.

drag in *vb.* (*tr., adv.*) to introduce or mention (a topic, name, etc.) with slight or no pretext.

drag·line ('drægˌlaɪn) *n.* **1.** another word for **dragrope** (sense 2). **2.** Also called: **dragline crane, dragline excavator.** a machine for dredging or excavating.

drag link *n.* a link for conveying motion between cranks on parallel shafts that are slightly offset. It is used in cars to connect the steering gear to the steering arm.

drag·net ('drægˌnɛt) *n.* **1.** a heavy or weighted net used to scour the bottom of a pond, river, etc., as when searching for something. **2.** any system of coordinated efforts by police forces to track down wanted persons.

dra·go·man ('drægəʊmən) *n., pl.* **-mans** *or* **-men.** (in some Middle Eastern countries, esp. formerly) a professional interpreter or guide. [C14: from French, from Italian *dragomano,* from Medieval Greek *dragoumanos,* from Arabic *targumān* an interpreter, from Aramaic *tūrgemānā,* of Akkadian origin]

drag·on ('drægən) *n.* **1.** a mythical monster usually represented as breathing fire and having a scaly reptilian body, wings, claws, and a long tail. **2.** *Informal.* a fierce or intractable person, esp. a woman. **3.** any of various very large lizards, esp. the Komodo dragon. **4.** *Archaic.* a large snake. **5.** any of various North American aroid plants, esp. the green dragon. **6.** *Christianity.* a manifestation of Satan or an attendant devil. [C13: from Old French, from Latin *dracō,* from Greek *drakōn;* related to *drakos* eye] —**'drag·on·ess** *fem. n.* —**'drag·on·ish** *adj.*

drag·on·et ('drægənɪt) *n.* any small spiny-finned fish of the family *Callionymidae,* having a flat head and a slender tapering brightly coloured body and living at the bottom of shallow seas. [C14 (meaning: small dragon): from French; applied to fish C18]

drag·on·fly ('drægənˌflaɪ) *n., pl.* **-flies. 1.** any predatory insect of the suborder *Anisoptera,* having a large head and eyes, a long slender body, two pairs of iridescent wings that are outspread at rest, and aquatic larvae: order *Odonata.* See also **damselfly. 2.** any other insect of the order *Odonata.*

drag·on·head ('drægənˌhɛd) *or* **drag·on's-head** *n.* **1.** any plant of the genus *Dracocephalum,* of Europe, Asia, and North America, having dense spikes of white or bluish flowers: family *Labiatae* (labiates). **2.** any North American plant of the related genus *Physostegia,* having pink or purplish flowers.

drag·on·nade (ˌdrægə'neɪd) *n.* **1.** *History.* the persecution of French Huguenots during the reign of Louis XIV by dragoons quartered in their villages and homes. **2.** subjection by military force. ~*vb.* **3.** (*tr.*) to subject to persecution by military troops. [C18: from French, from *dragon* DRAGOON]

drag·on·root ('drægənˌruːt) *n.* **1.** a North American aroid plant, *Arisaema dracontium,* having a greenish spathe and a long pointed spadix. **2.** the tuberous root of this plant, formerly used in medicine.

drag·on's blood *n.* **1.** a red resinous substance obtained from the fruit of a Malaysian palm, *Daemonorops* (or *Calamus*) *draco:* formerly used medicinally and now used in varnishes and lacquers. **2.** any of several similar resins obtained from other trees, esp. from the dragon tree.

drag·on tree *n.* a liliaceous tree, *Dracaena draco,* of the Canary Islands, having clusters of sword-shaped leaves at the tips of its branches: a source of dragon's blood.

dra·goon (drə'guːn) *n.* **1.** (originally) a mounted infantryman armed with a carbine. **2.** (*sometimes cap.*) a domestic fancy pigeon. **3. a.** a type of cavalryman. **b.** (*pl.; cap. when part of a name*): *the Royal Dragoons.* ~*vb.* (*tr.*) **4.** to coerce; force: *he was dragooned into admitting it.* **5.** to persecute by military force. [C17: from French *dragon* (special use of DRAGON), soldier armed with a carbine, perhaps suggesting that a carbine, like a dragon, breathed forth fire] —**dra·'goon·age** *n.*

drag out of *vb.* (*tr., adv.* + *prep.*) to obtain or extract (a confession, statement, etc.), esp. by force: *we dragged the name out of him. Also:* **drag from.**

drag race *n.* a type of motor race in which specially built or modified cars are timed over a measured course. —**drag rac·er** *n.* —**drag rac·ing** *n.*

drag·rope ('drægˌrəʊp) *n.* **1.** a rope used to drag military equipment, esp. artillery. **2.** Also called: **dragline, guide rope.** a rope trailing from a balloon or airship for mooring or braking purposes.

drag sail *n.* another term for **sea anchor.**

drag·ster ('drægstə) *n.* a car specially built or modified for drag racing.

drag up *vb.* (*tr., adv.*) *Informal.* **1.** to rear (a child) poorly and in an undisciplined manner. **2.** to introduce or revive (an unpleasant fact or story).

drail (dreɪl) *n.* **1.** *Angling.* a weighted hook used in trolling. ~*vb.* **2.** (*intr.*) to fish with a drail. [C16: apparently from TRAIL, influenced by DRAW]

drain (dreɪn) *n.* **1.** a pipe or channel that carries off water, sewage, etc. **2.** an instance or cause of continuous diminution in resources or energy; depletion. **3.** *Surgery.* a device, such as a tube, for insertion into a wound, incision, or bodily cavity to drain off pus, etc. **4.** *Electronics.* the electrode region in a field-effect transistor into which majority carriers flow from the interelectrode conductivity channel. **5. down the drain.** wasted. ~*vb.* **6.** (*tr.;* often foll. by *off*) to draw off or remove (liquid) from: *to drain water from vegetables; to drain vegetables.* **7.** (*intr.;* often foll. by *away*) to flow (away) or filter (off). **8.** (*intr.*) to dry or be emptied as a result of liquid running off or flowing away: *leave the dishes to drain.* **9.** (*tr.*) to drink the entire contents of (a glass, cup, etc.). **10.** (*tr.*) to consume or make constant demands on (resources, energy, etc.); exhaust; sap. **11.** (*intr.*) to disappear or leave, esp. gradually: *the colour drained from his face.* **12.** (*tr.*) (of a river, etc.) to carry off the surface water from an area. **13.** (*intr.*) (of an area) to discharge its surface water into rivers, streams, etc. [Old English *drēahnian;* related to Old Norse *drangr* dry wood; see DRY] —**'drain·a·ble** *adj.* —**'drain·er** *n.*

drain·age ('dreɪnɪdʒ) *n.* **1.** the process or a method of draining. **2.** a system of watercourses or drains. **3.** liquid, sewage, etc., that is drained away.

drain·age ba·sin *or* **ar·e·a** *n.* another name for **catchment area.**

drain·ing board *n.* a sloping grooved surface at one side of a sink, used for draining washed dishes, etc. Also called: **drainer.**

drain·pipe ('dreɪnˌpaɪp) *n.* a pipe for carrying off rainwater, sewage, etc.; downpipe.

drain·pipes ('dreɪnˌpaɪps) *pl. n.* very narrow men's trousers, worn in Britain during the 1950s, esp. by Teddy boys.

drake¹ (dreɪk) *n.* the male of any duck. [C13: perhaps from Low German; compare Middle Dutch *andrake,* Old High German *antrahho*]

drake² (dreɪk) *n.* **1.** *Angling.* an artificial fly resembling a mayfly. **2.** *History.* a small cannon. **3.** an obsolete word for **dragon.** [Old English *draca,* ultimately from Latin *dracō* DRAGON]

Drake (dreɪk) *n.* Sir **Fran·cis.** ?1540–96, English navigator and buccaneer, the first Englishman to sail around the world (1577–80). He commanded a fleet against the Spanish Armada (1588) and contributed greatly to its defeat.

Dra+kens+berg ('drɑːkənz,bɜːg) *n.* a mountain range in southern Africa, extending through Lesotho, E South Africa, and Swaziland. Highest peak: Thabana Ntlenyana, 3482 m (11 425 ft.). Sotho name: **Quathlamba.**

Drake Pas+sage *n.* a strait between S South America and the South Shetland Islands, connecting the Atlantic and Pacific Oceans.

dram (dræm) *n.* **1.** one sixteenth of an ounce (avoirdupois). 1 dram is equivalent to 0.0018 kilogram. **2.** Also called: **drachm, drachma.** *U.S.* one eighth of an apothecaries' ounce; 60 grains. 1 dram is equivalent to 0.0039 kilogram. **3.** a small amount of an alcoholic drink, esp. a spirit; tot. [C15: from Old French *dragme,* from Late Latin *dragma,* from Greek *drakhmē;* see DRACHMA]

dra+ma ('drɑːmə) *n.* **1.** a work to be performed by actors on stage, radio, or television; play. **2.** the genre of literature represented by works intended for the stage. **3.** the art of the writing and production of plays. **4.** a situation or sequence of events that is highly emotional, tragic, or turbulent. [C17: from Late Latin: a play, from Greek: something performed, from *dran* to do]

Dra+ma+mine ('dræmə,miːn) *n.* a trademark for **dimenhydrinate.**

dra+mat+ic (drə'mætɪk) *adj.* **1.** of or relating to drama. **2.** like a drama in suddenness, emotional impact, etc. **3.** striking; effective. **4.** acting or performed in a flamboyant way. **5.** *Music.* (of a voice) powerful and marked by histrionic quality. —**dra+'mat·i·cal+ly** *adv.*

dra+mat+ic i·ron·y *n. Theatre.* the irony occurring when the implications of a situation, speech, etc., are understood by the audience but not by the characters in the play.

dra+mat+ics (drə'mætɪks) *n.* **1.** (*functioning as sing. or pl.*) the art of acting or producing plays. **2.** dramatic productions. **3.** histrionic behaviour.

dra+ma+tis per+so+nae ('drɑːmətɪs pə'səʊnaɪ) *n.* **1.** the characters or a list of characters in a play or story. **2.** the main personalities in any situation or event. [C18: from New Latin]

dram·a·tist ('dræmətɪst) *n.* a writer of plays; playwright.

dram·a·ti+za+tion *or* **dram·a·ti+sa+tion** (,dræmətaɪ'zeɪʃən) *n.* **1.** the reconstruction of an event, novel, story, etc. in a form suitable for dramatic presentation. **2.** the art or act of dramatizing.

dram·a·tize *or* **dram·a+tise** ('dræmə,taɪz) *vb.* **1.** (*tr.*) to put into dramatic form. **2.** to express or represent (something) in a dramatic or exaggerated way: *he dramatizes his illness.* —**'dram·a+,tiz+a·ble** *or* **'dram·a+,tis+a·ble** *adj.* —**'dram·a+,tiz+er** *or* **'dram·a+,tis+er** *n.*

dram·a+turge ('dræmə,tɜːdʒ) *or* **dram·a+tur+gist** *n.* a dramatist, esp. one associated with a particular company or theatre. [C19: probably from French, from Greek *dramatourgos* playwright, from DRAMA + *ergon* work]

dram·a+tur+gy ('dræmə,tɜːdʒɪ) *n.* the art and technique of the theatre; dramatics. —**,dram·a+'tur+gic** *or* **,dram·a+'tur+gi+cal** *adj.* —**,dram·a+'tur+gi+cal+ly** *adv.*

Dram+men (*Norwegian* 'dramən) *n.* a port in S Norway. Pop.: 49 808 (1970).

Dran+cy (*French* drɑ̃'si) *n.* a residential suburb of NE Paris. Pop.: 64 494 (1975).

drank (dræŋk) *vb.* the past tense of **drink.**

drape (dreɪp) *vb.* **1.** (*tr.*) to hang or cover with flexible material or fabric, usually in folds; adorn. **2.** to hang or arrange or be hung or arranged, esp. in folds. **3.** (*tr.*) to place casually and loosely; hang: *she draped her arm over the back of the chair.* ~*n.* **4.** (*often pl.*) a cloth or hanging that covers something in folds; drapery. **5.** the way in which fabric hangs. [C15: from Old French *draper,* from *drap* piece of cloth; see DRAB[1]] —**'drap+a·ble** *or* **'drape+a·ble** *adj.*

drap+er ('dreɪpə) *n.* **1.** *Brit.* a dealer in fabrics and sewing materials. **2.** *Archaic.* a maker of cloth.

Dra·per ('dreɪpə) *n.* **1. Hen·ry.** 1837–82, U.S. astronomer, who contributed to stellar classification and spectroscopy. **2.** his father, **John Wil·liam.** 1811–82, U.S. chemist and historian, born in England, made the first photograph of the moon.

dra+per·y ('dreɪpərɪ) *n., pl.* **+per·ies. 1.** fabric or clothing arranged and draped. **2.** (*often pl.*) curtains or hangings that drape. **3.** *Brit.* the occupation or shop of a draper. **4.** fabrics and cloth collectively. —**'dra+per+ied** *adj.*

drapes (dreɪps) *or* **dra+per·ies** ('dreɪpərɪz) *pl. n. Chiefly U.S.* curtains, esp. ones of heavy fabric.

dras+tic ('dræstɪk) *adj.* extreme or forceful; severe. [C17: from Greek *drastikos,* from *dran* to do, act] —**'dras+ti+cal+ly** *adv.*

drat (dræt) *interj. Slang.* an exclamation of annoyance (also in the phrases **drat it! drat you!** etc.). [C19: probably alteration of *God rot*]

drat+ted ('drætɪd) *adj.* (*prenominal*) *Informal.* wretched; annoying.

draught *or U.S.* **draft** (drɑːft) *n.* **1.** a current of air, esp. one intruding into an enclosed space. **2. a.** the act of pulling a load, as by a vehicle or animal. **b.** (*as modifier*): *a draught horse.* **3.** the load or quantity drawn. **4.** a portion of liquid to be drunk, esp. a dose of medicine. **5.** the act or an instance of drinking; a gulp or swallow. **6.** the act or process of drawing air, smoke, etc., into the lungs. **7.** the amount of air, smoke, etc., inhaled in one breath. **8. a.** beer, wine, etc., stored in bulk, esp. in a cask, as opposed to being bottled. **b.** (*as modifier*): *draught beer.* **c. on draught.** drawn from a cask or keg. **9.** Also called: **draughtsman.** any one of the 12 flat thick discs used by each player in the game of draughts. U.S. equivalent: **checker. 10.** the depth of a loaded vessel in the water, taken from the level of the waterline to the lowest point of the hull. **11. feel the draught.** to be short of money. Usual U.S. spelling **draft.** [C14: probably from Old Norse *drahtr,* of Germanic origin; related to DRAW] —**'draught+er** *or U.S.* **'draft+er** *n.*

draught+board ('drɑːft,bɔːd) *n.* a square board divided into 64 squares of alternating colours, used for playing draughts or chess.

draughts (drɑːfts) *n.* a game for two players using a draughtboard and 12 draughtsmen each. The object is to jump over and capture the opponent's pieces. U.S. name: **checkers.** [C14: plural of DRAUGHT (in obsolete sense: a chess move)]

draughts+man *or U.S.* **drafts+man** ('drɑːftsmən) *n., pl.* **+men. 1.** a person who practises or is qualified in mechanical drawing, employed to prepare detailed scale drawings of machinery, buildings, devices, etc. **2.** a person skilled in drawing. **3.** *Brit.* any of the 12 flat thick discs used by each player in the game of draughts. U.S. equivalent: **checker.** —**'draughts+man+,ship** *or U.S.* **'drafts+man+,ship** *n.*

draught·y *or U.S.* **draft·y** ('drɑːftɪ) *adj.* **draught·i+er, draught·i+est** *or U.S.* **draft·i+er, draft·i·est.** characterized by or exposed to draughts of air. —**'draught·i+ly** *or U.S.* **'draft·i+ly** *adv.* —**'draught·i+ness** *or U.S.* **'draft·i+ness** *n.*

Dra+va *or* **Dra+ve** ('drɑːvə) *n.* a river in S central Europe, rising in N Italy and flowing east through Austria, then southeast as part of the border between Yugoslavia and Hungary to join the River Danube. Length: 725 km (450 miles). German name: **Drau** (draʊ).

Dra+vid+i·an (drə'vɪdɪən) *n.* **1.** a family of languages spoken in S and central India and Ceylon, including Tamil, Malayalam, Telugu, Kannada, and Gondi. **2.** a member of one of the aboriginal races of India, pushed south by the Indo-Europeans and now mixed with them. ~*adj.* **3.** denoting, belonging to, or relating to this family of languages or these peoples.

draw (drɔː) *vb.* **draws, draw+ing, drew, drawn. 1.** to cause (a person or thing) to move towards or away by pulling. **2.** to bring, take, or pull (something) out, as from a drawer, holster, etc. **3.** (*tr.*) to extract or pull or take out: *to draw teeth; to draw a card from a pack.* **4.** (*tr.;* often foll. by *off*) to take (liquid) out of a cask, keg, tank, etc., by means of a tap. **5.** (*intr.*) to move, go, or proceed, esp. in a specified direction: *to draw alongside.* **6.** (*tr.*) to attract or elicit: *to draw a crowd; draw attention.* **7.** (*tr.*) to cause to flow: *to draw blood.* **8.** to depict or sketch (a form, figure, picture, etc.) in lines, as with a pencil or pen, esp. without the use of colour; delineate. **9.** (*tr.*) to make, formulate, or derive: *to draw conclusions, comparisons, parallels.* **10.** (*tr.*) to write (a legal document) in proper form. **11.** (*tr.;* sometimes foll. by *in*) to suck or take in (air, liquid, etc.): *to draw a breath.* **12.** (*intr.*) to induce or allow a draught to carry off air, smoke, etc.: *the flue draws well.* **13.** (*tr.*) to take or receive from a source: *to draw money from the bank.* **14.** (*tr.*) to earn: *draw interest.* **15.** (*tr.*) *Finance.* to write out (a bill of exchange or promissory note): *to draw a cheque.* **16.** (*tr.*) to choose at random: *to draw lots.* **17.** (*tr.*) to reduce the diameter of (a wire or metal rod) by pulling it through a die. **18.** (*tr.*) to shape (a sheet of metal or glass) by rolling, by pulling it through a die or by stretching. **19.** *Archery.* to bend (a bow) by pulling the string. **20.** to steep (tea) or (of tea) to steep in boiling water. **21.** (*tr.*) to disembowel: *draw a chicken.* **22.** (*tr.*) to cause (pus, blood, etc.) to discharge from an abscess or wound. **23.** (*intr.*) (of two teams, contestants, etc.) to finish a game with an equal number of points, goals, etc.; tie. **24.** (*tr.*) *Bridge, whist.* to keep leading a suit in order to force out (all outstanding cards). **25. draw trumps.** *Bridge, whist.* to play the trump suit until the opponents have none left. **26.** (*tr.*) *Billiards.* to cause (the cue ball) to spin back after a direct impact with another ball by applying backspin when making the stroke. **27.** (*tr.*) to search (a place) in order to find wild animals, game, etc., for hunting. **28.** *Golf.* to drive (the ball) too far to the left. **29.** (*tr.*) *Curling.* to deliver (the stone) gently. **30.** (*tr.*) *Nautical.* (of a vessel) to require (a certain depth) in which to float. **31. draw (a) blank.** to be unsuccessful; fail. **32. draw and quarter.** to disembowel and dismember (a person) after hanging. **33. draw stumps.** *Cricket.* to close play, as by pulling out the stumps. **34. draw the line.** *Informal.* **a.** to fix a limit. **b.** to refuse to do. **35. draw the shot.** *Bowls.* to deliver the bowl in such a way that it approaches the jack. ~*n.* **36.** the act of drawing. **37.** *U.S.* a sum of money advanced to finance anticipated expenses. **38.** *Informal.* an event, occasion, act, etc., that attracts a large audience. **39.** a raffle or lottery. **40.** something taken or chosen at random, as a ticket in a raffle or lottery. **41.** a contest or game ending in a tie. **42.** *U.S.* a small natural drainage way or gully. **43.** a defect found in metal castings due to the contraction of the metal on solidification. ~See also **drawback, draw in, draw off, draw on, draw out, draw up.** [Old English *dragan;* related to Old Norse *draga;* Old Frisian *draga,* Old Saxon *dragan,* Old High German *tragan* to carry] —**'draw+a·ble** *adj.*

draw+back ('drɔː,bæk) *n.* **1.** a disadvantage or hindrance. **2.** a refund of certain excise duties paid on imported goods that are re-exported or used in the production of manufactured exports. ~*vb.* **draw back.** (*intr., adv.;* often foll. by *from*) **3.** to retreat; move backwards. **4.** to turn aside from an undertaking.

draw+bar ('drɔː,bɑː) *n.* a strong metal bar on a tractor, locomotive, etc., bearing a hook or link and pin to attach a trailer, wagon, etc.

draw·bridge ('drɔːˌbrɪdʒ) *n.* a bridge that may be raised to prevent access or to enable vessels to pass.
draw·ee (drɔːˈiː) *n.* the person or organization on which a cheque or other order for payment is drawn.
draw·er ('drɔːə) *n.* **1.** a person or thing that draws, esp. a draughtsman. **2.** a person who draws a cheque. **3.** a person who draws up a commercial paper. **4.** *Archaic.* a person who draws beer, etc., in a bar. **5.** (drɔː). a boxlike container in a chest, table, etc., made for sliding in and out.
drawers (drɔːz) *pl. n.* a legged undergarment for either sex, worn below the waist. Also called: **underdrawers.**
draw gear *n. Brit.* an apparatus for coupling railway cars.
draw in *vb.* (*intr., adv.*) **1.** (of hours of daylight) to become shorter. **2.** (of a train) to arrive at a station.
draw·ing ('drɔːɪŋ) *n.* **1.** a picture or plan made by means of lines on a surface, esp. one made with a pencil or pen without the use of colour. **2.** a sketch, plan, or outline. **3.** the art of making drawings; draughtsmanship.
draw·ing ac·count *n. U.S.* an account out of which an employee, partner, or salesman may make withdrawals to meet expenses or as advances against expected income.
draw·ing board *n.* **1.** a smooth flat rectangular board on which paper, canvas, etc., is placed for making drawings. **2. back to the drawing board.** return to an earlier stage in an enterprise because a planned undertaking has failed.
draw·ing card *n. U.S. theatre.* a performer, act, etc., certain to attract a large audience.
draw·ing pin *n. Brit.* a short tack with a broad smooth head for fastening papers to a drawing board, etc. U.S. names: **thumbtack, pushpin.**
draw·ing room *n.* **1.** a room where visitors are received and entertained; living room; sitting room. **2.** *Archaic.* a ceremonial or formal reception, esp. at court.
draw·knife ('drɔːˌnaɪf) *or* **draw·shave** *n., pl.* **·knives** *or* **·shaves.** a woodcutting tool with two handles at right angles to the blade, used to shave wood. U.S. name: **spokeshave.**
drawl (drɔːl) *vb.* **1.** to speak or utter (words) slowly, esp. prolonging the vowel sounds. ~*n.* **2.** the way of speech of someone who drawls. [C16: probably frequentative of DRAW] —'**drawl·er** *n.* —'**drawl·y** *adj.*
drawn (drɔːn) *adj.* haggard, tired, or tense in appearance.
drawn but·ter *n.* melted butter often with seasonings.
drawn work *n.* ornamental needlework done by drawing threads out of the fabric and using the remaining threads to form lacelike patterns. Also called: **drawn-thread work.**
draw off *vb.* (*adv.*) **1.** (*tr.*) to cause (a liquid) to flow from something. **2.** to withdraw (troops).
draw on *vb.* **1.** (*intr., prep.*) to use or exploit (a source, fund, etc.): *to draw on one's experience.* **2.** (*intr., adv.*) to come near: *the time for his interview drew on.* **3.** (*tr., prep.*) to withdraw (money) from (an account). **4.** (*tr., adv.*) to put on (clothes). **5.** (*tr., adv.*) to lead further; entice or encourage: *the prospect of nearing his goal drew him on.*
draw out *vb.* (*adv.*) **1.** to extend or cause to be extended: *he drew out his stay.* **2.** (*tr.*) to cause (a person) to talk freely: *she's been quiet all evening—see if you can draw her out.* **3.** (*tr.*; foll. by *of*) Also: **draw from.** to elicit (information) (from): *he managed to draw out of his son where he had been.* **4.** (*tr.*) to withdraw (money) as from a bank account or a business. **5.** (*intr.*) (of hours of daylight) to become longer. **6.** (*intr.*) (of a train) to leave a station. **7.** (*tr.*) to extend (troops) in line; lead from camp. **8.** (*intr.*) (of troops) to proceed from camp.
draw·plate ('drɔːˌpleɪt) *n.* a plate having conical holes through which wire is drawn to reduce its diameter.
draw·string ('drɔːˌstrɪŋ) *n.* **a.** a cord, ribbon, etc., run through a hem around an opening, as on the bottom of a sleeve or at the mouth of a bag, so that when it is pulled tighter, the opening closes. **b.** (*as modifier*): *a drawstring neckline.*
draw·tube ('drɔːˌtjuːb) *n.* a tube, such as one of the component tubes of a telescope, fitting coaxially within another tube through which it can slide.
draw up *vb.* (*adv.*) **1.** to come or cause to come to a halt. **2.** (*tr.*) **a.** to prepare a draft of (a legal document, etc.). **b.** to formulate and write out in appropriate form: *to draw up a contract.* **3.** (*used reflexively*) to straighten oneself. **4.** to form or arrange (a body of soldiers, etc.) in order or formation.
dray (dreɪ) *n.* **1. a.** a low cart without fixed sides, used for carrying heavy loads. **b.** (*in combination*): *a drayman.* **2.** any other vehicle or sledge used to carry a heavy load. [Old English *dræge* dragnet; related to Old Norse *draga* load of timber carried on horseback and trailing on the ground; see DRAW]
dray·horse ('dreɪˌhɔːs) *n.* a large powerful horse used for drawing a dray.
Dray·ton ('dreɪtᵊn) *n.* **Mi·chael.** 1563–1631, English poet; his work includes odes and pastorals, and *Poly-Olbion* (1613–22), on the topography of England.
dread (drɛd) *vb.* (*tr.*) **1.** to anticipate with apprehension or terror. **2.** to fear greatly. **3.** *Archaic.* to be in awe of. ~*n.* **4.** great fear; horror. **5.** an object of terror. **6.** *Archaic.* deep reverence. [Old English *ondrǣdan;* related to Old Saxon *antdrādan,* Old High German *intrātan*]
dread·ful ('drɛdfʊl) *adj.* **1.** extremely disagreeable, shocking, or bad: *what a dreadful play.* **2.** (intensifier): *this is a dreadful waste of time.* **3.** causing dread; terrifying. **4.** *Archaic.* inspiring awe. —'**dread·ful·ness** *n.*
dread·ful·ly ('drɛdfʊlɪ) *adv.* **1.** in a shocking, or disagreeable manner. **2.** (intensifier): *you're dreadfully kind.*
dread·nought *or* **dread·naught** ('drɛdˌnɔːt) *n.* **1.** a battleship armed with heavy guns of uniform calibre. **2.** an overcoat made of heavy cloth. **3.** *Slang.* a heavyweight boxer. **4.** a person who fears nothing.
dream (driːm) *n.* **1. a.** mental activity, usually in the form of an imagined series of events, occurring during certain phases of sleep. **b.** (*as modifier*): *a dream sequence.* **c.** (*in combination*): *dreamland.* **2. a.** a sequence of imaginative thoughts indulged in while awake; daydream; fantasy. **b.** (*as modifier*): *a dream world.* **3.** a person or thing seen or occurring in a dream. **4.** a cherished hope; ambition; aspiration. **5.** a vain hope. **6.** a person or thing that is as pleasant, or seemingly unreal as a dream. **7. go like a dream.** to move, develop, or work very well. ~*vb.* **dreams, dream·ing, dreamt** *or* **dreamed. 8.** (*may take a clause as object*) to undergo or experience (a dream or dreams). **9.** (*intr.*) to indulge in daydreams. **10.** to suffer delusions; be unrealistic: *you're dreaming if you think you can win.* **11.** (when *intr.*, foll. by *of* or *about*) to have an image (of) or fantasy (about) in or as if in a dream. **12.** (*intr.*; foll. by *of*) to consider the possibility (of): *I wouldn't dream of troubling you.* [Old English *drēam* song; related to Old High German *troum,* Old Norse *draumr,* Greek *thrulos* noise] —'**dream·ful** *adj.* —'**dream·ful·ly** *adv.* —'**dream·ing·ly** *adv.* —'**dream·less** *adj.* —'**dream·less·ly** *adv.* —'**dream·less·ness** *n.* —'**dream·ˌlike** *adj.*
dream·er ('driːmə) *n.* **1.** a person who dreams habitually. **2.** a person who lives in or escapes to a world of fantasy or illusion; escapist. **3.** *Archaic.* a prophet; visionary.
dream time *n.* another name for **alcheringa.**
dream up *vb.* (*tr., adv.*) *Informal.* to invent by ingenuity and imagination: *to dream up an excuse for leaving.*
dream·y ('driːmɪ) *adj.* **dream·i·er, dream·i·est. 1.** vague or impractical. **2.** resembling a dream in quality. **3.** relaxing; gentle: *dreamy music.* **4.** *Informal.* wonderful. **5.** having dreams, esp. daydreams. —'**dream·i·ly** *adv.* —'**dream·i·ness** *n.*
drear·y ('drɪərɪ) *adj.* **drear·i·er, drear·i·est. 1.** sad or dull; dismal. **2.** wearying; boring. **3.** *Archaic.* miserable. ~Also (literary): **drear.** [Old English *drēorig* gory; related to Old High German *trūreg* sad] —'**drear·i·ly** *adv.* —'**drear·i·ness** *n.*
dredge¹ (drɛdʒ) *n.* **1.** Also called: **dredger.** a machine, in the form of a bucket ladder, grab, or suction device, used to remove material from a riverbed, channel, etc. **2.** another name for **dredger¹** (sense 1). ~*vb.* **3.** to remove (material) from a riverbed, channel, etc., by means of a dredge. **4.** (*tr.*) to search for (a submerged object) with or as if with a dredge; drag. [C16: perhaps ultimately from Old English *dragan* to DRAW; see DRAG]
dredge² (drɛdʒ) *vb.* to sprinkle or coat (food) with flour, sugar, etc. [C16: from Old French *dragie,* perhaps from Latin *tragēmata* spices, from Greek]
dredg·er¹ ('drɛdʒə) *n.* **1.** Also called: **dredge.** a vessel used for dredging, often bargelike and usually equipped with retractable steel piles that are driven into the bottom for stability. **2.** another name for **dredge¹** (sense 1).
dredg·er² ('drɛdʒə) *n.* a container with a perforated top for sprinkling flour, sugar, etc.
dredge up *vb.* (*tr., adv.*) **1.** *Informal.* to bring to notice, esp. with considerable effort and from an obscure, remote, or unlikely source: *to dredge up worthless ideas.* **2.** to raise with or as if with a dredge: *they dredged up the corpse from the lake.*
dree (driː) *Scot., literary.* ~*vb.* **drees, dree·ing, dreed. 1.** (*tr.*) to endure. ~*adj.* **2.** another word for **dreich.** [Old English *drēogan;* related to Old Norse *drȳgja* to perpetrate]
dreg (drɛg) *n.* **1.** a small quantity: *not a dreg of pity.* [see DREGS]
dreg·gy ('drɛgɪ) *adj.* **·gi·er, ·gi·est.** like or full of dregs.
D re·gion *or* **lay·er** *n.* the lowest region of the ionosphere, extending from a height of about 60 kilometres to about 90 kilometres: contains a low concentration of free electrons and reflects low-frequency radio waves. See also **ionosphere.**
dregs (drɛgz) *pl. n.* **1.** solid particles that tend to settle at the bottom of some liquids, such as wine or coffee. **2.** residue or remains. **3.** *Brit. slang.* a despicable person. [C14 *dreg,* from Old Norse *dregg;* compare Icelandic *dreggjar* dregs, Latin *fracēs* oil dregs]
Drei·bund *German.* ('draɪbʊnt) *n.* a triple alliance, esp. that formed between Germany, Austria-Hungary, and Italy (1882–1915). [from *drei* THREE + *Bund* union, alliance]
dreich *or* **dreigh** (driːx) *adj. Scot. dialect.* dreary. [Middle English *dreig, drih* enduring, from Old English *drēog* (unattested); see DREE]
Drei·ser ('draɪsə, -zə) *n.* **The·o·dore (Herman Albert).** 1871–1945, U.S. novelist; his works include *Sister Carrie* (1900) and *An American Tragedy* (1925).
drench (drɛntʃ) *vb.* (*tr.*) **1.** to make completely wet; soak. **2.** to give liquid medicine to (an animal), esp. by force. ~*n.* **3.** the act or an instance of drenching. **4.** a dose of liquid medicine given to an animal. [Old English *drencan* to cause to drink; related to Old High German *trenken*] —'**drench·er** *n.*
Dren·the (*Dutch* 'drɛntə) *n.* a province of the NE Netherlands: a low plateau, with many raised bogs, partially reclaimed; agricultural, with oil deposits. Capital: Assen. Pop.: 386 400 (1973 est.). Area: 2647 sq. km (1032 sq. miles).
Dres·den ('drɛzdᵊn) *n.* **1.** an industrial city in SE East Germany, on the River Elbe: capital of Saxony from the 16th century until 1952; it was severely damaged in the Seven Years' War (1760); the baroque city was almost totally destroyed in World War II

by Allied bombing (1945). Pop.: 508 298 (1975 est.). ~*adj.* **2.** relating to, designating, or made of Dresden china.

Dres+den chi+na *n.* porcelain ware, esp. delicate and elegantly decorative objects and figures of high quality made at Meissen, near Dresden, since 1710.

dress (drɛs) *vb.* **1.** to put clothes on (oneself or another); attire. **2.** (*intr.*) to change one's clothes, esp. to more formal attire. **3.** (*tr.*) to provide (someone) with clothing; clothe. **4.** (*tr.*) to arrange merchandise in (a shop window) for effective display. **5.** (*tr.*) to comb out or arrange (the hair) into position. **6.** (*tr.*) to apply protective or therapeutic covering to (a wound, sore, etc.). **7.** (*tr.*) to prepare (food, esp. fowl and fish) for cooking or serving by cleaning, trimming, gutting, etc. **8.** (*tr.*) to put a finish on (the surface of stone, metal, etc.). **9.** (*tr.*) to till and cultivate (land), esp. by applying manure, compost, or fertilizer. **10.** (*tr.*) to prune and trim (trees, bushes, etc.). **11.** (*tr.*) to groom (an animal, esp. a horse). **12.** (*tr.*) to convert (tanned hides) into leather. **13.** *Military.* to bring (troops) into line or (of troops) to come into line (esp. in the phrase **dress ranks**). **14. dress ship.** *Nautical.* to decorate a vessel by displaying all signal flags on lines run from the bow to the stern over the mast trucks. ~*n.* **15.** a one-piece garment for a woman, consisting of a skirt and bodice. **16.** complete style of clothing; costume: *formal dress; military dress.* **17.** (*modifier*) suitable or required for a formal occasion: *a dress shirt.* **18.** the outer covering or appearance, esp. of living things: *trees in their spring dress of leaves.* ~See also **dress down, dress up.** [C14: from Old French *drecier,* ultimately from Latin *dīrigere* to DIRECT]

dres+sage ('drɛsɑːʒ) *n* **1.** the method of training a horse to perform manoeuvres in response to the rider's body signals. **2.** the manoeuvres performed by a horse trained in this method. [French: preparation, from Old French *dresser* to prepare; see DRESS]

dress cir+cle *n.* a tier of seats in a theatre or other auditorium, usually the first gallery above the ground floor.

dress coat *n.* a man's formal tailcoat with a cutaway skirt.

dress down *vb.* (*tr., adv.*) *Informal.* to reprimand severely or scold (a person).

dress+er[1] ('drɛsə) *n.* **1.** a set of shelves, usually also with cupboards or drawers, for storing or displaying dishes, etc. **2.** a chest of drawers for storing clothing in a bedroom or dressing room, often having a mirror on the top. [C15 *dressour,* from Old French *dreceore,* from *drecier* to arrange; see DRESS]

dress+er[2] ('drɛsə) *n.* **1.** a person who dresses in a specified way: *a fashionable dresser.* **2.** *Theatre.* a person employed to assist actors in putting on and taking off their costumes. **3.** a tool used for dressing stone or other materials. **4.** *Brit.* a person who assists a surgeon during operations. **5.** *Brit.* See **window-dresser.**

dress+ing ('drɛsɪŋ) *n.* **1.** a sauce for food, esp. for salad. **2.** the U.S. name for **stuffing** (sense 2). **3.** a covering for a wound, sore, etc. **4. a.** manure or artificial fertilizer spread on land. **5.** size used for stiffening textiles. **6.** the processes in the conversion of certain rough tanned hides into leather ready for use.

dress·ing-down *n. Informal.* a severe scolding or thrashing.

dress+ing gown *n.* a full robe worn before dressing or for lounging.

dress+ing room *n.* **1.** *Theatre.* a room backstage for an actor to change clothing and to make up. **2.** any room used for changing clothes, such as one at a sports ground or off a bedroom.

dress+ings ('drɛsɪŋz) *pl. n.* dressed stonework, mouldings, and carved ornaments used to form quoins, keystones, sills, and similar features.

dress+ing sta+tion *n. Military.* a first-aid post close to a combat area.

dress+ing ta+ble *n.* a piece of bedroom furniture with a mirror and a set of drawers for clothes, cosmetics, etc.

dress+mak·er ('drɛsˌmeɪkə) *n.* a person whose occupation is making clothes, esp. for women. —'**dress+ˌmak·ing** *n.*

dress pa+rade *n. Military.* a formal parade of sufficient ceremonial importance for the wearing of dress uniform.

dress re+hears+al *n.* **1.** the last complete rehearsal of a play or other work, using costumes, scenery, lighting, etc., as for the first night. **2.** any full-scale practice.

dress shield *n.* a fabric pad worn under the armpits or attached to the armhole of a garment to prevent sweat from showing on or staining the clothing.

dress shirt *n.* a man's evening shirt, worn as part of formal evening dress.

dress suit *n.* a man's evening suit, esp. tails.

dress u·ni+form *n. Military.* formal ceremonial uniform.

dress up *vb.* (*adv.*) **1.** to attire (oneself or another) in one's best clothes. **2.** to put fancy dress, disguise, etc., on (oneself or another), as in children's games: *let's dress up as ghosts!* **3.** (*tr.*) to improve the appearance or impression of: *it's no good trying to dress up the facts.*

dress·y ('drɛsɪ) *adj.* **dress·i+er, dress·i+est.** *Informal.* **1.** (of clothes) elegant. **2.** (of persons) dressing stylishly. **3.** over-elegant. —'**dress·i+ly** *adv.* —'**dress·i+ness** *n.*

drew (druː) *vb.* the past tense of **draw.**

Drey·fus ('dreɪfəs; *French* drɛ'fys) *n.* **Al+fred** (al'frɛd). 1859–1935, French army officer, a Jew whose false imprisonment for treason (1894) raised issues of anti-semitism and militarism that dominated French politics until his release (1906).

drib+ble ('drɪbᵊl) *vb.* **1.** (*usually intr.*) to flow or allow to flow in a thin stream or drops; trickle. **2.** (*intr.*) to allow saliva to trickle from the mouth. **3.** (in soccer, basketball, hockey, etc.) to propel (the ball) by repeatedly tapping it with the hand, foot, or stick. ~*n.* **4.** a small quantity of liquid falling in drops or flowing in a thin stream. **5.** a small quantity or supply. **6.** an act or instance of dribbling. [C16: frequentative of *drib,* variant of DRIP] —'**drib+bler** *n.* —'**drib+bly** *adj.*

drib+let *or* **drib+blet** ('drɪblɪt) *n.* a small quantity or amount, as of liquid. [C17: from obsolete *drib* to fall bit by bit + -LET]

dribs and drabs *n. Informal.* small sporadic amounts.

dried (draɪd) *vb.* the past tense or past participle of **dry.**

dri+er[1] ('draɪə) *adj.* the comparative of **dry.**

dri+er[2] ('draɪə) *n.* a variant spelling of **dryer**[1].

dri+est ('draɪɪst) *adj.* the superlative of **dry.**

drift (drɪft) *vb.* (*mainly intr.*) **1.** (*also tr.*) to be carried along by or as if by currents of air or water or (of a current) to carry (a vessel, etc.) along. **2.** to move aimlessly from place to place or from one activity to another. **3.** to wander or move gradually away from a fixed course or point; stray. **4.** (*also tr.*) (of snow, sand, etc.) to accumulate in heaps or banks or to drive (snow, sand, etc.) into heaps or banks. ~*n.* **5.** something piled up by the wind or current, such as a snowdrift. **6.** tendency, trend, meaning, or purport: *the drift of the argument.* **7.** a state of indecision or inaction. **8.** the extent to which a vessel, aircraft, projectile, etc. is driven off its course by adverse winds, tide, or current. **9.** a general tendency of surface ocean water to flow in the direction of the prevailing winds: *North Atlantic Drift.* **10.** a driving movement, force, or influence; impulse. **11.** a controlled four-wheel skid, used by racing drivers to take bends at high speed. **12.** a loose unstratified deposit of sand, gravel, etc., esp. one transported and deposited by a glacier or ice sheet. **13.** a horizontal passage in a mine that follows the mineral vein. **14.** something, esp. a group of animals, driven along by human or natural agencies: *a drift of cattle.* **15.** Also called: **driftpin.** a tapering steel tool driven into holes to enlarge or align them before bolting or riveting. **16.** an uncontrolled slow change in some operating characteristic of a piece of equipment, esp. an electronic circuit or component. **17.** *Linguistics.* gradual change in a language, esp. in so far as this is influenced by the internal structure of the language rather than by contact with other languages. **18.** *S. African.* a ford. [C13: from Old Norse: snowdrift; related to Old High German *trift* pasturage] —'**drift·y** *adj.*

drift+age ('drɪftɪdʒ) *n.* **1.** the act of drifting. **2.** matter carried along or deposited by drifting. **3.** the amount by which an aircraft or vessel has drifted from its intended course.

drift an+chor *n.* another term for **sea anchor.**

drift+er ('drɪftə) *n.* **1.** a person or thing that drifts. **2.** *Informal.* a person who moves aimlessly from place to place, usually without a regular job. **3.** a boat used for drift-net fishing. **4.** *Nautical.* a large jib of thin material used in light breezes.

drift ice *n.* masses of ice floating in the open sea.

drift net *n.* a large fishing net supported by floats or attached to a drifter that is allowed to drift with the tide or current.

drift tran+sis+tor *n.* a transistor in which the impurity concentration in the base increases from the collector-base junction to the emitter-base junction, producing a resistivity gradient that greatly increases its high-frequency response.

drift tube *n. Physics.* a hollow cylindrical electrode to which a radio-frequency voltage is applied in a linear accelerator.

drift+wood ('drɪftˌwʊd) *n.* wood floating on or washed ashore by the sea or other body of water.

drill[1] (drɪl) *n.* **1.** a rotating tool that is inserted into a drilling machine or tool for boring cylindrical holes. **2.** a hand tool, either manually or electrically operated, for drilling holes. **3.** *Military.* training in procedures or movements, as for ceremonial parades or the use of weapons. **4.** strict and often repetitious training or exercises used as a method of teaching. **5.** *Informal.* correct procedure or routine. **6.** a marine gastropod mollusc, *Urosalpinx cinera,* closely related to the whelk, that preys on oysters. ~*vb.* **7.** to pierce, bore, or cut (a hole) in (material) with or as if with a drill: *to drill a hole; to drill metal.* **8.** to instruct or be instructed in military procedures or movements. **9.** (*tr.*) to teach by rigorous exercises or training. **10.** (*tr.*) *Slang.* to hit (a ball) in a straight line at great speed. **11.** (*tr.*) *Informal.* to riddle with bullets. [C17: from Middle Dutch *drillen;* related to Old High German *drāen* to turn] —'**drill+a·ble** *adj.* —'**drill+er** *n.*

drill[2] (drɪl) *n.* **1.** a machine for planting seeds in rows or depositing fertilizer. **2.** a small furrow in which seeds are sown. **3.** a row of seeds planted using a drill. ~*vb.* **4.** to plant (seeds) by means of a drill. [C18: of uncertain origin; compare German *Rille* furrow] —'**drill+er** *n.*

drill[3] (drɪl) *or* **drill+ing** *n.* a hard-wearing twill-weave cotton cloth, used for uniforms, etc. [C18: variant of German *Drillich,* from Latin *trilīx,* from TRI- + *līcium* thread]

drill[4] (drɪl) *n.* an Old World monkey, *Mandrillus leucophaeus,* of W Africa, related to the mandrill but smaller and less brightly coloured. [C17: from a West African word; compare MANDRILL]

drill+mas·ter ('drɪlˌmɑːstə) *n.* **1.** Also called: **drill sergeant.** a military drill instructor. **2.** a person who instructs in a strict manner.

drill press *n.* a machine tool for boring holes, having a fixed stand and work table with facilities for lowering the rotating tool to the workpiece.

drill+stock ('drɪlˌstɒk) *n.* the part of a machine tool that holds the shank of a drill or bit; chuck.

dri+ly ('draɪlɪ) *adv.* a variant spelling of **dryly.**

Drin (drɪn) *n.* a river in S Europe, rising on the border between

Albania and Yugoslavia and flowing north and west into the Adriatic Sea. Length: about 270 km (170 miles).

drink (drɪŋk) *vb.* **drinks, drink·ing, drank, drunk.** **1.** to swallow (a liquid); imbibe. **2.** (*tr.*) to take in or soak up (liquid); absorb: *this plant drinks a lot of water.* **3.** (*tr.*; usually foll. by *in*) to pay close attention (to); be fascinated (by): *he drank in the speaker's every word.* **4.** (*tr.*) to bring (oneself into a certain condition) by consuming alcohol. **5.** (*tr.*; often foll. by *away*) to dispose of or ruin by excessive expenditure on alcohol: *he drank away his fortune.* **6.** (*intr.*) to consume alcohol, esp. to excess. **7.** (when *intr.*, foll. by *to*) to drink (a toast) in celebration, honour, or hope (of). **8. drink (someone) under the table.** to be able to drink more intoxicating beverage than (someone). **9. drink the health of.** to salute or celebrate with a toast. **10. drink with the flies.** *Austral. informal.* to drink alone. ~*n.* **11.** liquid suitable for drinking; any beverage. **12.** alcohol or its habitual or excessive consumption. **13.** an amount or portion of liquid for drinking; draught. **14. the drink.** *Informal.* the sea. [Old English *drincan;* related to Old Frisian *drinka,* Gothic *drigkan,* Old High German *trinkan*] —**drink·a·ble** *adj.*

drink·er ('drɪŋkə) *n.* a person who drinks, esp. a person who drinks alcohol habitually.

drink·ing foun·tain *n.* a device for providing a flow or jet of drinking water, usually in public places.

drink·ing-up time *n.* (in Britain) a short time allowed for finishing drinks before closing time in a public house.

drink·ing wa·ter *n.* water reserved or suitable for drinking.

Drink·wa·ter ('drɪŋkˌwɔːtə) *n.* **John.** 1882–1937, English dramatist, poet, and critic; author of chronicle plays such as *Abraham Lincoln* (1918) and *Mary Stuart* (1921).

drip (drɪp) *vb.* **drips, drip·ping, dripped.** **1.** to fall or let fall in drops. ~*n.* **2.** the formation and falling of drops of liquid. **3.** the sound made by falling drops. **4.** *Architect.* a projection at the front lower edge of a sill or cornice designed to throw water clear of the wall below. **5.** *Informal.* an inane, insipid person. **6.** *Med.* the usually intravenous drop-by-drop administration of a therapeutic solution, as of salt or sugar. [Old English *dryppan,* from *dropa* DROP]

drip-dry *adj.* designating clothing or a fabric that will dry relatively free of creases if hung up when wet.

drip·ping ('drɪpɪŋ) *n.* **1.** the fat that exudes from meat while it is being roasted or fried, used for basting or as shortening, etc. **2.** (*often pl.*) liquid that falls in drops. ~*adv.* **3.** (intensifier)*: dripping wet.*

drip·ping pan *or* **drip pan** *n.* a shallow pan placed under roasting meat to catch the dripping.

drip·py ('drɪpɪ) *adj.* **·pi·er, ·pi·est.** **1.** tending to drip. **2.** *Informal.* mawkish, insipid, or inane.

drip·stone ('drɪpˌstəʊn) *n.* **1.** the form of calcium carbonate existing in stalactites or stalagmites. **2.** Also called: **label, hood mould.** *Architect.* a drip made of stone.

drive (draɪv) *vb.* **drives, driv·ing, drove, driv·en.** **1.** to push, propel, or be pushed or propelled. **2.** to control and guide the movement of (a vehicle, draught animal, etc.): *to drive a car.* **3.** (*tr.*) to compel or urge to work or act, esp. excessively. **4.** (*tr.*) to goad or force into a specified attitude or state: *work drove him to despair.* **5.** (*tr.*) to cause (an object) to make or form (a hole, crack, etc.): *his blow drove a hole in the wall.* **6.** to move or cause to move rapidly by striking or throwing with force. **7.** *Sport.* to hit (a ball) very hard and straight, as (in cricket) with the bat swinging more or less vertically. **8.** *Golf.* to strike (the ball) with a driver, as in teeing off. **9.** (*tr.*) **a.** to chase (game) from cover into more open ground. **b.** to search (an area) for game. **10.** to transport or be transported in a driven vehicle. **11.** (*intr.*) to rush or dash violently, esp. against an obstacle or solid object: *the waves drove against the rock.* **12.** (*tr.*) to carry through or transact with vigour (esp. in the phrase **drive a hard bargain**). **13.** (*tr.*) to force (a component) into or out of its location by means of blows or a press. **14.** (*tr.*) *Mining.* to excavate horizontally. **15. drive home. a.** to cause to penetrate to the fullest extent. **b.** to make clear by special emphasis. ~*n.* **16.** the act of driving. **17.** a trip or journey in a driven vehicle. **18. a.** a road for vehicles, esp. a private road leading to a house. **b.** (*cap. when part of a street name*)*: Woodland Drive.* **19.** vigorous or urgent pressure, as in business. **20.** a united effort, esp. directed towards a common goal: *a charity drive.* **21.** *Brit.* a large gathering of persons to play whist, bridge, etc. **22.** energy, ambition, or initiative. **23.** a sustained and powerful military offensive. **24. a.** the means by which force, torque, motion, or power is transmitted in a mechanism: *fluid drive.* **b.** (*as modifier*)*: a drive shaft.* **25.** *Sport.* a hard straight shot or stroke. **26.** a search for and chasing of game towards waiting guns. [Old English *drīfan;* related to Old Frisian *drīva,* Old Norse *drīfa,* Gothic *dreiban,* Old High German *trīban*] —'**driv·a·ble** *or* '**drive·a·ble** *adj.*

drive at *vb.* (*intr., prep.*) *Informal.* to aim at; to intend or mean: *what are you driving at?*

drive-in *n. Chiefly U.S.* **a.** a cinema, designed to be used by patrons seated in their cars. **b.** (*modifier*) a public facility or service designed for use in such a manner: *a drive-in restaurant.*

driv·el ('drɪvəl) *vb.* **·els, ·el·ling, ·elled** *or U.S.* **·els, ·el·ing, ·eled.** **1.** to allow (saliva) to flow from the mouth; dribble. **2.** (*intr.*) to speak foolishly or childishly. **3.** *Archaic.* to flow or trickle: *a wound drivelling blood.* ~*n.* **4.** foolish or senseless talk. **5.** saliva flowing from the mouth; slaver. [Old English *dreflian* to slaver; see DRAFF] —'**driv·el·ler** *n.*

driv·en ('drɪvən) *vb.* the past participle of **drive.**

driv·er ('draɪvə) *n.* **1.** a person who drives a vehicle. **2.** a person who drives animals. **3.** a mechanical component that exerts a force on another to produce motion. **4.** *Golf.* a club, a No. 1 wood, with a large head and deep face for tee shots. **5.** *Electronics.* a circuit whose output provides the input of another circuit. —'**driv·er·less** *adj.*

driv·er ant *n.* any of various tropical African predatory ants of the subfamily *Dorylinae,* which live in temporary nests and travel in vast hordes preying on other animals. See also **army ant.**

drive·way ('draɪvˌweɪ) *n.* a private road for vehicles, often connecting a house or garage with a public road; drive.

driv·ing ('draɪvɪŋ) *adj.* **1.** having or moving with force and violence: *driving rain.* **2.** forceful or energetic. **3.** relating to the controlling of a motor vehicle in motion: *driving test.*

driv·ing li·cence *n.* an official document or certificate authorizing a person to drive a motor vehicle.

driv·ing wheel *n.* **1.** a wheel, esp. a gear wheel, that causes other wheels to rotate. **2.** any wheel of a vehicle that transforms torque into a tractive force.

driz·zle ('drɪzəl) *n.* **1.** very light rain, specifically consisting of droplets less than 0.5 mm in diameter. ~*vb.* **2.** (*intr.*) to rain lightly. **3.** (*tr.*) to moisten with tiny droplets. [Old English *drēosan* to fall; related to Old Saxon *driosan,* Gothic *driusan,* Norwegian *drjōsa*] —'**driz·zly** *adj.*

Drog·he·da ('drɔɪɪdə) *n.* a port in NE Ireland, in Co. Louth near the mouth of the River Boyne: captured by Cromwell in 1649 and its inhabitants massacred. Pop.: 20 095 (1971).

drogue (drəʊg) *n.* **1.** any funnel-like device, esp. one of canvas, used as a sea anchor. **2. a.** a small parachute released behind a jet aircraft to reduce its landing speed. **b.** a small parachute released before a heavier main parachute during the landing of a spacecraft. **3.** a device towed behind an aircraft as a target for firing practice. **4.** a funnel-shaped device on the end of the refuelling hose of a tanker aircraft, to assist stability and the location of the probe of the receiving aircraft. **5.** another name for **windsock.** [C18: probably based ultimately on Old English *dragan* to DRAW]

droit (drɔɪt; *French* drwa) *n., pl.* **droits** (drɔɪts; *French* drwa). a legal or moral right or claim; due. [C15: from French: legal right, from Medieval Latin *dīrēctum* law, from Latin: a straight line; see DIRECT]

droit du sei·gneur (*French* drwɑ dy sɛˈɲœːr) *n.* in feudal times, the right of a lord to have sexual intercourse with a vassal's bride on her wedding night. [literally: the right of the lord]

droll (drəʊl) *adj.* amusing in a quaint or odd manner; comical. [C17: from French *drôle* scamp, from Middle Dutch: imp] —'**droll·ness** *n.* —'**drol·ly** *adv.*

droll·er·y ('drəʊlərɪ) *n., pl.* **·er·ies.** **1.** humour; comedy. **2.** *Rare.* a droll act, story, or remark.

Drôme (*French* droːm) *n.* a department of SE France, in Rhône-Alpes region. Capital: Valence. Pop.: 370 571 (1975). Area: 6561 sq. km (2559 sq. miles).

-drome *n. combining form.* **1.** a course, race course: *hippodrome.* **2.** a large place for a special purpose: *aerodrome.* [via Latin from Greek *dromos* race, course]

drom·e·dar·y ('drʌmədərɪ, -drɪ, 'drɒm-) *n., pl.* **·dar·ies.** **1.** a type of Arabian camel bred for racing and riding, having a single hump and long slender legs. **2.** another name for **Arabian camel.** [C14: from Late Latin *dromedārius* (*camēlus*), from Greek *dromas* running]

drom·ond ('drɒmənd, 'drʌm-) *or* **drom·on** ('drɒmən, 'drʌm-) *n.* a large swift sailing vessel of the 12th to 15th centuries. [C13: from Anglo-French *dromund,* ultimately from Late Greek *dromōn* light swift ship, from *dromos* a running]

-dro·mous *adj. combining form.* moving or running: *anadromous; catadromous.* [via New Latin from Greek *-dromos,* from *dromos* a running]

drone[1] (drəʊn) *n.* **1.** a male bee in a colony of social bees, whose sole function is to mate with the queen. **2.** *Brit.* a person who lives off the work of others. **3.** a pilotless radio-controlled aircraft. [Old English *drān;* related to Old High German *treno* drone, Gothic *drunjus* noise, Greek *tenthrēnē* wasp; see DRONE[2]] —'**dron·ish** *adj.*

drone[2] (drəʊn) *vb.* **1.** (*intr.*) to make a monotonous low dull sound; buzz or hum. **2.** (when *intr.*, often foll. by *on*) to utter (words) in a monotonous tone, esp. to talk without stopping. ~*n.* **3.** a monotonous low dull sound. **4.** *Music.* **a.** a sustained bass note or chord of unvarying pitch accompanying a melody. **b.** (*as modifier*)*: a drone bass.* **5.** *Music.* one of the single-reed pipes in a set of bagpipes, used for accompanying the melody played on the chanter. **6.** a person who speaks in a low monotonous tone. [C16: related to DRONE[1] and Middle Dutch *drōnen,* German *dröhnen*] —'**dron·ing·ly** *adv.*

dron·go ('drɒŋgəʊ) *n., pl.* **·gos.** **1.** Also: **drongo shrike.** any insectivorous songbird of the family *Dicruridae,* of the Old World tropics, having a glossy black plumage, a forked tail, and a stout bill. **2.** *Austral. slang.* a slow-witted person. [C19: from Malagasy]

droob (druːb) *n. Austral. slang.* a pathetic person. [C20: of unknown origin]

drool (druːl) *vb.* **1.** (*intr.*; often foll. by *over*) to show excessive enthusiasm (for) or pleasure (in); gloat (over). ~*vb., n.* **2.** another word for **drivel** (senses 1, 2, 5). [C19: probably alteration of DRIVEL]

droop (druːp) *vb.* **1.** to sag or allow to sag, as from weakness or exhaustion; hang down; sink. **2.** (*intr.*) to be overcome by weariness; languish; flag. **3.** (*intr.*) to lose courage; become dejected. ~*n.* **4.** the act or state of drooping. [C13: from Old Norse *drūpa;* see DROP] —'**droop·ing·ly** *adv.* —'**droop·y** *adj.* —'**droop·i·ly** *adv.* —'**droop·i·ness** *n.*

drop (drɒp) *n.* **1.** a small quantity of liquid that forms or falls in a spherical or pear-shaped mass; globule. **2.** a very small quantity of liquid. **3.** a very small quantity of anything. **4.** something resembling a drop in shape or size, such as a decorative pendant or small sweet. **5.** the act or an instance of falling; descent. **6.** a decrease in amount or value; slump: *a drop in prices.* **7.** the vertical distance that anything may fall. **8.** a steep or sheer incline or slope. **9.** the act of unloading troops, equipment, or supplies by parachute. **10.** *Theatre.* See **drop curtain. 11.** another word for **trap door** or **gallows. 12.** *Chiefly U.S.* a slot or aperture through which an object can be dropped to fall into a receptacle. **13.** *Nautical.* the midships height of a sail bent to a fixed yard. Compare **hoist** (sense 5). **14.** *Austral. cricket slang.* a fall of the wicket. **15.** See **drop shot. 16. a drop in the bucket** (*or* **in the ocean**). *Informal.* an amount very small in relation to what is needed or desired. **17. at the drop of a hat.** without hesitation or delay. **18. have had a drop too much.** to be drunk. ~*vb.* **drops, drop+ping, dropped. 19.** (of liquids) to fall or allow to fall in globules. **20.** to fall or allow to fall vertically. **21.** (*tr.*) to allow to fall by letting go of. **22.** to sink or fall or cause to sink or fall to the ground, as from a blow, wound, shot, weariness, etc. **23.** (*intr.;* foll. by *back, behind,* etc.) to fall, move, or go in a specified manner, direction, etc. **24.** (*intr.;* foll. by *in, by,* etc.) *Informal.* to pay a casual visit (to). **25.** to decrease or cause to decrease in amount or value: *the cost of living never drops.* **26.** to sink or cause to sink to a lower position, as on a scale. **27.** to make or become less in strength, volume, etc. **28.** (*intr.*) to sink or decline in health or condition. **29.** (*intr.;* sometimes foll. by *into*) to pass easily into a state or condition: *to drop into a habit.* **30.** (*intr.*) to move along gently as with a current of water or air. **31.** (*tr.*) to allow to pass casually in conversation: *to drop a hint.* **32.** (*tr.*) to leave out (a word or letter). **33.** (*tr.*) to set down or unload (passengers or goods). **34.** (*tr.*) *Informal.* to send or post: *drop me a line.* **35.** (*tr.*) *Informal.* to discontinue; terminate: *let's drop the matter.* **36.** (*tr.*) *Informal.* to cease to associate or have to do with. **37.** (*tr.*) *Slang, chiefly U.S.* to cease to employ: *he was dropped from his job.* **38.** (*tr.;* sometimes foll. by *in, off,* etc.) *Informal.* to leave or deposit, esp. at a specified place. **39.** (of animals) to give birth to (offspring). **40.** *Slang, chiefly U.S.* to lose (money), esp. when gambling. **41.** (*tr.*) to lengthen (a hem, etc.). **42.** (*tr.*) to unload (troops, equipment, or supplies) by parachute. **43.** (*tr.*) *Nautical.* to leave behind; sail out of sight of. **44.** (*tr.*) *Sport.* to omit (a player) from a team. **45.** (*tr.*) to lose (a score, game, or contest): *the champion dropped his first service game.* **46.** (*tr.*) *Golf, basketball, etc.* to hit or throw (a ball) into a goal: *he dropped a 30 foot putt.* **47.** (*tr.*) to hit (a ball) with a drop shot. **48. drop astern.** *Nautical.* to fall back to the stern (of another vessel). **49.** (*tr.*) *Motor racing slang.* to spin (the car) and (usually) crash out of the race. **50.** (*tr.*) *Slang.* to swallow (a drug, esp. barbiturates or LSD). **51. drop dead!** *Slang.* an exclamation of contempt. ~*n., vb.* **52.** *Rugby.* short for **drop kick** or **drop-kick.** ~See also **drop away, drop off, dropout.** [Old English *dropian;* related to Old High German *triofan* to DRIP]

drop a·way *vb.* (*intr., adv.*) to fall or go away gradually.

drop can+non *n. Billiards.* a shot in which the first object ball joins or gathers with the cue ball and the other object ball, esp. at the top of the table.

drop cur+tain *n. Theatre.* a curtain that is suspended from the flies and can be raised and lowered onto the stage. Also called: **drop cloth, drop.**

drop forge *n.* **1.** Also called: **drop hammer.** a device for forging metal between two dies, one of which is fixed, the other acting by gravity or by steam or hydraulic pressure. ~*vb.* **drop-forge. 2.** (*tr.*) to forge (metal) into (a component) by the use of a drop forge.

drop goal *n. Rugby.* a goal scored with a drop kick during the run of play.

drop ham+mer *n.* another name for **drop forge.**

drop+head cou+pé *n. Brit.* a two-door four-seater car with a folding roof and a sloping back.

drop kick *n.* **1.** a kick in certain sports such as rugby, in which the ball is dropped and kicked as it bounces from the ground. Compare **punt**², **place kick. 2.** a wrestling attack, illegal in amateur wrestling, in which a wrestler leaps in the air and kicks his opponent in the face or body with both feet. ~*vb.* **drop-kick. 3.** to kick (a ball, etc.) using a drop kick. **4.** to kick (an opponent in wrestling) by the use of a drop kick.

drop leaf *n.* **a.** a hinged flap on a table that can be raised and supported by a bracket or additional pivoted leg to extend the surface. **b.** (*as modifier*): *a drop-leaf table.*

drop+let (ˈdrɒplɪt) *n.* a tiny drop.

drop+light (ˈdrɒpˌlaɪt) *n.* an electric light that may be raised or lowered by means of a pulley or other mechanism.

drop off *vb.* (*adv.*) **1.** (*intr.*) to grow smaller or less; decline. **2.** (*tr.*) to allow to alight; set down. **3.** (*intr.*) *Informal.* to fall asleep. ~*n.* **drop-off. 4.** a steep or vertical descent. **5.** a sharp decrease.

drop+out (ˈdrɒpˌaʊt) *n.* **1.** a student who fails to complete a school or college course. **2.** a person who rejects conventional society. **3. drop-out.** *Rugby.* a drop kick taken by the defending team to restart play, as after a touchdown. ~*vb.* **drop out.** (*intr., adv.;* often foll. by *of*) **4.** to abandon or withdraw from (a school, social group, job, etc.).

drop+per (ˈdrɒpə) *n.* **1.** a small tube having a rubber bulb at one end for drawing up and dispensing drops of liquid. **2.** a person or thing that drops.

drop+pings (ˈdrɒpɪŋz) *pl. n.* the dung of certain animals, such as rabbits, sheep, and birds.

drops (drɒps) *pl. n.* any liquid medication applied by means of a dropper.

drop scone *n.* a scone made by dropping a spoonful of batter on a griddle. Also called: **girdlecake, griddlecake, Scotch pancake.**

drop ship+ment *n.* a consignment invoiced to a wholesaler or other middleman but sent directly to the retailer by a manufacturer.

drop shot *n.* **1.** *Tennis, squash, etc.* a softly-played return that drops abruptly after clearing the net, intended to give an opponent no chance of reaching the ball and usually achieved by imparting backspin. **2.** a type of shot made by permitting molten metal to percolate through a sieve and then dropping it into a tank of water.

drop+sonde (ˈdrɒpsɒnd) *n. Meteorol.* a radiosonde dropped by parachute. [C20: DROP + (RADIO)SONDE]

drop+sy (ˈdrɒpsɪ) *n. Pathol.* a condition characterized by an accumulation of watery fluid in the tissues or in a body cavity. [C13: shortened from *ydropesie,* from Latin *hydrōpisis,* from Greek *hudrōps,* from *hudōr* water] —**drop+si+cal** (ˈdrɒpsɪkᵊl) *or* ˈ**drop+sied** *adj.* —ˈ**drop+si+cal+ly** *adv.*

drop tank *n.* an external aircraft tank, usually containing fuel, that can be detached and dropped in flight.

drop+wort (ˈdrɒpˌwɜːt) *n.* **1.** a Eurasian rosaceous plant, *Filipendula vulgaris,* with finely divided leaves and clusters of white or reddish flowers. See also **meadowsweet** (sense 1). **2. water dropwort.** any of several umbelliferous marsh plants of the genus *Oenanthe,* esp. *O. fistulosa,* with umbrella-shaped clusters of white flowers.

drosh+ky (ˈdrɒʃkɪ) *or* **dros+ky** (ˈdrɒskɪ) *n., pl.* **+kies.** an open four-wheeled horse-drawn passenger carriage, formerly used in Russia. [C19: from Russian *drozhki,* diminutive of *drogi* a wagon, from *droga* shaft]

dro+soph·i+la (drɒˈsɒfɪlə) *n., pl.* **+las** *or* **+lae** (-ˌliː). any small dipterous fly of the genus *Drosophila,* esp. *D. melanogaster* which is widely used in laboratory genetics studies: family *Drosophilidae.* They feed on plant sap, decaying fruit, etc. Also called: **fruit fly, vinegar fly.** [C19: New Latin, from Greek *drosos* dew, water + *-phila;* see -PHILE]

dross (drɒs) *n.* **1.** the scum formed, usually by oxidation, on the surfaces of molten metals. **2.** worthless matter; waste. [Old English *drōs* dregs; related to Old High German *truosana*] —ˈ**dross·y** *adj.* —ˈ**dross·i+ness** *n.*

drought (draʊt) *n.* **1.** a prolonged period of scanty rainfall. **2.** a prolonged shortage. **3.** an archaic or dialect word for **thirst.** Archaic form: **drouth.** [Old English *drūgoth;* related to Dutch *droogte;* see DRY] —ˈ**drought·y** *adj.*

drove¹ (drəʊv) *vb.* the past tense of **drive.**

drove² (drəʊv) *n.* **1.** a herd of livestock being driven together. **2.** (*often pl.*) a moving crowd of people. **3.** Also called: **drove chisel.** a chisel with a broad edge used for dressing stone. ~*vb.* **4. a.** (*tr.*) to drive (a group of livestock), usually for a considerable distance. **b.** (*intr.*) to be employed as a drover. **5.** to work (a stone surface) with a drove. [Old English *drāf* herd; related to Middle Low German *drēfwech* cattle pasture; see DRIVE, DRIFT]

drov+er (ˈdrəʊvə) *n.* a person whose occupation is the driving of sheep or cattle, esp. to and from market.

drown (draʊn) *vb.* **1.** to die or kill by immersion in liquid. **2.** (*tr.*) to destroy or get rid of as if by submerging: *he drowned his sorrows in drink.* **3.** (*tr.*) to drench thoroughly; inundate; flood. **4.** (*tr.;* sometimes foll. by *out*) to render (a sound) inaudible by making a loud noise. [C13: probably from Old English *druncnian;* related to Old Norse *drukna* to be drowned] —ˈ**drown+er** *n.*

drowse (draʊz) *vb.* **1.** to be or cause to be sleepy, dull, or sluggish. ~*n.* **2.** the state of being drowsy. [C16: probably from Old English *drūsian* to sink; related to *drēosan* to fall]

drows·y (ˈdraʊzɪ) *adj.* **drows·i+er, drows·i+est. 1.** heavy with sleepiness; sleepy. **2.** inducing sleep; soporific. **3.** sluggish or lethargic; dull. —ˈ**drows·i+ly** *adv.* —ˈ**drows·i+ness** *n.*

drub (drʌb) *vb.* **drubs, drub+bing, drubbed.** (*tr.*) **1.** to beat as with a stick; cudgel; club. **2.** to defeat utterly, as in a contest. **3.** to drum or stamp (the feet). **4.** to instil with force or repetition: *the master drubbed Latin into the boys.* ~*n.* **5.** a blow, as from a stick. [C17: probably from Arabic *dáraba* to beat] —ˈ**drub+ber** *n.*

drudge (drʌdʒ) *n.* **1.** a person, such as a servant, who works hard at wearisome menial tasks. ~*vb.* **2.** (*intr.*) to toil at such tasks. [C16: perhaps from *druggen* to toil] —ˈ**drudg+er** *n.* —ˈ**drudg+ing+ly** *adv.*

drudg+er·y (ˈdrʌdʒərɪ) *n., pl.* **+er·ies.** hard, menial, and monotonous work.

druf+fen (ˈdrʌfᵊn) *adj. Northern Brit. dialect.* inebriated; drunk. [of obscure origin]

drug (drʌg) *n.* **1.** any synthetic or natural chemical substance used in the treatment, prevention, or diagnosis of disease. Related adj.: **pharmaceutical. 2.** a chemical substance, esp. a narcotic, taken for the pleasant effects it produces. **3. drug on the market.** a commodity available in excess of the demands of the market. ~*vb.* **drugs, drug+ging, drugged.** (*tr.*) **4.** to mix a drug with (food, drink, etc.). **5.** to administer a drug to. **6.** to stupefy or poison with or as if with a drug. [C14: from Old French *drogue,* probably of Germanic origin]

drug ad+dict *n.* any person who is abnormally dependent on narcotic drugs. See **addiction.**

drug+get (ˈdrʌgɪt) *n.* a coarse fabric used as a protective floor-

covering, etc. [C16: from French *droguet* useless fabric, from *drogue* trash]
drug·gist ('drʌgɪst) *n.* a U.S. term for a **pharmacist.**
drug·store ('drʌgˌstɔː) *n. U.S.* a shop where medical prescriptions are made up and a wide variety of goods and usually light meals are sold.
dru·id ('druːɪd) *n.* (*sometimes cap.*) **1.** a member of an ancient order of priests in Gaul, Britain, and Ireland in the pre-Christian era. **2.** a member of any of several modern movements attempting to revive druidism. [C16: from Latin *druides* of Gaulish origin; compare Old Irish *druid* wizards] —**dru·id·ess** ('druːɪdɪs) *n. fem.* —**dru·'id·ic** *or* **dru·'id·i·cal** *adj.* —**'dru·id·ˌism** *n.*
drum[1] (drʌm) *n.* **1.** *Music.* a percussion instrument sounded by striking a membrane stretched across the opening of a hollow cylinder or hemisphere. **2.** the sound produced by a drum or any similar sound. **3.** an object that resembles a drum in shape, such as a large spool or a cylindrical container. **4.** *Architect.* **a.** one of a number of cylindrical blocks of stone used to construct the shaft of a column. **b.** the wall or structure supporting a dome or cupola. **5.** short for **eardrum. 6.** Also called: **drumfish.** any of various North American marine and freshwater sciaenid fishes, such as *Equetus pulcher* (**striped drum**), that utter a drumming sound. **7.** a cylindrical object or hollow cylindrical structure, esp. the centre body of an axial-flow compressor rotor to which the rotor blades are attached. **8.** Also called: **magnetic drum.** *Computer technol.* a rotating cylindrical device on which data may be stored for later retrieval. Compare **disk** (sense 2). **9.** *Archaic.* a drummer. **10.** *Austral. slang.* a brothel. **11. run a drum.** *Austral. slang.* (of a racehorse) to perform as tipped. **12. the drum.** *Austral. informal.* the necessary information (esp. in the phrase **give (someone) the drum.** ~*vb.* **drums, drum·ming, drummed. 13.** to play (music) on or as if on a drum. **14.** to beat or tap (the fingers) rhythmically or regularly. **15.** (*intr.*) (of birds) to produce a rhythmical sound, as by beating the bill against a tree, branch, etc. **16.** (*tr.*; sometimes foll. by *up*) to summon or call by drumming. **17.** (*tr.*) to instil by constant repetition: *to drum an idea into someone's head.* **18. beat the drum for.** *Informal.* to attempt to arouse interest in. [C16: probably from Middle Dutch *tromme*, of imitative origin]
drum[2] (drʌm) *n. Scot., Irish.* a narrow ridge or hill. [C18: from Scottish Gaelic *druim*]
drum·beat ('drʌmˌbiːt) *n.* the sound made by beating a drum.
drum brake *n.* a type of brake used on the wheels of vehicles, consisting of two pivoted shoes that rub against the inside walls of the brake drum when the brake is applied.
drum·fire ('drʌmˌfaɪə) *n.* heavy, rapid, and continuous gunfire, the sound of which resembles rapid drumbeats.
drum·fish ('drʌmˌfɪʃ) *n., pl.* **·fish** *or* **·fish·es.** another name for **drum**[1] (sense 6).
drum·head ('drʌmˌhɛd) *n.* **1.** *Music.* the part of a drum that is actually struck with a stick or the hand. **2.** the head of a capstan, pierced with holes for the capstan bars. **3.** another name for **eardrum.**
drum·head court-mar·tial *n.* a military court convened to hear urgent charges of offences committed in action. [C19: from the use of a drumhead as a table around which the court-martial was held]
drum·lin ('drʌmlɪn) *n.* a streamlined mound of glacial drift, rounded or elongated in the direction of the original flow of ice. [C19: from Irish Gaelic *druim* ridge + *-lin* -LING[1]]
drum ma·jor *n.* the noncommissioned officer, usually of sergeant major's rank, who commands the corps of drums of a military band and who is in command of both the drums and the band when paraded together.
drum ma·jor·ette *n. Chiefly U.S.* a girl who marches at the head of a procession, twirling a baton.
drum·mer ('drʌmə) *n.* **1.** a person who plays a drum or set of drums. **2.** *Chiefly U.S.* a salesman, esp. a travelling salesman. **3.** *Austral. slang.* the slowest shearer in a team.
drum out *vb.* (*tr., adv*; usually foll. by *of*) **a.** to expel from a club, association, etc. **b.** (formerly) to dismiss from military service to the beat of a drum.
drum·stick ('drʌmˌstɪk) *n.* **1.** a stick used for playing a drum. **2.** the lower joint of the leg of a cooked fowl.
drum up *vb.* (*tr., adv.*) to evoke or obtain (support, business, etc.) by solicitation or canvassing.
drunk (drʌŋk) *adj.* **1.** intoxicated with alcohol to the extent of losing control over normal physical and mental functions. **2.** overwhelmed by strong influence or emotion: *drunk with power.* ~*n.* **3.** a person who is drunk or drinks habitually to excess. **4.** *Informal.* a drinking bout.
drunk·ard ('drʌŋkəd) *n.* a person who is frequently or habitually drunk.
drunk·en ('drʌŋkən) *adj.* **1.** intoxicated with or as if with alcohol. **2.** frequently or habitually drunk. **3.** (*prenominal*) caused by or relating to alcoholic intoxication: *a drunken brawl.* —**'drunk·en·ly** *adv.* —**'drunk·en·ness** *n.*
drunk·om·e·ter (drʌŋ'kɒmɪtə) *n.* the usual U.S. name for **breathalyzer.**
drupe (druːp) *n.* an indehiscent fruit consisting of outer epicarp, fleshy or fibrous mesocarp, and stony endocarp enclosing a single seed. It occurs in the peach, plum, and cherry. [C18: from Latin *druppa* wrinkled over-ripe olive, from Greek: olive] —**dru·pa·ceous** (druː'peɪʃəs) *adj.*
drupe·let ('druːplɪt) *or* **dru·pel** ('druːpᵊl) *n.* a small drupe, usually one of a number forming a compound fruit.
Dru·ry Lane ('drʊərɪ) *n.* a street in the West End of London, formerly famous for its theatres.
druse (druːz) *n.* an aggregate of small crystals within a cavity, esp. those lining a cavity in a rock or mineral. [C19: from German, from Old High German *druos* bump]
Druse *or* **Druze** (druːz) *n.* a member of a religious sect in Syria and Lebanon, having certain characteristics in common with the Muslims. [C18: from Arabic *Durūz* the Druses, after *Ismail al-Darazi* Ismail the tailor, 11th-century Muslim leader who founded the sect] —**'Dru·se·an, 'Dru·si·an** *or* **'Dru·ze·an, 'Dru·zi·an** *adj.*
dry (draɪ) *adj.* **dri·er, dri·est** *or* **dry·er, dry·est. 1.** lacking moisture; not damp or wet. **2.** having little or no rainfall. **3.** not in or under water: *dry land.* **4.** having the water drained away or evaporated: *a dry river.* **5.** not providing milk: *a dry cow.* **6.** (of the eyes) free from tears. **7. a.** in need of a drink; thirsty. **b.** causing thirst: *dry work.* **8.** eaten without butter, jam, etc.: *dry toast.* **9.** (of a wine, cider, etc.) not sweet. **10.** *Pathol.* not accompanied by or producing a mucous or watery discharge: *a dry cough.* **11.** consisting of solid as opposed to liquid substances or commodities. **12.** without adornment; plain: *dry facts.* **13.** lacking interest or stimulation: *a dry book.* **14.** lacking warmth or emotion; cold: *a dry greeting.* **15.** (of wit or humour) shrewd and keen in an impersonal, sarcastic, or laconic way. **16.** *Informal.* opposed to or prohibiting the sale of alcoholic liquor for human consumption: *a dry country.* ~*vb.* **dries, dry·ing, dried. 17.** to make or become dry or free from moisture. **18.** (*tr.*) to preserve (meat, vegetables, fruit, etc.) by removing the moisture. ~*n., pl.* **drys** *or* **dries. 19. the dry.** *Austral. informal.* the dry season. **20.** *U.S.* an informal word for **prohibitionist.** ~See also **dry out, dry up.** [Old English *drȳge*; related to Old High German *truckan*, Old Norse *draugr* dry wood] —**'dry·a·ble** *adj.* —**'dry·ly** *or* **'dri·ly** *adv.* —**'dry·ness** *n.*
dry·ad ('draɪəd, -æd) *n., pl.* **·ads** *or* **·a·des** (-əˌdiːz). *Greek myth.* a nymph or divinity of the woods. [C14: from Latin *Dryas*, from Greek *Druas*, from *drus* tree] —**dry·ad·ic** (draɪ'ædɪk) *adj.*
dry bat·ter·y *n.* an electric battery consisting of two or more dry cells.
dry-blowing *n. Austral.* **1.** *Mining.* the use of the wind for separating gold from ore. **2.** *Informal.* any tedious activity.
dry-bone ore *n.* a mining term for **smithsonite.**
dry-bulb ther·mom·e·ter *n.* an ordinary thermometer used alongside a wet-bulb thermometer to obtain relative humidity. See also **psychrometer.**
dry cell *n.* a primary cell in which the electrolyte is in the form of a paste or is treated in some way to prevent it from spilling. Compare **wet cell.**
dry-clean *vb.* (*tr.*) to clean (clothing, fabrics, etc.) with a solvent other than water, such as trichloroethylene. —ˌ**dry-'clean·er** *n.* —ˌ**dry-'clean·ing** *n.*
Dry·den ('draɪdᵊn) *n.* **John.** 1631–1700, English poet, dramatist, and critic of the Augustan period, commonly regarded as the chief exponent of heroic tragedy. His major works include the tragedy *All for Love* (1677), the verse satire *Absalom and Achitophel* (1681), and the *Essay of Dramatick Poesie* (1668).
dry dis·til·la·tion *n.* another name for **destructive distillation.**
dry dock *n.* **1.** a basin-like structure that is large enough to admit a ship and that can be pumped dry for work on the ship's bottom. ~*vb.* **dry-dock. 2.** to put (a ship) into a dry dock, or (of a ship) to go into a dry dock.
dry·er[1] ('draɪə) *n.* **1.** a person or thing that dries. **2.** an apparatus for removing moisture by forced draught, heating, or centrifuging. **3.** any of certain chemicals added to oils such as linseed oil to accelerate their drying when used as bases in paints, etc.
dry·er[2] ('draɪə) *adj.* a variant spelling of **drier**[1].
dry farm·ing *n.* a system of growing crops in arid or semiarid regions without artificial irrigation, by reducing evaporation and by special methods of tillage. —**dry farm·er** *n.*
dry fly *n. Angling.* **a.** an artificial fly designed and prepared to be floated or skimmed on the surface of the water. **b.** (*as modifier*): *dry-fly fishing.* ~Compare **wet fly.**
dry goods *n.* textile fabrics and related merchandise. Also called: **soft goods.**
dry ice *n.* solid carbon dioxide, which sublimates at –78.5°C: used as a refrigerant. Also called: **carbon dioxide snow.**
dry·ing oil *n.* one of a number of animal or vegetable oils, such as linseed oil, that harden by oxidation on exposure to air: used as a base for some paints and varnishes.
dry kiln *n.* an oven in which cut timber is dried and seasoned.
dry law *n. U.S.* a law prohibiting the sale of alcoholic beverages.
dry·ly *or* **dri·ly** ('draɪlɪ) *adv.* in a dry manner.
dry mar·ti·ni *n.* a cocktail of between four and ten parts gin to one part dry vermouth.
dry meas·ure *n.* a unit or a system of units for measuring dry goods, such as fruit, grains, etc.
dry nurse *n.* **1.** a nurse who cares for a child without suckling it. Compare **wet nurse.** ~*vb.* **dry-nurse. 2.** to care for (a baby or young child) without suckling.
dry·o·pith·e·cine (ˌdraɪəʊ'pɪθəˌsiːn) *n.* any extinct Old World ape of the genus *Dryopithecus*, common in Miocene and Pliocene times: thought to be the ancestors of modern apes. [C20: from New Latin *Dryopithēcus*, from Greek *drus* tree + *pithēkos* ape]
dry out *vb.* (*adv.*) **1.** to make or become dry. **2.** *Informal.* to

undergo or cause to undergo treatment for alcoholism or drug addiction.

dry point *n.* **1.** a technique of intaglio engraving with a hard steel needle, without acid, on a copper plate. **2.** the sharp steel needle used in this process. **3.** an engraving or print produced by this method.

dry rot *n.* **1.** crumbling and drying of timber, bulbs, potatoes, or fruit, caused by saprophytic basidiomycetous fungi. **2.** any fungus causing this decay, esp. of the genus *Merulius*. **3.** *Informal.* corrupt practices, esp. when previously unsuspected.

dry run *n.* **1.** *Military.* practice in weapon firing without live ammunition. **2.** *Informal.* a trial or practice, esp. in simulated conditions; rehearsal.

dry-salt *vb.* to preserve (food) by salting and removing moisture.

dry+salt·er ('draɪˌsɔːltə) *n. Obsolete.* a dealer in certain chemical products, such as dyestuffs and gums, and in dried, tinned, or salted foods and edible oils.

Drys+dale ('draɪzdeɪl) *n.* Sir **George Rus·sell.** 1912–81, Australian painter, esp. of landscapes.

dry steam *n.* steam that does not contain droplets of water.

dry-stone *adj.* (of a wall) made without mortar.

Dry Tor+tu+gas (tɔː'tuːgəz) *n.* a group of eight coral islands at the entrance to the Gulf of Mexico: part of Florida.

dry up *vb.* (*adv.*) **1.** (*intr.*) to become barren or unproductive; fail: *in middle age his inspiration dried up.* **2.** to dry (dishes, cutlery, etc.) with a tea towel after they have been washed. **3.** (*intr.*) *Informal.* to stop talking or speaking: *when I got on the stage I just dried up; dry up!*

D.S. *or* **d.s.** *Music. abbrev. for* dal segno.

D.Sc. *abbrev. for* Doctor of Science.

D.S.C. *Military. abbrev. for* Distinguished Service Cross.

D.S.M. *Military. abbrev. for* Distinguished Service Medal.

D.S.O. *Brit. military. abbrev. for* Distinguished Service Order.

d.s.p. *abbrev. for* decessit sine prole. [Latin: died without issue]

D.S.T. *abbrev. for* Daylight Saving Time.

DTL *Electronics. abbrev. for* diode transistor logic: a stage in the development of electronic logic circuits.

D.T.'s *Informal. abbrev. for* delirium tremens.

Du. *abbrev. for:* **1.** Duke. **2.** Dutch.

du·ad ('djuːæd) *n.* a rare word for **pair.** [C17: from Greek *duas* two, a pair]

du·al ('djuːəl) *adj.* **1.** relating to or denoting two. **2.** twofold; double. **3.** (in the grammar of Old English, Ancient Greek, and certain other languages) denoting a form of a word indicating that exactly two referents are being referred to. ~*n.* **4.** *Grammar.* **a.** the dual number. **b.** a dual form of a word. [C17: from Latin *duālis* concerning two, from *duo* two] —**'du·al+ly** *adv.*

Du+a·la (dʊ'ɑːlə, -lɑː) *n.* **1.** (*pl.* **·la** *or* **·las**) a member of a Negroid people of W Africa living chiefly in Cameroon. **2.** the language of this people, belonging to the Bantu group of the Niger-Congo family.

Du·al Al+li+ance *n.* **1.** the alliance between France and Russia (1893–1917). **2.** the secret Austro-German alliance against Russia (1879) later expanded to the Triple Alliance.

du·al car·riage+way *n. Brit.* a road on which traffic travelling in opposite directions is separated by a central strip of turf, etc. U.S. name: **divided highway.**

du·al+ism ('djuːəˌlɪzəm) *n.* **1.** the state of being twofold or double. **2.** *Philosophy.* the doctrine, as opposed to idealism and materialism, that reality consists of two basic principles, usually taken to be mind and matter. Compare **monism, pluralism. 3.** *Theol.* **a.** the theory that the universe has been ruled from its origins by two conflicting powers, one good and one evil, both existing as equally ultimate first causes. **b.** the theory that there are two personalities, one human and one divine, in Christ. —**'du·al+ist** *n.* —**du·al+'is·tic** *adj.* —**ˌdu·al+'is+ti+cal+ly** *adv.*

du·al+i·ty (djuː'ælɪtɪ) *n., pl.* **·ties. 1.** the state or quality of being two or in two parts; dichotomy. **2.** *Physics.* the property or phenomenon associated with matter and electromagnetic radiation and characterized by the fact that some properties are best explained by a wave theory and others by a corpuscular theory. **3.** *Geom.* the interchangeability of the roles of the point and the plane in statements and theorems in projective geometry.

Du·al Mon+ar+chy *n.* the monarchy of Austria-Hungary from 1867 to 1918.

du·al-pur·pose *adj.* having or serving two functions.

dub[1] (dʌb) *vb.* **dubs, dub+bing, dubbed. 1.** (*tr.*) to invest (a person) with knighthood by the ritual of tapping on the shoulder with a sword. **2.** (*tr.*) to invest with a title, name, or nickname. **3.** (*tr.*) to dress (leather) by rubbing. **4.** *Angling.* to dress (a fly). ~*n.* **5.** the sound of a drum. [Old English *dubbian;* related to Old Norse *dubba* to dub a knight, Old High German *tubili* plug, peg]

dub[2] (dʌb) *Films.* ~*vb.* **dubs, dub+bing, dubbed. 1.** to alter the soundtrack of (an old recording, film, etc.). **2.** (*tr.*) to substitute for the soundtrack of (a film) a new soundtrack, esp. in a different language. **3.** (*tr.*) to provide (a film or tape) with a soundtrack. ~*n.* **4.** the new sounds added. [C20: shortened from DOUBLE]

dub[3] (dʌb) *U.S. informal.* ~*n.* **1.** a clumsy or awkward person or player. ~*vb.* **dubs, dub+bing, dubbed. 2.** to bungle (a shot, etc.), as in golf. [C19: of uncertain origin]

dub[4] (dʌb) *n. Northern Brit. dialect.* a pool of water; puddle. [C16: Scottish dialect *dubbe;* related to Middle Low German *dobbe*]

Du+bai (duː'baɪ) *n.* a sheikdom in the NE Arab Emirates, consisting principally of the port of Dubai, on the Persian Gulf: oilfields. Pop.: 75 000 (1972 est.).

du Bar·ry (djuː'bærɪ; *French* dy ba'ri) *n.* **Com·tesse** (kɔ̃'tɛs). original name *Marie Jeanne Bécu.* ?1743–93, mistress of Louis XV, guillotined in the French Revolution.

dub+bin ('dʌbɪn) *or* **dub+bing** *n. Brit.* a greasy mixture of tallow and oil applied to leather to soften it and make it waterproof. [C18: from *dub* to dress leather; see DUB[1]]

dub+bing[1] ('dʌbɪŋ) *n. Films.* **1.** the replacement of a soundtrack in one language by one in another language. **2.** the combination of several soundtracks into a single track. **3.** the addition of a soundtrack to a film or broadcast.

dub+bing[2] ('dʌbɪŋ) *n.* **1.** *Angling.* the dressing for an artificial fly. **2.** a variant spelling of **dubbin.**

Dub·ček (*Czech* 'duptʃɛk) *n.* **A·le·xan·der** ('aleksandᵊr). born 1921, Czechoslovak statesman. His reforms as first secretary of the Czechoslovak Communist Party (1968–69) prompted the Russian occupation (1968) and his enforced resignation.

du Bel·lay (*French* dy bɛ'lɛ) *n.* See (Joachim du) **Bellay.**

du·bi·e·ty (djuː'baɪɪtɪ) *or* **du+bi+os+i·ty** (ˌdjuːbɪ'ɒsɪtɪ) *n., pl.* **·ties. 1.** the state of being doubtful. **2.** a doubtful matter. [C18: from Late Latin *dubietās,* from Latin *dubius* DUBIOUS]

du·bi+ous ('djuːbɪəs) *adj.* **1.** marked by or causing doubt: *a dubious reply.* **2.** unsettled in mind; uncertain; doubtful. **3.** of doubtful quality; untrustworthy: *a dubious reputation.* **4.** not certain in outcome. [C16: from Latin *dubius* wavering] —**'du+bi+ous+ly** *adv.* —**'du+bi+ous+ness** *n.*

du+bi+ta·ble ('djuːbɪtəbᵊl) *adj.* open to doubt. [C17: from Latin *dubitāre* to DOUBT] —**'du+bi·ta·bly** *adv.*

du+bi+ta+tion (ˌdjuːbɪ'teɪʃən) *n.* another word for **doubt.**

Dub+lin ('dʌblɪn) *n.* **1.** the capital of the Republic of Ireland, on **Dublin Bay:** under English rule from 1171 until 1922; commercial and cultural centre; contains one of the world's largest breweries and exports whiskey, stout, and agricultural produce. Pop.: 567 866 (1971). Gaelic name: **Baile Átha Cliath. 2.** a county in E Ireland, in Leinster on the Irish Sea: mountainous in the south but low-lying in the north and centre. County seat: Dublin. Pop.: 862 219 (1971). Area: 922 sq. km (356 sq. miles).

Dub+lin Bay prawn *n.* a large prawn usually used in a dish of scampi.

du+bon+net (djuː'bɒneɪ) *n.* **a.** a dark purplish-red colour. **b.** (*as adj.*): *a dubonnet coat.* [from DUBONNET]

Du+bon+net (djuː'bɒneɪ) *n. Trademark.* a sweet usually red apéritif wine flavoured with quinine and bark.

Du+brov+nik (dʊ'brɒvnɪk) *n.* a port in S Yugoslavia, in Croatia on the Dalmatian coast: an important commercial centre in the Middle Ages; tourist centre. Pop.: 30 000 (1972 est.). Former Italian name (until 1918): **Ragusa.**

Du·buf·fet (*French* dyby'fe) *n.* **Jean** (ʒɑ̃). born 1901, French painter, inspired by graffiti and the untrained art of children and psychotics.

du+cal ('djuːkᵊl) *adj.* of or relating to a duke or duchy. [C16: from French, from Late Latin *ducālis* of a leader, from *dux* leader] —**'du+cal+ly** *adv.*

duc+at ('dʌkət) *n.* **1.** any of various former European gold or silver coins, esp. those used in Italy or the Netherlands. **2.** (*often pl.*) *Informal.* any coin or money. [C14: from Old French, from Old Italian *ducato* coin stamped with the doge's image, from *duca* doge, from Latin *dux* leader]

Duc·cio di Buo·nin·se·gna (*Italian* 'duttʃo diː ˌbwonɪn'seɲɲa) *n.* ?1255–?1318, Italian painter; founder of the Sienese school.

du·ce ('duːtʃɪ; *Italian* 'duːtʃe) *n.* leader. [C20: from Italian, from Latin *dux*]

Du·ce (*Italian* 'duːtʃe) *n.* **Il.** the title assumed by Benito Mussolini as leader of Fascist Italy (1922–43).

Du·champ (*French* dy'ʃɑ̃) *n.* **Mar·cel** (mar'sɛl). 1887–1968, U.S. painter and sculptor, born in France; noted as a leading exponent of Dada. His best-known work is *Nude Descending a Staircase* (1912).

duch+ess ('dʌtʃɪs) *n.* **1.** the wife or widow of a duke. **2.** a woman who holds the rank of duke in her own right. [C14: from Old French *duchesse,* feminine of *duc* DUKE]

duch·y ('dʌtʃɪ) *n., pl.* **duch·ies.** the territory of a duke or duchess; dukedom. [C14: from Old French *duche,* from *duc* DUKE]

duck[1] (dʌk) *n., pl.* **ducks** *or* **duck. 1.** any of various small aquatic birds of the family *Anatidae,* typically having short legs, webbed feet, and a broad blunt bill: order *Anseriformes.* **2.** the flesh of this bird, used as food. **3.** the female of such a bird, as opposed to the male (drake). **4.** any other bird of the family *Anatidae,* including geese, and swans. **5.** Also: **ducks.** *Brit. informal.* dear or darling: used as a term of endearment or of general address. **6.** *Informal.* a person, esp. one regarded as odd or endearing. **7.** *Cricket.* a score of nothing by a batsman. **8. like water off a duck's back.** *Informal.* without effect. **9. take to something like a duck to water.** *Informal.* to become adept at or attracted to something very quickly. [Old English *dūce* duck, diver; related to DUCK[2]]

duck[2] (dʌk) *vb.* **1.** to move (the head or body) quickly downwards or away, esp. so as to escape observation or evade a blow. **2.** to submerge or plunge suddenly and often briefly under water. **3.** (when *intr.,* often foll. by *out*) *Informal.* to dodge or escape (a person, duty, etc.). **4.** (*intr.*) *Bridge.* to play a low card when possessing a higher one rather than trying to win a trick. ~*n.* **5.** the act or an instance of ducking. [C14: related to Old High German *tūhhan* to dive, Middle Dutch *dūken*] —**'duck+er** *n.*

duck[3] (dʌk) *n.* a heavy cotton fabric of plain weave, used for

clothing, tents, etc. [C17: from Middle Dutch *doek;* related to Old High German *tuoh* cloth]
duck[4] (dʌk) *n.* an amphibious vehicle used in World War II. [C20: from code name DUKW]
duck-billed plat·y·pus *n.* an amphibious egg-laying mammal, *Ornithorhynchus anatinus,* of E Australia, having dense fur, a broad bill and tail, and webbed feet: family *Ornithorhynchidae.* Sometimes shortened to **duckbill, platypus.** See also **monotreme.**
duck·board (ˈdʌkˌbɔːd) *n.* a board or boards laid so as to form a floor or path over wet or muddy ground.
duck-egg blue *n.* **a.** a pale greenish-blue colour. **b.** (*as adj.*): *duck-egg blue walls.*
duck hawk *n.* a variety of peregrine falcon, *Falco peregrinus anatum,* occurring in North America.
duck·ing stool *n. History.* a chair or stool used for the punishment of offenders by plunging them into water.
duck·ling (ˈdʌklɪŋ) *n.* a young duck.
ducks (dʌks) *pl. n.* clothing made of duck, esp. white trousers for sports.
ducks and drakes *n.* **1.** a game in which a flat stone is bounced across the surface of water. **2. make ducks and drakes of** *or* **play (at) ducks and drakes with.** *Informal.* to use recklessly; squander or waste.
duck's arse *n.* a type of haircut in which the hair is trimmed and swept back to resemble a duck's tail. Also called: **D.A.**
duck soup *n. U.S. slang.* something that is easy to do.
duck·weed (ˈdʌkˌwiːd) *n.* any of various small stemless aquatic plants of the family *Lemnaceae,* esp. any of the genus *Lemna,* that have rounded leaves and occur floating on still water in temperate regions.
duck·y *or* **duck·ie** (ˈdʌkɪ) *Informal.* ~*n., pl.* **duck·ies. 1.** *Brit.* darling or dear: used as a term of endearment among women, but now often used in imitation of the supposed usage of homosexual men. ~*adj.* **2.** delightful; fine.
duct (dʌkt) *n.* **1.** a tube, pipe, or canal by means of which a substance, esp. a fluid or gas, is conveyed. **2.** any bodily passage, esp. one conveying secretions or excretions. **3.** a narrow tubular cavity in plants, often containing resin or some other substance. **4.** Also called: **conduit.** a channel or pipe carrying electric cable or wires. **5.** a passage through which air can flow, as in air conditioning. **6.** the ink reservoir in a printing press. [C17: from Latin *ductus* a leading (in Medieval Latin: aqueduct), from *dūcere* to lead] —**ˈduct·less** *adj.*
duc·tile (ˈdʌktaɪl) *adj.* **1.** (of a metal, such as gold or copper) able to sustain large deformations without fracture and able to be hammered into sheets or drawn out into wires. **2.** able to be moulded; pliant; plastic. **3.** easily led or influenced; tractable. [C14: from Old French, from Latin *ductilis,* from *dūcere* to lead] —**ˈduc·tile·ly** *adv.* —**duc·til·i·ty** (dʌkˈtɪlɪtɪ) *or* **ˈduc·tile·ness** *n.*
duct·less gland *n. Anatomy.* See **endocrine gland.**
dud (dʌd) *Informal.* ~*n.* **1.** a person or thing that proves ineffectual or a failure. **2.** a shell, etc., that fails to explode. **3.** (*pl.*) clothes or other personal belongings. ~*adj.* **4.** failing in its purpose or function. [C15 (in the sense: an article of clothing, a thing, used disparagingly): of unknown origin]
dude (djuːd) *n. Informal.* **1.** *Western U.S.* a city dweller, esp. one holidaying on a ranch. **2.** *U.S.* a dandy. **3.** *U.S.* any person. [C19: of unknown origin] —**ˈdud·ish** *adj.* —**ˈdud·ish·ly** *adv.*
du·deen (duːˈdiːn) *n.* a clay pipe with a short stem. [C19: from Irish *dūidīn* a little pipe, from *dūd* pipe]
dude ranch *n. U.S.* a ranch used as a holiday resort offering activities such as riding and camping.
dudg·eon[1] (ˈdʌdʒən) *n.* anger or resentment (archaic, except in the phrase **in high dudgeon**). [C16: of unknown origin]
dudg·eon[2] (ˈdʌdʒən) *n.* **1.** *Obsolete.* a wood used in making the handles of knives, etc. **2.** *Archaic.* a dagger, knife, etc., with a dudgeon hilt. [C15: from Anglo-Norman *digeon,* of obscure origin]
Dud·ley[1] (ˈdʌdlɪ) *n.* a town in W central England, in the West Midlands: wrought-iron industry. Pop.: 185 535 (1971).
Dud·ley[2] (ˈdʌdlɪ) *n.* **Rob·ert.** See (Earl of) **Leicester.**
due (djuː) *adj.* **1.** (*postpositive*) immediately payable. **2.** (*postpositive*) owed as a debt, irrespective of any date for payment. **3.** requisite; fitting; proper. **4.** (*prenominal*) adequate or sufficient; enough. **5.** (*postpositive*) expected or appointed to be present or arrive: *the train is now due.* **6. due to.** attributable to or caused by. ~*n.* **7.** something that is owed, required, or due. **8. give (a person) his due.** to give or allow what is deserved or right. ~*adv.* **9.** directly or exactly; straight: *a course due west.* ~See also **dues.** [C13: from Old French *deu,* from *devoir* to owe, from Latin *debēre;* see DEBT, DEBIT]
Usage. There is considerable controversy over the use of *due to* and *owing to* as compound prepositions equivalent to *because of.* Careful users of English prefer *because of* or *on account of,* at least in formal contexts, and restrict *due* to its adjectival function. There is no dispute about the postpositive adjectival use of *due to* to mean *caused by* (*the error was due to carelessness*), but *owing to* is not ordinarily used in this way.
due bill *n. Chiefly U.S.* a document acknowledging indebtedness, exchangeable for goods or services.
du·el (ˈdjuːəl) *n.* **1.** a prearranged combat with deadly weapons between two people following a formal procedure in the presence of seconds and traditionally fought until one party was wounded or killed, usually to settle a quarrel involving a point of honour. **2.** a contest or conflict between two persons or parties. ~*vb.* **du·els, du·el·ling, du·elled** *or U.S.* **du·els, du·el·ing, du·eled.** (*intr.*) **3.** to fight in a duel. **4.** to contest closely. [C15: from Medieval Latin *duellum,* from Latin, poetical variant of *bellum* war; associated by folk etymology with Latin *duo* two] —**ˈdu·el·ler** *or* **ˈdu·el·list** *n.*
du·el·lo (djuːˈɛləʊ) *n., pl.* **·los. 1.** the art of duelling. **2.** the code of rules for duelling. [C16: from Italian; see DUEL]
du·en·na (djuːˈɛnə) *n.* (in Spain and Portugal, etc.) an elderly woman retained by a family to act as governess and chaperon to young girls. [C17: from Spanish *dueña,* from Latin *domina* lady, feminine of *dominus* master]
due pro·cess of law *n.* the administration of justice in accordance with established rules and principles.
Due·ro (ˈdwero) *n.* the Spanish name for the **Douro.**
dues (djuːz) *pl. n.* (*sometimes sing.*) charges, as for membership of a club or organization; fees.
du·et *or* **du·ette** (ˈdjuːɛt, djuːˈɛt) *n.* **1.** Also called (esp. for instrumental compositions): **duo.** a musical composition for two performers or voices. **2.** a pair of closely connected individuals; duo. [C18: from Italian *duetto* a little duet, from *duo* duet, from Latin: two] —**duˈet·tist** *n.*
duff[1] (dʌf) *n.* **1.** a thick flour pudding, often flavoured with currants, citron, etc., and boiled in a cloth bag: *plum duff.* **2. up the duff.** *Slang, chiefly Austral.* pregnant. [C19: Northern English variant of DOUGH]
duff[2] (dʌf) *Slang.* ~*vb.* (*tr.*) **1.** to change the appearance of or give a false appearance to (old or stolen goods); fake. **2.** *Austral.* to steal (cattle), altering the brand. **3.** Also: **sclaff.** *Golf.* to bungle a shot by hitting the ground behind the ball. ~*adj.* **4.** *Brit.* bad or useless, as by not operating correctly; dud: *a duff engine.* ~See also **duff up.** [C19: probably back formation from DUFFER]
duff[3] (dʌf) *n. Slang.* the rump or buttocks. [C20: special use of DUFF[1]]
duf·fel *or* **duf·fle** (ˈdʌfəl) *n.* **1.** a heavy woollen cloth with a thick nap. **2.** *Chiefly U.S.* equipment or supplies, esp. those of a camper. [C17: after *Duffel,* Belgian town]
duf·fel bag *n.* a cylindrical drawstring canvas bag, originally used esp. by sailors for carrying personal articles.
duf·fel coat *n.* a knee-length or short wool coat, usually with a hood and fastened with toggles.
duf·fer (ˈdʌfə) *n.* **1.** *Informal.* a dull or incompetent person. **2.** *Slang.* something worthless. **3.** *Brit. dialect.* a peddler or hawker. **4.** *Austral. slang.* **a.** a mine that proves unproductive. **b.** a person who steals cattle. [C19: of uncertain origin]
duff up *vb.* (*tr., adv.*) *Brit. slang.* to beat or thrash (a person) severely.
Du·fy (*French* dyˈfi) *n.* **Ra·oul** (raˈul). 1877–1953, French painter and designer whose style is characterized by swift calligraphic draughtsmanship and bright colouring.
dug[1] (dʌg) *vb.* the past tense or past participle of **dig.**
dug[2] (dʌg) *n.* **1.** the nipple, teat, udder, or breast of a female mammal. **2.** a human breast, esp. when old and withered. [C16: of Scandinavian origin; compare Danish *dægge* to coddle, Gothic *daddjan* to give suck]
Du Gard (*French* dy ˈgar) *n.* See (Roger) **Martin du Gard.**
du·gong (ˈduːgɒŋ) *n.* a whalelike sirenian mammal, *Dugong dugon,* occurring in shallow tropical waters from E Africa to Australia: family *Dugongidae.* [C19: from Malay *duyong*]
dug·out (ˈdʌgˌaʊt) *n.* **1.** a canoe, made by hollowing out a log. **2.** *Military.* a covered excavation dug to provide shelter. **3.** *Slang.* a retired officer, former civil servant, etc., recalled to employment. **4.** *Baseball.* the place where players wait when not on the field.
Du Gues·clin ((*French* dy geˈklɛ̃) *n.* **Ber·trand** (bɛrˈtrɑ̃). ?1320–80, French military leader; as constable of France (1370–80), he helped to drive the English from France.
Du·ha·mel (*French* dyaˈmɛl) *n.* **Georges** (ʒɔrʒ). 1884–1966, French novelist, poet, and dramatist; author of *La Chronique des Pasquier* (1933–45).
dui·ker *or* **duy·ker** (ˈdaɪkə) *n., pl.* **·kers** *or* **·ker. 1.** Also: **duikerbok.** any small antelope of the genera *Cephalophus* and *Sylvicapra,* occurring throughout Africa south of the Sahara, having short straight backward-pointing horns, pointed hooves, and an arched back. **2.** *S. African.* any of several cormorants, esp. the long-tailed shag (*Phalacrocorax africanus*). [C18: via Afrikaans from Dutch *duiker* diver, from *duiken* to dive; see DUCK[2]]
Duis·burg (*German* ˈdyːsbʊrk) *n.* an industrial city in NW West Germany, in North Rhine-Westphalia at the confluence of the Rivers Rhine and Ruhr: one of the world's largest and busiest inland ports. Pop.: 435 281 (1974 est.).
du·ka (ˈduːka) *n. E. African.* a shop; store. [C20: from Swahili]
Du·kas (*French* dyˈka) *n.* **Paul** (pɔl). 1865–1935, French composer best known for the orchestral scherzo *The Sorcerer's Apprentice* (1897).
duke (djuːk) *n.* **1.** a nobleman of high rank: in the British Isles standing above the other grades of the nobility. **2.** the prince or ruler of a small principality or duchy. [C12: from Old French *duc,* from Latin *dux* leader]
duke·dom (ˈdjuːkdəm) *n.* **1.** another name for a **duchy. 2.** the title, rank, or position of a duke.
dukes (djuːks) *pl. n. Slang.* the fists. [C19: from *Duke of Yorks* rhyming slang for *forks* (fingers)]
Du·kho·bors (ˈduːkəʊˌbɔːz) *pl. n.* a variant spelling of **Doukhobors.**
dul·cet (ˈdʌlsɪt) *adj.* (of a sound) soothing or pleasant; sweet. [C14: from Latin *dulcis* sweet] —**ˈdul·cet·ly** *adv.* —**ˈdul·cet·ness** *n.*

dul·ci·an·a (ˌdʌlsɪˈɑːnə) *n.* a sweet-toned organ stop, controlling metal pipes of narrow scale. [C18: from Latin *dulcis* sweet]

dul·ci·fy (ˈdʌlsɪˌfaɪ) *vb.* **·fies, ·fy·ing, ·fied.** (*tr.*) **1.** *Rare.* to make pleasant or agreeable. **2.** a rare word for **sweeten.** [C16: from Late Latin *dulcificāre,* from Latin *dulcis* sweet + *facere* to make] —ˌ**dul·ci·fi·ˈca·tion** *n.*

dul·ci·mer (ˈdʌlsɪmə) *n. Music.* **1.** a tuned percussion instrument consisting of a set of strings of graduated length stretched over a sounding board and struck with a pair of hammers. **2.** an instrument used in U.S. folk music, consisting of an elliptical body, a fretted fingerboard, and usually three strings plucked with a goose quill. [C15: from Old French *doulcemer,* from Old Italian *dolcimelo,* from *dolce* sweet, from Latin *dulcis* + *-melo,* perhaps from Greek *melos* song]

dul·cin·e·a (ˌdʌlsɪˈnɪə) *n.* a man's sweetheart. [C18: from the name of Don Quixote's mistress Dulcinea del Toboso in Cervantes' novel; from Spanish *dulce* sweet]

du·li·a (ˈdjuːlɪə) *n. Theol.* the veneration accorded to saints in the Roman Catholic and Eastern Churches, as contrasted with hyperdulia and latria. [C17: from Medieval Latin: service, from Greek *douleia* slavery, from *doulos* slave]

dull (dʌl) *adj.* **1.** slow to think or understand; stupid. **2.** lacking in interest. **3.** lacking in perception or the ability to respond; insensitive. **4.** lacking sharpness; blunt. **5.** not acute, intense, or piercing. **6.** (of weather) not bright or clear; cloudy. **7.** not active, busy, or brisk. **8.** lacking in spirit or animation; listless. **9.** (of colour) lacking brilliance or brightness; sombre. **10.** not loud or clear; muffled. ~*vb.* **11.** to make or become dull. [Old English *dol;* related to Old Norse *dul* conceit, Old High German *tol* foolish, Greek *tholeros* confused] —ˈ**dull·ish** *adj.* —ˈ**dull·ness** *or* ˈ**dul·ness** *n.* —ˈ**dul·ly** *adv.*

dull·ard (ˈdʌləd) *n.* a dull or stupid person.

Dul·les (ˈdʌlɪs) *n.* **John Fos·ter.** 1888–1959, U.S. statesman and lawyer; secretary of state (1953–59).

dulls·ville (ˈdʌlzvɪl) *n. Slang.* **1.** a thing, place, or activity that is boring or dull. **2.** the state of being bored.

du·lo·sis (djuːˈləʊsɪs) *n.* a practice of some ants, in which one species forces members of a different species to do the work of the colony. Also called: **helotism.** [C20: from Greek: enslavement, from *doulos* slave] —**du·lot·ic** (djuːˈlɒtɪk) *adj.*

dulse (dʌls) *n.* any of several seaweeds, esp. *Rhodymenia palmata,* that occur on rocks and have large red edible fronds. [C17: from Old Irish *duilesc* seaweed]

Du·luth (dəˈluːθ) *n.* a port in E Minnesota, at the W end of Lake Superior. Pop.: 100 578 (1970).

du·ly (ˈdjuːlɪ) *adv.* **1.** in a proper or fitting manner. **2.** at the proper time; punctually. [C14: see DUE, -LY]

du·ma *or* **dou·ma** *Russian.* (ˈdumə) *n. Russian history.* **1.** (*usually cap.*) the elective legislative assembly established by Tsar Nicholas II in 1905: overthrown by the Bolsheviks in 1917. **2.** (before 1917) any official assembly or council. [C20: from *duma* thought, of Germanic origin; related to Gothic *dōms* judgment]

Du·mas (*French* dyˈmɑ) *n.* **1. A·le·xan·dre** (alɛkˈsɑ̃dr), known as *Dumas père.* 1802–70, French novelist and dramatist, noted for his historical romances *The Count of Monte Cristo* (1844) and *The Three Musketeers* (1844). **2.** his son, **A·le·xan·dre,** known as *Dumas fils.* 1824–95, French novelist and dramatist, noted esp. for the play he adapted from an earlier novel, *La Dame aux camélias* (1852). **3. Jean-Bap·tiste An·dré** (ʒɑ̃ batist ɑ̃ˈdre). 1800–84, French chemist, noted for his research on vapour density and atomic weight.

Du Mau·ri·er (djuː ˈmɒrɪˌeɪ) *n.* **1. Daph·ne.** born 1907, English novelist; author of *Rebecca* (1938) and *My Cousin Rachel* (1951). **2.** her grandfather, **George Lou·is Pal·mel·la Bus·son** (ˈpælmɛlə ˈbjuːsᵊn). 1834–96, English novelist, caricaturist, and illustrator; author of *Peter Ibbetson* (1891) and *Trilby* (1894).

dumb (dʌm) *adj.* **1.** lacking the power to speak, either because of defects in the vocal organs or because of hereditary deafness; mute. **2.** lacking the power of human speech: *dumb animals.* **3.** temporarily lacking or bereft of the power to speak: *struck dumb.* **4.** refraining from speech; uncommunicative. **5.** producing no sound; silent: *a dumb piano.* **6.** made, done, or performed without speech. **7.** *Informal, chiefly U.S.* **a.** slow to understand; dim-witted. **b.** foolish; stupid. [Old English; related to Old Norse *dumbr,* Gothic *dumbs,* Old High German *tump*] —ˈ**dumb·ly** *adv.* —ˈ**dumb·ness** *n.*

dumb a·gue *n.* an irregular form of malarial fever (ague) lacking the typically symptomatic chill.

Dum·bar·ton (dʌmˈbɑːtᵊn) *n.* a town in W Scotland, in Strathclyde region near the confluence of the Rivers Leven and Clyde: centred around the **Rock of Dumbarton,** an important stronghold since ancient times; shipbuilding, engineering, and distilling. Pop.: 25 640 (1971).

Dum·bar·ton Oaks (ˈdʌmbɑːtᵊn) *n.* an estate in the District of Columbia in the U.S.: scene of conferences in 1944 concerned with creating the United Nations.

dumb·bell (ˈdʌmˌbɛl) *n.* **1.** *Gymnastics, etc.* an exercising weight consisting of a single bar with a heavy ball or disc at either end. **2.** *Slang, chiefly U.S.* a fool.

dumb-cane *n.* an aroid plant, *Dieffenbachia seguine,* that occurs in the West Indies and induces speechlessness in anyone who chews the stem.

dumb·found *or* **dum·found** (dʌmˈfaʊnd) *vb.* (*tr.*) to strike dumb with astonishment; amaze. [C17: from DUMB + (CON)FOUND]

dumb show *n.* **1.** a part of a play acted in pantomime, popular in early English drama. **2.** meaningful gestures; mime.

dumb·struck (ˈdʌmˌstrʌk) *or* **dumb·strick·en** *adj.* temporarily deprived of speech through shock or surprise.

dumb·wait·er (ˈdʌmˌweɪtə) *n.* **1.** *Brit.* **a.** a stand placed near a dining table to hold food. **b.** a revolving circular tray placed on a table to hold food. U.S. name: **lazy Susan. 2.** a lift for carrying food, rubbish, etc., between floors.

dum·dum (ˈdʌmˌdʌm) *n.* a soft-nosed or hollow-nosed small-arms bullet that expands on impact and inflicts extensive laceration. Also: **dumdum bullet.** [C19: named after *Dum-Dum,* town near Calcutta where these bullets were made]

Dum·fries (dʌmˈfriːs) *n.* **1.** a town in S Scotland, administrative centre of Dumfries and Galloway region on the River Nith. Pop.: 29 384 (1971). **2.** (until 1975) a county in S Scotland, on the Solway Firth, now part of Dumfries and Galloway region: the Southern Uplands in the north slope down to the coast; chiefly agricultural.

Dum·fries and Gal·lo·way Re·gion *n.* a local government region in SW Scotland. Administrative centre: Dumfries. Pop.: 143 585 (1976 est.). Area: 6475 sq. km (2500 sq. miles).

dum·my (ˈdʌmɪ) *n., pl.* **·mies. 1.** a figure representing the human form, used for displaying clothes, in a ventriloquist's act, as a target, etc. **2. a.** a copy or imitation of an object, often lacking some essential feature of the original. **b.** (*as modifier*): *a dummy drawer.* **3.** *Slang.* a stupid person; fool. **4.** *Derogatory, slang.* a person without the power of speech; mute. **5.** *Informal.* a person who says or does nothing. **6. a.** a person who appears to act for himself while acting on behalf of another. **b.** (*as modifier*): *a dummy buyer.* **7.** *Military.* a blank round. **8.** *Bridge.* **a.** the hand exposed on the table by the declarer's partner and played by the declarer. **b.** the declarer's partner. **9. a.** a prototype of a proposed book, indicating the general appearance and dimensions of the finished product. **b.** a designer's layout of a page indicating the positions for illustrations, etc. **10.** a feigned pass or move in a sport such as football or rugby. **11.** *Brit.* a rubber teat for babies to suck or bite on. U.S. equivalent: **pacifier. 12.** (*modifier*) counterfeit; sham. **13.** (*modifier*) (of a card game) played with one hand exposed or unplayed. ~*vb.* **·mies, ·my·ing, ·mied. 14.** to prepare a dummy of a proposed book, page, etc. **15.** Also: **sell (someone) a dummy.** *Sport.* to use a dummy pass in order to trick an opponent. [C16: see DUMB, -Y[3]]

dum·my var·i·a·ble *n.* a variable or constant appearing in a mathematical expression that can be replaced by any arbitrary variable or constant, not occurring in the expression, without affecting the value of the whole.

du·mor·ti·e·rite (djuːˈmɔːtɪəˌraɪt) *n.* a hard fibrous blue or green mineral consisting of hydrated aluminium borosilicate. Formula: $Al_8BSi_3O_{19}(OH)$. [C19: named after Eugène *Dumortier,* 19th-century French palaeontologist who discovered it]

dump[1] (dʌmp) *vb.* **1.** to drop, fall, or let fall heavily or in a mass. **2.** (*tr.*) to empty (objects or material) out of a container. **3.** to unload, empty, or make empty (a container), as by tilting or overturning. **4.** (*tr.*) *Informal.* to dispose of. **5.** *Commerce.* **a.** to market (goods) in bulk and at low prices. **b.** to offer for sale large quantities of (goods) on foreign markets at low prices in order to maintain a high price in the home market and obtain a share of the foreign markets. **6.** (*tr.*) to store (supplies, arms, etc.) temporarily. **7.** (*tr.*) *Austral.* (of a wave) to hurl a swimmer or surfer down. **8.** (*tr.*) *Austral.* to compact (bales of wool) by hydraulic pressure. **9.** (*tr.*) *Computer technol.* to record (the contents of part or all of the memory) on a storage device, such as magnetic tape, at a series of points during a computer run. ~*n.* **10. a.** a place or area where waste materials are dumped. **b.** (*in combination*): *rubbish dump.* **11.** a pile or accumulation of rubbish. **12.** the act of dumping. **13.** *Informal.* a dirty or unkempt place. **14.** *Military.* a place where weapons, supplies, etc., are stored. [C14: probably of Scandinavian origin; compare Norwegian *dumpa* to fall suddenly, Middle Low German *dumpeln* to duck] —ˈ**dump·er** *n.*

dump[2] (dʌmp) *n. Obsolete.* a mournful song; lament. [C16: see DAMP]

dump·ling (ˈdʌmplɪŋ) *n.* **1.** a small ball of dough cooked and served with stew. **2.** a pudding consisting of a ball of dough filled with fruit: *apple dumpling.* **3.** *Informal.* a short plump person. [C16: *dump-,* perhaps variant of LUMP[1] + -LING[1]]

dumps (dʌmps) *pl. n. Informal.* a state of melancholy or depression (esp. in the phrase **down in the dumps**). [C16: probably from Middle Dutch *domp* haze, mist; see DAMP]

dump truck *or* **dump·er-truck** *n.* another name for **tipper truck.**

dump·y[1] (ˈdʌmpɪ) *adj.* **dump·i·er, dump·i·est.** short and plump; squat. [C18: perhaps related to DUMPLING] —ˈ**dump·i·ly** *adv.* —ˈ**dump·i·ness** *n.*

dump·y[2] (ˈdʌmpɪ) *or* **dump·ish** *adj. Rare.* in low spirits; depressed; morose. [C17: from C16 *dump;* see DUMPS]

dump·y lev·el *n. Surveying.* a levelling instrument consisting of a horizontal telescope with various rotational arrangements and a spirit level.

Dum·yat (dumˈjæt) *n.* the Arabic name for **Damietta.**

dun[1] (dʌn) *vb.* **duns, dun·ning, dunned. 1.** (*tr.*) to press or importune (a debtor) for the payment of a debt. ~*n.* **2.** a person, esp. a hired agent, who importunes another for the payment of a debt. **3.** a demand for payment, esp. one in writing. [C17: of unknown origin]

dun[2] (dʌn) *n.* **1.** a brownish-grey colour. **2.** a horse of this colour. **3.** *Angling.* an immature adult mayfly, esp. one of the genus *Ephemera.* ~*adj.* **dun·ner, dun·nest. 4.** of a dun colour. **5.** dark and gloomy. [Old English *dunn;* related to Old Norse *dunna* wild duck, Middle Irish *doun* dark; see DUSK]

Du·na ('dunɔ) *n.* the Hungarian name for the **Danube.**
Dü+na+burg ('dy:naˌbʊrk) *n.* the German name (until 1893) for **Daugavpils.**
Du+naj ('dunaj) *n.* the Czech name for the **Danube.**
Du·nant (*French* dy'nã) *n.* **Jean Hen·ri** (ʒã ã'ri). 1828–1910, Swiss humanitarian, founder of the International Red Cross (1864): shared the Nobel peace prize 1901.
Du+nă+rea ('dunərjɑ) *n.* the Rumanian name for the **Danube.**
Dun+bar[1] (dʌn'bɑ:) *n.* a port and resort in SE Scotland, in Lothian region: scene of Cromwell's defeat of the Scots (1650). Pop.: 4586 (1971).
Dun·bar[2] (dʌn'bɑ:) *n.* **Wil·liam.** ?1460–?1520, Scottish poet, noted for his satirical and humorous verse.
Dun+bar+ton (dʌn'bɑ:tᵊn) *n.* (until 1975) a county of W Scotland, now part of Strathclyde region.
Dun·can ('dʌŋkən) *n.* **Is·a·do·ra.** 1878–1927, U.S. dancer and choreographer, who influenced modern ballet by introducing greater freedom of movement.
Dun·can I ('dʌŋkən) *n.* died 1040, king of Scotland (1034–40); murdered by Macbeth.
Dun·can Phyfe ('dʌŋkən 'faɪf) *n.* (*modifier*) *U.S. furniture.* of or in the manner of Duncan Phyfe, esp. in that which followed the Sheraton and Directoire styles.
dunce (dʌns) *n.* a person who is stupid or slow to learn. [C16: from *Dunses* or *Dunsmen,* term of ridicule applied to the followers of John DUNS SCOTUS especially by 16th-century humanists] —**'dunce+ˌlike** *adj.*
dunce cap *or* **dunce's cap** *n.* a conical paper hat, formerly placed on the head of a dull child at school.
Dun+dalk (dʌn'dɔ:k) *n.* a town in NE Ireland, on **Dundalk Bay:** county town of Co. Louth. Pop.: 23 816 (1971).
Dun+dee (dʌn'di:) *n.* a port in E Scotland, administrative centre of Tayside region on the Firth of Tay: centre of the British jute industry. Pop.: 182 084 (1971).
Dun+dee cake *n. Chiefly Brit.* a fairly rich fruit cake decorated with almonds.
dun·der+head ('dʌndəˌhɛd) *or* **dun·der+pate** *n.* a stupid or slow-witted person; dunce. [C17: probably from Dutch *donder* thunder + HEAD; compare BLOCKHEAD] —**'dun·der+ˌhead·ed** *adj.* —**'dun·der+ˌhead·ed+ness** *n.*
dune (dju:n) *n.* a mound or ridge of drifted sand, occurring on the sea coast and in deserts. [C18: via Old French from Middle Dutch *dūne;* see DOWN[3]]
Dun+e·din (dʌn'i:dɪn) *n.* a port in New Zealand, on SE South Island: founded (1848) by Scottish settlers. Pop.: 83 600 (1974 est.).
Dun+ferm+line (dʌn'fɜ:mlɪn) *n.* a city in E Scotland, in SW Fife: ruined palace, a former residence of Scottish kings. Pop.: 49 882 (1971).
dun fly *n. Angling.* a drab-coloured artificial fly intended to simulate the larva of various insects, esp. the mayfly.
dung (dʌŋ) *n.* **1. a.** excrement, esp. of animals; manure. **b.** (*as modifier*): *dung cart.* **2.** something filthy. ~*vb.* **3.** (*tr.*) to cover (ground) with manure. [Old English: prison; related to Old High German *tunc* cellar roofed with dung, Old Norse *dyngja* manure heap] —**'dung·y** *adj.*
dun+ga+ree (ˌdʌŋgə'ri:) *n.* **1.** a coarse cotton fabric used chiefly for work clothes, etc. **2.** (*pl.*) **a.** a suit of workman's overalls made of this material. **b.** a child's playsuit. **3.** *U.S.* trousers. [C17: from Hindi *dungrī,* after *Dungrī,* district of Bombay, where this fabric originated]
dun·gas ('dʌŋgəz) *pl. n. Austral. informal.* short for **dungarees.**
dung bee+tle *or* **chaf+er** *n.* any of the various beetles of the family *Scarabaeidae* and related families that feed on or breed in dung.
Dun+ge+ness (ˌdʌndʒə'nɛs) *n.* a low shingle headland on the S coast of England, in Kent: lighthouse.
dun+geon ('dʌndʒən) *n.* **1.** a close prison cell, often underground. **2.** a variant spelling of **donjon.** [C14: from Old French *donjon;* related to Latin *dominus* master]
dung+hill ('dʌŋˌhɪl) *n.* **1.** a heap of dung. **2.** a foul place, condition, or person.
dun+ite ('dʌnaɪt) *n.* an ultrabasic igneous rock consisting mainly of olivine. [C19: named after Dun Mountain, a mountain in New Zealand where it is abundant]
du+ni+was+sal ('du:nɪˌwɑsᵊl) *n.* (in Scotland) a minor nobleman. [C16: from Gaelic *duine* man + *uasal* noble]
dunk (dʌŋk) *vb.* **1.** to dip (bread, etc.) in tea, soup, etc., before eating. **2.** to submerge or be submerged in liquid. [C20: from Pennsylvania Dutch, from Middle High German *dunken,* from Old High German *dunkōn;* see DUCK[2], TINGE] —**'dunk+er** *n.*
Dunk+er ('dʌŋkə) *or* **Dun+kard** ('dʌŋkəd) *n.* a member of the German Baptist Brethren. [C18: from German *Tunker,* ducker]
Dun+kerque (*French* dœ̃'kɛrk) *n.* a port in N France, on the Strait of Dover: scene of the evacuation of British and other Allied troops after the fall of France in 1940; industrial centre with an oil refinery and naval shipbuilding yards. Pop.: 83 759 (1975). English name: **Dunkirk.**
Dun Laoghai·re (dʌn 'lɛərə) *n.* a port in E Ireland, on Dublin Bay. Pop.: 53 171 (1971). Former names: **Dunleary** (until 1821), **Kingstown** (1821–1921).
dun+lin ('dʌnlɪn) *n.* a small sandpiper, *Calidris* (or *Erolia*) *alpina,* of northern and arctic regions, having a brown back and black breast in summer. Also called: **red-backed sandpiper.** [C16: DUN[2] + -LING[1]]
Dun·lop ('dʌnlɒp) *n.* **John Boyd.** 1840–1921, Scottish veterinary surgeon, who devised the first successful pneumatic tyre, which was manufactured by the company named after him.
dun+nage ('dʌnɪdʒ) *n.* loose material used for packing cargo. [C14: of uncertain origin]
dun+na+kin ('dʌnəkɪn) *n. Brit. dialect.* a lavatory. Also called: **dunny.** [of obscure origin; but perhaps related to DUNG]
dun+nite ('dʌnaɪt) *n.* an explosive containing ammonium picrate. [C20: named after Colonel B. W. *Dunn* (1860–1936), American army officer who invented it]
dun+no (dʌ'nəʊ, dʊ-, də-) *Slang. contraction of* (I) do not know.
dun+nock ('dʌnək) *n.* another name for **hedge sparrow.** [C15: from DUN[2] + -OCK]
dun+ny ('dʌnɪ) *n., pl.* **+nies. 1.** *Scot. dialect.* a cellar or basement. **2.** *Brit. dialect.* another word for **dunnakin. 3.** *Austral. informal.* **a.** a lavatory. **b.** (*as modifier*)*: a dunny roll; a dunny seat.* [C20: of obscure origin; but see DUNNAKIN]
Du·nois (*French* dy'nwa) *n.* **Jean** (ʒã), Comte de Dunois, called *the Bastard of Orléans.* ?1403–68, French military commander, who defended Orléans against the English until the siege was raised by Joan of Arc (1429).
Du+noon (də'nu:n) *n.* a town and resort in W Scotland, in central Strathclyde on the Firth of Clyde. Pop.: 9824 (1971).
Dun·sa·ny (dʌn'seɪnɪ) *n.* **18th Bar·on,** title of *Edward John Moreton Drax Plunkett.* 1878–1957, Irish dramatist and short-story writer.
Dun+si+nane ('dʌnsɪˌneɪn) *n.* a hill in central Scotland, in the Sidlaw Hills: the ruined fort at its summit is regarded as Macbeth's castle. Height: 303 m (1012 ft.).
Duns Scot·us ('dʌnz 'skɒtəs) *n.* **John.** ?1265–1308, Scottish scholastic theologian and Franciscan priest: opposed the theology of St. Thomas Aquinas. See also **Scotism.**
Dun+sta+ble[1] ('dʌnstəbᵊl) *n.* an industrial town in SE central England, in central Bedfordshire. Pop.: 31 790 (1971).
Dun·sta·ble[2] ('dʌnstəbᵊl) *n.* **John.** died 1453, English composer, esp. of motets and mass settings, noted for his innovations in harmony and rhythm.
Dun·stan ('dʌnstən) *n.* **Saint.** ?909–988 A.D., English prelate and statesman; archbishop of Canterbury (959–988). He revived monasticism in England on Benedictine lines and promoted education. Feast day: May 19.
dunt (dʌnt, dʊnt) *Northern Brit. dialect.* ~*n.* **1.** a blow; thump. **2.** the injury caused by such a blow. ~*vb.* **3.** to strike or hit. [C15: perhaps variant of DINT]
Dun+troon (dʌn'tru:n) *n.* a suburb of Canberra: seat of the Royal Military College of Australia.
du·o ('dju:əʊ) *n., pl.* **du·os** *or* **du·i** ('dju:i:). **1.** *Music.* **a.** a pair of performers. **b.** another word for **duet. 2.** a pair of actors, entertainers, etc. **3.** *Informal.* a pair of closely connected individuals. [C16: via Italian from Latin: two]
du·o- *combining form.* indicating two: *duotone.* [from Latin]
du·o·dec·i+mal (ˌdju:əʊ'dɛsɪməl) *adj.* **1.** relating to twelve or twelfths. ~*n.* **2.** a twelfth. **3.** one of the numbers used in a duodecimal number system. —**ˌdu·o·'dec·i+mal+ly** *adv.*
du·o·dec·i+mo (ˌdju:əʊ'dɛsɪˌməʊ) *n., pl.* **+mos. 1.** a book size resulting from folding a sheet of paper into twelve leaves. Also called: **twelvemo.** Often written: **12mo, 12°. 2.** a book of this size. [C17: from Latin phrase *in duodecimō* in twelfth, from *duodecim* twelve]
du·o·de·na·ry (ˌdju:əʊ'di:nərɪ) *adj.* of or relating to the number 12; duodecimal. [C17: from Latin *duodēnārius* containing twelve]
du·o+de·ni·tis (ˌdju:əʊdɪ'naɪtɪs) *n.* inflammation of the duodenum.
du·o+de·num (ˌdju:əʊ'di:nəm) *n., pl.* **+na** (-nə) *or* **+nas.** the first part of the small intestine, between the stomach and the jejunum. [C14: from Medieval Latin, shortened from *intestinum duodenum digitorum* intestine of twelve fingers' length, from Latin *duodēnī* twelve each] —**ˌdu·o+'denal** *adj.*
du·o+logue *or U.S.* (*sometimes*) **du·o+log** ('dju:əˌlɒg) *n.* **1.** a part or all of a play in which the speaking roles are limited to two actors. **2.** a less common word for **dialogue.**
duo+mo ('dwəʊməʊ) *n., pl.* **+mos.** a cathedral. [Italian, literally: dome]
du·o+tone ('dju:əˌtəʊn) *n. Printing.* **1.** a process for producing halftone illustrations using two shades of a single colour or black and a colour. **2.** a picture produced by this process.
dup (dʌp) *vb.* **dups, dup+ping, dupped.** (*tr.*) *Archaic or Brit. dialect.* to open. [C16: contraction of DO[1] + UP]
dup. *abbrev. for* duplicate.
Du·parc (*French* dy'park) *n.* **Hen·ri** (ã'ri), full name *Marie Eugène Henri Fouques Duparc.* 1848–1933, French composer of songs noted for their sad brooding quality.
du+pat+ta (dʊ'pʌtə) *n.* a scarf worn in India.
dupe (dju:p) *n.* **1.** a person who is easily deceived. **2.** a person who unwittingly serves as the tool of another person or power. ~*vb.* **3.** (*tr.*) to deceive, esp. by trickery; make a dupe or tool of; cheat; fool. [C17: from French, from Old French *duppe,* contraction of *de huppe* of (a) hoopoe (from Latin *upupa*); from the bird's reputation for extreme stupidity] —**'dup+a·ble** *adj.* —**ˌdup+a·'bil+i·ty** *n.* —**'dup+er** *n.* —**'dup+er·y** *n.*
du+pi·on 'dju:pɪən, -'pi:ɒn) *n.* a silk fabric made from the threads of double cocoons. [C19: from French *doupion,* from Italian *doppione* double]
du+ple ('dju:pᵊl) *adj.* **1.** a less common word for **double. 2.** *Music.* (of time or music) having two beats in a bar. [C16: from Latin *duplus* twofold, double]
Du·pleix (*French* dy'plɛks) *n.* Marquis **Jo·seph Fran·çois** (ʒozɛf frã'swa). 1697–1763, French governor general in India (1742–54). His plan to establish a French empire in India was frustrated by Clive.

Du·ples·sis-Mor·nay (*French* dyplɛsimɔr'nɛ) *n.* a variant of (Philippe de) **Mornay.**
du+plet ('dju:plɪt) *n.* **1.** a pair of electrons shared between two atoms in a covalent bond. **2.** *Music.* a group of two notes played in the time of three.
du+ple time *n.* musical time with two beats in each bar.
du+plex ('dju:plɛks) *n.* **1.** *U.S.* a duplex apartment or house. ~*adj.* **2.** having two parts. **3.** *Machinery.* having pairs of components of independent but identical function. **4.** permitting the transmission of simultaneous signals in both directions in a radio or telecommunications channel. Compare **diplex, simplex** (sense 1). [C19: from Latin: twofold, from *duo* two + *-plex* -FOLD] **—du+'plex+i·ty** *n.*
du+plex a+part+ment *n. U.S.* an apartment on two floors.
du+plex house *n. U.S.* a house divided into two separate dwellings. Also called: **semidetached.**
du+pli+cate *adj.* ('dju:plɪkɪt). **1.** copied exactly from an original. **2.** identical. **3.** existing as a pair or in pairs; twofold. ~*n.* ('dju:plɪkɪt). **4.** an exact copy; double. **5.** something additional or supplementary of the same kind. **6.** two exact copies (esp. in the phrase **in duplicate**). ~*vb.* ('dju:plɪ,keɪt). **7.** (*tr.*) to make a replica of. **8.** (*tr.*) to do or make again. **9.** (*tr.*) to make in a pair; make double. **10.** (*intr.*) *Biology.* to reproduce by dividing into two identical parts: *the chromosomes duplicated in mitosis.* [C15: from Latin *duplicāre* to double, from *duo* two + *plicāre* to fold] **—du+pli+ca·ble** ('dju:plɪkəbᵊl) *adj.* **—,du+pli+ca·'bil+i·ty** *n.* **—'du+pli+cate+ly** *adv.* **—'du+pli+ca+tive** *adj.*
du+pli+cate bridge *n.* a form of contract bridge in which a team of four players in two pairs plays identical hands at two separate tables.
du+pli+ca+tion (,dju:plɪ'keɪʃən) *n.* **1.** the act of duplicating or the state of being duplicated. **2.** a copy; duplicate.
du+pli+ca+tor ('dju:plɪ,keɪtə) *n.* an apparatus for making replicas of an original, such as a machine using a stencil wrapped on an ink-loaded drum.
du+plic+i·ty (dju:'plɪsɪtɪ) *n., pl.* **·ties.** deception; double-dealing. [C15: from Old French *duplicite,* from Late Latin *duplicitās* a being double, from Latin DUPLEX] **—du+'plic+it+ous** *adj.*
du+pon+di·us (dju:'pɒndɪəs) *n., pl.* **+di·i** (-dɪ,aɪ). a brass coin of ancient Rome worth half a sesterce. [from Latin, from *duo* two + *pondus* weight]
dup+py ('dʌpi) *n., pl.* **+pies.** *Caribbean.* a spirit or ghost. [C18: probably of African origin]
Du·pré (*French* dy'pre) *n.* **Mar·cel** (mar'sɛl). 1886–1971, French organist and composer, noted as an improviser.
Du+que de Ca+xi+as (*Portuguese* 'duke de ka'ʃias) *n.* a city in SE Brazil, near Rio de Janeiro. Pop.: 256 582 (1970).
Dur. *abbrev. for* Durham.
du+ra·ble ('djuərəbᵊl) *adj.* long-lasting; enduring: *a durable fabric.* [C14: from Old French, from Latin *dūrābilis,* from *dūrāre* to last; see ENDURE] **—,du+ra·'bil+i·ty** *or* **'du+ra·ble+ness** *n.* **—'du+ra·bly** *adv.*
du+ra·ble goods *pl. n.* goods, such as most producer goods and some consumer goods, that require infrequent replacement. Compare **perishables.** Also called: **durables.**
dur+a·ble press *n.* **a.** another term for **permanent press. b.** (*as modifier*): *durable-press skirts.*
Du+ral·u+min (djʊ'ræljʊmɪn) *n. Trademark.* a light strong aluminium alloy containing 3.5–4.5 per cent of copper with small quantities of silicon, magnesium, and manganese; used in aircraft manufacture.
du+ra ma+ter ('djuərə 'meɪtə) *n.* the outermost and toughest of the three membranes (see **meninges**) covering the brain and spinal cord. Often shortened to **dura.** [C15: from Medieval Latin, hard mother]
du+ra+men (djʊ'reɪmɛn) *n.* another name for **heartwood.** [C19: from Latin: hardness, from *dūrāre* to harden]
du+rance ('djuərəns) *n. Archaic or literary.* **1.** imprisonment. **2.** duration. [C15: from Old French, from *durer* to last, from Latin *dūrāre*]
Du+rance (*French* dy'rɑ̃s) *n.* a river in S France, rising in the Alps and flowing generally southwest into the Rhône. Length: 304 km (189 miles).
Du+ran+go (djʊ'ræŋgəʊ; *Spanish* du'raŋgo) *n.* **1.** a state in N central Mexico: high plateau, with the Sierra Madre Occidental in the west; irrigated agriculture (esp. cotton) and rich mineral resources. Capital: Durango. Pop.: 939 208 (1970). Area: 119 648 sq. km (46 662 sq. miles). **2.** a city in NW central Mexico, capital of Durango state: mining centre. Pop.: 191 034 (1975 est.). Official name: **Victoria de Durango.**
du+ra+tion (djʊ'reɪʃən) *n.* the length of time that something lasts, or continues. [C14: from Medieval Latin *dūrātiō,* from Latin *dūrāre* to last] **—du+'ra+tion+al** *adj.*
du+ra+tive ('djuərətɪv) *Grammar.* ~*adj.* **1.** denoting an aspect of verbs that includes the imperfective and the progressive. ~*n.* **2. a.** the durative aspect of a verb. **b.** a verb in this aspect.
Du+raz+zo (du'rattso) *n.* the Italian name for **Durrës.**
Dur+ban ('dɜ:bᵊn) *n.* a port in E South Africa, in E Natal on the Indian Ocean: University of Natal (1909); resort and industrial centre, with oil refineries, shipbuilding yards, etc. Pop.: 495 458 (1970).
dur+bar ('dɜ:bɑ:, ,dɜ:'bɑ:) *n.* **a.** (formerly) the court of a native ruler or a governor in India and British Colonial West Africa. **b.** a levée at such a court. [C17: from Hindi *darbār* court, from Persian, from *dar* door + *bār* entry, audience]
Dü+ren (*German* 'dy:rən) *n.* a city in W West Germany, in North Rhine-Westphalia. Pop.: 53 800 (1970).
Dü·rer (*German* 'dy:rər) *n.* **Al·brecht** ('albrɛçt). 1471–1528, German painter and engraver, regarded as the greatest artist of the German Renaissance and noted particularly as a draughtsman and for his copper engravings and woodcuts.
du+ress (djʊ'rɛs, djʊə-) *n.* **1.** compulsion by use of force or threat; constraint; coercion (often in the phrase **under duress**). **2.** *Law.* the illegal exercise of coercion. **3.** confinement; imprisonment. [C14: from Old French *duresse,* from Latin *dūritia* hardness, from *dūrus* hard]
Du+rex ('djuərɛks) *n., pl.* **+rex.** *Trademark.* **1.** a brand of condom. **2.** *Austral.* a brand of adhesive tape.
dur+gah ('dɜ:gɑ:) *n.* a variant spelling of **dargah.**
Dur+ham ('dʌrəm) *n.* **1.** a county of NE England, on the North Sea: rises to the N Pennines in the west, with a coalfield to the east. Administrative centre: Durham. Pop.: 610 400 (1976 est.). Area: 2496 sq. km (964 sq. miles). Abbrev.: **Dur. 2.** a city in NE England, administrative centre of Co. Durham, on the River Wear: Norman cathedral; 11th-century castle (founded by William the Conqueror), now occupied by the University of Durham (1832). Pop.: 24 744 (1971). **3.** a variety of shorthorn cattle. See **shorthorn.**
du+ri·an *or* **du+ri+on** ('djuərɪən) *n.* **1.** a SE Asian bombacaceous tree, *Durio zibethinus,* having edible oval fruits with a hard spiny rind. **2.** the fruit of this tree, which has an offensive smell but a pleasant taste. [C16: from Malay, from *duri* thorn]
dur+ing ('djuərɪŋ) *prep.* **1.** concurrently with (some other activity): *kindly don't sleep during my lectures!* **2.** within the limit of (a period of time): *during the day.* [C14: from *duren* to last, ultimately from Latin *dūrāre* to last]
Durk·heim ('dɜ:khaɪm; *French* dyr'kɛm) *n.* **É·mile** (e'mil). 1858–1917, French sociologist, whose pioneering works include *De la Division du travail social* (1893).
dur+mast *or* **durmast oak** ('dɜ:,mɑ:st) *n.* **1.** Also called: **sessile oak.** a large Eurasian oak tree, *Quercus petraea,* with lobed leaves and sessile acorns. Compare **pedunculate oak. 2.** the heavy elastic wood of this tree, used in building and cabinet-work. [C18: probably alteration of *dun mast;* see DUN², MAST²]
du+ro ('dʊərəʊ) *n., pl.* **·ros.** the silver peso of Spain or Spanish America. [from Spanish, shortened from *peso duro* hard peso, ultimately from Latin *dūrus* hard]
Du+roc ('djuərɒk) *n.* an American breed of red lard pig. [C19: from *Duroc,* name of a stallion owned by the man who developed this breed]
dur+ra ('dʌrə), **dou+ra,** *or* **dou+rah** ('duərə) *n.* an Old World variety of sorghum, *Sorghum vulgare durra,* with erect hairy flower spikes and round seeds: cultivated for grain and fodder. Also called: **Guinea corn, Indian millet.** [C18: from Arabic *dhurah* grain]
Dur·rell ('dʌrəl) *n.* **Law·rence (George).** born 1912, English poet and novelist; author of *The Alexandria Quartet* of novels, consisting of *Justine* (1957), *Balthazar* (1958), *Mountolive* (1958), and *Clea* (1960).
Dür·ren·matt ('dyrən,mat) *n.* **Frie·drich** ('fri:drɪç). born 1921, Swiss dramatist and writer of detective stories, noted for his grotesque and paradoxical treatment of the modern world: author of *The Visit* (1956) and *The Physicists* (1962).
Dur+rës ('durrəs) *n.* a port in W Albania, on the Adriatic. Pop.: 53 800 (1970). Ancient names: **Epidamnus, Dyrrachium.** Italian name: **Durazzo.**
durst (dɜ:st) *vb.* a past tense of **dare.**
du+rum *or* **du+rum wheat** ('djuərəm) *n.* a variety of wheat, *Triticum durum,* with a high gluten content, cultivated mainly in the Mediterranean region, and used chiefly to make pastas. [C20: short for New Latin *trīticum dūrum,* literally: hard wheat]
dur+zi ('dɜ:rzɪ) *n.* an Indian tailor. [C19: from Hindi, from Persian *darzi* from *darz* sewing]
Du+shan+be (du:'ʃɑ:nbɪ) *n.* an industrial city in the SW Soviet Union, capital of the Tadzhik SSR. Pop.: 436 000 (1975 est.). Former name (1929–61): **Stalinabad.**
dusk (dʌsk) *n.* **1.** twilight or the darker part of twilight. **2.** *Poetic.* gloom; shade. ~*adj.* **3.** *Poetic.* shady; gloomy. ~*vb.* **4.** *Poetic.* to make or become dark. [Old English *dox;* related to Old Saxon *dosan* brown, Old High German *tusin* yellow, Norwegian *dusmen* misty, Latin *fuscus* dark brown]
dusk·y ('dʌskɪ) *adj.* **dusk·i·er, dusk·i·est. 1.** dark in colour; swarthy. **2.** dim. **—'dusk·i+ly** *adv.* **—'dusk·i·ness** *n.*
Düs+sel+dorf ('dʊsəl,dɔ:f; *German* 'dysəl,dɔrf) *n.* an industrial city in W West Germany, capital of North Rhine-Westphalia, on the Rhine: commercial centre of the Rhine-Ruhr industrial area. Pop.: 628 498 (1974 est.).
dust (dʌst) *n.* **1.** dry fine powdery material, such as particles of dirt, earth or pollen. **2.** a cloud of such fine particles. **3.** the powdery particles to which something is thought to be reduced by death, decay, or disintegration. **4.** *Theol.* **a.** the mortal body of man. **b.** the corpse of a dead person. **5.** the earth; ground. **6.** *Informal.* a disturbance; fuss (esp. in the phrases **kick up a dust, raise a dust**). **7.** something of little or no worth. **8.** *Informal.* (in mining parlance) silicosis or any similar respiratory disease. **9.** short for **gold dust. 10.** ashes or household refuse. **11. bite the dust.** *Informal.* **a.** to suffer complete defeat. **b.** to die. **12. dust and ashes.** something that is very disappointing. **13. lick the dust.** *Informal.* to be forced to be humble; grovel. **14. shake the dust off one's feet.** to depart angrily. **15. throw dust in the eyes of.** to confuse or mislead. ~*vb.* **16.** (*tr.*) to sprinkle or cover (something) with (dust or some other powdery substance): *to dust a cake with sugar; to dust sugar onto a cake.* **17.** to remove dust by wiping, sweeping, or brushing. **18.** to make or become dirty with dust. [Old English *dūst;* related to Danish *dyst* flour dust, Middle Dutch *dūst* dust, meal dust, Old High German *tunst* storm] **—'dust+less** *adj.*

dust-bath *n.* the action of a bird of driving dust into its feathers, which may dislodge parasites.
dust+bin ('dʌstˌbɪn) *n.* a large, usually cylindrical container for rubbish, esp. one used by a household. U.S. names: **garbage can, trash can.**
dust bowl *n.* a semiarid area in which the surface soil is exposed to wind erosion and dust storms occur.
Dust Bowl *n.* **the.** the area of the south central U.S. that became denuded of topsoil by wind erosion during the droughts of the mid-1930s.
dust+cart ('dʌstˌkɑːt) *n.* a road vehicle for collecting domestic refuse. U.S. name: **garbage truck.**
dust coat *n. Brit.* a loose lightweight coat worn for early open motor-car riding. U.S. name: **duster.**
dust cov+er *n.* **1.** another name for a **dustsheet. 2.** another name for **dust jacket. 3.** a perspex cover for a gramophone turntable.
dust dev+il *n.* a strong miniature whirlwind that whips up dust, litter, leaves, etc., into the air.
dust down *vb.* (*tr., adv.*). **1.** to remove dust from by brushing or wiping. **2.** to reprimand severely. **—dust+ing down** *n.*
dust+er ('dʌstə) *n.* **1.** a cloth used for dusting furniture, etc. U.S. name: **dust cloth. 2.** a machine for blowing out dust over trees or crops. **3.** a person or thing that dusts.
dust+er coat *n.* a woman's loose summer coat with wide sleeves and no buttons, popular in the mid-20th century.
dust+ing-pow+der *n.* fine powder (such as talcum powder) used to absorb moisture, etc.
dust jack+et *or* **cov+er** *n.* a removable paper cover used to protect a bound book. Also called: **book jacket, jacket.**
dust+man ('dʌstmən) *n., pl.* **+men.** *Brit.* a man whose job is to collect domestic refuse.
dust+pan ('dʌstˌpæn) *n.* a short-handled hooded shovel into which dust is swept from floors, etc.
dust+sheet ('dʌstˌʃiːt) *n. Brit.* a large cloth or sheet used for covering furniture to protect it from dust. Also called: **dust cover.**
dust shot *n.* the smallest size of shot for a shotgun.
dust storm *n.* a windstorm that whips up clouds of dust.
dust-up *Informal.* ~*n.* **1.** a quarrel, fight, or argument. ~*vb.* **dust up. 2.** (*tr., adv.*) to attack or assault (someone).
dust·y ('dʌstɪ) *adj.* **dust·i+er, dust·i+est. 1.** covered with or involving dust. **2.** like dust in appearance or colour. **3.** (of a colour) tinged with grey; pale: *dusty pink.* **4.** dull or unsatisfactory. **—'dust·i·ly** *adv.* **—'dust·i·ness** *n.*
dust·y mill+er *n.* **1.** Also called: **snow-in-summer.** a caryophyllaceous plant, *Cerastium tomentosum,* of SE Europe and Asia, having white flowers and downy stems and leaves: cultivated as a rock plant. **2.** a plant, *Artemisia stelleriana,* of NE Asia and E North America, having small yellow flower heads and downy stems and leaves: family *Compositae* (composites). **3.** any of various other downy plants, such as the rose campion.
dutch (dʌtʃ) *n. Cockney slang.* wife. [C19: short for *duchess*]
Dutch (dʌtʃ) *n.* **1.** the language of the Netherlands, belonging to the West Germanic branch of the Indo-European family and quite closely related to German and English. See also **Flemish, Afrikaans. 2. the Dutch.** (*functioning as pl.*) the natives, citizens, or inhabitants of the Netherlands. **3.** See **Pennsylvania Dutch. 4.** See **double Dutch. 5. in Dutch.** *Slang.* in trouble. ~*adj.* **6.** of, relating to, or characteristic of the Netherlands, its inhabitants, or their language. ~*adv.* **7. go Dutch.** *Informal.* to share expenses equally.
Dutch auc+tion *n.* an auction in which the price is lowered by stages until a buyer is found.
Dutch barn *n. Brit.* a farm building consisting of a steel frame and a curved roof.
Dutch cap *n.* **1.** a woman's lace cap with triangular flaps, characteristic of Dutch national dress. **2.** a contraceptive device for women. See **diaphragm** (sense 2).
Dutch cheese *n.* any of various small round hard cheeses of the Netherlands, esp. Edam and Gouda.
Dutch cour+age *n.* **1.** false courage gained from drinking alcohol. **2.** alcoholic drink.
Dutch doll *n.* a jointed wooden doll.
Dutch door *n.* the U.S. name for **stable door.**
Dutch East In+dies *n.* **The.** a former name (1798–1945) of **Indonesia.** Also called: **Netherlands East Indies.**
Dutch elm *n.* a widely planted hybrid elm tree, *Ulmus hollandica,* with spreading branches and a short trunk.
Dutch elm dis+ease *n.* a disease of elm trees caused by the fungus *Ceratocystis ulmi* and characterized by withering of the foliage and stems and eventual death of the tree.
Dutch Gui+an·a *or* **Neth+er+lands Gui+an·a** *n.* the former name of **Surinam.**
Dutch hoe *n.* a type of hoe in which two prongs are joined by a crosspiece.
Dutch+man ('dʌtʃmən) *n., pl.* **+men. 1.** a native, citizen, or inhabitant of the Netherlands. **2.** a piece of wood, metal, etc., used to repair or patch faulty workmanship.
Dutch·man's-breech·es *n.* (*functioning as sing.*) a North American plant, *Dicentra cucullaria,* with finely divided basal leaves and pink flowers: family *Fumariaceae.* Also called: **colicweed.**
Dutch·man's-pipe *n.* a woody climbing plant, *Aristolochia sipho,* of the eastern U.S., cultivated for its greenish-brown mottled flowers, which are shaped like a curved pipe: family *Aristolochiaceae.*
Dutch met+al *or* **gold** *n.* a substitute for gold leaf, consisting of thin sheets of copper that have been turned yellow by exposure to the fumes of molten zinc.
Dutch New Guin·ea *n.* the former name (until 1963) of **West Irian.**
Dutch ov·en *n.* **1.** an iron or earthenware container with a cover used for stews, etc. **2.** a metal box, open in front, for cooking in front of an open fire.
Dutch Re+formed Church *n.* any of the three Calvinist Churches to which most Afrikaans-speaking South Africans belong.
Dutch rush *n.* (*sometimes not cap.*) a horsetail, *Equisetum hyemale,* whose siliceous stems have been used for polishing and scouring pots and pans. Also called: **scouring rush.**
Dutch treat *n. Informal.* an entertainment, meal, etc., where each person pays for himself.
Dutch un+cle *n. Informal.* a person who criticizes or reproves frankly and severely.
Dutch West In+dies *n.* **The.** a former name of the **Netherlands Antilles.**
du+te·ous ('djuːtɪəs) *adj. Formal or archaic.* dutiful; obedient. **—'du+te·ous+ly** *adv.* **—'du+te·ous+ness** *n.*
du+ti+a·ble ('djuːtɪəbᵊl) *adj.* (of goods, etc.) liable to duty. **—ˌdu+ti+a·'bil+i·ty** *n.*
du+ti+ful ('djuːtɪfʊl) *adj.* **1.** exhibiting or having a sense of duty. **2.** characterized by or resulting from a sense of duty: *a dutiful answer.* **—'du+ti+ful+ly** *adv.* **—'du+ti+ful+ness** *n.*
du·ty ('djuːtɪ) *n., pl.* **·ties. 1.** a task or action that a person is bound to perform for moral or legal reasons. **2.** respect or obedience due to a superior, older persons, etc.: *filial duty.* **3.** the force that binds one morally or legally to one's obligations. **4.** a government tax, esp. on imports. **5.** *Brit.* **a.** the quantity of work for which a machine is designed. **b.** a measure of the efficiency of a machine. **6.** the quantity of water necessary to irrigate an area of land to grow a particular crop. **7.** a job or service allocated. **8. do duty for.** to act as a substitute for. **9. on** (*or* **off**) **duty.** at (*or* not at) work. [C13: from Anglo-French *dueté,* from Old French *deu* DUE]
du·ty-bound *adj.* morally obliged as a matter of duty.
du·ty-free *adj., adv.* with exemption from customs or excise duties.
du·ty-free shop *n.* a shop, esp. one at a port or on board a ship, that sells perfume, tobacco, etc., at duty-free prices.
du·ty of+fic+er *n.* an officer (in the armed forces, police, etc.) on duty at a particular time.
du+um+vir (djuː'ʌmvə) *n., pl.* **+virs** *or* **+vi+ri** (-vɪˌriː). **1.** *Roman history.* one of two coequal magistrates or officers. **2.** either of two men who exercise a joint authority. [C16: from Latin, from *duo* two + *vir* man]
du+um+vi+rate (djuː'ʌmvɪrɪt) *n.* the office of or government by duumvirs.
Du·va·lier (*French* dyva'lje) *n.* **1. Fran·çois** (frɑ̃'swa), known as *Papa Doc.* 1907–71, president of Haiti (1957–71). **2.** his son, **Jean-Claude** (ʒɑ̃'kloːd). born 1951, Haitian statesman; life president of Haiti since 1971.
du+vet ('duːveɪ) *n.* another name for **continental quilt.** [C18: from French, from earlier *dumet,* from Old French *dum* DOWN²]
du+ve·tyn, du+ve·tine, *or* **du+ve·tyne** ('djuːvəˌtiːn) *n.* a soft napped velvety fabric of cotton, silk, wool, or rayon. [C20: from French *duvetine,* from *duvet* down + -INE¹]
dux (dʌks) *n.* (in Scottish and certain other schools) the top pupil in a class or school. [Latin: leader]
duy+ker ('daɪkə) *n.* a variant spelling of **duiker.**
D.V. *abbrev. for:* **1.** Deo volente. [Latin: God willing] **2.** Douay Version (of the Bible).
dvan+dva ('dvɑːndvɑː) *n.* **1.** a class of compound words consisting of two elements having a coordinate relationship as if connected by *and.* **2.** a compound word of this type, such as *Austro-Hungarian, tragicomic.* [from Sanskrit *dvamdva* a pair, from the reduplication of *dva* TWO]
Dvi+na (*Russian* dvi'na) *n.* **1. Northern.** a river in the NW Soviet Union, formed by the confluence of the Sukhona and Yug Rivers and flowing northwest to *Dvina Bay* in the White Sea. Length: 750 km (466 miles). Russian name: **Severnaya Dvina. 2. Western.** a river in the W Soviet Union, rising in the Valdai Hills and flowing south and southwest then northwest to the Gulf of Riga. Length: 1021 km (634 miles). Russian name: **Zapadnaya Dvina.** Latvian name: **Daugava.**
Dvi+na Bay *or* **Dvi+na Gulf** *n.* an inlet of the White Sea, off the coast of the NW Soviet Union.
Dvinsk (dvinsk) *n.* transliteration of the former Russian name for **Daugavpils.**
D.V.M. *or* **DVM** *abbrev. for* Doctor of Veterinary Medicine.
Dvo·řák ('dvɔːʒæk; *Czech* 'dvɔrʒaːk) *n.* **An·to·nín** ('antɔniːn), known as *Anton Dvořák.* 1841–1904, Czech composer, much of whose work reflects the influence of folk music. His best-known work is the *Symphony No. 9 From the New World* (1893).
D/W *abbrev. for* dock warrant.
dwale (dweɪl) *n.* another name for **deadly nightshade.** [C14: perhaps of Scandinavian origin]
dwarf (dwɔːf) *n., pl.* **dwarfs** *or* **dwa+rves** (dwɔːvz). **1.** an abnormally undersized person, esp. one with a large head and short arms and legs. Compare **midget. 2. a.** an animal or plant much below the average height for the species. **b.** (*as modifier*): *a dwarf tree.* **3.** (in folklore) a small ugly manlike creature, often possessing magical powers. **4.** *Astronomy.* short for **dwarf star.** ~*vb.* **5.** to become or cause to become small in size, importance, etc. **6.** (*tr.*) to stunt the growth of. [Old English *dweorg;* related to Old Norse *dvergr,* Old High German

twerc] —'**dwarf+ish** *adj.* —'**dwarf+ish+ly** *adv.* —'**dwarf+ish+ness** *n.*
dwarf bean *n.* another name for **French bean.**
dwarf chest+nut *n.* **1.** the edible nut of the chinquapin tree. **2.** another name for **chinquapin** (sense 1).
dwarf cor+nel *n.* an arctic and subarctic cornaceous plant, *Chamaepericlymenum suecicum* (or *Cornus suecica*), having small purple flowers surrounded by petal-like bracts.
dwarf+ism ('dwɔːfɪzəm) *n.* the condition of being a dwarf.
dwarf mal+low *n.* a European malvaceous plant, *Malva neglecta* (or *M. rotundifolia*), having rounded leaves and small pinkish-white flowers.
dwarf star *n.* any of a class of faint stars lying in the main sequence of the Hertzsprung-Russell diagram and having a very high density and small diameter compared to the much brighter class of stars, **giant stars.** Both types belong to the same spectral classes (G, K, and M). Sometimes shortened to **dwarf.** See **red dwarf, white dwarf.**
dwell (dwɛl) *vb.* **dwells, dwell+ing, dwelt** *or* **dwelled.** (*intr.*) **1.** *Formal, literary.* to live as a permanent resident. **2.** to live (in a specified state): *to dwell in poverty.* ~*n.* **3.** a regular pause in the operation of a machine. **4.** a flat or constant-radius portion on a linear or rotary cam. [Old English *dwellan* to seduce, get lost; related to Old Saxon *bidwellian* to prevent, Old Norse *dvelja,* Old High German *twellen* to prevent] —'**dwell+er** *n.*
dwell+ing ('dwɛlɪŋ) *n. Formal, literary.* a place of residence.
dwell on *or* **up·on** *vb.* (*intr., prep.*) to think, speak, or write at length: *he dwells on his misfortunes.*
dwelt (dwɛlt) *vb.* the past tense of **dwell.**
dwin+dle ('dwɪndᵊl) *vb.* to grow or cause to grow less in size, intensity, or number; diminish or shrink gradually. [C16: from Old English *dwīnan* to waste away; related to Old Norse *dvīna* to pine away]
dwt *or* **dwt.** *Obsolete. abbrev. for* pennyweight. [*d,* from Latin *denarius* penny]
d.w.t. *abbrev. for* deadweight tonnage.
DX *Telegraphy, telephony.* **1.** *symbol for* long distance. **2.** (of a radio station) indicating that it is far away.
Dy *the chemical symbol for* dysprosium.
dy·ad ('daɪæd) *n.* **1.** *Maths.* an operator that is the unspecified product of two vectors. It can operate on a vector to produce either a scalar or vector product. **2.** an atom or group that has a valency of two. [C17: from Late Latin *dyas,* from Greek *duas* two, a pair]
dy+ad+ic (daɪ'ædɪk) *adj.* **1.** of or relating to a dyad. **2.** relating to or based on two; twofold. ~*n.* **3.** *Maths.* the sum of two or more dyads.
Dy·ak *or* **Day+ak** ('daɪæk) *n., pl.* **·aks** *or* **·ak.** a member of a Malaysian people of the interior of Borneo: noted for their long houses. [from Malay *Dayak* upcountry, from *darat* land]
dy+ar+chy ('daɪɑːkɪ) *n., pl.* **+chies.** a variant spelling of **diarchy.** —**dy+'ar+chic, dy+'ar+chi+cal,** *or* **dy+'ar+chal** *adj.*
dyb+buk ('dɪbək; *Hebrew* di'buk) *n., pl.* **+buks** *or* **+buk+kim** (*Hebrew* -bu'kim). *Judaism.* (in the folklore of the cabala) the soul of a dead sinner that has transmigrated into the body of a living person. [from Yiddish *dibbūk* devil, from Hebrew *dibbūq;* related to *dābhaq* to hang on, cling]
dye (daɪ) *n.* **1.** a staining or colouring substance, such as a natural or synthetic pigment. **2.** a liquid that contains a colouring material and can be used to stain fabrics, skins, etc. **3.** the colour or shade produced by dyeing. ~*vb.* **dyes, dye+ing, dyed. 4.** (*tr.*) to impart a colour or stain to (something, such as fabric or hair) by or as if by the application of a dye. [Old English *dēagian,* from *dēag* a dye; related to Old High German *tugōn* to change, Lettish *dūkans* dark] —'**dy+a·ble** *or* '**dye+a·ble** *adj.* —'**dy·er** *n.*
dyed-in-the-wool *adj.* **1.** extreme or unchanging in attitude, opinion, etc. **2.** (of a fabric) made of dyed yarn.
dye+ing ('daɪɪŋ) *n.* the process or industry of colouring yarns, fabric, etc.
dye+line ('daɪ,laɪn) *adj.* another word for **diazo** (sense 2).
dy·er's-green·weed *or esp. U.S.* **dy·er's-broom** *n.* a small Eurasian papilionaceous shrub, *Genista tinctoria,* whose yellow flowers yield a yellow dye, formerly mixed with woad to produce the colour Kendal green. Also called: **woadwaxen, woodwaxen.**
dy·er's rock+et *n.* a Eurasian resedaceous plant, *Reseda luteola,* with a spike of yellowish-green flowers and long narrow leaves: formerly cultivated as the source of a yellow dye, used with woad to make Lincoln green. Also called: **weld.**
dy·er's-weed *n.* any of several plants that yield a dye, such as woad, dyer's rocket, and dyer's-greenweed.
dye+stuff ('daɪ,stʌf) *n.* a substance that can be used as a dye or from which a dye can be obtained.
dye+wood ('daɪ,wʊd) *n.* any wood, such as brazil, from which dyes and pigments can be obtained.
Dyf+ed ('dʌvɛd) *n.* a county in SW Wales, formed in 1974 from Cardiganshire, Pembrokeshire, and Carmarthenshire: coastal lowlands rising to a high plateau in the north and mountains in the south. Administrative centre: Carmarthen. Pop.: 323 100 (1976 est.). Area: 5762 sq. km (2280 sq. miles).
dy+ing ('daɪɪŋ) *vb.* **1.** the present participle of **die**[1]. ~*adj.* **2.** relating to or occurring at the moment of death: *a dying wish.*
dyke[1] *or esp. U.S.* **dike** (daɪk) *n.* **1.** an embankment constructed to prevent flooding or keep out the sea. **2.** a ditch or water-course. **3.** a bank made of earth excavated for and placed alongside a ditch. **4.** a barrier or obstruction. **5.** a wall-like mass of igneous rock intruded into cracks in older sedimentary rock. **6.** *Austral. informal.* **a.** a lavatory. **b.** (*as modifier*): *a dyke roll.* ~*vb.* **7.** (*tr.*) to protect, enclose, or drain (land) with a dyke. [C13: modification of Old English *dīc* ditch; compare Old Norse *dīki* ditch]
dyke[2] *or* **dike** (daɪk) *n. Slang.* a lesbian. [C20: of unknown origin]
Dyl·an ('dɪlən) *n.* **Bob.** original name *Robert Zimmerman.* born 1941, U.S. folk singer and songwriter, noted for his protest songs in the 1960s. His albums include *The Freewheelin' Bob Dylan* (1961), *The Times they are a-changin'* (1963), *Bringing it All Back Home* (1965), *Highway 61 Revisited* (1965), *Blonde on Blonde* (1966), *John Wesley Harding* (1968), *Nashville Skyline* (1969), *Before the Flood* (1974), *Blood on the Tracks* (1975), and *Desire* (1976).
dy+nam+e·ter (daɪ'næmɪtə) *n.* an instrument for determining the magnifying power of telescopes.
dy+nam+ic (daɪ'næmɪk) *adj.* **1.** of or concerned with energy or forces that produce motion, as opposed to *static.* **2.** of or concerned with dynamics. **3.** Also: **dy+nam·i+cal.** characterized by force of personality, ambition, energy, new ideas, etc. **4.** *Music.* of, relating to, or indicating dynamics: *dynamic range; dynamic marks.* **5.** *Computer technol.* (of a memory) needing its contents refreshed periodically. Compare **static** (sense 8). [C19: from French *dynamique,* from Greek *dunamikos* powerful, from *dunamis* power, from *dunasthai* to be able] —**dy+'nam·i+cal+ly** *adv.*
dy+nam+ic psy+chol+o·gy *n. Psychol.* any method or system concerned with explaining motives and impulses.
dy+nam+ics (daɪ'næmɪks) *n.* **1.** (*functioning as sing.*) the branch of mechanics concerned with the forces that change or produce the motions of bodies. Compare **statics, kinematics. 2.** (*functioning as sing.*) the branch of mechanics that includes statics and kinetics. See **statics, kinetics. 3.** (*functioning as sing.*) the branch of any science concerned with forces. **4.** those forces that produce change in any field or system. **5.** *Music.* **a.** the various degrees of loudness called for in performance. **b.** Also called: **dynamic marks, dynamic markings.** directions and symbols used to indicate degrees of loudness.
dy+na+mism ('daɪnə,mɪzəm) *n.* **1.** *Philosophy.* any of several theories that attempt to explain phenomena in terms of an immanent force or energy. Compare **mechanism** (sense 5), **vitalism. 2.** the forcefulness of an energetic personality. —'**dy+na+mist** *n.* —,**dy+na+'mis+tic** *adj.*
dy+na+mite ('daɪnə,maɪt) *n.* **1.** an explosive consisting of nitroglycerin or ammonium nitrate mixed with kieselguhr, sawdust, or wood pulp. **2.** *Informal.* a spectacular or potentially dangerous person or thing. ~*vb.* **3.** (*tr.*) to mine or blow up with dynamite. [C19 (coined by Alfred Nobel): from DYNAMO- + -ITE[1]] —'**dy+na+,mit+er** *n.*
dy+na+mo ('daɪnə,məʊ) *n., pl.* **+mos. 1.** a device for converting mechanical energy into electrical energy, esp. one that produces direct current. Compare **generator** (sense 1). **2.** *Informal.* an energetic hard-working person. [C19: short for *dynamo-electric machine*]
dy·na·mo- *or sometimes before a vowel* **dy·nam-** *combining form.* indicating power: *dynamoelectric; dynamite.* [from Greek, from *dunamis* power]
dy+na+mo+e·lec+tric (,daɪnəməʊɪ'lɛktrɪk) *or* **dy+na+mo+e·lec+tri+cal** *adj.* of or concerned with the interconversion of mechanical and electrical energy.
dy+na+mom+e·ter (,daɪnə'mɒmɪtə) *n.* any of a number of instruments for measuring power.
dy+na+mom+e·try (,daɪnə'mɒmɪtrɪ) *n.* **1.** the science of power measurement. **2.** the manufacture and use of dynamometers. —**dy+na+mo+met+ric** (,daɪnəməʊ'mɛtrɪk) *or* ,**dy+na+mo+'met+ri+cal** *adj.*
dy+na+mo+tor ('daɪnə,məʊtə) *n.* an electrical machine having a single magnetic field and two independent armature windings of which one acts as a motor and the other a generator: used to convert direct current from an accumulator into alternating current.
dyn+ast ('dɪnəst, -æst) *n.* a ruler, esp. a hereditary one. [C17: from Latin *dynastēs,* from Greek *dunastēs,* from *dunasthai* to be powerful]
dyn+as+ty ('dɪnəstɪ) *n., pl.* **+ties. 1.** a sequence of hereditary rulers: *an Egyptian dynasty.* **2.** any sequence of powerful leaders of the same family: *the Kennedy dynasty.* [C15: via Late Latin from Greek *dunasteia,* from *dunastēs* DYNAST] —**dy+nas+tic** (dɪ'næstɪk) *or* **dy+'nas+ti+cal** *adj.* —**dy+'nas+ti+cal+ly** *adv.*
dy+na+tron os+cil+la+tor ('daɪnə,trɒn) *n. Electronics.* an oscillator containing a tetrode in which the screen grid is more positive than the anode, causing the anode current to decrease as its voltage increases. [C20: from DYNA(MO)- + -TRON]
dyne (daɪn) *n.* the cgs unit of force; the force that imparts an acceleration of 1 centimetre per second per second to a mass of 1 gram. 1 dyne is equivalent to 10^{-5} newton or 7.233×10^{-5} poundal. [C19: from French, from Greek *dunamis* power, force]
dy+node ('daɪnəʊd) *n.* an electrode onto which a beam of electrons can fall, causing the emission of a greater number of electrons by secondary emission. They are used in photomultipliers, etc., to amplify the signal.
dys- *prefix.* **1.** diseased, abnormal, or faulty: *dysentery; dyslexia.* **2.** difficult or painful: *dysuria.* **3.** unfavourable or bad: *dyslogistic.* [via Latin from Greek *dus-*]
dys+cra+si·a (dɪs'kreɪzɪə) *n. Obsolete.* any abnormal physiological condition, esp. of the blood. [C19: New Latin, from Medieval Latin: an imbalance of humours, from Greek, from DYS- + *-krasia,* from *krasis* a mixing]
dys+en+ter·y ('dɪsᵊntrɪ) *n.* infection of the intestine with

bacteria or amoebae, marked chiefly by severe diarrhoea with the passage of mucus and blood. [C14: via Latin from Greek *dusenteria,* from *dusentera,* literally: bad bowels, from DYS- + *enteron* intestine] —**dys+en+ter+ic** (ˌdɪsᵊnˈtɛrɪk) *adj.*

dys+func+tion (dɪsˈfʌŋkʃən) *n. Med.* any disturbance or abnormality in the function of an organ or part. —ˌ**dys+ˈfunc+tion+al** *adj.*

dys+gen+ic (dɪsˈdʒɛnɪk) *adj.* **1.** of, relating to, or contributing to a degeneration or deterioration in the fitness and quality of a race or strain. **2.** of or relating to dysgenics.

dys+gen+ics (dɪsˈdʒɛnɪks) *n.* (*functioning as sing.*) the study of factors capable of reducing the quality of a race or strain, esp. the human race. Also called: **cacogenics.**

dys+graph·i·a (dɪsˈgræfɪə) *n.* impaired ability to write, esp. as a result of a brain lesion. —**dys+ˈgraph+ic** *adj.*

dys+lex·i·a (dɪsˈlɛksɪə) *n.* impaired ability to read, due to a disorder of the brain. Nontechnical name: **word blindness.** [C19: New Latin, from DYS- + *-lexia,* from *legein* to speak] —**dys+lec+tic** (dɪsˈlɛktɪk) *adj., n.* —**dys+ˈlex+ic** *adj.*

dys+lo+gis+tic (ˌdɪsləˈdʒɪstɪk) *adj. Rare.* disapproving. [C19: from DYS- + *-logistic,* as in *eulogistic*] —ˌ**dys+lo+ˈgis+ti+cal+ly** *adv.*

dys+men+or+rhoe·a *or esp. U.S.* **dys+men+or+rhe·a** (ˌdɪsmɛnəˈrɪə, dɪsˌmɛn-) *n.* abnormally difficult or painful menstruation. —ˌ**dys+men+or+ˈrhoe·al** *or esp. U.S.* ˌ**dys+men+or+ˈrhe·al** *adj.*

dys+pep+si·a (dɪsˈpɛpsɪə) *or* **dys+pep+sy** (dɪsˈpɛpsɪ) *n.* indigestion or upset stomach. [C18: from Latin, from Greek *duspepsia,* from DYS- + *pepsis* digestion]

dys+pep+tic (dɪsˈpɛptɪk) *adj. also* **dys+pep+ti+cal. 1.** relating to or suffering from dyspepsia. **2.** irritable. ~*n.* **3.** a person suffering from dyspepsia. —**dys+ˈpep+ti+cal+ly** *adv.*

dys+pha+gi·a (dɪsˈfeɪdʒɪə) *n.* difficulty in swallowing, caused by obstruction or spasm of the oesophagus. —**dys+phag+ic** (dɪsˈfædʒɪk) *adj.*

dys+pha+si·a (dɪsˈfeɪzɪə) *n.* impaired coordination of speech caused by a brain lesion. —**dys+ˈpha+sic** *adj., n.*

dys+phe+mism (ˈdɪsfɪˌmɪzəm) *n.* **1.** substitution of a derogatory or offensive word or phrase for an innocuous one. **2.** the word or phrase so substituted. [C19: DYS- + EUPHEMISM] —**dys+phe+ˈmis+tic** *adj.*

dys+pho+ni·a (dɪsˈfəʊnɪə) *n.* any impairment in the ability to speak normally, as from spasm or strain of the vocal cords. [C18: New Latin, from Greek: harshness of sound, from DYS- + *-phōnia* -PHONY] —**dys+phon+ic** (dɪsˈfɒnɪk) *adj.*

dys+pho+ri·a (dɪsˈfɔːrɪə) *n.* a feeling of being ill at ease. [C20: New Latin, from Greek DYS- + *-phoria,* from *pherein* to bear] —**dys+phor+ic** (dɪsˈfɒrɪk) *adj.*

dys+pla+si·a (dɪsˈpleɪzɪə) *n.* abnormal development of an organ or part of the body, including congenital absence. [C20: New Latin, from DYS- + *-plasia,* from Greek *plasis* a moulding] —**dys+plas+tic** (dɪsˈplæstɪk) *adj.*

dysp+noe·a *or U.S.* **dysp+ne·a** (dɪspˈniːə) *n.* difficulty in breathing or in catching the breath. Compare **eupnoea.** [C17: via Latin from Greek *duspnoia,* from DYS- + *pnoē* breath, from *pnein* to breathe] —**dysp+ˈnoe·al, dysp+ˈnoe+ic** *or U.S.* **dysp+ˈne·al, dysp+ˈne+ic** *adj.*

dys+pro+si·um (dɪsˈprəʊsɪəm) *n.* a soft silvery-white metallic element of the lanthanide series: used in laser materials and as a neutron absorber in nuclear control rods. Symbol: Dy; atomic no.: 66; atomic wt.: 162.50; valency: 3; relative density: 8.56; melting pt.: 1407°C; boiling pt.: 2335°C. [C20: New Latin, from Greek *dusprositos* difficult to get near + -IUM]

dys+tel+e·ol+o·gy (ˌdɪstɛlɪˈɒlədʒɪ, -tiːlɪ-) *n. Philosophy.* the denial of purpose in life. Compare **teleology.** —**dys+ˌtel·e·o+ˈlog·i·cal** *adj.* —ˌ**dys+tel+e·ˈol·o·gist** *n.*

dys+thy+mi·a (dɪsˈθaɪmɪə) *n. Psychiatry.* **1.** the characteristics of the neurotic and introverted, including anxiety, depression, and compulsive behaviour. **2.** *Obsolete.* a relatively mild depression. [C19: New Latin, from Greek *dusthumia,* from DYS- + *thumos* mind] —**dys+ˈthy+mic** *adj.*

dys+to+pi·a (dɪsˈtəʊpɪə) *n.* an imaginary place where everything is as bad as it can be. [C19 (coined by J. S. Mill): from DYS- + UTOPIA] —**dys+ˈto+pi·an** *adj., n.*

dys+tro+phy (ˈdɪstrəfɪ) *or* **dys+tro+phi·a** (dɪˈstrəʊfɪə) *n.* **1.** any of various bodily disorders, characterized by wasting of tissues. See also **muscular dystrophy. 2.** *Ecology.* a condition of lake water when it is too acidic and poor in oxygen to support life, resulting from excessive humus content. [C19: New Latin *dystrophia,* from DYS- + Greek *trophē* food] —**dys+troph+ic** (dɪsˈtrɒfɪk) *adj.*

dys+u·ri·a (dɪsˈjʊərɪə) *n.* difficult or painful urination. [C14: via Latin from Greek *dusouria*] —**dys+ˈu·ric** *adj.*

dy+tis+cid (dɪˈtɪsɪd, daɪ-) *n.* **1.** any carnivorous aquatic beetle of the family *Dytiscidae,* having large flattened back legs used for swimming. ~*adj.* **2.** of, relating to, or belonging to the *Dytiscidae.* [C19: from New Latin *Dytiscus* genus name, changed from Greek *dutikos* able to dive, from *duein* to dive]

Dy·u·la (diːˈuːlə, ˈdjuːlə) *n.* **1.** (*pl.* **+la** *or* **+las**) a member of a negroid people of W Africa, living chiefly in the rain forests of the Ivory Coast, where they farm rice, etc. **2.** the language of this people, belonging to the Mande branch of the Niger-Congo family.

dz. *abbrev. for* dozen.

DZ *international car registration for* Algeria. [from Arabic *Djazir*]

Dzau+dzhi+kau (dzaʊˈdʒɪkaʊ) *n.* the former name (1944–54) of **Ordzhonikidze.**

Dzer+zhinsk (*Russian* dzɪrˈʒinsk) *n.* an industrial city in the central Soviet Union. Pop.: 240 000 (1975 est.).

Dzham+bul (*Russian* dʒamˈbul) *n.* a city in the S central Soviet Union, in the Kazakh SSR: chemical manufacturing. Pop.: 239 000 (1975 est.). Former name (until 1938): **Auliye-Ata.**

dzig+ge+tai (ˈdʒɪgɪˌtaɪ) *n.* a variant spelling of **chigetai.**

dzo (zəʊ) *n., pl.* **dzos** *or* **dzo.** a variant spelling of **zo.**

Dzong+ka (ˈzɒŋkə) *n.* the official language of Bhutan, probably a member of the Sino-Tibetan family.

Dzun+ga+ri·a *or* **Zun+ga+ri·a** (dzʊŋˈgɛərɪə, zʊŋ-) *n.* an arid region of W China, in N Sinkiang-Uighur between the Altai Mountains and the Tien Shan.

E

e *or* **E** (iː) *n., pl.* **e's, E's,** *or* **Es. 1.** the fifth letter and second vowel of the modern English alphabet. **2.** any of several speech sounds represented by this letter, in English as in *he, bet,* or *below.*

e *symbol for:* **1.** *Maths.* a transcendental number, fundamental to mathematics, that is the limit of $(1 + 1/n)^n$ as n increases to infinity: used as the base of natural logarithms. Approximate value: 2.718 282...; relation to π: $e^{\pi i} = -1$, where $i = \sqrt{-1}$. **2.** electron.

E *symbol for:* **1.** *Music.* **a.** a note having a frequency of 329.63 hertz (**E above middle C**) or this value multiplied or divided by any power of 2; the third note of the scale of C major. **b.** a key, string, or pipe producing this note. **c.** the major or minor key having this note as its tonic. **2.** *Physics.* **a.** energy. **b.** electromotive force. **c.** Young's modulus (of elasticity). **3.** East. **4.** English. **5.** Egypt(ian). ~ **6.** *international car registration for* Spain. [from Spanish *España*]

e. *abbrev. for* engineer(ing).

E. *abbrev. for* Earl.

ea. *abbrev. for* each.

each (iːtʃ) *determiner.* **1. a.** every (one) of two or more considered individually: *each day; each person.* **b.** (*as pronoun*): *each gave according to his ability.* ~*adv.* **2.** for, to, or from each one; apiece: *four apples each.* [Old English *ǣlc;* related to Old High German *ēogilīh,* Old Frisian *ellik,* Dutch *elk*]

each oth+er *pron.* used when the action, attribution, etc., is reciprocal: *furious with each other.*

Usage. *Each other* and *one another* are interchangeable in modern British usage, despite recommendations by some authorities that the meaning of the former be restricted to each of two and the latter to each of three or more.

EACSO (iːˈɑːksəʊ) *n. acronym for* East African Common Services Organization.

ea·ger[1] (ˈiːɡə) *adj.* **1.** (*postpositive;* often foll. by *to* or *for*) impatiently desirous (of); anxious or avid (for): *he was eager to see her departure.* **2.** characterized by or feeling expectancy or great desire: *an eager look.* **3.** *Archaic.* tart or biting; sharp. [C13: from Old French *egre,* from Latin *acer* sharp, keen] —**ˈea·ger+ly** *adv.* —**ˈea·ger+ness** *n.*

ea·ger[2] (ˈeɪɡə) *n.* a variant spelling of **eagre.**

ea·ger bea+ver *n. Informal.* a person who displays conspicuous diligence, esp. one who volunteers for extra work.

ea·gle (ˈiːɡᵊl) *n.* **1.** any of various birds of prey of the genera *Aquila, Harpia,* etc. (see **golden eagle, harpy eagle**), having large broad wings and strong soaring flight: family *Accipitridae* (hawks, etc.). See also **sea eagle.** Related adj.: **aquiline. 2.** a representation of an eagle used as an emblem, etc., esp. representing power: *the Roman eagle.* **3.** a standard, seal, etc., bearing the figure of an eagle. **4.** *Golf.* a score of two strokes under par for a hole. **5.** a former U.S. gold coin worth ten dollars: withdrawn from circulation in 1934. **6.** the shoulder insignia worn by a U.S. full colonel or equivalent rank. [C14: from Old French *aigle,* from Old Provençal *aigla,* from Latin *aquila,* perhaps from *aquilus* dark]

ea·gle-eyed *adj.* having keen or piercing eyesight.

ea·gle-hawk *n.* **1.** Also called: **wedge-tailed eagle.** a large aggressive Australian eagle, *Aquila audax.* ~*vb.* (*intr.*). **2.** *Austral. slang.* to pluck wool from a sheep's dead body.

ea·gle owl *n.* a large owl, *Bubo bubo,* of Europe and Asia. It has brownish speckled plumage and large ear tufts.

ea·gle ray *n.* any of various rays of the family *Myliobatidae,* related to the stingrays but having narrower pectoral fins and a projecting snout with heavily browed eyes.

ea·gle+stone (ˈiːɡᵊlˌstəʊn) *n.* a hollow oval nodule of clay ironstone, formerly thought to have magical properties.

ea·glet (ˈiːɡlɪt) *n.* a young eagle.

ea·gle+wood (ˈiːɡᵊlˌwʊd) *n.* **1.** an Asian thymelaeaceous tree, *Aquilaria agallocha,* having fragrant wood that yields a resin used as a perfume. **2.** the wood of this tree. ~Also called: **aloes, aloes wood, agalloch, lignaloes.**

ea·gre *or* **ea·ger** (ˈeɪɡə) *n.* a tidal bore, esp. of the Humber or Severn estuaries. [C17: perhaps from Old English *ēagor* flood; compare Old English *ēa* river, water]

EAK *international car registration for* East Africa Kenya.

eal·dor+man (ˈɔːldəmən) *n., pl.* **+men.** an official of Anglo-Saxon England, appointed by the king, who was responsible for law, order, and justice in his shire and for leading his local fyrd in battle. [Old English *ealdor* lord + MAN]

Ea·ling (ˈiːlɪŋ) *n.* a borough of W Greater London, formed in 1965 from Acton, Ealing, and Southall. Pop.: 293 800 (1976 est.).

EAM *n.* (in World War II) the leftist resistance in German-occupied Greece. [C20: from Modern Greek *Ethniko Apeleutherotiko Metopo* National Liberation Front]

-e·an *suffix forming adjectives.* variant of **-an:** *Caesarean.*

E.& O.E. *abbrev. for* errors and omissions excepted.

Ea·nes (*Portuguese* eˈanɛʃ) *n.* **An·tó·ni·o (dos Santos Ramalho)** (ɐnˈtɔnju). born 1935, Portuguese statesman and general; president of Portugal since 1976.

ear[1] (ɪə) *n.* **1.** the organ of hearing and balance in higher vertebrates and of balance only in fishes. In man and other mammals it consists of three parts (see **external ear, middle ear, inner ear**). Related adj.: **aural. 2.** the outermost cartilaginous part of the ear (pinna) in mammals, esp. man. **3.** the sense of hearing. **4.** sensitivity to musical sounds, poetic diction, etc.: *he has an ear for music.* **5.** attention, esp. favourable attention; consideration; heed (esp. in the phrases **give ear to, lend an ear**). **6.** an object resembling the external ear in shape or position, such as a handle on a jug. **7.** Also called (esp. Brit.): **earpiece.** a display box at the head of a newspaper page, esp. the front page, for advertisements, etc. **8. all ears.** *Informal.* very attentive; listening carefully. **9. by ear.** without reading from written music. **10. fall on deaf ears.** to be ignored or pass unnoticed. **11. have hard ears.** *Caribbean.* to be stubbornly disobedient. **12. a flea in one's ear.** *Informal.* a sharp rebuke. **13. have the ear of.** to be in a position to influence: *he has the ear of the president.* **14. head over ears.** tumultuously; with a powerful and confusing effect: *head over ears in love.* **15. in one ear and out the other.** *Informal.* heard but unheeded. **16. keep** (*or* **have**) **one's ear to the ground.** *Informal.* to be or try to be well informed about current trends and opinions. **17. make a pig's ear of.** *Informal.* to ruin disastrously. **18. one's ears are burning.** one is aware of being the topic of another's conversation. **19. out on one's ear.** *Informal.* dismissed unceremoniously. **20. play by ear. a.** *Informal.* to act according to the demands of a situation rather than to a plan; improvise. **b.** to perform a musical piece on an instrument without written music. **21. prick up one's ears.** to start to listen attentively; become interested. **22. set by the ears.** to cause disagreement or commotion. **23. a thick ear.** *Informal.* a blow on the ear. **24. turn a deaf ear.** *Informal.* to be unwilling to pay attention. **25. up to one's ears.** *Informal.* deeply involved, as in work or debt. **26. wet behind the ears.** *Informal.* youthful in manner or attitudes; naive; immature. [Old English *ēare;* related to Old Norse *eyra,* Old High German *ōra,* Gothic *ausō,* Greek *ous,* Latin *auris*] —**ˈear+less** *adj.* —**ˈear+ˌlike** *adj.*

ear[2] (ɪə) *n.* **1.** the part of a cereal plant, such as wheat or barley, that contains the seeds, grains, or kernels. ~*vb.* **2.** (*intr.*) (of cereal plants) to develop such parts. [Old English *ēar;* related to Old High German *ahar,* Old Norse *ax,* Gothic *ahs* ear, Latin *acus* chaff, Greek *akros* pointed]

ear+ache (ˈɪərˌeɪk) *n.* pain in the middle or inner ear. Technical name: **otalgia.** Compare **otitis.**

ear+bash (ˈɪəbæʃ) *vb.* (*intr.*) *Austral. slang.* to talk incessantly.—**ˈear+ˌbash+er** *n.* —**ˈear+ˌbash+ing** *n.*

ear+drop (ˈɪəˌdrɒp) *n.* a pendant earring.

ear+drops (ˈɪəˌdrɒps) *pl. n.* liquid medication for inserting into the external ear.

ear+drum (ˈɪəˌdrʌm) *n.* the nontechnical name for **tympanic membrane.**

eared (ɪəd) *adj.* **a.** having an ear or ears. **b.** (*in combination*): *long-eared; two-eared.*

eared seal *n.* any seal of the pinniped family *Otariidae,* typically having visible earflaps and conspicuous hind limbs that can be used for locomotion on land. Compare **earless seal.**

ear+flap (ˈɪəˌflæp) *n.* **1.** Also called: **earlap.** either of two pieces of fabric or fur attached to a cap, which can be let down to keep the ears warm. **2.** *Zoology.* a small flap of skin forming the pinna of such animals as seals.

ear+ful (ˈɪəfʊl) *n. Informal.* **1.** something heard or overheard. **2.** a rebuke or scolding, esp. a lengthy or severe one.

Ear·hart (ˈɛəhɑːt) *n.* **A·mel·ia.** 1898–1937, U.S. aviatrix: the first woman to fly the Atlantic (1928). She disappeared on a Pacific flight (1937).

ear+ing (ˈɪərɪŋ) *n. Nautical.* a line fastened to a corner of a sail for reefing.

earl (ɜːl) *n.* **1.** (in the British Isles) a nobleman ranking below a marquess and above a viscount. Female equivalent: **countess. 2.** (in Anglo-Saxon England) a royal governor of any of the large divisions of the kingdom, such as Wessex. [Old English *eorl;* related to Old Norse *jarl* chieftain, Old Saxon *erl* man]

ear+lap (ˈɪəˌlæp) *n.* **1.** another word for **earflap** (sense 1). **2.** *Rare.* **a.** the external ear. **b.** the ear lobe.

earl+dom (ˈɜːldəm) *n.* **1.** the rank, title, or dignity of an earl or countess. **2.** the lands of an earl or countess.

ear+less seal *n.* any seal of the pinniped family *Phocidae,* typically having rudimentary hind limbs, no external earflaps, and a body covering of hair with no underfur. Also called: **hair seal.** Compare **eared seal.**

Earl Mar+shal *n.* an officer of the English peerage who presides over the College of Heralds and organizes royal processions and other important ceremonies.

ear lobe *n.* the fleshy lower part of the external ear.

ear+ly (ˈɜːlɪ) *adj.* **-li+er, -li+est,** *adv.* **1.** before the expected or usual time. **2.** occurring in or characteristic of the first part of a period or sequence. **3.** occurring in or characteristic of a period far back in time. **4.** occurring in the near future. **5. at the earliest.** not before the time or date mentioned. **6. early days.** *Brit. informal.* not yet time for some expected occurrence. [Old English *ǣrlīce,* from *ǣr* ERE + *-līce* -LY; related to Old Norse *arliga*] —**'ear·li·ness** *n.*

ear·ly bird *n. Informal.* a person who rises early or arrives in good time.

Ear·ly Bird *n.* one of a number of communications satellites, the first of which was launched in 1965 into a stationary orbit and provided telephone channels between Europe and the U.S. See also **Intelsat.**

Ear·ly Chris·tian *adj.* denoting or relating to the style of architecture that started in Italy in the 3rd century A.D. and spread through the Roman empire until the 5th century.

ear·ly clos·ing *n. Brit.* **1. a.** the shutting of most of the shops in a town one afternoon each week. **b.** (*as adj.*): *early-closing day.* **2.** the day on which this happens: *Thursday is early closing in Aylesbury.*

Ear·ly Eng·lish *n.* a style of architecture used in England in the 12th and 13th centuries, characterized by lancet arches, narrow openings, and plate tracery.

ear·ly pur·ple or·chid *n.* another name for **blue butcher.**

Ear·ly Re·nais·sance *n.* **the.** the period from about 1400 to 1500 in European, esp. Italian, painting, sculpture, and architecture, when naturalistic styles and humanist theories were evolved from the study of classical sources, notably by Donatello, Masaccio, and Alberti.

ear·ly warn·ing *n.* advance notice of some impending event or development, esp. detection by radar, etc., of an attack by enemy aircraft or missiles.

ear·mark ('ɪəˌmɑːk) *vb.* (*tr.*) **1.** to set aside or mark out for a specific purpose. **2.** to make an identification mark on the ear of (a domestic animal). ~*n.* **3.** a mark of identification on the ear of a domestic animal. **4.** any distinguishing mark or characteristic.

ear·muff ('ɪəˌmʌf) *n.* one of a pair of pads of fur or cloth, joined by a headband, for keeping the ears warm.

earn (ɜːn) *vb.* **1.** to gain or be paid (money or other payment) in return for work or service. **2.** (*tr.*) to acquire, merit, or deserve through behaviour or action: *he has earned a name for duplicity.* **3.** (*tr.*) (of securities, investments, etc.) to gain (interest, return, profit, etc.). [Old English *earnian;* related to Old High German *arnēn* to reap, Old Saxon *asna* salary, tithe] —**'earn·er** *n.*

earned in·come *n.* income derived from paid employment and comprising mainly wages and salaries.

ear·nest[1] ('ɜːnɪst) *adj.* **1.** serious in mind or intention: *an earnest student.* **2.** showing or characterized by sincerity of intention: *an earnest promise.* **3.** demanding or receiving serious attention. ~*n.* **4. in earnest.** with serious or sincere intentions. [Old English *eornost;* related to Old High German *ernust* seriousness, Old Norse *ern* energetic, efficient, Gothic *arniba* secure] —**'ear·nest·ly** *adv.* —**'ear·nest·ness** *n.*

ear·nest[2] ('ɜːnɪst) *n.* **1.** a part or portion of something given in advance as a guarantee of the remainder. **2.** Also called: **earnest money.** *Contract law.* something given, usually a nominal sum of money, to confirm a contract. **3.** any token of something to follow; pledge; assurance. [C13: from Old French *erres* pledges, plural of *erre* earnest money, from Latin *arrha,* shortened from *arrabō* pledge, from Greek *arrabon,* from Hebrew *'ērābhōn* pledge, from *'ārabh* he pledged]

earn·ings ('ɜːnɪŋz) *pl. n.* **1.** money or other payment earned. **2. a.** the profits of an enterprise. **b.** an individual's investment income.

Earn·ings Re·lat·ed Sup·ple·ment *or* **Ben·e·fit** *n.* (in the British National Insurance scheme) a payment based on earnings in the previous tax year, payable (in addition to unemployment or sickness benefit) for about six months to a sick or unemployed person. Abbrev.: **ERS.**

EAROM ('ɪərɒm) *Computer technol. n. acronym for* electrically alterable read only memory.

ear·phone ('ɪəˌfəʊn) *n.* a device for converting electric currents into sound waves, held close to or inserted into the ear.

ear·piece ('ɪəˌpiːs) *n.* the earphone in a telephone receiver.

ear·plug ('ɪəˌplʌg) *n.* a small piece of soft material, such as wax, placed in the ear to keep out noise or water.

ear·ring ('ɪəˌrɪŋ) *n.* an ornament for the ear, usually clipped onto the lobe or fastened through a hole pierced in the lobe.

ear shell *n.* another name for the **abalone.**

ear·shot ('ɪəˌʃɒt) *n.* the range or distance within which sound may be heard.

ear-split·ting *or* **ear-pierc·ing** *adj.* so loud or shrill as to hurt the ears.

earth (ɜːθ) *n.* **1.** (*sometimes cap.*) the third planet from the sun, the only planet on which life is known to exist. It is not quite spherical, being flattened at the poles, and consists of three geological zones, the core, mantle, and thin outer crust. The surface, covered with large areas of water, is enveloped by an atmosphere principally of nitrogen (78 per cent), oxygen (21 per cent), and some water vapour. The age is estimated at over four thousand million years. Distance from sun: 149.6 million kilometres; equatorial diameter: 12 756 km; mass: 5.976×10^{24} kg; sidereal period of axial rotation: 23 hours 56 minutes 4 seconds; sidereal period of revolution: 365.256 days. Related adjs.: **terrestrial, telluric. 2.** the inhabitants of this planet: *the whole earth rejoiced.* **3.** the dry surface of this planet as distinguished from sea or sky; land; ground. **4.** the loose soft material that makes up a large part of the surface of the ground and consists of disintegrated rock particles, mould, clay, etc.; soil. **5.** worldly or temporal matters as opposed to the concerns of the spirit. **6.** the hole in which a burrowing animal, esp. a fox, lives. **7.** *Chem.* See **rare earth** and **alkaline earth. 8. a.** a connection between an electrical circuit or device and the earth, which is at zero potential. **b.** a terminal to which this connection is made. U.S. equivalent: **ground. 9.** Also called: **earth colour.** any of various brown pigments composed chiefly of iron oxides. **10.** (*modifier*) *Astrology.* of or relating to a group of three signs of the zodiac, Taurus, Virgo, and Capricorn. Compare **air** (sense 18), **fire** (sense 24), **water** (sense 12). **11. cost the earth.** *Informal.* to be very expensive. **12. come back** *or* **down to earth.** to return to reality from a fantasy or daydream. **13. on earth.** used as an intensifer in such phrases as **what on earth, who on earth,** etc. **14. run to earth. a.** to hunt (an animal, esp. a fox) to its earth and trap it there. **b.** to hunt (a criminal, etc.) down. ~*vb.* **15.** (*intr.*) (of a hunted fox) to go to ground. **16.** (*tr.*) to connect (a circuit, device, etc.) to earth. ~See also **earth up.** [Old English *eorthe;* related to Old Norse *jorth,* Old High German *ertha,* Gothic *airtha,* Greek *erā*]

earth·born ('ɜːθˌbɔːn) *adj. Chiefly poetic.* **1.** of earthly origin. **2.** human; mortal.

earth·bound ('ɜːθˌbaʊnd) *adj.* **1.** confined to the earth. **2.** lacking in imagination; pedestrian or dull. **3.** moving or heading towards the earth.

earth clos·et *n.* a type of lavatory in which earth is used to cover excreta.

earth·en ('ɜːθən) *adj.* (*prenominal*) **1.** made of baked clay: *an earthen pot.* **2.** made of earth.

earth·en·ware ('ɜːθənˌwɛə) *n.* **1. a.** vessels, etc., made of baked clay. **b.** (*as adj.*): *an earthenware pot.*

earth in·duc·tor com·pass *n.* a compass that depends on the current induced in a coil revolving in the earth's magnetic field. Also called: **inductor compass.**

earth·light ('ɜːθˌlaɪt) *n.* another name for **earthshine.**

earth·ling ('ɜːθlɪŋ) *n.* (esp. in poetry or science fiction) an inhabitant of the earth; human being.

earth·ly ('ɜːθlɪ) *adj.* **·li·er, ·li·est. 1.** of or characteristic of the earth as opposed to heaven; material or materialistic; worldly. **2.** (*usually used with a negative*) *Informal.* conceivable or possible; feasible (in such phrases as **not an earthly (chance),** etc.). —**'earth·li·ness** *n.*

earth·man ('ɜːθˌmæn) *n., pl.* **·men.** (esp. in science fiction) an inhabitant or native of the earth.

earth moth·er *n.* **1.** (in various mythologies) **a.** a female goddess considered as the source of fertility and life. **b.** the earth personified. **2.** *Informal.* a sensual or fecund woman.

earth·nut ('ɜːθˌnʌt) *n.* **1.** Also called: **pignut.** a perennial umbelliferous plant, *Conopodium majus,* of Europe and Asia, having edible dark brown tubers. **2.** any of various plants having an edible root, tuber, underground pod, or similar part, such as the peanut or truffle.

earth pil·lar *n.* a landform consisting of a column of clay or earth capped and protected from erosion by a boulder.

earth·quake ('ɜːθˌkweɪk) *n.* a series of vibrations at the surface of the earth caused by movement along a fault plane, volcanic activity, etc. Related adj.: **seismic.**

earth·rise ('ɜːθˌraɪz) *n.* the rising of the earth above the lunar horizon, as seen from the moon or a spacecraft.

earth sci·ence *n.* any of various sciences, such as geology, geography, and geomorphology, that are concerned with the structure, age, and other aspects of the earth.

Earth·shak·er ('ɜːθˌʃeɪkə) *n.* **the.** *Classical myth.* Poseidon (or Neptune) in his capacity as the bringer of earthquakes.

earth·shak·ing ('ɜːθˌʃeɪkɪŋ) *adj. Informal.* of enormous importance or consequence; momentous.

earth·shine ('ɜːθˌʃaɪn) *or* **earth·light** *n.* the ashen light reflected from the earth, which illuminates the new moon when it is not receiving light directly from the sun.

earth·star ('ɜːθˌstɑː) *n.* any of various basidiomycetous saprophytic woodland fungi of the genus *Geastrum,* whose brown onion-shaped reproductive body splits into a star shape to release the spores.

earth up *vb.* (*tr., adv.*) to cover (part of a plant, esp. the stem) with soil in order to protect from frost, light, etc.

earth·ward ('ɜːθwəd) *adj.* **1.** directed towards the earth. ~*adv.* **2.** a variant of **earthwards.**

earth·wards ('ɜːθwədz) *or* **earth·ward** *adv.* towards the earth.

earth wax *n.* another name for **ozocerite.**

earth·work ('ɜːθˌwɜːk) *n.* **1.** excavation of earth, as in engineering construction. **2.** a fortification made of earth.

earth·worm ('ɜːθˌwɜːm) *n.* **1.** any of numerous oligochaete worms of the genera *Lumbricus, Allolobophora, Eisenia,* etc., which burrow in the soil and help aerate and break up the ground. **2.** *Archaic.* a grovelling person.

earth·y ('ɜːθɪ) *adj.* **earth·i·er, earth·i·est. 1.** of, composed of, or characteristic of earth. **2.** robust, lusty, or uninhibited. **3.** unrefined, coarse, or crude. **4.** an archaic word for **worldly** (sense 1). —**'earth·i·ly** *adv.* —**'earth·i·ness** *n.*

ear trum·pet *n.* a trumpet-shaped instrument that amplifies sounds and is held to the ear: an old form of hearing aid.

ear·wax ('ɪəˌwæks) *n.* the nontechnical name for **cerumen.**

ear·wig ('ɪəˌwɪg) *n.* **1.** any of various insects of the order *Dermaptera,* esp. *Forficula auricularia* (**common European earwig**), which typically have an elongated body with small leathery forewings, semicircular membranous hindwings, and curved forceps at the tip of the abdomen. ~*vb.* **·wigs, ·wig·ging, ·wigged. 2.** (*tr.*) *Archaic.* to attempt to influence (a person) by private insinuation. [Old English *ēarwicga*, from *ēare* EAR[1] + *wicga* beetle, insect; probably from a superstition that the insect crept into human ears]

ease (i:z) *n.* **1.** freedom from discomfort, worry, or anxiety. **2.** lack of difficulty, labour, or awkwardness; facility. **3.** rest, leisure, or relaxation. **4.** freedom from poverty or financial embarrassment; affluence: *a life of ease.* **5.** lack of restraint, embarrassment, or stiffness: *his ease of manner disarmed us.* **6. at ease. a.** *Military.* (of a standing soldier, etc.) in a relaxed position rather than at attention. **b.** a command to adopt such a position. **c.** in a relaxed attitude or frame of mind. ~*vb.* **7.** to make or become less burdensome. **8.** (*tr.*) to relieve (a person) of worry or care; comfort. **9.** (*tr.*) to make comfortable or give rest to. **10.** (*tr.*) to make less difficult; facilitate. **11.** to move or cause to move into, out of, etc., with careful manipulation: *to ease a car into a narrow space.* **12.** (when *intr.*, often foll. by *off* or *up*) to lessen or cause to lessen in severity, pressure, tension, or strain; slacken, loosen, or abate. **13. ease oneself** *or* **ease nature.** *Archaic, euphemistic.* to urinate or defecate. **14. ease the helm.** *Nautical.* to relieve the pressure on the rudder of a vessel, esp. by bringing the bow into the wind. [C13: from Old French *aise* ease, opportunity, from Latin *adjacēns* neighbouring (area); see ADJACENT] —**'eas·er** *n.*

ease·ful ('i:zfʊl) *adj.* characterized by or bringing ease; peaceful; tranquil. —**'ease·ful·ly** *adv.* —**'ease·ful·ness** *n.*

ea·sel ('i:zᵊl) *n.* a frame, usually in the form of an upright tripod, used for supporting or displaying an artist's canvas, blackboard, etc. [C17: from Dutch *ezel* ASS[1]; related to Gothic *asilus*, German *Esel*, Latin *asinus* ass]

ease·ment ('i:zmənt) *n.* **1.** *Property law.* the right enjoyed by a landowner of making limited use of his neighbour's land, as by crossing it to reach his own property. **2.** the act of easing or something that brings ease.

eas·i·ly ('i:zɪlɪ) *adv.* **1.** with ease; without difficulty or exertion. **2.** by far; beyond question; undoubtedly: *he is easily the best in the contest.* **3.** probably; almost certainly: *he may easily come first.*
Usage. See at **easy.**

eas·i·ness ('i:zɪnɪs) *n.* **1.** the quality or condition of being easy to accomplish, do, obtain, etc. **2.** ease or relaxation of manner; nonchalance.

east (i:st) *n.* **1.** one of the four cardinal points of the compass, 90° clockwise from north and 180° from west. **2.** the direction along a parallel towards the sunrise, at 90° to north; the direction of the earth's rotation. **3. the east.** (*often cap.*) any area lying in or towards the east. Related adj.: **oriental.** ~*adj.* **4.** situated in, moving towards, or facing the east. **5.** (esp. of the wind) from the east. ~*adv.* **6.** in, to, towards, or (esp. of the wind) from the east. ~Abbrev.: **E** [Old English *ēast*; related to Old High German *ōstar* to the east, Old Norse *austr*, Latin *aurora* dawn, Greek *eōs*, Sanskrit *usās* dawn, morning]

East (i:st) *n.* **the. 1.** the continent of Asia regarded as culturally distinct from Europe and the West; the Orient. **2.** the countries under Communist rule, lying mainly in the E hemisphere. Compare **West**[1] (sense 2). **3.** (in the U.S.) **a.** the area north of the Ohio and east of the Mississippi. **b.** the area north of Maryland and east of the Alleghenies. ~*adj.* **4. a.** of or denoting the eastern part of a specified country, area, etc. **b.** (*as part of a name*): *East Germany.*

East Af·ri·ca *n.* a region of Africa comprising Kenya, Uganda, and Tanzania. —**East Af·ri·can** *adj., n.*

East Af·ri·can Com·mun·i·ty *n.* an association established in 1967 by Kenya, Uganda, and Tanzania to promote closer economic and social ties between member states: dissolved in 1977.

East An·gli·a ('æŋglɪə) *n.* **1.** a region of E England south of the Wash: consists of Norfolk and Suffolk, and parts of Essex and Cambridgeshire. **2.** an Anglo-Saxon kingdom that consisted of Norfolk and Suffolk in the 6th century A.D.; became a dependency of Mercia in the 8th century. —**East An·gli·an** *adj., n.*

East Ben·gal *n.* the part of the former Indian province of Bengal assigned to Pakistan in 1947 (now Bangladesh). —**East Ben·ga·li** *adj., n.*

East Ber·lin *n.* the part of Berlin under East German control. —**East Ber·lin·er** *n.*

east·bound ('i:st,baʊnd) *adj.* going or leading towards the east.

East·bourne ('i:st,bɔ:n) *n.* a resort in SE England, in East Sussex on the English Channel. Pop.: 70 495 (1971).

east by north *n.* **1.** one point on the compass north of east, 78° 45′ clockwise from north. ~*adj., adv.* **2.** in, from, or towards this direction.

east by south *n.* **1.** one point on the compass south of east, 101° 15′ clockwise from north. ~*adj., adv.* **2.** in, from, or towards this direction.

East Cape *n.* **1.** the easternmost point of New Guinea, on Milne Bay. **2.** the easternmost point of New Zealand, on North Island. **3.** the former name for Cape **Dezhnev.**

East Chi·na Sea *n.* part of the N Pacific, between the E coast of China and the Ryukyu Islands.

East End *n.* **the.** a densely populated part of E London containing slums and industrial and dock areas. —**East End·er** *n.*

East·er ('i:stə) *n.* **1.** a festival of the Christian Church commemorating the Resurrection of Christ: falls on the Sunday following the first full moon after the vernal equinox. **2.** Also called: **Easter Sunday, Easter Day.** the day on which this festival is celebrated. **3.** the period between Good Friday and Easter Monday. Related adj.: **paschal.** [Old English *ēastre*, after a Germanic goddess *Eostre*; related to Old High German *ōstarūn* Easter, Old Norse *austr* to the EAST, Old Slavonic *ustru* like summer]

East·er egg *n.* an egg given to children at Easter, usually a chocolate egg or a hen's egg with its shell painted.

East·er Is·land *n.* an isolated volcanic island in the Pacific, 3700 km (2300 miles) west of Chile: discovered on Easter Sunday, 1722; annexed by Chile in 1888; noted for the remains of an aboriginal culture, which includes gigantic stone figures. Pop.: 1135 (1960). Area: 166 sq. km (64 sq. miles). Also called: **Rapa Nui.** —**East·er Is·land·er** *n.*

East·er-ledg·es *n.* **1.** (*functioning as sing.*) another name for **bistort** (sense 1). **2. Easter-ledge pudding.** *Northern English dialect.* a pudding made from the young leaves of the bistort.

East·er lil·y *n.* any of various lilies, esp. *Lilium longiflorum*, that have large showy white flowers.

east·er·ly ('i:stəlɪ) *adj.* **1.** of, relating to, or situated in the east. ~*adv., adj.* **2.** towards or in the direction of the east. **3.** from the east: *an easterly wind.* ~*n., pl.* **·lies. 4.** a wind from the east.

east·ern ('i:stən) *adj.* **1.** situated in or towards the east. **2.** facing or moving towards the east.

East·ern Church *n.* **1.** any of the Christian Churches of the former Byzantine Empire. **2.** any Church owing allegiance to the Orthodox Church and in communion with the Greek patriarchal see of Constantinople. **3.** any Church, including Uniat Churches, having Eastern forms of liturgy and institutions.

East·ern·er ('i:stənə) *n.* (*sometimes not cap.*) a native or inhabitant of the east of any specified region, esp. of the Orient or of the eastern states of the U.S.

East·ern Ghats *pl. n.* a mountain range in S India, parallel to the Bay of Bengal: united with the Western Ghats by the Nilgiri Hills; forms the E margin of the Deccan plateau.

east·ern hem·i·sphere *n.* (*often caps.*) **1.** that half of the globe containing Europe, Asia, Africa, and Australia, lying east of the Greenwich meridian. **2.** the lands in this, esp. Asia.

east·ern·most ('i:stən,məʊst) *adj.* situated or occurring farthest east.

East·ern Or·tho·dox Church *n.* another name for the **Orthodox Church.**

East·ern rite *n.* the rite and liturgy of an Eastern Church or of a Uniat Church.

East·ern Ro·man Em·pire *n.* the eastern of the two empires created by the division of the Roman Empire in 395 A.D. See also **Byzantine Empire.**

East·ern Stand·ard Time *n.* one of the standard times used in North America, five hours behind Greenwich Mean Time. Abbrev.: **E.S.T.**

East·ern Town·ships *n.* an area of central Canada, in S Quebec: consists of 11 townships south of the St. Lawrence.

East·er·tide ('i:stə,taɪd) *n.* the Easter season.

East Flan·ders *n.* a province of W Belgium: low-lying, with reclaimed land in the northeast: textile industries. Capital: Ghent. Pop.: 1 325 419 (1975 est.). Area: 2979 sq. km (1150 sq. miles).

East Ger·man·ic *n.* a subbranch of the Germanic languages: now extinct. The only member of which records survive is Gothic.

East Ger·ma·ny *n.* a republic in N central Europe, on the Baltic: established in 1949 and declared a sovereign state by the Soviet Union in 1954; low-lying in the north, with many lakes; mountainous and forested in the south. Language: German. Currency: East German mark. Capital: East Berlin. Pop.: 16 850 000 (1975 est.). Area: 108 178 sq. km (42 189 sq. miles). Official name: **German Democratic Republic.** Abbrevs.: **DDR, GDR.** See also **Germany.** —**East Ger·man** *adj., n.*

East In·di·a Com·pa·ny *n.* **1.** the company chartered in 1600 by the British government to trade in the East Indies: dissolved in 1874. **2.** any similar trading company, such as any of those founded by the Dutch, French, and Danes in the 17th and 18th centuries.

East Ind·i·an *n.* **1.** *Caribbean.* an immigrant to the West Indies who is of Indian origin; an Asian West Indian. ~*adj.* **2.** *U.S.* of, relating to, or originating in the East Indies.

East In·dies *n.* **the. 1.** the Malay Archipelago, including or excluding the Philippines. **2.** SE Asia in general.

east·ing ('i:stɪŋ) *n.* **1.** *Nautical.* the net distance eastwards made by a vessel moving towards the east. **2.** *Cartography.* **a.** the distance eastwards of a point from a given meridian indicated by the first half of a map grid reference. **b.** a longitudinal grid line. Compare **northing** (sense 3).

East Kil·bride (kɪl'braɪd) *n.* a town in W Scotland, near Glasgow: designated a new town in 1947. Pop.: 63 505 (1971).

East·leigh ('i:st,li:) *n.* a town in S England, in S Hampshire: railway engineering industry. Pop.: 45 320 (1971).

East Lon·don *n.* a port in S South Africa, in SE Cape Province. Pop.: 118 298 (1970).

East Lo·thi·an *n.* (until 1975) a county of E central Scotland, now part of Lothian region.

East·man ('i:stmən) *n.* **George.** 1854–1932, U.S. manufacturer of photographic equipment: noted for the introduction of roll film and developments in colour photography.

east-north·east *n.* **1.** the point on the compass or the direction midway between northeast and east, 67° 30′ clockwise from north. ~*adj., adv.* **2.** in, from, or towards this direction. ~Abbrev.: **ENE**

East Pa·ki·stan *n.* the former name (until 1971) of **Bangladesh.** —**East Pa·ki·sta·ni** *adj., n.*

East Prus·sia *n.* a former province of NE Germany on the Baltic Sea: separated in 1919 from the rest of Germany by the Polish Corridor and Danzig: in 1945 Poland received the south part, the Soviet Union the north. German name: **Ostpreussen.** —**East Prus·sian** *adj., n.*

East Rid·ing *n.* (until 1974) an administrative division of Yorkshire, now mostly in Humberside.

east-south·east *n.* **1.** the point on the compass or the direction midway between east and southeast, 112° 30′ clockwise from north. ~*adj., adv.* **2.** in, from, or towards this direction. ~Abbrev.: **ESE**

East Sus·sex *n.* a county of SE England comprising part of the former county of Sussex: mainly undulating agricultural land, with the South Downs and seaside resorts in the south. Administrative centre: Lewes. Pop.: 655 600 (1976 est.). Area: 1836 sq. km (710 sq. miles).

east·ward ('i:stwəd) *adj.* **1.** situated or directed towards the east. ~*adv.* **2.** a variant of **eastwards.** ~*n.* **3.** the eastward part, direction, etc. —**'east·ward·ly** *adv., adj.*

east·wards ('i:stwədz) *or* **east·ward** *adv.* towards the east.

eas·y ('i:zɪ) *adj.* **eas·i·er, eas·i·est. 1.** not requiring much labour or effort; not difficult; simple: *an easy job.* **2.** free from pain, care, or anxiety: *easy in one's mind.* **3.** not harsh or restricting; lenient: *easy laws.* **4.** tolerant and undemanding; easy-going: *an easy disposition.* **5.** readily influenced or persuaded; pliant: *she was an easy victim of his wiles.* **6.** not tight or constricting; loose: *an easy fit.* **7.** not strained or extreme; moderate; gentle: *an easy pace; an easy ascent.* **8.** *Economics.* **a.** readily obtainable. **b.** (of a market) characterized by low demand or excess supply with prices tending to fall. Compare **tight** (sense 10). **9.** *Informal.* ready to fall in with any suggestion made; not predisposed: *he is easy about what to do.* **10. easy on the eye.** *Informal.* pleasant to look at; attractive, esp. sexually. **11. Easy Street.** *Informal.* a state of financial security. **12. woman of easy virtue.** a sexually available woman, esp. a prostitute. ~*adv.* **13.** *Informal.* in any easy or relaxed manner. **14. easy does it.** *Informal.* go slowly and carefully; be careful. **15. go easy.** (*usually imperative;* often foll. by *on*) *Informal.* to exercise moderation. **16. stand easy.** *Military.* a command to soldiers standing at ease that they may relax further. **17. take it easy.** *Informal.* **a.** to avoid stress or undue hurry. **b.** to remain calm; not become agitated or angry. ~*vb.* **eas·ies, eas·y·ing, eas·ied. 18.** (*usually imperative*) Also: **easy-oar.** to stop rowing. [C12: from Old French *aisié,* past participle of *aisier* to relieve, EASE]

Usage. *Easy* is not used as an adverb by careful speakers and writers except in certain set phrases: *to take it easy; easy does it.* Where a fixed expression is not involved, the usual adverbial form of *easy* is preferred: *this polish goes on more easily* (not *easier*) *than the other.*

eas·y chair *n.* a comfortable upholstered armchair.

eas·y game *or* **eas·y mark** *n. Informal.* a person who is easily deceived or taken advantage of.

eas·y-go·ing ('i:zɪ'gəʊɪŋ) *adj.* **1.** relaxed in manner or attitude; inclined to be excessively tolerant. **2.** moving at a comfortable pace: *an easy-going horse.*

eat (i:t) *vb.* **eats, eat·ing, ate, eat·en. 1.** to take into the mouth and swallow (food, etc.), esp. after biting and chewing. **2.** (*tr.;* often foll. by *away* or *up*) to destroy as if by eating: *the damp had eaten away the woodwork.* **3.** (often foll. by *into*) to use up or waste: *taxes ate into his inheritance.* **4.** (often foll. by *into* or *through*) to make (a hole, passage, etc.) by eating or gnawing: *rats ate through the floor.* **5.** to take or have (a meal or meals): *we always eat at six.* **6.** (*tr.*) to include as part of one's diet: *he doesn't eat fish.* **7.** (*tr.*) *Informal.* to cause to worry; make anxious: *what's eating you?* **8.** (*tr.*) *Taboo slang.* to perform cunnilingus or fellatio upon. **9. eat one's hat if.** *Informal.* to be greatly surprised if (something happens). **10. eat one's heart out.** *Informal.* to brood or pine with grief or longing. **11. eat one's words.** to take back something said; recant; retract. **12. eat out of (someone's) hand.** to be entirely obedient to (someone). **13. eat (someone) out of house and home.** *Informal.* to ruin (someone, esp. one's parent or one's host) by consuming all his food. [Old English *etan;* related to Gothic *itan,* Old High German *ezzan,* Latin *edere,* Greek *edein,* Sanskrit *admi*] —**'eat·er** *n.*

eat·a·ble ('i:təbᵊl) *adj.* fit or suitable for eating; edible.

eat·a·bles ('i:təbᵊlz) *pl. n.* (*sometimes sing.*) food.

eat·age ('i:tɪdʒ) *n. Northern Brit. dialect.* grazing rights.

eat·en ('i:tᵊn) *vb.* the past participle of **eat.**

eat·ing ('i:tɪŋ) *n.* **1.** food, esp. in relation to its quality or taste: *this fruit makes excellent eating.* ~*adj.* **2.** relating to or suitable for eating, esp. uncooked: *eating pears.* **3.** relating to or for eating: *an eating house.*

eat out *vb.* (*intr., adv.*) to eat away from home, esp. in a restaurant.

eats (i:ts) *pl. n. Slang.* articles of food; provisions.

eat up *vb.* (*adv., mainly tr.*) **1.** (*also intr.*) to eat or consume entirely: often used as an exhortation to children. **2.** *Informal.* to listen to with enthusiasm or appreciation: *the audience ate up the speaker's every word.* **3.** *Informal.* to absorb eagerly: *some women eat up flattery.* **4.** (*often passive*) *Informal.* to affect grossly: *she was eaten up by jealousy.* **5.** *Informal.* to travel (a distance) quickly: *we just ate up the miles.*

EAU *international car registration for* East Africa Uganda.

eau de Co·logne (ˌəʊ də kə'ləʊn) *n.* See **cologne.** [French, literally: water of Cologne]

eau de Ja·velle (ˌəʊ də ʒæ'vɛl, ʒə-; *French* od ʒa'vɛl) *n.* another name for **Javel water.**

eau de nil (ˌəʊ də 'ni:l) *n., adj.* **a.** a pale yellowish-green colour. **b.** (*as adj.*): *eau-de-nil walls.* [from French, literally: water of (the) Nile]

eau de vie (ˌəʊ də 'vi:; *French* od 'vi) *n.* brandy or other spirits. [French, literally: water of life]

eaves (i:vz) *pl. n.* the edge of a roof that projects beyond the wall. [Old English *efes;* related to Gothic *ubizwa* porch, Greek *hupsos* height]

eaves·drop ('i:vzˌdrɒp) *vb.* **·drops, ·drop·ping, ·dropped.** (*intr.*) to listen secretly to the private conversation of others. [C17: back formation from earlier *evesdropper,* from Old English *yfesdrype* water dripping from the eaves; see EAVES, DROP; compare Old Norse *upsardropi*] —**'eaves·ˌdrop·per** *n.*

ebb (ɛb) *vb.* (*intr.*) **1.** (of tide water) to flow back or recede. Compare **flow** (sense 9). **2.** to fall away or decline. ~*n.* **3. a.** the flowing back of the tide from high to low water or the period in which this takes place. **b.** (*as modifier*): *the ebb tide.* Compare **flood** (sense 3). **4. at a low ebb.** in a state or period of weakness, lack of vigour, or decline. [Old English *ebba;* related to Old Norse *efja* river bend, Gothic *ibuks* moving backwards, Old High German *ippihōn* to roll backwards, Middle Dutch *ebbe* ebb]

Ebbw Vale ('ɛbu: 'veɪl) *n.* a town in S Wales, in W Gwent: coal mines. Pop.: 26 049 (1971).

EBCDIC ('ɛpsɪˌdɪk) *n. acronym for* extended binary-coded decimal-interchange code: a computer code for representing alphanumeric characters.

E·bert (*German* 'e:bərt) *n.* **Frie·drich** ('fri:drɪç). 1871–1925, German Social Democratic statesman; first president of the German Republic (1919–25).

Eb·lis ('ɛblɪs) *n.* the chief evil jinni in Islamic mythology. [Arabic *Iblīs,* from Greek *diabolos* slanderer, DEVIL]

E-boat *n.* (in World War II) an enemy torpedo boat, esp. a German one.

eb·on ('ɛbᵊn) *adj., n.* a poetic word for **ebony.** [C14: from Latin *hebenus;* see EBONY]

eb·on·ite ('ɛbəˌnaɪt) *n.* another name for **vulcanite.**

eb·on·ize *or* **eb·on·ise** ('ɛbəˌnaɪz) *vb.* (*tr.*) to stain or otherwise finish in imitation of ebony.

eb·on·y ('ɛbənɪ) *n., pl.* **·on·ies. 1.** any of various tropical and subtropical trees of the genus *Diospyros,* esp. *D. ebenum* of S India, that have hard dark wood: family *Ebenaceae.* See also **persimmon. 2.** the wood of such a tree, much used for cabinetwork. **3. a.** a black colour, sometimes with a dark olive tinge. **b.** (*as adj.*): *an ebony skin.* [C16 *hebeny,* from Late Latin *ebeninus* from Greek *ebeninos,* from *ebenos* ebony, of Egyptian origin]

E·bor·a·cum (i:'bɒrəkəm, ˌi:bɔ:'rɑ:kəm) *n.* the Roman name for **York**[1] (sense 1).

e·brac·te·ate (ɪ'bræktɪˌeɪt, -tɪɪt) *adj.* (of plants) having no bracts. [C19: from New Latin *ebracteātus;* see EX-, BRACTEATE]

E·bro ('i:brəʊ; *Spanish* 'eβro) *n.* the second largest river in Spain, rising in the Cantabrian Mountains and flowing southeast to the Mediterranean. Length: 910 km (565 miles).

e·bul·lient (ɪ'bʌljənt, ɪ'bʊl-) *adj.* **1.** overflowing with enthusiasm or excitement; exuberant. **2.** boiling. [C16: from Latin *ēbullīre* to bubble forth, be boisterous, from *bullīre* to BOIL[1]] —**e·'bul·lience** *or* **e·'bul·lien·cy** *n.* —**e·'bul·lient·ly** *adv.*

e·bul·li·os·co·py (ɪˌbʌlɪ'ɒskəpɪ, ɪˌbʊl-) *n. Chem.* a technique for finding molecular weights of substances by measuring the extent to which they change the boiling point of a solvent. [C19: from *ebullioscope,* from Latin *ebullire* to boil over + -SCOPE] —**e·bul·li·o·scop·ic** (ɪˌbʌlɪə'skɒpɪk, ɪˌbʊl-) *adj.* —**e·ˌbul·li·o·'scop·i·cal·ly** *adv.*

e·bul·li·tion (ˌɛbə'lɪʃən) *n.* **1.** the process of boiling. **2.** a sudden outburst, as of intense emotion. [C16: from Late Latin *ēbullītiō;* see EBULLIENT]

e·bur·na·tion (ˌi:bə'neɪʃən, ˌɛb-) *n.* a degenerative condition of bone or cartilage characterized by unusual hardness. [C19: from Latin *eburnus* of ivory, from *ebur* ivory]

ec- *combining form.* out from; away from: *ecbolic; eccentric; ecdysis.* [from Greek *ek* (before a vowel *ex*) out of, away from; see EX-[1]]

EC 1. *abbrev. for* East central. ~ **2.** *international car registration for* Ecuador.

e·cad ('i:kæd) *n.* an organism whose form has been affected by its environment. [C20: from EC(OLOGY) + -AD[1]]

é·car·té (eɪ'kɑ:teɪ; *French* ekar'te) *n.* **1.** a card game for two, played with 32 cards and king high. **2.** *Ballet.* **a.** a body position in which one arm and the same leg are extended at the side of the body. **b.** (*as adj.*): *the écarté position.* [C19: from French, from *écarter* to discard, from *carte* CARD[1]]

Ec·bat·a·na (ɛk'bætənə) *n.* an ancient city in Iran, on the site of modern Hamadān; capital of Media and royal residence of the Persians and Parthians.

ec·bol·ic (ɛk'bɒlɪk) *adj.* **1.** hastening labour or abortion. ~*n.* **2.** a drug or agent that hastens labour or abortion. [C18: from Greek *ekbolē* a throwing out, from *ekballein* to throw out, from *ballein* to throw]

Ec·ce Ho·mo ('ɛkeɪ 'həʊməʊ, 'ɛksɪ) *n.* a picture or sculpture of Christ crowned with thorns. [Latin: behold the man, the words of Pontius Pilate to his accusers (John 19:5)]

ec·cen·tric (ɪk'sɛntrɪk) *adj.* **1.** deviating or departing from convention, esp. in a bizarre manner; irregular or odd. **2.** situated away from the centre or the axis. **3.** not having a common centre: *eccentric circles.* Compare **concentric. 4.** not precisely circular. ~*n.* **5.** a person who deviates from normal forms of behaviour esp. in a bizarre manner. **6.** a device for converting rotary motion to reciprocating motion. [C16: from

Medieval Latin *eccentricus,* from Greek *ekkentros* out of centre, from *ek-* EX- + *kentron* centre] —**ec+'cen+tri+cal+ly** *adv.*

ec+cen+tri·ci·ty (ˌɛksɛn'trɪsɪtɪ) *n., pl.* **·ties. 1.** unconventional or irregular behaviour. **2.** deviation from a circular path or orbit. **3.** a measure of the elongation of an elliptical orbit, esp. of a planet or satellite: the distance between the foci divided by the length of the major axis. **4.** *Geom.* a number that expresses the shape of a conic section: the ratio of the distance of a point on the curve from a fixed point (the focus) to the distance of the point from a fixed line (the directrix). **5.** the degree of displacement of the geometric centre of a part from the true centre, esp. of the axis of rotation of a wheel.

ec+chy+mo+sis (ˌɛkɪ'məʊsɪs) *n., pl.* **+ses** (-si:z). discoloration of the skin through bruising. [C16: from New Latin, from Greek *ekkhumōsis,* from *ekkhumousthai* to pour out, from *khumos* juice] —**ec+chy+mosed** ('ɛkɪˌməʊzd, -ˌməʊst) *or* **ec+chy+mot+ic** (ˌɛkɪ'mɒtɪk) *adj.*

eccl. *or* **eccles.** *abbrev. for* ecclesiastic(al).

Ec+cles ('ɛkᵊlz) *n.* a town in NW England, in Greater Manchester. Pop.: 38 413 (1971).

Eccles. *or* **Eccl.** *Bible. abbrev. for* Ecclesiastes.

Ec+cles cake *n. Brit.* a pastry with a filling of dried fruit.

ec+cle+si·a (ɪ'kli:zɪə) *n., pl.* **+si·ae** (-zɪˌi:). **1.** (in formal Church usage) a congregation. **2.** the assembly of citizens of an ancient Greek state. [C16: from Medieval Latin, from Late Greek *ekklēsia* assembly, from *ekklētos* called, from *ekkalein* to call out, from *kalein* to call]

ecclesiast. *abbrev. for* ecclesiastical.

Ec+cle+si+as+tes (ɪˌkli:zɪ'æsti:z) *n.* a book of the Old Testament, probably written about 250 B.C. [via Late Latin, from Greek *ekklēsiastēs* member of the assembly; see ECCLESIA]

ec+cle+si+as+tic (ɪˌkli:zɪ'æstɪk) *n.* **1.** a clergyman or other person in holy orders. ~*adj.* **2.** of or associated with the Christian Church or clergy.

ec+cle+si+as+ti+cal (ɪˌkli:zɪ'æstɪkᵊl) *adj.* of or relating to the Christian Church. —**ec+ˌcle+si+'as+ti+cal+ly** *adv.*

Ec+cle+si+as+ti+cal Com+mis+sion+ers *pl. n.* the administrators of the properties of the Church of England from 1836 to 1948, when they were combined with Queen Anne's Bounty to form the Church Commissioners.

ec+cle+si+as+ti+cism (ɪˌkli:zɪ'æstɪˌsɪzəm) *n.* exaggerated attachment to the practices or principles of the Christian Church.

Ec+cle+si+as+ti+cus (ɪˌkli:zɪ'æstɪkəs) *n.* one of the books of the Apocrypha, written around 180 B.C. and also called **The Wisdom of Jesus, the son of Sirach.**

ec+cle+si+ol·a·try (ɪˌkli:zɪ'ɒlətrɪ) *n.* obsessional devotion to ecclesiastical traditions. —**ec+ˌcle+si+'ol·a·ter** *n.*

ec+cle+si+ol+o·gy (ɪˌkli:zɪ'ɒlədʒɪ) *n.* **1.** the study of the Christian Church. **2.** the study of Church architecture and decoration. —**ec+cle+si·o·log·i·cal** (ɪˌkli:zɪə'lɒdʒɪkᵊl) *adj.* —**ec+ˌcle+si·o+'log·i·cal+ly** *adv.* —**ec+ˌcle+si+'ol·o·gist** *n.*

Ecclus. *abbrev. for* Ecclesiasticus.

ec+crine ('ɛkrɪn) *adj.* of or denoting glands that secrete externally, esp. the numerous sweat glands on the human body. Compare **apocrine.** [from Greek *ekkrinein* to secrete, from *ek-* EC- + *krinein* to separate]

ec+crin+ol+o·gy (ˌɛkrɪ'nɒlədʒɪ) *n.* the branch of medical science concerned with secretions of the eccrine glands.

ec+dys·i·ast (ɛk'dɪzɪˌæst) *n.* a facetious word for **stripper** (sense 1). [C20: (coined by H. L. Mencken) from ECDYSIS + *-ast,* variant of -IST]

ec+dy+sis ('ɛkdɪsɪs) *n., pl.* **+ses** (-ˌsi:z). the periodic shedding of the cuticle in insects and other arthropods or the outer epidermal layer in reptiles. See also **ecdysone.** [C19: New Latin, from Greek *ekdusis,* from *ekduein* to strip, from *ek-* EX- + *duein* to put on] —**ec+'dys·i·al** *adj.*

ec+dy+sone (ɛk'daɪˌsəʊn) *n.* a hormone secreted by the prothoracic gland of insects that controls ecdysis and stimulates metamorphosis.

e·ce·sis (ɪ'si:sɪs) *n.* the establishment of a plant in a new environment. [C20: from Greek *oikēsis* a dwelling in, from *oikein* to inhabit; related to *oikos* a house]

E·ce·vit ('ɛtʃəvɪt) *n.* **Bü·lent** ('bulənt). born 1925, Turkish statesman; prime minister (1974; 1978-79).

E.C.G. *abbrev. for:* **1.** electrocardiogram. **2.** electrocardiograph.

ec+hard ('ɛkɑ:d) *n.* water that is present in the soil but cannot be absorbed or otherwise utilized by plants. [C20: from Greek *ekhein* to hold back + *ardein* to water]

e·che+lon ('ɛʃəˌlɒn) *n.* **1.** a level of command, responsibility, etc. (esp. in the phrase **the upper echelons**). **2.** *Military.* **a.** a formation in which units follow one another but are offset sufficiently to allow each unit a line of fire ahead. **b.** a group formed in this way. **3.** *Physics.* a type of diffraction grating consisting of a series of plates of equal thickness arranged stepwise with a constant offset. ~*vb.* **4.** to assemble in echelon. [C18: from French *échelon,* literally: rung of a ladder, from Old French *eschiele* ladder, from Latin *scāla;* see SCALE³]

ech+e·ve+ri·a (ˌɛtʃɪ'vɪərɪə) *n.* any of various tropical American crassulaceous plants of the genus *Echeveria,* cultivated for their colourful foliage. [named after M. *Echeveri,* 19th-cent. Mexican botanical artist]

e·chid+na (ɪ'kɪdnə) *n., pl.* **+nas** *or* **+nae** (-ni:). any of the spine-covered monotreme mammals of the genera *Tachyglossus* of Australia and *Zaglossus* of New Guinea: family *Tachyglossidae.* They have a long snout and claws for hunting ants and termites. Also called: **spiny anteater.** [C19: from New Latin, from Latin: viper, from Greek *ekhidna*]

ech·i+nate ('ɛkɪˌneɪt) *or* **ech·i+nat+ed** *adj. Biology.* covered with spines, bristles, or bristle-like outgrowths.

e·chi·no- *or before a vowel* **e·chin-** *combining form* indicating spiny or prickly: *echinoderm.* [from New Latin, via Latin from Greek *ekhinos* sea urchin, hedgehog]

e·chi+no+coc+cus (ɪˌkaɪnə'kɒkəs) *n.* any of the tapeworms constituting the genus *Echinococcus,* the larvae of which are parasitic in man and domestic animals.

e·chi+no+derm (ɪ'kaɪnəʊˌdɜ:m) *n.* any of the marine invertebrate animals constituting the phylum *Echinodermata,* characterized by tube feet, a calcite body-covering (test), and a five-part symmetrical body. The group includes the starfish, sea urchins, and sea cucumbers. —**e·ˌchi+no+'der+mal** *or* **e·ˌchi+no+'der+ma+tous** *adj.*

e·chi+noid (ɪ'kaɪnɔɪd, 'ɛkə-) *n.* **1.** any of the echinoderms constituting the class *Echinoidea,* typically having a rigid ovoid body. The class includes the sea urchins and sand dollars. ~*adj.* **2.** of or belonging to this class.

e·chi+nus (ɪ'kaɪnəs) *n., pl.* **+ni** (-naɪ). **1.** *Architect.* an ovolo moulding between the shaft and the abacus of a Doric column. **2.** any of the sea urchins of the genus *Echinus,* such as *E. esculentus* (**edible sea urchin**) of the Mediterranean. [C14: from Latin, from Greek *ekhinos*]

ech·o ('ɛkəʊ) *n., pl.* **·oes. 1. a.** the reflection of sound or other radiation by a reflecting medium, esp. a solid object. **b.** the sound so reflected. **2.** a repetition or imitation, esp. an unoriginal reproduction of another's opinions. **3.** something that evokes memories, esp. of a particular style or era. **4.** (*sometimes pl.*) an effect that continues after the original cause has disappeared; repercussion: *the echoes of the French Revolution.* **5.** a person who copies another, esp. one who obsequiously agrees with another's opinions. **6. a.** the signal reflected by a radar target. **b.** the trace produced by such a signal on a radar screen. **7.** the repetition of certain sounds or syllables in a verse line. **8.** the quiet repetition of a musical phrase. **9.** Also called: **echo organ** *or* **echo stop.** a manual or stop on an organ that controls a set of quiet pipes that give the illusion of sounding at a distance. **10.** an electronic effect in recorded music that adds vibration or resonance. ~*vb.* **·oes, ·o·ing, +oed. 11.** to resound or cause to resound with an echo: *the cave echoed their shouts.* **12.** (*intr.*) (of sounds) to repeat or resound by echoes; reverberate. **13.** (*tr.*) (of persons) to repeat (words, opinions, etc.), in imitation, agreement, or flattery. **14.** (*tr.*) (of things) to resemble or imitate (another style, earlier model, etc.). [C14: via Latin from Greek *ēkhō;* related to Greek *ēkhē* sound] —**'ech·o+less** *adj.* —**'ech·o-ˌlike** *adj.*

Ech·o[1] ('ɛkəʊ) *n.* either of two U.S. passive communications satellites, the first of which was launched in 1960.

Ech·o[2] ('ɛkəʊ) *n. Greek myth.* a nymph who, spurned by Narcissus, pined away until only her voice remained.

ech·o cham+ber *n.* **1.** Also called: **reverberation chamber.** a room with walls that reflect sound. It is used to make acoustic measurements and as a recording studio when echo effects are required. **2.** an electronic device producing a similar effect.

ech·o·ic (ɛ'kəʊɪk) *adj.* **1.** characteristic of or resembling an echo. **2.** onomatopoeic; imitative.

e·cho+ism ('ɛkəʊˌɪzəm) *n.* **1.** onomatopoeia as a source of word formation. **2.** phonetic assimilation of one vowel to the vowel in the preceding syllable.

ech·o+la+li·a (ˌɛkəʊ'leɪlɪə) *n. Psychiatry.* the tendency to repeat mechanically words just spoken by another person: occurs in cases of schizophrenia. [C19: from New Latin, from ECHO + Greek *lalia* talk, chatter, from *lalein* to chatter] —**ech·o+la+lic** (ˌɛkəʊ'lælɪk) *adj.*

ech·o+lo·ca·tion (ˌɛkəʊləʊ'keɪʃən) *n.* determination of the position of an object by measuring the time taken for an echo to return from it and its direction.

ech·o+prax·i·a (ˌɛkəʊ'præksɪə) *or* **ech·o+prax+is** *n. Psychiatry.* the tendency to repeat automatically movements recently performed by another person: occurs in cases of schizophrenia. [C20: from New Latin, from ECHO + *-praxia,* from Greek *praxis* deed, action] —**ech·o+prac+tic** (ˌɛkəʊ'præktɪk) *adj.*

ech·o sound+er *n.* a device for determining depth by measuring the time taken for a pulse of high-frequency sound to reach the sea bed or a submerged object and for the echo to return. Also called: **sonar, asdic.** —**ech·o sound+ing** *n.*

ech·o+vi+rus *or* **ECHO vi+rus** ('ɛkəʊˌvaɪrəs) *n.* any of a group of viruses that can cause symptoms of mild meningitis, the common cold, or infections of the intestinal and respiratory tracts. [C20: from the initials of *Enteric Cytopathic Human Orphan* ("orphan" because originally believed to be unrelated to any disease) + VIRUS]

echt *German.* (ɛçt; *English* ɛkt) *adj.* real; genuine; authentic.

Eck (ɛk) *n.* **Jo·hann** ('jo:han), original name *Johann Mayer.* 1486–1543, German Roman Catholic theologian; opponent of Luther and the Reformation.

Eck·hart (*German* 'ɛkart) *n.* **Jo·han·nes** (jo'hanəs), called *Meister Eckhart.* ?1260–?1327, German Dominican theologian, mystic, and preacher.

é·clair (eɪ'klɛə, ɪ'klɛə) *n.* a finger-shaped cake of choux pastry, usually filled with cream and covered with chocolate. [C19: from French, literally: lightning (probably so called because it does not last long), from *éclairer,* from Latin *clārāre* to make bright, from *clārus* bright]

ec+lamp+si·a (ɪ'klæmpsɪə) *n. Pathol.* a toxic condition of unknown cause that sometimes develops in the last three months of pregnancy, characterized by high blood pressure, abnormal weight gain and convulsions. Compare **pre-**

eclampsia. [C19: from New Latin, from Greek *eklampsis* a shining forth, from *eklampein*, from *lampein* to shine] —**ec·'lamp·tic** *adj.*

é·clat (eɪ'klɑː; *French* e'kla) *n.* **1.** brilliant or conspicuous success, effect, etc. **2.** showy display; ostentation. **3.** social distinction. **4.** approval; acclaim; applause. [C17: from French, from *éclater* to burst; related to Old French *esclater* to splinter, perhaps of Germanic origin; compare SLIT]

ec·lec·tic (ɪ'klɛktɪk, ɛ'klɛk-) *adj.* **1.** (in art, philosophy, etc.) selecting what seems best from various styles, doctrines, ideas, methods, etc. **2.** composed of elements drawn from a variety of sources, styles, etc. ~*n.* **3.** a person who favours an eclectic approach, esp. in art or philosophy. [C17: from Greek *eklektikos*, from *eklegein* to select, from *legein* to gather] —**ec·'lec·ti·cal·ly** *adv.*

ec·lec·ti·cism (ɪ'klɛktɪˌsɪzəm, ɛ'klɛk-) *n.* **1.** an eclectic system or method. **2.** the use or advocacy of such a system.

e·clipse (ɪ'klɪps) *n.* **1.** the total or partial obscuring of one celestial body by another. A **solar eclipse** occurs when the moon passes between the sun and the earth; a **lunar eclipse** when the earth passes between the sun and the moon. See also **total eclipse, partial eclipse, annular eclipse.** Compare **occultation. 2.** the period of time during which such a phenomenon occurs. **3.** any dimming or obstruction of light. **4.** a loss of importance, power, fame, etc., esp. through overshadowing by another. ~*vb.* (*tr.*) **5.** to cause an eclipse of. **6.** to cast a shadow upon; darken; obscure. **7.** to overshadow or surpass in importance, power, etc. [C13: back formation from Old English *eclypsis*, from Latin *eclīpsis*, from Greek *ekleipsis* a forsaking, from *ekleipein* to abandon, from *leipein* to leave] —**e'clips·er** *n.*

e·clipse plum·age *n.* seasonal plumage that occurs in certain birds after the breeding plumage and before the winter plumage: is characterized by dull coloration.

e·clips·ing bi·na·ry *or* **var·i·a·ble** *n.* a binary star whose orbital plane lies in or near the line of sight so that one component is regularly eclipsed by its companion. See also **variable star.**

e·clip·sis (ɪ'klɪpsɪs) *n.* *Linguistics.* **1.** a rare word for **ellipsis. 2.** (in Gaelic) phonetic change of an initial consonant under the influence of a preceding word. Unvoiced plosives become voiced, while voiced plosives are changed to nasals.

e·clip·tic (ɪ'klɪptɪk) *n.* **1.** *Astronomy.* **a.** the great circle on the celestial sphere representing the apparent annual path of the sun relative to the stars. It is inclined at 23.45° to the celestial equator. The **poles of the ecliptic** lie on the celestial sphere due north and south of the plane of the ecliptic. **b.** (*as modifier*): *the ecliptic plane.* **2.** an equivalent great circle, opposite points of which pass through the Tropics of Cancer and Capricorn, on the terrestrial globe. ~*adj.* **3.** of or relating to an eclipse. —**e'clip·ti·cal·ly** *adv.*

ec·lo·gite ('ɛkləˌdʒaɪt) *n.* a rare coarse-grained basic rock consisting of large bright red garnets in a greenish mixture of pyroxene, quartz, feldspar, etc. Its origin is thought to be intermediate between igneous and metamorphic. [C19: from Greek *eklogē* a selection]

ec·logue ('ɛklɒg) *n.* a pastoral or idyllic poem, usually in the form of a conversation or soliloquy. [C15: from Latin *ecloga* short poem, collection of extracts, from Greek *eklogē* selection, from *eklēgein* to select; see ECLECTIC]

e·clo·sion (ɪ'kləʊʒən) *n.* the emergence of an insect larva from the egg or an adult from the pupal case. [C19: from French *éclosion*, from *éclore* to hatch, ultimately from Latin *exclūdere* to shut out, EXCLUDE]

e·co- *combining form.* denoting ecology or ecological: *ecocide; ecosphere.*

e·co·cide ('iːkəˌsaɪd, 'ɛkə-) *n.* total destruction of an area of the natural environment, esp. by human agency.

ecol. *abbrev. for:* **1.** ecological. **2.** ecology.

e·col·o·gy (ɪ'kɒlədʒɪ) *n.* **1.** the study of the relationships between living organisms and their environment. **2.** the set of relationships of a particular organism with its environment. **3. human ecology.** the study of the relationships between human groups and their physical environment. ~Also called (for senses 1, 2): **bionomics.** [C19: from German *Ökologie*, from Greek *oikos* house (hence, environment)] —**e·co·log·i·cal** (ˌiːkə'lɒdʒɪkəl) *adj.* —ˌ**e·co·'log·i·cal·ly** *adv.* —**e'col·o·gist** *n.*

econ. *abbrev. for:* **1.** economical. **2.** economics. **3.** economy.

e·con·o·met·rics (ɪˌkɒnə'mɛtrɪks) *n.* the application of mathematical and statistical techniques to economic problems and theories. —**e**ˌ**con·o·'met·ric** *or* **e**ˌ**con·o·'met·ri·cal** *adj.* —**e·con·o·me·tri·cian** (ɪˌkɒnəmə'trɪʃən) *or* **e**ˌ**con·o·'met·rist** *n.*

e·co·nom·ic (ˌiːkə'nɒmɪk, ˌɛkə-) *adj.* **1.** of or relating to an economy, economics, or finance: *economic development; economic theories.* **2.** *Brit.* capable of being produced, operated, etc., for profit; profitable: *the firm is barely economic.* **3.** concerning or affecting material resources or welfare: *economic pests.* **4.** concerned with or relating to the necessities of life; utilitarian. **5.** variant of **economical. 6.** *Informal.* inexpensive; cheap.

e·co·nom·i·cal (ˌiːkə'nɒmɪkəl, ˌɛkə-) *adj.* **1.** using the minimum required; not wasteful of time, effort, resources, etc.: *an economical car; an economical style.* **2.** frugal; thrifty: *she was economical by nature.* **3.** variant of **economic** (senses 1–4).

e·co·nom·i·cal·ly (ˌiːkə'nɒmɪklɪ, ˌɛkə-) *adv.* **1.** with economy or thrift; without waste. **2.** with regard to the economy of a person, country, etc.

e·co·nom·ic de·ter·min·ism *n.* a doctrine that states that all cultural, social, political, and intellectual activities are a product of the economic organization of society.

e·co·nom·ic ge·og·ra·phy *n.* the study of the geographical distribution of economic resources and their use.

e·co·nom·ic rent *n.* *Economics.* the return derived from cultivated land in excess of that derived from the poorest land cultivated under similar conditions.

e·co·nom·ics (ˌiːkə'nɒmɪks, ˌɛkə-) *n.* **1.** (*functioning as sing.*) the social science concerned with the production and consumption of goods and services and the analysis of the commercial activities of a society. See also **macroeconomics, microeconomics. 2.** (*pl.*) financial aspects: *the economics of the project are very doubtful.*

e·con·o·mist (ɪ'kɒnəmɪst) *n.* **1.** a specialist in economics. **2.** *Archaic.* a person who advocates or practises frugality.

e·con·o·mize *or* **e·con·o·mise** (ɪ'kɒnəˌmaɪz) *vb.* (often foll. by *on*) to limit or reduce (expense, waste, etc.). —**e**ˌ**con·o·mi·'za·tion** *or* **e**ˌ**con·o·mi·'sa·tion** *n.*

e·con·o·miz·er *or* **e·con·o·mis·er** (ɪ'kɒnəˌmaɪzə) *n.* **1.** a device that uses the waste heat from a boiler flue to preheat the feed water. **2.** a person or thing that economizes.

E·con·o·mo's dis·ease (ɪ'kɒnəməʊz) *n.* *Pathol.* another name for **sleeping sickness** (sense 2). [C20: named after K. von *Economo* (1876–1931), Austrian neurologist]

e·con·o·my (ɪ'kɒnəmɪ) *n., pl.* **·mies. 1.** careful management of resources to avoid unnecessary expenditure or waste; thrift. **2.** a means or instance of this; saving. **3.** sparing, restrained, or efficient use, esp. to achieve the maximum effect for the minimum effort: *economy of language.* **4. a.** the complex of human activities undertaken for profit and concerned with the production, distribution, and consumption of goods and services. **b.** a particular type or branch of such production, distribution, and consumption: *a socialist economy; an agricultural economy.* **5.** the management of the resources, finances, income, and expenditure of a community, business enterprise, etc. **6.** Also called: **tourist. a.** a class of travel in aircraft, providing less luxurious accommodation than first class at a lower fare. **b.** (*as modifier*): *economy class.* **7.** (*modifier*) offering or purporting to offer a larger quantity for a lower price: *economy pack.* **8.** the orderly interplay between the parts of a system or structure: *the economy of nature.* **9.** *Archaic.* the management of household affairs; domestic economy. [C16: via Latin from Greek *oikonomia* domestic management, from *oikos* house + *-nomia*, from *nemein* to manage]

é·cor·ché (ˌeɪkɔː'ʃeɪ) *n.* an anatomical figure without the skin, so that the muscular structure is visible. [French, literally: skinned]

e·co·spe·cies ('iːkəʊˌspiːʃiːz, -spiːsiːz, 'ɛkəʊ-) *n.* *Ecology.* a species of plant or animal that can be divided into several ecotypes. [C20: from ECO(LOGY) + SPECIES] —**e·co·spe·cif·ic** (ˌiːkəʊspɪ'sɪfɪk, ˌɛkəʊ-) *adj.*

e·co·sphere ('iːkəʊˌsfɪə, 'ɛkəʊ-) *n.* the parts of the universe, esp. on the earth, in which life can exist.

é·coss·aise (ˌeɪkɒ'seɪz; *French* ekɔ'sɛːz) *n.* **1.** a lively dance in two-four time. **2.** the tune for such a dance. [literally: Scottish (dance)]

e·co·sys·tem ('iːkəʊˌsɪstəm, 'ɛkəʊ-) *n.* *Ecology.* a system involving the interactions between a community and its nonliving environment. [C20: from ECO(LOGY) + SYSTEM]

e·co·tone ('iːkəˌtəʊn, 'ɛkə-) *n.* the zone between two major ecological communities. [C20: from ECO(LOGY) + *-tone*, from Greek *tonos* tension, TONE] —'**e·co**ˌ**ton·al** *adj.*

e·co·type ('iːkəˌtaɪp, 'ɛkə-) *n.* *Ecology.* a group of organisms within a species that are adapted to different environmental conditions and therefore differ from one another in structure and physiology. —**e·co·typ·ic** (ˌiːkə'tɪpɪk, ˌɛkə-) *adj.* —ˌ**e·co·'typ·i·cal·ly** *adv.*

ECOWAS (ɛ'kəʊəs) *n.* *acronym for* Economic Community of West African States; an economic association established in 1975 among Benin, Gambia, Ghana, Guinea, Guinea-Bissau, Ivory Coast, Liberia, Mali, Mauritania, Niger, Nigeria, Senegal, Sierra Leone, Togo, and Upper Volta.

é·cra·seur (ˌeɪkrɑː'zɜː) *n.* a surgical device consisting of a heavy wire loop placed around a part to be removed and tightened until it cuts through. [C19: from French, from *écraser* to crush]

ec·ru ('ɛkruː, 'eɪkruː) *n.* **1.** a greyish-yellow to a light greyish colour; the colour of unbleached linen. ~*adj.* **2.** of the colour ecru. [C19: from French, from *é-* (intensive) + *cru* raw, from Latin *crūdus*; see CRUDE]

E.C.S.C. *abbrev. for* European Coal and Steel Community.

ec·sta·sy ('ɛkstəsɪ) *n., pl.* **·sies. 1.** (*often pl.*) a state of exalted delight, joy, etc.; rapture. **2.** intense emotion of any kind: *an ecstasy of rage.* **3.** *Psychol.* overpowering emotion characterized by loss of self-control and sometimes a temporary loss of consciousness: often associated with orgasm, religious mysticism, and the use of certain drugs. **4.** *Archaic.* a state of prophetic inspiration, esp. of poetic rapture. [C14: from Old French *extasie*, via Medieval Latin from Greek *ekstasis* displacement, trance, from *existanai* to displace, from *ex-* out + *histanai* to cause to stand]

ec·stat·ic (ɛk'stætɪk) *adj.* **1.** in a trancelike state of great rapture or delight. **2.** showing or feeling great enthusiasm: *ecstatic applause.* ~*n.* **3.** a person who has periods of intense trancelike joy. —**ec·'stat·i·cal·ly** *adv.*

ec·stat·ics (ɛk'stætɪks) *pl. n.* fits of delight or rapture.

E.C.T. *abbrev. for* electroconvulsive therapy.

ec·thy·ma ('ɛkθɪmə) *n.* *Pathol.* a local inflammation of the skin characterized by flat ulcerating pustules. [C19: from New Latin, from Greek *ekthuma* pustule, from *ekthuein* to break out, from *ek-* out + *thuein* to seethe]

ec·to- *combining form.* indicating outer, outside, external: *ectoplasm.* [from Greek *ektos* outside, from *ek, ex* out]

ec+to+blast ('ɛktəʊ,blæst) *n.* another name for **ectoderm** or **epiblast.** —ˌ**ec+to+'blas+tic** *adj.*

ec+to+crine ('ɛktəʊ,kri:n, -,krɪn) *n.* a substance that is released by an organism into the external environment and influences the development, behaviour, etc., of members of the same or different species. [C20: from ECTO + *-crine,* as in *endocrine*]

ec+to+derm ('ɛktəʊ,dɜ:m) *or* **ex·o+derm** *n.* the outer germ layer of an animal embryo, which gives rise to epidermis and nervous tissue. See also **mesoderm** and **endoderm.** —ˌ**ec+to+'der+mal** *or* ˌ**ec+to+'der+mic** *adj.*

ec+to+en+zyme (ˌɛktəʊ'ɛnzaɪm) *n.* any of a group of enzymes secreted from the cells in which they are produced into the surrounding medium; extracellular enzyme. Also called: **exo-enzyme.**

ec+tog+e·nous (ɛk'tɒdʒɪnəs) *or* **ec+to+gen+ic** (ˌɛktəʊ'dʒɛnɪk) *adj.* (of certain bacteria and other parasites) able to grow outside the body of the host. —ˌ**ec+to+'gen+e·sis** *n.*

ec+to+mere ('ɛktəʊ,mɪə) *n. Embryol.* any of the blastomeres that later develop into ectoderm. —**ec+to+mer+ic** (ˌɛktəʊ'mɛrɪk) *adj.*

ec+to+morph ('ɛktəʊ,mɔ:f) *n.* a type of person having a body build characterized by thinness, weakness, and a lack of weight: said to be correlated with a character type in which intellectual processes, inhibition and alertness predominate. Compare **endomorph, mesomorph.** —ˌ**ec+to+'mor+phic** *adj.* —'**ec+to+ˌmorph·y** *n.*

-ec·to·my *n. combining form.* indicating surgical excision of a part: *appendectomy.* [from New Latin *-ectomia,* from Greek *ek-* out + -TOMY]

ec+to+par·a+site (ˌɛktəʊ'pærə,saɪt) *n.* a parasite, such as the flea, that lives on the outer surface of its host. —**ec+to+par·a+sit+ic** (ˌɛktəʊˌpærə'sɪtɪk) *adj.*

ec+to+phyte ('ɛktəʊ,faɪt) *n.* a parasitic plant that lives on the surface of its host.

ec+to+pi·a (ɛk'təʊpɪə) *n. Med.* congenital displacement or abnormal positioning of an organ or part. [C19: from New Latin, from Greek *ektopos* out of position, from *ek-* out of + *topos* place] —**ec+top+ic** (ɛk'tɒpɪk) *adj.*

ec+top+ic preg+nan+cy *n. Pathol.* the abnormal development of a fertilized egg outside the cavity of the uterus, usually within a Fallopian tube.

ec+to+plasm ('ɛktəʊ,plæzəm) *n.* **1.** *Cytology.* the outer layer of cytoplasm that differs in many cells from the inner cytoplasm (see **endoplasm**) in being a clear gel. **2.** *Spiritualism.* the substance supposedly emanating from the body of a medium during trances. —ˌ**ec+to+'plas+mic** *adj.*

ec+to+proct ('ɛktəʊ,prɒkt) *n., adj.* another word for **bryozoan.** [from ECTO- + *-proct,* from Greek *prōktos* rectum]

ec+to+sarc ('ɛktəʊ,sɑ:k) *n. Zoology.* the ectoplasm of an amoeba or any other protozoan. [C19: ECTO- + *-sarc,* from Greek *sarx* flesh] —ˌ**ec+to+'sar+cous** *adj.*

ec+type ('ɛk,taɪp) *n.* **1.** a copy as distinguished from a prototype. **2.** *Architect.* a cast embossed or in relief. [C17: from Greek *ektupos* worked in relief, from *ek-* out of + *tupos* mould; see TYPE] —**ec+ty+pal** ('ɛktɪpᵊl) *adj.*

é·cu (eɪ'kju:; *French* e'ky) *n.* **1.** any of various former French gold or silver coins. **2.** a small shield. [C18: from Old French *escu,* from Latin *scūtum* shield]

Ecua. *abbrev. for* Ecuador.

Ec·ua+dor ('ɛkwə,dɔ:) *n.* a republic in South America, on the Pacific: under the Incas when Spanish colonization began in 1532; gained independence in 1822; declared a republic in 1830. It consists chiefly of a coastal plain in the west, separated from the densely forested upper Amazon basin (Oriente) by ranges and plateaus of the Andes. Official language: Spanish; Quechua is also widely spoken. Religion: Roman Catholic. Currency: sucre. Capital: Quito. Pop.: 6 500 845 (1974). Area: 283 560 sq. km (109 483 sq. miles). —ˌ**Ec·ua+'do+ri·an** *or* ˌ**Ec·ua+'do+ran** *adj., n.*

e·cu+men·i+cal, oe·cu+men·i+cal (ˌi:kjʊ'mɛnɪkᵊl, ˌɛk-) *or* **e·cu+men+ic, oe·cu+men+ic** *adj.* **1.** of or relating to the Christian Church throughout the world, esp. with regard to its unity. **2. a.** tending to promote unity among Churches. **b.** of or relating to the international movement initiated among non-Catholic Churches in 1910 aimed at Christian unity: embodied, since 1937, in the World Council of Churches. **3.** *Rare.* universal; general; worldwide. [C16: via Late Latin from Greek *oikoumenikos,* from *oikein* to inhabit, from *oikos* house] —ˌ**e·cu+'men·i·cal+ly** *or* ˌ**oe·cu+'men·i·cal+ly** *adv.*

e·cu+men·i·cal coun+cil *n. R.C. Church.* an assembly of the bishops, convened by the pope to reach binding decisions on matters of faith and morals.

e·cu+men·i+cal+ism (ˌi:kjʊ'mɛnɪkə,lɪzəm, ˌɛk-) *or* **e·cu+men·i+cism** *n.* the aim of unity among all Christian churches throughout the world.

é·cu+rie (*French* eky'ri) *n.* a team of motor-racing cars. [C20: French, literally: a stable]

ec+ze+ma ('ɛksɪmə) *n. Pathol.* a skin inflammation with lesions that scale, crust, or ooze a serous fluid, often accompanied by intense itching or burning. [C18: from New Latin, from Greek *ekzema,* from *ek-* out + *zein* to boil; see YEAST] —**ec+zem·a+tous** (ɛk'sɛmətəs) *adj.*

ed. *abbrev. for:* **1.** edited. **2.** (*pl.* **eds.**) edition. **3.** (*pl.* **eds.**) editor. **4.** education.

-ed[1] *suffix.* forming the past tense of most English verbs. [Old English *-de, -ede, -ode, -ade*]

-ed[2] *suffix.* forming the past participle of most English verbs. [Old English *-ed, -od, -ad*]

-ed[3] *suffix forming adjectives from nouns.* possessing or having the characteristics of: *salaried; red-blooded.* [Old English *-ede*]

e·da+cious (ɪ'deɪʃəs) *adj. Chiefly humorous.* devoted to eating; voracious; greedy. [C19: from Latin *edāx* voracious, from *edere* to eat] —**e'da+cious+ly** *adv.* —**e·dac+i·ty** (ɪ'dæsɪtɪ) *or* **e'da+cious+ness** *n.*

E·dam ('i:dæm) *n.* a hard round mild-tasting Dutch cheese, dark yellow in colour with a red outside covering.

e·daph+ic (ɪ'dæfɪk) *adj.* of or relating to the physical and chemical conditions of the soil, esp. in relation to the plant and animal life it supports. [C20: from Greek *edaphos* bottom, soil] —**e'daph·i·cal+ly** *adv.*

E.D.C. *abbrev. for* European Defence Community.

Ed·da ('ɛdə) *n.* **1.** Also called: **Elder Edda, Poetic Edda.** a collection of mythological Old Norse poems made in the 12th century. **2.** Also called: **Younger Edda, Prose Edda.** a treatise on versification together with a collection of Scandinavian myths, legends, and poems compiled by Snorri Sturluson. [C18: Old Norse] —**Ed+da+ic** (ɛ'deɪɪk) *adj.*

Ed·ding·ton ('ɛdɪŋtən) *n.* Sir **Ar+thur Stan·ley.** 1882–1944, English astronomer and physicist, noted for his research on the motion, internal constitution, and luminosity of stars and for his elucidation of the theory of relativity.

ed·do *or* **Chi+nese ed·do** ('ɛdəʊ) *n., pl.* **ed·does.** variants of **taro.**

ed·dy ('ɛdɪ) *n., pl.* **·dies. 1.** a movement in a stream of air, water, or other fluid in which the current doubles back on itself causing a miniature whirlwind or whirlpool. **2.** a deviation from or disturbance in the main trend of thought, life, etc., esp. one that is relatively unimportant. ~*vb.* **·dies, +dy+ing, +died. 3.** to move or cause to move against the main current. [C15: probably of Scandinavian origin; compare Old Norse *itha;* related to Old English *ed-* again, back, Old High German *it-*]

Ed·dy ('ɛdɪ) *n.* **Mar·y Ba·ker.** 1821–1910, U.S. religious leader; founder of the Christian Science movement (1866).

ed·dy cur+rent *n.* an electric current induced in a massive conductor, such as the core of an electromagnet, transformer, etc., by an alternating magnetic field. Also called: **Foucault current.**

Ed+dy+stone Rocks ('ɛdɪstən) *n.* a dangerous group of rocks at the W end of the English Channel, southwest of Plymouth: lighthouse.

E·de ('eɪdə) *n.* a city in the central Netherlands, in Gelderland province. Pop.: 77 589 (1973 est.).

e·del+weiss ('eɪdᵊl,vaɪs) *n.* a small alpine flowering plant, *Leontopodium alpinum,* having white woolly oblong leaves and a tuft of attractive floral leaves surrounding the flowers: family *Compositae* (composites). [C19: German, literally: noble white]

e·de+ma (ɪ'di:mə) *n., pl.* **+ma+ta** (-mətə). the usual U.S. spelling of **oedema.** —**e·dem·a+tous** (ɪ'dɛmətəs) *or* **e'dem·a+ˌtose** *adj.*

E·den[1] ('i:dᵊn) *n.* **1.** Also called: **Garden of Eden.** *Old Testament.* the garden in which Adam and Eve were placed at the Creation. **2.** a delightful place, region, dwelling, etc.; paradise. **3.** a state of great delight, happiness, or contentment; bliss. [C14: from Late Latin, from Hebrew *'ēdhen* place of pleasure]

E·den[2] ('i:dᵊn) *n.* Sir **(Robert) An·tho·ny,** Earl of Avon. 1897–1977, British Conservative statesman; foreign secretary (1935–38; 1940–45; 1951–55) and prime minister (1955–57). He resigned after the controversy caused by the occupation of the Suez Canal zone by British and French forces (1956).

e·den+tate (i:'dɛnteɪt) *n.* **1.** any of the placental mammals that constitute the order *Edentata,* which inhabit tropical regions of Central and South America. The order includes anteaters, sloths, and armadillos. ~*adj.* **2.** of, relating to, or belonging to the order *Edentata.* [C19: from Latin *ēdentātus* lacking teeth, from *ēdentāre* to render toothless, from *e-* out + *dēns* tooth]

e·den+tu+lous (i:'dɛntʃʊləs) *or* **e·den+tu+late** (i:'dɛntʃʊlɪt) *adj.* having no teeth.

E·des+sa (ɪ'dɛsə) *n.* **1.** an ancient city on the N edge of the Syrian plateau, founded as a Macedonian colony by Seleucus I: a centre of early Christianity. Modern name: **Urfa. 2.** a market town in Greece: ancient capital of Macedonia. Pop.: 13 967 (1971). Ancient name: **Aegae.** Modern Greek name: **Edhessa.**

Ed·gar ('ɛdgə) *n.* 944–975 A.D., king of Mercia and Northumbria (957–975) and of England (959–975).

Ed·gar Ath·e·ling ('æθɪlɪŋ) *n.* ?1050–?1125, grandson of Edmund II; Anglo-Saxon pretender to the English throne in 1066.

edge (ɛdʒ) *n.* **1.** the border, brim, or margin of a surface, object, etc. **2.** a brink or verge: *the edge of a cliff; the edge of a breakthrough.* **3.** a line along which two faces or surfaces of a solid meet. **4.** the sharp cutting side of a blade. **5.** keenness, sharpness, or urgency: *the walk gave an edge to his appetite.* **6.** force, effectiveness, or incisiveness: *the performance lacked edge.* **7.** *Dialect, chiefly northern Brit.* **a.** a cliff, ridge, or hillside. **b.** (*cap.*) (in place names): *Hade Edge.* **8. have the edge on** *or* **over.** to have a slight advantage or superiority (over). **9. on edge. a.** nervously irritable; tense. **b.** nervously excited or eager. **10. set (someone's) teeth on edge.** to make someone acutely irritated or uncomfortable. ~*vb.* **11.** (*tr.*) to provide an edge or border for. **12.** (*tr.*) to shape or trim (the edge or border of something), as with a knife or scissors: *to edge a pie.* **13.** to push (one's way, someone, something, etc.) gradually, esp. edgeways. **14.** (*tr.*) *Cricket.* to hit (a bowled ball) with the edge of the bat. **15.** (*tr.*) to tilt (a ski) sideways so that one edge digs into the snow. **16.** (*tr.*) to sharpen (a knife, etc.). [Old English *ecg*; related to Old Norse *egg*, Old High German *ecka* edge, Latin *aciēs* sharpness, Greek *akis* point] —**'edge·less** *adj.* —**'edg·er** *n.*

Edge·hill (ˌɛdʒ'hɪl) *n.* a ridge in S Warwickshire: site of the indecisive first battle between Charles I and the Parliamentarians (1642) in the Civil War.

edge tool *n.* a tool with one or more cutting edges.

edge·ways ('ɛdʒˌweɪz) *or esp. U.S.* **edge·wise** ('ɛdʒˌwaɪz) *adv.* **1.** with the edge forwards or uppermost: *they carried the piano in edgeways.* **2.** on, by, with, or towards the edge: *he held it edgeways.* **3. get a word in edgeways.** (*usually used with a negative*) *Informal.* to succeed in interrupting a conversation in which someone else is talking incessantly.

Edge·worth ('ɛdʒwɜːθ) *n.* **Ma·ri·a.** 1767–1849, English novelist: her works include *Castle Rackrent* (1800), and *The Absentee* (1812).

edg·ing ('ɛdʒɪŋ) *n.* **1.** anything placed along an edge to finish it, esp. as an ornament, fringe, or border on clothing or along a path in a garden. **2.** the act of making an edge. ~*adj.* **3.** relating to or used for making an edge: *edging shears.*

edg·y ('ɛdʒɪ) *adj.* **·i·er, ·i·est.** **1.** (*usually postpositive*) nervous, irritable, tense, or anxious. **2.** (of paintings, drawings, etc.) excessively defined. —**'edg·i·ly** *adv.* —**'edg·i·ness** *n.*

edh *or* **eth** (ɛð) *n.* a character of the runic alphabet (ð) used to represent the voiced dental fricative as in *then, mother, bathe.* It is used in modern phonetic transcription for the same purpose. Compare **thorn** (sense 4).

E·dhes·sa (*Greek* 'ɛðɛsa) *n.* transliteration of the Modern Greek name for **Edessa.**

ed·i·ble ('ɛdɪbᵊl) *adj.* fit to be eaten; eatable. [C17: from Late Latin *edibilis*, from Latin *edere* to eat] —**ˌed·i'bil·i·ty** *or* **'ed·i·ble·ness** *n.*

ed·i·bles ('ɛdɪbᵊlz) *pl. n.* articles fit to eat; food.

e·dict ('iːdɪkt) *n.* **1.** a decree, order, or ordinance issued by a sovereign, state, or any other holder of authority. **2.** any formal or authoritative command, proclamation, etc. [C15: from Latin *ēdictum*, from *ēdīcere* to declare] —**e'dic·tal** *adj.* —**e'dic·tal·ly** *adv.*

E·dict of Nantes *n.* the law granting religious and civil liberties to the French Protestants, promulgated by Henry IV in 1598 and revoked by Louis XIV in 1685.

ed·i·fi·ca·tion (ˌɛdɪfɪ'keɪʃən) *n.* **1.** improvement, instruction, or enlightenment, esp. when morally or spiritually uplifting. **2.** the act of edifying or state of being edified. —**ˌe·dif·i'ca·to·ry** *adj.*

ed·i·fice ('ɛdɪfɪs) *n.* **1.** a building, esp. a large or imposing one. **2.** a complex or elaborate institution or organization. [C14: from Old French, from Latin *aedificium*, from *aedificāre* to build; see EDIFY] —**ed·i·fi·cial** (ˌɛdɪ'fɪʃəl) *adj.*

ed·i·fy ('ɛdɪˌfaɪ) *vb.* **·fies, ·fy·ing, ·fied.** (*tr.*) to improve the morality, intellect, etc., of, esp. by instruction. [C14: from Old French *edifier*, from Latin *aedificāre* to construct, from *aedēs* a dwelling, temple + *facere* to make] —**'ed·iˌfi·er** *n.* —**'ed·iˌfy·ing·ly** *adv.*

e·dile ('iːdaɪl) *n.* a variant spelling of **aedile.**

Ed·in·burgh[1] ('ɛdɪnbərə, -brə) *n.* the capital of Scotland, on the S side of the Firth of Forth: became the capital in the 15th century; university (1583); commercial and cultural centre, noted for its annual festival. Pop.: 453 422 (1971).

Ed·in·burgh[2] ('ɛdɪnbərə, -brə) *n.* **Duke of,** title of Prince *Philip Mountbatten.* born 1921, husband of Queen Elizabeth II of England.

E·dir·ne (ɛ'dɪrnɛ) *n.* a city in NW Turkey: a Thracian town, rebuilt and renamed by the Roman emperor Hadrian. Pop.: 54 885 (1970). Former name: **Adrianople.**

Ed·i·son ('ɛdɪsᵊn) *n.* **Thom·as Al·va.** 1847–1931, U.S. inventor. He patented more than a thousand inventions, including the phonograph, the incandescent electric lamp, the microphone, and the kinetoscope.

ed·it ('ɛdɪt) *vb.* (*tr.*) **1.** to prepare (text) for publication by checking and improving its accuracy, clarity, etc. **2.** to be in charge of (a publication, esp. a periodical): *he edits the local newspaper.* **3.** to prepare (a film, tape, etc.) by rearrangement, selection, or rejection of previously filmed or taped material. **4.** (often foll. by *out*) to remove (incorrect or unwanted matter), as from a manuscript or film. ~*n.* **5.** *Informal.* an act of editing: *give the book a final edit.* [C18: back formation from EDITOR]

edit. *abbrev. for:* **1.** edited. **2.** edition. **3.** editor.

e·di·tion (ɪ'dɪʃən) *n.* **1.** *Printing.* **a.** the entire number of copies of a book, newspaper, or other publication printed at one time from a single setting of type. **b.** a single copy from this number: *a first edition; the evening edition.* **2.** one of a number of printings of a book or other publication, issued at separate times with alterations, amendments, etc. Compare **impression** (sense 6). **3. a.** an issue of a work identified by its format: *a leather-bound edition of Shakespeare.* **b.** an issue of a work identified by its editor or publisher: *the Oxford edition of Shakespeare.* [C16: from Latin *ēditiō* a bringing forth, publishing, from *ēdere* to give out; see EDITOR]

e·di·ti·o prin·ceps (ɪ'dɪʃɪəʊ 'prɪnsɛps) *n., pl.* **e·di·ti·o·nes prin·ci·pes** (ɪˌdɪʃɪ'əʊniːz 'prɪnsɪˌpiːz). *Latin.* the first printed edition of a work.

ed·i·tor ('ɛdɪtə) *n.* **1.** a person who edits written material for publication. **2.** a person in overall charge of the editing and often the policy of a newspaper or periodical. **3.** a person in charge of one section of a newspaper or periodical: *the sports editor.* **4.** *Films.* **a.** a person who makes a selection and arrangement of individual shots in order to construct the flowing sequence of images for a film. **b.** a device for editing film, including a viewer and a splicer. [C17: from Late Latin: producer, exhibitor, from *ēdere* to give out, publish, from *ē-* out + *dāre* to give] —**'ed·i·tor·ˌship** *n.*

ed·i·to·ri·al (ˌɛdɪ'tɔːrɪəl) *adj.* **1.** of or relating to editing or editors. **2.** of, relating to, or expressed in an editorial. **3.** of or relating to the content of a publication rather than its commercial aspects. ~*n.* **4.** an article in a newspaper, etc., expressing the opinion of the editor or the publishers. —**ˌed·i'to·ri·al·ist** *n.* —**ˌed·i'to·ri·al·ly** *adv.*

ed·i·to·ri·al·ize *or* **ed·i·to·ri·al·ise** (ˌɛdɪ'tɔːrɪəˌlaɪz) *vb.* (*intr.*) **1.** to express an opinion in or as in an editorial. **2.** to insert one's personal opinions into an otherwise objective account. —**ˌed·iˌto·ri·al·i'za·tion** *or* **ˌed·iˌto·ri·al·i'sa·tion** *n.* —**ˌed·i'to·ri·alˌiz·er** *or* **ˌed·i'to·ri·alˌis·er** *n.*

ed·i·tor in chief *n.* the controlling editor of a publication.

Ed·mon·ton ('ɛdməntən) *n.* a city in W Canada, capital of Alberta: oil industry. Pop.: 438 152 (1971).

Ed·mund I ('ɛdmənd) *n.* ?922–946 A.D., king of England (940–946).

Ed·mund II *n.* called *Edmund Ironside.* ?980–1016, king of England in 1016. His succession was contested by Canute and they divided the kingdom between them.

Ed·o ('ɛdəʊ) *n.* **1.** (*pl.* **Ed·o** *or* **Ed·os**) a member of a Negroid people of SW Nigeria around Benin, noted for their 16th-century bronze sculptures. **2.** Also called: **Bini.** the language of this people, belonging to the Kwa branch of the Niger-Congo family.

E·dom ('iːdəm) *n.* **1.** a nomadic people descended from Esau. **2.** the son of Esau who was the supposed ancestor of this nation. **3.** the ancient kingdom of this people, situated between the Dead Sea and the Gulf of Aqaba.

E·dom·ite ('iːdəˌmaɪt) *n.* **1.** an inhabitant of the ancient kingdom of Edom, whose people were hostile to the Israelites in Old Testament times. **2.** the ancient Semitic language of this people, closely related to Hebrew. —**'E·dom·ˌit·ish** *or* **E·dom·it·ic** (ˌiːdə'mɪtɪk) *adj.*

E.D.P. *or* **e.d.p.** *abbrev. for* electronic data processing.

E.D.T. (in the U.S.) *abbrev. for* Eastern Daylight Time.

EDTA *n.* ethylenediaminetetra-acetic acid; a colourless crystalline slightly soluble organic compound used in inorganic chemistry and biochemistry. It is a powerful chelating agent. Formula: $[(HOOCCH_2)_2NCH_2]_2$.

educ. *abbrev. for:* **1.** educated. **2.** education(al).

ed·u·ca·ble ('ɛdjʊkəbᵊl) *or* **ed·u·cat·a·ble** ('ɛdjʊˌkeɪtəbᵊl) *adj.* capable of being trained or educated; able to learn. —**ˌed·u·ca'bil·i·ty** *or* **ˌed·u·ˌcat·a'bil·i·ty** *n.*

ed·u·cate ('ɛdjʊˌkeɪt) *vb.* (*mainly tr.*) **1.** (*also intr.*) to impart knowledge by formal instruction to (a pupil); teach. **2.** to provide education for (children); pay for the schooling of: *I have educated my children at the best schools.* **3.** to improve or develop (a person, judgment, taste, skills, etc.). **4.** to train for some particular purpose or occupation. [C15: from Latin *ēducāre* to rear, educate, from *dūcere* to lead]

ed·u·cat·ed ('ɛdjʊˌkeɪtɪd) *adj.* **1.** having an education, esp. a good one. **2.** displaying culture, taste, and knowledge; cultivated. **3.** (*prenominal*) based on experience or information (esp. in the phrase **an educated guess**).

ed·u·ca·tion (ˌɛdjʊ'keɪʃən) *n.* **1.** the act or process of acquiring knowledge, esp. systematically during childhood and adolescence. **2.** the knowledge or training acquired by this process: *his education has been invaluable to him.* **3.** the act or process of imparting knowledge to, esp. at a school, college, or university: *education is my profession.* **4.** the theory of teaching and learning: *a course in education.* **5.** a particular kind of instruction or training: *a university education; consumer education.*

ed·u·ca·tion·al (ˌɛdjʊ'keɪʃənᵊl) *adj.* **1.** providing knowledge; instructive or informative: *an educational toy.* **2.** of or relating to education. —**ˌed·u'ca·tion·al·ly** *adv.*

ed·u·ca·tion·al·ist (ˌɛdjʊ'keɪʃənəlɪst) *or* **ed·u·ca·tion·ist** *n.* a specialist in educational theory or administration.

ed·u·ca·tive ('ɛdjʊkətɪv) *adj.* producing or resulting in education: *an educative experience.*

ed·u·ca·tor ('ɛdjʊˌkeɪtə) *n.* **1.** a person who educates; teacher. **2.** a specialist in education; educationalist.

ed·u·ca·to·ry ('ɛdjʊkətərɪ, -trɪ; ˌɛdjʊ'keɪtərɪ, -trɪ) *adj.* educative or educational: *an educatory procedure.*

e·duce (ɪ'djuːs) *vb.* (*tr.*) *Rare.* **1.** to evolve or develop, esp. from a latent or potential state. **2.** to draw out or elicit (information, solutions, etc.). **3.** *Logic.* to deduce (a proposition). [C15: from Latin *ēdūcere* to draw out, from *ē-* out + *dūcere* to lead] —**e'duc·i·ble** *adj.* —**e·duc·tive** (ɪ'dʌktɪv) *adj.*

e·duct ('iːdʌkt) *n.* a substance separated from another substance without chemical change. Compare **product.** [C18: from Latin *ēductus*; see EDUCE]

e·duc·tion (ɪ'dʌkʃən) *n.* **1.** something educed. **2.** the act or process of educing. **3.** the exhaust stroke of a steam or internal-combustion engine. Compare **induction.** [C17: from Latin *ēductiō*, from *ēdūcere* to EDUCE]

e·dul·co·rate (ɪ'dʌlkəˌreɪt) *vb.* (*tr.*) to free from soluble impurities by washing. [C17: from Medieval Latin *ēdulcorāre*, from *dulcor* sweetness] —**eˌdul·co'ra·tion** *n.*

Ed·ward[1] ('ɛdwəd) *n.* **Lake.** a lake in central Africa, between

Uganda and Zaïre in the Great Rift Valley: empties through the Semliki River into Lake Albert. Area: about 2150 sq. km (830 sq. miles). Official name: **Lake Amin.**

Ed·ward[2] ('ɛdwəd) *n.* called *the Black Prince.* 1330–76, Prince of Wales, the son of Edward III of England. He won victories over the French at Crécy (1346) and Poitiers (1356) in the Hundred Years' War.

Ed·ward I *n.* 1239–1307, king of England (1272–1307); son of Henry III. He conquered Wales (1284) but failed to subdue Scotland.

Ed·ward II *n.* 1284–1327, king of England (1307–27); son of Edward I. He invaded Scotland but was defeated by Robert Bruce at Bannockburn (1314). He was deposed by his wife Isabella and Roger Mortimer; died in prison.

Ed·ward III *n.* 1312–77, king of England (1327–77); son of Edward II. His claim to the French throne in right of his mother Isabella provoked the Hundred Years' War (1337).

Ed·ward IV *n.* 1442–83, king of England (1461–70; 1471–83); son of Richard, duke of York. He defeated Henry VI in The Wars of the Roses and became king (1461). In 1470 Henry was restored to the throne, but Edward recovered the crown by his victory at Tewkesbury.

Ed·ward V *n.* 1470–?83, king of England in 1483; son of Edward IV. He was deposed by his uncle, Richard, Duke of Gloucester (Richard III), and is thought to have been murdered with his brother in the Tower of London.

Ed·ward VI *n.* 1537–53, king of England (1547–53), son of Henry VIII and Jane Seymour. His uncle the Duke of Somerset was regent until 1552, when he was executed. Edward then came under the control of Dudley, Duke of Northumberland.

Ed·ward VII *n.* 1841–1910, king of Great Britain and Ireland (1901–10); son of Queen Victoria.

Ed·ward VIII *n.* 1894–1972, king of Great Britain and Ireland in 1936; son of George V and brother of George VI. He abdicated in order to marry an American divorcee, Mrs. Wallis Simpson; created Duke of Windsor (1937).

Ed+ward+i·an (ɛd'wɔːdɪən) *adj.* denoting, relating to, or having the style of life, architecture, dress, etc., current in Britain during the reign of Edward VII. —**Ed+'ward+i·an+ism** *n.*

Ed·wards ('ɛdwədz) *n.* **1. Gar·eth (Owen).** born 1947, British Rugby Union footballer: halfback for Wales (since 1967) and the British Lions (1968–74). **2. Jon·a·than.** 1703–58, American Calvinist theologian and metaphysician; author of *The Freedom of the Will* (1754).

Ed·ward the Con·fes·sor *n.* **Saint.** ?1002–66, king of England (1042–66); son of Ethelred II; founder of Westminster Abbey. Feast day: Oct. 13.

Ed·win ('ɛdwɪn) *n.* ?585–633 A.D., king of Northumbria (617–633) and overlord of all England except Kent.

e.e. *abbrev. for* errors excepted.

E.E. *abbrev. for:* **1.** Early English. **2.** electrical engineer *or* electrical engineering.

-ee *suffix forming nouns.* **1.** indicating a person who is the recipient of an action (as opposed, esp. in legal terminology, to the agent, indicated by *-or* or *-er*): *assignee; grantee; lessee.* **2.** indicating a person in a specified state or condition: *absentee; employee.* **3.** indicating a diminutive form of something: *bootee.* [via Old French *-e, -ee,* past participial endings, from Latin *-ātus, -āta* -ATE[1]]

E.E. & M.P. *abbrev. for* Envoy Extraordinary and Minister Plenipotentiary.

EEC *abbrev. for* European Economic Community (the Common Market).

EEG *abbrev. for:* **1.** electroencephalogram. **2.** electroencephalograph.

eel (iːl) *n.* **1.** any teleost fish of the order *Apodes* (or *Anguilliformes*), such as the European freshwater species *Anguilla anguilla,* having a long snakelike body, a smooth slimy skin, and reduced fins. **2.** any of various other animals with a long body and smooth skin, such as the mud eel and the electric eel. **3.** an evasive or untrustworthy person. [Old English *ǣl;* related to Old Frisian *ēl,* Old Norse *āll,* Old High German *āl*] —**'eel-ˌlike** *adj.* —**'eel·y** *adj.*

eel+grass ('iːlˌgrɑːs) *n.* **1.** any of several perennial submerged marine plants of the genus *Zostera,* esp. *Z. marina,* having grasslike leaves: family *Zosteraceae.* **2.** another name for **tape grass.**

eel+pout ('iːlˌpaʊt) *n.* **1.** any marine eel-like blennioid fish of the family *Zoarcidae,* such as *Zoarces viviparus* (**viviparous eelpout** or blenny). **2.** another name for **burbot.** [Old English *ǣlepūte;* related to Middle Dutch *aalpuit*]

eel+worm ('iːlˌwɜːm) *n.* any of various nematode worms, esp. the wheat worm and the vinegar eel.

e'en (iːn) *adv., n.* a contraction of **even**[2] or **evening.**

-eer *or* **-ier** *suffix.* **1.** (*forming nouns*) indicating a person who is concerned with or who does something specified: *auctioneer; engineer; profiteer; mutineer.* **2.** (*forming verbs*) to be concerned with something specified: *electioneer.* [from Old French *-ier,* from Latin *-arius* -ARY]

e'er (ɛə) *adv. Poetic or archaic.* a contraction of **ever.**

ee·rie ('ɪərɪ) *adj.* **ee·ri+er, ee·ri+est.** (esp. of places, an atmosphere, etc.) mysteriously or uncannily frightening or disturbing; weird; ghostly. [C13: originally Scottish and Northern English, probably from Old English *earg* cowardly, miserable] —**'ee·ri+ly** *adv.* —**'ee·ri+ness** *n.*

eff (ɛf) *vb.* euphemism for **fuck** (esp. in the phrase **eff off**).

ef+fa·ble ('ɛfəbᵊl) *adj. Archaic.* capable of being expressed in words. [C17: from Old French, from Late Latin *effābilis,* from Latin *effārī,* from *ex-* out + *fārī* to speak]

ef+face (ɪ'feɪs) *vb.* (*tr.*) **1.** to obliterate or make dim: *to efface a memory.* **2.** to make (oneself) inconspicuous or humble through modesty, cowardice, or obsequiousness. **3.** to rub out (a line, drawing, etc.); erase. [C15: from French *effacer,* literally: to obliterate the face; see FACE] —**ef+'face+a·ble** *adj.* —**ef+'face+ment** *n.* —**ef+'fac+er** *n.*

ef+fect (ɪ'fɛkt) *n.* **1.** something that is produced by a cause or agent; result. **2.** power or ability to influence or produce a result; efficacy: *with no effect.* **3.** the condition of being operative (esp. in the phrases **in** or **into effect**): *the law comes into effect at midnight.* **4. take effect.** to become operative or begin to produce results. **5.** basic meaning or purpose (esp. in the phrase **to that effect**). **6.** an impression, usually one that is artificial or contrived (esp. in the phrase **for effect**). **7.** a scientific phenomenon: *the Doppler effect.* **8. in effect. a.** in fact; actually. **b.** for all practical purposes. **9.** the overall impression or result: *the effect of a painting.* ~*vb.* **10.** (*tr.*) to cause to occur; bring about; accomplish. [C14: from Latin *effectus* a performing, tendency, from *efficere* to accomplish, from *facere* to do] —**ef+'fect+er** *n.* —**ef+'fect+i·ble** *adj.*

ef+fec+tive (ɪ'fɛktɪv) *adj.* **1.** productive of or capable of producing a result. **2.** in effect; operative: *effective from midnight.* **3.** producing a striking impression; impressive: *an effective entrance.* **4.** (*prenominal*) actual rather than theoretical; real: *the effective income after deductions.* **5.** (of a military force, etc.) equipped and prepared for action. **6.** *Physics.* (of an alternating quantity) having a value that is the square root of the mean of the squares of the magnitude measured at each instant over a defined period of time, usually one cycle. —**ef+'fec+tive+ly** *adv.* —**ef+'fec+tive+ness** *n.*

ef+fec+tor *or* **ef+fec+ter** (ɪ'fɛktə) *n. Physiol.* a nerve ending that terminates in a muscle or gland and provides neural stimulation causing contraction or secretion.

ef+fects (ɪ'fɛkts) *pl. n.* **1.** Also called: **personal effects.** personal property or belongings. **2.** Also called: **special effects. a.** lighting, sounds, etc., to accompany and enhance a stage, film, or broadcast production. **b.** the devices used to produce these.

ef+fec+tu·al (ɪ'fɛktjʊəl) *adj.* **1.** capable of or successful in producing an intended result; effective. **2.** (of documents, agreements, etc.) having legal force. —**ef+ˌfec+tu+'al+i·ty** *or* **ef+'fec+tu+al+ness** *n.*

ef+fec+tu+al+ly (ɪ'fɛktjʊəlɪ) *adv.* **1.** with the intended effect; thoroughly. **2.** to all practical purposes; in effect.

ef+fec+tu+ate (ɪ'fɛktjuːˌeɪt) *vb.* (*tr.*) to cause to happen; effect; accomplish. —**ef+ˌfec+tu+'a·tion** *n.*

ef+fem·i+nate (ɪ'fɛmɪnɪt) *adj.* **1.** (of a man or boy) displaying characteristics regarded as typical of a woman; not manly. **2.** lacking firmness or vigour: *an effeminate piece of writing.* [C14: from Latin *effēmināre* to make into a woman, from *fēmina* woman] —**ef+'fem·i+na+cy** *or* **ef+'fem·i+nate+ness** *n.* —**ef+'fem·i+nate+ly** *adv.*

ef+fen+di (ɛ'fɛndɪ) *n., pl.* **+dis. 1.** (in the Ottoman Empire) a title of respect used to address men of learning or social standing. **2.** (in Turkey since 1934) the oral title of address equivalent to *Mr.* [C17: from Turkish *efendi* master, from Modern Greek *aphentēs,* from Greek *authentēs* lord, doer; see AUTHENTIC]

ef+fer+ent ('ɛfərənt) *adj.* carrying or conducting outwards from a part or an organ of the body, esp. from the brain or spinal cord. Compare **afferent.** [C19: from Latin *efferre* to bear off, from *ferre* to bear] —**'ef+fer+ence** *n.* —**'ef+fer+ent+ly** *adv.*

ef+fer+vesce (ˌɛfə'vɛs) *vb.* (*intr.*) **1.** (of a liquid) to give off bubbles of gas. **2.** (of a gas) to issue in bubbles from a liquid. **3.** to exhibit great excitement, vivacity, etc. [C18: from Latin *effervescere* to foam up, from *fervescere* to begin to boil, from *fervēre* to boil, ferment] —**ˌef+fer+'ves+ci·ble** *adj.*

ef+fer+ves+cent (ˌɛfə'vɛsᵊnt) *adj.* **1.** (of a liquid) giving off bubbles of gas; bubbling. **2.** high-spirited; vivacious. —**ˌef+fer+'ves+cence** *n.* —**ˌef+fer+'ves+cent+ly** *adv.* —**ˌef+fer+'ves+cing+ly** *adv.*

ef+fete (ɪ'fiːt) *adj.* **1.** weak, ineffectual, or decadent as a result of overrefinement: *an effete academic.* **2.** exhausted of vitality or strength; worn out; spent. **3.** (of animals or plants) no longer capable of reproduction. [C17: from Latin *effētus* having produced young, hence, exhausted by bearing, from *fētus* having brought forth; see FETUS] —**ef+'fete+ly** *adv.* —**ef+'fete+ness** *n.*

ef+fi+ca+cious (ˌɛfɪ'keɪʃəs) *adj.* capable of or successful in producing an intended result; effective as a means, remedy, etc. [C16: from Latin *efficāx* powerful, efficient, from *efficere* to achieve; see EFFECT] —**ˌef+fi+'ca+cious+ly** *adv.* —**ef+fi+ca+cy** ('ɛfɪkəsɪ) *or* **ˌef+fi+'ca+cious+ness** *n.*

ef+fi+cien+cy (ɪ'fɪʃənsɪ) *n., pl.* **+cies. 1.** the quality or state of being efficient; competence; effectiveness. **2.** the ratio of the energy output of a machine, engine, device, etc., to the energy supplied to it, often expressed as a percentage. See also **thermal efficiency.**

ef+fi+cien+cy a·part+ment *n. U.S.* a small flat or bedsitter.

ef+fi+cient (ɪ'fɪʃənt) *adj.* **1.** functioning or producing effectively and with the least waste of effort; competent. **2.** *Philosophy.* producing a direct effect; causative. [C14: from Latin *efficiēns* effecting] —**ef+'fi+cient+ly** *adv.*

ef+fi+gy ('ɛfɪdʒɪ) *n., pl.* **+gies. 1.** a portrait of a person, esp. as a monument or architectural decoration. **2.** a crude representation of someone, used as a focus for contempt or ridicule and often hung up or burnt in public (often in the phrases **burn** or **hang in effigy).** [C18: from Latin *effigiēs,* from *effingere* to form, portray, from *fingere* to shape] —**ef+fig+i·al** (ɪ'fɪdʒɪəl) *adj.*

ef+flo+resce (ˌɛflɔː'rɛs) *vb.* (*intr.*) **1.** to burst forth into or as if into flower; bloom. **2.** to become powdery by loss of water or crystallization. 3. to become encrusted with powder or crystals as a result of chemical change or the evaporation of a solution. [C18: from Latin *efflōrēscere* to blossom, from *flōrēscere,* from *flōs* flower]

ef·flo·res·cence (ˌɛflɔːˈrɛsəns) *n.* **1.** a bursting forth or flowering. **2.** *Chem, geology.* **a.** the process of efflorescing. **b.** the powdery substance formed as a result of this process, esp. on the surface of rocks. **3.** any skin rash or eruption. —ˌ**ef·flo·ˈres·cent** *adj.*

ef·flu·ence (ˈɛflʊəns) *or* **ef·flux** (ˈɛflʌks) *n.* **1.** the act or process of flowing out. **2.** something that flows out.

ef·flu·ent (ˈɛflʊənt) *n.* **1.** liquid discharged as waste, as from an industrial plant or sewage works. **2.** radioactive waste released from a nuclear power station. **3.** a stream that flows out of another body of water. **4.** something that flows out or forth. ~*adj.* **5.** flowing out or forth. [C18: from Latin *effluere* to run forth, from *fluere* to flow]

ef·flu·vi·um (ɛˈfluːvɪəm) *n., pl.* **·vi·a** (-vɪə) *or* **·vi·ums.** an unpleasant smell or exhalation, as of gaseous waste or decaying matter. [C17: from Latin: a flowing out; see EFFLUENT] —**efˈflu·vi·al** *adj.*

ef·fort (ˈɛfət) *n.* **1.** physical or mental exertion, usually considerable when unqualified: *the rock was moved with effort.* **2.** a determined attempt: *our effort to save him failed.* **3.** achievement; creation: *a great literary effort.* **4.** *Physics.* an applied force acting against inertia. [C15: from Old French *esfort,* from *esforcier* to force, ultimately from Latin *fortis* strong; see FORCE] —**ˈef·fort·ful** *adj.*

ef·fort·less (ˈɛfətlɪs) *adj.* **1.** requiring or involving little effort; easy. **2.** *Archaic.* making little effort; passive. —**ˈef·fort·less·ly** *adv.* —**ˈef·fort·less·ness** *n.*

ef·fron·ter·y (ɪˈfrʌntərɪ) *n., pl.* **·ies.** shameless or insolent boldness; impudent presumption; audacity; temerity. [C18: from French *effronterie,* from Old French *esfront* barefaced, shameless, from Late Latin *effrons,* literally: putting forth one's forehead; see FRONT]

ef·ful·gent (ɪˈfʌldʒənt) *adj.* radiant; brilliant. [C18: from Latin *effulgēre* to shine forth, from *fulgēre* to shine] —**efˈful·gence** *n.* —**efˈful·gent·ly** *adv.*

ef·fuse *vb.* (ɪˈfjuːz). **1.** to pour or flow out. **2.** to spread out; diffuse. **3.** (*intr.*) to talk profusely, esp. in an excited manner. **4.** to cause (a gas) to flow or (of a gas) to flow under pressure. ~*adj.* (ɪˈfjuːs). **5.** *Botany.* (esp. of an inflorescence) spreading out loosely. [C16: from Latin *effūsus* poured out, from *effundere* to shed, from *fundere* to pour]

ef·fu·si·om·e·ter (ɪˌfjuːzɪˈɒmɪtə) *n. Physics.* an apparatus for determining rates of effusion of gases, usually used for measuring molecular weights.

ef·fu·sion (ɪˈfjuːʒən) *n.* **1.** an unrestrained outpouring in speech or words. **2.** the act or process of being poured out. **3.** something that is poured out. **4.** the flow of a gas through a small aperture under pressure, esp. when the density is such that the mean distance between molecules is large compared to the diameter of the aperture.

ef·fu·sive (ɪˈfjuːsɪv) *adj.* **1.** extravagantly demonstrative of emotion; gushing. **2.** (of rock) formed by the solidification of magma. —**efˈfu·sive·ly** *adv.* —**efˈfu·sive·ness** *n.*

Ef·ik (ˈɛfɪk) *n.* **1.** (*pl.* **Ef·iks** *or* **Ef·ik**) a member of a subgroup of the Ibibio people of SE Nigeria. **2.** the language spoken by this people: the chief literary dialect of Ibibio.

eft[1] (ɛft) *n.* **1.** a dialect or archaic name for a **newt. 2.** any of certain terrestrial newts, such as *Diemictylus viridescens* (**red eft**) of the eastern U.S. [Old English *efeta*]

eft[2] (ɛft) *adv. Archaic* **a.** again. **b.** afterwards. [Old English; see AFT, AFTER]

EFTA (ˈɛftə) *n. acronym for* European Free Trade Association; established in 1960 to eliminate trade tariffs on industrial products; comprised Britain, Denmark, Norway, Sweden, Switzerland, Austria, and Portugal. Finland became an associate member in 1961 and Iceland joined in 1970. Britain and Denmark left EFTA to join the EEC in 1972.

eft·soons (ɛftˈsuːnz) *adv. Archaic.* **1.** soon afterwards. **2.** repeatedly. [Old English *eft sōna,* literally: afterwards soon]

Eg. *abbrev. for:* **1.** Egypt(ian). **2.** Egyptology.

e.g. *abbrev. for* exempli gratia. [Latin: for example]

e·gad (ɪˈgæd, iːˈgæd) *interj. Archaic.* a mild oath or expression of surprise. [C17: probably variant of *Ah God!*]

e·gal·i·tar·i·an (ɪˌgælɪˈtɛərɪən) *adj.* **1.** of, relating to, or upholding the doctrine of the equality of mankind and the desirability of political, social, and economic equality. ~*n.* **2.** an adherent of egalitarian principles. [C19: alteration of *equalitarian,* through influence of French *égal* EQUAL] —**e·ˌgal·i·ˈtar·i·an·ˌism** *n.*

Eg·bert (ˈɛgbɜːt) *n.* ?775–839 A.D., king of Wessex (802–839); first overlord of all England (829–830).

E·ger *n.* **1.** (*Hungarian* ˈɛgɛr). a city in N central Hungary. Pop.: 45 000 (1970). **2.** (ˈeːgər). the German name for **Cheb.**

E·ge·ri·a (ɪˈdʒɪərɪə) *n.* a female adviser. [C17: name of the mythical adviser of Numa Pompilius, king of Rome]

e·gest (iːˈdʒɛst) *vb.* (*tr.*) to excrete (waste material, etc.). [C17: from Latin *ēgerere* to carry out, from *gerere* to carry] —**eˈges·tion** *n.* —**eˈges·tive** *adj.*

e·ges·ta (iːˈdʒɛstə) *pl. n.* anything egested, as waste material from the body; excrement. [C18: from Latin, literally: (things) carried out; see EGEST]

egg[1] (ɛg) *n.* **1.** the oval or round reproductive body laid by the females of birds, reptiles, fishes, insects, and some other animals, consisting of a developing embryo, its food store, and sometimes jelly or albumen, all surrounded by an outer shell or membrane. **2.** Also called: **egg cell.** any female gamete; ovum. **3.** the egg of the domestic hen used as food. **4.** something resembling an egg, esp. in shape or in being in an early stage of development. **5. good** (*or* **bad**) **egg.** *Old-fashioned slang.* **a.** a good (or bad) person. **b.** an exclamation of delight (or dismay). **6. lay an egg.** *Slang, chiefly U.S.* **a.** to make a joke or give a performance, etc., that fails completely. **b.** (of a joke, performance, etc.) to fail completely; flop. **7. put** *or* **have all one's eggs in one basket.** to stake everything on a single venture. **8. teach one's grandmother to suck eggs.** *Informal.* to presume to teach someone something that he knows already. ~*vb.* (*tr.*) **9.** to dip (food) in beaten egg before cooking. **10.** *U.S. informal.* to throw eggs at. [C14: from Old Norse *egg;* related to Old English *ǣg,* Old High German *ei*]

egg[2] (ɛg) *vb.* (*tr.;* usually foll. by *on*) to urge or incite, esp. to daring or foolish acts. [Old English *eggian,* from Old Norse *eggja* to urge; related to Old English *ecg* EDGE, Middle Low German *eggen* to harrow]

egg and dart, egg and tongue, *or* **egg and an·chor** *n.* (in architecture and cabinetwork) **a.** an ornamental moulding in which a half egg shape alternates with a dart, tongue, or anchor shape. **b.** (*as modifier*): *egg-and-dart moulding.*

egg-and-spoon race *n.* a race in which runners carry an egg balanced in a spoon.

egg·beat·er (ˈɛgˌbiːtə) *n.* **1.** Also called: **eggwhisk.** a kitchen utensil for beating eggs, whipping cream, etc.; whisk. **2.** *Chiefly U.S.* an informal name for **helicopter.**

egg cup *n.* a small cuplike container, used for holding a boiled egg while it is being eaten.

eg·ger *or* **eg·gar** (ˈɛgə) *n.* any of various widely distributed moths of the family *Lasiocampidae,* such as *Lasiocampa quercus* (**oak egger**) of Europe, having brown bodies and wings. [C18: from EGG, from the egg-shaped cocoon]

egg·head (ˈɛgˌhɛd) *n. Informal.* an intellectual; highbrow.

egg·nog (ˌɛgˈnɒg) *or* **egg-nog·gin** *n.* a drink that can be served hot or cold, made of eggs, milk, sugar, spice, and brandy, rum, or other spirit. Also called **egg flip.**

egg·plant (ˈɛgˌplɑːnt) *n.* another name (esp. U.S.) for **aubergine.**

egg roll *n.* a Chinese-American dish consisting of egg dough filled with a minced mixture of pork, bamboo shoots, onions, etc., and browned in deep fat.

eggs Ben·e·dict *n.* a dish consisting of toast, covered with a slice of ham, poached egg, and hollandaise sauce.

egg·shell (ˈɛgˌʃɛl) *n.* **1.** the hard porous protective outer layer of a bird's egg, consisting of calcite and protein. **2.** a yellowish-white colour. **3.** a type of paper with a slightly rough finish. **4.** (*modifier*) (of paint) having little gloss; possessing a matt finish similar to that of an egg. ~*adj.* **5.** of a yellowish-white colour.

egg·shell porce·lain *or* **chi·na** *n.* a type of very thin translucent porcelain originally made in China.

egg slice *n.* a spatula for removing omelettes, fried eggs, etc., from a pan.

egg spoon *n.* a small spoon for eating a boiled egg.

egg tim·er *n.* a device, typically a miniature hour-glass, for timing the boiling of an egg.

egg tooth *n.* (in embryo birds and reptiles) a temporary tooth or (in birds) projection of the beak used for piercing the eggshell.

egg white *n.* the white of an egg; albumen.

Eg·ham (ˈɛgəm) *n.* a town in S England, in N Surrey on the River Thames. Pop.: 30 510 (1971).

e·gis (ˈiːdʒɪs) *n.* a rare spelling of **aegis.**

eg·lan·tine (ˈɛglənˌtaɪn) *n.* another name for **sweetbrier.** [C14: from Old French *aiglent,* ultimately from Latin *acus* needle, from *acer* sharp, keen]

Eg·mont[1] (ˈɛgmɒnt) *n.* an extinct volcano in New Zealand, in W central North Island in the **Egmont National Park:** an almost perfect cone. Height: 2478 m (8260 ft.).

Eg·mont[2] (ˈɛgmɒnt) *n.* **La·mo·ral** (ˈlamɔral), Count of Egmont, Prince of Gavre. 1522–68, Flemish statesman and soldier. He attempted to secure limited reforms and religious tolerance in the Spanish government of the Netherlands, refused to join William the Silent's rebellion, but was nevertheless executed for treason by the Duke of Alva.

e·go (ˈiːgəʊ, ˈɛgəʊ) *n., pl.* **e·gos. 1.** the self of an individual person; the conscious subject. **2.** *Psychoanal.* the conscious mind, based on perception of the environment from birth onwards: responsible for modifying the antisocial instincts of the id and itself modified by the conscience (superego). **3.** *Informal.* one's image of oneself; morale: *to boost one's ego.* **4.** *Informal.* egotism; conceit. [C19: from Latin: I]

e·go·cen·tric (ˌiːgəʊˈsɛntrɪk, ˌɛg-) *adj.* **1.** regarding everything only in relation to oneself; self-centred; selfish. **2.** *Philosophy.* **a.** believing that the study of the self should be the starting point in philosophy. **b.** real, valid, or known only as perceived by the individual mind. ~*n.* **3.** a self-centred person; egotist. —ˌ**e·go·cen·ˈtric·i·ty** *n.*

e·go·cen·trism (ˌiːgəʊˈsɛntrɪzəm, ˌɛgəʊ-) *n.* **1.** the condition or fact of being egocentric. **2.** *Psychol.* a stage in a child's development characterized by lack of awareness that other people's points of view differ from his own.

e·go i·deal *n. Psychoanal.* an internal ideal of personal perfection that represents what one wants to be rather than what one ought to be and is derived from one's early relationship with one's parents. See also **superego.**

e·go·ism (ˈiːgəʊˌɪzəm, ˈɛg-) *n.* **1.** concern for one's own interests and welfare. **2.** *Ethics.* the theory that the pursuit of one's own welfare is the highest good. Compare **altruism.** **3.** self-centredness; egotism.

e·go·ist ('iːgəʊɪst, 'ɛg-) *n.* **1.** a person who is preoccupied with his own interests; a selfish person. **2.** a conceited person; egotist. **3.** *Ethics.* a person who lives by the values of egoism. —ˌ**e·go·'is·tic** *or* ˌ**e·go·'is·ti·cal** *adj.* —ˌ**e·go·'is·ti·cal·ly** *adv.*

e·go·ma·ni·a (ˌiːgəʊ'meɪnɪə, ˌɛg-) *n. Psychiatry.* **1.** obsessive love for oneself and regard for one's own needs. **2.** any action dictated by this point of view. —ˌ**e·go·'ma·ni·ˌac** *n.* —**e·go·ma·ni·a·cal** (ˌiːgəʊmə'naɪɪkᵊl, ˌɛg-) *adj.*

e·go·tism ('iːgəˌtɪzəm, 'ɛgə-) *n.* **1.** an inflated sense of self-importance or superiority; self-centredness. **2.** excessive reference to oneself. [C18: from Latin *ego* I + -ISM]

e·go·tist ('iːgətɪst, 'ɛg-) *n.* **1.** a conceited boastful person. **2.** a self-interested person; egoist. —ˌ**e·go·'tis·tic** *or* ˌ**e·go·'tis·ti·cal** *adj.* —ˌ**e·go·'tis·ti·cal·ly** *adv.*

e·go trip *Informal. n.* **1.** something undertaken to boost or draw attention to a person's own image or appraisal of himself. ~*vb.* **e·go-trip, -trips, -trip·ping, -tripped.** (*intr.*) **2.** to act in this way.

e·gre·gious (ɪ'griːdʒəs, -dʒɪəs) *adj.* **1.** outstandingly bad; flagrant: *an egregious lie.* **2.** *Archaic.* distinguished; eminent. [C16: from Latin *ēgregius* outstanding (literally: standing out from the herd), from *ē-* out + *grex* flock, herd] —**e'gre·gious·ly** *adv.* —**e'gre·gious·ness** *n.*

e·gress *n.* ('iːgrɛs) **1.** Also: **egression.** the act of going or coming out; emergence. **2.** a way out, such as a path; exit. **3.** the right or permission to go out or depart. **4.** *Astronomy.* another name for **emersion** (sense 2). ~*vb.* (ɪ'grɛs). **5.** (*intr.*) to go forth; issue. [C16: from Latin *ēgredī* to come forth, depart, from *gradī* to move, step]

e·gret ('iːgrɪt) *n.* any of various wading birds of the genera *Egretta, Hydranassa,* etc., that are similar to herons but usually have a white plumage and, in the breeding season, long feathery plumes (see **aigrette**): family *Ardeidae,* order *Ciconiiformes.* [C15: from Old French *aigrette,* from Old Provençal *aigreta,* from *aigron* heron, of Germanic origin; compare Old High German *heigaro* HERON]

E·gypt ('iːdʒɪpt) *n.* a republic in NE Africa, on the Mediterranean and Red Sea: its history dates back about 5000 years. Occupied by the British from 1882, it became an independent kingdom in 1922 and a republic in 1953. Over 96 per cent of the total area is desert, with the chief areas of habitation and cultivation in the Nile delta and valley. Cotton is the main export. Language: Arabic. Religion: chiefly Sunni Muslim. Currency: pound. Capital: Cairo. Pop.: 38 228 180 (1976). Area: 1 002 000 sq. km (386 900 sq. miles). Official name: **Arab Republic of Egypt.**

Egypt. *abbrev. for* Egyptian.

E·gyp·tian (ɪ'dʒɪpʃən) *adj.* **1.** of, relating to, or characteristic of Egypt, its inhabitants, or their dialect of Arabic. **2.** of, relating to, or characteristic of the ancient Egyptians, their language, or culture. **3.** (of type) having square slab serifs. **4.** *Archaic.* of or relating to the Gypsies. ~*n.* **5.** a native or inhabitant of Egypt. **6.** a member of an indigenous non-Semitic people who established an advanced civilization in Egypt that flourished from the late fourth millennium B.C. **7.** the extinct language of the ancient Egyptians, belonging to the Afro-Asiatic family of languages. It is recorded in hieroglyphic inscriptions, the earliest of which date from before 3000 B.C. It was extinct by the fourth century A.D. See also **Coptic. 8.** a large size of drawing paper. **9.** an archaic name for a **Gypsy.**

E·gyp·tol·o·gy (ˌiːdʒɪp'tɒlədʒɪ) *n.* the study of the archaeology and language of ancient Egypt. —**E·gyp·to·log·i·cal** (ɪˌdʒɪptə'lɒdʒɪkᵊl) *adj.* —ˌ**E·gyp·'tol·o·gist** *n.*

eh (eɪ) *interj.* an exclamation used to express questioning surprise or to seek the repetition or confirmation of a statement or question: *Eh? What did you say?*

EHF *abbrev. for* extremely high frequency.

Eh·ren·burg *or* **E·ren·burg** ('ɛrənbɜːg; *Russian* erɪn'burk) *n.* **Il·ya Gri·gor·ie·vich** (ilj'ja gri'gɔrjɪvitʃ). 1891–1967, Soviet novelist and journalist. His novel *The Thaw* (1954) was the first published in the Soviet Union to deal with repression under Stalin.

Ehr·lich (*German* 'eːrlɪç) *n.* **Paul** (paʊl). 1854–1915, German bacteriologist, noted for his pioneering work in immunology and chemotherapy and for his discovery of a remedy for syphilis: Nobel prize for physiology and medicine 1908.

E.I. *abbrev. for:* **1.** East Indian. **2.** East Indies.

Ei·chen·dorff (*German* 'aɪçᵊnˌdɔrf) *n.* **Jo·seph** ('joːzɛf), Freiherr von Eichendorff. 1788–1857, German poet and novelist, regarded as one of the greatest German romantic lyricists.

Eich·mann (*German* 'aɪçˌman) *n.* **(Karl) A·dolf** ('aːdɔlf). 1902–62, Austrian Nazi official. He escaped to Argentina after World War II, but was captured and executed in Israel as a war criminal.

ei·der *or* **ei·der duck** ('aɪdə) *n.* any of several sea ducks of the genus *Somateria,* esp. *S. mollissima,* and related genera, which occur in the N hemisphere. The male has black and white plumage, and the female is the source of eiderdown. [C18: from Old Norse *æthr;* related to Swedish *ejder,* Dutch, German *Eider*]

ei·der·down ('aɪdəˌdaʊn) *n.* **1.** the breast down of the female eider duck, with which it lines the nest, used for stuffing pillows, quilts, etc. **2.** a thick warm cover for a bed, made of two layers of material enclosing a soft filling. **3.** *U.S.* a warm cotton fabric having a woollen nap.

ei·det·ic (aɪ'dɛtɪk) *adj. Psychol.* **1.** (of visual images, esp. those experienced in childhood) imagined and unreal, but so vivid and sharp that they may be mistaken for reality. **2.** relating to or subject to such imagery. [C20: from Greek *eidētikos,* from *eidos* shape, form] —**ei·'det·i·cal·ly** *adv.*

ei·do·lon (aɪ'dəʊlɒn) *n., pl.* **·la** (-lə) *or* **·lons. 1.** an unsubstantial image; apparition; phantom. **2.** an ideal or idealized figure. [C19: from Greek: phantom, IDOL]

Eif·fel ('aɪfᵊl; *French* ɛ'fɛl) *n.* **A·le·xan·dre Gus·tave** (alɛk'sɑːdr gys'tav). 1832–1923, French engineer.

Eif·fel Tow·er ('aɪfᵊl) *n.* a tower in Paris: designed by A. G. Eiffel; erected for the 1889 Paris Exposition. Height: 295 m (984 ft.), raised in 1959 to 315 m (1052 ft.).

ei·gen- *n. combining form.* characteristic; proper: *eigenvalue.* [from German, literally: own]

ei·gen·fre·quen·cy ('aɪgənˌfriːkwənsɪ) *n., pl.* **·cies.** *Physics.* a resonance frequency of a system.

ei·gen·func·tion ('aɪgənˌfʌŋkʃən) *n. Maths, physics.* a function satisfying a differential equation, esp. an allowed function for a system in wave mechanics.

ei·gen·val·ue ('aɪgənˌvæljuː) *n. Maths, physics.* a solution of a differential equation satisfying given conditions.

Ei·ger (*German* 'aɪgər) *n.* a mountain in central Switzerland, in the Bernese Alps. Height: 3970 m (13 101 ft.).

eight (eɪt) *n.* **1.** the cardinal number that is the sum of one and seven and the product of two and four. See also **number** (sense 1). **2.** a numeral 8, VIII, etc., representing this number. **3.** *Music.* the numeral 8 used as the lower figure in a time signature to indicate that the beat is measured in quavers. **4.** the amount or quantity that is one greater than seven. **5.** something representing, represented by, or consisting of eight units, such as a playing card with eight symbols on it. **6.** *Rowing.* **a.** a racing shell propelled by eight oarsmen. **b.** the crew of such a shell. **7.** Also called: **eight o'clock.** eight hours after noon or midnight. **8. have one over the eight.** *Slang.* to be drunk. **9.** See **figure of eight.** ~*determiner.* **10. a.** amounting to eight. **b.** (*as pronoun*): *I could only find eight.* ~Related prefixes: **octa-, octo-.** [Old English *eahta;* related to Old High German *ahto,* Old Norse *ātta,* Old Irish *ocht,* Latin *octō,* Greek *okto,* Sanskrit *astau*]

eight·een ('eɪ'tiːn) *n.* **1.** the cardinal number that is the sum of ten and eight and the product of two and nine. See also **number** (sense 1). **2.** a numeral 18, XVIII, etc., representing this number. **3.** the amount or quantity that is eight more than ten. **4.** something represented by, representing, or consisting of 18 units. **5.** (*functioning as sing. or pl.*) a team of 18 players in Australian Rules football. ~*determiner.* **6. a.** amounting to eighteen: *eighteen weeks.* **b.** (*as pronoun*): *eighteen of them knew.* [Old English *eahtatēne;* related to Old Norse *attjan,* Old High German *ahtozehan*]

eight·een·mo ('eɪ'tiːnməʊ) *n., pl.* **·mos. 1.** Also called: **octodecimo.** a book size resulting from folding a sheet of paper into 18 leaves or 36 pages. Often written: **18mo, 18°. 2.** a book of this size.

eight·eenth ('eɪ'tiːnθ) *adj.* **1.** (*usually prenominal*) **a.** coming after the seventeenth in numbering or counting order, position, time, etc.; being the ordinal number of *eighteen:* often written 18th. **b.** (*as n.*): *come on the eighteenth.* ~*n.* **2. a.** one of 18 approximately equal parts of something. **b.** (*as modifier*): *an eighteenth part.* **3.** the fraction that is equal to one divided by 18 (1/18).

eight·fold ('eɪtˌfəʊld) *adj.* **1.** equal to or having eight times as many or as much. **2.** composed of eight parts. ~*adv.* **3.** by or up to eight times as much.

eighth (eɪtθ) *adj.* **1.** (*usually prenominal*) **a.** coming after the seventh and before the ninth in numbering or counting order, position, time, etc.; being the ordinal number of *eight:* often written 8th. **b.** (*as n.*): *the eighth in line.* ~*n.* **2. a.** one of eight equal or nearly equal parts of an object, quantity, measurement, etc. **b.** (*as modifier*): *an eighth part.* **3.** the fraction equal to one divided by eight (1/8). **4.** another word for **octave.** ~*adv.* **5.** Also: **eighthly.** after the seventh person, position, event, etc.

eighth note *n.* the usual U.S. name for **quaver** (sense 4).

eight·i·eth ('eɪtɪɪθ) *adj.* **1.** (*usually prenominal*) **a.** being the ordinal number of *eighty* in numbering or counting order, position, time, etc.: often written 80th. **b.** (*as n.*): *the eightieth in succession.* ~*n.* **2. a.** one of 80 approximately equal parts of something. **b.** (*as modifier*): *an eightieth part.* **3.** the fraction equal to one divided by 80 (1/80).

eight·some reel ('eɪtsəm) *n.* a Scottish dance for eight people.

eight·vo ('eɪtvəʊ) *n., pl.* **·vos.** *Bookbinding.* another word for **octavo.**

eight·y ('eɪtɪ) *n., pl.* **·ies. 1.** the cardinal number that is the product of ten and eight. See also **number** (sense 1). **2.** a numeral 80, LXXX, etc., representing this number. **3.** (*pl.*) the numbers 80-89, esp. the 80th to the 89th year of a person's life or of a particular century. **4.** the amount or quantity that is eight times as big as ten. **5.** something represented by, representing, or consisting of 80 units. ~*determiner.* **6. a.** amounting to eighty: *eighty pages of nonsense.* **b.** (*as pronoun*): *eighty are expected.* [Old English *eahtatig;* related to Old Frisian *achtig,* Old High German *ahtozug*]

Eijk·man (*Dutch* 'ɛjkman) *n.* **Chris·ti·aan** ('kriːstiːˌaːn). 1858–1930, Dutch physician, who discovered that beriberi is caused by nutritional deficiency: Nobel prize for medicine 1929.

ei·kon ('aɪkɒn) *n.* a variant spelling of **icon.**

Ei·lat (eɪ'lɑːt) *n.* a port in S Israel, on the Gulf of Aqaba: Israel's only outlet to the Red Sea. Pop.: 12 800 (1972).

Eind·ho·ven ('aɪntˌhəʊvᵊn, *Dutch* 'ɛjntˌhoːvə) *n.* a city in the SE Netherlands, in North Brabant province: radio and electrical industry. Pop.: 191 942 (1974 est.).

ein+korn ('aɪnˌkɔːn) *n.* a variety of wheat, *Triticum monococcum*, of Greece and SW Asia, having pale red kernels, and cultivated in hilly regions as grain for horses. [German, literally: one kernel]

Ein·stein ('aɪnstaɪn) *n.* **Al·bert.** 1879–1955, U.S. physicist and mathematician, born in Germany. He formulated the special theory of relativity (1905) and the general theory of relativity (1916); he is noted also for his work for world peace: Nobel prize for physics 1921. —**Ein+'stein+i·an** *adj.*

ein+stein+i·um (aɪn'staɪnɪəm) *n.* a metallic transuranic element artificially produced from plutonium. Symbol: Es; atomic no.: 99; half-life of most stable isotope, ^{254}Es: 276 days. [C20: New Latin, named after Albert EINSTEIN]

Ein·stein shift *n. Astron.* a small displacement towards the red in the spectra, caused by the interaction between the radiation and the gravitational field of a massive body, such as the sun.

Ein·stein's law *n.* **1.** the principle that mass (m) and energy (E) are equivalent according to the equation $E = mc^2$, where c is the velocity of light. **2.** the principle that the maximum energy of a photoelectron is $h\nu - \Phi$, where ν is the frequency of the incident radiation, h is the Planck constant, and Φ is the work function.

Eir·e ('ɛərə) *n.* the Gaelic name for (the Republic of) **Ireland.** [from Old Irish *Ériu*]

ei·ren+ic (aɪ'riːnɪk) *adj.* a variant spelling of **irenic.**

ei·re·ni+con *or* **i·re·ni+con** (aɪ'riːnɪˌkɒn) *n.* a proposition that attempts to harmonize conflicting viewpoints. [C19: from Greek, from *eirēnikos* of or concerning peace, from *eirēnē* peace]

eis+e·ge·sis (ˌaɪsə'dʒiːsɪs) *n., pl.* **·ses** (-siːz) the interpretation of a text, esp. a biblical text, using one's own ideas. Compare **exegesis.** [C19: from Greek *eis* into, in + *-egesis*, as in EXEGESIS]

Ei·sen+ach (*German* 'aɪzənax) *n.* a city in SW East Germany, in Erfurt district. Pop.: 50 674 (1972 est.).

Ei·sen·how·er ('aɪzənˌhauə) *n.* **Dwight Da·vid,** nickname *Ike.* 1890–1969, U.S. general and Republican statesman; Supreme Commander of the Allied Expeditionary Force (1943–45) and 34th president of the U.S. (1953–61). He commanded Allied forces in Europe and North Africa (1942), directed the invasion of Italy (1943), and was Supreme Commander of the combined land forces of NATO (1950–52).

Ei·sen+stadt (*German* 'aɪzənˌʃtat) *n.* a town in E Austria, capital of Burgenland province: Hungarian until 1921. Pop.: 10 059 (1971).

Ei·sen·stein ('aɪzənˌstaɪn; *Russian* ejzɪn'ʃtjejn) *n.* **Ser·gei Mi·khai·lo·vich** (sɪr'gjej mi'xajləvitʃ). 1898–1948, Soviet film director. His films include *Battleship Potemkin* (1925), *Alexander Nevsky* (1938), and *Ivan the Terrible* (1944).

Eisk *or* **Eysk** (*Russian* jejsk) *n.* variant spellings of **Yeisk.**

ei·stedd+fod (aɪ'stɛdfəd; *Welsh* aɪ'stɛðvɒd, eɪ-) *n., pl.* **+fods** *or* **+fod·au** (*Welsh* aɪˌstɛð'vɒdaɪ, ˌeɪstɛð-). any of a number of annual festivals in Wales, esp. the **Royal National Eisteddfod,** in which competitions are held in music, poetry, drama, and the fine arts. [C19: from Welsh, literally: session, from *eistedd* to sit (from *sedd* seat) + *-fod*, from *bod* to be] —**ˌei·stedd+'fod+ic** *adj.*

ei·ther ('aɪðə) *determiner.* **1. a.** one or the other (of two): *either coat will do.* **b.** (*as pronoun*): *either is acceptable.* **2.** both one and the other: *there were ladies at either end of the table.* ~*conj.* **3.** (*coordinating*) used preceding two or more possibilities joined by "*or*": *you may have either cheese or a sweet.* ~*adv.* (*sentence modifier*) **4.** (*used with a negative*) used to indicate that the clause immediately preceding is a partial reiteration of a previous clause: *John isn't a liar, but he isn't exactly honest either.* [Old English *ǣgther*, short for *ǣghwæther* each of two; related to Old Frisian *ēider*, Old High German *ēogihweder*; see EACH, WHETHER]

Usage. *Either* is followed by a singular verb in good usage: *either is good; either of these books is useful.* Careful writers and speakers are cautious in using *either* to mean *both* or *each* because of the possible ambiguity, as in the following sentence: *a ship could be moored on either side of the channel.* Agreement between the verb and its subject in *either... or...* constructions follows the pattern given for *neither... nor...* See at **neither.**

ei·ther-or *adj.* presenting an unavoidable need to choose between two alternatives: *an either-or situation.*

e·jac·u·late *vb.* (ɪ'dʒækjʊˌleɪt). **1.** to eject or discharge (semen) in orgasm. **2.** (*tr.*) to utter abruptly; blurt out. ~*n.* (ɪ'dʒækjʊlɪt). **3.** another word for **semen.** [C16: from Latin *ējaculārī* to hurl out, from *jaculum* javelin, from *jacere* to throw] —**e·'jac·u+ˌla+tor** *n.*

e·jac·u+la·tion (ɪˌdʒækjʊ'leɪʃən) *n.* **1.** an abrupt emphatic utterance or exclamation. **2.** a discharge of semen. —**e·'jac·u+la·to·ry** *or* **e·'jac·u·la+tive** *adj.*

e·ject (ɪ'dʒɛkt) *vb.* **1.** (*tr.*) to drive or force out; expel or emit. **2.** (*tr.*) to compel (a person) to leave; evict; dispossess. **3.** (*tr.*) to dismiss, as from office. **4.** (*intr.*) to leave an aircraft rapidly, using an ejection seat or capsule. **5.** (*tr.*) *Psychiatry.* to attribute (one's own motivations and characteristics) to others. [C15: from Latin *ejicere*, from *jacere* to throw] —**e·'jec+tion** *n.*

e·jec+ta (ɪ'dʒɛktə) *pl. n.* matter thrown out by an erupting volcano. [Latin, literally: (things) ejected; see EJECT]

e·jec+tion seat *or* **e·jec+tor seat** *n.* a seat, esp. as fitted to military aircraft, that is fired by a cartridge or rocket to eject the occupant from the aircraft in an emergency.

e·jec+tive (ɪ'dʒɛktɪv) *adj.* **1.** relating to or causing ejection. **2.** *Phonetics.* (of a plosive or fricative consonant, as in some African languages) pronounced with a glottal stop. ~*n.* **3.** *Phonetics.* an ejective consonant. —**e·'jec+tive+ly** *adv.*

e·ject+ment (ɪ'dʒɛktmənt) *n.* **1.** *Property law.* (formerly) an action brought by a wrongfully dispossessed owner seeking to recover possession of his land. **2.** the act of ejecting or state of being ejected; dispossession.

e·jec+tor (ɪ'dʒɛktə) *n.* **1.** a person or thing that ejects. **2.** the mechanism in a firearm that ejects the empty cartridge or shell after firing.

E·ka+te+rin+burg (*Russian* jɪkətɪrim'burk) *n.* a variant spelling of **Yekaterinburg.**

E·ka+te+ri+no+dar (*Russian* jɪkətɪrina'dar) *n.* the former name (until 1920) of **Krasnodar.**

E·ka+te+ri+no+slav (*Russian* jɪkətɪrina'slaf) *n.* the former name (1787–96, 1802–1926) of **Dnepropetrovsk.**

eke[1] (iːk) *vb.* (*tr.*) *Archaic.* to increase, enlarge, or lengthen. [Old English *eacan*; related to Old Norse *auka* to increase, Latin *augēre* to increase]

eke[2] (iːk) *sentence connector. Archaic.* also; moreover. [Old English *eac*; related to Old Norse, Gothic *auk* also, Old High German *ouh*, Latin *autem* but, *aut* or]

eke out *vb.* (*tr., adv.*) **1.** to make (a supply) last, esp. by frugal use: *they eked out what little food was left.* **2.** to support (existence) with difficulty and effort. **3.** to add to (something insufficient), esp. with effort: *to eke out an income with evening work.*

e·kis·tics (ɪ'kɪstɪks) *n.* the science or study of human settlements. [C20: from Greek *oikistikos* of or concerning settlements, from *oikizein* to settle (a colony), from *oikos* a house] —**e·'kis·ti+cal** *or* **e·'kis·tic** *adj.* —**ˌe·kis+'ti·cian** *n.*

el (ɛl) *n. Informal.* a shortened form of **elevated railway.**

El Aai·ún (ɛl aɪ'juːn) *n.* a city in Western Sahara: the former capital of Spanish Sahara; port facilities begun in 1967 at **Playa de El Aaiún,** 20 km (12 miles) away, following the discovery of rich phosphate deposits. Pop.: 18 212 (1970 est.).

e·lab·o+rate *adj.* (ɪ'læbərɪt). **1.** planned or executed with care and exactness; detailed. **2.** marked by complexity, ornateness, or detail. ~*vb.* (ɪ'læbəˌreɪt). **3.** (*intr.*; usually foll. by *on* or *upon*) to add information or detail (to an account); expand (upon). **4.** (*tr.*) to work out in detail; develop. **5.** (*tr.*) to make more complicated or ornate. **6.** (*tr.*) to produce by careful labour; create. **7.** (*tr.*) *Physiol.* to change (food or simple substances) into more complex substances for use in the body. [C16: from Latin *ēlabōrāre* to take pains, from *labōrāre* to toil] —**e·'lab·o·rate+ly** *adv.* —**e·'lab·o·rate+ness** *n.* —**e·ˌlab·o+'ra·tion** *n.* —**e·lab·o·ra+tive** (ɪ'læbərətɪv) *adj.* —**e·'lab·o+ˌra+tor** *n.*

el+ae·op+tene (ˌɛlɪ'ɒptiːn) *n.* a variant spelling of **eleoptene.**

El·a·gab·a·lus (ˌɛlə'gæbələs, ˌiːlə-) *n.* a variant of **Heliogabalus.**

E·laine (ɪ'leɪn) *n. Arthurian legend.* **1.** the half sister of Arthur and mother by him of Modred. **2.** the mother of Sir Galahad.

El Al·a+mein *or* **Al·a+mein** (ɛl 'æləˌmeɪn) *n.* a village on the N coast of Egypt, about 112 km (70 miles) west of Alexandria: scene of a decisive Allied victory over the Germans (1942).

E·lam ('iːləm) *n.* an ancient kingdom east of the River Tigris: established before 4000 B.C.; probably inhabited by a non-Semitic people.

E·lam+ite ('iːləˌmaɪt) *n.* **1.** an inhabitant of the ancient kingdom of Elam. **2.** Also called: **Elamitic, Susian.** the extinct language of this people, of no known relationship, recorded in cuneiform inscriptions dating from the 25th to the 4th centuries B.C. ~*adj.* **3.** of or relating to Elam, its people, or their language.

é·lan (eɪ'lɑːn, eɪ'læn; *French* e'lɑ̃) *n.* a combination of style and vigour: *he performed the concerto with élan.* [C19: from French, from *élancer* to throw forth, ultimately from Latin *lancea* LANCE]

e·land ('iːlənd) *n.* **1.** a large spiral-horned antelope, *Taurotragus oryx*, inhabiting bushland in eastern and southern Africa. It has a dewlap and a hump on the shoulders and is light brown with vertical white stripes. **2. giant eland.** a similar but larger animal, *T. derbianus*, living in wooded areas of central and W Africa. [C18: via Afrikaans from Dutch *eland* elk; related to Old Slavonic *jeleni* stag, Greek *ellos* fawn]

é·lan vi·tal *French.* (elã vi'tal) *n.* a creative principle held by Henri Bergson to be present in all organisms and responsible for evolution. Compare **Bergsonism.** [literally: vital impetus]

el·a+pid ('ɛləpɪd) *n.* **1.** any venomous snake of the mostly tropical family *Elapidae*, having fixed poison fangs at the front of the upper jaw and including the cobras, coral snakes, and mambas. ~*adj.* **2.** of, relating to, or belonging to the *Elapidae.* [C19: from New Latin *Elapidae*, from Medieval Greek *elaps*, *elops* a fish, sea serpent; perhaps related to *lepis* scale]

e·lapse (ɪ'læps) *vb.* (*intr.*) (of time) to pass by. [C17: from Latin *ēlābī* to slip away, from *lābī* to slip, glide]

e·las+mo+branch (ɪ'læsməˌbræŋk, ɪ'læz-) *n.* **1.** any cartilaginous fish of the subclass *Elasmobranchii* (or *Selachii*), which includes the sharks, rays, dogfish, and skates. ~*adj.* **2.** of, relating to, or belonging to the *Elasmobranchii.* ~Also called: **selachian.** [C19: from New Latin *elasmobranchii*, from Greek *elasmos* metal plate + *brankhia* gills]

e·las+mo+saur (ɪ'læzməˌsɔː) *n.* a very long-necked extinct marine reptile: a type of plesiosaur. [C19: from Greek *elasmos* metal plate + *sauros* lizard]

e·las+tance (ɪ'læstəns) *n. Physics.* the reciprocal of capacitance. It is measured in reciprocal farads (darafs).

e·las+tic (ɪ'læstɪk) *adj.* **1.** (of a body or material) capable of returning to its original shape after compression, expansion, stretching, or other deformation. **2.** capable of adapting to change: *an elastic schedule.* **3.** quick to recover from fatigue, dejection, etc.; buoyant. **4.** springy or resilient: *an elastic walk.* **5.** (of gases) capable of expanding spontaneously. **6.** *Physics.* (of collisions) involving no overall change in translational kinetic energy. **7.** made of elastic. ~*n.* **8.** tape, cord, or fabric containing interwoven strands of flexible rubber or similar substance allowing it to stretch and return to its original shape. **9.** *Chiefly U.S.* something made of elastic, such as a garter or a rubber band. [C17: from New Latin *elasticus* impulsive, from Greek *elastikos,* from *elaunein* to beat, drive] —**e'las·ti·cal·ly** *adv.*

e·las·ti·cate (ɪ'læstɪˌkeɪt) *vb.* (*tr.*) to insert elastic sections or thread into (a fabric or garment): *an elasticated waistband.* —**eˌlas·ti·'ca·tion** *n.*

e·las·tic band *n.* another name for **rubber band.**

e·las·tic·i·ty (ˌɪlæ'stɪsɪtɪ, ˌi:læ-) *n.* **1.** the property of a body or substance that enables it to resume its original shape or size when a distorting force is removed. See also **elastic limit. 2.** the state or quality of being elastic; flexibility or buoyancy.

e·las·ti·cize *or* **e·las·ti·cise** (ɪ'læstɪˌsaɪz) *vb.* **1.** to make elastic. **2.** another word for **elasticate.**

e·las·tic lim·it *n.* the greatest stress that can be applied to a material without causing permanent deformation.

e·las·tic mod·u·lus *n.* another name for **modulus of elasticity.**

e·las·tin (ɪ'læstɪn) *n. Biochem.* a fibrous scleroprotein constituting the major part of elastic tissue, such as the walls of arteries. [C19: from ELASTIC + -IN]

e·las·to·mer (ɪ'læstəmə) *n.* any material, such as natural or synthetic rubber, that is able to resume its original shape when a deforming force is removed. [C20: from ELASTIC + -MER] —**e·las·to·mer·ic** (ɪˌlæstə'mɛrɪk) *adj.*

E·las·to·plast (ɪ'læstəˌplɑ:st) *n. Trademark.* a gauze surgical dressing backed by adhesive tape.

E·lat *or* **E·lath** (eɪ'lɑ:t) *n.* variant spellings of **Eilat.**

e·late (ɪ'leɪt) *vb.* (*tr.*) to fill with high spirits, exhilaration, pride or optimism. [C16: from Latin *efferre* to bear away, from *ferre* to carry] —**e·'lat·ed·ly** *adv.* —**e·'lat·ed·ness** *n.*

el·a·ter ('ɛlətə) *n.* **1.** an elaterid beetle. **2.** *Botany.* a spirally thickened filament, occurring in liverwort capsules and horsetails, thought to aid dispersal of spores. [C17: via New Latin from Greek: driver, from *elaunein* to beat, drive; compare ELASTIC]

e·lat·er·id (ɪ'lætərɪd) *n.* **1.** any of the beetles constituting the widely distributed family *Elateridae* (click beetles). The group includes the wireworms and certain fireflies. ~*adj.* **2.** of, relating to, or belonging to the family *Elateridae.* [C19: from New Latin *Elateridae,* from ELATER]

e·lat·er·in (ɪ'lætərɪn) *n.* a white crystalline substance found in elaterium, used as a purgative. [C19: from ELATERIUM + -IN]

e·lat·er·ite (ɪ'lætəˌraɪt) *n.* a dark brown naturally occurring bitumen resembling rubber.

el·a·te·ri·um (ˌɛlə'tɪərɪəm) *n.* a greenish sediment prepared from the juice of the squirting cucumber, used as a purgative. [C16: from Latin, from Greek *elatērion* squirting cucumber, from *elatērios* purgative, from *elaunein* to drive]

e·la·tion (ɪ'leɪʃən) *n.* joyfulness or exaltation of spirit, as from success, pleasure, or relief; high spirits.

e·la·tive ('i:ləˌtɪv) *adj.* **1.** (in the grammar of Finnish and other languages) denoting a case of nouns expressing a relation of motion or direction, usually translated by the English prepositions *out of* or *away from.* Compare **illative** (sense 3). ~*n.* **2. a.** the elative case. **b.** an elative word or speech element. [C19: from Latin *ēlātus,* past participle of *efferre* to carry out; see ELATE]

E lay·er *n.* another name for **E region.**

El·ba ('ɛlbə) *n.* a mountainous island off the W coast of Italy, in the Mediterranean: Napoleon Bonaparte's first place of exile (1814–15). Pop.: 27 543 (1971). Area: 223 sq. km (86 sq. miles).

El·be (ɛlb; *German* 'ɛlbə) *n.* a river in central Europe, rising in N Czechoslovakia and flowing generally northwest through East and West Germany to the North Sea at Hamburg. Length: 1165 km (724 miles). Czech name: **Labe.**

El·bert ('ɛlbət) *n.* **Mount.** a mountain in central Colorado, in the Sawatch range. Height: 4329 m (14 431 ft.).

El·bląg (*Polish* 'ɛlblɔŋk) *n.* a port in N Poland: metallurgical industries. Pop.: 92 600 (1972 est.). German name: **El·bing** ('ɛlbɪŋ).

el·bow ('ɛlbəʊ) *n.* **1.** the joint between the upper arm and the forearm, formed by the junction of the radius and ulna with the humerus. **2.** the corresponding joint or bone of birds or mammals. **3.** the part of a garment that covers the elbow. **4.** something resembling an elbow, such as a sharp bend in a road or river. **5. at one's elbow.** within easy reach. **6. out at elbow(s).** ragged or impoverished. **7. up to the elbows with** *or* **in.** busily occupied with; deeply immersed in. ~*vb.* **8.** to make (one's way) by shoving, jostling, etc. **9.** (*tr.*) to knock or shove with or as if with the elbow. [Old English *elnboga;* see ELL², BOW²; related to Old Norse *olbogi,* Old High German *elinbogo*]

el·bow grease *n. Informal.* vigorous physical labour.

el·bow·room ('ɛlbəʊˌru:m, -ˌrʊm) *n.* sufficient scope to move or function.

El·brus (ɪl'bru:s) *n.* a mountain in the S Soviet Union, in the Caucasus Mountains, with two extinct volcanic peaks: the highest mountain in Europe. Height: 5633 m (18 476 ft.).

El·burz Moun·tains (ɛl'bʊəz) *pl. n.* a mountain range in N Iran, parallel to the SW and S shores of the Caspian Sea. Highest peak: 5604 m (18 376 ft.).

El Cap·i·tan (ɛl ˌkapɪ'tæn) *n.* a mountain in E central California, in the Sierra Nevada: a monolith with a precipice rising over 1100 m (3600 ft.) above the floor of the Yosemite Valley. Height: 2306 m (7564 ft.).

El Cid Cam·pe·a·dor (*Spanish* ˌkampea'ðor) *n.* See (El) **Cid.**

eld (ɛld) *n. Archaic.* **1.** old age. **2.** olden days; antiquity. [Old English *eldu;* related to Old Norse *elli;* see OLD]

el·der[1] ('ɛldə) *adj.* **1.** born earlier; senior. Compare **older. 2.** (in piquet and similar card games) denoting or relating to the nondealer (the **elder hand**), who has certain advantages in the play. **3.** *Archaic.* **a.** prior in rank, position, or office. **b.** of a previous time; former. ~*n.* **4.** an older person; one's senior. **5.** *Anthropol.* a senior member of a tribe who has influence or authority. **6.** (in certain Protestant Churches) a lay office having teaching, pastoral, or administrative functions. **7.** another word for **presbyter.** [Old English *eldra,* comparative of *eald* OLD; related to Old Norse *ellri,* Old High German *altiro,* Gothic *althiza*] —**'el·der·ˌship** *n.*

el·der[2] ('ɛldə) *n.* **1.** Also called: **elderberry.** any of various caprifoliaceous shrubs or small trees of the genus *Sambucus,* having clusters of small white flowers and red, purple, or black berry-like fruits. **2.** any of various unrelated plants, such as box elder and marsh elder. ~Compare **alder.** [Old English *ellern;* related to Old Norse *elrir,* Old High German *erlīn,* Old Slavonic *jelĭcha,* Latin *alnus*]

eld·er·ber·ry ('ɛldəˌbɛrɪ) *n., pl.* **-ries. 1.** the berry-like fruit of the elder, used for making wines, jellies, etc. **2.** another name for **elder**[2] (sense 1).

el·der·ly ('ɛldəlɪ) *adj.* (of people) **a.** quite old; past middle age. **b.** (*as collective n.* preceded by *the*): *the elderly.* —**'el·der·li·ness** *n.*

el·der states·man *n.* an old, experienced, and eminent person, esp. a politician, whose advice is often sought.

eld·est ('ɛldɪst) *adj.* being the oldest, esp. the oldest surviving child of the same parents. [Old English *eldesta,* superlative of *eald* OLD]

ELDO ('ɛldəʊ) *acronym for* European Launcher Development Organization.

El Do·ra·do (ɛl dɒ'rɑ:dəʊ; *Spanish* el do'raðo) *n.* **1.** a fabled city in South America, rich in treasure and sought by Spanish explorers in the 16th century. **2.** Also: **eldorado.** any place of great riches or fabulous opportunity. [C16: from Spanish, literally: the gilded (place)]

el·dritch *or* **el·drich** ('ɛldrɪtʃ) *adj. Poetic.* unearthly; weird. [C16: perhaps from Old English *ælf* ELF + *rīce* realm; see RICH]

E·le·a ('i:lɪə) *n.* (in ancient Italy) a Greek colony on the Tyrrhenian coast of Lucana.

El·ea·nor of Aq·ui·taine ('ɛlɪnə, -ˌnɔ:) *n.* ?1122–1204, queen of France (1137–52) by her marriage to Louis VII and queen of England (1154–89) by her marriage to Henry II; mother of the English kings Richard I and John.

El·e·at·ic (ˌɛlɪ'ætɪk) *adj.* **1.** denoting or relating to a school of philosophy founded in Elea in Greece in the 6th century B.C. by Xenophanus, Parmenides, and Xeno. It held that one pure immutable Being is the only object of knowledge and that information obtained by the senses is illusory. ~*n.* **2.** a follower of this school. —**El·e·at·i·cism** (ˌɛlɪ'ætɪsɪzəm) *n.*

el·e·cam·pane (ˌɛlɪkæm'peɪn) *n.* a perennial flowering plant, *Inula helenium,* of Europe, Asia, and North America having large hairy leaves and narrow yellow petals: family *Compositae* (composites). [C16: from Medieval Latin *enula campāna,* from *enula* (from Greek *helenion*) + *campānus* of the field]

e·lect (ɪ'lɛkt) *vb.* **1.** (*tr.*) to choose (someone) to be (a representative or a public official) by voting: *they elected him Mayor.* **2.** to select; choose: *to elect to die rather than surrender.* **3.** (*tr.*) (of God) to select or predestine for the grace of salvation. ~*adj.* **4.** (*immediately postpositive*) voted into office but not yet installed: *the president elect.* **5. a.** chosen or choice; selected or elite. **b.** (*as collective n.* preceded by *the*): *the elect.* **6.** *Theol.* **a.** selected or predestined by God to receive salvation; chosen. **b.** (*as collective n.* preceded by *the*): *the elect.* [C15: from Latin *ēligere* to select, from *legere* to choose]

elect. *or* **elec.** *abbrev. for:* **1.** electric(al). **2.** electricity.

e·lec·tion (ɪ'lɛkʃən) *n.* **1.** the selection by vote of a person or persons from among candidates for a position, esp. a political office. **2.** a public vote on an official proposition. **3.** the act or an instance of choosing. **4.** *Theol.* **a.** the doctrine of Calvin that God chooses certain individuals for salvation without reference to their faith or works. **b.** the doctrine of Arminius and others that God chooses for salvation those who, by grace, persevere in faith and works.

e·lec·tion·eer (ɪˌlɛkʃə'nɪə) *vb.* (*intr.*) **1.** to be active in a political election or campaign. ~*n.* **2.** a person who engages in this activity. —**eˌlec·tion·'eer·ing** *n., adj.*

e·lec·tive (ɪ'lɛktɪv) *adj.* **1.** of or based on selection by vote: *elective procedure.* **2.** selected by vote: *an elective official.* **3.** having the power to elect. **4.** open to choice; optional: *an elective course of study.* —**e·'lec·tive·ly** *adv.* —**e·lec·tiv·i·ty** (ˌi:lɛk'tɪvɪtɪ) *or* **e·'lec·tive·ness** *n.*

e·lec·tor (ɪ'lɛktə) *n.* **1.** someone who is eligible to vote in the election of a government. **2.** (*often cap.*) a member of the U.S. electoral college. **3.** (*often cap.*) (in the Holy Roman Empire) any of the German princes entitled to take part in the election of a new emperor. —**e·'lec·tor·ˌship** *n.* —**e·'lec·tress** *fem. n.*

e·lec·tor·al (ɪ'lɛktərəl) *adj.* relating to or consisting of electors. —**e·'lec·tor·al·ly** *adv.*

e·lec·to·ral col·lege *n.* **1.** (*often cap.*) *U.S.* a body of electors chosen by the voters who formally elect the president and vice-president. **2.** any body of electors.

e·lec·tor·ate (ɪ'lɛktərɪt) *n.* **1.** the body of all qualified voters. **2.** the rank, position, or territory of an elector of the Holy Roman

Empire. **3.** *Austral.* the area represented by a Member of Parliament.

E·lec·tra (ɪˈlɛktrə) *n. Greek myth.* the daughter of Agamemnon and Clytemnestra. She persuaded her brother Orestes to avenge their father by killing his murderess Clytemnestra and her lover Aegisthus.

E·lec·tra com+plex *n. Psychoanal.* the sexual attachment of a female child to her father. See also **penis envy.**

e·lec+tret (ɪˈlɛktrət) *n.* a permanently polarized dielectric material; its electric field is similar to the magnetic field of a permanent magnet. [C20: from *electr(icity + magn)et*]

e·lec+tric (ɪˈlɛktrɪk) *adj.* **1.** of, derived from, produced by, producing, transmitting, or powered by electricity: *electric current; an electric cord; an electric blanket; an electric fence; an electric fire.* **2.** (of a musical instrument) amplified electronically: *an electric guitar; an electric mandolin.* **3.** very tense or exciting; emotionally charged: *an electric atmosphere.* ~*n.* **4.** *Informal.* an electric train, car, etc. **5.** *Brit., not standard.* electricity or electrical power. [C17: from New Latin *electricus* amber-like (because friction causes amber to become charged), from Latin *ēlectrum* amber, from Greek *ēlektron,* of obscure origin]

Usage. See at **electronic.**

e·lec+tri+cal (ɪˈlɛktrɪkᵊl) *adj.* of, relating to, or concerned with electricity. **—e·ˈlec+tri+cal+ly** *adv.* **—e·ˈlec+tri+cal+ness** *n.*

Usage. See at **electronic.**

e·lec+tri+cal en+gi+neer+ing *n.* the branch of engineering concerned with the practical applications of electricity. **—e·lec+tri+cal en+gi+neer** *n.*

e·lec+tric blue *n., adj.* **a.** a strong metallic blue colour. **b.** (*as adj.*): *an electric-blue evening dress.*

e·lec+tric chair *n.* (in the U.S.) **a.** an electrified chair for executing criminals. **b.** (usually preceded by *the*) execution by this method.

e·lec+tric charge *n.* another name for **charge** (sense 25).

e·lec+tric con+stant *n.* the permittivity of free space, which has the value 8.854 185 × 10^{-12} farad per metre. Symbol: ϵ_0 Also called: **absolute permittivity.**

e·lec+tric cur+rent *n.* another name for **current** (sense 8).

e·lec+tric eel *n.* an eel-like freshwater cyprinoid fish, *Electrophorus electricus,* of N South America, having electric organs in the body: family *Electrophoridae.*

e·lec+tric eye *n.* **1.** another name for **photocell. 2.** Also called: **magic eye.** a miniature cathode-ray tube in some radio receivers, on the screen of which a pattern is displayed in order to assist tuning.

e·lec+tric field *n.* a field of force surrounding a charged particle within which another charged particle experiences a force. Compare **magnetic field.**

e·lec+tric field strength *n.* the strength or intensity of an electric field at any point, usually measured in volts per metre. Symbol: ***E***

e·lec+tric fur+nace *n.* any furnace in which the heat is provided by an electric current.

e·lec+tric gui+tar *n.* an electrically amplified guitar, used mainly in pop music. Compare **acoustic guitar.**

e·lec+tric hare *n.* (in greyhound racing) a model of a hare, mounted on an electrified rail, which the dogs chase.

e·lec+tri+cian (ɪlɛkˈtrɪʃən, ˌiːlɛk-) *n.* a person whose occupation is the installation, maintenance, and repair of electrical devices.

e·lec+tric+i·ty (ɪlɛkˈtrɪsɪtɪ, ˌiːlɛk-) *n.* **1.** a form of energy associated with stationary or moving electrons, protons, or other charged particles. **2.** the science concerned with electricity. **3.** an electric current or charge: *a motor powered by electricity.* **4.** emotional tension or excitement, esp. between or among people.

e·lec+tric nee+dle *n.* a surgical instrument for cutting tissue by the application of a high-frequency current.

e·lec+tric or+gan *n.* **1.** *Music.* **a.** a pipe organ operated by electrical means. **b.** another name for **electronic organ. 2.** a small group of modified muscle cells on the body of certain fishes, such as the electric eel, that gives an electric shock to any animal touching them.

e·lec+tric po+ten+tial *n.* **a.** the work required to transfer a unit positive electric charge from an infinite distance to a given point. **b.** the potential difference between the point and some other reference point. Symbol: *V* or ϕ Sometimes shortened to **potential.**

e·lec+tric ray *n.* any ray of the order *Torpediniformes,* of tropical and temperate seas, having a flat rounded body with an electric organ in each of the fins, close to the head.

e·lec+tric shock *n.* the physiological reaction, characterized by pain and muscular spasm, to the passage of an electric current through the body. It can affect the respiratory system and heart rhythm. Sometimes shortened to **shock.**

e·lec+tric storm *n.* a violent atmospheric disturbance in which the air is highly charged with static electricity, causing a storm. Compare **thunderstorm.**

e·lec+tri+fy (ɪˈlɛktrɪˌfaɪ) *vb.* **+fies, +fy+ing, +fied.** (*tr.*) **1.** to adapt or equip (a system, device, etc.) for operation by electrical power. **2.** to charge with or subject to electricity. **3.** to startle or excite intensely; shock or thrill. **—e·ˈlec+tri+ˌfi+a·ble** *adj.* **—e·ˌlec+tri+fi+ˈca+tion** *n.* **—e·ˈlec+tri+ˌfi+er** *n.*

e·lec+tro (ɪˈlɛktrəʊ) *n., pl.* **+tros.** short for **electroplate** or **electrotype.**

e·lec·tro- *or sometimes before a vowel* **e·lectr-** *combining form.* **1.** electric or electrically: *electrocardiograph; electrocute.* **2.** electrolytic: *electroanalysis.* [from New Latin, from Latin *ēlectrum* amber, from Greek *ēlektron*]

e·lec+tro+a·cous+tics (ɪˌlɛktrəʊəˈkuːstɪks) *n.* (*functioning as sing.*) the branch of technology concerned with the interconversion of electrical and acoustic energy, as by a transducer. **—e·ˌlec+tro+a·ˈcous+tic** *or* **e·ˌlec+tro+a·ˈcous+ti+cal** *adj.* **—e·ˌlec+tro+a·ˈcous+ti+cal+ly** *adv.*

e·lec+tro+a·nal·y+sis (ɪˌlɛktrəʊəˈnælɪsɪs) *n.* chemical analysis by electrolysis or electrodeposition. **—e·lec+tro+an·a+lyt·ic** (ɪˌlɛktrəʊˌænəˈlɪtɪk) *or* **e·ˌlec+tro+ˌan·a+ˈlyt·i+cal** *adj.*

e·lec+tro+car+di·o+gram (ɪˌlɛktrəʊˈkɑːdɪəʊˌgræm) *n.* a tracing of the electric currents that initiate the heartbeat, used to diagnose possible heart disorders. Abbrev.: **ECG**

e·lec+tro+car+di·o+graph (ɪˌlɛktrəʊˈkɑːdɪəʊˌgrɑːf, -ˌgræf) *n.* an instrument for recording the electrical activity of the heart. Abbrev.: **E.C.G. —e·ˌlec+tro+ˌcar+di·o+ˈgraph+ic** *or* **e·ˌlec+tro+ˌcar+di·o+ˈgraph·i+cal** *adj.* **—e·lec+tro+car+di+og+ra+phy** (ɪˌlɛktrəʊˌkɑːdɪˈɒgrəfɪ) *n.*

e·lec+tro+chem·i+cal se+ries *n.* another name for **electromotive series.**

e·lec+tro+chem+is+try (ɪˌlɛktrəʊˈkɛmɪstrɪ) *n.* the branch of chemistry concerned with the study of electric cells and electrolysis. **—e·lec+tro+chem·i+cal** (ɪˌlɛktrəʊˈkɛmɪkᵊl) *adj.* **—e·ˌlec+tro+ˈchem·i+cal+ly** *adv.* **—e·ˌlec+tro+ˈchem+ist** *n.*

e·lec+tro+con+vul+sive ther·a+py (ɪˌlɛktrəʊkənˈvʌlsɪv) *n. Med.* the treatment of certain psychotic conditions by passing an electric current through the brain to induce coma or convulsions. Abbrev.: **E.C.T.** Also called: **electroshock therapy.** See also **shock therapy.**

e·lec+tro+cor+ti+co+gram (ɪˌlɛktrəʊˈkɔːtɪkəʊˌgræm) *n.* a record of brain waves obtained by placing electrodes directly on the surface of the exposed cerebral cortex. Compare **electroencephalogram, electroencephalograph.**

e·lec+tro+cute (ɪˈlɛktrəˌkjuːt) *vb.* (*tr.*) **1.** to kill as a result of an electric shock. **2.** *U.S.* to execute in the electric chair. [C19: from ELECTRO- + (EXE)CUTE] **—e·ˌlec+tro+ˈcu+tion** *n.*

e·lec+trode (ɪˈlɛktrəʊd) *n.* **1.** a conductor through which an electric current enters or leaves an electrolyte, an electric arc, or an electronic valve or tube. **2.** an element in a semiconducting device that emits, collects, or controls the movement of electrons or holes.

e·lec+tro+de+pos+it (ɪˌlɛktrəʊdɪˈpɒzɪt) *vb.* **1.** (*tr.*) to deposit (a metal) by electrolysis. ~*n.* **2.** the deposit so formed. **—e·lec+tro+dep·o+si+tion** (ɪˌlɛktrəʊˌdɛpəˈzɪʃən) *n.*

e·lec+trode po+ten+tial *n. Chem.* the potential difference developed when an electrode of an element is placed in a solution containing ions of that element.

e·lec+tro+di+al·y+sis (ɪˌlɛktrəʊdaɪˈælɪsɪs) *n.* dialysis in which electrolytes are removed from a colloidal solution by a potential difference between two electrodes separated by one or more membranes.

e·lec+tro+dy+nam+ic (ɪˌlɛktrəʊdaɪˈnæmɪk) *or* **e·lec+tro+dy+nam·i+cal** *adj.* **1.** operated by an electromotive force between current-carrying coils: *an electrodynamic wattmeter.* **2.** of or relating to electrodynamics.

e·lec+tro+dy+nam+ics (ɪˌlɛktrəʊdaɪˈnæmɪks) *n.* (*functioning as sing.*) the branch of physics concerned with the interactions between electrical and mechanical forces.

e·lec+tro+dy+na+mom+e+ter (ɪˌlɛktrəʊˌdaɪnəˈmɒmɪtə) *n.* an instrument that uses the interaction of the magnetic fields of two coils to measure electric current, voltage, or power.

e·lec+tro+en+ceph·a+lo+gram (ɪˌlɛktrəʊɛnˈsɛfələˌgræm) *n. Med.* the tracing obtained from an electroencephalograph. Abbrev.: **EEG**

e·lec+tro+en+ceph·a+lo+graph (ɪˌlɛktrəʊɛnˈsɛfələˌgrɑːf, -ˌgræf) *n.* an instrument for recording the electrical activity of the brain, usually by means of electrodes placed on the scalp: used to diagnose tumours of the brain, to study brain waves, etc. Abbrev.: **EEG** See also **brain wave. —e·ˌlec+tro+en+ˌceph·a+lo+ˈgraph+ic** *adj.* **—e·ˌlec+tro+en+ˌceph·a+lo+ˈgraph·i+cal+ly** *adv.* **—e·lec+tro+en+ceph·a+log+ra+phy** (ɪˌlɛktrəʊɛnˌsɛfəˈlɒgrəfɪ) *n.*

e·lec+tro+form (ɪˈlɛktrəˌfɔːm) *vb.* to form (a metallic object) by electrolytic deposition on a mould or matrix.

e·lec+tro+graph (ɪˈlɛktrəʊˌgrɑːf, ˌgræf) *n.* **1.** an apparatus for engraving metal printing cylinders, esp. in gravure printing. **2.** the equipment used for the electrical transmission of pictures. **3. a.** a recording electrometer. **b.** a graph produced by this instrument. **4.** a visual record of the surface composition of a metal, obtained by placing an electrolyte-soaked paper over the metal and passing a current through the paper to an electrode on the other side. **—e+lec+tro+graph+ic** (ɪˌlɛktrəʊˈgræfɪk) *adj.* **—e·ˌlec+tro+ˈgraph·i+cal+ly** *adv.* **—e·lec+trog+ra+phy** (ɪlɛkˈtrɒgrəfɪ, ˌiːlɛk-) *n.*

e·lec+tro+jet (ɪˈlɛktrəʊˌdʒɛt) *n.* a narrow belt of fast-moving ions in the ionosphere, under the influence of the earth's magnetic field, causing auroral displays.

e·lec+tro+ki+net+ic (ɪˌlɛktrəʊkɪˈnɛtɪk, -kaɪ-) *adj.* of or relating to the motion of charged particles and its effects.

e·lec+tro+ki+net+ics (ɪˌlɛktrəʊkɪˌnɛtɪks, -kaɪ-) *n.* (*functioning as sing.*) the branch of physics concerned with the motion of charged particles.

e·lec+tro+lu+mi+nes+cence (ɪˌlɛktrəʊˌluːmɪˈnɛsᵊns) *n. Physics.* **a.** the emission of light by a phosphor when activated by an alternating field or by a gas when activated by an electric discharge. **b.** the light emitted by this process. **—e·ˌlec+tro+ˌlu+mi+ˈnes+cent** *n.*

e·lec+tro+lyse *or U.S.* **e·lec+tro+lyze** (ɪˈlɛktrəʊˌlaɪz) *vb.* (*tr.*) **1.** to decompose (a chemical compound) by electrolysis. **2.** to destroy (living tissue, such as hair roots) by electrolysis. **—e·ˌlec+tro+ly+ˈsa+tion** *n.* **—e·ˈlec+tro+ˌlys+er** *n.*

e·lec·trol·y·sis (ɪlɛk'trɒlɪsɪs) *n.* **1.** the conduction of electricity by a solution or melt, esp. the use of this process to induce chemical changes. **2.** the destruction of living tissue, such as hair roots, by an electric current, usually for cosmetic reasons.

e·lec·tro·lyte (ɪ'lɛktrəʊ,laɪt) *n.* a solution or molten substance that conducts electricity.

e·lec·tro·lyt·ic (ɪ,lɛktrəʊ'lɪtɪk) *or* **e·lec·tro·lyt·i·cal** *adj.* **1.** *Physics.* **a.** of, concerned with, or produced by electrolysis or electrodeposition. **b.** of, relating to, or containing an electrolyte. ~*n.* **2.** *Electronics.* Also called: **electrolytic capacitor.** a small capacitor consisting of two electrodes separated by an electrolyte. —**e·,lec·tro·'lyt·i·cal·ly** *adv.*

e·lec·tro·lyt·ic cell *n.* any device in which electrolysis occurs. Sometimes shortened to **cell.**

e·lec·tro·lyt·ic gas *n.* a mixture of two parts of hydrogen and one part of oxygen by volume, formed by the electrolysis of water.

e·lec·tro·mag·net (ɪ,lɛktrəʊ'mægnɪt) *n.* a magnet consisting of an iron or steel core wound with a coil of wire, through which a current is passed.

e·lec·tro·mag·net·ic (ɪ,lɛktrəʊmæg'nɛtɪk) *adj.* **1.** of, containing, or operated by an electromagnet: *an electromagnetic pump.* **2.** of, relating to, or consisting of electromagnetism: *electromagnetic moment.* **3.** of or relating to electromagnetic radiation: *the electromagnetic spectrum.* —**e·,lec·tro·mag·'net·i·cal·ly** *adv.*

e·lec·tro·mag·net·ic field *n.* a field of force equivalent to an electric field and a magnetic field at right angles to each other and to the direction of propagation.

e·lec·tro·mag·net·ic in·ter·ac·tion *n. Physics.* an interaction between charged particles arising from their electric and magnetic fields; its strength is about 100 times weaker than the strong interaction.

e·lec·tro·mag·net·ic mo·ment *n.* a measure of the magnetic strength of a magnet or current-carrying coil, expressed as the torque produced when the magnet or coil is set with its axis perpendicular to unit magnetic flux density. It is measured in ampere metres squared. Symbol: *m* Also called: **magnetic moment.** Compare **magnetic dipole moment.**

e·lec·tro·mag·net·ic pump *n.* a device for pumping liquid metals by placing a pipe between the poles of an electromagnet and passing a current through the liquid metal.

e·lec·tro·mag·net·ic ra·di·a·tion *n.* radiation consisting of an electric and magnetic field at right angles to each other and to the direction of propagation. It requires no supporting medium and travels through empty space at 2.9979×10^8 metres per second. See also **photon.**

e·lec·tro·mag·net·ic spec·trum *n.* the complete range of electromagnetic radiation from the longest radio waves (wavelength 10^5 metres) to the shortest gamma radiation (wavelength 10^{-13} metre).

e·lec·tro·mag·net·ic u·nit *n.* any unit that belongs to a system of electrical cgs units in which the magnetic constant is given the value of unity and is taken as a pure number. Abbrev.: EMU, e.m.u. Compare **electrostatic unit.**

e·lec·tro·mag·net·ic wave *n.* a wave of energy propagated in an electromagnetic field. See also **electromagnetic radiation.**

e·lec·tro·mag·ne·tism (ɪ,lɛktrəʊ'mægnɪ,tɪzəm) *n.* **1.** magnetism produced by an electric current. **2.** the branch of physics concerned with magnetism produced by electric currents and with the interaction of electric and magnetic fields.

e·lec·tro·me·chan·i·cal (ɪ,lɛktrəʊmɪ'kænɪkᵊl) *adj.* of, relating to, or concerning an electrically operated mechanical device. —**e·,lec·tro·me·'chan·i·cal·ly** *adv.*

e·lec·tro·mer·ism (ɪ,lɛktrəʊ'mɛrɪzəm) *n. Chem.* a type of tautomerism in which the isomers (**electromers**) differ in the distribution of charge in their molecules. [C20: from ELECTRO- + (ISO)MERISM]

e·lec·tro·met·al·lur·gy (ɪ,lɛktrəʊmɪ'tælədʒɪ, -'mɛtə,lɜːdʒɪ) *n.* metallurgy involving the use of electric-arc furnaces, electrolysis, and other electrical operations. —**e·,lec·tro·,met·al·'lur·gi·cal** *adj.* —**e·,lec·tro·me·t'al·lur·gist** *n.*

e·lec·trom·e·ter (ɪlɛk'trɒmɪtə, ,iːlɛk-) *n.* an instrument for detecting or determining the magnitude of a potential difference or charge by the electrostatic forces between charged bodies. —**e·lec·tro·met·ric** (ɪ,lɛktrəʊ'mɛtrɪk) *or* **e·,lec·tro·'met·ri·cal** *adj.* —**e·,lec·tro·'met·ri·cal·ly** *adv.* —**e·lec·'trom·e·try** *n.*

e·lec·tro·mo·tive (ɪ,lɛktrəʊ'məʊtɪv) *adj.* of, concerned with, producing, or tending to produce an electric current.

e·lec·tro·mo·tive force *n. Physics.* **a.** a source of energy that can cause a current to flow in an electrical circuit or device. **b.** the rate at which energy is drawn from this source when unit current flows through the circuit or device, measured in volts. Abbrev.: emf Symbol: *E* Compare **potential difference.**

e·lec·tro·mo·tive se·ries *n. Chem.* a series of the metals, together with hydrogen, ranged in the order of their electrode potentials.

e·lec·tron (ɪ'lɛktrɒn) *n.* a stable elementary particle present in all atoms, orbiting the nucleus in numbers equal to the atomic number of the element; a lepton with a negative charge of 1.6022×10^{-19} coulomb, a rest mass of 9.1096×10^{-31} kilogram, a radius of 2.818×10^{-15} metre, and a spin of ½. [C19: from ELECTRO- + -ON]

e·lec·tron af·fin·i·ty *n.* a measure of the ability of an atom or molecule to form a negative ion, expressed as the energy released when an electron is attached. Symbol: *A*

e·lec·tron cam·e·ra *n.* an iconoscope or similar device for converting an optical image into an electric current.

e·lec·tro·neg·a·tive (ɪ,lɛktrəʊ'nɛgətɪv) *adj.* **1.** having a negative electric charge. **2.** (of an atom, group, molecule, etc.) tending to gain or attract electrons and form negative ions or polarized bonds. Compare **electropositive.**

e·lec·tro·neg·a·tiv·i·ty (ɪ,lɛktrəʊ,nɛgə'tɪvɪtɪ) *n.* **1.** the state of being electronegative. **2.** a measure of the ability of a specified atom to attract electrons in a molecule.

e·lec·tron gun *n.* a heated cathode with an associated system of electrodes and coils for producing and focusing a beam of electrons, used esp. in cathode-ray tubes.

e·lec·tron·ic (ɪlɛk'trɒnɪk, ,iːlɛk-) *adj.* **1.** of, concerned with, using, or operated by devices, such as transistors or valves, in which electrons are conducted through a semiconductor, vacuum, or gas. **2.** of or concerned with electronics. **3.** of or concerned with electrons or an electron: *an electronic energy level in a molecule.* —**e·lec·'tron·i·cal·ly** *adv.*

Usage. *Electronic* is used to refer to equipment, such as television sets, computers, etc., in which the current is controlled by transistors, valves, and similar components and also to the components themselves. *Electrical* is used in a more general sense, often to refer to the use of electricity as a whole as opposed to other forms of energy: *electrical engineering; an electrical appliance. Electric,* in many cases used interchangeably with *electrical,* is often restricted to the description of particular devices or to concepts relating to the flow of current: *electric fire; electric charge.*

e·lec·tron·ic da·ta pro·ces·sing *n.* data processing largely performed by electronic equipment, such as computers. Abbrev.: **E.D.P., e.d.p.** Compare **automatic data processing.**

e·lec·tron·ic flash *n. Photog.* an electronic device for producing a very bright flash of light by means of an electric discharge in a gas-filled tube.

e·lec·tron·ic mu·sic *n.* a form of music consisting of sounds produced by oscillating electric currents either controlled from an instrument panel or keyboard or prerecorded on magnetic tape.

e·lec·tron·ic or·gan *n. Music.* an electrophonic instrument played by means of a keyboard, in which sounds are produced and amplified by any of various electronic or electrical means. See also **Moog synthesizer.**

e·lec·tron·ics (ɪlɛk'trɒnɪks, ,iːlɛk-) *n.* **1.** (*functioning as sing.*) the science and technology concerned with the development, behaviour, and applications of electronic devices and circuits. **2.** (*functioning as pl.*) the circuits and devices of a piece of electronic equipment: *the electronics of a television set.*

e·lec·tron lens *n.* a system, such as an arrangement of electrodes or magnets, that produces a field for focusing a beam of electrons.

e·lec·tron mi·cro·scope *n.* a powerful type of microscope that uses electrons, rather than light, and electron lenses to produce a magnified image.

e·lec·tron mul·ti·pli·er *n. Physics.* a device for amplifying and measuring a flux of electrons. Each electron hits an anode surface and releases secondary electrons that are accelerated to a second surface; after several such stages a measurable pulse of current is obtained.

e·lec·tron op·tics *n.* the study and use of beams of electrons and of their deflection and focusing by electric and magnetic fields.

e·lec·tron probe mi·cro·a·nal·y·sis *n.* a technique for the analysis of a very small amount of material by bombarding it with a narrow beam of electrons and examining the resulting x-ray emission spectrum.

e·lec·tron spin res·o·nance *n.* a technique for investigating paramagnetic substances by subjecting them to high-frequency radiation in a strong magnetic field. Changes in the spin of unpaired electrons cause radiation to be absorbed at certain frequencies. Abbrev.: **ESR.** See also **nuclear magnetic resonance.**

e·lec·tron tel·e·scope *n.* an astronomical telescope with an attachment for converting the infrared radiation emitted from the surface of planets into a visible image.

e·lec·tron tube *n.* an electrical device, such as a valve, in which a flow of electrons between electrodes takes place. Sometimes shortened to **tube.**

e·lec·tron·volt (ɪ,lɛktrɒn'vəʊlt) *n.* a unit of energy equal to the work done on an electron accelerated through a potential difference of 1 volt. 1 electronvolt is equivalent to 1.602×10^{-9} joule. Symbol: eV

e·lec·tro·phil·ic (ɪ,lɛktrəʊ'fɪlɪk) *adj. Chem.* having or involving an affinity for negative charge. Electrophilic reagents (**electrophiles**) are atoms, molecules, and ions that behave as electron acceptors. Compare **nucleophilic.** —**e·lec·tro·phile** (ɪ'lɛktrəʊ,faɪl) *n.*

e·lec·tro·phone (ɪ'lɛktrə,fəʊn) *n. Music.* any instrument whose sound is produced by the oscillation of an electric current, such as an electronic organ, Moog synthesizer, etc. —**e·lec·tro·phon·ic** (ɪ,lɛktrə'fɒnɪk) *adj.*

e·lec·tro·pho·re·sis (ɪ,lɛktrəʊfə'riːsɪs) *n.* the motion of charged particles in a colloid under the influence of an applied electric field. Also called: **cataphoresis.** —**e·lec·tro·pho·ret·ic** (ɪ,lɛktrəʊfə'rɛtɪk) *adj.*

e·lec·troph·o·rus (ɪlɛk'trɒfərəs, ,iːlɛk-) *n.* an apparatus for generating static electricity. It consists of an insulating plate charged by friction and used to charge a metal plate by induction. [C18: from ELECTRO- + *-phorus,* from Greek *-phoros* bearing, from *pherein* to bear]

e·lec·tro·phys·i·ol·o·gy (ɪ,lɛktrəʊ,fɪzɪ'ɒlədʒɪ) *n.* the branch of medical science concerned with the electrical activity associated with bodily processes. —**eˌlec+tro+ˌphys·i·o+'log·i+cal** *adj.* —**eˌlec+tro+ˌphys·i+'ol·o+gist** *n.*

e·lec+tro+plate (ɪ'lɛktrəʊˌpleɪt) *vb.* **1.** (*tr.*) to plate (an object) by electrolysis. ~*n.* **2.** electroplated articles collectively, esp. when plated with silver. ~*adj.* **3.** coated with metal by electrolysis; electroplated. —**e'lec+tro+ˌplat+er** *n.*

e·lec+tro+po+si+tive (ɪˌlɛktrəʊ'pɒzɪtɪv) *adj.* **1.** having a positive electric charge. **2.** (of an atom, group, molecule, etc.) tending to release electrons and form positive ions or polarized bonds. Compare **electronegative.**

e·lec+tro+scope (ɪ'lɛktrəʊˌskəʊp) *n.* an apparatus for detecting an electric charge, typically consisting of a rod holding two gold foils that separate when a charge is applied. —**e·lec+tro+scop+ic** (ɪˌlɛktrəʊ'skɒpɪk) *adj.*

e·lec+tro+shock ther+a+py (ɪ'lɛktrəʊˌʃɒk) *n.* another name for **electroconvulsive therapy.**

e·lec+tro+stat+ic (ɪˌlɛktrəʊ'stætɪk) *adj.* **1.** of, concerned with, producing, or caused by static electricity. **2.** concerned with electrostatics. —**eˌlec+tro+'stat·i+cal+ly** *adv.*

e·lec+tro+stat+ic gen+er+a+tor *n.* any device for producing a high voltage by building up a charge of static electricity.

e·lec+tro+stat+ic lens *n.* an electron lens consisting of a system of metal electrodes, the electrostatic field of which focuses the charged particles.

e·lec+tro+stat+ic pre+cip+i+ta+tion *n. Chem.* the removal of suspended solid particles from a gas by giving them an electric charge and attracting them to charged plates.

e·lec+tro+stat+ics (ɪˌlɛktrəʊ'stætɪks) *n.* the branch of physics concerned with static electricity.

e·lec+tro+stat+ic u+nit *n.* any unit that belongs to a system of electrical cgs units in which the electric constant is given the value of unity and is taken as a pure number. Abbrevs.: **ESU, e.s.u.** Compare **electromagnetic unit.**

e·lec+tro+stric+tion (ɪˌlɛktrəʊ'strɪkʃən) *n.* the change in dimensions of a dielectric occurring as an elastic strain when an electric field is applied.

e·lec+tro+sur+ger+y (ɪˌlɛktrəʊ'sɜːdʒərɪ) *n.* the surgical use of electricity, as in cauterization. —**eˌlec+tro+'sur+gi+cal** *adj.*

e·lec+tro+tech+nol+o+gy (ɪˌlɛktrəʊtɛk'nɒlədʒɪ) *n.* the technological use of electric power.

e·lec+tro+ther+a+peu+tics (ɪˌlɛktrəʊˌθɛrə'pjuːtɪks) *n.* the branch of medical science concerned with the use of electricity (**electrotherapy**) in treating certain disorders or diseases. —**eˌlec+tro+ˌther+a+'peu+tic** *or* **eˌlec+tro+ˌther+a+'peu+ti+cal** *adj.* —**eˌlec+tro+'ther+a+pist** *n.*

e·lec+tro+ther+mal (ɪˌlɛktrəʊ'θɜːməl) *adj.* concerned with both electricity and heat, esp. the production of electricity by heat.

e·lec+trot+o+nus (ɪlɛk'trɒtənəs, ˌiːlɛk-) *n. Physiol.* the change in the state of irritability and conductivity of a nerve or muscle caused by the passage of an electric current. [C19: from New Latin, from ELECTRO- + Latin *tonus* TONE] —**e·lec+tro+ton+ic** (ɪˌlɛktrəʊ'tɒnɪk) *adj.*

e·lec+tro+type (ɪ'lɛktrəʊˌtaɪp) *n.* **1.** a duplicate printing plate made by electrolytically depositing a layer of copper or nickel onto a mould of the original. Sometimes shortened to **electro.** ~*vb.* **2.** (*tr.*) to make an electrotype of (printed matter, illustrations, etc.). —**e'lec+tro+ˌtyp+er** *n.*

e·lec+tro+va+len+cy (ɪˌlɛktrəʊ'veɪlənsɪ) *or* **e·lec+tro+va+lence** *n. Chem.* the valency of a substance in forming ions, equal to the number of electrons gained or lost. —**eˌlec+tro+'va+lent** *adj.* —**eˌlec+tro+'va+lent+ly** *adv.*

e·lec+tro+va+lent bond *n.* a type of chemical bond in which one atom loses an electron to form a positive ion and the other atom gains the electron to form a negative ion. The resulting ions are held together by electrostatic attraction. Also called: **ionic bond.** Compare **covalent bond.**

e·lec+trum (ɪ'lɛktrəm) *n.* an alloy of gold (55–88 per cent) and silver used for jewellery and ornaments. [C14: from Latin, from Greek *ēlektron* amber]

e·lec+tu+ar+y (ɪ'lɛktjʊərɪ) *n., pl.* **+ar+ies.** *Medicine.* a paste taken orally, containing a drug mixed with syrup or honey. [C14: from Late Latin *ēlēctuārium,* probably from Greek *ēkleikton* electuary, from *leikhein* to lick out, from *leikhein* to lick]

el+e+e·mos·y+nar·y (ˌɛlɪiː'mɒsɪnərɪ) *adj.* **1.** of, concerned with, or dependent on charity. **2.** given as an act of charity. [C17: from Church Latin *eleēmosyna* ALMS]

el+e+gance ('ɛlɪgəns) *or* **el+e+gan+cy** *n., pl.* **·ganc·es** *or* **·gan+cies. 1.** dignified grace in appearance, movement, or behaviour. **2.** good taste in design, style, arrangement, etc. **3.** something elegant; a refinement.

el+e+gant ('ɛlɪgənt) *adj.* **1.** tasteful in dress, style, or design. **2.** dignified and graceful in appearance, behaviour, etc. **3.** cleverly simple; ingenious: *an elegant solution to a problem.* [C16: from Latin *ēlegāns* tasteful, related to *ēligere* to select; see ELECT] —**'el+e+gant+ly** *adv.*

el+e+gi+ac (ˌɛlɪ'dʒaɪək) *adj.* **1.** resembling, characteristic of, relating to, or appropriate to an elegy. **2.** lamenting; mournful; plaintive. **3.** denoting or written in elegiac couplets or elegiac stanzas. ~*n.* **4.** (*often pl.*) an elegiac couplet or stanza.

el+e+gi+ac coup+let *n. Classical prosody.* a couplet composed of a dactylic hexameter followed by a dactylic pentameter.

el+e+gi+ac stan+za *n. Prosody.* a quatrain in iambic pentameters with alternate lines rhyming.

el+e+gize *or* **el+e+gise** ('ɛlɪˌdʒaɪz) *vb.* to compose an elegy or elegies (in memory of). —**'el+e+gist** *n.*

el+e+gy ('ɛlɪdʒɪ) *n., pl.* **·gies. 1.** a mournful or plaintive poem or song, esp. a lament for the dead. **2.** poetry or a poem written in elegiac couplets or stanzas. [C16: via French and Latin from Greek *elegeia,* from *elegos* lament sung to flute accompaniment]

E·lei·a ('iːlɪə) *n.* a variant spelling of **Elia**[1].

elem. *abbrev. for:* **1.** element(s). **2.** elementary.

el+e+ment ('ɛlɪmənt) *n.* **1.** any of the 105 known substances (of which 93 occur naturally) that consist of atoms with the same number of protons in their nuclei. Compare **compound**[1] (sense 1). **2.** one of the fundamental or irreducible components making up a whole. **3.** any group that is part of a larger unit, such as a military formation. **4.** a small amount; hint: *an element of sarcasm in her voice.* **5.** a distinguishable section of a social group: *he belonged to the stable element in the expedition.* **6.** the most favourable environment for an animal or plant. **7.** the situation in which a person is happiest or most effective (esp. in the phrases **in** or **out of one's element**). **8.** the resistance wire and its former that constitute the electrical heater in a cooker, heater, etc. **9.** *Electronics.* another name for **component** (sense 2). **10.** one of the four substances thought in ancient and medieval cosmology to constitute the universe (earth, air, water, or fire). **11.** (*pl.*) atmospheric conditions or forces, esp. wind, rain, and cold: *exposed to the elements.* **12.** *Geom.* a point, line, plane, or part of a geometric figure. **13.** *Maths.* **a.** any of the terms in the array of a determinant or matrix. **b.** the expression following the integral sign in a definite integral: *in* $\int_a^b f(x)dx$, *f(x)dx is an element of area.* **c.** a member of a set. **14.** *Christianity.* the bread or wine consecrated in the Eucharist. **15.** *Astronomy.* any of the numerical quantities, such as the major axis or eccentricity, used in describing the orbit of a planet, satellite, etc. [C13: from Latin *elementum* a first principle, alphabet, element, of uncertain origin]

el+e+ment+al (ˌɛlɪ'mɛntᵊl) *adj.* **1.** fundamental; basic; primal: *the elemental needs of man.* **2.** motivated by or symbolic of primitive and powerful natural forces or passions: *elemental rites of worship.* **3.** of or relating to earth, air, water, and fire considered as elements. **4.** of or relating to atmospheric forces, esp. wind, rain, and cold. **5.** of, relating to, or denoting a chemical element. ~*n.* **6.** *Rare.* a disembodied spirit. —**ˌel+e+'men+tal+ly** *adv.* —**ˌel+e+'men+tal+ˌism** *n.*

el+e+men+ta+ry (ˌɛlɪ'mɛntərɪ, -trɪ) *adj.* **1.** not difficult; simple; rudimentary. **2.** of or concerned with the first principles of a subject; introductory or fundamental. **3.** *Maths.* (of a function) having the form of an algebraic, exponential, trigonometric, or a logarithmic function, or any combination of these. **4.** *Chem.* another word for **elemental** (sense 5). —**ˌel+e+'men+ta+ri+ly** *adv.* —**ˌel+e+'men+ta+ri+ness** *n.*

el+e+men+ta+ry par+ti+cle *n.* any of several entities, such as electrons, neutrons, or protons, that are less complex than atoms and are regarded as the constituents of all matter. Also called: **fundamental particle.**

el+e+men+ta+ry school *n.* **1.** *Brit.* a former name for **primary school. 2.** Also called: **grade school, grammar school.** *U.S.* a state school in which instruction is given for the first six to eight years of a child's education.

el+e+mi ('ɛlɪmɪ) *n., pl.* **·mis.** any of various fragrant resins obtained from tropical trees, esp. trees of the family *Burseraceae:* used in making varnishes, ointments, inks, etc. [C16: via Spanish from Arabic *al-lāmi* the elemi]

e·len+chus (ɪ'lɛŋkəs) *n., pl.* **+chi** (-kaɪ). *Logic.* refutation of an argument by proving the contrary of its conclusion, esp. syllogistically. [C17: from Latin, from Greek *elenkhos* refutation, from *elenkhein* to put to shame, refute]

e·lenc+tic (ɪ'lɛŋktɪk) *adj. Logic.* refuting an argument by proving the opposite. Compare **deictic** (sense 1).

el+e+op+tene *or* **el+ae+op+tene** (ˌɛlɪ'ɒptiːn) *n.* the liquid part of a volatile oil. [C20: from Greek *elaion* oil + *ptēnos* having wings, volatile; related to Greek *petesthai* to fly]

el+e+phant ('ɛlɪfənt) *n., pl.* **·phants** *or* **·phant. 1.** either of the two proboscidean mammals of the family *Elephantidae.* The **African elephant** (*Loxodonta africana*) is the larger species, with large flapping ears and a less humped back than the **Indian elephant** (*Elephas maximus*), of S and SE Asia. **2.** *Chiefly Brit.* a size of writing paper, 23 by 28 inches. [C13: from Latin *elephantus,* from Greek *elephas* elephant, ivory, of uncertain origin] —**'el+e+phan+ˌtoid** *adj.*

el+e+phant bird *n.* another name for **aepyornis.**

el+e+phant grass *n.* any of various stout tropical grasses or grasslike plants, esp. *Pennisetum purpureum,* and *Typha elephantina,* a type of reed mace.

el+e+phan+ti+a+sis (ˌɛlɪfən'taɪəsɪs) *n. Pathol.* a complication of chronic filariasis, in which nematode worms block the lymphatic vessels, usually in the legs or scrotum, causing extreme enlargement of the affected area. See also **filariasis.** [C16: via Latin from Greek, from *elephas* ELEPHANT + -IASIS] —**el+e+phan+ti+as+ic** (ˌɛlɛˌfæntɪ'æsɪk, -fən'taɪəsɪk) *adj.*

el+e+phan+tine (ˌɛlɪ'fæntaɪn) *adj.* **1.** denoting, relating to, or characteristic of an elephant or elephants. **2.** huge, clumsy, or ponderous.

el+e+phant seal *n.* either of two large earless seals, *Mirounga leonina* of southern oceans or *M. angustirostris* of the N Atlantic, the males of which have a long trunklike snout.

el+e+phant's-ear *n.* **1.** any aroid plant of the genus *Colocasia,* of tropical Asia and Polynesia, having very large heart-shaped leaves: grown for ornament and for their edible tubers. See also **taro. 2.** any of various cultivated begonias with large showy leaves.

el+e+phant's-foot *or* **el+e+phant foot** *n.* a monocotyledonous plant, *Testudinaria elephantipes,* of southern Africa, with a very large starchy tuberous stem, covered in corky scales: family *Dioscoreaceae.*

el+e+phant shrew *n.* any small active African mammal of the family *Macroscelididae,* having an elongated nose, large ears, and long hind legs: order *Insectivora* (insectivores).

El·eu·sin·i·an mys·ter·ies *pl. n.* a mystical religious festival, held in September at Eleusis in classical times, in which initiates celebrated Persephone, Demeter, and Dionysus.

E·leu·sis (ɪ'luːsɪs) *n.* a town in Greece, in Attica about 23 km (14 miles) west of Athens, of which it is now an industrial suburb. Modern Greek name: **Elevsís.** —**El·eu·sin·i·an** (ˌɛljʊ'sɪnɪən) *n., adj.*

elev. *or* **el.** *abbrev. for* elevation.

el·e·vate ('ɛlɪˌveɪt) *vb.* (*tr.*) **1.** to move to a higher place. **2.** to raise in rank or status; promote. **3.** to put in a cheerful mood; elate. **4.** to put on a higher cultural plane; uplift: *to elevate the tone of a conversation.* **5.** to raise the axis of a gun. **6.** to raise the intensity or pitch of (the voice). **7.** *R.C. Church.* to lift up (the Host) at Mass for adoration. [C15: from Latin *ēlevāre* from *levāre* to raise, from *levis* (adj.) light] —ˌ**el·e·'va·to·ry** *adj.*

el·e·vat·ed ('ɛlɪˌveɪtɪd) *adj.* **1.** raised to or being at a higher level. **2.** inflated or lofty; exalted: *an elevated opinion of oneself.* **3.** in a cheerful mood; elated. **4.** *Informal.* slightly drunk.

el·e·va·tion (ˌɛlɪ'veɪʃən) *n.* **1.** the act of elevating or the state of being elevated. **2.** the height of something above a given or implied place, esp. above sea level. **3.** a raised area; height. **4.** nobleness or grandeur; loftiness: *elevation of thought.* **5.** a drawing to scale of the external face of a building or structure. Compare **plan** (sense 3), **ground plan** (sense 1). **6.** the external face of a building or structure. **7.** a ballet dancer's ability to leap high. **8.** *R.C. Church.* the lifting up of the Host at Mass for adoration. **9.** *Astronomy.* another name for **altitude** (sense 3). **10.** the angle formed between the muzzle of a gun and the horizontal. **11.** *Surveying.* the angular distance between the plane through a point of observation and an object above it. Compare **depression** (sense 7). **12.** *Linguistics.* another term for **amelioration.** —ˌ**el·e·'va·tion·al** *adj.*

el·e·va·tor ('ɛlɪˌveɪtə) *n.* **1.** a person or thing that elevates. **2.** a mechanical hoist for raising something, esp. grain or coal, often consisting of a chain of scoops linked together on a conveyor belt. **3.** the U.S. name for **lift** (sense 15). **4.** *Chiefly U.S.* a granary equipped with mechanical devices for hoisting grain. **5.** a surgical instrument for lifting a part. **6.** a control surface on the tailplane of an aircraft, for making it climb or descend.

e·lev·en (ɪ'lɛvᵊn) *n.* **1.** the cardinal number that is the sum of ten and one. **2.** a numeral 11, XI, etc., representing this number. **3.** something representing, represented by, or consisting of 11 units. **4.** (*functioning as sing. or pl.*) a team of 11 players in football, cricket, hockey, etc. **5.** Also called: **eleven o'clock.** eleven hours after noon or midnight. ~*determiner.* **6. a.** amounting to eleven: *eleven chances.* **b.** (*as pronoun*)*: have another eleven today.* [Old English *endleofan;* related to Old Norse *ellefo,* Gothic *ainlif,* Old Frisian *andlova,* Old High German *einlif*]

e·lev·en-plus *n.* (esp. formerly) an examination, taken in England and Wales by children aged 11 or 12, that selects suitable candidates for grammar schools.

e·lev·en·ses (ɪ'lɛvᵊnzɪz) *pl. n. Brit. informal.* a light snack, usually with tea or coffee, taken in mid-morning.

e·lev·enth (ɪ'lɛvᵊnθ) *adj.* **1. a.** coming after the tenth in order, position, time, etc.; often written 11th. **b.** (*as pronoun*)*: the eleventh in succession.* ~*n.* **2. a.** one of 11 equal or nearly equal parts of an object, quantity, measurement, etc. **b.** (*as modifier*)*: an eleventh part.* **3.** the fraction equal to one divided by 11 (1/11). **4.** *Music.* **a.** an interval of one octave plus one fourth. **b.** See **eleventh chord.**

e·lev·enth chord *n.* a chord much used in jazz, consisting of a major or minor triad upon which are superimposed the seventh, ninth, and eleventh above the root.

e·lev·enth hour *n.* **a.** the latest possible time; last minute. **b.** (*as modifier*)*: an eleventh-hour decision.*

el·e·von ('ɛlɪˌvɒn) *n.* an aircraft control surface that combines the functions of an elevator and aileron, usually fitted to tailless or delta-wing aircraft. [C20: from ELEV(ATOR + AILER)ON]

E·lev·sís (ˌɛlɛf'sis) *n.* transliteration of the Modern Greek name for **Eleusis.**

elf (ɛlf) *n., pl.* **elves** (ɛlvz). **1.** (in folklore) one of a kind of legendary beings, usually characterized as small, manlike, and mischievous. **2.** a mischievous or whimsical child or girl. [Old English *ælf;* related to Old Norse *elfr* elf, Middle Low German *alf* incubus, Latin *albus* white]

El Fai·yûm (ɛl faɪ'juːm) *or* **Al Fai·yûm** *n.* a city in N Egypt: a site of towns going back at least to the 12th dynasty. Pop.: 167 700 (1974 est.).

El Fer·rol (*Spanish* el fe'rrol) *n.* a port in NW Spain, on the Atlantic: fortified naval base, with a deep natural harbour. Pop.: 87 736 (1970). Official name (since 1939): **El Fer·rol del Cau·di·llo** (del kaʊ'ðiʎo).

elf·ish ('ɛlfɪʃ) *or* **elv·ish** ('ɛlvɪʃ) *adj.* **1.** Also: **elfin.** of, relating to, or like an elf or elves; charmingly mischievous or sprightly; impish. ~*n.* **2.** the supposed language of elves. —'**elf·ish·ly** *or* '**elv·ish·ly** *adv.* —'**elf·ish·ness** *or* '**elv·ish·ness** *n.*

elf·land ('ɛlfˌlænd) *n.* another name for **fairyland.**

elf·lock ('ɛlfˌlɒk) *n.* a lock of hair, fancifully regarded as having been tangled by the elves.

El·gar ('ɛlgɑː) *n.* Sir **Ed·ward (William).** 1857–1934, English composer, whose works include the *Enigma Variations* (1899), the oratorio *The Dream of Gerontius* (1900), two symphonies, a cello concerto, and a violin concerto.

El·gin mar·bles ('ɛlgɪn) *n.* a group of fifth-century B.C. Greek sculptures originally decorating the Parthenon in Athens, brought to England by Thomas Bruce, seventh Earl of Elgin (1766–1841), and now at the British Museum.

El Gî·za (ɛl 'giːzə) *n.* a city in NE Egypt, on the W bank of the Nile opposite Cairo: nearby are the Great Pyramid of Cheops (Khufu) and the Sphinx. Pop.: 853 700 (1974 est.).

El·gon ('ɛlgɒn) *n.* **Mount.** an extinct volcano in E Africa, on the Kenya-Uganda border. Height: 4321 m (14 178 ft.).

El Gre·co (ɛl 'grɛkəʊ) *n.* original name *Domenikos Theotocopoulos.* 1541–1614, Spanish painter, noted for his elongated human forms and dramatic use of colour.

E·li ('iːlaɪ) *n. Old Testament.* the highest priest at Shiloh and teacher of Samuel (I Samuel 1–3).

E·li·a[1] ('iːlɪə) *n.* a department of SW Greece, in the W Peloponnese: in ancient times most of the region formed the state of Elis. Pop.: 165 056 (1971). Area: 2681 sq. km (1046 sq. miles). Modern Greek name: **Ilía.**

E·li·a[2] ('iːlɪə) *n.* the pen name of (Charles) **Lamb.**

E·li·as (ɪ'laɪəs) *n. Bible.* the Douay spelling of **Elijah.**

e·lic·it (ɪ'lɪsɪt) *vb.* (*tr.*) **1.** to give rise to; evoke: *to elicit a sharp retort.* **2.** to bring to light: *to elicit the truth.* [C17: from Latin *ēlicere* to lure forth, from *licere* to entice] —**e·'lic·it·a·ble** *adj.* —**e·ˌlic·i·'ta·tion** *n.* —**e·'lic·i·tor** *n.*

e·lide (ɪ'laɪd) *vb. Phonetics.* to undergo or cause to undergo elision. [C16: from Latin *ēlīdere* to knock, from *laedere* to hit, wound] —**e·'lid·i·ble** *adj.*

el·i·gi·ble ('ɛlɪdʒəbᵊl) *adj.* **1.** fit, worthy, or qualified, as for an office or function. **2.** desirable and worthy of being chosen, esp. as a spouse: *an eligible young man.* [C15: from Late Latin *ēligibilis* able to be chosen, from *ēligere* to ELECT] —ˌ**el·i·gi·'bil·i·ty** *n.* —'**el·i·gi·bly** *adv.*

E·li·jah (ɪ'laɪdʒə) *n. Old Testament.* a Hebrew prophet of the ninth century B.C., who was persecuted for denouncing Ahab and Jezebel. (I Kings 17–21: 21; II Kings 1–2:18).

E·li·kón (ɛli'kɔn) *n.* transliteration of the Modern Greek name for **Helicon.**

e·lim·i·nate (ɪ'lɪmɪˌneɪt) *vb.* (*tr.*) **1.** to remove or take out; get rid of. **2.** to reject as trivial or irrelevant; omit from consideration. **3.** to remove (a competitor, team, etc.) from a contest, usually by defeat. **4.** *Slang.* to murder in a cold-blooded manner. **5.** *Physiol.* to expel (waste matter) from the body. **6.** *Maths.* to remove (an unknown variable) from two or more simultaneous equations. [C16: from Latin *ēlīmināre* to turn out of the house, from *e-* out + *līmen* threshold] —**e·'lim·i·na·ble** *adj.* —**e·ˌlim·i·na·'bil·i·ty** *n.* —**e·'lim·i·nant** *n.* —**e·ˌlim·i·'na·tion** *n.* —**e·'lim·i·na·tive** *or* **e·'lim·i·na·to·ry** *adj.* —**e·'lim·i·ˌna·tor** *n.*

El·i·ot ('ɛlɪət) *n.* **1. George,** pen name of *Mary Ann Evans.* 1819–80, English novelist, noted for her analysis of provincial Victorian society. Her best-known novels include *Adam Bede* (1859), *The Mill on the Floss* (1860), *Silas Marner* (1861), and *Middlemarch* (1872). **2.** Sir **John.** 1592–1632, English statesman, a leader of parliamentary opposition to Charles I. **3. T(homas) S(tearns).** 1888–1965, British poet, dramatist, and critic, born in the U.S. His poetry includes *Prufrock and Other Observations* (1917), *The Waste Land* (1922), *Ash Wednesday* (1930), and *Four Quartets* (1944). Among his verse plays are *Murder in the Cathedral* (1935), *The Family Reunion* (1939), *The Cocktail Party* (1950), and *The Confidential Clerk* (1954): Nobel prize for literature 1948.

E·lis ('iːlɪs) *n.* an ancient city-state of SW Greece, in the NW Peloponnese: site of the ancient Olympic games.

E·lis·a·beth (ɪ'lɪzəbəθ) *n.* a variant spelling of **Elizabeth**[2] (sense 1).

E·lis·a·beth·ville (ɪ'lɪzəbəθˌvɪl) *n.* the former name (until 1966) of **Lubumbashi.**

E·li·sa·vet·grad (*Russian* jɪliza'vjɛtgrət) *n.* the former name (until 1924) of **Kirovograd.**

E·li·sa·vet·pol (*Russian* jɪliza'vjɛtpəlj) *n.* a former name (until 1920) of **Kirovabad.**

E·li·sha (ɪ'laɪʃə) *n. Old Testament.* a Hebrew prophet of the 9th century B.C.: successor of Elijah (II Kings 3–9).

e·li·sion (ɪ'lɪʒən) *n.* omission of a syllable or vowel at the beginning or end of a word, esp. when a word ending with a vowel is next to one beginning with a vowel. [C16: from Latin *ēlīsiō,* from *ēlīdere* to ELIDE]

e·lite *or* **é·lite** (ɪ'liːt, eɪ-) *n.* **1.** (*sometimes functioning as pl.*) the most powerful, rich, gifted, or educated members of a group, community, etc. **2.** a typewriter typesize having 12 characters to the inch. ~*adj.* **3.** of, relating to, or suitable for an elite; exclusive. [C18: from French, from Old French *eslit* chosen, from *eslire* to choose, from Latin *ēligere* to ELECT]

e·lit·ism (ɪ'liːtɪzəm, eɪ-) *n.* **1. a.** the belief that society should be governed by a select group of gifted and highly educated individuals. **b.** such government. **2.** pride in or awareness of being one of an elite group. —**e·'lit·ist** *n.*

e·lix·ir (ɪ'lɪksə) *n.* **1.** an alchemical preparation supposed to be capable of prolonging life indefinitely **(elixir of life)** or of transmuting base metals into gold. **2.** anything that purports to be a sovereign remedy; panacea. **3.** an underlying principle; quintessence. **4.** a liquid containing a medicinal drug with syrup, glycerin, or alcohol added to mask its unpleasant taste. [C14: from Medieval Latin, from Arabic *al iksīr* the elixir, probably from Greek *xērion* powder used for drying wounds, from *xēros* dry]

Eliz. *abbrev. for* Elizabethan.

E·liz·a·beth[1] (ɪ'lɪzəbəθ) *n.* **1.** a city in NE New Jersey, on

Newark Bay. Pop.: 110 303 (1973 est.). **2.** a town in SE South Australia, near Adelaide. Pop.: 33 389 (1971).

E·liz·a·beth[2] (ɪ'lɪzəbəθ) *n.* **1.** *New Testament.* the wife of Zacharias, mother of John the Baptist, and kinswoman of the Virgin Mary. **2.** pen name *Carmen Sylva.* 1843–1916, queen of Rumania (1881–1914) and author. **3.** Russian name *Yelizaveta Petrovna.* 1709–62, empress of Russia (1741–62); daughter of Peter the Great. **4. Saint.** 1207–31, Hungarian princess who devoted herself to charity and asceticism. Feast day: Nov. 19. **5.** title *The Queen Mother*; original name Lady *Elizabeth Bowes-Lyon.* born 1900, queen of Great Britain and Northern Ireland (1936–52) as the wife of George VI; mother of Elizabeth II.

E·liz·a·beth I *n.* 1533–1603, queen of England (1558–1603); daughter of Henry VIII and Anne Boleyn. She established the Church of England (1559) and put an end to Catholic plots, notably by executing Mary Queen of Scots (1587) and defeating the Spanish Armada (1588). Her reign was notable for commercial growth, maritime expansion, and the flourishing of literature, music, and architecture.

E·liz·a·beth II *n.* born 1926, queen of Great Britain and Northern Ireland since 1952; daughter of George VI.

E·liz·a+be·than (ɪˌlɪzə'bi:θən) *adj.* **1.** of, characteristic of, or relating to England or its culture in the age of Elizabeth I or II. **2.** of, relating to, or designating a style of architecture used in England during the reign of Elizabeth I, characterized by moulded and sculptured ornament based on German and Flemish models. ~*n.* **3.** a person who lived in England during the reign of Elizabeth I.

E·liz·a·be·than son+net *n.* another term for **Shakespearean sonnet.**

elk (ɛlk) *n., pl.* **elks** *or* **elk. 1.** a large deer, *Alces alces,* of N Europe and Asia, having large flattened palmate antlers: also occurs in North America, where it is called a moose. **2. American elk.** another name for **wapiti. 3.** a stout pliable waterproof leather made from calfskin or horsehide. [Old English *eolh;* related to Old Norse *elgr,* Old High German *elaho,* Latin *alcēs,* Greek *alkē, elaphos* deer]

El Kha+lil (æl xɒ'li:l) *n.* transliteration of the Arabic name for **Hebron.**

elk+hound ('ɛlkˌhaʊnd) *n.* a powerful breed of dog with a thick grey coat and tightly curled tail. Also called: **Norwegian elkhound.**

ell[1] (ɛl) *n.* an obsolete unit of length equal to approximately 45 inches. [Old English *eln* the forearm (the measure originally being from the elbow to the fingertips); related to Old High German *elina,* Latin *ulna,* Greek *ōlenē*]

ell[2] (ɛl) *n.* **1.** an extension to a building, usually at right angles and located at one end. **2.** a pipe fitting, pipe, or tube with a sharp right-angle bend. [C20: a spelling of *L,* indicating a right angle]

El+lás (ɛ'las) *n.* transliteration of the Modern Greek name for **Greece.**

Elles+mere Is+land ('ɛlzmɪə) *n.* a Canadian island in the Arctic Ocean: part of the Northwest Territories; mountainous, with many glaciers. Area: 212 688 sq. km (82 119 sq. miles).

Elles+mere Port *n.* a port in NW England, in NW Cheshire on the Manchester Ship Canal. Pop.: 61 556 (1971).

El+lice Is+lands ('ɛlɪs) *pl. n.* the former name (until 1975) of **Tuvalu.**

El·ling·ton ('ɛlɪŋtən) *n.* **Duke,** nickname of *Edward Kennedy Ellington.* 1899–1974, U.S. jazz composer, pianist, and conductor, famous for such works as *Mood Indigo* and *Take the A Train.*

el+lipse (ɪ'lɪps) *n.* a closed conic section shaped like a flattened circle and formed by an inclined plane that does not cut the base of the cone. Standard equation: $x^2/a^2 + y^2/b^2 = 1$, where $2a$ and $2b$ are the lengths of the major and minor axes. Area: πab. [C18: back formation from ELLIPSIS]

el+lip+sis (ɪ'lɪpsɪs) *n., pl.* **+ses** (-si:z). **1.** Also called: **eclipsis.** omission of parts of a word or sentence. **2.** *Printing.* a sequence of three dots (...) indicating an omission in text. [C16: from Latin, from Greek *elleipsis* omission, from *elleipein* to leave out, from *leipein* to leave]

el+lip+soid (ɪ'lɪpsɔɪd) *n.* **a.** a geometric surface, symmetrical about the three coordinate axes, whose plane sections are ellipses or circles. Standard equation: $x^2/a^2 + y^2/b^2 + z^2/c^2 = 1$, where $\pm a$, $\pm b$, $\pm c$ are the intercepts on the *x-*, *y-*, and *z-*axes. **b.** a solid having this shape: *the earth is an ellipsoid.* —**el+lip+soi+dal** (ɪlɪp'sɔɪdᵊl, ˌɛl-) *adj.*

el+lip+ti+cal (ɪ'lɪptɪkᵊl) *adj.* **1.** relating to or having the shape of an ellipse. **2.** relating to or resulting from ellipsis. **3.** (of speech, literary style, etc.) **a.** very condensed or concise, often so as to be obscure or ambiguous. **b.** circumlocutory or long-winded. ~Also (for senses 1 and 2): **el+lip+tic.** —**el+'lip+ti+cal+ly** *adv.* —**el+'lip+ti+cal+ness** *n.*

Usage. The use of *elliptical* to mean *circumlocutory* is avoided by many careful speakers and writers.

el+lip+tic ge+om+e+try *n.* another name for **Riemannian geometry.**

el+lip+ti·ci·ty (ɪlɪp'tɪsɪtɪ, ˌɛl-) *n.* the degree of deviation from a circle or sphere of an elliptical or ellipsoidal shape or path, measured as the ratio of the major to the minor axes.

El+lis ('ɛlɪs) *n.* **1. Al·ex·an·der John.** 1814–90, English philologist: made the first systematic survey of the phonology of British dialects. **2. (Henry) Have·lock.** 1859–1939. English essayist: author of works on the psychology of sex.

elm (ɛlm) *n.* **1.** any ulmaceous tree of the genus *Ulmus,* occurring in the N hemisphere, having serrated leaves and winged fruits (samaras): cultivated for shade, ornament, and timber. **2.** the hard heavy wood of this tree. ~See also **slippery elm, wahoo**[1]**, wych-elm.** [Old English *elm;* related to Old Norse *almr,* Old High German *elm,* Latin *ulmus*]

El Man+su+ra (ɛl mæn'sʊərə) *or* **Al Man+su+rah** *n.* a city in NE Egypt: scene of a battle (1250) in which the Crusaders were defeated by the Mamelukes and Louis IX of France was captured; cotton-manufacturing centre. Pop.: 232 400 (1974 est.).

El Min+ya (ɛl 'mɪnjə) *n.* a river port in central Egypt on the Nile. Pop.: 122 100 (1970 est.).

El Mis+ti (ɛl 'mi:sti:) *n.* a volcano in S Peru, in the Andes. Height: 5822 m (19 096 ft.).

El O·beid (ɛl əʊ'beɪd) *n.* a city in the central Sudan, in Kordofan province: scene of the defeat of a British and Egyptian army by the Mahdi (1883). Pop.: 89 789 (1973).

el·o+cu+tion (ˌɛlə'kju:ʃən) *n.* the art of public speaking, esp. of voice production, delivery, and gesture. [C15: from Latin *ēlocūtiō* a speaking out, from *ēloquī,* from *loquī* to speak] —**ˌel·o+'cu+tion+ar·y** *adj.* —**ˌel·o+'cu+tion+ist** *n.*

E·lo+him (ɛ'ləʊhɪm, ˌɛləʊ'hi:m) *n. Old Testament.* a Hebrew word for God or gods. [C17: from Hebrew *'Elōhim,* plural of *'Elōah* God; probably related to *'El* God]

E·lo+hist (ɛ'ləʊhɪst) *n. Old Testament.* the author or authors of one of the four main strands of text of the Pentateuch, identified chiefly by the use of the word *Elohim* for God instead of *YHVH* (Jehovah).

e·loign *or* **e·loin** (ɪ'lɔɪn) *vb.* (*tr.*) *Archaic.* to remove (oneself, property, etc.) to a distant place. [C16: from Anglo-French *esloigner* to go far away; related to Latin *longē* (adv.) far; compare ELONGATE] —**e·'loign+er** *or* **e·'loin+er** *n.* —**e·'loign+ment** *or* **e·'loin+ment** *n.*

e·lon+gate ('i:lɒŋgeɪt) *vb.* **1.** to make or become longer; stretch. ~*adj.* **2.** long and narrow; slender: *elongate leaves.* **3.** lengthened or tapered. [C16: from Late Latin *ēlongāre* to keep at a distance, from *ē-* away + Latin *longē* (adv.) far, but also later: to lengthen, as if from *ē-* + Latin *longus* (adj.) long] —**'e·lon+ˌga+tive** *adj.*

e·lon+ga+tion (ˌi:lɒŋ'geɪʃən) *n.* **1.** the act of elongating or state of being elongated; lengthening. **2.** something that is elongated. **3.** *Astronomy.* the difference between the celestial longitude of the sun and that of a planet or the moon.

e·lope (ɪ'ləʊp) *vb.* (*intr.*) to run away secretly with a lover, esp. in order to marry. [C16: from Anglo-French *aloper,* perhaps from Middle Dutch *lōpen* to run; see LOPE] —**e·'lope+ment** *n.* —**e·'lop+er** *n.*

el·o+quence ('ɛləkwəns) *n.* **1.** ease in using language to best effect. **2.** powerful and effective language. **3.** the quality of being persuasive or moving.

el·o+quent ('ɛləkwənt) *adj.* **1.** (of speech, writing, etc.) characterized by fluency and persuasiveness. **2.** visibly or vividly expressive, as of an emotion: *an eloquent yawn.* [C14: from Latin *ēloquēns,* from *ēloquī* to speak out, from *loquī* to speak] —**'el·o+quent+ly** *adv.* —**'el·o+quent+ness** *n.*

El Pas·o (ɛl 'pæsəʊ) *n.* a city in W Texas, on the Rio Grande opposite Ciudad Juárez, Mexico. Pop.: 353 226 (1973 est.).

El Sal+va+dor (ɛl 'sælvəˌdɔ:) *n.* a republic in Central America, on the Pacific: colonized by the Spanish from 1524; declared independence in 1841, becoming a republic in 1856. It consists of coastal lowlands rising to a central plateau. Coffee constitutes about half of the total exports. Language: Spanish. Religion: Roman Catholic. Currency: colón. Capital: San Salvador. Pop.: 3 549 260 (1971). Area: 21 330 sq. km (8236 sq. miles). —**ˌSal+va+'dor+an** *or* **ˌSal+va+'do+ri+an** *adj., n.*

El+san ('ɛlsæn) *n. Trademark.* a type of portable lavatory in which chemicals are used to kill bacteria and deodorize the sludge. [C20: from the initials of *E. L.* Jackson, the manufacturer + SAN(ITATION)]

El+sass ('ɛlzas) *n.* the German name for **Alsace.**

El·sass-Lo·thring+en ('ɛlzas 'lo:trɪŋən) *n.* the German name for **Alsace-Lorraine.**

else (ɛls) *determiner.* (*postpositive; used after an indefinite pronoun or an interrogative*) **1.** in addition; more: *there is nobody else here.* **2.** other; different: *where else could he be?* ~*adv.* **3. or else. a.** if not, then: *go away or else I won't finish my work today.* **b.** or something terrible will result: used as a threat: *sit down, or else!* [Old English *elles,* genitive of *el-* strange, foreign; related to Old High German *eli-* other, Gothic *alja,* Latin *alius,* Greek *allos*]

Usage. The possessive of the expressions *anybody else, everybody else, nobody else,* etc., is formed by adding *'s* to *else: this must be somebody else's letter. Who else* is an exception in that *whose else* is an acceptable alternative to *who else's: whose else can it be?* or *who else's can it be?* Careful writers and speakers avoid *whose else's* since it contains two possessives, one of which is redundant.

else+where (ˌɛls'wɛə) *adv.* in or to another place; somewhere else. [Old English *elles hwǣr;* see ELSE, WHERE]

El+si+nore ('ɛlsɪˌnɔ:, ˌɛlsɪ'nɔ:) *n.* the English name for **Helsingør.**

ELT *abbrev. for* European letter telegram.

É·lu·ard (*French* e'lɥa:r) *n.* **Paul** (pɔl). 1895–1952, French surrealist poet, noted for his political and love poems.

e·lu+ci+date (ɪ'lu:sɪˌdeɪt) *vb.* to make clear (something obscure or difficult); clarify. [C16: from Late Latin *ēlūcidāre* to enlighten; see LUCID] —**eˌlu+ci+'da+tion** *n.* —**e·'lu+ci+ˌda+tive** *or* **e·'lu+ci+ˌda+to+ry** *adj.* —**e·'lu+ci+ˌda+tor** *n.*

e·lude (ɪ'lu:d) *vb.* (*tr.*) **1.** to escape or avoid (capture, one's pursuers, etc.), esp. by cunning. **2.** to avoid fulfilment of (a responsibility, obligation, etc.); evade. **3.** to escape discovery, or understanding by; baffle: *the solution eluded her.* [C16: from Latin *ēlūdere* to deceive, from *lūdere* to play] —**e·'lud·er** *n.* —**e·lu·sion** (ɪ'luːʒən) *n.*

el·u·ent *or* **el·u·ant** ('ɛljuːənt) *n.* a solvent used for eluting.

E·lul *Hebrew.* (ɛ'luːl) *n. Judaism.* the twelfth month of the civil year and the sixth of the ecclesiastical year in the Jewish calendar, falling approximately in August and September.

e·lu·sive (ɪ'luːsɪv) *adj.* **1.** difficult to catch: *an elusive thief.* **2.** preferring or living in solitude and anonymity. **3.** difficult to remember: *an elusive thought.* **4.** avoiding the issue; evasive: *an elusive answer.* —**e·'lu·sive·ly** *adv.* —**e·'lu·sive·ness** *n.*

e·lute (iː'luːt, ɪ'luːt) *vb.* (*tr.*) to wash out (a substance) by the action of a solvent, as in chromatography. [C18: from Latin *ēlūtus* rinsed out, from *ēluere* to wash clean, from *luere* to wash, LAVE] —**e·'lu·tion** *n.*

e·lu·tri·ate (ɪ'luːtrɪˌeɪt) *vb.* (*tr.*) to purify or separate (a substance or mixture) by washing and straining or decanting. [C18: from Latin *ēlūtriāre* to wash out, from *ēluere*, from *ē-* out + *lavere* to wash] —**e·'lu·tri·ant** *n.* —**e·ˌlu·tri·'a·tion** *n.* —**e·'lu·tri·ˌa·tor** *n.*

e·lu·vi·a·tion (ɪˌluːvɪ'eɪʃən) *n.* the process by which material suspended in water is removed from one layer of soil to another by the action of rainfall or chemical decomposition. [C20: from ELUVIUM]

e·lu·vi·um (ɪ'luːvɪəm) *n., pl.* **-vi·a** (-vɪə). a mass of sand, silt, etc.: a product of the erosion of rocks that has remained in its place of origin. [C19: New Latin, from Latin *ēluere* to wash out] —**e·'lu·vi·al** *adj.*

el·ver ('ɛlvə) *n.* a young eel, esp. one migrating up a river from the sea. See also **leptocephalus.** [C17: variant of *eelfare* migration of young eels, literally: eel-journey; see EEL, FARE]

elves (ɛlvz) *n.* the plural of **elf.**

elv·ish ('ɛlvɪʃ) *adj.* a variant spelling of **elfish.**

E·ly ('iːlɪ) *n.* **1.** a cathedral city in E England, in E Cambridgeshire on the River Ouse. Pop.: 9969 (1971). **2. Isle of.** a former county of E England, part of Cambridgeshire since 1965.

El·y·ot ('ɛlɪət) *n.* Sir **Thom·as.** ?1490–1546, English scholar and diplomat; author of *The Boke named the Governour* (1531), a treatise in English on education.

É·ly·sée (ˌeɪliː'zeɪ) *n.* a palace in Paris, in the Champs Elysées: official residence of the president of France.

E·ly·si·an (ɪ'lɪzɪən) *adj.* **1.** of or relating to Elysium. **2.** *Literary.* delightful; glorious; blissful.

E·ly·si·um (ɪ'lɪzɪəm) *n.* **1.** Also called: **Elysian fields.** *Greek myth.* the dwelling place of the blessed after death. See also **Islands of the Blessed. 2.** a state or place of perfect bliss. [C16: from Latin, from Greek *Ēlusion pedion* Elysian (that is, blessed) fields]

el·y·tron ('ɛlɪˌtrɒn) *or* **el·y·trum** ('ɛlɪtrəm) *n., pl.* **-tra** (-trə). either of the horny front wings of beetles and some other insects, which cover and protect the hind wings. [C18: from Greek *elutron* sheath, covering] —**'el·y·ˌtroid** *or* **'el·y·trous** *adj.*

em (ɛm) *n. Printing.* **1.** Also called: **mutton, mut.** the square of a body of any size of type, used as a unit of measurement. **2.** Also called: **pica em, pica.** a unit of measurement used in printing, equal to one sixth of an inch.

em- *prefix.* variant of **en-**[1] and **en-**[2] before *b, m,* and *p.*

'em (əm) *pron.* an informal variant of **them.**

e·ma·ci·ate (ɪ'meɪsɪˌeɪt) *vb.* (*usually tr.*) to become or cause to become abnormally thin. [C17: from Latin *ēmaciāre* to make lean, from *macer* thin] —**e·ˌma·ci·'a·tion** *n.*

em·a·nate ('ɛməˌneɪt) *vb.* **1.** (*intr.;* often foll. by *from*) to issue or proceed from or as from a source. **2.** (*tr.*) to send forth; emit. [C18: from Latin *ēmānāre* to flow out, from *mānāre* to flow] —**em·a·na·tive** ('ɛmənətɪv) *adj.* —**'em·a·ˌna·tor** *n.* —**em·a·na·to·ry** ('ɛməˌneɪtərɪ, -trɪ) *adj.*

em·a·na·tion (ˌɛmə'neɪʃən) *n.* **1.** an act or instance of emanating. **2.** something that emanates or is produced; effusion. **3.** a gaseous product of radioactive decay, such as radon. —**ˌem·a·'na·tion·al** *adj.*

e·man·ci·pate (ɪ'mænsɪˌpeɪt) *vb.* (*tr.*) **1.** to free from restriction or restraint, esp. social or legal restraint. **2.** (*often passive*) to free from the inhibitions imposed by conventional morality. **3.** to liberate (a slave) from bondage. [C17: from Latin *ēmancipāre* to give independence (to a son), from *mancipāre* to transfer property, from *manceps* a purchaser; see MANCIPLE] —**e·'man·ci·ˌpa·tive** *adj.* —**e·'man·ci·pist** *or* **e·'man·ci·ˌpa·tor** *n.* —**e·man·ci·pa·to·ry** (ɪ'mænsɪpətərɪ, -trɪ) *adj.*

e·man·ci·pa·tion (ɪˌmænsɪ'peɪʃən) *n.* **1.** the act of freeing or state of being freed; liberation. **2.** *Informal.* freedom from inhibition and convention. —**e·ˌman·ci·'pa·tion·ist** *n.*

e·mar·gi·nate (ɪ'mɑːdʒɪˌneɪt) *or* **e·mar·gi·nat·ed** *adj.* having a notched tip or edge: *emarginate leaves.* [C17: from Latin *ēmargināre* to deprive of its edge, from *margō* MARGIN] —**e·'mar·gi·ˌnate·ly** *adv.* —**e·ˌmar·gi·'na·tion** *n.*

e·mas·cu·late *vb.* (ɪ'mæskjʊˌleɪt). (*tr.*) **1.** to remove the testicles of; castrate; geld. **2.** to deprive of vigour, effectiveness, etc. ~*adj.* (ɪ'mæskjʊlɪt, -ˌleɪt). **3.** castrated; gelded. **4.** deprived of strength, effectiveness, etc. [C17: from Latin *ēmasculāre*, from *masculus* male; see MASCULINE] —**e·ˌmas·cu·'la·tion** *n.* —**e·'mas·cu·la·tive** *or* **e·'mas·cu·la·to·ry** *adj.* —**e·'mas·cu·ˌla·tor** *n.*

em·balm (ɪm'bɑːm) *vb.* (*tr.*) **1.** to treat (a dead body) with preservatives, as by injecting formaldehyde into the blood vessels, to retard putrefaction. **2.** to preserve or cherish the memory of. **3.** *Poetic.* to give a sweet fragrance to. [C13: from Old French *embaumer;* see BALM] —**em·'balm·er** *n.* —**em·'balm·ment** *n.*

em·bank (ɪm'bæŋk) *vb.* (*tr.*) to protect, enclose, or confine (a waterway, road, etc.) with an embankment.

em·bank·ment (ɪm'bæŋkmənt) *n.* a man-made ridge of earth or stone that carries a road or railway or confines a waterway. See also **levee**[1].

em·bar·go (ɛm'bɑːgəʊ) *n., pl.* **-goes. 1.** a government order prohibiting the departure or arrival of merchant ships in its ports. **2.** any legal stoppage of commerce: *an embargo on arms shipments.* **3.** a restraint, hindrance, or prohibition. ~*vb.* **-goes, -go·ing, -goed.** (*tr.*) **4.** to lay an embargo upon. **5.** to seize for use by the state. [C16: from Spanish, from *embargar*, from Latin IM- + *barra* BAR[1]]

em·bark (ɛm'bɑːk) *vb.* **1.** to board (a ship or aircraft). **2.** (*intr.;* usually foll. by *on* or *upon*) to commence or engage (in) a new project, venture, etc. [C16: via French from Old Provençal *embarcar*, from EM- + *barca* boat, BARQUE] —**ˌem·bar·'ka·tion** *n.* —**em·'bark·ment** *n.*

em·bar·ras de rich·esses *French.* (ãbara də ri'ʃɛs) *n.* a superfluous abundance of options, from which one finds it difficult to select. Also called: ***em·bar·ras de choix*** (də 'ʃwa). [literally: embarrassment of riches]

em·bar·rass (ɪm'bærəs) *vb.* (*mainly tr.*) **1.** (*also intr.*) to feel or cause to feel confusion or self-consciousness; disconcert; fluster. **2.** (*usually passive*) to involve in financial difficulties. **3.** *Archaic.* to make difficult; complicate. **4.** *Archaic.* to impede; obstruct; hamper. [C17 (in the sense: to impede): via French and Spanish from Italian *imbarrazzare*, from *imbarrare* to confine within bars; see EN-[1], BAR[1]] —**em·'bar·rass·ing** *adj.* —**em·'bar·rass·ing·ly** *adv.*

em·bar·rass·ment (ɪm'bærəsmənt) *n.* **1.** the state of being embarrassed. **2.** something that embarrasses. **3.** a financial predicament. **4.** an excessive amount; superfluity.

em·bas·sy ('ɛmbəsɪ) *n., pl.* **-sies. 1.** the residence or place of official business of an ambassador. **2.** an ambassador and his entourage collectively. **3.** the position, business, or mission of an ambassador. **4.** any important or official mission, duty, etc., esp. one undertaken by an agent. [C16: from Old French *ambassee*, from Old Italian *ambasciata*, from Old Provençal *ambaisada*, ultimately of Germanic origin; see AMBASSADOR]

em·bat·tle (ɪm'bætᵊl) *vb.* (*tr.*) **1.** to deploy (troops) for battle. **2.** to strengthen or fortify (a position, town, etc.). **3.** to provide (a building) with battlements. [C14: from Old French *embataillier;* see EN-[1], BATTLE]

em·bat·tled (ɪm'bætᵊld) *adj.* **1.** prepared for or engaged in conflict, controversy, or battle. **2.** *Heraldry.* having an indented edge resembling battlements.

em·bay (ɪm'beɪ) *vb.* (*tr.*) (*usually passive*) **1.** to form into a bay. **2.** to enclose in or as if in a bay. **3.** (esp. of the wind) to force (a ship, esp. a sailing ship) into a bay.

em·bay·ment (ɪm'beɪmənt) *n.* a shape resembling a bay.

em·bed *or* **im·bed** (ɪm'bɛd) *vb.* **-beds, -bed·ding, -bed·ded. 1.** (usually foll. by *in*) to fix or become fixed firmly and deeply in a surrounding solid mass: *to embed a nail in wood.* **2.** (*tr.*) to surround closely: *hard rock embeds the roots.* **3.** (*tr.*) to fix or retain (a thought, idea, etc.) in the mind. **4.** (*tr.*) *Grammar.* to insert (a subordinate clause) into a sentence. —**em·'bed·ment** *or* **im·'bed·ment** *n.*

em·bel·lish (ɪm'bɛlɪʃ) *vb.* (*tr.*) **1.** to improve or beautify by adding detail or ornament; adorn. **2.** to make (a story, etc.) more interesting by adding detail. **3.** to provide (a melody, part, etc.) with ornaments. See **ornament** (sense 5). [C14: from Old French *embelir*, from *bel* beautiful, from Latin *bellus*] —**em·'bel·lish·er** *n.* —**em·'bel·lish·ment** *n.*

em·ber ('ɛmbə) *n.* **1.** a glowing or smouldering piece of coal or wood, as in a dying fire. **2.** the fading remains of a past emotion: *the embers of his love.* [Old English *ǣmyrge;* related to Old Norse *eimyrja* ember, *eimr* smoke, Old High German *eimuria* ember]

Em·ber days *pl. n. R.C. and Anglican Church.* any of four groups of three days (always Wednesday, Friday, and Saturday) of prayer and fasting, the groups occurring after Pentecost, after the first Sunday of Lent, after the feast of St. Lucy (Dec. 13), and after the feast of the Holy Cross (Sept. 14). [Old English *ymbrendæg*, from *ymbren*, perhaps from *ymbryne* a (recurring) period, from *ymb* around + *ryne* a course + *dæg* day]

em·ber goose *n.* (*not in ornithological use*) another name for the **great northern diver.** See **diver** (the bird). [C18: from Norwegian *emmer-gaas*]

Em·ber week *n.* a week in which Ember days fall.

em·bez·zle (ɪm'bɛzᵊl) *vb.* to convert (money or property entrusted to one) fraudulently to one's own use. [C15: from Anglo-French *embeseiller* to destroy, from Old French *beseiller* to make away with, of uncertain origin] —**em·'bez·zle·ment** *n.* —**em·'bez·zler** *n.*

em·bit·ter (ɪm'bɪtə) *vb.* (*tr.*) **1.** to make (a person) resentful or bitter. **2.** to aggravate (an already hostile feeling, difficult situation, etc.). —**em·'bit·ter·er** *n.* —**em·'bit·ter·ment** *n.*

em·blaze (ɪm'bleɪz) *vb.* (*tr.*) *Archaic.* **1.** to cause to light up; illuminate. **2.** to set fire to.

em·bla·zon (ɪm'bleɪzᵊn) *vb.* (*tr.*) **1.** to describe, portray, or colour (arms) according to the conventions of heraldry. **2.** to portray heraldic arms on (a shield, one's notepaper, etc.). **3.** to make bright or splendid, as with colours, flowers, etc. **4.** to glorify, praise, or extol, often so as to attract great publicity: *his feat was emblazoned on the front page.* —**em·'bla·zon·ment** *n.*

em+bla+zon+ry (ɪm'bleɪzᵊnrɪ) *n.* another name for **blazonry.**

em+blem ('ɛmbləm) *n.* **1.** a visible object or representation that symbolizes a quality, type, group, etc., esp. the concrete symbol of an abstract idea: *the dove is an emblem of peace.* **2.** an allegorical picture containing a moral lesson, often with an explanatory motto or verses, esp. one printed in an **emblem book.** [C15: from Latin *emblēma* raised decoration, mosaic, from Greek, literally: something inserted, from *emballein* to insert, from *ballein* to throw] —ˌ**em+blem+'at+ic** *or* ˌ**em+blem+'at·i+cal** *adj.* —ˌ**em+blem+'at·i+cal+ly** *adv.*

em+blem·a+tize (ɛm'blɛməˌtaɪz), **em+blem+ize** ('ɛmbləˌmaɪz), *or* **em+blem·a+tise, em+blem+ise** *vb. (tr.)* **1.** to function as an emblem of; symbolize. **2.** to represent by or as by an emblem.

em+ble+ments ('ɛmbləmənts) *pl. n. Law.* **1.** annual crops and vegetable products cultivated by man's labour. **2.** the profits from such crops. [C15: from Old French *emblaement,* from *emblaer* to sow with grain, from Medieval Latin *imblādāre,* from *blāda* grain, of Germanic origin; compare Old English *blǣd* grain]

em+bod·y (ɪm'bɒdɪ) *vb.* **+bod+ies, +bod·y+ing, +bod+ied.** *(tr.)* **1.** to give a tangible, bodily, or concrete form to (an abstract concept). **2.** to be an example of or express (an idea, principle, etc.), esp. in action: *his gentleness embodies a Christian ideal.* **3.** (often foll. by *in*) to collect or unite in a comprehensive whole, system, etc.; comprise; include: *all the different essays were embodied in one long article.* **4.** *Theol.* to invest (a spiritual entity) with a body or with bodily form; render incarnate. —**em+'bod·i+ment** *n.*

em+bold+en (ɪm'bəʊldᵊn) *vb. (tr.)* to encourage; make bold.

em+bo+lec+to+my (ˌɛmbə'lɛktəmɪ) *n., pl.* **+mies.** the surgical removal of an embolus that is blocking a blood vessel.

em+bol+ic (ɛm'bɒlɪk) *adj.* **1.** of or relating to an embolus or embolism. **2.** *Embryol.* of, relating to, or resulting from invagination.

em+bo+lism ('ɛmbəˌlɪzəm) *n.* **1.** the occlusion of a blood vessel by an embolus. **2.** the insertion of one or more days into a calendar, esp. the Jewish calendar; intercalation. **3.** *R.C. Church.* a prayer inserted in the canon of the Mass between the Lord's Prayer and the breaking of the bread. **4.** another name (not in technical use) for **embolus.** [C14: from Medieval Latin *embolismus,* from Late Greek *embolismos* intercalary; see EMBOLUS] —ˌ**em+bo+'lis+mic** *adj.*

em+bo+lus ('ɛmbələs) *n., pl.* **+li** (-ˌlaɪ). material, such as part of a blood clot or an air bubble, that is transported by the blood stream until it becomes lodged within a small vessel and impedes the circulation. Compare **thrombus.** [C17: via Latin from Greek *embolos* stopper, from *emballein* to insert, from *ballein* to throw; see EMBLEM]

em+bo+ly ('ɛmbəlɪ) *n., pl.* **+lies.** another name for **invagination** (sense 3). [C19: from Greek *embolē* an insertion, from *emballein* to throw in; see EMBLEM]

em+bon+point *French.* (ɑ̃bɔ̃'pwɛ̃) *n.* **1.** plumpness or stoutness. ~*adj.* **2.** plump; stout. [C18: from phrase *en bon point* in good condition]

em+bos+om (ɪm'bʊzəm) *vb. (tr.) Archaic.* **1.** to enclose or envelop, esp. protectively. **2.** to clasp to the bosom; hug. **3.** to cherish.

em+boss (ɪm'bɒs) *vb.* **1.** to mould or carve (a decoration or design) on (a surface) so that it is raised above the surface in low relief. **2.** to cause to bulge; make protrude. [C14: from Old French *embocer,* from EM- + *boce* BOSS[2]] —**em+'boss+er** *n.* —**em+'boss+ment** *n.*

em+bou+chure (ˌɒmbʊ'ʃʊə) *n.* **1.** the mouth of a river or valley. **2.** *Music.* **a.** the correct application of the lips and tongue in playing a wind instrument. **b.** the mouthpiece of a wind instrument, esp. of the brass family. [C18: from French, from Old French *emboucher* to put to one's mouth, from *bouche* mouth, from Latin *bucca* cheek]

em+bow (ɪm'bəʊ) *vb. (tr.)* to design or create (a structure) in the form of an arch or vault. —**em+'bow+ment** *n.*

em+bow+el (ɪm'baʊəl) *vb. Obsolete.* **1.** to bury or embed deeply. **2.** another word for **disembowel.**

em+bow+er (ɪm'baʊə) *vb. (tr.) Archaic.* to enclose in or as in a bower.

em+brace[1] (ɪm'breɪs) *vb. (mainly tr.)* **1.** *(also intr.)* (of a person) to take or clasp (another person) in the arms, or (of two people) to clasp each other, as in affection, greeting, etc.; hug. **2.** to accept (an opportunity, challenge, etc.) willingly or eagerly. **3.** to take up (a new idea, faith, etc.); adopt: *to embrace Judaism.* **4.** to comprise or include as an integral part: *geology embraces the science of mineralogy.* **5.** to encircle or enclose: *an island embraced by the ocean.* **6.** *Rare.* to perceive or understand. ~*n.* **7.** the act of embracing. **8.** *(often pl.) Euphemistic.* sexual intercourse. [C14: from Old French *embracier,* from EM- + *brace* a pair of arms, from Latin *bracchia* arms] —**em+'brace+a·ble** *adj.* —**em+'brace+ment** *n.* —**em+'brac+er** *n.*

em+brace[2] (ɪm'breɪs) *vb. (tr.) Criminal law.* to commit or attempt to commit embracery against (a jury, etc.). [C15: back formation from EMBRACEOR]

em+brace+or *or* **em+brac+er** (ɪm'breɪsə) *n. Criminal law.* a person guilty of embracery. [C15: from Old French *embraseor,* from *embraser* to instigate, literally: to set on fire, from *braser* to burn, from *brese* live coals]

em+brac+er·y (ɪm'breɪsərɪ) *n. Criminal law.* the offence of attempting by corrupt means to influence a jury or juror, as by bribery or threats.

em+branch+ment (ɪm'brɑːntʃmənt) *n.* **1.** the process of branching out, esp. by a river. **2.** a branching out or ramification, as of a river or mountain range.

em+bran+gle (ɪm'bræŋgᵊl) *vb. (tr.) Rare.* to confuse or entangle. [C17: from EM- + obsolete *brangle* to wrangle, perhaps a blend of BRAWL + WRANGLE] —**em+'bran+gle+ment** *n.*

em+bra+sure (ɪm'breɪʒə) *n.* **1.** *Fortifications.* an opening or indentation, as in a battlement, for shooting through. **2.** an opening forming a door or window, having splayed sides that increase the width of the opening in the interior. [C18: from French, from obsolete *embraser* to widen, of uncertain origin] —**em+'bra+sured** *adj.*

em+brec+to+my (ɛm'brɛktəmɪ) *n., pl.* **+mies.** surgical removal of an embryo, esp. in cases of ectopic pregnancy.

em+bro+cate ('ɛmbrəʊˌkeɪt) *vb. (tr.)* to apply a liniment or lotion to (a part of the body). [C17: from Medieval Latin *embrocāre,* from *embrocha* poultice, from Greek *embrokhē* lotion, infusion, from *brokhē* a moistening]

em+bro+ca+tion (ˌɛmbrəʊ'keɪʃən) *n.* a drug or agent for rubbing into the skin; liniment.

em+broi+der (ɪm'brɔɪdə) *vb.* **1.** to do decorative needlework upon (cloth, etc.). **2.** to add fictitious or fanciful detail to (a story). **3.** to add exaggerated or improbable details to (an account of an event, etc.). [C15: from Old French *embroder;* see *em-* EN-[1], BROIDER] —**em+'broi+der+er** *n.*

em+broi+der·y (ɪm'brɔɪdərɪ) *n., pl.* **+der·ies. 1.** decorative needlework done usually on loosely woven cloth or canvas, often being a picture or pattern. **2.** elaboration or exaggeration, esp. in writing or reporting; embellishment.

em+broil (ɪm'brɔɪl) *vb. (tr.)* **1.** to involve (a person, oneself, etc.) in trouble, conflict, or argument. **2.** to throw (affairs, etc.) into a state of confusion or disorder; complicate; entangle. [C17: from French *embrouiller,* from *brouiller* to mingle, confuse] —**em+'broil+er** *n.* —**em+'broil+ment** *n.*

em+brue (ɪm'bruː) *vb.* **+brues, +bru+ing, +brued.** a variant spelling of **imbrue.** —**em+'brue+ment** *n.*

em+bry+ec+to+my (ˌɛmbrɪ'ɛktəmɪ) *n., pl.* **+mies.** surgical removal of an embryo.

em+bry·o ('ɛmbrɪˌəʊ) *n., pl.* **+bry·os. 1.** an animal in the early stages of development following cleavage of the zygote and ending at birth or hatching. **2.** the human product of conception up to approximately the end of the second month of pregnancy. Compare **fetus. 3.** a plant in the early stages of development: in higher plants, the plumule, cotyledons, and radicle within the seed. **4.** an undeveloped or rudimentary state (esp. in the phrase **in embryo**). **5.** something in an early stage of development: *an embryo of an idea.* [C16: from Late Latin, from Greek *embruon,* from *bruein* to swell] —**'em+bry+ˌoid** *adj.*

em+bry+og+e+ny (ˌɛmbrɪ'ɒdʒɪnɪ) *n.* **1.** Also called: **embryogenesis** (ˌɛmbrɪəʊ'dʒɛnəsɪs). the formation and development of an embryo. **2.** the study of these processes. —**em+bry·o+gen+ic** (ˌɛmbrɪəʊ'dʒɛnɪk) *adj.*

embryol. *abbrev. for* embryology.

em+bry+ol+o·gy (ˌɛmbrɪ'ɒlədʒɪ) *n.* **1.** the branch of science concerned with the study of embryos. **2.** the structure and development of the embryo of a particular organism. —**em+bry·o·log+i+cal** (ˌɛmbrɪə'lɒdʒɪkᵊl) *or* ˌ**em+bry·o+'log+ic** *adj.* —ˌ**em+bry·o+'log·i+cal+ly** *adv.* —ˌ**em+bry+'ol·o+gist** *n.*

em+bry+on+ic (ˌɛmbrɪ'ɒnɪk) *or* **em+bry·o+nal** ('ɛmbrɪənᵊl) *adj.* **1.** of or relating to an embryo. **2.** in an early stage; rudimentary; undeveloped. —ˌ**em+bry+'on·i+cal+ly** *adv.*

em+bry·o sac *n.* the structure within a plant ovule that contains the egg cell; the megaspore of seed plants: contains the embryo plant and endosperm after fertilization.

em+bus (ɪm'bʌs) *vb.* **+bus·es, +bus+ing, +bused** *or* **+bus·ses, +bus+sing, +bussed.** *Military.* to cause (troops) to board or (of troops) to board a transport vehicle.

em+bus+qué *French.* (ɑ̃bys'ke) *n., pl.* **+qués** (-'ke). a man who avoids military conscription by obtaining a government job. [from *embusquer* to lie in ambush, shirk]

em+cee (ˌɛm'siː) *Informal.* ~*n.* **1.** a master of ceremonies. ~*vb.* **+cees, +cee+ing, +ceed. 2.** to act as master of ceremonies (for or at). [from the abbreviation M.C.]

em dash *n. Printing.* a dash (—) one em long.

Em+den (*German* 'ɛmdᵊn) *n.* a port in NW West Germany, in Lower Saxony at the mouth of the River Ems. Pop.: 49 500 (1970).

-eme *suffix forming nouns. Linguistics.* indicating a minimal distinctive unit of a specified type in a language: *morpheme; phoneme.* [C20: via French, abstracted from PHONEME]

e·mend (ɪ'mɛnd) *vb. (tr.)* to make corrections or improvements in (a text) by critical editing. [C15: from Latin *ēmendāre* to correct, from *ē-* out + *mendum* a mistake] —**e·'mend+a·ble** *adj.*

e·men+da·tion (ˌiːmɛn'deɪʃən) *n.* **1.** a correction or improvement in a text. **2.** the act or process of emending. —**'e·men+ˌda·tor** *n.* —**e·men+da·to·ry** (ɪ'mɛndətərɪ, -trɪ) *adj.*

em+er+ald ('ɛmərəld, 'ɛmrəld) *n.* **1.** a green transparent variety of beryl: highly valued as a gem. **2. a.** the clear green colour of an emerald. **b.** *(as adj.): an emerald carpet.* **3.** (formerly) a size of printer's type approximately equal to 6½ point. [C13: from Old French *esmeraude,* from Latin *smaragdus,* from Greek *smaragdos;* related to Sanskrit *marakata* emerald]

Em+er+ald Isle *n.* a poetic name for **Ireland.**

e·merge (ɪ'mɜːdʒ) *vb. (intr.;* often foll. by *from)* **1.** to come up to the surface of or rise from water or other liquid. **2.** to come into view, as from concealment or obscurity: *he emerged from the cave.* **3.** (foll. by *from*) to come out (of) or live (through a difficult experience, etc.): *he emerged from his ordeal with dignity.* **4.** to become apparent: *several interesting things* *emerged from the report.* [C17: from Latin *ēmergere* to rise up from, from *mergere* to dip]

e·mer+gence (ɪˈmɜːdʒəns) *n.* **1.** the act or process of emerging. **2.** an outgrowth, such as a prickle, that contains no vascular tissue and does not develop into stem, leaf, etc.

e·mer+gen+cy (ɪˈmɜːdʒənsɪ) *n., pl.* **+cies. 1. a.** an unforeseen or sudden occurrence, esp. of a danger demanding immediate remedy or action. **b.** (*as modifier*): *an emergency exit.* **2. a.** a patient requiring urgent treatment. **b.** (*as modifier*): *an emergency ward.* **3. state of emergency.** a condition, declared by a government, in which martial law applies, usually because of civil unrest or natural disaster.

e·mer+gent (ɪˈmɜːdʒənt) *adj.* **1.** coming into being or notice: *an emergent political structure.* **2.** (of a nation) recently independent. ~*n.* **3.** an aquatic plant with stem and leaves above the water. **—e'mer+gent+ly** *adv.* **—e'mer+gent+ness** *n.*

e·mer+gent e·vo+lu+tion *n. Philosophy.* the doctrine that, in the course of evolution, some entirely new properties, such as life and consciousness, appear at certain critical points, usually because of an unpredictable rearrangement of the already existing entities.

e·mer·i+tus (ɪˈmɛrɪtəs) *adj.* (*postpositive*) retired or honourably discharged from full-time work, but retaining one's title on an honorary basis: *a professor emeritus.* [C19: from Latin, from *merēre* to deserve; see MERIT]

e·mersed (ɪˈmɜːst) *adj.* (of the leaves or stems of aquatic plants) protruding above the surface of the water.

e·mer+sion (ɪˈmɜːʃən) *n.* **1.** the act or an instance of emerging. **2.** Also called: **egress.** *Astronomy.* the reappearance of a celestial body after an eclipse or occultation. [C17: from Latin *ēmersus,* from *ēmergere;* see EMERGE]

Em·er·son (ˈɛməsᵊn) *n.* **Ralph Wal·do.** 1803–82, U.S. poet, essayist, and transcendentalist.

em+er·y (ˈɛmərɪ) *n.* **a.** a hard greyish-black mineral consisting of corundum with either magnetite or haematite: used as an abrasive and polishing agent, esp. as a coating on paper, cloth, etc. Formula: Al_2O_3. **b.** (*as modifier*): *emery paper.* [C15: from Old French *esmeril,* ultimately from Greek *smuris* powder for rubbing]

em+er·y board *n.* a strip of cardboard or wood with a rough surface of crushed emery, for filing one's nails.

em+er·y wheel *n.* a grinding or polishing wheel the surface of which is coated with abrasive emery particles.

em+e·sis (ˈɛmɪsɪs) *n.* the technical name for **vomiting.** [C19: via New Latin from Greek, from *emein* to vomit]

e·met+ic (ɪˈmɛtɪk) *adj.* **1.** causing vomiting. ~*n.* **2.** an emetic agent or drug. [C17: from Late Latin *ēmeticus,* from Greek *emetikos,* from *emein* to vomit] **—e'met·i·cal+ly** *adv.*

em+e·tine (ˈɛməˌtiːn, -tɪn) *or* **em+e·tin** (ˈɛmətɪn) *n.* a white bitter poisonous alkaloid obtained from ipecac: the hydrochloride is used to treat amoebic infections. Formula: $C_{29}H_{40}O_4N_2$. [C19: from French *émétine;* see EMETIC, -INE²]

emf *or* **EMF** *abbrev. for* electromotive force.

-e·mi·a *n. combining form.* U.S. variant of **-aemia.**

em·i+grant (ˈɛmɪgrənt) *n.* **a.** a person who leaves one place or country, esp. a native country, to settle in another. Compare **immigrant. b.** (*as modifier*): *an emigrant worker.*

em·i+grate (ˈɛmɪˌgreɪt) *vb.* (*intr.*) to leave one place or country, esp. one's native country, in order to settle in another. Compare **immigrate.** [C18: from Latin *ēmīgrāre,* from *mīgrāre* to depart, MIGRATE] **—'em·i+ˌgra+tive** *or* **'em·i+ˌgra+to·ry** *adj.*

em·i·gra+tion (ˌɛmɪˈgreɪʃən) *n.* **1.** the act or an instance of emigrating. **2.** emigrants considered collectively.

é·mi·gré (ˈɛmɪˌgreɪ; *French* emiˈgre) *n.* an emigrant, esp. one forced to leave his native country for political reasons. [C18: from French, from *émigrer* to EMIGRATE]

E·mil·i·a-Ro·ma·gna (ɪˈmiːlɪəˌ rəʊˈmɑːnjə; *Italian* eˈmiːlja roˈmaɲɲa) *n.* a region of N central Italy, on the Adriatic: rises from the plains of the Po valley in the north to the Apennines in the south. Capital: Bologna. Pop.: 3 841 103 (1971). Area: 22 123 sq. km. (8628 sq. miles).

em·i+nence (ˈɛmɪnəns) *or* **em·i+nen+cy** *n., pl.* **+nenc·es** *or* **+nen+cies. 1.** a position of superiority, distinction, high rank, or fame. **2.** a high or raised piece of ground. **3.** *Anatomy.* a projection of an organ or part. [C17: from French, from Latin *ēminentia* a standing out; see EMINENT]

Em·i+nence (ˈɛmɪnəns) *or* **Em·i+nen+cy** *n., pl.* **+nenc·es** *or* **+nen+cies.** (preceded by *Your* or *His*) a title used to address or refer to a cardinal.

é·mi+nence grise *French.* (eminɑ̃s ˈgriːz) *n., pl.* ***é·mi+nences grises*** (eminɑ̃s ˈgriːz). a person who wields power and influence unofficially or behind the scenes. [literally: grey eminence, originally applied to Père Joseph (François Le Clerc du Tremblay; died 1638), French monk, secretary of Cardinal Richelieu]

em·i+nent (ˈɛmɪnənt) *adj.* **1.** above others in rank, merit, or reputation; distinguished: *an eminent scientist.* **2.** (*prenominal*) noteworthy, conspicuous, or outstanding: *eminent good sense.* **3.** projecting or protruding; prominent. [C15: from Latin *ēminēre* to project, stand out, from *minēre* to stand] **—'em·i+nent+ly** *adv.*

em·i+nent do+main *n. Law.* the right of a state to confiscate private property for public use, payment usually being made to the owners in compensation.

e·mir (ɛˈmɪə) *n.* (in the Islamic world) **1.** an independent ruler or chieftain. **2.** a military commander or governor. **3.** a descendant of Mohammed. ~Also spelled: **amir.** [C17: via French from Spanish *emir,* from Arabic *'amīr* commander]

e·mir+ate (ɛˈmɪərɪt) *n.* **1.** the rank or office of an emir. **2.** the government, jurisdiction, or territory of an emir.

Em·i+scan (ˌɛmɪˈskæn) *n. Trademark.* a computerized radiological technique for examining the soft tissues of the body, esp. the brain, to detect the presence of tumours, abscesses, etc.

em+is+sar·y (ˈɛmɪsərɪ, -ɪsrɪ) *n., pl.* **+sar·ies. 1. a.** an agent or messenger sent on a mission, esp. one who represents a government or head of state. **b.** (*as modifier*): *an emissary delegation.* **2.** an agent sent on a secret mission, as a spy. [C17: from Latin *ēmissārius* emissary, spy, from *ēmittere* to send out; see EMIT]

e·mis+sion (ɪˈmɪʃən) *n.* **1.** the act of emitting or sending forth. **2.** energy, in the form of heat, light, radio waves, etc., emitted from a source. **3.** a substance, fluid, etc., that is emitted; discharge. **4.** a measure of the number of electrons emitted by a cathode or electron gun: *at 1000°C the emission is 3 mA.* See also **secondary emission, thermionic emission. 5.** *Physiol.* any bodily discharge, esp. an involuntary release of semen during sleep. **6.** an issue, as of currency. [C17: from Latin *ēmissiō,* from *ēmittere* to send forth, EMIT] **—e'mis+sive** *adj.*

e·mis+sion spec+trum *n.* the continuous spectrum or pattern of bright lines or bands seen when the electromagnetic radiation emitted by a substance is passed into a spectrometer. The spectrum is characteristic of the emitting substance and the type of excitation to which it is subjected. Compare **absorption spectrum.**

e·mis+siv+i·ty (ˌɪmɪˈsɪvɪtɪ, ˌɛm-) *n.* a measure of the ability of a surface to radiate energy as measured by the ratio of the radiant flux per unit area to that radiated by a black body at the same temperature. Symbol: ϵ

e·mit (ɪˈmɪt) *vb.* **e·mits, e·mit+ting, e·mit+ted.** (*tr.*) **1.** to give or send forth; discharge: *the pipe emitted a stream of water.* **2.** to give voice to; utter: *she emitted a shrill scream.* **3.** *Physics.* to give off (radiation or particles). **4.** to put (currency) into circulation. [C17: from Latin *ēmittere* to send out, from *mittere* to send]

e·mit+ter (ɪˈmɪtə) *n.* **1.** a person or thing that emits. **2.** a radioactive substance that emits radiation: *a beta emitter.* **3.** the region in a transistor in which the charge-carrying holes or electrons originate.

Em·man·u·el (ɪˈmænjʊəl) *n.* a variant spelling of **Immanuel.**

Em+men (ˈɛmən; *Dutch* ˈɛmə) *n.* a city in the NE Netherlands, in Drenthe province: a new town developed since World War II. Pop.: 82 574 (1973 est.).

em+men·a+gogue (ɪˈmɛnəˌgɒg, -ˈmiː-) *n.* **1.** a drug or agent that increases menstrual flow. ~*adj.* also **em+men·a+gog+ic** (ɪˌmɛnəˈgɒdʒɪk). **2.** inducing or increasing menstrual flow. [C18: from Greek *emmēna* menses, (from *mēn* month) + -AGOGUE]

Em+men+thal (ˈɛmənˌtɑːl) *or* **Em+men+thal+er** *n.* a hard Swiss cheese with holes in it, similar to Gruyère. [named after *Emmenthal,* a valley in Switzerland]

em+mer (ˈɛmə) *n.* a variety of wheat, *Triticum dicoccum,* grown in mountainous parts of Europe as a cereal crop and for livestock food: thought to be an ancestor of many other varieties of wheat. [from German; related to Old High German *amari* spelt]

em+met (ˈɛmɪt) *n. Brit.* an archaic or dialect word for **ant.** [Old English *ǣmette* ANT; related to Old Norse *meita,* Old High German *āmeiza,* Gothic *maitan*]

em+me+tro·pi·a (ˌɛmɪˈtrəʊpɪə) *n.* the normal condition of perfect vision, in which parallel light rays are focused on the retina without the need for accommodation. [C19: from New Latin, from Greek *emmetros* in due measure + -OPIA] **—em+me+trop+ic** (ˌɛmɪˈtrɒpɪk) *adj.*

Em·my (ˈɛmɪ) *n., pl.* **·mys** *or* **·mies.** *U.S.* one of the gold-plated statuettes awarded annually for outstanding television performances and productions. [C20: alteration of *Immy,* short for *image orthicon tube*]

e·mol+lient (ɪˈmɒljənt) *adj.* **1.** softening or soothing, esp. to the skin. ~*n.* **2.** any preparation or substance that has a softening or soothing effect, esp. when applied to the skin. [C17: from Latin *ēmollīre* to soften, from *mollis* soft] **—e'mol+lience** *n.*

e·mol·u·ment (ɪˈmɒljʊmənt) *n.* the profit arising from an office or employment, usually in the form of fees or wages. [C15: from Latin *ēmolumentum* benefit; originally, fee paid to a miller, from *ēmolere,* from *molere* to grind]

e·mote (ɪˈməʊt) *vb.* (*intr.*) *Informal.* to display exaggerated emotion, as in acting; behave theatrically. [C20: back formation from EMOTION] **—e'mot+er** *n.*

e·mo+tion (ɪˈməʊʃən) *n.* any strong feeling, as of joy, sorrow, or fear. [C16: from French, from Old French *esmovoir* to excite, from Latin *ēmovēre* to disturb, from *movēre* to MOVE] **—e'mo+tion+less** *adj.*

e·mo+tion+al (ɪˈməʊʃənᵊl) *adj.* **1.** of, characteristic of, or expressive of emotion. **2.** readily or excessively affected by emotion. **3.** appealing to or arousing emotion: *an emotional piece of music.* **4.** caused, determined, or actuated by emotion rather than reason: *an emotional argument.* **—e,mo+tion+'al+i·ty** *n.* **—e'mo+tion+al+ly** *adv.*

e·mo+tion+al+ism (ɪˈməʊʃənəˌlɪzəm) *n.* **1.** emotional nature, character, or quality. **2.** a tendency to yield readily to the emotions. **3.** an appeal to the emotions, esp. an excessive appeal, as to an audience. **4.** a doctrine stressing the value of deeply felt responses in ethics and the arts. **—e'mo+tion+al+ist** *n.* **—e,mo+tion+al+'is+tic** *adj.*

e·mo+tion+al+ize *or* **e·mo+tion+al+ise** (ɪˈməʊʃənəˌlaɪz) *vb.* (*tr.*) to make emotional; subject to emotional treatment. **—e,mo+tion+al·i+'za+tion** *or* **e,mo+tion+al·i+'sa+tion** *n.*

e·mo·tive (ɪ'məʊtɪv) *adj.* **1.** tending or designed to arouse emotion. **2.** of or characterized by emotion. —**e·'mo·tive·ly** *adv.* —**e·'mo·tive·ness** *or* **,e·mo·'tiv·i·ty** *n.*

e·mo·ti·vism (ɪ'məʊtɪ,vɪzəm) *n. Ethics.* the theory that moral utterances do not have a truth value but express the feelings of the speaker. Compare **prescriptivism, descriptivism.**

Emp. *abbrev. for:* **1.** Emperor. **2.** Empire. **3.** Empress.

em·pale (ɪm'peɪl) *vb.* a less common spelling of **impale.** —**em·'pale·ment** *n.* —**em·'pal·er** *n.*

em·pan·el *or* **im·pan·el** (ɪm'pænᵊl) *vb.* **·els, ·el·ling, ·elled** *or U.S.* **·els, ·el·ing, eled.** (*tr.*) *Law.* **1.** to enter on a list (names of persons to be summoned for jury service). **2.** to select (a jury) from the names on such a list. —**em·'pan·el·ment** *or* **im·'pan·el·ment** *n.*

em·path·ic (ɛm'pæθɪk) *or* **em·pa·thet·ic** (,ɛmpə'θɛtɪk) *adj.* of or relating to empathy. —**em·'path·i·cal·ly** *or* **,em·pa·'thet·i·cal·ly** *adv.*

em·pa·thize *or* **em·pa·thise** ('ɛmpə,θaɪz) *vb.* (*intr.*) to engage in or feel empathy.

em·pa·thy ('ɛmpəθɪ) *n.* **1.** the power of understanding and imaginatively entering into another person's feelings. See also **identification** (sense 3b.). **2.** the attribution to an object, such as a work of art, of one's own emotional or intellectual feelings about it. [C20: from Greek *empatheia* affection, passion, intended as a rendering of German *Einfühlung,* literally: a feeling in; see EN-², -PATHY] —**'em·path·ist** *n.*

Em·ped·o·cles (ɛm'pɛdə,kli:z) *n.* ?490–430 B.C., Greek philosopher and scientist, who held that the world is composed of four elements, air, fire, earth, and water, which are governed by the opposing forces of love and discord.

em·pen·nage (ɛm'pɛnɪdʒ; *French* ɑ̃pɛ'na:ʒ) *n.* the rear part of an aircraft, comprising the fin, rudder, and tailplane. [C20: from French: feathering, from *empenner* to feather an arrow, from *penne* feather, from Latin *pinna*]

em·per·or ('ɛmpərə) *n.* **1.** a monarch who rules or reigns over an empire. **2.** Also called: **emperor moth.** any of several large saturniid moths with eyelike markings on each wing, esp. *Saturnia pavonia* of Europe. **3. purple emperor.** any of several Old World nymphalid butterflies of the genus *Apatura,* esp. *A. iris,* having mottled purple-and-brown wings. **4.** *Chiefly Brit.* a size of drawing or writing paper, 48 by 72 inches. [C13: from Old French *empereor,* from Latin *imperātor* commander-in-chief, from *imperāre* to command, from IM- + *parāre* to make ready] —**'em·per·or·,ship** *n.*

em·per·or pen·guin *n.* an Antarctic penguin, *Aptenodytes forsteri,* with orange-yellow patches on the neck: the largest penguin, reaching a height of 1.3 m (4 ft.).

em·per·y ('ɛmpərɪ) *n., pl.* **·per·ies.** *Archaic.* dominion or power; empire. [C13 (in the sense: the status of an emperor): from Anglo-French *emperie,* from Latin *imperium* power; see EMPIRE]

em·pha·sis ('ɛmfəsɪs) *n., pl.* **·ses** (-si:z). **1.** special importance or significance. **2.** an object, idea, etc., that is given special importance or significance. **3.** stress made to fall on a particular syllable, word, or phrase in speaking. **4.** force or intensity of expression: *he spoke with special emphasis on the subject of civil rights.* **5.** sharpness or clarity of form or outline: *the sunlight gave emphasis to the shape of the mountain.* [C16: via Latin from Greek: meaning, (in rhetoric) significant stress; see EMPHATIC]

em·pha·size *or* **em·pha·sise** ('ɛmfə,saɪz) *vb.* (*tr.*) to give emphasis or prominence to; stress.

em·phat·ic (ɪm'fætɪk) *adj.* **1.** expressed, spoken, or done with emphasis. **2.** forceful and positive; definite; direct: *an emphatic personality.* **3.** sharp or clear in form, contour, or outline. **4.** important or significant; stressed: *the emphatic points in an argument.* **5.** *Phonetics.* denoting certain dental consonants of Arabic that are pronounced with accompanying pharyngeal constriction. ~*n.* **6.** *Phonetics.* an emphatic consonant, as used in Arabic. [C18: from Greek *emphatikos* expressive, forceful, from *emphainein* to exhibit, display, from *phainein* to show] —**em·'phat·i·cal·ly** *adv.*

em·phy·se·ma (,ɛmfɪ'si:mə) *n. Pathol.* **1.** Also called: **pulmonary emphysema.** a condition in which the air sacs of the lungs are grossly enlarged, causing breathlessness and wheezing. **2.** the abnormal presence of air in a tissue or part. [C17: from New Latin, from Greek *emphusēma,* a swelling up, from *emphusan* to inflate, from *phusan* to blow] —**em·phy·sem·a·tous** (,ɛmfɪ'sɛmətəs, -'si:-) *adj.*

em·pire ('ɛmpaɪə) *n.* **1.** an aggregate of peoples and territories, often of great extent, under the rule of a single person, oligarchy, or sovereign state. **2.** any monarchy that for reasons of history, prestige, etc., has an emperor rather than a king as head of state. **3.** the period during which a particular empire exists. **4.** supreme power; sovereignty. **5.** a large industrial organization with many ramifications, esp. a multinational corporation. [C13: from Old French, from Latin *imperium* rule, from *imperāre* to command, from *parāre* to prepare]

Em·pire ('ɛmpaɪə) *n.* **the. 1.** See **British Empire. 2.** *French history.* **a.** the period of imperial rule in France from 1804 to 1815 under Napoleon Bonaparte. **b.** Also called: **Second Empire.** the period from 1852 to 1870 when Napoleon III ruled as emperor. ~*adj.* **3.** denoting, characteristic of, or relating to the British Empire. **4.** denoting, characteristic of, or relating to either French Empire, esp. the first: in particular, denoting the neoclassical style of architecture and furniture and the high-waisted style of women's dresses characteristic of the period.

em·pire-build·er *n. Informal.* a person who seeks extra power for its own sake, esp. by increasing the number of his subordinates or staff. —**'em·pire-,build·ing** *n., adj.*

Em·pire Day *n.* the former name of **Commonwealth Day.**

Em·pire State *n.* nickname of **New York** (state).

em·pir·ic (ɛm'pɪrɪk) *n.* **1.** a person who relies on empirical methods. **2.** a medical quack; charlatan. ~*adj.* **3.** a variant of **empirical.** [C16: from Latin *empīricus,* from Greek *empeirikos* practised, from *peiran* to attempt]

em·pir·i·cal (ɛm'pɪrɪkᵊl) *adj.* **1.** derived from or relating to experiment and observation rather than theory. **2.** (of medical treatment) based on practical experience rather than scientific proof. **3.** *Philosophy.* **a.** (of knowledge) derived from experience rather than by logic from first principles. Compare **a priori, a posteriori. b.** (of a proposition) subject, at least theoretically, to verification. Compare **analytic** (sense 4), **synthetic** (sense 4). **4.** of or relating to medical quackery. —**em·'pir·i·cal·ly** *adv.* —**em·'pir·i·cal·ness** *n.*

em·pir·i·cal for·mu·la *n.* **1.** a chemical formula indicating the proportion of each element present in a molecule: $C_6H_{12}O_6$ *is the molecular formula of sucrose whereas* CH_2O *is its empirical formula.* Compare **molecular formula, structural formula. 2.** a formula or expression obtained from experimental data rather than theory.

em·pir·i·cism (ɛm'pɪrɪ,sɪzəm) *n.* **1.** *Philosophy.* the doctrine that all knowledge derives from experience. Compare **intuitionism, rationalism. 2.** the use of empirical methods. **3.** medical quackery; charlatanism. —**em·'pir·i·cist** *n., adj.*

em·place (ɪm'pleɪs) *vb.* (*tr.*) to put in place or position.

em·place·ment (ɪm'pleɪsmənt) *n.* **1.** a prepared position for the siting of a gun or other weapon. **2.** the act of putting or state of being put in place. [C19: from French, from obsolete *emplacer* to put in position, from PLACE]

em·plane (ɪm'pleɪn) *vb.* to board or put on board an aeroplane.

em·ploy (ɪm'plɔɪ) *vb.* (*tr.*) **1.** to engage or make use of the services of (a person) in return for money; hire. **2.** to provide work or occupation for; keep busy; occupy: *collecting stamps employs a lot of his time.* **3.** to use as a means: *to employ secret measures to get one's ends.* ~*n.* **4.** the state of being employed (esp. in the phrase **in someone's employ**). [C15: from Old French *emploier,* from Latin *implicāre* to entangle, engage, from *plicāre* to fold] —**em·'ploy·a·ble** *adj.* —**em·,ploy·a·'bil·i·ty** *n.*

em·ploy·ee (ɛm'plɔɪi:, ,ɛmplɔɪ'i:) *or* **em·ploy·é** *n.* a person who is hired to work for another or for a business, firm, etc., in return for payment.

em·ploy·er (ɪm'plɔɪə) *n.* **1.** a person, business, firm, etc., that employs workers. **2.** a person who employs; user.

em·ploy·ment (ɪm'plɔɪmənt) *n.* **1.** the act of employing or state of being employed. **2.** the work or occupation in which a person is employed. **3.** the purpose for which something is used.

em·ploy·ment a·gen·cy *n. Brit.* a private firm whose business is placing people in jobs.

em·ploy·ment ex·change *n. Brit.* a former name for the **Employment Service Agency.**

Em·ploy·ment Ser·vice A·gen·cy *n. Brit.* the section of the Department of Employment responsible for finding jobs for the unemployed, paying unemployment benefits, collecting labour statistics, etc. Former names: **employment exchange, labour exchange.** See also **Jobcentre.**

em·poi·son (ɪm'pɔɪzᵊn) *vb.* (*tr.*) **1.** *Rare.* to embitter or corrupt. **2.** an archaic word for **poison** (senses 6–9). —**em·'poi·son·ment** *n.*

em·pol·der (ɪm'pəʊldə) *vb.* a variant spelling of **impolder.**

em·po·ri·um (ɛm'pɔ:rɪəm) *n., pl.* **·ri·ums** *or* **·ri·a** (-rɪə). a large and often ostentatious retail shop offering for sale a wide variety of merchandise. [C16: from Latin, from Greek *emporion,* from *emporos* merchant, from *poros* a journey]

em·pov·er·ish (ɪm'pɒvərɪʃ) *vb.* a less common spelling of **impoverish.** —**em·'pov·er·ish·er** *n.* —**em·'pov·er·ish·ment** *n.*

em·pow·er (ɪm'paʊə) *vb.* (*tr.*) **1.** to give or delegate power or authority to; authorize. **2.** to give ability to; enable or permit. —**em·'pow·er·ment** *n.*

em·press ('ɛmprɪs) *n.* **1.** the wife or widow of an emperor. **2.** a woman who holds the rank of emperor in her own right. **3.** *Informal.* a woman of great power and influence. [C12: from Old French *empereriz,* from Latin *imperātrix* feminine of *imperātor* EMPEROR]

em·prise (ɛm'praɪz) *n. Archaic.* **1.** a chivalrous or daring enterprise; adventure. **2.** chivalrous daring or prowess. [C13: from Old French, from *emprendre* to undertake; see ENTERPRISE]

Emp·son ('ɛmpsᵊn) *n.* **Wil·liam.** born 1906, English poet and critic; author of *Seven Types of Ambiguity* (1930).

empt (ɛmpt, ɛmt) *vb.* (*tr.*) *Brit. dialect.* to empty. [from Old English *ǣmtian* to be without duties; compare EMPTY]

emp·ty ('ɛmptɪ) *adj.* **·ti·er, ·ti·est. 1.** containing nothing. **2.** without inhabitants; vacant or unoccupied. **3.** carrying no load, passengers, etc. **4.** without purpose, substance, or value: *an empty life.* **5.** insincere or trivial: *empty words.* **6.** not expressive or vital; vacant: *she has an empty look.* **7.** *Informal.* hungry. **8.** (*postpositive,* foll. by *of*) devoid; destitute: *a life empty of happiness.* **9.** *Informal.* drained of energy or emotion: *after the violent argument he felt very empty.* **10.** *Maths, logic.* (of a set or class) containing no members. ~*vb.* **·ties, ·ty·ing, ·tied. 11.** to make or become empty. **12.** (when *intr.,* foll. by *into*) to discharge (contents). **13.** (*tr.;* often foll. by *of*) to unburden or rid (oneself): *to empty oneself of emotion.* ~*n.,* *pl.* -ties. 14. *Informal.* an empty container, esp. a bottle or can. [Old English *ǣmtig,* from *ǣmetta* free time, from *ǣ-* without + *-metta,* from *mōtan* to be obliged to; see MUST] —'emp·ti·a·ble *adj.* —'emp·ti·er *n.* —'emp·ti·ly *adv.* —'emp·ti·ness *n.*

emp·ty-hand·ed *adj.* 1. carrying nothing in the hands. 2. having gained nothing: *they returned from the negotiations empty-handed.*

emp·ty-head·ed *adj.* lacking intelligence or sense; frivolous.

Emp·ty Quar·ter *n.* another name for **Rub' al Khali.**

em·py·e·ma (ˌɛmpaɪ'iːmə) *n.* a collection of pus in a body cavity, esp. in the chest. [C17: from Medieval Latin, from Greek *empuēma* abscess, from *empuein* to suppurate, from *puon* pus] —ˌem·py·'e·mic *adj.*

em·py·re·an (ˌɛmpaɪ'riːən) *n.* 1. *Archaic.* the highest part of the (supposedly spherical) heavens, thought in ancient times to contain the pure element of fire and by early Christians to be the abode of God and the angels. 2. *Poetic.* the heavens or sky. ~*adj. also* **em·py·re·al.** 3. of or relating to the sky, the heavens, or the empyrean. 4. heavenly or sublime. 5. *Archaic.* composed of fire.

em·py·reu·ma (ˌɛmpɪ'ruːmə) *n.* the smell and taste associated with burning vegetable and animal matter. [C17: from Greek, from *empureuein* to set on fire]

Ems (ɛmz) *n.* 1. a town in W West Germany, in the Rhineland-Palatinate: famous for the **Ems Telegram** (1870), Bismarck's dispatch that led to the outbreak of the Franco-Prussian War. Pop.: 10 000 (1970 est.). 2. a river in West Germany, rising in the Teutoburger Wald and flowing generally north to the North Sea. Length: about 370 km (230 miles).

e·mu ('iːmjuː) *n.* a large Australian flightless bird, *Dromaius novaehollandiae,* similar to the ostrich but with three-toed feet and grey or brown plumage: order *Casuariiformes.* See also **ratite.** [C17: changed from Portuguese *ema* ostrich, perhaps from Moluccan *eme*]

emu *or* **E.M.U.** *abbrev. for* electromagnetic unit.

e·mu bush *n.* any of various Australian shrubs, esp. those of the genus *Eremophila* (family Myoporaceae), whose fruits are eaten by emus.

em·u·late ('ɛmjʊˌleɪt) *vb.* (*tr.*) 1. to attempt to equal or surpass, esp. by imitation. 2. to rival or compete with. [C16: from Latin *aemulārī,* from *aemulus* competing with; probably related to *imitārī* to IMITATE] —'em·u·la·tive *adj.* —'em·u·la·tive·ly *adv.* —'em·u·ˌla·tor *n.*

e·mu·la·tion (ˌɛmjʊ'leɪʃən) *n.* 1. the act of emulating or imitating. 2. the effort or desire to equal or surpass another or others. 3. *Archaic.* jealous rivalry.

em·u·lous ('ɛmjʊləs) *adj.* 1. desiring or aiming to equal or surpass another; competitive. 2. characterized by or arising from emulation or imitation. 3. *Archaic.* envious or jealous. [C14: from Latin *aemulus* rivalling; see EMULATE] —'em·u·lous·ly *adv.* —'em·u·lous·ness *n.*

e·mul·si·fy (ɪ'mʌlsɪˌfaɪ) *vb.* -fies, -fy·ing, -fied. to make or form into an emulsion. —e·ˌmul·si·'fi·a·ble *or* e·'mul·si·ble *adj.* —e·ˌmul·si·fi·'ca·tion *n.* —e·'mul·si·ˌfi·er *n.*

e·mul·sion (ɪ'mʌlʃən) *n.* 1. *Photog.* a light-sensitive coating on a base, such as paper or film, consisting of fine grains of silver bromide suspended in gelatin. 2. *Chem.* a colloid in which both phases are liquids: *an oil-in-water emulsion.* 3. Also called: **emulsion paint.** a type of paint in which the pigment is suspended in a vehicle, usually a synthetic resin, that is dispersed in water as an emulsion. 4. *Pharmacol.* a mixture in which an oily medicine is dispersed in another liquid. 5. any liquid resembling milk. [C17: from New Latin *ēmulsiō,* from Latin *ēmulsus* milked out, from *ēmulgēre* to milk out, drain out, from *mulgēre* to milk] —e·'mul·sive *adj.*

e·mul·soid (ɪ'mʌlsɔɪd) *n. Chem.* a sol with a liquid disperse phase.

e·munc·to·ry (ɪ'mʌŋktərɪ) *adj.* 1. of or relating to a bodily organ or duct having an excretory function. ~*n., pl.* -ries. 2. an excretory organ or duct, such as a skin pore. [C16: from New Latin *ēmunctōrium,* from Latin *ēmungere* to wipe clean, from *mungere* to wipe]

e·mu-wren *n.* any Australian wren of the genus *Stipiturus,* having long plumy tail feathers.

en (ɛn) *n. Printing.* half the width of an em. Also called: **nut.** See also **ennage.**

en-[1] *or* **em-** *prefix forming verbs.* 1. (*from nouns*) a. put in or on: *entomb; enthrone.* b. go on or into: *enplane.* c. surround or cover with: *enmesh.* d. furnish with: *empower.* 2. (*from adjectives and nouns*) cause to be in a certain condition: *enable; encourage; enrich; enslave.* [via Old French from Latin *in-* IN-[2]]

en-[2] *or* **em-** *prefix forming nouns and adjectives.* in; into; inside: *endemic.* [from Greek (often via Latin); compare IN-[1], IN-[2]]

-en[1] *suffix forming verbs from adjectives and nouns.* cause to be; become; cause to have: *blacken; heighten.* [Old English *-n-,* as in *fæst-n-ian* to fasten, of common Germanic origin; compare Icelandic *fastna*]

-en[2] *suffix forming adjectives from nouns.* of; made of; resembling: *ashen; earthen; wooden.* [Old English *-en;* related to Gothic *-eins,* Latin *-īnus* -INE[1]]

en·a·ble (ɪn'eɪbᵊl) *vb.* (*tr.*) 1. to provide (someone) with adequate power, means, opportunity, or authority (to do something). 2. to make possible or easy. —en·'a·bler *n.*

en·a·bling act *n.* a legislative act conferring certain specified powers on a person or organization.

en·act (ɪn'ækt) *vb.* (*tr.*) 1. to make into an act or statute. 2. to establish by law; ordain or decree. 3. to represent or perform in or as if in a play; to act out. —en·'act·a·ble *adj.* —en·'ac·tive *or* en·'ac·to·ry *adj.* —en·'act·ment *or* en·'ac·tion *n.* —en·'ac·tor *n.*

e·nam·el (ɪ'næməl) *n.* 1. a coloured glassy substance, translucent or opaque, fused to the surface of articles made of metal, glass, etc., for ornament or protection. 2. an article or articles ornamented with enamel. 3. an enamel-like paint or varnish. 4. any smooth glossy coating resembling enamel. 5. another word for **nail polish.** 6. the hard white calcified substance that covers the crown of each tooth. 7. (*modifier*) a. decorated or covered with enamel: *an enamel ring.* b. made with enamel: *enamel paste.* ~*vb.* -els, -el·ling, -elled *or U.S.* -els, -el·ing, -eled. (*tr.*) 8. to inlay, coat, or otherwise decorate with enamel. 9. to ornament with glossy variegated colours, as if with enamel. 10. to portray in enamel. [C15: from Old French *esmail,* of Germanic origin; compare Old High German *smalz* lard; see SMELT[1]] —e·'nam·el·ler, e·'nam·el·list *or U.S.* e·'nam·el·er, e·'nam·el·ist *n.* —e·'nam·el·ˌwork *n.*

en·am·our *or U.S.* **en·am·or** (ɪn'æmə) *vb.* (*tr.; usually passive and foll. by of*) to inspire with love; captivate; charm. [C14: from Old French *enamourer,* from *amour* love, from Latin *amor*] —en·'am·oured *or U.S.* en·'am·ored *adj.*

en·an·ti·o·morph (ɛn'æntɪəˌmɔːf) *n.* either of the two crystal forms of a substance that are mirror images of each other. [C19: from Greek *enantios* opposite + -MORPH] —en·ˌan·ti·o·'mor·phic *adj.* —en·ˌan·ti·o·'mor·phism *n.*

en·ar·thro·sis (ˌɛnɑː'θrəʊsɪs) *n., pl.* -ses (-siːz). *Anatomy.* a ball-and-socket joint, such as that of the hip. [C17: via New Latin from Greek, from *arthrōsis,* from *arthron* a joint + -OSIS] —ˌen·ar·'thro·di·al *adj.*

e·nate ('iːneɪt) *adj. also* **e·nat·ic** (iː'nætɪk). 1. *Biology.* growing out or outwards. 2. related on the side of the mother. ~*n.* 3. a relative on the mother's side. [C17: from Latin *ēnātus,* from *ēnāscī* to be born from, from *nāscī* to be born]

en at·ten·dant *French.* (ɑ̃ natɑ̃'dɑ̃) *adv.* in the mean time; while waiting.

en bloc *French.* (ɑ̃ 'blɔk) *adv.* in a lump or block; as a body or whole; all together.

en bro·chette *French.* (ɑ̃ brɔ'ʃɛt) *adj., adv.* (esp. of meat) roasted or grilled on a skewer. [French, literally: on a skewer]

en brosse *French.* (ɑ̃ 'brɔs) *adj., adv.* (of the hair) cut very short so that the hair stands up stiffly. [French, literally: in the style of a brush]

enc. *abbrev. for:* 1. enclosed. 2. enclosure.

en·cae·ni·a (ɛn'siːnɪə) *n. Rare.* a festival of dedication or commemoration. [C14: via Late Latin from Greek *enkainia,* from *kainos* new]

en·cage (ɪn'keɪdʒ) *vb.* (*tr.*) to confine in or as in a cage.

en·camp (ɪn'kæmp) *vb.* to lodge or cause to lodge in a camp.

en·camp·ment (ɪn'kæmpmənt) *n.* 1. the act of setting up a camp. 2. the place where a camp, esp. a military camp, is set up.

en·cap·su·late *or* **in·cap·su·late** (ɪn'kæpsjʊˌleɪt) *vb.* 1. to enclose or be enclosed in or as if in a capsule. 2. (*tr.*) to put in a short or concise form; condense; abridge. —en·ˌcap·su·'la·tion *or* in·ˌcap·su·'la·tion *n.*

en·car·nal·ize *or* **en·car·nal·ise** (ɪn'kɑːnəˌlaɪz) *vb.* (*tr.*) *Rare.* 1. to provide with a bodily form; incarnate. 2. to make carnal, gross, or sensual.

en·case *or* **in·case** (ɪn'keɪs) *vb.* (*tr.*) to place or enclose in or as if in a case. —en·'case·ment *or* in·'case·ment *n.*

en·cash (ɪn'kæʃ) *vb.* (*tr.*) *Brit., formal.* to exchange (a cheque) for cash. —en·'cash·a·ble *adj.* —en·'cash·ment *n.*

en·caus·tic (ɪn'kɒstɪk) *Ceramics, etc.* ~*adj.* 1. decorated by any process involving burning in colours, esp. by inlaying coloured clays and baking or by fusing wax colours to the surface. ~*n.* 2. the process of burning in colours. 3. a product of such a process. [C17: from Latin *encausticus,* from Greek *enkaustikos,* from *enkaiein* to burn in, from *kaiein* to burn] —en·'caus·ti·cal·ly *adv.*

-ence *or* **-en·cy** *suffix forming nouns.* indicating an action, state, condition, or quality: *benevolence; residence; patience.* [via Old French from Latin *-entia,* from *-ēns,* present participial ending]

en·ceinte[1] (ɒn'sænt; *French* ɑ̃'sɛ̃ːt) *adj.* another word for **pregnant.** [C17: from French, from Latin *inciēns* pregnant; related to Greek *enkuos,* from *kuein* to be pregnant]

en·ceinte[2] (ɒn'sænt; *French* ɑ̃'sɛ̃ːt) *n.* 1. a boundary wall enclosing a defended area. 2. the area enclosed. [C18: from French: enclosure, from *enceindre* to encompass, from Latin *incingere, from cingere* to gird]

En·cel·a·dus (ɛn'sɛlədəs) *n.* 1. *Greek myth.* a giant who was punished for his rebellion against the gods by a fatal blow from a stone cast by Athena. He was believed to be buried under Mount Etna in Sicily. 2. one of the smallest of the ten satellites of the planet Saturn.

en·ce·phal·ic (ˌɛnsɪ'fælɪk) *adj.* of or relating to the brain.

en·ceph·a·lin (ɛn'sɛfəlɪn) *or* **en·keph·a·lin** (ɛn'kɛfəlɪn) *n.* a chemical occurring in the brain, having effects similar to those of morphine.

en·ceph·a·li·tis (ˌɛnsɛfə'laɪtɪs) *n.* inflammation of the brain. —**en·ceph·a·lit·ic** (ˌɛnsɛfə'lɪtɪk) *adj.*

en·ceph·a·li·tis le·thar·gi·ca (lɪ'θɑːdʒɪkə) *n. Pathol.* a technical name for **sleeping sickness** (sense 2).

en·ceph·a·lo- *or before a vowel* **en·ceph·al-** *combining form.* indicating the brain: *encephalogram; encephalitis.* [from New Latin, from Greek *enkephalos,* from *en-* in + *kephale* head]

en·ceph·a·lo·gram (ɛn'sɛfələˌgræm) *n.* 1. an x-ray photograph of the brain, esp. one (a **pneumoencephalogram**) taken after replacing some of the cerebrospinal fluid with air or oxygen so that the brain cavities show clearly. **2.** short for **electroencephalogram.**

en·ceph·a·lo·graph (ɛnˈsɛfələˌgrɑːf, -ˌgræf) *n.* **1.** another name for **electroencephalograph. 2.** another name for **encephalogram.**

en·ceph·a·log·ra·phy (ˌɛnsɛfəˈlɒgrəfɪ) *n.* **1.** the branch of medical science concerned with taking and analysing x-ray photographs of the brain. **2.** another name for **electroencephalography.** —**en·ceph·a·lo·graph·ic** (ɛnˌsɛfələˈgræfɪk) *or* **enˌceph·a·lo·ˈgraph·i·cal** *adj.* —**enˌceph·a·lo·ˈgraph·i·cal·ly** *adv.*

en·ceph·a·lo·ma (ˌɛnsɛfəˈləʊmə) *n., pl.* **·mas** *or* **·ma·ta** (-mətə). a brain tumour.

en·ceph·a·lo·my·e·li·tis (ɛnˌsɛfələʊˌmaɪəˈlaɪtɪs) *n.* acute inflammation of the brain and spinal cord. —**en·ceph·a·lo·my·e·lit·ic** (ɛnˌsɛfələʊˌmaɪəˈlɪtɪk) *adj.*

en·ceph·a·lon (ɛnˈsɛfəˌlɒn) *n., pl.* **·la** (-lə). a technical name for **brain.** [C18: from New Latin, from Greek *enkephalos* brain (literally: that which is in the head), from EN-[2] + *kephalē* head] —**enˈceph·a·lous** *adj.*

en·chain (ɪnˈtʃeɪn) *vb. (tr.)* **1.** to bind with chains. **2.** to hold fast or captivate (the attention, etc.). —**enˈchain·ment** *n.*

en·chant (ɪnˈtʃɑːnt) *vb. (tr.)* **1.** to cast a spell on; bewitch. **2.** to delight or captivate utterly; fascinate; charm. [C14: from Old French *enchanter,* from Latin *incantāre* to chant a spell, from *cantāre* to chant, from *canere* to sing] —**enˈchant·er** *n.* —**enˈchant·ress** *fem. n.*

en·chant·er's night·shade *n.* any of several onagraceous plants of the genus *Circaea,* esp. *C. lutetiana,* having small white flowers and bristly fruits.

en·chant·ing (ɪnˈtʃɑːntɪŋ) *adj.* pleasant; delightful. —**enˈchant·ing·ly** *adv.*

en·chant·ment (ɪnˈtʃɑːntmənt) *n.* **1.** the act of enchanting or state of being enchanted. **2.** a magic spell or act of witchcraft. **3.** great charm or fascination.

en·chase (ɪnˈtʃeɪs) *vb. (tr.)* a less common word for **chase**[3]. [C15: from Old French *enchasser* to enclose, set, from EN-[1] + *casse* CASE[2]] —**enˈchas·er** *n.*

en·chi·la·da (ˌɛntʃɪˈlɑːdə) *n.* a Mexican dish consisting of a tortilla fried in hot fat, filled with meat, and served with a chilli sauce. [American Spanish, feminine of *enchilado* seasoned with chilli, from *enchilar* to spice with chilli, from *chile* CHILLI]

en·chi·rid·i·on (ˌɛnkaɪˈrɪdɪən) *n., pl.* **·i·ons** *or* **·i·a** (-ɪə). *Rare.* a handbook or manual. [C16: from Late Latin, from Greek *enkheiridion,* from EN-[2] + *kheir* hand]

en·chon·dro·ma (ˌɛnkənˈdrəʊmə) *n., pl.* **·mas** *or* **·ma·ta** (-mətə). *Pathol.* a benign cartilaginous tumour, most commonly in the bones of the hands or feet. —**ˌen·chonˈdrom·a·tous** *adj.*

en·cho·ri·al (ɛnˈkɔːrɪəl) *or* **en·cho·ric** *adj.* of or used in a particular country: used esp. of the popular (demotic) writing of the ancient Egyptians. [C19: via Late Latin from Greek *enkhōrios,* from EN-[2] + *khōra* country]

-en·chy·ma *combining form.* denoting cellular tissue: *aerenchyma.* [C20: abstracted from PARENCHYMA]

en·ci·pher (ɪnˈsaɪfə) *vb. (tr.)* to convert (a message, document, etc.) from plain text into code or cipher; encode. —**enˈci·pher·er** *n.* —**enˈci·pher·ment** *n.*

en·cir·cle (ɪnˈsɜːkᵊl) *vb. (tr.)* to form a circle around; enclose within a circle; surround. —**enˈcir·cle·ment** *n.*

encl. *abbrev. for:* **1.** enclosed. **2.** enclosure.

en clair *French.* (ɑ̃ ˈklɛːr) *adv., adj.* in ordinary language; not in cipher. [literally: in clear]

en·clasp (ɪnˈklɑːsp) *vb. (tr.)* to clasp; embrace.

en·clave (ˈɛnkleɪv) *n.* a part of a country entirely surrounded by foreign territory: viewed from the position of the surrounding territories. Compare **exclave.** [C19: from French, from Old French *enclaver* to enclose, from Vulgar Latin *inclāvāre* (unattested) to lock up, from Latin IN-[2] + *clavis* key]

en·clit·ic (ɪnˈklɪtɪk) *adj.* **1. a.** denoting or relating to a monosyllabic word or form that is treated as a suffix of the preceding word, as Latin *-que* in *populusque.* **b.** (in classical Greek) denoting or relating to a word that throws an accent back onto the preceding word. ~*n.* **2.** an enclitic word or linguistic form. ~Compare **proclitic.** [C17: from Late Latin *encliticus,* from Greek *enklitikos,* from *enklinein* to cause to lean, from EN-[2] + *klinein* to lean] —**enˈclit·i·cal·ly** *adv.*

en·close *or* **in·close** (ɪnˈkləʊz) *vb. (tr.)* **1.** to close; hem in; surround. **2.** to surround (land) with or as if with a fence. **3.** to put in an envelope or wrapper, esp. together with a letter. **4.** to contain or hold. —**enˈclos·a·ble** *or* **inˈclos·a·ble** *adj.* —**enˈclos·er** *or* **inˈclos·er** *n.*

en·closed or·der *n.* a Christian religious order that does not permit its members to go into the outside world.

en·clo·sure *or* **in·clo·sure** (ɪnˈkləʊʒə) *n.* **1.** the act of enclosing or state of being enclosed. **2.** a region or area enclosed by or as if by a fence. **3.** the act of appropriating land, esp. common land, by setting up a fence or barrier around it. **4.** a fence, wall, etc., that serves to enclose. **5.** something, esp. a supporting document, enclosed within an envelope or wrapper, esp. together with a letter. **6.** *Brit.* a section of a sports ground, race course, etc., allotted to certain spectators.

en·code (ɪnˈkəʊd) *vb. (tr.)* to convert (a message) from plain text into code. —**enˈcode·ment** *n.* —**enˈcod·er** *n.*

en·co·mi·ast (ɛnˈkəʊmɪˌæst) *n.* a person who speaks or writes an encomium. [C17: from Greek *enkōmiastēs,* from *enkōmiazein* to utter an ENCOMIUM] —**enˌco·mi·ˈas·tic** *or* **enˌco·mi·ˈas·ti·cal** *adj.* —**enˌco·mi·ˈas·ti·cal·ly** *adv.*

en·co·mi·um (ɛnˈkəʊmɪəm) *n., pl.* **·mi·ums** *or* **·mi·a** (-mɪə). a formal expression of praise; eulogy; panegyric. [C16: from Latin, from Greek *enkōmion,* from EN-[2] + *kōmos* festivity]

en·com·pass (ɪnˈkʌmpəs) *vb. (tr.)* **1.** to enclose within a circle; surround. **2.** to bring about; cause to happen; contrive: *he encompassed the enemy's ruin.* **3.** to include entirely or comprehensively: *this book encompasses the whole range of knowledge.* —**enˈcom·pass·ment** *n.*

en·core (ˈɒŋkɔː) *interj.* **1.** again; once more: used by an audience to demand an extra or repeated performance. ~*n.* **2.** an extra or repeated performance given in response to enthusiastic demand. ~*vb.* **3.** *(tr.)* to demand an extra or repeated performance of (a work, piece of music, etc.) by (a performer). [C18: from French: still, again, perhaps from Latin *in hanc hōram* until this hour]

en·coun·ter (ɪnˈkaʊntə) *vb.* **1.** to come upon or meet casually or unexpectedly. **2.** to come into conflict with (an enemy, army, etc.) in battle or contest. **3.** *(tr.)* to be faced with; contend with: *he encounters many obstacles in his work.* ~*n.* **4.** a meeting with a person or thing, esp. when casual or unexpected. **5.** a hostile meeting; contest or conflict. [C13: from Old French *encontrer,* from Vulgar Latin *incontrāre* (unattested), from Latin IN-[2] + *contrā* against, opposite] —**enˈcoun·ter·er** *n.*

en·coun·ter group *n.* a group of people who meet in order to develop self-awareness and mutual understanding by openly expressing their feelings, by confrontation, physical contact, etc.

en·cour·age (ɪnˈkʌrɪdʒ) *vb. (tr.)* **1.** to inspire (someone) with the courage or confidence (to do something). **2.** to stimulate (something or someone to do something) by approval or help; support. —**enˈcour·age·ment** *n.* —**enˈcour·ag·er** *n.* —**enˈcour·ag·ing·ly** *adv.*

en·cri·nite (ˈɛnkrɪˌnaɪt) *n.* a fossil crinoid, esp. one of the genus *Encrinus.* Sometimes shortened to **crinite.** [C19: from New Latin *encrinus* (from Greek EN-[2] + *krinon* lily) + -ITE[1]]

en·croach (ɪnˈkrəʊtʃ) *vb. (intr.)* **1.** (often foll. by *on* or *upon*) to intrude gradually, stealthily, or insidiously upon the rights, property, etc., of another. **2.** to advance beyond the usual or proper limits. [C14: from Old French *encrochier* to seize, literally: fasten upon with hooks, from EN-[1] + *croc* hook, of Germanic origin; see CROOK] —**enˈcroach·er** *n.* —**enˈcroach·ing·ly** *adv.* —**enˈcroach·ment** *n.*

en·crust *or* **in·crust** (ɪnˈkrʌst) *vb.* **1.** *(tr.)* to cover or overlay with or as with a crust or hard coating. **2.** to form or cause to form a crust or hard coating. **3.** *(tr.)* to decorate lavishly, as with jewels. —**enˈcrust·ant** *or* **inˈcrust·ant** *adj., n.* —**ˌen·crusˈta·tion** *or* **ˌin·crusˈta·tion** *n.*

en·cul·tu·ra·tion (ɛnˌkʌltʃʊˈreɪʃən) *n.* another word for **socialization.** —**en·cul·tu·ra·tive** (ɛnˈkʌltʃʊrətɪv) *adj.*

en·cum·ber *or* **in·cum·ber** (ɪnˈkʌmbə) *vb. (tr.)* **1.** to hinder or impede; make difficult; hamper: *encumbered with parcels after going shopping at Christmas; his stupidity encumbers his efforts to learn.* **2.** to fill with superfluous or useless matter. **3.** to burden with debts, obligations, etc. [C14: from Old French *encombrer,* from EN-[1] + *combre* a barrier, from Late Latin *combrus,* of uncertain origin] —**enˈcum·ber·ing·ly** *or* **inˈcum·ber·ing·ly** *adv.*

en·cum·brance *or* **in·cum·brance** (ɪnˈkʌmbrəns) *n.* **1.** a thing that impedes or is burdensome; hindrance. **2.** *Law.* a burden or charge upon property, such as a mortgage or lien. **3.** *Rare.* a dependent person, esp. a child.

en·cum·branc·er (ɪnˈkʌmbrənsə) *n. Law.* a person who holds an encumbrance on property belonging to another.

ency., encyc., *or* **encycl.** *abbrev. for* encyclopedia.

-en·cy *suffix forming nouns.* variant of **-ence:** *fluency; permanency.*

en·cyc·li·cal (ɛnˈsɪklɪkᵊl) *n.* **1.** a letter sent by the pope to all Roman Catholic bishops throughout the world. ~*adj. also* **en·cyc·lic. 2.** (of letters) intended for general or wide circulation. [C17: from Late Latin *encyclicus,* from Greek *enkuklios* general, from *kuklos* circle]

en·cy·clo·pe·di·a *or* **en·cy·clo·pae·di·a** (ɛnˌsaɪkləʊˈpiːdɪə) *n.* a book, often in many volumes, containing articles on various topics, often arranged in alphabetical order, dealing either with the whole range of human knowledge or with one particular subject: *a medical encyclopedia.* [C16: from New Latin *encyclopaedia,* erroneously for Greek *enkuklios paideia* general education, from *enkuklios* general, (see ENCYCLICAL) + *paideia* education, from *pais* child]

en·cy·clo·pe·dic *or* **en·cy·clo·pae·dic** (ɛnˌsaɪkləʊˈpiːdɪk) *adj.* **1.** of, characteristic of, or relating to an encyclopedia. **2.** covering a wide range of knowledge; comprehensive. —**enˌcy·cloˈpe·di·cal·ly** *or* **enˌcy·cloˈpae·di·cal·ly** *adv.*

en·cy·clo·pe·dist *or* **en·cy·clo·pae·dist** (ɛnˌsaɪkləʊˈpiːdɪst) *n.* a person who compiles or contributes to an encyclopedia. —**enˌcy·cloˈpe·dism** *or* **enˌcy·cloˈpae·dism** *n.*

en·cyst (ɛnˈsɪst) *vb. Biology.* to enclose or become enclosed by a cyst, thick membrane, or shell. —**enˈcyst·ment** *or* **ˌen·cysˈta·tion** *n.*

end[1] (ɛnd) *n.* **1.** the extremity of the length of something, such as a road, line, etc. **2.** the surface at either extremity of a three-dimensional object. **3.** the extreme extent, limit, or degree of something. **4.** the most distant place or time that can be imagined: *the ends of the earth.* **5.** the time at which something is concluded. **6. a.** the last section or part. **b.** (*as modifier*): *the end office.* **7.** a share or part: *his end of the bargain; to keep one's end up.* **8.** (*often pl.*) a remnant or fragment (esp. in the phrase **odds and ends**). **9.** a final state, esp. death; destruction. **10.** the purpose of an action or existence. **11.** *Sport.* either of the two defended areas of a playing field, rink, etc. **12.** *Bowls.* a section of play from one side of the green to the other. **13.** *American football.* a player at the extremity of the playing line; wing. **14. all ends up.** totally or completely. **15. a sticky end.** *Informal.* an unpleasant death. **16. at a loose end** *or* (*U.S.*) **at loose ends.** without purpose or occupation. **17. at an end.** exhausted. **18. come to an end.** to become completed or exhausted. **19. end on. a.** with the end pointing towards one. **b.** with the end adjacent to the end of another object. **20. go off the deep end.** *Informal.* to lose one's temper; react angrily. **21. in the end.** finally. **22. make (both) ends meet.** to spend no more than the money one has. **23. no end (of).** *Informal.* (intensifier): *I had no end of work.* **24. on end.** *Informal.* without pause or interruption. **25. the end.** *Slang.* **a.** the worst, esp. something that goes beyond the limits of endurance. **b.** *Chiefly U.S.* the best in quality. **26. the end of the road.** the point beyond which survival or continuation is impossible. Related adjs.: **final, terminal, ultimate.** ~*vb.* **27.** to bring or come to a finish; conclude. **28.** to die or cause to die. **29.** (*tr.*) surpass; outdo: *a novel to end all novels.* **30. end it all.** *Informal.* to commit suicide. ~See also **end up.** [Old English *ende;* related to Old Norse *endir,* Gothic *andeis,* Old High German *endi,* Latin *antiae* forelocks, Sanskrit *antya* last] **—'end+er** *n.*

end[2] (ɛnd) *vb.* (*tr.*) *Brit.* to put (hay or grain) into a barn or stack. [Old English *innian;* related to Old High German *innōn;* see INN]

end- *combining form.* variant of **endo-** before a vowel.

-end *suffix forming nouns.* See **-and.**

end-all *n.* short for **be-all and end-all.**

en+dam+age (ɛn'dæmɪdʒ) *vb.* (*tr.*) to cause injury to; damage. **—en+'dam+age+ment** *n.*

en+da+moe·ba *or U.S.* **en+da+me·ba** (ˌɛndə'miːbə) *n., pl.* **·bae** (-biː) *or* **·bas.** variant spellings of **entamoeba.**

en+dan+ger (ɪn'deɪndʒə) *vb.* (*tr.*) to put in danger or peril; imperil. **—en+'dan+ger+ment** *n.*

end+arch ('ɛndˌɑːk) *adj. Botany.* (of a xylem strand) having the first-formed xylem internal to that formed later. Compare **exarch[2], mesarch.** [C20: see ENDO-, ARCH]

en dash *n. Printing.* a dash (-) one en long.

end-blown *adj. Music.* (of a recorder, etc.) held downwards and blown through one end.

end+brain ('ɛndˌbreɪn) *n. Anatomy.* another name for **telencephalon.**

en+dear (ɪn'dɪə) *vb.* (*tr.*) to cause to be beloved or esteemed. **—en+'dear+ing+ly** *adv.*

en+dear+ment (ɪn'dɪəmənt) *n.* **1.** something that endears, such as an affectionate utterance. **2.** the act or process of endearing or the condition of being endeared.

en+deav+our *or U.S.* **en+deav+or** (ɪn'dɛvə) *vb.* **1.** to try (to do something). ~*n.* **2.** an effort to do or attain something. [C14 *endeveren,* from EN-[1] + *-deveren* from *dever* duty, from Old French *deveir;* see DEVOIR] **—en+'deav+our+er** *or U.S.* **en+'deav+or+er** *n.*

en+dem+ic (ɛn'dɛmɪk) *adj. also* **en+dem·i+al** (ɛn'dɛmɪəl) *or* **en+dem·i+cal. 1.** present within a localized area or peculiar to persons in such an area. ~*n.* **2.** an endemic disease or plant. [C18: from New Latin *endēmicus,* from Greek *endēmos* native, from EN-[2] + *dēmos* the people] **—en+'dem·i+cal+ly** *adv.* **—'en+de+mism** *or* **ˌen+de+'mic+i+ty** *n.*

En+der+by Land ('ɛndəbɪ) *n.* part of the coastal region of Antarctica, between Kempland and Queen Maud Land: the westernmost part of the Australian Antarctic Territory; discovered in 1831.

en+der+mic (ɛn'dɜːmɪk) *adj.* (of a medicine, etc.) acting by absorption through the skin. [C19: from EN-[2] + Greek *derma* skin]

end+game ('ɛndˌgeɪm) *n.* **1.** the closing stage of a game of chess, in which only a few pieces are left on the board. **2.** the closing stage of any of certain other games.

end+ing ('ɛndɪŋ) *n.* **1.** the act of bringing to or reaching an end. **2.** the last part of something, as a book, film, etc. **3.** the final part of a word, esp. a suffix.

en+dive ('ɛndaɪv) *n.* a plant, *Cichorium endivia,* cultivated for its crisp curly leaves, which are used in salads: family *Compositae* (composites). Compare **chicory.** [C15: from Old French, from Medieval Latin *endīvia,* variant of Latin *intubus, entubus,* of uncertain origin]

end+less ('ɛndlɪs) *adj.* **1.** having or seeming to have no end; eternal or infinite. **2.** continuing too long or continually recurring. **3.** formed with the ends joined: *an endless belt.* **—'end+less+ly** *adv.* **—'end+less+ness** *n.*

end+long ('ɛndˌlɒŋ) *adv. Archaic.* lengthways or on end.

end mat+ter *n.* another name for **back matter.**

end+most ('ɛndˌməʊst) *adj.* nearest the end; most distant.

en·do- *or before a vowel* **end-** *combining form.* inside; within: *endocrine.* [from Greek, from *endon* within]

en·do+blast ('ɛndəʊˌblæst) *n.* **1.** *Embryol.* a less common name for **endoderm. 2.** another name for **hypoblast** (sense 1). **—ˌen·do+'blas+tic** *adj.*

en·do+car+di·al (ˌɛndəʊ'kɑːdɪəl) *or* **en·do+car+di+ac** *adj.* **1.** of or relating to the endocardium. **2.** within the heart.

en·do+car+di+tis (ˌɛndəʊkɑː'daɪtɪs) *n.* inflammation of the endocardium. **—en·do+car+dit+ic** (ˌɛndəʊkɑː'dɪtɪk) *adj.*

en·do+car+di·um (ˌɛndəʊ'kɑːdɪəm) *n., pl.* **+di·a** (-dɪə). the membrane that lines the cavities of the heart and forms part of the valves. [C19: from New Latin, from ENDO- + Greek *kardia* heart]

en·do+carp ('ɛndəˌkɑːp) *n.* the inner, usually woody, layer of the pericarp of a fruit, such as the stone of a peach or cherry. **—ˌen·do+'car+pal** *or* **ˌen·do+'car+pic** *adj.*

en·do+cen+tric (ˌɛndəʊ'sɛntrɪk) *adj. Grammar.* (of a construction) fulfilling the grammatical role of one of its constituents; as in *three blind mice,* where the whole noun phrase fulfils the same role as its head noun *mice.* Compare **exocentric.**

en·do+cra+ni+um (ˌɛndəʊ'kreɪnɪəm) *n., pl.* **+nia** (-nɪə). *Anatomy.* the thick fibrous membrane that lines the cranial cavity and forms the outermost layer of the dura mater.

en·do+crine ('ɛndəʊˌkraɪn, -krɪn) *adj. also* **en·do+cri+nal** (ˌɛndəʊ'kraɪnᵊl), **en·do+crin+ic** (ˌɛndəʊ'krɪnɪk), *or* **en+doc+ri+nous** (ɛn'dɒkrɪnəs). **1.** of or denoting endocrine glands or their secretions: *endocrine disorders.* ~*n.* **2.** an endocrine gland. ~Compare **exocrine.** [C20: from ENDO- + *-crine,* from Greek *krinein* to separate]

en+do+crine gland *n.* any of the glands that secrete hormones directly into the blood stream, including the pituitary, pineal, thyroid, parathyroid, adrenal, testes, ovaries, and the pancreatic islets of Langerhans. Also called: **ductless gland.**

en·do+cri+nol+o·gy (ˌɛndəʊkraɪ'nɒlədʒɪ, -krɪ-) *n.* the branch of medical science concerned with the endocrine glands and their secretions. **—en·do+crin+o+log+ic** (ˌɛndəʊˌkrɪnə'lɒdʒɪk) *or* **ˌen·do+ˌcrin·o+'log·i+cal** *adj.* **—ˌen·do+cri+'nol·o+gist** *n.*

en·do+derm ('ɛndəʊˌdɜːm) *or* **en+to+derm** *n.* the inner germ layer of an animal embryo, which gives rise to the lining of the digestive and respiratory tracts. See also **ectoderm** and **mesoderm. —ˌen·do+'der+mal, ˌen·do+'der+mic** *or* **ˌen+to+'der+mal, ˌen+to+'der+mic** *adj.*

en·do+derm+is (ˌɛndəʊ'dɜːmɪs) *n. Botany.* the specialized innermost layer of cortex in roots and some stems, which controls the passage of water and dissolved substances between the cortex and stele. [C19: from New Latin, from ENDO- + Greek *derma* skin]

en·do+don+tics (ˌɛndəʊ'dɒntɪks) *n.* (*functioning as sing.*) the branch of dentistry concerned with diseases of the dental pulp. [C19: from New Latin *endodontia,* from ENDO- + Greek *odōn* tooth] **—ˌen·do+'don+tic** *adj.* **—ˌen·do+'don+tist** *n.*

en·do+en+zyme (ˌɛndəʊ'ɛnzaɪm) *n.* **1.** any of a group of enzymes, esp. endopeptidases, that act upon inner chemical bonds in a chain of molecules. Compare **exoenzyme** (sense 1). **2.** *Becoming rare.* any of a group of enzymes that act within a cell.

en·do+er+gic (ˌɛndəʊ'ɜːdʒɪk) *adj.* (of a nuclear reaction) occurring with absorption of energy, as opposed to *exoergic.* Compare **endothermic.**

end of steel *n. Canadian.* **1.** a point up to which railway tracks have been laid. **2.** a town located at such a point.

en+dog·a+my (ɛn'dɒgəmɪ) *n.* **1.** *Anthropol.* marriage within one's own tribe or similar unit. Compare **exogamy** (sense 1). **2.** pollination between two flowers on the same plant. **—en+'dog·a+mous** *or* **en·do+gam+ic** (ˌɛndəʊ'gæmɪk) *adj.*

en·do+gen ('ɛndəʊˌdʒɛn) *n.* a former name for **monocotyledon.**

en+dog+e+nous (ɛn'dɒdʒɪnəs) *adj. Biology.* developing or originating within an organism or part of an organism. **—en+'dog+e+nous+ly** *adv.* **—en+'dog+e+ny** *n.*

en·do+lymph ('ɛndəʊˌlɪmf) *n.* the fluid that fills the membranous labyrinth of the internal ear. **—en·do+lym+phat+ic** (ˌɛndəʊlɪm'fætɪk) *adj.*

en·do+me+tri·o+sis (ˌɛndəʊˌmiːtrɪ'əʊsɪs) *n. Pathol.* the presence of endometrium in areas other than the lining of the uterus, as on the ovaries, resulting in premenstrual pain.

en·do+me+tri+um (ˌɛndəʊ'miːtrɪəm) *n., pl.* **·tri·a** (-trɪə). the mucous membrane that lines the uterus. [C19: New Latin, from ENDO- + Greek *mētra* uterus] **—ˌen·do+'me+tri+al** *adj.*

en·do+morph ('ɛndəʊˌmɔːf) *n.* **1.** a type of person having a body build characterized by roundness, fatness, and heaviness. Compare **ectomorph, mesomorph. 2.** a mineral that naturally occurs enclosed within another mineral, as within quartz. **—ˌen·do+'mor+phic** *adj.* **—'en·do+ˌmor+phy** *n.*

en·do+mor+phism (ˌɛndəʊ'mɔːˌfɪzəm) *n. Geology.* a type of metamorphism in which changes are induced in the cooling molten rock material by contact with the older rocks surrounding it.

en·do+neu+ri+um (ˌɛndəʊ'njʊərɪəm) *n.* the delicate connective tissue surrounding nerve fibres within a bundle.

en·do+par·a+site (ˌɛndəʊ'pærəˌsaɪt) *n.* a parasite, such as the tapeworm, that lives within the body of its host. **—en·do+par·a+sit+ic** (ˌɛndəʊˌpærə'sɪtɪk) *adj.*

en·do+pep+ti+dase (ˌɛndəʊ'pɛptɪˌdeɪz) *n.* any proteolytic enzyme, such as pepsin, that splits a protein into smaller peptide fragments. Also called: **proteinase.** Compare **exopeptidase.**

en·do+phyte ('ɛndəʊˌfaɪt) *n.* any plant, such as a parasitic fungus, that lives within another plant. **—en·do+phyt+ic** (ˌɛndəʊ'fɪtɪk) *adj.* **—ˌen·do+'phyt·i+cal+ly** *adv.*

en·do+plasm ('ɛndəʊˌplæzəm) *n. Cytology.* the inner cytoplasm that in many cells is more granular and fluid than the outer cytoplasm (see **ectoplasm** (sense 1)). **—ˌen·do+'plas+mic** *adj.*

en·do+plas+mic re+tic+u+lum *n.* a network of membranes in the cytoplasm of most cells, functioning in intracellular transport. It is sometimes covered with numerous particles (ribosomes).

end or+gan *n. Anatomy.* the expanded end of a peripheral motor or sensory nerve.

en+dorse *or* **in+dorse** (ɪn'dɔːs) *vb.* (*tr.*) **1.** to give approval or sanction to. **2.** to sign (one's name) on the back of (a cheque, etc.) to specify oneself as payee. **3.** *Commerce.* **a.** to sign the back of (a negotiable document) to transfer ownership of the rights to a specified payee. **b.** to specify (a designated sum) as transferable to another as payee. **4.** to write (a qualifying comment, recommendation, etc.) on the back of a document. **5.** to sign a document, as when confirming receipt of payment. **6.** *Chiefly Brit.* to record (a conviction) on (a driving licence). [C16: from Old French *endosser* to put on the back, from EN-[1] + *dos* back, from Latin *dorsum*] **—en+'dors+a·ble** *or* **in+'dors+a·ble** *adj.* **—en+'dors+er, en+'dor+sor** *or* **in+'dors+er, in+'dor+sor** *n.*

en+dor+see (ɪnˌdɔːˈsiː, ˌɛndɔː-) *or* **in+dor+see** *n.* the person in whose favour a negotiable instrument is endorsed.

en+dorse+ment *or* **in+dorse+ment** (ɪnˈdɔːsmənt) *n.* **1.** the act or an instance of endorsing. **2.** something that endorses, such as a signature or qualifying comment. **3.** approval or support. **4.** a record of a motoring offence on a driving licence. **5.** *Insurance.* a clause in or amendment to an insurance policy allowing for alteration of coverage.

en·do+scope (ˈɛndəʊˌskəʊp) *n.* a long slender medical instrument for examining the interior of a hollow organ such as the urinary bladder. **—en·do+scop+ic** (ˌɛndəʊˈskɒpɪk) *adj.* **—en+dos+co+pist** (ɛnˈdɒskəpɪst) *n.* **—en+'dos+co+py** *n.*

en·do+skel+e·ton (ˌɛndəʊˈskɛlɪtᵊn) *n.* the internal skeleton of an animal, esp. the bony or cartilaginous skeleton of vertebrates. Compare **exoskeleton.** **—ˌen·do+'skel+e·tal** *adj.*

en+dos+mo+sis (ˌɛndɒsˈməʊsɪs, -dɒz-) *n. Biology.* osmosis in which water enters a cell or organism from the surrounding solution. Compare **exosmosis.** **—en+dos+mot+ic** (ˌɛndɒsˈmɒtɪk, -dɒz-) *adj.* **—ˌen+dos+'mot·i·cal+ly** *adv.*

en·do+some (ˈɛndəʊˌsəʊm) *n. Cytology.* any dense particle of chromatin within a nucleus, esp. a nucleolus.

en·do+sperm (ˈɛndəʊˌspɜːm) *n.* the tissue within the seed of a flowering plant that surrounds and nourishes the developing embryo. **—ˌen·do+'sper+mic** *adj.*

en·do+spore (ˈɛndəʊˌspɔː) *n.* **1.** a small asexual spore produced by some bacteria and algae. **2.** the innermost wall of a spore or pollen grain. **—en+dos+por+ous** (ɛnˈdɒspərəs, ˌɛndəʊˈspɔːrəs) *adj.*

en+dos+te·um (ɛnˈdɒstɪəm) *n., pl.* **+te·a** (-tɪə). a highly vascular membrane lining the internal surface of long bones, such as the femur and humerus. [C19: New Latin, from ENDO- + Greek *osteon* bone] **—en+'dos+te·al** *adj.*

en+dos+to+sis (ˌɛndɒsˈtəʊsɪs) *n., pl.* **+ses** (-siːz). the conversion of cartilage into bone.

en·do·the·ci·um (ˌɛndəʊˈθiːʃɪəm, -sɪəm) *n., pl.* **·ci·a** (-ʃɪə, -sɪə). *Botany.* **1.** the inner mass of cells of the developing capsule in mosses. **2.** the fibrous tissue of the inner wall of an anther. [C19: New Latin, from ENDO- + Greek *thēkion* case; see THECA] **—ˌen·do+'the·ci·al** *adj.*

en·do·the·li·o·ma (ˌɛndəʊˌθiːlɪˈəʊmə) *n., pl.* **+ma·ta** (-mətə). *Pathol.* a tumour originating in endothelial tissue, such as the lining of blood vessels.

en·do·the·li·um (ˌɛndəʊˈθiːlɪəm) *n., pl.* **·li·a** (-lɪə). a tissue consisting of a single layer of cells that lines the blood and lymph vessels, heart, and some other cavities. [C19: New Latin, from ENDO- + *-thelium*, from Greek *thēlē* nipple] **—ˌen·do+'the·li·al** *adj.* **—ˌen·do+'the·li+ˌoid** *adj.*

en·do·ther+mic (ˌɛndəʊˈθɜːmɪk) *or* **en·do·ther+mal** *adj.* (of a chemical reaction or compound) occurring or formed with the absorption of heat. Compare **exothermic, endoergic.** **—ˌen·do+'ther+mi·cal+ly** *adv.* **—ˌen·do+'ther+mism** *n.*

en·do·tox+in (ˌɛndəʊˈtɒksɪn) *n.* a toxin contained within the protoplasm of an organism, esp. a bacterium, and liberated only at death. **—ˌen·do+'tox+ic** *adj.*

end+o·ver (ˈɛndˌəʊvə) *n. Skateboarding.* a movement in a straight line by means of a series of spins through 180° all in the same direction.

en+dow (ɪnˈdaʊ) *vb. (tr.)* **1.** to provide with or bequeath a source of permanent income. **2.** (usually foll. by *with*) to provide (with qualities, characteristics, etc.). **3.** *Obsolete.* to provide with a dower. [C14: from Old French *endouer*, from EN-[1] + *douer* from Latin *dōtāre*, from *dōs* dowry] **—en+'dow+er** *n.*

en+dow+ment (ɪnˈdaʊmənt) *n.* **1. a.** the source of income with which an institution, etc., is endowed. **b.** the income itself. **2.** the act or process of endowing. **3.** (*usually pl.*) natural talents or qualities.

en+dow+ment as+sur+ance *or* **in+sur+ance** *n.* a form of life insurance that provides for the payment of a specified sum directly to the policyholder at a designated date or to his beneficiary should he die before this date.

end+pa·per (ˈɛndˌpeɪpə) *n.* either of two leaves at the front and back of a book pasted to the inside of the board covers and the first leaf of the book to secure the binding.

end pin *n. Music.* the adjustable metal spike attached to the bottom of a cello, double bass, etc., that supports it while it is being played.

end+plate (ˈɛndˌpleɪt) *n.* **1.** any usually flat platelike structure at the end of something. **2.** *Physiol.* the flattened end of a motor nerve fibre, which transmits impulses to muscle.

end+play (ˈɛndˌpleɪ) *Bridge.* ~*n.* **1.** a way of playing the last few tricks in a hand so that an opponent is forced to make a particular lead. ~*vb. (tr.).* **2.** to force (an opponent) to make a particular lead near the end of a hand: *declarer endplayed West for the jack of spades.*

end point *n.* **1.** *Chem.* the point at which a titration is complete, usually marked by a change in colour of an indicator. **2.** the point at which anything is complete.

end prod+uct *n.* the final result or outcome of a process, series, endeavour, etc., esp. in manufacturing.

end-stopped *adj.* (of verse) having a pause at the end of each line.

en+due *or* **in+due** (ɪnˈdjuː) *vb.* **+dues, +du+ing, +dued.** *(tr.)* **1.** (usually foll. by *with*) to invest or provide, as with some quality or trait. **2.** *Rare.* to don or assume. **3.** *Rare.* (foll. by *with*) to clothe or dress (in). [C15: from Old French *enduire*, from Latin *indūcere*, from *dūcere* to lead]

end up *vb. (adv.)* **1.** (*copula*) to become eventually; turn out to be: *he ended up a thief.* **2.** (*intr.*) to arrive, esp. by a circuitous or lengthy route or process: *to end up in prison.*

en+dur+ance (ɪnˈdjʊərəns) *n.* **1.** the capacity, state, or an instance of enduring. **2.** something endured; a hardship, strain, or privation.

en+dure (ɪnˈdjʊə) *vb.* **1.** to undergo (hardship, strain, privation, etc.) without yielding; bear. **2.** (*tr.*) to permit or tolerate. **3.** (*intr.*) to last or continue to exist. [C14: from Old French *endurer*, from Latin *indūrāre* to harden, from *dūrus* hard] **—en+'dur+a·ble** *adj.* **—en+ˌdur+a·'bil+i·ty** *or* **en+'dur+a·ble+ness** *n.* **—en+'dur+a·bly** *adv.*

en+dur+ing (ɪnˈdjʊərɪŋ) *adj.* **1.** permanent; lasting. **2.** having forbearance; long-suffering. **—en+'dur+ing+ly** *adv.* **—en+'dur+ing+ness** *n.*

end+ways (ˈɛndˌweɪz) *or esp. U.S.* **end+wise** (ˈɛndˌwaɪz) *adv.* **1.** having the end forwards or upwards. ~*adj.* **2.** vertical or upright. **3.** lengthways. **4.** standing or lying end to end.

En·dym·i·on (ɛnˈdɪmɪən) *n. Greek myth.* a handsome youth who was visited every night by the moon goddess Selene, who loved him.

ENE *abbrev. for* east-northeast.

-ene *n. combining form.* (in chemistry) indicating an unsaturated compound containing double bonds: *benzene; ethylene.* [from Greek *-ēnē*, feminine patronymic suffix]

en+e·ma (ˈɛnɪmə) *n., pl.* **·mas** *or* **·ma·ta** (-mətə). *Med.* **1.** the introduction of liquid into the rectum to evacuate the bowels, medicate, or nourish. **2.** the liquid so introduced. [C15: from New Latin, from Greek: injection, from *enienai* to send in, from *hienai* to send]

en+e·my (ˈɛnəmɪ) *n., pl.* **·mies.** **1.** a person hostile or opposed to a policy, cause, person, or group, esp. one who actively tries to do damage; opponent. **2. a.** an armed adversary; opposing military force. **b.** (*as modifier*): *enemy aircraft.* **3. a.** a hostile nation or people. **b.** (*as modifier*): *an enemy alien.* **4.** something that harms or opposes; adversary: *courage is the enemy of failure.* ~Related adj.: **inimical.** [C13: from Old French *enemi*, from Latin *inimīcus* hostile, from IN-[1] + *amīcus* friend]

en+er+get+ic (ˌɛnəˈdʒɛtɪk) *adj.* having or showing much energy or force; vigorous. **—ˌen+er+'get·i·cal+ly** *adv.*

en+er+get+ics (ˌɛnəˈdʒɛtɪks) *n.* (*functioning as sing.*) the branch of science concerned with energy and its transformations. **—ˌen+er+'get·i·cist** *n.*

en+er+gid (ˈɛnədʒɪd) *n.* a biological unit that consists of nucleus and cytoplasm but does not constitute a cell.

en+er+gize *or* **en+er+gise** (ˈɛnəˌdʒaɪz) *vb.* **1.** to have or cause to have energy; invigorate. **2.** (*tr.*) to apply a source of electric current or electromotive force to (a circuit, field winding, etc.). **—'en+er+ˌgiz+er** *or* **'en+er+ˌgis+er** *n.*

en+er+gu+men (ˌɛnəˈgjuːmɛn) *n.* **1.** a person thought to be possessed by an evil spirit. **2.** a fanatic or zealot. [C18: via Late Latin from Greek *energoumenos* having been worked on, from *energein* to be in action, from *energos* effective; see ENERGY]

en+er+gy (ˈɛnədʒɪ) *n., pl.* **+gies.** **1.** intensity or vitality of action or expression; forcefulness. **2.** capacity or tendency for intense activity; vigour. **3.** vigorous or intense action; exertion. **4.** *Physics.* **a.** the capacity of a body or system to do work. **b.** a measure of this capacity, expressed as the work that it does in changing to some specified reference state. It is measured in joules (SI units). Symbol: *E* See also **kinetic energy, potential energy.** [C16: from Late Latin *energīa*, from Greek *energeia* activity, from *energos* effective, from EN-[2] + *ergon* work]

en+er+gy band *n.* a range of energy levels associated with the electrons in a crystalline solid, the distribution of which determines the conducting properties of the solid.

en+er+gy lev+el *or* **state** *n. Physics.* **1.** one of the states of constant energy in which a system may exist. Each level is separated by finite amounts of energy. **2.** the energy of such a state.

en+er+vate *vb.* (ˈɛnəˌveɪt). **1.** (*tr.*) to deprive of strength or vitality; weaken physically or mentally; debilitate. ~*adj.* (ɪˈnɜːvɪt). **2.** deprived of strength or vitality; weakened. [C17: from Latin *ēnervāre* to remove the nerves from, from *nervus* nerve, sinew] **—ˌen+er+'va+tion** *n.* **—'en+er+ˌva+tive** *adj.* **—'en+er+ˌva+tor** *n.*

E·ne·sco (ɛˈnɛskəʊ) *n.* **Georges** (ʒɔrʒ). original name *George Enescu.* 1881–1955, Rumanian violinist and composer.

en+face (ɪnˈfeɪs) *vb. (tr.)* to write, print, or stamp (something) on the face of (a document). **—en+'face+ment** *n.*

en face *French.* (ɑ̃ ˈfas) *adj.* **1.** facing forwards. **2.** opposite; facing.

en fa+mille *French.* (ɑ̃ faˈmij) *adv.* **1.** with one's family; at home. **2.** in a casual way; informally.

en+fant ter+ri+ble *French.* (ɑ̃fɑ̃ tɛˈribl) *n., pl.* ***en+fants ter+ri+bles*** (ɑ̃fɑ̃ tɛˈribl). a person given to unconventional conduct or indiscreet remarks. [C19: from French, literally: terrible child]

en+fee+ble (ɪnˈfiːbᵊl) *vb. (tr.)* to make weak; deprive of strength. **—en+'fee+ble+ment** *n.* **—en+'fee+bler** *n.*

en+feoff (ɪnˈfiːf) *vb. (tr.)* **1.** *Property law.* to invest (a person) with possession of a freehold estate in land. **2.** (in feudal society) to take (someone) into vassalage by giving a fee or fief in return for certain services. [C14: from Anglo-French *enfeoffer*; see FIEF] —en+'feoff+ment *n.*

en fête *French.* (ã 'fɛt) *adv.* **1.** dressed for a festivity. **2.** engaged in a festivity. [literally: in festival]

En+field ('ɛnfi:ld) *n.* a borough of Greater London: a N residential suburb. Pop.: 260 900 (1976 est.).

En+field ri+fle *n.* **1.** a breech-loading bolt-action magazine rifle of varying calibres, formerly used by the British and U.S. armies. **2.** a nineteenth-century muzzle-loading musket used by the British army. [C19: from ENFIELD, where it was first made]

en+fi+lade (ˌɛnfɪ'leɪd) *Military.* ~*n.* **1.** a position or formation subject to fire directed along the length as opposed to the breadth of its front. ~*vb.* (*tr.*) **2.** to attack (a position or formation) with enfilade. [C18: from French: suite, from *enfiler* to thread on string, from *fil* thread]

en+fleu+rage *French.* (ãflœ'ra:ʒ) *n.* the process of exposing odourless oils to the scent of fresh flowers, used in perfume-making.

en+fold *or* **in+fold** (ɪn'fəʊld) *vb.* (*tr.*) **1.** to cover by enclosing. **2.** to embrace. **3.** to form with or as with folds. —**en+'fold+er** *or* **in+'fold+er** *n.* —**en+'fold+ment** *or* **in+'fold+ment** *n.*

en+force (ɪn'fɔ:s) *vb.* (*tr.*) **1.** to ensure observance of or obedience to (a law, decision, etc.). **2.** to impose (obedience, loyalty, etc.) by or as by force. **3.** to emphasize or reinforce (an argument, demand, etc.). —**en+'force+a·ble** *adj.* —**en+ˌforce+a·'bil+i+ty** *n.* —**en+forc+ed+ly** (ɪn'fɔ:sɪdlɪ) *adv.* —**en+'force+ment** *n.* —**en+'forc+er** *n.*

en+fran+chise (ɪn'fræntʃaɪz) *vb.* (*tr.*) **1.** to grant the power of voting to, esp. as a right of citizenship. **2.** to liberate, as from servitude. **3.** (in England) to invest (a town, city, etc.) with the right to be represented in Parliament. **4.** *English law.* (formerly) to convert (copyhold land) to freehold. —**en+'fran+chise+ment** *n.* —**en+'fran+chis+er** *n.*

eng (ɛŋ) *n. Phonetics.* another name for **agma.**

eng. *abbrev. for:* **1.** engine. **2.** engineer. **3.** engineering. **4.** engraved. **5.** engraver. **6.** engraving.

Eng. *abbrev. for:* **1.** England. **2.** English.

En+ga+dine ('ɛŋgəˌdi:n) *n.* the upper part of the valley of the River Inn in Switzerland, in Graubünden canton: tourist and winter sports centre.

en+gage (ɪn'geɪdʒ) *vb.* (*mainly tr.*) **1.** to secure the services of; employ. **2.** to secure for use; reserve: *engage a room.* **3.** to involve (a person or his attention) intensely; engross; occupy. **4.** to attract (the affection) of (a person): *her innocence engaged him.* **5.** to draw (somebody) into conversation. **6.** (*intr.*) to take part; participate: *he engages in many sports.* **7.** to promise (to do something). **8.** (*also intr.*) *Military.* to begin an action with (an enemy). **9.** to bring (a mechanism) into operation: *he engaged the clutch.* **10.** (*also intr.*) to undergo or cause to undergo interlocking, as of the components of a driving mechanism, such as a gear train. **11.** *Machinery.* to locate (a locking device) in its operative position or to advance (a tool) into a workpiece to commence cutting. [C15: from Old French *engagier*, from EN-[1] + *gage* a pledge, see GAGE[1]] —**en+'gag+er** *n.*

en+ga+gé *or* (*fem.*) ***en+ga+gée*** *French.* (ãga'ʒe) *adj.* (of a writer or artist) morally or politically committed to some ideology.

en+gaged (ɪn'geɪdʒd) *adj.* **1.** pledged to be married; betrothed. **2.** employed, occupied, or busy. **3.** *Architect.* built against or attached to a wall or similar structure: *an engaged column.* **4.** (of a telephone line) already in use. —**en+gag+ed+ly** (ɪn'geɪdʒɪdlɪ) *adv.*

en+gaged tone *n. Brit.* a repeated single note heard on a telephone when the number called is already in use. U.S. equivalent: **busy signal.** Compare **ringing tone, dialling tone.**

en+gage+ment (ɪn'geɪdʒmənt) *n.* **1.** a pledge of marriage; betrothal. **2.** an appointment or arrangement, esp. for business or social purposes. **3.** the act of engaging or condition of being engaged. **4.** a promise, obligation, or other condition that binds. **5.** a period of employment, esp. a limited period. **6.** an action; battle. **7.** (*pl.*) financial obligations.

en+gage+ment ring *n.* a ring given by a man to a woman as a token of their betrothal.

en+gag+ing (ɪn'geɪdʒɪŋ) *adj.* pleasing, charming, or winning. —**en+'gag+ing+ly** *adv.* —**en+'gag+ing+ness** *n.*

en garde *French.* (ã 'gard) *interj.* **1.** on guard; a call to a fencer to adopt a defensive stance in readiness for an attack or bout. ~*adj.* **2.** (of a fencer) in such a stance.

En+gels (*German* 'ɛŋəls) *n.* **Frie·drich** ('fri:drɪç). 1820–95, German socialist leader and political philosopher, in England from 1849. He collaborated with Marx on *The Communist Manifesto* (1848) and his own works include *Condition of the Working Classes in England* (1844) and *The Origin of the Family, Private Property and the State* (1884).

en+gen+der (ɪn'dʒɛndə) *vb.* **1.** (*tr.*) to bring about or give rise to; produce or cause. **2.** to be born or cause to be born; bring or come into being. [C14: from Old French *engendrer*, from Latin *ingenerāre*, from *generāre* to beget] —**en+'gen+der+er** *n.* —**en+'gen+der+ment** *n.*

engin. *abbrev. for* engineering.

en+gine ('ɛndʒɪn) *n.* **1.** any machine designed to convert energy, esp. thermal energy, into mechanical work: *a steam engine; a petrol engine.* **2. a.** a railway locomotive. **b.** (*as modifier*): *the engine cab.* **3.** *Military.* any of various pieces of equipment formerly used in warfare, such as a battering ram or gun. **4.** any instrument or device: *engines of torture.* [C13: from Old French *engin*, from Latin *ingenium* nature, talent, ingenious contrivance, from IN-[2] + *-genium*, related to *gignere* to beget, produce]

en+gine driv+er *n. Chiefly Brit.* a man who drives a railway locomotive; train driver.

en+gi+neer (ˌɛndʒɪ'nɪə) *n.* **1.** a person trained in any branch of the profession of engineering. **2.** the originator or manager of a situation, system, etc. **3.** a mechanic; one who repairs or services machines. **4.** *U.S.* the driver of a railway locomotive. **5.** an officer responsible for a ship's engines. **6.** *Informal* name: **sapper.** a member of the armed forces, esp. the army, trained in engineering and construction work. ~*vb.* (*tr.*) **7.** to originate, cause, or plan in a clever or devious manner: *he engineered the minister's downfall.* **8.** to design, plan, or construct as a professional engineer. [C14 *enginer*, from Old French *engigneor*, from *engignier* to contrive, ultimately from Latin *ingenium* skill, talent; see ENGINE]

en+gi+neer+ing (ˌɛndʒɪ'nɪərɪŋ) *n.* the profession of applying scientific principles to the design, construction, and maintenance of engines, cars, machines, etc. (**mechanical engineering**), buildings, bridges, roads, etc. (**civil engineering**), electrical machines and communication systems (**electrical engineering**), chemical plant and machinery (**chemical engineering**), or aircraft (**aeronautical engineering**). See also **military engineering.**

en+gine room *n.* **1.** a place where engines are housed, esp. on a ship. **2.** *Informal.* a place where heavy or productive work is done.

en+gine+ry ('ɛndʒɪnrɪ) *n., pl.* **+ries. 1.** a collection or assembly of engines; machinery. **2.** engines employed in warfare. **3.** *Rare.* skilful manoeuvring or contrivance.

en+gla+ci+al (ɪn'gleɪsɪəl) *adj.* embedded in, carried by, or running through a glacier: *englacial drift; an englacial river.* —**en+'gla+ci+al+ly** *adv.*

Eng+land ('ɪŋglənd) *n.* the largest division of Great Britain, bordering on Scotland and Wales: unified in the mid-tenth century and conquered by the Normans in 1066; united with Wales in 1536 and Scotland in 1707; monarchy overthrown in 1649 but restored in 1660; became the world's leading colonial power in the 18th century; the first country to undergo the Industrial Revolution. Capital: London. Pop.: 46 417 600 (1976 est.). Area: 130 360 sq. km (50 332 sq. miles). See **United Kingdom, Great Britain.** Related adj.: **Anglican.**

Eng+lish ('ɪŋglɪʃ) *n.* **1.** the official language of Britain, the U.S., most parts of the Commonwealth, and certain other countries. It is the native language of over 280 million people and is acquired as a second language by many more. It is an Indo-European language belonging to the West Germanic branch. **2. the English.** (*functioning as pl.*) the natives or inhabitants of England or (loosely) of Great Britain collectively. **3.** (formerly) a size of printer's type approximately equal to 14 point. **4.** an old style of black-letter typeface. **5.** (*often not cap.*) the usual U.S. term for **side** (in billiards). ~*adj.* **6.** denoting, using, or relating to the English language. **7.** relating to or characteristic of England or the English. ~*vb.* (*tr.*) **8.** *Archaic.* to translate or adapt into English. —**'Eng+lish+ness** *n.*

Eng+lish bond *n.* a bond used in brickwork that has a course of headers alternating with a course of stretchers.

Eng+lish Chan+nel *n.* an arm of the Atlantic Ocean between S England and N France, linked with the North Sea by the Strait of Dover. Length: about 560 km (350 miles). Width: between 32 km (20 miles) and 161 km (100 miles).

Eng+lish flute *n. Music.* another name for **recorder** (sense 4).

Eng+lish horn *n. Music.* another name for **cor anglais.**

Eng+lish+ism ('ɪŋglɪˌʃɪzəm) *n. Chiefly U.S.* **1.** an English custom, practice, etc. **2.** a word or expression not found in forms of English other than British English; Anglicism. **3.** high regard for English customs, institutions, etc.

Eng·lish+man ('ɪŋglɪʃmən) *or* (*fem.*) **Eng·lish+wom·an** *n., pl.* **+men** *or* **+wom·en. 1.** a native or inhabitant of England. **2.** (loosely) a citizen of the United Kingdom.

Eng·lish+man's tie *or* **knot** *n.* a type of knot for tying together heavy ropes.

Eng·lish+ry ('ɪŋglɪʃrɪ) *n. Now rare.* **1.** people of English descent, esp. in Ireland. **2.** the fact or condition of being an Englishman or Englishwoman, esp. by birth.

Eng+lish set+ter *n.* a breed of setter having a soft silky coat, usually with a good deal of white in it, and a plumed tail.

en+glut (ɪn'glʌt) *vb.* **+gluts, +glut+ting, +glut+ted.** (*tr.*) *Literary.* **1.** to devour ravenously; swallow eagerly. **2.** to glut or sate (oneself); surfeit; satiate.

en+gorge (ɪn'gɔ:dʒ) *vb.* (*tr.*) **1.** *Pathol.* to congest with blood. **2.** to eat (food) ravenously or greedily. **3.** to gorge (oneself); glut; satiate. —**en+'gorge+ment** *n.*

engr. *abbrev. for:* **1.** engineer. **2.** engraved. **3.** engraver.

en+graft *or* **in+graft** (ɪn'grɑ:ft) *vb.* (*tr.*) **1.** to graft (a shoot, bud, etc.) onto a stock. **2.** to incorporate in a firm or permanent way; implant: *they engrafted their principles into the document.* —**ˌen+graf+'ta+tion, ˌin+graf+'ta+tion** *or* **en+'graft+ment, in+'graft+ment** *n.*

en+grail (ɪn'greɪl) *vb.* (*tr.*) to decorate or mark (the edge of) (a coin, etc.) with small carved notches. [C14: from Old French *engresler*, from EN-[1] + *gresle* slim, from Latin *gracilis* slender, graceful] —**en+'grail+ment** *n.*

en+grain (ɪn'greɪn) *vb.* a variant spelling of **ingrain.**

en+gram ('ɛngræm) *n. Psychol.* the physical basis of an individual memory in the brain. Also called: **neurogram.** See also **memory trace.** [C20: from German *Engramm*, from Greek *en-* IN + *gramma* letter] —**en+'gram+mic** *or* **ˌen+gram+'mat+ic** *adj.*

en+grave (ɪn'greɪv) *vb.* (*tr.*) **1.** to inscribe (a design, writing, etc.) onto (a block, plate, or other surface used for printing) by carving, etching with acid, or other process. **2.** to print (designs or characters) from a printing plate so made. **3.** to fix deeply or permanently in the mind. [C16: from EN-^{1} + GRAVE^3, on the model of French *engraver*] —**en+'grav+er** *n.*

en+grav+ing (ɪn'greɪvɪŋ) *n.* **1.** the art of a person who engraves. **2.** a block, plate, or other surface that has been engraved. **3.** a print made from such a surface.

en+gross (ɪn'grəʊs) *vb.* (*tr.*) **1.** to occupy one's attention completely; absorb. **2.** to write or copy (manuscript) in large legible handwriting. **3.** *Law.* to write or type out formally (a deed, agreement, or other document) preparatory to execution. **4.** another word for **corner** (sense 19b). [C14 (in the sense: to buy up wholesale): from Old French *en gros* in quantity; C15 (in the sense: to write in large letters): probably from Medieval Latin *ingrossāre;* both from Latin *grossus* thick, GROSS] —**en+gross+ed+ly** (ɪn'grəʊsɪdlɪ) *adv.* —**en+'gross+er** *n.*

en+gross+ment (ɪn'grəʊsmənt) *n.* **1.** a deed or other document that has been engrossed. **2.** the state of being engrossed.

en+gulf *or* **in+gulf** (ɪn'gʌlf) *vb.* (*tr.*) **1.** to immerse, plunge, bury, or swallow up. **2.** (*often passive*) to overwhelm: *engulfed by debts.* —**en+'gulf+ment** *n.*

en+hance (ɪn'hɑːns) *vb.* (*tr.*) to intensify or increase in quality, value, etc.; improve; augment. [C14: from Old French *enhaucier,* from EN-^{1} + *haucier* to raise, from Vulgar Latin *altiāre* (unattested), from Latin *altus* high] —**en+'hance+ment** *n.* —**en+'hanc+er** *n.* —**en+'hanc+ive** *adj.*

en+har+mon+ic (ˌɛnhɑː'mɒnɪk) *adj. Music.* **1.** denoting or relating to a small difference in pitch between two notes such as A flat and G sharp: not present in instruments of equal temperament such as the piano, but significant in the intonation of stringed and wind instruments. **2.** denoting or relating to enharmonic modulation. [C17: from Latin *enharmonicus,* from Greek *enarmonios,* from EN-^{2} + *harmonia;* see HARMONY] —ˌ**en+har+'mon+i+cal+ly** *adv.*

en+har+mon+ic mod+u+la+tion *n. Music.* a change of key achieved by regarding a note in one key as an equivalent note in another. Thus E flat in the key of A flat could be regarded as D sharp in the key of B major.

E+nid ('iːnɪd) *n.* (in Arthurian legend) the faithful wife of Geraint.

e+nig+ma (ɪ'nɪgmə) *n.* a person, thing, or situation that is mysterious, puzzling, or ambiguous. [C16: from Latin *aenigma,* from Greek *ainigma,* from *ainissesthai* to speak in riddles, from *ainos* fable, story] —**en+ig+mat+ic** (ˌɛnɪg'mætɪk) *or* ˌ**en+ig+'mat+i+cal** *adj.* —ˌ**en+ig+'mat+i+cal+ly** *adv.*

e+nig+ma+tize *or* **e+nig+ma+tise** (ɪ'nɪgməˌtaɪz) *vb.* (*tr.*) to make enigmatic.

en+isle (ɪn'aɪl) *vb.* (*tr.*) *Poetic.* to put on or make into an island.

En+i+we+tok (ˌɛnə'wiːtɒk, ə'niːwɪˌtɔːk) *n.* an atoll in the W Pacific Ocean, in the NW Marshall Islands: taken by the U.S. from Japan in 1944; became a naval base and later a testing ground for atomic weapons.

en+jamb+ment *or* **en+jambe+ment** (ɪn'dʒæmmənt; *French* ɑ̃ʒɑ̃b'mɑ̃) *n. Prosody.* the running over of a sentence from one line of verse into the next. [C19: from French, literally: a straddling, from *enjamber* to straddle, from EN-^{1} + *jambe* leg; see JAMB] —**en+'jambed** *adj.*

en+join (ɪn'dʒɔɪn) *vb.* (*tr.*) **1.** to order (someone) to do (something); urge strongly; command. **2.** to impose or prescribe (a condition, mode of behaviour, etc.). **3.** *Law.* to require (a person) to do or refrain from doing (some act), esp. by issuing an injunction. [C13: from Old French *enjoindre,* from Latin *injungere* to fasten to, from IN-^{2} + *jungere* to JOIN] —**en+'join+er** *n.* —**en+'join+ment** *n.*

en+joy (ɪn'dʒɔɪ) *vb.* (*tr.*) **1.** to receive pleasure from; take joy in. **2.** to have the benefit of; use with satisfaction. **3.** to have as a condition; experience: *the land enjoyed a summer of rain.* **4.** *Archaic.* to have sexual intercourse with. **5. enjoy oneself.** to have a good time. [C14: from Old French *enjoir,* from EN-^{1} + *joir* to find pleasure in, from Latin *gaudēre* to rejoice] —**en+'joy+a+ble** *adj.* —**en+'joy+a+ble+ness** *n.* —**en+'joy+a+bly** *adv.* —**en+'joy+er** *n.*

en+joy+ment (ɪn'dʒɔɪmənt) *n.* **1.** the act or condition of receiving pleasure from something. **2.** the use or possession of something that is satisfying or beneficial. **3.** something that provides joy or satisfaction. **4.** the possession or exercise of a legal right.

en+kin+dle (ɪn'kɪndᵊl) *vb.* (*tr.*) **1.** to set on fire; kindle. **2.** to excite to activity or ardour; arouse. —**en+'kin+dler** *n.*

enl. *abbrev. for:* **1.** enlarge(d). **2.** enlisted.

en+lace (ɪn'leɪs) *vb.* (*tr.*) **1.** to bind or encircle with or as with laces. **2.** to entangle; intertwine. —**en+'lace+ment** *n.*

en+large (ɪn'lɑːdʒ) *vb.* **1.** to make or grow larger in size, scope, etc.; increase or expand. **2.** (*tr.*) to make (a photographic print) of a larger size than the negative. **3.** (*intr.;* foll. by *on* or *upon*) to speak or write (about) in greater detail; expatiate (on). —**en+'large+a+ble** *adj.* —**en+'larg+er** *n.*

en+large+ment (ɪn'lɑːdʒmənt) *n.* **1.** the act of enlarging or the condition of being enlarged. **2.** something that enlarges or is intended to enlarge. **3.** a photographic print that is larger than the negative from which it is made.

en+larg+er (ɪn'lɑːdʒə) *n.* an optical instrument for making enlarged photographic prints in which a negative is brightly illuminated and its enlarged image is focused onto a sheet of sensitized paper.

en+light+en (ɪn'laɪtᵊn) *vb.* (*tr.*) **1.** to give information or understanding to; instruct; edify. **2.** to give spiritual or religious revelation to. **3.** *Poetic.* to shed light on. —**en+'light+en+er** *n.* —**en+'light+en+ing+ly** *adv.*

en+light+en+ment (ɪn'laɪtᵊnmənt) *n.* **1.** the act or means of enlightening or the state of being enlightened. **2.** *Buddhism.* the awakening to ultimate truth by which man is freed from the endless cycle of personal reincarnations to which all men are otherwise subject. **3.** *Hinduism.* a state of transcendent divine experience represented by Vishnu: regarded as a goal of all religion.

En+light+en+ment (ɪn'laɪtᵊnmənt) *n.* **the.** an 18th-century philosophical movement stressing the importance of reason and the critical reappraisal of existing ideas and social institutions.

en+list (ɪn'lɪst) *vb.* **1.** to enter or persuade to enter into an engagement to serve in the armed forces. **2.** (*tr.*) to engage or secure (a person, his services, or his support) for a venture, cause, etc. **3.** (*intr.;* foll. by *in*) to enter into or join an enterprise, cause, etc. —**en+'list+er** *n.* —**en+'list+ment** *n.*

en+list+ed man *n. U.S.* a serviceman who holds neither a commission nor a warrant and is not under training for officer rank as a cadet or midshipman.

en+liv+en (ɪn'laɪvᵊn) *vb.* (*tr.*) **1.** to make active, vivacious, or spirited; invigorate. **2.** to make cheerful or bright; gladden or brighten. —**en+'liv+en+er** *n.* —**en+'liv+en+ing+ly** *adv.* —**en+'liv+en+ment** *n.*

en masse (*French* ɑ̃ 'mas) *adv.* in a group, body, or mass; as a whole; all together. [C19: from French]

en+mesh, in+mesh (ɪn'mɛʃ), *or* **im+mesh** *vb.* (*tr.*) to catch or involve in or as if in a net or snare; entangle. —**en+'mesh+ment** *n.*

en+mi+ty ('ɛnmɪtɪ) *n., pl.* **·ties.** a feeling of hostility or ill will, as between enemies; antagonism. [C13: from Old French *enemistié,* from *enemi* ENEMY]

en+nage ('ɛnɪdʒ) *n. Printing.* the total number of ens in a piece of matter to be set in type.

en+ne+ad ('ɛnɪˌæd) *n.* **1.** a group or series of nine. **2.** the sum of or number nine. [C17: from Greek *enneas,* from *ennea* nine] —ˌ**en+ne+'ad+ic** *adj.*

en+ne+a+gon ('ɛnɪəgən) *n.* another name for **nonagon.**

en+ne+a+he+dron (ˌɛnɪə'hiːdrən) *n., pl.* **+drons** *or* **+dra** (-drə). a solid figure having nine plane faces. See also **polyhedron.** —ˌ**en+ne+a+'he+dral** *adj.*

En+ner+dale Wa+ter ('ɛnəˌdeɪl) *n.* a lake in NW England, in Cumbria in the Lake District. Length: 4 km (2.5 miles).

En+nis ('ɛnɪs) *n.* a town in the W Republic of Ireland, county town of Co. Clare. Pop.: 5972 (1971).

En+nis+kil+len (ˌɛnɪs'kɪlɪn) *or* (*formerly*) **In+nis+kil+ling** *n.* a town in SW Northern Ireland, county town of Fermanagh, on an island in the River Erne: scene of the defeat of James II's forces in 1689. Pop.: 6553 (1971).

En+ni+us ('ɛnɪəs) *n.* **Quin+tus** ('kwɪntəs). 239–169 B.C., Roman epic poet and dramatist.

en+no+ble (ɪ'nəʊbᵊl) *vb.* (*tr.*) **1.** to make noble, honourable, or excellent; dignify; exalt. **2.** to raise to a noble rank; confer a title of nobility upon. —**en+'no+ble+ment** *n.* —**en+'no+bler** *n.* —**en+'no+bling+ly** *adv.*

en+nui ('ɒnwiː; *French* ɑ̃'nɥi) *n.* a feeling of listlessness and general dissatisfaction resulting from lack of activity or excitement. [C18: from French: apathy, from Old French *enui* annoyance, vexation; see ANNOY]

E+noch ('iːnɒk) *n. Old Testament.* **1.** the eldest son of Cain after whom the first city was named (Genesis 4:17). **2.** the father of Methuselah: said to have walked with God and to have been taken by God at the end of his earthly life (Genesis 5:24).

e+nol ('iːnɒl) *n.* any organic compound containing the group -CH:CO-, often existing in chemical equilibrium with the corresponding keto form. See **keto-enol tautomerism.** [C19: from -ENE + -OL] —**e'nol+ic** *adj.*

e+nor+mi+ty (ɪ'nɔːmɪtɪ) *n., pl.* **·ties. 1.** the quality or character of being outrageous; extreme wickedness. **2.** an act of great wickedness; atrocity. **3.** *Informal.* vastness of size or extent. [C15: from Old French *enormite,* from Late Latin *ēnormitās* hugeness; see ENORMOUS]

Usage. In careful usage, the noun *enormity* is not employed to convey the idea of great size, but that of something outrageous or horrifying: *the enormity of this crime leaves one astonished. The immensity* (rather than *enormity*) *of the area covered by the lake is astonishing.*

e+nor+mous (ɪ'nɔːməs) *adj.* **1.** unusually large in size, extent, or degree; immense; vast. **2.** *Archaic.* extremely wicked; heinous. [C16: from Latin *ēnormis,* from *ē-* out of, away from + *norma* rule, pattern] —**e'nor+mous+ly** *adv.* —**e'nor+mous+ness** *n.*

E+nos ('iːnɒs) *n. Old Testament.* a son of Seth (Genesis 4:26; 5:6).

en+o+sis ('ɛnəʊsɪs) *n.* the union of Greece and Cyprus: the aim of a group of Greek Cypriots. [C20: Modern Greek: from Greek *henoun* to unite, from *heis* one]

e+nough (ɪ'nʌf) *determiner.* **1. a.** sufficient to answer a need, demand, supposition, or requirement; adequate: *enough cake.* **b.** (*as pronoun*): *enough is now known.* **2. that's enough!** that will do: used to put an end to an action, speech, performance, etc. ~*adv.* **3.** so as to be adequate or sufficient; as much as necessary: *you have worked hard enough.* **4.** (*not used with a negative*) very or quite; rather: *she was pleased enough to see me.* **5.** (intensifier): *oddly enough; surprisingly enough.* **6.** just adequately; tolerably: *he did it well enough.* [Old English *genōh;* related to Old Norse *gnōgr,* Gothic *ganōhs,* Old High German *ginuog*]

e·nounce (ɪ'naʊns) *vb. (tr.) Formal.* **1.** to enunciate. **2.** to pronounce. [C19: from French *énoncer,* from Latin *ēnuntiāre* ENUNCIATE] —**e·'nounce·ment** *n.*
e·now (ɪ'naʊ) *adj., adv.* an archaic word for **enough.**
en pas·sant (ɒn pæ'sɑːnt; *French* ã pa'sã) *adv.* in passing: in chess, said of capturing a pawn that has made an initial move of two squares to its fourth rank, bypassing the square where an enemy pawn on its own fifth rank could capture it. The capture is made as if the captured pawn had moved one square instead of two. [C17: from French]
en pen·sion *French.* (ã pã'sjɔ̃) *adv.* in lodgings with all meals provided.
en·phy·tot·ic (ˌɛnfaɪ'tɒtɪk) *adj.* (of plant diseases) causing a constant amount of damage each year. [C20: from EN-[2] + -PHYTE + -OTIC]
en·plane (ɛn'pleɪn) *vb. (intr.)* to board an aircraft.
en plein (*French* ã 'plɛ̃) *adj. (postpositive), adv.* (of a gambling bet) placed entirely on a single number, etc. [from French: in full]
en prise (*French* ã 'priːz) *adj. (postpositive), adv.* (of a chess piece) exposed to capture. [French; see PRIZE[1]]
en·quire (ɪn'kwaɪə) *vb.* (often foll. by *of*) **1.** to seek (information) by questioning; ask. **2.** See **inquire.** —**en·'quir·er** *n.* —**en·'quir·y** *n.*
en·rage (ɪn'reɪdʒ) *vb. (tr.)* to provoke to fury; put into a rage; anger. —**en·rag·ed·ly** (ɪn'reɪdʒɪdlɪ) *adv.* —**en·'rage·ment** *n.*
en rap·port *French.* (ã ra'pɔːr) *adj. (postpositive), adv.* in sympathy, harmony, or accord.
en·rap·ture (ɪn'ræptʃə) *vb. (tr.)* to fill with delight; enchant.
en·rich (ɪn'rɪtʃ) *vb. (tr.)* **1.** to increase the wealth of. **2.** to endow with fine or desirable qualities: *to enrich one's experience by travelling.* **3.** to make more beautiful; adorn; decorate: *a robe enriched with jewels.* **4.** to improve in quality, colour, flavour, etc. **5.** to increase the food value of by adding nutrients: *to enrich dog biscuits with calcium.* **6.** to make (soil) more productive, esp. by adding fertilizer. **7.** *Physics.* to increase the concentration or abundance of one component or isotope in (a solution or mixture); concentrate: *to enrich a solution by evaporation; enrich a nuclear fuel.* —**en·'rich·er** *n.* —**en·'rich·ment** *n.*
en·robe (ɪn'rəʊb) *vb. (tr.)* to dress in or as if in a robe; attire. —**en·'rob·er** *n.*
en·rol *or U.S.* **en·roll** (ɪn'rəʊl) *vb.* **·rols** *or U.S.* **·rolls, ·rol·ling ·rolled.** *(mainly tr.)* **1.** to record or note in a roll or list. **2.** (*also intr.*) to become or cause to become a member; enlist; register. **3.** to put on record; record. **4.** *Rare.* to roll or wrap up. —ˌ**en·rol·'lee** *n.* —**en·'rol·ler** *n.*
en·rol·ment *or U.S.* **en·roll·ment** (ɪn'rəʊlmənt) *n.* **1.** the act of enrolling or state of being enrolled. **2.** a list of people enrolled. **3.** the total number of people enrolled.
en·root (ɪn'ruːt) *vb. (tr.; usually passive)* **1.** to establish (plants) by fixing their roots in the earth. **2.** to fix firmly, implant, or embed: *to enroot an idea in the mind.*
en route (ɒn 'ruːt; *French* ã 'rut) *adv.* on or along the way; on the road.
ens (ɛnz) *n., pl.* **en·ti·a** ('ɛnʃɪə). *Metaphysics.* **1.** being or existence in the most general abstract sense. **2.** a real thing, esp. as opposed to an attribute; entity. [C16: from Late Latin, literally: being, from Latin *esse* to be]
Ens. *abbrev. for* Ensign.
en·sam·ple (ɛn'sɑːmpᵊl) *n.* an archaic word for **example.**
en·san·guine (ɪn'sæŋgwɪn) *vb. (tr.) Literary.* to cover or stain with or as with blood.
En·sche·de (*Dutch* 'ɛnsxəˌdeː) *n.* a city in the E Netherlands, in Overijssel province: a major centre of the Dutch cotton industry. Pop.: 141 575 (1974 est.).
en·sconce (ɪn'skɒns) *vb. (tr.; often passive)* **1.** to establish or settle firmly or comfortably: *ensconced in a chair.* **2.** to place in safety; hide. [C16: see EN-[1], SCONCE[2]]
en·sem·ble (ɒn'sɒmbᵊl; *French* ã'sãbl) *n.* **1.** all the parts of something considered together and in relation to the whole. **2.** a person's complete costume; outfit. **3. a.** the cast of a play other than the principals; supporting players. **b.** (*as modifier*): *an ensemble role.* **4.** *Music.* **a.** a group of soloists singing or playing together. **b.** (*as modifier*): *an ensemble passage.* **5.** *Music.* the degree of precision and unity exhibited by a group of instrumentalists or singers performing together: *the ensemble of the strings is good.* **6.** the general or total effect of something made up of individual parts. **7.** *Physics.* **a.** a set of systems (such as a set of collections of atoms) that are identical in all respects apart from the motions of their constituents. **b.** a single system (such as a collection of atoms) in which the properties are determined by the statistical behaviour of its constituents. ~*adv.* **8.** all together or at once. [C15: from French: together, from Latin *insimul,* from IN-[2] + *simul* at the same time]
en·shrine *or* **in·shrine** (ɪn'ʃraɪn) *vb. (tr.)* **1.** to place or enclose in or as if in a shrine. **2.** to hold as sacred; cherish; treasure. —**en·'shrine·ment** *n.*
en·shroud (ɪn'ʃraʊd) *vb. (tr.)* to cover or hide with or as if with a shroud: *the sky was enshrouded in mist.*
en·si·form ('ɛnsɪˌfɔːm) *adj. Biology.* shaped like a sword blade: *ensiform leaves.* [C16: from Latin *ensis* sword]
en·sign ('ɛnsaɪn) *n.* **1.** (*also* 'ɛnsən). a flag flown by a ship, branch of the armed forces, etc., to indicate nationality, allegiance, etc. See also **Red Ensign, White Ensign. 2.** any flag, standard, or banner. **3.** a standard-bearer. **4.** a symbol, token, or emblem; sign. **5.** (in the U.S. Navy) a commissioned officer of the lowest rank. **6.** (formerly in the British infantry) a commissioned officer of the lowest rank. [C14: from Old French *enseigne,* from Latin INSIGNIA] —**'en·sign·ˌship** *or* **'en·sign·cy** *n.*
en·si·lage ('ɛnsɪlɪdʒ) *n.* **1.** the process of ensiling green fodder. **2.** a less common name for **silage.**
en·sile (ɛn'saɪl, 'ɛnsaɪl) *vb. (tr.)* **1.** to store and preserve (green fodder) in an enclosed pit or silo. **2.** to turn (green fodder) into silage by causing it to ferment in a closed pit or silo. [C19: from French *ensiler,* from Spanish *ensilar,* from EN-[1] + *silo* SILO] —**en·ˌsi·la·'bil·i·ty** *n.*
en·slave (ɪn'sleɪv) *vb. (tr.)* to make a slave of; reduce to slavery; subjugate. —**en·'slave·ment** *n.* —**en·'slav·er** *n.*
en·snare *or* **in·snare** (ɪn'snɛə) *vb. (tr.)* to catch or trap in or as if in a snare. —**en·'snare·ment** *n.* —**en·'snar·er** *n.*
En·sor ('ɛnsɔː) *n.* **James.** 1860–1949, Belgian expressionist painter, noted for his macabre subjects.
en·soul *or* **in·soul** (ɪn'səʊl) *vb. (tr.) Literary.* **1.** to endow with a soul. **2.** to cherish within the soul.
en·sphere *or* **in·sphere** (ɪn'sfɪə) *vb. (tr.)* **1.** to enclose in or as if in a sphere. **2.** to make spherical in form.
en·sta·tite ('ɛnstəˌtaɪt) *n.* a grey, green, yellow, or brown pyroxene mineral consisting of magnesium silicate in orthorhombic crystalline form. Formula: $Mg_2Si_2O_6$. [C19: from Greek *enstatēs* adversary (referring to its refractory quality) + -ITE[1]]
en·sue (ɪn'sjuː) *vb.* **·sues, ·su·ing, ·sued. 1.** (*intr.*) to follow subsequently or in order; come next or afterwards. **2.** (*intr.*) to follow or occur as a consequence; result. **3.** (*tr.*) *Obsolete.* to pursue. [C14: from Anglo-French *ensuer,* from Old French *ensuivre,* from EN-[1] + *suivre* to follow, from Latin *sequī*] —**en·'su·ing·ly** *adv.*
en suite *French.* (ã 'sɥit) *adv.* as part of a set; forming a unit: *a hotel room with bathroom en suite.* [literally: in sequence]
en·sure (ɛn'ʃʊə, -'ʃɔː) *or (esp. U.S.)* **in·sure** *vb. (tr.)* **1.** (*may take a clause as object*) to make certain or sure; guarantee: *this victory will ensure his happiness.* **2.** to make safe or secure; protect. —**en·'sur·er** *n.*
en·swathe (ɪn'sweɪð) *vb. (tr.)* to bind or wrap; swathe. —**en·'swathe·ment** *n.*
E.N.T. *Med. abbrev. for* ear, nose, and throat.
-ent *suffix forming adjectives and nouns.* causing or performing an action or existing in a certain condition; the agent that performs an action: *astringent; dependent.* [from Latin *-ent-, -ens,* present participial ending]
en·tab·la·ture (ɛn'tæblətʃə) *n. Architect.* **1.** the part of a classical temple above the columns, having an architrave, a frieze, and a cornice. **2.** any construction of similar form. [C17: from French, from Italian *intavolatura* something put on a table, hence, something laid flat, from *tavola* table, from Latin *tabula* TABLE]
en·ta·ble·ment (ɪn'teɪbᵊlmənt) *n.* the platform of a pedestal, above the dado, that supports a statue. [C17: from Old French]
en·tail (ɪn'teɪl) *vb. (tr.)* **1.** to bring about or impose by necessity; have as a necessary consequence: *this task entails careful thought.* **2.** *Property law.* to restrict (the descent of an estate) to a designated line of heirs. ~*n.* **3.** *Property law.* **a.** such a limitation. **b.** an estate that has been entailed. [C14 *entaillen,* from EN-[1] + *taille* limitation, TAIL[2]] —**en·'tail·er** *n.* —**en·'tail·ment** *n.*
en·ta·moe·ba (ˌɛntə'miːbə), **en·da·moe·ba** *or U.S.* **en·ta·me·ba, en·da·me·ba** *n., pl.* **·bae** (-biː) *or* **·bas.** any parasitic amoeba of the genus *Entamoeba* (or *Endamoeba*), esp. *E. histolytica,* which lives in the intestines of man and causes amoebic dysentery.
en·tan·gle (ɪn'tæŋgᵊl) *vb. (tr.)* **1.** to catch or involve in or as if in a tangle; ensnare or enmesh. **2.** to make tangled or twisted; snarl. **3.** to make complicated; confuse. **4.** to involve in difficulties; entrap. —**en·'tan·gler** *n.*
en·tan·gle·ment (ɪn'tæŋgᵊlmənt) *n.* **1.** something that entangles or is itself entangled. **2.** a sexual relationship regarded as unfortunate, damaging, or compromising.
en·ta·sis ('ɛntəsɪs) *n., pl.* **·ses** (-siːz). **1.** a slightly convex curve given to the shaft of a column, pier, or similar structure, to correct the illusion of concavity produced by a straight shaft. **2.** Also called: **en·ta·sia** (ɛn'teɪzɪə). *Physiol.* an involuntary or spasmodic muscular contraction. [C18: from Greek, from *enteinein* to stretch tight, from *teinein* to stretch]
En·teb·be (ɛn'tɛbɪ) *n.* a town in S Uganda, on Lake Victoria: British administrative centre of Uganda (1893–1958); international airport. Pop.: 21 096 (1969).
en·tel·e·chy (ɛn'tɛlɪkɪ) *n., pl.* **·chies.** *Metaphysics.* **1.** (in the philosophy of Aristotle) actuality as opposed to potentiality. **2.** (in the system of Leibnitz) the soul or principle of perfection of an object or person; a monad or basic constituent. **3.** something that contains or realizes a final cause, esp. the vital force thought to direct the life of an organism. [C17: from Late Latin *entelechia,* from Greek *entelekheia,* from EN-[2] + *telos* goal, completion + *ekhein* to have]
en·tel·lus (ɛn'tɛləs) *n.* an Old World monkey, *Presbytes entellus,* of S Asia. This langur is regarded as sacred in India. Also called: **hanuman.** [C19: New Latin, apparently from the name of the aged Sicilian character in Book V of Virgil's *Aeneid*]
en·tente (*French* ã'tãːt) *n.* **1.** short for **entente cordiale. 2.** the parties to an entente cordiale collectively.
en·tente cor·diale (*French* ã'tãt kɔr'djal) *n.* **1.** a friendly understanding between political powers: less formal than an

alliance. **2.** (*often caps.*) the understanding reached by France and Britain in April 1904, which settled outstanding colonial disputes. [C19: French: cordial understanding]

en·ter ('ɛntə) *vb.* **1.** to come or go into (a place, house, etc.). **2.** to penetrate or pierce. **3.** (*tr.*) to introduce or insert. **4.** to join (a party, organization, etc.). **5.** (when *intr.*, foll. by *into*) to become involved or take part (in): *to enter a game; to enter into an agreement.* **6.** (*tr.*) to record (an item such as a commercial transaction) in a journal, account, register, etc. **7.** (*tr.*) to record (a name, etc.) on a list. **8.** (*tr.*) to present or submit: *to enter a proposal.* **9.** (*intr.*) *Theatre.* to come on stage: used as a stage direction: *enter Juliet.* **10.** (when *intr.*, often foll. by *into, on,* or *upon*) to begin; start: *to enter upon a new career.* **11.** (*intr.;* often foll. by *upon*) to come into possession (of). **12.** (*tr.*) to place (evidence, a plea, etc.) before a court of law or upon the court records. **13.** (*tr.*) *Law.* **a.** to go onto and occupy (land). **b.** *Chiefly U.S.* to file a claim to (public lands). [C13: from Old French *entrer,* from Latin *intrāre* to go in, from *intrā* within] —**'en·ter·a·ble** *adj.* —**'en·ter·er** *n.*

en·ter·ic (ɛn'tɛrɪk) *or* **en·ter·al** ('ɛntərəl) *adj.* intestinal. [C19: from Greek *enterikos,* from *enteron* intestine] —**'en·ter·al·ly** *adv.*

en·ter·ic fe·ver *n.* another name for **typhoid fever.**

en·ter in·to *vb.* (*intr., prep.*) **1.** to be considered as a necessary part of (one's plans, calculations, etc.). **2.** to be in sympathy with: *he enters into his patient's problems.*

en·ter·i·tis (ˌɛntə'raɪtɪs) *n.* inflammation of the intestine.

en·ter·o- *or before a vowel* **en·ter-** *combining form.* indicating an intestine: *enterovirus; enteritis.* [from New Latin, from Greek *enteron* intestine]

en·ter·o·gas·trone (ˌɛntərəʊ'gæstrəʊn) *n.* a hormone liberated by the upper intestinal mucosa when stimulated by fat: reduces peristalsis and secretion in the stomach. [C20: from ENTERO- + GASTRO- + (HORM)ONE]

en·ter·o·ki·nase (ˌɛntərəʊ'kaɪneɪz) *n.* an enzyme in intestinal juice that converts trypsinogen to trypsin.

en·ter·on ('ɛntəˌrɒn) *n., pl.* **·ter·a** (-tərə). the alimentary canal, esp. of an embryo or a coelenterate. [C19: via New Latin from Greek: intestine; related to Latin *inter* between]

en·ter·os·to·my (ˌɛntə'rɒstəmɪ) *n., pl.* **·mies.** surgical formation of a permanent opening into the intestine through the abdominal wall, used as an artificial anus, for feeding, etc.

en·ter·ot·o·my (ˌɛntə'rɒtəmɪ) *n., pl.* **·mies.** surgical incision into the intestine.

en·ter·o·vi·rus (ˌɛntərəʊ'vaɪrəs) *n., pl.* **·vi·rus·es.** any of a group of viruses that occur in and cause diseases of the gastrointestinal tract.

en·ter·prise ('ɛntəˌpraɪz) *n.* **1.** a project or undertaking, esp. one that requires boldness or effort. **2.** participation in such projects. **3.** readiness to embark on new ventures; boldness and energy. **4.** a business unit; a company or firm. [C15: from Old French *entreprise* (n.), from *entreprendre* from *entre-* between (from Latin: INTER-) + *prendre* to take, from Latin *prehendere* to grasp] —**'en·ter·ˌpris·er** *n.*

en·ter·pris·ing ('ɛntəˌpraɪzɪŋ) *adj.* ready to embark on new ventures; full of boldness and initiative. —**'en·ter·ˌpris·ing·ly** *adv.*

en·ter·tain (ˌɛntə'teɪn) *vb.* **1.** to provide amusement for (a person or audience). **2.** to show hospitality to (guests). **3.** (*tr.*) to hold in the mind: *to entertain an idea.* [C15: from Old French *entretenir,* from *entre-* mutually + *tenir* to hold, from Latin *tenēre*]

en·ter·tain·er (ˌɛntə'teɪnə) *n.* **1.** a professional singer, comedian, or other performer who takes part in public entertainments. **2.** any person who entertains.

en·ter·tain·ing (ˌɛntə'teɪnɪŋ) *adj.* serving to entertain or give pleasure; diverting; amusing. —**ˌen·ter·'tain·ing·ly** *adv.*

en·ter·tain·ment (ˌɛntə'teɪnmənt) *n.* **1.** the act or art of entertaining or state of being entertained. **2.** an act, production, etc., that entertains; diversion; amusement.

en·thal·py ('ɛnθəlpɪ, ɛn'θæl-) *n.* a thermodynamic property of a system equal to the sum of its internal energy and the product of its pressure and volume. Symbol: *H* Also called: **heat content, total heat.** [C20: from Greek *enthalpein* to warm in, from EN-[2] + *thalpein* to warm]

en·thet·ic (ɛn'θɛtɪk) *adj.* (esp. of infectious diseases) introduced into the body from without. [C19: from Greek *enthetikos,* from *entithenai* to put in]

en·thral *or U.S.* **en·thrall** (ɪn'θrɔːl) *vb.* **·thrals** *or U.S.* **·thralls, ·thral·ling, ·thralled.** (*tr.*) **1.** to hold spellbound; enchant; captivate. **2.** *Obsolete.* to hold as thrall; enslave. —**en·'thral·ler** *n.* —**en·'thral·ling·ly** *adv.* —**en·'thral·ment** *or U.S.* **en·'thrall·ment** *n.*

en·throne (ɛn'θrəʊn) *vb.* (*tr.*) **1.** to place on a throne. **2.** to honour or exalt. **3.** to assign authority to. —**en·'throne·ment** *n.*

en·thuse (ɪn'θjuːz) *vb.* to feel or show or cause to feel or show enthusiasm.

en·thu·si·asm (ɪn'θjuːzɪˌæzəm) *n.* **1.** ardent and lively interest or eagerness. **2.** an object of keen interest; passion. **3.** *Archaic.* extravagant or unbalanced religious fervour. [C17: from Late Latin *enthūsiasmus,* from Greek *enthousiasmos,* from *enthousiazein* to be possessed by a god, from *entheos* inspired, from EN-[2] + *theos* god]

en·thu·si·ast (ɪn'θjuːzɪˌæst) *n.* **1.** a person filled with or motivated by enthusiasm; fanatic. **2.** *Archaic.* a religious visionary, esp. one whose zeal for religion is extravagant or unbalanced. —**en·ˌthu·si·'as·tic** *adj.* —**en·ˌthu·si·'as·ti·cal·ly** *adv.*

en·thy·meme ('ɛnθɪˌmiːm) *n. Logic.* an incomplete syllogism, in which one or more premisses are unexpressed as their truth is considered to be self-evident. [C16: via Latin from Greek *enthumēma,* from *enthumeisthai* to infer (literally: to have in the mind), from EN-[2] + *thumos* mind] —**ˌen·thy·me·'mat·ic** *or* **ˌen·thy·me·'mat·i·cal** *adj.*

en·tice (ɪn'taɪs) *vb.* (*tr.*) to attract or draw towards oneself by exciting hope or desire; tempt; allure. [C13: from Old French *enticier,* from Vulgar Latin *intitiāre* (unattested) to incite, from Latin *titiō* firebrand] —**en·'tice·ment** *n.* —**en·'tic·er** *n.* —**en·'tic·ing·ly** *adv.* —**en·'tic·ing·ness** *n.*

en·tire (ɪn'taɪə) *adj.* **1.** (*prenominal*) whole; complete: *the entire project is going well.* **2.** (*prenominal*) without reservation or exception; total: *you have my entire support.* **3.** not broken or damaged; intact. **4.** consisting of a single piece or section; undivided; continuous. **5.** (of leaves, petals, etc.) having a smooth margin not broken up into teeth or lobes. **6.** not castrated: *an entire horse.* **7.** *Obsolete.* of one substance or kind; unmixed; pure. ~*n.* **8.** a less common word for **entirety. 9.** an uncastrated horse. **10.** *Philately.* **a.** a complete item consisting of an envelope, postcard, or wrapper with stamps affixed. **b. on entire.** (of a stamp) placed on an envelope, postcard, etc., and bearing postal directions. [C14: from Old French *entier,* from Latin *integer* whole, from IN-[1] + *tangere* to touch] —**en·'tire·ness** *n.*

en·tire·ly (ɪn'taɪəlɪ) *adv.* **1.** without reservation or exception; wholly; completely. **2.** solely or exclusively; only.

en·tire·ty (ɪn'taɪərɪtɪ) *n., pl.* **·ties. 1.** the state of being entire or whole; completeness. **2.** a thing, sum, amount, etc., that is entire; whole; total.

en·ti·tle (ɪn'taɪtᵊl) *vb.* (*tr.*) **1.** to give (a person) the right to do or have something; qualify; allow. **2.** to give a name or title to. **3.** to confer a title of rank or honour upon. [C14: from Old French *entituler,* from Late Latin *intitulāre,* from Latin *titulus* TITLE] —**en·'ti·tle·ment** *n.*

en·ti·ty ('ɛntɪtɪ) *n., pl.* **·ties. 1.** something having real or distinct existence; a thing, esp. when considered as independent of other things. **2.** existence or being. **3.** the essence or real nature. [C16: from Medieval Latin *entitās,* from *ēns* being; see ENS] —**en·ti·ta·tive** ('ɛntɪtətɪv) *adj.*

en·to- *combining form.* inside; within: *entoderm.* [New Latin, from Greek *entos* within]

en·to·blast ('ɛntəʊˌblæst) *n.* **1.** *Embryol.* a less common name for **endoderm. 2.** a less common name for **hypoblast.** —**en·to·blas·tic** (ˌɛntəʊ'blæstɪk) *adj.*

en·to·derm ('ɛntəʊˌdɜːm) *n. Embryol.* another name for **endoderm.** —**ˌen·to·'der·mal** *or* **ˌen·to·'der·mic** *adj.*

en·toil (ɪn'tɔɪl) *vb.* (*tr.*) an archaic word for **ensnare.** —**en·'toil·ment** *n.*

en·tomb (ɪn'tuːm) *vb.* (*tr.*) **1.** to place in or as if in a tomb; bury; inter. **2.** to serve as a tomb for. —**en·'tomb·ment** *n.*

en·tom·ic (ɛn'tɒmɪk) *adj.* denoting or relating to insects. [C19: from Greek *entomon* (see ENTOMO-) + -IC]

en·to·mo- *combining form.* indicating an insect: *entomology.* [from Greek *entomon* insect (literally: creature cut into sections), from *en-* in + *-tomon,* from *temnein* to cut]

entomol. *or* **entom.** *abbrev. for* entomology.

en·to·mo·lo·gize *or* **en·to·mo·lo·gise** (ˌɛntə'mɒləˌdʒaɪz) *vb.* (*intr.*) to collect or study insects.

en·to·mol·o·gy (ˌɛntə'mɒlədʒɪ) *n.* the branch of science concerned with the study of insects. —**en·to·mo·log·i·cal** (ˌɛntəmə'lɒdʒɪkᵊl) *or* **ˌen·to·mo·'log·ic** *adj.* —**ˌen·to·mo·'log·i·cal·ly** *adv.* —**ˌen·to·'mol·o·gist** *n.*

en·to·moph·a·gous (ˌɛntə'mɒfəgəs) *adj.* feeding mainly on insects; insectivorous.

en·to·moph·i·lous (ˌɛntə'mɒfɪləs) *adj.* (of flowering plants such as orchids) pollinated by insects. Compare **anemophilous.** —**ˌen·to·'moph·i·ly** *n.*

en·to·mo·stra·can (ˌɛntə'mɒstrəkən) *n.* **1.** any small crustacean of the group (formerly subclass) *Entomostraca,* including the branchiopods, ostracods, and copepods. ~*adj.* **2.** of, relating to, or belonging to the *Entomostraca.* [C19: from New Latin ENTOMO- + Greek *ostrakon* shell; see OSTRACIZE] —**ˌen·to·'mos·tra·cous** *adj.*

en·to·phyte ('ɛntəʊˌfaɪt) *n. Botany.* a variant spelling of **endophyte.** —**en·to·phyt·ic** (ˌɛntəʊ'fɪtɪk) *adj.*

en·top·ic (ɛn'tɒpɪk) *adj. Anatomy.* situated in its normal place or position. See also **ectopia.** [from Greek *entopos* in a place, from *topos* place]

en·tou·rage (ɒntʊ'rɑːʒ; *French* ɑ̃tu'raːʒ) *n.* **1.** a group of attendants or retainers, esp. such as surround an important person; retinue. **2.** surroundings or environment. [C19: from French, from *entourer* to surround, from *entour* around, from *tour* circuit; see TOUR, TURN]

en·to·zo·ic (ˌɛntəʊ'zəʊɪk) *adj.* **1.** of or relating to an entozoon. **2.** living inside an animal: *entozoic fungi.*

en·to·zo·on (ˌɛntəʊ'zəʊɒn) *or* **en·to·zo·an** *n., pl.* **·zo·a** (-'zəʊə). any animal, such as a tapeworm, that lives within another animal, usually as a parasite.

en·tr'acte (ɒn'trækt; *French* ɑ̃'trakt) *n.* **1.** an interval between two acts of a play or opera. **2.** (esp. formerly) an entertainment during an interval, such as dancing between acts of an opera. [C19: French, literally: between-act]

en·trails ('ɛntreɪlz) *pl. n.* **1.** the internal organs of a person or animal; intestines; guts. **2.** the innermost parts of anything. [C13: from Old French *entrailles,* from Medieval Latin *intrālia,* changed from Latin *interānea* intestines, ultimately from *inter* between]

en+train[1] (ɪnˈtreɪn) *vb.* to board or put aboard a train. —**en+ˈtrain+ment** *n.*

en+train[2] (ɪnˈtreɪn) *vb.* (*tr.*) (of a liquid or gas) to carry along (drops of liquid, bubbles, etc.), as in certain distillations.

en+tram+mel (ɪnˈtræməl) *vb.* **+mels, +mel+ling, +melled.** (*tr.*) to hamper or obstruct by entangling.

en+trance[1] (ˈɛntrəns) *n.* **1.** the act or an instance of entering; entry. **2.** a place for entering, such as a door or gate. **3. a.** the power, liberty, or right of entering; admission. **b.** (*as modifier*): *an entrance fee.* **4.** the coming of an actor or other performer onto a stage. [C16: from French, from *entrer* to ENTER]

en+trance[2] (ɪnˈtrɑːns) *vb.* (*tr.*) **1.** to fill with wonder and delight; enchant. **2.** to put into a trance; hypnotize. —**en+ˈtrance+ment** *n.* —**en+ˈtranc+ing+ly** *adv.*

en+trant (ˈɛntrənt) *n.* **1.** a person who enters. **2.** a new member of a group, society, or association. **3.** a person who enters a competition or contest; competitor. [C17: from French, literally: entering, from *entrer* to ENTER]

en+trap (ɪnˈtræp) *vb.* **+traps, +trap+ping, +trapped.** (*tr.*) **1.** to catch or snare in or as if in a trap. **2.** to lure or trick into danger, difficulty, or embarrassment. —**en+ˈtrap+ment** *n.*

en+treat *or* **in+treat** (ɪnˈtriːt) *vb.* **1.** to ask (a person) earnestly; beg or plead with; implore. **2.** to make an earnest request or petition for (something). **3.** an archaic word for **treat** (sense 4). [C15: from Old French *entraiter*, from EN-[1] + *traiter* to TREAT] —**en+ˈtreat+ing+ly** *or* **in+ˈtreat+ing+ly** *adv.* —**en+ˈtreat+ment** *or* **in+ˈtreat+ment** *n.*

en+treat·y (ɪnˈtriːtɪ) *n., pl.* **+treat·ies.** an earnest request or petition; supplication; plea.

en+tre+chat (*French* ãtrəˈʃa) *n.* a leap in ballet during which the dancer repeatedly crosses his feet or beats them together. [C18: from French, from earlier *entrechase*, changed by folk etymology from Italian (*capriola*) *intrecciata*, literally: entwined (caper), from *intrecciare* to interlace, from IN-[2] + *treccia* TRESS]

en+tre+côte (*French* ãtrəˈkoːt) *n.* a beefsteak cut from between the ribs. [French *entrecôte*, from *entre-* INTER- + *côte* rib, from Latin *costa*]

En·tre-Deux-Mers (*French* ãtrə døˈmɛːr) *n.* any wine produced in the area of the Gironde between the rivers Dordogne and Garonne in S France.

en+trée (ˈɒntreɪ) *n.* **1.** a dish served before a main course. **2.** *Chiefly U.S.* the main course of a meal. **3.** the power or right of entry. [C18: from French, from *entrer* to ENTER; in cookery, so called because formerly the course was served after an intermediate course called the *relevé* (remove)]

en+tre+mets (*French* ãtrəˈmɛ) *n., pl.* **+mets** (*French* -ˈmɛ). **1.** a dessert. **2.** a light dish, formerly served at formal dinners between the main course and the dessert. [C18: from French, from Old French *entremes*, from *entre-* between, INTER- + *mes* dish, MESS]

en+trench *or* **in+trench** (ɪnˈtrɛntʃ) *vb.* **1.** (*tr.*) to construct (a defensive position) by digging trenches around it. **2.** (*tr.*) to fix or establish firmly, esp. so as to prevent removal or change. **3.** (*intr.*; foll. by *on* or *upon*) to trespass or encroach; infringe. —**en+ˈtrench+er** *or* **in+ˈtrench+er** *n.*

en+trench+ment *or* **in+trench+ment** (ɪnˈtrɛntʃmənt) *n.* **1.** the act of entrenching or state of being entrenched. **2.** a position protected by trenches. **3.** one of a series of deep trenches constructed as a shelter from gunfire.

en+tre nous (*French* ãtrə ˈnu) *adv.* between ourselves; in confidence.

en+tre+pôt (*French* ãtrəˈpo) *n.* **1.** a warehouse for commercial goods. **2. a.** a trading centre or port at a geographically convenient location, at which goods are imported and re-exported without incurring liability for duty. **b.** (*as modifier*): *the entrepôt trade.* [C18: French, from *entreposer* to put in, from *entre-* between, INTER- + *poser* to place (see POSE); formed on the model of DEPOT]

en+tre+pre+neur (ˌɒntrəprəˈnɜː; *French* ãtrəprəˈnœːr) *n.* **1.** the owner or manager of a business enterprise who, by risk and initiative, attempts to make profits. **2.** a middleman or commercial intermediary. [C19: from French, from *entreprendre* to undertake; see ENTERPRISE] —**ˌen+tre+pre+ˈneur+i·al** *adj.* —**ˌen+tre+pre+ˈneur+ship** *n.*

en+tre+sol (ˌɒntrəˈsɒl; *French* ãtrəˈsɔl) *n.* another name for **mezzanine.** [C18: from French, literally: between floors, from *entre-* INTER- + *sol* floor, ground, from Latin *solum*]

en+tro+py (ˈɛntrəpɪ) *n., pl.* **+pies. 1.** a thermodynamic quantity that changes in a reversible process by an amount equal to the heat absorbed or emitted divided by the thermodynamic temperature. It is measured in joules per kelvin. Symbol: S See also **law of thermodynamics** (sense 1). **2.** a statistical measure of the disorder of a closed system expressed by $S = k\log P + c$ where P is the probability that a particular state of the system exists, k is the Boltzmann constant, and c is another constant. **3.** lack of pattern or organization; disorder. **4.** a measure of the efficiency of a system, such as a code or language, in transmitting information. [C19: from EN-[2] + -TROPE]

en+trust *or* **in+trust** (ɪnˈtrʌst) *vb.* (*tr.*) **1.** (usually foll. by *with*) to invest or charge (with a duty, responsibility, etc.). **2.** (often foll. by *to*) to put into the care or protection of someone. —**en+ˈtrust+ment** *or* **in+ˈtrust+ment** *n.*

en+try (ˈɛntrɪ) *n., pl.* **+tries. 1.** the act or an instance of entering; entrance. **2.** a point or place for entering, such as a door, gate, etc. **3. a.** the right or liberty of entering; admission; access. **b.** (*as modifier*): *an entry permit.* **4.** the act of recording an item, such as a commercial transaction, in a journal, account, register, etc. **5.** an item recorded, as in a diary, dictionary, or account. **6. a.** a person, horse, car, etc., entering a competition or contest; competitor. **b.** (*as modifier*): *an entry fee.* **7.** the competitors entering a contest considered collectively: *a good entry this year for the speed trials.* **8.** the action of an actor in going on stage or his manner of doing this. **9.** *Criminal law.* the act of unlawfully going onto the premises of another with the intention of committing a crime. **10.** *Property law.* the act of going upon another person's land with the intention of asserting the right to possession. **11.** any point in a piece of music, esp. a fugue, at which a performer commences or resumes playing or singing. **12.** *Cards.* a card with which a player or hand can win a trick and so gain the lead. **13.** *Northern Brit. dialect.* a passage between the backs of two rows of terraced houses. [C13: from Old French *entree*, past participle of *entrer* to ENTER]

en+twine *or* **in+twine** (ɪnˈtwaɪn) *vb.* (of two or more things) to twine together or (of one or more things) to twine around (something else). —**en+ˈtwine+ment** *or* **in+ˈtwine+ment** *n.*

e·nu+cle·ate *vb.* (ɪˈnjuːklɪˌeɪt). (*tr.*) **1.** *Biology.* to remove the nucleus from (a cell). **2.** *Surgery.* to remove (a tumour or other structure) from its capsule without rupturing it. **3.** *Archaic.* to explain or disclose. ~*adj.* (ɪˈnjuːklɪɪt, -ˌeɪt). **4.** (of cells) deprived of their nuclei. [C16: from Latin *ēnūcleāre* to remove the kernel, from *nūcleus* kernel] —**e·ˌnu+cle·ˈa+tion** *n.* —**e·ˈnu+cle·ˌa+tor** *n.*

E·nu+gu (ɛˈnuːguː) *n.* a city in S Nigeria, capital of Anambra state: capital of the former Eastern region and of the breakaway state of Biafra during the Civil War (1967–70): coal-mining. Pop.: 187 000 (1975 est.).

e·nu+mer+ate (ɪˈnjuːməˌreɪt) *vb.* (*tr.*) **1.** to mention separately or in order; name one by one; list. **2.** to determine the number of; count. [C17: from Latin *ēnumerāre*, from *numerāre* to count, reckon; see NUMBER] —**e·ˈnu+mer+a·ble** *adj.* —**e·ˌnu+mer·ˈa+tion** *n.* —**e·ˈnu+mer·a+tive** *adj.*

e·nu+mer·a·tor (ɪˈnjuːməˌreɪtə) *n.* **1.** a person or thing that enumerates. **2.** *Canadian.* a person who compiles the voting list for an area. **3.** *Brit.* a person who issues and retrieves forms during a census of population.

e·nun+ci+a·ble (ɪˈnʌnsɪəbᵊl) *adj.* capable of being enunciated. —**e·ˌnun+ci+a·ˈbil+i·ty** *n.*

e·nun+ci+ate (ɪˈnʌnsɪˌeɪt) *vb.* **1.** to articulate or pronounce (words), esp. clearly and distinctly. **2.** (*tr.*) to state precisely or formally. [C17: from Latin *ēnuntiāre* to declare, from *nuntiāre* to announce, from *nuntius* messenger] —**e·ˌnun+ci·ˈa+tion** *n.* —**e·ˈnun+ci·a+tive** *or* **e·ˈnun+ci·a·to·ry** *adj.* —**e·ˈnun+ci·a+tive+ly** *adv.* —**e·ˈnun+ci·ˌa+tor** *n.*

en+ure (ɪˈnjʊə) *vb.* a variant spelling of **inure.** —**en+ˈure+ment** *n.*

en·u+re·sis (ˌɛnjʊˈriːsɪs) *n.* involuntary discharge of urine, esp. during sleep. [C19: from New Latin, from Greek EN-[2] + *ourein* to urinate, from *ouron* urine] —**en·u+ret+ic** (ˌɛnjʊˈrɛtɪk) *adj.*

en+vel+op (ɪnˈvɛləp) *vb.* (*tr.*) **1.** to wrap or enclose in or as if in a covering. **2.** to conceal or obscure, as from sight or understanding: *a plan enveloped in mystery.* **3.** to surround or partially surround (an enemy force). [C14: from Old French *envoluper*, from EN-[1] + *voluper*, *voloper*, of obscure origin] —**en+ˈvel+op+ment** *n.*

en+ve·lope (ˈɛnvəˌləʊp, ˈɒn-) *n.* **1.** a flat covering of paper, usually rectangular in shape and with a flap that can be folded over and sealed, used to enclose a letter, etc. **2.** any covering or wrapper. **3.** *Biology.* any enclosing structure, such as a membrane, shell, or skin. **4.** the bag enclosing the gas in a balloon. **5.** *Maths.* a curve or surface that is tangential to each one of a group of curves or surfaces. **6.** *Electronics.* the sealed glass or metal housing of a valve, electric light, etc. [C18: from French *enveloppe*, from *envelopper* to wrap around; see ENVELOP]

en+ven+om (ɪnˈvɛnəm) *vb.* (*tr.*) **1.** to fill or impregnate with venom; make poisonous. **2.** to fill with bitterness or malice.

En·ver Pa·sha (ˈɛnvə ˈpɑːʃə) *n.* 1881–1922, Turkish soldier and leader of the Young Turks.

en+vi+a·ble (ˈɛnvɪəbᵊl) *adj.* exciting envy; fortunate or privileged. —**ˈen+vi+a·ble+ness** *n.* —**ˈen+vi+a·bly** *adv.*

en+vi·ous (ˈɛnvɪəs) *adj.* feeling, showing, or resulting from envy. [C13: from Anglo-Norman, ultimately from Latin *invidiōsus* full of envy, INVIDIOUS; see ENVY] —**ˈen+vi+ous+ly** *adv.* —**ˈen+vi+ous+ness** *n.*

en+vi+ron (ɪnˈvaɪrən) *vb.* (*tr.*) to encircle or surround. [C14: from Old French *environner* to surround, from *environ* around, from EN-[1] + *viron* a circle, from *virer* to turn, VEER]

en+vi+ron+ment (ɪnˈvaɪrənmənt) *n.* **1.** external conditions or surroundings, esp. those in which people live or work. **2.** *Ecology.* the external surroundings in which a plant or animal lives, which tend to influence its development and behaviour. **3.** the state of being environed; encirclement. —**en+ˌvi+ron+ˈmen+tal** *adj.* —**en+ˌvi+ron+ˈmen+tal+ly** *adv.*

en+vi+ron+men+tal+ism (ɪnˌvaɪrənˈmɛntəˌlɪzəm) *n.* *Psychol.* the belief that a person's behaviour is affected chiefly by his environment. Compare **hereditarianism.**

en+vi+ron+men+tal+ist (ɪnˌvaɪrənˈmɛntəˌlɪst) *n.* **1.** an adherent of environmentalism. **2.** a specialist in the maintenance of ecological balance and the conservation of the environment.

en+vi+rons (ɪnˈvaɪrənz) *pl. n.* a surrounding area or region, esp. the suburbs or outskirts of a town or city; vicinity.

en+vis+age (ɪnˈvɪzɪdʒ) *vb.* (*tr.*) **1.** to form a mental image of; visualize; contemplate. **2.** to conceive of as a possibility in the future; foresee. **3.** *Archaic.* to look in the face of; confront. [C19: from French *envisager*, from EN-[1] + *visage* face, VISAGE] —**en+ˈvis+age+ment** *n.*

Usage. *Envisage*, followed by *that* and a clause, has come to be used in place of such verbs as *expect* and *think: the board envisages that there will be a high profit.* American writers in particular tend to prefer *envision* for this usage. In careful English, *envisage* is usually used with a direct object rather than a clause to refer to conceptions of future possibilities: *he envisaged great success for his project.*

en+vi+sion (ɪn'vɪʒən) *vb.* (*tr.*) to conceive of as a possibility, esp. in the future; foresee.

en+voy[1] ('ɛnvɔɪ) *n.* **1.** Formal name: **envoy extraordinary and minister plenipotentiary.** a diplomat of the second class, ranking between an ambassador and a minister resident. **2.** an accredited messenger, agent, or representative. [C17: from French *envoyé*, literally: sent, from *envoyer* to send, from Vulgar Latin *inviāre* (unattested) to send on a journey, from IN-[2] + *via* road] —**'en+voy+ship** *n.*

en+voy[2] *or* **en+voi** ('ɛnvɔɪ) *n.* **1.** a brief dedicatory or explanatory stanza concluding certain forms of poetry, notably ballades. **2.** a postscript in other forms of verse or prose. [C14: from Old French *envoye*, from *envoyer* to send; see ENVOY[1]]

en·vy ('ɛnvɪ) *n., pl.* **·vies. 1.** a feeling of grudging or somewhat admiring discontent aroused by the possessions, achievements, or qualities of another. **2.** the desire to have for oneself something possessed by another; covetousness. **3.** an object of envy. ~*vb.* **·vies, ·vy+ing, ·vied. 4.** to be envious of (a person or thing). [C13: via Old French from Latin *invidia*, from *invidēre* to eye maliciously, from IN-[2] + *vidēre* to see] —**'en+vi+er** *n.* —**'en+vy+ing+ly** *adv.*

en+wind (ɪn'waɪnd) *vb.* **+winds, +wind+ing, +wound.** (*tr.*) to wind or coil around; encircle.

en+womb (ɪn'wu:m) *vb.* (*tr.; often passive*) to enclose in or as if in a womb.

en+wrap *or* **in+wrap** (ɪn'ræp) *vb.* **+wraps, +wrap+ping, +wrapped.** (*tr.*) **1.** to wrap or cover up; envelop. **2.** (*usually passive*) to engross or absorb: *enwrapped in thought.*

en+wreath (ɪn'ri:ð) *vb.* (*tr.*) to surround or encircle with or as with a wreath or wreaths.

En+zed (ɛn'zɛd) *n. Austral., N.Z. informal.* **1.** New Zealand. **2.** Also called: **En+zed+der.** a New Zealander.

en+zo+ot+ic (ˌɛnzəʊ'ɒtɪk) *adj.* **1.** (of diseases) affecting animals within a limited region. ~*n.* **2.** an enzootic disease. ~Compare **epizootic.** [C19: from EN-[2] + Greek *zōion* animal + -OTIC] —ˌ**en·zo+'ot+i+cal+ly** *adv.*

en+zyme ('ɛnzaɪm) *n.* any of a group of complex proteins or conjugated proteins that are produced by living cells and act as catalysts in specific biochemical reactions. [C19: from Medieval Greek *enzumos* leavened, from Greek EN-[2] + *zumē* leaven] —**en+zy+mat+ic** (ˌɛnzaɪ'mætɪk, -zɪ-) *or* **en+zy+mic** (ɛn-'zaɪmɪk, -'zɪm-) *adj.*

en+zy+mol+o+gy (ˌɛnzaɪ'mɒlədʒɪ) *n.* the branch of science concerned with the study of enzymes. —**en+zy+mo+log+i+cal** (ˌɛnzaɪmə'lɒdʒɪkəl) *adj.* —ˌ**en+zy+'mol+o+gist** *n.*

en+zy+mol+y+sis (ˌɛnzaɪ'mɒlɪsɪs) *or* **en+zy+mo+sis** (ˌɛnzaɪ-'məʊsɪs) *n.* a biochemical decomposition, such as a fermentation, that is catalysed by an enzyme. —**en+zy+mo+lyt+ic** (ˌɛnzaɪmə'lɪtɪk) *adj.*

e.o. *abbrev. for* ex officio.

e·o- *combining form.* early or primeval: *Eocene; eohippus.* [from Greek, from *ēos* dawn]

e·o·bi+ont (ˌi:əʊ'baɪənt) *n.* a hypothetical chemical precursor of a living cell.

E·o·cene ('i:əʊˌsi:n) *adj.* **1.** of, denoting, or formed in the second epoch of the Tertiary period, which lasted for 20 000 000 years, during which hooved mammals appeared. ~*n.* **2. the Eocene.** the Eocene epoch or rock series. [C19: from EO- + -CENE]

E·o·gene ('i:əʊˌdʒi:n) *adj., n.* another word for **Palaeogene.**

e·o·hip+pus (ˌi:əʊ'hɪpəs) *n., pl.* **+pus·es.** the earliest horse: an extinct Eocene dog-sized animal of the genus *Hyracotherium*, with four-toed forelegs, three-toed hindlegs, and teeth specialized for browsing. [C19: New Latin, from EO- + Greek *hippos* horse]

E·o·li·an (i:'əʊlɪən) *adj., n.* a variant spelling of **Aeolian.**

E·ol+ic (i:'ɒlɪk, ɪ'əʊlɪk) *adj., n.* a variant spelling of **Aeolic.**

e·ol·i+pile (i:'ɒlɪˌpaɪl) *n.* a variant spelling of **aeolipile.**

e·o·lith ('i:əʊlɪθ) *n.* a stone, usually crudely broken, used as a primitive tool in Eolithic times.

E·o·lith+ic (ˌi:əʊ'lɪθɪk) *adj.* denoting, relating to, or characteristic of the early part of the Stone Age, characterized by the use of crude stone tools.

e.o.m. *Commerce. abbrev. for* end of the month.

e·on ('i:ən, 'i:ɒn) *n.* the usual U.S. spelling of **aeon.**

e·o·ni·an (i:'əʊnɪən) *adj.* the usual U.S. spelling of **aeonian.**

e·o·nism ('i:əˌnɪzəm) *n. Psychiatry.* the adoption of female dress and behaviour by a male. See also **transvestite.** [C19: named after Charles *Eon* de Beaumont (died 1810), French transvestite]

E·os ('i:ɒs) *n. Greek myth.* the winged goddess of the dawn, the daughter of Hyperion. Roman counterpart: **Aurora.**

e·o·sin ('i:əʊsɪn) *or* **e·o·sine** ('i:əʊsɪn, -ˌsi:n) *n.* **1.** Also called: **bromeosin.** a red crystalline water-insoluble derivative of fluorescein. Its soluble salts are used as dyes. Formula: $C_{20}H_8Br_4O_5$. **2.** any of several similar dyes. [C19: from Greek *ēos* dawn + -IN; referring to the colour it gives to silk] —ˌ**e·o·'sin+ic** *adj.* —**'e·o·sin-ˌlike** *adj.*

e·o·sin·o+phil (ˌi:əʊ'sɪnəfɪl) *or* **e·o·sin·o·phile** (ˌi:əʊ'sɪnəˌfaɪl) *n.* a leucocyte with a bilobed nucleus and coarse granular cytoplasm that stains readily with acidic dyes such as eosin. —ˌ**e·o·ˌsin·o·'phil+ic** *or* **e·o·si+noph·i·lous** (ˌi:əʊsɪ'nɒfɪləs) *adj.*

-e·ous *suffix of adjectives.* relating to or having the nature of: *gaseous.* Compare **-ious.** [from Latin *-eus*]

E·o·zo+ic (ˌi:əʊ'zəʊɪk) *adj.* of or formed in the part of the Precambrian era during which life first appeared.

EP *n.* **1.** Also called: **maxisingle.** an extended-play gramophone record: usually 7 inches (18 cm) in diameter with a longer recording on it than a single, designed to be played at 45 or 33 1/3 revolutions per minute. ~*adj.* **2.** denoting such a record.

Ep. *abbrev. for* Epistle.

e.p. *Chess. abbrev. for* en passant.

ep- *prefix.* variant of **epi-** before a vowel: *epexegesis.*

EPA *abbrev. for* education priority area.

e·pact ('i:pækt) *n.* **1.** the difference in time, about 11 days, between the solar year and the lunar year. **2.** the number of days between the beginning of the calendar year and the new moon immediately preceding this. **3.** the difference in time between the calendar month and the synodic month. [C16: via Late Latin from Greek *epaktē*, from *epagein* to bring in, intercalate, from *agein* to lead]

E·pam·i·non·das (ɛˌpæmɪ'nɒndæs) *n.* ?418–362 B.C., Greek Theban statesman and general: defeated the Spartans at Leuctra (371) and Mantinea (362) and restored power in Greece to Thebes.

ep+arch ('ɛpɑ:k) *n.* **1.** a bishop or metropolitan in charge of an eparchy (sense 1). **2.** a government official in charge of an eparchy (senses 2 or 3). [C17: from Greek *eparkhos*, from *epi-* over, on + -ARCH]

ep+ar+chy ('ɛpɑ:kɪ) *or* **ep+ar+chate** ('ɛpɑ:kɪt) *n., pl.* **+chies** *or* **+chates. 1.** a diocese of the Eastern Christian Church. **2.** (in ancient Greece) a province. **3.** (in modern Greece) a subdivision of a province. —**ep+'ar+chi·al** *adj.*

é·pa+tant *French.* (epa'tã) *adj.* startling or shocking, esp. through being unconventional.

ep+au·let *or* **ep+au+lette** ('ɛpəˌlɛt, -lɪt) *n.* a piece of ornamental material on the shoulder of a garment, esp. a military uniform. [C18: from French *épaulette*, from *épaule* shoulder, from Latin *spatula* shoulder blade; see SPATULA]

é·pée ('ɛpeɪ; *French* e'pe) *n.* a sword similar to the foil but with a larger guard and a heavier blade of triangular cross section. [French: sword, from Latin *spatha*, from Greek *spathē* blade; see SPADE[1]]

é·pée+ist ('ɛpeɪɪst) *n. Fencing.* one who uses or specializes in using an épée.

ep+ei+rog+e·ny, ep·i+rog+e·ny (ˌɛpaɪ'rɒdʒɪnɪ), *or* **e·pei+ro+gen+e·sis** (ɪˌpaɪrəʊ'dʒɛnɪsɪs) *n.* the formation and submergence of continents by broad relatively slow displacements of the earth's crust. [C19: from Greek *ēpeiros* continent + -GENY] —**e·pei+ric** (ɪ'paɪrɪk), **e·pei+ro+gen+ic** (ɪˌpaɪrəʊ-'dʒɛnɪk), *or* **e·pei+ro+ge+net+ic** (ɪˌpaɪrəʊdʒɪ'nɛtɪk) *adj.*

ep+en+ceph·a·lon (ˌɛpɛn'sɛfəˌlɒn) *n., pl.* **+la** (-lə). *Anatomy.* **1.** the cerebellum and pons Varolii. **2.** the part of the embryonic brain that develops into this; metencephalon. [C19: New Latin; see EPI-, ENCEPHALON] —ˌ**ep+en+ce·phal+ic** (ˌɛpɛnsɪ'fælɪk) *adj.*

e·pen+the·sis (ɛ'pɛnθɪsɪs) *n., pl.* **·ses** (-ˌsi:z). the insertion of a vowel or consonant into a word to make its pronunciation easier. [C17: via Late Latin from Greek, from *epentithenai* to insert, from EPI- + EN-[2] + *tithenai* to place] —**ep+en+thet+ic** (ˌɛpɛn'θɛtɪk) *adj.*

e·pergne (ɪ'pɜ:n) *n.* an ornamental centrepiece for a table: a stand with holders for sweetmeats, fruit, flowers, etc. [C18: probably from French *épargne* a saving, from *épargner* to economize, of Germanic origin; compare SPARE]

ep+ex+e·ge·sis (ɛˌpɛksɪ'dʒi:sɪs) *n., pl.* **·ses** (-ˌsi:z). *Rhetoric.* **1.** the addition of a phrase, clause, or sentence to a text to provide further explanation. **2.** the phrase, clause, or sentence added for this purpose. [C17: from Greek; see EPI-, EXEGESIS] —**ep+ex+e·get+ic** (ɛˌpɛksɪ'dʒɛtɪk) *or* **ep+ˌex+e·'get·i·cal** *adj.* —**ep+ˌex+e·'get·i·cal+ly** *adv.*

Eph. *or* **Ephes.** *Bible. abbrev. for* Ephesians.

eph- *prefix.* variant of **epi-** before an aspirate: *ephedra; ephedrine.*

e·phah *or* **e·pha** ('i:fə) *n.* a Hebrew unit of dry measure equal to approximately one bushel or about 33 litres. [C16: from Hebrew *'ephāh*, of Egyptian origin]

e·phebe (ɪ'fi:b, 'ɛfi:b) *n.* (in ancient Greece) a youth about to enter full citizenship, esp. one undergoing military training. [C19: from Latin *ephēbus*, from Greek *ephēbos*, from *hēbē* young manhood] —**e·'phe+bic** *adj.*

e·phed+ra (ɪ'fɛdrə) *n.* any gymnosperm shrub of the genus *Ephedra*, of warm regions of America and Eurasia: the source of ephedrine: family *Ephedraceae*, order *Gnetales.* [C18: New Latin, from Latin, from Greek *ephedros* a sitting upon, from EPI- + *hedra* seat]

e·phed+rine *or* **e·phed+rin** (ɪ'fɛdrɪn, 'ɛfɪˌdri:n, -drɪn) *n.* a white crystalline alkaloid obtained from plants of the genus *Ephedra:* used for the treatment of asthma and hay fever; l-phenyl-2-methylaminopropanol. Formula: $C_6H_5CH(OH)CH(NHCH_3)CH_3$. [C19: from New Latin EPHEDRA + INE[2]]

e·phem+er·a (ɪ'fɛmərə) *n., pl.* **+er·as** *or* **+er·ae** (-əˌri:). **1.** a mayfly, esp. one of the genus *Ephemera.* **2.** something transitory or short-lived. **3.** a plural of **ephemeron.** [C16; see EPHEMERAL]

e·phem+er+al (ɪ'fɛmərəl) *adj.* **1.** lasting for only a short time; transitory; short-lived: *ephemeral pleasure.* ~*n.* **2.** a short-lived organism, such as the mayfly. [C16: from Greek *ephēmeros* lasting only a day, from *hēmera* day] —**e·'phem+er+al+ly** *adv.* —**e·ˌphem+er+'al+i·ty** *or* **e·'phem+er·al+ness** *n.*

e·phem+er+id (ɪ'fɛmərɪd) *n.* any insect of the order *Ephemeroptera* (or *Ephemerida*), which comprises the mayflies. [C19:

from New Latin *Ephēmerida*, from Greek *ephēmeros* short-lived + -ID[2]]

e·phem·er·is (ɪˈfɛmərɪs) *n., pl.* **eph·e·mer·i·des** (ˌɛfɪˈmɛrɪˌdiːz). **1.** a table giving the future positions of a planet, comet, or satellite. **2.** an annual publication giving the positions of the sun, moon, and planets during the course of a year, information concerning eclipses, astronomical constants, etc. **3.** *Obsolete.* a diary or almanac. [C16: from Latin, from Greek: diary, journal; see EPHEMERAL]

e·phem·er·is time *n.* time based on the orbit of the earth around the sun rather than the axial rotation of the earth, one **ephemeris second** being 1/315 556 925.9747 of the tropical year 1960. It is used in astronomy in preference to mean solar time.

e·phem·er·on (ɪˈfɛməˌrɒn) *n., pl.* **·er·a** (-ərə) *or* **·er·ons.** (*usually pl.*). something transitory or short-lived. [C16; see EPHEMERAL]

E·phe·sian (ɪˈfiːʒən) *adj.* **1.** of or relating to Ephesus. ~*n.* **2.** an inhabitant or native of Ephesus.

E·phe·sians (ɪˈfiːʒənz) *n.* (*functioning as sing.*) a book of the New Testament (in full **The Epistle of Paul the Apostle to the Ephesians**), containing an exposition of the divine plan for the world and the consummation of this in Christ.

Eph·e·sus (ˈɛfɪsəs) *n.* (in ancient Greece) a major trading city on the W coast of Asia Minor: famous for its temple of Artemis (Diana); sacked by the Goths (262 A.D.).

e·phod (ˈiːfɒd) *n. Old Testament.* an embroidered vestment believed to resemble an apron with shoulder straps, worn by priests in ancient Israel. [C14: from Hebrew *ēphōdh*]

eph·or (ˈɛfɔː) *n., pl* **·ors** *or* **·o·ri** (-əˌraɪ). (in ancient Greece) one of a board of senior magistrates in any of several Dorian states, esp. the five Spartan ephors, who were elected by vote of all full citizens and who wielded effective power. [C16: from Greek *ephoros*, from *ephoran* to supervise, from EPI- + *horan* to look] —ˈ**eph·or·al** *adj.* —ˈ**eph·or·ate** *n.*

E·phra·im (ˈiːfreɪɪm) *n. Old Testament.* **1. a.** the younger son of Joseph, who received the principal blessing of his grandfather Jacob (Genesis 48:8–22). **b.** the tribe descended from him. **c.** the territory of this tribe, west of the River Jordan. **2.** the northern kingdom of Israel after the kingdom of Solomon had been divided into two.

E·phra·im·ite (ˈiːfreɪɪˌmaɪt) *n.* a member of the tribe of Ephraim.

ep·i-, eph-, *or before a vowel* **ep-** *prefix.* **1.** on; upon; above; over: *epidermis; epicentre.* **2.** in addition to: *epiphenomenon.* **3.** after: *epigenesis; epilogue.* **4.** near; close to: *epicalyx.* [from Greek, from *epi* (prep.)]

ep·i·blast (ˈɛpɪˌblæst) *n. Embryol.* the outermost layer of an embryo, which becomes the ectoderm at gastrulation. Also called: **ectoblast.** —ˌ**ep·i·ˈblas·tic** *adj.*

e·pib·o·ly (ɪˈpɪbəlɪ) *n., pl.* **·lies.** *Embryol.* a process that occurs during gastrulation in vertebrates, in which cells on one side of the blastula grow over and surround the remaining cells and yolk and eventually form the ectoderm. [C19: from Greek *epibolē* a laying on, from *epiballein* to throw on, from EPI- + *ballein* to throw] —**ep·i·bol·ic** (ˌɛpɪˈbɒlɪk) *adj.*

ep·ic (ˈɛpɪk) *n.* **1.** a long narrative poem recounting in elevated style the deeds of a legendary hero, esp. one originating in oral folk tradition. **2.** the genre of epic poetry. **3.** any work of literature, film, etc., having heroic deeds for its subject matter or having other qualities associated with the epic: *a Hollywood epic.* **4.** an episode in the lives of men in which heroic deeds are performed or attempted: *the epic of Scott's expedition to the South Pole.* ~*adj.* **5.** denoting, relating to, or characteristic of an epic or epics. **6.** of heroic or impressive proportions: *an epic voyage.* [C16: from Latin *epicus*, from Greek *epikos*, from *epos* speech, word, song]

ep·i·ca·lyx (ˌɛpɪˈkeɪlɪks, -ˈkæl-) *n., pl.* **·lyx·es** *or* **·ly·ces** (-lɪˌsiːz). *Botany.* a series of small sepal-like bracts forming an outer calyx beneath the true calyx in some flowers.

ep·i·can·thus (ˌɛpɪˈkænθəs) *n., pl.* **·thi** (-θaɪ). a fold of skin extending vertically over the inner angle of the eye: characteristic of Mongolian peoples and a congenital anomaly among other races. Also called: **epicanthic fold.** [C19: New Latin, from EPI- + Latin *canthus* corner of the eye, from Greek *kanthos*] —ˌ**ep·i·ˈcan·thic** *adj.*

ep·i·car·di·um (ˌɛpɪˈkɑːdɪəm) *n., pl.* **·di·a** (-dɪə). *Anatomy.* the innermost layer of the pericardium, in direct contact with the heart. [C19: New Latin, from EPI- + Greek *kardia* heart] —ˌ**ep·i·ˈcar·di·ac** *or* ˌ**ep·i·ˈcar·di·al** *adj.*

ep·i·carp (ˈɛpɪˌkɑːp) *or* **ex·o·carp** *n.* the outermost layer of the pericarp of fruits: forms the skin of a peach or grape. [C19: from French *épicarpe*, from EPI- + Greek *karpos* fruit]

ep·i·ce·di·um (ˌɛpɪˈsiːdɪəm) *n., pl.* **·di·a** (-dɪə). *Rare.* a funeral ode. [C16: Latin, from Greek *epikēdeion*, from EPI- + *kēdos* care]

ep·i·cene (ˈɛpɪˌsiːn) *adj.* **1.** having the characteristics of both sexes; hermaphroditic. **2.** of neither sex; sexless. **3.** effeminate. **4.** *Grammar.* **a.** denoting a noun that may refer to a male or a female, such as *teacher* as opposed to *businessman* or *shepherd.* **b.** (in Latin, Greek, etc.) denoting a noun that retains the same grammatical gender regardless of the sex of the referent. ~*n.* **5.** an epicene person or creature. **6.** an epicene noun. [C15: from Latin *epicoenus* of both genders, from Greek *epikoinos* common to many, from *koinos* common] —ˌ**ep·i·ˈcen·ism** *n.*

ep·i·cen·tre *or U.S.* **ep·i·cen·ter** (ˈɛpɪˌsɛntə), *n., pl.* **·tres** *or U.S.* **·ters.** the area immediately above the origin of earthquake vibrations. [C19: from New Latin *epicentrum*, from Greek *epikentros* over the centre, from EPI- + *kentron* needle; see CENTRE] —ˌ**ep·i·ˈcen·tral** *adj.*

ep·i·cle·sis (ˌɛpɪˈkliːsɪs) *n., pl.* **·ses** (-siːz). *Christianity.* the invocation of the Holy Spirit to consecrate the bread and wine of the Eucharist. [from Greek, from EPI- + *klēsis* a prayer, from *kalein* to call]

ep·i·con·ti·nen·tal (ˌɛpɪˌkɒntɪˈnɛntᵊl) *adj.* (esp. of a sea) situated on a continental shelf or continent.

ep·i·cot·yl (ˌɛpɪˈkɒtɪl) *n.* the part of an embryo plant stem above the cotyledons but beneath the terminal bud.

e·pic·ri·sis[1] (ɪˈpɪkrɪsɪs) *n. Rare.* a critical evaluation, esp. of a literary work. [C19: from Greek *epikrisis* a judgment, from *epikrinein* to decide, from EPI- + *krinein* to judge]

ep·i·cri·sis[2] (ˈɛpɪˌkraɪsɪs) *n. Pathol.* a secondary crisis occurring in the course of a disease. [C20: from EPI- + CRISIS]

ep·i·crit·ic (ˌɛpɪˈkrɪtɪk) *adj.* (of certain nerve fibres of the skin) serving to perceive and distinguish fine variations of temperature or touch. [C20: from Greek *epikritikos* decisive; see EPICRISIS[1]]

ep·ic sim·i·le *n.* an extended simile, as used in the epic poetry of Homer and other writers.

Ep·ic·te·tus (ˌɛpɪkˈtiːtəs) *n.* ?50–?120 A.D., Greek Stoic philosopher, who stressed self-renunciation and the brotherhood of man.

ep·i·cure (ˈɛpɪˌkjʊə) *n.* **1.** a person who cultivates a discriminating palate for the enjoyment of good food and drink; gourmet. **2.** a person devoted to sensual pleasures. [C16: from Medieval Latin *epicūrus*, after EPICURUS] —ˈ**ep·i·cur·ˌism** *n.*

ep·i·cu·re·an (ˌɛpɪkjʊˈriːən) *adj.* **1.** devoted to sensual pleasures, esp. food and drink; hedonistic. **2.** suitable for an epicure: *an epicurean feast.* ~*n.* **3.** an epicure; gourmet. —ˌ**ep·i·cu·ˈre·an·ism** *n.*

Ep·i·cu·re·an (ˌɛpɪkjʊˈriːən) *adj.* **1.** of or relating to the philosophy of Epicurus. ~*n.* **2.** a follower of the philosophy of Epicurus. —ˌ**Ep·i·cu·ˈre·an·ism** *n.*

Ep·i·cu·rus (ˌɛpɪˈkjʊərəs) *n.* 341–270 B.C., Greek philosopher, who held that the highest good is pleasure and that the world is a series of fortuitous combinations of atoms.

ep·i·cy·cle (ˈɛpɪˌsaɪkᵊl) *n.* **1.** *Astronomy.* (in the Ptolemaic system) a small circle, around which a planet was thought to revolve, whose centre describes a larger circle (the **deferent**) centred on the earth. **2.** a circle that rolls around the inside or outside of another circle, so generating an epicycloid or hypocycloid. [C14: from Late Latin *epicyclus*, from Greek *epikuklos*; see EPI-, CYCLE] —**ep·i·cy·clic** (ˌɛpɪˈsaɪklɪk, -ˈsɪklɪk) *or* ˌ**ep·i·ˈcy·cli·cal** *adj.*

ep·i·cy·clic train *n.* a cluster of gears consisting of a central gear wheel with external teeth (the sun), a coaxial gear wheel of greater diameter with internal teeth (the annulus), and one or more planetary gears engaging with both of them to provide a large gear ratio in a compact space.

ep·i·cy·cloid (ˌɛpɪˈsaɪklɔɪd) *n.* the curve described by a point on the circumference of a circle as this circle rolls around the outside of another fixed circle, the two circles being coplanar. Compare **hypocycloid, cycloid** (sense 4). —ˌ**ep·i·cy·ˈcloid·al** *adj.*

ep·i·cy·cloi·dal wheel *n.* one of the planetary gears of an epicyclic train.

Ep·i·daur·us (ˌɛpɪˈdɔːrəs) *n.* an ancient port in Greece, in the NE Peloponnese, in Argolis on the Saronic Gulf.

ep·i·deic·tic (ˌɛpɪˈdaɪktɪk) *or* **ep·i·dic·tic** (ˌɛpɪˈdɪktɪk) *adj.* designed to display something, esp. the skill of the speaker in rhetoric. [C18: from Greek *epideiktikos*, from *epideiknunai* to display, show off, from *deiknunai* to show]

ep·i·dem·ic (ˌɛpɪˈdɛmɪk) *adj.* **1.** (esp. of a disease) attacking or affecting many persons simultaneously in a community or area. ~*n.* **2.** a widespread occurrence of a disease: *an influenza epidemic.* **3.** a rapid development, spread, or growth of something, esp. something unpleasant: *an epidemic of strikes.* [C17: from French *épidémique*, via Late Latin from Greek *epidēmia* literally: among the people, from EPI- + *dēmos* people] —ˌ**ep·i·ˈdem·i·cal·ly** *adv.*

ep·i·dem·ic en·ceph·a·li·tis *n. Pathol.* a technical name for **sleeping sickness** (sense 2).

ep·i·dem·ic men·in·gi·tis *n.* another name for **cerebrospinal meningitis.**

ep·i·dem·ic par·o·ti·tis *n.* another name for **mumps.**

ep·i·de·mi·ol·o·gy (ˌɛpɪˌdiːmɪˈɒlədʒɪ) *n.* the branch of medical science concerned with the occurrence, transmission, and control of epidemic diseases. —**ep·i·de·mi·o·log·i·cal** (ˌɛpɪˌdiːmɪəˈlɒdʒɪkᵊl) *adj.* —ˌ**ep·i·ˌde·mi·o·ˈlog·i·cal·ly** *adv.* —ˌ**ep·i·ˌde·mi·ˈol·o·gist** *n.*

ep·i·der·mis (ˌɛpɪˈdɜːmɪs) *n.* **1.** Also called: **cuticle.** the thin protective outer layer of the skin, composed of stratified epithelial tissue. **2.** the outer layer of cells of an invertebrate. **3.** the outer protective layer of cells of a plant, which may be thickened by a cuticle. [C17: via Late Latin from Greek, from EPI- + *derma* skin] —ˌ**ep·i·ˈder·mal,** ˌ**ep·i·ˈder·mic,** *or* ˌ**ep·i·ˈder·moid** *adj.*

ep·i·di·a·scope (ˌɛpɪˈdaɪəˌskəʊp) *n.* an optical device for projecting a magnified image onto a screen. See also **episcope.**

ep·i·did·y·mis (ˌɛpɪˈdɪdɪmɪs) *n., pl.* **·di·dym·i·des** (-dɪˈdɪmɪˌdiːz). *Anatomy.* a convoluted tube situated along the posterior margin of each testis, in which spermatozoa are stored and conveyed to the vas deferens. [C17: from Greek *epididumis*, from EPI- + *didumos* twin, testicle; see DIDYMOUS] —ˌ**ep·i·ˈdid·y·mal** *adj.*

ep·i·dote (ˈɛpɪˌdəʊt) *n.* a green mineral consisting of hydrated calcium iron aluminium silicate in monoclinic crystalline form: common in metamorphic rocks. Formula: $Ca_2(Al,Fe)_3(SiO_4)_3(OH)$. [C19: from French *épidote*, ultimately from

Greek *epididonai* to increase, from *didonai* to give; so called because two sides of its crystal are longer than the other two sides] —**ep·i·dot·ic** (ˌɛpɪˈdɒtɪk) *adj.*

e·pi·dur·al (ˌɛpɪˈdjʊərəl) *adj.* **1.** upon or outside the dura mater. ~*n.* **2.** Also: **epidural anaesthesia. a.** injection of anaesthetic into the space outside the dura mater enveloping the spinal cord. **b.** anaesthesia induced by this method. [C19: from EPI- + DUR(A MATER) + -AL[1]]

ep·i·fo·cal (ˌɛpɪˈfəʊkəl) *adj. Geology.* situated or occurring at an epicentre.

ep·i·gas·tri·um (ˌɛpɪˈgæstrɪəm) *n., pl.* **-tri·a** (-trɪə). the upper middle part of the abdomen, above the navel and below the breast. [C17: from New Latin, from Greek EPI- + *gastrion*, from *gastēr* stomach] —ˌ**ep·i·ˈgas·tri·al** *or* ˌ**ep·i·ˈgas·tric** *adj.*

ep·i·ge·al (ˌɛpɪˈdʒiːəl), **ep·i·ge·an,** *or* **ep·i·ge·ous** *adj.* **1.** of or relating to seed germination in which the cotyledons appear above the ground because of the growth of the hypocotyl. **2.** living or growing on or close to the surface of the ground. [C19: from Greek *epigeios* of the earth, from EPI- + *gē* earth]

ep·i·gene (ˈɛpɪˌdʒiːn) *adj.* formed or taking place at the surface of the earth. Compare **hypogene.** [C19: from French *épigène*, ultimately from Greek *epigignesthai* to be born after, from *gignesthai* to be born]

ep·i·gen·e·sis (ˌɛpɪˈdʒɛnɪsɪs) *n.* **1.** the widely accepted theory that an individual animal or plant develops by the gradual differentiation and elaboration of a fertilized egg cell. Compare **preformation** (sense 2). **2.** the formation of ore deposits after the surrounding rock has been formed. **3.** alteration of the mineral composition of a rock by external agents: a type of metamorphism. —ˌ**ep·i·ˈgen·e·sist** *or* **e·pig·e·nist** (ɪˈpɪdʒɪnɪst) *n.* —**ep·i·ge·net·ic** (ˌɛpɪdʒɪˈnɛtɪk) *adj.* —ˌ**ep·i·ge·ˈnet·i·cal·ly** *adv.*

e·pig·e·nous (ɪˈpɪdʒɪnəs) *adj. Biology.* growing on the surface, esp. the upper surface, of an organism or part: *an epigenous fungus.*

ep·i·ge·ous (ˌɛpɪˈdʒiːəs) *adj.* a variant of **epigeal.**

ep·i·glot·tis (ˌɛpɪˈglɒtɪs) *n., pl.* **-tis·es** *or* **-ti·des** (-tɪˌdiːz). a thin cartilaginous flap that covers the entrance to the larynx during swallowing, preventing food from entering the trachea. —ˌ**ep·i·ˈglot·tal** *or* ˌ**ep·i·ˈglot·tic** *adj.*

ep·i·gone (ˈɛpɪˌgəʊn) *or* **ep·i·gon** (ˈɛpɪˌgɒn) *n. Rare.* an inferior follower or imitator. [C19: from Greek *epigonos* one born after, from *epigignesthai;* see EPIGENE]

E·pig·o·ni (ɪˈpɪgəˌnaɪ) *pl. n., sing.* **-o·nus** (-ənəs). *Greek myth.* the descendants of the Seven against Thebes, who undertook a second expedition against the city and eventually captured and destroyed it. [from Greek *epigonoi* those born after]

ep·i·gram (ˈɛpɪˌgræm) *n.* **1.** a witty, often paradoxical remark, concisely expressed. **2.** a short, pungent, and often satirical poem, esp. one having a witty and ingenious ending. [C15: from Latin *epigramma,* from Greek: inscription, from *epigraphein* to write upon, from *graphein* to write] —ˌ**ep·i·gram·ˈmat·ic** *adj.* —ˌ**ep·i·gram·ˈmat·i·cal·ly** *adv.*

ep·i·gram·ma·tize *or* **ep·i·gram·ma·tise** (ˌɛpɪˈgræməˌtaɪz) *vb.* to make an epigram or epigrams (about). —ˌ**ep·i·ˈgram·ma·tism** *n.* —ˌ**ep·i·ˈgram·ma·tist** *n.*

ep·i·graph (ˈɛpɪˌgrɑːf, -ˌgræf) *n.* **1.** a quotation at the beginning of a book, chapter, etc., suggesting its theme. **2.** an inscription on a monument or building. [C17: from Greek *epigraphē;* see EPIGRAM] —**ep·i·graph·ic** (ˌɛpɪˈgræfɪk) or ˌ**ep·i·ˈgraph·i·cal** *adj.* —**ep·i·ˈgraph·i·cal·ly** *adv.*

e·pig·ra·phy (ɪˈpɪgrəfɪ) *n.* **1.** the study of ancient inscriptions. **2.** epigraphs collectively. —**e·ˈpig·ra·phist** *or* **e·ˈpig·ra·pher** *n.*

e·pig·y·nous (ɪˈpɪdʒɪnəs) *adj.* (of flowers) having the receptacle enclosing and fused with the gynoecium so that the other floral parts arise above it. [C19: from EPI- + Greek *gunē* (female organ, pistil) + -OUS] —**e·ˈpig·y·ny** *n.*

ep·i·late (ˈɛpɪˌleɪt) *vb. (tr.) Rare.* to remove hair from. [C19: from French *épiler* (modelled on *dépiler* DEPILATE) + -ATE[1]] —ˌ**ep·i·ˈla·tion** *n.*

ep·i·lep·sy (ˈɛpɪˌlɛpsɪ) *n.* a disorder of the central nervous system characterized by periodic loss of consciousness with or without convulsions. In some cases it is due to brain damage but in others the cause is unknown. See also **grand mal, petit mal.** [C16: from Late Latin *epilēpsia,* from Greek, from *epilambanein* to attack, seize, from *lambanein* to take]

ep·i·lep·tic (ˌɛpɪˈlɛptɪk) *adj.* **1.** of, relating to, or having epilepsy. ~*n.* **2.** a person who has epilepsy. —ˌ**ep·i·ˈlep·ti·cal·ly** *adv.*

ep·i·lep·toid (ˌɛpɪˈlɛptɔɪd) *or* **ep·i·lep·ti·form** (ˌɛpɪˈlɛptɪˌfɔːm) *adj.* resembling epilepsy.

ep·i·lim·ni·on (ˌɛpɪˈlɪmnɪən) *n.* the upper layer of water in a lake. [C20: from EPI- + Greek *limnion,* diminutive of *limnē* lake]

ep·i·logue (ˈɛpɪˌlɒg) *n.* **1. a.** a speech, usually in verse, addressed to the audience by an actor at the end of a play. **b.** the actor speaking this. **2.** a short postscript to any literary work, such as a brief description of the fates of the characters in a novel. **3.** *Brit.* the concluding programme of the day on a radio or television station, often having a religious content. [C15: from Latin *epilogus,* from Greek *epilogos,* from *logos* word, speech] —**e·pil·o·gist** (ɪˈpɪlədʒɪst) *n.*

ep·i·mere (ˈɛpɪˌmɪə) *n. Embryol.* the dorsal part of the mesoderm of a vertebrate embryo, consisting of a series of segments (somites).

e·pim·er·ism (ɪˈpɪməˌrɪzəm) *n.* optical isomerism in which isomers (**epimers**) can form about asymmetric atoms within the molecule, esp. in carbohydrates. [C20: from German *Epimer* (see EPI-, -MER) + -ISM] —**ep·i·mer·ic,** (ˌɛpɪˈmɛrɪk) *adj.*

ep·i·mor·pho·sis (ˌɛpɪmɔːˈfəʊsɪs) *n.* a type of development in animals, such as certain insect larvae, in which segmentation of the body is complete before hatching. —ˌ**ep·i·ˈmor·phic** *adj.*

e·pi·my·si·um (ˌɛpɪˈmɪzɪəm) *n., pl.* **-si·a** (-zɪə). *Anatomy.* the sheath of connective tissue that encloses a skeletal muscle. [from New Latin, from EPI- + Greek *mus* mouse, MUSCLE]

ep·i·nas·ty (ˈɛpɪˌnæstɪ) *n., pl.* **-ties.** increased growth of the upper surface of a plant part, such as a leaf, resulting in a downward bending of the part. Compare **hyponasty.** [C19: from EPI- + *-nasty,* from Greek *nastos* pressed down, from *nassein* to press] —ˌ**ep·i·ˈnas·tic** *adj.*

ep·i·neph·rine (ˌɛpɪˈnɛfrɪn, -riːn) *or* **ep·i·neph·rin** *n.* a U.S. name for **adrenaline.** [C19: from EPI- + *nephro-* + -INE[2]]

ep·i·neu·ri·um (ˌɛpɪˈnjʊərɪəm) *n.* a sheath of connective tissue around two or more bundles of nerve fibres. [C19: from New Latin, from EPI- + Greek *neuron* nerve + -IUM] —ˌ**ep·i·ˈneu·ri·al** *adj.*

Epiph. *abbrev. for* Epiphany.

e·piph·a·ny (ɪˈpɪfənɪ) *n., pl.* **-nies. 1.** the manifestation of a supernatural or divine reality. **2.** any moment of great or sudden revelation. [C17: via Church Latin from Greek *epiphaneia* an appearing, from EPI- + *phainein* to show] —**ep·i·phan·ic** (ˌɛpɪˈfænɪk) *adj.*

E·piph·a·ny (ɪˈpɪfənɪ) *n., pl.* **-nies.** a Christian festival held on Jan. 6, commemorating, in the Western Church, the manifestation of Christ to the Magi and, in the Eastern Church, the baptism of Christ.

ep·i·phe·nom·e·nal·ism (ˌɛpɪfɪˈnɒmɪnəˌlɪzəm) *n.* the doctrine that consciousness is merely a by-product of physiological processes and that it has no power to affect them. —ˌ**ep·i·phe·ˈnom·e·nal·ist** *n.*

ep·i·phe·nom·e·non (ˌɛpɪfɪˈnɒmɪnən) *n., pl.* **-na** (-nə). **1.** a secondary or additional phenomenon; by-product. **2.** *Philosophy.* consciousness regarded as a by-product of the biological activity of the human brain. **3.** *Pathol.* an unexpected or atypical symptom or occurrence during the course of a disease. —ˌ**ep·i·phe·ˈnom·e·nal** *adj.* —ˌ**ep·i·phe·ˈnom·e·nal·ly** *adv.*

ep·i·phragm (ˈɛpɪˌfræm) *n.* a disc of calcium phosphate and mucilage secreted by snails over the aperture of their shells before hibernation. [C19: via New Latin from Greek *epiphragma* a lid, from *epiphrassein,* from EPI- + *phrassein* to place in an enclosure]

e·piph·y·sis (ɪˈpɪfɪsɪs) *n., pl.* **-ses** (-ˌsiːz). **1.** the end of a long bone, initially separated from the shaft (diaphysis) by a section of cartilage that eventually ossifies so that the two portions fuse together. **2.** Also called: **epiphysis cerebri.** the technical name for **pineal gland.** [C17: via New Latin from Greek: a growth upon, from EPI- + *phusis* growth, from *phuein* to bring forth, produce] —**ep·i·phys·e·al** *or* **ep·i·phys·i·al** (ˌɛpɪˈfɪzɪəl) *adj.*

ep·i·phyte (ˈɛpɪˌfaɪt) *n.* a plant, such as a moss, that grows on another plant but is not parasitic on it. —**ep·i·phyt·ic** (ˌɛpɪˈfɪtɪk), ˌ**ep·i·ˈphyt·al,** *or* ˌ**ep·i·ˈphyt·i·cal** *adj.* —ˌ**ep·i·ˈphyt·i·cal·ly** *adv.*

ep·i·phy·tot·ic (ˌɛpɪfaɪˈtɒtɪk) *adj.* (of plant diseases and parasites) affecting plants over a wide geographical region.

ep·i·rog·e·ny (ˌɛpaɪˈrɒdʒɪnɪ) *n.* a variant spelling of **epeirogeny.** —**e·pi·ro·gen·ic** (ɪˌpaɪrəʊˈdʒɛnɪk) *or* **e·pi·ro·ge·net·ic** (ɪˌpaɪrəʊdʒɪˈnɛtɪk) *adj.*

E·pi·rus (ɪˈpaɪrəs) *n.* **1.** a region of NW Greece, part of ancient Epirus ceded to Greece after independence in 1830. **2.** (in ancient Greece) a region between the Pindus mountains and the Ionian Sea, straddling the modern border with Albania.

Epis. *abbrev. for:* **1.** Also: **Episc.** Episcopal or Episcopalian. **2.** Epistle.

e·pis·co·pa·cy (ɪˈpɪskəpəsɪ) *n., pl.* **-cies. 1.** government of a Church by bishops. **2.** another word for **episcopate.**

e·pis·co·pal (ɪˈpɪskəpəl) *adj.* of, denoting, governed by, or relating to a bishop or bishops. [C15: from Church Latin *episcopālis,* from *episcopus* BISHOP] —**e·ˈpis·co·pal·ly** *adv.*

E·pis·co·pal (ɪˈpɪskəpəl) *adj.* belonging to or denoting the Episcopal Church. —**E·ˈpis·co·pal·ly** *adv.*

E·pis·co·pal Church *n.* an autonomous branch of the Anglican Communion in Scotland and the U.S.

e·pis·co·pa·li·an (ɪˌpɪskəˈpeɪlɪən) *adj. also* **e·pis·co·pal. 1.** practising or advocating the principle of Church government by bishops. ~*n.* **2.** an advocate of such Church government. —**e·ˌpis·co·ˈpa·li·an·ism** *n.*

E·pis·co·pa·li·an (ɪˌpɪskəˈpeɪlɪən) *adj.* **1.** belonging to or denoting the Episcopal Church. . ~*n.* **2.** a member or adherent of this Church.

e·pis·co·pal·ism (ɪˈpɪskəpəˌlɪzəm) *n.* the belief that a Church should be governed by bishops.

e·pis·co·pate (ɪˈpɪskəpɪt, -ˌpeɪt) *n.* **1.** the office, status, or term of office of a bishop. **2.** bishops collectively.

ep·i·scope (ˈɛpɪˌskəʊp) *n. Brit.* an optical device that projects an enlarged image of an opaque object, such as a printed page or photographic print, onto a screen by means of reflected light. U.S. name: **opaque projector.** See also **epidiascope.**

ep·i·se·mat·ic (ˌɛpɪsɪˈmætɪk) *adj. Zoology.* (esp. of coloration) aiding recognition between animals of the same species.

ep·i·si·ot·o·my (əˌpiːzɪˈɒtəmɪ) *n., pl.* **-mies.** surgical incision into the perineum during the late stages of labour to prevent its laceration during childbirth. [C20: from *episio-,* from Greek *epision* pubic region + -TOMY]

ep·i·sode (ˈɛpɪˌsəʊd) *n.* **1.** an incident, event, or series of events. **2.** any one of the sections into which a serialized novel or radio or television programme is divided. **3.** an incident, sequence, or scene that forms part of a narrative but may be a digression from the main story. **4.** (in ancient Greek tragedy) a section between two choric songs. **5.** *Music.* a contrasting section between statements of the subject, as in a fugue or rondo. [C17: from Greek *epeisodion* something added, from *epi-* (in addition) + *eisodios* coming in, from *eis-* in + *hodos* road]

ep·i·sod·ic (ˌɛpɪˈsɒdɪk) *or* **ep·i·sod·i·cal** *adj.* **1.** resembling or relating to an episode. **2.** divided into or composed of episodes. **3.** irregular, occasional, or sporadic. —ˌ**ep·i·ˈsod·i·cal·ly** *adv.*

ep·i·some (ˈɛpɪˌsəʊm) *n.* any of various genetic particles, esp. viruses, that occur in bacteria and replicate either independently or in association with the chromosome.

ep·i·spas·tic (ˌɛpɪˈspæstɪk) *Med.* ~*adj.* **1.** producing a serous discharge or a blister. ~*n.* **2.** an epispastic agent. [C17: from Greek *epispastikos*, from *epispan* to attract, from *span* to draw; alluding to the ancient belief that blisters consisted of humours drawn to the surface of the skin]

Epist. *Bible. abbrev. for* Epistle.

e·pi·sta·sis (ɪˈpɪstəsɪs) *n.* **1.** scum on the surface of a liquid, esp. on an old specimen of urine. **2.** *Med.* the arrest or checking of a bodily discharge, esp. bleeding. **3.** Also called: **hypostasis.** *Genetics.* the suppression by a gene of the effect of another gene that is not its allele. [C19: from Greek: a stopping, from *ephistanai* to stop, from EPI- + *histanai* to put] —**ep·i·stat·ic** (ˌɛpɪˈstætɪk) *adj.*

e·pi·stax·is (ˌɛpɪˈstæksɪs) *n.* the technical name for **nosebleed.** [C18: from Greek: a dropping, from *epistazein* to drop on, from *stazein* to drip]

ep·is·tem·ic (ˌɛpɪˈstiːmɪk) *adj.* **1.** of or relating to knowledge or epistemology. **2.** denoting the branch of modal logic that deals with the formalization of certain epistemological concepts, such as knowledge, certainty, and ignorance. ~See also **doxastic.** [C20: from Greek *epistēmē* knowledge] —ˌ**ep·is·ˈtem·i·cal·ly** *adv.*

e·pis·te·mol·o·gy (ɪˌpɪstɪˈmɒlədʒɪ) *n.* the theory of knowledge, esp. the critical study of its validity, methods, and scope. [C19: from Greek *epistēmē* knowledge] —**e·pis·te·mo·log·i·cal** (ɪˌpɪstɪməˈlɒdʒɪkəl) *adj.* —**e**ˌ**pis·te·mo·ˈlog·i·cal·ly** *adv.* —**e**ˌ**pis·te·ˈmol·o·gist** *n.*

ep·i·ster·num (ˌɛpɪˈstɜːnəm) *n., pl.* **-na** (-nə). **1.** the manubrium of the sternum in mammals. **2.** another name for **interclavicle.** —ˌ**ep·i·ˈster·nal** *adj.*

e·pis·tle (ɪˈpɪsəl) *n.* **1.** a letter, esp. one that is long, formal, or didactic. **2.** a literary work in letter form, esp. a dedicatory verse letter of a type originated by Horace. [Old English *epistol*, via Latin from Greek *epistolē*, from *epistellein* to send to, from *stellein* to prepare, send]

E·pis·tle (ɪˈpɪsəl) *n.* **1.** *New Testament.* any of the apostolic letters of Saints Paul, Peter, James, Jude, or John. **2.** a reading from one of the Epistles, forming part of the Eucharistic service in many Christian Churches.

e·pis·tler (ɪˈpɪslə, ɪˈpɪstlə), **e·pis·to·ler** (ɪˈpɪstələ), *or* **e·pis·to·list** *n.* (*often cap.*) **1.** a writer of an epistle or epistles. **2.** the person who reads the Epistle in a Christian religious service.

e·pis·to·lar·y (ɪˈpɪstələrɪ), **ep·i·stol·ic** (ˌɛpɪˈstɒlɪk), *or* **e·pis·to·la·to·ry** *adj.* **1.** relating to, denoting, conducted by, or contained in letters. **2.** (of a novel or other work) constructed in the form of a series of letters.

e·pis·tro·phe (ɪˈpɪstrəfɪ) *n.* *Rhetoric.* repetition of a word at the end of successive clauses or sentences. [C17: New Latin, from Greek, from EPI- + *strophē* a turning]

ep·i·style (ˈɛpɪˌstaɪl) *n.* another name for **architrave** (sense 1). [C17: via Latin *epistȳlium* from Greek *epistulion*, from EPI- + *stulos* column, STYLE]

ep·i·taph (ˈɛpɪˌtɑːf, -ˌtæf) *n.* **1.** a commemorative inscription on a tombstone or monument. **2.** a speech or written passage composed in commemoration of a dead person. **3.** a final judgment on a person or thing. [C14: via Latin from Greek *epitaphion*, from *epitaphios* over a tomb, from EPI- + *taphos* tomb] —**ep·i·taph·ic** (ˌɛpɪˈtæfɪk) *adj.* —ˈ**ep·i**ˌ**taph·ist** *n.*

e·pit·a·sis (ɪˈpɪtəsɪs) *n.* (in classical drama) the part of a play in which the main action develops. Compare **protasis, catastrophe** (sense 2). [C16: from Greek: a stretching, intensification, from *teinein* to stretch]

ep·i·tax·i·al tran·sis·tor (ˌɛpɪˈtæksɪəl) *n.* a transistor made by depositing a thin pure layer of semiconductor material (**epitaxial layer**) onto a crystalline support by epitaxy. The layer acts as one of the electrode regions, usually the collector.

ep·i·tax·y (ˈɛpɪˌtæksɪ) *or* **ep·i·tax·is** *n.* the growth of a thin layer on the surface of a crystal so that the layer has the same structure as the underlying crystal. —**ep·i·tax·i·al** (ˌɛpɪˈtæksɪəl) *adj.*

ep·i·tha·la·mi·um (ˌɛpɪθəˈleɪmɪəm) *or* **ep·i·tha·la·mi·on** *n., pl.* **-mi·a** (-mɪə). a poem or song written to celebrate a marriage; nuptial ode. [C17: from Latin, from Greek *epithalamion* marriage song, from *thalamos* bridal chamber] —**ep·i·tha·lam·ic** (ˌɛpɪθəˈlæmɪk) *adj.*

ep·i·the·li·o·ma (ˌɛpɪˌθiːlɪˈəʊmə) *n., pl.* **-mas** *or* **-ma·ta** (-mətə). *Pathol.* a malignant tumour of epithelial tissue. —**ep·i·the·li·om·a·tous** (ˌɛpəˌθiːlɪˈɒmətəs) *adj.*

ep·i·the·li·um (ˌɛpɪˈθiːlɪəm) *n., pl.* **-li·ums** *or* **-li·a** (-lɪə). an animal tissue consisting of one or more layers of closely packed cells covering the external and internal surfaces of the body. The cells vary in structure according to their function, which may be protective, secretory, or absorptive. [C18: New Latin, from EPI- + Greek *thēlē* nipple] —ˌ**ep·i·ˈthe·li·al** *or* ˌ**ep·i·ˈthe·li·oid** *adj.*

ep·i·thet (ˈɛpɪˌθɛt) *n.* a descriptive word or phrase added to or substituted for a person's name: *"Lackland" is an epithet for King John.* [C16: from Latin *epitheton*, from Greek, from *epitithenai* to add, from *tithenai* to put] —ˌ**ep·i·ˈthet·ic** *or* ˌ**ep·i·ˈthet·i·cal** *adj.*

e·pit·o·me (ɪˈpɪtəmɪ) *n.* **1.** a typical example of a characteristic or class; embodiment; personification: *he is the epitome of sloth.* **2.** a summary of a written work; abstract. [C16: via Latin from Greek *epitomē*, from *epitemnein* to abridge, from EPI- + *temnein* to cut] —**ep·i·tom·i·cal** (ˌɛpɪˈtɒmɪkəl) *or* ˌ**ep·i·ˈtom·ic** *adj.*

e·pit·o·mize *or* **e·pit·o·mise** (ɪˈpɪtəˌmaɪz) *vb.* (*tr.*) **1.** to be a personification of; typify. **2.** to make an epitome of. —**e·ˈpit·o·mist** *n.* —**e**ˌ**pit·o·mi·ˈza·tion** *or* **e**ˌ**pit·o·mi·ˈsa·tion** *n.* —**e·ˈpit·o**ˌ**miz·er** *or* **e·ˈpit·o**ˌ**mis·er** *n.*

ep·i·zo·ic (ˌɛpɪˈzəʊɪk) *adj.* (of an animal or plant) growing or living on the exterior of a living animal. —ˌ**ep·i·ˈzo·ism** *n.* —**ep·i·zo·ite** (ˌɛpɪˈzəʊaɪt) *n.*

ep·i·zo·on (ˌɛpɪˈzəʊɒn) *n., pl.* **-zo·a** (-ˈzəʊə). an animal, such as a parasite, that lives on the body of another animal. [C19: New Latin, from EPI- + Greek *zōion* animal]

ep·i·zo·ot·ic (ˌɛpɪzəʊˈɒtɪk) *adj.* **1.** (of a disease) suddenly and temporarily affecting a large number of animals. ~*n.* **2.** an epizootic disease. Compare **enzootic.** —ˌ**ep·i·zo·ˈot·i·cal·ly** *adv.*

E.P.N.S. *abbrev. for* electroplated nickel silver.

e·poch (ˈiːpɒk) *n.* **1.** a point in time beginning a new or distinctive period: *the invention of nuclear weapons marked an epoch in the history of warfare.* **2.** a long period of time marked by some predominant or typical characteristic; era. **3.** *Astronomy.* a precise date to which information, such as coordinates, relating to a celestial body is referred. **4.** *Geology.* a unit of geological time within a period during which a series of rocks is formed: *the Pleistocene epoch.* **5.** *Physics.* the displacement of an oscillating or vibrating body at zero time. [C17: from New Latin *epocha*, from Greek *epokhē* cessation; related to *ekhein* to hold, have] —**ep·och·al** (ˈɛpˌɒkəl) *adj.* —ˈ**ep**ˌ**och·al·ly** *adv.*

e·poch-mak·ing *adj.* of great importance; momentous.

ep·ode (ˈɛpəʊd) *n.* *Greek prosody.* **1.** the part of a lyric ode that follows the strophe and the antistrophe. **2.** a type of lyric poem composed of couplets in which a long line is followed by a shorter one, invented by Archilochus. [C16: via Latin from Greek *epōidos* a singing after, from *epaidein* to sing after, from *aidein* to sing]

ep·o·nym (ˈɛpənɪm) *n.* **1.** a name, esp. a place name, derived from the name of a real or mythical person, as for example *Constantinople* from *Constantine I.* **2.** the name of the person from which such a name is derived: *in the Middle Ages, "Brutus" was thought to be the eponym of "Britain".* [C19: from Greek *epōnumos* giving a significant name] —**e·pon·y·mous** (ɪˈpɒnɪməs) *or* ˌ**ep·o·ˈnym·ic** *adj.* —**e·ˈpon·y·mous·ly** *or* ˌ**ep·o·ˈnym·i·cal·ly** *adv.*

e·pon·y·my (ɪˈpɒnɪmɪ) *n.* the derivation of names of places, etc., from those of persons.

ép·o·pée (ˈɛpəʊˌpiː; *French* epɔˈpe) *or* **ep·o·poe·ia** (ˌɛpəˈpiːə) *n.* **1.** an epic poem. **2.** epic poetry in general. [C17: from French *épopée*, from Greek *epopoiia*, from EPOS + *poiein* to make]

ep·os (ˈɛpɒs) *n.* **1.** a body of poetry in which the tradition of a people is conveyed, esp. a group of poems concerned with a common epic theme. **2.** another word for **epic** (sense 1). [C19: via Latin from Greek: speech, word, epic poem, song; related to Latin *vōx* VOICE]

e·pox·ide (ɪˈpɒksaɪd) *n.* **a.** a compound containing an oxygen atom joined to two different groups that are themselves joined to other groups. **b.** (*as modifier*): *epoxide resin.* [C20: from EPI- + OXIDE]

e·pox·y (ɪˈpɒksɪ) *adj. Chem.* **1.** of, consisting of, or containing an oxygen atom joined to two different groups that are themselves joined to other groups: *epoxy group.* **2.** of, relating to, or consisting of an epoxy resin. ~*n., pl.* **e·pox·ies. 3.** short for **epoxy resin.** [C20: from EPI- + OXY-]

e·pox·y *or* **e·pox·ide res·in** *n.* any of various tough resistant thermosetting synthetic resins containing epoxy groups: used in surface coatings, laminates, and adhesives.

Ep·ping For·est (ˈɛpɪŋ) *n.* a forest in E England, northeast of London: formerly a royal hunting ground.

EPROM (ˈiːprɒm) *Computer technol. n. acronym for* erasable programmable read only memory.

ep·si·lon (ˈɛpsɪˌlɒn, ɛpˈsaɪlən) *n.* the fifth letter of the Greek alphabet (Ε, ϵ), a short vowel, transliterated as *e.* [Greek *e psilon*, literally: simple *e*]

Ep·si·lon (ˈɛpsɪˌlɒn, ɛpˈsaɪlən) *n.* (*foll. by the genitive case of a specified constellation*) the fifth brightest star in a constellation: *Epsilon Aurigae.*

Ep·som (ˈɛpsəm) *n.* a town in SE England, in Surrey: famous for its mineral springs and for horse racing. Pop. (with Ewell): 72 054 (1971).

Ep·som salts *n.* a medicinal preparation of hydrated magnesium sulphate, used as a purgative, to reduce inflammation, etc. [C18: named after EPSOM, where they occur naturally in the water]

Ep·stein (ˈɛpstaɪn) *n.* Sir **Ja·cob.** 1880–1959, British sculptor, born in the U.S. of Russo-Polish parents.

e·pyl·li·on (ɪˈpɪlɪən) *n., pl.* **-li·a** (-lɪə). a miniature epic. [C19: from Greek, diminutive of EPOS]

eq. *abbrev. for:* **1.** equal. **2.** equation. **3.** equivalent.

eq+ua·ble ('ɛkwəbᵊl) *adj.* **1.** even-tempered; placid. **2.** unvarying; uniform: *an equable climate.* [C17: from Latin *aequābilis,* from *aequāre* to make equal] —ˌ**eq+ua·'bil+i·ty** *or* '**eq+ua·ble+ness** *n.* —'**eq+ua·bly** *adv.*

e·qual ('i:kwəl) *adj.* **1.** (often foll. by *to* or *with*) identical in size, quantity, degree, intensity, etc.; the same (as). **2.** having identical privileges, rights, status, etc.: *all men are equal before the law.* **3.** having uniform effect or application: *equal opportunities.* **4.** evenly balanced or proportioned: *the game was equal between the teams.* **5.** (usually foll. by *to*) having the necessary or adequate strength, ability, means, etc. (for): *to be equal to one's work.* **6.** another word for **equivalent** (sense 3a.). **7.** *Archaic.* tranquil; placid. ~*n.* **8.** a person or thing equal to another, esp. in merit, ability, etc.: *he has no equal when it comes to boxing.* ~*vb.* **e·quals, e·qual+ling, e·qualled** *or U.S.* **e·quals, e·qual+ing, e·qualed. 9.** (*tr.*) to be equal to; correspond to; match: *my offer equals his.* **10.** (*intr.;* usually foll. by *out*) to become equal or level. **11.** (*tr.*) to make, perform, or do something equal to: *to equal the world record.* **12.** (*tr.*) *Archaic.* to make equal. [C14: from Latin *aequālis,* from *aequus* level, of obscure origin] —'**e·qual+ly** *adv.*

e·qual-ar·e·a *n.* (*modifier*) (of a map projection) showing area accurately and therefore distorting shape and direction. Also: **homolographic.**

e·qual·i+tar+i·an (ɪˌkwɒlɪ'tɛərɪən) *adj., n.* a less common word for **egalitarian.** —eˌ**qual·i+'tar+i·an+ism** *n.*

e·qual·i+ty (ɪ'kwɒlɪtɪ) *n., pl.* **+ties. 1.** the state of being equal. **2.** *Maths.* a statement, usually an equation, indicating that quantities or expressions on either side of an equal sign are equal in value.

e·qual+ize *or* **e·qual+ise** ('i:kwəˌlaɪz) *vb.* **1.** (*tr.*) to make equal or uniform; regularize. **2.** (*intr.*) (in sports) to reach the same score as one's opponent or opponents. —ˌ**e·qual·i+'za+tion** *or* ˌ**e·qual·i+'sa+tion** *n.*

e·qual+iz+er *or* **e·qual+is+er** ('i:kwəˌlaɪzə) *n.* **1.** a person or thing that equalizes, esp. a device to counterbalance opposing forces. **2.** an electronic network introduced into a transmission circuit to alter its response, esp. to reduce distortion by equalizing its response over a specified frequency range. **3.** *Sport.* a goal, point, etc., that levels the score. **4.** *U.S. slang.* a weapon, esp. a gun.

e·qual sign *or* **e·quals sign** *n.* the symbol =, used to indicate a mathematical equality.

e·qua+nim+i·ty (ˌi:kwə'nɪmɪtɪ, ˌɛkwə-) *n.* calmness of mind or temper; composure. [C17: from Latin *aequanimitās,* from *aequus* even, EQUAL + *animus* mind, spirit] —**e·quan·i+mous** (ɪ'kwænɪməs) *adj.* —**e·'quan·i+mous+ly** *adv.*

e·quate (ɪ'kweɪt) *vb.* (*mainly tr.*) **1.** to make or regard as equivalent or similar, esp. in order to compare or balance. **2.** *Maths.* to indicate the equality of; form an equation from. **3.** (*intr.*) to be equal; correspond. [C15: from Latin *aequāre* to make EQUAL] —**e·'quat+a·ble** *adj.* —**eˌquat+a·'bil+i·ty** *n.*

e·qua+tion (ɪ'kweɪʒən, -ʃən) *n.* **1.** a mathematical statement that two expressions are equal: it is either an **identity,** in which the variables can assume any value, or a **conditional equation,** in which the variables have only certain values (roots). **2.** the act of regarding as equal; equating. **3.** the act of making equal or balanced; equalization. **4.** the state of being equal, equivalent, or equally balanced. **5.** See **chemical equation. 6.** *Astronomy.* See **personal equation.** —**e·'qua+tion+al** *adj.* —**e·'qua+tion+al+ly** *adv.*

e·qua+tion of time *n.* the difference between apparent solar time and mean solar time, being at a maximum in February (over 14 minutes) and November (over 16 minutes).

e·qua+tor (ɪ'kweɪtə) *n.* **1.** the great circle of the earth with a latitude of 0°, lying equidistant from the poles; dividing the N and S hemispheres. **2.** a circle dividing a sphere or other surface into two equal symmetrical parts. **3.** See **magnetic equator. 4.** *Astronomy.* See **celestial equator.** [C14: from Medieval Latin (*circulus*) *aequātor* (*diei et noctis*) (circle) that equalizes (the day and night), from Latin *aequāre* to make EQUAL]

e·qua+to+ri·al (ˌɛkwə'tɔ:rɪəl) *adj.* **1.** of, like, or existing at or near the equator. **2.** *Astronautics.* lying in the plane of the equator: *an equatorial orbit.* ~*n.* **3.** an equatorial telescope or the mounting of such a telescope. —ˌ**e·qua+'to+ri·al+ly** *adv.*

E·qua+to+ri·al Guin·ea *n.* a republic of W Africa, consisting of Rio Muni on the mainland and the island of Macias Nguema in the Gulf of Guinea, with four smaller islands: ceded by Portugal to Spain in 1778; gained independence in 1968. Official language: Spanish. Currency: peseta. Capital: Malabo. Pop.: 310 000 (1975 UN est.). Area: 28 049 sq. km (10 830 sq. miles). Former name (until 1964): **Spanish Guinea.**

e·qua+to+ri·al tel·e+scope *n.* an astronomical telescope that is mounted on two mutually perpendicular axes, one of which is parallel to the earth's axis.

eq+uer+ry (ɪ'kwɛrɪ) *n., pl.* **+ries. 1.** an officer attendant upon the British sovereign. **2.** an officer in a royal household responsible for the horses. [C16: alteration (through influence of Latin *equus* horse) of earlier *escuirie,* from Old French: stable, group of squires, from *escuyer* SQUIRE]

e·ques+tri·an (ɪ'kwɛstrɪən) *adj.* **1.** of or relating to horses and riding. **2.** on horseback; mounted. **3.** depicting or representing a person on horseback: *an equestrian statue.* **4.** of, relating to, or composed of Roman equites. **5.** of, relating to, or composed of knights, esp. the imperial free knights of the Holy Roman Empire. ~*n.* **6.** a person skilled in riding and horsemanship. [C17: from Latin *equestris,* from *eques* horseman, knight, from *equus* horse] —**e·'ques+tri·an+ism** *n.*

e·ques+tri+enne (ɪˌkwɛstrɪ'ɛn) *n.* a female rider on horseback, esp. one in a circus who performs acrobatics.

eq·ui- *combining form.* equal or equally: *equidistant; equilateral.*

e·qui+an+gu+lar (ˌi:kwɪ'æŋgjʊlə) *adj.* having all angles equal.

e·qui+dis+tant (ˌi:kwɪ'dɪstənt) *adj.* distant by equal amounts from two or more places. —ˌ**e·qui+'dis+tance** *n.* —ˌ**e·qui+'dis+tant+ly** *adv.*

e·qui+lat+e·ral (ˌi:kwɪ'lætərəl) *adj.* **1.** having all sides of equal length: *an equilateral triangle.* ~*n.* **2.** a geometric figure having all its sides of equal length. **3.** a side that is equal in length to other sides. —ˌ**e·qui+'lat+er+al+ly** *adv.*

e·quil·i+brant (ɪ'kwɪlɪbrənt) *n.* a force capable of balancing another force and producing equilibrium.

e·quil·i+brate (ˌi:kwə'laɪbreɪt, ɪ'kwɪlɪˌbreɪt) *vb.* to bring to or be in equilibrium; balance. [C17: from Late Latin *aequilībrāre,* from *aequilībris* in balance; see EQUILIBRIUM] —**e·qui+li+bra+tion** (ˌi:kwɪlaɪ'breɪʃən, ɪˌkwɪlɪ-) *n.* —**e·qui+li+bra+tor** (ɪ'kwɪlɪˌbreɪtə) *n.*

e·quil·i+brist (ɪ'kwɪlɪbrɪst) *n.* a person who performs balancing feats, esp. on a high wire. —**eˌquil·i·'bris+tic** *adj.*

e·qui+lib+ri·um (ˌi:kwɪ'lɪbrɪəm) *n., pl.* **+ri·ums** *or* **+ri·a** (-rɪə). **1.** a stable condition in which forces cancel one another. **2.** any unchanging condition or state of a body, system, etc., resulting from the balance or cancelling out of the influences or processes to which it is subjected. See **thermodynamic equilibrium. 3.** *Physics.* a state of rest or uniform motion in which there is no resultant force on a body. **4.** *Chem.* the condition existing when a chemical reaction and its reverse reaction take place at equal rates. **5.** *Physics.* the condition of a system that has its total energy distributed among its component parts in the statistically most probable manner. **6.** *Physiol.* a state of bodily balance, maintained primarily by special receptors in the inner ear. **7.** the economic condition in which there is neither excess demand nor excess supply in a market. [C17: from Latin *aequilībrium,* from *aequi-* EQUI- + *lībra* pound, balance]

e·qui+mo+lec·u·lar (ˌi:kwɪmə'lɛkjʊlə) *adj.* (of substances, solutions, etc.) containing equal numbers of molecules.

eq·uine ('ɛkwaɪn) *adj.* **1.** of, relating to, or resembling a horse. **2.** of, relating to, or belonging to the family *Equidae,* which comprises horses, zebras, and asses. [C18: from Latin *equīnus,* from *equus* horse] —'**eq·uine+ly** *adv.* —**e·'quin+i·ty** *n.*

eq·uine dis+tem+per *n.* another name for **strangles.**

e·qui+noc+tial (ˌi:kwɪ'nɒkʃəl) *adj.* **1.** relating to or occurring at either or both equinoxes. **2.** (of a plant) having flowers that open and close at specific regular times. **3.** *Astronomy.* of or relating to the celestial equator. ~*n.* **4.** a storm or gale at or near an equinox. **5.** another name for **celestial equator.** [C14: from Latin *aequinoctiālis* concerning the EQUINOX]

e·qui+noc+tial cir+cle *or* **line** *n.* another name for **celestial equator.**

e·qui+noc+tial point *n.* either of the two points at which the celestial equator intersects the ecliptic.

e·qui+noc+tial year *n.* another name for **solar year.** See **year** (sense 4).

e·qui+nox ('i:kwɪˌnɒks) *n.* **1.** either of the two occasions, six months apart, when day and night are of equal length. See **vernal equinox, autumnal equinox. 2.** another name for **equinoctial point.** [C14: from Medieval Latin *equinoxium,* changed from Latin *aequinoctium,* from *aequi-* EQUI- + *nox* night]

e·qui-NP-de·le·tion *n.* (in transformational grammar) a rule that deletes repeated noun phrases in complement clauses, thus deriving a sentence like *John claims to be a genius* from some such structure as *John claims John is a genius.* Often shortened to **equi.**

e·quip (ɪ'kwɪp) *vb.* **e·quips, e·quip+ping, e·quipped.** (*tr.*) **1.** to furnish with (necessary supplies, etc.). **2.** (*usually passive*) to provide with abilities, understanding, etc.: *her son was never equipped to be a scholar.* **3.** to dress out; attire. [C16: from Old French *eschiper* to embark, fit out (a ship), of Germanic origin; compare Old Norse *skipa* to put in order, *skip* SHIP] —**e·'quip+ment** *n.* —**e·'quip+per** *n.*

eq·ui+page ('ɛkwɪpɪdʒ) *n.* **1.** a horse-drawn carriage, esp. one elegantly equipped and attended by liveried footmen. **2.** the stores and equipment of a military unit. **3.** *Archaic.* **a.** a set of useful articles. **b.** a group of attendants; retinue.

eq·ui+par+ti+tion (ˌɛkwɪpɑ:'tɪʃən) *n.* the equal division of the energy of a system in thermal equilibrium between different degrees of freedom.

eq·ui+poise ('ɛkwɪˌpɔɪz) *n.* **1.** even balance of weight or other forces; equilibrium. **2.** a counterbalance; counterpoise. ~*vb.* **3.** (*tr.*) to offset or balance in weight or force; balance.

e·qui+pol+lent (ˌi:kwɪ'pɒlənt) *adj.* **1.** equal or equivalent in significance, power, or effect. **2.** *Logic.* (of two propositions) logically deducible from each other. ~*n.* **3.** something that is equipollent. [C15: from Latin *aequipollēns* of equal importance, from EQUI- + *pollēre* to be able, be strong] —ˌ**e·qui+'pol+lence** *or* ˌ**e·qui+'pol+len+cy** *n.* —ˌ**e·qui+'pol+lent+ly** *adv.*

e·qui+pon+der+ate (ˌi:kwɪ'pɒndəˌreɪt) *vb.* (*tr.*) to equal or balance in weight, power, force, etc.; offset; counterbalance. [C17: from Medieval Latin *aequiponderāre,* from Latin EQUI- + *ponderāre* to weigh] —ˌ**e·qui+'pon+der+ance** *or* ˌ**e·qui+'pon+der+an+cy** *n.* —ˌ**e·qui+'pon+der+ant** *adj.*

e·qui+po+ten+tial (ˌi:kwɪpə'tɛnʃəl) *adj.* **1.** having the same electric potential or uniform electric potential. **2.** Also: **e·qui+po+tent** (ˌi:kwɪ'pəʊtᵊnt). equivalent in power or effect. ~*n.* **3.** an equipotential line or surface. —ˌ**e·qui+po+ˌten+ti+'al+i·ty** *n.*

e·qui+prob+a·ble (ˌiːkwɪˈprɒbəbᵊl) *adj.* equally probable. —**ˌe·qui+ˌprob·a+ˈbil+i·ty** *n.*

eq·ui+se·tum (ˌɛkwɪˈsiːtəm) *n., pl.* **·tums** *or* **·ta** (-tə). any pteridophyte plant of the genus *Equisetum,* which comprises the horsetails. [C19: New Latin, changed from Latin *equisaetum,* from *equus* horse + *saeta* bristle]

eq·ui+ta·ble (ˈɛkwɪtəbᵊl) *adj.* **1.** impartial or reasonable; fair; just: *an equitable decision.* **2.** *Law.* relating to or valid in equity, as distinct from common law or statute law. **3.** *Law.* (formerly) recognized in a court of equity only, as claims, rights, etc. [C17: from French *équitable,* from *équité* EQUITY] —**ˈeq·ui+ta·ble+ness** *n.* —**ˈeq·ui+ta·bly** *adv.*

eq·ui+tant (ˈɛkwɪtᵊnt) *adj.* (of a leaf) having the base folded around the stem so that it overlaps the leaf above and opposite. [C19: from Latin *equitāns* riding, from *equitāre* to ride, from *equus* horse]

eq·ui+ta+tion (ˌɛkwɪˈteɪʃən) *n.* the study and practice of riding and horsemanship. [C16: from Latin *equitātiō,* from *equitāre* to ride, from *equus* horse]

eq·ui+tes (ˈɛkwɪˌtiːz) *pl. n.* (in ancient Rome) **1.** the cavalry. **2.** members of a social order distinguished by wealth and ranking just below the senators. ~Also called: **knights.** [from Latin, plural of *eques* horseman, from *equus* horse]

eq·ui+ties (ˈɛkwɪtɪz) *pl. n.* another name for **ordinary shares.**

eq·ui+ty (ˈɛkwɪtɪ) *n., pl.* **+ties.** **1.** the quality of being impartial or reasonable; fairness. **2.** an impartial or fair act, decision, etc. **3.** *Law.* a system of jurisprudence founded on principles of natural justice and fair conduct. It supplements the common law and mitigates its inflexibility, as by providing a remedy where none exists at law. **4.** *Law.* an equitable right or claim: *equity of redemption.* **5.** the interest of ordinary shareholders in a company. **6.** the market value of a debtor's property in excess of all debts to which it is liable. [C14: from Old French *equite,* from Latin *aequitās,* from *aequus* level, EQUAL]

Eq·ui+ty (ˈɛkwɪtɪ) *n. Brit.* the actors' trade union. Full name: **Actors' Equity Association.**

eq·ui+ty of re+demp+tion *n. Property law.* the right that a mortgager has in equity to redeem his property on payment of the sum owing, even though the sum is overdue. See also **foreclose.**

equiv. *abbrev. for* equivalent.

e·quiv·a+lence (ɪˈkwɪvələns) *or* **e·quiv·a+len+cy** *n.* **1.** the state of being equivalent or interchangeable. **2.** *Maths, logic.* a relation, interpreted as meaning *if and only if,* between two single or compound propositions, which are either both true or both false and such that each implies the other. Symbol: ≡ or ↔, as in $-(p \wedge q) \equiv -p \vee -q$. **3.** *Logic.* a function of two propositions that takes the value *true* either when both propositions are true or both are false, and the value *false* otherwise. ~Also called (for senses 2, 3): **biconditional.**

eq·ui+va+len+cy (ˌɛkwɪˈveɪlənsɪ) *or* **eq·ui+va+lence** *n. Chem.* the state of having equal valencies. —**ˌeq·ui+ˈva+lent** *adj.*

e·quiv·a+lent (ɪˈkwɪvələnt) *adj.* **1.** equal or interchangeable in value, quantity, significance, etc. **2.** having the same or a similar effect or meaning. **3.** *Maths.* **a.** (of two geometric figures) having a particular property in common; equal. **b.** (of two equations or inequalities) having the same set of solutions. **c.** (of two sets) having the same cardinal number. **4.** *Maths, logic.* (of two propositions) having an equivalence between them. ~*n.* **5.** something that is equivalent. **6.** short for **equivalent weight.** [C15: from Late Latin *aequivalēns,* from *aequivalēre* to be equally significant, from Latin *aequi-* EQUI- + *valēre* to be worth] —**eˈquiv·a+lent+ly** *adv.*

e·quiv·a+lent cir+cuit *n.* an arrangement of simple electrical components that is electrically equivalent to a complex circuit and is used to simplify circuit analysis.

e·quiv·a+lent fo+cal length *n. Optics.* the ratio of the size of an image of a small distant object near the optical axis to the angular distance of the object in radians.

e·quiv·a+lent weight *n.* the weight of an element or compound that will combine with or displace 8 grams of oxygen or 1.007 97 grams of hydrogen. Also called: **gram equivalent.**

e·quiv·o+cal (ɪˈkwɪvəkᵊl) *adj.* **1.** capable of varying interpretations; ambiguous. **2.** deliberately misleading or vague; evasive. **3.** of doubtful character or sincerity; dubious. [C17: from Late Latin *aequivocus,* from Latin EQUI- + *vōx* voice] —**eˈquiv·o+cal+ly** *adv.* —**eˌquiv·o+ˈcal+i·ty** *or* **e·quiv·o·ca+cy** (ɪˈkwɪvəkəsɪ) *n.* —**eˈquiv·o+cal+ness** *n.*

e·quiv·o+cate (ɪˈkwɪvəˌkeɪt) *vb.* (*intr.*) to use vague or ambiguous language, esp. in order to avoid speaking directly or honestly; hedge. [C15: from Medieval Latin *aequivocāre,* from Late Latin *aequivocus* ambiguous, EQUIVOCAL] —**eˈquiv·o+ˌcat+ing+ly** *adv.* —**eˌquiv·o+ˈca+tion** *n.* —**eˈquiv·o+ˌca+tor** *n.* —**eˈquiv·o+ca·to·ry** *adj.*

eq·ui+voque *or* **eq·ui+voke** (ˈɛkwɪˌvəʊk) *n.* **1.** a play on words; pun. **2.** an ambiguous phrase or expression. **3.** double meaning; ambiguity. [C14 *equivoc* EQUIVOCAL]

E·quul+e·us (ɛˈkwʊlɪəs) *n., Latin genitive* **E·quul·e·i** (ɛˈkwʊlɪˌaɪ). a small faint constellation in the N hemisphere between Pegasus and Aquarius. [from Latin: a young horse, from *equus* horse]

er (ə, ɜː) *interj.* a sound made when hesitating in speech.

Er *the chemical symbol for* erbium.

E.R. *abbrev. for:* **1.** Elizabeth Regina. [Latin: Queen Elizabeth] **2.** Eduardus Rex. [Latin: King Edward]

-er[1] *suffix forming nouns.* **1.** a person or thing that performs a specified action: *reader; decanter; lighter.* **2.** a person engaged in a profession, occupation, etc.: *writer; baker; bootlegger.* **3.** a native or inhabitant of: *islander; Londoner; villager.* **4.** a person or thing having a certain characteristic: *newcomer; double-decker; fiver.* [Old English *-ere;* related to German *-er,* Latin *-ārius*]

-er[2] *suffix.* forming the comparative degree of adjectives (*deeper, freer, sunnier,* etc.) and adverbs (*faster, slower,* etc.). [Old English *-rd, -re* (adj.), *-or* (adv.)]

e·ra (ˈɪərə) *n.* **1.** a period of time considered as being of a distinctive character; epoch. **2.** an extended period of time the years of which are numbered from a fixed point or event: *the Christian era.* **3.** a point in time, esp. one beginning a new or distinctive period: *the discovery of antibiotics marked an era in modern medicine.* **4.** *Geology.* a major division of geological time, divided into several periods: *the Mesozoic era.* [C17: from Latin *aera* counters, plural of *aes* brass, pieces of brass money]

e·ra+di+ate (ɪˈreɪdɪˌeɪt) *vb.* a less common word for **radiate.** Compare **irradiate.** —**eˌra+di·ˈa+tion** *n.*

e·rad·i+cate (ɪˈrædɪˌkeɪt) *vb.* (*tr.*) **1.** to obliterate; stamp out. **2.** to pull or tear up by the roots. [C16: from Latin *ērādīcāre* to uproot, from EX- + *rādīx* root] —**eˈrad·i+ca·ble** *adj.* —**eˈrad·i+ca·bly** *adv.* —**eˌrad·i+ˈca+tion** *n.* —**eˈrad·i+ca+tive** *adj.* —**eˈrad·i+ˌca+tor** *n.*

e·rase (ɪˈreɪz) *vb.* **1.** to obliterate or rub out (something written, typed, etc.). **2.** (*tr.*) to destroy all traces of; remove completely: *time erases grief.* **3.** to remove (a recording) from (magnetic tape). **4.** (*tr.*) *Computer technol.* to replace (data) on a storage device with characters representing an absence of data. [C17: from Latin *ērādere* to scrape off, from EX- + *rādere* to scratch, scrape] —**eˈras+a·ble** *adj.*

e·ras+er (ɪˈreɪzə) *n.* an object, such as a piece of rubber or felt, used for erasing something written, typed, etc.: *a pencil eraser.*

e·ra+sion (ɪˈreɪʒən) *n.* **1.** the act of erasing; erasure. **2.** the surgical scraping away of tissue, esp. of bone.

E·ras·mus (ɪˈræzməs) *n.* **Des·i·der·i·us** (ˌdɛzɪˈdɪərɪəs), original name *Gerhard Gerhards.* ?1466–1536, Dutch humanist, the leading scholar of the Renaissance in northern Europe. He published the first Greek edition of the New Testament in 1516; his other works include the satirical *Encomium Moriae* (1509); *Colloquia* (1519), a series of dialogues; and an attack on the theology of Luther, *De Libero Arbitrio* (1524).

E·ras·ti·an+ism (ɪˈræstɪəˌnɪzəm) *n.* the theory that the state should have authority over the church in ecclesiastical matters. [C17: named after Thomas *Erastus* (1524–83), Swiss theologian to whom such views were attributed] —**Eˈras+ti·an** *adj.*

e·ras+ure (ɪˈreɪʒə) *n.* **1.** the act or an instance of erasing. **2.** the place or mark, as on a piece of paper, where something has been erased.

Er·a·to (ˈɛrəˌtəʊ) *n. Greek myth.* the Muse of love poetry.

Er·a·tos·the·nes (ˌɛrəˈtɒsθɪˌniːz) *n.* ?276–?194 B.C., Greek mathematician and astronomer, who calculated the circumference of the earth by observing the angle of the sun's rays at different places.

Er+bil, Ir+bil (ˈɜːbɪl), *or* **Ar+bil** *n.* a city in N Iraq: important in Assyrian times. Pop.: 107 400 (1970 est.). Ancient name: **Arbela.**

er+bi·um (ˈɜːbɪəm) *n.* a soft malleable silvery-white element of the lanthanide series of metals: used in special alloys, room-temperature lasers, and as a pigment. Symbol: Er; atomic no.: 68; atomic wt.: 167.26; valency: 3; relative density: 9.045; melting pt.: 1522°C; boiling pt.: 2510°C. [C19: from New Latin, from (*Ytt*)*erb*(*y*), Sweden, where it was first found + -IUM]

Er+ci+yas Da·ği (*Turkish* ˈɛrdʒijɑs dɑːˈɪ) *n.* an extinct volcano in central Turkey. Height 3916 m (12 923 ft.).

ere (ɛə) *conj., prep.* a poetic word for **before.** [Old English *ǣr;* related to Old Norse *ār* early, Gothic *airis* earlier, Old High German *ēr* earlier, Greek *eri* early]

Er·e·bus[1] (ˈɛrɪbəs) *n. Greek myth.* **1.** the god of darkness, son of Chaos and brother of Night. **2.** the darkness below the earth, thought to be the abode of the dead or the region they pass through on their way to Hades.

Er+e·bus[2] (ˈɛrɪbəs) *n.* **Mount.** a volcano in Antarctica, on Ross Island: discovered by Sir James Ross in 1841 and named after his ship. Height: 3794 m (12 520 ft.).

E·rech·the·um (ɪˈrɛkθɪəm, ˌɛrəkˈθiːəm) *or* **E·rech+thei+on** (ɪˈrɛkθɪən, ˌɛrəkˈθiːən) *n.* a temple on the Acropolis at Athens, which has a porch of caryatids.

E·rech·theus (ɛˈrɛkθjuːs, -θɪəs) *n. Greek myth.* a king of Athens who sacrificed one of his daughters because the oracle at Delphi said this was the only way to win the war against the Eleusinians.

e·rect (ɪˈrɛkt) *adj.* **1.** upright in posture or position; not bent or leaning: *an erect stance.* **2.** (of an optical image) having the same orientation as the object; not inverted. **3.** *Physiol.* (of the penis, clitoris, or nipples) firm or rigid after swelling with blood, esp. as a result of sexual excitement. **4.** (of plant parts) growing vertically or at right angles to the parts from which they arise. ~*vb.* (*mainly tr.*) **5.** to put up; construct; build. **6.** to raise to an upright position; lift up: *to erect a flagpole.* **7.** to found or form; set up. **8.** (*also intr.*) *Physiol.* to become or cause to become firm or rigid by filling with blood. **9.** to hold up as an ideal; exalt. **10.** *Optics.* to change (an inverted image) to an upright position. **11.** to draw or construct (a line, figure, etc.) on a given line or figure, esp. at right angles to it. [C14: from Latin *ērigere* to set up, from *regere* to control, govern] —**eˈrect+a·ble** *adj.* —**eˈrect+er** *n.* —**eˈrect+ly** *adv.* —**eˈrect+ness** *n.*

e·rec+tile (ɪˈrɛktaɪl) *adj.* **1.** *Physiol.* (of tissues or organs, such as the penis or clitoris) capable of becoming rigid or erect as the result of being filled with blood. **2.** capable of being erected. —**e·rec+til+i·ty** (ɪrɛk'tɪlɪtɪ, ˌi:rɛk-) *n.*

e·rec+tion (ɪ'rɛkʃən) *n.* **1.** the act of erecting or the state of being erected. **2.** something that has been erected; a building or construction. **3.** *Physiol.* the enlarged state or condition of erectile tissues or organs, esp. the penis, when filled with blood. **4.** an erect penis.

e·rec+tor *or* **e·rect+er** (ɪ'rɛktə) *n.* **1.** *Anatomy.* any muscle that raises a part or makes it erect. **2.** a person or thing that erects.

E re+gion *or* **lay+er** *n.* a region of the ionosphere, extending from a height of 90 to about 150 kilometres. It reflects radio waves of medium wavelength. Also called: **Heaviside layer, Kennelly-Heaviside layer.** See also **ionosphere.**

ere+long (ɛə'lɒŋ) *adv. Archaic or poetic.* before long; soon.

er+e·mite ('ɛrɪˌmaɪt) *n.* a Christian hermit or recluse. Compare **coenobite.** [C13: see HERMIT] —**er+e·mit+ic** (ˌɛrɪ'mɪtɪk) or **ˌer+e·'mit·i+cal** *adj.* —**er+e·mit+ism** ('ɛrɪmaɪˌtɪzəm) *n.*

E·ren·burg ('ɛrənbɜ:g; *Russian* ɛrɪn'burk) *n.* a variant spelling of (Ilya Grigorievich) **Ehrenburg.**

e·rep+sin (ɪ'rɛpsɪn) *n.* a mixture of proteolytic enzymes secreted by the small intestine. [C20: *er-*, from Latin *ēripere* to snatch (from *rapere* to seize) + (P)EPSIN]

er+e·thism ('ɛrɪˌθɪzəm) *n.* **1.** *Physiol.* an abnormally high degree of irritability or sensitivity in any part of the body. **2.** *Psychiatry.* an abnormal tendency to become aroused quickly, esp. sexually, as the result of a verbal or psychic stimulus. [C18: from French *éréthisme,* from Greek *erethismos* irritation, from *erethizein* to excite, irritate] —**ˌer+e·'this+mic, ˌer+e·'this+tic,** *or* **ˌer+e·'thit+ic** *adj.*

E·re+van (*Russian* jɪrɪ'van) *n.* a variant spelling of **Yerevan.**

ere+while (ɛə'waɪl) *or* **ere+whiles** *adv. Archaic.* a short time ago; a little while before.

Er+furt (*German* 'ɛrfurt) *n.* an industrial city in SW East Germany: university (1392). Pop.: 203 190 (1975 est.).

erg[1] (ɜ:g) *n.* the cgs unit of work or energy; the work done when the point of application of a force of 1 dyne is displaced through 1 centimetre in the direction of the force. 1 erg is equivalent to 10^{-7} joule. [C19: from Greek *ergon* work]

erg[2] (ɜ:g) *n., pl.* **ergs** *or* **a·reg.** an area of shifting sand dunes in a desert, esp. the Sahara. [C19: from Arabic *'irj*]

er+gas+to+plasm (ɜ:'gæstəˌplæzəm) *n.* a former name for **endoplasmic reticulum.**

er+ga+toc+ra+cy (ˌɜ:gə'tɒkrəsɪ) *n., pl.* **+cies.** *Rare.* government by the workers. [C20: from Greek *ergatēs* a workman, from *ergon* work, deed + -CRACY]

er·go ('ɜ:gəʊ) *sentence connector.* therefore; hence. [C14: from Latin: therefore]

er+go+graph ('ɜ:gəˌgrɑ:f, -ˌgræf) *n.* an instrument that measures and records the amount of work a muscle does during contraction, its rate of fatigue, etc.

er+gom+e·ter (ɜ:'gɒmɪtə) *n.* a dynamometer. [C20: from Greek *ergon* work + -METER]

er+go+nom+ics (ˌɜ:gə'nɒmɪks) *n.* (*functioning as sing.*) the study of the relationship between workers and their environment. U.S. name: **biotechnology.** [C20: from Greek *ergon* work + (ECO)NOMICS] —**ˌer+go+'nom+ic** *adj.* —**er+gon·o+mist** (ɜ:'gɒnəmɪst) *n.*

er+gos+te·rol (ɜ:'gɒstəˌrɒl) *n.* a plant sterol that is converted into vitamin D by the action of ultraviolet radiation. Formula: $C_{28}H_{43}OH$.

er+got ('ɜ:gət, -gɒt) *n.* **1.** a disease of cereals and other grasses caused by ascomycete fungi of the genus *Claviceps,* esp. *C. purpurea,* in which the seeds or grain of the plants are replaced by the spore-containing bodies (sclerotia) of the fungus. **2.** any fungus causing this disease. **3.** the dried sclerotia of *C. purpurea,* used as the source of certain alkaloids used to treat haemorrhage, facilitate uterine contraction in childbirth, etc. [C17: from French: spur (of a cock), of unknown origin]

er+got+ism ('ɜ:gəˌtɪzəm) *n.* ergot poisoning, producing either burning pains and eventually gangrene in the limbs or itching skin and convulsions. Also called: **Saint Anthony's fire.**

Er·hard (*German* 'e:rhart) *n.* **Lud·wig** ('lu:tvɪç). 1897–1977, German statesman: chief architect of the *Wirtschaftswunder* ("economic miracle") of West Germany's recovery after World War II; chancellor (1963–66).

er·ic *or* **er+iach** ('ɛrɪk) *n.* (in old Irish law) a fine paid by a murderer to the family of his victim. Compare **wergild.** [C16: from Irish *eiric*]

er·i+ca ('ɛrɪkə) *n.* any shrub of the ericaceous genus *Erica,* including the heaths and some heathers. [C19: via Latin from Greek *ereikē* heath]

er·i+ca+ceous (ˌɛrɪ'keɪʃəs) *adj.* of, relating to, or belonging to the *Ericaceae,* a family of trees and shrubs with typically bell-shaped flowers: includes heather, rhododendron, azalea, and arbutus. [C19: from New Latin *Erīcāceae,* from Latin *erīca* heath, from Greek *ereikē*]

Er·ic·son *or* **Er·ics·son** ('ɛrɪksᵊn) *n.* **Leif** (li:f). 10th–11th centuries A.D., Norse navigator, who discovered Vinland (?1000), variously identified as the coast of New England, Labrador, or Newfoundland; son of Eric the Red.

Er·ic the Red ('ɛrɪk) *n.* ?940–?1010 A.D., Norse navigator: discovered and colonized Greenland; father of Leif Ericson.

E·rid·a+nus (ɛ'rɪdənəs) *n., Latin genitive* **E·rid·a·ni** (ɛ'rɪdəˌnaɪ). a long twisting constellation in the S hemisphere extending from Orion to Hydrus and containing the first magnitude star Achernar. [from Greek *Eridanos* river in Italy (sometimes identified with the Po) into which, according to legend, Phaëthon fell]

E·rie[1] ('ɪərɪ) *n.* **1.** (*pl.* **E·ries** *or* **E·rie**) a member of a North American Indian people formerly living in the region south of Lake Erie. **2.** the language of this people, belonging to the Iroquoian family.

E·rie[2] ('ɪərɪ) *n.* **1. Lake.** a lake between the U.S. and Canada: the southernmost and the shallowest of the Great Lakes; empties by the Niagara River into Lake Ontario. Area: 25 718 sq. km (9930 sq. miles). **2.** a port in NW Pennsylvania, on Lake Erie. Pop.: 130 084 (1973 est.).

E·rie Ca+nal *n.* a canal in New York State between Albany and Buffalo, linking the Hudson River with Lake Erie. Length: 579 km (360 miles).

e·rig+er+on (ɪ'rɪdʒərən, -'rɪg-) *n.* any plant of the genus *Erigeron,* whose flowers resemble asters but have narrower rays: family *Compositae* (composites). See also **fleabane** (sense 1). [C17: via Latin from Greek, from *ēri* early + *gerōn* old man; from the white down characteristic of some species]

E·rin ('ɪərɪn, 'ɛərɪn) *n.* an archaic or poetic name for **Ireland.** [from Old Irish *Ērinn,* dative of *Ēriu* Ireland]

er·i+na+ceous (ˌɛrɪ'neɪʃəs) *adj.* of, relating to, or resembling hedgehogs. [C18: from Latin *ērināceus* hedgehog]

e·rin+go (ɪ'rɪŋgəʊ) *n., pl.* **+goes** *or* **+gos.** a variant spelling of **eryngo.**

E·rin·y+es (ɪ'rɪnɪˌi:z) *pl. n., sing.* **E·rin+ys** (ɪ'rɪnɪs, ɪ'raɪ-). *Myth.* another name for the **Furies.**

Er·is ('ɛrɪs) *n. Greek myth.* the goddess of discord, sister of Ares.

er+is+tic (ɛ'rɪstɪk) *adj. also* **er+is+ti·cal. 1.** of, relating, or given to controversy or logical disputation, esp. for its own sake. ~*n.* **2.** a person who engages in logical disputes; a controversialist. **3.** the art or practice of logical disputation, esp. if specious. [C17: from Greek *eristikos,* from *erizein* to wrangle, from *eris* discord]

Er·i+tre·a (ˌɛrɪ'treɪə) *n.* a province of N Ethiopia, on the Red Sea: became an Italian colony in 1890; federated with Ethiopia in 1952; secessionist movements have been engaged in civil war with the government since 1974; consists of hot and arid coastal lowlands, rising to the foothills of the Ethiopian highlands. Capital: Asmara. Pop.: 1 837 000 (1970 est.). Area: 117 600 sq. km (45 405 sq. miles). —**ˌEr·i+'tre·an** *n.*

E·ri+van (*Russian* jɪrɪ'van) *n.* a variant spelling of **Yerevan.**

erk (ɜ:k) *n. Brit. slang.* an aircraftman or naval rating. [C20: perhaps a corruption of *A.C.* (aircraftman)]

Er+lang ('ɜ:læŋ) *n.* a unit of traffic intensity in a telephone system equal to the intensity for a specific period when the average number of simultaneous calls is unity. [C20: named after A. K. *Erlang* (died 1929), Danish mathematician]

Er+lan+gen (*German* 'ɛrlaŋən) *n.* a town in SW West Germany, in Bavaria: university (1743). Pop.: 85 100 (1970).

Er·lang·er ('ɜ:læŋə) *n.* **Jo·seph.** 1874–1965, U.S. physiologist. He shared a Nobel prize for medicine (1944) with Gasser for their work on the electrical signs of nervous activity.

Er·len·mey·er flask ('ɜ:lənˌmaɪə) *n.* a flask, for use in a laboratory, with a narrow neck, wide base, and conical shape; conical flask. [C19: named after Emil *Erlenmeyer* (1825–1909), German chemist]

erl+king ('ɜ:lˌkɪŋ) *n. German myth.* a malevolent spirit who carries children off to death. [C18: from German *Erlkönig,* literally: alder king, coined in 1778 by Herder, a mistranslation of Danish *ellerkonge* king of the elves]

Er·man·a·ric (ə'mænərɪk) *n.* died ?375 A.D., king of the Ostrogoths: ruled an extensive empire in eastern Europe, which was overrun by the Huns in the 370s.

er+mine ('ɜ:mɪn) *n., pl.* **+mines** *or* **+mine. 1.** the stoat in northern regions, where it has a white winter coat with a black-tipped tail. **2.** the fur of this animal. **3.** one of the two principal furs used on heraldic shields, conventionally represented by a white field flecked with black ermine tails. Compare **vair. 4.** the dignity or office of a judge, noble, or king. [C12: from Old French *hermine,* from Medieval Latin *Armenius* (*mūs*) Armenian (mouse)]

erne *or* **ern** (ɜ:n) *n.* another name for the (European) **sea eagle.** [Old English *earn;* related to Old Norse *örn* eagle, Old High German *aro* eagle, Greek *ornis* bird]

Erne (ɜ:n) *n.* a river in N central Ireland, rising in County Cavan and flowing north across the border, through **Upper Lough Erne** and **Lower Lough Erne,** and then west to Donegal Bay. Length: about 96 km (60 miles).

Er+nie ('ɜ:nɪ) *n.* (in Britain) a computer that randomly selects winning numbers of Premium Bonds. [C20: acronym of Electronic Random Number Indicator Equipment]

Ernst (*German* ɛrnst) *n.* **Max** (maks). 1891–1976, German painter, resident in France and the U.S., a prominent exponent of dada and surrealism: developed the technique of collage.

e·rode (ɪ'rəʊd) *vb.* **1.** to grind or wear down or away or become ground or worn down or away. **2.** to deteriorate or cause to deteriorate: *jealousy eroded the relationship.* **3.** (*tr.; usually passive*) *Pathol.* to remove (tissue) by ulceration. [C17: from Latin *ērōdere,* from EX-[1] + *rōdere* to gnaw] —**e·'rod+ent** *adj.* —**e·'rod+i·ble** *adj.*

e·rog+e·nous (ɪ'rɒdʒɪnəs) *or* **er·o·gen+ic** (ˌɛrə'dʒɛnɪk) *adj.* **1.** sensitive to sexual stimulation: *erogenous zones of the body.* **2.** arousing sexual desire or giving sexual pleasure. [C19: from Greek *erōs* love, desire + -GENOUS] —**e·ro+ge·ne·i·ty** (ˌɛrədʒɪ'ni:ɪtɪ) *n.*

E·ros[1] ('ɪərɒs, 'ɛrɒs) *n.* **1.** *Greek myth.* the god of love, son of Aphrodite. Roman counterpart: **Cupid. 2.** Also called: **life instinct.** (in Freudian theory) the group of instincts, esp. sexual, that govern acts of self-preservation and that tend towards uninhibited enjoyment of life. Compare **Thanatos.** [Greek: desire, sexual love]

E·ros^{2} ('ɪərɒs, 'ɛrɒs) *n.* an asteroid with a mean distance from the earth of 217 million kilometres, though it may come within 25 million kilometres.

e·rose (ɪ'rəʊs, -'rəʊz) *adj.* jagged or uneven, as though gnawed or bitten: *erose leaves.* [C18: from Latin *ērōsus* eaten away, from *ērōdere* to ERODE] —**e'rose·ly** *adv.*

e·ro·sion (ɪ'rəʊʒən) *n.* **1.** the wearing away of rocks and other deposits on the earth's surface by the action of water, ice, wind, etc. **2.** the act or process of eroding or the state of being eroded. —**e'ro·sive** *or* **e'ro·sion·al** *adj.*

er·o·te·ma (ˌɛrəʊ'ti:mə), **er·o·teme** ('ɛrəʊˌti:m), *or* **er·o·te·sis** (ˌɛrəʊ'ti:sɪs) *n. Rhetoric.* a rhetorical question. [C16: New Latin, from Greek, from *erōtaein* to ask] —**er·o·te·mat·ic** (ɛˌrəʊtɪ'mætɪk) *or* **er·o·tet·ic** (ˌɛrəʊ'tɛtɪk) *adj.*

e·rot·ic (ɪ'rɒtɪk) *adj.* also **e·rot·i·cal. 1.** of, concerning, or arousing sexual desire or giving sexual pleasure. **2.** marked by strong sexual desire or being especially sensitive to sexual stimulation. ~*n.* **3.** a person who has strong sexual desires or is especially responsive to sexual stimulation. [C17: from Greek *erōtikos* of love, from *erōs* love] —**e'rot·i·cal·ly** *adv.*

e·rot·i·ca (ɪ'rɒtɪkə) *n.* explicitly sexual literature or art. [C19: from Greek *erōtika,* neuter plural of *erōtikos* EROTIC]

e·rot·i·cism (ɪ'rɒtɪˌsɪzəm) *or* **er·o·tism** ('ɛrəˌtɪzəm) *n.* **1.** erotic quality or nature. **2.** the use of sexually arousing or pleasing symbolism in literature or art. **3.** sexual excitement or desire. **4.** a tendency to exalt sex. **5.** *Psychol.* an overt display of sexual behaviour.

e·ro·to- *combining form.* denoting erotic desire, excitement, etc.: *erotogenic; erotology.* [from Greek *erōt-, erōs* love]

e·ro·to·gen·ic (ɪˌrɒtə'dʒɛnɪk) *adj.* originating from or causing sexual stimulation; erogenous.

e·rot·ol·o·gy (ˌɛrə'tɒlədʒɪ) *n.* **1.** the study of erotic stimuli and sexual behaviour. **2.** a description of such stimuli and behaviour. —**e·rot·o·log·i·cal** (ˌɛrətə'lɒdʒɪkᵊl) *adj.* —ˌ**e·rot'ol·o·gist** *n.*

e·ro·to·ma·ni·a (ɪˌrɒtəʊ'meɪnɪə) *n.* abnormally strong sexual desire. —**e**ˌ**ro·to'ma·ni·ac** *n.*

err (ɜ:) *vb. (intr.)* **1.** to make a mistake; be incorrect. **2.** to act with bias, esp. favourable bias: *to err on the side of justice.* [C14 *erren* to wander, stray, from Old French *errer,* from Latin *errāre*]

er·ran·cy ('ɛrənsɪ) *n., pl.* **·cies. 1.** the state or an instance of erring or a tendency to err. **2.** *Christianity.* the holding of views at variance with accepted doctrine.

er·rand ('ɛrənd) *n.* **1.** a short trip undertaken to perform a necessary task or commission (esp. in the phrase **run errands**). **2.** the purpose or object of such a trip. [Old English *ǣrende;* related to *ār* messenger, Old Norse *erendi* message, Old High German *ārunti,* Swedish *ärende*]

er·rand boy *n.* (in Britain, esp. formerly) a boy employed by a shopkeeper to deliver goods and run other errands.

er·rant ('ɛrənt) *adj. (often postpositive)* **1.** *Archaic or literary.* wandering in search of adventure. **2.** erring or straying from the right course or accepted standards. [C14: from Old French: journeying, from Vulgar Latin *iterāre* (unattested), from Latin *iter* journey; influenced by Latin *errāre* to ERR] —**'er·rant·ly** *adv.*

er·rant·ry ('ɛrəntrɪ) *n., pl.* **·ries.** the way of life of a knight errant.

er·ra·ta (ɪ'rɑ:tə) *n.* the plural of **erratum.**

Usage. *Errata* is sometimes used to mean a list of errata (in a book). Careful writers and speakers usually treat the word as plural: *the errata for this book are* (not *is*) *complete.*

er·rat·ic (ɪ'rætɪk) *adj.* **1.** irregular in performance, behaviour, or attitude; inconsistent and unpredictable. **2.** having no fixed or regular course; wandering. ~*n.* **3.** a piece of rock that differs in composition, shape, etc., from the rock surrounding it, having been transported from its place of origin, esp. by glacial action. **4.** an erratic person or thing. [C14: from Latin *errāticus,* from *errāre* to wander, ERR] —**er'rat·i·cal·ly** *adv.*

er·ra·tum (ɪ'rɑ:təm) *n., pl.* **·ta** (-tə). **1.** an error in writing or printing. **2.** another name for **corrigendum.** [C16: from Latin: mistake, from *errāre* to ERR]

er·rhine ('ɛraɪn, 'ɛrɪn) *Med.* ~*adj.* **1.** causing nasal secretion. ~*n.* **2.** an errhine drug or agent. [C17: from Greek *errhinos,* from EN-^{2} + *rhis* nose]

Er Rif (ɛə 'rɪf) *n.* a mountainous region of N Morocco, near the Mediterranean coast.

er·ro·ne·ous (ɪ'rəʊnɪəs) *adj.* based on or containing error; mistaken; incorrect. [C14 (in the sense: deviating from what is right), from Latin *errōneus,* from *errāre* to wander] —**er'ro·ne·ous·ly** *adv.* —**er'ro·ne·ous·ness** *n.*

er·ror ('ɛrə) *n.* **1.** a mistake or inaccuracy, as in action or speech: *a typing error.* **2.** an incorrect belief or wrong judgment. **3.** the condition of deviating from accuracy or correctness, as in belief, action, or speech: *he was in error about the train times.* **4.** deviation from a moral standard; wrongdoing: *he saw the error of his ways.* [C13: from Latin, from *errāre* to ERR] —**'er·ror-**ˌ**free** *adj.*

er·ror of clo·sure *n. Surveying.* the amount by which a computed, plotted, or observed quantity or position differs from the true or established one, esp. when plotting a closed traverse. Also called: **closing error.**

ERS *abbrev. for* earnings related supplement.

er·satz ('ɛəzæts, 'ɜ:-) *adj.* **1.** made in imitation of some natural or genuine product; artificial. ~*n.* **2.** an ersatz substance or article. [C20: German, from *ersetzen* to substitute]

Erse (ɜ:s) *n.* **1.** another name for **Gaelic.** ~*adj.* **2.** of or relating to the Gaelic language. [C14: from Lowland Scots *Erisch* Irish; Irish being regarded as the literary form of Gaelic]

Er·skine ('ɜ:skɪn) *n.* **Thom·as,** 1st Baron Erskine. 1750–1823, Scottish lawyer: noted as a defence advocate, esp. in cases involving civil liberties.

erst (ɜ:st) *adv. Archaic.* **1.** long ago; formerly. **2.** at first. [Old English *ǣrest* earliest, superlative of *ǣr* early; see ERE; related to Old High German *ērist,* Dutch *eerst*]

erst·while ('ɜ:stˌwaɪl) *adj.* **1.** former; one-time: *my erstwhile companions.* ~*adv.* **2.** *Archaic.* long ago; formerly.

er·u·bes·cence (ˌɛrʊ'bɛsᵊns) *n.* the process of growing red or a condition of redness. [C18: from Latin *ērubescentia* blushing, from *rubēscere* to grow red, from *ruber* red] —ˌ**er·u'bes·cent** *adj.*

e·ruct (ɪ'rʌkt) *or* **e·ruc·tate** *vb.* **1.** to raise (gas and often a small quantity of acid) from the stomach; belch. **2.** (of a volcano) to pour out (fumes or volcanic matter). [C17: from Latin *ēructāre,* from *ructāre* to belch] —**e·ruc·ta·tion** (ɪˌrʌk'teɪʃən, ˌi:rʌk-) *n.* —**e·ruc·ta·tive** (ɪ'rʌktətɪv) *adj.*

er·u·dite ('ɛrʊˌdaɪt) *adj.* having or showing extensive scholarship; learned. [C15: from Latin *ērudītus,* from *ērudīre* to polish, from EX- + *rudis* unpolished, rough] —**'er·u**ˌ**dite·ly** *adv.* —**er·u·di·tion** (ˌɛrʊ'dɪʃən) *or* **'er·u**ˌ**dite·ness** *n.*

e·rum·pent (ɪ'rʌmpənt) *adj.* bursting out or (esp. of plant parts) developing as though bursting through an overlying structure. [C17: from Latin *ērumpere* to burst forth, from *rumpere* to shatter, burst]

e·rupt (ɪ'rʌpt) *vb.* **1.** to eject (steam, water, and volcanic material such as lava and ash) violently or (of volcanic material, etc.) to be so ejected. **2.** *(intr.)* (of a skin blemish) to appear on the skin; break out. **3.** *(intr.)* (of a tooth) to emerge through the gum and become visible during the normal process of tooth development. **4.** *(intr.)* to burst forth suddenly and violently, as from restraint: *to erupt in anger.* [C17: from Latin *ēruptus* having burst forth, from *ērumpere,* from *rumpere* to burst] —**e'rupt·i·ble** *adj.* —**e'rup·tion** *n.*

e·rup·tive (ɪ'rʌptɪv) *adj.* **1.** erupting or tending to erupt. **2.** resembling or of the nature of an eruption. **3.** (of rocks) formed by solidification of magma; igneous. **4.** (of a disease) characterized by skin eruptions. —**e'rup·tive·ly** *adv.* —**e**ˌ**rup'tiv·i·ty** *or* **e'rup·tive·ness** *n.*

-er·y *or* **-ry** *suffix forming nouns.* **1.** indicating a place of business or some other activity: *bakery; brewery; refinery.* **2.** indicating a class or collection of things: *cutlery; greenery.* **3.** indicating qualities or actions collectively: *snobbery; trickery.* **4.** indicating a practice or occupation: *husbandry.* **5.** indicating a state or condition: *slavery.* [from Old French *-erie;* see -ER^{1}, -Y^{3}]

Er·y·man·thi·an boar (ˌɛrɪ'mænθɪən) *n. Greek myth.* a wild boar that savaged the district around Mount Erymanthus: captured by Hercules as his fourth labour.

Er·y·man·thus (ˌɛrɪ'mænθəs) *n.* **Mount.** a mountain in SW Greece, in the NW Pelopponese. Height: 2224 m (7339 ft.). Modern Greek name: **E·ri·man·thos** (e'rimanθɔs).

e·ryn·go *or* **e·rin·go** (ɪ'rɪŋgəʊ) *n., pl.* **·goes** *or* **·gos.** any umbelliferous plant of the genus *Eryngium,* such as the sea holly, having toothed or lobed leaves. [C16: from Latin *ēryngion* variety of thistle, from Greek *ērungion,* diminutive of *ērungos* thistle]

er·y·sip·e·las (ˌɛrɪ'sɪpɪləs) *n.* an acute streptococcal infectious disease of the skin, characterized by fever, headache, vomiting, and purplish raised lesions, esp. on the face. Also called: **Saint Anthony's fire.** [C16: from Latin, from Greek *erusipelas,* from Greek *erusi-* red + *-pelas* skin] —**er·y·si·pel·a·tous** (ˌɛrɪsɪ'pɛlətəs) *adj.*

er·y·sip·e·loid (ˌɛrɪ'sɪpɪˌlɔɪd) *n.* an infective dermatitis mainly affecting the hands, characterized by inflammation and caused by the microorganism *Erysipelothrix rhusiopathiae* on contaminated meat, poultry, or fish: most prevalent among fishermen and butchers.

er·y·the·ma (ˌɛrɪ'θi:mə) *n. Pathol.* redness of the skin, usually occurring in patches, caused by irritation or injury to the tissue. [C18: from New Latin, from Greek *eruthēma,* from *eruthros* red] —**er·y·the·mat·ic** (ˌɛrɪθɪ'mætɪk), **er·y·them·a·tous** (ˌɛrɪ'θi:mətəs), *or* **er·y'the·mal** *adj.*

e·ryth·rism (ɪ'rɪθrɪzəm) *n.* abnormal red coloration, as in plumage or hair. —**er·y·thris·mal** (ˌɛrɪ'θrɪzməl) *adj.*

e·ryth·rite (ɪ'rɪθraɪt) *n.* **1.** Also called: **cobalt bloom.** a pink to purple secondary mineral consisting of hydrated cobalt arsenate in monoclinic crystalline form. Formula: $Co_3(AsO_4)_2.8H_2O$. **2.** another name for **erythritol.**

e·ryth·ri·tol (ɪ'rɪθrɪˌtɒl) *or* **e·ryth·rite** *n.* a sweet crystalline compound extracted from certain algae and lichens and used in medicine to dilate the blood vessels of the heart; 1,2,3,4-butanetetrol. Formula: $C_4H_{10}O_4$.

e·ryth·ro- *or before a vowel* **e·rythr-** *combining form.* red: *erythrocyte.* [from Greek *eruthros* red]

e·ryth·ro·blast (ɪ'rɪθrəʊˌblæst) *n.* a nucleated cell in bone marrow that develops into an erythrocyte. —**e**ˌ**ryth·ro'blas·tic** *adj.*

e·ryth·ro·blas·to·sis (ɪˌrɪθrəʊblæ'stəʊsɪs) *n.* **1.** the abnormal presence of erythroblasts in the circulating blood. **2.** an anaemic blood disease of a fetus or newborn child, characterized by erythroblasts in the circulating blood: caused by a blood incompatibility between mother and fetus.

e·ryth·ro·cyte (ɪ'rɪθrəʊˌsaɪt) *n.* a blood cell of vertebrates that transports oxygen and carbon dioxide, combined with the red pigment haemoglobin, to and from the tissues. Also called: **red blood cell.** —**e·ryth·ro·cyt·ic** (ɪˌrɪθrəʊˈsɪtɪk) *adj.*

e·ryth·ro·cy·tom·e·ter (ɪˌrɪθrəʊsaɪˈtɒmɪtə) *n.* an instrument for counting the number or measuring the size of red blood cells in a sample of blood. —**e·ˌryth·ro·cy·ˈtom·e·try** *n.*

e·ryth·ro·my·cin (ɪˌrɪθrəʊˈmaɪsɪn) *n.* an antibiotic used in treating infections caused by Gram-positive bacteria. It is obtained from the bacterium *Streptomyces erythreus.* Formula: $C_{37}M_{67}NO_{13}$.

e·ryth·ro·poi·e·sis (ɪˌrɪθrəʊpɔɪˈiːsɪs) *n. Physiol.* the formation of red blood cells. [C19: from ERYTHRO- + Greek *poiēsis* a making, from *poiein* to make] —**e·ˌryth·ro·poi·ˈet·ic** *adj.*

Erz·ge·bir·ge (*German* ˈɛrtsgəˌbɪrgə) *pl. n.* a mountain range on the border between East Germany and Czechoslovakia: formerly rich in mineral resources. Highest peak: Mount Klínovec (Keilberg), 1244 m (4105 ft.). Czech name: **Krušné Hory.** Also called: **Ore Mountains.**

Er·zu·rum (ˈɛəzʊrʊm) *n.* a city in E Turkey: a strategic centre; scene of two major battles against Russian forces (1877 and 1916); important military base, and a closed city to unofficial visitors. Pop.: 162 973 (1975).

Es *the chemical symbol for* einsteinium.

-es *suffix.* **1.** variant of **-s**[1] for nouns ending in *ch, s, sh, z,* postconsonantal *y,* for some nouns ending in a vowel, and nouns in *f* with *v* in the plural: *ashes; heroes; calves.* **2.** variant of **-s**[2] for verbs ending in *ch, s, sh, z,* postconsonantal *y,* or a vowel: *preaches; steadies; echoes.*

E·sa·ki di·ode (ɪˈsɑːkɪ) *n.* another name for **tunnel diode.** [named after L. *Esaki,* its Japanese designer]

E·sau (ˈiːsɔː) *n. Bible.* son of Isaac and Rebecca and twin brother of Jacob, to whom he sold his birthright (Genesis 25).

ESB *abbrev for* electrical stimulation of the brain.

Es·bjerg (*Danish* ˈɛsbjɛr) *n.* a port in SW Denmark, in Jutland on the North Sea: Denmark's chief fishing port. Pop.: 63 906 (1970).

es·ca·drille (ˌɛskəˈdrɪl; *French* ɛskaˈdrij) *n.* **1.** a French squadron of aircraft, esp. in World War I. **2.** a small squadron of ships. [from French: flotilla, from Spanish *escuadrilla,* from *escuadra* SQUADRON]

es·ca·lade (ˌɛskəˈleɪd) *n.* **1.** an assault by the use of ladders, esp. on a fortification. ~*vb.* **2.** to gain access to (a place) by the use of ladders. [C16: from French, from Italian *scalata,* from *scalare* to mount, SCALE[3]] —ˌ**es·ca·ˈlad·er** *n.*

es·ca·late (ˈɛskəˌleɪt) *vb.* to increase or be increased in extent, intensity, or magnitude: *to escalate a war; prices escalated because of inflation.* [C20: back formation from ESCALATOR] —ˌ**es·ca·ˈla·tion** *n.*

Usage. *Escalate,* as in *after the arrival of the troops the violence escalated,* is very commonly used in journalistic contexts in the sense of gradually increasing the intensity or scope of a war, etc. This word is, however, not yet completely accepted as appropriate in formal English.

es·ca·la·tor (ˈɛskəˌleɪtə) *n.* **1.** a moving staircase consisting of stair treads fixed to a conveyor belt, for transporting passengers between levels, esp. between the floors of a building. **2.** short for **escalator clause.** [C20: originally a trademark]

es·ca·la·tor clause *n.* a clause in a contract stipulating an adjustment in wages, prices, etc., in the event of specified changes in conditions, such as a large rise in the cost of living or price of raw materials. Compare **threshold agreement.**

es·cal·lo·ni·a (ˌɛskəˈləʊnɪə) *n.* any evergreen shrub of the South American saxifragaceous genus *Escallonia,* with white or red flowers: cultivated for ornament. [C19: from *Escallon,* eighteenth-century Spanish traveller who discovered it]

es·cal·lop (ɛˈskɒləp, ɛˈskæl-) *n., vb.* another word for **scallop.**

es·ca·lope (ˈɛskəˌlɒp) *n.* a thin slice of meat, usually veal, coated with egg and breadcrumbs, fried, and served with a rich sauce. [from Old French: shell]

es·ca·pade (ˈɛskəˌpeɪd, ˌɛskəˈpeɪd) *n.* **1.** a wild or exciting adventure, esp. one that is mischievous or unlawful; scrape. **2.** any lighthearted or carefree episode; prank; romp. [C17: from French, from Old Italian *scappata,* from Vulgar Latin *excappāre* (unattested) to ESCAPE]

es·cape (ɪˈskeɪp) *vb.* **1.** to get away or break free from (confinements, captors, etc.): *the lion escaped from the zoo.* **2.** to manage to avoid (imminent danger, punishment, evil, etc.): *to escape death.* **3.** (*intr.;* usually foll. by *from*) (of gases, liquids, etc.) to issue gradually, as from a crack or fissure; seep; leak: *water was escaping from the dam.* **4.** (*tr.*) to elude; be forgotten by: *the actual figure escapes me.* **5.** (*tr.*) to be articulated inadvertently or involuntarily: *a roar escaped his lips.* **6.** (*intr.*) (of cultivated plants) to grow wild. ~*n.* **7.** the act of escaping or state of having escaped. **8.** avoidance of injury, harm, etc.: *a narrow escape.* **9. a.** a means or way of escape. **b.** (*as modifier*): *an escape route.* **10.** a means of distraction or relief, esp. from reality or boredom: *angling provides an escape for many city dwellers.* **11.** a gradual outflow; leakage; seepage. **12.** Also called: **escape valve, escape cock.** a valve that releases air, steam, etc., above a certain pressure; relief valve. **13.** a plant that was originally cultivated but is now growing wild. [C14: from Old Northern French *escaper,* from Vulgar Latin *excappāre* (unattested) to escape (literally: to remove one's cloak, hence free oneself), from EX-[1] + Late Latin *cappa* cloak] —**es·ˈcap·a·ble** *adj.* —**es·ˈcap·er** *n.*

es·cape clause *n.* a clause in a contract freeing one of the parties from his obligations in certain circumstances.

es·cap·ee (ɪˌskeɪˈpiː) *n.* a person who has escaped, esp. an escaped prisoner.

es·cape hatch *n.* a means of escape in an emergency, esp. from a submarine.

es·cape mech·an·ism *n. Psychol.* any emotional or mental mechanism that enables a person to avoid acknowledging unpleasant or threatening realities. See also **escapism.**

es·cape·ment (ɪˈskeɪpmənt) *n.* **1.** *Horology.* a mechanism consisting of an escape wheel and anchor, used in timepieces to provide periodic impulses to the pendulum or balance. **2.** any similar mechanism that regulates movement, usually consisting of toothed wheels engaged by rocking levers. **3.** an overflow channel. **4.** *Rare.* an act or means of escaping.

es·cape pipe *n.* a pipe for overflowing water, escaping steam, etc.

es·cape road *n.* a road, usually ending in a pile of sand, provided on a hill for a driver to drive into if his brakes fail or on a bend if he loses control of the turn.

es·cape shaft *n.* a shaft in a mine through which miners can escape if the regular shaft is blocked.

es·cape ve·loc·i·ty *n.* the minimum velocity that a body must have in order to escape from the gravitational field of the earth or other celestial body.

es·cape wheel *n. Horology.* a toothed wheel that engages intermittently with a balance wheel or pendulum, causing the mechanism to oscillate and thereby moving the hands of a clock or watch. Also called: **scapewheel.**

es·cap·ism (ɪˈskeɪpɪzəm) *n.* an inclination to or habit of retreating from unpleasant reality, as through diversion or fantasy. —**es·ˈcap·ist** *n., adj.*

es·ca·pol·o·gist (ˌɛskəˈpɒlədʒɪst) *n.* an entertainer who specializes in freeing himself from confinement. Also called: **escape artist.** —ˌ**es·ca·ˈpol·o·gy** *n.*

es·car·got *French.* (ɛskarˈgo) *n.* a variety of edible snail, usually eaten with a sauce made of melted butter and garlic.

es·carp (ɪˈskɑːp) *n.* **1.** *Fortifications.* the inner side of the ditch separating besiegers and besieged. Compare **counterscarp.** ~*vb.* **2.** a rare word for **scarp** (sense 3). [C17: from French *escarpe;* see SCARP]

es·carp·ment (ɪˈskɑːpmənt) *n.* **1. a.** the long continuous steep face of a ridge or plateau formed by erosion; scarp. **b.** any steep slope, such as one resulting from faulting. **2.** a steep artificial slope made around a fortified place.

Es·caut (ɛsˈko) *n.* the French name for the **Scheldt.**

-es·cent *suffix forming adjectives.* beginning to be, do, show, etc.: *convalescent; luminescent.* [via Old French from Latin *-ēscent-,* stem of present participial suffix of *-ēscere,* ending of inceptive verbs] —**-es·cence** *suffix forming nouns.*

esch·a·lot (ˈɛʃəˌlɒt, ˌɛʃəˈlɒt) *n.* another name for a **shallot.** [C18: from Old French *eschalotte* a little SCALLION]

es·char (ˈɛskɑː) *n.* a dry scab or slough, esp. one following a burn or cauterization of the skin. [C16: from Late Latin *eschara* scab, from Greek *eskhara* hearth, pan of hot coals (which could inflict burns); see SCAR[1]]

es·cha·rot·ic (ˌɛskəˈrɒtɪk) *Med.* ~*adj.* **1.** capable of producing an eschar. ~*n.* **2.** a caustic or corrosive agent.

es·cha·tol·o·gy (ˌɛskəˈtɒlədʒɪ) *n.* the branch of theology or biblical exegesis concerned with the end of the world. [C19: from Greek *eskhatos* last] —**es·cha·to·log·i·cal** (ˌɛskətəˈlɒdʒɪkᵊl) *adj.* —ˌ**es·cha·to·ˈlog·i·cal·ly** *adv.* —ˌ**es·cha·ˈtol·o·gist** *n.*

es·cheat (ɪsˈtʃiːt) *Law.* ~*n.* **1.** (before 1926) the reversion of property to the Crown in the absence of legal heirs. **2.** (in feudal times) the reversion of property to the feudal lord in the absence of legal heirs or upon outlawry of the tenant. **3.** the property so reverting. ~*vb.* **4.** to take (land) by escheat or (of land) to revert by escheat. [C14: from Old French *eschete,* from *escheoir* to fall to the lot of, from Late Latin *excadere* (unattested), from Latin *cadere* to fall] —**es·ˈcheat·a·ble** *adj.* —**es·ˈcheat·age** *n.*

es·chew (ɪsˈtʃuː) *vb.* (*tr.*) to keep clear of or abstain from (something disliked, injurious, etc.); shun; avoid. [C14: from Old French *eschiver,* of Germanic origin; compare Old High German *skiuhan* to frighten away; see SHY[1], SKEW] —**es·ˈchew·al** *n.* —**es·ˈchew·er** *n.*

Es·cof·fier (*French* ɛskɔˈfje) *n.* **Au·guste** (oˈgyst). 1846–1935, French chef at the Savoy Hotel, London (1890–99).

es·co·lar (ˌɛskəˈlɑː) *n., pl.* **·lars** *or* **·lar.** any slender spiny-finned fish of the family *Gempylidae,* of warm and tropical seas: similar and closely related to the scombroid fishes. Also called: **snake mackerel.** [from Spanish: SCHOLAR; so called from the rings round its eyes, suggestive of spectacles]

Es·co·ri·al (ˌɛskɒrɪˈɑːl, ɛˈskɔːrɪəl) *or* **Es·cu·ri·al** *n.* a village in central Spain, northwest of Madrid: site of an architectural complex containing a monastery, palace, and college, built by Philip II between 1563 and 1584.

es·cort *n.* (ˈɛskɔːt). **1.** one or more persons, soldiers, vehicles, etc., accompanying another or others for protection or guidance or as a mark of honour. **2.** a man or youth who accompanies a woman or girl: *he was her escort for the evening.* **3. a.** a person, esp. a young woman, who may be hired to accompany another for entertainment, etc. **b.** (*as modifier*): *an escort agency.* ~*vb.* (ɪsˈkɔːt). **4.** (*tr.*) to accompany or attend as an escort. [C16: from French *escorte,* from Italian *scorta,* from *scorgere* to guide, from Latin *corrigere* to straighten; see CORRECT]

e·scribe (ɪˈskraɪb) *vb.* (*tr.*) to draw (a circle) so that it is tangential to one side of a triangle and to the other two sides produced. [C16 (meaning: to write out): from EX-[1] + Latin *scribere* to write]

es·cri·toire (ˌɛskrɪˈtwɑː) *n.* a writing desk with compartments and drawers, concealed by a hinged flap, on a chest of drawers or plain stand. [C18: from French, from Medieval Latin *scriptōrium* writing room in a monastery, from Latin *scrībere* to write]

es+crow ('ɛskrəʊ, ɛ'skrəʊ) *n. Law.* **1.** money, goods, or a written document, such as a contract bond, delivered to a third party and held by him pending fulfilment of some condition. **2.** the state or condition of being an escrow (esp. in the phrase **in escrow**). ~*vb. (tr.)* **3.** to place (a document, etc.) in escrow. [C16: from Old French *escroe*, of Germanic origin; see SCREED, SHRED, SCROLL]

es+cu+age ('ɛskjʊɪdʒ) *n.* (in medieval Europe) another word for **scutage.** [C16: from Old French, from *escu* shield, from Latin *scūtum*]

es+cu+do (ɛ'skuːdəʊ; *Portuguese* ɪ'ʃkudu) *n., pl.* **+dos** (-dəʊz; *Portuguese* -duʃ). **1.** the standard monetary unit of Portugal, divided into 100 centavos. **2.** the standard monetary unit of Chile, divided into 100 centesimos. **3.** an old Spanish silver coin worth 10 reals. [C19: Spanish, literally: shield, from Latin *scūtum*]

es+cu+lent ('ɛskjʊlənt) *n.* **1.** any edible substance. ~*adj.* **2.** edible. [C17: from Latin *ēsculentus* good to eat, from *ēsca* food, from *edere* to eat]

Es+cu+ri·al (ɛˌskjʊərɪ'ɑːl, ɛ'skjʊərɪəl) *n.* a variant of **Escorial.**

es+cutch+eon (ɪ'skʌtʃən) *n.* **1.** a shield, esp. a heraldic one that displays a coat of arms. **2.** Also called: **escutcheon plate.** a plate or shield that surrounds a keyhole, door handle, light switch, etc., esp. an ornamental one protecting a door or wall surface. **3.** the place on the stern or transom of a vessel where the name is shown. **4. blot on one's escutcheon.** a stain on one's honour. [C15: from Old Northern French *escuchon*, ultimately from Latin *scūtum* shield] —**es+'cutch+eoned** *adj.*

Esd. *Bible. abbrev. for* Esdras.

Es+dra+e·lon (ˌɛsdreɪ'iːlɒn) *n.* a plain in N Israel, east of Mount Carmel. Also called: (Plain of) **Jezreel.**

Es·dras ('ɛzdræs) *n.* **1.** either of two books of the Apocrypha, **I** and **II Esdras,** called **III** and **IV Esdras** in the Douay Bible. **2.** either of two books of the Douay Bible Old Testament, **I** and **II Esdras,** corresponding to the books of Ezra and Nehemiah in the Authorized Version.

ESE *abbrev. for* east-southeast.

-ese *suffix forming adjectives and nouns.* indicating place of origin, language, or style: *Cantonese; Japanese; journalese.*

es+em+plas+tic (ˌɛsɛm'plæstɪk) *adj. Literature.* making into one; unifying. [C19 (first used by Samuel Taylor Coleridge): from Greek *es, eis* into + *em,* from *hen,* neuter of *heis* one + -PLASTIC]

es+er+ine ('ɛsəriːn, -rɪn) *n.* another name for **physostigmine.** [C19: *eser-*, of African origin + -INE²]

Eş+fa+han (ˌɛʃfə'hɑːn) *n.* a variant spelling of **Isfahan.**

E·sher ('iːʃə) *n.* a town in SE England, in NE Surrey near London: racecourse. Pop.: 64 186 (1971).

es+ker ('ɛskə) *or* **es+kar** ('ɛskɑː, -kə) *n.* a long winding ridge of gravel, sand, etc., originally deposited by a meltwater stream running under a glacier. Also called: **os.** [C19: from Old Irish *escir* ridge]

E·skils+tu+na (*Swedish* 'ɛskilstuːna) *n.* an industrial city in SE Sweden. Pop.: 94 076 (1970).

Es+ki+mo ('ɛskɪˌməʊ) *n.* **1.** (*pl.* **+mos** *or* **+mo**) a member of a group of peoples inhabiting N Canada, Greenland, Alaska, and E Siberia, having a material culture adapted to an extremely cold climate. **2.** the language of these peoples. **3.** a family of languages that includes Eskimo and Aleut. ~*adj.* **4.** relating to, denoting, or characteristic of the Eskimos. ~Former spelling: **Esquimau.** [C18 *Esquimawes:* related to Abnaki *esquimantsic* eaters of raw flesh]

Es+ki+mo dog *n.* a large powerful breed of sled dog with a long thick coat and curled tail.

Es+ki+şe·hir (*Turkish* ɛs'kiʃɛˌhir) *n.* an industrial city in NW Turkey: founded around hot springs in Byzantine times. Pop.: 259 952 (1975).

Es·ky ('ɛskɪ) *n., pl.* **·kies.** (*sometimes not cap.*) *Austral. trademark.* a portable insulated container for keeping food and drink cool. [C20: from ESKIMO, alluding to the Eskimos' cold habitat]

E.S.N. *abbrev. for* educationally subnormal; used to designate a person of limited intelligence who needs special schooling.

e·soph·a·gus (iː'sɒfəgəs) *n., pl.* **+gi** (-ˌdʒaɪ) *or* **+gus·es.** the U.S. spelling of **oesophagus.** —**e·soph·a·ge·al** (iːˌsɒfə'dʒiːəl) *adj.*

es·o+ter+ic (ˌɛsəʊ'tɛrɪk) *adj.* **1.** restricted to or intended for an enlightened or initiated minority, esp. because of abstruseness or obscurity: *an esoteric cult.* Compare **exoteric. 2.** difficult to understand; abstruse: *an esoteric statement.* **3.** not openly admitted; private: *esoteric aims.* [C17: from Greek *esōterikos*, from *esōterō* inner] —ˌ**es·o+'ter·i+cal+ly** *adv.* —ˌ**es·o+'ter·i+ˌcism** *n.*

E.S.P. *abbrev. for* extrasensory perception.

esp. *abbrev. for* especially.

es+pa+drille (ˌɛspə'drɪl) *n.* a light shoe with a canvas upper, esp. with a braided cord sole. [C19: from French, from Provençal *espardilho*, diminutive of *espart* ESPARTO; so called from the use of esparto for the soles of such shoes]

es+pal+ier (ɪ'spæljə) *n.* **1.** an ornamental shrub or fruit tree that has been trained to grow flat, as against a wall. **2.** the trellis, framework, or arrangement of stakes on which such plants are trained. **3.** the method used to produce such plants. ~*vb.* **4.** (*tr.*) to train (a plant) on an espalier. [C17: from French: trellis, from Old Italian: shoulder supports, from *spalla* shoulder, from Late Latin SPATULA]

Es+pa+ña (es'paɲa) *n.* the Spanish name for **Spain.**

es+par+to *or* **es+par+to grass** (ɛ'spɑːtəʊ) *n., pl.* **+tos.** any of various grasses, esp. *Stipa tenacissima* of S Europe and N Africa, that yield a fibre used to make ropes, mats, etc. [C18: from Spanish, via Latin from Greek *sparton* rope made of rushes, from *spartos* a kind of rush]

es+pe+cial (ɪ'spɛʃəl) *adj.* (*prenominal*) **1.** unusual; notable; exceptional: *he paid especial attention to her that evening.* **2.** applying to one person or thing in particular; not general; specific; peculiar: *he had an especial dislike of relatives.* [C14: from Old French, from Latin *speciālis* individual; see SPECIAL] —**es+'pe+cial+ly** *adv.*

Usage. *Especial* and *especially* have a more limited use than *special* and *specially. Special* is always used in preference to *especial* when the sense is one of being out of the ordinary: *a special lesson; he has been specially trained. Special* is also used when something is referred to as being for a particular purpose: *the word was specially underlined for you.* Where an idea of preeminence or individuality is involved, either *especial* or *special* may be used: *he is my especial* (or *special*) *friend; he is especially* (or *specially*) *good at his job.* In informal English, however, *special* is usually preferred in all contexts.

es+per+ance ('ɛspərəns) *n. Archaic.* hope or expectation. [C15: from Old French, from Vulgar Latin *sperantia* (unattested), from Latin *spērāre* to hope, from *spēs* hope]

Es+pe+ran+to (ˌɛspə'ræntəʊ) *n.* an artificial language based on words common to the chief European languages, invented in 1887. [C19: literally: the one who hopes, pseudonym of Dr. L. L. Zamenhof (1859–1917), Polish philologist who invented it] —ˌ**Es+pe+'ran+tist** *n., adj.*

es+pi·al (ɪ'spaɪəl) *n. Archaic.* **1.** the act or fact of being seen or discovered. **2.** the act of noticing. **3.** the act of spying upon; secret observation.

es+pi·o+nage (ˌɛspɪə'nɑːʒ, 'ɛspɪəˌnɑːʒ, 'ɛspɪənɪdʒ) *n.* **1.** the systematic use of spies to obtain secret information, esp. by governments to discover military or political secrets. **2.** the act or practice of spying. [C18: from French *espionnage*, from *espionner* to spy, from *espion* spy, from Old Italian *spione*, of Germanic origin; compare German *spähen* to SPY]

Es+pí+ri+to San+to (*Portuguese* is'piritu 'sɑ̃ntu) *n.* a state of E Brazil, on the Atlantic: swampy coastal plain with mountains in the west; heavily forested. Capital: Vitória. Pop.: 1 599 333 (1970). Area: 45 597 sq. km (17 782 sq. miles).

Es+pi+ri+tu San+to (ɛs'pɪrɪtuː 'sæntəʊ) *n.* an island in the SW Pacific: the largest and westernmost of the New Hebrides Islands. Area: 4856 sq. km (1875 sq. miles).

es+pla+nade (ˌɛsplə'neɪd) *n.* **1.** a long open level stretch of ground for walking along, esp. beside the sea shore. Compare **promenade** (sense 1). **2.** an open area in front of a fortified place, in which attackers are exposed to the defenders' fire. [C17: from French, from Old Italian *spianata*, from *spianare* to make level, from Latin *explānāre*; see EXPLAIN]

Es+poo (*Finnish* 'ɛspoː) *n.* a city in S Finland. Pop.: 110 107 (1973 est.).

es+pous+al (ɪ'spaʊzᵊl) *n.* **1.** adoption or support: *an espousal of new beliefs.* **2.** (*sometimes pl.*) *Archaic.* a marriage or betrothal ceremony.

es+pouse (ɪ'spaʊz) *vb.* (*tr.*) **1.** to adopt or give support to (a cause, ideal, etc.): *to espouse socialism.* **2.** *Archaic.* (esp. of a man) to take as spouse; marry. [C15: from Old French *espouser*, from Latin *spōnsāre* to affiance, espouse] —**es+'pous+er** *n.*

es+pres+so (ɛ'sprɛsəʊ) *n., pl.* **+sos. 1.** strong coffee made by forcing steam or boiling water through ground coffee beans. **2.** an apparatus for making coffee in this way. [Italian, short for *caffè espresso*, literally: pressed coffee]

es+prit (ɛ'spriː) *n.* spirit and liveliness, esp. in wit. [C16: from French, from Latin *spīritus* a breathing, SPIRIT]

es+prit de corps (ɛ'spriː də 'kɔː; *French* ɛsprid 'kɔːr) *n.* consciousness of and pride in belonging to a particular group; the sense of shared purpose and fellowship.

es·py (ɪ'spaɪ) *vb.* **·pies, +py+ing, +pied.** (*tr.*) to catch sight of or perceive (something distant or previously unnoticed); detect: *to espy a ship on the horizon.* [C14: from Old French *espier* to SPY, of Germanic origin] —**es+'pi+er** *n.*

Esq. *abbrev. for* esquire: used esp. in correspondence.

-esque *suffix forming adjectives.* indicating a specified character, manner, style, or resemblance: *picturesque; Romanesque; statuesque; Chaplinesque.* [via French from Italian *-esco*, of Germanic origin; compare -ISH]

Es+qui+line ('ɛskwəˌlaɪn) *n.* one of the seven hills on which ancient Rome was built.

Es+qui+mau ('ɛskɪˌməʊ) *n., pl.* **+maus** *or* **+mau,** *adj.* a former spelling of **Eskimo.**

es+quire (ɪ'skwaɪə) *n.* **1.** *Chiefly Brit.* a title of respect, usually abbreviated *Esq.*, placed after a man's name. **2.** (in medieval England) the attendant and shield bearer of a knight, subsequently often knighted himself. **3.** *Rare.* a male escort. ~*vb.* **4.** (*tr.*) *Rare.* to escort (a woman). [C15: from Old French *escuier*, from Late Latin *scūtārius* shield bearer, from Latin *scūtum* shield]

ESR *abbrev. for* electron spin resonance.

ESRO ('ɛzrəʊ) *n. acronym for* European Space Research Organization.

-ess *suffix forming nouns.* indicating a female: *actress; lioness.* [via Old French from Late Latin *-issa*, from Greek]

Es+sa+oui+ra (ˌɛsə'wɪərə) *n.* a port in SW Morocco on the Atlantic. Pop.: 30 061 (1971). Former name (until 1956): **Mogador.**

es+say *n.* ('ɛseɪ; *defs. 2,3 also* ɛ'seɪ). **1.** a short literary composition dealing with a subject analytically or speculatively. **2.** an attempt or endeavour; effort. **3.** a test or trial. ~*vb.* (ɛ'seɪ). (*tr.*) **4.** to attempt or endeavour; try. **5.** to test or try out. [C15: from Old French *essaier* to attempt, from *essai* an attempt, from Late Latin *exagium* a weighing, from Latin *agere* to do, compel, influenced by *exigere* to investigate]

es+say+ist ('ɛseɪɪst) *n.* a person who writes essays.

Es+sen (*German* 'ɛsᵊn) *n.* a city in W West Germany, in North Rhine-Westphalia: the leading industrial centre of the Ruhr, with extensive iron and steel factories. Pop.: 674 000 (1974 est.).

es+sence ('ɛsᵊns) *n.* **1.** the characteristic or intrinsic feature of a thing, which determines its identity; fundamental nature. **2.** the most distinctive element of a thing: *the essence of a problem.* **3.** a perfect or complete form of something, esp. a person who typifies an abstract quality: *he was the essence of gentility.* **4.** *Philosophy.* the unchanging inward nature of something as opposed to its attributes and existence. **5.** *Theol.* an immaterial or spiritual entity. **6. a.** the constituent of a plant, usually an oil, alkaloid, or glycoside, that determines its chemical or pharmacological properties. **b.** an alcoholic solution of such a substance. **7.** a rare word for **perfume.** [C14: from Medieval Latin *essentia*, from Latin: the being (of something), from *esse* to be]

Es+sene ('ɛsi:n, ɛ'si:n) *n. Judaism.* a member of an ascetic sect that flourished in Palestine from the second century B.C. to the second century A.D., living in strictly organized communities. —**Es+se+ni·an** (ɛ'si:nɪən) *or* **Es+sen+ic** (ɛ'sɛnɪk) *adj.*

es+sen+tial (ɪ'sɛnʃəl) *adj.* **1.** vitally important; absolutely necessary. **2.** basic; fundamental: *the essential feature.* **3.** completely realized; absolute; perfect: *essential beauty.* **4.** *Biochem.* (of an amino acid) necessary for the normal growth of an organism but not synthesized by the organism. **5.** derived from or relating to an extract of a plant, drug, etc.: *an essential oil.* **6.** *Music.* denoting or relating to a note that belongs to the fundamental harmony of a chord or piece. ~*n.* **7.** something fundamental or indispensable: *a sharp eye is an essential for a printer.* **8.** *Music.* an essential note. —**es+sen+ti·al+i·ty** (ɪ,sɛnʃɪ'ælɪtɪ) *or* **es+'sen+tial+ness** *n.* —**es+'sen+tial+ly** *adv.*

es+sen+tial+ism (ɪ'sɛnʃə,lɪzəm) *n.* **1.** *Philosophy.* the doctrine that material objects have an essence that is distinguishable from their perceivable attributes and their existence. **2.** the doctrine that education should concentrate on teaching basic skills and encouraging intellectual self-discipline. —**es+'sen+tial+ist** *n.*

es+sen+tial oil *n.* any of various volatile organic oils present in plants, usually containing terpenes and esters and having the odour or flavour of the plant from which they are extracted: used in flavouring and perfumery. Compare **fixed oil.** See also **oleoresin.**

Es+se·qui+bo (,ɛsɪ'kwi:bəʊ) *n.* a river in Guyana, rising near the Brazilian border and flowing north to the Atlantic: drains over half of Guyana. Length: 1014 km (630 miles).

Es+sex[1] ('ɛsɪks) *n.* **1.** a county of SE England, on the North Sea and the Thames estuary. Administrative centre: Chelmsford. Pop.: 1 426 200 (1976 est.). Area: 3957 sq. km (1528 sq. miles). **2.** an Anglo-Saxon kingdom that in the early 7th century A.D. comprised the modern county of Essex and much of Hertfordshire and Surrey. By the late 8th century, Essex had become a dependency of the kingdom of Mercia.

Es·sex[2] ('ɛsɪks) *n.* **Earl of,** title of *Robert Devereux.* ?1566–1601, English soldier and favourite of Queen Elizabeth I; executed for treason.

es+so+nite ('ɛsə,naɪt) *n.* a variant spelling of **hessonite.**

Es+sonne (*French* ɛ'sɔn) *n.* a department of N France, south of Paris in Île-de-France region: formed in 1964. Capital: Ivry. Pop.: 932 619 (1975). Area: 1811 sq. km (706 sq. miles).

E.S.T. *abbrev. for:* **1.** (in the U.S.) Eastern Standard Time. **2.** electric-shock treatment.

est. *abbrev. for:* **1.** Also: **estab.** established. **2.** *Law.* estate. **3.** estimate(d). **4.** estuary.

-est[1] *suffix.* forming the superlative degree of adjectives and adverbs: *shortest; fastest.* [Old English *-est, -ost*]

-est[2] *or* **-st** *suffix.* forming the archaic second person singular present and past indicative tense of verbs: *thou goest; thou hadst.* [Old English *-est, -ast*]

es+tab+lish (ɪ'stæblɪʃ) *vb.* (*tr.*) **1.** to make secure or permanent in a certain place, condition, job, etc.: *to establish one's usefulness; to establish a house.* **2.** to create or set up (an organization, etc.) on or as if on a permanent basis: *to establish a company.* **3.** to prove correct or free from doubt; validate: *to establish a fact.* **4.** to cause (a principle, theory, etc.) to be widely or permanently accepted: *to establish a precedent.* **5.** to give (a Church) the status of a national institution. **6.** *Cards.* to make winners of (the remaining cards of a suit) by forcing out opponents' top cards. [C14: from Old French *establir*, from Latin *stabilīre* to make firm, from *stabilis* STABLE[2]] —**es+'tab+lish+er** *n.*

Es+tab+lished Church *n.* a Church that is officially recognized as a national institution, esp. the Church of England.

es+tab+lish+ment (ɪ'stæblɪʃmənt) *n.* **1.** the act of establishing or state of being established. **2. a.** a business organization or other large institution. **b.** the place where a business is carried on. **3.** the staff and equipment of a commercial or other organization. **4.** any large organization, institution, or system. **5.** a household or place of residence. **6.** a body of employees or servants.

Es+tab+lish+ment (ɪ'stæblɪʃmənt) *n.* **the.** a group or class of people having institutional authority within a society, esp. those who control the civil service, the government, the armed forces, and the Church: usually identified with a conservative outlook.

es+tab+lish+men+tar+i·an (ɪ,stæblɪʃmən'tɛərɪən) *adj.* **1.** denoting or relating to an Established Church, esp. the Church of England. **2.** denoting or relating to the principle of a Church being officially recognized as a national institution. ~*n.* **3.** an upholder of this principle, esp. as applied to the Church of England. —**es+,tab+lish+men+'tar·i·an+ism** *n.*

es+ta+mi+net *French.* (ɛstami'nɛ) *n.* a small café, bar, or bistro, esp. a shabby one. [C19: from French, perhaps from Walloon dialect *staminet* manger]

es+tan+ci·a (ɪ'stænsɪə; *Spanish* e'stanθja) *n.* (in Spanish America) a large estate or cattle ranch. [C18: from American Spanish, from Spanish: dwelling, from Vulgar Latin *stantia* (unattested) a remaining, from Latin *stāre* to stand]

es+tate (ɪ'steɪt) *n.* **1.** a large piece of landed property, esp. in the country. **2.** *Chiefly Brit.* a large area of property development, esp. of new houses or (**trading estate**) of factories. **3.** *Property law.* **a.** property or possessions. **b.** the nature of interest that a person has in land or other property, esp. in relation to the right of others. **c.** the total extent of the real and personal property of a deceased person or bankrupt. **4.** Also called: **estate of the realm.** an order or class of persons in a political community, regarded collectively as a part of the body politic: usually regarded as being the lords temporal (peers), lords spiritual and commons. See also **States General, fourth estate.** **5.** state, period, or position in life, esp. with regard to wealth or social standing: *youth's estate; a poor man's estate.* **6.** *Archaic.* pomp; ceremony; grandeur. [C13: from Old French *estat*, from Latin *status* condition, STATE]

es+tate a·gent *n.* **1.** *Brit.* an agent concerned with the valuation, management, lease, and sale of property. Usual U.S. name: **realtor.** **2.** the administrator of a large landed property, acting on behalf of its owner; estate manager.

es+tate car *n. Brit.* a car with a comparatively long body containing a large carrying space, reached through a rear door: usually the back seats can be folded forward to increase the carrying space. Also called (esp. U.S.): **station wagon.**

es+tate du·ty *n.* another name for **death duty.**

Es+tates Gen+er+al *n.* See **States General.**

Es·te ('ɛstɛ) *n.* a noble family of Italy founded by Alberto Azzo II (996–1097), who was invested with the town of Este in NE Italy as a fief of the Holy Roman Empire. The family governed Ferrara (13th–16th centuries), Modena, and Reggio (13th–18th centuries).

es+teem (ɪ'sti:m) *vb.* (*tr.*) **1.** to have great respect or high regard for: *to esteem a colleague.* **2.** *Formal.* to judge or consider; deem: *to esteem an idea improper.* ~*n.* **3.** high regard or respect; good opinion. **4.** *Archaic.* judgment; opinion. [C15: from Old French *estimer*, from Latin *aestimāre* ESTIMATE]

es+ter ('ɛstə) *n. Chem.* any of a class of compounds produced by reaction between acids and alcohols with the elimination of water. Esters with low molecular weights, such as ethyl acetate, are usually volatile fragrant liquids; fats are solid esters. [C19: from German, probably a contraction of *Essigäther* acetic ether, from *essig* vinegar (ultimately from Latin *acētum*) + *äther* ETHER]

es+ter+ase ('ɛstə,reɪs, -,reɪz) *n.* any of a group of enzymes that hydrolyse esters into alcohols and acids.

es+ter·i+fy (ɛ'stɛrə,faɪ) *vb.* **+fies, +fy+ing, +fied.** *Chem.* to change or cause to change into an ester. —**es+,ter·i+fi+'ca+tion** *n.*

Esth. *Bible. abbrev. for* Esther.

Es+ther ('ɛstə) *n. Old Testament.* **1.** a beautiful Jewess who became queen of Persia and saved her people from massacre. **2.** the book in which this episode is recounted.

es+the·si·a (i:s'θi:zɪə) *n.* a U.S. spelling of **aesthesia.**

es+thete ('i:sθi:t) *n.* a U.S. spelling of **aesthete.** —**es+thet+ic** (ɛs'θɛtɪk) *or* **es+'thet·i·cal** *adj.* —**es+'thet·i·cal+ly** *adv.* —**es+the·ti+cian** (,i:sθɪ'tɪʃən) —**es+'thet·i+,cism** *n.* —**es+'thet+ics** *n.*

Es+tho+ni·a (ɛ'stəʊnɪə, ɛ'sθəʊ-) *n.* See **Estonian Soviet Socialist Republic.**

Es·tienne *or* **É·tienne** (*French* e'tjɛn) *n.* a family of French printers, scholars, and dealers in books, including **Hen·ri** (ã'ri), ?1460–1520, who founded the printing business in Paris, his son **Ro·bert** (rɔ'bɛ:r), 1503–59, and his grandson **Hen·ri,** 1528–98.

es+ti+ma·ble ('ɛstɪməbᵊl) *adj.* **1.** worthy of respect; deserving of admiration: *my estimable companion.* **2.** *Rare.* (of amounts, numbers, etc.) capable of being calculated. —**'es+ti+ma·ble+ness** *n.* —**'es+ti+ma·bly** *adv.*

es+ti+mate *vb.* ('ɛstɪ,meɪt). **1.** to form an approximate idea of (distance, size, cost, etc.); calculate roughly; gauge. **2.** (*tr.; may take a clause as object*) to form an opinion about; judge: *to estimate one's chances.* **3.** to submit (an approximate price) for (a job) to a prospective client. **4.** (*tr.*) to derive a statistical estimate for (a population parameter). ~*n.* ('ɛstɪmɪt). **5.** an approximate calculation. **6.** a statement indicating the likely charge for or cost of certain work. **7.** a judgment; appraisal; opinion. [C16: from Latin *aestimāre* to assess the worth of, of obscure origin] —**'es+ti+,ma+tor** *n.* —**'es+ti+ma+tive** *adj.*

es+ti+ma+tion (,ɛstɪ'meɪʃən) *n.* **1.** a considered opinion; judgment: *what is your estimation of the situation?* **2.** esteem; respect. **3.** the act of estimating.

e·stip·u·late (ɪ'stɪpjʊlɪt, -,leɪt) *adj.* a variant spelling of **exstipulate.**

es+ti+val (i:'staɪvᵊl, 'ɛstɪ-) *adj.* the usual U.S. spelling of **aestival.**

es+ti+vate ('i:stɪ,veɪt, 'ɛs-) *vb.* (*intr.*) the usual U.S. spelling of **aestivate.** —**'es+ti+,va+tor** *n.*

es+ti+va+tion (ˌiːstɪˈveɪʃən, ˌɛs-) *n.* the usual U.S. spelling of **aestivation.**

Es+to+ni+an *or* **Es+tho+ni+an** (ɛˈstəʊnɪən, ɛˈsθəʊ-) *adj.* **1.** of, relating to, or characteristic of the Estonian SSR, its people, or their language. ~*n.* **2.** an official language of the Estonian SSR, along with Russian: belongs to the Finno-Ugric family. **3.** a native or inhabitant of Estonia.

Es+to+ni+an So+vi+et So+cial+ist Re+pub+lic *n.* a constituent republic of the W Soviet Union, on the Gulf of Finland and the Baltic: low-lying with many lakes and forests. As **Es+to+ni+a** or **Es+tho+ni+a** it was under Scandinavian and Teutonic rule from the 13th century to 1721, when it passed to Russia: it was an independent republic from 1920 to 1940, when it was annexed by the Soviet Union. Capital: Tallinn. Pop.: 1 356 079 (1970). Area: 45 100 sq. km (17 410 sq. miles).

es+top (ɪˈstɒp) *vb.* **+tops, +top+ping, +topped.** (*tr.*) **1.** *Law.* to preclude by estoppel. **2.** *Archaic.* to stop. [C15: from Old French *estoper* to plug, ultimately from Latin *stuppa* tow; see STOP] —**es+ˈtop+page** *n.*

es+top+pel (ɪˈstɒpəl) *n. Law.* a rule of evidence whereby a person is precluded from denying the truth of a statement of facts he has previously asserted. See also **conclusion.** [C16: from Old French *estoupail* plug, from *estoper* to stop up; see ESTOP]

es+to+vers (ɛˈstəʊvəz) *pl. n. Law.* necessaries allowed by law to tenant of land, esp. wood for fuel and repairs. [C15: from Anglo-French, plural of *estover*, n. use of Old French *estovoir* to be necessary, from Latin *est opus* there is need]

es+trade (ɪsˈtrɑːd) *n.* a dais or raised platform. [C17: from French, from Spanish *estrado* carpeted floor, from Latin: STRATUM]

es+tra+di+ol (ˌɛstrəˈdaɪɒl, ˌiːstrə-) *n.* the usual U.S. spelling of **oestradiol.**

es+tra+gon (ˈɛstrəˌgɒn) *n.* another name for **tarragon.**

es+trange (ɪˈstreɪndʒ) *vb.* (*tr.*) to antagonize or lose the affection of (someone previously friendly); alienate. [C15: from Old French *estranger*, from Late Latin *extrāneāre* to treat as a stranger, from Latin *extrāneus* foreign; see STRANGE] —**es+ˈtrange+ment** *n.* —**es+ˈtrang+er** *n.*

es+tray (ɪˈstreɪ) *n. Law.* a stray domestic animal of unknown ownership. [C16: from Anglo-French, from Old French *estraier* to STRAY]

es+treat (ɪˈstriːt) *Law.* ~*n.* **1.** a true copy of or extract from a court record. ~*vb.* (*tr.*) **2.** to enforce (a recognizance that has been forfeited) by sending an extract of the court record to the proper authority. [C14: from Old French *estraite*, feminine of *estrait* extracted, from *estraire* to EXTRACT]

Es+tre+ma+du+ra (*Portuguese* ˌɪʃtrəməˈdurə) *n.* **1.** a region of W Spain: arid and sparsely populated except in the valleys of the Tagus and Guadiana Rivers. Area: 41 593 sq. km (16 059 sq. miles). Spanish name: **Extremadura. 2.** a province in Portugal around Lisbon. Pop.: 1 600 000 (1970 est.). Area: 5348 sq. km (2065 sq. miles).

es+trin (ˈɛstrɪn, ˈiːstrɪn) *n.* the U.S. spelling of **oestrin.**

es+tri+ol (ˈɛstrɪˌɒl, ˈiːstrɪ-) *n.* the usual U.S. spelling of **oestriol.**

es+tro+gen (ˈɛstrədʒən, ˈiːstrə-) *n.* the usual U.S. spelling of **oestrogen.** —**es+tro+gen+ic** (ˌɛstrəˈdʒɛnɪk, ˌiːstrə-) *adj.* —ˌ**es+tro+ˈgen+i+cal+ly** *adv.*

es+trone (ˈɛstrəʊn, ˈiːstrəʊn) *n.* the usual U.S. spelling of **oestrone.**

es+trus (ˈɛstrəs, ˈiːstrəs) *n.* the usual U.S. spelling of **oestrus.** —**ˈes+trous** *adj.*

es+tu+a+rine (ˈɛstjʊəˌraɪn, -rɪn) *adj.* **1.** formed or deposited in an estuary: *estuarine muds.* **2.** growing in, inhabiting, or found in an estuary: *an estuarine fauna.*

es+tu+ar+y (ˈɛstjʊərɪ) *n., pl.* **+ar+ies. 1.** the widening channel of a river where it nears the sea, with a mixing of fresh water and salt (tidal) water. **2.** an inlet of the sea. [C16: from Latin *aestuārium* marsh, channel, from *aestus* tide, billowing movement, related to *aestās* summer] —**es+tu+ar+i+al** (ˌɛstjʊˈɛərɪəl) *adj.*

e.s.u. *or* **E.S.U.** *abbrev. for* electrostatic unit.

e+su+ri+ent (ɪˈsjʊərɪənt) *adj.* greedy; voracious. [C17: from Latin *ēsurīre* to be hungry, from *edere* to eat] —**e+ˈsu+ri+ence** *or* **e+ˈsu+ri+en+cy** *n.* —**e+ˈsu+ri+ent+ly** *adv.*

Et *the chemical symbol for* ethyl.

-et *suffix of nouns.* small or lesser: *islet; baronet.* [from Old French *-et, -ete*]

e+ta[1] (ˈiːtə) *n.* the seventh letter in the Greek alphabet (Η, η), a long vowel sound, transliterated as *e* or *ē.* [Greek, of Phoenician origin; compare Hebrew HETH]

e+ta[2] (ˈeɪtə) *n., pl.* **e+ta** or **e+tas.** (in Japan, formerly) a member of a class of outcasts who did menial and dirty tasks. [Japanese]

E.T.A. *abbrev. for* estimated time of arrival.

e+tae+ri+o (ɛˈtɪərɪəʊ) *n.* an aggregate fruit, as one consisting of drupes (raspberry) or achenes (traveller's joy). [C19: from French *etairion*, from Greek *hetaireia* association]

é+ta+gère *French.* (etaˈʒɛːr) *n.* a stand with open shelves for displaying ornaments, etc. [C19: from French, from *étage* shelf; see STAGE]

et al. *abbrev. for:* **1.** et alibi. [Latin: and elsewhere] **2.** et alii. [Latin: and others]

et+a+lon (ˈɛtəˌlɒn) *n. Physics.* a device used in spectroscopy to measure wavelengths by interference effects produced by multiple reflections between parallel half-silvered glass or quartz plates. [C20: French *étalon* a fixed standard of weights and measures, from Old French *estalon;* see also STALLION]

et+a+mine (ˈɛtəˌmiːn) *or* **et+a+min** (ˈɛtəmɪn) *n.* a cotton or worsted fabric of loose weave, used for clothing, curtains, etc. [C18: from French, from Latin *stāminea*, from *stāmineus* made of threads, from *stamen* thread, warp]

et+a+oin shrd+lu (ˈɛtɪˌɔɪn ˈʃɜːdluː) *n. Printing.* a Linotype slug, used as a marker, produced by running the fingers down the first two rows of the keyboard.

etc. *abbrev. for* et cetera.

et cet+er+a (ɪt ˈsɛtrə) **1.** and the rest; and others; and so forth: used at the end of a list to indicate that other items of the same class or type should be considered or included. **2.** or the like; or something else similar. Abbrev.: **etc., &c.** [from Latin, from *et* and + *cetera* the other (things)]

Usage. Since *et cetera* (or *etc.*) means *and other things*, careful writers do not use the expression *and etc.* because *and* is redundant. The repetition of *etc.*, as in *he brought paper, ink, notebooks, etc., etc.*, is avoided except in informal contexts.

et+cet+er+as (ɪtˈsɛtrəz) *pl. n.* miscellaneous extra things or persons.

etch (ɛtʃ) *vb.* **1.** (*tr.*) to wear away the surface of (a metal, glass, etc.) by chemical action, esp. the action of an acid. **2.** to cut or corrode (a design, decoration, etc.) on (a metal or other plate to be used for printing) by using the action of acid on parts not covered by wax or other acid-resistant coating. **3.** (*tr.*) to cut with or as if with a sharp implement: *he etched his name on the table.* **4.** (*tr.; usually passive*) to imprint vividly: *the event was etched on her memory.* [C17: from Dutch *etsen*, from Old High German *azzen* to feed, bite] —**ˈetch+er** *n.*

etch+ant (ˈɛtʃənt) *n.* any acid or corrosive used for etching.

etch+ing (ˈɛtʃɪŋ) *n.* **1.** the art, act, or process of preparing etched surfaces or of printing designs from them. **2.** an etched plate. **3.** an impression made from an etched plate.

E.T.D. *abbrev. for* estimated time of departure.

E+te+o+cles (ɪˈtiːəˌkliːz, ˈɛtɪə-) *n. Greek myth.* a son of Oedipus and Jocasta. He expelled his brother Polynices from Thebes; they killed each other in single combat when Polynices returned as leader of the Seven against Thebes.

e+ter+nal (ɪˈtɜːnəl)) *adj.* **1. a.** without beginning or end; lasting for ever: *eternal life.* **b.** (*as n.*): *the eternal.* **2.** (*often cap.*) denoting or relating to that which is without beginning and end, regarded as an attribute of God. **3.** unchanged by time, esp. being true or valid for all time; immutable: *eternal truths.* **4.** seemingly unceasing; occurring again and again: *eternal bickering.* [C14: from Late Latin *aeternālis*, from Latin *aeternus;* related to Latin *aevum* age] —ˌ**e+ter+ˈnal+i+ty** *or* **e+ˈter+nal+ness** *n.* —**e+ˈter+nal+ly** *adv.*

E+ter+nal Cit+y *n.* Rome.

e+ter+nal+ize (ɪˈtɜːnəˌlaɪz), **e+ter+nize** (ɪˈtɜːnaɪz) *or* **e+ter+nal+ise, e+ter+nise** *vb.* (*tr.*) **1.** to make eternal. **2.** to make famous for ever; immortalize. —**e+ˌter+nal+i+ˈza+tion, e+ˌter+ni+ˈza+tion** *or* **e+ˌter+nal+i+ˈsa+tion, e+ˌter+ni+ˈsa+tion** *n.*

e+ter+nal tri+an+gle *n.* an emotional relationship in which there are conflicts involving a man and two women or a woman and two men.

e+terne (ɪˈtɜːn) *adj.* an archaic or poetic word for **eternal.** [C14: from Old French, from Latin *aeternus*]

e+ter+ni+ty (ɪˈtɜːnɪtɪ) *n., pl.* **+ties. 1.** endless or infinite time. **2.** the quality, state, or condition of being eternal. **3.** (*usually pl.*) any of the aspects of life and thought that are considered to be timeless, esp. timeless and true. **4.** *Theol.* the condition of timeless existence, believed by some to characterize the afterlife. **5.** a seemingly endless period of time: *an eternity of waiting.*

e+ter+ni+ty ring *n.* a ring given as a token of lasting affection, esp. one set all around with stones to symbolize continuity.

e+te+si+an (ɪˈtiːʒɪən) *adj.* (of NW winds) recurring annually in the summer in the E Mediterranean. [C17: from Latin *etēsius* yearly, from Greek *etēsios*, from *etos* year]

eth (ɛð, ɛθ) *n.* a variant spelling of **edh.**

Eth. *abbrev. for:* **1.** Ethiopia(n). **2.** Ethiopic.

-eth[1] *suffix.* forming the archaic third person singular present indicative tense of verbs: *goeth; taketh.* [Old English *-eth, -th*]

-eth[2] *or* **-th** *suffix forming ordinal numbers.* variant of **-th**[2]: *twentieth.*

e+thane (ˈiːθeɪn, ˈɛθ-) *n.* a colourless odourless flammable gaseous alkane obtained from natural gas and petroleum: used as a fuel and in the manufacture of organic chemicals. Formula: C_2H_6. [C19: from ETH(YL) + -ANE]

e+thane+di+o+ic ac+id (ˌiːθeɪndaɪˈəʊɪk, ˌɛθ-) *n.* the technical name for **oxalic acid.** [C20: from ETHANE + DI-[1] + -OIC]

e+thane+di+ol (ˈiːθeɪnˌdaɪɒl, ˈɛθ-) *n.* a clear colourless syrupy soluble liquid substance, used as an antifreeze and solvent. Formula: CH_2OHCH_2OH. Also called: **glycol, ethylene glycol.** [C20: from ETHANE + DI-[1] + -OL[1]]

eth+a+nol (ˈɛθəˌnɒl, ˈiːθə-) *n.* the technical name for **alcohol** (sense 1).

Eth+el+bert (ˈɛθəlˌbɜːt) *or* **Æth+el+bert** (ˈæθəlˌbɜːt) *n.* ?552–616 A.D., king of Kent (560–616): converted to Christianity by St. Augustine; issued the earliest known code of English laws.

Eth+el+red II (ˈɛθəlˌrɛd) *or* **Æth+el+red** (ˈæθəlˌrɛd) *n.* known as *Ethelred the Unready.* ?968–1016 A.D., king of England (978–1016). He was temporarily deposed by the Danish king Sweyn (1013) but was recalled on Sweyn's death (1014).

eth+ene (ˈɛθiːn) *n.* the technical name for **ethylene.**

e+ther (ˈiːθə) *n.* **1.** Also called: **diethyl ether, ethyl ether, ethoxyethane.** a colourless volatile highly flammable liquid with a characteristic sweetish odour, made by the reaction of sulphuric acid with ethanol: used as a solvent and anaesthetic. Formula: $C_2H_5OC_2H_5$. **2.** any of a class of organic compounds with the general formula ROR′, as in diethyl ether $C_2H_5OC_2H_5$. **3. the ether.** the hypothetical medium formerly believed to fill all space and to support the propagation of electromagnetic waves. **4.** *Greek myth.* the upper regions of the atmosphere; clear sky or heaven. **5.** a rare word for **air.** ~Also (for senses 3–5): **aether.** [C17: from Latin *aether,* from Greek *aithēr,* from *aithein* to burn] —**e·ther·ic** (iːˈθɛrɪk) *adj.*

e·the·re·al (ɪˈθɪərɪəl) *adj.* **1.** extremely delicate or refined; exquisite. **2.** almost as light as air; impalpable; airy. **3.** celestial or spiritual. **4.** of, containing, or dissolved in an ether, esp. diethyl ether: *an ethereal solution.* **5.** of or relating to the ether. [C16: from Latin *aethereus,* from Greek *aitherios,* from *aithēr* ETHER] —**e,the·re'al·i·ty** *or* **e'the·re·al·ness** *n.* —**e'the·re·al·ly** *adv.*

e·the·re·al·ize *or* **e·the·re·al·ise** (ɪˈθɪərɪə,laɪz) *vb.* (*tr.*) **1.** to make or regard as being ethereal. **2.** to add ether to or make into ether or something resembling ether. —**e,the·re·al·i'za·tion** *or* **e,the·re·al·i'sa·tion** *n.*

Eth·er·ege (ˈɛθərɪdʒ) *n.* Sir **George.** ?1635–?92, English Restoration dramatist; author of the comedies *The Comical Revenge* (1664), *She would if she could* (1668), and *The Man of Mode* (1676).

e·ther·i·fy (ˈiːθərɪ,faɪ, iːˈθɛrɪ-) *vb.* **-fies, -fy·ing, -fied.** (*tr.*) to change (a compound, such as an alcohol) into an ether. —**e,ther·i·fi'ca·tion** *n.*

e·ther·ize *or* **e·ther·ise** (ˈiːθə,raɪz) *vb.* (*tr.*) *Obsolete.* to subject (a patient, etc.) to the anaesthetic influence of ether fumes; anaesthetize. —**,e·ther·i'za·tion** *or* **,e·ther·i'sa·tion** *n.* —**'e·ther,iz·er** *or* **'e·ther,is·er** *n.*

eth·ic (ˈɛθɪk) *n.* **1.** a moral principle or set of moral values held by an individual or group: *the Puritan ethic.* ~*adj.* **2.** another word for **ethical.** [C15: from Latin *ēthicus,* from Greek *ēthikos,* from *ēthos* custom; see ETHOS]

eth·i·cal (ˈɛθɪkᵊl) *adj.* **1.** in accordance with principles of conduct that are considered correct, esp. those of a given profession or group. **2.** of or relating to ethics. **3.** (of a medicinal agent) available legally only with a doctor's prescription or consent. —**'eth·i·cal·ly** *adv.* —**'eth·i·cal·ness** *or* **,eth·i'cal·i·ty** *n.*

eth·i·cize *or* **eth·i·cise** (ˈɛθɪ,saɪz) *vb.* (*tr.*) to make or consider as ethical.

eth·ics (ˈɛθɪks) *n.* **1.** (*functioning as sing.*) the philosophical study of the moral value of human conduct and of the rules and principles that ought to govern it; moral philosophy. **2.** (*functioning as pl.*) a social, religious, or civil code of behaviour considered correct, esp. that of a particular group, profession, or individual. **3.** (*functioning as pl.*) the moral fitness of a decision, course of action, etc.: *he doubted the ethics of their verdict.* —**'eth·i·cist** *n.*

E·thi·op (ˈiːθɪ,ɒp) *or* **E·thi·ope** (ˈiːθɪ,əʊp) *adj.* an archaic word for **Negro.**

E·thi·o·pi·a (,iːθɪˈəʊpɪə) *n.* a state in NE Africa, on the Red Sea: consolidated as an empire under Menelik II (1889–1913); federated with Eritrea in 1952; Emperor Haile Selassie was deposed by the military in 1974 and the monarchy was abolished in 1975; secessionist movements in Eritrea have been engaged in civil war with the government since 1974; lies along the Great Rift Valley and consists of deserts in the southeast and northeast and a high central plateau with many rivers (including the Blue Nile) and mountains rising over 4500 m (15 000 ft.); the main export is coffee. Official language: Amharic. Currency: birr. Capital: Addis Ababa. Pop.: 27 946 000 (1975 UN est.). Area: 1 221 894 sq. km (471 776 sq. miles). Former name: **Abyssinia.**

E·thi·o·pi·an (,iːθɪˈəʊpɪən) *adj.* **1.** of, relating to, or characteristic of Ethiopia, its people, or any of their languages. **2.** of or denoting a zoogeographical region consisting of Africa south of the Sahara. **3.** *Anthropol., obsolete.* of or belonging to a postulated racial group characterized by dark skin, an oval elongated face, and thin lips, living chiefly in Africa south of the Sahara. ~*n.* **4.** a native or inhabitant of Ethiopia. **5.** any of the languages of Ethiopia, esp. Amharic. ~*n., adj.* **6.** an archaic word for **Negro.**

E·thi·o·pic (,iːθɪˈɒpɪk, -ˈəʊpɪk) *n.* **1.** the ancient language of Ethiopia, belonging to the Semitic subfamily of the Afro-Asiatic family: a Christian liturgical language. See also **Ge'ez. 2.** the group of languages developed from this language, including Amharic, Tigre, and Tigrinya. ~*adj.* **3.** denoting or relating to this language or group of languages. **4.** a less common word for **Ethiopian.**

eth·moid (ˈɛθmɔɪd) *adj. also* **eth·moi·dal. 1.** *Anatomy.* denoting or relating to a bone of the skull that forms part of the eye socket and the nasal cavity. ~*n.* **2.** the ethmoid bone. [C18: from Greek *ēthmoeidēs* like a sieve, from *ēthmos* sieve, from *ēthein* to sift]

eth·narch (ˈɛθnɑːk) *n.* the ruler of a people or province, as in parts of the Roman and Byzantine Empires. [C17: from Greek *ethnarkhēs,* from *ethnos* nation + *arkhein* to rule] —**'eth·nar·chy** *n.*

eth·nic (ˈɛθnɪk) *or* **eth·ni·cal** *adj.* **1.** relating to or characteristic of a human group having racial, religious, linguistic, and certain other traits in common. **2.** relating to the classification of mankind into groups, esp. on the basis of racial characteristics. **3.** denoting or deriving from the cultural traditions of a group of people: *the ethnic dances of Bosnia.* [C14 (in the senses: heathen, Gentile): from Late Latin *ethnicus,* from Greek *ethnikos,* from *ethnos* race] —**'eth·ni·cal·ly** *adv.* —**eth·nic·i·ty** (ɛθˈnɪsɪtɪ) *n.*

eth·no- *combining form.* indicating race, people, or culture: *ethnology.* [via French from Greek *ethnos* race]

eth·no·bot·a·ny (,ɛθnəʊˈbɒtənɪ) *n.* the branch of botany concerned with the use of plants in folklore, religion, etc.

eth·no·cen·trism (,ɛθnəʊˈsɛn,trɪzəm) *n.* belief in the intrinsic superiority of the nation, culture, or group to which one belongs, often accompanied by feelings of dislike and contempt for other groups. —**,eth·no'cen·tric** *adj.* —**,eth·no'cen·tri·cal·ly** *adv.* —**,eth·no·cen'tric·i·ty** *n.*

eth·nog·e·ny (ɛθˈnɒdʒɪnɪ) *n.* the branch of ethnology that deals with the origin of races or peoples. —**eth·no·gen·ic** (,ɛθnəʊˈdʒɛnɪk) *adj.* —**eth'nog·e·nist** *n.*

eth·nog·ra·phy (ɛθˈnɒgrəfɪ) *n.* the branch of anthropology that deals with the scientific description of individual human societies. —**eth'nog·ra·pher** *n.* —**eth·no·graph·ic** (,ɛθnəʊˈgræfɪk) *or* **,eth·no'graph·i·cal** *adj.* —**,eth·no'graph·i·cal·ly** *adv.*

ethnol. *abbrev. for* ethnology.

eth·nol·o·gy (ɛθˈnɒlədʒɪ) *n.* the branch of anthropology that deals with races and peoples, their relations to one another, their origins, and their distinctive characteristics. —**eth·no·log·ic** (,ɛθnəˈlɒdʒɪk) *or* **,eth·no'log·i·cal** *adj.* —**,eth·no'log·i·cal·ly** *adv.* —**eth'nol·o·gist** *n.*

e·thol·o·gy (ɪˈθɒlədʒɪ) *n.* the study of the behaviour of animals in their normal environment. [C17 (in the sense: mimicry): via Latin from Greek *ēthologia,* from *ēthos* character; current sense, C19] —**eth·o·log·i·cal** (,ɛθəˈlɒdʒɪkᵊl) *adj.* —**,eth·o'log·i·cal·ly** *adv.* —**e'thol·o·gist** *n.*

eth·o·none (ˈɛθə,nəʊn) *n.* another name for **ketene.**

e·thos (ˈiːθɒs) *n.* the distinctive character, spirit, and attitudes of a people, culture, era, etc.: *the revolutionary ethos.* [C19: from Late Latin: habit, from Greek]

eth·ox·ide (iːˈθɒksaɪd) *n.* any of a class of saltlike compounds with the formula MOC_2H_5, where M is a metal atom. Also called: **ethylate.** [C20: from *ethox(yl)* (from ETH(YL) + OX(YGEN) + -YL) + -IDE]

eth·ox·y·e·thane (ɛ,θɒksɪˈiːθeɪn) *n.* the technical name for **ether** (sense 1). [C20: from ETH(YL) + OXY- + ETHANE]

e·thyl (ˈiːθaɪl, ˈɛθɪl) *n.* (*modifier*) of, consisting of, or containing the monovalent group C_2H_5-: *ethyl group or radical.* [C19: from ETH(ER) + -YL] —**e·thyl·ic** (ɪˈθɪlɪk) *adj.*

e·thyl ac·e·tate *n.* a colourless volatile flammable fragrant liquid ester, made from acetic acid and ethanol: used in perfumes and flavourings and as a solvent for plastics, lacquers, etc. Formula: $CH_3COOC_2H_5$.

e·thyl al·co·hol *n.* another name for **alcohol** (sense 1).

eth·yl·ate (ˈɛθɪ,leɪt) *vb.* **1.** to undergo or cause to undergo a chemical reaction in which an ethyl group is introduced into a molecule. ~*n.* **2.** another name for an **ethoxide.** —**,eth·yl'a·tion** *n.*

e·thyl car·ba·mate *n.* a colourless odourless crystalline ester used in the manufacture of pesticides, fungicides, and pharmaceuticals. Formula: $CO(NH_2)OC_2H_5$. Also called: **urethane.**

eth·yl·ene (ˈɛθɪ,liːn) *or* **eth·ene** (ˈɛθiːn) *n.* a colourless flammable gaseous alkene with a sweet odour, obtained from petroleum and natural gas and used in the manufacture of polythene and many other chemicals. Formula: $CH_2{:}CH_2$. Also called: **ethene.** —**eth·yl·e·nic** (,ɛθɪˈliːnɪk) *adj.*

eth·yl·ene gly·col *n.* another name for **ethanediol.**

eth·yl·ene group *or* **rad·i·cal** *n. Chem.* the divalent group, $-CH_2CH_2-$, derived from ethylene.

eth·yl·ene se·ries *n. Chem.* the homologous series of unsaturated hydrocarbons that contain one double bond and have the general formula, C_nH_{2n}; alkene series.

e·thyl e·ther *n.* a more formal name for **ether** (sense 1).

e·thyne (ˈiːθaɪn, ˈɛθaɪn) *n.* another name for **acetylene.** [C20: from ETHYL + -INE]

É·tienne (*French* eˈtjɛn) *n.* a variant spelling of **Estienne.**

e·ti·o·late (ˈiːtɪəʊ,leɪt) *vb.* **1.** *Botany.* to whiten (a green plant) through lack of sunlight. **2.** to become or cause to become pale and weak, as from malnutrition. [C18: from French *étioler* to make pale, probably from Old French *estuble* straw, from Latin *stipula*] —**,e·ti·o'la·tion** *n.*

e·ti·ol·o·gy (,iːtɪˈɒlədʒɪ) *n., pl.* **-gies.** the usual U.S. spelling of **aetiology.** —**e·ti·o·log·i·cal** (,iːtɪəˈlɒdʒɪkᵊl) *adj.* —**,e·ti·o'log·i·cal·ly** *adv.* —**,e·ti'ol·o·gist** *n.*

et·i·quette (ˈɛtɪ,kɛt, ,ɛtɪˈkɛt) *n.* **1.** the customs or rules governing behaviour regarded as correct or acceptable in social or official life. **2.** a conventional but unwritten code of practice followed by members of any of certain professions or groups: *medical etiquette.* [C18: from French, from Old French *estiquette* label, from *estiquier* to attach; see STICK[2]]

Et·na (ˈɛtnə) *n.* **Mount.** an active volcano in E Sicily: the highest volcano in Europe and the highest peak in Italy south of the Alps. Height: 3263 m (10 500 ft.).

E·ton (ˈiːtᵊn) *n.* **1.** a town in S England, in Berkshire near the River Thames: site of **Eton College,** a public school for boys founded in 1440. Pop.: 3954 (1971). **2.** this college. —**E·to·ni·an** (iːˈtəʊnɪən) *adj., n.*

E·ton col·lar *n.* a broad stiff white collar worn outside an Eton jacket.

E·ton crop *n.* a very short mannish hair style worn by women in the 1920s.

E·ton jack·et *n.* a waist-length jacket with a V-shaped back, open in front, formerly worn by pupils of Eton College.

é·tri·er (*French* etriˈe) *n. Mountaineering.* a short rope ladder with two or three wooden or metal rungs. [French: stirrup]

E·tru·ri·a (ɪˈtrʊərɪə) *n.* **1.** an ancient country of central Italy, between the Rivers Arno and Tiber **2.** a pottery factory established in Staffordshire by Josiah Wedgwood in 1769.

E·trus·can (ɪˈtrʌskən) *or* **E·tru·ri·an** (ɪˈtrʊərɪən) *n.* **1.** a member of an ancient people of central Italy whose civilization greatly influenced the Romans, who had suppressed them by about 200 B.C. **2.** the non-Indo-European language of the ancient Etruscans, whose few surviving records have not been fully interpreted. ~*adj.* **3.** of, relating to, or characteristic of Etruria, the Etruscans, their culture, or their language.

et seq. *abbrev. for:* **1.** et sequens [Latin: and the following] **2.** Also: **et seqq.** et sequentia [Latin: and those that follow]

-ette *suffix of nouns.* **1.** small: *cigarette; kitchenette.* **2.** female: *majorette; suffragette.* **3.** (esp. in trade names) imitation: *Leatherette.* [from French, feminine of -ET]

é·tude ('eɪtjuːd; *French* e'tyd) *n.* a short musical composition for a solo instrument, esp. one designed as an exercise or exploiting technical virtuosity. [French: STUDY]

é·tui (ɛ'twiː) *n., pl.* **é·tuis.** a small usually ornamented case for holding needles, cosmetics, or other small articles. [C17: from French, from Old French *estuier* to enclose; see TWEEZERS]

ety., etym., *or* **etymol.** *abbrev. for:* **1.** etymological. **2.** etymology.

et·y·mol·o·gize *or* **et·y·mol·o·gise** (ˌɛtɪ'mɒləˌdʒaɪz) *vb.* to trace, state, or suggest the etymology of (a word).

et·y·mol·o·gy (ˌɛtɪ'mɒlədʒɪ) *n., pl.* **·gies. 1.** the study of the sources and development of words and morphemes. **2.** an account of the source and development of a word or morpheme. [C14: via Latin from Greek *etumologia;* see ETYMON, -LOGY] —**et·y·mo·log·i·cal** (ˌɛtɪmə'lɒdʒɪkᵊl) *adj.* —ˌ**et·y·mo·'log·i·cal·ly** *adv.* —ˌ**et·y·'mol·o·gist** *n.*

et·y·mon ('ɛtɪˌmɒn) *n., pl.* **·mons** *or* **·ma** (-mə). a form of a word or morpheme, usually the earliest recorded form or a reconstructed form, from which another word or morpheme is derived: *the etymon of English "ewe" is Indo-European "*owi".* [C16: via Latin, from Greek *etumon* basic meaning, from *etumos* true, actual]

Et·zel ('ɛtsᵊl) *n. German legend.* a great king who, according to the *Nibelungenlied,* was the second husband of Kriemhild after the death of Siegfried: identified with Attila the Hun. Compare **Atli.**

Eu *the chemical symbol for* europium.

eu- *prefix.* well, pleasant, or good: *eupeptic; euphony.* [via Latin from Greek, from *eus* good]

eu·bac·te·ri·a (ˌjuːbæk'tɪərɪə) *pl. n., sing.* **·ri·um** (-rɪəm). a large group of bacteria characterized by a rigid cell wall and, in motile types, flagella; the true bacteria. [C20: via New Latin from Greek, from EU- (in the sense: true) + BACTERIUM]

Eu·boe·a (juː'bɪə) *n.* an island in the W Aegean Sea: the largest island after Crete of the Greek archipelago; linked with the mainland by a bridge across the Euripus channel. Capital: Chalcis. Pop.: 165 369 (1971). Area: 3908 sq. km (1524 sq. miles). Modern Greek name: **Évvoia.** Former English name: **Negropont.** —**Eu·'boe·an** *adj., n.*

eu·caine (juː'keɪn) *n.* a crystalline optically active substance formerly used as a local anaesthetic. Formula: $C_{15}H_{21}NO_2$.

eu·ca·lyp·tol (ˌjuːkə'lɪptɒl) *or* **eu·ca·lyp·tole** (ˌjuːkə'lɪptəʊl) *n.* a colourless oily liquid with a camphor-like odour and a spicy taste, obtained from eucalyptus oil and used in perfumery and as a flavouring. Formula: $C_{10}H_{18}O$. Also called: **cineol.**

eu·ca·lyp·tus (ˌjuːkə'lɪptəs) *or* **eu·ca·lypt** ('juːkəˌlɪpt) *n., pl.* **·lyp·tus·es, ·lyp·ti** (-'lɪptaɪ), *or* **·lypts.** any myrtaceous tree of the mostly Australian genus *Eucalyptus,* such as the blue gum and ironbark, widely cultivated for the medicinal oil in their leaves (**eucalyptus oil**), timber, and ornament. [C19: New Latin, from EU- + Greek *kaluptos* covered, from *kaluptein* to cover, hide]

eu·cha·ris ('juːkərɪs) *n.* any amaryllidaceous plant of the South American genus *Eucharis,* cultivated for their large white fragrant flowers. [C19: New Latin, from Late Latin: charming, from Greek *eukharis,* from EU- + *kharis* grace]

Eu·cha·rist ('juːkərɪst) *n.* **1.** the Christian sacrament in which Christ's Last Supper is commemorated by the consecration of bread and wine. **2.** the consecrated elements of bread and wine offered in the sacrament. [C14: via Church Latin from Greek *eukharistia,* from *eukharistos* thankful, from EU- + *kharizesthai* to show favour, from *kharis* favour] —ˌ**Eu·cha·'ris·tic** *or* ˌ**Eu·cha·'ris·ti·cal** *adj.* —ˌ**Eu·cha·'ris·ti·cal·ly** *adv.*

eu·chlo·rine (juː'klɔːriːn) *or* **eu·chlo·rin** (juː'klɔːrɪn) *n.* an explosive gaseous mixture of chlorine and chlorine dioxide.

eu·chre ('juːkə) *n.* **1.** a U.S. card game similar to écarté for two, three, or four players, using a poker pack with joker and jack high. **2.** an instance of euchring another player, preventing him from making his contracted tricks. ~*vb.* (*tr.*) **3.** to prevent (a player) from making his contracted tricks. **4.** (usually foll. by *out*) *U.S. informal.* to outwit or cheat. **5.** *Austral. informal.* to ruin or exhaust. [C19: of unknown origin]

eu·chro·ma·tin (juː'krəʊmətɪn) *n.* the part of a chromosome that constitutes the major genes and does not stain strongly with basic dyes when the cell is not dividing. Compare **heterochromatin.** —**eu·chro·mat·ic** (ˌjuːkrəʊ'mætɪk) *adj.*

Euc·ken (*German* 'ɔɪkᵊn) *n.* **Ru·dolph Chris·toph** ('ruːdɔlf 'krɪstɔf). 1846–1926, German idealist philosopher: Nobel prize for literature 1908.

Eu·clid ('juːklɪd) *n.* **1.** 3rd century B.C., Greek mathematician of Alexandria; author of *Elements,* which sets out the principles of geometry and remained a text until the 19th century at least. **2.** the works of Euclid, esp. his system of geometry. —**Eu·clid·e·an** *or* **Eu·clid·i·an** (juː'klɪdɪən) *adj.*

eu·de·mon *or* **eu·dae·mon** (juː'diːmən) *n.* a benevolent spirit or demon. [C17: from Greek *eudaimōn,* from EU- + *daimōn* in-dwelling spirit; see DEMON]

eu·de·mo·ni·a *or* **eu·dae·mo·ni·a** (ˌjuːdɪ'məʊnɪə) *n.* happiness, esp. (in the philosophy of Aristotle) that resulting from a rational active life.

eu·de·mon·ics *or* **eu·dae·mon·ics** (ˌjuːdɪ'mɒnɪks) *n.* (*functioning as sing.*) **1.** the art or theory of happiness. **2.** another word for **eudemonism.** —ˌ**eu·de·'mon·ic** *or* ˌ**eu·dae·'mon·ic** *adj.*

eu·de·mon·ism *or* **eu·dae·mon·ism** (juː'diːməˌnɪzəm) *n. Philosophy.* an ethical doctrine holding that the value of moral action lies in its capacity to produce happiness. —**eu·'de·mon·ist** *or* **eu·'dae·mon·ist** *n.* —**eu·ˌde·mon·'is·tic, eu·ˌdae·mon·'is·tic** *or* **eu·ˌde·mon·'is·ti·cal, eu·ˌdae·mon·'is·ti·cal** *adj.* —**eu·ˌde·mon·'is·ti·cal·ly** *or* **eu·ˌdae·mon·'is·ti·cal·ly** *adv.*

eu·di·om·e·ter (ˌjuːdɪ'ɒmɪtə) *n.* a graduated glass tube used in the study and volumetric analysis of gas reactions. [C18: from Greek *eudios,* literally: clear skied (from EU- + *Dios,* genitive of *Zeus* god of the heavens) + -METER] —**eu·di·o·met·ric** (ˌjuːdɪə'mɛtrɪk) *or* ˌ**eu·di·o·'met·ri·cal** *adj.* —ˌ**eu·di·o·'met·ri·cal·ly** *adv.* —ˌ**eu·di·'om·e·try** *n.*

Eu·dox·us of Cni·dus (juː'dɒksəs; 'naɪdəs) *n.* ?406–?355 B.C., Greek astronomer and mathematician; believed to have calculated the length of the solar year.

Eu·gène (*French* øʒɛn) *n.* **Prince,** title of *François Eugène de Savoie-Carignan.* 1663–1736, Austrian general, born in France: with Marlborough defeated the French at Blenheim (1704), Oudenaarde (1708), and Malplaquet (1709).

eu·gen·ics (juː'dʒɛnɪks) *n.* (*functioning as sing.*) the study of methods of improving the quality of the human race, esp. by selective breeding. [C19: from Greek *eugenēs* wellborn, from EU- + *-genēs* born; see -GEN] —**eu·'gen·ic** *adj.* —**eu·'gen·i·cal·ly** *adv.* —**eu·'gen·i·cist** *n.*

Eu·gé·nie (*French* øʒe'ni) *n.* original name *Eugénia Maria de Montijo de Guzman, Comtesse de Téba.* 1826–1920, Empress of France (1853–71) as wife of Napoleon III.

eu·ge·nol ('juːdʒɪˌnɒl) *n.* a colourless or pale yellow oily liquid substance with a spicy taste and an odour of cloves, used in perfumery; 4-allyl-2-methoxyphenol. Formula: $C_{10}H_{12}O_2$. [C19: *eugen-,* from *Eugenia caryophyllata* kind of clove from which oil may be obtained + -OL]

eu·gle·na (juː'gliːnə) *n.* any freshwater flagellate protozoan of the genus *Euglena,* typically having holophytic nutrition. Because it has some plant characteristics *Euglena* is sometimes classified as an alga. [C19: from New Latin, from EU- + Greek *glēnē* eyeball, socket of a joint]

eu·he·mer·ism (juː'hiːməˌrɪzəm) *n.* **1.** the theory that gods arose out of the deification of historical heroes. **2.** any interpretation of myths that derives the gods from outstanding men and seeks the source of mythology in history. [C19: named after *Euhemerus* (?300 B.C.), Greek philosopher who propounded this theory] —**eu·'he·mer·ist** *n.* —**eu·ˌhe·mer·'is·tic** *adj.* —**eu·ˌhe·mer·'is·ti·cal·ly** *adv.*

eu·he·mer·ize *or* **eu·he·mer·ise** (juː'hiːməˌraɪz) *vb.* to deal with or explain (myths) by euhemerism.

eu·la·chon ('juːləˌkɒn) *or* **eu·la·chan** *n., pl.* **·chons, ·chon** *or* **·chans, ·chan.** another name for **candlefish.** [from Chinook Jargon *ulâkân*]

Eu·ler (*German* 'ɔɪlər) *n.* **Le·on·hard** ('leːɔnˌhart). 1707–83, Swiss mathematician, noted esp. for his work on the calculus of variation: considered the founder of modern mathematical analysis.

eu·lo·gi·a (juː'ləʊdʒɪə) *n.* **1.** *Eastern Christian Church.* blessed bread distributed to members of the congregation after the liturgy, esp. to those who have not communed. **2.** *Archaic.* a blessing or something blessed. [C18: from Greek: blessing; see EULOGY]

eu·lo·gize *or* **eu·lo·gise** ('juːləˌdʒaɪz) *vb.* to praise (a person or thing) highly in speech or writing. —**'eu·lo·gist, 'eu·lo·ˌgiz·er,** *or* **'eu·lo·ˌgis·er** *n.* —ˌ**eu·lo·'gis·tic** *or* ˌ**eu·lo·'gis·ti·cal** *adj.* —ˌ**eu·lo·'gis·ti·cal·ly** *adv.*

eu·lo·gy ('juːlədʒɪ) *n., pl.* **·gies. 1.** a formal speech or piece of writing praising a person or thing, esp. a person who has recently died. **2.** high praise or commendation. ~Also called (archaic): **eu·lo·gi·um** (juː'ləʊdʒɪəm). [C16: from Late Latin *eulogia,* from Greek: praise, from EU- + -LOGY; influenced by Latin *ēlogium* short saying, inscription]

Eu·men·i·des (juː'mɛnɪˌdiːz) *pl. n.* another name for the **Furies,** used by the Greeks as a euphemism. [from Greek, literally: the benevolent ones, from *eumenēs* benevolent, from EU- + *menos* spirit]

eu·nuch ('juːnək) *n.* **1.** a man who has been castrated, esp. (formerly) for some office such as a guard in a harem. **2.** *Informal.* an ineffective man: *a political eunuch.* [C15: via Latin from Greek *eunoukhos* attendant of the bedchamber, from *eunē* bed + *ekhein* to have, keep]

eu·on·y·mus (juː'ɒnɪməs) *or* **e·von·y·mus** *n.* any tree or shrub of the N temperate genus *Euonymus,* such as the spindle tree, whose seeds are each enclosed in a fleshy, typically red, aril: family *Celastraceae.* [C18: from Latin: spindle tree, from Greek *euōnumos* fortunately named, from EU- + *onoma* NAME]

eu·pa·to·ri·um (ˌjuːpə'tɔːrɪəm) *n.* any plant of the genus *Eupatorium,* of tropical America and the West Indies: cultivated for their ornamental clusters of purple, pink, or white flowers: family *Compositae* (composites). [C16: from New Latin, from Greek *eupatorion* hemp agrimony, from *Eupator* surname of Mithridates VI, king of Pontus and traditionally the first to have used it medicinally]

eu·pat·rid (juː'pætrɪd) *n., pl.* **·pat·ri·dae** (-'pætrɪˌdiː) *or* **·pat·rids.** (in ancient Greece) a hereditary noble or landowner. [C19: via Latin from Greek *eupatridēs,* literally: having a good father, from EU- + *patēr* father]

Eu·pen and Mal·mé·dy (*French* ø'pɛn; malme'di) *n.* a region of Belgium in Liège province: ceded by Germany in 1919. Pop.: of Eupen 14 879 (1970); of Malmédy 6464 (1970).

eu·pep·si·a (juː'pɛpsɪə) *or* **eu·pep·sy** (juː'pɛpsɪ) *n. Physiol.* good digestion. [C18: from New Latin, from Greek, from EU- + *pepsis* digestion, from *peptein* to digest] —**eu·pep·tic** (juː'pɛptɪk) *adj.*

eu·phau·si·id (juː'fɔːzɪɪd) *n.* any small pelagic shrimplike crustacean of the order *Euphausiacea:* an important constituent of krill. [C19: from New Latin *Euphausiacea,* perhaps from Greek EU- + *pha-* from *phainein* to reveal, show + *ousia* substance, stuff]

eu·phe·mism ('juːfɪˌmɪzəm) *n.* **1.** an inoffensive word or phrase substituted for one considered offensive or hurtful, esp. one concerned with religion, sex, death, or excreta. Examples of euphemisms are: *sleep with* for *have sexual intercourse with; departed* for *dead; relieve oneself* for *urinate.* **2.** the use of such inoffensive words or phrases. [C17: from Greek *euphēmismos,* from EU- + *phēmē* speech] —'**eu·phe·mist** *n.* —ˌ**eu·phe·'mis·tic** *adj.* —ˌ**eu·phe·'mis·ti·cal·ly** *adv.*

eu·phe·mize *or* **eu·phe·mise** ('juːfɪˌmaɪz) *vb.* to speak in euphemisms or refer to by means of a euphemism. —'**eu·phe·ˌmiz·er** *or* '**eu·phe·ˌmis·er** *n.*

eu·phon·ic (juː'fɒnɪk) *or* **eu·pho·ni·ous** (juː'fəʊnɪəs) *adj.* **1.** denoting or relating to euphony; pleasing to the ear. **2.** (of speech sounds) altered for ease of pronunciation. —**eu·'phon·i·cal·ly** *or* **eu·'pho·ni·ous·ly** *adv.* —**eu·'pho·ni·ous·ness** *n.*

eu·pho·ni·um (juː'fəʊnɪəm) *n.* a brass musical instrument with four valves; the tenor of the tuba family. It is used mainly in brass bands. [C19: New Latin, from EUPH(ONY + HARM)ONIUM]

eu·pho·nize *or* **eu·pho·nise** ('juːfəˌnaɪz) *vb.* **1.** to make pleasant to hear; render euphonious. **2.** to change (speech sounds) so as to facilitate pronunciation.

eu·pho·ny ('juːfənɪ) *n., pl.* **-nies. 1.** the alteration of speech sounds, esp. by assimilation, so as to make them easier to pronounce. **2.** a pleasing sound, esp. in speech. [C17: from Late Latin *euphōnia,* from Greek, from EU- + *phōnē* voice]

eu·phor·bi·a (juː'fɔːbɪə) *n.* any plant of the genus *Euphorbia,* such as the spurges and poinsettia: family *Euphorbiaceae.* [C14: *euforbia,* from Latin *euphorbea* African plant named after *Euphorbus,* first-century A.D. Greek physician]

eu·phor·bi·a·ceous (juːˌfɔːbɪ'eɪʃəs) *adj.* of, relating to, or belonging to the *Euphorbiaceae,* a family of plants typically having capsular fruits: includes the spurges, the castor oil and cassava plants, cascarilla, and poinsettia.

eu·pho·ri·a (juː'fɔːrɪə) *n.* a feeling of great elation, esp. when exaggerated. [C19: from Greek: good ability to endure, from EU- + *pherein* to bear] —**eu·phor·ic** (juː'fɒrɪk) *adj.*

eu·pho·ri·ant (juː'fɔːrɪənt) *adj.* **1.** relating to or able to produce euphoria. ~*n.* **2.** a euphoriant drug or agent.

eu·pho·tic (juː'fəʊtɪk, -'fɒt-) *adj. Ecology.* denoting or relating to the uppermost part of a sea or lake down to about 100 metres depth, which receives enough light to enable photosynthesis to take place. [C20: from EU- + PHOTIC]

eu·phra·sy ('juːfrəsɪ) *n., pl.* **-sies.** another name for **eyebright.** [C15 *eufrasie,* from Medieval Latin *eufrasia,* from Greek *euphrasia* gladness, from *euphrainein* to make glad, from EU- + *phrēn* mind]

Eu·phra·tes (juː'freɪtiːz) *n.* a river in SW Asia, rising in E Turkey and flowing south across Syria and Iraq to join the Tigris, forming the Shatt-al-Arab, which flows to the head of the Persian Gulf: important in ancient times for the extensive irrigation of its valley (in Mesopotamia). Length: 3598 km (2235 miles).

eu·phroe *or* **u·phroe** ('juːfrəʊ, -vrəʊ) *n. Nautical.* a wooden block with holes through which the lines of a crowfoot are rove. [C19: from Dutch *juffrouw* maiden, earlier *joncfrouwe* (from *jonc* YOUNG + *frouwe* woman)]

Eu·phros·y·ne (juː'frɒzɪˌniː) *n. Greek myth.* one of the three Graces.

eu·phu·ism ('juːfjuːˌɪzəm) *n.* **1.** an artificial prose style of the Elizabethan period, marked by extreme use of antithesis, alliteration, and extended similes and allusions. **2.** any stylish affectation in speech or writing, esp. a rhetorical device or expression. [C16: after *Ephues,* prose romance by John Lyly] —'**eu·phu·ist** *n.* —ˌ**eu·phu·'is·tic** *or* ˌ**eu·phu·'is·ti·cal** *adj.* —ˌ**eu·phu·'is·ti·cal·ly** *adv.*

eu·plas·tic (juː'plæstɪk) *adj.* healing quickly and well. [C19: from Greek *euplastos* readily moulded; see EU-, PLASTIC]

eu·ploid ('juːplɔɪd) *Biology.* ~*adj.* **1.** having chromosomes present in an exact multiple of the haploid number. ~*n.* **2.** a euploid cell or individual. ~Compare **aneuploid.** [C20: from EU- + *-ploid,* as in HAPLOID] —'**eu·ploid·y** *n.*

eup·noe·a *or U.S.* **eup·ne·a** (juːp'nɪə) *n. Physiol.* normal relaxed breathing. Compare **dyspnoea.** [C18: from New Latin, from Greek *eupnoia,* from *eupnous* breathing easily, from EU- + *pnoē,* from *pnein* to breathe] —**eup·'noe·ic** *or U.S.* **eup·'ne·ic** *adj.*

Eur. *abbrev. for* Europe(an).

Eur- *combining form.* variant of **Euro-** before a vowel.

Eur·a·sia (jʊə'reɪʃə, -ʒə) *n.* the continents of Europe and Asia considered as a whole.

Eur·a·sian (jʊə'reɪʃən, -ʒən) *adj.* **1.** of or relating to Eurasia. **2.** of mixed European and Asian descent. ~*n.* **3.** a person of mixed European and Asian descent.

Eur·at·om (jʊə'rætəm) *n.* short for **European Atomic Energy Commission;** an authority established by the Common Market to develop peaceful uses of nuclear energy.

Eure (*French* œːr) *n.* a department of N France, in Haute-Normandie region. Capital: Évreux. Pop.: 433 529 (1975). Area: 6037 sq. km (2354 sq. miles).

Eure-et-Loir (*French* œr e 'lwaːr) *n.* a department of N central France, in Centre region. Capital: Chartres. Pop.: 342 281 (1975). Area: 5940 sq. km (2317 sq. miles).

eu·re·ka (jʊ'riːkə) *interj.* an exclamation of triumph on discovering or solving something. [C17: from Greek *heurēka* I have found (it), from *heuriskein* to find; traditionally the exclamation of Archimedes when he realized, during bathing, that the volume of an irregular solid could be calculated by measuring the water displaced when it was immersed]

Eu·re·ka Stock·ade *n.* a violent incident in Ballarat, Australia, in 1854 between gold miners and the military, as a result of which the miners won their democratic rights in the state parliament.

eu·rhyth·mic (juː'rɪðmɪk), **eu·rhyth·mi·cal** *or esp. U.S.* **eu·ryth·mic, eu·ryth·mi·cal** *adj.* **1.** having a pleasing and harmonious rhythm, order, or structure. **2.** of or relating to eurhythmics.

eu·rhyth·mics *or esp. U.S.* **eu·ryth·mics** (juː'rɪðmɪks) *n.* (*functioning as sing.*) **1.** a system of training through physical movement to music, originally taught by Émile Jaques-Dalcroze, to develop grace and musical understanding. **2.** dancing of this style, expressing the rhythm and spirit of the music through body movements.

eu·rhyth·my *or esp. U.S. or* **eu·ryth·my** (juː'rɪðmɪ) *n.* **1.** rhythmical movement. **2.** harmonious structure. [C17: from Latin *eurythmia,* from Greek *eurhuthmia,* from EU- + *rhuthmos* proportion, RHYTHM]

Eu·rip·i·des (jʊ'rɪpɪˌdiːz) *n.* ?480–406 B.C., Greek tragic dramatist. His plays, 18 of which are extant, include *Alcestis, Medea, Hippolytus, Hecuba, Trojan Women, Electra, Iphigeneia in Tauris, Iphigeneia in Aulis,* and *Bacchae.*

eu·ri·pus (jʊ'raɪpəs) *n., pl.* **-pi** (-paɪ). **1.** a strait or channel with a strong current or tide. **2.** *Rare.* a state of violent fluctuation. [C17: from Latin, from Greek *Euripos* the strait between Boeotia and Euboea, from *ripē* force, rush]

Eu·ro- ('jʊərəʊ-) *or before a vowel* **Eur-** *combining form.* Europe or European: *Eurodollar.*

Eu·roc·ly·don (jʊ'rɒklɪˌdɒn) *n.* **1.** a stormy wind from the north or northeast that occurs in the Levant, which caused the ship in which St. Paul was travelling to be wrecked (Acts 27:14). **2.** any stormy wind. [C17: from Greek *eurokludōn,* from *Euros* EURUS + Greek *akulōn* (unattested) north wind, from Latin *aquilō*]

Eu·ro·com·mun·ism (ˌjʊərəʊ'kɒmjʊˌnɪzəm) *n.* the policies, doctrines, and practices of Communist Parties in Western Europe, esp. insofar as these favour nonalignment with Russia or China. —ˌ**Eu·ro·'com·mun·ist** *n., adj.*

Eu·ro·crat ('jʊərəˌkræt) *n.* a member, esp. a senior member, of the administration of the Common Market.

Eu·ro·dol·lar ('jʊərəʊˌdɒlə) *n.* a U.S. dollar as part of a European holding: they are used as a source of short or medium-term finance, esp. in international trade, because of their easy convertibility.

Eu·ro·mar·ket ('jʊərəʊˌmɑːkɪt) *or* **Eu·ro·mart** *n.* other names for the **Common Market.**

Eu·ro·pa[1] (jʊ'rəʊpə) *n. Greek myth.* a Phoenician princess who had three children by Zeus in Crete, where he had taken her after assuming the guise of a white bull. Their offspring were Rhadamanthys, Minos, and Sarpedon.

Eu·ro·pa[2] (jʊ'rəʊpə) *n.* the fourth largest of the twelve satellites of Jupiter and the third nearest to the planet.

Eu·rope ('jʊərəp) *n.* **1.** the second smallest continent, forming the W peninsula of the land mass of Eurasia: the border with Asia runs from the Urals to the Caspian and the Black Sea. The coastline is generally extremely indented and there are several peninsulas (notably Scandinavia, Italy, and Iberia) and offshore islands (including the British Isles and Iceland). It contains a series of great mountain systems in the south (Pyrenees, Alps, Apennines, Carpathians, Caucasus), a large central plain, and a N region of lakes and mountains in Scandinavia. Pop.: 458 067 000 (1969 est.). Area: about 10 400 000 sq. km (4 000 000 sq. miles). **2.** *Brit.* the continent of Europe except for the British Isles: *we're going to Europe for our holiday.* **3.** *Brit.* the Common Market: *when did Britain go into Europe?*

Eu·ro·pe·an (ˌjʊərə'pɪən) *adj.* **1.** of or relating to Europe or its inhabitants. **2.** native to or derived from Europe. ~*n.* **3.** a native or inhabitant of Europe. **4.** a person of European descent. —ˌ**Eu·ro·'pe·an·ism** *n.*

Eu·ro·pe·an E·co·nom·ic Com·mu·ni·ty *n.* the official name for the **Common Market.** Abbrev.: **EEC**

Eu·ro·pe·an Free Trade As·so·ci·a·tion *n.* See **EFTA.**

Eu·ro·pe·an·ize *or* **Eu·ro·pe·an·ise** (ˌjʊərə'pɪəˌnaɪz) *vb.* (*tr.*) **1.** to make European in culture, dress, etc. **2.** to integrate (a country, economy, etc.) into the Common Market. —ˌ**Eu·ro·ˌpe·an·i·'za·tion** *or* ˌ**Eu·ro·ˌpe·an·i·'sa·tion** *n.*

Eu·ro·pe·an let·ter tel·e·gram *n.* a letter telegram sent from the U.K. to a European country. Abbrev.: **ELT**

Eu·ro·pe·an plan *n. U.S.* a hotel rate of charging covering room and service but not meals. Compare **American plan.**

Eu·ro·pe·an Re·cov·er·y Pro·gramme *n.* the official name for the **Marshall Plan.**

eu·ro·pi·um (jʊ'rəʊpɪəm) *n.* a soft ductile reactive silvery-white element of the lanthanide series of metals: used as the red phosphor in colour television and in lasers. Symbol: Eu; atomic no.: 63; atomic wt.: 151.96; valency: 2 or 3; relative density: 5.25; melting pt.: 826°C; boiling pt.: 1439°C. [C20: named after EUROPE + -IUM]

Eu·ro·poort (*Dutch* 'øːroːpoːrt) *n.* a port in the Netherlands near Rotterdam: developed in the 1960s; handles chiefly oil.

Eu·ro·vis·ion ('jʊərəʊˌvɪʒən) *n.* **a.** the network of the European Broadcasting Union for the exchange of news and television programmes amongst its member organizations and for the relay of news and programmes from outside the network. **b.** (*as modifier*): *the Eurovision song contest.*

Eu·rus ('jʊərəs) *n.* *Greek myth.* the east or southeast wind personified. [Latin, from Greek *euros*]

eu·ry- *combining form.* broad or wide: *eurythermal.* [New Latin, from Greek, from *eurus* wide]

Eu·ry·a·le (jʊ'raɪəlɪ) *n.* *Greek myth.* one of the three Gorgons.

Eu·ryd·i·ce (jʊ'rɪdɪsɪ) *n.* *Greek myth.* a dryad married to Orpheus, who sought her in Hades after she died. She would have been able to leave Hades with him had he not broken his pact and looked back at her.

eu·ryp·ter·id (jʊ'rɪptərɪd) *n.* any large extinct scorpion-like aquatic arthropod of the group *Eurypterida,* of Palaeozoic times, thought to be related to the horseshoe crabs. [C19: from New Latin *Eurypterida,* from EURY- + Greek *pteron* wing, feather]

Eu·rys·theus (jʊ'rɪsθjuːs, -θɪəs) *n.* *Greek myth.* a grandson of Perseus, who, through the favour of Hera, inherited the kingship of Mycenae, which Zeus had intended for Hercules.

eu·ry·ther·mal (ˌjʊərɪ'θɜːməl), **eu·ry·ther·mic,** *or* **eu·ry·ther·mous** *adj.* (of organisms) able to tolerate a wide range of temperatures in the environment.

eu·ryth·mics (juː'rɪðmɪks) *n.* a variant spelling (esp. U.S.) of **eurhythmics.** —**eu'ryth·mic** *or* **eu'ryth·mi·cal** *adj.* —**eu'ryth·my** *n.*

eu·ry·trop·ic (ˌjʊərɪ'trɒpɪk) *adj.* *Ecology.* (of a species, etc.) able to tolerate a wide range of environmental changes. Compare **stenotropic.** [C20: from EURY- + -TROPIC]

Eu·se·bi·us (juː'siːbɪəs) *n.* ?265–?340 A.D., bishop of Caesarea: author of a history of the Christian Church to 324 A.D.

eu·spo·ran·gi·ate (ˌjuːspɔː'rændʒɪɪt) *adj.* (of ferns) having each sporangium developing from a group of cells rather than a single cell. [from New Latin *eusporangiātus* (unattested), from EU- + SPORANGIUM]

Eu·sta·chian tube (juː'steɪʃən) *n.* a tube that connects the middle ear with the nasopharynx and equalizes the pressure between the two sides of the eardrum. [C18: named after Bartolomeo *Eustachio,* 16th-century Italian anatomist]

eu·stat·ic (juː'stætɪk) *adj.* denoting or relating to worldwide changes in sea level, caused by the melting of ice sheets, movements of the ocean floor, sedimentation, etc. [C20: from Greek, from EU- + STATIC] —**eu·sta·sy** ('juːstəsɪ) *n.* —**eu'stat·i·cal·ly** *adv.*

eu·tec·tic (juː'tɛktɪk) *adj.* **1.** (of a mixture of substances, esp. an alloy) having the lowest freezing point of all possible mixtures of the substances. **2.** concerned with or suitable for the formation of eutectic mixtures. ~*n.* **3.** a eutectic mixture. **4.** the temperature on a phase diagram at which a eutectic mixture forms. [C19: from Greek *eutēktos* melting readily, from EU- + *tēkein* to melt]

eu·tec·toid (juː'tɛktɔɪd) *adj.* another word for **eutectic.**

Eu·ter·pe (juː'tɜːpɪ) *n.* *Greek myth.* the Muse of lyric poetry and music. —**Eu'ter·pe·an** *adj.*

eu·tha·na·si·a (ˌjuːθə'neɪzɪə) *n.* the act of killing someone painlessly, esp. to relieve suffering from an incurable illness. Also called: **mercy killing.** [C17: via New Latin from Greek: easy death, from EU- + *thanatos* death]

eu·then·ics (juː'θɛnɪks) *n.* (*functioning as sing.*) the study of the control of the environment, esp. with a view to improving the health and living standards of the human race. [C20: from Greek *euthēnein* to thrive] —**eu'then·ist** *n.*

eu·the·ri·an (juː'θɪərɪən) *adj.* **1.** of, relating to, or belonging to the *Eutheria,* a subclass of mammals all of which have a placenta and reach an advanced state of development before birth. The group includes all mammals except monotremes and marsupials. ~*n.* **2.** any eutherian mammal. ~Compare **metatherian, prototherian.** [C19: from New Latin *Euthēria,* from Greek EU- + *thēria,* plural of *thērion* beast]

eu·troph·ic (juː'trɒfɪk, -'trəʊ-) *adj.* (of lakes, etc.) rich in organic and mineral nutrients and supporting an abundant plant life. Compare **oligotrophic.** [C18: probably from *eutrophy,* from Greek *eutrophia* sound nutrition, from *eutrophos* well-fed, from EU- + *trephein* to nourish] —**eu,troph·i'ca·tion** *n.* —'**eu·troph·y** *n.*

eux·e·nite ('juːksɪˌnaɪt) *n.* a rare brownish-black mineral containing erbium, cerium, uranium, columbium, and yttrium. [C19: from Greek *euxenos* hospitable (literally: well-disposed to strangers), from EU- + *xenos* stranger; from its containing a number of rare elements]

Eux·ine Sea ('juːksaɪn) *n.* another name for the **Black Sea.**

eV *abbrev. for* electronvolt.

E.V. *abbrev. for* English Version (of the Bible).

EVA *Astronautics. abbrev. for* extravehicular activity.

e·vac·u·ant (ɪ'vækjʊənt) *adj.* **1.** serving to promote excretion, esp. of the bowels. ~*n.* **2.** an evacuant agent.

e·vac·u·ate (ɪ'vækjʊˌeɪt) *vb.* (*mainly tr.*) **1.** (*also intr.*) to withdraw or cause to withdraw from (a place of danger) to a place of greater safety. **2.** to make empty by removing the contents of. **3.** (*also intr.*) *Physiol.* **a.** to eliminate or excrete (faeces); defecate. **b.** to discharge (any waste product) from (a part of the body). **4.** (*tr.*) to create a vacuum in (a bulb, flask, reaction vessel, etc.). [C16: from Latin *ēvacuāre* to void, from *vacuus* empty] —**e,vac·u'a·tion** *n.* —**e'vac·u·a·tive** *adj.* —**e'vac·u,a·tor** *n.*

e·vac·u·ee (ɪˌvækjʊ'iː) *n.* a person evacuated from a place of danger, esp. in wartime.

e·vade (ɪ'veɪd) *vb.* (*mainly tr.*) **1.** to get away from or avoid (imprisonment, captors, etc.); escape. **2.** to get around, shirk, or dodge (the law, a duty, etc.). **3.** (*also intr.*) to avoid answering (a question). [C16: from French *évader,* from Latin *ēvādere* to go forth, from *vādere* to go] —**e'vad·a·ble** *adj.* —**e'vad·er** *n.* —**e'vad·ing·ly** *adv.*

e·vag·i·nate (ɪ'vædʒɪˌneɪt) *vb.* (*tr.*) *Med.* to turn (an organ or part) inside out; turn the outer surface (of an organ or part) back on itself. [C17: from Late Latin *ēvāgīnāre* to unsheath, from *vāgīna* sheath] —**e,vag·i'na·tion** *n.*

e·val·u·ate (ɪ'væljʊˌeɪt) *vb.* (*tr.*) **1.** to ascertain or set the amount or value of. **2.** to judge or assess the worth of; appraise. [C19: back formation from *evaluation,* from French, from *evaluer* to evaluate; see VALUE] —**e,val·u'a·tion** *n.* —**e'val·u·a·tive** *adj.* —**e'val·u,a·tor** *n.*

ev·a·nesce (ˌɛvə'nɛs) *vb.* (*intr.*) (of smoke, mist, etc.) to fade gradually from sight; vanish. [C19: from Latin *ēvānēscere* to disappear; see VANISH]

ev·a·nes·cent (ˌɛvə'nɛsᵊnt) *adj.* **1.** passing out of sight; fading away; vanishing. **2.** ephemeral or transitory. —**,ev·a'nes·cent·ly** *adv.* —**,ev·a'nes·cence** *n.*

evang. *or* **evan.** (*often cap.*) *abbrev. for* evangelical.

e·van·gel (ɪ'vændʒəl) *n.* **1.** *Archaic.* the gospel of Christianity. **2.** (*often cap.*) any of the four Gospels of the New Testament. **3.** any body of teachings regarded as central or basic. **4.** a rare word for **evangelist.** [C14: from Church Latin *ēvangelium,* from Greek *evangelion* good news, from EU- + *angelos* messenger; see ANGEL]

e·van·gel·i·cal (ˌiːvæn'dʒɛlɪkᵊl) *Christianity.* ~*adj.* **1.** of, based upon, or following from the Gospels. **2.** denoting or relating to any of certain Protestant sects or parties, which emphasize the importance of personal conversion and faith in atonement through the death of Christ as a means of salvation. **3.** another word for **evangelistic.** ~*n.* **4.** an upholder of evangelical doctrines or a member of an evangelical sect or party, esp. the Low-Church party of the Church of England. —**,e·van'gel·i·cal·ism** *n.* —**,e·van'gel·i·cal·ly** *adv.*

e·van·ge·lism (ɪ'vændʒɪˌlɪzəm) *n.* **1.** the practice of spreading the Christian gospel. **2.** ardent or missionary zeal for a cause. **3.** the work, methods, or characteristic outlook of a revivalist or evangelist preacher. **4.** a less common word for **evangelicalism.**

e·van·ge·list (ɪ'vændʒɪlɪst) *n.* **1.** an occasional preacher, sometimes itinerant and often preaching at meetings in the open air. **2.** a preacher of the Christian gospel. **3.** any zealous advocate of a cause. **4.** another word for **revivalist** (sense 1).

E·van·ge·list (ɪ'vændʒɪlɪst) *n.* **1.** any of the writers of the New Testament Gospels: Matthew, Mark, Luke, or John. **2.** a senior official or dignitary of the Mormon Church.

e·van·ge·lis·tic (ɪˌvændʒɪ'lɪstɪk) *adj.* **1.** denoting, resembling, or relating to evangelists or their methods and attitudes: *evangelistic zeal.* **2.** zealously advocating a cause. **3.** (*often cap.*) of or relating to all or any of the four Evangelists. —**e,van·ge'lis·ti·cal·ly** *adv.*

e·van·ge·lize *or* **e·van·ge·lise** (ɪ'vændʒɪˌlaɪz) *vb.* **1.** to preach the Christian gospel or a particular interpretation of it (to). **2.** (*intr.*) to advocate a cause with the object of making converts. —**e,van·ge·li'za·tion** *or* **e,van·ge·li'sa·tion** *n.* —**e'van·ge,liz·er** *or* **e'van·ge,lis·er** *n.*

e·van·ish (ɪ'vænɪʃ) *vb.* a poetic word for **vanish.** [C15: from Old French *esvanir,* from Latin *ēvānēscere* to VANISH] —**e'van·ish·ment** *n.*

Ev·ans ('ɛvənz) *n.* **1.** Sir **Ar·thur John.** 1851–1941, English archaeologist, whose excavations of the palace of Knossos in Crete provided evidence for the existence of the Minoan civilization. **2.** **(Arthur) Mos·tyn,** known as *Moss.* born 1925, British trade-union leader; general secretary of the Transport and General Workers' Union since 1978. **3.** Dame **E·dith.** 1888–1976, English actress. **4.** Sir **Ger·aint (Llewellyn).** born 1922, Welsh operatic baritone. **5. Her·bert Mc·Lean.** 1882–1971, U.S. anatomist and embryologist; discoverer of vitamin E (1922). **6. Mar·y Ann.** original name of (George) **Eliot.**

Ev·ans·ton ('ɛvənstən) *n.* a city in NE Illinois, on Lake Michigan north of Chicago: Northwestern University (1851). Pop.: 79 808 (1970).

Ev·ans·ville ('ɛvənzˌvɪl) *n.* a city in SW Indiana, on the Ohio River. Pop.: 136 165 (1973 est.).

e·vap·o·rate (ɪ'væpəˌreɪt) *vb.* **1.** to change or cause to change from a liquid or solid state to a vapour. Compare **boil**[1] (sense 1). **2.** to lose or cause to lose liquid by vaporization leaving a more concentrated residue. **3.** to disappear or cause to disappear; fade away or cause to fade away: *all her doubts evaporated.* **4.** (*tr.*) to deposit (a film, metal, etc.) by vaporization of a liquid or solid and the subsequent condensation of its vapour. [C16: from Late Latin *ēvapōrāre,* from Latin *vapor* steam; see VAPOUR] —**e'vap·o·ra·ble** *adj.* —**e,vap·o·ra'bil·i·ty** *n.* —**e,vap·o'ra·tion** *n.* —**e'vap·o·ra·tive** *adj.* —**e'vap·o,ra·tor** *n.*

e·vap·o·rat·ed milk *n.* thick unsweetened tinned milk from which some of the water has been evaporated.

e·vap·o·rim·e·ter (ɪˌvæpə'rɪmɪtə) *or* **e·vap·o·rom·e·ter** (ɪˌvæpə'rɒmɪtə) *n.* another name for **atmometer.**

e·vap·o·rite (ɪ'væpəˌraɪt) *n.* any sedimentary rock, such as rock salt, gypsum, or anhydrite, formed by evaporation of former seas or salt-water lakes. [C20: EVAPORATION + -ITE[1]]

e·vap·o·tran·spi·ra·tion (ɪˌvæpəʊˌtrænspə'reɪʃən) *n.* the return of water vapour to the atmosphere by evaporation from land and water surfaces and by the transpiration of vegetation.

e·va+sion (ɪˈveɪʒən) *n.* **1.** the act of evading or escaping, esp. from a distasteful duty, responsibility, etc., by trickery, cunning, or illegal means: *tax evasion.* **2.** trickery, cunning, or deception used to dodge a question, duty, etc.; means of evading. [C15: from Late Latin *ēvāsiō*, from Latin *ēvādere* to go forth; see EVADE]

e·va+sive (ɪˈveɪsɪv) *adj.* **1.** tending or seeking to evade; avoiding the issue; not straightforward. **2.** avoiding or seeking to avoid trouble or difficulties: *to take evasive action.* **3.** hard to catch or obtain; elusive. —**e·ˈva+sive+ly** *adv.* —**e·ˈva+sive+ness** *n.*

eve (iːv) *n.* **1. a.** the evening or day before some special event or festival. **b.** (*cap. when part of a name*): *New Year's Eve.* **2.** the period immediately before an event: *on the eve of civil war.* **3.** an archaic word for **evening.** [C13: variant of EVEN²]

Eve (iːv) *n. Old Testament.* the first woman; mother of the human race, fashioned by God from the rib of Adam (Genesis 2:18-25).

e·vec+tion (ɪˈvɛkʃən) *n.* irregularity in the moon's motion caused by perturbations of the sun and planets. [C17: from Latin *ēvectiō* a going up, from *ēvehere* to lead forth, from *vehere* to carry] —**e·ˈvec+tion+al** *adj.*

Eve·lyn (ˈiːvlɪn, ˈɛv-) *n.* **John.** 1620–1706, English author, noted chiefly for his diary (1640–1706).

e·ven¹ (ˈiːvᵊn) *adj.* **1.** level and regular; flat: *an even surface.* **2.** (*postpositive;* foll. by *with*) on the same level or in the same plane (as): *one surface even with another.* **3.** without variation or fluctuation; regular; constant: *an even rate of progress.* **4.** not readily moved or excited; placid; calm: *an even temper.* **5.** equally balanced between two sides: *an even game.* **6.** equal or identical in number, quantity, etc.: *two even spoonfuls of sugar.* **7. a.** (of a number) divisible by two. **b.** characterized or indicated by such a number: *maps are on the even pages.* Compare **odd** (sense 4). **8.** relating to or denoting two or either of two alternatives, events, etc., that have an equal probability: *an even chance of missing or catching a train.* **9.** having no balance of debt; neither owing nor being owed. **10.** just and impartial; fair: *an even division.* **11.** exact in number, amount, or extent: *an even pound.* **12.** equal, as in score; level: *now the teams are even.* **13.** *Maths.* (of a function) unchanged in value when the sign of the independent variable is changed, as in $y = z^2$. Compare **odd** (sense 8). **14. even money. a.** a bet that wins an identical sum if it succeeds. **b.** (*as modifier*): *the even-money favourite.* **15. get even (with).** *Informal.* to exact revenge (on). **16. of even date.** *Legal, formal, or obsolete.* of the same or today's date. ~*adv.* **17.** (intensifier; used to suggest that the content of a statement is unexpected or paradoxical): *even an idiot can do that.* **18.** (intensifier; used with comparative forms): *this is even better.* **19.** notwithstanding; in spite of: *even having started late she soon caught him up.* **20.** used to introduce a more precise version of a word, phrase, or statement: *he is base, even depraved.* **21.** used preceding a clause of supposition or hypothesis to emphasize the implication that whether or not the condition in it is fulfilled, the statement in the main clause remains valid: *even if she died he wouldn't care.* **22.** *Archaic.* that is to say; namely (used for emphasis): *he, even he, hath spoken these things.* **23.** *Archaic.* all the way; fully: *I love thee even unto death.* **24. even as.** (*conj.*) at the very same moment or in the very same way that: *even as I spoke, it thundered.* **25. even so. a.** in spite of any assertion to the contrary; nevertheless. **b.** *Archaic.* yes; (that is) correct. ~See also **break even, even out, even up.** [Old English *efen;* related to Old Norse *jafn* even, equal, Gothic *ibns,* Old High German *eban*] —**ˈe·ven+er** *n.* —**ˈe·ven+ly** *adv.* —**ˈe·ven+ness** *n.*

e·ven² (ˈiːvᵊn) *n.* an archaic word for **eve** or **evening.** [Old English *ǣfen;* related to Old Frisian *ēvend,* Old High German *āband*]

e·ven+fall (ˈiːvᵊnˌfɔːl) *n. Archaic.* early evening; dusk.

e·ven-hand·ed *adj.* dealing fairly with all; impartial. —**ˌe·ven-ˈhand·ed+ly** *adv.* —**ˌe·ven-ˈhand·ed+ness** *n.*

eve+ning (ˈiːvnɪŋ) *n.* **1.** the latter part of the day, esp. from late afternoon until nightfall. **2.** the latter or concluding period: *the evening of one's life.* **3.** the early part of the night spent in a specified way: *an evening at the theatre.* **4.** an entertainment, meeting, or reception held in the early part of the night. **5.** *Southern U.S. and Brit. dialect.* the period between noon and sunset. **6.** (*modifier*) of, used, or occurring in the evening: *the evening papers.* [Old English *ǣfnung;* related to Old Frisian *ēvend,* Old High German *āband*]

eve+ning class *n.* a class held in the evenings at certain colleges, normally for adults.

eve+ning dress *n.* attire for wearing at a formal occasion during the evening, esp. (for men) a dinner jacket and black tie, or (less commonly, for women) a floor-length gown.

eve+ning prim+rose *n.* any onagraceous plant of the American genus *Oenothera,* esp. *O. biennis,* typically having yellow flowers that open in the evening.

eve+nings (ˈiːvnɪŋz) *adv. Informal.* in the evening, esp. regularly.

eve+ning star *n.* a planet, usually Venus, seen shining brightly in the west just after sunset. Compare **morning star.**

e·ven out *vb.* (*adv.*) to make or become even, as by the removal of bumps, inequalities, etc.: *the land evens out beyond that rise.*

e·vens (ˈiːvᵊnz) *adj., adv.* **1.** (of a bet) winning an identical sum if successful. **2.** (of a runner) offered at such odds.

e·ven+song (ˈiːvᵊnˌsɒŋ) *n.* **1.** Also called: **Evening Prayer.** *Church of England.* the daily evening service of Bible readings and prayers prescribed in the Book of Common Prayer. **2.** *Archaic.* another name for **vespers. 3.** an archaic or poetic word for **evening.**

e·vent (ɪˈvɛnt) *n.* **1.** anything that takes place or happens, esp. something important; happening; incident. **2.** the actual or final outcome; result (esp. in the phrases **in the event, after the event**). **3.** any one contest in a programme of sporting or other contests: *the high jump is his event.* **4.** *Philosophy.* an occurrence not caused by human agency. Compare **act** (sense 8). **5. at all events** *or* **in any event.** regardless of circumstances; in any case. **6. in the event of.** in case of; if (such a thing) happens: *in the event of rain the race will be cancelled.* **7. in the event that.** if it should happen that. [C16: from Latin *ēventus* a happening, from *ēvenīre* to come forth, happen, from *venīre* to come]

e·ven-tem·pered *adj.* not easily angered or excited; calm.

e·vent+ful (ɪˈvɛntfʊl) *adj.* full of events or incidents: *an eventful day.* —**e·ˈvent+ful+ly** *adv.* —**e·ˈvent+ful+ness** *n.*

e·vent ho+ri+zon *n. Astronomy.* the spherical surface around a black hole enclosing the space from which electromagnetic radiation cannot escape due to excessive gravitational attraction. The radius is proportional to the mass of the black hole.

e·ven+tide (ˈiːvᵊnˌtaɪd) *n. Archaic or poetic.* another word for **evening.**

e·ven+tu·al (ɪˈvɛntʃʊəl) *adj.* **1.** (*prenominal*) happening in due course of time; ultimate: *the eventual outcome was his defeat.* **2.** *Archaic.* contingent or possible.

e·ven+tu+al+i·ty (ɪˌvɛntʃʊˈælɪtɪ) *n., pl.* **·ties.** a possible event, occurrence, or result; contingency.

e·ven+tu+al+ly (ɪˈvɛntʃʊəlɪ) *adv.* **1.** at the very end; finally. **2.** (*as sentence modifier*) after a long time or long delay: *eventually, he arrived.*

e·ven+tu+ate (ɪˈvɛntʃʊˌeɪt) *vb.* (*intr.*) **1.** (often foll. by *in*) to result ultimately (in). **2.** to come about as a result: *famine eventuated from the crop failure.* —**e·ˌven+tu·ˈa+tion** *n.*

e·ven up *vb.* (*adv.*) to make or become equal, esp. in respect of claims or debts; settle or balance.

ev·er (ˈɛvə) *adv.* **1.** at any time: *have you ever seen it?* **2.** by any chance; in any case: *how did you ever find out?* **3.** at all times; always: *ever busy.* **4.** in any possible way or manner: *come as fast as ever you can.* **5.** *Informal, chiefly Brit.* (intensifier, in the phrases **ever so, ever such,** and **ever such a**): *ever so good; ever such bad luck; ever such a waste.* **6. ever and again** (*or* **anon**). *Archaic.* now and then; from time to time. **7. is he** *or* **she ever!** *U.S. slang.* he *or* she displays the quality concerned in abundance. ~See also **for ever.** [Old English *ǣfre,* of uncertain origin]

Ev+er+est (ˈɛvərɪst) *n.* **1. Mount.** a mountain in S Asia on the border between Nepal and Tibet, in the Himalayas: the highest mountain in the world; first climbed by a British expedition (1953). Height: 8848 m (29 028 ft.). **2.** any high point of ambition or achievement. [C19: named after Sir G. *Everest* (died 1866), Surveyor-General of India]

Ev·er+glades (ˈɛvəˌgleɪdz) *pl. n.* **the.** a subtropical marshy region of Florida, south of Lake Okeechobee: contains the **Everglades National Park,** established to preserve the flora and fauna of the swamps. Area: over 13 000 sq. km (5000 sq. miles).

ev·er+green (ˈɛvəˌgriːn) *adj.* **1.** (of certain trees and shrubs) bearing foliage throughout the year; continually shedding and replacing leaves. Compare **deciduous. 2.** remaining fresh and vital. ~*n.* **3.** an evergreen tree or shrub.

ev·er+last·ing (ˌɛvəˈlɑːstɪŋ) *adj.* **1.** never coming to an end; eternal. **2.** lasting for an indefinitely long period. **3.** lasting so long or occurring so often as to become tedious; incessant: *I cannot bear her everlasting complaints.* ~*n.* **4.** endless duration; eternity. **5.** Also called: **everlasting flower.** another name for **immortelle.** —**ˌev·er+ˈlast·ing+ly** *adv.* —**ˌev·er+ˈlast·ing+ness** *n.*

ev·er+more (ˌɛvəˈmɔː) *adv.* (often preceded by *for*) all time to come.

e·vert (ɪˈvɜːt) *vb.* (*tr.*) to turn (an eyelid, the intestines, or some other bodily part) outwards or inside out. [C16: from Latin *ēvertere* to overthrow, from *vertere* to turn] —**e·ˈver+si·ble** *adj.* —**e·ˈver+sion** *n.*

Ev·ert Lloyd (ˈɛvət lɔɪd) *n.* **Chris·tine,** known as *Chrissie.* born 1954, U.S. tennis player: Wimbledon champion 1974 and 1976; U.S. champion 1975–78.

e·vert+or (ɪˈvɜːtə) *n.* any muscle that turns a part outwards.

eve·ry (ˈɛvrɪ) *determiner.* **1.** each one (of the class specified), without exception: *every child knows it.* **2.** (*not used with a negative*) the greatest or best possible: *every hope of success.* **3.** each: used before a noun phrase to indicate the recurrent, intermittent, or serial nature of a thing: *every third day; every now and then; every so often.* **4. every bit.** (used in comparisons with *as*) quite; just; equally: *every bit as funny as the other show.* **5. every other.** each alternate; every second: *every other day.* **6. every which way.** *U.S.* **a.** in all directions; everywhere: *I looked every which way for you.* **b.** from all sides: *stones coming at me every which way.* [C15 *everich,* from Old English *ǣfre ǣlc,* from *ǣfre* EVER + *ǣlc* EACH]

eve·ry+bod·y (ˈɛvrɪˌbɒdɪ) *pron.* every person; everyone. **Usage.** See at **everyone.**

eve·ry+day (ˈɛvrɪˌdeɪ) *adj.* **1.** happening each day; daily. **2.** commonplace or usual; ordinary. **3.** suitable for or used on ordinary days as distinct from Sundays or special days.

Eve·ry+man (ˈɛvrɪˌmæn) *n.* **1.** a medieval English morality play in which the central figure represents mankind, whose earthly destiny is dramatized from the Christian viewpoint. **2.** (*often not cap.*) the ordinary person; common man.

eve·ry one *pron.* each person or thing in a group, without exception: *every one of the large cats is a fast runner.*

eve·ry+one ('ɛvrɪ,wʌn, -wən) *pron.* every person; everybody.
Usage. *Everyone* and *everybody* are interchangeable, as are *no one* and *nobody*, and *someone* and *somebody*. *Everybody, everyone, none, no one, nobody, somebody, someone,* and *each* function as singular in careful English: *everyone nodded his head* (not *their heads*). The use of *their* in such constructions is, however, common in informal English. Careful writers distinguish between *everyone* and *someone* as single words and *every one* and *some one* as two words, using the latter form to refer to each individual person or thing in a particular group: *every one of them is wrong.*

eve·ry+place ('ɛvrɪ,pleɪs) *adv. U.S.* an informal word for **everywhere.**

eve·ry+thing ('ɛvrɪ,θɪŋ) *pron.* **1.** the entirety of a specified or implied class: *she lost everything in the War.* **2.** a great deal, esp. of something very important: *she means everything to me.*

eve·ry+where ('ɛvrɪ,wɛə) *adv.* to or in all parts or places.

Eve+sham ('iːvʃəm) *n.* a town in W central England, in E Hereford and Worcester, on the River Avon: scene of the Battle of Evesham in 1265 (Lord Edward's defeat of Simon de Montfort and the barons); centre of the **Vale of Evesham,** famous for market gardens and orchards. Pop.: 13 847 (1971).

Eve's pud+ding *n. Brit.* a baked sponge pudding with a layer of fruit at the bottom.

e·vict (ɪ'vɪkt) *vb.* (*tr.*) **1.** to expel (a tenant) from property by process of law. **2.** to recover (property or the title to property) by judicial process or by virtue of a superior title. [C15: from Late Latin *ēvincere,* from Latin: to vanquish utterly, from *vincere* to conquer] **—e·'vic+tion** *n.* **—e·'vic+tor** *n.*

ev·i+dence ('ɛvɪdəns) *n.* **1.** ground for belief or disbelief; data on which to base proof or to establish truth or falsehood. **2.** a mark or sign that makes evident; indication: *his pallor was evidence of ill health.* **3.** *Law.* matter produced before a court of law in an attempt to prove or disprove a point in issue, such as the statements of witnesses, documents, material objects, etc. See also **circumstantial evidence, direct evidence. 4. turn queen's (king's, state's) evidence.** (of an accomplice) to act as witness for the prosecution and testify against those associated with him in crime. **5. in evidence.** on display; apparent; conspicuous: *her engagement ring was in evidence.* ~*vb.* (*tr.*) **6.** to make evident; show clearly. **7.** to give proof of or evidence for.

ev·i+dent ('ɛvɪdənt) *adj.* easy to see or understand; readily apparent. [C14: from Latin *ēvidēns,* from *vidēre* to see]

ev·i+den+tial (,ɛvɪ'dɛnʃəl) *adj.* relating to, serving as, or based on evidence. **—,ev·i·'den+tial+ly** *adv.*

ev·i+dent+ly ('ɛvɪdəntlɪ) *adv.* **1.** without question; clearly; undoubtedly. **2.** to all appearances; apparently: *they are evidently related.*

e·vil ('iːvəl) *adj.* **1.** morally wrong or bad; wicked: *an evil ruler.* **2.** causing harm or injury; harmful: *an evil plan.* **3.** marked or accompanied by misfortune; unlucky: *an evil fate.* **4.** (of temper, disposition, etc.) characterized by anger or spite. **5.** not in high esteem; infamous: *an evil reputation.* **6.** offensive or unpleasant: *an evil smell.* ~*n.* **7.** the quality or an instance of being morally wrong; wickedness: *the evils of war.* **8.** (*sometimes cap.*) a force or power that brings about wickedness or harm: *evil is strong in the world.* **9.** *Archaic.* an illness or disease, esp. scrofula (the **king's evil**). ~*adv.* **10.** (*now usually in combination*) in an evil manner; badly: *evil-smelling.* [Old English *yfel,* of Germanic origin; compare Old Frisian *evel,* Old High German *ubil* evil, Old Irish *adbal* excessive] **—'e·vil+ly** *adv.* **—'e·vil+ness** *n.*

e·vil+do·er ('iːvəl,duːə) *n.* a person who does evil. **—'e·vil+,do·ing** *n.*

e·vil eye *n.* **the. 1.** a look or glance superstitiously supposed to have the power of inflicting harm or injury. **2.** the power to inflict harm, etc., by such a look. **—,e·vil-'eyed** *adj.*

e·vil-mind·ed *adj.* inclined to evil thoughts; malicious or spiteful. **—,e·vil-'mind·ed+ly** *adv.* **—,e·vil-'mind·ed+ness** *n.*

E·vil One *n.* **the.** the devil; Satan.

e·vince (ɪ'vɪns) *vb.* (*tr.*) to make evident; show (something, such as an emotion) clearly. [C17: from Latin *ēvincere* to overcome; see EVICT] **—e·'vin+ci·ble** *adj.* **—e·'vin+cive** *adj.*

e·vis+cer+ate (ɪ'vɪsə,reɪt) *vb.* **1.** (*tr.*) to remove the internal organs of; disembowel. **2.** (*tr.*) to deprive of meaning or significance. **3.** (*tr.*) *Surgery.* to remove the contents of (the eyeball or other organ). **4.** (*intr.*) *Surgery.* (of the viscera) to protrude through a weakened abdominal incision after an operation. ~*adj.* **5.** having been disembowelled. [C17: from Latin *ēviscerāre* to disembowel, from *viscera* entrails] **—e·,vis+cer·'a+tion** *n.* **—e·'vis+cer·,a+tor** *n.*

ev·i+ta·ble ('ɛvɪtəbəl) *adj. Rare.* able to be avoided. [C16: from Latin *ēvītābilis,* from *ēvītāre,* from *vītāre* to avoid]

e·vite (ɪ'vaɪt) *vb.* (*tr.*) an archaic word for **avoid.**

ev·o+ca+tion (,ɛvə'keɪʃən) *n.* **1.** the act or an instance of evoking. **2.** *French law.* the transference of a case from an inferior court for adjudication by a higher tribunal. **3.** another word for **induction** (sense 5). [C17: from Latin *ēvocātiō* a calling forth, from *ēvocāre* to EVOKE]

e·voc·a·tive (ɪ'vɒkətɪv) *adj.* tending or serving to evoke. **—e·'voc·a·tive+ly** *adv.* **—e·'voc·a·tive+ness** *n.*

ev·o+ca+tor ('ɛvə,keɪtə) *n.* **1.** a person or thing that evokes. **2.** *Embryol.* a substance or tissue that induces morphogenesis.

e·voke (ɪ'vəʊk) *vb.* (*tr.*) **1.** to call or summon up (a memory, feeling, etc.), esp. from the past. **2.** to call forth or provoke; produce; elicit: *his words evoked an angry reply.* **3.** to cause (spirits) to appear; conjure up. [C17: from Latin *ēvocāre* to call forth, from *vocāre* to call] **—ev·o+ca·ble** ('ɛvəkəbəl) *adj.* **—e·'vok+er** *n.*

ev·o+lute ('ɛvə,luːt) *n.* a geometric curve that describes the locus of the centres of curvature of another curve (the **involute**). The tangents to the evolute are normal to the involute. [C19: from Latin *ēvolūtus* unrolled, from *ēvolvere* to roll out, EVOLVE]

e·vo+lu+tion (,iːvə'luːʃən) *n.* **1.** *Biology.* a gradual change in the characteristics of a population of animals or plants over successive generations: accounts for the origin of existing species from ancestors unlike them. See also **natural selection. 2.** a gradual development, esp. to a more complex form: *the evolution of modern art.* **3.** the act of throwing off, as heat, gas, vapour, etc. **4.** a pattern formed by a series of movements or something similar. **5.** an algebraic operation in which the root of a number, expression, etc., is extracted. Compare **involution** (sense 6). **6.** *Military.* an exercise carried out in accordance with a set procedure or plan. [C17: from Latin *ēvolūtiō* an unrolling, from *ēvolvere* to EVOLVE] **—,e·vo+'lu+tion+ar·y** *or* **,e·vo+'lu+tion+al** *adj.*

e·vo+lu+tion+ist (,iːvə'luːʃənɪst) *n.* **1.** a person who believes in a theory of evolution, esp. Darwin's theory of the evolution of plant and animal species. ~*adj.* **2.** of or relating to a theory of evolution. **—,e·vo+'lu+tion+ism** *n.* **—,e·vo+lu+tion+'is+tic** *adj.*

e·volve (ɪ'vɒlv) *vb.* **1.** to develop or cause to develop gradually. **2.** (of animal or plant species) to undergo evolution of (organs or parts). **3.** (*tr.*) to yield, emit, or give off (heat, gas, vapour, etc.). [C17: from Latin *ēvolvere* to unfold, from *volvere* to roll] **—e·'volv+a·ble** *adj.* **—e·'volve+ment** *n.* **—e·'volv+er** *n.*

e·von·y·mus (ɛ'vɒnɪməs) *n.* another name for **euonymus.**

É·vo+ra (*Portuguese* 'ɛvura) *n.* a city in S central Portugal: ancient Roman settlement; occupied by the Moors from 712 to 1166; residence of the Portuguese court in 15th and 16th centuries. Pop.: 50 235 (1970). Ancient name: **Ebora.**

É·vreux (*French* e'vrø) *n.* an industrial town in NW France: severely damaged in World War II; cathedral (12th–16th centuries). Pop.: 50 358 (1975).

Év+ros ('ɛvrɔs) *n.* transliteration of the Modern Greek name for the (River) **Maritsa.**

e·vul+sion (ɪ'vʌlʃən) *n. Rare.* the act of extracting by force. [C17: from Latin *ēvulsiō,* from *ēvellere,* from *vellere* to pluck]

Év+voi·a ('ɛvia) *n.* transliteration of the Modern Greek name for **Euboea.**

ev+zone ('ɛvzəʊn) *n.* a soldier in an elite Greek infantry regiment. [C19: from Modern Greek, from Greek *euzōnos* literally: well-girt, from EU- + *zōnē* girdle]

ewe (juː) *n.* **a.** a female sheep. **b.** (*as modifier*): *a ewe lamb.* [Old English *ēowu;* related to Old Norse *ǣr* ewe, Old High German *ou,* Latin *ovis* sheep, Sanskrit *avi*]

E·we ('ɛwɛ) *n.* **1.** (*pl.* **E·we** *or* **E·wes**) a member of a Negroid people of W Africa living chiefly in the forests of E Ghana, Togo, and Benin. **2.** the language of this people, belonging to the Kwa branch of the Niger-Congo family.

ewe-neck *n.* **1.** a condition in horses in which the neck is straight and sagging rather than arched. **2.** a horse or other animal with this condition. **—'ewe-,necked** *adj.*

ew·er ('juːə) *n.* a large jug or pitcher with a wide mouth. [C14: from Old French *evier,* from Latin *aquārius* water carrier, from *aqua* water]

ex[1] (ɛks) *prep.* **1.** *Finance.* not participating in; excluding; without: *ex dividend; ex interest.* **2.** *Commerce.* without charge to the buyer until removed from: *ex warehouse.* [C19: from Latin: out of, from]

ex[2] (ɛks) *n. Informal.* short for **ex-wife, ex-husband, ex-girlfriend,** etc.

ex-[1] *prefix.* **1.** out of; outside of; from: *exclosure; exurbia.* **2.** former: *ex-wife.* [from Latin, from *ex* (prep.), identical in meaning and origin with Greek *ex, ek;* see EC-]

ex-[2] *combining form.* variant of **exo-** before a vowel: *exergonic.*

ex. *abbrev. for:* **1.** examination. **2.** examined. **3.** example. **4.** except(ed). **5.** exception. **6.** exchange. **7.** excursion. **8.** executed. **9.** executive. **10.** express. **11.** extra.

Ex. *Bible. abbrev. for* Exodus.

exa- *prefix.* denoting 10^{18}: *exametres.* Symbol: E

ex+ac+er+bate (ɪg'zæsə,beɪt, ɪk'sæs-) *vb.* (*tr.*) **1.** to make (pain, disease, emotion, etc.) more intense; aggravate. **2.** to exasperate or irritate (a person). [C17: from Latin *exacerbāre* to irritate, from *acerbus* bitter] **—ex+'ac+er+,bat+ing+ly** *adv.* **—ex+,ac+er+'ba+tion** *n.*

ex+act (ɪg'zækt) *adj.* **1.** correct in every detail; strictly accurate: *an exact copy.* **2.** precise, as opposed to approximate; neither more nor less: *the exact sum.* **3.** (*prenominal*) specific; particular: *this exact spot.* **4.** operating with very great precision: *exact instruments.* **5.** allowing no deviation from a standard; rigorous; strict: *an exact mind.* **6.** based mainly on measurement and the formulation of laws, as opposed to description and classification: *physics is an exact science.* ~*vb.* (*tr.*) **7.** to force or compel (payment or performance); extort: *to exact tribute.* **8.** to demand as a right; insist upon: *to exact respect from one's employees.* **9.** to call for or require: *this work exacts careful effort.* [C16: from Latin *exactus* driven out, from *exigere* to drive forth, from *agere* to drive] **—ex+'act+a·ble** *adj.* **—ex+'act+ness** *n.* **—ex+'ac+tor** *or* **ex+'act+er** *n.*

ex+act+ing (ɪg'zæktɪŋ) *adj.* making rigorous or excessive demands: *an exacting job.* **—ex+'act+ing+ly** *adv.* **—ex+'act+ing+ness** *n.*

ex+ac+tion (ɪg'zækʃən) *n.* **1.** the act or an instance of exacting, esp. money. **2.** an excessive or harsh demand, esp. for money; extortion. **3.** a sum or payment exacted.

ex·act·i·tude (ɪg'zæktɪˌtjuːd) *n.* the quality of being exact; precision; accuracy.

ex·act·ly (ɪg'zæktlɪ) *adv.* **1.** in an exact manner; accurately or precisely. **2.** in every respect; just: *it is exactly what he wants.* ~*interj.* **3.** just so! precisely! **4. not exactly.** *Ironical.* not at all; by no means.

ex·ag·ger·ate (ɪg'zædʒəˌreɪt) *vb.* **1.** to regard or represent as larger or greater, more important or more successful, etc., than is true. **2.** (*tr.*) to make greater, more noticeable, etc., than usual: *his new clothes exaggerated his awkwardness.* [C16: from Latin *exaggerāre* to magnify, from *aggerāre* to heap, from *agger* heap] —**ex·'ag·ger·ˌat·ing·ly** *adv.* —**ex·ˌag·ger·'a·tion** *n.* —**ex·'ag·ger·a·tive** *or* **ex·'ag·ger·a·to·ry** *adj.* —**ex·'ag·ger·ˌa·tor** *n.*

ex·ag·ger·at·ed (ɪg'zædʒəˌreɪtɪd) *adj.* **1.** unduly or excessively magnified; enlarged beyond truth or reasonableness. **2.** *Pathol.* abnormally enlarged: *an exaggerated spleen.* —**ex·'ag·ger·ˌat·ed·ly** *adv.*

ex·alt (ɪg'zɔːlt) *vb.* (*tr.*) **1.** to raise or elevate in rank, position, dignity, etc. **2.** to praise highly; glorify; extol. **3.** to stimulate the mind or imagination of; excite. **4.** to increase the intensity of (a colour, etc.). **5.** to fill with joy or delight; elate. **6.** *Obsolete.* to lift up physically. [C15: from Latin *exaltāre* to raise, from *altus* high] —**ex·'alt·er** *n.*

ex·al·ta·tion (ˌegzɔːl'teɪʃən) *n.* **1.** the act of exalting or state of being exalted. **2.** a feeling of intense well-being or exhilaration; elation; rapture. **3.** a flock of larks.

ex·alt·ed (ɪg'zɔːltɪd) *adj.* **1.** high or elevated in rank, position, dignity, etc. **2.** elevated in character; noble; lofty: *an exalted ideal.* **3.** *Informal.* excessively high; inflated: *he has an exalted opinion of himself.* **4.** intensely excited; elated. —**ex·'alt·ed·ly** *adv.* —**ex·'alt·ed·ness** *n.*

ex·am (ɪg'zæm) *n.* short for **examination.**

ex·a·men (ɪg'zeɪmɛn) *n. R.C. Church.* an examination of conscience, usually made daily by Jesuits and others. [C17: from Latin: tongue of a balance, from *exigere* to thrust out, from *agere* to thrust]

ex·am·i·na·tion (ɪgˌzæmɪ'neɪʃən) *n.* **1.** the act of examining or state of being examined. **2.** *Education.* **a.** written exercises, oral questions, or practical tasks, set to test a candidate's knowledge and skill. **b.** (*as modifier*): *an examination paper.* **3.** *Med.* **a.** physical inspection of a patient or parts of his body, in order to verify health or diagnose disease. **b.** laboratory study of secretory or excretory products, tissue samples, etc., esp. in order to diagnose disease. **4.** *Law.* the formal interrogation of a person on oath, esp. of an accused or a witness. —**ex·ˌam·i·'na·tion·al** *adj.*

ex·am·ine (ɪg'zæmɪn) *vb.* (*tr.*) **1.** to look at, inspect, or scrutinize carefully or in detail; investigate. **2.** *Education.* to test the knowledge or skill of (a candidate) in (a subject or activity) by written or oral questions or by practical tests. **3.** *Law.* to interrogate (a witness or accused person) formally on oath. **4.** *Med.* to investigate the state of health of (a patient). [C14: from Old French *examiner,* from Latin *exāmināre* to weigh, from *exāmen* means of weighing; see EXAMEN] —**ex·'am·in·a·ble** *adj.* —**ex·'am·in·er** *n.*

ex·am·i·nee (ɪgˌzæmɪ'niː) *n.* a person who takes an examination.

ex·am·ine-in-chief *vb.* (*tr.*) *Law.* to examine (one's own witness) in attempting to adduce a case. Compare **cross-examine.** —**ex·ˌam·i·'na·tion-in-chief** *n.*

ex·am·ple (ɪg'zɑːmpᵊl) *n.* **1.** a specimen or instance that is typical of the group or set of which it forms part; sample. **2.** a person, action, thing, etc., that is worthy of imitation; pattern: *you must set an example to the younger children.* **3.** a precedent, illustration of a principle, or model: *an example in a maths book.* **4.** a punishment or the recipient of a punishment serving or intended to serve as a warning: *the headmaster made an example of him.* **5. for example.** as an illustration; for instance. ~*vb.* **6.** (*tr.; now usually passive*) to present an example of; exemplify. [C14: from Old French, from Latin *exemplum* pattern, from *eximere* to take out, from EX- + *emere* to purchase]

ex·an·i·mate (ɪg'zænɪmɪt, -ˌmeɪt) *adj. Rare.* lacking life; inanimate. [C16: from Latin *exanimāre* to deprive of air, kill, from *anima* breath, spirit] —**ex·ˌan·i·'ma·tion** *n.*

ex·an·the·ma (ˌɛksæn'θiːmə) *or* **ex·an·them** (ɛk'sænθəm) *n., pl.* **·the·ma·ta** (-'θiːmətə), **·the·mas,** *or* **·thems.** a skin eruption or rash occurring as a symptom in a disease such as measles or scarlet fever. [C17: via Late Latin from Greek, from *exanthein* to burst forth, from *anthein* to blossom, from *anthos* flower] —**ex·an·the·ma·tous** (ˌɛksæn'θɛmətəs) *or* **ex·an·the·mat·ic** (ɛkˌsænθɪ'mætɪk) *adj.*

ex·a·rate ('ɛksəˌreɪt) *adj.* (of the pupa of such insects as ants and bees) having the legs, wings, antennae, etc., free and movable. [C19: from Latin *exarātus,* literally: ploughed up (apparently referring to the way this type of pupa throws off the larval skin), from *exarāre,* from *arā* plough]

ex·arch[1] ('ɛksɑːk) *n.* **1.** the head of certain autonomous Orthodox Christian Churches, such as that of Bulgaria and Cyprus. **2.** any of certain Eastern Orthodox bishops, lower in rank than a patriarch but higher than a metropolitan. **3.** the governor of a province in the Byzantine Empire. [C16: from Late Latin *exarchus* overseer, from Greek *exarkhos,* from *exarkhein* to take the lead, from *arkhein* to rule] —**ex·'arch·al** *adj.*

ex·arch[2] ('ɛksɑːk) *adj. Botany.* (of a xylem strand) having the first-formed xylem external to that formed later. Compare **endarch, mesarch.** [C19: from EX- (outside) + Greek *arkhē* beginning, origin]

ex·ar·chate ('ɛksɑːˌkeɪt, ɛk'sɑːkeɪt) *or* **ex·ar·chy** ('ɛksɑːkɪ) *n., pl.* **·chates** *or* **·chies.** the office, rank, or jurisdiction of an exarch.

ex·as·per·ate (ɪg'zɑːspəˌreɪt) *vb.* (*tr.*) **1.** to cause great irritation or anger to; infuriate. **2.** to cause (an unpleasant feeling, condition, etc.) to worsen; aggravate. ~*adj.* **3.** *Botany.* having a rough prickly surface because of the presence of hard projecting points. [C16: from Latin *exasperāre* to make rough, from *asper* rough] —**ex·'as·per·ˌat·ed·ly** *adv.* —**ex·'as·per·ˌat·er** *n.* —**ex·'as·per·ˌat·ing·ly** *adv.* —**ex·ˌas·per·'a·tion** *n.*

exc. *abbrev. for:* **1.** excellent. **2.** except(ed). **3.** exception. **4.** excursion.

Exc. *abbrev. for* Excellency.

Ex·cal·i·bur (ɛk'skælɪbə) *n.* (in Arthurian legend) the magic sword of King Arthur. [C14: from Old French *Escalibor,* from Medieval Latin *Caliburnus,* from Welsh *Caledvwlch,* perhaps related to Irish *Caladbolg* a legendary sword (literally: hard belly, hence, voracious)]

ex ca·the·dra (ɛks kə'θiːdrə) *adj., adv.* **1.** with authority. **2.** *R.C. Church.* (of doctrines of faith or morals) defined by the pope as infallibly true, to be accepted by all Catholics. [Latin, literally: from the chair]

ex·cau·date (ɛks'kɔːdeɪt) *adj. Zoology.* having no tail or tail-like process; tailless.

ex·ca·vate ('ɛkskəˌveɪt) *vb.* **1.** to remove (soil, earth, etc.) by digging; dig out. **2.** to make (a hole, cavity, or tunnel) in (solid matter) by hollowing or removing the centre or inner part: *to excavate a tooth.* **3.** to unearth (buried objects) methodically in an attempt to discover information about the past. [C16: from Latin *excavāre,* from *cavāre* to make hollow, from *cavus* hollow] —**ˌex·ca·'va·tion** *n.*

ex·ca·va·tor ('ɛkskəˌveɪtə) *n.* **1.** a powered machine for digging earth, gravel, sand, etc., esp. a caterpillar tractor so equipped. **2.** any person, animal, or thing that excavates.

ex·ceed (ɪk'siːd) *vb.* **1.** to be superior to (a person or thing), esp. in size or quality; excel. **2.** (*tr.*) to go beyond the limit or bounds of: *to exceed one's income; exceed a speed limit.* **3.** to be greater in degree or quantity than (a person or thing). [C14: from Latin *excēdere* to go beyond, from *cēdere* to go] —**ex·'ceed·a·ble** *adj.* —**ex·'ceed·er** *n.*

ex·ceed·ing (ɪk'siːdɪŋ) *adj.* **1.** very great; exceptional or excessive. ~*adv.* **2.** an archaic word for **exceedingly.**

ex·ceed·ing·ly (ɪk'siːdɪŋlɪ) *adv.* to a very great or unusual degree; extremely; exceptionally.

ex·cel (ɪk'sɛl) *vb.* **·cels, ·cel·ling, ·celled.** **1.** to be superior to (another or others); surpass. **2.** (*intr.*; foll. by *in* or *at*) to be outstandingly good or proficient: *he excels at tennis.* [C15: from Latin *excellere* to rise up]

ex·cel·lence ('ɛksələns) *n.* **1.** the state or quality of excelling or being exceptionally good; extreme merit; superiority. **2.** an action, characteristic, feature, etc., in which a person excels. —**'ex·cel·lent** *adj.* —**'ex·cel·lent·ly** *adv.*

Ex·cel·len·cy ('ɛksələnsɪ) *or* **Ex·cel·lence** *n., pl.* **·len·cies** *or* **·lenc·es.** **1.** (usually preceded by *Your, His,* or *Her*) a title used to address or refer to a high-ranking official, such as an ambassador or governor. **2.** *R.C. Church.* a title of bishops and archbishops in many non-English-speaking countries.

ex·cel·si·or (ɪk'sɛlsɪˌɔː) *interj., adv., n.* **1.** excellent: used as a motto and as a trademark for various products. **2.** upwards. [C19: from Latin: higher]

ex·cept (ɪk'sɛpt) *prep.* **1.** Also: **except for.** other than; apart from; with the exception of: *he likes everyone except you; except for this mistake, you did very well.* **2. except that.** (*conj.*) but for the fact that; were it not true that. ~*conj.* **3.** an archaic word for **unless.** **4.** *Informal; not standard in the U.S.* except that; but for the fact that: *I would have arrived earlier, except I lost my way.* ~*vb.* **5.** (*tr.*) to leave out; omit; exclude. **6.** (*intr.*; often foll. by *to*) *Rare.* to take exception; object. [C14: from Old French *excepter* to leave out, from Latin *exceptāre,* from *excipere* to take out, from *capere* to take] —**ex·'cept·a·ble** *adj.*

ex·cept·ing (ɪk'sɛptɪŋ) *prep.* **1.** excluding; except; except for (esp. in the phrase **not excepting**). ~*conj.* **2.** an archaic word for **unless.**

ex·cep·tion (ɪk'sɛpʃən) *n.* **1.** the act of excepting or fact of being excepted; omission. **2.** anything excluded from or not in conformance with a general rule, principle, class, etc. **3.** criticism, esp. when it is adverse; objection. **4.** *Law.* (formerly) a formal objection in the course of legal proceedings. **5.** *Law.* a clause or term in a document that restricts the usual legal effect of the document. **6. take exception. a.** (usually foll. by *to*) to make objections (to); demur (at). **b.** (often foll. by *at*) to be offended (by); be resentful (at).

ex·cep·tion·a·ble (ɪk'sɛpʃənəbᵊl) *adj.* open to or subject to objection; objectionable. —**ex·'cep·tion·a·ble·ness** *n.* —**ex·'cep·tion·a·bly** *adv.*

ex·cep·tion·al (ɪk'sɛpʃənᵊl) *adj.* **1.** forming an exception; not ordinary. **2.** having much more than average intelligence, ability, or skill. —**ex·'cep·tion·al·ly** *adv.*

ex·cep·tive (ɪk'sɛptɪv) *adj.* **1.** relating to or forming an exception. **2.** *Rare.* tending to take exception or find fault.

ex·cerpt *n.* ('ɛksɜːpt). **1.** a part or passage taken from a book, speech, play, etc., and considered on its own; extract. ~*vb.* (ɛk'sɜːpt). **2.** (*tr.*) to take (a part or passage) from a book, speech, play, etc. [C17: from Latin *excerptum,* literally: (something) picked out, from *excerpere* to select, from *carpere* to pluck] —**ex·'cerpt·er** *or* **ex·'cerp·tor** *n.* —**ex·'cerpt·i·ble** *adj.* —**ex·'cerp·tion** *n.*

ex·cess *n.* (ɪk'sɛs, 'ɛksɛs). **1.** the state or act of going beyond normal, sufficient, or permitted limits. **2.** an immoderate or abnormal amount, number, extent, or degree too much or too many: *an excess of tolerance.* **3.** the amount, number, extent, or degree by which one thing exceeds another. **4.** *Chem.* a quantity of a reagent that is greater than the quantity required to complete a reaction: *add an excess of acid.* **5.** overindulgence or intemperance. **6.** *Insurance, chiefly Brit.* a specified contribution towards the cost of a claim, stipulated on certain insurance policies as being payable by the policyholder. **7. in excess of.** of more than; over: *baggage in excess of 40 kilos is charged extra.* **8. to excess.** to an inordinate extent; immoderately: *he drinks to excess.* ~*adj.* ('ɛksɛs, ɪk'sɛs). (*usually prenominal*) **9.** more than normal, necessary, or permitted; surplus: *excess weight.* **10.** payable as a result of previous underpayment: *excess postage; an excess fare for a railway journey.* [C14: from Latin *excessus*, from *excēdere* to go beyond; see EXCEED]

ex·cess de·mand *n. Economics.* a situation in which the market demand for a commodity is greater than its market supply, thus causing its market price to rise.

ex·ces·sive (ɪk'sɛsɪv) *adj.* exceeding the normal or permitted extents or limits; immoderate; inordinate. —**ex·'ces·sive·ly** *adv.* —**ex·'ces·sive·ness** *n.*

ex·cess sup·ply *n. Economics.* a situation in which the market supply of a commodity is greater than the market demand for it, thus causing its market price to fall.

exch. *abbrev. for:* **1.** exchange. **2.** exchequer.

ex·change (ɪks'tʃeɪndʒ) *vb.* **1.** (*tr.*) to give up, part with, or transfer (one thing) for an equivalent: *to exchange gifts; to exchange francs for dollars.* **2.** (*tr.*) to give and receive (information, ideas, etc.); interchange. **3.** (*tr.*) to replace (one thing) with another, esp. to replace unsatisfactory goods. **4.** to transfer or hand over (goods) in return for the equivalent value in kind rather than in money; barter; trade. **5.** (*tr.*) *Chess.* to capture and surrender (pieces, usually of the same value) in a single sequence of moves. ~*n.* **6.** the act or process of exchanging. **7. a.** anything given or received as an equivalent, replacement, or substitute for something else. **b.** (*as modifier*): *an exchange student.* **8.** an argument or quarrel; altercation: *the two men had a bitter exchange.* **9.** Also called: **telephone exchange.** a switching centre in which telephone lines are interconnected. **10. a.** a place where securities or commodities are sold, bought, or traded, esp. by brokers or merchants: *a stock exchange; a corn exchange.* **b.** (*as modifier*): *an exchange broker.* **11. a.** the system by which commercial debts between parties in different places are settled by commercial documents, esp. bills of exchange, instead of by direct payment of money. **b.** the percentage or fee charged for accepting payment in this manner. **12.** a transfer or interchange of sums of money of equivalent value, as between different national currencies or different issues of the same currency. **13.** (*often pl.*) the cheques, drafts, bills, etc., exchanged or settled between banks in a clearing house. **14.** *Chess.* the capture by both players of pieces of equal value, usually on consecutive moves. **15. win** (*or* **lose**) **the exchange.** *Chess.* to win (or lose) a rook in return for a bishop or knight. **16.** *Med.* another word for **transfusion** (sense 2). **17.** *Physics.* a process in which a particle is transferred between two nucleons, such as the transfer of a meson between two nucleons. ~See also **bill of exchange, exchange rate, foreign exchange, labour exchange.** [C14: from Anglo-French *eschaungier*, from Vulgar Latin *excambiāre* (unattested), from Latin *cambīre* to barter] —**ex·'change·a·ble** *adj.* —**ex·,change·a·'bil·i·ty** *n.* —**ex·'change·a·bly** *adv.* —**ex·'chang·er** *n.*

ex·change force *n. Physics.* **1.** a force between two elementary particles resulting from the exchange of a virtual particle. **2.** the force causing the alignment of the magnetic dipole moments of atoms in ferromagnetic materials.

ex·change rate *n.* the rate at which the currency unit of one country may be exchanged for that of another.

ex·cheq·uer (ɪks'tʃɛkə) *n.* **1.** (*often cap.*) *Government.* (in Britain and certain other countries) the accounting department of the Treasury, responsible for receiving and issuing funds. **2.** *Informal.* personal funds; finances. [C13 (in the sense: chessboard, counting table): from Old French *eschequier*, from *eschec* CHECK]

Ex·cheq·uer (ɪks'tʃɛkə) *n.* See **Court of Exchequer.**

ex·cide (ɪk'saɪd) *vb.* (*tr.*) *Rare.* to cut out; excise. [C18: from Latin *excīdere* to cut off, from *caedere* to cut]

ex·cip·i·ent (ɪk'sɪpɪənt) *n.* an inert substance, such as sugar or gum, used to prepare drugs in a form suitable for oral administration. [C18: from Latin *excipiēns* excepting, from *excipere* to EXCEPT]

ex·cis·a·ble (ɪk'saɪzəbᵊl) *adj.* liable to an excise tax.

ex·cise[1] *n.* ('ɛksaɪz, ɛk'saɪz). **1.** Also called: **excise tax.** a tax on goods, such as spirits, produced for the home market. **2.** a tax paid for a licence to carry out various trades, sports, etc. **3.** *Brit.* that section of the government service responsible for the collection of excise, now the Board of Customs and Excise. ~*vb.* (ɪk'saɪz). **4.** (*tr.*) *Rare.* to compel (a person) to pay excise. [C15: probably from Middle Dutch *excijs*, probably from Old French *assise* a sitting, assessment, from Latin *assidēre* to sit beside, assist in judging, from *sedēre* to sit] —**ex·ci·sion** (ɛk'sɪʒən) *n.*

ex·cise[2] (ɪk'saɪz) *vb.* (*tr.*) **1.** to delete (a passage, sentence, etc.); expunge. **2.** to remove (an organ, structure, or part) surgically. [C16: from Latin *excīdere* to cut down; see EXCIDE] —**ex·'cis·a·ble** *adj.*

ex·cise·man ('ɛksaɪz,mæn) *n., pl.* **·men.** *Brit.* (formerly) a government agent whose function was to collect excise and prevent smuggling.

ex·cit·a·ble (ɪk'saɪtəbᵊl) *adj.* **1.** easily excited; volatile. **2.** (esp. of a nerve) ready to respond to a stimulus. —**ex·,cit·a·'bil·i·ty** *or* **ex·'cit·a·ble·ness** *n.* —**ex·'cit·a·bly** *adv.*

ex·cit·ant (ɪk'saɪtᵊnt, 'ɛksɪtənt) *adj. also* **ex·cit·a·tive** *or* **ex·cit·a·to·ry. 1.** able to excite or stimulate. ~*n.* **2.** something, such as a drug or other agent, able to excite; stimulant.

ex·ci·ta·tion (,ɛksɪ'teɪʃən) *n.* **1.** the act or process of exciting or state of being excited. **2.** a means of exciting or cause of excitement. **3. a.** the current in a field coil of a generator, motor, etc., or the magnetizing current in a transformer. **b.** (*as modifier*): *an excitation current.* **4.** the action of a stimulus on an animal or plant organ, inducing it to respond.

ex·cite (ɪk'saɪt) *vb.* (*tr.*) **1.** to arouse (a person) to strong feeling, esp. to pleasurable anticipation or nervous agitation. **2.** to arouse or elicit (an emotion, response, etc.); evoke: *her answers excited curiosity.* **3.** to cause or bring about; stir up: *to excite a rebellion.* **4.** to arouse sexually. **5.** *Physiol.* to cause a response in or increase the activity of (an organ, tissue, or part); stimulate. **6.** to raise (an atom, molecule, electron, nucleus, etc.) from the ground state to a higher energy level. **7.** to supply electricity to (the coils of a generator or motor) in order to create a magnetic field. **8.** to supply a signal to a stage of a valve or transistor circuit. [C14: from Latin *excitāre*, from *excīere* to stimulate, from *ciēre* to set in motion, rouse]

ex·cit·ed (ɪk'saɪtɪd) *adj.* **1.** emotionally aroused, esp. to pleasure or agitation. **2.** characterized by excitement: *an excited dance.* **3.** sexually aroused. **4.** (of an atom, molecule, etc.) having an energy level above the ground state. —**ex·'cit·ed·ly** *adv.* —**ex·'cit·ed·ness** *n.*

ex·cite·ment (ɪk'saɪtmənt) *n.* **1.** the state of being excited. **2.** a person or thing that excites; stimulation or thrill.

ex·cit·er (ɪk'saɪtə) *n.* **1.** a person or thing that excites. **2.** a small generator that excites a larger machine. **3.** an oscillator producing a transmitter's carrier wave.

ex·cit·ing (ɪk'saɪtɪŋ) *adj.* causing excitement; stirring; stimulating. —**ex·'cit·ing·ly** *adv.*

ex·ci·ton ('ɛksaɪ,tɒn) *n.* a mobile neutral entity in a crystalline solid consisting of an excited electron bound to the hole produced by its excitation. [C20: from EXCIT(ATION) + -ON]

ex·ci·tor (ɪk'saɪtə) *n.* **1.** a nerve that, when stimulated, causes increased activity in the organ or part it supplies. **2.** a variant spelling of **exciter.**

excl. *abbrev. for:* **1.** exclamation. **2.** excluding. **3.** exclusive.

ex·claim (ɪk'skleɪm) *vb.* to cry out or speak suddenly or excitedly, as from surprise, delight, horror, etc. [C16: from Latin *exclāmāre*, from *clāmāre* to shout] —**ex·'claim·er** *n.*

ex·cla·ma·tion (,ɛksklə'meɪʃən) *n.* **1.** an abrupt, emphatic, or excited cry or utterance; interjection; ejaculation. **2.** the act of exclaiming. —**,ex·cla·'ma·tion·al** *adj.*

ex·cla·ma·tion mark *or U.S.* **point** *n.* **1.** the punctuation mark **!** used after exclamations and vehement commands. **2.** this mark used for any other purpose, as to draw attention to an obvious mistake, in road warning signs, (in chess commentaries) beside the notation of a move considered a good one, (in mathematics) as a symbol of the factorial function, or (in logic) occurring with an existential quantifier.

ex·clam·a·to·ry (ɪk'sklæmətərɪ, -trɪ) *adj.* using, containing, or relating to exclamations. —**ex·'clam·a·to·ri·ly** *adv.*

ex·claus·tra·tion (,ɛksklɔː'streɪʃən) *n.* the return of a monk or nun to the outside world after being released from his or her religious vows.

ex·clave ('ɛkskleɪv) *n.* a part of a country entirely surrounded by foreign territory: viewed from the position of the home country. Compare **enclave.** [C20: from EX-[1] + *-clave*, on the model of ENCLAVE]

ex·clo·sure (ɪk'skləʊʒə) *n.* an area of land, esp. in a forest, fenced round to keep out unwanted animals.

ex·clude (ɪk'skluːd) *vb.* (*tr.*) **1.** to keep out; prevent from entering. **2.** to reject or not consider; leave out. **3.** to expel forcibly; eject. [C14: from Latin *exclūdere*, from *claudere* to shut] —**ex·'clud·a·ble** *or* **ex·'clud·i·ble** *adj.* —**ex·'clud·er** *n.*

ex·clu·sion (ɪk'skluːʒən) *n.* the act or an instance of excluding or the state of being excluded. —**ex·'clu·sion·ar·y** *adj.*

ex·clu·sion·ist (ɪk'skluːʒənɪst) *adj.* **1.** *Chiefly U.S.* denoting or relating to a policy of excluding various types of immigrants, imports, etc. ~*n.* **2.** a supporter of a policy of exclusion. —**ex·'clu·sion·,ism** *n.*

ex·clu·sion prin·ci·ple *n.* See **Pauli exclusion principle.**

ex·clu·sive (ɪk'skluːsɪv) *adj.* **1.** excluding all else; rejecting other considerations, possibilities, events, etc.: *an exclusive preoccupation with money.* **2.** belonging to a particular individual or group and to no other; not shared: *exclusive rights; an exclusive story.* **3.** belonging to or catering for a privileged minority, esp. a fashionable clique: *an exclusive restaurant.* **4.** (*postpositive;* foll. by *to*) limited (to); found only (in): *the kilt is exclusive to Scotland.* **5.** single; unique; only: *the exclusive means of transport on the island was the bicycle.* **6.** separate and incompatible: *mutually exclusive principles.* **7.** (*immediately postpositive*) not including the numbers, dates, letters, etc., mentioned: *1980–84 exclusive.* **8.** (*postpositive;* foll. by *of*) except (for); not taking account (of): *exclusive of bonus payments, you will earn this amount.* **9.** *Commerce.* (of a contract, agreement, etc.) binding the parties to do business only with each other with respect to a class of goods or services. **10.** *Logic.* (of a disjunction) true if only one rather than both of its component propositions is true. Compare **inclusive** (sense 4). ~*n.* **11.** an exclusive story; a story reported in only one newspaper. —**ex+'clu+sive+ly** *adv.* —**ex+'clu+sive+ness** *or* **ex+clu+siv·i+ty** (ˌɛkskluːˈsɪvɪtɪ) *n.*

Ex+clu+sive Breth+ren *pl. n.* one of the two main divisions of the Plymouth Brethren, which, in contrast to the Open Brethren, restricts its members' contacts with those outside the sect.

ex+clu+sive or *n. Logic.* the connective that gives the value *true* to a disjunction if one or other, but not both, of the disjuncts are true. Also called: **exclusive disjunction.** Compare **inclusive or.**

ex+clu+sive OR cir+cuit *or* **gate** *n. Electronics.* a computer logic circuit having two or more input wires and one output wire and giving a high-voltage output signal if a low-voltage signal is fed to one or more, but not all, of the input wires. Compare **OR circuit.**

ex+cog·i+tate (ɛksˈkɒdʒɪˌteɪt) *vb.* (*tr.*) **1.** to devise, invent, or contrive. **2.** to think out in detail. [C16: from Latin *excōgitāre,* from *cōgitāre* to ponder, COGITATE] —**ex+'cog·i+ta·ble** *adj.* —**ex+ˌcog·i+'ta+tion** *n.* —**ex+'cog·i+ta+tive** *adj.* —**ex+'cog·i+ˌta+tor** *n.*

ex+com+mun·i+cate *R.C. Church.* ~*vb.* (ˌɛkskəˈmjuːnɪˌkeɪt). **1.** (*tr.*) to sentence (a member of the Church) to exclusion from the communion of believers and from the privileges and public prayers of the Church. ~*adj.* (ˌɛkskəˈmjuːnɪkɪt, -ˌkeɪt). **2.** having incurred such a sentence. ~*n.* (ˌɛkskəˈmjuːnɪkɪt, -ˌkeɪt). **3.** an excommunicated person. [C15: from Late Latin *excommūnicāre,* literally: to exclude from the community, from Latin *commūnis* COMMON] —ˌ**ex+com+'mun·i·ca·ble** *adj.* —ˌ**ex+com+ˌmu+ni+'ca+tion** *n.* —ˌ**ex+com+'mu+ni+ca+tive** *or* ˌ**ex+com+'mu+ni+ca+to·ry** *adj.* —ˌ**ex+com+'mu+ni+ca+tor** *n.*

ex+co+ri+ate (ɪkˈskɔːrɪˌeɪt) *vb.* (*tr.*) **1.** to strip (the skin) from (a person or animal); flay. **2.** to denounce vehemently; censure severely. [C15: from Late Latin *excoriāre* to strip, flay, from Latin *corium* skin, hide] —**ex+ˌco+ri+'a+tion** *n.*

ex+cre+ment (ˈɛkskrɪmənt) *n.* waste matter discharged from the body, esp. faeces; excreta. [C16: from Latin *excrēmentum,* from *excernere* to sift, EXCRETE] —**ex+cre+men+tal** (ˌɛkskrɪˈmɛntᵊl) *or* **ex+cre+men+ti+tious** (ˌɛkskrɪmɛnˈtɪʃəs) *adj.* —ˌ**ex+cre+'men+tal+ly** *adv.*

ex+cres+cence (ɪkˈskrɛsᵊns) *n.* a projection or protuberance, esp. an outgrowth from an organ or part of the body. —**ex+cres+cen+tial** (ˌɛkskrɪˈsɛnʃəl) *adj.*

ex+cres+cen+cy (ɪkˈskrɛsənsɪ) *n., pl.* **+cies. 1.** the state or condition of being excrescent. **2.** another word for **excrescence.**

ex+cres+cent (ɪkˈskrɛsᵊnt) *adj.* **1.** denoting, relating to, or resembling an abnormal outgrowth. **2.** uselessly added; not essential; superfluous. **3.** denoting or relating to a speech sound or letter inserted into a word without etymological justification, such as the *b* in *nimble.* [C17: from Latin *excrēscēns,* from *excrēscere,* from *crēscere* to grow] —**ex+'cres+cent+ly** *adv.*

ex+cre+ta (ɪkˈskriːtə) *pl. n.* waste matter, such as urine, faeces, or sweat, discharged from the body; excrement. [C19: New Latin, from Latin *excernere* to EXCRETE] —**ex+'cre+tal** *adj.*

ex+crete (ɪkˈskriːt) *vb.* **1.** to discharge (waste matter, such as urine, sweat, carbon dioxide, or faeces) from the body through the kidneys, skin, lungs, bowels, etc. **2.** (of plants) to eliminate (waste matter, such as carbon dioxide and salts) through the leaves, roots, etc. [C17: from Latin *excernere* to separate, discharge, from *cernere* to sift] —**ex+'cret+er** *n.* —**ex+'cre+tion** *n.* —**ex+'cre+tive** *or* **ex+'cre+to+ry** *adj.*

ex+cru+ci+ate (ɪkˈskruːʃɪˌeɪt) *vb.* (*tr.*) **1.** to inflict mental suffering on; torment. **2.** *Obsolete.* to inflict physical pain on; torture. [C16: from Latin *excruciāre,* from *cruciāre* to crucify, from *crux* cross] —**ex+ˌcru+ci+'a+tion** *n.*

ex+cru+ci+at+ing (ɪkˈskruːʃɪˌeɪtɪŋ) *adj.* **1.** unbearably painful; agonizing. **2.** intense; extreme: *he took excruciating pains to do it well.* **3.** *Informal.* irritating; trying. —**ex+'cru+ci+ˌat+ing+ly** *adv.*

ex+cul+pate (ˈɛkskʌlˌpeɪt, ɪkˈskʌlpeɪt) *vb.* (*tr.*) to free from blame or guilt; vindicate or exonerate. [C17: from Medieval Latin *exculpāre,* from Latin EX-[1] + *culpāre* to blame, from *culpa* fault, blame] —**ex+cul+pa·ble** (ɪkˈskʌlpəbᵊl) *adj.* —ˌ**ex+cul+'pa+tion** *n.* —**ex+'cul+pa+to+ry** *adj.*

ex+cur+rent (ɛkˈskʌrənt) *adj.* **1.** *Zoology.* having an outward flow, as certain pores in sponges, ducts, etc. **2.** *Botany.* **a.** (of veins) extending beyond the margin of the leaf. **b.** having an undivided main stem or trunk, as the spruce and other conifers. **3.** flowing or running in an outward direction. [C19: from Latin *excurrere* to run forth; see EXCURSION]

ex+cur+sion (ɪkˈskɜːʃən, -ʒən) *n.* **1.** a short outward and return journey, esp. for relaxation, sightseeing, etc.; outing. **2.** a group of people going on such a journey. **3.** (*modifier*) of or relating to special reduced rates offered on certain journeys by rail: *an excursion ticket.* **4.** a digression or deviation; diversion: *an excursion into politics.* **5.** (formerly) a raid or attack. **6.** *Physics.* **a.** a movement from an equilibrium position, as in an oscillation. **b.** the magnitude of this displacement. **7.** the normal movement of a movable bodily organ or part from its resting position, such as the lateral movement of the lower jaw. **8.** *Machinery.* the locus of a point on a moving part, esp. the deflection of a whirling shaft. [C16: from Latin *excursiō* an attack, from *excurrere* to run out, from *currere* to run]

ex+cur+sion+ist (ɪkˈskɜːʃənɪst, -ʒənɪst) *n.* a person who goes on an excursion.

ex+cur+sive (ɪkˈskɜːsɪv) *adj.* **1.** tending to digress. **2.** involving detours; rambling. [C17: from Latin *excursus,* from *excurrere* to run forth] —**ex+'cur+sive+ly** *adv.* —**ex+'cur+sive+ness** *n.*

ex+cur+sus (ɛkˈskɜːsəs) *n., pl.* **+sus·es** *or* **+sus.** an incidental digression from the main topic under discussion or from the main story in a narrative. [C19: from Latin: a running forth, from *excurrere* to run out]

ex+cus·a+to·ry (ɪkˈskjuːzətərɪ, -trɪ) *adj.* tending to or intended to excuse; apologetic.

ex+cuse *vb.* (ɪkˈskjuːz). (*tr.*) **1.** to pardon or forgive: *he always excuses her unpunctuality.* **2.** to seek pardon or exemption for (a person, esp. oneself): *to excuse oneself for one's mistakes.* **3.** to make allowances for; judge leniently: *to excuse someone's ignorance.* **4.** to serve as an apology or explanation for; vindicate or justify: *her age excuses her behaviour.* **5.** to exempt from a task, obligation, etc.: *you are excused making breakfast.* **6.** to dismiss or allow to leave: *he asked them to excuse him.* **7.** to seek permission for (someone, esp. oneself) to leave: *he excused himself and left.* **8. be excused.** *Euphemistic.* to go to the lavatory. **9. excuse me!** an expression used to catch someone's attention or to apologize for an interruption, disagreement, or social indiscretion. ~*n.* (ɪkˈskjuːs). **10.** an explanation offered in defence of some fault or offensive behaviour or as a reason for not fulfilling an obligation, etc.: *he gave no excuse for his rudeness.* **11.** *Informal.* an inferior example of something specified; makeshift substitute: *she is a poor excuse for a hostess.* **12.** the act of excusing. [C13: from Latin *excusāre,* from EX-[1] + *-cūsare,* from *causa* cause, accusation] —**ex+'cus+a·ble** *adj.* —**ex+'cus+a·ble+ness** *n.* —**ex+'cus+a·bly** *adv.*

ex·cuse-me *n.* a dance in which a person may take another's partner.

ex-di·rec·to·ry *adj. Chiefly Brit.* not listed in a telephone directory, by request, and not disclosed to enquirers. U.S. term: **unlisted.**

ex div. *abbrev. for* ex dividend.

ex div·i+dend without the right to the current dividend: *to quote shares ex dividend.* Compare **cum dividend.**

ex+e·at (ˈɛksɪæt) *n. Brit.* **1.** leave of absence from school or some other institution. **2.** a bishop's permission for a priest to leave his diocese in order to take up an appointment elsewhere. [C18: Latin, literally: he may go out, from *exīre*]

exec. *abbrev. for:* **1.** executive. **2.** executor.

ex+e·cra·ble (ˈɛksɪkrəbᵊl) *adj.* **1.** deserving to be execrated; abhorrent. **2.** of very poor quality: *an execrable meal.* [C14: from Latin *exsecrābilis,* from *exsecrārī* to EXECRATE] —**'ex+e·cra·ble+ness** *n.* —**'ex+e·cra·bly** *adv.*

ex+e·crate (ˈɛksɪˌkreɪt) *vb.* **1.** (*tr.*) to loathe; detest; abhor. **2.** (*tr.*) to profess great abhorrence for; denounce; deplore. **3.** to curse (a person or thing); damn. [C16: from Latin *exsecrārī* to curse, from EX-[1] + *-secrārī* from *sacer* SACRED] —ˌ**ex+e+'cra+tion** *n.* —**'ex+e·ˌcra+tive** *or* **'ex+e·ˌcra+to·ry** *adj.* —**'ex+e·ˌcra+tive+ly** *adv.*

ex+ec·u+tant (ɪɡˈzɛkjʊtənt) *n.* a performer, esp. of musical works.

ex+e·cute (ˈɛksɪˌkjuːt) *vb.* (*tr.*) **1.** to put (a condemned person) to death; inflict capital punishment upon. **2.** to carry out; complete; perform; do: *to execute an order.* **3.** to perform; accomplish; effect: *to execute a pirouette.* **4.** to make or produce: *to execute a drawing.* **5.** to carry into effect (a judicial sentence, the law, etc.); enforce. **6.** *Law.* to comply with legal formalities in order to render (a deed, etc.) effective, as by signing, sealing, and delivering. **7.** to sign (a will) in the presence of witnesses and in accordance with other legal formalities. **8.** to carry out the terms of (a contract, will, etc.). [C14: from Old French *executer,* back formation from *executeur* EXECUTOR] —**'ex+e·ˌcut+a·ble** *adj.* —**'ex+e·ˌcut+er** *n.*

ex+e·cu+tion (ˌɛksɪˈkjuːʃən) *n.* **1.** the act or process of executing. **2.** the carrying out or undergoing of a sentence of death. **3.** the style or manner in which something is accomplished or performed; technique: *as a pianist his execution is poor.* **4. a.** the enforcement of the judgment of a court of law. **b.** the writ ordering such enforcement.

ex+e·cu·tion+er (ˌɛksɪˈkjuːʃənə) *n.* **1.** an official charged with carrying out the death sentence passed upon a condemned person. **2.** an assassin, esp. one appointed by a political or criminal organization.

ex+ec·u+tive (ɪɡˈzɛkjʊtɪv) *n.* **1. a.** a person or group responsible for the administration of a project, activity, or business. **b.** (*as modifier*): *executive duties; an executive position.* **2. a.** the branch of government responsible for carrying out laws, decrees, etc.; administration. **b.** any administration. Compare **judiciary, legislature.** ~*adj.* **3.** having the function or purpose of carrying plans, orders, laws, etc., into practical effect. —**ex+'ec·u+tive+ly** *adv.*

Ex+ec·u+tive Coun+cil *n.* (in Australia) a body consisting of ministers of the Crown presided over by the Governor or Governor-General that formally approves Cabinet decisions, etc.

ex+ec·u+tive of+fic+er *n.* **1.** the second-in-command of any of certain military units. **2.** (formerly) a specialist seaman officer of the British and certain other navies.

ex+ec·u+tive ses+sion *n. U.S. government.* a session of the Senate for the discussion of executive business, such as the ratification of treaties: formerly held in secret.

ex+ec·u+tor (ɪɡˈzɛkjʊtə) *n.* **1.** *Law.* a person appointed by a testator to carry out the wishes expressed in his will. **2.** a person who executes. —**ex+ˌec·u+'to+ri·al** *adj.* —**ex+'ec·u+tor+ˌship** *n.*

ex+ec·u+to·ry (ɪɡˈzɛkjʊtərɪ, -trɪ) *adj.* **1.** (of a law, agreement, etc.) coming into operation at a future date; not yet effective: *an executory contract.* **2.** executive; administrative.

ex·ec·u·trix (ɪɡ'zɛkjʊˌtrɪks) *n., pl.* **ex·ec·u·tri·ces** (ɪɡˌzɛkjʊ'traɪsiːz) *or* **ex·ec·u·trix·es.** *Law.* a female executor.

ex·e·dra ('ɛksɪdrə, ɛk'siː-) *n.* **1.** a building, room, portico, or apse containing a continuous bench, used in ancient Greece and Rome for holding discussions. **2.** an outdoor bench in a recess. [C18: via Latin from Greek, from *hedra* seat]

ex·e·ge·sis (ˌɛksɪ'dʒiːsɪs) *n., pl.* **·ses** (-siːz). explanation or critical interpretation of a text, esp. of the Bible. Compare **eisegesis.** [C17: from Greek, from *exēgeisthai* to interpret, from EX-[1] + *hēgeisthai* to guide]

ex·e·gete ('ɛksɪˌdʒiːt) *or* **ex·e·ge·tist** (ˌɛksɪ'dʒiːtɪst, -'dʒɛt-) *n.* a person who practises exegesis. [C18: from Greek *exēgētēs*, from *exēgeisthai* to interpret; see EXEGESIS]

ex·e·get·ic (ˌɛksɪ'dʒɛtɪk) *or* **ex·e·get·i·cal** *adj.* of or relating to exegesis; expository. —ˌ**ex·e'get·i·cal·ly** *adv.*

ex·e·get·ics (ˌɛksɪ'dʒɛtɪks) *n.* (*functioning as sing.*) the scientific study of exegesis and exegetical methods.

ex·em·plar (ɪɡ'zɛmplə, -plɑː) *n.* **1.** a person or thing to be copied or imitated; model. **2.** a typical specimen or instance; example. **3.** a copy of a book or text on which further printings have been based. [C14: from Latin *exemplarium* model, from *exemplum* EXAMPLE]

ex·em·pla·ry (ɪɡ'zɛmplərɪ) *adj.* **1.** fit for imitation; model: *an exemplary performance.* **2.** serving as a warning; admonitory: *an exemplary jail sentence.* **3.** representative; typical: *an action exemplary of his conduct.* —**ex'em·pla·ri·ly** *adv.* —**ex'em·pla·ri·ness** *n.*

ex·em·pla·ry dam·ag·es *pl. n. Law.* damages awarded to a plaintiff above the value of actual loss sustained so that they serve also as a punishment to the defendant and a deterrent to others.

ex·em·pli·fy (ɪɡ'zɛmplɪˌfaɪ) *vb.* **·fies, ·fy·ing, ·fied.** (*tr.*) **1.** to show by example. **2.** to serve as an example of. **3.** *Law.* **a.** to make an official copy of (a document from public records) under seal. **b.** to transcribe (a legal document). [C15: via Old French from Medieval Latin *exemplificāre*, from Latin *exemplum* EXAMPLE + *facere* to make] —**ex'em·pli·ˌfi·a·ble** *adj.* —**exˌem·pli·fi'ca·tion** *n.* —**ex'em·pli·fiˌca·tive** *adj.* —**ex'em·pliˌfi·er** *n.*

ex·em·pli gra·ti·a *Latin.* (ɪɡ'zɛmplaɪ 'ɡrɑːtɪˌɑː) for the sake of example. Abbrev.: **e.g.**

ex·em·plum (ɪɡ'zɛmpləm) *n., pl.* **·pla** (-plə). **1.** an anecdote that supports a moral point or sustains an argument, used esp. in medieval sermons. **2.** an example or illustration. [from Latin: EXAMPLE]

ex·empt (ɪɡ'zɛmpt) *vb.* **1.** (*tr.*) to release from an obligation, liability, tax, etc.; excuse: *to exempt a soldier from drill.* ~*adj.* (*postpositive*) **2.** freed from or not subject to an obligation, liability, tax, etc.; excused. **3.** *Obsolete.* set apart; remote. ~*n.* **4.** a person who is exempt from an obligation, tax, etc. [C14: from Latin *exemptus* removed, from *eximere* to take out, from *emere* to buy, obtain] —**ex'empt·i·ble** *adj.* —**ex'emp·tion** *n.*

ex·en·ter·ate *vb.* (ɪɡ'zɛntəˌreɪt). (*tr.*) **1.** *Surgery.* to remove (internal organs, an eyeball, etc.); eviscerate. **2.** a rare word for **disembowel.** ~*adj.* (ɪɡ'zɛntəˌreɪt, -rɪt). **3.** *Rare.* having been disembowelled. [C17: from Latin *exenterāre*, from EX-[1] + Greek *enteron* intestine] —**exˌen·ter'a·tion** *n.*

ex·e·qua·tur (ˌɛksɪ'kweɪtə) *n.* **1.** an official authorization issued by a host country to a consular agent, permitting him to perform his official duties. **2.** an act by which the civil governments of certain nations permit the laws of the Roman Catholic Church to take effect in their territories. [C18: from Latin, literally: let him perform, from *exequī* to perform, from EX-[1] + *sequī* to follow]

ex·e·quies ('ɛksɪkwɪz) *pl. n., sing.* **·quy.** the rites and ceremonies used at funerals. [C14: from Latin *exequiae* (plural) funeral procession, rites, from *exequī* to follow to the end, from *sequī* to follow]

ex·er·cise ('ɛksəˌsaɪz) *vb.* (*mainly tr.*) **1.** to put into use; employ: *to exercise tact.* **2.** (*intr.*) to take exercise or perform exercises; exert one's muscles, etc., esp. in order to keep fit. **3.** to practise using in order to develop or train: *to exercise one's voice.* **4.** to perform or make proper use of: *to exercise one's rights.* **5.** to bring to bear; exert: *to exercise one's influence.* **6.** (*often passive*) to occupy the attentions of, esp. so as to worry or vex: *to be exercised about a decision.* **7.** *Military.* to carry out or cause to carry out practice, manoeuvres, drill, etc. ~*n.* **8.** physical exertion, esp. for the purpose of development, training, or keeping fit. **9.** mental or other activity or practice, esp. in order to develop a skill. **10.** a set of movements, questions, tasks, etc., designed to train, improve, or test one's ability in a particular field: *piano exercises.* **11.** a performance or work of art done as practice or to demonstrate a technique. **12.** the performance of a function; discharge: *the exercise of one's rights; the object of the exercise is to win.* **13.** (*usually pl.*) *Military.* practice, manoeuvres, or drill carried out to increase efficiency. **14.** (*usually pl.*) *U.S.* a ceremony, usually including speeches, formal processions, etc., at the graduation of students: *graduation exercises.* **15.** *Gymnastics.* a particular type of event, such as performing on the horizontal bar. [C14: from Old French *exercice*, from Latin *exercitium*, from *exercēre* to drill, from EX-[1] + *arcēre* to ward off] —'**ex·erˌcis·a·ble** *adj.*

ex·er·cis·er ('ɛksəˌsaɪzə) *n.* **1.** a device with springs or elasticated cords for muscular exercise. **2.** a person or thing that exercises.

ex·er·ci·ta·tion (ɪɡˌzɜːsɪ'teɪʃən) *n.* a rare word for **exercise.** [C14: from Latin *exercitātiō*, from *exercitāre* frequentative of *exercēre* to EXERCISE]

ex·ergue (ɛk'sɜːɡ) *n.* a space on the reverse of a coin or medal below the central design, often containing the date, place of minting, etc. [C17: from French, from Medieval Latin *exergum*, from Greek *ex* outside + *ergon* work] —**ex'ergu·al** *adj.*

ex·ert (ɪɡ'zɜːt) *vb.* (*tr.*) to apply (oneself) diligently; make a strenuous effort. [C17 (in the sense: push forth, emit): from Latin *exserere* to thrust out, from EX-[1] + *serere* to bind together, entwine] —**ex'er·tion** *n.* —**ex'er·tive** *adj.*

Ex·e·ter ('ɛksɪtə) *n.* a city in SW England, administrative centre of Devon; university (1955). Pop.: 95 598 (1971).

ex·e·unt ('ɛksɪˌʌnt) *Latin.* they go out: used as a stage direction.

ex·e·unt om·nes ('ɛksɪˌʌnt 'ɒmneɪz) *Latin.* they all go out: used as a stage direction.

ex·fo·li·ate (ɛks'fəʊlɪˌeɪt) *vb.* **1.** (of bark, skin, etc.) to peel off in (layers, flakes, or scales). **2.** (*intr.*) (of rocks or minerals) to shed the thin outermost layer because of weathering or heating. **3.** (of some minerals, esp. mica) to split or cause to split into thin flakes: *a factory to exfoliate vermiculite.* [C17: from Late Latin *exfoliāre* to strip off leaves, from Latin *folium* leaf] —**exˌfo·li'a·tion** *n.* —**ex'fo·li·a·tive** *adj.*

ex gra·tia ('ɡreɪʃə) *adj.* given as a favour or gratuitously where no legal obligation exists: *an ex gratia payment.* [New Latin, literally: out of kindness]

ex·hal·ant (ɛks'heɪlənt, ɪɡ'zeɪ-) *adj.* **1.** emitting a vapour or liquid; exhaling: *an exhalant siphon; exhalant duct.* ~*n.* **2.** an organ or vessel that emits a vapour or liquid.

ex·hale (ɛks'heɪl, ɪɡ'zeɪl) *vb.* **1.** to expel (breath, tobacco smoke, etc.) from the lungs; breathe out. **2.** to give off (air, vapour, fumes, etc.) or (of air, etc.) to be given off; emanate. [C14: from Latin *exhālāre* to breathe out, from *hālāre* to breathe] —**ex'hal·a·ble** *adj.* —ˌ**ex·ha'la·tion** *n.*

ex·haust (ɪɡ'zɔːst) *vb.* (*mainly tr.*) **1.** to drain the energy of; tire out: *to exhaust someone by constant questioning.* **2.** to deprive of resources, etc.: *a nation exhausted by war.* **3.** to deplete totally; expend; consume: *to exhaust food supplies.* **4.** to empty (a container) by drawing off or pumping out (the contents). **5.** to develop or discuss thoroughly so that no further interest remains: *to exhaust a topic of conversation.* **6.** to remove gas from (a vessel, etc.) in order to reduce the pressure or create a vacuum; evacuate. **7.** to remove or use up the active ingredients from (a drug, solution, etc.). **8.** to destroy the fertility of (soil) by excessive cultivation. **9.** (*intr.*) (of steam or other gases) to be emitted or to escape from an engine after being expanded. ~*n.* **10.** gases ejected from an engine as waste products. **11. a.** the expulsion of expanded gas or steam from an engine. **b.** (*as modifier*): *exhaust stroke.* **12. a.** the parts of an engine through which the exhausted gases or steam pass. **b.** (*as modifier*): *exhaust valve; exhaust pipe.* [C16: from Latin *exhaustus* made empty, from *exhaurīre* to draw out, from *haurīre* to draw, drain] —**ex'haust·er** *n.* —**ex'haust·i·ble** *adj.* —**exˌhaust·i'bil·i·ty** *n.*

ex·haus·tion (ɪɡ'zɔːstʃən) *n.* **1.** extreme tiredness; fatigue. **2.** the condition of being used up; consumption: *exhaustion of the earth's resources.* **3.** the act of exhausting or the state of being exhausted.

ex·haus·tive (ɪɡ'zɔːstɪv) *adj.* **1.** comprehensive in scope; thorough: *an exhaustive survey.* **2.** tending to exhaust. —**ex'haust·ive·ly** *adv.* —**ex'haust·ive·ness** *n.*

ex·hib·it (ɪɡ'zɪbɪt) *vb.* (*mainly tr.*) **1.** (*also intr.*) to display (something) to the public for interest or instruction: *this artist exhibits all over the world.* **2.** to manifest; display; show: *the child exhibited signs of distress.* **3.** *Law.* to produce (a document or object) in court to serve as evidence. ~*n.* **4.** an object or collection exhibited to the public. **5.** *Law.* a document or object produced in court and referred to or identified by a witness in giving evidence. [C15: from Latin *exhibēre* to hold forth, from *habēre* to have] —**ex'hib·i·to·ry** *adj.*

ex·hi·bi·tion (ˌɛksɪ'bɪʃən) *n.* **1.** a public display of art, products, skills, activities, etc.: *a judo exhibition.* **2.** the act of exhibiting or the state of being exhibited. **3. make an exhibition of oneself.** to behave so foolishly in public that one excites notice or ridicule. **4.** *Brit.* an allowance or scholarship awarded to a student at a university or school.

ex·hi·bi·tion·er (ˌɛksɪ'bɪʃənə) *n. Brit.* a student who has been awarded an exhibition.

ex·hi·bi·tion·ism (ˌɛksɪ'bɪʃəˌnɪzəm) *n. Psychiatry.* **1.** a compulsive desire to attract attention to oneself, esp. by absurd or exaggerated behaviour or boasting. **2.** a compulsive desire to expose one's genital organs publicly. —ˌ**ex·hi'bi·tion·ist** *n.* —ˌ**ex·hiˌbi·tion'is·tic** *adj.*

ex·hib·i·tive (ɪɡ'zɪbɪtɪv) *adj.* (*usually postpositive* and foll. by *of*) illustrative or demonstrative: *a masterpiece exhibitive of his talent.* —**ex'hib·i·tive·ly** *adv.*

ex·hib·i·tor (ɪɡ'zɪbɪtə) *n.* **1.** a person or thing that exhibits. **2.** an individual or company that shows films, esp. the manager or owner of a cinema.

ex·hil·ar·ant (ɪɡ'zɪlərənt) *adj.* **1.** exhilarating; invigorating. ~*n.* **2.** something that exhilarates.

ex·hil·a·rate (ɪɡ'zɪləˌreɪt) *vb.* (*tr.*) to make lively and cheerful; gladden; elate. [C16: from Latin *exhilarāre*, from *hilarāre* to cheer; see HILARITY] —**ex'hil·aˌrat·ing·ly** *adv.* —**exˌhil·a'ra·tion** *n.* —**ex'hil·a·ra·tive** *or* **ex'hil·a·ra·to·ry** *adj.* —**ex'hil·aˌra·tor** *n.*

ex·hort (ɪɡ'zɔːt) *vb.* to urge or persuade (someone) earnestly; advise strongly. [C14: from Latin *exhortārī*, from *hortārī* to urge] —**ex·hor·ta·tive** (ɪɡ'zɔːtətɪv) *or* **ex'hor·ta·to·ry** *adj.* —**ex'hort·er** *n.*

ex·hor·ta·tion (ˌɛɡzɔː'teɪʃən) *n.* **1.** the act or process of ex-

horting. **2.** a speech or written passage intended to persuade, inspire, or encourage.
ex+hume (ɛks'hju:m) *vb.* (*tr.*) **1.** to dig up (something buried, esp. a corpse); disinter. **2.** to reveal; disclose; unearth: *don't exhume that old argument.* [C18: from Medieval Latin *exhumāre,* from Latin EX-[1] + *humāre* to bury, from *humus* the ground] —**ex+hu+ma+tion** (ˌɛkshjʊ'meɪʃən) *n.* —**ex+'hum+er** *n.*
ex hy+poth+e+si (ɛks haɪ'pɒθəsɪ) *adv.* in accordance with or following from the hypothesis stated. [C17: New Latin]
ex·i+gen+cy ('ɛksɪdʒənsɪ, ɪg'zɪdʒənsɪ) *or* **ex·i+gence** ('ɛksɪdʒəns) *n., pl.* **+gen+cies** *or* **+genc·es. 1.** the state of being exigent; urgency. **2.** (*often pl.*) an urgent demand; pressing requirement. **3.** an emergency.
ex·i+gent ('ɛksɪdʒənt) *adj.* **1.** urgent; pressing. **2.** exacting; demanding. [C15: from Latin *exigere* to drive out, weigh out, from *agere* to drive, compel] —**'ex·i+gent+ly** *adv.*
ex·i·gi·ble ('ɛksɪdʒəbᵊl) *adj.* liable to be exacted or required: *part of the debt is exigible this month.* [C17: from French, from *exiger* to demand, from Latin *exigere;* see EXIGENT]
ex+ig·u·ous (ɪg'zɪgjʊəs, ɪk'sɪg-) *adj.* scanty or slender; meagre: *an exiguous income.* [C17: from Latin *exiguus,* from *exigere* to weigh out; see EXIGENT] —**ex·i+gu·i·ty** (ˌɛksɪ'gju:ɪtɪ) *or* **ex+'ig·u·ous+ness** *n.* —**ex+'ig·u·ous+ly** *adv.*
ex+ile ('ɛgzaɪl, 'ɛksaɪl) *n.* **1.** a prolonged, usually enforced absence from one's home or country; banishment. **2.** the expulsion of a person from his native land by official decree. **3.** a person banished or living away from his home or country; expatriate. ~*vb.* **4.** to expel from home or country, esp. by official decree as a punishment; banish. [C13: from Latin *exsilium* banishment, from *exsul* banished person; perhaps related to Greek *alasthai* to wander] —**ex+il+ic** (ɛg'zɪlɪk, ɛk'sɪlɪk) *or* **ex+'il·i·an** *adj.*
Ex+ile ('ɛgzaɪl, 'ɛksaɪl) *n.* **the.** another name for the **Babylonian captivity** (of the Jews).
ex+im·i·ous (ɛg'zɪmɪəs) *adj. Rare.* select and distinguished; eminent. [C16: from Latin *eximius,* from *eximere* to take out, from *emere* to purchase] —**ex+'im·i·ous+ly** *adv.*
ex+ine ('ɛksɪn, -aɪn) *n.* another name for **extine.**
ex int. *Banking. abbrev. for* without [Latin *ex*] interest.
ex+ist (ɪg'zɪst) *vb.* (*intr.*) **1.** to have being or reality; to be. **2.** to eke out a living; stay alive; survive: *he could barely exist on such a low wage.* **3.** to be living; live. **4.** to be present under specified conditions or in a specified place: *sharks exist in the Pacific.* **5.** *Philosophy.* to have contingent being while free, responsible, and aware of one's situation. [C17: from Latin *exsistere* to step forth, from EX-[1] + *sistere* to stand]
ex+ist+ence (ɪg'zɪstəns) *n.* **1.** the fact or state of existing; being. **2.** the continuance or maintenance of life; living, esp. in adverse circumstances: *a struggle for existence; she has a wretched existence.* **3.** something that exists; a being or entity. **4.** everything that exists, esp. that is living.
ex+ist+ent (ɪg'zɪstənt) *adj.* **1.** in existence; extant; current. **2.** having existence; living. ~*n.* **3.** a person or a thing that exists.
Usage. See at **extant.**
ex+is+ten+tial (ˌɛgzɪ'stɛnʃəl) *adj.* **1.** of or relating to existence, esp. human existence. **2.** *Philosophy.* based on personal experience; empirical as opposed to theoretical; concrete as opposed to abstract. **3.** *Logic.* denoting or relating to a formula or proposition asserting the existence of at least one object fulfilling a given condition. **4.** of or relating to existentialism. —ˌ**ex+is+'ten+tial+ly** *adv.*
ex+is+ten+tial+ism (ˌɛgzɪ'stɛnʃəˌlɪzəm) *n.* a modern philosophical movement stressing the importance of personal experience and responsibility and the demands that they make on the individual, who is seen as a free agent in a deterministic and seemingly meaningless universe. —ˌ**ex+is+'ten+tial+ist** *adj., n.*
ex+it ('ɛgzɪt, 'ɛksɪt) *n.* **1.** a way out; door or gate by which people may leave. **2.** the act or an instance of going out; departure. **3. a.** the act of leaving or right to leave a particular place. **b.** (*as modifier*): *an exit visa.* **4.** departure from life; death. **5.** *Theatre.* the act of going offstage. **6.** *Bridge, whist, etc.* **a.** the act of losing the lead deliberately. **b.** a card enabling one to do this. ~*vb.* (*intr.*) **7.** to go away or out; depart; leave. **8.** *Theatre.* to go offstage: used as a stage direction: *exit Hamlet.* **9.** *Bridge, whist, etc.* to lose the lead deliberately. [C17: from Latin *exitus* a departure, from *exīre* to go out, from EX-[1] + *īre* to go]
ex·i+tance ('ɛksɪtəns) *n.* a measure of the ability of a surface to emit radiation. See **luminous exitance, radiant exitance.**
ex. lib. *abbrev. for* ex libris.
ex li+bris (ɛks 'li:brɪs) **1.** from the collection or library of: frequently printed on bookplates. ~*n.* **ex-li·bris. 2.** a bookplate bearing the owner's name, coat of arms, etc. [C19: from Latin, literally: from the books (of)]
Ex+moor ('ɛksˌmʊə, -ˌmɔ:) *n.* **1.** a high moorland in SW England, in NW Somerset and Devon: largely forested until the 19th century, now chiefly grazing ground for Exmoor ponies, sheep, and red deer. **2.** a small stocky breed of pony with a fawn-coloured nose, originally from Exmoor.
ex·o- *combining form.* external, outside, or beyond: *exobiology; exothermal.* [from Greek *exō* outside]
ex·o·bi·ol·o·gy (ˌɛksəʊbaɪ'ɒlədʒɪ) *n.* another name for **astrobiology.** —ˌ**ex·o·bi+'ol·o+gist** *n.*
ex·o·carp ('ɛksəʊˌkɑ:p) *n.* another name for **epicarp.**
ex·o·cen+tric (ˌɛksəʊ'sɛntrɪk) *adj. Grammar.* (of a construction) not fulfilling the grammatical role of any of its constituents; as in *until last Easter,* where the constituents are prepositional, adjectival, and nominal, while the whole construction is adverbial. Compare **endocentric.**
ex·o+crine ('ɛksəʊˌkraɪn) *adj.* **1.** of or relating to exocrine glands or their secretions. ~*n.* **2.** an exocrine gland. ~Compare **endocrine.** [C20: EXO- + *-crine* from Greek *krinein* to separate]
ex·o+crine gland *n.* any gland, such as a salivary or sweat gland, that secretes its products through a duct onto an epithelial surface.
Exod. *Bible. abbrev. for* Exodus.
ex·o+derm ('ɛksəʊˌdɜ:m) *n. Embryol.* another name for **ectoderm.**
ex·o·don+tics (ˌɛksəʊ'dɒntɪks) *n.* the branch of dental surgery concerned with the extraction of teeth. [C20: New Latin, from EX-[1] + *-odontia,* from Greek *odōn* tooth] —ˌ**ex·o+'don+tist** *n.*
ex·o+dus ('ɛksədəs) *n.* the act or an instance of going out. [C17: via Latin from Greek *exodos* from EX-[1] + *hodos* way]
Ex·o+dus ('ɛksədəs) *n.* **1. the.** the departure of the Israelites from Egypt led by Moses. **2.** the second book of the Old Testament, recounting the events connected with this and the divine visitation of Moses at Mount Sinai.
ex·o·en+zyme (ˌɛksəʊ'ɛnzaɪm) *n.* **1.** any enzyme, esp. an exopeptidase, that acts upon terminal chemical bonds in a chain of molecules. Compare **endoenzyme** (sense 1). **2.** another name for **ectoenzyme.**
ex·o·er+gic (ˌɛksəʊ'ɜ:dʒɪk) *adj.* (of a nuclear reaction) occurring with evolution of energy. Compare **endoergic, exothermic.** [EXO- + *-ergic,* from Greek *ergon* work]
ex of·fi·ci·o ('ɛks ə'fɪʃɪəʊ, ə'fɪsɪəʊ) *adv., adj.* by right of position or office. Abbrev.: **ex. off.**
ex+og·a+my (ɛk'sɒgəmɪ) *n.* **1.** *Sociol, anthropol.* the custom or an act of marrying a person belonging to another tribe, clan, or similar social unit. Compare **endogamy. 2.** *Biology.* fusion of gametes from parents that are not closely related. —**ex+og·a+mous** (ɛk'sɒgəməs) *or* **ex·o+gam+ic** (ˌɛksəʊ'gæmɪk) *adj.*
ex+og·e·nous (ɛk'sɒdʒɪnəs) *adj.* **1.** having an external origin. **2.** *Biology.* **a.** developing or originating outside an organism or part of an organism. **b.** of or relating to external factors, such as light, that influence an organism. —**ex+'og·e·nous+ly** *adv.*
ex·on ('ɛksɒn) *n. Brit.* one of the four officers who command the Yeomen of the Guard. [C17: a pronunciation spelling of French *exempt* EXEMPT]
ex·on+er+ate (ɪg'zɒnəˌreɪt) *vb.* (*tr.*) **1.** to clear or absolve from blame or a criminal charge. **2.** to relieve from an obligation or task; exempt. [C16: from Latin *exonerāre* to free from a burden, from *onus* a burden] —**ex+ˌon+er+'a+tion** *n.* —**ex+'on+er·a+tive** *adj.* —**ex+'on+er·ˌa+tor** *n.*
ex·o+nym ('ɛksəˌnɪm) *n.* a name given to a place by foreigners: *Londres is an exonym of London.* [C20: from Greek EX-[1] + -ONYM]
ex·o·pep+ti+dase (ˌɛksəʊ'pɛptɪˌdeɪz) *n.* any proteolytic enzyme, such as erepsin, that acts on the terminal bonds in a peptide chain. Compare **endopeptidase.**
ex+oph+thal+mic goi+tre *n.* a form of hyperthyroidism characterized by enlargement of the thyroid gland, protrusion of the eyeballs, increased basal metabolic rate, and weight loss. Also called: **Graves' disease.**
ex+oph+thal+mos (ˌɛksɒf'θælmɒs), **ex+oph+thal+mus** (ˌɛksɒf'θælməs), *or* **ex+oph+thal+mi·a** (ˌɛksɒf'θælmɪə) *n.* abnormal protrusion of the eyeball, as caused by hyperthyroidism. Also called: **proptosis, ocular proptosis.** [C19: via New Latin from Greek, from EX-[1] + *ophthalmos* eye] —ˌ**ex+oph+'thal+mic** *adj.*
ex·o+plasm ('ɛksəʊˌplæzəm) *n.* another name for **ectoplasm.**
exor. ('ɛksɔ:) *Brit. abbrev. for* executor.
ex·o+ra·ble ('ɛksərəbᵊl) *adj.* able to be persuaded or moved by pleading. [C16: from Latin *exōrābilis,* from *exōrāre* to persuade, from *ōrāre* to beseech] —ˌ**ex·o·ra·'bil·i·ty** *n.*
ex+or+bi+tant (ɪg'zɔ:bɪtᵊnt) *adj.* (of prices, demands, etc.) in excess of what is reasonable; excessive; extravagant; immoderate. [C15: from Late Latin *exorbitāre* to deviate, from Latin *orbita* track] —**ex+'or+bi+tance** *n.* —**ex+'or+bi+tant+ly** *adv.*
ex+or+cise *or* **ex+or+cize** ('ɛksɔ:ˌsaɪz) *vb.* (*tr.*) to expel or attempt to expel (one or more evil spirits) from (a person or place believed to be possessed or haunted), by prayers, adjurations, and religious rites. [C15: from Late Latin *exorcizāre,* from Greek *exorkizein,* from EX-[1] + *horkizein* to adjure] —**'ex+or+ˌcis+er** *or* **'ex+or+ˌciz+er** *n.* —**'ex+or+cism** *n.* —**'ex+or+cist** *n.*
ex+or+di·um (ɛk'sɔ:dɪəm) *n., pl.* **+di·ums** *or* **+di·a** (-dɪə). an introductory part or beginning, esp. of an oration or discourse. [C16: from Latin, from *exōrdīrī* to begin, from *ōrdīrī* to begin] —**ex+'or+di·al** *adj.*
ex·o+skel+e·ton (ˌɛksəʊ'skɛlɪtᵊn) *n.* the protective or supporting structure covering the outside of the body of many animals, such as the thick cuticle of arthropods. Compare **endoskeleton.** —ˌ**ex·o+'skel+e·tal** *adj.*
ex+os+mo+sis (ˌɛksɒz'məʊsɪs, -sɒs-) *n. Biology.* osmosis in which water flows from a cell or organism into the surrounding solution. Compare **endosmosis.** —**ex+os+mot+ic** (ˌɛksɒz'mɒtɪk, -sɒs-) *or* **ex+os+mic** (ɛk'sɒzmɪk, -'sɒs-) *adj.*
ex·o+sphere ('ɛksəʊˌsfɪə) *n.* the outermost layer of the earth's atmosphere. It extends from about 400 kilometres above the earth's surface.
ex·o+spore ('ɛksəʊˌspɔ:) *n.* the outer layer of the spores of some algae and fungi. —ˌ**ex·o+'spor+ous** *adj.*
ex+os+to+sis (ˌɛksɒ'stəʊsɪs) *n., pl.* **+ses** (-si:z). an abnormal bony outgrowth from the surface of a bone. [C18: via New Latin from Greek, from EX-[1] + *osteon* bone]

ex·o·ter·ic (ˌɛksəʊ'tɛrɪk) *adj.* **1.** intelligible to or intended for more than a select or initiated minority: *an exoteric account of a philosophical doctrine.* **2.** external; exterior. [C17: from Latin *exōtericus* external, from Greek *exōterikos,* from *exōterō* further outside; see EXO-] —ˌ**ex·o·'ter·i·cal·ly** *adv.* —ˌ**ex·o·'ter·i·ˌcism** *n.*

ex·o·ther·mic (ˌɛksəʊ'θɜːmɪk) *or* **ex·o·ther·mal** *adj.* (of a chemical reaction or compound) occurring or formed with the evolution of heat. Compare **endothermic, exoergic.** —ˌ**ex·o·'ther·mi·cal·ly** *or* ˌ**ex·o·'ther·mal·ly** *adv.*

ex·ot·ic (ɪg'zɒtɪk) *adj.* **1.** originating in a foreign country, esp. one in the tropics; not native: *an exotic plant.* **2.** having a strange or bizarre allure, beauty, or quality. ~*n.* **3.** an exotic person or thing. [C16: from Latin *exōticus,* from Greek *exōtikos* foreign, from *exō* outside] —**ex·'ot·i·cal·ly** *adv.* —**ex·'ot·i·ˌcism** *n.* —**ex·'ot·ic·ness** *n.*

ex·ot·i·ca (ɪg'zɒtɪkə) *pl. n.* exotic objects, esp. when forming a collection. [C19: Latin, neuter plural of *exōticus; see* EXOTIC]

ex·ot·ic danc·er *n.* a striptease dancer or belly dancer.

ex·o·tox·in (ˌɛksəʊ'tɒksɪn) *n.* a toxin produced by a micro-organism and secreted into the surrounding medium. —ˌ**ex·o·'tox·ic** *adj.*

exp *Maths. abbrev. for* exponential (sense 2).

exp. *abbrev. for:* **1.** expenses. **2.** experiment(al). **3.** expired. **4.** export(ed). **5.** exporter. **6.** express.

ex·pand (ɪk'spænd) *vb.* **1.** to make or become greater in extent, volume, size, or scope; increase. **2.** to spread out or be spread out; unfold; stretch out. **3.** (*intr.; often foll. by on*) to enlarge or expatiate on (a story, topic, etc.) in detail. **4.** (*intr.*) to become increasingly relaxed, friendly, or talkative. **5.** *Maths.* to express (a function or expression) as the sum or product of terms. [C15: from Latin *expandere* to spread out, from *pandere* to spread, extend] —**ex·'pand·a·ble** *or* **ex·'pand·i·ble** *adj.* —**ex·'pand·er** *n.*

ex·pand·ed (ɪk'spændɪd) *adj.* **1.** Also: **extended.** (of printer's type) wider than usual for a particular height. Compare **condensed. 2.** (of a plastic) having been foamed during manufacture by the introduction of a gas in order to make a light packaging material or heat insulator: *expanded polystyrene.* See also **expanded metal.**

ex·pand·ed met·al *n.* an open mesh of metal produced by stamping out alternating slots in a metal sheet and stretching it into an open pattern. It is used for reinforcing brittle or friable materials and in fencing.

ex·pand·er (ɪk'spændə) *n.* **1.** a device for exercising and developing the muscles of the body: *a chest expander.* **2.** an electronic device for increasing the variations in signal amplitude in a transmission system according to a specified law. Compare **compressor** (sense 5), **compander.**

ex·pand·ing u·ni·verse the·o·ry *n.* the theory, developed from the observed red shifts of celestial bodies, that all the galaxies are receding from each other at velocities that increase as the distance from earth increases. See also **oscillating universe theory.**

ex·panse (ɪk'spæns) *n.* **1.** an uninterrupted surface of something that spreads or extends, esp. over a wide area; stretch: *an expanse of water.* **2.** expansion or extension. [C17: from New Latin *expansum* the heavens, from Latin *expansus* spread out, from *expandere* to EXPAND]

ex·pan·si·ble (ɪk'spænsəbᵊl) *adj.* able to expand or be expanded. —**ex·ˌpan·si·'bil·i·ty** *n.*

ex·pan·sile (ɪk'spænsaɪl) *adj.* **1.** able to expand or cause expansion. **2.** of or relating to expansion.

ex·pan·sion (ɪk'spænʃən) *n.* **1.** the act of expanding or the state of being expanded. **2.** something expanded; an expanded surface or part. **3.** the degree, extent, or amount by which something expands. **4.** an increase, enlargement, or development, esp. in the activities of a company. **5.** *Maths.* **a.** the form of an expression or function when it is written as the sum or product of its terms. **b.** the act or process of determining this expanded form. **6.** the part of an engine cycle in which the working fluid does useful work by increasing in volume. **7.** the increase in the dimensions of a body or substance when subjected to an increase in temperature, internal pressure, etc. —**ex·'pan·sion·ar·y** *adj.*

ex·pan·sion bolt *n.* a bolt that expands on tightening, enabling it to be secured into an unthreaded hole.

ex·pan·sion·ism (ɪk'spænʃəˌnɪzəm) *n.* the doctrine or practice of expanding the economy or territory of a country. —**ex·'pan·sion·ist** *n., adj.* —**ex·ˌpan·sion·'is·tic** *adj.*

ex·pan·sive (ɪk'spænsɪv) *adj.* **1.** able or tending to expand or characterized by expansion. **2.** wide; extensive. **3.** friendly, open, or talkative: *an expansive person.* **4.** grand or extravagant: *an expansive way of life.* **5.** *Psychiatry.* lacking restraint in the expression of feelings, esp. in having delusions of grandeur or being inclined to overvalue oneself or one's work. —**ex·'pan·sive·ly** *adv.* —**ex·'pan·sive·ness** *or* **ex·pan·siv·it·y** (ˌɛkspæn'sɪvɪtɪ) *n.*

ex par·te (ɛks 'pɑːtɪ) *adj. Law.* (of an application in a judicial proceeding) on behalf of one side or party only: *an ex parte injunction.*

ex·pa·ti·ate (ɪk'speɪʃɪˌeɪt) *vb.* (*intr.*) **1.** (foll. by *on* or *upon*) to enlarge (on a theme, topic, etc.) at length or in detail; elaborate (on). **2.** *Rare.* to wander about. [C16: from Latin *exspatiārī* to digress, from *spatiārī* to walk about] —**ex·ˌpa·ti·'a·tion** *n.* —**ex·'pa·ti·ˌa·tor** *n.*

ex·pat·ri·ate *adj.* (ɛks'pætrɪɪt, -ˌeɪt). **1.** exiled or banished from one's native country: *an expatriate American.* ~*n.* (ɛks'pætrɪɪt, -ˌeɪt). **2.** an exile; expatriate person. ~*vb.* (ɛks'pætrɪˌeɪt). (*tr.*) **3.** to exile (oneself) from one's native country or cause (another) to go into exile. **4.** to deprive (oneself or another) of citizenship. [C18: from Medieval Latin *expatriāre,* from Latin EX-[1] + *patria* native land] —**ex·ˌpat·ri·'a·tion** *n.*

ex·pect (ɪk'spɛkt) *vb.* (*tr.; may take a clause as object or an infinitive*) **1.** to regard as probable or likely; anticipate: *he expects to win.* **2.** to look forward to or be waiting for: *we expect good news today.* **3.** to decide that (something) is requisite or necessary; require: *the teacher expects us to work late today.* ~See also **expecting.** [C16: from Latin *exspectāre* to watch for, from *spectāre* to look at] —**ex·'pect·a·ble** *adj.* —**ex·'pect·a·bly** *adv.*

ex·pec·tan·cy (ɪk'spɛktənsɪ) *or* **ex·pec·tance** *n.* **1.** something expected, esp. on the basis of a norm or average: *his life expectancy was 30 years.* **2.** anticipation; expectation. **3.** the prospect of a future interest or possession, esp. in property: *an estate in expectancy.*

ex·pec·tant (ɪk'spɛktənt) *adj.* **1.** expecting, anticipating, or hopeful: *an expectant glance.* **2.** having expectations, esp. of possession of something or prosperity. **3.** pregnant: *an expectant mother.* ~*n.* **4.** a person who expects something. **5.** *Obsolete.* a candidate for office, esp. for ecclesiastical preferment. —**ex·'pect·ant·ly** *adv.*

ex·pec·ta·tion (ˌɛkspɛk'teɪʃən) *n.* **1.** the act or state of expecting or the state of being expected. **2.** (*usually pl.*) something looked forward to, whether feared or hoped for: *we have great expectations for his future; their worst expectations.* **3.** an attitude of expectancy or hope; anticipation: *to regard something with expectation.* **4.** *Statistics.* **a.** the numerical probability that an event will occur. **b.** another term for **expected value.** —**ex·pec·ta·tive** (ɪk'spɛktətɪv) *adj.*

ex·pect·ed val·ue *n. Statistics.* the sum or integral of all possible values of a variable multiplied by their respective probabilities. It is equivalent to the mean of the distribution of the variable. Also called: **mathematical expectation.**

ex·pect·ing (ɪk'spɛktɪŋ) *adj. Informal.* pregnant.

ex·pec·to·rant (ɪk'spɛktərənt) *Med.* ~*adj.* **1.** promoting the secretion, liquefaction, or expulsion of sputum from the respiratory passages. ~*n.* **2.** an expectorant drug or agent.

ex·pec·to·rate (ɪk'spɛktəˌreɪt) *vb.* to cough up and spit out (sputum from the respiratory passages). [C17: from Latin *expectorāre,* literally: to drive from the breast, expel, from *pectus* breast] —**ex·ˌpec·to·'ra·tion** *n.* —**ex·'pec·to·ˌra·tor** *n.*

ex·pe·di·en·cy (ɪk'spiːdɪənsɪ) *or* **ex·pe·di·ence** *n., pl.* **·en·cies** *or* **·enc·es. 1.** appropriateness; suitability. **2.** the use of or inclination towards methods that are advantageous rather than fair or just. **3.** another word for **expedient** (sense 3).

ex·pe·di·ent (ɪk'spiːdɪənt) *adj.* **1.** suitable to the circumstances; appropriate. **2.** inclined towards methods or means that are advantageous rather than fair or just. ~*n. also* **expediency. 3.** something suitable or appropriate, esp. something used during an urgent situation. [C14: from Latin *expediēns* setting free; see EXPEDITE] —**ex·'pe·di·ent·ly** *adv.*

ex·pe·di·en·tial (ɪkˌspiːdɪ'ɛnʃəl) *adj.* denoting, based on, or involving expediency. —**ex·ˌpe·di·'en·tial·ly** *adv.*

ex·pe·dite ('ɛkspɪˌdaɪt) *vb.* (*tr.*) **1.** to facilitate the progress of; hasten or assist. **2.** to do or process (something, such as business matters) with speed and efficiency. **3.** *Rare.* to dispatch (documents, messages, etc.). ~*adj. Obsolete.* **4.** unimpeded or prompt; expeditious. **5.** alert or prepared. [C17: from Latin *expedīre,* literally: to free the feet (as from a snare), hence, liberate, from EX-[1] + *pēs* foot] —'**ex·pe·ˌdit·er** *or* '**ex·pe·ˌdi·tor** *n.*

ex·pe·di·tion (ˌɛkspɪ'dɪʃən) *n.* **1.** an organized journey or voyage for a specific purpose, esp. for exploration or for a scientific or military purpose. **2.** the people and equipment comprising an expedition. **3.** a pleasure trip; excursion. **4.** promptness in acting; dispatch. [C15: from Latin *expeditiō,* from *expedīre* to prepare, EXPEDITE]

ex·pe·di·tion·ar·y (ˌɛkspɪ'dɪʃənərɪ) *adj.* relating to or constituting an expedition, esp. a military one: *an expeditionary force.*

ex·pe·di·tious (ˌɛkspɪ'dɪʃəs) *adj.* characterized by or done with speed and efficiency; prompt; quick. —ˌ**ex·pe·'di·tious·ly** *adv.* —ˌ**ex·pe·'di·tious·ness** *n.*

ex·pel (ɪk'spɛl) *vb.* **·pels, ·pel·ling, ·pelled.** (*tr.*) **1.** to eject or drive out with force. **2.** to deprive of participation in or membership of a school, club, etc. [C14: from Latin *expellere* to drive out, from *pellere* to thrust, drive] —**ex·'pel·la·ble** *adj.* —**ex·pel·lee** (ˌɛkspɛ'liː) *n.* —**ex·'pel·ler** *n.*

ex·pel·lant *or* **ex·pel·lent** (ɪk'spɛlənt) *adj.* **1.** forcing out or having the capacity to force out. ~*n.* **2.** a medicine used to expel undesirable substances or organisms from the body, esp. worms from the digestive tract.

ex·pel·lers (ɪk'spɛləz) *pl. n.* the residue remaining after an oilseed has been crushed to expel the oil, used for animal fodder: *groundnut expellers.* Compare **extractions.**

ex·pend (ɪk'spɛnd) *vb.* (*tr.*) **1.** to spend; disburse. **2.** to consume or use up. [C15: from Latin *expendere,* from *pendere* to weigh] —**ex·'pend·er** *n.*

ex·pend·a·ble (ɪk'spɛndəbᵊl) *adj.* **1.** that may be expended or used up. **2.** not essential; not worth preserving. **3.** able to be sacrificed to achieve an objective, esp. a military one. ~*n.* **4.** something that is expendable. —**ex·ˌpend·a·'bil·i·ty** *n.*

ex·pend·i·ture (ɪk'spɛndɪtʃə) *n.* **1.** something expended, such as time or money. **2.** the act of expending.

ex·pense (ɪk'spɛns) *n.* **1.** a particular payment of money; expenditure. **2.** money needed for individual purchases; cost; charge. **3.** (*pl.*) incidental money spent in the performance of a job, commission, etc., usually reimbursed by an employer or allowable against tax. **4.** something requiring money for its purchase or upkeep: *the car was more of an expense than he had expected.* **5. at the expense of.** to the detriment of: *he succeeded at the expense of his health.* ~*vb.* **6.** (*tr.*) *U.S.* to treat as an expense for book-keeping or tax purposes. [C14: from Late Latin *expēnsa,* from Latin *expēnsus* weighed out; see EXPEND]

ex+pense ac+count *n.* **1.** an arrangement by which expenses incurred in the course of a person's work are refunded by his employer or deducted from his income for tax purposes. **2.** a record of such expenses. **3.** (*modifier*) *Informal.* paid for by an employer or by money allowable against tax: *an expense-account lunch.*

ex+pen+sive (ɪk'spɛnsɪv) *adj.* high-priced; costly; dear. —**ex+'pen+sive+ly** *adv.* —**ex+'pen+sive+ness** *n.*

ex+pe·ri+ence (ɪk'spɪərɪəns) *n.* **1.** direct personal participation or observation; actual knowledge or contact: *experience of prison life.* **2.** a particular incident, feeling, etc., that a person has undergone: *an experience to remember.* **3.** accumulated knowledge, esp. of practical matters: *a man of experience.* **4.** the impact made on an individual by the culture of a people, nation, etc.: *the American experience.* **5.** *Philosophy.* the totality of a person's perceptions, thoughts, memories, and encounters. ~*vb.* (*tr.*) **6.** to participate in or undergo. **7.** to be emotionally or aesthetically moved by; feel: *to experience beauty.* [C14: from Latin *experientia,* from *experīrī* to prove; related to Latin *perīculum* PERIL] —**ex+'pe·ri+ence+a·ble** *adj.*

ex+pe·ri+enced (ɪk'spɪərɪənst) *adj.* having become skilful or knowledgeable from extensive contact or participation or observation.

ex+pe·ri+ence ta+ble *n.* *Insurance.* an actuarial table, esp. a mortality table based on past statistics.

ex+pe·ri+en+tial (ɪkˌspɪərɪ'ɛnʃəl) *adj.* relating to or derived from experience; empirical. —**ex+ˌpe·ri+'en+tial+ly** *adv.*

ex+pe·ri+en+tial+ism (ɪkˌspɪərɪ'ɛnʃəˌlɪzəm) *n.* the philosophical doctrine that all knowledge is based on experience. Also called: **experiential philosophy.** —**ex+ˌpe·ri+'en+tial+ist** *n.*

ex+per·i+ment *n.* (ɪk'spɛrɪmənt). **1.** a test or investigation, esp. one planned to provide evidence for or against a hypothesis: *a scientific experiment.* **2.** the act of conducting such an investigation or test; experimentation; research. **3.** an attempt at something new or different; an effort to be original: *a poetic experiment.* **4.** an obsolete word for **experience.** ~*vb.* (ɪk'spɛrɪˌmɛnt). **5.** (*intr.*) to make an experiment or experiments. [C14: from Latin *experīmentum* proof, trial, from *experīrī* to test; see EXPERIENCE] —**ex+'per·i+ˌment+er** *n.*

ex+per·i+men+tal (ɪkˌspɛrɪ'mɛntᵊl) *adj.* **1.** relating to, based on, or having the nature of experiment: *an experimental study.* **2.** based on or derived from experience; empirical: *experimental evidence.* **3.** tending to experiment: *an experimental artist.* **4.** tentative or provisional: *an experimental rule in football.* —**ex+ˌper·i+'men+tal+ly** *adv.*

ex+per·i+men+tal+ism (ɪkˌspɛrɪ'mɛntəˌlɪzəm) *n.* employment of or reliance upon experiments; empiricism. —**ex+ˌper·i+'men+tal+ist** *n.*

ex+per·i+men+tal+ize *or* **ex+per·i+men+tal+ise** (ɪkˌspɛrɪ'mɛntəˌlaɪz) *vb.* (*intr.*) to engage in experiments.

ex+per·i+men+ta+tion (ɪkˌspɛrɪmɛn'teɪʃən) *n.* the act, process, or practice of experimenting.

ex+per·i+ment+er ef+fect *n.* *Psychol.* the influence of an experimenter's expectations on his results.

ex+pert ('ɛkspɜːt) *n.* **1.** a person who has extensive skill or knowledge in a particular field. **2. the expert.** *Austral. informal.* the worker in a sheep-shearing shed responsible for the care of machinery. ~*adj.* **3.** skilful or knowledgeable. **4.** of, involving, or done by an expert: *an expert job.* [C14: from Latin *expertus* known by experience, from *experīrī* to test; see EXPERIENCE] —**'ex+pert+ly** *adv.* —**'ex+pert+ness** *n.*

ex+per+tise (ˌɛkspɜː'tiːz) *n.* special skill, knowledge, or judgment; expertness. [C19: from French: expert skill, from EXPERT]

ex+pert+ize *or* **ex+pert+ise** ('ɛkspɜːˌtaɪz) *vb.* *U.S.* to act as an expert or give an expert opinion (on).

ex+pi+a·ble ('ɛkspɪəbᵊl) *adj.* capable of being expiated or atoned for.

ex+pi+ate ('ɛkspɪˌeɪt) *vb.* (*tr.*) to atone for or redress (sin or wrongdoing); make amends for. [C16: from Latin *expiāre,* from *pius* dutiful; see PIOUS] —**'ex+pi·ˌa+tor** *n.*

ex+pi·a+tion (ˌɛkspɪ'eɪʃən) *n.* the act, process, or a means of expiating; atonement.

ex+pi·a·to·ry ('ɛkspɪətərɪ, -trɪ) *adj.* **1.** capable of making expiation. **2.** given or offered in expiation.

ex+pi+ra+tion (ˌɛkspɪ'reɪʃən) *n.* **1.** the finish of something; ending; expiry. **2.** the act, process, or sound of breathing out. **3.** *Rare.* a last breath; death.

ex+pir·a·to·ry (ɪk'spaɪərətərɪ, -trɪ) *adj.* relating to the expulsion of air from the lungs during respiration.

ex+pire (ɪk'spaɪə) *vb.* **1.** (*intr.*) to finish or run out; cease; come to an end. **2.** to breathe out (air); exhale. **3.** (*intr.*) to die. [C15: from Old French *expirer,* from Latin *exspīrāre* to breathe out, from *spīrāre* to breathe] —**ex+'pir+er** *n.*

ex+pi+ry (ɪk'spaɪərɪ) *n., pl.* **+ries. 1. a.** a coming to an end, esp. of a contract period; termination: *expiry of a lease.* **b.** (*as modifier*): *the expiry date.* **2.** death.

ex+plain (ɪk'spleɪn) *vb.* **1.** (when *tr., may take a clause as object*) to make (something) comprehensible, esp. by giving a clear and detailed account of the relevant structure, operation, surrounding circumstances, etc. **2.** (*tr.*) to justify or attempt to justify (oneself) by giving reasons for one's actions or words. [C15: from Latin *explānāre* to flatten, from *plānus* level] —**ex+'plain+a·ble** *adj.* —**ex+'plain+er** *n.*

ex+plain a·way *vb.* (*tr., adv.*) to offer excuses or reasons for (bad conduct, mistakes, etc.).

ex+pla+na+tion (ˌɛksplə'neɪʃən) *n.* **1.** the act or process of explaining. **2.** a statement or occurrence that explains. **3.** a clarification of disputed terms or points; reconciliation.

ex+plan·a·to·ry (ɪk'splænətərɪ, -trɪ) *or* **ex+plan·a·tive** *adj.* serving or intended to serve as an explanation. —**ex+'plan·a+to+ri+ly** *adv.*

ex+plant (ɛks'plɑːnt) *vb.* **1.** to transfer (living tissue) from its natural site to a culture medium. ~*n.* **2.** a piece of tissue treated in this way. —**ˌex+plan+'ta+tion** *n.*

ex+ple·tive (ɪk'spliːtɪv) *n.* **1.** an exclamation or swearword; an oath or a sound expressing an emotional reaction rather than any particular meaning. **2.** any syllable, word, or phrase conveying no independent meaning, esp. one inserted in a line of verse for the sake of the metre. ~*adj.* *also* **ex+ple·to·ry** (ɪk'spliːtərɪ). **3.** expressing no particular meaning, esp. when filling out a line of verse. [C17: from Late Latin *explētīvus* for filling out, from *explēre,* from *plēre* to fill] —**ex+'ple·tive+ly** *adv.*

ex+pli+ca·ble ('ɛksplɪkəbᵊl, ɪk'splɪk-) *adj.* capable of being explained.

ex+pli+cate ('ɛksplɪˌkeɪt) *vb.* (*tr.*) *Formal.* **1.** to make clear or explicit; explain. **2.** to formulate or develop (a theory, hypothesis, etc.). [C16: from Latin *explicāre* to unfold, from *plicāre* to fold] —**ex+pli+ca+tive** (ɪk'splɪkətɪv) *or* **ex+pli+ca+to·ry** (ɪk'splɪkətərɪ, -trɪ) *adj.* —**'ex+pli+ˌca+tor** *n.*

ex+pli+ca+tion (ˌɛksplɪ'keɪʃən) *n.* **1.** the act or process of explicating. **2.** analysis or interpretation, esp. of a literary passage or work or philosophical doctrine. **3.** a comprehensive exposition or description.

ex+pli+ca+tion de texte *French.* (ɛksplikasjɔ̃ də 'tɛkst) *n., pl.* ***ex+pli+ca+tions de texte*** (ɛksplikasjɔ̃ də 'tɛkst). a close textual analysis of a literary work. [literally: explanation of (the) text]

ex+plic+it[1] (ɪk'splɪsɪt) *adj.* **1.** precisely and clearly expressed, leaving nothing to implication; fully stated: *explicit instructions.* **2.** openly expressed without reservations; unreserved. **3.** *Maths.* (of a function) having an equation of the form $y = f(x)$, in which y is expressed directly in terms of x, as in $y = x^4 + x + z$. Compare **implicit** (sense 4). [C17: from Latin *explicitus* unfolded, from *explicāre;* see EXPLICATE] —**ex+'plic+it+ly** *adv.* —**ex+'plic+it+ness** *n.*

ex+plic+it[2] (ɪk'splɪsɪt) the end; an indication, used esp. by medieval scribes, of the end of a book, part of a manuscript, etc. [Late Latin, probably short for *explicitus est liber* the book is unfolded (or complete); shortened by analogy with INCIPIT]

ex+plode (ɪk'spləʊd) *vb.* **1.** to burst or cause to burst with great violence as a result of internal pressure, esp. through the detonation of an explosive; blow up. **2.** to destroy or be destroyed in this manner: *to explode a bridge.* **3.** (of a gas) to undergo or cause (a gas) to undergo a sudden violent expansion, accompanied by heat, light, a shock wave, and a loud noise, as a result of a fast uncontrolled exothermic chemical or nuclear reaction. **4.** (*intr.*) to react suddenly or violently with emotion, etc.: *to explode with anger.* **5.** (*intr.*) (esp. of a population) to increase rapidly. **6.** (*tr.*) to show (a theory, etc.) to be baseless; refute and make obsolete. **7.** (*tr.*) *Phonetics.* to pronounce (a stop) with audible plosion. ~Compare **implode.** [C16: from Latin *explōdere* to drive off by clapping, hiss (an actor) off, from EX-[1] + *plaudere* to clap] —**ex+'plod+er** *n.*

ex+plod+ed view *n.* a drawing or photograph of a complicated mechanism that shows the individual parts separately, usually indicating their relative positions.

ex+plod+ing star *n.* an irregular variable star, such as a nova, supernova, or flare star, in which rapid increases in luminosity occur, caused by some form of explosion.

ex+ploit *n.* ('ɛksplɔɪt). **1.** a notable deed or feat, esp. one that is noble or heroic. ~*vb.* (ɪk'splɔɪt). (*tr.*) **2.** to take advantage of (a person, situation, etc.), esp. unethically or unjustly for one's own advantage. **3.** to make the best use of: *to exploit natural resources.* [C14: from Old French: accomplishment, from Latin *explicitum* (something) unfolded, from *explicāre* to EXPLICATE] —**ex+'ploit+a·ble** *adj.* —**ˌex+ploi+'ta+tion** *n.* —**ex+'ploit+ive** *or* **ex+'ploit·a·tive** *adj.*

ex+plo+ra+tion (ˌɛksplə'reɪʃən) *n.* **1.** the act or process of exploring. **2.** *Med.* examination of an organ or part for diagnostic purposes. **3.** an organized trip into unfamiliar regions, esp. for scientific purposes; expedition. —**ex+plor·a+to·ry** (ɪk'splɒrətərɪ, -trɪ) *or* **ex+'plor·a+tive** *adj.*

ex+plore (ɪk'splɔː) *vb.* **1.** (*tr.*) to examine or investigate, esp. systematically. **2.** to travel to or into (unfamiliar or unknown regions), esp. for organized scientific purposes. **3.** (*tr.*) *Med.* to examine (an organ or part) for diagnostic purposes. **4.** (*tr.*) *Obsolete.* to search for or out. [C16: from Latin *explōrāre,* from EX-[1] + *plōrāre* to cry aloud; probably from the shouts of hunters sighting prey] —**ex+'plor+er** *n.*

Ex+plor+er[1] (ɪk'splɔːrə) *n.* *U.S.* a member of the senior branch of the Scouts. Brit. equivalent: **Venture Scout.**

Ex+plor+er[2] (ɪk'splɔːrə) *n.* any of the first series of U.S. satellites. **Explorer 1,** launched in 1958, confirmed the existence of intense radiation belts around the earth.

ex+plo+sion (ɪk'spləʊʒən) *n.* **1.** the act or an instance of exploding. **2.** a violent release of energy resulting from a rapid chemical or nuclear reaction, esp. one that produces a shock wave, loud noise, heat, and light. Compare **implosion. 3.** a sudden or violent outburst of activity, noise, emotion, etc. **4.** a rapid increase, esp. in a population. **5.** *Phonetics.* another word for **plosion.** [C17: from Latin *explōsiō*, from *explōdere* to EXPLODE]

ex·plo·sive (ɪk'spləʊsɪv) *adj.* **1.** of, involving, or characterized by an explosion or explosions. **2.** capable of exploding or tending to explode. **3.** potentially violent or hazardous; dangerous: *an explosive situation.* **4.** *Phonetics.* another word for **plosive.** ~*n.* **5.** a substance that decomposes rapidly under certain conditions with the production of gases, which expand by the heat of the reaction. The energy released is used in firearms, blasting, and rocket propulsion. **6.** a plosive consonant; stop. —**ex·'plo·sive·ly** *adv.* —**ex·'plo·sive·ness** *n.*

ex·po ('ɛkspəʊ) *n., pl.* **·pos.** *Informal.* short for **exposition** (sense 3).

ex·po·nent (ɪk'spəʊnənt) *n.* **1.** (usually foll. by *of*) a person or thing that acts as an advocate (of an idea, cause, etc.). **2.** a person or thing that explains or interprets. **3.** a performer or interpretive artist, esp. a musician. **4.** Also called: **power, index.** *Maths.* a number or variable placed as a superscript to the right of another number or quantity indicating the number of times the number or quantity is to be multiplied by itself. ~*adj.* **5.** offering a declaration, explanation, or interpretation. [C16: from Latin *expōnere* to set out, expound, from *pōnere* to set, place]

ex·po·nen·tial (ˌɛkspəʊ'nɛnʃəl) *adj.* **1.** *Maths.* (of a function, curve, series, or equation) of, containing, or involving one or more numbers or quantities raised to an exponent, esp. e^x. **2.** *Maths.* raised to the power of e, the base of natural logarithms. Abbrev.: **exp 3.** of or involving an exponent or exponents. ~*n.* **4.** *Maths.* an exponential function, etc. —ˌ**ex·po·'nen·tial·ly** *adv.*

ex·po·nen·tial dis·tri·bu·tion *n. Statistics.* a continuous single-parameter distribution used esp. when making statements about the length of life of certain materials.

ex·pon·i·ble (ɪk'spəʊnəbᵊl) *adj.* (of a proposition, etc.) requiring explanation or revision to be intelligible.

ex·port *n.* ('ɛkspɔːt). **1.** (*often pl.*) **a.** goods (**visible exports**) or services (**invisible exports**) sold to a foreign country or countries. **b.** (*as modifier*): *an export licence; export finance.* ~*vb.* (ɪk'spɔːt, 'ɛkspɔːt). **2.** to sell (goods or services) or ship (goods) to a foreign country or countries. **3.** (*tr.*) to transmit or spread (an idea, social institution, etc.) abroad. ~Compare **import.** [C15: from Latin *exportāre* to carry away, from *portāre* to carry] —**ex·'port·a·ble** *adj.* —**ex·ˌport·a·'bil·i·ty** *n.* —**ex·'port·er** *n.*

ex·por·ta·tion (ˌɛkspɔː'teɪʃən) *n.* **1.** the act, business, or process of exporting goods or services. **2.** *Chiefly U.S.* an exported product or service.

ex·port re·ject *n.* an article that fails to meet a standard of quality required for export and that is sold on the home market.

ex·pose (ɪk'spəʊz) *vb.* (*tr.*) **1.** to display for viewing; exhibit. **2.** to bring to public notice; disclose; reveal: *to expose the facts.* **3.** to divulge the identity of; unmask. **4.** (foll. by *to*) to make subject or susceptible (to attack, criticism, etc.). **5.** to abandon (a child, animal, etc.) in the open to die. **6.** (foll. by *to*) to introduce (to) or acquaint (with): *he was exposed to the classics at an early age.* **7.** *Photog.* to subject (a photographic film or plate) to light, x-rays, or some other type of actinic radiation. **8.** *R.C. Church.* to exhibit (the consecrated Eucharistic Host or a relic) for public veneration. **9. expose oneself.** to display one's sexual organs in public. [C15: from Old French *exposer*, from Latin *expōnere* to set out; see EXPONENT] —**ex·'pos·a·ble** *adj.* —**ex·'pos·al** *n.* —**ex·'pos·er** *n.*

ex·po·sé (ɛks'pəʊzeɪ) *n.* **1.** the act or an instance of bringing a scandal, crime, etc., to public notice. **2.** an article, book, or statement that discloses a scandal, crime, etc.

ex·posed (ɪk'spəʊzd) *adj.* **1.** not concealed; displayed for viewing. **2.** without shelter from the elements. **3.** susceptible to attack or criticism; vulnerable. —**ex·pos·ed·ness** (ɪk'spəʊzɪdnɪs) *n.*

ex·po·si·tion (ˌɛkspə'zɪʃən) *n.* **1.** a systematic, usually written statement about, commentary on, or explanation of a specific subject. **2.** the act of expounding or setting forth information or a viewpoint. **3.** a large public exhibition, esp. of industrial products or arts and crafts. **4.** the act of exposing or the state of being exposed. **5.** the part of a play, novel, etc., in which the theme and main characters are introduced. **6.** *Music.* the first statement of the subjects or themes of a movement in sonata form or a fugue. **7.** *R.C. Church.* the exhibiting of the consecrated Eucharistic Host or a relic for public veneration. [C14: from Latin *expositiō* a setting forth, from *expōnere* to display; see EXPONENT] —ˌ**ex·po·'si·tion·al** *adj.*

ex·pos·i·tor (ɪk'spɒzɪtə) *n.* a person who expounds.

ex·pos·i·to·ry (ɪk'spɒzɪtərɪ, -trɪ) *or* **ex·pos·i·tive** *adj.* of, involving, or assisting in exposition; explanatory. —**ex·'pos·i·to·ri·ly** *or* **ex·'pos·i·tive·ly** *adv.*

ex post fac·to (ɛks 'pəʊst 'fæktəʊ) *adj.* having retrospective effect: *an ex post facto law.* [C17: from Latin *ex* from + *post* afterwards + *factus* done, from *facere* to do]

ex·pos·tu·late (ɪk'spɒstjʊˌleɪt) *vb.* (*intr.*; usually foll. by *with*) to argue or reason (with), esp. in order to dissuade from an action or intention. [C16: from Latin *expostulāre* to require, from *postulāre* to demand; see POSTULATE] —**ex·'pos·tu·ˌlat·ing·ly** *adv.* —**ex·ˌpos·tu·'la·tion** *n.* —**ex·'pos·tu·ˌla·tor** *n.* —**ex·'pos·tu·la·to·ry** *or* **ex·'pos·tu·la·tive** *adj.*

ex·po·sure (ɪk'spəʊʒə) *n.* **1.** the act of exposing or the condition of being exposed. **2.** the position or outlook of a house, building, etc.; aspect: *the bedroom has a southern exposure.* **3.** lack of shelter from the weather, esp. the cold: *to die of exposure.* **4.** a surface that is exposed: *an exposure of granite.* **5.** *Photog.* **a.** the act of exposing a photographic film or plate to light, x-rays, etc. **b.** an area on a film or plate that has been exposed to light, etc. **c.** (*as modifier*): *exposure control.* **6.** *Photog.* **a.** the intensity of light falling on a photographic film or plate multiplied by the time for which it is exposed. **b.** a combination of lens aperture and shutter speed used in taking a photograph: *he used the wrong exposure.* **7.** appearance or presentation before the public, as in a theatre, on television, or in films. **8.** See **indecent exposure.**

ex·po·sure me·ter *n. Photog.* an instrument for measuring the intensity of light, usually by means of a photocell, so that the suitable camera settings of shutter speed and f-number (or lens aperture) can be determined. Also called: **light meter.**

ex·pound (ɪk'spaʊnd) *vb.* (when *intr.*, foll. by *on* or *about*) to explain or set forth (an argument, theory, etc.) in detail: *to expound on one's theories; he expounded his reasoning.* [C13: from Old French *espondre*, from Latin *expōnere* to set forth, from *pōnere* to put] —**ex·'pound·er** *n.*

ex·press (ɪk'sprɛs) *vb.* (*tr.*) **1.** to transform (ideas) into words; utter; verbalize. **2.** to show or reveal; indicate: *tears express grief.* **3.** to communicate (emotion, etc.) without words, as through music, painting, etc. **4.** to indicate through a symbol, formula, etc. **5.** to force or squeeze out: *to express the juice from an orange.* **6.** to send by rapid transport or special messenger. **7. express oneself.** to communicate one's thoughts or ideas. ~*adj.* (*prenominal*) **8.** clearly indicated or shown; explicitly stated: *an express wish.* **9.** done or planned for a definite reason or goal; particular: *an express purpose.* **10.** of, concerned with, or designed for rapid transportation of people, merchandise, mail, money, etc.: *express delivery; an express depot.* ~*n.* **11. a.** a system for sending merchandise, mail, money, etc., rapidly. **b.** merchandise, mail, etc., conveyed by such a system. **c.** *Chiefly U.S.* an enterprise operating such a system. **12.** Also called: **express train.** a fast train stopping at none or only a few of the intermediate stations between its two termini. **13.** See **express rifle.** ~*adv.* **14.** by means of a special delivery or express delivery: *it went express.* [C14: from Latin *expressus*, literally: squeezed out, hence, prominent, from *exprimere* to force out, from EX-[1] + *premere* to press] —**ex·'press·er** *n.* —**ex·'press·i·ble** *adj.*

ex·press·age (ɪk'sprɛsɪdʒ) *n.* **1.** the conveyance of merchandise by express. **2.** the fee charged for such conveyance.

ex·pres·sion (ɪk'sprɛʃən) *n.* **1.** the act or an instance of transforming ideas into words. **2.** a manifestation of an emotion, feeling, etc., without words: *tears are an expression of grief.* **3.** communication of emotion through music, painting, etc. **4.** a look on the face that indicates mood or emotion: *a joyful expression.* **5.** the choice of words, phrases, syntax, intonation, etc., in communicating. **6.** a particular phrase used conventionally to express something: *a dialect expression.* **7.** the act or process of forcing or squeezing out a liquid. **8.** *Maths.* a variable, function, or some combination of constants, variables, or functions. **9.** *Genetics.* the effect of a particular gene on the phenotype. —**ex·'pres·sion·al** *adj.* —**ex·'pres·sion·less** *adj.* —**ex·'pres·sion·less·ly** *adv.*

ex·pres·sion·ism (ɪk'sprɛʃəˌnɪzəm) *n.* (*sometimes cap.*) an artistic and literary movement originating in Germany at the beginning of the 20th century, which sought to express emotions rather than to represent external reality: characterized by the use of symbolism and of exaggeration and distortion. —**ex·'pres·sion·ist** *n., adj.* —**ex·ˌpres·sion·'is·tic** *adj.*

ex·pres·sion mark *n.* one of a set of musical directions, usually in Italian, indicating how a piece or passage is to be performed.

ex·pres·sive (ɪk'sprɛsɪv) *adj.* **1.** of, involving, or full of expression. **2.** (*postpositive*; foll. by *of*) indicative or suggestive (of): *a look expressive of love.* **3.** having a particular meaning, feeling, or force; significant. —**ex·'pres·sive·ly** *adv.* —**ex·'pres·sive·ness** *n.*

ex·pres·siv·i·ty (ˌɛksprɛ'sɪvɪtɪ) *n.* **1.** (esp. of a work of art) the quality of being expressive. **2.** *Genetics.* the strength of the effect of a gene on the phenotype.

ex·press·ly (ɪk'sprɛslɪ) *adv.* **1.** for an express purpose; with specific intentions. **2.** plainly, exactly, or unmistakably.

ex·press·o (ɪk'sprɛsəʊ) *n.* variant of **espresso.**

ex·press ri·fle *n. U.S.* a hunting rifle designed to kill large game at close range.

ex·press·way (ɪk'sprɛsˌweɪ) *n. Chiefly U.S.* an urban motorway.

ex·pro·pri·ate (ɛks'prəʊprɪˌeɪt) *vb.* (*tr.*) to deprive (an owner) of (property), esp. by taking it for public use. See also **eminent domain.** [C17: from Medieval Latin *expropriāre* to deprive of possessions, from *proprius* own] —**ex·'pro·pri·a·ble** *adj.* —**ex·ˌpro·pri·'a·tion** *n.* —**ex·'pro·pri·ˌa·tor** *n.*

exptl. *abbrev. for* experimental.

ex·pul·sion (ɪk'spʌlʃən) *n.* the act of expelling or the fact or condition of being expelled. [C14: from Latin *expulsiō* a driving out, from *expellere* to EXPEL]

ex·pul·sive (ɪk'spʌlsɪv) *adj.* tending or serving to expel.

ex·punge (ɪk'spʌndʒ) *vb.* (*tr.*) **1.** to delete or erase; blot out; obliterate. **2.** to wipe out or destroy. [C17: from Latin *expungere* to blot out, from *pungere* to prick] —**ex·punc·tion** (ɪk'spʌŋkʃən) *n.* —**ex·'pung·er** *n.*

ex·pur·gate ('ɛkspəˌgeɪt) *vb.* (*tr.*) to amend (a book, text, etc.) by removing (obscene or offensive sections). [C17: from Latin *expurgāre* to clean out, from *purgāre* to purify; see PURGE] —ˌ**ex·pur·'ga·tion** *n.* —**'ex·pur·ˌga·tor** *n.* —**ex·pur·ga·to·ry** (ɛks'pɜːgətərɪ, -trɪ) *or* **ex·pur·ga·to·ri·al** (ɪkˌspɜːgə'tɔːrɪəl) *adj.*

ex·quis·ite (ɪk'skwɪzɪt, 'ɛkskwɪzɪt) *adj.* **1.** possessing qualities of unusual delicacy and fine craftsmanship: *jewels in an* *exquisite setting.* **2.** extremely beautiful and pleasing: *an exquisite face.* **3.** outstanding or excellent: *an exquisite victory.* **4.** sensitive; discriminating: *exquisite taste.* **5.** fastidious and refined. **6.** intense or sharp in feeling: *exquisite pleasure.* ~*n.* **7.** *Obsolete.* a dandy. [C15: from Latin *exquīsītus* excellent, from *exquīrere* to search out, from *quaerere* to seek] —**ex+'quis+ite+ly** *adv.* —**ex+'quis+ite+ness** *n.*

exr. *abbrev. for* executor.

ex+san+gui+nate (ɪk'sæŋgwɪneɪt) *vb. (tr.) Rare.* to drain the blood from. [C19: from Latin *exsanguināre*] —**ex+,san+guin+'a+tion** *n.*

ex+san+guine (ɪk'sæŋgwɪn) *or* **ex+san+gui+nous** *adj.* without blood; bloodless or anaemic. [C17: from Latin *exsanguis,* from *sanguis* blood] —**,ex+san+'guin+i+ty** *n.*

ex+scind (ɛk'sɪnd) *vb. (tr.)* to cut off or out; excise. [C17 *exscind,* from Latin *exscindere* to extirpate, destroy, from *scindere* to cut, tear, split]

ex+sect (ɛk'sɛkt) *vb. (tr.)* to cut out. [C17 *exsect,* from Latin *exsecāre* to cut away, from *secāre* to cut] —**ex+sec+tion** (ɛk'sɛkʃən) *n.*

ex+sert (ɛk'sɜ:t) *vb.* **1.** *(tr.)* to thrust out; protrude. ~*adj. also* **ex+sert+ed.** **2.** protruded, stretched out, or (esp. of stamens) projecting beyond the corolla of a flower. [C19: from Latin *exserere* to thrust out; see EXERT] —**ex+ser+tion** *n.* —**ex+ser+tile** (ɛk'sɜ:taɪl) *adj.*

ex-serv·ice *adj.* having formerly served in the army, navy, or air force.

ex-serv·ice+man *n., pl.* **+men.** a man who has served in the army, navy, or air force.

ex+sic+cate ('ɛksɪ,keɪt) *vb.* to dry up; desiccate. [C15: from Latin *exsiccāre,* from *siccus* dry] —**,ex+sic+'ca+tion** *n.* —**'ex+sic+ca+tive** *adj.* —**'ex+sic+,ca+tor** *n.*

ex si+len+ti+o *Latin.* (ɛks sɪ'lɛnʃɪ,əʊ) *adv., adj.* (of a theory, assumption, etc.) based on a lack of evidence to the contrary. [literally: from silence]

ex+stip·u+late (ɛk'stɪpjʊlɪt, -,leɪt) *or* **es+tip·u+late** *adj.* (of a flowering plant) having no stipules.

ex+stro+phy ('ɛkstrəfɪ) *n. Med.* congenital eversion of a hollow organ, esp. the urinary bladder. [C19: from Greek EX-[1] + *strophein* to turn]

ext. *abbrev. for:* **1.** extension. **2.** external(ly). **3.** extinct. **4.** extra. **5.** extract.

ex+tant (ɛk'stænt, 'ɛkstənt) *adj.* **1.** still in existence; surviving. **2.** *Archaic.* standing out; protruding. [C16: from Latin *exstāns* standing out, from *exstāre,* from *stāre* to stand]

Usage. Careful writers distinguish between *extant* and *existent.* Both are used of that which exists at the present time, but *extant* has a further connotation of survival. *Extant* is therefore used of that which still exists, although there would be reason for believing that it might have disappeared: *the species was believed extinct, but a small population was found to be still extant in Africa; in the existent circumstances this is impossible.*

ex+tem+po+ra+ne+ous (ɪk,stɛmpə'reɪnɪəs) *or* **ex+tem+po+rar+y** (ɪk'stɛmpərərɪ, -prərɪ) *adj.* **1.** spoken, performed, etc., without planning or preparation; impromptu; extempore. **2.** done in a temporary manner; improvised. —**ex+,tem+po+'ra+ne+ous+ly** *or* **ex+'tem+po+rar+i+ly** *adv.* —**ex+,tem+po+'ra+ne+ous+ness** *or* **ex+'tem+po+rar+i+ness** *n.*

ex+tem+po+re (ɪk'stɛmpərɪ) *adv., adj.* without planning or preparation; impromptu. [C16: from Latin *ex tempore* instantaneously, from EX-[1] out of + *tempus* time]

ex+tem+po+rize *or* **ex+tem+po+rise** (ɪk'stɛmpə,raɪz) *vb.* **1.** to perform, speak, or compose (an act, speech, piece of music, etc.) without planning or preparation. **2.** to use (a temporary solution) for an immediate need; improvise. —**ex+,tem+po+ri+'za+tion** *or* **ex+,tem+po+ri+'sa+tion** *n.* —**ex+'tem+po+,riz+er** *or* **ex+'tem+po+,ris+er** *n.*

ex+tend (ɪk'stɛnd) *vb.* **1.** to draw out or be drawn out; stretch. **2.** to last for a certain time: *his schooling extended for three years.* **3.** *(intr.)* to reach a certain point in time or distance: *the land extends five miles.* **4.** *(intr.)* to exist or occur: *the trees extended throughout the area.* **5.** *(tr.)* to increase (a building, etc.) in size or area; add to or enlarge. **6.** *(tr.)* to broaden the meaning or scope of: *the law was extended.* **7.** *(tr.)* to put forth, present, or offer: *to extend greetings.* **8.** to stretch forth (an arm, etc.). **9.** *(tr.)* to lay out (a body) at full length. **10.** *(tr.)* to strain or exert (a person or animal) to the maximum. **11.** *(tr.)* to prolong (the time originally set) for payment of (a debt or loan), completion of (a task), etc. **12.** *(tr.) Book-keeping.* **a.** to carry forward. **b.** to calculate the amount of (a total, balance, etc.). **13.** *(tr.) Law.* (formerly in England) to value or assess (land). [C14: from Latin *extendere* to stretch out, from *tendere* to stretch] —**ex+'tend+i+ble** *or* **ex+'tend+a+ble** *adj.* —**ex+,tend+i+'bil+i+ty** *or* **ex+,tend+a+'bil+i+ty** *n.*

ex+tend+ed (ɪk'stɛndɪd) *adj.* **1.** stretched out in time, space, influence, application, etc. **2.** (of a horse's pace) free-moving and with long steps: *an extended trot.* **3.** *Printing.* another word for **expanded** (sense 1). —**ex+'tend+ed+ly** *adv.* —**ex+'tend+ed+ness** *n.*

ex+tend+ed fam+i+ly *n. Sociol., anthropol.* a social unit that contains the nuclear family together with blood relatives, often spanning three or more generations.

ex+tend·ed-play *adj.* denoting an EP record.

ex+tend+er (ɪk'stɛndə) *n.* **1.** a person or thing that extends. **2.** a substance, such as French chalk or china clay, added to paints to give them body and decrease their rate of settlement. **3.** a substance added to glues and resins to dilute them or to modify their viscosity. **4.** a substance added to elastomers to assist the plasticizer.

ex+ten+si+ble (ɪk'stɛnsəbᵊl) *or* **ex+ten+sile** (ɪk'stɛnsaɪl) *adj.* capable of being extended. —**ex+,ten+si+'bil+i+ty** *or* **ex+'ten+si+ble+ness** *n.*

ex+ten+sion (ɪk'stɛnʃən) *n.* **1.** the act of extending or the condition of being extended. **2.** something that can be extended or that extends another object. **3.** the length, range, etc., over which something is extended; extent. **4.** an additional telephone set connected to the same telephone line as another set or other sets. **5.** a room or rooms added to an existing building. **6.** a delay, esp. one agreed by all parties, in the date originally set for payment of a debt or completion of a contract. **7.** the property of matter by which it occupies space; size. **8.** **a.** the act of straightening or extending an arm or leg. **b.** its position after being straightened or extended. **9.** *Med.* a steady pull applied to a fractured or dislocated arm or leg to restore it to its normal position. See also **traction** (sense 3). **10.** **a.** a service by which some of the facilities of an educational establishment, library, etc., are offered to outsiders. **b.** *(as modifier): a university extension course.* **11.** Also called: **denotation.** *Logic.* the class of entities to which a given word correctly applies: thus, the extension of *satellite of Mars* is the set containing only Deimos and Phobos. Compare **intension** (sense 1). [C14: from Late Latin *extensiō* a stretching out; see EXTEND] —**ex+'ten+sion+al** *adj.* —**ex+,ten+sion+'al+i+ty** *or* **ex+'ten+sion+al+,ism** *n.* —**ex+'ten+sion+al+ly** *adv.*

ex+ten+si+ty (ɪk'stɛnsɪtɪ) *n.* **1.** *Psychol.* that part of sensory perception relating to the spatial aspect of objects. **2.** *Rare.* the condition of being extensive or extended.

ex+ten+sive (ɪk'stɛnsɪv) *adj.* **1.** having a large extent, area, scope, degree, etc.; vast: *extensive deserts; an extensive inheritance.* **2.** widespread: *extensive coverage in the press.* **3.** *Agriculture.* involving or farmed with minimum expenditure of capital or labour. Compare **intensive** (sense 3). **4.** *Physics.* of or relating to a property, measurement, etc., that is dependent on mass: *heat is an extensive property.* Compare **intensive** (sense 7). **5.** of or relating to logical extension. —**ex+'ten+sive+ly** *adv.* —**ex+'ten+sive+ness** *n.*

ex+ten+som+e+ter (,ɛkstɛn'sɒmɪtə) *or* **ex+ten+sim+e+ter** (,ɛkstɛn'sɪmɪtə) *n.* an apparatus for studying small changes of length, as in the thermal expansion or mechanical compression of a solid.

ex+ten+sor (ɪk'stɛnsə, -sɔ:) *n.* any muscle that stretches or extends an arm, leg, or other bodily part. Compare **flexor.** [C18: from New Latin, from Latin *extensus* stretched out]

ex+tent (ɪk'stɛnt) *n.* **1.** the range over which something extends; scope: *the extent of the damage.* **2.** an area or volume: *a vast extent of concrete.* **3.** *U.S. law.* a writ authorizing a person to whom a debt is due to assume temporary possession of his debtor's lands. **4.** *Logic.* another word for **extension** (sense 11). [C14: from Old French *extente,* from Latin *extentus* extensive, from *extendere* to EXTEND]

ex+ten·u+ate (ɪk'stɛnjʊ,eɪt) *vb. (tr.)* **1.** to represent (an offence, fault, etc.) as being less serious than it appears, as by showing mitigating circumstances. **2.** to cause to be or appear less serious; mitigate. **3.** to underestimate or make light of. **4.** *Archaic.* **a.** to emaciate or weaken. **b.** to dilute or thin out. [C16: from Latin *extenuāre* to make thin, from *tenuis* thin, frail] —**ex+'ten·u+,at+ing+ly** *adv.* —**ex+,ten·u+'a+tion** *n.* —**ex+'ten·u+,a+tor** *n.* —**ex+'ten·u+a+to·ry** *adj.*

ex+te+ri+or (ɪk'stɪərɪə) *n.* **1.** a part, surface, or region that is on the outside. **2.** the observable outward behaviour or appearance of a person. **3.** a film or scene shot outside a studio. ~*adj.* **4.** of, situated on, or suitable for the outside: *exterior cleaning.* **5.** coming or acting from without; external: *exterior complications.* **6.** of or involving foreign nations. [C16: from Latin, comparative of *exterus* on the outside, from *ex* out of] —**ex+'te+ri+or+ly** *adv.*

ex+te+ri+or an+gle *n.* **1.** an angle of a polygon contained between one side extended and the adjacent side. **2.** any of the four angles made by a transversal that are outside the region between the two intersected lines.

ex+te+ri+or+ize *or* **ex+te+ri+or+ise** (ɪk'stɪərɪə,raɪz) *vb. (tr.)* **1.** *Surgery.* to expose (an attached organ or part) outside a body cavity, esp. in order to remove it from an operating area. **2.** another word for **externalize.** —**ex+,te+ri+or+i+'za+tion** *or* **ex+,te+ri+or+i+'sa+tion** *n.*

ex+ter+mi+nate (ɪk'stɜ:mɪ,neɪt) *vb. (tr.)* to destroy (living things, esp. pests or vermin) completely; annihilate; eliminate. [C16: from Latin *extermināre* to drive away, from *terminus* boundary] —**ex+'ter+mi+na+ble** *adj.* —**ex+,ter+mi+'na+tion** *n.* —**ex+'ter+mi+na+tive** *or* **ex+'ter+mi+na+to+ry** *adj.* —**ex+'ter+mi+,na+tor** *n.*

ex+tern *or* **ex+terne** ('ɛkstɜ:n, ɪk'stɜ:n) *n. U.S.* a person, such as a physician at a hospital, who has an official connection with an institution but does not reside in it. [C16: from Latin *externus* EXTERNAL]

ex+ter+nal (ɪk'stɜ:nᵊl) *adj.* **1.** of, situated on, or suitable for the outside; outer. **2.** coming or acting from without: *external evidence from an independent source.* **3.** of or involving foreign nations; foreign. **4.** of, relating to, or designating a medicine that is applied to the outside of the body. **5.** *Anatomy.* situated on or near the outside of the body: *the external ear.* **6.** *Philosophy.* (of objects, etc.) taken to exist independently of a perceiving mind. ~*n.* **7.** *(often pl.)* an external circumstance or aspect, esp. one that is superficial or inessential. [C15: from Latin *externus* outward, from *exterus* on the outside, from *ex* out of] —**ex+'ter+nal+ly** *adv.*

ex+ter+nal-com+bus+tion en+gine *n.* an engine, such as a steam engine, in which the fuel is burned outside the combustion chamber.

ex·ter·nal ear *n.* the part of the ear consisting of the auricle and the auditory canal.

ex·ter·nal·ism (ɪk'stɜːnəˌlɪzəm) *n.* **1.** exaggerated emphasis on outward form, esp. in religious worship. **2.** a philosophical doctrine holding that only objects that can be perceived by the senses are real; phenomenalism. —**ex·'ter·nal·ist** *n.*

ex·ter·nal·i·ty (ˌɛkstɜː'nælɪtɪ) *n., pl.* **·ties. 1.** the state or condition of being external. **2.** something external. **3.** *Philosophy.* the quality of existing independently of a perceiving mind.

ex·ter·nal·ize (ɪk'stɜːnəˌlaɪz), **ex·te·ri·or·ize** (ɪk'stɪərɪəˌraɪz) *or* **ex·ter·nal·ise, ex·te·ri·or·ise** *vb.* (*tr.*) **1.** to make external; give outward shape to. **2.** *Psychol.* to attribute (one's own feelings) to one's surroundings. —**ex·ˌter·nal·i·'za·tion, ex·ˌte·ri·or·i·'za·tion** *or* **ex·ˌter·nal·i·'sa·tion, ex·ˌte·ri·or·i·'sa·tion** *n.*

ex·ter·o·cep·tor ('ɛkstərəʊˌsɛptə) *n.* any sensory organ or part of the body, such as the eye, able to receive stimuli from outside the body. [C20: *extero-*, from Latin *exterus* EXTERIOR outward + (RE)CEPTOR] —**ˌex·ter·o·'cep·tive** *adj.*

ex·ter·ri·to·ri·al (ˌɛkstɛrɪ'tɔːrɪəl) *adj.* a variant of **extraterritorial.** —**ex·ˌter·ri·ˌto·ri·'al·i·ty** *n.* —**ˌex·ter·ri·'to·ri·al·ly** *adv.*

ex·tinct (ɪk'stɪŋkt) *adj.* **1.** (of an animal or plant species) having no living representative; having died out. **2.** quenched or extinguished. **3.** (of a volcano) no longer liable to erupt; inactive. **4.** void or obsolete: *an extinct political office.* [C15: from Latin *exstinctus* quenched, from *exstinguere* to EXTINGUISH]

ex·tinc·tion (ɪk'stɪŋkʃən) *n.* **1.** the act of making extinct or the state of being extinct. **2.** the act of extinguishing or the state of being extinguished. **3.** complete destruction; annihilation. **4.** *Physics.* reduction of the intensity of radiation as a result of absorption or scattering by matter. **5.** *Astronomy.* the absorption of light from a planet or star by the earth's atmosphere. **6.** *Psychol.* a process in which the frequency or intensity of a response is decreased as a result of reinforcement being withdrawn.

ex·tinc·tive (ɪk'stɪŋktɪv) *adj.* tending or serving to extinguish or make extinct.

ex·tine ('ɛkstɪn, -tiːn, -taɪn) *or* **ex·ine** ('ɛksɪn, -aɪn) *n. Botany.* the outermost coat of a pollen grain or a spore. Compare **intine.** [C19: from Latin *extimus* outermost + -INE[1]]

ex·tin·guish (ɪk'stɪŋgwɪʃ) *vb.* (*tr.*) **1.** to put out or quench (a light, flames, etc.). **2.** to remove or destroy entirely; annihilate. **3.** *Archaic.* to eclipse or obscure by or as if by superior brilliance. **4.** *Law.* to discharge (a debt). [C16: from Latin *exstinguere*, from *stinguere* to quench] —**ex·'tin·guish·a·ble** *adj.* —**ex·'tin·guish·er** *n.* —**ex·'tin·guish·ment** *n.*

ex·tin·guish·ant (ɪk'stɪŋgwɪʃənt) *n.* a substance, such as a liquid, foam, powder, etc., used in extinguishing fires.

ex·tir·pate ('ɛkstəˌpeɪt) *vb.* (*tr.*) **1.** to remove or destroy completely. **2.** to pull up or out; uproot. **3.** to remove (an organ or part) surgically. [C16: from Latin *exstirpāre* to root out, from *stirps* root, stock] —**ˌex·tir·'pa·tion** *n.* —**'ex·tir·ˌpa·tive** *adj.* —**'ex·tir·ˌpa·tor** *n.*

ex·tol *or U.S.* **ex·toll** (ɪk'stəʊl) *vb.* **·tols, ·tol·ling, ·tolled** *or U.S.* **·tolls, ·toll·ing, ·tolled.** (*tr.*) to praise lavishly; exalt. [C15: from Latin *extollere* to elevate, from *tollere* to raise] —**ex·'tol·ler** *n.* —**ex·'tol·ling·ly** *adv.* —**ex·'tol·ment** *n.*

ex·tort (ɪk'stɔːt) *vb.* (*tr.*) **1.** to secure (money, favours, etc.) by intimidation, violence, or the misuse of influence or authority. **2.** to obtain by importunate demands: *the children extorted a promise of a trip to the zoo.* **3.** to overcharge for (something, esp. interest on a loan). [C16: from Latin *extortus* wrenched out, from *extorquēre* to wrest away, from *torquēre* to twist, wrench] —**ex·'tor·tion** *n.* —**ex·'tor·tion·er, ex·'tor·tion·ist,** *or* **ex·'tort·er** *n.* —**ex·'tor·tive** *adj.*

ex·tor·tion·ate (ɪk'stɔːʃənɪt) *adj.* **1.** (of prices, etc.) excessive; exorbitant. **2.** (of persons) using extortion. —**ex·'tor·tion·ate·ly** *adv.*

ex·tra ('ɛkstrə) *adj.* **1.** being more than what is usual or expected; additional. ~*n.* **2.** a person or thing that is additional. **3.** something for which an additional charge is made: *the new car had many extras.* **4.** an additional edition of a newspaper, esp. to report a new development or crisis. **5.** *Films.* an actor or person temporarily engaged, usually for crowd scenes. **6.** *Cricket.* a run not scored from the bat, such as a wide, no-ball, bye, or leg bye. **7.** *U.S.* something that is better than usual in quality. ~*adv.* **8.** unusually; exceptionally: *an extra fast car.* [C18: shortened from EXTRAORDINARY]

ex·tra- *prefix.* outside or beyond an area or scope: *extrasensory; extraterritorial.* [from Latin *extrā* outside, beyond, changed from *extera*, from *exterus* outward]

ex·tra·ca·non·i·cal (ˌɛkstrəkə'nɒnɪkəl) *adj. Christianity.* not included in the canon of Scripture.

ex·tra·cel·lu·lar (ˌɛkstrə'sɛljʊlə) *adj. Biology.* situated or occurring outside a cell or cells. —**ˌex·tra·'cel·lu·lar·ly** *adv.*

ex·tra·cor·por·e·al (ˌɛkstrəkɔː'pɔːrɪəl) *adj.* outside the body.

ex·tra cov·er *n. Cricket.* a fielding position between cover and mid-off.

ex·tract *vb.* (ɪk'strækt). (*tr.*) **1.** to withdraw, pull out, or uproot by force. **2.** to remove or separate. **3.** to derive (pleasure, information, etc.) from some source or situation. **4.** to deduce or develop (a doctrine, policy, etc.). **5.** *Informal.* to extort (money, etc.). **6.** to obtain (a substance) from a mixture or material by a chemical or physical process, such as digestion, distillation, the action of a solvent, or mechanical separation. **7.** to cut out or copy out (an article, passage, quotation, etc.) from a publication. **8.** to determine the value of (the root of a number). ~*n.* ('ɛkstrækt). **9.** something extracted, such as a part or passage from a book, speech, etc. **10.** a preparation containing the active principle or concentrated essence of a material: *beef extract; yeast extract.* **11.** *Pharmacol.* a solution of plant or animal tissue containing the active principle. [C15: from Latin *extractus* drawn forth, from *extrahere*, from *trahere* to drag] —**ex·'tract·a·ble** *adj.* —**ex·ˌtract·a·'bil·i·ty** *n.*

ex·trac·tion (ɪk'strækʃən) *n.* **1.** the act of extracting or the condition of being extracted. **2.** something extracted; an extract. **3. a.** the act or an instance of extracting a tooth or teeth. **b.** a tooth or teeth extracted. **4.** origin, descent, lineage, or ancestry: *of German extraction.*

ex·trac·tions (ɪk'strækʃənz) *pl. n.* the residue remaining after an oilseed has had the oil extracted by a solvent. Used as a feed for animals: *groundnut extractions.* Compare **expellers.**

ex·trac·tive (ɪk'stræktɪv) *adj.* **1.** tending or serving to extract. **2.** of, involving, or capable of extraction. ~*n.* **3.** something extracted or capable of being extracted. **4.** the part of an extract that is insoluble.

ex·trac·tor (ɪk'stræktə) *n.* **1.** a person or thing that extracts. **2.** an instrument for pulling something out or removing tight-fitting components. **3.** a device for extracting liquid from a solid, esp. a centrifugal dryer. **4.** Also called: **extractor fan.** a device for extracting air or other gases from a room, building, etc.

ex·tra·cur·ric·u·lar (ˌɛkstrəkə'rɪkjʊlə) *adj.* **1.** taking place outside the normal school timetable: *extracurricular activities.* **2.** beyond the regular duties, schedule, etc.

ex·tra·dit·a·ble ('ɛkstrəˌdaɪtəbəl) *adj.* **1.** (of a crime, etc.) rendering the offender liable to extradition: *an extraditable offence.* **2.** (of a person) subject to extradition.

ex·tra·dite ('ɛkstrəˌdaɪt) *vb.* (*tr.*) **1.** to surrender (an alleged offender) for trial to a foreign state. **2.** to procure the extradition of. [C19: back formation from EXTRADITION]

ex·tra·di·tion (ˌɛkstrə'dɪʃən) *n.* the surrender of an alleged offender or fugitive to the state in whose territory the alleged offence was committed. [C19: from French, from Latin *trāditiō* a handing over; see TRADITION]

ex·tra·dos (ɛk'streɪdɒs) *n., pl.* **·dos** (-dəʊz) *or* **·dos·es.** *Architect.* the outer curve or surface of an arch or vault. Compare **intrados.** [C18: from French, from EXTRA- + *dos* back, from Latin *dorsum*]

ex·tra·ga·lac·tic (ˌɛkstrəgə'læktɪk) *adj.* occurring or existing beyond the Galaxy.

ex·tra·ga·lac·tic neb·u·la *n.* the former name for **galaxy.**

ex·tra·ju·di·cial (ˌɛkstrədʒuː'dɪʃəl) *adj.* **1.** outside the ordinary course of legal proceedings: *extrajudicial evidence.* **2.** beyond the jurisdiction or authority of the court: *an extrajudicial opinion.* —**ˌex·tra·ju·'di·cial·ly** *adv.*

ex·tra·mar·i·tal (ˌɛkstrə'mærɪtəl) *adj.* (esp. of sexual relations) occurring outside marriage.

ex·tra·mun·dane (ˌɛkstrə'mʌndeɪn) *adj.* not of the physical world or universe.

ex·tra·mu·ral (ˌɛkstrə'mjʊərəl) *adj.* **1.** connected with but outside the normal courses or programme of a university, college, etc.: *extramural studies.* **2.** located beyond the boundaries or walls of a city, castle, etc. —**ˌex·tra·'mu·ral·ly** *adv.*

ex·tra·ne·ous (ɪk'streɪnɪəs) *adj.* **1.** not essential. **2.** not pertinent or applicable; irrelevant. **3.** coming from without; of external origin. **4.** not belonging; unrelated to that to which it is added or in which it is contained. [C17: from Latin *extrāneus* external, from *extrā* outside] —**ex·'tra·ne·ous·ly** *adv.* —**ex·'tra·ne·ous·ness** *n.*

ex·tra·nu·cle·ar (ˌɛkstrə'njuːklɪə) *adj. Biology.* situated or occurring in part of a cell outside the nucleus.

ex·traor·di·nar·y (ɪk'strɔːdənrɪ, -dənərɪ) *adj.* **1.** very unusual, remarkable, or surprising. **2.** not in an established manner, course, or order. **3.** employed for particular events or purposes. **4.** (*usually postpositive*) (of an official, etc.) additional or subordinate to the usual one: *a minister extraordinary.* [C15: from Latin *extraordinārius* beyond what is usual; see ORDINARY] —**ex·'traor·di·nar·i·ly** *adv.* —**ex·'traor·di·nar·i·ness** *n.*

ex·traor·di·nar·y ray *n. Optics.* the plane-polarized ray of light that does not obey the laws of refraction in a doubly refracting crystal. See **double refraction.** Compare **ordinary ray.**

ex·trap·o·late (ɪk'stræpəˌleɪt) *vb.* **1.** *Maths.* to estimate (a value of a function or measurement) beyond the values already known, by the extension of a curve. Compare **interpolate** (sense 4). **2.** to infer (something not known) by using but not strictly deducing from the known facts. [C19: EXTRA + *-polate*, as in INTERPOLATE] —**ex·ˌtrap·o·'la·tion** *n.* —**ex·'trap·o·la·tive** *or* **ex·'trap·o·la·to·ry** *adj.* —**ex·'trap·o·ˌla·tor** *n.*

ex·tra·po·si·tion (ˌɛkstrəpə'zɪʃən) *n.* **1.** placement of something outside something else. **2.** *Transformational grammar.* a rule that moves embedded clauses out to the end of the main clause, converting, for example, *A man who will help has just arrived* into *A man has just arrived who will help.*

ex·tra·sen·so·ry (ˌɛkstrə'sɛnsərɪ) *adj.* of or relating to extrasensory perception.

ex·tra·sen·so·ry per·cep·tion *n.* the supposed ability of certain individuals to obtain information about the environment without the use of normal sensory channels. Also called: **cryptaesthesia.** See also **clairvoyance, telepathy.** Abbrev.: **ESP**

ex·tra·ter·res·tri·al (ˌɛkstrətɪˈrɛstrɪəl) *adj.* occurring or existing beyond the earth's atmosphere.

ex·tra·ter·ri·to·ri·al (ˌɛkstrəˌtɛrɪˈtɔːrɪəl) *or* **ex·ter·ri·to·ri·al** *adj.* **1.** beyond the limits of a country's territory. **2.** of, relating to, or possessing extraterritoriality. —**ˌex·tra·ˌter·ri·ˈto·ri·al·ly** *or* **ˌex·ter·ri·ˈto·ri·al·ly** *adv.*

ex·tra·ter·ri·to·ri·al·i·ty (ˌɛkstrəˌtɛrɪˌtɔːrɪˈælɪtɪ) *n. International law.* **1.** the privilege granted to some aliens, esp. diplomats, of being exempt from the jurisdiction of the state in which they reside. **2.** the right or privilege of a state to exercise authority in certain circumstances beyond the limits of its territory.

ex·tra time *n. Sport.* an additional period played at the end of a match, to compensate for time lost through injury or (in certain circumstances) to allow the teams to achieve a conclusive result.

ex·tra·u·ter·ine (ˌɛkstrəˈjuːtəˌraɪn) *adj.* situated or developing outside the cavity of the uterus.

ex·trav·a·gance (ɪkˈstrævɪɡəns) *n.* **1.** excessive outlay of money; wasteful spending. **2.** immoderate or absurd speech or behaviour.

ex·trav·a·gant (ɪkˈstrævɪɡənt) *adj.* **1.** spending money excessively or immoderately. **2.** going beyond usual bounds; unrestrained: *extravagant praise.* **3.** ostentatious; showy. **4.** exorbitant in price; overpriced. [C14: from Medieval Latin *extravagāns,* from Latin EXTRA- + *vagārī* to wander] —**exˈtrav·a·gant·ly** *adv.*

ex·trav·a·gan·za (ɪkˌstrævəˈɡænzə) *n.* **1.** an elaborately staged and costumed light entertainment. **2.** any lavish or fanciful display, literary or other composition, etc. [C18: from Italian: EXTRAVAGANCE]

ex·trav·a·gate (ɪkˈstrævəˌɡeɪt) *vb. (intr.) Archaic.* **1.** to exceed normal limits or propriety. **2.** to roam at will. [C17: from Latin *extravagārī;* see EXTRAVAGANT] —**ex·ˌtrav·a·ˈga·tion** *n.*

ex·trav·a·sate (ɪkˈstrævəˌseɪt) *vb.* **1.** *Pathol.* to cause (blood or lymph) to escape or (of blood or lymph) to escape into the [illegible]ounding tissues from their proper vessels. **2.** to exude [illegible]ten material, such as lava) or (of molten material) to be [illegible]d. ~*n.* **3.** *Pathol.* the material extravasated. [C17: from [illegible]A- + *vās* vessel] —**ex·ˌtrav·a·ˈsa·tion** *n.*

[illegible]**as·cu·lar** (ˌɛkstrəˈvæskjʊlə) *adj. Anatomy.* situated or [illegible]ing outside a lymph or blood vessel.

ex·tra·ve·hic·u·lar (ˌɛkstrəviːˈhɪkjʊlə) *adj.* occurring or used outside a spacecraft, either in space or on the surface of the moon or another planet: *extravehicular activity.*

ex·tra·ver·sion (ˌɛkstrəˈvɜːʃən) *n.* a variant spelling of **extroversion.** —**ˌex·tra·ˈver·sive** *adj.*

ex·tra·vert (ˈɛkstrəˌvɜːt) *n.* a variant spelling of **extrovert.**

Ex·tre·ma·du·ra (ˌestremaˈðura) *n.* the Spanish name for **Estremadura.**

ex·treme (ɪkˈstriːm) *adj.* **1.** being of a high or of the highest degree or intensity: *extreme cold; extreme difficulty.* **2.** exceeding what is usual or reasonable; immoderate: *extreme behaviour.* **3.** very strict, rigid, or severe; drastic: *an extreme measure.* **4.** (*prenominal*) farthest or outermost in direction: *the extreme boundary.* **5.** *Meteorol.* of, relating to, or characteristic of a **continental climate.** ~*n.* **6.** the highest or furthest degree (often in the phrases **in the extreme, go to extremes**). **7.** (*often pl.*) either of the two limits or ends of a scale or range of possibilities: *extremes of temperature.* **8.** *Maths.* **a.** the first or last term of a series or a proportion. **b.** a maximum or minimum value of a function. **9.** *Logic.* the subject or predicate of the conclusion of a syllogism. [C15: from Latin *extrēmus* outermost, from *exterus* on the outside; see EXTERIOR] —**exˈtreme·ness** *n.*

ex·treme·ly (ɪkˈstriːmlɪ) *adv.* **1.** to the extreme; exceedingly. **2.** (intensifier): *she behaved extremely badly.* **Usage.** See at **very.**

ex·treme·ly high fre·quen·cy *n.* a radio frequency between 30 000 and 300 000 megahertz. Abbrev.: **EHF**

ex·treme unc·tion *n. R.C. Church.* a sacrament in which a person who is seriously ill or dying is anointed by a priest with consecrated oil.

ex·trem·ist (ɪkˈstriːmɪst) *n.* **1.** a person who favours or resorts to immoderate, uncompromising, or fanatical methods or behaviour, esp. in being politically radical. ~*adj.* **2.** of, relating to, or characterized by immoderate or excessive actions, opinions, etc. —**exˈtrem·ism** *n.*

ex·trem·i·ty (ɪkˈstrɛmɪtɪ) *n., pl.* **·ties. 1.** the farthest or outermost point or section; termination. **2.** the greatest or most intense degree. **3.** an extreme condition or state, as of adversity or disease. **4.** a limb, such as a leg, arm, or wing, or the part of such a limb farthest from the trunk. **5.** (*usually pl.*) *Archaic.* a drastic or severe measure.

ex·tri·cate (ˈɛkstrɪˌkeɪt) *vb. (tr.)* **1.** to remove or free from complication, hindrance, or difficulty; disentangle. **2.** *Rare.* to free (a substance, gas, liquid, etc.) from chemical combination; liberate. [C17: from Latin *extrīcāre* to disentangle, from EX-[1] + *trīcae* trifles, vexations] —**ˈex·tri·ca·ble** *adj.* —**ˌex·tri·ˈca·tion** *n.*

ex·trin·sic (ɛkˈstrɪnsɪk) *adj.* **1.** not contained or included within; extraneous. **2.** originating or acting from outside; external. [C16: from Late Latin *extrinsecus* (adj.) outward, from Latin (adv.) from without, on the outward side, from *exter* outward + *secus* alongside, related to *sequī* to follow] —**exˈtrin·si·cal·ly** *adv.*

ex·trorse (ɛkˈstrɔːs) *or* **ex·tror·sal** *adj. Botany.* turned or opening outwards or away from the axis: *extrorse anthers.* [C19: from Late Latin *extrorsus* in an outward direction, from Latin EXTRA- + *versus* turned towards]

ex·tro·ver·sion *or* **ex·tra·ver·sion** (ˌɛkstrəˈvɜːʃən) *n.* **1.** *Psychol.* the directing of one's interest outwards, esp. towards social contacts. **2.** *Pathol.* a turning inside out of an organ or part. ~Compare **introversion.** [C17: from *extro-* (variant of EXTRA-, contrasting with INTRO-) + *-version,* from Latin *vertere* to turn] —**ˌex·tro·ˈver·sive** *or* **ˌex·tra·ˈver·sive** *adj.* —**ˌex·tro·ˈver·sive·ly** *or* **ˌex·tra·ˈver·sive·ly** *adv.*

ex·tro·vert *or* **ex·tra·vert** (ˈɛkstrəˌvɜːt) *Psychol.* ~*n.* **1.** a person concerned more with external reality than inner feelings. ~*adj.* **2.** of or characterized by extroversion: *extrovert tendencies.* ~Compare **introvert.** [C20: from *extro-* (variant of EXTRA-, contrasting with INTRO-) + *-vert,* from Latin *vertere* to turn] —**ˈex·tro·ˌvert·ed** *or* **ˈex·tra·ˌvert·ed** *adj.*

ex·trude (ɪkˈstruːd) *vb.* **1.** (*tr.*) to squeeze or force out. **2.** (*tr.*) to produce (moulded sections of plastic, metal, etc.) by ejection under pressure from a suitably shaped nozzle or die. **3.** a less common word for **protrude.** [C16: from Latin *extrūdere* to thrust out, from *trūdere* to push, thrust]

ex·tru·sion (ɪkˈstruːʒən) *n.* **1.** the act or process of extruding. **2. a.** the movement of magma through volcano craters and cracks in the earth's crust, forming igneous rock. **b.** any igneous rock formed in this way. [C16: from Medieval Latin *extrūsiō,* from *extrūdere* to EXTRUDE] —**exˈtru·si·ble** *adj.*

ex·tru·sive (ɪkˈstruːsɪv) *adj.* **1.** tending to extrude. **2.** (of igneous rocks) formed from magma issuing from volcanoes or cracks in the earth's crust; volcanic. Compare **intrusive** (sense 2).

ex·u·ber·ant (ɪɡˈzjuːbərənt) *adj.* **1.** abounding in vigour and high spirits; full of vitality. **2.** lavish or effusive; excessively elaborate: *exuberant compliments.* **3.** growing luxuriantly or in profusion. [C15: from Latin *exūberāns,* from *ūberāre* to be fruitful, from *ūber* fertile] —**exˈu·ber·ance** *n.* —**exˈu·ber·ant·ly** *adv.*

ex·u·ber·ate (ɪɡˈzjuːbəˌreɪt) *vb. (intr.) Rare.* **1.** to be exuberant. **2.** to abound or grow in profusion. [C15: from Latin *exūberāre* to be abundant; see EXUBERANT]

ex·u·da·tion (ˌɛksjʊˈdeɪʃən) *n.* **1.** the act of exuding or oozing out. **2.** Also called: **ex·u·date** (ˈɛksjʊˌdeɪt). an exuded substance, such as sweat or cellular debris. —**ex·u·da·tive** (ɪɡˈzjuːdətɪv) *adj.*

ex·ude (ɪɡˈzjuːd) *vb.* **1.** to release or be released through pores, incisions, etc., as sweat from the body or sap from trees. **2.** (*tr.*) to make apparent by mood or behaviour: *he exuded confidence.* [C16: from Latin *exsūdāre,* from *sūdāre* to sweat]

ex·ult (ɪɡˈzʌlt) *vb. (intr.)* **1.** to be joyful or jubilant, esp. because of triumph or success; rejoice. **2.** (often foll. by *over*) to triumph (over); show or take delight in the defeat or discomfiture (of). [C16: from Latin *exsultāre* to jump or leap for joy, from *saltāre* to leap] —**ex·ul·ta·tion** (ˌɛɡzʌlˈteɪʃən) *n.* —**exˈult·ing·ly** *adv.*

ex·ult·ant (ɪɡˈzʌltənt) *adj.* elated or jubilant, esp. because of triumph or success. —**exˈult·ant·ly** *adv.*

ex·ur·bi·a (ɛksˈɜːbɪə) *n. U.S.* the region outside the suburbs of a city, consisting of residential areas (**exurbs**) that are occupied predominantly by rich commuters (**exurbanites**). Compare **stockbroker belt.** —**exˈur·ban** *adj.*

ex·u·vi·ae (ɪɡˈzjuːvɪˌiː) *pl. n.* layers of skin or cuticle shed by animals during ecdysis. [C17: from Latin: something stripped off (the body), from *exuere* to strip off] —**exˈu·vi·al** *adj.*

ex·u·vi·ate (ɪɡˈzjuːvɪˌeɪt) *vb.* to shed (a skin or similar outer covering). —**ex·ˌu·vi·ˈa·tion** *n.*

ex vo·to *Latin.* (ɛksˈvəʊtəʊ) *adv., adj.* in accordance with a vow.

ex works *adv., adj.* (**ex-works** *when prenominal*) *Brit.* (of a price, value, etc.) excluding the cost of delivery from the factory and sometimes excluding the commission or profit of the distributor or retailer: *the price is £500 ex works.*

-ey *suffix.* variant of **-y**[1] and **-y**[2].

ey·as (ˈaɪəs) *n.* a nestling hawk or falcon, esp. one reared for training in falconry. [C15: mistaken division of earlier *a nyas,* from Old French *niais* nestling, from Latin *nīdus* nest]

eye[1] (aɪ) *n.* **1.** the organ of sight of animals, containing light-sensitive cells associated with nerve fibres, so that light entering the eye is converted to nervous impulses that reach the brain. In man and other vertebrates the iris controls the amount of light entering the eye and the lens focuses the light onto the retina. Related adjs.: **ocular, ophthalmic. 2.** (*often pl.*) the ability to see; sense of vision: *weak eyes.* **3.** the visible external part of an eye, often including the area around it: *heavy-lidded eyes; piercing eyes.* **4.** a look, glance, expression, or gaze: *a stern eye.* **5.** a sexually inviting or provocative look (esp. in the phrases **give (someone) the (glad) eye; make eyes at**). **6.** attention or observation (often in the phrases **catch someone's eye; keep an eye on; cast an eye over**). **7.** ability to recognize, judge, or appreciate: *an eye for antiques.* **8.** (*often pl.*) opinion, judgment, point of view, or authority: *in the eyes of the law.* **9.** a structure or marking having the appearance of an eye, such as the bud on a twig or potato tuber or a spot on a butterfly wing. **10.** a small loop or hole, as at one end of a needle. **11.** a small area of low pressure and calm in the centre of a tornado. **12.** See **electric eye. 13.** *Informal.* See **private eye. 14. all eyes.** *Informal.* acutely vigilant or observant: *the children were all eyes.* **15. (all) my eye.** *Informal.* rubbish; nonsense. **16. an eye for an eye.** retributive or vengeful justice; retaliation. **17. cut one's eye after, at,** *or* **on (someone).** *Caribbean.* to look rudely at (a person) and then turn one's face away sharply while closing one's eyes: a **gesture of** contempt. **18. get one's eye in.** *Chiefly sports.* to become accustomed to the conditions, light, etc., with a consequent improvement in one's performance. **19. half an eye. a.** a modicum of perceptiveness: *anyone with half an eye can see she's in love.* **b.** continuing unobtrusive observation or awareness: *the dog had half an eye on the sheep.* **20. have eyes for.** to be interested in: *she has eyes only for him.* **21. in one's mind's eye.** pictured within the mind; imagined or remembered vividly. **22. in the public eye.** exposed to public curiosity or publicity. **23. keep an eye open** *or* **out (for).** to watch with special attention (for). **24. keep one's eyes skinned.** to watch vigilantly. **25. lay, clap,** *or* **set eyes on.** (*usually used with a negative*) to see: *she had never laid eyes on him before.* **26. look (someone) in the eye.** to look openly and without shame or embarrassment at. **27. make sheep's eyes (at).** *Archaic.* to ogle amorously. **28. more than meets the eye.** hidden motives, meaning, or facts. **29. pick the eyes out (of).** *Austral.* to select the best parts or pieces (of). **30. see eye to eye (with).** to agree (with). **31. shut one's eyes to** *or* **turn a blind eye to.** to overlook or ignore deliberately. **32. the eye of the wind.** *Nautical.* the direction from which the wind is blowing. **33. up to one's eyes (in).** extremely busy (with). **34. with a...eye.** in a...manner: *he regards our success with a jealous eye.* **35. with** *or* **having an eye to.** (*prep.*) **a.** regarding; with reference to: *with an eye to one's own interests.* **b.** with the intention or purpose of: *with an eye to reaching agreement.* **36. with one's eyes open.** in the full knowledge of all relevant facts. **37. with one's eyes shut. a.** with great ease, esp. as a result of thorough familiarity: *I could drive home with my eyes shut.* **b.** without being aware of all the facts. ~*vb.* **eyes, eye+ing** *or* **ey+ing, eyed.** (*tr.*) **38.** to look at carefully or warily. **39.** to look at in a manner indicating sexual interest; ogle. ~See also **eyes.** [Old English *ēage;* related to Old Norse *auga,* Old High German *ouga,* Sanskrit *akṣi*] —**'eye+less** *adj.* —**'eye+,like** *adj.*

eye[2] (aɪ) *n.* another word for **nye.**

eye+ball ('aɪ,bɔːl) *n.* **1.** the entire ball-shaped part of the eye. **2. eyeball to eyeball.** in close confrontation.

eye+bath ('aɪ,bɑːθ) *n.* a small vessel with a rim shaped to fit round the eye, used for applying medicated or cleansing solutions to the eyeball.

eye+black ('aɪ,blæk) *n.* another name for **mascara.**

eye+bolt ('aɪ,bəult) *n.* a threaded bolt, the head of which is formed into a ring or eye for lifting, pulling, or securing.

eye+bright ('aɪ,braɪt) *n.* any scrophulariaceous annual plant of the genus *Euphrasia,* esp. *E. nemorosa,* having small white-and-purple two-lipped flowers: formerly used in the treatment of eye disorders. Also called: **euphrasy.**

eye+brow ('aɪ,brau) *n.* **1.** the transverse bony ridge over each eye. **2.** the arch of hair that covers this ridge.

eye-catch·ing *adj.* tending to attract attention; striking. —**'eye-,catch·er** *n.*

eye+cup ('aɪ,kʌp) *n.* a U.S. name for an **eyebath.**

eyed (aɪd) *adj.* **a.** having an eye or eyes (as specified). **b.** (*in combination*): *one-eyed; brown-eyed.*

eye+ful ('aɪ,fʊl) *n. Informal.* **1.** a view, glance, or gaze: *he got an eyeful of the secret before they blindfolded him.* **2.** a very beautiful or attractive sight, esp. a woman.

eye+glass ('aɪ,glɑːs) *n.* **1.** a lens for aiding or correcting defective vision, esp. a monocle. **2.** another word for **eyepiece** or **eyebath.**

eye+glass·es ('aɪ,glɑːsɪz) *pl. n. Now chiefly U.S.* another word for **spectacles.**

eye+hole ('aɪ,həul) *n.* **1.** a hole through which something, such as a rope, hook, or bar, is passed. **2.** *Informal.* the cavity that contains the eyeball; eye socket. **3.** another word for **peephole.**

eye+hook ('aɪ,hʊk) *n.* a hook attached to a ring at the extremity of a rope or chain.

eye+lash ('aɪ,læʃ) *n.* **1.** any one of the short curved hairs that grow from the edge of the eyelids. **2.** a row or fringe of these hairs.

eye+let ('aɪlɪt) *n.* **1.** a small hole for a lace or cord to be passed through or for a hook to be inserted into. **2.** a small metal ring or tube with flared ends bent back, reinforcing an eyehole in fabric. **3.** a chink or small opening, such as a peephole in a wall. **4.** *Embroidery.* **a.** a small hole with finely stitched edges, forming part of an ornamental pattern. **b.** Also called: **eyelet embroidery.** a piece of embroidery decorated with such work. **5.** fabric decorated with such work produced by machine. **6.** a small eye or eyelike marking. ~*vb.* **7.** (*tr.*) to supply with an eyelet or eyelets. [C14: from Old French *oillet,* literally: a little eye, from *oill* eye, from Latin *oculus* eye; see EYE]

eye+let+eer (,aɪlɪ'tɪə) *n.* a small bodkin or other pointed tool for making eyelet holes.

eye+lid ('aɪ,lɪd) *n.* **1.** either of the two muscular folds of skin that can be moved to cover the exposed portion of the eyeball. **2.** Also called: **clamshell.** *Aeronautics.* a set of movable parts at the rear of a jet engine that redirect the exhaust flow to assist braking during landing.

eye+lin·er ('aɪ,laɪnə) *n.* a cosmetic used to outline the eyes.

eye of day *n. Poetic.* the sun.

eye-o·pen·er *n. Informal.* **1.** something startling or revealing. **2.** *U.S.* an alcoholic drink taken early in the morning.

eye+piece ('aɪ,piːs) *n.* the lens or combination of lenses in an optical instrument nearest the eye of the observer.

eye rhyme *n.* a rhyme involving words that are similar in spelling but not in sound, such as *stone* and *none.*

eyes (aɪz) *pl. n. Nautical.* the part of the bows of a ship that are furthest forward at the level of the main deck.

eyes front *interj.* **1.** *Military.* a command to troops to look ahead. **2.** a demand for attention.

eye+shade ('aɪ,ʃeɪd) *n.* an opaque or tinted translucent visor, worn on the head like a cap to protect the eyes from glare.

eye shad+ow *n.* a coloured cosmetic put around the eyes so as to enhance their colour or shape.

eye+shot ('aɪ,ʃɒt) *n.* range of vision; view.

eye+sight ('aɪ,saɪt) *n.* the ability to see; faculty of sight.

eyes left *interj. Military.* a command to troops to look left, esp. as a salute when marching.

eye sock+et *n.* the nontechnical name for **orbit** (sense 3).

eye+sore ('aɪ,sɔː) *n.* something very ugly.

eye splice *n.* an eye formed in a rope by splicing the end into its standing part.

eye+spot ('aɪ,spɒt) *n.* **1.** a small area of light-sensitive pigment in some protozoans and algae and in other simple organisms. **2.** an eyelike marking, as on the wings of certain butterflies.

eyes right *interj. Military.* a command to troops to look right, esp. as a salute when marching.

eye+stalk ('aɪ,stɔːk) *n.* a movable stalk bearing a compound eye at its tip: occurs in crustaceans and some molluscs.

eye+strain ('aɪ,streɪn) *n.* fatigue or irritation of the eyes, resulting from excessive use, as from prolonged reading of small print, or uncorrected defects of vision.

Eye+tie ('aɪtaɪ) *n., adj. Brit. slang, offensive.* Italian. [C20: based on a jocular mispronunciation of *Italian*]

eye+tooth ('aɪ,tuːθ) *n., pl.* **+teeth. 1.** either of the two canine teeth in the upper jaw. **2. give one's eyeteeth for.** *Informal.* to go to any lengths to achieve or obtain (something): *I'd give my eyeteeth for a radio as good as that.*

eye+wash ('aɪ,wɒʃ) *n.* **1.** a mild solution for applying to the eyes for relief of irritation, etc. **2.** *Informal.* nonsense; rubbish.

eye+wit·ness ('aɪ,wɪtnɪs) *n.* **a.** a person present at an event who can describe what happened. **b.** (*as modifier*): *an eyewitness account.*

eyot (aɪt) *n. Brit., obsolete except in placenames.* island. [variant of AIT]

ey·ra ('ɛərə, 'aɪərə) *n.* a reddish-brown variety of the jaguarondi. [from American Spanish, from Tupi *eirara*]

eyre (ɛə) *n. English legal history.* **1.** any of the circuit courts held in each shire from 1176 until the late 13th century. **2. justices in eyre.** the justices travelling on circuit and presiding over such courts. [C13: from Old French *erre* journey, from *errer* to travel, from Latin *errāre* to wander]

Eyre (ɛə) *n.* **Lake.** a shallow salt lake in NE central South Australia, about 10 m (35 ft.) below sea level. Area: 9600 sq. km (3700 sq. miles). [C19: named after E. J. *Eyre* (1815–1901), English explorer, who discovered it]

Eyre Pen+in+su+la *n.* a peninsula of South Australia, between the Great Australian Bight and Spencer Gulf.

ey+rie ('ɪərɪ, 'ɛərɪ, 'aɪərɪ) *or* **aer·ie** *n.* **1.** the nest of an eagle or other bird of prey, built in a high inaccessible place. **2.** the brood of a bird of prey, esp. an eagle. **3.** any high isolated position or place. [C16: from Medieval Latin *airea,* from Latin *ārea* open field, hence nest]

ey+rir ('eɪrɪə) *n., pl.* **au·rar** ('ɔɪrɑː). an Icelandic monetary unit worth one hundredth of a krona. [Old Norse: ounce (of silver), money; related to Latin *aureus* golden]

Ey·senck ('aɪzɛŋk) *n.* **Hans Jür·gen** (hænz 'jɜːgən). born 1916, British psychologist, born in Germany, who developed a dimensional theory of personality that stressed the influence of heredity.

Ez. *or* **Ezr.** *Bible. abbrev. for* Ezra.

Ezek. *Bible. abbrev. for* Ezekiel.

E·ze·ki·el (ɪ'ziːkɪəl) *n. Old Testament.* **1.** a Hebrew prophet of the 6th century B.C., exiled to Babylon in 597 B.C. **2.** the book containing his oracles, which describe the downfall of Judah and Jerusalem and their subsequent restoration. Douay spelling: **E·ze·chi·el.**

Ez·ra ('ɛzrə) *n. Old Testament.* **1.** a Jewish priest of the 5th century B.C., who was sent from Babylon by the Persian king Artaxerxes I to reconstitute observance of the Jewish law and worship in Jerusalem after the captivity. **2.** the book recounting his efforts to perform this task.

F

f *or* **F** (ɛf) *n., pl.* **f's, F's,** *or* **Fs. 1.** the sixth letter and fourth consonant of the modern English alphabet. **2.** a speech sound represented by this letter, usually a voiceless labio-dental fricative, as in *fat.*

f *symbol for:* **1.** *Music.* forte: an instruction to play loudly. **2.** *Physics.* frequency. **3.** (in the Netherlands) guilder. [from Dutch: florin] **4.** *Maths.* function (of). **5.** *Physics.* femto-.

f, f/, *or* **f:** *symbol for* f number.

f. *or* **F.** *abbrev. for:* **1.** female. **2.** *Grammar.* feminine. **3.** *Metallurgy.* fine. **4.** filly. **5.** (*pl.* **ff.** *or* **FF.**) folio. **6.** (*pl.* **ff.**) following (page). **7.** franc(s). **8.** *Sport.* foul.

F *symbol for:* **1.** *Music.* a note having a frequency of 349.23 hertz (**F above middle C**) or this value multiplied or divided by any power of 2; the fourth note of the scale of C major. **2.** Fahrenheit. **3.** Fellow. **4.** *Chem.* fluorine. **5.** Helmholtz function. **6.** *Physics.* force. **7.** farad(s). **8.** *Genetics.* a generation of filial offspring, F_1 being the first generation of offspring, F_2 being the second generation, etc. ~ **9.** *international car registration for* France.

F- (of U.S. military aircraft) *abbrev. for* fighter: *F-106.*

fa *or* **fah** (fɑː) *Music.* **1.** (in the fixed system of solmization) the note F. **2.** (in tonic sol-fa) the fourth degree of any major scale; subdominant. [C14: see GAMUT]

FA *abbrev. for:* **1.** *Military.* field artillery. **2.** (in Britain) Football Association. See also **FA Cup.**

f.a. *or* **F.A.** *abbrev. for:* **1.** freight agent. **2.** fanny adams.

fab (fæb) *adj., interj. Informal. Chiefly Brit.* short for **fabulous:** an expression of approval or enthusiasm.

fa+ba+ceous (fəˈbeɪʃəs) *adj.* a less common term for **leguminous.** [C18: from Late Latin *fabāceus* of beans, from Latin *faba* bean]

Fa·ber·gé (ˈfæbəˌʒeɪ) *n.* **Pe·ter Carl.** 1846–1920, Russian goldsmith, known for the golden Easter eggs and other ornate and fanciful objects that he created for the Russian and other royal families.

Fa·bi·an (ˈfeɪbɪən) *adj.* **1.** of, relating to, or resembling the delaying tactics of Q. Fabius Maximus; cautious; circumspect. ~*n.* **2.** a member of or sympathizer with the Fabian Society. [C19: from Latin *Fabiānus* of Fabius]

Fa+bi+an+ism (ˈfeɪbɪəˌnɪzəm) *n.* the beliefs, principles, or practices of the Fabian Society. —**ˈFa+bi+an+ist** *n., adj.*

Fa+bi+an So+ci+e+ty *n.* an association of British socialists advocating the establishment of democratic socialism by gradual reforms within the law: founded in 1884.

Fa·bi·us Max·i·mus (ˈfeɪbɪəs ˈmæksɪməs) *n.* full name *Quintus Fabius Maximus Verrucosus,* called *Cunctator* (the delayer). died 203 B.C., Roman general and statesman. As commander of the Roman army during the Second Punic War, he withstood Hannibal by his strategy of harassing the Carthaginians while avoiding a pitched battle.

fa·ble (ˈfeɪbᵊl) *n.* **1.** a short moral story, esp. one with animals as characters. **2.** a false, fictitious, or improbable account; fiction or lie. **3.** a story or legend about supernatural or mythical characters or events. **4.** legends or myths collectively. **5.** *Archaic.* the plot of a play or of an epic or dramatic poem. ~*vb.* **6.** to relate or tell (fables). **7.** (*intr.*) to speak untruthfully; tell lies. **8.** (*tr.*) to talk about or describe in the manner of a fable: *ghosts are fabled to appear at midnight.* [C13: from Latin *fābula* story, narrative, from *fārī* to speak, say] —**ˈfa+bler** *n.*

fa+bled (ˈfeɪbᵊld) *adj.* **1.** made famous in fable. **2.** fictitious.

fab+li+au (ˈfæblɪˌəʊ; *French* fabliˈo) *n., pl.* **fab+li·aux** (ˈfæblɪˌəʊz; *French* fabliˈo). a comic usually ribald verse tale, of a kind popular in France in the 12th and 13th centuries. [C19: from French: a little tale, from *fable* tale]

Fa·bre (*French* ˈfabr) *n.* **Jean Hen·ri** (ʒã ãˈri). 1823–1915, French entomologist; author of many works on insect life, remarkable for their vivid and minute observation, esp. *Souvenirs Entomologiques* (1879–1907). Nobel prize for literature 1910.

fab+ric (ˈfæbrɪk) *n.* **1.** any cloth made from yarn or fibres by weaving, knitting, felting, etc. **2.** the texture of a cloth. **3.** a structure or framework: *the fabric of society.* **4.** a style or method of construction. **5.** *Rare.* a building. **6.** the texture, arrangement, and orientation of the constituents of a rock. [C15: from Latin *fabrica* workshop, from *faber* craftsman]

fab+ri+cant (ˈfæbrɪkənt) *n. Archaic.* a manufacturer.

fab+ri+cate (ˈfæbrɪˌkeɪt) *vb.* (*tr.*) **1.** to make, build, or construct. **2.** to devise, invent, or concoct (a story, lie, etc.). **3.** to fake or forge. [C15: from Latin *fabricāre* to build, make, from *fabrica* workshop; see FABRIC] —**ˌfab+ri+ˈca+tion** *n.* —**ˈfab+ri+ca+tive** *adj.* —**ˈfab+ri+ˌca+tor** *n.*

Fab+ri+koid (ˈfæbrɪˌkɔɪd) *n. Trademark.* a waterproof fabric made of cloth coated with pyroxylin.

fab·u+list (ˈfæbjʊlɪst) *n.* **1.** a person who invents or recounts fables. **2.** a person who lies or falsifies.

fab·u+lous (ˈfæbjʊləs) *adj.* **1.** almost unbelievable; astounding; legendary: *fabulous wealth.* **2.** *Informal.* extremely good: *a fabulous time at the party.* **3.** of, relating to, or based upon fable: *a fabulous beast.* [C15: from Latin *fābulōsus* celebrated in fable, from *fābula* FABLE] —**ˈfab·u·lous+ly** *adv.* —**ˈfab·u+lous+ness** *n.*

fac. *abbrev. for:* **1.** facsimile. **2.** factor. **3.** factory.

fa+çade *or* **fa+cade** (fəˈsɑːd, fæ-) *n.* **1.** the face of a building, esp. the main front. **2.** a front or outer appearance, esp. a deceptive one. [C17: from French, from Italian *facciata,* from *faccia* FACE]

face (feɪs) *n.* **1. a.** the front of the head from the forehead to the lower jaw; visage. **b.** (*as modifier*): *face flannel; face cream.* **2. a.** the expression of the countenance; look: *a sad face.* **b.** a distorted expression, esp. to indicate disgust; grimace: *she made a face.* **3.** *Informal.* make-up (esp. in the phrase **put one's face on.**) **4.** outward appearance: *the face of the countryside is changing.* **5.** appearance or pretence (esp. in the phrases **put a bold, good, bad,** etc., **face on**). **6.** worth in the eyes of others; dignity (esp. in the phrases **lose** or **save face**). **7.** *Informal.* impudence or effrontery. **8.** the main side of an object, building, etc., or the front: *the face of a palace; a cliff face.* **9.** the marked surface of an instrument, esp. the dial of a timepiece. **10.** the functional or working side of an object, as of a tool or playing card. **11. a.** the exposed area of a mine from which coal, ore, etc., may be mined. **b.** (*as modifier*): *face worker.* **12.** the uppermost part or surface: *the face of the earth.* **13.** Also called: **side.** any one of the plane surfaces of a crystal or other solid figure. **14.** either of the surfaces of a coin, esp. the one that bears the head of a ruler. **15.** Also called: **typeface.** *Printing.* **a.** the printing surface of any type character. **b.** the style, the design, or sometimes the size of the character on the type. **c.** the print made from the type. **16.** *Nautical, aeronautics.* the aft or near side of a propeller blade. **17. face to face.** in confrontation. **18. fly in the face of.** to act in defiance of. **19. in one's face.** directly opposite or against one. **20. in (the) face of.** despite. **21. look (someone) in the face.** look directly at a person without fear or shame. **22. on the face of it.** to all appearances. **23. set one's face against.** to oppose with determination. **24. show one's face.** to make an appearance. **25. to someone's face.** in someone's presence; directly and openly: *I told him the truth to his face.* ~*vb.* **26.** (when *intr.,* often foll. by *to, towards,* or *on*) to look or be situated or placed (in a specified direction): *the house faces on the square.* **27.** to be opposite: *facing page 9.* **28.** (*tr.*) to meet or be confronted by: *in his work he faces many problems.* **29.** (*tr.*) to provide with a surface of a different material: *the cuffs were faced with velvet.* **30.** to dress the surface of (stone or other material). **31.** (*tr.*) to expose (a card) with the face uppermost. **32.** *Military, chiefly U.S.* to order (a formation) to turn in a certain direction or (of a formation) to turn as required: *right face!* **33.** *Ice hockey.* **a.** (of the referee) to drop (the puck) between two opposing players, as when starting or restarting play. See also **face-off. b.** to start or restart play in this manner. **34. face the music.** *Informal.* to confront the consequences of one's actions. ~See also **face out, face up to.** [C13: from Old French, from Vulgar Latin *facia* (unattested), from Latin *faciēs* form, related to *facere* to make] —**ˈface·a·ble** *adj.*

face-ache *n.* **1.** neuralgia. **2.** *Slang.* an ugly or miserable-looking person.

face+bar (ˈfeɪsˌbɑː) *n.* a wrestling hold in which a wrestler stretches the skin on his opponent's face backwards.

face card *n.* the usual U.S. term for **court card.**

face-cen·tred *adj.* (of a crystal) having a lattice point at the centre of each face of each unit cell as well as at the corners. Compare **body-centred.**

face cloth *n.* a flannel used to wash the face and hands.

face-hard·en *vb.* (*tr.*) to harden the surface of (steel or iron) by the addition of carbon at high temperature.

face+less (ˈfeɪslɪs) *adj.* **1.** without a face. **2.** without identity; anonymous. —**ˈface+less+ness** *n.*

face-lift *n.* **1.** cosmetic surgery for tightening sagging skin and smoothing unwanted wrinkles on the face. **2.** any improvement or renovation, as of a building, etc.

face-off *Ice hockey, etc.* ~*n.* **1.** the method of starting a game, in which the referee drops the puck, etc. between two opposing players. ~*vb.* **face off.** (*adv.*) **2.** to start play by (a face-off).

face out *vb.* (*tr., adv.*) **1.** to endure (trouble). **2.** to defy or act boldly in spite of (criticism, blame, etc.). **3.** Also (*esp. U.S.*): **face down.** to cause to concede by a bold stare.

face pack *n.* a cream treatment that cleanses and tones the skin.

face+plate (ˈfeɪsˌpleɪt) *n.* **1.** a perforated circular metal plate, attached to the headstock of a lathe, on which a workpiece can be mounted. **2.** Also called: **surface plate.** a flat rigid plate used to check the the flatness and squareness of the faces of a component.

face pow·der *n.* a flesh-tinted cosmetic powder worn to make the face look less shiny, softer, etc.

fac+er (ˈfeɪsə) *n.* **1.** a person or thing that faces. **2.** a lathe tool used to turn a face perpendicular to the axis of rotation. **3.** *Brit. informal.* a difficulty or problem.

face-sav·ing *adj.* maintaining dignity or prestige.

fac+et ('fæsɪt) *n.* **1.** any of the surfaces of a cut gemstone. **2.** an aspect or phase, as of a subject or personality. **3.** *Architect.* the raised surface between the flutes of a column. **4.** any of the lenses that make up the compound eye of an insect or other arthropod. **5.** *Anatomy.* any small smooth area on a hard surface, as on a bone. ~*vb.* **+ets, +et+ing, +et+ed** *or* **+ets, +et+ting, +et+ted. 6.** (*tr.*) to cut facets in (a gemstone). [C17: from French *facette* a little FACE]

fa+ce·ti·ae (fə'si:ʃɪ,i:) *pl. n.* **1.** humorous or witty sayings. **2.** obscene or coarsely witty books. [C17: from Latin: jests, plural of *facētia* witticism, from *facētus* elegant]

fa+ce·tious (fə'si:ʃəs) *adj.* **1.** characterized by levity of attitude and love of joking: *a facetious person.* **2.** jocular or amusing, esp. at inappropriate times: *facetious remarks.* [C16: from Old French *facetieux,* from *facetie* witty saying; see FACETIAE] **—fa+'ce·tious+ly** *adv.* **—fa+'ce·tious+ness** *n.*

face up to *vb.* (*intr., adv.* + *prep.*) to accept (an unpleasant fact, reality, etc.).

face va+lid+i·ty *n. Psychol.* the extent to which a psychological test appears to measure what it is intended to measure.

face val·ue *n.* **1.** the value written or stamped on the face of a commercial paper or coin. **2.** apparent worth or value, as opposed to real worth.

fa+ci·a ('feɪʃɪə) *n.* a variant spelling of **fascia.** **—'fa+ci·al** *adj.*

fa+cial ('feɪʃəl) *adj.* **1.** of or relating to the face. ~*n.* **2.** a beauty treatment for the face, involving cleansing, massage, and cosmetic packs. **—'fa+cial+ly** *adv.*

fa+cial an+gle *n.* the angle formed between a line from the base of the nose to the opening of the ear and a line from the base of the nose to the most prominent part of the forehead: often used in comparative anthropology.

fa+cial in+dex *n.* the ratio of the length of the face to the width of the face multiplied by 100: often used in comparative anthropology. Compare **cranial index.**

fa+cial nerve *n.* the seventh cranial nerve, supplying the muscles controlling facial expression, glands of the palate and nose, and the taste buds in the anterior two-thirds of the tongue.

-fa·cient *suffix forming adjectives and nouns.* indicating a state or quality: *absorbefacient; rubefacient.* [from Latin *facient-, faciēns,* present participle of *facere* to do]

fa+ci·es ('feɪʃɪ,i:z) *n., pl.* **+ci·es. 1.** the general form and appearance of an individual or a group of plants or animals. **2.** the characteristics of a rock or series of rocks reflecting their appearance, composition, and conditions of formation. **3.** *Med.* the general facial expression of a patient, esp. when typical of a specific disease or disorder. [C17: from Latin: appearance, FACE]

fac+ile ('fæsaɪl) *adj.* **1.** easy to perform or achieve. **2.** working or moving easily or smoothly. **3.** without depth; superficial: *a facile solution.* **4.** relaxed in manner; easygoing. [C15: from Latin *facilis* easy, from *facere* to do] **—'fac+ile+ly** *adv.* **—'fac+ile+ness** *n.*

fac+ile prin+ceps *Latin.* ('fæsɪlɪ 'prɪnsɛps) *n.* an obvious leader. [literally: easily first]

fa+cil+i·tate (fə'sɪlɪ,teɪt) *vb.* (*tr.*) to make easier; assist the progress of. **—fa+'cil·i·ta·tive** *adj.* **—fa+'cil·i+,ta·tor** *n.*

fa+cil·i·ta+tion (fə,sɪlɪ'teɪʃən) *n.* **1.** the act or process of facilitating. **2.** *Physiol.* the increased ease of transmission of impulses in a nerve fibre, caused by prior excitation.

fa+cil+i·ty (fə'sɪlɪtɪ) *n., pl.* **·ties. 1.** ease of action or performance; freedom from difficulty. **2.** ready skill or ease deriving from practice or familiarity. **3.** (*often pl.*) the means or equipment facilitating the performance of an action. **4.** *Rare.* easy-going disposition. **5.** *Military.* an organization or building offering supporting capability. **6.** (*usually pl.*) a euphemistic word for **lavatory.** [C15: from Latin *facilitās,* from *facilis* easy; see FACILE]

fac+ing ('feɪsɪŋ) *n.* **1.** a piece of material used esp. to conceal the seam of a garment and prevent fraying. **2.** (*usually pl.*) a piece of additional cloth, esp. in a different colour, the collar, cuffs, etc., of the jacket of a military uniform. **3.** an outer layer or coat of material applied to the surface of a wall.

fac+sim·i+le (fæk'sɪmɪlɪ) *n.* **1. a.** an exact copy or reproduction. **b.** (*as modifier*): *a facsimile publication.* **2.** a telegraphic system in which a written, printed, or pictorial document is scanned photoelectrically, the resulting signals being transmitted and reproduced photographically after reception. **3.** an image produced by this means. ~*vb.* **+les, +le+ing, +led. 4.** (*tr.*) to make an exact copy of. [C17: from Latin *fac simile!* make something like it!, from *facere* to make + *similis* similar, like]

fact (fækt) *n.* **1.** an event or thing known to have happened or existed. **2.** a truth verifiable from experience or observation. **3.** a piece of information: *get me all the facts of this case.* **4.** *Law.* (*often pl.*) an actual event, happening, etc., as distinguished from its legal consequences. Questions of fact are decided by the jury, questions of law by the court or judge. **5. after** (*or* **before**) **the fact.** *Criminal law.* after (or before) the commission of the offence: *an accessory after the fact.* **6. as a matter of fact, in fact, in point of fact.** in reality or actuality. **7. fact of life.** an inescapable truth, esp. an unpleasant one. **8. the fact of the matter.** the truth. [C16: from Latin *factum* something done, from *factus* made, from *facere* to make] **—'fact+ful** *adj.*

fac+tice ('fæktɪs) *n.* a soft rubbery material made by reacting sulphur or sulphur chloride with vegetable oil.

fac+tion ('fækʃən) *n.* **1.** a group of people forming a minority within a larger body, esp. a dissentious group. **2.** strife or dissension within a group. [C16: from Latin *factiō* a making, from *facere* to make, do] **—'fac+tion+al** *adj.* **—'fac+tion+al+,ism** *n.* **—'fac+tion+al+ist** *n.*

fac+tious ('fækʃəs) *adj.* given to, producing, or characterized by faction. **—'fac+tious+ly** *adv.* **—'fac+tious+ness** *n.*

fac+ti+tious (fæk'tɪʃəs) *adj.* **1.** artificial rather than natural: *factitious demands created by the mass media.* **2.** not genuine; sham: *factitious enthusiasm.* [C17: from Latin *factīcius,* from *facere* to make, do] **—fac+'ti+tious+ly** *adv.* **—fac+'ti+tious+ness** *n.*

fac+ti+tive ('fæktɪtɪv) *adj. Grammar.* denoting a verb taking a direct object as well as a noun in apposition, as for example *elect* in *They elected John president,* where *John* is the direct object and *president* is the complement. [C19: from New Latin *factitīvus,* from Latin *factitāre* to do frequently, from *facere* to do] **—'fac+ti+tive+ly** *adv.*

fac+tor ('fæktə) *n.* **1.** an element or cause that contributes to a result. **2.** *Maths.* **a.** one of two or more integers or polynomials whose product is a given integer or polynomial: *2 and 3 are factors of 6.* **b.** an integer or polynomial that can be exactly divided into another integer or polynomial: *1, 2, 3, and 6 are all factors of 6.* **3.** a person who acts on another's behalf, esp. one who transacts business for another. **4.** *Commerce.* a business that makes loans in return for or on security of trade debts. **5.** former name for a **gene. 6.** *Commercial law.* a person to whom goods are consigned for sale and who is paid a factorage. **7.** (in Scotland) the manager of an estate. ~*vb.* **8.** (*intr.*) to engage in the business of a factor. [C15: from Latin: one who acts, from *facere* to do] **—'fac+tor+a·ble** *adj.* **—,fac+tor+a·'bil+i·ty** *n.* **—'fac+tor+,ship** *n.*

fac+tor+age ('fæktərɪdʒ) *n.* the commission payable to a factor.

fac+tor a·nal·y+sis *n. Statistics.* any of several techniques for deriving from a number of given variables a smaller number of different, more useful, variables.

fac+tor cost *n.* (in social accounting) valuation of goods and services at their overall commercial cost, including markups but excluding indirect taxes and subsidies.

fac+to·ri·al (fæk'tɔ:rɪəl) *Maths.* ~*n.* **1.** the product of all the positive integers from one up to and including a given integer. Factorial zero is assigned the value of one: *factorial four is* $1 \times 2 \times 3 \times 4$. Symbol: $n!$, $\underline{n|}$, where n is the given integer. ~*adj.* **2.** of or involving factorials or factors. **—fac+'to+ri+al+ly** *adv.*

fac+tor+ing ('fæktərɪŋ) *n.* the business of a factor.

fac+tor+ize *or* **fac+tor+ise** ('fæktə,raɪz) *vb.* (*tr.*) *Maths.* to resolve (an integer or polynomial) into factors. **—,fac+tor·i+'za+tion** *or* **,fac+tor·i+'sa+tion** *n.*

fac+tor of pro+duc+tion *n.* a resource or input entering the production of wealth, such as land, labour, capital, etc. Also called: **agent of production.**

fac+tor of safe+ty *n.* the ratio of the breaking stress of a material or structure to the calculated maximum stress when in use. Also called: **safety factor.**

fac+to+ry ('fæktərɪ) *n., pl.* **+ries. 1. a.** a building or group of buildings containing a plant assembly for the manufacture of goods. **b.** (*as modifier*): *a factory worker.* **2.** *Rare.* a trading station maintained by factors in a foreign country. [C16: from Late Latin *factorium*; see FACTOR] **—'fac·to·ry-,like** *adj.*

fac+to+ry farm *n.* a farm in which animals are bred and fattened using modern industrial methods. **—fac+to+ry farm+ing** *n.*

fac+to+ry ship *n. Whaling.* a vessel that processes whale carcasses supplied by a whale catcher.

fac+to+tum (fæk'təutəm) *n.* a person employed to do all kinds of work. [C16: from Medieval Latin, from Latin *fac!* do! + *tōtum,* from *tōtus* (adj.) all]

facts and fig+ures *pl. n.* details; precise information.

facts of life *pl. n.* **the.** the details of sexual behaviour and reproduction, esp. as told to children.

fac+tu·al ('fæktʃuəl) *adj.* **1.** of, relating to, or characterized by facts. **2.** of the nature of fact; real; actual. **—'fac+tu+al+ism** *n.* **—'fac+tu+al+ist** *n.* **—,fac+tu+al+'is+tic** *adj.* **—'fac+tu+al+ly** *adv.* **—'fac+tu+al+ness** *or* **,fac+tu+'al+i+ty** *n.*

fac+ture ('fæktʃə) *n. Rare.* **1.** construction. **2.** workmanship; quality. [C15: from Old French, from Latin *factūra*]

fac·u+la ('fækjulə) *n., pl.* **+lae** (-,li:). any of the bright areas on the sun's surface, usually appearing just before a sunspot and subject to the same 11-year cycle. [C18: from Latin: little torch, from *fax* torch] **—'fac·u·lar** *adj.*

fac+ul+ta+tive ('fækəltətɪv) *adj.* **1.** empowering but not compelling the doing of an act. **2.** *Philosophy.* that may or may not occur. **3.** *Biology.* able to exist under more than one set of environmental conditions: *a facultative parasite can exist as a parasite or a saprophyte.* Compare **obligate** (sense 4). **4.** of or relating to a faculty. **—'fac+ul+ta+tive+ly** *adv.*

fac+ul+ty ('fækəltɪ) *n., pl.* **+ties. 1.** one of the inherent powers of the mind or body, such as reason, memory, sight, or hearing. **2.** any ability or power, whether acquired or inherent. **3.** a conferred power or right. **4. a.** a department within a university or college devoted to a particular branch of knowledge. **b.** the staff of such a department. **c.** *Chiefly U.S.* all administrative and teaching staff at a university, college, school, etc. **5.** all members of a learned profession. **6.** *Archaic.* occupation. [C14 (in the sense: department of learning): from Latin *facultās* capability; related to Latin *facilis* easy]

Fac+ul+ty of Ad+vo+cates *n. Law.* the college or society of advocates in Scotland.

FA Cup *n. Soccer.* (in England) **1.** an annual knockout competition for a silver trophy, open to all member teams of the Football Association. **2.** the trophy itself.

fad (fæd) *n. Informal.* **1.** an intense but short-lived fashion; craze. **2.** a personal idiosyncrasy or whim. [C19: of uncertain origin] —'**fad+dish** *or* '**fad+dy** *adj.* —'**fad+dish+ness** *n.* —'**fad+dism** *n.* —'**fad+dist** *n.*

FAD *n. Biochem.* flavin adenine dinucleotide: an ester of riboflavin with ADP that acts as the prosthetic group for many flavoproteins. See also **FMN.**

Fad·den ('fædᵊn) *n.* Sir **Ar·thur Wil·liam.** 1895–1973, Australian statesman; prime minister of Australia (1941).

fade (feɪd) *vb.* **1.** to lose or cause to lose brightness, colour, or clarity. **2.** (*intr.*) to lose freshness, vigour, or youth; wither. **3.** (*intr.;* usually foll. by *away* or *out*) to vanish slowly; die out. **4.** to decrease the brightness or volume of (a television or radio programme or film sequence) or (of a television programme, etc.) to decrease in this way. **5.** (*intr.*) (of the brakes of a vehicle) to lose power. **6.** to cause (a golf ball) to veer from a straight line or (of a golf ball) to veer from a straight flight. *~n.* **7.** the act or an instance of fading. [C14: from *fade* (adj.) dull, from Old French, from Vulgar Latin *fatidus* (unattested), probably blend of Latin *vapidus* VAPID + Latin *fatuus* FATUOUS] —'**fad+a·ble** *adj.* —'**fad+ed+ness** *n.* —'**fad+er** *n.*

fade-in *n.* **1.** *Films.* an optical effect in which a shot appears gradually out of darkness. **2.** a gradual increase in the volume in a radio or television broadcast. *~vb.* **fade in** (*adv.*). **3.** Also: **fade up.** to increase or cause to increase gradually, as vision or sound in a film or broadcast.

fade+less ('feɪdlɪs) *adj.* not subject to fading.

fade-out *n.* **1.** *Films.* an optical effect in which a shot slowly disappears into darkness. **2.** a gradual reduction in signal strength in a radio or television broadcast. **3.** a gradual and temporary loss of a received radio or television signal due to atmospheric disturbances, magnetic storms, etc. **4.** a slow or gradual disappearance. *~vb.* **fade out.** (*adv.*) **5.** to decrease or cause to decrease gradually, as vision or sound in a film or broadcast.

fadge (fædʒ) *vb.* (*intr.*) *Archaic or Brit. dialect.* **1.** to agree. **2.** to succeed. [C16: of uncertain origin]

fad+ing ('feɪdɪŋ) *n.* a variation in the strength of received radio signals due to variations in the conditions of the transmission medium.

fa·do *Portuguese.* ('fadu) *n.* a type of melancholy Portuguese folk song. [literally: FATE]

fae+cal *or esp. U.S.* **fe+cal** ('fiːkᵊl) *adj.* of, relating to, or consisting of faeces.

fae+ces *or esp. U.S.* **fe+ces** ('fiːsiːz) *pl. n.* bodily waste matter derived from ingested food and the secretions of the intestines and discharged through the anus. [C15: from Latin *faecēs*, plural of *faex* sediment, dregs]

fa+e·na *Spanish.* (fa'ena) *n. Bullfighting.* the matador's final series of passes with sword and cape before the kill. [literally: task, from obsolete Catalan (modern *feina*), from Latin *facienda* things to be done, from *facere* to do]

Fa+en+za (*Italian* fa'ɛntsa) *n.* a city in N Italy, in Emilia-Romagna: famous in the 15th and 16th centuries for its majolica earthenware, esp. faience. Pop.: 54 703 (1971).

fa·e+rie *or* **fa·e+ry** ('feɪərɪ, 'fɛərɪ) *n., pl.* **+ries.** *Archaic or poetic.* **1.** the land of fairies. **2.** enchantment. *~adj., n.* **3.** a variant spelling of **fairy.**

Fae+roes *or* **Fa+roes** ('fɛərəuz) *pl. n.* a group of 21 basalt islands in the North Atlantic between Iceland and the Shetland Islands: a self-governing community within the kingdom of Denmark; fishing. Capital: Thorshavn. Pop.: 41 000 (1975 est.). Area: 1400 sq. km (540 sq. miles). Also called: **Faeroe Islands** or **Faroe Islands.**

Faer·o+ese *or* **Far·o+ese** (ˌfɛərəu'iːz) *adj.* **1.** of, relating to, or characteristic of the Faeroes, their inhabitants, or their language. *~n.* **2.** the chief language of the Faeroes, closely related to Icelandic, although they are not mutually intelligible. **3.** (*pl.* **+ese**) a native or inhabitant of the Faeroes.

faff (fæf) *vb.* (*intr.;* often foll. by *about*) *Brit. informal.* to dither or fuss.

Faf·nir ('fæfnɪə, 'fæv-) *n. Norse myth.* the son of Hreidmar, whom he killed to gain the cursed treasure of Andvari. He became a dragon and was slain by Sigurd while guarding the treasure.

fag[1] (fæg) *n.* **1.** *Informal.* a boring or wearisome task: *it's a fag having to walk all that way.* **2.** *Brit.* (esp. formerly) a young public school boy who performs menial chores for an older boy or prefect. *~vb.* **fags, fag+ging, fagged. 3.** (when *tr.*, often foll. by *out*) *Informal.* to become or cause to become exhausted by hard toil or work. **4.** (*usually intr.*) *Brit.* to do or cause to do menial chores in a public school.: *Brown fags for Lee.* [C18: of obscure origin]

fag[2] (fæg) *n.* **1.** *Brit.* a slang word for **cigarette. 2.** a fag end, as of cloth. [C16 (in the sense: something hanging loose, flap): of obscure origin]

fag[3] (fæg) *n. Slang, chiefly U.S.* short for **faggot**[2].

fa+ga+ceous (fə'geɪʃəs) *adj.* of, relating to, or belonging to the *Fagaceae,* a family of trees, including beech, oak, and chestnut, whose fruit is partly or wholly enclosed in a husk (cupule). [C19: from New Latin *Fāgāceae*, from Latin *fāgus* beech]

fag end *n.* **1.** the last and worst part, esp. when it is of little use. **2.** *Brit. informal.* the stub of a cigarette. [C17: see FAG[2]]

fag+got[1] *or esp. U.S.* **fag+ot** ('fægət) *n.* **1.** a bundle of sticks or twigs, esp. when bound together and used as fuel. **2.** a bundle of iron bars, esp. a box formed by four pieces of wrought iron and filled with scrap to be forged into wrought iron. **3.** a ball of chopped meat, usually pork liver, bound with herbs and bread and eaten fried. **4.** a bundle of anything. *~vb.* (*tr.*) **5.** to collect into a bundle or bundles. **6.** *Needlework.* to do faggoting on (a garment, piece of cloth, etc.). [C14: from Old French, perhaps from Greek *phakelos* bundle]

fag+got[2] ('fægət) *n. Slang, chiefly U.S.* a male homosexual. Often shortened to **fag.** [C20: special use of FAGGOT[1]]

fag+got+ing *or esp. U.S.* **fag+ot+ing** ('fægətɪŋ) *n.* **1.** decorative needlework done by tying vertical threads together in bundles. **2.** a decorative way of joining two hems by crisscross stitches.

Fah. *or* **Fahr.** *abbrev. for* Fahrenheit.

Fahd ibn Ab·dul Az·iz (fɑːd 'ɪbᵊn 'æbdʊl ə'ziːz) *n.* born 1922, king and President of the Council of Ministers of Saudi Arabia from 1982.

fahl+band ('fɑːlˌbænd) *n.* a thin bed of schistose rock impregnated with metallic sulphides. [C19: from German: pale band]

Fahr+en+heit[1] ('færənˌhaɪt) *adj.* of or measured according to the Fahrenheit scale of temperature. Symbol: **F**

Fahr·en+heit[2] (*German* 'faːrənˌhaɪt) *n.* **Ga·bri·el Da·ni·el** ('gaːbriˌeːl 'daːnjeːl). 1686–1736, German physicist, who invented the mercury thermometer and devised the temperature scale that bears his name.

Fahr+en+heit scale *n.* a scale of temperatures in which 32° represents the melting point of ice and 212° represents the boiling point of pure water under standard atmospheric pressure. Compare **Celsius scale.**

Fai+al *or* **Fay+al** (*Portuguese* fə'jal) *n.* an island in the central Azores archipelago. Chief town: Horta. Area: 171 sq. km (66 sq. miles).

faï+ence (faɪ'ɑːns, feɪ-) *n.* **a.** tin-glazed earthenware, usually that of French, German, Italian, or Scandinavian origin. **b.** (*as modifier*): *a faïence cup.* [C18: from French, strictly: pottery from FAENZA]

fail (feɪl) *vb.* **1.** to be unsuccessful in an attempt (at something or to do something). **2.** (*intr.*) to stop operating or working properly: *the steering failed suddenly.* **3.** to judge or be judged as being below the officially accepted standard required for success in (a course, examination, etc.). **4.** (*tr.*) to prove disappointing, undependable, or useless to (someone). **5.** (*tr.*) to neglect or be unable (to do something). **6.** (*intr.*) to prove partly or completely insufficient in quantity, duration, or extent. **7.** (*intr.*) to weaken; fade away. **8.** (*intr.*) to go bankrupt or become insolvent. *~n.* **9.** a failure to attain the required standard, as in an examination. **10. without fail.** definitely; with certainty. [C13: from Old French *faillir,* ultimately from Latin *fallere* to disappoint; probably related to Greek *phēlos* deceitful]

fail+ing ('feɪlɪŋ) *n.* **1.** a weak point; flaw. *~prep.* **2.** (*used to express a condition*) in default of: *failing a solution this afternoon, the problem will have to wait until Monday.*

faille (feɪl; *French* faj) *n.* a soft light ribbed fabric of silk, rayon, or taffeta. [C16: from French: head covering, hence, fabric used for this, of obscure origin]

fail-safe *adj.* **1.** able to return to a safe condition in the event of a failure or malfunction. **2.** (of a nuclear weapon) capable of being deactivated in the event of failure or accident.

fail+ure ('feɪljə) *n.* **1.** the act or an instance of failing. **2.** a person or thing that is unsuccessful or disappointing: *the evening was a failure.* **3.** nonperformance of something required or expected: *failure to attend will be punished.* **4.** cessation of normal operation; breakdown: *a power failure.* **5.** an insufficiency or shortage: *a crop failure.* **6.** a decline or loss, as in health or strength. **7.** the fact of not reaching the required standard in an examination, test, course, etc. **8.** the act or process of becoming bankrupt or the state of being bankrupt.

fain (feɪn) *adv.* **1.** (usually with *would*) *Archaic.* willingly; gladly: *she would fain be dead.* *~adj.* **2.** *Obsolete.* **a.** willing or eager. **b.** compelled. [Old English *fægen;* related to Old Norse *fegiun* happy, Old High German *gifehan* to be glad, Gothic *fahehs* joy; see FAWN[2]]

fai+né+ant ('feɪnɪənt; *French* fɛne'ɑ̃) *n.* **1.** a lazy person; idler. *~adj.* **2.** indolent. [C17: from French, modification of earlier *fait-nient* (he) does nothing, by folk etymology from Old French *faignant* shirker, from *faindre* to be lazy] —'**fai+ne+ance** *n.*

faint (feɪnt) *adj.* **1.** lacking clarity, brightness, volume, etc.: *a faint noise.* **2.** lacking conviction or force; weak: *faint praise.* **3.** feeling dizzy or weak as if about to lose consciousness. **4.** without boldness or courage; timid (esp. in the combination **faint-hearted**). *~vb.* (*intr.*) **5.** to lose consciousness, esp. momentarily, as through weakness. **6.** *Archaic or poetic.* to fail or become weak, esp. in hope or courage. *~n.* **7.** a sudden spontaneous loss of consciousness, usually momentary, caused by an insufficient supply of blood to the brain. Technical name: **syncope.** [C13: from Old French, from *faindre* to be idle] —'**faint+er** *n.* —'**faint+ing+ly** *adv.* —'**faint+ish** *adj.* —'**faint+ish+ness** *n.* —'**faint+ly** *adv.* —'**faint+ness** *n.*

fair[1] (fɛə) *adj.* **1.** free from discrimination, dishonesty, etc.; just; impartial. **2.** in conformity with rules or standards; legitimate: *a fair fight.* **3.** (of the hair or complexion) light in colour. **4.** beautiful or lovely to look at. **5.** moderately or quite good: *a fair piece of work.* **6.** unblemished; untainted. **7.** (of the tide or wind) favourable to the passage of a vessel. **8.** sunny, fine, or cloudless. **9.** (*prenominal*) *Informal.* thorough; real: *a fair battle to get to the counter.* **10.** pleasant or courteous. **11.** apparently good or valuable, but really false: *fair words.* **12.** open or unobstructed: *a fair passage.* **13.** (of handwriting, etc.) clear and legible. **14. fair and square.** in a correct or just way. **15. fair enough!** an expression of agreement. **16. fair to middling.** about average. **17. fair go.** *Austral.* fair treatment or a fair chance. *~adv.* **18.** in a fair way; correctly: *act fair, now!* **19.** absolutely or squarely; quite: *the question caught him* fair off his guard. **20.** *Austral.* really or very: *fair tired.* ~*vb.* **21.** (*intr.*) *Dialect.* (of the weather) to become fine and mild. ~*n.* **22.** *Archaic.* a person or thing that is beautiful or valuable, esp. a woman. [Old English *fæger;* related to Old Norse *fagr,* Old Saxon, Old High German *fagar,* Gothic *fagrs* suitable] —**'fair·ness** *n.*

fair[2] (fɛə) *n.* **1.** a travelling entertainment with sideshows, rides, etc., esp. one that visits places at the same time each year. **2.** a gathering of producers of and dealers in a given class of products to facilitate business: *a world fair.* **3.** an event including sale of goods and amusements, esp. for a charity; bazaar. **4.** a regular assembly at a specific place for the sale of goods, esp. livestock. [C13: from Old French *feire,* from Late Latin *fēria* holiday, from Latin *fēriae* days of rest: related to *festus* FESTAL]

Fair·banks[1] ('fɛə,bæŋks) *n.* a city in central Alaska, at the terminus of the Alaska Highway. Pop.: 14 771 (1970).

Fair·banks[2] ('fɛə,bæŋks) *n.* **1. Doug·las.** 1883–1939, U.S. film actor. **2. Doug·las, Jnr.** born 1909, U.S. film actor, son of Douglas Fairbanks.

fair cop·y *n.* a clean copy of a document on which all corrections have been made.

Fair·fax ('fɛəfæks) *n.* **Thom·as,** 3rd Baron Fairfax. 1612–71, English general and statesman: commanded the Parliamentary army (1645–50), defeating Charles I at Naseby (1645). He was instrumental in restoring Charles II to the throne (1660).

fair game *n.* **1.** a legitimate object for ridicule or attack. **2.** *Hunting, archaic.* quarry that may legitimately be pursued according to the rules of a particular sport.

fair·ground ('fɛə,graʊnd) *n.* an open space used for a fair or exhibition.

fair-haired boy *n.* the usual U.S. name for **blue-eyed boy.**

fair·ing[1] ('fɛərɪŋ) *n.* an external metal structure fitted around parts of an aircraft, car, vessel, etc., to reduced drag. Also called: **fillet.** Compare **cowling.** [C20: FAIR[1] + -ING[1]]

fair·ing[2] ('fɛərɪŋ) *n.* **1.** *Archaic.* a present, esp. from a fair. **2.** a sweet circular biscuit made with butter.

fair·ish ('fɛərɪʃ) *adj.* **1.** moderately good, well, etc. **2.** (of the hair, complexion, etc.) moderately light in colour.

Fair Isle *n.* an intricate multicoloured pattern knitted with Shetland wool into various garments, such as sweaters. [C19: named after one of the Shetland Islands where the pattern originated]

fair·lead ('fɛə,li:d) *or* **fair·lead·er** *n. Nautical.* a block or ring through which a line is rove to keep it clear of obstructions, prevent chafing, or maintain it at an angle.

fair·ly ('fɛəlɪ) *adv.* **1.** (*not used with a negative*) moderately. **2.** as deserved; justly. **3.** (*not used with a negative*) positively; absolutely: *the hall fairly rang with applause.* **4.** *Archaic.* clearly. **5.** *Obsolete.* courteously.

fair-mind·ed *adj.* just or impartial. —**,fair-'mind·ed·ness** *n.*

fair play *n.* **1.** an established standard of decency, honesty, etc. **2.** abidance by this standard.

fair sex *n.* **the.** women collectively.

fair-spo·ken *adj.* civil, courteous, or elegant in speech. —**,fair-'spo·ken·ness** *n.*

fair·way ('fɛə,weɪ) *n.* Also called: **fair green. 1.** (on a golf course) the areas of shorter grass between the tees and greens, esp. the avenue approaching a green bordered by rough. 2. *Nautical.* **a.** the navigable part of a river, harbour, etc. **b.** the customary course followed by vessels.

fair-weath·er *adj.* **1.** suitable for use in fair weather only. **2.** not reliable or present in situations of hardship or difficulty (esp. in the phrase **fair-weather friend**).

Fair·weath·er ('fɛə,wɛðə) *n.* **Mount.** a mountain in W North America, on the border between Alaska and British Columbia. Height: 4596 m (15 320 ft.).

fair·y ('fɛərɪ) *n., pl.* **fair·ies. 1.** an imaginary supernatural being, usually represented in diminutive human form and characterized as clever, playful, and having magical powers. **2.** *Slang.* a male homosexual. ~*adj.* (*prenominal*) **3.** of or relating to a fairy or fairies. **4.** resembling a fairy or fairies, esp. in being enchanted or delicate. [C14: from Old French *faerie* fairyland, from *feie* fairy, from Latin *Fāta* the Fates; see FATE, FAY[1]] —**'fair·y-,like** *adj.*

fair·y cy·cle *n.* a child's bicycle.

fair·y·floss ('fɛərɪ,flɒs) *n.* the Australian word for **candyfloss.**

fair·y god·moth·er *n.* **1.** a character in certain fairy stories who brings unexpected benefits to the hero or heroine. **2.** any benefactress, esp. an unknown one.

fair·y·land ('fɛərɪ,lænd) *n.* **1.** the imaginary domain of the fairies; an enchanted or wonderful place. **2.** a fantasy world, esp. one resulting from a person's wild imaginings.

fair·y pen·guin *n.* a small penguin, *Eudyptula minor,* with a bluish head and back, found on the Australian coast. Also called: **little** or **blue penguin.**

fair·y ring *n.* a ring of dark luxuriant vegetation in grassy ground corresponding to the outer edge of an underground fungal mycelium: seasonally marked by a ring of mushrooms.

fair·y shrimp *n.* any small freshwater branchiopod crustacean of the genera *Chirocephalus, Artemia,* etc., having a transparent body with many appendages and habitually swimming on its back: order *Anostraca.*

fair·y swal·low *n.* (*sometimes cap.*) a variety of domestic fancy pigeon having blue-and-white plumage and heavily muffed feet.

fair·y tale *or* **sto·ry** *n.* **1.** a story about fairies or other mythical or magical beings, esp. one of traditional origin told to children. **2.** a highly improbable account.

Fai·sal I *or* **Fei·sal I** ('faɪsᵊl) *n.* 1885–1933, king of Syria (1920) and first king of Iraq (1921–33).

Fai·sal II *or* **Fei·sal II** *n.* 1935–58, last king of Iraq (1939–58).

fait ac·com·pli *French.* (fɛ takɔ̃'pli) *n., pl.* ***faits ac·com·plis*** (fɛ takɔ̃'pli). something already done and beyond alteration. [literally: accomplished fact]

faites vos jeux *French.* (fɛt vo 'ʒø) place your bets! (a phrase used by croupiers in roulette and other casino gambling games).

faith (feɪθ) *n.* **1.** strong or unshakeable belief in something, esp. without proof or evidence. **2.** a specific system of religious beliefs: *the Jewish faith.* **3.** *Christianity.* trust in God and in his actions and promises. **4.** a conviction of the truth of certain doctrines of religion, esp. when this is not based on reason. **5.** complete confidence or trust in a person, remedy, etc. **6.** any set of firmly held principles or beliefs. **7.** allegiance or loyalty, as to a person or cause (esp. in the phrases **keep faith, break faith**). **8. bad faith.** insincerity or dishonesty. **9. good faith.** honesty or sincerity, as of intention in business (esp. in the phrase **in good faith**). **10.** (*modifier*) using, concerned with, or relating to the supposed ability to cure bodily ailments by means of religious faith: *a faith cure; a faith healer.* ~*interj.* **11.** *Archaic.* indeed; really (also in the phrases **by my faith, in faith**). [C12: from Anglo-French *feid,* from Latin *fidēs* trust, confidence]

faith·ful ('feɪθfʊl) *adj.* **1.** having faith; remaining true, constant, or loyal. **2.** maintaining sexual loyalty to one's lover or spouse. **3.** consistently reliable: *a faithful worker.* **4.** reliable or truthful: *a faithful source.* **5.** accurate in detail: *a faithful translation.* ~*n.* **6. the faithful. a.** the believers in and loyal adherents of a religious faith, esp. Christianity. **b.** any group of loyal and steadfast followers. —**'faith·ful·ly** *adv.* —**'faith·ful·ness** *n.*

faith·less ('feɪθlɪs) *adj.* **1.** unreliable or treacherous. **2.** dishonest or disloyal. **3.** having no faith or trust. **4.** lacking faith, esp. religious faith. —**'faith·less·ly** *adv.* —**'faith·less·ness** *n.*

fai·tour ('feɪtə) *n. Obsolete.* an imposter. [C14: from Anglo-French: cheat, from Old French *faitor,* from Latin: FACTOR]

Fai·yum *or* **Fa·yum** (faɪ'ju:m) *n.* See **El Faiyum.**

Faiz·a·bad (,faɪzə'bæd) *n.* **1.** a city in NE Afghanistan. Pop.: 65 000 (1971 est.). **2.** a variant spelling of **Fyzabad.**

fake[1] (feɪk) *vb.* **1.** (*tr.*) to cause (something inferior or not genuine) to appear more valuable, desirable, or real by fraud or pretence. **2.** to pretend to have (an illness, emotion, etc.): *to fake a headache.* **3.** to improvise (music, stage dialogue, etc.). ~*n.* **4.** an object, person, or act that is not genuine; sham, counterfeit, or forgery. ~*adj.* **5.** not genuine; spurious. [C19: of uncertain origin] —**'fak·er** *n.*

fake[2] (feɪk) *Nautical.* ~*vb.* **1.** (*tr.;* usually foll. by *down*) to coil (a rope) on deck. ~*n.* **2.** one round of a coil of rope. [Middle English *faken*]

fa·kir, fa·qir (fə'kɪə, 'feɪkə), *or* **fa·keer** (fə'kɪə) *n.* **1.** a member of any religious order of Islam. **2.** a Hindu ascetic mendicant or holy man. [C17: from Arabic *faqīr* poor]

fa-la *or* **fal la** (fɑ:'lɑ:) *n.* (esp. in 16th-century songs) a refrain sung to the syllables *fa-la-la.*

Fa·lange ('fælændʒ; *Spanish* fa'laŋxe) *n.* the Fascist movement founded in Spain in 1933; the one legal party in Spain under the Franco regime. [Spanish: PHALANX] —**Fa·'lan·gist** *n., adj.*

fal·ba·la ('fælbələ) *n.* a gathered flounce, frill, or ruffle. [C18: from French, from (dialect) *ferbelà;* see FURBELOW]

fal·cate ('fælkeɪt) *or* **fal·ci·form** ('fælsɪ,fɔ:m) *adj. Biology.* shaped like a sickle. [C19: from Latin *falcātus,* from *falx* sickle]

fal·chion ('fɔ:ltʃən, 'fɔ:lʃən) *n.* **1.** a short and slightly curved medieval sword. **2.** an archaic word for **sword.** [C14: from Italian *falcione,* from *falce,* from Latin *falx* sickle]

fal·con ('fɔ:lkən, 'fɔ:kən) *n.* **1.** any diurnal bird of prey of the family *Falconidae,* esp. any of the genus *Falco* (gyrfalcon, peregrine falcon, etc.), typically having pointed wings and a long tail. **2. a.** any of these or related birds, trained to hunt small game. **b.** the female of such a bird (compare **tercel**). **3.** a light-medium cannon used from the 15th to 17th centuries. [C13: from Old French *faucon,* from Late Latin *falcō* hawk, probably of Germanic origin; perhaps related to Latin *falx* sickle]

fal·con·er ('fɔ:lkənə, 'fɔ:kə-) *n.* a person who breeds or trains hawks or who follows the sport of falconry.

fal·con·et ('fɔ:lkə,nɛt, 'fɔ:kə-) *n.* **1.** any of various small falcons, esp. any of the Asiatic genus *Microhierax.* **2.** a small light cannon used from the 15th to 17th centuries.

fal·con-gen·tle *or* **fal·con-gen·til** *n. Falconry.* a female falcon, esp. a female peregrine falcon. [C14: from Old French *faucon-gentil* literally: noble falcon]

fal·con·i·form (fæl'kəʊnɪ,fɔ:m) *adj.* of, relating to, or belonging to the order *Falconiformes,* which includes the vultures, hawks, eagles, buzzards, and falcons.

fal·con·ine ('fɔ:lkə,naɪn, 'fɔ:kə-) *adj.* **1.** of, relating to, or resembling a falcon. **2.** of, relating to, or belonging to the family *Falconidae,* which includes the falcons.

fal·con·ry ('fɔ:lkənrɪ, 'fɔ:kən-) *n.* **1.** the art of keeping falcons and training them to return from flight to a lure or to hunt quarry. **2.** the sport of causing falcons to return from flight to their trainer and to hunt quarry under his direction.

fal·de·ral ('fældɪ,ræl), **fal·de·rol** ('fældɪ,rɒl), *or* **fol·de·rol** ('fɒldɪ,rɒl) *n.* **1.** a showy but worthless trifle. **2.** foolish nonsense. **3.** a nonsensical refrain in old songs.

fald·stool ('fɔ:ld,stu:l) *n.* a backless seat, sometimes capable of being folded, used by bishops and certain other prelates. [C11 *fyldestol*, probably a translation of Medieval Latin *faldistolium* folding stool, of Germanic origin; compare Old High German *faldstuol*]

Fa·le·ri·i (fəˈlɪərɪˌaɪ) *n.* an ancient city of S Italy, in Latium: important in pre-Roman times.

Fa·lis·can (fəˈlɪskən) *n.* an ancient language of Italy, spoken in the area north of the Tiber. It was closely related to Latin, which displaced it before 200 B.C.

Fal·kirk (ˈfɔːlkɜːk) *n.* a town in Scotland, in the Central region: scene of Edward I's defeat of Wallace (1298) and Prince Charles Edward's defeat of General Hawley (1746); iron works. Pop.: 37 587 (1971).

Falk·land Is·lands (ˈfɔːklənd) *n.* a group of over 100 islands in the S Atlantic: a British crown colony. Chief town: Stanley. Pop.: 2045 (1970). Area: about 12 200 sq. km (4700 sq. miles). Spanish name: **Islas Malvinas.**

Falk·land Is·lands De·pend·en·cies *n.* a group of almost uninhabited islands south of the Falkland Islands: consisting of the South Sandwich Islands and South Georgia. Area: 4090 sq. km (1580 sq. miles).

Falk·ner (ˈfɔːknə) *n.* a variant spelling of (William) **Faulkner.**

fall (fɔːl) *vb.* **falls, fall·ing, fell, fall·en.** (*mainly intr.*) **1.** to descend by the force of gravity from a higher to a lower place. **2.** to drop suddenly from an erect position. **3.** to collapse to the ground, esp. in pieces. **4.** to become less or lower in number, quality, etc.: *prices fell in the summer.* **5.** to become lower in pitch. **6.** to extend downwards: *her hair fell to her waist.* **7.** to be badly wounded or killed. **8.** to slope in a downward direction. **9.** *Christianity.* to yield to temptation or sin. **10.** to diminish in status, estimation, etc. **11.** to yield to attack: *the city fell under the assault.* **12.** to lose power: *the government fell after the riots.* **13.** to pass into or take on a specified condition: *to fall asleep; fall in love.* **14.** to adopt a despondent expression: *her face fell.* **15.** to be averted: *her gaze fell.* **16.** to come by chance or presumption: *suspicion fell on the butler.* **17.** to occur; take place: *night fell; Easter falls early this year.* **18.** (of payments) to be due. **19.** to be directed to a specific point. **20.** (foll. by *back, behind,* etc.) to move in a specified direction. **21.** to occur at a specified place: *the accent falls on the last syllable.* **22.** (foll. by *to*) to return (to); be inherited (by): *the estate falls to the eldest son.* **23.** (often foll. by *into, under,* etc.) to be classified or included: *the subject falls into two main areas.* **24.** to issue forth: *a curse fell from her lips.* **25.** (of animals, esp. lambs) to be born. **26.** *Brit. dialect.* to become pregnant. **27.** (*tr.*) *Austral. and dialect.* to fell (trees). **28.** *Cricket.* (of a batsman's wicket) to be taken by the bowling side: *the sixth wicket fell for 96.* **29.** *Archaic.* to begin to do: *fall a-doing; fall to doing.* **30. fall flat.** to fail to achieve a desired effect. **31. fall foul of. a.** *Nautical.* to come into collision with. **b.** to come into conflict with. **32. fall short. a.** to prove inadequate. **b.** (often foll. by *of*) to fail to reach or measure up to (a standard). ~*n.* **33.** an act or instance of falling. **34.** something that falls: *a fall of snow.* **35.** *Chiefly U.S.* autumn. **36.** the distance that something falls: *a hundred-foot fall.* **37.** a sudden drop from an upright position. **38.** (*often pl.*) **a.** a waterfall or cataract. **b.** (*cap. when part of a name*): *Niagara Falls.* **39.** a downward slope or decline. **40.** a decrease in value, number, etc. **41.** a decline in status or importance. **42.** a moral lapse or failing. **43.** a capture or overthrow: *the fall of the city.* **44.** a long false hairpiece; switch. **45.** a piece of loosely hanging material, such as a veil on a hat. **46.** *Machinery, nautical.* the end of a tackle to which power is applied to hoist it. **47.** *Nautical.* one of the lines of a davit for holding, lowering, or raising a boat. **48.** Also called: **pinfall.** *Wrestling.* a scoring move, pinning both shoulders of one's opponent to the floor for a specified period. **49.** *Hunting.* **a.** another word for **deadfall. b.** (*as modifier*): *a fall trap.* **50. a.** the birth of an animal. **b.** the animals produced at a single birth. ~See also **fall about, fall among, fall away, fall back, fall behind, fall down, fall for, fall in, fall off, fall on, fallout, fall over, fall through, fall to.** [Old English *feallan;* related to Old Norse *falla,* Old Saxon, Old High German *fallan* to fall; see FELL[2]]

Fall (fɔːl) *n.* **the.** *Theol.* Adam's sin of disobedience and the state of innate sinfulness ensuing from this for himself and all mankind. See also **original sin.**

Fal·la (*Spanish* ˈfaʎa) *n.* **Ma·nuel de** (maˈnwel ðe). 1876–1946, Spanish composer and pianist, composer of the opera *La Vida Breve* (1905), the ballet *The Three-Cornered Hat* (1919), guitar and piano music, and songs.

fall a·bout *vb.* (*intr., adv.*) to behave in an uncontrolled manner: *we fell about laughing when we saw him.*

fal·la·cious (fəˈleɪʃəs) *adj.* **1.** containing or involving a fallacy; illogical; erroneous. **2.** tending to mislead. **3.** delusive or disappointing: *a fallacious hope.* **—fal·ˈla·cious·ly** *adv.* **—fal·ˈla·cious·ness** *n.*

fal·la·cy (ˈfæləsɪ) *n., pl.* **·cies. 1.** an incorrect or misleading notion or opinion based on inaccurate facts or invalid reasoning. **2.** unsound or invalid reasoning. **3.** the tendency to mislead. **4.** *Logic.* an error in reasoning that renders an argument logically invalid. [C15: from Latin *fallācia,* from *fallax* deceitful, from *fallere* to deceive]

fal·lal (fælˈlæl) *n.* a showy ornament, trinket, or article of dress. [C18: perhaps based on FALBALA] **—fal·ˈlal·er·y** *n.*

fall a·mong *vb.* (*intr., prep.*) to enter the company of (a group of people), esp. by chance: *he fell among thieves.*

fall a·way *vb.* (*intr., adv.*) **1.** (of friendship, etc.) to be withdrawn. **2.** to slope down.

fall back *vb.* (*intr., adv.*) **1.** to recede or retreat. **2.** (foll. by *on* or *upon*) to have recourse (to). ~*n.* **fall-back. 3.** a retreat. **4.** a reserve, esp. money, that can be called upon in need.

fall be·hind *vb.* (*intr., adv.*) **1.** to drop back; fail to keep up. **2.** to be in arrears, as with a payment.

fall down *vb.* (*intr., adv.*) **1.** to drop suddenly or collapse. **2.** (often foll. by *on*) *Informal.* to prove unsuccessful; fail.

fall·en (ˈfɔːlən) *vb.* **1.** the past participle of **fall.** ~*adj.* **2.** having sunk in reputation or honour: *a fallen woman.* **3.** killed in battle with glory: *our fallen heroes.* **4.** defeated.

fall·en arch *n.* collapse of the arch formed by the instep of the foot, resulting in flat feet.

fall·er (ˈfɔːlə) *n.* **1.** any device that falls or operates machinery by falling, as in a spinning machine. **2.** one that falls, esp. a horse that falls at a fence in a steeplechase. **3.** *Austral.* a person who fells trees.

fall·fish (ˈfɔːlˌfɪʃ) *n., pl.* **·fish** *or* **·fish·es.** a large North American freshwater cyprinid fish, *Semotilus corporalis,* resembling the chub.

fall for *vb.* (*intr., prep.*) **1.** to become infatuated with (a person). **2.** to allow oneself to be deceived by (a lie, trick, etc.).

fall guy *n. Informal, chiefly U.S.* a person who is the victim of a confidence trick.

fal·li·ble (ˈfælɪbᵊl) *adj.* **1.** capable of being mistaken; erring. **2.** liable to mislead. [C15: from Medieval Latin *fallibilis,* from Latin *fallere* to deceive] **—ˌfal·li·ˈbil·i·ty** *or* **ˈfal·li·ble·ness** *n.* **—ˈfal·li·bly** *adv.*

fall in *vb.* (*intr., adv.*) **1.** to collapse; no longer act as a support. **2.** to adopt a military formation, esp. as a soldier taking his place in a line. **3.** (of a lease) to expire. **4.** (of land) to come into the owner's possession on the expiry of the lease. **5.** (often foll. by *with*) **a.** to meet and join. **b.** to agree with or support a person, suggestion, etc. **6.** *Austral.* to make a mistake or come to grief.

fall·ing band *n.* a man's large flat collar, often lace-trimmed, worn during the 17th century.

fall·ing sick·ness *or* **e·vil** *n.* a former name (nontechnical) for **epilepsy.**

fall·ing star *n.* an informal name for **meteor.**

fall line *n.* **1.** *Skiing.* the natural downward course between two points on a slope. **2.** the edge of a plateau.

Fall Line *n.* a natural junction, running parallel to the E coast of the U.S., between the hard rocks of the Appalachians and the softer coastal plain, along which rivers form falls and rapids.

fall off *vb.* (*intr.*) **1.** to drop unintentionally to the ground from (a high object, bicycle, etc.), esp. after losing one's balance. **2.** (*adv.*) to diminish in size, intensity, etc.; decline or weaken: *business fell off after Christmas.* **3.** (*adv.*) *Nautical.* to allow or cause a vessel to sail downwind of her former heading.

fall on *vb.* (*intr., prep.*) **1.** Also: **fall upon.** to attack or snatch (an army, booty, etc.). **2. fall flat on one's face.** to fail, esp. in a ridiculous or humiliating manner. **3. fall on one's feet.** to emerge unexpectedly well from a difficult situation.

Fal·lo·pi·an tube (fəˈləʊpɪən) *n.* either of a pair of slender tubes through which ova pass from the ovaries to the uterus in female mammals. See **oviduct.** [C18: named after Gabriello *Fallopio* (1523–62), Italian anatomist who first described the tubes]

fall·out (ˈfɔːlˌaʊt) *n.* **1.** the descent of solid material in the atmosphere onto the earth, esp. of radioactive material following a nuclear explosion. **2.** any solid particles that so descend. ~*vb.* **fall out.** (*intr., adv.*) **3.** *Informal.* to quarrel or disagree. **4.** (*intr.*) to happen or occur. **5.** *Military.* to leave a parade or disciplinary formation.

fall o·ver *vb.* (*intr., adv.*) **1.** to lose one's balance and collapse to the ground. **2.** to fall from an upright position: *the vase fell over.* **3. fall over oneself.** to do everything within one's power: *he fell over himself to be as helpful as possible.*

fal·low[1] (ˈfæləʊ) *adj.* **1.** (of land) left unseeded after being ploughed and harrowed to regain fertility for a crop. **2.** (of an idea, state of mind, etc.) undeveloped or inactive, but potentially useful. ~*n.* **3.** land treated in this way. ~*vb.* **4.** (*tr.*) to leave (land) unseeded after ploughing and harrowing it. [Old English *fealga;* related to Greek *polos* ploughed field] **—ˈfal·low·ness** *n.*

fal·low[2] (ˈfæləʊ) *adj.* of a light yellowish-brown colour. [Old English *fealu;* related to Old Norse *fölr,* Old Saxon, Old High German *falo,* Latin *pallidus* Greek *polios* grey]

fal·low deer *n.* either of two deer, *Dama dama* or *D. mesopotamica,* native to the Mediterranean region and Persia respectively. The antlers are flattened and the summer coat is reddish with white spots.

fall through *vb.* (*intr., adv.*) to miscarry or fail.

fall to *vb.* (*intr.*) **1.** (*adv.*) to begin some activity, as eating, working, or fighting. **2.** (*prep.*) to devolve on (a person): *the task fell to me.* **3. fall to the ground.** (of a plan, theory, etc.) to be rendered invalid, esp. because of lack of necessary information.

Fal·mouth (ˈfælməθ) *n.* a port and resort in SW England, in S Cornwall. Pop.: 17 883 (1971).

false (fɔːls) *adj.* **1.** not in accordance with the truth or facts. **2.** irregular or invalid: *a false argument; a false start.* **3.** untruthful or lying: *a false account.* **4.** not genuine, real, or natural; artificial; fake: *false eyelashes.* **5.** being or intended to be misleading or deceptive: *a false rumour; a false alarm.* **6.** disloyal or treacherous: *a false friend.* **7.** based on mistaken or irrelevant ideas or facts: *false pride; a false hope.* **8.** (*prenominal*) (esp. of plants) superficially resembling the species specified: *false hellebore.* **9.** serving to supplement or replace, often temporarily: *a false keel.* **10.** *Music.* **a.** (of a note, interval, etc.) out of tune. **b.** (of the interval of a perfect fourth or fifth) decreased by a semitone. **c.** (of a cadence) interrupted or imperfect. *~adv.* **11.** in a false or dishonest manner (esp. in the phrase **play (someone) false**). [Old English *fals*, from Latin *falsus*, from *fallere* to deceive] —**'false+ly** *adv.* —**'false+ness** *n.*

False Bay *n.* a bay in SW South Africa, near the Cape of Good Hope.

false bed+ding *n.* another name for **cross bedding.**

false-card ('fɔːlsˌkɑːd) *vb.* (*intr.*) *Bridge.* to play a misleading card, esp. a high loser, in order to deceive an opponent.

false cir+rus *n.* a type of thick cirrus cloud spreading from the top of a cumulonimbus cloud.

false col+ours *pl. n.* **1.** a flag to which one is not entitled, flown esp. in order to deceive: *the ship was sailing under false colours.* **2.** an assumed or misleading name or guise: *to trade under false colours.*

false dawn *n.* zodiacal light appearing just before sunrise.

false fruit *n.* another name for **pseudocarp.**

false+hood ('fɔːlsˌhʊd) *n.* **1.** the quality of being untrue. **2.** an untrue statement; lie. **3.** the act of deceiving or lying.

false im+pris+on+ment *n. Law.* the restraint of a person's liberty without lawful authority.

false keel *n.* an extension to the keel of a vessel either for protecting the keel from damage or for reducing leeway.

false po+si+tion *n.* a situation in which a person is forced to act or seems to be acting against his principles or interests.

false pre+tenc+es *pl. n.* **1.** *Criminal law.* a former name for **deception** (see **obtaining by deception**). **2.** a similar misrepresentation used to obtain anything, such as trust or affection (esp. in the phrase **under false pretences**).

false re+la+tion *n. Music.* a harmonic clash that occurs when a note in one part sounds simultaneously with or immediately before or after its chromatically altered (sharpened or flattened) equivalent appearing in another part. Also called (esp. U.S.): **cross relation.**

false ribs *pl. n.* any of the lower five pairs of ribs in man, attached behind to the thoracic vertebrae but in front not attached directly to the breastbone. See **floating rib.**

false step *n.* **1.** an unwise action. **2.** a stumble; slip.

false teeth *pl. n.* a denture, esp. a removable complete set of artificial teeth for one or both jaws.

fal+set+to (fɔːl'sɛtəʊ) *n., pl.* **+tos.** a form of vocal production used by male singers to extend their range upwards beyond its natural compass by limiting the vibration of the vocal cords. [C18: from Italian, from *falso* FALSE]

false vam+pire *n.* any large insectivorous bat of the family *Megadermatidae*, of Africa, S and SE Asia, and Australia. They eat insects and small vertebrates but do not feed on blood.

false+work ('fɔːlsˌwɜːk) *n.* a framework supporting something under construction.

fal+sies ('fɔːlsɪz) *pl. n. Informal.* pads of soft material, such as foam rubber, worn to exaggerate the size of or simulate the appearance of a woman's breasts.

fal+si+fy ('fɔːlsɪˌfaɪ) *vb.* **+fies, +fy+ing, +fied. 1.** (*tr.*) to make (a report, evidence, accounts, etc.) false or inaccurate by alteration. **2.** to render (the truth or facts) false or inaccurate in order to deceive; misrepresent; distort. **3.** (*tr.*) to prove false; disprove or disappoint. [C15: from Old French *falsifier*, from Late Latin *falsificāre*, from Latin *falsus* FALSE + *facere* to make] —**'fal+si+ˌfi+a+ble** *adj.* —**fal+si+fi+ca+tion** (ˌfɔːlsɪfɪ'keɪʃən) *n.* —**'fal+si+ˌfi+er** *n.*

fal+si+ty ('fɔːlsɪtɪ) *n., pl.* **+ties. 1.** the state of being false or untrue. **2.** something false; a lie or deception.

Fal+staff+ian (fɔːl'stɑːfɪən) *adj.* jovial, plump, and dissolute. [C19: after *Sir John Falstaff*, a character in Shakespeare's play *Henry IV* 1597–98]

Fal+ster ('fɑːlstə) *n.* an island in the Baltic Sea, part of SE Denmark. Chief town: Nykøbing. Pop.: 44 697 (1970). Area: 513 sq. km (198 sq. miles).

falt+boat ('fæltˌbəʊt) *n.* a collapsible boat made of waterproof material stretched over a light framework. [German *Faltboot*, from *falten* to FOLD + *Boot* BOAT]

fal+ter ('fɔːltə) *vb.* **1.** (*intr.*) to be hesitant, weak, or unsure; waver. **2.** (*intr.*) to move unsteadily or hesitantly; stumble. **3.** to utter haltingly or hesitantly; stammer. *~n.* **4.** uncertainty or hesitancy in speech or action. **5.** a quavering or irregular sound. [C14: probably of Scandinavian origin; compare Icelandic *faltrast*] —**'fal+ter+er** *n.* —**'fal+ter+ing+ly** *adv.*

Fa+lun (ˌfɑː'lʌn) *n.* a city in central Sweden: iron and pyrites mines. Pop.: 46 846 (1970).

fam. *abbrev. for:* **1.** familiar. **2.** family.

F.A.M. *abbrev. for* Free and Accepted Masons. See **Freemason.**

Fa+ma+gu+sta (ˌfæmə'gʊstə) *n.* a port in E Cyprus, on **Famagusta Bay:** became one of the richest cities in Christendom in the 14th century. Pop.: 38 960 (1973).

fame (feɪm) *n.* **1.** the state of being widely known or recognized; renown; celebrity. **2.** *Archaic.* rumour or public report. *~vb.* **3.** (*tr.; now usually passive*) to make known or famous; celebrate: *he was famed for his ruthlessness.* [C13: from Latin *fāma* report; related to *fārī* to say] —**'fame+less** *adj.*

fa+mil+i+al (fə'mɪlɪəl) *adj.* **1.** of or relating to the family. **2.** transmitted between individuals of a family: *a familial disease.*

fa+mil+i+ar (fə'mɪlɪə) *adj.* **1.** well-known; easily recognized: *a familiar figure.* **2.** frequent or customary: *a familiar excuse.* **3.** (*postpositive;* foll. by *with*) acquainted. **4.** friendly; informal. **5.** close; intimate. **6.** more intimate than is acceptable; presumptuous. **7.** an archaic word for **familial.** *~n.* **8.** Also called: **familiar spirit.** a supernatural spirit often assuming animal form, supposed to attend and aid a witch, wizard, etc. **9.** a person, attached to the household of the pope or a bishop, who renders service in return for support. **10.** an officer of the Inquisition who arrested accused persons. **11.** a friend or frequent companion. [C14: from Latin *familiāris* domestic, from *familia* FAMILY] —**fa+'mil+i+ar+ly** *adv.* —**fa+'mil+i+ar+ness** *n.*

fa+mil+i+ar+i+ty (fəˌmɪlɪ'ærɪtɪ) *n., pl.* **+ties. 1.** reasonable knowledge or acquaintance, as with a subject or place. **2.** close acquaintanceship or intimacy. **3.** undue intimacy. **4.** (*sometimes pl.*) an instance of unwarranted intimacy.

fa+mil+iar+ize *or* **fa+mil+iar+ise** (fə'mɪljəˌraɪz) *vb.* (*tr.*) **1.** to make (oneself or someone else) familiar, as with a particular subject. **2.** to make (something) generally known or accepted. —**fa+ˌmil+iar+i+'za+tion** *or* **fa+ˌmil+iar+i+'sa+tion** *n.* —**fa+'mil+iar+ˌiz+er** *or* **fa+'mil+iar+ˌis+er** *n.*

Fam+i+list ('fæmɪlɪst) *n.* a member of the Family of Love, a mystical Christian religious sect of the 16th and 17th centuries based upon love. —**'Fam+i+lism** *n.*

fa+mille *French.* (fa'mij) *n.* a type of Chinese porcelain characterized either by a design on a background of yellow (***famille jaune***) or black (***famille noire***) or by a design in which the predominant colour is pink (***famille rose***) or green (***famille verte***). [C19: literally: family]

fam+i+ly ('fæmɪlɪ, 'fæmlɪ) *n., pl.* **+lies. 1. a.** a primary social group consisting of parents and their offspring, the principal function of which is provision for its members. **b.** (*as modifier*): *family quarrels; a family unit.* **2.** one's wife or husband and one's children. **3.** one's children, as distinguished from one's husband or wife. **4.** a group of persons related by blood; a group descended from a common ancestor. Compare **extended family. 5.** all the persons living together in one household. **6.** any group of related things or beings, esp. when scientifically categorized. **7.** *Biology.* any of the taxonomic groups into which an order is divided and which contains one or more genera. *Felidae* (cat family) and *Canidae* (dog family) are two families of the order *Carnivora.* **8.** *Ecology.* a group of organisms of the same species living together in a community. **9.** a group of historically related languages assumed to derive from one original language. **10.** *Chiefly U.S.* an independent local group of the Mafia. **11.** *Maths.* a group of curves or surfaces whose equations differ from a given equation only in the values assigned to one or more constants in each curve: *a family of concentric circles.* **12. in the family way.** *Informal.* pregnant. [C15: from Latin *familia* a household, servants of the house, from *famulus* servant]

fam+i+ly al+low+ance *n.* (in Britain) a former name for **child benefit.**

fam+i+ly Bi+ble *n.* a large Bible used for family worship in which births, marriages, and deaths are recorded.

fam+i+ly cir+cle *n.* **1.** members of a family regarded as a closed group. **2.** *Chiefly U.S.* the cheap seating area in a theatre behind or above the dress circle.

Fam+i+ly Com+pact *n. Canadian.* **1. the.** the ruling oligarchy in Upper Canada in the early 19th century. **2.** (*often not cap.*) any influential clique.

Fam+i+ly Di+vi+sion *n. Brit. law.* a division of the High Court of Justice dealing with divorce, the custody of and rights of access to children, etc.

fam+i+ly doc+tor *n.* See **general practitioner.**

fam+i+ly group+ing *n.* a system, used usually in the infant school, of grouping children of various ages together, esp. for project work. Also called: **vertical grouping.**

fam+i+ly man *n.* a man who is married and has children, esp. one who is devoted to his family.

fam+i+ly name *n.* **1.** a surname, esp. when regarded as representing the family honour. **2.** a first or middle name frequently used in a family, often originally a surname.

fam+i+ly plan+ning *n.* the control of the number of children in a family and of the intervals between them, esp. by the use of contraceptives. See also **birth control.**

fam+i+ly skel+e+ton *n.* a closely guarded family secret.

fam+i+ly tree *n.* a chart showing the genealogical relationships and lines of descent of a family. Also called: **genealogical tree.**

fam+ine ('fæmɪn) *n.* **1.** a severe shortage of food, as through crop failure or overpopulation. **2.** acute shortage of anything. **3.** violent hunger. [C14: from Old French, via Vulgar Latin, from Latin *famēs* hunger]

fam+ish ('fæmɪʃ) *vb.* **1.** (*now usually passive*) to be or make very hungry or weak. **2.** *Archaic.* to die or cause to die from starvation. [C14: from Old French *afamer*, via Vulgar Latin, from Latin *famēs* FAMINE] —**'fam+ish+ment** *n.*

fa+mous ('feɪməs) *adj.* **1.** known to or recognized by many people; renowned. **2.** *Informal.* excellent; splendid. **3.** *Archaic.* of ill repute. [C14: from Latin *fāmōsus;* see FAME] —**'fa+mous+ly** *adv.* —**'fa+mous+ness** *n.*

fam+u+lus ('fæmjʊləs) *n., pl.* **+li** (-ˌlaɪ). (formerly) the attendant of a sorcerer or scholar. [C19: from Latin: servant]

fan[1] (fæn) *n.* **1. a.** any device for creating a current of air by movement of a surface or number of surfaces, esp. a rotating device consisting of a number of blades attached to a central hub. **b.** a machine that rotates such a device. **2.** any of various hand-agitated devices for cooling onself, esp. a collapsible semicircular series of flat segments of paper, ivory, etc. **3.** something shaped like such a fan, such as the tail of certain birds. **4.** *Agriculture.* **a.** a kind of basket formerly used for winnowing grain. **b.** a machine equipped with a fan for winnowing or cleaning grain. *~vb.* **fans, fan+ning, fanned.** (*mainly tr.*) **5.** to cause a current of air, esp. cool air, to blow upon, as by means of a fan: *to fan one's face.* **6.** to agitate or move (air, smoke, etc.) with or as if with a fan. **7.** to make fiercer, more ardent, etc.: *fan one's passion.* **8.** (*also intr.*; often foll. by *out*) to spread out or cause to spread out in the shape of a fan. **9. a.** to fire (an automatic gun) continuously by keeping the trigger depressed. **b.** to fire (a nonautomatic gun) several times by repeatedly chopping back the hammer with the palm. **10.** to winnow (grain) by blowing the chaff away from it. [Old English *fann,* from Latin *vannus*] —'**fan+like** *adj.* —'**fan+ner** *n.*

fan[2] (fæn) *n.* **1.** an ardent admirer of a pop star, film actor, football team, etc. **2.** a devotee of a sport, hobby, etc.

Fan·a·ga+lo ('fænəgələʊ) *or* **Fan·a+ka+lo** *n.* a pidgin language widely used in southern Africa, having English, Afrikaans, and Zulu components. [C20: from Fanagalo *fana ga lo,* literally: do it like this; compare Zulu *fana,* be like, *ka-lo* of this]

fa+nat+ic (fə'nætɪk) *n.* **1.** a person whose enthusiasm or zeal for something is extreme or beyond normal limits. **2.** *Informal.* a person devoted to a particular hobby or pastime; fan: *a jazz fanatic.* ~*adj.* **3.** a variant of **fanatical.** [C16: from Latin *fānāticus* belonging to a temple, hence, inspired by a god, frenzied, from *fānum* temple]

fa+nat·i+cal (fə'nætɪkᵊl) *adj.* surpassing what is normal or accepted in enthusiasm for or belief in something; excessively or unusually dedicated or devoted. —**fa+'nat·i+cal+ly** *adv.*

fa+nat·i+cism (fə'nætɪˌsɪzəm) *n.* wildly excessive or irrational devotion, dedication, or enthusiasm.

fa+nat·i+cize *or* **fa+nat·i+cise** (fə'nætɪˌsaɪz) *vb.* to make or become fanatical.

fan belt *n.* any belt that drives a fan, esp. the belt that drives a cooling fan together with a dynamo or alternator in a car engine.

fan+cied ('fænsɪd) *adj.* **1.** imaginary; unreal. **2.** thought likely to win or succeed: *a fancied runner.*

fan+ci+er ('fænsɪə) *n.* **1.** a person with a special interest in something. **2.** a person who breeds plants or animals, often as a pastime: *a bird fancier.*

fan+ci+ful ('fænsɪful) *adj.* **1.** not based on fact; dubious or imaginary: *fanciful notions.* **2.** made or designed in a curious, intricate, or imaginative way. **3.** indulging in or influenced by fancy; whimsical. —'**fan+ci+ful+ly** *adv.* —'**fan+ci+ful+ness** *n.*

fan+cy ('fænsɪ) *adj.* **+ci+er, +ci+est. 1.** not plain; ornamented or decorative: *a fancy cake; fancy clothes.* **2.** requiring skill to perform; intricate: *a fancy dance routine.* **3.** arising in the imagination; capricious or illusory. **4.** (often used ironically) superior in quality or impressive: *a fancy course in business administration.* **5.** higher than expected: *fancy prices.* **6.** (of a domestic animal) bred for particular qualities. ~*n., pl.* **+cies. 7.** a sudden capricious idea; whim. **8.** a sudden or irrational liking for a person or thing. **9.** the power to conceive and represent decorative and novel imagery, esp. in poetry. Fancy was held by Coleridge to be more casual and superficial than imagination. See **imagination** (sense 4). **10.** an idea or thing produced by this. **11.** a mental image. **12.** taste or judgment, as in art of dress. **13.** Also called: **fantasy, fantasia.** *Music.* a composition for solo lute, keyboard, etc, current during the 16th and 17th centuries. **14. the fancy.** *Archaic.* those who follow a particular sport, esp. prize fighting. ~*vb.* **+cies, +cy+ing, +cied.** (*tr.*) **15.** to picture in the imagination. **16.** to suppose; imagine: *I fancy it will rain.* **17.** (*often used with a negative*) to like: *I don't fancy your chances!* **18.** (*reflexive*) to have a high or ill-founded opinion of oneself: *he fancied himself as a doctor.* **19.** *Informal.* to have a wish for; desire: *she fancied some chocolate.* **20.** *Brit. informal.* to be physically attracted to (another person). **21.** to breed (animals) for particular characteristics. ~*interj.* **22.** Also: **fancy that!** an exclamation of surprise or disbelief. [C15 *fantsy,* shortened from *fantasie;* see FANTASY] —'**fan+ci+ly** *adv.* —'**fan+ci+ness** *n.*

fan+cy dress *n.* **a.** costume worn at masquerades, etc., usually representing a particular role, historical figure, etc. **b.** (*as modifier*): *a fancy-dress ball.*

fan·cy-free *adj.* having no commitments; carefree.

fan+cy goods *pl. n.* small decorative gifts; knickknacks.

fan+cy man *n. Slang.* **1.** a woman's lover. **2.** a pimp.

fan+cy wom+an *n. Slang.* a mistress or prostitute.

fan·cy+work ('fænsɪˌwɜːk) *n.* any ornamental needlework, such as embroidery or crochet.

fan dance *n.* a dance in which large fans are manipulated in front of the body, partially revealing or suggesting nakedness.

fan+dan+gle (fæn'dæŋgᵊl) *n. Informal.* **1.** elaborate ornament. **2.** nonsense. [C19: perhaps from FANDANGO]

fan+dan+go (fæn'dæŋgəʊ) *n., pl.* **+gos. 1.** an old Spanish courtship dance in triple time between a couple who dance closely and provocatively. **2.** a piece of music composed for or in the rhythm of this dance. [C18: from Spanish, of uncertain origin]

fane (feɪn) *n. Archaic or poetic.* a temple or shrine. [C14: from Latin *fānum*]

Fan·fa·ni (*Italian* fan'faːni) *n.* **A·min·to·re** (a'mintore). born 1908, Italian statesman; premier 1954, 1958–59, 1960–63.

fan+fare ('fænfɛə) *n.* **1.** a flourish or short tune played on brass instruments, used as a military signal, at a ceremonial event, etc. **2.** an ostentatious flourish or display. [C17: from French, back formation from *fanfarer* to play a flourish on trumpets; see FANFARONADE]

fan+fa+ro+nade (ˌfænfærə'nɑːd) *n. Rare.* boasting or flaunting behaviour; bluster. [C17: via French from Spanish *fanfaronada,* from *fanfarron* boaster, from Arabic *farfār* garrulous]

fang (fæŋ) *n.* **1.** the long pointed hollow or grooved tooth of a venomous snake through which venom is injected. **2.** any large pointed tooth, esp. the canine or carnassial tooth of a carnivorous mammal. **3.** the root of a tooth. **4.** (*usually pl.*) *Brit. informal.* tooth: *clean your fangs.* [Old English *fang* what is caught, prey; related to Old Norse *fang* a grip, German *Fang* booty] —**fanged** *adj.* —'**fang+less** *adj.* —'**fang+ˌlike** *adj.*

Fang (fæŋ, fɑːŋ) *n.* **1.** (*pl.* **Fangs** *or* **Fang**) a member of a Negroid people of W Africa, living chiefly in the rain forests of Gabon and Rio Muni: noted for their use of iron and copper money and for their sculpture. **2.** the language of this people, belonging to the Bantu group of the Niger-Congo family.

Fan·gi·o (*Spanish* 'faŋxjo) *n.* **Juan Ma·nuel** (xwan ma'nwel). born 1911, Argentinian racing driver who won the World Championship five times between 1951 and 1957.

fan+go ('fæŋgəʊ) *n.* mud from thermal springs in Italy, used in the treatment of rheumatic disease. [from Italian]

fan heat+er *n.* a space heater consisting of an electrically heated element with an electrically driven fan to disperse the heat by forced convection.

fan+ion ('fænjən) *n.* a small flag used by surveyors to mark stations. [C18: from French, from *fanon* maniple, of Germanic origin]

fan+jet ('fænˌdʒɛt) *n.* another name for **turbofan** (senses 1, 2).

fan+kle ('fæŋkᵊl) *vb.* (*tr.*) *Scot. dialect.* to entangle. [from *fank* a coil of rope, from *fang* an obsolete variant of VANG]

fan+light ('fænˌlaɪt) *n.* **1.** a semicircular window over a door or window, often having sash bars like the ribs of a fan. **2.** a small rectangular window over a door. U.S name: **transom. 3.** another name for **skylight.**

fan mail *n.* mail sent to a famous person, such as a pop musician or film star, by admirers.

fan+ny ('fænɪ) *n., pl.* **+nies.** *Slang.* **1.** *Taboo, Brit.* the female pudendum. **2.** *Chiefly U.S.* the buttocks. [C20: perhaps from *Fanny,* pet name from *Frances*]

fan+ny ad+ams *n. Brit. slang.* **1.** (usually preceded by *sweet*) absolutely nothing at all. Often shortened to **f.a. 2.** *Chiefly nautical.* (formerly) tinned meat, esp. mutton. [C19: from the name of a young murder victim whose body was cut up into small pieces. For sense 1: a euphemism for *fuck all*]

fan+on ('fænən) *n. R.C. Church.* **1.** a collar-shaped vestment worn by the pope when celebrating mass. **2.** (formerly) various pieces of embroidered fabric used in the liturgy. [Middle English, of Germanic origin; related to Old High German *fano* cloth]

fan palm *n.* any of various palm trees, such as the talipot and palmetto, that have fan-shaped leaves. Compare **feather palm.**

fan+tail ('fænˌteɪl) *n.* **1.** a breed of domestic pigeon having a large tail that can be opened like a fan. **2.** any Old World flycatcher of the genus *Rhipidura,* of Australia and SE Asia, having a broad fan-shaped tail. **3.** a tail shaped like an outspread fan. **4.** *Architect.* a part or structure having a number of components radiating from a common centre. **5.** a burner that ejects fuel to produce a wide flat flame in a lamp or furnace. **6.** a flat jet of air and coal dust projected into the air stream of a pulverized-coal furnace. **7.** an auxiliary sail on the upper portion of a windmill that turns the mill to face the wind. **8.** *U.S.* a curved part of the deck projecting aft of the sternpost of a ship. —'**fan-ˌtailed** *adj.*

fan-tan *n.* **1.** a Chinese gambling game in which a random number of counters are placed under a bowl and wagers laid on how many will remain after they have been divided by four. **2.** a card game played in sequence, the winner being the first to use up all his cards. [C19: from Chinese (Cantonese) *fan t'an* repeated divisions, from *fan* times + *t'an* division]

fan+ta+si·a (fæn'teɪzɪə, ˌfæntə'zɪə) *n.* **1.** any musical composition of a free or improvisatory nature. **2.** a potpourri of popular tunes woven freely into a loosely bound•composition. **3.** another word for **fancy** (sense 13). [C18: from Italian: fancy; see FANTASY]

fan+ta+size *or* **fan+ta+sise** ('fæntəˌsaɪz) *vb.* **1.** (when *tr.,* takes a clause as object) to conceive extravagant or whimsical ideas, images, etc. **2.** (*intr.*) to conceive pleasant or satisfying mental images.

fan+tasm ('fæntæzəm) *n.* an archaic spelling of **phantasm.** —**fan+'tas+mal** *or* **fan+'tas+mic** *adj.* —**fan+'tas+mal+ly** *or* **fan+'tas+mi+cal+ly** *adv.*

fan+tast ('fæntæst) *n.* a dreamer or visionary. [C16: from German *Phantast,* from Greek *phantastēs* boaster; English word influenced in meaning by FANTASTIC]

fan+tas+tic (fæn'tæstɪk) *adj. also* **fan+tas+ti+cal. 1.** strange, weird, or fanciful in appearance, conception, etc. **2.** created in the mind; illusory. **3.** extravagantly fanciful; unrealistic: *fantastic plans.* **4.** incredible or preposterous; absurd: *a fantastic verdict.* **5.** *Informal.* very large or extreme; great: *a fantastic fortune; he suffered fantastic pain.* **6.** *Informal.* very good; excellent. **7.** of, given to, or characterized by fantasy. **8.** not constant; capricious; fitful: *given to fantastic moods.* ~*n.* **9.** *Archaic.* a person who dresses or behaves eccentrically. [C14 *fantastik* imaginary, via Late Latin from Greek *phantastikos* capable of imagining, from *phantazein* to make visible] —**ˌfan+tas+ti+'cal+i+ty** *or* **fan+'tas+ti+cal+ness** *n.*

fan+tas+ti+cal+ly (fæn'tæstɪklɪ) *adv.* **1.** in a fantastic manner. **2.** *Informal.* (intensifier): *it's fantastically cheap.*

fan+ta+sy *or* **phan+ta+sy** ('fæntəsɪ) *n., pl.* **+sies. 1. a.** imagination unrestricted by reality. **b.** (*as modifier*): *a fantasy world.* **2.** a creation of the imagination, esp. a weird or bizarre one. **3.** *Psychol.* **a.** a series of pleasing mental images, usually serving to fulfil a need not gratified in reality. **b.** the activity of forming such images. **4.** a whimsical or far-fetched notion. **5.** an illusion, hallucination, or phantom. **6.** a highly elaborate imaginative design or creation. **7.** *Music.* another word for **fantasia** (senses 1, 2), **fancy** (sense 13), or (rare) **development** (sense 5). **8. a.** literature having a large fantasy content. **b.** a prose or dramatic composition of this type. ~*vb.* **+sies, +sy+ing, +sied. 9.** a less common word for **fantasize.** [C14 *fantasie,* from Latin *phantasia,* from Greek *phantazein* to make visible]

Fan+ti ('fæntɪ) *n.* **1.** a language of Ghana: one of the two chief dialects of Akan. Compare **Twi. 2.** (*pl.* **+tis** *or* **+ti**) a member of a Negroid people who speak this language, inhabiting the rain forests of Ghana and the Ivory Coast.

Fan·tin-La·tour (*French* fɑ̃tɛ̃ la'tu:r) *n.* **(Ignace) Hen·ri (Joseph Théodore)** (ɑ̃'ri). 1836–1904, French painter, noted for his still-lifes and portrait groups.

fan+toc+ci+ni (ˌfæntə'tʃi:nɪ) *pl. n.* **1.** marionettes. **2.** puppet shows in which they are used. [C18: from Italian: little puppets, plural of *fantoccino,* from *fantoccio* puppet, from *fante* boy, from Latin *infāns* INFANT]

fan+tod ('fæntəd) *n.* **1.** crotchety or faddish behaviour. **2.** (*pl.*) a state of restlessness or unease. [C19: of uncertain origin]

fan+tom ('fæntəm) *n.* an archaic spelling of **phantom.**

fan trac+er·y *n. Architect.* the carved ornamentation on fan vaulting.

fan vault+ing *n. Architect.* vaulting having ribs that radiate like those of a fan and spring from the top of a capital or corbel. Also called: **palm vaulting.**

fan worm *n.* any tube-dwelling polychaete worm of the family *Sabellidae,* having long tentacles that spread into a fan when the worm emerges from its tube.

FAO *abbrev. for* Food and Agriculture Organization (of the United Nations).

f.a.q. *Austral. informal. abbrev. for* fair average quality.

fa+qir (fə'kɪə, 'feikə) *n.* a variant spelling of **fakir.**

far (fɑ:) *adv., adj.* **far+ther** *or* **fur+ther, far+thest** *or* **fur+thest.** *adv.* **1.** at, to, or from a great distance. **2.** at or to a remote time: *far in the future.* **3.** to a considerable degree; very much: *a far better plan.* **4. as far as. a.** to the degree or extent that. **b.** to the distance or place of. **5. by far.** by a considerable margin. **6. far and away.** by a very great margin. **7. far and wide.** over great distances; everywhere. **8. far be it from me.** I would not presume; on no account: *far be it from me to tell you what to do.* **9. far gone. a.** in an advanced state of deterioration. **b.** *Informal.* extremely drunk. **10. few and far between.** infrequent. **11. go far. a.** to be successful; achieve much: *your son will go far.* **b.** to be sufficient or last long: *the wine didn't go far.* **12. go too far.** to exceed reasonable limits. **13. how far?** to what extent, distance, or degree? **14. in so far.** a variant form (esp. Brit.) of **insofar. 15. so far. a.** up to the present moment. **b.** up to a certain point, extent, degree, etc. **16. so far, so good.** an expression of satisfaction with progress made. ~*adj.* (*prenominal*) **17.** remote in space or time: *a far country; in the far past.* **18.** extending a great distance; long. **19.** more distant: *the far end of the room.* **20. a far cry.** very different. **21. far from.** in a degree, state, etc., remote from: *he is far from happy.* [Old English *feorr;* related to Old Frisian *fīr,* Old High German *ferro,* Latin *porro* forwards, Greek *pera* further] —**'far+ness** *n.*

far+ad ('færəd, -æd) *n. Physics.* the derived SI unit of electric capacitance; the capacitance of a capacitor between the plates of which a potential of 1 volt is created by a charge of 1 coulomb. Symbol: F [C19: named after Michael FARADAY]

far·a·day ('færəˌdeɪ) *n.* a quantity of electricity, used in electrochemical calculations, equivalent to unit amount of substance of electrons. It is equal to the product of the Avogadro number and the charge on the electron and has the value 96 487 coulombs per mole. Symbol: *F* [C20: named after Michael FARADAY]

Far·a·day ('færəˌdeɪ) *n.* **Mi·chael.** 1791–1867, English physicist and chemist who discovered electromagnetic induction, leading to the invention of the dynamo. He also carried out research into the principles of electrolysis.

fa+rad+ic (fə'rædɪk) *adj.* of or concerned with an intermittent asymmetric alternating current such as that induced in the secondary winding of an induction coil. [C19: from French *faradique,* from Michael FARADAY]

far·a·dism ('færəˌdɪzəm) *n.* the therapeutic use of faradic currents.

far·a·dize *or* **far·a·dise** ('færəˌdaɪz) *vb.* (*tr.*) to treat (an organ or part) with faradic currents. —ˌ**far·a·di+'za+tion** *or* ˌ**far·a·di+'sa+tion** *n.* —**'far·a+ˌdiz+er** *or* **'far·a+ˌdis+er** *n.*

far+an+dole ('færənˌdəʊl; *French* farɑ̃'dɔl) *n.* **1.** a lively dance in six-eight or four-four time from Provence. **2.** a piece of music composed for or in the rhythm of this dance. [C19: from French, from Provençal *farandoulo,* of uncertain origin; compare Spanish *farándula* itinerant group of actors]

far+a·way ('fɑ:rəˌweɪ) *adj.* **(far a·way** *when postpositive*). **1.** very distant; remote. **2.** dreamy or absent-minded.

farce (fɑ:s) *n.* **1.** a broadly humorous play based on the exploitation of improbable situations. **2.** the genre of comedy represented by works of this kind. **3.** a ludicrous situation or action. **4.** Also: **farcemeat.** another name for **forcemeat.** ~*vb.* (*tr.*) *Obsolete.* **5.** to enliven (a speech, etc.) with jokes. **6.** to stuff (meat, fowl, etc.) with forcemeat. [C14 (in the sense: stuffing): from Old French, from Latin *farcīre* to stuff, interpolate passages (in the mass, in religious plays, etc.)]

far+ceur (*French* far'sœ:r) *n.* **1.** a writer of or performer in farces. **2.** a joker. —**far+'ceuse** *fem. n.*

far+ci (fɑ:'si:) *adj.* (of food) stuffed. [French: stuffed; see FARCE]

far+ci+cal ('fɑ:sɪkᵊl) *adj.* **1.** ludicrous; absurd. **2.** of or relating to farce. —ˌ**far+ci+'cal+i·ty** *or* **'far+ci+cal+ness** *n.* —**'far+ci+cal+ly** *adv.*

far+cy ('fɑ:sɪ) *n., pl.* **+cies.** *Vet. science.* a form of glanders in which lymph vessels near the skin become thickened, with skin lesions and abscess-forming nodules. [C15: from Old French *farcin,* from Late Latin *farcīminum* glanders, from Latin *farcīmen* a sausage, from *farcīre* to stuff]

fard (fɑ:d) *n. Archaic.* paint for the face, esp. white paint. [C15: from Old French *farder* to use facial cosmetics, of Germanic origin]

far+del ('fɑ:dᵊl) *n. Archaic.* a bundle or burden. [C13: from Old French *farde,* ultimately from Arabic *fardah*]

fare (fɛə) *n.* **1.** the sum charged or paid for conveyance in a bus, train, aeroplane, etc. **2.** a paying passenger, esp. when carried by taxi. **3.** a range of food and drink; diet. ~*vb.* (*intr.*) **4.** to get on (as specified); manage: *he fared well.* **5.** (with *it* as a subject) to turn out or happen as specified: *it fared badly with him.* **6.** *Archaic.* to eat: *we fared sumptuously.* **7.** (often foll. by *forth*) *Archaic.* to go or travel. [Old English *faran;* related to Old Norse *fara* to travel, Old High German *faran* to go, Greek *poros* ford] —**'far+er** *n.*

Far East *n.* **the.** the countries of E Asia, including China, Japan, North and South Korea, E Siberia, Indochina, and adjacent islands: sometimes extended to include all territories east of Afghanistan. —**Far East+ern** *adj.*

Fare+ham ('fɛərəm) *n.* a market town in S England, in S Hampshire. Pop.: 80 296 (1971).

fare-thee-well *or* **fare-you-well** *n. Informal.* a state of perfection: *the steak was cooked to a fare-thee-well.*

fare+well (ˌfɛə'wɛl) *sentence substitite.* **1.** goodbye; adieu. ~*n.* **2.** a parting salutation. **3.** an act of departure; leave-taking. **4.** (*modifier*) expressing leave-taking: *a farewell speech.* ~*vb.* (*tr.*) **5.** *Austral.* to honour (a person) at his departure, retirement, etc.

far-fetched *adj.* improbable in nature; unlikely.

far-flung *adj.* **1.** widely distributed. **2.** far distant; remote.

fa+ri+na (fə'ri:nə) *n.* **1.** flour or meal made from any kind of cereal grain. **2.** *Chiefly Brit.* starch, esp. prepared from potato flour. [C18: from Latin *fār* spelt, coarse meal]

far·i+na+ceous (ˌfærɪ'neɪʃəs) *adj.* **1.** consisting or made of starch, such as bread, macaroni, and potatoes. **2.** having a mealy texture or appearance. **3.** containing starch: *farinaceous seeds.*

far·i+nose ('færɪˌnəʊs, -ˌnəʊz) *adj.* **1.** similar to or yielding farina. **2.** *Botany.* covered with very short hairs resembling a whitish mealy dust. —**'far·i+ˌnose+ly** *adv.*

farl *or* **farle** (fɑ:l) *n.* a thin cake of oatmeal, often triangular in shape. [C18: from earlier *fardel* fourth part, from Old English *fēortha* fourth + Middle English *del* part]

farm (fɑ:m) *n.* **1. a.** a tract of land, usually with house and buildings, cultivated as a unit or used to rear livestock. **b.** (*as modifier*): *farm produce.* **c.** (*in combination*): *farmland.* **2.** a unit of land or water devoted to the growing or rearing of some particular type of vegetable, fruit, animal, or fish: *a fish farm.* **3.** an installation for storage. **4.** a district of which one or more taxes are leased. **5.** *History.* **a.** a fixed sum paid by an individual or group for the right of collecting and retaining taxes, rents, etc. **b.** a fixed sum paid regularly by a town, county, etc., in lieu of taxes. **c.** the leasing of a source of revenue to an individual or group. **d.** a fixed tax, rent, etc., paid regularly. ~*vb.* **6.** (*tr.*) **a.** to cultivate (land). **b.** to rear (stock, etc.) on a farm. **7.** (*intr.*) to engage in agricultural work, esp. as a way of life. **8.** (*tr.*) to look after a child for a fixed sum. **9. a.** to collect the moneys due and retain the profits from (a tax district, business, etc.) for a specified period on payment of a sum or sums. **b.** to operate (a franchise) under similar conditions. ~See also **farm out.** [C13: from Old French *ferme* rented land, ultimately from Latin *firmāre* to settle] —**'farm+a·ble** *adj.*

farm+er ('fɑ:mə) *n.* **1.** a person who operates or manages a farm. **2.** a person who obtains the right to collect and retain a tax, rent, etc., or operate a franchise for a specified period on payment of a fee. **3.** a person who looks after a child for a fixed sum.

Far·mer ('fɑ:mə) *n.* **John.** ?1565–1605, English madrigal composer and organist.

farm·er-gen·er·al *n., pl.* **farm·ers-gen·er·al.** (in France before 1789) a member of a group allowed to farm certain taxes. —**'farm·er-'gen·er·al+ˌship** *n.*

farm hand *n.* a person who is hired to work on a farm.

farm+house ('fɑ:mˌhaʊs) *n.* **1.** a house attached to a farm, esp. the dwelling from which the farm is managed. **2.** Also called: **farmhouse loaf.** *Brit.* a large white loaf, baked in a tin, with slightly curved sides and top.

farm+ing ('fɑ:mɪŋ) *n.* **a.** the business, art, or skill of agriculture. **b.** (*as modifier*): *farming methods.*

farm+land ('fɑ:mˌlænd) *n.* land used or suitable for farming.

farm out *vb.* (*tr., adv.*) **1.** to send (work) to be done by another person, firm, etc.; subcontract. **2.** to put (a child, etc.) into the care of a private individual; foster. **3.** to lease to another for a rent or fee the right to operate (a business for profit, land, etc.) or the right to collect (taxes).

farm+stead ('fɑ:mˌstɛd) *n.* a farm or the part of a farm comprising its main buildings together with adjacent grounds.

farm+yard ('fɑ:mˌjɑ:d) *n.* **a.** an area surrounded by or adjacent to farm buildings. **b.** (*as modifier*): *farmyard animals.*

Farn+bor+ough ('fɑ:nbərə, -brə) *n.* a town in S England, in NE Hampshire: military base, with an aeronautical research centre. Pop.: 41 233 (1971).

Far·ne·se (*Italian* far'ne:se) *n.* **1. A·les·san·dro** (ˌales'sandro).

original name of (Pope) **Paul III.** **2.** **A·les·san·dro,** duke of Parma and Piacenza. 1545–92, Italian general, statesman, and diplomat in the service of Philip II of Spain. As governor of the Netherlands (1578–92), he successfully suppressed revolts against Spanish rule.

far+ne·sol ('fɑːnɪˌsɒl) *n.* a colourless aromatic sesquiterpene alcohol found in many essential oils and used in the form of its derivatives in perfumery; 3,7,11-trimethyl-2,6,10-dodecatrienol. Formula: $C_{15}H_{26}O$. [C20: from New Latin (*Acacia*) *farnesiāna;* named after Odoardo *Farnese,* C17 Italian cardinal]

Farn+ham ('fɑːnəm) *n.* a town in S England, in NW Surrey. Pop.: 31 175 (1971).

Far North *n.* **the.** the Arctic and sub-Arctic regions of the world.

far·o ('fɛərəʊ) *n.* a gambling game in which players bet against the dealer on what cards he will turn up. [C18: probably spelling variant of *Pharoah*]

Far·oes ('fɛərəʊz) *n.* a variant spelling of **Faeroes.** —**Far·o+ese** (ˌfɛərəʊ'iːz) *adj., n.*

far-off *adj.* (**far off** *when postpositive*). remote in space or time; distant.

fa+rouche *French.* (fa'ruʃ) *adj.* sullen or remote. [C18: from French, from Old French *faroche,* from Late Latin *forasticus* from without, from Latin *foras* out of doors]

Fa·rouk I *or* **Fa·ruk I** (fə'ruːk) *n.* 1920–65, last king of Egypt (1936–52). He was forced to abdicate (1952).

far-out *Slang.* ~*adj.* (**far out** *when postpositive*) **1.** bizarre or avant-garde. **2.** excellent; wonderful. ~*interj.* **far out. 3.** an expression of amazement or delight.

Far·quhar ('fɑːkwə, -kə) *n.* **George.** 1678–1707, Irish-born dramatist; author of comedies such as *The Recruiting Officer* (1706) and *The Beaux' Stratagem* (1707).

Far+quhar Is+lands ('fɑːkwə, -kə) *n.* an island group in the Indian Ocean: administratively part of the Seychelles.

far+ra+go (fə'rɑːgəʊ) *n., pl.* **+goes.** a hotchpotch. [C17: from Latin: mash for cattle (hence, a mixture), from *fār* spelt] —**far+rag·i·nous** (fə'rædʒɪnəs) *adj.*

far-reach·ing *adj.* extensive in influence, effect, or range.

far+ri+er ('færɪə) *n.* *Chiefly Brit.* **1.** a person who shoes horses. **2.** another name for **veterinary surgeon. 3.** *Military.* a noncommissioned officer who looks after horses. [C16: from Old French *ferrier,* from Latin *ferrārius* smith, from *ferrum* iron]

far+ri·er·y ('færɪərɪ) *n., pl.* **+er·ies.** *Chiefly Brit.* the art, work, or establishment of a farrier.

far+row[1] ('færəʊ) *n.* **1.** a litter of piglets. ~*vb.* **2.** (of a sow) to give birth to (a litter). [Old English *fearh;* related to Old High German *farah* young pig, Latin *porcus* pig, Greek *porkos*]

far+row[2] ('færəʊ) *adj.* (of a cow) not calving in a given year. [C15: from Middle Dutch *verwe-* (unattested) cow that has ceased to bear; compare Old English *fearr* ox]

far-see·ing *adj.* having shrewd judgment; far-sighted.

far-sight·ed *adj.* **1.** possessing prudence and foresight. **2.** *Med.* of, relating to, or suffering from hyperopia. **3.** another word for **long-sighted.** —ˌ**far-'sight·ed+ly** *adv.* —ˌ**far-'sight·ed+ness** *n.*

fart (fɑːt) *Taboo.* ~*n.* **1.** an emission of intestinal gas from the anus, esp. an audible one. **2.** *Slang.* a contemptible person. ~*vb.* (*intr.*) **3.** to expel intestinal gas from the anus; to break wind. **4. fart about** *or* **around.** *Slang.* **a.** to behave foolishly or aimlessly. **b.** to waste time. [Middle English *farten;* related to Old Norse *freta,* Old High German *ferzan* to break wind, Sanskrit *pardatē* he breaks wind]

far+ther ('fɑːðə) *adv.* **1.** to or at a greater distance in space or time. **2.** in addition. ~*adj.* **3.** more distant or remote in space or time. **4.** additional. [C13: see FAR, FURTHER]

Usage. In careful usage, *farther* and *farthest* are preferred when referring to literal distance: *the farthest planet. Further* and *furthest* are regarded as more correct for figurative senses denoting greater or additional amount, time, etc.: *further to my letter. Further* and *furthest* are also preferred for figurative distance.

far·ther+most ('fɑːðəˌməʊst) *adj.* most distant or remote.

far+thest ('fɑːðɪst) *adv.* **1.** to or at the greatest distance in space or time. ~*adj.* **2.** most distant in space or time. **3.** most extended. [C14 *ferthest,* from *ferther* FURTHER]

far+thing ('fɑːðɪŋ) *n.* **1.** a former British bronze coin worth a quarter of an old penny that ceased to be legal tender in 1961. **2.** something of negligible value; jot. [Old English *fēorthing* from *fēortha* FOURTH + -ING[1]]

far+thin+gale ('fɑːðɪŋˌgeɪl) *n.* a hoop or framework worn under skirts, esp. in the Elizabethan period, to shape and spread them. [C16: from French *verdugale,* from Old Spanish *verdugado,* from *verdugo* rod]

fart+lek ('fɑːtlɛk) *n.* *Sport.* another name for **interval training.** [Swedish, literally: speed play]

Fa·ruk I (fə'ruːk) *n.* a variant spelling of **Farouk I.**

F.A.S. *or* **f.a.s.** *abbrev. for* free alongside ship.

fas+ces ('fæsiːz) *pl. n., sing.* **+cis** (-sɪs). **1.** (in ancient Rome) one or more bundles of rods containing an axe with its blade protruding; a symbol of a magistrate's power. **2.** (in modern Italy) such an object used as the symbol of Fascism. [C16: from Latin, plural of *fascis* bundle]

fas+ci·a *or* **fa+ci·a** ('feɪʃɪə) *n., pl.* **+ci·ae** (-ʃɪˌiː). **1.** the flat surface above a shop window. **2.** *Architect.* a flat band or surface, esp. a part of an architrave or cornice. **3.** ('fæʃɪə). fibrous connective tissue occurring in sheets beneath the surface of the skin and between muscles and groups of muscles. **4.** *Biology.* a distinctive band of colour, as on an insect or plant. **5.** *Brit.* a less common name for **dashboard** (sense 1). [C16: from Latin: band: related to *fascis* bundle; see FASCES] —**'fas·ci·al** *or* **'fa·ci·al** *adj.*

fas+ci+ate ('fæʃɪˌeɪt) *or* **fas+ci+at+ed** *adj.* **1.** *Botany.* **a.** (of stems and branches) abnormally flattened due to coalescence. **b.** growing in a bundle. **2.** (of birds, insects, etc.) marked by distinct bands of colour. [C17: probably from New Latin *fasciātus* (unattested) having bands; see FASCIA] —**'fas+ci+ˌate+ly** *adv.*

fas+ci·a+tion (ˌfæʃɪ'eɪʃən) *n.* *Botany.* an abnormal flattening of stems due to failure of the lateral branches to separate from the main stem.

fas+ci+cle ('fæsɪkəl) *n.* **1.** a bundle or cluster of branches, leaves, etc. **2.** Also called: **fasciculus.** *Anatomy.* a small bundle of fibres, esp. nerve fibres. **3.** *Printing.* another name for **fascicule. 4.** any small bundle or cluster. [C15: from Latin *fasciculus* a small bundle, from *fascis* a bundle] —**'fas+ci+cled** *adj.* —**fas+cic·u+lar** (fə'sɪkjʊlə) *or* **fas+cic·u+late** (fə'sɪkjʊˌleɪt, -lɪt) *adj.* —**fas+'cic·u+late+ly** *adv.* —**fas+ˌcic·u+'la+tion** *n.*

fas+ci+cule ('fæsɪˌkjuːl) *n.* one part of a printed work that is published in instalments. Also called: **fascicle, fasciculus.**

fas+ci+cu+lus (fə'sɪkjʊləs) *n., pl.* **+li** (-ˌlaɪ). another name for **fascicle** (sense 2) or **fascicule.**

fas+ci+nate ('fæsɪˌneɪt) *vb.* (*mainly tr.*) **1.** to attract and delight by arousing interest or curiosity: *his stories fascinated me for hours.* **2.** to render motionless, as with a fixed stare or by arousing terror or awe. **3.** *Archaic.* to put under a spell. [C16: from Latin *fascināre,* from *fascinum* a bewitching] —**'fas+ci+ˌnat+ed+ly** *adv.* —ˌ**fas+ci+'na+tion** *n.* —**'fas+ci+na+tive** *adj.*

fas+ci+nat+ing ('fæsɪˌneɪtɪŋ) *adj.* **1.** arousing great interest. **2.** enchanting or alluring: *a fascinating woman.* —**'fas+ci+ˌnat+ing+ly** *adv.*

fas+ci+na+tor ('fæsɪˌneɪtə) *n.* *Rare.* a lace or crocheted head covering for women.

fas+cine (fæ'siːn, fə-) *n.* a bundle of long sticks used in the construction of embankments, roads, fortifications, etc. [C17: from French, from Latin *fascīna;* see FASCES]

fas+cism ('fæʃɪzəm) *n.* (*sometimes cap.*) **1.** any ideology or movement inspired by Italian Fascism, such as German National Socialism; any right-wing nationalist ideology or movement with an authoritarian and hierarchical structure that is fundamentally opposed to democracy and liberalism. **2.** any ideology, movement, programme, tendency, etc., that may be characterized as right-wing, chauvinist, authoritarian, etc. [C20: from Italian *fascismo,* from *fascio* political group, from Latin *fascis* bundle; see FASCES]

Fas+cism ('fæʃɪzəm) *n.* the political movement, doctrine, system, or regime of Benito Mussolini. Fascism encouraged militarism and nationalism, organizing the country along hierarchical authoritarian lines.

fas+cist ('fæʃɪst) (*sometimes cap.*) ~*n.* **1.** an adherent or practitioner of fascism. **2.** any person regarded as having right-wing authoritarian views. ~*adj. also* **fa+scis+tic** (fə'ʃɪstɪk). **3.** characteristic of or relating to fascism. —**fa+'scis+ti+cal+ly** *adv.*

Fas+cist ('fæʃɪst) *n.* **1.** a supporter or member of the Italian Fascist movement. ~*adj.* **2.** of or relating to Italian Fascism.

fash (fæʃ) *Scot.* ~*n.* **1.** worry; trouble; bother. ~*vb.* **2.** to trouble; bother; annoy. [C16: from obsolete French *fascher* to annoy, ultimately from Latin *fastīdium* disgust, aversion]

fash+ion ('fæʃən) *n.* **1. a.** style in clothes, cosmetics, behaviour, etc., esp. the latest or most admired style. **b.** (*as modifier*): *a fashion magazine.* **2. a.** manner of performance; mode; way: *in a striking fashion.* **b.** (*in combination*): *crab-fashion.* **3.** a way of life that revolves around the activities, dress, interests, etc., that are most fashionable. **4.** shape, appearance, or form. **5.** sort; kind; type. **6. after** *or* **in a fashion. a.** in some manner, but not very well: *I mended it, after a fashion.* **b.** of a low order; of a sort: *he is a poet, after a fashion.* **7. after the fashion of.** like; similar to. **8. of fashion.** of high social standing. ~*vb.* (*tr.*) **9.** to give a particular form to. **10.** to make suitable or fitting. **11.** *Obsolete.* to contrive; manage. [C13 *facioun* form, manner, from Old French *faceon,* from Latin *factiō* a making, from *facere* to make] —**'fash+ion+er** *n.*

fash+ion+a+ble ('fæʃənəbəl) *adj.* **1.** conforming to fashion; in vogue. **2.** of, characteristic of, or patronized by people of fashion: *a fashionable café.* **3.** (usually foll. by *with*) patronized (by); popular (with). —**'fash+ion+a+ble+ness** *n.* —**'fash+ion+a+bly** *adv.*

fash+ion house *n.* an establishment in which fashionable clothes are designed, made, and sold.

fash+ion plate *n.* an illustration of the latest fashion in dress.

Fa+sho+da (fə'ʃəʊdə) *n.* a small town in SE Sudan: scene of an incident (1898) that caused a crisis between France and England. Modern name: **Kodok.**

Fass·bin·der (*German* fasbɪndər) *n.* **Rai·ner Wer·ner** ('raɪnər 'vɛrnər). 1946-82, West German film director. His films include *The Bitter Tears of Petra von Kant* (1972), *Fear eats the Soul* (1973), and *Effi Briest* (1974).

fast[1] (fɑːst) *adj.* **1.** acting or moving or capable of acting or moving quickly; swift. **2.** accomplished in or lasting a short time: *fast work; a fast visit.* **3.** (*prenominal*) adapted to or facilitating rapid movement: *the fast lane of a motorway.* **4.** requiring rapidity of action or movement: *a fast sport.* **5.** (of a clock, etc.) indicating a time in advance of the correct time. **6.** given to an active dissipated life. **7.** of or characteristic of such activity: *a fast life.* **8.** not easily moved; firmly fixed; secure. **9.** firmly fastened, secured, or shut. **10.** steadfast; constant (esp. in the phrase **fast friends**). **11.** *Sport.* (of a playing surface, running track, etc.) conducive to rapid speed, as of a ball used on it or of competitors playing or racing on it. **12.** that will not fade or change colour readily: *a fast dye.* **13. a.** proof against fading: *the colour is fast to sunlight.* **b.** (*in combination*): *washfast.* **14.** *Photog.* **a.** requiring a relatively short time of exposure to produce a given density: *a fast film.* **b.** permitting a short exposure time: *a fast shutter.* **15.** *Cricket.* (of a bowler) characteristically delivering the ball rapidly. **16.** *Informal.* glib or unreliable; deceptive: *a fast talker.* **17.** *Archaic.* sound; deep: *a fast sleep.* **18. a fast one.** *Informal.* a deceptive or unscrupulous trick (esp. in the phrase **pull a fast one**). **19. fast worker.** a person who achieves results quickly, esp. in seductions. ~*adv.* **20.** quickly; rapidly. **21.** soundly; deeply: *fast asleep.* **22.** firmly; tightly. **23.** in quick succession. **24.** in advance of the correct time: *my watch is running fast.* **25.** in a reckless or dissipated way. **26. fast by** *or* **beside.** *Archaic.* close or hard by; very near. **27. play fast and loose.** *Informal.* to behave in an insincere or unreliable manner. ~*interj.* **28.** *Archery.* (said by the Field Captain to archers) stop shooting! [Old English *fæst* strong, tight; related to Old High German *festi* firm, Old Norse *fastr*]

fast[2] (fɑːst) *vb.* **1.** (*intr.*) to abstain from eating all or certain foods or meals, esp. as a religious observance. ~*n.* **2.** an act or period of fasting. [Old English *fæstan;* related to Old High German *fastēn* to fast, Gothic *fastan*] —**'fast+er** *n.*

fast+back ('fɑːstˌbæk) *n.* **1.** a car having a back that forms one continuous slope from roof to rear. **2.** *Brit.* a type of pig developed from the landrace or large white and bred for lean meat.

fast-breed·er re+ac+tor *n.* a nuclear reactor that uses little or no moderator and produces more fissionable material than it consumes. See also **breeder reactor, fast reactor.**

fas+ten ('fɑːsᵊn) *vb.* **1.** to make or become fast or secure. **2.** to make or become attached or joined. **3.** to close or become closed by fixing firmly in place, locking, etc. **4.** (*tr.;* foll. by *in* or *up*) to enclose or imprison. **5.** (*tr.;* usually foll. by *on*) to cause (blame, a nickname, etc.) to be attached (to); place (on) or impute (to). **6.** (usually foll. by *on* or *upon*) to direct or be directed in a concentrated way; fix: *he fastened his gaze on the girl.* **7.** (*intr.;* usually foll. by *on*) take firm hold (of). [Old English *fæstnian;* related to Old Norse *fastna* to pledge, Old High German *fastinōn* to make fast; see FAST[1]] —**'fas+ten+er** *n.*

fas+ten+ing ('fɑːsᵊnɪŋ) *n.* something that fastens, such as a clasp or lock.

fas+tid·i·ous (fæ'stɪdɪəs) *adj.* **1.** very critical; hard to please. **2.** excessively particular about details. **3.** exceedingly delicate; easily disgusted. [C15: from Latin *fastīdiōsus* scornful, from *fastīdium* loathing, from *fastus* pride, + *taedium* weariness] —**fas+'tid·i+ous+ly** *adv.* —**fas+'tid·i·ous+ness** *n.*

fas+tig·i+ate (fæ'stɪdʒɪɪt, -ˌeɪt) *or* **fas+tig·i+at+ed** *adj. Biology.* **1.** (of plants) having erect branches, often appearing to form a single column with the stem. **2.** (of parts or organs) united in a tapering group. [C17: from Medieval Latin *fastīgiātus* lofty, from Latin *fastīgium* height]

fast mo+tion *n. Films.* action that appears to have occurred at a faster speed than that at which it was filmed. Compare **slow motion** (sense 1).

fast+ness ('fɑːstnɪs) *n.* **1.** a stronghold; fortress. **2.** the state or quality of being firm or secure. **3.** the ability of a dye to remain permanent and not run or fade. **4.** *Archaic.* swiftness. [Old English *fæstnes;* see FAST[1]]

fast neu+tron *n. Physics.* **a.** a neutron produced by nuclear fission that has lost little energy by collision; a neutron with a kinetic energy in excess of 0.1 MeV. **b.** a neutron with a kinetic energy in excess of 1.5 MeV, the fission threshold of uranium-238.

fast re+ac+tor *n.* a nuclear reactor using little or no moderator, fission being caused by fast neutrons.

fast talk *Slang.* ~*n.* **1.** fervent, deceptive patter. ~*vb.* **fast-talk. 2.** to influence (a person) by means of such patter.

fat (fæt) *n.* **1.** any of a class of naturally occurring soft greasy solids that are esters of glycerol and certain fatty acids. They are present in some plants and in the adipose tissue of animals, forming a reserve energy source, and are used in making soap and paint and in the food industry. See also **oil** (sense 1). **2.** vegetable or animal tissue containing fat. **3.** corpulence, obesity, or plumpness. **4.** the best or richest part of something. **5.** a part in a play that gives an actor a good opportunity to show his talents. **6. chew the fat.** *Slang.* to chat. **7. the fat is in the fire.** an irrevocable action has been taken, esp. one from which dire consequences are expected. **8. the fat of the land.** the best that is obtainable. ~*adj.* **fat+ter, fat+test. 9.** having much or too much flesh or fat. **10.** consisting of or containing fat; greasy: *fat pork.* **11.** profitable; lucrative: *a fat year.* **12.** affording great opportunities: *a fat part in the play.* **13.** fertile or productive: *a fat land.* **14.** thick, broad, or extended: *a fat log of wood.* **15.** having a high content of a particular material or ingredient, such as resin in wood or oil in paint. **16.** plentifully supplied: *a fat larder.* **17.** *Slang.* empty; stupid: *get this into your fat head.* **18.** *Slang.* very little or none; minimal (in phrases such as **a fat chance, a fat lot of good,** etc.). ~*vb.* **fats, fat+ting, fat+ted. 19.** to make or become fat; fatten. [Old English *fǣtt,* past participle of *fǣtan* to cram; related to Old Norse *feita,* Old High German *feizen* to fatten; compare Gothic *fētjan* to adorn] —**'fat+less** *adj.* —**'fat+ˌlike** *adj.* —**'fat+ly** *adv.* —**'fat+ness** *n.* —**'fat+tish** *adj.*

Fa+tah ('fætə) *n.* **Al.** a Palestinian terrorist organization, founded in 1956, with the aim of destroying the state of Israel.

fa+tal ('feɪtᵊl) *adj.* **1.** resulting in or capable of causing death: *a fatal accident.* **2.** bringing ruin; disastrous. **3.** decisively important; fateful. **4.** decreed by fate; destined; inevitable.

fa+tal+ism ('feɪtəˌlɪzəm) *n.* **1.** the philosophical doctrine that all events are predetermined so that man is powerless to alter his destiny. **2.** the acceptance of and submission to this doctrine. **3.** a lack of effort or action in the face of difficulty. —**'fa+tal+ist** *n.* —**ˌfa+tal+'is+tic** *adj.* —**ˌfa+tal+'is+ti+cal+ly** *adv.*

fa+tal+i·ty (fə'tælɪtɪ) *n., pl.* **·ties. 1.** an accident or disaster resulting in death. **2.** a person killed in an accident or disaster. **3.** the power of causing death or disaster; deadliness. **4.** the quality or condition of being fated. **5.** something caused or dictated by fate.

fa+tal+ly ('feɪtəlɪ) *adv.* **1.** resulting in death or disaster. **2.** as decreed by fate; inevitably.

Fa·ta Mor·ga·na *Italian.* ('fata mor'gana) *n.* a mirage, esp. one in the Strait of Messina attributed to the sorcery of Morgan le Fay. [C19: from Italian: MORGAN LE FAY]

fat+back ('fætˌbæk) *n.* the fat, usually salted, from the upper part of a side of pork.

fat cat *n. Slang, chiefly U.S.* a very wealthy or influential person.

fate (feɪt) *n.* **1.** the ultimate agency that predetermines the course of events. **2.** the inevitable fortune that befalls a person or thing; destiny. **3.** the end or final result. **4.** a calamitous or unfavourable outcome or result; death, destruction, or downfall. ~*vb.* **5.** (*tr.; usually passive*) to predetermine; doom: *he was fated to lose the game.* [C14: from Latin *fātum* oracular utterance, from *fārī* to speak]

fat+ed ('feɪtɪd) *adj.* **1.** destined. **2.** doomed to death or destruction.

fate+ful ('feɪtfʊl) *adj.* **1.** having important consequences; decisively important. **2.** bringing death or disaster. **3.** controlled by or as if by fate. **4.** prophetic. —**'fate+ful+ly** *adv.* —**'fate+ful+ness** *n.*

Fates (feɪts) *pl. n.* **1.** *Greek myth.* the three goddesses who control the destinies of the lives of man, which are likened to skeins of thread that they spin, measure out, and at last cut. See **Atropos, Clotho, Lachesis. 2. Norse myth.** another name for the **Norns.**

fath. *abbrev. for* fathom.

fat+head ('fætˌhɛd) *n. Informal.* a stupid person; fool. —**'fat+ˌhead·ed** *adj.*

fat hen *n.* a common plant, *Chenopodium album,* with small green flowers and whitish scales on the stem and leaves: family *Chenopodiaceae* (chenopods). Also called (U.S.): **pigweed, lamb's-quarters.**

fa+ther ('fɑːðə) *n.* **1.** a male parent. **2.** a person who founds a line or family; forefather. **3.** any male acting in a paternal capacity. **4.** (*often cap.*) a respectful term of address for an old man. **5.** a male who originates something: *the father of modern psychology.* **6.** a leader of an association, council, etc.; elder: *a city father.* **7.** *Brit.* the eldest or most senior member in a society, profession, etc.: *father of the House.* **8.** (*often pl.*) a senator or patrician in ancient Rome. **9. the father of.** *Informal.* a very large, severe, etc., example of a specified kind: *the father of a whipping.* ~*vb.* (*tr.*) **10.** to procreate or generate (offspring); beget. **11.** to create, found, originate, etc. **12.** to act as a father to. **13.** to acknowledge oneself as father or originator of. **14.** (foll. by *on* or *upon*) to impose or place without a just reason. [Old English *fæder;* related to Old Norse *fathir,* Old Frisian *feder,* Old High German *fater,* Latin *pater,* Greek *patēr,* Sanskrit *pitr*] —**'fa·ther-ˌlike** *adj.*

Fa+ther ('fɑːðə) *n.* **1.** God, esp. when considered as the first person of the Christian Trinity. **2.** Also called: **Church Father.** any of the writers on Christian doctrine of the pre-Scholastic period. **3.** a title used for Christian priests.

Fa+ther Christ+mas *n.* another name for **Santa Claus.**

fa+ther con+fes+sor *n.* **1.** *Christianity.* a priest who hears confessions and advises on religious or moral matters. **2.** any person to whom one tells private matters.

fa·ther+hood ('fɑːðəˌhʊd) *n.* the state or responsibility of being a father.

fa·ther-in-law *n., pl.* **fa·thers-in-law.** the father of one's wife or husband.

fa·ther+land ('fɑːðəˌlænd) *n.* **1.** a person's native country. **2.** the country of a person's ancestors.

fa+ther lash+er *n.* a large sea scorpion, *Myoxocephalus scorpius,* occurring in British and European coastal waters. Also called: **short-spined sea scorpion.**

fa+ther+less ('fɑːðəlɪs) *adj.* having no father.

fa+ther+ly ('fɑːðəlɪ) *adj.* of, resembling, or suitable to a father. —**'fa+ther+li+ness** *n.*

fa·ther of the chap+el *n.* (in British trade unions in the publishing and printing industries) a shop steward. Abbrev.: F.o.C.

Fa+ther's Day *n.* the third Sunday in June, observed as a day in honour of fathers.

Fa+ther Time *n.* time personified as an old bearded man, usually carrying a scythe and an hourglass.

fath+om ('fæðəm) *n.* **1.** a unit of length equal to six feet, used to measure depths of water. **2.** *Mining.* a unit of volume usually equal to six cubic feet, used in measuring ore bodies. ~*vb.* (*tr.*) **3.** to measure the depth of, esp. with a sounding line; sound. **4.** to penetrate (a mystery, problem, etc.); discover the meaning of. [Old English *fæthm;* related to Old Frisian *fethem* outstretched arms, Old Norse *fathmr* embrace, Old High German *fadum* cubit, Latin *patēre* to gape] —**'fath+om+a·ble** *adj.* —**'fath+om+er** *n.*

Fa·thom·e·ter (fəˈðɒmɪtə) *n. Trademark.* a type of echo sounder used for measuring the depth of water.
fath·om·less (ˈfæðəmlɪs) *adj.* another word for **unfathomable.** —ˈ**fath·om·less·ly** *adv.* —ˈ**fath·om·less·ness** *n.*
fa·tid·ic (feɪˈtɪdɪk) *or* **fa·tid·i·cal** *adj. Rare.* prophetic. [C17: from Latin *fātidicus*, from *fātum* FATE + *dīcere* to say] —**fa·ˈtid·i·cal·ly** *adv.*
fa·tigue (fəˈtiːg) *n.* **1.** physical or mental exhaustion due to exertion. **2.** a tiring activity or effort. **3.** *Physiol.* the temporary inability of an organ or part to respond to a stimulus because of overactivity. **4.** the weakening of a material subjected to alternating stresses, esp. vibrations. **5. a.** any of the mainly domestic duties performed by military personnel, esp. as a punishment. **b.** (*as modifier*): *fatigue duties.* **6.** (*pl.*) special clothing worn by military personnel to carry out such duties. ~*vb.* ·**tigues, ·tigu·ing, ·tigued. 7.** to make or become weary or exhausted. **8.** to weaken or break (a material or part) by inducing fluctuating stresses in it, or (of a metal or part) to become weakened or fail as a result of fluctuating stresses. [C17: from French, from *fatiguer* to tire, from Latin *fatigāre*] —**fa·tig·a·ble** (ˈfætɪgəbᵊl) *adj.* —**fa·ˈtigue·less** *adj.*
Fat·i·ma (ˈfætɪmə) *n.* ?606–632 A.D., daughter of Mohammed; wife of Ali.
Fát·i·ma (*Portuguese* ˈfatimə) *n.* a village in central Portugal: Roman Catholic shrine and pilgrimage centre.
Fat·i·mid (ˈfætɪmɪd) *n.* **1.** a member of the Moslem dynasty, descended from Fatima and Ali, that ruled over North Africa and parts of Egypt and Syria (909–1171). **2.** Also called: **Fat·i·mite** (ˈfætɪˌmaɪt). a descendant of Fatima and Ali.
fat·ling (ˈfætlɪŋ) *n.* a young farm animal fattened for killing.
fat mouse *n.* any nocturnal African mouse of the genus *Steatomys*, of dry regions: eaten as a delicacy by Africans because of their high fat content: family *Muridae.*
Fat·shan (ˈfɑːtˈʃɑːn) *n.* a city in SE China, in W Kwantung province. Pop.: 122 500 (1953). Also called: **Namhoi.**
fat·so (ˈfætsəʊ) *n., pl.* ·**sos** *or* ·**soes.** *Slang.* a fat person: used as an insulting or disparaging term of address.
fat-sol·u·ble *adj.* soluble in nonpolar substances, such as ether, chloroform, and oils. Fat-soluble compounds are often insoluble in water.
fat stock *n.* livestock fattened and ready for market.
fat·ten (ˈfætᵊn) *vb.* **1.** to grow or cause to grow fat or fatter. **2.** (*tr.*) to cause (an animal or fowl) to become fat by feeding it. **3.** (*tr.*) to make fuller or richer. **4.** (*tr.*) to enrich (soil) by adding fertilizing agents. —ˈ**fat·ten·a·ble** *adj.* —ˈ**fat·ten·er** *n.*
fat·ty (ˈfætɪ) *adj.* ·**ti·er,** ·**ti·est. 1.** containing, consisting of, or derived from fat. **2.** having the properties of fat; greasy; oily. **3.** (esp. of tissues, organs, etc.) characterized by the excessive accumulation of fat. ~*n., pl.* ·**ties. 4.** *Informal.* a fat person. —ˈ**fat·ti·ly** *adv.* —ˈ**fat·ti·ness** *n.*
fat·ty ac·id *n.* **1.** any of a class of aliphatic carboxylic acids, such as palmitic acid, stearic acid, and oleic acid, that form part of a lipid molecule. **2.** another name for **carboxylic acid,** esp. a naturally occurring one.
fat·ty de·gen·er·a·tion *n. Pathol.* the abnormal formation of tiny globules of fat within the cytoplasm of a cell.
fat·ty oil *n.* another name for **fixed oil.**
fa·tu·i·ty (fəˈtjuːɪtɪ) *n., pl.* ·**ties. 1.** complacent foolishness; inanity. **2.** a fatuous remark, act, sentiment, etc. **3.** *Archaic.* idiocy. —**fa·ˈtu·i·tous** *adj.*
fat·u·ous (ˈfætjʊəs) *adj.* complacently or inanely foolish. [C17: from Latin *fatuus;* related to *fatiscere* to gape] —ˈ**fat·u·ous·ly** *adv.* —ˈ**fat·u·ous·ness** *n.*
fau·bourg (ˈfəʊbʊəg; *French* foˈbur) *n.* a suburb or quarter, esp. of a French city. [C15: from French *fauxbourg*, perhaps a modification through folk etymology of Old French *forsborc*, from Latin *foris* outside + Old French *borc* BURG]
fau·cal (ˈfɔːkᵊl) *or* **fau·cial** (ˈfɔːʃəl) *adj.* **1.** *Anatomy.* of or relating to the fauces. **2.** *Phonetics.* articulated in that part of the vocal tract between the back of the mouth and the larynx; pharyngeal.
fau·ces (ˈfɔːsiːz) *n., pl.* ·**ces.** *Anatomy.* the area between the cavity of the mouth and the pharynx, including the surrounding tissues. [C16: from Latin: throat]
fau·cet (ˈfɔːsɪt) *n.* the U.S. name for a **tap.**
faugh (fɔː) *interj.* an exclamation of disgust, scorn, etc.
Faulk·ner *or* **Falk·ner** (ˈfɔːknə) *n.* **Wil·liam.** 1897–1962, U.S. novelist and short-story writer. Most of his works portray the problems of the southern U.S., esp. the novels set in the imaginary county of Yoknapatawpha in Mississippi. Other novels include *The Sound and the Fury* (1929) and *Light in August* (1932): Nobel prize for literature 1949.
fault (fɔːlt) *n.* **1.** an imperfection; failing or defect; flaw. **2.** a mistake or error. **3.** an offence; misdeed. **4.** responsibility for a mistake or misdeed; culpability. **5.** *Electronics.* a defect in a circuit, component, or line, such as a short circuit. **6.** *Geology.* a fracture in the earth's crust resulting in the relative displacement and loss of continuity of the rocks on either side of it. **7.** *Tennis, squash, etc.* an invalid serve, such as one that lands outside a prescribed area. **8.** (in showjumping) a device that records foul jumps. **9.** *Hunting.* an instance of the hounds losing the scent. **10.** deficiency; lack; want. **11. at fault. a.** guilty of error; culpable. **b.** perplexed. **c.** (of hounds) having temporarily lost the scent. **12. find fault (with).** to seek out minor imperfections or errors (in); carp (at). **13. to a fault.** excessively. ~*vb.* **14.** *Geology.* to undergo or cause to undergo a fault. **15.** (*tr.*) to find a fault in, criticize, or blame. **16.** (*intr.*) to commit a fault. [C13: from Old French *faute*, from Vulgar Latin *fallita* (unattested), ultimately from Latin *fallere* to fail]
fault-find·ing *n.* **1.** continual and usually trivial criticism. ~*adj.* **2.** given to finding fault. —ˈ**fault-ˌfind·er** *n.*
fault·less (ˈfɔːltlɪs) *adj.* without fault; perfect or blameless. —ˈ**fault·less·ly** *adv.* —ˈ**fault·less·ness** *n.*
fault plane *n. Geology.* the surface of a fault fracture along which the rocks have been displaced.
fault·y (ˈfɔːltɪ) *adj.* **fault·i·er, fault·i·est. 1.** defective or imperfect. **2.** *Archaic.* culpable. —ˈ**fault·i·ly** *adv.* —ˈ**fault·i·ness** *n.*
faun (fɔːn) *n.* (in Roman legend) a rural deity represented as a man with a goat's ears, horns, tail, and hind legs. [C14: back formation from *Faunes* (plural), from Latin FAUNUS] —ˈ**faun·ˌlike** *adj.*
fau·na (ˈfɔːnə) *n., pl.* ·**nas** *or* ·**nae** (-niː). **1.** all the animal life of a given place or time, esp. when distinguished from the plant life (flora). **2.** a descriptive list of such animals. [C18: from New Latin, from Late Latin *Fauna* a goddess, sister of FAUNUS] —ˈ**fau·nal** *adj.* —ˈ**fau·nal·ly** *adv.*
Fau·nus (ˈfɔːnəs) *n.* an ancient Italian deity of pastures and forests, later identified with the Greek Pan.
Fau·ré (ˈfɔːreɪ; *French* foˈre) *n.* **Ga·bri·el (Urbain)** (gabriˈɛl). 1845–1924, French composer and teacher, noted particularly for his song settings of French poems, esp. those of Verlaine, his piano music, and his *Messe de Requiem* (1887).
Faust (faʊst) *or* **Faust·us** (ˈfaʊstəs) *n. German legend.* a magician and alchemist who sells his soul to the devil in exchange for knowledge and power. —ˈ**Faust·i·an** *adj.*
faute de mieux *French.* (fot də ˈmjø; *English* ˈfəʊt də ˈmjɜː) for lack of anything better.
fau·teuil (ˈfəʊtɜːɪ; *French* foˈtœj) *n.* an armchair, the sides of which are not upholstered. [C18: from French, from Old French *faudestuel*, folding chair, of Germanic origin; see FALDSTOOL]
Fauve (*French* foːv) *n.* **1.** one of a group of French painters prominent from 1905, including Matisse, Vlaminck, and Derain, characterized by the use of bright colours and simplified forms. ~*adj.* **2.** (*often not cap.*) of this group or its style. [C20: from French, literally: wild beast, alluding to the violence of colours, etc.] —ˈ**Fauv·ism** *n.* —ˈ**Fauv·ist** *n., adj.*
faux-naïf (*French* fo naˈif) *adj.* **1.** appearing or seeking to appear simple and unsophisticated: *a faux-naïf narration.* ~*n.* **2.** a person who pretends to be naïve. [French: false naïve]
faux pas (fəʊ ˈpɑː; *French* fo ˈpɑ) *n., pl.* **faux pas** (fəʊ ˈpɑːz; *French* fo ˈpɑ). a social blunder or indiscretion. [C17: from French: false step]
fa·ve·o·late (fəˈviːəˌleɪt) *adj.* pitted with cell-like cavities. [C19: from New Latin *faveolus* a little honeycomb, blend of Latin *favus* honeycomb + *alveolus* a small hollow]
fa·vo·ni·an (fəˈvəʊnɪən) *adj.* **1.** of or relating to the west wind. **2.** *Poetic.* favourable. [C17: from Latin *Favōniānus*]
fa·vor·ite son *n. U.S.* a politician popular in his home state but little admired beyond it.
fa·vour *or U.S.* **fa·vor** (ˈfeɪvə) *n.* **1.** an approving attitude; good will. **2.** an act performed out of good will, generosity, or mercy. **3.** prejudice and partiality; favouritism. **4.** a condition of being regarded with approval or good will (esp. in the phrases **in favour, out of favour**). **5.** a token of love, good will, etc. **6.** a small gift or toy given to a guest at a party. **7.** *History.* a badge or ribbon worn or given to indicate loyalty, often bestowed on a knight by a lady. **8.** *Obsolete, chiefly Brit.* a communication, esp. a business letter. **9.** *Archaic.* appearance. **10. find favour with.** to be approved of by someone. **11. in favour of. a.** approving. **b.** to the benefit of. **c.** (of a cheque, etc.) made out to. **d.** in order to show preference for: *I rejected him in favour of George.* ~*vb.* (*tr.*) **12.** to regard with especial kindness or approval. **13.** to treat with partiality or favouritism. **14.** to support; advocate. **15.** to perform a favour for; oblige. **16.** to help; facilitate. **17.** *Informal.* to resemble: *he favours his father.* **18.** to wear habitually: *she favours red.* **19.** to treat gingerly or with tenderness; spare: *a footballer favouring an injured leg.* [C14: from Latin, from *favēre* to protect] —ˈ**fa·vour·er** *or U.S.* ˈ**fa·vor·er** *n.* —ˈ**fa·vour·ing·ly** *or U.S.* ˈ**fa·vor·ing·ly** *adv.*
fa·vour·a·ble *or U.S.* **fa·vor·a·ble** (ˈfeɪvərəbᵊl, ˈfeɪvrə-) *adj.* **1.** encouraging or promising. **2.** giving consent. —ˈ**fa·vour·a·ble·ness** *or U.S.* ˈ**fa·vor·a·ble·ness** *n.* —ˈ**fa·vour·a·bly** *or U.S.* ˈ**fa·vor·a·bly** *adv.*
-fa·voured *adj.* (*in combination*) having an appearance (as specified): *ill-favoured.*
fa·vour·ite *or U.S.* **fa·vor·ite** (ˈfeɪvərɪt, ˈfeɪvrɪt) *adj.* **1.** (*prenominal*) most liked; preferred above all others. ~*n.* **2. a.** a person or thing regarded with especial preference or liking. **b.** (*as modifier*): *a favourite book.* **3.** *Sport.* a competitor thought likely to win. [C16: from Italian *favorito*, from *favorire* to favour, from Latin *favēre*]
fa·vour·it·ism *or U.S.* **fa·vor·it·ism** (ˈfeɪvərɪˌtɪzəm, ˈfeɪvrɪ-) *n.* **1.** the practice of giving special treatment to a person or group. **2.** the state of being treated as a favourite.
fa·vours *or U.S.* **fa·vors** (ˈfeɪvəz) *pl. n.* sexual intimacy, as when consented to by a woman.
Fav·rile glass (fəˈvriːl) *n.* a type of iridescent glass developed by L.C. Tiffany.
fa·vus (ˈfeɪvəs) *n.* an infectious fungal skin disease of man and some domestic animals, characterized by formation of a honeycomb-like mass of roundish dry cup-shaped crusts. [C19: from New Latin, from Latin: honeycomb]

Fawkes (fɔːks) *n.* **Guy.** 1570–1606, English conspirator, executed for his part in the Gunpowder Plot to blow up King James I and the Houses of Parliament (1605). Effigies of him, "guys", are burnt in England on Guy Fawkes Day (Nov. 5).

fawn[1] (fɔːn) *n.* **1.** a young deer of either sex aged under one year. **2. a.** a light greyish-brown colour. **b.** (*as adj.*): *a fawn raincoat.* **3. in fawn.** (of deer) pregnant. ~*vb.* **4.** (*tr.*) (of deer) to bear young. [C14: from Old French *faon,* from Latin *fētus* offspring; see FETUS] —ˈ**fawn**+ˌ**like** *adj.*

fawn[2] (fɔːn) *vb.* (*intr.;* often foll. by *on* or *upon*) **1.** to seek attention and admiration (from) by cringing and flattering. **2.** (of animals, esp. dogs) to try to please by a show of extreme friendliness and fondness (towards). [Old English *fægnian* to be glad, from *fægen* glad; see FAIN] —ˈ**fawn**+**er** *n.* —ˈ**fawn**+**ing**+**ly** *adv.* —ˈ**fawn**+**ing**+**ness** *n.*

fawn lil·y *n.* another name for **dogtooth violet.**

fay[1] (feɪ) *n.* **1.** a fairy or sprite. ~*adj.* **2.** of or resembling a fay. **3.** *Informal.* pretentious or precious. [C14: from Old French *feie,* ultimately from Latin *fātum* FATE]

fay[2] (feɪ) *vb.* to fit or be fitted closely or tightly. [Old English *fēgan* to join; related to Old High German *fuogen,* Latin *pangere* to fasten]

fay[3] (feɪ) *n.* an obsolete word for **faith.** [C13: from Anglo-French *feid;* see FAITH]

Fay+**al** (*Portuguese* fəˈjal) *n.* a variant spelling of **Faial.**

fay+**al**+**ite** (ˈfeɪəˌlaɪt, faɪˈɑːlaɪt) *n.* a rare brown or black mineral of the olivine group, consisting of iron silicate. Formula: Fe_2SiO_4. [C19: named after FAYAL]

Fa+**yum** (faɪˈjuːm) *n.* See **El Faiyum.**

faze (feɪz) *vb.* (*tr.*) *U.S. informal.* to disconcert; worry; disturb. [C19: variant of FEEZE]

F.B.A. *abbrev. for* Fellow of the British Academy.

F.B.I. (in the U.S.) *abbrev. for* Federal Bureau of Investigation; an agency of the Justice Department responsible for investigating violations of Federal laws.

f.c. *Printing. abbrev. for* follow copy.

F.C. (in Britain) *abbrev. for* Football Club.

F.C.A. (in Britain) *abbrev. for* Fellow of the Institute of Chartered Accountants.

F clef *n.* another name for **bass clef.**

F.C.O. *abbrev. for* Foreign and Commonwealth Office.

F.D. *abbrev. for* Fidei Defensor. [Latin: Defender of the Faith]

F dis+**tri**+**bu**+**tion** *n. Statistics.* a continuous distribution obtained from the ratio of two chi-square distributions and used esp. to test the equality of the variances of two normally distributed variances.

Fe *the chemical symbol for* iron. [from New Latin *ferrum*]

feal (fiːl) *adj.* an archaic word for **faithful.** [C16: from Old French *feeil,* from Latin *fidēlis*]

fe+**al**+**ty** (ˈfiːəltɪ) *n., pl.* +**ties.** (in feudal society) the loyalty sworn to one's lord on becoming his vassal. See **homage** (sense 2). [C14: from Old French *fealte,* from Latin *fidēlitās* FIDELITY]

fear (fɪə) *n.* **1.** a feeling of distress, apprehension, or alarm caused by impending danger, pain, etc. **2.** a cause of this feeling. **3.** awe; reverence: *fear of God.* **4.** concern; anxiety. **5.** possibility; chance: *there is no fear of that happening.* **6. for fear of, that** *or* **lest.** to forestall or avoid. **7. no fear.** certainly not. **8. put the fear of God into.** to frighten. ~*vb.* **9.** to be afraid (to do something) or of (a person or thing); dread. **10.** (*tr.*) to revere; respect. **11.** (*tr.; takes a clause as object*) to be sorry: used to lessen the effect of an unpleasant statement: *I fear that you have not won.* **12.** (*intr.;* foll. by *for*) to feel anxiety about something. **13.** an archaic word for **frighten.** [Old English *fǣr;* related to Old High German *fāra,* Old Norse *fār* hostility, Latin *perīculum* danger] —ˈ**fear**+**er** *n.* —ˈ**fear**+**less** *adj.* —ˈ**fear**+**less**+**ly** *adv.* —ˈ**fear**+**less**+**ness** *n.*

fear+**ful** (ˈfɪəfʊl) *adj.* **1.** having fear; afraid. **2.** causing fear; frightening. **3.** *Informal.* very unpleasant or annoying: *a fearful cold.* —ˈ**fear**+**ful**+**ness** *n.*

fear+**ful**+**ly** (ˈfɪəfʊlɪ) *adv.* **1.** in a fearful manner. **2.** (intensifier): *you're fearfully kind.*

fear+**nought** *or* **fear**+**naught** (ˈfɪəˌnɔːt) *n.* **1.** a heavy woollen fabric. **2.** a coat made of such fabric.

fear+**some** (ˈfɪəsəm) *adj.* **1.** frightening. **2.** timorous; afraid. —ˈ**fear**+**some**+**ly** *adv.* —ˈ**fear**+**some**+**ness** *n.*

fea+**si**+**ble** (ˈfiːzəbᵊl) *adj.* **1.** able to be done or put into effect; possible. **2.** likely; probable: *a feasible excuse.* [C15: from Anglo-French *faisible,* from *faire* to do, from Latin *facere*] —ˌ**fea**+**si**+ˈ**bil**+**i**+**ty** *or* ˈ**fea**+**si**+**ble**+**ness** *n.* —ˈ**fea**+**si**+**bly** *adv.*

feast (fiːst) *n.* **1.** a large and sumptuous meal, usually given as an entertainment for several people. **2.** a periodic religious celebration. **3.** something extremely pleasing or sumptuous: *a feast for the eyes.* **4. moveable feast.** a festival of variable date. ~*vb.* **5.** (*intr.*) **a.** to eat a feast. **b.** (usually foll. by *on*) to enjoy the eating (of), as if feasting: *to feast on cakes.* **6.** (*tr.*) to give a feast to. **7.** (*intr.;* foll. by *on*) to take great delight (in): *to feast on beautiful paintings.* **8.** (*tr.*) to regale or delight: *to feast one's mind or one's eyes.* [C13: from Old French *feste,* from Latin *festa,* neuter plural (later assumed to be feminine singular) of *festus* joyful; related to Latin *fānum* temple, *fēriae* festivals] —ˈ**feast**+**er** *n.*

Feast of Ded+**i**+**ca**+**tion** *n. Judaism.* another name for **Hanukkah.**

Feast of Lan+**terns** *n.* **1.** *Hinduism.* a five-day festival usually taking place in October or November, dedicated to the goddess of wealth. **2.** Also called: **Festival of Lanterns.** *Japanese Buddhism.* another name for **Bon.**

Feast of Tab+**er**+**na**+**cles** *n. Judaism.* another name for **Sukkoth.**

Feast of Weeks *n.* **the.** *Judaism.* another name for **Shabuoth.**

feat[1] (fiːt) *n.* a remarkable, skilful, or daring action; exploit; achievement: *feats of strength.* [C14: from Anglo-French *fait,* from Latin *factum* deed; see FACT]

feat[2] (fiːt) *adj. Archaic.* **1.** another word for **skilful. 2.** another word for **neat** or **suitable.** [C14: from Old French *fet,* from Latin *factus* made, from *facere* to make] —ˈ**feat**+**ly** *adv.*

feath+**er** (ˈfɛðə) *n.* **1.** any of the flat light waterproof epidermal structures forming the plumage of birds, each consisting of a hollow shaft having a vane of barbs on either side. They are essential for flight and help maintain body temperature. **2.** something resembling a feather, such as a tuft of hair or grass. **3.** *Archery.* **a.** a bird's feather or artificial substitute fitted to an arrow to direct its flight. **b.** the feathered end of an arrow, opposite the head. **4.** a strip, spline, or tongue of wood fitted into a groove. **5.** the wake created on the surface of the water by the raised periscope of a submarine. **6.** *Rowing.* the position of an oar turned parallel to the water between strokes. Compare **square** (sense 6). **7.** a step in ballroom dancing in which a couple maintain the conventional hold but dance side by side. **8.** condition of spirits; fettle: *in fine feather.* **9.** something of negligible value; jot: *I don't care a feather.* **10. birds of a feather.** people of the same type, character, or interests. **11. feather in one's cap.** a cause for pleasure at one's achievements: *your promotion is a feather in your cap.* **12. in full feather.** in good spirits. **13. white feather.** a sign of cowardice. ~*vb.* **14.** (*tr.*) to fit, cover, or supply with feathers. **15.** *Rowing.* to turn (an oar) parallel to the water during recovery between strokes, principally in order to lessen wind resistance. Compare **square** (sense 38). **16.** (in canoeing) to turn (a paddle) parallel to the direction of the canoe between strokes, while keeping it in the water, principally in order to move silently. **17.** to change the pitch of (an aircraft propeller) so that the chord lines of the blades are in line with the airflow. **18.** (*tr.*) to join (two boards) by means of a tongue-and-groove joint. **19.** (*intr.*) (of a bird) to grow feathers. **20.** (*intr.*) to move or grow like feathers. **21. feather one's nest.** to provide oneself with comforts, esp. financial. [Old English *fether;* related to Old Frisian *fethere,* Old Norse *fjöthr* feather, Old High German *fedara* wing, Greek *petesthai* to fly, Sanskrit *patati* he flies] —ˈ**feath**+**er**+**less** *adj.* —ˈ**feath·er**+ˌ**like** *adj.* —ˈ**feath**+**er·y** *adj.*

feath·er bed *n.* **1.** a mattress filled with feathers or down. ~*vb.* **feath·er**+**bed,** +**beds,** +**bed·ding,** +**bed·ded. 2.** (*tr.*) to pamper; spoil. **3.** *U.S.* to be subject to or engage in feather bedding.

feath·er+**bed·ding** (ˈfɛðəˌbɛdɪŋ) *n.* the practice of limiting production, duplicating work, or overmanning, esp. in accordance with a union contract, in order to prevent redundancies or create jobs.

feath·er+**brain** (ˈfɛðəˌbreɪn) *or* **feath·er**+**head** *n.* a frivolous or forgetful person. —ˈ**feath·er**+ˌ**brained** *or* ˈ**feath·er**+ˌ**head·ed** *adj.*

feath·er+**edge** (ˈfɛðərˌɛdʒ) *n.* a board or plank that tapers to a thin edge at one side. —ˈ**feath·er**+ˌ**edged** *adj.*

feath+**er grass** *n.* a perennial grass, *Stipa pennata,* native to the steppes of Europe and N Asia, cultivated as an ornament for its feathery inflorescence.

feath+**er**+**ing** (ˈfɛðərɪŋ) *n.* the plumage of a bird; feathers.

feath+**er palm** *n.* any of various palm trees, such as the wax palm and date palm, that have pinnate or feather-like leaves. Compare **fan palm.**

feath+**ers** (ˈfɛðəz) *pl. n.* **1.** the plumage of a bird. **2.** the long hair on the legs or tail of certain horses and dogs. **3.** *Informal.* dress; attire: *her best feathers.*

feath+**er star** *n.* any free-swimming crinoid echinoderm of the genus *Antedon* and related genera, living on muddy sea bottoms and having ten feathery arms radiating from a small central disc.

feath·er+**stitch** (ˈfɛðəˌstɪtʃ) *n.* **1.** a zigzag embroidery stitch. ~*vb.* **2.** to decorate (cloth) with featherstitch.

feath·er-veined *adj.* (of a leaf) having a network of veins branching from the midrib to the margin.

feath·er+**weight** (ˈfɛðəˌweɪt) *n.* **1. a.** something very light or of little importance. **b.** (*as modifier*): *featherweight considerations.* **2. a.** a professional boxer weighing 118–126 pounds (53.5–57 kg). **b.** an amateur boxer weighing 54–57 kg (119–126 pounds). **c.** (*as modifier*): *the featherweight challenger.* **3.** a wrestler in a similar weight category (usually 126–139 pounds (57–63 kg)).

feat+**ly** (ˈfiːtlɪ) *adv. Archaic.* **1.** neatly. **2.** fitly. —ˈ**feat**+**li**+**ness** *n.*

fea+**ture** (ˈfiːtʃə) *n.* **1.** any one of the parts of the face, such as the nose, chin, or mouth. **2.** a prominent or distinctive part or aspect, as of a landscape, building, book, etc. **3.** the principal film in a programme at a cinema. **4.** an item or article appearing at intervals in a newspaper, magazine, etc.: *a gardening feature.* **5.** Also called: **feature story.** a prominent story in a newspaper, etc.: *a feature on prison reform.* **6.** a programme given special prominence on radio or television as indicated by attendant publicity. **7.** an article offered for sale as a special attraction, as in a large retail establishment. **8.** *Archaic.* general form or make-up. ~*vb.* **9.** (*tr.*) to have as a feature or make a feature of. **10.** to give prominence to (an actor, famous event, etc.) in a film or (of an actor, etc.) to have prominence in a film. **11.** (*tr.*) to draw the main features or parts of. **12.** (*tr.*) *U.S. informal.* to imagine; consider: *I can't feature that happening.* **13.** (*tr.*) *Informal.* to resemble in looks. **14.** (*intr.;*

often foll. by *with*) *Slang.* to have sexual intercourse (with). [C14: from Anglo-French *feture,* from Latin *factūra* a making, from *facere* to make]

-fea·tured *adj.* (*in combination*) having features as specified: *heavy-featured.*

fea·ture-length *adj.* (of a film or programme) similar in extent to a feature although not classed as such.

fea+ture+less ('fi:tʃəlɪs) *adj.* without distinctive points or qualities; undistinguished. —'**fea+ture+less+ness** *n.*

feaze[1] (fi:z) *vb. Nautical.* to make or become unravelled or frayed. [C16: perhaps from obsolete Dutch *vese* fringe, from Middle Dutch *vese, veze* fringe; related to Old English *fæs*]

feaze[2] (fi:z) *vb., n.* a variant of **feeze** or **faze.**

Feb. *abbrev. for* February.

feb·ri- *combining form.* indicating fever: *febrifuge.* [from Latin *febris* fever]

fe+bric+i·ty (fɪ'brɪsɪtɪ) *n. Rare.* the condition of having a fever. [C19: from Medieval Latin *febricitās,* from Latin *febris* fever]

feb+ri+fa+cient (ˌfɛbrɪ'feɪʃənt) *adj.* **1.** producing fever. ~*n.* **2.** something that produces fever.

fe+brif+ic (fɪ'brɪfɪk) *or* **fe+brif+er+ous** *adj.* causing or having a fever.

feb+ri+fuge ('fɛbrɪˌfju:dʒ) *n.* **1.** any drug or agent for reducing fever. ~*adj.* **2.** serving to reduce fever. [C17: from Medieval Latin *febrifugia* feverfew; see FEBRI-, -FUGE] —**fe+brif·u+gal** (fɪ'brɪfjʊgᵊl, ˌfɛbrɪ'fju:gᵊl) *adj.*

fe+brile ('fi:braɪl) *adj.* of or relating to fever; feverish. [C17: from medical Latin *febrīlis,* from Latin *febris* fever] —**fe+bril+i·ty** (fɪ'brɪlɪtɪ) *n.*

Feb+ru+ar·y ('fɛbrʊərɪ) *n., pl.* **+ar·ies.** the second month of the year, consisting of 28 or (in a leap year) 29 days. [C13: from Latin *Februārius mēnsis* month of expiation, from *februa* Roman festival of purification held on February 15, from plural of *februum* a purgation]

Feb+ru+ar·y Rev·o+lu+tion *n.* another name for the **Russian Revolution** (sense 1).

fec. *abbrev. for* fecit.

fe+cal ('fi:kᵊl) *adj.* the usual U.S. spelling of **faecal.**

fe+ces ('fi:si:z) *pl. n.* the usual U.S. spelling of **faeces.**

Fech·ner (*German* 'fɛçnər) *n.* **Gus·tav The·o·dor** ('gʊstaf 'te:oˌdo:r). 1801–87, German physicist, philosopher, and psychologist, noted particularly for his work on the relationship between physiology and psychology, *Elemente der Psychophysik* (1860).

fe+cit *Latin.* ('feɪkɪt) (he or she) made it: used formerly on works of art next to the artist's name.

feck (fɛk) *n. Scot. obsolete.* **a.** worth; value. **b.** amount; quantity. **c.** the greater part; the majority. [C15 (Scottish dialect) *fek,* short for EFFECT]

feck+less ('fɛklɪs) *adj.* feeble; weak; ineffectual. [C16: from obsolete *feck* value, effect + -LESS] —'**feck+less+ly** *adv.* —'**feck+less+ness** *n.*

fec·u+la ('fɛkjʊlə) *n., pl.* **+lae** (-ˌli:). **1.** starch obtained by washing the crushed parts of plants, such as the potato. **2.** faecal material, esp. of insects. [C17: from Latin: burnt tartar, appearing as a crust in wine, from *faex* sediment]

fec·u+lent ('fɛkjʊlənt) *adj.* **1.** filthy, scummy, muddy, or foul. **2.** of the nature of or containing waste matter. [C15: from Latin *faeculentus;* see FAECES] —'**fec·u+lence** *n.*

fe+cund ('fi:kənd, 'fɛk-) *adj.* **1.** greatly productive; fertile. **2.** intellectually productive; prolific. [C14: from Latin *fēcundus;* related to Latin *fētus* offspring]

fe+cun+date ('fi:kənˌdeɪt, 'fɛk-) *vb.* (*tr.*) **1.** to make fruitful. **2.** to fertilize; impregnate. [C17: from Latin *fēcundāre* to fertilize] —ˌ**fe+cun+'da+tion** *n.* —'**fe+cun+ˌda+tor** *n.* —**fe+cun+da+to+ry** (fɪ'kʌndətərɪ, -trɪ) *adj.*

fe+cun+di·ty (fɪ'kʌndɪtɪ) *n.* **1.** fertility; fruitfulness. **2.** intellectual fruitfulness; creativity.

fed[1] (fɛd) *vb.* **1.** the past tense or past participle of **feed. 2. fed to death** *or* **fed (up) to the (back) teeth.** *Informal.* bored or annoyed.

fed[2] (fɛd) *n. U.S. slang.* an agent of the F.B.I.

Fed. *or* **fed.** *abbrev. for:* **1.** Federal. **2.** Federation. **3.** Federated.

fe+da+yee (fə'dɑ:ji:) *n., pl.* **+yeen** (-ji:n). (*sometimes cap.*) (in Arab states) a commando, esp. one fighting against Israel. [from Arabic *fidā'i* one who risks his life in a cause, from *fidā'* redemption]

fed+er+al ('fɛdərəl) *adj.* **1.** of or relating to a form of government or a country in which power is divided between one central and several regional governments. **2.** of or relating to a treaty between provinces, states, etc., that establishes a political unit in which power is so divided. **3.** of or relating to the central government of a federation. **4.** of or relating to any union or association of parties or groups that retain some autonomy. ~*n.* **5.** a supporter of federal union or federation. [C17: from Latin *foedus* league] —'**fed+er+al+ly** *adv.*

Fed+er+al ('fɛdərəl) *adj.* **1. a.** of or relating to the Federalist party or Federalism. **b.** characteristic of or supporting the Union government during the American Civil War. ~*n.* **2. a.** a supporter of the Union government during the American Civil War. **b.** a Federalist.

Fed+er+al Bu+reau of In+ves+ti+ga+tion *n.* See **F.B.I.**

fed+er+al dis+trict *or* **ter+ri+to+ry** *n.* an area used as the seat of central government in a federal system.

fed+er+al+ism ('fɛdərəˌlɪzəm) *n.* **1.** the principle or a system of federal union. **2.** advocacy of federal union. —'**fed+er+al+ist** *n., adj.* —ˌ**fed+er+al+'is+tic** *adj.*

Fed+er+al+ism ('fɛdərəˌlɪzəm) *n. U.S. history.* the principles and policies of the Federalist party.

Fed+er+al+ist ('fɛdərəlɪst) *U.S. history.* ~*n.* **1.** a supporter or member of the Federalist party. ~*adj.* also **Fed+er+al+is+tic. 2.** characteristic of the Federalists.

Fed+er+al+ist Par+ty *or* **Fed+er+al Par+ty** *n.* the American political party founded in 1787 and led initially by Alexander Hamilton. It took an active part in the shaping of the U.S. Constitution and thereafter favoured strong centralized government and business interests.

fed+er+al+ize *or* **fed+er+al+ise** ('fɛdərəˌlaɪz) *vb.* (*tr.*) **1.** to unite in a federation or federal union; federate. **2.** to subject to federal control. —ˌ**fed+er+al·i+'za+tion** *or* ˌ**fed+er+al·i+'sa+tion** *n.*

Fed+er+al Re+pub+lic of Ger+ma+ny *n.* the official name of **West Germany.**

Fed+er+al Re+serve note *n.* a bank note issued by the Federal Reserve Banks and now serving as the prevailing paper currency in circulation in the U.S.

Fed+er+al Re+serve Sys+tem *n.* (in the U.S.) a banking system consisting of twelve **Federal Reserve Districts,** each containing member banks regulated and served by a **Federal Reserve Bank.** It operates under the supervision of the **Federal Reserve Board** and performs functions similar to those of the Bank of England.

fed+er+ate *vb.* ('fɛdəˌreɪt). **1.** to unite or cause to unite in a federal union. ~*adj.* ('fɛdərɪt). **2.** federal; federated. —'**fed+er·a+tive** *adj.*

Fed+er+at+ed Ma+lay States *n.* See **Malay States.**

fed+er·a+tion (ˌfɛdə'reɪʃən) *n.* **1.** the act of federating. **2.** the union of several provinces, states, etc., to form a federal union. **3.** a political unit formed in such a way. **4.** any league, alliance, or confederacy. **5.** a union of several parties, groups, etc. **6.** any association or union for common action.

Fed+er+a+tion of Rho+de·sia and Ny+as+a+land *n.* a federation (1953–63) of Northern Rhodesia, Southern Rhodesia, and Nyasaland.

fe+do+ra (fɪ'dɔ:rə) *n.* a soft felt or velvet medium-brimmed hat, usually with a band. [C19: allegedly named after *Fédora* (1882), play by Victorien Sardou (1831–1908)]

fed up *adj.* (*usually postpositive*) annoyed or bored: *I'm fed up with your conduct.*

fee (fi:) *n.* **1.** a payment asked by professional people or public servants for their services: *a doctor's fee; school fees.* **2.** a charge made for a privilege: *an entrance fee.* **3.** *Property law.* **a.** an interest in land capable of being inherited. See **fee simple, fee tail. b.** the land held in fee. **4.** (in feudal Europe) the land granted by a lord to his vassal. **5.** an obsolete word for a **gratuity. 6. in fee. a.** *Law.* (of land) in absolute ownership. **b.** *Archaic.* in complete subjection. ~*vb.* **fees, fee+ing, feed. 7.** *Rare.* to give a fee to. **8.** *Chiefly Scot.* to hire for a fee. [C14: from Old French *fie,* of Germanic origin; see FIEF] —'**fee+less** *adj.*

fee+ble ('fi:bᵊl) *adj.* **1.** lacking in physical or mental strength; frail; weak. **2.** inadequate; unconvincing: *feeble excuses.* **3.** easily influenced or indecisive. [C12: from Old French *feble, fleible,* from Latin *flēbilis* to be lamented, from *flēre* to weep] —'**fee+ble+ness** *n.* —'**fee+bly** *adv.*

fee·ble-mind·ed *adj.* **1.** lacking in intelligence; stupid. **2.** mentally defective. **3.** lacking decision; irresolute. —ˌ**fee·ble-'mind·ed+ly** *adv.* —ˌ**fee·ble-'mind·ed·ness** *n.*

feed (fi:d) *vb.* **feeds, feed+ing, fed.** (*mainly tr.*) **1.** to give food to: *to feed the cat.* **2.** to give as food: *to feed meat to the cat.* **3.** (*intr.*) to eat food: *the horses feed at noon.* **4.** to provide food for: *these supplies can feed 10 million people.* **5.** to provide what is necessary for the existence or development of: *to feed one's imagination.* **6.** to gratify; satisfy: *to feed one's eyes on a beautiful sight.* **7.** (*also intr.*) to supply (a machine, furnace, etc.) with (the necessary materials or fuel) for its operation, or (of such materials) to flow or move forwards into a machine, etc. **8.** to use (land) as grazing. **9.** *Theatre, informal.* to cue (an actor, esp. a comedian) with lines or actions. **10.** *Sport.* to pass a ball to (a teammate). **11.** *Electronics.* to introduce (electrical energy) into a circuit, esp. by means of a feeder. **12.** (*also intr.;* foll. by *on* or *upon*) to eat or cause to eat. ~*n.* **13.** the act or an instance of feeding. **14.** food, esp. that of animals or babies. **15.** the process of supplying a machine or furnace with a material or fuel. **16.** the quantity of material or fuel so supplied. **17.** the rate of advance of a cutting tool in a lathe, drill, etc. **18.** a mechanism that supplies material or fuel or controls the rate of advance of a cutting tool. **19.** *Theatre, informal.* a performer, esp. a straight man, who provides cues. **20.** an informal word for **meal**[1]. [Old English *fēdan;* related to Old Norse *fœtha* to feed, Old High German *fuotan,* Gothic *fōthjan;* see FOOD, FODDER] —'**feed+a·ble** *adj.*

feed+back ('fi:dˌbæk) *n.* **1. a.** the return of part of the output of an electronic circuit, device, or mechanical system to its input, so modifying its characteristics. In **negative feedback** a rise in output energy reduces the input energy; in **positive feedback** an increase in output energy reinforces the input energy. **b.** that part of the output signal fed back into the input. **2.** the return of part of the sound output by a loudspeaker to the microphone, esp. in a public-address system, so that a high-pitched whistle is produced. **3.** the whistling noise so produced. **4. a.** the effect of a product or action in a cyclic biological reaction on another stage in the same reaction. **b.** the substance or reaction causing such an effect, such as the release of a hormone in a biochemical pathway. **5.** information in response to an enquiry, experiment, etc.: *there was little feedback from our questionnaire.* ~*vb.* **feed back.** (*adv.*) **6.** (*tr.*) to return (part of the output of a system) to its input. **7.** to offer or suggest (information, ideas, etc.) in reaction to an enquiry, experiment, etc.

feed·bag ('fiːdˌbæg) *n.* **1.** any bag in which feed for livestock is sacked. **2.** the usual U.S. name for **nosebag.**

feed·er ('fiːdə) *n.* **1.** a person or thing that feeds or is fed. **2.** a child's feeding bottle or bib. **3.** *Agriculture, chiefly U.S.* a head of livestock being fattened for slaughter. **4.** a person or device that feeds the working material into a system or machine. **5.** a tributary channel. **6. a.** a road, service, etc., that links secondary areas to the main traffic network. **b.** (*as modifier*): *a feeder bus.* **7. a.** a transmission line connecting an aerial to a transmitter or receiver. **b.** a power line for transmitting electrical power from a generating station to a distribution network.

feed·ing bot·tle *n.* a bottle fitted with a rubber teat from which infants or young animals suck liquids. Also called: **nursing bottle.**

feed·lot ('fiːdˌlɒt) *n.* an area or building where livestock are fattened rapidly for market.

feel (fiːl) *vb.* **feels, feel·ing, felt. 1.** to perceive (something) by touching. **2.** to have a physical or emotional sensation of (something): *to feel heat; to feel anger.* **3.** (*tr.*) to examine (something) by touch. **4.** (*tr.*) to find (one's way) by testing or cautious exploration. **5.** (*copula*) to seem or appear in respect of the sensation given: *I feel tired; it feels warm.* **6.** to have an indistinct, esp. emotional conviction; sense (esp. in the phrase **feel in one's bones**). **7.** (*intr.*; foll. by *for*) to show sympathy or compassion (towards): *I feel for you in your sorrow.* **8.** (*tr.*) *Slang.* to pass one's hands over the sexual organs of. **9. feel like.** to have an inclination (for something or doing something): *I don't feel like going to the pictures.* **10. feel (quite) oneself.** to be fit and sure of oneself. **11. feel up to.** (*usually used with a negative or in a question*) to be fit enough for (something or doing something): *I don't feel up to going out tonight.* ~*n.* **12.** the act or an instance of feeling, esp. by touching. **13.** the quality of or an impression from something perceived through feeling: *the house has a homely feel about it.* **14.** the sense of touch: *the fabric is rough to the feel.* [Old English *fēlan;* related to Old High German *fuolen,* Old Norse *fālma* to grope, Latin *palma* PALM[1]]

Usage. The verbs *feel, look,* and *smell* can be followed by an adverb or an adjective according to the sense in which they are used. Where a quality of the subject is involved, an adjective is used: *I feel sick; he looks strong; this medicine smells bad.* For other senses an adverb would be used: *she feels strongly about that; I must look closely at his record; this animal smells inefficiently although its sight is well developed.*

feel·er ('fiːlə) *n.* **1.** a person or thing that feels. **2.** an organ in certain animals, such as an antenna or tentacle, that is sensitive to touch. **3.** a remark designed to probe the reactions or intentions of other people.

feel·er gauge *n.* a thin metal strip of known thickness used to measure a narrow gap or to set a gap between two parts.

feel·ing ('fiːlɪŋ) *n.* **1.** the sense of touch. **2. a.** the ability to experience physical sensations, such as heat, pain, etc. **b.** the sensation so experienced. **3.** a state of mind. **4.** a physical or mental impression: *a feeling of warmth.* **5.** fondness; sympathy: *to have a great deal of feeling for someone.* **6.** an ability to feel deeply: *a person of feeling.* **7.** a sentiment: *a feeling that the project is feasible.* **8.** an impression or mood; atmosphere: *the feeling of a foreign city.* **9.** an emotional disturbance, esp. anger or dislike: *a lot of bad feeling about the increase in taxes.* **10.** intuitive appreciation and understanding: *a feeling for words.* **11.** sensibility in the performance of something. **12.** (*pl.*) emotional or moral sensitivity, as in relation to principles or personal dignity (esp. in the phrase **hurt** or **injure the feelings of**). ~*adj.* **13.** sentient; sensitive. **14.** expressing or containing emotion. **15.** warm-hearted; sympathetic. —**'feel·ing·ly** *adv.*

fee sim·ple *n. Property law.* an absolute interest in land over which the holder has complete freedom of disposition during his life. Compare **fee tail.** [C15: from Anglo-French: fee (or fief) simple]

feet (fiːt) *n.* **1.** the plural of **foot. 2. at (someone's) feet.** as someone's disciple. **3. be run** *or* **rushed off one's feet.** to be very busy. **4. carry** *or* **sweep off one's feet.** to fill with enthusiasm. **5. feet of clay.** a weakness that is not widely known. **6. get one's feet wet.** to begin to participate in something. **7. have (***or* **keep) one's feet on the ground.** to be practical and reliable. **8. on one's** *or* **its feet. a.** standing up. **b.** in good health. **c.** (of a business, company, etc.) thriving. **9. put one's feet up.** to rest. **10. to stand on one's own feet.** to be independent. —**'feet·less** *adj.*

fee tail *n. Property law.* **a.** a freehold interest in land restricted to a particular line of heirs. **b.** an estate in land subject to such restriction. Compare **fee simple.** [C15: from Anglo-French *fee tailé* fee (or fief) determined, from *taillier* to cut]

feeze *or* **feaze** (fiːz) *Dialect.* ~*vb.* **1.** (*tr.*) to beat. **2.** to drive off. **3.** *Chiefly U.S.* to disconcert; worry. ~*n.* **4.** a rush. **5.** *Chiefly U.S.* a state of agitation. [Old English *fēsian*]

feign (feɪn) *vb.* **1.** to put on a show of (a quality or emotion); pretend: *to feign innocence.* **2.** (*tr.*) to make up; invent: *to feign an excuse.* **3.** (*tr.*) to copy; imitate: *to feign someone's laugh.* **4.** (*tr.*) *Archaic.* to portray. [C13: from Old French *feindre* to pretend, from Latin *fingere* to form, shape, invent] —**'feign·er** *n.* —**'feign·ing·ly** *adv.*

Fein·ing·er ('faɪnɪŋə) *n.* **Ly·o·nel.** 1871–1956, U.S. artist, who worked at the Bauhaus, noted for his use of superimposed translucent planes of colour.

feint[1] (feɪnt) *n.* **1.** a mock attack or movement designed to distract an adversary, as in a military manoeuvre or in boxing, fencing, etc. **2.** a misleading action or appearance. ~*vb.* **3.** (*intr.*) to make a feint. [C17: from French *feinte,* from *feint* pretended, from Old French *feindre* to FEIGN]

feint[2] (feɪnt) *Printing.* ~*n.* the narrowest rule used in the production of ruled paper. [C19: variant of FAINT]

feints *or* **faints** (feɪnts) *pl. n.* the leavings of the second distillation of Scotch malt whisky.

Fei·sal ('faɪsᵊl) *n.* a variant spelling of **Faisal.**

feist·y ('faɪstɪ) *adj.* **feist·i·er, feist·i·est.** *U.S., chiefly southern.* **1.** frisky. **2.** irritable. [C19: from dialect *feist, fist* small dog; related to Old English *fisting* breaking wind]

fel·a·fel (fɛl'ɑːfəl) *n.* bread stuffed with spiced vegetables. [C20: from Arabic *felāfil*]

feld·sher, feld·scher, *or* **feld·schar** ('fɛldʃə) *n.* (in Russia) a medical doctor's assistant. [C19: Russian, from German *Feldscher* a field surgeon, from *Feld* field + *Scherer,* surgeon, from *scheren* to shear]

feld·spar ('fɛldˌspɑː, 'fɛlˌspɑː) *or* **fel·spar** *n.* any of a group of hard rock-forming minerals consisting of aluminium silicates of potassium, sodium, calcium, or barium: the principal constituents of igneous rocks. The group includes orthoclase, microcline, and the plagioclase minerals. —**feld·spath·ic** (fɛld'spæθɪk, fɛl'spæθ-), **'feld·spath·ˌose** *or* **fel·'spath·ic, 'fel·spath·ˌose** *adj.*

fe·li·cif·ic (ˌfiːlɪ'sɪfɪk) *adj.* making or tending to make happy. [C19: from Latin *fēlix* happy + *facere* to make]

fe·lic·i·tate (fɪ'lɪsɪˌteɪt) *vb.* **1.** to wish joy to; congratulate. **2.** *Archaic.* to please. —**fe·'lic·i·ˌta·tor** *n.*

fe·lic·i·ta·tion (fɪˌlɪsɪ'teɪʃən) *n.* a less common word for **congratulation.**

fe·lic·i·tous (fɪ'lɪsɪtəs) *adj.* **1.** well-chosen; apt. **2.** possessing an agreeable style. **3.** producing or marked by happiness. —**fe·'lic·i·tous·ly** *adv.* —**fe·'lic·i·tous·ness** *n.*

fe·lic·i·ty (fɪ'lɪsɪtɪ) *n., pl.* **·ties. 1.** happiness; joy. **2.** a cause of happiness. **3.** an appropriate expression or style. **4.** the quality or display of such expressions or style. [C14: from Latin *fēlīcitās* happiness, from *fēlix* happy]

fe·line ('fiːlaɪn) *adj.* **1.** of, relating to, or belonging to the *Felidae,* a family of predatory mammals, including cats, lions, leopards, and cheetahs, typically having a round head and retractile claws: order *Carnivora* (carnivores). **2.** resembling or suggestive of a cat, esp. in stealth or grace. ~*n. also* **fe·lid** ('fiːlɪd). **3.** any animal belonging to the family *Felidae;* a cat. [C17: from Latin *fēlīnus,* from *fēlēs* cat] —**'fe·line·ly** *adv.* —**'fe·line·ness** *or* **fe·lin·i·ty** (fɪ'lɪnɪtɪ) *n.*

fell[1] (fɛl) *vb.* the past tense of **fall.**

fell[2] (fɛl) *vb.* (*tr.*) **1.** to cut or knock down: *to fell a tree; to fell an opponent.* **2.** *Needlework.* to fold the edges of a seam under and sew them flat. ~*n.* **3.** *U.S.* the timber felled in one season. **4.** a seam finished by felling. [Old English *fellan;* related to Old Norse *fella,* Old High German *fellen;* see FALL] —**'fell·a·ble** *adj.*

fell[3] (fɛl) *adj.* **1.** *Archaic.* cruel or fierce; terrible. **2.** *Archaic.* destructive or deadly: *a fell disease.* **3. one fell swoop.** a single hasty action or occurrence. [C13 *fel,* from Old French: cruel, from Medieval Latin *fellō* villain; see FELON[1]] —**'fell·ness** *n.*

fell[4] (fɛl) *n.* an animal skin or hide. [Old English; related to Old High German *fel* skin, Old Norse *berfjall* bearskin, Latin *pellis* skin; see PEEL[1]]

fell[5] (fɛl) *n.* (*often pl.*) *Northern Brit.* **a.** a mountain, hill, or moor. **b.** (*in combination*): *fell-walking.* [C13: from Old Norse *fjall;* related to Old High German *felis* rock]

fel·lah ('fɛlə) *n., pl.* **fel·lahs, fel·la·hin,** *or* **fel·la·heen** (ˌfɛlə'hiːn). a peasant in Arab countries. [C18: from Arabic, dialect variant of *fallāh,* from *falaha* to cultivate]

fel·la·ti·o (fɪ'leɪʃɪəʊ, fɛ-) *or* **fel·la·tion** *n.* a sexual activity in which the penis is stimulated by the mouth. Compare **cunnilingus.** [C19: New Latin, from Latin *fellāre* to suck] —**fel·'la·tor** *n.* —**fel·'la·trix** *fem. n.*

fell·er[1] ('fɛlə) *n.* **1.** a person or thing that fells. **2.** an attachment on a sewing machine for felling seams.

fel·ler[2] ('fɛlə) *n.* a nonstandard spelling of **fellow.**

Fel·ling ('fɛlɪŋ) *n.* a coal-mining town in N England, in Tyneside. Pop.: 38 595 (1971).

Fel·li·ni (fə'liːnɪ) *n.* **Fe·de·ri·co** (ˌfede'riːko). born 1920, Italian film director; his films include *La Dolce Vita* (1960) and *8½* (1963).

fell·mon·ger ('fɛlˌmʌŋgə) *n.* a person who deals in animal skins or hides. —**'fell·ˌmon·ger·ing** *or* **'fell·ˌmon·ger·y** *n.*

fel·loe ('fɛləʊ) *or* **fel·ly** *n., pl.* **·loes** *or* **·lies.** a segment or the whole rim of a wooden wheel to which the spokes are attached and onto which a metal tyre is usually shrunk. [Old English *felge;* related to Old High German *felga,* Middle Dutch *velge,* of unknown origin]

fel·low ('fɛləʊ) *n.* **1.** a man or boy. **2.** an informal word for **boyfriend. 3.** *Informal.* one or oneself: *a fellow has to eat.* **4.** a person considered to be of little importance or worth. **5. a.** (*often pl.*) a companion; comrade; associate. **b.** (*as modifier*): *fellow travellers.* **6.** (at Oxford and Cambridge universities) a member of the governing body of a college, who is usually a member of the teaching staff. **7.** a member of the governing body or established teaching staff at any of various universities or colleges. **8.** a postgraduate student employed, esp. for a fixed period, to undertake research and, often, to do some teaching. **9. a.** a person in the same group, class, or condition: *the surgeon asked his fellows.* **b.** (*as modifier*): *fellow students; a fellow sufferer.* **10.** one of a pair; counterpart; mate: *looking for the glove's fellow.* ~*vb.* (*tr.*) *Rare.* **11.** to produce a counterpart for; match. **12.** to place on a par with; make equal to. [Old English *fēolaga,* from Old Norse *fēlagi,* one who lays down money, from *fē* money + *lag* a laying down]

Fel·low ('fɛləʊ) *n.* a member of any of various learned societies: *Fellow of the British Academy.*

fel·low feel·ing *n.* **1.** mutual sympathy or friendship. **2.** an opinion held in common.

fel·low·ship ('fɛləʊˌʃɪp) *n.* **1.** the state of sharing mutual interests, experiences, activities, etc. **2.** a society of people sharing mutual interests, experiences, activities, etc.; club. **3.** companionship; friendship. **4.** the state or relationship of being a fellow. **5. a.** mutual trust and charitableness between Christians. **b.** a Church or religious association. **6.** *Education.* **a.** a financed research post providing study facilities, privileges, etc., often in return for teaching services. **b.** a foundation endowed to support a postgraduate research student. **c.** an honorary title carrying certain privileges awarded to a postgraduate student. **7.** (*often cap.*) the body of fellows in a college, university, etc.

fel·low trav·el·ler *n.* **1.** a companion on a journey. **2.** a non-Communist who sympathizes with Communism.

fe·lo de se ('fi:ləʊ dɪ 'si:, 'fɛləʊ) *n., pl.* **fe·lo·nes de se** ('fi:ləʊˌni:z dɪ 'si:, 'fɛl-) *or* **fe·los de se.** *Law.* **a.** suicide. **b.** a person who commits suicide. [C17: from Anglo-Latin, from *felō* felon, + Latin *dē* of, + *sē* oneself]

fel·on[1] ('fɛlən) *n.* **1.** *Criminal law.* (formerly) a person who has committed a felony. **2.** *Obsolete.* a wicked person. ~*adj.* **3.** *Archaic or poetic.* evil; cruel. [C13: from Old French: villain, from Medieval Latin *fellō,* of uncertain origin]

fel·on[2] ('fɛlən) *n.* a purulent inflammation of the end joint of a finger, sometimes affecting the bone. [C12: from Medieval Latin *fellō* sore, perhaps from Latin *fel* poison]

fe·lo·ni·ous (fɪ'ləʊnɪəs) *adj.* **1.** *Criminal law.* of, involving, or constituting a felony. **2.** *Obsolete.* wicked; base. —**fe·'lo·ni·ous·ly** *adv.* —**fe·'lo·ni·ous·ness** *n.*

fel·on·ry ('fɛlənrɪ) *n., pl.* **·ries. 1.** felons collectively. **2.** (formerly) the convict population of a penal colony, esp. in Australia.

fel·o·ny ('fɛlənɪ) *n., pl.* **·nies. 1.** *Criminal law.* (formerly) a serious crime, such as murder or arson. All distinctions between felony and misdemeanour were abolished in England in 1967.

fel·site ('fɛlsaɪt) *or* **fel·stone** ('fɛlˌstəʊn) *n.* any fine-grained igneous rock consisting essentially of quartz and feldspar. [C18: FELS(PAR) + -ITE[1]] —**fel·sit·ic** (fɛl'sɪtɪk) *adj.*

fel·spar ('fɛlˌspɑ:) *n.* a variant spelling (esp. Brit.) of **feldspar.** —**fel·spath·ic** (fɛl'spæθɪk) *or* **'fel·spath·ˌose** *adj.*

felt[1] (fɛlt) *vb.* the past tense or past participle of **feel.**

felt[2] (fɛlt) *n.* **1. a.** a matted fabric of wool, hair, etc., made by working the fibres together under pressure or by heat or chemical action. **b.** (*as modifier*): *a felt hat.* **2.** any material, such as asbestos, made by a similar process of matting. ~*vb.* **3.** (*tr.*) to make into or cover with felt. **4.** (*intr.*) to become matted. [Old English; related to Old Saxon *filt,* Old High German *filz* felt, Latin *pellere* to beat, Greek *pelas* close; see ANVIL, FILTER]

felt·ing ('fɛltɪŋ) *n.* **1.** felted material; felt. **2.** the process of making felt. **3.** materials for making felt.

fe·luc·ca (fɛ'lʌkə) *n.* a narrow lateen-rigged vessel of the Mediterranean. [C17: from Italian *felucca,* probably from obsolete Spanish *faluca,* probably from Arabic *fulūk* ships, from Greek *epholkion* small boat, from *ephelkein* to tow]

fel·wort ('fɛlˌwɜ:t) *n.* a biennial gentianaceous plant, *Gentianella amarella,* of Europe and SW China, having purple flowers and rosettes of leaves. [Old English *feldwyrt;* see FIELD, WORT]

fem. *abbrev. for:* **1.** female. **2.** feminine.

fe·male ('fi:meɪl) *adj.* **1.** of, relating to, or designating the sex producing gametes (ova) that can be fertilized by male gametes (spermatozoa). **2.** of, relating to, or characteristic of a woman: *female charm.* **3.** for or composed of women or girls: *female suffrage; a female choir.* **4.** (of reproductive organs such as the ovary and carpel) capable of producing female gametes. **5.** (of gametes such as the ovum) capable of being fertilized by a male gamete in sexual reproduction. **6.** (of flowers) lacking, or having nonfunctional, stamens. **7.** having an internal cavity into which a projecting male counterpart can be fitted: *a female thread.* ~*n.* **8. a.** a female animal or plant. **b.** *Mildly offensive.* a woman or girl. [C14: from earlier *femelle* (influenced by *male*), from Latin *fēmella* a young woman, from *fēmina* a woman] —**'fe·male·ness** *n.*

fe·male im·per·son·a·tor *n.* a male theatrical performer who acts as a woman.

fe·male suf·frage *n. Chiefly U.S.* another name for **women's suffrage.**

feme (fɛm) *n. Law.* a woman or wife. [C16: from Anglo-French, ultimately from Latin *fēmina* woman]

feme cov·ert *n. Law.* a married woman. [C16: from Anglo-French: a covered woman, one protected by marriage]

feme sole *n. Law.* **1.** a single woman, whether spinster, widow, or divorcee. **2.** a woman separated from her husband, or otherwise independent of him, as by owning her own property. [C16: from Anglo-French: a woman alone]

fem·in·e·i·ty (ˌfɛmɪ'neɪɪtɪ) *n.* the quality of being feminine; womanliness.

fem·i·nine ('fɛmɪnɪn) *adj.* **1.** suitable to or characteristic of a woman: *a feminine fashion.* **2.** possessing qualities or characteristics considered typical of or appropriate to a woman. **3.** effeminate; womanish. **4.** *Grammar.* **a.** denoting or belonging to a gender of nouns, occurring in many inflected languages, that includes all kinds of referents as well as some female animate referents. **b.** (*as n.*): *German* Zeit *"time" and* Ehe *"marriage" are feminines.* [C14: from Latin *fēminīnus,* from *fēmina* woman] —**'fem·i·nine·ly** *adv.* —**'fem·i·nine·ness** *n.*

fem·i·nine end·ing *n. Prosody.* an unstressed syllable at the end of a line of verse.

fem·i·nine rhyme *n. Prosody.* a rhyme between words in which one, two, or more unstressed syllables follow a stressed one, as in *elation, nation* or *merrily, verily.* Compare **masculine rhyme.**

fem·i·nin·i·ty (ˌfɛmɪ'nɪnɪtɪ) *n.* **1.** the quality of being feminine. **2.** womanhood.

fem·i·nism ('fɛmɪˌnɪzəm) *n.* a doctrine or movement that advocates equal rights for women. —**'fem·i·nist** *n., adj.*

fem·i·nize *or* **fem·i·nise** ('fɛmɪˌnaɪz) *vb.* **1.** to make or become feminine. **2.** to cause (a male animal) to develop female characteristics. —**ˌfem·i·ni·'za·tion** *or* **ˌfem·i·ni·'sa·tion** *n.*

femme *French.* (fam; *English* fɛm) *n.* a woman or wife.

femme de cham·bre *French.* (fam də 'ʃɑ̃br) *n., pl.* ***femmes de cham·bre*** (fam də 'ʃɑ̃br). **1.** a chambermaid. **2.** *Rare.* a personal maid. [C18: woman of the bedroom]

femme fa·tale *French.* (fam fa'tal; *English* 'fɛm fə'tæl, -'tɑ:l) *n., pl.* ***femmes fa·tales*** (fam fa'tal; *English* 'fɛm fə'tælz, -'tɑ:lz). an alluring or seductive woman, esp. one who causes men to love her to their own distress. [fatal woman]

fem·o·ral ('fɛmərəl) *adj.* of or relating to the thigh or femur.

fem·to- *prefix.* denoting 10^{-15}: *femtometer.* Symbol: f [from Danish or Norwegian *femten* fifteen]

fe·mur ('fi:mə) *n., pl.* **fe·murs** *or* **fem·o·ra** ('fɛmərə). **1.** the longest thickest bone of the human skeleton, articulating with the pelvis above and the knee below. Nontechnical name: **thighbone. 2.** the corresponding bone in other vertebrates. **3.** the segment of an insect's leg nearest to the body. [C18: from Latin: thigh]

fen[1] (fɛn) *n.* low-lying flat land that is marshy or artificially drained. [Old English *fenn;* related to Old High German *fenna,* Old Norse *fen,* Gothic *fani* clay, Sanskrit *panka* mud] —**fen·ny** *adj.*

fen[2] (fɛn) *n., pl.* **fen.** a monetary unit of the People's Republic of China worth one hundredth of a yuan. [from Mandarin Chinese]

fence (fɛns) *n.* **1.** a structure that serves to enclose an area such as a garden or field, usually made of posts of timber, concrete, or metal connected by wire, netting, rails, or boards. **2.** *Slang.* a dealer in stolen property. **3.** an obstacle for a horse to jump in steeplechasing or showjumping. **4.** *Machinery.* a guard or guide, esp. in a circular saw or plane. **5.** a projection usually fitted to the top surface of a sweptback aircraft wing to prevent movement of the airflow towards the wing tips. **6. mend one's fences.** *Chiefly U.S.* to restore a position or reputation that has been damaged, esp. in politics. **7. (sit) on the fence.** (to be) unable or unwilling to commit oneself. ~*vb.* **8.** (*tr.*) to construct a fence on or around (a piece of land, etc.). **9.** (*tr.;* foll. by *in* or *off*) to close (in) or separate (off) with or as if with a fence: *he fenced in the livestock.* **10.** (*intr.*) to fight using swords or foils. **11.** (*intr.*) to evade a question or argument, esp. by quibbling over minor points. **12.** (*intr.*) to engage in skilful or witty debate, repartee, etc. **13.** (*intr.*) *Slang.* to receive stolen property. **14.** (*tr.*) *Archaic.* to ward off or keep out. [C14 *fens,* shortened from *defens* DEFENCE] —**'fence·less** *adj.* —**'fence·ˌlike** *adj.*

fenc·er ('fɛnsə) *n.* **1.** a person who fights with a sword, esp. one who practises the art of fencing. **2.** *Chiefly Australian.* a person who erects and repairs fences.

fen·ci·ble ('fɛnsəbəl) *adj.* **1.** a Scot. word for **defensible.** ~*n.* **2.** (formerly) a person who undertook military service in immediate defence of his homeland only.

fenc·ing ('fɛnsɪŋ) *n.* **1.** the practice, art, or sport of fighting with swords, esp. the sport of using foils, épées, or sabres under a set of rules to score points. **2. a.** wire, stakes, etc., used as fences. **b.** fences collectively. **3.** skilful or witty debate. **4.** the avoidance of direct answers; evasiveness. **5.** *Slang.* the business of buying and selling stolen property.

fend (fɛnd) *vb.* **1.** (*tr.;* foll. by *for*) to give support (to someone, esp. oneself); provide (for). **2.** (*tr.;* usually foll. by *off*) to ward off or turn aside (blows, questions, attackers, etc.). **3.** (*tr.*) *Archaic.* to defend or resist. **4.** (*intr.*) *Scot. and northern English dialect.* to struggle; strive. ~*n.* **5.** *Scot. and northern English dialect.* a shift or effort. [C13 *fenden,* shortened from *defenden* to DEFEND]

fend·er ('fɛndə) *n.* **1.** a low metal frame which confines falling coals to the hearth. **2.** a metal frame fitted to the front of locomotives to absorb shock, clear the track, etc. **3.** a cushion-like device, such as a bundle of rope or car tyre hung over the side of a vessel for protection against collision. **4.** the U.S. name for **wing** (sense 10) or **mudguard.** —**'fend·ered** *adj.*

Fé·ne·lon (*French* fen'lɔ̃) *n.* **Fran·çois de Sa·li·gnac de La Mothe** (frɑ̃swa də saliɲak də la 'mɔt). 1651–1715, French theologian and writer; author of *Maximes des saints* (1697), a defence of quietism, and *Les aventures de Télémaque* (1699), which was construed as criticizing the government of Louis XIV.

fen·es·tel·la (ˌfɛnɪ'stɛlə) *n., pl.* **·lae** (-li:). **1.** *R.C. Church.* a small aperture in the front of an altar, containing relics. **2.** *Ecclesiast.* a niche in the side wall of a chancel, in which the credence or piscina are set. **3.** *Architect.* a small window or an opening in a wall. [C18: from Latin: a little window, from *fenestra* window]

fe·nes·tra (fɪ'nɛstrə) *n., pl.* **·trae** (-tri:). **1.** *Biology.* a small opening, esp. either of two openings between the middle and inner ears. **2.** *Zoology.* a transparent marking or spot, as on the wings of moths. [C19: via New Latin from Latin: wall opening, window] —**fe·'nes·tral** *adj.*

fe·nes·trat·ed (fɪ'nɛstreɪtɪd, 'fɛnɪˌstreɪtɪd) *or* **fe·nes·trate** *adj.* **1.** *Architect.* having windows or window-like openings. **2.** *Biology.* perforated or having fenestrae.

fen·es·tra·tion (ˌfɛnɪ'streɪʃən) *n.* **1.** the arrangement and design of windows in a building. **2.** a surgical operation to restore hearing by making an artificial opening into the labyrinth of the ear.

Fe·ni·an ('fiːnɪən, 'fɛnjən) *n.* **1.** (formerly) a member of an Irish revolutionary organization founded in the U.S. in the 19th century to fight for an independent Ireland. **2.** Also called: **Fianna.** one of a legendary band of Irish warriors noted for their heroic exploits, attributed to the 2nd and 3rd centuries A.D. —*adj.* **3.** of or relating to the Fenians. [C19: from Irish Gaelic *fēinne,* plural of *fiann* band of Fenians, after *Fiann* Irish folk hero] —**'Fe·ni·an·ism** *n.*

fen·nec ('fɛnɛk) *n.* a very small nocturnal fox, *Fennecus zerda,* inhabiting deserts of N Africa and Arabia, having pale fur and enormous ears. [C18: from Arabic *fenek* fox]

fen·nel ('fɛnᵊl) *n.* **1.** a strong-smelling yellow-flowered umbelliferous plant, *Foeniculum vulgare,* whose seeds and feathery leaves are used to season and flavour food. See also **finochio. 2. dog fennel.** another name for **mayweed.** [Old English *fenol,* from Latin *faeniculum* fennel, diminutive of *faenum* hay]

fen·nel·flow·er ('fɛnᵊlˌflaʊə) *n.* any of various Mediterranean ranunculaceous plants of the genus *Nigella,* having finely divided leaves and white, blue, or yellow flowers. See also **love-in-a-mist.**

fen·ny ('fɛnɪ) *adj.* **1.** boggy or marshy: *fenny country.* **2.** found in, characteristic of, or growing in fens.

Fen·rir ('fɛnrɪə), **Fen·ris** ('fɛnrɪs), *or* **Fen·ris·wolf** ('fɛnrɪsˌwʊlf) *n. Norse myth.* an enormous wolf, fathered by Loki, which killed Odin.

Fens (fɛnz) *pl. n.* **the.** a flat low-lying area of E England, west and south of the Wash: consisted of marshes until reclaimed in the 17th to 19th centuries.

fen·u·greek ('fɛnjʊˌgriːk) *n.* an annual heavily scented Mediterranean leguminous plant, *Trigonella foenum-graecum,* with hairy stems and white flowers: cultivated for forage and for its medicinal seeds. [Old English *fēnogrēcum,* from Latin *fenum Graecum* literally: Greek hay]

feoff (fiːf) *Medieval history.* ~*n.* **1.** a variant spelling of **fief.** ~*vb.* **2.** (*tr.*) to invest with a benefice or fief. [C13: from Anglo-French *feoffer,* from *feoff* a FIEF] —**'feof·for** *or* **'feoff·er** *n.*

feoff·ee (fɛ'fiː, fiː'fiː) *n.* (in feudal society) a vassal granted a fief by his lord.

feoff·ment ('fiːfmənt) *n.* (in medieval Europe) a lord's act of granting a fief to his man.

-fer *n. combining form.* indicating a person or thing that bears something specified: *crucifer; conifer.* [from Latin, from *ferre* to bear]

fe·ral¹ ('fɪərəl, 'fɛr-) *or* **fe·rine** *adj.* **1.** (of animals and plants) existing in a wild or uncultivated state, esp. after being domestic or cultivated. **2.** savage; brutal. [C17: from Medieval Latin *ferālis,* from Latin *fera* a wild beast, from *ferus* savage] —**fer·i·ty** ('fɛrɪtɪ) *n.*

fe·ral² ('fɪərəl, 'fɛr-) *adj. Archaic.* **1.** *Astrology.* associated with death. **2.** gloomy; funereal. [C17: from Latin *fērālis* relating to corpses; perhaps related to *ferre* to carry]

fer·bam ('fɜːbæm) *n.* a black slightly water-soluble fluffy powder used as a fungicide. Formula: $[(CH_3)_2NCSS]_3Fe$. [C20: from *fer*(*ric dimethyldithiocar*)*bam*(*ate*)]

fer-de-lance (ˌfɛədə'lɑːns) *n.* a large highly venomous tropical American snake, *Trimeresurus* (or *Bothops*) *atrox,* with a greyish-brown mottled coloration: family *Crotalidae* (pit vipers). [C19: from French, literally: iron (head) of a lance]

Fer·di·nand ('fɜːdɪˌnænd; *German* 'fɛrdɪˌnant) *n.* See **Franz Ferdinand.**

Fer·di·nand I ('fɜːdɪˌnænd) *n.* **1.** called *the Great.* ?1016–65, king of Castile (1035–65) and León (1037–65): achieved control of the Moorish kings of Saragossa, Seville, and Toledo. **2.** 1503–64, king of Hungary and Bohemia (1526–64); Holy Roman Emperor (1558–64), bringing years of religious warfare to an end. **3.** 1751–1825, king of the Two Sicilies (1816–25); king of Naples (1759–1806; 1815–25), as Ferdinand IV, being dispossessed by Napoleon (1806–15). **4.** 1793–1875, king of Hungary (1830–48) and emperor of Austria (1835–48); abdicated after the Revolution of 1848 in favour of his nephew, Franz Josef I. **5.** 1861–1948, ruling prince of Bulgaria (1887–1908) and tsar from 1908 until his abdication in 1918. **6.** 1865–1927, king of Rumania (1914–27); sided with the Allies in World War I.

Fer·di·nand II *n.* **1.** 1578–1637, Holy Roman Emperor (1619–37); king of Bohemia (1617–19; 1620–37) and of Hungary (1617–37). His anti-Protestant policies led to the Thirty Years' War. **2.** title as king of Aragon and Sicily of **Ferdinand V.**

Fer·di·nand III *n.* **1.** 1608–57, Holy Roman Emperor (1637–57) and king of Hungary (1625–57); son of Ferdinand II. **2.** title as king of Naples of **Ferdinand V.**

Fer·di·nand V *n.* called *the Catholic.* 1452–1516, king of Castile (1474–1504); as Ferdinand II, king of Aragon (1479–1516) and Sicily (1468–1516); as Ferdinand III, king of Naples (1504–16). His marriage to Isabella I of Castile (1469) led to the union of Aragon and Castile and his reconquest of Granada from the Moors (1492) completed the unification of Spain. He introduced the Inquisition (1478), expelled the Jews from Spain (1492), and financed Columbus' voyage to the New World.

fere (fɪə) *n. Archaic.* **1.** a companion. **2.** a husband or wife. [Old English *gefēra,* from *fēran* to travel; see FARE]

fer·e·to·ry ('fɛrɪtərɪ, -trɪ) *n., pl.* **·ries.** *Chiefly R.C. Church.* **1.** a shrine, usually portable, for a saint's relics. **2.** the chapel in which a shrine is kept. [C14: from Middle French *fiertre,* from Latin *feretrum* a bier, from Greek *pheretron,* from *pherein* to bear]

Fer·ga·na *or* **Fer·gha·na** (fə'gɑːnə) *n.* **1.** a region of W central Asia, surrounded by high mountains and accessible only from the west; mainly in the Uzbek SSR and partly in the Tadzhik and Kirgiz SSRs. **2.** the chief city of this region, in the E Uzbek SSR. Pop.: 128 000 (1975 est.).

Fer·gus ('fɜːgəs) *n.* (in Irish legend) a warrior king of Ulster, who was supplanted by Conchobar.

fe·ri·a ('fɪərɪə) *n., pl.* **·ri·as** *or* **·ri·ae** (-rɪˌiː). *R.C. Church.* a weekday, other than Saturday, on which no feast occurs. [C19: from Late Latin: day of the week (as in *prīma fēria* Sunday), singular of Latin *fēriae* festivals]

fe·ri·al ('fɪərɪəl) *adj.* **1.** of or relating to a feria. **2.** *Rare.* of or relating to a holiday.

fe·rine ('fɪəraɪn) *adj.* another word for **feral**¹. [C17: from Latin *ferīnus* of wild animals, from *fera* wild beast]

fer·i·ty ('fɛrɪtɪ) *n., pl.* **·ties.** *Rare.* **1.** the state of being wild or uncultivated. **2.** savagery; ferocity. [C16: from Latin *feritās,* from *ferus* savage, untamed]

Fer·man·agh (fə'mænə) *n.* a county of SW Northern Ireland: contains the Upper and Lower Lough Erne. County town: Enniskillen. Pop.: 49 960 (1971). Area (excluding water): 1691 sq. km (653 sq. miles).

Fer·mat (*French* fɛr'ma; *English* fɜː'mæt) *n.* **Pierre de** ('pjɛːr də). 1601–65, French mathematician, regarded as the founder of the modern theory of numbers. He studied the properties of whole numbers and, with Pascal, investigated the theory of probability.

fer·ma·ta (fə'mɑːtə) *n., pl.* **·tas** *or* **·te** (-tɪ). *Music.* another word for **pause** (sense 5). [from Italian, from *fermare* to stop, from Latin *firmāre* to establish; see FIRM¹]

Fer·mat's last the·o·rem *n.* (in number theory) the hypothesis that the equation $x^n + y^n = z^n$ has no integral solutions for n greater than two.

Fer·mat's prin·ci·ple *n. Physics.* the principle that a ray of light passes from one point to another in such a way that the time taken is a minimum.

fer·ment *n.* ('fɜːmɛnt) **1.** any agent or substance, such as a bacterium, mould, yeast, or enzyme, that causes fermentation. **2.** another word for **fermentation. 3.** commotion; unrest. ~*vb.* (fə'mɛnt). **4.** to undergo or cause to undergo fermentation. **5.** to stir up or seethe with excitement. [C15: from Latin *fermentum* yeast, from *fervēre* to seethe] —**fer·'ment·a·ble** *adj.* —**fer·ˌment·a·'bil·i·ty** *n.* —**fer·'ment·er** *n.*

fer·men·ta·tion (ˌfɜːmɛn'teɪʃən) *n.* a chemical reaction in which a ferment causes an organic molecule to split into simpler substances, esp. the anaerobic conversion of sugar to ethyl alcohol by yeast. Also called: **ferment.** —**fer·'ment·a·tive** *adj.* —**fer·'ment·a·tive·ly** *adv.* —**fer·'ment·a·tive·ness** *n.*

fer·men·ta·tion lock *n.* a valve placed on the top of bottles of fermenting wine to allow bubbles to escape.

fer·mi ('fɜːmɪ) *n.* a unit of length used in nuclear physics equal to 10^{-15} metre.

Fer·mi ('fɜːmɪ; *Italian* 'fermi) *n.* **En·ri·co** (en'riːko). 1901–54, Italian nuclear physicist, in the U.S. from 1939. He was awarded a Nobel prize for physics in 1938 for his work on radioactive substances and nuclear bombardment and headed the group that produced the first controlled nuclear reaction (1942).

Fer·mi-Di·rac sta·tis·tics *n. Physics.* the branch of quantum statistics used to calculate the permitted energy arrangements of the particles in a system in terms of the exclusion principle. Compare **Bose-Einstein statistics.** [C20: named after Enrico FERMI and Paul DIRAC]

fer·mi·on ('fɜːmɪˌɒn) *n.* any of a group of elementary particles, such as a nucleon, that has half-integral spin and obeys Fermi-Dirac statistics. Compare **boson.** [C20: named after Enrico FERMI; see -ON]

fer·mi·um ('fɜːmɪəm) *n.* a transuranic element artificially produced by neutron bombardment of plutonium. Symbol: Fm; atomic no.: 100; half-life of most stable isotope, ^{257}Fm: 80 days (approx.). [C20: named after Enrico FERMI]

fern (fɜːn) *n.* **1.** any pteridophyte plant of the order *Filicales,* having roots, stems, and fronds and reproducing by spores formed in structures (sori) on the fronds. See also **tree fern. 2.** any of certain similar but unrelated plants, such as the sweet fern. [Old English *fearn;* related to Old High German *farn,* Sanskrit *parnā* leaf] —**'fern·ˌlike** *adj.* —**'fern·y** *adj.*

Fer·nan·del (*French* fɛrnã'dɛl) *n.* original name *Fernand Contandin.* 1903–71, French comic film actor.

Fer·nan·do de No·ro·nha (*Portuguese* fer'nandu di no'roŋa) *n.* a volcanic island in the S Atlantic northeast of Cape São Roque: constitutes a federal territory of Brazil; a penal colony since the 18th century. Pop.: 1241 (1970). Area: 26 sq. km (10 sq. miles).

Fer·nan·do Po (fə'nændəʊ 'pəʊ) *n.* the former name (until 1973) of **Macías Nguema.**

fern·er·y ('fɜːnərɪ) *n., pl.* **·er·ies. 1.** a place where ferns are grown. **2.** a collection of ferns grown in such a place.

fern seed *n.* the minute particles by which ferns reproduce themselves, formerly thought to be invisible. Possession of them was thought to make a person invisible.

fe+ro+cious (fəˈrəʊʃəs) *adj.* savagely fierce or cruel: *a ferocious tiger; a ferocious argument.* [C17: from Latin *ferox* fierce, untamable, warlike] —**fe+ˈro+cious+ly** *adv.* —**fe+roc+i·ty** (fəˈrɒsɪtɪ) *or* **fe+ˈro+cious+ness** *n.*

-fer·ous *adj. combining form.* bearing or producing: *coniferous; crystalliferous.* Compare **-gerous.** [from -FER + -OUS]

Fer+ra+ra (fəˈrɑːrə; *Italian* ferˈraːra) *n.* a city in N Italy, in Emilia-Romagna: a centre of the Renaissance under the House of Este; university (1391). Pop.: 155 175 (1975 est.).

Fer·ra·ri (*Italian* ferˈraːri) *n.* **En·zo** (ˈɛntso). born 1898, Italian designer and manufacturer of racing cars.

fer+rate (ˈfɛreɪt) *n.* a salt containing the divalent ion, FeO_4^{2-}. Ferrates are derivatives of the hypothetical acid H_2FeO_4. [C19: from Latin *ferrum* iron]

fer+re·ous (ˈfɛrɪəs) *adj.* containing or resembling iron: *a ferreous alloy; a ferreous substance.* [C17: from Latin *ferreus* made of iron, from *ferrum* iron]

fer+ret[1] (ˈfɛrɪt) *n.* **1.** a domesticated albino variety of the polecat *Mustela putorius*, bred for hunting rats, rabbits, etc. **2. black-footed ferret.** a musteline mammal, *Mustela nigripes*, of W North America, closely related to the weasels. ~*vb.* **3.** to hunt (rabbits, rats, etc.) with ferrets. **4.** (*tr.*; usually foll. by *out*) to drive from hiding: *to ferret out snipers.* **5.** (*tr.*; usually foll. by *out*) to find by persistent investigation. **6.** (*intr.*) to search around. [C14: from Old French *furet*, from Latin *fur* thief] —ˈ**fer+ret+er** *n.* —ˈ**fer+ret·y** *adj.*

fer+ret[2] (ˈfɛrɪt) *or* **fer+ret+ing** *n.* silk binding tape. [C16: from Italian *fioretti* floss silk, plural of *fioretto:* a little flower, from *fiore* flower, from Latin *flōs*]

fer+ret badg+er *n.* any small badger of the genus *Melogale*, of SE Asia, resembling a ferret in appearance and smell.

fer·ri- *combining form.* indicating the presence of iron, esp. in the trivalent state: *ferricyanide; ferriferous.* Compare **ferro-.** [from Latin *ferrum* iron]

fer+ri+age (ˈfɛrɪɪdʒ) *n.* **1.** transportation by ferry. **2.** the fee charged for passage on a ferry.

fer+ric (ˈfɛrɪk) *adj.* of or containing iron in the trivalent state: *ferric oxide.* [C18: from Latin *ferrum* iron]

fer+ric ox+ide *n.* a red crystalline insoluble oxide of iron that occurs as haematite and rust and is made by heating ferrous sulphate: used as a pigment and metal polish (**jewellers' rouge**). Formula: Fe_2O_3.

fer+ri+cy+an+ic ac·id (ˌfɛrɪsaɪˈænɪk) *n.* a brown soluble unstable solid tribasic acid, usually known in the form of ferricyanide salts. Formula: $H_3Fe(CN)_6$.

fer+ri+cy·a+nide (ˌfɛrɪˈsaɪəˌnaɪd) *n.* any salt of ferricyanic acid.

fer+rif+er+ous (fɛˈrɪfərəs) *adj.* producing or yielding iron; iron-bearing: *a ferriferous rock.*

fer+ri+mag+net+ism (ˌfɛrɪˈmægnɪˌtɪzəm) *n.* a phenomenon exhibited by certain substances, such as ferrites, in which the magnetic moments of neighbouring ions are antiparallel and unequal in magnitude. The substances behave like ferromagnetic materials. See also **antiferromagnetism.** —**fer+ri+mag+ˈnet+ic** (ˌfɛrɪmægˈnɛtɪk) *adj.*

Fer+ris wheel (ˈfɛrɪs) *n.* a fairground wheel having seats freely suspended from its rim; the seats remain horizontal throughout its rotation. [C19: named after G.W.G. *Ferris* (1859–96), American engineer]

fer+rite (ˈfɛraɪt) *n.* **1.** any of a group of ferromagnetic highly resistive ceramic compounds with the formula MFe_2O_4, where M is usually a metal such as cobalt or zinc. **2.** any of the body-centred cubic allotropes of iron, such as alpha iron, occurring in steel, cast iron, etc. **3.** any of various microscopic grains, probably composed of iron compounds, in certain igneous rocks. [C19: from FERRI- + -ITE[1]]

fer+rite-rod aer+i·al *n.* a type of aerial, normally used in radio reception, consisting of a small coil of wire mounted on a ferrite core, the coil serving as a tuning inductance.

fer+ri+tin (ˈfɛrɪtɪn) *n. Biochem.* a protein that contains iron and plays a part in the storage of iron in the body. It occurs in the liver and spleen. [C20: from FERRITE + -IN]

fer·ro- *combining form.* **1.** indicating a property of iron or the presence of iron: *ferromagnetism; ferromanganese.* **2.** indicating the presence of iron in the divalent state: *ferrocyanide.* Compare **ferri-.** [from Latin *ferrum* iron]

fer+ro+cene (ˈfɛrəʊˌsiːn) *n.* a reddish-orange insoluble crystalline compound. Its molecules have an iron atom sandwiched between two cyclopentadiene rings. Formula: $Fe(C_5H_5)_2$. [C20: from FERRO- + C(YCLOPENTADI)ENE]

fer+ro+chro+mi·um (ˌfɛrəʊˈkrəʊmɪəm) *or* **fer+ro+chrome** *n.* an alloy of iron and chromium (60–72 per cent), used in the production of very hard steel.

fer+ro+con+crete (ˌfɛrəʊˈkɒŋkriːt) *n.* another name for **reinforced concrete.**

fer+ro+cy+an+ic ac·id (ˌfɛrəʊsaɪˈænɪk) *n.* a white volatile unstable solid tetrabasic acid, usually known in the form of ferrocyanide salts. Formula: $H_4Fe(CN)_6$.

fer+ro+cy·a+nide (ˌfɛrəʊˈsaɪəˌnaɪd) *n.* any salt of ferrocyanic acid, such as potassium ferrocyanide, $K_4Fe(CN)_6$.

fer+ro+e·lec+tric (ˌfɛrəʊɪˈlɛktrɪk) *adj.* **1.** (of a substance) exhibiting spontaneous polarization that can be reversed by the application of a suitable electric field. **2.** of or relating to ferroelectric substances. ~*n.* **3.** a ferroelectric substance. —ˌ**fer+ro+e·ˈlec+tri+cal+ly** *adv.* —**fer+ro+e·lec+tric+i·ty** (ˌfɛrəʊɪlɛkˈtrɪsɪtɪ, -ˌiːlɛk-) *n.*

Fer+rol (*Spanish* feˈrrol) *n.* See **El Ferrol.**

fer+ro+mag+ne+sian (ˌfɛrəʊmægˈniːʒən) *adj.* (of minerals such as biotite) containing a high proportion of iron and magnesium.

fer+ro+mag+net+ism (ˌfɛrəʊˈmægnɪˌtɪzəm) *n.* the phenomenon exhibited by substances, such as iron, that have relative permeabilities much greater than unity and increasing magnetization with applied magnetizing field. Certain of these substances retain their magnetization in the absence of the applied field. The effect is caused by the alignment of electron spin in regions called domains. Compare **diamagnetism, paramagnetism.** See also **magnet, Curie-Weiss Law.** —**fer+ro+mag+net+ic** (ˌfɛrəʊmægˈnɛtɪk) *adj.*

fer+ro+man+ga+nese (ˌfɛrəʊˈmæŋgəˌniːz) *n.* an alloy of iron and manganese, used in making additions of manganese to cast iron and steel.

fer+ro+sil·i+con (ˌfɛrəʊˈsɪlɪkən) *n.* an alloy of iron and silicon, used in making cast iron and steel.

fer+ro+type (ˈfɛrəʊˌtaɪp) *n.* **1.** a photographic print produced directly in a camera by exposing a sheet of iron or tin coated with a sensitized enamel. **2.** the process by which such a print is produced. ~Also called: **tintype.**

fer+rous (ˈfɛrəs) *adj.* of or containing iron in the divalent state. [C19: from FERRI- + -OUS]

fer+rous sul+phate *n.* an iron salt with a saline taste, usually obtained as greenish crystals of the heptahydrate, which are converted to the white monohydrate above 100°C: used in inks, tanning, water purification, and in the treatment of anaemia. Formula: $FeSO_4$. Also called: **copperas, green vitriol.**

fer+ru+gi+nous (fɛˈruːdʒɪnəs) *adj.* **1.** (of minerals, rocks, etc.) containing iron: *a ferruginous clay.* **2.** rust-coloured. [C17: from Latin *ferrūgineus* of a rusty colour, from *ferrūgō* iron rust, from *ferrum* iron]

fer+ru+gi+nous duck *n.* a common European duck, *Aythyra nyroca*, having reddish-brown plumage with white wing bars.

fer+rule *or* **fer+ule** (ˈfɛruːl, -rəl) *n.* **1.** a metal ring, tube, or cap placed over the end of a stick, handle, or post for added strength or to increase wear. **2.** a side opening in a pipe that gives access for inspection or cleaning. **3.** a bush, gland, small length of tube, etc., esp. one used for making a joint. ~*vb.* **4.** (*tr.*) to equip (a stick, etc.,) with a ferrule. [C17: from Middle English *virole*, from Old French *virol*, from Latin *viriola* a little bracelet, from *viria* bracelet; influenced by Latin *ferrum* iron]

fer+ry (ˈfɛrɪ) *n., pl.* **+ries. 1.** Also called: **ferryboat.** a vessel for transporting passengers and usually vehicles across a body of water, esp. as a regular service. **2. a.** such a service. **b.** (*in combination*): *a ferryman.* **3.** a legal right to charge for transporting passengers by boat. **4.** the act or method of delivering aircraft by flying them to their destination. ~*vb.* **+ries, +ry+ing, +ried. 5.** to transport or go by ferry. **6.** to deliver (an aircraft) by flying it to its destination. **7.** (*tr.*) to convey (passengers, goods, etc.): *the guests were ferried to the church in taxis.* [Old English *ferian* to carry, bring; related to Old Norse *ferja* to transport, Gothic *farjan;* see FARE]

fer+tile (ˈfɜːtaɪl) *adj.* **1.** capable of producing offspring. **2. a.** (of land) having nutrients capable of sustaining an abundant growth of plants. **b.** (of farm animals) capable of breeding stock. **3.** *Biology.* **a.** capable of undergoing growth and development: *fertile seeds; fertile eggs.* **b.** (of plants) capable of producing gametes, spores, seeds, or fruits. **4.** producing many offspring; prolific. **5.** highly productive; rich; abundant: *a fertile brain.* **6.** *Physics.* (of a substance) able to be transformed into fissile or fissionable material, esp. in a nuclear reactor. **7.** conducive to productiveness: *fertile rain.* [C15: from Latin *fertilis*, from *ferre* to bear] —ˈ**fer+tile+ly** *adv.* —ˈ**fer+tile+ness** *n.*

Fer+tile Cres+cent *n.* an area of fertile land in the Middle East, extending around the Rivers Tigris and Euphrates in a semicircle from Israel to the Persian Gulf, where the Sumerian, Babylonian, Assyrian, Phoenician, and Hebrew civilizations flourished.

fer+til+i+ty (fɜːˈtɪlɪtɪ) *n.* **1.** the ability to produce offspring, esp. abundantly. **2.** the state or quality of being fertile.

fer+til+i+ty cult *n.* the practice in some settled agricultural communities of performing religious or magical rites to ensure good weather and crops and the perpetuity of the tribe.

fer+til+i+ty sym+bol *n.* an object, esp. a phallic symbol, used in fertility-cult ceremonies to symbolize regeneration.

fer+ti+li+za+tion *or* **fer+ti+li+sa+tion** (ˌfɜːtɪlaɪˈzeɪʃən) *n.* **1.** the union of male and female gametes, during sexual reproduction, to form a zygote. **2.** the act or process of fertilizing. **3.** the state of being fertilized.

fer+ti+lize *or* **fer+ti+lise** (ˈfɜːtɪˌlaɪz) *vb.* (*tr.*) **1.** to provide (an animal, plant, or egg cell) with sperm or pollen to bring about fertilization. **2.** to supply (soil or water) with mineral and organic nutrients to aid the growth of plants. **3.** to make fertile or productive. —ˈ**fer+ti+ˌliz+a·ble** *or* ˈ**fer+ti+ˌlis+a·ble** *adj.*

fer+ti+liz+er *or* **fer+ti+lis+er** (ˈfɜːtɪˌlaɪzə) *n.* **1.** any substance, such as manure or a mixture of nitrates, added to soil or water to increase its productivity. **2.** an object or organism such as an insect that fertilizes an animal or plant.

fer·u·la (ˈfɛrʊlə, ˈfɛrjʊ-) *n., pl.* **+las** *or* **+lae** (-ˌliː). **1.** any large umbelliferous plant of the Mediterranean genus *Ferula*, having thick stems and dissected leaves: cultivated as the source of several strongly scented gum resins, such as galbanum. **2.** a rare word for **ferule**[1]. [C14: from Latin: giant fennel] —**fer·u+la+ceous** (ˌfɛruːˈleɪʃəs, ˌfɛrjuː-) *adj.*

fer+ule[1] (ˈfɛruːl, -rəl) *n.* **1.** a flat piece of wood, such as a ruler, used in some schools to cane children on the hand. ~*vb.* **2.** (*tr.*) *Rare.* to punish with a ferule. [C16: from Latin *ferula* giant fennel, whip, rod; the stalk of the plant was used for punishment]

fer·ule[2] ('fɛruːl, -rəl) *n.* a variant spelling of **ferrule.**
fer·ven·cy ('fɜːvənsɪ) *n., pl.* **·cies.** another word for **fervour.**
fer·vent ('fɜːvənt) *or* **fer·vid** ('fɜːvɪd) *adj.* **1.** intensely passionate; ardent: *a fervent desire to change society.* **2.** *Archaic or poetic.* boiling, burning, or glowing: *fervent heat.* [C14: from Latin *fervēre* to boil, glow] —'**fer·vent·ly** *or* '**fer·vid·ly** *adv.* —'**fer·vent·ness** *or* '**fer·vid·ness** *n.*
Fer·vi·dor *French.* (fɛrvi'dɔːr) *n.* another name for **Thermidor.** [probably from *ferveur* heat + THERMIDOR]
fer·vour *or U.S.* **fer·vor** ('fɜːvə) *n.* **1.** great intensity of feeling or belief; ardour; zeal. **2.** *Rare.* intense heat. [C14: from Latin: heat, from *fervēre* to glow, boil]
Fès (fɛs) *or* **Fez** *n.* a city in N central Morocco, traditional capital of the north: became an independent kingdom in the 11th century, at its height in the 14th century; religious centre; university (850). Pop.: 325 327 (1971).
Fes·cen·nine ('fɛsɪˌnaɪn) *adj. Rare.* scurrilous or obscene. [C17: from Latin *Fescennīnus* of *Fescennia,* a city in Etruria noted for the production of mocking or obscene verse]
fes·cue ('fɛskjuː) *or* **fes·cue grass** *n.* any grass of the genus *Festuca:* widely cultivated as pasture and lawn grasses, having stiff narrow leaves. See also **meadow fescue, sheep's fescue.** [C14: from Old French *festu,* ultimately from Latin *festūca* stem, straw]
fesse *or* **fess** (fɛs) *n. Heraldry.* an ordinary consisting of a horizontal band across a shield, conventionally occupying a third of its length and being wider than a bar. [C15: from Anglo-French *fesse,* from Latin *fascia* band, fillet]
fesse point *n. Heraldry.* the midpoint of a shield.
fes·tal ('fɛstᵊl) *adj.* another word for **festive.** [C15: from Latin *festum* holiday, banquet; see FEAST] —'**fes·tal·ly** *adv.*
fes·ter ('fɛstə) *vb.* **1.** to form or cause to form pus. **2.** (*intr.*) to become rotten; decay. **3.** to become or cause to become bitter, irritated, etc., esp. over a long period of time; rankle: *resentment festered his imagination.* **4.** (*intr.*) *Informal, chiefly Brit.* to be idle or inactive. ~*n.* **5.** a small ulcer or sore containing pus. [C13: from Old French *festre* suppurating sore, from Latin: FISTULA]
fes·ti·na·tion (ˌfɛstɪ'neɪʃən) *n.* an involuntary quickening of gait, as in some persons with Parkinson's disease.
fes·ti·val ('fɛstɪvᵊl) *n.* **1.** a day or period set aside for celebration or feasting, esp. one of religious significance. **2.** any occasion for celebration, esp. one which commemorates an anniversary or other significant event. **3.** an organized series of special events and performances, usually in one place: *a festival of drama.* **4.** *Archaic.* a time of revelry; merrymaking. **5.** (*modifier*) relating to or characteristic of a festival. [C14: from Church Latin *fēstivālis* of a feast, from Latin *festīvus* FESTIVE]
fes·tive ('fɛstɪv) *adj.* appropriate to or characteristic of a holiday, etc.; merry. [C17: from Latin *festīvus* joyful, from *festus* of a FEAST] —'**fes·tive·ly** *adv.* —'**fes·tive·ness** *n.*
fes·tiv·i·ty (fɛs'tɪvɪtɪ) *n., pl.* **·ties. 1.** merriment characteristic of a festival, party, etc. **2.** any festival or other celebration. **3.** (*pl.*) festive proceedings; celebrations.
fes·toon (fɛ'stuːn) *n.* **1.** a decorative chain of flowers, ribbons, etc., suspended in loops; garland. **2.** a carved or painted representation of this, as in architecture, furniture, or pottery. **3. a.** the scalloped appearance of the gums where they meet the teeth. **b.** a design carved on the base material of a denture to simulate this. ~*vb.* (*tr.*) **4.** to decorate or join together with festoons. **5.** to form into festoons. [C17: from French *feston,* from Italian *festone* ornament for a feast, from *festa* FEAST]
fes·toon·er·y (fɛ'stuːnərɪ) *n.* an arrangement of festoons.
fest·schrift ('fɛstˌʃrɪft) *n., pl.* **·schrift·en** (-ˌʃrɪftən) *or* **·schrifts.** a collection of essays or learned papers contributed by a number of people to honour an eminent scholar, esp. a colleague. [German, from *Fest* celebration, FEAST + *Schrift* writing]
FET *abbrev. for* field-effect transistor.
fet·a ('fɛtə) *n.* a white sheep or goat cheese popular in Greece. [Modern Greek, from the phrase *turi pheta,* from *turi* cheese + *pheta,* from Italian *fetta* a slice]
fe·tal *or* **foe·tal** ('fiːtᵊl) *adj.* of, relating to, or resembling a fetus.
fe·tal di·ag·no·sis *n.* prenatal determination of genetic or chemical abnormalities in a fetus, esp. by amniocentesis.
fe·ta·tion *or* **foe·ta·tion** (fiː'teɪʃən) *n.* **1.** the state of pregnancy. **2.** the process of development of a fetus.
fetch[1] (fɛtʃ) *vb.* (*mainly tr.*) **1.** to go after and bring back; get: *to fetch help.* **2.** to cause to come; bring or draw forth: *the noise fetched him from the cellar.* **3.** (*also intr.*) to cost or sell for (a certain price): *the table fetched six hundred pounds.* **4.** to utter (a sigh, groan, etc.). **5.** *Informal.* to deal (a blow, slap, etc.). **6.** (*also intr.*) *Nautical.* to arrive at or proceed by sailing. **7.** *Informal.* to attract: *to be fetched by an idea.* **8.** (used esp. as a command to dogs) to retrieve (shot game, an object thrown, etc.). **9.** *Rare.* to draw in (a breath, gasp, etc.), esp. with difficulty. **10. fetch and carry.** to perform menial tasks or run errands. ~*n.* **11.** the reach, stretch, etc., of a mechanism. **12.** a trick or stratagem. [Old English *feccan;* related to Old Norse *feta* to step, Old High German *sih fazzōn* to climb] —'**fetch·er** *n.*
fetch[2] (fɛtʃ) *n.* the ghost or apparition of a living person. [C18: of unknown origin]
fetch·ing ('fɛtʃɪŋ) *adj. Informal.* **1.** attractively befitting: *a fetching hat.* **2.** charming: *a fetching personality.* —'**fetch·ing·ly** *adv.*
fetch up *vb.* (*adv.*) **1.** (*intr.; usually foll. by at or in*) *Informal.* to arrive (at) or end up (in): *to fetch up in New York.* **2.** (*intr.*) *Nautical.* to stop suddenly, as from running aground: *to fetch up on a rock.* **3.** *Slang.* to vomit (food, etc.). **4.** (*tr.*) *Brit. dialect.* to rear (children, animals, etc.).
fête *or* **fete** (feɪt) *n.* **1.** a gala, bazaar, or similar entertainment, esp. one held outdoors in aid of charity. **2.** a feast day or holiday, esp. one of religious significance. **3.** *Caribbean informal.* an organized group entertainment, esp. a party or a dance. ~*vb.* **4.** (*tr.*) to honour or entertain with or as if with a fête: *the author was fêted by his publishers.* **5.** (*intr.*) *Caribbean informal.* to join in a fête. [C18: from French: FEAST]
fête cham·pê·tre *French.* (fɛt ʃɑ̃'pɛtr) *n., pl.* ***fêtes cham·pê·tres*** (fɛt ʃɑ̃'pɛtr). **1.** a garden party, picnic, or similar outdoor entertainment. **2.** Also called: ***fête ga·lante*** ('fɛt ga'lɑ̃t). *Arts.* **a.** a genre of painting popular in France from the early 18th century, characterized by the depiction of figures in pastoral settings. Watteau was its most famous exponent. **b.** a painting in this genre. [C18: from French, literally: country festival]
fe·tial ('fiːʃəl) *n., pl.* **·ti·a·les** (ˌfiːʃi'eɪliːz). **1.** (in ancient Rome) any of the 20 priestly heralds involved in declarations of war and in peace negotiations. ~*adj.* **2.** of or relating to the fetiales. **3.** a less common word for **heraldic.** [C16: from Latin *fētiālis,* probably from Old Latin *fētis* treaty]
fe·ti·cide *or* **foe·ti·cide** ('fiːtɪˌsaɪd) *n.* the destruction of a fetus in the uterus; aborticide. —ˌ**fe·ti·'cid·al** *or* ˌ**foe·ti·'cid·al** *adj.*
fet·id *or* **foet·id** ('fɛtɪd, 'fiː-) *adj.* having a stale nauseating smell, as of decay. [C16: from Latin *fētidus,* from *fētēre* to stink; related to *fūmus* smoke] —'**fet·id·ly** *or* '**foet·id·ly** *adv.* —'**fet·id·ness** *or* '**foet·id·ness** *n.*
fe·tip·a·rous *or* **foe·tip·a·rous** (fɪ'tɪpərəs) *adj.* (of marsupials, such as the kangaroo) giving birth to incompletely developed offspring. [C19: from FETUS + -PAROUS]
fet·ish *or* **fet·ich** ('fɛtɪʃ, 'fiːtɪʃ) *n.* **1.** something, esp. an inanimate object, that is believed in certain cultures to be the embodiment or habitation of a spirit or magical powers. **2. a.** a form of behaviour involving fetishism. **b.** any object that is involved in fetishism. **3.** any object, activity, etc., to which one is excessively or irrationally devoted: *to make a fetish of cleanliness.* [C17: from French *fétiche,* from Portuguese *feitiço* (n.) sorcery, from adj.: artificial, from Latin *factīcius* made by art, FACTITIOUS] —'**fet·ish-ˌlike** *or* '**fet·ich-ˌlike** *adj.*
fet·ish·ism *or* **fet·ich·ism** ('fɛtɪˌʃɪzəm, 'fiː-) *n.* **1.** a condition in which the handling of an inanimate object or a specific part of the body other than the sexual organs is a source of sexual satisfaction. **2.** belief in or recourse to a fetish for magical purposes. **3.** excessive attention or attachment to something. —'**fet·ish·ist** *or* '**fet·ich·ist** *n.* —ˌ**fet·ish·'is·tic** *or* ˌ**fet·ich·'is·tic** *adj.*
fet·lock ('fɛtˌlɒk) *or* **fet·ter·lock** *n.* **1.** a projection behind and above a horse's hoof: the part of the leg between the cannon bone and the pastern. **2.** Also called: **fetlock joint.** the joint at this part of the leg. **3.** the tuft of hair growing from this part. [C14 *fetlak;* related to Middle High German *vizzeloch* fetlock, from *vizzel* pastern + *-och;* see FOOT]
fe·tor *or* **foe·tor** ('fiːtə, -tɔː) *n.* an offensive stale or putrid odour; stench. [C15: from Latin, from *fētēre* to stink]
fet·ter ('fɛtə) *n.* **1.** (*often pl.*) a chain or bond fastened round the ankle; shackle. **2.** (*usually pl.*) a check or restraint: *in fetters.* ~*vb.* (*tr.*) **3.** to restrict or confine. **4.** to bind in fetters. [Old English *fetor;* related to Old Norse *fjöturr* fetter, Old High German *fezzera,* Latin *pedica* fetter, *impedīre* to hinder] —'**fet·ter·er** *n.* —'**fet·ter·less** *adj.*
fet·ter bone *n.* another name for **pastern** (sense 2).
fet·ter·lock ('fɛtəˌlɒk) *n.* another name for **fetlock.**
fet·tle ('fɛtᵊl) *vb.* (*tr.*) **1.** to remove (excess moulding material and casting irregularities) from a cast component. **2.** to line or repair (the walls of a furnace). **3.** *Brit. dialect.* **a.** to prepare or arrange (a thing, oneself, etc.), esp. to put a finishing touch to. **b.** to repair or mend (something). ~*n.* **4.** state of health, spirits, etc. (esp. in the phrase **in fine fettle**). **5.** another name for **fettling.** [C14 (in the sense: to put in order): back formation from *fetled* girded up, from Old English *fetel* belt]
fet·tling ('fɛtlɪŋ) *n.* a refractory material used to line the hearth of puddling furnaces. Also called: **fettle.**
fet·tu·ci·ne, fet·tuc·ci·ne, *or* **fet·tu·ci·ni** (ˌfɛtuː'tʃiːnɪ) *n.* a type of pasta in the form of narrow ribbons. [Italian *fettuccine,* plural of *fettuccina,* diminutive of *fetta* slice]
fe·tus *or* **foe·tus** ('fiːtəs) *n.* the embryo of a mammal in the later stages of development, when it shows all the main recognizable features of the mature animal, esp. a human embryo from the end of the second month of pregnancy until birth. Compare **embryo** (sense 2). [C14: from Latin: offspring, brood]
feu (fjuː) *n. Scot. legal history.* **a.** a feudal tenure of land for which rent was paid in money or grain instead of by the performance of military service. **b.** the land so held. [C15: from Old French; see FEE]
feu·ar ('fjuə) *n. Scot. legal history.* the tenant of a feu.
Feucht·wang·er (*German* 'fɔɪçtvaŋər) *n.* **Li·on** ('liːɔn). 1884–1958, German novelist and dramatist, lived in the U.S. (1940–58): noted for his historical novels, including *Die hässliche Herzogin* (1923) and *Jud Süss* (1925).
feud[1] (fjuːd) *n.* **1.** long and bitter hostility between two families, clans, or individuals; vendetta. **2.** a quarrel or dispute. ~*vb.* **3.** (*intr.*) to take part in or carry on a feud. [C13 *fede,* from Old French *feide,* from Old High German *fēhida;* related to Old English *fæhth* hostility; see FOE]
feud[2] *or* **feod** (fjuːd) *n. Feudal law.* land held in return for

service. [C17: from Medieval Latin *feodum*, of Germanic origin; see FEE]
feu·dal[1] ('fju:dᵊl) *adj.* **1.** of, resembling, relating to, or characteristic of feudalism or its institutions. **2.** of, characteristic of, or relating to a fief. Compare **allodial. 3.** *Disparaging.* old-fashioned, reactionary, etc. [C17: from Medieval Latin *feudālis*, from *feudum* FEUD[2]]
feu·dal[2] ('fju:dᵊl) *adj.* of or relating to a feud or quarrel.
feu·dal·ism ('fju:də,lɪzəm) *n.* **1.** Also called: **feudal system.** the legal and social system that evolved in W Europe in the 8th and 9th centuries, in which vassals were protected and maintained by their lords, usually through the granting of fiefs, and were required to serve under them in war. See also **vassalage, fief. 2.** any social system or society, such as medieval Japan or Ptolemaic Egypt, that resembles medieval European feudalism. —**'feu·dal·ist** *n.* —**,feu·dal·'is·tic** *adj.*
feu·dal·i·ty (fju:'dælɪtɪ) *n., pl.* **·ties. 1.** the state or quality of being feudal. **2.** a fief or fee.
feu·dal·ize *or* **feu·dal·ise** ('fju:də,laɪz) *vb.* (*tr.*) to make feudal; create feudal institutions in (a society, etc.). —**,feu·dal·i·'za·tion** *or* **,feu·dal·i·'sa·tion** *n.*
feu·da·to·ry ('fju:dətərɪ, -trɪ) (in feudal Europe) ~*n.* **1.** a person holding a fief; vassal. ~*adj.* **2.** relating to or characteristic of the relationship between lord and vassal. **3.** (esp. of a kingdom) under the overlordship of another sovereign. [C16: from Medieval Latin *feudātor*]
feud·ist ('fju:dɪst) *n. U.S.* a person who takes part in a feud or quarrel.
Feu·er·bach (*German* 'fɔɪərbax) *n.* **Lud·wig An·dre·as** ('lu:tvɪç an'dre:as). 1804–72, German materialist philosopher: in *The Essence of Christianity* (1841), translated into English by George Eliot (1853), he maintained that God is merely an outward projection of man's inner self.
Feuil·lant *French.* (fœ'jã) *n. French history.* a member of a club formed in 1791 by Lafayette advocating a limited constitutional monarchy: forced to disband in 1792 as the revolution became more violent and antimonarchical. [from the convent of Notre Dame des *Feuillants*, where meetings were held]
feuil·le·ton ('fɜɪ,tɒn; *French* fœj'tɔ̃) *n.* **1.** the part of a European newspaper carrying reviews, serialized fiction, etc. **2.** such a review or article. [C19: from French, from *feuillet* sheet of paper, diminutive of *feuille* leaf, from Latin *folium*] —**'feuil·le·ton·ism** *n.* —**'feuil·le·ton·ist** *n.* —**,feuil·le·ton·'is·tic** *adj.*
fe·ver ('fi:və) *n.* **1.** an abnormally high body temperature, accompanied by a fast pulse rate, dry skin, etc. Related adj.: **febrile. 2.** any of various diseases, such as yellow fever or scarlet fever, characterized by a high temperature. **3.** intense nervous excitement or agitation: *she was in a fever about her party.* ~*vb.* **4.** (*tr.*) to affect with or as if with fever. [Old English *fēfor*, from Latin *febris*] —**'fe·vered** *adj.* —**'fe·ver·less** *adj.*
fe·ver blis·ter *or* **sore** *n.* another name for **cold sore.**
fe·ver·few ('fi:və,fju:) *n.* a bushy European strong-scented perennial plant, *Chrysanthemum parthenium*, with white flower heads, formerly used medicinally: family *Compositae* (composites). [Old English *feferfuge*, from Late Latin *febrifugia*, from Latin *febris* fever + *fugāre* to put to flight]
fe·ver·ish ('fi:vərɪʃ) *or* **fe·ver·ous** *adj.* **1.** suffering from fever, esp. a slight fever. **2.** in a state of restless excitement. **3.** of, relating to, caused by, or causing fever. —**'fe·ver·ish·ly** *or* **'fe·ver·ous·ly** *adv.* —**'fe·ver·ish·ness** *n.*
fe·ver pitch *n.* a state of intense excitement: *things were at fever pitch with the election coming up.*
fe·ver ther·a·py *n.* a former method of treating disease by raising the body temperature. Compare **cryotherapy.**
fe·ver tree *n.* **1.** any of several trees that produce a febrifuge or tonic, esp. *Pinckneya pubens*, a rubiaceous tree of SE North America. **2.** a tall mimosaceous swamp tree, *Acacia xanthophloea*, of southern Africa, with fragrant yellow flowers.
fe·ver·wort ('fi:və,wɜ:t) *n.* any of several plants considered to have medicinal properties, such as horse gentian and boneset.
few (fju:) *determiner.* **1. a.** a small number of; hardly any: *few men are so cruel.* **b.** (*as pronoun; functioning as pl.*): *many are called but few are chosen.* **2.** (preceded by *a*) **a.** a small number of: *a few drinks.* **b.** (*as pronoun; functioning as pl.*): *a few of you.* **3. a good few.** *Informal.* several. **4. few and far between. a.** at great intervals; widely spaced. **b.** not abundant; scarce. **5. have a few (too many).** to consume several (*or* too many) alcoholic drinks. **6. not** *or* **quite a few.** *Informal.* several. ~*n.* **7. the few.** a small number of people considered as a class: *the few who fell at Thermopylae.* Compare **many** (sense 4). [Old English *fēawa*; related to Old High German *fao* little, Old Norse *fār* little, silent] —**'few·ness** *n.*
Usage. See at **less.**
fey (feɪ) *adj.* **1.** interested in or believing in the supernatural; whimsical. **2.** attuned to the supernatural; clairvoyant; visionary. **3.** *Chiefly Scot.* fated to die; doomed. **4.** *Chiefly Scot.* in a state of high spirits or unusual excitement, formerly believed to presage death. [Old English *fæge* marked out for death; related to Old Norse *feigr* doomed, Old High German *feigi*] —**'fey·ness** *n.*
Fey·deau (*French* fɛ'do) *n.* **Georges** (ʒɔrʒ). 1862–1921, French dramatist, noted for his farces, esp. *La Dame de chez Maxim* (1899) and *Occupe-toi d'Amélie* (1908).
fez (fɛz) *n., pl.* **fez·zes.** an originally Turkish brimless felt or wool cap, shaped like a truncated cone, usually red and with a tassel. [C19: via French from Turkish, from FEZ] —**fezzed** *adj.*
Fez (fɛz) *n.* a variant spelling of **Fès.**
Fez·zan (fɛ'zɑ:n) *n.* a region of SW Libya, in the Sahara: a former province (until 1963).
ff *Music. symbol for* fortissimo. See f
ff. **1.** *abbrev. for* folios. **2.** *symbol for* and the following (pages, lines, etc.).
f.f.a. *Commerce. abbrev. for* free from alongside (ship).
F.I. *abbrev. for* Falkland Islands.
fi·a·cre (fɪ'ɑ:krə) *n.* a small four-wheeled horse-drawn carriage, usually with a folding roof. [C17: named after the Hotel de St. *Fiacre*, Paris, where these vehicles were first hired out]
fi·an·cé *or* (*fem.*) **fi·an·cée** (fɪ'ɒnseɪ) *n.* a person who is engaged to be married. [C19: from French, from Old French *fiancier* to promise, betroth, from *fiance* a vow, from *fier* to trust, from Latin *fīdere*]
Fi·an·na ('fi:ənə) *n. Irish myth.* another word for **Fenian** (sense 2).
Fi·an·na Fail (fɔɪl) *n.* one of the major Irish political parties, founded by de Valera in 1926 as an anti-British republican party. [Irish, from *Fianna* Fenians + *Fāil* of the earth, from *fāl* earth, sod]
fi·as·co (fɪ'æskəʊ) *n., pl.* **·cos** *or* **·coes.** a complete failure, esp. one that is ignominious or humiliating. [C19: from Italian, literally: FLASK; sense development obscure]
fi·at ('faɪət, -æt) *n.* **1.** official sanction; authoritative permission. **2.** an arbitrary order or decree. **3.** *Chiefly literary.* any command, decision, or act of will that brings something about. [C17: from Latin, literally: let it be done, from *fierī* to become]
fi·at mon·ey *n. Chiefly U.S.* money declared by a government to be legal tender though it is not convertible into standard specie.
fib (fɪb) *n.* **1.** a trivial and harmless lie. ~*vb.* **fibs, fib·bing, fibbed. 2.** (*intr.*) to tell such a lie. [C17: perhaps from *fibble-fable* an unlikely story; see FABLE] —**'fib·ber** *n.*
fi·ber ('faɪbə) *n.* the usual U.S. spelling of **fibre.**
Fib·o·nac·ci se·quence *or* **se·ries** (,fɪbə'nɑ:tʃɪ) *n.* the infinite sequence of numbers, 0, 1, 1, 2, 3, 5, 8, etc., in which each member (**Fibonacci number**) is the sum of the previous two. [named after Leonardo *Fibonacci* (?1170–?1250), Florentine mathematician]
fi·bre *or U.S.* **fi·ber** ('faɪbə) *n.* **1.** a natural or synthetic filament that may be spun into yarn, such as cotton or nylon. **2.** cloth or other material made from such yarn. **3.** a long fine continuous thread or filament. **4.** the structure of any material or substance made of or as if of fibres; texture. **5.** essential substance or nature: *all the fibres of his being were stirred.* **6.** strength of character (esp. in the phrase **moral fibre**). **7.** *Botany.* **a.** a narrow elongated thick-walled cell: a constituent of sclerenchyma tissue. **b.** such tissue extracted from flax, hemp, etc., used to make linen, rope, etc. **c.** a very small root or twig. **8.** *Anatomy.* any thread-shaped structure, such as a nerve fibre. [C14: from Latin *fibra* filament, entrails] —**'fi·bred** *or U.S.* **'fi·bered** *adj.* —**'fi·bre·less** *or U.S.* **'fi·ber·less** *adj.*
fi·bre·board *or U.S.* **fi·ber·board** ('faɪbə,bɔ:d) *n.* a building material made of compressed wood or other plant fibres, esp. one in the form of a thin semirigid sheet.
fi·bre·fill *or U.S.* **fi·ber·fill** ('faɪbə,fɪl) *n.* a synthetic fibre used as a filling for pillows, quilted materials, etc.
fi·bre·glass ('faɪbə,glɑ:s) *n.* **1.** material consisting of matted fine glass fibres, used as insulation in buildings, in fireproof fabrics, etc. **2.** a fabric woven from this material or a light strong material made by bonding fibreglass with a synthetic resin; used for car bodies, boat hulls, etc.
fi·bre op·tics *n.* the use of bundles of long transparent glass fibres in transmitting light, esp. optical images.
fi·bri·form ('faɪbrɪ,fɔ:m, 'fɪb-) *adj.* having the form of a fibre or fibres.
fi·bril ('faɪbrɪl) *or* **fi·bril·la** (faɪ'brɪlə, fɪ-) *n., pl.* **·brils** *or* **·bril·lae** (-'brɪli:). **1.** a small fibre or part of a fibre. **2.** *Biology.* a threadlike structure, such as a root hair or a thread of muscle tissue. [C17: from New Latin *fibrilla* a little FIBRE] —**'fi·bri·lar, fi·'bril·lar,** *or* **fi·'bril·lose** *adj.* —**fi·'bril·li·,form** *adj.*
fi·bril·la·tion (,faɪbrɪ'leɪʃən, ,fɪb-) *n.* **1.** a local and uncontrollable twitching of muscle fibres, not affecting the entire muscle. **2.** irregular twitchings of the muscular wall of the heart, often interfering with the normal rhythmical contractions.
fi·brin ('fɪbrɪn) *n.* a white insoluble elastic protein formed from fibrinogen when blood clots: forms a network that traps red cells and platelets.
fi·brin·o·gen (fɪ'brɪnədʒən) *n.* a soluble protein, a globulin, in blood plasma, converted to fibrin by the action of the enzyme thrombin when blood clots. —**fi·brin·o·gen·ic** (,faɪbrɪnəʊ'dʒɛnɪk) *or* **fi·brin·o·gen·ous** (,faɪbrɪ'nɒdʒənəs) *adj.*
fi·bri·nol·y·sin (,fɪbrɪ'nɒlɪsɪn) *n.* a proteolytic enzyme that causes fibrinolysis in blood clots. Also called: **plasmin.**
fi·bri·nol·y·sis (,fɪbrɪ'nɒlɪsɪs) *n.* the breakdown of fibrin in blood clots, esp. by enzymes. —**fi·bri·no·lyt·ic** (,faɪbrɪnəʊ'lɪtɪk) *adj.*
fi·brin·ous ('fɪbrɪnəs) *adj.* of, containing, or resembling fibrin.
fi·bro ('faɪbrəʊ) *n. Austral. informal.* **1. a.** short for **fibrocement. b.** (*as modifier*): *a fibro shack.* **2.** a house built of fibrocement.
fi·bro- *combining form.* **1.** indicating fibrous tissue: *fibroin; fibrosis.* **2.** indicating fibre: *fibrocement.* [from Latin *fibra* FIBRE]
fi·bro·blast ('faɪbrəʊ,blæst) *n.* a cell in connective tissue that synthesizes collagen. —**,fi·bro·'blas·tic** *adj.*
fi·bro·ce·ment (,faɪbrəʊsɪ'mɛnt) *n.* cement combined with asbestos fibre, used esp. in sheets for building.

fi·broid ('faɪbrɔɪd) *adj.* **1.** *Anatomy.* (of structures or tissues) containing or resembling fibres. ~*n.* **2.** another word for **fibroma.**

fi·bro·in ('faɪbrəʊɪn) *n.* a tough elastic protein that is the principal component of spiders' webs and raw silk.

fi·bro·ma (faɪ'brəʊmə) *n., pl.* ·**ma·ta** (-mətə) *or* ·**mas.** a benign tumour derived from fibrous connective tissue. —**fi·brom·a·tous** (faɪ'brɒmətəs) *adj.*

fi·bro·sis (faɪ'brəʊsɪs) *n.* the formation of an abnormal amount of fibrous tissue in an organ or part as the result of inflammation, irritation, or healing. —**fi·brot·ic** (faɪ'brɒtɪk) *adj.*

fi·bro·si·tis (ˌfaɪbrə'saɪtɪs) *n.* inflammation of white fibrous tissue, esp. that of muscle sheaths.

fi·brous ('faɪbrəs) *adj.* consisting of, containing, or resembling fibres: *fibrous tissue.* —'**fi·brous·ly** *adv.* —'**fi·brous·ness** *n.*

fi·bro·vas·cu·lar (ˌfaɪbrəʊ'væskjʊlə) *adj. Botany.* (of a vascular bundle) surrounded by sclerenchyma or within sclerenchymatous tissue.

fib·u·la ('fɪbjʊlə) *n., pl.* ·**lae** (-ˌliː) *or* ·**las. 1.** the outer and thinner of the two bones between the knee and ankle of the human leg. Compare **tibia. 2.** the corresponding bone in other vertebrates. **3.** a metal brooch resembling a safety pin, often highly decorated, common in Europe after 1300 B.C. [C17: from Latin: clasp, probably from *fīgere* to fasten] —'**fib·u·lar** *adj.*

-fic *suffix forming adjectives.* causing, making, or producing: *honorific.* [from Latin *-ficus,* from *facere* to do, make]

fiche (fiːʃ) *n.* See **microfiche** or **ultrafiche.**

Fich·te (*German* 'fɪçtə) *n.* **Jo·hann Gott·lieb** ('joːhan 'gɔtliːp). 1762–1814, German philosopher: expounded ethical idealism.

fich·u ('fɪːʃuː) *n.* a woman's shawl or scarf of some light material, worn esp. in the 18th century. [C19: from French: small shawl, from *ficher* to fix with a pin, from Latin *fīgere* to fasten, FIX]

Fi·ci·no (*Italian* fi'tʃiːno) *n.* **Mar·si·lio** (mar'siːljo). 1433–99, Italian Neoplatonist philosopher: attempted to integrate Platonism with Christianity.

fick·le ('fɪkᵊl) *adj.* changeable in purpose, affections, etc.; capricious. [Old English *ficol* deceitful; related to *fician* to wheedle, *befician* to deceive] —'**fick·le·ness** *n.*

fi·co ('fiːkəʊ) *n., pl.* ·**coes.** *Archaic.* **1.** a worthless trifle. **2.** another word for **fig**[1] (sense 7). [C16: from Italian: FIG[1]]

fic·tile ('fɪktaɪl) *adj.* **1.** moulded or capable of being moulded from clay; plastic. **2.** made of clay by a potter. **3.** relating to the craft of pottery. [C17: from Latin *fictilis* that can be moulded, hence, made of clay, from *fingere* to shape]

fic·tion ('fɪkʃən) *n.* **1.** literary works invented by the imagination, such as novels or short stories. **2.** an invented story or explanation; lie. **3.** the act of inventing a story or explanation. **4.** *Law.* something assumed to be true for the sake of convenience, though probably false. [C14: from Latin *fictiō* a fashioning, hence something imaginary, from *fingere* to shape] —'**fic·tion·al** *adj.* —'**fic·tion·al·ly** *adv.* —ˌ**fic·tio·'neer** *or* '**fic·tion·ist** *n.*

fic·tion·al·ize *or* **fic·tion·al·ise** ('fɪkʃənəˌlaɪz) *vb. (tr.)* to make into fiction or give a fictional aspect to. —ˌ**fic·tion·al·i·'za·tion** *or* ˌ**fic·tion·al·i·'sa·tion** *n.*

fic·ti·tious (fɪk'tɪʃəs) *adj.* **1.** not genuine or authentic; assumed; false: *to give a fictitious address.* **2.** of, related to, or characteristic of fiction; created by the imagination. —**fic·'ti·tious·ly** *adv.* —**fic·'ti·tious·ness** *n.*

fic·tive ('fɪktɪv) *adj.* **1.** *Rare.* of, relating to, or able to create fiction. **2.** a rare word for **fictitious.** —'**fic·tive·ly** *adv.*

fid (fɪd) *n. Nautical.* **1.** a spike for separating strands of rope in splicing. **2.** a wooden or metal bar for supporting the heel of a topmast. [C17: of unknown origin]

-fid *adj. combining form.* divided into parts or lobes: *bifid; pinnatifid.* [from Latin *-fidus,* from *findere* to split]

Fid. Def. *abbrev. for* Fidei Defensor.

fid·dle ('fɪdᵊl) *n.* **1.** *Informal or disparaging.* any instrument of the viol or violin family, esp. the violin. **2.** time-wasting or trifling behaviour; nonsense; triviality. **3.** *Nautical.* a small railing around the top of a table to prevent objects from falling off it in bad weather. **4.** *Brit. informal.* an illegal or fraudulent transaction or arrangement. **5. face as long as a fiddle.** *Informal.* a dismal or gloomy facial expression. **6. fit as a fiddle.** *Informal.* in very good health. **7. play second fiddle.** *Informal.* to be subordinate; play a minor part. ~*vb.* **8.** to play (a tune) on the fiddle. **9.** (*intr.;* often foll. by *with*) to make restless or aimless movements with the hands. **10.** (when *intr.,* often foll. by *about* or *around*) *Informal.* to spend (time) or act in a careless or inconsequential manner; waste (time). **11.** (often foll. by *with*) *Informal.* to tamper or interfere (with). **12.** *Informal.* to contrive to do (something) by illicit means or deception: *he fiddled his way into a position of trust.* **13.** (*tr.*) *Informal.* to falsify (accounts, etc.); swindle. [Old English *fithele,* probably from Medieval Latin *vītula,* from Latin *vītulārī* to celebrate; compare Old High German *fidula* fiddle; see VIOLA[1]]

fid·dle-back *n.* **1.** a chair with a fiddle-shaped back. **2.** a chasuble with a fiddle-shaped front.

fid·dle-de-dee, fid·dle·de·dee, *or* **fid·dle·dee·dee** (ˌfɪdᵊldɪ'diː) *interj. Rare.* an exclamation of impatience, disbelief, or disagreement.

fid·dle-fad·dle ('fɪdᵊlˌfædᵊl) *n., interj.* **1.** trivial matter; nonsense. ~*vb.* **2.** (*intr.*) to fuss or waste time, esp. over trivial matters. [C16: reduplication of FIDDLE] —'**fid·dle-ˌfad·dler** *n.*

fid·dle·head ('fɪdᵊlˌhɛd) *or* **fid·dle·neck** *n.* **1.** *Nautical.* an ornamental carving, in the shape of the scroll at the head end of a fiddle, fitted to the top of the stem or cutwater. **2.** *U.S.* the edible coiled tip of a young fern frond.

fid·dle pat·tern *n.* the style of a spoon or fork with a violin-shaped handle.

fid·dler ('fɪdlə) *n.* **1.** a person who plays the fiddle, esp. in folk music. **2.** See **fiddler crab. 3.** a person who wastes time or acts aimlessly. **4.** *Informal.* a cheat or petty rogue.

fid·dler crab *n.* any of various burrowing crabs of the genus *Uca* of American coastal regions, the males of which have one of their anterior pincer-like claws very much enlarged. [C19: referring to the rapid fiddling movement of the enlarged anterior claw of the males, used to attract females]

fid·dle·stick ('fɪdᵊlˌstɪk) *n.* **1.** *Informal.* a violin bow. **2.** any meaningless or inconsequential thing; trifle. **3.** (*pl.*) *interj.* used to express annoyance or disagreement.

fid·dle·wood ('fɪdᵊlˌwʊd) *n.* **1.** any of various tropical American verbenaceous trees of the genus *Citharexylum* and related genera. **2.** the hard durable wood of any of these trees.

fid·dling ('fɪdlɪŋ) *adj.* trifling or insignificant; petty.

fid·dly *adj.* ·**dli·er,** ·**dli·est.** small and awkward to do or handle.

F.I.D.E. *abbrev. for* Fédération Internationale des Echecs: International Chess Federation.

fid·e·i·com·mis·sar·y (ˌfɪdɪaɪ'kɒmɪsərɪ) *Civil law. n., pl.* ·**sar·ies. 1.** a person who receives a fideicommissum. ~*adj.* **2.** of, relating to, or resembling a fideicommissum.

fid·e·i·com·mis·sum (ˌfɪdɪaɪkə'mɪsəm) *n., pl.* ·**sa** (-sə). *Civil law.* a gift of property, usually by will, to be held on behalf of another who cannot receive the gift directly. [C18: from Late Latin: (something) bequeathed in trust, from Latin *fidēs* trust, faith + *committere* to entrust]

Fi·de·i De·fen·sor *Latin.* ('faɪdɪˌaɪ dɪ'fɛnsɔː) *n.* defender of the faith; a title given to Henry VIII by Pope Leo X, and appearing on Brit. coins as FID DEF (before decimalization) or FD (after decimalization).

fi·de·ism ('fiːdeɪˌɪzəm) *n.* trust placed in faith rather than in reason. [C19: from Latin *fidēs* faith] —'**fi·de·ist** *n.* —ˌ**fi·de·'is·tic** *adj.*

Fi·del·ism (fiː'dɛlɪzəm) *n.* belief in, adherence to, or advocacy of the principles of Fidel Castro. Also called: **Castroism.** —**Fi·'del·ist** *n.*

fi·del·i·ty (fɪ'dɛlɪtɪ) *n., pl.* ·**ties. 1.** devotion to duties, obligations, etc.; faithfulness. **2.** loyalty or devotion, as to a person or cause. **3.** faithfulness to one's spouse, lover, etc. **4.** adherence to truth; accuracy in reporting detail. **5.** *Electronics.* the degree to which the output of a system, such as an amplifier or radio, accurately reproduces the characteristics of the input signal. See also **high fidelity.** [C15: from Latin *fidēlitās,* from *fidēlis* faithful, from *fidēs* faith, loyalty]

fidge (fɪdʒ) *vb.* (*intr.*) an obsolete word for **fidget.** [C18: probably variant of dialect *fitch* to FIDGET]

fidg·et ('fɪdʒɪt) *vb.* **1.** (*intr.*) to move about restlessly. **2.** (*intr.;* often foll. by *with*) to make restless or uneasy movements (with something); fiddle: *he fidgeted with his pen.* **3.** (*tr.*) to cause to fidget. ~*n.* **4.** (*often pl.*) a state of restlessness or unease, esp. as expressed in continual motion: *he's got the fidgets.* **5.** a person who fidgets. [C17: from earlier *fidge,* probably from Old Norse *fīkjast* to desire eagerly] —'**fidg·et·ing·ly** *adv.* —'**fidg·et·y** *adj.*

fi·du·ci·al (fɪ'djuːʃɪəl) *adj.* **1.** *Physics.* used as a standard of reference or measurement: *a fiducial point.* **2.** of or based on trust or faith. **3.** *Law.* a less common word for **fiduciary.** [C17: from Late Latin *fīdūciālis,* from Latin *fīdūcia* confidence, reliance, from *fīdere* to trust] —**fi·'du·ci·al·ly** *adv.*

fi·du·ci·ar·y (fɪ'duːʃɪərɪ) *Law.* ~*n.* **1.** a person bound to act for another's benefit, as a trustee in relation to his beneficiary. ~*adj.* **2. a.** having the nature of a trust. **b.** of or relating to a trust or trustee. [C17: from Latin *fīdūciārius* relating to something held in trust, from *fīdūcia* trust; see FIDUCIAL] —**fi·'du·ci·ar·i·ly** *adv.*

fi·du·ci·ar·y is·sue *n.* an issue of bank notes not backed by gold.

fi·dus A·cha·tes ('faɪdəs ə'keɪtiːz) *n.* a faithful friend or companion. [Latin, literally: faithful Achates, the name of the faithful companion of Aeneas in Virgil's *Aeneid*]

fie (faɪ) *interj. Obsolete or facetious.* an exclamation of distaste or mock dismay. [C13: from Old French *fi,* from Latin *fī,* exclamation of disgust]

fief *or* **feoff** (fiːf) *n.* (in feudal Europe) the property or fee granted to a vassal for his maintenance by his lord in return for service. [C17: from Old French *fie,* of Germanic origin; compare Old English *fēo* cattle, money, Latin *pecus* cattle, *pecūnia* money, Greek *pokos* fleece]

field (fiːld) *n.* **1.** an open tract of uncultivated grassland; meadow. Related adj.: **campestral. 2.** a piece of land cleared of trees and undergrowth, usually enclosed with a fence or hedge and used for pasture or growing crops: *a field of barley.* **3.** a limited or marked off area, usually of mown grass, on which any of various sports, athletic competitions, etc., are held: *a soccer field.* **4.** an area that is rich in minerals or other natural resources: *a coalfield.* **5.** short for **battlefield** and **airfield. 6.** the mounted followers that hunt with a pack of hounds. **7.** *Horse racing.* all the runners in a particular race. **8.** *Cricket.* the fielders collectively, esp. with regard to their positions. **9.** a wide or open expanse: *a field of snow.* **10. a.** an area of human activity: *the field of human knowledge.* **b.** a sphere or division of knowledge, interest, etc.: *his field is physics.* **11. a.** a place away from the laboratory, office, library, etc., usually out of doors, where practical work is done or original material or data collected. **b.** (*as modifier*): *a field course.* **12.** the surface or background, as of a flag, coin, or heraldic shield, on which a design is displayed. **13.** Also called: **field of view.** the area within which an object may be observed with a telescope, microscope, etc. **14.** *Physics.* **a.** See **field of force. b.** a region of space that is a vector field. **c.** a region of space under the influence of some scalar quantity, such as temperature. **15.** *Maths.* **a.** a set of numbers in which the sum, difference, product, and quotient of any two members, excluding division by zero, are themselves members of the set. **b.** a set of entities subject to two binary operations, addition and multiplication, such that the set is a commutative group under addition and the set, minus the zero, is a commutative group under multiplication. **16.** *Computer technol.* **a.** a set of one or more characters comprising a unit of information. **b.** the characters in a vertical column of a punched card. **17.** *Obsolete.* the open country: *beasts of the field.* **18. hold** *or* **keep the field.** to maintain one's position in the face of opposition. **19. in the field. a.** *Military.* in an area in which operations are in progress. **b.** actively or closely involved with or working on something (rather than being in a more remote or administrative position). **20. leave the field.** *Informal.* to back out of a competition, contest, etc. **21. take the field.** to begin or carry on activity, esp. in sport or military operations. **22. play the field.** *Informal.* to disperse one's interests or attentions among a number of activities, people, or objects. **23.** (*modifier*) *Military.* of or relating to equipment, personnel, etc., specifically designed or trained for operations in the field: *a field gun; a field army.* ~*vb.* **24.** (*tr.*) *Sport.* to stop, catch, or return (the ball) as a fielder. **25.** (*tr.*) *Sport.* to send (a player or team) onto the field to play. **26.** (*intr.*) *Sport.* (of a player or team) to act or take turn as a fielder or fielders. **27.** (*tr.*) *Informal.* to deal with or handle, esp. adequately and by making a reciprocal gesture: *to field a question.* [Old English *feld;* related to Old Saxon, Old High German *feld,* Old English *fold* earth, Greek *platus* broad]

Field (fiːld) *n.* **John.** 1782–1837, Irish composer and pianist, lived in Russia from 1803: invented the nocturne.

field ar·til·ler·y *n.* artillery capable of deployment in support of front-line troops, due mainly to its mobility.

field bat·ter·y *n.* a small unit of usually four field guns.

field boot *n.* a close-fitting knee-length boot.

field cap·tain *n.* the senior official at an archery meeting, responsible for safety.

field corn *n. U.S.* any variety of corn that is grown as a feed for livestock.

field day *n.* **1.** a day spent in some special outdoor activity, such as nature study or sport. **2.** a day-long competition between amateur radio operators using battery or generator power, the aim being to make the most contacts with other operators around the world. **3.** *Military.* a day devoted to manoeuvres or exercises, esp. before an audience. **4.** *Informal.* a day or time of exciting or successful activity: *the children had a field day with their new toys.*

field-ef·fect tran·sis·tor *n.* a unipolar transistor consisting of three or more electrode regions, the source, one or more gates, and the drain. A current flowing in a channel between the highly doped source and drain is controlled by the electric field arising from a voltage applied between source and gate. Abbrev.: **FET.** See also **JUGFET, IGFET.**

field e·mis·sion *n.* the emission of electrons from a solid or liquid subjected to a high electric field.

field·er ('fiːldə) *n. Cricket, baseball, etc.* **a.** a player in the field. **b.** a member of the fielding rather than the batting side.

field e·vent *n.* a competition, such as the discus, high jump, etc., that takes place on a field or similar area as opposed to those on the running track.

field·fare ('fiːldˌfɛə) *n.* a large Old World thrush, *Turdus pilaris,* having a pale grey head and rump, brown wings and back, and a blackish tail. [Old English *feldefare;* see FIELD, FARE]

field glass·es *pl. n.* another name for **binoculars.**

field goal *n.* **1.** *Basketball.* a goal worth two points scored while the ball is in normal play rather than from a free throw. **2.** *American football.* a score of three points made by kicking the ball over the opponent's crossbar.

field guid·ance *n.* a method of guiding a missile to a point within a gravitational or radio field by means of the properties of the field.

field gun *n.* a gun specially designed for service in direct support of front-line troops.

field hock·ey *n. Chiefly U.S.* hockey played on a field, as distinguished from ice hockey.

field-hol·ler *n.* a cry employing falsetto, portamento, and sudden changes of pitch, used in Negro work songs, later integrated into the techniques of the blues.

field hos·pi·tal *n.* a temporary hospital set up on an isolated battle field for emergency treatment; first-aid station.

Field·ing ('fiːldɪŋ) *n.* **Hen·ry.** 1707–54, English novelist and dramatist, noted particularly for his picaresque novel *Tom Jones* (1749), a comic masterpiece, *Joseph Andrews* (1742), which starts as a parody of Richardson's *Pamela,* and *Amelia* (1751).

field mag·net *n.* a permanent magnet or an electromagnet that produces the magnetic field in a generator, electric motor, or similar device.

field mar·shal *n.* an officer holding the highest rank in the British and certain other armies.

field·mouse ('fiːldˌmaʊs) *n., pl.* **·mice. 1.** any nocturnal mouse of the genus *Apodemus,* inhabiting woods, fields, and gardens of the Old World: family *Muridae.* They have yellowish-brown fur and feed on fruit, vegetables, seeds, etc. **2.** a former name for **vole.**

field of·fic·er *n.* an officer holding **field rank,** namely that of major, lieutenant colonel, or colonel.

field of force *n.* the region of space surrounding a body, such as a charged particle or a magnet, within which it can exert a force on another similar body not in contact with it. See also **electric field, magnetic field, gravitational field.**

field of hon·our *n.* the place or scene of a battle or duel, esp. of jousting tournaments in medieval times.

field·piece ('fiːldˌpiːs) *n.* (formerly) a field gun.

field pop·py *n.* another name for **corn poppy.**

Fields (fiːldz) *n.* **1. Gra·cie.** original name *Grace Stansfield.* 1898-1979, English popular singer and comedienne. **2. W.C.** original name *William Claude Dukenfield.* 1880-1946, U.S. film actor, noted for his portrayal of comic roles.

fields·man ('fiːldzmən) *n., pl.* **·men.** *Cricket.* another name for **fielder.**

field span·iel *n.* a breed of spaniel developed by crossing the cocker spaniel with the Sussex spaniel.

field sports *pl. n.* sports carried on in the open countryside, such as hunting, shooting, or fishing.

field·stone ('fiːldˌstəʊn) *n.* building stone found in fields.

field tri·al *n.* **1.** *Hunting.* a test of or contest between gun dogs to determine their proficiency and standard of training in retrieving or pointing. **2.** (*often pl.*) a test to display performance, efficiency, or durability, as of a vehicle or invention.

field trip *n.* an expedition, as by a group of students or research workers, to study something at first hand.

field wind·ing ('waɪndɪŋ) *n.* the insulated current-carrying coils on a field magnet that produce the magnetic field intensity required to set up the electrical excitation in a generator or motor.

field·work ('fiːldˌwɜːk) *n. Military.* a temporary structure used in defending or fortifying a place or position.

field work *n.* an investigation or search for material, data, etc., made in the field as opposed to the classroom, laboratory, or official headquarters. —**field work·er** *n.*

fiend (fiːnd) *n.* **1.** an evil spirit; demon; devil. **2.** a person who is extremely wicked, esp. in being very cruel or brutal. **3.** *Informal.* **a.** a person who is intensely interested in or fond of something: *a fresh-air fiend; he is a fiend for cards.* **b.** an addict: *a drug fiend.* **4.** *Informal.* a mischievous or spiteful person, esp. a child. [Old English *fēond;* related to Old Norse *fjāndi* enemy, Gothic *fijands,* Old High German *fiant*] —**'fiend·ˌlike** *adj.*

Fiend (fiːnd) *n.* **the.** the devil; Satan.

fiend·ish ('fiːndɪʃ) *adj.* **1.** of or like a fiend. **2.** diabolically wicked or cruel. **3.** *Informal.* extremely difficult or unpleasant: *a fiendish problem.* —**'fiend·ish·ly** *adv.* —**'fiend·ish·ness** *n.*

fierce (fɪəs) *adj.* **1.** having a violent and unrestrained nature; savage: *a fierce dog.* **2.** wild or turbulent in force, action, or intensity: *a fierce storm.* **3.** vehement, intense, or strong: *fierce competition.* **4.** *Informal.* very disagreeable or unpleasant. [C13: from Old French *fiers,* from Latin *ferus*] —**'fierce·ly** *adv.* —**'fierce·ness** *n.*

fi·er·i fa·ci·as ('faɪəˌraɪ 'feɪʃɪæs) *n. Law.* a writ ordering a levy on the belongings of an adjudged debtor to satisfy the debt. [C15: from Latin, literally: cause (it) to be done]

fier·y ('faɪərɪ) *adj.* **1.** of, containing, or composed of fire. **2.** resembling fire in heat, colour, ardour, etc.: *a fiery desert wind; a fiery speaker.* **3.** easily angered or aroused: *a fiery temper.* **4.** (of food) producing a burning sensation: *a fiery curry.* **5.** (of the skin or a sore) inflamed. **6.** flammable or containing flammable gas. **7.** (of a cricket pitch) making the ball bounce dangerously high.

fier·y cross *n.* **1.** a burning cross, used as a symbol by the Ku Klux Klan. **2.** a wooden cross with ends charred or dipped in blood formerly used by Scottish Highlanders to summon the clans to battle.

Fie·so·le[1] (*Italian* 'fjɛːzole) *n.* a town in central Italy, in Tuscany near Florence: Etruscan and Roman remains. Pop.: 114 111 (1971). Ancient name: **Faesulae.**

Fie·so·le[2] (*Italian* 'fjɛːzole) *n.* **Gio·van·ni da** (dʒo'vanni da). the monastic name of (Fra) **Angelico.**

fi·es·ta (fɪ'ɛstə; *Spanish* 'fjesta) *n.* (esp. in Spain and Latin America) **1.** a religious festival or celebration, esp. on a saint's day. **2.** a holiday or carnival. [Spanish, from Latin *festa,* plural of *festum* festival; see FEAST]

FIFA ('fiːfə) *n. acronym for* Fédération Internationale de Football Association. [from French]

fife (faɪf) *n.* **1.** a small high-pitched flute similar to the piccolo and usually having no keys, used esp. in military bands. ~*vb.* **2.** to play (music) on a fife. [C16: from Old High German *pfīfa;* see PIPE[1]] —**'fif·er** *n.*

Fife (faɪf) *n.* **1.** a local government region of E central Scotland, bordering on the North Sea between the Firths of Tay and Forth: coastal lowlands in the north and east, with several ranges of hills; mainly agricultural. Administrative centre: Glenrothes. Pop.: 338 734 (1976 est.). Area: 1305 sq. km (504 sq. miles). **2.** (until 1975) a county of E central Scotland, coextensive with Fife region.

fife rail *n. Nautical.* a rail at the base of a mast of a sailing vessel, fitted with pins for belaying running rigging. Compare **pin rail.** [C18: of unknown origin]

fif·teen ('fɪf'tiːn) *n.* **1.** the cardinal number that is the sum of ten and five. **2.** a numeral 15, XV, etc., representing this number. **3.** something represented by, representing, or consisting of 15 units. **4.** a rugby football team. ~*determiner.* **5. a.**

amounting to fifteen: *fifteen jokes.* **b.** (*as pronoun*): *fifteen of us danced.* [Old English *fiftēne*]

fif·teenth ('fɪf'ti:nθ) *adj.* **1. a.** coming after the fourteenth in order, position, time, etc. Often written 15th. **b.** (*as n.*): *the fifteenth of the month.* ~*n.* **2. a.** one of 15 equal or nearly equal parts of something. **b.** (*as modifier*): *a fifteenth part.* **3.** the fraction equal to one divided by 15 (1/15). **4. a.** an interval of two octaves. **b.** one of two notes constituting such an interval in relation to the other, esp. the one higher in pitch. **c.** an organ stop of diapason quality sounding a note two octaves higher than that normally produced by the key depressed; a two-foot stop.

fifth (fɪfθ) *adj.* (*usually prenominal*) **1. a.** coming after the fourth in order, position, time, etc. Often written 5th. **b.** (*as n.*): *he came on the fifth.* ~*n.* **2. a.** one of five equal or nearly equal parts of an object, quantity, measurement, etc. **b.** (*as modifier*): *a fifth part.* **3.** the fraction equal to one divided by five (1/5). **4.** *Music.* **a.** the interval between one note and another five notes away from it counting inclusively along the diatonic scale. **b.** one of two notes constituting such an interval in relation to the other. See also **perfect** (sense 9), **diminished** (sense 2), **interval** (sense 5). **5.** an additional high gear fitted to some vehicles, esp. certain sports cars. ~*adv.* **6.** Also: **fifthly.** after the fourth person, position, event, etc. ~*sentence connector.* **7.** Also: **fifthly.** as the fifth point: linking what follows with the previous statements, as in a speech or argument. [Old English *fīfta*]

fifth col·umn *n.* **1.** (originally) a group of Falangist sympathizers in Madrid during the Spanish Civil War who were prepared to join the four columns of insurgents marching on the city. **2.** any group of hostile or subversive infiltrators; an enemy in one's midst. —**fifth col·umn·ist** *n.*

Fifth Re·pub·lic *n.* the French republic established in 1958 as the successor to the Fourth Republic. Its constitution is characterized by the strong position of the president.

fifth wheel *n.* **1.** a spare wheel for a four-wheeled vehicle. **2.** a steering bearing that enables the front axle of a horse-drawn vehicle to rotate relative to the body. **3.** a superfluous or unnecessary person or thing.

fif·ti·eth ('fɪftɪɪθ) *adj.* **1. a.** being the ordinal number of *fifty* in order, position, time, etc. Often written 50th. **b.** (*as n.*): *the fiftieth in the series.* ~*n.* **2. a.** one of 50 equal or approximately equal parts of something. **b.** (*as modifier*): *a fiftieth part.* **3.** the fraction equal to one divided by 50 (1/50).

fif·ty ('fɪftɪ) *n., pl.* **·ties. 1.** the cardinal number that is the product of ten and five. **2.** a numeral 50, L, etc., representing this number. **3.** something represented by, representing, or consisting of 50 units. ~*determiner.* **4. a.** amounting to fifty: *fifty people.* **b.** (*as pronoun*): *fifty should be sufficient.* [Old English *fīftig*]

fif·ty-fif·ty *adj., adv. Informal.* shared or sharing equally; in equal parts.

fig[1] (fɪg) *n.* **1.** any moraceous tree or shrub of the tropical and subtropical genus *Ficus* that produces a closed pear-shaped receptacle which becomes fleshy and edible when mature. **2.** the receptacle of any of these trees, esp. of *F. carica,* having sweet flesh containing numerous seedlike fruits. **3.** any of various plants or trees having a fruit similar to this. **4. Hottentot** *or* **sour fig.** a succulent plant, *Mesembryanthemum edule,* of southern Africa, having a capsular fruit containing edible pulp: family *Aizoaceae.* **5.** (*used with a negative*) something of negligible value; jot: *I don't care a fig for your opinion.* **6.** Also: **feg.** *Dialect.* a piece or segment from an orange. **7.** Also called: **fico.** an insulting gesture made with the thumb between the first two fingers or under the upper teeth. [C13: from Old French *figue,* from Old Provençal *figa,* from Latin *fīcus* fig tree]

fig[2] (fɪg) *Slang.* ~*vb.* **figs, fig·ging, figged.** (*tr.*) **1.** (foll. by *out* or *up*) to dress (up) or rig (out). **2.** to administer stimulating drugs to (a horse). ~*n.* **3.** dress, appearance, or array (esp. in the phrase **in full fig**). **4.** physical condition or form: *in bad fig.* [C17 *feague,* of uncertain origin]

fig. *abbrev. for:* **1.** figurative(ly). **2.** figure.

fig-bird *n.* any Australian oriole of the genus *Sphecotheres,* feeding on figs and other fruit.

fight (faɪt) *vb.* **fights, fight·ing, fought. 1.** to oppose or struggle against (an enemy) in battle. **2.** to oppose or struggle against (a person, thing, cause, etc.) in any manner. **3.** (*tr.*) to engage in or carry on (a battle, contest, etc.). **4.** (when *intr.,* often foll. by *for*) to uphold or maintain (a cause, ideal, etc.) by fighting or struggling: *to fight for freedom.* **5.** (*tr.*) to make or achieve (a way) by fighting. **6.** (*intr.*) *Boxing.* **a.** to box, as for a living. **b.** to use aggressive rough tactics. **7.** to engage (another or others) in combat. **8. fight it out.** to contend or struggle until a decisive result is obtained. **9. fight shy.** to keep aloof from. ~*n.* **10.** a battle, struggle, or physical combat. **11.** a quarrel, dispute, or contest. **12.** resistance (esp. in the phrase **to put up a fight**). **13.** the desire to take part in physical combat (esp. in the phrase **to show fight**). 14. a boxing match. [Old English *feohtan;* related to Old Frisian *fiuchta,* Old Saxon, Old High German *fehtan* to fight]

fight·er ('faɪtə) *n.* **1.** a person who fights, esp. a professional boxer. **2.** a person who has determination. **3.** *Military.* an armed aircraft designed for destroying other aircraft.

fight·er-bomb·er *n.* a high-performance aircraft that combines the roles of fighter and bomber.

fight·ing chance *n.* a slight chance of success dependent on a struggle.

fight·ing cock *n.* **1.** another name for **gamecock. 2.** a pugnacious person.

fight·ing fish *n.* any of various labyrinth fishes of the genus *Betta,* esp. the Siamese fighting fish.

fight·ing top *n.* one of the gun platforms on the lower masts of sailing men-of-war, used for observation.

fight off *vb.* (*tr., adv.*) to struggle to avoid or repress: *to fight off a cold.*

fig leaf *n.* **1.** a leaf from a fig tree. **2.** a representation of a fig leaf used in painting or sculpture to cover the genitals of nude figures. **3.** a device intended to conceal something regarded as shameful or indecent.

fig mar·i·gold *n.* any plant of the genus *Mesembryanthemum,* of southern Africa, having white, yellow, or pink flowers and fleshy leaves: family *Aizoaceae.*

fig·ment ('fɪgmənt) *n.* a fantastic notion, invention, or fabrication: *a figment of the imagination.* [C15: from Late Latin *figmentum* a fiction, from Latin *fingere* to shape]

fig·u·line ('fɪgjʊ,laɪn) *Rare.* ~*adj.* **1.** of or resembling clay. ~*n.* **2.** an article made of clay. [C17: from Latin *figulīnus* of a potter, from *figulus* a potter, from *fingere* to mould]

fig·u·ral ('fɪgərəl) *adj.* composed of or relating to human or animal figures.

fig·u·rant ('fɪgjʊrənt) *n.* **1.** a ballet dancer who does group work but no solo roles. **2.** *Theatre.* a minor character, esp. one who does not speak. [C18: from French, from *figurer* to represent, appear, FIGURE] —**fig·u·rante** (,fɪgjʊ'rɒnt) *fem. n.*

fig·ur·ate ('fɪgjʊrɪt) *adj.* **1.** *Music.* exhibiting or produced by figuration; florid or decorative. **2.** having a definite or particular shape or figure. [C15: from Latin *figūrāre* to shape] —'**fig·ur·ate·ly** *adv.*

fig·ur·a·tion (,fɪgə'reɪʃən) *n.* **1.** *Music.* **a.** the employment of characteristic patterns of notes, esp. in variations on a theme. **b.** decoration or florid ornamentation in general. **2.** the act or an instance of representing figuratively, as by means of allegory or emblem. **3.** a figurative or emblematic representation. **4.** the act of decorating with a design.

fig·ur·a·tive ('fɪgərətɪv) *adj.* **1.** of the nature of, resembling, or involving a figure of speech; not literal; metaphorical. **2.** using or filled with figures of speech. **3.** representing by means of an emblem, likeness, figure, etc. **4.** (in painting, sculpture, etc.) of, relating to, or characterized by the naturalistic representation of the external world. —'**fig·ur·a·tive·ly** *adv.* —'**fig·ur·a·tive·ness** *n.*

fig·ure ('fɪgə; *U.S.* 'fɪgjər) *n.* **1.** any written symbol other than a letter, esp. a whole number. **2.** another name for **digit** (sense 2). **3.** an amount expressed numerically: *a figure of £1800 was suggested.* **4.** (*pl.*) calculations with numbers: *he's good at figures.* **5.** visible shape or form; outline. **6.** the human form, esp. as regards size or shape: *a girl with a slender figure.* **7.** a slim bodily shape (esp. in the phrases **keep** *or* **lose one's figure**). **8.** a character or personage, esp. a prominent or notable one; personality: *a figure in politics.* **9.** the impression created by a person through behaviour (esp. in the phrase **to cut a fine, bold,** etc., **figure**). **10. a.** a person as impressed on the mind: *the figure of Napoleon.* **b.** (*in combination*): *father-figure.* **11.** a representation in painting or sculpture, esp. of the human form. **12.** a representative object or symbol; emblem. **13.** a pattern or design, as on fabric or in wood. **14.** a predetermined set of movements in dancing or skating. **15.** *Geom.* any combination of points, lines, curves, or planes. A **plane figure,** such as a circle, encloses an area; a **solid figure,** such as a sphere, encloses a volume. **16.** *Rhetoric.* See **figure of speech. 17.** *Logic.* one of four possible arrangements of the terms in the major and minor premisses of a syllogism that give the same conclusion. **18.** *Music.* **a.** a numeral written above or below a note in a part. See **figured bass, thorough bass. b.** a characteristic short pattern of notes. ~*vb.* **19.** (when *tr.,* often foll. by *up*) to calculate or compute (sums, amounts, etc.). **20.** (*tr.; usually takes a clause as object*) *Informal, chiefly U.S.* to think or conclude; consider. **21.** (*tr.*) to represent by a diagram or illustration. **22.** (*tr.*) to pattern or mark with a design. **23.** (*tr.*) to depict or portray in a painting, etc. **24.** (*tr.*) *Rhetoric.* to express by means of a figure of speech. **25.** (*tr.*) to imagine. **26.** (*tr.*) *Music.* **a.** to decorate (a melody line or part) with ornamentation. **b.** to provide figures above or below (a bass part) as an indication of the accompanying harmonies required. See **figured bass, thorough bass. 27.** (*intr.;* usually foll. by *in*) to be included: *his name figures in the article.* **28.** (*intr.*) *Informal.* to accord with expectation; be logical: *it figures that he wouldn't come.* ~See also **figure on, figure out.** [C13: from Latin *figūra* a shape, from *fingere* to mould] —'**fig·ure·less** *adj.* —'**fig·ur·er** *n.*

fig·ured ('fɪgəd) *adj.* **1.** depicted as a figure in graphic art, painting, or sculpture. **2.** decorated or patterned with a design. **3.** having a form. **4.** *Music.* **a.** ornamental. **b.** (of a bass part) provided with numerals indicating accompanying harmonies.

fig·ured bass (beɪs) *n.* a shorthand method of indicating a thorough-bass part in which each bass note is accompanied by figures indicating the intervals to be played in the chord above it in the realization.

fig·ure-ground *n.* a concept in Gestalt psychology referring to the way in which a perceptual field is divided into an inseparable outstanding object and a background that form the basis of various optical illusions.

fig·ure·head ('fɪgə,hɛd) *n.* **1.** a person nominally having a prominent position, but no real authority. **2.** a carved bust or full-length figure at the upper end of the stems of some sailing vessels.

fig·ure of eight *or* **fig·ure eight** *n.* **1.** an outline of the number 8 traced on ice by a skater. **2.** a flight manoeuvre by an

F G

aircraft outlining a figure 8. **3.** a knot in the shape of a figure 8 made to prevent the unreeving of a rope.

fig·ure of speech *n.* an expression of language, such as simile, metaphor, or personification, by which the usual or literal meaning of a word is abandoned.

fig·ure on *or* **up·on** *vb.* (*intr., prep.*) *Informal, chiefly U.S.* **1.** to depend on (support or help.) **2.** to take into consideration.

fig·ure out *vb.* (*tr., adv.; may take a clause as object*) *Informal.* **1.** to calculate or reckon. **2.** to understand.

fig·ure skat·ing *n.* ice skating in which the skater traces outlines of selected patterns. —**fig·ure skat·er** *n.*

fig·u·rine (ˌfɪgəˈriːn) *n.* a small carved or moulded figure; statuette. [C19: from French, from Italian *figurina* a little FIGURE]

fig·wort (ˈfɪgˌwɜːt) *n.* any scrophulariaceous plant of the N temperate genus *Scrophularia,* having square stems and small greenish flowers.

Fi·ji (ˈfiːdʒiː, fiːˈdʒiː) *n.* **1.** an independent state within the British Commonwealth, consisting of 844 islands (chiefly Viti Levu and Vanua Levu) in the SW Pacific: a British colony (1874-1970); the large islands are of volcanic origin, surrounded by coral reefs; smaller ones are of coral. Official language: English. Religion: Christian and Hindu. Currency: dollar. Capital: Suva. Pop.: 588 068 (1976). Area: 18 272 sq. km (7055 sq. miles). **2.** (*also adj.*) another word for **Fijian.**

Fi·ji·an (fiːˈdʒiːən) *n.* **1.** a member of the indigenous people of mixed Melanesian and Polynesian descent inhabiting Fiji. **2.** the language of this people, belonging to the Malayo-Polynesian family. ~*adj.* **3.** of, relating to, or characteristic of Fiji or its inhabitants. ~Also: **Fiji.**

fil·a·gree (ˈfɪləˌgriː) *n., adj., vb.* a less common spelling of **filigree.**

fil·a·ment (ˈfɪləmənt) *n.* **1.** the thin wire, usually tungsten, inside a light bulb that emits light when heated to incandescence by an electric current. **2.** *Electronics.* a high-resistance wire or ribbon, forming the cathode in some valves. **3.** a single strand of a natural or synthetic fibre; fibril. **4.** *Botany.* **a.** the stalk of a stamen. **b.** any of the long slender chains of cells into which some algae and fungi are divided. **5.** *Ornithol.* the barb of a down feather. **6.** *Anatomy.* any slender structure or part, such as the tail of a spermatozoon; filum. [C16: from New Latin *filāmentum,* from Medieval Latin *filāre* to spin, from Latin *fīlum* thread] —**fil·a·men·ta·ry** (ˌfɪləˈmɛntərɪ, -trɪ) *or* ˌ**fil·a·ˈmen·tous** *adj.*

fi·lar (ˈfaɪlə) *adj.* **1.** of thread. **2.** (of an optical instrument) having fine threads across the eyepiece forming a reticle or set of cross wires. [C19: from Latin *fīlum* thread]

fi·lar·i·a (fɪˈlɛərɪə) *n., pl.* **·i·ae** (-ɪˌiː). any parasitic nematode worm of the family *Filariidae,* living in the blood and tissues of vertebrates and transmitted by insects: the cause of filariasis. [C19: New Latin (former name of genus), from Latin *fīlum* thread] —**fi·ˈlar·i·al** *or* **fi·ˈlar·i·an** *adj.*

fil·a·ri·a·sis (ˌfɪləˈraɪəsɪs, fɪˌlɛərɪˈeɪsɪs) *n.* a disease common in tropical and subtropical countries resulting from infestation of the lymphatic system with the nematode worms *Wuchereria bancrofti* or *Brugia malayi,* transmitted by mosquitoes: characterized by inflammation and obstruction of the lymphatic vessels. See also **elephantiasis.** [C19: from New Latin; see FILARIA]

fil·a·ture (ˈfɪlətʃə) *n.* **1.** the act or process of spinning silk, etc., into threads. **2.** the reel used for this. **3.** a place where such spinning or reeling is done. [C18: from Medieval Latin *filātūra* the art of spinning, from *filāre* to spin thread; see FILAMENT]

fil·bert (ˈfɪlbət) *n.* **1.** any of several N temperate shrubs of the genus *Corylus,* esp. *C. maxima,* that have edible rounded brown nuts: family *Corylaceae.* **2.** Also called: **hazelnut,** and in the U.S.: **cobnut.** the nut of any of these shrubs. ~See also **hazel** (sense 1). [C14: named after St. *Philbert,* 7th-century Frankish abbot, because the nuts are ripe around his feast day, Aug. 22]

filch (fɪltʃ) *vb.* (*tr.*) to steal or take surreptitiously in small amounts; pilfer. [C16 *filchen* to steal, attack, perhaps from Old English *gefylce* band of men] —ˈ**filch·er** *n.*

file[1] (faɪl) *n.* **1.** a folder, box, etc., used to keep documents or other items in order. **2.** the documents, etc., kept in this way. **3.** documents or information about a specific subject, person, etc.: *we have a file on every known thief.* **4.** an orderly line or row. **5.** a line of people in marching formation, one behind another. Compare **rank**[1] (sense 4). **6.** any of the eight vertical rows of squares on a chessboard. **7.** Also called: **data set.** *Computer technol.* a block of data that can be accessed by means of its unique address from a storage device. **8.** *Obsolete.* a list or catalogue. **9. on file.** recorded or catalogued for reference, as in a file. ~*vb.* **10.** to place (a document, letter, etc.) in a file. **11.** (*tr.*) to put on record, esp. to place (a legal document) on public or official record; register. **12.** (*tr.*) to bring (a suit, esp. a divorce suit) in a court of law. **13.** (*tr.*) to submit (copy) to a newspaper or news agency. **14.** (*intr.*) to march or walk in a file or files: *the ants filed down the hill.* [C16 (in the sense: string on which documents are hung): from Old French *filer,* from Medieval Latin *filāre;* see FILAMENT] —ˈ**fil·er** *n.*

file[2] (faɪl) *n.* **1.** a hand tool consisting essentially of a steel blade with small cutting teeth on some or all of its faces. It is used for shaping or smoothing metal, wood, etc. **2.** *Rare, Brit. slang.* a cunning or deceitful person. ~*vb.* **3.** (*tr.*) to shape or smooth (a surface) with a file. [Old English *fīl;* related to Old Saxon *fīla,* Old High German *fīhala* file, Greek *pikros* bitter, sharp] —ˈ**fil·er** *n.*

file[3] (faɪl) *vb.* (*tr.*) *Obsolete.* to pollute or defile. [Old English *fȳlan;* related to Middle Low German *vülen;* see DEFILE, FILTH, FOUL]

file·card (ˈfaɪlˌkɑːd) *n.* a type of brush with sharp steel bristles, used for cleaning the teeth of a file.

file·fish (ˈfaɪlˌfɪʃ) *n., pl.* **·fish** *or* **·fish·es.** any tropical triggerfish, such as *Alutera scripta,* having a narrow compressed body and a very long dorsal spine. [C18: referring to its file-like scales]

fi·let (ˈfɪlɪt, ˈfɪleɪ; *French* fiˈlɛ) *n.* a variant spelling of **fillet** (senses 1-3). [C20: from French: net, from Old Provençal *filat,* from *fil* thread, from Latin *fīlum*]

fi·let mi·gnon (ˈfɪleɪ ˈmiːnjɒn) *n.* a small tender boneless cut of beef from the inside of the loin. [from French, literally: dainty fillet]

fil·ial (ˈfɪljəl) *adj.* **1.** of, resembling, or suitable to a son or daughter: *filial affection.* **2.** *Genetics.* designating any of the generations following the parental generation. Abbrev.: F; F_1 indicates the first filial generation, F_2 the second, etc. [C15: from Late Latin *filiālis,* from Latin *filius* son] —ˈ**fil·ial·ly** *adv.* —ˈ**fil·ial·ness** *n.*

fil·i·ate (ˈfɪlɪˌeɪt) *vb.* (*tr.*) **1.** *Law.* to fix judicially the paternity of (a child, esp. one born out of wedlock). **2.** *Law.* a less common word for **affiliate. 3.** *Archaic.* to affiliate or associate. [C18: from Medieval Latin *filiātus* acknowledged as a son, from Latin *fīlius* son]

fil·i·a·tion (ˌfɪlɪˈeɪʃən) *n.* **1.** line of descent; lineage; derivation. **2.** the fact of being the child of certain parents. **3.** *Law.* the act or process of filiating. **4.** *Law.* a less common word for **affiliation. 5.** the set of rules governing the attachment of children to their parents and its social consequences.

fil·i·beg, fil·li·beg, *or* **phil·i·beg** (ˈfɪlɪˌbɛg) *n.* the kilt worn by Scottish Highlanders. [C18: from Scottish Gaelic *fēileadh-beag,* from *fēileadh* kilt + *beag* small]

fil·i·bus·ter (ˈfɪlɪˌbʌstə) *n.* **1.** *Chiefly U.S.* the process or an instance of obstructing legislation by means of long speeches and other delaying tactics. **2.** Also called: **filibusterer.** *Chiefly U.S.* a legislator who engages in such obstruction. **3.** a buccaneer, freebooter, or irregular military adventurer, esp. a revolutionary in a foreign country. ~*vb.* **4.** *Chiefly U.S.* to obstruct (legislation) with delaying tactics. **5.** (*intr.*) to engage in unlawful and private military action. [C16: from Spanish *filibustero,* from French *flibustier,* probably from Dutch *vrijbuiter* pirate, literally: one plundering freely; see FREEBOOTER] —ˈ**fil·i·ˌbus·ter·er** *n.* —ˈ**fil·i·ˌbus·ter·ism** *n.*

fil·i·cide (ˈfɪlɪˌsaɪd) *n.* **1.** the act of killing one's own son or daughter. **2.** a person who does this. [C17: from Latin *fīlius* son or *fīlia* daughter + -CIDE] —ˌ**fil·i·ˈcid·al** *adj.*

fil·i·form (ˈfɪlɪˌfɔːm, ˈfaɪ-) *adj. Biology.* having the form of a thread. [C18: from Latin *fīlum* thread]

fil·i·gree (ˈfɪlɪˌgriː), **fil·a·gree,** *or* **fill·a·gree** *n.* **1.** delicate ornamental work of twisted gold, silver, or other wire. **2.** any fanciful delicate ornamentation. ~*adj.* **3.** made of or as if with filigree. ~*vb.* **·grees, ·gree·ing, ·greed. 4.** (*tr.*) to decorate with or as if with filigree. [C17: from earlier *filigreen,* from French *filigrane,* from Latin *fīlum* thread + *grānum* GRAIN]

fil·ing clerk *n.* an employee who maintains office files.

fil·ings (ˈfaɪlɪŋz) *pl. n.* shavings or particles removed by a file: *iron filings.*

Fil·i·pi·no (ˌfɪlɪˈpiːnəʊ) *n., pl.* **·nos. 1.** a native or inhabitant of the Philippines. **2.** another name for **Tagalog.** ~*adj.* **3.** of or relating to the Philippines or their inhabitants.

fill (fɪl) *vb.* (*mainly tr.*; often foll. by *up*) **1.** (*also intr.*) to make or become full: *to fill up a bottle; the bath fills in two minutes.* **2.** to occupy the whole of: *the party filled two floors of the house.* **3.** to plug (a gap, crevice, cavity, etc.). **4.** to meet (a requirement or need) satisfactorily. **5.** to cover (a page or blank space) with writing, drawing, etc. **6.** to hold and perform the duties of (an office or position). **7.** to appoint or elect an occupant to (an office or position). **8.** *Building trades.* to build up (ground) with fill. **9.** (*also intr.*) to swell or cause to swell with wind, as in manoeuvring the sails of a sailing vessel. **10.** to increase the bulk of by adding an inferior substance. **11.** *Poker.* to complete (a full house, etc.) by drawing the cards needed. **12.** *Chiefly U.S.* to put together the necessary materials for (a prescription or order). **13. fill the bill.** *Informal.* to serve or perform adequately. ~*n.* **14.** material such as gravel, stones, etc., used to bring an area of ground up to a required level. **15. one's fill.** the quantity needed to satisfy one: *to eat your fill.* ~See also **fill away, fill in, fill out, fill up.** [Old English *fyllan;* related to Old Frisian *fella,* Old Norse *fylla,* Gothic *fulljan,* Old High German *fullen;* see FULL[1], FULFIL]

fill·a·gree (ˈfɪləˌgriː) *n., adj., vb.* a less common spelling of **filigree.**

fill a·way *vb.* (*intr., adv.*) *Nautical.* to cause a vessel's sails to fill, either by steering it off the wind or by bracing the yards.

fille de joie *French.* (fij də ˈʒwa) *n., pl.* ***filles de joie*** (fij də ˈʒwa). a prostitute. [girl of pleasure]

filled gold *n.* another name (esp. U.S.) for **rolled gold.**

fill·er (ˈfɪlə) *n.* **1.** a person or thing that fills. **2.** an object or substance used to add weight or size to something or to fill in a gap. **3.** a paste, used for filling in cracks, holes, etc., in a surface before painting. **4.** *Architect.* a small joist inserted between and supported by two beams. **5. a.** the inner portion of a cigar. **b.** the cut tobacco for making cigarettes. **6.** *Journalism.* articles, photographs, etc., to fill space between more important articles in the layout of a newspaper or magazine. **7.** *Informal.* something, such as a musical selection, to fill time in a broadcast or stage presentation.

fill·er cap *n.* a device sealing the filling pipe to the petrol tank in a motor vehicle.

fil·let ('fɪlɪt) *n.* **1. a.** Also called: **fillet steak.** a strip of boneless meat, esp. the undercut of a sirloin of beef. **b.** the boned side of a fish. **c.** the white meat of breast and wing of a chicken. **2.** a narrow strip of any material. **3.** a thin strip of ribbon, lace, etc., worn in the hair or around the neck. **4.** a narrow flat moulding, esp. one between other mouldings. **5.** a narrow band between two adjacent flutings on the shaft of a column. **6.** a narrow strip of welded metal used to join steel members. **7.** *Heraldry.* a horizontal division of a shield, one quarter of the depth of the chief. **8.** Also called: **listel, list.** the top member of a cornice. **9.** *Anatomy.* a band of sensory nerve fibres in the brain connected to the thalamus. Technical name: **lemniscus. 10. a.** a narrow decorative line, impressed on the cover of a book. **b.** a wheel tool used to impress such lines. **11.** another name for **fairing**[1]. ~*vb.* (*tr.*) **12.** to cut or prepare (meat or fish) as a fillet. **13.** to cut fillets from (meat or fish). **14.** to bind or decorate with or as if with a fillet. ~ Also (for senses 1-3): **filet.** [C14: from Old French *filet,* from *fil* thread, from Latin *filum*]

fill in *vb.* (*adv.*) **1.** (*tr.*) to complete (a form, drawing, etc.). **2.** (*intr.*) to act as a substitute: *a girl is filling in while the typist is away.* **3.** (*tr.*) to put material into (a hole or cavity), esp. so as to make it level with a surface. **4.** (*tr.*) *Informal.* to inform with facts or news. **5.** (*tr.*) *Brit. slang.* to attack and injure severely. ~*n.* **fill-in. 6.** a substitute. **7.** *U.S. informal.* a briefing to complete one's understanding.

fill·ing ('fɪlɪŋ) *n.* **1.** the substance or thing used to fill a space or container: *pie filling.* **2.** *Dentistry.* any of various substances (metal, plastic, etc.) for inserting into the prepared cavity of a tooth. **3.** *Textiles.* another term for **weft.**

fill·ing sta·tion *n.* a place where petrol and other supplies for motorists are sold.

fil·lip ('fɪlɪp) *n.* **1.** something that adds stimulation or enjoyment. **2.** the action of holding a finger towards the palm with the thumb and suddenly releasing it outwards to produce a snapping sound. **3.** a quick blow or tap made by a finger snapped in this way. ~*vb.* **4.** (*tr.*) to stimulate or excite. **5.** (*tr.*) to strike or project sharply with a fillip. **6.** (*intr.*) to make a fillip. [C15: *philippe,* of imitative origin]

fil·lis·ter, fil·is·ter, *or* **fil·les·ter** ('fɪlɪstə) *n.* **1.** Also called: **fillister plane.** an adjustable plane for cutting rabbets, grooves, etc. **2.** Also called: **sash fillister.** a rabbet or groove, esp. one in a window sash bar for a pane of glass. [C19: of unknown origin]

Fill·more ('fɪlmɔː) *n.* **Mil·lard.** 1800–74, 13th president of the U.S. (1850-53); a leader of the Whig Party.

fill out *vb.* (*adv.*) **1.** to make or become fuller, thicker, or rounder: *her figure has filled out since her marriage.* **2.** to make more substantial: *the writers were asked to fill their stories out.* **3.** (*tr.*) *U.S.* to complete (a form, application, etc.).

fill up *vb.* (*adv.*) **1.** (*tr.*) to complete (a form, application, etc.). **2.** to make or become completely full. ~*n.* **fill-up. 3.** the act of filling something completely, esp. the petrol tank of a car.

fil·ly ('fɪlɪ) *n., pl.* **·lies. 1.** a female horse or pony under the age of four. **2.** *Informal, rare.* a spirited girl or young woman. [C15: from Old Norse *fylja;* related to Old High German *fulihha;* see FOAL]

film (fɪlm) *n.* **1. a.** a sequence of images of moving objects photographed by a camera and providing the optical illusion of continuous movement when projected onto a screen. **b.** a form of entertainment, information, etc., composed of such a sequence of images and shown in a cinema, etc. **c.** (*as modifier*): *film techniques.* **2.** a thin flexible strip of cellulose coated with a photographic emulsion, used to make negatives and transparencies. **3.** a thin coating or layer. **4.** a thin sheet of any material, as of plastic for packaging. **5.** a fine haze, mist, or blur. **6.** a gauzy web of filaments or fine threads. **7.** *Pathol.* an abnormally opaque tissue, such as the cornea in some eye diseases. ~*vb.* **8. a.** to photograph with a cine camera. **b.** to make a film of (a screenplay, event, etc.). **9.** to cover or become covered or coated with a film. [Old English *filmen* membrane; related to Old Frisian *filmene,* Greek *pelma* sole of the foot; see FELL[4]] —'**film·ic** *adj.*

film li·brar·y *n.* a collection of films as archives or for loan or hire.

fil·mog·ra·phy (fɪl'mɒgrəfɪ) *n.* **1.** a list of the films made by a particular director, actor, etc. **2.** any writing that deals with films or the cinema.

film pack *n.* a box containing several sheets of film for use in a plate camera.

film·set ('fɪlm,sɛt) *vb.* (*tr.*) *Brit.* to set (type matter) by filmsetting. —'**film·,set·ter** *n.*

film·set·ting ('fɪlm,sɛtɪŋ) *n. Brit., printing.* typesetting by exposing type characters onto photographic film from which printing plates are made. U.S. name: **photocomposition.**

film star *n.* a popular film actor or actress.

film strip *n.* a strip of film composed of different images projected separately as slides.

film·y ('fɪlmɪ) *adj.* **film·i·er, film·i·est. 1.** composed of or resembling film; transparent or gauzy. **2.** covered with or as if with a film; hazy; blurred. —'**film·i·ly** *adv.* —'**film·i·ness** *n.*

film·y fern *n.* any fern of the family *Hymenophyllaceae,* growing in humid regions and having thin translucent leaves.

fil·o·plume ('fɪlə,pluːm, 'faɪ-) *n. Ornithol.* any of the hairlike feathers that lack vanes and occur between the contour feathers. [C19: from New Latin *filoplūma,* from Latin *filum* thread + *plūma* feather]

fi·lose ('faɪləʊs, -ləʊz) *adj. Biology.* resembling or possessing a thread or threadlike process: *filose pseudopodia.* [C19: from Latin *filum* thread]

fil·o·selle (,fɪləʊ'sɛl) *n.* soft silk thread, used esp. for embroidery. [C17: from French: silk, silkworm, from Italian *filosello,* perhaps from Latin *foliculus* little bag]

fils[1] *French.* (fis) an addition to a French surname to specify the son rather than the father of the same name: *a book by Dumas fils.* Compare **père.** [French: son]

fils[2] (fɪls) *or* **fil** (fɪl) *n., pl.* **fils.** a fractional monetary unit of Iraq, Jordan, Kuwait, and Southern Yemen worth one thousandth of a dinar. [from Arabic]

fil·ter ('fɪltə) *n.* **1.** a porous substance, such as paper or sand, that allows fluid to pass but retains suspended solid particles: used to clean fluids or collect solid particles. **2.** any device containing such a porous substance for separating suspensions from fluids. **3.** any of various porous substances built into the mouth end of a cigarette or cigar for absorbing impurities such as tar. **4.** any electronic, optical, or acoustic device that blocks signals or radiations of certain frequencies while allowing others to pass. See also **band-pass filter. 5.** any transparent disc of gelatin or glass used to eliminate or reduce the intensity of given frequencies from the light leaving a lamp, entering a camera, etc. **6.** *Brit.* a traffic signal at a road junction consisting of a green arrow which when illuminated permits vehicles to turn either left or right when the main signals are red. ~*vb.* **7.** (often foll. by *out*) to remove or separate (suspended particles, wavelengths of radiation, etc.) from (a liquid, gas, radiation, etc.) by the action of a filter. **8.** (*tr.*) to obtain by filtering. **9.** (*intr.;* foll. by *through*) to pass (through a filter or something like a filter): *dust filtered through the screen.* **10.** (*intr.*) to flow slowly; trickle. ~See also **filter out.** [C16 *filtre,* from Medieval Latin *filtrum* piece of felt used as a filter, of Germanic origin; see FELT[2]]

fil·ter·a·ble ('fɪltərəbᵊl) *or* **fil·tra·ble** *adj.* **1.** capable of being filtered. **2.** (of most viruses and certain bacteria) capable of passing through the pores of a fine filter. —,**fil·ter·a·'bil·i·ty** *or* '**fil·ter·a·ble·ness** *n.*

fil·ter bed *n.* **1.** a layer of sand or gravel in a tank or reservoir through which a liquid is passed so as to purify it. Compare **bacteria bed. 2.** any layer of material through which a liquid is passed so as to filter it.

fil·ter out *or* **through** *vb.* (*intr., adv.*) to become known gradually; leak: *rumours filtered out about the divorce.*

fil·ter pa·per *n.* a porous paper used for filtering liquids.

fil·ter press *n.* an apparatus used for filtration consisting of a set of frames covered with filter cloth on both sides, between which the liquid to be filtered is pumped.

fil·ter pump *n.* a vacuum pump used to assist laboratory filtrations in which a jet of water inside a glass tube entrains air molecules from the system to be evacuated.

fil·ter tip *n.* **1.** an attachment to the mouth end of a cigarette for trapping impurities such as tar during smoking. It consists of any of various dense porous substances, such as cotton. **2.** a cigarette having such an attachment. —'**fil·ter-,tipped** *adj.*

filth (fɪlθ) *n.* **1.** foul or disgusting dirt; refuse. **2.** extreme physical or moral uncleanliness; pollution. **3.** vulgarity or obscenity, as in language. [Old English *fȳlth;* related to Old Saxon, Old High German *fūlitha;* see FOUL, DEFILE]

filth·y ('fɪlθɪ) *adj.* **filth·i·er, filth·i·est. 1.** characterized by or full of filth; very dirty or obscene. **2.** offensive or vicious: *that was a filthy trick to play.* **3.** *Informal, chiefly Brit.* extremely unpleasant: *filthy weather.* —'**filth·i·ly** *adv.* —'**filth·i·ness** *n.*

fil·trate ('fɪltreɪt) *n.* **1.** a liquid or gas that has been filtered. ~*vb.* **2.** another name for **filter** (sense 7). [C17: from Medieval Latin *filtrāre* to FILTER] —'**fil·trat·a·ble** *adj.*

fil·tra·tion (fɪl'treɪʃən) *n.* the act or process of filtering.

fi·lum ('faɪləm) *n., pl.* **·la** (-lə). *Anatomy.* any threadlike structure or part. [Latin: thread, cord, fibre]

fim·ble ('fɪmbᵊl) *n.* the male plant of the hemp, which matures before the female plant. [C15: from Middle Dutch *femeel,* from Old French *chanvre femelle* female hemp, from *chanvre* hemp + *femelle* FEMALE]

fim·bri·a ('fɪmbrɪə) *n., pl.* **·bri·ae** (-brɪ,iː). *Anatomy.* a fringe or fringelike margin or border, esp. at the opening of the Fallopian tubes. [C18: from Late Latin, from Latin *fimbriae* threads, shreds] —'**fim·bri·al** *adj.*

fim·bri·ate ('fɪmbrɪɪt, -,eɪt), **fim·bri·at·ed,** *or* **fim·bril·late** ('fɪmbrɪlɪt, -,leɪt) *adj.* having a fringed margin, as some petals, antennae, etc. —,**fim·bri·'a·tion** *n.*

fin[1] (fɪn) *n.* **1.** any of the firm appendages that are the organs of locomotion and balance in fishes and some other aquatic animals. Most fishes have paired and unpaired fins, the former corresponding to the limbs of higher vertebrates. **2.** a part or appendage that resembles a fin. **3. a.** *Brit.* a vertical surface to which the rudder is attached, usually placed at the rear of an aeroplane to give stability about the vertical axis. U.S. name: **vertical stabilizer. b.** an aerofoil fixed to a rocket or missile to give stability. **4.** *Nautical.* a fixed or adjustable blade projecting under water from the hull of a vessel to give it stability or control. **5.** a projecting rib to dissipate heat from the surface of an engine cylinder, motor casing, or radiator. **6.** (*often pl.*) another name for **flipper** (sense 2). ~*vb.* **fins, fin·ning, finned. 7.** (*tr.*) to provide with fins. **8.** (*tr.*) to remove the fins from (a dead fish). **9.** (*intr.*) (esp. of a whale) to agitate the fins violently in the water. [Old English *finn;* related to Middle Dutch *vinne,* Old Swedish *fina,* Latin *pinna* wing] —'**fin·less** *adj.*

fin[2] (fɪn) *n. U.S. slang.* a five-dollar bill. [from Yiddish *finf* five, ultimately from Old High German *funf, finf*]

fin. *abbrev. for:* **1.** finance. **2.** financial. **3.** finish.

Fin. *abbrev. for:* **1.** Finland. **2.** Finnish.
fin·a·ble *or* **fine·a·ble** ('faɪnəbᵊl) *adj.* liable to a fine. —'**fin·a·ble·ness** *or* '**fine·a·ble·ness** *n.*
fi·na·gle (fɪ'neɪgᵊl) *vb. Informal.* **1.** (*tr.*) to get or achieve by trickery, craftiness, or persuasion; wangle. **2.** to use trickery or craftiness on (a person). [C20: probably changed from FAINAIGUE] —**fi·'na·gler** *n.*
fi·nal ('faɪnᵊl) *adj.* **1.** of or occurring at the end; concluding; ultimate; last. **2.** having no possibility for further discussion, action, or change; conclusive; decisive: *a final decree of judgment.* **3.** relating to or constituting an end or purpose: *a final clause may be introduced by "in order to".* **4.** *Phonetics.* at the end of a word: *"cat" has a final "t".* Compare **medial** (sense 1), **initial** (sense 1). **5.** *Music.* another word for **perfect** (sense 9b.). ~*n.* **6.** a terminal or last thing; end. **7.** a deciding contest between the winners of previous rounds in a competition. **8.** *Music.* the tonic note of a church mode. [C14: from Latin *fīnālis,* from *fīnis* limit, boundary]
fi·nal cause *n. Philosophy.* the end or purpose of a thing or process.
fi·na·le (fɪ'nɑːlɪ) *n.* **1.** the concluding part of any performance or presentation. **2.** the closing section or movement of a musical composition. [C18: from Italian, n. use of adj. *finale,* from Latin *fīnālis* FINAL]
fi·nal·ism ('faɪnəˌlɪzəm) *n. Philosophy.* the doctrine that final causes determine the course of all events. —**fi·na·'lis·tic** *adj.*
fi·nal·ist ('faɪnəlɪst) *n.* a contestant who has reached the last and decisive stage of a sports or other competition.
fi·nal·i·ty (faɪ'nælɪtɪ) *n., pl.* **·ties. 1.** the condition or quality of being final or settled; conclusiveness: *the finality of death.* **2.** a final or conclusive act. **3.** *Metaphysics.* the doctrine of the efficacy of final causes. Compare **teleology.**
fi·nal·ize *or* **fi·nal·ise** ('faɪnəˌlaɪz) *vb.* **1.** (*tr.*) to put into final form; settle: *to finalize plans for the merger.* **2.** (*intr.*) to complete arrangements or negotiations; reach agreement on a transaction. —ˌ**fi·na·li·'za·tion** *or* ˌ**fi·na·li·'sa·tion** *n.*
Usage. Although *finalize* has been in widespread use for some time, it carries strong associations of bureaucratic or commercial jargon for many careful speakers and writers, who usually prefer *complete, conclude,* or *make final,* esp. in formal contexts.
fi·nal·ly ('faɪnəlɪ) *adv.* **1.** after a long delay; at last; eventually. **2.** at the end or final point; lastly. **3.** completely; conclusively; irrevocably. ~*sentence connector.* **4.** in the end; lastly: *finally, he put his tie on.* **5.** as the last or final point: linking what follows with the previous statements, as in a speech or argument.
fi·nals ('faɪnᵊlz) *pl. n.* **1.** the deciding part or parts of a sports or other competition. **2.** *Education.* the last examination series in an academic or professional course.
fi·nance (fɪ'næns, 'faɪnæns) *n.* **1.** the system of money, credit, etc., esp. with respect to government revenues and expenditures. **2.** funds or the provision of funds. **3.** (*pl.*) funds; financial condition. ~*vb.* **4.** (*tr.*) to provide or obtain funds, capital, or credit for. **5.** (*intr.*) to manage or secure financial resources. [C14: from Old French, from *finer* to end, settle by payment]
fi·nance bill *n.* a legislative bill providing money for the public treasury.
fi·nance com·pa·ny *or* **house** *n.* an enterprise engaged in the loan of money against collateral or speculatively to manufacturers and retailers, esp. one specializing in the financing of hire-purchase contracts.
fi·nan·cial (fɪ'nænʃəl, faɪ-) *adj.* **1.** of or relating to finance or finances. **2.** of or relating to persons who manage money, capital, or credit. —**fi·'nan·cial·ly** *adv.*
fi·nan·cial year *n. Brit.* **1.** any annual period at the end of which a firm's accounts are made up. **2.** the annual period ending April 5, over which Budget estimates are made by the British Government and which functions as the income-tax year. ~U.S. equivalent: **fiscal year.**
fi·nan·ci·er (fɪ'nænsɪə, faɪ-) *n.* a person who is engaged or skilled in large-scale financial operations.
fin·back ('fɪnˌbæk) *n.* another name for **rorqual.**
finch (fɪntʃ) *n.* **1.** any songbird of the family *Fringillidae,* having a short stout bill for feeding on seeds and, in most species, a bright plumage in the male. Common examples are the goldfinch, bullfinch, chaffinch, siskin, and canary. **2.** any of various similar or related birds. [Old English *finc;* related to Old High German *finko,* Middle Dutch *vinker,* Greek *spingos*]
Finch·ley ('fɪntʃlɪ) *n.* a residential district of N London, part of the Greater London borough of Barnet since 1965.
find (faɪnd) *vb.* **finds, find·ing, found.** (*mainly tr.*) **1.** to meet with or discover by chance. **2.** to discover or obtain, esp. by search or effort: *to find happiness.* **3.** (*may take a clause as object*) to become aware of; realize: *he found that nobody knew.* **4.** (*may take a clause as object*) to regard as being; consider: *I find this wine a little sour.* **5.** to look for and point out (something to be criticized): *to find fault.* **6.** (*also intr.*) *Law.* to determine an issue after judicial inquiry and pronounce a verdict (upon): *the court found the accused guilty.* **7.** to regain (something lost or not functioning): *to find one's tongue.* **8.** to reach (a target): *the bullet found its mark.* **9.** to provide, esp. with difficulty: *we'll find room for you too.* **10.** to be able to pay: *I can't find that amount of money.* **11. find oneself.** to accept and make use of one's personality and interests. **12. find one's feet.** to become capable or confident, as in a new job. ~*n.* **13.** a person, thing, etc., that is found, esp. a valuable or fortunate discovery. [Old English *findan;* related to Old Norse *finna,* Gothic *finthan,* Old High German *fintan* to find) —'**find·a·ble** *adj.*
find·er ('faɪndə) *n.* **1.** a person or thing that finds. **2.** *Physics.* a small low-power wide-angle telescope fitted to a more powerful larger telescope, used to locate celestial objects to be studied by the larger instrument. **3.** *Photog.* short for **viewfinder. 4. finders keepers.** *Informal.* whoever finds something has the right to keep it.
fin de siè·cle *French.* (fɛ̃ də 'sjɛkl) *n.* **1.** the end of the 19th century, when traditional social, moral, and artistic values were in transition. ~*adj.* ***fin-de-siè·cle.*** **2.** of or relating to the close of the 19th century. **3.** decadent, esp. in artistic tastes.
find·ing ('faɪndɪŋ) *n.* **1.** a thing that is found or discovered. **2.** *Law.* the conclusion reached after a judicial inquiry; verdict. **3.** (*pl.*) the tools and equipment of an artisan.
find out *vb.* (*adv.*) **1.** to gain knowledge of (something); learn: *he found out what he wanted.* **2.** to detect the crime, deception, etc., of (someone).
find the la·dy *n.* another name for **three-card trick.**
fine[1] (faɪn) *adj.* **1.** excellent or choice in quality; very good of its kind: *a fine speech.* **2.** superior in skill, ability, or accomplishment: *a fine violinist.* **3.** (of weather) clear and dry. **4.** enjoyable or satisfying: *a fine time.* **5.** (*postpositive*) *Informal.* quite well; in satisfactory health: *I feel fine.* **6.** of delicate composition or careful workmanship: *fine crystal.* **7.** (of precious metals) pure or having a high or specified degree of purity: *fine silver; gold 98 per cent fine.* **8.** subtle in perception; discriminating: *a fine eye for antique brasses.* **9.** abstruse or subtle: *a fine point in argument.* **10.** very thin or slender: *fine hair.* **11.** very small: *fine dust; fine print.* **12.** (of edges, blades, etc.) sharp; keen. **13.** ornate, showy, or smart. **14.** good-looking; handsome: *a fine young woman.* **15.** polished, elegant, or refined: *a fine gentleman.* **16.** morally upright and commendable: *a fine man.* **17.** *Cricket.* (of a fielding position) oblique to and behind the wicket: *fine leg.* **18.** (*prenominal*) *Informal.* disappointing or terrible: *a fine mess.* ~*adv.* **19.** *Informal.* quite well; all right: *that suits me fine.* **20.** a nonstandard word for **finely. 21.** *Billiards, etc.* (of a stroke on the cue ball) so as to merely brush the object ball. **22. cut it fine.** to allow little margin of time, space, etc. ~*vb.* **23.** to make or become finer; refine. **24.** (often foll. by *down* or *away*) to make or become smaller. **25.** (*tr.*) to clarify (wine, etc.) by adding finings. **26.** (*tr.*) *Billiards.* to hit (a cue ball) fine. **27.** (*intr.; foll by up*) *Austral. informal.* (of the weather) to become fine. [C13: from Old French *fin,* from Latin *fīnis* end, boundary, as in *fīnis honōrum* the highest degree of honour]
fine[2] (faɪn) *n.* **1.** a certain amount of money exacted as a penalty: *a parking fine.* **2.** a payment made by a tenant at the start of his tenancy to reduce his subsequent rent; premium. **3.** *Feudal law.* a sum of money paid by a man to his lord, esp. for a privilege. **4.** a method of transferring land in England by bringing a fictitious law suit: abolished 1833. **5.** *Archaic.* a penalty of any sort. **6. in fine. a.** in short; briefly. **b.** in conclusion; finally. ~*vb.* **7.** (*tr.*) to impose a fine on. [C12 (in the sense: conclusion, settlement): from Old French *fin;* see FINE[1]]
fi·ne[3] ('fiːneɪ) *n. Music.* **1.** the point at which a piece is to end, usually after a *da capo* or *dal segno.* **2.** an ending or finale. [Italian, from Latin *fīnis* end]
fine[4] *French.* (fin) *n.* brandy of ordinary quality. [literally: fine]
fine·a·ble ('faɪnəbᵊl) *adj.* a variant spelling of **finable.** —'**fine·a·ble·ness** *n.*
fine art *n.* **1.** art produced chiefly for its aesthetic value, as opposed to applied art. **2.** (*often pl.*) Also called: **beaux arts.** any of the fields in which such art is produced, such as painting, sculpture, and engraving.
fine-cut *adj.* (of tobacco) finely cut or shredded.
fine-draw *vb.* **-draws, -draw·ing, -drew, -drawn.** (*tr.*) **1.** to sew together so finely that the join is scarcely noticeable. **2.** to carry out the last drawing-out operation on (wire, tube, etc.) to reduce its diameter.
fine-drawn *adj.* **1.** (of arguments, distinctions, etc.) precise or subtle. **2.** (of wire, etc.) drawn out until very fine; attenuated. **3.** (of features, etc.) delicate or refined.
Fi·ne Gael ('fɪnə 'geɪl) *n.* one of the major political parties in the Republic of Ireland.
fine-grain *adj. Photog.* having or producing an image with grain of inconspicuous size: *a fine-grain image; a fine-grain developer.*
fine-grained *adj.* (of wood, leather, etc.) having a fine smooth even grain.
fine·ly ('faɪnlɪ) *adv.* **1.** into small pieces; minutely. **2.** precisely or subtly. **3.** splendidly or delicately.
fine·ness ('faɪnnɪs) *n.* **1.** the state or quality of being fine. **2.** a measurement of the purity of precious metal, expressed as the number of parts per thousand that is precious metal.
fine print *n.* matter set in small type, as in a contract, esp. considered as containing unfavourable conditions that the signer might overlook. Also called: **small print.**
fin·er·y[1] ('faɪnərɪ) *n.* elaborate or showy decoration, esp. clothing and jewellery.
fin·er·y[2] ('faɪnərɪ) *n., pl.* **·er·ies.** a hearth for converting cast iron into wrought iron. [C17: from Old French *finerie,* from *finer* to refine; see FINE[1]]
fines herbes (*French* fin 'zɛrb) *pl. n.* a mixture of finely chopped herbs, used to flavour omelettes, salads, etc.
fine·spun ('faɪn'spʌn) *adj.* **1.** spun or drawn out to a fine thread. **2.** excessively subtle or refined; not practical.
fi·nesse (fɪ'nɛs) *n.* **1.** elegant skill in style or performance. **2.** subtlety and tact in handling difficult situations. **3.** *Bridge,*

whist. an attempt to win a trick when opponents hold a high card in the suit led by playing a lower card, hoping the opponent who has already played holds the missing card. **4.** a trick, artifice, or strategy. ~*vb.* **5.** to manage or bring about with finesse. **6.** to play (a card) as a finesse. [C15: from Old French, from *fin* fine, delicate; see FINE[1]]

fine struc·ture *n.* the splitting of a spectral line into two or more closely spaced components as a result of interaction between the spin and orbital angular momenta of the atomic electrons. Compare **hyperfine structure.**

fine-tooth comb *or* **fine-toothed comb** *n.* **1.** a comb with fine teeth set closely together. **2. go over** *or* **through with a fine-tooth(ed) comb.** to examine very thoroughly.

fin·foot ('fɪnˌfʊt) *n., pl.* **·foots.** any aquatic bird of the tropical and subtropical family *Heliornithidae*, having broadly lobed toes, a long slender head and neck, and pale brown plumage: order *Gruiformes* (cranes, rails etc.). Also called: **sungrebe.**

Fin·gal's Cave ('fɪŋgəlz) *n.* a cave in W Scotland, on Staffa Island in the Inner Hebrides: basaltic pillars. Length: 68 m (227 ft.). Height: 35 m (117 ft.).

fin·ger ('fɪŋgə) *n.* **1. a.** any of the digits of the hand, often excluding the thumb. Technical name: **digitus manus. b.** (*as modifier*): *a finger bowl.* **c.** (*in combination*): *a fingernail.* Related adj.: **digital. 2.** the part of a glove made to cover a finger. **3.** something that resembles a finger in shape or function: *a finger of land.* **4.** Also called: **digit.** the length or width of a finger used as a unit of measurement. **5.** a quantity of liquid in a glass, etc., as deep as a finger is wide; tot. **6.** a projecting machine part, esp. one serving as an indicator. **7. burn one's fingers.** to suffer as a result of incautious or meddlesome action. **8. get** *or* **pull one's finger out.** *Brit. informal.* to begin or speed up activity, esp. after initial delay or slackness. **9. have a** (*or* **one's**) **finger in the pie. a.** to have an interest in or take part in some activity. **b.** to meddle or interfere. **10. lay a finger on.** (*usually negative*) to harm. **11. lay** *or* **put one's finger on.** to indicate, identify, or locate accurately. **12. not lift** (*or* **raise**) **a finger.** (*foll. by an infinitive*) not to make any effort (to do something). **13. let slip through one's fingers.** to allow to escape; miss narrowly. **14. twist** *or* **wrap around one's little finger.** to have easy and complete control or influence over. **15. put the finger on.** *Informal, chiefly U.S.* **a.** to inform on or identify, esp. for the police. **b.** to choose (the victim or location of an intended crime). ~*vb.* **16.** (*tr.*) to touch or manipulate with the fingers; handle. **17.** (*tr.*) *Informal, chiefly U.S.* to put the finger on (see sense 15). **18.** (*intr.*) to extend like a finger. **19.** to use one's fingers in playing (an instrument, such as a piano or clarinet). **20.** to indicate on (a composition or part) the fingering required by a pianist, harpsichordist, etc. **21.** (*tr.; usually passive*) to arrange the keys of (a clarinet, flute, etc.) for playing in a certain way. [Old English; related to Old Norse *fingr*, Gothic *figgrs*, Old High German *fingar*; see FIVE, FIST] —'**fin·ger·er** *n.* —'**fin·ger·less** *adj.*

fin·ger·board ('fɪŋgəˌbɔːd) *n.* the long strip of hard wood on a violin, guitar, or related stringed instrument upon which the strings are stopped by the fingers.

fin·ger bowl *n.* a small bowl filled with water for rinsing the fingers at the table after a meal.

fin·ger·breadth ('fɪŋgəˌbrɛdθ, -ˌbrɛtθ) *or* **fin·ger's breadth** *n.* the width of a finger, used as an indication of length.

fin·gered ('fɪŋgəd) *adj.* **1.** marked or dirtied by handling. **2. a.** having a finger or fingers. **b.** (*in combination*): *nine-fingered; red-fingered.* **3.** (of a musical part) having numerals indicating the necessary fingering.

fin·ger·ing ('fɪŋgərɪŋ) *n.* **1.** the technique or art of using one's fingers in playing a musical instrument, esp. the piano. **2.** the numerals in a musical part indicating this.

fin·ger·ling ('fɪŋgəlɪŋ) *n.* **1.** a very young fish, esp. the parr of salmon or trout. **2.** a diminutive creature or object.

fin·ger·mark ('fɪŋgəˌmɑːk) *n.* a mark left by dirty or greasy fingers on paintwork, walls, etc.

fin·ger·nail ('fɪŋgəˌneɪl) *n.* a thin horny translucent plate covering part of the dorsal surface of the end joint of each finger.

fin·ger paint·ing *n.* **1.** the process or art of painting with **finger paints** of starch, glycerin, and pigments, using the fingers, hand, or arm. **2.** a painting made in this way.

fin·ger post *n.* a signpost showing a pointing finger or hand.

fin·ger·print ('fɪŋgəˌprɪnt) *n.* **1.** an impression of the pattern of ridges on the palmar surface of the end joint of each finger and thumb. **2.** any identifying characteristic. ~*vb.* **3.** (*tr.*) to take an inked impression of the fingerprints of (a person).

fin·ger·stall ('fɪŋgəˌstɔːl) *n.* a protective covering for a finger. Also called: **cot, fingertip.**

fin·ger tight *adj.* made as tight as possible by hand.

fin·ger·tip ('fɪŋgəˌtɪp) *n.* **1.** the end joint or tip of a finger. **2.** another term for **fingerstall. 3. at one's fingertips.** readily available and within one's mental grasp.

fin·ger wave *n. Hairdressing.* a wave set in wet hair by using fingers and comb only.

Fin·go ('fɪŋgəʊ) *n., pl.* **·go** *or* **·gos.** a member of a Xhosa-speaking people settled in southern Africa in the Ciskei and Transkei: originally refugees from the Zulu wars of conquest.

fi·ni·al ('faɪnɪəl) *n.* **1.** an ornament on top of a spire, gable, etc., esp. in the form of a foliated fleur-de-lis. **2.** an ornament at the top of a piece of furniture, etc. [C14: from *finial* (adj.), variant of FINAL] —'**fi·ni·aled** *adj.*

fin·ick·y ('fɪnɪkɪ) *or* **fin·ick·ing** *adj.* **1.** excessively particular, as in tastes or standards; fussy. **2.** full of trivial detail; overelaborate. [C19: from *finical*, from FINE[1]]

fin·ing ('faɪnɪŋ) *n.* **1.** the process of removing undissolved gas bubbles from molten glass. **2.** the process of clarifying liquors by the addition of a coagulant. **3.** (*pl.*) a substance, such as isinglass, added to wine, beer, etc., to clarify it. [C17: from FINE[1] (in the sense: to clarify, refine)]

fin·is ('fɪnɪs) the end; finish: used at the end of books, films, etc. [C15: from Latin]

fin·ish ('fɪnɪʃ) *vb.* (*mainly tr.*) **1.** to bring to an end; complete, conclude, or stop. **2.** (*intr.;* sometimes foll. by *up*) to be at or come to the end. **3.** to bring to a desired or complete condition. **4.** to put a particular surface texture on (wood, cloth, etc.). **5.** (often foll. by *off*) to destroy or defeat completely. **6.** to train (a person) in social graces and talents. **7.** (*intr.;* foll. by *with*). **a.** to end a relationship or association. **b.** to stop punishing a person: *I haven't finished with you yet!* ~*n.* **8.** the final or last stage or part; end. **9. a.** the death, destruction, or absolute defeat of a person or one side in a conflict: *a fight to the finish.* **b.** the person, event, or thing that brings this about. **10. a.** the surface texture or appearance of wood, cloth, etc.: *a rough finish.* **b.** a preparation, such as varnish, used to produce such a texture. **11.** a thing, event, etc., that completes. **12.** completeness and high quality of workmanship. **13.** refinement in social graces. **14.** *Sport.* ability to sprint at the end of a race: *he has a good finish.* [C14: from Old French *finir*, from Latin *fīnīre* see FINE[1]] —'**fin·ish·er** *n.*

fin·ished ('fɪnɪʃt) *adj.* **1.** perfected. **2.** (*predicative*) at the end of a task, activity, etc.: *they were finished by four.* **3.** (*predicative*) without further hope of success or continuation: *she was finished as a prima ballerina.*

fin·ish·ing school *n.* a private school for girls that prepares them for society by teaching social graces and accomplishments.

Fin·is·tère (ˌfɪnɪ'stɛə; *French* finis'tɛːr) *n.* a department of NW France, at the tip of the Breton peninsula. Capital: Quimper. Pop.: 832 158 (1975). Area: 7029 sq. km (2741 sq. miles).

Fin·is·terre (ˌfɪnɪ'stɛə) *n.* **1. Cape.** a headland in NW Spain: the westernmost point of the Spanish mainland. **2.** an English name for **Finistère.**

fi·nite ('faɪnaɪt) *adj.* **1.** bounded in magnitude or spatial or temporal extent: *a finite difference.* **2.** *Maths.* having a limited or countable number of digits, terms, etc. Compare **infinite** (sense 5b. and c.). **3. a.** limited or restricted in nature: *human existence is finite.* **b.** (*as n.*): *the finite.* **4.** denoting any form or occurrence of a verb inflected for grammatical features such as person, number, and tense. [C15: from Latin *fīnītus* limited, from *fīnīre* to limit, end] —'**fi·nite·ly** *adv.* —'**fi·nite·ness** *n.*

fink (fɪŋk) *Slang, chiefly U.S.* ~*n.* **1.** a strikebreaker; blackleg. **2.** an informer, such as one working for the police; spy. **3.** an unpleasant, disappointing, or contemptible person. ~*vb.* **4.** (*intr.;* often foll. by *on*) to inform (on someone), as to the police. [C20: of uncertain origin]

fin keel *n.* a projection from the keel of a vessel to give it additional stability.

fink out *vb.* (*intr., adv.*) *Slang, chiefly U.S.* to fail to carry something out or through; give up.

Fin·land ('fɪnlənd) *n.* **1.** a republic in N Europe, on the Baltic Sea: ceded to Russia by Sweden in 1809; gained independence in 1917; Soviet invasion successfully withstood in 1939–40, with the loss of Karelia. It is generally low-lying, with about 50 000 lakes, extensive forests, and peat bogs. Official language: Finnish; Swedish is also widely spoken. Religion: chiefly Lutheran. Currency: markka. Capital: Helsinki. Pop.: 4 707 000 (1975 est.). Area: 337 000 sq. km (130 120 sq. miles). Finnish name: **Suomi. 2. Gulf of.** an arm of the Baltic Sea between Finland and the Soviet Union.

Finn[1] (fɪn) *n.* **1.** a native, inhabitant, or citizen of Finland. **2.** a speaker of a Finnic language, esp. one of the original inhabitants of Russia, who were pushed northwards during the Slav migrations. [Old English *Finnas* (plural); related to Old Norse *Finnr* Finn, Latin *Fennī* the Finns, Greek *Phinnoi*]

Finn[2] (fɪn) *n.* called *Finn MacCool.* (in Irish legend) chief of the Fianna, father of the heroic poet Ossian.

fin·nan had·dock ('fɪnən) *or* **had·die** *n.* smoked haddock. [C18: *finnan* after River *Findhorn*, confused with *Findon*, a village in the Grampian region of Scotland + HADDOCK]

finned (fɪnd) *adj.* having one or more fins or finlike parts.

fin·ner ('fɪnə) *n.* another name for **rorqual.** [C18: from FIN[1] + -ER[1]]

Fin·ney ('fɪnɪ) *n.* **Al·bert.** born 1936, English stage and film actor.

Finn·ic ('fɪnɪk) *n.* **1.** one of the two branches of the Finno-Ugric family of languages, including Finnish and several languages of the N Soviet Union in Europe. Compare **Ugric.** ~*adj.* **2.** of or relating to this group of languages or to the Finns.

Finn·ish ('fɪnɪʃ) *adj.* **1.** of, relating to, or characteristic of Finland, the Finns, or their language. ~*n.* **2.** the official language of Finland, also spoken in the NW Soviet Union, belonging to the Finno-Ugric family.

Finn·mark ('fɪnˌmɑːk) *n.* a county of N Norway: the largest, northernmost, and least populated county; mostly a barren plateau. Capital: Vadsø. Pop.: 76 354 (1971). Area: 48 649 sq. km (18 973 sq. miles).

Fin·no-U·gric ('fɪnəʊ'uːgrɪk, -'juː-) *or* **Fin·no-U·gri·an** *n.* **1.** a family of languages spoken in Scandinavia, Hungary, and the Soviet Union, including Finnish, Estonian, Hungarian, Ostyak, and Vogul: sometimes regarded as a subfamily of a Uralic family. See also **Ural-Altaic.** ~*adj.* **2.** of, relating to, or belonging to this family of languages.

fin·ny ('fɪnɪ) *adj.* **·ni·er, ·ni·est. 1.** *Poetic.* relating to or containing many fishes. **2.** having or resembling a fin or fins.

fi·no ('fiːnəʊ) *n.* a very dry sherry. [from Spanish: FINE[1]]

fi·noch·i·o *or* **fi·noc·chi·o** (fɪ'nɒkɪˌəʊ) *n.* a variety of fennel, *Foeniculum vulgare dulce,* with thickened stalks that resemble celery and are eaten as a vegetable, esp. in S Europe. [C18: from Italian: FENNEL]

Fin·sen (*Danish* 'fensən) *n.* **Niels Ry·berg** (neːls 'ryber). 1860–1904, Danish physician; founder of phototherapy: Nobel prize for physiology or medicine 1903.

Fin·ster·aar·horn (ˌfɪnstər'ɑːhɔːn) *n.* a mountain in S central Switzerland: highest peak in the Bernese Alps. Height: 4274 m (14 014 ft.).

fiord (fjɔːd) *n.* a variant spelling of **fjord.**

fi·o·rin ('faɪərɪn) *n.* a temperate perennial grass, *Agrostis stolonifera.* Also called: **creeping bent grass.** See **bent grass.** [C19: from Irish Gaelic *fiorthann* wheat grass]

fip·ple ('fɪpᵊl) *n.* **1.** a wooden plug forming a flue in the end of a pipe, as the mouthpiece of a recorder. **2.** a similar device in an organ pipe with a flutelike tone. [C17: of unknown origin]

fip·ple flute *n.* an end-blown flute provided with a fipple, such as the recorder or flageolet.

fir (fɜː) *n.* **1.** any pyramidal coniferous tree of the N temperate genus *Abies,* having single needle-like leaves and erect cones: family *Pinaceae.* See also **red fir, silver fir, balsam fir. 2.** any of various other trees of the family *Pinaceae,* such as the Douglas fir. **3.** the wood of any of these trees. [Old English *furh;* related to Old Norse *fura,* Old High German *foraha* fir, Latin *quercus* oak]

Fir·bank ('fɜːbænk) *n.* **(Arthur Annesley) Ro·nald.** 1886–1926, English novelist, whose works include *Valmouth* (1919), *The Flower beneath the Foot* (1923), and *Concerning the Eccentricities of Cardinal Pirelli* (1926).

Fir·dau·si (fɪə'daʊsɪ) *or* **Fir·du·si** (fɪə'duːsɪ) *n.* pen name of *Abul Qasim Mansur.* ?935–1020 A.D., Persian epic poet; author of *Shah Nama* (*The Book of Kings*), a chronicle of the legends and history of Persia.

fire (faɪə) *n.* **1.** the state of combustion in which inflammable material burns, producing heat, flames, and often smoke. **2. a.** a mass of burning coal, wood, etc., used esp. in a hearth to heat a room. **b.** (*in combination*): *firewood; firelighter.* **3.** a destructive conflagration, as of a forest, building, etc. **4.** a device for heating a room, etc. **5.** something resembling a fire in light or brilliance: *a diamond's fire.* **6.** a flash or spark of or as if of fire. **7. a.** the act of discharging weapons, artillery, etc. **b.** the shells, etc., fired. **8.** a burst or rapid volley: *a fire of questions.* **9.** intense passion; ardour. **10.** liveliness, as of imagination, thought, etc. **11.** a burning sensation sometimes produced by drinking strong alcoholic liquor. **12.** fever and inflammation. **13.** a severe trial or torment (esp. in the phrase **go through fire and water**). **14. between two fires.** under attack from two sides. **15. catch fire.** to ignite. **16. hang fire. a.** to delay firing. **b.** to delay or be delayed. **17. no smoke without fire.** the evidence strongly suggests something has indeed happened. **18. on fire. a.** in a state of ignition. **b.** ardent or eager. **19. open fire.** to start firing a gun, artillery, etc. **20. play with fire.** to be involved in something risky. **21. set fire to** *or* **set on fire. a.** to ignite. **b.** to arouse or excite. **22. set the world** *or* (*Brit.*) **the Thames on fire.** *Informal.* to cause a great sensation. **23. under fire.** being attacked, as by weapons or by harsh criticism. **24.** (*modifier*) *Astrology.* of or relating to a group of three signs of the zodiac, Aries, Leo, and Sagittarius. Compare **earth** (sense 10), **air** (sense 18), **water** (sense 12). ~*vb.* **25.** to discharge (a firearm or projectile) or (of a firearm, etc.) to be discharged. **26.** to detonate (an explosive charge or device), or (of such a charge or device) to be detonated. **27.** (*tr.*) *Informal.* to dismiss from employment. **28.** (*tr.*) *Ceramics.* to bake in a kiln to harden the clay, fix the glaze, etc. **29.** to kindle or be kindled; ignite. **30.** (*tr.*) to provide with fuel: *oil fires the heating system.* **31.** (*intr.*) to tend a fire. **32.** (*tr.*) to subject to heat. **33.** (*tr.*) to heat slowly so as to dry. **34.** (*tr.*) to arouse to strong emotion. **35.** to glow or cause to glow. **36.** (*intr.*) (of grain) to become blotchy or yellow before maturity. **37.** *Vet. science.* another word for **cauterize. 38.** (*intr.*) *Austral. slang.* (of a sportsman, etc.) to play well or with enthusiasm. ~*interj.* **39.** a cry to warn others of a fire. [Old English *fȳr;* related to Old Saxon *fiur,* Old Norse *fūrr,* Old High German *fūir,* Greek *pur*] —**'fire·a·ble** *adj.* —**'fire·less** *adj.* —**'fir·er** *n.*

fire a·larm *n.* **1.** a device to give warning of fire, esp. a bell, siren, or hooter. **2.** a shout to warn that a fire has broken out.

fire-and-brim·stone *adj.* (of a sermon, preacher, etc.) zealous, esp. in threatening eternal damnation.

fire ant *n.* any mound-building predatory ant of the genus *Solenopsis,* of tropical and subtropical America, that can inflict a painful sting.

fire·arm ('faɪərˌɑːm) *n.* a weapon, esp. a portable gun or pistol, from which a projectile can be discharged by an explosion caused by igniting gunpowder, etc.

fire a·way *vb.* (*intr., adv.; often imperative*) *Informal.* to begin to speak or to ask questions.

fire·back ('faɪəˌbæk) *n.* **1.** Also called: **reredos.** an ornamental iron slab against the back wall of a hearth. **2.** any pheasant of the genus *Lophura,* of SE Asia.

fire·ball ('faɪəˌbɔːl) *n.* **1.** a ball-shaped discharge of lightning. **2.** the bright spherical region of hot ionized gas at the centre of a nuclear explosion. **3.** *Astronomy.* another name for **bolide. 4.** *Slang.* an energetic person.

fire·bird ('faɪəˌbɜːd) *n. Chiefly U.S.* any of various songbirds having a bright red plumage, esp. the Baltimore oriole.

fire blight *n.* a disease of apples, pears, and similar fruit trees, caused by the bacterium *Erwinia amylovora* and characterized by blackening of the blossoms and leaves, and cankers on the branches.

fire·boat ('faɪəˌbəʊt) *n.* a motor vessel equipped with fire-fighting apparatus.

fire·bomb ('faɪəˌbɒm) *n.* another name for **incendiary** (sense 6).

fire·box ('faɪəˌbɒks) *n.* **1.** the furnace chamber of a boiler in a steam locomotive. **2.** an obsolete word for **tinderbox.**

fire·brand ('faɪəˌbrænd) *n.* **1.** a piece of burning or glowing wood or other material. **2.** a person who causes unrest or is very energetic.

fire·brat ('faɪəˌbræt) *n.* a small primitive wingless insect, *Thermobia domestica,* that occurs in warm buildings, feeding on starchy food scraps, fabric, etc.: order *Thysanura* (bristletails).

fire·break ('faɪəˌbreɪk), **fire·guard** ('faɪəˌgɑːd), *or* **fire line** *n.* a strip of open land in forest or prairie, serving to arrest the advance of a fire.

fire·brick ('faɪəˌbrɪk) *n.* a refractory brick made of fire clay, used for lining furnaces, flues, etc.

fire bri·gade *n. Chiefly Brit.* an organized body of firemen.

fire·bug ('faɪəˌbʌg) *n. Informal.* a person who deliberately sets fire to property.

fire clay *n.* a heat-resistant clay used in the making of firebricks, furnace linings, etc.

fire com·pa·ny *n.* **1.** an insurance company selling policies relating to fire risk. **2.** *U.S.* an organized body of firemen.

fire con·trol *n. Military.* the procedures by which weapons are brought to engage a target.

fire·crack·er ('faɪəˌkrækə) *n.* a small cardboard container filled with explosive powder and lit by a fuse.

fire·crest ('faɪəˌkrɛst) *n.* a small European warbler, *Regulus ignicapillus,* having a crown striped with yellow, black, and white.

fire-cure *vb.* (*tr*). to cure (tobacco) by exposure to the smoke and heat of an open fire.

fire·damp ('faɪəˌdæmp) *n.* a mixture of hydrocarbons, chiefly methane, formed in coal mines. It forms explosive mixtures with air. See also **afterdamp.**

fire de·part·ment *n. U.S.* the department of a local authority responsible for the prevention and extinguishing of fires.

fire·dog ('faɪəˌdɒg) *n.* either of a pair of decorative metal stands used to support logs in an open fire.

fire·drake ('faɪəˌdreɪk) *or* **fire·drag·on** ('faɪəˌdrægən) *n. Myth.* a fire-breathing dragon.

fire drill *n.* a rehearsal of duties or escape procedures to be followed in case of fire.

fire-eat·er *n.* **1.** a performer who simulates the swallowing of fire. **2.** a belligerent person. —**'fire-ˌeat·ing** *n., adj.*

fire en·gine *n.* a heavy road vehicle that carries firemen and fire-fighting equipment to a fire.

fire es·cape *n.* a means of evacuating persons from a building in the event of fire, esp. a metal staircase outside the building.

fire-ex·tin·guish·er *n.* a portable device for extinguishing fires, usually consisting of a canister with a directional nozzle used to direct a spray of water, chemically generated foam, inert gas, or fine powder onto the fire.

fire·fly ('faɪəˌflaɪ) *n., pl.* **·flies. 1.** any nocturnal beetle of the family *Lampyridae,* common in warm and tropical regions, having luminescent abdominal organs. See also **glow-worm. 2.** any tropical American click beetle of the genus *Pyrophorus,* esp. *P. noctiluca,* that have luminescent thoracic organs.

fire·guard ('faɪəˌgɑːd) *n.* **1.** Also called: **fire screen.** a metal panel or meshed frame put before an open fire to protect against falling logs, sparks, etc. **2.** a less common word for **firebreak.**

fire hy·drant *n.* a hydrant for use as an emergency supply for fighting fires, esp. one in a street. Also called (U.S.): **fireplug.**

fire in·sur·ance *n.* insurance covering damage or loss caused by fire or lightning.

fire i·rons *pl. n.* metal fireside implements, such as poker, shovel, and tongs.

fire·less cook·er *n.* an insulated container that retains enough heat to cook food or keep it warm.

fire·lock ('faɪəˌlɒk) *n.* **1.** an obsolete type of gunlock with a priming mechanism ignited by sparks. **2.** a gun or musket having such a lock.

fire·man ('faɪəmən) *n., pl.* **·men. 1.** a person who fights fires, usually a trained volunteer or public employee. **2. a.** (on steam locomotives) the man who stokes the fire and controls the injectors feeding water to the boiler. **b.** (on diesel and electric locomotives) the driver's assistant. **3.** a man who tends furnaces; stoker. **4.** Also called: **deputy.** a mine official responsible for safety precautions. U.S. equivalent: **fire boss. 5.** *U.S. Navy.* a junior rating who works on marine engineering equipment.

fire mar·shal *n. U.S.* **1.** a public official responsible for investigating the causes of fires, enforcing fire prevention laws, etc. **2.** the head of a fire prevention organization.

Fi·ren·ze (fi'rɛntse) *n.* the Italian name for **Florence.**

fire o·pal *n.* an orange-red translucent variety of opal, valued as a gemstone.

fire·pan ('faɪəˌpæn) *n.* a metal container for a fire in a room.

fire·place ('faɪəˌpleɪs) *n.* an open recess in a wall of a room, at the base of a chimney, etc., for a fire; hearth.

fire·plug ('faɪəˌplʌg) *n. U.S.* another name for **fire hydrant.**

fire pow+er *n. Military.* the capability of delivering fire.
fire+proof ('faɪə,pruːf) *adj.* **1.** capable of resisting damage by fire. ~*vb.* **2.** (*tr.*) to make resistant to fire.
fire rais+er *n.* a person who deliberately sets fire to property, etc. —**fire rais+ing** *n.*
fire screen *n.* **1.** a decorative screen placed in the hearth when there is no fire. **2.** a screen placed before a fire to protect the face from intense heat.
fire ship *n.* a vessel loaded with explosives and used, esp. formerly, as a bomb by igniting it and directing it to drift among an enemy's warships.
fire+side ('faɪə,saɪd) *n.* **1.** the hearth. **2.** family life; the home.
fire sta+tion *n.* a building where fire-fighting vehicles and equipment are stationed and where firemen on duty wait. Also called (U.S.): **firehouse, station house.**
fire+stone ('faɪə,stəʊn) *n.* a sandstone that withstands intense heat, esp. one used for lining kilns, furnaces, etc.
fire+storm ('faɪə,stɔːm) *n.* a storm in which violent winds are drawn into the column of rising hot air over an area that has been severely bombed.
fire+thorn ('faɪə,θɔːn) *n.* any rosaceous evergreen spiny shrub of the genus *Pyracantha,* of SE Europe and Asia, having bright red or orange fruits: cultivated for ornament.
fire+trap ('faɪə,træp) *n.* a building that would burn easily or one without fire escapes.
fire walk+ing *n.* a religious rite in which people walk barefoot over white-hot ashes, stones, etc.
fire wall *n.* a fireproof wall or partition used to impede the progress of a fire, as from one room or compartment to another.
fire+ward·en ('faɪə,wɔːdᵊn) *n. U.S.* an officer responsible for fire prevention and control in an area, esp. in a forest.
fire watch+er *n.* a person who watches for fires, esp. those caused by aerial bombardment.
fire+wa·ter ('faɪə,wɔːtə) *n.* any strong spirit, esp. whisky.
fire+weed ('faɪə,wiːd) *n.* **1.** any of various plants that appear as first vegetation in burnt-over areas. **2.** Also called: **pilewort.** a weedy North American plant, *Erechtites hieracifolia,* having small white or greenish flowers: family *Compositae* (composites). **3.** another name for **rosebay willowherb.** See **rosebay** (sense 2).
fire+work ('faɪə,wɜːk) *n.* a device, such as a Catherine wheel, Roman candle, or rocket, in which combustible materials are ignited and produce coloured flames, sparks, and smoke, sometimes accompanied by bangs.
fire+works ('faɪə,wɜːks) *pl. n.* **1.** a show in which large numbers of fireworks are let off simultaneously. **2.** *Informal.* an exciting or spectacular exhibition, as of musical virtuosity or wit. **3.** *Informal.* a burst of temper.
fir+ing ('faɪərɪŋ) *n.* **1.** the process of baking ceramics, etc., in a kiln or furnace: *a second firing.* **2.** the act of stoking a fire or furnace. **3.** a discharge of a firearm. **4.** something used as fuel, such as coal or wood. **5.** *U.S.* a scorching of plants, as a result of disease, drought, or heat.
fir+ing line *n.* **1.** *Military.* **a.** the positions from which fire is delivered. **b.** the soldiers occupying these positions. **2.** the leading or most advanced position in an activity.
fir+ing or+der *n.* the sequence of ignition in the cylinders of an internal-combustion engine.
fir+ing par+ty *n.* **1.** a military detachment detailed to fire a salute at a funeral. **2.** another name for **firing squad.**
fir+ing pin *n.* the part of the firing mechanism of a firearm that ignites the charge by striking the primer.
fir+ing squad *n.* a small military detachment formed to implement a death sentence by shooting.
fir+kin ('fɜːkɪn) *n.* **1.** a small wooden barrel or similar container. **2.** *Brit.* a unit of capacity equal to nine gallons. [C14: *fir,* from Middle Dutch *vierde* FOURTH + -KIN]
firm[1] (fɜːm) *adj.* **1.** not soft or yielding to a touch or pressure; rigid; solid. **2.** securely in position; stable or stationary. **3.** definitely established; decided; settled. **4.** enduring or steady; constant. **5.** having determination or strength; resolute. **6.** (of prices, markets, etc.) tending to rise. ~*adv.* **7.** in a secure, stable, or unyielding manner: *he stood firm over his obligation to pay.* ~*vb.* **8.** (sometimes foll. by *up*) to make or become firm. **9.** (*intr.*) *Austral. horse racing.* (of a horse) to shorten in odds. [C14: from Latin *firmus*] —**'firm+ly** *adv.* —**'firm+ness** *n.*
firm[2] (fɜːm) *n.* **1.** a commercial enterprise. **2.** a team of doctors and their assistants. [C16 (in the sense: signature): from Spanish *firma* signature, title of a partnership or business concern, from *firmar* to sign, from Latin *firmāre* to confirm, from *firmus* firm]
fir+ma+ment ('fɜːməmənt) *n.* the expanse of the sky; heavens. [C13: from Late Latin *firmāmentum* sky (considered as fixed above the earth), from Latin: prop, support, from *firmāre* to make FIRM[1]] —**fir+ma+men+tal** (,fɜːmə'mɛntᵊl) *adj.*
fir+mer chis+el ('fɜːmə) *n.* a chisel or gouge with a thin blade, used on wood. Sometimes shortened to **firmer.**
firm+ware ('fɜːm,wɛə) *n. Computer technol.* a series of fixed instructions that requires computer hardware to change it.
firn (fɪən) *n.* another name for **névé** (sense 1). [C19: from German (Swiss dialect) *firn* of the previous year, from Old High German *firni* old]
fir+ry ('fɜːrɪ) *adj.* **1.** of, relating to, or made from fir trees. **2.** abounding in or dominated by firs.
first (fɜːst) *adj.* (*usually prenominal*) **1. a.** coming before all others; earliest, best, or foremost. **b.** (*as n.*)*: I was the first to arrive.* **2.** preceding all others in numbering or counting order; the ordinal number of *one.* Often written: 1st. **3.** rated, graded, or ranked above all other levels. **4.** denoting the lowest forward ratio of a gearbox in a motor vehicle. **5.** *Music.* **a.** denoting the highest part assigned to one of the voice parts in a chorus or one of the sections of an orchestra: *first soprano; the first violins.* **b.** denoting the principal player in a specific orchestral section: *he plays first horn.* **6. first thing.** as the first action of the day: *I'll see you first thing tomorrow.* **7. first things first.** things must be done in order of priority. **8. the first thing, idea, etc.** (*in negative constructions*) even one thing, etc.: *he doesn't know the first thing about me.* ~*n.* **9.** the beginning; outset: *I knew you were a rogue from the first; I couldn't see at first because of the mist.* **10.** *Education, chiefly Brit.* an honours degree of the highest class. Full term: **first-class honours degree.** **11.** the lowest forward ratio of a gearbox in a motor vehicle; low gear. **12.** *Music.* **a.** the highest part in a particular section of a chorus or orchestra. **b.** the instrument or voice taking such a part. **c.** the chief or leading player in a section of an orchestra; principal. **13.** *Music.* a rare word for **prime** (sense 11). ~*adv.* **14.** Also: **firstly.** before anything else in order, time, preference, importance, etc.: *do this first.* **15. first and last.** on the whole; overall. **16. from first to last.** throughout. **17.** for the first time: *I've loved you since I first saw you.* **18.** (*sentence modifier*) in the first place or beginning of a series of actions: *first I want to talk about criminality.* [Old English *fyrest;* related to Old Saxon *furist,* Old Norse *fyrstr,* German *Fürst* prince, one who is first in rank]
first aid *n.* **1. a.** immediate medical assistance given in an emergency. **b.** (*as modifier*)*: first-aid box.* **2.** (in Barbados) a small shop that sells domestic items after hours.
first base *n.* **1.** *Baseball.* **a.** the base that a runner must reach safely to score a hit, and the first of the three bases he must reach safely on the way to home plate in order to score a run. **b.** the fielding position nearest this base. **2. get to first base.** *Informal, chiefly U.S.* to accomplish the first step of an undertaking.
first-born *adj.* **1.** eldest of the children in a family. ~*n.* **2.** the eldest child in a family.
first cause *n.* **1.** a source or cause of something. **2.** (*often caps.*) (esp. in philosophy) God considered as the uncaused creator of all beings apart from himself.
first class *n.* **1.** the class or grade of the best or highest value, quality, etc. ~*adj.* (**first-class** *when prenominal*). **2.** of the best or highest class or grade: *a first-class citizen.* **3.** excellent; first-rate. **4.** of or denoting the most comfortable and expensive class of accommodation in a hotel, aircraft, train, etc. **5. a.** (in Britain) of or relating to letters that are handled faster than second-class letters. **b.** (in the U.S. and Canada) of or relating to mail that consists mainly of written letters, cards, etc. **6.** *Education.* See **first** (sense 10). ~*adv.* **first-class.** **7.** by first-class mail, means of transportation, etc.
first-day cov+er *n. Philately.* a cover, usually an envelope, postmarked on the first day of the issue of its stamps.
first-de·gree burn *n. Pathol.* See **burn**[1] (sense 19).
First Em+pire *n.* the period of imperial rule in France (1804–14) under Napoleon Bonaparte.
first es+tate *n.* the first of the three estates of the realm, such as the Lords Spiritual in England or the clergy in France until the revolution.
first floor *n.* **1.** *Brit.* the floor or storey of a building immediately above the ground floor. U.S. term: **second floor.** **2.** *U.S.* another term for **ground floor.**
first-foot *Chiefly Scot.* ~*n. also* **first-foot·er.** **1.** the first person to enter a household in the New Year. By Hogmanay tradition a dark-haired person who crosses the threshold at midnight brings good luck. ~*vb.* **2.** to enter (a house) as first-foot. —**'first-'foot·ing** *n.*
first fruits *pl. n.* **1.** the first results, products, or profits of an undertaking. **2.** fruit that ripens first.
first-hand *adj., adv.* **1.** from the original source; direct or directly: *first-hand news; he got the news first-hand.* **2. at first hand.** from the original source; directly.
First In+ter+na+tion+al *n.* an association of socialists and labour leaders founded in London in 1864 and dissolved in Philadelphia in 1876. Official name: **International Working-men's Association.**
first la·dy *n.* (*often caps.*) **1.** *U.S.* the wife or official hostess of a chief executive, esp. of a state governor or a president. **2.** a woman considered to be at the top of her profession or art: *the first lady of jazz.*
first lieu+ten+ant *n.* **1.** the officer responsible for the upkeep and maintenance of a warship, esp. the executive officer of a smaller ship in the Royal Navy. **2.** an officer holding commissioned rank in the U.S. Army, Air Force, Marine Corps, or in certain other forces, senior to a second lieutenant and junior to a captain.
first+ling ('fɜːstlɪŋ) *n.* the first, esp. the first offspring.
first+ly ('fɜːstlɪ) *adv.* another word for **first** (sense 14).
first mate *n.* an officer second in command to the captain of a merchant ship. Also called: **first officer.**
first mort+gage *n.* a mortgage that has priority over other mortgages on the same property, except for taxation and other statutory liabilities.
first name *n.* another term for Christian name.
first night *n.* **a.** the first public performance of a play or other production. **b.** (*as modifier*)*: first-night nerves.*
first-night·er *n.* a member of an opening night audience, esp. one who habitually attends first nights.
first of+fend+er *n.* a person convicted of any criminal offence for the first time.

first of·fic·er *n.* **1.** another name for **first mate. 2.** the member of an aircraft crew who is second in command to the captain.
first-past-the-post (*modifier*) of or relating to a voting system in which a candidate may be elected by a simple majority rather than an absolute majority.
first per·son *n.* a grammatical category of pronouns and verbs used by the speaker to refer to or talk about himself, either alone (**first person singular**) or together with others (**first person plural**).
first post *n. Brit.* the first of two military bugle calls ordering or giving notice of the time to retire for the night. The second is called **last post.**
first prin·ci·ple *n.* (*usually pl.*) one of the fundamental assumptions, axioms, laws, etc., that form the basis of a scientific, mathematical, or logical argument or theory.
first quar·ter *n.* one of the four principal phases of the moon, occurring between new moon and full moon, when half of the lighted surface is visible from earth. Compare **last quarter.**
first-rate *adj.* **1.** of the best or highest rated class or quality. **2.** *Informal.* very good; excellent. ~*adv.* **3.** *Not standard.* very well; excellently.
first read·ing *n.* the introduction of a bill in a legislative assembly.
first re·fus·al *n.* the chance of buying a house, merchandise, etc., before the offer is made to other potential buyers.
First Re·pub·lic *n.* the republic in France, which lasted from the abolition of the monarchy in 1792 until Napoleon Bonaparte proclaimed himself emperor in 1804.
firsts (fɜːsts) *pl. n.* saleable goods of the highest quality.
first school *n. Brit.* a school for children aged between 5 and 8 or 9. Compare **middle school.**
first string ~*n.* **1.** the top player of a team in an individual sport, such as squash. ~*adj.* **first-string. 2.** being a regular member of a team rather than a substitute or reserve. **3.** being the top player of a team in an individual sport. **4.** of high rating; first-class.
first wa·ter *n.* **1.** the finest quality of diamond or other precious stone. **2.** the highest grade or best quality. **3.** the most extreme kind: *a fool of the first water.*
First World War *n.* another name for **World War I.**
firth (fɜːθ) *or* **frith** *n.* a relatively narrow inlet of the sea, esp. in Scotland. [C15: from Old Norse *fjörthr* FIORD]
fisc (fɪsk) *n. Rare.* a state or royal treasury. [C16: from Latin *fiscus* treasury, originally money-bag]
fis·cal ('fɪskᵊl) *adj.* **1.** of or relating to government finances, esp. tax revenues. **2.** of or involving financial matters. ~*n.* **3. a.** (in some countries) a public prosecutor. **b.** *Scot.* short for **procurator fiscal. 4.** a postage or other stamp signifying payment of a tax. [C16: from Latin *fiscālis* concerning the state treasury, from *fiscus* public money; see FISC] —**'fis·cal·ly** *adv.*
fis·cal year *n.* the U.S. term for **financial year.**
Fisch·er (*German* 'fɪʃər) *n.* **1. E·mil Her·mann** ('eːmiːl 'hɛrman). 1852–1919, German chemist noted particularly for his work on synthetic sugars and the purine group: Nobel prize for chemistry 1902. **2. Hans** (hans). 1881–1945, German chemist, noted particularly for his work on chlorophyll, haemin, and the porphyrins: Nobel prize for chemistry 1930. **3.** ('fɪʃə). **Rob·ert James,** called *Bobby.* born 1943, U.S. chess player; world champion 1972–75.
Fisch·er-Die·skau (*German* 'fɪʃər 'diːskaʊ) *n.* **Die·trich** ('diːtrɪç). born 1925, German baritone, noted particularly for his interpretation of Schubert's song cycles.
fish (fɪʃ) *n., pl.* **fish** *or* **fish·es. 1. a.** any of a large group of cold-blooded aquatic vertebrates having jaws, gills, and usually fins and a skin covered in scales: includes the sharks and rays (class *Chondrichthyes:* **cartilaginous fishes**) and the teleosts, lungfish, etc. (class *Osteichthyes:* **bony fishes**). **b.** (*in combination*): *fishpond.* Related adj.: **piscine. 2.** any of various similar but jawless vertebrates, such as the hagfish and lamprey. **3.** (*not in technical use*) any of various aquatic invertebrates, such as the cuttlefish, jellyfish, and crayfish. **4.** the flesh of fish used as food. **5.** *Informal.* a person of little emotion or intelligence: *a poor fish.* **6.** short for **fishplate. 7.** Also called: **tin fish.** an informal word for **torpedo** (sense 1). **8. a fine kettle of fish.** a great problem; trouble. **9. drink like a fish.** to drink to excess. **10. have other fish to fry.** to have other activities to do, esp. more important ones. **11. like a fish out of water.** out of one's usual place. **12. neither fish, flesh, nor fowl.** neither this nor that. ~*vb.* **13.** (*intr.*) to attempt to catch fish, as with a line and hook or with nets, traps, etc. **14.** (*tr.*) to fish in (a particular area of water). **15.** to search (a body of water) for something or to search for something, esp. in a body of water. **16.** (*intr.; foll. by* *for*) to seek something indirectly: *to fish for compliments.* **17. fish in troubled water.** to try to take advantage of confusion or trouble. ~See also **fish out.** [Old English *fisc;* related to Old Norse *fiskr,* Gothic *fiscs,* Russian *piskar,* Latin *piscis*] —**'fish·a·ble** *adj.* —**'fish·,like** *adj.*
fish and chips *n.* fish fillets coated with batter and deep-fried, eaten with potato chips.
fish-and-chip shop *n.* (in Britain) a place where fish and chips are cooked and sold.
fish·bolt ('fɪʃ,bəʊlt) *n.* a bolt used for fastening a fishplate to a rail.
fish·bowl ('fɪʃ,bəʊl) *n.* another name for **goldfish bowl.**
fish cake *n.* a fried ball of flaked fish mixed with mashed potatoes.
fish ea·gle *n.* another name for the **osprey.**
fish·er ('fɪʃə) *n.* **1.** a person who fishes; fisherman. **2.** Also called: **pekan. a.** a large North American marten, *Martes pennanti,* having thick dark brown fur. **b.** the fur of this animal. **3. fisher of men.** an evangelist.
Fish·er ('fɪʃə) *n.* **1. An·drew.** 1862–1928, Australian statesman, born in Scotland: prime minister of Australia (1908–09; 1910–13; 1914–15). **2. Geof·frey Fran·cis,** Baron Fisher of Lambeth. 1887–1972, archbishop of Canterbury (1945–61). **3. Saint John.** ?1469–1535, English prelate and scholar: executed for refusing to acknowledge Henry VIII as supreme head of the church. Feast day: June 20. **4. John Ar·buth·not,** 1st Baron Fisher of Kilverstone. 1841–1920, British admiral; First Sea Lord (1904–10; 1914–15); introduced the dreadnought.
fish·er·man ('fɪʃəmən) *n., pl.* **·men. 1.** a person who fishes as a profession or for sport. **2.** a vessel used for fishing.
fish·er·man's bend *n.* a knot used to fasten a rope to an anchor, ring, or spar.
fish·er·y ('fɪʃərɪ) *n., pl.* **·er·ies. 1. a.** the industry of catching, processing, and selling fish. **b.** a place where this is carried on. **2.** a place where fish are reared. **3.** a fishing ground. **4.** *Law.* another word for **piscary.**
Fish·es ('fɪʃɪz) *n.* **the.** the constellation Pisces, the twelfth sign of the zodiac.
fish-eye lens *n. Photog.* a lens of small focal length, having a highly curved protruding front element, that covers an angle of view of almost 180°. It yields a circular image having considerable linear distortion.
fish·fin·ger ('fɪʃ'fɪŋgə) *or U.S.* **fish stick** *n.* an oblong piece of filleted or minced fish coated in breadcrumbs.
fish flake *n. Canadian.* a platform on which fish are dried.
fish·gig ('fɪʃ,gɪg) *n.* a pole with barbed prongs for impaling fish. Also: **fizgig.** [C17: of uncertain origin; perhaps altered from Spanish *fisga* harpoon]
fish hawk *n.* another name for the **osprey.**
fish-hook *n.* a sharp hook used in angling, esp. one with a barb.
fish·ing ('fɪʃɪŋ) *n.* **1. a.** the occupation of catching fish. **b.** (*as modifier*): *a fishing match.* **2.** another word for **piscary** (sense 2).
fish·ing rod *n.* a long tapered flexible pole, often in jointed sections, for use with a fishing line and, usually, a reel.
fish·ing tack·le *n.* all the equipment, such as rods, lines, bait, etc., used in angling.
fish joint *n.* a connection formed by fishplates at the meeting point of two rails, beams, etc., as on a railway.
fish lad·der *n.* a row of ascending pools or weirs connected by short falls to allow fish to pass barrages or dams.
fish louse *n.* any small flat rounded crustacean of the subclass *Branchiura,* having sucking mouth parts: parasites of fish.
fish meal *n.* ground dried fish used as feed for farm animals, as a fertilizer, etc.
fish·mon·ger ('fɪʃ,mʌŋgə) *n. Chiefly Brit.* a retailer of fish.
fish·net ('fɪʃ,nɛt) *n.* **1.** *Chiefly U.S.* a net for catching fish. **2. a.** an open mesh fabric resembling netting. **b.** (*as modifier*): *fishnet tights.*
fish out *vb.* (*tr., adv.*) to find or extract (something): *to fish keys out of a pocket.*
fish·plate ('fɪʃ,pleɪt) *n.* a flat piece of metal joining one rail or beam to the next, esp. on railway tracks.
fish·skin dis·ease ('fɪʃ,skɪn) *n. Pathol.* a nontechnical name for **ichthyosis.**
fish·tail ('fɪʃ,teɪl) *n.* **1.** an aeroplane manoeuvre in which the tail is moved from side to side to reduce speed. **2.** a nozzle having a long narrow slot at the top, placed over a Bunsen burner to produce a thin fanlike flame. ~*vb.* **3.** (*intr.*) to slow an aeroplane by moving the tail from side to side.
fish tail *n.* a step in ballroom dancing in which the feet are quickly crossed.
fish·wife ('fɪʃ,waɪf) *n., pl.* **·wives. 1.** a woman who sells fish. **2.** a coarse scolding woman.
fish·y ('fɪʃɪ) *adj.* **fish·i·er, fish·i·est. 1.** of, involving, or suggestive of fish. **2.** abounding in fish. **3.** *Informal.* suspicious, doubtful, or questionable: *their leaving at the same time looked fishy.* **4.** dull and lifeless: *a fishy look.* —**'fish·i·ly** *adv.* —**'fish·i·ness** *n.*
fis·si- *combining form.* indicating a splitting or cleft: *fissirostral.* [from Latin *fissus,* past participle of *findere* to split]
fis·sile ('fɪsaɪl) *adj.* **1.** *Brit.* capable of undergoing nuclear fission as a result of the impact of slow neutrons. **2.** another word (esp. U.S.) for **fissionable. 3.** tending to split or capable of being split. [C17: from Latin *fissilis,* from *fissus* split; see FISSI-] —**fis·sil·i·ty** (fɪ'sɪlɪtɪ) *n.*
fis·sion ('fɪʃən) *n.* **1.** the act or process of splitting or breaking into parts. **2.** *Biology.* a form of asexual reproduction in single-celled animals and plants involving a division into two or more equal parts that develop into new cells. **3.** short for **nuclear fission.** [C19: from Latin *fissiō* a cleaving]
fis·sion·a·ble ('fɪʃənəbᵊl) *adj.* capable of undergoing nuclear fission as a result of any process. Compare **fissile** (sense 1). —**,fis·sion·a·'bil·i·ty** *n.*
fis·sion bomb *n.* a bomb in which the energy is supplied by nuclear fission. See **atom bomb.**
fis·sion-fu·sion bomb *n.* another name for **fusion bomb.**
fis·sion re·ac·tor *n.* a nuclear reactor in which a fission reaction takes place.
fis·si·pal·mate (,fɪsɪ'pælmeɪt) *adj.* (of some birds' feet) partially webbed, having lobes and fringes on separate toes.
fis·sip·a·rous (fɪ'sɪpərəs) *adj. Biology.* reproducing by fission. —**fis·'sip·a·rous·ly** *adv.* —**fis·'sip·a·rous·ness** *n.*
fis·si·ped ('fɪsɪ,pɛd) *adj. also* **fis·sip·e·dal** (fɪ'sɪpɪdᵊl, ,fɪsɪ-

'pi:dᵊl). **1.** having toes that are separated from one another, as dogs, cats, bears, and similar carnivores. ~*n.* **2.** a fissiped animal. ~Compare **pinniped.**

fis+si+ros+tral (ˌfɪsɪ'rɒstrəl) *adj.* **1.** (of the beaks of some birds) broad and deeply cleft. **2.** having such a beak, as swifts and swallows.

fis+sure ('fɪʃə) *n.* **1.** any long narrow cleft or crack, esp. in a rock. **2.** a weakness or flaw indicating impending disruption or discord: *fissures in a decaying empire.* **3.** *Anatomy.* a narrow split or groove that divides an organ such as the brain, lung, or liver into lobes. See also **sulcus. 4.** a small unnatural crack in the skin or mucous membrane, as between the toes or at the anus. **5.** a minute crack in the surface of a tooth, caused by imperfect joining of enamel during development. ~*vb.* **6.** to crack or split apart. [C14: from medical Latin *fissūra,* from Latin *fissus* split]

fis+sure of Ro·lan·do (rəʊ'lændəʊ) *n.* another name for **central sulcus.** [C19: named after L. *Rolando* (died 1831), Italian anatomist]

fis+sure of Syl·vi·us ('sɪlvɪəs) *n.* a deep horizontal cleft in each cerebral hemisphere: marks the separation of the temporal lobe from the frontal and parietal lobes. [named after Franciscus *Sylvius* (died 1652), German anatomist]

fist (fɪst) *n.* **1.** a hand with the fingers clenched into the palm, as for hitting. **2.** Also called: **fist+ful.** the quantity that can be held in a fist or hand. **3.** an informal word for **hand** or **index** (sense 9). ~*vb.* **4.** (*tr.*) to hit with the fist. [Old English *fȳst;* related to Old Frisian *fest,* Old Saxon, Old High German *fūst;* see FIVE]

fist+ic ('fɪstɪk) *adj.* of or relating to fisticuffs or boxing.

fist·i·cuffs ('fɪstɪˌkʌfs) *pl. n.* combat with the fists. [C17: probably from *fisty* with the fist + CUFF[2]]

fist+mele ('fɪstˌmi:l) *n. Archery.* a measure of the width of a hand and the extended thumb, used to calculate the approximate height of the string of a braced bow. [C17: from FIST + *mele,* variant of obsolete *meal* measure]

fis+tu+la ('fɪstjʊlə) *n., pl.* **+las** *or* **+lae** (-ˌli:). **1.** *Pathol.* an abnormal opening between one hollow organ and another or between a hollow organ and the surface of the skin, caused by ulceration, congenital malformation, etc. **2.** *Obsolete.* any musical wind instrument; a pipe. [C14: from Latin: pipe, tube, hollow reed, ulcer]

fis+tu+lous ('fɪstjʊləs), **fis+tu+lar,** *or* **fis+tu+late** ('fɪstjʊlɪt) *adj.* **1.** *Pathol.* containing, relating to, or resembling a fistula. **2.** hollow, esp. slender and hollow; reedlike or tubular. **3.** containing tubes or tubelike parts.

fit[1] (fɪt) *vb.* **fits, fit+ting, fit+ted. 1.** to be appropriate or suitable for (a situation, etc.). **2.** to be of the correct size or shape for (a connection, container, etc.). **3.** (*tr.*) to adjust in order to render appropriate: *they had to fit the idea to their philosophy.* **4.** (*tr.*) to supply with that which is needed. **5.** (*tr.*) to try clothes on (someone) in order to make adjustments if necessary. **6.** (*tr.*) to make competent or ready: *the experience helped to fit him for the task.* **7.** (*tr.*) to locate with care. **8.** (*intr.*) to correspond with the facts or circumstances. ~*adj.* **fit+ter, fit+test. 9.** suitable to a purpose or design; appropriate. **10.** having the right qualifications; qualifying. **11.** in good health. **12.** worthy or deserving: *a book fit to be read.* **13.** (*foll. by an infinitive*) *Informal.* strongly disposed (to): *she was fit to scream.* ~*n.* **14.** the manner in which something fits. **15.** the act or process of fitting. ~See also **fit in, fit out, fit up.** [C14: probably from Middle Dutch *vitten;* related to Old Norse *fitja* to knit] —**'fit+ness** *n.* —**'fit+ta·ble** *adj.*

fit[2] (fɪt) *n.* **1.** *Pathol.* a sudden attack or convulsion, such as an epileptic seizure. **2.** a sudden spell of emotion: *a fit of anger.* **3.** an impulsive period of activity or lack of activity; mood: *a fit of laziness.* **4. by fits (and starts).** in spasmodic spells; irregularly. **5. give (a person) a fit.** to surprise (a person) in an outrageous manner. **6. have** *or* **throw a fit.** *Informal.* to become very angry or excited. [Old English *fitt* conflict; see FIT[3]]

fit[3] (fɪt) *n. Archaic.* a story or song or a section of a story or song. [Old English *fitt;* related to Old Norse *fit* hem, Old High German *fizza* yarn]

fitch (fɪtʃ) *or* **fitch+et** ('fɪtʃɪt) *n.* **1.** another name for **polecat** (sense 1). **2.** the fur of the polecat. [C16: probably from *ficheux* FITCHEW]

fitch+ew ('fɪtʃu:) *n.* an archaic name for **polecat.** [C14 *ficheux,* from Old French *ficheau,* from Middle Dutch *vitsau,* of obscure origin]

fit+ful ('fɪtfʊl) *adj.* characterized by or occurring in irregular spells: *fitful sleep.* —**'fit+ful+ly** *adv.* —**'fit+ful+ness** *n.*

fit in *vb.* **1.** (*tr.*) to give a place or time to: *if my schedule allows it, I'll fit you in.* **2.** (*intr., adv.*) to belong or conform, esp. after adjustment: *he didn't fit in with their plans.*

fit+ly ('fɪtlɪ) *adv.* in a proper manner or place or at a proper time.

fit+ment ('fɪtmənt) *n.* **1.** *Machinery.* an accessory attached to an assembly of parts. **2.** *Chiefly Brit.* a detachable part of the furnishings of a room.

fit out *vb.* (*tr., adv.*) to equip; supply with necessary or new equipment, clothes, etc.

fit+ted ('fɪtɪd) *adj.* **1.** designed for excellent fit: *a fitted suit.* **2.** (of a carpet) cut, sewn, or otherwise adapted to cover a floor completely. **3.** (of furniture) built to fit a particular space: *a fitted cupboard.* **4.** having accessory parts.

fit+ter ('fɪtə) *n.* **1.** a person who fits a garment, esp. when it is made for a particular person. **2.** a person who is skilled in the assembly and adjustment of machinery, esp. of a specified sort: *an electrical fitter.* **3.** a person who supplies something for an expedition, activity, etc.

fit+ting ('fɪtɪŋ) *adj.* **1.** appropriate or proper; suitable. ~*n.* **2.** an accessory or part: *an electrical fitting.* **3.** (*pl.*) furnishings or accessories in a building. **4.** work carried out by a fitter. **5.** the act of trying on clothes so that they can be adjusted to fit. **6.** *Brit.* size in clothes or shoes: *a narrow fitting.* —**'fit+ting+ly** *adv.* —**'fit+ting+ness** *n.*

Fit·ti·pal·di (ˌfɪtɪ'pældɪ) *n.* **E·mer·son.** born 1946, Brazilian motor-racing driver: world champion in 1972 and 1974.

fit up *vb.* (*tr., adv.;* often foll. by *with*) to equip or provide: *the optician will soon fit you up with a new pair of glasses.*

Fitz·ger·ald (fɪts'dʒerəld) *n.* **1. Ed·ward.** 1809–83, English poet, noted particularly for his free translation of the *Rubáiyát of Omar Khayyám* (1859). **2. El·la.** born 1918, U.S. jazz singer, noted for her vocal range, clarity, and rhythm. **3. F(rancis) Scott (Key).** 1896–1940, U.S. novelist and short-story writer, noted particularly for his portrayal of the 1920s in *The Great Gatsby* (1925) and *Tender is the Night* (1934). **4. Gar·rett.** born 1927. Irish politician; prime minister of the Republic of Ireland 1981-82.

Fitz·sim·mons (ˌfɪt'sɪmənz) *n.* **Bob.** 1862–1917, New Zealand boxer, born in England: world middleweight (1891–97), heavyweight (1897–99), and light-heavyweight (1903–05) champion.

Fiu+me ('fju:me) *n.* the Italian name for **Rijeka.**

five (faɪv) *n.* **1.** the cardinal number that is the sum of four and one. **2.** a numeral, 5, V, etc., representing this number. **3.** the amount or quantity that is one greater than four. **4.** something representing, represented by, or consisting of five units, such as a playing card with five symbols on it. ~*determiner.* **5. a.** amounting to five: *five minutes; five nights.* **b.** (*as pronoun*): *choose any five you like.* ~Related prefixes: **penta-, quinque-.** [Old English *fīf;* related to Old Norse *fimm,* Gothic *fimf,* Old High German *finf,* Latin *quinque,* Greek *pente,* Sanskrit *pañca*]

five-eighth *n. Austral., N.Z.* a rugby player positioned between the half-backs and three-quarters.

five-faced bish+op *n. Brit.* another name for **moschatel.**

five-fin·ger *n.* any of various plants having five-petalled flowers or five lobed leaves, such as cinquefoil and Virginia creeper.

five+fold ('faɪvˌfəʊld) *adj.* **1.** equal to or having five times as many or as much. **2.** composed of five parts. ~*adv.* **3.** by or up to five times as many or as much.

five hun+dred *n.* a card game for three players, with 500 points for game.

Five Na+tions *pl. n.* (formerly) a confederacy of North American Indian peoples living mainly in and around present-day New York state, consisting of the Cayugas, Mohawks, Oneidas, Onondagas, and Senecas. Also called: **Iroquois.** See also **Six Nations.**

five-o'clock shad+ow *n.* beard growth visible late in the day on a man's shaven face.

five+pen·ny ('faɪfpənɪ) *adj.* (*prenominal*) *U.S.* (of a nail) one and three-quarters of an inch in length.

five+pins ('faɪvˌpɪnz) *n.* (*functioning as sing.*) a bowling game using five pins, played esp. in Canada. —**'five+ˌpin** *adj.*

fiv+er ('faɪvə) *n. Informal.* **1.** *Brit.* a five-pound note. **2.** *U.S.* a five-dollar bill.

fives (faɪvz) *n.* (*functioning as sing.*) a ball game similar to squash but played with bats or the hands.

five-spot *n. U.S.* a five-dollar bill.

five-star *adj.* (of a hotel, etc.) first class, top quality, or offering exceptional luxury.

five stones *n.* the game of jacks played with five stones.

Five-Year Plan *n.* (in socialist economies) a government plan for economic development over a period of five years.

fix (fɪks) *vb.* (*mainly tr.*) **1.** (*also intr.*) to make or become firm, stable, or secure. **2.** to attach or place permanently: *fix the mirror to the wall.* **3.** (often foll. by *up*) to settle definitely; decide: *let us fix a date.* **4.** to hold or direct (eyes, attention, etc.) steadily: *he fixed his gaze on the woman.* **5.** to call to attention or rivet. **6.** to make rigid: *to fix one's jaw.* **7.** to place or ascribe: *to fix the blame on someone.* **8.** to mend or repair. **9.** *Informal.* to provide with: *how are you fixed for supplies?* **10.** *Informal.* to influence (a person, outcome of a contest, etc.) unfairly, as by bribery. **11.** *Slang.* to take revenge on; get even with, esp. by killing. **12.** *Informal.* to give (someone) his just deserts: *that'll fix him.* **13.** *Informal, chiefly U.S.* to arrange or put in order: *to fix one's hair.* **14.** *Informal, chiefly U.S.* to prepare: *to fix a meal.* **15.** *Dialect or informal.* to spay or castrate (an animal). **16.** *U.S. dialect or informal.* to prepare oneself: *I'm fixing to go out.* **17.** *Photog.* to treat (a film, plate, or paper) with fixer to make permanent the image rendered visible by developer. **18.** *Cytology.* to kill, preserve, and harden (tissue, cells, etc.) for subsequent microscopic study. **19.** to convert (atmospheric nitrogen) into nitrogen compounds, as in the manufacture of fertilizers or the action of bacteria in the soil. **20.** to reduce (a substance) to a solid or condensed state or a less volatile state. **21.** (*intr.*) *Slang.* to inject a narcotic drug. ~*n.* **22.** *Informal.* a predicament; dilemma. **23.** the ascertaining of the navigational position, as of a ship, by radar, observation, etc. **24.** *Slang.* an intravenous injection of a narcotic such as heroin. **25.** *Informal.* an act or instance of bribery. ~See also **fix up.** [C15: from Medieval Latin *fixāre,* from Latin *fixus* fixed, from Latin *fīgere*] —**'fix+a·ble** *adj.* —**'fix+er** *n.*

fix+ate ('fɪkseɪt) *vb.* **1.** to become or cause to become fixed. **2.** *Chiefly U.S.* to concentrate (the eyes, attention, etc.). **3.** *Psychol.* to engage in fixation. **4.** (*tr.; usually passive*) *Informal.* to obsess or preoccupy. [C19: from Latin *fixus* fixed + -ATE[1]]

fix·a·tion (fɪk'seɪʃən) *n.* **1.** the act of fixing or the state of being fixed. **2.** a preoccupation or obsession. **3.** *Psychol.* **a.** the situation of being set in a certain way of thinking or acting. **b.** (in psychoanalytical schools) a strong attachment of a person to another person or an object in early life. **4.** *Chem.* **a.** the conversion of nitrogen in the air into a compound, esp. a fertilizer. **b.** the conversion of a free element into one of its compounds. **5.** the reduction of a substance from a volatile or fluid form to a nonvolatile or solid form.

fix·a·tive ('fɪksətɪv) *adj.* **1.** serving or tending to fix. ~*n.* **2.** a fluid usually consisting of a transparent resin, such as shellac, dissolved in alcohol and sprayed over drawings to prevent smudging. **3.** *Cytology.* a fluid, such as formaldehyde or ethanol, that fixes tissues and cells for microscopic study. **4.** a substance added to a liquid, such as a perfume, to make it less volatile.

fixed (fɪkst) *adj.* **1.** attached or placed so as to be immovable. **2.** not subject to change; stable: *fixed prices.* **3.** steadily directed: *a fixed expression.* **4.** established as to relative position: *a fixed point.* **5.** not fluctuating; always at the same time: *a fixed holiday.* **6.** (of ideas, notions, etc.) firmly maintained. **7.** (of an element) held in chemical combination: *fixed nitrogen.* **8.** (of a substance) nonvolatile. **9.** arranged. **10.** *Astrology.* of, relating to, or belonging to the group consisting of the four signs of the zodiac Taurus, Leo, Scorpio, and Aquarius, which are associated with stability. Compare **cardinal** (sense 8), **mutable** (sense 2). **11.** *Informal.* equipped or provided for, as with money, possessions, etc. **12.** *Informal.* illegally arranged: *a fixed trial.* —**fix+ed+ly** ('fɪksɪdlɪ) *adv.* —'**fix+ed+ness** *n.*

fixed as+sets *pl. n.* nontrading business assets of a relatively permanent nature, such as plant, fixtures, or goodwill. Also called: **capital assets.** Compare **current assets.**

fixed charge *n.* **1.** an invariable expense usually at regular intervals, such as rent. **2.** a legal charge on specific assets or property, as of a company.

fixed costs *pl. n.* **1.** another name for **overheads. 2.** costs that do not vary with output.

fixed-head cou+pé *n.* another name (esp. Brit.) for **coupé** (sense 1).

fixed i·de·a *n.* an idea, esp. one of an obsessional nature, that is persistently maintained and not subject to change. Also called: *idée fixe.*

fixed oil *n.* a natural animal or vegetable oil that is not volatile: a mixture of esters of fatty acids, usually triglycerides. Also called: **fatty oil.** Compare **essential oil.**

fixed point *n.* **1.** *Physics.* a reproducible invariant temperature; the boiling point, freezing point, or triple point of a substance, such as water, that is used to calibrate a thermometer or define a temperature scale. **2.** *Maths.* a point that is not moved by a given transformation.

fixed-point rep+re+sen+ta+tion *n. Computer technol.* the representation of numbers by a single set of digits such that the radix point has a predetermined location, the value of the number depending on the position of each digit relative to the radix point. Compare **floating-point representation.**

fixed sat+el+lite *n.* a satellite revolving in a stationary orbit so that it appears to remain over a fixed point on the earth's surface.

fixed star *n.* **1.** any of the stars in the Ptolemaic system, all of which were thought to be attached to an outer crystal sphere thus explaining their apparent lack of movement. **2.** an extremely distant star whose position appears to be almost stationary over a long period of time.

fix+er ('fɪksə) *n.* **1.** *Photog.* a solution containing one or more chemical compounds that is used, in fixing, to dissolve unexposed silver halides. It sometimes has an additive to stop the action of developer. **2.** *Slang.* a person who makes arrangements, esp. by underhand or illegal means.

fix+ings *pl. n. Chiefly U.S.* **1.** apparatus or equipment. **2.** accompaniments for a dish; trimmings.

fix+i·ty ('fɪksɪtɪ) *n., pl.* **·ties. 1.** the state or quality of being fixed; stability. **2.** something that is fixed; a fixture.

fix+ture ('fɪkstʃə) *n.* **1.** an object firmly fixed in place, esp. a household appliance. **2.** a person or thing regarded as fixed in a particular place or position. **3.** *Property law.* an article attached to land and regarded as part of it. **4.** a device to secure a workpiece in a machine tool. **5.** *Chiefly Brit.* **a.** a sports match or social occasion. **b.** the date of such an event. **6.** *Rare.* the act of fixing. [C17: from Late Latin *fixūra* a fastening (with *-t-* by analogy with *mixture*)] —'**fix+ture+less** *adj.*

fix up *vb.* (*tr., adv.*) **1.** to arrange: *let's fix up a date.* **2.** (often foll. by *with*) to provide: *I'm sure we can fix you up with a room.* **3.** *Informal, chiefly U.S.* to repair or rearrange: *to fix up one's house.*

fiz+gig ('fɪz,gɪg) *n.* **1.** a frivolous or flirtatious girl. **2.** a firework or whirling top that fizzes as it moves. **3.** a variant spelling of **fishgig.** [C16: probably from obsolete *fise* a breaking of wind + *gig* girl]

fizz (fɪz) *vb.* (*intr.*) **1.** to make a hissing or bubbling sound. **2.** (of a drink) to produce bubbles of carbon dioxide, either through fermentation or artificially introduced. ~*n.* **3.** a hissing or bubbling sound. **4.** the bubbly quality of a drink; effervescence. **5.** any effervescent drink. [C17: of imitative origin] —'**fizz·y** *adj.* —'**fizz·i+ness** *n.*

fiz+zer ('fɪzə) *n.* **1.** anything that fizzes. **2.** *Austral. slang.* a person or thing that disappoints, fails to succeed, etc.: *the horse proved to be a fizzer.*

fiz+zle ('fɪzᵊl) *vb.* (*intr.*) **1.** to make a hissing or bubbling sound. **2.** (often foll. by *out*) *Informal.* to fail or die out, esp. after a promising start. ~*n.* **3.** a hissing or bubbling sound; fizz. **4.** *Informal.* an outright failure; fiasco. [C16: probably from obsolete *fist* to break wind]

fjeld *or* **field** (fjɛld) *n.* a high rocky plateau with little vegetation in Scandinavian countries. [C19: Norwegian; related to Old Norse *fjall* mountain; see FELL[5]]

fjord *or* **fiord** (fjɔːd) *n.* a long narrow inlet of the sea between high steep cliffs. It is common in Norway and was probably formed by glacial action. [C17: from Norwegian, from Old Norse *fjörthr;* see FIRTH, FORD]

FL *international car registration for* Liechtenstein. [from German *Fürstentum Liechtenstein* Principality of Liechtenstein]

fl. *abbrev. for:* **1.** floor. **2.** floruit. **3.** fluid. ~**4.** (in the Netherlands) *symbol for* guilder.

Fl. *abbrev. for:* **1.** Flanders. **2.** Flemish.

Fla. *abbrev. for* Florida.

flab (flæb) *n.* unsightly or unwanted fat on the body; flabbiness. [C20: back formation from FLABBY]

flab+ber+gast ('flæbə,gɑːst) *vb.* (*tr.; usually passive*) *Informal.* to overcome with astonishment; amaze utterly; astound. [C18: of uncertain origin]

flab+by ('flæbɪ) *adj.* **+bi+er, +bi+est. 1.** lacking firmness; loose or yielding: *flabby muscles.* **2.** having flabby flesh, esp. through being overweight. **3.** lacking vitality; weak; ineffectual. [C17: alteration of FLAPPY; compare Dutch *flabbe* drooping lip] —'**flab+bi+ly** *adv.* —'**flab+bi+ness** *n.*

fla+bel+late (flə'bɛlɪt, -eɪt) *or* **fla+bel+li+form** (flə'bɛlɪ,fɔːm) *adj. Biology.* shaped like a fan.

fla+bel+lum (flə'bɛləm) *n., pl.* **+la** (-lə). **1.** a fan-shaped organ or part, such as the tip of the proboscis of a honeybee. **2.** *R.C. Church.* a large ceremonial fan. [C19: from Latin: small fan, from *flābra* breezes, from *flāre* to blow]

flac+cid ('flæksɪd, 'flæs-) *adj.* lacking firmness; soft and limp; flabby. [C17: from Latin *flaccidus,* from *flaccus*] —**flac+'cid+i·ty** *or* '**flac+cid+ness** *n.* —'**flac+cid+ly** *adv.*

flack (flæk) *n.* a variant spelling of **flak.**

fla+con (*French* fla'kɔ̃) *n.* a small stoppered bottle or flask, such as one used for perfume. [C19: from French; see FLAGON]

flag[1] (flæg) *n.* **1.** a piece of cloth, esp. bunting, often attached to a pole or staff, decorated with a design and used as an emblem, symbol, or standard or as a means of signalling. **2.** *Informal.* short for **flag officer** and **flagship. 3.** *Journalism.* another name for **masthead** (sense 2). **4.** the conspicuously marked or shaped tail of a deer or of certain dogs. **5.** a less common name for **bookmark. 6.** *Brit., Austral.* the part of a taximeter that is raised when a taxi is for hire. **7. show the flag. a.** to assert a claim, as to a territory or stretch of water, by military presence. **b.** *Informal.* to be present; make an appearance. **8. strike** (*or* **lower**) **the flag. a.** to relinquish command, esp. of a ship. **b.** to submit or surrender. ~*vb.* **flags, flag+ging, flagged.** (*tr.*) **9.** to decorate or mark with a flag or flags. **10.** (often foll. by *down*) to warn or signal (a vehicle) to stop. **11.** to send or communicate (messages, information, etc.) by flag. **12.** to decoy (game or wild animals) by waving a flag or similar object so as to attract their attention. **13.** to mark (a page in a book, card, etc.) for attention by attaching a small tab or flag. [C16: of uncertain origin] —'**flag+ger** *n.* —'**flag+less** *adj.*

flag[2] (flæg) *n.* **1.** any of various plants that have long swordlike leaves, esp. the iris *Iris pseudacorus* (**yellow flag**). **2.** the leaf of any such plant. ~See also **sweet flag.** [C14: probably of Scandinavian origin; compare Dutch *flag,* Danish *flæg* yellow iris]

flag[3] (flæg) *vb.* **flags, flag+ging, flagged.** (*intr.*) **1.** to hang down; become limp; droop. **2.** to decline in strength or vigour; become weak or tired. [C16: of unknown origin]

flag[4] (flæg) *n.* **1.** short for **flagstone.** ~*vb.* **flags, flag+ging, flagged. 2.** (*tr.*) to furnish (a floor, etc.) with flagstones.

flag cap+tain *n.* the captain of a flagship.

flag day *n.* a day on which money is collected by a charity and small flags or emblems are given to contributors.

Flag Day *n.* June 14, the annual holiday in the U.S. to celebrate the adoption in 1777 of the Stars and Stripes.

flag+el+lant ('flædʒɪlənt, flə'dʒɛlənt) *or* **flag+el+la+tor** ('flædʒɪ,leɪtə) *n.* **1.** a person who whips himself or others either as part of a religious penance or for sexual gratification. **2.** (*often cap.*) (in medieval Europe) a member of a religious sect who whipped themselves in public. [C16: from Latin *flagellāre* to whip, from FLAGELLUM] —'**flag+el+lant+ism** *n.*

flag+el+late *vb.* ('flædʒɪ,leɪt). **1.** (*tr.*) to whip; scourge; flog. ~*adj.* ('flædʒɪlɪt, -,leɪt), *also* **flag+el+lat+ed. 2.** possessing one or more flagella. **3.** resembling a flagellum; whiplike. ~*n.* ('flædʒɪlɪt, -,leɪt). **4.** a flagellate organism, esp. any protozoan of the class *Mastigophora.* —,**flag+el+'la+tion** *n.*

fla+gel+li+form (flə'dʒɛlɪ,fɔːm) *adj.* slender, tapering, and whiplike, as the antennae of certain insects.

fla+gel+lum (flə'dʒɛləm) *n., pl.* **+la** (-lə) *or* **+lums. 1.** *Biology.* a long whiplike outgrowth from a cell that acts as an organ of locomotion: occurs in some protozoans, gametes, spores, etc. **2.** *Botany.* a long thin supple shoot or runner. **3.** *Entomol.* the terminal whiplike part of the antenna of many insects. [C19: from Latin: a little whip, from *flagrum* a whip, lash] —**fla+'gel+lar** *adj.*

flag·eo+let (,flædʒə'lɛt) *n.* a high-pitched musical instrument of the recorder family having six or eight finger holes. [C17: from French, modification of Old French *flajolet* a little flute, from *flajol* flute, from Vulgar Latin *flabeolum* (unattested), from Latin *flāre* to blow]

flag fall *n. Austral.* the minimum charge for hiring a taxi.

flag+ging ('flægɪŋ) *n.* flagstones or a flagged area.

flag+gy[1] ('flægɪ) *adj.* **+gi+er, +gi+est.** drooping; limp.

flag+gy[2] ('flægɪ) *adj.* made of or similar to flagstone.

fla+gi+tious (flə'dʒɪʃəs) *adj.* atrociously wicked; vicious; outrageous. [C14: from Latin *flāgitiōsus* infamous, from *flāgitium* a shameful act; related to Latin *flagrum* whip] —**fla+'gi+tious+ly** *adv.* —**fla+'gi+tious+ness** *n.*

flag lieu+ten+ant *n.* an admiral's A.D.C.

flag+man ('flægmən) *n., pl.* **+men.** a person who has charge of, carries, or signals with a flag, esp. a railway employee.

flag of con+ven·i+ence *n.* a national flag flown by a ship registered in that country to gain financial or legal advantage.

flag of+fic+er *n.* an officer in certain navies of the rank of rear admiral or above and entitled to fly its flag.

flag of truce *n.* a white flag indicating the peaceful intent of its bearer or an invitation to an enemy to negotiate.

flag+on ('flægən) *n.* **1.** a large bottle of wine, cider, etc. **2.** a vessel having a handle, spout, and narrow neck. [C15: from Old French *flascon*, from Late Latin *flascō*, probably of Germanic origin; see FLASK]

flag+pole ('flæg,pəʊl) *or* **flag+staff** ('flæg,stɑ:f) *n., pl.* **+poles, +staffs,** *or* **+staves** (-,steɪvz). a pole or staff on which a flag is hoisted and displayed.

flag rank *n.* the rank of a flag officer.

fla+grant ('fleɪgrənt) *adj.* **1.** blatant; glaring; outrageous. **2.** *Obsolete.* burning or blazing. [C15: from Latin *flagrāre* to blaze, burn] —**'fla+gran+cy, 'fla+grance,** *or* **'fla+grant+ness** *n.* —**'fla+grant+ly** *adv.*

fla+gran+te de+lic+to (flə'græntɪ dɪ'lɪktəʊ) *adv. Chiefly law.* while committing the offence; red-handed. Also: **in flagrante delicto.** [from Latin: with the crime still blazing]

flags (flægz) *pl. n. Rare.* the long feathers on the leg of a hawk or falcon.

flag+ship ('flæg,ʃɪp) *n.* **1.** a ship, esp. in a fleet, aboard which the commander of the fleet is quartered. **2.** the most important ship belonging to a shipping company.

Flag·stad ('flægstæd; *Norwegian* 'flaksta) *n.* **Kir·sten** ('çirstən). 1895–1962, Norwegian operatic soprano, noted particularly for her interpretations of Wagner.

flag+stone ('flæg,stəʊn) *or* **flag** *n.* **1.** a hard fine-textured rock, such as a sandstone or shale, that can be split up into slabs for paving. **2.** a slab of such a rock. [C15 *flag* (in the sense: sod, turf), from Old Norse *flaga* slab; compare Old English *flæcg* plaster, poultice]

flag-wav·ing *n. Informal.* **a.** an emotional appeal or display intended to arouse patriotic or nationalistic feeling. **b.** (*as modifier*): *a flag-waving speech.* —**'flag-,wav·er** *n.*

flail (fleɪl) *n.* **1.** an implement used for threshing grain, consisting of a wooden handle with a free-swinging metal or wooden bar attached to it. **2.** a weapon so shaped used in the Middle Ages. ~*vb.* **3.** (*tr.*) to beat or thrash with or as if with a flail. **4.** to move or be moved like a flail; thresh about: *with arms flailing.* [C12 *fleil*, ultimately from Late Latin *flagellum* flail, from Latin: whip]

flair (flɛə) *n.* **1.** natural ability; talent; aptitude. **2.** instinctive discernment; perceptiveness. **3.** *Informal.* stylishness or elegance; dash: *to dress with flair.* **4.** *Hunting, rare.* **a.** the scent left by quarry. **b.** the sense of smell of a hound. [C19: from French, literally: sense of smell, from Old French: scent, from *flairier* to give off a smell, ultimately from Latin *frāgrāre* to smell sweet; see FRAGRANT]

flak *or* **flack** (flæk) *n.* **1.** antiaircraft fire or artillery. **2.** *Informal.* a great deal of adverse criticism. [C20: from German *Fl(ieger)a(bwehr)k(anone)* literally: aircraft defence gun]

flake[1] (fleɪk) *n.* **1.** a small thin piece or layer chipped off or detached from an object or substance; scale. **2.** a small piece or particle: *a flake of snow.* **3.** a thin layer or stratum. **4.** *Archaeol.* **a.** a fragment removed by chipping or hammering from a larger stone used as a tool or weapon. See also **blade. b.** (*as modifier*): *flake tool.* ~*vb.* **5.** to peel or cause to peel off in flakes; chip. **6.** to cover or become covered with or as with flakes. **7.** (*tr.*) to form into flakes. [C14: of Scandinavian origin; compare Norwegian *flak* disc, Middle Dutch *vlacken* to flutter] —**'flak+er** *n.*

flake[2] (fleɪk) *n.* a rack for drying fish or other produce. [C14: from Old Norse *flaki;* related to Dutch *vlaak* hurdle]

flake[3] (fleɪk) *vb. Nautical.* another word for **fake**[2].

flake out *vb.* (*intr., adv.*) *Informal.* to become unconscious as through extreme exhaustion.

flake white *n.* a pigment made from flakes of white lead.

flak jack+et *n.* a reinforced sleeveless jacket for protection against gunfire worn by soldiers, policemen, etc.

flak·y ('fleɪkɪ) *adj.* **flak·i+er, flak·i+est. 1.** like or made of flakes. **2.** tending to peel off or break easily into flakes. —**'flak·i+ly** *adv.* —**'flak·i+ness** *n.*

flak·y pas+try *n.* a rich pastry in the form of very thin layers, used for making pies, small cakes, etc.

flam[1] (flæm) *Now chiefly dialect.* ~*n.* **1.** a falsehood, deception, or sham. **2.** nonsense; drivel. ~*vb.* **flams, flam+ming, flammed. 3.** (*tr.*) to cheat or deceive. [C16: probably short for FLIMFLAM]

flam[2] (flæm) *n.* a drumbeat in which both sticks strike the head almost simultaneously but are heard to do so separately. [C18: probably imitative of the sound]

flam+bé *or* **flam+bée** ('flɑ:mbeɪ, 'flæm-; *French* flã'be) *adj.* (of food, such as steak or pancakes) served in flaming brandy, etc. [French, past participle of *flamber* to FLAME]

flam+beau ('flæmbəʊ) *n., pl.* **+beaux** (-bəʊ, -bəʊz) *or* **+beaus. 1.** a burning torch, as used in night processions, etc. **2.** a large ornamental candlestick. [C17: from Old French: torch, literally: a little flame, from *flambe* FLAME]

Flam+bor+ough Head ('flæmbərə -brə) *n.* a chalk promontory in NE England, on the coast of Humberside.

flam+boy+ant (flæm'bɔɪənt) *adj.* **1.** elaborate or extravagant; florid; showy. **2.** rich or brilliant in colour; resplendent. **3.** of, denoting, or relating to the French Gothic style of architecture characterized by flamelike tracery and elaborate carving. ~*n.* **4.** another name for **royal poinciana.** [C19: from French: flaming, from *flamboyer* to FLAME] —**flam+'boy+ance** *or* **flam+'boy+an+cy** *n.* —**flam+'boy+ant+ly** *adv.*

flame (fleɪm) *n.* **1.** a hot usually luminous body of burning gas often containing small incandescent particles, typically emanating in flickering streams from burning material or produced by a jet of ignited gas. **2.** (*often pl.*) the state or condition of burning with flames: *to burst into flames.* **3.** a brilliant light; fiery glow. **4. a.** a strong reddish-orange colour. **b.** (*as adj.*): *a flame carpet.* **5.** intense passion or ardour; burning emotion. **6.** *Informal.* a lover or sweetheart (esp. in the phrase **an old flame**). —*vb.* **7.** to burn or cause to burn brightly; give off or cause to give off flame. **8.** (*intr.*) to burn or glow as if with fire; become red or fiery: *his face flamed with anger.* **9.** (*intr.*) to show great emotion; become angry or excited. **10.** (*tr.*) to apply a flame to (something). **11.** (*tr.*) *Archaic.* to set on fire, either physically or with emotion. [C14: from Anglo-French *flaume*, from Old French *flambe*, modification of *flamble*, from Latin *flammula* a little flame, from *flamma* flame] —**'flam+er** *n.* —**'flame+less** *adj.* —**'flame+let** *n.* —**'flame+,like** *adj.* —**'flam·y** *adj.*

flame cell *n.* an organ of excretion in flatworms: a hollow cup-shaped cell containing a bunch of cilia, whose movement draws in waste products and wafts them to the outside through a connecting tubule.

flame gun *n.* a type of flame-thrower for destroying garden weeds, etc.

fla+men ('fleɪmɛn) *n., pl.* **fla+mens** *or* **fla+mi+nes** ('flæmɪ,ni:z). (in ancient Rome) any of 15 priests who each served a particular deity. [C14: from Latin; probably related to Old English *blōtan* to sacrifice, Gothic *blotan* to worship]

fla+men+co (flə'mɛŋkəʊ) *n., pl.* **+cos. 1.** a type of dance music for vocal soloist and guitar, characterized by elaborate melody and sad mood. **2.** the dance performed to such music. [from Spanish: like a gipsy, literally: Fleming, from Middle Dutch *Vlaminc* Fleming]

flame-of-the-for·est *n.* **1.** (esp. in Malaysia) another name for **royal poinciana. 2.** a papilionaceous tree, *Butea frondosa*, native to E India and Burma, having hanging clusters of scarlet flowers.

flame+out ('fleɪm,aʊt) *n.* **1.** the failure of an aircraft jet engine in flight due to extinction of the flame. ~*vb.* **flame out.** (*adv.*) **2.** (of a jet engine) to fail in flight or to cause (a jet engine) to fail in flight.

flame+proof ('fleɪm,pru:f) *adj.* **1.** not liable to catch fire or be damaged by fire. **2.** (of electrical apparatus) designed so that an internal explosion will not ignite external flammable gas.

flame test *n.* a test for detecting the presence of certain metals in compounds by the coloration they give to a flame. Sodium, for example, turns a flame yellow.

flame-throw·er *n.* a weapon that ejects a stream or spray of burning fluid.

flame tree *n.* any of various tropical trees with red or orange flowers, such as flame-of-the-forest.

flam+ing ('fleɪmɪŋ) *adj.* **1.** burning with or emitting flames. **2.** glowing brightly; brilliant. **3.** intense or ardent; vehement; passionate: *a flaming temper.* **4.** *Informal.* (intensifier): *you flaming idiot.* **5.** an obsolete word for **flagrant.** —**'flam+ing+ly** *adv.*

fla+min+go (flə'mɪŋgəʊ) *n., pl.* **+gos** *or* **+goes. 1.** any large wading bird of the family *Phoenicopteridae*, having a pink-and-red plumage and downward-bent bill and inhabiting brackish lakes: order *Ciconiiformes.* **2. a.** a reddish-orange colour. **b.** (*as adj.*): *flamingo gloves.* [C16: from Portuguese *flamengo*, from Provençal *flamenc*, from Latin *flamma* flame + Germanic suffix *-ing* denoting descent from or membership of; compare -ING[3]]

Fla+min+i·an Way (flə'mɪnɪən) *n.* an ancient road in Italy, extending north from Rome to Rimini: constructed in 220 B.C. by Gaius Flaminius. Length: over 322 km (200 miles). Latin name: **Via Flaminia.**

Flam·i·ni·nus (,flæmɪ'naɪnəs) *n.* **Ti·tus Quinc·ti·us** ('taɪtəs 'kwɪŋktɪəs). ?230–?174 B.C. Roman general and statesman: defeated Macedonia (197) and proclaimed the independence of the Greek states (196).

Fla·min·i·us (flə'mɪnɪəs) *n.* **Gai·us** ('gaɪəs). died 217 B.C., Roman statesman and general: built the Flaminian Way; defeated by Hannibal at Trasimene (217).

flam+ma·ble ('flæməbᵊl) *adj.* liable to catch fire; readily combustible; inflammable. —**,flam+ma·'bil+i·ty** *n.*

Usage. *Flammable* and *inflammable* are interchangeable when used of the properties of materials. *Flammable* is, however, often preferred for warning labels as there is less likelihood of misunderstanding (*inflammable* being sometimes taken to mean *not flammable*). *Inflammable* is preferred in figurative contexts: *his temperament could be described as inflammable.*

Flam·steed ('flæm,sti:d) *n.* **John.** 1646–1719, English astronomer: the first Astronomer Royal and first director of the Royal Observatory, Greenwich (1675). He increased the accuracy of existing stellar catalogues, greatly aiding navigation.

flan (flæn) *n.* **1.** an open pastry or sponge tart filled with fruit or a savoury mixture. **2.** a piece of metal ready to receive the die or stamp in the production of coins; shaped blank; planchet. [C19: from French, from Old French *flaon,* from Late Latin *fladō* flat cake, of Germanic origin]

flanch (flæntʃ) *n.* a variant spelling of **flaunch.**

Flan·ders ('flɑːndəz) *n.* a powerful medieval principality in the SW part of the Low Countries, now in the Belgian provinces of East and West Flanders, the Netherlands province of Zeeland, and the French department of the Nord; scene of battles in many wars.

Flan·ders pop·py *n.* another name for **corn poppy.**

flâne·rie *French.* (flan'ri) *n.* aimless strolling or lounging; idleness. [C19: from *flâner* to stroll, dawdle, ultimately from Old Norse *flana* to wander about]

flâ·neur *French.* (fla'nœːr) *n.* an idler or loafer. [C19: see FLÂNERIE]

flange (flændʒ) *n.* **1.** a radially projecting collar or rim on an object for locating or strengthening it or for attaching it to another object. **2.** a flat outer face of a rolled-steel joist, esp. of an I- or H-beam. **3.** a tool for forming a flange. ~*vb.* **4.** (*tr.*) to attach or provide (a component) with a flange. **5.** (*intr.*) to take the form of a flange. [C17: probably changed from earlier *flaunche* curved segment at side of a heraldic field, from French *flanc* FLANK] —**'flange·less** *adj.* —**'flang·er** *n.*

flank (flæŋk) *n.* **1.** the side of a man or animal between the ribs and the hip. **2.** (loosely) the outer part of the human thigh. **3.** a cut of beef from the flank. **4.** the side of anything, such as a mountain or building. **5.** the side of a naval or military formation. ~*vb.* **6.** (when *intr.*, often foll. by *on* or *upon*) to be located at the side of (an object, building, etc.). **7.** *Military.* to position or guard on or beside the flank of (a formation, etc.). **8.** *Military.* to move past or go round (a flank). [C12: from Old French *flanc,* of Germanic origin; see LANK]

flank·er ('flæŋkə) *n.* **1.** one of a detachment of soldiers detailed to guard the flanks, esp. of a formation. **2.** a projecting fortification, used esp. to protect or threaten a flank.

flan·nel ('flænᵊl) *n.* **1.** a soft light woollen fabric with a slight nap, used for clothing, etc. **2.** (*pl.*) trousers or other garments made of flannel. **3.** See **cotton flannel. 4.** *Brit.* a small piece of cloth used to wash the face and hands; face cloth. U.S. equivalent: **washcloth. 5.** *Brit. informal.* indirect or evasive talk; deceiving flattery. ~*vb.* **·nels, ·nel·ling, ·nelled** *or U.S.* **·nels, ·nel·ing, ·neled.** (*tr.*) **6.** to cover or wrap with flannel. **7.** to rub, clean, or polish with flannel. **8.** *Brit. informal.* to talk evasively to; flatter in order to mislead. [C14: probably variant of *flanen* sackcloth, from Welsh *gwlanen* woollen fabric, from *gwlân* wool] —**'flan·nel·ly** *adj.*

flan·nel·ette (ˌflænᵊ'lɛt) *n.* a cotton imitation of flannel.

flan·nel flow·er *n.* any Australian plant of the umbelliferous genus *Actinotus* having white flannel-like bracts beneath the flowers.

flap (flæp) *vb.* **flaps, flap·ping, flapped. 1.** to move (wings or arms) up and down, esp. in or as if in flying, or (of wings or arms) to move in this way. **2.** to move or cause to move noisily back and forth or up and down: *the curtains flapped in the breeze.* **3.** (*intr.*) *Informal.* to become agitated or flustered; panic. **4.** to deal (a person or thing) a blow with a broad flexible object. **5.** (*tr.*; sometimes foll. by *down*) to toss, fling, slam, etc., abruptly or noisily. **6.** (*tr.*) *Phonetics.* to pronounce (an (r) sound) by allowing the tongue to give a single light tap against the alveolar ridge or uvula. ~*n.* **7.** the action, motion, or noise made by flapping: *with one flap of its wings the bird was off.* **8.** a piece of material, etc., attached at one edge and usually used to cover an opening, as on a tent, envelope, or pocket. **9.** a blow dealt with a flat object; slap. **10.** a movable surface fixed to the trailing edge of an aircraft wing that increases lift during takeoff and drag during landing. **11.** *Surgery.* a piece of tissue partially connected to the body, either following an amputation or to be used as a graft. **12.** *Informal.* a state of panic, distress, or agitation. **13.** *Phonetics.* an (r) produced by allowing the tongue to give a single light tap against the alveolar ridge or uvula. [C14: probably of imitative origin]

flap·doo·dle ('flæpˌduːdᵊl) *n. Slang.* foolish talk; nonsense. [C19: of unknown origin]

flap·jack ('flæpˌdʒæk) *n.* **1.** a chewy biscuit made with rolled oats. **2.** *Chiefly U.S.* another word for **pancake.**

flap·per ('flæpə) *n.* **1.** a person or thing that flaps. **2.** (in the 1920s) a young woman, esp. one flaunting her unconventional dress and behaviour.

flare (flɛə) *vb.* **1.** to burn or cause to burn with an unsteady or sudden bright flame. **2.** to spread or cause to spread outwards from a narrow to a wider shape. **3.** (*tr.*) to make a conspicuous display of. **4.** to increase the temperature of (a molten metal or alloy) until a gaseous constituent of the melt burns with a characteristic flame or (of a molten metal or alloy) to show such a flame. ~*n.* **5.** an unsteady flame. **6.** a sudden burst of flame. **7. a.** a blaze of light or fire used to illuminate, identify, alert, etc. **b.** the device producing such a blaze. **8.** a spreading shape or anything with a spreading shape: *a skirt with a flare.* **9.** a sudden outburst, as of emotion. **10.** *Optics.* **a.** the unwanted light reaching the image region of an optical device by reflections inside the instrument, etc. **b.** the fogged area formed on a negative by such reflections. **11.** *Astronomy.* short for **solar flare.** [C16 (to spread out): of unknown origin]

flare star *n.* a red dwarf star in which outbursts, thought to be analogous to solar flares, occur, increasing the luminosity by several magnitudes in a few minutes.

flare-up *n.* **1.** a sudden burst of fire or light. **2.** *Informal.* a sudden burst of emotion or violence. ~*vb.* **flare up.** (*intr., adv.*). **3.** to burst suddenly into fire or light. **4.** *Informal.* to burst into anger.

flash (flæʃ) *n.* **1.** a sudden short blaze of intense light or flame: *a flash of sunlight.* **2.** a sudden occurrence or display, esp. one suggestive of brilliance: *a flash of understanding.* **3.** a very brief space of time: *over in a flash.* **4.** an ostentatious display: *a flash of her diamonds.* **5.** Also called: **news flash.** a short news announcement concerning a new event. **6.** *Chiefly Brit.* an insignia or emblem worn on a uniform, vehicle, etc., to identify its military formation. **7.** a patch of bright colour on a dark background, such as light marking on an animal. **8.** a volatile mixture of inorganic salts used to produce a glaze on bricks or tiles. **9. a.** a sudden rush of water down a river or watercourse. **b.** a device, such as a sluice, for producing such a rush. **10.** *Photog., informal.* short for **flashlight** (sense 2) or **flash photography. 11.** a ridge of thin metal or plastic formed on a moulded object by the extrusion of excess material between dies. **12.** *Yorkshire and Lancashire dialect.* a pond, esp. one produced as a consequence of subsidence. **13.** (*modifier*) involving, using, or produced by a flash of heat, light, etc.: *flash blindness; flash distillation.* **14. flash in the pan.** a project, person, etc., that enjoys only short-lived success, notoriety, etc. ~*adj.* **15.** *Informal.* ostentatious or vulgar. **16.** *Informal.* of or relating to gamblers and followers of boxing and racing. **17.** sham or counterfeit. **18.** *Informal.* relating to or characteristic of the criminal underworld. ~*vb.* **19.** to burst or cause to burst suddenly or intermittently into flame. **20.** to emit or reflect or cause to emit or reflect light suddenly or intermittently. **21.** (*intr.*) to move very fast: *he flashed by on his bicycle.* **22.** (*intr.*) to come rapidly (into the mind or vision). **23.** (*intr.*; foll. by *out* or *up*) to appear like a sudden light: *his anger really flashes out at times.* **24. a.** to signal or communicate very fast: *to flash a message.* **b.** to signal by use of a light, such as car headlights. **25.** (*tr.*) *Informal.* to display ostentatiously: *to flash money around.* **26.** (*tr.*) *Informal.* to show suddenly and briefly. **27.** (*intr.*) *Brit. slang.* to expose oneself indecently. **28.** (*tr.*) to cover (a roof) with flashing. **29.** to send a sudden rush of water down (a river, etc.), or to carry (a vessel) down by this method. **30.** (in the making of glass) to coat (glass) with a thin layer of glass of a different colour. **31.** (*tr.*) to subject to a brief pulse of heat or radiation. **32.** (*tr.*) to change (a liquid) to a gas by causing it to hit a hot surface. **33.** *Obsolete.* to splash or dash (water). [C14 (in the sense: to rush, as of water): of unknown origin]

flash·back ('flæʃˌbæk) *n.* **1.** a transition in a novel, film, etc., to an earlier scene or event. ~*vb.* **flash back. 2.** (*intr., adv.*) to return in a novel, film, etc., to a past event.

flash·board ('flæʃˌbɔːd) *n.* a board or boarding that is placed along the top of a dam to increase its height and capacity.

flash·bulb ('flæʃˌbʌlb) *n. Photog.* a small expendable glass light bulb that is triggered, usually electrically to produce a bright flash of light. Also called: **photoflash.** Compare **electronic flash.**

flash burn *n. Pathol.* a burn caused by momentary exposure to intense radiant heat.

flash card *n.* a card on which are written or printed words for children to look at briefly, used as an aid to learning.

flash·cube ('flæʃˌkjuːb) *n.* a boxlike camera attachment, holding four flashbulbs, that turns so that each flashbulb can be used in quick succession.

flash·er ('flæʃə) *n.* **1.** something that flashes, such as a direction indicator on a vehicle. **2.** *Brit. slang.* a person who indecently exposes himself.

flash flood *n.* a sudden short-lived torrent, usually caused by a heavy storm, esp. in desert regions.

flash gun *n.* a device, attachable to or sometimes incorporated in a camera, for holding and electrically firing a flashbulb as the shutter opens. Compare **electronic flash.**

flash·ing ('flæʃɪŋ) *n.* a weatherproof material, esp. thin sheet metal, used to cover the valleys between the slopes of a roof, the junction between a chimney and a roof, etc.

flash·light ('flæʃˌlaɪt) *n.* **1.** another word (esp. U.S.) for **torch. 2.** *Photog.* the brief bright light emitted by a flashbulb or electronic flash. Sometimes shortened to **flash. 3.** *Chiefly U.S.* a bright flashing light or its source.

flash·o·ver ('flæʃˌəʊvə) *n.* an electric discharge over or around the surface of an insulator.

flash pho·tog·ra·phy *n.* photography in which a flashbulb or electronic flash is used to provide momentary illumination of a dark or insufficiently lit subject.

flash pho·tol·y·sis *n. Physics.* a technique for producing and investigating free radicals. A low-pressure gas is subjected to a flash of radiation to produce the radicals, subsequent flashes being used to identify them and assess their lifetimes by absorption spectroscopy.

flash point *or* **flash·ing point** *n.* **1.** the lowest temperature at which the vapour above a liquid can be ignited in air. **2.** a critical moment beyond which a situation will inevitably erupt into violence: *the political mood has reached flash point.*

flash·y ('flæʃɪ) *adj.* **flash·i·er, flash·i·est. 1.** brilliant and dazzling, esp. for a short time or in a superficial way. **2.** cheap and ostentatious. —**'flash·i·ly** *adv.* —**'flash·i·ness** *n.*

flask (flɑːsk) *n.* **1.** a bottle with a narrow neck, esp. used in a laboratory or for wine, oil, etc. **2.** Also called: **hip flask.** a small flattened container of glass or metal designed to be carried in a pocket, esp. for liquor. **3.** See **powder flask. 4.** a container packed with sand to form a mould in a foundry. **5.** See **vacuum flask.** [C14: from Old French *flasque, flaske,* from Medieval Latin *flasca, flasco,* perhaps of Germanic origin; compare Old English *flasce, flaxe*]

flask·et ('flɑːskɪt) *n.* **1.** a long shallow basket. **2.** a small flask. [C15: from Old French *flasquet* a little FLASK]

flat[1] (flæt) *adj.* **flat·ter, flat·test. 1.** horizontal; level: *flat ground; a flat roof.* **2.** even or smooth, without projections or depressions: *a flat surface.* **3.** lying stretched out at full length; prostrate: *he lay flat on the ground.* **4.** having little depth or thickness; shallow: *a flat dish.* **5.** (*postpositive;* often foll. by *against*) having a surface or side in complete contact with another surface: *flat against the wall.* **6.** spread out, unrolled, or levelled. **7.** (of a tyre) deflated, either partially or completely. **8.** (of shoes) having an unraised or only slightly raised heel. **9.** *Chiefly Brit.* **a.** (of races, racetracks, or racecourses) not having obstacles to be jumped. **b.** of, relating to, or connected with flat racing as opposed to steeplechasing and hurdling: *flat jockeys earn more.* **10.** without qualification; total: *a flat denial.* **11.** without possibility of change; fixed: *a flat rate.* **12.** (*prenominal or immediately postpositive*) neither more nor less; exact: *he did the journey in thirty minutes flat; a flat thirty minutes.* **13.** unexciting or lacking point or interest: *a flat joke.* **14.** without variation or resonance; monotonous: *a flat voice.* **15.** (of food) stale or tasteless. **16.** (of beer, sparkling wines, etc.) having lost effervescence, as by exposure to air. **17.** (of trade, business, a market, etc.) commercially inactive; sluggish. **18.** (of a battery) fully discharged; dead. **19.** (of a print, photograph, or painting) lacking contrast or shading between tones. **20.** (of paint) without gloss or lustre; matt. **21.** (of a painting) lacking perspective. **22.** *Music.* **a.** (*immediately postpositive*) denoting a note of a given letter name (or the sound it represents) that has been lowered in pitch by one chromatic semitone: *B flat.* **b.** (of an instrument, voice, etc.) out of tune by being too low in pitch. Compare **sharp** (sense 12). **23.** *Phonetics.* another word for **lenis. 24.** *Phonetics.* **flat a.** the vowel sound of *a* as in the usual U.S. or S Brit. pronunciation of *hand, cat,* usually represented by the symbol (æ). ~*adv.* **25.** in or into a prostrate, level, or flat state or position: *he held his hand out flat.* **26.** completely or utterly; absolutely: *he went flat against the rules.* **27.** *Music.* **a.** lower than a standard pitch. **b.** too low in pitch: *she sings flat.* Compare **sharp** (sense 16). **28. fall flat.** to prove a failure, not amusing, etc. **29. flat out.** *Informal.* **a.** with the maximum speed or effort. **b.** totally exhausted. ~*n.* **30.** a flat object, surface, or part. **31.** a low-lying tract of land, esp. a marsh or swamp. **32.** a mud bank exposed at low tide. **33.** *Music.* **a.** an accidental that lowers the pitch of the following note by one chromatic semitone. Usual symbol: ♭ **b.** a note affected by this accidental. Compare **sharp** (sense 17). **34.** *Theatre.* a rectangular wooden frame covered with painted canvas, etc., used to form part of a stage setting. **35.** a punctured car tyre. **36.** (*often cap.;* preceded by *the*) *Chiefly Brit.* **a.** flat racing, esp. as opposed to steeplechasing and hurdling. **b.** the season of flat racing. **37.** *Nautical.* a flatboat or lighter. ~*vb.* **flats, flat·ting, flat·ted. 38.** to make or become flat. **39.** *Music.* the usual U.S. word for **flatten** (sense 3). [C14: from Old Norse *flatr;* related to Old High German *flaz* flat, Greek *platus* flat, broad] —**'flat·ly** *adv.* —**'flat·ness** *n.*

flat[2] (flæt) *n.* **1.** a set of rooms comprising a residence entirely on one floor of a building. Usual U.S. name: **apartment. 2.** *Canadian.* a set of rooms that is run-down, old-fashioned, not self-contained, or in an old building. ~*vb.* (*intr.*) **3.** *Austral. informal.* to live in a flat (with someone). [Old English *flett* floor, hall, house; related to FLAT[1]]

flat-bed press *n.* a printing machine on which the type forme is carried on a flat bed under a revolving paper-bearing cylinder. Also called: **cylinder press.**

flat·boat ('flæt,bəʊt) *n.* any boat with a flat bottom, usually for transporting goods on a canal or river.

flat cap *n.* **1.** another name for **cloth cap** (sense 1). **2.** an Elizabethan man's hat with a narrow down-turned brim.

flat·ette (,flæt'ɛt) *n. Austral.* a small flat.

flat·fish ('flæt,fɪʃ) *n., pl.* **·fish** *or* **·fish·es.** any marine spiny-finned fish of the order *Heterosomata,* including the halibut, plaice, turbot, and sole, all of which (when adult) swim along the sea floor on one side of the body, which is highly compressed and has both eyes on the uppermost side.

flat·foot ('flæt,fʊt) *n.* **1.** a condition in which the entire sole of the foot is able to touch the ground because of flattening of the instep arch. **2.** (*pl.* **·foots** *or* **·feet.**) a slang word (usually derogatory) for a **policeman.**

flat-foot·ed (,flæt'fʊtɪd) *adj.* **1.** having flatfoot. **2.** *Brit. informal.* **a.** clumsy or awkward. **b.** downright and uncompromising. **3.** *Informal.* off guard or unawares (often in the phrase **catch flat-footed**). —**,flat-'foot·ed·ly** *adv.* —**,flat-'foot·ed·ness** *n.*

flat·head ('flæt,hɛd) *n., pl.* **·head** *or* **·heads.** any Pacific scorpaenoid food fish of the family *Platycephalidae,* which resemble gurnards.

flat·i·ron ('flæt,aɪən) *n.* (formerly) an iron for pressing clothes that was heated by being placed on a stove, etc.

flat knot *n.* another name for **reef knot.**

flat·let ('flætlɪt) *n.* a flat having only a few rooms.

flat·ling ('flætlɪŋ) *Archaic or dialect.* ~*adv.* **1.** in a flat or prostrate position. ~*adj., adv.* **2.** with the flat side, as of a sword. ~Also (for adv.): **flat·lings.**

flat·mate ('flæt,meɪt) *n. Brit.* a person with whom one shares a flat.

flat rac·ing *n.* **a.** the racing of horses on racecourses without jumps. **b.** (*as modifier*): *the flat-racing season.*

flats (flæts) *pl. n.* shoes with a flat heel or no heel.

flat spin *n.* **1.** an aircraft spin in which the longitudinal axis is more nearly horizontal than vertical. **2.** *Informal.* a state of confusion; dither.

flat·ten ('flætᵊn) *vb.* **1.** (sometimes foll. by *out*) to make or become flat or flatter. **2.** (*tr.*) *Informal.* **a.** to knock down or injure; prostrate. **b.** to crush or subdue: *failure will flatten his self-esteem.* **3.** (*tr.*) *Music.* to lower the pitch of (a note) by one chromatic semitone. Usual U.S. word: **flat. 4.** (*intr.;* foll. by *out*) to manoeuvre an aircraft into horizontal flight, esp. after a dive. —**'flat·ten·er** *n.*

flat·ter[1] ('flætə) *vb.* **1.** to praise insincerely, esp. in order to win favour or reward. **2.** to show to advantage: *that dress flatters her.* **3.** (*tr.*) to make to appear more attractive, etc., than in reality. **4.** to play upon or gratify the vanity of (a person): *it flatters her to be remembered.* **5.** (*tr.*) to beguile with hope; encourage, esp. falsely: *this success flattered him into believing himself a champion.* **6.** (*tr.*) to congratulate or deceive (oneself): *I flatter myself that I am the best.* [C13: probably from Old French *flater* to lick, fawn upon, of Frankish origin] —**'flat·ter·a·ble** *adj.* —**'flat·ter·er** *n.* —**'flat·ter·ing·ly** *adv.*

flat·ter[2] ('flætə) *n.* **1.** a blacksmith's tool, resembling a flat-faced hammer, that is placed on forged work and struck to smooth the surface of the forging. **2.** a die with a narrow rectangular orifice for drawing flat sections.

flat·ter·y ('flætərɪ) *n., pl.* **·ter·ies. 1.** the act of flattering. **2.** excessive or insincere praise.

flat·ting ('flætɪŋ) *n. Metallurgy.* the process of flattening metal into a sheet by rolling.

flat·tish ('flætɪʃ) *adj.* somewhat flat.

flat·top ('flæt,tɒp) *n. U.S.* an informal name for **aircraft carrier.**

flat·u·lent ('flætjʊlənt) *adj.* **1.** suffering from or caused by an excessive amount of gas in the alimentary canal, producing uncomfortable distension. **2.** generating excessive gas in the alimentary canal. **3.** pretentious or windy in style. [C16: from New Latin *flātulentus,* from Latin: FLATUS] —**'flat·u·lence** *or* **'flat·u·len·cy** *n.* —**'flat·u·lent·ly** *adv.*

fla·tus ('fleɪtəs) *n., pl.* **·tus·es.** gas generated in the alimentary canal. [C17: from Latin: a blowing, snorting, from *flāre* to breathe, blow]

flat·ware ('flæt,wɛə) *n.* plates, saucers, etc.

flat·ways ('flæt,weɪz) *or U.S.* **flat·wise** *adv.* with the flat or broad side down or in contact with another surface.

flat·worm ('flæt,wɜːm) *n.* any parasitic or free-living invertebrate of the phylum *Platyhelminthes,* including planarians, flukes, and tapeworms, having a flattened body with no circulatory system and only one opening to the intestine.

flat-wo·ven *adj.* (of a carpet) woven without pile.

Flau·bert ('fləʊbɛə; *French* flo'bɛːr) *n.* **Gus·tave** (gys'tav). 1821–80, French novelist and short-story writer, regarded as a leader of the 19th-century naturalist school. His most famous novel, *Madame Bovary* (1857), for which he was prosecuted (and acquitted) on charges of immorality, and *L'Education sentimentale* (1869) deal with the conflict of romantic attitudes and bourgeois society. His other major works include *Salammbô* (1862), *La Tentation de Saint Antoine* (1874), and *Trois Contes* (1877).

flaunch (flɔːntʃ) *n.* a cement or mortar slope around a chimney top, manhole, etc., to throw off water. Also called: **flaunching.** [C18: variant of FLANGE]

flaunt (flɔːnt) *vb.* **1.** to display (possessions, oneself, etc.) ostentatiously; show off. **2.** to wave or cause to wave freely; flutter. ~*n.* **3.** the act of flaunting. [C16: perhaps of Scandinavian origin; compare Norwegian dialect *flanta* to wander about] —**'flaunt·er** *n.* —**'flaunt·ing·ly** *adv.*

flaunt·y ('flɔːntɪ) *adj.* **flaunt·i·er, flaunt·i·est.** *Chiefly U.S.* characterized by or inclined to ostentatious display or flaunting. —**'flaunt·i·ly** *adv.* —**'flaunt·i·ness** *n.*

flau·tist ('flɔːtɪst) *or U.S.* **flut·ist** ('fluːtɪst) *n.* a player of the flute. [C19: from Italian *flautista,* from *flauto* FLUTE]

fla·ves·cent (flə'vɛsᵊnt) *adj.* turning yellow; yellowish. [C19: from Latin *flāvēscere* to become yellow, from *flāvēre* to be yellow, from *flāvus* yellow]

fla·vin *or* **fla·vine** ('fleɪvɪn) *n.* **1.** a heterocyclic ketone that forms the nucleus of certain natural yellow pigments, such as riboflavin. Formula: $C_{10}H_6N_4O_2$. See **flavoprotein. 2.** any yellow pigment based on flavin. **3.** another name for **quercetin.** [C19: from Latin *flāvus* yellow]

fla·vine ('fleɪvɪn) *n.* **1.** another name for **acriflavine hydrochloride. 2.** a variant spelling of **flavin.**

fla·vone ('fleɪvəʊn) *n.* **1.** a crystalline compound occurring in plants. Formula: $C_{15}H_{10}O_2$. **2.** any of a class of yellow plant pigments derived from flavone. [C19: from German *Flavon,* from Latin *flāvus* yellow + -ONE]

fla·vo·pro·tein (,fleɪvəʊ'prəʊtiːn) *n.* any of a group of enzymes that contain a derivative of riboflavin linked to a protein and catalyse oxidation in cells. Also called: **cytochrome reductase.** See also **FMN, FAD.** [C20: from FLAVIN + PROTEIN]

fla·vo·pur·pu·rin (,fleɪvəʊ'pɜːpjʊrɪn) *n.* a yellow crystalline dye derived from anthraquinone. Formula: $C_{14}H_5O_2(OH)_3$. [C20: from Latin *flāvus* yellow + PURPURIN]

fla·vor·ous ('fleɪvərəs) *adj.* having flavour; tasty.

fla·vour *or U.S.* **fla·vor** ('fleɪvə) *n.* **1.** taste perceived in food or liquid in the mouth. **2.** a substance added to food, etc., to impart a specific taste. **3.** a distinctive quality or atmosphere; suggestion: *a poem with a Shakespearian flavour.* ~*vb.* **4.** (*tr.*) to impart a flavour, taste, or quality to. [C14: from Old French *flaour,* from Late Latin *flātor* (unattested) bad smell, breath, from Latin *flāre* to blow] —**'fla·vour·er** *or U.S.* **'fla·vor·er** *n.* —**'fla·vour·less** *or U.S.* **'fla·vor·less** *adj.* —**'fla·vour·some** *or U.S.* **'fla·vor·some** *adj.*

fla+vour+ful *or U.S.* **fla+vor+ful** ('fleɪvəfʊl) *adj.* having a full pleasant taste or flavour. —**'fla+vour+ful+ly** *or U.S.* **'fla+vor+ful+ly** *adv.*

fla+vour+ing *or U.S.* **fla+vor+ing** ('fleɪvərɪŋ) *n.* a substance used to impart a particular flavour to food: *rum flavouring.*

flaw[1] (flɔː) *n.* **1.** an imperfection, defect, or blemish. **2.** a crack, breach, or rift. **3.** *Law.* an invalidating fault or defect in a document or proceeding. ~*vb.* **4.** to make or become blemished, defective, or imperfect. [C14: probably from Old Norse *flaga* stone slab; related to Swedish *flaga* chip, flake, flaw] —**'flaw+less** *adj.* —**'flaw+less+ly** *adv.* —**'flaw+less+ness** *n.*

flaw[2] (flɔː) *n.* **1. a.** a sudden short gust of wind; squall. **b.** a spell of bad, esp. windy, weather. **2.** *Obsolete.* an outburst of strong feeling. [C16: of Scandinavian origin; related to Norwegian *flaga* squall, gust, Middle Dutch *vlāghe*] —**'flaw·y** *adj.*

flax (flæks) *n.* **1.** any herbaceous plant or shrub of the genus *Linum*, esp. *L. usitatissimum*, which has blue flowers and is cultivated for its seeds (flaxseed) and for the fibres of its stems: family *Linaceae*. **2.** the fibre of this plant, made into thread and woven into linen fabrics. **3.** any of various similar plants. [Old English *fleax;* related to Old Frisian *flax*, Old High German *flahs* flax, Greek *plekein* to plait]

flax+en ('flæksən) *or* **flax·y** *adj.* **1.** of, relating to, or resembling flax. **2.** of a soft yellow colour: *flaxen hair.*

Flax·man ('flæksmən) *n.* **John.** 1755–1826, English neoclassical sculptor and draughtsman, noted particularly for his monuments and his engraved illustrations for the *Iliad*, the *Odyssey*, and works by Dante and Aeschylus.

flax+seed ('flæks,siːd) *n.* the seed of the flax plant, which yields linseed oil. Also called: **linseed.**

flay (fleɪ) *vb.* (*tr.*) **1.** to strip off the skin or outer covering of, esp. by whipping; skin. **2.** to attack with savage criticism. **3.** to strip of money or goods, esp. by cheating or extortion. [Old English *flēan;* related to Old Norse *flā* to peel, Lithuanian *plėšti* to tear] —**'flay+er** *n.*

fld. *abbrev. for* field.

fl. dr. *abbrev. for* fluid dram.

flea (fliː) *n.* **1.** any small wingless parasitic blood-sucking insect of the order *Siphonaptera*, living on the skin of mammals and birds and noted for their powers of leaping. **2.** any of various invertebrates that resemble fleas, such as the water flea and flea beetle. **3. flea in one's ear.** *Informal.* a sharp rebuke. [Old English *flēah;* related to Old Norse *flō*, Old High German *flōh*]

flea+bag ('fliː,bæg) *n. Slang.* **1.** *Brit.* a dirty or unkempt person, esp. a woman. **2.** *U.S.* a cheap or dirty hotel.

flea+bane ('fliː,beɪn) *n.* **1.** any of several plants of the genus *Erigeron*, such as *E. acer*, having purplish tubular flower heads with orange centres: family *Compositae* (composites). **2.** any of several plants of the related genus *Pulicaria*, esp. the Eurasian *P. dysenterica*, which has yellow daisy-like flower heads. **3. Canadian fleabane.** a related plant, *Conyza* (or *Erigeron*) *canadensis*, with small white tubular flower heads. U.S. name: **horseweed. 4.** any of various other plants reputed to ward off fleas.

flea bee+tle *n.* any small common beetle of the genera *Phyllotreta*, *Chalcoides*, etc., having enlarged hind legs and capable of jumping: family *Chrysomelidae*. The larvae of many species are very destructive to turnips and other cruciferous vegetables.

flea+bite ('fliː,baɪt) *n.* **1.** the bite of a flea. **2.** a slight or trifling annoyance or discomfort.

flea-bit·ten *adj.* **1.** bitten by or infested with fleas. **2.** *Informal.* shabby or decrepit; mean. **3.** (of the coat of a horse) having reddish-brown spots on a lighter background.

fleam (fliːm) *n.* a lancet used for letting blood. [C16: from Old French *flieme*, alteration of Late Latin *phlebotomus* lancet (literally: vein cutter); see PHLEBOTOMY]

flea mar+ket *n.* an open-air market selling cheap and often second-hand goods.

flea+pit ('fliː,pɪt) *n. Informal.* a shabby cinema or theatre.

flea+wort ('fliː,wɜːt) *n.* **1.** any of various plants of the genus *Senecio*, esp. *S. integrifolius*, a European species with yellow daisy-like flowers and rosettes of downy leaves: family *Compositae* (composites). **2.** a Eurasian plantain, *Plantago psyllium* (or *P. indica*), whose seeds resemble fleas and were formerly used as a flea repellent. **3.** another name for **ploughman's spikenard.**

flèche (fleɪʃ, flɛʃ) *n.* **1.** Also called: **spirelet.** a slender spire, esp. over the intersection of the nave and transept ridges of a church roof. **2.** a pointed part of a fortification directed towards the attackers. [C18: from French: spire (literally: arrow), probably of Germanic origin; related to Middle Low German *flieke* long arrow]

flé+chette (fleɪ'ʃɛt) *n.* a steel dart or missile dropped from an aircraft, as in World War I. [from French; see FLÈCHE]

fleck (flɛk) *n.* **1.** a small marking or streak; speckle. **2.** a small particle; speck: *a fleck of dust.* ~*vb.* **3.** (*tr.*) Also: **flecker.** to mark or cover with flecks; speckle. [C16: probably from Old Norse *flekkr* stain, spot; related to Old High German *flec* spot, plot of land]

Fleck·er ('flɛkə) *n.* **James El·roy.** 1884–1915, English poet and dramatist; author of *Hassan* (1922).

flec+tion ('flɛkʃən) *n.* **1.** the act of bending or the state of being bent. **2.** something bent; bend. **3.** *Grammar.* a less common word for **inflection.** ~See also **flexion.** [C17: from Latin *flexiō* a bending, from *flectere* to curve, bow] —**'flec+tion+al** *adj.* —**'flec+tion+less** *adj.*

fled (flɛd) *vb.* the past tense or past participle of **flee.**

fledge (flɛdʒ) *vb.* **1.** (*tr.*) to feed and care for (a young bird) until it is able to fly. **2.** (*tr.*) Also called: **fletch.** to fit (something, esp. an arrow) with a feather or feathers. **3.** (*intr.*) (of a young bird) to grow feathers. **4.** (*tr.*) to cover or adorn with or as if with feathers. [Old English *-flycge*, as in *unflycge* unfledged; related to Old High German *flucki* able to fly; see FLY[1]]

fledg+ling *or* **fledge+ling** ('flɛdʒlɪŋ) *n.* **1.** a young bird that has just fledged. **2.** a young and inexperienced person.

fledg·y ('flɛdʒɪ) *adj.* **fledg·i·er, fledg·i+est.** *Rare.* feathery or feathered.

flee (fliː) *vb.* **flees, flee+ing, fled. 1.** to run away from (a place, danger, etc.); fly: *to flee the country.* **2.** (*intr.*) to run or move quickly; rush; speed: *she fled to the door.* [Old English *flēon;* related to Old Frisian *fliā*, Old High German *fliohan*, Gothic *thliuhan*] —**'fle+er** *n.*

fleece (fliːs) *n.* **1.** the coat of wool that covers the body of a sheep or similar animal and consists of a mass of crinkly hairs. **2.** the wool removed from a single sheep. **3.** something resembling a fleece in texture or warmth. **4.** sheepskin or a fabric with soft pile, used as a lining for coats, etc. ~*vb.* (*tr.*) **5.** to defraud or charge exorbitantly; swindle. **6.** another term for **shear** (sense 1). [Old English *flēos;* related to Middle High German *vlius*, Dutch *vlies* fleece, Latin *plūma* feather, down]

fleec·y ('fliːsɪ) *adj.* **fleec·i·er, fleec·i·est.** of or resembling fleece; woolly. —**'fleec·i+ly** *adv.* —**'fleec·i+ness** *n.*

fleer (flɪə) *Archaic.* ~*vb.* **1.** to grin or laugh at; scoff; sneer. ~*n.* **2.** a derisory glance or grin. [C14: of Scandinavian origin; compare Norwegian *flire* to snigger] —**'fleer+ing+ly** *adv.*

fleet[1] (fliːt) *n.* **1.** a number of warships organized as a tactical unit. **2.** all the warships of a nation. **3.** a number of aircraft ships, buses, etc., operating together or under the same ownership. [Old English *flēot* ship, flowing water, from *flēotan* to FLOAT]

fleet[2] (fliːt) *adj.* **1.** rapid in movement; swift. **2.** *Poetic.* fleeting; transient. ~*vb.* **3.** (*intr.*) to move rapidly. **4.** (*intr.*) *Archaic.* to fade away smoothly; glide. **5.** (*tr.*) *Nautical.* **a.** to change the position of (a hawser). **b.** to pass (a messenger or lead) to a hawser from a winch for hauling in. **c.** to spread apart (the blocks of a tackle). **6.** (*intr.*) *Obsolete.* to float or swim. **7.** (*tr.*) *Obsolete.* to cause (time) to pass rapidly. [probably Old English *flēotan* to float, glide rapidly; related to Old High German *fliozzan* to flow, Latin *pluere* to rain] —**'fleet+ly** *adv.* —**'fleet+ness** *n.*

fleet[3] (fliːt) *n. Chiefly southeastern Brit.* a small coastal inlet; creek. [Old English *flēot* flowing water; see FLEET[1]]

Fleet (fliːt) *n.* **the. 1.** a stream that formerly ran into the Thames between Ludgate Hill and Fleet Street and is now a covered sewer. **2.** Also called: **Fleet Prison.** (formerly) a London prison, esp. used for holding debtors.

fleet ad+mi+ral *n.* an officer holding the most senior commissioned rank in the U.S. and certain other navies.

Fleet Air Arm *n.* (formerly) the aviation branch of the Royal Navy.

fleet+ing ('fliːtɪŋ) *adj.* rapid and transient: *a fleeting glimpse of the sea.* —**'fleet+ing+ly** *adv.* —**'fleet+ing+ness** *n.*

Fleet Street *n.* **1.** a street in central London in which many newspaper offices are situated. **2.** British journalism or journalists collectively.

Fleet+wood ('fliːt,wʊd) *n.* a fishing port in NW England, in Lancashire. Pop.: 28 584 (1971).

Fleet+wood Mac ('fliːtwʊd 'mæk) *n.* Anglo-American rock group (formed 1967): comprising Mick Fleetwood (born 1947; drums), John McVie (born 1945; bass guitar), Christine McVie (born 1947; keyboard and vocals; joined 1971), Stevie Nicks (born 1948; vocals; joined 1975), and Lindsey Buckingham (born 1949; guitar; joined 1975). Former members include Peter Green (born 1946; guitar; quit 1970) and Jeremy Spencer (born 1948; slide guitar; quit 1971).

Flem. *abbrev. for* Flemish.

Flem+ing[1] ('flɛmɪŋ) *n.* a native or inhabitant of Flanders or a Flemish-speaking Belgian. Compare **Walloon.** [C14: from Middle Dutch *Vlaminc*]

Flem·ing[2] ('flɛmɪŋ) *n.* **1.** Sir **Al·ex·an·der.** 1881–1955, Scottish bacteriologist: discovered lysozyme (1922) and penicillin (1928): shared the Nobel prize for medicine in 1945. **2. I·an (Lancaster).** 1908–64, English author of spy novels; creator of the secret agent James Bond. **3.** Sir **John Am·brose.** 1849–1945, English electrical engineer: invented the thermionic valve (1904).

Flem·ing's rules *pl. n. Physics.* two rules used as mnemonics for the relationship between the directions of current flow, motion, and magnetic field in electromagnetic induction. The hand is held with the thumb, first, and second fingers at right angles, respectively indicating the directions of motion, field, and electric current. The left hand is used for electric motors and the right hand for dynamos. [C19: named after Sir John Ambrose FLEMING, who devised them]

Flem+ish ('flɛmɪʃ) *n.* **1.** one of the two official languages of Belgium, almost identical in form with Dutch. **2. the.** (*functioning as pl.*) the Flemings collectively. ~*adj.* **3.** of, relating to, or characteristic of Flanders, the Flemings, or their language.

Flem+ish bond *n.* a bond used in brickwork that has alternating stretchers and headers in each course, each header being placed centrally over a stretcher.

Flens+burg (*German* 'flɛnsbʊrk) *n.* a port in N West Germany, in Schleswig-Holstein: taken from Denmark by Prussia in 1864; voted to remain German in 1920. Pop.: 95 400 (1970).

flense (flɛns), **flench** (flɛntʃ), *or* **flinch** (flɪntʃ) *vb.* (*tr.*) to strip (a whale, seal, etc.) of (its blubber or skin). [C19: from Danish *flense;* related to Dutch *flensen*] —**'flens+er, 'flench+er,** *or* **'flinch+er** *n.*

flesh (flɛʃ) *n.* **1.** the soft part of the body of an animal or human, esp. muscular tissue, as distinct from bone and viscera. **2.** *Informal.* excess weight; fat. **3.** *Archaic.* the edible tissue of animals as opposed to that of fish or, sometimes, fowl; meat. **4.** the thick usually soft part of a fruit or vegetable, as distinct from the skin, core, stone, etc. **5.** the human body and its physical or sensual nature as opposed to the soul or spirit. Related adj.: **carnal. 6.** mankind in general. **7.** animate creatures in general. **8.** one's own family; kin (esp. in the phrase **one's own flesh and blood**). **9.** a yellowish-pink to greyish-yellow colour. **10.** *Christian Science.* erroneous belief on the physical plane, esp. the belief that matter has sensation. **11.** (*modifier*) *Tanning.* of or relating to the inner or under layer of a skin or hide: *a flesh split.* **12. in the flesh.** in person; actually present. **13. make one's flesh creep.** (esp. of something ghostly) to frighten and horrify one. ~*vb.* **14.** (*tr.*) *Hunting.* to stimulate the hunting instinct of (hounds or falcons) by giving them small quantities of raw flesh. **15.** to wound the flesh of with a weapon. **16.** *Archaic or poetic.* to accustom or incite to bloodshed or battle by initial experience. **17.** *Tanning.* to remove the flesh layer of (a hide or skin). **18.** to fatten; fill out. [Old English *flǣsc;* related to Old Norse *flesk* ham, Old High German *fleisk* meat, flesh]

flesh+er ('flɛʃə) *n.* **1.** a person or machine that fleshes hides or skins. **2.** *Scot.* a person who sells meat; butcher.

flesh fly *n.* any dipterous fly of the genus *Sarcophaga,* esp. *S. carnaria,* whose larvae feed on carrion or the tissues of living animals: family *Calliphoridae.*

flesh+ings ('flɛʃɪŋz) *pl. n.* **1.** flesh-coloured tights. **2.** bits of flesh scraped from the hides or skins of animals.

flesh+ly ('flɛʃlɪ) *adj.* **+li+er, +li+est. 1.** relating to the body, esp. its sensual nature; carnal: *fleshly desire.* **2.** worldly as opposed to spiritual. **3.** fleshy; fat. —**'flesh+li+ness** *n.*

flesh+pots ('flɛʃˌpɒts) *pl. n. Often facetious.* **1.** luxurious or self-indulgent living. **2.** places, such as striptease clubs, where bodily desires are gratified or titillated. [C16: from the Biblical use as applied to Egypt (Exodus 16:3)]

flesh wound (wu:nd) *n.* a wound affecting superficial tissues.

flesh·y ('flɛʃɪ) *adj.* **flesh·i+er, flesh·i+est. 1.** fat; plump. **2.** related to or resembling flesh. **3.** *Botany.* (of some fruits, leaves, etc.) thick and pulpy. —**'flesh·i+ness** *n.*

fletch (flɛtʃ) *vb.* another word for **fledge** (sense 2). [C17: probably back formation from FLETCHER]

fletch+er ('flɛtʃə) *n.* a person who makes arrows. [C14: from Old French *flechier,* from *fleche* arrow; see FLÈCHE]

Fletch·er ('flɛtʃə) *n.* **John.** 1579–1625, English Jacobean dramatist, noted for his romantic tragicomedies written in collaboration with Francis Beaumont, esp. *Philaster* (1610) and *The Maid's Tragedy* (1611).

Fletch+er+ism ('flɛtʃəˌrɪzəm) *n.* the practice of chewing food thoroughly and drinking liquids in small sips to aid digestion. [C20: named after Horace *Fletcher* (1849–1919), American nutritionist]

fletch+ings ('flɛtʃɪŋz) *pl. n.* arrow feathers. [plural of *fletching,* from FLETCH]

fleur-de-lis *or* **fleur-de-lys** (ˌflɜ:də'li:) *n., pl.* **fleurs-de-lis** *or* **fleurs-de-lys** (ˌflɜ:də'li:z). **1.** *Heraldry.* a charge representing a lily with three distinct petals. **2.** another name for **iris** (sense 2). [C19: from Old French *flor de lis,* literally: lily flower]

fleu+rette *or* **fleu+ret** (flʊə'rɛt, flɜ:-) *n.* an ornament or motif resembling a flower. [C19: French, literally: a small flower, from *fleur* flower]

fleur+on ('flʊərɒn, -rən, 'flɜ:-) *n.* **1.** another name for **flower** (sense 8). **2.** *Cookery.* a decorative piece of pastry. [C14: from French, from Old French *floron,* from *flor* FLOWER]

Fleu·ry (*French* flœ'ri) *n.* **An·dré Her·cule de** (ɑ̃dre ɛr'kyl də). 1653–1743, French cardinal and statesman: Louis XV's chief adviser and virtual ruler of France (1726–43).

flew[1] (flu:) *vb.* the past tense of **fly**[1].

flew[2] (flu:) *n.* a variant spelling of **flue**[3].

flews (flu:z) *n.* the fleshy hanging upper lip of a bloodhound or similar dog. [C16: of unknown origin]

flex (flɛks) *n.* **1.** *Brit.* a flexible insulated electric cable, used esp. to connect appliances to mains. U.S. name: **cord. 2.** *Informal.* flexibility or pliability. ~*vb.* **3.** to bend or be bent: *he flexed his arm; his arm flexed.* **4.** to contract (a muscle) or (of a muscle) to contract. [C16: from Latin *flexus* bent, winding, from *flectere* to bend, bow]

flex+i·ble ('flɛksɪbᵊl) *adj.* **1.** Also **flex+ile** ('flɛksaɪl). able to be bent easily without breaking; pliable. **2.** adaptable or variable: *flexible working hours.* **3.** able to be persuaded easily; tractable. —ˌ**flex·i+'bil+i·ty** *or* **'flex+i·ble+ness** *n.* —**'flex+i·bly** *adv.*

flex+ion ('flɛkʃən) *n.* **1.** the act of bending a joint or limb. **2.** the condition of the joint or limb so bent. **3.** a variant spelling of **flection.** —**'flex+ion+al** *adj.* —**'flex+ion+less** *adj.*

flex·i·time ('flɛksɪˌtaɪm) *n. Brit.* a system permitting flexibility of working hours at the beginning or end of each day, provided an agreed number of hours (**core time**) are spent at work.

flex·o ('flɛksəʊ) *n., adj., adv.* short for **flexography, flexographic,** or **flexographically.**

flex+og+ra+phy (flɛk'sɒgrəfɪ) *n.* **1.** a method of rotary letterpress printing using a resilient printing plate and solvent-based ink: used characteristically for printing on metal foil or plastic. **2.** matter printed by this method. ~Abbrev.: **flexo.** —**flex+o+graph+ic** (ˌflɛksə'græfik) *adj.* —ˌ**flex+o+'graph+ic+al+ly** *adv.*

flex+or ('flɛksə) *n.* any muscle whose contraction serves to bend a joint or limb. Compare **extensor.** [C17: New Latin; see FLEX]

flex·u+ous ('flɛksjʊəs) *or* **flex·u+ose** ('flɛksjʊˌəʊs) *adj.* **1.** full of bends or curves; winding. **2.** variable; unsteady. [C17: from Latin *flexuōsus* full of bends, tortuous, from *flexus* a bending; see FLEX] —**'flex·u+ous+ly** *adv.*

flex+ure ('flɛkʃə) *n.* **1.** the act of flexing or the state of being flexed. **2.** a bend, turn, or fold. —**'flex+ur+al** *adj.*

fley *or* **flay** (fleɪ) *vb. Northern Brit. dialect.* **1.** to be afraid or cause to be afraid. **2.** (*tr.*) to frighten away; scare. [Old English *āflēgan* to put to flight; related to Old Norse *fleygja*]

fley+some ('fleɪsəm) *adj. Northern Brit. dialect.* frightening.

flib+ber+ti+gib+bet ('flɪbətɪˌdʒɪbɪt) *n.* an irresponsible, silly, or gossipy person. [C15: of uncertain origin]

flick[1] (flɪk) *vb.* **1.** (*tr.*) to touch with or as if with the finger or hand in a quick jerky movement. **2.** (*tr.*) to propel or remove by a quick jerky movement, usually of the fingers or hand: *to flick a piece of paper at someone.* **3.** to move or cause to move quickly or jerkily. **4.** (intr.; foll. by *through*) to read or look at (a book, newspaper, etc.) quickly or idly. **5.** to snap or click (the fingers) to produce a sharp sound. ~*n.* **6.** a tap or quick stroke with the fingers, a whip, etc. **7.** the sound made by such a stroke. **8.** a fleck, streak, or particle. [C15: of imitative origin; compare French *flicflac*]

flick[2] (flɪk) *n. Slang.* **1.** a cinema film. **2.** (*pl.*) **the.** the cinema: *what's on at the flicks tonight?*

flick+er[1] ('flɪkə) *vb.* **1.** (*intr.*) to shine with an unsteady or intermittent light: *a candle flickers.* **2.** (*intr.*) to move quickly to and fro; quiver, flutter, or vibrate. **3.** (*tr.*) to cause to flicker. ~*n.* **4.** an unsteady or brief light or flame. **5.** a swift quivering or fluttering movement. **6.** a visual sensation, often seen in a television image, produced by periodic fluctuations in the brightness of light at a frequency below that covered by the persistence of vision. [Old English *flicorian;* related to Dutch *flikkeren,* Old Norse *flökra* to flutter] —**'flick+er+ing+ly** *adv.* —**'flick+er·y** *adj.*

flick+er[2] ('flɪkə) *n.* any North American woodpecker of the genus *Colaptes,* esp. *C. auratus* (**yellow-shafted flicker**), which has a yellow undersurface to the wings and tail. [C19: perhaps imitative of the bird's call]

flick knife *n.* a knife with a retractable blade that springs out when a button is pressed. U.S. word: **switchblade.**

fli+er *or* **fly+er** ('flaɪə) *n.* **1.** a person or thing that flies or moves very fast. **2.** an aviator or pilot. **3.** *Informal.* a long flying leap; bound. **4.** a fast-moving machine part, esp. one having periodic motion. **5.** a rectangular step in a straight flight of stairs. Compare **winder** (sense 5). **6.** *Athletics.* an informal word for **flying start.**

flight[1] (flaɪt) *n.* **1.** the act, skill, or manner of flying. **2.** a journey made by a flying animal or object. **3.** a group of flying birds or aircraft: *a flight of swallows.* **4.** the basic tactical unit of a military air force. **5.** a journey through space, esp. of a spacecraft. **6.** rapid movement or progress. **7.** a soaring mental journey above or beyond the normal everyday world: *a flight of fancy.* **8. a.** a single line of hurdles across a track in a race. **b.** a series of such hurdles. **9.** a bird's wing or tail feather; flight feather. **10.** a feather or plastic attachment fitted to an arrow or dart to give it stability in flight. **11.** See **flight arrow. 12.** the distance covered by a flight arrow. **13.** *Sport, esp. cricket.* **a.** a flighted movement imparted to a ball, dart, etc. **b.** the ability to flight a ball. **14.** *Angling.* a device on a spinning lure that revolves rapidly. **15.** a set of steps or stairs between one landing or floor and the next. **16.** a large enclosed area attached to an aviary or pigeon loft where the birds may fly but not escape. ~*vb.* **17.** (*tr.*) *Sport.* to cause (a ball, dart, etc.) to float slowly or deceptively towards its target. **18.** (*intr.*) (of wild fowl) to fly in groups. **19.** (*tr.*) to shoot (a bird) in flight. **20.** (*tr.*) to fledge (an arrow or dart). [Old English *flyht;* related to Middle Dutch *vlucht,* Old Saxon *fluht*]

flight[2] (flaɪt) *n.* **1.** the act of fleeing or running away, as from danger. **2. put to flight.** to cause to run away; rout. **3. take (to) flight.** to run away or withdraw hastily; flee. [Old English *flyht* (unattested); related to Old Frisian *flecht,* Old High German *fluht,* Old Norse *flōtti*]

flight ar+row *n.* a long thin arrow used for shooting long distances. Often shortened to **flight.**

flight deck *n.* **1.** the crew compartment in an airliner. Compare **cockpit** (sense 1). **2.** the upper deck of an aircraft carrier from which aircraft take off and on which they land.

flight en+gi+neer *n.* the member of an aircraft crew who is responsible for the operation of the aircraft's systems, including the engines, during flight.

flight feath+er *n.* any of the large stiff feathers that cover the wings and tail of a bird and are adapted for flying.

flight for+ma+tion *n.* two or more aircraft flying together in a set pattern.

flight+less ('flaɪtlɪs) *adj.* (of certain birds and insects) unable to fly. See also **ratite.**

flight lieu+ten+ant *n.* an officer holding a commissioned rank senior to a flying officer and junior to a squadron leader in the R.A.F. and certain other air forces.

flight line *n.* an area of an airfield or airport on which aircraft, esp. military aircraft, are parked and serviced.

flight path *n.* the course through the air of an aircraft, rocket, or projectile. Compare **approach** (sense 10), **glide path.**

flight plan *n.* a written statement of the details of a proposed aircraft flight.

flight re+cord+er *n.* an electronic device fitted to an aircraft for collecting and storing information concerning its performance in flight. It is often used to determine the cause of a crash. Also called: **black box.**

flight sim·u·la·tor *n.* a ground-training device that reproduces exactly the conditions experienced on the flight deck of an aircraft. Compare **Link trainer.**

flight strip *n.* **1.** a strip of cleared land used as an emergency runway for aircraft. **2.** another name for **runway** (sense 1). **3.** a strip of continuous aerial photographs.

flight sur·geon *n.* a medical officer specializing in aviation medicine in the U.S. and certain other air forces.

flight·y ('flaɪtɪ) *adj.* **flight·i·er, flight·i·est. 1.** frivolous and irresponsible; capricious; volatile. **2.** mentally erratic, unstable, or wandering. **3.** flirtatious; coquettish. —'**flight·i·ly** *adv.* —'**flight·i·ness** *n.*

flim·flam ('flɪmˌflæm) *Informal.* ~*n.* **1. a.** nonsense; rubbish; foolishness. **b.** (*as modifier*): *flimflam arguments.* **2.** a deception; trick; swindle. ~*vb.* **·flams, ·flam·ming, ·flammed. 3.** (*tr.*) to deceive; trick; swindle; cheat. [C16: probably of Scandinavian origin; compare Old Norse *flīm* mockery, Norwegian *flire* to giggle] —'**flim·ˌflam·mer** *n.*

flim·sy ('flɪmzɪ) *adj.* **·si·er, ·si·est. 1.** not strong or substantial; fragile: *a flimsy building.* **2.** light and thin: *a flimsy dress.* **3.** unconvincing or inadequate; weak: *a flimsy excuse.* ~*n.* **4.** thin paper used for making carbon copies of a letter, etc. **5.** a copy made on such paper. [C17: of uncertain origin] —'**flim·si·ly** *adv.* —'**flim·si·ness** *n.*

flinch[1] (flɪntʃ) *vb.* (*intr.*) **1.** to draw back suddenly, as from pain, shock, etc.; wince: *he flinched as the cold water struck him.* **2.** (often foll. by *from*) to avoid contact (with); shy away: *he never flinched from his duty.* ~*n.* **3.** the act or an instance of drawing back. **4.** a card game in which players build sequences. [C16: from Old French *flenchir;* related to Middle High German *lenken* to bend, direct; see LANK] —'**flinch·er** *n.* —'**flinch·ing·ly** *adv.*

flinch[2] (flɪntʃ) *vb.* (*tr.*) a variant spelling of **flense.**

flin·ders ('flɪndəz) *pl. n. Rare.* small fragments or splinters (esp. in the phrase **fly into flinders**). [C15: probably of Scandinavian origin; compare Norwegian *flindra* thin piece of stone]

Flin·ders bar ('flɪndəz) *n. Navigation.* a bar of soft iron mounted on a binnacle to compensate for local magnetism causing error to the compass. [C19: named after Matthew *Flinders* (died 1814), English navigator]

Flin·ders Is·land ('flɪndəz) *n.* an island off the coast of NE Tasmania: the largest of the Furneaux Islands. Pop.: 967 (1971). Area: 2077 sq. km (802 sq. miles).

Flin·ders Range *n.* a mountain range in E South Australia, between Lake Torrens and Lake Frome. Highest peak: 1170 m (3900 ft.).

fling (flɪŋ) *vb.* **flings, fling·ing, flung.** (*mainly tr.*) **1.** to throw, esp. with force or abandon; hurl or toss. **2.** to put or send without warning or preparation: *to fling someone into jail.* **3.** (*also intr.*) to move (oneself or a part of the body) with abandon or speed: *he flung himself into a chair.* **4.** (usually foll. by *into*) to apply (oneself) diligently and with vigour (to). **5.** to cast aside; disregard: *she flung away her scruples.* **6.** to utter violently or offensively. **7.** *Poetic.* to give out; emit. ~*n.* **8.** the act or an instance of flinging; toss; throw. **9.** a period or occasion of unrestrained, impulsive, or extravagant behaviour: *to have a fling.* **10.** any of various vigorous Scottish reels full of leaps and turns, such as the Highland fling. **11.** a trial; try: *to have a fling at something different.* [C13: of Scandinavian origin; related to Old Norse *flengja* to flog, Swedish *flänga,* Danish *flænge*] —'**fling·er** *n.*

flint (flɪnt) *n.* **1.** an impure opaque microcrystalline greyish-black form of quartz that occurs in chalk. It produces sparks when struck with steel and is used in the manufacture of pottery, flint glass, and road-construction materials. Formula: SiO_2. **2.** any piece of flint, esp. one used as a primitive tool or for striking fire. **3.** a small cylindrical piece of an iron alloy, used in cigarette lighters. **4.** Also called: **flint glass, white flint.** colourless glass other than plate glass. **5.** See **optical flint.** ~*vb.* **6.** (*tr.*) to fit or provide with a flint. [Old English; related to Old High German *flins,* Old Swedish *flinta* splinter of stone, Latin *splendēre* to shine]

Flint (flɪnt) *n.* **1.** a town in NE Wales, in Clwyd, on the Dee estuary. Pop.: 14 660 (1971). **2.** a city in SE Michigan: car production. Pop.: 181 684 (1973 est.).

flint glass *n.* another name for **optical flint, flint** (sense 4).

flint·lock ('flɪntˌlɒk) *n.* **1.** an obsolete gunlock in which the charge is ignited by a spark produced by a flint in the hammer. **2.** a firearm having such a lock.

Flint·shire ('flɪntʃɪə, -ʃə) *n.* (until 1974) a county of NE Wales, now part of Clwyd.

flint·y ('flɪntɪ) *adj.* **flint·i·er, flint·i·est. 1.** of, relating to, or resembling flint. **2.** hard or cruel; obdurate; unyielding. —'**flint·i·ly** *adv.* —'**flint·i·ness** *n.*

flip (flɪp) *vb.* **flips, flip·ping, flipped. 1.** to throw (something light or small) carelessly or briskly; toss: *he flipped me an envelope.* **2.** to throw or flick (an object such as a coin) so that it turns or spins in the air. **3.** to propel by a sudden movement of the finger; flick: *to flip a crumb across the room.* **4.** (foll. by *through*) to read or look at (a book, newspaper, etc.) quickly, idly, or incompletely. **5.** (*intr.*) (of small objects) to move or bounce jerkily. **6.** (*intr.*) to make a snapping movement or noise with the finger and thumb. **7.** (*intr.*) *Slang, chiefly U.S.* to fly into a rage or an emotional outburst (also in the phrases **flip one's lid, flip one's top**). 8. (*intr.*) *Slang, chiefly U.S.* to become ecstatic or very excited: *he flipped over the jazz group.* ~*n.* **9.** a snap or tap, usually with the fingers. **10.** a rapid jerk. **11.** a somersault, esp. one performed in the air, as in a dive, rather than from a standing position. **12.** any alcoholic drink containing beaten egg. ~*adj.* **13.** *U.S. informal.* impertinent, flippant, or pert. [C16: probably of imitative origin; see FILLIP]

flip-flop *n.* **1.** a backward handspring. **2.** an electronic device or circuit that can assume either of two stable states by the application of a suitable pulse. **3.** a complete change of opinion, policy, etc. **4.** a repeated flapping or banging noise. **5.** Also called (esp. U.S.): **thong.** a rubber-soled sandal attached to the foot by a thong between the big toe and the next toe. ~*vb.* **-flops, -flop·ping, -flopped. 6.** (*intr.*) to move with repeated flaps. ~*adv.* **7.** with repeated flappings: *to go flip-flop.* [C16: reduplication of FLIP]

flip·pant ('flɪpənt) *adj.* **1.** marked by inappropriate levity; frivolous or offhand. **2.** impertinent; saucy. **3.** *Obsolete.* talkative or nimble. [C17: perhaps from FLIP] —'**flip·pan·cy** *n.* —'**flip·pant·ly** *adv.*

flip·per ('flɪpə) *n.* **1.** the flat broad limb of seals, whales, penguins, and other aquatic animals, specialized for swimming. **2.** (*often pl.*) Also called: **fin.** either of a pair of rubber paddle-like devices worn on the feet as an aid in swimming, esp. underwater.

flip·ping ('flɪpɪŋ) *adj., adv. Brit. slang.* (intensifier): *a flipping idiot; it's flipping cold.* [C19: perhaps a euphemism for FUCKING]

flip side *n.* the less important side of a pop record.

flirt (flɜːt) *vb.* **1.** (*intr.*) to behave or act amorously without emotional commitment; toy or play with another's affections; dally. **2.** (*intr.;* usually foll. by *with*) to deal playfully or carelessly (with something dangerous or serious); trifle: *the motorcyclist flirted with death.* **3.** (*intr.;* usually foll. by *with*) to think casually (about); toy (with): *to flirt with the idea of leaving.* **4.** (*intr.*) to move jerkily; dart; flit. **5.** (*tr.*) to subject to a sudden swift motion; flick or toss. ~*n.* **6.** a person who acts flirtatiously. [C16: of uncertain origin] —'**flirt·er** *n.* —'**flirt·ing·ly** *adv.*

flir·ta·tion (flɜːˈteɪʃən) *n.* **1.** behaviour intended to arouse sexual feelings or advances without emotional commitment; coquetry. **2.** any casual involvement without commitment: *a flirtation with journalism.*

flir·ta·tious (flɜːˈteɪʃəs) *adj.* **1.** given to flirtation. **2.** expressive of playful sexual invitation: *a flirtatious glance.* —**flir·'ta·tious·ly** *adv.* —**flir·'ta·tious·ness** *n.*

flit (flɪt) *vb.* **flits, flit·ting, flit·ted.** (*intr.*) **1.** to move along rapidly and lightly; skim or dart. **2.** to fly rapidly and lightly; flutter. **3.** to pass quickly; fleet: *a memory flitted into his mind.* **4.** *Scot. and northern English dialect.* to move house. **5.** *Brit. informal.* to depart hurriedly and stealthily in order to avoid obligations. **6.** an informal word for **elope.** ~*n.* **7.** the act or an instance of flitting. **8.** *Slang, chiefly U.S.* a male homosexual. **9.** *Brit. informal.* a hurried and stealthy departure in order to avoid obligations (esp. in the phrase **do a flit**). **10.** moonlight flit. *Brit. informal.* a departure in this manner at night, esp. from rented accommodation to avoid payment of rent owed. [C12: from Old Norse *flytja* to carry] —'**flit·ter** *n.*

flitch (flɪtʃ) *n.* **1.** a side of pork salted and cured. **2.** a steak cut from the side of certain fishes, esp. halibut. **3.** a piece of timber cut lengthways from a tree trunk, esp. one that is larger than 4 by 12 inches. ~*vb.* **4.** (*tr.*) to cut (a tree trunk) into flitches. [Old English *flicce;* related to Old Norse *flikki,* Middle Low German *vlicke,* Norwegian *flika;* see FLESH]

flite *or* **flyte** (flaɪt) *Scot. and northern Brit. dialect.* ~*vb.* **1.** (*tr.*) to scold or rail at. ~*n.* **2.** a dispute or scolding. [Old English *flītan* to wrangle, of Germanic origin; related to Old Frisian *flīt* strife, Old High German *flīz* strife]

flit·ter ('flɪtə) *vb.* a less common word for **flutter.**

flit·ter·mouse ('flɪtəˌmaʊs) *n., pl.* **·mice.** a dialect name for **bat**[2] (the animal). [C16: translation of German *Fledermaus;* see FLITTER, MOUSE]

fliv·ver ('flɪvə) *n.* an old, cheap, or battered car. [C20: of unknown origin]

float (fləʊt) *vb.* **1.** to rest or cause to rest on the surface of a fluid or in a fluid or space without sinking; be buoyant or cause to exhibit buoyancy: *oil floats on water; to float a ship.* **2.** to move or cause to move buoyantly, lightly, or freely across a surface or through air, water, etc.; drift: *fog floated across the road.* **3.** to move about aimlessly, esp. in the mind: *thoughts floated before him.* **4.** to suspend or be suspended without falling; hang: *lights floated above them.* **5.** (*tr.*) **a.** to launch or establish (a commercial enterprise, etc.). **b.** to offer for sale (stock or bond issues, etc.) on the stock market. **6.** (*tr.*) *Finance.* to allow (a currency) to fluctuate against other currencies in accordance with market forces. **7.** (*tr.*) to flood, inundate, or irrigate (land), either artificially or naturally. **8.** (*tr.*) to spread, smooth, or level (a surface of plaster, rendering, etc.). ~*n.* **9.** something that floats. **10.** *Angling.* an indicator attached to a baited line that sits on the water and moves when a fish bites. **11.** a small hand tool with a rectangular blade used for floating plaster, etc. **12.** *Chiefly U.S.* any buoyant object, such as a platform or inflated tube, used offshore by swimmers or, when moored alongside a pier, as a dock by vessels. **13.** Also called: **paddle.** a blade of a paddle wheel. **14.** *Brit.* a buoyant garment or device to aid a person in staying afloat. **15.** a hollow watertight structure fitted to the underside of an aircraft to allow it to land on water. **16.** another name for **air bladder** (sense 2). **17.** an exhibit carried in a parade, esp. a religious parade. **18.** a motor vehicle used to carry a tableau or exhibit in a parade, esp. a civic parade. **19.** a small delivery vehicle, esp. one powered by batteries: *a milk float.* **20.** *Austral.* a vehicle for transporting horses. **21.** *Banking, chiefly U.S.* the total value of uncollected cheques and other commercial papers. **22.** *Chiefly U.S.* a sum to be applied to minor expenses; petty cash. **23.** a sum of money used by shopkeepers to provide change at the start of the day's business, this sum being subtracted from the total at the end of the day when calculating the day's takings. **24.** the hollow floating ball of a ballcock. **25.** *Chiefly U.S.* a milk shake or other drink with a scoop of ice cream in it. **26.** (in textiles) a single thread brought to or above the surface of a woven fabric, esp. to form a pattern. [Old English *flotian;* related to Old Norse *flota,* Old Saxon *flotōn;* see FLEET[2]] —'**float·a·ble** *adj.* —ˌ**float·a·'bil·i·ty** *n.*

float·age ('fləʊtɪdʒ) *n.* a variant spelling of **flotage.**

float·a·tion (fləʊ'teɪʃən) *n.* a variant spelling of **flotation.**

float·er ('fləʊtə) *n.* **1.** a person or thing that floats. **2.** *U.S.* **a.** a person of no fixed political opinion. **b.** a person who votes illegally in more than one district at one election. **c.** a voter who can be bribed. **3.** Also called: **floating policy.** *Insurance, U.S.* a policy covering loss or theft of or damage to movable property, such as jewels or furs, regardless of its location. **4.** *U.S. informal.* a person who often changes employment, residence, etc.; drifter.

float-feed *adj.* (of a fuel system) controlled by a float operating a needle valve.

float glass *n.* a type of flat polished transparent glass made by allowing the molten glass to harden as it floats on liquid of higher density.

float·ing ('fləʊtɪŋ) *adj.* **1.** having little or no attachment. **2.** (of an organ or part) displaced from the normal position or abnormally movable: *a floating kidney.* **3.** not definitely attached to one place or policy; uncommitted or unfixed: *floating voters.* **4.** *Finance.* **a.** (of capital) not allocated or invested; available for current use. **b.** (of debt) short-term and unfunded, usually raised by a government or company to meet current expenses. **c.** (of a currency) free to fluctuate against other currencies in accordance with market forces. **5.** *Machinery.* operating smoothly through being free from external constraints. **6.** (of an electronic circuit or device) not connected to a source of voltage. —'**float·ing·ly** *adv.*

float·ing as·sets *pl. n.* another term for **current assets.**

float·ing charge *n. Chiefly Brit.* an unsecured charge on the assets of an enterprise that allows such assets to be used commercially until the enterprise ceases to operate or the creditor intervenes to demand collateral.

float·ing dock *n.* a large boxlike structure that can be submerged to allow a vessel to enter it and then floated to raise the vessel out of the water for maintenance or repair. Also called: **floating dry dock.**

float·ing heart *n.* any perennial aquatic freshwater plant of the genus *Nymphoides,* esp. *N. lacunosum,* having floating heart-shaped leaves: family *Menyanthaceae.*

float·ing is·land *n.* a mass of soil held together by vegetation and floating like an island.

float·ing-point rep·re·sen·ta·tion *n. Computer technol.* the representation of numbers by two sets of digits (a, b), the set a indicating the significant digits, the set b giving the position of the radix point. The number is the product ar^b, where r is the base of the number system used. Compare **fixed-point representation.**

float·ing pol·i·cy *n.* **1.** (in marine insurance) a policy covering loss of or damage to specified goods irrespective of the ship in which they are consigned. **2.** another term for **floater** (sense 3).

float·ing rib *n.* any one of the lower two pairs of ribs in man, which are not attached to the breastbone.

floats (fləʊts) *pl. n. Theatre.* another word for **footlights.**

float·y ('fləʊtɪ) *adj.* **float·i·er, float·i·est. 1.** filmy and light: *floaty material.* **2.** capable of floating; buoyant. **3.** (of a vessel) riding high in the water; of shallow draught.

floc (flɒk) *n.* another word for **floccule.** [C20: from Latin *floccus* a tuft of wool, FLOCK[2]]

floc·cose ('flɒkəʊs) *adj.* consisting of or covered with woolly tufts or hairs: *floccose growths of bacteria.* [C18: from Latin *floccōsus* full of flocks of wool]

floc·cu·lant ('flɒkjʊlənt) *n.* a substance added to colloids to prevent coagulation of their suspended particles.

floc·cu·late ('flɒkjʊˌleɪt) *vb.* to form or be formed into an aggregated flocculent mass. —ˌ**floc·cu·'la·tion** *n.*

floc·cule ('flɒkju:l), **floc·cu·lus, flock,** *or* **floc** *n.* **1.** a small aggregate of flocculent material. **2.** something resembling a tuft of wool. [C19: from Late Latin *flocculus* a little tuft; see FLOCK[2]]

floc·cu·lent ('flɒkjʊlənt) *adj.* **1.** like wool; fleecy. **2.** *Chem.* aggregated in woolly cloudlike masses: *a flocculent precipitate.* **3.** *Biology.* covered with tufts or flakes of a waxy or wool-like substance. —'**floc·cu·lence** *or* '**floc·cu·len·cy** *n.* —'**floc·cu·lent·ly** *adv.*

floc·cu·lus ('flɒkjʊləs) *n., pl.* **·li** (-ˌlaɪ). **1.** a marking on the sun's surface or in its atmosphere, as seen on a spectroheliogram. It consists of calcium when lighter than the surroundings and of hydrogen when darker. **2.** *Anatomy.* a tiny ovoid prominence on each side of the cerebellum. **3.** another word for **floccule.**

floc·cus ('flɒkəs) *n., pl.* **floc·ci** ('flɒksaɪ). **1.** a downy or woolly covering, as on the young of certain birds. **2.** a small woolly tuft of hair. ~*adj.* **3.** (of a cloud) having the appearance of woolly tufts at odd intervals in its structure. [C19: from Latin: tuft of hair or wool, FLOCK[2]]

flock[1] (flɒk) *n.* (*sometimes functioning as pl.*) **1.** a group of animals of one kind, esp. sheep or birds. **2.** a large number of people; crowd. **3.** a body of Christians regarded as the pastoral charge of a priest, a bishop, the pope, etc. **4.** *Rare.* a band of people; group. ~*vb.* (*intr.*) **5.** to gather together or move in a flock. **6.** to go in large numbers: *people flocked to the church.* [Old English *flocc;* related to Old Norse *flokkr* crowd, Middle Low German *vlocke*]

flock[2] (flɒk) *n.* **1.** a tuft, as of wool, hair, cotton, etc. **2. a.** waste from fabrics such as cotton, wool, or other cloth used for stuffing mattresses, upholstered chairs, etc. **b.** (*as modifier*): *flock mattress.* **3.** very small tufts of wool applied to fabrics, wallpaper, etc., to give a raised pattern. **4.** another word for **floccule.** ~*vb.* **5.** (*tr.*) to fill, cover, or ornament with flock. [C13: from Old French *floc,* from Latin *floccus;* probably related to Old High German *floccho* down, Norwegian *flugsa* snowflake] —'**flock·y** *adj.*

Flod·den ('flɒdᵊn) *n.* a hill in Northumberland where invading Scots were defeated by the English in 1513 and James IV of Scotland was killed. Also called: **Flodden Field.**

floe (fləʊ) *n.* See **ice floe.** [C19: probably from Norwegian *flo* slab, layer, from Old Norse; see FLAW[1]]

flog (flɒg) *vb.* **flogs, flog·ging, flogged. 1.** (*tr.*) to beat harshly, esp. with a whip, strap, etc. **2.** *Brit. slang.* to sell. **3.** (*intr.*) (of a sail) to flap noisily in the wind. **4.** (*intr.*) to make progress by painful work. **5. flog a dead horse.** to pursue a line of attack or argument from which no results can come. **6. flog to death.** to persuade a person so persistently of the value of (an idea or venture) that he loses interest in it. [C17: probably from Latin *flagellāre;* see FLAGELLANT] —'**flog·ger** *n.*

flong (flɒŋ) *n.* **1.** *Printing.* a material used for making moulds in stereotyping. **2.** *Journalism, slang.* material that is not urgently topical. [C20: variant of FLAN]

flood (flʌd) *n.* **1. a.** the inundation of land that is normally dry through the overflowing of a body of water, esp. a river. **b.** the state of a river that is at an abnormally high level (esp. in the phrase **in flood**). Related adj.: **diluvial. 2.** a great outpouring or flow: *a flood of words.* **3. a.** the rising of the tide from low to high water. **b.** (*as modifier*): *the flood tide.* Compare **ebb** (sense 3). **4.** *Theatre.* short for **floodlight. 5.** *Archaic.* a large body of water, as the sea or a river. ~*vb.* **6.** (of water) to inundate or submerge (land) or (of land) to be inundated or submerged. **7.** to fill or be filled to overflowing, as with a flood: *the children's home was flooded with gifts.* **8.** (*intr.*) to flow; surge: *relief flooded through him.* **9.** to supply an excessive quantity of petrol to (a carburettor or petrol engine) or (of a carburettor, etc.) to be supplied with such an excess. **10.** (*intr.*) to rise to a flood; overflow. **11.** (*intr.*) **a.** to bleed profusely from the uterus, as following childbirth. **b.** to have an abnormally heavy flow of blood during a menstrual period. [Old English *flōd;* related to Old Norse *flōth,* Gothic *flōdus,* Old High German *fluot* flood, Greek *plōtos* navigable; see FLOW, FLOAT] —'**flood·a·ble** *adj.* —'**flood·er** *n.* —'**flood·less** *adj.*

Flood (flʌd) *n. Old Testament.* **the.** the flood extending over all the earth from which Noah and his family and livestock were saved in the ark. (Genesis 7–8); the Deluge.

flood con·trol *n.* the technique or practice of preventing or controlling floods with dams, artificial channels, etc.

flood·gate ('flʌdˌgeɪt) *n.* **1.** Also called: **head gate, water gate.** a gate in a sluice that is used to control the flow of water. See also **sluicegate. 2.** (*often pl.*) a control or barrier against an outpouring or flow: *to open the floodgates to immigration.*

flood·light ('flʌdˌlaɪt) *n.* **1.** a broad intense beam of artificial light, esp. as used in the theatre or to illuminate the exterior of buildings. **2.** the lamp or source producing such light. ~*vb.* **·lights, ·light·ing, ·lit. 3.** (*tr.*) to illuminate by or as if by a floodlight.

flood plain *n.* the flat area bordering a river, composed of sediment deposited during flooding.

floor (flɔ:) *n.* **1.** Also called: **flooring.** the inner lower surface of a room. **2.** a storey of a building: *the second floor.* **3.** a flat bottom surface in or on any structure: *the floor of a lift; a dance floor.* **4.** the bottom surface of a tunnel, cave, river, sea, etc. **5.** *Mining.* an underlying stratum. **6.** *Nautical.* the bottom, or the lowermost framing members at the bottom, of a vessel. **7.** that part of a legislative hall in which debate and other business is conducted. **8.** the right to speak in a legislative or deliberative body (esp. in the phrases **get, have,** or **be given the floor**). **9.** the room in a stock exchange where trading takes place. **10.** the earth; ground. **11.** a minimum price charged or paid: *a wage floor.* **12. take the floor.** to begin dancing on a dance floor. ~*vb.* **13.** to cover with or construct a floor. **14.** (*tr.*) to knock to the floor or ground. **15.** (*tr.*) *Informal.* to disconcert, confound, or defeat: *to be floored by a problem.* [Old English *flōr;* related to Old Norse *flōrr,* Middle Low German *vlōr* floor, Latin *plānus* level, Greek *planan* to cause to wander]

floor·age ('flɔ:rɪdʒ) *n.* an area of floor; floor space.

floor·board ('flɔ:ˌbɔ:d) *n.* one of the boards forming a floor.

floor·ing ('flɔ:rɪŋ) *n.* **1.** the material used in making a floor, esp. the surface material. **2.** another word for **floor** (sense 1).

floor·ing saw *n.* a type of saw curved at the end for cutting through floorboards.

floor lead·er *n. U.S. government.* a member of a legislative body who organizes his party's activities.

floor man·ag·er *n.* **1.** the stage manager employed in the production of a television programme. **2.** a person in overall charge of one floor of a large shop or department store.

floor plan *n.* a drawing to scale of the arrangement of rooms on one floor of a building. Compare **elevation** (sense 5).

floor show *n.* a series of entertainments, such as singing, dancing, and comedy acts, performed in a nightclub.

floor-walker *n.* the U.S. name for **shopwalker.**

floo·zy, floo·zie, *or* **floo·sie** ('flu:zɪ) *n., pl.* **·zies** *or* **·sies.** *Slang.* a disreputable woman. [C20: of unknown origin]
flop (flɒp) *vb.* **flops, flop·ping, flopped.** **1.** (*intr.*) to bend, fall, or collapse loosely or carelessly: *his head flopped backwards.* **2.** (when *intr.*, often foll. by *into, onto,* etc.) to fall, cause to fall, or move with a sudden noise: *the books flopped onto the floor.* **3.** (*intr.*) *Informal.* to fail; be unsuccessful: *the scheme flopped.* **4.** (*intr.*) to fall flat onto the surface of water, hitting it with the front of the body. **5.** (*intr.; often foll. by out*) *Slang.* to go to sleep. ~*n.* **6.** the act of flopping. **7.** *Informal.* a complete failure. **8.** *U.S. slang.* a place to sleep. **9.** *Athletics.* See **Fosbury flop.** [C17: variant of FLAP]
flop·house ('flɒp,haʊs) *n. Slang.* the U.S. word for **dosshouse.**
flop·py ('flɒpɪ) *adj.* **·pi·er, ·pi·est.** limp or hanging loosely: *a dog with floppy ears.* —**'flop·pi·ly** *adv.* —**'flop·pi·ness** *n.*
flor. *abbrev. for* floruit.
flo·ra ('flɔ:rə) *n., pl.* **·ras** *or* **·rae** (-ri:). **1.** all the plant life of a given place or time. **2.** a descriptive list of such plants, often including a key for identification. **3.** short for **intestinal flora.** [C18: from New Latin, from Latin *Flōra* goddess of flowers, from *flōs* FLOWER]
Flo·ra ('flɔ:rə) *n.* the Roman goddess of flowers. [C16: from Latin, from *flōs* flower]
flo·ral ('flɔ:rəl) *adj.* **1.** decorated with or consisting of flowers or patterns of flowers. **2.** of, relating to, or associated with flowers: *floral leaves.* —**'flo·ral·ly** *adv.*
flo·ral en·ve·lope *n.* the part of a flower that surrounds the stamens and pistil: the calyx and corolla (considered together) or the perianth.
Flo·ré·al *French.* (flɔre'al) *n.* the month of flowers: the eighth month of the French revolutionary calendar, extending from April 21 to May 20. [C19: ultimately from Latin *flōreus* of flowers, from *flōs* a flower]
flo·re·at *Latin.* ('flɒrɪæt) *vb.* (*intr.*) *pl.* ***flo·re·ant.*** may (a person, institution, etc.) flourish: *floreat Oxonia!*
flo·re·at·ed ('flɔ:rɪ,eɪtɪd) *adj.* a variant spelling of **floriated.**
Flor·ence ('flɒrəns) *n.* a city in central Italy, on the River Arno in Tuscany: became an independent republic in the 14th century; under Austrian and other rule intermittently from 1737 to 1859; capital of Italy 1865–70. It was the major cultural and artistic centre of the Renaissance and is still one of the world's chief art centres. Pop.: 465 823 (1975 est.). Ancient name: **Florentia.** Italian name: **Firenze.**
Flor·ence flask *n.* a round flat-bottomed glass flask with a long neck, used in chemical experiments.
Flor·en·tine ('flɒrən,taɪn) *adj.* **1.** of or relating to Florence. **2.** (*usually postpositive*) (of food) served or prepared with spinach. ~*n.* **3.** a native or inhabitant of Florence. **4.** a biscuit containing nuts and dried fruit and coated with chocolate. **5.** a type of domestic fancy pigeon somewhat resembling the Modena.
Flo·res ('flɔ:rɛs) *n.* **1.** an island in Indonesia, one of the Lesser Sunda Islands, between the Flores Sea and the Savu Sea: mountainous, with active volcanoes and unexplored forests. Chief town: Ende. Area: 17 150 sq. km (6622 sq. miles). **2.** (*also Portuguese* 'floriʃ). an island in the Atlantic, the westernmost of the Azores. Chief town: Santa Cruz. Area: 142 sq. km (55 sq. miles).
flo·res·cence (flɔ:'rɛsəns) *n.* the process, state, or period of flowering. [C18: from New Latin *flōrēscentia,* from Latin *flōrēscere* to come into flower]
Flo·res Sea *n.* a part of the Pacific Ocean in Indonesia between Celebes and the Lesser Sunda Islands.
flo·ret ('flɔ:rɪt) *n.* a small flower, esp. one of many making up the head of a composite flower. [C17: from Old French *florete* a little flower, from *flor* FLOWER]
Flo·rey ('flɔ:rɪ) *n.* **How·ard Wal·ter,** Baron Florey. 1898–1968, British pathologist: shared the Nobel prize for medicine (1945) with E. B. Chain and Alexander Fleming for their work on penicillin.
Flo·ria·nóp·o·lis (*Portuguese* ,florjə'nɔpulis) *n.* a port in S Brazil, capital of Santa Caterina state, on the W coast of Santa Caterina Island. Pop.: 115 665 (1970).
flo·ri·at·ed *or* **flo·re·at·ed** ('flɔ:rɪ,eɪtɪd) *adj. Architect.* having ornamentation based on flowers and leaves. [C19: from Latin *flōs* FLOWER]
flo·ri·bun·da (,flɔ:rɪ'bʌndə) *n.* any of several varieties of cultivated hybrid roses whose flowers grow in large sprays. [C19: from New Latin, feminine of *flōribundus* flowering freely]
flo·ri·cul·ture ('flɔ:rɪ,kʌltʃə) *n.* the cultivation of flowering plants. —**,flo·ri·'cul·tur·al** *adj.* —**,flo·ri·'cul·tur·ist** *n.*
flor·id ('flɒrɪd) *adj.* **1.** having a red or flushed complexion. **2.** excessively ornate; flowery: *florid architecture.* **3.** an archaic word for **flowery.** [C17: from Latin *flōridus* blooming] —**flo·'rid·i·ty** *or* **'flor·id·ness** *n.* —**'flor·id·ly** *adv.*
Flor·i·da ('flɒrɪdə) *n.* **1.** a state of the southeastern U.S., between the Atlantic and the Gulf of Mexico: consists mostly of a low-lying peninsula ending in the **Florida Keys,** a chain of small islands off the coast of S Florida, extending southwest for over 160 km (100 miles). Capital: Tallahassee. Pop.: 6 789 443 (1970). Area: 143 900 sq. km (55 560 sq. miles). Abbrevs.: **Fla.** or (with zip code) **FL 2. Straits of.** a sea passage between the Florida Keys and Cuba, linking the Atlantic with the Gulf of Mexico. —**Flo·'rid·i·an** *adj.*
flo·ri·gen ('flɒrɪdʒən) *n.* the hypothetical plant hormone that induces flowering, thought to be synthesized in the leaves as a photoperiodic response and transmitted to the flower buds. [C20: from Latin *flor-, flos* FLOWER + -GEN]
flo·ri·le·gi·um (,flɔ:rɪ'li:dʒɪəm) *n., pl.* **·gi·a** (-dʒɪə). **1.** (formerly) a lavishly illustrated book on flowers. **2.** *Rare.* an anthology. [C17: Modern Latin, from Latin *florilegus* flower-collecting, from *flos* flower + *legere* to collect]
flor·in ('flɒrɪn) *n.* **1.** a former British coin, originally silver and later cupronickel, equivalent to ten (new) pence. **2.** (formerly) another name for **guilder** (sense 1). **3.** any of various gold coins of Florence, Britain, or Austria. [C14: from French, from Old Italian *fiorino* Florentine coin, from *fiore* flower, from Latin *flōs*]
Flo·ri·o ('flɔ:rɪ,əʊ) *n.* **John.** ?1553–?1625, English lexicographer, noted for his translation of Montaigne's *Essays* (1603).
flo·rist ('flɒrɪst) *n.* a person who grows or deals in flowers.
flo·ris·tic (flɒ'rɪstɪk) *adj.* of or relating to flowers or a flora. —**flo·'ris·ti·cal·ly** *adv.*
flo·ris·tics (flɒ'rɪstɪks) *n.* (*functioning as sing.*) the branch of botany concerned with the types, numbers, and distribution of plant species in a particular area.
-flo·rous *adj. combining form.* indicating number or type of flowers: *tubuliflorous.*
flo·ru·it *Latin.* ('flɒru:ɪt) *vb.* (he or she) flourished: used to indicate the period when a historical figure, whose birth and death dates are unknown, was most active.
flo·ry ('flɔ:rɪ) *or* **fleu·ry** ('fluərɪ, 'flɜ:rɪ) *adj.* (*usually postpositive*) *Heraldry.* containing a fleur-de-lis. [C15: from Old French *floré,* from *flor* FLOWER]
flos fer·ri ('flɒs 'fɛrɪ) *n.* a variety of aragonite that is deposited from hot springs in the form of a white branching mass. [C18: from New Latin, literally: flower of iron]
floss (flɒs) *n.* **1.** the mass of fine silky fibres obtained from cotton and similar plants. **2.** any similar fine silky material, such as the hairlike styles and stigmas of maize or the fibres prepared from silkworm cocoons. **3.** untwisted silk thread used in embroidery, etc. **4.** Also called: **dental floss.** a waxed thread used to remove food particles from between teeth. [C18: perhaps from Old French *flosche* down]
floss·y ('flɒsɪ) *adj.* **floss·i·er, floss·i·est. 1.** consisting of or resembling floss. **2.** *U.S. slang.* (esp. of dress) showy.
flo·tage *or* **float·age** ('fləʊtɪdʒ) *n.* **1.** the act or state of floating; flotation. **2.** buoyancy; power or ability to float. **3.** objects or material that float on the surface of the water; flotsam.
flo·ta·tion *or* **float·a·tion** (fləʊ'teɪʃən) *n.* **1. a.** the launching or financing of a commercial enterprise by bond or share issues. **b.** the raising of a loan or new capital by bond or share issues. **2.** power or ability to float; buoyancy. **3.** Also called: **froth flotation.** a process to concentrate the valuable ore in low-grade ores. The ore is ground to a powder, mixed with water containing surface-active chemicals, and vigorously aerated. The bubbles formed trap the required ore and carry them to the surface froth, which is then skimmed off.
flo·til·la (flə'tɪlə) *n.* a small fleet or a fleet of small vessels. [C18: from Spanish *flota* fleet, from French *flotte,* ultimately from Old Norse *floti*]
Flo·tow (*German* 'flo:to) *n.* **Frie·drich von** ('fri:drɪç fɔn). 1812–83, German composer of operas, esp. *Martha* (1847).
flot·sam ('flɒtsəm) *n.* **1.** wreckage from a ship found floating. Compare **jetsam, lagan. 2.** useless or discarded objects; odds and ends (esp. in the phrase **flotsam and jetsam**). **3.** vagrants. [C16: from Anglo-French *floteson,* from *floter* to FLOAT]
flounce[1] (flaʊns) *vb.* **1.** (*intr.; often foll. by about, away, out,* etc.) to move or go with emphatic or impatient movements. ~*n.* **2.** the act of flouncing. [C16: of Scandinavian origin; compare Norwegian *flunsa* to hurry, Swedish *flunsa* to splash]
flounce[2] (flaʊns) *n.* an ornamental gathered ruffle sewn to a garment by its top edge. [C18: from Old French *fronce* wrinkle, from *froncir* to wrinkle, of Germanic origin]
flounc·ing ('flaʊnsɪŋ) *n.* material, such as lace or embroidered fabric, used for making flounces.
floun·der[1] ('flaʊndə) *vb.* (*intr.*) **1.** to struggle; to move with difficulty, as in mud. **2.** to behave awkwardly; make mistakes. ~*n.* **3.** the act of floundering. [C16: probably a blend of FOUNDER[2] + BLUNDER; perhaps influenced by FLOUNDER[2]]
floun·der[2] ('flaʊndə) *n., pl.* **·der** *or* **·ders. 1.** a European flatfish, *Platichthys flesus,* having a greyish-brown body covered with prickly scales: family *Pleuronectidae:* an important food fish. **2.** *U.S.* any flatfish of the families *Bothidae* (turbot, etc.) and *Pleuronectidae* (plaice, halibut, sand dab, etc.). [C14: probably of Scandinavian origin; compare Old Norse *flythra,* Norwegian *flundra*]
flour ('flaʊə) *n.* **1.** a powder, which may be either fine or coarse, prepared by sifting and grinding the meal of a grass, esp. wheat. **2.** any finely powdered substance. ~*vb.* **3.** (*tr.*) to make (grain, etc.) into flour. **4.** (*tr.*) to dredge or sprinkle (food or cooking utensils) with flour. **5.** (of mercury) to break into fine particles on the surface of a metal rather than amalgamating, or to produce such an effect on (a metal). The effect is caused by impurities, esp. sulphur. [C13 *flur* finer portion of meal, FLOWER] —**'flou·r·y** *adj.*
flour·ish ('flʌrɪʃ) *vb.* **1.** (*intr.*) to thrive; prosper. **2.** (*intr.*) to be at the peak of condition. **3.** (*intr.*) to be healthy: *plants flourish in the light.* **4.** to wave or cause to wave in the air with sweeping strokes. **5.** to display or make a display. **6.** to play (a fanfare, etc.) on a musical instrument. **7.** (*intr.*) to embellish writing, characters, etc., with ornamental strokes. **8.** to add decorations or embellishments to (speech or writing). **9.** (*intr.*) an obsolete word for **blossom.** ~*n.* **10.** the act of waving or brandishing. **11.** a showy gesture: *he entered with a flourish.* **12.** an ornamental embellishment in writing. **13.** a display of ornamental language or speech. **14.** a grandiose passage of music. **15.** an ostentatious display or parade. **16.**

Obsolete. **a.** the state of flourishing. **b.** the state of flowering. [C13: from Old French *florir,* ultimately from Latin *flōrēre* to flower, from *flōs* a flower] —**'flour+ish+er** *n.*

flout (flaʊt) *vb.* (when *intr.,* usually foll. by *at*) to show contempt (for); scoff or jeer (at). [C16: perhaps from Middle English *flouten* to play the flute, from Old French *flauter;* compare Dutch *fluiten;* see FLUTE] —**'flout+er** *n.* —**'flout+ing+ly** *adv.*

flow (fləʊ) *vb.* (*mainly intr.*) **1.** (of liquids) to move or be conveyed as in a stream. **2.** (of blood) to circulate around the body. **3.** to move or progress freely as if in a stream: *the crowd flowed into the building.* **4.** to proceed or be produced continuously and effortlessly: *ideas flowed from her pen.* **5.** to show or be marked by smooth or easy movement. **6.** to hang freely or loosely: *her hair flowed down her back.* **7.** to be present in abundance: *wine flows at their parties.* **8.** an informal word for **menstruate. 9.** (of tide water) to advance or rise. Compare **ebb** (sense 1). **10.** (*tr.*) to cover or swamp with liquid; flood. **11.** (of rocks such as slate) to yield to pressure without breaking so that the structure and arrangement of the constituent minerals are altered. ~*n.* **12.** the act, rate, or manner of flowing: *a fast flow.* **13.** a continuous stream or discharge. **14.** continuous progression. **15.** the advancing of the tide. **16.** a stream of molten or solidified lava. **17.** the amount of liquid that flows in a given time. **18.** an informal word for **menstruation. 19.** *Scot.* **a.** a marsh or swamp. **b.** an inlet or basin of the sea. **c.** (cap. when part of a name): *Scapa Flow.* **20. flow of spirits.** natural happiness. [Old English *flōwan;* related to Old Norse *flōa,* Middle Low German *vlōien,* Greek *plein* to float, Sanskrit *plavate* he swims]

flow+age ('fləʊɪdʒ) *n.* **1.** the act of flowing or overflowing or the state of having overflowed. **2.** the liquid that flows or overflows. **3.** a gradual deformation or motion of certain solids, such as asphalt, which flow without fracture.

flow chart *or* **sheet** *n.* a diagrammatic representation of the sequence of operations or equipment in an industrial process, computer program, etc.

flow+er ('flaʊə) *n.* **1. a.** a bloom or blossom on a plant. **b.** a plant that bears blooms or blossoms. **2.** the reproductive structure of angiosperm plants, consisting of stamens and carpels surrounded by petals and sepals all borne on the receptacle. In some plants it is conspicuous and brightly coloured and attracts insects for pollination. Related adj.: **floral. 3.** any similar reproductive structure in other plants. **4.** the prime; peak: *in the flower of his youth.* **5.** the choice or finest product, part, or representative: *the flower of the young men.* **6.** a decoration or embellishment. **7.** *Printing.* a type ornament, used with others in borders, chapter headings, etc. **8.** Also called: **fleuron.** an embellishment or ornamental symbol depicting a flower. **9.** (*pl.*) fine powder, usually produced by sublimation: *flowers of sulphur.* ~*vb.* **10.** (*intr.*) to produce flowers; bloom. **11.** (*intr.*) to reach full growth or maturity. **12.** (*tr.*) to deck or decorate with flowers or floral designs. [C13: from Old French *flor,* from Latin *flōs;* see BLOW[3]] —**'flow·er-ˌlike** *adj.*

flow+er+age ('flaʊərɪdʒ) *n.* **1.** a mass of flowers. **2.** *Now rare.* the process or act of flowering.

flow·er+bed ('flaʊəˌbɛd) *n.* a plot of ground in which flowers are grown in a garden, park, etc.

flow·er-de-luce ('flaʊədəˈluːs) *n., pl.* **flow·ers-de-luce.** an archaic name for the **iris** (sense 2) and **lily** (sense 1). [C16: anglicized variant of French *fleur de lis*]

flow+ered ('flaʊəd) *adj.* **1.** having or abounding in flowers. **2.** decorated with flowers or a floral design.

flow+er+er ('flaʊərə) *n.* a plant that flowers at a specified time or in a specified way: *a late flowerer.*

flow+er+et ('flaʊərɪt) *n.* another name for **floret.**

flow+er girl *n.* **1.** a girl or woman who sells flowers in the street. **2.** *Chiefly U.S.* a young girl who carries flowers in a procession, esp. at weddings.

flow+er head *n.* an inflorescence in which stalkless florets are crowded together at the tip of the stem.

flow+er+ing ('flaʊərɪŋ) *adj.* (of certain species of plants) capable of producing conspicuous flowers: *a flowering ash.*

flow+er+ing ma+ple *n.* any tropical shrub of the malvaceous genus *Abutilon,* esp. *A. hybridum,* having lobed leaves like those of the maple and brightly coloured flowers.

flow+er+less ('flaʊəlɪs) *adj.* designating any plant that does not produce seeds. See **cryptogam.**

flow·er-of-an-hour *n.* a malvaceous Old World herbaceous plant, *Hibiscus trionum,* having pale yellow flowers with a bladder-like calyx. Also called: **bladder ketmia.**

flow·er-peck·er *n.* any small songbird of the family *Dicaeidae,* of SE Asia and Australasia, typically feeding on nectar, berries, and insects.

flow·er+pot ('flaʊəˌpɒt) *n.* a pot in which plants are grown.

flow+er pow+er *n. Informal.* a youth cult of the late 1960s advocating peace and love, using the flower as a symbol; associated with drug-taking. Its adherents were known as **flower children** or **flower people.**

flow+er·y ('flaʊərɪ) *adj.* **1.** abounding in flowers. **2.** decorated with flowers or floral patterns. **3.** like or suggestive of flowers: *a flowery scent.* **4.** (of language or style) elaborate; ornate. —**'flow+er·i+ness** *n.*

flown[1] (fləʊn) *vb.* the past participle of **fly**[1].

flown[2] (fləʊn) *adj.* relating to coloured (usually blue) decoration on porcelain that, during firing, has melted into the surrounding glaze giving a halo-like effect. [probably from the obsolete past participle of FLOW]

flow-on *n. Austral.* a wage or salary increase granted to one group of workers as a consequence of a similar increase granted to another group.

flow sheet *n.* another name for **flow chart.**

Floyd (flɔɪd) *n.* See **Pink Floyd.**

fl. oz. *abbrev. for* fluid ounce.

flu (fluː) *n. Informal.* **1.** (often preceded by *the*) short for **influenza. 2.** any of various viral infections, esp. a respiratory or intestinal infection.

fluc+tu+ant ('flʌktjʊənt) *adj.* inclined to vary or fluctuate; unstable.

fluc+tu+ate ('flʌktjʊˌeɪt) *vb.* **1.** to change or cause to change position constantly; be or make unstable; waver or vary. **2.** (*intr.*) to rise and fall like a wave; undulate. [C17: from Latin *fluctuāre,* from *fluctus* a wave, from *fluere* to flow]

fluc+tu·a+tion (ˌflʌktjʊˈeɪʃən) *n.* **1.** constant change; vacillation; instability. **2.** undulation. **3.** a variation in an animal or plant that is determined by environment rather than heredity.

flue[1] (fluː) *n.* **1.** a shaft, tube, or pipe, esp. as used in a chimney, to carry off smoke, gas, etc. **2.** *Music.* the passage in an organ pipe or flute within which a vibrating air column is set up. See also **flue pipe.** [C16: of unknown origin]

flue[2] (fluː) *n.* loose fluffy matter; down. [C16: from Flemish *vluwe,* from Old French *velu* shaggy] —**'flue·y** *adj.*

flue[3] *or* **flew** (fluː) *n.* a type of fishing net. [Middle English, from Middle Dutch *vlūwe*]

flue[4] (fluː) *n.* another word for **fluke**[1] (senses 1, 3). —**flued** *adj.*

flue-cure *vb.* (*tr.*) to cure (tobacco) by means of radiant heat from pipes or flues connected to a furnace.

flu+en+cy ('fluːənsɪ) *n.* the quality of being fluent, esp. facility in speech or writing.

flu+ent ('fluːənt) *adj.* **1.** able to speak or write a specified foreign language with facility. **2.** spoken or written with facility: *his French is fluent.* **3.** easy and graceful in motion or shape. **4.** flowing or able to flow freely. [C16: from Latin: flowing, *fluere* to flow] —**'flu+ent+ly** *adv.*

flue pipe *or* **flue** *n.* an organ pipe or tubular instrument of the flute family whose sound is produced by the passage of air across a sharp-edged fissure in the side. This sets in motion a vibrating air column within the pipe or instrument.

flue stop *n.* an organ stop controlling a set of flue pipes.

fluff (flʌf) *n.* **1.** soft light particles, such as the down or nap of cotton or wool. **2.** any light downy substance. **3.** an object, matter, etc., of little importance; trifle. **4.** *Informal.* a mistake, esp. in speaking or reading lines or performing music. **5.** *Informal.* a young woman (esp. in the phrase **a bit of fluff**). ~*vb.* **6.** to make or become soft and puffy by shaking or patting; puff up. **7.** *Informal.* to make a mistake in performing (an action, dramatic speech, music, etc.). [C18: perhaps from FLUE[2]]

fluff·y ('flʌfɪ) *adj.* **fluff·i+er, fluff·i+est. 1.** of, resembling, or covered with fluff. **2.** soft and light: *fluffy hair.* —**'fluff·i·ly** *adv.* —**'fluff·i+ness** *n.*

flu+gel+horn ('fluːgəlˌhɔːn) *n.* a type of valved brass instrument consisting of a tube of conical bore with a cup-shaped mouthpiece, used esp. in brass bands. It is a transposing instrument in B flat or C, and has the same range as the cornet in B flat. [German *Flügelhorn,* from *Flügel* wing + *Horn* HORN]

flu+id ('fluːɪd) *n.* **1.** a substance, such as a liquid or gas, that can flow, has no fixed shape, and offers little resistance to an external stress. ~*adj.* **2.** capable of flowing and easily changing shape. **3.** of, concerned with, or using a fluid or fluids. **4.** constantly changing or apt to change. **5.** smooth in shape or movement; flowing. [C15: from Latin *fluidus,* from *fluere* to flow] —**'flu+id+al** *adj.* —**flu+'id+i·ty** *or* **'flu+id+ness** *n.* —**'flu+id+ly** *or* **'flu+id+al+ly** *adv.*

flu+id dram *n.* another name for **drachm.**

flu+id drive *n.* a type of coupling for transmitting power from the engine of a motor vehicle to the transmission, using a torque converter. Also called: **fluid coupling, fluid clutch, fluid flywheel.**

flu·id+ex·tract (ˌfluːɪdˈɛkstrækt) *n.* an alcoholic solution of a vegetable drug, one millilitre of which has an equivalent activity to one gram of the powdered drug.

flu+id+ics (fluːˈɪdɪks) *n.* (*functioning as sing.*) the study and use of systems in which the flow of fluids in tubes simulates the flow of electricity in conductors. Such systems are used in place of electronics in certain applications, such as the control of apparatus. —**flu+'id+ic** *adj.*

flu+id+ize *or* **flu+id+ise** ('fluːɪˌdaɪz) *vb.* (*tr.*) to make fluid, esp. to make (solids) fluid by pulverizing them so that they can be transported in a stream of gas as if they were liquids: *fluidized coal.* —ˌ**flu+id·i+'za+tion** *or* ˌ**flu+id·i+'sa+tion** *n.* —**'flu+id+ˌiz+er** *or* **'flu+id+ˌis+er** *n.*

flu+id me+chan+ics *n.* (*functioning as sing.*) the study of the mechanical and flow properties of fluids, esp. as they apply to practical engineering. Also called: **hydraulics.** See also **hydrodynamics, hydrostatics, hydrokinetics.**

flu+id ounce *n.* **1.** *Brit.* a unit of capacity equal to one twentieth of an Imperial pint. **2.** *U.S.* a unit of capacity equal to one sixteenth of a U.S. pint.

flu+id pres+sure *n.* the pressure exerted by a fluid at any point inside it, determined by the product of its density and the height of the fluid above the point.

fluke[1] (fluːk) *n.* **1.** Also called: **flue.** a flat bladelike projection at the end of the arm of an anchor. **2.** either of the two lobes of the tail of a whale or related animal. **3.** the barb or barbed head of a harpoon, arrow, etc. [C16: perhaps a special use of FLUKE[3] (in the sense: a flounder)]

fluke[2] (flu:k) *n.* **1.** an accidental stroke of luck. **2.** any chance happening. ~*vb.* **3.** (*tr.*) to gain, make, or hit by a fluke. [C19: of unknown origin]

fluke[3] (flu:k) *n.* any parasitic flatworm, such as the blood fluke and liver fluke, of the classes *Monogenea* and *Digenea* (formerly united in a single class *Trematoda*). [Old English *flōc;* related to Old Norse *flōki* flounder, Old Saxon *flaka* sole, Old High German *flah* smooth]

fluk·y *or* **fluk+ey** (ˈflu:kɪ) *adj.* **fluk·i+er, fluk·i+est.** *Informal.* **1.** done or gained by an accident, esp. a lucky one. **2.** variable; uncertain: *fluky weather.* —ˈ**fluk·i+ness** *n.*

flume (flu:m) *n.* **1.** a ravine through which a stream flows. **2.** a narrow artificial channel made for providing water for power, floating logs, etc. ~*vb.* **3.** (*tr.*) to transport (logs) in a flume. [C12: from Old French *flum,* ultimately from Latin *flūmen* stream, from *fluere* to flow]

flum+mer·y (ˈflʌmərɪ) *n., pl.* **+mer·ies. 1.** *Informal.* meaningless flattery; nonsense. **2.** *Chiefly Brit.* a cold pudding of oatmeal, etc. [C17: from Welsh *llymru*]

flum+mox (ˈflʌməks) *vb.* (*tr.*) to perplex or bewilder. [C19: of unknown origin]

flung (flʌŋ) *vb.* the past tense or past participle of **fling.**

flunk (flʌŋk) *Informal, chiefly U.S.* ~*vb.* **1.** to fail or cause to fail to reach the required standard in (an examination, course, etc.). **2.** (*intr.;* foll. by *out*) to be dismissed from a school or college through failure in examinations. ~*n.* **3.** a low grade below the pass standard. [C19: perhaps from FLINCH[1] + FUNK]

flunk·y *or* **flunk+ey** (ˈflʌŋkɪ) *n., pl.* **flunk·ies** *or* **flunk+eys. 1.** a servile or fawning person. **2.** a person who performs menial tasks. **3.** *Usually derogatory.* a manservant in livery. [C18: of unknown origin]

flu+or (ˈflu:ɔ:) *n.* another name for **fluorspar.** [C17: from Latin: a flowing; so called from its use as a metallurgical flux]

flu·or- *combining form.* variant of **fluoro-** before a vowel: *fluorene; fluorine.*

flu·o+rene (ˈflʊəri:n) *n.* a white insoluble crystalline solid used in making dyes. Formula: $(C_6H_4)_2CH_2$.

flu·o+resce (ˌflʊəˈrɛs) *vb.* (*intr.*) to exhibit fluorescence. [C19: back formation from FLUORESCENCE]

flu·o+res·ce·in *or* **flu·o+res·ce·ine** (ˌflʊəˈrɛsɪɪn) *n.* an orange-red crystalline compound that in aqueous solution exhibits a greenish-yellow fluorescence in reflected light and is reddish-orange in transmitted light: used as a marker in sea water and as an indicator. Formula: $C_{20}H_{12}O_5$.

flu·o+res+cence (ˌflʊəˈrɛsəns) *n.* **1.** *Physics.* **a.** the emission of light or other radiation from atoms or molecules that are bombarded by particles, such as electrons, or by radiation from a separate source. The bombarding radiation produces excited atoms, molecules, or ions and these emit photons as they fall back to the ground state. **b.** such an emission of photons that ceases as soon as the bombarding radiation is discontinued. **c.** such an emission of photons for which the average lifetime of the excited atoms and molecules is less than about 10^{-8} seconds. **2.** the radiation emitted as a result of fluorescence. Compare **phosphorescence.** [C19: FLUOR + *-escence* (as in *opalescence*)]

flu·o+res+cent (ˌflʊəˈrɛsᵊnt) *adj.* exhibiting or having the property of fluorescence.

flu·o+res+cent lamp *n.* **1.** a type of lamp in which an electrical gas discharge is maintained in a tube with a thin layer of phosphor on its inside surface. The gas, which is often mercury vapour, emits ultraviolet radiation causing the phosphor to fluoresce. **2.** a type of lamp in which an electrical discharge is maintained in a tube containing a gas such as neon, mercury vapour, or sodium vapour at low pressure. Gas atoms in the discharge are struck by electrons and fluoresce.

flu+or+ic (flu:ˈɔ:rɪk) *adj.* of, concerned with, or produced from fluorine or fluorspar.

fluor·i+date (ˈflʊərɪˌdeɪt) *vb.* to subject (water) to fluoridation.

fluor·i+da+tion (ˌflʊərɪˈdeɪʃən) *n.* the addition of about one part per million of fluorides to the public water supply as a protection against tooth decay.

flu·o+ride (ˈflʊəˌraɪd) *n.* **1.** any salt of hydrofluoric acid, containing the fluoride ion, F^-. **2.** any compound containing fluorine, such as methyl fluoride.

fluor·i+nate (ˈflʊərɪˌneɪt) *vb.* to treat or combine with fluorine. —ˌ**fluor·i·ˈna+tion** *n.*

flu·o+rine (ˈflʊəri:n) *or* **flu·o+rin** *n.* a toxic pungent pale yellow gas of the halogen group that is the most electronegative and reactive of all the elements, occurring principally in fluorspar and cryolite: used in the production of uranium, fluorocarbons, and other chemicals. Symbol: F; atomic no.: 9; atomic wt.: 18.998; valency: 1; density: 1.696 kg/m^3; freezing pt.: −219.62°C; boiling pt.: −188.14°C.

flu·o+rite (ˈflʊəraɪt) *n.* the U.S. name for **fluorspar.**

flu·o+ro- *or before a vowel* **flu·or-** *combining form.* **1.** indicating the presence of fluorine: *fluorocarbon.* **2.** indicating fluorescence: *fluoroscope.*

flu·o+ro+car+bon (ˌflʊərəʊˈkɑ:bᵊn) *n.* any compound derived by replacing all or some of the hydrogen atoms in hydrocarbons by fluorine atoms. Many of them are used as lubricants, solvents, and coatings. See also **Freon, polytetrafluoroethylene.**

flu·o+rom+e·ter (ˌflʊəˈrɒmɪtə) *or* **flu·o+rim+e·ter** (ˌflʊəˈrɪmɪtə) *n.* **1.** an instrument for inducing fluorescence by irradiation and for examination of the emission spectrum of the resulting fluorescent light. **2.** a device for detecting and measuring ultraviolet radiation by determining the amount of fluorescence that it produces from a phosphor. —**flu·o+ro+met+ric** (ˌflʊərəʊˈmɛtrɪk) *or* **flu·o+ri+met+ric** (ˌflʊərɪˈmɛtrɪk) *adj.* —ˌ**flu·o+ˈrom+e·try** *or* ˌ**flu·o+ˈrim+e·try** *n.*

fluor·o+scope (ˈflʊərəˌskəʊp) *n.* a device consisting of a fluorescent screen and an x-ray source that enables an x-ray image of an object, person, or part to be observed directly. —**fluor·o+scop+ic** (ˌflʊərəˈskɒpɪk) *adj.* —ˌ**fluor·o+ˈscop·i·cal+ly** *adv.*

fluor+os+co+py (flʊəˈrɒskəpɪ) *n.* examination of a person or object by means of a fluoroscope.

fluo+ro+sis (flʊəˈrəʊsɪs) *n.* fluoride poisoning, due to ingestion of too much fluoride in drinking water over a long period or to ingestion of pesticides containing fluoride salts. Chronic fluorosis results in mottling of the teeth of children.

flu+or+spar (ˈflʊəˌspɑ:), **flu+or,** *or U.S.* **flu·o+rite** *n.* a soft often fluorescent mineral consisting of calcium fluoride in cubic crystalline form, widespread in veins of metallic ores or in sedimentary rock: the chief source of fluorine and its compounds. Formula: CaF_2.

flur+ry (ˈflʌrɪ) *n., pl.* **+ries. 1.** a sudden commotion. **2.** a light gust of wind or rain or fall of snow. **3.** *Stock exchange.* a sudden brief increase in trading or fluctuation in stock prices. **4.** the death spasms of a harpooned whale. ~*vb.* **+ries, +ry+ing, +ried. 5.** to confuse or bewilder or be confused or bewildered. [C17: from obsolete *flurr* to scatter, perhaps formed on analogy with HURRY]

flush[1] (flʌʃ) *vb.* **1.** to blush or cause to blush. **2.** to flow or flood or cause to flow or flood with or as if with water. **3.** to glow or shine or cause to glow or shine with a rosy colour. **4.** to send a volume of water quickly through (a pipe, channel, etc.) or into (a toilet) for the purpose of cleansing, emptying, etc. **5.** (*tr.; usually passive*) to excite or elate. ~*n.* **6.** a rosy colour, esp. in the cheeks; blush. **7.** a sudden flow or gush, as of water. **8.** a feeling of excitement or elation: *the flush of success.* **9.** early bloom; freshness: *the flush of youth.* **10.** redness of the skin, esp. of the face, as from the effects of a fever, alcohol, etc. ~*adj.* **11.** having a ruddy or heightened colour. [C16 (in the sense: to gush forth): perhaps from FLUSH[3]] —ˈ**flush+er** *n.*

flush[2] (flʌʃ) *adj.* (*usually postpositive*) **1.** level or even with another surface. **2.** directly adjacent; continuous. **3.** *Informal.* having plenty of money. **4.** *Informal.* abundant or plentiful, as money. **5.** full of vigour. **6.** full to the brim or to the point of overflowing. **7.** *Printing.* having an even margin, right or left, with no indentations. **8.** (of a blow) accurately delivered. **9.** (of a vessel) having no superstructure built above the flat level of the deck. ~*adv.* **10.** so as to be level or even. **11.** directly or squarely. ~*vb.* (*tr.*) **12.** to cause (surfaces) to be on the same level or in the same plane. **13.** to enrich the diet of (a ewe) during the breeding season. ~*n.* **14.** a period of fresh growth of leaves, shoots, etc. [C18: probably from FLUSH[1] (in the sense: spring out)] —ˈ**flush+ness** *n.*

flush[3] (flʌʃ) *vb.* (*tr.*) to rouse (game, wild creatures, etc.) and put to flight. [C13 *flusshen,* perhaps of imitative origin]

flush[4] (flʌʃ) *n.* (in poker and similar games) a hand containing only one suit. [C16: from Old French *flus,* from Latin *fluxus* FLUX]

Flush+ing (ˈflʌʃɪŋ) *n.* a port in the SW Netherlands, in Zeeland province, on Walcheren Island, at the mouth of the West Scheldt river: the first Dutch city to throw off Spanish rule (1572). Pop.: 41 085 (1971). Dutch name: **Vlissingen.**

flus+ter (ˈflʌstə) *vb.* **1.** to make or become confused, nervous, or upset. ~*n.* **2.** a state of confusion or agitation. [C15: probably of Scandinavian origin; compare Icelandic *flaustr* to hurry, *flaustra* to bustle]

flute (flu:t) *n.* **1.** a wind instrument consisting of an open cylindrical tube of wood or metal having holes in the side stopped either by the fingers or by pads controlled by keys. The breath is directed across a mouth hole cut in the side, causing the air in the tube to vibrate. Range: about three octaves upwards from middle C. **2.** any pipe blown directly on the principle of a flue pipe, either by means of a mouth hole or through a fipple. **3.** *Architect.* a rounded shallow concave groove on the shaft of a column, pilaster, etc. **4.** a groove or furrow in cloth, etc. **5.** anything shaped like a flute. ~*vb.* **6.** to produce or utter (sounds) in the manner or tone of a flute. **7.** (*tr.*) to make grooves or furrows in. [C14: from Old French *flahute,* via Old Provençal, from Vulgar Latin *flabeolum* (unattested); perhaps also influenced by Old Provençal *laut* lute; see FLAGEOLET] —ˈ**flute+ˌlike** *adj.* —ˈ**flut·y** *adj.*

flut+ed (ˈflu:tɪd) *adj.* **1.** (esp. of the shaft of a column) having flutes. **2.** sounding like a flute.

flut+er (ˈflu:tə) *n.* **1.** a craftsman who makes flutes or fluting. **2.** a tool used to make flutes or fluting. **3.** a less common word, used esp. in folk music, for **flautist.**

flut+ing (ˈflu:tɪŋ) *n.* **1.** a design or decoration of flutes on a column, pilaster, etc. **2.** grooves or furrows, as in cloth.

flut+ist (ˈflu:tɪst) *n. Now chiefly U.S.* a variant spelling of **flautist.**

flut+ter (ˈflʌtə) *vb.* **1.** to wave or cause to wave rapidly; flap. **2.** (*intr.*) (of birds, butterflies, etc.) to flap the wings. **3.** (*intr.*) to move, esp. downwards, with an irregular motion. **4.** (*intr.*) *Pathol.* (of the auricles of the heart) to beat abnormally rapidly, esp. in a regular rhythm. **5.** to be or make nervous or restless. **6.** (*intr.*) to move about restlessly. **7.** *Swimming.* to cause (the legs) to move up and down in a flutter kick or (of the legs) to move in this way. **8.** (*tr.*) *Brit. informal.* to wager or gamble (a small amount of money). ~*n.* **9.** a quick flapping or vibrating motion. **10.** a state of nervous excitement or confusion. **11.** excited interest; sensation; stir. **12.** *Brit. informal.* a modest bet or wager. **13.** *Pathol.* an abnormally rapid beating of the auricles of the heart (200 to 400 beats per minute), esp. in a regular rhythm, sometimes resulting in heart block. **14.** *Electronics.* a slow variation in pitch in a sound-reproducing system, similar to wow but occurring at higher frequencies. **15.** a potentially dangerous oscillation of an aircraft, or part of an aircraft, caused by the interaction of aerodynamic forces, structural elastic reactions, and inertia. **16.** *Swimming.* See **flutter kick. 17.** Also called: **flutter tonguing.** *Music.* a method of sounding a wind instrument, esp. the flute, with a rolling movement of the tongue. [Old English *floterian* to float to and fro; related to German *flattern;* see FLOAT] —**'flut·ter·er** *n.* —**'flut·ter·ing·ly** *adv.* —**'flut·ter·y** *adj.*

flut·ter·board ('flʌtəˌbɔːd) *n. U.S.* an oblong board or piece of polystyrene plastic used by swimmers in training or practice. Brit. word: **float.**

flut·ter kick *n.* a type of kick used in certain swimming strokes, such as the crawl, in which the legs are held straight and alternately moved up and down rapidly in the water.

flu·vi·al ('fluːvɪəl) *or* **flu·vi·a·tile** ('fluːvɪəˌtaɪl, -tɪl) *adj.* of, relating to, or occurring in a river: *fluvial deposits.* [C14: from Latin *fluviālis,* from *fluvius* river, from *fluere* to flow]

flu·vi·o·ma·rine (ˌfluːvɪˌəʊmə'riːn) *adj.* **1.** (of deposits) formed by joint action of the sea and a river or stream. **2.** (esp. of fish) able to live in both rivers and the sea. [C19: *fluvio-,* from Latin *fluvius* river + MARINE]

flux (flʌks) *n.* **1.** a flow or discharge. **2.** continuous change; instability. **3.** a substance, such as borax or salt, that gives a low melting-point mixture with a metal oxide. It is used for cleaning metal surfaces during soldering, etc., and for protecting the surfaces of liquid metals. **4.** *Metallurgy.* a chemical used to increase the fluidity of refining slags in order to promote the rate of chemical reaction. **5.** a similar substance used in the making of glass. **6.** *Physics.* **a.** the rate of flow of particles, energy, or a fluid, such as that of neutrons (**neutron flux**) or of light energy (**luminous flux**). **b.** the strength of a field in a given area expressed as the product of the area and the component of the field strength at right angles to the area: *magnetic flux; electric flux.* **7.** *Pathol.* an excessive discharge of fluid from the body, such as watery faeces in diarrhoea. **8.** the act or process of melting; fusion. ~*vb.* **9.** to make or become fluid. **10.** (*tr.*) to apply flux to (a metal, soldered joint, etc.). **11.** (*tr.*) an obsolete word for **purge.** [C14: from Latin *fluxus* a flow, from *fluere* to flow]

flux den·si·ty *n. Physics.* the amount of flux per unit of cross-sectional area.

flux·ion ('flʌkʃən) *n.* **1.** *Maths, obsolete.* the rate of change of a function; derivative. **2.** a less common word for **flux** (senses 1, 2). [C16: from Late Latin *fluxiō* a flowing] —**'flux·ion·al** *or* **'flux·ion·ar·y** *adj.* —**'flux·ion·al·ly** *adv.*

flux·me·ter ('flʌksˌmiːtə) *n.* any instrument for measuring magnetic flux, usually by measuring the current that it induces in a coil.

fly[1] (flaɪ) *vb.* **flies, fly·ing, flew, flown. 1.** (*intr.*) (of birds, aircraft, etc.) to move through the air in a controlled manner using aerodynamic forces. **2.** to travel over (an area of land or sea) in an aircraft. **3.** to operate (an aircraft or spacecraft). **4.** to float, flutter, or be displayed in the air or cause to float, etc., in this way: *to fly a kite; they flew the flag.* **5.** to transport or be transported by or through the air by aircraft, wind, etc. **6.** (*intr.*) to move or be moved very quickly, forcibly, or suddenly: *she came flying towards me; the door flew open.* **7.** (*intr.*) to pass swiftly: *time flies.* **8.** to escape from (an enemy, place, etc.); flee: *he flew the country.* **9.** (*intr.;* may be foll. by *at* or *upon*) to attack a person. **10.** (*intr.*) to have a sudden outburst: *he flew into a rage again.* **11.** (*intr.*) (of money, etc.) to vanish rapidly. **12.** (*tr.*) *Falconry.* (of hawks) to fly at (quarry) in attack: *peregrines fly rooks.* **13.** (*tr.*) *Theatre.* to suspend (scenery) above the stage so that it may be lowered into view. **14. fly a kite. a.** to procure money by an accommodation bill. **b.** to experiment with something. **15. fly high.** *Informal.* **a.** to have a high aim. **b.** to prosper or flourish. **16. fly in the face of.** See **face** (sense 18). **17. fly off the handle.** *Informal.* to lose one's temper. **18. fly the coop.** *U.S. informal.* to leave suddenly. **19. go fly a kite.** *U.S. informal.* go away. **20. let fly.** *Informal.* **a.** to lose one's temper (with a person): *she really let fly at him.* **b.** to shoot or throw (an object). ~*n., pl.* **flies. 21.** (*often pl.*) Also called: **fly front.** a closure that conceals a zip, buttons, or other fastening, by having one side overlapping, as on trousers. **22. a.** a flap forming the entrance to a tent. **b.** a piece of canvas drawn over the ridgepole of a tent to form an outer roof. **23.** short for **flywheel. 24.** the horizontal weighted arm of a fly press. **25. a.** the outer edge of a flag. **b.** the distance from the outer edge of a flag to the staff. Compare **hoist** (sense 8). **26.** *Brit.* a light one-horse covered carriage formerly let out on hire. **27.** *Printing.* **a.** a device for transferring printed sheets from the press to a flat pile. **b.** Also called: **flyhand.** a person who collects and stacks printed matter from a printing press. **c.** a piece of paper folded once to make four pages, with printing only on the first page. **28.** (*pl.*) *Theatre.* the space above the stage out of view of the audience, used for storing scenery, etc. **29.** *Rare.* the act of flying. [Old English *flēogan;* related to Old Frisian *fliāga,* Old High German *fliogan,* Old Norse *fljūga*] —**'fly·a·ble** *adj.*

fly[2] (flaɪ) *n., pl.* **flies. 1.** any dipterous insect, esp. the housefly, characterized by active flight. See also **horsefly, blowfly, tsetse fly, crane fly. 2.** any of various similar but unrelated insects, such as the caddis fly, firefly, dragonfly, and chalcid fly. **3.** *Angling.* a lure made from a fish-hook dressed with feathers, tinsel, etc., to resemble any of various flies or nymphs: used in fly-fishing. See also **dry fly, wet fly. 4.** (in southern Africa) an area that is infested with the tsetse fly. **5. drink with the flies.** *Austral. slang.* to drink alone. **6. fly in the ointment.** *Informal.* a slight flaw that detracts from value, completeness, or enjoyment. **7. fly on the wall.** a person who watches others, while not being noticed himself. **8. there are no flies on him, her,** etc. *Informal.* he, she, etc., is no fool. [Old English *flēoge;* related to Old Norse *fluga,* Old High German *flioga;* see FLY[1]] —**'fly·less** *adj.*

fly[3] (flaɪ) *adj. Slang, chiefly Brit.* knowing and sharp; smart. [C19: of uncertain origin]

fly ag·a·ric *n.* a saprophytic agaricaceous woodland fungus, *Amanita muscaria,* having a scarlet cap with white warts and white gills: poisonous but rarely fatal. See also **amanita.** [so named from its use as a poison on flypaper]

fly ash *n.* fine solid particles of ash carried into the air during combustion, esp. the combustion of pulverized fuel in power stations.

fly·a·way ('flaɪəˌweɪ) *adj.* **1.** (of hair or clothing) loose and fluttering. **2.** frivolous or flighty; giddy. ~*n.* **3.** a person who is frivolous or flighty.

fly·back ('flaɪˌbæk) *n.* the fast return of the spot on a cathode-ray tube after completion of each trace.

fly·blow ('flaɪˌbləʊ) *vb.* **·blows, ·blow·ing, ·blew, ·blown. 1.** (*tr.*) to contaminate, esp. with the eggs or larvae of the blowfly; taint. ~*n.* **2.** (*usually pl.*) the egg or young larva of a blowfly, deposited on meat, paper, etc.

fly·blown ('flaɪˌbləʊn) *adj.* **1.** covered with flyblows. **2.** contaminated; tainted.

fly·boat ('flaɪˌbɒat) *n.* any small swift boat.

fly·book ('flaɪˌbʊk) *n.* a small case or wallet used by anglers for storing artificial flies.

fly·by ('flaɪˌbaɪ) *n., pl.* **·bys.** a flight past a particular position or target, esp. the close approach of a spacecraft to a planet or satellite for investigation of conditions.

fly-by-night *Informal.* ~*adj.* **1.** unreliable or untrustworthy, esp. in finance. **2.** brief; impermanent. ~*n.* **3.** an untrustworthy person, esp. one who departs secretly or by night to avoid paying debts. **4.** a person who goes out at night to places of entertainment.

fly·catch·er ('flaɪˌkætʃə) *n.* **1.** any small insectivorous songbird of the Old World subfamily *Muscicapinae,* having small slender bills fringed with bristles: family *Muscicapidae.* See also **spotted flycatcher. 2.** any American passerine bird of the family *Tyrannidae.*

fly·er ('flaɪə) *n.* a variant spelling of **flier.**

fly-fish *vb.* (*intr.*) *Angling.* to fish using artificial flies as lures. See **dry fly, wet fly.** —**'fly-ˌfish·er** *n.* —**'fly-ˌfish·ing** *n.*

fly half *n. Rugby.* another name for **stand-off half.**

fly·ing ('flaɪɪŋ) *adj.* **1.** (*prenominal*) hurried; fleeting: *a flying visit.* **2.** (*prenominal*) designed for fast action. **3.** hanging, waving, or floating freely: *flying hair.* **4.** *Nautical.* (of a sail) not hauled in tight against the wind. ~*n.* **5.** the act of piloting, navigating, or travelling in an aircraft. **6.** (*modifier*) relating to, capable of, accustomed to, or adapted for flight: *a flying machine.* **7.** (*modifier*) moving or passing quickly on or as if on wings: *flying hours.* ~*adv.* **8.** *Nautical.* freely flapping in the wind.

fly·ing boat *n.* a seaplane in which the fuselage consists of a hull that provides buoyancy in the water.

fly·ing bridge *n.* an auxiliary bridge of a vessel, usually built above or far outboard of the main bridge.

fly·ing but·tress *n.* a buttress supporting a wall or other structure by an arch or part of an arch that transmits the thrust outwards and downwards. Also called: **arc-boutant.**

fly·ing cir·cus *n.* **1.** an exhibition of aircraft aerobatics. **2.** the aircraft and men who take part in such exhibitions.

fly·ing col·ours *pl. n.* conspicuous success; triumph: *he passed his test with flying colours.*

fly·ing doc·tor *n.* (in areas of sparse or scattered population) a doctor who visits patients by aircraft.

Fly·ing Dutch·man *n. Legend.* **1.** a phantom ship sighted in bad weather, esp. off the Cape of Good Hope. **2.** the captain of this ship.

fly·ing field *n.* a small airport; an airfield.

fly·ing fish *n.* any marine teleost fish of the family *Exocoetidae,* common in warm and tropical seas, having enlarged winglike pectoral fins used for gliding above the surface of the water.

fly·ing fox *n.* **1.** any large fruit bat, esp. any of the genus *Pteropus* of tropical Africa and Asia: family *Pteropodidae.* **2.** *Austral.* a cable mechanism used for transportation across a river, gorge, etc.

fly·ing frog *n.* any of several tropical frogs of the family *Rhacophoridae,* esp. *Rhacophorus reinwardtii* of Malaya, that glide between trees by means of long webbed digits.

fly·ing gur·nard *n.* any marine spiny-finned gurnard-like fish of the mostly tropical family *Dactylopteridae,* having enlarged fan-shaped pectoral fins used to glide above the surface of the sea.

fly·ing jib *n.* the jib set furthest forward or outboard on a vessel with two or more jibs.

fly·ing le·mur *n.* either of the two arboreal mammals of the genus *Cynocephalus,* family *Cynocephalidae,* and order *Dermoptera,* of S and SE Asia. They resemble lemurs but have a fold of skin between the limbs enabling movement by gliding leaps. Also called: **colugo.**

fly·ing liz·ard *or* **drag·on** *n.* any lizard of the genus *Draco,* of S and SE Asia, having an extensible fold of skin on each side of the body, used to make gliding leaps: family *Agamidae* (agamas).

fly+ing mare *n.* a wrestling throw in which a wrestler seizes his opponent's arm or head (**flying head mare**) and turns to throw him over his shoulder.

fly+ing of+fic+er *n.* an officer holding commissioned rank senior to a pilot officer but junior to a flight lieutenant in the British and certain other air forces.

fly+ing pha+lan+ger *n.* any nocturnal arboreal phalanger of the genus *Petaurus,* of E Australia and New Guinea, having black-striped greyish fur and moving with gliding leaps using folds of skin between the hind limbs and forelimbs.

fly+ing sau+cer *n.* any unidentified disc-shaped flying object alleged to come from outer space.

fly+ing squad *n.* a small group of police, soldiers, etc., ready to move into action quickly.

fly+ing squir+rel *n.* any nocturnal sciurine rodent of the subfamily *Petauristinae,* of Asia and North America. Furry folds of skin between the forelegs and hind legs enable these animals to move by gliding leaps.

fly+ing start *n.* **1.** Also called (informal): **flier.** (in sprinting) a start by a competitor anticipating the starting signal. **2.** a start to a race or time trial in which the competitor is already travelling at speed as he passes the starting line. **3.** any promising beginning. **4.** an initial advantage over others.

fly+ing wing *n.* an aircraft consisting mainly of one large wing and no fuselage.

fly+leaf ('flaɪˌliːf) *n., pl.* **+leaves.** the inner leaf of the endpaper of a book, pasted to the first leaf.

fly+o·ver ('flaɪˌəʊvə) *n.* **1.** Also called: **overpass.** *Brit.* **a.** an intersection of two roads at which one is carried over the other by a bridge. **b.** such a bridge. **2.** the U.S. name for a **fly-past.**

fly+pa·per ('flaɪˌpeɪpə) *n.* paper with a sticky and poisonous coating, usually hung from the ceiling to trap flies.

fly-past *n.* a ceremonial flight of aircraft over a given area. Also called (esp. in the U.S.): **flyover.**

fly press *n.* a hand-operated press in which a horizontal beam with heavy steel balls attached to the ends gives additional momentum to the descending member.

Fly Riv+er *n.* a river in W Papua New Guinea, flowing southeast to the Gulf of Papua. Length: about 1300 km (800 miles).

fly rod *n.* a light flexible rod, now usually made of fibreglass or split cane, used in fly-fishing.

Flysch (flɪʃ) *n.* (*sometimes not cap.*) deposits of late Cretaceous and early Tertiary age that occur in the Alps, consisting of sandstones, marls, shales, and clays. [Swiss German]

fly sheet *n.* **1. a.** a flap forming the entrance to a tent. **b.** a piece of canvas drawn over the ridgepole of a tent to form an outer roof. **2.** a short handbill or circular.

fly+speck ('flaɪˌspɛk) *n.* **1.** the small speck of the excrement of a fly. **2.** a small spot or speck. ~*vb.* **3.** (*tr.*) to mark with flyspecks.

fly spray *n.* a liquid used to destroy flies and other insects, sprayed from an aerosol.

flyte (flaɪt) *vb.* a variant spelling of **flite.**

fly+trap ('flaɪˌtræp) *n.* **1.** any of various insectivorous plants, esp. Venus's flytrap. **2.** a device for catching flies.

fly way *n.* the usual route used by birds when migrating.

fly+weight ('flaɪˌweɪt) *n.* **1. a.** a professional boxer weighing not more than 112 pounds (51 kg). **b.** an amateur boxer weighing 48–51 kg (106-112 pounds). **c.** (*as modifier*): *a flyweight contest.* **2.** (in Olympic wrestling) a wrestler not more than 115 pounds (52 kg).

fly+wheel ('flaɪˌwiːl) *n.* a heavy wheel that stores kinetic energy and smoothes the operation of a reciprocating engine by maintaining a constant speed of rotation over the whole cycle.

Fm *the chemical symbol for* fermium.

FM *abbrev. for* frequency modulation.

fm. *abbrev. for:* **1.** Also: **fm** fathom. **2.** from.

F.M. *abbrev. for* Field Marshal.

FMN *n. Biochem.* flavin mononucleotide; a phosphoric ester of riboflavin that acts as the prosthetic group for many flavoproteins. See also **FAD.**

f-num+ber *or* **f num+ber** *n. Photog.* the numerical value of the relative aperture. If the relative aperture is f8, 8 is the f-number and indicates that the focal length of the lens is 8 times the size of the lens aperture. See also **T-number.**

fo. *abbrev. for* folio.

F.O. *abbrev. for:* **1.** *Army.* Field Officer. **2.** *Air Force.* Flying Officer. **3.** Foreign Office.

foal (fəʊl) *n.* **1.** the young of a horse or related animal. ~*vb.* **2.** to give birth to (a foal). [Old English *fola;* related to Old Frisian *fola,* Old High German *folo* foal, Latin *pullus* young creature, Greek *pōlos* foal]

foam (fəʊm) *n.* **1.** a mass of small bubbles of gas formed on the surface of a liquid, such as the froth produced by agitating a solution of soap or detergent in water. **2.** frothy saliva sometimes formed in and expelled from the mouth, as in rabies. **3.** the frothy sweat of a horse or similar animal. **4. a.** any of a number of light cellular solids made by creating bubbles of gas in the liquid material and solidifying it: used as insulators and in packaging. **b.** (*as modifier*): *foam rubber; foam plastic.* **5.** a colloid consisting of a gas suspended in a liquid. **6.** a mixture of chemicals sprayed from a fire extinguisher onto a burning substance to create a stable layer of bubbles which smothers the flames. **7.** a poetic word for the **sea.** ~*vb.* **8.** to produce or cause to produce foam; froth. **9.** (*intr.*) to be very angry (esp. in the phrase **foam at the mouth**). [Old English *fām;* related to Old High German *feim,* Latin *spūma,* Sanskrit *phena*] —**'foam+less** *adj.* —**'foam+ˌlike** *adj.*

foam+flow·er ('fəʊmˌflaʊə) *n.* a perennial saxifragaceous plant, *Tiarella cordifolia,* of North America and Asia, having spring-blooming white flowers.

foam·y ('fəʊmɪ) *adj.* **foam·i+er, foam·i+est.** of, resembling, consisting of, or covered with foam. —**'foam·i+ly** *adv.* —**'foam·i+ness** *n.*

fob[1] (fɒb) *n.* **1.** a chain or ribbon by which a pocket watch is attached to a waistcoat. **2.** any ornament hung on such a chain. **3.** a small pocket in a man's waistcoat, etc., for holding a watch. [C17: probably of Germanic origin; compare German dialect *Fuppe* pocket]

fob[2] (fɒb) *vb.* **fobs, fob+bing, fobbed.** (*tr.*) an archaic word for **cheat.** [C15: probably from German *foppen* to trick]

f.o.b. *or* **F.O.B.** *Commerce. abbrev. for* free on board.

fob off *vb.* (*tr., adv.*) **1.** to appease or trick (a person) with lies or excuses. **2.** to dispose of (goods) by trickery.

F.o.C. *abbrev. for* father of the chapel.

fo+cal ('fəʊkᵊl) *adj.* **1.** of or relating to a focus. **2.** situated at, passing through, or measured from the focus. —**'fo+cal+ly** *adv.*

fo+cal in+fec+tion *n.* a bacterial infection limited to a specific part of the body, such as the tonsils or a gland.

fo+cal+ize *or* **fo+cal+ise** ('fəʊkəˌlaɪz) *vb.* a less common word for **focus.** —ˌ**fo+cal·i+'za+tion** *or* ˌ**fo+cal·i+'sa+tion** *n.*

fo+cal length *or* **dis+tance** *n.* the distance from the focal point of a lens or mirror to the reflecting surface of the mirror or the centre point of the lens.

fo+cal plane *n.* **1.** the plane that is perpendicular to the axis of a lens or mirror and passes through the focal point. **2.** the plane in a telescope, camera, or other optical instrument in which a real image is in focus.

fo+cal point *n.* **1.** Also called: **principal focus, focus.** the point on the axis of a lens or mirror to which parallel rays of light converge or from which they appear to diverge after refraction or reflection. **2.** a central point of attention or interest.

fo+cal ra+ti·o *n. Photog.* another name for **f-number.**

Foch (*French* fɔʃ) *n.* **Fer·di·nand** (fɛrdiˈnɑ̃). 1851–1929, marshal of France; commander in chief of Allied armies on the Western front in World War I (1918).

fo'c's'le *or* **fo'c'sle** ('fəʊksᵊl) *n.* a variant spelling of **forecastle.**

fo+cus ('fəʊkəs) *n., pl.* **+cus·es** *or* **+ci** (-saɪ). **1.** a point of convergence of light or other electromagnetic radiation, particles, sound waves, etc., or a point from which they appear to diverge. **2.** another name for **focal point** or **focal length. 3.** *Optics.* the state of an optical image when it is distinct and clearly defined or the state of an instrument producing this image: *the picture is in focus; the telescope is out of focus.* **4.** a point upon which attention, activity, etc., is directed or concentrated. **5.** *Geom.* a fixed reference point on the concave side of a conic section, used when defining its eccentricity. **6.** the point beneath the earth's surface at which an earthquake originates. **7.** *Pathol.* the main site of an infection or a localized region of diseased tissue. ~*vb.* **+cus·es, +cus+ing, +cused. 8.** to bring or come to a focus or into focus. **9.** (*tr.; often foll. by on*) to fix attention (on); concentrate. [C17: via New Latin from Latin: hearth, fireplace] —**'fo+cus+a·ble** *adj.* —**'fo+cus+er** *n.*

fod+der ('fɒdə) *n.* **1.** bulk feed for livestock, esp. hay, straw, etc. **2.** raw experience or material: *fodder for the imagination.* ~*vb.* **3.** (*tr.*) to supply (livestock) with fodder. [Old English *fōdor;* related to Old Norse *fōthr,* Old High German *fuotar;* see FOOD, FORAGE]

foe (fəʊ) *n. Formal or literary.* another word for **enemy.** [Old English *fāh* hostile; related to Old High German *fēhan* to hate, Old Norse *feikn* dreadful; see FEUD[1]]

foehn (fɜːn; *German* føːn) *n. Meteorol.* a variant spelling of **föhn.**

foe+man ('fəʊmən) *n., pl.* **+men.** *Archaic and poetic.* an enemy in war; foe.

foe+tal ('fiːtᵊl) *adj.* a variant spelling of **fetal.**

foe+ta+tion (fiːˈteɪʃən) *n.* a variant spelling of **fetation.**

foe+ti+cide ('fiːtɪˌsaɪd) *n.* a variant spelling of **feticide.** —ˌ**foe+ti+'cid+al** *adj.*

foet+id ('fɛtɪd, 'fiː-) *adj.* a variant spelling of **fetid.** —**'foet+id+ly** *adv.* —**'foet+id+ness** *n.*

foe+tor ('fiːtə) *n.* a variant spelling of **fetor.**

foe+tus ('fiːtəs) *n., pl.* **+tus·es.** a variant spelling of **fetus.**

fog[1] (fɒg) *n.* **1.** a mass of droplets of condensed water vapour suspended in the air, often greatly reducing visibility, corresponding to a cloud but at a lower level. **2.** a cloud of any substance in the atmosphere reducing visibility. **3.** a state of mental uncertainty or obscurity. **4.** *Photog.* a blurred or discoloured area on a developed negative, print, or transparency caused by the action of extraneous light, incorrect development, etc. **5.** a colloid or suspension consisting of liquid particles dispersed in a gas. ~*vb.* **fogs, fog+ging, fogged. 6.** to envelop or become enveloped with or as if with fog. **7.** to confuse or become confused: *to fog an issue.* **8.** *Photog.* to produce fog on (a negative, print, or transparency) or (of a negative, print, or transparency) to be affected by fog. [C16: perhaps back formation from *foggy* damp, boggy, from FOG[2]]

fog[2] (fɒg) *n. Chiefly northern Brit.* **a.** a second growth of grass after the first mowing. **b.** grass left to grow long in winter. [C14: probably of Scandinavian origin; compare Norwegian *fogg* rank grass]

fog bank *n.* a distinct mass of fog, esp. at sea.

fog+bound ('fɒgˌbaʊnd) *adj.* **1.** prevented from operation by fog: *the airport was fogbound.* **2.** obscured by or enveloped in fog: *the skyscraper was fogbound.*

fog·bow ('fɒg,bəʊ) *n.* a faint arc of light sometimes seen in a fog bank. Also called: **seadog, white rainbow.**
fog·dog ('fɒg,dɒg) *n.* a whitish spot sometimes seen in fog near the horizon. Also called: **seadog.**
fogged (fɒgd) *or* **fog·gy** *adj. Photog.* affected or obscured by fog.
Fog·gia (*Italian* 'fɔddʒa) *n.* a city in SE Italy, in Apulia: seat of Emperor Frederick II; centre for Carbonari revolutionary societies in the revolts of 1820, 1848, and 1860. Pop.: 151 203 (1975 est.).
fog·gy ('fɒgɪ) *adj.* **·gi·er, ·gi·est. 1.** thick with fog. **2.** obscure or confused. **3.** another word for **fogged.** —**'fog·gi·ly** *adv.* —**'fog·gi·ness** *n.*
fog·horn ('fɒg,hɔːn) *n.* **1.** a mechanical instrument sounded at intervals to serve as a warning to vessels in fog. **2.** *Informal.* a loud deep resounding voice.
fog lev·el *n.* the density produced by the development of photographic materials that have not been exposed to light or other actinic radiation. It forms part of the characteristic curve of a particular material.
fog sig·nal *n.* a signal used to warn railway engine drivers in fog, consisting of a detonator placed on the line.
fo·gy *or* **fo·gey** ('fəʊgɪ) *n., pl.* **·gies** *or* **·geys.** an extremely fussy, old-fashioned, or conservative person (esp. in the phrase **old fogy**). [C18: of unknown origin] —**'fo·gy·ish** *or* **'fo·gey·ish** *adj.* —**'fo·gy·ism** *or* **'fo·gey·ism** *n.*
föhn *or* **foehn** (fɜːn; *German* føːn) *n.* a warm dry wind blowing down the northern slopes of the Alps. It originates as moist air blowing from the Mediterranean, rising on reaching the Alps and cooling at the saturated adiabatic lapse rate, and descending on the leeward side, warming at the dry adiabatic lapse rate, thus gaining heat. See also **lapse rate.** [German, from Old High German *phōnno,* from Latin *favōnius;* related to *fovēre* to warm]
foi·ble ('fɔɪbᵊl) *n.* **1.** a slight peculiarity or minor weakness; idiosyncrasy. **2.** the most vulnerable part of a sword's blade, from the middle to the tip. Compare **forte**[1] (sense 2). [C17: from obsolete French, from obsolete adj.: FEEBLE]
foie gras (*French* fwa'grɑ) *n.* See **pâté de foie gras.**
foil[1] (fɔɪl) *vb. (tr.)* **1.** to baffle or frustrate (a person, attempt, etc.). **2.** *Hunting.* (of hounds, hunters, etc.) to obliterate the scent left by a hunted animal or (of a hunted animal) to run back over its own trail. **3.** *Archaic.* to repulse or defeat (an attack or assailant). ~*n.* **4.** *Hunting.* any scent that obscures the trail left by a hunted animal. **5.** *Archaic.* a setback or defeat. [C13 *foilen* to trample, from Old French *fouler,* from Old French *fuler* tread down, FULL[2]] —**'foil·a·ble** *adj.*
foil[2] (fɔɪl) *n.* **1.** metal in the form of very thin sheets: *gold foil; tin foil.* **2.** the thin metallic sheet forming the backing of a mirror. **3.** a thin leaf of shiny metal set under a gemstone to add brightness or colour. **4.** a person or thing that gives contrast to another. **5.** *Architect.* a small arc between cusps, esp. as used in Gothic window tracery. **6.** short for **aerofoil** or **hydrofoil.** ~*vb. (tr.)* **7.** to back or cover with foil. **8.** Also: **foliate.** *Architect.* to ornament (windows, etc.) with foils. **9.** *Rare.* to act as a foil to. [C14: from Old French *foille,* from Latin *folia* leaves, plural of *folium*]
foil[3] (fɔɪl) *n.* a light slender flexible sword tipped by a button and usually having a bell-shaped guard. [C16: of unknown origin]
foils·man ('fɔɪlzmən) *n., pl.* **·men.** *Fencing.* a person who uses or specializes in using a foil.
foin (fɔɪn) *Archaic.* ~*n.* **1.** a thrust or lunge with a weapon. ~*vb.* **2.** to thrust with a weapon. [C14: probably from Old French *foine,* from Latin *fuscina* trident]
Fo·ism ('fəʊ,ɪzəm) *n.* Chinese Buddhism, the version introduced from India from the 4th century A.D. onwards and essentially belonging to the Mahayana school. [from Mandarin Chinese *fo* BUDDHA] —**'Fo·ist** *n., adj.*
foi·son ('fɔɪzᵊn) *n. Archaic or poetic.* a plentiful supply or yield. [C13: from Old French, from Latin *fūsiō* a pouring out, from *fundere* to pour; see FUSION]
foist (fɔɪst) *vb. (tr.)* **1.** (often foll. by *off* or *on*) to sell or pass off (something, esp. an inferior article) as genuine, valuable, etc. **2.** (usually foll. by *in* or *into*) to insert surreptitiously or wrongfully. [C16: probably from obsolete Dutch *vuisten* to enclose in one's hand, from Middle Dutch *vuist* fist]
Fo·kine (*Russian* 'fɔkin; *French* fɔ'kin) *n.* **Mi·chel** (mi'ʃɛl). 1880–1942, Russian choreographer, regarded as the creator of modern ballet. He worked with Diaghilev as director of the Ballet Russe (1909–15), producing works such as *Les Sylphides* and *Petrushka.*
Fok·ker ('fɒkə; *Dutch* 'fɔkər) *n.* **An·tho·ny Her·man Ge·rard** (an'toːniː 'hɛrman 'xeːrɑrt). 1890–1939, Dutch designer and builder of aircraft.
fol. *abbrev. for:* **1.** folio. **2.** followed. **3.** following.
fol·a·cin ('fɒləsɪn) *n.* another name for **folic acid.** [C20: from FOL(IC) AC(ID) + -IN]
fold[1] (fəʊld) *vb.* **1.** to bend or be bent double so that one part covers another: *to fold a sheet of paper.* **2.** *(tr.)* to bring together and intertwine (the arms, legs, etc.): *she folded her hands.* **3.** *(tr.)* (of birds, insects, etc.) to close (the wings) together from an extended position. **4.** *(tr.; often foll. by up or in)* to enclose in or as if in a surrounding material. **5.** *(tr.; foll. by in)* to clasp (a person) in the arms. **6.** *(tr.; usually foll. by round, about, etc.)* to wind (around); entwine. **7.** *(tr.) Poetic.* to cover completely: *night folded the earth.* **8.** Also: **fold in.** *(tr.)* to mix (a whisked mixture) with other ingredients by gently turning one part over the other with a spoon. **9.** to produce a bend (in stratified rock) or (of stratified rock) to display a bend. **10.** *(intr.; often foll. by up) Informal.* to collapse; fail: *the business folded.* ~*n.* **11.** a piece or section that has been folded: *a fold of cloth.* **12.** a mark, crease, or hollow made by folding. **13.** a hollow in undulating terrain. **14.** a bend in stratified rocks that results from movements within the earth's crust and produces such structures as anticlines and synclines. **15.** *Anatomy.* another word for **plica** (sense 1). **16.** a coil, as in a rope, etc. **17.** an act of folding. [Old English *fealdan;* related to Old Norse *falda,* Old High German *faldan,* Latin *duplus* double, Greek *haploos* simple] —**'fold·a·ble** *adj.*
fold[2] (fəʊld) *n.* **1. a.** a small enclosure or pen for sheep or other livestock, where they can be gathered. **b.** the sheep or other livestock gathered in such an enclosure. **c.** a flock of sheep. **2.** a church or the members of it. **3.** any group or community sharing a way of life or holding the same values. ~*vb.* **4.** *(tr.)* to gather or confine (sheep or other livestock) in a fold. [Old English *falod;* related to Old Saxon *faled,* Middle Dutch *vaelt*]
-fold *suffix forming adjectives and adverbs.* having so many parts, being so many times as much or as many, or multiplied by so much or so many: *threefold; three-hundredfold.* [Old English *-fald, -feald*]
fold·a·way ('fəʊldə,weɪ) *adj. (prenominal)* (of a bed, etc.) able to be folded and put away when not in use.
fold·boat ('fəʊld,bəʊt) *n.* another name for **faltboat.**
fold·ed di·pole *n.* a type of aerial, widely used with television and frequency-modulated receivers, consisting of two parallel dipoles connected together at their outer ends and fed at the centre of one of them. The length is usually half the operating wavelength.
fold·er ('fəʊldə) *n.* **1.** a binder or file for holding loose papers, etc. **2.** a folded circular. **3.** a machine for folding printed sheets. **4.** a person or thing that folds.
fol·de·rol ('fɒldə,rɒl) *n.* a variant spelling of **falderal.**
fold·ing door *n.* a door in the form of two or more vertical hinged leaves that can be folded one against another.
fold·ing mon·ey *n. U.S. informal.* paper money.
fold·ing press *n.* a fall in wrestling won by folding one's opponent's legs up to his head and pressing his shoulders to the floor.
fold·out *n. Printing.* another name for **gatefold.**
fold up *vb. (adv.)* **1.** *(tr.)* to make smaller or more compact. **2.** *(intr.)* to collapse, as with laughter or pain.
fo·li·a ('fəʊlɪə) *n.* the plural of **folium.**
fo·li·a·ceous (,fəʊlɪ'eɪʃəs) *adj.* **1.** having the appearance of the leaf of a plant. **2.** bearing leaves or leaflike structures. **3.** *Geology.* (of certain rocks, esp. schists) consisting of thin layers. [C17: from Latin *foliāceus*]
fo·li·age ('fəʊlɪɪdʒ) *n.* **1.** the green leaves of a plant. **2.** sprays of leaves used for decoration. **3.** an ornamental leaf-like design. [C15: from Old French *fuellage,* from *fuelle* leaf; influenced in form by Latin *folium*] —**'fo·li·aged** *adj.*
fo·li·ar ('fəʊlɪə) *adj.* of or relating to a leaf or leaves. [C19: from French *foliaire,* from Latin *folium* leaf]
fo·li·ate *adj.* ('fəʊlɪɪt, -,eɪt). **1. a.** relating to, possessing, or resembling leaves. **b.** *(in combination): trifoliate.* **2.** (of certain metamorphic rocks, esp. schists) having the constituent minerals arranged in thin leaflike layers. ~*vb.* ('fəʊlɪ,eɪt). **3.** *(tr.)* to ornament with foliage or with leaf forms such as foils. **4.** to hammer or cut (metal) into thin plates or foil. **5.** *(tr.)* to coat or back (glass, etc.) with metal foil. **6.** *(tr.)* to number the leaves of (a book, manuscript, etc.). Compare **paginate. 7.** *(intr.)* (of plants) to grow leaves. [C17: from Latin *foliātus* leaved, leafy]
fo·li·at·ed ('fəʊlɪ,eɪtɪd) *adj.* **1.** *Architect.* ornamented with or made up of foliage or foils. **2.** (of rocks and minerals, esp. schists) composed of thin easily separable layers. **3.** (esp. of parts of animals or plants) resembling a leaf.
fo·li·a·tion (,fəʊlɪ'eɪʃən) *n.* **1.** *Botany.* **a.** the process of producing leaves. **b.** the state of being in leaf. **c.** the arrangement of leaves in a leaf bud; vernation. **2.** *Architect.* **a.** ornamentation consisting of foliage. **b.** ornamentation consisting of cusps and foils. **3.** any decoration with foliage. **4.** the consecutive numbering of the leaves of a book. **5.** *Geology.* the arrangement of the constituents of a rock in leaflike layers, as in schists.
fo·lic ac·id ('fəʊlɪk, 'fɒl-) *n.* any of a group of vitamins of the B complex, including pteroylglutamic acid and its derivatives: used in the treatment of megaloblastic anaemia. Also called: **folacin.** [C20: from Latin *folium* leaf; so called because it may be obtained from green leaves]
fo·lie à deux ('fɒlɪ æ 'dɜː) *n. Psychiatry.* the occurrence of mental illness simultaneously in two persons who are close to each other. [French: madness involving two (people)]
fo·lie de gran·deur *French.* (fɔli də grɑ̃'dœːr) *n.* delusions of grandeur. [literally: madness of grandeur]
fo·li·o ('fəʊlɪəʊ) *n., pl.* **·li·os. 1.** a sheet of paper folded in half to make two leaves for a book or manuscript. **2.** a book or manuscript of the largest common size made up of such sheets. **3.** a leaf of paper or parchment numbered on the front side only. **4.** *Law.* a unit of measurement of the length of legal documents, determined by the number of words, generally 72 or 90 in Britain and 100 in the U.S. ~*adj.* **5.** relating to or having the format of a folio: *a folio edition.* ~*vb.* **·li·os, ·li·o·ing, ·li·oed. 6.** *(tr.)* to number the leaves of (a book) consecutively. [C16: from Latin phrase *in foliō* in a leaf, from *folium* leaf]
fo·li·o·late ('fəʊlɪə,leɪt; fəʊ'lɪəlɪt, -,leɪt) *adj. Botany.* possessing

or relating to leaflets. [C19: from Late Latin *foliolum* little leaf, from Latin *folium* leaf]

fo·li·ose ('fəʊlɪˌəʊs, -ˌəʊz) *adj.* another word for **foliaceous** (senses 1, 2). [C18: from Latin *foliōsus* full of leaves]

fo·li·um ('fəʊlɪəm) *n., pl.* **·li·a** (-lɪə). **1.** a plane geometrical curve consisting of a loop whose two ends, intersecting at a node, are asymptotic to the same line. Standard equation: $x^3 + y^3 = 3axy$ where $x = y + a$ is the equation of the line. **2.** any thin leaflike layer, esp. of some metamorphic rocks. [C19: from Latin, literally: leaf]

folk (fəʊk) *n., pl.* **folk** *or* **folks.** **1.** (*functioning as pl.; often pl. in form*) people in general, esp. those of a particular group or class: *country folk.* **2.** (*functioning as pl.; usually pl. in form*) *Informal.* members of a family. **3.** (*functioning as sing.*) *Informal.* short for **folk music. 4.** a people or tribe. **5.** (*modifier*) relating to, originating from, or traditional to the common people of a country: *a folk song.* [Old English *folc;* related to Old Saxon, Old Norse, Old High German *folk*] —**'folk·ish** *adj.* —**'folk·ish·ness** *n.*

folk dance *n.* **1.** any of various traditional rustic dances often originating from festivals or rituals. **2.** a piece of music composed for such a dance. ~*vb.* **folk-dance. 3.** to perform a folk dance. —**folk danc·ing** *n.*

Folke·stone ('fəʊkstən) *n.* a port and resort in SE England, in E Kent. Pop.: 43 760 (1971).

Fol·ke·ting ('fəʊlkətɪŋ; *Danish* 'fɔlgəteŋ) *n.* the lower chamber of the Danish parliament. [Danish, from *folk* the people, FOLK + Old Norse *thing* assembly]

folk et·y·mol·o·gy *n.* **1.** the gradual change in the form of a word through the influence of a more familiar word or phrase with which it becomes associated, as for example *sparrow-grass* for *asparagus.* **2.** a popular but erroneous conception of the origin of a word.

folk·lore ('fəʊkˌlɔː) *n.* **1.** the unwritten literature of a people as expressed in folk tales, proverbs, riddles, songs, etc. **2.** the anthropological discipline concerned with the study of such materials. —**'folk·ˌlor·ic** *adj.* —**'folk·ˌlor·ist** *n., adj.* —**ˌfolk·lor·'is·tic** *adj.*

folk med·i·cine *n.* the traditional art of medicine as practised among rustic communities and primitive peoples, consisting typically of the use of herbal remedies, fruits and vegetables thought to have healing power, etc.

folk mem·o·ry *n.* the memory of past events as preserved in a community.

folk·moot ('fəʊkˌmuːt), **folk·mote,** *or* **folk·mot** ('fəʊkˌməʊt) *n.* (in early medieval England) an assembly of the people of a district, town, or shire. [Old English *folcmōt,* from *folc* FOLK + *mōt* from *mǣtan* to MEET]

folk mu·sic *n.* **1.** music that is passed on from generation to generation by oral tradition. Compare **art music. 2.** any music composed in the idiom of this oral tradition.

folk-rock *n.* a combination of folk-orientated lyrics with a pop accompaniment.

folk sing·er *n.* a person who sings folk songs or other songs in the folk idiom. —**folk sing·ing** *n.*

folk song *n.* **1.** a song of which the music and text have been handed down by oral tradition among the common people. **2.** a modern song which employs or reflects the folk idiom.

folk·sy ('fəʊksɪ) *adj.* **·si·er, ·si·est.** *Informal, chiefly U.S.* **1.** of or like ordinary people; sometimes used derogatorily to describe affected simplicity. **2.** friendly; affable. **3.** of or relating to folk art. —**'folk·si·ness** *n.*

folk tale *or* **sto·ry** *n.* a tale or legend originating among a people and typically becoming part of an oral tradition.

folk·ways ('fəʊkˌweɪz) *pl. n. Sociol.* traditional and customary ways of living.

folk weave *n.* a type of fabric with a loose weave.

foll. *abbrev. for:* **1.** followed. **2.** following.

fol·li·cle ('fɒlɪk°l) *n.* **1.** any small sac or cavity in the body having an excretory, secretory, or protective function: *a hair follicle.* **2.** *Botany.* a dry fruit, formed from a single carpel, that splits along one side only to release its seeds: occurs in larkspur and columbine. [C17: from Latin *folliculus* small bag, from *follis* pair of bellows, leather money-bag] —**fol·lic·u·lar** (fɒ'lɪkjʊlə), **fol·lic·u·late** (fɒ'lɪkjʊˌleɪt), *or* **fol·'lic·u·ˌlat·ed** *adj.*

fol·li·cle-stim·u·lat·ing hor·mone *n.* a gonadotropic hormone secreted by the pituitary gland that stimulates maturation of ovarian follicles in female mammals and growth of seminiferous tubules in males. Abbrev.: **FSH.** See also **luteinizing hormone, prolactin.**

fol·lic·u·lin (fɒ'lɪkjʊlɪn) *n.* another name for **oestrone.**

fol·low ('fɒləʊ) *vb.* **1.** to go or come after in the same direction: *he followed his friend home.* **2.** (*tr.*) to accompany; attend: *she followed her sister everywhere.* **3.** to come after as a logical or natural consequence. **4.** (*tr.*) to keep to the course or track of: *she followed the towpath.* **5.** (*tr.*) to act in accordance with; obey: *to follow instructions.* **6.** (*tr.*) to accept the ideas or beliefs of (a previous authority, etc.): *he followed Donne in most of his teachings.* **7.** to understand (an explanation, argument, etc.): *the lesson was difficult to follow.* **8.** to watch closely or continuously: *she followed his progress carefully.* **9.** (*tr.*) to have a keen interest in: *to follow athletics.* **10.** (*tr.*) to help in the cause of or accept the leadership of: *the men who followed Napoleon.* **11.** (*tr.*) *Rare.* to earn a living at or in: *to follow the Navy.* **12. follow suit. a.** *Cards.* to play a card of the suit led. **b.** to do the same as someone else. ~*n.* **13.** *Billiards, etc.* **a.** forward spin imparted to a cue ball causing it to roll after the object ball. **b.** a shot made in this way. [Old English *folgian;* related to Old Frisian *folgia,* Old Saxon *folgōn,* Old High German *folgēn*] —**'fol·low·a·ble** *adj.*

fol·low·er ('fɒləʊə) *n.* **1.** a person who accepts the teachings of another; disciple; adherent: *a follower of Marx.* **2.** an attendant or henchman. **3.** an enthusiast or supporter, as of a sport or team. **4.** (esp. formerly) a male admirer. **5.** *Rare.* a pursuer. **6.** a machine part that derives its motion by following the motion of another part.

fol·low·ing ('fɒləʊɪŋ) *adj.* **1. a.** (*prenominal*) about to be mentioned, specified, etc.: *the following items.* **b.** (*as n.*): *will the following please raise their hands?* **2.** (of winds, currents, etc.) moving in the same direction as the course of a vessel. ~*n.* **3.** a group of supporters or enthusiasts: *he attracted a large following wherever he played.*

fol·low-my-lead·er *n.* a game in which the players must repeat the actions of the leader. U.S. name: **follow-the-leader.**

fol·low-on *Cricket.* ~*n.* **1.** an immediate second innings forced on a team scoring a prescribed number of runs fewer than its opponents in the first innings. ~*vb.* **fol·low on. 2.** (*intr., adv.*) (of a team) to play a follow-on.

fol·low out *vb.* (*tr., adv.*) to implement (an idea or action) to a conclusion.

fol·low through *vb.* (*adv.*) **1.** *Sport.* to complete (a stroke or shot) by continuing the movement to the end of its arc. **2.** (*tr.*) to pursue (an aim) to a conclusion. ~*n.* **fol·low-through. 3.** *Sport.* **a.** the act of following through. **b.** the part of the stroke after the ball has been hit. **4.** the completion of a procedure, esp. after a first action.

fol·low up *vb.* (*tr., adv.*) **1.** to pursue or investigate (a person, evidence, etc.) closely. **2.** to continue (action) after a beginning, esp. to increase its effect. ~*n.* **fol·low-up. 3. a.** something done to reinforce an initial action. **b.** (*as modifier*): *a follow-up letter.* **4.** *Med.* a routine examination of a patient at various intervals after medical or surgical treatment.

fol·ly ('fɒlɪ) *n., pl.* **·lies. 1.** the state or quality of being foolish; stupidity; rashness. **2.** a foolish action, mistake, idea, etc. **3.** a building in the form of a castle, temple, etc., built to satisfy a fancy or conceit, often of an eccentric kind. **4.** (*pl.*) *Theatre.* an elaborately costumed review. **5.** *Archaic.* **a.** evil; wickedness. **b.** lewdness; wantonness. [C13: from Old French *folie* madness, from *fou* mad; see FOOL[1]]

Fol·som man ('fɒlsəm) *n.* a type of early man from a North American culture of the Pleistocene period, thought to have used flint tools and to have subsisted mainly by hunting bison. [C20: named after *Folsom,* a settlement in New Mexico, where archaeological evidence was found]

Fo·mal·haut ('fəʊməˌləʊt) *n.* the brightest star in the constellation Piscis Austrinus. Distance: 24 light years. [C16: from Arabic *fum'l-hūt* mouth of the fish, referring to its position in the constellation]

fo·ment (fə'mɛnt) *vb.* (*tr.*) **1.** to encourage or instigate (trouble, discord, etc.); stir up. **2.** *Med.* to apply heat and moisture to (a part of the body) to relieve pain and inflammation. [C15: from Late Latin *fōmentāre,* from Latin *fōmentum* a poultice, ultimately from *fovēre* to foster] —**fo·men·ta·tion** (ˌfəʊmɛn'teɪʃən) *n.* —**fo·'ment·er** *n.*

fond[1] (fɒnd) *adj.* **1.** (*postpositive;* foll. by *of*) predisposed (to); having a liking (for). **2.** loving; tender: *a fond embrace.* **3.** indulgent; doting: *a fond mother.* **4.** *Archaic or dialect.* **a.** foolish. **b.** credulous. [C14 *fonned,* from *fonnen* to be foolish, from *fonne* a fool] —**'fond·ly** *adv.* —**'fond·ness** *n.*

fond[2] (fɒnd; *French* fɔ̃) *n.* **1.** the background of a design, as in lace. **2.** *Obsolete.* fund; stock. [C17: from French, from Latin *fundus* bottom; see FUND]

Fon·da ('fɒndə) *n.* **1. Hen·ry.** 1905–82, U.S. film actor and director: films as an actor include *The Grapes of Wrath* (1940) and *War and Peace* (1956) and, as a director, *Twelve Angry Men* (1957). **2.** his daughter **Jane.** born 1937, U.S. film actress, noted for her role in *Barbarella* (1968), an extravaganza of sexual fantasy, and subsequent more serious roles in *Klute* (1971) and *Julia* (1977). **3.** his son **Peter.** born 1939, U.S. film actor, who made his name in *Easy Rider* (1969).

fon·dant ('fɒndənt) *n.* **1.** a thick flavoured paste of sugar and water, used in sweets and icings. **2.** a sweet made of this mixture. [C19: from French, literally: melting, from *fondre* to melt, from Latin *fundere;* see FOUND[3]]

fon·dle ('fɒnd°l) *vb.* **1.** (*tr.*) to touch or stroke tenderly; caress. **2.** (*intr.*) *Archaic.* to act in a loving manner. [C17: from (obsolete) vb. *fond* to fondle; see FOND[1]] —**'fon·dler** *n.* —**'fon·dling·ly** *adv.*

fon·due ('fɒndjuː; *French* fɔ̃'dy) *n.* a Swiss dish, consisting of cheese melted in white wine or cider, into which small pieces of bread are dipped and then eaten. [C19: from French, feminine of *fondu* melted, from *fondre* to melt; see FONDANT]

fon·due Bour·gui·gnonne ('bʊəgɪˌnjɒn; *French* burgi'ɲɔn) *n.* a dish consisting of pieces of steak impaled on forks, cooked in oil at the table and dipped in sauces. [French: Burgundy fondue]

Fon·se·ca (*Spanish* fon'seka) *n.* **Gulf of.** an inlet of the Pacific Ocean in W Central America.

fons et or·i·go *Latin.* (fɒnz ɛt 'ɒrɪgəʊ) *n.* the source and origin.

font[1] (fɒnt) *n.* **1.** a large bowl for baptismal water, usually mounted on a pedestal. **2.** the reservoir for oil in an oil lamp. **3.** *Archaic or poetic.* a fountain or well. [Old English, from Church Latin *fons* from Latin: fountain] —**'font·al** *adj.*

font[2] (fɒnt) *n. Printing.* another name (esp. in the U.S.) for **fount**[2].

Fon·taine·bleau ('fɒntɪnˌbləʊ; *French* fɔ̃tɛn'blo) *n.* a town in N France, in the **Forest of Fontainebleau:** famous for its palace (now a museum), one of the largest royal residences in France, built largely by Francis I (16th century). Pop.: 19 595 (1975).

fon·ta·nelle *or* **fon·ta·nel** (ˌfɒntəˈnɛl) *n. Anatomy.* any of several soft membranous gaps between the bones of the skull in a fetus or infant. [C16 (in the sense: hollow between muscles): from Old French *fontanele,* literally: a little spring, from *fontaine* FOUNTAIN]

Fon·teyn (fɒnˈteɪn) *n.* Dame **Mar·got.** original name *Margaret Hookham.* born 1919, English classical ballerina.

Foo·chow *or* **Fu-chou** (ˈfuːˈtʃaʊ) *n.* a port in SE China, capital of Fukien province, on the Min Chiang: one of the original five treaty ports (1842). Pop.: 680 000 (1970 est.).

food (fuːd) *n.* **1.** any substance containing nutrients, such as carbohydrates, proteins, and fats, that can be ingested by a living organism and metabolized into energy and body tissue. Related adj.: **alimentary. 2.** nourishment in more or less solid form as opposed to liquid form: *food and drink.* **3.** anything that provides mental nourishment or stimulus. [Old English *fōda;* related to Old Frisian *fōdia* to nourish, feed, Old Norse *fœthi,* Gothic *fōdeins* food; see FEED, FODDER] —**ˈfood·less** *adj.*

food chain *n. Ecology.* a series of organisms in a community, each member of which feeds on another in the chain and is eaten in turn by another member.

food poi·son·ing *n.* an acute illness typically characterized by gastrointestinal inflammation, vomiting, and diarrhoea, caused by food that is either naturally poisonous or contaminated by pathogenic bacteria (esp. *Salmonella*).

food·stuff (ˈfuːdˌstʌf) *n.* any material, substance, etc., that can be used as food.

fool[1] (fuːl) *n.* **1.** a person who lacks sense or judgement. **2.** a person who is made to appear ridiculous. **3.** (formerly) a professional jester living in a royal or noble household. **4.** *Obsolete.* an idiot or imbecile: *the village fool.* **5. act** *or* **play the fool.** to deliberately act foolishly; indulge in buffoonery. **6. form the fool.** *Caribbean.* to play the fool or behave irritatingly. **7. no fool.** a wise or sensible person. ~*vb.* **8.** (*tr.*) to deceive (someone), esp. in order to make him look ridiculous. **9.** (*intr.;* foll. by *with, around with,* or *about with*) *Informal.* to act or play (with) irresponsibly or aimlessly: *to fool around with a woman.* **10.** (*intr.*) to speak or act in a playful, teasing, or jesting manner. **11.** (*tr.;* foll. by *away*) to squander; fritter: *he fooled away a fortune.* **12.** *U.S.* **fool along.** to move or proceed in a leisurely way. ~*adj.* **13.** *Informal.* short for **foolish.** [C13: from Old French *fol* mad person, from Late Latin *follis* empty-headed fellow, from Latin: bellows; related to Latin *flāre* to blow]

fool[2] (fuːl) *n. Chiefly Brit.* a dessert made from a purée of fruit with cream or custard: *gooseberry fool.* [C16: perhaps from FOOL[1]]

fool·er·y (ˈfuːlərɪ) *n., pl.* **·er·ies. 1.** foolish behaviour. **2.** an instance of this, esp. a prank or trick.

fool·hard·y (ˈfuːlˌhɑːdɪ) *adj.* **·hard·i·er, ·hard·i·est.** heedlessly rash or adventurous. [C13: from Old French *fol hardi,* from *fol* foolish + *hardi* bold] —**ˈfool·ˌhar·di·ly** *adv.* —**ˈfool·ˌhar·di·ness** *n.*

fool·ish (ˈfuːlɪʃ) *adj.* **1.** unwise; silly. **2.** resulting from folly or stupidity. **3.** ridiculous or absurd; not worthy of consideration. **4.** weak-minded; simple. **5.** an archaic word for **insignificant.** —**ˈfool·ish·ly** *adv.* —**ˈfool·ish·ness** *n.*

fool·proof (ˈfuːlˌpruːf) *adj. Informal.* **1.** proof against failure; infallible: *a foolproof idea.* **2.** (esp. of machines, etc.) proof against human misuse, error, etc.

fool's cap *n.* **1.** a hood or cap with bells or tassels, worn by court jesters. **2.** a dunce's cap.

fools·cap (ˈfuːlzˌkæp) *n.* **1.** *Chiefly Brit.* a size of writing or printing paper, 13½ by 17 inches or 13½ by 16½ inches. **2.** a book size, 4¼ by 6¾ inches (**foolscap octavo**) or (chiefly Brit.) 6¾ by 8½ inches (**foolscap quarto**). **3.** a variant spelling of **fool's cap.** [C17: see FOOL[1], CAP; so called from the watermark formerly used on this kind of paper]

fool's er·rand *n.* a fruitless undertaking.

fool's gold *n.* any of various yellow minerals, esp. pyrite or chalcopyrite, that can be mistaken for gold.

fool's par·a·dise *n.* illusory happiness.

fool's-pars·ley *n.* an evil-smelling Eurasian umbelliferous plant, *Aethusa cynapium,* with small white flowers: contains the poison coniine.

foot (fʊt) *n., pl.* **feet** (fiːt). **1.** the part of the vertebrate leg below the ankle joint that is in contact with the ground during standing and walking. Related adj.: **pedal. 2.** any of various organs of locomotion or attachment in invertebrates, including molluscs. **3.** *Botany.* the lower part of some plants or plant structures, as of developing moss or fern sporophytes. **4.** a unit of length equal to one third of a yard or 12 inches. 1 foot is equivalent to 0.3048 metre. **5.** any part resembling a foot in form or function: *the foot of a chair.* **6.** the lower part of something; base; bottom: *the foot of the page; the foot of a hill.* **7.** the end of a series or group: *the foot of the list.* **8.** manner of walking or moving; tread; step: *a heavy foot.* **9. a.** infantry, esp. in the British army. **b.** (*as modifier*): *a foot soldier.* **10.** any of various attachments on a sewing machine that hold the fabric in position, such as a presser foot for ordinary sewing and a zipper foot. **11.** *Music.* **a.** a unit used in classifying organ pipes according to their pitch, in terms of the length of an equivalent column of air. **b.** this unit applied to stops and registers on other instruments. **12.** *Printing.* **a.** the margin at the bottom of a page. **b.** the undersurface of a piece of type. **13.** *Prosody.* a group of two or more syllables in which one syllable has the major stress, forming the basic unit of poetic rhythm. **14. a foot in the door.** an action, appointment, etc., that provides an initial step towards a desired goal, esp. one that is not easily attainable. **15. have one's foot on the ground.** to be practical. **16. kick with the wrong foot.** *Scot., Irish.* to be of the opposite religion to that of the person who is speaking. **17. my foot!** an expression of disbelief, often of the speaker's own preceding statement: *he didn't know, my foot! Of course he did!* **18. of foot.** *Archaic.* in manner of movement: *fleet of foot.* **19. on foot. a.** walking or running. **b.** in progress; astir; afoot. **20. one foot in the grave.** *Informal.* near to death. **21. on the wrong** (*or* **right**) **foot.** *Informal.* in an inauspicious (or auspicious) manner. **22. put a foot wrong.** to make a mistake. **23. put one's best foot forward.** *Informal.* **a.** to try to do one's best, esp. in order to give a good impression. **b.** to hurry. **24. put one's foot down.** *Informal.* to act firmly. **25. put one's foot in it.** *Informal.* to blunder. **26. set on foot.** to initiate or start (something). **27. tread under foot.** to oppress. **28. under foot.** on the ground; beneath one's feet. ~*vb.* **29.** to dance to music (esp. in the phrase **foot it**). **30.** (*tr.*) to walk over or set foot on; traverse (esp. in the phrase **foot it**). **31.** (*tr.*) to pay the entire cost of (esp. in the phrase **foot the bill**). **32.** (usually foll. by *up*) *Archaic or dialect.* to add up. [Old English *fōt;* related to Old Norse *fōtr,* Gothic *fōtus,* Old High German *fuoz,* Latin *pēs,* Greek *pous,* Sanskrit *pad*] —**ˈfoot·less** *adj.*

Foot (fʊt) *n.* **Mi·chael.** born 1913, British Labour politician, and a leader of the left-wing *Tribune* group; secretary of state for employment (1974–76); leader of the House of Commons (1976–79); leader of the Labour Party 1980–83.

foot·age (ˈfʊtɪdʒ) *n.* **1.** a length or distance measured in feet. **2. a.** the extent of film material shot and exposed. **b.** the sequences of filmed material. **3. a.** payment, by the linear foot of work done. **b.** the amount paid.

foot-and-mouth dis·ease *n.* an acute highly infectious viral disease of cattle, pigs, sheep, and goats, characterized by the formation of vesicular eruptions in the mouth and on the feet, esp. around the hoofs. Also called: **hoof-and-mouth disease.**

foot·ball (ˈfʊtˌbɔːl) *n.* **1. a.** any of various games played with a round or oval ball and usually based on two teams competing to kick, butt, carry, or otherwise propel the ball into each other's goal, territory, etc. See **association football, rugby, Australian football, American football, Gaelic football. b.** (*as modifier*): *a football ground; a football supporter.* **2.** the ball used in any of these games or their variants. **3.** a problem, issue, etc., that is passed from one group or person to another. —**ˈfoot·ˌball·er** *n.*

foot·board (ˈfʊtˌbɔːd) *n.* **1.** a treadle or foot-operated lever on a machine. **2.** a vertical board at the foot of a bed.

foot·boy (ˈfʊtˌbɔɪ) *n.* a boy servant; page.

foot brake *n.* a brake operated by applying pressure to a foot pedal. Also called: **pedal brake.**

foot·bridge (ˈfʊtˌbrɪdʒ) *n.* a narrow bridge for the use of pedestrians.

foot-can·dle *n.* a former unit of illumination, equal to one lumen per square foot or 10.764 lux.

foot·cloth (ˈfʊtˌklɒθ) *n.* **1.** *Archaic.* a carpet or rug. **2.** an obsolete word for **caparison** (sense 1).

-foot·ed *adj.* **1.** having a foot or feet as specified: *four-footed.* **2.** having a tread as specified: *heavy-footed.*

foot·er[1] (ˈfʊtə) *n.* **1.** *Archaic.* a person who goes on foot; walker. **2.** (*in combination*) a person or thing of a specified length or height in feet: *a six-footer.*

foot·er[2] (ˈfʊtə) *n. Brit. informal.* short for **football** (the game).

foot·fall (ˈfʊtˌfɔːl) *n.* the sound of a footstep.

foot fault *n. Tennis.* a fault that occurs when the server fails to keep both feet behind the baseline until he has served.

foot·gear (ˈfʊtˌgɪə) *n.* another name for **footwear.**

foot·hill (ˈfʊtˌhɪl) *n.* (*often pl.*) a lower slope of a mountain or a relatively low hill at the foot of a mountain.

foot·hold (ˈfʊtˌhəʊld) *n.* **1.** a ledge, hollow, or other place affording a secure grip for the foot, as during climbing. **2.** a secure position from which further progress may be made: *a foothold for a successful career.*

foot·ie *n.* a variant spelling of **footy.**

foot·ing (ˈfʊtɪŋ) *n.* **1.** the basis or foundation on which something is established: *the business was on a secure footing.* **2.** the relationship or status existing between two persons, groups, etc.: *the two countries were on a friendly footing.* **3.** a secure grip by or for the feet. **4.** the lower part of a foundation of a column, wall, building, etc. **5.** *Chiefly U.S.* **a.** the act of adding a column of figures. **b.** the total obtained. **6.** *Rare.* a fee paid upon entrance into a craft, society, etc., or such an entrance itself.

foot-lam·bert *n.* a former unit of luminance equal to the luminance of a surface emitting or reflecting 1 lumen per square foot. A completely reflecting surface illuminated by 1 foot-candle has a luminance of 1 foot-lambert. Symbol: **ft-L.**

foot·le (ˈfuːtᵊl) *Informal.* ~*vb.* **1.** (*intr.;* often foll. by *around* or *about*) to loiter aimlessly; potter. **2.** (*intr.*) to talk nonsense. ~*n.* **3.** *Rare.* foolishness. [C19: probably from French *foutre* to copulate with, from Latin *futuere*]

foot·lights (ˈfʊtˌlaɪts) *pl. n. Theatre.* **1.** lights set in a row along the front of the stage floor and shielded on the audience side. **2.** *Informal.* the acting profession; the stage.

foot·ling (ˈfuːtlɪŋ) *adj. Informal.* silly, trivial, or petty.

foot·loose (ˈfʊtˌluːs) *adj.* **1.** free to go or do as one wishes. **2.** eager to travel; restless: *to feel footloose.*

foot·man (ˈfʊtmən) *n., pl.* **·men. 1.** a male servant, esp. one in livery. **2.** a low four-legged metal stand used in a fireplace for utensils, etc. **3.** (formerly) a foot soldier.

foot+mark (ˈfʊtˌmɑːk) *n.* a mark or trace of mud, wetness, etc., left by a person's foot on a surface.

foot+note (ˈfʊtˌnəʊt) *n.* **1.** a note printed at the bottom of a page, to which attention is drawn by means of a reference mark in the body of the text. **2.** an additional comment, as to a main statement. ~*vb.* **3.** (*tr.*) to supply (a page, book, etc.) with footnotes.

foot+pace (ˈfʊtˌpeɪs) *n.* **1.** a normal or walking pace. **2.** Also called (in the Roman Catholic Church): **predella.** the platform immediately before an altar at the top of the altar steps.

foot+pad (ˈfʊtˌpæd) *n. Archaic.* a robber or highwayman, on foot rather than horseback.

foot+path (ˈfʊtˌpɑːθ) *n.* a narrow path for walkers only.

foot+plate (ˈfʊtˌpleɪt) *n. Chiefly Brit.* **a.** a platform in the cab of a locomotive on which the crew stand to operate the controls. **b.** (*as modifier*): *a footplate man.*

foot-pound *n.* an fps unit of work or energy equal to the work done when a force of 1 pound moves through a distance of 1 foot. Abbrev.: **ft-lb.**

foot-pound·al *n.* a unit of work or energy equal to the work done when a force of one poundal moves through a distance of one foot: it is equal to 0.042 14 joule.

foot-pound-sec·ond *n.* See **fps units.**

foot+print (ˈfʊtˌprɪnt) *n.* **1.** an indentation or outline of the foot of a person or animal on a surface. **2.** an identifying characteristic on land or water, such as the area in which an aircraft's sonic boom can be heard or the area covered by the down-blast of a hovercraft.

foot+rest (ˈfʊtˌrɛst) *n.* something that provides a support for the feet, such as a low stool, rail, etc.

foot+rope (ˈfʊtˌrəʊp) *n. Nautical.* **1.** the part of a boltrope to which the foot of a sail is stitched. **2.** a rope fixed so as to hang below a yard to serve as a foothold.

foot rot *n. Vet. science.* See **rot**[1] (sense 11).

foot rule *n.* a rigid measure, one foot in length.

foots (fʊts) *pl. n.* (*sometimes sing.*) the sediment that accumulates at the bottom of a vessel containing any of certain liquids, such as vegetable oil or varnish; dregs.

foot+sie (ˈfʊtsɪ) *n. Informal.* flirtation involving the touching together of feet, knees, etc. (esp. in the phrase **play footsie**).

foot+slog (ˈfʊtˌslɒg) *vb.* **+slogs, +slog+ging, +slogged.** (*intr.*) to march; tramp. —**ˈfoot+ˌslog+ger** *n.*

foot sol+dier *n.* an infantryman.

foot+sore (ˈfʊtˌsɔː) *adj.* having sore or tired feet, esp. from much walking. —**ˈfoot+ˌsore+ness** *n.*

foot+stalk (ˈfʊtˌstɔːk) *n.* a small supporting stalk in animals and plants; a pedicel, peduncle, or pedicle.

foot+stall (ˈfʊtˌstɔːl) *n.* **1.** the pedestal, plinth, or base of a column, pier, or statue. **2.** the stirrup on a sidesaddle.

foot+step (ˈfʊtˌstɛp) *n.* **1.** the action of taking a step in walking. **2.** the sound made by stepping or walking. **3.** the distance covered with a step; pace. **4.** a footmark. **5.** a single stair; step. **6. follow in someone's footsteps.** to continue the tradition or example of another.

foot+stock (ˈfʊtˌstɒk) *n.* another name for **tailstock.**

foot+stool (ˈfʊtˌstuːl) *n.* a low stool used for supporting or resting the feet of a seated person.

foot-ton *n.* a unit of work or energy equal to 2240 foot-pounds.

foot+wall (ˈfʊtˌwɔːl) *n.* the rocks on the lower side of an inclined fault plane or mineral vein. Compare **hanging wall.**

foot+way (ˈfʊtˌweɪ) *n.* a way or path for pedestrians, such as a raised walk along the edge of a bridge.

foot+wear (ˈfʊtˌwɛə) *n.* anything worn to cover the feet.

foot+work (ˈfʊtˌwɜːk) *n.* skilful use of the feet, as in sports, dancing, etc.

foot+worn (ˈfʊtˌwɔːn) *adj.* **1.** Also: **foot+wear·y.** footsore. **2.** worn away by the feet: *a footworn staircase.*

foot·y *or* **foot·ie** (fʊtɪ) *n. Informal, chiefly Austral. and N.Z.* **a.** football. **b.** (*as modifier*): *footy boots.*

foo yong (ˈfuː ˈjɒŋ), **foo yoong, foo yung,** *or* **fu yung** (ˈfuː ˈjʊŋ) *n.* a Chinese dish made of eggs mixed with chicken, crab meat, etc., and cooked like an omelette. [from Chinese *fu yung* hibiscus]

foo+zle (ˈfuːzᵊl) *Chiefly golf.* ~*vb.* **1.** to bungle (a shot, etc.). ~*n.* **2.** a bungled shot, etc. [C19: perhaps from German dialect *fuseln* to do slipshod work] —**ˈfoo+zler** *n.*

fop (fɒp) *n.* a man who is excessively concerned with fashion and elegance. [C15: related to German *foppen* to trick; see FOB[2]] —**ˈfop+pish** *adj.* —**ˈfop+pish+ly** *adv.* —**ˈfop+pish+ness** *n.*

fop+per·y (ˈfɒpərɪ) *n., pl.* **+per·ies.** the clothes, affectations, obsessions, etc., of or befitting a fop.

for (fɔː; *unstressed* fə) *prep.* **1.** intended to reach; directed or belonging to: *there's a phone call for you.* **2.** to the advantage of: *I only did it for you.* **3.** in the direction of: *heading for the border.* **4.** over a span of (time or distance): *working for six days; the river ran for six miles.* **5.** in favour of; in support of: *those for the proposal; vote for me.* **6.** in order to get or achieve: *I do it for money; he does it for pleasure; what did you do that for?* **7.** appropriate to; designed to meet the needs of; meant to be used in: *these kennels are for puppies.* **8.** in exchange for; at a cost of; to the amount of: *I got it for hardly any money.* **9.** such as explains or results in: *his reason for changing his job was not given.* **10.** in place of: *a substitute for the injured player.* **11.** because of; through: *she wept for pure relief.* **12.** with regard or consideration to the usual characteristics of: *he's short for a man; it's cool for this time of year.* **13.** concerning; as regards: *desire for money.* **14.** as being: *we took him for the owner; I know that for a fact.* **15.** at a specified time: *a date for the next evening.* **16.** to do or partake of: *an appointment for supper.* **17.** in the duty or task of: *that's for him to say.* **18.** to allow of: *too big a job for us to handle.* **19.** despite; notwithstanding: *she's a good wife, for all her nagging.* **20.** in order to preserve, retain, etc.: *to fight for survival.* **21.** as a direct equivalent to: *word for word; weight for weight.* **22.** in order to become or enter: *to go for a soldier; to train for the priesthood.* **23.** in recompense for: *I paid for it last week; he took the punishment for his crime.* **24. for it.** *Brit. informal.* liable for punishment or blame: *you'll be for it if she catches you.* **25. not long for this world.** almost dead. **26. nothing for it.** it can't be helped; it must be so. ~*conj.* **27.** (*coordinating*) for the following reason; because; seeing that: *I couldn't stay, for the area was violent.* [Old English; related to Old Norse *fyr* for, Old High German *fora* before, Latin *per* through, *prō* before, Greek *pro* before, in front]

for. *abbrev. for:* **1.** foreign. **2.** forestry.

f.o.r. *or* **F.O.R.** *Commerce. abbrev. for* free on rail.

for- *prefix.* **1.** indicating rejection or prohibition: *forbear; forbid.* **2.** indicating falsity or wrongness: *forswear.* **3.** used to give intensive force: *forgive; forlorn.* [Old English *for-*; related to German *ver-*, Latin *per-*, Greek *peri-*]

for+age (ˈfɒrɪdʒ) *n.* **1.** food for horses or cattle, esp. hay or straw. **2.** the act of searching for food or provisions. **3.** *Military.* a raid or incursion. ~*vb.* **4.** to search (the countryside or a town) for food, provisions, etc. **5.** (*intr.*) *Military.* to carry out a raid. **6.** (*tr.*) to obtain by searching about. **7.** (*tr.*) to give food or other provisions to. **8.** (*tr.*) to feed (cattle or horses) with such food. [C14: from Old French *fourrage,* probably of Germanic origin; see FOOD, FODDER] —**ˈfor+ag+er** *n.*

for+age cap *n.* a soldier's undress cap.

fo+ra+men (fɒˈreɪmɛn) *n., pl.* **+ram+i+na** (-ˈræmɪnə) *or* **+ra+mens.** a natural hole, esp. one in a bone through which nerves and blood vessels pass. [C17: from Latin, from *forāre* to bore, pierce] —**fo+ram+i+nal** (fɒˈræmɪnᵊl) *adj.*

fo+ra+men mag+num *n.* the large opening at the base of the skull through which the spinal cord passes. [New Latin: large hole]

for·a·min·i·fer (ˌfɒrəˈmɪnɪfə) *n.* any rhizopod protozoan of the order *Foraminifera,* having a shell with numerous openings through which the pseudopodia protrude. See also **globigerina, nummulite.** [C19: from New Latin, from FORAMEN + -FER] —**fo+ram·i·nif+er+al** (fɒˌræmɪˈnɪfərəl) *or* **fo+ˌram·i+ˈnif+er+ous** *adj.*

for+as+much as (fərəzˈmʌtʃ) *conj.* (*subordinating*) *Archaic or legal.* seeing that; since.

for+ay (ˈfɒreɪ) *n.* **1.** a short raid or incursion. **2.** a first attempt or new undertaking. ~*vb.* **3.** to raid or ravage (a town, district, etc.). [C14: from *forrayen* to pillage, from Old French *forreier,* from *forrier* forager, from *fuerre* fodder; see FORAGE] —**ˈfor+ay+er** *n.*

forb (fɔːb) *n.* any herbaceous plant that is not a grass. [C20: from Greek *phorbē* food, from *pherbein* to graze]

for+bade (fəˈbæd, -ˈbeɪd) *or* **for+bad** (fəˈbæd) *vb.* the past tense of **forbid.**

for+bear[1] (fɔːˈbɛə) *vb.* **+bears, +bear+ing, +bore, +borne. 1.** (when *intr.,* often foll. by *from* or an infinitive) to cease or refrain (from doing something). **2.** *Archaic.* to tolerate or endure (misbehaviour, mistakes, etc.). [Old English *forberan;* related to Gothic *frabairan* to endure] —**for+ˈbear+er** *n.* —**for+ˈbear+ing+ly** *adv.*

for+bear[2] (ˈfɔːˌbɛə) *n.* a variant spelling of **forebear.**

for+bear+ance (fɔːˈbɛərəns) *n.* **1.** the act of forbearing. **2.** self-control; patience. **3.** *Law.* abstention from or postponement of the enforcement of a legal right, esp. by a creditor allowing his debtor time to pay.

Forbes (fɔːbz) *n.* **George Wil+liam.** 1869–1947, New Zealand statesman; prime minister of New Zealand (1930–35).

for+bid (fəˈbɪd) *vb.* **+bids, +bid+ding, +bade** *or* **+bad, +bid+den** *or* **+bid.** (*tr.*) **1.** to prohibit (a person) in a forceful or authoritative manner (from doing something or having something). **2.** to make impossible; hinder. **3.** to shut out or exclude. **4. God forbid!** may it not happen. [Old English *forbēodan;* related to Old High German *farbiotan,* Gothic *faurbiudan;* see FOR-, BID] —**for+ˈbid+dance** *n.* —**for+ˈbid+der** *n.*

for+bid+den (fəˈbɪdᵊn) *adj.* **1.** not permitted by order or law. **2.** *Physics.* involving a change in quantum numbers that is not permitted by certain rules derived from quantum mechanics, esp. rules for changes in the electrical dipole moment of the system.

For+bid+den Cit·y *n.* **the. 1.** Lhasa, Tibet: once famed for its inaccessibility and hostility to strangers. **2.** a walled section of Peking, China, enclosing the Imperial Palace and associated buildings of the former Chinese Empire.

for+bid+den fruit *n.* any pleasure or enjoyment regarded as illicit, esp. sexual indulgence.

for+bid+ding (fəˈbɪdɪŋ) *adj.* **1.** hostile or unfriendly. **2.** dangerous or ominous. —**for+ˈbid+ding+ly** *adv.* —**for+ˈbid+ding+ness** *n.*

for+bore (fɔːˈbɔː) *vb.* the past tense of **forbear**[1].

for+borne (fɔːˈbɔːn) *vb.* the past participle of **forbear**[1].

for+by *or* **for+bye** (fɔːˈbaɪ) *prep., adv. Scot.* **1.** besides; in addition (to). **2.** *Obsolete.* near; nearby.

force[1] (fɔːs) *n.* **1.** strength or energy; might; power: *the force of the blow; a gale of great force.* **2.** exertion or the use of exertion against a person or thing that resists; coercion. **3.** *Physics.* **a.** a dynamic influence that changes a body from a state of rest to one of motion or changes its rate of motion. The magnitude of the force is equal to the product of the mass of the body and its acceleration. **b.** a static influence that produces an elastic strain in a body or system or bears weight. Symbol: *F* **4.** *Physics.* any operating influence that produces or tends to produce a change in a physical quantity: *electromotive force; coercive force.* **5. a.** intellectual, social, political, or moral influence or strength: *the force of his argument; the forces of evil.* **b.** a person or thing with such influence: *he was a force in the land.* **6.** a group of persons organized for military or police functions: *armed forces.* **7.** (*sometimes cap.;* preceded by *the*) *Informal.* the police force. **8.** a group of persons organized for particular duties or tasks: *a work force.* **9.** *Criminal law.* violence unlawfully committed or threatened. **10. in force. a.** (of a law) having legal validity or binding effect. **b.** in great strength or numbers. **11. join forces.** to combine strengths, efforts, etc. ~*vb.* (*tr.*) **12.** to compel or cause (a person, group, etc.) to do something through effort, superior strength, etc.; coerce. **13.** to acquire, secure, or produce through effort, superior strength, etc.: *to force a confession.* **14.** to propel or drive despite resistance: *to force a nail into wood.* **15.** to break down or open (a lock, safe, door, etc.). **16.** to impose or inflict: *he forced his views on them.* **17.** to cause (plants or farm animals) to grow or fatten artificially at an increased rate. **18.** to strain or exert to the utmost: *to force the voice.* **19.** to rape; ravish. **20.** *Cards.* **a.** to compel (a player) to trump in order to take a trick. **b.** to compel a player by the lead of a particular suit to play (a certain card). **c.** (in bridge) to induce (a bid) from one's partner by bidding in a certain way. **21. force down.** to compel an aircraft to land. **22. force a smile.** to make oneself smile. **23. force the pace.** to adopt a high speed or rate of procedure. [C13: from Old French, from Vulgar Latin *fortia* (unattested), from Latin *fortis* strong] —**'force·a·ble** *adj.* —**'force·less** *adj.* —**'forc·er** *n.* —**'forc·ing·ly** *adv.*

force[2] (fɔːs) *n. Northern Brit.* a waterfall. [C17: from Old Norse *fors*]

forced (fɔːst) *adj.* **1.** done because of force; compulsory: *forced labour.* **2.** false or unnatural: *a forced smile.* **3.** due to an emergency or necessity: *a forced landing.* **4.** *Physics.* caused by an external agency: *a forced vibration; a forced draught.* —**forc·ed·ly** ('fɔːsɪdlɪ) *adv.* —**'forc·ed·ness** *n.*

forced march *n. Military.* a march in which normal needs are subordinated to the need for speed.

force-feed *vb.* **-feeds, -feed·ing, -fed.** (*tr.*) **1.** to force (a person or animal) to eat or swallow (food). **2.** to force (someone) to receive (opinions, propaganda, etc.). ~*n.* **force feed. 3.** a method of lubrication in which a pump forces oil into the bearings of an engine, etc.

force·ful ('fɔːsfʊl) *adj.* **1.** powerful. **2.** persuasive or effective. —**'force·ful·ly** *adv.* —**'force·ful·ness** *n.*

force ma·jeure ('fɔːs mæ'ʒɜː, -'dʒʊə) *n. Law.* irresistible force or compulsion such as will excuse a party from performing his part of a contract. [from French: superior force]

force·meat ('fɔːsˌmiːt) *n.* a mixture of chopped or minced ingredients used for stuffing. Also called: **farce, farcemeat.** [C17: from *force* (see FARCE) + MEAT]

for·ceps ('fɔːsɪps) *n. pl.* **·ceps** *or* **·ci·pes** (-sɪˌpiːz) **1. a.** a surgical instrument in the form of a pair of pincers, used esp. in the delivery of babies. **b.** (*as modifier*): *a forceps baby.* **2.** any pincer-like instrument. **3.** any part or structure of an organism shaped like a forceps. [C17: from Latin, from *formus* hot + *capere* to seize] —**'for·ceps-ˌlike** *adj.*

force pump *n.* a pump that ejects fluid under pressure. Compare **lift pump.**

force-ripe *Caribbean.* ~*adj.* **1.** (of fruit) prematurely picked and ripened by squeezing or warm storage. **2.** precocious, esp. sexually. ~*vb.* **3.** (*tr.*) to ripen (prematurely picked fruit) by squeezing or warm storage.

Forc·es ('fɔːsɪz) *pl. n.* (usually preceded by *the*) the armed services of a nation.

for·ci·ble ('fɔːsəbᵊl) *adj.* **1.** done by, involving, or having force. **2.** convincing or effective: *a forcible argument.* —**'for·ci·ble·ness** *or* **ˌfor·ci·'bil·i·ty** *n.* —**'for·ci·bly** *adv.*

forc·ing bid *n. Contract bridge.* a bid at a higher level than required, obliging the bidder's partner to reply.

forc·ing house *n.* a place where growth or maturity (as of fruit, animals, etc.) is artificially hastened.

ford (fɔːd) *n.* **1.** a shallow area in a river that can be crossed by car, horseback, etc. ~*vb.* **2.** (*tr.*) to cross (a river, brook, etc.) over a shallow area. [Old English; related to Old Frisian *forda*, Old High German *furt* ford, Latin *porta* door, *portus* PORT[1]] —**'ford·a·ble** *adj.*

Ford (fɔːd) *n.* **1. Ford Mad·ox** ('mædəks), original name *Ford Madox Hueffer.* 1873–1939, English novelist, editor, and critic; works include *The Good Soldier* (1915), the war tetralogy *Parade's End* (1924–28). **2. Ger·ald.** born 1913, U.S. politician; 38th president of the U.S. (1974–77). **3. Hen·ry.** 1863–1947, U.S. car manufacturer, who pioneered mass production. **4. John.** 1586–?1639, English dramatist; author of revenge tragedies such as *'Tis Pity She's a Whore* (1633). **5. John.** 1895–1973, U.S. film director, esp. of Westerns such as *Stagecoach* (1939) and *How the West was Won* (1962).

for·do *or* **fore·do** (fɔː'duː) *vb.* **·does, ·do·ing, ·did, ·done.** (*tr.*) *Archaic.* **1.** to destroy. **2.** to exhaust. [Old English *fordōn;* related to Old Saxon *fardōn*, Old High German *fartuon*, Dutch *verdoen;* see FOR-, DO[1]]

for·done *or* **fore·done** (fɔː'dʌn) *vb.* the past participle of **fordo.**

fore[1] (fɔː) *adj.* **1.** (*usually in combination*) located at, in, or towards the front: *the forelegs of a horse.* ~*n.* **2.** the front part. **3.** something located at, in, or towards the front. **4.** short for **foremast. 5. fore and aft.** located at or directed towards both ends of a vessel: *a fore-and-aft rig.* **6. to the fore.** to or into the front or conspicuous position. ~*adv.* **7.** at or towards a ship's bow. **8.** *Obsolete.* before. ~*prep., conj.* **9.** a less common word for **before.** [Old English; related to Old Saxon, Old High German *fora*, Gothic *faura*, Greek *para*, Sanskrit *pura*]

fore[2] (fɔː) *interj.* (in golf) a warning shout made by a player about to make a shot. [C19: probably short for BEFORE]

fore- *prefix.* **1.** before in time or rank: *foresight; forefather; foreman.* **2.** at or near the front; before in place: *forehead; forecourt.* [Old English, from *fore* (adv.)]

fore-and-aft·er *n. Nautical.* **1.** any vessel with a fore-and-aft rig. **2.** a double-ended vessel.

fore·arm[1] ('fɔːrˌɑːm) *n.* the part of the arm from the elbow to the wrist. [C18: from FORE- + ARM[1]]

fore·arm[2] (fɔːr'ɑːm) *vb.* (*tr.*) to prepare or arm (someone, esp. oneself) in advance. [C16: from FORE- + ARM[2]]

fore·arm smash *n.* a blow like a punch delivered with the forearm in certain types of wrestling.

fore·bear *or* **for·bear** ('fɔːˌbɛə) *n.* an ancestor; forefather.

fore·bode (fɔː'bəʊd) *vb.* **1.** to warn of or indicate (an event, result, etc.) in advance. **2.** to have an intuition or premonition of (an event). —**fore·'bod·er** *n.*

fore·bod·ing (fɔː'bəʊdɪŋ) *n.* **1.** a feeling of impending evil, disaster, etc. **2.** an omen or portent. ~*adj.* **3.** presaging something. —**fore·'bod·ing·ly** *adv.* —**fore·'bod·ing·ness** *n.*

fore·brain ('fɔːˌbreɪn) *n.* the nontechnical name for **prosencephalon.**

fore·cast ('fɔːˌkɑːst) *vb.* **·casts, ·cast·ing, ·cast** *or* **·cast·ed. 1.** to predict or calculate (weather, events, etc.), in advance. **2.** (*tr.*) to serve as an early indication of. **3.** (*tr.*) to plan in advance. ~*n.* **4.** a statement of probable future weather conditions calculated from meteorological data. **5.** a prophecy or prediction. **6.** the practice or power of forecasting. —**'fore·ˌcast·er** *n.*

fore·cas·tle, fo'c's'le, *or* **fo'c'sle** ('fəʊksᵊl) *n.* the part of a vessel at the bow where the crew is quartered and stores, machines, etc., may be stowed.

fore·close (fɔː'kləʊz) *vb.* **1.** *Law.* to deprive (a mortgagor, etc.) of the right to redeem (a mortgage or pledge). **2.** (*tr.*) to shut out; bar. **3.** (*tr.*) to prevent or hinder. **4.** (*tr.*) to answer or settle (an obligation, promise, etc.) in advance. **5.** (*tr.*) to make an exclusive claim to. [C15: from Old French *forclore*, from *for-* out + *clore* to close, from Latin *claudere*] —**fore·'clos·a·ble** *adj.* —**fore·clo·sure** (fɔː'kləʊʒə) *n.*

fore·course ('fɔːˌkɔːs) *n. Nautical.* the lowest foresail on a square-rigged vessel.

fore·court ('fɔːˌkɔːt) *n.* **1.** a courtyard in front of a building, as one in a filling station. **2.** Also called: **front court.** the front section of the court in tennis, badminton, etc., esp. the area between the service line and the net.

fore·deck ('fɔːˌdɛk) *n. Nautical.* the deck between the bridge and the forecastle.

fore·do (fɔː'duː) *vb.* **·does, ·do·ing, ·did, ·done.** (*tr.*) a variant spelling of **fordo.**

fore·doom (fɔː'duːm) *vb.* (*tr.*) to doom or condemn beforehand.

fore-edge *n.* the outer edge of the pages of a book.

fore·fa·ther ('fɔːˌfɑːðə) *n.* an ancestor, esp. a male. —**'fore·ˌfa·ther·ly** *adj.*

fore·fend (fɔː'fɛnd) *vb.* (*tr.*) a variant spelling of **forfend.**

fore·fin·ger ('fɔːˌfɪŋgə) *n.* the finger next to the thumb. Also called: **index finger.**

fore·foot ('fɔːˌfʊt) *n., pl.* **·feet. 1.** either of the front feet of a quadruped. **2.** *Nautical.* the forward end of the keel.

fore·front ('fɔːˌfrʌnt) *n.* **1.** the extreme front. **2.** the position of most prominence, responsibility, or action.

fore·gath·er (fɔː'gæðə) *vb.* a variant spelling of **forgather.**

fore·go[1] (fɔː'gəʊ) *vb.* **·goes, ·go·ing, ·went, ·gone.** to precede in time, place, etc. [Old English *foregān*] —**fore·'go·er** *n.*

fore·go[2] (fɔː'gəʊ) *vb.* **·goes, ·go·ing, ·went, ·gone.** (*tr.*) a variant spelling of **forgo.** —**fore·'go·er** *n.*

fore·go·ing (fɔː'gəʊɪŋ) *adj.* (*prenominal*) (esp. of writing or speech) going before; preceding.

fore·gone (fɔː'gɒn, 'fɔːˌgɒn) *adj.* gone or completed; past. —**fore·'gone·ness** *n.*

fore·gone con·clu·sion *n.* an inevitable result or conclusion.

fore·ground ('fɔːˌgraʊnd) *n.* **1.** the part of a scene situated towards the front or nearest to the viewer. **2.** the area of space in a perspective picture, depicted as nearest the viewer. **3.** a conspicuous or active position.

fore·gut ('fɔːˌgʌt) *n.* **1.** the anterior part of the digestive tract of vertebrates, between the buccal cavity and the bile duct. **2.** the anterior part of the digestive tract of arthropods. ~See also **midgut, hindgut.**

fore·hand ('fɔːˌhænd) *adj.* (*prenominal*) **1.** *Tennis, squash, etc.* **a.** (of a stroke) made with the palm of the hand facing the direction of the stroke. **b.** of or relating to the right side of a right-handed player or the left side of a left-handed player. **2.** foremost or paramount. **3.** done or given beforehand. ~*n.* **4.** *Tennis, squash, etc.* **a.** a forehand stroke. **b.** the side on which such strokes are made. **5.** the part of a horse in front of the saddle. **6.** a frontal position. ~*adv.* **7.** *Tennis, squash, etc.* with a forehand stroke. ~*vb.* **8.** to play (a shot) forehand.

fore·hand·ed (ˌfɔː'hændɪd) *adj.* **1.** *U.S.* **a.** thrifty. **b.** well-off. ~*adv., adj.* **2.** *Tennis, squash, etc.* a less common word for **forehand.** —**ˌfore·'hand·ed·ly** *adv.* —**ˌfore·'hand·ed·ness** *n.*

fore·head ('fɒrɪd) *n.* the part of the face between the natural hair line and the eyes, formed skeletally by the frontal bone of the skull; brow. Related adj.: **frontal.** [Old English *forhēafod;* related to Old Frisian *forhāfd,* Middle Low German *vorhōved*]

fore·hock ('fɔːˌhɒk) *n.* a foreleg cut of bacon or pork.

for·eign ('fɒrɪn) *adj.* **1.** of, involving, located in, or coming from another country, area, people, etc.: *a foreign resident.* **2.** dealing or concerned with another country, area, people, etc.: *a foreign office.* **3.** not pertinent or related: *a matter foreign to the discussion.* **4.** not familiar: strange. **5.** in an abnormal place or position: *foreign matter.* **6.** *Law.* outside the jurisdiction of a particular state; alien. [C13: from Old French *forain,* from Vulgar Latin *forānus* (unattested) situated on the outside, from Latin *foris* outside] —'**for·eign·ly** *adv.* —'**for·eign·ness** *n.*

for·eign af·fairs *pl. n.* **1.** matters abroad that involve the homeland, such as relations with another country. **2.** matters that do not involve the homeland.

for·eign aid *n.* economic and other assistance given by one country to another.

for·eign bill *or* **draft** *n.* a bill of exchange that is drawn in one country and made payable in another: used extensively in foreign trade. Compare **inland bill.**

for·eign cor·res·pond·ent *n. Journalism.* a reporter who visits or resides in a foreign country in order to report on its affairs.

for·eign·er ('fɒrɪnə) *n.* **1.** a person from a foreign country; alien. **2.** an outsider or interloper. **3.** something from a foreign country, such as a ship or product.

for·eign ex·change *n.* **1.** the system by which one currency is converted into another, enabling international transactions to take place without the physical transportation of gold. **2.** foreign bills and currencies.

for·eign·ism ('fɒrɪˌnɪzəm) *n.* **1.** a custom, mannerism, idiom, etc., that is foreign. **2.** imitation of something foreign.

for·eign le·gion *n.* a body of foreign volunteers serving in an army, esp. that of France.

for·eign min·is·ter *or* **sec·re·ta·ry** *n.* (*often caps.*) a cabinet minister who is responsible for a country's dealings with other countries. U.S. equivalent: **secretary of state.** —**for·eign min·is·try** *n.*

for·eign mis·sion *n.* **1.** a body of persons sent to a non-Christian country in order to propagate Christianity. **2.** a diplomatic or other mission sent by one country to another.

for·eign of·fice *n.* the ministry of a country or state that is concerned with dealings with other states. U.S. equivalent: **state department.**

for·eign serv·ice *n. Chiefly U.S.* the diplomatic and usually consular personnel of a foreign affairs ministry or foreign office collectively who represent their country abroad, deal with foreign diplomats at home, etc.

fore·judge[1] (fɔː'dʒʌdʒ) *vb.* to judge (someone or an event, circumstance, etc.) before the facts are known; prejudge.

fore·judge[2] (fɔː'dʒʌdʒ) *vb. Law.* a variant spelling of **forjudge.** —**fore·'judge·ment** *n.*

fore·know (fɔː'nəʊ) *vb.* **·knows, ·know·ing, ·knew, ·known.** (*tr.*) to know in advance. —**fore·'know·a·ble** *adj.* —**fore·'knowl·edge** *n.* —**fore·'know·ing·ly** *adv.*

fore·land ('fɔːlənd) *n.* **1.** a headland, cape, or promontory. **2.** land lying in front of something, such as water.

Fore·land ('fɔːlənd) *n.* either of two headlands (**North Foreland** and **South Foreland**) in SE England, on the coast of Kent.

fore·leg ('fɔːˌlɛg) *n.* either of the front legs of a horse, sheep, or other quadruped.

fore·limb ('fɔːˌlɪm) *n.* either of the front or anterior limbs of a four-limbed vertebrate: a foreleg, flipper, or wing.

fore·lock[1] ('fɔːˌlɒk) *n.* **1.** a lock of hair growing or falling over the forehead. **2.** a lock of a horse's mane that grows forwards between the ears.

fore·lock[2] ('fɔːˌlɒk) *n.* **1.** a wedge or peg passed through the tip of a bolt to prevent withdrawal. ~*vb.* **2.** (*tr.*) to secure (a bolt) by means of a forelock.

fore·man ('fɔːmən) *n., pl.* **·men. 1.** a person, often experienced, who supervises other workmen. Female equivalent: **forewoman. 2.** *Law.* the principal juror, who presides at the deliberations of a jury. —'**fore·man·ˌship** *n.*

fore·mast ('fɔːˌmɑːst; *Nautical* 'fɔːməst) *n.* the mast nearest the bow on vessels with two or more masts.

fore·most ('fɔːˌməʊst) *adj., adv.* first in time, place, rank, etc. [Old English *formest,* from *forma* first; related to Old Saxon *formo* first, Old High German *fruma* advantage]

fore·name ('fɔːˌneɪm) *n.* another term for **Christian name.**

fore·named ('fɔːˌneɪmd) *adj.* (*prenominal*) named or mentioned previously; aforesaid.

fore·noon ('fɔːˌnuːn) *n.* **a.** the daylight hours before or just before noon. **b.** (*as modifier*): *a forenoon conference.*

fo·ren·sic (fə'rɛnsɪk) *adj.* relating to, used in, or connected with a court of law: *forensic science.* [C17: from Latin *forēnsis* public, from FORUM] —**fo·ren·si·cal·i·ty** (fəˌrɛnsɪ'kælɪtɪ) *n.* —**fo·'ren·si·cal·ly** *adv.*

fo·ren·sic med·i·cine *n.* the applied use of medical knowledge or practice, esp. pathology, to the purposes of the law, as in determining the cause of death. Also called: **medical jurisprudence, legal medicine.**

fo·ren·sics (fə'rɛnsɪks) *n.* (*functioning as sing. or pl.*) the art or study of formal debating.

fore·or·dain (ˌfɔːrɔː'deɪn) *vb.* (*tr.; may take a clause as object*) to determine (events, results, etc.) in the future. —ˌ**fore·or·'dain·ment** *or* **fore·or·di·na·tion** (ˌfɔːrɔːdɪ'neɪʃən) *n.*

fore·part ('fɔːˌpɑːt) *n.* the first or front part in place, order, or time.

fore·paw ('fɔːˌpɔː) *n.* either of the front feet of most land mammals that do not have hoofs.

fore·peak ('fɔːˌpiːk) *n. Nautical.* the interior part of a vessel that is furthest forward.

fore·play ('fɔːˌpleɪ) *n.* mutual sexual stimulation preceding sexual intercourse.

fore·quar·ter ('fɔːˌkwɔːtə) *n.* the front portion, including the leg, of half of a carcass, as of beef or lamb.

fore·quar·ters ('fɔːˌkwɔːtəz) *pl. n.* the part of the body of a horse or similar quadruped that consists of the forelegs, shoulders, and adjoining parts.

fore·reach (fɔː'riːtʃ) *vb.* **1.** (*intr.*) *Nautical.* to keep moving under momentum without engine or sails. **2.** (*tr.*) to surpass or outdo.

fore·run (fɔː'rʌn) *vb.* **·runs, ·run·ning, ·ran, ·run.** (*tr.*) **1.** to serve as a herald for. **2.** to go before; precede. **3.** to prevent or forestall.

fore·run·ner ('fɔːˌrʌnə) *n.* **1.** a person or thing that precedes another; precursor. **2.** a person or thing coming in advance to herald the arrival of someone or something; harbinger. **3.** an indication beforehand of something to follow; omen; portent.

fore·said ('fɔːˌsɛd) *adj.* a less common word for **aforesaid.**

fore·sail ('fɔːˌseɪl; *Nautical* 'fɔːsᵊl) *n. Nautical.* **1.** the aftermost headsail of a fore-and-aft rigged vessel. **2.** the lowest sail set on the foremast of a square-rigged vessel.

fore·see (fɔː'siː) *vb.* **·sees, ·see·ing, ·saw, ·seen.** (*tr.; may take a clause as object*) to see or know beforehand: *he did not foresee that.* —**fore·'see·a·ble** *adj.* —**fore·'se·er** *n.*

fore·shad·ow (fɔː'ʃædəʊ) *vb.* (*tr.*) to show, indicate, or suggest in advance; presage. —**fore·'shad·ow·er** *n.*

fore·shank ('fɔːˌʃæŋk) *n.* **1.** the top of the front leg of an animal. **2.** a cut of meat from this part.

fore·sheet ('fɔːˌʃiːt) *n.* **1.** the sheet of a foresail. **2.** (*pl.*) the part forward of the foremost thwart of a boat.

fore·shock ('fɔːˌʃɒk) *n. Chiefly U.S.* a minor earthquake preceding and associated with a larger one.

fore·shore ('fɔːˌʃɔː) *n.* the part of the shore that lies between the limits for high and low tides.

fore·short·en (fɔː'ʃɔːtᵊn) *vb.* (*tr.*) **1.** to represent (a line, form, object, etc.) as shorter than actual length in order to give an illusion of recession or projection, in accordance with the laws of linear perspective. **2.** to make shorter or more condensed; reduce or abridge.

fore·show (fɔː'ʃəʊ) *vb.* **·shows, ·show·ing, ·showed, ·shown.** (*tr.*) *Archaic.* to indicate in advance; foreshadow.

fore·side ('fɔːˌsaɪd) *n.* **1.** the front or upper side or part. **2.** *U.S.* land extending along the sea.

fore·sight ('fɔːˌsaɪt) *n.* **1.** provision for or insight into future problems, needs, etc. **2.** the act or ability of foreseeing. **3.** the act of looking forward. **4.** *Surveying.* a reading taken looking forwards to a new station, esp. in levelling from a point of known elevation to a point the elevation of which is to be determined. Compare **backsight. 5.** a sight on a firearm's muzzle. —ˌ**fore·'sight·ed** *adj.* —ˌ**fore·'sight·ed·ly** *adv.* —ˌ**fore·'sight·ed·ness** *n.*

fore·skin ('fɔːˌskɪn) *n. Anatomy.* the nontechnical name for **prepuce** (sense 1).

fore·speak (fɔː'spiːk) *vb.* **·speaks, ·speak·ing, ·spoke, ·spo·ken.** (*tr.*) *Rare.* **1.** to predict; foresee. **2.** to arrange or speak of in advance.

fore·spent (fɔː'spɛnt) *adj.* a variant spelling of **forspent.**

for·est ('fɒrɪst) *n.* **1.** a large wooded area having a thick growth of trees and plants. **2.** the trees of such an area. **3.** something resembling a large wooded area, esp. in density: *a forest of telegraph poles.* **4.** *Law.* (formerly) an area of woodland, esp. one owned by the sovereign and set apart as a hunting ground with its own laws and officers. Compare **park** (sense 4). **5.** (*modifier*) of, involving, or living in a forest or forests: *a forest glade.* ~*vb.* **6.** (*tr.*) to create a forest; plant with trees. [C13: from Old French, from Medieval Latin *forestis* unfenced woodland, from Latin *foris* outside] —'**for·est·al** *or* **fo·res·te·al** (fə'rɛstɪəl) *adj.* —'**for·est·ed** *adj.* —'**for·est·less** *adj.* —'**for·est·ˌlike** *adj.*

fore·stall (fɔː'stɔːl) *vb.* (*tr.*) **1.** to delay, stop, or guard against beforehand. **2.** to anticipate. **3. a.** to prevent or hinder sales at (a market, etc.) by buying up merchandise in advance, etc. **b.** to buy up merchandise for profitable resale. Compare **corner** (sense 19). [C14 *forestallen* to waylay, from Old English *foresteall* an ambush, from *fore-* in front of + *steall* place] —**fore·'stall·er** *n.* —**fore·'stal·ment** *or esp. U.S.* **fore·'stall·ment** *n.*

for·est·a·tion (ˌfɒrɪ'steɪʃən) *n.* the planting of trees over a wide area.

fore·stay ('fɔːˌsteɪ) *n. Nautical.* an adjustable stay leading from the truck of the foremast to the deck, stem, or bowsprit, for controlling the motion or bending of the mast.

fore·stay·sail (fɔː'steɪˌseɪl; *Nautical* fɔː'steɪsᵊl) *n. Nautical.* the triangular headsail set aftermost on a vessel.

for·est·er ('fɒrɪstə) *n.* **1.** a person skilled in forestry or in charge of a forest. **2.** any of various Old World moths of the genus *Ino,* characterized by brilliant metallic green wings: family *Zygaenidae.* **3.** a person or animal that lives in a forest. **4.** (*cap.*) a member of the Ancient Order of Foresters, a friendly society.

For·est·er ('fɒrɪstə) *n.* **C(ecil) S(cott).** 1899–1966, English novelist; creator of *Captain Horatio Hornblower* in a series of novels on the Napoleonic Wars.

for·est rang·er *n. Chiefly U.S.* a government official who patrols and protects forests, wildlife, etc.

for·est·ry ('fɒrɪstrɪ) *n.* **1.** the science of planting and caring for trees. **2.** the planting and management of forests. **3.** *Rare.* forest land.

fore·taste *n.* ('fɔːˌteɪst). **1.** an early but limited experience or awareness of something to come. ~*vb.* (fɔː'teɪst) **2.** (*tr.*) to have a foretaste of.

fore·tell (fɔː'tɛl) *vb.* **·tells, ·tell·ing, ·told.** (*tr.; may take a clause as object*) to tell or indicate (an event, result, etc.) beforehand; predict. —**fore·'tell·er** *n.*

fore·thought ('fɔːˌθɔːt) *n.* **1.** advance consideration or deliberation. **2.** thoughtful anticipation of future events. —**fore·'thought·ful** *adj.* —**fore·'thought·ful·ly** *adv.* —**fore·'thought·ful·ness** *n.*

fore·time ('fɔːˌtaɪm) *n.* time already gone; the past.

fore·to·ken *n.* ('fɔːˌtəʊkən). **1.** a sign of a future event. ~*vb.* (fɔː'təʊkən). **2.** (*tr.*) to foreshadow.

fore·tooth ('fɔːˌtuːθ) *n., pl.* **·teeth.** *Dentistry.* another word for an **incisor.**

fore·top ('fɔːˌtɒp; *Nautical* 'fɔːtəp) *n. Nautical.* a platform at the top of the foremast.

fore-top·gal·lant (ˌfɔːtɒp'gælənt; *Nautical* ˌfɔːtə'gælənt) *adj. Nautical.* of, relating to, or being the topmost portion of a foremast, above the topmast: *the fore-topgallant mast.*

fore-top·mast (fɔː'tɒpˌmɑːst; *Nautical* fɔː'tɒpməst) *n. Nautical.* a mast stepped above a foremast.

fore-top·sail (fɔː'tɒpˌseɪl; *Nautical* fɔː'tɒpsᵊl) *n. Nautical.* a sail set on a fore-topmast.

fore·tri·an·gle ('fɔːtraɪˌæŋgᵊl) *n.* the triangular area formed by the deck, foremast, and headstay of a sailing vessel.

for ev·er *or* **for·ev·er** (fɔː'rɛvə, fə-) *adv.* **1.** without end; everlastingly; eternally. **2.** at all times; incessantly. **3.** *Informal.* for a very long time: *he went on speaking for ever.* ~*n.* **for·ev·er. 4.** (*as object*) *Informal.* a very long time: *it took him forever to reply.* **5. ... for ever!** an exclamation expressing support or loyalty: *Scotland for ever!*

for ev·er·more *or* **for·ev·er·more** (fɔːˌrɛvə'mɔː, fə-) *adv.* a more emphatic or emotive term for **for ever.**

fore·warn (fɔː'wɔːn) *vb.* (*tr.*) to warn beforehand. —**fore·'warn·er** *n.* —**fore·'warn·ing·ly** *adv.*

fore·went (fɔː'wɛnt) *vb.* the past tense of **forego.**

fore·wind ('fɔːˌwɪnd) *n. Nautical.* a favourable wind.

fore·wing ('fɔːˌwɪŋ) *n.* either wing of the anterior pair of an insect's two pairs of wings.

fore·word ('fɔːˌwɜːd) *n.* an introductory statement to a book. [C19: literal translation of German *Vorwort*]

fore·worn (fɔː'wɔːn) *adj.* a variant spelling of **forworn.**

fore·yard ('fɔːˌjɑːd) *n. Nautical.* a yard for supporting the foresail of a square-rigger.

For·far ('fɔːfər, -fɑː) *n.* **1.** a market town in E Scotland, in Tayside region: site of a castle, residence of Scottish kings between the 11th and 14th centuries. Pop.: 10 349 (1971).

for·feit ('fɔːfɪt) *n.* **1.** something lost or given up as a penalty for a fault, mistake, etc. **2.** the act of losing or surrendering something in this manner. **3.** *Law.* something confiscated as a penalty for an offence, breach of contract, etc. **4.** (*sometimes pl.*) **a.** a game in which a player has to give up an object, perform a specified action, etc., if he commits a fault. **b.** an object so given up. ~*vb.* **5.** (*tr.*) to lose or be liable to lose in consequence of a mistake, fault, etc. **6.** (*tr.*) *Law.* **a.** to confiscate as punishment. **b.** to surrender (something exacted as a penalty). ~*adj.* **7.** surrendered or liable to be surrendered as a penalty. [C13: from Old French *forfet* offence, from *forfaire* to commit a crime, from Medieval Latin *foris facere* to act outside (what is lawful), from Latin *foris* outside + *facere* to do] —**'for·feit·a·ble** *adj.* —**'for·feit·er** *n.*

for·fei·ture ('fɔːfɪtʃə) *n.* **1.** something forfeited. **2.** the act of forfeiting or paying a penalty.

for·fend *or* **fore·fend** (fɔː'fɛnd) *vb.* (*tr.*) **1.** *U.S.* to protect or secure. **2.** *Obsolete.* to prohibit or prevent.

for·fi·cate ('fɔːfɪkɪt, -ˌkeɪt) *adj.* (esp. of the tails of certain birds) deeply forked. [C19: from Latin *forfex* scissors]

for·gat (fə'gæt) *vb. Archaic.* a past tense of **forget.**

for·gath·er *or* **fore·gath·er** (fɔː'gæðə) *vb.* (*intr.*) **1.** to gather together; assemble. **2.** *Rare.* to meet, esp. unexpectedly. **3.** (foll. by *with*) to socialize.

for·gave (fə'geɪv) *vb.* the past tense of **forgive.**

forge[1] (fɔːdʒ) *n.* **1.** a place in which metal is worked by heating and hammering; smithy. **2.** a hearth or furnace used for heating metal. **3.** a machine used to shape metals by hammering. ~*vb.* **4.** (*tr.*) to shape (metal) by heating and hammering. **5.** (*tr.*) to form, shape, make, or fashion (objects, articles, etc.). **6.** (*tr.*) to invent or devise (an agreement, understanding, etc.). **7.** to make or produce a fraudulent imitation of (a signature, banknote, etc.) or to commit forgery. [C14: from Old French *forgier* to construct, from Latin *fabricāre,* from *faber* craftsman] —**'forge·a·ble** *adj.* —**'forg·er** *n.*

forge[2] (fɔːdʒ) *vb.* (*intr.*) **1.** to move at a steady and persevering pace. **2. forge ahead.** to increase speed; spurt. [C17: of unknown origin]

for·ger·y ('fɔːdʒərɪ) *n., pl.* **·ger·ies. 1.** the act of reproducing something for a deceitful or fraudulent purpose. **2.** something forged, such as a work of art or an antique. **3.** *Criminal law.* **a.** the false making or altering of a document, such as a cheque, banknote, etc., with intent to defraud. **b.** something forged. **4.** *Criminal law.* the counterfeiting of a seal or die with intention to defraud.

for·get (fə'gɛt) *vb.* **·gets, ·get·ting, ·got, ·got·ten** *or* **·got. 1.** (when *tr., may take a clause as object or an infinitive*) to fail to recall (someone or something once known); be unable to remember. **2.** (*tr.; may take a clause as object or an infinitive*) to neglect, usually as the result of an unintentional error. **3.** (*tr.*) to leave behind by mistake. **4.** (*tr.*) to disregard intentionally. **5.** (when *tr., may take a clause as object*) to fail to mention. **6. forget oneself. a.** to act in an improper manner. **b.** to be unselfish. **c.** to be deep in thought. **7. forget it!** an exclamation of annoyed or forgiving dismissal of a matter or topic. [Old English *forgietan;* related to Old Frisian *forgeta,* Old Saxon *fargetan,* Old High German *firgezzan*] —**for·'get·ta·ble** *adj.* —**for·'get·ter** *n.*

for·get·ful (fə'gɛtfʊl) *adj.* **1.** tending to forget. **2.** (*often postpositive;* foll. by *of*) inattentive (to) or neglectful (of). **3.** *Poetic.* causing loss of memory. —**for·'get·ful·ly** *adv.* —**for·'get·ful·ness** *n.*

for·get-me-not *n.* any temperate low-growing plants of the mainly European boraginaceous genus *Myosotis,* esp. *M. scorpioides,* having clusters of small typically blue flowers. Also called: **scorpion grass.**

forg·ing ('fɔːdʒɪŋ) *n.* **1.** the process of producing a metal component by hammering. **2.** the act of a forger. **3.** a metal component produced by this process. **4.** the collision of a horse's hind shoe and fore shoe.

for·give (fə'gɪv) *vb.* **·gives, ·giv·ing, ·gave, ·giv·en. 1.** to cease to blame or hold resentment against (someone or something). **2.** to grant pardon for (a mistake, wrongdoing, etc.). **3.** (*tr.*) to free or pardon (someone) from penalty. **4.** (*tr.*) to free from the obligation of (a debt, payment, etc.). [Old English *forgiefan;* see FOR-, GIVE] —**for·'giv·a·ble** *adj.* —**for·'giv·a·bly** *adv.* —**for·'giv·er** *n.*

for·giv·en (fə'gɪvᵊn) *vb.* the past participle of **forgive.**

for·give·ness (fə'gɪvnɪs) *n.* **1.** the act of forgiving or the state of being forgiven. **2.** willingness to forgive.

for·giv·ing (fə'gɪvɪŋ) *adj.* willing to forgive; merciful. —**for·'giv·ing·ly** *adv.* —**for·'giv·ing·ness** *n.*

for·go *or* **fore·go** (fɔː'gəʊ) *vb.* **·goes, ·go·ing, ·went, ·gone.** (*tr.*) **1.** to give up or do without. **2.** *Archaic.* to leave. [Old English *forgān;* see FOR-, GO[1]] —**for·'go·er** *or* **fore·'go·er** *n.*

for·got (fə'gɒt) *vb.* **1.** the past tense of **forget. 2.** *Archaic or dialect.* a past participle of **forget.**

for·got·ten (fə'gɒtᵊn) *vb.* the past participle of **forget.**

for·int (*Hungarian* 'forint) *n.* the standard monetary unit of Hungary, divided into 100 fillér. [from Hungarian, from Italian *fiorino* FLORIN]

for·judge *or* **fore·judge** (fɔː'dʒʌdʒ) *vb.* (*tr.*) *Law.* **1.** to deprive of a right by the judgment of a court. **2.** *Chiefly U.S.* to expel (an officer or attorney) from court for misconduct. —**for·'judg·ment** *or* **fore·'judg·ment** *n.*

fork (fɔːk) *n.* **1.** a small usually metal implement consisting of two, three, or four long thin prongs on the end of a handle, used for lifting food to the mouth or turning it in cooking, etc. **2.** an agricultural tool consisting of a handle and three or four metal prongs, used for lifting, digging, etc. **3.** a pronged part of any machine, device, etc. **4.** (of a road, river, etc.) **a.** a division into two or more branches. **b.** the point where the division begins. **c.** such a branch. **5.** *Chiefly U.S.* the main tributary of a river. **6.** *Chess.* a position in which two pieces are forked. ~*vb.* **7.** (*tr.*) to pick up, dig, etc., with a fork. **8.** (*tr.*) *Chess.* to place (two enemy pieces) under attack with one of one's own pieces, esp. a knight. **9.** (*tr.*) to make into the shape of a fork. **10.** (*intr.*) to be divided into two or more branches. **11.** to take one or other branch at a fork in a road, river, etc. [Old English *forca,* from Latin *furca*] —**'fork·ful** *n.*

forked (fɔːkt, 'fɔːkɪd) *adj.* **1. a.** having a fork or forklike parts. **b.** (*in combination*): *two-forked.* **2.** having sharp angles; zigzag. **3.** insincere or equivocal (esp. in the phrase **forked tongue**). —**fork·ed·ly** ('fɔːkɪdlɪ) *adv.* —**'fork·ed·ness** *n.*

forked light·ning *n.* a zigzag form of lightning. Also called: **chain lightning.**

fork-lift truck *n.* a vehicle having two power-operated horizontal prongs that can be raised and lowered for loading, transporting, and unloading goods, esp. goods that are stacked on wooden pallets.

fork out, over, *or* **up** *vb.* (*adv.*) *Slang.* to pay (money, goods, etc.), esp. with reluctance.

For·lì (*Italian* for'li) *n.* a city in N Italy, in Emilia-Romagna. Pop.: 108 888 (1975 est.). Ancient name: **Forum Livii.**

for·lorn (fə'lɔːn) *adj.* **1.** miserable, wretched, or cheerless; desolate. **2.** deserted; forsaken. **3.** (*postpositive;* foll. by *of*) destitute; bereft: *forlorn of hope.* **4.** desperate: *the last forlorn attempt.* [Old English *forloren* lost, from *forlēosan* to lose; related to Old Saxon *farliosan,* Gothic *fraliusan,* Greek *luein* to release] —**for·'lorn·ly** *adv.* —**for·'lorn·ness** *n.*

for·lorn hope *n.* **1.** a hopeless or desperate enterprise. **2.** a faint hope. **3.** *Obsolete.* a group of soldiers assigned to an extremely dangerous duty. [C16 (in the obsolete sense): changed (by folk etymology) from Dutch *verloren hoop* lost troop, from *verloren,* past participle of *verliezen* to lose + *hoop* troop (literally: heap)]

form (fɔːm) *n.* **1.** the shape or configuration of something as distinct from its colour, texture, etc. **2.** the particular mode, appearance, etc., in which a thing or person manifests itself: *water in the form of ice; in the form of a bat.* **3.** a type or kind: *imprisonment is a form of punishment.* **4. a.** a printed document, esp. one with spaces in which to insert facts or answers: *an application form.* **b.** (*as modifier*): *a form letter.* **5.** physical or mental condition, esp. good condition, with reference to ability to perform: *off form.* **6.** the previous record of a horse, athlete, etc., esp. with regard to fitness. **7.** style, arrangement, or design in the arts, as opposed to content. **8.** a fixed mode of artistic expression or representation in literary, musical, or other artistic works: *sonata form; sonnet form.* **9.** a mould, frame, etc., that gives shape to something. **10.** *Education, chiefly Brit.* a group of children who are taught together; class. **11.** manner, method, or style of doing something, esp. with regard to recognized standards. **12.** behaviour or procedure, esp. as governed by custom or etiquette: *good form.* **13.** formality or ceremony. **14.** a prescribed set or order of words, terms, etc., as in a religious ceremony or legal document. **15.** *Philosophy.* **a.** the essence of something, esp. as distinguished from *matter.* **b.** (in the philosophy of Aristotle) that which makes a thing belong to its particular class. **16.** *Logic.* **a.** the pattern of an argument by which the reasoning can be shown to be logically valid or invalid. **b.** the related pattern of a set of propositions or arguments all of which have different subject matter. **17.** *Brit.* a bench, esp. one that is long, low, and backless. **18.** the nest or hollow in which a hare lives. **19.** a group of organisms within a species that differ from similar groups by trivial differences, as of colour. **20.** *Linguistics.* **a.** the phonological or orthographic shape or appearance of a linguistic element, such as a word. **b.** a linguistic element considered from the point of view of its shape or sound rather than, for example, its meaning. **21.** *Crystallog.* See **crystal form.** ~*vb.* **22.** to give shape or form to or to take shape or form, esp. a specified or particular shape. **23.** to come or bring into existence: *a scum formed on the surface.* **24.** to make, produce, or construct or be made, produced, or constructed. **25.** to construct or develop in the mind: *to form an opinion.* **26.** (*tr.*) to train, develop, or mould by instruction, discipline, or example. **27.** (*tr.*) to acquire, contract, or develop: *to form a habit.* **28.** (*tr.*) to be an element of, serve as, or constitute: *this plank will form a bridge.* **29.** (*tr.*) to draw up; organize: *to form a club.* [C13: from Old French *forme,* from Latin *forma* shape, model] —**'form+a·ble** *adj.*

Form (fɔːm) *n. Philosophy.* a Platonic idea. See **idea** (sense 7).

-form *adj. combining form.* having the shape or form of or resembling: *cruciform; vermiform.* [from New Latin *-formis,* from Latin, from *fōrma* FORM]

for+mal[1] ('fɔːməl) *adj.* **1.** of, according to, or following established or prescribed forms, conventions, etc.: *a formal document.* **2.** characterized by observation of conventional forms of ceremony, behaviour, dress, etc.: *a formal dinner.* **3.** methodical, precise, or stiff. **4.** suitable for occasions organized according to conventional ceremony: *formal dress.* **5.** denoting or characterized by idiom, vocabulary, etc., used by educated speakers and writers of a language. **6.** acquired by study in academic institutions: *a formal education.* **7.** regular or symmetrical in form: *a formal garden.* **8.** of or relating to the appearance, form, etc., of something as distinguished from its substance. **9.** logically deductive: *formal proof.* **10.** *Philosophy.* **a.** of or relating to form as opposed to matter. **b.** (in the writings of Aristotle) essential. **11.** denoting a second-person pronoun in some languages used when the addressee is a stranger, social superior, etc.: *in French the pronoun "vous" is formal, while "tu" is informal.* [C14: from Latin *formālis*] —**'for+mal+ly** *adv.* —**'for+mal+ness** *n.*

for+mal[2] ('fɔːmæl) *n.* another name for **methylal.** [C19: from FORM(IC) + -AL[3]]

for+mal+de+hyde (fɔː'mældɪˌhaɪd) *n.* a colourless poisonous irritating gas with a pungent characteristic odour, made by the oxidation of methanol and used as formalin and in the manufacture of synthetic resins. Formula: HCHO. Also called: **methanal.** [C19: FORM(IC) + ALDEHYDE; on the model of German *Formaldehyd*]

for+ma+lin ('fɔːməlɪn) *or* **for+mol** ('fɔːmɒl) *n.* a 40-per-cent solution of formaldehyde in water, used as a disinfectant, preservative for biological specimens, etc.

for+mal+ism ('fɔːməˌlɪzəm) *n.* **1.** scrupulous or excessive adherence to outward form at the expense of inner reality or content. **2.** the mathematical or logical structure of a scientific argument as distinguished from its subject matter. **3.** *Theatre.* a stylised mode of production. **4.** (in Marxist criticism, etc.) excessive concern with artistic technique at the expense of social values, etc. **5.** the philosophical theory that a mathematical statement has no meaning but that its symbols, regarded as physical objects, exhibit a structure that has useful applications. Compare **logicism, intuitionism.** —**'for+mal+ist** *n.* —**ˌfor+mal+'is+tic** *adj.* —**ˌfor+mal+'is+ti+cal+ly** *adv.*

for+mal+i·ty (fɔː'mælɪtɪ) *n., pl.* **·ties. 1.** a requirement of rule, custom, etiquette, etc. **2.** the condition or quality of being formal or conventional. **3.** strict or excessive observance of form, ceremony, etc. **4.** an established, proper, or conventional method, act, or procedure.

for+mal+ize *or* **for+mal+ise** ('fɔːməˌlaɪz) *vb.* **1.** to be or make formal. **2.** (*tr.*) to make official or valid. **3.** (*tr.*) to give a definite shape or form to. —**ˌfor+mal·i·'za+tion** *or* **ˌfor+mal·i+'sa+tion** *n.* —**'for+mal+ˌiz+er** *or* **'for+mal+ˌis+er** *n.*

for+mal lan+guage *n.* a language designed for use in situations in which natural language is unsuitable, as for example in mathematics, logic, or computer programming. The symbols and formulas of such languages stand in precisely specified syntactic and semantic relations to one another.

for+mal log+ic *n.* a branch of logic concerned with the analysis of the structure of propositions and with the deductive processes by which conclusions are drawn from propositions. See also **symbolic logic.**

for+mant ('fɔːmənt) *n. Acoustics, phonetics.* any of several frequency ranges within which the partials of a sound, esp. a vowel sound, are at their strongest, thus imparting to the sound its own special quality, tone colour, or timbre.

for+mat ('fɔːmæt) *n.* **1.** the general appearance of a publication, including type style, paper, binding, etc. **2.** an approximate indication of the size of a publication as determined by the number of times the original sheet of paper is folded to make a leaf. See also **duodecimo, quarto. 3.** style, plan, or arrangement, as of a television programme. **4.** *Computer technol.* the arrangement of data on magnetic tape, paper tape, etc., to comply with a computer's specific input device. ~*vb.* **+mats, +mat+ting, +mat+ted.** (*tr.*) **5.** to arrange (a book, page, etc.) into a specified format. [C19: via French from German, from Latin *liber formātus* volume formed]

for+mate ('fɔːmeɪt) *n.* any salt or ester of formic acid containing the ion $HCOO^-$ or the group HCOO-. [C19: from FORM(IC) + -ATE[1]]

for+ma+tion (fɔː'meɪʃən) *n.* **1.** the act of giving or taking form, shape, or existence. **2.** something that is formed. **3.** the manner in which something is formed or arranged. **4.** a formal arrangement of a number of persons or things acting as a unit, such as a troop of soldiers, aircraft in flight, or a football team. **5.** a series of rocks with certain characteristics in common. **6.** *Ecology.* a community of plants, such as a tropical rain forest, extending over a very large area. —**for+'ma+tion+al** *adj.*

form·a+tive ('fɔːmətɪv) *adj.* **1.** of or relating to formation, development, or growth: *formative years.* **2.** shaping; moulding: *a formative experience.* **3.** (of tissues and cells in certain parts of an organism) capable of growth and differentiation. **4.** functioning in the formation of derived, inflected, or compound words. ~*n.* **5.** an inflectional or derivational affix. **6.** (in generative grammar) any of the minimum units of a sentence that have syntactic function. —**'form·a+tive+ly** *adv.* —**'form·a+tive+ness** *n.*

form class *n.* **1.** another term for **part of speech. 2.** a group of words distinguished by common inflections, such as the weak verbs of English.

form drag *n.* the drag on a body moving through a fluid as a result of the shape of the body. It can be reduced by streamlining.

forme *or U.S.* **form** (fɔːm) *n. Printing.* type matter, blocks, etc., assembled in a chase and ready for printing. [C15: from French: FORM]

for+mer[1] ('fɔːmə) *adj.* (*prenominal*) **1.** belonging to or occurring in an earlier time: *former glory.* **2.** having been at a previous time: *a former colleague.* **3.** denoting the first or first mentioned of two: *in the former case.* **4.** near the beginning. ~*n.* **5. the former.** the first or first mentioned of two: distinguished from *latter.*

form+er[2] ('fɔːmə) *n.* **1.** a person or thing that forms or shapes. **2.** *Electrical engineering.* a tool for giving a coil or winding the required shape, sometimes consisting of a frame on which the wire can be wound, the frame then being removed.

for+mer+ly ('fɔːməlɪ) *adv.* **1.** at or in a former time; in the past. **2.** *Obsolete.* in the immediate past; just now.

form ge+nus *n.* a group of species (**form species**) that have similar structural characteristics but are not closely related.

for+mic ('fɔːmɪk) *adj.* **1.** of, relating to, or derived from ants. **2.** of, containing, or derived from formic acid. [C18: from Latin *formīca* ant; the acid occurs naturally in ants]

For+mi+ca (fɔː'maɪkə) *n. Trademark.* any of various laminated plastic sheets, containing melamine, used esp. for heat-resistant surfaces that can be easily cleaned.

for+mic ac+id *n.* a colourless corrosive liquid carboxylic acid found in some insects, esp. ants, and many plants: used in dyeing textiles and the manufacture of insecticides and refrigerants. Formula: HCOOH.

for+mi+car·y ('fɔːmɪkərɪ) *or* **for+mi+car+i·um** *n., pl.* **+car+ies** *or* **+car·i·a** (-'kɛərɪə). less common names for **ant hill.** [C19: from Medieval Latin *formīcārium;* see FORMIC]

for+mi+cate ('fɔːmɪˌkeɪt) *vb.* (*intr.*) *Now rare.* **1.** to crawl around like ants. **2.** to swarm with ants or other crawling things. [C17: from Latin *formīcāre,* from *formīca* ant]

for+mi+ca+tion (ˌfɔːmɪ'keɪʃən) *n.* a sensation of insects crawling on the skin; symptom of a nerve disorder.

for+mi+da·ble ('fɔːmɪdəbᵊl) *adj.* **1.** arousing or likely to inspire fear or dread. **2.** extremely difficult to defeat, overcome, manage, etc.: *a formidable problem.* **3.** tending to inspire awe or admiration because of great size, strength, excellence, etc. [C15: from Latin *formīdābilis,* from *formīdāre* to dread, from *formīdō* fear] —**ˌfor+mi+da·'bil+i+ty** *or* **'for+mi+da·ble+ness** *n.* —**'for+mi+da·bly** *adv.*

form+less ('fɔːmlɪs) *adj.* without a definite shape or form; amorphous. —**'form+less+ly** *adv.* —**'form+less+ness** *n.*

form let+ter *n.* a single copy of a letter that has been mechanically reproduced in large numbers for circulation.

For+mo+sa (fɔː'məʊsə) *n.* the former name of **Taiwan.**

For+mo+sa Strait *n.* an arm of the Pacific between Taiwan and mainland China, linking the East and South China Seas. Also called: **Taiwan Strait.**

for+mu+la ('fɔːmjʊlə) *n., pl.* **+las** *or* **+lae** (-ˌliː). **1.** an established form or set of words, as used in religious ceremonies, legal proceedings, etc. **2.** *Maths, physics.* a general relationship, principle, or rule stated, often as an equation, in the form of symbols. **3.** *Chem.* a representation of molecules, radicals, ions, etc., expressed in the symbols of the atoms of their constituent elements. See **molecular formula, empirical formula, structural formula. 4.** a method or rule for doing or producing something, often one proved to be successful. **5.**

U.S. **a.** a prescription for making up a medicine, baby's food, etc. **b.** a substance prepared according to such a prescription. **6.** *Motor racing.* the specific category in which a particular type of car competes, judged according to engine size, weight, and fuel capacity. [C17: from Latin: diminutive of *forma* FORM] —**for·mu·la·ic** (ˌfɔːmjʊˈleɪɪk) *adj.*

for·mu·lar·ize *or* **for·mu·lar·ise** (ˈfɔːmjʊləˌraɪz) *vb.* a less common word for **formulate** (sense 1). —ˌ**for·mu·lar·i·ˈza·tion** *or* ˌ**for·mu·lar·i·ˈsa·tion** *n.* —ˈ**for·mu·lar·ˌiz·er** *or* ˈ**for·mu·lar·ˌis·er** *n.*

for·mu·lar·y (ˈfɔːmjʊlərɪ) *n., pl.* **·lar·ies. 1.** a book or system of prescribed formulas, esp. relating to religious procedure or doctrine. **2.** a formula. **3.** *Pharmacol.* a book containing a list of pharmaceutical products with their formulas and means of preparation. ~*adj.* **4.** of, relating to, or of the nature of a formula.

for·mu·late (ˈfɔːmjʊˌleɪt) *vb.* (*tr.*) **1.** to put into or express in systematic terms; express in or as if in a formula. **2.** to devise. —ˌ**for·mu·ˈla·tion** *n.* —ˈ**for·mu·ˌla·tor** *n.*

for·mu·lism (ˈfɔːmjʊˌlɪzəm) *n.* adherence to or belief in formulas. —ˈ**for·mu·list** *n., adj.* —ˌ**for·mu·ˈlis·tic** *adj.*

form·work (ˈfɔːmˌwɜːk) *n.* an arrangement of wooden boards, bolts, etc., used to shape reinforced concrete while it is setting. Also called (esp. Brit.): **shuttering.**

for·myl (ˈfɔːmaɪl) *n.* (*modifier*) of, consisting of, or containing the monovalent group HCO-: *a formyl group or radical.* [C19: from FORM(IC) + -YL]

For·nax (ˈfɔːnæks) *n., Latin genitive* **For·na·cis** (fɔːˈneɪsɪs, -ˈnæs-). a faint constellation in the S hemisphere lying between Cetus and Phoenix. [Latin: oven, kiln]

for·nenst (fɔːˈnɛnst) *prep. Scot. and northeast English dialect.* situated against or facing towards [from Scottish, from FORE[1] + *anenst* a variant of archaic ANENT]

for·ni·cate[1] (ˈfɔːnɪˌkeɪt) *vb.* (*intr.*) to indulge in or commit fornication. [C16: from Late Latin *fornicārī*, from Latin *fornix* vault, brothel situated therein] —ˈ**for·ni·ˌca·tor** *n.*

for·ni·cate[2] (ˈfɔːnɪkɪt, -ˌkeɪt) *or* **for·ni·cat·ed** *adj. Biology.* arched or hoodlike in form. [C19: from Latin *fornicātus* arched, from *fornix* vault]

for·ni·ca·tion (ˌfɔːnɪˈkeɪʃən) *n.* **1.** voluntary sexual intercourse outside marriage. **2.** *Law.* voluntary sexual intercourse between two persons of the opposite sex, where one or both are unmarried. **3.** *Bible.* sexual immorality in general, esp. adultery.

for·nix (ˈfɔːnɪks) *n., pl.* **·ni·ces** (-nɪˌsiːz). *Anatomy.* any archlike structure, esp. the arched band of white fibres at the base of the brain. [C17: from Latin; see FORNICATE[2]] —ˈ**for·ni·cal** *adj.*

For·rest (ˈfɒrɪst) *n.* **John,** 1st Baron Forrest. 1847–1918, Australian statesman and explorer; first prime minister of Western Australia (1890–1901).

for·sake (fəˈseɪk) *vb.* **·sakes, ·sak·ing, ·sook, ·sak·en.** (*tr.*) **1.** to abandon. **2.** to give up (something valued or enjoyed). [Old English *forsacan*] —**for·ˈsak·er** *n.*

for·sak·en (fəˈseɪkən) *vb.* **1.** the past participle of **forsake.** ~*adj.* **2.** completely deserted or helpless; abandoned. —**for·ˈsak·en·ly** *adv.* —**for·ˈsak·en·ness** *n.*

for·sook (fəˈsʊk) *vb.* the past tense of **forsake.**

for·sooth (fəˈsuːθ) *adv. Archaic.* in truth; indeed. [Old English *forsōth*]

for·speak (fɔːˈspiːk) *vb.* **·speaks, ·speak·ing, ·spoke, ·spo·ken.** (*tr.*) *Scot. archaic.* to bewitch.

for·spent *or* **fore·spent** (fɔːˈspɛnt) *adj. Archaic.* tired out; exhausted.

For·ster (ˈfɔːstə) *n.* **E(dward) M(organ).** 1879–1970, English novelist, short-story writer, and essayist. His best-known novels are *A Room with a View* (1908), *Howard's End* (1910), and *A Passage to India* (1924), in all of which he stresses the need for sincerity and sensitivity in human relationships and criticizes English middle-class values.

for·ster·ite (ˈfɔːstəˌraɪt) *n.* a white, yellow, or green mineral of the olivine group consisting of magnesium silicate. Formula: Mg_2SiO_4. [C19: named after J. R. *Forster* (1729–98), German naturalist]

for·swear (fɔːˈswɛə) *vb.* **·swears, ·swear·ing, ·swore, ·sworn. 1.** (*tr.*) to reject or renounce with determination or as upon oath. **2.** (*tr.*) to deny or disavow absolutely or upon oath: *he forswore any knowledge of the crime.* **3.** to perjure (oneself). [Old English *forswearian*] —**for·ˈswear·er** *n.*

for·sworn (fɔːˈswɔːn) *vb.* the past participle of **forswear.** —**for·ˈsworn·ness** *n.*

for·syth·i·a (fɔːˈsaɪθɪə) *n.* any oleaceous shrub of the genus *Forsythia,* native to China, Japan, and SE Europe but widely cultivated for its showy yellow bell-shaped flowers, which appear in spring before the foliage. [C19: New Latin, named after William *Forsyth* (1737–1804), English botanist and superintendent of the Royal Gardens, Kensington]

fort (fɔːt) *n.* **1.** a fortified enclosure, building, or position able to be defended against an enemy. **2. hold the fort.** *Informal.* to maintain or guard something temporarily. [C15: from Old French, from *fort* (adj.) strong, from Latin *fortis*]

fort. *abbrev. for:* **1.** fortification. **2.** fortified.

For·ta·le·za (*Portuguese* ˌfortaˈleza) *n.* a port in NE Brazil, capital of Ceará state. Pop.: 520 175 (1970). Also called: **Ceará.**

for·ta·lice (ˈfɔːtəlɪs) *n.* a small fort or outwork of a fortification. [C15: from Medieval Latin *fortalitia,* from Latin *fortis* strong; see FORTRESS]

Fort-de-France (*French* fɔr də ˈfrɑ̃ːs) *n.* the capital of Martinique, a port on the W coast: commercial centre of the French Antilles. Pop.: 99 051 (1967).

forte[1] (fɔːt, ˈfɔːteɪ) *n.* **1.** something at which a person excels; strong point: *cooking is my forte.* **2.** *Fencing.* the stronger section of a sword blade, between the hilt and the middle. Compare **foible.** [C17: from French *fort,* from *fort* (adj.) strong, from Latin *fortis*]

for·te[2] (ˈfɔːtɪ) *Music.* ~*adj., adv.* **1.** loud or loudly. ~*n.* **2.** a loud passage in music. Symbol: *f* [C18: from Italian, from Latin *fortis* strong]

for·te·pi·an·o (ˌfɔːtɪpɪˈænəʊ) *n.* an early type of piano popular in the late 18th century. [from Italian, loud-soft]

for·te-pia·no (ˌfɔːtɪˈpjɑːnəʊ) *Music.* ~*adj., adv.* **1.** loud and then immediately soft. ~*n.* **2.** a note played in this way. Symbol: *fp*

forth (fɔːθ) *adv.* **1.** forward in place, time, order, or degree. **2.** out, as from concealment, seclusion, or inaction. **3.** away, as from a place or country. **4. and so forth.** and so on; etcetera. ~*prep.* **5.** *Archaic.* out of; away from. [Old English; related to Middle High German *vort;* see FOR, FURTHER]

Forth (fɔːθ) *n.* **1. Firth of.** an inlet of the North Sea in SE Scotland: spanned by a cantilever railway bridge 1600 m (almost exactly 1 mile) long (1889), and by a road bridge (1964). **2.** a river in S Scotland, flowing generally east to the Firth of Forth. Length: about 104 km (65 miles).

forth·com·ing (ˈfɔːθˈkʌmɪŋ) *adj.* **1.** approaching in time: *the forthcoming debate.* **2.** about to appear: *his forthcoming book.* **3.** available or ready: *the money wasn't forthcoming.* **4.** open or sociable. —ˈ**forth·ˈcom·ing·ness** *n.*

forth·right *adj.* (ˈfɔːθˌraɪt). **1.** direct and outspoken. ~*adv.* (ˌfɔːθˈraɪt, ˈfɔːθˌraɪt), *also* **forth·right·ly. 2.** in a direct manner; frankly. **3.** at once. —ˈ**forth·ˌright·ness** *n.*

forth·with (ˌfɔːθˈwɪθ, -ˈwɪð) *adv.* at once; immediately.

for·ti·eth (ˈfɔːtɪɪθ) *adj.* **1. a.** being the ordinal number of *forty* in numbering or counting order, position, time, etc.: often written 40th. **b.** (*as n.*): *he was the fortieth.* ~*n.* **2. a.** one of 40 approximately equal parts of something. **b.** (*as modifier*): *a fortieth part.* **3.** the fraction that is equal to one divided by 40 (1/40). [Old English *fēowertigotha*]

for·ti·fi·ca·tion (ˌfɔːtɪfɪˈkeɪʃən) *n.* **1.** the act, art, or science of fortifying or strengthening. **2. a.** a wall, mound, etc., used to fortify a place. **b.** such works collectively. **3.** any place that can be militarily defended.

for·ti·fied wine *n.* wine treated by the addition of brandy or alcohol, such as port, marsala, and sherry.

for·ti·fy (ˈfɔːtɪˌfaɪ) *vb.* **·fies, ·fy·ing, ·fied.** (*mainly tr.*) **1.** (*also intr.*) to make (a place) defensible, as by building walls, digging trenches, etc. **2.** to strengthen physically, mentally, or morally. **3.** to strengthen, support, or reinforce (a garment, structure, etc.). **4.** to add spirits or alcohol to (wine), in order to produce sherry, port, etc. **5.** to increase the nutritious value of (a food), as by adding vitamins and minerals. **6.** to support or confirm: *to fortify an argument with facts.* [C15: from Old French *fortifier,* from Late Latin *fortificāre,* from Latin *fortis* strong + *facere* to make] —ˈ**for·ti·ˌfi·a·ble** *adj.* —ˈ**for·ti·ˌfi·er** *n.* —ˈ**for·ti·ˌfy·ing·ly** *adv.*

for·tis (ˈfɔːtɪs) *Phonetics.* ~*adj.* **1.** (of a consonant) articulated with considerable muscular tension of the speech organs or with a great deal of breath pressure or plosion. ~*n., pl.* **·tes** (-tiːz). **2.** a consonant, such as English *p* or *f,* pronounced with considerable muscular force or breath pressure. ~Compare **lenis.** [Latin: strong]

for·tis·si·mo (fɔːˈtɪsɪˌməʊ) *Music.* ~*adj., adv.* **1.** very loud. ~*n.* **2.** a very loud passage in music. Symbol: *ff* [C18: from Italian, from Latin *fortissimus,* from *fortis* strong]

for·ti·tude (ˈfɔːtɪˌtjuːd) *n.* strength and firmness of mind; resolute endurance. [C15: from Latin *fortitūdō* courage] —ˌ**for·ti·ˈtu·di·nous** *adj.*

Fort Knox (nɒks) *n.* a military reservation in N Kentucky: site of the U.S. Gold Bullion Depository. Pop.: 37 608 (1970).

Fort La·my (ˈfɔːt ˈlɑːmɪ; *French* fɔr laˈmi) *n.* the former name (until 1973) of **Ndjamena.**

Fort Lau·der·dale (ˈlɔːdəˌdeɪl) *n.* a city in SE Florida, on the Atlantic. Pop.: 155 605 (1973 est.).

fort·night (ˈfɔːtˌnaɪt) *n.* a period of 14 consecutive days; two weeks. [Old English *fēowertīene niht* fourteen nights]

fort·night·ly (ˈfɔːtˌnaɪtlɪ) *Chiefly Brit.* ~*adj.* **1.** occurring or appearing once each fortnight. ~*adv.* **2.** once a fortnight. ~*n., pl.* **·lies. 3.** a publication issued at intervals of two weeks.

FORTRAN (ˈfɔːtræn) *n.* a high-level computer programming language for mathematical and scientific purposes, designed to facilitate and speed up the solving of complex problems. [C20: from *for*(*mula*) *tran*(*slation*)]

for·tress (ˈfɔːtrɪs) *n.* **1.** a large fort or fortified town. **2.** a place or source of refuge or support. ~*vb.* **3.** (*tr.*) to protect with or as if with a fortress. [C13: from Old French *forteresse,* from Medieval Latin *fortalitia,* from Latin *fortis* strong]

Fort Sum·ter (ˈsʌmtə) *n.* a fort in SE South Carolina, guarding Charleston Harbour. Its capture by Confederate forces (1861) was the first action of the Civil War.

for·tu·i·tism (fɔːˈtjuːɪˌtɪzəm) *n. Philosophy.* the doctrine that evolutionary adaptations are the result of chance. Compare **tychism.** —**for·ˈtu·i·tist** *n., adj.*

for·tu·i·tous (fɔːˈtjuːɪtəs) *adj.* happening by chance, esp. by a lucky chance; unplanned; accidental. [C17: from Latin *fortuitus* happening by chance, from *forte* by chance, from *fors* chance, luck] —**for·ˈtu·i·tous·ly** *adv.* —**for·ˈtu·i·tous·ness** *n.*

for·tu·i·ty (fɔːˈtjuːɪtɪ) *n., pl.* **·ties. 1.** a chance or accidental occurrence. **2.** fortuitousness. **3.** chance or accident.

For·tu·na (fɔːˈtjuːnə) *n.* the Roman goddess of fortune and good luck. Greek counterpart: **Tyche.**

for·tu·nate (ˈfɔːtʃənɪt) *adj.* **1.** having good luck; lucky. **2.** occurring by or bringing good fortune or luck; auspicious. —ˈ**for·tu·nate·ly** *adv.* —ˈ**for·tu·nate·ness** *n.*

for·tune (ˈfɔːtʃən) *n.* **1.** an amount of wealth or material prosperity, esp., when unqualified, a great amount. **2. small fortune.** a large sum of money. **3.** a power or force, often personalized, regarded as being responsible for human affairs; chance. **4.** luck, esp. when favourable. **5.** (*often pl.*) a person's lot or destiny. ~*vb.* **6.** *Archaic.* **a.** (*tr.*) to endow with great wealth. **b.** (*intr.*) to happen by chance. [C13: from Old French, from Latin *fortūna,* from *fors* chance] —ˈ**for·tune·less** *adj.*

for·tune-hunt·er *n.* a person who seeks to secure a fortune, esp. through marriage. —ˈ**for·tune-ˌhunt·ing** *adj., n.*

for·tune-tell·er *n.* a person who makes predictions about the future as by looking into a crystal ball, reading palms, etc. —ˈ**for·tune-ˌtell·ing** *adj., n.*

Fort Wayne (weɪn) *n.* a city in NE Indiana. Pop.: 185 488 (1973 est.).

Fort Wil·liam *n.* a town in W Scotland, in the Highland region at the head of Loch Linnhe: tourist centre; the fort itself, built in 1655 and renamed after William III in 1690, was demolished in 1866. Pop.: 4195 (1971).

Fort Worth (wɜːθ) *n.* a city in N Texas, at the junction of the Clear and West forks of the Trinity River. Pop.: 359 542 (1973 est.).

for·ty (ˈfɔːtɪ) *n., pl.* **·ties. 1.** the cardinal number that is the product of ten and four. See also **number** (sense 1). **2.** a numeral, 40, XL, etc., representing this number. **3.** something representing, represented by, or consisting of 40 units. ~*determiner.* **4. a.** amounting to forty: *forty thieves.* **b.** (*as pronoun*): *there were forty in the herd.* [Old English *fēowertig*]

for·ty-five *n.* **1.** a gramophone record played at 45 revolutions per minute. **2.** *U.S.* a pistol having .45 calibre.

For·ty-Five *n.* **the.** *British history.* another name for the **Jacobite Rebellion.**

for·ty-nin·er *n.* (*sometimes cap.*) *U.S. history.* a prospector who took part in the California goldrush of 1849.

for·ty winks *n.* (*functioning as sing. or pl.*) *Informal.* a short light sleep; nap.

fo·rum (ˈfɔːrəm) *n., pl.* **·rums** *or* **·ra** (-rə). **1.** a meeting or assembly for the open discussion of subjects of public interest. **2.** a medium for open discussion, such as a magazine. **3.** a public meeting place for open discussion. **4.** a court; tribunal. **5.** (in ancient Italy) an open space, usually rectangular in shape, serving as a city's marketplace and centre of public business. [C15: from Latin: public place; related to Latin *foris* outside]

Fo·rum *or* **Fo·rum Ro·ma·num** (rəʊˈmɑːnəm) *n.* **the.** the main forum of ancient Rome, situated between the Capitoline and the Palatine Hills.

for·ward (ˈfɔːwəd) *adj.* **1.** directed or moving ahead. **2.** lying or situated in or near the front part of something. **3.** presumptuous, pert, or impudent: *a forward remark.* **4.** well developed or advanced, esp. in physical, material, or intellectual growth or development: *forward ideas.* **5.** (*often postpositive*) ready, eager, or willing. **6. a.** of or relating to the future or favouring change; progressive. **b.** (*in combination*): *forward-looking.* ~*n.* **7. a.** an attacking player in any of various sports, such as soccer, hockey, or basketball. **b.** (in American football) a lineman. ~*adv.* **8.** a variant of **forwards. 9.** (ˈfɔːwəd; *Nautical* ˈfɒrəd). towards the front or bow of an aircraft or ship. **10.** into prominence or a position of being subject to public scrutiny; out; forth: *the witness came forward.* ~*vb.* (*tr.*) **11.** to send forward or pass on to an ultimate destination: *the letter was forwarded from a previous address.* **12.** to advance, help, or promote: *to forward one's career.* **13.** *Bookbinding.* to prepare (a book) for the finisher. [Old English *foreweard*] —ˈ**for·ward·ly** *adv.*

for·ward bi·as *or* **volt·age** *n.* a voltage applied to a circuit or device, esp. a semiconductor device, in the direction that produces the larger current.

for·ward de·liv·er·y *n.* (in commerce) delivery at a future date.

for·ward·er (ˈfɔːwədə) *n.* **1.** a person or thing that forwards. **2.** a person engaged in the bookbinding process of forwarding. **3.** See **forwarding agent.**

for·ward·ing (ˈfɔːwədɪŋ) *n.* all the processes involved in the binding of a book subsequent to cutting and up to the fitting of its cover.

for·ward·ing a·gent *n.* a person, agency, or enterprise engaged in the collection, shipment, and delivery of goods.

for·ward·ness (ˈfɔːwədnɪs) *n.* **1.** lack of modesty; presumption; boldness. **2.** willing readiness; eagerness. **3.** a state or condition of advanced progress or development.

for·ward pass *n. Rugby.* an illegal pass towards the opponent's dead-ball line. Also called: **throw-forward.**

for·ward quo·ta·tion *n.* (in commerce) the price quoted for goods sent on forward delivery.

for·ward roll *n.* a gymnastic movement in which the body is turned heels over head with the back of the neck resting on the ground.

for·wards (ˈfɔːwədz) *or* **for·ward** *adv.* **1.** towards or at a place ahead or in advance, esp. in space but also in time. **2.** towards the front.

for·went (fɔːˈwɛnt) *vb.* the past tense of **forgo.**

for·why (fɔːˈwaɪ) *Archaic.* ~*adv.* **1.** for what reason; why. ~*conj.* **2.** (*subordinating*) because. [Old English *for hwī*]

for·worn *or* **fore·worn** (fɔːˈwɔːn) *adj. Archaic.* weary. [C16: past participle of obsolete *forwear* to wear out, from Middle English *forweren* to hollow out]

for·zan·do (fɔːˈtsændəʊ) *adj., adv., n.* another word for **sforzando.**

Fos·bur·y flop (ˈfɒzbərɪ, -brɪ) *n. Athletics.* a modern high-jumping technique whereby the jumper clears the bar headfirst and backwards. [C20: named after Dick *Fosbury,* American winner of men's high jump at Mexico Olympics in 1968, who perfected the technique]

fos·sa[1] (ˈfɒsə) *n., pl.* **·sae** (-siː). an anatomical depression, trench, or hollow area. [C19: from Latin: ditch, from *fossus* dug up, from *fodere* to dig up]

fos·sa[2] (ˈfɒsə) *n.* a large primitive catlike viverrine mammal, *Cryptoprocta ferox,* inhabiting the forests of Madagascar: order *Carnivora* (carnivores). It has thick reddish-brown fur and preys on lemurs, poultry, etc. [from Malagasy]

fosse *or* **foss** (fɒs) *n.* a ditch or moat, esp. one dug as a fortification. [C14: from Old French, from Latin *fossa;* see FOSSA]

fos·sette (fɒˈsɛt) *n.* **1.** *Anatomy.* a small depression or fossa, as in a bone. **2.** *Pathol.* a small deep ulcer of the cornea. [C19: from French: dimple, from *fosse* ditch]

Fosse Way (fɒs) *n.* a Roman road in Britain between Lincoln and Exeter, with a fosse on each side.

fos·sick (ˈfɒsɪk) *vb. Austral.* **1.** (*intr.*) to search for gold or precious stones in abandoned workings, rivers, etc. **2.** to rummage or search for (something). [C19: Australian, probably from English dialect *fussock* to bustle about, from English FUSS] —ˈ**fos·sick·er** *n.*

fos·sil (ˈfɒsᵊl) *n.* **1. a.** a relic, remnant, or representation of a plant or animal that existed in a past geological age, occurring in the form of mineralized bones, shells, etc., as casts, impressions, and moulds, and as frozen perfectly preserved organisms. **b.** (*as modifier*): *fossil insects.* **2.** *Informal, derogatory.* **a.** a person, idea, thing, etc., that is outdated or incapable of change. **b.** (*as modifier*): *fossil politicians.* **3.** *Linguistics.* a form once current but now appearing only in one or two special contexts, as for example *stead,* which is found now only in *instead* (*of*) and in phrases like *in his stead.* **4.** *Obsolete.* any rock or mineral dug out of the earth. [C17: from Latin *fossilis* dug up, from *fodere* to dig]

fos·sil fu·el *n.* any naturally occurring carbon or hydrocarbon fuel, such as coal, petroleum, peat, and natural gas, formed by the decomposition of prehistoric organisms.

fos·sil·if·er·ous (ˌfɒsɪˈlɪfərəs) *adj.* (of sedimentary rocks) containing fossils.

fos·sil·ize *or* **fos·sil·ise** (ˈfɒsɪˌlaɪz) *vb.* **1.** to convert or be converted into a fossil. **2.** to become or cause to become antiquated or inflexible. —ˈ**fos·sil·ˌiz·a·ble** *or* ˈ**fos·sil·ˌis·a·ble** *adj.* —ˌ**fos·sil·i·ˈza·tion** *or* ˌ**fos·sil·i·ˈsa·tion** *n.*

fos·so·ri·al (fɒˈsɔːrɪəl) *adj.* **1.** (of the forelimbs and skeleton of burrowing animals) adapted for digging. **2.** (of burrowing animals, such as the mole and armadillo) having limbs of this type. [C19: from Medieval Latin *fossōrius* from Latin *fossor* digger, from *fodere* to dig]

fos·ter (ˈfɒstə) *vb.* (*tr.*) **1.** to promote the growth or development of. **2.** to bring up (a child, etc.); rear. **3.** to cherish (a plan, hope, etc.) in one's mind. **4.** *Chiefly Brit.* **a.** to place (a child) in the care of foster parents. **b.** to bring up under fosterage. ~*adj.* **5.** (*in combination*) of or involved in the rearing of a child by persons other than his natural or adopted parents: *foster father; foster home.* [Old English *fōstrian* to feed, from *fōstor* FOOD] —ˈ**fos·ter·er** *n.* —ˈ**fos·ter·ing·ly** *adv.*

Fos·ter (ˈfɒstə) *n.* **Ste·phen Col·lins.** 1826–64, U.S. composer of songs such as *The Old Folks at Home* and *Oh Susanna.*

fos·ter·age (ˈfɒstərɪdʒ) *n.* **1.** the act of caring for or bringing up a foster child. **2.** the condition or state of being a foster child. **3.** the act of encouraging or promoting.

fos·ter child *n.* a child looked after temporarily or brought up by people other than its natural or adopted parents.

fos·ter·ling (ˈfɒstəlɪŋ) *n.* a less common word for **foster child.**

Foth·er·ing·hay (ˈfɒðərɪŋˌgeɪ) *n.* a village in E England, in NE Northamptonshire: ruined castle, scene of the imprisonment and execution of Mary Queen of Scots (1587).

Fou·cault (*French* fuˈko) *n.* **Jean Ber·nard Lé·on** (ʒɑ̃ bɛrnaːr leˈɔ̃). 1819–68, French physicist. He determined the velocity of light and proved that light travels more slowly in water than in air (1850). He demonstrated by means of the pendulum named after him the rotation of the earth on its axis (1851) and invented the gyroscope (1852).

Fou·cault cur·rent *n.* another name for **eddy current.**

Fouc·quet (*French* fuˈkɛ) *n.* a variant spelling of (Nicolas) **Fouquet.**

fou·droy·ant (fuːˈdrɔɪənt) *adj.* **1.** (of a disease) occurring suddenly and with great severity. **2.** *Rare.* stunning, dazzling, or overwhelming. [C19: from French, from *foudroyer* to strike with lightning, from Old French *foudre* lightning, from Latin *fulgur*]

fouet·té *French.* (fwɛˈte) *n.* a step in ballet in which the dancer stands on one foot and makes a whiplike movement with the other. [C19: French, past participle of *fouetter* to whip, from *fouet* a whip]

fought (fɔːt) *vb.* the past tense or past participle of **fight.**

foul (faʊl) *adj.* **1.** offensive to the senses; revolting. **2.** offensive in odour; stinking. **3.** charged with or full of dirt or offensive matter; filthy. **4.** (of food) putrid; rotten. **5.** morally or spiritually offensive; wicked; vile. **6.** obscene; vulgar: *foul language.* **7.** not in accordance with accepted standards or established rules; unfair: *to resort to foul means.* **8.** (esp. of weather) unpleasant or adverse. **9.** blocked or obstructed with dirt or foreign matter: *a foul drain.* **10.** entangled or impeded: *a foul anchor.* **11.** (of the bottom of a vessel) covered with barnacles and other growth that slow forward motion. **12.** *Printing.* (of a typecase) having type distributed in the wrong compartments. **13.** *Informal.* unsatisfactory or uninteresting; bad: *a foul book.* **14.** *Archaic.* ugly. ~*n.* **15.** *Sport.* **a.** a violation of the rules. **b.** (*as modifier*): *a foul shot; a foul blow.* **16.** something foul. **17.** an entanglement or collision, esp. in sailing or fishing. ~*vb.* **18.** to make or become dirty or polluted. **19.** to become or cause to become entangled or snarled. **20.** (*tr.*) to disgrace or dishonour. **21.** to become or cause to become clogged or choked. **22.** (*tr.*) *Nautical.* (of underwater growth) to cling to (the bottom of a vessel) so as to slow its motion. **23.** (*tr.*) *Sport.* to commit a foul against (an opponent). **24.** (*tr.*) *Baseball.* to hit (a ball) in an illegal manner. **25.** (*intr.*) *Sport.* to infringe the rules. **26.** to collide (with a boat, etc.). ~*adv.* **27.** in a foul or unfair manner. **28.** **fall foul of. a.** to get into trouble with. **b.** (of ships) to collide with. [Old English *fūl;* related to Old Norse *fūll,* Gothic *fūls* smelling offensively, Latin *pūs* PUS, Greek *puol* pus] —**'foul·ly** *adv.*

fou·lard (fuːˈlɑːd, ˈfuːlɑː) *n.* **1.** a soft light fabric of plain-weave or twill-weave silk or rayon, usually with a printed design. **2.** something made of this fabric, esp. a scarf or handkerchief. [C19: from French, of unknown origin]

foul-mouthed *adj.* given to using obscene, abusive, or blasphemous language.

foul·ness (ˈfaʊlnɪs) *n.* **1.** the state or quality of being foul. **2.** obscenity; vulgarity. **3.** viciousness or inhumanity. **4.** foul matter; filth.

Foul·ness (faʊlˈnɛs) *n.* a flat marshy island in SE England, in Essex north of the Thames estuary.

foul play *n.* **1.** unfair or treacherous conduct esp. with violence. **2.** a violation of the rules in a game or sport.

foul shot *n. Basketball.* another term (esp. U.S.) for **free throw.**

foul up ~*vb.* (*adv.*) **1.** (*tr.*) to bungle; mismanage. **2.** (*tr.*) to make dirty; contaminate. **3.** to be or cause to be blocked, choked, or entangled. ~*n.* **foul-up.** *U.S.* **4.** a confusion or botch.

found[1] (faʊnd) *vb.* **1.** the past tense or past participle of **find.** ~*adj.* **2.** furnished, or fitted out: *the boat is well found.* **3.** *Brit.* with meals, heating, bed linen, etc., provided without extra charge (esp. in the phrase **all found**).

found[2] (faʊnd) *vb.* **1.** (*tr.*) to bring into being, set up, or establish (something, such as an institution, society, etc.). **2.** (*tr.*) to build or establish the foundation or basis of. **3.** (*also intr.;* foll. by *on* or *upon*) to have a basis (in); depend (on). [C13: from Old French *fonder,* from Latin *fundāre,* from *fundus* bottom]

found[3] (faʊnd) *vb.* (*tr.*) **1.** to cast (a material, such as metal or glass) by melting and pouring into a mould. **2.** to shape or make (articles) in this way; cast. [C14: from Old French *fondre,* from Latin *fundere* to melt]

foun·da·tion (faʊnˈdeɪʃən) *n.* **1.** that on which something is founded; basis. **2.** (*often pl.*) a construction below the ground that distributes the load of a building, wall, etc. **3.** the base on which something stands. **4.** the act of founding or establishing or the state of being founded or established. **5. a.** an endowment or legacy for the perpetual support of an institution such as a school or hospital. **b. on the foundation.** entitled to benefit from the funds of a foundation. **6.** an institution supported by an endowment, often one that provides funds for charities, research, etc. **7.** the charter incorporating or establishing a society or institution and the statutes or rules governing its affairs. **8.** a cosmetic in cream or cake form used as a base for make-up. **9.** See **foundation garment. 10.** *Cards.* a card on which a sequence may be built. —**foun·'da·tion·al** *adj.* —**foun·'da·tion·al·ly** *adv.* —**foun·'da·tion·ar·y** *adj.*

foun·da·tion gar·ment *n.* a woman's undergarment worn to shape and support the figure; brassiere or corset.

foun·da·tion stone *n.* a stone laid at a ceremony to mark the foundation of a new building.

found·er[1] (ˈfaʊndə) *n.* a person who establishes an institution, company, society, etc. [C14: see FOUND[2]]

found·er[2] (ˈfaʊndə) *vb.* (*intr.*) **1.** (of a ship, etc.) to sink. **2.** to break down or fail: *the project foundered.* **3.** to sink into or become stuck in soft ground. **4.** to fall in or give way; collapse. **5.** (of a horse) to stumble or go lame. **6.** (of animals, esp. livestock) to become ill from overeating. ~*n.* **7.** *Vet. science.* another name for **laminitis.** [C13: from Old French *fondrer* to submerge, from Latin *fundus* bottom; see FOUND[2]]

found·er[3] (ˈfaʊndə) *n.* **a.** a person who makes metal castings. **b.** (*in combination*): *an iron founder.* [C15: see FOUND[3]]

foun·ders' shares *pl. n.* shares awarded to the founders of a company and often granting special privileges.

found·er's type *n. Printing.* type cast by a typefounder for hand composition.

found·ing fa·ther *n.* (*often caps.*) a person who founds or establishes an important institution, esp. a member of the U.S. Constitutional Convention (1787).

found·ling (ˈfaʊndlɪŋ) *n.* an abandoned infant whose parents are not known. [C13: *foundeling;* see FIND]

found·ry (ˈfaʊndrɪ) *n., pl.* **·ries. 1.** a place in which metal castings are produced. **2.** the science or practice of casting metal. **3.** cast-metal articles collectively. [C17: from Old French *fonderie,* from *fondre;* see FOUND[3]]

found·ry proof *n. Printing.* a proof taken from a forme before duplicate plates are made from it.

fount[1] (faʊnt) *n.* **1.** *Poetic.* a spring or fountain. **2.** source or origin. [C16: back formation from FOUNTAIN]

fount[2] (faʊnt, fɒnt) *n. Printing.* a complete set of type of one style and size. Also called (esp. U.S.): **font.** [C16: from Old French *fonte* a founding, casting, from Vulgar Latin *funditus* (unattested) a casting, from Latin *fundere* to melt; see FOUND[3]]

foun·tain (ˈfaʊntɪn) *n.* **1.** a jet or spray of water or some other liquid. **2.** a structure from which such a jet or a number of such jets spurt, often incorporating figures, basins, etc. **3.** a natural spring of water, esp. the source of a stream. **4.** a stream, jet, or cascade of sparks, lava, etc. **5.** a principal source or origin. **6.** a reservoir or supply chamber, as for oil in a lamp. **7.** short for **drinking fountain** or **soda fountain.** [C15: from Old French *fontaine,* from Late Latin *fontāna,* from Latin *fons* spring, source] —**'foun·tained** *adj.* —**'foun·tain·less** *adj.* —**'foun·tain-,like** *adj.*

foun·tain·head (ˈfaʊntɪn,hɛd) *n.* **1.** a spring that is the source of a stream. **2.** a principal or original source.

foun·tain pen *n.* a pen the nib of which is supplied with ink from a cartridge or a reservoir in its barrel.

Fou·qué (*German* fuˈkeː) *n.* **Frie·drich Hein·rich Karl** (ˈfriːdrɪç ˈhaɪnrɪç karl), Baron de la Motte. 1777–1843, German romantic writer; author of *Undine* (1811).

Fou·quet (*French* fuˈkɛ) *n.* **1. Jean** (ʒɑ̃). ?1420–?80, French painter and miniaturist. **2.** Also: **Foucquet. Ni·co·las** (nikɔˈlɑ), *Marquis de Belle-Isle.* 1615–80, French statesman; superintendent of finance (1653–61) under Louis XIV. He was imprisoned for embezzlement, having been denounced by Colbert.

Fou·quier-Tin·ville (*French* fukje tɛ̃ˈvil) *n.* **An·toine Quen·tin** (ɑ̃twan kɑ̃ˈtɛ̃). 1746–95, French revolutionary; as public prosecutor (1793–94) during the Reign of Terror, he sanctioned the guillotining of Desmoulins, Danton, and Robespierre.

four (fɔː) *n.* **1.** the cardinal number that is the sum of three and one. **2.** a numeral, 4, IV, etc., representing this number. **3.** something representing, represented by, or consisting of four units, such as a playing card with four symbols on it. **4.** Also called: **four o'clock.** four hours after noon or midnight. **5.** *Cricket.* **a.** a shot that crosses the boundary after hitting the ground. **b.** the four runs scored for such a shot. **6.** *Rowing.* **a.** a racing shell propelled by four oarsmen pulling one oar each, with or without a cox. **b.** the crew of such a shell. ~*determiner.* **7. a.** amounting to four: *four thousand eggs; four times.* **b.** (*as pronoun*): *four are ready.* ~Related prefixes: **quadri-, tetra-.** [Old English *fēower;* related to Old Frisian *fiūwer,* Old Norse *fjōrir,* Old High German *fior,* Latin *quattuor,* Greek *tessares,* Sanskrit *catur*]

four-ball *n. Golf.* a match for two pairs in which each of the four players tees off and after selecting the better drive the partners of each pair play each stroke alternately.

four·chette (fʊəˈʃɛt) *n.* **1.** *Anatomy.* the bandlike fold of skin, about one inch from the anus, forming the posterior margin of the vulva. **2.** a less common name for **furcula** or **frog**[3]. [C18: from French: a little fork, from Old French *forche,* from Latin *furca* FORK]

four-col·our *n.* (*modifier*) (of a print or photographic process) using the principle in which four colours (magenta, cyan, yellow, and black) are used in combination to produce almost any other colour.

four-cy·cle *n.* (*modifier*) the U.S. word for **four-stroke.**

four-deal bridge *n.* a version of bridge in which four hands only are played, the players then cutting for new partners.

four-di·men·sion·al *adj.* having or specified by four dimensions, esp. the three spatial dimensions and the dimension of time: *a four-dimensional continuum.*

Four·drin·i·er (fʊəˈdrɪnɪə) *n.* a particular type of paper-making machine that forms the paper in a continuous web. [C19: named after Henry (died 1854) and Sealy (died 1847) *Fourdrinier,* English paper-makers]

four-eyed fish *n.* either of two viviparous tropical American freshwater cyprinodont fishes, *Anableps anableps* or *A. microlepis,* that swim at the surface of the water and have half of each eye specialized for seeing in air, the other half for seeing in water.

four flush *n.* **1.** a useless poker hand, containing four of a suit and one odd card. ~*vb.* **four-flush.** (*intr.*) **2.** to bid confidently on a poor hand such as a four flush. **3.** *U.S.* a slang word for **bluff.**

four·fold (ˈfɔː,fəʊld) *adj.* **1.** equal to or having four times as many or as much. **2.** composed of four parts. ~*adv.* **3.** by or up to four times as many or as much.

four-four time *n. Music.* a form of simple quadruple time in which there are four crotchets to the bar, indicated by the time signature $\frac{4}{4}$. Often shortened to **four-four.** Also called: **common time.**

four·gon *French.* (furˈgɔ̃) *n.* a long covered wagon, used mainly for carrying baggage, supplies, etc. [C19: from French: from Old French *forgon* poker, from *furgier* to search, ultimately from Latin *fūr* thief]

four-hand·ed *adj.* **1.** (of a card game) arranged for four players. **2.** (of a musical composition) written for two performers at the same piano. —**,four-'hand·ed·ly** *adv.*

Four Hun·dred *n.* **the.** *U.S.* the most exclusive or affluent social clique in a particular place.

Fou·ri·er (ˈfʊərɪ,eɪ; *French* fuˈrje) *n.* **1. (François Marie) Charles** (ʃarl). 1772–1837, French social reformer: propounded a system of cooperatives known as Fourierism, esp. in his work *Le Nouveau Monde industriel* (1829–30). **2. Jean Bap·tiste Jo·seph** (ʒɑ̃ batist ʒoˈzɛf). 1768–1830, French mathematician, Egyptologist, and administrator, noted particularly for his research on the theory of heat and the method of analysis named after him.

Fou·ri·er a·nal·y·sis *n.* the analysis of a periodic function into its simple sinusoidal or harmonic components, whose sum forms a Fourier series.

Fou+ri+er+ism (ˈfʊərɪəˌrɪzəm) *n.* the system of Charles Fourier under which society was to be organized into self-sufficient cooperatives. —**ˈFou+ri+er+ist** *or* **Fou+ri+er+ite** (ˈfʊərɪəˌraɪt) *n., adj.* —**ˌFou+ri+er+ˈis+tic** *adj.*

Fou·ri·er se+ries *n.* an infinite trigonometric series of the form $\frac{1}{2}a_0 + a_1\cos x + b_1\sin x + a_2\cos 2x + b_2\sin 2x + \ldots$, where a_0, a_1, b_1, a_2, b_2 ... are the **Fourier coefficients.** It is used, esp. in mathematics and physics, to represent or approximate any single-valued periodic function by assigning suitable values to the coefficients. [C19: named after Baron Jean Baptiste Joseph FOURIER]

four-in-hand *n.* **1.** Also called: **tally-ho.** a road vehicle drawn by four horses and driven by one driver. **2.** a four-horse team in a coach or carriage. **3.** a long narrow tie formerly worn tied in a flat slipknot with ends dangling.

four-leaf clo+ver *or* **four-leaved clo+ver** *n.* **1.** a clover with four leaves rather than three, supposed to bring good luck. **2.** another name for **cloverleaf** (sense 1).

four-let·ter word *n.* any of several short English words referring to sex or excrement: often used as swearwords and regarded generally as offensive or obscene.

four-o'clock *n.* **1.** Also called: **marvel-of-Peru.** a tropical American nyctaginaceous plant, *Mirabilis jalapa,* cultivated for its tubular yellow, red, or white flowers that open in late afternoon. **2.** an Australian name for **friarbird,** esp. the noisy friarbird (*Philemon corniculatus*).

four-part *adj. Music.* arranged for four voices or instruments.

four+pence (ˈfɔːpəns) *n.* a former English silver coin then worth four pennies.

four+pen·ny (ˈfɔːpənɪ) *adj.* **fourpenny one.** *Brit. slang.* a blow, esp. with the fist.

four-post·er *n.* a bed with posts at each corner supporting a canopy and curtains. Also called: **four-poster bed.**

four+ra+gère (ˈfʊərəˌʒɛə; *French* furaˈʒɛːr) *n.* an ornamental cord worn on the shoulder of a uniform for identification or as an award, esp. in the U.S. and French Armies. [French, feminine adj. of *fourrager* relating to forage, from *fourrage* FORAGE]

four+score (ˌfɔːˈskɔː) *determiner.* an archaic word for **eighty.**

four+some (ˈfɔːsəm) *n.* **1.** a set or company of four. **2.** Also called: **fourball.** *Sport.* a game between two pairs of players, esp. in golf. **3.** (*modifier*) of or performed by a company of four: *a foursome competition.*

four+square (ˌfɔːˈskwɛə) *adv.* **1.** squarely; firmly. ~*adj.* **2.** solid and strong. **3.** forthright; honest. **4.** a rare word for **square.** —**ˌfour+ˈsquare+ly** *adv.* —**ˌfour+ˈsquare+ness** *n.*

four-stroke *adj.* relating to or designating an internal-combustion engine in which the piston makes four strokes for every explosion. U.S. name: **four-cycle.** Compare **two-stroke.**

four+teen (ˈfɔːˈtiːn) *n.* **1.** the cardinal number that is the sum of ten and four. **2.** a numeral, 14, XIV, etc., representing this number. **3.** something represented by, representing, or consisting of 14 units. ~*determiner.* **4. a.** amounting to fourteen: *fourteen cats.* **b.** (*as pronoun*): *the fourteen who remained.* [Old English *fēowertīene*]

Four+teen Points *pl. n.* the principles expounded by President Wilson in 1918 as war aims of the U.S.

four+teenth (ˈfɔːˈtiːnθ) *adj.* **1. a.** coming after the thirteenth in order, position, time etc. Often written: 14th. **b.** (*as n.*): *the fourteenth in succession.* ~*n.* **2. a.** one of 14 equal or nearly equal parts of something. **b.** (*as modifier*): *a fourteenth part.* **3.** the fraction equal to one divided by 14 (1/14).

fourth (fɔːθ) *adj.* (*usually prenominal*) **1. a.** coming after the third in order, position, time, etc. Often written: 4th. **b.** (*as n.*): *the fourth in succession.* **2.** denoting the highest forward ratio of a gearbox in most motor vehicles. ~*n.* **3.** *Music.* **a.** the interval between one note and another four notes away from it counting inclusively along the diatonic scale. **b.** one of two notes constituting such an interval in relation to the other. See also **perfect** (sense 9), **interval** (sense 5), **diminished** (sense 2). **4.** the fourth forward ratio of a gearbox in a motor vehicle, usually the highest gear in cars; top gear: *he changed into fourth as soon as he had passed me.* **5.** a less common word for **quarter** (sense 2). ~*adv. also:* **fourth+ly. 6.** after the third person, position, event, etc. ~*also:* **fourth+ly. 7.** *sentence connector.* as the fourth point: linking what follows with the previous statements, as in a speech or argument.

fourth-class *U.S.* ~*adj.* **1.** of or relating to mail that is carried at the lowest rate. ~*adv.* **2.** by fourth-class mail.

fourth di+men+sion *n.* **1.** the dimension of time, which is necessary in addition to three spatial dimensions to specify fully the position and behaviour of a point or particle. **2.** the concept in science fiction of a dimension in addition to three spatial dimensions, used to explain supranatural phenomena, events, etc. —**ˌfourth-di·ˈmen·sion·al** *adj.*

fourth es+tate *n.* (*sometimes caps.*) journalists or their profession; the press. See **estate** (sense 4).

Fourth In+ter+na+tion+al *n.* another name for any of the **Trotskyist Internationals.**

Fourth of Ju·ly *n.* (preceded by *the*) a holiday in the United States, traditionally celebrated with fireworks: the day of the adoption of the Declaration of Independence in 1776. Official name: **Independence Day.**

Fourth Re+pub+lic *n.* the fourth period of republican government in France or the republic itself (1945–58).

four-way *adj.* (*usually prenominal*) **1.** giving passage in four directions. **2.** made up of four elements.

four-wheel drive *n.* a system used in motor vehicles in which all four wheels are connected to the source of power.

fo+ve·a (ˈfəʊvɪə) *n., pl.* **+ve·ae** (-vɪˌiː). **1.** *Anatomy.* any small pit or depression in the surface of a bodily organ or part. **2.** See **fovea centralis.** [C19: from Latin: a small pit] —**ˈfo+ve·al** *adj.* —**ˈfo+ve·ate** *or* **ˈfo+ve·ˌat+ed** *adj.*

fo+ve·a cen+tra+lis (sɛnˈtrɑːlɪs) *n.* a small depression in the back of the retina, in the centre, that contains only cone cells and is therefore the area of sharpest vision. [C19: from New Latin: central fovea]

fo+ve·o+la (fəʊˈviːələ) *n., pl.* **+lae** (-ˌliː). *Biology.* a small fovea. [C19: from New Latin, diminutive of FOVEA] —**fo+ˈve·o+lar** *adj.* —**fo+ve·o+late** (ˈfəʊvɪəˌleɪt) *or* **ˈfo+ve·o+ˌlat+ed** *adj.*

Fowey (fɔɪ) *n.* a resort and fishing village in SW England, in Cornwall, linked administratively with St. Austell in 1968. Pop. (with St. Austell): 32 252 (1971).

fowl (faʊl) *n.* **1.** See **domestic fowl. 2.** any other bird, esp. any gallinaceous bird, that is used as food or hunted as game. See also **waterfowl, wildfowl. 3.** the flesh or meat of fowl, esp. of chicken. **4.** an archaic word for any **bird.** ~*vb.* **5.** (*intr.*) to hunt or snare wildfowl. [Old English *fugol;* related to Old Frisian *fugel,* Old Norse *fogl,* Gothic *fugls,* Old High German *fogal*]

Fow·ler (ˈfaʊlə) *n.* **Hen·ry Wat·son.** 1858–1933, English lexicographer and grammarian; compiler of *Modern English Usage* (1926).

Fow·liang *or* **Fou-liang** (ˈfuːˈljæŋ) *n.* a city in SE China, in NE Kiangsi province east of Lake Poyang: famous for its porcelain industry, established in the sixth century. Pop.: 92 000 (1953 est.).

fowl+ing (ˈfaʊlɪŋ) *n.* the shooting or trapping of birds for sport or as a livelihood. —**ˈfowl+er** *n.*

fowl pest *n.* **1.** an acute and usually fatal viral disease of domestic fowl, characterized by refusal to eat, high temperature, and discoloration of the comb and wattles. **2.** another name for **Newcastle disease.**

fox (fɒks) *n., pl.* **fox·es** *or* **fox. 1.** any canine mammal of the genus *Vulpes* and related genera. They are mostly predators that do not hunt in packs and typically have large pointed ears, a pointed muzzle, and a bushy tail. **2.** the fur of any of these animals, usually reddish-brown or grey in colour. **3.** a person who is cunning and sly. **4.** *Bible.* **a.** a jackal. **b.** an image of a false prophet. **5.** *Nautical.* small stuff made from yarns twisted together and then tarred. ~*vb.* **6.** (*tr.*) *Informal.* to perplex or confound: *to fox a person with a problem.* **7.** to cause (paper, wood, etc.) to become discoloured with spots, or (of paper, etc.) to become discoloured, as through mildew. **8.** (*tr.*) to trick; deceive. **9.** (*intr.*) to act deceitfully or craftily. **10.** (*tr.*) *Austral. informal.* to pursue stealthily; tail. **11.** (*tr.*) *Austral. informal.* to chase and retrieve (a ball). **12.** (*tr.*) *Obsolete.* to befuddle with alcoholic drink. [Old English; related to Old High German *fuhs,* Old Norse *fōa* fox, Sanskrit *puccha* tail; see VIXEN] —**ˈfox+ˌlike** *adj.*

Fox[1] (fɒks) *n.* **1.** (*pl.* **Fox** *or* **Fox·es**) a member of a North American Indian people formerly living west of Lake Michigan along the Fox River. **2.** the language of this people, belonging to the Algonquian family.

Fox[2] (fɒks) *n.* **1. Charles James.** 1749–1806, English Whig statesman and orator. He opposed North over taxation of the American colonies and Pitt over British intervention against the French Revolution. He advocated parliamentary reform and the abolition of the slave trade. **2. George.** 1624–91, English religious leader; founder (1647) of the Society of Friends (Quakers). **3. Sir Wil·liam.** 1812–93, New Zealand statesman, born in England: prime minister of New Zealand (1856; 1861–62; 1869–72; 1873).

Foxe (fɒks) *n.* **John.** 1516–87, English Protestant clergyman; author of *History of the Acts and Monuments of the Church* (1563), popularly known as the *Book of Martyrs.*

Foxe Ba+sin *n.* an arm of the Atlantic in NE Canada, between Melville Peninsula and Baffin Island.

fox+fire (ˈfɒksˌfaɪə) *n.* a luminescent glow emitted by certain fungi on rotting wood. See also **bioluminescence.**

fox+glove (ˈfɒksˌglʌv) *n.* any Eurasian scrophulariaceous plant of the genus *Digitalis,* esp. *D. purpurea,* having spikes of purple or white thimble-like flowers. The soft wrinkled leaves are a source of digitalis.

fox grape *n.* a common wild grape, *Vitis labrusca* of the northern U.S., having purplish-black fruit and woolly leaves: the source of many cultivated grapes, including the catawba.

fox+hole (ˈfɒksˌhəʊl) *n. Military.* a small pit dug during an action to provide individual shelter against hostile fire.

fox+hound (ˈfɒksˌhaʊnd) *n.* either of two breeds (the English and the American) of short-haired hound, usually kept for hunting foxes.

fox hunt *n.* **1. a.** the hunting of foxes with hounds. **b.** an instance of this. **2.** an organization for fox hunting within a particular area.

fox-hunt·ing *n.* a sport in which hunters follow a pack of hounds in pursuit of a fox. —**ˈfox-ˌhunt·er** *n.*

fox·ie (ˈfɒksɪ) *Austral.* an informal name for **fox terrier.**

fox·ing ('fɒksɪŋ) *n.* a piece of leather, etc., used to reinforce or trim part of the upper of a shoe.
fox squir·rel *n.* a large squirrel, *Sciurus niger,* occurring in E North America.
fox·tail ('fɒks,teɪl) *n.* **1.** any grass of the genus *Alopecurus,* esp. *A. pratensis,* of Europe, Asia, and South America, having soft cylindrical spikes of flowers: cultivated as a pasture grass. **2.** any of various similar and related grasses, esp. any of the genus *Setaria.*
Fox Tal·bot (fɒks 'tɔ:lbət) *n.* **Wil·liam Hen·ry.** 1800–77, English physicist; a pioneer of photography.
fox ter·ri·er *n.* either of two breeds of small black-and-white terrier, the wire-haired and the smooth.
fox·trot ('fɒks,trɒt) *n.* **1.** a ballroom dance in quadruple time, combining short and long steps in various sequences. ~*vb.* **·trots, ·trot·ting, ·trot·ted. 2.** (*intr.*) to perform this dance.
fox·y ('fɒksɪ) *adj.* **fox·i·er, fox·i·est. 1.** of or resembling a fox, esp. in craftiness. **2.** smelling strongly, like a fox. **3.** of a reddish-brown colour. **4.** (of paper, wood, etc.) spotted, esp. by mildew. **5.** (of wine) having the flavour of fox grapes. —**'fox·i·ly** *adv.* —**'fox·i·ness** *n.*
foy·boat ('fɔɪ,bəut) *n. Tyneside dialect.* **a.** a small rowing boat. **b.** (*in combination*): *a foyboatman.* [C19: from *foy* to provide aid for ships, esp. those in distress]
foy·er ('fɔɪeɪ, 'fɔɪə) *n.* a hall, lobby, or anteroom, used for reception and as a meeting place, as in a hotel, theatre, cinema, etc. [C19: from French: fireplace, from Medieval Latin *focārius,* from Latin *focus* fire]
fp *Music. abbrev. for* forte-piano.
f.p. *or* **fp** *abbrev. for:* **1.** freezing point. **2.** fine point.
F.P. *or* **f.p.** *abbrev. for:* **1.** Also: **fp** freezing point. **2.** fully paid.
F.P.A. *abbrev. for* Family Planning Association.
f.p.s. *abbrev. for:* **1.** feet per second. **2.** foot-pound-second. **3.** *Photog.* frames per second.
fps u·nits *n.* an Imperial system of units based on the foot, pound, and second as the units of length, mass, and time. For scientific and most technical purposes these units have been replaced by SI units.
Fr *the chemical symbol for* francium.
fr. *abbrev. for:* **1.** fragment. **2.** franc. **3.** from.
Fr. *abbrev. for:* **1.** *Christianity.* **a.** Father. **b.** Frater. [Latin: brother] **c.** Friar. **2.** France. **3.** French. ~**4.** the German equivalent of **Mrs.** [from German *Frau*]
Fra (frɑ:) *n.* brother: a title given to an Italian monk or friar. [Italian, short for *frate* brother (in either natural or religious sense), from Latin *frāter* BROTHER]
fra·cas ('frækɑ:) *n.* a noisy quarrel; brawl. [C18: from French, from *fracasser* to shatter, from Latin *frangere* to break, influenced by *quassāre* to shatter]
frac·tion ('frækʃən) *n.* **1.** *Maths.* **a.** a ratio of two expressions or numbers other than zero. **b.** any rational number that can be expressed as the ratio of two integers, *a/b,* where *b* does not equal *a,* 1, or 0, and *a* does not equal 0. **2.** any part or subdivision: *a substantial fraction of the nation.* **3.** a small piece; fragment. **4.** *Chem.* a component of a mixture separated by a fractional process, such as fractional distillation. **5.** *Christianity.* the formal breaking of the bread in Communion. **6.** the act of breaking. ~*vb.* **7.** (*tr.*) to divide. [C14: from Late Latin *fractiō* a breaking into pieces, from Latin *fractus* broken, from *frangere* to break]
frac·tion·al ('frækʃənᵊl) *adj.* **1.** relating to, containing, or constituting one or more fractions. **2.** of or denoting a process in which components of a mixture are separated by exploiting differences in their physical properties, such as boiling points, solubility, etc.: *fractional distillation; fractional crystallization.* **3.** very small or insignificant. **4.** broken up; fragmented. ~Also called: **frac·tion·ar·y** ('frækʃənərɪ). —**'frac·tion·al·ly** *adv.*
frac·tion·al cur·ren·cy *n.* paper or metal money of smaller denomination than the standard monetary unit.
frac·tion·al dis·til·la·tion *n.* **1.** the process of separating the constituents of a liquid mixture by heating it and condensing separately the components according to their different boiling points. **2.** a distillation in which the vapour is brought into contact with a countercurrent of condensed liquid to increase the purity of the final products. ~Sometimes shortened to **distillation.**
frac·tion·ate ('frækʃə,neɪt) *vb.* **1.** to separate or cause to separate into constituents or into fractions containing concentrated constituents. **2.** (*tr.*) *Chem.* to obtain (a constituent of a mixture) by a fractional process. —**,frac·tion·'a·tion** *n.* —**'frac·tion·,a·tor** *n.*
frac·tion·ize *or* **frac·tion·ise** ('frækʃə,naɪz) *vb.* to divide (a number or quantity) into fractions. —**,frac·tion·i·'za·tion** *or* **,frac·tion·i·'sa·tion** *n.*
frac·tious ('frækʃəs) *adj.* **1.** irritable. **2.** unruly. [C18: from (obsolete) *fraction* discord + -OUS] —**'frac·tious·ly** *adv.* —**'frac·tious·ness** *n.*
frac·to·cu·mu·lus (,fræktəu'kju:mjuləs) *n., pl.* **·li** (-,laɪ). low ragged slightly bulbous cloud, often appearing below nimbostratus clouds during rain. Also called: **fractocumulus cloud.** [C19: from Latin *fractus* broken + CUMULUS]
frac·to·stra·tus (,fræktəu'strɑ:təs, -'stræt-) *n., pl.* **·ti** (-taɪ). low ragged layered cloud often appearing below nimbostratus clouds during rain. [C19: from Latin *fractus* broken + STRATUS]
frac·ture ('fræktʃə) *n.* **1.** the act of breaking or the state of being broken. **2. a.** the breaking or cracking of a bone or the tearing of a cartilage. **b.** the resulting condition. See also **Colles' fracture, comminuted fracture, compound fracture, greenstick fracture, impacted fracture, simple fracture. 3.** a division, split, or breach. **4.** *Mineralogy.* **a.** the characteristic appearance of the surface of a freshly broken mineral or rock. **b.** the way in which a mineral or rock naturally breaks. ~*vb.* **5.** to break or cause to break; split. **6.** to break or crack (a bone) or (of a bone) to become broken or cracked. **7.** to tear (a cartilage) or (of a cartilage) to become torn. [C15: from Old French, from Latin *fractūra,* from *frangere* to break] —**'frac·tur·a·ble** *adj.* —**'frac·tur·al** *adj.*
frae (freɪ) *prep.* a Scot. word for **from.**
frae·num *or* **fre·num** ('fri:nəm) *n., pl.* **·na** (-nə). a fold of membrane or skin, such as the fold beneath the tongue, that supports an organ. [C18: from Latin: bridle]
frag (fræg) *vb.* **frags, frag·ging, fragged.** (*tr.*) *U.S. military slang.* to kill or wound (a fellow soldier or superior officer) deliberately with an explosive device. [C20: short for *fragmentation grenade,* as used in Vietnam] —**'frag·ging** *n.*
frag·ile ('frædʒaɪl) *adj.* **1.** able to be broken easily. **2.** in a weakened physical state. **3.** delicate; light: *a fragile touch.* **4.** slight; tenuous: *a fragile link with the past.* [C17: from Latin *fragilis,* from *frangere* to break] —**'frag·ile·ly** *adv.* —**fra·gil·i·ty** (frə'dʒɪlɪtɪ) *or* **'fra·gile·ness** *n.*
frag·ment *n.* ('frægmənt). **1.** a piece broken off or detached: *fragments of rock.* **2.** an incomplete piece; portion: *fragments of a novel.* **3.** a scrap; morsel; bit. ~*vb.* (fræg'mɛnt), *also U.S.* **frag·ment·ize** ('frægmən,taɪz). **4.** to break or cause to break into fragments. [C15: from Latin *fragmentum,* from *frangere* to break]
frag·men·tal (fræg'mɛntᵊl) *adj.* **1.** (of rocks or deposits) composed of fragments of pre-existing rocks and minerals. **2.** another word for **fragmentary.** —**frag·'men·tal·ly** *adv.*
frag·men·tar·y ('frægməntərɪ, -trɪ) *adj.* made up of fragments; disconnected; incomplete. Also: **fragmental.** —**'frag·men·tar·i·ly** *adv.* —**'frag·men·tar·i·ness** *n.*
frag·men·ta·tion (,frægmɛn'teɪʃən) *n.* **1.** the act of fragmenting or the state of being fragmented. **2.** the disintegration of norms regulating behaviour, thought, and social relationships. **3.** the steel particles of an exploded projectile. **4.** (*modifier*) of or relating to a weapon designed to explode into many small pieces, esp. as an antipersonnel weapon: *a fragmentation bomb.*
Fra·go·nard (*French* fragɔ'na:r) *n.* **Jean Ho·no·ré** (ʒɑ̃ ɔnɔ're). 1732–1806, French artist, noted for richly coloured paintings typifying the frivolity of 18th-century French court life.
fra·grance ('freɪgrəns) *or* **fra·gran·cy** *n., pl.* **·granc·es** *or* **·gran·cies. 1.** a pleasant or sweet odour; scent; perfume. **2.** the state of being fragrant.
fra·grant ('freɪgrənt) *adj.* having a pleasant or sweet smell. [C15: from Latin *frāgrāns,* from *frāgrāre* to emit a smell] —**'fra·grant·ly** *adv.*
frail[1] (freɪl) *adj.* **1.** physically weak and delicate. **2.** fragile: *a frail craft.* **3.** easily corrupted or tempted. [C13: from Old French *frele,* from Latin *fragilis,* FRAGILE] —**'frail·ly** *adv.* —**'frail·ness** *n.*
frail[2] (freɪl) *n.* **1.** a rush basket for figs or raisins. **2.** a quantity of raisins or figs equal to between 50 and 75 pounds. [C13: from Old French *fraiel,* of uncertain origin]
frail·ty ('freɪltɪ) *n., pl.* **·ties. 1.** physical or moral weakness. **2.** (*often pl.*) a fault symptomatic of moral weakness.
fraise (freɪz) *n.* **1.** a neck ruff worn during the 16th century. **2.** a sloping or horizontal rampart of pointed stakes. **3. a.** a tool for enlarging a drill hole. **b.** a tool for cutting teeth on watch wheels. [C18: from French: mesentery of a calf, from Old French *fraiser* to remove a shell, from Latin *frendere* to crush]
Frak·tur (*German* frak'tu:r) *n.* a style of typeface, formerly used in German typesetting for many printed works. [German, from Latin *fractūra* a breaking, FRACTURE; from the curlicues that seem to interrupt the continuous line of a word]
fram·boe·si·a *or U.S.* **fram·be·si·a** (fræm'bi:zɪə) *n. Pathol.* another name for **yaws.** [C19: from New Latin, from French *framboise* raspberry; see FRAMBOISE; so called because of its raspberry-like excrescences]
fram·boise *French.* (frɑ̃'bwaz) *n.* a brandy distilled from raspberries in the Alsace-Lorraine region. [C16: from Old French: raspberry, probably of Germanic origin]
frame (freɪm) *n.* **1.** an open structure that gives shape and support to something, such as the transverse stiffening ribs of a ship's hull or an aircraft's fuselage or the skeletal beams and uprights of a building. **2.** an enclosing case or border into which something is fitted: *the frame of a picture.* **3.** the system around which something is built up: *the frame of government.* **4.** the structure of the human body. **5.** a condition; state (esp. in the phrase **frame of mind**). **6. a.** one of a series of individual exposures on a strip of film used in making motion pictures. **b.** an individual exposure on a film used in still photography. **c.** an individual picture in a comic strip. **7. a.** a television picture scanned by one or more electron beams at a particular frequency. **b.** the area of the picture so formed. **8.** *Snooker, etc.* **a.** the wooden triangle used to set up the balls. **b.** the balls when set up. **c.** a single game finished when all the balls have been potted. U.S. equivalent (for **a.** and **b.**): **rack**[1] (sense 6). **9.** short for **cold frame. 10.** one of the sections of which a beehive is composed, esp. one designed to hold a honeycomb. **11.** a machine or part of a machine over which yarn is stretched in the production of textiles. **12.** (in language teaching, etc.) a syntactic construction with a gap in it, used for assigning words to syntactic classes by seeing which words may fill the gap. **13.** (in telecommunications, computers, etc.) one cycle of a regularly recurring number of pulses in a pulse

train. **14.** *Slang.* another word for **frame-up. 15.** *Obsolete.* shape; form. ~*vb.* (*mainly tr.*) **16.** to construct by fitting parts together. **17.** to draw up the plans or basic details for; outline: *to frame a policy.* **18.** to compose, contrive, or conceive: *to frame a reply.* **19.** to provide, support, or enclose with a frame: *to frame a picture.* **20.** to form (words) with the lips, esp. silently. **21.** *Slang.* to conspire to incriminate (someone) on a false charge. **22.** *Slang.* to contrive the dishonest outcome of (a contest, match, etc.); rig. **23.** (*intr.*) *Yorkshire and northeastern English dialect.* **a.** (*usually imperative or dependent imperative*) to make an effort. **b.** to have ability. [Old English *framiae* to avail; related to Old Frisian *framia* to carry out, Old Norse *frama*] —'**fram·a·ble** *or* '**frame·a·ble** *adj.* —'**frame·less** *adj.* —'**fram·er** *n.*

frame aer·i·al *n.* another name for **loop aerial.**

frame house *n.* a house that has a structural framework of timber.

frame line *n. Films.* a black horizontal bar appearing between successive picture images.

frame of ref·er·ence *n.* **1.** *Sociol.* a set of basic assumptions or standards that determines and sanctions behaviour. **2.** any set of planes or curves, such as the three coordinate axes, used to locate or measure movement of a point in space.

frame-up *n. Slang.* **1.** a conspiracy to incriminate someone on a false charge. **2.** a plot to bring about a dishonest result, as in a contest.

frame·work ('freɪm,wɜːk) *n.* **1.** a structural plan or basis of a project. **2.** a structure or frame supporting or containing something. **3.** frames collectively. **4.** work such as embroidery or weaving done in or on a frame.

fram·ing ('freɪmɪŋ) *n.* **1.** a frame, framework, or system of frames. **2.** the way in which something is framed.

franc (fræŋk; *French* frɑ̃) *n.* **1.** the standard monetary unit of France, French dependencies, and Monaco, divided into 100 centimes. **2.** the standard monetary and currency unit of Belgium and Luxembourg, divided into 100 centimes. **3.** the standard monetary and currency unit of Switzerland and Liechtenstein, divided into 100 centimes. **4.** the standard monetary and currency unit, comprising 100 centimes, of the following countries: Burundi, Cameroon, the Central African Republic, Chad, Dahomey, Gabon, Guinea, the Ivory Coast, Mauritania, the Malagasy Republic, Niger, the Republic of Congo, Senegal, Togo, Upper Volta, Mali, and Rwanda. **5.** a Moroccan monetary unit worth one hundredth of a dirham. [C14: from Old French; from the Latin phrase *Rex Francōrum* King of the Franks, inscribed on 14th-century francs]

France[1] (frɑːns) *n.* a republic in W Europe, between the English Channel, the Mediterranean, and the Atlantic: the largest country wholly in Europe; became a republic in 1793 after the French Revolution and an empire in 1804 under Napoleon; reverted to a monarchy (1815–48), followed by the Second Republic (1848–52), the Second Empire (1852–70), the Third Republic (1870–1940), and the Fourth and Fifth Republics (1946 and 1958); a member of the Common Market. It is generally flat or undulating in the north and west and mountainous in the south and east. Language: French. Religion: mostly Roman Catholic. Currency: franc. Capital: Paris. Pop.: 52 655 802 (1975). Area: (including Corsica) 551 600 sq. km (212 973 sq. miles). Related adj.: **Gallic.**

France[2] (*French* frɑ̃s) *n.* **A·na·tole** (ana'tɔl), pen name of *Anatole François Thibault.* 1844–1924, French novelist, short-story writer, and critic. His works include *Le Crime de Sylvestre Bonnard* (1881), *L'Île des Pingouins* (1908), and *La Révolte des anges* (1914): Nobel prize for literature 1921.

Fran·ces·ca (*Italian* fran'tʃeska) *n.* See **Piero della Francesca.**

Franche-Com·té (*French* frɑ̃ʃ kɔ̃'te) *n.* a region of E France, covering the Jura and the low country east of the Saône: part of the Kingdom of Burgundy (6th cent. A.D.–1137); autonomous as the Free County of Burgundy (1137–1384); under Burgundian rule again (1384–1477) and Hapsburg rule (1493–1674); annexed by France (1678).

fran·chise ('fræntʃaɪz) *n.* **1.** (usually preceded by *the*) the right to vote, esp. for representatives in a legislative body; suffrage. **2.** any exemption, privilege, or right granted to an individual or group by a public authority, such as the right to use public property for a business. **3.** *Commerce.* authorization granted by a manufacturing enterprise to a distributor to market the manufacturer's products. **4.** the full rights of citizenship. **5.** (in marine insurance) a sum or percentage stated in a policy, below which the insurer disclaims all liability. ~*vb.* **6.** (*tr.*) *Commerce, chiefly U.S.* to grant (a person, firm, etc.) a franchise. **7.** an obsolete word for **enfranchise.** [C13: from Old French, from *franchir* to set free, from *franc* free; see FRANK] —**fran·chise·ment** ('fræntʃɪzmənt) *n.*

Fran·cis I ('frɑːnsɪs) *n.* **1.** 1494–1547, king of France (1515–47). His reign was dominated by his rivalry with Emperor Charles V for the control of Italy. He was a noted patron of the arts and learning. **2.** title as emperor of Austria of **Francis II.**

Fran·cis II *n.* 1768–1835, last Holy Roman Emperor (1792–1806) and, as Francis I, first emperor of Austria (1804–35). The Holy Roman Empire was dissolved (1806) following his defeat by Napoleon at Austerlitz.

Fran·cis·can (fræn'sɪskən) *n.* a member of any of several Christian religious orders of mendicant friars or nuns tracing their origins back to Saint Francis of Assisi; a Grey Friar.

Fran·cis of As·si·si *n.* **Saint.** original name *Giovanni di Bernardone.* ?1181–1226, Italian monk; founder of the Franciscan order of friars. He is remembered for his humility and love for all creation and, according to legend, he received the stigmata (1224). Feast day: Oct. 4.

Fran·cis of Sales *n.* **Saint.** 1567–1622, French ecclesiastic and theologian; bishop of Geneva (1602–22) and an opponent of Calvinism; author of *Introduction to a Devout Life* (1609) and founder of the Order of the Visitation (1610). Feast day: Jan. 29.

Fran·cis Xa·vi·er ('zeɪvɪə) *n.* **Saint.** See (Saint Francis) **Xavier.**

fran·ci·um ('frænsɪəm) *n.* an unstable radioactive element of the alkali-metal group, occurring in minute amounts in uranium ores. Symbol: Fr; atomic no.: 87; half-life of most stable isotope, ^{223}Fr: 22 minutes; valency: 1. [C20: from New Latin, from FRANCE + -IUM; so-called because first found in France]

Franck *n.* **1.** (*French* frɑ̃k). **Cé·sar (Auguste)** (se'zaːr). 1822–90, French composer, organist, and teacher, born in Belgium. His works, some of which make use of cyclic form, include a violin sonata, a string quartet, the *Symphony in D Minor* (1888), and much organ music. **2.** (fræŋk). **James.** 1882–1964, U.S. physicist, born in Germany: shared Nobel prize for physics with Gustav Hertz (1925) for work on the quantum theory, particularly the effects of bombarding atoms with electrons.

Fran·co ('fræŋkəʊ; *Spanish* 'fraŋko) *n.* **Fran·cis·co** (fran'θisko), called *el Caudillo.* 1892–1975, Spanish general and statesman; head of state (1939–1975). He was commander-in-chief of the Falangists in the Spanish Civil War (1936–39), defeating the republican government and establishing a dictatorship (1939). He kept Spain neutral in World War II.

Fran·co- ('fræŋkəʊ-) *combining form.* indicating France or French: *Franco-Prussian.* [from Medieval Latin *Francus,* from Late Latin: FRANK]

fran·co·lin ('fræŋkəʊlɪn) *n.* any African or Asian partridge of the genus *Francolinus.* [C17: from French, from Old Italian *francolino,* of unknown origin]

Fran·co·ni·a (fræŋ'kəʊnɪə) *n.* a medieval duchy of Germany, inhabited by the Franks from the 7th century, now chiefly in Bavaria, Hesse, and Baden-Württemberg.

Fran·co·ni·an (fræŋ'kəʊnɪən) *n.* **1.** a group of medieval Germanic dialects spoken by the Franks in an area from N Bavaria and Alsace to the mouth of the Rhine. **Low Franconian** developed into Dutch, while **Upper Franconian** contributed to High German, of which it remains a recognizable dialect. See also **Old Low German, Old High German, Frankish.** ~*adj.* **2.** of or relating to Franconia, the Franks, or their languages.

Fran·co·phile ('fræŋkəʊ,faɪl) *or* **Fran·co·phil** ('fræŋkəʊfɪl) *n.* (*sometimes not cap.*) a person who admires France and the French.

Fran·co·phobe ('fræŋkəʊ,fəʊb) *n.* (*sometimes not cap.*) a person who hates or despises France or its people.

Fran·co·phone ('fræŋkəʊ,fəʊn) (*often not cap.*) ~*n.* **1.** a person who speaks French, esp. a native speaker. ~*adj.* **2.** speaking French as a native language. **3.** using French as a lingua franca. ~Compare **Anglophone.**

Fran·co-Prus·sian War *n.* the war of 1870–71 between France and Prussia culminating in the fall of the French Second Empire and the founding of the German empire.

franc-ti·reur *French.* (frɑ̃ti'rœːr) *n.* **1.** a sniper. **2.** a guerrilla or irregular soldier. [C19: from *franc* free + *tireur* shooter, from *tirer* to shoot, of unknown origin]

frang·er ('fræŋə) *n. Austral. taboo slang.* a condom. [C20: perhaps related to FRENCH LETTER]

fran·gi·ble ('frændʒɪbᵊl) *adj.* breakable or fragile. [C15: from Old French, ultimately from Latin *frangere* to break] —,**fran·gi·'bil·i·ty** *or* '**fran·gi·ble·ness** *n.*

fran·gi·pane ('frændʒɪ,peɪn) *n.* **1. a.** a pastry filled with cream and flavoured with almonds. **b.** a rich cake mixture containing ground almonds. **2.** a variant spelling of **frangipani** (the perfume).

fran·gi·pan·i (,frændʒɪ'pɑːnɪ) *n., pl.* **·pan·is** *or* **·pan·i. 1.** any tropical American apocynaceous shrub of the genus *Plumeria,* esp. *P. rubra,* cultivated for its waxy typically white or pink flowers, which have a sweet overpowering scent. **2.** a perfume prepared from this plant or resembling the odour of its flowers. **3. native frangipani.** *Austral.* an Australian evergreen tree, *Hymenosporum flavum,* with large fragrant yellow flowers: family *Pittosporaceae.* [C17: via French from Italian: perfume for scenting gloves, named after the Marquis Muzio *Frangipani,* 16th-century Roman nobleman who invented it]

Frang·lais (*French* frɑ̃'glɛ) *n.* informal French containing a high proportion of words of English origin. [C20: from French *français* French + *anglais* English]

frank (fræŋk) *adj.* **1.** honest and straightforward in speech or attitude: *a frank person.* **2.** outspoken or blunt. **3.** open and avowed; undisguised: *frank interest.* **4.** an obsolete word for **free** or **generous.** ~*vb.* **5.** *Chiefly Brit.* to put a mark on (a letter, parcel, etc.), either cancelling the postage stamp or in place of a stamp, ensuring free carriage. See also **postmark. 6.** to mark (a letter, parcel, etc.) with an official mark or signature, indicating the right of free delivery. **7.** (*tr.*) to facilitate or assist (a person) to come and go, pass, or enter easily. **8.** (*tr.*) to obtain immunity for or exempt (a person). ~*n.* **9.** an official mark or signature affixed to a letter, parcel, etc., ensuring free delivery or delivery without stamps. **10.** the privilege, issued to certain people and establishments, entitling them to delivery without postage stamps. [C13: from Old French *franc,* from Medieval Latin *francus* free; identical with FRANK (in Frankish Gaul only members of this people enjoyed full freedom)] —'**frank·a·ble** *adj.* —'**frank·er** *n.* —'**frank·ness** *n.*

Frank[1] (fræŋk) *n.* a member of a group of West Germanic peoples who spread from the east bank of the middle Rhine into the Roman Empire in the late 4th century A.D., gradually conquering most of Gaul and Germany. The Franks achieved their greatest power under Charlemagne. [Old English *Franca;* related to Old High German *Franko;* perhaps from the name of a typical Frankish weapon (compare Old English *franca* javelin)]

Frank² (*Dutch* fraŋk) *n.* **Anne.** 1929–45, Dutch Jewess, whose *Diary* (1947) recorded the experiences of her family while in hiding from the Nazis in Amsterdam (1942–44). They were betrayed and she died in a concentration camp.

frank·al·moign ('fræŋkəl,mɔɪn) *n. English legal history.* a form of tenure by which religious bodies held lands, esp. on condition of praying for the soul of the donor. [C16: from Anglo-French *fraunke almoigne,* from *fraunke* FRANK + *almoign* church treasury, alms chest]

Frank·en·stein ('fræŋkɪn,staɪn) *n.* **1.** a person who creates something that brings about his ruin. **2.** Also called: **Frankenstein's monster.** a thing that destroys its creator. [C19: after Baron *Frankenstein,* who created a destructive monster from parts of corpses in the novel by Mary Shelley (1818)]

Frank·fort ('fræŋkfət) *n.* **1.** a city in N Kentucky: the state capital. Pop.: 21 356 (1970). **2.** *Now rare.* an English spelling of **Frankfurt.**

Frank·furt (am Main) (*German* 'fraŋkfurt am 'maɪn) *n.* a city in central West Germany, in Hesse on the Main River: a Roman settlement in the 1st century; a free imperial city (1372–1806); seat of the federal assembly (1815–66); university (1914); trade fairs since the 13th century. Pop.: 663 422 (1974 est.).

Frank·furt (an der O·der) (*German* 'fraŋkfurt an dɛr 'o:dər) *n.* a city in E East Germany on the Polish border: member of the Hanseatic League (1368–1450). Pop.: 65 072 (1972 est.).

frank·fur·ter ('fræŋk,fɜ:tə) *n.* a light brown smoked sausage, made of finely minced pork or beef, often served in a bread roll. [C20: short for German *Frankfurter Wurst* sausage from FRANKFURT (AM MAIN)]

Frank·fur·ter ('fræŋk,fɜ:tə) *n.* an inhabitant or native of Frankfurt.

frank·in·cense ('fræŋkɪn,sɛns) *n.* an aromatic gum resin obtained from trees of the burseraceous genus *Boswellia,* which occur in Asia and Africa. Also called: **olibanum.** [C14: from Old French *franc* free, pure + *encens* INCENSE; see FRANK]

Frank·ish ('fræŋkɪʃ) *n.* **1.** the ancient West Germanic language of the Franks, esp. the dialect that contributed to the vocabulary of modern French. See also **Franconian, Old High German.** ~*adj.* **2.** of or relating to the Franks or their language.

frank·lin ('fræŋklɪn) *n.* (in 14th- and 15th-century England) a substantial landholder of free but not noble birth. [C13: from Anglo-French *fraunclein,* from Old French *franc* free, on the model of CHAMBERLAIN]

Frank·lin¹ ('fræŋklɪn) *n.* an administrative district of the Northwest Territories of Canada: consists mostly of Arctic islands; extends to the North Pole. Pop.: (mainly Eskimo) 7747 (1971). Area: 1 422 565 sq. km (549 253 sq. miles).

Frank·lin² ('fræŋklɪn) *n.* **1. A·re·tha** (ə'ri:θə). born 1942, U.S. soul singer, whose recordings include *I never loved a Man the Way I loved you* (1966), *Respect* (1968), *Think* (1969), and *Sweet Passion* (1977). **2. Ben·ja·min.** 1706–90, American statesman, scientist, and author. He helped draw up the Declaration of Independence (1776) and, as ambassador to France (1776–85), he negotiated an alliance with France and a peace settlement with Britain. As a scientist, he is noted particularly for his researches in electricity, esp. his invention of the lightning conductor. **3.** Sir **John.** 1786–1847, English explorer of the Arctic.

frank·lin·ite ('fræŋklɪ,naɪt) *n.* a black mineral consisting of an oxide of iron, manganese, and zinc: a source of iron and zinc. Formula: $(Fe,Mn,Zn)(Fe,Mn)_2O_4$. [C19: from *Franklin,* New Jersey, where it is found, + -ITE¹]

frank·ly ('fræŋklɪ) *adv.* **1.** (*sentence modifier*) in truth; to be honest: *frankly, I can't bear him.* **2.** in a frank manner.

frank·pledge ('fræŋk,plɛdʒ) *n.* (in medieval England) **1.** the corporate responsibility of members of a tithing for the good behaviour of each other. **2.** a member of a tithing. **3.** a tithing itself. [C15: via Anglo-French from Old French *franc* free (see FRANK) + *plege* PLEDGE]

fran·tic ('fræntɪk) *adj.* **1.** distracted with fear, pain, joy, etc. **2.** *Archaic.* insane. [C14: from Old French *frenetique,* from Latin *phrenēticus* mad, FRENETIC] —**'fran·ti·cal·ly** *or* **'fran·tic·ly** *adv.* —**'fran·tic·ness** *n.*

Franz Fer·di·nand (*German* frants 'fɛrdi,nant) *n.* English name *Francis Ferdinand.* 1863–1914, archduke of Austria; heir apparent of Franz Josef I. His assassination contributed to the outbreak of World War I.

Franz Jo·sef I (*German* frants 'jo:zɛf) *n.* English name *Francis Joseph I.* 1830–1916, emperor of Austria (1848–1916) and king of Hungary (1867–1916).

Franz Jo·sef Land *n.* an archipelago of over 100 islands in the Arctic Ocean, administratively part of the Soviet Union. Area: about 21 000 sq. km (8000 sq. miles). Russian name: **Zem·lya Fran·tsa Io·si·fa** (zji'mlja 'frantsə 'jɔsifə).

frap (fræp) *vb.* **fraps, frap·ping, frapped.** (*tr.*) *Nautical.* to lash down or together. [C14: from Old French *fraper* to hit, probably of imitative origin]

frap·pé ('fræpeɪ; *French* fra'pe) *n.* **1.** a drink consisting of a liqueur, etc., poured over crushed ice. ~*adj.* **2.** (*postpositive*) (esp. of drinks) chilled; iced. [C19: from French, from *frapper* to strike, hence, chill; see FRAP]

Fra·ser¹ ('freɪzə) *n.* a river in SW Canada, in S central British Columbia, flowing northwest, south, and west through spectacular canyons in the Coast Mountains to the Strait of Georgia. Length: 1370 km (850 miles).

Fra·ser² ('freɪzə) *n.* **1. (John) Mal·colm.** born 1930, Australian statesman; prime minister of Australia since 1975. **2. Pe·ter.** 1884–1950, New Zealand statesman, born in Scotland; prime minister (1940–49).

frass (fræs) *n.* excrement or other refuse left by insects and insect larvae. [C19: from German, from *fressen* to devour]

fratch·y ('frætʃɪ) *adj.* **fratch·i·er, fratch·i·est.** *Informal.* quarrelsome; irritable. [C19: from obsolete *fratch* to make a harsh noise; perhaps of imitative origin]

fra·ter¹ ('freɪtə) *n.* a mendicant friar or a lay brother in a monastery or priory. [C16: from Latin: BROTHER]

fra·ter² ('freɪtə) *n. Archaic.* a refectory. [C13: from Old French *fraiteur,* aphetic variant of *refreitor,* from Late Latin *rēfectōrium* REFECTORY]

fra·ter·nal (frə'tɜ:nəl) *adj.* **1.** of or suitable to a brother; brotherly. **2.** of or relating to a fraternity. **3.** designating either or both of a pair of twins of the same or opposite sex that developed from two separate fertilized ova. Compare **identical** (sense 3). [C15: from Latin *frāternus,* from *frāter* brother] —**fra·'ter·nal·ism** *n.* —**fra·'ter·nal·ly** *adv.*

fra·ter·ni·ty (frə'tɜ:nɪtɪ) *n., pl.* **·ties. 1.** a body of people united in interests, aims, etc.: *the teaching fraternity.* **2.** brotherhood. **3.** *U.S.* a secret society joined by male students, usually functioning as a social club and bearing a name composed of Greek letters.

frat·er·nize *or* **frat·er·nise** ('frætə,naɪz) *vb.* **1.** (*intr.;* often foll. by *with*) to associate on friendly terms. **2.** (*tr.*) *Rare.* to cause fraternal relations between. —**,frat·er·ni·'za·tion** *or* **,frat·er·ni·'sa·tion** *n.* —**'frat·er·,niz·er** *or* **'frat·er·,nis·er** *n.*

frat·ri·cide ('frætrɪ,saɪd, 'freɪ-) *n.* **1.** the act of killing one's brother. **2.** a person who kills his brother. [C15: from Latin *frātricīda;* see FRATER¹, -CIDE] —**,frat·ri·'cid·al** *adj.*

Frau (fraʊ) *n., pl.* **Frau·en** ('fraʊən) *or* **Fraus.** a married German woman: usually used as a title equivalent to *Mrs.* and sometimes extended to older unmarried women. [from Old High German *frouwa;* related to Dutch *vrouw*]

fraud (frɔ:d) *n.* **1.** deliberate deception, trickery, or cheating intended to gain an advantage. **2.** an act or instance of such deception. **3.** something false or spurious: *his explanation was a fraud.* **4.** *Informal.* a person who acts in a false or deceitful way. [C14: from Old French *fraude,* from Latin *fraus* deception]

fraud·u·lent ('frɔ:djʊlənt) *adj.* **1.** acting with or having the intent to deceive. **2.** relating to or proceeding from fraud or dishonest action. [C15: from Latin *fraudulentus* deceitful] —**'fraud·u·lence** *or* **'fraud·u·len·cy** *n.* —**'fraud·u·lent·ly** *adv.*

Frau·en·feld (*German* 'fraʊən,fɛlt) *n.* a town in NE Switzerland, capital of Thurgau canton. Pop.: 17 576 (1970).

fraught (frɔ:t) *adj.* **1.** (*usually postpositive* and foll. by *with*) filled or charged; attended: *a venture fraught with peril.* **2.** *Archaic.* (*usually postpositive* and foll. by *with*) freighted. ~*n.* **3.** an obsolete word for **freight.** [C14: from Middle Dutch *vrachten,* from *vracht* FREIGHT]

Fräu·lein (*German* 'frɔɪlaɪn; *English* 'frɔ:laɪn, 'fraʊ-) *n., pl.* **·lein** *or English* **·leins.** an unmarried German woman: often used as a title equivalent to *Miss.* Abbrev.: **Frl.** [from Middle High German *vrouwelīn,* diminutive of *vrouwe* lady]

Fraun·ho·fer (*German* 'fraʊnho:fər) *n.* **Jo·seph von** ('jo:zɛf fɔn). 1787–1826, German physicist and optician, who investigated spectra of the sun, planets, and fixed stars, and improved telescopes and other optical instruments.

Fraun·ho·fer lines *pl. n.* a set of dark lines appearing in the continuous emission spectrum of the sun. It is caused by the absorption of light of certain wavelengths coming from the hotter region of the sun by elements in the cooler outer atmosphere.

frax·i·nel·la (,fræksɪ'nɛlə) *n.* another name for **gas plant.** [C17: from New Latin: a little ash tree, from Latin *fraxinus* ash]

fray¹ (freɪ) *n.* **1.** a noisy quarrel. **2.** a fight or brawl. **3.** an archaic word for **fright.** ~*vb. Archaic.* **4.** (*intr.*) to fight or disturb the peace. **5.** (*tr.*) to frighten. [C14: short for AFFRAY]

fray² (freɪ) *vb.* **1.** to wear or cause to wear away into tatters or loose threads, esp. at an edge or end. **2.** to make or become strained or irritated. **3.** to rub or chafe (another object) or (of two objects) to rub against one another. ~*n.* **4.** a frayed place, as in cloth. [C14: from French *frayer* to rub, from Latin *fricāre;* see FRICTION, FRIABLE]

Fra·zer ('freɪzə) *n.* Sir **James George.** 1854–1941, Scottish anthropologist; author of many works on primitive religion, and magic, esp. *The Golden Bough* (1890).

Fra·zier ('freɪzjə) *n.* **Joe.** born 1944, U.S. boxer: won the world heavyweight title in 1970 and was the first to beat Muhammad Ali professionally (1971).

fra·zil ('freɪzɪl) *n.* spikes of ice that form in water moving turbulently enough to prevent the formation of a sheet of ice. [C19: from Canadian French *frasil,* from French *fraisil* cinders, ultimately from Latin *fax* torch]

fraz·zle ('fræzəl) *vb.* **1.** *Informal.* to make or become exhausted or weary; tire out. **2.** a less common word for **fray²** (sense 1). ~*n.* **3.** *Informal.* the state of being frazzled or exhausted. **4.** a frayed end or remnant. **5. to a frazzle.** *Informal.* absolutely; completely (esp. in the phrase **burnt to a frazzle**). [C19: probably from Middle English *faselen* to fray, from *fasel* fringe; influenced by FRAY²]

F.R.C.M. (in Britain) *abbrev. for* Fellow of the Royal College of Music.

F.R.C.O. (in Britain) *abbrev. for* Fellow of the Royal College of Organists.
F.R.C.P. (in Britain) *abbrev. for* Fellow of the Royal College of Physicians.
F.R.C.S. (in Britain) *abbrev. for* Fellow of the Royal College of Surgeons.
freak[1] (fri:k) *n.* **1.** a person, animal, or plant that is abnormal or deformed; monstrosity. **2. a.** an object, event, etc., that is abnormal or extremely unusual. **b.** (*as modifier*): *a freak storm.* **3.** a personal whim or caprice. **4.** *Slang.* a person who acts or dresses in a markedly unconventional or strange way. **5.** *Slang.* a person who is obsessed with something specified: *a jazz freak.* ~*vb.* **6.** See **freak out.** [C16: of obscure origin]
freak[2] (fri:k) *Rare.* ~*n.* **1.** a fleck or streak of colour. ~*vb.* **2.** (*tr.*) to streak with colour; variegate. [C17: from earlier *freaked,* probably coined by Milton, based on STREAK + obsolete *freckt* freckled; see FRECKLE]
freak+ish ('fri:kɪʃ) *adj.* **1.** of, related to, or characteristic of a freak; abnormal or unusual. **2.** unpredictable or changeable: *freakish weather.* —**'freak+ish+ly** *adv.* —**'freak+ish+ness** *n.*
freak out *Informal.* ~*vb.* (*adv.*) **1.** to experience or cause to experience radically altered perception characterized by disorientation, hallucinations, etc., esp. under the influence of drugs. **2.** to be or cause to be in a heightened emotional state, such as that of anger, excitement, etc. **3.** (*intr.*) to withdraw from society and adopt an unconventional way of life. ~*n.* **freak+out. 4.** a wild experience, esp. one induced by hallucinogenic drugs.
freak·y ('fri:kɪ) *adj.* **freak·i·er, freak·i·est. 1.** *Slang.* strange; unconventional; bizarre. **2.** another word for **freakish.** —**'freak·i·ly** *adv.* —**'freak·i·ness** *n.*
freck+le ('frɛkᵊl) *n.* **1.** a small brownish spot on the skin: a localized deposit of the pigment melanin, developed by exposure to sunlight. Technical name: **lentigo. 2.** any small area of discoloration; a spot. ~*vb.* **3.** to mark or become marked with freckles or spots. [C14: from Old Norse *freknur* freckles; related to Swedish *fräkne,* Danish *fregne*] —**'freck+led** *or* **'freck+ly** *adj.*
Fre+de+ri+cia (*Danish* freðəˈredsja) *n.* a port in Denmark, in E Jutland at the N end of the Little Belt. Pop.: 33 364 (1970).
Fred·er·ick I ('frɛdrɪk) *n.* **1.** See **Frederick Barbarossa. 2.** 1657–1713, first king of Prussia (1701–13); son of Frederick William.
Fred·er·ick II *n.* **1.** 1194–1250, Holy Roman Emperor (1220–50), king of Germany (1212–50), and king of Sicily (1198–1250). **2.** See **Frederick the Great.**
Fred·er·ick III *n.* called *the Wise.* 1463–1525, elector of Saxony (1486–1525). He protected Martin Luther in Wartburg Castle after the Diet of Worms (1521).
Fred·er·ick IX *n.* 1899–1972, king of Denmark (1947–72).
Fred·er·ick Bar·ba·ros·sa (ˌbɑ:bəˈrɒsə) *n.* official title *Frederick I.* ?1123–90, Holy Roman Emperor (1155–90), king of Germany (1152–90). His attempt to assert imperial rights in Italy ended in his defeat at Legnano (1176) and the independence of the Lombard cities (1183).
Fred·er·ick the Great *n.* official title *Frederick II.* 1712–86, king of Prussia (1740–86); son of Frederick William I. He gained Silesia during the War of Austrian Succession (1740–48) and his military genius during the Seven Years' War (1756–63) established Prussia as a European power. He was also a noted patron of the arts.
Fred·er·ick Wil·liam *n.* called *the Great Elector.* 1620–88, elector of Brandenburg (1640–88).
Fred·er·ick Wil·liam I *n.* 1688–1740, king of Prussia (1713–40); son of Frederick I: reformed the Prussian army.
Fred·er·ick Wil·liam III *n.* 1770–1840, king of Prussia (1797–1840).
Fred·er·ick Wil·liam IV *n.* 1795–1861, king of Prussia (1840–61). He submitted to the 1848 Revolution but refused the imperial crown offered by the Frankfurt Parliament (1849). In 1857 he became insane and his brother, William I, became regent (1858–61).
Fred+er+ic+ton ('frɛdrɪktən) *n.* a city in SE Canada, capital of New Brunswick, on the St. John River. Pop.: 24 254 (1971).
Fred+er+iks+berg (*Danish* ˌfrɛðregsˈbɛr) *n.* a city in E Denmark, within the area of greater Copenhagen: founded in 1651 by King Frederick III. Pop.: 101 899 (1970).
Fred+rik+stad (*Norwegian* 'frɛdrikˌsta) *n.* a port in SE Norway at the entrance to Oslo Fjord. Pop.: 30 009 (1970).
free (fri:) *adj.* **fre+er, fre+est. 1.** able to act at will; not under compulsion or restraint. **2. a.** having personal rights or liberty; not enslaved or confined. **b.** (*as n.*): *land of the free.* **3.** (*often postpositive* and foll. by *from*) not subject (to) or restricted (by some regulation, constraint, etc.); exempt: *a free market; free from pain.* **4.** (of a country, etc.) autonomous or independent. **5.** exempt from external direction or restriction; not forced or induced: *free will.* **6.** not subject to conventional constraints: *free verse.* **7.** (of jazz) totally improvised, with no preset melodic, harmonic, or rhythmic basis. **8.** not exact or literal: *a free translation.* **9.** costing nothing; provided without charge: *free entertainment.* **10.** *Law.* (of property) **a.** not subject to payment of rent or performance of services; freehold. **b.** not subject to any burden or charge, such as a mortgage or lien; unencumbered. **11.** (*postpositive;* often foll. by *of* or *with*) ready or generous in using or giving; liberal; lavish: *free with advice.* **12.** unrestrained by propriety or good manners; licentious. **13.** not occupied or in use; available: *a free cubicle.* **14.** open or available to all; public. **15.** not fixed or joined; loose: *the free end of a chain.* **16.** without obstruction or impediment: *free passage.* **17.** *Chem.* chemically uncombined: *free nitrogen.* **18.** *Phonetics.* denoting a vowel that can occur in an open syllable, as the vowel in *see* as opposed to the vowel in *cat.* **19.** *Grammar.* denoting a morpheme that can occur as a separate word. Compare **bound**[1] (sense 8). **20.** *Logic.* denoting an occurrence of a variable not bound by a quantifier. Compare **bound**[1] (sense 9). **21.** (of some materials, such as certain kinds of stone) easily worked. **22.** *Nautical.* (of the wind) blowing from the quarter. **23. free and easy.** casual or tolerant; easygoing. **24. for free.** *Nonstandard.* without charge or cost. ~*adv.* **25.** in a free manner; freely. **26.** without charge or cost. **27.** *Nautical.* with the wind blowing from the quarter: *a yacht sailing free.* **28. make free with.** to take liberties with; behave too familiarly towards. ~*vb.* **frees, free+ing, freed.** (*tr.*) **29.** to set at liberty; release. **30.** to remove obstructions, attachments, or impediments from; disengage. **31.** (often foll. by *of* or *from*) to relieve or rid (of obstacles, pain, etc.). [Old English *frēo;* related to Old Saxon, Old High German *frī,* Gothic *freis* free, Sanskrit *priya* dear] —**'fre+er** *n.* —**'free+ly** *adv.* —**'free+ness** *n.*
-free (-fri:) *adj. combining form.* free from: *trouble-free; lead-free petrol.*
free a·gent *n.* a person whose actions are not constrained by others.
free a·long+side ship *adj.* (of a shipment of goods) delivered to the dock without charge to the buyer, but excluding the cost of loading onto the vessel. Compare **free on board.** Abbrevs.: **F.A.S., f.a.s.** Also: **free alongside vessel.**
free as+so+ci·a+tion *n.* **1.** *Psychoanal.* a method of exploring a person's unconscious by eliciting words and thoughts that are associated with key words provided by a psychoanalyst. **2.** a spontaneous mental process whereby ideas, words, or images suggest other ideas, etc., in a nonlogical chain reaction.
free+bie ('fri:bɪ) *U.S. slang.* ~*n.* **1.** something provided without charge. ~*adj.* **2.** without charge; free.
free+board ('fri:ˌbɔ:d) *n.* the space or distance between the deck of a vessel and the waterline.
free+boot ('fri:ˌbu:t) *vb.* (*intr.*) to act as a freebooter; pillage.
free+boot·er ('fri:ˌbu:tə) *n.* **1.** a person, such as a pirate, living from plunder. **2.** *Informal.* a person, esp. an itinerant, who seeks pleasure, wealth, etc., without responsibility. [C16: from Dutch *vrijbuiter,* from *vrijbuit* booty; see FILIBUSTER]
free+born ('fri:ˌbɔ:n) *adj.* **1.** not born in slavery. **2.** of, relating to, or suitable for people not born in slavery.
Free Church *n.* **1.** *Chiefly Brit.* any Protestant Church, esp. the Presbyterian, other than the Established Church. **2.** (*as modifier*): *Free-Church attitudes.*
free cit·y *n.* a sovereign or autonomous city; city-state.
free coin+age *n. U.S.* coinage of bullion brought to the mint by any individual.
free com+pan+ion *n.* (in medieval Europe) a member of a company of mercenary soldiers.
free com+pan·y *n. European history.* a band of mercenary soldiers during the Middle Ages.
freed+man ('fri:dˌmæn) *n., pl.* **+men.** a man who has been freed from slavery. —**'freed+ˌwom·an** *fem. n.*
free+dom ('fri:dəm) *n.* **1.** personal liberty, as from slavery, bondage, serfdom, etc. **2.** liberation or deliverance, as from confinement or bondage. **3.** the quality or state of being free, esp. to enjoy political and civil liberties. **4.** (usually foll. by *from*) the state of being without something unpleasant or bad; exemption or immunity: *freedom from taxation.* **5.** the right or privilege of unrestricted use or access: *the freedom of a city.* **6.** autonomy, self-government, or independence. **7.** the power or liberty to order one's own actions. **8.** *Philosophy.* the quality, esp. of the will or the individual, of being unrestrained by physical determinants, destiny, etc. **9.** ease or frankness of manner; candour: *she talked with complete freedom.* **10.** excessive familiarity of manner; boldness. **11.** ease and grace, as of movement; lack of effort. [Old English *frēodōm*]
free+dom fight+er *n.* a militant revolutionary.
Free+dom+ites ('fri:dəˌmaɪts) *pl. n.* another name for **Sons of Freedom.**
free+dom of the seas *n. International law.* **1.** the right of ships of all nations to sail the high seas in peacetime. **2.** (in wartime) the immunity accorded to neutral ships from attack. **3.** the exclusive jurisdiction possessed by a state over its own ships sailing the high seas in peacetime.
free+dom rid+er *n. U.S.* a person who participated, esp. in the 1960s, in an organized tour, usually by public transport in the South, in order to protest against racialism and put federal laws on integration to the test.
free en+er+gy *n.* a thermodynamic property that expresses the capacity of a system to perform work under certain conditions. See **Gibbs function, Helmholtz function.**
free en+ter+prise *n.* an economic system in which commercial organizations compete for profit with little state control.
free fall *n.* **1.** free descent of a body in which the gravitational force is the only force acting on it. **2.** the part of a parachute descent before the parachute opens.
free flight *n.* the flight of a rocket, missile, etc., when its engine has ceased to produce thrust.
free-float·ing *adj.* unattached or uncommitted, as to a cause, a party, etc. —**ˌfree-'float·er** *n.*
free-for-all *n. Informal.* a disorganized brawl or argument, usually involving all those present.
free form *Arts.* ~*n.* **1.** an irregular flowing shape, often used in industrial or fabric design. ~*adj.* **free-form. 2.** freely flowing, spontaneous.

free gift *n.* something given away, esp. as an incentive to a purchaser.

free gold *n.* **1.** gold, uncombined with other minerals, found in a pure state. **2.** *U.S.* the excess of gold held by the Federal Reserve Banks over the legal reserve.

free hand *n.* **1.** unrestricted freedom to act (esp. in the phrase **give (someone) a free hand**). *~adj., adv.* **free+hand. 2.** (done) by hand without the use of guiding instruments: *a freehand drawing.*

free-hand·ed *adj.* generous or liberal; unstinting. —ˌ**free-'hand·ed+ly** *adv.* —ˌ**free-'hand·ed+ness** *n.*

free-heart·ed *adj.* frank and spontaneous; open; generous. —ˌ**free-'heart·ed+ly** *adv.* —ˌ**free-'heart·ed+ness** *n.*

free+hold ('fri:ˌhəʊld) *Property law.* *~n.* **1. a.** tenure by which land is held in fee simple, fee tail, or for life. **b.** an estate held by such tenure. *~adj.* **2.** relating to or having the nature of freehold.

free+hold·er ('fri:ˌhəʊldə) *n. Property law.* a person in possession of a freehold building or estate in land.

free house *n. Brit.* a public house not bound to sell only one brewer's products.

free kick *n. Soccer.* a place kick awarded for a foul or infringement, either direct, from which a goal may be scored, or indirect, from which the ball must be touched by at least one other player for a goal to be allowed.

free la+bour *n.* **1.** the labour of workers who are not members of trade unions. **2.** such workers collectively.

free+lance ('fri:ˌlɑ:ns) *n.* **1. a.** Also called: **freelancer.** a self-employed person, esp. a writer or artist, who is not employed continuously but hired to do specific assignments. **b.** (*as modifier*): *a freelance journalist.* **2.** a person, esp. a politician, who supports several causes or parties without total commitment to any one. **3.** (in medieval Europe) a mercenary soldier or adventurer. *~vb.* **4.** to work as a freelance on (an assignment, etc.). *~adv.* **5.** as a freelance. [C19 (in sense 3): later applied to politicians, writers, etc.]

free list *n.* **1.** *Commerce, chiefly U.S.* a list of commodities not subject to tariffs. **2.** a list of people admitted free.

free-liv·ing *adj.* **1.** given to ready indulgence of the appetites. **2.** (of animals and plants) not parasitic; existing independently. —ˌ**free-'liv·er** *n.*

free+load ('fri:ˌləʊd) *vb.* (*intr.*) *U.S. slang.* to act as a freeloader; sponge.

free+load·er ('fri:ˌləʊdə) *n. U.S. slang.* a person who habitually depends on the charity of others for food, shelter, etc. —**'free+ˌload·ing** *n.*

free love *n.* the practice of sexual relationships without fidelity to a single partner or without formal or legal ties.

free+man ('fri:mən) *n., pl.* **+men. 1.** a person who is not a slave or in bondage. **2.** a person who enjoys political and civil liberties; citizen. **3.** a person who enjoys a privilege or franchise, such as the freedom of a city.

free+mar·tin ('fri:ˌmɑ:tɪn) *n.* the female of a pair of twin calves of unlike sex that is imperfectly developed and sterile, probably due to the influence of the male hormones of its twin during development in the uterus. [C17: of uncertain origin]

free+ma·son ('fri:ˌmeɪsᵊn) *n. Medieval history.* a member of a guild of itinerant skilled stonemasons, who had a system of secret signs and passwords with which they recognized each other. —**free+ma·son·ic** (ˌfri:mə'sɒnɪk) *adj.*

Free+ma·son ('fri:ˌmeɪsᵊn) *n.* a member of the widespread secret order, founded in London in 1717, of **Free and Accepted Masons,** pledged to brotherliness and mutual aid. —**Free+ma·son·ic** (ˌfri:mə'sɒnɪk) *adj.*

free+ma·son·ry ('fri:ˌmeɪsᵊnrɪ) *n.* natural or tacit sympathy and understanding.

Free+ma·son·ry ('fri:ˌmeɪsᵊnrɪ) *n.* **1.** the institutions, rites, practices, etc., of Freemasons. **2.** Freemasons collectively.

free on board *adj.* (of a shipment of goods) delivered on board ship or other carrier without charge to the buyer. Compare **free alongside ship.** Abbrevs.: **F.O.B., f.o.b.**

free on rail *adj.* (of a consignment of goods) delivered to a railway station and loaded onto a train without charge to the buyer. Abbrevs.: **F.O.R., f.o.r.**

free port *n.* **1.** a port open to all commercial vessels on equal terms. **2.** Also called: **free zone.** a zone adjoining a port that permits the duty-free entry of foreign goods intended for re-export.

free rad·i+cal *n.* an atom or group of atoms containing at least one unpaired electron and existing for a brief period of time before reacting to produce a stable molecule. Sometimes shortened to **radical.** Compare **group** (sense 10).

free-range *adj. Chiefly Brit.* kept or produced in natural nonintensive conditions: *free-range hens; free-range eggs.*

free-se·lect *vb.* (*tr.*) *Austral. history.* to select (areas of crown land) and acquire the freehold by a series of annual payments. —**'free-se·'lec+tion** *n.* —**'free-se·'lec+tor** *n.*

free+sheet ('fri:ˌʃi:t) *n.* a newspaper that is distributed free, paid for by its advertisers. Also called: **giveaway.**

free+si·a ('fri:zɪə) *n.* any iridaceous plant of the genus *Freesia,* of southern Africa, cultivated for their white, yellow, or pink tubular fragrant flowers. [C19: New Latin, named after F. H. T. *Freese* (died 1876), German physician]

free sil+ver *n.* the unlimited minting of silver coins, esp. when at a fixed ratio to gold.

Free Soil Par+ty *n.* a former U.S. political party opposing slavery from 1848 until 1854 when it merged with the Republican party.

free speech *n.* the right to express one's opinions publicly.

free-spo·ken *adj.* speaking frankly or without restraint. —ˌ**free-'spo·ken+ly** *adv.* —ˌ**free-'spo·ken+ness** *n.*

free+stand·ing (ˌfri:'stændɪŋ) *adj.* standing apart; not attached to or supported by another object.

Free State *n.* **1.** *U.S. history.* (before the Civil War). any state prohibiting slavery. **2.** short for the **Irish Free State.**

free+stone ('fri:ˌstəʊn) *n.* **1. a.** any fine-grained stone, esp. sandstone or limestone, that can be cut and worked in any direction without breaking. **b.** (*as modifier*): *a freestone house.* **2.** *Botany.* **a.** a fruit, such as a peach, in which the flesh separates readily from the stone. **b.** (*as modifier*): *a freestone peach.* Compare **clingstone.**

free+style ('fri:ˌstaɪl) *n.* **1.** a competition or race, as in swimming, in which each participant may use a style of his or her choice instead of a specified style. **2.** a wrestling style in which any hold or throw is permitted. **3.** a series of acrobatics performed in skiing, skateboarding, etc. **4.** (*as modifier*): *a freestyle event.*

free-swim·ming *adj.* (of aquatic animals or larvae) not sessile or attached to any object and therefore able to swim freely in the water. —ˌ**free-'swim·mer** *n.*

free+think·er (ˌfri:'θɪŋkə) *n.* a person who forms his ideas and opinions independently of authority or accepted views, esp. in matters of religion. —ˌ**free+'think·ing** *n., adj.*

free thought *n.* thought unrestrained and uninfluenced by dogma or authority, esp. in religious matters.

free throw *n. Basketball.* an unimpeded shot at the basket from the **free-throw line,** given for a technical fault (one free shot) or a foul (two free shots).

Free+town ('fri:ˌtaʊn) *n.* the capital and chief port of Sierra Leone: founded in 1787 for slaves freed and destitute in England. Pop.: 178 600 (1970 est.).

free trade *n.* **1.** international trade that is free of such government interference as import quotas, export subsidies, protective tariffs, etc. Compare **protection** (sense 3). **2.** *Archaic.* illicit trade; smuggling.

free-trad·er *n.* **1.** a person who supports or advocates free trade. **2.** *Archaic.* a smuggler or smuggling vessel.

free verse *n.* unrhymed verse without a metrical pattern.

free vote *n. Chiefly Brit.* a parliamentary division in which members are not constrained by a party whip.

free+way ('fri:ˌweɪ) *n. U.S.* a major road that can be used without paying a toll.

free+wheel (ˌfri:'wi:l) *n.* **1.** a ratchet device in the rear hub of a bicycle wheel that permits the wheel to rotate freely while the pedals are stationary. **2.** a device in the transmission of some vehicles that automatically disengages the drive shaft when it rotates more rapidly than the engine shaft, so that the drive shaft can turn freely. *~vb.* **3.** (*intr.*) to coast in a vehicle or on a bicycle using the freewheel.

free+wheel·ing (ˌfri:'wi:lɪŋ) *adj.* **1.** relating to, operating as, or having a freewheel; coasting. **2.** *Informal, chiefly U.S.* free of restraints; carefree or uninhibited.

free will *n.* **1. a.** the apparent human ability to make choices that are not externally determined. **b.** the doctrine that human beings have such freedom of choice. Compare **determinism. c.** (*as modifier*): *a free-will decision.* **2.** the ability to make a choice without outside coercion: *he left of his own free will: I did not influence him.*

Free World *n.* **the.** the non-Communist countries collectively, esp. those that are actively anti-Communist.

freeze (fri:z) *vb.* **freez·es, freez+ing, froze, fro+zen. 1.** to change (a liquid) into a solid as a result of a reduction in temperature, or (of a liquid) to solidify in this way, esp. to convert or be converted into ice. **2.** (when *intr.,* sometimes foll. by *over* or *up*) to cover, clog, or harden with ice, or become so covered, clogged, or hardened: *the lake froze over last week.* **3.** to fix fast or become fixed (to something) because of the action of frost. **4.** (*tr.*) to preserve (food) by subjection to extreme cold, as in a freezer. **5.** to feel or cause to feel the sensation or effects of extreme cold. **6.** to die or cause to die of frost or extreme cold. **7.** to become or cause to become paralysed, fixed, or motionless, esp. through fear, shock, etc.: *he froze in his tracks.* **8.** (*tr.*) to cause (moving film) to stop at a particular frame. **9.** to decrease or cause to decrease in animation or vigour. **10.** to make or become formal, haughty, etc., in manner. **11.** (*tr.*) to fix (prices, incomes, etc.) at a particular level, usually by government direction. **12.** (*tr.*) to forbid by law the exchange, liquidation, or collection of (loans, assets, etc.). **13.** (*tr.*) to prohibit the manufacture, sale, or use of (something specified). **14.** (*tr.*) to stop (a process) at a particular stage of development. **15.** (*tr.*) *Informal.* to render (tissue or a part of the body) insensitive, as by the application or injection of a local anaesthetic. **16.** (*intr.;* foll. by *onto*) *Informal, chiefly U.S.* to cling. *~n.* **17.** the act of freezing or state of being frozen. **18.** *Meteorol.* a spell of temperatures below freezing point, usually over a wide area. **19.** the fixing of incomes, prices, etc., by legislation. **20.** another word for **frost.** [Old English *frēosan;* related to Old Norse *frjōsa,* Old High German *friosan,* Latin *prūrīre* to itch; see FROST] —**'freez+a·ble** *adj.*

freeze-dry *vb.* **-dries, -dry·ing, -dried.** (*tr.*) to preserve (a substance) by rapid freezing and subsequently drying in a vacuum.

freeze out *vb.* (*tr., adv.*) *Informal, chiefly U.S.* to force out or exclude, as by unfriendly behaviour, boycotting, etc.

freez+er ('fri:zə) *n.* **1.** Also called: **deepfreeze.** a device that freezes or chills, esp. an insulated cold-storage cabinet for long-term storage of perishable foodstuffs. **2.** a former name for a **refrigerator.**

freeze-up *n. Informal.* **1.** a period of freezing or extremely cold weather. **2.** *U.S., Canadian.* **a.** the freezing of lakes, rivers, and topsoil in autumn or early winter. **b.** the time of year when this occurs. Compare **break-up.**

freez·ing mix·ture *n.* a mixture of two substances, usually salt and ice, to give a temperature below 0°C.

freez·ing point *n.* the temperature below which a liquid turns into a solid. It is equal to the melting point.

freez·ing works *n. Austral.* a slaughterhouse at which animal carcasses are frozen for export.

free zone *n.* an area at a port where certain customs restrictions are not implemented. See also **free port.**

F re·gion *n.* the highest region of the ionosphere, extending from a height of about 150 kilometres to about 1000 kilometres. It contains the highest proportion of free electrons and is the most useful region for long-range radio transmission. Also called: **Appleton layer.** See also **ionosphere.**

Frei (*Spanish* frej) *n.* **E·duar·do** (e'ðwarðo). 1911-82, Chilean Christian-Democrat statesman; president (1964-70).

Frei·burg (*German* 'fraɪbʊrk) *n.* **1.** a city in West Germany, in SW Baden-Württemberg: under Austrian rule (1368–1805); university (1457). Pop.: 174 997 (1974 est.). Official name: **Frei·burg im Breis·gau** (ˌɪm 'braɪsgaʊ). **2.** the German name for **Fribourg.**

freight (freɪt) *n.* **1. a.** commercial transport that is slower and cheaper than express. **b.** the price charged for such transport. **c.** goods transported by this means. **d.** (*as modifier*): *freight transport.* **2.** *Chiefly Brit.* a ship's cargo or part of it. ~*vb.* (*tr.*) **3.** to load with goods for transport. **4.** *Chiefly U.S.* to convey commercially as or by freight. **5.** to load or burden; charge. [C16: from Middle Dutch *vrecht;* related to French *fret,* Spanish *flete,* Portuguese *frete*] —**'freight·less** *adj.*

freight·age ('freɪtɪdʒ) *n.* **1.** the commercial conveyance of goods. **2.** the goods so transported. **3.** the price charged for such conveyance.

freight·er ('freɪtə) *n.* **1.** a ship or aircraft designed for transporting cargo. **2.** a person concerned with the loading or chartering of a ship.

freight·lin·er ('freɪtˌlaɪnə) *n.* a type of goods train carrying containers that can be transferred onto lorries or ships.

freight ton *n.* the full name for **ton**[1] (sense 4).

Fre·man·tle ('friːˌmænt°l) *n.* a port in SW Western Australia, on the Indian Ocean. Pop.: 25 990 (1971).

fremd (frɛmd, freɪmd) *adj. Archaic.* alien or strange. [Old English *fremde;* related to Old High German *fremidi*]

frem·i·tus ('frɛmɪtəs) *n., pl.* **·tus.** *Med.* a vibration felt by the hand when placed on a part of the body, esp. the chest, when the patient is speaking or coughing. [C19: from Latin: a roaring sound, a humming, from *fremere* to make a low roaring, murmur]

French[1] (frɛntʃ) *n.* **1.** the official language of France: also an official language of Switzerland, Belgium, Canada, and certain other countries. It is the native language of approximately 70 million people; also used for diplomacy. Historically, French is an Indo-European language belonging to the Romance group. See also **Old French, Anglo-French. 2.** (preceded by *the; functioning as pl.*) the natives, citizens, or inhabitants of France collectively. **3.** See **French vermouth.** ~*adj.* **4.** relating to, denoting, or characteristic of France, the French, or their language. [Old English *Frencisc* French, Frankish; see FRANK[1]] —**'French·ness** *n.*

French[2] (frɛntʃ) *n.* Sir **John Den·ton Pink·stone,** 1st Earl of Ypres. 1852–1925, British field marshal in World War I: commanded the British Expeditionary Force in France and Belgium (1914–15); Lord Lieutenant of Ireland (1918–21).

French A·cad·e·my *n.* an association of 40 French scholars and writers, founded by Cardinal Richelieu in 1635, devoted chiefly to preserving the purity of the French language.

French and In·di·an War *n.* the war (1755–60) between the French and British, each aided by different Indian tribes, that formed part of the North American Seven Years' War.

French bean *n.* **1.** a small twining bushy or annual bean plant, *Phaseolus vulgaris,* with white or lilac flowers and slender green edible pods. **2.** the pod of this plant. See also **haricot.** ~Also called: **dwarf bean, kidney bean.**

French bread *n.* white bread in a long slender loaf that is made from a water dough and has a crisp brown crust.

French bull·dog *n.* a small stocky breed of dog with a sleek coat and a large square head.

French Cam·e·roons *pl. n.* the part of Cameroon formerly administered by France (1919–60).

French Can·a·da *n.* the areas of Canada, esp. in the province of Quebec, where French Canadians predominate.

French Ca·na·di·an *n.* **1.** a Canadian citizen whose native language is French. ~*adj.* **French-Ca·na·di·an. 2.** of or relating to French Canadians or their language.

French chalk *n.* a compact variety of talc used to mark cloth or remove grease stains from materials.

French Com·mun·i·ty *n.* an international association consisting of France and a number of former French colonies: founded in 1958 as a successor to the French Union.

French crick·et *n.* a child's game resembling cricket, in which the batsman's legs are used as the wicket.

French cuff *n.* a double cuff formed by a backward fold of the material.

French curve *n.* a thin plastic sheet with profiles of several curves, used by draughtsmen for drawing curves.

French doors *pl. n.* the U.S. name for **French windows.**

French dress·ing *n.* a salad dressing made from oil and vinegar with seasonings.

French E·qua·to·ri·al Af·ri·ca *n.* the former French overseas territories of Chad, Gabon, Middle Congo, and Ubangi-Shari (1910–58).

French For·eign Le·gion *n.* a unit of the French Army serving outside France, esp. formerly in French North African colonies. It is largely recruited from foreigners.

French fried po·ta·toes *pl. n.* a more formal name for **chips.** Also called (U.S.): **French fries.**

French Gui·an·a *n.* a French overseas region in NE South America, on the Atlantic: colonized by the French in about 1637; tropical forests. Capital: Cayenne. Pop.: 52 000 (1975). Area: about 91 000 sq. km (23 000 sq. miles). —**French Gui·a·nese** *or* **Gui·an·an** *adj., n.*

French Guin·ea *n.* a former French territory of French West Africa: became independent as Guinea in 1958.

French heel *n.* a fairly high and narrow-waisted heel on women's shoes. —ˌ**French-'heeled** *adj.*

French horn *n. Music.* a valved brass instrument with a funnel-shaped mouthpiece and a tube of conical bore coiled into a spiral. It is a transposing instrument in F. Range: about three and a half octaves upwards from B on the second leger line below the bass staff. See **horn.**

French·i·fy ('frɛntʃɪˌfaɪ) *vb.* **·fies, ·fy·ing, ·fied.** *Informal.* to make or become French in appearance, behaviour, etc. —ˌ**French·i·fi·'ca·tion** *n.*

French In·di·a *n.* a former French overseas territory in India, including Chandernagore and Pondicherry: restored to India between 1949 and 1954.

French In·do·chi·na *n.* the territories of SE Asia that were colonized by France and held mostly until 1954: included Cochin China, Annam, and Tonkin (now largely Vietnam), Cambodia, Laos, and Kuang-Chou Wan (returned to China in 1945, now Chan Chiang).

French kiss *n.* a kiss involving insertion of the tongue into the partner's mouth.

French knick·ers *pl. n.* women's wide-legged underpants.

French knot *n.* an ornamental stitch made by looping the thread three or four times around the needle before putting it into the fabric.

French leave *n.* an unauthorized or unannounced absence or departure. [C18: alluding to a custom in France of leaving without saying goodbye to one's host or hostess]

French let·ter *n. Brit.* a slang term for **condom.**

French li·lac *n.* another name for **goat's-rue** (sense 1).

French·man ('frɛntʃmən) *n., pl.* **·men.** a native, citizen, or inhabitant of France. —**'French·ˌwom·an** *fem. n.*

French Mo·roc·co *n.* a former French protectorate in NW Africa, united in 1956 with Spanish Morocco and Tangier to form the kingdom of Morocco.

French mus·tard *n.* a mild mustard paste made with vinegar rather than water.

French na·vy *n.* **a.** a dark dull navy blue. **b.** (*as adj.*): *a French-navy dress.*

French North Af·ri·ca *n.* the former French possessions of Algeria, French Morocco, and Tunisia.

French O·ce·an·i·a *n.* a former name of **French Polynesia.**

French pas·try *n.* a rich pastry made esp. from puff pastry and filled with cream, fruit, etc.

French pleat *or* **roll** *n.* a woman's hair style with the hair gathered at the back into a cylindrical roll.

French-pol·ish *vb.* to treat with French polish or give a French polish (to).

French pol·ish *n.* **1.** a varnish for wood consisting of shellac dissolved in alcohol. **2.** the gloss finish produced by repeated applications of this polish.

French Pol·y·ne·sia *n.* a French Overseas Territory in the S Pacific Ocean, including the Society Islands, the Tuamotu group, the Gambier group, the Tubuai Islands, and the Marquesas Islands. Capital: Papeete, on Tahiti. Pop.: 113 279 (1971). Area: about 4000 sq. km (1500 sq. miles). Former name (until 1958): **French Oceania.**

French Rev·o·lu·tion *n.* the anticlerical and republican revolution in France from 1789 until 1799, when Napoleon seized power.

French Rev·o·lu·tion·ar·y cal·en·dar *n.* the full name for the **Revolutionary calendar.**

French seam *n.* a seam in which the edges are not visible.

French sixth *n.* (in musical harmony) an augmented sixth chord having a major third and an augmented fourth between the root and the augmented sixth.

French So·ma·li·land *n.* a former name (until 1967) of **Djibouti.**

French stick *n. Brit.* a long straight notched stick loaf. Also called: **French stick loaf.**

French Su·dan *n.* a former name (1898–1959) of **Mali.**

French toast *n.* **1.** *Brit.* toast cooked on one side only. **2.** bread dipped in beaten egg and lightly fried.

French To·go·land *n.* a former United Nations Trust Territory in W Africa, administered by France (1946–60), now the independent republic of Togo.

French Un·ion *n.* a union of France with its dependencies (1946–58): replaced by the French Community.

French ver·mouth *n.* a dry aromatic white wine. Also called: **French.**

French West Af·ri·ca *n.* a former group (1895–1960) of French Overseas Territories: consisted of Senegal, Mauritania,

French Sudan, Upper Volta, Niger, French Guinea, the Ivory Coast, and Dahomey.

French West In·dies *pl. n.* **the.** a group of islands in the Lesser Antilles, administered by France. Pop.: 632 754 (1967). Area: 2792 sq. km (1077 sq. miles).

French win·dows *pl. n.* (*sometimes sing.*) *Brit.* a pair of casement windows extending to floor level and opening onto a balcony, garden, etc. U.S. name: **French doors.**

French·y ('frɛntʃɪ) *adj.* **·i·er, ·i·est. 1.** *Informal.* characteristic of or resembling the French. ~*n., pl.* **·ies. 2.** an informal word for **Frenchman.**

fre·net·ic (frɪ'nɛtɪk) *adj.* distracted or frantic; frenzied. [C14: via Old French *frenetique* from Latin *phrenēticus,* from Greek *phrenetikos,* from *phrenitis* insanity, from *phrēn* mind] —**fre·'net·i·cal·ly** *adv.* —**fre·'net·ic·ness** *n.*

fren·u·lum ('frɛnjʊləm) *n., pl.* **·la** (-lə). **1.** a strong bristle or group of bristles on the hindwing of some moths and other insects, by which the forewing and hindwing are united during flight. **2.** a small fraenum. [C18: New Latin, diminutive of Latin *frēnum* bridle]

fre·num ('fri:nəm) *n., pl.* **·na** (-nə). a variant spelling (esp. U.S.) of **fraenum.**

fren·zied ('frɛnzɪd) *adj.* filled with or as if with frenzy; wild; frantic. —**'fren·zied·ly** *adv.*

fren·zy ('frɛnzɪ) *n., pl.* **·zies. 1.** violent mental derangement. **2.** wild excitement or agitation; distraction. ~*vb.* **·zies, ·zy·ing, ·zied. 3.** (*tr.*) to make frantic; drive into a frenzy. [C14: from Old French *frenesie,* from Late Latin *phrēnēsis* madness, delirium, from Late Greek, ultimately from Greek *phrēn* mind; compare FRENETIC]

Fre·on ('fri:ɒn) *n. Trademark.* any of a group of chemically unreactive gaseous or liquid derivatives of methane in which hydrogen atoms have been replaced by chlorine and fluorine atoms: used as aerosol propellants, refrigerants, and solvents.

freq. *abbrev. for:* **1.** frequent(ly). **2.** frequentative.

fre·quen·cy ('fri:kwənsɪ) *n., pl.* **·cies. 1.** the state of being frequent; frequent occurrence. **2.** the number of times that an event occurs within a given period; rate of recurrence. **3.** *Physics.* **a.** the number of times that a periodic function or vibration repeats itself in a specified time, often 1 second. It is usually measured in hertz. Symbol: ν or *f.* **b.** the quotient of the length of the given time interval to the period of the function. **4.** *Statistics.* **a.** the number of individuals in a class (**absolute frequency**). **b.** the ratio of this number to the total number of individuals under survey (**relative frequency**). ~Also called (for senses 1, 2): **frequence.** [C16: from Latin *frequentia* a large gathering, from *frequēns* numerous, crowded]

fre·quen·cy band *n.* a continuous range of frequencies, esp. in the radio spectrum, between two limiting frequencies.

fre·quen·cy dis·tri·bu·tion *n. Statistics.* a set of values of a variable divided into classes with associated frequencies.

fre·quen·cy mod·u·la·tion *n.* a method of transmitting information using a radio-frequency carrier wave. The frequency of the carrier wave is varied in accordance with the amplitude and polarity of the input signal, the amplitude of the carrier remaining unchanged. Abbrevs.: **FM, fm.** Compare **amplitude modulation.**

fre·quent *adj.* ('fri:kwənt). **1.** recurring at short intervals. **2.** constant or habitual. ~*vb.* (frɪ'kwɛnt). **3.** (*tr.*) to visit repeatedly or habitually. [C16: from Latin *frequēns* numerous; perhaps related to Latin *farcīre* to stuff] —**fre·'quent·a·ble** *adj.* —**fre·'quent·er** *n.* —**'fre·quent·ly** *adv.* —**'fre·quent·ness** *n.*

fre·quen·ta·tion (ˌfri:kwɛn'teɪʃən) *n.* the act or practice of frequenting or visiting often.

fre·quen·ta·tive (frɪ'kwɛntətɪv) *Grammar.* ~*adj.* **1.** denoting an aspect of verbs in some languages used to express repeated or habitual action. **2.** (in English) denoting a verb or an affix having meaning that involves repeated or habitual action, such as the verb *wrestle,* from *wrest.* ~*n.* **3. a.** a frequentative verb or affix. **b.** the frequentative aspect of verbs.

fres·co ('frɛskəʊ) *n., pl.* **·coes** *or* **·cos. 1.** a very durable method of wall-painting using watercolours on wet plaster or, less properly, dry plaster (**fresco secco**), with a less durable result. **2.** a painting done in this way. [C16: from Italian: fresh plaster, coolness, from *fresco* (adj.) fresh, cool, of Germanic origin]

Fres·co·bal·di (*Italian* fresko'baldi) *n.* **Gi·ro·la·mo** (dʒi'rɔ:lamo). 1583–1643, Italian organist and composer, noted esp. for his organ and harpsichord music.

fresh (frɛʃ) *adj.* **1.** not stale or deteriorated; newly made, harvested, etc.: *fresh bread; fresh strawberries.* **2.** newly acquired, created, found, etc.: *fresh publications.* **3.** novel; original: *a fresh outlook.* **4.** latest; most recent: *fresh developments.* **5.** further; additional; more: *fresh supplies.* **6.** not canned, frozen, or otherwise preserved: *fresh fruit.* **7.** (of water) not salt. **8.** bright or clear: *a fresh morning.* **9.** chilly or invigorating: *a fresh breeze.* **10.** not tired; alert; refreshed. **11.** not worn or faded: *fresh colours.* **12.** having a healthy or ruddy appearance. **13.** newly or just arrived; straight: *fresh from the presses.* **14.** youthful or inexperienced. **15.** *Chiefly U.S.* designating a female farm animal, esp. a cow, that has recently given birth. **16.** *Informal.* presumptuous or disrespectful; forward. **17.** *Northern English dialect.* partially intoxicated; tipsy. **18. fresh out of.** *Informal, chiefly U.S.* having just run out of supplies of. ~*n.* **19.** the fresh part or time of something. **20.** another name for **freshet.** ~*vb.* **21.** *Obsolete.* to make or become fresh; freshen. ~*adv.* **22.** in a fresh manner; freshly. [Old English *fersc* fresh, unsalted; related to Old High German *frisc,* Old French *freis,* Old Norse *ferskr*] —**'fresh·ly** *adv.* —**'fresh·ness** *n.*

fresh breeze *n.* a fairly strong breeze of force five on the Beaufort scale.

fresh·en ('frɛʃən) *vb.* **1.** to make or become fresh or fresher. **2.** (often foll. by *up*) to refresh (oneself), esp. by washing. **3.** (*intr.*) (of the wind) to increase. **4.** to lose or cause to lose saltiness. **5.** (*intr.*) *Chiefly U.S.* **a.** (of farm animals) to give birth. **b.** (of cows) to commence giving milk after calving. —**'fresh·en·er** *n.*

fresh·er ('frɛʃə) *or* **fresh·man** ('frɛʃmən) *n., pl.* **·ers** *or* **·men.** a first-year student at college or university.

fresh·et ('frɛʃɪt) *n.* **1.** the sudden overflowing of a river caused by heavy rain or melting snow. **2.** a stream of fresh water emptying into the sea.

fresh gale *n.* a gale of force eight on the Beaufort scale.

fresh-run *adj.* (of fish) newly migrated upstream from the sea, esp. to spawn.

fresh·wa·ter ('frɛʃˌwɔ:tə) *n.* (*modifier*) **1.** of, relating to, or living in fresh water. **2.** (esp. of a sailor who has not sailed on the sea) unskilled or inexperienced. **3.** *U.S.* small and little known: *a freshwater school.*

fres·nel ('freɪnɛl; *French* frɛ'nɛl) *n.* a unit of frequency equivalent to 10^{12} hertz. [C20: named after A. J. FRESNEL]

Fres·nel (*French* frɛ'nɛl) *n.* **Au·gus·tin Jean** (ogystɛ̃ 'ʒɑ̃). 1788–1827, French physicist: worked on the interference of light, contributing to the wave theory of light.

Fres·nel lens *n.* a lens consisting of a number of smaller lenses arranged to give a flat surface of short focal length. [C20: named after A. J. FRESNEL]

Fres·no ('frɛznəʊ) *n.* a city in central California, in the San Joaquin Valley. Pop.: 174 882 (1973 est.).

fret[1] (frɛt) *vb.* **frets, fret·ting, fret·ted. 1.** to distress or be distressed; worry. **2.** to rub or wear away. **3.** to irritate or be irritated; feel or give annoyance or vexation. **4.** to eat away or be eaten away by chemical action; corrode. **5.** (*intr.*) (of a road surface) to become loose so that potholes develop; scab. **6.** to agitate (water) or (of water) to be agitated. **7.** (*tr.*) to make by wearing away; erode. ~*n.* **8.** a state of irritation or anxiety. **9.** the result of fretting; corrosion. **10.** a hole or channel caused by fretting. [Old English *fretan* to EAT; related to Old High German *frezzan,* Gothic *fraitan,* Latin *peredere*]

fret[2] (frɛt) *n.* **1.** a repetitive geometrical figure, esp. one used as an ornamental border. **2.** such a pattern made in relief and with numerous small openings; fretwork. **3.** *Heraldry.* a charge on a shield consisting of a mascle crossed by a saltire. ~*vb.* **frets, fret·ting, fret·ted. 4.** (*tr.*) to ornament with fret or fretwork. [C14: from Old French *frete* interlaced design used on a shield, probably of Germanic origin] —**'fret·less** *adj.*

fret[3] (frɛt) *n.* any of several small metal bars set across the fingerboard of a musical instrument of the lute, guitar, or viol family at various points along its length so as to produce the desired notes when the strings are stopped by the fingers. [C16: of unknown origin] —**'fret·less** *adj.*

fret·ful ('frɛtfʊl) *adj.* peevish, irritable, or upset. —**'fret·ful·ly** *adv.* —**'fret·ful·ness** *n.*

fret saw *n.* a fine-toothed saw with a long thin narrow blade, used for cutting designs in thin wood or metal.

fret·ted ('frɛtɪd) *adj.* **1.** ornamented with angular designs or frets. **2.** decorated with fretwork.

fret·work ('frɛtˌwɜ:k) *n.* **1.** decorative geometrical carving or openwork. **2.** any similar pattern of light and dark. **3.** ornamental work of three-dimensional frets.

Freud (frɔɪd) *n.* **Sig·mund** ('zikmʊnt). 1856–1939, Austrian psychiatrist; originator of psychoanalysis, based on free association of ideas and analysis of dreams. He stressed the importance of infantile sexuality in later development, evolving the concept of the Oedipus complex. His works include *The Interpretation of Dreams* (1900) and *The Ego and the Id* (1923).

Freud·i·an ('frɔɪdɪən) *adj.* **1.** of or relating to Sigmund Freud or his ideas. ~*n.* **2.** a person who follows or believes in the basic ideas of Sigmund Freud. —**'Freud·i·an·ism** *n.*

Freud·i·an slip *n.* any action, such as a slip of the tongue, that may reveal an unconscious thought.

Frey (freɪ) *or* **Freyr** (freɪə) *n. Norse myth.* the god of earth's fertility and dispenser of prosperity.

Frey·a *or* **Frey·ja** ('freɪə) *n. Norse myth.* the goddess of love and fecundity, sister of Frey.

Frey·tag (*German* 'fraɪta:k) *n.* **Gus·tav** ('gʊstaf). 1816–95, German novelist and dramatist; author of the comedy *Die Journalisten* (1853) and *Soll und Haben* (1855), a novel about German commercial life.

F.R.G.S. (in Britain) *abbrev. for* Fellow of the Royal Geographical Society.

Fri. *abbrev. for* Friday.

fri·a·ble ('fraɪəbᵊl) *adj.* easily broken up; crumbly. [C16: from Latin *friābilis,* from *friāre* to crumble; related to Latin *fricāre* to rub down] —ˌ**fri·a·'bil·i·ty** *or* **'fri·a·ble·ness** *n.*

fri·ar ('fraɪə) *n.* a member of any of various chiefly mendicant religious orders of the Roman Catholic Church, the main orders being the **Black Friars** (Dominicans), **Grey Friars** (Franciscans), **White Friars** (Carmelites), and **Austin Friars** (Augustinians). [C13 *frere,* from Old French: brother, from Latin *frāter* BROTHER] —**'fri·ar·ly** *adj.*

fri·ar·bird ('fraɪəˌbɜ:d) *n.* any of various Australian honeyeaters of the genus *Philemon,* having a naked head.

Fri·ar Mi·nor *n., pl.* **Fri·ars Mi·nor.** *Christianity.* a member of either of two of the three orders into which the order founded by St. Francis of Assisi came to be divided, namely the **Order of Friars Minor** and the **Order of Friars Minor Conventual.** Compare **Capuchin.**

fri+ar's bal+sam *n.* a compound containing benzoin, mixed with hot water and used as an inhalant to relieve colds and sore throats.

fri+ar's lan+tern *n.* another name for **will-o'-the-wisp.**

Fri+ar Tuck *n. English legend.* a jolly friar who joined Robin Hood's band and aided their exploits.

fri+ar·y ('fraɪərɪ) *n., pl.* **+ar·ies.** *Christianity.* a convent or house of friars.

frib+ble ('frɪbᵊl) *vb.* **1.** (*tr.*) to fritter away; waste. **2.** (*intr.*) to act frivolously; trifle. ~*n.* **3.** a wasteful or frivolous person or action. ~*adj.* **4.** frivolous; trifling. [C17: of unknown origin] —**'frib+bler** *n.*

Fri+bourg (*French* fri'bu:r) *n.* **1.** a canton in W Switzerland. Capital: Fribourg. Pop.: 180 309 (1970). Area: 1676 sq. km (645 sq. miles). **2.** a town in W Switzerland, capital of Fribourg canton: university (1889). Pop.: 39 695 (1970). ~German name: **Freiburg.**

fric+an+deau *or* **fric+an+do** ('frɪkənˌdəʊ) *n., pl.* **+deaus, +deaux,** *or* **+does** (-ˌdəʊz). a larded and braised veal fillet. [C18: from Old French, probably based on FRICASSEE]

fric+as+see (ˌfrɪkə'si:, 'frɪkəsɪ, 'frɪkəˌseɪ) *n.* **1.** stewed meat, esp. chicken or veal, and vegetables, served in a thick white sauce. ~*vb.* **+sees, +see+ing, +seed. 2.** (*tr.*) to prepare (meat, etc.) as a fricassee. [C16: from Old French, from *fricasser* to fricassee; probably related to *frire* to FRY[1]]

fric·a+tive ('frɪkətɪv) *n.* **1.** a continuant consonant produced by partial occlusion of the airstream, such as (f) or (z). ~*adj.* **2.** relating to or denoting a fricative. [C19: from New Latin *fricātivus,* from Latin *fricāre* to rub]

fric+tion ('frɪkʃən) *n.* **1.** a resistance encountered when one body moves relative to another body with which it is in contact. **2.** the act, effect, or an instance of rubbing one object against another. **3.** disagreement or conflict; discord. **4.** *Phonetics.* the hissing element of a speech sound, such as a fricative. **5.** perfumed alcohol used on the hair to stimulate the scalp. [C16: from French, from Latin *frictiō* a rubbing, from *fricāre* to rub, rub down; related to Latin *friāre* to crumble] —**'fric+tion+al** *adj.* —**'fric+tion+less** *adj.*

fric+tion clutch *n.* a mechanical clutch in which the drive is transmitted by the friction between surfaces, lined with cork, asbestos, or other fibrous materials, attached to the driving and driven shafts.

fric+tion match *n.* a match that ignites as a result of the heat produced by friction when it is struck on a rough surface. See also **safety match.**

fric+tion tape *n.* the U.S. name for **insulating tape.**

Fri+day ('fraɪdɪ) *n.* the sixth day of the week; fifth day of the working week. [Old English *Frīgedæg,* literally: Freya's day; related to Old Frisian *frīadei,* Old High German *frīatag*]

fridge (frɪdʒ) *n. Informal.* short for **refrigerator.**

fried (fraɪd) *vb.* the past tense or past participle of **fry**[1].

Frie·drich (*German* 'fri:drɪç) *n.* **Cas·par Da·vid** ('kaspar 'da:fɪt). 1774–1840, German romantic landscape painter, noted for his skill in rendering changing effects of light.

friend (frɛnd) *n.* **1.** a person known well to another and regarded with liking, affection, and loyalty; an intimate. **2.** an acquaintance or associate. **3.** an ally in a fight or cause; supporter. **4.** a fellow member of a party, society, etc. **5.** a patron or supporter: *a friend of the opera.* **6. be friends (with).** to be friendly (with). **7. make friends (with).** to become friendly (with). ~*vb.* **8.** (*tr.*) an archaic word for **befriend.** [Old English *frēond;* related to Old Saxon *friund,* Old Norse *frǣndi,* Gothic *frijōnds,* Old High German *friunt*] —**'friend+less** *adj.* —**'friend+less+ness** *n.* —**'friend+ship** *n.*

Friend (frɛnd) *n.* a member of the Society of Friends; Quaker.

friend at court *n.* an influential acquaintance who can promote one's interests.

friend+ly ('frɛndlɪ) *adj.* **+li+er, +li+est. 1.** showing or expressing liking, goodwill, or trust: *a friendly smile.* **2.** tending or disposed to help or support; favourable: *a friendly breeze helped them escape.* ~*n., pl.* **+lies. 3.** Also called: **friendly match.** *Sport.* a match played for its own sake, and not as part of a competition, etc. —**'friend+li+ly** *adv.* —**'friend+li+ness** *n.*

Friend+ly Is+lands *pl. n.* another name for **Tonga**[2].

friend+ly so+ci+e·ty *n. Brit.* an association of people who pay regular dues or other sums in return for old-age pensions, sickness benefits, etc. U.S. term: **benefit society.**

fri+er ('fraɪə) *n.* a variant spelling of **fryer.**

Frie+sian[1] ('fri:ʒən) *n. Brit.* any of several breeds of black-and-white dairy cattle having a high milk yield. Usual U.S. name: **Holstein.**

Frie+sian[2] ('fri:ʒən) *n., adj.* a variant spelling of **Frisian.**

Fries+land ('fri:zlənd; *Dutch* 'fri:sˌlɑnt) *n.* a province of the N Netherlands, on the IJsselmeer and the North Sea: includes four of the West Frisian Islands; flat, with sand dunes and fens (under reclamation), canals, and lakes. Capital: Leeuwarden. Pop.: 539 200 (1973 est.). Area: 3319 sq. km (1294 sq. miles).

frieze[1] (fri:z) *n.* **1.** *Architect.* **a.** the horizontal band between the architrave and cornice of a classical entablature, esp. one that is decorated with sculpture. **b.** the upper part of the wall of a room, below the cornice, esp. one that is decorated. **2.** any ornamental band or strip on a wall. [C16: from French *frise,* perhaps from Medieval Latin *frisium,* changed from Latin *Phrygium* Phrygian (work), from *Phrygia* Phrygia, famous for embroidery in gold]

frieze[2] (fri:z) *n.* a heavy woollen fabric with a long nap, used for coats, etc. [C15: from Old French *frise,* from Middle Dutch *friese, vriese,* perhaps from *Vriese* Frisian]

frig (frɪg) *vb.* **frigs, frig+ging, frigged.** *Taboo slang.* **1.** to have sexual intercourse with. **2.** to masturbate. **3.** (*intr.;* foll. by *around,* etc.) to behave foolishly or aimlessly. [C15 (in the sense: to wriggle): of uncertain origin; perhaps related to obsolete *frike* strong, or to Old English *frīgan* to love]

frig+ate ('frɪgɪt) *n.* **1.** a medium-sized square-rigged warship of the 18th and 19th centuries. **2. a.** *Brit.* a warship larger than a corvette and smaller than a destroyer. **b.** *U.S.* a warship larger than a destroyer and smaller than a cruiser. [C16: from French *frégate,* from Italian *fregata,* of unknown origin]

frig+ate bird *n.* any bird of the genus *Fregata* and family *Fregatidae,* of tropical and subtropical seas, having a long bill with a downturned tip, a wide wingspan, and a forked tail: order *Pelecaniformes* (pelicans, cormorants, etc.). Also called: **man-of-war bird.**

Frigg (frɪg) *or* **Frig·ga** ('frɪgə) *n. Norse myth.* the wife of Odin; goddess of the heavens and married love.

frig+ging ('frɪgɪŋ) *adj. Taboo slang.* (intensifier, used as a milder word for *fucking*): *you frigging idiot.*

fright (fraɪt) *n.* **1.** sudden intense fear or alarm. **2.** a sudden alarming shock. **3.** *Informal.* a horrifying, grotesque, or ludicrous person or thing: *she looks a fright in that hat.* **4. take fright.** to become frightened. ~*vb.* **5.** (*tr.*) a poetic word for **frighten.** [Old English *fryhto;* related to Gothic *faurhtei,* Old Frisian *fruchte,* Old High German *forhta*]

fright+en ('fraɪtᵊn) *vb.* (*tr.*) **1.** to cause fear in; terrify; scare. **2.** to drive or force to go (away, off, out, in, etc.) by making afraid. —**'fright+en+a·ble** *adj.* —**'fright+en+er** *n.* —**'fright+en+ing+ly** *adv.*

fright+ful ('fraɪtfʊl) *adj.* **1.** very alarming, distressing, or horrifying. **2.** unpleasant, annoying, or extreme: *a frightful hurry.* —**'fright+ful+ness** *n.*

fright+ful+ly ('fraɪtfʊlɪ) *adv.* (intensifier): *I'm frightfully glad.*

frig+id ('frɪdʒɪd) *adj.* **1.** formal or stiff in behaviour or temperament; lacking in affection or warmth. **2.** (esp. of women) **a.** lacking sexual responsiveness. **b.** averse to sexual intercourse or unable to achieve orgasm during intercourse. **3.** characterized by physical coldness: *a frigid zone.* [C15: from Latin *frigidus* cold, from *frīgēre* to be cold, freeze; related to Latin *frīgus* frost] —**fri+'gid+i·ty** *or* **'frig+id+ness** *n.* —**'frig+id+ly** *adv.*

Frig+id Zone *n.* the cold region inside the Arctic or Antarctic Circle where the sun's rays are very oblique.

frig·o+rif+ic (ˌfrɪgə'rɪfɪk) *adj. Obsolete.* causing cold or freezing. [C17: from French *frigorifique,* from Latin *frīgorificus,* from *frīgus* cold, coldness + *facere* to make]

fri+jol ('fri:həʊl; *Spanish* fri'xol) *n., pl.* **+joles** (-həʊlz; *Spanish* -'xoles). a variety of bean, esp. of the French bean, extensively cultivated for food in Mexico. [C16: from Spanish, ultimately from Latin *phaseolus,* diminutive of *phasēlus,* from Greek *phasēlos* bean with edible pod]

frill (frɪl) *n.* **1.** a gathered, ruched, or pleated strip of cloth sewn on at one edge only, as on garments, as ornament, or to give extra body. **2.** a ruff of hair or feathers around the neck of a dog or bird or a fold of skin around the neck of a reptile or amphibian. **3.** Full name: **oriental frill.** (*often cap.*) a variety of domestic fancy pigeon having a ruff of curled feathers on the chest and crop. **4.** *Photog.* a wrinkling or loosening of the emulsion at the edges of a negative or print. **5.** (*often pl.*) *Informal.* a superfluous or pretentious thing or manner; affectation: *he made a plain speech with no frills.* ~*vb.* **6.** (*tr.*) to adorn or fit with a frill or frills. **7.** to form into a frill or frills. **8.** (*intr.*) *Photog.* (of an emulsion) to develop a frill. [C14: perhaps of Flemish origin] —**'frill·i+ness** *n.* —**'frill·y** *adj.*

frilled liz+ard *n.* a large arboreal insectivorous Australian lizard, *Chlamydosaurus kingi,* having an erectile fold of skin around the neck: family *Agamidae* (agamas).

Fri+maire *French.* (fri'mɛ:r) *n.* the frosty month: the third month of the French Revolutionary calendar, extending from Nov. 22 to Dec. 21. [C19: from French, from *frimas* hoarfrost, from Old French *frim,* of Germanic origin; related to Old Norse *hrīm* RIME[1]]

fringe (frɪndʒ) *n.* **1.** an edging consisting of hanging threads, tassels, etc. **2. a.** an outer edge; periphery. **b.** (*as modifier*): *fringe dwellers; a fringe area.* **3.** (*modifier*) unofficial; not conventional in form: *fringe theatre.* **4.** *Chiefly Brit.* a section of the front hair cut short over the forehead. **5.** an ornamental border or margin. **6.** *Physics.* any of the light and dark or coloured bands produced by diffraction or interference of light. ~*vb.* (*tr.*) **7.** to adorn or fit with a fringe or fringes. **8.** to be a fringe for: *fur fringes the satin.* [C14: from Old French *frenge,* ultimately from Latin *fimbria* fringe, border; see FIMBRIA] —**'fringe+less** *adj.* —**'fring·y** *adj.*

fringe ben+e+fit *n.* an incidental or additional advantage, esp. a benefit provided by an employer to supplement an employee's regular pay, such as a pension.

fringed or+chis *n.* any orchid of the genus *Habenaria,* having yellow, white, purple, or greenish flowers with fringed petals. See also **purple-fringed orchid.**

fringe tree *n.* either of two ornamental oleaceous shrubs or small trees of the genus *Chionanthus,* of North America and China, having clusters of white narrow-petalled flowers.

frin+gil+line (frɪn'dʒɪlaɪn, -ɪn) *or* **frin+gil+lid** (frɪn'dʒɪlɪd) *adj.* of, relating to, or belonging to the *Fringillidae,* a family of songbirds that includes the finches. [C19: from New Latin *Fringilla* type genus, from Latin *fringilla* a small bird, perhaps a chaffinch]

fring·ing reef *n.* a coral reef close to the shore to which it is attached, having a steep seaward edge.

frip·per·y ('frɪpərɪ) *n., pl.* **·per·ies. 1.** ornate or showy clothing or adornment. **2.** showiness; ostentation. **3.** unimportant considerations; trifles; trivia. [C16: from Old French *freperie,* from *frepe* frill, rag, old garment, from Medieval Latin *faluppa* a straw, splinter, of obscure origin]

frip·pet ('frɪpɪt) *n.* **1.** a frivolous or flamboyant young woman. **2.** *Informal.* young womanhood (esp. in the phrase **a (nice) bit of frippet**). [C20: of uncertain origin]

Fris. *abbrev. for* Frisian.

Fris·bee ('frɪzbiː) *n. Trademark.* a light plastic disc, usually 20–25 centimetres in diameter, thrown with a spinning motion for recreation or in competition.

Frisch (frɪʃ) *n.* **1. Max** (maks). born 1911, Swiss dramatist and novelist. His works are predominantly satirical and include the plays *Biedermann und die Brandstifter* (1953) and *Andorra* (1961), and the novel *Stiller* (1954). **2. Ot·to.** 1904-79, British nuclear physicist, born in Austria.

Frisch·es Haff ('frɪʃəs 'haf) *n.* the German name for **Vistula** (sense 2).

Fris·co ('frɪskəʊ) *n.* an informal name for **San Francisco.**

fri·sé ('friːzeɪ) *n.* a fabric with a long normally uncut nap used for upholstery and rugs. [from French, literally: curled]

fri·sette *or* **fri·zette** (frɪ'zɛt) *n.* a curly or frizzed fringe, often an artificial hairpiece, worn by women on the forehead. [C19: from French, literally: little curl, from *friser* to curl, shrivel up, probably from *frire* to fry[1]]

fri·seur *French.* (fri'zœːr) *n.* a hairdresser. [C18: literally: one who curls (hair); see FRISETTE]

Fri·sian ('frɪʒən) *or* **Frie·sian** *n.* **1.** a language spoken in the NW Netherlands and adjacent islands, belonging to the West Germanic branch of the Indo-European family: the nearest relative of the English language. **2.** a speaker of this language; a native or inhabitant of Friesland. ~*adj.* **3.** of or relating to this language or its speakers. [C16: from Latin *Frīsiī* people of northern Germany]

Fri·sian Is·lands *pl. n.* a chain of islands in the North Sea along the coasts of the Netherlands, West Germany, and Denmark: separated from the mainland by shallows.

frisk (frɪsk) *vb.* **1.** (*intr.*) to leap, move about, or act in a playful manner; frolic. **2.** (*tr.*) (esp. of animals) to whisk or wave briskly: *the dog frisked its tail.* **3.** (*tr.*) *Informal.* **a.** to search (someone) by feeling for concealed weapons, etc. **b.** to rob by searching in this way. ~*n.* **4.** a playful antic or movement; frolic. **5.** *Informal.* the act or an instance of frisking a person. [C16: from Old French *frisque,* of Germanic origin; related to Old High German *frisc* lively, FRESH] —**'frisk·er** *n.* —**'frisk·ing·ly** *adv.*

frisk·et ('frɪskɪt) *n. Printing.* a light rectangular frame, attached to the tympan of a hand-printing press, that carries a parchment sheet to protect the non-printing areas. [C17: from French *frisquette,* of obscure origin]

frisk·y ('frɪskɪ) *adj.* **frisk·i·er, frisk·i·est.** lively, high-spirited, or playful. —**'frisk·i·ly** *adv.* —**'frisk·i·ness** *n.*

fris·son *French.* (fri'sɔ̃) *n.* a shudder or shiver; thrill. [C18 (but in common use only from C20): literally: shiver]

frit *or* **fritt** (frɪt) *n.* **1. a.** the basic materials, partially or wholly fused, for making glass, glazes for pottery, enamel, etc. **b.** a glassy substance used in some soft-paste porcelain. **2.** the material used for making the glaze for artificial teeth. ~*vb.* **frits** *or* **fritts, frit·ting, frit·ted. 3.** (*tr.*) to fuse (materials) in making frit. [C17: from Italian *fritta,* literally: fried, from *friggere* to fry, from Latin *frīgere*]

frit fly *n.* a small black dipterous fly, *Oscinella frit,* whose larvae are destructive to barley, wheat, rye, oats, etc.: family *Chloropidae.*

fri·til·lar·y (frɪ'tɪlərɪ) *n., pl.* **·lar·ies. 1.** any N temperate liliaceous plant of the genus *Fritillaria,* having purple or white drooping bell-shaped flowers, typically marked in a chequered pattern. See also **snake's head. 2.** any of various nymphalid butterflies of the genera *Argynnis, Boloria,* etc., having brownish wings chequered with black and silver. [C17: from New Latin *fritillāria,* from Latin *fritillus* dice box; probably with reference to the spotted markings]

frit·ter[1] ('frɪtə) *vb.* (*tr.*) **1.** (usually foll. by *away*) to waste or squander: *to fritter away time.* **2.** to break or tear into small pieces; shred. ~*n.* **3.** a small piece; shred. [C18: probably from obsolete *fitter* to break into small pieces, ultimately from Old English *fitt* a piece] —**'frit·ter·er** *n.*

frit·ter[2] ('frɪtə) *n.* a piece of food, such as apple or clam, that is dipped in batter and fried in deep fat. [C14: from Old French *friture,* from Latin *frictus* fried, roasted, from *frīgere* to fry, parch]

Fri·u·li (*Italian* fri'uːli) *n.* a historic region of SW Europe, between the Carnic Alps and the Gulf of Venice: the W part (**Venetian Friuli**) was ceded by Austria to Italy in 1866 and **Eastern Friuli** in 1919; in 1947 Eastern Friuli (except Gorizia) was ceded to Yugoslavia.

Fri·u·li·an (frɪ'uːlɪən) *n.* **1.** the Rhaetian dialect spoken in parts of Friuli. See also **Ladin, Romansch. 2.** an inhabitant of Friuli or a speaker of Friulian. ~*adj.* **3.** of or relating to Friuli, its inhabitants, or their language.

Fri·u·li-Ve·ne·zi·a Giu·lia (*Italian* 'dʒuːlja) *n.* a region of NE Italy, formed in 1947 from **Venetian Friuli** and part of **Eastern Friuli.** Capital: Trieste. Pop.: 1 209 810 (1971). Area: 7851 sq. km (3031 sq. miles).

friv·ol ('frɪvəl) *vb.* **·ols, ·ol·ling, ·olled** *or U.S.* **·ols, ·ol·ing, ·oled.** *Informal.* **1.** (*intr.*) to behave frivolously; trifle. **2.** (*tr.*; often foll. by *away*) to waste on frivolous pursuits. [C19: back formation from FRIVOLOUS] —**'friv·ol·ler** *or U.S.* **'friv·ol·er** *n.*

friv·o·lous ('frɪvələs) *adj.* **1.** not serious or sensible in content, attitude, or behaviour; silly: *a frivolous remark.* **2.** unworthy of serious or sensible treatment; unimportant: *frivolous details.* [C15: from Latin *frīvolus* silly, worthless] —**'friv·o·lous·ly** *adv.* —**'friv·o·lous·ness** *or* **fri·vol·i·ty** (frɪ'vɒlɪtɪ) *n.*

fri·zette (frɪ'zɛt) *n.* a variant spelling of **frisette.**

frizz (frɪz) *vb.* **1.** (of the hair, nap, etc.) to form or cause (the hair, etc.) to form tight wiry curls or crisp tufts. ~*n.* **2.** hair that has been frizzed. **3.** the state of being frizzed. [C19: from French *friser* to curl, shrivel up (see FRISETTE): influenced by FRIZZLE[1]] —**'frizz·er** *n.*

friz·zle[1] ('frɪzəl) *vb.* **1.** to form (the hair) into tight crisp curls; frizz. ~*n.* **2.** a tight crisp curl. [C16: probably related to Old English *frīs* curly, Old Frisian *frēsle* curl, ringlet] —**'friz·zler** *n.* —**'friz·zly** *adj.*

friz·zle[2] ('frɪzəl) *vb.* **1.** to scorch or be scorched, esp. with a sizzling noise. **2.** (*tr.*) to fry (bacon, etc.) until crisp. [C16: probably blend of FRY[1] + SIZZLE]

friz·zy ('frɪzɪ) *or* **friz·zly** ('frɪzlɪ) *adj.* **·zi·er, ·zi·est** *or* **·zli·er, ·zli·est.** (of the hair) in tight crisp wiry curls. —**'friz·zi·ly** *adv.* —**'friz·zi·ness** *or* **'friz·zli·ness** *n.*

Frl. *abbrev. for* Fräulein. [German: Miss]

fro (frəʊ) *adv.* back or from. See **to and fro.** [C12: from Old Norse *frā;* related to Old English *fram* FROM]

Fro·bish·er ('frəʊbɪʃə) *n.* Sir **Mar·tin.** ?1535–94, English navigator and explorer: made three unsuccessful voyages in search of the Northwest Passage (1576; 1577; 1578), visiting Labrador and Baffin Island.

Fro·bish·er Bay *n.* an inlet of the Atlantic in NE Canada, in the SE coast of Baffin Island.

frock (frɒk) *n.* **1.** a girl's or woman's dress. **2.** a loose garment of several types, such as a peasant's smock. **3.** a coarse wide-sleeved outer garment worn by members of some religious orders. ~*vb.* **4.** (*tr.*) to invest (a person) with the office or status of a cleric. [C14: from Old French *froc;* related to Old Saxon, Old High German *hroc* coat]

frock coat *n.* a man's single- or double-breasted skirted coat, as worn in the 19th century.

frock·ing ('frɒkɪŋ) *n.* coarse material suitable for making frocks or work clothes.

froe *or* **frow** (frəʊ) *n.* a cutting tool with handle and blade at right angles, used for stripping young trees, etc.

Froe·bel *or* **Frö·bel** (*German* 'frøːbəl) *n.* **Frie·drich (Wilhelm August)** ('friːdrɪç). 1782–1852, German educator: founded the first kindergarten (1840).

frog[1] (frɒg) *n.* **1.** any insectivorous anuran amphibian of the family *Ranidae,* such as *Rana temporaria* of Europe, having a short squat tailless body with a moist smooth skin and very long hind legs specialized for hopping. **2.** any of various similar amphibians of related families, such as the tree frog. **3.** any spiked or perforated object used to support plant stems in a flower arrangement. **4.** a recess in a brick to reduce its weight. **5. a frog in one's throat.** phlegm on the vocal cords that affects one's speech. ~*vb.* **frogs, frog·ging, frogged. 6.** (*intr.*) to hunt or catch frogs. [Old English *frogga;* related to Old Norse *froskr,* Old High German *forsk*] —**'frog·gy** *adj.*

frog[2] (frɒg) *n.* **1.** (*often pl.*) a decorative fastening of looped braid or cord, as on the front of a 19th-century military uniform. **2.** a loop or other attachment on a belt to hold the scabbard of a sword, etc. **3.** *Music.* another name (esp. U.S.) for **nut** (sense 10). [C18: perhaps ultimately from Latin *floccus* tuft of hair, FLOCK[2]]

frog[3] (frɒg) *n.* a tough elastic horny material in the centre of the sole of a horse's foot. [C17: of uncertain origin]

frog[4] (frɒg) *n.* a grooved plate of iron or steel placed to guide train wheels over an intersection of railway lines. [C19: of uncertain origin; perhaps a special use of FROG[1]]

Frog (frɒg) *or* **Frog·gy** ('frɒgɪ) *n., pl.* **Frogs** *or* **Frog·gies.** *Brit. slang.* a derogatory word for a French person.

frog-bit *n.* a floating aquatic Eurasian plant, *Hydrocharis morsus-ranae,* with heart-shaped leaves and white flowers: family *Hydrocharitaceae.*

frog·fish ('frɒg,fɪʃ) *n., pl.* **·fish** *or* **·fish·es.** any angler (fish) of the family *Antennariidae,* in which the body is covered with fleshy processes, including a fleshy lure on top of the head.

frogged (frɒgd) *adj.* (of a coat) fitted with ornamental frogs.

frog·ging ('frɒgɪŋ) *n.* the ornamental frogs on a coat collectively.

frog·hop·per ('frɒg,hɒpə) *n.* any small leaping herbivorous homopterous insect of the family *Cercopidae,* whose larvae secrete a protective spittle-like substance around themselves. Also called: **spittle insect, spittlebug.**

frog kick *n.* a type of kick used in swimming, as in the breast stroke, in which the legs are simultaneously drawn towards the body and bent at the knees with the feet together, straightened out with the legs apart, and then brought together again quickly.

frog·man ('frɒgmən) *n., pl.* **·men.** a swimmer equipped with a rubber suit, flippers, and breathing equipment for working underwater.

frog·march ('frɒg,mɑːtʃ) *Chiefly Brit.* ~*n.* **1.** a method of carrying a resisting person in which each limb is held by one person and the victim is carried horizontally and face downwards. **2.** any method of making a resisting person move forward against his will. ~*vb.* **3.** (*tr.*) to carry in a frogmarch or cause to move forward unwillingly.

frog+mouth ('frɒg,maʊθ) *n.* any nocturnal insectivorous bird of the genera *Podargus* and *Batrachostomus,* of SE Asia and Australia, similar to the nightjars: family *Podargidae,* order *Caprimulgiformes.*

frog+spawn ('frɒg,spɔ:n) *n.* a mass of fertilized frogs' eggs or developing tadpoles, each egg being surrounded by a protective nutrient jelly.

frog spit *or* **spit+tle** *n.* **1.** another name for **cuckoo spit. 2.** a foamy mass of threadlike green algae floating on ponds.

Frois·sart (*French* frwa'sa:r) *n.* **Jean** (ʒã). ?1333–?1400, French chronicler and poet, noted for his *Chronique,* a vivid history of Europe from 1325 to 1400.

frol+ic ('frɒlɪk) *n.* **1.** a gay or light-hearted entertainment or occasion. **2.** light-hearted activity; gaiety; merriment. *~vb.* **+ics, +ick+ing, +icked. 3.** (*intr.*) to caper about; act or behave playfully. *~adj.* **4.** *Archaic or literary.* full of merriment or fun; gay. [C16: from Dutch *vrolijk,* from Middle Dutch *vro* happy, glad; related to Old High German *frō* happy] —**'frol+ick+er** *n.*

frol+ic+some ('frɒlɪksəm) *or* **frol+ick·y** *adj.* given to frolicking; merry and playful. —**'frol+ic+some+ly** *adv.* —**'frol+ic+some+ness** *n.*

from (frɒm; *unstressed* frəm) *prep.* **1.** used to indicate the original location, situation, etc.: *from Paris to Rome; from behind the bushes; from childhood to adulthood.* **2.** in a period of time starting at: *he lived from 1910 to 1970.* **3.** used to indicate the distance between two things or places: *a hundred miles from here.* **4.** used to indicate a lower amount: *from five to fifty pounds.* **5.** showing the model of: *painted from life.* **6.** used with the gerund to mark prohibition, restraint, etc.: *nothing prevents him from leaving.* **7.** because of: *exhausted from his walk.* [Old English *fram;* related to Old Norse *frā,* Old Saxon, Old High German, Gothic *fram* from, Greek *promos* foremost]
Usage. See at **off.**

Frome (frəʊm) *n.* **Lake.** a shallow salt lake in NE South Australia: intermittently filled with water. Length: 100 km (60 miles). Width: 48 km (30 miles).

fro+men+ty ('frəʊməntɪ) *n.* a variant spelling of **frumenty.**

Fromm (frɒm) *n.* **Er·ich** ('e:rɪç). 1900-80, U.S. psychoanalyst and sociologist born in Germany. His works include *Escape from Freedom* (1941) and *The Sane Society* (1955).

frond (frɒnd) *n.* **1.** the compound leaf of a fern. **2.** the leaf of a palm or a cycad. **3.** the thallus of a seaweed or a lichen. [C18: from Latin *frōns*] —**'frond+ed** *adj.* —**'frond+less** *adj.*

Fronde (frɒnd; *French* frɔ̃d) *n. French history.* either of two rebellious movements against the ministry of Cardinal Mazarin in the reign of Louis XIV, the first led by the parlement of Paris (1648–49) and the second by the princes (1650–53). [C18: from French, literally: sling, the insurgent parliamentarians being likened to naughty schoolboys using slings]

fron+des+cence (frɒn'dɛsəns) *n.* **1.** the process or state of producing leaves. **2.** a less common name for **foliage.** [C19: from New Latin *frondēscentia,* from Latin *frondēscere* to put forth leaves, from *frōns* foliage; see FROND] —**fron+'des+cent, 'fron+dose,** *or* **'fron+dous** *adj.*

Fron+deur (frɒn'dɜ:; *French* frɔn'dœ:r) *n.* **1.** *French history.* a member of the Fronde. **2.** any malcontent or troublemaker.

frons (frɒnz) *n., pl.* **fron+tes** ('frɒnti:z). an anterior cuticular plate on the head of some insects, in front of the clypeus. [C19: from Latin: forehead, brow, FRONT]

front (frʌnt) *n.* **1.** that part or side that is forward, prominent, or most often seen or used. **2.** a position or place directly before or ahead: *a fountain stood at the front of the building.* **3.** the beginning, opening, or first part: *the front of the book.* **4.** the position of leadership; forefront; vanguard: *in the front of scientific knowledge.* **5.** land bordering a lake, street, etc. **6.** land along a seashore or large lake, esp. a promenade. **7.** *Military.* **a.** the total area in which opposing armies face each other. **b.** the lateral space in which a military unit or formation is operating: *to advance on a broad front.* **8.** *Meteorol.* the dividing line or plane between two air masses of different origins and having different characteristics. See also **warm front, cold front. 9.** outward aspect or bearing, as when dealing with a situation: *a bold front.* **10.** assurance, over-confidence, or effrontery. **11.** *Informal.* a business or other activity serving as a respectable cover for another, usually criminal, organization. **12.** *Chiefly U.S.* a nominal leader of an organization, etc., who lacks real power or authority; figurehead. **13.** *Informal.* outward appearance of rank or wealth. **14.** a particular field of activity involving some kind of struggle: *on the wages front.* **15.** a group of people with a common goal: *a national liberation front.* **16.** a false fill-in for a jacket; a dickey. **17.** *Archaic.* the forehead or the face. *~adj.* (*prenominal*) **18.** of, at, or in the front: *a front seat.* **19.** *Phonetics.* of, relating to, or denoting a vowel articulated with the blade of the tongue brought forward and raised towards the hard palate, as for the sound of *ee* in English *see* or *a* in English *hat.* *~vb.* **20.** (when *intr.,* foll. by *on* or *onto*) to be opposite (to); face (onto): *this house fronts the river.* **21.** (*tr.*) to be a front of or for. **22.** (*tr.*) to confront, esp. in hostility or opposition. **23.** to supply a front for. **24.** (*intr.;* often foll. by *up*) *Austral. informal.* to appear (at): *to front up at the police station.* [C13 (in the sense: forehead, face): from Latin *frōns* forehead, foremost part] —**'front+less** *adj.*

front. *abbrev. for* frontispiece.

front+age ('frʌntɪdʒ) *n.* **1.** the façade of a building or the front of a plot of ground. **2.** the extent of the front of a shop, plot of land, etc., esp. along a street, river, etc. **3.** the direction in which a building faces: *a frontage on the river.*

front+al ('frʌntᵊl) *adj.* **1.** of, at, or in the front. **2.** of or relating to the forehead: *frontal artery.* **3.** *Meteorol.* of, relating to, or resulting from a front or its passage: *frontal rainfall.* *~n.* **4.** a decorative hanging for the front of an altar. **5.** See **frontal lobe, frontal bone. 6.** another name for **frontlet** (sense 1). [C14 (in the sense: adornment for forehead, altarcloth): via Old French *frontel,* from Latin *frontālia* (pl.) ornament worn on forehead, *frontellum* altarcloth, both from *frōns* forehead, FRONT] —**'fron+tal+ly** *adv.*

front+al bone *n.* the bone that forms the front part of the skull.

fron+tal+i·ty (frʌn'tælɪtɪ) *n. Fine arts.* a frontal view, as in a painting or other work of art.

front+al lobe *n. Anatomy.* the anterior portion of each cerebral hemisphere, situated in front of the central sulcus.

front bench *n. Brit.* **a.** the foremost bench of either the Government or Opposition in the House of Commons. **b.** the leadership (**frontbenchers**) of either group, who occupy this bench. **c.** (*as modifier*): *a front-bench decision.*

front door *n.* **1.** the main entrance to a house. **2.** an open legitimate means of obtaining a job, position, etc.: *to get in by the front door.*

Fronte·nac (*French* frɔ̃t'nak) (et Palluau) *n.* **Comte de** (kɔ̃t də). title of *Louis de Buade.* 1620–98, governor of New France (1672–82; 1689–98).

fron+tier ('frʌntɪə, frʌn'tɪə) *n.* **1. a.** the region of a country bordering on another or a line, barrier, etc., marking such a boundary. **b.** (*as modifier*): *a frontier post.* **2.** *U.S.* **a.** the edge of the settled area of a country. **b.** (*as modifier*): *the frontier spirit.* **3.** (*often pl.*) the limit of knowledge in a particular field: *the frontiers of physics have been pushed back.* **4.** *Maths.* the part of the closure of a topological set that lies outside its interior. [C14: from Old French *frontiere,* from *front* (in the sense: part which is opposite); see FRONT]

fron+tiers+man ('frʌntɪəzmən, frʌn'tɪəz-) *n., pl.* **+men.** (formerly) a man living on a frontier, esp. in a newly pioneered territory of the U.S.

fron+tis+piece ('frʌntɪs,pi:s) *n.* **1.** an illustration facing the title page of a book. **2.** the principal façade of a building; front. **3.** a pediment, esp. an ornamented one, over a door, window, etc. [C16 *frontispice,* from French, from Late Latin *frontispicium* façade, inspection of the forehead, from Latin *frōns* forehead + *specere* to look at; influenced by PIECE]

front+let ('frʌntlɪt) *n.* **1.** Also called: **frontal.** a small decorative loop worn on a woman's forehead, projecting from under her headdress, in the 15th century. **2.** the forehead of an animal, esp. of a bird when it is a different colour from the rest of the head. **3.** the decorated border of an altar frontal. **4.** *Judaism.* **a.** a band worn on the forehead to bind a phylactery in position. **b.** a phylactery attached to the forehead. [C15: from Old French *frontelet* a little FRONTAL]

front line *n.* **1.** *Military.* the most advanced military units or elements in a battle. **2.** the most advanced, exposed, or conspicuous element in any activity or situation. **3.** (*modifier*) **a.** of, relating to, or suitable for the front line of a military formation: *frontline troops.* **b.** to the fore; advanced, conspicuous, etc.: *frontline news.*

front man *n. Informal.* a nominal leader of an organization, etc., who lacks real power or authority, esp. one who lends respectibility to some nefarious activity.

front mat+ter *n.* another name for **prelims** (sense 1).

front of house *n.* the areas of a theatre, opera house, etc., used by the audience.

fron+to+gen+e·sis (,frʌntəʊ'dʒɛnɪsɪs) *n. Meteorol.* the formation or development of a front through the meeting of air masses from different origins. —**fron+to+ge+net+ic** (,frʌntəʊdʒə'nɛtɪk) *adj.* —**,fron+to+ge+'net+ic+al+ly** *adv.*

fron+tol·y+sis (frʌn'tɒlɪsɪs) *n. Meteorol.* the weakening or dissipation of a front.

fron+ton ('frɒntɒn, frɒn'tɒn) *n.* a wall against which pelota or jai alai is played. [C17: from Spanish *frontón,* from *frente* forehead, from Latin *frōns*]

front-page *n.* (*modifier*) important or newsworthy enough to be put on the front page of a newspaper.

front+run·ner ('frʌnt,rʌnə) *n. Informal.* the leader or a favoured contestant in a race, election, etc.

front+wards ('frʌntwədz) *or* **front+ward** *adv.* towards the front.

frore (frɔ:) *adj. Archaic.* very cold or frosty. [C13 *froren,* past participle of Old English *frēosan* to FREEZE]

frost (frɒst) *n.* **1.** a white deposit of ice particles, esp. one formed on objects out of doors at night. See also **hoarfrost. 2.** an atmospheric temperature of below freezing point, characterized by the production of this deposit. **3. degrees of frost.** degrees below freezing point: eight degrees of frost indicates a temperature of either −8°C or 24°F. **4.** *Informal.* something given a cold reception; failure. **5.** *Informal.* coolness of manner. **6.** the act of freezing. *~vb.* **7.** to cover or be covered with frost. **8.** (*tr.*) to give a frostlike appearance to (glass, etc.), as by means of a fine-grained surface. **9.** (*tr.*) *Chiefly U.S.* to decorate (cakes, etc.) with icing or frosting. **10.** (*tr.*) to kill or damage (crops, etc.) with frost. [Old English *frost;* related to Old Norse, Old Saxon, Old High German *frost;* see FREEZE] —**'frost+,like** *adj.*

Frost (frɒst) *n.* **Rob·ert (Lee).** 1874–1963, U.S. poet, noted for his lyrical verse on country life in New England. His books include *A Boy's Will* (1913), *North of Boston* (1914), and *New Hampshire* (1923).

frost+bite ('frɒst,baɪt) *n.* destruction of tissues, esp. those of the fingers, ears, toes, and nose, by freezing, characterized by tingling, blister formation, and gangrene.

frost+bit·ten ('frɒst,bɪtᵊn) *adj.* of or affected with frostbite.

frost+ed ('frɒstɪd) *adj.* **1.** covered or injured by frost. **2.** covered with icing, as a cake. **3.** (of glass, etc.) having a surface roughened, as if covered with frost, to prevent clear vision through it.

frost heave *n.* the upthrust and cracking of a ground surface through the freezing and expansion of water underneath. Also called: **frost heaving.**

frost+ing ('frɒstɪŋ) *n.* **1.** a soft icing based on sugar and egg whites. **2.** another word (esp. U.S.) for **icing. 3.** a rough or matt finish on glass, silver, etc.

frost line *n.* **1.** the deepest point in the ground to which frost will penetrate. **2.** the limit towards the equator beyond which frosts do not occur.

frost+work ('frɒst,wɜ:k) *n.* **1.** the patterns made by frost on glass, metal, etc. **2.** similar artificial ornamentation.

frost·y ('frɒstɪ) *adj.* **frost·i·er, frost·i·est. 1.** characterized by frost: *a frosty night.* **2.** covered by or decorated with frost. **3.** lacking warmth or enthusiasm: *the new plan had a frosty reception.* **4.** like frost in appearance or colour; hoary. —**'frost·i+ly** *adv.* —**'frost·i·ness** *n.*

froth (frɒθ) *n.* **1.** a mass of small bubbles of air or a gas in a liquid, produced by fermentation, detergent, etc. **2.** a mixture of saliva and air bubbles formed at the lips in certain diseases, such as rabies. **3.** trivial ideas, talk, or entertainment. ~*vb.* **4.** to produce or cause to produce froth. **5.** (*tr.*) to give out in the form of froth. **6.** (*tr.*) to cover with froth. [C14: from Old Norse *frotha* or *frauth;* related to Old English *āfrēothan* to foam, Sanskrit *prothati* he snorts] —**'froth·y** *adj.* —**'froth·i+ly** *adv.* —**'froth·i+ness** *n.*

froth flo+ta+tion *n.* another name for **flotation** (in metallurgy).

frott+age ('frɒtɑ:ʒ; *French* frɔ'taʒ) *n.* **1.** the act or process of taking a rubbing from a rough surface, such as wood, for a work of art. **2.** sexual excitement obtained by rubbing against another person's clothed body. [French, from *frotter* to rub]

Froude (fru:d) *n.* **James An·tho·ny.** 1818–94, English historian; author of a controversial biography (1882–84) of Carlyle.

frou+frou ('fru:,fru:) *n.* **1.** a swishing sound, as made by a long silk dress. **2.** elaborate dress or ornamentation, esp. worn by women. [C19: from French, of imitative origin]

frow (frəʊ) *n.* a variant spelling of **froe.**

fro+ward ('frəʊəd) *adj.* obstinate; contrary. [C14: see FRO, -WARD] —**'fro+ward+ly** *adv.* —**'fro+ward+ness** *n.*

frown (fraʊn) *vb.* **1.** (*intr.*) to draw the brows together and wrinkle the forehead, esp. in worry, anger, or concentration. **2.** (*intr.;* foll. by *on* or *upon*) to have a dislike (of); look disapprovingly (upon): *the club frowned upon political activity by its members.* **3.** (*tr.*) to express (worry, etc.) by frowning. **4.** (*tr.;* often foll. by *down*) to force, silence, etc., by a frowning look. ~*n.* **5.** the act of frowning. **6.** a show of dislike or displeasure. [C14: from Old French *froigner,* of Celtic origin; compare Welsh *ffroen* nostril, Middle Breton *froan*] —**'frown+er** *n.* —**'frown+ing+ly** *adv.*

frowst (fraʊst) *n. Brit. informal.* a hot and stale atmosphere; fug. [C19: back formation from *frowsty* musty, stuffy, variant of FROWZY]

frows+ty ('fraʊstɪ) *adj.* ill-smelling; stale; musty.

frowz·y, frouz·y, *or* **frows·y** ('fraʊzɪ) *adj.* **frowz·i·er, frowz·i+est; frouz·i+er, frouz·i+est;** *or* **frows·i+er, frows·i+est. 1.** untidy or unkempt in appearance; shabby. **2.** ill-smelling; frowsty. [C17: of unknown origin] —**'frowz·i·ness, 'frouz·i·ness,** *or* **'frows·i+ness** *n.*

froze (frəʊz) *vb.* the past tense of **freeze.**

fro+zen ('frəʊzᵊn) *vb.* **1.** the past participle of **freeze.** ~*adj.* **2.** turned into or covered with ice. **3.** obstructed or blocked by ice. **4.** killed, injured, or stiffened by extreme cold. **5.** (of a region or climate) icy or snowy. **6.** (of food) preserved by a freezing process. **7. a.** (of prices, wages, etc.) arbitrarily pegged at a certain level. **b.** (of business assets) not convertible into cash, as by government direction or business conditions. **8.** frigid, unfeeling, or disdainful in manner. **9.** motionless or unyielding: *he was frozen with horror.* —**'fro+zen+ly** *adv.* —**'fro+zen+ness** *n.*

Frs. *abbrev. for* Frisian.

F.R.S. (in Britain) *abbrev. for* Fellow of the Royal Society.

frt. *abbrev. for* freight.

Fruc+ti+dor *French.* (frykti'dɔ:r) *n.* the month of fruit: the twelfth month of the French Revolutionary calendar, extending from Aug. 19 to Sept. 22. [C18: from Latin *frūctus* fruit + Greek *dōron* gift]

fruc+tif+er+ous (frʌk'tɪfərəs, frʊk-) *adj.* (of plants or trees) bearing or yielding fruit. —**fruc+'tif+er+ous+ly** *adv.*

fruc·ti+fi+ca+tion (,frʌktɪfɪ'keɪʃən, ,frʊk-) *n.* **1.** the act or state of fructifying. **2.** the fruit of a seed-bearing plant. **3.** any spore-bearing structure in ferns, mosses, fungi, etc.

fruc·ti+fy ('frʌktɪ,faɪ, 'frʊk-) *vb.* **+fies, +fy+ing, +fied. 1.** to bear or cause to bear fruit. **2.** to make or become productive or fruitful. [C14: from Old French *fructifier,* from Late Latin *frūctificāre* to bear fruit, from Latin FRUCTI- + *facere* to make, produce] —**'fruc·ti+,fi+er** *n.*

fruc+tose ('frʌktəʊs, -təʊz, 'frʊk-) *n.* a white crystalline water-soluble sugar occurring in honey and many fruits. Formula: $C_6H_{12}O_6$. Also called: **laevulose, fruit sugar.** [C19: from FRUCTI- + -OSE[2]]

fruc+tu+ous ('frʌktjʊəs, 'frʊk-) *adj.* productive or fruitful; fertile. [C14: from Latin *frūctuōsus,* from *frūctus* fruit + -OUS] —**'fruc+tu+ous+ly** *adv.* —**'fruc+tu+ous+ness** *n.*

fru+gal ('fru:gᵊl) *adj.* **1.** practising economy; living without waste; thrifty. **2.** not costly; meagre. [C16: from Latin *frūgālis,* from *frūgī* useful, temperate, from *frux* fruit] —**fru+'gal+i·ty** *or* **'fru+gal+ness** *n.* —**'fru+gal+ly** *adv.*

fru+giv+or+ous (fru:'dʒɪvərəs) *adj.* feeding on fruit; fruit-eating. [C18: from *frugi-* (as in FRUGAL) + -VOROUS]

fruit (fru:t) *n.* **1.** *Botany.* the ripened ovary of a flowering plant, containing one or more seeds. It may be dry, as in the poppy, or fleshy, as in the peach. **2.** any fleshy part of a plant, other than the above structure, that supports the seeds and is edible, such as the strawberry. **3.** the spore-producing structure of plants that do not bear seeds. **4.** any plant product useful to man, including grain, vegetables, etc. **5.** (*often pl.*) the result or consequence of an action or effort. **6.** *Brit. slang, old-fashioned.* chap; fellow: used as a term of address. **7.** *Slang, chiefly Brit.* a person considered to be eccentric or insane. **8.** *Slang, chiefly U.S.* a male homosexual. **9.** *Archaic.* offspring of man or animals; progeny. ~*vb.* **10.** to bear or cause to bear fruit. [C12: from Old French, from Latin *frūctus* enjoyment, profit, fruit, from *fruī* to enjoy] —**'fruit+,like** *adj.*

fruit+age ('fru:tɪdʒ) *n.* **1.** the process, state, or season of producing fruit. **2.** fruit collectively.

frui+tar+i·an (fru:'tɛərɪən) *n.* **1.** a person who eats only fruit. ~*adj.* **2.** of or relating to a fruitarian: *a fruitarian diet.* —**frui+'tar+i·an+ism** *n.*

fruit bat *n.* any large Old World bat of the suborder *Megachiroptera,* occurring in tropical and subtropical regions and feeding on fruit. Compare **insectivorous bat.**

fruit bod·y *n.* the part of a fungus in which the spores are produced.

fruit+cake ('fru:t,keɪk) *n.* **1.** a rich cake containing mixed dried fruit, lemon peel, nuts, etc. **2.** *Slang, chiefly Brit.* a person considered to be eccentric or insane.

fruit cock+tail *n.* fruit salad consisting of small or diced fruits.

fruit cup *n.* a variety of fruits served in a cup or glass as an appetizer or dessert.

fruit+er ('fru:tə) *n.* **1.** a fruit grower. **2.** any tree that bears fruit, esp. edible fruit.

fruit+er+er ('fru:tərə) *n. Chiefly Brit.* a fruit dealer or seller.

fruit fly *n.* **1.** any small dipterous fly of the family *Trypetidae,* which feed on and lay their eggs in plant tissues. See also **gallfly. 2.** any dipterous fly of the genus *Drosophila.* See **drosophila.**

fruit+ful ('fru:tfʊl) *adj.* **1.** bearing fruit in abundance. **2.** productive or prolific, esp. in bearing offspring. **3.** causing or assisting prolific growth. **4.** producing results or profits: *a fruitful discussion.* —**'fruit+ful+ly** *adv.* —**'fruit+ful+ness** *n.*

fru·i·tion (fru:'ɪʃən) *n.* **1.** the attainment or realization of something worked for or desired; fulfilment. **2.** enjoyment of this. **3.** the act or condition of bearing fruit. [C15: from Late Latin *fruitiō* enjoyment, from Latin *fruī* to enjoy]

fruit knife *n.* a small stainless knife for cutting fruit.

fruit+less ('fru:tlɪs) *adj.* **1.** yielding nothing or nothing of value; unproductive; ineffectual. **2.** without fruit. —**'fruit+less+ly** *adv.* —**'fruit+less+ness** *n.*

fruit ma+chine *n. Brit.* a gambling machine that pays out when certain combinations of diagrams, usually of fruit, appear on a dial.

fruit sal+ad *n.* a dish consisting of sweet fruits cut up and served in their juice: often sold canned.

fruit sug+ar *n.* another name for **fructose.**

fruit tree *n.* any tree that bears edible fruit.

fruit·y ('fru:tɪ) *adj.* **fruit·i·er, fruit·i·est. 1.** of or resembling fruit. **2.** (of a voice) mellow or rich. **3.** ingratiating or unctuous. **4.** *Informal, chiefly Brit.* erotically stimulating; salacious. **5.** *Slang.* eccentric or insane. **6.** *Chiefly U.S.* a slang word for **homosexual.** —**'fruit·i+ness** *n.*

fru+men+ta+ceous (,fru:mɛn'teɪʃəs) *adj.* resembling or made of wheat or similar grain. [C17: from Late Latin *frūmentāceus,* from Latin *frūmentum* corn, grain]

fru+men+ty ('fru:məntɪ), **fro+men+ty,** *or* **fur+men+ty** *n. Brit.* a kind of porridge made from hulled wheat boiled with milk, sweetened, and spiced. [C14: from Old French *frumentee,* from *frument* grain, from Latin *frūmentum*]

frump (frʌmp) *n.* a woman who is dowdy, drab, or unattractive. [C16 (in the sense: to be sullen; C19: dowdy woman): from Middle Dutch *verrompelen* to wrinkle, RUMPLE] —**'frump+ish** *or* **'frump·y** *adj.* —**'frump+ish+ly** *or* **'frump·i+ly** *adv.* —**'frump+ish+ness** *or* **'frump·i+ness** *n.*

Frun+ze (*Russian* 'frunzɪ) *n.* a city in the SW Soviet Union, capital of the Kirghiz SSR. Pop.: 486 000 (1975 est.). Former name (until 1926): **Pishpek.**

frus+trate (frʌ'streɪt) *vb.* (*tr.*) **1.** to hinder or prevent (the efforts, plans, or desires) of; thwart. **2.** to upset, agitate, or tire: *her constant complaints began to frustrate him.* ~*adj.* **3.** *Archaic.* frustrated or thwarted; baffled. [C15: from Latin *frustrāre* to cheat, from *frustrā* in error] —**frus+'trat+er** *n.*

frus+tra+tion (frʌ'streɪʃən) *n.* **1.** the condition of being frustrated. **2.** something that frustrates. **3.** *Psychol.* **a.** the prevention or hindering of a potentially satisfying activity. **b.** the emotional reaction to such prevention that may involve aggression.

frus+tule ('frʌstju:l) *n. Botany.* the hard siliceous cell wall of a diatom. [C19: from French, from Late Latin *frustulum* a small piece, from *frustum* a bit]

frus+tum ('frʌstəm) *n., pl.* **+tums** *or* **+ta** (-tə). **1.** *Geom.* **a.** the part of a solid, such as a cone or pyramid, contained between the base and a plane parallel to the base that intersects the solid. **b.** the part of such a solid contained between two parallel planes intersecting the solid. **2.** *Architect.* a single drum of a column or a single stone used to construct a pier. [C17: from Latin: piece; probably related to Old English *brȳsan* to crush, BRUISE]

fru·tes·cent (fruːˈtɛsᵊnt) *or* **fru·ti·cose** (ˈfruːtɪˌkəʊs, -ˌkəʊz) *adj.* having the appearance or habit of a shrub; shrubby. [C18: from Latin *frutex* shrub, bush] —**fru'tes·cence** *n.*

fry[1] (fraɪ) *vb.* **fries, fry·ing, fried. 1.** (when *tr.*, sometimes foll. by *up*) to cook or be cooked in fat, oil, etc., usually over direct heat. **2.** (*intr.*) *Informal.* to be excessively hot. **3.** *Slang, chiefly U.S.* to kill or be killed by electrocution, esp. in the electric chair. ~*n., pl.* **fries. 4.** a dish of something fried, esp. the offal of a specified animal: *pig's fry.* **5.** *U.S.* a social occasion, often outdoors, at which the chief food is fried. **6. fry-up.** *Brit. informal.* the act of preparing a mixed fried dish or the dish itself. [C13: from Old French *frire*, from Latin *frīgere* to roast, fry]

fry[2] (fraɪ) *pl. n.* **1.** the young of various species of fish. **2.** the young of certain other animals, such as frogs. **3.** young children. ~See also **small fry.** [C14 (in the sense: young, offspring): perhaps via Norman French from Old French *freier* to spawn, rub, from Latin *fricāre* to rub]

Fry (fraɪ) *n.* **1. Chris·to·pher.** born 1907, English dramatist; author of the verse dramas *A Phoenix Too Frequent* (1946), *The Lady's Not For Burning* (1948) and *Venus Observed* (1950). **2. E·liz·a·beth.** 1780–1845, English prison reformer and Quaker. **3. Rog·er El·i·ot.** 1866–1934, English art critic and painter who helped to introduce the post-impressionists to Britain. His books include *Vision and Design* (1920) and *Cézanne* (1927).

fry·er *or* **fri·er** (ˈfraɪə) *n.* **1.** a person or thing that fries. **2.** a young chicken suitable for frying.

fry·ing pan *or U.S.* **fry-pan** *n.* **1.** a long-handled shallow pan used for frying. **2. out of the frying pan into the fire.** from a bad situation to a worse one.

f.s. *abbrev. for* foot-second.

F.S.A. *abbrev. for* Fellow of the Society of Antiquaries.

FSH *abbrev. for* follicle-stimulating hormone.

FSK *Computer technol. abbrev. for* Frequency Shift Keying.

ft. *abbrev. for:* **1.** foot *or* feet. **2.** fort. **3.** fortification.

fth. *or* **fthm.** *abbrev. for* fathom.

ft-lb *abbrev. for* foot-pound.

Fu·ad I (fuːˈɑːd) *n.* original name *Ahmed Fuad Pasha.* 1868–1936, sultan of Egypt (1917–22) and king (1922–36).

fub·sy (ˈfʌbzɪ) *adj.* **·si·er, ·si·est.** *Archaic or dialect.* short and stout; squat. [C18: from obsolete *fubs* plump person]

Fu-chou (ˈfuːˈtʃaʊ) *n.* a variant spelling of **Foochow.**

Fuchs (fʊks, fuːks) *n.* **1. Klaus E·mil** (klaʊs ˈemɪl). born 1911, East German physicist. He was born in Germany, became a British citizen (1942), and was imprisoned (1950–59) for giving secret atomic research information to the Soviet Union. **2.** Sir **Viv·i·an Er·nest.** born 1908, English explorer and geologist: led the Commonwealth Trans-Antarctic Expedition (1955–58).

fuch·sia (ˈfjuːʃə) *n.* **1.** any onagraceous shrub of the mostly tropical genus *Fuchsia*, widely cultivated for their showy drooping purple, red, or white flowers. **2.** Also called: **California fuchsia.** a North American onagraceous plant, *Zauschneria californica*, with tubular scarlet flowers. **3. a.** a reddish-purple to purplish-pink colour. **b.** (*as adj.*): *a fuchsia dress.* [C18: from New Latin, named after Leonhard *Fuchs* (1501–66), German botanist]

fuch·sin (ˈfuːksɪn) *or* **fuch·sine** (ˈfuːksiːn, -sɪn) *n.* a greenish crystalline substance, the quaternary chloride of rosaniline, forming a red solution in water: used as a textile dye and a biological stain. Formula: $C_{20}H_{19}N_3HCl$. Also called: **magenta.** [C19: from FUCHS(IA) + -IN; from its similarity in colour to the flower]

fuck (fʌk) *Taboo.* ~*vb.* **1.** to have sexual intercourse with (someone). ~*n.* **2.** an act of sexual intercourse. **3.** *Slang.* a partner in sexual intercourse, esp. one of specified competence or experience: *she was a good fuck.* **4. not care** *or* **give a fuck.** not to care at all. ~*interj.* **5.** *Offensive.* an expression of strong disgust or anger (often in exclamatory phrases such as **fuck you! fuck it!** etc.). [C16: of Germanic origin; related to Middle Dutch *fokken* to strike]

fuck a·bout *or* **a·round** *vb.* (*adv.*) *Offensive taboo slang.* **1.** (*intr.*) to act in a stupid or aimless manner. **2.** (*tr.*) to treat (someone) in an inconsiderate or selfish way.

fuck·er (ˈfʌkə) *n. Taboo.* **1.** *Slang.* a despicable or obnoxious person. **2.** *Slang.* a person; fellow. **3.** a person who fucks.

fuck·ing (ˈfʌkɪŋ) *adj.* (*prenominal*), *adv. Taboo slang.* (intensifier): *a fucking good time.*

fuck off *Offensive taboo slang.* ~*interj.* **1.** a forceful expression of dismissal or contempt. ~*vb.* **2.** (*intr., adv.*) to go away.

fuck up *Offensive taboo slang.* ~*vb.* (*tr., adv.*) **1.** to damage or bungle: *to fuck up a machine.* **2.** to make confused. ~*n.* **fuck-up. 3.** an act or an instance of bungling.

fuck·wit (ˈfʌkwɪt) *n. Austral. taboo slang.* a fool or idiot.

fu·coid (ˈfjuːkɔɪd) *adj. also* **fu·coid·al** *or* **fu·cous** (ˈfjuːkəs). **1.** of, relating to, or resembling seaweeds of the genus *Fucus.* ~*n.* **2.** any seaweed of the genus *Fucus.*

fu·cus (ˈfjuːkəs) *n., pl.* **·ci** (-saɪ) *or* **·cus·es.** any seaweed of the genus *Fucus*, common in the intertidal regions of many shores and typically having greenish-brown slimy fronds. See also **wrack**[2] (sense 2). [C16: from Latin: rock lichen, from Greek *phukos* seaweed, dye, of Semitic origin]

fud·dle (ˈfʌdᵊl) *vb.* **1.** (*tr.; often passive*) to cause to be confused or intoxicated. **2.** (*intr.*) to drink excessively; tipple. ~*n.* **3.** a muddled or confused state. [C16: of unknown origin]

fud·dy-dud·dy (ˈfʌdɪˌdʌdɪ) *n., pl.* **·dies.** *Informal.* a person, esp. an elderly one, who is extremely conservative or dull. [C20: of uncertain origin]

fudge[1] (fʌdʒ) *n.* a soft variously flavoured sweet made from sugar, butter, cream, etc. [C19: of unknown origin]

fudge[2] (fʌdʒ) *n.* **1.** foolishness; nonsense. ~*interj.* **2.** a mild exclamation of annoyance. ~*vb.* **3.** (*intr.*) to talk foolishly or emptily. [C18: of uncertain origin]

fudge[3] (fʌdʒ) *n.* **1.** a small section of type matter in a box in a newspaper allowing late news to be included without the whole page having to be remade. **2.** the box in which such type matter is placed. **3.** the late news so inserted. **4.** a machine attached to a newspaper press for printing this. ~*vb.* **5.** (*tr.*) to make or adjust in a false or clumsy way. **6.** to misrepresent; falsify. **7.** to evade (a problem, issue, etc.); dodge; avoid. [C19: see FADGE]

Fu·eg·i·an (fjuːˈiːdʒɪən, ˈfweɪdʒ-) *adj.* **1.** of or relating to Tierra del Fuego or its indigenous Indians. ~*n.* **2.** an Indian of Tierra del Fuego.

fuel (fjʊəl) *n.* **1.** any substance burned as a source of heat or power, such as coal or petrol. **2.** the material, containing a fissile substance such as uranium-235, that produces energy in a nuclear reactor. **3.** something that nourishes or builds up emotion, action, etc. ~*vb.* **fuels, fuel·ling, fuelled** *or U.S.* **fuels, fuel·ing, fueled. 4.** to supply with or receive fuel. [C14: from Old French *feuaile*, from *feu* fire, ultimately from Latin *focus* fireplace, hearth] —**'fuel·ler** *or U.S.* **'fuel·er** *n.*

fuel cell *n.* a cell in which the energy produced by oxidation of a fuel is converted directly into electrical energy.

fuel el·e·ment *n.* a can containing nuclear fuel for use in a reactor.

fuel in·jec·tion *n.* a system for introducing atomized liquid fuel under pressure directly into the combustion chambers of an internal-combustion engine without the use of a carburettor.

fuel oil *n.* a liquid petroleum product having a flash point above 37.8°C: used as a substitute for coal in industrial furnaces, domestic heaters, ships, and locomotives.

fug (fʌg) *n. Chiefly Brit.* a hot, stale, or suffocating atmosphere. [C19: perhaps variant of FOG[1]] —**'fug·gy** *adj.*

fu·ga·cious (fjuːˈgeɪʃəs) *adj.* **1.** passing quickly away; transitory; fleeting. **2.** *Botany.* lasting for only a short time: *fugacious petals.* [C17: from Latin *fugax* inclined to flee, swift, from *fugere* to flee; see FUGITIVE] —**fu'ga·cious·ly** *adv.* —**fu'ga·cious·ness** *n.*

fu·gac·i·ty (fjuːˈgæsɪtɪ) *n.* **1.** Also called: **escaping tendency.** *Thermodynamics.* a property of a gas that expresses its tendency to escape or expand, given by $d(\log_e f) = d\mu/RT$, where μ is the chemical potential, R the gas constant, and T the thermodynamic temperature. Symbol: f **2.** the state or quality of being fugacious.

fu·gal (ˈfjuːgᵊl) *adj.* of, relating to, or in the style of a fugue. —**'fu·gal·ly** *adv.*

Fu·gard (ˈfuːgɑːd) *n.* **A·thol** (ˈæθɒl). born 1932, South African dramatist and theatre director. His plays include *Blood-Knot* (1961), *The Trials of Brother Jero* (1966), *The Island* (1973), *Statements after an Arrest under the Immorality Act* (1974), and *Dimetos* (1976).

fu·ga·to (fjʊˈgɑːtəʊ) *Music.* ~*adv., adj.* **1.** in the manner or style of a fugue. ~*n.* **2.** a movement, section, or piece in this style. [C19: from Italian, from *fugare* to compose in the style of a FUGUE]

-fuge *n. combining form.* indicating an agent or substance that expels or drives away: *vermifuge.* [from Latin *fugāre* to expel, put to flight] —**-fu·gal** *adj. combining form.*

Fug·ger (*German* ˈfʊgər) *n.* a German family of merchants and bankers, prominent in 15th- and 16th-century Europe.

fu·gi·o (ˈfjuːdʒɪəʊ) *n., pl.* **·gi·os.** a former U.S. copper coin worth one dollar, the first authorized by Congress (1787). [C18: Latin: I flee; one of the words inscribed on the coin]

fu·gi·tive (ˈfjuːdʒɪtɪv) *n.* **1.** a person who flees. **2.** a thing that is elusive or fleeting. ~*adj.* **3.** fleeing, esp. from arrest or pursuit. **4.** not permanent; fleeting; transient. **5.** moving or roving about. [C14: from Latin *fugitīvus* fleeing away, from *fugere* to take flight, run away] —**'fu·gi·tive·ly** *adv.* —**'fu·gi·tive·ness** *n.*

fu·gle·man (ˈfjuːgᵊlmən) *n., pl.* **·men. 1.** (formerly) a soldier used as an example for those learning drill. **2.** any person who acts as a leader or example. [C19: from German *Flügelmann*, from *Flügel* wing, flank + *Mann* MAN]

fugue (fjuːg) *n.* **1.** a musical form consisting essentially of a theme repeated a fifth above or a fourth below the continuing first statement. **2.** *Psychiatry.* a dreamlike altered state of consciousness, lasting from a few hours to several days, during which a person wanders away with loss of memory. [C16: from French, from Italian *fuga*, from Latin: a running away, flight] —**'fugue,like** *adj.*

fu·guist (ˈfjuːgɪst) *n.* a composer of fugues.

Füh·rer *or* ***Fueh·rer*** *German.* (ˈfyːrər; *English* ˈfjʊərə) *n.* a leader: applied esp. to Adolf Hitler (***der Führer***) while he was Chancellor. [German, from *führen* to lead]

Fu·ji (ˈfuːdʒiː) *n.* **Mount.** an extinct volcano in central Japan, in S central Honshu: the highest mountain in Japan, famous for its symmetrical snow-capped cone. Height: 3776 m (12 388 ft.). Also called: **Fujiyama** or **Fuji-san.**

Fu·kien (ˈfuːˈkjɛn) *n.* **1.** a province of SE China: mountainous and forested, drained chiefly by the Min River; noted for the production of flower-scented teas. Capital: Foochow. Pop.: 18 000 000 (1967–71 est.). Area: 123 000 sq. km (47 970 sq. miles). **2.** any of the Chinese dialects of this province. See also **Min.**

Fu·ku·da ('fu:ku:də) *n.* **Ta·ke·o** ('tækeɪəʊ). born 1905, Japanese statesman; prime minister (1976–78).

Fu+ku·o+ka (ˌfu:ku:'əʊkə) *n.* an industrial city and port in SW Japan, in N Kyushu: an important port in ancient times; site of Kyushu university. Pop.: 1 000 000 (1975).

Fu+ku+shi+ma (ˌfu:ku:'ʃi:mə) *n.* a city in Japan, in N central Honshu. Pop.: 243 083 (1974 est.).

-ful *suffix.* **1.** (*forming adjectives*) full of or characterized by: *painful; spiteful; restful.* **2.** (*forming adjectives*) able or tending to: *helpful; useful.* **3.** (*forming nouns*) indicating as much as will fill the thing specified: *mouthful; spoonful.* [Old English *-ful, -full,* from FULL]

Usage. Where the amount held by a spoon, etc., is used as a rough unit of measurement, the correct form is *spoonful,* etc.: *take a spoonful of this medicine every day. Spoon full* is used in a sentence such as *he left a spoon full of treacle,* where *full of* describes the spoon. The plural of a word like *spoonful* is *spoonfuls* and not *spoonsful.*

Fu·la ('fu:lə) *or* **Fu+lah** ('fu:lɑ:) *n.* **1.** (*pl.* **·la, ·las** *or* **+lah, +lahs**) a member of a pastoral nomadic people of W and central Africa, living chiefly in the sub-Sahara region from Senegal to N Cameroon: a racial mixture of light-skinned Berber peoples of the North and darker-skinned W Africans. **2.** the language of this people; Fulani.

Fu+la+ni (fu:'lɑ:nɪ, 'fu:lənɪ) *n.* **1.** the language of the Fula, belonging to the West Atlantic branch of the Niger-Congo family, widely used as a trade pidgin in W Africa. **2.** another name for **Fula** (the people). **3.** a humped breed of cattle from W Africa. ~*adj.* **4.** of or relating to the Fula or their language.

ful+crum ('fʊlkrəm, 'fʌl-) *n., pl.* **+crums** *or* **+cra** (-krə). **1.** the pivot about which a lever turns. **2.** something that supports or sustains; prop. **3.** a spinelike scale occurring in rows along the anterior edge of the fins in primitive bony fishes such as the sturgeon. [C17: from Latin: foot of a couch, bedpost, from *fulcire* to prop up]

ful+fil *or U.S.* **ful+fill** (fʊl'fɪl) *vb.* **+fils** *or U.S.* **+fills, +fil+ling, +filled.** (*tr.*) **1.** to bring about the completion or achievement of (a desire, promise, etc.). **2.** to carry out or execute (a request, etc.). **3.** to conform with or satisfy (regulations, demands, etc.). **4.** to finish or reach the end of: *he fulfilled his prison sentence.* **5. fulfil oneself.** to achieve one's potentials or desires. [Old English *fulfyllan*] **—ful+'fil+ler** *n.* **—ful+'fil+ment** *or U.S.* **ful+'fill+ment** *n.*

ful+gent ('fʌldʒənt) *or* **ful+gid** ('fʌldʒɪd) *adj. Poetic.* shining brilliantly; resplendent; gleaming. [C15: from Latin *fulgēre* to shine, flash] **—'ful+gent+ly** *adv.*

ful+gu+rate ('fʌlgjʊˌreɪt) *vb.* (*intr.*) *Rare.* to flash like lightning. [C17: from Latin *fulgurāre,* from *fulgur* lightning] **—'ful+gu+rant** ('fʌlgjʊrənt) *adj.*

ful+gu+rat+ing ('fʌlgjʊˌreɪtɪŋ) *adj.* **1.** *Pathol.* (of pain) sudden and sharp; piercing. **2.** *Surgery.* of or relating to fulguration.

ful+gu+ra+tion (ˌfʌlgjʊ'reɪʃən) *n. Surgery.* destruction of tissue by means of high-frequency (more than 10 000 per second) electric sparks.

ful+gu+rite ('fʌlgjʊˌraɪt) *n.* a tube of glassy mineral matter found in sand and rock, formed by the action of lightning. [C19: from Latin *fulgur* lightning]

ful+gu+rous ('fʌlgjʊrəs) *adj. Rare.* flashing like or resembling lightning; fulgurant. [C17: from Latin *fulgur* lightning]

Ful+ham ('fʊləm) *n.* a district of the Greater London borough of Hammersmith (since 1965): contains **Fulham Palace** (16th century), residence of the Bishop of London.

fu+lig·i+nous (fju:'lɪdʒɪnəs) *adj.* **1.** sooty or smoky. **2.** of the colour of soot; dull greyish-black or brown. [C16: from Late Latin *fūlīginōsus* full of soot, from Latin *fūlīgō* soot] **—fu+'lig·i+nous+ly** *adv.* **—fu+'lig·i+nous+ness** *n.*

full[1] (fʊl) *adj.* **1.** holding or containing as much as possible; filled to capacity or near capacity. **2.** abundant in supply, quantity, number, etc.: *full of energy.* **3.** having consumed enough food or drink. **4.** (esp. of the face or figure) rounded or plump; not thin. **5.** (*prenominal*) with no part lacking; complete: *a full dozen.* **6.** (*prenominal*) with all privileges, rights, etc.; not restricted: *a full member.* **7.** (*prenominal*) of, relating to, or designating a relationship established by descent from the same parents: *full brother.* **8.** filled with emotion or sentiment: *a full heart.* **9.** (*postpositive;* foll. by *of*) occupied or engrossed (with): *full of his own projects.* **10.** *Music.* **a.** powerful or rich in volume and sound. **b.** completing a piece or section; concluding: *a full close.* **11.** (of a garment, esp. a skirt) containing a large amount of fabric; of ample cut. **12.** (of sails, etc.) distended by wind. **13.** (of wine, such as a burgundy) having a heavy body. **14.** (of a colour) containing a large quantity of pure hue as opposed to white or grey; rich; saturated. **15.** *Austral. informal.* drunk. **16. full and by.** *Nautical.* another term for **close-hauled. 17. full of oneself.** full of pride or conceit; egoistic. **18. full up.** filled to capacity: *the cinema was full up.* **19. in full cry.** (of a pack of hounds) in full pursuit of quarry. **20. in full swing.** at the height of activity: *the party was in full swing.* ~*adv.* **21. a.** completely; entirely. **b.** (*in combination*): *full-grown; full-fledged.* **22.** exactly; directly; right: *he hit him full in the stomach.* **23.** very; extremely (esp. in the phrase **full well**). **24. full out.** with maximum effort or speed. ~*n.* **25.** the greatest degree, extent, etc. **26.** *Brit.* a ridge of sand or shingle along a sea shore. **27. in full.** without omitting, decreasing, or shortening: *we paid in full for our mistake.* **28. to the full.** to the greatest extent; thoroughly; fully. ~*vb.* **29.** (*tr.*) *Needlework.* to gather or tuck. **30.** (*intr.*) (of the moon) to be fully illuminated. [Old English; related to Old Norse *fullr,* Old High German *foll,* Latin *plēnus,* Greek *plērēs;* see FILL] **—'full+ness** *or esp. U.S.* **'ful+ness** *n.*

full[2] (fʊl) *vb.* (of cloth, yarn, etc.) to become or to make (cloth, yarn, etc.) heavier and more compact during manufacture through shrinking and beating or pressing. [C14: from Old French *fouler,* ultimately from Latin *fullō* a FULLER[1]]

full+back ('fʊlˌbæk) *n.* **1.** *Soccer, hockey.* one of two defensive players positioned in front of the goalkeeper. **2.** *Rugby.* a defensive player positioned close to his own line. **3.** the position held by any of these players.

full blood *n.* **1.** an individual, esp. a horse or similar domestic animal, of unmixed race or breed. **2.** the relationship between individuals having the same parents.

full-blood·ed *adj.* **1.** (esp. of horses) of unmixed ancestry; thoroughbred. **2.** having great vigour or health; hearty; virile. **—ˌfull-'blood·ed+ness** *n.*

full-blown *adj.* **1.** characterized by the fullest, strongest, or best development. **2.** in full bloom.

full board *n.* **a.** the provision by a hotel of a bed and all meals. **b.** (*as modifier*): *full board accommodation.*

full-bod·ied *adj.* having a full rich flavour or quality.

full-bot·tomed *adj.* (of a wig) long at the back.

full-cream *adj.* denoting or made with whole unskimmed milk.

full dress *n.* **a.** a formal or ceremonial style of dress, such as white tie and tails for a man and a full-length evening dress for a woman. **b.** (*as modifier*): *full-dress uniform.*

full+er[1] ('fʊlə) *n.* a person who fulls cloth for his living. [Old English *fullere,* from Latin *fullō*]

full+er[2] ('fʊlə) *n.* **1.** Also called: **fullering tool.** a tool for forging a groove. **2.** a tool for caulking a riveted joint. ~*vb.* **3.** (*tr.*) to forge (a groove) or caulk (a riveted joint) with a fuller. [C19: perhaps from the name *Fuller*]

Ful·ler ('fʊlə) *n.* **1.** (**Richard**) **Buck·min·ster.** born 1895, U.S. architect and engineer: developed the geodesic dome. **2. Roy.** born 1912, English poet, whose collections of poetry include *The Middle of a War* (1942) and *A Lost Season* (1944), both of which are concerned with World War II, and *Epitaphs and Occasions* (1949), *Brutus's Orchard* (1957), and *New Poems* (1968). **3. Thom·as.** 1608–61, English clergyman and antiquarian; author of *The Worthies of England* (1662).

full+er's earth *n.* a natural absorbent clay used, after heating, for decolorizing oils and fats, fulling cloth, etc.

full+er's tea+sel *n.* **1.** a Eurasian teasel plant, *Dipsacus fullonum,* whose prickly flower heads are used for raising the nap on woollen cloth. **2.** a similar and related plant, *Dipsacus sativum.*

full-faced *adj.* **1.** having a round full face. **2.** facing towards the spectator or in a specific direction. **3.** another name for **bold face. —'full+'face** *n., adv.*

full-fledged *adj.* See **fully fledged.**

full-fron·tal *adj.* **1.** *Informal.* (of a nude person or a photograph of a nude person) exposing the genitals to full view. ~*n.* **full fron+tal. 2.** a full-frontal photograph.

full house *n.* **1.** *Poker.* a hand with three cards of the same value and another pair. **2.** a theatre, etc., filled to capacity. **3.** (in bingo, etc.) the set of numbers needed to win.

full-length *n.* (*modifier*) **1.** extending to or showing the complete length: *a full-length mirror.* **2.** of the original or normal length; not abridged.

full moon *n.* **1.** one of the four phases of the moon, occurring when the earth lies between the sun and the moon so that the moon is visible as a fully illuminated disc. **2.** the moon in this phase. **3.** the time at which this occurs.

full-mouthed *adj.* **1.** (of livestock) having a full adult set of teeth. **2.** uttered loudly: *a full-mouthed oath.*

full nel+son *n.* a wrestling hold, illegal in amateur wrestling, in which a wrestler places both arms under his opponent's arms from behind and exerts pressure with both palms on the back of the neck. Compare **half-nelson.**

full pitch *or* **full toss** *n. Cricket.* a bowled ball that reaches the batsman without bouncing.

full pro+fes+sor *n. U.S.* another name for **professor** (sense 1).

full ra+di+a·tor *n. Physics.* another name for **black body.**

full-rigged *adj.* **1.** (of a sailing vessel) having three or more masts rigged square. **2.** *Rare.* fully equipped.

full sail *adv.* **1.** at top speed. ~*adj.* (*postpositive*), *adv.* **2.** with all sails set. **—ˌfull-'sailed** *adj.*

full-scale *n.* (*modifier*) **1.** (of a plan, etc.) of actual size; having the same dimensions as the original. **2.** done with thoroughness or urgency; using all resources; all-out.

full score *n.* the entire score of a musical composition, showing each part separately.

full stop *or* **full point** *n.* the punctuation mark (.) used at the end of a sentence that is not a question or exclamation, after abbreviations, etc. U.S. term: **period.**

full time *n.* the end of a football or other match. Compare **half time.**

full-time *adj.* **1.** for the entire time appropriate to an activity: *a full-time job; a full-time student.* ~*adv.* **full time. 2.** on a full-time basis: *he works full time.* ~Compare **part-time. —full-'tim+er** *n.*

full toss *n. Cricket.* another term for **full pitch.**

ful+ly ('fʊlɪ) *adv.* **1.** to the greatest degree or extent; totally; entirely. **2.** amply; sufficiently; adequately: *they were fully fed.* **3.** at least: *it was fully an hour before she came.*

ful·ly fash·ioned *adj.* (of stockings, seams, knitwear, etc.) shaped so as to fit closely.
ful·ly fledged *or* **full-fledged** *adj.* **1.** (of a young bird) having acquired its adult feathers and thus able to fly. **2.** developed or matured to the fullest degree. **3.** of full rank or status.
ful·mar ('fʊlmə) *n.* any heavily built short-tailed oceanic bird of the genus *Fulmarus* and related genera, of polar regions: family *Procellariidae*, order *Procellariiformes* (petrels). [C17: of Scandinavian origin; related to Old Norse *fūlmār*, from *fūll* foul + *mār* gull]
ful·mi·nant ('fʌlmɪnənt, 'fʊl-) *adj.* **1.** sudden and violent; fulminating. **2.** *Pathol.* (of pain) sudden and sharp; piercing. [C17: from Latin *fulmināre* to cause lightning, from *fulmen* lightning that strikes]
ful·mi·nate ('fʌlmɪˌneɪt, 'fʊl-) *vb.* **1.** (*intr.*; often foll. by *against*) to make severe criticisms or denunciations; rail. **2.** to explode with noise and violence. **3.** (*intr.*) *Archaic.* to thunder and lighten. ~*n.* **4.** any salt or ester of fulminic acid, esp. the mercury salt, which is used as a detonator. [C15: from Medieval Latin *fulmināre*; see FULMINANT] —**ˌful·mi·'na·tion** *n.* —**'ful·mi·ˌna·tor** *n.* —**'ful·mi·ˌna·to·ry** *adj.*
ful·mi·nat·ing pow·der *n.* powder that detonates by percussion.
ful·min·ic ac·id (fʌl'mɪnɪk, fʊl-) *n.* an unstable volatile acid known only in solution and in the form of its salts and esters. Formula: HONC. Compare **cyanic acid.** [C19: from Latin *fulmen* lightning]
ful·mi·nous ('fʌlmɪnəs, 'fʊl-) *adj. Rare.* **1.** harshly critical. **2.** of, involving, or resembling thunder and lightning.
ful·some ('fʊlsəm) *adj.* **1.** excessive or insincere, esp. in an offensive or distasteful way: *fulsome compliments.* **2.** *Archaic.* disgusting; loathsome. —**'ful·some·ly** *adv.* —**'ful·some·ness** *n.*
Ful·ton ('fʊltᵊn) *n.* **Rob·ert.** 1765–1815, U.S. engineer and inventor: designed the first commercially successful steamboat (1807) and the first steam warship (1814).
ful·vous ('fʌlvəs, 'fʊl-) *adj.* of a dull brownish-yellow colour; tawny. [C17: from Latin *fulvus* reddish yellow, gold-coloured, tawny; probably related to *fulgēre* to shine]
fu·mar·ic ac·id (fju:'mærɪk) *n.* a colourless crystalline acid with a fruity taste, found in some plants and manufactured from benzene; *trans*-butenedioic acid: used esp. in synthetic resins. Formula: HCOOCH:CHCOOH. [C19: from New Latin *Fumāria* name of genus, from Late Latin: fumitory, from Latin *fūmus* smoke]
fu·ma·role ('fju:məˌrəʊl) *n.* a vent in or near a volcano from which hot gases, esp. steam, are emitted. [C19: from French *fumerolle*, from Late Latin *fūmāriolum* smoke hole, from Latin *fūmus* smoke] —**fu·ma·rol·ic** (ˌfju:mə'rɒlɪk) *adj.*
fu·ma·to·ri·um (ˌfju:mə'tɔ:rɪəm) *n., pl.* **·ri·ums** *or* **·ri·a** (-rɪə). an airtight chamber in which insects and fungi on organic matter or plants are destroyed by fumigation. Also called: **fumatory.** [New Latin, from Latin *fūmāre* to smoke]
fu·ma·to·ry ('fju:mətərɪ, -trɪ) *adj.* **1.** of or relating to smoking or fumigation. ~*n., pl.* **·ries. 2.** another name for a **fumatorium.**
fum·ble ('fʌmbᵊl) *vb.* **1.** (*intr.*; often foll. by *for* or *with*) to grope about clumsily or blindly, esp. in searching: *he was fumbling in the dark for the money he had dropped.* **2.** (*intr.*; foll. by *at* or *with*) to finger or play with, esp. in an absent-minded way. **3.** to say or do hesitantly or awkwardly: *he fumbled the introduction badly.* **4.** to fail to catch or grasp (a ball, etc.) cleanly. ~*n.* **5.** the act of fumbling. [C16: probably of Scandinavian origin; related to Swedish *fumla*] —**'fum·bler** *n.* —**'fum·bling·ly** *adv.* —**'fum·bling·ness** *n.*
fume (fju:m) *vb.* **1.** (*intr.*) to be overcome with anger or fury; rage. **2.** to give off (fumes) or (of fumes) to be given off, esp. during a chemical reaction. **3.** (*tr.*) to subject to or treat with fumes; fumigate. ~*n.* **4.** (*often pl.*) a pungent or toxic vapour, gas, or smoke. **5.** a sharp or pungent odour. **6.** a condition of anger or fury. [C14: from Old French *fum*, from Latin *fūmus* smoke, vapour] —**'fume·less** *adj.* —**'fume·ˌlike** *adj.* —**'fum·er** *n.* —**'fum·ing·ly** *adv.* —**'fum·y** *adv.*
fume cup·board *n.* a ventilated enclosure for storing or experimenting with chemicals with harmful vapours.
fumed (fju:md) *adj.* (of wood, esp. oak) having a dark colour and distinctive grain from exposure to ammonia fumes.
fu·mi·gant ('fju:mɪgənt) *n.* a substance used for fumigating.
fu·mi·gate ('fju:mɪˌgeɪt) *vb.* to treat (something contaminated or infected) with fumes or smoke. [C16: from Latin *fūmigāre* to smoke, steam, from *fūmus* smoke + *agere* to drive, produce] —**ˌfu·mi·'ga·tion** *n.* —**'fu·mi·ˌga·tor** *n.*
fum·ing sul·phur·ic ac·id *n.* a mixture of pyrosulphuric acid, $H_2S_2O_7$, and other condensed acids, made by dissolving sulphur trioxide in concentrated sulphuric acid. Also called: **oleum, Nordhausen acid.**
fu·mi·to·ry ('fju:mɪtərɪ, -trɪ) *n., pl.* **·ries.** any plant of the chiefly European genus *Fumaria*, esp. *F. officinalis*, having spurred flowers and formerly used medicinally: family *Fumariaceae*. [C14: from Old French *fumetere*, from Medieval Latin *fūmus terrae*, literally: smoke of the earth; see FUME]
fun (fʌn) *n.* **1.** a source of enjoyment, amusement, diversion, etc. **2.** pleasure, gaiety, or merriment. **3.** jest or sport (esp. in the phrases **in** or **for fun**). **4. fun and games.** *Ironic or facetious.* gay amusement; frivolous activity. **5. like fun.** (*interj.*) *U.S. informal.* not at all! certainly not! **6. make fun of** or **poke fun at.** to ridicule or deride. **7.** (*modifier*) full of amusement, diversion, gaiety, etc.: *a fun sport.* ~*vb.* **funs, fun·ning, funned. 8.** (*intr.*) *Informal.* to act or say in a joking or sporting manner. [C17: perhaps from obsolete *fon* to make a fool of; see FOND[1]]
fu·nam·bu·list (fju:'næmbjʊlɪst) *n.* a tightrope walker. [C18: from Latin *fūnambulus* rope-dancer, from *fūnis* rope + *ambulāre* to walk] —**fu·'nam·bu·lism** *n.*
Fun·chal (*Portuguese* fũ'ʃal) *n.* the capital and chief port of the Madeira Islands, on the S coast of Madeira. Pop.: 105 791 (1970).
func·tion ('fʌŋkʃən) *n.* **1.** the natural action or intended purpose of a person or thing in a specific role: *the function of a hammer is to hit nails into wood.* **2.** an official or formal social gathering or ceremony. **3.** a factor dependent upon another or other factors: *whether he comes to the party is a function of whether his wife is well enough.* **4.** *Maths.* **a.** a variable or expression that can take a set of values each of which is associated with the value of an independent variable or variables: *y is a function of x, written* $y = f(x)$. **b.** Also called: **map, mapping.** a relation between two sets such that a member of one set (the range) can be associated with a member of the other (the domain). ~*vb.* (*intr.*) **5.** to operate or perform as specified; work properly. **6.** (foll. by *as*) to perform the action or role (of something or someone else): *a coin may function as a screwdriver.* [C16: from Latin *functiō*, from *fungī* to perform, discharge] —**'func·tion·less** *adj.*
func·tion·al ('fʌŋkʃənᵊl) *adj.* **1.** of, involving, or containing a function or functions. **2.** practical rather than decorative; utilitarian: *functional architecture.* **3.** capable of functioning; working. **4.** *Psychol.* **a.** relating to the purpose or context of a behaviour. **b.** denoting a disorder without structural change. ~*n.* **5.** *Maths.* a function whose domain is a set of functions and whose range is another set of functions that can be a set of numbers. —**'func·tion·al·ly** *adv.*
func·tion·al cal·cu·lus *n.* another name for **predicate calculus.**
func·tion·al dis·ease *n.* a disease in which there is no observable change in the structure of an organ or part. Compare **organic disease.**
func·tion·al group *n. Chem.* the group of atoms in a compound, such as the hydroxyl group in an alcohol, that determines the chemical behaviour of the compound.
func·tion·al il·lit·er·ate *n.* a person whose literacy is insufficient for most work and normal daily situations. —**func·tion·al il·lit·er·a·cy** *n.*
func·tion·al·ism ('fʌŋkʃənəˌlɪzəm) *n.* **1.** the theory of design that the form of a thing should be determined by its use. **2.** any doctrine that stresses utility or purpose. **3.** *Psychol.* a system of thought based on the premise that all mental processes derive from their usefulness to the organism in adapting to the environment. —**'func·tion·al·ist** *n., adj.*
func·tion·ar·y ('fʌŋkʃənərɪ) *n., pl.* **·ar·ies. 1.** a person acting in an official capacity, as for a government; an official. ~*adj.* **2.** a less common word for **functional** or **official.**
func·tion shift *or* **change** *n.* **1.** *Grammar.* a change in the syntactic function of a word, as when the noun *mushroom* is used as an intransitive verb. **2.** *Linguistics.* sound change involving a realignment of the phonemic system of a language.
func·tion word *n. Grammar.* a word, such as *the*, with a particular grammatical role but little identifiable meaning. Compare **content word, grammatical meaning.**
fund (fʌnd) *n.* **1.** a reserve of money, etc., set aside for a certain purpose. **2.** a supply or store of something; stock: *it exhausted his fund of wisdom.* ~*vb.* (*tr.*) **3.** to furnish money to in the form of a fund. **4.** to place or store up in a fund. **5.** to convert (short-term floating debt) into long-term debt bearing fixed interest and represented by bonds. **6.** to provide a fund for the redemption of principal or payment of interest. **7.** to accumulate a fund for the discharge of (a recurrent liability): *to fund a pension plan.* **8.** to invest (money) in government securities. [C17: from Latin *fundus* the bottom, piece of land, estate; compare FOND[2]]
fun·da·ment ('fʌndəmənt) *n.* **1.** *Euphemistic or facetious.* the buttocks. **2.** the natural features of the earth's surface, unaltered by man. **3.** a base or foundation, esp. of a building. **4.** a theory, principle, or underlying basis. [C13: from Latin *fundāmentum* foundation, from *fundāre* to FOUND[2]]
fun·da·men·tal (ˌfʌndə'mentᵊl) *adj.* **1.** of, involving, or comprising a foundation; basic. **2.** of, involving, or comprising a source; primary. **3.** *Music.* denoting or relating to the principal or lowest note of a harmonic series. **4.** of or concerned with the component of lowest frequency in a complex vibration. ~*n.* **5.** a principle, law, etc., that serves as the basis of an idea or system. **6. a.** the principal or lowest note of a harmonic series. **b.** the bass note of a chord in root position. **7.** Also called: **fundamental frequency, first harmonic.** *Physics.* **a.** the component of lowest frequency in a complex vibration. **b.** the frequency of this component. —**ˌfun·da·men·'tal·i·ty** *or* **ˌfun·da·'men·tal·ness** *n.* —**ˌfun·da·'men·tal·ly** *adv.*
fun·da·men·tal·ism (ˌfʌndə'mentəˌlɪzəm) *n. Christianity.* (esp. among certain Protestant sects) interpretation of every word of the Bible as literal truth. —**ˌfun·da·'men·tal·ist** *n., adj.* —**ˌfun·da·ˌmen·tal·'is·tic** *adj.*
fun·da·men·tal law *n.* the law determining the constitution of the government of a state; organic law.
fun·da·men·tal par·ti·cle *n.* another name for **elementary particle.**
fun·da·men·tal u·nit *n.* one of a set of unrelated units that form the basis of a system of units. For example, the metre, kilogram, and second are fundamental units of the SI system.
fund·ed debt *n.* a long-term bonded debt with at least a year to maturity, issued usually by the government.

fun+di ('fʊndi:) *n. E. African.* a person skilled in repairing or maintaining machinery; mechanic. [C20: from Swahili]
funds (fʌndz) *pl. n.* **1.** money that is readily available. **2.** British government securities representing national debt.
fun+dus ('fʌndəs) *n., pl.* **+di** (-daɪ). *Anatomy.* the base of an organ or the part farthest away from its opening. [C18: from Latin, literally: the bottom, a farm, estate] —**'fun+dic** *adj.*
Fun+dy ('fʌndɪ) *n.* **Bay of.** an inlet of the Atlantic in SE Canada, between S New Brunswick and W Nova Scotia: remarkable for its swift tides of up to 21 m (70 ft.).
Fü+nen ('fy:nən) *n.* the German name for **Fyn.**
fu+ner+al ('fju:nərəl) *n.* **1. a.** a ceremony at which a dead person is buried or cremated. **b.** (*as modifier*): *a funeral service.* **2.** a procession of people escorting a corpse to burial. **3.** *Informal.* worry; concern; affair: *that's your funeral.* [C14: from Medieval Latin *fūnerālia,* from Late Latin *fūnerālis* (adj.), from Latin *fūnus* funeral]
fu+ner+al di+rec+tor *n.* an undertaker.
fu+ner+al par+lour *n.* a place where the dead are prepared for burial or cremation. Usual U.S. name: **funeral home.**
fu+ner+ar·y ('fju:nərərɪ) *adj.* of, relating to, or for a funeral.
fu+ne·re·al (fju:'nɪərɪəl) *adj.* suggestive of a funeral; gloomy or mournful. Also: **funebrial.** [C18: from Latin *fūnereus*] —**fu+'ne·re·al+ly** *adv.*
fun+fair ('fʌn,fɛə) *n. Brit.* an amusement park or fairground.
fun+gal ('fʌŋgᵊl) *adj.* of, derived from, or caused by a fungus or fungi: *fungal spores; a fungal disease.*
fun+gi ('fʌndʒaɪ, 'fʌŋgaɪ) *n.* the plural of **fungus.**
fun·gi- *or before a vowel* **fung-** *combining form.* fungus: *fungicide; fungoid.*
fun+gi·ble ('fʌndʒɪbᵊl) *Law.* ~*n.* **1.** (*often pl.*) moveable perishable goods of a sort that may be estimated by number or weight, such as grain, wine, etc. ~*adj.* **2.** having the nature or quality of fungibles. [C18: from Medieval Latin *fungibilis,* from Latin *fungī* to perform; see FUNCTION] —**,fun+gi·'bil+i·ty** *n.*
fun+gi+cide ('fʌndʒɪ,saɪd) *n.* a substance or agent that destroys or is capable of destroying fungi. —**,fun+gi+'cid+al** *adj.* —**,fun+gi+'cid+al+ly** *adv.*
fun+gi+form ('fʌndʒɪ,fɔ:m) *adj.* shaped like a mushroom or similar fungus: *the fungiform papillae of the tongue.*
fun+gi+stat ('fʌndʒɪ,stæt) *n.* a substance that inhibits the growth of fungi. —**,fun+gi+'stat+ic** *adj.*
fun+goid ('fʌŋgɔɪd) *adj.* resembling a fungus or fungi: *a fungoid growth.*
fun+gous ('fʌŋgəs) *adj.* **1.** appearing suddenly and spreading quickly like a fungus, but not lasting. **2.** a less common word for **fungal.**
fun+gus ('fʌŋgəs) *n., pl.* **fun+gi** ('fʌndʒaɪ, 'fʌŋgaɪ, 'fʌŋgɪ:) *or* **fun+gus·es. 1.** any plant of the division *Fungi,* lacking chlorophyll, leaves, true stems, and roots, reproducing by spores, and living as a saprophyte or parasite. The group includes moulds, mildews, rusts, yeasts, and mushrooms. **2.** something resembling a fungus, esp. in suddenly growing and spreading rapidly. **3.** *Pathol.* any soft tumorous growth. [C16: from Latin: mushroom, fungus; probably related to Greek *spongos* SPONGE] —**fun+gic** ('fʌndʒɪk) *adj.* —**'fun·gus-,like** *adj.*
fu+ni+cle ('fju:nɪkᵊl) *n. Botany.* the stalk that attaches an ovule or seed to the wall of the ovary. Also called: **funiculus.** [C17: from Latin *fūniculus* a thin rope, from *fūnis* rope] —**fu+nic·u+late** (fjʊ'nɪkjʊlɪt, -,leɪt) *adj.*
fu+nic·u+lar (fju:'nɪkjʊlə) *n.* **1.** Also called: **funicular railway.** a railway up the side of a mountain, consisting of two counterbalanced cars at either end of a cable passing round a driving wheel at the summit. ~*adj.* **2.** relating to or operated by a rope, cable, etc. **3.** of or relating to a funicle.
fu+nic·u+lus (fju:'nɪkjʊləs) *n., pl.* **+li** (-,laɪ). **1.** *Anatomy.* a cordlike part or structure, esp. a small bundle of nerve fibres in the spinal cord. **2.** a variant of **funicle.** [C17: from Latin; see FUNICLE]
funk[1] (fʌŋk) *Informal, chiefly Brit.* ~*n.* **1.** Also called: **blue funk.** a state of nervousness, fear, or depression (esp. in the phrase **in a funk**). **2.** a coward. ~*vb.* **3.** to flinch from (responsibility, etc.) through fear. **4.** (*tr.; usually passive*) to make afraid. [C18: university slang, perhaps related to FUNK[2]] —**'funk+er** *n.*
funk[2] (fʌŋk) *n. U.S. slang.* a strong foul odour. [C17 (in the sense: tobacco smoke): from *funk* (vb.) to smoke (tobacco), probably of French dialect origin; compare Old French *funkier* to smoke, from Latin *fūmigāre*]
Funk (fʊŋk) *n.* **Cas·i·mir** ('kæzɪ,mɪə). 1884–1967, U.S. biochemist, born in Poland: studied and named vitamins.
funk hole *n. Informal.* **1.** *Military.* a dugout. **2.** a job that affords exemption from military service.
funk·y[1] ('fʌŋkɪ) *adj.* **funk·i+er, funk·i+est.** *Informal.* **1.** (of jazz, pop, etc.) passionate and soulful, reminiscent of early blues. **2.** pleasing or attractive, esp. in an exaggerated or camp manner. [C20: from FUNK[2], perhaps alluding to music that was smelly, that is, earthy (like the early blues)]
funk·y[2] ('fʌŋkɪ) *adj.* **funk·i+er, funk·i+est.** *Slang, chiefly U.S.* evil-smelling; foul. [C18: from FUNK[2]]
fun+nel ('fʌnᵊl) *n.* **1.** a hollow utensil with a wide mouth tapering to a small hole, used for pouring liquids, powders, etc., into a narrow-necked vessel. **2.** something resembling this in shape or function. **3.** a smokestack for smoke and exhaust gases, as on a steamship or steam locomotive. **4.** a shaft or tube, as in a building, for ventilation. ~*vb.* **+nels, +nel+ling, +nelled** *or U.S.* **+nels, +nel+ing, +neled. 5.** to move or cause to move or pour through or as if through a funnel. **6.** to concentrate or focus or be concentrated or focused in a particular direction: *they funnelled their attention on the problem.* **7.** (*intr.*) to take on a funnel-like shape. [C15: from Old Provençal *fonilh,* ultimately from Latin *infundibulum* funnel, hopper (in a mill), from *infundere* to pour in] —**'fun·nel-,like** *adj.*
fun+nel cloud *n.* a whirling column of cloud extending downwards from the base of a cumulonimbus cloud: part of a waterspout or tornado.
fun·nel-web *n. Austral.* any large poisonous black spider of the family *Dipluridae,* constructing funnel-shaped webs.
fun+nies ('fʌnɪz) *pl. n. U.S. informal.* comic strips in a newspaper.
fun+ny ('fʌnɪ) *adj.* **+ni+er, +ni+est. 1.** causing amusement or laughter; humorous; comical. **2.** peculiar; odd. **3.** suspicious or dubious (esp. in the phrase **funny business**). **4.** *Informal.* faint or ill: *to feel funny.* ~*n., pl.* **+nies. 5.** *Informal.* a joke or witticism. —**'fun+ni+ly** *adv.* —**'fun+ni+ness** *n.*
fun+ny bone *n.* the area near the elbow where the ulnar nerve is close to the surface of the skin: when it is struck, a sharp tingling sensation is experienced along the forearm. Also called (U.S.): **crazy bone.**
fun+ny farm *n. Facetious.* a mental institution.
fun+ny pa+per *n. U.S.* a section or separate supplement of a newspaper, etc., containing comic strips.
fur (fɜ:) *n.* **1.** the dense coat of fine silky hairs on such mammals as the cat, seal, and mink. **2. a.** the dressed skin of certain fur-bearing animals, with the hair left on. **b.** (*as modifier*): *a fur coat.* **3.** a garment made of fur, such as a coat or stole. **4. a.** a pile fabric made in imitation of animal fur. **b.** a garment made from such a fabric. **5.** *Heraldry.* any of various stylized representations of animal pelts or their tinctures, esp. ermine or vair, used in coats of arms. **6. make the fur fly.** to cause a scene or disturbance. **7.** *Informal.* a whitish coating of cellular debris on the tongue, caused by excessive smoking, an upset stomach, etc. **8.** *Brit.* a whitish-grey deposit consisting chiefly of calcium carbonate precipitated from hard water onto the insides of pipes, boilers, and kettles. ~*vb.* **furs, fur+ring, furred. 9.** (*tr.*) to line or trim a garment, etc., with fur. **10.** (often foll. by *up*) to cover or become covered with a furlike lining or deposit. **11.** (*tr.*) to clothe (a person) in a fur garment or garments. [C14: from Old French *forrer* to line a garment, from *fuerre* sheath, of Germanic origin; related to Old English *fōdder* case, Old Frisian *fōder* coat lining] —**'fur+less** *adj.*
fur. *abbrev. for* furlong.
fur+al+de+hyde (fjə'rældə,haɪd) *n.* either of two aldehydes derived from furan, esp. **2-furaldehyde** (see **furfuraldehyde**). [C20: shortened from *furfuraldehyde,* from *furfurol* (see FURFUR, -OL[1]) + ALDEHYDE]
fu+ran ('fjʊəræn, fjʊə'ræn) *n.* a colourless flammable toxic liquid heterocyclic compound, used in the synthesis of nylon. Formula: C_4H_4O. Also called: **furfuran.** [C19: shortened form of *furfuran,* from FURFUR]
fur+be·low ('fɜ:bɪ,ləʊ) *n.* **1.** a flounce, ruffle, or other ornamental trim. **2.** (*often pl.*) showy ornamentation. ~*vb.* **3.** (*tr.*) to put a furbelow on (a garment, etc.). [C18: by folk etymology from French dialect *farbella;* see FALBALA]
fur+bish ('fɜ:bɪʃ) *vb.* (*tr.*) **1.** to make bright by polishing; burnish. **2.** (often foll. by *up*) to improve the appearance or condition of; renovate; restore. [C14: from Old French *fourbir* to polish, of Germanic origin] —**'fur+bish+er** *n.*
fur bri+gade *n. Canadian.* (formerly) a convoy of canoes, horses, or dog sleighs that transported furs and other goods between trading posts and towns or factories.
fur+cate *vb.* ('fɜ:keɪt). **1.** to divide into two parts; fork. ~*adj.* ('fɜ:keɪt, -kɪt) *or* **fur+cat+ed. 2.** forked or divided: *furcate branches.* [C19: from Late Latin *furcātus* forked, from Latin *furca* a fork] —**fur+'ca+tion** *n.*
fur+cu+la ('fɜ:kjʊlə) *or* **fur+cu+lum** ('fɜ:kjʊləm) *n., pl.* **+lae** (-,li:) *or* **+la** (-lə). any forklike part or organ, esp. the fused clavicles (wishbone) of birds. [C19: from Latin: a forked support for a wall, diminutive of *furca* fork]
fur+fur ('fɜ:fə) *n., pl.* **fur+fur·es** ('fɜ:fjʊ,ri:z, -fə,ri:z). **1.** a scaling of the skin; dandruff. **2.** any scale of the epidermis. [C17: from Latin: bran, scurf]
fur+fu+ra+ceous (,fɜ:fjʊ'reɪʃəs, -fə'reɪ-) *adj.* **1.** relating to or resembling bran. **2.** *Med.* resembling dandruff; scaly. —**,fur+fu+'ra+ceous+ly** *adv.*
fur+fur+al+de+hyde (,fɜ:fjə'rældə,haɪd) *n.* a colourless flammable soluble mobile liquid with a penetrating odour, present in oat and rice hulls; 2-furaldehyde: used as a solvent and in the manufacture of resins. Formula: $C_5H_4O_2$. Also called: **furfural.**
fur+fu+ran ('fɜ:fə,ræn, 'fɜ:fjʊ-) *n.* another name for **furan.**
Fu·ries ('fjʊərɪz) *pl. n., sing.* **Fu·ry.** *Classical myth.* the snake-haired goddesses of vengeance, usually three in number, who pursued unpunished criminals. Also called: **Erinyes, Eumenides.**
fu+ri·o·so (,fjʊərɪ'əʊsəʊ) *Music.* ~*adj., adv.* **1.** in a frantically rushing manner. ~*n.* **2.** a passage or piece to be performed in this way. [C19: Italian, literally: furious; see FURY]
fu+ri+ous ('fjʊərɪəs) *adj.* **1.** extremely angry or annoyed; raging. **2.** violent, wild, or unrestrained, as in speed, vigour, energy, etc. —**'fu+ri+ous+ly** *adv.* —**'fu+ri+ous+ness** *n.*
furl (fɜ:l) *vb.* **1.** to roll up (an umbrella, flag, etc.) neatly and securely or (of an umbrella, flag, etc.) to be rolled up in this way. **2.** (*tr.*) *Nautical.* to gather in (a square sail). **3.** (*intr.*) *Rare.* to disappear; vanish. ~*n.* **4.** the act or an instance of furling. **5.** a single rolled-up section. [C16: from Old French *ferlier* to bind tightly, from *ferm* tight (from Latin *firmus*

FIRM[1]) + *lier* to tie, bind, from Latin *ligāre*] —**'furl·a·ble** *adj.* —**'furl·er** *n.*

fur·long ('fɜːˌlɒŋ) *n.* a unit of length equal to 220 yards (201.168 metres). [Old English *furlang,* from *furh* FURROW + *lang* LONG]

fur·lough ('fɜːləʊ) *U.S.* ~*n.* **1.** leave of absence from military duty. **2.** a temporary laying off of employees, usually because there is insufficient work to occupy them. ~*vb.* (*tr.*) **3.** to grant a furlough to. **4.** to lay off (staff) temporarily. [C17: from Dutch *verlof,* from *ver-* FOR- + *lof* leave, permission; related to Swedish *förlof*]

fur·men·ty ('fɜːməntɪ) *or* **fur·me·ty** ('fɜːmɪtɪ) *n.* variants of **frumenty.**

fur·nace ('fɜːnɪs) *n.* **1.** an enclosed chamber in which heat is produced to generate steam, destroy refuse, smelt or refine ores, etc. **2.** a very hot or stifling place. [C13: from Old French *fornais,* from Latin *fornax* oven, furnace; related to Latin *formus* warm] —**'fur·nace-ˌlike** *adj.*

Fur·ness ('fɜːnɪs) *n.* a region in NW England in Cumbria, forming a peninsula between the Irish Sea and Morecambe Bay.

fur·nish ('fɜːnɪʃ) *vb.* (*tr.*) **1.** to provide (a house, room, etc.) with furniture, carpets, etc. **2.** to equip with what is necessary; fit out. **3.** to give; supply: *the records furnished the information required.* [C15: from Old French *fournir,* of Germanic origin; related to Old High German *frummen* to carry out] —**'fur·nish·er** *n.*

fur·nish·ings ('fɜːnɪʃɪŋz) *pl. n.* **1.** furniture and accessories, including carpets and curtains, with which a room, house, etc., is furnished. **2.** *U.S.* articles of dress and accessories.

fur·ni·ture ('fɜːnɪtʃə) *n.* **1.** the movable, generally functional, articles that equip a room, house, etc. **2.** the equipment necessary for a ship, factory, etc. **3.** *Printing.* lengths of wood, plastic, or metal, used in assembling formes to create the blank areas and to surround the type. **4.** *Obsolete.* the full armour, trappings, etc., for a man and horse. **5.** Also called: **door furniture.** locks, handles, etc., designed for use on doors. [C16: from French *fourniture,* from *fournir* to equip, FURNISH]

Fur·ni·vall ('fɜːnɪvᵊl) *n.* **Fred·er·ick James.** 1825–1910, English philologist: founder of the Early English Text Society and one of the founders of the *Oxford English Dictionary.*

fu·ro·re (fjʊ'rɔːrɪ) *or esp. U.S.* **fu·ror** ('fjʊərɔː) *n.* **1.** a public outburst, esp. of protest; uproar. **2.** a sudden widespread enthusiasm for something; craze. **3.** frenzy; rage; madness. [C15: from Latin: frenzy, rage, from *furere* to rave]

fur·phy ('fɜːfɪ) *n., pl.* **·phies.** *Austral. slang.* a rumour or fictitious story. [C20: from *Furphy* carts (used for water or sewage in World War I), made at a foundry established by the Furphy family]

furred (fɜːd) *adj.* **1.** made of, lined with, or covered in fur. **2.** wearing fur. **3.** (of animals) having fur. **4.** another word for **furry** (sense 4). **5.** Also: **furry.** provided with furring strips. **6.** (of a pipe, kettle, etc.) lined with hard lime or other salts deposited from water.

fur·ri·er ('fʌrɪə) *n.* a person whose occupation is selling, making, dressing, or repairing fur garments. [C14: *furour,* from Old French *fourrer* to trim or line with FUR]

fur·ri·er·y ('fʌrɪərɪ) *n., pl.* **·er·ies. 1.** the occupation of a furrier. **2.** furs worn as a garment or trim collectively.

fur·ring ('fɜːrɪŋ) *n.* **1. a.** short for **furring strip. b.** the fixing of furring strips. **c.** furring strips collectively. **2.** the formation of fur on the tongue. **3.** trimming of animal fur, as on a coat or other garment, or furs collectively.

fur·ring strip *n.* a strip of wood or metal fixed to a wall, floor, or ceiling to provide a surface for the fixing of plasterboard, floorboards, etc. Sometimes shortened to **furring.**

fur·row ('fʌrəʊ) *n.* **1.** a long narrow trench made in the ground by a plough or a trench resembling this. **2.** any long deep groove, esp. a deep wrinkle on the forehead. ~*vb.* **3.** to develop or cause to develop furrows or wrinkles. **4.** to make a furrow or furrows in (land). [Old English *furh;* related to Old Frisian *furch,* Old Norse *for,* Old High German *furuh* furrow, Latin *porca* ridge between furrows] —**'fur·row·er** *n.* —**'fur·row·less** *adj.* —**'fur·row-ˌlike** *or* **'fur·row·y** *adj.*

fur·ry ('fɜːrɪ) *adj.* **·ri·er, ·ri·est. 1.** covered with fur or something furlike. **2.** of, relating to, or resembling fur. **3.** another word for **furred** (sense 5). **4.** Also: **furred.** (of the tongue) coated with whitish cellular debris. —**'fur·ri·ly** *adv.* —**'fur·ri·ness** *n.*

fur seal *n.* any of various eared seals, esp. of the genus *Arctocephalus,* that have a fine dense underfur and are hunted as a source of sealskin.

Fur Seal Is·lands *pl. n.* another name for the **Pribilof Islands.**

Fürth (*German* fyrt) *n.* a city in S West Germany, in Bavaria northwest of Nuremberg. Pop.: 103 559 (1974 est.).

fur·ther ('fɜːðə) *adv.* **1.** in addition; furthermore. **2.** to a greater degree or extent. **3.** to or at a more advanced point. **4.** to or at a greater distance in time or space; farther. ~*adj.* **5.** additional; more. **6.** more distant or remote in time or space; farther. ~*vb.* **7.** (*tr.*) to assist the progress of; promote. ~See also **far, furthest.** [Old English *furthor;* related to Old Frisian *further,* Old Saxon *furthor,* Old High German *furdar;* see FORTH] —**'fur·ther·er** *n.*

Usage. See at **farther.**

fur·ther·ance ('fɜːðərəns) *n.* **1.** the act of furthering; advancement. **2.** something that furthers or advances.

fur·ther ed·u·ca·tion *n.* (in Britain) formal education beyond school other than at a university or polytechnic.

fur·ther·more ('fɜːðəˌmɔː) *adv.* in addition; moreover.

fur·ther·most ('fɜːðəˌməʊst) *adj.* most distant; furthest.

fur·thest ('fɜːðɪst) *adv.* **1.** to the greatest degree or extent. **2.** to or at the greatest distance in time or space; farthest. ~*adj.* **3.** most distant or remote in time or space; farthest.

fur·tive ('fɜːtɪv) *adj.* characterized by stealth; sly and secretive. [C15: from Latin *furtīvus* stolen, clandestine, from *furtum* a theft, from *fūr* a thief; related to Greek *phōr* thief] —**'fur·tive·ly** *adv.* —**'fur·tive·ness** *n.*

Furt·wäng·ler (*German* 'fʊrtˌvɛŋglər) *n.* **Wil·helm** ('vɪlhɛlm). 1886–1954, German conductor, noted for his interpretations of Wagner.

fu·run·cle ('fjʊərʌŋkᵊl) *n. Pathol.* the technical name for **boil**[2]. [C17: from Latin *fūrunculus* pilferer, petty thief, sore on the body, from *fūr* thief] —**fu·run·cu·lar** (fjʊ'rʌŋkjʊlə) *or* **fu·'run·cu·lous** *adj.*

fu·run·cu·lo·sis (fjʊˌrʌŋkjʊ'ləʊsɪs) *n.* a skin condition characterized by the presence of multiple boils.

fu·ry ('fjʊərɪ) *n., pl.* **·ries. 1.** violent or uncontrolled anger; wild rage. **2.** an outburst of such anger. **3.** a person, esp. a woman, with a violent temper. **4.** See **Furies. 5. like fury.** *Informal.* violently; furiously: *they rode like fury.* [C14: from Latin *furia* rage, from *furere* to be furious]

furze (fɜːz) *n.* another name for **gorse.** [Old English *fyrs*] —**'furz·y** *adj.*

fu·sain (fjuː'zeɪn; *French* fy'zɛ̃) *n.* **1.** a fine charcoal pencil or stick made from the spindle tree. **2.** a drawing done with such a pencil. **3.** a dull black brittle form of carbon resembling charcoal, found in certain coals. [C19: from French: spindle tree or charcoal made from it, from Vulgar Latin *fūsāgō* (unattested) a spindle (generally made from the spindle tree), from Latin *fūsus*]

fus·cous ('fʌskəs) *adj.* of a brownish-grey colour. [C17: from Latin *fuscus* dark, swarthy, tawny]

fuse[1] *or U.S.* **fuze** (fjuːz) *n.* **1.** a lead of combustible black powder in a waterproof covering (**safety fuse**), or a lead containing an explosive (**detonating fuse**), used to fire an explosive charge. **2.** any device by which an explosive charge is ignited. ~*vb.* **3.** (*tr.*) to provide or equip with such a fuse. [C17: from Italian *fuso* spindle, from Latin *fūsus*] —**'fuse·less** *adj.*

fuse[2] (fjuːz) *vb.* **1.** to unite or become united by melting, esp. by the action of heat: *to fuse borax and copper sulphate at a high temperature.* **2.** to become or cause to become liquid, esp. by the action of heat; melt. **3.** to join or become combined; integrate. **4.** (*tr.*) to equip (an electric circuit, plug, etc.) with a fuse. **5.** *Brit.* to fail or cause to fail as a result of the blowing of a fuse: *the lights fused.* ~*n.* **6. a.** a protective device for safeguarding electric circuits, etc., containing a wire that melts and breaks the circuit when the current exceeds a certain value. **b.** any device performing a similar function, such as a switch that automatically breaks the circuit when the load is excessive. [C17: from Latin *fūsus* melted, cast, poured out, from *fundere* to pour out, shed; sense 5 influenced by FUSE[1]]

fuse box *n.* a housing for electric fuses.

fu·see *or* **fu·zee** (fjuː'ziː) *n.* **1.** (in early clocks and watches) a spirally grooved spindle, functioning as an equalizing force on the unwinding of the mainspring. **2.** a friction match with a large head, capable of remaining alight in a wind. **3.** an explosive fuse. [C16: from French *fusée* spindleful of thread, from Old French *fus* spindle, from Latin *fūsus*]

fu·se·lage ('fjuːzɪˌlɑːʒ) *n.* the main body of an aircraft, excluding the wings, tailplane, and fin. [C20: from French, from *fuseler* to shape like a spindle, from Old French *fusel* spindle; see FUSEE]

fu·sel oil *or* **fu·sel** ('fjuːzᵊl) *n.* a mixture of amyl alcohols, propanol, and butanol: a by-product in the distillation of fermented liquors used as a source of amyl alcohols.

Fu·shih *or* **Fu-shih** ('fuː'ʃiː) *n.* another name for **Yenan.**

Fu·shun ('fuː'ʃʌn) *n.* a city in NE China, in central Liaoning province near Shenyang: situated on one of the richest coalfields in the world; site of the largest thermal power plant in NE Asia. Pop.: 1 000 000 (1965 Western est.).

fu·si·ble ('fjuːzəbᵊl) *adj.* capable of being fused or melted. —**ˌfu·si·'bil·i·ty** *or* **'fu·si·ble·ness** *n.* —**'fu·si·bly** *adv.*

fu·si·ble met·al *or* **al·loy** *n.* any of various alloys with low melting points that contain bismuth, lead, and tin. They are used as solders and in safety devices.

fu·si·form ('fjuːzɪˌfɔːm) *adj.* elongated and tapering at both ends; spindle-shaped. [C18: from Latin *fūsus* spindle]

fu·sil[1] ('fjuːzɪl) *n.* a light flintlock musket. [C16 (in the sense: steel for a tinderbox): from Old French *fuisil,* from Vulgar Latin *focīlis* (unattested), from Latin *focus* fire]

fu·sil[2] ('fjuːzɪl) *n. Heraldry.* a charge shaped like a lengthened lozenge. [C15: from Old French *fusel,* ultimately from Latin *fūsus* spindle, FUSE[1] (the heraldic lozenge originally represented a spindle covered with tow for spinning)]

fu·sil[3] ('fjuːzɪl) *adj.* a variant spelling of **fusile.**

fu·sile ('fjuːzaɪl) *or* **fu·sil** *adj.* **1.** easily melted; fusible. **2.** formed by casting or melting; founded. [C14: from Latin *fūsilis* molten, from *fundere* to pour out, melt]

fu·si·lier (ˌfjuːzɪ'lɪə) *n.* **1.** (formerly) an infantryman armed with a light musket. **2.** Also: **fusileer. a.** a soldier, esp. a private, serving in any of certain British or other infantry regiments. **b.** (*pl.; cap. when part of a name*): *the Royal Welsh Fusiliers.* [C17: from French; see FUSIL[1]]

fu·sil·lade (ˌfjuːzɪ'leɪd, -'lɑːd) *n.* **1.** a simultaneous or rapid continual discharge of firearms. **2.** a sudden outburst, as of criticism. ~*vb.* **3.** (*tr.*) to attack with a fusillade. [C19: from French, from *fusiller* to shoot; see FUSIL[1]]

fu·sion ('fju:ʒən) *n.* **1.** the act or process of fusing or melting together; union. **2.** the state of being fused. **3.** something produced by fusing. **4.** See **nuclear fusion. 5.** the merging of juxtaposed speech sounds, morphemes, or words. **6.** a coalition of political parties or other groups, esp. to support common candidates at an election. **7.** *Psychol.* the combination of two or more perceptual elements in which the original elements cannot be distinguished. [C16: from Latin *fūsiō* a pouring out, melting, casting, from *fundere* to pour out, FOUND[3]]

fu·sion bomb *n.* a type of bomb in which most of the energy is provided by nuclear fusion, esp. the fusion of hydrogen isotopes. Also called: **thermonuclear bomb, fission-fusion bomb.** See also **hydrogen bomb.**

fu·sion·ism ('fju:ʒəˌnɪzəm) *n.* the favouring of coalitions among political groups. —**'fu·sion·ist** *n., adj.*

fu·sion re·ac·tor *n.* a nuclear reactor in which a thermonuclear fusion reaction takes place.

fuss (fʌs) *n.* **1.** nervous activity or agitation, esp. when disproportionate or unnecessary. **2.** complaint or objection: *he made a fuss over the bill.* **3.** an exhibition of affection or admiration, esp. if excessive: *they made a great fuss over the new baby.* **4.** a quarrel; dispute. ~*vb.* **5.** (*intr.*) to worry unnecessarily. **6.** (*intr.*) to be excessively concerned over trifles. **7.** (when *intr.*, usually foll. by *over*) to show great or excessive concern, affection, etc. (for). **8.** (*intr.*; foll. by *with*) *Jamaican.* to quarrel violently. **9.** (*tr.*) to bother (a person). [C18: of uncertain origin] —**'fuss·er** *n.*

fuss·pot ('fʌsˌpɒt) *n. Brit. informal.* a person who fusses unnecessarily. Also called (U.S.): **fuss-budg·et.**

fuss·y ('fʌsɪ) *adj.* **fuss·i·er, fuss·i·est. 1.** inclined to fuss over minor points. **2.** very particular about detail. **3.** characterized by overelaborate detail: *the furniture was too fussy to be elegant.* —**'fuss·i·ly** *adv.* —**'fuss·i·ness** *n.*

fus·ta·nel·la (ˌfʌstə'nɛlə) *or* **fus·ta·nelle** *n.* a white knee-length pleated skirt worn by men in Greece and Albania. [C19: from Italian, from Modern Greek *phoustani,* probably from Italian *fustagno* FUSTIAN]

fus·ti·an ('fʌstɪən) *n.* **1. a.** a hard-wearing fabric of cotton mixed with flax or wool with a slight nap. **b.** (*as modifier*): *a fustian jacket.* **2.** pompous or pretentious talk or writing. ~*adj.* **3.** cheap; worthless. **4.** pompous; bombastic. [C12: from Old French *fustaigne,* from Medieval Latin *fustāneum,* from Latin *fustis* cudgel]

fus·tic ('fʌstɪk) *n.* **1.** Also called: **old fustic.** a large tropical American moraceous tree, *Chlorophora tinctoria.* **2.** the yellow dye obtained from the wood of this tree. **3.** any of various trees or shrubs that yield a similar dye, esp. *Rhus cotinus* (**young fustic**), a European sumach. [C15: from French *fustoc,* from Spanish, from Arabic *fustuq,* from Greek *pistakē* pistachio tree]

fus·ti·gate ('fʌstɪˌgeɪt) *vb.* (*tr.*) *Archaic.* to beat; cudgel. [C17: from Late Latin *fūstīgāre* to cudgel to death, from Latin *fūstis* cudgel] —ˌ**fus·ti·'ga·tion** *n.* —**'fus·ti·ˌga·tor** *n.* —ˌ**fus·ti·'ga·to·ry** *adj.*

fus·ty ('fʌstɪ) *adj.* **·ti·er, ·ti·est. 1.** smelling of damp or mould; musty. **2.** old-fashioned in attitude. [C14: from *fust* wine cask, from Old French: cask, tree trunk, from Latin *fūstis* cudgel, club] —**'fus·ti·ly** *adv.* —**'fus·ti·ness** *n.*

fut. *abbrev. for* future.

fu·thark, fu·tharc ('fu:θɑ:k) *or* **fu·thorc, fu·thork** ('fu:θɔ:k) *n.* a phonetic alphabet consisting of runes. [C19: from the first six letters: *f, u, th, a, r, k;* compare ALPHABET]

fu·tile ('fju:taɪl) *adj.* **1.** having no effective result; unsuccessful. **2.** pointless; unimportant; trifling. **3.** inane or foolish: *don't be so futile!* [C16: from Latin *futtilis* pouring out easily, worthless, from *fundere* to pour out] —**'fu·tile·ly** *adv.* —**'fu·tile·ness** *n.*

fu·til·i·tar·i·an (fju:ˌtɪlɪ'tɛərɪən) *adj.* **1.** of or relating to the belief that human endeavour can serve no useful purpose. ~*n.* **2.** one who holds this belief. [C19: facetious coinage from FUTILE + UTILITARIAN] —**fu**ˌ**til·i·'tar·i·an·ism** *n.*

fu·til·i·ty (fju:'tɪlɪtɪ) *n., pl.* **·ties. 1.** lack of effectiveness or success. **2.** lack of purpose or meaning. **3.** something futile.

fut·tock ('fʌtək) *n. Nautical.* one of the ribs in the frame of a wooden vessel. [C13: perhaps variant of *foothook*]

fut·tock plate *n. Nautical.* a horizontal metal disc fixed at the top of a lower mast for holding the futtock shrouds.

fut·tock shroud *n. Nautical.* any of several metal rods serving as a brace between the futtock plate on a lower mast and the topmast.

fu·ture ('fju:tʃə) *n.* **1.** the time yet to come. **2.** undetermined events that will occur in that time. **3.** the condition of a person or thing at a later date: *the future of the school is undecided.* **4.** likelihood of later improvement or advancement: *he has a future as a singer.* **5.** *Grammar.* **a.** a tense of verbs used when the action or event described is to occur after the time of utterance. **b.** a verb in this tense. **6. in future.** from now on; henceforth. ~*adj.* **7.** that is yet to come or be. **8.** of or expressing time yet to come. **9.** (*prenominal*) destined to become: *a future president.* **10.** *Grammar.* in or denoting the future as a tense of verbs. [C14: from Latin *fūtūrus* about to be, from *esse* to be] —**'fu·ture·less** *adj.*

fu·ture life *n.* a life after death; afterlife.

fu·ture per·fect *Grammar.* ~*adj.* **1.** denoting a tense of verbs describing an action that will have been performed by a certain time. In English this is formed with *will have* or *shall have* plus the past participle. ~*n.* **2. a.** the future perfect tense. **b.** a verb in this tense.

fu·tures ('fju:tʃəz) *pl. n.* commodities bought or sold at an agreed price for delivery at a specified future date.

fu·tur·ism ('fju:tʃəˌrɪzəm) *n.* an artistic movement that arose in Italy in 1909 to replace traditional aesthetic values with the characteristics of the machine age. —**'fu·tur·ist** *n., adj.*

fu·tur·is·tic (ˌfju:tʃə'rɪstɪk) *adj.* **1.** denoting or relating to design, technology, etc., that is thought likely to be current or fashionable at some future time; ultramodern. **2.** of or relating to futurism. —ˌ**fu·tur·'is·ti·cal·ly** *adv.*

fu·tur·i·ty (fju:'tjʊərɪtɪ) *n., pl.* **·ties. 1.** a less common word for **future. 2.** the quality of being in the future. **3.** a future event.

fu·tur·ol·o·gy (ˌfju:tʃə'rɒlədʒɪ) *n.* the study or prediction of the future of mankind. —ˌ**fu·tur·'ol·o·gist** *n.*

fuze (fju:z) *n. U.S.* a variant spelling of **fuse**[1].

fu·zee (fju:'zi:) *n.* a variant spelling of **fusee.**

fuzz[1] (fʌz) *n.* **1.** a mass or covering of fine or curly hairs, fibres, etc. **2.** a blur. **3.** *Informal.* (in pop music) a distortion of sound produced by adding overtones in an electronic device (**fuzz box**). ~*vb.* **4.** to make or become fuzzy. **5.** to make or become indistinct; blur. [C17: perhaps from Low German *fussig* loose]

fuzz[2] (fʌz) *n.* a slang word for **police** or **policeman.** [C20: of uncertain origin]

fuzz·y ('fʌzɪ) *adj.* **fuzz·i·er, fuzz·i·est. 1.** of, resembling, or covered with fuzz. **2.** indistinct; unclear or distorted. **3.** not clearly thought out or expressed. **4.** (of the hair) tightly curled or very wavy. —**'fuzz·i·ly** *adv.* —**'fuzz·i·ness** *n.*

fuzz·y-wuzz·y ('fʌzɪˌwʌzɪ) *n., pl.* **·ies** *or* **·y. 1.** *Informal.* (formerly) a Sudanese soldier. **2.** *Slang.* a coloured fuzzy-haired native of any of certain areas of the world.

f.v. *abbrev. for* folio verso. [Latin: on the reverse (that is left-hand) page]

fwd. *abbrev. for* forward.

f.w.d. *abbrev. for:* **1.** four-wheel drive. **2.** front-wheel drive.

-fy *suffix forming verbs.* to make or become: *beautify; simplify; liquefy.* [from Old French *-fier,* from Latin *-ficāre,* verbal ending formed from *-ficus* -FIC]

fyke (faɪk) *n. U.S.* a fish trap consisting of a net suspended over a series of hoops, laid horizontally in the water. [C19: from Middle Dutch *fuycke*]

Fylde (faɪld) *n.* a region in NW England in Lancashire between the Wyre and Ribble estuaries.

fyl·fot ('fɪlfɒt) *n.* a rare word for **swastika.** [C16 (apparently meaning: a sign or device for the lower part or foot of a painted window): from *fillen* to FILL + *fot* FOOT]

Fyn (*Danish* fy:n) *n.* the second largest island of Denmark, between the Jutland peninsula and the island of Sjælland. Pop.: 398 255 (1970). Area: 3481 sq. km (1344 sq. miles). German name: **Fünen.**

fyrd (fɪəd, faɪəd) *n. History.* the local militia of an Anglo-Saxon shire, in which all freemen had to serve.

Fyz·a·bad *or* **Faiz·a·bad** (ˌfaɪzə'bæd) *n.* a city in N India, in E central Uttar Pradesh on the Gogra River. Pop.: 102 835 (1971).

F.Z.S. *abbrev. for* Fellow of the Zoological Society.

G

g *or* **G** (dʒiː) *n., pl.* **g's, G's,** *or* **Gs. 1.** the seventh letter and fifth consonant of the modern English alphabet. **2.** a speech sound represented by this letter, in English usually either a voiced velar stop, as in *grass,* or a voiced palato-alveolar affricate, as in *page.*

g *symbol for:* **1.** gallon(s). **2.** gram(s). **3.** acceleration of free fall (due to gravity).

G *symbol for:* **1.** *Music.* **a.** a note having a frequency of 392 hertz (**G above middle C**) or this value multiplied or divided by any power of 2; the fifth note of the scale of C major. **b.** a key, string, or pipe producing this note. **c.** the major or minor key having this note as its tonic. **2.** gravitational constant. **3.** *Physics.* conductance. **4.** German. **5.** giga. **6.** good. **7.** *Slang, chiefly U.S.* grand (a thousand dollars or pounds).

G. *or* **g.** *abbrev. for:* **1.** gauges. **2.** gauss. **3.** gelding. **4.** Gulf. **5.** guilder(s). **6.** guinea(s).

Ga *the chemical symbol for* gallium.

Ga *or* **Gã** (gɑː) *n.* **1.** (*pl.* **Ga, Gas** *or* **Gã, Gãs**) a member of a Negroid people of W Africa living chiefly in S Ghana. **2.** the language of this people, belonging to the Kwa branch of the Niger-Congo family.

Ga. *abbrev. for* Georgia.

G.A. *abbrev. for:* **1.** General Assembly (of the United Nations). **2.** general average.

gab[1] (gæb) *Informal.* ~*vb.* **gabs, gab+bing, gabbed. 1.** (*intr.*) to talk excessively or idly, esp. about trivial matters; gossip; chatter. ~*n.* **2.** idle or trivial talk. **3. gift of the gab.** ability to speak effortlessly, glibly, or persuasively. [C18: variant of Northern dialect *gob* mouth, probably from Irish Gaelic *gob* beak, mouth] —**'gab+ber** *n.*

gab[2] (gæb) *n.* a fork, prong, or toothed part that engages periodically with a slotted link or rod in a mechanism. [C18: probably from Flemish *gabbe* notch, gash]

Ga+bar ('gɑːbə), **Ghe+ber,** *or* **Ghe+bre** *n.* **1.** a member of an Iranian religious sect practising a modern version of Zoroastrianism. ~*adj.* **2.** of, relating to, or characterizing the Gabar sect or its beliefs.

gab+ar+dine ('gæbəˌdiːn, ˌgæbə'diːn) *n.* a variant spelling of **gaberdine** (esp. sense 2).

gab+ble ('gæbᵊl) *vb.* **1.** to utter (words, etc.) rapidly and indistinctly; jabber. **2.** (*intr.*) (of geese and some other birds or animals) to utter rapid cackling noises. ~*n.* **3.** rapid and indistinct speech or noises. [C17: from Middle Dutch *gabbelen,* of imitative origin] —**'gab+bler** *n.*

gab+bro ('gæbrəʊ) *n., pl.* **+bros.** a dark coarse-grained basic plutonic igneous rock consisting of plagioclase feldspar, pyroxene, and often olivine. [C19: from Italian, probably from Latin *glaber* smooth, bald] —**gab+'bro+ic** *or* **ˌgab+bro+'it+ic** *adj.*

gab+by ('gæbɪ) *adj.* **+bi+er, +bi+est.** *Informal.* inclined to chatter; talkative.

ga+belle (gæ'bɛl) *n. French history.* a salt tax levied until 1790. [C15: from Old Italian *gabella,* from Arabic *qabālah* tribute, from *qabala* he received] —**ga+'belled** *adj.*

gab+er+dine ('gæbəˌdiːn, ˌgæbə'diːn) *n.* **1.** a twill-weave worsted, cotton, or spun-rayon fabric. **2.** Also called: **gabardine.** an ankle-length loose coat or frock worn by men, esp. by Jews, in the Middle Ages. **3.** any of various other garments made of gaberdine, esp. a child's raincoat. [C16: from Old French *gauvardine* pilgrim's garment, from Middle High German *wallewart* pilgrimage; related to Spanish *gabardina*]

gab+er+lun+zie (ˌgæbə'lʌnzɪ, -'luːnjɪ) *n. Scot. archaic or literary.* a wandering beggar. Also: **gaberlunzie-man.** [C16: variant of earlier *gaberlungy*]

Gab+e+ro+nes (ˌgæbə'rəʊnɛs) *n.* the former name for **Gaborone.**

Ga+bès ('gɑːbɛs; *French* ga'bɛs) *n.* **1.** a port in E Tunisia. Pop.: 76 356 (1966). Ancient name: **Tacape. 2. Gulf of.** an inlet of the Mediterranean on the E coast of Tunisia. Ancient name: **Syrtis Minor.**

gab+fest ('gæbfɛst) *n. Informal, chiefly U.S.* **1.** prolonged gossiping or conversation. **2.** an informal gathering for conversation.

ga+bi+on ('geɪbɪən) *n.* **1.** a cylindrical metal container filled with stones, used in the construction of underwater foundations. **2.** a wickerwork basket filled with stones or earth, used (esp. formerly) as part of a fortification. [C16: from French: basket, from Italian *gabbione,* from *gabbia* cage, from Latin *cavea;* see CAGE]

ga+bi+on+ade *or* **ga+bi+on+nade** (ˌgeɪbɪə'neɪd) *n.* **1.** a row of gabions submerged in a waterway, stream, river, etc., to control the flow of water. **2.** a fortification constructed of gabions. [C18: from French; see GABION]

ga+ble ('geɪbᵊl) *n.* **1.** Also called: **gable end.** the triangular upper part of a wall between the sloping ends of a pitched roof (**gable roof**). **2.** a triangular ornamental feature in the form of a gable, esp. as used over a door or window. **3.** the triangular wall on both ends of a gambrel roof. [C14: Old French *gable,* probably from Old Norse *gafl;* related to Old English *geafol* fork, Old High German *gibil* gable] —**'ga+bled** *adj.* —**'ga+ble-ˌlike** *adj.*

Ga+ble ('geɪbᵊl) *n.* **Clark.** 1901–60, U.S. film actor; his films include *It Happened One Night* (1934), *Gone with the Wind* (1939), *Mogambo* (1953), *Band of Angels* (1957), and *The Misfits* (1960).

ga+blet ('geɪblɪt) *n.* a small gable.

ga+ble win+dow *n.* a window positioned in a gable or having a small gable over it.

Ga+bo ('gɑːbəʊ, -bə) *n.* **Naum** (naʊm). 1890-1977, U.S. sculptor born in Russia: a leading constructivist.

Ga+bon (gə'bɒn; *French* ga'bɔ̃) *n.* a republic in W central Africa, on the Atlantic: settled by the French in 1839; made part of the French Congo in 1888; became independent in 1960; almost wholly forested. Official language: French. Religion: Christian and animist. Currency: franc. Capital: Libreville. Pop.: 530 000 (1975 UN est.). Area: 267 675 sq. km (103 350 sq. miles). —**Gab·o·nese** (ˌgæbə'niːz) *adj., n.*

Ga+bor (gə'bɔː) *n.* **Den+nis.** 1900-1979, British electrical engineer, born in Hungary. He invented holography: Nobel prize for physics 1971.

Gab·o+ro+ne (ˌgæbə'rəʊnɪ) *n.* the capital of Botswana (since 1964), in the extreme southeast. Pop.: 17 718 (1971). Former name: **Gaberones.**

Ga+bri+el[1] ('geɪbrɪəl) *n. Bible.* one of the archangels, the messenger of good news (Daniel 8:16–26; Luke 1:11–20, 26–38).

Ga+bri+el[2] (*French* gabri'ɛl) *n.* **Jacques-Ange** (ʒɑːk 'ɑ̃ːʒ). 1698–1782, French architect: designed the Petit Trianon at Versailles.

ga+by ('geɪbɪ) *n., pl.* **+bies.** *Informal, chiefly Brit.* a simpleton.

gad[1] (gæd) *vb.* **gads, gad+ding, gad+ded. 1.** (*intr.;* often foll. by *about* or *around*) to go out in search of pleasure, esp. in an aimless manner; gallivant. ~*n.* **2.** carefree adventure (esp. in the phrase **on** *or* **upon the gad**). [C15: back formation from obsolete *gadling* companion, from Old English, from *gæd* fellowship; related to Old High German *gatuling*] —**'gad+der** *n.*

gad[2] (gæd) *n.* **1.** *Mining.* a short chisel-like instrument for breaking rock or coal from the face. **2.** a goad for driving cattle. **3.** a western U.S. word for **spur** (sense 1). ~*vb.* **gads, gad+ding, gad+ded. 4.** (*tr.*) *Mining.* to break up or loosen with a gad. [C13: from Old Norse *gaddr* spike; related to Old High German *gart,* Gothic *gazds* spike]

Gad[1] (gæd) *n., interj.* an archaic euphemism for **God:** used as or in an oath.

Gad[2] (gæd) *n. Old Testament.* **1. a.** Jacob's sixth son, whose mother was Zilpah, Leah's maid. **b.** the Israelite tribe descended from him. **c.** the territory of this tribe, lying to the east of the Jordan and extending southwards from the Sea of Galilee. **2.** a prophet and admonisher of David (I Samuel 22; II Samuel 24).

gad+a+bout ('gædəˌbaʊt) *n. Informal.* a person who restlessly seeks amusement, etc.

Gad+a+rene ('gædəˌriːn) *adj.* relating to or engaged in a headlong rush. [C19: via Late Latin from Greek *Gadarēnos,* of Gadara (Palestine), alluding to the Biblical Gadarene swine (Matthew 8:28ff.)]

Gad+da+fi *or* **Qad+da+fi** (gə'dɑːfɪ) *n.* **Mo+am+mar al** ('məʊəˌmɑːˌæl). born 1942, Libyan army officer and statesman; chairman of the Revolutionary Command Council of Libya since 1969.

gad+fly ('gædˌflaɪ) *n., pl.* **+flies. 1.** any of various large dipterous flies, esp. the horsefly, that annoy livestock by sucking their blood. **2.** a constantly irritating or harassing person. [C16: from GAD[2] (sting) + FLY]

gadg+et ('gædʒɪt) *n.* **1.** a small mechanical device or appliance. **2.** any object that is interesting for its ingenuity or novelty rather than for its practical use. [C19: of uncertain origin] —**'gadg+et·y** *adj.*

gadg+e+teer (ˌgædʒɪ'tɪə) *n.* a person who delights in gadgetry.

gadg+et+ry ('gædʒɪtrɪ) *n.* **1.** gadgets collectively. **2.** use of or preoccupation with gadgets and their design.

Gad+hel+ic (gæd'hɛlɪk) *n., adj.* another term for **Gaelic.** [from Irish *Gaedheal* Gael]

ga+did ('geɪdɪd) *n.* **1.** any marine teleost fish of the family *Gadidae,* which includes the cod, haddock, whiting, and pollack. ~*adj.* **2.** of, relating to, or belonging to the *Gadidae.* [C19: see GADOID]

ga+doid ('geɪdɔɪd) *adj.* **1.** of, relating to, or belonging to the *Anacanthini,* an order of marine soft-finned fishes typically having the pectoral and pelvic fins close together and small cycloid scales. The group includes gadid fishes and hake. ~*n.* **2.** any gadoid fish. [C19: from New Latin *Gadidae,* from *gadus* cod; see -OID]

gad+o+lin+ite ('gædəlɪˌnaɪt) *n.* a rare brown or black mineral consisting of a silicate of iron, beryllium, and yttrium in monoclinic crystalline form. Formula: $2BeO.FeO.Y_2O_3.2SiO_2$. Also called: **ytterbite.** [C19: named after Johan *Gadolin* (1760–1852), Finnish mineralogist]

gad+o+lin+i+um (ˌgædə'lɪnɪəm) *n.* a ductile malleable silvery-white ferromagnetic element of the lanthanide series of metals: occurs principally in monazite and bastnaesite. Symbol: Gd; atomic no.: 64; atomic wt.: 157.25; valency: 3; relative density: 7.898; melting pt.: 1312°C; boiling pt.: 3000°C (approx.). [C19: New Latin, from GADOLINITE] —ˌ**gad·o·'lin·ic** *adj.*

ga·droon *or* **go·droon** (gəˈdruːn) *n.* **1.** a moulding composed of a series of convex flutes and curves joined to form a decorative pattern, used esp. as an edge to silver articles. **2.** *Architect.* a carved ornamental moulding having a convex cross section. [C18: from French *godron,* perhaps from Old French *godet* cup, goblet, drinking vessel] —**ga·'drooned** *or* **go·'drooned** *adj.*

Gads·den Pur·chase (ˈgædzdən) *n.* an area of about 30 000 square miles (77 000 square kilometres) in present-day Arizona and New Mexico, bought by the U.S. from Mexico for 10 million dollars in 1853. The purchase was negotiated by James Gadsden (1788–1858), U.S. diplomat.

gad·wall (ˈgædˌwɔːl) *n., pl.* **·walls** *or* **·wall.** a duck, *Anas strepera,* related to the mallard. The male has a grey body and black tail. [C17: of unknown origin]

gad·zooks (gædˈzuːks) *interj. Archaic.* a mild oath. [C17: perhaps from *God's hooks* (the nails of the cross); see GAD[1]]

Gae·a (ˈdʒiːə), **Gai·a** (ˈgeɪə), *or* **Ge** (dʒiː, giː) *n. Greek myth.* the goddess of the earth, who bore Uranus and by him Oceanus, Cronus and the Titans. [from Greek *gaia* earth]

Gaek·war *or* **Gaik·war** (ˈgaɪkwɑː) *n. History.* the title of the ruler of the former native state of Baroda in India. [C19: from Marathi *Gaekvād,* literally: Guardian of the Cows, from Sanskrit *gauh* cow + *-vad* guardian]

Gael (geɪl) *n.* a person who speaks a Gaelic language, esp. a Highland Scot or a southern Irishman. [C19: from Gaelic *Gaidheal;* related to Old Irish *goidel,* Old Welsh *gwyddel* Irishman] —**'Gael·dom** *n.*

Gael·ic (ˈgeɪlɪk, ˈgæl-) *n.* **1.** any of the closely related languages of the Celts in Ireland, Scotland, or the Isle of Man. Compare **Goidelic.** ~*adj.* **2.** of, denoting, or relating to the Celtic people of Ireland, Scotland, or the Isle of Man or their language or customs.

Gael·ic cof·fee *n.* coffee with Irish whiskey and cream.

Gael·ic foot·ball *n.* a game played in Eire and parts of the U.S. with 15 men on each side and goals resembling rugby posts with a net on the bottom part. Players are allowed to kick, punch, and bounce the ball and attempt to get it over the bar or in the net.

Gael·tacht (ˈgeɪlˌtɑːxt) *n.* any of the regions in Ireland in which Irish is the vernacular speech. [C20: from Irish]

gaff[1] (gæf) *n.* **1.** *Angling.* a stiff pole with a stout prong or hook attached for landing large fish. **2.** *Nautical.* a boom hoisted aft of a mast to support a gaffsail. **3.** a metal spur fixed to the leg of a gamecock. ~*vb.* **4.** (*tr.*) *Angling.* to hook or land (a fish) with a gaff. **5.** (*tr.*) *Slang.* to cheat; hoax. [C13: from French *gaffe,* from Provençal *gaf* boat hook]

gaff[2] (gæf) *n.* **1.** *Slang.* foolish talk; nonsense. **2. blow the gaff.** *Brit. slang.* to divulge a secret. **3. stand the gaff.** *Slang, chiefly U.S.* to endure ridicule, difficulties, etc. [C19: of unknown origin]

gaff[3] (gæf) *n. Brit. slang, archaic.* **1.** a person's home, esp. a flat. **2.** Also called: **penny-gaff.** a cheap or low-class place of entertainment, esp. a cheap theatre or music hall in Victorian England. [C18: of unknown origin]

gaffe (gæf) *n.* a social blunder, esp. a tactless remark. [C19: from French]

gaf·fer (ˈgæfə) *n.* **1.** an old man, esp. one living in the country: often used affectionately or patronizingly. Compare **gammer. 2.** *Informal, chiefly Brit.* a boss, foreman, or owner of a factory, etc. **3.** the senior electrician on a television or film set. [C16: alteration of GODFATHER]

gaff-rigged *adj.* (of a sailing vessel) rigged with one or more gaffsails.

gaff·sail (ˈgæfˌseɪl, -səl) *n.* a quadrilateral fore-and-aft sail on a sailing vessel.

gaff-top·sail *n.* a sail set above a gaffsail.

gag[1] (gæg) *vb.* **gags, gag·ging, gagged. 1.** (*tr.*) to stop up (a person's mouth), esp. with a piece of cloth, etc., to prevent him from speaking or crying out. **2.** (*tr.*) *Informal.* to suppress or censor (free expression, information, etc.). **3.** *Slang.* to retch or cause to retch. **4.** (*intr.*) *Slang.* to struggle for breath; choke. **5.** (*tr.*) to hold (the jaws) of (a person or animal) apart with a surgical gag. **6.** (*tr.*) to apply a gag-bit to (a horse). ~*n.* **7.** a piece of cloth, rope, etc., stuffed into or tied across the mouth. **8.** *Informal.* any restraint on or suppression of information, free speech, etc. **9.** a surgical device for keeping the jaws apart, as during a tonsillectomy. **10.** *Parliamentary procedure.* another word for **closure** (sense 4). [C15 *gaggen;* perhaps imitative of a gasping sound]

gag[2] (gæg) *Slang.* ~*n.* **1.** a joke or humorous story, esp. one told by a professional comedian. **2.** a hoax, practical joke, etc.: *he did it for a gag.* ~*vb.* **gags, gag·ging, gagged. 3.** (*intr.*) to tell jokes or funny stories, as comedians in nightclubs, etc. **4.** (often foll. by *up*) *Theatre.* **a.** to interpolate lines or business not in the actor's stage part, usually comic and improvised. **b.** to perform a stage jest, either spoken or based on movement. [C19: perhaps special use of GAG[1]]

ga·ga (ˈgɑːgɑː) *adj. Slang.* **1.** senile; doting. **2.** slightly crazy. [C20: from French, of imitative origin]

Ga·ga·rin (*Russian* gaˈgarin) *n.* **Yu·ri** (ˈjʊrɪ). 1934–68, Soviet cosmonaut: made the first manned space flight (1961).

Ga·gau·zi (gəˈgɔːzɪ) *n.* a language spoken in the Soviet Union, chiefly on the NW coast of the Black Sea, belonging to the Turkic branch of the Altaic family.

gag-bit *n.* a powerful type of bit used in breaking horses.

gage[1] (geɪdʒ) *n.* **1.** something deposited as security against the fulfilment of an obligation; pledge. **2.** (formerly) a glove or other object thrown down to indicate a challenge to combat. ~*vb.* **3.** (*tr.*) *Archaic.* to stake, pledge, or wager. [C14: from Old French *gage,* of Germanic origin; compare Gothic *wadi* pledge]

gage[2] (geɪdʒ) *n.* short for **greengage.**

gage[3] (geɪdʒ) *n. Slang, chiefly U.S.* marijuana or a marijuana cigarette. [C20: of uncertain origin; compare GANJA]

gage[4] (geɪdʒ) *n., vb. U.S.* a variant spelling (esp. in technical senses) of **gauge.**

Gage (geɪdʒ) *n.* **Thom·as.** 1721–87, British general and governor in America; commander in chief of British forces at Bunker Hill (1775).

gag·er (ˈgeɪdʒə) *n.* a variant spelling of **gauger.**

gag·ger (ˈgægə) *n.* **1.** a person or thing that gags. **2.** a wedge for a core in a casting mould.

gag·gle (ˈgægəl) *vb.* **1.** (*intr.*) (of geese) to cackle. ~*n.* **2.** a flock of geese. **3.** *Informal.* a disorderly group of people. **4.** a gabbling or cackling sound. [C14: of Germanic origin; compare Old Norse *gagl* gosling, Dutch *gaggelen* to cackle, all of imitative origin]

gag rule *or* **res·o·lu·tion** *n. U.S.* any closure regulation adopted by a deliberative body.

gahn·ite (ˈgɑːnaɪt) *n.* a dark green mineral of the spinel group consisting of zinc aluminium oxide. Formula: $ZnAl_2O_4$. [C19: named after J. G. *Gahn* (1745–1818), Swedish chemist; see -ITE[1]]

Gai·a (ˈgeɪə) *n.* a variant spelling of **Gaea.**

gai·e·ty (ˈgeɪətɪ) *n., pl.* **·ties. 1.** the state or condition of being gay. **2.** festivity; merrymaking. **3.** colourful bright appearance. ~Also: **gayety.**

Gaik·war (ˈgaɪkwɑː) *n.* a variant spelling of **Gaekwar.**

Gail·lard Cut (gɪlˈjɑːd, ˈgeɪlɑːd) *n.* the SE section of the Panama Canal, cut through Culebra Mountain. Length: about 13 km (8 miles). Former name: **Culebra Cut.** [C19: named after David Du Bose *Gaillard* (1859–1913), American army engineer in charge of the work]

gail·lar·di·a (geɪˈlɑːdɪə) *n.* any plant of the North American genus *Gaillardia,* having ornamental flower heads with yellow or red rays and purple discs: family *Compositae* (composites). [C19: from New Latin, named after *Gaillard* de Marentonneau, 18th-century French amateur botanist]

gai·ly (ˈgeɪlɪ) *adv.* **1.** in a gay manner; merrily. **2.** with bright colours; showily.

gain[1] (geɪn) *vb.* **1.** (*tr.*) to acquire (something desirable); obtain. **2.** (*tr.*) to win in competition: *to gain the victory.* **3.** to increase, improve, or advance: *the car gained speed; the shares gained in value.* **4.** (*tr.*) to earn (a wage, living, etc.). **5.** (*intr.;* usually foll. by *on* or *upon*) **a.** to get nearer (to) or catch up (on). **b.** to get farther away (from). **6.** (*tr.*) (esp. of ships) to get to; reach: *the steamer gained port.* **7.** (of a timepiece) to operate too fast, so as to indicate a time ahead of the true time: *this watch gains; it gains ten minutes a day.* **8. gain ground.** to make progress or obtain an advantage. **9. gain time.** to obtain extra time by a delay or postponement. ~*n.* **10.** something won, acquired, earned, etc.; profit; advantage. **11.** an increase in size, amount, etc. **12.** the act of gaining; attainment; acquisition. **13.** Also called: **amplification.** *Electronics.* the ratio of the output power of an amplifier to the power fed into it, usually measured in decibels. [C15: from Old French *gaaignier,* of Germanic origin; related to Old High German *weidenen* to forage, hunt] —**'gain·a·ble** *adj.*

gain[2] (geɪn) *n.* **1.** a notch, mortise, or groove, esp. one cut to take the flap of a butt hinge. ~*vb.* **2.** (*tr.*) to cut a gain or gains in. [C17: of obscure origin]

gain·er (ˈgeɪnə) *n.* **1.** a person or thing that gains. **2.** Also called: **full gainer.** a type of dive in which the diver leaves the board facing forward and completes a full backward somersault to enter the water feet first with his back to the diving board. Compare **half gainer.**

gain·ful (ˈgeɪnfʊl) *adj.* profitable; lucrative: *gainful employment.* —**'gain·ful·ly** *adv.* —**'gain·ful·ness** *n.*

gain·ings (ˈgeɪnɪŋz) *pl. n.* profits or earnings.

gain·ly (ˈgeɪnlɪ) *Obsolete or dialect.* ~*adj.* **1.** graceful or well-formed; shapely. ~*adv.* **2.** conveniently or suitably. —**'gain·li·ness** *n.*

gains (geɪnz) *pl. n.* profits or winnings: *ill-gotten gains.*

gain·say (geɪnˈseɪ) *vb.* **·says, ·say·ing, ·said.** (*tr.*) *Archaic or literary.* to deny (an allegation, statement, etc.); contradict. [C13 *gainsaien,* from *gain-* AGAINST + *saien* to SAY] —**gain'say·er** *n.*

Gains·bor·ough (ˈgeɪnzbərə, -brə) *n.* **Thom·as.** 1727–88, English painter, noted particularly for his informal portraits and for his naturalistic landscapes.

'gainst *or* **gainst** (gɛnst, geɪnst) *prep. Poetic.* short for **against.**

Gai·ser·ic (ˈgaɪzərɪk) *n.* a variant of **Genseric.**

gait (geɪt) *n.* **1.** manner of walking or running, esp. the manner in which a horse walks or runs, as the walk, trot, canter, etc. ~*vb.* **2.** (*tr.*) to teach (a horse) a particular gait. [C16: variant of GATE[1]]

-gait·ed (-ˈgeɪtɪd) *adj.* (*in combination*) having a gait as specified: *slow-gaited.*

gait·er (ˈgeɪtə) *n.* (*often pl.*) **1.** a cloth or leather covering for the leg or ankle buttoned on one side and usually strapped under the foot. **2.** Also called: **spat.** a similar covering extending from the ankle to the instep. [C18: from French *guêtre*, probably of Germanic origin and related to WRIST] —**'gait+er+less** *adj.*

Gait·skell ('geɪtskɪl) *n.* **Hugh Todd Nay·lor.** 1906–63, English politician; leader of the Labour Party (1955–63).

Gai·us ('gaɪəs) *or* **Cai·us** *n.* **1.** ?110–?180 A.D., Roman jurist. His *Institutes* were used as the basis for those of Justinian. **2. Gaius Caesar.** See **Caligula.**

gal[1] (gæl) *n. Slang.* a girl.

gal[2] (gæl) *n.* a unit of acceleration equal to 1 centimetre per second per second. [C20: named after GALILEO]

gal *or* **gal.** *abbrev. for* gallon.

Gal. *abbrev. for* Galatians.

ga·la ('gɑːlə, 'geɪlə) *n.* **1. a.** a celebration; festive occasion. **b.** (*as modifier*): *a gala occasion.* **2.** *Chiefly Brit.* a sporting occasion involving competitions in several events: *a swimming gala.* [C17: from French or Italian, from Old French *gale* pleasure, from Old French *galer* to make merry, probably of Germanic origin; compare GALLANT]

ga+lac+ta+gogue (gəˈlæktəˌgɒg) *adj.* **1.** inducing milk secretion. ~*n.* **2.** a galactagogue agent. [C19: from GALACT- + -AGOGUE]

ga+lac+tic (gəˈlæktɪk) *adj.* **1.** *Astronomy.* of or relating to a galaxy, esp. the Galaxy: *the galactic plane.* **2.** *Med.* of or relating to milk. [C19: from Greek *galaktikos*; see GALAXY]

ga+lac+tic e·qua+tor *or* **cir+cle** *n.* the great circle on the celestial sphere containing the galactic plane.

ga+lac+tic plane *n.* the plane passing through the spiral arms of the Galaxy.

ga+lac+tic poles *pl. n.* the two points on the celestial sphere, diametrically opposite each other, that can be joined by an imaginary line perpendicular to the galactic plane.

ga·lac·to- *or before a vowel* **ga·lact-** *combining form.* milk or milky: *galactometer.* [from Greek *galakt-, gala*]

gal+ac+tom+e+ter (ˌgæləkˈtɒmɪtə) *n.* an instrument, similar to a hydrometer, for measuring the relative density of milk. It is used to determine the fat content. —**ˌgal+ac+'tom+e+try** *n.*

ga+lac+to+poi+et+ic (gəˌlæktəʊpɔɪˈɛtɪk) *adj.* **1.** inducing or increasing the secretion of milk. ~*n.* **2.** a galactopoietic agent. —**ga+lac+to+poi+e+sis** (gəˌlæktəʊpɔɪˈiːsɪs) *n.*

ga+lac+tose (gəˈlæktəʊz, -əʊs) *n.* a white water-soluble monosaccharide found in lactose. Formula: $C_6H_{12}O_6$.

ga+la+go (gəˈlɑːgəʊ) *n., pl.* **+gos.** another name for **bushbaby.** [C19: from New Latin, perhaps from Wolof *golokh* monkey]

ga+lah (gəˈlɑː) *n.* **1.** an Australian cockatoo, *Kakatoe roseicapilla*, having grey wings, back, and crest and a pink body. **2.** *Austral. slang.* a fool or simpleton. [C19: from a native Australian language]

Gal·a·had ('gæləˌhæd) *n.* **1. Sir.** (in Arthurian legend) the most virtuous knight of the Round Table, destined to regain the Holy Grail; son of Lancelot and Elaine. **2.** a pure or noble man.

ga+lan+gal (gəˈlæŋgəl) *n.* **1.** another name for **galingale. 2.** a zingiberaceous plant, *Alpinia officinarum,* of China and the East Indies. **3.** the pungent aromatic root of this plant, dried and used as a seasoning and in medicine.

gal+an+tine ('gælənˌtiːn) *n.* a cold dish of meat or poultry, which is boned, cooked, stuffed, then pressed into a neat shape and glazed. [C14: from Old French, from Medieval Latin *galatina,* probably from Latin *gelātus* frozen, set; see GELATIN]

ga+lan+ty show (gəˈlæntɪ) *n.* (formerly) a pantomime shadow play, esp. one in miniature using figures cut from paper. [C19: perhaps from Italian *galante* GALLANT]

Ga+lá+pa+gos Is+lands (gəˈlæpəgəs; *Spanish* gaˈlapaˌɣos) *pl. n.* a group of 15 islands in the Pacific west of Ecuador, of which they form a province: discovered (1535) by the Spanish; main settlement on San Cristóbal. Pop.: 4000 (1973 est.). Area: 7844 sq. km (3059 sq. miles). Official Spanish name: **Archipiélago de Colón.**

Gal·a+shiels (ˌgæləˈʃiːlz) *n.* a town in SE Scotland, in the central Borders region. Pop.: 12 605 (1971).

Ga+la+ta ('gælətə) *n.* a port in NW Turkey, a suburb and the chief business section of Istanbul.

gal·a·te·a (ˌgæləˈtɪə) *n.* a strong twill-weave cotton fabric, striped or plain, for clothing. [C19: named after the man-of-war H.M.S. *Galatea,* (the fabric was at one time in demand for children's sailor suits)]

Gal·a·te·a (ˌgæləˈtɪə) *n. Greek myth.* a statue of a maiden brought to life by Aphrodite in response to the prayers of the sculptor Pygmalion, who had fallen in love with his creation.

Ga+lați (*Rumanian* gaˈlatsj) *n.* an inland port in SE Rumania, on the River Danube. Pop.: 197 853 (1974 est.).

Ga+la+tia (gəˈleɪʃə, -ʃɪə) *n.* an ancient region in central Asia Minor, conquered by Gauls 278–277 B.C.: later a Roman province. —**Ga+'la+tian** *adj., n.*

Ga+la+tians (gəˈleɪʃənz, -ʃɪənz) *n.* (*functioning as sing.*) a book of the New Testament (in full **The Epistle of Paul the Apostle to the Galatians**).

gal+ax·y ('gæləksɪ) *n., pl.* **+ax·ies. 1.** any of a vast number of star systems held together by gravitational attraction in an asymmetric shape (an **irregular galaxy**) or, more usually, in a symmetrical shape (a **regular galaxy**), which is either a spiral or an ellipse. Former names: **island universe, extragalactic nebula. 2.** a splendid gathering, esp. one of famous or distinguished people. [C14 (in the sense: the Milky Way), from Medieval Latin *galaxia,* from Latin *galaxias,* from Greek, from *gala* milk; related to Latin *lac* milk]

Gal+ax·y ('gæləksɪ) *n.* **the.** the spiral galaxy, approximately 100 000 light years in diameter, that contains the solar system about three fifths of the distance from its centre. Also called: the **Milky Way System.** See also **Magellanic Cloud.**

Gal·ba ('gælbə) *n.* **Ser·vi·us Sul·pi·cius** ('sɜːvɪəs sʌlˈpɪʃəs). ?3 B.C.–69 A.D., Roman emperor (68–69) after the assassination of Nero.

gal+ba+num ('gælbənəm) *n.* a bitter aromatic gum resin extracted from any of several Asian umbelliferous plants of the genus *Ferula,* esp. *F. galbaniflua,* and used in incense and medicinally as a counterirritant. [C14: from Latin, from Greek *khalbanē,* from Hebrew *helbenāh*]

Gal·braith ('gælbreɪθ) *n.* **John Ken·neth.** born 1908, U.S. economist and diplomat; author of *The Affluent Society* (1958) and *The New Industrial State* (1967).

gale[1] (geɪl) *n.* **1.** a strong wind, specifically one of force seven to ten on the Beaufort scale or from 45 to 90 kilometres per hour. **2.** (*often pl.*) *Informal.* a loud outburst, esp. of laughter. **3.** *Archaic and poetic.* a gentle breeze. [C16: of unknown origin]

gale[2] (geɪl) *n.* short for **sweet gale.** [Old English *gagel;* related to Middle Low German *gagel*]

ga+le·a ('geɪlɪə) *n., pl.* **+le·ae** (-lɪˌiː). a part or organ shaped like a helmet or hood, such as the petals of certain flowers. [C18: from Latin: helmet] —**'ga+le·ˌate** *or* **'ga+le·ˌat+ed** *adj.* —**'ga+le·i+ˌform** *adj.*

Ga·len ('geɪlən) *n.* Latin name *Claudius Galenus.* ?130–?200 A.D., Greek physician, anatomist, and physiologist. He codified existing medical knowledge and his authority continued until the Renaissance.

ga+le·na (gəˈliːnə) *or* **ga+le·nite** (gəˈliːnaɪt) *n.* a soft heavy bluish-grey or black mineral consisting of lead sulphide in cubic crystalline form, found principally in ore veins: the chief source of lead. Formula: PbS. [C17: from Latin: lead ore, dross left after melting lead]

Ga+len+ic (geɪˈlɛnɪk, gə-) *adj.* of or relating to Galen or his teachings or methods.

ga+len·i·cal (geɪˈlɛnɪkəl, gə-) *Pharmacol.* ~*n.* **1.** any drug obtained from plant or animal tissue, esp. vegetables, rather than being chemically synthesized. ~*adj.* **2.** denoting or belonging to this group of drugs. [C17: after GALEN]

Ga+len+ism ('geɪlɪˌnɪzəm) *n.* a system of medicine based on the 84 surviving technical treatises of Galen, including the theory of the four bodily humours. —**'Ga+len+ist** *adj., n.*

ga+lère *French.* (gaˈlɛːr) *n.* **1.** a group of people having a common interest, esp. a coterie of undesirable people. **2.** an unpleasant situation. [C18: literally: a galley]

Ga+li+bi (gɑːˈliːbɪ) *n.* **1.** (*pl.* **+bi** *or* **+bis**) a member of an American Indian people of French Guiana. **2.** the language of this people, belonging to the Carib family.

Ga+li+ci·a *n.* **1.** (gəˈlɪʃɪə, -ˈlɪʃə). a region of E central Europe on the N side of the Carpathians, now in SE Poland and the SW Soviet Union. **2.** (*Spanish* gaˈlɪθja). a region and former kingdom of NW Spain, on the Bay of Biscay and the Atlantic.

Ga+li·ci·an (gəˈlɪʃɪən, -ʃən) *adj.* **1.** of or relating to Galicia in E central Europe. **2.** of or relating to Galicia in NW Spain. ~*n.* **3.** a native or inhabitant of either Galicia. **4.** the Romance language or dialect of Spanish Galicia, sometimes regarded as a dialect of Spanish, although historically it is more closely related to Portuguese.

Gal·i+le·an[1] (ˌgælɪˈliːən) *n.* **1.** a native or inhabitant of Galilee. **2. a. the.** an epithet of Jesus Christ. **b.** (*often pl.*) a Christian. ~*adj.* **3.** of Galilee.

Gal·i+le·an[2] (ˌgælɪˈleɪən) *adj.* of or relating to Galileo.

Gal·i+le·an tel·e·scope *n.* a type of telescope with a convex objective lens and a concave eyepiece; it produces an erect image and is suitable for terrestrial use.

gal·i+lee ('gælɪˌliː) *n.* a porch or chapel at the entrance to some medieval churches and cathedrals in England.

Gal·i+lee ('gælɪˌliː) *n.* **1. Sea of.** Also called: Lake **Tiberias.** a lake in NE Israel, 209 m (696 ft.) below sea level, through which the River Jordan flows. Area: 165 sq. km (64 sq. miles). **2.** a northern region of Israel: scene of Christ's early ministry.

Gal·i·le·o (ˌgælɪˈleɪəʊ) *n.* full name *Galileo Galilei.* 1564–1642, Italian mathematician, astronomer and physicist. He discovered the isochronism of the pendulum and demonstrated that falling bodies of different weights descend at the same rate. He perfected the refracting telescope, which led to his discovery of Jupiter's satellites, sunspots, and craters on the moon. He was forced by the Inquisition to recant his support of the Copernican system.

gal·i·ma+ti+as (ˌgælɪˈmeɪʃɪəs, -ˈmætɪəs) *n. Rare.* confused talk; gibberish. [C17: from French, of unknown origin]

gal+in+gale ('gælɪŋˌgeɪl) *or* **ga+lan+gal** *n.* a European cyperaceous plant, *Cyperus longus,* with rough-edged leaves, reddish spikelets of flowers, and aromatic roots. [C13: from Old French *galingal,* from Arabic *khalanjān,* from Chinese *kaoliang-chiang,* from *Kaoliang* district in Kwangtung province + *chiang* ginger]

gal·i+ot *or* **gal+li+ot** ('gælɪət) *n.* **1.** a small swift galley formerly sailed on the Mediterranean. **2.** a shallow-draught ketch formerly used along the coasts of Germany and the Netherlands. [C14: from Old French *galiote,* from Italian *galeotta,* from Medieval Latin *galea* GALLEY]

gal·i+pot *or* **gal+li+pot** ('gælɪˌpɒt) *n.* a resin obtained from several species of pine, esp. from the S European *Pinus pinaster.* [C18: from French, of unknown origin]

gall[1] (gɔːl) *n.* **1.** *Informal.* impudence. **2.** bitterness; rancour. **3.** something bitter or disagreeable. **4.** *Physiol.* an obsolete term for **bile. 5.** an obsolete term for **gall bladder.** [from Old Norse, replacing Old English *gealla;* related to Old High German *galla,* Greek *kholē*]

gall[2] (gɔːl) *n.* **1.** a sore on the skin caused by chafing. **2.** something that causes vexation or annoyance: *a gall to the spirits.* **3.** irritation; exasperation. ~*vb.* **4.** *Pathol.* to abrade (the skin, etc.) as by rubbing. **5.** (*tr.*) to irritate or annoy; vex. [C14: of Germanic origin; related to Old English *gealla* sore on a horse, and perhaps to GALL[1]]

gall[3] (gɔːl) *n.* an abnormal outgrowth in plant tissue caused by certain parasitic insects, fungi, bacteria, or mechanical injury. [C14: from Old French *galle,* from Latin *galla*]

gall. *abbrev. for* gallon.

Gal+la ('gælə) *n.* **1.** (*pl.* **+las** *or* **+la**) a member of a tall dark-skinned people inhabiting Somalia and SE Ethiopia. **2.** the language of this people, belonging to the Cushitic subfamily of the Afro-Asiatic family of languages.

gal+lant *adj.* ('gælənt). **1.** brave and high-spirited; courageous and honourable; dashing: *a gallant warrior.* **2.** (gə'lænt, 'gælənt). (of a man) attentive to women; chivalrous. **3.** imposing; dignified; stately: *a gallant ship.* **4.** *Archaic.* showy in dress. ~*n.* ('gælənt, gə'lænt). **5.** a woman's lover or suitor. **6.** a dashing or fashionable young man, esp. one who pursues women. **7.** a brave, high-spirited, or adventurous man. ~*vb.* (gə'lænt, 'gælənt). *Rare.* **8.** (when *intr.,* usually foll. by *with*) to court or flirt (with). **9.** (*tr.*) to attend or escort (a woman). [C15: from Old French *galant,* from *galer* to make merry, from *gale* enjoyment, pleasure, of Germanic origin; related to Old English *wela* WEAL[2]] —'**gal+lant+ly** *adv.* —'**gal+lant+ness** *n.*

gal+lant+ry ('gæləntrɪ) *n., pl.* **+ries. 1.** conspicuous courage, esp. in war: *the gallantry of the troops.* **2.** polite attentiveness to women. **3.** a gallant action, speech, etc.

gal+lant sol+dier *n.* a South American plant, *Galinsoga parviflora,* widely distributed as a weed, having small daisy-like flowers surrounded by silvery scales: family *Compositae* (composites). Also called: **Joey Hooker.** [C20: by folk etymology from New Latin *Galinsoga*]

gall blad+der *n.* a muscular sac, attached to the right lobe of the liver, that stores bile and ejects it into the duodenum.

Gal+le ('gɑːlə) *n.* a port in SW Sri Lanka. Pop.: 73 000 (1971). Former name: **Point de Galle.**

gal+le·ass *or* **gal+li+ass** ('gælɪˌæs) *n. Nautical.* a three-masted lateen-rigged galley used as a warship in the Mediterranean from the 15th to the 18th centuries. [C16: from French *galleasse,* from Italian *galeazza,* from *galea* GALLEY]

gal+le·on ('gælɪən) *n. Nautical.* a large sailing ship having three or more masts, lateen-rigged on the after masts and square-rigged on the foremast and mainmast, used as a warship or trader from the 15th to the 18th centuries. [C16: from Spanish *galeón,* from French *galion,* from Old French *galie* GALLEY]

gal+ler·y ('gælərɪ) *n., pl.* **+ler·ies. 1.** a covered passageway open on one side or on both sides. See also **colonnade** (sense 1). **2. a.** a balcony running along or around the inside wall of a church, hall, etc. **b.** a covered balcony, sometimes with columns on the outside. **3.** *Theatre.* **a.** an upper floor that projects from the rear over the main floor and contains the cheapest seats. **b.** the seats there. **c.** the audience seated there. **4.** a long narrow room, esp. one used for a specific purpose: *a shooting gallery.* **5.** a room or building for exhibiting works of art. **6.** *Chiefly U.S.* a building or room where articles are sold at auction. **7.** an underground passage, as in a mine, the burrow of an animal, etc. **8.** *Theatre.* a narrow raised platform at the side or along the back of the stage for the use of technicians and stagehands. **9.** *Nautical.* a balcony or platform at the quarter or stern of a ship, sometimes used as a gun emplacement. **10.** a small ornamental metal or wooden balustrade or railing on a piece of furniture, esp. one surrounding the top of a desk, table, etc. **11.** any group of spectators, as at a golf match. **12. play to the gallery.** to try to gain popular favour, esp. by crude appeals. [C15: from Old French *galerie,* from Medieval Latin *galeria,* probably from *galilea* GALILEE] —'**gal+ler+ied** *adj.*

gal+ler·y for+est *n.* a stretch of forest along a river in an area of otherwise open country.

gal+ley ('gælɪ) *n.* **1.** any of various kinds of ship propelled by oars or sails used in ancient or medieval times as a warship or as a trader. **2.** the kitchen of a ship, boat, or aircraft. **3.** any of various long rowing boats. **4.** *Printing.* **a.** (in hot-metal composition) a tray open at one end for holding composed type. **b.** short for **galley proof.** [C13: from Old French *galie,* from Medieval Latin *galea,* from Greek *galaia,* of unknown origin; the sense development apparently is due to the association of a galley or slave ship with a ship's kitchen and hence with a hot furnace, trough, printer's tray, etc.]

gal+ley proof *n.* a printer's proof, esp. one taken on a long strip of paper from type in a galley, used to make corrections before the matter has been split into pages. Often shortened to **galley.**

gal+ley slave *n.* **1.** a criminal or slave condemned to row in a galley. **2.** *Informal.* a drudge.

gal·ley-west *adv. Slang, chiefly U.S.* into confusion, inaction, or unconsciousness (esp. in the phrase **knock (someone** *or* **something) galley-west**). [C19: from English dialect *collywest* awry, perhaps from *Collyweston,* a village in Northamptonshire]

gall+fly ('gɔːlˌflaɪ) *n., pl.* **+flies.** any of several small insects that produce galls in plant tissues, such as the gall wasp and gall midge.

Gal+li·a ('gælɪə) *n.* the Latin name of **Gaul.**

gal+li+am+bic (ˌgælɪ'æmbɪk) *Prosody.* ~*adj.* **1.** of or relating to a metre consisting of four lesser Ionics, used by Callimachus and Catullus and imitated by Tennyson in *Boadicea.* ~*n.* **2.** a verse in this metre. [C19: from Latin *galliambus* song of the *Galli* (priests of Cybele)]

gal+liard ('gæljəd) *n.* **1.** a spirited dance in triple time for two persons, popular in the 16th and 17th centuries. **2.** a piece of music composed for this dance. ~*adj.* **3.** *Archaic.* lively; spirited. [C14: from Old French *gaillard* valiant, perhaps of Celtic origin]

gal+lic[1] ('gælɪk) *adj.* of or containing gallium in the trivalent state. [C18: from GALL(IUM) + -IC]

gal+lic[2] ('gælɪk) *adj.* of, relating to, or derived from plant galls. [C18: from French *gallique;* see GALL[3]]

Gal+lic ('gælɪk) *adj.* **1.** of or relating to France. **2.** of or relating to ancient Gaul or the Gauls.

gal+lic ac·id *n.* a colourless crystalline compound obtained from tannin: used as a tanning agent and in making inks, paper, and pyrogallol; 3,4,5-trihydroxybenzoic acid. Formula: $C_6H_2(OH)_3COOH$.

Gal+li+can ('gælɪkən) *adj.* **1.** of or relating to Gallicanism. ~*n.* **2.** an upholder of Gallicanism.

Gal+li+can+ism ('gælɪkəˌnɪzəm) *n.* a movement among French Roman Catholic clergy that favoured the restriction of papal control and greater autonomy for the French church. Compare **ultramontanism.**

Gal+li·ce ('gælɪsɪ) *adv.* in French. [C19: from Latin]

Gal+li+cism ('gælɪˌsɪzəm) *n.* a word or idiom borrowed from French.

Gal+li+cize *or* **Gal+li+cise** ('gælɪˌsaɪz) *vb.* to make or become French in attitude, language, etc. —ˌ**Gal+li+ci+'za+tion** *or* ˌ**Gal+li+ci+'sa+tion** *n.* —'**Gal+li+ˌciz+er** *or* '**Gal+li+ˌcis+er** *n.*

gal+li+gas+kins *or* **gal+ly+gas+kins** (ˌgælɪ'gæskɪnz) *pl. n.* **1.** loose wide breeches or hose, esp. as worn by men in the 17th century. **2.** leather leggings, as worn in the 19th century. [C16: from obsolete French *gargues*q*ues,* from Italian *grechesco* Greek, from Latin *Graecus*]

gal+li+mau+fry (ˌgælɪ'mɔːfrɪ) *n., pl.* **+fries.** *Chiefly U.S.* a jumble; hotchpotch. [C16: from French *galimafrée* ragout, hash, of unknown origin]

gal+li+na+cean (ˌgælɪ'neɪʃən) *n.* any gallinaceous bird.

gal+li+na+ceous (ˌgælɪ'neɪʃəs) *adj.* **1.** of, relating to, or belonging to the *Galliformes,* an order of birds, including domestic fowl, pheasants, grouse, etc., having a heavy rounded body, short bill, and strong legs. **2.** of, relating to, or resembling the domestic fowl. [C18: from Latin *gallīnāceus,* from *gallīna* hen]

Ga+lli+nas Point (gɑː'jiːnəs) *n.* a cape in NE Colombia: the northernmost point of South America. Spanish name: **Pun+ta Ga+lli+nas** ('punta ga'jinas).

gall+ing ('gɔːlɪŋ) *adj.* **1.** irritating, exasperating, or bitterly humiliating. **2.** *Obsolete.* rubbing painfully; chafing. —'**gall+ing+ly** *adv.*

gal+li+nule ('gælɪˌnjuːl) *n.* **1.** any of various aquatic birds of the genera *Porphyrio* and *Porphyrula,* typically having a dark plumage, red bill, and a red shield above the bill: family *Rallidae* (rails). **2. common gallinule.** the U.S. name for **moorhen** (sense 1). [C18: from New Latin *Gallīnula* genus name, from Late Latin: pullet, chicken, from Latin *gallīna* hen]

gal+li+ot ('gælɪət) *n.* a variant spelling of **galiot.**

Gal+lip·o+li (gə'lɪpəlɪ) *n.* **1.** a peninsula in NW Turkey, between the Dardanelles and the Gulf of Saros: scene of a costly but unsuccessful Allied campaign in World War I. **2.** a port in NW Turkey, at the entrance to the Sea of Marmara: historically important for its strategic position. Pop.: 14 600 (1970). Turkish name: **Gelibolu.**

gal+li+pot[1] ('gælɪˌpɒt) *n.* a small earthenware pot used by pharmacists as a container for ointments, etc. [C16: probably from GALLEY + POT[1]; so called because imported in galleys]

gal+li+pot[2] ('gælɪˌpɒt) *n.* a variant spelling of **galipot.**

gal+li·um ('gælɪəm) *n.* a silvery metallic element that is liquid for a wide temperature range. It occurs in trace amounts in some ores and is used in high-temperature thermometers, semiconductors, and low-melting alloys. Symbol: Ga; atomic no.: 31; atomic wt.: 69.72; valency: 2 or 3; relative density: 5.91; melting pt.: 29.78°C; boiling pt.: 2403°C. [C19: from New Latin, from Latin *gallus* cock, translation of French *coq* in the name of its discoverer, *Lecoq* de Boisbaudran, 19th-century French chemist]

gal+li+vant, gal·i+vant, *or* **gal·a+vant** ('gælɪˌvænt) *vb.* (*intr.*) to go about in search of pleasure, etc.; gad about. [C19: perhaps whimsical modification of GALLANT]

Gäl+li+va+re (*Swedish* 'jɛlɪˌvaːrə) *n.* a town in N Sweden, within the Arctic Circle: iron mines. Pop.: 25 417 (1970).

gal+li+wasp ('gælɪˌwɒsp) *n.* any lizard of the Central American genus *Diploglossus,* esp. *D. monotropis* of the West Indies: family *Anguidae.* [C18: of unknown origin]

gall midge *n.* any of various small fragile mosquito-like dipterous flies constituting the widely distributed family *Cecidomyidae,* many of which have larvae that produce galls on plants. Also called: **gallfly, gall gnat.** See also **Hessian fly.**

gall+nut ('gɔːlˌnʌt) *or* **gall-ap·ple** *n.* a type of plant gall that resembles a nut.

Gal·lo- ('gæləʊ-) *combining form.* denoting Gaul or France: *Gallo-Roman.* [from Latin *Gallus* a Gaul]

gal+lo+glass *or* **gal+low+glass** ('gæləʊˌglɑːs) *n.* any heavily armed military retainer of a chieftain in a Celtic country, esp. in Ireland from the 14th to the 16th century. [C16: from Irish Gaelic *gallóglach,* from *gall* foreigner + *óglach,* servant]

gal+lon ('gælən) *n.* **1.** Also called: **imperial gallon.** *Brit.* a unit of capacity equal to 277.42 cubic inches. 1 Brit. gallon is equivalent to 1.20 U.S. gallons or 4.55 litres. **2.** *U.S.* a unit of capacity equal to 231 cubic inches. 1 U.S. gallon is equivalent to 0.83 Brit. gallon or 3.79 litres. [C13: from Old Northern French *galon* (Old French *jalon*), perhaps of Celtic origin]

gal+lon+age ('gælənɪdʒ) *n.* **1.** a capacity measured in gallons. **2.** the rate of pumping, transmission, or consumption of a fluid in gallons per unit of time.

gal+loon (gə'lu:n) *n.* a narrow band of cord, embroidery, silver or gold braid, etc., used on clothes and furniture. [C17: from French *galon*, from Old French *galonner* to trim with braid, of unknown origin] **—gal+'looned** *adj.*

gal+loot (gə'lu:t) *n.* a variant spelling of **galoot.**

gal+lop ('gæləp) *vb.* **1.** (of a horse or other quadruped) to run fast with a two-beat stride in which all four legs are off the ground at once. **2.** to ride (a horse, etc.) at a gallop. **3.** (*intr.*) *Informal.* to move, read, talk, etc., rapidly; hurry. *~n.* **4.** the fast two-beat gait of horses and other quadrupeds. **5.** an instance of galloping. [C16: from Old French *galoper*, of uncertain origin] **—'gal+lop+er** *n.*

gal+lo+pade *or* **gal+o+pade** (ˌgælə'peɪd) *n.* another word for **galop.**

gal+lop+ing ('gæləpɪŋ) *adj.* (*prenominal*) progressing at or as if at a gallop: *galloping consumption.*

Gal·lo-Ro·mance *or* **Gal·lo-Ro·man** *n.* **1.** the vernacular language or group of dialects, of which few records survive, spoken in France between about 600 A.D. and 900 A.D.; the intermediate stage between Vulgar Latin and Old French. *~adj.* **2.** denoting or relating to this language or the period during which it was spoken.

gal+lous ('gæləs) *adj.* of or containing gallium in the divalent state.

Gal+lo+way ('gæləˌweɪ) *n.* **1.** an area of SW Scotland, on the Solway Firth: consists of the former counties of Kirkcudbright and Wigtown, now part of Dumfries and Galloway region; in the west is a large peninsula, the **Rhinns of Galloway,** with the **Mull of Galloway,** a promontory, at the south end of it (the southernmost point of Scotland). Related adj.: **Galwegian. 2.** a breed of hardy black cattle originally bred in Galloway.

gal+lows ('gæləʊz) *n., pl.* **+lows·es** *or* **+lows. 1.** a wooden structure usually consisting of two upright posts with a crossbeam from which a rope is suspended, used for hanging criminals. **2.** any timber structure resembling this, such as (in Australia) a frame for hoisting up the bodies of slaughtered cattle. **3. the gallows.** execution by hanging. [C13: from Old Norse *galgi*, replacing Old English *gealga;* related to Old High German *galgo*]

gal+lows bird *n. Informal.* a person considered deserving of hanging.

gal+lows hu+mour *n.* sinister and ironic humour.

gal+lows tree *or* **gal+low tree** *n.* another name for **gallows.**

gall+stone ('gɔ:lˌstəʊn) *n. Pathol.* a small hard concretion of cholesterol, bile pigments, and lime salts, formed in the gall bladder or its ducts. Also called: **bilestone.**

Gal·lup ('gæləp) *n.* **George Hor·ace.** born 1901, U.S. statistician: devised the Gallup Poll; founded the American Institute of Public Opinion (1935) and its British counterpart (1936).

Gal+lup Poll ('gæləp) *n.* a sampling by the American Institute of Public Opinion or its British counterpart of the views of a representative cross-section of the population, used esp. as a means of forecasting voting.

gal+lus·es ('gæləsɪz) *pl. n. Dialect.* braces for trousers. [C18: variant spelling of *gallowses*, from GALLOWS (in the obsolete sense: braces)]

gall wasp *n.* any small solitary wasp of the family *Cynipidae* and related families that produces galls in plant tissue, which provide shelter and food for the larvae.

Gal·ois the·o+ry ('gælwɑ:) *n. Maths.* the theory applying group theory to solving algebraic equations. [C19: named after Évariste *Galois* (1811–32), French mathematician]

ga+loot *or* **gal+loot** (gə'lu:t) *n. Slang, chiefly U.S.* a clumsy or uncouth person. [C19: of unknown origin]

gal+op ('gæləp) *n.* **1.** a 19th-century couple dance in quick duple time. **2.** a piece of music composed for this dance. *~*Also: **gallopade.** [C19: from French; see GALLOP]

ga+lore (gə'lɔ:) *determiner.* (*immediately postpositive*) *Informal.* in great numbers or quantity: *there were daffodils galore in the park.* [C17: from Irish Gaelic *go leór* to sufficiency]

ga+losh·es *or* **go+losh·es** (gə'lɒʃɪz) *pl. n.* (*sometimes sing.*) a pair of waterproof overshoes. [C14 (in the sense: wooden shoe): from Old French *galoche*, from Late Latin *gallicula* Gallic shoe]

Gals·wor·thy ('gɔ:lzˌwɜ:ðɪ) *n.* **John.** 1867–1933, English novelist and dramatist, noted for *The Forsyte Saga* (1906–28): Nobel prize for literature 1932.

Gal·ton ('gɔ:ltən) *n.* Sir **Fran·cis.** 1822–1911, English explorer and scientist, a cousin of Charles Darwin, noted for his researches in heredity, meteorology, and statistics. He founded the study of eugenics and the theory of anticyclones.

ga+lumph (gə'lʌmpf, -'lʌmf) *vb.* (*intr.*) *Informal.* to leap or move about clumsily or joyfully. [C19 (coined by Lewis Carroll): probably a blend of GALLOP + TRIUMPH]

galv. *abbrev. for:* **1.** galvanic. **2.** galvanism.

Gal·va·ni (*Italian* gal'va:ni) *n.* **Lu·i·gi** (lʊ'i:dʒi). 1737–98, Italian physiologist: observed that muscles contracted on contact with dissimilar metals. This led to the galvanic cell and the electrical theory of muscle control by nerves.

gal+van+ic (gæl'vænɪk) *or* **gal+van·i+cal** *adj.* **1.** Also called: **voltaic.** of, producing, or concerned with an electric current, esp. a direct current produced chemically: *a galvanic cell.* **2.** *Informal.* resembling the effect of an electric shock; convulsive, startling, or energetic: *galvanic reflexes.* **—gal+'van·i+cal+ly** *adv.*

gal+van+ic pile *n.* another name for **voltaic pile.**

gal+va+nism ('gælvəˌnɪzəm) *n.* **1.** *Obsolete.* electricity, esp. when produced by chemical means as in a cell or battery. **2.** *Med.* treatment involving the application of electric currents to tissues. [C18: via French from Italian *galvanismo*, after GALVANI]

gal+va+nize *or* **gal+va+nise** ('gælvəˌnaɪz) *vb.* (*tr.*) **1.** to stimulate to action; excite; startle. **2.** to cover (iron, steel, etc.) with a protective zinc coating by dipping into molten zinc or by electrodeposition. **3.** to stimulate by application of an electric current. *~n.* **4.** *Caribbean.* galvanized iron, usually in the form of corrugated sheets as used in roofing. **—ˌgal+va+ni+'za+tion** *or* **ˌgal+va+ni+'sa+tion** *n.* **—'gal+va+ˌniz+er** *or* **'gal+va+ˌnis+er** *n.*

gal·van·o- *combining form.* indicating a galvanic current: *galvanometer.*

gal+va+nom+e·ter (ˌgælvə'nɒmɪtə) *n.* any sensitive instrument for detecting or measuring small electric currents. **—gal+va+no+met+ric** (ˌgælvənəʊ'mɛtrɪk, gælˌvænə-) *or* **ˌgal+va+no+'met+ri+cal** *adj.* **—ˌgal+va+no+'met+ri+cal+ly** *adv.* **—ˌgal+va+'nom+e·try** *n.*

gal+va+no+scope ('gælvənəˌskəʊp, gæl'vænə-) *n.* a galvanometer that depends for its action on the deflection of a magnetic needle in a magnetic field produced by the electric current that is to be detected. **—gal+va+no+scop+ic** (ˌgælvənə'skɒpɪk, gælˌvænə-) *adj.* **—ˌgal+va+'nos+co+py** *n.*

gal+va+not+ro+pism (ˌgælvə'nɒtrəˌpɪzəm) *n.* the directional growth of an organism, esp. a plant, in response to an electrical stimulus. **—gal+va+no+trop+ic** (ˌgælvənəʊ'trɒpɪk, gælˌvænəʊ-) *adj.*

Gal+ves+ton plan ('gælvɪstən) *n.* another term for **commission plan.**

gal+vo ('gælvəʊ) *n., pl.* **+vos.** an informal name for a **galvanometer.**

Gal+way[1] ('gɔ:lweɪ) *n.* **1.** a county of W Ireland, in S Connacht, on **Galway Bay** and the Atlantic: it has a deeply indented coastline and many offshore islands, including the Aran Islands. County town: Galway. Pop.: 149 223 (1971). Area: 5939 sq. km (2293 sq. miles). **2.** a port in W Ireland, county town of Co. Galway, on Galway Bay: important fisheries (esp. for salmon). Pop.: 27 726 (1971).

Gal·way[2] ('gɔ:lweɪ) *n.* **James.** born 1939, Irish flautist.

Gal+we+gian (gæl'wi:dʒən) *n.* **1.** a native or inhabitant of Galloway. *~adj.* **2.** of or relating to Galloway. [C18: influenced by *Norway, Norwegian*]

gal+yak *or* **gal+yac** ('gæljæk, gæl'jæk) *n.* a smooth glossy fur obtained from the skins of newborn or premature lambs and kids. [from Russian (Uzbekistan dialect)]

gam[1] (gæm) *n.* **1.** a school of whales. **2.** *Nautical.* an informal visit between crew members of whalers. *~vb.* **gams, gam+ming, gammed. 3.** (*intr.*) (of whales) to form a school. **4.** *Nautical.* (of members of the crews of whalers) to visit (each other) informally. **5.** (*tr.*) *U.S. informal.* to visit or exchange visits with. [C19: perhaps dialect variant of GAME[1]]

gam[2] (gæm) *n. Slang.* a leg, esp. a woman's shapely leg. [C18: probably from Old Northern French *gambe;* see JAMB]

Ga·ma ('ga:mə) *n.* **Vas·co da** ('væskəʊ də). ?1469–1524, Portuguese navigator, who discovered the sea route from Portugal to India around the Cape of Good Hope (1498).

ga·ma grass ('gɑ:mə) *n.* a tall perennial grass, *Tripsacum dactyloides*, of SE North America: cultivated for fodder. [C19: *gama*, probably changed from GRAMA]

gam+ba ('gæmbə) *n.* short for **viola da gamba.**

gam+ba+do[1] (gæm'beɪdəʊ) *n., pl.* **+dos** *or* **+does. 1.** either of two leather holders for the feet attached to a horse's saddle like stirrups. **2.** either of a pair of leggings. [C17: from Italian *gamba* leg, from Late Latin: leg, hoof; see JAMB]

gam+ba+do[2] (gæm'beɪdəʊ) *or* **gam+bade** (gæm'beɪd, -'bɑ:d) *n., pl.* **+ba+dos, +ba+does,** *or* **+bades. 1.** *Dressage.* another word for **curvet. 2.** a leap or gambol; caper. [C19: from French *gambade* spring (of a horse), ultimately from Spanish or Italian *gamba* leg]

gam+ba stop ('gæmbə) *n.* an organ stop with a tone resembling that of stringed instruments.

gam+be·son ('gæmbɪsᵊn) *n.* a quilted and padded or stuffed leather or cloth garment worn under chain mail in the Middle Ages and later as a doublet by men and women. [C13: from Old French, of Germanic origin; related to Old High German *wamba* belly; see WOMB]

Gam·bet·ta (gæm'bɛtə; *French* gɑ̃bɛ'ta) *n.* **Lé·on** (le'ɔ̃). 1838–82, French statesman; prime minister (1881–82). He organized resistance during the Franco-Prussian War (1870–71) and was a founder of the Third Republic (1871).

Gam+bi·a ('gæmbɪə) *n.* a republic in W Africa, entirely surrounded by Senegal except for an outlet to the Atlantic: sold to English merchants by the Portuguese in 1588; became a British colony in 1843; gained independence within the Commonwealth in 1965; consists of a strip of land about 16 km (10 miles) wide, on both banks of the **Gambia River,** extending inland for about 480 km (300 miles). Official language: English. Religion: Muslim majority. Currency: dalasi. Capital: Banjul. Pop.: 493 197 (1973). Area: 11 295 sq. km (4361 sq. miles). Official name: **The Gambia. —'Gam+bi·an** *adj., n.*

gam+bier *or* **gam+bir** ('gæmbɪə) *n.* an astringent resinous substance obtained from a rubiaceous tropical Asian woody climbing plant, *Uncaria gambir* (or *U. gambier*): used as an astringent and tonic and in tanning. [C19: from Malay]

Gam+bier Is+lands ('gæmbɪə) *pl. n.* a group of islands in the S Pacific Ocean, in French Polynesia. Chief settlement: Rikitéa. Pop.: 1562 (1971). Area: 30 sq. km (11 sq. miles).

gam+bit ('gæmbɪt) *n.* **1.** *Chess.* an opening move in which a chessman, usually a pawn, is sacrificed to secure an advantageous position. **2.** an opening comment, manoeuvre, etc., intended to secure an advantage or promote a point of view. [C17: from French, from Italian *gambetto* a tripping up, from *gamba* leg]

gam+ble ('gæmbᵊl) *vb.* **1.** (*intr.*) to play games of chance to win money, etc. **2.** to risk or bet (money, etc.) on the outcome of an event, sport, etc. **3.** (*intr.;* often foll. by *on*) to act with the expectation of: *to gamble on its being a sunny day.* **4.** (often foll. by *away*) to lose by or as if by betting; squander. ~*n.* **5.** a risky act or venture. **6.** a bet, wager, or other risk or chance taken for possible monetary gain. [C18: probably variant of GAME[1]] —'**gam+bler** *n.* —'**gam+bling** *n.*

gam+boge (gæm'bəʊdʒ, -'buːʒ) *n.* **1. a.** a gum resin used as the source of a yellow pigment and as a purgative. **b.** the pigment made from this resin. **2. gamboge tree.** any of several tropical Asian trees of the genus *Garcinia,* esp. *G. hanburyi,* that yield this resin: family *Guttiferae.* **3.** a strong yellow colour. ~Also called (for senses 1, 2): **cambogia.** [C18: from New Latin *gambaugium,* from CAMBODIA] —**gam+'bo+gi+an** *adj.*

gam+bol ('gæmbᵊl) *vb.* **+bols, +bol+ling, +bolled** *or U.S.* **+bols, +bol+ing, +boled. 1.** (*intr.*) to skip or jump about in a playful manner; frolic. ~*n.* **2.** a playful antic; frolic. [C16: from French *gambade;* see GAMBADO[2], JAMB]

gam+brel ('gæmbrəl) *n.* **1.** the hock of a horse or similar animal. **2.** a frame of wood or metal shaped like a horse's hind leg, used by butchers for suspending carcasses of meat. **3.** short for **gambrel roof.** [C16: from Old Northern French *gamberel,* from *gambe* leg]

gam+brel roof *n.* **1.** *Chiefly Brit.* a hipped roof having a small gable at both ends. **2.** *Chiefly U.S.* a roof having two slopes on both sides, the lower slopes being steeper than the upper. Compare **mansard** (sense 1). ~Sometimes shortened to **gambrel.** —'**gam·brel-,roofed** *adj.*

Gam·bri·nus (gæm'braɪnəs) *n.* a legendary Flemish king who was said to have invented beer.

game[1] (geɪm) *n.* **1.** an amusement or pastime; diversion. **2.** a contest with rules, the result being determined by skill, strength, or chance. **3.** a single period of play in such a contest, sport, etc. **4.** the score needed to win a contest. **5.** a single contest in a series; match. **6.** equipment needed for playing certain games. **7.** style or ability in playing a game: *he is a keen player but his game is not good.* **8.** a scheme, proceeding, etc., practised like a game: *the game of politics.* **9.** an activity undertaken in a spirit of levity; joke: *marriage is just a game to him.* **10. a.** wild animals, including birds and fish, hunted for sport, food, or profit. **b.** (*as modifier*): *game laws.* **11.** the flesh of such animals, used as food. **12.** an object of pursuit; quarry; prey (esp. in the phrase **fair game**). **13.** *Informal.* work or occupation. **14.** *Informal.* a trick, strategy, or device: *I can see through your little game.* **15.** *Obsolete.* pluck or courage; bravery. **16.** *Slang, chiefly Brit.* prostitution (esp. in the phrase **on the game**). **17. give the game away.** to reveal one's intentions or a secret. **18. make (a) game of.** to make fun of; ridicule; mock. **19. on** (*or* **off**) **one's game.** playing well (or badly). **20. play the game.** *Informal.* to behave fairly or in accordance with rules. **21. the game is up.** there is no longer a chance of success. ~*adj.* **22.** *Informal.* full of fighting spirit; plucky; brave. **23.** (usually foll. by *for*) *Informal.* prepared or ready; willing: *I'm game for a try.* ~*vb.* **24.** (*intr.*) to play games of chance for money, stakes, etc.; gamble. [Old English *gamen;* related to Old Norse *gaman,* Old High German *gaman* amusement] —'**game+,like** *adj.* —'**game+ly** *adv.* —'**game+ness** *n.*

game[2] (geɪm) *adj.* a less common word for **lame** (esp. in the phrase **game leg**). [C18: of unknown origin]

game bird *n.* a bird of any species hunted as game.

game chips *pl. n.* round thin potato chips served with game.

game+cock ('geɪm,kɒk) *n.* a cock bred and trained for fighting. Also called: **fighting cock.**

game fish *n.* any fish providing sport for the angler.

game fowl *n.* any of several breeds of domestic fowl reared for cock-fighting.

game+keep·er ('geɪm,kiːpə) *n.* a person employed to take care of game and wildlife, as on an estate. —'**game+,keep·ing** *n.*

gam+e·lan ('gæmɪ,læn) *n.* a type of percussion orchestra common in the East Indies. [from Javanese]

game laws *pl. n.* laws governing the hunting and preservation of game.

game+ly ('geɪmlɪ) *adv.* in a brave or sporting manner.

game+ness ('geɪmnɪs) *n.* courage or bravery; pluck.

game point *n. Tennis, etc.* a point that would enable one player or side to win a game.

games+man+ship ('geɪmzmən,ʃɪp) *n. Informal.* the art of winning games or defeating opponents by clever or cunning practices without actually cheating. —'**games+man** *n.*

game+some ('geɪmsəm) *adj.* full of merriment; sportive. —'**game+some+ly** *adv.* —'**game+some+ness** *n.*

game+ster ('geɪmstə) *n.* a person who habitually plays games for money; gambler.

games the·o+ry *n.* a mathematical theory concerned with the optimum choice of strategy in situations involving a conflict of interest. Also called: **theory of games.**

gam+e·tan+gi·um (,gæmɪ'tændʒɪəm) *n., pl.* **+gi·a** (-dʒɪə). *Botany.* an organ or cell in which gametes are produced, esp. in algae and fungi. [C19: New Latin, from GAMETO- + Greek *angeion* vessel] —,**gam+e·'tan+gi·al** *adj.*

gam+ete ('gæmiːt, gə'miːt) *n.* a haploid reproductive cell, such as a spermatozoon or ovum, that can undergo fertilization. [C19: from New Latin, from Greek *gametē* wife, from *gamos* marriage] —**ga+'met+al** *or* **ga+met+ic** (gə'mɛtɪk) *adj.*

ga·me·to- *or sometimes before a vowel* **ga·met-** *combining form.* gamete: *gametocyte.*

ga+me·to+cyte (gə'miːtəʊ,saɪt) *n.* an animal or plant cell that develops into gametes by meiosis. See also **oocyte, spermatocyte.**

gam+e·to+gen+e·sis (,gæmɪtəʊ'dʒɛnɪsɪs) *or* **gam+e·tog+e·ny** (,gæmɪ'tɒdʒɪnɪ) *n.* the formation and maturation of gametes. See also **spermatogenesis, oogenesis.** —,**gam+e·to+'gen+ic** *or* ,**gam+e·'tog+e·nous** *adj.*

ga+me·to+phore (gə'miːtəʊ,fɔː) *n.* the part of a plant that bears the reproductive organs. —**ga+,me·to+'phor+ic** *adj.*

ga+me·to+phyte (gə'miːtəʊ,faɪt) *n.* the plant body, in species showing alternation of generations, that produces the gametes. Compare **sporophyte.** —**gam+e·to+phyt+ic** (,gæmɪtəʊ'fɪtɪk) *adj.*

game war+den *n.* a person who looks after game, as in a game reserve.

gam+ic ('gæmɪk) *adj.* (esp. of reproduction) requiring the fusion of gametes; sexual. [C19: from Greek *gamikos* of marriage; see GAMETE]

gam+in ('gæmɪn; *French* ga'mɛ̃) *n.* a street urchin; waif. [from French]

gam+ine ('gæmiːn; *French* ga'min) *n.* a slim and boyish girl or young woman; an elfish tomboy. [from French]

gam+ing ('geɪmɪŋ) *n.* **a.** gambling on games of chance. **b.** (*as modifier*): *gaming house; gaming losses.*

gam+ma ('gæmə) *n.* **1.** the third letter in the Greek alphabet (Γ, γ), a consonant, transliterated as *g.* When double, it is transcribed and pronounced as *ng.* **2.** the third highest grade or mark, as in an examination. **3.** a unit of magnetic field strength equal to 10^{-5} oersted. 1 gamma is equivalent to $0.795\,775 \times 10^{-3}$ ampere per metre. **4.** *Photog.* the numerical value of the slope of the characteristic curve of a photographic emulsion; a measure of the contrast reproduced in a photographic image. **5.** (*modifier*) **a.** involving or relating to photons of very high energy: *a gamma detector.* **b.** relating to one of two or more allotropes or crystal structures of a solid: *gamma iron.* **c.** relating to one of two or more isomeric forms of a chemical compound, esp. one in which a group is attached to the carbon atom next but one to the atom to which the principal group is attached. [C14: from Greek; related to Hebrew *gīmel* third letter of the Hebrew alphabet (probably: camel)]

Gam+ma ('gæmə) *n.* (*foll. by the genitive case of a specified constellation*) the third brightest star in a constellation: *Gamma Leonis.*

gam+ma+di+on (gæ'meɪdɪən) *n., pl.* **+di·a** (-dɪə). a decorative figure composed of a number of Greek capital gammas, esp. radiating from a centre, as in a swastika. [C19: from Late Greek, literally: little GAMMA]

gam+ma dis+tri+bu+tion *n. Statistics.* a continuous two-parameter distribution from which the chi-square and exponential distributions are derived.

gam+ma glob·u·lin *n.* any of a group of proteins in blood plasma that includes most known antibodies.

gam+ma i·ron *n.* an allotrope of iron that is nonmagnetic and exists between 910°C and 1400°C.

gam+ma ra+di·a·tion *n.* electromagnetic radiation of shorter wavelength and higher energy than x-rays, esp. the portion of the electromagnetic spectrum with a frequency greater than about 3×10^{19} hertz.

gam+ma rays *pl. n.* streams of gamma radiation.

gam+mer ('gæmə) *n. Rare, chiefly Brit.* a dialect word for an old woman: now chiefly humorous or contemptuous. Compare **gaffer** (sense 1). [C16: probably alteration of GODMOTHER or GRANDMOTHER]

gam+mon[1] ('gæmən) *n.* **1.** *Archaic.* the game of backgammon. **2.** a double victory in backgammon in which one player throws off all his pieces before his opponent throws any. ~*vb.* **3.** (*tr.*) to score such a victory over. [C18: probably special use of Middle English *gamen* GAME[1]]

gam+mon[2] ('gæmən) *n.* **1.** a cured or smoked ham. **2.** the hindquarter of a side of bacon, cooked either whole or cut into large rashers. [C15: from Old Northern French *gambon,* from *gambe* leg; see GAMBREL]

gam+mon[3] ('gæmən) *Brit. informal.* ~*n.* **1.** deceitful nonsense; humbug. ~*vb.* **2.** to deceive (a person). [C18: perhaps special use of GAMMON[1]] —'**gam+mon+er** *n.*

gam+mon[4] ('gæmən) *vb.* (*tr.*) *Nautical.* to fix (a bowsprit) to the stemhead of a vessel. [C18: perhaps related to GAMMON[2], with reference to the tying up of a ham]

gam+my ('gæmɪ) *adj.* **+mi+er, +mi+est.** *Brit. slang.* (esp. of the leg) malfunctioning, injured, or lame; game. U.S. equivalent: **gimpy.** [C19: dialect variant of GAME[2]]

gam·o- *or before a vowel* **gam-** *combining form.* **1.** indicating sexual union or reproduction: *gamogenesis.* **2.** united or fused: *gamopetalous.* [from Greek *gamos* marriage]

gam·o+gen+e·sis (,gæməʊ'dʒɛnɪsɪs) *n.* another name for **sexual reproduction.** —**gam·o·ge·net+ic** (,gæməʊdʒɪ'nɛtɪk) *or* ,**gam·o+ge·'net·i·cal** *adj.* —,**gam·o·ge·'net·i·cal+ly** *adv.*

gam·o+pet+al+ous (,gæməʊ'pɛtələs) *adj.* (of flowers) having petals that are united or partly united, as the primrose. Also: **sympetalous.** Compare **polypetalous.**

gam·o·phyl·lous (ˌgæməʊˈfɪləs) *adj.* (of flowers) having united leaves or perianth segments.

gam·o·sep·al·ous (ˌgæməʊˈsɛpələs) *adj.* (of flowers) having sepals that are united or partly united, as the primrose. Compare **polysepalous.**

gamp (gæmp) *n. Brit. informal.* an umbrella. [C19: after Mrs. Sarah *Gamp,* a nurse in Dickens' *Martin Chuzzlewit,* who carried a faded cotton umbrella]

gam·ut (ˈgæmət) *n.* **1.** entire range or scale, as of emotions. **2.** *Music.* **a.** a scale, esp. (in medieval theory) one starting on the G on the bottom line of the bass staff. **b.** the whole range of notes. [C15: from Medieval Latin, changed from *gamma ut,* from *gamma,* the lowest note of the hexachord as established by Guido d'Arezzo + *ut* (now, *doh*), the first of the notes of the scale *ut, re, mi, fa, sol, la, si,* derived from a Latin hymn to St. John: *Ut* queant laxis *re*sonare fibris, *Mi*ra gestorum *fa*muli tuorum, *Sol*ve polluti *la*bi reatum, *S*ancte *I*ohannes]

gam·y *or* **gam·ey** (ˈgeɪmɪ) *adj.* **gam·i·er, gam·i·est. 1.** having the smell or flavour of game, esp. high game. **2.** *Informal.* spirited; plucky; brave. —**ˈgam·i·ly** *adv.* —**ˈgam·i·ness** *n.*

-ga·my *n. combining form.* denoting marriage or sexual union: *bigamy.* [from Greek *-gamia,* from *gamos* marriage] —**-ga·mous** *adj. combining form.*

gan[1] (gæn) *vb. Archaic or poetic.* a past tense of **begin.**

gan[2] (gæn) *vb.* **gans, gan·ning, ganned.** (*intr.*) *Northeast English dialect.* to go. [from Old English *gangan;* related to Old Norse *ganga.* See GANG[1]]

Gance (*French* gɑ̃:s) *n.* **A·bel** (aˈbɛl). 1889-1981, French film director, whose works include *J'accuse* (1919, 1937) and *Napoléon* (1926), which introduced the split-screen technique.

Gand (gɑ̃) *n.* the French name for **Ghent.**

Gan·da (ˈgændə) *n.* **1.** (*pl.* **-das** *or* **-da**) a member of the Buganda people of Uganda, whose kingdom was formerly the largest in E Africa. See also **Luganda. 2.** the Luganda language of this people.

gan·der (ˈgændə) *n.* **1.** a male goose. **2.** *Informal.* a quick look (esp. in the phrase **take** (*or* **have**) **a gander**). **3.** *Informal.* a simpleton. [Old English *gandra, ganra;* related to Low German and Dutch *gander* and to GANNET]

Gan·dhi (ˈgændɪ) *n.* **1.** Mrs. **In·di·ra** (ɪnˈdɪərə, ˈɪndərə), daughter of Jawaharlal Nehru. born 1917, Indian stateswoman; prime minister of India (1966–77; since 1980). **2. Mo·han·das Kar·am·chand** (ˌməʊhənˈdʌs ˌkʌrəmˈtʃʌnd), known as *Mahatma Gandhi.* 1869–1948, Indian political and spiritual leader and social reformer. He played a major part in India's struggle for home rule and was frequently imprisoned by the British for organizing acts of civil disobedience. He advocated passive resistance and hunger strikes as means of achieving reform, campaigned for the untouchables, and attempted to unite Muslims and Hindus. He was assassinated by a Hindu extremist. —**Gan·dhi·an** (ˈgændɪən) *adj.*

Gan·dhi cap *n.* a cap made of white hand-woven cloth worn by some men in India.

Gan·dhi·ism (ˈgændɪˌɪzəm) *or* **Gan·dhism** *n.* the political principles of M. K. Gandhi, esp. civil disobedience and passive resistance as means of achieving reform.

gan·dy danc·er (ˈgændɪ) *n. Slang.* a railway track maintenance worker. [C20: of uncertain origin]

Gan·dzha (*Russian* ganˈdʒa) *n.* a former name (until 1813 and 1920–35) of **Kirovabad.**

ga·nef, ga·nev, ga·nof (ˈgɑ:nəf), **gon·if,** *or* **gon·of** *n. U.S. slang.* an unscrupulous opportunist who stoops to sharp practice. [from Yiddish, from Hebrew *gannābh* thief, from *gānnabh* he stole]

Ga·ne·sa (gæˈni:sə) *n.* the Hindu god of prophecy, represented as having an elephant's head.

gang[1] (gæŋ) *n.* **1.** a group of people who associate together or act as an organized body, esp. for criminal or illegal purposes. **2.** an organized group of workmen. **3.** a herd of buffalos or elks or a pack of wild dogs. **4. a.** a series of similar tools arranged to work simultaneously in parallel. **b.** (*as modifier*): *a gang saw.* ~*vb.* **5.** to form into, become part of, or act as a gang. **6.** (*tr.*) *Electronics.* to mount (two or more components, such as variable capacitors) on the same shaft, permitting adjustment by a single control. ~See also **gang up.** [Old English *gang* journey; related to Old Norse *gangr,* Old High German *gang,* Sanskrit *jangha* foot] —**ganged** *adj.*

gang[2] (gæŋ) *n.* a variant spelling of **gangue.**

Gan·ga jal (ˈgʌŋgɑ: ˈdʒʌl) *n.* sacred water from the River Ganges in India. [Hindi, from *Ganga* GANGES + *jal* water]

gang·bang (ˈgæŋˌbæŋ) *Slang.* ~*n.* **1.** an instance of sexual intercourse between one woman and several men one after the other, esp. against her will. ~*vb.* **2.** (*tr.*) to force (a woman) to take part in a gangbang. **3.** (*intr.*) to take part in a gangbang. ~Also called: **gang·shag.**

gang·er (ˈgæŋə) *n. Chiefly Brit.* the foreman of a gang of labourers.

Gan·ges (ˈgændʒi:z) *n.* the great river of N India and central Bangladesh: rises in two headstreams in the Himalayas and flows southeast to Allahabad, where it is joined by the Jumna; continues southeast into Bangladesh, where it enters the Bay of Bengal in a great delta; the most sacred river to Hindus, with many places of pilgrimage, esp. Varanasi. Length: 2507 km (1557 miles). Hindi name: **Gan·ga** (ˈgʌŋgə, ˈgɑ:ŋ-). —**Gan·get·ic** (gænˈdʒɛtɪk) *adj.*

gang·land (ˈgæŋˌlænd, -lənd) *n. Informal.* the criminal underworld.

gan·gling (ˈgæŋglɪŋ) *or* **gan·gly** *adj.* tall, lanky, and awkward in movement. [perhaps related to GANGREL; see GANG[1]]

gan·gli·on (ˈgæŋglɪən) *n., pl.* **-gli·a** (-glɪə) *or* **-gli·ons. 1.** an encapsulated collection of nerve-cell bodies, usually located outside the brain and spinal cord. **2.** any concentration or centre of energy, activity, or strength. **3.** a cystic tumour on a tendon sheath or joint capsule. [C17: from Late Latin: swelling, from Greek: cystic tumour] —**ˈgan·gli·al** *or* **ˈgan·gli·ar** *adj.* —**ˌgan·gli·ˈon·ic** *or* **ˈgan·gli·ˌat·ed** *adj.*

Gang of Four *n.* **the.** a radical faction within the Chinese Communist Party that emerged as a political force in the spring of 1976 and was suppressed later that year. Its members, Chang Ch'un-ch'iao, Wong Hung-wen, Yao Wen-yan, and Chiang Ch'ing, were tried and imprisoned (1981).

gang·plank (ˈgæŋˌplæŋk) *or* **gang·way** *n. Nautical.* a portable bridge for boarding and leaving a vessel at dockside.

gang plough *n.* a plough having two or more shares, coulters, and mouldboards designed to work simultaneously.

gan·grel (ˈgæŋgrəl, ˈgæŋrəl) *n. Scot. archaic or literary.* **1.** a wandering beggar. **2.** a child just able to walk; toddler. [C16: from Old English *gangan* to GO]

gan·grene (ˈgæŋgri:n) *n.* **1.** death and decay of tissue as the result of interrupted blood supply, disease, or injury. **2.** moral decay or corruption. [C16: from Latin *gangraena,* from Greek *gangraina* an eating sore; related to Greek *gran* to gnaw] —**gan·gre·nous** (ˈgæŋgrɪnəs) *adj.*

gang saw *n.* a saw having several parallel blades making simultaneous cuts. —**gang saw·yer** *n.*

gang·ster (ˈgæŋstə) *n.* a member of an organized gang of criminals, esp. one who resorts to violence.

Gang·tok (ˈgʌŋtɒk) *n.* a city in NE India: capital of Sikkim state. Pop.: 9000 (1968 est.).

gangue *or* **gang** (gæŋ) *n.* valueless and undesirable material, such as quartz in small quantities, in an ore. [C19: from French *gangue,* from German *Gang* vein of metal, course; see GANG[1]]

gang up *vb.* (often foll. by *on* or *against*) *Informal.* to combine in a group (against).

gang·way (ˈgæŋˌweɪ) *n.* **1.** Also called: **logway.** *Chiefly U.S.* a ramp for logs leading into a sawmill. **2.** another word for **gangplank. 3.** *Brit.* an aisle between rows of seats. **4.** a main passage in a mine. **5.** temporary planks over mud or earth, as on a building site. ~*interj.* **6.** clear a path!

gan·is·ter *or* **gan·nis·ter** (ˈgænɪstə) *n.* **1.** a highly refractory siliceous sedimentary rock occurring beneath coal seams: used for lining furnaces. **2.** a similar material synthesized from ground quartz and fireclay. [C19: of unknown origin]

gan·ja (ˈgɑ:ndʒə) *n.* a highly potent form of cannabis, usually used for smoking. [from Hindi *gājā,* from Sanskrit *grñja*]

gan·net (ˈgænɪt) *n.* any of several heavily built marine birds of the genus *Morus* (or *Sula*), having a long stout bill and typically white plumage with dark markings: family *Sulidae,* order *Pelecaniformes* (pelicans, cormorants, etc.). See also **booby** (sense 3). [Old English *ganot;* related to Old High German *gannazzo* gander]

ga·nof (ˈgɑ:nəf) *n.* a variant spelling of **ganef.**

gan·oid (ˈgænɔɪd) *adj.* **1.** (of the scales of certain fishes) consisting of an inner bony layer and an outer layer of an enamel-like substance (ganoin). **2.** denoting fishes, including the sturgeon and bowfin, having such scales. ~*n.* **3.** a ganoid fish. [C19: from French *ganoïde,* from Greek *ganos* brightness + -OID]

gan·sey (ˈgænzɪ) *n. Brit. dialect.* a jersey or pullover. [from the island of GUERNSEY]

gant·let[1] (ˈgæntlɪt, ˈgɔ:nt-) *n.* **1.** a section of a railway where two tracks overlap. **2.** *U.S.* a variant spelling of **gauntlet**[2]. [C17 *gantlope* (modern spelling influenced by GAUNTLET[1]), from Swedish *gatlopp,* literally: passageway, from *gata* way (related to GATE[3]) + *lop* course]

gant·let[2] (ˈgæntlɪt, ˈgɔ:nt-) *n.* a variant spelling of **gauntlet**[1].

gant·line (ˈgæntˌlaɪn, -lɪn) *n. Nautical.* a line rove through a sheave for hoisting men or gear. [C19: variant of *girtline;* see GIRT[1], LINE]

gan·try (ˈgæntrɪ) *or* **gaun·try** *n., pl.* **-tries. 1.** a bridgelike framework used to support a travelling crane, signals over a railway track, etc. **2.** Also called: **gantry scaffold.** the framework tower used to attend to a large rocket on its launching pad. **3.** a supporting framework for a barrel or cask. [C16 (in the sense: wooden platform for barrels): from Old French *chantier,* from Medieval Latin *cantārius,* changed from Latin *canthērius* supporting frame, pack ass; related to Greek *kanthēlios* pack ass]

Gan·y·mede[1] (ˈgænɪˌmi:d) *n. Classical myth.* a beautiful Trojan youth who was abducted by Zeus to Olympus and made the cupbearer of the gods.

Gan·y·mede[2] (ˈgænɪˌmi:d) *n.* the largest of the 12 satellites of Jupiter and the fourth nearest to the planet. Approximate diameter: 5000 km (3100 miles).

Ga·o (ˈgɑ:əʊ, gaʊ) *n.* a town in E Mali, on the River Niger: a small river port. Pop.: 15 400 (1967 est.).

gaol (dʒeɪl) *n., vb. Brit.* a variant spelling of **jail.** —**ˈgaol·er** *n.*

gap (gæp) *n.* **1.** a break or opening in a wall, fence, etc. **2.** a break in continuity; interruption; hiatus: *there is a serious gap in the accounts.* **3.** a break in a line of hills or mountains affording a route through. **4.** *Chiefly U.S.* a gorge or ravine. **5.** a divergence or difference; disparity: *there is a gap between his version of the event and hers; the generation gap.* **6.** *Electronics.* **a.** a break in a magnetic circuit that increases the inductance and saturation point of the circuit. **b.** See **spark gap. 7. bridge, close, fill,** *or* **stop a gap.** to remedy a deficiency. ~*vb.* **gaps, gap·ping, gapped. 8.** (*tr.*) to make a breach or opening in. [C14: from Old Norse *gap* chasm; related to *gapa* to GAPE, Swedish *gap*, Danish *gab* open mouth, opening] —'**gap+less** *adj.*

gape (geɪp) *vb.* (*intr.*) **1.** to stare in wonder or amazement, esp. with the mouth open. **2.** to open the mouth wide, esp. involuntarily, as in yawning or hunger. **3.** to be or become wide open: *the crater gaped under his feet.* ~*n.* **4.** the act of gaping. **5.** a wide opening; breach. **6.** the width of the widely opened mouth of a vertebrate. **7.** a stare or expression of astonishment. [C13: from Old Norse *gapa;* related to Middle Dutch *gapen*, Danish *gabe*] —'**gap+er** *n.* —'**gap+ing+ly** *adv.*

gapes (geɪps) *n.* (*functioning as sing.*) **1.** a disease of young domestic fowl, characterized by gaping or gasping for breath and caused by gapeworms. **2.** *Informal.* a fit of yawning. —'**gap·y** *adj.*

gape+worm ('geɪpˌwɜːm) *n.* a parasitic nematode worm, *Syngamus trachea*, that lives in the trachea of birds and causes gapes in domestic fowl: family *Syngamidae.*

gapped scale *n. Music.* a scale, such as a pentatonic scale, containing fewer than seven notes.

gap+ping ('gæpɪŋ) *n.* (in transformational grammar) a rule that deletes repetitions of a verb, as in the sentence *Bill voted for Smith, Sam for McKay, and Dave for Harris.*

gap-toothed *adj.* having wide spaces between the teeth.

gar (gɑː) *n., pl.* **gar** *or* **gars.** short for **garpike** (sense 1).

G.A.R. *abbrev. for* Grand Army of the Republic; an association of Unionist veterans of the American Civil War.

gar+age ('gærɑːʒ, -rɪdʒ) *n.* **1.** a building or part of a building used to house a motor vehicle. **2.** a commercial establishment in which motor vehicles are repaired, serviced, bought, and sold, and which usually also sells motor fuels. ~*vb.* **3.** (*tr.*) to put into, keep in, or take to a garage. [C20: from French, from *garer* to dock (a ship), from Old French: to protect, from Old High German *warōn;* see BEWARE]

ga+ram ma+sa+la ('gɑːrəm mɑː'sɑːlə) *n.* an aromatic mixture of spices, extensively used in curries, etc. [from Hindi]

Gar·a+mond ('gærəmɒnd) *n.* a typeface, designed by Claude Garamond (?1480–1561), French typefounder.

Gar+and ri+fle ('gærənd, gə'rænd) *n.* another name for **M-1 rifle.** [C20: named after John C. *Garand* (1888–1974), U.S. gun designer]

garb (gɑːb) *n.* **1.** clothes, esp. the distinctive attire of an occupation or profession: *clerical garb.* **2.** style of dress; fashion. **3.** external appearance, covering, or attire. ~*vb.* **4.** (*tr.*) to clothe or cover; attire. [C16: from Old French *garbe* graceful contour, from Old Italian *garbo* grace, probably of Germanic origin] —'**garb+less** *adj.*

gar+bage ('gɑːbɪdʒ) *n.* **1.** worthless, useless, or unwanted matter. **2.** another word (esp. U.S.) for **rubbish.** [C15: probably from Anglo-French *garbelage* removal of discarded matter, of uncertain origin; compare Old Italian *garbuglio* confusion]

gar+bage can *n.* a U.S. word for **dustbin.** Also called: **ash bin, ash can, trash can.**

gar+bage truck *n.* the U.S. name for **dustcart.**

gar+ban+zo (gɑː'bænzəʊ) *n., pl.* **+zos.** another name for **chick-pea.** [C18: from Spanish, from *arvanço*, probably of Germanic origin; compare Old High German *araweiz* pea]

gar+ble ('gɑːbᵊl) *vb.* (*tr.*) **1.** to jumble (a story, quotation, etc.), esp. unintentionally. **2.** to distort the meaning of (an account, text, etc.), as by making misleading omissions; corrupt. **3.** *Rare.* to select the best part of. ~*n.* **4. a.** the act of garbling. **b.** garbled matter. [C15: from Old Italian *garbellare* to strain, sift, from Arabic *gharbala*, from *ghirbāl* sieve, from Late Latin *cribellum* small sieve, from *crībrum* sieve] —'**gar+bler** *n.*

gar+bo ('gɑːbəʊ) *n., pl.* **gar+bos.** *Austral. informal.* a dustman. [C20: from GARBAGE]

Gar·bo ('gɑːbəʊ) *n.* **Gret·a** ('grɛtə). original name *Greta Louisa Gustafsson.* born 1905, U.S. film actress, born in Sweden: her films include *Grand Hotel* (1932), *Queen Christina* (1933), *Anna Karenina* (1935), *Camille* (1936), and *Ninotchka* (1939).

gar+board ('gɑːˌbɔːd) *n. Nautical.* the bottommost plank of a vessel's hull. Also called: **garboard plank, garboard strake.** [C17: from Dutch *gaarboord*, probably from Middle Dutch *gaderen* to GATHER + *boord* BOARD]

gar+boil ('gɑːbɔɪl) *n. Archaic.* confusion or disturbance; uproar. [C16: from Old French *garbouil*, from Old Italian *garbuglio*, ultimately from Latin *bullīre* to boil, hence, seethe with indignation]

Gar·cí·a Lor·ca (*Spanish* gar'θia 'lorka) *n.* See (Federico García) **Lorca.**

gar+çon (*French* gar'sɔ̃) *n.* a waiter or male servant, esp. if French. [C19: from Old French *gars* lad, probably of Germanic origin]

Gard (*French* gaːr) *n.* a department of S France, in Languedoc-Roussillon region. Capital: Nîmes. Pop.: 506 607 (1975). Area: 5881 sq. km (2294 sq. miles).

Gar+da ('gɑːdə) *n.* **Lake.** a lake in N Italy: the largest lake in the country. Area: 370 sq. km (143 sq. miles).

gar+dant ('gɑːdᵊnt) *adj.* a less common spelling of **guardant.**

gar+den ('gɑːdᵊn) *n.* **1.** *Brit.* **a.** an area of land, usually planted with grass, trees, flowerbeds, etc., adjoining a house. U.S. word: **yard. b.** (*as modifier*): *a garden chair.* **2. a.** an area of land used for the cultivation of ornamental plants, herbs, fruit, vegetables, trees, etc. **b.** (*as modifier*): *garden tools.* Related adj.: **horticultural. 3.** (*often pl.*) such an area of land that is open to the public, sometimes part of a park: *botanical gardens.* **4. a.** a fertile and beautiful region. **b.** (*as modifier*): *a garden paradise.* **5.** (*modifier*) provided with or surrounded by a garden or gardens: *a garden flat.* **6. lead (a person) up the garden path.** *Informal.* to mislead or deceive. **7. common or garden.** *Informal.* ordinary or commonplace. ~*vb.* **8.** to work in, cultivate, or take care of (a garden, plot of land, etc.). [C14: from Old French *gardin*, of Germanic origin; compare Old High German *gart* enclosure; see YARD[2] (sense 1)] —'**gar+den+less** *adj.* —'**gar·den-ˌlike** *adj.*

gar+den cen+tre *n.* a place where gardening tools and equipment, plants, seeds, etc., are sold.

gar+den cit·y *n. Brit.* a planned town of limited size surrounded by a rural belt. See also **garden suburb.**

gar+den cress *n.* a pungent-tasting cruciferous plant, *Lepidium sativum*, with white or reddish flowers: cultivated for salads, as a garnish, etc.

gar+den+er ('gɑːdnə) *n.* **1.** a person who works in or takes care of a garden as an occupation or pastime. **2.** any bowerbird of the genus *Amblyornis.*

gar+den frame *n.* another name for a **cold frame.**

gar+de·ni·a (gɑː'diːnɪə) *n.* **1.** any evergreen shrub or tree of the Old World tropical rubiaceous genus *Gardenia*, cultivated for their large fragrant waxlike typically white flowers. **2.** the flower of any of these shrubs. [C18: New Latin, named after Dr. Alexander *Garden* (1730–91), American botanist]

Gar+den of E·den *n.* the full name for **Eden.**

gar+den par+ty *n.* a social gathering held in the grounds of a house, school, etc., usually with light refreshments.

gar+den sub+urb *n. Brit.* a suburb of a large established town or city, planned along the lines of a garden city.

gar+den war+bler *n.* any of several small brownish-grey European songbirds of the genus *Sylvia* (warblers), esp. *S. borin*, common in woods and hedges: in some parts of Europe they are esteemed as a delicacy.

garde+robe ('gɑːdˌrəʊb) *n. Archaic.* **1.** a wardrobe or the contents of a wardrobe. **2.** a bedroom or private room. [C14: from French, from *garder* to keep + *robe* dress, clothing; see WARDROBE]

Gar·di·ner ('gɑːdnə) *n.* **Ste·phen.** ?1483–1555, English bishop and statesman; lord chancellor (1553–55). He opposed Protestantism, supporting the anti-Reformation policies of Mary I.

Gar·field ('gɑːˌfiːld) *n.* **James A·bram.** 1831–81, 20th president of the U.S. (1881); assassinated in office.

gar+fish ('gɑːˌfɪʃ) *n., pl.* **+fish** *or* **+fish·es. 1.** another name for **garpike. 2.** an elongated European marine teleost fish, *Belone belone*, with long toothed jaws: related to the flying fishes. [Old English *gār* spear + FISH]

gar+ga+ney ('gɑːgənɪ) *n.* a small Eurasian duck, *Anas querquedula*, closely related to the mallard. The male has a white stripe over each eye. [C17: from Italian dialect *garganei*, of imitative origin]

Gar·gan·tu·a (gɑː'gæntjʊə) *n.* a gigantic king noted for his great capacity for food and drink, in Rabelais' satire *Gargantua and Pantagruel* (1534).

gar+gan+tu·an (gɑː'gæntjʊən) *adj.* (*sometimes cap.*) huge; enormous.

gar+get ('gɑːgɪt) *n.* inflammation of the mammary gland of domestic animals, esp. cattle. [C16 (in the sense: throat): from Old French *gargate*, perhaps from Latin *gurges* gulf] —'**gar+get·y** *adj.*

gar+gle ('gɑːgᵊl) *vb.* **1.** to rinse the mouth and throat with (a liquid, esp. a medicinal fluid) by slowly breathing through the liquid. **2.** to utter (words, sounds, etc.) with the throaty bubbling noise of gargling. ~*n.* **3.** the liquid used for gargling. **4.** the sound produced by gargling. [C16: from Old French *gargouiller* to gargle, make a gurgling sound, from *gargouille* throat, perhaps of imitative origin] —'**gar+gler** *n.*

gar+goyle ('gɑːgɔɪl) *n.* **1.** a waterspout carved in the form of a grotesque face or creature and projecting from a roof gutter, esp. of a Gothic church. **2.** any grotesque ornament or projection, esp. on a building. **3.** a person with a grotesque appearance. [C15: from Old French *gargouille* gargoyle, throat; see GARGLE] —'**gar+goyled** *adj.*

gar·i+bal+di (ˌgærɪ'bɔːldɪ) *n.* **1.** a woman's loose blouse with long sleeves popular in the 1860s, copied from the red flannel shirt worn by Garibaldi's soldiers. **2.** *Brit.* a type of biscuit having a layer of currants in the centre.

Ga·ri·bal·di (ˌgærɪ'bɔːldɪ) *n.* **Giu·sep·pe** (dʒu'zɛppe). 1807–82, Italian patriot; a leader of the Risorgimento. He fought against the Austrians and French in Italy (1848–49; 1859) and, with 1000 volunteers, conquered Sicily and Naples for the emerging kingdom of Italy (1860).

gar+ish ('gɛərɪʃ) *adj.* gay or colourful in a crude or vulgar manner; gaudy. [C16: from earlier *gaure* to stare + -ISH] —'**gar+ish+ly** *adv.* —'**gar+ish+ness** *n.*

gar+land ('gɑːlənd) *n.* **1.** a wreath or festoon of flowers, leaves, etc., worn round the head or neck or hung up. **2.** a representation of such a wreath, as in painting, sculpture, etc. **3.** a collection of short literary pieces, such as ballads or poems; miscellany or anthology. **4.** *Nautical.* a ring or grommet of rope. ~*vb.* **5.** (*tr.*) to deck or adorn with a garland or garlands. [C14: from Old French *garlande*, perhaps of Germanic origin]

gar+lic ('gɑːlɪk) *n.* **1.** a hardy widely cultivated Asian alliaceous plant, *Allium sativum*, having a stem bearing whitish flowers and bulbils. **2. a.** the bulb of this plant, made up of small segments (cloves) that have a strong odour and pungent taste and are used in cooking. **b.** (*as modifier*): *a garlic taste.* **3.** any of various other plants of the genus *Allium.* [Old English *gārlēac*, from *gār* spear + *lēac* LEEK]

gar+lick·y ('gɑːlɪkɪ) *adj.* containing or resembling the taste or odour of garlic.

gar+lic mus+tard *n.* a cruciferous plant, *Alliaria petiolata*, of N temperate regions, with small white flowers and an odour of garlic. Also called: **jack-by-the-hedge, hedge garlic.** Compare **garlic.**

gar+ment ('gɑːmənt) *n.* **1.** (*often pl.*) an article of clothing. **2.** outer covering. ~*vb.* **3.** (*tr.; usually passive*) to cover or clothe. [C14: from Old French *garniment*, from *garnir* to equip; see GARNISH] —'**gar+ment+less** *adj.*

gar+ner ('gɑːnə) *vb.* (*tr.*) **1.** to gather or store in or as if in a granary. ~*n.* **2.** an archaic word for **granary. 3.** a place for storage or safekeeping. [C12: from Old French *gernier* granary, from Latin *grānārium*, from *grānum* grain]

Gar·ner ('gɑːnə) *n.* **Er·roll.** 1921–77, U.S. jazz pianist and songwriter.

gar+net[1] ('gɑːnɪt) *n.* any of a group of hard glassy red, yellow, or green minerals consisting of the silicates of calcium, iron, manganese, chromium, magnesium, and aluminium in cubic crystalline form: used as a gemstone and abrasive. Formula: $A_3B_2(SiO_4)_3$ where A is a divalent metal and B is a trivalent metal. [C13: from Old French *grenat*, from *grenat* (adj.) red, from *pome grenate* POMEGRANATE] —'**gar·net-**ˌ**like** *adj.*

gar+net[2] ('gɑːnɪt) *n. Nautical.* a tackle used for lifting cargo. [C15: probably from Middle Dutch *garnaat*]

Gar·nett ('gɑːnɪt) *n.* **Con·stance.** 1862–1946, English translator of Russian novels.

gar+ni·er+ite ('gɑːnɪəˌraɪt) *n.* a green amorphous mineral consisting of hydrated nickel magnesium silicate: a source of nickel. [C19: named after Jules *Garnier* (died 1904), French geologist]

gar+nish ('gɑːnɪʃ) *vb.* (*tr.*) **1.** to decorate; trim. **2.** to add something to (food) in order to improve its appearance or flavour. **3.** *Law.* **a.** to serve with notice of proceedings; warn. **b.** *Obsolete.* to summon to proceedings already in progress. **c.** to attach (a debt). **4.** *Slang.* to extort money from. ~*n.* **5.** a decoration; trimming. **6.** something, such as parsley, added to a dish for its flavour or decorative effect. **7.** *Slang.* a payment illegally extorted, as from a prisoner by his jailer. [C14: from Old French *garnir* to adorn, equip, of Germanic origin; compare Old High German *warnōn* to pay heed] —'**gar+nish+er** *n.*

gar+nish·ee (ˌgɑːnɪ'ʃiː) *Law.* ~*n.* **1.** a person upon whom a garnishment has been served. ~*vb.* **+nish·ees, +nish·ee+ing, +nish·eed.** (*tr.*) **2.** to attach (a debt or other property) by garnishment. **3.** to serve (a person) with a garnishment.

gar+nish+ment ('gɑːnɪʃmənt) *n.* **1.** the act of garnishing. **2.** decoration or embellishment; garnish. **3.** *Law.* **a.** a notice or warning. **b.** a summons to court proceedings already in progress. **c.** a notice warning a person holding money or property belonging to a debtor whose debt has been attached to hold such property until directed by the court to apply it.

gar+ni+ture ('gɑːnɪtʃə) *n.* decoration or embellishment. [C16: from French, from *garnir* to GARNISH]

Ga+ronne (*French* ga'rɔn) *n.* a river in SW France, rising in the central Pyrenees in Spain and flowing northeast then northwest into the Gironde estuary. Length: 580 km (360 miles).

ga+rotte (gə'rɒt) *n., vb.* a variant spelling of **garrotte.** —**ga+'rot+ter** *n.*

gar+pike ('gɑːˌpaɪk) *n.* **1.** Also called: **garfish, gar.** any primitive freshwater elongated bony fish of the genus *Lepisosteus*, of North and Central America, having very long toothed jaws and a body covering of thick scales. **2.** another name for **garfish** (sense 2).

gar+ret ('gærɪt) *n.* another word for **attic** (sense 1). [C14: from Old French *garite*, watchtower, from *garir* to protect, of Germanic origin; see WARY]

Gar·rick ('gærɪk) *n.* **Da·vid.** 1717–79, English actor and theatre manager.

gar+ri+son ('gærɪsᵊn) *n.* **1.** the troops who maintain and guard a base or fortified place. **2. a.** the place itself. **b.** (*as modifier*): *garrison town.* ~*vb.* **3.** (*tr.*) to station (troops) in (a fort, etc.). [C13: from Old French *garison*, from *garir* to defend, of Germanic origin; compare Old Norse *verja* to defend, Old English, Old High German *werian*]

gar+rotte, gar+rote, *or* **ga+rotte** (gə'rɒt) *n.* **1.** a Spanish method of execution by strangulation or by breaking the neck. **2.** the device, usually an iron collar, used in such executions. **3.** *Obsolete.* strangulation of one's victim while committing robbery. ~*vb.* (*tr.*) **4.** to execute by means of the garrotte. **5.** to strangle, esp. in order to commit robbery. [C17: from Spanish *garrote*, perhaps from Old French *garrot* cudgel; of obscure origin] —**gar+'rott+er, gar+'rot+er,** *or* **ga+'rott+er** *n.*

gar+ru+lous ('gærʊləs) *adj.* **1.** given to constant and frivolous chatter; loquacious; talkative. **2.** wordy or diffuse; prolix. [C17: from Latin *garrulus*, from *garrīre* to chatter] —'**gar+ru+lous+ly** *adv.* —'**gar+ru+lous+ness** *or* **gar+ru+li·ty** (gæ'ruːlɪtɪ) *n.*

gar+ry·a ('gærɪə) *n.* any ornamental catkin-bearing evergreen shrub of the North American genus *Garrya:* family *Garryaceae.* [C19: named after Nicholas *Garry* (1781–1856), an officer of the Hudson's Bay Company]

gar+ter ('gɑːtə) *n.* **1.** a band, usually of elastic, worn round the arm or leg to hold up a shirt sleeve, sock, or stocking. **2.** the U.S. word for **suspender.** ~*vb.* **3.** (*tr.*) to fasten, support, or secure with or as if with a garter. [C14: from Old Northern French *gartier*, from *garet* bend of the knee, probably of Celtic origin]

Gar+ter ('gɑːtə) *n.* **the. 1.** See **Order of the Garter. 2.** (*sometimes not cap.*) **a.** the badge of this Order. **b.** membership of this Order.

gar+ter snake *n.* any nonvenomous North American colubrid snake of the genus *Thamnophis*, typically marked with longitudinal stripes.

gar+ter stitch *n.* knitting in which all the rows are knitted in plain stitch instead of alternating with purl rows.

garth[1] (gɑːθ) *n.* **1.** a courtyard surrounded by a cloister. **2.** *Archaic.* a yard or garden. [C14: from Old Norse *garthr;* related to Old English *geard* YARD[2]]

garth[2] (gɑːθ) *n. Northern English dialect.* a child's hoop, often the rim of a bicycle wheel. [dialect variant of GIRTH]

Gar·y ('gærɪ) *n.* a port in NW Indiana, on Lake Michigan: a major world steel producer. Pop.: 177 925 (1973 est.).

gas (gæs) *n., pl.* **gas·es** *or* **gas+ses. 1.** a substance in the physical state in which the attractive forces between its constituent atoms or molecules are not sufficiently strong to have a marked effect on their positions or mobility. **2.** any substance that is gaseous at room temperature and atmospheric pressure. **3.** any gaseous substance that is above its critical temperature and therefore not liquefiable by pressure alone. Compare **vapour** (sense 2). **4. a.** a fossil fuel in the form of a gas, used as a source of domestic and industrial heat. See also **coal gas, natural gas. b.** (*as modifier*): *a gas cooker; gas fire.* **5.** a gaseous anaesthetic, such as nitrous oxide. **6.** *Mining.* firedamp or the explosive mixture of firedamp and air. **7.** the usual U.S. word for **petrol. 8. step on the gas.** *Informal.* **a.** to increase the speed of a motor vehicle; accelerate. **b.** to hurry. **9.** a toxic, etc., substance in suspension in air used against an enemy, etc. **10.** *Slang.* **a.** idle talk or boasting. **b.** *Chiefly U.S.* a delightful or successful person or thing: *his latest record is a gas.* ~*vb.* **gas·es** *or* **gas+ses, gas+sing, gassed. 11.** (*tr.*) to provide or fill with gas. **12.** (*tr.*) to subject to gas fumes, esp. so as to asphyxiate or render unconscious. **13.** (*intr.*) to give off gas, as in the charging of a battery. **14.** (*tr.*) (in textiles) to singe (fabric) with a flame from a gas burner to remove unwanted fibres. **15.** (*intr.; foll. by to*) *Informal.* to talk in an idle or boastful way (to a person). **16.** (*tr.*) *Slang, chiefly U.S.* to thrill or delight. [C17 (coined by J. B. van Helmont (1577–1644), Flemish chemist): modification of Greek *khaos* atmosphere] —'**gas+less** *adj.*

gas+bag ('gæsˌbæg) *n. Slang.* a person who talks in a vapid or empty way.

gas black *n.* finely powdered carbon produced by burning natural gas. It is used as a pigment in paints, etc.

gas burn+er *n.* **1.** Also called: **gas jet.** a jet or nozzle from which a combustible gas issues in order to form a stable flame. **2.** an assembly of such jets or nozzles, used esp. in cooking.

gas cham+ber *or* **ov·en** *n.* an airtight room into which poison gas is introduced to kill people or animals.

gas chro+ma+tog+ra+phy *n.* a technique for analysing a mixture of volatile substances in which the mixture is carried by an inert gas through a column packed with a selective adsorbent and a detector records on a moving strip the conductivity of the gas leaving the tube. Peaks on the resulting graph indicate the presence of a particular component. Also called: **gas-liquid chromatography.**

gas coal *n.* coal that is rich in volatile hydrocarbons, making it a suitable source of domestic gas.

gas+con ('gæskən) *n. Rare.* a boaster; braggart. [C14: from Old French *gascoun;* compare Latin *Vascōnēs* Basque]

Gas+con ('gæskən) *n.* **1.** a native or inhabitant of Gascony. **2.** the dialect of French spoken in Gascony. ~*adj.* **3.** of or relating to Gascony, its inhabitants, or their dialect of French.

gas+con+ade (ˌgæskə'neɪd) *Rare.* ~*n.* **1.** boastful talk, bragging, or bluster. ~*vb.* **2.** (*intr.*) to boast, brag, or bluster. [C18: from French *gasconnade*, from *gasconner* to chatter, boast like a GASCON] —ˌ**gas+con+'ad+er** *n.*

gas con+stant *n.* the constant in the gas equation. It is equal to 8.3143 joules per kelvin per mole. Symbol: *R* Also called: **universal gas constant.**

Gas+co+ny ('gæskənɪ) *n.* a former province of SW France. French name: **Gas+cogne** (ga'skɔɲ).

gas-cooled re+ac+tor *n.* a nuclear reactor using a gas as the coolant. In the Mark I type the coolant is carbon dioxide, the moderator is graphite, and the fuel is uranium cased in magnox. See also **advanced gas-cooled reactor.**

gas+e·lier (ˌgæsə'lɪə) *n.* a variant spelling of **gasolier.**

gas en+gine *n.* a type of internal-combustion engine using a flammable gas, such as coal gas or natural gas, as fuel.

gas+e·ous ('gæsɪəs, -ʃəs, -ʃɪəs, 'geɪ-) *adj.* of, concerned with, or having the characteristics of a gas. —'**gas+e·ous+ness** *n.*

gas e·qua+tion *n.* an equation, obtained by combining Boyle's and Charles' laws, that equates the product of the pressure and the volume of an ideal gas to the product of its thermodynamic temperature and the **gas constant.** Also called: **ideal gas equation or law.**

gas fix+ture *n.* a wall or ceiling attachment for holding a gaslight.

gas gan+grene *n.* gangrene resulting from infection of a wound by anaerobic bacteria (esp. *Clostridium welchii*) that cause gas bubbles and swelling in the surrounding tissues.

gash (gæʃ) *vb.* **1.** (*tr.*) to make a long deep cut or wound in; slash. ~*n.* **2.** a long deep cut or wound. [C16: from Old French *garser* to scratch, wound, from Vulgar Latin *charissāre* (unattested), from Greek *kharassein* to scratch]

gas+hold·er ('gæsˌhəʊldə) *n.* **1.** Also called: **gasometer.** a large tank for storing coal gas or natural gas prior to distribution to users. **2.** any vessel for storing or measuring a gas.

gas·i+form ('gæsɪˌfɔːm) *adj.* in a gaseous form.

gas·i·fy ('gæsɪˌfaɪ) *vb.* **-fies, -fy·ing, -fied. 1.** to make into or become a gas. **2.** to subject (coal, etc.) to destructive distillation to produce gas, esp. for use as a fuel. —**'gas·i·ˌfi·a·ble** *adj.* —**ˌgas·i·fi·'ca·tion** *n.* —**'gas·i·ˌfi·er** *n.*
Gas·kell ('gæskᵊl) *n.* **Mrs.** married name of *Elizabeth Cleghorn Stevenson.* 1810–65, English novelist. Her novels include *Mary Barton* (1848), an account of industrial life in Manchester, and *Cranford* (1853), a social study of a country village.
gas·ket ('gæskɪt) *n.* **1.** a compressible packing piece of paper, rubber, asbestos, etc., sandwiched between the metal faces of a joint to provide a seal. **2.** *Nautical.* a piece of line used as a sail stop. **3. blow a gasket.** *Slang.* to burst out in anger. [C17 (in the sense: rope lashing a furled sail): probably from French *garcette* rope's end, literally: little girl, from Old French *garce* girl, feminine of *gars* boy, servant]
gas·kin ('gæskɪn) *n.* the lower part of a horse's thigh, between the hock and the stifle. [C16: perhaps shortened from GALLIGASKINS]
gas laws *pl. n.* the physical laws obeyed by gases, esp. Boyle's law and Charles' law. See also **gas equation.**
gas·light ('gæsˌlaɪt) *n.* **1.** a type of lamp in which the illumination is produced by an incandescent mantle heated by a jet of gas. **2.** the light produced by such a lamp.
gas light·er *n.* **1.** a device for igniting a jet of gas. **2.** a cigarette lighter using a gas as fuel.
gas main *n.* a large pipeline in which gas is carried for distribution through smaller pipes to consumers.
gas·man ('gæsˌmæn) *n., pl.* **-men.** a man employed to read household gas meters, supervise gas fittings, etc.
gas man·tle *n.* a mantle for use in a gaslight. See **mantle** (sense 3).
gas mask *n.* a mask fitted with a chemical filter to enable the wearer to breathe air free of poisonous or corrosive gases: used for military or industrial purposes. Also called (in Brit.): **respirator.**
gas me·ter *n.* an apparatus for measuring and recording the amount of gas passed through it.
gas oil *n.* a fuel oil obtained in the distillation of petroleum, intermediate in viscosity and boiling point between paraffin and lubricating oils. It boils above about 250°C.
gas·o·lier *or* **gas·e·lier** (ˌgæsə'lɪə) *n.* a branched hanging fitting for gaslights. [C19: from GAS + (CHAND)ELIER]
gas·o·line *or* **gas·o·lene** ('gæsəˌli:n) *n.* the U.S. name for **petrol.** —**gas·o·lin·ic** (ˌgæsə'lɪnɪk) *adj.*
gas·om·e·ter (gæs'ɒmɪtə) *n.* a nontechnical name for **gasholder.** —**gas·o·met·ric** (ˌgæsə'mɛtrɪk) *or* **ˌgas·o·'met·ri·cal** *adj.*
gas·om·e·try (gæs'ɒmɪtrɪ) *n.* the measurement of quantities of gases.
gas ov·en *n.* **1.** a domestic oven heated by gas. **2.** a gas-fuelled cremation chamber. **3.** another name for **gas chamber.**
gasp (gɑ:sp) *vb.* **1.** (*intr.*) to draw in the breath sharply, convulsively, or with effort, esp. in expressing awe, horror, etc. **2.** (*intr.;* foll. by *after* or *for*) to crave. **3.** (*tr.;* often foll. by *out*) to utter or emit breathlessly. ~*n.* **4.** a short convulsive intake of breath. **5.** a short convulsive burst of speech. **6. at the last gasp. a.** at the point of death. **b.** at the last moment. [C14: from Old Norse *geispa* to yawn; related to Swedish dialect *gispa,* Danish *gispe*] —**'gasp·ing·ly** *adv.*
Gas·par ('gæspə, 'gæspɑ:) *n.* a variant of **Caspar.**
Gas·pé Pen·in·su·la (gæ'speɪ; *French* ga'spe) *n.* a peninsula in E Canada, in SE Quebec between the St. Lawrence River and New Brunswick: mountainous and wooded with many lakes and rivers. Area: about 29 500 sq. km (11 400 sq. miles).
gasp·er ('gɑ:spə) *n.* **1.** a person who gasps. **2.** *Brit. slang.* a cheap cigarette.
gas plant *n.* an aromatic white-flowered Eurasian rutaceous plant, *Dictamnus albus,* that emits a vapour capable of being ignited. Also called: **burning bush, dittany, fraxinella.**
gas pok·er *n.* a long tubular gas burner used to kindle a fire.
gas ring *n.* a circular assembly of gas jets, used esp. for cooking.
gas·ser ('gæsə) *n.* a drilling or well that yields natural gas.
Gas·ser ('gæsə) *n.* **Her·bert Spen·cer.** 1888–1963, U.S. physiologist: shared a Nobel prize for medicine (1944) with Erlanger for work on electrical signs of nervous activity.
gas·sing ('gæsɪŋ) *n.* **1.** the act or process of supplying or treating with gas. **2.** the affecting or poisoning of persons with gas or fumes. **3.** the evolution of a gas, esp. in electrolysis.
gas sta·tion *n. Chiefly U.S.* another term for **filling station.**
gas·sy ('gæsɪ) *adj.,* **-si·er, -si·est. 1.** filled with, containing, or resembling gas. **2.** *Slang.* full of idle or vapid talk. —**'gas·si·ness** *n.*
gas·ter·o·pod ('gæstərəˌpɒd) *n., adj.* a variant spelling of **gastropod.**
gas ther·mom·e·ter *n.* a device for measuring temperature by observing the pressure of gas at a constant volume or the volume of a gas kept at a constant pressure.
gas·tight ('gæsˌtaɪt) *adj.* not allowing gas to enter or escape.
gas·tral·gi·a (gæs'trældʒɪə) *n.* pain in the stomach. —**gas·'tral·gic** *adj.*
gas·trec·to·my (gæs'trɛktəmɪ) *n., pl.* **-mies.** surgical removal of all or part of the stomach.
gas·tric ('gæstrɪk) *adj.* of, relating to, near, or involving the stomach: *gastric pains.*
gas·tric juice *n.* a digestive fluid secreted by the stomach, containing hydrochloric acid, pepsin, rennin, etc.
gas·tric ul·cer *n.* an ulcer of the mucous membrane lining the stomach. Compare **peptic ulcer.**
gas·trin ('gæstrɪn) *n.* a polypeptide hormone secreted by the stomach: stimulates secretion of gastric juice.
gas·tri·tis (gæs'traɪtɪs) *n.* inflammation of the stomach. —**gas·trit·ic** (gæs'trɪtɪk) *adj.*
gas·tro- *or often before a vowel* **gastr-** *combining form.* stomach: *gastroenteritis; gastritis.* [from Greek *gastēr*]
gas·tro·en·ter·ic (ˌgæstrəuɛn'tɛrɪk) *adj.* another word for **gastrointestinal.**
gas·tro·en·ter·i·tis (ˌgæstrəuˌɛntə'raɪtɪs) *n.* inflammation of the stomach and intestines. —**gas·tro·en·ter·it·ic** (ˌgæstrəuˌɛntə'rɪtɪk) *adj.*
gas·tro·en·ter·ol·o·gy (ˌgæstrəuˌɛntə'rɒlədʒɪ) *n.* the branch of medical science concerned with diseases of the stomach and intestines. —**ˌgas·tro·ˌen·ter·'ol·o·gist** *n.*
gas·tro·en·ter·os·to·my (ˌgæstrəuˌɛntə'rɒstəmɪ) *n., pl.* **-mies.** surgical formation of an artificial opening between the stomach and the small intestine.
gas·tro·in·tes·ti·nal (ˌgæstrəuɪn'tɛstɪnᵊl) *adj.* of or relating to the stomach and intestinal tract.
gas·tro·lith ('gæstrəlɪθ) *n. Pathol.* a stone in the stomach; gastric calculus.
gas·trol·o·gy (gæs'trɒlədʒɪ) *n.* another name for **gastroenterology.** —**gas·tro·log·i·cal** (ˌgæstrə'lɒdʒɪkᵊl) *adj.* —**gas·'trol·o·gist** *n.*
gas·tro·nome ('gæstrəˌnəum), **gas·tron·o·mer** (gæs'trɒnəmə), *or* **gas·tron·o·mist** *n.* less common words for **gourmet.**
gas·tron·o·my (gæs'trɒnəmɪ) *n.* **1.** the art of good eating. **2.** the type of cookery of a particular region: *the gastronomy of Provence.* [C19: from French *gastronomie,* from Greek *gastronomia,* from *gastēr* stomach; see -NOMY] —**gas·tro·nom·ic** (ˌgæstrə'nɒmɪk) *or* **ˌgas·tro·'nom·i·cal** *adj.* —**ˌgas·tro·'nom·i·cal·ly** *adv.*
gas·tro·pod ('gæstrəˌpɒd) *or* **gas·ter·o·pod** ('gæstərəˌpɒd) *n.* **1.** any mollusc of the class *Gastropoda,* typically having a flattened muscular foot for locomotion and a head that bears stalked eyes. The class includes the snails, whelks, limpets, and slugs. ~*adj.* **2.** of, relating to, or belonging to the *Gastropoda.* —**gas·trop·o·dan** (gæs'trɒpədᵊn) *adj., n.* —**gas·'trop·o·dous** *adj.*
gas·tro·scope ('gæstrəˌskəup) *n.* a medical instrument for examining the interior of the stomach. —**gas·tro·scop·ic** (ˌgæstrə'skɒpɪk) *adj.* —**gas·tros·co·pist** (gæs'trɒskəpɪst) *n.* —**gas·'tros·co·py** *n.*
gas·tros·to·my (gæs'trɒstəmɪ) *n., pl.* **-mies.** surgical formation of an artificial opening into the stomach from the skin surface: used for feeding.
gas·tro·to·my (gæs'trɒtəmɪ) *n., pl.* **-mies.** surgical incision into the stomach.
gas·tro·trich ('gæstrətrɪk) *n.* any minute aquatic multicellular animal of the phylum *Gastrotricha,* having a wormlike body covered with cilia and bristles.
gas·tro·vas·cu·lar (ˌgæstrəu'væskjulə) *adj.* (esp. of the body cavities of coelenterates) functioning in digestion and circulation.
gas·tru·la ('gæstrulə) *n., pl.* **-las** *or* **-lae** (-ˌli:). a saclike animal embryo consisting of three layers of cells (see **ectoderm, mesoderm,** and **endoderm**) surrounding a central cavity (archenteron) with a small opening (blastopore) to the exterior. [C19: New Latin: little stomach, from Greek *gastēr* belly] —**'gas·tru·lar** *adj.*
gas·tru·la·tion (ˌgæstru'leɪʃən) *n. Embryol.* the process in which a gastrula is formed from a blastula by the inward migration of cells.
gas tur·bine *n.* an internal-combustion engine in which the expanding gases emerging from one or more combustion chambers drive a turbine. A rotary compressor driven by the turbine compresses the air used for combustion, power being taken either as torque from the turbine or thrust from the expanding gases.
gas well *n.* a well for obtaining natural gas.
gas·works ('gæsˌwɜ:ks) *n.* (*functioning as sing.*) a plant in which gas, esp. coal gas, is made.
gat[1] (gæt) *vb. Archaic.* a past tense of **get.**
gat[2] (gæt) *n. Slang, chiefly U.S.* a pistol or revolver. [C20: shortened from GATLING GUN]
gat[3] (gæt) *n.* a narrow channel of water. [C18: probably from Old Norse *gat* passage; related to GATE[1]]
gate[1] (geɪt) *n.* **1.** a movable barrier, usually hinged, for closing an opening in a wall, fence, etc. **2.** an opening to allow passage into or out of an enclosed place. **3.** any means of entrance or access. **4.** a mountain pass or gap, esp. one providing entry into another country or region. **5.** a valve with a sliding or swinging component that regulates the flow of a liquid or gas in a pipe, etc. **6. a.** the number of people admitted to a sporting event or entertainment. **b.** the total entrance money received from them. **7.** (in a large airport) any of the numbered exits leading to the airfield or aircraft: *passengers for Paris should proceed to gate 14.* **8.** *Horse racing.* short for **starting gate. 9.** *Electronics.* **a.** a logic circuit having one or more input terminals and one output terminal, the output being switched between two voltage levels determined by the combination of input signals. **b.** a circuit used in radar, etc., that allows only a fraction of the input signal to pass. **10.** the electrode region or regions in a field-effect transistor that is biased to control the conductivity of the channel between the source and drain. **11.** a component in a motion-picture camera or projector that holds each frame flat and momentarily stationary behind the lens. **12.** a slotted metal frame that controls the positions of the gear lever in a motor vehicle. **13.** *Rowing.* a hinged clasp to

prevent the oar from jumping out of a rowlock. **14.** a frame surrounding the blade or blades of a saw. ~*vb.* **15.** (*tr.*) *Brit.* to restrict (a student) to the school or college grounds as a punishment. [Old English *geat;* related to Old Frisian *jet* opening, Old Norse *gat* opening, passage] —**'gate+less** *adj.* —**'gate+,like** *adj.*

gate[2] (geɪt) *n. Dialect.* **1.** the channels by which molten metal is poured into a mould. **2.** the metal that solidifies in such channels. [C17: probably related to Old English *gyte* a pouring out, *geotan* to pour]

gate[3] (geɪt) *n. Archaic or northern English dialect.* **1.** a way, road, or path. **2.** a way or method of doing something. [C13: from Old Norse *gata* path; related to Old High German *gazza* road, street]

gâ+teau ('gætəʊ) *n., pl.* **+teaux** (-təʊz). any of various elaborate and rich cakes. [French: cake]

gate-crash *vb. Informal.* to gain entry to (a party, concert, etc.) without invitation or payment. —**'gate-,crash·er** *n.*

gate+fold ('geɪt,fəʊld) *n.* an oversize page in a book or magazine that is folded in. Also called: **foldout.**

gate+house ('geɪt,haʊs) *n.* **1.** a house built at or over a gateway, used as a fortification, etc. **2.** a structure that houses the controls operating lock gates or dam sluices.

gate+keep·er ('geɪt,ki:pə) *n.* **1.** a person who has charge of a gate and controls who may pass through it. **2.** any of several Eurasian butterflies of the genus *Pyronia,* esp. *P. tithonus,* having brown-bordered orange wings with a black-and-white eyespot on each forewing: family *Satyridae.*

gate-leg ta+ble *or* **gate-legged ta+ble** *n.* a table with one or two drop leaves that are supported when in use by a hinged leg swung out from the frame.

gate mon+ey *n.* the total receipts taken for admission to a sporting event or other entertainment.

gate+post ('geɪt,pəʊst) *n.* **1. a.** the post on which a gate is hung. **b.** the post to which a gate is fastened when closed. **2. between you, me, and the gatepost.** confidentially.

Gates (geɪts) *n.* **Ho·ra·ti·o.** ?1728–1806, American Revolutionary general: defeated the British at Saratoga (1777).

Gates+head ('geɪts,hɛd) *n.* a port in NE England, in Tyne and Wear: engineering works. Pop.: 94 457 (1971).

gate+way ('geɪt,weɪ) *n.* **1.** an entrance that may be closed by or as by a gate. **2.** a means of entry or access: *Bombay, gateway to India.*

Gath (gæθ) *n. Old Testament.* one of the five cities of the Philistines, from which Goliath came (I Samuel 17:4) and near which Saul fell in battle (II Samuel 1:20). Douay spelling: **Geth** (gɛθ).

Ga+tha ('gɑ:tə) *n. Zoroastrianism.* any of a number of versified sermons in the Avesta that are in a more ancient dialect than the rest. [from Avestan *gāthā-;* related to Sanskrit *gāthā* song]

gath+er ('gæðə) *vb.* **1.** to assemble or cause to assemble. **2.** to collect or be collected gradually; muster. **3.** (*tr.*) to learn from information given; conclude or assume. **4.** (*tr.*) to pick or harvest (flowers, fruit, etc.). **5.** (*tr.; foll. by to or into*) to clasp or embrace: *the mother gathered the child into her arms.* **6.** (*tr.*) to bring close (to) or wrap (around): *she gathered her shawl about her shoulders.* **7.** to increase or cause to increase gradually, as in force, speed, intensity, etc. **8.** to contract (the brow) or (of the brow) to become contracted into wrinkles; knit. **9.** (*tr.*) to assemble (sections of a book) in the correct sequence for binding. **10.** (*tr.*) to collect by making a selection. **11.** (*tr.*) to prepare or make ready: *to gather one's wits.* **12.** to draw (material) into a series of small tucks or folds by passing a thread through it and then pulling it tight. **13.** (*intr.*) *Informal.* (of a boil or other sore) to come to a head; form pus. **14. be gathered to one's fathers.** *Euphemistic.* to die. ~*n.* **15. a.** the act of gathering. **b.** the amount gathered. **16.** a small fold in material, as made by a tightly pulled stitch; tuck. **17.** *Printing.* an informal name for **section** (sense 15). [Old English *gadrian;* related to Old Frisian *gaderia,* Middle Low German *gaderen*] —**'gath+er+a·ble** *adj.* —**'gath+er+er** *n.*

gath+er+ing ('gæðərɪŋ) *n.* **1.** a group of people, things, etc., that are gathered together; assembly. **2.** *Sewing.* a gather or series of gathers in material. **3.** *Informal.* **a.** the formation of pus in a boil. **b.** the pus so formed. **4.** *Printing.* an informal name for **section** (sense 15).

Gat·ling gun ('gætlɪŋ) *n.* a machine-gun equipped with a rotating cluster of barrels that are fired in succession. [C19: named after R. J. *Gatling* (1818–1903), U.S. inventor]

GATT (gæt) *n. acronym for* General Agreement on Tariffs and Trade: a multilateral international treaty signed in 1947 to promote trade, esp. by means of the reduction and elimination of tariffs and import quotas.

Ga+tún Lake (*Spanish* ga'tun) *n.* a lake in the Canal Zone, part of the Panama Canal: formed in 1912 on the completion of the **Gatún Dam** across the Chagres River. Area: 424 sq. km (164 sq. miles).

gauche (gəʊʃ) *adj.* lacking ease of manner; tactless. [C18: from French: awkward, left, from Old French *gauchir* to swerve, ultimately of Germanic origin; related to Old High German *wankōn* to stagger] —**'gauche+ly** *adv.* —**'gauche+ness** *n.*

gau+che·rie (,gəʊʃə'ri:, 'gəʊʃərɪ; *French* goʃ'ri) *n.* **1.** the quality of being gauche. **2.** a gauche act.

gau+cho ('gaʊtʃəʊ) *n., pl.* **+chos.** a cowboy of the South American pampas, usually one of mixed Spanish and Indian descent. [C19: from American Spanish, probably from Quechuan *wáhcha* orphan, vagabond]

gaud (gɔ:d) *n.* an article of cheap finery; trinket; bauble. [C14: probably from Old French *gaudir* to be joyful, from Latin *gaudēre*]

gaud+er·y ('gɔ:dərɪ) *n., pl.* **+er·ies.** cheap finery or display.

Gau·dí ('gaʊdɪ; *Spanish* gaʊ'ði) *n.* **An·to·nio** (an'tonjo). 1852–1926, Spanish architect, regarded as one of the most original exponents of art nouveau in Europe and noted esp. for the church of the Sagrada familia, Barcelona.

Gau·dier-Brzes·ka (*French* godje bʒɛs'ka) *n.* **Hen·ri** (ã'ri). 1891–1915, French vorticist sculptor.

gaud·y[1] ('gɔ:dɪ) *adj.* **gaud·i·er, gaud·i+est.** gay, bright, or colourful in a crude or vulgar manner; garish. [C16: from GAUD] —**'gaud·i+ly** *adv.* —**'gaud·i+ness** *n.*

gaud·y[2] ('gɔ:dɪ) *n., pl.* **gaud·ies.** *Brit.* a celebratory festival or feast held at some schools and colleges. [C16: from Latin *gaudium* joy, from *gaudēre* to rejoice]

gauf+fer ('gəʊfə) *n., vb.* a less common spelling of **goffer.**

gauge *or* **gage** (geɪdʒ) *vb.* (*tr.*) **1.** to measure or determine the amount, quantity, size, condition, etc., of. **2.** to estimate or appraise; judge. **3.** to check for conformity or bring into conformity with a standard measurement, etc. ~*n.* **4.** a standard measurement, dimension, capacity, or quantity. **5.** any of various instruments for measuring a quantity: *a pressure gauge.* **6.** any of various devices used to check for conformity with a standard measurement. **7.** a standard or means for assessing; test; criterion. **8.** scope, capacity, or extent. **9.** the diameter of the barrel of a gun, esp. a shotgun. **10.** the thickness of sheet metal or the diameter of wire. **11.** the distance between the rails of a railway track. **12.** the distance between two wheels on the same axle of a vehicle, truck, etc. **13.** *Nautical.* the position of a vessel in relation to the wind and another vessel. One vessel may be windward (**weather gauge**) or leeward (**lee gauge**) of the other. **14.** the proportion of plaster of Paris added to mortar to accelerate its setting. **15.** the distance between the nails securing the slates, tiles, etc., of a roof. **16.** a measure of the fineness of woven or knitted fabric, usually expressed as the number of needles used per inch. ~*adj.* **17.** (of a pressure measurement) measured on a pressure gauge that registers zero at atmospheric pressure; above or below atmospheric pressure: *5 bar gauge.* See also **absolute** (sense 10). [C15: from Old Northern French, probably of Germanic origin] —**'gauge+a·ble** *or* **'gage+a·ble** *adj.* —**'gauge+a·bly** *or* **'gage+a·bly** *adv.*

gaug+er *or* **gag+er** ('geɪdʒə) *n.* **1.** a person or thing that gauges. **2.** *Chiefly Brit.* a customs officer who inspects bulk merchandise, esp. liquor casks, for excise duty purposes. **3.** a collector of excise taxes.

Gau·guin (*French* go'gɛ̃) *n.* **Paul** (pɔl). 1848–1903, French postimpressionist painter, who worked in the South Pacific from 1891. Inspired by primitive art, his work is characterized by flat contrasting areas of pure colours.

Gau+ha+ti (gaʊ'hɑ:tɪ) *n.* a city in NE India, in Assam on the River Brahmaputra: centre of British administration in Assam (1826–74). Pop.: 123 784 (1971).

Gaul (gɔ:l) *n.* **1.** an ancient region of W Europe corresponding to N Italy, France, Belgium, part of Germany, and the S Netherlands: divided into Cisalpine Gaul, which became a Roman province before 100 B.C., and Transalpine Gaul, which was conquered by Julius Caesar (58–51 B.C.). Latin name: **Gallia. 2.** a native of ancient Gaul. **3.** a Frenchman.

Gau+lei+ter ('gaʊ,laɪtə) *n.* a provincial governor in Germany under Hitler. [German, from *Gau* district + *Leiter* LEADER]

Gaul+ish ('gɔ:lɪʃ) *n.* **1.** the extinct language of the pre-Roman Gauls, belonging to the Celtic branch of the Indo-European family. ~*adj.* **2.** of or relating to ancient Gaul, the Gauls, or their language.

Gaulle (gəʊl, gɔ:l; *French* go:l) *n.* **Charles de.** See (Charles) **de Gaulle.**

Gaull+ism ('gəʊlɪzəm, 'gɔ:-) *n.* **1.** the conservative French nationalist policies and principles associated with General de Gaulle. **2.** a political movement founded on and supporting General de Gaulle's principles and policies.

Gaull+ist ('gəʊlɪst, 'gɔ:-) *n.* **1.** a supporter of Gaullism. ~*adj.* **2.** of, characteristic of, supporting, or relating to Gaullism.

gaul+the·ri·a (gɔ:l'θɪərɪə) *n.* any aromatic evergreen shrub of the ericaceous genus *Gaultheria,* of America, Asia, and Australia, esp. the wintergreen. [C19: New Latin, after Jean-François *Gaultier,* 18th-century Canadian physician and botanist]

gaum+less (('gɔ:mlɪs) *adj.* a variant spelling of **gormless.**

gaunt (gɔ:nt) *adj.* **1.** bony and emaciated in appearance. **2.** (of places) bleak or desolate. [C15: perhaps of Scandinavian origin; compare Norwegian dialect *gand* tall lean person] —**'gaunt+ly** *adv.* —**'gaunt+ness** *n.*

gaunt+let[1] ('gɔ:ntlɪt) *or* **gant+let** *n.* **1.** a medieval armoured leather glove. **2.** a heavy glove with a long cuff. **3. take up** (*or* **throw down**) **the gauntlet.** to accept (or offer) a challenge. [C15: from Old French *gantelet,* diminutive of *gant* glove, of Germanic origin]

gaunt+let[2] ('gɔ:ntlɪt) *n.* **1.** a punishment in which the victim is forced to run between two rows of men who strike at him as he passes: formerly a military punishment. **2. run the gauntlet. a.** to suffer this punishment. **b.** to endure an onslaught or ordeal, as of criticism. **3.** a testing ordeal; trial. **4.** a variant spelling of **gantlet**[1] (sense 1). [C15: changed (through influence of GAUNTLET[1]) from earlier *gantlope;* see GANTLET[1]]

gaun+try ('gɔ:ntrɪ) *n., pl.* **+tries.** a variant spelling of **gantry.**

gaup (gɔ:p) *vb.* a variant spelling of **gawp.**

gaur (gaʊə) *n.* a large wild member of the cattle tribe, *Bos* *gaurus,* inhabiting mountainous regions of S Asia. [C19: from Hindi, from Sanskrit *gaura*]

gauss (gaʊs) *n., pl.* **gauss.** the cgs unit of magnetic flux density; the flux density that will induce an emf of 1 abvolt (10^{-8} volt) per centimetre in a wire moving across the field at a velocity of 1 centimetre per second. 1 gauss is equivalent to 10^{-4} tesla. [after K.F. GAUSS]

Gauss (*German* gaʊs) *n.* **Karl Frie·drich** (karl 'fri:drɪç). 1777–1855, German mathematician: developed the theory of numbers and applied mathematics to astronomy, electricity and magnetism, and geodesy. —**Gauss·i·an** ('gaʊsɪən) *adj.*

Gauss·i·an dis·tri·bu·tion *n.* another name for **normal distribution.**

gauss·me·ter ('gaʊs,mi:tə) *n.* an instrument for measuring the intensity of a magnetic field.

Gau·ta·ma ('gaʊtəmə) *n.* the Sanskrit form of the name assumed by Siddhartha, the future Buddha, when he became a monk.

Gau·tier (*French* go'tje) *n.* **Thé·o·phile** (teɔ'fil). 1811–72, French poet, novelist, and critic. His early extravagant romanticism gave way to a preocupation with poetic form and expression that anticipated the Parnassians.

gauze (gɔ:z) *n.* **1. a.** a transparent cloth of loose plain or leno weave. **b.** (*as modifier*): *a gauze veil.* **2.** a surgical dressing of muslin or similar material. **3.** any thin open-work material, such as wire. **4.** a fine mist or haze. [C16: from French *gaze,* perhaps from GAZA, where it was believed to originate]

gauz·y ('gɔ:zɪ) *adj.* **gauz·i·er, gauz·i·est.** resembling gauze; thin and transparent. —**'gauz·i·ly** *adv.* —**'gauz·i·ness** *n.*

ga·vage ('gævɑ:ʒ) *n.* forced feeding by means of a tube inserted into the stomach through the mouth. [C19: from French, from *gaver,* from Old French (dialect) *gave* throat]

gave (geɪv) *vb.* the past tense of **give.**

gav·el ('gævᵊl) *n.* **1.** a small hammer used by a chairman, auctioneer, etc., to call for order or attention. **2.** a hammer used by masons to trim rough edges off stones. [C19: of unknown origin]

gav·el·kind ('gævᵊl,kaɪnd) *n.* **1.** a former system of land tenure peculiar to Kent based on the payment of rent to the lord instead of the performance of services by the tenant. **2.** the land subject to such tenure. **3.** *English law.* (formerly) land held under this system. [C13: from Old English *gafol* tribute + *gecynd* KIND²]

ga·vi·al ('geɪvɪəl), **ghar·i·al,** *or* **gar·i·al** ('gærɪəl) *n.* **1.** a large fish-eating Indian crocodilian, *Gavialis gangeticus,* with a very long slender snout: family *Gavialidae.* **2. false gavial.** a SE Asian crocodile, *Tomistoma schlegeli,* similar to but smaller than the gavial. [C19: from French, from Hindi *ghariyāl*]

Gäv·le (*Swedish* 'jɛ:vlə) *n.* a port in E Sweden, on an inlet of the Gulf of Bothnia. Pop.: 84 625 (1970).

ga·votte *or* **ga·vot** (gə'vɒt) *n.* **1.** an old formal dance in quadruple time. **2.** a piece of music composed for or in the rhythm of this dance. [C17: from French, from Provençal *gavoto,* from *gavot,* mountaineer, dweller in the Alps (where the dance originated), from *gava* goitre (widespread in the Alps), from Old Latin *gaba* (unattested) throat]

gawk (gɔ:k) *n.* **1.** a clumsy stupid person; lout. ~*vb.* **2.** (*intr.*) to stare in a stupid way; gape. [C18: from Old Danish *gaukr;* probably related to GAPE]

gawk·y ('gɔ:kɪ) *or* **gawk·ish** *adj.* **gawk·i·er, gawk·i·est. 1.** clumsy or ungainly; awkward. **2.** *West Yorkshire dialect.* left-handed. —**'gawk·i·ly** *or* **'gawk·ish·ly** *adv.* —**'gawk·i·ness** *or* **'gawk·ish·ness** *n.*

gawp *or* **gaup** (gɔ:p) *vb.* (*intr.;* often foll. by *at*) *Brit. slang.* to stare stupidly; gape. [C14 *galpen;* probably related to Old English *gielpan* to boast, YELP. Compare Dutch *galpen* to yelp]

gay (geɪ) *adj.* **1.** carefree and merry: *a gay temperament.* **2.** brightly coloured; brilliant: *a gay hat.* **3.** given to pleasure, esp. in social entertainment: *a gay life.* **4.** rakish or dissolute; licentious: *a gay old dog.* **5. a.** *Informal.* homosexual (used esp. by homosexuals of themselves). **b.** (*as n.*): *a group of gays.* [C13: from Old French *gai,* from Old Provençal, of Germanic origin] —**'gay·ness** *n.*

Gay (geɪ) *n.* **John.** 1685–1732, English poet and dramatist; author of *The Beggar's Opera* (1728).

Ga·ya ('gɑ:jə, 'gaɪə) *n.* a city in NE India, in central Bihar: Hindu place of pilgrimage and one of the holiest sites of Buddhism. Pop.: 179 884 (1971).

Gay Gor·dons ('gɔ:dᵊnz) *n. Brit.* an old-time ballroom dance.

Gay-Lus·sac ('geɪ 'lu:sæk; *French* gɛ ly'sak) *n.* **Jo·seph Louis** (ʒozɛf 'lwi). 1778–1850, French physicist and chemist: discovered the law named after him (1808). He also investigated the effects of terrestrial magnetism, isolated boron and cyanogen, and discovered new methods of manufacturing sulphuric and oxalic acids.

Gay-Lus·sac's law *n.* **1.** the principle that gases react together in volumes (measured at the same temperature and pressure) that bear a simple ratio to each other and to the gaseous products. **2.** another name for **Charles' law.**

Ga·yo·mart (gɑ:'jəʊmɑ:t) *n. Zoroastrianism.* the first man, whose seed was buried in the earth for 40 years and then produced the first human couple.

gaz. *abbrev. for:* **1.** gazette. **2.** gazetteer.

Ga·za ('gɑ:zə) *n.* a city in the Gaza Strip: a Philistine city in biblical times. It was under Egyptian administration from 1949 until occupied by Israel (1967). Pop.: 118 272 (1967). Arabic name: **Ghazzah.**

Gaz·an·ku·lu (,gazaŋ'ku:lu:) *n.* a Bantustan in South Africa: consists of four exclaves, three in N Transvaal and one in E Transvaal. Capital: Giyani.

Ga·za Strip *n.* a coastal region on the SE corner of the Mediterranean: administered by Egypt from 1949; occupied by Israel in 1967. Pop. (with North Sinai): 390 700 (1967).

gaze (geɪz) *vb.* **1.** (*intr.*) to look long and fixedly, esp. in wonder or admiration. ~*n.* **2.** a fixed look; stare. [C14: from Swedish dialect *gasa* to gape at] —**'gaz·er** *n.*

ga·ze·bo (gə'zi:bəʊ) *n., pl.* **·bos** *or* **·boes.** a summerhouse, garden pavilion, or belvedere, sited to command a view. [C18: perhaps a pseudo-Latin coinage based on GAZE]

gaze·hound ('geɪz,haʊnd) *n.* a hound such as a greyhound that hunts by sight rather than by scent.

ga·zelle (gə'zɛl) *n., pl.* **·zelles** *or* **·zelle.** any small graceful usually fawn-coloured antelope of the genera *Gazella* and *Procapra,* of Africa and Asia, such as *G. thomsoni* (**Thomson's gazelle**). [C17: from Old French, from Arabic *ghazāl*] —**ga·'zelle-,like** *adj.*

ga·zette (gə'zɛt) *n.* **1. a.** a newspaper or official journal. **b.** (*cap. when part of the name of a newspaper, etc.*): *the Thame Gazette.* **2.** *Brit.* an official document containing public notices, appointments, etc. Abbrev.: **gaz.** ~*vb.* **3.** (*tr.*) *Brit.* to announce or report (facts or an event) in a gazette. [C17: from French, from Italian *gazzetta,* from Venetian dialect *gazeta* news sheet costing one *gazet* small copper coin, perhaps from *gaza* magpie, from Latin *gaia, gaius* jay]

ga·zet·ted of·fic·er *n.* (in India) a senior official whose appointment is published in the government gazette.

gaz·et·teer (,gæzɪ'tɪə) *n.* **1.** a book or section of a book that lists and describes places. Abbrev.: **gaz. 2.** *Archaic.* a writer for a gazette or newspaper; journalist.

Ga·zi·an·tep (,gɑ:zi:ɑ:n'tɛp) *n.* a city in S Turkey: base for Ibrahim Pasha's campaign against the Turks (1839) and centre of Turkish resistance to French forces (1921). Pop.: 300 882 (1975). Former name (until 1921): **Aintab.**

gaz·pa·cho (gəz'pɑ:tʃəʊ, gæs-) *n.* a Spanish soup made from tomatoes, peppers, etc., and served cold. [from Spanish]

ga·zump (gə'zʌmp) *Brit.* ~*vb.* **1.** to raise the price of something, esp. a house, after agreeing a price verbally with (an intending buyer). **2.** (*tr.*) to swindle or overcharge. ~*n.* **3.** the act or an instance of gazumping. [C20: of uncertain origin] —**ga·'zump·er** *n.*

GB *international car registration for* Great Britain.

G.B. *abbrev. for* Great Britain.

GBA *international car registration for* Alderney.

G.B.E. *abbrev. for* (Knight or Dame) Grand Cross of the British Empire (a Brit. title).

GBG *international car registration for* Guernsey.

G.B.H. *abbrev. for* grievous bodily harm.

GBJ *international car registration for* Jersey.

GBM *international car registration for* Isle of Man.

GBZ *international car registration for* Gibraltar.

G.C. *abbrev. for* George Cross (a Brit. award for bravery).

GCA 1. *Aeronautics. abbrev. for* ground control approach. **2.** *international car registration for* Guatemala.

G.C.B. *abbrev. for* (Knight) Grand Cross of the Bath (a Brit. title).

GCE 1. (in Britain) *abbrev. for* General Certificate of Education: either of two public examinations in specified subjects taken as school-leaving qualifications or as qualifying examinations for entry into a university. See also **O level, A level, S level.** ~*n.* **2.** *Informal.* any subject taken for one of these examinations, esp. for O level: *how many GCEs have you got?*

G.C.F. *or* **g.c.f.** *abbrev. for* greatest common factor.

G clef *n.* another name for **treble clef.**

G.C.M. *or* **g.c.m.** *abbrev. for* greatest common measure.

G.C.M.G. *abbrev. for* (Knight or Dame) Grand Cross of the Order of St. Michael and St. George (a Brit. title).

G.C.V.O. *or* **GCVO** *abbrev. for* (Knight or Dame) Grand Cross of the Royal Victorian Order (a Brit. title).

Gd *the chemical symbol for* gadolinium.

Gdańsk (*Polish* gdajnsk) *n.* **1.** the chief port of Poland, on the Baltic: a member of the Hanseatic league; under Prussian rule (1793–1807 and 1814–1919); a free city under the League of Nations from 1919 until annexed by Germany in 1939; returned to Poland in 1945. Pop.: 402 200 (1974 est.). German name: **Danzig. 2. Bay of.** a wide inlet of the Baltic sea on the N coast of Poland.

Gdns. *abbrev. for* Gardens.

GDR *abbrev. for* German Democratic Republic.

gds. *abbrev. for* goods.

Gdy·nia (*Polish* 'gdɪnja) *n.* a port in N Poland, near Gdańsk: developed 1924–39 as the outlet for trade through the Polish Corridor; naval base. Pop.: 211 900 (1974 est.).

Ge *the chemical symbol for* germanium.

Ge (dʒi:) *n.* another name for **Gaea.**

gean (gi:n) *n.* another name for **sweet cherry.**

ge·an·ti·cline (dʒi:'æntɪ,klaɪn) *n.* a gently sloping anticline covering a large area. [C19: from Greek *gē* earth, land + ANTICLINE] —**ge·,an·ti·'cli·nal** *adj.*

gear (gɪə) *n.* **1.** a toothed wheel that engages with another toothed wheel or with a rack in order to change the speed or direction of transmitted motion. **2.** a mechanism for transmitting motion by gears, esp. for a specific purpose: *the steering gear of a boat.* **3.** the engagement or specific ratio of a system of gears: *in gear; high gear.* **4.** equipment and supplies for a particular operation, sport, etc.: *fishing gear.* **5.** *Nautical.* all equipment or appurtenances belonging to a certain vessel, sailor, etc. **6.** short for **landing gear. 7.** *Slang.* **a.** up-to-date clothes and accessories, esp. those bought by young people. **b.**

stolen goods. **8.** a less common word for **harness** (sense 1). **9. out of gear.** out of order; not functioning properly. ~*vb.* **10.** (*tr.*) to adjust or adapt (one thing) so as to fit in or work with another: *to gear our output to current demand.* **11.** (*tr.*) to equip with or connect by gears. **12.** (*intr.*) to be or come into gear. **13.** (*tr.*) to equip with harness. [C13: from Old Norse *gervi;* related to Old High German *garawī* equipment, Old English *gearwe*] —**'gear·less** *adj.*

gear·box ('gɪəˌbɒks) *n.* **1.** the metal casing within which a train of gears is sealed. **2.** this metal casing and its contents, esp. in a motor vehicle.

gear down *vb.* (*adv.*) to adapt to a new situation by decreasing output, intensity of operations, etc.

gear·ing ('gɪərɪŋ) *n.* **1.** an assembly of gears designed to transmit motion. **2.** the act or technique of providing gears to transmit motion. **3.** *Accounting, Brit.* the ratio of a company's debt capital to its equity capital.

gear le·ver *or U.S.* **gear·shift** ('gɪəˌʃɪft) *n.* a lever used to move gear wheels relative to each other, esp. in a motor vehicle.

gear up *vb.* (*adv.*) **1.** (*tr.*) to equip with gears. **2.** to prepare, esp. for greater efficiency: *is our industry geared up for the eighties?*

gear·wheel ('gɪəˌwi:l) *n.* another name for **gear** (sense 1).

Ge·ber ('dʒi:bə) *n.* Latinized form of Jabir, assumed in honour of **Jabir ibn Hayyan** by a 14th-century alchemist, probably Spanish: he described the preparation of nitric and sulphuric acids.

geck·o ('gɛkəʊ) *n., pl.* **·os** *or* **·oes.** any small insectivorous terrestrial lizard of the family *Gekkonidae,* of warm regions. The digits have adhesive pads, which enable these animals to climb on smooth surfaces. [C18: from Malay *ge'kok,* of imitative origin]

ge·dact (gə'dɑ:kt, -'dækt) *or* **ge·deckt** (gə'dɛkt) *n. Music.* a flutelike stopped metal diapason organ pipe. [(*gedeckt*) from German: covered, from *decken* to cover]

gee[1] (dʒi:) *interj.* **1.** Also: **gee up!** an exclamation, as to a horse or draught animal, to encourage it to turn to the right, go on, or go faster. ~*vb.* **gees, gee·ing, geed. 2.** (usually foll. by *up*) to move (an animal, esp. a horse) ahead; urge on. ~*n.* **3.** *Slang.* See **gee-gee.**

gee[2] (dʒi:) *interj. U.S. informal.* a mild exclamation. Also: **gee whiz.** [C20: euphemism for JESUS]

gee-gee ('dʒi:ˌdʒi:) *n. Slang.* a horse. [C19: reduplication of GEE[1]]

geek (gi:k) *n.* a sideshow performer who bites the heads off or eats live animals. [C19: probably variant of Scottish *geck* fool, from Middle Low German *geck*]

Gee·long (dʒə'lɒŋ) *n.* a port in SE Australia, in S Victoria on Port Phillip Bay. Pop.: 129 651 (1975 est.).

gee·pound ('dʒi:ˌpaʊnd) *n.* another name for **slug**[2] (sense 1). [C20: from *gee,* representing G(RAVITY) + POUND[2]]

geese (gi:s) *n.* the plural of **goose.**

geest (gi:st) *n.* an area of sandy heathland in N Germany and adjacent areas. [C19: Low German *Geest* dry soil]

Ge'ez ('gi:ɛz) *n.* the classical form of the ancient Ethiopic language, having an extensive Christian literature and still used in Ethiopia as a liturgical language.

gee·zer ('gi:zə) *n. Informal.* a man, esp. an old one regarded as eccentric. [C19: probably from dialect pronunciation of *guiser,* from GUISE + -ER[1]]

ge·fil·te fish *or* **ge·füll·te fish** (gə'fɪltə) *n. Jewish cookery.* a dish consisting of fish and matzo meal rolled into balls and poached, formerly served stuffed into the skin of a fish. [Yiddish, literally: filled fish]

ge·gen·schein ('geɪgənˌʃaɪn) *n.* a faint glow in the sky, just visible at a position opposite to that of the sun and having a similar origin to zodiacal light. Also called: **counterglow.** [German, from *gegen* against, opposite + *Schein* light; see SHINE]

Ge·hen·na (gɪ'hɛnə) *n.* **1.** *Old Testament.* the valley below Jerusalem, where unclean things were burnt and where idolatry was practised (II Kings 23:10). **2.** *New Testament, Judaism.* a place where the wicked are punished after death. **3.** a place or state of pain and torment. [C16: from Late Latin, from Greek *Geena,* from Hebrew *Gê' Hinnōm,* literally: valley of Hinnom, symbolic of hell]

geh·len·ite ('geɪləˌnaɪt) *n.* a green mineral consisting of calcium aluminium silicate in tetragonal crystalline form. Formula: $Ca_2Al_2SiO_7$. [named after A.F. *Gehlen* (1775–1815), German chemist; see -ITE[1]]

Gei·ger ('gaɪgə) *n.* **Hans** (hans). 1882–1945, German physicist: developed the Geiger counter.

Gei·ger count·er *or* **Gei·ger-Mül·ler count·er** ('gaɪgə 'mʊlə) *n.* an instrument for detecting and measuring the intensity of high-energy radiation, consisting of a gas-filled tube containing two electrodes with a high potential difference between them. Each particle entering the tube causes gas atoms to ionize, the electrons liberated being attracted to the anode and registered by electronic equipment. [C20: named after Hans GEIGER and W. *Müller,* 20th-century German physicist]

Gei·sel (*Portuguese* 'gaɪzɛl) *n.* **Er·nes·to** (er'nɛstu). born 1907, Brazilian general and statesman; president of Brazil since 1974.

gei·sha ('geɪʃə) *n., pl.* **·sha** *or* **·shas.** a professional female companion for men in Japan, trained in music, dancing, and the art of conversation. [C19: from Japanese, from *gei* art + *sha* person, from Ancient Chinese *ngi* and *che*]

Geis·sler tube ('gaɪslə) *n.* a glass or quartz vessel, usually having two bulbs containing electrodes separated by a capillary tube, for maintaining an electric discharge in a low-pressure gas as a source of visible or ultraviolet light for spectroscopy, etc. [C19: named after Heinrich *Geissler* (1814–79), German mechanic]

gel (dʒɛl) *n.* **1.** a semirigid jelly-like colloid in which a liquid is dispersed in a solid: *nondrip paint is a gel.* **2.** *Theatre, informal.* See **gelatin** (sense 4). ~*vb.* **gels, gel·ling, gelled. 3.** to become or cause to become a gel. **4.** a variant spelling of **jell.** [C19: by shortening from GELATIN]

ge·la·da ('dʒɛlədə, 'gɛl-; dʒɪ'lɑ:də, gɪ-) *n.* a NE African baboon, *Theropithecus gelada,* with dark brown hair forming a mane over the shoulders, a bare red chest, and a ridge muzzle: family *Cercopithecidae.* Also called: **gelada baboon.** [probably from Arabic *qilādah* mane]

ge·län·de·sprung (gə'lɛndəˌsprʊŋ; *German* gə'lɛndəˌʃprʊŋ) *or* **ge·län·de jump** *n. Skiing.* a jump made in downhill skiing, usually over an obstacle. [from German *Geländesprung,* from *Gelände* terrain + *Sprung* jump]

gel·a·tin ('dʒɛlətɪn) *or* **gel·a·tine** ('dʒɛləˌti:n) *n.* **1.** a colourless or yellowish water-soluble protein prepared by boiling animal hides and bones: used in foods, glue, photographic emulsions, etc. **2.** an edible jelly made of this substance, sweetened and flavoured. **3.** any of various substances that resemble gelatin. **4.** Also called (informal): **gel.** a translucent substance used for colour effects in theatrical lighting. [C19: from French *gélatine,* from Medieval Latin *gelātina,* from Latin *gelāre* to freeze]

ge·lat·i·nize *or* **ge·lat·i·nise** (dʒɪ'lætɪˌnaɪz) *vb.* **1.** to make or become gelatinous. **2.** (*tr.*) *Photog.* to coat (glass, paper, etc.) with gelatin. —**ge·ˌlat·i·ni·'za·tion** *or* **ge·ˌlat·i·ni·'sa·tion** *n.* —**ge·'lat·i·ˌniz·er** *or* **ge·'lat·i·ˌnis·er** *n.*

ge·lat·i·noid (dʒɪ'lætɪˌnɔɪd) *adj.* **1.** resembling gelatin. ~*n.* **2.** a gelatinoid substance, such as collagen.

ge·lat·i·nous (dʒɪ'lætɪnəs) *adj.* **1.** consisting of or resembling jelly; viscous. **2.** of, containing, or resembling gelatin. —**ge·'lat·i·nous·ly** *adv.* —**ge·'lat·i·nous·ness** *n.*

ge·la·tion[1] (dʒɪ'leɪʃən) *n.* the act or process of freezing a liquid. [C19: from Latin *gelātiō* a freezing; see GELATIN]

ge·la·tion[2] (dʒɪ'leɪʃən) *n.* the act or process of forming into a gel. [C20: from GEL]

geld[1] (gɛld) *vb.* **gelds, geld·ing, geld·ed** *or* **gelt.** (*tr.*) **1.** to castrate (a horse or other animal). **2.** to deprive of virility or vitality; emasculate; weaken. [C13: from Old Norse *gelda,* from *geldr* barren] —**'geld·er** *n.*

geld[2] (gɛld) *n.* a tax on land levied in late Anglo-Saxon and Norman England. [Old English *gield* service, tax; related to Old Norse *gjald* tribute, Old Frisian *jeld,* Old High German *gelt* retribution, income]

Gel·der·land *or* **Guel·der·land** ('gɛldəˌlænd; *Dutch* 'xɛldərˌlɑnt) *n.* a province of the E Netherlands: formerly a duchy, belonging successively to several different European powers. Capital: Arnhem. Pop.: 1 580 000 (1973 est.). Area: 5014 sq. km (1955 sq. miles). Also called: **Guelders.**

geld·ing ('gɛldɪŋ) *n.* a castrated male horse. [C14: from Old Norse *geldingr;* see GELD[1], -ING[1]]

Ge·lée (*French* ʒə'le) *n.* **Claude** (klo:d). the original name of **Claude Lorrain.**

Ge·li·bo·lu (gɛ'liboˌlu) *n.* the Turkish name for **Gallipoli.**

gel·id ('dʒɛlɪd) *adj.* very cold, icy, or frosty. [C17: from Latin *gelidus* icy cold, from *gelu* frost] —**ge·'lid·i·ty** *or* **'gel·id·ness** *n.* —**'gel·id·ly** *adv.*

gel·ig·nite ('dʒɛlɪgˌnaɪt) *n.* a type of dynamite in which the nitrogelatin is absorbed in a base of wood pulp and potassium or sodium nitrate. Also called (informal): **gelly.** [C19: from GEL(ATIN) + Latin *ignis* fire + -ITE[1]]

Gel·li·gaer (*Welsh* ˌgɛhli:'gaɪr) *n.* a town in S Wales, in Mid Glamorgan. Pop.: 33 670 (1971).

gel·se·mi·um (dʒɛl'si:mɪəm) *n., pl.* **·mi·ums** *or* **·mi·a** (-mɪə). **1.** any climbing shrub of the loganiaceous genus *Gelsemium,* of SE Asia and North America, esp. the yellow jasmine, having fragrant yellow flowers. **2.** the powdered root of the yellow jasmine, formerly used as a sedative. [C19: New Latin, from Italian *gelsomino* JASMINE]

Gel·sen·kir·chen (*German* ˌgɛlzᵊn'kɪrçᵊn) *n.* an industrial city in W West Germany, in North Rhine-Westphalia. Pop.: 333 202 (1974 est.).

gelt[1] (gɛlt) *vb. Archaic or dialect.* a past tense or past participle of **geld**[1].

gelt[2] (gɛlt) *n. Slang, chiefly U.S.* cash or funds; money. [C19: from Yiddish, from Old High German *gelt* reward]

gem (dʒɛm) *n.* **1.** a precious or semiprecious stone used in jewellery as a decoration; jewel. **2.** a person or thing held to be a perfect example; treasure. **3.** a size of printer's type, approximately equal to 4 point. ~*vb.* **gems, gem·ming, gemmed. 4.** (*tr.*) to set or ornament with gems. [C14: from Old French *gemme,* from Latin *gemma* bud, precious stone] —**'gem·ˌlike** *adj.* —**'gem·my** *adj.*

Ge·ma·ra (gɛ'mɑ:rə; *Hebrew* gɛma'ra) *n. Judaism.* the later main part of the Talmud, being a commentary on the Mishnah. [C17: from Aramaic *gemārā* completion, from *gemār* to complete] —**Ge·'ma·ric** *adj.* —**Ge·'ma·rist** *n.*

ge·mein·schaft (*German* gə'maɪnˌʃaft) *n., pl.* **·schaf·ten** (*German* -ˌʃaftən). (*often cap.*) a social group united by common beliefs, family ties, etc. Compare: **gesellschaft.** [German, literally: community]

gem·i·nate *adj.* ('dʒɛmɪnɪt, -ˌneɪt) *also* **gem·i·nat·ed. 1.** combined in pairs; doubled: *a geminate leaf; a geminate consonant.* ~*vb.* ('dʒɛmɪˌneɪt). **2.** to arrange or be arranged in pairs: *the "t"s in Italian "gatto" are geminated.* [C17: from

Latin *gemināre* to double, from *geminus* born at the same time, twin] —ˈ**gem·i·nate·ly** *adv.*

gem·i·na·tion (ˌdʒɛmɪˈneɪʃən) *n.* **1.** the act or state of being doubled or paired. **2.** the doubling of a consonant. **3.** the immediate repetition of a word, phrase, or clause for rhetorical effect.

Gem·i·ni (ˈdʒɛmɪˌnaɪ, -ˈniː) *n., Latin genitive* **Gem·i·no·rum** (ˌdʒɛmɪˈnɔːrəm). **1.** *Astronomy.* a zodiacal constellation in the N hemisphere lying between Taurus and Cancer on the ecliptic and containing the stars Castor and Pollux. **2.** *Classical myth.* another name for **Castor and Pollux. 3.** *Astronautics.* any of a series of manned U.S. spacecraft launched between the Mercury and Apollo projects to improve orbital rendezvous and docking techniques. **4.** *Astrology.* **a.** Also called: the **Twins.** the third sign of the zodiac, symbol Π, having a mutable air classification and ruled by the planet Mercury. The sun is in this sign between about May 21 and June 20. **b.** a person born when the sun is in this sign. ~*adj.* **5.** *Astrology.* born under or characteristic of Gemini. ~Also (for senses 4b., 5): **Gem·i·ni·an** (ˌdʒɛmɪˈnaɪən).

gem·ma (ˈdʒɛmə) *n., pl.* **·mae** (-miː). **1.** a small asexual reproductive structure in liverworts, mosses, etc., that becomes detached from the parent and develops into a new individual. **2.** *Zoology.* another name for **gemmule** (sense 1). [C18: from Latin: bud, GEM] —**gem·ma·ceous** (dʒɛˈmeɪʃəs) *adj.*

gem·mate (ˈdʒɛmeɪt) *adj.* **1.** (of some plants and animals) having or reproducing by gemmae. ~*vb.* **2.** (*intr.*) to produce or reproduce by gemmae. —**gem·ˈma·tion** *n.*

gem·mip·a·rous (dʒɛˈmɪpərəs) *adj.* (of plants and animals) reproducing by gemmae or buds. —**gem·ˈmip·a·rous·ly** *adv.*

gem·mu·la·tion (ˌdʒɛmjʊˈleɪʃən) *n.* the process of reproducing by or bearing gemmules.

gem·mule (ˈdʒɛmjuːl) *n.* **1.** *Zoology.* a cell or mass of cells produced asexually by sponges and developing into a new individual; bud. **2.** *Botany.* a small gemma. **3.** a small hereditary particle postulated by Darwin in his theory of pangenesis. [C19: from French, from Latin *gemmula* a little bud; see GEM]

gem·ol·o·gy *or* **gem·mol·o·gy** (dʒɛˈmɒlədʒɪ) *n.* the branch of mineralogy that is concerned with gems and gemstones. —**gem·o·log·i·cal** *or* **gem·mo·log·i·cal** (ˌdʒɛməˈlɒdʒɪkəl) *adj.* —**gem·ˈol·o·gist** *or* **gem·ˈmol·o·gist** *n.*

ge·mot *or* **ge·mote** (gɪˈməʊt) *n.* (in Anglo-Saxon England) a legal or administrative assembly of a community, such as a shire or hundred. [Old English *gemōt* MOOT]

gems·bok *or* **gems·buck** (ˈgɛmzˌbʌk) *n., pl.* **·bok, ·boks** *or* **·buck, ·bucks.** an oryx, *Oryx gazella,* of southern Africa, marked with a broad black band along its flanks. [C18: from Afrikaans, from German *Gemsbock,* from *Gemse* chamois + *Bock* BUCK[1]]

gem·stone (ˈdʒɛmˌstəʊn) *n.* a precious or semiprecious stone, esp. one cut and polished for setting in jewellery.

ge·müt·lich *German.* (gəˈmyːtlɪç) *adj.* having a feeling or atmosphere of warmth and friendliness; cosy.

gen (dʒɛn) *n. Brit. informal.* information: *give me the gen on your latest project.* ~See also **gen up.** [C20: from *gen*(*eral information*)]

gen. *abbrev. for:* **1.** gender. **2.** general(ly). **3.** generator. **4.** generic. **5.** genitive. **6.** genus.

Gen. *abbrev. for:* **1.** General. **2.** *Bible.* Genesis.

-gen *suffix forming nouns.* **1.** producing or that which produces: *hydrogen.* **2.** something produced: *antigen.* [via French *-gène,* from Greek *-genēs* born]

ge·nappe (dʒəˈnæp) *n.* a smooth worsted yarn used for braid, etc. [C19: from *Genappe,* Belgium, where originally manufactured]

gen·darme (ˈʒɒndɑːm; *French* ʒɑ̃ˈdarm) *n.* **1.** a member of the police force in France or in countries influenced or controlled by France. **2.** a slang word for a **policeman. 3.** a sharp pinnacle of rock on a mountain ridge. [C16: from French, from *gens d'armes* people of arms]

gen·dar·me·rie *or* **gen·dar·me·ry** (ʒɒnˈdɑːmərɪ; *French* ʒɑ̃darməˈri) *n.* **1.** the whole corps of gendarmes. **2.** the headquarters or barracks of a body of gendarmes.

gen·der (ˈdʒɛndə) *n.* **1.** a set of two or more grammatical categories into which the nouns of certain languages are divided, sometimes but not necessarily corresponding to the sex of the referent when animate. See also **natural gender. 2.** any of the categories, such as masculine, feminine, neuter, or common, within such a set. **3.** *Informal.* the state of being male, female, or neuter. **4.** *Informal.* all the members of one sex: *the female gender.* [C14: from Old French *gendre,* from Latin *genus* kind] —ˈ**gen·der·less** *adj.*

gene (dʒiːn) *n.* a unit of heredity, capable of replication and mutation, occupying a fixed position on a chromosome and transmitted from parent to offspring during reproduction. It is thought to act by controlling the synthesis of a particular polypeptide chain in protein synthesis. [C20: from German *Gen,* shortened from *Pangen;* see PAN-, -GEN]

-gene *suffix forming nouns.* variant of **-gen.**

geneal. *abbrev. for* genealogy.

ge·ne·a·log·i·cal tree *n.* another name for a **family tree.**

ge·ne·al·o·gy (ˌdʒiːnɪˈælədʒɪ) *n., pl.* **·gies. 1.** the direct descent of an individual or group from an ancestor. **2.** the study of the evolutionary development of animals and plants from earlier forms. **3.** a chart showing the relationships and descent of an individual, group, etc. [C13: from Old French *genealogie,* from Late Latin *geneālogia,* from Greek, from *genea* race] —**ge·ne·a·log·i·cal** (ˌdʒiːnɪəˈlɒdʒɪkəl) *or* ˌ**ge·ne·a·ˈlog·ic** *adj.* —ˌ**ge·ne·a·ˈlog·i·cal·ly** *adv.* —ˌ**ge·ne·ˈal·o·gist** *n.*

gene flow *n.* the movement and exchange of genes between interbreeding populations.

gene fre·quen·cy *n.* the frequency of occurrence of a particular gene in a population in relation to the frequency of its alleles.

gene pool *n.* the sum of all the genes in an interbreeding population.

gen·er·a (ˈdʒɛnərə) *n.* the plural of **genus.**

gen·er·a·ble (ˈdʒɛnərəbəl) *adj.* able to be generated. [C15: from Late Latin *generābilis,* from Latin *generāre* to beget]

gen·er·al (ˈdʒɛnərəl, ˈdʒɛnrəl) *adj.* **1.** common; widespread: *a general feeling of horror at the crime.* **2.** of, including, applying to, or participated in by all or most of the members of a group, category, or community. **3.** relating to various branches of an activity, profession, etc.; not specialized: *general office work.* **4.** including various or miscellaneous items: *general knowledge; a general store.* **5.** not specific as to detail; overall: *a general description of the merchandise.* **6.** not definite; vague: *give me a general idea of when you will finish.* **7.** applicable or true in most cases; usual. **8.** (*prenominal or immediately postpositive*) having superior or extended authority or rank: *general manager; consul general.* **9.** Also: **pass.** designating a degree awarded at some universities, studied at a lower academic standard than an honours degree. See **honours** (sense 2). **10.** *Med.* relating to or involving the entire body or many of its parts; systemic. ~*n.* **11.** an officer of a rank senior to lieutenant general, esp. one who commands a large military formation. **12.** any person who applies strategy or tactics. **13.** a general condition or principle: opposed to *particular.* **14.** a title for the head of a religious order, congregation, etc. **15.** *Med.* short for **general anaesthetic. 16.** *Archaic.* the people; public. **17. in general.** generally; mostly or usually. [C13: from Latin *generālis* of a particular kind, from *genus* kind] —ˈ**gen·er·al·ness** *n.*

gen·er·al an·aes·thet·ic *n.* a drug producing anaesthesia of the entire body, with loss of consciousness.

Gen·er·al As·sem·bly *n.* **1.** the deliberative assembly of the United Nations. Abbrev.: **G.A. 2.** the parliament of New Zealand. **3.** the supreme governing body of certain religious denominations, esp. of the Presbyterian Church.

Gen·er·al Cer·tif·i·cate of Ed·u·ca·tion *n.* See **GCE.**

gen·er·al de·liv·er·y *n.* the U.S. and Canadian equivalent of **poste restante.**

gen·er·al e·lec·tion *n.* **1.** an election in which representatives are chosen in all constituencies of a state. **2.** *U.S.* a final election from which successful candidates are sent to a legislative body. Compare **primary. 3.** *U.S.* a national or state election in contrast to a local election.

gen·er·al hos·pi·tal *n.* a hospital not specializing in the treatment of particular illnesses or of patients of a particular sex or age group.

gen·er·al·is·si·mo (ˌdʒɛnərəˈlɪsɪˌməʊ, ˌdʒɛnrə-) *n., pl.* **·mos.** a supreme commander of combined military, naval, and air forces, esp. one who wields political as well as military power. [C17: from Italian, superlative of *generale* GENERAL]

gen·er·al·ist (ˈdʒɛnərəlɪst, ˈdʒɛnrə-) *n.* a person who is knowledgeable in many fields of study. Compare **specialist** (sense 1).

gen·er·al·i·ty (ˌdʒɛnəˈrælɪtɪ) *n., pl.* **·ties. 1.** a principle or observation having general application, esp. when imprecise or unable to be proved. **2.** the state or quality of being general. **3.** *Archaic.* the majority.

gen·er·al·i·za·tion *or* **gen·er·al·i·sa·tion** (ˌdʒɛnrəlaɪˈzeɪʃən) *n.* **1.** a principle, theory, etc., with general application. **2.** the act or an instance of generalizing. **3.** *Psychol.* the process of evoking by certain stimuli a response learned to a similar stimulus. See also **conditioning. 4.** *Logic.* a proposition asserting the truth of something either for all members of a class (**universal generalization**) or for one or more particular members of a class (**existential generalization**).

gen·er·al·ize *or* **gen·er·al·ise** (ˈdʒɛnrəˌlaɪz) *vb.* **1.** to form (general principles or conclusions) from (detailed facts, experience, etc.); infer. **2.** (*intr.*) to think or speak in generalities, esp. in a prejudiced way. **3.** (*tr.; usually passive*) to cause to become widely used or known. **4.** (*intr.*) (of a disease) **a.** to spread throughout the body. **b.** to change from a localized infection or condition to a systemic one. —ˈ**gen·er·al·ˌiz·er** *or* ˈ**gen·er·al·ˌis·er** *n.*

gen·er·al·ized oth·er *n. Psychol.* an individual's concept of other people.

gen·er·al·ly (ˈdʒɛnrəlɪ) *adv.* **1.** usually; as a rule. **2.** commonly or widely. **3.** without reference to specific details or facts; broadly.

gen·er·al of·fic·er *n.* an officer holding a commission of brigadier's rank or above in the army, air force, or marine corps.

gen·er·al pa·ral·y·sis of the in·sane *n.* a disease of the central nervous system: a late manifestation of syphilis, often occurring up to 15 years after the original infection, characterized by mental deterioration, speech defects, and progressive paralysis. Abbrev.: **GPI** Also called: **general paresis, dementia paralytica.**

Gen·er·al Post Of·fice *n.* **1.** (in Britain until 1969) the department of the central Government that provided postal and telephone services. **2.** the main post office in a locality.

gen·er·al prac·ti·tion·er *n.* a physician who does not specialize but has a medical practice (**general practice**) in which he treats all illnesses. Informal name: **family doctor.** Abbrev.: **G.P.**

gen+er+al se+man+tics *n.* (*functioning as sing.*) a school of thought, founded by Alfred Korzybski, that stresses the arbitrary nature of language and other symbols and the problems that result from misunderstanding their nature.

gen+er+al+ship ('dʒɛnrəl,ʃɪp) *n.* **1.** the art or duties of exercising command of a major military formation or formations. **2.** tactical or administrative skill.

gen+er+al staff *n.* officers assigned to advise senior officers in the planning and execution of military policy.

gen+er+al strike *n.* a strike by all or most of the workers of a country, province, city, etc., esp. (*caps.*) such a strike that took place in Britain in 1926.

Gen+er+al Syn+od *n.* the governing body, under Parliament, of the Church of England, made up of the bishops and elected clerical and lay representatives.

gen+er+al the·o+ry of rel·a+tiv+i·ty *n.* the theory of gravitation, developed by Einstein in 1916, extending the special theory of relativity to include acceleration and leading to the conclusion that gravitational forces are equivalent to forces caused by acceleration.

gen+er+ate ('dʒɛnə,reɪt) *vb.* (*mainly tr.*) **1.** to produce or bring into being; create. **2.** (*also intr.*) to produce (electricity), esp. in a power station. **3.** to produce (a substance) by a chemical process. **4.** *Mathematics, linguistics.* to provide a precise criterion or specification for membership in (a set): *these rules will generate all the noun phrases in English.* **5.** *Geom.* to trace or form by moving a point, line, or plane in a specific way: *circular motion of a line generates a cylinder.* [C16: from Latin *generāre* to beget, from *genus* kind]

gen+er·a+tion (,dʒɛnə'reɪʃən) *n.* **1.** the act or process of bringing into being; production or reproduction, esp. of offspring. **2.** a successive stage in natural descent of people or animals or the individuals produced at each stage. **3.** the normal or average time between two such generations of a species: about 35 years for humans. **4.** a phase or form in the life cycle of a plant or animal characterized by a particular type of reproduction: *the gametophyte generation.* **5.** all the people of approximately the same age, esp. when considered as sharing certain attitudes, etc. **6.** production of electricity, heat, etc. **7.** *Physics.* a set of nuclei formed directly from a preceding set in a chain reaction. **8.** (*modifier, in combination*) **a.** belonging to a generation specified as having been born in or as having parents, grandparents, etc., born in a given country: *a third-generation American.* **b.** belonging to a specified stage of development in manufacture, usually implying improvement: *a second-generation computer.*

gen+er·a+tion gap *n.* the years separating one generation from the generation that precedes or follows it, esp. when regarded as representing the difference in outlook and the lack of understanding between them.

gen+er·a+tive ('dʒɛnərətɪv) *adj.* **1.** of or relating to the production of offspring, parts, etc.: *a generative cell.* **2.** capable of producing or originating.

gen+er·a+tive gram+mar *n.* a description of a language in terms of explicit rules that ideally generate all and only the grammatical sentences of the language. Compare **transformational grammar.**

gen+er·a+tive se+man+tics *n.* (*functioning as sing.*) a school of semantic theory based on the doctrine that syntactic and semantic structure are of the same formal nature and that there is a single system of rules in the mind that relates surface structure to meaning. Compare **interpretive semantics.**

gen+er·a+tor ('dʒɛnə,reɪtə) *n.* **1.** *Physics.* **a.** any device for converting mechanical energy into electrical energy by electromagnetic induction, esp. a large one as in a power station. **b.** a device for producing a voltage electrostatically. **c.** any device that converts one form of energy into another form: *an acoustic generator.* **2.** an apparatus for producing a gas. **3.** a person or thing that generates.

gen+er·a+trix ('dʒɛnə,reɪtrɪks) *n., pl.* **gen+er·a+tri+ces** ('dʒɛnə,reɪtrɪ,si:z). a point, line, or plane that is moved in a specific way to produce a geometric figure.

ge+ner+ic (dʒɪ'nɛrɪk) *or* **ge+ner·i+cal** *adj.* **1.** applicable or referring to a whole class or group; general. **2.** *Biology.* of, relating to, or belonging to a genus: *the generic name.* **3.** (of a drug) not having a trademark. [C17: from French; see GENUS] —**ge+'ner·i·cal+ly** *adv.*

gen+er+os+i·ty (,dʒɛnə'rɒsɪtɪ) *n., pl.* **·ties. 1.** willingness and liberality in giving away one's money, time, etc.; magnanimity. **2.** freedom from pettiness in character and mind. **3.** a generous act. **4.** abundance; plenty.

gen+er+ous ('dʒɛnərəs, 'dʒɛnrəs) *adj.* **1.** willing and liberal in giving away one's money, time, etc.; munificent. **2.** free from pettiness in character and mind. **3.** full or plentiful: *a generous portion.* **4.** (of wine) rich in alcohol. **5.** (of a soil type) fertile. [C16: via Old French from Latin *generōsus* nobly born, from *genus* race; see GENUS] —**'gen+er+ous+ly** *adv.* —**'gen+er+ous+ness** *n.*

gen+e·sis ('dʒɛnɪsɪs) *n., pl.* **·ses** (-,si:z). a beginning or origin of anything. [Old English: via Latin from Greek; related to Greek *gignesthai* to be born]

Gen+e·sis ('dʒɛnɪsɪs) *n.* the first book of the Old Testament recounting the events from the Creation of the world to the sojourning of the Israelites in Egypt.

-gen·e·sis *n. combining form.* indicating genesis, development, or generation: *biogenesis; parthenogenesis.* [New Latin, from Latin: GENESIS] —**-ge·net·ic** *or* **-gen·ic** *adj. combining form.*

gen+et[1] ('dʒɛnɪt) *or* **ge+nette** (dʒɪ'nɛt) *n.* **1.** any agile catlike viverrine mammal of the genus *Genetta*, inhabiting wooded regions of Africa and S Europe, having an elongated head, thick spotted or blotched fur, and a very long tail. **2.** the fur of such an animal. [C15: from Old French *genette*, from Arabic *jarnayt*]

gen+et[2] ('dʒɛnɪt) *n.* an obsolete spelling of **jennet.**

Ge+net (*French* ʒə'nɛ) *n.* **Jean** (ʒɑ̃). born 1910, French dramatist and novelist; his novels include *Notre-Dame des Fleurs* (1944) and his plays, *Les Bonnes* (1947) and *Le Balcon* (1956).

ge+net+ic (dʒɪ'nɛtɪk) *or* **ge+net·i+cal** *adj.* of or relating to genetics, genes, or the origin of something. [C19: from GENESIS] —**ge+'net·i·cal+ly** *adv.*

ge+net+ic code *n. Biochem.* the order in which the nitrogenous bases of DNA are arranged in the molecule, which determines the type and amount of protein synthesized in the cell. The four bases are arranged in groups of three in a specific order, each group acting as a unit (codon), which specifies a particular amino acid. See also **messenger RNA, transfer RNA.**

ge+net+ic en+gi+neer+ing *n.* alteration of the structure of the chromosomes in living organisms so as to produce effects beneficial to man in agriculture, medicine, etc.

ge+net·i+cist (dʒɪ'nɛtɪsɪst) *n.* a person who studies or specializes in genetics.

ge+net+ics (dʒɪ'nɛtɪks) *n.* **1.** (*functioning as sing.*) the study of heredity and variation in organisms. **2.** the genetic features and constitution of a single organism, species, or group.

Ge·ne·va (dʒɪ'ni:və) *n.* **1.** a city in SW Switzerland, in the Rhône valley on Lake Geneva: centre of Calvinism; headquarters of the International Red Cross (1864), the International Labour Office (1925), the League of Nations (1929–46), the World Health Organization, and the European office of the United Nations; banking centre. Pop.: 159 200 (1975 est.). **2.** a canton in SW Switzerland. Capital: Geneva. Pop.: 331 599 (1970). Area: 282 sq. km (109 sq. miles). **3. Lake.** a lake between SW Switzerland and E France: fed and drained by the River Rhône, it is the largest of the Alpine lakes; the surface is subject to considerable changes of level. Area: 580 sq. km (224 sq. miles). French name: **Lac Léman.** German name: **Genfersee.** ~(for senses 1 and 2) French name: **Genève;** German name: **Genf.**

Ge+ne·va bands *pl. n.* a pair of white lawn or linen strips hanging from the front of the neck or collar of some ecclesiastical and academic robes. [C19: named after GENEVA, where originally worn by Swiss Calvinist clergy]

Ge+ne·va Con+ven+tion *n.* the international agreement, first formulated in 1864 at Geneva, establishing a code for wartime treatment of the sick or wounded: revised and extended on several occasions to cover maritime warfare and prisoners of war.

Ge+ne·va gown *n.* a long loose black gown with very wide sleeves worn by academics or Protestant clerics. [C19: named after GENEVA; see GENEVA BANDS]

Ge+ne·van (dʒɪ'ni:vən) *or* **Gen+e·vese** (,dʒɛnɪ'vi:z) *adj.* **1.** of, relating to, or characteristic of Geneva. **2.** *Theol.* of, adhering to, or relating to the teachings of Calvin or the Calvinists. ~*n., pl.* **·vans** *or* **·vese. 3.** a native or inhabitant of Geneva. **4.** a less common name for a **Calvinist.**

Ge+nève (ʒə'nɛ:v) *n.* the French name for **Geneva.**

Gen·e·viève ('dʒɛnɪ,vi:v; *French* ʒən'vjɛ:v) *n.* **Saint.** ?422–?512 A.D., French nun; patron saint of Paris. Feast day: Jan. 3.

Genf (gɛnf) *n.* the German name for **Geneva.**

Genf+er+see ('gɛnfər,ze:) *n.* the German name for (Lake) **Geneva.**

Gen·ghis Khan ('gɛŋgɪs 'kɑ:n) *n.* original name *Temuchin* or *Temujin.* ?1162–1227, Mongol ruler, whose empire stretched from the Black Sea to the Pacific. Also called: **Jinghis Khan, Jenghiz Khan.**

gen+ial[1] ('dʒi:njəl, -nɪəl) *adj.* **1.** cheerful, easygoing, and warm in manner or behaviour. **2.** pleasantly warm, so as to give life, growth, or health: *the genial sunshine.* [C16: from Latin *geniālis* relating to birth or marriage, from *genius* tutelary deity; see GENIUS] —**ge+ni+al+i·ty** (,dʒi:nɪ'ælɪtɪ) *or* **'gen+ial+ness** *n.* —**'gen+ial+ly** *adv.*

ge+ni+al[2] (dʒɪ'ni:əl) *adj. Anatomy.* of or relating to the chin. [C19: from Greek *geneion*, from *genus* jaw]

gen+ic ('dʒɛnɪk) *adj.* of or relating to a gene or genes.

-gen·ic *adj. combining form.* **1.** relating to production or generation: *antigenic.* **2.** well suited to or suitable for: *photogenic.* [from -GEN + -IC]

ge+nic·u+late (dʒɪ'nɪkjʊlɪt, -,leɪt) *adj.* **1.** *Biology.* bent at a sharp angle: *geniculate antennae.* **2.** having a joint or joints capable of bending sharply. [C17: from Latin *geniculātus* jointed, from *geniculum* a little knee, small joint, from *genu* knee] —**ge+'nic·u·late+ly** *adv.* —**ge+,nic·u+'la+tion** *n.*

ge+nie ('dʒi:nɪ) *n.* **1.** (in fairy tales and stories) a servant who appears by magic and fulfils a person's wishes. **2.** another word for **jinni.** [C18: from French *génie*, from Arabic *jinni* demon, influenced by Latin *genius* attendant spirit; see GENIUS]

ge+ni·i ('dʒi:nɪ,aɪ) *n.* the plural of **genius** (senses 5, 6).

gen+ip ('dʒɛnɪp) *n.* another word for **genipap.** [C18: from Spanish *genipa*, from French, from Guarani]

gen·i+pap ('dʒɛnɪ,pæp) *or* **gen+ip** *n.* **1.** an evergreen West Indian rubiaceous tree, *Genipa americana*, with reddish-brown edible orange-like fruits. **2.** the fruit of this tree. [C17: from Portuguese *genipapo*, from Tupi]

genit. *abbrev. for* genitive.

gen·i+tal ('dʒɛnɪtᵊl) *adj.* **1.** of or relating to the sexual organs or to reproduction. **2.** *Psychoanal.* relating to the mature stage of psychosexual development in which an affectionate relationship with one's sex partner is established. Compare **anal** (sense 2), **oral** (sense 7), **phallic** (sense 2). [C14: from Latin *genitālis* concerning birth, from *gignere* to beget]

gen·i·tals ('dʒɛnɪtᵊlz) *or* **gen·i·ta·li·a** (ˌdʒɛnɪ'teɪlɪə, -'teɪljə) *pl. n.* the sexual organs; the testicles and penis of a male or the labia, clitoris, and vagina of a female. —**gen·i·tal·ic** (ˌdʒɛnɪ'tælɪk) *adj.*

gen·i·tive ('dʒɛnɪtɪv) *Grammar.* ~*adj.* **1.** denoting a case of nouns, pronouns, and adjectives in inflected languages used to indicate a relation of ownership or association, usually translated by English *of.* ~*n.* **2. a.** the genitive case. **b.** a word or speech element in this case. [C14: from Latin *genetīvus,* relating to birth, from *gignere* to produce] —**gen·i·ti·val** (ˌdʒɛnɪ'taɪvᵊl) *adj.* —ˌ**gen·i·'ti·val·ly** *adv.*

gen·i·tor ('dʒɛnɪtə, -tɔː) *n.* the biological father as distinguished from the pater or legal father. [C15: from Latin, from *gignere* to beget]

gen·i·to·u·ri·nar·y (ˌdʒɛnɪtəʊ'jʊərɪnərɪ) *adj.* another name for **urogenital.**

ge·ni·us ('dʒiːnɪəs, -njəs) *n., pl.* **·us·es** *or* (for senses 5, 6) **ge·ni·i** ('dʒiːnɪˌaɪ). **1.** a person with exceptional ability, esp. of a highly original kind. **2.** such ability or capacity: *Mozart's musical genius.* **3.** the distinctive spirit or creative nature of a nation, era, language, etc. **4.** a person considered as exerting great influence of a certain sort: *an evil genius.* **5.** *Roman myth.* **a.** the guiding spirit who attends a person from birth to death. **b.** the guardian spirit of a place, group of people, or institution. **6.** *Arabic myth.* (*usually pl.*) a demon; jinn. [C16: from Latin, from *gignere* to beget]

ge·ni·us lo·ci *Latin.* ('dʒiːnɪəs 'ləʊsaɪ) *n.* **1.** the guardian spirit of a place. **2.** the special atmosphere of a particular place. [genius of the place]

ge·ni·zah (gɛ'niːzə) *n.* a room in a synagogue for storing books, sacred objects, etc. [C19: from Hebrew, literally: a hiding place, from *gānaz* to hide, set aside]

Genk *or* **Genck** (*Flemish* xɛŋk) *n.* a town in NE Belgium, in Limbourg province: coal-mining. Pop.: 57 913 (1970).

Genl. *or* **genl.** *abbrev. for* General *or* general.

gen·o·a ('dʒɛnəʊə) *n. Yachting.* a large triangular jib sail, often with a foot that extends as far aft as the clew of the mainsail. Also called: **genoa jib.** Sometimes shortened to **genny, jenny.**

Gen·o·a ('dʒɛnəʊə) *n.* a port in NW Italy, capital of Liguria, on the **Gulf of Genoa:** Italy's main port; an independent commercial city with many colonies in the Middle Ages; university (1243); heavy industries. Pop.: 805 855 (1975 est.). Italian name: **Genova.**

Gen·o·a cake *n.* a rich fruit cake, usually decorated with almonds.

gen·o·cide ('dʒɛnəʊˌsaɪd) *n.* the policy of deliberately killing a nationality or ethnic group. [C20: from *geno-,* from Greek *genos* race + -CIDE] —ˌ**gen·o·'cid·al** *adj.*

Gen·o·ese (ˌdʒɛnəʊ'iːz) *or* **Gen·o·vese** (ˌdʒɛnə'viːz) *n., pl.* **·ese** *or* **·vese.** **1.** a native or inhabitant of Genoa. ~*adj.* **2.** of or relating to Genoa or its inhabitants.

ge·nome *or* **ge·nom** ('dʒiːnəʊm) *n.* the complement of haploid chromosomes contained in a single gamete or nucleus. [C20: from German *Genom,* from *Gen* GENE + (CHROMOS)OME]

gen·o·type ('dʒɛnəʊˌtaɪp) *n.* **1.** the genetic constitution of an organism. **2.** a group of organisms with the same genetic constitution. ~Compare **phenotype.** —**gen·o·typ·ic** (ˌdʒɛnəʊ'tɪpɪk) *or* ˌ**gen·o·'typ·i·cal** *adj.* —ˌ**gen·o·'typ·i·cal·ly** *adv.* —**gen·o·ty·pic·i·ty** (ˌdʒɛnəʊtɪ'pɪsɪtɪ) *n.*

-gen·ous *adj. combining form.* **1.** yielding or generating: *androgenous; erogenous.* **2.** generated by or issuing from: *endogenous.* [from -GEN + -OUS]

Ge·no·va ('dʒɛːnoˌva) *n.* the Italian name for **Genoa.**

gen·re ('ʒɑːnrə) *n.* **1.** kind, category, or sort, esp. of literary or artistic work. **2. a.** a category of painting in which domestic scenes or incidents from everyday life are depicted. **b.** (*as modifier*): *genre painting.* [C19: from French, from Old French *gendre;* see GENDER]

gen·ro ('gɛn'rəʊ) *n.* **1.** (*functioning as sing. or pl.*) a group of highly respected elder statesmen in late 19th- and early 20th-century Japan. **2.** a member of this group. [C20: from Japanese, from Ancient Chinese *nguan lao,* from *nguan* first + *lao* elder]

gens (dʒɛnz) *n., pl.* **gen·tes** ('dʒɛntiːz). **1.** (in ancient Rome) any of a group of aristocratic families, having a common name and claiming descent from a common ancestor in the male line. **2.** *Anthropol.* a group based on descent in the male line. [C19: from Latin: race; compare GENUS, GENDER]

Gen·ser·ic ('gɛnsərɪk, 'dʒɛn-) *or* **Gai·ser·ic** *n.* ?390–477 A.D., king of the Vandals (428–77). He seized Roman lands, esp. extensive parts of N Africa, and sacked Rome (455).

Gent (xɛnt) *n.* the Flemish name for **Ghent.**

gent (dʒɛnt) *n. Informal.* short for **gentleman.**

gen·teel (dʒɛn'tiːl) *adj.* **1.** respectable, polite, and well-bred: *a genteel old lady.* **2.** appropriate to polite or fashionable society: *genteel behaviour.* **3.** affectedly proper or refined; excessively polite. [C16: from French *gentil* well-born; see GENTLE] —**gen·'teel·ly** *adv.* —**gen·'teel·ness** *n.*

gen·teel·ism (dʒɛn'tiːlɪzəm) *n.* a word or phrase used in place of a less genteel one.

gen·tian ('dʒɛnʃən) *n.* **1.** any gentianaceous plant of the genus *Gentiana,* having blue, yellow, white, or red showy flowers. **2.** the bitter-tasting dried rhizome and roots of *Gentiana lutea* (**European** *or* **yellow gentian**), which can be used as a tonic. **3.** any of several similar plants, such as the horse gentian. [C14: from Latin *gentiāna;* perhaps named after *Gentius,* a second-century B.C. Illyrian king, reputedly the first to use it medicinally]

gen·ti·a·na·ceous (ˌdʒɛnʃɪə'neɪʃəs) *adj.* of, relating to, or belonging to the *Gentianaceae,* a family of flowering plants that includes centaury, felwort, and gentian.

gen·tian blue *n.* **a.** a purplish-blue colour. **b.** (*as adj.*): *gentian-blue shoes.*

gen·tian·el·la (ˌdʒɛnʃə'nɛlə, -ʃɪə-) *n.* any of various gentianaceous plants, esp. the alpine species *Gentiana acaulis,* which has showy blue flowers. [C17: from New Latin, literally: a little GENTIAN]

gen·tian vi·o·let *n.* a greenish crystalline substance, obtained from rosaniline, that forms a violet solution in water, used as an indicator, antiseptic, and in the treatment of burns. Also called: **crystal violet.**

gen·tile ('dʒɛntaɪl) *adj.* **1.** denoting an adjective or proper noun used to designate a place or the inhabitants of a place, as *Spanish* and *Spaniard.* **2.** of or relating to a tribe or people. [C14: from Late Latin *gentīlis,* from Latin: one belonging to the same tribe or family; see GENS]

Gen·tile[1] ('dʒɛntaɪl) *n.* **1.** a person, esp. a Christian, who is not a Jew. **2.** a Christian, as contrasted with a Jew. **3.** a person who is not a member of one's own church: used esp. by Mormons. **4.** a heathen or pagan. ~*adj.* **5.** of or relating to a race or religion that is not Jewish. **6.** Christian, as contrasted with Jewish. **7.** not being a member of one's own church: used esp. by Mormons. **8.** pagan or heathen.

Gen·ti·le[2] (*Italian* dʒɛn'tiːle) *n.* **Gio·van·ni** (dʒo'vanni). 1875–1944, Italian Idealist philosopher and Fascist politician: minister of education (1922–24).

gen·ti·lesse ('dʒɛntᵊˌlɛs) *n. Archaic.* politeness or good breeding. [C14: from Old French *gentillesse;* see GENTEEL]

gen·til·i·ty (dʒɛn'tɪlɪtɪ) *n., pl.* **·ties.** **1.** respectability and polite good breeding. **2.** affected politeness. **3.** noble birth or ancestry. **4.** people of noble birth. [C14: from Old French *gentilite,* from Latin *gentīlitās* relationship of those belonging to the same tribe or family; see GENS]

gen·tle ('dʒɛntᵊl) *adj.* **1.** having a mild or kindly nature or character. **2.** soft or temperate; mild; moderate: *a gentle scolding.* **3.** gradual: *a gentle slope.* **4.** easily controlled; tame: *a gentle horse.* **5.** *Archaic.* of good breeding; noble: *gentle blood.* **6.** *Archaic.* gallant; chivalrous. ~*vb.* (*tr.*) **7.** to tame or subdue (a horse, etc.). **8.** to appease or mollify. **9.** *Obsolete.* to ennoble or dignify. ~*n.* **10.** a maggot, esp. when used as bait in fishing. **11.** *Archaic.* a person who is of good breeding. [C13: from Old French *gentil* noble, from Latin *gentīlis* belonging to the same family; see GENS] —'**gen·tly** *adv.*

gen·tle breeze *n. Meteorol.* a light breeze of force three on the Beaufort scale.

gen·tle·folk ('dʒɛntᵊlˌfəʊk) *or* **gen·tle·folks** *pl. n. Chiefly U.S.* persons regarded as being of good breeding.

gen·tle·man ('dʒɛntᵊlmən) *n., pl.* **·men.** **1.** a man regarded as having qualities of refinement associated with a good family. **2.** a man who is cultured, courteous, and well-educated. **3.** a polite name for a man. **4.** the personal servant of a gentleman (esp. in the phrase **gentleman's gentleman**). **5.** *British history.* a man of gentle birth, who was entitled to bear arms, ranking above a yeoman in social position. **6.** (formerly) a euphemistic word for a **smuggler.** —'**gen·tle·man·ly** *adj.* —'**gen·tle·man·li·ness** *n.*

gen·tle·man-at-arms *n., pl.* **gen·tle·men-at-arms.** a member of the guard who attend the British sovereign on ceremonial and state occasions.

gen·tle·man-farm·er *n., pl.* **gen·tle·men-farm·ers.** **1.** a person who engages in farming but does not depend on it for his living. **2.** a person who owns farmland but does not farm it personally.

gen·tle·men's a·gree·ment *or* **gen·tle·man's a·gree·ment** *n.* a personal understanding or arrangement based on honour and not legally binding.

gen·tle·ness ('dʒɛntᵊlnɪs) *n.* **1.** the quality of being gentle. **2.** *Physics.* a property of elementary particles, conserved in certain strong interactions. See also **charm** (sense 7).

gen·tle·wom·an ('dʒɛntᵊlˌwʊmən) *n., pl.* **·wom·en.** **1.** a woman regarded as being of good family or breeding; lady. **2.** a woman who is cultured, courteous, and well-educated. —'**gen·tle·ˌwom·an·ly** *adj.* —'**gen·tle·ˌwom·an·li·ness** *n.*

Gen·too ('dʒɛntuː) *n., pl.* **·toos.** (*sometimes not cap.*) *Archaic.* a Hindu, esp. as distinguished from a Muslim. [C17: from Portuguese *gentio* pagan (literally: GENTILE)]

gen·tri·fi·ca·tion (ˌdʒɛntrɪfɪ'keɪʃən) *n. Brit.* a process by which middle-class people take up residence in a traditionally working-class area of a city, changing the character of the area. [C20: from *gentrify* (to become GENTRY)]

gen·try ('dʒɛntrɪ) *n.* **1.** persons of high birth or social standing; aristocracy. **2.** *Brit.* persons just below the nobility in social rank. [C14: from Old French *genterie,* from *gentil* GENTLE]

gents (dʒɛnts) *n.* (*functioning as sing.*) *Brit. informal.* a men's public lavatory.

gen·u ('dʒɛnjuː) *n., pl.* **gen·u·a** ('dʒɛnjʊə). *Anatomy.* **1.** the technical name for the **knee.** **2.** any kneelike bend in a structure or part. [Latin: knee]

gen·u·flect ('dʒɛnjʊˌflɛkt) *vb.* (*intr.*) **1.** to act in a servile or deferential manner. **2.** *R.C. Church.* to bend one or both knees as a sign of reverence, esp. when passing before the Blessed Sacrament. [C17: from Medieval Latin *genūflectere,* from Latin *genu* knee + *flectere* to bend] —ˌ**gen·u·'flec·tion** *or* (esp. Brit.) ˌ**gen·u·'flex·ion** *n.* —'**gen·u·ˌflec·tor** *n.*

gen·u·ine ('dʒɛnjʊɪn) *adj.* **1.** not fake or counterfeit; original;

real; authentic. **2.** not pretending; frank; sincere. **3.** being of authentic or original stock. [C16: from Latin *genuīnus* inborn, hence (in Late Latin) authentic, from *gignere* to produce] —'**gen·u·ine·ly** *adv.* —'**gen·u·ine·ness** *n.*

gen up *vb.* **gens up, gen·ning up, genned up.** (*tr.; adv.; often passive*) *Brit. informal.* to brief (someone) in detail; give full information to: *I can only take over this job if I am properly genned up.*

ge·nus ('dʒiːnəs) *n., pl.* **gen·e·ra** ('dʒɛnərə) *or* **ge·nus·es. 1.** *Biology.* any of the taxonomic groups into which a family is divided and which contains one or more species. For example, *Vulpes* (foxes) is a genus of the dog family (*Canidae*). **2.** *Logic.* a class of objects or individuals that can be divided into two or more groups or species. **3.** a class, group, etc., with common characteristics. [C16: from Latin: race]

-gen·y *n. combining form.* indicating origin or manner of development: *phylogeny.* [from Greek *-geneia,* from *-genēs* born] —**-gen·ic** *adj. combining form.*

ge·o- *combining form.* indicating earth: *geomorphology.* [from Greek, from *gē* earth]

ge·o·cen·tric (ˌdʒiːəʊ'sɛntrɪk) *adj.* **1.** having the earth at its centre: *the Ptolemaic system postulated a geocentric universe.* **2.** measured from or relating to the centre of the earth. —ˌ**ge·o·'cen·tri·cal·ly** *adv.*

ge·o·cen·tric par·al·lax *n.* See **parallax** (sense 2).

ge·o·chem·is·try (ˌdʒiːəʊ'kɛmɪstrɪ) *n.* the chemistry of the earth's crust. —**ge·o·chem·i·cal** (ˌdʒiːəʊ'kɛmɪkᵊl) *adj.* —ˌ**ge·o·'chem·ist** *n.*

ge·o·chro·nol·o·gy (ˌdʒiːəʊkrə'nɒlədʒɪ) *n.* the branch of geology concerned with ordering events in the earth's history. —**ge·o·chron·o·log·i·cal** (ˌdʒiːəʊˌkrɒnᵊ'lɒdʒɪkᵊl) *adj.*

geod. *abbrev. for:* **1.** geodesy. **2.** geodetic.

ge·ode ('dʒiːəʊd) *n.* a cavity, usually lined with crystals, within a rock mass or nodule. [C17: from Latin *geōdēs* a precious stone, from Greek: earthlike; see GEO-, -ODE[1]] —**ge·od·ic** (dʒɪ'ɒdɪk) *adj.*

ge·o·des·ic (ˌdʒiːəʊ'dɛsɪk, -'diː-) *adj.* **1.** Also: **geodetic, geodesical.** relating to or involving the geometry of curved surfaces. ~*n.* **2.** Also called: **geodesic line.** the shortest line between two points on a curved or plane surface.

ge·o·des·ic dome *n.* a light structural framework arranged as a set of polygons in the form of a shell and covered with sheeting made of plastic, plywood, metal, etc.

ge·od·e·sy (dʒɪ'ɒdɪsɪ) *or* **ge·o·det·ics** (ˌdziːəʊ'dɛtɪks) *n.* the branch of science concerned with determining the exact position of geographical points and the shape and size of the earth. [C16: from French *géodésie,* from Greek *geōdaisia,* from GEO- + *daiein* to divide] —**ge·'od·e·sist** *n.*

ge·o·det·ic (ˌdʒiːəʊ'dɛtɪk) *adj.* **1.** of or relating to geodesy. **2.** another word for **geodesic.** —ˌ**ge·o·'det·i·cal·ly** *adv.*

ge·o·det·ic sur·vey·ing *n.* the surveying of the earth's surface, making allowance for its curvature and giving an accurate framework for lower-order surveys.

ge·o·dy·nam·ics (ˌdʒiːəʊdaɪ'næmɪks) *n.* (*functioning as sing.*) the study of the forces within the earth that affect the structure of the earth's crust. —ˌ**ge·o·dy·'nam·ic** *adj.* —ˌ**ge·o·dy·'nam·i·cist** *n.*

Geof·frey of Mon·mouth ('dʒɛfrɪ) *n.* ?1100–54, Welsh bishop and chronicler; author of *Historia Regum Britanniae,* the chief source of Arthurian legends.

geog. *abbrev. for:* **1.** geographer. **2.** geographic(al). **3.** geography.

ge·og·no·sy (dʒɪ'ɒgnəsɪ) *n.* the study of the structure and composition of the earth. [C18: from French *géognosie,* from GEO- + Greek *gnōsis* a seeking to know, knowledge] —**ge·og·nos·tic** (ˌdʒiːɒg'nɒstɪk) *adj.*

ge·o·graph·i·cal de·ter·min·ism *n. Sociol.* the theory that human activity is determined by geographical conditions.

ge·o·graph·i·cal mile *n.* another name for **nautical mile.**

ge·og·ra·phy (dʒɪ'ɒgrəfɪ) *n., pl.* **-phies. 1.** the study of the natural features of the earth's surface, including topography, climate, soil, vegetation, etc., and man's response to them. **2.** the natural features of a region. **3.** an arrangement of constituent parts; plan; layout. —**ge·'og·ra·pher** *n.* —**ge·o·graph·i·cal** (ˌdʒɪə'græfɪkᵊl) *or* ˌ**ge·o·'graph·ic** *adj.* —ˌ**ge·o·'graph·i·cal·ly** *adv.*

ge·oid ('dʒiːɔɪd) *n.* **1.** a hypothetical surface that corresponds to mean sea level and extends at the same level under the continents. **2.** the shape of the earth.

geol. *abbrev. for:* **1.** geologic(al). **2.** geologist. **3.** geology.

ge·ol·o·gize *or* **ge·ol·o·gise** (dʒɪ'ɒləˌdʒaɪz) *vb.* to study the geological features of (an area).

ge·ol·o·gy (dʒɪ'ɒlədʒɪ) *n.* **1.** the scientific study of the origin, history, structure, and composition of the earth. **2.** the geological features of a district or country. —**ge·o·log·i·cal** (ˌdʒɪə'lɒdʒɪkᵊl) *or* ˌ**ge·o·'log·ic** *adj.* —ˌ**ge·o·'log·i·cal·ly** *adv.* —**ge·'ol·o·gist** *or* **ge·'ol·o·ger** *n.*

geom. *abbrev. for:* **1.** geometric(al). **2.** geometry.

ge·o·mag·ne·tism (ˌdʒiːəʊ'mægnɪˌtɪzəm) *n.* **1.** the magnetic field of the earth. **2.** the branch of physics concerned with this. —**ge·o·mag·net·ic** (ˌdʒiːəʊmæg'nɛtɪk) *adj.*

ge·o·man·cy ('dʒiːəʊˌmænsɪ) *n.* prophecy from the pattern made when a handful of earth is cast down or dots are drawn at random and connected with lines. —'**ge·o·ˌman·cer** *n.* —ˌ**ge·o·'man·tic** *adj.*

ge·o·me·chan·ics (ˌdʒiːəʊmɪ'kænɪks) *n.* (*functioning as sing.*) the study and application of rock and soil mechanics.

ge·om·e·ter (dʒɪ'ɒmɪtə) *or* **ge·om·e·tri·cian** (dʒɪˌɒmɪ'trɪʃən, ˌdʒɪɒmɪ-) *n.* a person who is practised in or who studies geometry.

ge·o·met·ric (ˌdʒɪə'mɛtrɪk) *or* **ge·o·met·ri·cal** *adj.* **1.** of, relating to, or following the methods and principles of geometry. **2.** consisting of, formed by, or characterized by points, lines, curves, or surfaces: *a geometric figure.* **3.** (of design or ornamentation) composed predominantly of simple geometric forms, such as circles, rectangles, triangles, etc. —ˌ**ge·o·'met·ri·cal·ly** *adv.*

ge·o·met·ric mean *n.* the average value of a set of *n* integers, terms, or quantities, expressed as the *n*th root of their product. Compare **arithmetic mean.**

ge·o·met·ric pace *n.* a modern form of a Roman pace, a measure of length taken as 5 feet.

ge·o·met·ric pro·gres·sion *n.* a sequence of numbers, each of which differs from the succeeding one by a constant ratio, as 1, 2, 4, 8, ... Compare **arithmetic progression.**

ge·o·met·ric se·ries *n.* a geometric progression written as a sum, as in 1 + 2 + 4 + 8.

ge·om·e·trid (dʒɪ'ɒmɪtrɪd) *n.* **1.** any moth of the family *Geometridae,* the larvae of which are called measuring worms, inchworms, or loopers. ~*adj.* **2.** of, relating to, or belonging to the *Geometridae.* [C19: from New Latin *Geōmetridae,* from Latin, from Greek *geometrēs:* land measurer, from the looping gait of the larvae]

ge·om·e·trize *or* **ge·om·e·trise** (dʒɪ'ɒmɪˌtraɪz) *vb.* (*intr.*) **1.** to use or apply geometric methods or principles. **2.** to represent in geometric form.

ge·om·e·try (dʒɪ'ɒmɪtrɪ) *n.* **1.** the branch of mathematics concerned with the properties, relationships, and measurement of points, lines, curves, and surfaces. See also **analytical geometry, non-Euclidean geometry. 2. a.** any branch of geometry using a particular notation or set of assumptions: *analytical geometry.* **b.** any branch of geometry referring to a particular set of objects: *solid geometry.* **3.** a shape, configuration, or arrangement. **4.** *Arts.* the shape of a solid or a surface. [C14: from Latin *geōmetria,* from Greek, from *geōmetrein* to measure the land]

ge·o·mor·phic (ˌdʒiːəʊ'mɔːfɪk) *adj.* of, relating to, or resembling the earth's surface.

ge·o·mor·phol·o·gy (ˌdʒiːəʊmɔː'fɒlədʒɪ) *or* **ge·o·mor·phog·e·ny** (ˌdʒiːəʊmɔː'fɒdʒənɪ) *n.* the branch of geology that is concerned with the structure, origin, and development of the topographical features of the earth's crust. —**ge·o·mor·pho·log·i·cal** (ˌdʒiːəʊˌmɔːfə'lɒdʒɪkᵊl) *or* ˌ**ge·o·ˌmor·pho·'log·ic** *adj.* —ˌ**ge·o·ˌmor·pho·'log·i·cal·ly** *adv.*

ge·oph·a·gy (dʒɪ'ɒfədʒɪ), **ge·o·pha·gia** (ˌdʒɪə'feɪdʒə, -dʒɪə), *or* **ge·oph·a·gism** (dʒɪ'ɒfədʒɪzəm) *n.* the practice of eating earth, clay, chalk, etc., found in some primitive tribes. —**ge·'oph·a·gist** *n.* —**ge·oph·a·gous** (dzɪ'ɒfəgəs) *adj.*

ge·o·phys·ics (ˌdʒiːəʊ'fɪzɪks) *n.* (*functioning as sing.*) the branch of geology that uses physics to examine the properties of the earth. It includes seismology, meteorology, and oceanography. —ˌ**ge·o·'phys·i·cal** *adj.* —ˌ**ge·o·'phys·i·cist** *n.*

ge·o·phyte ('dʒiːəʊˌfaɪt) *n.* a perennial plant that propagates by means of buds below the soil surface. —**ge·o·phyt·ic** (ˌdʒiːəʊ'fɪtɪk) *adj.*

ge·o·pol·i·tics (ˌdʒiːəʊ'pɒlɪtɪks) *n.* **1.** (*functioning as sing.*) the study of the effect of geographical factors on politics, esp. international politics; political geography. **2.** (*functioning as pl.*) the combination of geographical and political factors affecting a country or area. —**ge·o·po·lit·i·cal** (ˌdʒiːəʊpə'lɪtɪkᵊl) *adj.* —ˌ**ge·o·ˌpol·i·'ti·cian** *n.*

ge·o·pon·ic (ˌdʒiːəʊ'pɒnɪk) *adj.* **1.** of or relating to agriculture, esp. as a science. **2.** rural; rustic. [C17: from Greek *geōponikos* concerning land cultivation, from *geōponein* to till the soil, from GEO- + *ponein* to labour]

ge·o·pon·ics (ˌdʒiːəʊ'pɒnɪks) *n.* (*functioning as sing.*) the science of agriculture.

Geor·die ('dʒɔːdɪ) *Brit.* ~*n.* **1.** a person who comes from or lives in Tyneside. **2.** the dialect spoken by these people. ~*adj.* **3.** of or relating to these people or their dialect. [C19: a diminutive of GEORGE]

George[1] (dʒɔːdʒ) *n.* **1. Da·vid Lloyd.** See **Lloyd George. 2. Hen·ry.** 1839–97, U.S. economist: advocated a single tax on land values, esp. in *Progress and Poverty* (1879). **3. Saint.** died ?303 A.D., Christian martyr, the patron saint of England; the hero of a legend in which he slew a dragon. Feast day: April 23. **4.** (*German* ge'ɔrgə). **Stef·an (Anton)** ('ʃtɛfan). 1868–1933, German poet and aesthete. Influenced by the French Symbolists, esp. Mallarmé and later by Nietzsche, he sought for an idealized purity of form in his verse. Refused Nazi honours and went into exile in 1933.

George[2] (dʒɔːdʒ) *n. Brit. informal.* the automatic pilot in an aircraft. [C20: originally a slang name for an airman]

George I *n.* 1660–1727, first Hanoverian king of Great Britain (1714–27) and elector of Hanover (1698–1727). His dependence in domestic affairs on his ministers led to the emergence of Walpole as the first prime minister.

George II *n.* **1.** 1683–1760, king of Great Britain and elector of Hanover (1727–60); son of George I. His victory over the French at Dettingen (1743) in the War of the Austrian Succession was the last appearance on a battlefield by a British king. **2.** 1890–1947, king of Greece (1922–24; 1935–47). He was overthrown by the republicans (1924) and exiled during the German occupation of Greece (1941–45).

George III *n.* 1738–1820, king of Great Britain and Ireland (1760–1820) and of Hanover (1815–20). During his reign the American colonies were lost. He became insane in 1811, and his son acted as regent for the rest of the reign.

George IV *n.* 1762–1830, king of Great Britain and Ireland (1820–30); regent (1811–20). He was on bad terms with his father (George III) because of his profligate ways, which undermined the prestige of the crown, and his association with the Whig opposition.

George V *n.* 1865–1936, king of Great Britain and Northern Ireland and emperor of India (1910–36).

George VI *n.* 1895–1952, king of Great Britain and Northern Ireland (1936–52) and emperor of India (1936–47). The second son of George V, he succeeded to the throne after the abdication of his brother, Edward VIII.

George Cross *n.* a British award for bravery. Abbrev.: **G.C.**

George Town *n.* a port in NW Malaysia, capital of Penang state, in NE Penang Island: the first chartered city of the Malayan federation. Pop.: 270 019 (1970). Also called: **Penang.**

George+town ('dʒɔːdʒˌtaʊn) *n.* **1.** the capital and chief port of Guyana, at the mouth of the Demerara River: became capital of the Dutch colonies of Essequibo and Demerara in 1784; seat of the University of Guyana. Pop.: 63 184 (1970). Former name (until 1812): **Stabroek. 2.** the capital of the Cayman Islands: a port on Grand Cayman Island. Pop.: 3975 (1970).

geor+gette *or* **geor+gette crepe** (dʒɔː'dʒɛt) *n.* **a.** a thin silk or cotton crepe fabric with a mat finish. **b.** (*as modifier*): *a georgette blouse.* [C20: from the name *Mme. Georgette,* a French modiste]

Geor+gia ('dʒɔːdʒjə) *n.* **1.** a state of the southeastern U.S., on the Atlantic: consists of coastal plains with forests and swamps, rising to the Cumberland Plateau and the Appalachians in the northwest. Capital: Atlanta. Pop.: 4 686 000 (1970). Area: 152 489 sq. km (58 876 sq. miles). Abbrevs.: **Ga.** or (with zip code) **GA 2.** short for the **Georgian Soviet Socialist Republic.**

Geor+gian ('dʒɔːdʒjən) *adj.* **1.** of, characteristic of, or relating to any or all of the four kings who ruled Great Britain from 1714 to 1830, or to their reigns: *Georgian architecture.* **2.** of or relating to George V of Great Britain or his reign (1910–36): *the Georgian poets.* **3.** of or relating to the Georgian SSR, its people, or their language. **4.** of or relating to the American State of Georgia or its inhabitants. **5.** (of furniture, furnishings, etc.) in or imitative of the style prevalent in England during the 18th century (reigns of George I, II, and III), represented typically by the designs of Sheraton. ~*n.* **6.** the official language of the Georgian SSR, belonging to the South Caucasian family. **7.** a native or inhabitant of the Georgian SSR. **8.** an aboriginal inhabitant of the Caucasus. **9.** a native or inhabitant of the American State of Georgia. **10.** a person belonging to or imitating the styles of either of the Georgian periods in England.

Geor+gian Bay *n.* a bay in S central Canada, in Ontario: the NE part of Lake Huron. Area: 15 000 sq. km (5800 sq. miles).

Geor+gian So+vi+et So+cial+ist Re+pub+lic *or* **Geor+gia** *n.* an administrative division of the SW Soviet Union, on the Black Sea: an independent kingdom for over 2000 years, at its height in the 12th and 13th centuries; joined the Soviet Union in 1921; a major source of manganese, coal, and oil. Capital: Tbilisi. Pop.: 4 686 358 (1970). Area: 69 700 sq. km (26 900 sq. miles).

geor+gic ('dʒɔːdʒɪk) *adj.* **1.** *Literary.* agricultural. ~*n.* **2.** a poem about rural or agricultural life. [C16: from Latin *geōrgicus,* from Greek *geōrgikos,* from *geōrgos* farmer, from *gē* land, earth + *-ourgos,* from *ergon* work]

ge·o+sci+ence (ˌdʒiːəʊ'saɪəns) *n.* **1.** any science, such as geology, geophysics, geochemistry, or geodesy, concerned with the earth; an earth science. **2.** these sciences collectively.

ge·o+sphere ('dʒiːəʊˌsfɪə) *n.* another name for **lithosphere.**

ge·o+stat+ic (ˌdʒiːəʊ'stætɪk) *adj.* **1.** denoting or relating to the pressure exerted by a mass of rock or a similar substance. **2.** (of a construction) able to resist the pressure of a mass of earth or similar material.

ge·o+stat+ics (ˌdʒiːəʊ'stætɪks) *n.* (*functioning as sing.*) the branch of physics concerned with the statics of rigid bodies, esp. the balance of forces within the earth.

ge·o+strat+e·gy (ˌdʒiːəʊ'strætədʒɪ) *n.* the study of geopolitics and strategics, esp. as they affect the analysis of a region.

ge·o+stroph+ic (ˌdʒiːəʊ'strɒfɪk) *adj.* of, relating to, or caused by the force produced by the rotation of the earth: *geostrophic wind.*

ge·o+syn+cline (ˌdʒiːəʊ'sɪnklaɪn) *n.* a broad elongated depression in the earth's crust containing great thicknesses of sediment. —ˌ**ge·o+syn+'cli+nal** *adj.*

ge·o+tax+is (ˌdʒiːəʊ'tæksɪs) *n.* movement of an organism in response to the stimulus of gravity. —ˌ**ge·o+'tac+tic** *adj.* —ˌ**ge·o+'tac+ti+cal+ly** *adv.*

ge·o+tec+ton+ic (ˌdʒiːəʊtɛk'tɒnɪk) *adj.* of or relating to the formation, arrangement, and structure of the rocks of the earth's crust.

ge·o+ther+mal (ˌdʒiːəʊ'θɜːməl) *or* **ge·o+ther+mic** *adj.* of or relating to the heat in the interior of the earth.

ge+ot+ro+pism (dʒɪ'ɒtrəˌpɪzəm) *n.* the response of a plant part to the stimulus of gravity. Plant stems, which grow upwards irrespective of the position in which they are placed, show **negative geotropism.** —**ge·o+trop+ic** (ˌdʒiːəʊ'trɒpɪk) *adj.* —ˌ**ge·o+'trop·i·cal+ly** *adv.*

ger. *abbrev. for:* **1.** gerund. **2.** gerundive.

Ger. *abbrev. for:* **1.** German. **2.** Germany.

Ge·ra (*German* 'geːra) *n.* an industrial city in S East Germany. Pop.: 114 117 (1975 est.).

ge+rah ('gɪərə) *n.* **1.** an ancient Hebrew unit of weight. **2.** an ancient Hebrew coin equal to one twentieth of a shekel. [C16: from Hebrew *gērāh* bean]

ge+ra·ni·a+ceous (dʒɪˌreɪnɪ'eɪʃəs) *adj.* of, relating to, or belonging to the *Geraniaceae,* a family of plants with typically hairy stems and beaklike fruits: includes the geranium, pelargonium, storksbill, and cranesbill. [C19: from New Latin *Geraniāceae;* see GERANIUM]

ge+ra+ni+al (dʒɪ'reɪnɪəl) *n.* the *cis-* isomer of citral. [C19: from GERANI(UM) + AL(DEHYDE)]

ge+ra+ni+ol (dʒɪ'reɪnɪˌɒl, dʒɪ'rɑː-) *n.* a colourless or pale yellow terpine alcohol with an odour of roses, found in many essential oils: used in perfumery. Formula: $C_{10}H_{18}O$. [C19: from GERANI(UM + ALCOH)OL]

ge+ra+ni·um (dʒɪ'reɪnɪəm) *n.* **1.** any cultivated geraniaceous plant of the genus *Pelargonium,* having scarlet, pink, or white showy flowers. See also **pelargonium, rose geranium, lemon geranium. 2.** any geraniaceous plant of the genus *Geranium,* such as cranesbill and herb Robert, having divided leaves and pink or purplish flowers. **3.** a strong red to a moderate or strong pink colour. [C16: from Latin: cranesbill, from Greek *geranion,* from *geranos* CRANE]

ger·a+tol+o·gy (ˌdʒɛrə'tɒlədʒɪ) *n.* the branch of medicine concerned with the elderly and the phenomena associated with ageing; geriatrics and gerontology. [C19: from *gerato-,* from Greek *gēras* old age + -LOGY] —**ger·a+to+log+ic** (ˌdʒɛrətə'lɒdʒɪk) *adj.*

ger+bil *or* **ger+bille** ('dʒɜːbɪl) *n.* any burrowing rodent of the subfamily *Gerbillinae,* inhabiting hot dry regions of Asia and Africa and having soft pale fur: family *Cricetidae.* [C19: from French *gerbille,* from New Latin *gerbillus* a little JERBOA]

ger+ent ('dʒɛrənt) *n. Rare.* a person who rules or manages. [C16: from Latin *gerēns* managing, from *gerere* to bear]

ger+e·nuk ('gɛrɪˌnʊk) *n.* a slender E African antelope, *Litocranius walleri,* with a long thin neck and backward-curving horns. [from Somali *garanug*]

ger+fal+con ('dʒɜːˌfɔːlkən, -ˌfɔːkən) *n.* a variant spelling of **gyrfalcon.**

ger·i+at+ric (ˌdʒɛrɪ'ætrɪk) *adj.* **1.** of or relating to geriatrics or to elderly people. ~*n.* **2.** an elderly person. [C20: from Greek *gēras* old age + -IATRIC]

ger·i·a+tri+cian (ˌdʒɛrɪə'trɪʃən) *or* **ger·i·at+rist** (ˌdʒɛrɪ'ætrɪst). *n.* a physician who specializes in geriatrics.

ger·i+at+rics (ˌdʒɛrɪ'ætrɪks) *n.* (*functioning as sing.*) the branch of medical science concerned with the diagnosis and treatment of diseases affecting elderly people. Compare **gerontology.**

Gé·ri·cault (*French* ʒeri'ko) *n.* (**Jean Louis André**) **Thé·o·dore** (teɔ'dɔːr). 1791–1824, French romantic painter, noted for his skill in capturing movement, esp. of horses.

Ger+la+chov+ka (*Czech* 'gɛrlaxɔfka) *n.* a mountain in E Czechoslovakia, in the Tatra Mountains: the highest peak of the Carpathian Mountains. Height: 2663 m (8736 ft.).

germ (dʒɜːm) *n.* **1.** a microorganism, esp. one that produces disease in animals or plants. **2.** (*often pl.*) the rudimentary or initial form of something: *the germs of revolution.* **3.** a simple structure, such as a fertilized egg, that is capable of developing into a complete organism. [C17: from French *germe,* from Latin *germen* sprig, bud, sprout, seed]

ger+man¹ ('dʒɜːmən) *n. U.S.* a dance consisting of complicated figures and changes of partners. [C19: shortened from *German cotillion*]

ger+man² ('dʒɜːmən) *adj.* **1.** (used in combination) **a.** having the same parents as oneself: *a brother-german.* **b.** having a parent that is a brother or sister of either of one's own parents: *cousin-german.* **2.** a less common word for **germane.** [C14: via Old French *germain,* from Latin *germānus* of the same race, from *germen* sprout, offshoot]

Ger+man ('dʒɜːmən) *n.* **1.** the official language of East and West Germany and Austria and one of the official languages of Switzerland; the native language of approximately 100 million people. It is an Indo-European language belonging to the West Germanic branch, closely related to English and Dutch. There is considerable diversity of dialects; modern standard German is a development of Old High German, influenced by Martin Luther's translation of the Bible. See also **Low German. 2.** a native, inhabitant, or citizen of East or West Germany. **3.** a person whose native language is German: *Swiss Germans; Volga Germans.* ~*adj.* **4.** denoting, relating to, or using the German language. **5.** relating to, denoting, or characteristic of any German state or its people.

Ger+man Bap+tist Breth+ren *pl. n.* a Protestant sect founded in 1708 in Germany but who migrated to the U.S. in 1719–29, the members of which (Dunkers) insist on adult baptism by total immersion. Also called: **Church of the Brethren.**

Ger+man cock+roach *n.* a small cockroach, *Blattella germanica:* a common household pest. Also called (U.S.): **Croton bug.**

Ger+man Dem·o+crat+ic Re+pub+lic *n.* the official name of **East Germany.** Abbrev.: **GDR.**

ger+man+der (dʒɜː'mændə) *n.* any of several plants of the genus *Teucrium,* esp. *T. chamaedrys* (**wall germander**) of Europe, having two-lipped flowers with a very small upper lip: family *Labiatae* (labiates). [C15: from Medieval Latin *germandrea,* from Late Greek *khamandrua,* from Greek *khamaidrus,* from *khamai* on the ground + *drus* oak tree]

ger+man+der speed+well *n.* a creeping scrophulariaceous Eurasian plant, *Veronica chamaedrys,* naturalized in North America, having small bright blue flowers with white centres. Usual U.S. name: **bird's-eye speedwell.**

ger+mane (dʒɜː'meɪn) *adj.* (*postpositive;* usually foll. by *to*) related (to the topic being considered); akin; relevant: *an idea* *germane to the conversation.* [variant of GERMAN[2]] —**ger+'mane+ly** *adv.* —**ger+'mane+ness** *n.*

Ger+man East Af+ri+ca *n.* a former German territory in E Africa, consisting of Tanganyika and Ruanda-Urundi: divided in 1919 between Great Britain and Belgium; now in Tanzania, Rwanda, and Burundi.

ger+man+ic (dʒɜː'mænɪk) *adj.* of or containing germanium in the tetravalent state.

Ger+man+ic (dʒɜː'mænɪk) *n.* **1.** a branch of the Indo-European family of languages that includes English, Dutch, German, the Scandinavian languages, and Gothic. See **East Germanic, West Germanic, North Germanic.** Abbrev.: **Gmc. 2.** the unrecorded language from which all of these languages developed; Proto-Germanic. ~*adj.* **3.** of, denoting, or relating to this group of languages. **4.** of, relating to, or characteristic of Germany, the German language, or any people that speaks a Germanic language.

Ger·man·i·cus Cae·sar (dʒɜː'mænɪkəs) *n.* 15 B.C.–19 A.D., Roman general; nephew of the emperor Tiberius; waged decisive campaigns against the Germans (14–16).

Ger+man+ism ('dʒɜːməˌnɪzəm) *n.* **1.** a word or idiom borrowed from or modelled on German. **2.** a German custom, trait, practice, etc. **3.** attachment to or high regard for German customs, institutions, etc.

ger+man+ite ('dʒɜːməˌnaɪt) *n.* a mineral consisting of a complex copper arsenic sulphide containing germanium, gallium, iron, zinc, and lead: an ore of germanium and gallium. [from GERMANIUM + -ITE[1]]

ger+ma+ni·um (dʒɜː'meɪnɪəm) *n.* a brittle crystalline grey element that is a semiconducting metalloid, occurring principally in zinc ores and argyrodite: used in transistors, as a catalyst, and to strengthen and harden alloys. Symbol: Ge; atomic no.: 32; atomic wt.: 72.59; valency: 2 or 4; relative density: 5.32; melting pt.: 937.4°C; boiling pt.: 2830°C. [C19: New Latin, named after GERMANY]

Ger+man+ize *or* **Ger+man+ise** ('dʒɜːməˌnaɪz) *vb.* to adopt or cause to adopt German customs, speech, institutions, etc. —**ˌGer+man+i+'za+tion** *or* **ˌGer+man·i+'sa+tion** *n.* —**'Ger+man+ˌiz+er** *or* **'Ger+man+ˌis+er** *n.*

Ger+man mea+sles *n.* a nontechnical name for **rubella.**

Ger+man O·cean *n.* a former name for the **North Sea.**

Ger+man·o+phile (dʒɜː'mænəˌfaɪl) *or* **Ger+man·o+phil** *n.* a person having admiration for or devotion to Germany and the Germans. —**Ger+man·o+phil·i·a** (dʒɜːˌmænə'fɪlɪə) *n.*

Ger+man·o+phobe (dʒɜː'mænəˌfəʊb) *n.* a person who hates Germany or its people. —**Ger+ˌman·o+'pho+bi·a** *n.*

ger+man+ous (dʒɜː'mænəs) *adj.* of or containing germanium in the divalent state.

Ger+man shep+herd *n.* the U.S. name for **Alsatian** (sense 1).

Ger+man sil+ver *n.* another name for **nickel silver.**

Ger+man sixth *n.* (in musical harmony) an augmented sixth chord having a major third and a perfect fifth between the root and the augmented sixth. Compare **Italian sixth, French sixth.**

Ger+ma+ny ('dʒɜːmənɪ) *n.* **1.** a country in central Europe: in the Middle Ages the centre of the Holy Roman Empire; dissolved into numerous principalities; united under the leadership of Prussia in 1871 after the Franco-Prussian War; became a republic with reduced size in 1919 after being defeated in World War I; under the dictatorship of Hitler from 1933 to 1945; defeated in World War II and divided by the Allied Powers into four zones, which became established as East and West Germany in the late 1940s. German name: **Deutschland.** See also **East Germany, West Germany.** Related adj.: **Teutonic. 2. Fed+er+al Re+pub+lic of.** the official name of **West Germany.**

germ cell *n.* a sexual reproductive cell; gamete. Compare **somatic cell.**

ger+men ('dʒɜːmən) *n., pl.* **+mens** *or* **+mi+na** (-mɪnə). *Biology.* the mass of undifferentiated cells that gives rise to the germ cells. [C17: from Latin; see GERM]

ger+mi+cide ('dʒɜːmɪˌsaɪd) *n.* any substance that kills germs or other microorganisms. —**ˌger+mi+'cid+al** *adj.*

ger+mi+nal ('dʒɜːmɪn³l) *adj.* **1.** of, relating to, or like germs or a germ cell. **2.** of, or in the earliest stage of development; embryonic. [C19: from New Latin *germinālis*, from Latin *germen* bud; see GERM] —**'ger+mi+nal+ly** *adv.*

Ger+mi+nal *French.* (ʒɛrmi'nal) *n.* the month of buds: the seventh month of the French revolutionary calendar, from March 22 to April 20.

ger+mi+nal disc *n. Embryol.* another name for **blastoderm.**

ger+mi+nal ves·i·cle *n. Biology.* the large nucleus of an oocyte before it develops into an ovum.

ger+mi+nant ('dʒɜːmɪnənt) *adj.* in the process of germinating; sprouting.

ger+mi+nate ('dʒɜːmɪˌneɪt) *vb.* **1.** to cause (seeds or spores) to sprout or (of seeds or spores) to sprout or form new tissue following increased metabolism. **2.** to grow or cause to grow; develop. **3.** to come or bring into existence; originate: *the idea germinated with me.* [C17: from Latin *germināre* to sprout; see GERM] —**'ger+mi+na·ble** *or* **'ger+mi+na+tive** *adj.* —**ˌger+mi+'na+tion** *n.* —**'ger+mi+ˌna+tor** *n.*

Ger+mis+ton ('dʒɜːmɪstən) *n.* a city in South Africa, in the S Transvaal, southeast of Johannesburg: industrial centre, with the world's largest gold refinery, serving the Witwatersrand mines. Pop.: 139 472 (1970).

germ lay+er *n. Embryol.* any of the three layers of cells formed during gastrulation. See **ectoderm, mesoderm, endoderm.**

germ plasm *n.* **1. a.** the part of a germ cell that contains hereditary material; the chromosomes and genes. **b.** the germ cells collectively. Compare **somatoplasm. 2.** (in early theories) a type of protoplasm found only in the germ cells that is transmitted unchanged from generation to generation and gives rise to the body cells.

germ the·o+ry *n.* **1.** the theory that all infectious diseases are caused by microorganisms. **2.** the theory that living organisms develop from other living organisms by the growth and differentiation of germ cells.

germ war+fare *n.* the use of bacteria against an enemy.

Ge+ro+na (*Spanish* xe'rona) *n.* a city in NE Spain: city walls and 14th-century cathedral; often besieged, in particular by the French (1809). Pop.: 50 338 (1970). Ancient name: **Gerunda.**

Ge·ron·i·mo (dʒə'rɒnɪˌməʊ) *n.* **1.** 1829–1909, Apache Indian: led a campaign against the White settlers until his final capture in 1886. ~*interj.* **2.** *U.S.* a shout given by paratroopers as they jump into battle.

ger·on·to- *or before a vowel* **ger·ont-** *combining form.* indicating old age: *gerontology; gerontophilia.* [from Greek *gerōn*, *geront-* old man]

ger+on+toc+ra+cy (ˌdʒɛrɒn'tɒkrəsɪ) *n., pl.* **+cies. 1.** government by old men. **2.** a governing body of old men. —**ge+ron+to+crat+ic** (dʒəˌrɒntə'krætɪk) *adj.*

ger+on+tol+o·gy (ˌdʒɛrɒn'tɒlədʒɪ) *n.* the scientific study of ageing and the problems associated with elderly people. Compare **geriatrics.** —**ger+on+to+log·i·cal** (ˌdʒɛrɒntə'lɒdʒɪk³l) *adj.* —**ˌger+on+'tol·o·gist** *n.*

-ger·ous *adj. combining form.* bearing or producing: *armigerous.* Compare **-ferous.** [from Latin *-ger* bearing + -OUS]

ger+ry+man+der ('dʒɛrɪˌmændə) *vb.* **1.** to divide the constituencies of (a voting area) so as to give one party an unfair advantage. **2.** to manipulate or adapt to one's advantage. ~*n.* **3.** an act or result of gerrymandering. [C19: from Elbridge *Gerry*, U.S. politician + (SALA)MANDER; from the salamander-like outline of an electoral district reshaped (1812) for political purposes while Gerry was governor of Massachusetts]

Gers (*French* ʒɛːr) *n.* a department of SW France, in Midi-Pyrénées region. Capital: Auch. Pop.: 180 501 (1975). Area: 6291 sq. km (2453 sq. miles).

Gersh·win ('gɜːʃwɪn) *n.* **George.** 1898–1937, U.S. composer: incorporated jazz into works such as *Rhapsody in Blue* (1924) for piano and jazz band and the opera *Porgy and Bess* (1935).

ger+und ('dʒɛrənd) *n.* a noun formed from a verb, denoting an action or state. In English, the gerund, like the present participle, is formed in *-ing: the living is easy.* [C16: from Late Latin *gerundium*, from Latin *gerundum* something to be carried on, from *gerere* to wage] —**ge+run+di·al** (dʒɪ'rʌndɪəl) *adj.*

ge+run+dive (dʒɪ'rʌndɪv) *n.* **1.** (in Latin grammar) an adjective formed from a verb, expressing the desirability, etc., of the activity denoted by the verb. ~*adj.* **2.** of or relating to the gerund or gerundive. [C17: from Late Latin *gerundīvus*, from *gerundium* GERUND] —**ger+un+di+val** (ˌdʒɛrən'daɪv³l) *adj.* —**ge+'run+dive+ly** *adv.*

Ge·ry·on ('gɛrɪən) *n. Greek myth.* a winged monster with three bodies joined at the waist, killed by Hercules, who stole the monster's cattle as his tenth labour.

ge+sell+schaft (*German* gə'zɛlˌʃaft) *n., pl.* **+schaf+ten** (*German* -ˌʃaftən). (*often cap.*) a social group held together by practical concerns, formal and impersonal relationships, etc. Compare **gemeinschaft.** [German, literally: society]

ges+so ('dʒɛsəʊ) *n.* **1.** a white ground of plaster and size, used esp. in the Middle Ages and Renaissance to prepare panels or canvas for painting or gilding. **2.** any white substance, esp. plaster of Paris, that forms a ground when mixed with water. [C16: from Italian: chalk, GYPSUM]

gest *or* **geste** (dʒɛst) *n. Archaic.* **1.** a notable deed or exploit. **2.** a tale of adventure or romance, esp. in verse. See also **Chanson de Geste.** [C14: from Old French, from Latin *gesta* deeds, from *gerere* to carry out]

ge+stalt (gə'ʃtælt) *n., pl.* **+stalts** *or* **+stal+ten** (-'ʃtælt³n). (*sometimes cap.*) a perceptual pattern or structure possessing qualities as a whole that cannot be described merely as a sum of its parts. See also **Gestalt psychology.** [C20: German: form, from Old High German *stellen* to shape]

Ge+stalt psy+chol+o·gy *n.* a system of thought, derived from experiments carried out by German psychologists, that regards all mental phenomena as being arranged in gestalts. Also called: **configurationism.**

Ge+sta+po (gɛ'stɑːpəʊ; *German* ge'ʃtaːpo) *n.* the secret state police in Nazi Germany, noted for its brutal methods of interrogation. [from German *Ge(heime) Sta(ats)po(lizei)* literally: secret state police]

Ges+ta Ro+ma+no+rum ('dʒɛstə ˌrəʊmə'nɔːrəm) *n.* a popular collection of tales in Latin with moral applications, compiled in the late 13th century as a manual for preachers. [Latin: deeds of the Romans]

ges+tate ('dʒɛsteɪt) *vb.* to carry (developing young) in the uterus during pregnancy. [C19: back formation from GESTATION]

ges+ta+tion (dʒɛ'steɪʃən) *n.* **1. a.** the development of the embryo of a viviparous mammal, between conception and birth: about 266 days in humans, 624 days in elephants, and 63 days in cats. **b.** (*as modifier*): *gestation period.* **2.** the development of an idea or plan in the mind. **3.** the period of such a development. [C16: from Latin *gestātiō* a bearing, from *gestāre* to bear, frequentative of *gerere* to carry] —**ges+'ta+tion+al** *or* **ges+ta+tive** ('dʒɛstətɪv, dʒɛ'steɪ-) *adj.* —**'ges+ta+to+ry** *adj.*

ges+ta+to+ri+al chair (ˌdʒɛstə'tɔːrɪəl) *n.* a ceremonial chair on which the pope is carried.

ges·tic·u·late (dʒɛˈstɪkjʊˌleɪt) *vb.* to express by or make gestures. [C17: from Latin *gesticulārī*, from Latin *gesticulus* (unattested except in Late Latin) gesture, diminutive of *gestus* gesture, from *gerere* to bear, conduct] **—ges'tic·u·la·tive** *adj.* **—ges'tic·u·la·tor** *n.*

ges·tic·u·la·tion (dʒɛˌstɪkjʊˈleɪʃən) *n.* **1.** the act of gesticulating. **2.** an animated or expressive gesture. **—ges'tic·u·la·to·ry** *adj.*

ges·ture (ˈdʒɛstʃə) *n.* **1.** a motion of the hands, head, or body to emphasize an idea or emotion, esp. while speaking. **2.** something said or done as a formality or as an indication of intention: *a political gesture.* **3.** *Obsolete.* the manner in which a person bears himself; posture. ~*vb.* **4.** to express by or make gestures; gesticulate. [C15: from Medieval Latin *gestūra* bearing, from Latin *gestus,* past participle of *gerere* to bear] **—'ges·tur·al** *adj.* **—'ges·tur·er** *n.*

Ge·su·al·do (*Italian* ˌdʒezuˈaldo) *n.* **Car·lo** (ˈkarlo), Prince of Venosa. ?1560–1613, Italian composer, esp. of madrigals.

ge·sund·heit (*German* gəˈzʊntˌhaɪt) *interj.* an expression used to wish good health to someone who has just sneezed. [from *gesund* healthy + *-heit* -HOOD; see SOUND[2]]

get (gɛt) *vb.* **gets, get·ting, got.** (*mainly tr.*) **1.** to come into possession of; receive or earn. **2.** to bring or fetch. **3.** to contract or be affected by: *he got a chill at the picnic.* **4.** to capture or seize: *the police finally got him.* **5.** (*also intr.*) to become or cause to become or act as specified: *to get a window open; get one's hair cut; get wet.* **6.** (*intr.;* foll. by a preposition or adverbial particle) to succeed in going, coming, leaving, etc.: *get off the bus.* **7.** (*takes an infinitive*) to manage or contrive: *how did you get to be captain?* **8.** to make ready or prepare: *to get a meal.* **9.** to hear, notice, or understand: *I didn't get your meaning.* **10.** *U.S. informal.* to learn or master by study. **11.** (*intr.;* often foll. by *to*) to come (to) or arrive (at): *we got home safely; to get to London.* **12.** to catch or enter: *to get a train.* **13.** to induce or persuade: *get him to leave at once.* **14.** to reach by calculation: *add 2 and 2 and you will get 4.* **15.** to receive (a broadcast signal). **16.** to communicate with (a person or place), as by telephone. **17.** (*also intr.;* foll. by *to*) *Informal.* to have an emotional effect (on): *that music really gets me.* **18.** *Informal.* to annoy or irritate: *her high voice gets me.* **19.** *Informal.* to bring a person into a difficult position from which he cannot escape. **20.** *Informal.* to hit: *the blow got him in the back.* **21.** *Informal.* to be revenged on, esp. by killing. **22.** *U.S. slang.* **a.** (foll. by *to*) to gain access (to a person) with the purpose of bribing him. **b.** (often foll. by *to*) to obtain access (to someone) and kill or silence him. **23.** *Informal.* to have the better of: *your extravagant habits will get you in the end.* **24.** (*intr.;* foll. by present participle) *Informal.* to begin: *get moving.* **25.** (used as a command) *Informal.* go! leave now! **26.** *Archaic.* to beget or conceive. **27. get even with.** *Informal.* to settle an account with; pay back. **28. get it (in the neck).** *Informal.* to suffer a reprimand, punishment, etc. **29. get with it.** *Slang.* to allow oneself to respond to new ideas, styles, etc. **30. get with child.** *Archaic.* to make pregnant. ~*n.* **31.** *Rare.* the act of begetting. **32.** *Rare.* something begotten; offspring. **33.** *Brit. slang.* a variant of **git. 34.** *Informal.* (in tennis, etc.) a successful return of a shot that was difficult to reach. ~See also **get about, get across, get ahead, get along, get at, get away, get back, get by, get down, get in, get into, get off, get on, get onto, get out, get over, get round, get through, get-together, get up, got, gotten.** [Old English *gietan;* related to Old Norse *geta* to get, learn, Old High German *bigezzan* to obtain] **—'get·a·ble** *or* **'get·ta·ble** *adj.*

get a·bout *or* **a·round** *vb.* (*intr., adv.*) **1.** to move around, as when recovering from an illness. **2.** to be socially active. **3.** (of news, rumour, etc.) to become known; spread.

get a·cross *vb.* **1.** to cross or cause or help to cross. **2.** (*adv.*) to be or cause to be readily understood. **3.** (*intr., prep.*) *Informal.* to annoy: *her constant interference really got across him.*

get a·head *vb.* (*intr.*) **1.** to be successful; prosper. **2.** (foll. by *of*) to surpass or excel.

get a·long *vb.* (*intr., adv.*) **1.** (often foll. by *with*) to be friendly or compatible: *my brother gets along well with everybody.* **2.** to manage, cope, or fare: *how are you getting along in your job?* **3.** (*also prep.; often imperative*) to go or move away; leave. ~*interj.* **4.** *Brit. informal.* an exclamation indicating mild disbelief.

get a·round *vb.* See **get about, get round.**

get at *vb.* (*intr., prep.*) **1.** to gain access to: *the dog could not get at the meat on the high shelf.* **2.** to mean or intend: *what are you getting at when you look at me like that?* **3.** to irritate or annoy persistently; criticize: *she is always getting at him.* **4.** to influence or seek to influence, esp. illegally by bribery, intimidation, etc.: *someone had got at the witness before the trial.*

get-at-a·ble *Informal.* accessible.

get a·way *vb.* (*adv., mainly intr.*) **1.** to make an escape; leave. **2.** to make a start. **3. get away with. a.** to steal and escape (with money, goods, etc.). **b.** to do (something wrong, illegal, etc.) without being discovered or punished or with only a minor punishment. ~*interj.* **4.** an exclamation indicating mild disbelief. ~*n.* **get·a·way. 5.** the act of escaping, esp. by criminals. **6.** a start or acceleration. **7.** (*modifier*) used for escaping: *a getaway car.*

get back *vb.* (*adv.*) **1.** (*tr.*) to recover or retrieve. **2.** (*intr.;* often foll. by *to*) to return, esp. to a former position or activity: *let's get back to the original question.* **3.** (*intr.;* foll. by *at*) to retaliate (against); wreak vengeance (on). **4. get one's own back.** *Informal.* to obtain one's revenge.

get by *vb.* **1.** to pass; go past or overtake. **2.** (*intr., adv.*) *Informal.* to manage, esp. in spite of difficulties: *I can get by with little money.* **3.** (*intr.*) to be accepted or permitted: *that book will never get by the authorities.*

get down *vb.* (*mainly adv.*) **1.** (*intr.; also prep.*) to dismount or descend. **2.** (*tr.; also prep.*) to bring down: *we could not get the wardrobe down the stairs.* **3.** (*tr.*) to write down. **4.** (*tr.*) to make depressed: *your nagging gets me down.* **5.** (*tr.*) to swallow: *he couldn't get the meal down.* **6.** (*intr.;* foll. by *to*) to attend seriously (to); concentrate (on) (esp. in the phrases **get down to business** *or* **brass tacks**).

Geth·sem·a·ne (gɛθˈsɛmənɪ) *n. New Testament.* the garden in Jerusalem where Christ was betrayed on the night before his Crucifixion (Matthew 26:36–56).

get in *vb.* (*mainly adv.*) **1.** (*intr.*) to enter a car, train, etc. **2.** (*intr.*) to arrive, esp. at one's home or place of work: *I got in at midnight.* **3.** (*tr.*) to bring in or inside: *get the milk in.* **4.** (*tr.*) to insert or slip in: *he got his suggestion in before anyone else.* **5.** (*tr.*) to gather or collect (crops, debts, etc.). **6.** (*tr.*) to ask (a person, esp. a specialist) to give a service: *shall I get the doctor in?* **7.** to be elected or cause to be elected: *he got in by 400 votes.* **8.** (*tr.*) to succeed in doing (something), esp. during a specified period: *I doubt if I can get this task in today.* **9.** (*intr.*) to obtain a place at university, college, etc. **10.** (foll. by *on*) to join or cause to join (an activity or organization). **11. get in with.** to be or cause to be on friendly terms with (a person). **12.** (*prep.*) See **get into.**

get in·to *vb.* (*prep.*) **1.** (*intr.*) to enter. **2.** (*intr.*) to reach (a destination): *the train got into London at noon.* **3.** to get dressed in (clothes). **4.** (*intr.*) to preoccupy or obsess (a person's emotions or thoughts): *what's got into him tonight?* **5.** to assume or cause to assume (a specified condition, habit, etc.): *to get into debt; get a person into a mess.* **6.** to be elected to or cause to be elected to: *to get into Parliament.* **7.** (*usually intr.*) *Informal.* to become or cause to become familiar with (a skill): *once you get into driving you'll enjoy it.* **8.** (*usually intr.*) *Informal.* to develop or cause to develop an absorbing interest in (a hobby, subject, or book).

get off *vb.* **1.** (*intr., adv.*) to escape the consequences of an action: *he got off very lightly in the accident.* **2.** (*adv.*) to be or cause to be acquitted: *a good lawyer got him off.* **3.** (*adv.*) to depart or cause to depart: *to get the children off to school.* **4.** (*intr.*) to descend (from a bus, train, etc.); dismount: *she got off at the terminus.* **5.** to move or cause to move to a distance (from): *get off the field.* **6.** (*tr.*) to remove; take off: *get your coat off.* **7.** (*adv.*) to go or send to sleep. **8.** (*adv.*) to send (letters) or (of letters) to be sent. **9. get off with.** *Brit. informal.* to establish a sexual relationship (with). **10.** (*intr., adv.*) *Slang.* to become high on heroin or some other drug. **11. tell (someone) where to get off.** *Informal.* to rebuke or criticize harshly.

get on *vb.* (*mainly adv.*) **1.** Also (*when prep.*): **get onto.** to board or cause or help to board (a bus, train, etc.). **2.** (*tr.*) to dress in (clothes as specified). **3.** (*intr.*) to grow late or (of time) to elapse: *it's getting on and I must go.* **4.** (*intr.*) (of a person) to grow old. **5.** (*intr.;* foll. by *for*) to approach (a time, age, amount, etc.): *she is getting on for seventy.* **6.** (*intr.*) to make progress, manage, or fare: *how did you get on in your exam?* **7.** (*intr.;* often foll. by *with*) to establish a friendly relationship: *he gets on well with other people.* **8.** (*intr.;* foll. by *with*) to continue to do: *get on with your homework!* **9.** (*intr.*) *Slang.* to take drugs for the first time. ~*interj.* **10.** I don't believe you!

get on·to *vb.* (*prep.*) **1.** Also: **get on.** to board or cause or help to board (a bus, train, etc.). **2.** (*intr.*) to make contact with; communicate with. **3.** (*intr.*) to become aware of (something illicit or secret): *the boss will get onto their pilfering unless they're careful.* **4.** to deliver a demand, request, or rebuke to: *I'll get onto the manufacturers to replace these damaged goods.* See usage note at **onto.**

get out (*adv.*) **1.** to leave or escape or cause to leave or escape: used in the imperative when dismissing a person. **2.** to make or become known; publish or be published. **3.** (*tr.*) to express with difficulty. **4.** (*tr.;* often foll. by *of*) to extract (information or money) (from a person): *to get a confession out of a criminal.* **5.** (*tr.*) to gain or receive something, esp. something of significance or value: *you get out of life what you put into it.* **6.** (foll. by *of*) to avoid or cause to avoid: *she always gets out of swimming.* **7.** (*tr.*) to solve (a puzzle or problem) successfully. **8.** *Cricket.* to dismiss or be dismissed. ~*n.* **get-out. 9.** an escape, as from a difficult situation.

get o·ver *vb.* **1.** to cross or surmount (something): *get the children over the fence.* **2.** (*intr., prep.*) to recover from (an illness, shock, etc.). **3.** (*intr., prep.*) to overcome or master (a problem): *you'll soon get over your shyness.* **4.** (*intr., prep.*) to appreciate fully: *I just can't get over seeing you again.* **5.** (*tr., adv.*) to communicate effectively: *he had difficulty getting the message over.* **6.** (*tr., adv.;* sometimes foll. by *with*) to bring (something necessary but unpleasant) to an end: *let's get this job over with quickly.*

get round *or* **a·round** *vb.* (*intr.*) **1.** (*prep.*) to circumvent or overcome: *he got round the problem by an ingenious trick.* **2.** (*prep.*) *Informal.* to have one's way with; cajole: *that girl can get round anyone.* **3.** (*prep.*) to evade (a law or rules). **4.** (*adv.;* foll. by *to*) to reach or come to at length: *I'll get round to that job in an hour.*

get·ter (ˈgɛtə) *n.* **1.** a person or thing that gets. **2.** a substance, usually a metal such as titanium, evaporated onto the walls of a vacuum tube, vessel, etc., to adsorb the residual gas and lower the pressure. ~*vb.* **3.** (*tr.*) to remove (a gas) by the action of a getter.

get through *vb.* **1.** to succeed or cause or help to succeed in an examination, test, etc. **2.** to bring or come to a destination, esp. after overcoming problems: *we got through the blizzards to the survivors.* **3.** (*adv.*) to contact or cause to contact, as by telephone. **4.** (*intr., prep.*) to use, spend, or consume (money, supplies, etc.). **5.** to complete or cause to complete (a task, process, etc.): *to get a bill through Parliament.* **6.** (*adv.; foll. by to*) to reach the awareness and understanding (of a person): *I just can't get the message through to him.* **7.** (*intr., adv.*) *U.S. slang.* to obtain drugs.

get-to·geth+er *Informal.* ~*n.* **1.** a small informal meeting or social gathering. ~*vb.* **get to+geth+er.** (*adv.*) **2.** (*tr.*) to gather or collect. **3.** (*intr.*) (of people) to meet socially. **4.** (*intr.*) to discuss, esp. in order to reach an agreement. **5. get it together.** *Informal.* **a.** to achieve one's full potential, either generally as a person or in a particular field of activity. **b.** to achieve a harmonious frame of mind.

Get·ty ('gɛtɪ) *n.* **J(ean) Paul.** 1892–1976, U.S. oil executive, millionaire, and art collector.

Get+tys+burg ('gɛtɪzˌbɜːg) *n.* a small town in S Pennsylvania, southwest of Harrisburg: scene of a crucial battle (1863) during the American Civil War, in which Meade's Union forces defeated Lee's Confederate army; site of the national cemetery dedicated by President Lincoln. Pop.: 7275 (1970).

Get+tys+burg Ad+dress *n. U.S. history.* the speech made by President Lincoln at the dedication of the national cemetery on the Civil War battlefield at Gettysburg in Nov. 1863.

get up *vb.* (*mainly adv.*) **1.** to wake and rise from one's bed or cause to wake and rise from bed. **2.** (*intr.*) to rise to one's feet; stand up. **3.** (*also prep.*) to ascend or cause to ascend: *the old van couldn't get up the hill.* **4.** to mount or help to mount (a bicycle, horse, etc.). **5.** to increase or cause to increase in strength: *the wind got up at noon.* **6.** (*tr.*) *Informal.* to dress (oneself) in a particular way, esp. showily or elaborately. **7.** (*tr.*) *Informal.* to devise or create: *to get up an entertainment for Christmas.* **8.** (*tr.*) *Informal.* to study or improve one's knowledge of: *I must get up my history.* **9.** (*intr.; foll. by to*) *Informal.* to be involved in: *he's always getting up to mischief.* ~*n.* **get-up. 10.** *Informal.* a costume or outfit, esp. one that is striking or bizarre. **11.** *Informal.* the arrangement or production of a book, etc.

get-up-and-go *n. Informal.* energy, drive, or ambition.

ge·um ('dʒiːəm) *n.* any herbaceous plant of the rosaceous genus *Geum,* having compound leaves and red, orange, yellow, or white flowers. See also **avens.** [C19: New Latin, from Latin: herb bennet, avens]

GeV *abbrev. for* giga-electronvolts (10^9 electronvolts). Sometimes written (esp. U.S.) **BeV** (billion electronvolts).

gew+gaw ('gjuːgɔː, 'guː-) ~*n.* **1.** a showy but valueless trinket. ~*adj.* **2.** showy and valueless; gaudy. [C15: of unknown origin]

gey (gaɪ) *adv. Scot. and Northumberland dialect.* (intensifier): *it's gey cold.* [variant of GAY]

gey+ser ('giːzə; *U.S.* 'gaɪzər)) *n.* **1.** a spring that discharges steam and hot water. **2.** *Brit.* a domestic gas water heater. [C18: from Icelandic *Geysir,* from Old Norse *geysa* to gush]

gey+ser+ite ('giːzəˌraɪt) *n.* a mineral form of hydrated silica resembling opal, deposited from the waters of geysers and hot springs. Formula: $SiO_2.nH_2O$.

Ge+zi+ra (dʒə'zɪərə) *n.* a region of the E central Sudan between the Blue and White Niles: site of a large-scale irrigation system.

G.G. *abbrev. for:* **1.** Girl Guides. **2.** Governor-General.

GH *international car registration for* Ghana.

Gha+na ('gɑːnə) *n.* a republic in W Africa, on the Gulf of Guinea: a powerful empire from the 4th to the 13th centuries; a major source of gold and slaves for Europeans after 1471; British colony of the Gold Coast established in 1874; united with British Togoland in 1957 and became a republic within the Commonwealth in 1960. Official language: English. Religions: Christian and animist. Currency: new cedi. Capital: Accra. Pop.: 8 559 313 (1970). Area: 238 539 sq. km (92 100 sq. miles). —**Gha+na+ian** (gɑː'neɪən) *or* '**Gha+ni+an** *adj., n.*

gha+ri·al ('gærɪəl) *n.* another name for **gavial.**

ghar+ry *or* **ghar+ri** ('gærɪ) *n., pl.* **+ries.** a horse-drawn vehicle used in India. [C19: from Hindi *gārī*]

ghast+ly ('gɑːstlɪ) *adj.* **+li+er, +li+est. 1.** *Informal.* very bad or unpleasant. **2.** deathly pale; wan. **3.** *Informal.* extremely unwell; ill: *they felt ghastly the day after the party.* **4.** terrifying; horrible. ~*adv.* **5.** unhealthily; sickly: *ghastly pale.* **6.** *Archaic.* in a horrible or hideous manner. [Old English *gāstlīc* spiritual; see GHOSTLY] —'**ghast+li+ness** *n.*

ghat (gɑːt) *n.* (in India) **1.** stairs or a passage leading down to a river. **2.** a place for bathing on the bank of a river. **3.** a mountain pass or mountain range. [C17: from Hindi *ghāt,* from Sanskrit *ghatta*]

Ghats (gɑːts) *n.* See **Eastern Ghats** and **Western Ghats.**

ghaut (gʌt) *n. Caribbean.* a small cleft in a hill through which a rivulet runs down to the sea. [C17 *gaot,* a mountain pass, from Hindi: GHAT]

gha+zi ('gɑːzɪ) *n., pl.* **+zis. 1.** a Muslim fighter against infidels. **2.** (*often cap.*) a Turkish warrior of high rank. [C18: from Arabic, from *ghazā* he made war]

Ghaz+zah ('gɑːzə, 'gʌzə) *n.* transliteration of the Arabic name **Gaza.**

Ghe+ber *or* **Ghe+bre** ('geɪbə, 'giː-) *n.* another word for **Gabar.**

ghee (giː) *n.* butter, clarified by boiling, used in Indian cookery. [C17: from Hindi *ghī,* from Sanskrit *ghri* sprinkle]

Ghent (gɛnt) *n.* an industrial city and port in NW Belgium, capital of East Flanders province, at the confluence of the Rivers Lys and Scheldt: formerly famous for its cloth industry; university (1816). Pop.: 148 166 (1971 est.). Flemish name: **Gent.** French name: **Gand.**

ghe+rao (gɛ'raʊ) *n.* a form of industrial action in India in which workers imprison their employers on the premises until their demands are met. [from Hindi *gherna* to besiege]

gher+kin ('gɜːkɪn) *n.* **1.** the small immature fruit of any of various cucumbers, used for pickling. **2. a.** a tropical American cucurbitaceous climbing plant, *Cucumis anguria.* **b.** the small spiny edible fruit of this plant. [C17: from early modern Dutch *agurkkijn,* diminutive of *gurk,* from Slavonic, ultimately from Greek *angourion*]

ghet+to ('gɛtəʊ) *n., pl.* **+tos** *or* **+toes. 1.** *Sociol.* a densely populated slum area of a city inhabited by a socially and economically deprived minority. **2.** an area in a European city in which Jews were formerly required to live. [C17: from Italian, perhaps shortened from *borghetto,* diminutive of *borgo* settlement outside a walled city]

Ghib+el+line ('gɪbɪˌlaɪn, -ˌliːn) *n.* **1.** a member of the political faction in medieval Italy originally based on support for the German emperor. **2.** (*modifier*) of or relating to the Ghibellines. Compare **Guelph**[1]. [C16: from Italian *Ghibellino,* probably from Middle High German *Waiblingen,* a Hohenstaufen estate] —'**Ghib+el+ˌlin+ism** *n.*

Ghi·ber·ti (*Italian* gi'bɛrti) *n.* **Lo·ren·zo** (lo'rɛntso). 1378–1455, Italian sculptor, painter, and goldsmith of the quattrocento: noted esp. for the bronze doors of the baptistry of Florence Cathedral.

ghib+li *or* **gib+li** ('gɪblɪ) *n.* a fiercely hot wind of North Africa. [C20: from Arabic *gibliy* south wind]

ghil+lie ('gɪlɪ) *n.* **1.** a type of tongueless shoe with lacing up the instep, originally worn by the Scots. **2.** a variant spelling of **gillie.** [from Scottish Gaelic *gille* boy]

Ghir·lan·da·io *or* **Ghir·lan·da·jo** (*Italian* ˌgirlan'daːjo) *n.* **Do·me·ni·co** (do'meːniko). original name *Domenico Bigordi.* 1449–94, Italian painter of frescoes.

ghost (gəʊst) *n.* **1.** the disembodied spirit of a dead person, supposed to haunt the living as a pale or shadowy vision; phantom. Related adj.: **spectral. 2.** a haunting memory: *the ghost of his former life rose up before him.* **3.** a faint trace or possibility of something; glimmer: *a ghost of a smile.* **4.** the spirit; soul (archaic, except in the phrase **the Holy Ghost**). **5.** *Physics.* **a.** a faint secondary image produced by an optical system. **b.** a similar image on a television screen, formed by reflection of the transmitting waves or by a defect in the receiver. **6.** See **ghost word. 7.** Also called: **ghost edition.** an entry recorded in a bibliography, etc., of which no actual proof exists. **8.** See **ghostwriter. 9. give up the ghost.** to die. ~*vb.* **10.** See **ghostwrite. 11.** (*tr.*). to haunt. [Old English *gāst;* related to Old Frisian *jēst,* Old High German *geist* spirit, Sanskrit *hēda* fury, anger] —'**ghost+ˌlike** *adj.*

ghost dance *n.* a religious dance of certain North American Indians, connected with a political movement (from about 1888) that looked to reunion with the dead and a return to an idealized state of affairs before Europeans came.

ghost gum *n. Austral.* a eucalyptus tree with white trunk and branches.

ghost+ly ('gəʊstlɪ) *adj.* **+li+er, +li+est. 1.** of or resembling a ghost; spectral: *a ghostly face appeared at the window.* **2.** suggesting the presence of ghosts; eerie. **3.** *Archaic.* of or relating to the soul or spirit. —'**ghost+li+ness** *n.*

ghost moth *n.* any of various large pale moths of the family *Hepialidae* that are active at dusk.

ghost town *n.* a deserted town, esp. one in the western U.S. that was formerly a boom town.

ghost word *n.* a word that has entered the language through the perpetuation, in dictionaries, etc., of an error.

ghost+write ('gəʊstˌraɪt) *vb.* **+writes, +writ+ing, +wrote, +writ+ten.** to write (an autobiographical or other article) on behalf of a person who is then credited as author. Often shortened to **ghost.** —'**ghost+ˌwrit+er** *n.*

ghoul (guːl) *n.* **1.** a malevolent spirit or ghost. **2.** a person interested in morbid or disgusting things. **3.** a person who robs graves. **4.** (in Muslim legend) an evil demon thought to eat human bodies, either stolen corpses or children. [C18: from Arabic *ghūl,* from *ghāla* he seized] —'**ghoul+ish** *adj.* —'**ghoul+ish+ly** *adv.* —'**ghoul+ish+ness** *n.*

G.H.Q. *Military. abbrev. for* General Headquarters.

ghyll (gɪl) *n.* a variant spelling of **gill**[3].

gi *abbrev. for* gill (unit of measure).

Gi *Electronics. abbrev. for* gilbert.

GI *n. U.S. informal.* **1.** (*pl.* **GIs** *or* **GI's**). a soldier in the U.S. Army, esp. an enlisted man. ~*adj.* **2.** conforming to U.S. Army regulations; of standard government issue. [C20: abbrev. of *government issue*]

G.I. *or* **g.i.** *abbrev. for* gastrointestinal.

Gia·co·met·ti (*Italian* ˌdʒako'metti) *n.* **Al·ber·to** (al'bɛrto). 1901–66, Swiss sculptor and painter, noted particularly for his long skeletal statues of isolated figures.

gi+ant ('dʒaɪənt) *n.* **1.** Also (fem.): **gi+ant+ess** ('dʒaɪəntɪs). a mythical figure of superhuman size and strength, esp. in folklore or fairy tales. **2.** a person or thing of exceptional size, reputation, etc.: *a giant in the world of nuclear physics.* **3.** *Greek myth.* any of the large and powerful offspring of Uranus (sky) and Gaea (earth) who rebelled against the Olympian gods but were defeated in battle. **4.** *Pathol.* a person suffering from gigantism. **5.** *Astronomy.* See **giant star. 6.** *Mining.* another word for **monitor** (sense 6). ~*adj.* **7.** remarkably or supernaturally large. **8.** *Architect.* another word for **colossal.** [C13: from Old French *geant,* from Vulgar Latin *gagās*

(unattested), from Latin *gigant-*, *gigās*, from Greek] —'gi·ant-,like *adj.*
gi+ant+ism ('dʒaɪən,tɪzəm) *n.* another term for **gigantism.**
gi+ant kill+er *n.* a person, sports team, etc., that defeats an apparently superior opponent.
gi+ant pan+da *n.* See **panda** (sense 1).
gi+ant plan+et *n.* any of the planets Jupiter, Saturn, Uranus, and Neptune, characterized by enormous mass, low density, and an extensive atmosphere.
gi+ant pow+der *n.* dynamite composed of trinitroglycerin absorbed in kieselguhr.
Gi+ant's Cause+way *n.* a promontory of columnar basalt on the N coast of Northern Ireland, in Co. Antrim: consists of several thousand pillars, mostly hexagonal, that were formed by the rapid cooling of lava.
gi+ant star *n.* any of a class of very bright stars, such as Capella and Arcturus, having an absolute magnitude between +2 and -2, a diameter up to 100 times that of the sun, and an extremely low mean density. Sometimes shortened to **giant.** Compare **supergiant.**
gi+ant tor+toise *n.* any of various very large tortoises of the genus *Testudo*, of the Galápagos, Seychelles, and certain other islands, weighing up to 225 kilograms (495 lbs.).
gia+our ('dʒaʊə) *n.* a derogatory term for a non-Muslim, esp. a Christian, used esp. by the Turks. [C16: from Turkish *giaur* unbeliever, from Persian *gaur*, variant of *gābr*]
gib[1] (gɪb) *n.* **1.** a metal wedge, pad, or thrust bearing, esp. a brass plate let into a steam engine crosshead. ~*vb.* **gibs, gib+bing, gibbed. 2.** (*tr.*) to fasten or supply with a gib. [C18: of unknown origin]
gib[2] (gɪb) *n.* a male cat, esp. a castrated one. [C14: probably a shortening and alteration of the proper name *Gilbert*]
Gib (dʒɪb) an informal name for **Gibraltar.**
gib+ber[1] ('dʒɪbə) *vb.* **1.** to utter rapidly and unintelligibly; prattle. **2.** (*intr.*) (of monkeys and related animals) to make characteristic chattering sounds. ~*n.* **3.** a less common word for **gibberish.** [C17: of imitative origin]
gib+ber[2] ('dʒɪbə) *n. Austral.* **1.** a stone or boulder. **2.** (*modifier*) of or relating to a dry flat area of land covered with wind-polished stones: *gibber plains.* [C19: from a native Australian language]
gib+ber+el+lic ac+id (,dʒɪbə'rɛlɪk) *n.* a slightly soluble crystalline hormone extracted from fungi and other plants: a giberellin. Formula: $C_{19}H_{22}O_6$.
gib+ber+el+lin (,dʒɪbə'rɛlɪn) *n.* any of several plant hormones isolated from the fungus *Gibberella fujikuroi*, whose main action is to cause elongation of the stem: used in promoting the growth of plants, in the malting of barley, etc. [C20: from New Latin *Gibberella*, literally: a little hump, from Latin *gibber* hump + -IN]
gib+ber+ish ('dʒɪbərɪʃ) *n.* **1.** rapid chatter like that of monkeys. **2.** incomprehensible talk; nonsense.
gib+bet ('dʒɪbɪt) *n.* **1. a.** a wooden structure resembling a gallows, from which the bodies of executed criminals were formerly hung to public view. **b.** a gallows. ~*vb.* (*tr.*) **2.** to put to death by hanging on a gibbet. **3.** to hang (a corpse) on a gibbet. **4.** to expose to public ridicule. [C13: from Old French *gibet* gallows, literally: little cudgel, from *gibe* cudgel; of uncertain origin]
gib+bon ('gɪbᵊn) *n.* any small agile arboreal anthropoid ape of the genus *Hylobates*, inhabiting forests in S Asia. [C18: from French, probably from an Indian dialect word]
Gib·bon ('gɪbᵊn) *n.* **Ed·ward.** 1737–94, English historian; author of *The History of the Decline and Fall of the Roman Empire* (1776–88), controversial in its historical criticism of Christianity.
Gib·bons ('gɪbᵊnz) *n.* **1. Grin·ling.** 1648–1721, English sculptor and wood-carver, noted for his delicate carvings of fruit, flowers, birds, etc. **2. Or·lan·do.** 1583–1625, English organist and composer, esp. of anthems, motets, and madrigals.
gib+bos+i·ty (gɪ'bɒsɪtɪ) *n., pl.* **·ties.** *Rare.* **1.** the state of being gibbous. **2.** *Biology.* a bulge or protuberance.
gib+bous ('gɪbəs) *or* **gib+bose** ('gɪbəʊs) *adj.* **1.** (of the moon or a planet) more than half but less than fully illuminated. **2.** having a hunchback; hunchbacked. **3.** bulging. [C17: from Late Latin *gibbōsus* hump-backed, from Latin *gibba* hump] —'**gib+bous+ly** *adv.* —'**gib+bous+ness** *n.*
Gibbs func+tion (gɪbz) *n.* a thermodynamic property of a system equal to the difference between its enthalpy and the product of its temperature and its entropy. It is usually measured in joules. Symbol: *G* or (esp. U.S.) *F* Also called: **Gibbs free energy, free enthalpy.** Compare **Helmholtz function.** [C19: named after Josiah Willard *Gibbs* (1839–1903), American mathematician and physicist]
gibbs+ite ('gɪbzaɪt) *n.* a mineral consisting of hydrated aluminium oxide: a constituent of bauxite and a source of alumina. Formula: $Al(OH)_3$. [C19: named after George *Gibbs* (died 1833), American mineralogist]
gibe[1] *or* **jibe** (dʒaɪb) *vb.* **1.** to make jeering or scoffing remarks at; taunt. ~*n.* **2.** a derisive or provoking remark. [C16: perhaps from Old French *giber* to treat roughly, of uncertain origin] —'**gib+er** *or* '**jib+er** *n.* —'**gib+ing+ly** *or* '**jib+ing+ly** *adv.*
gibe[2] (dʒaɪb) *vb., n. Nautical.* a variant spelling of **gybe.**
Gib+e+on ('gɪbɪən) *n.* an ancient town of Palestine probably about 9 kilometres (6 miles) northwest of Jerusalem.
Gib+e+on+ite ('gɪbɪə,naɪt) *n. Old Testament.* one of the inhabitants of the town of Gibeon, who were compelled by Joshua to serve the Hebrews (Joshua 9).
gib+lets ('dʒɪblɪts) *pl. n.* (*sometimes sing.*) the gizzard, liver, heart, and neck of a fowl. [C14: from Old French *gibelet* stew of game birds, probably from *gibier* game, of Germanic origin]
gib+li ('gɪblɪ) *n.* a variant spelling of **ghibli.**
Gi+bral+tar (dʒɪ'brɔ:ltə) *n.* **1. City of.** a city on the **Rock of Gibraltar,** a limestone promontory at the tip of S Spain: settled by Moors in 711 and taken by Spain in 1462; ceded to Britain in 1713; a British crown colony (1830–1969), still politically associated with Britain; a naval and air base of strategic importance. Pop.: 27 000 (1975 UN est.). Area: 6.5 sq. km (2.5 sq. miles). Ancient name: **Calpe. 2. Strait of.** a narrow strait between the S tip of Spain and the NW tip of Africa, linking the Mediterranean with the Atlantic. —**Gi+bral+tar+i·an** (,dʒɪbrɔ:l'tɛərɪən) *adj., n.*
Gi·bran (dʒɪ'brɑ:n) *n.* **Kah·lil** ('kɑ:li:l). 1883–1931, Syro-Lebanese poet, mystic, and painter, resident in the U.S. after 1910; author of *The Prophet* (1923).
Gib+son[1] ('gɪbsᵊn) *n. Chiefly U.S.* a cocktail consisting of four or more parts dry gin and one part dry vermouth, iced and served with a pickled pearl onion.
Gib·son[2] ('gɪbsᵊn) *n.* **Mike.** born 1942, Irish Rugby Union footballer: halfback for Ireland (since 1964) and the British Lions (1966–77).
Gib+son Des+ert *n.* a desert in W central Australia, between the Great Sandy Desert and the Victoria Desert: salt marshes, lakes, and scrub. Area: about 220 000 sq. km (85 000 sq. miles).
Gib·son girl *n.* the ideal fashionable American girl of the late 1890s and early 1900s, as portrayed in the drawings of Charles Dana Gibson, 1867–1944, U.S. illustrator.
gid (gɪd) *n.* a disease of sheep characterized by an unsteady gait and staggering, caused by infestation of the brain with tapeworms (*Taenia caenuris*). [C17: back formation from GIDDY]
gid+dap (gɪ'dæp) *or* **gid·dy-up** (,gɪdɪ'ʌp) *interj.* an exclamation used to make a horse go faster. [C20: colloquial form of *get up*]
gid+dy ('gɪdɪ) *adj.* **+di·er, +di·est. 1.** affected with a reeling sensation and feeling as if about to fall; dizzy. **2.** causing or tending to cause vertigo. **3.** impulsive; scatterbrained. **4. my giddy aunt.** exclamation of surprise. ~*vb.* **+dies, +dy+ing, +died. 5.** to make or become giddy. [Old English *gydig* mad, frenzied, possessed by God; related to GOD] —'**gid+di+ly** *adv.* —'**gid+di+ness** *n.*
Gide (*French* ʒid) *n.* **An·dré** (ɑ̃'dre). 1869–1951, French novelist, dramatist, critic, diarist, and translator, noted particularly for his exploration of the conflict between self-fulfilment and conventional morality. His novels include *L'Immoraliste* (1902), *La Porte étroite* (1909), and *Les Faux-Monnayeurs* (1926): Nobel prize for literature 1947.
Gid·e·on ('gɪdɪən) *n. Old Testament.* a Hebrew judge who led the Israelites to victory over their Midianite oppressors (Judges 6:11–8:35).
Gid·e·on Bi+ble *n.* a Bible purchased by members of a Christian organization (**Gideons**) and placed in a hotel room, hospital ward, etc.
gidg·ee *or* **gidj·ee** ('gɪdʒi:) *n. Austral.* a small acacia tree, *Acacia cambagei*, yielding useful timber. [C19: from a native Australian language]
gie (gi:) *vb.* a Scot. word for **give.**
Giel·gud ('gi:lgʊd) *n.* Sir **John.** born 1904, English stage and film actor and director.
Gie·rek ('gɪᵊrɛk; *Polish* 'gjɛrɛk) *n.* **Ed·ward** ('ɛdvart). born 1913, Polish statesman; first secretary of the Politburo since 1970.
Gies+sen (*German* 'gi:sᵊn) *n.* a city in W central West Germany, in Hesse: university (1607). Pop.: 75 500 (1970).
gift (gɪft) *n.* **1.** something given; a present. **2.** a special aptitude, ability, or power; talent. **3.** the power or right to give or bestow (esp. in the phrases **in the gift of, in (someone's) gift**). **4.** the act or process of giving. **5. look a gift-horse in the mouth.** (*usually negative*) to find fault with a free gift or chance benefit. ~*vb.* (*tr.*) **6.** to present (something) as a gift to (a person). **7.** *Rare.* to endow with; bestow. [Old English *gift* payment for a wife, dowry; related to Old Norse *gipt*, Old High German *gift*, Gothic *fragifts* endowment, engagement; see GIVE] —'**gift+less** *adj.*
gift+ed ('gɪftɪd) *adj.* having or showing natural talent or aptitude: *a gifted musician; a gifted performance.* —'**gift+ed+ly** *adv.* —'**gift+ed+ness** *n.*
gift of tongues *n.* an utterance, partly or wholly unintelligible, produced under the influence of ecstatic religious emotion and conceived to be a manifestation of the Holy Ghost: practised in certain Christian churches, usually called Pentecostal. Also called: **glossolalia.**
gift tax *n.* another name for **capital transfer tax.**
gift+wrap ('gɪft,ræp) *vb.* **+wraps, +wrap+ping, +wrapped.** to wrap (an article intended as a gift) attractively.
Gi·fu ('gi:fu:) *n.* a city in Japan, on central Honshu: hot springs. Pop.: 407 257 (1974 est.).
gig[1] (gɪg) *n.* **1.** a light two-wheeled one-horse carriage without a hood. **2.** *Nautical.* a light tender for a vessel, often for the personal use of the captain. **3.** a long light rowing boat, used esp. for racing. **4.** a machine for raising the nap of a fabric. ~*vb.* **gigs, gig+ging, gigged. 5.** (*intr.*) to travel in a gig. **6.** (*tr.*). to raise the nap of (fabric). [C13 (in the sense: flighty girl, spinning top): perhaps of Scandinavian origin; compare Danish *gig* top, Norwegian *giga* to shake about]
gig[2] (gɪg) *n.* **1.** a cluster of barbless hooks drawn through a shoal of fish to try and impale them. **2.** short for **fishgig.** ~*vb.* **gigs, gig+ging, gigged. 3.** to catch (fish) with a gig.
gig[3] (gɪg) *n. Informal.* **1.** a job, esp. a single booking for jazz or

pop musicians to play at a concert or club. **2.** the performance itself. [C20: of unknown origin]

gi·ga- *prefix.* denoting 10^9: *gigavolt.* Symbol: G [from Greek *gigas* GIANT]

gi+ga+hertz ('gaɪgəˌhɜːts, 'dʒɪg-) *n., pl.* **+hertz.** a unit of frequency equal to 10^9 hertz. Symbol: GHz

gi+gan+tic (dʒaɪ'gæntɪk) *adj.* **1.** very large; enormous: *a gigantic error.* **2.** Also: **gi+gan+tesque** (ˌdʒaɪgæn'tɛsk). of or suitable for giants. [C17: from Greek *gigantikos,* from *gigas* GIANT] —**gi+'gan+ti+cal+ly** *adv.* —**gi+'gan+tic+ness** *n.*

gi+gan+tism ('dʒaɪgænˌtɪzəm, dʒaɪ'gæntɪzəm) *n.* **1.** Also called: **giantism.** excessive growth of the entire body, caused by overproduction of growth hormone by the pituitary gland during childhood or adolescence. Compare **acromegaly. 2.** the state or quality of being gigantic.

gi+gan+tom·a+chy (ˌdʒaɪgæn'tɒməkɪ) *or* **gi+gan+to+ma+chi·a** (dʒaɪˌgæntəʊ'meɪkɪə) *n., pl.* **+chies** or **+chi·as. 1.** *Greek myth.* the war fought between the gods of Olympus and the rebelling giants. See **giant** (sense 3). **2.** any battle fought between or as if between giants. [C17: from Greek *gigantomakhia,* from *gigas* giant + *makhē* battle]

gig+gle ('gɪgᵊl) *vb.* **1.** (*intr.*) to laugh nervously or foolishly. ~*n.* **2.** such a laugh. **3. for a giggle.** *Informal.* as a joke or prank; not seriously. [C16: of imitative origin] —**'gig+gler** *n.* —**'gig+gling+ly** *adv.* —**'gig+gly** *adj.*

gig+gle house *n. Austral. slang.* a lunatic asylum.

Gi·gli (*Italian* 'dʒiʎʎi) *n.* **Be·nia·mi·no** (ˌbenja'miːno). 1890–1957, Italian operatic tenor.

gig·o+lo ('ʒɪgəˌləʊ) *n., pl.* **+los. 1.** a man who is kept by a woman, esp. an older woman. **2.** a man who is paid to dance with or escort women. [C20: from French, back formation from *gigolette* girl for hire as a dancing partner, prostitute, from *giguer* to dance, from *gigue* a fiddle; compare GIGOT, GIGUE, JIG]

gi+got ('ʒiːgəʊ, 'dʒɪgət) *n.* **1.** a leg of lamb or mutton. **2.** a leg-of-mutton sleeve. [C16: from Old French: leg, a small fiddle, from *gigue* a fiddle, of Germanic origin]

gigue (ʒiːg) *n.* **1.** a piece of music, usually in six-eight time and often fugal, incorporated into the classical suite. **2.** a formal couple dance of the 16th and 17th centuries, derived from the jig. [C17: from French, from Italian *giga* literally: a fiddle; see GIGOT]

GI Joe *n. U.S. informal.* a U.S. enlisted soldier; a GI.

Gi+jón (giː'hɔːn; *Spanish* xi'xon) *n.* a port in NW Spain, on the Bay of Biscay: capital of the kingdom of Asturias until 791. Pop.: 187 612 (1970). Ancient name: **Gigia.**

Gi·la mon+ster ('hiːlə) *n.* a large venomous brightly coloured lizard, *Heloderma suspectum,* inhabiting deserts of the southwestern U.S. and Mexico and feeding mostly on eggs and small mammals: family *Helodermatidae.*

gil+bert ('gɪlbət) *n.* a unit of magnetomotive force; the magnetomotive force resulting from the passage of 4π abamperes through one turn of a coil. 1 gilbert is equivalent to $10/4\pi$ = 0.795 775 ampere-turn. Abbrev.: Gb or Gi [C19: named after William GILBERT]

Gil·bert ('gɪlbət) *n.* **1.** Sir **Hum·phrey.** ?1539–83, English navigator: founded the colony at St. John's, Newfoundland (1583). **2. Wil·liam.** 1540–1603, English physician and physicist, noted for his study of terrestrial magnetism in *De Magnete* (1600). **3.** Sir **W(illiam) S(chwenck).** 1836–1911, English dramatist, humorist, and librettist. He collaborated (1871–96) with Arthur Sullivan on the famous series of comic operettas, including *The Pirates of Penzance* (1879), *Iolanthe* (1882), and *The Mikado* (1885).

Gil+ber+ti·an (gɪl'bɜːtɪən) *adj.* characteristic of or resembling the style or whimsical humour of Sir W. S. Gilbert.

Gil+bert Is+lands *pl. n.* a group of islands in the W Pacific: with Ocean Island, the Phoenix Islands, and three of the Line Islands they constitute an independent state; until 1975 they formed part of the British colony of **Gilbert and Ellice Islands;** achieved full independence in 1978; now known as **Kiribati.** Pop.: 53 000 (1975 est.). Area: 655 sq. km (253 sq. miles).

gild[1] (gɪld) *vb.* **gilds, gild+ing, gild+ed** *or* **gilt.** (*tr.*) **1.** to cover with or as if with gold. **2. gild the lily. a.** to adorn unnecessarily something already beautiful. **b.** to praise someone inordinately. **3.** to give a falsely attractive or valuable appearance to. **4.** *Archaic.* to smear with blood. [Old English *gyldan,* from *gold* GOLD; related to Old Norse *gylla,* Middle High German *vergülden*] —**'gild+er** *n.*

gild[2] (gɪld) *n.* a variant spelling of **guild** (sense 2). —**'gilds+man** *n.*

gil+der ('gɪldə) *n.* a variant spelling of **guilder.**

gild+ing ('gɪldɪŋ) *n.* **1.** the act or art of applying gilt to a surface. **2.** the surface so produced. **3.** another word for **gilt**[1] (sense 2).

Gil+e·ad[1] ('gɪlɪˌæd) *n.* a historic mountainous region east of the River Jordan, rising over 1200 m (4000 ft.).

Gil·e·ad[2] ('gɪlɪˌæd) *n. Old Testament.* a grandson of Manasseh; ancestor of the Coileadites (Numbers 26: 29–30).

Gil+e·ad+ite ('gɪlɪəˌdaɪt) *n.* **1.** an inhabitant of the region of Gilead. **2.** a descendant of Gilead (the man).

Giles (dʒaɪlz) *n.* **1. Saint.** 7th century A.D., Greek hermit in France; patron saint of cripples, beggars, and lepers. Feast day: Sept. 1. **2. Wil·liam Er·nest Pow·ell.** 1835–97, Australian explorer, born in England. He was noted esp. for his exploration of the western desert (1875–76).

gi+let (dʒɪ'leɪ) *n.* **1.** a bodice resembling a waistcoat in a woman's dress. **2.** such a bodice as part of a ballet dancer's costume. [C19: French, literally: waistcoat]

gil+gai ('gɪlgaɪ) *n. Austral.* a natural water hole. [C19: from a native Australian language]

Gil·ga·mesh ('gɪlgəˌmɛʃ) *n.* a legendary Sumerian king.

gill[1] (gɪl) *n.* **1.** the respiratory organ in many aquatic animals, consisting of a membrane or outgrowth well supplied with blood vessels. **External gills** occur in tadpoles, some molluscs, etc.; **internal gills,** within gill slits, occur in most fishes. **2.** any of the radiating leaflike spore-producing structures on the undersurface of the cap of a mushroom. ~*vb.* **3.** to catch (fish) or (of fish) to be caught in a gill net. **4.** (*tr.*) to gut (fish). [C14: of Scandinavian origin; compare Swedish *gäl,* Danish *gjælle,* Greek *khelunē* lip] —**gilled** *adj.* —**'gill-less** *adj.* —**'gill-ˌlike** *adj.*

gill[2] (dʒɪl) *n.* **1.** a unit of liquid measure equal to one quarter of a pint. **2.** *Northern Brit. dialect.* half a pint, esp. of beer. [C14: from Old French *gille* vat, tub, from Late Latin *gillō* cooling vessel for liquids, of obscure origin]

gill[3] *or* **ghyll** (gɪl) *n. Brit. dialect.* **1.** a narrow stream; rivulet. **2.** a wooded ravine. **3.** (*cap. when part of place name*) a deep natural hole in rock; pothole: *Gaping Gill.* [C11: from Old Norse *gil* steep-sided valley]

gill[4] (dʒɪl) *n.* **1.** *Archaic.* a girl or sweetheart. **2.** an archaic or dialect name for **ground ivy.** [C15: special use of *Gill,* short for *Gillian,* girl's name]

Gil·les·pie (gɪ'lɛspɪ) *n.* **Diz·zy,** nickname of *John Birks Gillespie.* born 1917, U.S. jazz trumpeter.

gill fun+gus (gɪl) *n.* any fungus of the basidiomycetous family *Agaricaceae,* in which the spores are produced on gills underneath a cap. See also **agaric.**

gil+lie, ghil+lie, *or* **gil+ly** ('gɪlɪ) *n., pl.* **+lies.** *Scot.* **1.** an attendant or guide for hunting or fishing. **2.** (formerly) a Highland chieftain's male attendant or personal servant. [C17: from Scottish Gaelic *gille* boy, servant]

Gil+ling+ham ('dʒɪlɪŋəm) *n.* a town in SE England, in N Kent on the Medway estuary: dockyards. Pop.: 86 714 (1971).

gil+lion ('dʒɪljən) *n. Brit.* one thousand million. U.S. equivalent: **billion.** [C20: from G(IGA-) + (M)ILLION]

gill net (gɪl) *n. Fishing.* a net suspended vertically in the water to trap fish by their gills in its meshes.

gill pouch (gɪl) *n.* any of a series of paired linear pouches in chordate embryos, arising as outgrowths of the wall of the pharynx. In fish and some amphibians they become the gill slits.

Gill·ray ('gɪlreɪ) *n.* **James.** 1757–1815, English caricaturist.

gills (gɪlz) *pl. n.* **1.** (*sometimes sing.*) the wattle of birds such as domestic fowl. **2. green around** *or* **about the gills.** *Informal.* looking or feeling nauseated.

gill slit (gɪl) *n.* any of a series of paired linear openings to the exterior from the sides of the pharynx in fishes and some amphibians. They contain the gills.

gil+ly+flow·er *or* **gil+li+flow·er** ('dʒɪlɪˌflaʊə) *n.* **1.** any of several plants having fragrant flowers, such as the stock and wallflower. **2.** an archaic name for **carnation.** [C14: changed (through influence of *flower*) from *gilofre,* from Old French *girofle,* from Medieval Latin, from Greek *karuophullon* clove tree, from *karuon* nut + *phullon* leaf]

Gi+lo+lo (dʒaɪ'ləʊləʊ, dʒɪ-) *n.* See **Halmahera.**

Gil+son+ite ('gɪlsəˌnaɪt) *n. Trademark.* a very pure form of asphalt found in Utah and Colorado; used for making paints, varnishes, and linoleum. [C19: named after S. H. *Gilson* of Salt Lake City, Utah, who discovered it]

gilt[1] (gɪlt) *vb.* **1.** a past tense or past participle of **gild.** ~*n.* **2.** gold or a substance simulating it, applied in gilding. **3.** another word for **gilding** (senses 1, 2). **4.** superficial or false appearance of excellence; glamour. **5.** a gilt-edged security. ~*adj.* **6.** covered with or as if with gold or gilt; gilded.

gilt[2] (gɪlt) *n.* a young female pig, esp. one that has not had a litter. [C15: from Old Norse *gyltr;* related to Old English *gelte,* Old High German *gelza,* Middle Low German *gelte*]

gilt-edged *adj.* **1.** (of securities) dated over a short, medium, or long term, characterized by minimum risk and by redemption at par, and usually issued by the Government. **2.** (of books, papers, etc.) having gilded edges.

gilt+head ('gɪltˌhɛd) *n.* **1.** a sparid fish, *Sparus aurata,* of Mediterranean and European Atlantic waters, having a gold-coloured band between the eyes. **2.** any similar or related fish.

gim+bals ('dʒɪmbᵊlz, 'gɪm-) *pl. n.* a device, consisting of two or three pivoted rings at right angles to each other, that provides free suspension in all planes for an object such as a gyroscope, compass, chronometer, etc. Also called: **gimbal ring.** [C16: variant of GEMEL]

gim+crack ('dʒɪmˌkræk) *adj.* **1.** cheap; shoddy. ~*n.* **2.** a cheap showy trifle or gadget. [C18: changed from C14 *gibecrake* little ornament, of unknown origin] —**'gim+ˌcrack+er·y** *n.*

gim+el ('gɪməl; *Hebrew* 'giːmɛl) *n.* the third letter of the Hebrew alphabet (ג) transliterated as *g* or, when final, *gh.* [literally: camel]

gim+let ('gɪmlɪt) *n.* **1.** a small hand tool consisting of a pointed spiral tip attached at right angles to a handle, used for boring small holes in wood. **2.** *U.S.* a cocktail consisting of half gin or vodka and half lime juice. ~*vb.* **3.** (*tr*). to make holes in (wood) using a gimlet. ~*adj.* **4.** penetrating; piercing (esp. in the phrase **gimlet-eyed**). [C15: from Old French *guimbelet,* of Germanic origin, see WIMBLE]

gim+mal ('gɪməl) *n.* any of a number of parts forming rotating joints for transmitting motion in light mechanisms. [C16: variant of GEMEL]

gim+me ('gɪmiː) *vb. Slang. contraction of* give me.

gim·mick ('gɪmɪk) *Informal.* ~*n.* **1.** something designed to attract extra attention, interest, or publicity. **2.** any clever device, gadget, or stratagem, esp. one used to deceive. **3.** *Chiefly U.S.* a device or trick of legerdemain that enables a magician to deceive the audience. [C20: originally U.S. slang, of unknown origin] —'**gim·mick·ry** *n.* —'**gim·mick·y** *adj.*

gimp *or* **guimpe** (gɪmp) *n.* a tapelike trimming of silk, wool, or cotton, often stiffened with wire. [C17: probably from Dutch *gimp*, of unknown origin]

gin[1] (dʒɪn) *n.* **1.** an alcoholic drink obtained by distillation and rectification of the grain of malted barley, rye, or maize, flavoured with juniper berries. **2.** any of various grain spirits flavoured with other fruit or aromatic essences: *sloe gin*. **3.** an alcoholic drink made from any rectified spirit. [C18: shortened from Dutch *genever* juniper, via Old French from Latin *jūniperus* JUNIPER]

gin[2] (dʒɪn) *n.* **1.** a primitive engine in which a vertical shaft is turned by horses driving a horizontal beam or yoke in a circle. **2.** Also called: **cotton gin.** a machine of this type used for separating seeds from raw cotton. **3.** a trap for catching small mammals, consisting of a noose of thin strong wire. ~*vb.* **gins, gin·ning, ginned.** (*tr.*) **4.** to free (cotton) of seeds with a gin. **5.** to trap or snare (game) with a gin. [C13 *gyn*, shortened from ENGINE] —'**gin·ner** *n.*

gin[3] (gɪn) *vb.* **gins, gin·ning, gan, gun.** an archaic word for **begin.**

gin[4] (dʒɪn) *n. Austral.* an Aboriginal woman. [C19: from a native Australian language]

gin·ger ('dʒɪndʒə) *n.* **1.** any of several zingiberaceous plants of the genus *Zingiber*, esp. *Z. officinale* of the East Indies, cultivated throughout the tropics for its spicy hot-tasting underground stem. See also **galangal.** Compare **wild ginger. 2.** the underground stem of this plant, which is powdered and used as a seasoning or sugared and eaten as a sweetmeat. **3.** any of certain related plants. **4. a.** a reddish-brown or yellowish-brown colour. **b.** (*as adj.*): *ginger hair*. **5.** *Informal.* liveliness; vigour. ~*vb.* **6.** (*tr.*) to add the spice ginger to (a dish). ~See also **ginger up.** [C13: from Old French *gingivre*, from Medieval Latin *gingiber*, from Latin *zinziberi*, from Greek *zingiberis*, probably from Sanskrit *śrṅgaveram*, from *śrṅga-* horn + *vera-* body, referring to its shape]

gin·ger ale *n.* a sweetened effervescent nonalcoholic drink flavoured with ginger extract.

gin·ger beer *n.* a slightly alcoholic drink made by fermenting a mixture of syrup and root ginger.

gin·ger·bread ('dʒɪndʒə,brɛd) *n.* **1.** a moist brown cake, flavoured with ginger and treacle or syrup. **2. a.** a rolled biscuit, similarly flavoured, cut into various shapes and sometimes covered with icing. **b.** (*as modifier*): *gingerbread man*. **3. a.** an elaborate but unsubstantial ornamentation. **b.** (*as modifier*): *gingerbread style of architecture*.

gin·ger·bread tree *n.* a W African rosaceous tree, *Parinarium macrophyllum*, with large mealy edible fruits (**gingerbread plums**): family *Chrysobalanaceae*.

gin·ger group *n. Chiefly Brit.* a group within a party, association, etc., that enlivens or radicalizes its parent body.

gin·ger·ly ('dʒɪndʒəlɪ) *adv.* **1.** in a cautious, reluctant, or timid manner. ~*adj.* **2.** cautious, reluctant, or timid. [C16: perhaps from Old French *gensor* dainty, from *gent* of noble birth; see GENTLE] —'**gin·ger·li·ness** *n.*

gin·ger snap *or* **nut** *n.* a crisp biscuit flavoured with ginger.

gin·ger up *vb.* (*tr., adv.*) to enliven (an activity, group, etc.).

gin·ger wine *n.* an alcoholic drink made from fermented bruised ginger, sugar, and water.

gin·ger·y ('dʒɪndʒərɪ) *adj.* **1.** like or tasting of ginger. **2.** of or like the colour ginger. **3.** full of vigour; high-spirited. **4.** pointed; biting: *a gingery remark*.

ging·ham ('gɪŋəm) *n. Textiles.* **a.** a cotton fabric, usually woven of two coloured yarns in a checked or striped design. **b.** (*as modifier*): *a gingham dress*. [C17: from French *guingan*, from Malay *ginggang* striped cloth]

gin·gi·li, gin·gel·li, *or* **gin·gel·ly** ('dʒɪndʒɪlɪ) *n.* **1.** the oil obtained from sesame seeds. **2.** another name for **sesame.** [C18: from Hindi *jingalī*]

gin·gi·va ('dʒɪndʒɪvə, dʒɪn'dʒaɪvə) *n., pl.* **-gi·vae** (-dʒə,viː, -'dʒaɪviː). *Anatomy.* the technical name for the **gum.** [from Latin] —'**gin·gi·val** *adj.*

gin·gi·vi·tis (,dʒɪndʒɪ'vaɪtɪs) *n.* inflammation of the gums.

gin·gly·mus ('dʒɪŋglɪməs, 'gɪŋ) *n., pl.* **-mi** (-,maɪ). *Anatomy.* a hinge joint. See **hinge** (sense 2). [C17: New Latin, from Greek *ginglumos* hinge]

gink (gɪŋk) *n. Slang.* a man or boy, esp. one considered to be odd. [C20: of unknown origin]

gink·go ('gɪŋkgəʊ) *or* **ging·ko** ('gɪŋkəʊ) *n., pl.* **-goes** *or* **-koes.** a widely planted ornamental Chinese gymnosperm tree, *Ginkgo biloba*, with fan-shaped deciduous leaves and fleshy yellow fruit. Also called: **maidenhair tree.** [C18: from Japanese *ginkyō*, from Ancient Chinese *ngien* silver + *hang* apricot]

gin·nel ('gɪn°l, 'dʒɪn-) *n. Northern English dialect.* a narrow passageway between buildings. [C17: perhaps a corruption of CHANNEL]

gin pal·ace (dʒɪn) *n.* (formerly) a gaudy drinking-house.

gin rum·my (dʒɪn) *n.* a version of rummy in which a player may go out if the odd cards outside his sequences total less than ten points. Often shortened to **gin.** [C20: from GIN[1] + RUMMY[1], apparently from a humorous allusion to gin and rum]

Gins·berg ('gɪnzbɜːg) *n.* **Al·len.** born 1926, U.S. poet of the beat generation. His poetry includes *Howl* (1956).

gin·seng ('dʒɪnsɛŋ) *n.* **1.** either of two araliaceous plants, *Panax schinseng* of China or *P. quinquefolius* of North America, whose forked aromatic roots are used medicinally in China. **2.** the root of either of these plants or a substance obtained from the roots. [C17: from Mandarin Chinese *jen shen*, from *jen* man (from a resemblance of the roots to human legs) + *shen* ginseng]

gin sling (dʒɪn) *n.* an iced drink made from gin and water, sweetened, and flavoured with lemon or lime juice.

Gio·con·da (*Italian* dʒo'konda) *n.* **La.** See **Mona Lisa.** [Italian: the smiling (lady)]

Gior·gio·ne (*Italian* dʒor'dʒoːne) *n.* **Il.** original name *Giorgio Barbarelli*. ?1478–1511, Italian painter of the Venetian school, who introduced a new unity between figures and landscape.

Gior·gi sys·tem ('dʒɔːdʒɪ) *n.* a system of units based on the metre, kilogram, second, and ampere, in which the magnetic constant has the value $4\pi \times 10^{-7}$ henries per metre. It was used as a basis for SI units. Also called: **MKSA system.** [C20: named after *Giovanni Giorgi* (1871–1950), Italian physicist]

Giot·to (*Italian* 'dʒɔtto) *n.* also known as *Giotto di Bondone*. ?1267–1337, Florentine painter, who broke away from the stiff linear design of the Byzantine tradition and developed the more dramatic and naturalistic style characteristic of the Renaissance: his work includes cycles of frescoes in Assisi, the Arena Chapel in Padua, and the Church of Santa Croce, Florence.

gip (dʒɪp) *vb.* **gips, gip·ping, gipped. 1.** a variant spelling of **gyp**[1]. ~*n.* **2.** a variant spelling of **gyp**[2].

gi·pon (dʒɪ'pɒn, 'dʒɪpɒn) *n.* another word for **jupon.**

Gipps·land ('gɪps,lænd) *n.* a fertile region of SE Australia, in SE Victoria, extending east along the coast from Melbourne to the New South Wales border. Area: 35 200 sq. km (13 600 sq. miles).

gip·py ('dʒɪpɪ) *Slang.* ~*n., pl.* **-pies. 1.** an Egyptian person or thing. **2.** Also called: **gip·po,** *pl.* **-poes.** a Gypsy. ~*adj.* **3.** Egyptian. **4. gippy tummy.** diarrhoea, esp. as experienced by visitors to hot climates. [C19: from GYPSY and EGYPTIAN]

Gip·sy ('dʒɪpsɪ) *n., pl.* **-sies.** (*sometimes not cap.*) a variant spelling of **Gypsy.** —'**Gip·sy,·dom** *n.* —'**Gip·sy,·hood** *n.* —'**Gip·sy-,like** *adj.* —'**Gip·sy·ish** *adj.*

gip·sy moth *n.* a European moth, *Lymantria dispar*, introduced into North America, where it is a serious pest of shade trees: family *Lymantriidae* (or *Liparidae*). See also **tussock moth.**

gip·sy·wort ('dʒɪpsɪ,wɜːt) *n.* a hairy Eurasian plant, *Lycopus europaeus*, having two-lipped white flowers with purple dots on the lower lip: family *Labiatae* (labiates). See also **bugleweed** (sense 1).

gi·raffe (dʒɪ'rɑːf, -'ræf) *n., pl.* **-raffes** *or* **-raffe.** a large ruminant mammal, *Giraffa camelopardalis*, inhabiting savannahs of tropical Africa: the tallest mammal, with very long legs and neck and a colouring of regular reddish-brown patches on a beige ground: family *Giraffidae*. [C17: from Italian *giraffa*, from Arabic *zarāfah*, probably of African origin]

Gi·ral·dus Cam·bren·sis (dʒɪ'rældəs kæm'brɛnsɪs) *n.* literary name of *Gerald de Barri*. ?1146–?1223, Welsh chronicler and churchman, noted for his accounts of his travels in Ireland and Wales.

gir·an·dole ('dʒɪrən,dəʊl) *or* **gi·ran·do·la** (dʒɪ'rændələ) *n.* **1.** an ornamental wall candle holder, usually incorporating a mirror. **2.** an earring, esp. one having a central gem surrounded by smaller ones. **3.** *Artillery.* a group of connected mines. [C17: from French, from Italian *girandola*, from *girare* to revolve, from Latin *gȳrāre* to GYRATE]

gir·a·sol, gir·o·sol, *or* **gir·a·sole** ('dʒɪrə,sɒl, -,səʊl) *n.* a type of opal that has a red or pink glow in bright light; fire opal. [C16: from Italian, from *girare* to revolve (see GYRATE) + *sole* the sun, from Latin *sōl*]

Gi·raud (*French* ʒi'ro) *n.* **Hen·ri Ho·no·ré** (ãri ɔnɔ're). 1879–1949, French general, who commanded French forces in North Africa (1942–43).

Gi·rau·doux (*French* ʒiro'du) *n.* **Jean** (ʒã). 1882–1944, French dramatist. His works, noted for their use of paradox and imagery, include the novel *Suzanne et le Pacifique* (1921) and the plays *Amphitryon 38* (1929) and *La Guerre de Troie n'aura pas lieu* (1935).

gird[1] (gɜːd) *vb.* **girds, gird·ing, gird·ed** *or* **girt.** (*tr.*) **1.** to put a belt, girdle, etc., around (the waist or hips). **2.** to bind or secure with or as if with a belt: *to gird on one's armour*. **3.** to surround; encircle. **4.** to prepare (oneself) for action (esp. in the phrase **gird (up) one's loins**). **5.** to endow with a rank, attribute, etc., esp. knighthood. [Old English *gyrdan*, of Germanic origin; related to Old Norse *gyrtha*, Old High German *gurten*]

gird[2] (gɜːd) *Northern Brit. dialect.* ~*vb.* **1.** (when *intr.*, foll. by *at*) to jeer (at someone); mock. **2.** (*tr.*) to strike (a blow at someone). **3.** (*intr.*) to move at high speed. ~*n.* **4. a.** a blow or stroke. **b.** a taunt; gibe. **5.** a display of bad temper or anger (esp. in the phrases **in a gird; throw a gird**). [C13 *girden* to strike, cut, of unknown origin]

gird·er ('gɜːdə) *n.* a large beam, esp. one made of steel, used in the construction of bridges, buildings, etc.

gir·dle[1] ('gɜːd°l) *n.* **1.** a woman's elastic corset covering the waist to the thigh. **2.** anything that surrounds or encircles. **3.** a belt or sash. **4.** *Jewellery.* the outer edge of a gem. **5.** *Anatomy.* any encircling structure or part. See **pectoral girdle, pelvic girdle. 6.** the mark left on a tree trunk after the removal of a ring of bark. ~*vb.* (*tr.*) **7.** to put a girdle on or around. **8.** to surround or encircle. **9.** to remove a ring of bark from (a tree or branch), thus causing it to die. [Old English *gyrdel*, of Germanic origin; related to Old Norse *gyrthill*, Old Frisian *gerdel*, Old High German *gurtila*; see GIRD[1]] —'**gir·dle-,like** *adj.*

gir+dle[2] ('gɜ:dᵊl) *n.* a less common word for **griddle.**

gir·dle+cake ('gɜ:dᵊl͵keɪk) *n.* a less common name for **drop scone.**

gir+dler ('gɜ:dlə) *n.* **1.** a person or thing that girdles. **2.** a maker of girdles. **3.** any insect, such as the twig girdler, that bores circular grooves around the stems or twigs in which it lays its eggs.

Gir+gen+ti (*Italian* dʒir'dʒɛnti) *n.* a former name of **Agrigento.**

girl (gɜ:l) *n.* **1.** a female child from birth to young womanhood. **2.** a young unmarried woman; lass; maid. **3.** *Informal.* a sweetheart or girlfriend. **4.** *Informal.* a woman of any age. **5.** an informal word for **daughter. 6.** a female employee, esp. a female servant. **7.** (*usually pl.* and preceded by *the*) *Informal.* a group of women, esp. acquaintances. [C13: of uncertain origin; perhaps related to Low German *Göre* boy, girl]

girl Fri+day *n.* a female employee who has a wide range of duties, usually including secretarial and clerical work.

girl+friend ('gɜ:l͵frɛnd) *n.* **1.** a female friend with whom a man or boy is romantically or sexually involved; sweetheart. **2.** any female friend.

Girl Guide *n.* See **Guide.**

girl+hood ('gɜ:l͵hʊd) *n.* the state or time of being a girl.

girl·ie ('gɜ:lɪ) *n.* (*modifier*) *Informal.* displaying or featuring nude or scantily dressed women: *a girlie magazine.*

girl+ish ('gɜ:lɪʃ) *adj.* of or like a girl in looks, behaviour, innocence, etc. —**'girl+ish+ly** *adv.* —**'girl+ish+ness** *n.*

Girl Scout *n. U.S.* a member of the equivalent organization for girls to the Scouts. Brit. equivalent: **Guide.**

gi·ro ('dʒaɪrəʊ) *n., pl.* **+ros.** the settlement of debts or other payments by transfers between accounts or by giro cheque, operated by post offices or banks. [C20: ultimately from Greek *guros* circuit]

gi+ron *or* **gy+ron** ('dʒaɪrɒn) *n. Heraldry.* a charge consisting of the lower half of a diagonally divided quarter, usually in the top left corner of the shield. [C16: from Old French *giron* a triangular piece of material, of Germanic origin; related to Old High German *gēro* triangular object; compare GORE[3]]

Gi+ronde (*French* ʒi'rɔ̃:d) *n.* **1.** a department of SW France, in Aquitaine region. Capital: Bordeaux. Pop.: 1 082 074 (1975). Area: 10 726 sq. km. (4183 sq. miles). **2.** an estuary in SW France, formed by the confluence of the Rivers Garonne and Dordogne. Length: 72 km (45 miles).

Gi+ron+dist (dʒɪ'rɒndɪst) *n.* **1.** a member of a party of moderate republicans during the French Revolution, many of whom came from Gironde: overthrown (1793) by their rivals the Jacobins. See also **Jacobin** (sense 1). ~*adj.* **2.** of or relating to the Girondists or their principles. —**Gi+'ron+dism** *n.*

gi+ron+ny *or* **gy+ron+ny** (dʒaɪ'rɒnɪ) *adj.* (*usually postpositive*) *Heraldry.* divided into segments from the fesse point.

gir+o+sol ('dʒɪrə͵sɒl, -͵səʊl) *n.* a variant spelling of **girasol.**

girt[1] (gɜ:t) *vb.* **1.** the past tense or past participle of **gird**[1]. ~*adj.* **2.** *Nautical.* moored securely to prevent swinging.

girt[2] (gɜ:t) *vb.* **1.** (*tr.*) to bind or encircle; gird. **2.** to measure the girth of (something).

girth (gɜ:θ) *n.* **1.** the distance around something; circumference. **2.** size or bulk: *a man of great girth.* **3.** a band around a horse's belly to keep the saddle in position. ~*vb.* **4.** (usually foll. by *up*) to fasten a girth on (a horse). **5.** (*tr.*) to encircle or surround. [C14: from Old Norse *gjörth* belt; related to Gothic *gairda* GIRDLE; see GIRD[1]]

gi+sarme (gɪ'zɑ:m) *n.* a long-shafted battle-axe with a sharp point on the back of the axe head. [C13: from Old French *guisarme,* probably from Old High German *getīsarn* weeding tool, from *getan* to weed + *īsarn* IRON]

Gis+borne ('gɪzbən) *n.* a port in N New Zealand, on E North Island on Poverty Bay. Pop.: 26 726 (1971).

Gis·card d'Es·taing (*French* ʒiskar dɛs'tɛ̃) *n.* **Va·lé·ry** (vale'ri). born 1926, French politician; minister of finance and economic affairs (1962–66; 1969–74): president (1974–81).

Gish (gɪʃ) *n.* **1. Dor·o·thy.** 1898–1968, U.S. film actress, chiefly in silent films. **2.** her sister, **Lil·li·an.** born 1896, U.S. film and stage actress; noted esp. for her roles in such silent films as *Birth of a Nation* (1914) and *Intolerance* (1916).

Gis·sing ('gɪsɪŋ) *n.* **George (Robert).** 1857–1903, English novelist, noted for his depiction of middle-class poverty. His works include *Demos* (1886) and *New Grub Street* (1891).

gist (dʒɪst) *n.* **1.** the point or substance of an argument, speech, etc. **2.** *Law.* the essential point of an action. [C18: from Anglo-French, as in *cest action gist en* this action consists in, literally: lies in, from Old French *gésir* to lie, from Latin *jacēre,* from *jacere* to throw]

git (gɪt) *n. Brit. slang.* **1.** a contemptible person, often a fool. **2.** a bastard. [C20: from GET (in the sense: *to beget,* hence a bastard, fool)]

git+tern ('gɪtɜ:n) *n. Music.* an obsolete medieval stringed instrument resembling the guitar. Compare **cittern.** [C14: from Old French *guiterne,* ultimately from Old Spanish *guitarra* GUITAR; see CITTERN]

Giu·li·ni (*Italian* dʒu'li:ni) *n.* **Car·lo Ma·ri·a** ('karlo ma'ri:a). born 1914, Italian orchestral conductor, esp. of opera.

Giu·lio Ro·ma·no (*Italian* 'dʒu:ljo ro'ma:no) *n.* ?1499–1546, Italian architect and painter; a founder of mannerism.

giu+sto ('dʒu:stəʊ) *adv. Music.* (of a tempo marking) **a.** to be observed strictly. **b.** to be observed appropriately: *allegro giusto.* [Italian: just, proper]

give (gɪv) *vb.* **gives, giv+ing, gave, giv+en.** (*mainly tr.*) **1.** (*also intr.*) to present or deliver voluntarily (something that is one's own) to the permanent possession of another or others. **2.** (often foll. by *for*) to transfer (something that is one's own, esp. money) to the possession of another as part of an exchange: *to give fifty pounds for a painting.* **3.** to place in the temporary possession of another: *I gave him my watch while I went swimming.* **4.** (when *intr.,* foll. by *of*) to grant, provide, or bestow: *give me some advice.* **5.** to administer: *to give a reprimand.* **6.** to award or attribute: *to give blame, praise, etc.* **7.** to be a source of: *he gives no trouble.* **8.** to impart or communicate: *to give news; give a person a cold.* **9.** to utter or emit: *to give a shout.* **10.** to perform, make, or do: *the car gave a jolt and stopped.* **11.** to sacrifice or devote: *he gave his life for his country.* **12.** to surrender: *to give place to others.* **13.** to concede or yield: *I will give you this game.* **14.** *Informal.* to happen: *what gives?* **15.** (often foll. by *to*) to cause; lead: *she gave me to believe that she would come.* **16.** to place value on: *I don't give anything for his promises.* **17.** to perform or present as an entertainment: *to give a play.* **18.** to propose as a toast: *I give you the Queen.* **19.** (*intr.*) to yield or break under force or pressure: *this surface will give if you sit on it; his courage will never give.* **20. give as good as one gets.** to respond to verbal or bodily blows to at least an equal extent as those received. **21. give battle.** to commence fighting. **22. give birth.** (often foll. by *to*) **a.** to bear (offspring). **b.** to produce, originate, or create (an idea, plan, etc.). **23. give ground.** to draw back or retreat. **24. give rise to.** to be the cause of. **25. give me.** *Informal.* I prefer: *give me hot weather any day!* **26. give or take.** plus or minus: *three thousand people came, give or take a few hundred.* **27. give way. a.** to yield or surrender. **b.** (often foll. by *to*) to allow precedence (to). **28. give (a person) what for.** *Informal.* to scold or reprimand (a person) severely. ~*n.* **29.** *Informal.* tendency to yield under pressure; resilience: *there's bound to be some give in a long plank; there is no give in his moral views.* ~See also **give away, give in, give off, give onto, give out, give over, give up.** [Old English *giefan;* related to Old Norse *gefa,* Gothic *giban,* Old High German *geban,* Swedish *giva*] —**'giv+a·ble** *or* **'give+a·ble** *adj.* —**'giv+er** *n.*

give-and-take *n.* **1.** mutual concessions, shared benefits, and cooperation. **2.** a smoothly flowing exchange of ideas and talk. ~*vb.* **give and take. 3.** to make mutual concessions.

give a·way *vb.* (*tr., adv.*) **1.** to donate or bestow as a gift, prize, etc. **2.** to sell very cheaply. **3.** to reveal or betray (esp. in the phrases **give the game** *or* **show away**). **4.** to fail to use (an opportunity) through folly or neglect. **5.** to present (a bride) formally to her husband in a marriage ceremony. *vb.* (*tr., adv.*) **6.** *Austral. informal.* to give up or abandon something. ~*n.* **give+a·way. 7.** a betrayal or disclosure of information esp. when unintentional. **8.** *Chiefly U.S.* something given, esp. with articles on sale, at little or no charge to increase sales, attract publicity, etc. **9.** *Journalism.* another name for **freesheet. 10.** *Chiefly U.S.* a radio or television programme characterized by the award of money and prizes. **11.** (*modifier*) very cheap (esp. in the phrase **giveaway prices**).

give in *vb.* (*adv.*) **1.** (*intr.*) to yield; admit defeat. **2.** (*tr.*) to submit or deliver (a document).

giv+en ('gɪvᵊn) *vb.* **1.** the past participle of **give.** ~*adj.* **2.** (*postpositive;* foll. by *to*) tending (to); inclined or addicted (to). **3.** specific or previously stated. **4.** assumed as a premiss. **5.** *Maths.* known or determined independently: *a given volume.* **6.** (on official documents) issued or executed, as on a stated date. ~*n.* **7.** an assumed fact.

giv+en name *n.* a name by which a person is distinguished from others of the same name: usually chosen by the parents of a child at birth; Christian name.

give off *vb.* (*tr., adv.*) to emit or discharge: *the mothballs gave off an acrid odour.*

give on·to *vb.* (*intr.; prep.*) to afford a view or prospect of: *their new house gives onto the sea.*

give out *vb.* (*adv.*) **1.** (*tr.*) to emit or discharge. **2.** (*tr.*) to publish or make known: *the chairman gave out that he would resign.* **3.** (*tr.*) to hand out or distribute: *they gave out free chewing gum on the street.* **4.** (*intr.*) to become exhausted; fail: *the supply of candles gave out.* **5.** (*tr.*) *Cricket.* (of an umpire) to declare (a batsman) dismissed.

give o·ver *vb.* (*adv.*) **1.** (*tr.*) to transfer, esp. to the care or custody of another. **2.** (*tr.*) to assign or resign to a specific purpose or function: *the day was given over to pleasure.* **3.** *Informal.* to cease (an activity): *give over fighting, will you!*

give up *vb.* (*adv.*) **1.** to abandon hope (for). **2.** (*tr.*) to renounce (an activity, belief, etc.): *I have given up smoking.* **3.** to relinquish or resign from: *he gave up the presidency.* **4.** (*tr.; usually reflexive*) to surrender: *the escaped convict gave himself up.* **5.** (*tr.*) to reveal or disclose (information). **6.** (*intr.*) to admit one's defeat or inability to do something. **7.** (*tr.; often passive or reflexive*) to devote completely (to): *she gave herself up to caring for the sick.*

Gî·za ('gi:zə) *n.* See **El Giza.**

giz+zard ('gɪzəd) *n.* **1.** the thick-walled part of a bird's stomach, in which hard food is broken up by muscular action and contact with grit and small stones. **2.** a similar structure in many invertebrates. **3.** *Informal.* the stomach and entrails generally. [C14: from Old North French *guisier* fowl's liver, alteration of Latin *gigēria* entrails of poultry when cooked, of uncertain origin]

Gk *or* **Gk.** *abbrev. for* Greek.

gl. *abbrev. for:* **1.** glass. **2.** gloss.

gla+bel+la (glə'bɛlə) *n., pl.* **+lae** (-li:). *Anatomy.* a smooth elevation of the frontal bone just above the bridge of the nose: a reference point in physical anthropology or craniometry. [C19: New Latin, from Latin *glabellus* smooth, from *glaber* bald, smooth] —**gla+'bel+lar** *adj.*

gla+brous ('gleɪbrəs) *or* **gla+brate** ('gleɪbreɪt, -brɪt) *adj.*

Biology. without hair or a similar growth; smooth: *a glabrous stem.* [C17 *glabrous,* from Latin *glaber*] —'**gla·brous·ness** *n.*

gla·cé ('glæsɪ) *adj.* **1.** crystallized or candied: *glacé cherries.* **2.** covered in icing. **3.** (of leather, silk, etc.) having a glossy finish. **4.** *Chiefly U.S.* frozen or iced. ~*vb.* **·cés, ·cé·ing, ·céed. 5.** (*tr.*) to ice or candy (cakes, fruits, etc.). [C19: from French *glacé,* literally: iced, from *glacer* to freeze, from *glace,* ice, from Latin *glaciēs*]

gla·ci·al ('gleɪsɪəl, -ʃəl) *adj.* **1.** characterized by the presence of masses of ice. **2.** relating to, caused by, or deposited by a glacier. **3.** extremely cold; icy. **4.** cold or hostile in manner: *a glacial look.* **5.** (of a chemical compound) of or tending to form crystals that resemble ice: *glacial acetic acid.* **6.** very slow in progress: *a glacial pace.* —'**gla·ci·al·ly** *adv.*

gla·ci·al a·ce·tic ac·id *n.* pure acetic acid (more than 99.8 per cent).

gla·ci·al·ist ('gleɪsɪəlɪst, -ʃəl-) *n.* a person who studies ice and its effects on the earth's surface.

gla·ci·al pe·ri·od *n.* **1.** any period of time during which a large part of the earth's surface was covered with ice, due to the advance of glaciers, as in the late Carboniferous period, and during most of the Pleistocene; glaciation. **2.** (*often caps.*) the Pleistocene epoch. ~Also called: **glacial epoch, ice age.**

gla·ci·ate ('gleɪsɪˌeɪt) *vb.* **1.** to cover or become covered with glaciers or masses of ice. **2.** (*tr.*) to subject to the effects of glaciers, such as denudation and erosion. —**gla·ci·'a·tion** *n.*

glac·i·er ('glæsɪə, 'gleɪs-) *n.* a slowly moving mass of ice originating from an accumulation of snow. It can either spread out from a central mass (**continental glacier**) or descend from a high valley (**alpine glacier**). [C18: from French (Savoy dialect), from Old French *glace* ice, from Late Latin *glacia,* from Latin *glaciēs* ice]

glac·i·er milk *n.* water flowing in a stream from the snout of a glacier and containing particles of rock.

glac·i·ol·o·gy (ˌglæsɪ'ɒlədʒɪ, ˌgleɪ-) *n.* the study of the distribution, character, and effects of glaciers. —**glac·i·o·log·i·cal** (ˌglæsɪə'lɒdʒɪkᵊl, ˌgleɪ-) *or* ˌ**glac·i·o·'log·ic** *adj.* —ˌ**glac·i·'ol·o·gist** *or* '**gla·ci·al·ist** *n.*

glac·is ('glæsɪs, 'glæsɪ, 'gleɪ-) *n., pl.* **·is·es** *or* **·is** (-iːz, -ɪz). **1.** a slight incline; slope. **2.** an open slope in front of a fortified place. [C17: from French, from Old French *glacier* to freeze, slip, from Latin *glaciāre,* from *glaciēs* ice]

glad[1] (glæd) *adj.* **glad·der, glad·dest. 1.** happy and pleased; contented. **2.** causing happiness or contentment. **3.** (*postpositive;* foll. by *to*) very willing: *he was glad to help.* ~*vb.* **4.** (*tr.*) an archaic word for **gladden.** [Old English *glæd;* related to Old Norse *glathr,* Old High German *glat* smooth, shining, Latin *glaber* smooth, Lithuanian *glodùs* fitting closely] —'**glad·ly** *adv.* —'**glad·ness** *n.*

glad[2] (glæd) *n. Informal.* short for **gladiolus.** Also (Austral.): **glad·die** ('glædɪ).

Glad·beck (*German* 'glatbɛk) *n.* a city in N West Germany, in North Rhine-Westphalia. Pop.: 83 100 (1970).

glad·den ('glædᵊn) *vb.* to make or become glad and joyful. —'**glad·den·er** *n.*

glad·don ('glædᵊn) *n.* another name for the **stinking iris.** [Old English, of uncertain origin]

glade (gleɪd) *n.* an open place in a forest; clearing. [C16: of uncertain origin; perhaps related to GLAD (in obsolete sense: bright); see GLEAM] —'**glade·ˌlike** *adj.*

glad eye *n. Informal.* an inviting or seductive glance (esp. in the phrase **give (someone) the glad eye**).

glad hand *n.* **1. a.** a welcoming hand. **b.** a welcome. ~*vb.* **glad-hand.** to welcome by or as if by offering a hand.

glad·i·ate ('glædɪɪt, -ˌeɪt, 'gleɪ-) *adj. Botany.* shaped like a sword: *gladiate leaves.* [C18: from Latin *gladius* sword]

glad·i·a·tor ('glædɪˌeɪtə) *n.* **1.** (in ancient Rome and Etruria) a man trained to fight in arenas to provide entertainment. **2.** a person who supports and fights publicly for a cause. [C16: from Latin: swordsman, from *gladius* sword]

glad·i·a·to·ri·al (ˌglædɪə'tɔːrɪəl) *adj.* of, characteristic of, or relating to gladiators, combat, etc.

glad·i·o·lus (ˌglædɪ'əʊləs) *n., pl.* **·lus, ·li** (-laɪ), *or* **·lus·es. 1.** Also called: **sword lily, gladiola.** any iridaceous plant of the widely cultivated genus *Gladiolus,* having sword-shaped leaves and spikes of funnel-shaped brightly coloured flowers. **2.** *Anatomy.* the large central part of the breastbone. [C16: from Latin: a small sword, sword lily, from *gladius* a sword]

glad·rags ('glædˌrægz) *pl. n. Slang.* best clothes or clothes used on special occasions.

glad·some ('glædsəm) *adj.* an archaic word for **glad.** —'**glad·some·ly** *adv.* —'**glad·some·ness** *n.*

Glad·stone[1] ('glædstən) *n.* a light four-wheeled horse-drawn vehicle. [C19: named after W. E. GLADSTONE]

Glad·stone[2] ('glædstən) *n.* **Wil·liam Ew·art.** 1809–98, British statesman. He became leader of the Liberal party in 1867 and was four times prime minister (1868–74; 1880–85; 1886; 1892–94). In his first ministry he disestablished the Irish Church (1869), introduced educational reform (1870), and the secret ballot (1872). He succeeded in carrying the Reform Act of 1884 but failed to gain support for a Home Rule Bill for Ireland, to which he devoted much of the latter part of his career.

Glad·stone bag *n.* a piece of hand luggage consisting of two equal-sized hinged compartments. [C19: named after W. E. GLADSTONE]

Glag·o·lit·ic (ˌglægə'lɪtɪk) *adj.* of, relating to, or denoting a Slavic alphabet whose invention is attributed to Saint Cyril, preserved only in certain Roman Catholic liturgical books found in Dalmatia. [C19: from New Latin *glagoliticus,* from Serbo-Croatian *glagolica* the Glagolitic alphabet; related to Old Church Slavonic *glagolŭ* word]

glaik·it *or* **glaik·et** ('gleɪkɪt) *adj. Scot.* foolish; silly; thoughtless. [C15: of obscure origin] —'**glaik·it·ness** *or* '**glaik·et·ness** *n.*

glair (glɛə) *n.* **1.** white of egg, esp. when used as a size, glaze, or adhesive, usually in bookbinding. **2.** any substance resembling this. ~*vb.* **3.** (*tr.*) to apply glair to (something). [C14: from Old French *glaire,* from Vulgar Latin *clāria* (unattested) CLEAR, from Latin *clārus*] —'**glair·y** *or* '**glair·e·ous** *adj.* —'**glair·i·ness** *n.*

glaive (gleɪv) *n.* an archaic word for **sword.** [C13: from Old French: javelin, from Latin *gladius* sword] —**glaived** *adj.*

Gla·mor·gan (glə'mɔːgən) *or* **Gla·mor·gan·shire** *n.* (until 1974) a county of SE Wales, now divided into West Glamorgan, Mid Glamorgan, and South Glamorgan.

glam·or·ize, glam·or·ise, *or U.S.* (*sometimes*) **glam·our·ize** ('glæməˌraɪz) *vb.* to cause to be or seem glamorous; romanticize or beautify. —ˌ**glam·or·i·'za·tion** *or* ˌ**glam·or·i·'sa·tion** *n.* —'**glam·or·ˌiz·er** *or* '**glam·or·ˌis·er** *n.*

glam·or·ous *or* **glam·our·ous** ('glæmərəs) *adj.* **1.** possessing glamour; alluring and fascinating: *a glamorous career.* **2.** beautiful and smart, esp. in a showy way: *a glamorous woman.* —'**glam·or·ous·ly** *or* '**glam·our·ous·ly** *adv.* —'**glam·or·ous·ness** *or* '**glam·our·ous·ness** *n.*

glam·our *or U.S.* (*sometimes*) **glam·or** ('glæmə) *n.* **1.** charm and allure; fascination. **2. a.** fascinating or voluptuous beauty, often dependent on artifice. **b.** (*as modifier*): *a glamour girl.* **3.** *Archaic.* a magic spell; charm. [C18: Scottish variant of GRAMMAR (hence a magic spell, because occult practices were popularly associated with learning)]

glance[1] (glɑːns) *vb.* **1.** (*intr.*) to look hastily or briefly. **2.** (*intr.;* foll. by *over, through,* etc.) to look over briefly: *to glance through a report.* **3.** (*intr.*) to reflect, glint, or gleam: *the sun glanced on the water.* **4.** (*intr.;* usually foll. by *off*) to depart (from an object struck) at an oblique angle: *the arrow glanced off the tree.* **5.** (*tr.*) to strike at an oblique angle: *the arrow glanced the tree.* ~*n.* **6.** a hasty or brief look; peep. **7. at a glance.** from one's first look; immediately. **8.** a flash or glint of light; gleam. **9.** the act or an instance of an object glancing or glancing off another. **10.** a brief allusion or reference. **11.** *Cricket.* a stroke in which the ball is deflected off the bat to the leg side; glide. [C15: modification of *glacen* to strike obliquely, from Old French *glacier* to slide (see GLACIS); compare Middle English *glenten* to make a rapid sideways movement, GLINT] —'**glanc·ing·ly** *adv.*

glance[2] (glɑːns) *n.* any mineral having a metallic lustre, esp. a simple sulphide: *copper glance.* [C19: from German *Glanz* brightness, lustre]

gland[1] (glænd) *n.* **1.** a cell or organ in man and other animals that synthesizes chemical substances and secretes them for the body to use or eliminate, either through a duct (see **exocrine gland**) or directly into the bloodstream (see **endocrine gland**). **2.** a structure, such as a lymph node, that resembles a gland in form. **3.** a cell or organ in plants that synthesizes and secretes a particular substance. [C17: from Latin *glāns* acorn] —'**gland·ˌlike** *adj.*

gland[2] (glænd) *n.* a device that prevents leakage of fluid from a point in a vessel, container, etc., at which a rotating or reciprocating shaft emerges. It often consists of a flanged metal sleeve bedding into a stuffing box. [C19: of unknown origin]

glan·ders ('glændəz) *n.* a highly infectious bacterial disease of horses, sometimes communicated to man, caused by *Actinobacillus mallei* and characterized by inflammation and ulceration of the mucous membranes of the air passages, skin and lymph glands. [C16: from Old French *glandres* enlarged glands, from Latin *glandulae* literally: little acorns, from *glāns* acorn; see GLAND[1]] —'**glan·dered** *adj.* —'**glan·der·ous** *adj.*

glan·du·lar ('glændjʊlə) *or* **glan·du·lous** ('glændjʊləs) *adj.* of, relating to, containing, functioning as, or affecting a gland: *glandular tissue.* [C18: from Latin *glandula,* literally: a little acorn; see GLANDERS] —'**glan·du·lar·ly** *or* '**glan·du·lous·ly** *adv.*

glan·du·lar fe·ver *n.* another name for **infectious mononucleosis.**

glan·dule ('glændjuːl) *n.* a small gland.

glans (glænz) *n., pl.* **glan·des** ('glændiːz). *Anatomy.* any small rounded body or glandlike mass, such as the head of the penis (**glans penis**). [C17: from Latin: acorn; see GLAND[1]]

glare[1] (glɛə) *vb.* **1.** (*intr.*) to stare angrily; glower. **2.** (*tr.*) to express by glowering. **3.** (*intr.*) (of light, colour, etc.) to be very bright and intense. **4.** (*intr.*) to be dazzlingly ornamented or garish. ~*n.* **5.** an angry stare. **6.** a dazzling light or brilliance. **7.** garish ornamentation or appearance; gaudiness. [C13: probably from Middle Low German, Middle Dutch *glaren* to gleam; probably related to Old English *glæren* glassy; see GLASS] —'**glare·less** *adj.* —'**glar·y** *adj.*

glare[2] (glɛə) *Chiefly Canadian and U.S. adj.* smooth and glassy: *glare ice.* [C16: special use of GLARE[1]]

glar·ing ('glɛərɪŋ) *adj.* **1.** conspicuous: *a glaring omission.* **2.** dazzling or garish. —'**glar·ing·ly** *adv.* —'**glar·ing·ness** *n.*

Gla·rus (*German* 'glaːrus) *n.* **1.** an Alpine canton of E central Switzerland. Capital: Glarus. Pop.: 38 155 (1970). Area 684 sq. km (267 sq. miles). **2.** a town in E central Switzerland, the capital of Glarus canton. Pop.: 6109 (1970). ~French name: **Gla·ris** (gla'ri).

Gla·ser ('gleɪzə) *n.* **Don·ald Ar·thur.** born 1926, U.S. physicist: invented the bubble chamber; Nobel prize for physics 1960.

Glas·gow ('glɑːzgəʊ, 'glæz-) *n.* a port in W central Scotland, administrative centre of Strathclyde region on the River Clyde:

the largest city in Scotland; centre of a major industrial region, chiefly shipbuilding and engineering; university (1451). Pop.: 896 958 (1971). Related adj.: **Glaswegian.**

glass (glɑːs) *n.* **1. a.** a hard brittle transparent or translucent noncrystalline solid, consisting of metal silicates or similar compounds. They are made from a fused mixture of oxides, such as lime, silicon dioxide, phosphorus pentoxide, etc., and are used for making windows, mirrors, bottles, etc. **b.** (*as modifier*): *a glass bottle.* Related adj.: **vitreous. 2.** any compound that has solidified from a molten state into a noncrystalline form. **3.** something made of glass, esp. a drinking vessel, a barometer, or a mirror. **4.** Also called: **glass+ful.** the amount or volume contained in a drinking glass: *he drank a glass of wine.* **5.** glassware collectively. **6.** See **volcanic glass. 7.** See **fibreglass.** ~*vb.* **8.** (*tr.*) to cover with, enclose in, or fit with glass. [Old English *glæs;* related to Old Norse *gler,* Old High German *glas,* Middle High German *glast* brightness; see GLARE[1]] —**'glass+less** *adj.* —**'glass+ˌlike** *adj.*

glass-blow·ing *n.* the process of shaping a mass of molten or softened glass into a vessel, shape, etc., by blowing air into it through a tube. —**'glass-ˌblow·er** *n.*

glass·es ('glɑːsɪz) *pl. n.* a pair of lenses for correcting faulty vision, in a frame that rests on the bridge of the nose and hooks behind the ears. Also called: **spectacles, eyeglasses.**

glass eye *n.* an artificial eye made of glass.

glass har+mon·i·ca *n.* a musical instrument of the 18th century consisting of a set of glass bowls of graduated pitches, played by rubbing the fingers over the moistened rims or by a keyboard mechanism. Sometimes shortened to **harmonica.** Also called: **musical glasses.**

glass+house ('glɑːsˌhaʊs) *n.* **1.** *Brit.* a glass building, esp. a greenhouse, used for growing plants in protected or controlled conditions. **2.** *Informal, chiefly Brit.* a military detention centre. **3.** *U.S.* another word for **glassworks.**

glass+ine (glæ'siːn) *n.* a glazed translucent paper used for book jackets.

glass jaw *n. Boxing, informal.* a jaw that is excessively fragile or susceptible to punches.

glass-mak·er *n.* a person who makes glass or glass objects. —**'glass-ˌmak·ing** *n.*

glass+man ('glɑːsmən) *n., pl.* **+men. 1.** a man whose work is making or selling glassware. **2.** a less common word for **glazier.**

glass snake *n.* any snakelike lizard of the genus *Ophisaurus,* of Europe, Asia, and North America, with vestigial hind limbs and a tail that breaks off easily: family *Anguidae.*

glass string *n.* (in Malaysia) the string of a kite used in kite fighting that has an abrasive coating of glue and crushed glass.

glass+ware ('glɑːsˌwɛə) *n.* articles made of glass, esp. drinking glasses.

glass wool *n.* fine spun glass massed into a wool-like bulk, used in insulation, filtering, etc.

glass+work ('glɑːsˌwɜːk) *n.* **1.** the production of glassware. **2.** the fitting of glass. **3.** articles of glass. —**'glass-ˌwork·er** *n.*

glass+works ('glɑːsˌwɜːks) *n.* (*functioning as sing.*) a factory for the moulding of glass.

glass+wort ('glɑːsˌwɜːt) *n.* **1.** Also called: **marsh samphire.** any plant of the chenopodiaceous genus *Salicornia,* of salt marshes, having fleshy stems and scalelike leaves: formerly used as a source of soda for glass-making. **2.** another name for **saltwort** (sense 1).

glass·y ('glɑːsɪ) *adj.* **glass·i·er, glass·i·est. 1.** resembling glass, esp. in smoothness, slipperiness, or transparency. **2.** void of expression, life, or warmth: *a glassy stare.* —**'glass·i+ly** *adv.* —**'glass·i·ness** *n.*

Glas+ton+bur·y ('glæstənbərɪ, -brɪ) *n.* a town in SW England, in Somerset: remains of prehistoric lake villages; the reputed burial place of King Arthur; site of a ruined Benedictine abbey, probably the oldest in England. Pop.: 6571 (1971).

Glas+we+gian (glæz'wiːdʒən) *adj.* **1.** of or relating to Glasgow or its inhabitants. ~*n.* **2.** a native or inhabitant of Glasgow. [C19: influenced by *Norwegian*]

Glau+ber's salt ('glaʊbəz) *or* **Glau+ber salt** *n.* the crystalline decahydrate of sodium sulphate. [C18: named after J. R. *Glauber* (1604–68), German chemist]

Glau·ce ('glɔːsɪ) *n. Greek myth.* **1.** the second bride of Jason, murdered on her wedding day by Medea, whom Jason had deserted. **2.** a sea nymph, one of the Nereids.

glau+co+ma (glɔː'kəʊmə) *n.* a disease of the eye in which increased pressure within the eyeball causes damage to the optic disc and impaired vision, sometimes progressing to blindness. [C17: from Latin, from Greek *glaukōma,* from *glaukos;* see GLAUCOUS] —**glau+'co+ma+tous** *adj.*

glau+co+nite ('glɔːkəˌnaɪt) *n.* a green mineral consisting of the hydrated silicate of iron, potassium, aluminium, and magnesium: found in greensand and similar rocks. Formula: $K_2(Mg,Fe)_2Al_6(Si_4O_{10})_3(OH)_{12}$. [C19: from Greek *glaukon,* neuter of *glaukos* bluish-green + -ITE[1]; see GLAUCOUS] —**glau+co+nit+ic** (ˌglɔːkə'nɪtɪk) *adj.*

glau+cous ('glɔːkəs) *adj.* **1.** *Botany.* covered with a waxy or powdery bloom. **2.** bluish-green. [C17: from Latin *glaucus* silvery, bluish-green, from Greek *glaukos*] —**'glau+cous+ly** *adv.*

glau+cous gull *n.* a gull, *Larus hyperboreus,* of northern and arctic regions, with a white head and tail and pale grey back and wings.

glaze (gleɪz) *vb.* **1.** (*tr.*) to fit or cover with glass. **2.** (*tr.*) *Ceramics.* to cover with a vitreous solution, rendering impervious to liquid and smooth to the touch. **3.** (*tr.*) to cover (a painting) with a layer of semitransparent colour to modify the tones. **4.** (*tr.*) to cover (foods) with a shiny coating by applying beaten egg, sugar, etc. **5.** (*tr.*) to make glossy or shiny. **6.** (when *intr.*, often foll. by *over*) to become or cause to become glassy: *his eyes were glazing over.* ~*n.* **7.** *Ceramics.* **a.** a vitreous or glossy coating. **b.** the substance used to produce such a coating. **8.** a semitransparent coating applied to a painting to modify the tones. **9.** a smooth lustrous finish on a fabric produced by applying various chemicals. **10.** something used to give a glossy surface to foods: *a syrup glaze.* [C14 *glasen,* from *glas* GLASS] —**'glaz+er** *n.* —**'glaz·y** *adj.*

glaze ice *or* **glazed frost** *n. Brit.* a thin clear layer of ice caused by the freezing of rain or water droplets in the air on impact with a cool surface or by refreezing after a thaw. Also called: **silver frost.** U.S. term: **glaze.**

gla+zi+er ('gleɪzɪə) *n.* a person who fits windows, etc., with glass. —**'gla+zi+er·y** *n.*

glaz+ing ('gleɪzɪŋ) *n.* **1.** the surface of a glazed object. **2.** glass fitted, or to be fitted, in a door, frame, etc.

glaz·ing-bar *n.* a supporting or strengthening bar for a glass window, door, etc. Usual U.S. word: **muntin.**

Gla·zu·nov ('glæzʊnɒf; *Russian* glɘzu'nɔf) *n.* **A·lek·sandr Kon·stan·ti·no·vich** (alɪk'sandr kənstan'tinəvitʃ). 1865–1936, Russian composer, in France from 1928. A pupil of Rimsky-Korsakov, he wrote eight symphonies and concertos for piano and for violin among other works.

G.L.C. *abbrev. for* Greater London Council.

gld. *abbrev. for* guilder.

gleam (gliːm) *n.* **1.** a small beam or glow of light, esp. reflected light. **2.** a brief or dim indication: *a gleam of hope.* ~*vb.* (*intr.*) **3.** to send forth or reflect a beam of light. **4.** to appear, esp. briefly: *intelligence gleamed in his eyes.* [Old English *glǣm;* related to Old Norse *gljā* to flicker, Old High German *gleimo* glow-worm, *glīmo* brightness, Old Irish *glē* bright] —**'gleam+ing+ly** *adv.* —**'gleam+less** *adj.* —**'gleam·y** *adj.*

glean (gliːn) *vb.* **1.** to gather (something) slowly and carefully in small pieces: *to glean information from the newspapers.* **2.** to gather (the useful remnants of a crop) from the field after harvesting. [C14: from Old French *glener,* from Late Latin *glennāre,* probably of Celtic origin] —**'glean·a·ble** *adj.* —**'glean+er** *n.*

glean+ings ('gliːnɪŋz) *pl. n.* the useful remnants of a crop that can be gathered from the field after harvesting.

glebe (gliːb) *n.* **1.** *Brit.* land granted to a clergyman as part of his benefice. **2.** *Poetic.* land, esp. when regarded as the source of growing things. [C14: from Latin *glaeba*]

glede (gliːd) *or* **gled** (glɛd) *n.* a former Brit. name for the **red kite.** See **kite** (sense 4). [Old English *glida;* related to Old Norse *gletha,* Middle Low German *glede*]

glee (gliː) *n.* **1.** great merriment; joy. **2.** a type of song originating in 18th-century England, sung by three or more unaccompanied voices. Compare **madrigal** (sense 1). [Old English *glēo;* related to Old Norse *glȳ*]

glee club *n. Now chiefly U.S.* a club or society organized for the singing of choral music.

glee+ful ('gliːfʊl) *adj.* full of glee; merry. —**'glee+ful+ly** *adv.* —**'glee+ful+ness** *n.*

glee+man ('gliːmən) *n., pl.* **+men.** *Obsolete.* a minstrel.

gleet (gliːt) *n.* **1.** inflammation of the urethra with a slight discharge of thin pus and mucus: a stage of chronic gonorrhoea. **2.** the pus and mucus discharged. [C14: from Old French *glette* slime, from Latin *glittus* sticky] —**'gleet·y** *adj.*

Glei+witz ('glaɪvɪts) *n.* the German name for **Gliwice.**

glen (glɛn) *n.* a narrow and deep mountain valley, esp. in Scotland or Ireland. [C15: from Scottish Gaelic *gleann,* from Old Irish *glend*] —**'glen+ˌlike** *adj.*

Glen Al+byn ('ælbɪn, 'ɔːl-) *n.* another name for the **Great Glen.**

Glen+coe (glɛn'kəʊ) *n.* a glen in W Scotland, in S Highland region: site of the massacre of the Macdonalds by the Campbells and English troops (1692).

Glen·dow·er (glɛn'daʊə) *n.* **Ow·en,** Welsh name *Owain Glyndŵr.* ?1350–?1416, Welsh chieftain, who led a revolt against Henry IV's rule in Wales (1400–15).

glen+gar+ry (glɛn'gærɪ) *n., pl.* **+ries.** a brimless Scottish woollen cap with a crease down the crown, often with ribbons dangling at the back. Also called: **glengarry bonnet.** [C19: after *Glengarry,* Scotland]

Glen More (mɔː) *n.* another name for the **Great Glen.**

gle+noid ('gliːnɔɪd) *adj. Anatomy.* **1.** resembling or having a shallow cavity. **2.** denoting the cavity in the shoulder blade into which the head of the upper arm bone fits. [C18: from Greek *glēnoeidēs,* from *glēnē* socket of a joint]

Glen+roth+es (glɛn'rɒθɪs) *n.* a new town in Scotland, in Fife region: founded in 1948. Pop.: 27 137 (1971).

gley (gleɪ) *n.* a bluish-grey compact sticky soil occurring in certain humid regions. [C20: from Russian *glei* clay]

gli·a ('gliːə) *n.* another name for **neuroglia.**

gli·a·din ('glaɪədɪn) *or* **gli·a·dine** ('glaɪəˌdiːn, -dɪn) *n.* a protein of cereals, esp. wheat, with a high proline content: forms a sticky mass with water that binds flour into dough. Compare **glutelin.** [C19: from Italian *gliadina,* from Greek *glia* glue]

glib (glɪb) *adj.* **glib+ber, glib+best.** fluent and easy, often in an insincere or deceptive way. [C16: probably from Middle Low German *glibberich* slippery] —**'glib+ly** *adv.* —**'glib+ness** *n.*

glide (glaɪd) *vb.* **1.** to move or cause to move easily without jerks or hesitations: *to glide in a boat down the river.* **2.** (*intr.*) to pass slowly or without perceptible change: *to glide into sleep.* **3.** to cause (an aircraft) to come into land without engine power, or (of an aircraft) to land in this way. **4.** (*intr.*) to fly a glider. **5.** *Music.* to execute a portamento from one note to another. 6. (*intr.*) *Phonetics.* to produce a glide. ~*n.* 7. a smooth easy movement. 8. a. any of various dances featuring gliding steps. b. a step in such a dance. 9. a manoeuvre in which an aircraft makes a gentle descent without engine power. See also **glide path.** 10. the act or process of gliding. 11. *Music.* a. a long portion of tubing slipped in and out of a trombone to increase its length for the production of lower harmonic series. See also **valve** (sense 5). b. a portamento or slur. 12. *Phonetics.* a. a transitional sound as the speech organs pass from the articulatory position of one speech sound to that of the next, as the (w) sound in some pronunciations of the word *doing.* b. another word for **semivowel.** 13. *Crystallog.* another name for **slip**[1] (sense 33). 14. *Cricket.* another word for **glance**[1] (sense 11). [Old English *glīdan;* related to Old High German *glītan*] —**'glid·ing·ly** *adv.*

glide path *n.* the course that an aeroplane takes during a glide.

glid·er ('glaɪdə) *n.* 1. an aircraft capable of gliding and soaring in air currents without the use of an engine. See also **sailplane.** 2. a person or thing that glides.

glim (glɪm) *n. Slang.* 1. a light or lamp. 2. an eye. [C17: probably short for GLIMMER; compare GLIMPSE]

glim·mer ('glɪmə) *vb.* (*intr.*) 1. (of a light, candle, etc.) to glow faintly or flickeringly. 2. to be indicated faintly: *hope glimmered in his face.* ~*n.* 3. a glow or twinkle of light. 4. a faint indication. [C14: compare Middle High German *glimmern,* Swedish *glimra,* Danish *glimre*] —**'glim·mer·ing·ly** *adv.*

glimpse (glɪmps) *n.* 1. a brief or incomplete view: *to catch a glimpse of the sea.* 2. a vague indication: *he had a glimpse of what the lecturer meant.* 3. *Archaic.* a glimmer of light. ~*vb.* 4. (when *intr.,* usually foll. by *at*) to catch sight (of) briefly or momentarily. [C14: of Germanic origin; compare Middle High German *glimsen* to glimmer] —**'glimps·er** *n.*

Glin·ka (*Russian* 'glinkə) *n.* **Mi·kha·il I·va·no·vich** (mixa'il i'vanəvitʃ). 1803–57, Russian composer who pioneered the Russian national school of music. His works include the operas *A Life for the Tsar* (1836) and *Russlan and Ludmilla* (1842).

glint (glɪnt) *vb.* 1. to gleam or cause to gleam brightly. 2. (*intr.*) *Archaic.* to move or pass quickly. ~*n.* 3. a bright gleam or flash. 4. brightness or gloss. 5. a brief indication. [C15: probably of Scandinavian origin; compare Swedish dialect *glänta, glinta* to gleam]

gli·o·ma (glaɪ'əʊmə) *n., pl.* **·ma·ta** (-mətə) *or* **·mas.** a tumour of the brain and spinal cord, composed of neuroglia cells and fibres. [C19: from New Latin, from Greek *glia* glue + -OMA] —**gli·'o·ma·tous** *adj.*

glis·sade (glɪ'sɑːd, -'seɪd) *n.* 1. a gliding step in ballet, in which one foot slides forwards, sideways, or backwards. 2. a controlled descent over snow or ice. ~*vb.* 3. (*intr.*) to perform a glissade. [C19: from French, from *glisser* to slip, from Old French *glicier,* of Frankish origin; compare Old High German *glītan* to GLIDE] —**glis·'sad·er** *n.*

glis·san·do (glɪ'sændəʊ) *n., pl.* **·di** (-diː) *or* **·dos.** 1. a rapidly executed series of notes on the harp or piano, each note of which is discretely audible. 2. a portamento, esp. as executed on the violin, viola, etc. [C19: probably Italianized variant of GLISSADE]

glis·ten ('glɪsən) *vb.* (*intr.*) 1. (of a wet or glossy surface, etc.) to gleam by reflecting light: *wet leaves glisten in the sunlight.* 2. (of light) to reflect with brightness: *the sunlight glistens on wet leaves.* ~*n.* 3. *Rare.* a gleam or gloss. [Old English *glisnian;* related to *glisian* to glitter, Middle High German *glistern*] —**'glis·ten·ing·ly** *adv.*

glis·ter ('glɪstə) *vb., n.* an archaic word for **glitter.** [C14: probably from Middle Dutch *glisteren*] —**'glis·ter·ing·ly** *adv.*

glit·ter ('glɪtə) *vb.* (*intr.*) 1. (of a hard, wet, or polished surface) to reflect light in bright flashes. 2. (of light) to be reflected in bright flashes. 3. (usually foll. by *with*) to be decorated or enhanced by the glamour (of): *the show glitters with famous actors.* ~*n.* 4. sparkle or brilliance. 5. show and glamour. [C14: from Old Norse *glitra;* related to Old High German *glīzan* to shine] —**'glit·ter·ing·ly** *adv.* —**'glit·ter·y** *adj.*

glit·ter ice *n. Canadian.* ice formed from freezing rain. Also called: **silver thaw.**

Gli·wi·ce (*Polish* gli'vitsɛ) *n.* an industrial city in S Poland. Pop.: 179 900 (1974 est.). German name: **Gleiwitz.**

gloam·ing ('gləʊmɪŋ) *n. Scot. or poetic.* twilight or dusk. [Old English *glōmung,* from *glōm;* related to Old Norse *glāmr* moon]

gloat (gləʊt) *vb.* 1. (*intr.;* often foll. by *over*) to dwell (on) with malevolent smugness or exultation. ~*n.* 2. the act of gloating. [C16: probably of Scandinavian origin; compare Old Norse *glotta* to grin, Middle High German *glotzen* to stare] —**'gloat·er** *n.* —**'gloat·ing·ly** *adv.*

glob (glɒb) *n. Informal.* a rounded mass of some thick fluid or pliable substance: *a glob of cream.* [C20: probably from GLOBE, influenced by BLOB]

glob·al ('gləʊbəl) *adj.* 1. covering, influencing, or relating to the whole world. 2. comprehensive. —**'glob·al·ly** *adv.*

glob·al rule *n.* (in transformational grammar) a rule that makes reference to nonconsecutive stages of a derivation.

glo·bate ('gləʊbeɪt) *or* **glo·bat·ed** *adj.* shaped like a globe.

globe (gləʊb) *n.* 1. a sphere on which a map of the world or the heavens is drawn or represented. 2. **the globe.** the world; the earth. 3. a planet or some other astronomical body. 4. an object shaped like a sphere, such as a glass lampshade or fish bowl. 5. *Chiefly Austral.* an electric light-bulb. 6. an orb, usually of gold, symbolic of authority or sovereignty. ~*vb.* 7. to form or cause to form into a globe. [C16: from Old French, from Latin *globus*] —**'globe·,like** *adj.*

globe ar·ti·choke *n.* See **artichoke** (senses 1, 2).

globe·fish ('gləʊb,fɪʃ) *n., pl.* **·fish** *or* **·fish·es.** another name for **puffer** (sense 2) or **porcupine fish.**

globe·flow·er ('gləʊb,flaʊə) *n.* any ranunculaceous plant of the genus *Trollius,* having pale yellow, white, or orange globe-shaped flowers.

globe·trot·ter ('gləʊb,trɒtə) *n.* a habitual worldwide traveller, esp. a tourist or businessman. —**'globe·,trot·ting** *n., adj.*

glo·big·er·i·na (gləʊ,bɪdʒə'raɪnə) *n., pl.* **·nas** *or* **·nae** (-niː). 1. any marine protozoan of the genus *Globigerina,* having a rounded shell with spiny processes: order *Foraminifera* (foraminifers). 2. **globigerina ooze.** a deposit on the ocean floor consisting of the shells of these protozoans. [C19: from New Latin, from Latin *globus* GLOBE + *gerere* to carry, bear]

glo·bin ('gləʊbɪn) *n. Biochem.* a histone that is the protein component of haemoglobin. [C19: from Latin *globus* ball, sphere + -IN]

glo·boid ('gləʊbɔɪd) *adj.* 1. shaped approximately like a globe. ~*n.* 2. a globoid body, such as any of those occurring in certain plant granules.

glo·bose ('gləʊbəʊs, gləʊ'bəʊs) *or* **glo·bous** ('gləʊbəs) *adj.* spherical or approximately spherical. [C15: from Latin *globōsus;* see GLOBE] —**'glo·bose·ly** *adv.* —**glo·bos·i·ty** (gləʊ'bɒsɪtɪ) *or* **'glo·bose·ness** *n.*

glob·u·lar ('glɒbjʊlə) *or* **glob·u·lous** *adj.* 1. shaped like a globe or globule. 2. having or consisting of globules. —**glob·u·lar·i·ty** (,glɒbjʊ'lærɪtɪ) *or* **'glob·u·lar·ness** *n.* —**'glob·u·lar·ly** *adv.*

glob·ule ('glɒbjuːl) *n.* a small globe, esp. a drop of liquid. [C17: from Latin *globulus,* diminutive of *globus* GLOBE]

glob·u·lif·er·ous (,glɒbjʊ'lɪfərəs) *adj.* producing, containing, or having globules.

glob·u·lin ('glɒbjʊlɪn) *n.* any of a group of simple proteins, including gamma globulin, that are generally insoluble in water but soluble in salt solutions and coagulated by heat.

glo·chid·i·um (gləʊ'kɪdɪəm) *n., pl.* **·chid·i·a** (-'kɪdɪə). 1. any of the barbed hairs among the spore masses of some ferns and on certain other plants. 2. a parasitic larva of certain freshwater mussels that attaches itself to the fins or gills of fish by hooks or suckers. [C19: from New Latin, from Greek *glōkhis* projecting point] —**glo·'chid·i·ate** *adj.*

glock·en·spiel ('glɒkən,spiːl, -,ʃpiːl) *n.* a percussion instrument consisting of a set of tuned metal plates played with a pair of small hammers. [C19: German, from *Glocken* bells + *Spiel* play]

glogg (glɒg) *n.* a hot alcoholic mixed drink, originally from Sweden, consisting of sweetened brandy, red wine, bitters or other flavourings, and blanched almonds. [from Swedish *glögg,* from *glödga* to burn]

glom·er·ate ('glɒmərɪt) *adj.* 1. gathered into a compact rounded mass. 2. wound up like a ball of thread. 3. *Anatomy.* (esp. of glands) conglomerate in structure. [C18: from Latin *glomerāre* to wind into a ball, from *glomus* ball]

glom·er·a·tion (,glɒmə'reɪʃən) *n.* a conglomeration or cluster.

glom·er·ule ('glɒmə,ruːl) *n. Botany.* 1. a cymose inflorescence in the form of a ball-like cluster of flowers. 2. a ball-like cluster of spores. [C18: from New Latin GLOMERULUS] —**glo·mer·u·late** (glɒ'mɛrʊlɪt, -,leɪt) *adj.*

glo·mer·u·lus (glɒ'mɛrʊləs) *n., pl.* **·li** (-,laɪ). 1. a knot of blood vessels in the kidney projecting into the capsular end of a urine-secreting tubule. 2. any cluster or coil of blood vessels, nerve fibres, etc., in the body. [C18: from New Latin, diminutive of *glomus* ball] —**glo·'mer·u·lar** *adj.*

Glom·ma (*Norwegian* 'glɔma) *n.* a river in SE Norway, rising near the border with Sweden flowing generally south to the Skagerrak: the largest river in Scandinavia; important for hydroelectric power and floating timber. Length: 588 km (365 miles).

gloom (gluːm) *n.* 1. partial or total darkness. 2. a state of depression or melancholy. 3. an appearance or expression of despondency or melancholy. 4. *Poetic.* a dim or dark place. ~*vb.* 5. (*intr.*) to look sullen or depressed. 6. to make or become dark or gloomy. [C14 *gloumben* to look sullen; related to Norwegian dialect *glome* to eye suspiciously] —**'gloom·ful** *adj.* —**'gloom·ful·ly** *adv.* —**'gloom·less** *adj.*

gloom·y ('gluːmɪ) *adj.* **gloom·i·er, gloom·i·est.** 1. dark or dismal. 2. causing depression, dejection, or gloom: *gloomy news.* 3. despairing; sad. —**'gloom·i·ly** *adv.* —**'gloom·i·ness** *n.*

glo·ri·a ('glɔːrɪə) *n.* 1. a silk, wool, cotton, or nylon fabric used esp. for umbrellas. 2. a halo or nimbus, esp. as represented in art. [C16: from Latin: GLORY]

Glo·ri·a ('glɔːrɪə, -,ɑː) *n.* 1. any of several doxologies beginning with the word *Gloria,* esp. the Greater and the Lesser Doxologies. 2. a musical setting of one of these.

Glo·ri·a in Ex·cel·sis De·o ('glɔːrɪə ɪn ɛk'sɛlsɪs 'deɪəʊ, 'glɔːrɪ,ɑː, ɛks'tʃɛlsɪs) *n.* 1. the Greater Doxology (see **Doxology**), beginning in Latin with these words. 2. a musical setting of this, usually incorporated into the Ordinary of the Mass. Often shortened to **Gloria.** [literally: glory to God in the highest]

Glo·ri·a Pa·tri ('glɔːrɪə 'pɑːtrɪ, 'glɔːrɪ,ɑː, 'pæt-) *n.* 1. the Lesser Doxology (see **Doxology**), beginning in Latin with these words. 2. a musical setting of this. [literally: glory to the father]

glo·ri·fi·ca·tion (,glɔːrɪfɪ'keɪʃən) *n.* 1. the act of glorifying or state of being glorified. 2. *Informal.* an enhanced or favourably exaggerated version or account. 3. *Brit. informal.* a celebration.

glo·ri·fy ('glɔːrɪ,faɪ) *vb.* **·fies, ·fy·ing, ·fied.** (*tr.*) 1. to make glorious. 2. to make more splendid; adorn. 3. to worship, exalt, or adore. 4. to extol. 5. to cause to seem more splendid or imposing than reality. —ˈ**glo+ri+ˌfi+a·ble** *adj.* —ˈ**glo+ri+ˌfi+er** *n.*

glo+ri+ole (ˈglɔːrɪˌəʊl) *n.* another name for a **halo** or **nimbus** (senses 2, 3). [C19: from Latin *glōriola*, literally: a small GLORY]

glo+ri+ous (ˈglɔːrɪəs) *adj.* **1.** having or full of glory; illustrious. **2.** conferring glory or renown: *a glorious victory.* **3.** brilliantly beautiful. **4.** *Informal.* delightful or enjoyable. —ˈ**glo+ri+ous+ly** *adv.* —ˈ**glo+ri+ous+ness** *n.*

Glo+ri+ous Rev·o+lu+tion *n.* the events of 1688–89 in England that resulted in the ousting of James II and the establishment of William III and Mary II as joint monarchs. Also called: **Bloodless Revolution.**

glo+ry (ˈglɔːrɪ) *n., pl.* **+ries. 1.** exaltation, praise, or honour, as that accorded by general consent: *the glory for the exploit went to the captain.* **2.** something that brings or is worthy of praise (esp. in the phrase **crowning glory**). **3.** thanksgiving, adoration, or worship: *glory be to God.* **4.** pomp; splendour: *the glory of the king's reign.* **5.** radiant beauty; resplendence: *the glory of the sunset.* **6.** the beauty and bliss of heaven. **7.** a state of extreme happiness or prosperity. **8.** another word for **halo** or **nimbus.** ~*vb.* **+ries, +ry+ing, +ried. 9.** (*intr.;* often foll. by *in*) to triumph or exult. **10.** (*intr.*) *Obsolete.* to brag. ~*interj.* **11.** *Informal.* a mild interjection to express pleasure or surprise (often in the exclamatory phrase **glory be!**). [C13: from Old French *glorie*, from Latin *glōria*, of obscure origin]

glo+ry box *n. Austral.* a box in which a young woman stores clothes, etc., in preparation for marriage.

glo+ry hole *n. Nautical.* another term for **lazaretto** (sense 2).

glo·ry-of-the-snow *n.* a small W Asian liliaceous plant, *Chionodoxa luciliae*, cultivated for its early-blooming blue flowers.

Glos. *abbrev. for* Gloucestershire.

gloss[1] (glɒs) *n.* **1.** lustre or sheen, as of a smooth surface. **2.** a superficially attractive appearance. ~*vb.* **3.** to give a gloss to or obtain a gloss. **4.** (*tr.;* often foll. by *over*) to hide under a deceptively attractive surface or appearance. [C16: probably of Scandinavian origin; compare Icelandic *glossi* flame, Middle High German *glosen* to glow] —ˈ**gloss+er** *n.* —ˈ**gloss+less** *adj.*

gloss[2] (glɒs) *n.* **1.** a short or expanded explanation or interpretation of a word, expression, or foreign phrase in the margin or text of a manuscript, etc. **2.** an intentionally misleading explanation or interpretation. **3.** short for **glossary.** ~*vb.* (*tr.*) **4.** to add glosses to. **5.** (often foll. by *over*) to give a false or misleading interpretation of. [C16: from Latin *glōssa* unusual word requiring explanatory note, from Ionic Greek] ˈ**gloss+er** *n.* —ˈ**gloss+ing+ly** *adv.*

gloss. *abbrev. for* glossary.

glos+sa (ˈglɒsə) *n., pl.* **+sae** (-siː) *or* **+sas. 1.** *Anatomy.* a technical word for the **tongue. 2.** a paired tonguelike lobe in the labium of an insect. —ˈ**glos+sal** *adj.*

glos+sa+ry (ˈglɒsərɪ) *n., pl.* **+ries.** an alphabetical list of terms peculiar to a field of knowledge with definitions or explanations. Sometimes called: **gloss.** [C14: from Late Latin *glossārium;* see GLOSS[2]] —**glos+sar+i+al** (glɒˈsɛərɪəl) *adj.* —**glos+ˈsar+i+al+ly** *adv.* —ˈ**glos+sa+rist** *n.*

glos+sa+tor (glɒˈseɪtə) *n.* **1.** Also called: **glossarist, glossist, glossographer.** a writer of glosses and commentaries, esp. (in the Middle Ages) an interpreter of Roman and Canon Law. **2.** a compiler of a glossary.

glos+sec+to+my (glɒˈsɛktəmɪ) *n., pl.* **+mies.** surgical removal of all or part of the tongue.

gloss+eme (ˈglɒsiːm) *n.* the smallest meaningful unit of a language, such as stress, form, etc. [C20: from Greek *glōssēma;* see GLOSS[2], -EME]

glos+si+tis (glɒˈsaɪtɪs) *n.* inflammation of the tongue. —**glos+sit+ic** (glɒˈsɪtɪk) *adj.*

glos·so- *or before a vowel* **gloss-** *combining form.* indicating a tongue or language: *glossolaryngeal.* [from Greek *glossa* tongue]

glos+sog+ra+phy (glɒˈsɒgrəfɪ) *n.* the art of writing textual glosses or commentaries. —**glos+ˈsog+ra+pher** *n.*

glos+so+la+li·a (ˌglɒsəˈleɪlɪə) *n.* another term for **gift of tongues.** [C19: New Latin, from GLOSSO- + Greek *lalein* to babble]

glos+sol+o·gy (glɒˈsɒlədʒɪ) *n.* an obsolete term for **linguistics.** —**glos+so+log·i·cal** (ˌglɒsəˈlɒdʒɪkəl) *adj.* —**glos+ˈsol·o·gist** *n.*

glos+so+pha+ryn+ge·al nerve (ˌglɒsəʊˌfærɪnˈdʒiːəl) *n.* the ninth cranial nerve, which supplies the muscles of the pharynx, the tongue, the middle ear, and the parotid gland.

gloss·y (ˈglɒsɪ) *adj.* **gloss·i·er, gloss·i·est. 1.** smooth and shiny; lustrous. **2.** superficially attractive; plausible. **3.** (of a magazine) lavishly produced on shiny paper and usually with many colour photographs. ~*n., pl.* **gloss·ies. 4.** Also called (U.S.): **slick.** an expensively produced magazine, typically a sophisticated fashion or glamour magazine, printed on shiny paper and containing high quality colour photography. Compare **pulp** (sense 3). **5.** a photograph printed on paper that has a smooth shiny surface. —ˈ**gloss·i·ly** *adv.* —ˈ**gloss·i·ness** *n.*

glot+tal (ˈglɒtəl) *adj.* **1.** of or relating to the glottis. **2.** *Phonetics.* articulated or pronounced at or with the glottis.

glot+tal stop *n.* a plosive speech sound produced as the sudden onset of a vowel in several languages, such as German, by first tightly closing the glottis and then allowing the air pressure to build up in the trachea before opening the glottis, causing the air to escape with force.

glot+tic (ˈglɒtɪk) *adj.* of or relating to the tongue or the glottis.

glot+tis (ˈglɒtɪs) *n., pl.* **+tis·es** *or* **+ti·des** (-tɪˌdiːz). the vocal apparatus of the larynx, consisting of the two true vocal cords and the opening between them. [C16: from New Latin, from Greek *glōttis*, from *glōtta*, Attic form of Ionic *glōssa* tongue; see GLOSS[2]] —**glot+tid+e·an** (glɒˈtɪdɪən) *adj.*

glot+to+chro+nol+o·gy (ˌglɒtəʊkrəˈnɒlədʒɪ) *n.* the use of lexicostatistics to establish that languages are historically related. [C20: *glotto-*, from Greek *glōtta* tongue]

Glouces+ter[1] (ˈglɒstə) *n.* a city in SW England, administrative centre of Gloucestershire, on the River Severn. Pop.: 90 134 (1971). Latin name: **Glevum.**

Glouces·ter[2] (ˈglɒstə) *n.* **1. Hum·phrey,** Duke of. 1391–1447, English soldier and statesman; son of Henry IV. He acted as protector during Henry VI's minority (1422–29) and was noted for his patronage of humanists. **2. Duke of.** See **Richard III. 3. Duke of.** See **Thomas of Woodstock.**

Glouces+ter+shire (ˈglɒstəˌʃɪə, -ʃə) *n.* a county of SW England, situated around the lower Severn valley: contains the Forest of Dean and the main part of the Cotswold Hills. Administrative centre: Gloucester. Pop.: 491 500 (1976 est.). Area: 2704 sq. km (1044 sq. miles). Abbrev.: **Glos.**

glove (glʌv) *n.* **1.** (*often pl.*) a shaped covering for the hand with individual sheaths for the fingers and thumb, made of leather, fabric, etc. See also **gauntlet**[1] (sense 2). **2.** any of various large protective hand covers worn in sports, such as a boxing glove. **3. hand in glove.** *Informal.* in an intimate relationship. **4. handle with kid gloves.** *Informal.* to treat with extreme care. ~*vb.* **5.** (*tr.*) to cover or provide with or as if with gloves. [Old English *glōfe;* related to Old Norse *glōfi*] —ˈ**glove+less** *adj.* —ˈ**glove+ˌlike** *adj.*

glove box *n.* a closed box in which toxic or radioactive substances can be handled by an operator who places his hands through protective gloves sealed to the box.

glove com+part+ment *n.* a small compartment in a car dashboard for the storage of miscellaneous articles.

glove pup+pet *n.* a small figure of a person or animal that fits over and is manipulated by the hand.

glov+er (ˈglʌvə) *n.* a person who makes or sells gloves.

glow (gləʊ) *n.* **1.** light emitted by a substance or object at a high temperature. **2.** a steady even light without flames. **3.** brilliance or vividness of colour. **4.** brightness or ruddiness of complexion. **5.** a feeling of well-being or satisfaction. **6.** intensity of emotion; ardour. ~*vb.* (*intr.*) **7.** to emit a steady even light without flames. **8.** to shine intensely, as if from great heat. **9.** to be exuberant or high-spirited, as from excellent health or intense emotion. **10.** to experience a feeling of well-being or satisfaction: *to glow with pride.* **11.** (esp. of the complexion) to show a strong bright colour, esp. a shade of red. **12.** to be very hot. [Old English *glōwan;* related to Old Norse *glōa*, Old High German *gluoen*, Icelandic *glōra* to sparkle]

glow dis+charge *n.* a silent luminous discharge of electricity through a low-pressure gas.

glow+er (ˈglaʊə) *vb.* **1.** (*intr.*) to stare hard and angrily. ~*n.* **2.** a sullen or angry stare. [C16: probably of Scandinavian origin; related to Middle Low German *glūren* to watch] —ˈ**glow+er+ing+ly** *adv.*

glow lamp *n.* a small light consisting of two or more electrodes in an inert gas, such as neon, at low pressure, across which an electrical discharge occurs when the voltage applied to the electrodes exceeds the ionization potential.

glow-worm *n.* **1.** a European beetle, *Lampyris noctiluca*, the females and larvae of which bear luminescent organs producing a soft greenish light: family *Lampyridae.* **2.** any of various other beetles or larvae of the family *Lampyridae.* ~See also **firefly** (sense 1).

glox+in·i·a (glɒkˈsɪnɪə) *n.* any of several tropical plants of the genus *Sinningia*, esp. the South American *S. speciosa*, cultivated for its large white, red, or purple bell-shaped flowers: family *Gesneriaceae.* [C19: named after Benjamin P. Gloxin, 18th-century German physician and botanist who first described it]

gloze (gləʊz) *Archaic.* ~*vb.* **1.** (*tr.;* often foll. by *over*) to explain away; minimize the effect or importance of. **2.** to make explanatory notes or glosses on (a text). **3.** to use flattery. ~*n.* **4.** flattery or deceit. **5.** an explanatory note or gloss. **6.** specious or deceptive talk or action. [C13: from Old French *glosser* to comment; see GLOSS[2]]

glt. *Bookbinding. abbrev. for* gilt.

glu+ca+gon (ˈgluːkəˌgɒn, -gən) *n.* a polypeptide hormone, produced in the pancreas by the islets of Langerhans, that stimulates the release of glucose into the blood. Compare **insulin.** [C20: from GLUC(OSE) + *-agon*, perhaps from Greek *agein* to lead]

glu+ci+num (gluːˈsaɪnəm) *or* **glu+cin+i·um** (gluːˈsɪnɪəm) *n.* a former name for **beryllium.** [C19: New Latin *glucina* beryllium oxide, from Greek *glukus* sweet + -IN; alluding to the sweet taste of some of the salts]

Gluck (*German* glʊk) *n.* **Chris·toph Wil·li·bald von** (ˈkrɪstɔf ˈvɪlibalt fɔn). 1714–87, German composer, esp. of operas, including *Orfeo ed Euridice* (1762) and *Alceste* (1767).

glu+co+cor+ti+coid (ˌgluːkəʊˈkɔːtɪˌkɔɪd) *n.* any of a class of corticosteroids that control carbohydrate, protein, and fat metabolism and have anti-inflammatory activity.

glu+co+ne·o+gen+e·sis (ˌgluːkəʊˌniːəʊˈdʒɛnɪsɪs) *n. Biochem.* the formation of glucose from non-carbohydrate sources, such as amino acids, pyruvic acid, or glycerol. Also called: **glyconeogenesis.**

glu+co+pro+tein (ˌgluːkəʊˈprəʊtiːn) *n.* another name for **glycoprotein.**

glu+cose (ˈgluːkəʊz, -kəʊs) *n.* **1.** a white crystalline monosaccharide sugar that has several optically active forms, the most abundant being dextrose: a major energy source in metabolism. Formula: $C_6H_{12}O_6$. **2.** a yellowish syrup (or, after desiccation, a solid) containing dextrose, maltose, and dextrin, obtained by incomplete hydrolysis of starch: used in confectionery, fermentation, etc. [C19: from French, from Greek *gleukos* sweet wine; related to Greek *glukus* sweet] —**glu+cos+ic** (glu:'kɒsɪk) *adj.*

glu+co+side ('glu:kəʊˌsaɪd) *n. Biochem.* any of a large group of glycosides that yield glucose on hydrolysis. —ˌ**glu+co+'sid+al** *or* **glu+co+sid+ic** (ˌglu:kəʊ'sɪdɪk) *adj.*

glu+co+su+ri·a (ˌglʊkəʊ'sjʊərɪə) *n. Pathol.* a less common word for **glycosuria.** —ˌ**glu+co+'su+ric** *adj.*

glue (glu:) *n.* **1.** any natural or synthetic adhesive, esp. a sticky gelatinous substance prepared by boiling animal products such as bones, skin, and horns. **2.** any other sticky or adhesive substance. ~*vb.* **glues, glu+ing, glued. 3.** (*tr.*) to join or stick together with or as if with glue. [C14: from Old French *glu*, from Late Latin *glūs;* compare Greek *gloios*] —'**glue+ˌlike** *adj.* —'**glu+er** *n.* —'**glue·y** *adj.*

glum (glʌm) *adj.* **glum+mer, glum+mest.** silent or sullen, as from gloom. [C16: variant of GLOOM] —'**glum+ly** *adv.* —'**glum+ness** *n.*

glume (glu:m) *n. Botany.* one of a pair of dry membranous bracts at the base of the inflorescence, esp. the spikelet, of grasses. [C18: from Latin *glūma* husk of corn; related to Latin *glūbere* to remove the bark from] —**glu+'ma+ceous** *adj.* —'**glume+ˌlike** *adj.*

glu+on ('glu:ɒn) *n.* a hypothetical particle believed to be exchanged between quarks in order to bind them together to form particles.

glut (glʌt) *n.* **1.** an excessive amount, as in the production of a crop, often leading to a fall in price. **2.** the act of glutting or state of being glutted. ~*vb.* **gluts, glut+ting, glut+ted.** (*tr.*) **3.** to feed or supply beyond capacity. **4.** to supply (a market, etc.) with a commodity in excess of the demand for it. **5.** to cram full or choke up: *to glut a passage.* [C14: probably from Old French *gloutir*, from Latin *gluttīre;* see GLUTTON[1]] —'**glut+ting+ly** *adv.*

glu+ta+mate ('glu:təˌmeɪt) *n.* any salt of glutamic acid, esp. its sodium salt (see **monosodium glutamate**). [C19: from GLUTAM(IC) + -ATE[1]]

glu+tam+ic ac·id (glu:'tæmɪk) *or* **glu+ta+min+ic ac·id** (ˌglu:tə'mɪnɪk) *n.* an amino acid, occurring in proteins, that plays an important part in the nitrogen metabolism of plants and animals; 2-aminopentanedioic acid. Formula: $HOOC(CH_2)_2CH(NH_2)COOH$.

glu+ta+mine ('glu:təˌmi:n -mɪn) *n.* an amino acid occurring in proteins: plays an important role in protein metabolism. Formula: $NH_2CO(CH_2)_2CH(NH_2)COOH$. [C19: from GLUT(EN) + -AMINE]

glu+ta+thi+one (ˌglu:tə'θaɪəʊn, -θaɪ'əʊn) *n. Biochem.* a tripeptide consisting of glutamic acid, cysteine, and glycine: important in biological oxidations and the activation of some enzymes. Formula: $C_{10}H_{17}N_3O_6S$. [C20: from GLUTA(MIC ACID) + THI- + -ONE]

glu+te·lin ('glu:tɪlɪn) *n.* any of a group of water-insoluble plant proteins found in cereals. They are precipitated by alcohol and are not coagulated by heat. Compare **gliadin.** [C20: See GLUTEN, -IN]

glu+ten ('glu:tᵊn) *n.* a protein consisting of a mixture of glutelin and gliadin, present in cereal grains, esp. wheat. A gluten-free diet is necessary in cases of coeliac disease. [C16: from Latin: GLUE] —'**glu+te·nous** *adj.*

glu+ten bread *n.* bread made from flour containing a high proportion of gluten.

glu+te·us *or* **glu+tae·us** (glʊ'ti:əs) *n., pl.* **+te·i** *or* **+tae·i** (-'ti:aɪ). any one of the three large muscles that form the human buttock and move the thigh, esp. the **gluteus maximus.** [C17: from New Latin, from Greek *gloutos* buttock, rump] —**glu+'te·al** *or* '**glu+tae·al** *adj.*

glu+ti+nous ('glu:tɪnəs) *adj.* resembling glue in texture; sticky. —'**glu+ti+nous+ly** *adv.* —'**glu+ti+nous+ness** *or* **glu+ti+nos+i·ty** (ˌglu:tɪ'nɒsɪtɪ) *n.*

glut+ton[1] ('glʌtᵊn) *n.* **1.** a person devoted to eating and drinking to excess; greedy person. **2.** *Often ironical.* a person who has or appears to have a voracious appetite for something: *a glutton for punishment.* [C13: from Old French *glouton*, from Latin *glutto*, from *gluttīre* to swallow] —'**glut+ton+ous** *adj.* —'**glut+ton+ous+ly** *adv.*

glut+ton[2] ('glʌtᵊn) *n.* another name for **wolverine.** [C17: from GLUTTON[1], apparently translating German *Vielfass* great eater]

glut+ton·y ('glʌtənɪ) *n., pl.* **+ton·ies.** the act or practice of eating to excess.

gly+cer+ic (glɪ'sɛrɪk) *adj.* of, containing, or derived from glycerol.

gly+cer+ic ac·id *n.* a viscous liquid carboxylic acid produced by the oxidation of glycerol; 2,3-dihydroxypropanoic acid. Formula: $C_3H_6O_4$.

glyc+er+ide ('glɪsəˌraɪd) *n.* any fatty-acid ester of glycerol. See **monoglyceride, diglyceride, triglyceride.**

glyc+er+in ('glɪsərɪn) *or* **glyc+er+ine** ('glɪsərɪn, ˌglɪsə'ri:n) *n.* another name (not in technical usage) for **glycerol.** [C19: from French *glycérine*, from Greek *glukeros* sweet + *-ine* -IN; related to Greek *glukus* sweet]

glyc+er+ol ('glɪsəˌrɒl) *n.* a colourless or pale yellow odourless sweet-tasting syrupy liquid; 1,2,3-propanetriol: a by-product of soap manufacture, used as a solvent, antifreeze, plasticizer, and sweetener. Formula: $C_3H_8O_3$. Also called (not in technical usage): **glycerin, glycerine.** [C19: from GLYCER(IN) + -OL[1]]

glyc+er+yl ('glɪsərɪl) *n.* (*modifier*) derived from glycerol by replacing or removing one or more of its hydroxyl groups: *a glyceryl group or radical.*

glyc+er+yl tri+ni+trate *n.* another name for **nitroglycerin.**

gly+cine ('glaɪsi:n, glaɪ'si:n) *n.* a white sweet crystalline amino acid occurring in most proteins; aminoacetic acid. Formula: CH_2NH_2COOH. [C19: GLYCO- + -INE[2]]

gly·co- *or before a vowel* **glyc-** *combining form.* indicating sugar: *glycogen.* [from Greek *glukus* sweet]

gly+co+gen ('glaɪkəʊdʒən, -dʒɛn) *n.* a polysaccharide consisting of glucose units: the form in which carbohydrate is stored in animals. It can easily be hydrolysed to glucose. Also called: **animal starch.** —**gly+co+gen+ic** (ˌglaɪkəʊ'dʒɛnɪk) *adj.*

gly+co+gen+e·sis (ˌglaɪkəʊ'dʒɛnɪsɪs) *n.* the formation of sugar, esp. (in animals) from glycogen. —**gly+co+ge·net+ic** (ˌglaɪkəʊdʒɪ'nɛtɪk) *adj.*

gly+col ('glaɪkɒl) *n.* another name (not in technical usage) for **ethanediol** or a **diol.** —**gly+col+ic** *or* **gly+col+lic** (glaɪ'kɒlɪk) *adj.*

gly+col+ic ac·id *n.* a colourless crystalline soluble hygroscopic compound found in sugar cane and sugar beet: used in tanning and in the manufacture of pharmaceuticals, pesticides, adhesives, and plasticizers; hydroxyacetic acid. Formula: $CH_2(OH)COOH$.

gly+col·y+sis (glaɪ'kɒlɪsɪs) *n. Biochem.* the breakdown of glucose by enzymes into pyruvic and lactic acids with the liberation of energy.

gly+co+ne·o+gen+e·sis (ˌglaɪkəʊˌni:əʊ'dʒɛnɪsɪs) *n.* another name for **gluconeogenesis.**

gly+co+pro+tein (ˌglaɪkəʊ'prəʊti:n), **glu+co+pro+tein,** *or* **gly+co+pep+tide** (ˌglaɪkəʊ'pɛptaɪd) *n.* any of a group of conjugated proteins containing small amounts of carbohydrates as prosthetic groups. See also **mucoprotein.**

gly+co+side ('glaɪkəʊˌsaɪd) *n.* any of a group of substances, such as digitoxin, derived from monosaccharides by replacing the hydroxyl group by another group. Many are important medicinal drugs. See also **glucoside.** —**gly+co+sid+ic** (ˌglaɪkəʊ'sɪdɪk) *adj.*

gly+co+su+ri·a (ˌglaɪkəʊ'sjʊərɪə) *or* **glu+co+su+ri·a** *n.* the presence of excess sugar in the urine, as in diabetes. [C19: from New Latin, from French *glycose* GLUCOSE + -URIA] —ˌ**gly+co+'su+ric** *or* ˌ**glu+co+'su+ric** *adj.*

gly+ox·a+line (glaɪ'ɒksəlɪn) *n.* another name (not in technical usage) for **imidazole.**

glyph (glɪf) *n.* **1.** a carved channel or groove, esp. a vertical one as used on a Doric frieze. **2.** *Now rare.* another word for **hieroglyphic.** [C18: from French *glyphe*, from Greek *gluphē* carving, from *gluphein* to carve] —'**glyph+ic** *adj.*

gly+phog+ra+phy (glɪ'fɒgrəfɪ) *n.* a platemaking process in which an electrotype is made from an engraved copper plate. [C19: from Greek *gluphē* carving + -GRAPHY] —**glyph·o+graph** ('glɪfəˌgrɑ:f) *n.* —**gly+'phog+ra+pher** *n.* —**glyph·o+graph+ic** (ˌglɪfə'græfɪk) *or* ˌ**glyph·o+'graph·i+cal** *adj.*

glyp+tal ('glɪptəl) *n.* an alkyd resin obtained from polyhydric alcohols and polybasic organic acids or their anhydrides; used for surface coatings. [C20: a trademark, perhaps from GLY(CEROL) + P(H)T(H)AL(IC)]

glyp+tic ('glɪptɪk) *adj.* of or relating to engraving or carving, esp. on precious stones. [C19: from French *glyptique*, from Greek *gluptikos*, from *gluptos*, from *gluphein* to carve]

glyp+tics ('glɪptɪks) *n.* the art of engraving precious stones.

glyp+to+dont ('glɪptəˌdɒnt) *n.* any extinct late Cenozoic edentate mammal of the genus *Glyptodon* and related genera, of South America, which resembled giant armadillos. [C19: from Greek *gluptos* carved + -ODONT]

glyp+tog+ra+phy (glɪp'tɒgrəfɪ) *n.* the art of carving or engraving upon gemstones. —**glyp+'tog+ra+pher** *n.* —**glyp+to+graph+ic** (ˌglɪptə'græfɪk) *or* ˌ**glyp+to+'graph·i+cal** *adj.*

G.M. *abbrev. for:* **1.** general manager. **2.** (in Britain) George Medal. **3.** Grand Master.

G-man *n., pl.* **G-men. 1.** *U.S. slang.* an FBI agent. **2.** *Irish.* a political detective.

G.M.B. *abbrev. for* Grand Master Bowman; the highest standard of archer.

Gmc *abbrev. for* Germanic.

G.M.C. *abbrev. for* General Medical Council.

GMT *abbrev. for* Greenwich Mean Time.

gnarl[1] (nɑ:l) *n.* **1.** any knotty protuberance or swelling on a tree. ~*vb.* **2.** (*tr.*) to knot or cause to knot. [C19: back formation from *gnarled*, probably variant of KNURLED]

gnarl[2] (nɑ:l) *or* **gnar** (nɑ:) *vb.* (*intr.*) *Obsolete.* to growl or snarl. [C16: of imitative origin]

gnarled (nɑ:ld) *or* **gnarl·y** *adj.* **1.** having gnarls: *the gnarled trunk of the old tree.* **2.** (esp. of hands) rough, twisted, and weather-beaten in appearance. **3.** perverse or ill-tempered.

gnash (næʃ) *vb.* **1.** to grind (the teeth) together, as in pain or anger. **2.** (*tr.*) to bite or chew as by grinding the teeth. ~*n.* **3.** the act of gnashing the teeth. [C15: probably of Scandinavian origin; compare Old Norse *gnastan* gnashing of teeth, *gnesta* to clatter] —'**gnash+ing+ly** *adv.*

gnat (næt) *n.* any of various small fragile biting dipterous insects of the suborder *Nematocera*, esp. *Culex pipiens* (**common gnat**), which abounds near stagnant water. [Old English *gnætt;* related to Middle High German *gnaz* scurf, German dialect *Gnitze* gnat] —'**gnat+ˌlike** *adj.*

gnat+catch·er ('nætˌkætʃə) *n.* any of various small American songbirds of the genus *Polioptila* and related genera, typically having a long tail and a pale bluish-grey plumage: family *Muscicapidae* (Old World flycatchers, etc.).

gnath+ic ('næθɪk) *or* **gnath+al** *adj. Anatomy.* of or relating to the jaw. [C19: from Greek *gnathos* jaw]

gna+thi+on ('neɪθɪˌɒn, 'næθ-) *n.* the lowest point of the midline of the lower jaw: a reference point in craniometry. [C19: from New Latin, from Greek *gnathos* jaw]

gna+thite ('neɪθaɪt, 'næθ-) *n. Zoology.* an appendage of an arthropod that is specialized for grasping or chewing; mouthpart. [C19: from Greek *gnathos* jaw]

gna+thon+ic (næ'θɒnɪk) *adj. Literary.* deceitfully flattering; sycophantic. [C17: from Latin *gnathōnicus*, from *Gnathō*, such a character in the *Eunuchus*, Roman comedy by Terence] —**gna+'thon·i·cal+ly** *adv.*

-gna·thous *adj. combining form.* indicating or having a jaw of a specified kind: *prognathous.* [from New Latin *-gnathus*, from Greek *gnathos* jaw]

gnaw (nɔː) *vb.* **gnaws, gnaw+ing, gnawed; gnawed** *or* **gnawn. 1.** (when *intr.*, often foll. by *at* or *upon*) to bite (at) or chew (upon) constantly so as to wear away little by little. **2.** (*tr.*) to form by gnawing: *to gnaw a hole.* **3.** to cause erosion of (something). **4.** (when *intr.*, often foll. by *at*) to cause constant distress or anxiety (to). ~*n.* **5.** the act or an instance of gnawing. [Old English *gnagan;* related to Old Norse *gnaga*, Old High German *gnagan*] —**'gnaw+a·ble** *adj.* —**'gnaw+er** *n.*

gnaw+ing ('nɔːɪŋ) *n.* a dull persistent pang or pain, esp. of hunger. —**'gnaw+ing+ly** *adv.*

gneiss (naɪs) *n.* any coarse-grained metamorphic rock that is banded or foliated: represents the last stage in the metamorphism of rocks before melting. [C18: from German *Gneis*, probably from Middle High German *ganeist* spark; related to Old Norse *gneista* to give off sparks] —**'gneiss+ic, 'gneiss+oid,** *or* **'gneiss+ose** *adj.*

gnoc+chi ('nɒkɪ, gə'nɒkɪ, 'gnɒkɪ) *pl. n.* dumplings made of pieces of semolina pasta, or sometimes potato, used to garnish soup, etc., or served alone with cheese sauce. [Italian, plural of *gnocco* lump, probably of Germanic origin; compare Middle High German *knoche* bone]

gnome[1] (nəʊm) *n.* **1.** one of a species of legendary creatures, usually resembling small misshapen old men, said to live in the depths of the earth and guard buried treasure. **2.** the statue of a gnome, esp. in a garden. **3.** a very small or ugly person. **4.** *Facetious or derogatory.* an international banker or financier (esp. in the phrase **gnomes of Zurich**). [C18: from French, from New Latin *gnomus*, coined by Paracelsus, of obscure origin] —**'gnom+ish** *adj.*

gnome[2] (nəʊm) *n.* a short pithy saying or maxim expressing a general truth or principle. [C16: from Greek *gnōmē*, from *gignōskein* to know]

gno+mic ('nəʊmɪk, 'nɒm-) *or* **gno+mi+cal** *adj.* **1.** consisting of, containing, or relating to gnomes or aphorisms. **2.** of or relating to a writer of such sayings. —**'gno+mi+cal+ly** *adv.*

gno+mon ('nəʊmɒn) *n.* **1.** the stationary arm that projects the shadow on a sundial. **2.** a geometric figure remaining after a parallelogram has been removed from one corner of a larger parallelogram. [C16: from Latin, from Greek: interpreter, from *gignōskein* to know] —**gno+'mon+ic** *adj.* —**gno+'mon·i·cal+ly** *adv.*

gno+sis ('nəʊsɪs) *n., pl.* **+ses** (-siːz). intuitive knowledge of various spiritual truths, esp. that said to have been possessed by ancient Gnostics. [C18: ultimately from Greek: knowledge, from *gignōskein* to know]

-gno·sis *n. combining form.* (esp. in medicine) recognition or knowledge: *prognosis; diagnosis.* [via Latin from Greek: GNOSIS] —**-gnos·tic** *adj. combining form.*

gnos+tic ('nɒstɪk) *or* **gnos+ti+cal** *adj.* of, relating to, or possessing knowledge, esp. esoteric spiritual knowledge. —**'gnos+ti+cal+ly** *adv.*

Gnos+tic ('nɒstɪk) *n.* **1.** an adherent of Gnosticism. ~*adj.* **2.** of or relating to Gnostics or to Gnosticism. [C16: from Late Latin *Gnosticī* the Gnostics, from Greek *gnōstikos* relating to knowledge, from *gnōstos* known, from *gignōskein* to know]

Gnos+ti+cism ('nɒstɪˌsɪzəm) *n.* a religious movement characterized by a belief in gnosis, through which the spiritual element in man could be released from its bondage in matter: regarded as a heresy by the Christian Church.

Gnos+ti+cize *or* **Gnos+ti+cise** ('nɒstɪˌsaɪz) *vb.* **1.** (*intr.*) to maintain or profess Gnostic views. **2.** to put a Gnostic interpretation upon (something). —**'Gnos+ti+ˌciz+er** *or* **'Gnos+ti+ˌcis+er** *n.*

gno+to+bi+ot+ics (ˌnəʊtəʊbaɪ'ɒtɪks) *n.* (*functioning as sing.*) the study of organisms living in germ-free conditions or when inoculated with known microorganisms. [C20: from Greek, from *gnōtos*, from *gignōskein* to know + *bios* known life] —**ˌgno+to+bi+'ot·i·cal+ly** *adv.*

G.N.P. *abbrev. for* gross national product.

gns. *abbrev. for* guineas.

gnu (nuː) *n., pl.* **gnus** *or* **gnu.** either of two sturdy antelopes, *Connochaetes taurinus* (**brindled gnu**) or the much rarer *C. gnou* (**white-tailed gnu**), inhabiting the savannas of Africa, having an oxlike head and a long tufted tail. Also called: **wildebeest.** [C18: from Kaffir *nqu*]

go[1] (gəʊ) *vb.* **goes, go+ing, went, gone.** (*mainly intr.*) **1.** to move or proceed, esp. to or from a point or in a certain direction: *to go to London; to go home.* **2.** (*tr.; takes an infinitive,* often with *to* omitted or replaced by *and*) to proceed towards a particular person or place with some specified intention or purpose: *I must go and get that book.* **3.** to depart: *we'll have to go at eleven.* **4.** to start, as in a race: often used in commands. **5.** to make regular journeys: *this train service goes to the East coast.* **6.** to operate or function effectively: *the radio won't go.* **7.** (*copula*) to become: *his face went red with embarrassment.* **8.** to make a noise as specified: *the gun went bang.* **9.** to enter into a specified state or condition: *to go into hysterics; to go into action.* **10.** to be or continue to be in a specified state or condition: *to go in rags; to go in poverty.* **11.** to lead, extend, or afford access: *this route goes to the North.* **12.** to proceed towards an activity: *to go to supper; to go to sleep.* **13.** (*tr.; takes an infinitive*) to serve or contribute: *this letter goes to prove my point.* **14.** to follow a course as specified; fare: *the lecture went badly.* **15.** to be applied or allotted to a particular purpose or recipient: *her wealth went to her son; his money went on drink.* **16.** to be sold or otherwise transferred to a recipient: *the necklace went for three thousand pounds.* **17.** to be ranked; compare: *this meal is good as my meals go.* **18.** to blend or harmonize: *these chairs won't go with the rest of your furniture.* **19.** (foll. by *by* or *under*) to be known (by a name or disguise). **20.** to fit or extend: *that skirt won't go around your waist.* **21.** to have a usual or proper place: *those books go on this shelf.* **22.** (of music, poetry, etc.) to be sounded; expressed, etc.: *how does that song go?* **23.** to fail or give way: *my eyesight is going.* **24.** to break down or collapse abruptly: *the ladder went at the critical moment.* **25.** to die: *the old man went at 2 a.m.* **26.** (often foll. by *by*) **a.** (of time, etc.) to elapse: *the hours go by so slowly at the office.* **b.** to travel past: *the train goes by her house at four.* **c.** to be guided (by). **27.** to occur: *happiness does not always go with riches.* **28.** to be eliminated, abolished, or given up: *this entry must go to save space.* **29.** to be spent or finished: *all his money has gone.* **30.** to circulate or be transmitted: *the infection went around the whole community.* **31.** to attend: *go to school; go to church.* **32.** to join a stated profession: *go to the bar; go on the stage.* **33.** (foll. by *to*) to have recourse (to); turn: *to go to arbitration.* **34.** (foll. by *to*) to subject or put oneself (to): *she goes to great pains to please him.* **35.** to proceed, esp. up to or beyond certain limits: *you will go too far one day and then you will be punished.* **36.** to be acceptable or tolerated: *anything goes in this place.* **37.** to carry the weight of final authority: *what the boss says goes.* **38.** (foll. by *into*) to be contained in: *four goes into twelve three times.* **39.** (often foll. by *for*) to endure or last out: *we can't go for much longer without water in this heat.* **40.** (*tr.*) *Cards.* to bet or bid: *I go two hearts.* **41.** (*tr.*) *Informal, chiefly U.S.* to have as one's weight: *I went eight stone a year ago.* **42.** *U.S.* (*usually used in commands;* takes an infinitive without *to*) **a.** to start to act so as to: *go shut the door.* **b.** to leave so as to: *go blow your brains out.* **43.** *Informal.* to perform well; be successful: *that group can really go.* **44. go and.** *Informal.* to be so foolish or unlucky as to: *then she had to go and lose her hat.* **45. be going.** to intend or be about to start (to do or be doing something): often used as an alternative future construction: *what's going to happen to us?* **46. go ape.** *Slang.* to become crazy or extremely enthusiastic about. **47. go astray.** to be mislaid; go missing. **48. go bail.** to act as surety. **49. go halves.** *Informal.* See **half** (sense 11). **50. go hard.** (often foll. by *with*) to cause trouble or unhappiness (to). **51. go it.** *Slang.* to do something or move energetically. **52. go it alone.** *Informal.* to act or proceed without allies or help. **53. go one better.** *Informal.* to surpass or outdo (someone). **54. go the whole hog.** *Informal.* See **hog** (sense 8). **55. let go. a.** to relax one's hold (on); release. **b.** *Euphemistic.* to dismiss (from employment). **c.** to discuss or consider no further. **56. let oneself go. a.** to act in an uninhibited manner. **b.** to lose interest in one's appearance, manners, etc. **57. to go. a.** remaining. **b.** *U.S. informal.* (of food served by a restaurant) for taking away. ~*n., pl.* **goes. 58.** the act of going. **59. a.** an attempt or try: *he had a go at the stamp business.* **b.** an attempt at stopping a person suspected of a crime: *the police are not always in favour of the public having a go.* **60.** a turn: *it's my go next.* **61.** *Informal.* the quality of being active and energetic: *she has much more go than I.* **62.** *Informal.* hard or energetic work: *it's all go.* **63.** *Informal.* a successful venture or achievement: *he made a go of it.* **64.** *Informal.* a bargain or agreement. **65. from the word go.** *Informal.* from the very beginning. **66. get-up-and-go.** *Informal.* energetic enthusiasm: *he's got plenty of get-up-and-go.* **67. no go.** *Informal.* impossible; abortive or futile: *it's no go, I'm afraid.* **68. on the go.** *Informal.* active and energetic. ~*adj.* **69.** (*postpositive*) *Informal.* functioning properly and ready for action: esp. used in astronautics: *all systems are go.* ~See also **go about, go against, go ahead, go along, go around, go at, go away, go back, go by, go down, go for, go forth, go in, going, go into, gone, go off, go on, go out, go over, go through, go to, go together, go under, go up, go with, go without.** [Old English *gān;* related to Old High German *gēn*, Greek *kikhanein* to reach, Sanskrit *jahāti* he forsakes]

go[2] (gəʊ) *or* **I-go** *n.* a game for two players in which counters are placed on a board marked with a grid, the object being to capture territory on the board. [from Japanese]

G.O. *Military. abbrev. for* general order.

go·a ('gəʊə) *n.* a gazelle, *Procapra picticaudata*, inhabiting the plains of the Tibetan plateau, having a brownish-grey coat and backward-curving horns. [C19: from Tibetan *dgoba*]

Go·a ('gəʊə) *n.* a district on the W coast of India: a Portuguese overseas territory from 1510 until annexed by India in 1961 and, along with Daman and Diu, established as a Union Territory. Area: 3496 sq. km (1363 sq. miles).

go a·bout *vb.* (*intr.*) **1.** (*adv.*) to move from place to place. **2.** (*prep.*) to busy oneself with: *to go about one's duties.* **3.** (*prep.*) to tackle (a problem or task). **4.** (*prep.*) to be actively and constantly engaged in (doing something): *he went about doing good.* **5.** to circulate (in): *there's a lot of flu going about.* **6.** (*adv.*) (of a sailing ship) to change from one tack to another.

goad (gəʊd) *n.* **1.** a sharp pointed stick for urging on cattle, etc. **2.** anything that acts as a spur or incitement. ~*vb.* **3.** (*tr.*) to drive with or as if with a goad; spur; incite. [Old English *gād*, of Germanic origin, related to Old English *gār*, Old Norse *geirr* spear] —**'goad+,like** *adj.*

Go·a, Da·man, and Di·u *n.* a Union Territory of India consisting of the widely separated districts of Goa and Daman and the island of Diu. Pop.: 857 771 (1971). Area: 3693 sq. km (1440 sq. miles).

go a·gainst *vb.* (*intr., prep.*) **1.** to be contrary to (principles or beliefs). **2.** to be unfavourable to (a person): *the case went against him.*

go a·head *vb.* **1.** (*intr., adv.*) to start or continue, often after obtaining permission. ~*n.* **go-a·head. 2.** (usually preceded by *the*) *Informal.* permission to proceed. ~*adj.* **go-a·head. 3.** enterprising or ambitious.

goal (gəʊl) *n.* **1.** the aim or object towards which an endeavour is directed. **2.** the terminal point of a journey or race. **3.** (in various sports) the net, basket, etc. into or over which players try to propel the ball, puck, etc., to score. **4.** *Sport.* **a.** a successful attempt at scoring. **b.** the score so made. **5.** (in soccer, hockey, etc.) the position of goalkeeper. [C16: perhaps related to Middle English *gol* boundary, Old English *gǣlan* to hinder, impede] —**'goal+less** *adj.*

goal ar·e·a *n. Soccer.* a rectangular area to the sides and front of the goal, measuring 20 × 6 yards on a full-sized pitch, from which goal kicks are taken. Also called: **six-yard area.**

goal·ie ('gəʊlɪ) *n. Informal.* short for **goalkeeper.**

goal+keep·er ('gəʊl,kiːpə) *n. Sport.* a player in the goal whose duty is to prevent the ball, puck, etc., from entering or crossing it. —**'goal+,keep·ing** *n.*

goal kick *n. Soccer.* a kick taken from the six-yard line by the defending team after the ball has been put out of play by an opposing player.

goal line *n. Sport.* the line marking each end of the pitch, on which the goals stand.

goal+mouth ('gəʊl,maʊθ) *n. Soccer, hockey, etc.* the area in front of the goal.

go a·long *vb.* (*intr., adv.*; often foll. by *with*) to refrain from disagreement; assent.

goal post *n.* either of two upright posts supporting the crossbar of a goal.

go+an+na (gəʊ'ænə) *n.* any of various Australian monitor lizards. [C19: changed from IGUANA]

Go·a pow+der *n.* another name for **araroba** (sense 2).

go a·round *or* **round** *vb.* (*intr.*) **1.** (*adv.*) to move about. **2.** (*adv.*; foll. by *with*) to frequent the society (of a person or group of people): *she went around with older men.* **3.** (*adv.*) to be sufficient: *are there enough sweets to go round?* **4.** to circulate (in): *measles is going round the school.* **5.** (*prep.*) to be actively and constantly engaged in (doing something): *she went around caring for the sick.* **6.** to be long enough to encircle: *will that belt go round you?*

goat (gəʊt) *n.* **1.** any sure-footed agile bovid mammal of the genus *Capra*, naturally inhabiting rough stony ground in Europe, Asia, and N Africa, typically having a brown-grey colouring and a beard. Domesticated varieties (*C. hircus*) are reared for milk, meat, and wool. Related adjs.: **capric, hircine. 2.** short for **Rocky Mountain goat. 3.** *Informal.* a lecherous man. **4.** a bad or inferior person or thing (esp. in the phrase **separate the sheep from the goats**). **5.** short for **scapegoat. 6. get (someone's) goat.** *Slang.* to cause annoyance to (someone). [Old English *gāt*; related to Old Norse *geit*, Old High German *geiz*, Latin *haedus* kid] —**'goat+,like** *adj.*

Goat (gəʊt) *n.* **the.** the constellation Capricorn, the tenth sign of the zodiac.

go at *vb.* (*intr., prep.*) **1.** to make an energetic attempt at (something). **2.** to attack vehemently.

goat an+te+lope *n.* any bovid mammal of the tribe *Rupicaprini*, including the chamois, goral, serow, and Rocky Mountain goat, having characteristics of both goats and antelopes.

goat·ee (gəʊ'tiː) *n.* a pointed tuftlike beard growing on the chin. [C19: from GOAT + *-ee* (see -Y²)] —**goat+'eed** *adj.*

goat+fish ('gəʊt,fɪʃ) *n., pl.* **+fish** *or* **+fish·es.** the U.S. name for the **red mullet.**

goat+herd ('gəʊt,hɜːd) *n.* a person employed to tend or herd goats.

goat+ish ('gəʊtɪʃ) *adj.* **1.** of, like, or relating to a goat. **2.** *Archaic or literary.* lustful or lecherous. —**'goat+ish+ly** *adv.* —**'goat+ish+ness** *n.*

goat moth *n.* a large European moth, *Cossus cossus*, with pale brownish-grey variably marked wings: family *Cossidae.*

goats+beard *or* **goat's-beard** ('gəʊts,bɪəd) *n.* **1.** Also called: **Jack-go-to-bed-at-noon.** a Eurasian plant, *Tragopogon pratensis*, with woolly stems and large heads of yellow rayed flowers surrounded by large green bracts: family *Compositae* (composites). **2.** an American rosaceous plant, *Aruncus sylvester*, with long spikes of small white flowers.

goat+skin ('gəʊt,skɪn) *n.* **1.** the hide of a goat. **2. a.** something made from the hide of a goat, such as leather or a container for wine. **b.** (*as modifier*): *a goatskin rug.*

goat's-rue *n.* **1.** Also called: **French lilac.** a Eurasian leguminous plant, *Galega officinalis*, cultivated for its white, mauve, or pinkish flowers: formerly used medicinally. **2.** a North American leguminous plant, *Tephrosia virginiana*, with pink-and-yellow flowers.

goat+suck·er ('gəʊt,sʌkə) *n.* the U.S. name for **nightjar.**

go a·way *vb.* (*intr., adv.*) to leave, as when starting from home on holiday.

go-a·way bird *n.* any of several touracos of the genus *Corythaixoides.* [C19: imitative of its call]

gob[1] (gɒb) *n.* **1.** a lump or chunk, esp. of a soft substance. **2.** (*often pl.*) *Informal.* a great quantity or amount. **3.** *Mining.* **a.** waste material such as clay, shale, etc. **b.** a worked-out area in a mine often packed with this. **4.** *Informal.* a globule of spittle or saliva. ~*vb.* **gobs, gob+bing, gobbed. 5.** (*intr.*) *Brit. informal.* to spit. [C14: from Old French *gobe* lump, from *gober* to gulp down; see GOBBET]

gob[2] (gɒb) *n.* an informal word (not in nautical use) for a **sailor.** [C20: of unknown origin]

gob[3] (gɒb) *n.* a slang word (esp. Brit.) for the **mouth.** [C16: perhaps from Gaelic *gob*]

go back *vb.* (*intr., adv.*) **1.** to return. **2.** (often foll. by *to*) to originate (in): *the links with France go back to the Norman Conquest.* **3.** (foll. by *on*) to change one's mind about; repudiate (esp. in the phrase **go back on one's word**). **4.** (of clocks and watches) to be set to an earlier time, as during British Summer Time: *when do the clocks go back this year?*

gob+bet ('gɒbɪt) *n.* a chunk, lump, or fragment, esp. of raw meat. [C14: from Old French *gobet*, from *gober* to gulp down]

Gob·bi (*Italian* 'gɔbbi) *n.* **Ti·to** ('tiːto). born 1915, Italian operatic baritone.

gob+ble[1] ('gɒbᵊl) *vb.* **1.** (when *tr.*, often foll. by *up*) to eat or swallow (food) hastily and in large mouthfuls. **2.** (*tr.*; often foll. by *up*) *Informal.* to snatch. [C17: probably from GOB[1]]

gob+ble[2] ('gɒbᵊl) *n.* **1.** the loud rapid gurgling sound made by male turkeys. ~*interj.* **2.** an imitation of this sound. ~*vb.* **3.** (*intr.*) (of a turkey) to make this sound. [C17: probably of imitative origin]

gob+ble+de+gook *or* **gob+ble+dy+gook** ('gɒbᵊldɪ,guːk) *n. Informal.* pretentious language, esp. as characterized by obscure phraseology. [C20: whimsical formation from GOBBLE[2]]

gob+bler ('gɒblə) *n. Informal.* a male turkey.

Go+be·lin ('gəʊbəlɪn; *French* gɔ'blɛ̃) *adj.* **1.** of or resembling tapestry made at the Gobelins' factory in Paris, having vivid pictorial scenes. ~*n.* **2.** a tapestry of this kind. [C19: from the *Gobelin* family, who founded the factory]

go-be·tween *n.* a person who acts as agent or intermediary for two people or groups in a transaction or dealing.

Go·bi ('gəʊbɪ) *n.* a desert in E Asia, mostly in the Mongolian People's Republic and the Inner Mongolian Autonomous Region of China: sometimes considered to include all the arid regions east of the Pamirs and north of the plateau of Tibet and the Great Wall of China: one of the largest deserts in the world. Length: about 1600 km (1000 miles). Width: about 1000 km (625 miles). Average height: 900 m (3000 ft.). Chinese name: **Shamo.** —**'Go+bi·an** *adj.*

go+bi+oid ('gəʊbɪ,ɔɪd) *adj.* **1.** of or relating to the *Gobioidea*, a suborder of spiny-finned teleost fishes that includes gobies and mudskippers (family *Gobiidae*) and sleepers (family *Eleotridae*). ~*n.* **2.** any gobioid fish. [C19: from New Latin *Gobioidea*, from Latin *gōbius* gudgeon]

gob+let ('gɒblɪt) *n.* **1.** a vessel for drinking, usually of glass or metal, with a base and stem but without handles. **2.** *Archaic.* a large drinking cup shaped like a bowl. [C14: from Old French *gobelet* a little cup, from *gobel* ultimately of Celtic origin]

gob+lin ('gɒblɪn) *n.* (in folklore) a small grotesque supernatural creature, regarded as malevolent towards human beings. [C14: from Old French, from Middle High German *kobolt*; compare COBALT]

go·bo ('gəʊbəʊ) *n., pl.* **·bos** *or* **·boes. 1.** a shield placed around a microphone to exclude unwanted sounds. **2.** a black screen placed around a camera lens, television lens, etc., to reduce the incident light. [C20: of unknown origin]

gob+stop·per ('gɒb,stɒpə) *n. Brit.* a large hard sweet that changes colour when sucked.

go·by ('gəʊbɪ) *n., pl.* **·by** *or* **·bies. 1.** any small spiny-finned fish of the family *Gobiidae*, of coastal or brackish waters, having a large head, an elongated tapering body, and the ventral fins modified as a sucker. **2.** any other gobioid fish. [C18: from Latin *gōbius* gudgeon, fish of little value, from Greek *kōbios*]

go-by *n. Slang.* a deliberate snub or slight (esp. in the phrase **give (a person) the go-by**).

go by *vb.* (*intr.*) **1.** to pass: *the cars went by; as the years go by we all get older; don't let those opportunities go by!* **2.** (*prep.*) to be guided by: *in the darkness we could only go by the stars.* **3.** (*prep.*) to use as a basis for forming an opinion or judgement: *it's wise not to go only by appearances.*

G.O.C. (-in-C.) *abbrev. for* General Officer Commanding (-in-Chief).

go-cart *n.* **1.** *Chiefly U.S.* a small wagon for young children to ride in or pull. **2.** *Chiefly U.S.* a light frame on casters or wheels that supports a baby while learning to walk. Brit. word: **baby-walker. 3.** *Motor racing.* See **kart. 4.** another word for **handcart.**

god (gɒd) *n.* **1.** a supernatural being, who is worshipped as the controller of some part of the universe or some aspect of life in the world or is the personification of some force. **2.** an image, idol, or symbolic representation of such a deity. **3.** any person or thing to which excessive attention is given: *money was his god.* **4.** a man who has qualities regarded as making him superior to other men. **5.** (*in pl.*) the gallery of a theatre. [Old

English *god;* related to Old Norse *goth,* Old High German *got,* Old Irish *guth* voice]

God (gɒd) *n.* **1.** *Theol.* the sole Supreme Being, eternal, spiritual, and transcendent, who is the Creator and ruler of all and is infinite in all attributes; the object of worship in monotheistic religions. **2.** *Christian Science.* the Supreme Being regarded as Infinite Mind, Spirit, Soul, Principle, Life, Truth, and Love. ~*interj.* **3.** an oath or exclamation used to indicate surprise, annoyance, etc. (and in such expressions as **My God!** or **God Almighty!**).

Go·dard (*French* gɔ'da:r) *n.* **Jean-Luc** (ʒã 'lyk). born 1930, French film director. Influenced by surrealism, his early works explored the political and documentary use of film. His works include *Pierrot le fou* (1965), *Weekend* (1967), and *Pravda* (1969).

Go+da+va+ri (gəʊ'dɑ:vərɪ) *n.* a river in central India, rising in the Western Ghats and flowing southeast to the Bay of Bengal: extensive delta, linked by canal with the Krishna delta; a sacred river to Hindus. Length: about 1500 km (900 miles).

god+child ('gɒd,tʃaɪld) *n., pl.* **+chil·dren.** a person, usually an infant, who is sponsored by adults at baptism.

god+damn ('gɒd'dæm) *Informal, chiefly U.S.* ~*interj. also* **God damn. 1.** an oath expressing anger, surprise, etc. ~*adv. also* **god+dam,** *adj. also* **god+dam** *or* **god+damned. 2.** (intensifier): *a goddamn fool.*

God·dard ('gɒdɑ:d) *n.* **Rob·ert Hutch·ings.** 1882–1945, U.S. physicist. He made the first workable liquid-fuelled rocket.

god+daugh·ter ('gɒd,dɔ:tə) *n.* a female godchild.

god+dess ('gɒdɪs) *n.* **1.** a female god. **2.** a woman who is adored or idealized, esp. by a man. —**'god+dess+,hood** *or* **'god+dess+,ship** *n.*

Gode·froy de Bouil·lon (*French* gɔdfrwa də bu'jɔ̃) *n.* ?1060–1100, French leader of the First Crusade (1096–99), becoming first ruler of the Latin kingdom of Jerusalem.

Gö·del ('gɜ:dᵊl) *n.* **Kurt** (kʊrt). 1906–78, U.S. logician and mathematician, born in Austria-Hungary. He showed (**Gödel's proof**) that in a formal axiomatic system, such as logic or mathematics, it is impossible to prove consistency without using methods from outside the system.

Gode·rich ('gəʊdrɪtʃ) **Vis·count,** title of **Frederick John Robinson,** 1st Earl of Ripon 1782–1859, English statesman; prime minister 1827–28.

Go+des+berg (*German* 'go:dəs,bɛrk) *n.* a town and spa in West Germany, in North Rhine-Westphalia on the Rhine: a SE suburb of Bonn. Pop.: 70 700 (1966). Official name: **Bad Godesberg.**

go+de·tia (gə'di:ʃə) *n.* any plant of the American onagraceous genus *Godetia,* esp. one grown as a showy-flowered annual garden plant. [C19: named after C. H. *Godet* (died 1879), Swiss botanist]

god+fa·ther ('gɒd,fɑ:ðə) *n.* a male godparent.

god-fear·ing *adj.* pious; devout: *a god-fearing people.*

god+for·sak·en ('gɒdfə,seɪkən, ,gɒdfə'seɪkən) *adj.* **1.** (*usually prenominal*) desolate; dreary; forlorn. **2.** wicked.

God+head ('gɒd,hɛd) *n.* (*sometimes not cap.*) **1.** the essential nature and condition of being God. **2. the Godhead.** God.

god+hood ('gɒd,hʊd) *n.* the state of being divine.

Go·di·va (gə'daɪvə) *n.* **La·dy.** ?1040–1080, wife of Leofric, Earl of Mercia. According to legend, she rode naked through Coventry in order to obtain remission for the townspeople from the heavy taxes imposed by her husband.

god+less ('gɒdlɪs) *adj.* **1.** wicked or unprincipled. **2.** lacking a god. **3.** refusing to acknowledge God. —**'god+less+ly** *adv.* —**'god+less+ness** *n.*

god+like ('gɒd,laɪk) *adj.* resembling or befitting a god or God; divine.

god+ly ('gɒdlɪ) *adj.* **+li+er, +li+est.** having a religious character; pious; devout: *a godly man.* —**'god+li+ness** *n.*

god+moth·er ('gɒd,mʌðə) *n.* a female godparent.

Go·dol·phin (gə'dɒlfɪn) *n.* **Sid·ney.** 1st Earl of Godolphin. 1645–1712, English statesman; as Lord Treasurer, he managed the financing of Marlborough's campaigns in the War of the Spanish Succession.

go+down ('gəʊ,daʊn) *n.* (in the East, esp. in India and Malaya) a warehouse. [C16: from Malay *godong*]

go down *vb.* (*intr., mainly adv.*) **1.** (*also prep.*) to move or lead to or as if to a lower place or level; sink, decline, decrease, etc., *the ship went down this morning; prices are going down; the path goes down to the sea.* **2.** to be defeated; lose. **3.** to be remembered or recorded (esp. in the phrase **go down in history**). **4.** to be received: *his speech went down well.* **5.** (of food) to be swallowed. **6.** *Bridge.* to fail to make the number of tricks previously contracted for. **7.** *Brit.* to leave (a college or university) at the end of a term or the academic year. **8.** (usually foll. by *with*) *Brit.* to fall ill; be infected. **9.** (of a celestial body) to sink or set: *the sun went down before we arrived.* **10.** *Brit. slang.* to go to prison, esp. for a specified period: *he went down for six months.*

god+par·ent ('gɒd,pɛərənt) *n.* a person who stands sponsor to another at baptism.

go+droon (gə'dru:n) *n.* a variant spelling of **gadroon.** —**go+'drooned** *adj.*

God's a·cre *n. Literary.* a churchyard or burial ground. [C17: translation of German *Gottesacker*]

god+send ('gɒd,sɛnd) *n.* a person or thing that comes unexpectedly but is particularly welcome. [C19: changed from C17 *God's send,* alteration of *goddes sand* God's message, from Old English *sand;* see SEND]

god+son ('gɒd,sʌn) *n.* a male godchild.

God+speed ('gɒd'spi:d) *interj., n.* an expression of one's good wishes for a person's success and safety. [C15: from *God spede* may God prosper (you)]

Godt+haab (*Danish* 'gɔd,hɔ:b) *n.* the capital of Greenland, in the southwest on **Godthaab Fiord:** the oldest Danish settlement in Greenland, founded in 1721. Pop.: 8209 (1970).

Go·du·nov ('gɒdə,nɒf, 'gʊd-; *Russian* gədu'nɔf) *n.* **Bo·ris Fyo·do·ro·vich** (ba'ris 'fjɔdərəvitʃ). ?1551–1605, Russian regent (1584–98) and tsar (1598–1605).

God·win ('gɒdwɪn) *n.* **1.** died 1053, Earl of Wessex. He was chief adviser to Canute and Edward the Confessor. His son succeeded Edward to the throne as Harold II. **2. Mar·y,** *née* **Woll·stone·craft.** 1759–97, English feminist and writer; author of *Vindication of the Rights of Women* (1792). **3.** her husband, **Wil·liam.** 1756–1836, English political philosopher and novelist. In *An Enquiry concerning Political Justice* (1793), he rejected government and social institutions, including marriage. His views greatly influenced English romantic writers.

God+win Aus+ten (,gɒdwɪn 'ɔ:stɪn) *n.* another name for **K2.**

god+wit ('gɒdwɪt) *n.* any large shore bird of the genus *Limosa,* of northern and arctic regions, having long legs and a long upturned bill: family *Scolopacidae* (sandpipers, etc.), order *Charadriiformes.* [C16: of unknown origin]

Goeb·bels (*German* 'gœbᵊls) *n.* **Paul Jo·seph** (paul 'jo:zɛf). 1897–1945, German Nazi politician; minister of propaganda (1933–45).

go·er ('gəʊə) *n.* **1. a.** a person who attends something regularly. **b.** (*in combination*): *filmgoer.* **2.** a person or thing that goes, esp. one that goes very fast. **3.** *Austral. informal.* an acceptable or feasible idea, proposal, etc. **4.** *Austral. informal.* a person trying to succeed.

Goe·ring (*German* 'gø:rɪŋ) *n.* See (Hermann Wilhelm) **Göring.**

Goe·the (*German* 'gø:tə) *n.* **Jo·hann Wolf·gang von** ('jo:han 'vɔlfgaŋ fɔn). 1749–1832, German poet, novelist, and dramatist, who settled in Weimar in 1775. His early works of the *Sturm und Drang* period include the play *Götz von Berlichingen* (1773) and the novel *The Sorrows of Young Werther* (1774). After a journey to Italy (1786–88) his writings, such as the epic play *Iphigenie auf Tauris* (1787) and the epic idyll *Hermann und Dorothea* (1797), showed the influence of classicism. Other works include the *Wilhelm Meister* novels (1796–1829) and his greatest masterpiece *Faust* (1808; 1832).

goe+thite *or* **gö+thite** ('gəʊθaɪt; *German* 'gø:taɪt) *n.* a black, brown, or yellow mineral consisting of hydrated iron oxide in the form of orthorhombic crystals or fibrous masses. Formula: FeO(OH). [C19: named after GOETHE]

gof+fer *or* **gauf+fer** ('gəʊfə) *vb.* **1.** (*tr.*) to press pleats into (a frill). **2.** (*tr.*) to decorate (the gilt edges of a book) with a repeating pattern. ~*n.* **3.** an ornamental frill made by pressing pleats. **4.** the decoration formed by goffering books. **5.** the iron or tool used in making goffers. [C18: from French *gaufrer* to impress a pattern, from *gaufre,* from Middle Low German *wāfel;* see WAFFLE, WAFER]

go for *vb.* (*intr., prep.*) **1.** to go somewhere in order to have or fetch: *he went for a drink; shall I go for a doctor?* **2.** to seek to obtain: *I'd go for that job if I were you.* **3.** to apply to: *what I told him goes for you too.* **4.** to prefer or choose; like: *I really go for that new idea of yours.* **5.** to be to the advantage of: *you'll have great things going for you in the new year.* **6.** to make a physical or verbal attack on. **7.** to be considered to be of a stated importance or value: *his twenty years went for nothing when he was made redundant.*

go forth *vb.* (*intr., adv.*) *Archaic or formal.* **1.** to be issued: *the command went forth that taxes should be collected.* **2.** to go out: *the army went forth to battle.*

Gog and Ma·gog (gɒg; 'meɪgɒg) *n.* **1.** *Old Testament.* a hostile prince and the land from which he comes to attack Israel (Ezekiel 38). **2.** *New Testament.* two kings, who are to attack the Church in a climactic battle, but are then to be destroyed by God (Revelation 20:8–10).

go-get·ter *n. Informal.* an ambitious enterprising person.

gog+ga ('xɒxə) *n. S. African informal.* any small animal that crawls or flies, esp. an insect. [C20: from Hottentot *xoxon* insects collectively]

gog+gle ('gɒgᵊl) *vb.* **1.** (*intr.*) to stare stupidly or fixedly, as in astonishment. **2.** to cause (the eyes) to roll or bulge or (of the eyes) to roll or bulge. ~*n.* **3.** a fixed or bulging stare. **4.** (*pl.*) spectacles, often of coloured glass or covered with gauze: used to protect the eyes. [C14: from *gogelen* to look aside, of uncertain origin; see AGOG] —**'gog+gly** *adj.*

gog·gle+box ('gɒgᵊl,bɒks) *n. Brit. slang.* a television set.

gog·gle-eyed *adj.* (*often postpositive*) with a surprised, staring, or fixed expression.

Gogh (gɒx; *Dutch* xɔx) *n.* See (Vincent) **van Gogh.**

gog+let ('gɒglɪt), **gurg+let,** *or* **gug+let** ('gʌglɪt) *n.* a long-necked water-cooling vessel of porous earthenware, used esp. in India. [C17: from Portuguese *gorgoleta* a little throat, from *gorja* throat; related to French *gargoule;* see GARGLE]

go-go danc+er *n.* a dancer, usually scantily dressed, who performs rhythmic and often erotic modern dance routines, esp. in a nightclub or discotheque.

Go·gol ('gəʊgɒl; *Russian* 'gɔgəlj) *n.* **Ni·ko·lai Va·sil·ie·vich** (nika'laj va'siljɪvitʃ). 1809–52, Russian novelist, dramatist, and short-story writer. His best-known works are *The Government Inspector* (1836), a comedy satirizing bureaucracy, and the novel *Dead Souls* (1842).

Gog+ra ('gɒgrə) *n.* a river in N India, rising in Tibet, in the Himalayas, and flowing southeast through Nepal as the Karnali, then through Uttar Pradesh to join the Ganges. Length: about 1000 km (600 miles).

Goi·â·ni·a (gɔɪ'ɑːnɪə; *Portuguese* go'jənja) *n.* a city in central Brazil, capital of Goiás state: planned in 1933 to replace the old capital, Goiás; two universities. Pop.: 362 152 (1970).

Goi·ás (*Portuguese* gɔ'jas) *n.* a state of central Brazil, in the Brazilian Highlands: contains Brasília, the new capital of Brazil. Capital: Goiânia. Pop.: 2 938 677 (1970). Area: 642 092 sq. km (250 416 sq. miles).

Goi·del ('gɔɪdᵊl) *n.* a Celt who speaks a Goidelic language; Gael. Compare **Brython.**

Goi·del·ic, Goi·dhel·ic (gɔɪ'dɛlɪk), *or* **Ga·dhel·ic** *n.* **1.** the N group of Celtic languages, consisting of Irish Gaelic, Scottish Gaelic, and Manx. Compare **Brythonic.** ~*adj.* **2.** of, relating to, or characteristic of this group of languages. [C19: from Old Irish *Goidel* a Celt, from Old Welsh *gwyddel,* from *gwydd* savage]

go in *vb.* (*intr., mainly adv.*) **1.** to enter. **2.** (*prep*) See **go into. 3.** (of the sun, etc.) to become hidden behind a cloud. **4.** to be assimilated or grasped: *nothing much goes in if I try to read in the evenings.* **5.** *Cricket.* to begin an innings. **6. go in for. a.** to enter as a competitor or contestant. **b.** to adopt as an activity, interest, or guiding principle: *she went in for nursing; some men go in for football in a big way.*

go·ing ('gəʊɪŋ) *n.* **1.** a departure or farewell. **2.** the condition of a surface such as a road or field with regard to walking, riding, etc.: *muddy going.* **3.** *Informal.* speed, progress, etc.: *we made good going on the trip.* ~*adj.* **4.** thriving (esp. in the phrase **a going concern**). **5.** current or accepted, as from past negotiations or commercial operation: *the going rate for electricians; the going value of the firm.* **6.** (*postpositive*) available: *the best going.* **7. going, going, gone!** a statement by an auctioneer that the bidding has almost finished.

Go·ing ('gəʊɪŋ) *n.* **Sid(ney Milton).** born 1943, New Zealand Rugby Union footballer: halfback for the All Blacks (1967–77).

go·ing-o·ver *n., pl.* **go·ings-o·ver.** *Informal.* **1.** a check, examination, or investigation. **2.** a castigation or thrashing.

go·ings-on *pl. n. Informal.* **1.** actions or conduct, esp. when regarded with disapproval. **2.** happenings or events, esp. when mysterious or suspicious: *there were strange goings-on up at the Hall.*

go in·to *vb.* (*intr., prep.*) **1.** to enter. **2.** to start a career in: *to go into publishing.* **3.** to investigate or examine: *to go into the problem of price increases.* **4.** to dress oneself differently in: *to go into mourning.* **5.** to hit: *the car had gone into a lamp post.* **6.** to go to live in or be admitted to, esp. temporarily: *she went into hospital on Tuesday.* **7.** to enter a specified state: *she went into fits of laughter.*

goi·tre *or U.S.* **goi·ter** ('gɔɪtə) *n. Pathol.* a swelling of the thyroid gland, in some cases nearly doubling the size of the neck, usually caused by under- or over-production of hormone by the gland. [C17: from French *goitre,* from Old French *goitron* ultimately from Latin *guttur* throat] —**'goi·tred** *or U.S.* **'goi·tered** *adj.* —**'goi·trous** *adj.*

go-kart *or* **go-cart** *n.* See **kart.**

Gol·con·da[1] (gɒl'kɒndə) *n.* a ruined town and fortress in S central India, in W Andhra Pradesh near Hyderabad city: capital of one of the five Muslim kingdoms of the Deccan from 1512 to 1687, then annexed to the Mogul empire; renowned for its diamonds.

Gol·con·da[2] (gɒl'kɒndə) *n.* (*sometimes not cap.*) a source of wealth or riches, esp. a mine.

gold (gəʊld) *n.* **1. a.** a dense inert bright yellow element that is the most malleable and ductile metal, occurring in rocks and alluvial deposits: used as a monetary standard and in jewellery, dentistry, and plating. The radioisotope gold-198 (**radiogold**), with a half-life of 2.69 days, is used in radiotherapy. Symbol: Au; atomic no.: 79; atomic wt.: 196.97; valency: 1 or 3; relative density: 19.32; melting pt.: 1063°C; boiling pt.: 2966°C. Related adjs.: **aurous, auric. b.** (*as modifier*): *a gold mine.* **2.** a coin or coins made of this metal. **3.** money; wealth. **4.** something precious, beautiful, etc., such as a noble nature (esp. in the phrase **heart of gold**). **5. a.** a deep yellow colour, sometimes with a brownish tinge. **b.** (*as adj.*): *a gold carpet.* **6.** *Archery.* the bull's eye of a target, scoring nine points. [Old English *gold;* related to Old Norse *gull,* Gothic *gulth,* Old High German *gold*]

gol·darn (gɒl'dɑːn) *interj., adv. U.S. slang.* a euphemistic variant of **goddamn.**

Gold·bach's con·jec·ture ('gəʊld,bɑːxs) *n.* the hypothesis that every even number greater than two is the sum of two prime numbers. [named after C. *Goldbach* (1690–1764), German mathematician]

gold ba·sis *n.* the gold standard as a criterion for the determination of prices.

gold·beat·er's skin *n.* animal membrane used to separate sheets of gold that are being hammered into gold leaf.

gold-beat·ing *n.* the act, process, or skill of hammering sheets of gold into gold leaf. —**'gold-,beat·er** *n.*

gold bee·tle *or* **gold·bug** ('gəʊld,bʌg) *n.* any American beetle of the family *Chrysomelidae* having a bright metallic lustre.

gold brick *n.* **1.** something with only a superficial appearance of value. **2.** *U.S. slang.* an idler or shirker.

gold cer·tif·i·cate *n. U.S.* **1.** a currency note issued exclusively to the Federal Reserve Banks by the U.S. Treasury. It forms a claim on gold reserves deposited by the Federal Reserve Banks at the Treasury and is used to transfer interbank balances within the Federal Reserve System. **2.** Also called: **gold note.** (formerly) a bank note issued by the U.S. Treasury to the public and redeemable in gold.

Gold Coast *n.* **1.** the former name (until 1957) of **Ghana. 2.** the former name of **Southport** (Australia).

gold·crest ('gəʊld,krɛst) *n.* a small Old World warbler, *Regulus regulus,* having a greenish plumage and a bright yellow-and-black crown.

gold-dig·ger *n.* **1.** a person who prospects or digs for gold. **2.** *Informal.* a woman who uses her sexual attractions to accumulate gifts and wealth or advance her social position. —**'gold-,dig·ging** *n.*

gold dust *n.* gold in the form of small particles or powder, as found in placer-mining.

gold·en ('gəʊldən) *adj.* **1.** of the yellowish or brownish-yellow metallic colour of gold: *golden hair.* **2.** made from or largely consisting of gold: *a golden statue.* **3.** happy or prosperous: *golden days.* **4.** (*sometimes cap.*) (of anniversaries) the 50th in a series: *Golden Jubilee; golden wedding.* **5.** *Informal.* very successful or destined for success: *the golden girl of tennis.* **6.** extremely valuable or advantageous: *a golden opportunity.* —**'gold·en·ly** *adv.* —**'gold·en·ness** *n.*

gold·en age *n.* **1.** *Classical myth.* the first and best age of mankind, when existence was happy, prosperous, and innocent. **2.** the most flourishing and outstanding period, esp. in the history of an art or nation: *the golden age of poetry.* **3.** the great classical period of Latin literature, occupying approximately the 1st century B.C. and represented by such writers as Cicero and Virgil.

gold·en as·ter *n.* any North American plant of the genus *Chrysopsis,* esp. *C. mariana* of the eastern U.S., having yellow rayed flowers: family *Compositae* (composites).

gold·en calf *n.* **1.** *Old Testament.* **a.** an idol made by Aaron and set up for the Israelites to worship (Exodus 32). **b.** either of two similar idols set up by Jeroboam I at Dan and Bethel in the northern kingdom (I Kings 12:28–30). **2.** *Informal.* the pursuit or idolization of material wealth.

gold·en chain *n.* another name for **laburnum.**

Gold·en De·li·cious *n.* a variety of eating apple having sweet flesh and greenish-yellow skin.

gold·en disc *n.* an award given to a musical artiste or group after the sale of one million copies of a record made by them.

gold·en ea·gle *n.* a large eagle, *Aquila chrysaetos,* of mountainous regions of the N hemisphere, having a plumage that is golden brown on the back and brown elsewhere.

gold·en·eye ('gəʊldən,aɪ) *n., pl.* **-eyes** *or* **-eye. 1.** either of two black-and-white diving ducks, *Bucephala clangula* or *B. islandica,* of northern regions. **2.** any lacewing of the family *Chrysopidae* that has a greenish body and eyes of a metallic lustre.

Gold·en Fleece *n. Greek myth.* the fleece of a winged ram that rescued Phrixus and brought him to Colchis, where he sacrificed it to Zeus. Phrixus gave the fleece to King Aeëtes who kept it in a sacred grove, whence Jason and the Argonauts stole it with the help of Aeëtes daughter. See also **Phrixus.**

Gold·en Gate *n.* a strait between the Pacific and San Francisco Bay: crossed by the **Golden Gate Bridge,** with a central span of 1260 m (4200 ft.).

gold·en goose *n.* a goose in folklore that laid a golden egg a day until its greedy owner killed it in an attempt to get all the gold at once.

gold·en hand·shake *n. Informal.* a sum of money, usually large, given to an employee, either on retirement in recognition of long or excellent service or as compensation for loss of employment.

Gold·en Horde *n.* the Mongol horde that devastated E Europe in the early 13th century. It established the westernmost Mongol khanate, which at its height ruled most of European Russia. Defeated by the power of Muscovy (1380), the realm split into four smaller khanates in 1405.

Gold·en Horn *n.* an inlet of the Bosporus in NW Turkey, forming the harbour of Istanbul. Turkish name: **Haliç.**

gold·en mean *n.* **1.** the middle course between extremes. **2.** another term for **golden section.**

gold·en num·ber *n.* a number between 1 and 19, used to indicate the position of any year in the Metonic cycle, calculated as the remainder when 1 is added to the given year and the sum is divided by 19. If the remainder is zero the number is 19: *the golden number of 1984 is 9.*

gold·en o·ri·ole *n.* a European oriole, *Oriolus oriolus,* the male of which has a bright yellow head and body with black wings and tail.

gold·en pheas·ant *n.* a brightly coloured pheasant, *Chrysolophus pictus,* of the mountainous regions of W and central Asia, the males of which have a crest and ruff.

gold·en plov·er *n.* any of several plovers of the genus *Pluvialis,* such as *P. apricaria* of Europe and Asia, that have golden brown back, head, and wings.

gold·en re·triev·er *n.* a variety of retriever with a long silky wavy coat of a yellow or golden colour.

gold·en·rod (,gəʊldən'rɒd) *n.* **1.** any plant of the genus *Solidago,* of North America, Europe, and Asia, having spikes of small yellow flowers: family *Compositae* (composites). See also **yellowweed. 2.** any of various similar related plants, such as *Brachychaeta sphacelata* (**false goldenrod**) of the southern U.S.

gold·en rule *n.* **1.** the rule of conduct formulated by Christ: *Whatsoever ye would that men should do to you, do ye even so to them* (Matthew 7:12). **2.** any important principle: *a golden rule of sailing is to wear a life jacket.* **3.** another name for **rule of three.**

gold·en·seal (,gəʊldən'siːl) *n.* a ranunculaceous woodland plant, *Hydrastis canadensis,* of E North America, whose thick yellow rootstock contains such alkaloids as berberine and hydrastine and was formerly used medicinally.

gold+en sec+tion *or* **mean** *n. Fine arts.* the proportion of the two divisions of a straight line or the two dimensions of a plane figure such that the smaller is to the larger as the larger is to the sum of the two.

gold+en syr+up *n. Brit.* a light golden coloured treacle produced by the evaporation of cane sugar juice, used to sweeten and flavour cakes, puddings, etc.

gold+en wat+tle *n.* **1.** an Australian yellow-flowered mimosaceous plant, *Acacia pycnantha,* that yields a useful gum and bark. **2.** any of several similar and related plants, esp. *Acacia longifolia* of Australia.

gold-ex·change stand+ard *n.* a monetary system by which one country's currency, which is not itself based on the gold standard, is kept at a par with another currency that is based on the gold standard.

gold+eye ('gəʊldˌaɪ) *n., pl.* **+eyes** *or* **+eye.** a North American clupeoid fish, *Hiodon alosoides,* with yellowish eyes, silvery sides, and a dark blue back: family *Hiodontidae* (mooneyes).

gold+finch ('gəʊldˌfɪntʃ) *n.* **1.** a common European finch, *Carduelis carduelis,* the male of which has a red-and-white face and yellow-and-black wings. **2.** any of several North American finches of the genus *Spinus,* esp. the yellow-and-black species *S. tristis.*

gold+fish ('gəʊldˌfɪʃ) *n., pl.* **+fish** *or* **+fish·es. 1.** a freshwater cyprinid fish, *Carassius auratus,* of E Europe and Asia, esp. China, widely introduced as a pond or aquarium fish. It resembles the carp and has a typically golden or orange-red coloration. **2.** any of certain similar ornamental fishes, esp. the golden orfe (see **orfe**).

gold+fish bowl *n.* **1.** Also called: **fishbowl.** a glass bowl, typically spherical, in which fish are kept as pets. **2.** a place or situation open to observation by onlookers.

gold foil *n.* thin gold sheet that is thicker than gold leaf.

gold·i+locks ('gəʊldɪˌlɒks) *n.* **1.** a Eurasian plant, *Aster linosyris* (or *Linosyris vulgaris*), with clusters of small yellow flowers: family *Compositae* (composites). **2.** a Eurasian ranunculaceous woodland plant, *Ranunculus auricomus,* with yellow flowers. See also **buttercup. 3.** (*sometimes cap.*) a person, esp. a girl, with light blond hair.

Gold·ing ('gəʊldɪŋ) *n.* **Wil·liam (Gerald).** born 1911, English novelist noted for his allegories of man's proclivity for evil. His novels include *Lord of the Flies* (1954) and *Free Fall* (1959).

gold leaf *n.* very thin gold sheet with a thickness between about 0.076 and 0.127 micrometre, produced by rolling or hammering gold and used for gilding woodwork, etc.

gold med+al *n.* a medal of gold, awarded to the winner of a competition or race. Compare **silver medal, bronze medal.**

gold mine *n.* **1.** a place where gold ore is mined. **2.** a source of great wealth, profit, etc. **—'gold-ˌmin·er** *n.* **—'gold-ˌmin·ing** *n.*

gold note *n. U.S.* another name for **gold certificate.**

gold-of-pleas·ure *n.* a yellow-flowered Eurasian cruciferous plant, *Camelina sativa,* widespread as a weed, esp. in flax fields: formerly cultivated for its oil-rich seeds.

Gol·do·ni (*Italian* gol'do:ni) *n.* **Car·lo** ('karlo). 1707–93, Italian dramatist; author of over 250 plays in Italian or French, including *La Locandiera* (1753). His work introduced realistic Italian comedy, superseding the commedia dell'arte.

gold plate *n.* **1.** a thin coating of gold, usually produced by electroplating. **2.** vessels or utensils made of gold.

gold-plate *vb.* (*tr.*) to coat (other metal) with gold, usually by electroplating.

gold point *n. Finance.* either of two exchange rates (the **gold export point** and the **gold import point**) at which it is as cheap to settle international accounts by exporting or importing gold bullion as by selling or buying bills of exchange. Also called: **specie point.**

gold re+serve *n.* the gold reserved by a central bank to support domestic credit expansion, to cover balance of payments deficits, and to protect currency.

gold rush *n.* a large-scale migration of people to a territory where gold has been found.

Gold·schmidt ('gəʊldˌʃmɪt) *n.* **Rich·ard Ben·e·dikt.** 1878–1958, U.S. geneticist, born in Germany. He advanced the theory that heredity is determined by the chemical configuration of the chromosome molecule rather than by the qualities of the individual genes.

gold+smith ('gəʊldˌsmɪθ) *n.* **1. a.** a dealer in articles made of gold. **b.** an artisan who makes such articles. **2.** (formerly) a dealer or manufacturer of gold articles who also engaged in banking or other financial business. **3.** (in Malaysia) a Chinese jeweller.

Gold·smith ('gəʊldˌsmɪθ) *n.* **Ol·i·ver.** 1728–74, Irish poet, dramatist, and novelist. His works include the novel *The Vicar of Wakefield* (1766), the poem *The Deserted Village* (1770), and the comedy *She Stoops to Conquer* (1773).

gold+smith bee+tle *n.* any of various scarabaeid beetles that have a metallic golden lustre, esp. the rose chafer.

gold stand+ard *n.* a monetary system in which the unit of currency is defined with reference to gold.

Gold Stick *n.* (*sometimes not caps.*) **1.** a gilt rod carried by the colonel of the Life Guards or the captain of the Gentlemen-at-arms. **2.** the bearer of this rod.

gold+stone ('gəʊldˌstəʊn) *n.* another name for **aventurine** (senses 2, 3).

gold-tail moth *n.* a European moth, *Euproctis chrysorrhoea* (or *similis*), having white wings and a soft white furry body with a yellow tail tuft: family *Lymantriidae.*

gold+thread ('gəʊldˌθrɛd) *n.* **1.** a North American woodland ranunculaceous plant, *Coptis trifolia* (or *C. groenlandica*), with slender yellow roots. **2.** the root of this plant, which yields a medicinal tonic and a dye.

go+lem ('gəʊlɛm) *n.* (in Jewish legend) an artificially created human being brought to life by supernatural means. [from Yiddish *goylem,* from Hebrew *gōlem* formless thing]

golf (gɒlf) *n.* **1. a.** a game played on a large open course, the object of which is to hit a ball using clubs, with as few strokes as possible, into each of usually 18 holes. **b.** (*as modifier*): *a golf bag.* ~*vb.* **2.** (*intr.*) to play golf. [C15: probably from Middle Dutch *colf* CLUB]

golf ball *n.* **1.** a small resilient white ball of strands of rubber wound at high tension around a core with a cover made of gutta-percha, etc., used in golf. **2.** (in some electric typewriters) a small detachable metal sphere, around the surface of which type characters are arranged.

golf club *n.* **1.** any of various long-shafted clubs with wood or metal heads used to strike a golf ball. **2. a.** an association of golf players, usually having its own course and facilities. **b.** the premises of such an association.

golf course *or* **links** *n.* a large area of open land on which golf is played.

golf+er ('gɒlfə) *n.* **1.** a person who plays golf. **2.** a type of cardigan.

Gol·gi (*Italian* 'gɔldʒi) *n.* **Ca·mil·lo** (ka'millo). 1844–1926, Italian neurologist and histologist, noted for his work on the central nervous system and his discovery in animal cells of the bodies known by his name: shared the Nobel prize for medicine 1906.

Gol·gi bod·y, ap·pa+rat+us, *or* **com+plex** *n.* a membranous complex of vesicles, vacuoles, and flattened sacs in the cytoplasm of most cells: involved in intracellular secretion and transport. [C20: named after C. GOLGI]

Gol+go+tha ('gɒlgəθə) *n.* **1.** another name for **Calvary. 2.** (*sometimes not cap.*) *Now rare.* a place of burial. [C17: from Late Latin, from Greek, from Aramaic, based on Hebrew *gulgōleth* skull]

gol+iard ('gəʊljəd) *n.* one of a number of wandering scholars in 12th- and 13th-century Europe famed for their riotous behaviour, intemperance, and composition of satirical and ribald Latin verse. [C15: from Old French *goliart* glutton, from Latin *gula* gluttony] **—gol+iar+dic** (gəʊl'jɑ:dɪk) *adj.*

gol+iard+er·y (gəʊl'jɑ:dərɪ) *n.* the poems of the goliards.

Go·li·ath (gə'laɪəth) *n. Old Testament.* a Philistine giant from Gath who terrorized the Hebrews until he was killed by David with a stone from his sling (I Samuel 17).

go+li+ath bee+tle *n.* any very large tropical scarabaeid beetle of the genus *Goliathus,* esp. *G. giganteus* of Africa, which may grow to a length of 20 centimetres.

go+li+ath frog *n.* the largest living frog, *Rana goliath,* which occurs in the Congo region of Africa and can grow to a length of 30 centimetres.

gol+li+wog *or* **gol+li+wogg** ('gɒlɪˌwɒg) *n.* a soft doll with a black face, usually made of cloth or rags. [C19: from the name of a doll character in children's books by the Americans Bertha Upton (died 1912), writer, and Florence Upton (died 1922), illustrator]

gol+lop ('gɒləp) *vb.* to eat or drink (something) quickly or greedily. [dialect variant of GULP] **—'gol+lop+er** *n.*

gol+ly[1] ('gɒlɪ) *interj.* an exclamation of mild surprise or wonder. [C19: originally a euphemism for GOD]

gol+ly[2] ('gɒlɪ) *n., pl.* **+lies.** *Brit. informal.* short for **golliwog:** used chiefly by children.

gol+ly[3] ('gɒlɪ) *Austral. slang.* ~*vb.* **+lies, +ly+ing, +lied. 1.** to spit. ~*n., pl.* **+lies. 2.** a gob of spit. [C20: altered from *gollion* a gob of phlegm, probably of imitative origin]

go+losh·es (gə'lɒʃɪz) *pl. n.* a less common spelling of **galoshes.**

Gom·berg ('gɒmbɜ:g) *n.* **Mo·ses.** 1866–1947, U.S. chemist, born in Russia, noted for his work on free radicals.

gom+broon (gɒm'bru:n) *n.* Persian and Chinese pottery and porcelain wares. [C17: named after *Gombroon,* Iran, from which it was originally exported]

Go+mel (*Russian* 'gɔmɪlj) *n.* an industrial city in the W Soviet Union, in the SE Byelorussian SSR: belonged to Lithuania until 1772. Pop.: 337 000 (1975 est.).

Go+mor+rah *or* **Go+mor+rha** (gə'mɒrə) *n.* **1.** *Old Testament.* one of two ancient cities near the Dead Sea, the other being Sodom, that were destroyed by God as a punishment for the wickedness of their inhabitants (Genesis 19:24). **2.** any place notorious for vice and depravity. **—Go+'mor+re·an** *or* **Go+'mor+rhe·an** *adj.*

Gom·pers ('gɒmpəz) *n.* **Sam·u·el.** 1850–1924, U.S. labour leader, born in England; a founder of the American Federation of Labor and its president (1886–94; 1896–1924).

gom+pho+sis (gɒm'fəʊsɪs) *n., pl.* **+ses** (-si:z). *Anatomy.* a form of immovable articulation in which a peglike part fits into a cavity, as in the setting of a tooth in its socket. [C16: from New Latin, from Greek *gomphoein* to bolt together, from *gomphos* tooth, peg]

Go·mul·ka (gə'mʊlkə) *n.* **Wła·dy·sław** (vwa'diswaf). 1905–82, Polish statesman; first secretary of the Polish Communist Party (1956–70).

go+mu+ti *or* **go+mu+ti palm** (gə'mu:tɪ) *n.* **1.** an East Indian feather palm, *Arenga pinnata,* whose sweet sap is a source of sugar. **2.** a black wiry fibre obtained from the leafstalks of this plant, used for making rope, etc. **3.** a Malaysian sago palm, *Metroxylon sagu.* [from Malay *gĕmuti*]

gon- *combining form.* variant of **gono-** before a vowel: *gonidium.*

-gon *n. combining form.* indicating a figure having a specified number of angles: *pentagon.* [from Greek *-gōnon,* from *gōnia* angle]

gon·ad ('gɒnæd) *n.* an animal organ in which gametes are produced, such as a testis or an ovary. [C19: from New Latin *gonas,* from Greek *gonos* seed] —'**gon·ad·al, go·na·di·al** (gɒ'neɪdɪəl), *or* **go·'nad·ic** *adj.*

gon·ad·o·tro·pin (ˌgɒnədəʊ'trəʊpɪn) *or* **gon·ad·o·trop·ic hor·mone** *n.* any of three glycoprotein hormones secreted by the pituitary gland and placenta that stimulate the gonads and control reproductive activity. See **follicle-stimulating hormone, luteinizing hormone, prolactin.** —ˌ**gon·ad·o·'troph·ic** *or* ˌ**gon·ad·o·'trop·ic** *adj.*

Go·na·ïves (*French* gɔna'iːv) *n.* a port in W Haiti, on the **Gulf of Gonaïves;** scene of the proclamation of Haiti's independence (1804). Pop.: 14 000 (1971 est.).

Gon·court (*French* gɔ̃'kuːr) *n.* **Ed·mond Louis An·toine Hu·ot de** (ɛdmɔ̃ lwi ɑ̃twan y'o də), 1822–96, and his brother, **Jules Al·fred Hu·ot de** (ʒyl al'frɛd), 1830–70, French writers, noted for their collaboration, esp. on their *Journal,* and for the Académie Goncourt founded by Edmond's will.

Gond (gɒnd) *n.* a member of a formerly tribal people now living in scattered enclaves throughout S central India.

Gon·dar ('gɒndɑː) *n.* a city in NW Ethiopia: capital of Ethiopia from the 17th century until 1868. Pop.: 36 570 (1971 est.).

Gon·di ('gɒndɪ) *n.* the language or group of languages spoken by the Gonds, belonging to the Dravidian family of languages.

gon·do·la ('gɒndələ) *n.* **1.** a long narrow flat-bottomed boat with a high ornamented stem and a platform at the stern where an oarsman stands and propels the boat by sculling or punting: traditionally used on the canals of Venice. **2. a.** a car or cabin suspended from an airship or balloon. **b.** a moving cabin suspended from a cable across a valley, etc. **3.** a flat-bottomed barge used on canals and rivers of the U.S. as far west as the Mississippi. **4.** *U.S.* a low, open, and flat-bottomed railway goods wagon. **5.** a set of island shelves in a self-service shop: used for displaying goods. [C16: from Italian (Venetian dialect), from Medieval Latin *gondula,* perhaps ultimately from Greek *kondu* drinking vessel]

gon·do·lier (ˌgɒndə'lɪə) *n.* a man who propels a gondola.

Gond·wa·na·land (gɒnd'wɑːnəˌlænd) *or* **Gond·wa·na** *n.* a hypothetical southern continental mass of the late Palaeozoic and Mesozoic eras that included Antarctica, South America, Africa, India, and Australia.

gone (gɒn) *vb.* **1.** the past participle of **go.** ~*adj.* (*usually postpositive*) **2.** ended; past. **3.** lost; ruined (esp. in the phrases **gone goose** *or* **gosling**). **4.** dead or near to death. **5.** spent; consumed; used up. **6.** *Informal.* faint or weak. **7.** *Informal.* having been pregnant (for a specified time): *six months gone.* **8.** (usually foll. by *on*) *Slang.* in love (with). **9.** *Slang.* in an exhilarated state, as through music or the use of drugs.

gon·er ('gɒnə) *n. Slang.* a person or thing beyond help or recovery, esp. a person who is dead or about to die.

gon·fa·lon ('gɒnfələn) *or* **gon·fa·non** ('gɒnfənən) *n.* **1.** a banner hanging from a crossbar, used esp. by certain medieval Italian republics or in ecclesiastical processions. **2.** a battle flag suspended crosswise on a staff, usually having a serrated edge to give the appearance of streamers. [C16: from Old Italian *gonfalone,* from Old French *gonfalon,* of Germanic origin; compare Old English *gūthfana* war banner, Old Norse *gunnfani*]

gon·fa·lon·ier (ˌgɒnfələ'nɪə) *n.* the chief magistrate or other official of a medieval Italian republic, esp. the bearer of the republic's gonfalon.

gong (gɒŋ) *n.* **1.** Also called: **tam-tam.** a percussion instrument of indefinite pitch, consisting of a metal platelike disc struck with a soft-headed drumstick. **2.** a rimmed metal disc, hollow metal hemisphere, or metal strip, tube, or wire that produces a note when struck. It may be used to give alarm signals when operated electromagnetically. **3.** a fixed saucer-shaped bell, as on an alarm clock, struck by a mechanically operated hammer. **4.** *Brit. slang.* a medal, esp. a military one. ~*vb.* **5.** (*intr.*) to sound a gong. **6.** (*tr.*) (of traffic police) to summon (a driver) to stop by sounding a gong. [C17: from Malay, of imitative origin] —'**gong·ˌlike** *adj.*

Gon·go·la (gɒŋ'gəʊlə) *n.* a state of E Nigeria, formed in 1976 from part of Northeastern State. Capital: Yola. Pop.: 1 585 200 (1976 est). Area: 13 664 sq. km (5275 sq. miles).

Gón·go·ra y Ar·go·te (*Spanish* 'goŋgora i ar'ɣote) *n.* **Luis de** (lwis ðe). 1561–1627, Spanish lyric poet, noted for the exaggerated pedantic style of works such as *Las Soledades.*

Gon·go·rism ('gɒŋgəˌrɪzəm) *n.* **1.** an affected literary style characterized by intricate language and obscurity. **2.** an example of this. [C19: from Spanish *gongorismo;* see GÓNGORA Y ARGOTE] —'**Gon·go·rist** *n.* —ˌ**Gon·go·'ris·tic** *adj.*

go·ni·a·tite ('gəʊnɪəˌtaɪt) *n.* any extinct cephalopod mollusc of the genus *Goniatites* and related genera, similar to ammonites: a common fossil of Devonian and Carboniferous rocks. [C19: from Greek *gōnia* angle, referring to the angular sutures in some species + -ITE[1]]

go·nid·i·um (gə'nɪdɪəm) *n., pl.* **·i·a** (-ɪə). **1.** a green algal cell in the thallus of a lichen. **2.** an asexual reproductive cell in some colonial algae. [C19: from New Latin, from GONO- + -IDIUM] —**go·'nid·i·al** *or* **go·'nid·ic** *adj.*

go·ni·om·e·ter (ˌgəʊnɪ'ɒmɪtə) *n.* **1.** an instrument for measuring the angles between the faces of a crystal. **2.** an instrument consisting of a transformer circuit connected to two directional aerials, used to determine the bearing of a distant radio station. [C18: via French from Greek *gōnia* angle] —**go·ni·o·met·ric** (ˌgəʊnɪə'mɛtrɪk) *or* ˌ**go·ni·o·'met·ri·cal** *adj.* —ˌ**go·ni·o·'met·ri·cal·ly** *adv.* —ˌ**go·ni·'om·e·try** *n.*

go·ni·on ('gəʊnɪən) *n., pl.* **·ni·a** (-nɪə). *Anatomy.* the point or apex of the angle of the lower jaw. [C19: from New Latin, from Greek *gōnia* angle]

-go·ni·um *n. combining form.* indicating a seed or reproductive cell: *archegonium.* [from New Latin *gonium,* from Greek *gonos* seed]

gonk (gɒŋk) *n.* a soft toy, typically egg-shaped with arms and legs attached. [C20: of unknown origin]

gon·na ('gɒnə) *vb. Slang. contraction of* going to.

gon·o- *or before a vowel* **gon-** *combining form.* sexual or reproductive: *gonorrhoea.* [New Latin, from Greek *gonos* seed]

gon·o·coc·cus (ˌgɒnəʊ'kɒkəs) *n., pl.* **·coc·ci** (-'kɒksaɪ). a spherical Gram-negative bacterium, *Neisseria gonorrhoeae,* that causes gonorrhoea: family *Neisseriaceae.* —ˌ**gon·o·'coc·cal** *or* ˌ**gon·o·'coc·cic** *adj.* —ˌ**gon·o·'coc·coid** *adj.*

gon·o·cyte ('gɒnəʊˌsaɪt) *n.* an oocyte or spermatocyte.

gon·of *or* **gon·if** ('gɒnəf) *n.* a variant spelling of **ganef.**

gon·o·phore ('gɒnəʊˌfɔː) *n.* **1.** *Zoology.* **a.** a polyp in certain coelenterates that bears gonads. **2.** *Botany.* an elongated structure in certain flowers that bears the stamens and pistil above the level of the other flower parts. —**gon·o·phor·ic** (ˌgɒnəʊ'fɒrɪk) *or* **go·noph·o·rous** (gəʊ'nɒfərəs) *adj.*

gon·o·pore ('gɒnəˌpɔː) *n.* an external pore in insects, earthworms, etc., through which the gametes are extruded.

gon·or·rhoe·a *or esp. U.S.* **gon·or·rhe·a** (ˌgɒnə'rɪə) *n.* an infectious venereal disease caused by a gonococcus, characterized by a burning sensation when urinating and a mucopurulent discharge from the urethra or vagina. —ˌ**gon·or·'rhoe·al,** ˌ**gon·or·'rhoe·ic** *or esp. U.S.* ˌ**gon·or·'rhe·al,** ˌ**gon·or·'rhe·ic** *adj.*

-go·ny *n. combining form.* genesis, origin, or production: *cosmogony.* [from Latin *-gonia,* from Greek *-goneia,* from *gonos* seed, procreation]

Gon·za·les (gən'zɑːlɪs) *n.* **Ri·car·do A·lon·zo** (rɪ'kɑːdəʊ ə'lɒnzəʊ), known as *Pancho.* born 1928, U.S. tennis player.

Gon·zá·lez (*Spanish* gon'θaleθ) *n.* **Ju·lio** ('xuljo). 1876–1942, Spanish sculptor: one of the first to create abstract geometric forms with soldered iron.

goo (guː) *n. Informal.* **1.** a sticky or viscous substance. **2.** coy or sentimental language or ideas. [C20: of uncertain origin]

goo·ber *or* **goo·ber pea** ('guːbə) *n.* another name for **peanut** (sense 1). [C19: of African (Angolan) origin; related to Kongo *nguba*]

good (gʊd) *adj.* **bet·ter, best. 1.** having admirable, pleasing, superior, or positive qualities; not negative, bad, or mediocre: *a good idea; a good teacher.* **2. a.** morally excellent or admirable; virtuous; righteous: *a good man.* **b.** (*as collective n.* preceded by *the*): *the good.* **3.** suitable or efficient for a purpose: *a good secretary; a good winter coat.* **4.** beneficial or advantageous: *vegetables are good for you.* **5.** not ruined or decayed; sound or whole: *the meat is still good.* **6.** kindly or approving: *you are good to him.* **7.** right or acceptable: *your qualifications are good for the job.* **8.** rich and fertile: *good land.* **9.** valid or genuine: *I would not do this without good reason.* **10.** honourable or held in high esteem: *a good family.* **11.** commercially or financially secure, sound, or safe: *good securities; a good investment.* **12.** (of a draft, etc.) drawn for a stated sum. **13.** (of debts) expected to be fully paid. **14.** clever, competent, or talented: *he's good at science.* **15.** obedient or well-behaved: *a good dog.* **16.** reliable, safe, or recommended: *a good make of clothes.* **17.** affording material pleasure or indulgence: *the good things in life; the good life.* **18.** having a well-proportioned, beautiful, or generally fine appearance: *a good figure; a good complexion.* **19.** complete; full: *I took a good ten minutes to reach the house.* **20.** propitious; opportune: *a good time to ask the manager for a rise.* **21.** satisfying or gratifying: *a good rest.* **22.** comfortable: *did you have a good night?* **23.** newest or of the best quality: *to keep the good plates for important guests.* **24.** fairly large, extensive, or long: *a good distance away.* **25.** sufficient; ample: *we have a good supply of food.* **26.** *U.S.* (of meat) of the third government grade, above *standard* and below *choice.* **27.** serious or intellectual: *good music.* **28.** used in a traditional description: *the good ship "Venus."* **29.** used in polite or patronizing phrases or to express anger (often intended ironically): *how is your good lady?; look here, my good man!* **30. a good one. a.** an unbelievable assertion. **b.** a very funny joke. **31. as good as.** virtually; practically: *it's as good as finished.* **32. be as** *or* **so good as to.** would you please. **33. come good.** *Austral. informal.* to succeed, esp. after a setback. **34. good and.** *Informal.* (intensifier): *good and mad.* **35.** (intensifier; used in mild oaths): *good grief! good heavens!* ~*interj.* **36.** an exclamation of approval, agreement, pleasure, etc. ~*n.* **37.** moral or material advantage or use; benefit or profit: *for the good of our workers; what is the good of worrying?* **38.** positive moral qualities; goodness; virtue; righteousness; piety. **39.** (*sometimes cap.*) the force that controls or effects positive moral qualities or virtue: *Good at work in the world.* **40.** a good thing. **41.** *Economics.* a commodity or service that satisfies a human need. **42. for good (and all).** forever; permanently: *I have left them for good.* **43. make good. a.** to recompense or repair damage or injury. **b.** to be successful. **c.** to demonstrate or prove the truth of (a statement or accusation). **d.** to secure and retain (a position). **e.** to effect or fulfil (something intended or promised). **44. good on you.** *Chiefly Austral.* well done, well said, etc.: a term of congratulation. ~See also **goods.** [Old English *gōd;* related to Old Norse *gōthr,* Old High German *guot* good] —'**good·ish** *adj.*

Usage. Careful speakers and writers of English do not use *good* and *bad* as adverbs: *she dances well* (not *good*); *he sings really badly* (not *really bad*).

good af·ter·noon *sentence substitute.* a conventional expression of greeting or farewell used in the afternoon.

good ar·vo ('ɑːvəʊ) *sentence substitute. Austral.* good afternoon.

Good Book *n.* a name for the **Bible**. Also called: **the Book.**

good·bye (ˌgʊd'baɪ) *sentence substitute.* **1.** farewell: a conventional expression used at leave-taking or parting with people and at the loss or rejection of things or ideas. ~*n.* **2.** a leave-taking; parting: *they prolonged their goodbyes for a few more minutes.* **3.** a farewell: *they said goodbyes to each other.* [C16: contraction of *God be with ye*]

good day *sentence substitute.* a conventional expression of greeting or farewell used during the day.

good eve·ning *sentence substitute.* a conventional expression of greeting or farewell used in the evening.

good-for-noth·ing *n.* **1.** an irresponsible or worthless person. ~*adj.* **2.** irresponsible; worthless.

Good Fri·day *n.* the Friday before Easter, observed as a commemoration of the Crucifixion of Jesus.

good hair *n. Caribbean.* hair showing evidence of some European strain in a person's blood.

Good Hope *n.* **Cape of.** See **Cape of Good Hope.**

good-hu·moured *adj.* being in or expressing a pleasant, tolerant, and kindly state of mind. —ˌ**good-'hu·moured·ly** *adv.* —ˌ**good-'hu·moured·ness** *n.*

good·ies ('gʊdɪz) *pl. n.* **1.** any food or foods considered a special delight. **2.** a choice selection of an item or collection: *I have some goodies from my stamp collection here.*

Good King Hen·ry *n.* a weedy chenopodiaceous plant, *Chenopodium bonus-henricus,* of N Europe, W Asia, and North America, having arrow-shaped leaves and clusters of small green flowers.

good-look·er *n.* a handsome or pretty person.

good-look·ing *adj.* handsome or pretty.

good·ly ('gʊdlɪ) *adj.* **·li·er, ·li·est. 1.** considerable: *a goodly amount of money.* **2.** attractive, pleasing, or fine: *a goodly man.* —'**good·li·ness** *n.*

good·man ('gʊdmən) *n., pl.* **·men.** *Archaic.* **1.** a husband. **2.** a man not of gentle birth: used as a title. **3.** a master of a household.

Good·man ('gʊdmən) *n.* **Ben·ny.** born 1909, U.S. jazz clarinettist and bandleader, whose treatment of popular songs created the jazz idiom known as swing.

good morn·ing *sentence substitute.* a conventional expression of greeting or farewell used in the morning.

good-na·tured *adj.* of a tolerant and kindly disposition. —ˌ**good-'na·tured·ly** *adv.* —ˌ**good-'na·tured·ness** *n.*

good·ness ('gʊdnɪs) *n.* **1.** the state or quality of being good. **2.** generosity; kindness. **3.** moral excellence; piety; virtue. ~*interj.* **4.** a euphemism for **God:** used as an exclamation of surprise (often in phrases such as **goodness knows! thank goodness!**).

good·ness of fit *n. Statistics.* the extent to which observed sample values of a variable approximate to values derived from a theoretical density.

good night *sentence substitute.* a conventional expression of farewell, or, rarely, of greeting, used in the late afternoon, the evening, or at night, esp. when departing to bed.

good-oh *or* **good-o** ('gʊdəʊ) *interj. Brit. informal.* an exclamation of pleasure, agreement, approval, etc.

good oil *n.* (usually preceded by *the*) *Austral. slang.* true or reliable facts, information, etc.

good peo·ple *pl. n.* **the.** *Informal.* fairies.

good ques·tion *n.* a question that is hard to answer immediately.

goods (gʊdz) *pl. n.* **1.** possessions and personal property. **2.** (*sometimes sing.*) *Economics.* commodities that are tangible, usually movable, and generally not consumed at the same time as they are produced. Compare **services. 3.** articles of commerce; merchandise. **4.** *Chiefly Brit.* **a.** merchandise when transported, esp. by rail; freight. **b.** (*as modifier*): *a goods train.* **5.** *Slang.* that which is expected: *to deliver the goods.* **6. the goods.** *Slang.* the real thing. **7.** *Slang.* a person, esp. a woman (esp. in the phrase **a piece of goods**). **8.** *U.S. slang.* incriminating evidence (esp. in the phrase: **have the goods on someone**).

Good Sa·mar·i·tan *n.* **1.** *New Testament.* a figure in one of Christ's parables (Luke 10:30–37) who is an example of compassion towards those in distress. **2.** a kindly person who helps another in difficulty or distress.

goods and chat·tels *pl. n.* any property that is not freehold, usually limited to include only moveable property.

Good Shep·herd *n. New Testament.* a title given to Jesus Christ in John 10:11–12.

good-sized *adj.* quite large.

good sort *n. Austral. informal.* an agreeable or attractive woman.

good-tem·pered *adj.* of a kindly and generous disposition.

good-time *adj.* (of a person) wildly seeking pleasure.

good turn *n.* a helpful and friendly act; good deed; favour.

good·wife ('gʊdˌwaɪf) *n., pl.* **·wives.** *Archaic.* **1.** the mistress of a household. **2.** a woman not of gentle birth: used as a title.

good will *n.* **1.** benevolence; kindliness. **2.** willingness or acquiescence. **3.** *Accounting.* an intangible asset taken into account in assessing the value of an enterprise and reflecting its commercial reputation, customer connections, etc.

Good·win Sands ('gʊdwɪn) *pl. n.* a dangerous stretch of shoals at the entrance to the Strait of Dover: separated from the E coast of Kent by the Downs roadstead.

good·y[1] ('gʊdɪ) *interj.* **1.** a child's exclamation of pleasure and approval. ~*n., pl.* **good·ies. 2.** short for **goody-goody. 3.** *Informal.* the hero in a film, book, etc.

good·y[2] ('gʊdɪ) *n., pl.* **good·ies.** *Archaic, literary.* a married woman of low rank: used as a title: *Goody Two-Shoes.* [C16: shortened from GOODWIFE]

Good·year ('gʊdˌjɪə) *n.* **Charles.** 1800–60, U.S. inventor of vulcanized rubber.

good·y-good·y *n., pl.* **-good·ies. 1.** *Informal.* a smugly virtuous or sanctimonious person. ~*adj.* **2.** smug and sanctimonious.

goo·ey ('guːɪ) *adj.* **goo·i·er, goo·i·est.** *Informal.* **1.** sticky, soft, and often sweet. **2.** oversweet and sentimental.

goof (guːf) *Informal.* ~*n.* **1.** a foolish error or mistake. **2.** a stupid person. ~*vb.* **3.** to bungle (something); botch. **4.** (*intr.;* often foll. by *about* or *around*) to fool (around); mess (about). **5.** (*tr.*) to dope with drugs. [C20: probably from (dialect) *goff* simpleton, from Old French *goffe* clumsy, from Italian *goffo,* of obscure origin]

goof·ball ('guːfˌbɔːl) *n. U.S. slang.* a barbiturate sleeping pill.

go off *vb.* (*intr.*) **1.** (*adv.*) (of power, a water supply, etc.) to cease to be available, running, or functioning: *the lights suddenly went off.* **2.** (*adv.*) to be discharged or activated; explode. **3.** (*adv.*) to occur as specified: *the meeting went off well.* **4.** to leave (a place): *the actors went off stage.* **5.** (*adv.*) (of a sensation) to gradually cease to be felt or perceived. **6.** (*adv.*) to fall asleep. **7.** (*prep.*) to become mad or crazy (esp. in the phrases **go off one's rocker** *or* **head**). **8.** (*adv.*) to enter a specified state or condition: *she went off into hysterics.* **9.** (*adv.;* foll. by *with*) to abscond (with). **10.** (*adv.*) (of concrete, mortar, etc.) to harden. **11.** (*adv.*) *Brit. informal.* (of food, etc.) to become stale or rotten. **12.** (*prep.*) *Brit. informal.* to cease to like: *she went off him after their marriage.* **13.** (*adv.*) *Taboo slang.* to have an orgasm.

goof·y ('guːfɪ) *adj.* **goof·i·er, goof·i·est.** *Informal.* **1.** foolish; silly; stupid. **2.** *Brit.* (of teeth) sticking out; protruding. —'**goof·i·ly** *adv.* —'**goof·i·ness** *n.*

goog·ly ('guːglɪ) *n., pl.* **·lies.** *Cricket.* an off break bowled with a leg break action. [C20: Australian, of unknown origin]

goo·gol ('guːgɒl, -gᵊl) *n.* the number represented as one followed by 100 zeros (10^{100}). [C20: coined by E. Kasner (1878–1955), American mathematician]

goo·gol·plex ('guːgɒlˌplɛks, -gᵊl-) *n.* the number represented as one followed by a googol (10^{100}) of zeros. [C20: from GOOGOL + (DU)PLEX]

gook (gʊk, guːk) *n. U.S.* **1.** *Slang.* a derogatory word for a person from a Far Eastern country. **2.** *Informal.* a messy sticky substance; muck. [C20: of uncertain origin]

Goole (guːl) *n.* an inland port in NE England, in Humberside at the confluence of the Ouse and Don Rivers, 75 km (47 miles) from the North Sea. Pop.: 18 066 (1971).

goon (guːn) *n.* **1.** a stupid or deliberately foolish person. **2.** *U.S. informal.* a thug hired to commit acts of violence or intimidation, esp. in an industrial dispute. [C20: partly from dialect *gooney* fool, partly after the character Alice the *Goon,* created by E. C. Segar (1894–1938), American cartoonist]

go on *vb.* (*intr., mostly adv.*) **1.** to continue or proceed. **2.** to happen or take place: *there's something peculiar going on here.* **3.** (of power, water supply, etc.) to start running or functioning. **4.** (*prep.*) to mount or board and ride on, esp. as a treat: *children love to go on donkeys at the seaside.* **5.** *Theatre.* to make an entrance on stage. **6.** to act or behave: *he goes on as though he's rich.* **7.** to talk excessively; chatter. **8.** to continue talking, esp. after a short pause: *"When I am Prime Minister," he went on, "we shall abolish taxes."* **9.** to criticize or nag: *stop going on at me all the time!* **10.** (*prep.*) to use as a basis for further thought or action: *the police had no evidence at all to go on in the murder case.* **11.** (often foll. by *for*) *Brit.* to approach (a time, age, amount, etc.): *he's going on for his hundredth birthday.* **12.** *Cricket.* to start to bowl. **13.** to take one's turn. **14.** (of clothes) to be capable of being put on. **15. go much on.** (*used with a negative*) *Brit.* to care for; like. **16. something to go on** *or* **to be going on with.** something that is adequate for the present time. ~*interj.* **17.** I don't believe what you're saying.

goo·ney bird ('guːnɪ) *n.* an informal name for **albatross,** esp. the black-footed albatross (*Diomedea nigripes*). [C19 *gony* (originally sailors' slang), probably from dialect *gooney* fool, of obscure origin; compare GOON]

goop (guːp) *n. U.S. slang.* a rude or ill-mannered person. [C20: coined by G. Burgess (1866–1951), American humorist] —'**goop·y** *adj.*

goos·an·der (guː'sændə) *n.* a common merganser (a duck), *Mergus merganser,* of Europe and North America, having a dark head and white body in the male. [C17: probably from GOOSE[1] + Old Norse *önd* (genitive *andar*) duck]

goose[1] (guːs) *n., pl.* **geese. 1.** any of various web-footed long-necked birds of the family *Anatidae:* order *Anseriformes.* They are typically larger and less aquatic than ducks and are gregarious and migratory. See also **brent, barnacle goose, greylag, snow goose. 2.** the female of such a bird, as opposed to the male (gander). **3.** *Informal.* a silly person. **4.** *pl.* **goos·es.** a pressing iron with a long curving handle, used esp. by tailors. **5.** the flesh of the goose, used as food. **6. all his geese are swans.** he constantly exaggerates the importance of a person or thing. **7. cook one's goose.** *Informal.* to spoil one's chances or plans completely. **8. kill the goose that lays the golden eggs.** to sacrifice future benefits for the sake of momentary present needs. [Old English *gōs;* related to Old Norse *gās,* Old High German *gans,* Old Irish *gēiss* swan, Greek *khēn,* Sanskrit *hainsas*]

goose[2] (gu:s) *U.S. slang.* ~*vb.* **1.** (*tr.*) to prod (a person) playfully in the behind. ~*n., pl.* **goos·es. 2.** a playful prod in the behind. [C19: from GOOSE[1], probably from a comparison with the jabbing of a goose's bill]

goose bar+na+cle *n.* any barnacle of the genus *Lepas,* living attached by a stalk to pieces of wood, having long feathery appendages (cirri) and flattened shells.

goose+ber·ry ('gʊzbərɪ, -brɪ) *n., pl.* **·ries. 1.** a Eurasian shrub, *Ribes uva-crispa* (or *R. grossularia*), having greenish, purple-tinged flowers and ovoid yellow-green or red-purple berries: family *Grossulariaceae.* See also **currant** (sense 2). **2. a.** the berry of this plant. **b.** (*as modifier*): *gooseberry jam.* **3.** *Brit. informal.* an unwanted single person in a group of couples, esp. a third person with a couple (often in the phrase **play gooseberry**). **4. Cape gooseberry.** a tropical American solanaceous plant, *Physalis peruviana,* naturalized in southern Africa, having yellow flowers and edible yellow berries. See also **ground cherry. 5. Chinese gooseberry.** another name for **kiwi** (sense 2).

goose+ber·ry bush *n.* **1.** See **gooseberry** (sense 1). **2. under a gooseberry bush.** used humorously in answering children's questions regarding their birth.

goose+fish ('gu:sˌfɪʃ) *n., pl.* **+fish** *or* **+fish·es.** *U.S.* another name for **monkfish** (sense 1).

goose flesh *n.* the bumpy condition of the skin induced by cold, fear, etc., caused by contraction of the muscles at the base of the hair follicles with consequent erection of papillae. Also called: **goose bumps, goose pimples, goose skin.**

goose+foot ('gu:sˌfʊt) *n., pl.* **+foots.** any typically weedy chenopodiaceous plant of the genus *Chenopodium,* having small greenish flowers and leaves shaped like a goose's foot. See also **Good King Henry, fat hen.**

goose+gog ('gʊzgɒg) *or* **goose+gob** *n. Brit.* a dialect word for **gooseberry.** [from *goose* in GOOSEBERRY + *gog,* variant of GOB[1]]

goose+grass ('gu:sˌgrɑ:s) *n.* another name for **cleavers.**

goose+neck ('gu:sˌnɛk) *n.* **1.** *Nautical.* a pivot between the forward end of a boom and a mast, to allow the boom to swing freely. **2.** something in the form of a neck of a goose. —**'goose+ˌnecked** *adj.*

goose step *n.* **1.** a military march step in which the leg is swung rigidly to an exaggerated height, esp. as in the German army in the Third Reich. ~*vb.* **goose-step, -steps, -step·ping, -stepped. 2.** (*intr.*) to march in goose step.

goos·y *or* **goos+ey** ('gu:sɪ) *adj.* **goos·i·er, goos·i·est. 1.** of or like a goose. **2.** having goose flesh. **3.** silly and foolish. —**'goos·i·ness** *n.*

go out *vb.* (*intr., adv.*) **1.** to depart from a room, house, country, etc. **2.** to cease to illuminate, burn, or function: *the fire has gone out.* **3.** to cease to be fashionable or popular: *that style went out ages ago!* **4.** to become unconscious or fall asleep: *she went out like a light.* **5.** (of a broadcast) to be transmitted. **6.** to go to entertainments, social functions, etc. **7.** (usually foll. by *with* or *together*) to associate (with a person of the opposite sex) regularly; date. **8.** (of workers) to begin to strike. **9.** (foll. by *to*) to be extended (to): *our sympathy went out to her on the death of her sister.* **10.** *Card games, etc.* to get rid of the last card, token, etc., in one's hand. **11. go all out.** to make a great effort to achieve or obtain something: *he went all out to pass the exam.*

go o·ver *vb.* (*intr.*) **1.** to be received in a specified manner: *the concert went over very well.* **2.** (*prep.*) Also: **go through.** to examine and revise as necessary: *he went over the accounts.* **3.** (*prep.*) Also: **go through.** to clean: *she went over the room before her mother came.* **4.** (*prep.*) to check and repair: *can you go over my car please?* **5.** (*prep.*) Also: **go through.** to rehearse: *I'll go over my lines before the play.* **6.** (*adv.;* foll. by *to*) **a.** to change (to a different practice or system): *will Britain ever go over to driving on the right?* **b.** to change one's allegiances. **7.** (*prep.*) *Slang.* to do physical violence to: *they went over him with an iron bar.*

G.O.P. *U.S. abbrev. for* Grand Old Party.

go+pak ('gəʊˌpæk) *n.* a spectacular high-leaping Russian peasant dance for men. [from Russian, from Ukrainian *hopak,* from *hop!* a cry in the dance, from German *hopp!*]

go+pher ('gəʊfə) *n.* **1.** Also called: **pocket gopher.** any burrowing rodent of the family *Geomyidae,* of North and Central America, having a thickset body, short legs, and cheek pouches. **2.** another name for **ground squirrel. 3.** any burrowing tortoise of the genus *Gopherus,* of SE North America. **4. gopher snake.** another name for **bull snake.** [C19: shortened from earlier *megopher* or *magopher,* of obscure origin]

go+pher wood *n.* the wood used in the construction of Noah's ark, thought to be a type of cypress (Genesis 6:14). [from Hebrew *gōpher*]

go·pher+wood ('gəʊfəˌwʊd) *n. U.S.* another name for **yellowwood** (sense 1).

Go+rakh+pur ('gɔ:rəkˌpʊə) *n.* a city in N India, in SE Uttar Pradesh: formerly an important Muslim garrison. Pop.: 230 911 (1971).

go+ral ('gɔ:rəl) *n.* a small goat antelope, *Naemorhedus goral,* inhabiting mountainous regions of S Asia. It has a yellowish-grey and black coat and small conical horns. [C19: from Hindi, probably of Sanskrit origin]

Gor+bals ('gɔ:bəlz) *n.* **the.** a suburb of Glasgow, formerly known for its slums.

gor+bli+mey (gɔ:'blaɪmɪ) *interj.* a variant spelling of **cor blimey.**

gor+cock ('gɔ:ˌkɒk) *n.* the male of the red grouse. [C17: *gor-* (of unknown origin) + COCK[1]]

Gor+di·an knot ('gɔ:dɪən) *n.* **1.** (in Greek legend) a complicated knot, tied by King Gordius of Phrygia, that Alexander the Great cut with a sword. **2.** a complicated and intricate problem (esp. in the phrase **cut the Gordian knot**).

Gor·don ('gɔ:dᵊn) *n.* **1. Charles George,** known as *Chinese Gordon.* 1833–85, British general and administrator. He helped to crush the Taiping rebellion (1863–64), and was governor of the Sudan (1877–80), returning in 1884 to aid Egyptian forces against the Mahdi. He was killed in the siege of Khartoum. **2.** Lord **George.** 1751–93, English religious agitator. He led the Protestant opposition to legislation relieving Roman Catholics of certain disabilities, which culminated in the Gordon riots (1780). **3. George Ham·il·ton.** See (4th Earl of) **Aberdeen.**

Gor+don set+ter *n.* a breed of setter originating in Scotland, with a black-and-tan coat. [C19: named after Alexander *Gordon,* (1743–1827), Scottish nobleman who promoted this breed]

gore[1] (gɔ:) *n.* **1.** blood shed from a wound, esp. when coagulated. **2.** *Informal.* killing, fighting, etc. [Old English *gor* dirt; related to Old Norse *gor* half-digested food, Middle Low German *göre,* Dutch *goor*]

gore[2] (gɔ:) *vb.* (*tr.*) (of an animal, such as a bull) to pierce or stab (a person or another animal) with a horn or tusk. [C16: probably from Old English *gār* spear]

gore[3] (gɔ:) *n.* **1.** a tapering or triangular piece of material used in making a shaped skirt, umbrella, etc. **2.** a similarly shaped piece, esp. of land. ~*vb.* **3.** (*tr.*) to make into or with a gore or gores. [Old English *gāra;* related to Old Norse *geiri* gore, Old High German *gēro*]

go+reng pi+sang ('gɔ:rɛŋ 'pi:sæŋ) *n.* (in Malaysia) a dish consisting of banana fritters. [Malay, from *goreng* fry + *pisang* banana]

gorge (gɔ:dʒ) *n.* **1.** a deep ravine, esp. one through which a river runs. **2.** the contents of the stomach. **3.** feelings of disgust or resentment (esp. in the phrase **one's gorge rises**). **4.** an obstructing mass: *an ice gorge.* **5.** *Fortifications.* a narrow passage at the back of an outwork. **6.** *Archaic.* the throat or gullet. ~*vb. also* **en+gorge. 7.** (*intr.*) *Falconry.* (of hawks) to eat until the crop is completely full. **8.** to swallow (food) ravenously. **9.** (*tr.*) to stuff (oneself) with food. [C14: from Old French *gorger* to stuff, from *gorge* throat, from Late Latin *gurga,* modification of Latin *gurges* whirlpool] —**'gorge+a·ble** *adj.* —**gorg+ed+ly** ('gɔ:dʒɪdlɪ) *adv.* —**'gorg+er** *n.*

gor+geous ('gɔ:dʒəs) *adj.* **1.** strikingly beautiful or magnificent: *gorgeous array; a gorgeous girl.* **2.** *Informal.* extremely pleasing, fine, or good: *gorgeous weather.* [C15: from Old French *gorgias* elegant, from *gorgias* wimple, from *gorge;* see GORGE] —**'gor+geous+ly** *adv.* —**'gor+geous+ness** *n.*

gor+ger+in ('gɔ:dʒərɪn) *n. Architect.* another name for **necking.** [C17: from French, from *gorge* throat; see GORGE]

gor+get ('gɔ:dʒɪt) *n.* **1.** a collar-like piece of armour worn to protect the throat. **2.** a part of a wimple worn by women to cover the throat and chest, esp. in the 14th century. **3.** a band of distinctive colour on the throat of an animal, esp. a bird. [C15: from Old French, from *gorge;* see GORGE] —**'gor+get+ed** *adj.*

Gor·gi·as ('gɔ:dʒɪəs) *n.* ?485–?380 B.C., Greek sophist and rhetorician, subject of a dialogue by Plato.

Gor+gon ('gɔ:gən) *n.* **1.** *Greek myth.* any of three winged monstrous sisters, Stheno, Euryale, and Medusa, who had live snakes for hair, huge teeth, and brazen claws. **2.** (*often not cap.*) *Informal.* a fierce or unpleasant woman. [via Latin *Gorgō* from Greek, from *gorgos* terrible]

gor+go+nei+on (ˌgɔ:gə'ni:ɒn) *n., pl.* **+nei·a** (-'ni:ə). a representation of a Gorgon's head, esp. Medusa's. [C19: from Greek, from *gorgoneios* of a GORGON]

gor+go+ni·an (gɔ:'gəʊnɪən) *n.* **1.** any coral of the order *Gorgonacea,* having a horny or calcareous branching skeleton: includes the sea fans and red corals. ~*adj.* **2.** of, relating to, or belonging to the *Gorgonacea.*

Gor+go+ni·an (gɔ:'gəʊnɪən) *adj.* of or resembling a Gorgon.

Gor+gon+zo+la *or* **Gor+gon+zo+la cheese** (ˌgɔ:gən'zəʊlə) *n.* a semihard blue-veined cheese of sharp flavour, made from pressed milk. [C19: named after *Gorgonzola,* Italian town where it originated]

Go+ri+ca ('gɔritsa) *n.* the Serbo-Croatian name for **Gorizia.**

go+ril+la (gə'rɪlə) *n.* **1.** the largest anthropoid ape, *Gorilla gorilla,* inhabiting the forests of central W Africa. It is stocky and massive, with a short muzzle and coarse dark hair. **2.** *Informal.* a large, strong, and brutal-looking man. [C19: New Latin, from Greek *Gorillai,* an African tribe renowned for their hirsute appearance] —**go·'ril·la-ˌlike** *adj.* —**go+'ril·li·an** *or* **go+ril+line** (gə'rɪlaɪn) *adj.* —**go+'ril+loid** *adj.*

Gö·ring *or* **Goe·ring** (*German* 'gø:rɪŋ) *n.* **Her·mann Wil·helm** ('hɛrman 'vɪlhɛlm). 1893–1946, German Nazi leader and field marshal. He commanded Hitler's storm troops (1923) and as Prussian prime minister and German commissioner for aviation (1933–45) he founded the Gestapo and mobilized Germany for war. Sentenced to death at Nuremberg, he committed suicide.

Go·ri+zia (*Italian* go'rittsja) *n.* a city in NE Italy, in Friuli-Venezia Giulia, on the Isonzo River: cultural centre under the Hapsburgs. Pop.: 42 980 (1971). German name: **Görz.** Serbo-Croatian name: **Gorica.**

Gor+ki[1] *or* **Gor+ky** (*Russian* 'gɔrjkij) *n.* an industrial city and port in the central Soviet Union, at the confluence of the Volga and Oka Rivers: situated on the Volga route from the Baltic to central Asia; birthplace of Maxim Gorki. Pop.: 1 283 000 (1975 est.). Former name (until 1932): **Nizhni Novgorod.**

Gor·ki[2] *or* **Gor·ky** (*Russian* 'gɔrjkij) *n.* **Max·im** (mak'sim), pen name of *Aleksey Maximovich Peshkov.* 1868–1936, Russian novelist, dramatist, and short-story writer, noted for his depiction of the outcasts of society. His works include the play *The Lower Depths* (1902), the novel *Mother* (1907), and an autobiographical trilogy (1913–23).

Gor·ky ('gɔːkɪ) *n.* **Ar·shile** ('ɑːʃɪl). 1904–48, U.S. abstract expressionist painter. Influenced by Picasso and Miró, his style is characterized by fluid lines and resonant colours.

Gör·litz (*German* 'gœrlɪts) *n.* a city in SE East Germany, on the Neisse River: divided in 1945, the area on the E bank of the river becoming the Polish town of **Zgorzelec.** Pop.: 86 421 (1972 est.).

Gor·lov·ka (*Russian* 'gɔrləfkə) *n.* a city in the SW Soviet Union, in the SE Ukrainian SSR in the centre of the Donets basin: a major coal-mining centre. Pop.: 342 000 (1975 est.).

gor·mand ('gɔːmənd) *n.* a less common spelling of **gourmand.**

gor·mand·ize *or* **gor·mand·ise** *vb.* ('gɔːmən,daɪz). **1.** to eat (food) greedily and voraciously. ~*n.* ('gɔːmən,diːz). **2.** a less common spelling of **gourmandise.** —'**gor·mand·,iz·er** *or* '**gor·mand·,is·er** *n.*

gorm·less ('gɔːmlɪs) *adj. Brit. informal.* stupid; dull. [C19: variant of C18 *gaumless* from dialect *gome,* from Old English *gom, gome,* from Old Norse *gaumr* heed]

Gor·no-Al·tai Au·ton·o·mous Re·gion ('gɔːnəʊ æl'taɪ, 'æltaɪ) *n.* an administrative division of the S central Soviet Union: mountainous, rising over 4350 m (14 500 ft.) in the Altai Mountains of the south. Capital: Gorno-Altaisk. Pop.: 168 261 (1970). Area: 92 600 sq. km (35 740 sq. miles).

Gor·no-Ba·dakh·shan Au·ton·o·mous Re·gion ('gɔːnəʊ bə'dækʃɑːn) *n.* an administrative division of the S Soviet Union, in the Tadzhik SSR: generally mountainous and inaccessible. Capital: Khorog. Pop.: 97 796 (1970). Area: 63 700 sq. km (24 590 sq. miles).

gorse (gɔːs) *n.* any evergreen shrub of the papilionaceous genus *Ulex,* esp. the European species *U. europeaus,* which has yellow flowers and thick green spines instead of leaves. Also called: **furze, whin.** [Old English *gors;* related to Old Irish *garb* rough, Latin *horrēre* to bristle, Old High German *gersta* barley, Greek *khēr* hedgehog] —'**gors·y** *adj.*

Gor·sedd ('gɔːsɛð) *n.* (in Wales) the bardic institution associated with the eisteddfod, esp. a meeting of bards and druids held daily before the eisteddfod. [from Welsh, literally: throne]

Gor·ton ('gɔːtᵊn) *n.* **John Grey.** born 1911, Australian statesman; prime minister (1968–71).

gor·y ('gɔːrɪ) *adj.* **gor·i·er, gor·i·est. 1.** horrific or bloodthirsty: *a gory story.* **2.** involving bloodshed and killing: *a gory battle.* **3.** covered in gore. —'**gor·i·ly** *adv.* —'**gor·i·ness** *n.*

Görz (gœrts) *n.* the German name for **Gorizia.**

gosh (gɒʃ) *interj.* an exclamation of mild surprise or wonder. [C18: euphemistic for *God,* as in *by gosh!*]

gos·hawk ('gɒs,hɔːk) *n.* a large hawk, *Accipiter gentilis,* of Europe, Asia, and North America, having a bluish-grey back and wings and paler underparts: used in falconry. [Old English *gōshafoc;* see GOOSE[1], HAWK]

Go·shen ('gəʊʃən) *n.* **1.** a region of ancient Egypt, east of the Nile delta: granted to Jacob and his descendants by the king of Egypt and inhabited by them until the Exodus (Genesis 45:10). **2.** a place of comfort and plenty.

gos·ling ('gɒzlɪŋ) *n.* **1.** a young goose. **2.** an inexperienced or youthful person. [C15: from Old Norse *gæslingr;* related to Danish *gäsling;* see GOOSE[1], -LING[1]]

go-slow *n.* **1.** *Brit.* **a.** a deliberate slackening of the rate of production by organized labour as a tactic in industrial conflict. **b.** (*as modifier*): *go-slow tactics.* U.S. equivalent: **slowdown.** ~*vb.* **go slow. 2.** (*intr.*) to work deliberately slowly as a tactic in industrial conflict.

gos·pel ('gɒspᵊl) *n.* **1.** Also called: **gospel truth.** an unquestionable truth: *to take someone's word as gospel.* **2.** a doctrine maintained to be of great importance. **3.** Black religious music originating in the churches of the Southern states of the United States. **4.** the message or doctrine of a religious teacher. **5. a.** the story of Christ's life and teachings as narrated in the Gospels. **b.** the good news of salvation in Jesus Christ. **c.** (*as modifier*): *the gospel story.* [Old English *gōdspell,* from *gōd* GOOD + *spell* message; see SPELL[2]; compare Old Norse *guthspjall,* Old High German *guotspell*]

Gos·pel ('gɒspᵊl) *n.* **1.** any of the first four books of the New Testament, namely Matthew, Mark, Luke, and John. **2.** a reading from one of these in a religious service.

gos·pel·ler ('gɒspələ) *n.* **1.** a person who reads or chants the Gospel in a religious service. **2.** a person who professes to preach a gospel held exclusively by him and others of a like mind.

gos·pel oath an oath sworn on the Gospels.

Gos·plan ('gɒs,plæn) *n.* the state planning commission of the Soviet Union or any of its constituent republics: responsible for coordination and development of the economy, social services, etc. [C20: from Russian *Gos*(*udarstvennaya*) *Plan*(*ovaya Comissiya*) State Planning Committee]

gos·po·din *Russian.* (gəspa'din) *n., pl.* **·po·da** (-pa'da). a Russian title of address, often indicating respect, equivalent to *sir* when used alone or to *Mr.* when before a name. [literally: lord]

Gos·port ('gɒs,pɔːt) *n.* a town in S England, in Hampshire on Portsmouth harbour: naval base since the 16th century. Pop.: 75 947 (1971).

gos·sa·mer ('gɒsəmə) *n.* **1.** a gauze or silk fabric of the very finest texture. **2.** a filmy cobweb often seen on foliage or floating in the air. **3.** anything resembling gossamer in fineness or filminess. **4.** (*modifier*) made of or resembling gossamer: *gossamer wings.* [C14 (in the sense: a filmy cobweb): probably from *gos* GOOSE[1] + *somer* SUMMER[1]; the phrase refers to *St. Martin's summer,* a period in November when goose was traditionally eaten; from the prevalence of the cobweb in the autumn; compare German *Gänsemonat,* literally: goosemonth, used for November]

Gosse (gɒs) *n.* Sir **Ed·mund Wil·liam.** 1849–1928, English critic and poet, noted particularly for his autobiographical work *Father and Son* (1907).

gos·sip ('gɒsɪp) *n.* **1.** casual and idle chat: *to have a gossip with a friend.* **2.** a conversation involving malicious chatter or rumours about other people: *a gossip about the neighbours.* **3.** Also called: **gossipmonger.** a person who habitually talks about others, esp. maliciously. **4.** light easy communication: *to write a letter full of gossip.* **5.** *Archaic.* a close woman friend. ~*vb.* **6.** (*intr.;* often foll. by *about*) to talk casually or maliciously (about other people). [Old English *godsibb* godparent, from GOD + SIB; the term came to be applied to familiar friends, esp. a woman's female friends at the birth of a child, hence a person, esp. a woman, fond of light talk] —'**gos·sip·er** *n.* —'**gos·sip·ing·ly** *adv.* —'**gos·sip·y** *adj.*

gos·sip·mon·ger ('gɒsɪp,mʌŋgə) *n.* a spreader of rumours.

gos·soon (gɒ'suːn) *n. Irish.* a boy, esp. a servant boy. [C17: from Old French *garçon*]

gos·ter ('gɒstə) *vb.* (*intr.*) *Northern English dialect.* to laugh uncontrollably. [C18: from earlier *gauster,* from Middle English *galstre,* of obscure origin]

got (gɒt) *vb.* **1.** the past tense or past participle of **get. 2. have got. a.** to possess: *he has got three apples.* **b.** (*takes an infinitive*) used as an auxiliary to express compulsion felt to be imposed by or upon the speaker: *I've got to get a new coat.* **3. have got it badly.** *Informal.* to be infatuated.

Gö·ta (*Swedish* 'jøːta) *n.* a river in S Sweden, draining Lake Vänern and flowing south-southwest to the Kattegat: forms part of the **Göta Canal,** which links Göteborg in the west with Stockholm in the east. Length: 93 km (58 miles).

Go·ta·ma ('gəʊtəmə) *n.* the Pali form of the name **Gautama.**

Gö·te·borg (*Swedish* ,jœtə'bɔrj) *or* **Goth·en·burg** *n.* a port in SW Sweden, at the mouth of the Göta River: the largest port and second largest city in the country; developed through the Swedish East India Company and grew through Napoleon's continental blockade and with the opening of the Göta Canal (1832); university (1891). Pop.: 445 704 (1974 est.).

Goth (gɒθ) *n.* **1.** a member of an East Germanic people from Scandinavia who settled south of the Baltic early in the first millennium A.D. They moved on to the Ukrainian steppes and raided and later invaded many parts of the Roman Empire from the 3rd to the 5th century. See also **Ostrogoth, Visigoth. 2.** a rude or barbaric person.

Goth. *abbrev. for* Gothic.

Go·tha ('gəʊθə; *German* 'goːta) *n.* a town in SW East Germany, on the N edge of the Thuringian forest: capital of Saxe-Coburg-Gotha (1826–1918); noted for the *Almanach de Gotha* (a record of the royal and noble houses of Europe, first published in 1764). Pop.: 57 038 (1972 est.).

Goth·am *n.* **1.** ('gəʊtəm, 'gɒtəm). a village in N central England, in Nottinghamshire near Nottingham: renowned for the legend of its early inhabitants, the Wise Men of Gotham, who feigned stupidity in order to dissuade King John from residing in their neighbourhood. **2.** ('gɒθəm, 'gəʊθəm). a nickname for the city of **New York.**

Goth·en·burg ('gɒθən,bɜːg) *n.* the English name for **Göteborg.**

Goth·ic ('gɒθɪk) *adj.* **1.** denoting, relating to, or resembling the style of architecture that was used in W Europe from the 12th to the 16th centuries, characterized by the lancet arch, the ribbed vault, and the flying buttress. **2.** of or relating to the style of sculpture, painting, or other arts as practised in W Europe from the 12th to the 16th centuries. **3.** (*sometimes not cap.*) of or relating to a literary style characterized by gloom, the grotesque, and the supernatural, popular esp. in the late 18th century. **4.** of, relating to, or characteristic of the Goths or their language. **5.** (*sometimes not cap.*) primitive and barbarous in style, behaviour, etc. **6.** of or relating to the Middle Ages. ~*n.* **7.** Gothic architecture or art. **8.** the extinct language of the ancient Goths, known mainly from fragments of a translation of the Bible made in the 4th century by Bishop Wulfila. See also **East Germanic. 9.** Also called (esp. Brit): **black letter.** the family of heavy script typefaces in use from about the 15th to 18th centuries. —'**Goth·i·cal·ly** *adv.*

Goth·ic arch *n.* another name for **lancet arch.**

Goth·i·cism ('gɒθɪ,sɪzəm) *n.* **1.** conformity to, use of, or imitation of the Gothic style, esp. in architecture. **2.** crudeness of manner or style.

Goth·i·cize *or* **Goth·i·cise** ('gɒθɪ,saɪz) *vb.* (*tr.*) to make Gothic in style. —'**Goth·i·,ciz·er** *or* '**Goth·i·,cis·er** *n.*

go through *vb.* (*intr.*) **1.** (*adv.*) to be approved or accepted: *the amendment went through.* **2.** (*prep.*) to consume; exhaust: *we went through our supplies in a day; some men go through a pair of socks in no time.* **3.** (*prep.*) Also: **go over.** to examine and revise as necessary: *he went through the figures.* **4.** (*prep.*) to suffer: *she went through tremendous pain.* **5.** (*prep.*) Also: **go over.** to rehearse: *let's just go through the details again.* **6.** (*prep.*) Also: **go over.** to clean: *she went through the cupboards in the spring cleaning.* **7.** (*prep.*) to participate in: *she went* through the degree ceremony without getting too nervous. **8.** (*adv.*; foll by *with*) to bring to a successful conclusion, often by persistence. **9.** (*prep.*) (of a book) to be published in: *that book has gone through three printings this year alone.*

Got+land ('gɒtlənd; *Swedish* 'gɔtlant), **Goth+land,** *or* **Gott+land** *n.* an island in the Baltic Sea, off the SE coast of Sweden: important trading centre since the Bronze Age; long disputed between Sweden and Denmark, finally becoming Swedish in 1645; tourism and agriculture now important. Capital: Visby. Pop.: (including associated islands) 53 780 (1970). Area: 3140 sq. km (1225 sq. miles).

go to *vb.* (*intr., prep.*) **1.** to be awarded to: *the Nobel prize last year went to a Scot.* **2. go to it.** to tackle a task vigorously. ~*interj.* **3.** *Archaic.* an exclamation expressing surprise, encouragement, etc.

go to+geth+er *vb.* (*intr., adv.*) **1.** to be mutually suited; harmonize: *the colours go well together.* **2.** *Informal.* (of two people of opposite sex) to associate frequently with each other: *they had been going together for two years.*

got+ta ('gɒtə) *vb. Slang. contraction of* got to.

got+ten ('gɒtᵊn) *vb. U.S.* **1.** the past participle of **get. 2. have gotten.** (*not usually in the infinitive*) **a.** to have obtained: *he had gotten a car for his 21st birthday.* **b.** to have become: *I've gotten sick of your constant bickering.*

Göt+ter+däm+mer+ung (ˌgɒtə'dɛməˌrʊŋ; *German* ˌgœtər'dɛməˌrʊŋ) *n. German myth.* the twilight of the gods; their ultimate destruction in a battle with the forces of evil. Norse equivalent: **Ragnarök.**

Gott·fried von Strass+burg (*German* 'gɔtfri:t fɔn 'ʃtra:sbʊrk) *n.* early 13th-century German poet; author of the incomplete epic *Tristan and Isolde,* the version of the legend that served as the basis of Wagner's opera.

Göt+tin+gen ('gœtɪŋən) *n.* a city in central West Germany, in Lower Saxony; important member of the Hanseatic League (14th century); university, founded in 1734 by George II of England. Pop.: 120 435 (1974 est.).

Götz von Ber+lich+ing+en (*German* gœts fɔn 'bɛrlɪçɪŋən). See **Berlichingen.**

gou·ache (gʊ'ɑ:ʃ) *n.* **1.** Also called: **body colour.** a painting technique using opaque watercolour paint in which the pigments are bound with glue and the lighter tones contain white. **2.** the paint used in this technique. **3.** a painting done by this method. [C19: from French, from Italian *guazzo* puddle, from Latin *aquātiō* a watering place, from *aqua* water]

Gou+da ('gaʊdə; *Dutch* 'xɔuda:) *n.* **1.** a town in the W Netherlands, in South Holland province: important medieval cloth trade; famous for its cheese. Pop.: 47 920 (1973 est.). **2.** a large flat round Dutch cheese, mild and similar in taste to Edam.

gouge (gaʊdʒ) *vb.* (*mainly tr.*) **1.** (usually foll. by *out*) to scoop or force (something) out of its position, esp. with the fingers or a pointed instrument. **2.** (sometimes foll. by *out*) to cut (a hole or groove) in (something) with a sharp instrument or tool. **3.** *U.S. informal.* to extort from. **4.** (*intr.*) *Austral.* to dig for (opal). ~*n.* **5.** a type of chisel with a blade that has a concavo-convex section. **6.** a mark or groove made with, or as if with, a gouge. **7.** *Geology.* a fine deposit of rock fragments, esp. clay, occurring between the walls of a fault or mineral vein. **8.** *U.S. informal.* extortion; swindling. [C15: from French, from Late Latin *gulbia* a chisel, of Celtic origin] **—'goug+er** *n.*

gou+lash ('gu:læʃ) *n.* **1.** Also called: **Hungarian goulash.** a rich stew, originating in Hungary, made of beef, lamb, or veal highly seasoned with paprika. **2.** *Bridge.* a method of dealing in threes and fours without first shuffling the cards, to produce freak hands. [C19: from Hungarian *gulyás hus* herdsman's meat, from *gulya* herd]

Gould (gu:ld) *n.* **Ben·ja·min Ap·thorp.** 1824–96, U.S. astronomer: the first to use the telegraph to determine longtitudes; founded the *Astronomical Journal* (1849).

go un+der *vb.* (*intr., mainly adv.*) **1.** (*also prep.*) to sink below (a surface). **2.** to founder or drown. **3.** to be conquered or overwhelmed: *the firm went under in the economic crisis.*

Gou·nod ('gu:nəʊ; *French* gu'no) *n.* **Charles Fran·çois** (ʃarl frã'swa). 1818–93, French composer of the operas *Faust* (1859) and *Romeo and Juliet* (1867).

go up *vb.* (*intr., mainly adv.*) **1.** (*also prep.*) to move or lead to or as if to a higher place or level; rise; increase: *prices are always going up; the curtain goes up at eight o'clock; new buildings are going up all around us.* **2.** to be destroyed: *the house went up in flames.* **3.** *Brit.* to go or return (to college or university) at the beginning of a term or academic year.

gou+ra+mi ('gʊərəmɪ) *n., pl.* **+mi** *or* **+mis. 1.** a large SE Asian labyrinth fish, *Osphronemus goramy,* used for food and (when young) as an aquarium fish. **2.** any of various other labyrinth fishes, such as *Helostoma temmincki* (**kissing gourami**), many of which are brightly coloured and popular aquarium fishes. [from Malay *gurami*]

gourd (gʊəd) *n.* **1.** the fruit of any of various cucurbitaceous or similar plants, esp. the bottle gourd and some squashes, whose dried shells are used for ornament, drinking cups, etc. **2.** any plant that bears this fruit. See also **sour gourd, dishcloth gourd, calabash. 3.** a bottle or flask made from the dried shell of the bottle gourd. **4.** a small bottle shaped like a gourd. [C14: from Old French *gourde,* ultimately from Latin *cucurbita*] **—'gourd+ˌlike** *adj.* **—'gourd+ˌshaped** *adj.*

gourde (gʊəd) *n.* the standard monetary unit of Haiti, divided into 100 centimes. [C19: from French, feminine of *gourd* heavy, from Latin *gurdus* a stupid person]

gour+mand ('gʊəmənd; *French* gur'mã) *or* **gor+mand** *n.* a person devoted to eating and drinking, esp. to excess. [C15: from Old French *gourmant,* of uncertain origin] **—'gour+mand+ˌism** *n.*

gour+man+dise *or* **gour+man+dize** (ˌgɔ:mən'di:z) *n.* a love of and taste for good food.

gour+met ('gʊəmeɪ; *French* gur'mɛ) *n.* a person who cultivates a discriminating palate for the enjoyment of good food and drink. [C19: from French, from Old French *gromet* serving boy]

Gour·mont (*French* gur'mɔ̃) *n.* **Re·my de** (rə'mi də). 1858–1915, French symbolist critic and novelist.

gout (gaʊt) *n.* **1.** a metabolic disease characterized by painful inflammation of certain joints, esp. of the big toe and foot, caused by deposits of sodium urate in them. **2.** *Archaic.* a drop or splash, esp. of blood. [C13: from Old French *goute* gout (thought to result from drops of humours), from Latin *gutta* a drop] **—'gout·y** *adj.* **—'gout·i+ly** *adv.* **—'gout·i·ness** *n.*

goût *French.* (gu) *n.* taste or good taste.

gout+weed ('gaʊtˌwi:d) *n.* a widely naturalized Eurasian umbelliferous plant, *Aegopodium podagraria,* with white flowers and creeping underground stems. Also called: **bishop's weed, ground elder, herb Gerard.**

Gov. *or* **gov.** *abbrev. for:* **1.** government. **2.** governor.

gov+ern ('gʌvᵊn) *vb.* (*mainly tr.*) **1.** (*also intr.*) to direct and control the actions, affairs, policies, functions, etc., of (a political unit, organization, nation, etc.); rule. **2.** to exercise restraint over; regulate or direct: *to govern one's temper.* **3.** to be a predominant influence on (something); decide or determine (something): *his injury governed his decision to avoid sports.* **4.** to control the speed of an (engine, machine, etc.) using a governor. **5.** to control the rate of flow of (a fluid) by using an automatic valve. **6.** (of a word) to determine the inflection of (another word): *Latin nouns govern adjectives that modify them.* [C13: from Old French *gouverner,* from Latin *gubernāre* to steer, from Greek *kubernan*] **—'gov+ern+a·ble** *adj.* **—ˌgov+ern+a·'bil+i·ty** *or* **'gov+ern+a·ble+ness** *n.*

gov+ern+ance ('gʌvənəns) *n.* **1.** government, control, or authority. **2.** the action, manner, or system of governing.

gov+er+ness ('gʌvənɪs) *n.* a woman teacher employed in a private household to teach and train the children.

gov+ern+ment ('gʌvənmənt) *n.* **1.** the exercise of political authority over the actions, affairs, etc., of a political unit, people, etc., as well as the performance of certain functions for this unit or body; the action of governing; political rule and administration. **2.** the system or form by which a community, etc., is ruled: *tyrannical government.* **3. a.** the executive policy-making body of a political unit, community, etc.; ministry or administration: *yesterday we got a new government.* **b.** (*cap. when of a specific country*): *the British Government.* **4. a.** the state and its administration: *blame it on the government.* **b.** (*as modifier*): *a government agency.* **5.** regulation; direction. **6.** *Grammar.* the determination of the form of one word by another word. **—gov+ern+men+tal** (ˌgʌvən'mɛntᵊl) *adj.* **—ˌgov+ern+'men+tal+ly** *adv.*

gov+ern+ment is+sue *adj. Chiefly U.S.* supplied by a government or government agency.

gov+er+nor ('gʌvənə) *n.* **1.** a person who governs. **2.** the ruler or chief magistrate of a colony, province, etc. **3.** the representative of the Crown in a British colony. **4.** *Brit.* the senior administrator or head of a society, prison, etc. **5.** the chief executive of any state in the U.S. **6.** a device that controls the speed of an engine, esp. by regulating the supply of fuel, etc., either to limit the maximum speed or to maintain a constant speed. **7.** *Brit. informal.* a name or title of respect to a father, employer, etc.

gov+er+nor gen+er+al *n., pl.* **gov+er+nors gen+er+al** *or* **gov+er+nor gen+er+als. 1.** the representative of the Crown in a dominion of the Commonwealth or a British colony; vicegerent. **2.** *Brit.* a governor with jurisdiction or precedence over other governors. **—ˌgov·er·nor-'gen·er·al+ˌship** *n.*

gov+er+nor+ship ('gʌvənəˌʃɪp) *n.* the office, jurisdiction, or term of a governor.

Govt. *or* **govt.** *abbrev. for* government.

gow+an ('gaʊən) *n. Scot.* any of various yellow or white flowers growing in fields, esp. the common daisy. [C16: variant of *gollan,* probably of Scandinavian origin; compare Old Norse *gullin* golden] **—'gow+aned** *adj.* **—'gow+an·y** *adj.*

Gow·er[1] ('gaʊə) *n.* **John.** ?1330–1408, English poet, noted particularly for his tales of love, the *Confessio Amantis.*

Gow+er[2] ('gaʊə) *n.* **the.** a peninsula in S Wales, in West Glamorgan in the Bristol Channel: mainly agricultural with several resorts.

go with *vb.* (*intr., prep.*) **1.** to accompany. **2.** to blend or harmonize: *that new wallpaper goes well with the furniture.* **3.** to be a normal part of: *three acres of land go with the house.* **4.** to be of the same opinion as: *I'm sorry I can't go with you on your new plan.* **5.** (of two people of the opposite sex) to associate frequently with each other.

go with+out *vb.* (*intr.*) **1.** *Chiefly Brit.* to be denied or deprived of (something, esp. food): *if you don't like your tea you can go without.* **2. that goes without saying.** that is obvious or self-evident.

gowk (gaʊk) *n. Scot. and northern English dialect.* a stupid person; fool. [from Old Norse *gaukr* cuckoo; related to Old High German *gouh*]

gown (gaʊn) *n.* **1.** any of various outer garments, such as a woman's elegant or formal dress, a dressing robe, or a protective garment, esp. one worn by surgeons during operations. **2.** a loose wide garment indicating status, such as worn by academics. **3.** the members of a university as opposed to the other residents of the university town. Compare **town** (sense 7). ~*vb.* **4.** (*tr.*) to supply with or dress in a gown. [C14: from Old French *goune,* from Late Latin *gunna* garment made of leather or fur, of Celtic origin]

Gow·on ('gauən) *n.* **Ya·ku·bu** ('jɑ:kʊ,bu:). born 1934, Nigerian general and statesman; head of state from 1966 until his overthrow in 1975.

goy (gɔɪ) *n., pl.* **goy+im** ('gɔɪɪm) *or* **goys.** *Slang.* a derogatory word used by Jews for a non-Jew. [from Yiddish, from Hebrew *goi* people] —'**goy+ish** *adj.*

Goy·a ('gɔɪə; *Spanish* 'goja) *n.* **Fran·cis·co de** (fran'θisko ðe), full name *Francisco José de Goya y Lucientes.* 1746–1828, Spanish painter and etcher; well known for his portraits, he became court painter to Charles IV of Spain (1799). He recorded the French invasion of Spain in a series of etchings *The Disasters of War* (1810–14) and two paintings *2 May 1808* and *3 May 1808* (1814).

G.P. *abbrev. for:* **1.** general practitioner. **2.** Gallup poll. **3.** (in Britain) graduated pension. **4.** Grand Prix. **5.** *Music.* general pause.

GPI *abbrev. for* general paralysis of the insane (general paresis).

G.P.O. *abbrev. for* general post office.

G.P.U. *abbrev. for* State Political Administration; the Soviet police and secret police from 1922 to 1923. [from Russian *Gosudarstvennoye politicheskoye upravlenie*]

GQ *Military. abbrev. for* general quarters.

GR *international car registration for* Greece.

gr. *abbrev. for:* **1.** grade. **2.** grain. **3.** gross. **4.** gunner. **5.** gram.

Gr. *abbrev. for:* **1.** Grecian. **2.** Greece. **3.** Greek.

Graaf+i·an fol+li+cle ('grɑ:fɪən) *n.* a fluid-filled vesicle in the mammalian ovary containing a developing egg cell. [C17: named after R. de *Graaf* (1641–73), Dutch anatomist]

grab (græb) *vb.* **grabs, grab+bing, grabbed. 1.** to seize hold of (something). **2.** (*tr.*) to seize illegally or unscrupulously. **3.** (*tr.*) to arrest; catch. **4.** (*intr.*) (of a brake or clutch in a vehicle) to grip and release intermittently causing juddering. **5.** (*tr.*) *Informal.* to catch the attention or interest of; impress. ~*n.* **6.** the act or an instance of grabbing. **7.** a mechanical device for gripping objects, esp. the hinged jaws of a mechanical excavator. **8.** something that is grabbed. [C16: probably from Middle Low German or Middle Dutch *grabben;* related to Swedish *grabba,* Sanskrit *grbhnāti* he seizes] —'**grab+ber** *n.*

grab+ble ('græbᵊl) *vb.* **1.** (*intr.*) to scratch or feel about with the hands. **2.** (*intr.*) to fall to the ground; sprawl. **3.** (*tr.*) *Caribbean.* to seize rashly. [C16: probably from Dutch *grabbelen,* from *grabben* to GRAB] —'**grab+bler** *n.*

gra+ben ('grɑ:bᵊn) *n.* an elongated trough of land produced by subsidence of the earth's crust between two faults. [C19: from German, from Old High German *graban* to dig]

Grac·chus ('grækəs) *n.* **Ti·be·ri·us Sem·pro·ni·us** (taɪ'bɪərɪəs sem'prəʊnɪəs). ?163–133 B.C., and his younger brother, **Gai·us Sem·pro·ni·us** ('gaɪəs), 153–121 B.C., known as *the Gracchi.* Roman tribunes and reformers. Tiberius attempted to redistribute public land among the poor but was murdered in the ensuing riot. Violence again occurred when the reform was revived by Gaius, and he too was killed.

grace (greɪs) *n.* **1.** elegance and beauty of movement, form, expression, or proportion. **2.** a pleasing or charming quality. **3.** goodwill or favour. **4.** the granting of a favour or the manifestation of goodwill, esp. by a superior. **5.** a sense of propriety and consideration for others. **6.** (*pl.*) **a.** affectation of manner (esp. in the phrase **airs and graces**). **b. in (someone's) good graces.** regarded favourably and with kindness by (someone). **7.** mercy; clemency. **8.** *Theol.* **a.** the free and unmerited favour of God shown towards man. **b.** the divine assistance and power given to man in spiritual rebirth and sanctification. **c.** the condition of being favoured or sanctified by God. **d.** an unmerited gift, favour, etc., granted by God. **9.** a short prayer recited before or after a meal to invoke a blessing upon the food or give thanks for it. **10.** *Music.* a melodic ornament or decoration. **11.** See **days of grace. 12. with (a) bad grace.** unwillingly or grudgingly. **13. with (a) good grace.** willingly or cheerfully. ~*vb.* **14.** (*tr.*) to add elegance and beauty to: *flowers graced the room.* **15.** (*tr.*) to honour or favour: *to grace a party with one's presence.* **16.** to ornament or decorate (a melody, part, etc.) with nonessential notes. [C12: from Old French, from Latin *grātia,* from *grātus* pleasing] —'**grace+less** *adj.*

Grace[1] (greɪs) *n.* (preceded by *your, his,* or *her*) a title used to address or refer to a duke, duchess, or archbishop.

Grace[2] (greɪs) *n.* **W(illiam) G(ilbert).** 1848–1915, English cricketer.

grace-and-fa·vour *n.* (*modifier*) *Brit.* (of a house, flat, etc.) owned by the sovereign and granted free of rent to a person to whom the sovereign wishes to express gratitude.

grace cup *n.* a cup, as of wine, passed around at the end of the meal for the final toast.

grace+ful ('greɪsfʊl) *adj.* characterized by beauty of movement, style, form, etc. —'**grace+ful+ly** *adv.* —'**grace+ful+ness** *n.*

grace note *n. Music.* a note printed in small type to indicate that it is melodically and harmonically nonessential.

Grac·es ('greɪsɪz) *pl. n. Greek myth.* three sisters, the goddesses Aglaia, Euphrosyne, and Thalia, givers of charm and beauty.

grac+ile ('græsaɪl) *adj.* **1.** gracefully thin or slender. **2.** a less common word for **graceful.** —**gra+cil+i·ty** (græ'sɪlɪtɪ) *or* '**grac+ile+ness** *n.*

gra+ci·o+so (,græsɪ'əʊsəʊ; *Spanish* gra'θjoso) *n., pl.* **+sos.** a clown in Spanish comedy. [C17: from Spanish: GRACIOUS]

gra+cious ('greɪʃəs) *adj.* **1.** characterized by or showing kindness and courtesy. **2.** condescendingly courteous, benevolent, or indulgent. **3.** characterized by or suitable for a life of elegance, ease, and indulgence: *gracious living; gracious furnishings.* **4.** merciful or compassionate. **5.** *Obsolete.* fortunate, prosperous, or happy. ~*interj.* **6.** an expression of mild surprise or wonder (often in exclamatory phrases such as **good gracious! gracious me!**). —'**gra+cious+ly** *adv.* —'**gra+cious+ness** *n.*

grack+le ('grækᵊl) *n.* **1.** Also called: **crow blackbird.** any American songbird of the genera *Quiscalus* and *Cassidix,* having a dark iridescent plumage: family *Icteridae* (American orioles). **2.** any of various starlings of the genus *Gracula,* such as *G. religiosa* (**Indian grackle** or **hill myna**). [C18: from New Latin *Grācula,* from Latin *grāculus* jackdaw]

grad (græd) *n. Informal.* a graduate.

grad. *abbrev. for:* **1.** *Maths.* gradient. **2.** *Education.* graduate(d).

grad+a·ble ('greɪdəbᵊl) *adj.* **1.** capable of being graded. **2.** *Linguistics.* denoting or relating to a word in whose meaning there is some implicit relationship to a standard: *"big" and "small" are gradable adjectives.* ~*n.* **3.** *Linguistics.* a word of this kind. —,**grad+a·'bil+i·ty** *or* '**grad+a·ble+ness** *n.*

gra+date (grə'deɪt) *vb.* **1.** to change or cause to change imperceptibly, as from one colour, tone, or degree to another. **2.** (*tr.*) to arrange in grades or ranks.

gra+da+tion (grə'deɪʃən) *n.* **1.** a series of systematic stages; gradual progression. **2.** (*often pl.*) a stage or degree in such a series or progression. **3.** the act or process of arranging or forming in stages, grades, etc., or of progressing evenly. **4.** (in painting, drawing, or sculpture) transition from one colour, tone, or surface to another through a series of very slight changes. **5.** *Linguistics.* any change in the quality or length of a vowel within a word indicating certain distinctions, such as inflectional or tense differentiations. See **ablaut. 6.** *Geology.* the natural levelling of land as a result of the building up or wearing down of pre-existing formations. —**gra+'da+tion+al** *adj.* —**gra+'da+tion+al+ly** *adv.*

grade (greɪd) *n.* **1.** a position or degree in a scale, as of quality, rank, size, or progression: *small-grade eggs; high-grade timber.* **2.** a group of people or things of the same category. **3.** *Chiefly U.S.* a military or other rank. **4.** a stage in a course of progression. **5.** a mark or rating indicating achievement or the worth of work done, as at school. **6.** *U.S.* a unit of pupils of similar age or ability taught together at school. **7.** another word (esp. U.S.) for **gradient** (senses 1, 2). **8.** a unit of angle equal to one hundredth of a right angle or 0.9 degree. **9.** *Stockbreeding.* **a.** an animal with one purebred parent and one of unknown or unimproved breeding. **b.** (*as modifier*): *a grade sheep.* Compare **crossbred, purebred** (sense 2). **10.** *Linguistics.* one of the forms of the vowel in a morpheme when this vowel varies because of gradation. **11. at grade. a.** on the same level. **b.** (of a river profile or land surface) at an equilibrium level and slope, because there is a balance between erosion and deposition. **12. make the grade.** *Informal.* **a.** to reach the required standard. **b.** to succeed. ~*vb.* **13.** (*tr.*) to arrange according to quality, rank, etc. **14.** (*tr.*) to determine the grade of or assign a grade to. **15.** (*intr.*) to achieve or deserve a grade or rank. **16.** to change or blend (something) gradually; merge. **17.** (*tr.*) to level (ground, a road, etc.) to a suitable gradient. **18.** (*tr.*) *Stockbreeding.* to cross (one animal) with another to produce a grade animal. [C16: from French, from Latin *gradus* step, from *gradī* to step]

-grade *adj. combining form.* indicating a kind or manner of movement or progression: *plantigrade; retrograde.* [via French from Latin *-gradus,* from *gradus* a step, from *gradī* to walk]

grade crick+et *n. Austral.* competitive cricket, in which cricket club teams are arranged in grades.

grade cros+sing *n.* the U.S. name for **level crossing.**

grad+ed post *n. Brit.* a position in a school, etc., having special responsibility for which additional payment is given.

grade+ly ('greɪdlɪ) *adj.* **+li+er, +li+est.** *Midland English dialect.* fine; excellent. [C13 *greithlic, greithli,* from Old Norse *greidhligr,* from *greidhr* ready]

grad+er ('greɪdə) *n.* **1.** a person or thing that grades. **2.** a machine, either self-powered or towed by a tractor, that levels earth, rubble, etc., as in road construction.

grade school *n. U.S.* another name for **elementary school.**

gra+di+ent ('greɪdɪənt) *n.* **1.** Also called (esp. U.S.): **grade.** a part of a railway, road, etc., that slopes upwards or downwards; inclination. **2.** Also called (esp. U.S.): **grade.** a measure of such a slope, esp. the ratio of the vertical distance between two points on the slope to the horizontal distance between them. **3.** *Physics.* a measure of the change of some physical quantity, such as temperature or electric potential, over a specified distance. **4.** *Maths.* **a.** (of a curve) the slope of the tangent at any point on a curve with respect to the horizontal axis. **b.** (of a function, $f(x, y, z)$) the vector whose components along the axes are the partial derivatives of the function with respect to each variable, and whose direction is that in which the derivative of the function has its maximum value. Usually written: grad f, ∇f. Compare **curl** (sense 12), **divergence** (sense 4). ~*adj.* **5.** sloping uniformly. [C19: from Latin *gradiēns* stepping, from *gradī* to go]

gra+din ('greɪdɪn) *or* **gra+dine** (grə'di:n) *n.* **1.** a ledge above or behind an altar on which candles, a cross, or other ornaments stand. **2.** one of a set of steps or seats arranged on a slope, as in an amphitheatre. [C19: from French, from Italian *gradino,* a little step, from *grado* step; see GRADE]

grad·u·al ('grædjʊəl) *adj.* **1.** occurring, developing, moving, etc., in small stages: *a gradual improvement in health.* **2.** not steep or abrupt: *a gradual slope.* ~*n.* **3.** *(often cap.) Christianity* **a.** an antiphon or group of several antiphons, usually from the Psalms, sung or recited immediately after the epistle at Mass. **b.** a book of plainsong containing the words and music of the parts of the Mass that are sung by the cantors and choir. [C16: from Medieval Latin *graduālis* relating to steps, from Latin *gradus* a step] —**'grad·u·al·ly** *adv.* —**'grad·u·al·ness** *n.*

grad·u·al·ism ('grædjʊəˌlɪzəm) *n.* the policy of seeking to change something or achieve a goal gradually rather than quickly or violently, esp. in politics. —**'grad·u·al·ist** *n., adj.* —**ˌgrad·u·al·'is·tic** *adj.*

grad·u·and ('grædjʊˌænd) *n. Chiefly Brit.* a person who is about to graduate. [C19: from Medieval Latin *graduandus,* gerundive of *graduārī* to GRADUATE]

grad·u·ate *n.* ('grædjʊɪt). **1. a.** a person who has been awarded a first degree from a university or college. **b.** *(as modifier): a graduate profession.* **2.** *U.S.* a student who has completed a course of studies at a high school and received a diploma. **3.** *U.S.* a container, such as a flask, marked to indicate its capacity. ~*vb.* ('grædjʊˌeɪt). **4.** to receive or cause to receive a degree or diploma. **5.** *Chiefly U.S.* to confer a degree, diploma, etc. upon. **6.** *(tr.)* to mark (a thermometer, flask, etc.) with units of measurement; calibrate. **7.** *(tr.)* to arrange or sort into groups according to type, quality, etc. **8.** *(intr.;* often foll. by *to)* to change by degrees (from something to something else). [C15: from Medieval Latin *graduārī* to take a degree, from Latin *gradus* a step] —**'grad·u·ˌa·tor** *n.*

grad·u·a·tion (ˌgrædjʊ'eɪʃən) *n.* **1.** the act of graduating or the state of being graduated. **2.** the ceremony at which school or college degrees and diplomas are conferred. **3.** a mark or division or all the marks or divisions that indicate measure on an instrument or vessel.

gra·dus ('greɪdəs) *n., pl.* **-dus·es. 1.** a book of études or other musical exercises arranged in order of increasing difficulty. **2.** *Prosody.* a dictionary or textbook of prosody for use in writing Latin or Greek verse. [C18: shortened from Latin *Gradus ad Parnassum* a step towards Parnassus, a dictionary of prosody used in the 18th and 19th centuries]

Grae·ae ('gri:i:) *or* **Grai·ae** *pl. n. Greek myth.* three aged sea deities, having only one eye and one tooth among them, guardians of their sisters, the Gorgons.

Grae·cism *or esp. U.S.* **Gre·cism** ('gri:sɪzəm) *n.* **1.** Greek characteristics or style. **2.** admiration for or imitation of these, as in sculpture or architecture. **3.** a form of words characteristic or imitative of the idiom of the Greek language.

Grae·cize, Grae·cise, *or esp. U.S.* **Gre·cize** ('gri:saɪz) *vb.* another word for **Hellenize.** [C17: from Latin *graecizāre* to imitate the Greeks, from Greek *graikizein*]

Grae·co- *or esp. U.S.* **Gre·co-** ('gri:kəʊ-, 'grɛkəʊ-) *combining form.* Greek: *Graeco-Roman.*

Grae·co-Ro·man *or esp. U.S.* **Gre·co-Ro·man** *adj.* **1.** of, characteristic of, or relating to Greek and Roman influences, as found in Roman sculpture. **2.** denoting a style of wrestling in which the legs may not be used to obtain a fall and no hold may be applied below the waist.

Graf *German.* (gra:f) *n., pl.* ***Graf·en*** ('gra:fᵊn). a German or Swedish count: often used as a title. [German, from Old High German *grāvo*]

graf·fi·to (græ'fi:təʊ) *n., pl.* **-ti** (-ti:). **1.** *Archaeol.* any inscription or drawing scratched or carved onto a surface, esp. rock or pottery. **2.** *(pl.)* drawings, messages, etc., often obscene, scribbled on the walls of public lavatories, advertising posters, etc. [C19: from Italian: a little scratch, from *graffio,* from Latin *graphium* stylus, from Greek *grapheion;* see GRAFT[1]]

graft[1] (grɑ:ft) *n.* **1.** *Horticulture.* **a.** a small piece of plant tissue (the scion) that is made to unite with an established plant (the stock), which supports and nourishes it. **b.** the plant resulting from the union of scion and stock. **c.** the point of union between the scion and the stock. **2.** *Surgery.* a piece of tissue or an organ transplanted from a donor or from the patient's own body to an area of the body in need of the tissue. **3.** the act of joining one thing to another by or as if by grafting. ~*vb.* **4.** *Horticulture.* **a.** to induce (a plant or part of a plant) to unite with another part or (of a plant or part of a plant) to unite in this way. **b.** to produce (fruit, flowers, etc.) by this means or (of fruit, etc.) to grow by this means. **5.** to transplant (tissue) or (of tissue) to be transplanted. **6.** to attach or incorporate or become attached or incorporated: *to graft a happy ending onto a sad tale.* [C15: from Old French *graffe,* from Medieval Latin *graphium,* from Latin: stylus, from Greek *grapheion,* from *graphein* to write] —**'graft·er** *n.* —**'graft·ing** *n.*

graft[2] (grɑ:ft) *n.* **1.** *Informal.* work. (esp. in the phrase **hard graft**). **2.** *Chiefly U.S.* **a.** the acquisition of money, power, etc., by dishonest or unfair means, esp. by taking advantage of a position of trust. **b.** something gained in this way, such as profit from government business. **c.** a payment made to a person profiting by such a practice. ~*vb.* **3.** *(intr.) Informal.* to work. **4.** *Chiefly U.S.* to acquire by or practise graft. [C19: of uncertain origin] —**'graft·er** *n.*

graft hy·brid *n.* a plant produced by grafting a scion and stock from dissimilar plants; chimera.

gra·ham ('greɪəm) *n. (modifier) Chiefly U.S.* made of graham flour: *graham crackers.* [C19: named after S. *Graham* (1794–1851), American dietetic reformer]

Gra·ham ('greɪəm) *n.* **1. Mar·tha.** born 1895, U.S. dancer and choreographer. **2. Wil·liam Frank·lin,** known as *Billy Graham.* born 1918, U.S. evangelist.

Gra·hame ('greɪəm) *n.* **Ken·neth.** 1859–1932, Scottish author, noted for the children's classic *The Wind in the Willows* (1908).

gra·ham flour *n. Chiefly U.S.* unbolted wheat flour ground from whole-wheat grain, similar to whole-wheat flour.

Gra·ham Land ('greɪəm) *n.* the N part of the Antarctic Peninsula: became part of the British Antarctic Territory in 1962 (formerly part of the Falkland Islands Dependencies).

Grai·ae ('greɪi:, 'graɪi:) *pl. n.* a variant spelling of **Graeae.**

Gra·ian Alps ('greɪən, 'graɪ-) *pl. n.* the N part of the Western Alps, in France and NW Piedmont, Italy. Highest peak: Gran Paradiso, 4061 m (13 323 ft.).

Grail (greɪl) *n.* see **Holy Grail.**

grain (greɪn) *n.* **1.** the small hard seedlike fruit of a grass, esp. a cereal plant. **2.** a mass of such fruits, esp. when gathered for food. **3.** the plants, collectively, from which such fruits are harvested. **4.** a small hard particle: *a grain of sand.* **5. a.** the general direction or arrangement of the fibrous elements in wood: *to saw across the grain.* **b.** the pattern or texture of wood resulting from such an arrangement: *the attractive grain of the table.* **6.** the relative size of the particles of a substance: *sugar of fine grain.* **7. a.** the granular texture of a rock, mineral, etc. **b.** the appearance of a rock, etc., determined by the size and arrangement of its constituents. **8. a.** the outer (hair-side) layer of a hide or skin from which the hair or wool has been removed. **b.** the pattern on the outer surface of such a hide or skin. **9.** a surface artificially imitating the grain of wood, leather, stone, etc.; graining. **10.** the smallest unit of weight in the avoirdupois, Troy, and apothecaries' systems, based on the weight of a grain of wheat: in the avoirdupois system it equals one seven-thousandth of a pound. 1 grain equals 0.0648 gram. Abbrev.: gr **11.** Also called: **metric grain.** a metric unit of weight used for pearls or diamonds, equal to 50 milligrams or one quarter of a carat. **12.** the threads or direction of threads in a woven fabric. **13.** *Photog.* any of a large number of particles in a photographic emulsion, the size of which limit the extent to which an image can be enlarged without serious loss of definition. **14.** cleavage lines in crystalline material, parallel to growth planes. **15.** *Chem.* any of a large number of small crystals forming a polycrystalline solid, each having a regular array of atoms that differs in orientation from that of the surrounding crystallites. **16.** a state of crystallization: *to boil syrup to the grain.* **17.** a very small amount: *a grain of truth.* **18.** natural disposition, inclination, or character (esp. in the phrase **go against the grain**). **19.** *Astronautics.* a homogenous mass of solid propellant in a form designed to give the required combustion characteristics for a particular rocket. **20.** *(not in technical usage)* kermes or a red dye made from this insect. **21.** *Dyeing.* an obsolete word for **colour. 22. with a grain** *or* **pinch of salt.** without wholly believing. ~*vb. (mainly tr.)* **23.** *(also intr.)* to form grains or cause to form into grains; granulate; crystallize. **24.** to give a granular or roughened appearance or texture to. **25.** to paint, stain, etc., in imitation of the grain of wood or leather. **26. a.** to remove the hair or wool from (a hide or skin) before tanning. **b.** to raise the grain pattern on (leather). [C13: from Old French, from Latin *grānum*] —**'grain·er** *n.* —**'grain·less** *adj.*

grain al·co·hol *n.* ethanol containing about 10 per cent of water, made by the fermentation of grain.

grain el·e·va·tor *n.* a machine for raising grain to a higher level, esp. one having an endless belt fitted with scoops.

Grain·ger ('greɪndʒə) *n.* **Per·cy Al·dridge.** 1882–1961, Australian pianist, composer, and collector of folk music on which many of his works are based.

grain·ing ('greɪnɪŋ) *n.* **1.** the pattern or texture of the grain of wood, leather, etc. **2.** the process of painting, printing, staining, etc., a surface in imitation of a grain. **3.** a surface produced by such a process.

grains of par·a·dise *pl. n.* the peppery seeds of either of two African zingiberaceous plants, *Aframomum melegueta* or *A. granum-paradisi* used as stimulants, diuretics, etc. Also called: **guinea grains.**

grain·y ('greɪnɪ) *adj.* **grain·i·er, grain·i·est. 1.** resembling, full of, or composed of grain; granular. **2.** resembling the grain of wood, leather, etc. **3.** *Photog.* having poor definition because of large grain size. —**'grain·i·ness** *n.*

gral·la·to·ri·al (ˌgrælə'tɔ:rɪəl) *adj.* of or relating to long-legged wading birds, such as cranes and storks. [C19: from New Latin *grallātōrius,* from Latin *grallātor* one who walks on stilts, from *grallae* stilts]

gram[1] *or* **gramme** (græm) *n.* a metric unit of mass equal to one thousandth of a kilogram. It is equivalent to 15.432 grains or 0.002 205 pounds. Abbrev.: g [C18: from French *gramme,* from Late Latin *gramma,* from Greek: small weight, from *graphein* to write]

gram[2] (græm) *n.* **1.** any of several leguminous plants, such as the beans *Phaseolus mungo* (**black gram** or **urd**) and *P. aureus* (**green gram**), whose seeds are used as food in India. **2.** the seed of any of these plants. [C18: from Portuguese *gram* (modern spelling: *grão*), from Latin *grānum* GRAIN]

gram[3] (grɑ:m) *n.* (in India) a village. [Hindi]

gram. *abbrev. for:* **1.** grammar. **2.** grammatical.

-gram *n. combining form.* indicating a drawing or something written or recorded: *hexagram; telegram.* [from Latin *-gramma,* from Greek, from *gramma* letter and *grammē* line]

gra·ma *or* **gra·ma grass** ('grɑ:mə) *n.* any of various grasses of the genus *Bouteloua,* of W North America and South America: often used as pasture grasses. [C19: from Spanish, ultimately from Latin *grāmen* grass]

gram·a·rye *or* **gram·a·ry** ('græmərɪ) *n. Archaic.* magic, necromancy, or occult learning. [C14: from Old French *gramaire* GRAMMAR]

gram at·om *or* **gram-a·tom·ic weight** *n.* an amount of an element equal to its atomic weight expressed in grams: now replaced by the mole. See **mole**[3].

gram cal·o·rie *n.* another name for **calorie.**

gram e·quiv·a·lent *or* **gram-e·quiv·a·lent weight** *n.* an amount of a substance equal to its equivalent weight expressed in grams.

gra·mer·cy (grəˈmɜːsɪ) *interj. Archaic.* **1.** many thanks. **2.** an expression of surprise, wonder, etc. [C13: from Old French *grand merci* great thanks]

gram·i·ci·din *or* **gram·i·ci·din D** (ˌgræmɪˈsaɪdɪn) *n.* an antibiotic used in treating local Gram-positive bacterial infections: obtained from the soil bacterium *Bacillus brevis.* [C20: from GRAM-(POSITIVE) + -CID(E) + -IN]

gra·min·e·ous (grəˈmɪnɪəs) *adj.* **1.** of, relating to, or belonging to the grass family, *Gramineae.* **2.** resembling a grass; grasslike. ~Also: **gra·min·a·ceous** (ˌgræmɪˈneɪʃəs). [C17: from Latin *grāmineus* of grass, grassy, from *grāmen* grass]

gram·i·niv·o·rous (ˌgræmɪˈnɪvərəs) *adj.* (of animals) feeding on grass. [C18: from Latin *grāmen* grass + -VOROUS]

gram·mar (ˈgræmə) *n.* **1.** the branch of linguistics that deals with syntax and morphology, sometimes also phonology and semantics. **2.** the abstract system of rules in terms of which a person's mastery of his native language can be explained. **3.** a systematic description of the grammatical facts of a language. **4.** a book containing an account of the grammatical facts of a language or recommendations as to rules for the proper use of a language. **5. a.** the use of language with regard to its correctness or social propriety, esp. in syntax: *the teacher told him to watch his grammar.* **b.** (*as modifier*): *a grammar book.* **6.** the elementary principles of a science or art: *the grammar of drawing.* [C14: from Old French *gramaire,* from Latin *grammatica,* from Greek *grammatikē* (*tekhnē*) the grammatical (art), from *grammatikos* concerning letters, from *gramma* letter] —**ˈgram·mar·less** *adj.*

gram·mar·i·an (grəˈmɛərɪən) *n.* **1.** a person whose occupation is the study of grammar. **2.** the author of a grammar.

gram·mar school *n.* **1.** *Brit.* a state-maintained secondary school providing an education with an academic bias for children who are selected by the eleven-plus examination, teachers' reports, or other means. Compare **secondary modern school, comprehensive school. 2.** *U.S.* another term for **elementary school.**

gram·mat·i·cal (grəˈmætɪkᵊl) *adj.* **1.** of or relating to grammar. **2.** (of a sentence) well formed; regarded as correct and acceptable by native speakers of the language. —**gramˈmat·i·cal·ly** *adv.* —**gramˈmat·i·cal·ness** *n.*

gram·mat·i·cal mean·ing *n.* the meaning of a word by reference to its function within a sentence rather than to a world outside the sentence. Compare **lexical meaning, function word.**

gram·ma·tol·o·gy (ˌgræməˈtɒlədʒɪ) *n.* the scientific study of writing systems. —**ˌgram·maˈtol·o·gist** *n.*

gramme (græm) *n.* a variant spelling of **gram.**

gram mol·e·cule *or* **gram-mo·lec·u·lar weight** *n.* an amount of a compound equal to its molecular weight expressed in grams: now replaced by the mole. See **mole**[3]. —**ˌgram-moˈlec·u·lar** *or* **gram-mo·lar** (ˌgræmˈməʊlə) *adj.*

Gram-neg·a·tive *adj.* designating bacteria that fail to retain the violet stain in Gram's method.

gram·o·phone (ˈgræməˌfəʊn) *n.* **1. a.** Also called: **record-player.** a device for reproducing the sounds stored on a record, consisting of a turntable, usually electrically driven, that rotates the record at a fixed speed of 33, 45, 16, or (esp. formerly) 78 revolutions per minute. A stylus vibrates in accordance with the undulations of the walls of the groove in the record: these vibrations are converted into electric currents, which, after amplification, are recreated in the form of sound by one or more loudspeakers. U.S. word: **phonograph. b.** (*as modifier*): *a gramophone record.* See also **monophonic, stereophonic, quadraphonic. 2.** Also called: **acoustic gramophone.** an antique instrument of this type, esp. one driven by clockwork and having a horn for amplification. [C19: originally a trademark, perhaps based on an inversion of *phonogram;* see PHONO-, -GRAM]

Gram·pi·an Moun·tains (ˈgræmpɪən) *pl. n.* **1.** a mountain system of central Scotland, extending from the southwest to the northeast and separating the Highlands from the Lowlands. Highest peak: Ben Nevis, 1343 m (4406 ft.). **2.** a mountain range in SE Australia, in W Victoria. ~Also called: **The Grampians.**

Gram·pi·an Re·gion *n.* a local government region in NE Scotland, formed in 1975 from Aberdeenshire, Kincardineshire, and most of Banffshire and Morayshire. Administrative centre: Aberdeen. Pop.: 453 829 (1976 est.). Area: 8700 sq. km (3360 sq. miles).

Gram-pos·i·tive *adj.* designating bacteria that retain the violet stain in Gram's method.

gram·pus (ˈgræmpəs) *n., pl.* **·pus·es. 1.** a widely distributed slaty-grey dolphin, *Grampus griseus,* with a blunt snout. **2.** another name for **killer whale.** [C16: from Old French *graspois,* from *gras* fat (from Latin *crassus*) + *pois* fish (from Latin *piscis*)]

Gram's meth·od *n. Bacteriol.* a staining technique used to classify bacteria, based on their ability to retain or lose a violet colour, produced by crystal violet and iodine, after treatment with a decolorizing agent. See also **Gram-negative, Gram-positive.** [C19: named after Hans Christian Joachim *Gram* (1853–1938), Danish physician]

Gra·na·da (grəˈnɑːdə) *n.* **1.** a former kingdom of S Spain, in Andalusia: founded in the 13th century and divided in 1833 into the present-day provinces of Granada, Almería, and Málaga. **2.** a city in S Spain, in Andalusia: capital of the Moorish kingdom of Granada from 1238 to 1492 and a great commercial and cultural centre, containing the Alhambra palace (13th and 14th centuries); university (1531). Pop.: 190 429 (1970). **3.** a city in SW Nicaragua, on the NW shore of Lake Nicaragua: the oldest city in the country, founded in 1523 by Córdoba; attacked frequently by pirates in the 17th century. Pop.: 51 500 (1971 est.).

gran·a·dil·la (ˌgrænəˈdɪlə) *n.* **1.** any of various passionflowers, such as *Passiflora quadrangularis* (**giant granadilla**), that have edible egg-shaped fleshy fruit. **2.** Also called: **passion fruit.** the fruit of such a plant. [C18: from Spanish, diminutive of *granada* pomegranate, from Late Latin *grānātum*]

Gra·na·dos (*Spanish* graˈnaðos) *n.* **En·ri·que** (enˈrike). full name *Enrique Granados y Campina.* 1867–1916, Spanish composer, noted for the *Goyescas* (1911) for piano, which formed the basis for an opera of the same name.

gran·a·ry (ˈgrænərɪ; *U.S.* ˈgreɪnərɪ) *n., pl.* **·ries. 1.** a building or store room for storing threshed grain, farm feed, etc. **2.** a region that produces a large amount of grain. [C16: from Latin *grānārium,* from *grānum* GRAIN]

Gran Ca·na·ria (ˈgraŋ kaˈnarja) *n.* the Spanish name for **Grand Canary.**

gran cas·sa (*Italian* ˈgran ˈkassa) *n. Music.* another name for **bass drum.** [Italian: great drum]

Gran Cha·co (*Spanish* ˈgran ˈtʃakɔ) *n.* a plain of S central South America, between the Andes and the Paraguay River in SE Bolivia, E Paraguay, and N Argentina: huge swamps and scrub forest. Area: about 780 000 sq. km (300 000 sq. miles). Often shortened to: **Chaco.**

grand (grænd) *adj.* **1.** large or impressive in size, extent, or consequence: *grand mountain scenery.* **2.** characterized by or attended with magnificence or display; sumptuous: *a grand feast.* **3.** of great distinction or pretension; dignified or haughty. **4.** designed to impress: *he punctuated his story with grand gestures.* **5.** very good; wonderful. **6.** comprehensive; complete: *a grand total.* **7.** worthy of respect; fine: *a grand old man.* **8.** large or impressive in conception or execution: *grand ideas.* **9.** most important; chief: *the grand arena.* ~*n.* **10.** See **grand piano. 11.** (*pl.* **grand**) *Slang, chiefly U.S.* a thousand pounds or dollars. [C16: from Old French, from Latin *grandis*] —**ˈgrand·ly** *adv.* —**ˈgrand·ness** *n.*

grand- *prefix.* (in designations of kinship) one generation removed in ascent or descent: *grandson; grandfather.* [from French *grand-,* on the model of Latin *magnus* in such phrases as *avunculus magnus* great-uncle]

gran·dam (ˈgrændəm, -dæm) *or* **gran·dame** (ˈgrændeɪm, -dəm) *n.* an archaic word for **grandmother.** [C13: from Anglo-French *grandame,* from Old French GRAND- + *dame* lady, mother]

grand·aunt (ˈgrændˌɑːnt) *n.* another name for **great-aunt.**

Grand Ba·ha·ma *n.* an island in the Atlantic, in the W Bahamas. Pop.: 225 859 (1970). Area: 1114 sq. km (430 sq. miles).

Grand Banks *n.* a part of the continental shelf in the Atlantic, extending for about 560 km (350 miles) off the SE coast of Newfoundland: meeting place of the cold Labrador Current and the warm Gulf Stream, producing frequent fogs and rich fishing grounds.

Grand Ca·nal *n.* **1.** a canal in E China, extending north from Hangchow to Tientsin: the longest canal in China, now partly silted up; central section, linking the Yangtze and Yellow Rivers, finished in 486 B.C.; north section finished by Kublai Khan between 1282 and 1292. Length: about 1600 km (1000 miles). Chinese name: **Yun-Ho Ta. 2.** a canal in Venice, forming the main water thoroughfare: noted for its bridges, the Rialto, and the fine palaces along its banks.

Grand Ca·nar·y *n.* an island in the Atlantic, in the Canary Islands: part of the Spanish province of Las Palmas. Capital: Las Palmas. Pop.: 489 881 (1970). Area: 1533 (592 sq. miles). Spanish name: **Gran Canaria.**

Grand Can·yon *n.* a gorge of the Colorado River in N Arizona, extending from its junction with the Little Colorado River to Lake Mead; cut by vertical river erosion through the multicoloured strata of a high plateau; partly contained in the **Grand Canyon National Park,** covering 2610 sq. km (1008 sq. miles). Length: 451 km (280 miles). Width: 6 km (4 miles) to 29 km (18 miles). Greatest depth: over 1.5 km (1 mile).

grand chain *n.* a figure in formation dances, such as the Lancers and Scottish Reels, in which couples split up and move around in a circle in opposite directions, passing all other dancers until reaching their original partners.

grand·child (ˈgrænˌtʃaɪld) *n., pl.* **·chil·dren.** the son or daughter of one's child.

Grand Cou·lee (ˈkuːlɪ) *n.* a canyon in central Washington State, over 120 m (400 ft.) deep, at the N end of which is situated the **Grand Coulee Dam,** on the Columbia River. Height of dam: 168 m (550 ft.). Length of dam: 1310 m (4300 ft.).

grand·dad (ˈgrænˌdæd) *or* **grand·dad·dy** *n., pl.* **·dads** *or* **·dad·dies.** an informal word for **grandfather.**

grand·daugh·ter (ˈgrænˌdɔːtə) *n.* a daughter of one's son or daughter.

grand duch·ess *n.* **1.** the wife or a widow of a grand duke. **2.** a woman who holds the rank of grand duke in her own right.

grand duch·y *n.* the territory, state, or principality of a grand duke or grand duchess.
grand duke *n.* **1.** a prince or nobleman who rules a territory, state, or principality. **2.** a son or a male descendant in the male line of a Russian tsar. **3.** a medieval Russian prince who ruled over other princes.
grande dame *French.* (grɑ̃d 'dam) *n.* a woman regarded as the most experienced, prominent, or venerable member of her profession, etc.: *the grande dame of fashion.*
gran+dee (græn'diː) *n.* a Spanish prince or nobleman of the highest rank. [C16: from Spanish *grande*] **—gran+'dee+ship** *n.*
Grande-Terre (*French* grɑ̃d 'tɛr) *n.* an island in the French West Indies, in the Lesser Antilles: one of the two islands which constitute Guadeloupe. Chief town: Pointe-à-Pitre.
gran+deur ('grændʒə) *n.* **1.** personal greatness, esp. when based on dignity, character, or accomplishments. **2.** magnificence; splendour. **3.** pretentious or bombastic behaviour.
Grand Falls *pl. n.* the former name (until 1965) of **Churchill Falls.**
grand+fa·ther ('græn,fɑːðə, 'grænd-) *n.* **1.** the father of one's father or mother. **2.** (*often pl.*) a male ancestor. **3.** (*often cap.*) a familiar term of address for an old man. **4.** *Brit. dialect.* a caterpillar or woodlouse.
grand+fa·ther clause *n.* **1.** *U.S. history.* a clause in the constitutions of several Southern states that waived electoral literacy requirements for lineal descendants of people voting before 1867, thus ensuring the franchise for illiterate whites: declared unconstitutional in 1915. **2.** a clause in legislation that forbids or regulates an activity so that those engaged in it are exempted from the ban.
grand+fa·ther clock *n.* any of various types of long-pendulum clocks in tall standing wooden cases. Also called: **longcase clock.**
grand+fa·ther+ly ('græn,fɑːðəlɪ, 'grænd-) *adj.* of, resembling, or suitable to a grandfather, esp. in being kindly.
grand fi+nal *n. Austral.* the final game of the season in any of various sports, esp. football.
Grand Gui+gnol *French.* (grɑ̃ gi'ɲɔl) *n.* **a.** a brief sensational play intended to horrify. **b.** (*modifier*) of, relating to, or like plays of this kind. [C20: after *Le Grand Guignol,* a small theatre in Montmartre, Paris]
gran+dil·o·quent (græn'dɪləkwənt) *adj.* inflated, pompous, or bombastic in style or expression. [C16: from Latin *grandiloquus,* from *grandis* great + *loquī* to speak] **—gran+'dil·o+quence** *n.* **—gran+'dil·o+quent+ly** *adv.*
gran+di+ose ('grændɪ,əʊs) *adj.* **1.** pretentiously grand or stately. **2.** imposing in conception or execution. [C19: from French, from Italian *grandioso,* from *grande* great; see GRAND] **—'gran+di+ose+ly** *adv.* **—gran+di+os+i·ty** (,grændɪ'ɒsɪtɪ) *n.*
gran·di·o+so (,grændɪ'əʊsəʊ) *adj., adv. Music.* to be played in a grand manner.
grand ju·ry *n. Law.* (esp. in the U.S.) a jury of between 12 and 23 persons summoned to enquire into accusations of crime and ascertain whether the evidence is adequate to found an indictment. Abolished in England in 1948. Compare **petit jury.**
Grand La·ma *n.* either of two high priests of Lamaism, the Dalai Lama or the Panchen Lama.
grand lar+cen·y *n.* **1.** (formerly in England) the theft of property valued at over 12 pence. Abolished in 1827. **2.** (in some states of the U.S.) the theft of property of which the value is above a specified figure, varying from state to state but usually being between $25 and $60. Compare **petit larceny.**
grand+ma, ('græn,mɑː, 'grænd-, 'græm-) **grand+ma·ma,** *or* **grand+mam·ma** ('grænmə,mɑː, 'grænd-) *n.* an informal word for **grandmother.**
grand mal ('grɒn 'mæl; *French* grɑ̃ 'mal) *n.* a form of epilepsy characterized by loss of consciousness for up to five minutes and violent convulsions. Compare **petit mal.** [French: great illness]
Grand·ma Mo·ses *n.* the nickname of (Anna Mary Robertson) **Moses.**
Grand Ma+nan (mə'næn) *n.* a Canadian island, off the SW coast of New Brunswick: separated from the coast of Maine by the **Grand Manan Channel.** Area: 147 sq. km (57 sq. miles).
grand+mas·ter ('grænd,mɑːstə) *n. Chess.* **1. a.** one of the top chess players of a particular country. **b.** (*cap. as part of title*): *Grandmaster of the USSR.* **2.** Also called: **International Grandmaster.** a player who has been awarded the highest title by the Fédération Internationale des Échecs.
Grand Mas+ter *n.* the title borne by the head of any of various societies, orders, and other organizations, such as the Templars or Freemasons.
grand+moth·er ('græn,mʌðə, 'grænd-) *n.* **1.** the mother of one's father or mother. **2.** (*often pl.*) a female ancestor. **3.** (*often cap.*) a familiar term of address for an old woman. **4. teach one's grandmother to suck eggs.** See **egg**[1] (sense 8).
grand+moth·er clock *n.* a longcase clock with a pendulum, about two thirds the size of a grandfather clock.
grand+moth·er+ly ('græn,mʌðəlɪ, 'grænd-) *adj.* of, resembling, or suitable to a grandmother, esp. in being protective, indulgent, or solicitous.
Grand Muf+ti *n.* **1.** the titular head of the Muslim community in Jerusalem and formerly the chief constitutional administrator there. **2.** (in Turkey) the former official head of the state religion.
Grand Na+tion+al *n.* **the.** an annual steeplechase run at Aintree, Liverpool, since 1839.
grand+neph·ew ('græn,nɛvjuː, -,nɛfjuː, 'grænd-) *n.* another name for **great-nephew.**
grand+niece ('græn,niːs, 'grænd-) *n.* another name for **great-niece.**
Grand Old Par+ty *n. U.S.* a nickname for the Republican Party since 1880. Abbrev.: **G.O.P.**
grand op+er·a *n.* an opera with a serious plot and fully composed text.
grand+pa ('græn,pɑː, 'grænd-, 'græm) *or* **grand+pa·pa** ('grænpə,pɑː, 'grænd-) *n.* informal words for **grandfather.**
grand+par·ent ('græn,pɛərənt, 'grænd-) *n.* the father or mother of either of one's parents.
grand pi·a+no *n.* a form of piano in which the strings are arranged horizontally. Grand pianos exist in three sizes (**concert grand, baby grand, boudoir grand**). Compare **upright piano.**
Grand Pré ('grɒn 'preɪ; *French* grɑ̃ 'pre) *n.* a village in SE Canada, in W Nova Scotia: setting of Longfellow's *Evangeline.*
Grand Prix (*French* grɑ̃ 'pri) *n.* **1. a.** any of a series of formula motor races held to determine the annual Driver's World Championship. **b.** (*as modifier*): *a Grand Prix car.* **2.** *Horse racing.* a race for three-year-old horses run at Maisons Lafitte near Paris. [French: great prize]
Grand Rap+ids *n.* a city in SW Michigan. Pop.: 190 696 (1973 est.).
Grand Re+mon+strance *n.* **the.** *English history.* the document prepared by the Long Parliament in 1640 listing the evils of the king's government, the abuses already rectified, and the reforms Parliament advocated.
grand sei+gneur *French.* (grɑ̃ sɛ'ɲœːr) *n., pl.* ***grands sei+gneurs*** (grɑ̃ sɛ'ɲœːr). *Often ironic.* a dignified or aristocratic man. [literally: great lord]
grand siè+cle *French.* (grɑ̃ 'sjɛkl) *n., pl.* ***grands siè+cles*** (grɑ̃ 'sjɛkl). the 17th century in French art and literature, esp. the classical period of Louis XIV. [literally: great century]
grand+sire[1] ('græn,saɪə, 'grænd-) *n.* an archaic word for **grandfather.**
grand+sire[2] ('grændsə, -,saɪə) *n.* a well-established method used in change-ringing. See **method** (sense 4).
grand slam *n.* **1.** *Bridge, etc.* the winning of 13 tricks by one player or side or the contract to do so. **2.** the winning of all major competitions in a season, esp. in tennis and golf.
grand+son ('grænsʌn, 'grænd-) *n.* a son of one's son or daughter.
grand+stand ('græn,stænd, 'grænd-) *n.* **1. a.** a terraced block of seats, usually under a roof, commanding the best view at racecourses, football pitches, etc. **b.** (*as modifier*): *grandstand tickets.* **2.** the spectators in a grandstand. **3.** (*modifier*) as if from a grandstand; unimpeded (esp. in the phrase **grandstand view**). ~*vb.* **4.** (*intr.*) *U.S. informal.* to behave ostentatiously in an attempt to impress onlookers. **—'grand+,stand·er** *n.*
grand tour *n.* **1.** (formerly) an extended tour through the major cities of Europe, esp. one undertaken by a rich or aristocratic Englishman to complete his education. **2.** *Informal.* an extended sightseeing trip, tour of inspection, etc.
grand+un·cle ('grænd,ʌŋkᵊl) *n.* another name for **great-uncle.**
grand vi+zier *n.* (formerly) the chief officer or minister of state in the Ottoman Empire and other Muslim countries.
grange (greɪndʒ) *n.* **1.** *Chiefly Brit.* a farm, esp. a farmhouse or country house with its various outbuildings. **2.** *History.* an outlying farmhouse in which a religious establishment or feudal lord stored crops and tithes in kind. **3.** *Archaic.* a granary or barn. [C13: from Anglo-French *graunge,* from Medieval Latin *grānica,* from Latin *grānum* GRAIN]
Grange (greɪndʒ) *n.* (in the U.S.) **1. the.** an association of farmers that strongly influenced state legislatures in the late 19th century. **2.** a lodge of this association.
Grange+mouth ('greɪndʒməθ) *n.* a port in Scotland, in the Central region: now Scotland's second port, with oil refineries, shipyards, and chemical industries. Pop.: 24 572 (1971).
grang+er+ize *or* **grang+er+ise** ('greɪndʒə,raɪz) *vb.* (*tr.*) **1.** to illustrate (a book) by inserting prints, drawings, etc., taken from other works. **2.** to raid (books, etc.) to acquire material for illustrating another book. [C19: named after Joseph *Granger,* 18th-century English writer, whose *Biographical History of England* (1769) included blank pages for illustrations to be supplied by the reader] **—'grang+er+ism** *n.* **—,grang+er·i+'za+tion** *or* **,grang+er·i+'sa+tion** *n.* **—'grang+er+,iz+er** *or* **'grang+er+,is+er** *n.*
gran·i- *combining form.* indicating grain: *graniform.* [from Latin, from *grānum* GRAIN]
Gra+ni+cus (grə'naɪkəs) *n.* an ancient river in NW Asia Minor where Alexander won his first major battle against the Persians (334 B.C.).
gran+ite ('grænɪt) *n.* **1.** a light-coloured coarse-grained acid plutonic igneous rock consisting of quartz, feldspars, and such ferromagnesian minerals as biotite or hornblende: widely used for building. **2.** great hardness, endurance, or resolution. **3.** another name for a **stone** (sense 9). [C17: from Italian *granito* grained, from *granire* to grain, from *grano* grain, from Latin *grānum*] **—'gran·ite-,like** *adj.* **—gra+nit+ic** (grə'nɪtɪk) *or* **'gran+it+,oid** *adj.*
gran·ite+ware ('grænɪt,wɛə) *n.* **1.** iron vessels coated with enamel of a granite-like appearance. **2.** a type of very durable white semivitreous pottery. **3.** a type of pottery with a speckled glaze.
gran+it+ite ('grænɪ,taɪt) *n.* any granite with a high content of biotite.
gra+niv·o+rous (græ'nɪvərəs) *adj.* (of animals) feeding on seeds and grain. **—gran·i+vore** ('grænɪ,vɔː) *n.*

gran+ny *or* **gran+nie** ('grænɪ) *n., pl.* **+nies. 1.** informal words for **grandmother.** Often shortened to **gran. 2.** *Informal.* an irritatingly fussy person. **3.** *Southern U.S.* a midwife or nurse. **4.** See **granny knot.**

gran+ny flat *n.* a flat built onto or constructed inside a house to accommodate an elderly parent.

gran+ny knot *or* **gran+ny's knot** *n.* a reef knot with the ends crossed the wrong way, making it liable to slip or jam.

Gran+ny Smith *n.* a variety of hard green-skinned apple eaten raw or cooked. [C19: named after Maria Ann Smith, called *Granny Smith* (died 1870)]

gran·o- *combining form.* of or resembling granite: *granolith.* [from German, from *Granit* GRANITE]

gran·o·di·o·rite (ˌgrænəʊ'daɪəˌraɪt) *n.* a coarse-grained acid igneous rock containing almost twice as much plagioclase as orthoclase: intermediate in structure between granite and diorite. [C19: from *grano* + DIORITE]

gran·o+lith ('grænəʊˌlɪθ) *n.* a paving material consisting of a mixture of cement and crushed granite or granite chippings. —**ˌgran·o+'lith+ic** *adj., n.*

gran·o+phyre ('grænəʊˌfaɪə) *n.* a fine-grained granitic rock in which irregular crystals of intergrown quartz and feldspar are embedded in a groundmass of these minerals. [C19: from GRAN(ITE) + -PHYRE] —**gran·o+phyr+ic** (ˌgrænəʊ'fɪrɪk) *adj.*

Gran Pa+ra+di+so (*Italian* gram para'di:zo) *n.* a mountain in NW Italy, in NW Piedmont: the highest peak of the Graian Alps. Height: 4061 m (13 323 ft.).

grant (grɑ:nt) *vb.* (*tr.*) **1.** to consent to perform or fulfil: *to grant a wish.* **2.** (*may take a clause as object*) to permit as a favour, indulgence, etc.: *to grant an interview.* **3.** (*may take a clause as object*) to acknowledge the validity of; concede: *I grant what you say is true.* **4.** to bestow, esp. in a formal manner. **5.** to transfer (property) to another, esp. by deed; convey. **6. take for granted. a.** to accept (something) as true and not requiring verification. **b.** to take advantage of the benefits of (something) without due appreciation. ~*n.* **7.** a sum of money provided by a government or public fund to finance educational study, overseas aid, etc. **8.** a privilege, right, etc., that has been granted. **9.** the act of granting. **10.** a transfer of property by deed or other written instrument; conveyance. **11.** *U.S.* a territorial unit in Maine, New Hampshire, and Vermont, originally granted to an individual or organization. [C13: from Old French *graunter,* from Vulgar Latin *credentāre* (unattested), from Latin *crēdere* to believe] —**'grant+a·ble** *adj.* —**'grant+er** *n.*

Grant (grɑ:nt) *n.* **U·lys·ses S(impson),** original name *Hiram Ulysses Grant.* 1822–85, 18th president of the U.S. (1869–77); commander in chief of Union forces in the American Civil War (1864–65).

Gran+ta ('græntə, 'grɑ:ntə) *n.* the local name for the River Cam as it flows through Cambridge.

grant·ee (grɑ:n'ti:) *n. Law.* a person to whom a grant is made.

Granth *or* **Grant Sa+hib** (grʌnt) *n.* the sacred scripture of the Sikhs, believed by them to be the embodiment of the gurus. [from Hindi, from Sanskrit *grantha* a book]

grant-in-aid *n., pl.* **grants-in-aid. 1.** a sum of money granted by one government to a lower level of government or to a dependency for a programme, etc. **2.** *Education.* a grant provided by the central government or local education authority to ensure consistent standards in buildings and other facilities.

grant of pro+bate *n. Law.* an instrument authorizing an executor to control and dispose of a deceased person's estate if a will has been made.

gran+tor (grɑ:n'tɔ:, 'grɑ:ntə) *n. Law.* a person who makes a grant.

gran tur+is+mo ('græn tʊə'rɪzməʊ) *n.* a touring car; a name given to some car models, usually sports cars capable of high speed. Usually abbreviated to **GT** [C20: from Italian]

gran·u+lar ('grænjʊlə) *adj.* **1.** of, like, containing, or resembling a granule or granules. **2.** having a grainy or granulated surface. —**gran·u·lar+i·ty** (ˌgrænjʊ'lærɪtɪ) *n.* —**'gran·u·lar+ly** *adv.*

gran·u+late ('grænjʊˌleɪt) *vb.* **1.** to make into grains. **2.** to make or become roughened in surface texture. **3.** (*intr.*) (of a wound, ulcer, etc.) to form granulation tissue. —**'gran·u+la+tive** *adj.* —**'gran·u+ˌla+tor** *or* **'gran·u+ˌlat+er** *n.*

gran·u·lat+ed sug+ar *n.* a coarsely ground white sugar.

gran·u+la+tion (ˌgrænjʊ'leɪʃən) *n.* **1.** the act or process of granulating. **2.** a granulated texture or surface. **3.** a single bump or grain in such a surface. **4.** see **granulation tissue. 5.** Also called: **granule.** *Astronomy.* any of numerous bright regions (approximate diameter 900 km) having a fine granular structure that can appear briefly on any part of the sun's surface.

gran·u+la+tion tis+sue *n.* a mass of new connective tissue and capillaries formed on the surface of a healing ulcer or wound, usually leaving a scar. Nontechnical name: **proud flesh.**

gran+ule ('grænju:l) *n.* **1.** a small grain. **2.** *Astronomy.* another name for **granulation** (sense 5). [C17: from Late Latin *grānulum* a small GRAIN]

gran·u+lite ('grænjʊˌlaɪt) *n.* a granular foliated metamorphic rock in which the minerals form a mosaic of equal-sized granules. —**gran·u·lit+ic** (ˌgrænjʊ'lɪtɪk) *adj.*

gran·u+lo+cyte ('grænjʊləʊˌsaɪt) *n.* any of a group of phagocytic leucocytes having cytoplasmic granules that take up various dyes. See also **eosinophil, neutrophil** (sense 1), **basophil** (sense 2). —**gran·u+lo+cyt+ic** (ˌgrænjʊlə'sɪtɪk) *adj.*

gran·u+lo+ma (ˌgrænjʊ'ləʊmə) *n., pl.* **+mas** *or* **+ma+ta** (-mətə). a tumour composed of granulation tissue. —**gran·u·lom·a·tous** (ˌgrænjʊ'lɒmətəs) *adj.*

gran·u+lose ('grænjʊˌləʊs, -ˌləʊz) *adj.* a less common word for **granular.**

Gran·ville-Bar·ker ('grænvɪl 'bɑ:kə) *n.* **Har·ley.** 1877–1946, English dramatist, theatre director, and critic, noted particularly for his *Prefaces to Shakespeare* (1927–47).

grape (greɪp) *n.* **1.** the fruit of the grapevine, which has a purple or green skin and sweet flesh: eaten raw, dried to make raisins, currants, or sultanas, or used for making wine. **2.** any of various plants that bear grapelike fruit, such as the Oregon grape. **3.** See **grapevine** (sense 1). **4. the grape.** slang for **wine. 5.** See **grapeshot.** [C13: from Old French *grape* bunch of grapes, of Germanic origin; compare Old High German *krāpfo;* related to CRAMP[2], GRAPPLE] —**'grape+less** *adj.* —**'grape+ˌlike** *adj.* —**'grap+ey** *or* **'grap·y** *adj.*

grape+fruit ('greɪpˌfru:t) *n., pl.* **+fruit** *or* **+fruits. 1.** a tropical or subtropical evergreen rutaceous tree, *Citrus paradisi.* **2.** the large round edible fruit of this tree, which has yellow rind and juicy slightly bitter pulp. ~Also called (esp. in the U.S.): **pomelo.**

grape hy·a·cinth *n.* any of various Eurasian liliaceous plants of the genus *Muscari,* esp. *M. botryoides,* with clusters of rounded blue flowers resembling tiny grapes.

grapes (greɪps) *n. Vet. science.* an abnormal growth, resembling a bunch of grapes, on the fetlock of a horse.

grape+shot ('greɪpˌʃɒt) *n.* ammunition for cannons consisting of a number of or cluster of small projectiles.

grape sug+ar *n.* another name for **dextrose.**

grape+vine ('greɪpˌvaɪn) *n.* **1.** any of several vitaceous vines of the genus *Vitis,* esp. *V. vinifera* of E Asia, widely cultivated for its fruit (grapes): family *Vitaceae.* **2.** *Informal.* an unofficial means of relaying information, esp. from person to person. **3.** a wrestling hold in which a wrestler entwines his own leg around his opponent's and exerts pressure against various joints.

graph (grɑ:f, græf) *n.* **1.** Also called: **chart.** a drawing depicting the relation between certain sets of numbers or quantities by means of a series of dots, lines, etc., plotted with reference to a set of axes. See also **bar graph. 2.** *Maths.* a drawing depicting a functional relation between two or three variables by means of a curve or surface containing only those points whose coordinates satisfy the relation. **3.** *Linguistics.* a symbol in a writing system not further subdivisible into other such symbols. ~*vb.* **4.** (*tr.*) to draw or represent in a graph. [C19: short for *graphic formula*]

-graph *n. combining form.* **1.** an instrument that writes or records: *telegraph.* **2.** a writing, record, or drawing: *autograph; lithograph.* [via Latin from Greek *-graphos,* from *graphein* to write] —**-graph·ic** *or* —**graph·i·cal** *adj. combining form.* —**graph·i·cal·ly** *adv. combining form.*

graph+eme ('græfi:m) *n. Linguistics.* a minimum unit of writing, such as a letter, that may take different shapes but is regarded as a representation of the same letter. [C20: from Greek *graphēma* a letter] —**gra+'phem·i·cal·ly** *adv.*

-graph·er *n. combining form.* **1.** indicating a person who writes about or is skilled in a subject: *geographer; photographer.* **2.** indicating a person who writes, records, or draws in a specified way: *stenographer; lithographer.*

graph+ic ('græfɪk) *or* **graph·i+cal** *adj.* **1.** vividly or clearly described: *a graphic account of the disaster.* **2.** of or relating to writing or other inscribed representations: *graphic symbols.* **3.** *Maths.* using, relating to, or determined by a graph: *a graphic representation of the figures.* **4.** of or relating to the graphic arts. **5.** *Geology.* having or denoting a texture formed by intergrowth of the crystals to resemble writing: *graphic granite.* [C17: from Latin *graphicus,* from Greek *graphikos,* from *graphein* to write; see CARVE] —**'graph·i+cal+ly** *or* **'graph+ic+ly** *adv.* —**'graph·i+cal+ness** *or* **'graph+ic+ness** *n.*

graph+ic arts *pl. n.* any of the fine or applied visual arts based on drawing or the use of line, as opposed to colour or relief, on a plane surface, esp. illustration and print-making of all kinds.

graph+ics ('græfɪks) *n.* **1.** (*functioning as sing.*) the process or art of drawing in accordance with mathematical principles. **2.** (*functioning as sing.*) the study of writing systems. **3.** (*functioning as pl.*) the drawings, photographs, etc., in the layout of a magazine or book.

graph+ite ('græfaɪt) *n.* a blackish soft allotropic form of carbon in hexagonal crystalline form: used in pencils, crucibles, and electrodes, as a lubricant, and as a moderator in nuclear reactors. Also called: **plumbago.** [C18: from German *Graphit;* from Greek *graphein* to write + -ITE[1]] —**gra+'phit+ic** (grə'fɪtɪk) *adj.*

graph·i·tize *or* **graph·i·tise** ('græfɪˌtaɪz) *vb.* (*tr.*) **1.** to convert (a substance) into graphite, usually by heating. **2.** to coat or impregnate with graphite. —**ˌgraph·i·ti·'za·tion** *or* **ˌgraph·i+ti+'sa·tion** *n.*

graph+ol+o·gy (græ'fɒlədʒɪ) *n.* **1.** the study of handwriting, esp. to analyse the writer's character. **2.** *Linguistics.* the study of writing systems. —**graph·o·log+ic** (ˌgræfə'lɒdʒɪk) *or* **ˌgraph·o·'log·i·cal** *adj.* —**graph+'ol·o·gist** *n.*

graph·o·mo+tor ('græfəˌməʊtə) *adj.* of or relating to the muscular movements used or required in writing.

graph pa+per *n.* paper printed with intersecting lines, usually horizontal and vertical and equally spaced, for drawing graphs, diagrams, etc.

-graph·y *n. combining form.* **1.** indicating a form or process of writing, representing, etc.: *calligraphy; photography.* **2.** indicating an art or descriptive science: *choreography; oceanography.* [via Latin from Greek *-graphia,* from *graphein* to write]

grap+nel ('græpn³l) *n.* **1.** a device with a multiple hook at one end and attached to a rope, which is thrown or hooked over a firm mooring to secure an object attached to the other end of the rope. **2.** a light anchor for small boats. [C14: from Old French *grapin* a little hook, from *grape* a hook; see GRAPE]

grap·pa ('grɑːpɑː) *n.* a spirit distilled from the fermented remains of grapes after pressing. [Italian: grape stalk, of Germanic origin; see GRAPE]

Grap·pel·li (grə'pɛlɪ) *n.* **Steph·ane** ('stɛfᵊn). born 1908, French jazz violinist: with Django Reinhardt, he led the Quintet of the Hot Club of France between 1934 and 1939.

grap·ple ('græpᵊl) *vb.* **1.** to come to grips with (one or more persons), esp. to struggle in hand-to-hand combat. **2.** (*intr.*; foll. by *with*) to cope or contend: *to grapple with a financial problem.* **3.** (*tr.*) to secure with a grapple. ~*n.* **4.** any form of hook or metal instrument by which something is secured, such as a grapnel. **5. a.** the act of gripping or seizing, as in wrestling. **b.** a grip or hold. **6.** a contest of grappling, esp. a wrestling match. [C16: from Old French *grappelle* a little hook, from *grape* hook; see GRAPNEL] —'**grap·pler** *n.*

grap·ple plant *n.* a herbaceous plant, *Harpagophytum procumbens*, of southern Africa, whose fruits are covered with large woody barbed hooks: family *Pedaliaceae*. Also called: **wait-a-bit.**

grap·pling ('græplɪŋ) *n.* **1.** the act of gripping or seizing, as in wrestling. **2.** a hook used for securing something.

grap·pling i·ron *or* **hook** *n.* a grapnel, esp. one used for securing ships.

grap·to·lite ('græptəˌlaɪt) *n.* any extinct Palaeozoic colonial animal of the class *Graptolithina*, usually regarded as related to the coelenterates: a common fossil. [C19: from Greek *graptos* written, from *graphein* to write + -LITE]

Gras·mere ('grɑːsˌmɪə) *n.* a village in NW England, in Cumbria at the head of **Lake Grasmere**: home of William Wordsworth and of Thomas de Quincey.

grasp (grɑːsp) *vb.* **1.** to grip (something) firmly with or as if with the hands. **2.** (when *intr.*, often foll. by *at*) to struggle, snatch, or grope (for). **3.** (*tr.*) to understand, esp. with effort. ~*n.* **4.** the act of grasping. **5.** a grip or clasp, as of a hand. **6.** the capacity to accomplish (esp. in the phrase **within one's grasp**). **7.** total rule or possession. **8.** understanding; comprehension. [C14: from Low German *grapsen*; related to Old English *græppian* to seize, Old Norse *grāpa* to steal] —'**grasp·a·ble** *adj.* —'**grasp·er** *n.*

grasp·ing ('grɑːspɪŋ) *adj.* greedy; avaricious; rapacious. —'**grasp·ing·ly** *adv.* —'**grasp·ing·ness** *n.*

grass (grɑːs) *n.* **1.** any monocotyledonous plant of the family *Gramineae*, having jointed stems sheathed by long narrow leaves, flowers in spikes, and seedlike fruits. The family includes cereals, bamboo, etc. **2.** such plants collectively, in a lawn, meadow, etc. Related adj.: **verdant.** **3.** any similar plant, such as knotgrass, deergrass, or scurvy grass. **4.** ground on which such plants grow; a lawn, field, etc. **5.** ground on which animals are grazed; pasture. **6.** a slang word for **marijuana.** **7.** *Brit. slang.* a person who informs, esp. on criminals. **8. let the grass grow under one's feet.** to squander time or opportunity. **9. put out to grass. a.** to retire (a racehorse). **b.** *Informal.* to retire (a person). ~*vb.* **10.** to cover or become covered with grass. **11.** to feed or be fed with grass. **12.** (*tr.*) to spread (cloth, etc.) out on grass for drying or bleaching in the sun. **13.** (*tr.*) *Sport, chiefly U.S.* to knock or bring down (an opponent). **14.** (*tr.*) to shoot down (a bird). **15.** (*tr.*) to land (a fish) on a river bank. **16.** (when *intr.*, usually foll. by *on*) *Brit. slang.* to inform, esp. to the police. [Old English *græs*; related to Old Norse, Gothic, Old High German *gras*, Middle High German *gruose* sap] —'**grass·less** *adj.* —'**grass·ˌlike** *adj.*

Grass (*German* gras) *n.* **Gün·ter** ('gyntər). born 1927, German novelist, dramatist, and poet, noted particularly for his novels *The Tin Drum* (1959) and *Dog Years* (1963).

grass box *n.* a container attached to a lawn mower that receives grass after it has been cut.

grass cloth *n.* a cloth made from plant fibres, such as jute or hemp.

grass court *n.* a tennis court covered with grass. See also **hard court.**

grass·finch ('grɑːsˌfɪntʃ) *n.* any Australian weaverbird of the genus *Poephila* and related genera, many of which are brightly coloured and kept as cage birds.

grass hock·ey *n. Canadian.* field hockey, as contrasted with ice hockey.

grass·hook ('grɑːsˌhʊk) *n.* another name for **sickle.**

grass·hop·per ('grɑːsˌhɒpə) *n.* **1.** any orthopterous insect of the families *Acrididae* (**short-horned grasshoppers**) and *Tettigoniidae* (**long-horned grasshoppers**), typically terrestrial, feeding on plants, and producing a ticking sound by rubbing the hind legs against the leathery forewings. See also **locust** (sense 1), **katydid.** **2.** an iced cocktail of equal parts of crème de menthe, crème de cacao, and cream.

grass·land ('grɑːsˌlænd) *n.* **1.** land, such as a prairie, on which grass predominates. **2.** land reserved for natural grass pasture.

grass-of-Par·nas·sus *n.* a herbaceous perennial N temperate marsh plant, *Parnassia palustris*, with solitary whitish flowers: family *Parnassiaceae*.

grass·quit ('grɑːsˌkwɪt) *n.* any tropical American finch of the genus *Tiaris* and related genera, such as *T. olivacea* (**yellow-faced grassquit**). [from GRASS + *quit*, a bird name in Jamaica]

grass roots *pl. n.* **1.** the essentials. **2. a.** people, esp. from rural areas, considered to represent fundamental and practical views, esp. in politics. **b.** such rural areas.

grass snake *n.* **1.** a harmless nonvenomous European colubrid snake, *Natrix natrix*, having a brownish-green body with variable markings. **2.** any of several similar related European snakes, such as *Natrix maura* (**viperine grass snake**).

grass tree *n.* **1.** Also called: **blackboy.** any liliaceous plant of the Australian genus *Xanthorrhoea*, having a woody stem, stiff grasslike leaves, and a spike of small white flowers. Some species produce fragrant resins. See also **acaroid gum.** **2.** any of several similar Australasian plants.

grass wid·ow *or* (*masc.*) **grass wid·ow·er** *n.* **1.** a person divorced, separated, or living away from his or her spouse. **2.** a person whose spouse is regularly away for a short period. [C16: perhaps an allusion to a grass bed as representing an illicit relationship; compare BASTARD]

grass·y ('grɑːsɪ) *adj.* **grass·i·er, grass·i·est.** covered with, containing, or resembling grass. —'**grass·i·ness** *n.*

grate[1] (greɪt) *vb.* **1.** (*tr.*) to reduce to small shreds by rubbing against a rough or sharp perforated surface: *to grate carrots.* **2.** to scrape (an object) against or (objects) together, producing a harsh rasping sound, or (of objects) to scrape with such a sound. **3.** (when *intr.*, foll. by *on* or *upon*) to annoy. **4.** (*tr.*) *Archaic.* to abrade; erode. ~*n.* **5.** a harsh rasping sound. [C15: from Old French *grater* to scrape, of Germanic origin; compare Old High German *krazzōn*]

grate[2] (greɪt) *n.* **1.** a framework of metal bars for holding fuel in a fireplace, stove, or furnace. **2.** a less common word for **fireplace.** **3.** another name for **grating**[1] (sense 1). **4.** *Mining.* a perforated metal screen for grading crushed ore. ~*vb.* **5.** (*tr.*) to provide with a grate or grates. [C14: from Old French *grate*, from Latin *crātis* hurdle]

grate·ful ('greɪtfʊl) *adj.* **1.** thankful for gifts, favours, etc.; appreciative. **2.** showing gratitude: *a grateful letter.* **3.** favourable or pleasant: *a grateful rest.* [C16: from obsolete *grate*, from Latin *grātus* + -FUL] —'**grate·ful·ly** *adv.* —'**grate·ful·ness** *n.*

grat·er ('greɪtə) *n.* **1.** a kitchen utensil with sharp-edged perforations for grating carrots, cheese, etc. **2.** a person or thing that grates.

Gra·ti·an ('greɪʃɪən) *n.* Latin name *Flavius Gratianus.* 359–383 A.D., Roman emperor (367–383): ruled the Western Roman Empire with his brother Valentinian II (375–83); appointed Theodosius I emperor of the Eastern Roman Empire (379).

grat·i·cule ('grætɪˌkjuːl) *n.* **1.** the grid of intersecting lines of latitude and longitude on which a map is drawn. **2.** a scale or network of fine lines in the eyepiece of a telescope or microscope, to assist in locating objects. [C19: from French, from Latin *crāticula*, from *crātis* wickerwork]

grat·i·fi·ca·tion (ˌgrætɪfɪ'keɪʃən) *n.* **1.** the act of gratifying or the state of being gratified. **2.** something that gratifies. **3.** an obsolete word for **gratuity.**

grat·i·fy ('grætɪˌfaɪ) *vb.* **·fies, ·fy·ing, ·fied.** (*tr.*) **1.** to satisfy or please. **2.** to yield to or indulge (a desire, whim, etc.). **3.** *Obsolete.* to reward. [C16: from Latin *grātificārī* to do a favour to, from *grātus* grateful + *facere* to make] —'**grat·i·ˌfi·er** *n.* —'**grat·i·ˌfy·ing** *adj.* —'**grat·i·ˌfy·ing·ly** *adv.*

grat·in (*French* gra'tɛ̃) See **au gratin.**

grat·ing[1] ('greɪtɪŋ) *n.* **1.** Also called: **grate.** a framework of metal bars in the form of a grille set into a wall, pavement, etc., serving as a cover or guard but admitting air and sometimes light. **2.** short for **diffraction grating.**

grat·ing[2] ('greɪtɪŋ) *adj.* **1.** (of sounds) harsh and rasping. **2.** annoying; irritating. ~*n.* **3.** (*often pl.*) something produced by grating. —'**grat·ing·ly** *adv.*

gra·tis ('greɪtɪs, 'grætɪs, 'grɑːtɪs) *adv., adj.* (*postpositive*) without payment; free of charge. [C15: from Latin: out of kindness, from *grātiīs* ablative pl. of *grātia* favour]

grat·i·tude ('grætɪˌtjuːd) *n.* a feeling of thankfulness or appreciation, as for gifts or favours. [C16: from Medieval Latin *grātitūdō*, from Latin *grātus* GRATEFUL]

Grat·tan ('grætᵊn) *n.* **Hen·ry.** 1746–1820, Irish statesman and orator: led the movement that secured legislative independence for Ireland (1782), opposed union with England (1800), and campaigned for Catholic emancipation.

gra·tu·i·tous (grə'tjuːɪtəs) *adj.* **1.** given or received without payment or obligation. **2.** without cause; unjustified. **3.** *Law.* given or made without receiving any value in return: *a gratuitous contract.* [C17: from Latin *grātuītus* from *grātia* favour] —**gra·'tu·i·tous·ly** *adv.* —**gra·'tu·i·tous·ness** *n.*

gra·tu·i·ty (grə'tjuːɪtɪ) *n., pl.* **·ties.** **1.** a gift or reward, usually of money, for services rendered; tip. **2.** something given without claim or obligation. **3.** *Military.* a financial award granted for long or meritorious service.

grat·u·late ('grætjʊˌleɪt) *vb.* (*tr.*) *Archaic.* **1.** to greet joyously. **2.** to congratulate. [C16: from Latin *grātulārī*, from *grātus* pleasing] —'**grat·u·lant** *adj.* —ˌ**grat·u·'la·tion** *n.* —'**grat·u·la·to·ry** *adj.*

Grau·bün·den (*German* grau'byndᵊn) *n.* an Alpine canton of E Switzerland: the largest of the cantons, but sparsely populated. Capital: Chur. Pop.: 162 086 (1970). Area: 7109 sq. km (2773 sq. miles). Italian name: **Grigioni.** Romansch name: **Grishun.** French name: **Grisons.**

grau·pel ('graʊpᵊl) *n.* soft hail or snow pellets. [German, from *Graupe*, probably from Serbo-Croatian *krupa*; related to Russian *krupá* peeled grain]

grav (græv) *n.* a unit of acceleration equal to the standard acceleration of free fall. 1 grav is equivalent to 9.806 65 metres per second per second. Symbol: G

gra·va·men (grə'veɪmɛn) *n., pl.* **·vam·i·na** (-'væmɪnə). **1.** *Law.* that part of an accusation weighing most heavily against an accused. **2.** *Law.* the substance or material grounds of a complaint. **3.** a rare word for **grievance.** [C17: from Late

Latin: trouble, from Latin *gravāre* to load, from *gravis* heavy; see GRAVE[2]]

grave[1] (greɪv) *n.* **1.** a place for the burial of a corpse, esp. beneath the ground and usually marked by a tombstone. Related adj.: **sepulchral. 2.** something resembling a grave or resting place: *the ship went to its grave.* **3.** (often preceded by *the*) a poetic term for **death. 4. have one foot in the grave.** to be old, weak, or near death. **5. to make (someone) turn (over) in his grave.** to do something that would have shocked or distressed a person now dead: *many modern dictionaries would make Dr. Johnson turn in his grave.* [Old English *græf;* related to Old Frisian *gref,* Old High German *grab,* Old Slavonic *grobŭ;* see GRAVE[3]]

grave[2] (greɪv) *adj.* **1.** serious and solemn: *a grave look.* **2.** full of or suggesting danger: *a grave situation.* **3.** important; crucial: *grave matters of state.* **4.** (of colours) sober or dull. **5.** (grɑːv). *Phonetics.* **a.** (of a vowel or syllable in some languages with a pitch accent, such as ancient Greek) spoken on a lower or falling musical pitch relative to neighbouring syllables or vowels. **b.** of or relating to an accent (`) over vowels, denoting a pronunciation with lower or falling musical pitch (as in ancient Greek), with certain special quality (as in French), or in a manner that gives the vowel status as a syllable nucleus not usually possessed by it in that position (as in English *agèd*). Compare **acute** (sense 8), **circumflex.** ~*n.* **6.** (grɑːv). a grave accent. [C16: from Old French, from Latin *gravis;* related to Greek *barus* heavy; see GRAVAMEN] —'**grave·ly** *adv.* —'**grave·ness** *n.*

grave[3] (greɪv) *vb.* **graves, grav·ing, graved; graved** *or* **grav·en.** (*tr.*) *Archaic.* **1.** to cut, carve, sculpt, or engrave. **2.** to fix firmly in the mind. [Old English *grafan;* related to Old Norse *grafa,* Old High German *graban* to dig]

grave[4] (greɪv) *vb.* (*tr.*) *Nautical.* to clean and apply a coating of pitch to (the bottom of a vessel). [C15: perhaps from Old French *grave* GRAVEL]

gra·ve[5] ('grɑːvɪ) *adj., adv. Music.* to be performed in a solemn manner. [C17: from Italian: heavy, from Latin *gravis*]

grave clothes *pl. n.* the wrappings in which a dead body is interred.

grav·el ('græv[ə]l) *n.* **1.** a mixture of rock fragments and pebbles that is coarser than sand. **2.** *Pathol.* small rough calculi in the kidneys or bladder. ~*vb.* **·els, ·el·ling, ·elled** *or U.S.* **·els, ·el·ing, ·eled.** (*tr.*) **3.** to cover with gravel. **4.** to confound or confuse. **5.** *U.S. informal.* to annoy or disturb. [C13: from Old French *gravele,* diminutive of *grave,* gravel, perhaps of Celtic origin] —'**grav·el·ish** *adj.*

grav·el-blind *adj. Literary.* almost entirely blind. [C16: from GRAVEL + BLIND, formed on the model of SANDBLIND]

grav·el·ly ('grævəlɪ) *adj.* **1.** consisting of or abounding in gravel. **2.** of or like gravel. **3.** (esp. of a voice) harsh and grating.

grav·en ('greɪv[ə]n) *vb.* **1.** a past participle of **grave**[3]. ~*adj.* **2.** strongly fixed.

Gra·ven·ha·ge (ˌsxraːvən'haːxə) *n.* **'s.** a Dutch name for (The) **Hague.**

grav·en im·age *n. Chiefly Bible.* a carved image used as an idol.

grav·er ('greɪvə) *n.* any of various engraving, chasing, or sculpting tools, such as a burin.

Graves (grɑːv) *n.* **1.** (*sometimes not cap.*) a white or red wine from the district around Bordeaux, France. **2.** a dry or medium sweet white wine from any country: *Spanish Graves.*

Graves (greɪvz) *n.* **Rob·ert (Ranke).** born 1895, English poet, novelist, and critic, whose works include his World War I autobiography, *Goodbye to All That* (1929), and the historical novels *I, Claudius* (1934) and *Claudius the God* (1934).

Graves' dis·ease *n.* another name for **exophthalmic goitre.** [C19: named after R. J. *Graves* (1796–1853), Irish physician]

Graves·end (ˌgreɪvz'ɛnd) *n.* a river port in SE England, in NW Kent on the Thames. Pop.: 54 044 (1971).

grave·stone ('greɪvˌstəʊn) *n.* a stone marking a grave and usually inscribed with the name and dates of the person buried.

Gra·vett·i·an (grə'vɛtɪən) *adj.* of, referring to, or characteristic of an Upper Palaeolithic culture, characterized esp. by small pointed blades with blunt backs. [C20: from *La Gravette* on the Dordogne, France]

grave-wax *n.* the nontechnical name for **adipocere.**

grave·yard ('greɪvˌjɑːd) *n.* a place for graves; a burial ground, esp. a small one or one in a churchyard.

grav·id ('grævɪd) *adj.* the technical word for **pregnant.** [C16: from Latin *gravidus,* from *gravis* heavy] —**gra·'vid·i·ty** *or* '**gra·vid·ness** *n.* —'**gra·vid·ly** *adv.*

gra·vim·e·ter (grə'vɪmɪtə) *n.* **1.** an instrument for measuring the earth's gravitational field at points on its surface. **2.** an instrument for measuring relative density. [C18: from French *gravimètre,* from Latin *gravis* heavy] —**gra·'vim·e·try** *n.*

grav·i·met·ric (ˌgrævɪ'mɛtrɪk) *or* **grav·i·met·ri·cal** *adj.* of, concerned with, or using measurement by weight. Compare **volumetric.** —ˌ**grav·i·'met·ri·cal·ly** *adv.*

grav·i·met·ric a·nal·y·sis *n. Chem.* quantitative analysis by weight, usually involving the precipitation, filtration, drying, and weighing of the precipitate. Compare **volumetric analysis.**

grav·ing dock *n.* another term for **dry dock.**

grav·i·tate ('grævɪˌteɪt) *vb.* (*intr.*) **1.** *Physics.* to move under the influence of gravity. **2.** (usually foll. by *to* or *towards*) to be influenced or drawn, as by strong impulses. **3.** to sink or settle. —'**grav·i·ˌtat·er** *n.*

grav·i·ta·tion (ˌgrævɪ'teɪʃən) *n.* **1.** the force of attraction that bodies exert on one another as a result of their mass. **2.** any process or result caused by this interaction, such as the fall of a body to the surface of the earth. ~Also called: **gravity.** See also **Newton's law of gravitation.** —ˌ**grav·i·'ta·tion·al** *adj.* —ˌ**grav·i·'ta·tion·al·ly** *adv.*

grav·i·ta·tion·al con·stant *n.* the factor relating force to mass and distance in Newton's law of gravitation. It is a universal constant with the value 6.670×10^{-11}N m[2] kg[−2]. Symbol: *G*

grav·i·ta·tion·al field *n.* the field of force surrounding a body of finite mass in which another body would experience an attractive force that is proportional to the product of the masses and inversely proportional to the square of the distance between them: *the gravitational field of the earth.*

grav·i·ta·tion·al in·ter·ac·tion *n.* an interaction between particles or bodies resulting from their mass. It is very weak and occurs at all distances. Compare **electromagnetic interaction, strong interaction, weak interaction.**

grav·i·ta·tion·al mass *n.* the mass of a body determined by the extent to which it responds to the force of gravity. Compare **inertial mass.**

grav·i·ta·tive ('grævɪˌteɪtɪv) *adj.* **1.** of, involving, or produced by gravitation. **2.** tending or causing to gravitate.

grav·i·ton ('grævɪˌtɒn) *n.* a postulated quantum of gravitational energy, usually considered to be a particle with zero charge and rest mass and a spin of 2. Compare **photon.**

grav·i·ty ('grævɪtɪ) *n., pl.* **·ties. 1.** the force of attraction that moves or tends to move bodies towards the centre of a celestial body, such as the earth or moon. **2.** the property of being heavy or having weight. See also **specific gravity, centre of gravity. 3.** another name for **gravitation. 4.** seriousness or importance, esp. as a consequence of an action or opinion. **5.** manner or conduct that is solemn or dignified. **6.** lowness in pitch. **7.** (*modifier*) of or relating to gravity or gravitation or their effects: *gravity wave; gravity feed.* [C16: from Latin *gravitās* weight, from *gravis* heavy]

grav·i·ty cell *n.* an electrolytic cell in which the electrodes lie in two different electrolytes, which are separated into two layers by the difference in their relative densities.

grav·i·ty fault *n.* a fault in which the rocks on the upper side of an inclined fault plane have been displaced downwards; normal fault.

gra·vure (grə'vjʊə) *n.* **1.** a method of intaglio printing using a plate with many small etched recesses. See also **rotogravure. 2.** See **photogravure. 3.** matter printed by this process. [C19: from French, from *graver* to engrave, of Germanic origin; see GRAVE[3]]

gra·vy ('greɪvɪ) *n., pl.* **·vies. 1. a.** the juices that exude from meat during cooking. **b.** the sauce made by thickening and flavouring such juices. **2.** *Slang, chiefly U.S.* money or gain acquired with little effort, esp. above that needed for ordinary living. [C14: from Old French *gravé,* of uncertain origin]

gra·vy boat *n.* a small often boat-shaped vessel for serving gravy or other sauces.

gra·vy train *n. Slang, chiefly U.S.* a job requiring comparatively little work for good pay, benefits, etc.

gray (greɪ) *adj., n., vb.* a variant spelling (now esp. U.S.) of **grey.** —'**gray·ish** *adj.* —'**gray·ly** *adv.* —'**gray·ness** *n.*

Gray (greɪ) *n.* **Thom·as.** 1716–71, English poet, best known for his *Elegy written in a Country Churchyard* (1751).

Gray code *n.* a modification of a number system, esp. a binary code, in which any adjacent pair of numbers, in counting order, differ in their digits at one position only, the absolute difference being the value 1. [named after Frank *Gray,* 20th-century American physicist]

gray·ling ('greɪlɪŋ) *n., pl.* **·ling** *or* **·lings. 1.** any freshwater salmonoid food fish of the genus *Thymallus* and family *Thymallidae,* of the N hemisphere, having a long spiny dorsal fin, a silvery back, and greyish-green sides. **2.** any butterfly of the satyrid genus *Hipparchia* and related genera, esp. *H. semele* of Europe, having grey or greyish-brown wings.

Gray's Inn *n.* (in England) one of the four legal societies in London that together form the Inns of Court.

Graz (*German* graːts) *n.* an industrial city in SE Austria, capital of Styria province: the second largest city in the country. Pop.: 248 500 (1971).

graze[1] (greɪz) *vb.* **1.** to allow (animals) to consume the vegetation on (an area of land), or (of animals, esp. cows and sheep) to feed thus. **2.** (*tr.*) to tend (livestock) while at pasture. [Old English *grasian,* from *græs* GRASS; related to Old High German *grasōn,* Dutch *grazen,* Norwegian *grasa*]

graze[2] (greɪz) *vb.* **1.** (when *intr.,* often foll. by *against* or *along*) to brush or scrape (against) gently, esp. in passing. **2.** (*tr.*) to break the skin of (a part of the body) by scraping. ~*n.* **3.** the act of grazing. **4.** a scrape or abrasion made by grazing. [C17: probably special use of GRAZE[1]; related to Swedish *gräsa*] —'**graz·er** *n.* —'**graz·ing·ly** *adv.*

gra·zi·er ('greɪzɪə) *n.* a rancher or farmer who rears or fattens cattle or sheep on grazing land.

graz·ing ('greɪzɪŋ) *n.* **1.** the vegetation on ranges or pastures that is available for livestock to feed upon. **2.** the land on which this is growing.

grease *n.* (griːs). **1.** animal fat in a soft or melted condition. **2.** any thick fatty oil, esp. one used as a lubricant for machinery, etc. **3.** Also called: **grease wool.** shorn fleece before it has been cleaned. **4.** *Vet. science.* inflammation of the skin of horses around the fetlocks, usually covered with an oily secretion. ~*vb.* (griːs, griːz). (*tr.*) **5.** to soil, coat, or lubricate with grease. **6.** to ease the course of: *his education greased his path to success.* **7. grease the palm** (*or* **hand**) **of.** *Slang.* to bribe;

influence by giving money to. [C13: from Old French *craisse,* from Latin *crassus* thick] —**'grease+less** *adj.*

grease cup *n.* a container that stores grease and feeds it through a small hole into a bearing.

grease gun *n.* a device for forcing grease through nipples into bearings, usually consisting of a cylinder with a plunger and nozzle fitted to it.

grease mon+key *n. Informal.* a mechanic, esp. one who works on cars or aircraft.

grease+paint ('gri:sˌpeɪnt) *n.* **1.** a waxy or greasy substance used as make-up by actors. **2.** theatrical make-up.

greas+er ('gri:sə) *n. Brit. slang.* **1.** a mechanic, esp. of motor vehicles. **2.** a young long-haired motorcyclist, usually one of a gang. **3.** an unpleasant person, esp. one who ingratiates himself with superiors.

grease+wood ('gri:sˌwʊd) *or* **grease+bush** *n.* **1.** Also called: **chico.** a spiny chenopodiaceous shrub, *Sarcobatus vermiculatus* of W North America, that yields an oil used as a fuel. **2.** any of various similar or related plants, such as the creosote bush.

greas·y ('gri:sɪ, -zɪ) *adj.* **greas·i+er, greas·i+est. 1.** coated or soiled with or as if with grease. **2.** composed of or full of grease. **3.** resembling grease. **4.** unctuous or oily in manner. —**'greas·i·ly** *adv.* —**'greas·i+ness** *n.*

greas·y spoon *n. Slang.* a small, cheap, and often unsanitary restaurant, usually specializing in fried foods.

great (greɪt) *adj.* **1.** relatively large in size or extent; big. **2.** relatively large in number; having many parts or members: *a great assembly.* **3.** of relatively long duration: *a great wait.* **4.** of larger size or more importance than others of its kind: *the great auk.* **5.** extreme or more than usual: *great worry.* **6.** of significant importance or consequence: *a great decision.* **7. a.** of exceptional talents or achievements; remarkable: *a great writer.* **b.** (*as n.*): *the great; one of the greats.* **8.** arising from or possessing idealism in thought, action, etc.; heroic: *great deeds.* **9.** illustrious or eminent: *a great history.* **10.** impressive or striking: *a great show of wealth.* **11.** much in use; favoured: *poetry was a great convention of the Romantic era.* **12.** active or enthusiastic: *a great walker.* **13.** (often foll. by *at*) skilful or adroit: *a great carpenter; you are great at singing.* **14.** *Informal.* excellent; fantastic. **15.** *Brit. informal.* (intensifier): *a dirty great smack in the face.* **16.** (*postpositive;* foll. by *with*) *Archaic.* **a.** pregnant: *great with child.* **b.** full (of): *great with hope.* **17.** (intensifier, used in mild oaths): *Great Scott!* **18. be great on.** *Informal.* **a.** to be informed about. **b.** to be enthusiastic about or for. ~*adv.* **19.** *U.S. informal.* very well; excellently: *it was working great.* ~*n.* **20.** Also called: **great organ.** the principal manual on an organ. Compare **choir** (sense 4), **swell** (sense 16). [Old English *grēat;* related to Old Frisian *grāt,* Old High German *grōz;* see GRIT, GROAT] —**'great+ly** *adv.* —**'great+ness** *n.*

great- *prefix.* **1.** being the parent of a person's grandparent (in the combinations **great-grandfather, great-grandmother, great-grandparent**). **2.** being the child of a person's grandchild (in the combinations **great-grandson, great-granddaughter, great-grandchild**).

great ape *n.* any of the larger anthropoid apes, such as the chimpanzee, orang-utan, or gorilla.

great auk *n.* a large flightless auk, *Pinguinus impennis,* extinct since the middle of the 19th century.

great-aunt *or* **grand+aunt** *n.* an aunt of one's father or mother; sister of one's grandfather or grandmother.

Great Aus+tral+i·an Bight *n.* a wide bay of the Indian Ocean, in S Australia, extending from Cape Pasley to the Eyre Peninsula: notorious for storms.

Great Bar+ri+er Reef *n.* a coral reef in the Coral Sea, off the NE coast of Australia, extending for about 2000 km (1250 miles) from the Torres Strait along the coast of Queensland; the largest coral reef in the world.

Great Ba+sin *n.* a semiarid region of the western U.S., between the Wasatch and the Sierra Nevada Mountains, having no drainage to the ocean: includes Nevada, W Utah, and parts of E California, S Oregon, and Idaho. Area: about 490 000 sq. km (189 000 sq. miles).

Great Bear *n.* **the.** the English name for **Ursa Major.**

Great Bear Lake *n.* a lake in NW Canada, in the Northwest Territories: the largest freshwater lake entirely in Canada; drained by the **Great Bear River,** which flows to the Mackenzie River. Area: 31 792 sq. km (12 275 sq. miles).

Great Belt *n.* a strait in Denmark, between Sjælland and Fyn islands, linking the Kattegat with the Baltic. Danish name: **Store Bælt.**

Great Brit+ain *n.* the largest island in Europe and in the British Isles, separated from the mainland of W Europe by the English Channel and the North Sea: consists of England, Scotland, and Wales; forms, with Northern Ireland, the United Kingdom of Great Britain and Northern Ireland. It is divided geologically along a line between the Tees and the Exe, the rocks to the north and west being generally old and resistant, constituting mountains and upland, the rocks to the south and east being younger, forming plains and low hills. It has an indented coastline and several groups of islands. Pop.: 53 821 364 (1971). Area: 229 523 sq. km (88 619 sq. miles). See also **United Kingdom.**

great cir+cle *n.* a circular section of a sphere that has a radius equal to that of the sphere. Compare **small circle.**

great+coat ('greɪtˌkəʊt) *n.* a heavy overcoat, now worn esp. by men in the armed forces. —**'great+ˌcoat·ed** *adj.*

great coun+cil *n.* (in medieval England) an assembly of the great nobles and prelates to advise the king.

great crest+ed grebe *n.* a European grebe, *Podiceps cristatus,* having blackish ear tufts and, in the breeding season, a dark brown frill around the head.

Great Dane *n.* one of a very large rangy breed of dog with a short coat.

Great Di+vide *n.* another name for the **Continental Divide.**

Great Di+vid+ing Range *pl. n.* a series of mountain ranges and plateaus roughly parallel to the E coast of Australia, in Queensland, New South Wales, and Victoria; the highest range is the Australian Alps, in the south.

Great Dog *n.* **the.** the English name for **Canis Major.**

great+en ('greɪtᵊn) *vb. Archaic.* to make or become great.

Great+er ('greɪtə) *adj.* (of a city) considered with the inclusion of the outer suburbs: *Greater London.*

Great+er An+til+les *pl. n.* **the.** a group of islands in the West Indies, including Cuba, Jamaica, Hispaniola, and Puerto Rico.

great+er cel+an+dine *n.* a Eurasian papaveraceous plant, *Chelidonium majus,* with yellow flowers and deeply divided leaves. Also called: **swallowwort.** Compare **lesser celandine.**

Great+er Lon+don *n.* See **London**[1] (sense 2).

Great+er Man+ches+ter *n.* a metropolitan county of NW England, comprising the districts of Wigan, Bolton, Bury, Rochdale, Salford, Manchester, Oldham, Trafford, Stockport, and Tameside. Administrative centre: Manchester. Pop.: 2 684 100 (1976 est.). Area: 1285 sq. km (496 sq. miles).

Great+er Sun+da Is+lands *pl. n.* a group of islands in the W Malay Archipelago, forming the larger part of the Sunda Islands: consists of Borneo, Sumatra, Java, and Celebes.

great+est ('greɪtɪst) *adj.* **1.** the superlative of **great.** ~*n.* **2. the greatest.** *Slang.* an exceptional person.

great+est com+mon di+vi+sor *n.* another name for **highest common factor.**

Great Glen *n.* **the.** a fault valley across the whole of Scotland, extending southwest from the Moray Firth in the east to Loch Linnhe and containing Loch Ness and Loch Lochy. Also called: **Glen More, Glen Albyn.**

great gross *n.* a unit of quantity equal to one dozen gross (or 1728).

great-heart·ed *adj.* benevolent or noble; magnanimous. —**ˌgreat-'heart·ed·ness** *n.*

Great In+di·an Des+ert *n.* another name for the **Thar Desert.**

Great Ka+roo *or* **Cen+tral Ka+roo** (kə'ru:) *n.* an arid plateau of S central South Africa, in Cape Province, separated from the Little Karoo to the southwest by the Swartberg range. Average height: 750 m (2500 ft.).

Great Lakes *pl. n.* a group of five lakes in central North America with connecting waterways: the largest group of lakes in the world: consists of Lakes Superior, Huron, Erie, and Ontario, which are divided by the border between the U.S. and Canada and Lake Michigan, which is wholly in the U.S.; constitutes the most important system of inland waterways in the world, discharging through the St. Lawrence into the Atlantic. Total length: 3767 km (2340 miles). Area: 246 490 sq. km (95 170 sq. miles).

Great Leap For+ward *n.* **the.** the attempt by the People's Republic of China in 1959–60 to solve the country's economic problems by labour-intensive industrialization.

Great Mo+gul *n.* any of the Muslim emperors of India (1526–1857).

great-neph·ew *or* **grand+neph·ew** *n.* a son of one's nephew or niece; grandson of one's brother or sister.

great-niece *or* **grand+niece** *n.* a daughter of one's nephew or niece; granddaughter of one's brother or sister.

great north+ern div+er *n.* a large northern bird, *Gavia immer,* with a black-and-white chequered back and a black head and neck in summer: family *Gaviidae* (divers).

Great Ouse *n.* See **Ouse** (sense 1).

Great Plains *pl. n.* a vast region of North America east of the Rocky Mountains, extending from the lowlands of the Mackenzie River (Canada), south to the Big Bend of the Rio Grande.

Great Pow+er *n.* a nation that has exceptional political influence, resources, and military strength.

great prim+er *n.* (formerly) a size of printer's type approximately equal to 18 point.

Great Re+bel+lion *n.* **the.** another name for the English **Civil War.**

Great Rift Val+ley *n.* the most extensive rift in the earth's surface, extending from the Jordan valley in Syria to Mozambique; marked by a chain of steep-sided lakes, volcanoes, and escarpments.

Great Rus+sian *n.* **1.** *Linguistics.* the technical name for **Russian.** Compare **Byelorussian, Ukrainian. 2.** a member of the chief East Slavonic people of Russia. ~*adj.* **3.** of or relating to this people or their language.

Greats (greɪts) *pl. n.* (at Oxford University) **1.** the Honour School of Literae Humaniores, involving the study of Greek and Roman history and literature and philosophy. **2.** the final examinations at the end of this course.

Great Salt Lake *n.* a shallow salt lake in NW Utah, in the Great Basin at an altitude of 1260 m (4200 ft.): the area has fluctuated from less than 2500 sq. km (1000 sq. miles) to over 5000 sq. km (2000 sq. miles).

Great Sand·y Des+ert *n.* **1.** a desert in NW Australia. Area: about 415 000 sq. km (160 000 sq. miles). **2.** the English name for the **Rub' al Khali.**

Great Schism *n.* the division within the Roman Catholic Church from 1378 to 1429, during which rival popes reigned at Rome and Avignon.

great seal *n.* (*often caps.*) the principal seal of a nation, sovereign, etc., used to authenticate signatures and documents of the highest importance.

Great Slave Lake *n.* a lake in NW Canada, in the Northwest Territories: drained by the Mackenzie River into the Arctic Ocean. Area: 28 440 sq. km (10 980 sq. miles).

Great Slave Riv+er *n.* another name for the **Slave River.**

Great Smok·y Moun+tains *or* **Great Smok·ies** *pl. n.* the W part of the Appalachians, in W North Carolina and E Tennessee. Highest peak: Clingman's Dome, 2024 m (6642 ft.).

Great St. Ber+nard Pass *n.* a pass over the W Alps, between SW central Switzerland and N Italy: noted for the hospice at the summit, founded in the 11th century. Height: 2433 m (8111 ft.).

great tit *n.* a large common Eurasian tit, *Parus major,* with yellow-and-black underparts and a black-and-white head.

Great Trek *n.* **the.** *South African history.* the migration of Boer farmers from the Cape Colony to the north and east from about 1836 to 1845 to escape British authority.

great-un·cle *or* **grand+un·cle** *n.* an uncle of one's father or mother; brother of one's grandfather or grandmother.

Great Vic+to+ri·a Des+ert *n.* a desert in S Australia, in SE Western Australia and W South Australia. Area: 323 750 sq. km (125 000 sq. miles).

Great Vow+el Shift *n. Linguistics.* a phonetic change that took place during the transition from Middle to Modern English, whereby the long vowels were raised (e: became i:, o: became u:, etc.). The vowels (i:) and (u:) underwent breaking and became the diphthongs (aɪ) and (aʊ).

Great Wall of Chi+na *n.* a defensive wall in N China, extending from W Kansu to the Gulf of Liaotung: constructed in the 3rd century B.C. as a defence against the Mongols; substantially rebuilt in the 15th century. Length: over 2400 km (1500 miles). Average height: 6 m (20 ft.). Average width: 6 m (20 ft.).

Great War *n.* another name for **World War I.**

Great Week *n. Eastern Church.* the week preceding Easter, the equivalent of Holy Week in the Western Church.

great white her+on *n.* **1.** a large white heron, *Ardea occidentalis,* of S North America. **2.** a widely distributed white egret, *Egretta* (or *Casmerodius*) *albus.*

Great Yar+mouth ('jɑːməθ) *n.* a port and resort in E England, in E Norfolk. Pop.: 50 152 (1971).

great year *n.* one complete cycle of the precession of the equinoxes; about 25 800 years.

greave (griːv) *n.* (*often pl.*) a piece of armour worn to protect the shin from the ankle to the knee. [C14: from Old French *greve,* perhaps from *graver* to part the hair, of Germanic origin] —**greaved** *adj.*

greaves (griːvz) *pl. n.* the residue left after the rendering of tallow. [C17: from Low German *greven;* related to Old High German *griubo*]

grebe (griːb) *n.* any aquatic bird, such as *Podiceps cristatus* (**great crested grebe**), of the order *Podicipediformes,* similar to the divers but with lobate rather than webbed toes and a vestigial tail. [C18: from French *grèbe,* of unknown origin]

Gre+cian ('griːʃən) *adj.* **1.** (esp. of beauty or architecture) conforming to Greek ideals, esp. in being classically simple. ~*n.* **2.** a scholar of or expert in the Greek language or literature. ~*adj., n.* **3.** another word for **Greek.**

Gre+cism ('griːˌsɪzəm) *n.* a variant spelling (esp. U.S.) of **Graecism.**

Gre+cize ('griːsaɪz) *vb.* a variant spelling (esp. U.S.) of **Graecize.**

Grec·o *n.* **1.** ('grɛkəʊ) **El.** See **El Greco. 2.** (*French* gre'ko) **Ju·li·ette** (ʒy'ljɛt). born 1927, French night-club singer.

Gre·co- ('griːkəʊ-, 'grɛkəʊ-) *combining form.* a variant (esp. U.S.) of **Graeco-.**

gree[1] (griː) *n. Scot. archaic.* **1.** superiority or victory. **2.** the prize for a victory. [C14: from Old French *gré,* from Latin *gradus* step]

gree[2] (griː) *n. Obsolete.* **1.** goodwill; favour. **2.** satisfaction for an insult or injury. [C14: from Old French *gré,* from Latin *grātum* what is pleasing; see GRATEFUL]

gree[3] (griː) *vb.* **grees, gree+ing, greed.** *Northern Brit. dialect.* to come or cause to come to agreement or harmony. [C14: variant of AGREE]

Greece (griːs) *n.* a republic in SE Europe, occupying the S part of the Balkan Peninsula and many islands in the Ionian and Aegean Seas; site of two of Europe's earliest civilizations (the Minoan and Mycenaean); in the classical era divided into many small independent city-states, the most important being Athens and Sparta; part of the Roman and Byzantine Empires; passed under Turkish rule in the late Middle Ages; became an independent kingdom in 1827; taken over by a military junta (1967–74); the monarchy was abolished in 1973; became a republic in 1975. Language: Greek. Religion: predominantly Greek Orthodox. Currency: drachma. Capital: Athens. Pop.: 9 046 000 (1975 est.). Area: 131 944 sq. km (50 944 sq. miles). Modern Greek name: **Ellás.** Related adj.: **Hellenic.**

greed (griːd) *n.* **1.** excessive consumption of or desire for food; gluttony. **2.** excessive desire, as for wealth or power. [C17: back formation from GREEDY] —**'greed+less** *adj.*

greed·y ('griːdɪ) *adj.* **greed·i+er, greed·i+est. 1.** excessively desirous of food or wealth, esp. in large amounts; voracious. **2.** (*postpositive;* foll. by *for*) eager (for): *a man greedy for success.* [Old English *grǣdig;* related to Old Norse *grāthugr,* Gothic *grēdags* hungry, Old High German *grātac*] —**'greed·i+ly** *adv.* —**'greed·i+ness** *n.*

greed·y guts *n. Slang.* a glutton.

gree+gree ('griːgriː) *n.* a variant spelling of **grigri.**

Greek (griːk) *n.* **1.** the official language of Greece, constituting the Hellenic branch of the Indo-European family of languages. See **Ancient Greek, Late Greek, Medieval Greek, Modern Greek. 2.** a native or inhabitant of Greece or a descendant of such a native. **3.** a member of the Greek Orthodox Church. **4.** *Informal.* anything incomprehensible (esp. in the phrase **it's (all) Greek to me). 5. Greek meets Greek.** equals meet. ~*adj.* **6.** denoting, relating to, or characteristic of Greece, the Greeks, or the Greek language; Hellenic. **7.** of, relating to, or designating the Greek Orthodox Church. —**'Greek+ness** *n.*

Greek Cath·o·lic *n.* **1.** a member of an Eastern Church in communion with the Greek patriarchal see of Constantinople. **2.** a member of one of the Uniat Greek Churches, which acknowledge the Pope's authority while retaining their own institutions, discipline, and liturgy.

Greek Church *n.* another name for the **Greek Orthodox Church.**

Greek cross *n.* a cross with each of the four arms of the same length.

Greek fire *n.* **1.** a Byzantine weapon employed in naval warfare from 672 or 673 A.D. It consisted of a mixture, usually shot from tubes, that caught fire when wetted. **2.** any of several other inflammable mixtures used in ancient and medieval warfare.

Greek Or+tho+dox Church *n.* **1.** Also called: **Greek Church.** the established Church of Greece, governed by the holy synod of Greece, in which the Metropolitan of Athens has primacy of honour. **2.** another name for **Orthodox Church.**

Greek Re+viv+al *n.* (*modifier*) denoting, relating to, or having the style of architecture used in Western Europe in the late 18th and early 19th centuries, based upon ancient Greek classical examples. —**Greek Re+viv+al+ism** *n.* —**Greek Re+viv+al+ist** *adj., n.*

Gree·ley ('griːlɪ) *n.* **Hor·ace.** 1811–72, U.S. journalist and political leader: founder (1841) and editor of the *New York Tribune,* which championed the abolition of slavery.

green (griːn) *n.* **1.** any of a group of colours, such as that of fresh grass, that lie between yellow and blue in the visible spectrum in the wavelength range 575–500 nanometres. Green is the complementary colour of magenta and with red and blue forms a set of primary colours. Related adj.: **verdant. 2.** a dye or pigment of or producing these colours. **3.** something of the colour green. **4.** a small area of grassland, esp. in the centre of a village. **5.** an area of ground used for a purpose: *a putting green.* **6.** (*pl.*) **a.** the edible leaves and stems of certain plants, eaten as a vegetable. **b.** freshly cut branches of ornamental trees, shrubs, etc., used as a decoration. **7.** *Slang.* money. **8.** *Slang.* marijuana of low quality. **9.** (*pl.*) *Slang.* sexual intercourse. **10. green in one's eye.** an indication of immaturity or gullibility. ~*adj.* **11.** of the colour green. **12.** greenish in colour or having parts or marks that are greenish: *green monkey.* **13.** vigorous; not faded: *a green old age.* **14.** envious or jealous. **15.** immature, unsophisticated, or gullible. **16.** characterized by foliage or green plants: *a green wood; a green salad.* **17.** fresh, raw, or unripe: *green bananas.* **18.** unhealthily pale in appearance: *he was green after his boat trip.* **19.** (of pottery, etc.) not fired. **20.** (of meat) not smoked or cured; unprocessed: *green bacon.* **21.** *Metallurgy.* (of a product, such as a sand mould or cermet) compacted but not yet fired; ready for firing. **22.** (of timber) freshly felled; not dried or seasoned. ~*vb.* **23.** to make or become green. [Old English *grēne;* related to Old High German *gruoni;* see GROW] —**'green+ish** *adj.* —**'green+ly** *adv.* —**'green+ness** *n.* —**'green·y** *adj.*

Green (griːn) *n.* **1. John Rich·ard.** 1837–83, English historian; author of *A Short History of the English People* (1874). **2. Thom·as Hill.** 1836–82, English idealist philosopher. His chief work, *Prolegomena to Ethics,* was unfinished at his death.

green al+gae *pl. n.* the algae of the family *Chlorophyceae,* which possess the green pigment chlorophyll. The group includes sea lettuce and spirogyra.

Green·a·way ('griːnəˌweɪ) *n.* **Kate.** 1846–1901, English painter, noted as an illustrator of children's books.

green+back ('griːnˌbæk) *n.* **1.** *U.S. informal.* an inconvertible legal-tender U.S. currency note originally issued during the Civil War in 1862. **2.** *U.S. slang.* a dollar bill.

Green+back Par+ty *n. U.S. history.* a political party formed after the Civil War advocating the use of fiat money and opposing the reduction of paper currency. —**'Green+ˌback·er** *n.* —**'Green+ˌback·ism** *n.*

green bean *n.* any bean plant, such as the French bean, having narrow green edible pods when unripe.

green belt *n.* a zone of farmland, parks, and open country surrounding a town or city: usually officially designated as such and preserved from urban development.

Green Be+ret *n.* an informal name for a British or American commando.

green+bot·tle ('griːnˌbɒtᵊl) *n.* a common dipterous fly, *Lucilia caesar,* that has a dark greenish body with a metallic lustre and lays its eggs in carrion: family *Calliphoridae.*

green+bri·er ('griːnˌbraɪə) *n.* any of several prickly climbing plants of the liliaceous genus *Smilax,* esp. *S. rotundifolia* of the eastern U.S., which has small green flowers and blackish berries. Also called: **cat brier.**

green card *n.* an insurance document covering motorists against accidents abroad.

green corn *n.* another name for **sweet corn** (sense 1).

Green Cross Code *n. Brit.* a code for children giving rules for road safety: first issued in 1971.

green drag+on *n.* a North American aroid plant, *Arisaema dracontium,* with a long slender spadix projecting from a green or white long narrow spathe. Also called: **dragonroot.**

Greene (gri:n) *n.* **1. Gra·ham.** born 1904, English novelist and dramatist; his works include the novels *Brighton Rock* (1938) and *The Power and the Glory* (1940), and the film script *The Third Man* (1949). **2. Rob·ert.** ?1558–92, English poet, dramatist, and prose writer, noted for his autobiographical tract *A Groatsworth of Wit bought with a Million of Repentance* (1592), which contains an attack on Shakespeare.

green+er·y ('gri:nərɪ) *n., pl.* **+er·ies. 1.** green foliage or vegetation, esp. when used for decoration. **2.** a place where such foliage grows.

green-eyed *adj.* **1.** jealous or envious. **2. the green-eyed monster.** jealousy or envy.

green+finch ('gri:nˌfɪntʃ) *n.* a common European finch, *Carduelis chloris,* the male of which has a dull green plumage with yellow patches on the wings and tail.

green fin+gers *pl. n.* considerable talent or ability to grow plants. U.S. equivalent: **green thumb.**

green+fly ('gri:nˌflaɪ) *n., pl.* **+flies.** a greenish aphid commonly occurring as a pest on garden and crop plants.

green+gage ('gri:nˌgeɪdʒ) *n.* **1.** a cultivated variety of plum tree, *Prunus domestica italica,* with edible green plumlike fruits. **2.** the fruit of this tree. [C18: GREEN + *-gage,* after Sir W. *Gage* (1777–1864), English botanist who brought it from France]

green gland *n.* one of a pair of excretory organs in some crustaceans that open at the base of each antenna.

green glass *n.* glass in its natural colour, usually greenish as a result of metallic substances in the raw materials.

green+gro·cer ('gri:nˌgrəʊsə) *n. Chiefly Brit.* a retail trader in fruit and vegetables. —**'green+ˌgro·cer·y** *n.*

green+heart ('gri:nˌhɑ:t) *n.* **1.** Also called: **bebeeru.** a tropical American lauraceous tree, *Ocotea* (or *Nectandra*) *rodiaei,* that has dark green durable wood and bark that yields the alkaloid bebeerine. **2.** any of various similar trees. **3.** the wood of any of these trees.

green her+on *n.* a small heron, *Butorides virescens,* of subtropical North America, with dark greenish wings and back.

green+horn ('gri:nˌhɔ:n) *n. Informal.* **1.** an inexperienced person, esp. one who is extremely gullible. **2.** a newcomer or immigrant. [C17: originally an animal with *green* (that is, young) horns]

green+house ('gri:nˌhaʊs) *n.* **1.** a building with transparent walls and roof, usually of glass, for the cultivation and exhibition of plants under controlled conditions. **2.** *Informal.* the part of an aircraft covered by a clear plastic dome.

green+house ef+fect *n.* **1.** an effect occurring in greenhouses, etc., in which radiant heat from the sun passes through the glass warming the contents, the radiant heat from inside being trapped by the glass. **2.** the application of this effect to the earth's atmosphere, which increases the temperature of the earth's surface.

green+ing ('gri:nɪŋ) *n.* any of several varieties of apples that are used for cooking and have greenish-yellow skin.

Green+land ('gri:nlənd) *n.* the largest island in the world, lying mostly within the Arctic Circle off the NE coast of N America: first settled by Icelanders in 986; resettled by Danes from 1721 onwards; integral part of Denmark (1953–79); granted internal autonomy 1979; mostly covered by an icecap up to 3300 m (11 000 ft.) thick, with icefree coastal strips and coastal mountains; fishing, hunting, and mining. Capital: Godthaab. Pop.: 54 000 (1975 UN est.). Area: 2 175 600 sq. km (840 000 sq. miles). Danish name: **Grønland.** —**'Green+land+er** *n.* —**Green+'land+ic** *adj., n.*

Green+land Sea *n.* the S part of the Arctic Ocean, off the NE coast of Greenland.

Green+land whale *n.* an arctic right whale, *Balaena mysticetus,* that is black with a cream-coloured throat.

green leek *n.* any of several Australian parrots with a green or mostly green plumage.

green+let ('gri:nlɪt) *n.* a vireo, esp. one of the genus *Hylophilus.*

green light *n.* **1.** a signal to go, esp. a green traffic light. **2.** permission to proceed with a project, etc.

green+ling ('gri:nlɪŋ) *n.* any scorpaenoid food fish of the family *Hexagrammidae* of the North Pacific Ocean.

green ma+nure *n.* **1.** a growing crop that is ploughed under to enrich the soil. **2.** manure that has not yet decomposed.

green mon+key *n.* a W African variety of a common guenon monkey, *Cercopithecus aethiops,* having greenish-brown fur and a dark face. Compare **grivet, vervet.**

green mould *n.* another name for **blue mould** (sense 1).

Green Moun+tain Boys *pl. n.* the members of the armed bands of Vermont organized in the 1770s to oppose New York's territorial claims. Under Ethan Allen they won fame in the War of American Independence.

Green Moun+tains *pl. n.* a mountain range in E North America, extending from Canada through Vermont into W Massachusetts: part of the Appalachian system. Highest peak: Mount Mansfield, 1338 m (4393 ft.).

Green+ock ('gri:nək, 'grɛnək) *n.* a port in SW Scotland, on the Firth of Clyde: shipbuilding and other marine industries. Pop.: 74 607 (1971).

green+ock+ite ('gri:nəˌkaɪt) *n.* a rare yellowish mineral consisting of cadmium sulphide in hexagonal crystalline form: the only ore of cadmium. Formula: CdS. [C19: named after Lord C. C. *Greenock,* 19th-century English soldier]

green pa+per *n.* (*often caps.*) (in Britain) a command paper containing policy proposals to be discussed, esp. by Parliament.

green pep+per *n.* **1.** the green unripe fruit of the sweet pepper, eaten raw or cooked. **2.** the unripe fruit of various other pepper plants, eaten as a green vegetable.

green plov+er *n.* another name for **lapwing.**

green pound *n.* a unit of account used in calculating Britain's contributions to and payments from the Community Agricultural Fund of the EEC.

green rev·o+lu+tion *n.* the introduction of high-yielding seeds and modern agricultural techniques in developing countries.

Green Riv+er *n.* a river in the western U.S., rising in W central Wyoming and flowing south into Utah, east through NW Colorado, re-entering Utah before joining the Colorado River. Length: 1175 km (730 miles).

green+room ('gri:nˌru:m, -ˌrʊm) *n.* (esp. formerly) a backstage room in a theatre where performers may rest or receive visitors. [C18: probably from its original colour]

green+sand ('gri:nˌsænd) *n.* an olive-green sandstone consisting mainly of quartz and glauconite.

Greens+bo·ro ('gri:nzbərə, -brə) *n.* a city in N central North Carolina. Pop.: 155 514 (1973 est.).

green+shank ('gri:nˌʃæŋk) *n.* a large European sandpiper, *Tringa nebularia,* with greenish legs and a slightly upturned bill.

green+sick·ness ('gri:nˌsɪknɪs) *n.* another name for **chlorosis.** —**'green+ˌsick** *adj.*

green soap *n. Med.* a soft or liquid alkaline soap made from vegetable oils, used in treating certain chronic skin diseases. Also called: **soft soap.**

green+stick frac+ture ('gri:nˌstɪk) *n.* a fracture in children in which the bone is partly bent and splinters only on the convex side of the bend. [C20: alluding to the similar way in which a green stick splinters]

green+stone ('gri:nˌstəʊn) *n.* **1.** any basic igneous rock that is dark green because of the presence of chlorite or epidote. **2.** a variety of jade used in New Zealand for ornaments and tools.

green+stuff ('gri:nˌstʌf) *n.* green vegetables, such as cabbage or lettuce.

green+sward ('gri:nˌswɔ:d) *n. Archaic or literary.* fresh green turf or an area of such turf.

green tea *n.* a sharp tea made from tea leaves that have been steamed and dried quickly without fermenting.

green tur+tle *n.* a mainly tropical edible turtle, *Chelonia mydas,* with greenish flesh used to prepare turtle soup: family *Chelonidae.*

green vit+ri+ol *n.* another name for **ferrous sulphate.**

Green+wich ('grɪnɪdʒ, -ɪtʃ, 'grɛn-) *n.* a Greater London borough on the Thames: site of a Royal Naval College and of the original Royal Observatory designed by Christopher Wren (1675), accepted internationally as the prime meridian of longitude since 1884, and the basis of Greenwich Mean Time. Pop.: 207 200 (1976 est.).

Green+wich Mean Time *or* **Green+wich Time** *n.* the local time of the 0° meridian passing through Greenwich, England: a standard time for Britain and a basis for calculating times throughout most of the world. Abbrev.: **GMT**

Green+wich Vil+lage ('grɛnɪtʃ, 'grɪn-) *n.* a part of New York City in the lower west side of Manhattan; traditionally the home of many artists and writers.

green+wood ('gri:nˌwʊd) *n.* a forest or wood when the leaves are green: the traditional setting of stories about English outlaws, esp. Robin Hood.

green wood+peck·er *n.* a European woodpecker, *Picus viridis,* with a dull green back and wings and a red crown.

greet[1] (gri:t) *vb. (tr.)* **1.** to meet or receive with expressions of gladness or welcome. **2.** to send a message of friendship to. **3.** to receive in a specified manner: *her remarks were greeted by silence.* **4.** to become apparent to: *the smell of bread greeted him.* [Old English *grētan;* related to Old High German *gruozzen* to address] —**'greet+er** *n.*

greet[2] (gri:t) *Archaic or dialect.* ~*vb.* **1.** *(intr.)* to weep; lament. ~*n.* **2.** weeping; lamentation. [from Old English *grētan,* northern dialect variant of *grætan;* compare Old Norse *grāta,* Middle High German *grazen*]

greet+ing ('gri:tɪŋ) *n.* **1.** the act or an instance of welcoming or saluting on meeting. **2.** (*often pl.*) **a.** an expression of friendly salutation. **b.** (*as modifier*): *a greetings card.*

greg·a+rine ('grɛgəˌri:n, -rɪn) *n.* **1.** any parasitic protozoan of the order *Gregarinida,* typically occurring in the digestive tract and body cavity of other invertebrates: class *Sporozoa* (sporozoans). ~*adj.* also **greg·a+rin+i·an** (ˌgrɛgə'rɪnɪən). **2.** of, relating to, or belonging to the *Gregarinida.* [C19: from New Latin *Gregarīna* genus name, from Latin *gregārius;* see GREGARIOUS]

gre+gar·i·ous (grɪ'gɛərɪəs) *adj.* **1.** enjoying the company of others. **2.** (of animals) living together in herds or flocks. Compare **solitary** (sense 6). **3.** (of plants) growing close together but not in dense clusters. **4.** of, relating to, or characteristic of crowds or communities. [C17: from Latin *gregārius* belonging to a flock, from *grex* flock] —**gre+'gar·i+ous+ly** *adv.* —**gre+'gar·i·ous·ness** *n.*

Gre+go+ri·an (grɪ'gɔ:rɪən) *adj.* relating to, associated with, or introduced by any of the popes named Gregory, esp. Gregory I or Gregory XIII.

Gre+go+ri·an cal+en·dar *n.* the revision of the Julian calendar introduced in 1582 by Pope Gregory XIII and still in force, whereby the ordinary year is made to consist of 365 days and a leap year occurs in every year whose number is divisible by four, except those centenary years, such as 1900, whose numbers are not divisible by 400.

Gre+go+ri·an chant *n.* another name for **plainsong.**

Gre+go+ri·an tel·e+scope *n.* a form of reflecting astronomical telescope with a concave secondary mirror and the eyepiece set in the centre of the parabolic primary mirror. [C18: named after J. *Gregory* (d.1675), Scottish mathematician who invented it]

Gre+go+ri·an tone *n.* a plainsong melody. See **tone** (sense 6).

Greg·o·ry (ˈgrɛgərɪ) *n.* Lady **(Isabella) Au·gus·ta (Persse).** 1852–1932, Irish dramatist; a founder and director of the Abbey Theatre, Dublin.

Greg·o·ry I *n.* **Saint,** called *the Great.* ?540–604 A.D., pope (590–604), who greatly influenced the medieval Church. He strengthened papal authority by centralizing administration, tightened discipline, and revised the liturgy. He appointed Saint Augustine missionary to England. Feast day: March 12.

Greg·o·ry VII *n.* **Saint,** monastic name *Hildebrand.* ?1020–85, pope (1073–85), who did much to reform abuses in the Church. His assertion of papal supremacy and his prohibition (1075) of lay investiture was opposed by the Holy Roman Emperor Henry IV, whom he excommunicated (1076). He was driven into exile when Henry captured Rome (1084). Feast day: May 25.

Greg·o·ry XIII *n.* 1502–85, pope (1572–85). He promoted the Counter-Reformation and founded seminaries. His reformed (Gregorian) calendar was issued in 1582.

Greg·o·ry of Tours *n.* **Saint.** ?538–?594 A.D., Frankish bishop and historian. His *Historia Francorum* is the chief source of knowledge of 6th-century Gaul. Feast day: Nov. 17.

greige (greɪʒ) *Chiefly U.S.* ~*adj.* **1.** (of a fabric or material) not yet dyed. ~*n.* **2.** an unbleached or undyed cloth or yarn. [C20: from French *grège* raw]

grei+sen (ˈgraɪzᵊn) *n.* a light-coloured metamorphic rock consisting mainly of quartz and white mica, formed by the pneumatolysis of granite. [C19: from German, from *greissen* to split]

gre+mi+al (ˈgriːmɪəl) *n. R.C. Church.* a cloth spread upon the lap of a bishop when seated during a solemn High Mass. [C17: from Latin *gremium* lap]

grem+lin (ˈgrɛmlɪn) *n.* **1.** an imaginary imp jokingly said to be responsible for mechanical troubles in aircraft, esp. in World War II. **2.** any mischievous troublemaker. [C20: of unknown origin]

Gre+na+da (grɛˈneɪdə) *n.* an island state in the West Indies, in the Windward Islands: formerly a British colony; since 1974 an independent state within the British Commonwealth. Capital: St. George's. Pop.: 96 000 (1975 UN est.). Area: 344 sq. km (133 sq. miles). —**Gre+ˈna+di·an** *n., adj.*

gre+nade (grɪˈneɪd) *n.* **1.** a small container filled with explosive thrown by hand or fired from a rifle. **2.** a sealed glass vessel that is thrown and shatters to release chemicals, such as tear gas or a fire extinguishing agent. [C16: from French, from Spanish *granada* pomegranate, from Late Latin *grānāta,* from Latin *grānātus* seedy; see GRAIN]

gren·a+dier (ˌgrɛnəˈdɪə) *n.* **1.** *Military.* **a.** (in the British Army) a member of the senior regiment of infantry in the Household Brigade. **b.** (formerly) a member of a special formation, usually selected for strength and height. **c.** (formerly) a soldier trained to throw grenades. **2.** Also called: **rat-tail.** any deep-sea gadoid fish of the family *Macrouridae,* typically having a large head and trunk and a long tapering tail. **3.** any of various African weaverbirds of the genus *Estrilda.* See **waxbill.** [C17: from French; see GRENADE]

gren·a+dine[1] (ˌgrɛnəˈdiːn) *n.* a light thin leno-weave fabric of silk, wool, rayon, or nylon, used for dresses, etc. [C19: from French, perhaps from *Granada* Spain]

gren·a+dine[2] (ˌgrɛnəˈdiːn, ˈgrɛnəˌdiːn) *n.* **1.** a syrup made from pomegranate juice, used as a sweetening and colouring agent in various drinks. **2. a.** a moderate reddish-orange colour. **b.** (*as adj.*): *a grenadine coat.* [C19: from French: a little pomegranate, from *grenade* pomegranate; see GRENADE]

Gren·a+dines (ˌgrɛnəˈdiːnz, ˈgrɛnəˌdiːnz) *pl. n.* **the.** a chain of about 600 islets in the West Indies, part of the Windward Islands, extending for about 100 km (60 miles) between St. Vincent and Grenada and divided administratively between the two states. Largest island: Carriacou.

Gren·del (ˈgrɛndᵊl) *n.* (in Old English legend) a man-eating monster defeated by the hero Beowulf.

Gre+no+ble (grəˈnəubᵊl; *French* grəˈnɔbl) *n.* a city in SE France, on the Isère River: university (1339). Pop.: 169 740 (1975).

Gren·ville (ˈgrɛnvɪl) *n.* **1. George.** 1712–70, British statesman; prime minister (1763–65). His policy of taxing the American colonies precipitated the War of Independence. **2.** Sir **Rich·ard.** ?1541–91, English naval commander. He was fatally wounded aboard his ship, the *Revenge,* during a lone battle with a fleet of Spanish treasure ships. **3. Wil·liam Wynd·ham,** Baron Grenville, son of George Grenville. 1759–1834, British statesman; prime minister (1806–07) of the coalition government known as the "ministry of all the talents."

Gresh·am (ˈgrɛʃəm) *n.* Sir **Thom·as.** ?1519–79, English financier, who founded the Royal Exchange in London (1568).

Gresh·am's law *or* **the·o+rem** *n.* the economic hypothesis that bad money drives good money out of circulation; the superior currency will tend to be hoarded and the inferior will thus dominate the circulation. [C16: named after Sir T. GRESHAM]

gres+so·ri·al (grɛˈsɔːrɪəl) *or* **gres+so+ri+ous** *adj.* **1.** (of the feet of certain birds) specialized for walking. **2.** (of birds, such as the ostrich) having such feet. [C19: from New Latin *gressōrius,* from *gressus* having walked, from *gradī* to step]

Gret+na Green (ˈgrɛtnə) *n.* a village in S Scotland on the border with England: famous smithy where eloping couples were married by the blacksmith from 1754 until 1940, when such marriages became illegal. Pop.: 5519 (1971).

Greuze (*French* grøːz) *n.* **Jean Bap·tiste** (ʒã baˈtist). 1725–1805, French genre and portrait painter.

grew (gruː) *vb.* the past tense of **grow.**

grey *or U.S.* **gray** (greɪ) *adj.* **1.** of a neutral tone, intermediate between black and white, that has no hue and reflects and transmits only a little light. **2.** greyish in colour or having parts or marks that are greyish. **3.** dismal or dark, esp. from lack of light; gloomy. **4.** neutral or dull, esp. in character or opinion. **5.** having grey hair. **6.** of or characteristic of old age; wise. **7.** ancient; venerable. **8.** (of textiles) natural, unbleached, undyed, and untreated. ~*n.* **9.** any of a group of grey tones. **10.** grey cloth or clothing: *dressed in grey.* **11.** an animal, esp. a horse, that is grey or whitish. ~*vb.* **12.** to become or make grey. [Old English *grǣg;* related to Old High German *grāo,* Old Norse *grar*] —ˈ**grey+ish** *or U.S.* ˈ**gray+ish** *adj.* —ˈ**grey+ly** *or U.S.* ˈ**gray+ly** *adv.* —ˈ**grey+ness** *or U.S.* ˈ**gray+ness** *n.*

Grey (greɪ) *n.* **1. Charles,** 2nd Earl Grey. 1764–1845, British statesman. As Whig prime minister (1830–34), he carried the Reform Bill of 1832 and the bill for the abolition of slavery throughout the British Empire (1833). **2.** Sir **Ed·ward,** 1st Viscount Grey of Fallodon. 1862–1933, British statesman; foreign secretary (1905–16). **3.** Sir **George.** 1812–98, English statesman and colonial administrator; prime minister of New Zealand (1877–79). **4.** Lady **Jane.** 1537–54, queen of England (July 9–19, 1553); great-granddaughter of Henry VII. Her father-in-law, the duke of Northumberland, persuaded Edward VI to alter the succession in her favour, but after ten days as queen she was imprisoned and later executed. **5. Zane.** 1875–1939, U.S. author of Westerns, including *Riders of the Purple Sage* (1912).

grey ar·e·a *n.* **1.** (in Britain) a region in which unemployment is relatively high. **2.** an area or part of something existing between two extremes and having mixed characteristics of both. **3.** an area, situation, etc., lacking clearly defined characteristics.

grey+back *or U.S.* **gray+back** (ˈgreɪˌbæk) *n.* any of various animals having a grey back, such as the grey whale and the hooded crow.

grey+beard *or U.S.* **gray+beard** (ˈgreɪˌbɪəd) *n.* **1.** an old man, esp. a sage. **2.** a large stoneware or earthenware jar or jug for spirits. —ˈ**grey+ˌbeard·ed** *or U.S.* ˈ**gray+ˌbeard·ed** *adj.*

grey em·i+nence *n.* the English equivalent of **éminence grise.**

grey fox *n.* **1.** a greyish American fox, *Urocyon cinereoargenteus,* inhabiting arid and woody regions from S North America to N South America. **2. island grey fox.** a similar and related animal, *U. littoralis,* inhabiting islands off North America.

Grey Fri+ar *n.* a Franciscan friar.

grey+hen (ˈgreɪˌhɛn) *n.* the female of the black grouse. Compare **blackcock.**

grey her+on *n.* a large European heron, *Ardea cinerea,* with grey wings and back and a long black drooping crest.

grey+hound (ˈgreɪˌhaund) *n.* a tall slender fast-moving breed of hound.

grey+hound rac+ing *n.* a sport in which a mechanically propelled dummy hare is pursued by greyhounds around a race track.

grey+lag *or* **grey+lag goose** (ˈgreɪˌlæg) *n.* a large grey Eurasian goose, *Anser anser:* the ancestor of many domestic breeds of goose. U.S. spelling: **graylag.** [C18: from GREY + LAG, from its migrating later than other species]

grey mar+ket *n.* a system involving the secret but not illegal sale of goods at excessive prices. Compare **black market.**

grey mat+ter *n.* **1.** the greyish tissue of the brain and spinal cord, containing nerve cell bodies, dendrites, and bare (unmyelinated) axons. Technical name: **substantia grisea.** Compare **white matter. 2.** *Informal.* brains or intellect.

grey mul+let *n.* any teleost food fish of the family *Mugilidae,* mostly occurring in coastal regions, having a spindle-shaped body and a broad fleshy mouth. U.S. name: **mullet.** Compare **red mullet.**

grey squir+rel *n.* a grey-furred squirrel, *Sciurus carolinensis,* native to E North America but now widely established.

grey-state *n.* (*modifier*) (of a fabric or material) not yet dyed.

grey+wack·e (ˈgreɪˌwækə) *n.* any dark sandstone or grit having a matrix of clay minerals. [C19: partial translation of German *Grauwacke;* see WACKE]

grey whale *n.* a large N Pacific whalebone whale, *Eschrichtius glaucus,* that is grey or black with white spots and patches: family *Eschrichtidae.*

grey wolf *n.* another name for **timber wolf.**

grib+ble (ˈgrɪbᵊl) *n.* any small marine isopod crustacean of the genus *Limnoria,* which bores into and damages wharves and other submerged wooden structures. [C19: perhaps related to GRUB]

grid (grɪd) *n.* **1.** See **gridiron. 2.** a network of horizontal and vertical lines superimposed over a map, building plan, etc., for locating points. **3. the grid.** the national network of transmission lines, pipes, etc., by which electricity, gas, or water is distributed. **4.** Also called: **control grid.** *Electronics.* **a.** an electrode situated between the cathode and anode of a valve usually consisting of a cylindrical mesh of wires, that controls the flow of electrons between cathode and anode. See also **screen grid, suppressor grid. b.** (*as modifier*): *the grid bias.* **5.** See **starting grid. 6.** any interconnecting system of links: *the* *bus service formed a grid across the country.* [C19: back formation from GRIDIRON] —ˈ**grid+ded** *adj.*

grid bi·as *n.* the fixed voltage applied between the control grid and cathode of a valve.

grid dec+li+na+tion *n.* the angular difference between true north and grid north on a map.

grid+dle (ˈgrɪdəl) *n.* **1.** Also called: **girdle.** *Brit.* a thick round iron plate with a half hoop handle over the top, for making scones, etc. **2.** any flat heated surface, esp. on the top of a stove, for cooking food. ~*vb.* **3.** (*tr.*) to cook (food) on a griddle. [C13: from Old French *gridil,* from Late Latin *crāticulum* (unattested) fine wickerwork; see GRILL[1]]

grid·dle+cake (ˈgrɪdəlˌkeɪk) *n.* another name for **drop scone.**

gride (graɪd) *vb.* **1.** (*intr.*) *Literary.* to grate or scrape harshly. **2.** *Obsolete.* to pierce or wound. ~*n.* **3.** *Literary.* a harsh or piercing sound. [C14: variant of *girde* GIRD[2]]

grid+i·ron (ˈgrɪdˌaɪən) *n.* **1.** a utensil of parallel metal bars, used to grill meat, fish, etc. **2.** any framework resembling this utensil. **3.** a framework above the stage in a theatre from which suspended scenery, lights, etc., are manipulated. **4. a.** the field of play in American football. **b.** (*as modifier*): *a gridiron hero.* ~Often shortened to **grid.** [C13 *gredire,* perhaps a variant (through influence of *ire* IRON) of *gredile* GRIDDLE]

grid var·i·a·tion *n. Navigation.* the angle between grid north and magnetic north at a point on a map or chart. Also called: **grivation.**

grief (gri:f) *n.* **1.** deep or intense sorrow or distress, esp. at the death of someone. **2.** something that causes keen distress or suffering. **3. come to grief.** *Informal.* to end unsuccessfully or disastrously. [C13: from Anglo-French *gref,* from *grever* to GRIEVE] —ˈ**grief+less** *adj.*

Grieg (gri:g) *n.* **Ed·vard (Hagerup)** (ˈɛdvard). 1843–1907, Norwegian composer. His works, often inspired by Norwegian folk music, include the incidental music for *Peer Gynt* (1876), a piano concerto, and many songs.

Grier·son (ˈgrɪəsən) *n.* **John.** 1898–1972, British film director. He coined the word *documentary,* of which genre his *Industrial Britain* (1931) and *Song of Ceylon* (1934) are notable examples.

griev+ance (ˈgri:vəns) *n.* **1.** a real or imaginary wrong causing resentment and regarded as grounds for complaint. **2.** a feeling of resentment or injustice at having been unfairly treated. **3.** *Obsolete.* affliction or hardship. [C15 *grevance,* from Old French, from *grever* to GRIEVE]

grieve (gri:v) *vb.* **1.** to feel or cause to feel great sorrow or distress, esp. at the death of someone. **2.** (*tr.*) *Obsolete.* to inflict injury, hardship, or sorrow on. [C13: from Old French *grever,* from Latin *gravāre* to burden, from *gravis* heavy] —ˈ**griev+er** *n.* —ˈ**griev+ing+ly** *adv.*

griev+ous (ˈgri:vəs) *adj.* **1.** very severe or painful: *a grievous injury.* **2.** very serious; heinous: *a grievous sin.* **3.** showing or marked by grief: *a grievous cry.* **4.** causing great pain or suffering: *a grievous attack.* —ˈ**griev+ous+ly** *adv.* —ˈ**griev+ous+ness** *n.*

griev+ous bod+i+ly harm *n. Criminal law.* really serious injury caused by one person to another.

griffe (grɪf) *n. Architect.* a carved ornament at the base of a column, often in the form of a claw. [C19: from French: claw, of Germanic origin]

grif+fin[1] (ˈgrɪfɪn), **grif+fon,** *or* **gryph+on** *n.* a winged monster with an eagle-like head and the body of a lion. [C14: from Old French *grifon,* from Latin *gryphus,* from Greek *grups,* from *grupos* hooked]

grif+fin[2] (ˈgrɪfɪn) *n.* a newcomer to the Orient, esp. one from W Europe. [C18: of unknown origin]

Grif·fith (ˈgrɪfɪθ) *n.* **D(avid Lewelyn) W(ark).** 1875–1948, U.S. film director. He introduced several cinematic techniques, including the flashback and the fade-out, in his masterpiece *The Birth of a Nation* (1915).

grif+fon[1] (ˈgrɪfən) *n.* **1.** any of various small wire-haired breeds of dog, originally from Belgium. **2.** any large vulture of the genus *Gyps,* of Africa, S Europe, and SW Asia, having a pale plumage with black wings: family *Accipitridae* (hawks). [C19: from French: GRIFFIN[1]]

grif+fon[2] (ˈgrɪfən) *n.* a variant spelling of **griffin**[1].

grig (grɪg) *n. Dialect.* **1.** a lively person. **2.** a shortlegged hen. **3.** a young eel. [C14: dwarf, perhaps of Scandinavian origin; compare Swedish *krik* a little creature]

Gri+gio+ni (griˈdʒo:ni) *n.* the Italian name for **Graubünden.**

Gri·gnard re+a·gent (ˈgri:njɑ:; *French* griˈɲa:r) *n. Chem.* any of a class of organometallic reagents, having the general formula RMgX, where R is an organic group and X is a halogen atom: used in the synthesis of organic compounds. [C20: named after Victor *Grignard* (1871–1934), French chemist]

gri+gri, gris-gris, *or* **gree+gree** (ˈgri:gri:) *n., pl.* **+gris** (-gri:z) *or* **+grees.** an African talisman, amulet, or charm. [of African origin]

Gri+kwa (ˈgri:kwə, ˈgrɪk-) *n., pl.* **+kwa** *or* **+kwas.** a variant spelling of **Griqua.**

grill[1] (grɪl) *vb.* **1.** to cook (meat, etc.) by direct heat, as under a grill or over a hot fire, or (of meat, etc.) to be cooked in this way. Usual U.S. word: **broil. 2.** (*tr., usually passive*) to torment with or as if with extreme heat: *the travellers were grilled by the scorching sun.* **3.** (*tr.*) *Informal.* to subject to insistent or prolonged questioning. ~*n.* **4.** a device with parallel bars of thin metal on which meat, etc., may be cooked by a fire; gridiron. **5.** a device on a cooker that radiates heat downwards for grilling meat, etc. **6.** food cooked by grilling. **7.** See **grillroom.** [C17: from French *gril* gridiron, from Latin *crāticula* fine wickerwork; see GRILLE] —ˈ**grill+er** *n.*

grill[2] (grɪl) *n.* a variant spelling of **grille.** [C17: see GRILLE]

gril+lage (ˈgrɪlɪdʒ) *n.* an arrangement of beams and crossbeams used as a foundation on soft ground. [C18: from French, from *griller* to furnish with a grille]

grille *or* **grill** (grɪl) *n.* **1.** Also called: **grillwork.** a framework, esp. of metal bars arranged to form an ornamental pattern, used as a screen or partition. **2.** Also called: **radiator grille.** a grating, often chromium-plated, that admits cooling air to the radiator of a motor vehicle. **3.** a metal or wooden openwork grating used as a screen or divider. **4.** a protective screen, usually plastic or metal, in front of the loudspeaker in a radio, record player, etc. **5.** *Real tennis.* the opening in one corner of the receiver's end of the court. **6.** a group of small pyramidal marks impressed in parallel rows into a stamp to prevent reuse. [C17: from Old French, from Latin *crāticula* fine hurdlework, from *crātis* a hurdle]

grilled (grɪld) *adj.* **1.** cooked on a grill or gridiron. **2.** having a grille.

Grill·par·zer (*German* ˈgrɪlˌpartsər) *n.* **Franz** (frants). 1791–1872, Austrian dramatist and poet, noted for his historical and classical tragedies, which include *Sappho* (1818), the trilogy *The Golden Fleece* (1819–22), and *The Jewess of Toledo* (1872).

grill+room (ˈgrɪlˌru:m, -ˌrʊm) *n.* a restaurant or room in a restaurant, etc., where grilled steaks and other meat are served.

grilse (grɪls) *n., pl.* **grils·es** *or* **grilse.** a salmon at the stage when it returns for the first time from the sea to fresh water. [C15 *grilles* (plural), of uncertain origin]

grim (grɪm) *adj.* **grim+mer, grim+mest. 1.** stern; resolute: *grim determination.* **2.** harsh or formidable in manner or appearance. **3.** harshly ironic or sinister: *grim laughter.* **4.** cruel, severe, or ghastly: *a grim accident.* **5.** *Archaic or poetic.* fierce: *a grim warrior.* **6.** *Informal.* unpleasant; disagreeable. **7. hold on like grim death.** to hold very firmly or resolutely. [Old English *grimm;* related to Old Norse *grimmr,* Old High German *grimm* savage, Greek *khremizein* to neigh] —ˈ**grim+ly** *adv.* —ˈ**grim+ness** *n.*

gri+mace (grɪˈmeɪs) *n.* **1.** an ugly or distorted facial expression, as of wry humour, disgust, etc. ~*vb.* **2.** (*intr.*) to contort the face. [C17: from French *grimace,* of Germanic origin; related to Spanish *grimazo* caricature; see GRIM] —**gri+ˈmac+er** *n.* —**gri+ˈmac+ing+ly** *adv.*

Gri+mal+di[1] (grɪˈmɔ:ldɪ) *n.* a large crater in the SE quadrant of the moon, about 190 kilometres in diameter, which is conspicuous because of its dark floor. [named after Francesco Maria *Grimaldi* (1618–63), Italian physicist]

Gri·mal·di[2] (grɪˈmɔ:ldɪ) *n.* **Jo·seph.** 1779–1837, English actor, noted as a clown in pantomime.

Gri+mal+di man *n. Anthropol.* a type of Aurignacian man having a negroid appearance, thought to be a race of Cro-Magnon man. [C20: named after the *Grimaldi* caves, Italy, where skeletons of this type were found]

gri+mal+kin (grɪˈmælkɪn, -ˈmɔ:l-) *n.* **1.** an old cat, esp. an old female cat. **2.** a crotchety or shrewish old woman. [C17: from GREY + MALKIN]

grime (graɪm) *n.* **1.** dirt, soot, or filth, esp. when thickly accumulated or ingrained. ~*vb.* **2.** (*tr.*) to make dirty or coat with filth. [C15: from Middle Dutch *grime;* compare Flemish *grijm,* Old English *grīma* mask] —ˈ**grim·y** *adj.*

Grimm (grɪm) *n.* **Ja·kob Lud·wig Karl** (ˈja:kɔp ˈlu:tvɪç ˈkarl), 1785–1863, and his brother, **Wil·helm Karl** (ˈvɪlhɛlm ˈkarl), 1786–1859, German philologists and folklorists, who collaborated on *Grimm's Fairy Tales* (1812–22) and began a German dictionary. Jakob is noted also for his philological work *Deutsche Grammatik* (1819–37), in which he formulated the law named after him.

Grimm's law *n.* the rules accounting for systematic correspondences between consonants in the Germanic languages and consonants in other Indo-European languages; it states that Proto-Indo-European voiced aspirated stops, voiced unaspirated stops, and voiceless stops became voiced unaspirated stops, voiceless stops, and voiceless fricatives respectively. [formulated by J. GRIMM]

Grims+by (ˈgrɪmzbɪ) *n.* a fishing port in E England, in S Humberside. Pop.: 95 685 (1971).

grin (grɪn) *vb.* **grins, grin+ning, grinned. 1.** to smile with the lips drawn back revealing the teeth or express (something) by such a smile: *to grin a welcome.* **2.** (*intr.*) to draw back the lips revealing the teeth, as in a snarl or grimace. **3. grin and bear it.** *Informal.* to suffer trouble or hardship without complaint. ~*n.* **4.** a broad smile. **5.** a snarl or grimace. [Old English *grennian;* related to Old High German *grennen* to snarl, Old Norse *grenja* to howl; see GRUNT] —ˈ**grin+ner** *n.* —ˈ**grin+ning+ly** *adv.*

grind (graɪnd) *vb.* **grinds, grind+ing, ground. 1.** to reduce or be reduced to small particles by pounding or abrading: *to grind corn; to grind flour.* **2.** (*tr.*) to smooth, sharpen, or polish by friction or abrasion: *to grind a knife.* **3.** to scrape or grate together (two things, esp. the teeth) with a harsh rasping sound or (of such objects) to be scraped together. **4.** (*tr.;* foll. by *out*) to speak or say something in a rough voice. **5.** (*tr.;* often foll. by *down*) to hold down; oppress; tyrannize. **6.** (*tr.*) to operate (a machine) by turning a handle. **7.** (*tr.;* foll. by *out*) to produce in a routine or uninspired manner: *he ground out his weekly article for the paper.* **8.** (*tr.;* foll. by *out*) to continue to play in a dull or insipid manner: *the band only ground out old tunes all evening.* **9.** (*tr.;* often foll. by *into*) to instil (facts, information, etc.) by persistent effort: *they ground into the recruits the need for vigilance.* **10.** (*intr.*) *Informal.* to study or work laboriously. **11.** (*intr.*) *Chiefly U.S.* to dance erotically by rotating the pelvis (esp. in the phrase **bump and grind**). ~*n.* **12.** *Informal.* laborious or routine work or study. **13.** *Slang.* a person, esp. a student, who works excessively hard. **14.** a specific grade of pulverization, as of coffee beans: *coarse grind.* **15.** *Brit. slang.* the act of sexual intercourse. **16.** *Chiefly U.S.* a dance movement involving an erotic rotation of the pelvis. **17.** the act or sound of grinding. [Old English *grindan;* related to Latin *frendere,* Lithuanian *grẽndu* I rub, Low German *grand* sand] —**'grind·ing·ly** *adv.*

grin·de·li·a (grɪnˈdiːlɪə) *n.* **1.** any coarse plant of the American genus *Grindelia,* having yellow daisy-like flower heads: family *Compositae* (composites). See also **gum plant. 2.** the dried leaves and tops of certain species of these plants, used in tonics and sedatives. [C19: named after David Hieronymus *Grindel* (1777–1836), Russian botanist]

Grin·del·wald (*German* ˈgrɪndəlˌvalt) *n.* a valley and resort in central Switzerland, in the Bernese Oberland: mountaineering centre, with the Wetterhorn and the Eiger nearby.

grind·er (ˈgraɪndə) *n.* **1.** a person who grinds, esp. one who grinds cutting tools. **2.** a machine for grinding. **3.** a molar tooth.

grind·er·y (ˈgraɪndərɪ) *n., pl.* **·er·ies. 1.** a place in which tools and cutlery are sharpened. **2.** the equipment of a shoemaker.

grind·ing wheel *n.* an abrasive wheel, usually a composite of hard particles in a resin filler, used for grinding.

grind on *vb.* (*intr., adv.*) to move further relentlessly: *the enemy's invasion ground slowly on.*

grind·stone (ˈgraɪndˌstəʊn) *n.* **1. a.** a machine having a circular block of stone or composite abrasive rotated for sharpening tools or grinding metal. **b.** the stone used in this machine. **c.** any stone used for sharpening; whetstone. **2.** another name for **millstone. 3. keep** *or* **have one's nose to the grindstone.** to work hard and perseveringly.

grin·go (ˈgrɪŋgəʊ) *n., pl.* **·gos.** a person from an English-speaking country: used as a derogatory term by Latin Americans. [C19: from Spanish: foreigner, probably from *griego* Greek, hence an alien; see GREEK]

grip[1] (grɪp) *n.* **1.** the act or an instance of grasping and holding firmly: *he lost his grip on the slope.* **2.** Also called: **handgrip.** the strength or pressure of such a grasp, as in a handshake: *a feeble grip.* **3.** the style or manner of grasping an object, such as a tennis racket. **4.** understanding, control, or mastery of a subject, problem, etc. (esp. in such phrases as **get** *or* **have a grip on**). **5. come** *or* **get to grips.** (often foll. by *with*) **a.** to deal with (a problem or subject). **b.** to tackle (an assailant). **6.** Also called: **handgrip.** a part by which an object is grasped; handle. **7.** Also called: **handgrip.** a travelling bag or holdall. **8.** See **hairgrip. 9.** any device that holds by friction, such as certain types of brake. **10.** a method of clasping or shaking hands used by members of secret societies to greet or identify one another. **11.** a spasm of pain: *a grip in one's stomach.* **12.** a worker in a camera crew or a stagehand who shifts sets and props, etc. ~*vb.* **grips, grip·ping, gripped** *or* **gript. 13.** to take hold of firmly or tightly, as by a clutch. **14.** to hold the interest or attention of: *to grip an audience.* [Old English *gripe* grasp; related to Old Norse *gripr* property, Old High German *grif*] —**'grip·per** *n.* —**'grip·ping·ly** *adv.*

grip[2] (grɪp) *n. Med.* a variant spelling of **grippe.**

gripe (graɪp) *vb.* **1.** (*intr.*) *Informal.* to complain, esp. in a persistent nagging manner. **2.** to cause sudden intense pain in the intestines of (a person) or (of a person) to experience this pain. **3.** (*intr.*) *Nautical.* (of a ship) to tend to come up into the wind in spite of the helm. **4.** *Archaic.* to clutch; grasp. **5.** (*tr.*) *Archaic.* to afflict. ~*n.* **6.** (*usually pl.*) a sudden intense pain in the intestines; colic. **7.** *Informal.* a complaint or grievance. **8.** *Now rare.* **a.** the act of gripping. **b.** a firm grip. **c.** a device that grips. **9.** (*in pl.*) *Nautical.* the lashings that secure a boat. [Old English *grīpan;* related to Gothic *greipan,* Old High German *grīfan* to seize, Lithuanian *greibiu*] —**'grip·er** *n.* —**'grip·ing·ly** *adv.*

gripe wa·ter *n. Brit.* a solution given to infants to relieve colic.

grippe *or* **grip** (grɪp) *n.* a former name for **influenza.** [C18: from French *grippe,* from *gripper* to seize, of Germanic origin; see GRIP[1]]

grip tape *n.* a rough tape for sticking to a surface to provide a greater grip.

Gri·qua *or* **Gri·kwa** (ˈgriːkwə, ˈgrɪk-) *n.* **1.** (*pl.* **·qua, ·quas** *or* **·kwa, ·kwas**) a member of a people of mixed ancestry, mainly European and Hottentot, living chiefly in Griqualand. **2.** the language or dialect of Hottentot spoken by this people, belonging to the Khoisan family.

Gri·qua·land East (ˈgriːkwəˌlænd, ˈgrɪk-) *n.* an area of South Africa, in E Cape Province: settled in 1861 by Griquas led by Adam Kok III; annexed to the Cape in 1879; became part of the Transkei in 1903. Chief town: Kokstad. Area: 17 100 sq. km (6602 sq. miles).

Gri·qua·land West *n.* an area of South Africa, in N Cape Province north of the Orange river: settled after 1803 by the Griquas; annexed by the British in 1871 following a dispute with the Orange Free State; became part of the Cape in 1880. Chief town: Kimberley. Area: 39 360 sq. km (15 197 sq. miles).

Gris (*Spanish* gris) *n.* **Juan** (xwan). 1887–1927, Spanish cubist painter, resident in France from 1906.

gri·saille (grɪˈzeɪl; *French* griˈzaːj) *n.* **1.** a technique of monochrome painting in shades of grey, as in an oil painting or a wall decoration, imitating the effect of relief. **2.** a painting, stained glass window, etc., in this manner. [C19: from French, from *gris* grey]

gris·e·o·ful·vin (ˌgrɪzɪəʊˈfʊlvɪn) *n.* an antibiotic used to treat fungal infections of the hair and skin. [C20: from New Latin, from *Penicillium griseofulvum dierckx* (fungus from which it was isolated), from Medieval Latin *griseus* grey + Latin *fulvus* reddish yellow]

gris·e·ous (ˈgrɪsɪəs, ˈgrɪz-) *adj.* streaked or mixed with grey; somewhat grey. [C19: from Medieval Latin *griseus,* of Germanic origin]

gri·sette (grɪˈzɛt) *n.* (esp. formerly) a French working girl, esp. a pretty or flirtatious one. [C18: from French, from *grisette* grey fabric used for dresses, from *gris* grey]

gris-gris (ˈgriːgriː) *n., pl.* **-gris** (-griːz). a variant spelling of **grigri.**

Gri·shun (griːˈʃʊn) *n.* the Romansch name for **Graubünden.**

gris·kin (ˈgrɪskɪn) *n. Brit.* the lean part of a loin of pork. [C17: probably from dialect *gris* pig, from Old Norse *griss*]

gris·ly[1] (ˈgrɪzlɪ) *adj.* **·li·er, ·li·est.** causing horror or dread; gruesome. [Old English *grislic;* related to Old Frisian *grislik,* Old High German *grīsenlīh*] —**'gris·li·ness** *n.*

gris·ly[2] (ˈgrɪzlɪ) *n., pl* **·lies.** *Obsolete.* a variant spelling of **grizzly.**

gri·son (ˈgraɪsən, ˈgrɪzən) *n.* either of two musteline mammals, *Grison* (or *Galictis*) *cuja* or *G. vittata,* of Central and South America, having a greyish back and black face and underparts. [C18: from French, from *grison* grey animal, from Old French *gris* grey]

Gri·sons (griˈzɔ̃) *n.* the French name for **Graubünden.**

grist (grɪst) *n.* **1. a.** grain intended to be or that has been ground. **b.** the quantity of such grain processed in one grinding. **2.** *Brewing.* malt grains that have been cleaned and cracked. **3. grist to** (*or* **for**) **the** (*or* **one's**) **mill.** anything that can be turned to profit or advantage. [Old English *grīst;* related to Old Saxon *grist-grimmo* gnashing of teeth, Old High German *grist-grimmōn*]

gris·tle (ˈgrɪsəl) *n.* cartilage, esp. when in meat. [Old English *gristle;* related to Old Frisian, Middle Low German *gristel*] —**'gris·tly** *adj.* —**'gris·tli·ness** *n.*

grist·mill (ˈgrɪstˌmɪl) *n.* a mill, esp. one equipped with large grinding stones for grinding grain.

grit (grɪt) *n.* **1.** small hard particles of sand, earth, stone, etc. **2.** Also called: **gritstone.** any coarse sandstone that can be used as a grindstone or millstone. **3.** the texture or grain of stone. **4.** indomitable courage, toughness, or resolution. ~*vb.* **grits, grit·ting, grit·ted. 5.** to clench or grind together (two objects, esp. the teeth). **6.** to cover (a surface, such as icy roads) with grit. [Old English *grēot;* related to Old Norse *grjōt* pebble, Old High German *grioz;* see GREAT, GROATS, GRUEL] —**'grit·less** *adj.*

Grit (grɪt) *n., adj. Canadian.* an informal word for **Liberal.**

grith (grɪθ) *n.* **1.** *English legal history.* security, peace, or protection, guaranteed either in a certain place, such as a church, or for a period of time. **2.** a place of safety or protection. [Old English *grith;* related to Old Norse *grith* home]

grits (grɪts) *pl. n.* **1.** hulled and coarsely ground grain. **2.** *U.S.* See **hominy grits.** [Old English *grytt;* related to Old High German *gruzzi;* see GREAT, GRIT]

grit·ty (ˈgrɪtɪ) *adj.* **·ti·er, ·ti·est. 1.** courageous; hardy; resolute. **2.** of, like, or containing grit. —**'grit·ti·ly** *adv.* —**'grit·ti·ness** *n.*

gri·va·tion (grɪˈveɪʃən) *n. Navigation.* short for **grid variation.**

griv·et (ˈgrɪvɪt) *n.* an E African variety of a common guenon monkey, *Cercopithecus aethiops,* having long white tufts of hair on either side of the face. Compare **green monkey, vervet.** [C19: from French, of unknown origin]

griz·zle[1] (ˈgrɪzəl) *vb.* **1.** to make or become grey. ~*n.* **2.** a grey colour. **3.** grey or partly grey hair. **4.** a grey wig. [C15: from Old French *grisel,* from *gris,* of Germanic origin; compare Middle High German *grīs* grey]

griz·zle[2] (ˈgrɪzəl) *vb.* (*intr.*) *Informal, chiefly Brit.* **1.** (esp. of a child) to fret; whine. **2.** to sulk or grumble. [C18: of Germanic origin; compare Old High German *grist-grimmōn* gnashing of teeth, German *Griesgram* unpleasant person] —**'griz·zler** *n.*

griz·zled (ˈgrɪzəld) *adj.* **1.** streaked or mixed with grey; grizzly; griseous. **2.** having grey or partly grey hair.

griz·zly (ˈgrɪzlɪ) *adj.* **·zli·er, ·zli·est. 1.** somewhat grey; grizzled. ~*n., pl.* **·zlies. 2.** See **grizzly bear.**

griz·zly bear *n.* a greyish-brown variety of the brown bear, formerly widespread in W North America. Often shortened to **grizzly.**

gro. *abbrev. for* gross (unit of quantity).

groan (grəʊn) *n.* **1.** a prolonged stressed dull cry expressive of agony, pain, or disapproval. **2.** a loud harsh creaking sound, as of a tree bending in the wind. **3.** *Informal.* a grumble or complaint, esp. a persistent one. ~*vb.* **4.** to utter (low inarticulate sounds) expressive of pain, grief, disapproval, etc.: *they all groaned at Larry's puns.* **5.** (*intr.*) to make a sound like a groan. **6.** (*intr.,* usually foll. by *beneath* or *under*) to be weighed down (by) or suffer greatly (under): *the country groaned under the dictator's rule.* **7.** (*intr.*) *Informal.* to complain or grumble. [Old English *grānian;* related to Old Norse *grīna,* Old High German *grīnan;* see GRIN] —**'groan·er** *n.* —**'groan·ing·ly** *adv.*

groat (grəʊt) *n.* an English silver coin worth four pennies, taken out of circulation in the 17th century. [C14: from Middle Dutch *groot,* from Middle Low German *gros,* from Medieval Latin (*denarius*) *grossus* thick (coin); see GROSCHEN]

groats (grəʊts) *pl. n.* **1.** the hulled and crushed grain of oats, wheat, or certain other cereals. **2.** the parts of oat kernels used as food. [Old English *grot* particle; related to *grota* fragment, as in *meregrota* pearl; see GRIT, GROUT]

gro·cer ('grəʊsə) *n.* a dealer in foodstuffs and other household supplies. [C15: from Old French *grossier*, from *gros* large; see GROSS]

gro·cer·ies ('grəʊsərɪz) *pl. n.* merchandise, esp. foodstuffs, sold by a grocer.

gro·cer·y ('grəʊsərɪ) *n., pl.* **·cer·ies.** the business or premises of a grocer.

grock·le ('grɒkᵊl) *n. Devonshire dialect.* a tourist, esp. one from the Midlands or the North of England. [C20: of unknown origin]

Grod·no (*Russian* 'grɔdnə) *n.* a city in the W central Soviet Union, in the Byelorussian SSR on the Neman River: part of Poland (1921–39). Pop.: 168 000 (1975 est.).

grog (grɒg) *n.* **1.** diluted spirit, usually rum, as an alcoholic drink. **2.** *Informal, chiefly Austral.* alcoholic drink in general, esp. spirits. [C18: from Old *Grog*, nickname of Edward Vernon (1684–1757), British admiral, who in 1740 issued naval rum diluted with water; his nickname arose from his grogram cloak]

grog·gy ('grɒgɪ) *adj.* **·gi·er, ·gi·est.** *Informal.* **1.** dazed or staggering, as from exhaustion, blows, or drunkenness. **2.** faint or weak. —'**grog·gi·ly** *adv.* —'**grog·gi·ness** *n.*

grog·ram ('grɒgrəm) *n.* a coarse fabric of silk, wool, or silk mixed with wool or mohair, often stiffened with gum, formerly used for clothing. [C16: from French *gros grain* coarse grain; see GROSGRAIN]

grog·shop ('grɒg,ʃɒp) *n.* **1.** *Rare.* a drinking place, esp. one of disreputable character. **2.** *Austral. informal.* a shop, etc., where liquor can be bought for drinking off the premises.

groin (grɔɪn) *n.* **1.** the depression or fold where the legs join the abdomen. **2.** *Euphemistic.* the genitals, esp. the testicles. **3.** a variant spelling (esp. U.S.) of **groyne. 4.** *Architect.* a curved arris formed where two intersecting vaults meet. ~*vb.* **5.** (*tr.*) *Architect.* to provide or construct with groins. [C15: perhaps from English *grynde* abyss; related to GROUND[1]]

Gro·li·er ('grəʊlɪə; *French* grɔ'lje) *adj.* relating to or denoting a decorative style of bookbinding using interlaced leather straps, gilded ornamental scrolls, etc. [C19: named after Jean *Grolier de Servières* (1479–1565), French bibliophile]

grom·met ('grɒmɪt) *or* **grum·met** *n.* a ring of rubber or plastic or a metal eyelet designed to line a hole to prevent a cable or pipe passed through it from chafing. [C15: from obsolete French *gourmette* chain linking the ends of a bit, from *gourmer* bridle, of unknown origin]

grom·well ('grɒmwəl) *n.* any of various hairy plants of the boraginaceous genus *Lithospermum*, esp. *L. officinale*, having small greenish-white, yellow, or blue flowers, and smooth nutlike fruits. See also **puccoon** (sense 1). [C13: from Old French *gromil*, from *gres* sandstone + *mil* millet, from Latin *milium*]

Gro·my·ko (*Russian* gra'mɪkə) *n.* **An·drei An·dre·ye·vich** (an'drjej an'drjejɪvitʃ). born 1909, Soviet statesman and diplomat; foreign minister since 1957.

Gro·ning·en ('grəʊnɪŋən; *Dutch* 'xro:nɪŋə) *n.* **1.** a province in the NE Netherlands: mainly agricultural. Capital: Groningen. Pop.: 530 400 (1973 est.). Area: 2350 sq. km (900 sq. miles). **2.** a city in the NE Netherlands, capital of Groningen province. Pop.: 165 777 (1974 est.).

Grøn·land ('grœn,lan) *n.* the Danish name for **Greenland.**

groom (gru:m, grʊm) *n.* **1.** a person employed to clean and look after horses. **2.** See **bridegroom. 3.** any of various officers of a royal or noble household. **4.** *Archaic.* a male servant or attendant. **5.** *Archaic and poetic.* a young man. ~*vb.* (*tr.*) **6.** to make or keep (clothes, appearance, etc.) clean and tidy. **7.** to rub down, clean, and smarten (a horse, dog, etc.). **8.** to train or prepare for a particular task, occupation, etc.: *to groom someone for the Presidency.* [C13 *grom* manservant; perhaps related to Old English *grōwan* to GROW] —'**groom·er** *n.*

grooms·man ('gru:mzmən, 'grʊmz-) *n., pl.* **·men.** a man who attends the bridegroom at a wedding, usually the best man.

groove (gru:v) *n.* **1.** a long narrow channel or furrow, esp. one cut into wood by a tool. **2.** the spiral channel, usually V-shaped, in a gramophone record. See also **microgroove. 3.** *Printing.* a channel across the bottom surface of a piece of type. **4.** one of the spiral cuts in the bore of a gun. **5.** *Anatomy.* any furrow or channel on a bodily structure or part; sulcus. **6.** a settled existence, routine, etc., to which one is suited or accustomed, esp. one from which it is difficult to escape. **7.** *Slang.* an experience, event, etc., that is groovy. **8. in the groove. a.** *Jazz.* playing well and apparently effortlessly, with a good beat, etc. **b.** *U.S.* fashionable. ~*vb.* **9.** (*tr.*) to form or cut a groove in. **10.** (*intr.*) *Slang.* to enjoy oneself or feel in rapport with one's surroundings. **11.** (*tr.*) *Slang.* to excite. **12.** (*intr.*) *Slang.* to progress or develop. **13.** (*intr.*) *Jazz.* to play well, with a good beat, etc. [C15: from obsolete Dutch *groeve*, of Germanic origin; compare Old High German *gruoba* pit, Old Norse *grof*] —'**groove·less** *adj.* —'**groove,like** *adj.*

groov·y ('gru:vɪ) *adj.* **groov·i·er, groov·i·est.** *Slang.* attractive, fashionable, or exciting.

grope (grəʊp) *vb.* **1.** (*intr.* usually foll. by *for*) to feel or search about uncertainly (for something) with the hands. **2.** (usually foll. by *for* or *after*) to search uncertainly or with difficulty (for a solution, answer, etc.). ~*n.* **3.** the act of groping. [Old English *grāpian*; related to Old High German *greifōn*, Norwegian *greipa;* compare GRIPE] —'**grop·er** *n.* —'**grop·ing·ly** *adv.*

Gro·pi·us ('grəʊpɪəs) *n.* **Wal·ter.** 1883–1969, U.S. architect, designer, and teacher, born in Germany. He founded (1919) and directed (1919–28) the Bauhaus in Germany. His influence stemmed from his adaptation of architecture to modern social needs and his pioneering use of industrial materials, such as concrete and steel. His buildings include the Fagus factory at Alfeld (1911) and the Bauhaus at Dessau (1926).

Gros (*French* gro) *n.* Baron **An·toine Jean** (ãtwan 'ʒã). 1771–1835, French painter, noted for his battle scenes.

gros·beak ('grəʊs,bi:k, 'grɒs-) *n.* **1.** any of various finches, such as *Pinicola enucleator* (**pine grosbeak**), that have a massive powerful bill. **2. cardinal grosbeak.** any of various mostly tropical American buntings, such as the cardinal and pyrrhuloxia, the males of which have brightly coloured plumage. [C17: from French *grosbec*, from Old French *gros* large, thick + *bec* BEAK]

gro·schen ('grəʊʃən) *n., pl.* **·schen. 1.** an Austrian monetary unit worth one hundredth of a schilling. **2.** a German coin worth ten pfennigs. **3.** a former German silver coin. [C17: from German: Bohemian dialect alteration of Middle High German *grosse*, from Medieval Latin (*denarius*) *grossus* thick (penny); see GROSS, GROAT]

gros de Lon·dres *French.* (gro də 'lõdr) *n.* a lightweight shiny ribbed silk fabric, the ribs alternating between wide and narrow between different colours or between different textures of yarn. [literally: heavy (fabric) from London]

gros·grain ('grəʊ,greɪn) *n.* a heavy ribbed silk or rayon fabric or tape for trimming clothes, etc. [C19: from French *gros grain* coarse grain; see GROSS, GRAIN]

gros point (grəʊ) *n.* **1.** a needlepoint stitch covering two horizontal and two vertical threads. **2.** work done in this stitch. ~Compare **petit point.**

gross (grəʊs) *adj.* **1.** repellently or excessively fat or bulky. **2.** with no deductions for expenses, tax, etc.; total: *gross sales.* Compare **net**[2] (sense 1). **3.** (of personal qualities, tastes, etc.) conspicuously coarse or vulgar. **4.** obviously or exceptionally culpable or wrong; flagrant: *gross inefficiency.* **5.** lacking in perception, sensitivity, or discrimination: *gross judgments.* **6.** (esp. of vegetation) dense; thick; luxuriant. **7.** *Obsolete.* coarse in texture or quality. **8.** *Rare.* rude; uneducated; ignorant. ~*n.* **9.** *pl.* **gross.** a unit of quantity equal to 12 dozen. **10.** *pl.* **gross·es. a.** the entire amount. **b.** the great majority. ~*vb.* (*tr.*) **11.** to earn as total revenue, before deductions for expenses, tax, etc. ~See also **gross up.** [C14: from Old French *gros* large, from Late Latin *grossus* thick] —'**gross·ly** *adv.* —'**gross·ness** *n.*

gross do·mes·tic prod·uct *n.* the total value of all goods and services produced domestically by a nation during a year. It is equivalent to gross national product minus net investment incomes from foreign nations. Abbrev.: **GDP**

Grosse·teste ('grəʊs,tɛst) *n.* **Rob·ert.** ?1175–1253, English prelate and scholar; bishop of Lincoln (1235–53). He attacked ecclesiastical abuses and wrote commentaries on Aristotle and treatises on theology, philosophy, and science.

gross na·tion·al prod·uct *n.* the total value of all final goods and services produced annually by a nation. Abbrev.: **GNP**

gross prof·it *n. Accounting.* the difference between total revenue from sales and the total cost of purchases or materials, with an adjustment for stock.

gross ton *n.* another name for **long ton.**

gros·su·lar·ite ('grɒsjʊlə,raɪt) *n.* a green or greenish-grey garnet, used as a gemstone. Formula: $Ca_3Al_2(SiO_4)_3$. [C19: from New Latin *grossulāria* gooseberry, from Old French *grosele* + -ITE[1]]

gross up *vb.* (*tr., adv.*) to increase (net income) to its pre-tax value.

Gross·war·dein (,gro:svar'daɪn) *n.* the German name for **Oradea.**

gross weight *n.* total weight of an article inclusive of the weight of the container and packaging.

grosz (grɔ:ʃ) *n., pl.* **gro·szy** ('grɔ:ʃɪ). a Polish monetary unit worth one hundredth of a zloty. [from Polish, from Czech *grosh;* see GROSCHEN]

Grosz (grəʊs) *n.* **George.** 1893–1959, German painter, in the U.S. from 1932, whose works satirized German militarism and bourgeois society.

grot (grɒt) *n.* a poetic word for **grotto.** [C16: from French *grotte*, from Old Italian *grotta;* see GROTTO]

Grote (grəʊt) *n.* **George.** 1794–1871, English historian, noted particularly for his *History of Greece* (1846–56).

gro·tesque (grəʊ'tɛsk) *adj.* **1.** strangely or fantastically distorted; bizarre: *a grotesque reflection in the mirror.* **2.** of or characteristic of the grotesque in art. **3.** absurdly incongruous; in a ludicrous context: *a grotesque turn of phrase.* ~*n.* **4.** a 16th-century decorative style in which parts of human, animal, and plant forms are distorted and mixed. **5.** a decorative device, as in painting or sculpture, in this style. **6.** *Printing.* the family of 19th-century sans serif display types. **7.** any grotesque person or thing. [C16: from French, from Old Italian (*pittura*) *grottesca* cave painting, from *grottesco* of a cave, from *grotta* cave; see GROTTO] —**gro'·tesque·ly** *adv.* —**gro'·tesque·ness** *n.*

gro·tes·quer·y *or* **gro·tes·quer·ie** (grəʊ'tɛskərɪ) *n., pl.* **·quer·ies. 1.** the state of being grotesque. **2.** something that is grotesque, esp. an object such as a sculpture.

Gro·ti·us ('grəʊtɪəs) *n.* **Hu·go,** original name *Huig de Groot.* 1583–1645, Dutch jurist and statesman, whose *De Jure Belli ac Pacis* (1625) is regarded as the foundation of modern international law. —'**Gro·ti·an** *adj.* —'**Gro·ti·an·ism** *n.*

grot·to ('grɒtəʊ) *n., pl.* **·toes** *or* **·tos. 1.** a small cave, esp. one with attractive features. **2.** a construction in the form of a cave, esp. as in landscaped gardens during the 18th century. [C17: from Old Italian *grotta*, from Late Latin *crypta* vault; see CRYPT]

grot+ty *adj.* +ti+er, +ti+est. *Brit. slang.* unpleasant, nasty, or unattractive. [C20: from GROTESQUE]

grouch (graʊtʃ) *Informal.* ~*vb.* **1.** to complain; grumble. ~*n.* **2.** a complaint, esp. a persistent one. **3.** a person who is always grumbling. [C20: from obsolete *grutch*, from Old French *grouchier* to complain; see GRUDGE] —**'grouch·y** *adj.* —**'grouch·i+ly** *adv.* —**'grouch·i+ness** *n.*

ground[1] (graʊnd) *n.* **1.** the land surface. **2.** earth or soil: *he dug into the ground outside his house.* **3.** (*pl.*) the land around a dwelling house or other building. **4.** (*sometimes pl.*) an area of land given over to a purpose: *football ground; burial grounds.* **5.** land having a particular characteristic: *level ground; high ground.* **6.** matter for consideration or debate; field of research or enquiry: *the lecture was familiar ground to him; the report covered a lot of ground.* **7.** a position or viewpoint, as in an argument or controversy (esp. in the phrases **give ground, hold, stand,** *or* **shift one's ground**). **8.** position or advantage, as in a subject or competition (esp. in the phrases **gain ground, lose ground,** etc.). **9.** (*often pl.*) reason; justification: *grounds for complaint.* **10.** *Arts.* **a.** the prepared surface applied to the support of a painting, such as a wall, canvas, etc., to prevent it reacting with or absorbing the paint. **b.** the support of a painting. **c.** the background of a painting or main surface against which the other parts of a work of art appear superimposed. **11. a.** the first coat of paint applied to a surface. **b.** (*as modifier*): *ground colour.* **12.** the bottom of a river or the sea. **13.** (*pl.*) sediment or dregs, esp. from coffee. **14.** *Chiefly Brit.* the floor of a room. **15.** *Cricket.* **a.** the area from the popping crease back past the stumps, in which a batsman may legally stand. **b.** ground staff. **16.** See **ground bass. 17.** a mesh or network supporting the main pattern of a piece of lace. **18.** *Electrical.* the usual U.S. word for **earth** (sense 8). **19. above ground.** alive. **20. below ground.** dead and buried. **21. break new ground.** to do something that has not been done before. **22. common ground.** a subject about which there is agreement or similar thinking. **23. cut the ground from under someone's feet.** to anticipate someone's action and thus make it irrelevant or meaningless. **24. (down) to the ground.** *Brit. informal.* completely; absolutely: *it suited him down to the ground.* **25. get off the ground.** *Informal.* to make a beginning, esp. one that is successful. **26. home ground.** a familiar area or topic. **27. into the ground.** beyond what is requisite or can be endured; to exhaustion. **28. meet someone on his own ground.** to meet someone according to terms he has laid down himself. **29. touch ground. a.** (of a ship) to strike the sea bed. **b.** to arrive at something solid or stable after discussing or dealing with indistinct subjects, etc. **30.** (*modifier*) situated on, living on, used on, or concerned with the ground: *ground frost; ground forces.* ~*vb.* **31.** (*tr.*) to put or place on the ground. **32.** (*tr.*) to instruct in fundamentals. **33.** (*tr.*) to provide a basis or foundation for; establish. **34.** (*tr.*) to confine (an aircraft, pilot, etc.) to the ground. **35.** the usual U.S. word for **earth** (sense 16). **36.** (*tr.*) *Nautical.* to run (a vessel) aground. **37.** (*tr.*) to cover (a surface) with a preparatory coat of paint. **38.** (*intr.*) to hit or reach the ground. [Old English *grund;* related to Old Norse *grunn* shallow, *grunnr, grund* plain, Old High German *grunt*]

ground[2] (graʊnd) *vb.* **1.** the past tense or past participle of **grind.** ~*adj.* **2.** having the surface finished, thickness reduced, or an edge sharpened by grinding. **3.** reduced to fine particles by grinding.

ground+age ('graʊndɪdʒ) *n. Brit.* a fee levied on a vessel entering a port or anchored off a shore.

ground bait *n. Angling.* bait, such as scraps of bread, maggots, etc., thrown into an area of water to attract fish. See **chum**[2].

ground bass *or* **ground** (beɪs) *n. Music.* a short melodic bass line that is repeated over and over again.

ground bee+tle *n.* **1.** any beetle of the family *Carabidae,* often found under logs, stones, etc., having long legs and a dark coloration. **2.** any beetle of the family *Tenebrionidae,* feeding on plants and plant products. **3.** any of various other beetles that live close to or beneath the ground.

ground cher+ry *n.* any of various American solanaceous plants of the genus *Physalis,* esp. *P. pubescens,* having round fleshy fruit enclosed in a bladder-like husk. See also **winter cherry, gooseberry** (sense 4).

ground con+trol *n.* **1.** the personnel, radar, computers, etc., on the ground that monitor the progress of aircraft or spacecraft. **2.** a system for feeding continuous radio messages to an aircraft pilot to enable him to make a blind landing.

ground cov+er *n.* the mass of dense low herbaceous plants and shrubs that grow over the surface of the ground, esp. in a forest, preventing soil erosion.

ground el+der *n.* another name for **goutweed.**

ground floor *n.* **1.** the floor of a building level or almost level with the ground. **2. get in on** (*or* **start from**) **the ground floor.** *Informal.* **a.** to enter a business, organization, etc., at the lowest level. **b.** to be in a project, undertaking, etc., from its inception.

ground glass *n.* **1.** glass that has a rough surface produced by grinding, used for diffusing light. **2.** glass in the form of fine particles produced by grinding, used as an abrasive.

ground hog *n.* another name for **woodchuck.**

ground ice *n.* ice formed below the surface of a body of water, either on the ground or on a submerged object.

ground i·vy *n.* a creeping or trailing Eurasian aromatic herbaceous plant, *Glechoma* (or *Nepeta*) *hederacea,* with scalloped leaves and purplish-blue flowers: family *Labiatae* (labiates).

ground+less ('graʊndlɪs) *adj.* without reason or justification. *his suspicions were groundless.* —**'ground+less+ly** *adv.* —**'ground+less+ness** *n.*

ground+ling ('graʊndlɪŋ) *n.* **1.** any animal or plant that lives close to the ground or at the bottom of a lake, river, etc. **2. a.** (in Elizabethan theatre) a spectator standing in the yard in front of the stage and paying least. **b.** a spectator in the cheapest section of any theatre. **3.** a person on the ground as distinguished from one in an aircraft.

ground loop *n.* a sudden uncontrolled turn by an aircraft on the ground, while moving under its own power.

ground+mass ('graʊnd,mæs) *n.* the matrix of igneous rocks, such as porphyry, in which larger crystals (phenocrysts) are embedded.

ground+nut ('graʊnd,nʌt) *n.* **1.** a North American climbing leguminous plant, *Apios tuberosa,* with fragrant brown flowers and small edible underground tubers. **2.** the tuber of this plant. **3.** any of several other plants having underground nutlike parts. **4.** *Brit.* another name for **peanut** (sense 1).

ground pine *n.* **1.** a hairy plant, *Ajuga chamaepitys,* of Europe and N Africa, having two-lipped yellow flowers marked with red spots: family *Labiatae* (labiates). It smells of pine when crushed. See also **bugle**[2]. **2.** any of certain North American club mosses, esp. *Lycopodium obscurum.*

ground plan *n.* **1.** a drawing of the ground floor of a building, esp. one to scale. See also **plan** (sense 3). Compare **elevation** (sense 5). **2.** a preliminary or basic outline.

ground plate *n.* a joist forming the lowest member of a timber frame. Also called: **groundsill, soleplate.**

ground plum *n.* **1.** a North American leguminous plant, *Astragalus caryocarpus,* with purple or white flowers and green thick-walled plumlike edible pods. **2.** the pod of this plant.

ground pro+vi+sions *pl. n. Caribbean.* starchy vegetables, esp. root crops and plantains.

ground rent *n. Law.* the rent reserved by a lessor on granting a lease, esp. one for a long period of years to enable the lessee to develop the land.

ground rule *n.* a procedural rule or principle.

ground+sel ('graʊnsəl) *n.* **1.** any of certain plants of the genus *Senecio,* esp. *S. vulgaris,* a Eurasian weed with heads of small yellow flowers: family *Compositae* (composites). See also **ragwort. 2. groundsel tree.** a shrub, *Baccharis halimifolia,* of E North America, with white plumelike fruits: family *Compositae.* [Old English *grundeswelge,* changed from *gundeswilge,* from *gund* pus + *swelgan* to swallow; after its use in poultices on abscesses]

ground+sheet ('graʊnd,ʃi:t) *or* **ground cloth** *n.* **1.** a waterproof rubber, plastic, or polythene sheet placed on the ground in a tent, etc., to keep out damp. **2.** a similar sheet put over a sports field to protect it against rain.

ground+sill ('graʊnd,sɪl) *n.* another name for **ground plate.**

grounds+man ('graʊndzmən) *n., pl.* **+men.** a person employed to maintain a sports ground, park, etc.

ground+speed ('graʊnd,spi:d) *n.* the speed of an aircraft relative to the ground. Compare **airspeed.**

ground squir+rel *n.* any burrowing sciurine rodent of the genus *Citellus* and related genera, resembling chipmunks and occurring in North America, E Europe, and Asia. Also called: **gopher.**

ground state *or* **lev+el** *n.* the lowest energy state of an atom, molecule, particle, etc. Compare **excited** (sense 4).

ground stroke *n. Tennis.* any return made to a ball that has touched the ground, as opposed to a volley.

ground swell *n.* a considerable swell of the sea, often caused by a distant storm or earthquake or by the passage of waves into shallow water.

ground wa+ter *n.* underground water that has come mainly from the seepage of surface water and is held in the soil and in pervious rocks.

ground wave *or* **ray** *n.* a radio wave that travels directly between a transmitting and a receiving aerial. Compare **sky wave.**

ground+work ('graʊnd,wɜ:k) *n.* **1.** preliminary work as a foundation or basis. **2.** the ground or background of a painting, etc.

ground ze·ro *n.* a point on the ground directly below the centre of a nuclear explosion.

group (gru:p) *n.* **1.** a number of persons or things considered as a collective unit. **2. a.** a number of persons bound together by common social standards, interests, etc. **b.** (*as modifier*): *group behaviour.* **3.** a small band of players or singers, esp. of pop music. **4.** a number of animals or plants considered as a unit because of common characteristics, habits, etc. **5.** *Grammar.* another word for **phrase** (sense 1). **6.** an association of companies under a single ownership and control, consisting of a holding company, subsidiary companies, and sometimes associated companies. **7.** two or more figures or objects forming a design or unit in a design, in a painting or sculpture. **8.** a military formation comprising complementary arms and services, usually for a purpose: *a brigade group.* **9.** an air force organization of higher level than a squadron. **10.** Also called: **radical.** *Chem.* two or more atoms that are bound together in a molecule and behave as a single unit: *a methyl group* $-CH_3$. Compare **free radical. 11.** a vertical column of elements in the periodic table that all have similar electronic structures, properties, and valencies. Compare **period** (sense 8). **12.** *Geology.* any stratigraphical unit, esp. the unit for two or more formations. **13.** *Maths.* a set under an operation involving any two members of the set such that the set is closed, associative, and contains both an identity and the inverse of each member. **14.** See **blood group.** ~*vb.* **15.** to arrange or place (things, people, etc.) in or into a group, or (of things, etc.) to form into a group. [C17: from French *groupe*, of Germanic origin; compare Italian *gruppo;* see CROP]

group cap·tain *n.* an officer holding commissioned rank senior to a squadron leader but junior to an air commodore in the British R.A.F. and certain other air forces.

group dy·nam·ics *n.* (*functioning as sing.*) *Psychol.* a field of social psychology concerned with the nature of human groups, their development, and their interactions with individuals, other groups, and larger organizations.

group·er ('gru:pə) *n., pl.* **·er** *or* **·ers.** any large marine serranid fish of the genus *Epinephelus* and related genera, of warm and tropical seas. [C17: from Portuguese *garupa*, probably from a South American Indian word]

group·ie ('gru:pɪ) *n. Slang.* an ardent fan of pop groups, esp. a girl who follows them on tour in order to have sexual relations with them.

group·ing ('gru:pɪŋ) *n.* a planned arrangement of things, people, etc., within a group.

group in·sur·ance *n. Chiefly U.S.* insurance relating to life, health, or accident and covering several persons, esp. the employees of a firm, under a single contract at reduced premiums.

group mar·riage *n.* an arrangement in which several males live together with several females, forming a conjugal unit.

group prac·tice *n.* a medical practice undertaken by a group of associated doctors who work together as partners or as specialists in different areas.

group ther·a·py *n. Psychiatry.* the simultaneous treatment of a number of individuals who are members of a natural group or who are brought together to share their problems in group discussion.

grouse[1] (graʊs) *n., pl.* **grouse** *or* **grous·es. 1.** any gallinaceous bird of the family *Tetraonidae,* occurring mainly in the N hemisphere, having a stocky body and feathered legs and feet. They are popular game birds. See also **black grouse, red grouse.** ~*adj.* **2.** *Austral. slang.* excellent. [C16: of unknown origin] —'**grouse·ˌlike** *adj.*

grouse[2] (graʊs) *vb.* **1.** (*intr.*) to grumble; complain. ~*n.* **2.** a persistent complaint. [C19: of unknown origin] —'**grous·er** *n.*

grout (graʊt) *n.* **1.** a thin mortar for filling joints between tiles, masonry, etc. **2.** a fine plaster used as a finishing coat. **3.** coarse meal or porridge. ~*vb.* **4.** (*tr.*) to fill (joints) or finish (walls, etc.) with grout. [Old English *grūt;* related to Old Frisian *grēt* sand, Middle High German *grūz,* Middle Dutch *grūte* coarse meal; see GRIT, GROATS] —'**grout·er** *n.*

grouts (graʊts) *pl. n.* **1.** *Chiefly Brit.* sediment or grounds, as from making coffee. **2.** a variant spelling of **groats.**

grout·y ('graʊtɪ) *adj.* **grout·i·er, grout·i·est.** *Scot. and northern English dialect.* **1.** muddy; dirty. **2.** (of people's manners) rough; unpolished.

grove (grəʊv) *n.* **1.** a small wooded area or plantation. **2. a.** a road lined with houses and often trees, esp. in a suburban area. **b.** (*cap. as part of a street name*): *Ladbroke Grove.* [Old English *grāf;* related to *grǣfa* thicket, GREAVE, Norwegian *greivla* to intertwine]

grov·el ('grɒvᵊl) *vb.* **·els, ·el·ling, ·elled** *or U.S.* **·els, ·el·ing, ·eled.** (*intr.*) **1.** to humble or abase oneself, as in making apologies or showing respect. **2.** to lie or crawl face downwards, as in fear or humility. **3.** (often foll. by *in*) to indulge or take pleasure (in sensuality or vice). [C16: back formation from obsolete *groveling* (adv.), from Middle English *on grufe* on the face, of Scandinavian origin; compare Old Norse *ā grūfu,* from *grūfa* prone position; see -LING[2]] —'**grov·el·ler** *n.* —'**grov·el·ling·ly** *adv.*

Groves (grəʊvz) *n.* Sir **Charles.** born 1915, English orchestral conductor.

grov·et ('grɒvət) *n.* a wrestling hold in which a wrestler in a kneeling position grips the head of his kneeling opponent with one arm and forces his shoulders down with the other.

grow (grəʊ) *vb.* **grows, grow·ing, grew, grown. 1.** (of an organism or part of an organism) to increase in size or develop (hair, leaves, or other structures). **2.** (*intr.;* usually foll. by *out of* or *from*) to originate, as from an initial cause or source: *the federation grew out of the Empire.* **3.** (*intr.*) to increase in size, number, degree, etc.: *the population is growing rapidly.* **4.** (*intr.*) to change in length or amount in a specified direction: *some plants grow downwards; profits over the years grew downwards.* **5.** (*copula; may take an infinitive*) (esp. of emotions, physical states, etc.) to develop or come into existence or being gradually: *to grow cold; to grow morose; he grew to like her.* **6.** (*intr.;* usually foll. by *up*) to come into existence: *a close friendship grew up between them.* **7.** (*intr.;* foll. by *together*) to be joined gradually by or as by growth: *the branches on the tree grew together.* **8.** (*intr.;* foll. by *away, together,* etc.) to develop a specified state of friendship: *the lovers grew together gradually; many friends grow apart over the years.* **9.** (when *intr.,* foll. by *with*) to become covered with a growth: *the path grew with weeds.* **10.** to produce (plants) by controlling or encouraging their growth, esp. for home consumption or on a commercial basis. [Old English *grōwan;* related to Old Norse *grōa,* Old Frisian *grōia,* Old High German *gruoen;* see GREEN, GRASS] —'**grow·a·ble** *adj.*

grow·er ('grəʊə) *n.* **1.** a person who grows plants: *a vegetable grower.* **2.** a plant that grows in a specified way: *a fast grower.*

grow·ing pains *pl. n.* **1.** pains in muscles or joints sometimes experienced by children during a period of unusually rapid growth. **2.** difficulties besetting a new enterprise in the early stages of its development.

grow in·to *vb.* (*intr., prep.*) to become big or mature enough for: *his clothes were always big enough for him to grow into.*

growl (graʊl) *vb.* **1.** (of animals, esp. when hostile) to utter (sounds) in a low inarticulate manner: *the dog growled at us.* **2.** to utter (words) in a gruff or angry manner: *he growled an apology.* **3.** (*intr.*) to make sounds suggestive of an animal growling: *the thunder growled around the lake.* ~*n.* **4.** the act or sound of growling. **5.** *Jazz.* an effect resembling a growl, produced at the back of the throat when playing a wind instrument. [C18: from earlier *grolle,* from Old French *grouller* to grumble] —'**growl·ing·ly** *adv.*

growl·er ('graʊlə) *n.* **1.** a person, animal, or thing that growls. **2.** *Brit. slang, obsolete.* a four-wheeled hansom cab. **3.** *Canadian.* a small iceberg that can prove hazardous to shipping. **4.** *U.S. slang.* any container, such as a can, for draught beer.

grown (grəʊn) *adj.* **a.** developed or advanced: *fully grown.* **b.** (*in combination*): *half-grown.*

grown-up *adj.* **1.** having reached maturity; adult. **2.** suitable for or characteristic of an adult. ~*n.* **3.** an adult.

grow on *vb.* (*intr., prep.*) to become progressively more acceptable or pleasant to: *I don't think much of your new record, but I suppose it will grow on me.*

grow out of *vb.* (*intr., adv. + prep.*) to become too big or mature for: *she soon grew out of her girlish ways.*

growth (grəʊθ) *n.* **1.** the process or act of growing, esp. this process in organisms following assimilation of food. **2.** an increase in size, number, significance, etc. **3.** something grown or growing: *a new growth of hair.* **4.** a stage of development: *a full growth.* **5.** any abnormal tissue, such as a tumour. **6.** (*modifier*) of, relating to, or characterized by growth: *a growth industry.*

growth ring *n.* another name for **annual ring.**

growth shares *pl. n. Finance.* ordinary shares with good prospects of appreciation in yield and value.

grow up *vb.* (*intr., adv.*) **1.** to reach maturity; become adult. **2.** to come into existence; develop.

groyne *or esp. U.S.* **groin** (grɔɪn) *n.* a wall or jetty built out from a riverbank or seashore to control erosion. Also called: **spur, breakwater.**

groz·ing i·ron ('grəʊzɪŋ) *n.* an iron for smoothing joints between lead pipes. [C17: part translation of Dutch *gruisijzer,* from *gruizen* to crush, from *gruis* gravel + *yzer* iron]

Groz·ny (*Russian* 'grɔznɪj) *n.* a city in the S Soviet Union, capital of the Chechen-Ingush ASSR: a major oil centre. Pop.: 375 000 (1975 est.).

grub (grʌb) *vb.* **grubs, grub·bing, grubbed. 1.** (when *tr.,* often foll. by *up* or *out*) to search for and pull up (roots, stumps, etc.) by digging in the ground. **2.** to dig up the surface of (ground, soil, etc.), esp. to clear away roots, stumps, etc. **3.** (*intr.;* often foll. by *in* or *among*) to search carefully. **4.** (*intr.*) to work unceasingly, esp. at a dull task or research. **5.** *Slang.* to provide (a person) with food or (of a person) to take food. **6.** (*tr.*) *Slang, chiefly U.S.* to scrounge: *to grub a cigarette.* ~*n.* **7.** the short legless larva of certain insects, esp. beetles. **8.** *Slang.* food; victuals. **9.** a person who works hard, esp. in a dull plodding way. **10.** *Brit. informal.* a dirty child. [C13: of Germanic origin; compare Old High German *grubilōn* to dig, German *grübeln* to rack one's brain, Middle Dutch *grobben* to scrape together; see GRAVE, GROOVE]

grub·ber ('grʌbə) *n.* **1.** a person who grubs. **2.** another name for **grub hoe.**

grub·by ('grʌbɪ) *adj.* **·bi·er, ·bi·est. 1.** dirty; slovenly. **2.** mean; beggarly. **3.** infested with grubs. —'**grub·bi·ly** *adv.* —'**grub·bi·ness** *n.*

grub hoe *or* **grub·bing hoe** *n.* a heavy hoe for grubbing up roots. Also called: **grubber.**

grub screw *n.* a small headless screw used to secure a collar or other part to a shaft.

grub·stake ('grʌbˌsteɪk) *n.* **1.** *U.S. informal.* supplies provided for a prospector on the condition that the donor has a stake in any finds. ~*vb.* (*tr.*) **2.** to furnish with such supplies. **3.** *Chiefly U.S.* to supply (a person) with a stake in a gambling game. —'**grub·ˌstak·er** *n.*

Grub Street *n.* **1.** a former street in London frequented by literary hacks and needy authors. **2.** the world or class of literary hacks, etc. ~*adj. also* **Grub·street. 3.** (*sometimes not cap.*) relating to or characteristic of hack literature.

grudge (grʌdʒ) *n.* **1.** a persistent feeling of resentment, esp. one due to some cause, such as an insult or injury. ~*vb.* **2.** (*tr.*) to accept unwillingly. **3.** to feel resentful or envious about (someone else's success, possessions, etc.). [C15: from Old French *grouchier* to grumble, probably of Germanic origin; compare Old High German *grunnizōn* to grunt] —'**grudge·less** *adj.* —'**grudg·er** *n.* —'**grudg·ing·ly** *adv.*

gru·el ('gru:əl) *n.* a drink or thin porridge, made by boiling meal, esp. oatmeal, in water or milk. [C14: from Old French, of Germanic origin; see GROUT]

gru·el·ling *or U.S.* **gru·el·ing** ('gru:əlɪŋ) *adj.* **1.** extremely severe or tiring: *a gruelling interview.* ~*n.* **2.** *Informal.* a severe or tiring experience, esp. punishment.

grue·some *or* **grew·some** ('gru:səm) *adj.* inspiring repugnance and horror; ghastly. [C16: originally Northern English and Scottish, of Scandinavian origin; compare Old Swedish *grua,* Old Danish *grue;* related to German *graven,*

Dutch *gruwen* to abhor; see -SOME[1]] —'**grue+some+ly** *or* '**grew+some+ly** *adv.* —'**grue+some+ness** *or* '**grew+some+ness** *n.*

gruff (grʌf) *adj.* **1.** rough or surly in manner, speech, etc.: *a gruff reply.* **2.** (of a voice, bark, etc.) low and throaty. [C16: originally Scottish, from Dutch *grof,* of Germanic origin; compare Old High German *girob;* related to Old English *hrēof,* Lithuanian *kraupùs*] —'**gruff+ish** *adj.* —'**gruff+ly** *adv.* —'**gruff+ness** *n.*

gru+gru ('gruːgruː) *n.* **1.** any of several tropical American palms, esp. *Acrocomia sclerocarpa,* which has a spiny trunk and leaves and edible nuts. **2.** the large edible wormlike larva of a weevil, *Rhynchophorus palmarum,* that infests this palm. [C18: from American Spanish (Puerto Rican dialect) *grugrú,* of Cariban origin]

grum+ble ('grʌmbᵊl) *vb.* **1.** to utter (complaints) in a nagging or discontented way. **2.** (*intr.*) to make low dull rumbling sounds. ~*n.* **3.** a complaint; grouse. **4.** a low rumbling sound. [C16: from Middle Low German *grommelen,* of Germanic origin; see GRIM] —'**grum+bler** *n.* —'**grum+bling+ly** *adv.* —'**grum+bly** *adj.*

grum+met ('grʌmɪt) *n.* another word for **grommet.**

gru+mous ('gruːməs) *or* **gru+mose** ('gruːməʊs) *adj.* (esp. of plant parts) consisting of granular tissue. [C17: from *grume* a clot of blood, from Latin *grumus* a little heap; related to CRUMB]

grump (grʌmp) *Informal, chiefly U.S.* ~*n.* **1.** a surly or bad-tempered person. **2.** (*pl.*) a sulky or morose mood (esp. in the phrase **have the grumps**). ~*vb.* **3.** (*intr.*) to complain or grumble. [C18: dialect *grump* surly remark, probably of imitative origin]

grump·y ('grʌmpɪ) *or* **grump+ish** *adj.* **grump·i+er, grump·i+est.** peevish; sulky. [C18: from GRUMP + -Y[1]] —'**grump·i+ly** *or* '**grump+ish+ly** *adv.* —'**grump·i+ness** *or* '**grump+ish+ness** *n.*

Grun+dy ('grʌndɪ) *n.* a narrow-minded person who keeps critical watch on the propriety of others. [C18: named after Mrs. *Grundy,* the character in T. Morton's play *Speed the Plough* (1798)] —'**Grun+dy+ism** *n.* —'**Grun+dy+ist** *or* '**Grun+dy+ite** *n.*

Grü·ne·wald (*German* 'gryːnəˌvalt) *n.* **Mat·thi·as** (ma'tiːas), original name *Mathis Gothardt.* ?1470–1528, German painter, the greatest exponent of late Gothic art in Germany. The *Isenheim Altarpiece* is regarded as his masterpiece.

grun+ion ('grʌnjən) *n.* a Californian marine teleost fish, *Leuresthes tenuis,* that spawns on beaches: family *Atherinidae* (silversides). [C20: probably from Spanish *gruñón* a grunter]

grunt (grʌnt) *vb.* **1.** (*intr.*) (esp. of pigs and some other animals) to emit a low short gruff noise. **2.** (when *tr., may take a clause as object*) to express something gruffly: *he grunted his answer.* ~*n.* **3.** the characteristic low short gruff noise of pigs, etc., or a similar sound, as of disgust. **4.** any of various mainly tropical marine sciaenid fishes, such as *Haemulon macrostomum* (**Spanish grunt**), that utter a grunting sound when caught. [Old English *grunnettan,* probably of imitative origin; compare Old High German *grunnizōn, grunni* moaning, Latin *grunnīre*] —'**grunt+ing+ly** *adv.*

grunt+er ('grʌntə) *n.* **1.** a person or animal that grunts, esp. a pig. **2.** another name for **grunt** (sense 4). **3.** *Austral. slang.* a promiscuous woman.

grun+tled ('grʌntᵊld) *adj. Informal.* happy or contented; satisfied. [C20: back formation from DISGRUNTLED]

Grus (grʊs) *n., Latin genitive* **Gru+is** ('gruːɪs). a constellation in the S hemisphere lying near Phoenix and Piscis Austrinus and containing two second magnitude stars. [via New Latin from Latin: crane]

Gru+yère *or* **Gru+yère cheese** ('gruːjɛə; *French* gry'jɛːr) *n.* a hard flat whole-milk cheese, pale yellow in colour and with holes. [C19: after *Gruyère,* Switzerland where it originated]

gr. wt. *abbrev. for* gross weight.

gryph+on ('grɪfᵊn) *n.* a variant spelling of **griffin**[1].

grys+bok ('graɪsˌbɒk) *n.* either of two small antelopes, *Raphicerus melanotis* or *R. sharpei,* of central and southern Africa, having small straight horns. [C18: Afrikaans, from Dutch *grijs* grey + *bok* BUCK[1]]

G.S. *abbrev. for:* **1.** General Secretary. **2.** General Staff.

gs. *abbrev. for* guineas.

G-string *n.* **1.** a piece of cloth worn by striptease artistes covering the pubic area only and attached to a very narrow waistband. **2.** a strip of cloth attached to the front and back of a waistband and covering the loins. **3.** *Music.* a string tuned to G, such as the lowest string of a violin.

G-suit *n.* a close-fitting garment covering the legs and abdomen that is worn by the crew of high-speed aircraft and can be pressurized to prevent blackout during certain manoeuvres. Also called: **anti-G suit.** [C20: from *g(ravity) suit*]

GT *abbrev. for* gran turismo.

gt. *abbrev. for:* **1.** *Bookbinding.* gilt. **2.** great. **3.** (*pl.* **gtt.**) *Pharmacy.* gutta.

G.T.C. *or* **g.t.c.** (on a commercial order for goods) *abbrev. for* good till cancelled (*or* countermanded).

gtd. *abbrev. for* guaranteed.

g.u. *or* **GU** *abbrev. for* genitourinary.

gua+ca+mo+le *or* **gua+cha+mo+le** (ˌgwɑːkə'məʊlɪ) *n.* **1.** a spread of mashed avocado, tomato pulp, mayonnaise, and seasoning. **2.** any of various Mexican or South American salads containing avocado. [from American Spanish, from Nahuatl *ahuacamolli,* from *ahuacatl* avocado + *molli* sauce]

gua+cha+ro ('gwɑːtʃəˌrəʊ) *n., pl.* **+ros.** another name for **oilbird.** [C19: from Spanish *guácharo*]

gua+co ('gwɑːkəʊ) *n., pl.* **+cos. 1.** any of several tropical American plants whose leaves are used as an antidote to snakebite, esp. the climbers *Mikania guaco,* family *Compositae* (composites), or *Aristolochia maxima* (*A. serpentina*), family *Aristolochiaceae.* **2.** the leaves of any of these plants. [C19: from American Spanish]

Gua+da+la+ja+ra (ˌgwɑːdᵊlə'hɑːrə; *Spanish* ˌgwaðala'xara) *n.* **1.** a city in W Mexico, capital of Jalisco state: the second largest city of Mexico: centre of the Indian slave trade until its abolition, declared here in 1810; two universities (1792 and 1935). Pop.: 1 560 805 (1975 est.). **2.** a city in central Spain, in New Castile. Pop.: 31 917 (1970).

Gua+dal+ca+nal (ˌgwɑːdᵊlkə'næl; *Spanish* ˌgwaðalka'nal) *n.* a mountainous island in the SW Pacific, the largest of the Solomon Islands: under British Protection until 1977; occupied by the Japanese (1942–43). Pop.: 23 996 (1970). Area: 6475 sq. km (2500 sq. miles).

Gua+dal+qui+vir (ˌgwɑːdᵊlkwɪ'vɪə; *Spanish* ˌgwaðalki'βir) *n.* the chief river of S Spain, rising in the Sierra de Segura and flowing west and southwest to the Gulf of Cádiz: navigable by ocean-going vessels to Seville. Length: 560 km (348 miles).

Gua+da+lupe Hi+dal+go (ˌgwɑːdᵊ'luːp hɪ'dælgəʊ; *Spanish* ˌgwaða'lupe i'ðalγo) *n.* a city in central Mexico, northwest of Mexico City: became the foremost pilgrimage centre in the Americas after an Indian convert reported seeing a vision of the Virgin Mary here in 1531. Pop.: 153 454 (1970). Former name (1931–71): **Gustavo A. Madero.**

Gua+de+loupe (ˌgwɑːdᵊ'luːp) *n.* an overseas region of France in the E Caribbean, in the Leeward Islands, formed by the islands of Basse Terre and Grande Terre and their five dependencies. Capital: Basse-Terre. Pop.: 334 900 (1975). Area: 1702 sq. km (657 sq. miles).

Gua+dia+na (*Spanish* gwa'ðjana; *Portuguese* gwə'ðjənə) *n.* a river in SW Europe, rising in S central Spain and flowing west, then south as part of the border between Spain and Portugal, to the Gulf of Cádiz. Length: 578 km (359 miles).

guai·a+col ('gwaɪəˌkɒl) *n.* a yellowish oily creosote-like liquid extracted from guaiacum resin and hardwood tar, used medicinally as an expectorant. Formula: $C_7H_8O_2$. [from GUAIAC(UM) + -OL[2]]

guai·a+cum *or* **guai·o+cum** ('gwaɪəkəm) *n.* **1.** any tropical American evergreen tree of the zygophyllaceous genus *Guaiacum,* such as the lignum vitae. **2.** the hard heavy wood of any of these trees. **3.** Also called: **guai+ac** ('gwaɪæk). a brownish resin obtained from the lignum vitae, used medicinally and in making varnishes. [C16: New Latin, from Spanish *guayaco,* of Taino origin]

Guam (gwɑːm) *n.* an island in the N Pacific, the largest and southernmost of the Marianas: belonged to Spain from the 17th century until 1898, when it was ceded to the U.S.; site of naval and air force bases. Capital: Agaña. Pop.: 99 000 (1975 est.). Area: 450 sq. km (209 sq. miles). —**Gua+ma+ni+an** (gwɑː'meɪnɪən) *n., adj.*

guan (gwɑːn) *n.* any gallinaceous bird of the genera *Penelope, Pipile,* etc., of Central and South America: family *Cracidae* (curassows). [C18: from American Spanish]

Gua+na+ba+ra (*Portuguese* ˌgwəna'bara) *n.* (until 1975) a state of SE Brazil, on the Atlantic and **Guanabara Bay,** now amalgamated with the state of Rio de Janeiro.

gua+na+co (gwɑː'nɑːkəʊ) *n., pl.* **+cos.** a cud-chewing South American artiodactyl mammal, *Lama guanicoe,* closely related to the domesticated llama: family *Camelidae.* [C17: from Spanish, from Quechuan *huanacu*]

Gua+na+jua+to (*Spanish* ˌgwana'xwato) *n.* **1.** a state of central Mexico, on the great central plateau: mountainous in the north, with fertile plains in the south; important mineral resources. Capital: Guanajuato. Pop.: 2 270 370 (1970). Area: 30 588 sq. km (11 810 sq. miles). **2.** a city in central Mexico, capital of Guanajuato state: founded in 1554, it became one of the world's richest silver-mining centres. Pop.: 65 258 (1970).

gua+nase ('gwɑːneɪz) *n.* an enzyme that converts guanine to xanthine by removal of an amino group. [C20: from GUAN(INE) + -ASE]

guan·i+dine ('gwɑːnɪˌdiːn, -dɪn, 'gwænɪ-) *or* **guan·i+din** ('gwɑːnɪdɪn, 'gwænɪ-) *n.* a strongly alkaline crystalline substance, soluble in water and found in plant and animal tissues. It is used in organic synthesis. Formula: $HNC(NH_2)_2$. Also called: **carbamidine, iminourea.** [C19: from GUANO + -ID[3] + -INE[2]]

gua+nine ('gwɑːniːn, 'guːəˌniːn) *n.* a white almost insoluble compound: one of the purine bases in nucleic acids. Formula: $C_5H_5N_5O$. [C19: from GUANO + -INE[2]]

gua+no ('gwɑːnəʊ) *n., pl.* **+nos. 1.** the dried excrement of fish-eating sea birds, deposited in rocky coastal regions of South America: contains the urates, oxalates, and phosphates of ammonium and calcium and is used as a fertilizer. **2.** any similar but artificially produced fertilizer. [C17: from Spanish, from Quechuan *huano* dung]

gua+no+sine ('gwɑːnəˌsiːn, -ˌziːn) *n. Biochem.* a nucleoside consisting of guanine and ribose.

Guan+tá+na+mo (*Spanish* gwan'tanamo) *n.* a city in SE Cuba, on **Guantánamo Bay.** Pop.: 161 739 (1970).

Gua+po+ré (*Portuguese* gwapo'rɛ) *n.* **1.** a river in W central South America, rising in SW Brazil and flowing northwest as part of the border between Brazil and Bolivia, to join the Mamoré River. Length: 1750 km (1087 miles). Spanish name: **Iténez. 2.** the former name (until 1956) of **Rondônia.**

guar. *abbrev. for* guaranteed.

gua+ra+ni ('gwɑːrənɪ) *n., pl.* **+ni** *or* **+nis.** the standard monetary unit of Paraguay, divided into 100 centimos.

Gua+ra+ni (ˌgwɑːrəˈniː) *n.* **1.** (*pl.* **+ni** *or* **+nis**) a member of a South American Indian people of Paraguay, S Brazil, and Bolivia. **2.** the language of this people, belonging to the Tupi-Guarani family; one of the official languages of Paraguay, along with Spanish.

guar+an+tee (ˌgærənˈtiː) *n.* **1.** a formal assurance, esp. in writing, that a product, service, etc., will meet certain standards or specifications. **2.** *Law.* a promise, esp. a collateral agreement, to answer for the debt, default, or miscarriage of another. **3. a.** a person, company, etc., to whom a guarantee is made. **b.** a person, company, etc., who gives a guarantee. **4.** a person who acts as a guarantor. **5.** something that makes a specified condition or outcome certain. **6.** a variant spelling of **guaranty.** ~*vb.* **+tees, +tee+ing, +teed.** (*mainly tr.*) **7.** (*also intr.*) to take responsibility for (someone else's debts, obligations, etc.). **8.** to serve as a guarantee for. **9.** to secure or furnish security for: *a small deposit will guarantee any dress.* **10.** (usually foll. by *from* or *against*) to undertake to protect or keep secure, as against injury, loss, etc. **11.** to ensure: *good planning will guarantee success.* **12.** (*may take a clause as object or an infinitive*) to promise or make certain. [C17: perhaps from Spanish *garante* or French *garant,* of Germanic origin; compare WARRANT]

guar+an+tor (ˌgærənˈtɔː) *n.* a person who gives or is bound by a guarantee or guaranty; surety.

guar+an+ty (ˈgærəntɪ) *n., pl.* **+ties. 1.** a pledge of responsibility for fulfilling another person's obligations in case of that person's default. **2.** a thing given or taken as security for a guaranty. **3.** the act of providing security. **4.** a person who acts as a guarantor. ~*vb.* **+ties, +ty+ing, +tied. 5.** a variant spelling of **guarantee.** [C16: from Old French *garantie,* variant of *warantie,* of Germanic origin; see WARRANTY]

guard (gɑːd) *vb.* **1.** to watch over or shield (a person or thing) from danger or harm; protect. **2.** to keep watch over (a prisoner or other potentially dangerous person or thing), as to prevent escape. **3.** (*tr.*) to control: *to guard one's tongue.* **4.** (*intr.;* usually foll. by *against*) to take precautions. **5.** to control entrance and exit through (a gate, door, etc.). **6.** (*tr.*) to provide (machinery, etc.) with a device to protect the operator. **7.** (*tr.*) **a.** *Chess, cards.* to protect or cover (a chess man or card) with another. **b.** *Curling, bowling.* to protect or cover (a stone or bowl) by placing one's own stone or bowl between it and another player. **8.** (*tr.*) *Archaic.* to accompany as a guard. ~*n.* **9.** a person or group who keeps a protecting, supervising, or restraining watch or control over people, such as prisoners, things, etc. Related adj.: **custodial. 10.** a person or group of people, such as soldiers, who form a ceremonial escort. **11.** *Brit.* the official in charge of a train. **12. a.** the act or duty of protecting, restraining, or supervising. **b.** (*as modifier*): *guard duty.* **13.** a device, part, or attachment on an object, such as a weapon or machine tool, designed to protect the user against injury, as on the hilt of a sword or the trigger of a firearm. **14.** anything that provides or is intended to provide protection: *a guard against infection.* **15. a.** a chain on the fastening of a bracelet to ensure that the band cannot open enough to fall off the wrist or arm. **b.** a long neck chain often holding a chatelaine. **16.** See **guard ring. 17.** *Sport.* an article of light tough material worn to protect any of various parts of the body. **18.** *Basketball.* **a.** the position of either of the two defensive players in a team. **b.** a player in this position. **19.** the posture of defence or readiness in fencing, boxing, cricket, etc. **20. take guard.** *Cricket.* (of a batsman) to choose a position in front of the wicket to receive the bowling, esp. by requesting the umpire to indicate his position relative to the stumps. **21. give guard.** *Cricket.* (of an umpire) to indicate such a position to a batsman. **22. off (one's) guard.** having one's defences down; unprepared. **23. on (one's) guard.** prepared to face danger, difficulties, etc. **24. stand guard.** (of a military sentry, etc.) to keep watch. **25. mount guard.** *Chiefly military.* (of a sentry, etc.) to begin to keep watch. [C15: from Old French *garde,* from *garder* to protect, of Germanic origin; compare Spanish *guardar;* see WARD] —**ˈguard+a+ble** *adj.* —**ˈguard+er** *n.* —**ˈguard+less** *adj.* —**ˈguard+ˌlike** *adj.*

Guar+da+fu+i (ˌgwɑːdəˈfuːɪ) *n.* **Cape.** a cape at the NE tip of the Somali Republic, extending into the Indian Ocean.

guar+dant *or* **gar+dant** (ˈgɑːdᵊnt) *adj.* (*usually postpositive*) *Heraldry.* (of a beast) shown full face. [C16: from French *gardant* guarding, from *garder* to GUARD]

guard cell *n. Botany.* one of a pair of crescent-shaped cells that surround a pore (stoma) in the epidermis. Changes in the turgidity of the cells cause the opening and closing of the stoma.

guard+ed (ˈgɑːdɪd) *adj.* **1.** protected or kept under surveillance. **2.** prudent, restrained, or noncommittal: *a guarded reply.* —**ˈguard+ed+ly** *adv.* —**ˈguard+ed+ness** *n.*

guard hair *n.* any of the coarse hairs that form the outer fur in certain mammals, rising above the underfur.

guard+house (ˈgɑːdˌhaʊs) *n. Military.* a building serving as the headquarters or a post for military police and in which military prisoners are detained.

guard·i·an (ˈgɑːdɪən) *n.* **1.** one who looks after, protects, or defends: *the guardian of public morals.* **2.** *Law.* someone legally appointed to manage the affairs of a person incapable of acting for himself, as an infant or person of unsound mind. **3.** (*often cap.*) (in England) another word for **custos.** ~*adj.* **4.** protecting or safeguarding. —**ˈguard·i·an+ˌship** *n.*

guard+rail (ˈgɑːdˌreɪl) *n.* **1.** a railing placed alongside a staircase, road, etc., as a safety barrier. **2.** Also called (Brit.): **checkrail.** *Railways.* a short metal rail fitted to the inside of the main rail to provide additional support in keeping a train's wheels on the track.

guard ring *n.* **1.** Also called: **guard, keeper ring.** *Jewellery.* an extra ring worn to prevent another from slipping off the finger. **2.** an electrode used to counteract distortion of the electric fields at the edges of other electrodes in a capacitor or electron lens.

guard+room (ˈgɑːdˌruːm, -ˌrʊm) *n.* **1.** a room used by guards. **2.** a room in which prisoners are confined under guard.

Guards (gɑːdz) *pl. n.* **a.** (esp. in European armies) any of various regiments responsible for ceremonial duties and, formerly, the protection of the head of state: *the Life Guards; the Grenadier Guards.* **b.** (*as modifier*): *a Guards regiment.*

guards+man (ˈgɑːdzmən) *n., pl.* **+men. 1.** (in Britain) a member of a Guards battalion or regiment. **2.** (in the U.S.) a member of the National Guard. **3.** a guard.

guard's van *n. Railways, Brit.* the van in which the guard travels, usually attached to the rear of a train. U.S. equivalent: **caboose.**

Guar·ne·ri (gwɑːˈnɪərɪ; *Italian* gwarˈnɛːri), **Guar·nie·ri** (*Italian* gwarˈnjɛːri), *or* **Guar·ne·ri·us** (gwɑːˈnɛərɪəs) *n.* **1.** an Italian family of 17th- and 18th-century violin-makers. **2.** any violin made by a member of this family.

Guat. *abbrev. for* Guatemala.

Gua+te+ma+la (ˌgwɑːtəˈmɑːlə) *n.* a republic in Central America: original Maya Indians conquered by the Spanish in 1523; became the centre of Spanish administration in Central America; gained independence and was annexed to Mexico in 1821, becoming an independent republic in 1839. Official language: Spanish. Religion: Roman Catholic. Currency: quetzal. Capital: Guatemala City. Pop.: 5 175 400 (1973). Area: 108 889 sq. km (42 042 sq. miles). —**ˌGua+te+ˈma+lan** *adj., n.*

Gua+te+ma+la Cit·y *n.* the capital of Guatemala, in the southeast: founded in 1776 to replace the former capital, Antigua; university (1676). Pop.: 706 920 (1973).

gua+va (ˈgwɑːvə) *n.* **1.** any of various tropical American trees of the myrtaceous genus *Psidium,* esp. *P. guajava,* grown in tropical regions for their edible fruit. **2.** the fruit of such a tree, having yellow skin and pink pulp: used to make jellies, jams, etc. [C16: from Spanish *guayaba,* from a South American Indian word]

Gua+ya+quil (*Spanish* ˌgwajaˈkil) *n.* a port in W Ecuador: the largest city in the country and its chief port; university (1867). Pop.: 701 227 (1969 est.).

gua+yu+le (gwəˈjuːlɪ) *n.* **1.** a bushy shrub, *Parthenium argentatum,* of the southwestern U.S.: family *Compositae* (composites). **2.** rubber derived from the sap of this plant. [from American Spanish, from Nahuatl *cuauhuli,* from *cuahuitl* tree + *uli* gum]

gub+bins (ˈgʌbɪnz) *n.* **1.** an object of little or no value. **2.** a small device or gadget. **3.** *Informal.* a silly person. [C16 (meaning: fragments): from obsolete *gobbon,* probably related to GOBBET]

gu+ber+na+to+ri+al (ˌgjuːbənəˈtɔːrɪəl, ˌguː-) *adj. Chiefly U.S.* of or relating to a governor. [C18: from Latin *gubernātor* governor]

gu+ber+ni+ya *Russian.* (guˈbjɛrnɪjə) *n.* **1.** a territorial division of imperial Russia. **2.** a territorial and administrative subdivision in the Soviet Union. [from Russian: government, ultimately from Latin *gubernāre* to GOVERN]

guck (gʌk, gʊk) *n.* slimy matter; gunk. [C20: perhaps a blend of GOO and MUCK]

gudg+eon[1] (ˈgʌdʒən) *n.* **1.** a small slender European freshwater cyprinid fish, *Gobio gobio,* with a barbel on each side of the mouth: used as bait by anglers. **2.** any of various other fishes, such as the goby. **3.** bait or enticement. **4.** *Slang.* a person who is easy to trick or cheat. ~*vb.* **5.** (*tr.*) *Slang.* to trick or cheat. [C15: from Old French *gougon,* probably from Latin *gōbius;* see GOBY]

gudg+eon[2] (ˈgʌdʒən) *n.* **1.** the female or socket portion of a pinned hinge. **2.** *Nautical.* one of two or more looplike sockets, fixed to the transom of a boat, into which the pintles of a rudder are fitted. [C14: from Old French *goujon,* perhaps from Late Latin *gulbia* chisel]

gudg+eon pin *n. Brit.* the pin through the skirt of a piston in an internal-combustion engine, to which the little end of the connecting rod is attached. U.S. name: **wrist pin.**

Gud+run (ˈgʊdruːn), **Guth+run** (ˈgʊðruːn), *or* **Kud+run** (ˈkʊdruːn) *n. Norse myth.* the wife of Sigurd and, after his death, of Atli, whom she slew for his murder of her brother Gunnar. She corresponds to Kriemhild in the *Nibelungenlied.*

guel·der-rose (ˈgɛldəˌrəʊz) *n.* a Eurasian caprifoliaceous shrub, *Viburnum opulus,* with clusters of white flowers and small red fruits. [C16: from Dutch *geldersche roos,* from *Gelderland* or *Gelders,* province of Holland]

Guel+ders (ˈgɛldəz) *n.* another name for **Gelderland.**

Guelph[1] *or* **Guelf** (gwɛlf) *n.* **1.** a member of the political faction in medieval Italy that supported the power of the pope against the German emperors. Compare **Ghibelline. 2.** a member of a secret society in 19th-century Italy opposed to foreign rule. —**ˈGuelph+ic** *or* **ˈGuelf+ic** *adj.* —**ˈGuelph+ism** *or* **ˈGuelf+ism** *n.*

Guelph[2] (gwɛlf) *n.* a city in Canada, in SE Ontario. Pop.: 60 087 (1971).

gue+non (gəˈnɒn) *n.* any slender agile Old World monkey of the genus *Cercopithecus,* inhabiting wooded regions of Africa and having long hind limbs and tail and long hair surrounding the face. [C19: from French, of unknown origin]

guer·don ('gɜːdᵊn) *Poetic.* ~*n.* **1.** a reward or payment. ~*vb.* **2.** (*tr.*) to give a guerdon to. [C14: from Old French *gueredon,* of Germanic origin; compare Old High German *widarlōn,* Old English *witherlēan;* final element influenced by Latin *dōnum* gift] —**'guer·don·er** *n.*

Guer·ni·ca (gɜː'niːkə, 'gɜːnɪkə; *Spanish* ger'nika) *n.* a town in N Spain: formerly the seat of a Basque parliament; destroyed in 1937 by German bombers during the Spanish Civil War, an event depicted in one of Picasso's most famous paintings. Pop.: 15 149 (1970).

Guern·sey ('gɜːnzɪ) *n.* **1.** an island in the English Channel: the second largest of the Channel Islands, which, with Alderney and Sark, Herm, Jethou, and some islets, forms the bailiwick of Guernsey; market gardening, dairy farming, and tourism. Capital: St. Peter Port. Pop.: 53 734 (1971). Area: 63 sq. km (24.5 sq. miles). **2.** a breed of dairy cattle producing rich creamy milk, originating from the island of Guernsey. **3.** (*sometimes not cap.*) a seaman's knitted woollen sweater. **4.** (*not cap.*) *Austral.* a sleeveless woollen shirt or jumper worn by a football player. **5. get a guernsey.** *Austral.* to be selected or gain recognition for something.

Guer·re·ro (*Spanish* ge'rrero) *n.* a mountainous state of S Mexico, on the Pacific: rich mineral resources. Capital: Chilpancingo. Pop.: 1 597 360 (1970). Area: 63 794 sq. km (24 631 sq. miles).

guer·ril·la *or* **gue·ril·la** (gə'rɪlə) *n.* **a.** a member of an irregular usually politically motivated armed force that combats stronger regular forces, such as the army or police. **b.** (*as modifier*): *guerrilla warfare.* [C19: from Spanish, diminutive of *guerra* WAR] —**guer·'ril·la·ism** *or* **gue·'ril·la·ism** *n.*

guess (gɛs) *vb.* (when *tr., may take a clause as object*) **1.** (when *intr.*, often foll. by *at* or *about*) to form or express an uncertain estimate or conclusion (about something), based on insufficient information: *guess what we're having for dinner.* **2.** to arrive at a correct estimate of (something) by guessing: *he guessed my age.* **3.** *Informal, chiefly U.S.* to believe, think, or suppose (something): *I guess I'll go now.* **4. anyone's guess.** something difficult to predict. **5. keep a person guessing.** to let a person remain in a state of uncertainty. ~*n.* **6.** an estimate or conclusion arrived at by guessing: *a bad guess.* **7.** the act of guessing. [C13: probably of Scandinavian origin; compare Old Swedish *gissa,* Old Danish *gitse,* Middle Dutch *gissen;* see GET] —**'guess·a·ble** *adj.* —**'guess·er** *n.* —**'guess·ing·ly** *adv.*

guess·ti·mate *or* **gues·ti·mate** *Informal.* ~*n.* ('gɛstɪmɪt). **1.** an estimate calculated mainly or only by guesswork. ~*vb.* ('gɛstɪˌmeɪt). **2.** to form a guesstimate of.

guess·work ('gɛsˌwɜːk) *n.* **1.** a set of conclusions, estimates, etc., arrived at by guessing. **2.** the process of making guesses.

guest (gɛst) *n.* **1.** a person who is entertained, taken out to eat, etc., and paid for by another. **2. a.** a person who receives hospitality at the home of another: *a weekend guest.* **b.** (*as modifier*): *the guest room.* **3. a.** a person who receives the hospitality of a government, establishment, or organization. **b.** (*as modifier*): *a guest speaker.* **4. a.** an actor, contestant, entertainer, etc., taking part as a visitor in a programme in which there are also regular participants. **b.** (*as modifier*): *a guest appearance.* **5.** a patron of a hotel, boarding house, restaurant, etc. **6.** *Zoology.* a nontechnical name for **inquiline. 7. be my guest.** *Informal.* do as you like. ~*vb.* **8.** (*intr.*) *Informal.* (in theatre and broadcasting) to be a guest: *to guest on a show.* [Old English *giest* guest, stranger, enemy; related to Old Norse *gestr,* Gothic *gasts,* Old High German *gast,* Old Slavonic *gostĭ,* Latin *hostis* enemy]

guest·house ('gɛstˌhaʊs) *n.* a private home or boarding house offering accommodation, esp. to travellers.

guest rope *n. Nautical.* any line sent or trailed over the side of a vessel as a convenience for boats drawing alongside, as an aid in warping or towing, etc.

Gue·va·ra (gə'vɑːrə; *Spanish* ge'βara) *n.* **Er·nes·to** (er'nesto), known as *Che Guevara.* 1928–67, Latin American politician and soldier, born in Argentina. He developed guerrilla warfare as a tool for revolution and was instrumental in Castro's victory in Cuba (1959), where he held government posts until 1965. He was killed while training guerrillas in Bolivia.

guff (gʌf) *n. Slang.* ridiculous or insolent talk. [C19: imitative of empty talk; compare dialect Norwegian *gufs* puff of wind]

guf·faw (gʌ'fɔː) *n.* **1.** a crude and boisterous laugh. ~*vb.* **2.** to laugh crudely and boisterously or express (something) in this way. [C18: of imitative origin]

Gui·an·a (gaɪ'ænə, gɪ'ɑːnə) *or* **The Gui·an·as** *n.* a region of NE South America, including Guyana, Surinam, French Guiana, and the **Guiana Highlands** (largely in SE Venezuela and partly in N Brazil). Area: about 1 787 000 sq. km (690 000 sq. miles). —**Gui·a·nese** (ˌgaɪə'niːz, ˌgɪə-) *or* **Gui·an·an** (gaɪ'ænən, gɪ'ɑːnən) *adj., n.*

guid·ance ('gaɪdᵊns) *n.* **1.** leadership, instruction, or direction. **2. a.** counselling or advice on educational, vocational, or psychological matters. **b.** (*as modifier*): *the marriage-guidance counsellor.* **3.** something that guides. **4.** any process by which the flight path of a missile is controlled in flight. See also **guided missile.**

guide (gaɪd) *vb.* **1.** to lead the way for (a person). **2.** to control the movement or course of (an animal, vehicle, etc.) by physical action; steer. **3.** to supervise or instruct (a person). **4.** (*tr.*) to direct the affairs of (a person, company, nation, etc.): *he guided the country through the war.* **5.** (*tr.*) to advise or influence (a person) in his standards or opinions: *let truth guide you always.* ~*n.* **6. a.** a person, animal, or thing that guides. **b.** (*as modifier*): *a guide dog.* **7.** a person, usually paid, who conducts tour expeditions, etc. **8.** a model or criterion, as in moral standards or accuracy. **9.** Also called: **guidebook.** a handbook with information for visitors to a place, as a foreign country. **10.** a book that instructs or explains the fundamentals of a subject or skill: *a guide to better living.* **11.** a mark used to direct the reader's eye to a place on a page of printing. **12.** any device that directs the motion of a tool or machine part. **13. a.** a mark, sign, etc., that points the way. **b.** (*in combination*): *guidepost.* **14.** *Spiritualism.* a spirit believed to influence a medium so as to direct what he utters and convey messages through him. **15. a.** *Naval.* a ship in a formation used as a reference for manoeuvres, esp. with relation to maintaining the correct formation and disposition. **b.** *Military.* a soldier stationed to one side of a column or line to regulate alignment, show the way, etc. [C14: from (Old) French *guider,* of Germanic origin; compare Old English *wītan* to observe] —**'guid·a·ble** *adj.* —**'guide·less** *adj.* —**'guid·er** *n.* —**'guid·ing·ly** *adv.*

Guide (gaɪd) *n.* (*sometimes not cap.*) a member of the organization for girls equivalent to the Scouts. U.S. equivalent: **Girl Scout.**

guid·ed mis·sile *n.* a missile, esp. one that is rocket-propelled, having a flight path controlled during flight either by radio signals or by internal preset or self-actuating homing devices. See also **command guidance, field guidance, homing guidance, inertial guidance, terrestrial guidance.**

guide·line ('gaɪdˌlaɪn) *n.* **1.** a principle put forward to set standards or determine a course of action. **2.** *Printing.* a lightly marked line used to facilitate the alignment of letters, drawings, etc.

guide·post ('gaɪdˌpəʊst) *n.* **1.** a sign on a post by a road indicating directions. **2.** a principle or guideline.

guide rope *n.* **1.** a stay or rope attached to another rope that is lifting a load, either to steady the load or guide the rope. **2.** another name for **dragrope** (sense 2).

Gui·do d'A·rez·zo (*Italian* 'gwiːdo da'rettso) *n.* ?995–?1050 A.D., Italian Benedictine monk and musical theorist: reputed inventor of solmization.

gui·don ('gaɪdᵊn) *n.* **1.** a small pennant, used as a marker or standard, esp. by cavalry regiments. **2.** the man or vehicle that carries this. [C16: from French, from Old Provençal *guidoo,* from *guida* GUIDE]

Gui·enne *or* **Guy·enne** (*French* gɥi'jɛn) *n.* a former province of SW France: formed, with Gascony, the duchy of Aquitaine during the 12th century.

guild *or* **gild** (gɪld) *n.* **1.** an organization, club, or fellowship. **2.** (esp. in medieval Europe) an association of men sharing the same interests, such as merchants or artisans: formed for mutual aid and protection and to maintain craft standards or pursue some other purpose such as communal worship. **3.** *Ecology.* a group of plants, such as a group of epiphytes, that share certain habits or characteristics. [C14: of Scandinavian origin; compare Old Norse *gjald* payment, *gildi* guild; related to Old English *gield* offering, Old High German *gelt* money]

guil·der ('gɪldə) *or* **gul·den** *n., pl.* **·ders, ·der** *or* **·dens, ·den. 1.** Also: **gilder.** the standard monetary unit of the Netherlands, divided into 100 cents. **2.** the standard monetary unit of the Netherlands Antilles and Surinam, divided into 100 cents. **3.** any of various former gold or silver coins of Germany, Austria, or the Netherlands. [C15: changed from Middle Dutch *gulden,* literally: GOLDEN]

Guild·ford ('gɪlfəd) *n.* a city in S England, on the River Wey: cathedral (1936-1968); seat of the University of Surrey (1966). Pop.: 56 887 (1971).

guild·hall ('gɪldˌhɔːl) *n.* **1.** *Brit.* **a.** the hall of a guild or corporation. **b.** a town hall. **2.** Also: **gildhall.** the meeting place of a medieval guild.

guilds·man, gilds·man ('gɪldzmən) *or* (*fem.*) **guilds·wom·an, gilds·wom·an** *n., pl.* **·men** *or* **·wom·en.** a member of a guild.

guild so·cial·ism *n.* a form of socialism advocated in Britain in the early 20th century. Industry was to be owned by the state but managed and controlled by worker-controlled guilds. —**guild so·cial·ist** *n.*

guile (gaɪl) *n.* clever or crafty character or behaviour. [C18: from Old French *guile,* of Germanic origin; see WILE] —**'guile·ful** *adj.* —**'guile·ful·ly** *adv.* —**'guile·ful·ness** *n.*

guile·less ('gaɪllɪs) *adj.* free from guile; ingenuous. —**'guile·less·ly** *adv.* —**'guile·less·ness** *n.*

Guil·laume de Lor·ris (*French* gi'joːm də lɔ'ris) *n.* 13th century French poet, who wrote the first 4 058 lines of the allegorical romance, the *Roman de la Rose,* continued by Jean de Meung.

guil·le·mot ('gɪlɪˌmɒt) *n.* any northern oceanic diving bird of the genera *Uria* and *Cepphus,* having a black-and-white plumage and long narrow bill: family *Alcidae* (auks, etc.), order *Charadriiformes.* [C17: from French, diminutive of *Guillaume* William]

guil·loche (gɪ'lɒʃ) *n.* an ornamental band or border with a repeating pattern of two or more interwoven wavy lines, as in architecture. [C19: from French: tool used in ornamental work, perhaps from *Guillaume* William]

guil·lo·tine *n.* ('gɪləˌtiːn). **1. a.** a device for beheading persons, consisting of a weighted blade set between two upright posts. **b. the guillotine.** execution by this instrument. **2.** a device for cutting or trimming sheet material, such as paper or sheet metal, consisting of a long rigid blade that descends onto the sheet. **3.** a surgical instrument for removing tonsils, growths in the throat, etc. **4.** Also called: **closure by compartment.** (in Parliament, etc.) a form of closure under which a bill is divided into compartments, groups of which must be completely dealt with each day. ~*vb.* (ˌgɪlə'tiːn). (*tr.*) **5.** to behead (a person) by guillotine. **6.** (in Parliament, etc.) to limit debate on (a bill, motion, etc.) by the guillotine. [C18: from French, named after Joseph Ignace *Guillotin* (1738–1814), French physician, who advocated its use in 1789] —ˌ**guil+lo+'tin+er** *n.*

guilt (gɪlt) *n.* **1.** the fact or state of having done wrong or committed an offence. **2.** responsibility for a criminal or moral offence deserving punishment or a penalty. **3.** remorse or self-reproach caused by feeling that one is responsible for a wrong or offence. **4.** *Archaic.* sin or crime. [Old English *gylt,* of obscure origin]

guilt+less ('gɪltlɪs) *adj.* free of all responsibility for wrongdoing or crime; innocent. —'**guilt+less+ly** *adv.* —'**guilt+less+ness** *n.*

guilt·y ('gɪltɪ) *adj.* **guilt·i+er, guilt·i+est. 1.** responsible for an offence or misdeed. **2.** *Law.* having committed an offence or adjudged to have done so: *the accused was found guilty.* **3. plead guilty.** *Law.* (of a person charged with an offence) to admit responsibility for; confess. **4.** of, showing, or characterized by guilt. —'**guilt·i·ly** *adv.* —'**guilt·i+ness** *n.*

guimpe (gɪmp, gæmp) *n.* **1.** a short blouse with sleeves worn under a pinafore dress. **2.** a fill-in for a low-cut dress. **3.** a piece of starched cloth covering the chest and shoulders of a nun's habit. [C19: variant of GIMP[1]]

Guin. *abbrev. for* Guinea.

guin·ea ('gɪnɪ) *n.* **1. a.** a British gold coin taken out of circulation in 1813, worth 21 shillings. **b.** the sum of 21 shillings (£1.05), still used in some contexts, as in quoting professional fees. **2.** See **guinea fowl. 3.** *U.S. slang, derogatory.* an Italian or a person of Italian descent. [C16: the coin was originally made of gold from Guinea]

Guin·ea ('gɪnɪ) *n.* **1.** a republic in West Africa, on the Atlantic: established as the colony of French Guinea in 1890 and became an independent republic in 1958. Official language: French. Religion: Muslim majority and animist. Currency: franc. Capital: Conakry. Pop.: 4 416 000 (1975 UN est.). Area: 245 855 sq. km (94 925 sq. miles). **2.** (formerly) the coastal region of West Africa, between Cape Verde and Moçâmedes (Angola): divided by a line of volcanic peaks into **Upper Guinea** (between Gambia and Cameroon) and **Lower Guinea** (between Cameroon and S Angola). **3. Gulf of.** a large inlet of the S Atlantic on the W coast of Africa, extending from Cape Palmas, Liberia, to Cape Lopez, Gabon: contains two large bays, the Bight of Biafra and the Bight of Benin, separated by the Niger delta. —'**Guin+e·an** *adj., n.*

Guin·ea-Bis·sau *n.* a republic in West Africa, on the Atlantic: first discovered by the Portuguese in 1446 and of subsequent importance in the slave trade; made a colony in 1879; became an independent republic in 1974; eventual union with the Cape Verde Islands is planned. Languages: Portuguese and Cape Verde creole. Religion: animist majority and Muslim. Currency: Guinean peso. Provisional capital: Madina do Boé. Pop.: 487 488 (1970). Area: 36 125 sq. km (13 948 sq. miles). Former name (until 1974): **Portuguese Guinea.**

Guin·ea corn *n.* another name for **durra.**

guin·ea fowl *or* **guin·ea** *n.* any gallinaceous bird, esp. *Numida meleagris,* of the family *Numididae* of Africa and SW Asia, having a dark plumage mottled with white, a naked head and neck, and a heavy rounded body.

guin·ea grains *pl. n.* another name for **grains of paradise.**

guin·ea hen *n.* a guinea fowl, esp. a female.

Guin·ea pep+per *n.* a variety of the pepper plant *Capsicum frutescens,* from which cayenne pepper is obtained.

guin·ea pig *n.* **1.** a domesticated cavy, probably descended from *Cavia porcellus,* commonly kept as a pet and used in scientific experiments. **2.** *Informal.* a person or thing used for experimentation.

Guin·ea worm *n.* a parasitic nematode worm, *Dracunculus medinensis,* that lives beneath the skin in man and other vertebrates and is common in India and Africa.

Guin·e·vere ('gwɪnɪˌvɪə), **Guen·e·vere** ('gwɛnɪˌvɪə), *or* **Guin·e·ver** ('gwɪnɪvə) *n.* (in Arthurian legend) the wife of King Arthur and paramour of Lancelot.

Guin·ness ('gɪnɪs) *n.* Sir **Al·ec.** born 1914, British stage and film actor; his films include *Kind Hearts and Coronets* (1949) and *The Bridge on the River Kwai* (1957).

gui+pure (gɪ'pjʊə) *n.* **1.** Also called: **guipure lace.** any of many types of heavy lace that have their pattern connected by brides, rather than supported on a net mesh. **2.** a heavy corded trimming; gimp. [C19: from Old French *guipure,* from *guiper* to cover with cloth, of Germanic origin; see WIPE, WHIP]

Guis·card (*French* gis'ka:r) *n.* **Ro·bert** (rɔ'bɛ:r). ?1015–85, Norman conqueror in S Italy.

guise (gaɪz) *n.* **1.** semblance or pretence: *under the guise of friendship.* **2.** external appearance in general. **3.** *Archaic.* manner or style of dress. **4.** *Obsolete.* customary behaviour or manner. ~*vb.* **5.** *Brit. dialect.* to disguise or be disguised in fancy dress. **6.** (*tr.*) *Archaic.* to dress or dress up. [C13: from Old French *guise,* of Germanic origin; see WISE[2]]

gui+tar (gɪ'tɑ:) *n. Music.* a plucked stringed instrument originating in Spain, usually having six strings, a flat sounding board with a circular sound hole in the centre, a flat back, and a fretted fingerboard. Range: more than three octaves upwards from E on the first leger line below the bass staff. See also **electric guitar, bass guitar, Hawaiian guitar.** [C17: from Spanish *guitarra,* from Arabic *qītār,* from Greek *kithara* KITHARA] —**gui+'tar+ist** *n.* —**gui+'tar-ˌlike** *adj.*

gui·tar+fish (gɪ'tɑ:ˌfɪʃ) *n., pl.* **+fish** *or* **+fish·es.** any marine sharklike ray of the family *Rhinobatidae,* having a guitar-shaped body with a stout tail and occurring at the bottom of the sea.

Gui·zot (*French* gi'zo) *n.* **Fran·çois Pierre Guil·laume** (frãswa pjɛ:r gi'jo:m). 1787–1874, French statesman and historian. As chief minister (1840–48), his reactionary policies contributed to the outbreak of the revolution of 1848.

Gu+ja+rat *or* **Gu+je+rat** (ˌgʊdʒə'rɑ:t) *n.* **1.** a state of W India: formed in 1960 from the N and W parts of Bombay State; one of India's most industrialized states. Capital: Gandhinagar. Pop.: 26 697 475 (1971). Area: 187 114 sq. km (72 245 sq. miles). **2.** a region of W India, north of the Narmada River: generally includes the areas north of Bombay city where Gujarati is spoken.

Gu+ja+ra+ti *or* **Gu+je+ra+ti** (ˌgʊdʒə'rɑ:tɪ) *n.* **1.** (*pl.* **+ti**) a member of a people of India living chiefly in Gujarat. **2.** the state language of Gujarat, belonging to the Indic branch of the Indo-European family. ~*adj.* **3.** of or relating to Gujarat, its people, or their language.

Guj+ran+wa+la (gu:dʒ'rɑ:n,wʌlə) *n.* a city in NE Pakistan: textile manufacturing. Pop.: 360 419 (1972).

Gu+lag ('gu:læg) *n.* the central administrative department of the Soviet security service, established in 1930, responsible for maintaining prisons and forced labour camps. [C20: from Russian *G(lavnoye) U(pravleniye Ispravitelno-Trudovykh) Lag(erei)* Main Administration for Corrective Labour Camps]

gu+lar ('gu:lə, 'gju:-) *adj. Anatomy.* of, relating to, or situated in the throat or oesophagus. [C19: from Latin *gula* throat]

Gul·ben·ki·an (gʊl'bɛnkɪən) *n.* **1. Ca·louste Sar·kis** (kæ'lu:st 'sɑ:kɪz). 1869–1955, British industrialist, born in Turkey. He endowed the international Gulbenkian Foundation for the advancement of the arts, science, and education. **2.** his son, **Nu·bar Sar·kis** ('nu:bɑ: 'sɑ:kɪz). 1896–1972, British industrialist, diplomat, and philanthropist.

gulch (gʌltʃ) *n. U.S.* a narrow ravine cut by a fast stream. [C19: of obscure origin]

gul+den ('gʊldᵊn) *n., pl.* **+dens** *or* **+den.** a variant spelling of **guilder.**

Gü+lek Bo+gaz (gu:'lɛk bəʊ'gɑ:z) *n.* the Turkish name for the **Cilician Gates.**

gules (gju:lz) *adj.* (*usually postpositive*), *n. Heraldry.* red. [C14: from Old French *gueules* red fur worn around the neck, from *gole* throat, from Latin *gula* GULLET]

gulf (gʌlf) *n.* **1.** a large deep bay. **2.** a deep chasm. **3.** something that divides or separates, such as a lack of understanding. **4.** something that engulfs, such as a whirlpool. ~*vb.* **5.** (*tr.*) to swallow up; engulf. [C14: from Old French *golfe,* from Italian *golfo,* from Greek *kolpos*] —'**gulf+ˌlike** *adj.* —'**gulf·y** *adj.*

Gulf (gʌlf) *n. Austral.* **a. the.** the Gulf of Carpentaria. **b.** (*modifier*) of, relating to, or adjoining the Gulf: *Gulf country.*

Gulf States *pl. n.* **the. 1.** the states of the U.S. that border on the Gulf of Mexico: Alabama, Florida, Louisiana, Mississippi, and Texas. **2.** the oil-producing states around the Persian Gulf: Iran, Iraq, Kuwait, Saudi Arabia, Bahrain, Qatar, the United Arab Emirates, and Oman.

Gulf Stream *n.* **1.** a relatively warm ocean current flowing northeastwards off the Atlantic coast of the U.S. from the Gulf of Mexico. **2.** another name for **North Atlantic Drift.**

gulf+weed ('gʌlf,wi:d) *n.* any brown seaweed of the genus *Sargassum,* esp. *S. bacciferum,* having air bladders and forming dense floating masses in tropical Atlantic waters, esp. the Gulf Stream. Also called: **sargasso, sargasso weed.**

gull[1] (gʌl) *n.* any aquatic bird of the genus *Larus* and related genera, such as *L. canus* (**common gull** or **mew**) having long pointed wings, short legs, and a mostly white plumage: family *Laridae,* order *Charadriiformes.* [C15: of Celtic origin; compare Welsh *gwylan*] —'**gull-ˌlike** *adj.*

gull[2] (gʌl) *Archaic.* ~*n.* **1.** a person who is easily fooled or cheated. ~*vb.* **2.** (*tr.*) to fool, cheat, or hoax. [C16: perhaps from dialect *gull* unfledged bird, probably from *gul,* from Old Norse *gulr* yellow]

Gul+lah ('gʌlə) *n.* **1.** (*pl.* **+lahs** *or* **+lah**) a member of a Negro people living on the Sea Islands or in the coastal regions of South Carolina, Georgia, and NE Florida. **2.** the creolized English spoken by these people.

gul+let ('gʌlɪt) *n.* **1.** a less formal name for the **oesophagus. 2.** the throat or pharynx. **3.** *Mining, quarrying.* a preliminary cut in excavating, wide enough to take the vehicle that removes the earth. [C14: from Old French *goulet,* diminutive of *goule* throat, from Latin *gula* throat]

gul+li·ble *or* **gul+la·ble** ('gʌləbᵊl) *adj.* easily taken in or tricked. —ˌ**gul+li+'bil+i+ty** *or* ˌ**gul+la+'bil+i+ty** *n.* —'**gul+li+bly** *or* '**gul+la+bly** *adv.*

gull-wing ('gʌl,wɪŋ) *adj.* **1.** (of a car door) opening upwards. **2.** (of an aircraft wing) having a short upward-sloping inner section and a longer horizontal outer section.

gul+ly[1] ('gʌlɪ) *n., pl.* **+lies. 1.** a channel or small valley, esp. one cut by heavy rainwater. **2.** *Cricket.* **a.** a fielding position between the slips and point. **b.** a fielder in this position. **3.** either of the two channels at the side of a tenpin bowling lane. **4.** *Northern Brit. dialect.* a path between fences or walls. ~*vb.* **+lies, +ly+ing, +lied. 5.** (*tr.*) to make (channels) in (the ground, sand, etc.). [C16: from French *goulet* neck of a bottle; see GULLET]

gul+ly[2] ('gʌlɪ) *n., pl.* **+lies.** *Scot.* a large knife, such as a butcher's knife. [C16: of obscure origin]

gu+los+i+ty (gjʊ'lɒsɪtɪ) *n. Archaic.* greed or gluttony. [C16: from Late Latin *gulōsitās,* from Latin *gulōsus* gluttonous, from *gula* gullet]

gulp (gʌlp) *vb.* **1.** (*tr.;* often foll. by *down*) to swallow rapidly, esp. in large mouthfuls: *to gulp down food.* **2.** (*tr.;* often foll. by *back*) to stifle or choke: *to gulp back sobs.* **3.** (*intr.*) to swallow air convulsively, as while drinking, because of nervousness, surprise, etc. **4.** (*intr.*) to make a noise, as when swallowing too quickly. ~*n.* **5.** the act of gulping. **6.** the quantity taken in a gulp. [C15: from Middle Dutch *gulpen,* of imitative origin] —**'gulp·er** *n.* —**'gulp·ing·ly** *adv.* —**'gulp·y** *adj.*

gulp·er eel *or* **fish** *n.* any deep-sea eel-like fish of the genera *Eurypharynx* and *Saccopharynx* and order *Lyomeri,* having the ability to swallow large prey.

gum[1] (gʌm) *n.* **1.** any of various sticky substances that exude from certain plants, hardening on exposure to air and dissolving or forming viscous masses in water. **2.** any of various products, such as adhesives, that are made from such exudates. **3.** any sticky substance used as an adhesive; mucilage; glue. **4.** See **chewing gum, bubble gum, original gum,** and **gumtree. 5.** *Chiefly Brit.* a gumdrop. ~*vb.* **gums, gum·ming, gummed. 6.** to cover or become covered, clogged, or stiffened with or as if with gum. **7.** (*tr.*) to stick together or in place with gum. **8.** (*intr.*) to emit or form gum. ~See also **gum up.** [C14: from Old French *gomme,* from Latin *gummi,* from Greek *kommi,* from Egyptian *kemai*] —**'gum·less** *adj.* —**'gum·,like** *adj.*

gum[2] (gʌm) *n.* the fleshy tissue that covers the jaw bones around the bases of the teeth. Technical name: **gingiva.** Related adj.: **gingival.** [Old English *gōma* jaw; related to Old Norse *gōmr,* Middle High German *gūme,* Lithuanian *gomurìs*]

gum[3] (gʌm) *n.* used in the mild oath *by gum!* [C19: euphemism for GOD]

gum ac·croi·des (əˈkrɔɪdiːz) *n.* another name for **acaroid gum.**

gum am·mo·ni·ac *n.* another name for **ammoniac**[2].

gum ar·a·bic *n.* a gum exuded by certain acacia trees, esp. *Acacia senegal:* used in the manufacture of ink, food thickeners, pills, emulsifiers, etc. Also called: **acacia, gum acacia.**

gum ben·zo·in *n.* another name for **benzoin.**

gum·bo *or* **gom·bo** (ˈgʌmbəʊ) *n., pl.* **·bos.** *U.S.* **1.** the mucilaginous pods of okra. **2.** another name for **okra. 3.** a soup or stew thickened with okra pods. **4.** a fine soil in the W prairies that becomes muddy when wet. [C19: from Louisiana French *gombo,* of Bantu origin]

Gum·bo (ˈgʌmbəʊ) *n.* (*sometimes not cap.*) a French patois spoken by Creoles in Louisiana and the West Indies. [see GUMBO]

gum·boil (ˈgʌm,bɔɪl) *n.* an abscess on the gums, often at the root of a decayed tooth. Also called: **parulis.**

gum·boots (ˈgʌm,buːts) *pl. n.* another name for **Wellington boots** (sense 1).

gum·bo·til (ˈgʌmbətɪl) *n.* a sticky clay formed by the weathering of glacial drift. [C20: from GUMBO + TIL(L)[4]]

gum·drop (ˈgʌm,drɒp) *n.* a small jelly-like sweet containing gum arabic and various colourings and flavourings. Also called (esp. Brit.): **gum.**

gum e·las·tic *n.* another name for **rubber**[1] (sense 1).

gum el·e·mi *n.* another name for **elemi.**

gum·ma (ˈgʌmə) *n., pl.* **·mas** *or* **·ma·ta** (-mətə). *Pathol.* a rubbery tumour characteristic of advanced syphilis, occurring esp. on the skin, liver, brain or heart. [C18: from New Latin, from Latin *gummi* GUM[1]] —**'gum·ma·tous** *adj.*

gum·mite (ˈgʌmaɪt) *n.* an orange or yellowish amorphous secondary mineral consisting of hydrated uranium oxides.

gum·mo·sis (gʌˈməʊsɪs) *n.* the abnormal production of excessive gum in certain trees, esp. fruit trees, as a result of wounding, infection, adverse weather conditions, severe pruning, etc. [C19: from New Latin; see GUMMA]

gum·mous (ˈgʌməs) *or* **gum·mose** (ˈgʌməʊs) *adj. Rare.* resembling or consisting of gum.

gum·my[1] (ˈgʌmɪ) *adj.* **·mi·er, ·mi·est. 1.** sticky or tacky. **2.** consisting of, coated with, or clogged by gum or a similar substance. **3.** producing gum. [C14: from GUM[1] + -Y[1]] —**'gum·mi·ness** *n.*

gum·my[2] (ˈgʌmɪ) *adj.* **·mi·er, ·mi·est. 1.** toothless; not showing one's teeth. ~*n., pl.* **·mies. 2.** *Austral.* a small crustacean-eating shark, *Mustelus antarcticus,* with flat crushing teeth. [C20: from GUM[2] + -Y[1]] —**'gum·mi·ly** *adv.*

gum nut *n. Austral.* the hardened seed container of the gum tree *Eucalyptus gummifera.*

gum plant *or* **gum·weed** (ˈgʌm,wiːd) *n.* any of several American yellow-flowered plants of the genus *Grindelia,* esp. *G. robusta,* that have sticky flower heads: family *Compositae* (composites).

gump·tion (ˈgʌmpʃən) *n. Informal.* **1.** *Brit.* common sense or resourcefulness. **2.** initiative or courage: *you haven't the gumption to try.* [C18: originally Scottish, of unknown origin]

gum res·in *n.* a mixture of resin and gum obtained from various plants and trees. See also **bdellium, gamboge.**

gum·shield (ˈgʌm,ʃiːld) *n.* a plate or strip of soft waxy substance used by boxers to protect the teeth and gums. Also called: **mouthpiece.**

gum·shoe (ˈgʌm,ʃuː) *n.* **1.** a waterproof overshoe. **2.** *U.S. slang.* a detective or one who moves about stealthily. **3.** *U.S. slang.* a stealthy action or movement. ~*vb.* **·shoes, ·shoe·ing, ·shoed. 4.** (*intr.*) *U.S. slang.* to act stealthily.

gum·tree (ˈgʌm,triː) *n.* **1.** any of various trees that yield gum, such as the eucalyptus, sweet gum, and sour gum. Sometimes shortened to **gum. 2.** Also called: **gumwood.** the wood of any of these trees. **3. up a gumtree.** *Slang.* in a very awkward position; in difficulties.

gum up *vb.* (*tr., adv.*) **1.** to cover, dab, or stiffen with gum. **2.** *Informal.* to make a mess of; bungle (often in the phrase **gum up the works**).

gun (gʌn) *n.* **1. a.** a weapon with a metallic tube or barrel from which a missile is discharged, usually by force of an explosion. It may be portable or mounted. **b.** (*as modifier*): *a gun barrel.* **2.** the firing of a gun as a salute or signal, as in military ceremonial. **3.** a member of or a place in a shooting party or syndicate. **4.** any device used to project something under pressure: *a grease gun; a spray gun.* **5.** *U.S. slang.* an armed criminal; gunman. **6.** *Austral. slang.* **a.** an expert. **b.** (*as modifier*): *a gun shearer; a gun batsman.* **7. big gun.** *Slang.* **a.** an important or influential person. **b.** a high-ranking officer. **8. give it the gun.** *Slang.* to increase speed, effort, etc., to a considerable or maximum degree. **9. go great guns.** *Slang.* to act or function with great speed, intensity, etc. **10. jump** *or* **beat the gun. a.** (of a runner, etc.) to set off before the starting signal is given. **b.** *Informal.* to act prematurely. **11. spike someone's guns.** to hinder or obstruct someone. **12. stick to one's guns.** *Informal.* to maintain one's opinions or intentions in spite of opposition. ~*vb.* **guns, gun·ning, gunned. 13.** (when *tr.,* often foll. by *down*) to shoot (someone) with a gun. **14.** (*tr.*) to press hard on the accelerator of (an engine): *to gun the engine of a car.* **15.** (*intr.*) to hunt with a gun. ~See also **gun for.** [C14: probably from a female pet name shortened from the Scandinavian name *Gunnhildr* (from Old Norse *gunnr* war + *hildr* war)]

gun·boat (ˈgʌn,bəʊt) *n.* a small shallow-draft vessel carrying mounted guns and used by coastal patrols, etc.

gun·boat di·plo·ma·cy *n.* diplomacy conducted by threats of military intervention, esp. by a major power against a militarily weak state.

gun car·riage *n.* a mechanical frame on which a gun is mounted for adjustment and firing.

gun·cot·ton (ˈgʌn,kɒtᵊn) *n.* cellulose nitrate containing a relatively large amount of nitrogen: used as an explosive.

gun dog *n.* **1.** a dog trained to work with a hunter or gamekeeper, esp. in retrieving, pointing at, or flushing game. **2.** a dog belonging to any breed adapted to these activities.

gun·fight (ˈgʌn,faɪt) *n. U.S.* a fight between persons using firearms. —**'gun,fight·er** *n.* —**'gun,fight·ing** *n.*

gun·fire (ˈgʌn,faɪə) *n.* **1.** the firing of one or more guns, esp. when done repeatedly. **2.** the use of firearms, as contrasted with other military tactics.

gun·flint (ˈgʌn,flɪnt) *n.* a piece of flint in a flintlock's hammer used to strike the spark that ignites the charge.

gun for *vb.* (*intr., prep.*) **1.** to search for in order to reprimand, punish, or kill. **2.** to try earnestly for: *he was gunning for promotion.*

gunge (gʌndʒ) *Informal.* ~*n.* **1.** sticky, rubbery, or congealed matter. ~*vb.* **2.** (*tr.; usually passive;* foll by *up*) to block or encrust with gunge; clog. [C20: of imitative origin, perhaps influenced by GOO and SPONGE] —**gun·gy** *adj.*

gung ho (ˈgʌŋ ˈhəʊ) *adj. U.S. slang.* excessively or foolishly enthusiastic. [C20: pidgin English, from Mandarin Chinese *kung* work + *ho* together]

gunk (gʌŋk) *n. Informal.* slimy, oily, or filthy matter. [C20: perhaps of imitative origin]

gun·lock (ˈgʌn,lɒk) *n.* the mechanism in some firearms that causes the charge to be exploded.

gun·man (ˈgʌnmən) *n., pl.* **·men. 1.** a man who is armed with a gun, esp. unlawfully. **2.** a man who is skilled with a gun. **3.** *U.S.* a person who makes, repairs, or has expert knowledge of guns. —**'gun·man·,ship** *n.*

gun·met·al (ˈgʌn,mɛtᵊl) *n.* **1.** a type of bronze containing copper (88 per cent), tin (8–10 per cent), and zinc (2–4 per cent): used for parts that are subject to wear or to corrosion, esp. by sea water. **2.** any of various dark grey metals used for toys, belt buckles, etc. **3.** a dark grey colour with a purplish or bluish tinge.

gun moll *n. U.S. slang.* a female criminal or a woman who associates with criminals.

Gun·nar (ˈgunɑː) *n. Norse myth.* brother of Gudrun and husband of Brynhild, won for him by Sigurd. He corresponds to Gunther in the *Nibelungenlied.*

gunned (gʌnd) *adj.* **a.** having a gun or guns as specified: *heavily gunned.* **b.** (*in combination*): *three-gunned.*

gun·nel[1] (ˈgʌnᵊl) *n.* any eel-like blennioid fish of the family *Pholidae,* occurring in coastal regions of northern seas. See also **butterfish.** [C17: of unknown origin]

gun·nel[2] (ˈgʌnᵊl) *n.* a variant spelling of **gunwale.**

gun·ner (ˈgʌnə) *n.* **1.** a serviceman who works with, uses, or specializes in guns. **2.** *Naval.* (formerly) a warrant officer responsible for the training of gun crews, their performance in action, and accounting for ammunition. **3.** (in the British Army) an artilleryman, esp. a private. **4.** a person who hunts with a rifle or shotgun. —**'gun·ner·,ship** *n.*

gun·ner·y (ˈgʌnərɪ) *n.* **1.** the art and science of the efficient design and use of ordnance, esp. artillery. **2.** guns collectively. **3.** the use and firing of guns. **4.** (*modifier*) of, relating to, or concerned with heavy guns, as in warfare: *a gunnery officer.*

gun·ning (ˈgʌnɪŋ) *n.* **1.** the act or an instance of shooting with guns. **2.** the art, practice, or act of hunting game with guns.

gun·ny (ˈgʌnɪ) *n., pl.* **·nies.** *Chiefly U.S.* **1.** a coarse hard-wearing fabric usually made from jute and used for sacks, etc. **2.** Also called: **gunny sack.** a sack made from this fabric. [C18: from Hindi *gōnī,* from Sanskrit *gonī* sack, probably of Dravidian origin]

gun·pa·per (ˈgʌn,peɪpə) *n.* a cellulose nitrate explosive made by treating paper with nitric acid.

gun·play (ˈgʌn,pleɪ) *n. Chiefly U.S.* the use of firearms, as by criminals, etc.

gun+point ('gʌn,pɔɪnt) *n.* **1.** the muzzle of a gun. **2. at gunpoint.** being under or using the threat of being shot.
gun+pow·der ('gʌn,paʊdə) *n.* an explosive mixture of potassium nitrate, charcoal, and sulphur (typical proportions are 75:15:10): used in time fuses and in fireworks. —'**gun+,pow·der·y** *adj.*
Gun+pow·der Plot *n.* the unsuccessful conspiracy to blow up James I and Parliament at Westminster on Nov. 5, 1605. See also **Guy Fawkes Day.**
gun+pow·der tea *n.* a fine variety of green tea, each leaf of which is rolled into a pellet.
gun room *n.* **1.** (esp. in the Royal Navy) the mess allocated to subordinate or junior officers. **2.** a room where guns are stored.
gun+run·ning ('gʌn,rʌnɪŋ) *n.* the smuggling of guns and ammunition or other weapons of war into a country. —'**gun+,run·ner** *n.*
gun+sel ('gʌnsᵊl) *n. U.S. slang.* **1.** a catamite. **2.** a stupid or inexperienced person, esp. a youth. **3.** a criminal who carries a gun. [C20: probably from Yiddish *genzel;* compare German *ganslein* gosling, from *gans* GOOSE]
gun+shot ('gʌn,ʃɒt) *n.* **1. a.** shot fired from a gun. **b.** (*as modifier*): *gunshot wounds.* **2.** the range of a gun. **3.** the shooting of a gun.
gun-shy *adj.* afraid of a gun or the sound it makes: *a gun-shy dog is useless for hunting.*
gun+sling·er ('gʌn,slɪŋə) *n. U.S. slang.* a gunfighter or gunman, esp. in the Old West. —'**gun+,sling·ing** *n.*
gun+smith ('gʌn,smɪθ) *n.* a person who manufactures or repairs firearms, esp. portable guns. —'**gun+,smith·ing** *n.*
gun+stock ('gʌn,stɒk) *n.* the wooden or metallic handle or support to which is attached the barrel of a rifle.
Gun·ter ('gʌntə) *n.* **Ed·mund.** 1581–1626, English mathematician and astronomer, who invented various measuring instruments, including Gunter's chain.
gun+ter rig ('gʌntə) *n. Nautical.* a type of gaffing in which the gaff is hoisted parallel to the mast. [C18: named after E. GUNTER] —'**gun·ter-,rigged** *adj.*
Gun·ter's chain *n. Surveying.* a measuring chain 22 yards in length, or this length as a unit. See **chain** (sense 6). [C17: named after E. GUNTER]
Gun·ther ('gʊntə) *n.* (in the *Nibelungenlied*) a king of Burgundy, allied with Siegfried, who won for him his wife Brunhild. He corresponds to Gunnar in Norse mythology.
Gun+tur (gʊn'tʊə) *n.* a city in E India, in central Andhra Pradesh: founded by the French in the 18th century; ceded to Britain in 1788. Pop.: 269 991 (1971).
gun+wale *or* **gun+nel** ('gʌnᵊl) *n. Nautical.* the top of the side of a boat or the topmost plank of a wooden vessel.
gun+yah ('gʌnjɑː) *n. Austral.* a bush hut or shelter. [C19: from a native Australian language]
Günz (gʊnts) *n.* the first major Pleistocene glaciation of the Alps. See also **Mindel, Riss, Würm.** [named after the river *Günz* in Germany]
gup+py ('gʌpɪ) *n., pl.* **+pies.** a small brightly coloured freshwater viviparous cyprinodont fish, *Lebistes reticulatus,* of N South America and the West Indies: a popular aquarium fish. [C20: named after R. J. L. *Guppy,* 19th-century clergyman of Trinidad who first presented specimens to the British Museum]
Gur (gʊə) *n.* a small group of languages of W Africa, spoken chiefly in Upper Volta, forming a branch of the Niger-Congo family. Also called: **Voltaic.**
gurd+wa+ra ('gɜːdwɑːrə) *n.* a Sikh place of worship. [C20: from Punjabi *gurduārā,* from Sanskrit *guru* teacher + *dvārā* DOOR]
gur+gi+ta+tion (,gɜːdʒɪ'teɪʃən) *n.* surging or swirling motion, esp. of water. [C16: from Late Latin *gurgitātus* engulfed, from *gurgitāre* to engulf, from Latin *gurges* whirlpool]
gur+gle ('gɜːgᵊl) *vb.* **1.** (*intr.*) (of liquids, esp. of rivers, streams, etc.) to make low bubbling noises when flowing. **2.** to utter low throaty bubbling noises, esp. as a sign of contentment: *the baby gurgled with delight.* ~*n.* **3.** the act or sound of gurgling. [C16: perhaps from Vulgar Latin *gurgulāre,* from Latin *gurguliō* gullet] —'**gur+gling+ly** *adv.*
gur+glet ('gɜːglɪt) *n.* another word for **goglet.**
gur+jun ('gɜːdʒən) *n.* **1.** any of several S or SE Asian dipterocarpaceous trees of the genus *Dipterocarpus* that yield a resin. **2.** Also: **gurjun balsam.** the resin from any of these trees, used as a varnish. [C19: from Bengali *garjon*]
Gur+kha ('gʊəkɑː, 'gɜːkə) *n., pl.* **+khas** *or* **+kha. 1.** a member of a Hindu people, descended from Brahmins and Rajputs, living chiefly in Nepal, where they achieved dominance after being driven from India by the Muslims. **2.** a member of this people serving as a soldier in the Indian or British army.
Gur+kha+li (,gʊə'kɑːlɪ, ,gɜː-) *n.* the language of the Gurkhas, belonging to the Indic branch of the Indo-European family.
Gur+mu+khi ('gʊəmʊkɪ) *n.* the script used for writing the Punjabi language. [Sanskrit, from *guru* teacher + *mukh* mouth]
gur+nard ('gɜːnəd) *or* **gur+net** ('gɜːnɪt) *n., pl.* **+nard, +nards** *or* **+net, +nets.** any European marine scorpaenoid fish of the family *Triglidae,* such as *Trigla lucerna* (**tub** or **yellow gurnard**), having a heavily armoured head and finger-like pectoral fins. [C14: from Old French *gornard* grunter, from *grognier* to grunt, from Latin *grunnīre*]
gu·ru ('gʊruː, 'guːruː) *n.* **1.** a Hindu or Sikh religious teacher or leader, giving personal spiritual guidance to his disciples. **2.** *Often derogatory.* a leader or chief theoretician of a movement, esp. a spiritual or religious cult. [C17: from Hindi *gurū,* from Sanskrit *guruh* weighty] —'**gu+ru+,ship** *n.*
gush (gʌʃ) *vb.* **1.** to pour out or cause to pour out suddenly and profusely, usually with a rushing sound. **2.** to act or utter in an overeffusive, affected, or sentimental manner. ~*n.* **3.** a sudden copious flow or emission, esp. of liquid. **4.** something that flows out or is emitted. **5.** an extravagant and insincere expression of admiration, sentiment, etc. [C14: probably of imitative origin; compare Old Norse *gjósa,* Icelandic *gusa*] —'**gush+ing+ly** *adv.*
gush+er ('gʌʃə) *n.* **1.** a person who gushes, as in being unusually effusive or sentimental. **2.** something, such as a spurting oil well, that gushes.
gush·y ('gʌʃɪ) *adj.* **gush·i+er, gush·i+est.** *Informal.* displaying excessive admiration or sentimentality. —'**gush·i·ly** *adv.* —'**gush·i+ness** *n.*
gus+set ('gʌsɪt) *n.* **1.** an inset piece of material used esp. to strengthen or enlarge a garment. **2.** a triangular metal plate for strengthening a corner joist between two structural members. **3.** a piece of mail fitted between armour plates or into the leather or cloth underclothes worn with armour, to give added protection. ~*vb.* **4.** (*tr.*) to put a gusset in (a garment). [C15: from Old French *gousset* a piece of mail, a diminutive of *gousse* pod, of unknown origin]
gust (gʌst) *n.* **1.** a sudden blast of wind. **2.** a sudden rush of smoke, sound, etc. **3.** an outburst of emotion. [C16: from Old Norse *gustr;* related to *gjōsa* to GUSH; see GEYSER]
gus+ta+tion (gʌ'steɪʃən) *n.* the act of tasting or the faculty of taste. [C16: from Latin *gustātiō,* from *gustāre* to taste] —**gust+ta+to·ry** ('gʌstətərɪ, -trɪ) *or* '**gus+ta+tive** *adj.*
Gus+ta+vo A. Ma+de·ro (*Spanish* gus'taβo 'a ma'ðero) *n.* the former name (1931–71) of **Guadalupe Hidalgo.**
Gus·ta·vus I (gʊ'stɑːvəs) *n.* called *Gustavus Vasa.* ?1496–1560, king of Sweden (1523–60). He was elected king after driving the Danes from Sweden (1520–23).
Gus·ta·vus II *n.* See **Gustavus Adolphus.**
Gus·ta·vus VI *n.* title of *Gustaf Adolf.* 1882–1973, king of Sweden (1950–73).
Gus·ta·vus A·dol·phus (ə'dɒlfəs) *or* **Gus·ta·vus II** *n.* 1594–1632, king of Sweden (1611–32). A brilliant general, he waged successful wars with Denmark, Russia, and Poland and in the Thirty Years' War led a Protestant army against the Catholic League and the Holy Roman Empire (1630–32). He defeated Tilly at Leipzig (1631) and Lech (1632) but was killed at the battle of Lützen.
gus+to ('gʌstəʊ) *n.* vigorous enjoyment, zest, or relish, esp. in the performance of an action: *the aria was sung with great gusto.* [C17: from Spanish: taste, from Latin *gustus* a tasting; see GUSTATION]
gust·y ('gʌstɪ) *adj.* **gust·i+er, gust·i+est. 1.** blowing or occurring in gusts or characterized by blustery weather: *a gusty wind.* **2.** given to sudden outbursts, as of emotion or temperament. —'**gust·i+ly** *adv.* —'**gust·i+ness** *n.*
gut (gʌt) *n.* **1. a.** the lower part of the alimentary canal; intestine. **b.** the entire alimentary canal. Related adj.: **visceral. 2.** (*often pl.*) the bowels or entrails, esp. of an animal. **3.** See **catgut. 4.** a silky fibrous substance extracted from silkworms, used in the manufacture of fishing tackle. **5.** a narrow channel or passage. **6.** (*pl.*) *Informal.* courage, willpower, or daring; forcefulness. **7.** (*pl.*) *Informal.* the essential part: *the guts of a problem.* **8. hate a person's guts.** *Informal.* to dislike a person very strongly. **9. sweat** *or* **work one's guts out.** to work very hard. ~*vb.* **guts, gut+ting, gut+ted.** (*tr.*) **10.** to remove the entrails from (fish, etc.). **11.** (esp. of fire) to destroy the inside of (a building). **12.** to plunder; despoil: *the raiders gutted the city.* **13.** to take out the central points of (an article, etc.), esp. in summary form. ~*adj.* **14.** *Informal.* arising from or characterized by what is basic, essential, or natural: *a gut problem; a gut reaction.* [Old English *gutt;* related to *gēotan* to flow; see FUSION] —'**gut+,like** *adj.*
gut+buck·et ('gʌt,bʌkɪt) *n.* a highly emotional style of jazz playing.
Gu·ten·berg ('guːtᵊn,bɜːg; *German* 'guːtᵊn,bɛrk) *n.* **Jo·hann** ('joːhan), original name *Johannes Gensfleisch.* ?1398–1468, German printer; inventor of printing by movable type.
Gü+ters+loh (*German* 'gyːtərs,loː) *n.* a town in NW West Germany, in North Rhine-Westphalia. Pop.: 75 900 (1970).
Guth·rie ('gʌθrɪ) *n.* **1. Sam·u·el.** 1782–1848, U.S. chemist: invented percussion priming powder and a punch lock for exploding it, and discovered chloroform (1831). **2.** Sir (**William**) **Ty·rone.** 1900–71, English theatrical director. **3. Wood·y,** original name *Woodrow Wilson Guthrie.* 1912–67, U.S. folk singer and songwriter. Compilations of his recordings include *Dust Bowl Ballads, Sacco and Vanzetti,* and the children's album *Songs to grow on/Poor Boy.*
Guth+run ('gʊðruːn) *n.* a variant of **Gudrun.**
gut+less ('gʌtlɪs) *adj. Informal.* lacking courage or determination.
gut+ser ('gʌtsə) *n.* **come a gutser.** *Austral. slang.* **1.** to fall heavily to the ground. **2.** to fail through error or misfortune. [C20: from *guts* + -ER[1]]
guts·y ('gʌtsɪ) *adj.* **guts·i+er, guts·i+est.** *Slang.* **1.** gluttonous; greedy. **2.** full of courage, determination, or boldness.
gut+ta ('gʌtə) *n., pl.* **+tae** (-tiː). **1.** *Architect.* one of a set of small droplike ornaments, esp. as used on the architrave of a Doric entablature. **2.** *Med.* (formerly used in writing prescriptions) a technical name for **drop.** Abbrev.: **gt.** [C16: from Latin: a drop]
gut·ta-per·cha ('gʌtə'pɜːtʃə) *n.* **1.** any of several tropical trees of the sapotaceous genera *Palaquium* and *Payena,* esp. *Palaquium gutta.* **2.** a whitish rubber substance derived from

the coagulated milky latex of any of these trees: used in electrical insulation, waterproofing and dentistry. [C19: from Malay *getah* gum + *percha* piece of cloth]

gut+tate ('gʌteɪt) *or* **gut+tat+ed** *adj. Biology.* **1.** (esp. of plants) covered with small drops or droplike markings, esp. oil glands. **2.** resembling a drop or drops. [C19: from Latin *guttātus* dappled, from *gutta* a drop] —**gut+'ta+tion** *n.*

gut+ter ('gʌtə) *n.* **1.** a channel along the eaves or on the roof of a building, used to collect and carry away rainwater. **2.** a channel running along the kerb or the centre of a road to collect and carry away rainwater. **3.** either of the two channels running parallel to a tenpin bowling lane. **4.** *Printing.* **a.** the space between two pages in a forme. **b.** the white space between the facing pages of an open book. **5.** the space left between stamps on a sheet in order to separate them. **6. the gutter.** *Informal.* a poverty-stricken, degraded, or criminal environment. ~*vb.* **7.** (*tr.*) to make gutters in. **8.** (*intr.*) to flow in a stream or rivulet. [C13: from Anglo-French *goutiere*, from Old French *goute* a drop, from Latin *gutta*] —**'gut·ter-ˌlike** *adj.*

gut+ter+ing ('gʌtərɪŋ) *n.* **1.** the gutters, downpipes, etc., that make up the rainwater disposal system on the outside of a building. **2.** the materials used in this system.

gut+ter press *n.* the section of the popular press that seeks sensationalism in its coverage.

gut·ter+snipe ('gʌtəˌsnaɪp) *n.* **1.** a child who spends most of his time in the streets, esp. in a slum area. **2.** a person regarded as having the behaviour, morals, etc., of one brought up in squalor. —**'gut·ter+ˌsnip+ish** *adj.*

gut+tur+al ('gʌtərəl) *adj.* **1.** *Anatomy.* of or relating to the throat. **2.** *Phonetics.* pronounced in the throat or the back of the mouth; velar or uvular. **3.** raucous. ~*n.* **4.** *Phonetics.* a guttural consonant. [C16: from New Latin *gutturālis* concerning the throat, from Latin *guttur* gullet] —**'gut+tur+al+ly** *adv.* —**'gut+tur+al+ness, ˌgut+tur+'al+i+ty** *or* **'gut+tur+al+ism** *n.*

gut+tur+al+ize *or* **gut+tur+al+ise** ('gʌtərəˌlaɪz) *vb.* (*tr.*) **1.** *Phonetics.* to change into a guttural speech sound or pronounce with guttural articulation or pharyngeal constriction. **2.** to speak or utter in harsh raucous tones. —**ˌgut+tur+al·i+'za+tion** *or* **ˌgut+tur+al·i+'sa+tion** *n.*

gut+ty ('gʌtɪ) *n., pl.* **+ties.** *Irish dialect.* an urchin or delinquent. [probably from GUTTER, perhaps from the compound GUTTERSNIPE]

guv (gʌv) *or* **guv'nor** ('gʌvnə) *n. Brit.* an informal name for **governor.**

guy[1] (gaɪ) *n.* **1.** *Informal.* a man or youth. **2.** *Brit.* a crude effigy of Guy Fawkes, usually made of old clothes stuffed with straw or rags, that is burnt on top of a bonfire on Guy Fawkes Day. **3.** *Brit.* a person in shabby or ludicrously odd clothes. ~*vb.* **4.** (*tr.*) to make fun of; ridicule. [C19: short for Guy FAWKES]

guy[2] (gaɪ) *n.* **1.** a rope, chain, wire, etc., for anchoring an object, such as a radio mast, in position or for steadying or guiding it while being hoisted or lowered. ~*vb.* **2.** (*tr.*) to anchor, steady, or guide with a guy or guys. [C14: probably from Low German; compare Dutch *gei* brail, *geiblok* pulley, Old French *guie* guide, from *guier* to GUIDE]

Guy+an·a (gaɪ'ænə) *n.* a republic in NE South America, on the Atlantic: colonized chiefly by the Dutch in the 17th and 18th centuries; became a British colony in 1831 and an independent republic within the Commonwealth in 1966. Official language: English. Religions: Christian and Hindu. Currency: dollar. Capital: Georgetown. Pop.: 791 000 (1975 UN est.). Area: about 215 000 sq. km (83 000 sq. miles). Former name (until 1966): **British Guiana.** —**Guy·a+nese** (ˌgaɪə'ni:z) *or* **Guy+'an+an** *adj., n.*

Guy+enne (*French* gɥi'jɛn) *n.* a variant spelling of **Guienne.**

Guy Fawkes Day *n.* the anniversary of the discovery of the Gunpowder Plot, celebrated on Nov. 5 in Britain with fireworks and bonfires.

guy+ot ('gi:ˌəʊ) *n.* (esp. in the Pacific Ocean) a flat-topped submarine mountain, probably of volcanic origin, rising to within half a mile of the surface. [C20: named after A. H. *Guyot* (1807–84), Swiss geographer]

Guz·mán Blan·co (*Spanish* guθ'man 'blaŋko) *n.* **An·to·nio** (an'tonjo). 1829–99, Venezuelan statesman; president (1873–77; 1879–84; 1886–87). He was virtual dictator of Venezuela from 1870 until his overthrow (1889).

guz+zle ('gʌz°l) *vb.* to consume (food or drink) excessively or greedily. [C16: of unknown origin] —**'guz+zler** *n.*

g.v. *abbrev. for* gravimetric volume.

Gwa+li+or ('gwɑ:lɪˌɔ:) *n.* **1.** a city in N central India, in Madhya Pradesh: built around the fort, which dates from before 525; industrial and commercial centre. Pop.: 384 772 (1971). **2.** a former princely state of central India, established in the 18th century: merged with Madhya Bharat in 1948, which in turn merged with Madhya Pradesh in 1956.

Gwe+lo ('gweɪləʊ) *n.* a city in central Rhodesia. Pop.: 51 000 (1970 est.).

Gwent (gwɛnt) *n.* a county in SE Wales, formed in 1974 from most of Monmouthshire, part of Breconshire, and the county borough of Newport: generally hilly. Administrative centre: Cwmbran. Pop.: 439 600 (1976 est.). Area: 1360 sq. km (531 sq. miles).

Gwyn (gwɪn) *n.* **Nell,** original name *Eleanor Gwynne.* 1650–87, English actress; mistress of Charles II.

Gwyn+edd ('gwɪnɛð) *n.* a county of NW Wales, formed in 1974 from Anglesey, Caernarvonshire, part of Denbighshire, and most of Merionethshire: the mainland is generally mountainous with many lakes, much of it lying in the Snowdonia National Park. Administrative centre: Caernarvon. Pop.: 225 100 (1976 est.). Area: 3823 sq. km (1493 sq. miles).

gwyn+i+ad ('gwɪnɪˌæd) *n.* a freshwater whitefish, *Coregonus pennantii*, occurring in Lake Bala in Wales.

Gya+ni ('gjɑ:nɪ) *n.* (in India) a title placed before the name of a Punjabi scholar. [Hindi, from Sanskrit *gyan* knowledge]

gybe *or* **jibe** (dʒaɪb) *Nautical.* ~*vb.* **1.** (*intr.*) (of a fore-and-aft sail) to shift suddenly from one side of the vessel to the other when running before the wind, as the result of allowing the wind to catch the leech. **2.** to cause (a sailing vessel) to gybe or (of a sailing vessel) to undergo gybing. ~*n.* **3.** an instance of gybing. [C17: from obsolete Dutch *gijben* (now *gijpen*), of obscure origin]

gym (dʒɪm) short for **gymnasium, gymnastics, gymnastic.**

gym+kha+na (dʒɪm'kɑ:nə) *n. Chiefly Brit.* **1.** an event in which horses and riders display skill and aptitude in various races and contests. **2.** the place where this event is held. [C19: from Hindi *gend-khānā*, literally: ball house, from *khāna* house; influenced by GYMNASIUM]

gym+na+si+arch (dʒɪm'neɪzɪˌɑ:k) *n. History.* the magistrate responsible for education in numerous Hellenistic cities.

gym+na+si+ast (dʒɪm'neɪzɪˌæst) *n.* a student in a gymnasium.

gym+na+si·um (dʒɪm'neɪzɪəm) *n., pl.* **+si·ums** *or* **+si·a** (-zɪə). **1.** a large room or hall equipped with bars, weights, ropes, etc., for games or physical training. **2.** (in various European countries) a secondary school that prepares pupils for university. [C16: from Latin: school for gymnastics, from Greek *gumnasion*, from *gumnazein* to exercise naked, from *gumnos* naked]

gym+nast ('dʒɪmnæst) *n.* a person who is skilled or trained in gymnastics.

gym+nas+tic (dʒɪm'næstɪk) *adj.* of, relating to, like, or involving gymnastics. —**gym+'nas+ti+cal+ly** *adv.*

gym+nas+tics (dʒɪm'næstɪks) *n.* **1.** (*functioning as sing.*) practice or training in exercises that develop physical strength and agility or mental capacity. **2.** (*functioning as pl.*) gymnastic exercises.

gym·no- *combining form.* naked, bare, or exposed: *gymnosperm.* [from Greek *gumnos* naked]

gym+nos·o+phist (dʒɪm'nɒsəfɪst) *n.* one of a sect of naked Indian ascetics who regarded food or clothing as detrimental to purity of thought. [C16: from Latin *gymnosophistae*, from Greek *gumnosophistai* naked philosophers] —**gym+'nos·o+phy** *n.*

gym+no+sperm ('dʒɪmnəʊˌspɜ:m, 'gɪm-) *n.* any seed-bearing plant of the division *Gymnospermae*, in which the ovules are borne naked on the surface of the megasporophylls, which are often arranged in cones; any conifer or related plant. Compare **angiosperm.** —**ˌgym+no+'sper+mous** *adj.*

gym shoe *n.* another name for **plimsoll.**

gym+slip ('dʒɪmˌslɪp) *n.* a tunic or pinafore dress worn by schoolgirls, often part of a school uniform.

gyn. *abbrev. for:* **1.** gynaecological. **2.** gynaecology.

gyn- *combining form.* variant of **gyno-** before a vowel.

gy+nae+ce·um (ˌdʒaɪnɪ'si:əm) *n., pl.* **-ce·a** (-'si:ə). **1.** (in ancient Greece and Rome) the inner section of a house, used as women's quarters. **2.** (dʒaɪ'ni:sɪəm, gaɪ-). a variant spelling of **gynoecium.** [C17: from Latin: women's apartments, from Greek *gunaikeion*, from *gunē* a woman]

gy·nae·co- *or U.S.* **gy·ne·co-** *combining form.* relating to women; female: *gynaecology.* [from Greek, from *gunē*, *gunaik-* woman, female]

gy+nae+coc+ra+cy *or U.S.* **gy+ne+coc+ra+cy** (ˌdʒaɪnɪ'kɒkrəsɪ, ˌgaɪ-) *n., pl.* **+cies.** government by women or by a single woman. Also called: **gynarchy.** —**gy+nae+co+crat+ic** *or U.S.* **gy+ne+co+crat+ic** (dʒaɪˌni:kə'krætɪk, gaɪ-) *adj.*

gy+nae+coid *or U.S.* **gy+ne+coid** ('dʒaɪnɪˌkɔɪd, 'gaɪ-) *adj.* resembling, relating to, or like a woman.

gynaecol. *abbrev. for:* **1.** gynaecological. **2.** gynaecology.

gy+nae+col+o·gy *or U.S.* **gy+ne+col+o·gy** (ˌgaɪnɪ'kɒlədʒɪ) *n.* the branch of medicine concerned with diseases in women, esp. those of the genitourinary tract. —**gy+nae+co+log·i+cal** (ˌgaɪnɪkə'lɒdʒɪk°l), **ˌgy+nae+co+'log+ic** *or U.S.* **ˌgy+ne+co+'log·i+cal ˌgy+ne+co+'log+ic** *adj.* —**ˌgy+nae+'col+o+gist** *or U.S.* **ˌgy+ne+'col+o+gist** *n.*

gy+nae+co+mas+ti·a *or U.S.* **gy+ne+co+mas+ti·a** (ˌgaɪnɪkəʊ'mæstɪə) *n.* abnormal overdevelopment of the breasts in a man. [C19: from GYNAECO- + Greek *mastos* breast]

gy+nan+dro+morph (dʒɪ'nændrəʊˌmɔ:f, gaɪ-, dʒaɪ-) *n.* an abnormal organism, esp. an insect, that has both male and female physical characteristics. Compare **hermaphrodite** (sense 1). —**gy+ˌnan+dro+'mor+phic** *or* **gy+ˌnan+dro+'mor+phous** *adj.* —**gy+ˌnan+dro+'morph+ism** *or* **gy+'nan+dro+ˌmor+phy** *n.*

gy+nan+drous (dʒaɪ'nændrəs, dʒɪ-, gaɪ-) *adj.* **1.** (of flowers such as the orchid) having the stamens and styles united in a column. **2.** hermaphroditic. [C19: from Greek *gunandros* of uncertain sex, from *gunē* woman + *anēr* man] —**gy+'nan+dry** *or* **gy+'nan+drism** *n.*

gyn+ar+chy ('dʒaɪˌnɑ:kɪ, 'gaɪ-) *n., pl.* **+chies.** another word for **gynaecocracy.**

gy+ne+ci+um (dʒaɪ'ni:sɪəm, gaɪ-) *n., pl.* **+ci·a** (-sɪə). a variant spelling (esp. U.S.) of **gynoecium.**

gy·ne·co- *combining form.* a variant (esp. U.S.) of **gynaeco-.**

gy+ni+at+rics (ˌdʒaɪnɪ'ætrɪks, ˌgaɪ-) *or* **gy+ni+at+ry** (dʒaɪ'naɪətrɪ, gaɪ-) *n. Med.* less common words for **gynaecology.**

gyn·o- *or before a vowel* **gyn-** *combining form.* **1.** relating to women; female: *gynarchy.* **2.** denoting a female reproductive organ: *gynophore.* [from Greek, from *gunē* woman]

gy+noe+ci+um, gy+nae+ce+um, gy+nae+ci+um, *or esp. U.S.*

gy+ne·ci·um (dʒaɪ'ni:sɪəm, gaɪ-) *n., pl.* **+ci·a** *or* **+ce·a** (-sɪə). the carpels of a flowering plant collectively. [C18: New Latin, from Greek *gunaikeion* women's quarters, from *gunaik-, gunē* woman + *-eion,* suffix indicating place]

gy+no+phore ('dʒaɪnəʊ,fɔ:, 'gaɪ-) *n.* a stalk in some plants that bears the gynoecium above the level of the other flower parts. —**gy+no+phor+ic** (,dʒaɪnəʊ'fɒrɪk, ,gaɪ-) *adj.*

-gy·nous *adj. combining form.* **1.** of or relating to women or females: *androgynous; misogynous.* **2.** relating to female organs: *epigynous.* [from New Latin *-gynus,* from Greek *-gunos,* from *gunē* woman] —**-gyn·y** *n. combining form.*

Györ (*Hungarian* djø:r) *n.* an industrial town in NW Hungary: medieval Benedictine abbey. Pop.: 114 709 (1974 est.).

gyp[1] *or* **gip** (dʒɪp) *Slang.* ~*vb.* **gyps, gyp+ping, gypped** *or* **gips, gip+ping, gipped. 1.** (*tr.*) to swindle, cheat, or defraud. ~*n.* **2.** an act of cheating. **3.** a person who gyps. [C18: back formation from GYPSY]

gyp[2] (dʒɪp) *n. Brit. slang.* severe pain; torture: *his arthritis gave him gyp.* [C19: probably a contraction of *gee up!;* see GEE[1]]

gyp+soph·i·la (dʒɪp'sɒfɪlə) *n.* any caryophyllaceous plant of the Mediterranean genus *Gypsophila,* such as baby's-breath, having small white or pink flowers. [C18: New Latin, from Greek *gupsos* chalk + *philos* loving]

gyp+sum ('dʒɪpsəm) *n.* a colourless, white, or tinted mineral consisting of hydrated calcium sulphate in monoclinic crystalline form: occurs in sedimentary rocks and clay and is used principally in making plasters and cements, esp. plaster of Paris. Formula: $CaSO_4.2H_2O$. [C17: from Latin, from Greek *gupsos* chalk, plaster, cement, of Semitic origin] —**gyp+se+ous** ('dʒɪpsɪəs) *adj.* —**gyp+sif+er+ous** (dʒɪp'sɪfərəs) *adj.*

Gyp+sy *or* **Gip+sy** ('dʒɪpsɪ) *n., pl.* **+sies.** (*sometimes not cap.*) **1. a.** a member of a people scattered throughout Europe and North America, who maintain a nomadic way of life in industrialized societies. They migrated from NW India from around the 9th century onwards. **b.** (*as modifier*): *a Gypsy fortune-teller.* **2.** the language of the Gypsies; Romany. **3.** a person who looks or behaves like a Gypsy. [C16: from EGYPTIAN, since they were thought to have come originally from Egypt] —**'Gyp+sy+ish** *or* **'Gip+sy+ish** *adj.* —**'Gyp·sy-,like** *or* **'Gip·sy-,like** *adj.*

gyp+sy moth *n.* a variant spelling of **gipsy moth.**

gy+ral ('dʒaɪrəl) *adj.* **1.** having a circular, spiral, or rotating motion; gyratory. **2.** *Anatomy.* of or relating to a convolution (gyrus) of the brain. —**'gy+ral+ly** *adv.*

gy+rate *vb.* (dʒɪ'reɪt, dʒaɪ-). **1.** (*intr.*) to rotate or spiral, esp. about a fixed point or axis. ~*adj.* ('dʒaɪrɪt, -reɪt). **2.** *Biology.* curved or coiled into a circle; circinate. [C19: from Late Latin *gȳrāre,* from Latin *gȳrus* circle, from Greek *guros*] —**'gy+ra+tor** *n.* —**gy+ra+to·ry** ('dʒaɪrətərɪ, -trɪ; dʒaɪ'reɪtərɪ) *adj.*

gy+ra+tion (dʒaɪ'reɪʃən) *n.* **1.** the act or process of gyrating; rotation. **2.** any one of the whorls of a spiral-shaped shell.

gyre (dʒaɪə) *Chiefly literary.* ~*n.* **1.** a circular or spiral movement or path. **2.** a ring, circle, or spiral. ~*vb.* **3.** (*intr.*) to whirl. [C16: from Latin *gȳrus* circle, from Greek *guros*]

gyr+fal+con *or* **ger+fal+con** ('dʒɜ:,fɔ:lkən, -,fɔ:kən) *n.* a very large rare falcon, *Falco rusticolus,* of northern and arctic regions: often used for hunting. [C14: from Old French *gerfaucon,* perhaps from Old Norse *geirfalki,* from *geirr* spear + *falki* falcon]

gy·ro ('dʒaɪrəʊ) *n., pl.* **·ros. 1.** See **gyrocompass. 2.** See **gyroscope.**

gy·ro- *or before a vowel* **gyr-** *combining form.* **1.** indicating rotating or gyrating motion: *gyroscope.* **2.** indicating a spiral. **3.** indicating a gyroscope: *gyrocompass.* [via Latin from Greek *guro-,* from *guros* circle]

gy+ro+com+pass ('dʒaɪrəʊ,kʌmpəs) *n. Navigation.* a nonmagnetic compass that uses a motor-driven gyroscope to indicate true north. Sometimes shortened to **gyro.**

gy·ro ho+ri+zon *n.* another name for **artificial horizon** (sense 1).

gy+ro+mag+net+ic (,dʒaɪrəʊmæg'nɛtɪk) *adj.* of or caused by magnetic properties resulting from the spin of a charged particle, such as an electron.

gy+ro+mag+net+ic ra+ti+o *n. Physics.* the ratio of the magnetic moment of a rotating charged particle, such as an electron, to its angular momentum.

gy+ron ('dʒaɪrɒn) *n.* a variant spelling of **giron.**

gy+ron+ny (dʒaɪ'rɒnɪ) *adj.* a variant spelling of **gironny.**

gy+ro+plane ('dʒaɪrə,pleɪn) *n.* another name for **autogiro.**

gy+ro+scope ('dʒaɪrə,skəʊp) *or* **gy+ro+stat** *n.* a device containing a disc rotating on an axis that can turn freely in any direction so that the disc resists the action of an applied couple and tends to maintain the same orientation in space irrespective of the movement of the surrounding structure. Sometimes shortened to **gyro.** —**gy+ro+scop+ic** (,dʒaɪrə'skɒpɪk) *adj.* —**,gy+ro+'scop+i+cal+ly** *adv.* —**,gy+ro+'scop+ics** *n.*

gy+rose ('dʒaɪrəʊz) *adj. Botany.* marked with sinuous lines.

gy+ro+sta+bi+liz+er *or* **gy+ro+sta+bi+lis+er** (,dʒaɪrəʊ'steɪbɪ,laɪzə) *n.* a gyroscopic device used to stabilize the rolling motion of a ship.

gy+ro+stat+ic (,dʒaɪrəʊ'stætɪk) *adj.* of or concerned with the gyroscope or with gyrostatics. —**,gy+ro+'stat+i+cal+ly** *adv.*

gy+ro+stat+ics (,dʒaɪrəʊ'stætɪks) *n.* (*functioning as sing.*) the science of rotating bodies.

gy+rus ('dʒaɪrəs) *n., pl.* **gy·ri** ('dʒaɪraɪ). another name for **convolution** (sense 3). [C19: from Latin; see GYRE]

gyve (dʒaɪv) *Archaic.* ~*vb.* **1.** (*tr.*) to shackle or fetter. ~*n.* **2.** (*usually pl.*) fetters. [C13: of unknown origin]

H

h *or* **H** (eɪtʃ) *n., pl.* **h's, H's,** *or* **Hs. 1.** the eighth letter and sixth consonant of the modern English alphabet. **2.** a speech sound represented by this letter, in English usually a voiceless glottal fricative, as in *hat.* **3. a.** something shaped like an H. **b.** (*in combination*): *an H-beam.*

h *symbol for:* **1.** *Physics.* Planck constant. **2.** hecto-.

H *symbol for:* **1.** *Chem.* hydrogen. **2.** *Physics.* **a.** magnetic field strength. **b.** Hamiltonian. **3.** *Electronics.* henry or henries. **4.** *Thermodynamics.* enthalpy. **5.** (on Brit. pencils, signifying degree of hardness of lead) hard: *H; 2H; 3H.* Compare **B** (sense 8). **6.** *Slang.* heroin. ~**7.** *international car registration for* Hungary.

h. *or* **H.** *abbrev. for:* **1.** harbour. **2.** hard(ness). **3.** height. **4.** high. **5.** *Music.* horn. **6.** hour. **7.** hundred. **8.** husband.

ha *or* **hah** (hɑː) *interj.* **1.** an exclamation expressing derision, triumph, surprise, etc., according to the intonation of the speaker. **2.** (*reiterated*) a representation of the sound of laughter.

ha. *abbrev. for* hectare.

h.a. *abbrev. for* hoc anno. [Latin: in this year]

HAA hepatitis-associated antigen; an antigen that occurs in the blood serum of some people, esp. those with serum hepatitis.

haaf (hɑːf) *n.* a deep-sea fishing ground off the Shetland and Orkney Islands. [Old English *hæf* sea; related to Old Norse *haf;* see HEAVE]

Haa·kon VII ('hɑːkɒn) *n.* 1872–1957, king of Norway (1905–57). During the Nazi occupation of Norway (1940–45), he led Norwegian resistance from England.

haar (hɑː) *n. Eastern Brit.* a cold sea mist or fog off the North Sea. [C17: related to Dutch dialect *harig* damp]

Haar+lem (*Dutch* 'haːrlɛm) *n.* a city in the W Netherlands, capital of North Holland province. Pop.: 167 052 (1974 est.).

Hab. *Bible. abbrev. for* Habakkuk.

Hab·ak·kuk ('hæbəkək) *n. Old Testament.* **1.** a Hebrew prophet. **2.** the book containing his oracles and canticle. Douay spelling: **Hab·a·cuc.**

Ha+ba+na (a'βana) *n.* the Spanish name for **Havana.**

ha+ba+ne·ra (ˌhæbə'nɛərə) *n.* **1.** a slow Cuban dance in duple time. **2.** a piece of music composed for or in the rhythm of this dance. [from Spanish *danza habanera* Havanan dance]

Ha+ba+ne·ro (*Spanish* aβa'nero) *n., pl.* **·ros** (-ros). a native or inhabitant of Havana.

ha+be·as cor+pus ('heɪbɪəs 'kɔːpəs) *n. Law.* a writ ordering a person to be brought before a court or judge, esp. so that the court may ascertain whether his detention is lawful. [C15: from the opening of the Latin writ, literally: you may have the body]

hab+er+dash+er ('hæbəˌdæʃə) *n.* **1.** *Brit.* a dealer in small articles for sewing, such as buttons, zips, and ribbons. **2.** *U.S.* a men's outfitter. [C14: from Anglo-French *hapertas* small items of merchandise, of obscure origin]

hab+er+dash+er·y ('hæbəˌdæʃərɪ) *n., pl.* **+er·ies.** the goods or business kept by a haberdasher.

hab+er+geon ('hæbədʒən) *or* **hau+ber+geon** *n.* a light sleeveless coat of mail worn in the 14th century under the plated hauberk. [C14: from Old French *haubergeon* a little HAUBERK]

Ha·ber pro+cess ('hɑːbə) *n.* an industrial process for producing ammonia by reacting atmospheric nitrogen with hydrogen at about 200 atmospheres (2×10^7 pascals) and 500°C in the presence of a catalyst, usually iron. [named after Fritz *Haber* (1868–1934), German chemist]

hab+ile ('hæbiːl) *adj.* **1.** *Rare.* skilful. **2.** *Obsolete.* fit. [C14: from Latin *habilis,* from *habēre* to have; see ABLE]

ha+bil·i+ment (hə'bɪlɪmənt) *n.* (*often pl.*) dress or attire. [C15: from Old French *habillement,* from *habiller* to dress, from *bille* log; see BILLET[2]]

ha+bil·i·tate (hə'bɪlɪˌteɪt) *vb.* (*tr.*) **1.** *U.S., chiefly Western.* to equip and finance (a mine). **2.** (*intr.*) to qualify for office. **3.** *Archaic.* to clothe. [C17: from Medieval Latin *habilitāre* to make fit, from Latin *habilitās* aptness, readiness; see ABILITY] —**ha+ˌbil·i+'ta+tion** *n.* —**ha+'bil·i+ˌta+tor** *n.*

hab+it ('hæbɪt) *n.* **1.** a tendency or disposition to act in a particular way. **2.** established custom, usual practice, etc. **3.** *Psychol.* a learned behavioural response that has become associated with a particular situation, esp. one frequently repeated. **4.** mental disposition or attitude: *a good working habit of mind.* **5. a.** a practice or substance to which a person is addicted: *drink has become a habit with him.* **b.** the state of being dependent on something, esp. a drug. **6.** *Botany, zoology.* the method of growth, type of existence, or general appearance of a plant or animal: *a climbing habit; a burrowing habit.* **7.** the customary apparel of a particular occupation, rank, etc., now esp. the costume of a nun or monk. **8.** Also called: **riding habit.** a woman's riding dress. **9.** *Crystallog.* short for **crystal habit.** ~*vb.* (*tr.*) **10.** to clothe. **11.** an archaic word for **inhabit** or **habituate.** [C13: from Latin *habitus* custom, from *habēre* to have]

hab+it+a·ble ('hæbɪtəbᵊl) *adj.* able to be lived in. —ˌ**hab+it+a·'bil+i+ty** *or* **'hab+it+a·ble+ness** *n.* —**'hab+it+a·bly** *adv.*

hab+it+ant ('hæbɪtᵊnt) *n.* **1.** a less common word for **inhabitant. 2.** ('hæbɪtᵊnt; *French* abi'tã). **a.** one of the original French settlers in Canada or Louisiana. **b.** a descendant of these settlers.

hab·i+tat ('hæbɪˌtæt) *n.* **1.** the natural home of an animal or plant. **2.** the place in which a person, group, class, etc., is normally found. [C18: from Latin: it inhabits, from *habitāre* to dwell, from *habēre* to have]

hab·i·ta+tion (ˌhæbɪ'teɪʃən) *n.* **1.** a dwelling place. **2.** occupation of a dwelling place. —ˌ**hab·i+'ta+tion+al** *adj.*

hab+it+ed ('hæbɪtɪd) *adj.* **1.** dressed in a habit. **2.** clothed.

hab·it-form·ing *adj.* (of an activity, indulgence, etc.) tending to become a habit or addiction.

ha+bit·u+al (hə'bɪtjʊəl) *adj.* **1.** (*usually prenominal*) done or experienced regularly and repeatedly: *the habitual Sunday walk.* **2.** (*usually prenominal*) by habit: *a habitual drinker.* **3.** customary; usual: *his habitual comment.* —**ha+'bit·u·al+ly** *adv.* —**ha+'bit·u·al+ness** *n.*

ha+bit·u+ate (hə'bɪtjʊˌeɪt) *vb.* **1.** to accustom; make used to. **2.** *U.S. informal.* to frequent. —**ha+ˌbit·u·'a+tion** *n.*

hab·i+tude ('hæbɪˌtjuːd) *n. Rare.* habit or tendency. —ˌ**hab·i+'tu+di·nal** *adj.*

ha+bit·u·é (hə'bɪtjʊˌeɪ) *n.* a frequent visitor to a place. [C19: from French, from *habituer* to frequent]

hab·i+tus ('hæbɪtəs) *n., pl.* **+tus. 1.** *Med.* general physical state, esp. with regard to susceptibility to disease. **2.** tendency or inclination, esp. of plant or animal growth; habit. [C19: from Latin: state, HABIT]

Habs·burg ('haːpsˌburk) *n.* the German name for **Hapsburg.**

ha·bu ('hɑːbuː) *n.* a large venomous snake, *Trimeresurus flavoviridis,* of Okinawa and other Ryukyu Islands: family *Crotalidae* (pit vipers). [the native name in the Ryukyu Islands]

H.A.C. *abbrev. for* Honourable Artillery Company.

há·ček ('hɑːtʃɛk) *n.* a diacritic mark (ˇ) placed over certain letters in order to modify their sounds, esp. used in Slavonic languages to indicate various forms of palatal articulation, as in the affricate č and the fricative trill ř used in Czech. [from Czech]

ha+chure (hæ'ʃjʊə) *n.* **1.** another word for **hatching. 2.** shading of short lines drawn on a relief map to indicate gradients. ~*vb.* **3.** (*tr.*) to mark or show by hachures. [C19: from French, from *hacher* to chop up, HATCH[3]]

hac·i+en+da (ˌhæsɪ'ɛndə) *n.* **1.** (in Spain or Spanish-speaking countries) **a.** a ranch or large estate. **b.** any substantial stock-raising, mining, or manufacturing establishment in the country. **2.** the main house on such a ranch or plantation. [C18: from Spanish, from Latin *facienda* things to be done, from *facere* to do]

hack[1] (hæk) *vb.* **1.** (when *intr.,* usually foll. by *at* or *away*) to cut or chop (at) irregularly, roughly, or violently. **2.** to cut and clear (a way, path, etc.), as through undergrowth. **3.** (in sport, esp. rugby) to foul (an opposing player) by kicking or striking his shins. **4.** *Basketball.* to commit the foul of striking (an opposing player) on the arm. **5.** (*intr.*) *Informal.* to cough in short dry spasmodic bursts. **6.** (*tr.*) to reduce or cut (a story, article, etc.) in a damaging way. **7.** (*tr.*) *U.S.* to tolerate: *I can't hack it.* **8. hack to bits.** to damage severely: *his reputation was hacked to bits.* ~*n.* **9.** a cut, chop, notch, or gash, esp. as made by a knife or axe. **10.** any tool used for shallow digging, such as a mattock or pick. **11.** a chopping blow. **12.** *Informal.* a dry spasmodic cough. **13.** a kick on the shins, as in rugby. **14.** a wound from a sharp kick. [Old English *haccian;* related to Old Frisian *hackia,* Middle High German *hacken*] —**'hack+er** *n.*

hack[2] (hæk) *n.* **1.** a horse kept for riding or (more rarely) for driving. **2.** an old, ill-bred, or overworked horse. **3.** a horse kept for hire. **4.** *Brit.* a country ride on horseback. **5.** a drudge. **6.** a person who produces mediocre literary or journalistic work. **7.** Also called: **hackney.** *U.S.* a coach or carriage that is for hire. **8.** Also called: **hackie.** *U.S. informal.* **a.** a cabdriver. **b.** a taxi. ~*vb.* **9.** *Brit.* to ride (a horse) cross-country for pleasure. **10.** (*tr.*) to let (a horse) out for hire. **11.** (*tr.*) *Informal.* to write (an article, etc.) as or in the manner of a hack. **12.** (*intr.*) *U.S. informal.* to drive a taxi. ~*adj.* (*prenominal*) **13.** banal, mediocre, or unoriginal: *hack writing.* [C17: short for HACKNEY]

hack[3] (hæk) *n.* **1.** a rack used for fodder for livestock. **2.** a board on which meat is placed for a hawk. **3.** a pile or row of unfired bricks stacked to dry. ~*vb.* (*tr.*) **4.** to place (fodder) in such a rack. **5.** to place (bricks) in a hack. [C16: variant of HATCH[2]]

hack·a+more ('hækəˌmɔː) *n. U.S.* a rope or rawhide halter used for unbroken foals. [C19: by folk etymology from Spanish *jáquima* headstall, from Old Spanish *xaquima,* from Arabic *shaqīmah*]

hack+ber·ry ('hækˌbɛrɪ) *n., pl.* **·ries. 1.** any American tree or shrub of the ulmaceous genus *Celtis,* having edible cherry-like fruits. **2.** the fruit or soft yellowish wood of such a tree. [C18:

variant of C16 *hagberry*, of Scandinavian origin; compare Old Norse *heggr* hackberry]

hack+but ('hækbʌt) *or* **hag+but** *n.* another word for **arquebus.** —,**hack+but+'eer, 'hack+but+ter,** *or* ,**hag+but+'eer, 'hag+but+ter** *n.*

hack ham+mer *n.* an adze-like tool, used for dressing stone.

hack+ing ('hækɪŋ) *adj.* (of a cough) harsh, dry, and spasmodic.

hack+ing jack+et *or* **coat** *n. Chiefly Brit.* a riding jacket with side or back vents and slanting pockets.

hack+le[1] ('hæk°l) *n.* **1.** any of the long slender feathers on the necks of the turkey, pheasant, etc. **2.** *Angling.* **a.** parts of an artificial fly made from hackle feathers, representing the legs of a real fly. **b.** short for **hackle fly. 3.** a steel flax comb. ~*vb.* (*tr.*) **4.** to comb (flax) using a hackle. [C15: variant of HECKLE] —'**hack+ler** *n.*

hack+le[2] ('hæk°l) *vb. Rare.* to hack or be hacked; mangle. [C16: from HACK[1]; related to Middle Dutch *hakkelen*]

hack+le fly *n. Angling.* an artificial fly made from the hackle feathers of a turkey, etc.

hack+les ('hæk°lz) *pl. n.* **1.** the hairs on the back of the neck and the back of a dog, cat, etc., which rise when the animal is angry or afraid. **2.** anger or resentment (esp. in the phrases **get one's hackles up, make one's hackles rise**).

hack+ney ('hæknɪ) *n.* **1.** a compact breed of harness horse with a high-stepping trot. **2. a.** a coach or carriage that is for hire. **b.** (*as modifier*): *a hackney carriage.* **3.** a popular term for **hack**[2] (sense 1). ~*vb.* **4.** (*tr.; usually passive*) to make commonplace and banal by too frequent use. [C14: probably after HACKNEY, where horses were formerly raised; sense 4 meaning derives from the allusion to a weakened hired horse] —'**hack+ney+ism** *n.*

Hack+ney ('hæknɪ) *n.* a borough of NE Greater London: formed in 1965 from the former boroughs of Shoreditch, Stoke Newington, and Hackney; nearby are **Hackney Marshes,** the largest recreation ground in London. Pop.: 192 500 (1976 est.).

hack+neyed ('hæknɪd) *adj.* (of phrases, fashions, etc.) used so often as to be trite, dull, and stereotyped.

hack+saw ('hæk,sɔ:) *n.* **1.** a handsaw for cutting metal, with a hard-steel blade in a frame under tension. ~*vb.* **+saws, +saw+ing, +sawed, +sawed** *or* **+sawn. 2.** (*tr.*) to cut with a hacksaw.

had (hæd) *vb.* the past tense or past participle of **have.**

ha+dal ('heɪd°l) *adj.* of, relating to, or constituting the parts of the ocean below about 6000 metres (18 000 ft.). [C20: from French, from *Hadès* HADES]

had·a+way (,hædə'weɪ) *interj. Northeastern English dialect.* an exclamation urging the hearer to refrain from delay in the execution of a task. [perhaps from HOLD[1] + AWAY]

had+dock ('hædək) *n., pl.* **+docks** *or* **+dock.** a North Atlantic gadoid food fish, *Melanogrammus aeglefinus:* similar to but smaller than the cod. [C14: of uncertain origin]

hade (heɪd) *n. Geology.* **1.** the angle made to the vertical by the plane of a fault or vein. ~*vb.* **2.** (*intr.*) (of faults, or veins) to incline from the vertical. [C18: of unknown origin]

Ha+des ('heɪdi:z) *n.* **1.** *Greek myth.* **a.** the underworld abode of the souls of the dead. **b.** Pluto, the god of the underworld, brother of Zeus and husband of Persephone. **2.** *New Testament.* the abode or state of the dead. **3.** (*often not cap.*) *Informal.* hell. —**Ha+de·an** (heɪ'di:ən, 'heɪdɪən) *adj.*

Ha+dhra+maut *or* **Ha+dra+maut** (,hɑ:drə'mɔ:t) *n.* a plateau region of the S Arabian Peninsula, in E Southern Yemen on the Indian Ocean: corresponds roughly to the former East Aden Protectorate. Area: about 151 500 sq. km (58 500 sq. miles).

Had+ith ('hædɪθ, hɑ:'di:θ) *n.* the body of tradition and legend about Mohammed and his followers. [Arabic]

hadj (hædʒ) *n., pl.* **hadj·es.** a variant spelling of **hajj.**

hadj·i ('hædʒɪ) *n., pl.* **hadj·is.** a variant spelling of **hajji.**

had·n't ('hæd°nt) *contraction of* had not.

Ha·dri·an ('heɪdrɪən) *or* **A·dri·an** *n.* Latin name *Publius Aelius Hadrianus.* 76–138 A.D., Roman emperor (117–138); adopted son and successor of Trajan. He travelled throughout the Roman empire, strengthening its frontiers and encouraging learning and architecture, and in Rome he reorganized the army and codified Roman law.

Ha·dri·an's Wall *n.* a fortified Roman wall across N England, of which substantial parts remain, extending from the Solway Firth in the west to the mouth of the River Tyne in the east. It was built in 120–123 A.D. on the orders of the emperor Hadrian as a defence against the N British tribes.

had+ron ('hædrɒn) *n.* any elementary particle, excluding leptons and photons, capable of taking part in a strong nuclear interaction. [C20: from Greek *hadros* heavy, from *hadēn* enough + -ON] —**had+'ron+ic** *adj.*

had+ro+saur ('hædrə,sɔ:) *or* **ha+dro+saur+us** (,hædrə'sɔ:rəs) *n.* any bipedal Upper Cretaceous dinosaur of the genus *Anatosaurus* and related genera: partly aquatic, with a duck-billed skull and webbed feet. [C19: from Greek *hadros* thick, fat + -SAUR]

hadst (hædst) *vb. Archaic or dialect.* (used with the pronoun *thou*) a singular form of the past tense (indicative mood) of **have.**

hae (heɪ, hæ) *vb.* a Scottish variant of **have.**

haec+ce+i·ty (hɛk'si:ɪtɪ, hi:k-) *n., pl.* **·ties.** *Philosophy.* something that makes an object unique. Compare **quiddity.** [C17: from Medieval Latin *haecceitas,* literally: thisness, from *haec,* feminine of *hic* this]

Haeck·el (*German* 'hɛk°l) *n.* **Ernst Hein·rich** ('ɛrnst 'haɪnrɪç). 1834–1919, German biologist and philosopher. He formulated the recapitulation theory of evolution and was an exponent of the philosophy of materialistic monism. —**Haeck+e·li·an** (hɛ'ki:lɪən). *adj.*

haem *or U.S.* **heme** (hi:m) *n. Biochem.* a complex red organic pigment containing ferrous iron, present in haemoglobin. [C20: shortened from HAEMATIN]

haem- *combining form.* a variant of **haemo-** before a vowel. Also (esp. U.S.): **hem-**

hae·ma- *combining form.* a variant of **haemo-.** Also (U.S.): **he·ma-**

hae·ma+chrome *or U.S.* **he·ma+chrome** ('hi:mə,krəʊm, 'hɛm-) *n.* variants of **haemochrome.**

hae·ma+cy+tom+e·ter *or U.S.* **he·ma+cy+tom+e·ter** (,hi:məsaɪ'tɒmɪtə) *n. Med.* variants of **haemocytometer.**

hae+mag+glu+tin+ate *or U.S.* **he+mag+glu+tin+ate** (,hi:mə'glu:tɪ,neɪt, ,hɛm-) *vb.* (*tr.*) to cause the clumping of red blood cells in (a blood sample, etc.).

hae+mag+glu+ti+nin *or U.S.* **he+mag+glu+ti+nin** (,hi:mə'glu:tɪnən, ,hɛm-) *n.* an antibody that causes the clumping of red blood cells.

hae·ma+gogue *or U.S.* **he·ma+gogue, he·ma+gog** ('hi:mə,gɒg) *adj.* **1.** promoting the flow of blood. ~*n.* **2.** a drug or agent that promotes the flow of blood, esp. the menstrual flow.

hae+mal *or U.S.* **he+mal** ('hi:məl) *adj.* **1.** of or relating to the blood or the blood vessels. **2.** denoting or relating to the region of the body containing the heart.

hae+ma+te·in *or U.S.* **he·ma+te·in** (,hi:mə'ti:ɪn, ,hɛm-) *n.* a dark purple water-insoluble crystalline substance obtained from logwood and used as an indicator and biological stain. Formula: $C_{16}H_{12}O_6$.

hae·ma+tem+e·sis *or U.S.* **he·ma+tem+e·sis** (,hi:mə'tɛmɪsɪs, ,hɛm-) *n.* vomiting of blood, esp. as the result of a bleeding ulcer. Compare **haemoptysis.** [C19: from HAEMATO- + Greek *emesis* vomiting]

hae+mat+ic *or U.S.* **he+mat+ic** (hi:'mætɪk) *adj.* **1.** Also: **haemic.** relating to, acting on, having the colour of, or containing blood. ~*n.* **2.** *Med.* another name for a **haematinic.**

haem·a+tin *or U.S.* **hem·a+tin** ('hɛmətɪn, 'hi:-) *n. Biochem.* a dark bluish or brownish pigment containing iron in the ferric state, obtained by the oxidation of haem.

haem·a+tin+ic *or U.S.* **hem·a+tin+ic** (,hɛmə'tɪnɪk, ,hi:-) *n.* **1.** Also called: **haematic.** an agent that stimulates the production of red blood cells or increases the amount of haemoglobin in the blood. ~*adj.* **2.** having the effect of enriching the blood.

haem·a+tite *or U.S.* **hem·a+tite** ('hi:mə,taɪt, 'hɛm-) *n.* a red or reddish-black mineral consisting of ferric oxide in hexagonal crystalline form: the principal ore of iron. Formula: Fe_2O_3. [C16: via Latin from Greek *haimatitēs* resembling blood, from *haima* blood] —**haem·a+tit+ic** *or U.S.* **hem·a+tit+ic** (,hi:mə'tɪtɪk, ,hɛm-) *adj.*

hae·ma·to- *or before a vowel* **hae·mat-** *combining form.* indicating blood: *haematolysis.* Also: **haemo-** or (U.S.): **he·ma·to-, he·mat-.** [from Greek *haima, haimat-* blood]

hae+mat·o+blast *or U.S.* **he+mat·o+blast** (hi:'mætəʊ,blæst) *n.* any of the undifferentiated cells in the bone marrow that develop into blood cells. —**hae+,mat·o+'blas+tic** *or U.S.* **he+,mat·o+'blas+tic** *adj.*

haem·a+to+cele *or U.S.* **hem·a+to+cele** ('hɛmətəʊ,si:l, 'hi:-) *n. Pathol.* a collection of blood in a body cavity, as in the space surrounding the testis; blood cyst.

haem·a+to+crit *or U.S.* **hem·a+to+crit** ('hɛmətəʊkrɪt, 'hi:-) *n.* **1.** a centrifuge for separating blood cells from plasma. **2.** Also called: **packed cell volume.** the ratio of the volume occupied by these cells, esp. the red cells, to the total volume of blood, expressed as a percentage. [C20: from HAEMATO- + -CRIT, from Greek *kritēs* judge, from *krinein* to separate]

haem·a+to+cry+al *or U.S.* **hem·a+to+cry+al** (,hɛmətəʊ'kraɪəl, ,hi:-) *adj. Zoology.* another word for **poikilothermal.**

haem·a+to+gen+e·sis *or U.S.* **hem·a+to+gen+e·sis** (,hɛmətəʊ'dʒɛnɪsɪs, ,hi:-) *n.* another name for **haematopoiesis.** —,**haem·a+to+'gen+ic, haem·a+to+ge+net+ic** (,hɛmətəʊdʒɪ'nɛtɪk, ,hi:-) *or U.S.* ,**hem·a+to+'gen+ic,** ,**hem·a+to+ge·'net+ic** *adj.*

haem·a+tog+e·nous *or U.S.* **hem·a+tog+e·nous** (,hɛmə'tɒdʒɪnəs, ,hi:-) *adj.* **1.** producing blood. **2.** produced by, derived from, or originating in the blood. **3.** (of bacteria, cancer cells, etc.) borne by or distributed by the blood.

hae·ma+toid ('hi:mə,tɔɪd, 'hɛm-), **hae+moid** *or U.S.* **he·ma+toid, he+moid** *adj.* resembling blood.

hae·ma+tol+o·gy *or U.S.* **he·ma+tol+o·gy** (,hi:mə'tɒlədʒɪ) *n.* the branch of medical science concerned with diseases of the blood and blood-forming tissues. —**hae·ma+to+log+ic** (,hi:mətə'lɒdʒɪk), ,**hae·ma+to+'log·i·cal** *or U.S.* ,**he·ma+to+'log+ic,** ,**he·ma+to+'log·i·cal** *adj.* —,**haema+'tol·o·gist** *or U.S.* ,**he·ma+'tol·o·gist** *n.*

hae·ma+tol·y+sis *or U.S.* **he·ma+tol·y+sis** (,hi:mə'tɒlɪsɪs) *n., pl.* **+ses** (-,si:z). another name for **haemolysis.**

hae·ma+to+ma *or U.S.* **he·ma+to+ma** (,hi:mə'təʊmə, ,hɛm-) *n., pl.* **+mas** *or* **+ma·ta** (-mətə). *Pathol.* a tumour of clotted or partially clotted blood.

haem·a+to+poi+e·sis (,hɛmətəʊpɔɪ'i:sɪs, ,hi:-), **hae·mo+poi+e·sis** *or U.S.* **hem·a+to+poi+e·sis, he·mo+poi+e·sis** *n. Physiol.* the formation of blood. Also called: **haematosis, haematogenesis.** —**haem·a+to+poi+et+ic** (,hɛmətəʊpɔɪ'ɛtɪk, ,hi:-), **hae·mo+poi+et+ic** (,hi:məpɔɪ'ɛtɪk, ,hɛm-) *or U.S.* ,**hem·a+to+poi+'et+ic,** ,**he·mo+poi+'et+ic** *adj.*

hae·ma+to+sis *or U.S.* **he·ma+to+sis** (,hi:mə'təʊsɪs, ,hɛm-) *n. Physiol.* **1.** another word for **haematopoiesis. 2.** the oxygenation of venous blood in the lungs.

haem·a+to+ther+mal *or U.S.* **hem·a+to+ther+mal** (,hɛmətəʊ'θɜ:məl, ,hi:-) *adj. Zoology.* another word for **homoiothermal.**

hae·ma+tox·y+lin or *U.S.* **he·ma+tox·y+lin** (ˌhiːməˈtɒksɪlɪn, ˌhɛm-) *n.* **1.** a colourless or yellowish crystalline compound that turns red on exposure to light: obtained from logwood and used in dyes and as a biological stain. Formula: $C_{16}H_{14}O_6.3H_2O$. **2.** a variant spelling of **haematoxylon.** [C19: from New Latin *Haematoxylon* genus name of logwood, from HAEMATO- + Greek *xulon* wood + -IN]

hae·ma+tox·y+lon (ˌhiːməˈtɒksɪlɒn) or **hae·ma+tox·y+lin** *n.* any thorny leguminous tree of the genus *Haematoxylon*, esp. the logwood, of tropical America and SW Africa. The heartwood yields the dye haematoxylin. [C19: see HAEMATOXYLIN] —**hae·ma+tox+yl+ic** (ˌhiːmətɒkˈsɪlɪk) *adj.*

hae·ma+to+zo+on or *U.S.* **he·ma+to+zo+on** (ˌhiːmətəʊˈzəʊɒn, ˌhɛm-) *n., pl.* **+zo·a** (-ˈzəʊə). any microorganism, esp. a protozoan, that is parasitic in the blood.

hae·ma+tu+ri·a or *U.S.* **he·ma+tu+ri·a** (ˌhiːməˈtjʊərɪə, ˌhɛm-) *n. Pathol.* the presence of blood or red blood cells in the urine. —ˌ**hae·ma+ˈtu+ric** or *U.S.* ˌ**he·ma+ˈtu+ric** *adj.*

-hae·mi·a or *esp. U.S.* **-he·mi·a** *n. combining form.* variants of **-aemia.**

hae+mic or *U.S.* **he+mic** (ˈhiːmɪk, ˈhɛm-) *adj.* another word for **haematic.**

hae+min or *U.S.* **he+min** (ˈhiːmɪn) *n. Biochem.* haematin chloride; insoluble reddish-brown crystals formed by the action of hydrochloric acid on haematin in a test for the presence of blood. [C20: from HAEMO- + -IN]

hae·mo-, hae·ma-, or *before a vowel* **haem-** *combining form.* denoting blood: *haemophobia.* Also: **haemato-** or (U.S.) **hemo-, hema-** or **hem-.** [from Greek *haima* blood]

hae·mo+chrome or *U.S.* **he·mo+chrome** (ˈhiːməˌkrəʊm, ˈhɛm-) *n.* a blood pigment, such as haemoglobin, that carries oxygen.

hae·mo+coel or *U.S.* **he·mo+coel** (ˈhiːməˌsiːl) *n.* the body cavity of many invertebrates, including arthropods and molluscs, developed from part of the blood system. [C19: from HAEMO- + *-coel*, variant of -COELE]

hae·mo+cy·a·nin or *U.S.* **he·mo+cy·a·nin** (ˌhiːməʊˈsaɪənɪn) *n.* a blue copper-containing respiratory pigment in crustaceans and molluscs that functions as haemoglobin.

hae·mo+cyte or *U.S.* **he·mo+cyte** (ˈhiːməʊˌsaɪt, ˈhɛm-) *n.* any blood cell, esp. a red blood cell.

hae·mo+cy+tom+e·ter (ˌhiːməʊsaɪˈtɒmɪtə), **hae·ma+cy+tom+e·ter** or *U.S.* **he·mo+cy+tom+e·ter, he·ma+cy+tom+e·ter** *n. Med.* an apparatus for counting the number of cells in a quantity of blood, typically consisting of a graduated pipette for drawing and diluting the blood and a ruled glass slide on which the cells are counted under a microscope.

hae·mo+di·al·y+sis or *U.S.* **he·mo+di·al·y+sis** (ˌhiːməʊdaɪˈælɪsɪs) *n., pl.* **+ses** (-ˌsiːz). *Med.* the filtering of circulating blood through a semipermeable membrane in an apparatus (**haemodialyser** or **artificial kidney**) to remove waste products: performed in cases of kidney failure. Also called: **extracorporeal dialysis.** See also **dialysis.** [C20: from HAEMO- + DIALYSIS]

hae·mo+flag+el+late or *U.S.* **he·mo+flag+el+late** (ˌhiːməˈflædʒəˌleɪt, ˌhɛm-) *n.* a flagellate protozoan, such as a trypanosome, that is parasitic in the blood.

hae·mo+glo+bin or *U.S.* **he·mo+glo+bin** (ˌhiːməʊˈgləʊbɪn, ˌhɛm-) *n.* a conjugated protein, consisting of haem and the protein globin, that gives red blood cells their characteristic colour. It combines reversibly with oxygen and is thus very important in the transportation of oxygen to tissues. See also **oxyhaemoglobin.** [C19: shortened from HAEMATOGLOBULIN]

hae·mo+glo+bi+nu+ri·a or *U.S.* **he·mo+glo+bi+nu+ri·a** (ˌhiːməˌgləʊbɪˈnjʊərɪə, ˌhɛm-) *n. Pathol.* the presence of haemoglobin in the urine.

hae+moid or *U.S.* **he+moid** (ˈhiːmɔɪd) *adj.* another word for **haematoid.**

hae·mo+ly+sin or *U.S.* **he·mo+ly+sin** (ˌhiːməʊˈlaɪsɪn, ˌhɛməʊ-; hɪˈmɒlɪsɪn) *n. Biochem.* any substance, esp. an antibody, that causes the breakdown of red blood cells.

hae+mol·y+sis (hɪˈmɒlɪsɪs), **hae·ma+tol·y+sis** or *U.S.* **he+mol·y+sis, he·ma+tol·y+sis** *n., pl.* **+ses** (-ˌsiːz). the disintegration of red blood cells, with the release of haemoglobin, occurring in the living organism or in a blood sample. —**hae·mo+lyt+ic** or *U.S.* **he·mo+lyt+ic** (ˌhiːməʊˈlɪtɪk, ˌhɛm-) *adj.*

hae·mo+phile or *U.S.* **he·mo+phile** (ˈhiːməʊˌfaɪl, ˈhɛm-) *n.* **1.** another name for **haemophiliac.** **2.** a haemophilic bacterium.

hae·mo+phil·i·a or *U.S.* **he·mo+phil·i·a** (ˌhiːməʊˈfɪlɪə, ˌhɛm-) *n.* an inheritable disease, usually affecting only males but transmitted by women to their male children, characterized by loss or impairment of the normal clotting ability of blood so that a minor wound may result in fatal bleeding. —ˌ**hae·mo+ˈphil·i+ˌoid** or *U.S.* ˌ**he·mo+ˈphil·i+ˌoid** *adj.*

hae·mo+phil·i+ac or *U.S.* **he·mo+phil·i+ac** (ˌhiːməʊˈfɪlɪˌæk, ˌhɛm-) *n.* a person having haemophilia. Nontechnical name: **bleeder.** Also called: **haemophile.**

hae·mo+phil+ic or *U.S.* **he·mo+phil+ic** (ˌhiːməʊˈfɪlɪk, ˌhɛm-) *adj.* **1.** of, relating to, or affected by haemophilia. **2.** (of bacteria) growing well in a culture medium containing blood.

hae·mo+poi+e·sis or *U.S.* **he·mo+poi+e·sis** (ˌhiːməʊpɔɪˈiːsɪs, ˌhɛm-) *n. Physiol.* another name for **haematopoiesis.** —**hae·mo+poi+et+ic** or *U.S.* **he·mo+poi+et+ic** (ˌhiːməʊpɔɪˈɛtɪk, ˌhɛm-) *adj.*

haem+op+ty+sis or *U.S.* **hem+op+ty+sis** (hɪˈmɒptɪsɪs) *n., pl.* **+ses** (-ˌsiːz). spitting or coughing up of blood or blood-streaked mucus, as in tuberculosis. Compare **haematemesis.** [C17: HAEMO- + *-ptysis*, from Greek *ptyein* to spit]

haem+or+rhage or *U.S.* **hem+or+rhage** (ˈhɛmərɪdʒ) *n.* **1.** profuse bleeding from ruptured blood vessels. ~*vb.* **2.** (*intr.*) to bleed profusely. [C17: from Latin *haemorrhagia;* see HAEMO-, -RRHAGIA] —**haem+or+rhag+ic** or *U.S.* **hem+or+rhag+ic** (ˌhɛməˈrædʒɪk) *adj.*

haem+or+rhoid+ec+to+my or *U.S.* **hem+or+rhoid+ec+to+my** (ˌhɛmərɔɪˈdɛktəmɪ) *n., pl.* **+mies.** surgical removal of haemorrhoids.

haem+or+rhoids or *U.S.* **hem+or+rhoids** (ˈhɛməˌrɔɪdz) *pl. n. Pathol.* swollen and twisted veins in the region of the anus and lower rectum, often painful and bleeding. Nontechnical name: **piles.** [C14: from Latin *haemorrhoidae* (plural), from Greek, from *haimorrhoos* discharging blood, from *haimo-* HAEMO- + *rhein* to flow] —ˌ**haem+or+ˈrhoi+dal** or *U.S.* ˌ**hem+or+ˈrhoi+dal** *adj.*

hae·mo+sta+sis (ˌhiːməʊˈsteɪsɪs, ˌhɛm-), **hae·mo+sta+si·a** (ˌhiːməʊˈsteɪʒɪə, -ʒə, ˌhɛm-) or *U.S.* **he·mo+sta+sis, he·mo+sta+si·a** *n.* **1.** the stopping of bleeding or arrest of blood circulation in an organ or part, as during a surgical operation. **2.** stagnation of the blood. [C18: from New Latin, from HAEMO- + Greek *stasis* a standing still]

hae·mo+stat or *U.S.* **he·mo+stat** (ˈhiːməʊˌstæt, ˈhɛm-) *n.* **1.** a surgical instrument that stops bleeding by compression of a blood vessel. **2.** a chemical agent that retards or stops bleeding.

hae·mo+stat+ic or *U.S.* **he·mo+stat+ic** (ˌhiːməʊˈstætɪk, ˌhɛm-) *adj.* **1.** retarding or stopping the flow of blood within the blood vessels. **2.** retarding or stopping bleeding. ~*n.* **3.** a drug or agent that retards or stops bleeding.

hae+re+mai (ˈhaɪrəˌmaɪ) *interj. N.Z.* a Maori expression of welcome. [C18: Maori, literally: come hither]

hae+res (ˈhɪəriːz) *n. pl.* **hae+re·des** (hɪˈriːdiːz). a variant spelling of **heres.**

Ha-erh-pin (ˈhɑːˈɛəˈpɪn) *n.* transliteration of the Chinese name for **Harbin.**

ha+fiz (ˈhɑːfɪz) *n. Islam.* **1.** a title for a person who knows the Koran by heart. **2.** the guardian of a mosque. [from Persian, from Arabic *hāfiz,* from *hafiza* to guard]

haf+ni·um (ˈhæfnɪəm) *n.* a bright metallic element found in zirconium ores: used in tungsten filaments and as a neutron absorber in nuclear reactors. Symbol: Hf; atomic no.: 72; atomic wt.: 178.49; valency: 4; relative density: 13.31; melting pt.: 2150°C; boiling pt.: 5400°C. [C20: New Latin, named after *Hafnia,* Latin name of Copenhagen + -IUM]

haft (hɑːft) *n.* **1.** the handle of an axe, knife, etc. ~*vb.* **2.** (*tr.*) to provide with a haft. [Old English *hæft;* related to Old Norse *hapt,* Old High German *haft* fetter, *hefti* handle] —ˈ**haft+er** *n.*

Haf+ta+rah or **Haph+ta+rah** (hɑːfˈtəʊrə; *Hebrew* haftaˈra) *n., pl.* **+ta+roth** (-ˈtəʊrəʊt; *Hebrew* -taˈrɔt) or **+ta+rahs.** *Judaism.* a reading from the Prophets recited or chanted during the services for Sabbaths, festivals, etc.

hag[1] (hæg) *n.* **1.** an unpleasant or ugly old woman. **2.** a witch. **3.** short for **hagfish.** **4.** *Obsolete.* a female demon. [Old English *hægtesse* witch; related to Old High German *hagazussa,* Middle Dutch *haghetisse*] —ˈ**hag+gish** *adj.* —ˈ**hag+gish+ly** *adv.* —ˈ**hag+gish+ness** *n.* —ˈ**hag+ˌlike** *adj.*

hag[2] (hæg, hɑːg) *n. Northern Brit. dialect.* **1.** a firm spot in a bog. **2.** a soft place in a moor. [C13: of Scandinavian origin; compare Old Norse *högg* gap; see HEW]

Hag. *Bible. abbrev. for* Haggai.

Ha·gar (ˈheɪgɑː, -gə) *n. Old Testament.* an Egyptian maid of Sarah, who bore Ishmael to Abraham, Sarah's husband.

hag+but (ˈhægbʌt) *n.* another word for **arquebus.** —ˌ**hag+but+ˈeer** or ˈ**hag+but+ter** *n.*

Ha+gen[1] (ˈhɑːgən) *n.* (in the *Nibelungenlied*) Siegfried's killer, who in turn is killed by Siegfried's wife, Kriemhild.

Ha+gen[2] (*German* ˈhaːgᵊn) *n.* an industrial city in NE West Germany, in North Rhine-Westphalia. Pop.: 196 764 (1974 est.).

Ha·gen[3] (ˈheɪgən) *n.* **Wal·ter.** 1892–1969, U.S. golfer.

hag+fish (ˈhægˌfɪʃ) *n., pl.* **+fish** or **+fish·es.** any eel-like marine cyclostome vertebrate of the family *Myxinidae,* having a round sucking mouth and feeding on the tissues of other animals and on dead organic material. Often shortened to **hag.**

Hag+ga+dah or **Hag+ga+da** (həˈgɑːdə; *Hebrew* hagaˈda, -gɔˈdɔ) *n., pl.* **+dahs, +das** or **+doth** (*Hebrew* -ˈdɔt) *Judaism.* **1.** the nonlegal part of the Talmudic literature and associated Jewish tradition, as contrasted with Halakah. **2. a.** the ritual recitation of the Exodus narrative at the Passover Seder service. **b.** the book containing this narrative. **3.** a traditional homiletic exposition of Scripture. [C19: from Hebrew *haggādāh* a story, from *hagged* to tell] —**hag+gad+ic** (həˈgædɪk, -ˈgɑː-) or **hag+ˈgad·i·cal** *adj.*

hag+ga+dist (həˈgɑːdɪst) *n. Judaism.* **1.** a writer of Haggadahs. **2.** an expert in or a student of haggadic literature. —**hag+ga+dist+ic** (ˌhægəˈdɪstɪk) *adj.*

Hag·ga·i (ˈhægeɪˌaɪ) *n. Old Testament.* **1. a.** a Hebrew prophet, whose oracles are usually dated between August and December of 520 B.C. **2.** the book in which these oracles are contained, chiefly concerned with the rebuilding of the Temple after the Exile. Douay spelling: **Ag·ge·us** (əˈjiːəs).

hag+gard (ˈhægəd) *adj.* **1.** careworn or gaunt, as from lack of sleep, anxiety, or starvation. **2.** wild or unruly. **3.** (of a hawk) having reached maturity in the wild before being caught. ~*n.* **4.** *Falconry.* a hawk that has reached maturity before being caught. Compare **eyas, passage hawk.** —ˈ**hag+gard+ly** *adv.* —ˈ**hag+gard+ness** *n.*

Hag+gard (ˈhægəd) *n.* Sir (**Henry**) **Ri·der.** 1856–1925, English author of romantic adventure stories, including *King Solomon's Mines* (1885).

hag+gis (ˈhægɪs) *n.* a Scottish dish made from sheep's or calf's offal, oatmeal, suet, and seasonings boiled in a skin made from the animal's stomach. [C15: perhaps from *haggen* to HACK[1]]

hag·gle ('hægəl) *vb.* **1.** (*intr.*; often foll. by *over*) to bargain or wrangle (over a price, terms of an agreement, etc.); barter. **2.** (*tr.*) *Rare.* to hack. [C16: of Scandinavian origin; compare Old Norse *haggva* to HEW] —'**hag·gler** *n.*

hag·i·arch·y ('hægɪˌɑːkɪ) *n., pl.* **·arch·ies. 1.** government by saints, holy men, or men in holy orders. **2.** an order of saints.

hag·i·o- *or before a vowel* **hag·i-** *combining form.* indicating a saint, saints, or holiness: *hagiography.* [via Late Latin from Greek, from *hagios* holy]

hag·i·oc·ra·cy (ˌhægɪ'ɒkrəsɪ) *n., pl.* **·cies. 1.** government by holy men. **2.** a state, community, etc., governed by holy men.

Hag·i·og·ra·pha (ˌhægɪ'ɒgrəfə) *n.* the third of the three main parts into which the books of the Old Testament are divided in Jewish tradition (the other two parts being the Law and the Prophets), comprising Psalms, Proverbs, Job, the Song of Solomon, Ruth, Lamentations, Ecclesiastes, Esther, Daniel, Ezra, Nehemiah, and Chronicles. Also called: **Writings.**

hag·i·og·ra·pher (ˌhægɪ'ɒgrəfə) *or* **hag·i·og·ra·phist** *n.* **1.** a person who writes about the lives of the saints. **2.** one of the writers of the Hagiographa.

hag·i·og·ra·phy (ˌhægɪ'ɒgrəfɪ) *n., pl.* **·phies. 1.** the writing of the lives of the saints. **2.** biography of the saints. **3.** any biography that idealizes or idolizes its subject. —**hag·i·o·graph·ic** (ˌhægɪə'græfɪk) *or* ˌ**hag·i·o·'graph·i·cal** *adj.*

hag·i·ol·a·try (ˌhægɪ'ɒlətrɪ) *n.* worship or veneration of saints. —ˌ**hag·i·'ol·a·ter** *n.* —ˌ**hag·i·'ol·a·trous** *adj.*

hag·i·ol·o·gy (ˌhægɪ'ɒlədʒɪ) *n., pl.* **·gies. 1.** literature concerned with the lives and legends of saints. **2. a.** a biography of a saint. **b.** a collection of such biographies. **3.** an authoritative canon of saints. **4.** a history of sacred writings. —**hag·i·o·log·ic** (ˌhægɪə'lɒdʒɪk) *or* ˌ**hag·i·o·'log·i·cal** *adj.* —ˌ**hag·i·'ol·o·gist** *n.*

hag·i·o·scope ('hægɪəˌskəʊp) *n. Architect.* another name for **squint** (sense 6). —**hag·i·o·scop·ic** (ˌhægɪə'skɒpɪk) *adj.*

hag·rid·den *adj.* **1.** tormented or worried, as if by a witch. **2.** *Facetious.* (of a man) harassed by women.

Hague (heɪg) *n.* **The.** the seat of government of the Netherlands and capital of South Holland province, situated about 3 km (2 miles) from the North Sea. Pop.: 488 788 (1974 est.). Dutch names: **'s Gravenhage, Den Haag.**

Hague Tri·bu·nal *n.* a tribunal of judges at The Hague, founded in 1899 to provide a panel of arbitrators for international disputes. It also chooses nominees for election by the United Nations to the International Court of Justice. Official name: **Permanent Court of Arbitration.**

hah (hɑː) *interj.* a variant spelling of **ha.**

ha-ha[1] *or* **haw-haw** *interj.* **1.** a representation of the sound of laughter. **2.** an exclamation expressing derision, mockery, surprise, etc.

ha-ha[2] *or* **haw-haw** *n.* a sunken fence bordering a garden or park, that allows uninterrupted views from within. [C18: from French *haha*, probably based on *ha!* ejaculation denoting surprise]

Hahn (*German* haːn) *n.* **Ot·to** ('ɔto). 1879–1968, German physicist: discovered the radioactive element protactinium with Meitner (1917); with Strassmann, demonstrated the nuclear fission of uranium, when it is bombarded with neutrons: Nobel prize for chemistry 1944.

Hah·ne·mann (*German* 'haːnəˌman) *n.* **(Christian Friedrich) Sa·mu·el** ('zaːmuɛl). 1755–1843, German physician; founder of homeopathy.

Hai·da ('haɪdə) *n.* **1.** (*pl.* **·das** *or* **·da**) a member of a seafaring group of North American Indian peoples inhabiting the coast of British Columbia and SW Alaska. **2.** the language of these peoples, belonging to the Na-Dene phylum. —'**Hai·dan** *adj.*

Hai·dar A·li ('haɪdər 'ɑːlɪ) *n.* a variant spelling of **Hyder Ali.**

Hai·duk, Hey·duck, *or* **Hei·duc** ('haɪdʊk) *n.* a rural brigand in the European part of the Ottoman Empire. [C17: from Hungarian *hajdúk* brigands]

Hai·fa ('haɪfə) *n.* a port in NW Israel, near Mount Carmel, on the Bay of Acre: Israel's chief port, with an oil refinery and other heavy industry. Pop.: 225 000 (1974 est.).

Haig (heɪg) *n.* **Doug·las,** 1st Earl Haig. 1861–1928, British field marshal; commander in chief of the British forces in France and Flanders (1915–18).

haik *or* **haick** (haɪk, heɪk) *n.* an outer garment of cotton, wool, or silk, for the head and body. [C18: from Arabic *hā'ik*]

hai·ku ('haɪkuː) *or* **hok·ku** *n., pl.* **·ku.** an epigrammatic Japanese verse form in 17 syllables. [from Japanese, from *hai* amusement + *ku* verse]

hail[1] (heɪl) *n.* **1.** small pellets of ice falling from cumulonimbus clouds when there are very strong rising air currents. **2.** a shower or storm of such pellets. **3.** words, ideas, etc., directed with force and in great quantity: *a hail of abuse.* **4.** a collection of objects, esp. bullets, spears, etc., directed at someone with violent force. ~*vb.* **5.** (*intr.*; with *it* as subject) to be the case that hail is falling. **6.** (often with *it* as subject) to fall or cause to fall as or like hail: *to hail criticism; bad language hailed about him.* [Old English *hægl*; related to Old Frisian *heil*, Old High German *hagal* hail, Greek *kakhlēx* pebble]

hail[2] (heɪl) *vb.* (*mainly tr.*) **1.** to greet, esp. enthusiastically: *the crowd hailed the actress with joy.* **2.** to acclaim or acknowledge: *they hailed him as their hero.* **3.** to attract the attention of by shouting or gesturing: *to hail a taxi; to hail a passing ship.* **4.** (*intr.*; foll. by *from*) to be a native of; originate in: *she hails from India.* ~*n.* **5.** the act or an instance of hailing. **6.** a shout or greeting. **7.** distance across which one can attract attention (esp. in the phrase **within hail**). ~*interj.* **8.** *Poetic.* an exclamation of greeting. [C12: from Old Norse *heill* WHOLE; see HALE[1], WASSAIL] —'**hail·er** *n.*

Hai·le Se·las·sie ('haɪlɪ sə'læsɪ) *n.* title of *Ras Tafari Makonnen.* 1892–1975, emperor of Ethiopia (1930–36; 1941–74). During the Italian occupation of Ethiopia (1936–41), he lived in exile in England. He was a prominent figure in the Pan-African movement: deposed 1974.

hail-fel·low-well-met *adj.* genial and familiar, esp. in an offensive or ingratiating way: *a hail-fellow-well-met slap on the back.*

Hail Mar·y *n.* another term for the **Ave Maria.**

hail·stone ('heɪlˌstəʊn) *n.* a pellet of hail.

hail·storm ('heɪlˌstɔːm) *n.* a storm during which hail falls.

Hail·wood ('heɪlwʊd) *n.* **Mike.** 1940–81, English racing motorcyclist: world champion (250 cc.) 1961 and 1966–67; (350 cc.) 1966–67; and (500 cc.) 1962–65.

Hai·nan ('haɪ'næn) *or* **Hai·nan Tao** (taʊ) *n.* an island in the South China Sea, separated from the mainland of S China by **Hainan Strait:** administratively part of Kwantung province; China's second largest offshore island. Pop.: 2 700 000 (1956 est.). Area: 33 991 sq. km (13 124 sq. miles).

Hai·naut *or* **Hai·nault** (*French* ɛ'no) *n.* a province of SW Belgium: stretches from the Flanders Plain in the north to the Ardennes in the south; coal mines. Capital: Mons. Pop.: 1 321 846 (1975 est.). Area: 3797 sq. km (1466 sq. miles).

hain't (heɪnt) *Archaic or dialect. contraction of* has not, have not, *or* is not.

Hai·phong ('haɪ'fɒŋ) *n.* a port in N Vietnam, on the Red River delta: a major industrial centre. Pop.: 1 190 900 (1976 est.).

hair (hɛə) *n.* **1.** any of the threadlike pigmented structures that grow from follicles beneath the skin of mammals and consist of layers of dead keratinized cells. **2.** a growth of such structures, as on the human head or animal body, which helps prevent heat loss from the body. **3.** *Botany.* any threadlike outgrowth from the epidermis, such as a root hair. **4. a.** a fabric or material made from the hair of some animals. **b.** (*as modifier*): *a hair carpet; a hair shirt.* **5.** another word for **hair's-breadth:** *to lose by a hair.* **6. get in someone's hair.** *Informal.* to annoy someone persistently. **7. hair of the dog (that bit one).** an alcoholic drink taken as an antidote to a hangover. **8. keep your hair on!** *Brit. informal.* keep calm. **9. let one's hair down.** to behave without reserve. **10. not turn a hair.** to show no surprise, anger, fear, etc. **11. split hairs.** to make petty and unnecessary distinctions. [Old English *hær*; related to Old Norse *hār*, Old High German *hār* hair, Norwegian *herren* stiff, hard, Lettish *sari* bristles, Latin *crescere* to grow] —'**hair·less** *adj.* —'**hair·**ˌ**like** *adj.*

hair·ball ('hɛəˌbɔːl) *n.* a compact mass of hair that forms in the stomach of cats, calves, etc., as a result of licking and swallowing the fur, and causes indigestion and convulsions.

hair·brush ('hɛəˌbrʌʃ) *n.* a brush for grooming the hair.

hair·cloth ('hɛəˌklɒθ) *n.* a cloth woven from horsehair, used in upholstery, etc.

hair·cut ('hɛəˌkʌt) *n.* **1.** the act or an instance of cutting the hair. **2.** the style in which hair has been cut.

hair·do ('hɛəˌduː) *n., pl.* **·dos.** the arrangement of a woman's hair, esp. after styling and setting.

hair·dress·er ('hɛəˌdrɛsə) *n.* **1.** a person whose business is cutting, curling, colouring and arranging hair, esp. that of women. **2.** a hairdresser's establishment. ~Related· adj.: **tonsorial.** —'**hair·**ˌ**dress·ing** *n.*

-haired *adj.* having hair as specified: *long-haired.*

hair fol·li·cle *n.* a narrow tubular cavity that contains the root of a hair, formed by an infolding of the epidermis and corium of the skin.

hair grass *n.* any grass of the genera *Aira, Deschampsia,* etc., having very narrow stems and leaves.

hair·grip ('hɛəˌgrɪp) *n. Chiefly Brit.* a small tightly bent metal hair clip. Also called (esp. U.S.): **bobby pin.**

hair·if ('hɛərɪf) *n.* another name for **cleavers.**

hair·line ('hɛəˌlaɪn) *n.* **1.** the natural margin formed by hair on the head. **2. a.** a very narrow line. **b.** (*as modifier*): *a hairline crack.* **3.** *Printing.* **a.** a thin stroke in a typeface. **b.** any typeface consisting of such strokes. **c.** thin lines beside a character, produced by worn or poorly cast type. **4.** a rope or line of hair.

hair·net ('hɛəˌnɛt) *n.* any of several kinds of light netting worn over the hair to keep it in place.

hair·piece ('hɛəˌpiːs) *n.* **1.** a wig or toupee. **2.** Also called: **postiche.** a section of extra hair attached to a woman's real hair to give it greater bulk or length.

hair·pin ('hɛəˌpɪn) *n.* **1.** a thin double-pronged pin used by women to fasten the hair. **2.** (*modifier*) (esp. of a bend in a road) curving very sharply.

hair-rais·ing *adj.* inspiring horror; terrifying: *a hair-raising drop of 600 feet.* —'**hair-**ˌ**rais·er** *n.*

hair re·stor·er *n.* a lotion claimed to promote hair growth.

hair's-breadth *n.* **a.** a very short or imperceptible margin or distance. **b.** (*as modifier*): *a hair's-breadth escape.*

hair seal *n.* any earless seal, esp. the harbour seal, having a coat of stiff hair with no underfur.

hair sheep *n.* any variety of sheep growing hair instead of wool, yielding hides with a finer and tougher grain than those of wool sheep.

hair slide *n.* a hinged clip with a tortoiseshell, bone, or similar back, used to fasten a girl's hair.

hair space *n. Printing.* the thinnest of the metal spaces used in setting type to separate letters or words.

hair·split·ting ('hɛəˌsplɪtɪŋ) *n.* **1.** the making of petty distinctions. ~*adj.* **2.** occupied with or based on petty distinctions. —**'hair·ˌsplit·ter** *n.*

hair·spring ('hɛəˌsprɪŋ) *n. Horology.* a very fine spiral spring in a timepiece, used to regulate the balance wheel.

hair·streak ('hɛəˌstriːk) *n.* any small butterfly of the genus *Callophrys* and related genera, having fringed wings marked with narrow white streaks: family *Lycaenidae.*

hair stroke *n.* a very fine line in a written character.

hair·style ('hɛəˌstaɪl) *n.* a particular mode of arranging, cutting, or setting the hair. —**'hair·ˌstyl·ist** *n.*

hair·tail ('hɛəˌteɪl) *n.* any marine spiny-finned fish of the family *Trichiuridae,* most common in warm seas, having a long whiplike scaleless body and long sharp teeth. Usual U.S. name: **cutlass fish.**

hair trig·ger *n.* **1.** a trigger of a firearm that responds to very slight pressure. **2.** *Informal.* **a.** any mechanism, reaction, etc., set in operation by slight provocation. **b.** (*as modifier*): *a hair-trigger temper.*

hair·weav·ing ('hɛəˌwiːvɪŋ) *n.* the interweaving of false hair with the hair on a balding person's head.

hair·worm ('hɛəˌwɜːm) *n.* **1.** any hairlike nematode worm of the family *Trichostrongylidae,* such as the stomach worm, parasitic in the intestines of vertebrates. **2.** Also called: **horsehair worm.** any very thin long worm of the phylum (or class) *Nematomorpha,* the larvae of which are parasitic in arthropods.

hair·y ('hɛərɪ) *adj.* **hair·i·er, hair·i·est. 1.** having or covered with hair. **2.** *Slang.* **a.** difficult or problematic. **b.** scaring, dangerous, or exciting. —**'hair·i·ness** *n.*

hair·y frog *n.* a W African frog, *Astylosternus robustus,* the males of which have glandular hairlike processes on the flanks.

hair·y wil·low·herb *n.* another name for **codlins-and-cream.**

Hai·ti ('heɪtɪ, hɑː'iːtɪ) *n.* **1.** a republic occupying the W part of the island of Hispaniola in the Caribbean, the E part consisting of the Dominican Republic: ceded by Spain to France in 1697 and became one of the richest colonial possessions in the world, with numerous plantations; slaves rebelled under Toussaint L'Ouverture in 1793 and defeated the French; taken over by the U.S. (1915–41) after long political and economic chaos; under the authoritarian regime of François Duvalier (1957–71). Official language: French; Haitian creole is the common spoken language. Religions: Roman Catholic and voodoo. Currency: gourde. Capital: Port-au-Prince. Pop.: 4 314 628 (1971). Area: 27 749 sq. km (10 714 sq. miles). **2.** a former name for **Hispaniola.**

Hai·tian or **Hay·tian** ('heɪʃɪən, hɑː'iːʃən) *adj.* **1.** relating to or characteristic of Haiti, its inhabitants, or their language. ~*n.* **2.** a native, citizen, or inhabitant of Haiti. **3.** the creolized French spoken in Haiti.

Hai·tink ('haɪtɪŋk) *n.* Sir **Bern·ard.** born 1929, Dutch orchestral conductor.

hajj or **hadj** (hædʒ) *n., pl.* **hajj·es** or **hadj·es.** the pilgrimage to Mecca that every Muslim is required to make at least once in his life. [from Arabic *hajj* pilgrimage]

haj·ji, hadj·i, or **haj·i** ('hædʒɪ) *n., pl.* **haj·jis, hadj·is,** or **haj·is. 1.** a Muslim who has made a pilgrimage to Mecca: also used as a title. **2.** a Christian of the Greek Orthodox or Armenian Churches who has visited Jerusalem.

hake[1] (heɪk) *n., pl.* **hake** or **hakes. 1.** any gadoid food fish of the genus *Merluccius,* such as *M. merluccius* (European hake), of the N hemisphere, having an elongated body with a large head and two dorsal fins. **2.** any North American fish of the genus *Urophycis,* similar and related to *Merluccius* species. **3.** *Austral.* another name for **barracouta.** [C15: perhaps from Old Norse *haki* hook; compare Old English *hacod* pike; see HOOK]

hake[2] (heɪk) *n.* a wooden frame for drying cheese or fish. [C18: variant of HECK[2]]

ha·ke·a ('hɑːkɪə, 'heɪkɪə) *n.* any shrub or tree of the Australian genus *Hakea,* having a hard woody fruit and often yielding a useful wood: family *Proteaceae.*

Ha·ken·kreuz *German* ('hɑːkənˌkrɔɪts) *n.* the swastika. [literally: hooked cross]

ha·kim or **ha·keem** (hɑː'kiːm, 'hɑːkiːm) *n.* **1.** a Muslim judge, ruler, or administrator. **2.** a Muslim physician. [C17: from Arabic, from *hakama* to rule]

Hak·luyt ('hækluːt) *n.* **Rich·ard.** ?1552–1616, English geographer, who compiled *The Principal Navigations, Voyages, and Discoveries of the English Nation* (1589).

Ha·ko·da·te (ˌhɑːkəʊ'dɑːteɪ) *n.* a port in N Japan, on S Hokkaido: fishing industry and shipbuilding. Pop.: 241 663 (1970).

hal- *combining form.* variant of **halo-** before a vowel.

Ha·la·fi·an (hə'lɑːfɪən) *adj.* of or relating to the Neolithic culture extending from Iran to the Mediterranean.

Ḥa·la·kah or **Ha·la·cha** (ˌhɑːlə'kɑː, hə'lɑːkə; *Hebrew* hala'ka) *n.* that part of traditional Jewish literature concerned with the law, as contrasted with Haggadah. [C19: from Hebrew *hălākhāh* way, from *hālakh* to go] —**Ha·lak·ic** or **Ha·lach·ic** (hə'lækɪk) *adj.*

hal·al or **hall·al** (hɑː'lɑːl) *vb.* **1.** (*tr.*) to kill (animals) following Muslim law. ~*n.* **2.** meat killed in this way. [from Arabic: lawful]

ha·la·tion (hə'leɪʃən) *n. Photog.* fogging usually seen as a bright ring surrounding a source of light: caused by reflection from the back of the film. [C19: from HALO + -ATION]

hal·berd ('hælbəd) or **hal·bert** *n.* a spear fitted with an axe head, used in 15th- and 16th-century warfare. [C15: from Old French *hallebarde,* from Middle High German *helm* handle, HELM[1] + *barde* axe, from Old High German *bart* BEARD] —ˌ**hal·ber·'dier** *n.*

hal·cy·on ('hælsɪən) *adj.* also **hal·cy·o·ni·an** (ˌhælsɪ'əʊnɪən) or **hal·cy·on·ic** (ˌhælsɪ'ɒnɪk). **1.** peaceful, gentle, and calm. **2.** happy and carefree. ~*n.* **3.** *Greek myth.* a fabulous bird associated with the winter solstice. **4.** a poetic name for the **kingfisher. 5. halcyon days.** a fortnight of calm weather during the winter solstice. [C14: from Latin *alcyon,* from Greek *alkuōn* kingfisher, of uncertain origin]

Hal·cy·o·ne (hæl'saɪənɪ) *n.* a variant spelling of **Alcyone**[1].

Hal·dane ('hɔːldeɪn) *n.* **1. J(ohn) B(urdon) S(anderson).** 1892–1964, Scottish biochemist, geneticist, and writer on science. **2.** his father, **John Scott.** 1860–1936, Scottish physiologist, noted particularly for his research into industrial diseases. **3. Rich·ard Bur·don,** 1st Viscount Haldane of Cloan. 1856–1928, British statesman and jurist. As secretary of state for war (1905–12) he reorganized the army and set up the territorial reserve.

hale[1] (heɪl) *adj.* **1.** healthy and robust (esp. in the phrase **hale and hearty**). **2.** *Scot. and northern English dialect.* whole. [Old English *hæl* WHOLE] —**'hale·ness** *n.*

hale[2] (heɪl) *vb.* (*tr.*) **1.** to pull or drag; haul. **2.** *Rare.* to compel. [C13: from Old French *haler,* of Germanic origin; compare Old High German *halōn* to fetch, Old English *geholian* to acquire] —**'hal·er** *n.*

Hale (heɪl) *n.* **1. George El·ler·y.** 1868–1938, U.S. astronomer: undertook research into sunspots and invented the spectroheliograph. **2.** Sir **Mat·thew.** 1609–76, English judge and scholar; Lord Chief Justice (1671–76).

Ha·le·a·ka·la (ˌhɑːliːˌɑːkɑː'lɑː) *n.* a volcano in Hawaii, on E Mani Island. Height: 3057 m (10 032 ft.). Area of crater: 49 sq. km (19 sq. miles). Depth of crater: 829 m (2720 ft.).

ha·ler ('hɑːlə) *n., pl.* **·lers** or **·le·ru** (-ləˌruː). a Czech monetary unit worth one hundredth of a koruna. Also called: **heller.** [Czech, from Middle High German *haller* a silver coin, after *Hall,* Swabian town where the coins were minted]

Hales·ow·en (heɪlz'əʊɪn) *n.* a town in W central England, in the SW West Midlands. Pop.: 53 933 (1971).

Ha·lé·vy (*French* ale'vi) *n.* **Lu·do·vic** (lydɔ'vik). 1834–1908, French dramatist and novelist, who collaborated with Meilhac on opera libretti.

half (hɑːf) *n., pl.* **halves** (hɑːvz). **1. a.** either of two equal or corresponding parts that together comprise a whole. **b.** a quantity equalling such a part: *half a dozen.* **2.** half a pint, esp. of beer. **3.** *Football, hockey, etc.* the half of the pitch regarded as belonging to one team. **4.** *Golf.* an equal score on a hole or round with an opponent. **5.** (in various games) either of two periods of play separated by an interval (the **first half** and **second half**). **6.** a half-price ticket on a bus, etc. **7.** short for **half-hour. 8.** *Sport.* short for **halfback. 9.** *Obsolete.* a half-year period. **10. better half.** *Informal.* a person's wife or husband. **11. by halves.** (*used with a negative*) without being thorough or exhaustive: *we don't do things by halves.* **12. go halves.** (often foll. by *on, in,* etc.) **a.** to share the expenses (of something with one other person). **b.** to share the whole amount (of something with another person): *to go halves on an orange.* ~*determiner.* **13. a.** being a half or approximately a half: *half the kingdom.* **b.** (*as pronoun; functioning as sing. or pl.*): *half of them came.* ~*adj.* **14.** not perfect or complete; partial: *he only did a half job on it.* ~*adv.* **15.** to the amount or extent of a half. **16.** to a great amount or extent. **17.** partially; to an extent. **18. by half.** by an excessive amount or to an excessive degree: *he's too arrogant by half.* **19. half two, etc.** *Informal.* 30 minutes after two o'clock. **20. have half a mind to.** to have the intention of. **21. not half.** *Informal.* **a.** not in any way: *he's not half clever enough.* **b.** *Brit.* really; very; indeed: *he isn't half stupid.* ~ **c.** *sentence substitute.* certainly; yes, indeed. [Old English *healf;* related to Old Norse *halfr,* Old High German *halb,* Dutch *half*]

half-a-crown *n.* another name for a **half-crown.**

half-a-dol·lar *n. Brit. slang.* another name for a **half-crown.**

half-and-half *n.* **1.** a mixture of half one thing and half another thing. **2.** a drink consisting of equal parts of beer (or ale) and porter. ~*adj.* **3.** of half one thing and half another thing. ~*adv.* **4.** in two equal parts.

half-assed *adj. U.S. slang.* **1.** incompetent; inept. **2.** lacking efficiency or organization.

half·back ('hɑːfˌbæk) *n.* **1.** *Soccer.* any of three players positioned behind the line of forwards and in front of the fullbacks. **2.** *Rugby.* either the scrum half or the stand-off half. **3.** any of certain similar players in other team sports. **4.** the position of a player who is halfback.

half-baked *adj.* **1.** insufficiently baked. **2.** *Informal.* foolish; stupid. **3.** *Informal.* poorly planned or conceived.

half-ball *n.* **a.** a contact in billiards, etc., in which the player aims through the centre of the cue ball to the edge of the object ball, so that half the object ball is covered. **b.** (*as modifier*): *a half-ball stroke.*

half·beak ('hɑːfˌbiːk) *n.* any marine and freshwater teleost fish of the tropical and subtropical family *Hemiramphidae,* having an elongated body with a short upper jaw and a long protruding lower jaw.

half-bind·ing *n.* a type of bookbinding in which the backs are bound in one material and the sides in another.

ˌhalf-a-'fraid *adj.*
ˌhalf-a-'live *adj.*
ˌhalf-'an·gli·ˌcized or ˌhalf-'an·gli·ˌcised *adj.*
ˌhalf-a-'shamed *adj.*
ˌhalf-a-'sleep *adj.*
ˌhalf-a-'wake *adj.*
ˌhalf-'bar·rel *n.*

half-blood *n.* **1. a.** the relationship between individuals having only one parent in common. **b.** an individual having such a relationship. **2.** a less common name for a **half-breed. 3.** a half-blooded domestic animal.

half-blood·ed *adj.* **1.** being related to another individual through only one parent. **2.** having parents of different races. **3.** (of a domestic animal) having only one parent of known pedigree.

half-blue *n. Brit.* (at Oxford and Cambridge universities) a sportsman who substitutes for a full blue or who represents the university in a minor sport. Compare **blue.**

half-board *n.* a manoeuvre by a sailing ship enabling it to gain distance to windward by luffing up into the wind.

half board *n.* **a.** the daily provision by a hotel of bed, breakfast, and one main meal. **b.** (*as modifier*): *half-board accommodation.* Also called: **demi-pension.**

half-boot *n.* a boot reaching to the midcalf.

half-bound *adj.* (of a book) having a half-binding.

half-breed *n.* **1.** a person whose parents are of different races, esp. the offspring of a White person and an American Indian. ~*adj. also* **half-bred. 2.** of, relating to, or designating offspring of people or animals of different races or breeds.

half-broth·er *n.* the son of either of one's parents by another partner.

half-butt *n.* a cue of length between that of a long butt and an ordinary cue.

half-caste *n.* **1.** a person having parents of different races, esp. the offspring of a European and an Indian. ~*adj.* **2.** of, relating to, or designating such a person.

half-cock *n.* **1.** the halfway position of a firearm's hammer when the trigger is fixed and cannot be pulled. **2. go off at half-cock** *or* **half-cocked. a.** to fail as a result of inadequate preparation or premature starting. **b.** to act or function prematurely.

half-cocked *adj.* (of a firearm) at half-cock.

half-crown *n.* a British silver or cupronickel coin worth two shillings and sixpence (now equivalent to 12½ p), taken out of circulation in 1970. Also called: **half-a-crown.**

half-dead *adj. Brit. informal.* very tired.

half-dol·lar *n.* (in the U.S. and Canada) a 50-cent piece.

half ea·gle *n.* a former U.S. gold coin worth five dollars.

half-for+ward *n. Australian Rules football.* any of three forwards positioned between the centre line and the forward line.

half frame *n.* **a.** a photograph taking up half the normal area of a frame on a particular film, taken esp. on 35 millimetre film. **b.** (*as modifier*): *a half-frame camera.*

half gain+er *n.* a type of dive in which the diver completes a half backward somersault to enter the water headfirst facing the diving board. Compare **gainer.**

half-har·dy *adj.* (of a cultivated plant) able to survive out of doors except during severe frost.

half-heart·ed *adj.* without enthusiasm or determination. —ˌ**half-ˈheart·ed+ly** *adv.* —ˌ**half-ˈheart·ed+ness** *n.*

half-hitch *n.* a knot made by passing the end of a piece of rope around itself and through the loop thus made.

half hol·i·day *n.* a day of which either the morning or the afternoon is a holiday.

half-hour *n.* **1. a.** a period of 30 minutes. **b.** (*as modifier*): *a half-hour stint.* **2. a.** the point of time 30 minutes after the beginning of an hour. **b.** (*as modifier*): *a half-hour chime.* —ˌ**half-ˈhour·ly** *adv., adj.*

half-hunt·er *n.* a watch with a hinged lid in which a small circular opening or crystal allows the approximate time to be read. See **hunter** (sense 5).

half-jack *n. S African informal.* a flat pocket-sized bottle of alcohol. [C20: *jack,* probably from C16 *jack* a leather-covered vessel, from Old French *jaque,* of uncertain origin]

half land+ing *n.* a landing halfway up a flight of stairs.

half-leath·er *n.* a type of half-binding in which the backs and corners of a book are bound in leather.

half-length *adj.* **1.** (of a portrait) showing only the body from the waist up and including the hands. **2.** of half the entire or original length. ~*n.* **3.** a half-length portrait.

half-life *n.* **1.** the time taken for half of the atoms in a radioactive material to undergo decay. Symbol: τ. **2.** the time required for half of a quantity of radioactive material absorbed by a living tissue or organism to be naturally eliminated (**biological half-life**) or removed by both elimination and decay (**effective half-life**).

half-light *n.* a dim light, as at dawn or dusk.

half-mast *n.* **1.** the halfway position to which a flag is lowered on a mast to mourn the dead or signal distress. ~*vb.* **2.** (*tr.*) to put (a flag) in this position.

half meas+ure *n.* (*often pl.*) an inadequate measure.

half-mil·er *n.* a runner who specializes in running races over half a mile.

half-moon *n.* **1.** the moon at first or last quarter when half its face is illuminated. **2.** the time at which a half-moon occurs. **3. a.** something shaped like a half-moon. **b.** (*as modifier*): *half-moon spectacles.* **4.** *Anatomy.* a nontechnical name for **lunula.**

half-mourn·ing *n.* dark grey clothes worn by some during a period after full formal mourning.

half-nel·son *n.* a wrestling hold in which a wrestler places an arm under one of his opponent's arms from behind and exerts pressure with his palm on the back of his opponent's neck. Compare **full nelson.**

half-note *n.* the usual U.S. name for **minim** (sense 2).

half+pen·ny (ˈheɪpnɪ) *n.* **1.** (*pl.* **+pen·nies.**) a small British coin worth half a new penny. **2.** (*pl.* **+pen·nies.**) an old British coin worth half an old penny. **3.** (*pl.* **+pence.**) the sum represented by half a penny. **4.** (*pl.* **+pence**) something of negligible value. **5.** (*modifier*) having the value or price of a halfpenny. **6.** (*modifier*) of negligible value. —**half+pen·ny+worth** (ˈheɪpəθ) *n.*

half-pint *n. Slang.* a small or insignificant person.

half-plate *n. Photography.* a size of plate measuring 16.5 cm by 10.8 cm.

half-price *adj., adv.* for half the normal price: *children go half-price.*

half-quar·tern *n. Brit.* a loaf having a weight, when baked, of 800 g.

half-rhyme *n.* a rhyme in which the vowel sounds are not identical, such as *years* and *yours.* See **consonance** (sense 2).

half seas o·ver *adj. Brit. informal.* drunk.

half-sis·ter *n.* the daughter of either of one's parents by another partner.

half-size *n.* any size, esp. in clothing, that is halfway between two sizes.

half-slip *n.* a woman's topless slip that hangs from the waist. Also called: **waist-slip.**

half-sole *n.* **1.** a sole from the shank of a shoe to the toe. ~*vb.* **2.** (*tr.*) to replace the half-sole of a shoe.

half-step *n. Music, U.S.* another word for **semitone.**

half term *n. Brit. education.* a short holiday midway through an academic term.

half-tide *n.* the state of the tide between flood and ebb.

half-tim·bered *or* **half-tim·ber** *adj.* (of a building, wall, etc.) having an exposed timber framework filled with brick, stone, or plastered laths, as in Tudor architecture. —ˌ**half-ˈtim·ber+ing** *n.*

half-time *n. Sport.* a rest period between the two halves of a game.

half-ti·tle *n.* **1.** the short title of a book as printed on the right-hand page preceding the title page. **2.** a title on a separate page preceding a section of a book.

half+tone (ˈhɑːfˌtəʊn) *n.* **1. a.** a process used to reproduce an illustration by photographing it through a fine screen to break it up into dots. **b.** the etched plate thus obtained. **c.** the print obtained from such a plate. **2.** *Arts.* a tonal value midway between highlight and dark shading. ~*adj.* **3.** relating to, used in, or made by halftone.

half-track *n.* a vehicle with caterpillar tracks on the wheels that supply motive power only. —ˈ**half-ˌtracked** *adj.*

ˌ**half-ˈbeg·ging** *adj.*
ˌ**half-be·ˈgun** *adj.*
ˌ**half-ˈbent** *adj.*
ˌ**half-ˈblind** *adj.*
ˌ**half-ˈbur·ied** *adj.*
ˌ**half-ˈcen·tu·ry** *n., pl.* **-ies.**
ˌ**half-ˈciv·il·ly** *adv.*
ˌ**half-ˈciv·il·ˌized** *or* ˌ**half-ˈciv·il·ˌised** *adj.*
ˌ**half-ˈclad** *adj.*
ˌ**half-ˈclosed** *adj.*
ˌ**half-ˈclothed** *adj.*
ˌ**half-com·ˈplet·ed** *adj.*
ˌ**half-con·ˈcealed** *adj.*
ˌ**half-ˈcon·scious** *adj.*
ˌ**half-ˈcon·scious+ly** *adv.*
ˌ**half-con·ˈsumed** *adj.*
ˌ**half-con·ˈvinced** *adj.*
ˌ**half-con·ˈvinc·ing** *adj.*
ˌ**half-con·ˈvinc+ing+ly** *adv.*
ˌ**half-ˈcooked** *adj.*
ˌ**half-ˈcov·ered** *adj.*
ˌ**half-ˈcra·zy** *adj.*
ˌ**half-ˈday** *n.*
ˌ**half-ˈdazed** *adj.*
ˌ**half-ˈdaz·ed·ly** *adv.*
ˌ**half-ˈdeaf** *adj.*
ˌ**half-ˈdeaf·ened** *adj.*
ˌ**half-de·ˈment+ed** *adj.*
ˌ**half-de·ˈsert+ed** *adj.*
ˌ**half-de·ˈvel·oped** *adj.*
ˌ**half-di·ˈgest+ed** *adj.*
ˌ**half-ˈdone** *adj.*
ˌ**half-ˈdressed** *adj.*
ˌ**half-ˈdried** *adj.*
ˌ**half-ˈdrowned** *adj.*
ˌ**half-ˈdrunk** *adj.*
ˌ**half-ˈeat·en** *adj.*
ˌ**half-ˈed·u·ˌcat+ed** *adj.*
ˌ**half-ˈEng·lish** *adj.*
ˌ**half-ex·ˈpect+ant** *adj.*
ˌ**half-ex·ˈpect+ant+ly** *adv.*
ˌ**half-ˈfam·ished** *adj.*
ˌ**half-ˈfilled** *adj.*
ˌ**half-ˈfin·ished** *adj.*
ˌ**half-for·ˈgot+ten** *adj.*
ˌ**half-ˈformed** *adj.*
ˌ**half-ˈfro·zen** *adj.*
ˌ**half-ful·ˈfilled** *adj.*
ˌ**half-ˈfull** *adj.*
ˌ**half-ˈgrown** *adj.*
ˌ**half-ˈheard** *adj.*
ˌ**half-ˈhu·man** *adj.*
ˌ**half-in·ˈclined** *adj.*
ˌ**half-in·ˈformed** *adj.*
ˌ**half-in·ˈstinc+tive** *adj.*
ˌ**half-in·ˈstinc+tive+ly** *adv.*
ˌ**half-in·ˈtox·i·ˌcat+ed** *adj.*
ˌ**half-ˈjok·ing** *adj.*
ˌ**half-ˈjok·ing+ly** *adv.*
ˌ**half-ˈlearned** *adj.*
ˌ**half-ˈlie** *n.*
ˌ**half-ˈmad** *adj.*
ˌ**half-ˈmeant** *adj.*
ˌ**half-ˈmonth·ly** *adj., adv.*
ˌ**half-ˈna·ked** *adj.*
ˌ**half-ob·ˈlit·er+ˌat+ed** *adj.*
ˌ**half-ˈo·pen** *adj.*
ˌ**half-ˈpa·gan** *adj., n.*
ˌ**half-ˈpet·ri+ˌfied** *adj.*
ˌ**half-ˈplay·ful** *adj.*
ˌ**half-ˈplay·ful+ly** *adv.*
ˌ**half-ˈpleased** *adj.*
ˌ**half-pro·ˈtest+ing** *adj.*
ˌ**half-ˈproved** *adj.*
ˌ**half-ˈprov·en** *adj.*
ˌ**half-ˈques·tion+ing** *adj.*
ˌ**half-ˈques·tion+ing+ly** *adv.*
ˌ**half-ˈraw** *adj.*
ˌ**half-re·ˈluc·tant** *adj.*
ˌ**half-re·ˈluc·tant+ly** *adv.*
ˌ**half-re·ˈmem·bered** *adj.*
ˌ**half-re·ˈpent+ant** *adj.*
ˌ**half-ˈright** *adj.*
ˌ**half-ˈrot·ted** *adj.*
ˌ**half-ˈrot·ten** *adj.*
ˌ**half-ˈru·ined** *adj.*
ˌ**half-ˈsav·age** *adj.*
ˌ**half-ˈsav·age+ly** *adv.*
ˌ**half-ˈseen** *adj.*
ˌ**half-ˈsensed** *adj.*
ˌ**half-ˈse·ri·ous** *adj.*
ˌ**half-ˈse·ri·ous+ly** *adv.*
ˌ**half-ˈshut** *adj.*
ˌ**half-ˈstarved** *adj.*
ˌ**half-ˈstat·ed** *adj.*

half-truth *n.* a partially true statement intended to mislead. —'**half-'true** *adj.*

half vol·ley *Sport.* ~*n.* **1.** a stroke or shot in which the ball is hit immediately after it bounces. ~*vb.* **half-vol·ley. 2.** to hit or kick (a ball) immediately after it bounces.

half·way (ˌhɑːfˈweɪ) *adv., adj.* **1.** at or to half the distance; at or to the middle. **2.** in or of an incomplete manner or nature. **3. meet halfway.** to compromise with.

half·way house *n.* **1.** a place to rest midway on a journey. **2.** the halfway point in any progression. **3.** a centre or hostel designed to facilitate the readjustment to private life of released prisoners, mental patients, etc.

half·wit (ˈhɑːfˌwɪt) *n.* **1.** a feeble-minded person. **2.** a foolish or inane person. —ˌ**half·'wit·ted** *adj.* —ˌ**half·'wit·ted·ly** *adv.* —ˌ**half·'wit·ted·ness** *n.*

hal·i·but (ˈhælɪbət) *or* **hol·i·but** (ˈhɒlɪbət) *n., pl.* **·buts** *or* **·but. 1.** the largest flatfish: a dark green North Atlantic species, *Hippoglossus hippoglossus,* that is a very important food fish: family *Pleuronectidae.* **2.** any of several similar and related flatfishes, such as *Reinhardtius hippoglossoides* (**Greenland halibut**). [C15: from *hali* HOLY (because it was eaten on holy days) + *butte* flat fish, from Middle Dutch *butte*]

Ha·liç (haˈliːtʃ) *n.* the Turkish name for the **Golden Horn.**

Hal·i·car·nas·sus (ˌhælɪkɑːˈnæsəs) *n.* a Greek colony on the SW coast of Asia Minor: one of the major Hellenistic cities. —ˌ**Hal·i·car·'nas·si·an** *adj.*

hal·ide (ˈhælaɪd) *or* **hal·id** (ˈhælɪd) *n.* **1.** any binary salt of a halogen acid; a chloride, bromide, iodide, or fluoride. **2.** any organic compound containing halogen atoms in its molecules.

hal·i·dom (ˈhælɪdəm) *n. Archaic.* a holy place or thing. [Old English *hāligdōm;* see HOLY, -DOM]

Hal·i·fax[1] (ˈhælɪˌfæks) *n.* **1.** a port in SE Canada, capital of Nova Scotia, on the Atlantic: founded in 1749 as a British stronghold. Pop.: 122 035 (1971). **2.** a town in N England, in West Yorkshire: textiles. Pop.: 91 171 (1971).

Hal·i·fax[2] (ˈhælɪˌfæks) *n.* **1. Charles Mon·ta·gu,** Earl of Halifax. 1661–1715, English statesman; founder of the National Debt (1692) and the Bank of England (1694). **2. Ed·ward Fred·er·ick Lind·ley Wood,** Earl of Halifax. 1881–1959, British Conservative statesman. He was viceroy of India (1926–31), foreign secretary (1938–40), and ambassador to the U.S. (1941–46).

hal·ite (ˈhælaɪt) *n.* a mineral consisting of sodium chloride in cubic crystalline form, occurring in sedimentary beds and dried salt lakes: an important source of table salt and other sodium compounds. Formula: NaCl. Also called: **rock salt.** [C19: from New Latin *halītes;* see HALO-, -ITE[2]]

hal·i·to·sis (ˌhælɪˈtəʊsɪs) *n.* the state or condition of having bad breath. [C19: New Latin, from Latin *hālitus* breath, from *hālāre* to breathe]

hall (hɔːl) *n.* **1.** a room serving as an entry area within a house or building. **2.** (*sometimes cap.*) a building for public meetings. **3.** (*often cap.*) the great house of an estate; manor. **4.** a large building or room used for assemblies, worship, concerts, dances, etc. **5.** a residential building in a university. **6. a.** a large room, esp. for dining, in a college or university. **b.** a meal eaten in this room. **7.** the large room of a house, castle, etc. **8.** *U.S.* a passage or corridor into which rooms open. **9.** (*often pl.*) *Informal.* short for **music hall.** [Old English *heall;* related to Old Norse *höll,* Old High German *halla* hall, Latin *cela* CELL, Old Irish *cuile* cellar, Sanskrit *śālā* hut; see HELL]

Hall (hɔːl) *n.* **1. Charles Mar·tin.** 1863–1914, U.S. chemist: discovered the electrolytic process for producing aluminium. **2.** Sir **John.** 1824–1907, New Zealand statesman, born in England: prime minister of New Zealand (1879–82). **3.** Sir **Pe·ter.** born 1930, English stage director: director of the Royal Shakespeare Company (1960–73) and of the National Theatre (since 1973).

hal·lah (ˈhɑːlə; *Hebrew* xaˈla) *n., pl.* **·lahs** *or* **·lot** (*Hebrew* -ˈlɔt). a variant spelling of **challah.**

Hal·le (*German* ˈhalə) *n.* a city in SW East Germany, on the River Saale: early saltworks; a Hanseatic city in the late Middle Ages; university (1694). Pop.: 239 181 (1975 est.). Official name: **Halle an der Saale** (an deːr zaːlə).

Hall ef·fect *n.* the production of a potential difference across a conductor carrying an electric current when a magnetic field is applied in a direction perpendicular to that of the current flow. [named after Edwin Herbert *Hall* (1855–1938), American physicist who discovered it]

Hal·lel (hɑːˈleɪl) *n. Judaism.* a liturgical chant of praise used at Passover and other Jewish festivals. [C18: from Hebrew *hallēl,* from *hellēl* to praise]

hal·le·lu·jah, hal·le·lu·iah (ˌhælɪˈluːjə), *or* **al·le·lu·ia** (ˌælɪˈluːjə) *interj.* **1.** an exclamation of praise to God. **2.** an expression of relief or a similar emotion. ~*n.* **3.** an exclamation of "Hallelujah." **4.** a musical composition that uses the word *Hallelujah* as its text. [C16: from Hebrew *hallelūyāh* praise the Lord, from *hellēl* to praise + *yāh* the Lord, YAHWEH]

Hal·ler (*German* ˈhalər) *n.* **Al·brecht von** (ˈalbrɛçt fɔn). 1708–77, Swiss biologist: founder of experimental physiology.

Hal·ley (ˈhælɪ) *n.* **Ed·mund.** 1656–1742, English astronomer and mathematician. He predicted the return of the comet now known as Halley's comet, constructed charts of magnetic declination, and produced the first wind maps.

Hal·ley's Com·et *n.* a comet revolving around the sun in a period of about 76 years and last seen in 1910.

hal·liard (ˈhæljəd) *n.* a variant spelling of **halyard.**

Hall-Jones (ˈhɔːl ˈdʒəʊnz) *n.* Sir **Wil·liam.** 1851–1936, New Zealand statesman, born in England: prime minister of New Zealand (1906).

hall·mark (ˈhɔːlˌmɑːk) *n.* **1.** *Brit.* an official series of marks stamped by the London Guild of Goldsmiths on gold, silver, or platinum articles to guarantee purity, date of manufacture, etc. **2.** a mark or sign of authenticity or excellence. **3.** an outstanding or distinguishing feature. ~*vb.* **4.** (*tr.*) to stamp with or as if with a hallmark. ~Also (for senses 1 and 4): **platemark.** [C18: named after Goldsmiths' *Hall* in London, where items were graded and stamped]

hal·lo (həˈləʊ) *interj., n.* **1.** a variant spelling of **hello.** ~*interj., n., vb.* **2.** a variant spelling of **halloo.**

Hall of Fame *n. Chiefly U.S.* **1.** (*sometimes not cap.*) a building containing plaques or busts honouring famous people. **2.** (*sometimes not cap.*) a group of famous people.

hall of res·i·dence *n.* a residential block in or attached to a university, polytechnic, college, etc.

hal·loo (həˈluː), **hal·lo,** *or* **hal·loa** (həˈləʊ) *sentence substitute.* **1.** a shout to attract attention, esp. to call hounds at a hunt. ~*n., pl.* **·loos, ·los,** *or* **·loas. 2.** a shout of "halloo." ~*vb.* **·loos, ·loo·ing, ·looed; ·los, ·lo·ing, ·loed,** *or* **·loas, ·loa·ing, ·loaed. 3.** to shout (something) to (someone). **4.** (*tr.*) to urge on or incite (dogs) with shouts. [C16: perhaps variant of *hallow* to encourage hounds by shouting]

hal·low (ˈhæləʊ) *vb.* (*tr.*) **1.** to consecrate or set apart as being holy. **2.** to venerate as being holy. [Old English *hālgian,* from *hālig* HOLY] —'**hal·low·er** *n.*

hal·lowed (ˈhæləʊd; *liturgical* ˈhæləʊɪd) *adj.* **1.** set apart as sacred. **2.** consecrated or holy. —'**hal·lowed·ness** *n.*

Hal·low·e'en *or* **Hal·low·een** (ˌhæləʊˈiːn) *n.* the eve of All Saints' Day celebrated on Oct. 31 by masquerading; Allhallows Eve. [C18: see ALLHALLOWS, EVEN[2]]

Hal·low·mas *or* **Hal·low·mass** (ˈhæləʊˌmæs) *n. Archaic.* the feast celebrating All Saints' Day. [C14: see ALLHALLOWS, MASS]

hall stand *or esp. U.S.* **hall tree** *n.* a piece of furniture for hanging coats, hats, etc., on.

Hall·statt (ˈhælstæt) *or* **Hall·stat·ti·an** (hælˈstætɪən) *adj.* of or relating to a late Bronze Age culture extending from central Europe to Britain and lasting from the 9th to the 5th century B.C., characterized by distinctive burial customs, bronze and iron tools, etc. [C19: named after *Hallstatt,* Austrian village where remains were found]

hal·lu·ci·nate (həˈluːsɪˌneɪt) *vb.* (*intr.*) to experience hallucinations. [C17: from Latin *ālūcinārī* to wander in mind; compare Greek *aluein* to be distraught] —**hal·'lu·ci·ˌna·tor** *n.*

hal·lu·ci·na·tion (həˌluːsɪˈneɪʃən) *n.* the alleged perception of an object when no object is present, occurring under hypnosis, in some mental disorders, etc. —**hal·ˌlu·ci·'na·tion·al, hal·'lu·ci·na·tive** *or* **hal·'lu·ci·na·to·ry** *adj.*

hal·lu·cin·o·gen (həˈluːsɪnəˌdʒɛn) *n.* any drug, such as LSD or mescaline, that induces hallucinations. —**hal·lu·ci·no·gen·ic** (həˌluːsɪnəʊˈdʒɛnɪk) *adj.*

hal·lu·ci·no·sis (həˌluːsɪˈnəʊsɪs) *n. Psychiatry.* a mental disorder the symptom of which is hallucinations, commonly associated with the ingestion of alcohol or other drugs.

hal·lux (ˈhæləks) *n.* the first digit on the hind foot of a mammal, bird, reptile, or amphibian; the big toe of man. [C19: New Latin, from Late Latin *allex* big toe]

hal·lux val·gus *n.* an abnormal bending or deviation of the big toe towards the other toes of the same foot.

hall·way (ˈhɔːlˌweɪ) *n. U.S.* a hall or corridor.

halm (hɔːm) *n.* a variant spelling of **haulm.**

hal·ma (ˈhælmə) *n.* a board game in which players attempt to transfer their pieces from their own to their opponents' bases. [C19: from Greek *halma* leap, from *hallesthai* to leap]

Hal·ma·he·ra (ˌhælməˈhɪərə) *n.* an island in NE Indonesia, the largest of the Moluccas: consists of four peninsulas enclosing three bays; mountainous and forested. Area: 17 780 sq. km (6865 sq. miles). Dutch name: **Djailolo, Gilolo,** or **Jilolo.**

Halm·stad (*Swedish* ˈhalmˌstɑːd) *n.* a port in SW Sweden, on the Kattegat. Pop.: 47 298 (1970).

ha·lo (ˈheɪləʊ) *n., pl.* **·loes** *or* **·los. 1.** a disc or ring of light around the head of an angel, saint, etc., as in painting or sculpture. **2.** the aura surrounding an idealized, famous, or admired person, thing, or event. **3.** a circle of light around the sun or moon, caused by the refraction of light by particles of ice. **4.** *Astronomy.* a spherical cloud of stars surrounding the Galaxy and other spiral galaxies. ~*vb.* **·loes** *or* **·los, ·lo·ing, ·loed. 5.** to surround with or form a halo. [C16: from Medieval Latin, from Latin *halōs* circular threshing floor, from Greek] —'**ha·lo-ˌlike** *adj.*

hal·o- *or before a vowel* **hal-** *combining form.* **1.** indicating salt or the sea: *halophyte.* **2.** relating to or containing a halogen: *halothane.* [from Greek *hals, hal-* sea, salt]

ha·lo·bi·ont (ˌhæləʊˈbaɪɒnt) *n.* a plant or animal that lives in a salty environment such as the sea. [C20: from HALO- + *-biont* from Greek *bios* life]

hal·o·gen (ˈhæləˌdʒɛn) *n.* any of the chemical elements fluorine, chlorine, bromine, iodine, and astatine. They are all monovalent and readily form negative ions. [C19: from Swedish; see HALO-, -GEN] —'**hal·o·gen·ˌoid** *adj.* —**ha·log·e·nous** (həˈlɒdʒɪnəs) *adj.*

hal·o·gen·ate (ˈhælədʒəˌneɪt) *vb. Chem.* to treat or combine with a halogen. —ˌ**hal·o·gen·'a·tion** *n.*

ˌ**half-sub·'merged** *adj.*
ˌ**half-'trained** *adj.*
ˌ**half-un·der·'stood** *adj.*
ˌ**half-'used** *adj.*
ˌ**half-'ver·i·ˌfied** *adj.*
ˌ**half-'wild** *adj.*
ˌ**half-'wild·ly** *adv.*
ˌ**half-'wrong** *adj.*

hal·oid ('hælɔɪd) *Chem.* ~*adj.* **1.** resembling or derived from a halogen: *a haloid salt.* ~*n.* **2.** a compound containing halogen atoms in its molecules; halide.

hal·o·phyte ('hælə͵faɪt) *n.* a plant that grows in very salty soil, as in a salt marsh. —**hal·o·phyt·ic** (͵hælə'fɪtɪk) *adj.* —'**hal·o·phyt·ism** *n.*

hal·o·thane ('hæləʊ͵θeɪn) *n.* a colourless volatile slightly soluble liquid with an odour resembling that of chloroform; 2-bromo-2-chloro-1,1,1-trifluoroethane: a general anaesthetic. Formula: $CF_3CHBrCl$. [C20: from HALO- + *-thane,* as in METHANE]

Hals (*Dutch* hɑls) *n.* **Frans** (frɑns). ?1580–1666, Dutch portrait and genre painter: his works include *The Laughing Cavalier* (1624).

Häl·sing·borg *or* **Hel·sing·borg** (*Swedish* ͵hɛlsiŋ'bɔrj) *n.* a port in SW Sweden, on the Sound opposite Helsingör, Denmark: changed hands several times between Denmark and Sweden, finally becoming Swedish in 1710; shipbuilding. Pop.: 102 137 (1974 est.).

halt[1] (hɔ:lt) *n.* **1.** an interruption or end to activity, movement, or progress. **2.** *Chiefly Brit.* a minor railway station, without permanent buildings. **3. call a halt (to).** to put an end (to something); stop. ~*n., interj.* **4.** a command to halt, esp. as an order when marching. ~*vb.* **5.** to come or bring to a halt. [C17: from the phrase *to make halt,* translation of German *halt machen,* from *halten* to HOLD[1], stop]

halt[2] (hɔ:lt) *vb.* (*intr.*) **1.** (esp. of logic or verse) to falter or be defective. **2.** to waver or be unsure. **3.** *Archaic.* to be lame. ~*adj.* **4.** *Archaic.* lame. ~*n.* **5. the halt.** *Archaic.* lame persons collectively. **6.** *Archaic.* lameness. [Old English *healt* lame; related to Old Norse *haltr,* Old High German *halz* lame, Greek *kólos* maimed, Old Slavonic *kladivo* hammer]

Hal·tem·price ('hɔ:ltəm͵praɪs) *n.* a township in NE England, in Humberside: a residential suburb of Hull. Pop.: 52 239 (1971).

hal·ter ('hɔ:ltə) *n.* **1.** a rope or canvas headgear for a horse, usually with a rope for leading. **2.** a style of woman's top fastened behind the neck and waist, leaving the back and arms bare. **3.** a rope having a noose for hanging a person. **4.** death by hanging. ~*vb.* (*tr.*) **5.** to secure with or put on a halter. **6.** to hang (someone). [Old English *hælfter;* related to Old High German *halftra,* Middle Dutch *heliftra*] —'**hal·ter·**͵**like** *adj.*

hal·tere ('hæltɪə) *or* **hal·ter** ('hæltə) *n., pl.* **hal·te·res** (hæl'tɪəri:z). one of a pair of short projections in dipterous insects that are modified hind wings, used for maintaining equilibrium during flight. Also called: **balancer.** [C18: from Greek *haltēres* (plural) hand-held weights used as balancers or to give impetus in leaping, from *hallesthai* to leap]

halt·ing ('hɔ:ltɪŋ) *adj.* **1.** hesitant: *halting speech.* **2.** lame. —'**halt·ing·ly** *adv.* —'**halt·ing·ness** *n.*

ha·lutz *or* ***cha·lutz*** *Hebrew.* (xa'lu:ts; *English* hɑ:'lʊts) *n.* a member of an organization of immigrants to Israeli agricultural settlements. [literally: pioneer, fighter]

hal·vah, hal·va ('hælvɑ:), *or* **ha·la·vah** ('hæləvɑ:) *n.* a Middle Eastern or Indian sweetmeat containing sesame seeds, nuts, rose water, saffron, etc. [from Yiddish *halva,* from Rumanian, from Turkish *helve,* from Arabic *halwā* sweetmeat]

halve (hɑ:v) *vb.* (*tr.*) **1.** to divide into two approximately equal parts. **2.** to share equally. **3.** to reduce by half, as by cutting. **4.** *Golf.* to take the same number of strokes on (a hole or round) as one's opponent. [Old English *hielfan;* related to Middle High German *helben;* see HALF]

halve to·geth·er *vb.* (*tr., adv.*) to join (two timbers) by cutting each to half its thickness.

hal·yard *or* **hal·liard** ('hæljəd) *n. Nautical.* a line for hoisting or lowering a sail, flag, or spar. [C14 *halier,* influenced by YARD[1]; see HALE[2]]

ham[1] (hæm) *n.* **1.** the part of the hindquarters of a pig or similar animal between the hock and the hip. **2.** the meat of this part, esp. when salted or smoked. **3.** *Informal.* **a.** the back of the leg above the knee. **b.** the space or area behind the knee. **4.** *Needlework.* a cushion used for moulding curves. [Old English *hamm;* related to Old High German *hamma* haunch, Old Irish *cnāim* bone, *camm* bent, Latin *camur* bent]

ham[2] (hæm) *n.* **1.** *Theatre, informal.* **a.** an actor who overacts or relies on stock gestures or mannerisms. **b.** overacting or clumsy acting. **c.** (*as modifier*): *a ham actor.* **2.** *Informal.* **a.** a licensed amateur radio operator. **b.** (*as modifier*): *a ham licence.* ~*vb.* **hams, ham·ming, hammed. 3.** *Informal.* to overact. [C19: special use of HAM[1]; in some senses probably influenced by AMATEUR]

Ha·ma ('hɑ:mɑ:) *n.* a city in W Syria, on the Orontes River: an early Hittite settlement; famous for its huge water wheels, used for irrigation since the Middle Ages. Pop.: 137 421 (1970). Biblical name: **Ha·math.**

Ham·a·dān *or* **Ham·e·dān** ('hæmə͵dæn) *n.* city in W central Iran, at an altitude of over 1830 m (6000 ft.): changed hands several times since the 17th century between Iraq, Persia, and Turkey; trading centre. Pop.: 144 000 (1973 est.).

ham·a·dry·ad (͵hæmə'draɪəd, -æd) *n.* **1.** *Classical myth.* one of a class of nymphs, each of which inhabits a tree and dies with it. **2.** another name for **king cobra.** [C14: from Latin *Hamādryas,* from Greek *Hamadruas,* from *hama* together with + *drus* tree; see DRYAD]

ham·a·dry·as (͵hæmə'draɪəs) *n.* a baboon, *Papio* (or *Comopithecus*) *hamadryas,* of Arabia and NE Africa, having long silvery hair on the head, neck, and chest: regarded as sacred by the ancient Egyptians: family *Cercopithecidae.* Also called: **hamadryas baboon, sacred baboon.** [C19: via New Latin from Latin; see HAMADRYAD]

ha·mal, ham·mal, *or* **ha·maul** (hə'mɑ:l) *n.* (in the Orient) a porter, bearer, or servant. [from Arabic *hamala* to carry]

Ha·ma·ma·tsu (͵hæmə'mætsu:) *n.* a city in central Japan, in S central Honshu: cotton textiles and musical instruments. Pop.: 466 933 (1974 est.).

ham·a·me·li·da·ceous (͵hæmə͵mi:lɪ'deɪʃəs, -͵mɛlɪ-) *adj.* of, relating to, or belonging to the *Hamamelidaceae,* a chiefly subtropical family of trees and shrubs that includes the witch hazel. [C19: from New Latin *Hamamelis* type genus, from Greek: medlar, from *hama* together with + *mēlon* fruit]

ha·mate ('heɪmeɪt) *adj. Rare.* hook-shaped. [C18: from Latin *hāmātus,* from *hāmus* hook]

Ham·ble·to·ni·an (͵hæmbᵊl'təʊnɪən) *n.* one of a superior breed of trotting horses descended from a stallion named Hambletonian.

Ham·burg ('hæmbɜ:g) *n.* a city-state and port in N West Germany, on the River Elbe: the largest port in Germany; a founder member of the Hanseatic League; became a free imperial city in 1510 and a state of the German empire in 1871; university (1919); extensive shipyards. Pop.: 1 751 621 (1974 est.).

ham·burg·er ('hæm͵bɜ:gə) *or* **ham·burg** *n.* a flat fried cake of minced beef, often served in a bread roll. Also called: **Hamburger steak, beefburger.** [C20: shortened from *Hamburger steak* (that is, steak in the fashion of HAMBURG)]

hame (heɪm) *n.* either of the two curved bars holding the traces of the harness, attached to the collar of a draught animal. [C14: from Middle Dutch *hame;* related to Middle High German *hame* fishing-rod]

Ham·e·lin ('hæməlɪn, 'hæmlɪn) *n.* the English name for **Hameln.**

Ha·meln (*German* 'ha:mᵊln) *n.* an industrial town in N West Germany, in Lower Saxony on the Weser River: famous for the legend of the Pied Piper (supposedly took place in 1284). Pop.: 46 800 (1970). English name: **Hamelin.**

Ham·ers·ley Range ('hæməzlɪ) *n.* a mountain range in N Western Australia: iron-ore deposits. Highest peak: 1236 m (4056 ft.).

ham-hand·ed *or* **ham-fist·ed** *adj.* **1.** *Informal.* lacking dexterity or elegance; clumsy. **2.** having large hands.

Ham·hung *or* **Ham·heung** ('hɑ:m'hʊŋ) *n.* an industrial city in central North Korea: commercial and governmental centre of NE Korea during the Yi dynasty (1392–1910).

Ha·mil·car Bar·ca (hæ'mɪlkɑ: 'bɑ:kə, 'hæmɪl͵kɑ:) *n.* died ?228 B.C., Carthaginian general; father of Hannibal. He held command (247–41) during the first Punic War and established Carthaginian influence in Spain (237–?228).

Ham·il·ton[1] ('hæməltən) *n.* **1.** a port in central Canada, in S Ontario on Lake Ontario: iron and steel industry. Pop.: 309 173 (1971). **2.** a city in New Zealand, on central North Island. Pop.: 74 784 (1971). **3.** a town in S Scotland, near Glasgow. Pop.: 46 347 (1971). **4.** the capital and chief port of Bermuda. Pop.: 2060 (1970). **5.** the former name of the **Churchill** River.

Ham·il·ton[2] ('hæməltən) *n.* **1. Al·ex·an·der.** ?1757–1804, American statesman. He was a leader of the Federalists and as first secretary of the Treasury (1789–95) established a federal bank. **2.** Lady **Em·ma.** ?1765–1815, mistress of Nelson. **3.** Sir **Wil·liam Ro·wan.** 1805–65, Irish mathematician: founded Hamiltonian mechanics and formulated the theory of quaternions.

Ham·il·to·ni·an (͵hæməl'təʊnɪən) *Physics, maths.* ~*n.* **1.** a mathematical function of the coordinates and momenta of a system of particles used to express their equations of motion. **2.** a mathematical operator that generates such a function. Symbol: **H** ~*adj.* **3.** denoting or relating to Sir William Rowan Hamilton, or the theory of mechanics or mathematical operator devised by him.

Ham·ite ('hæmaɪt) *n.* a member of a group of peoples of N Africa supposedly descended from Noah's son Ham (Genesis 5:32, 10:6), including the ancient Egyptians, the Berbers, the Tuaregs, etc.

Ham·it·ic (hæ'mɪtɪk, hə-) *n.* **1.** a group of N African languages related to Semitic. They are now classified in four separate subfamilies of the Afro-Asiatic family: Egyptian, Berber, Cushitic, and Chadic. ~*adj.* **2.** denoting, relating to, or belonging to this group of languages. **3.** denoting, belonging to, or characteristic of the Hamites.

Ham·i·to-Se·mit·ic *n.* **1.** a former name for the **Afro-Asiatic** family of languages. ~*adj.* **2.** denoting or belonging to this family of languages.

ham·let ('hæmlɪt) *n.* **1.** a small village or group of houses. **2.** (in Britain) a village without its own church. [C14: from Old French *hamelet,* diminutive of *hamel,* from *ham,* of Germanic origin; compare Old English *hamm* plot of pasture, Low German *hamm* enclosed land; see HOME]

Hamm (*German* ham) *n.* an industrial city in NW West Germany, in North Rhine-Westphalia: a Hanse town from 1417; severely damaged in World War II. Pop.: 84 600 (1970).

Ham·mar·skjöld ('hæmə͵ʃʊld; *Swedish* 'hamar͵ʃœld) *n.* **Dag (Hjalmar Agne Carl)** (dɑ:g). 1905–61, Swedish statesman; secretary-general of the United Nations (1953–61): Nobel peace prize 1961.

ham·mer ('hæmə) *n.* **1.** a hand tool consisting of a heavy usually steel head held transversely on the end of a handle, used for driving in nails, beating metal, etc. **2.** any tool or device with a similar function, such as the moving part of a door knocker, the striking head on a bell, etc. **3.** a power-driven striking tool, esp. one used in forging. A **pneumatic hammer** delivers a repeated blow from a pneumatic ram, a **drop hammer** uses the energy of a falling weight. **4.** a part of a gunlock that strikes the primer or percussion cap when the trigger is pulled. **5.** *Field sports.* **a.** a heavy metal ball attached to a flexible wire: thrown in competitions. **b.** the event or sport of throwing the hammer. **6.** an auctioneer's gavel. **7.** a device on a piano that is made to strike a string or group of strings causing them to vibrate. **8.** *Anatomy.* the nontechnical name for **malleus. 9. go** (or **come**) **under the hammer.** to be offered for sale by an auctioneer. **10. hammer and tongs.** with great effort or energy: *fighting hammer and tongs.* ~*vb.* **11.** to strike or beat (a nail, wood, etc.) with or as if with a hammer. **12.** (*tr.*) to shape or fashion with or as if with a hammer. **13.** (when *intr.*, foll. by *away*) to impress or force (facts, ideas, etc.) into (someone) through constant repetition. **14.** (*intr.*) to feel or sound like hammering: *his pulse was hammering.* **15.** (*intr.*; often foll. by *away*) to work at constantly. **16.** (*tr.*) *Brit.* **a.** to question in a relentless manner. **b.** to criticize severely. **17.** *Informal.* to inflict a defeat on. **18.** (*tr.*) *Stock Exchange.* **a.** to announce the default of (a member). **b.** to cause prices of (securities, the market, etc.) to fall by bearish selling. [Old English *hamor;* related to Old Norse *hamarr* crag, Old High German *hamar* hammer, Old Slavonic *kamy* stone] —**'ham·mer·er** *n.* —**'ham·mer-,like** *adj.*

ham·mer and sick·le *n.* **1.** the emblem on the flag of the Soviet Union, representing the industrial workers and the peasants respectively. **2.** a symbolic representation of the Soviet Union or of Communism in general.

ham·mer beam *n.* either of a pair of short horizontal beams that project from opposite walls to support arched braces and struts.

ham·mer drill *n.* a rock drill operated by compressed air in which the boring bit is not attached to the reciprocating piston.

Ham·mer·fest (*Norwegian* 'hamər,fɛst) *n.* a port in N Norway, on the W coast of Kvaløy Island: the northernmost town in the world, with uninterrupted daylight from May 17 to July 19 and no sun between Nov. 21 and Jan. 21; fishing and tourist centre. Pop.: 6974 (1970).

ham·mer·head ('hæmə,hɛd) *n.* **1.** any ferocious shark of the genus *Sphyrna* and family *Sphyrnidae,* having a flattened hammer-shaped head. **2.** a heavily built tropical African wading bird, *Scopus umbretta,* related to the herons, having a dark plumage and a long backward-pointing crest: family *Scopidae,* order *Ciconiiformes.* **3.** a large African fruit bat, *Hypsignathus monstrosus,* with a large square head and hammer-shaped muzzle. —**'ham·mer,head·ed** *adj.*

ham·mer·less ('hæməlɪs) *adj.* (of a firearm) having the hammer enclosed so that it is not visible.

ham·mer·lock *n.* a wrestling hold in which a wrestler twists his opponent's arm upwards behind his back.

ham·mer out *vb.* (*tr., adv.*) **1.** to shape or remove with or as if with a hammer. **2.** to settle or reconcile (differences, problems, etc.) after much dispute or conflict.

Ham·mer·smith ('hæmə,smɪθ) *n.* a borough of Greater London on the River Thames in the south: established in 1965 by the amalgamation of Fulham and Hammersmith. Pop.: 170 000 (1976 est.).

Ham·mer·stein II ('hæmə,staɪn) *n.* **Os·car.** 1895–1960, U.S. librettist and songwriter: collaborated with the composer Richard Rodgers in musicals such as *South Pacific* (1949) and *The Sound of Music* (1959).

ham·mer·toe ('hæmə,təʊ) *n.* **1.** a deformity of the bones of a toe causing the toe to be bent in a clawlike arch. **2.** such a toe.

ham·mock[1] ('hæmək) *n.* a length of canvas, net, etc., suspended at the ends and used as a bed. [C16: from Spanish *hamaca,* of Taino origin] —**'ham·mock-,like** *adj.*

ham·mock[2] (hæmək) *n.* a variant spelling of **hummock** (sense 3).

Ham·mond[1] ('hæmənd) *n.* a city in NW Indiana, adjacent to Chicago. Pop.: 106 383 (1973 est.).

Ham·mond[2] ('hæmənd) *n.* **1.** Dame **Joan.** born 1912, Australian operatic singer. **2. Wal·ter Reg·i·nald,** known as *Wally Hammond.* 1903–65, English cricketer. An all-rounder, he played for England 85 times between 1928 and 1946.

Ham·mu·ra·bi (,hæmʊ'rɑːbɪ) *or* **Ham·mu·ra·pi** *n.* ?18th century B.C., king of Babylonia; promulgator of one of the earliest known codes of law.

ham·my ('hæmɪ) *adj.* **·mi·er, ·mi·est.** *Informal.* **1.** (of an actor) overacting or tending to overact. **2.** (of a play, performance, etc.) overacted or exaggerated.

Hamp·den ('hæmpdən, 'hæmdən) *n.* **John.** 1594–1643, English statesman; one of the leaders of the Parliamentary opposition to Charles I.

ham·per[1] ('hæmpə) *vb.* **1.** (*tr.*) to prevent the progress or free movement of. ~*n.* **2.** *Nautical.* gear aboard a vessel that, though essential, is often in the way. [C14: of obscure origin; perhaps related to Old English *hamm* enclosure, *hemm* HEM[1]] —**'ham·pered·ness** *n.* —**'ham·per·er** *n.*

ham·per[2] ('hæmpə) *n.* **1.** a large basket, usually with a cover. **2.** *Brit.* such a basket and its contents, usually food. **3.** *U.S.* a laundry basket. [C14: variant of HANAPER]

Hamp·shire ('hæmpʃɪə, -ʃə) *n.* a county of S England, on the English Channel: crossed by the **Hampshire Downs** and the South Downs, with the New Forest in the southwest and many prehistoric and Roman remains. Administrative centre: Winchester. Pop.: 1 456 100 (1976 est.). Abbrev.: **Hants.**

Hamp·stead ('hæmpstɪd) *n.* a residential district in N London: part of the Greater London borough of Camden since 1965; nearby is **Hampstead Heath,** a popular recreation area.

Hamp·ton ('hæmptən) *n.* **1.** a city in SE Virginia, on the harbour of **Hampton Roads** on Chesapeake Bay. Pop.: 128 119 (1973 est.). **2.** a district of the Greater London borough of Richmond-upon-Thames, on the River Thames: famous for **Hampton Court Palace** (built in 1515 by Cardinal Wolsey).

ham·shack·le ('hæm∫æk^{ə}l) *vb.* (*tr.*) to hobble (a cow, horse, etc.) by tying a rope around the head and one of the legs.

ham·ster ('hæmstə) *n.* any Eurasian burrowing rodent of the tribe *Cricetini,* such as *Mesocricetus auratus* (**golden hamster**), having a stocky body, short tail, and cheek pouches: family *Cricetidae.* They are popular pets. [C17: from German, from Old High German *hamustro,* of Slavic origin]

ham·string ('hæm,strɪŋ) *n.* **1.** *Anatomy.* one of the tendons at the back of the knee. **2.** the large tendon at the back of the hock in the hind leg of a horse, etc. ~*vb.* **·strings, ·string·ing, ·strung. 3.** to cripple by cutting the hamstring of. **4.** to ruin or thwart. [C16: HAM[1] + STRING]

Ham·sun (*Norwegian* 'hamsʊn) *n.* **Knut** (knuːt), pen name of *Knut Pedersen.* 1859–1952, Norwegian novelist, whose works include *The Growth of the Soil* (1917): Nobel prize for literature 1920.

ham·u·lus ('hæmjʊləs) *n., pl.* **·li** (-,laɪ). *Biology.* a hook or hooklike process at the end of some bones or between the fore and hind wings of a bee or similar insect. [C18: from Latin: a little hook, from *hāmus* hook] —**'ham·u·lar, 'ham·u·,late, 'ham·u·,lose,** *or* **'ham·u·lous** *adj.*

ham·za *or* **ham·zah** ('hɑːmzɑː, -zə) *n.* the sign used in Arabic to represent the glottal stop. [from Arabic *hamzah,* literally: a compression]

Han[1] (hæn) *n.* **1.** the imperial dynasty that ruled China for most of the time from 206 B.C. to 221 A.D., expanding its territory and developing its bureaucracy. **2.** the Chinese people as contrasted to Mongols, Manchus, etc.

Han[2] (hæn) *n.* a river in E central China, rising in S Shensi and flowing southeast through Hupeh to the Yangtze River at Wuhan. Length: about 1450 km (900 miles).

han·a·per ('hænəpə) *n.* a small wickerwork basket, often used to hold official papers. [C15: from Old French *hanapier,* from *hanap* cup, of Germanic origin; compare Old High German *hnapf* bowl, Old English *hnæp*]

Ha·nau (*German* 'haːnaʊ) *n.* a city in central West Germany, in Hesse east of Frankfurt am Main: a centre of the jewellery industry. Pop.: 55 500 (1970).

hance (hæns) *n.* a variant spelling of **haunch** (sense 3).

Han Cit·ies (hɑːn) *pl. n.* a group of three cities in E central China, in SE Hupeh at the confluence of the Han and Yangtze Rivers: Hanyang, Hankow, and Wuchang; united in 1950 to form the conurbation of Wuhan, the capital of Hupeh province.

Han·cock ('hænkɒk) *n.* **John.** 1737–93, American statesman; first signatory of the Declaration of Independence.

hand (hænd) *n.* **1. a.** the prehensile part of the body at the end of the arm, consisting of a thumb, four fingers, and a palm. **b.** the bones of this part. Related adj.: **manual. 2.** the corresponding or similar part in animals. **3.** something resembling this in shape or function. **4. a.** the cards dealt to one or all players in one round of a card game. **b.** a player holding such cards. **c.** one round of a card game. **5.** agency or influence: *the hand of God.* **6.** a part in something done: *he had a hand in the victory.* **7.** assistance: *to give someone a hand with his work.* **8.** a pointer on a dial, indicator, or gauge, esp. on a clock: *the minute hand.* **9.** acceptance or pledge of partnership, as in marriage: *he asked for her hand; he gave me his hand on the merger.* **10.** a position or direction indicated by its location to the side of an object or the observer: *on the right hand; on every hand.* **11.** a contrastive aspect, condition, etc. (in the phrases **on the one hand, on the other hand**). **12.** (preceded by an ordinal number) source or origin: *a story heard at third hand.* **13.** a person, esp. one who creates something: *a good hand at painting.* **14.** a labourer or manual worker: *we've just taken on a new hand at the farm.* **15.** a member of a ship's crew: *all hands on deck.* **16.** *Printing.* another name for **index** (sense 9). **17.** a person's handwriting: *the letter was in his own hand.* **18.** a round of applause: *give him a hand.* **19.** ability or skill: *a hand for woodwork.* **20.** a manner or characteristic way of doing something: *the hand of a master.* **21.** a unit of length measurement equalling four inches, used for measuring the height of horses, usually from the front hoof to the withers. **22.** a cluster or bundle, esp. of bananas. **23.** a shoulder of pork. **24.** one of the two possible mirror-image forms of an asymmetric object, such as the direction of the helix in a screw thread. **25. a free hand.** freedom to do as desired. **26. a heavy hand.** tyranny, persecution, or oppression: *he ruled with a heavy hand.* **27. a high hand.** an oppressive or dictatorial manner. **28.** (**near**) **at hand.** very near or close, esp. in time. **29. at someone's hand(s).** from: *the acts of kindness received at their hands.* **30. by hand. a.** by manual rather than mechanical means. **b.** by messenger or personally: *the letter was delivered by hand.* **31. come to hand.** to become available; be received. **32. force someone's hand.** to force someone to act. **33. from hand to hand.** from one person to another. **34. from hand to mouth. a.** in poverty: *living from hand to mouth.* **b.** without preparation or planning. **35. hand and foot.** in all ways possible; completely: *they waited on him hand and foot.* **36. hand in glove.** in close association. **37. hand in hand. a.** together; jointly. **b.** clasping each other's hands. **38. hand over fist. a.** in an easy manner. **b.** in large amounts: *he squanders money hand over fist.* **39. hold one's hand.** to stop or postpone a planned action or punishment. **40. hold someone's hand.** to support, help, or guide someone, esp. by giving sympathy or moral support. **41. in hand. a.** in possession. **b.** under control. **c.** receiving attention or being acted on. **d.** available for use; in reserve. **e.** with deferred payment: *he works a week in hand.* **42. keep one's**

hand in. to continue or practise. **43. on hand.** close by; present: *I'll be on hand to help you.* **44. out of hand. a.** beyond control. **b.** without reservation or deeper examination: *he condemned him out of hand.* **45. set one's hand to. a.** to sign (a document). **b.** to start (a task or undertaking). **46. show one's hand.** to reveal one's stand, opinion, or plans. **47. take in hand.** to discipline; control. **48. throw one's hand in.** to give up or discontinue a venture, game, etc. **49. to hand.** accessible. **50. try one's hand.** to attempt to do something. **51.** (*modifier*) **a.** of or involving the hand: *a hand grenade.* **b.** made to be carried in or worn on the hand: *hand luggage.* **c.** operated by hand: *a hand drill.* **52.** (*in combination*) made by hand rather than by a machine: *hand-sewn.* ~*vb.* (*tr.*) **53.** to transmit or offer by the hand or hands. **54.** to help or lead with the hand. **55.** *Nautical.* to furl (a sail). **56. hand it to someone.** to give credit to someone. ~See also **hand down, hand in, hand-off, hand on, hand-out, hand over, hands.** [Old English *hand;* related to Old Norse *hönd,* Gothic *handus,* Old High German *hant*] —'**hand·less** *adj.* —'**hand·,like** *adj.*

hand·bag ('hænd,bæg) *n.* **1.** Also called: **bag, purse** (U.S.), **pocketbook** (U.S.). a woman's small bag carried to contain personal articles. **2.** a small suitcase that can be carried by hand.

hand·ball ('hænd,bɔ:l) *n.* **1.** a game in which two or four people strike a ball against a wall or walls with the hand, usually gloved. **2.** the small hard rubber ball used in this game. ~*vb.* (*tr.*) **3.** *Australian Rules football.* to pass (the ball) with a blow of the fist. —'**hand·,ball·er** *n.*

hand·bar·row ('hænd,bærəʊ) *n.* a flat tray for transporting loads, usually carried by two men.

hand·bell ('hænd,bɛl) *n.* a bell rung by hand, esp. one of a tuned set used in musical performance.

hand·bill ('hænd,bɪl) *n.* a small printed notice for distribution by hand.

hand·book ('hænd,bʊk) *n.* a reference book listing brief facts on a subject or place or directions for maintenance or repair, as of a car: *a tourists' handbook.*

hand·brake ('hænd,breɪk) *n.* **1.** a brake operated by a hand lever. **2.** the lever that operates the handbrake.

hand·breadth ('hænd,brɛtθ, -,brɛdθ) *or* **hand's-breadth** *n.* the width of a hand used as an indication of length.

h. and c. *abbrev. for* hot and cold (water).

hand·cart ('hænd,kɑ:t) *n.* a simple cart, usually with one or two wheels, pushed or drawn by hand.

hand·clasp ('hænd,klɑ:sp) *n. U.S.* another word for **handshake.**

hand·craft ('hænd,krɑ:ft) *n.* **1.** another word for **handicraft.** ~*vb.* **2.** (*tr.*) to make by handicraft.

hand·cuff ('hænd,kʌf) *vb.* **1.** (*tr.*) to put handcuffs on (a person); manacle. ~*n.* **2.** (*pl.*) a pair of locking metal rings joined by a short bar or chain for securing prisoners, etc.

hand down *vb.* (*tr., adv.*) **1.** to leave to a later period or generation; bequeath. **2.** to pass (an outgrown garment) on from one member of a family to a younger one. **3.** *U.S. law.* to announce or deliver (a verdict).

-hand·ed *adj.* having a hand or hands as specified: *broad-handed; a four-handed game of cards.*

Han·del ('hændᵊl) *n.* **George Fred·er·ick.** German name *Georg Friedrich Händel.* 1685–1759, German composer, resident in England, noted particularly for his oratorios, including the *Messiah* (1741) and *Samson* (1743). Other works include over 40 operas, 12 concerti grossi, organ concertos, chamber and orchestral music, esp. *Water Music* (1717).

hand·fast ('hænd,fɑ:st) *Archaic.* ~*n.* **1.** an agreement, esp. of marriage, confirmed by a handshake. **2.** a firm grip. ~*vb.* (*tr.*) **3.** to betroth or marry (two persons or another person) by joining the hands. **4.** to grip with the hand.

hand·fast·ing ('hænd,fɑ:stɪŋ) *n.* **1.** an archaic word for **betrothal. 2.** (formerly) a kind of trial marriage marked by the formal joining of hands.

hand·feed ('hænd,fi:d) *vb.* **·feeds, ·feed·ing, ·fed.** (*tr.*) **1.** to feed (a person or an animal) by hand. **2.** *Agriculture.* to give food to (poultry or livestock) in fixed amounts and at fixed times, rather than use a self-feeding system.

hand·ful ('hænd,fʊl) *n., pl.* **·fuls. 1.** the amount or number that can be held in the hand. **2.** a small number or quantity. **3.** *Informal.* a person or thing difficult to manage or control.

hand glass *n.* **1.** a magnifying glass with a handle. **2.** a small mirror with a handle. **3.** a small glazed frame for seedlings or plants.

hand gre·nade *n.* a small metal canister containing explosives, usually activated by a short fuse and used in close combat.

hand·grip ('hænd,grɪp) *n.* **1.** another word for **grip**[1] (senses 2, 6, and 7). **2.** *Tennis, golf, etc.* a covering, usually of towelling or rubber, that makes the handle of a racket or club easier to hold.

hand·gun ('hænd,gʌn) *n. U.S.* a firearm that can be held, carried, and fired with one hand, such as a pistol.

hand-held *adj.* (of a film camera) held rather than mounted, as in close-up action shots.

hand·hold ('hænd,həʊld) *n.* **1.** an object, crevice, etc., that can be used as a grip or support, as in climbing. **2.** a grip or secure hold with the hand or hands.

hand·i·cap ('hændɪ,kæp) *n.* **1.** something that hampers or hinders. **2.** a contest, esp. a race, in which competitors are given advantages or disadvantages of weight, distance, time, etc., in an attempt to equalize their chances of winning. **3.** the advantage or disadvantage prescribed: *a handicap of three strokes.* **4.** any physical disability, esp. one affecting the normal ability to move or manipulate objects. ~*vb.* **·caps, ·cap·ping, ·capped.** (*tr.*) **5.** to be a hindrance or disadvantage to. **6.** to assign a handicap or handicaps to. **7.** to organize (a contest) by handicapping. **8.** *U.S.* **a.** to attempt to forecast the winner of (a contest, esp. a horse race). **b.** to assign odds for or against (a contestant). [C17: probably from *hand in cap,* a lottery game in which players drew forfeits from a cap or deposited money in it] —'**hand·i·,cap·per** *n.*

hand·i·capped ('hændɪ,kæpt) *adj.* **1.** physically disabled. **2.** *Psychol.* denoting a person whose social behaviour or emotional reactions are in some way impaired. **3.** (of a competitor) assigned a handicap.

hand·i·cap·per ('hændɪ,kæpə) *n.* **1.** an official appointed to assign handicaps to competitors in such sports as golf and horse racing. **2.** a newspaper columnist employed to estimate the chances that horses have of winning races.

hand·i·craft ('hændɪ,krɑ:ft) *n.* **1.** skill or dexterity in working with the hands. **2.** a particular skill or art performed with the hands, such as weaving, pottery, etc. **3.** the work produced by such a skill or art: *local handicraft is on sale.* ~Also called: **handcraft.** [C15: changed from HANDCRAFT through the influence of HANDIWORK, which was analysed as if HANDY + WORK] —'**hand·i·,crafts·man** *n.*

hand·i·ly ('hændɪlɪ) *adv.* **1.** in a handy way or manner. **2.** conveniently or suitably: *handily nearby.* **3.** *U.S.* easily: *the horse won handily.*

hand in *vb.* (*tr., adv.*) to return or submit (something, such as an examination paper).

hand·i·work ('hændɪ,wɜ:k) *n.* **1.** work performed or produced by hand, such as embroidery or pottery. **2.** the result of the action or endeavours of a person or thing. [Old English *handgeweorc,* from HAND + *geweorc,* from *ge-* (collective prefix) + *weorc* WORK]

hand·ker·chief ('hæŋkətʃɪf, -tʃi:f) *n.* a small square of soft absorbent material, such as linen, silk, or soft paper, carried and used to wipe the nose, etc.

hand-knit *adj. also* **hand-knit·ted. 1.** knitted by hand, not on a machine. ~*vb.* **-knits, -knit·ting, -knit·ted** *or* **-knit. 2.** to knit (garments, etc.) by hand.

han·dle ('hændᵊl) *n.* **1.** the part of a utensil, drawer, etc., designed to be held in order to move, use, or pick up the object. **2.** *Slang.* a title put before a person's name. **3.** an opportunity, reason, or excuse for doing something: *his background served as a handle for their mockery.* **4.** the quality, as of textiles, perceived by touching or feeling. **5.** the total amount of a bet on a horse race or similar event. **6. fly off the handle.** *Informal.* to become suddenly extremely angry. ~*vb.* (*mainly tr.*) **7.** to pick up and hold, move, or touch with the hands. **8.** to operate or employ using the hands: *the boy handled the reins well.* **9.** to have power or control over: *my wife handles my investments.* **10.** to manage successfully: *a secretary must be able to handle clients.* **11.** to discuss (a theme, subject, etc.). **12.** to deal with or treat in a specified way: *I was handled with great tact.* **13.** to trade or deal in (specified merchandise). **14.** (*intr.*) to react or respond in a specified way to operation or control: *the car handles well on bends.* [Old English; related to Old Saxon *handlon* (vb.), Old High German *hantilla* towel] —'**han·dle·a·ble** *adj.* —'**han·dled** *adj.* —'**han·dle·less** *adj.*

han·dle·bar mous·tache ('hændᵊl,bɑ:) *n.* a bushy extended moustache with curled ends that resembles handlebars.

han·dle·bars ('hændᵊl,bɑ:z) *pl. n.* (*sometimes sing.*) a metal bar having its ends curved to form handles, used for steering a bicycle, motorcycle, etc.

han·dler ('hændlə) *n.* **1.** a person who holds or incites a dog, gamecock, etc., esp. in a race or contest. **2.** the trainer or second of a boxer.

han·dling ('hændlɪŋ) *n.* **1.** the act or an instance of picking up, turning over, or touching something. **2.** treatment, as of a theme in literature. **3. a.** the process by which a commodity is packaged, transported, etc. **b.** (*as modifier*): *handling charges.* **4.** *Law.* the act of receiving property that one knows or believes to be stolen.

hand·made (,hænd'meɪd) *adj.* made by hand, not by machine, esp. with care or craftsmanship.

hand·maid·en ('hænd,meɪdᵊn) *or* **hand·maid** *n.* **1.** a person or thing that serves a useful but subordinate purpose: *logic is the handmaid of philosophy.* **2.** *Archaic.* a female servant or attendant.

hand-me-down *n. Informal.* **1. a.** something, esp. an outgrown garment, passed down from one person to another. **b.** (*as modifier*): *a hand-me-down dress.* **2. a.** anything that has already been used by another. **b.** (*as modifier*): *hand-me-down ideas.*

hand-off *Rugby.* ~*n.* **1.** the act of warding off an opposing player with the open hand. ~*vb.* **hand off. 2.** (*tr., adv.*) to ward off (an opponent) using a hand-off.

hand on *vb.* (*tr., adv.*) to pass to the next in a succession.

hand or·gan *n.* another name for **barrel organ.**

hand-out *n.* **1.** clothing, food, or money given to a needy person. **2.** a leaflet, free sample, etc., given out to publicize something. **3.** a statement or other document distributed to the press or an audience to confirm, supplement, or replace an oral presentation. ~*vb.* **hand out. 4.** (*tr., adv.*) to distribute.

hand o·ver *vb.* (*tr., adv.*) to surrender possession of; transfer.

hand-pick *vb.* (*tr.*) to choose or select with great care, as for a special job or purpose. —,**hand-'picked** *adj.*

hand·rail ('hænd,reɪl) *n.* a rail alongside a stairway, etc., at a convenient height to be grasped to provide support.

hands (hændz) *n.* **1.** power or keeping: *your welfare is in his hands.* **2.** Also called: **handling.** *Soccer.* the infringement of touching the ball with any part of the hand or arm. **3. change**

hands. to pass from the possession of one person or group to another. **4. clean hands.** freedom from guilt. **5. hands down.** without effort; easily. **6. hands off.** do not touch or interfere. **7. hands up!** raise the hands above the level of the shoulders, an order usually given by an armed robber to a victim, etc. **8. have one's hands full. a.** to be completely occupied. **b.** to be beset with problems. **9. have one's hands tied.** to be wholly unable to act. **10. in good hands.** in protective care. **11. join hands. a.** to become married. **b.** to enter into partnership. **12. lay hands on** *or* **upon. a.** to seize or get possession of. **b.** to beat up; assault. **c.** to find: *I just can't lay my hands on it anywhere.* **d.** *Christianity.* to confirm or ordain by the imposition of hands. **13. off one's hands.** for which one is no longer responsible. **14. on one's hands. a.** for which one is responsible: *I've got too much on my hands to help.* **b.** to spare: *time on my hands.* **15. throw up one's hands.** to give up in despair. **16. wash one's hands of.** to have nothing more to do with.

hand·saw ('hænd,sɔː) *n.* any saw for use in one hand only.

hand's-breadth *n.* another name for **handbreadth.**

hand·sel *or* **han·sel** ('hænsᵊl) *Archaic or dialect.* ~*n.* **1.** a gift for good luck at the beginning of a new year, new venture, etc. ~*vb.* **·sels, ·sel·ling, ·selled** *or U.S.* **·sels, ·sel·ing, ·seled.** (*tr.*) **2.** to give a handsel to (a person). **3.** to begin (a venture) with ceremony; inaugurate. [Old English *handselen* delivery into the hand; related to Old Norse *handsal* promise sealed with a handshake, Swedish *handsöl* gratuity; see HAND, SELL]

hand·set ('hænd,sɛt) *n.* a telephone mouthpiece and earpiece mounted so that they can be held simultaneously to mouth and ear.

hand·shake ('hænd,ʃeɪk) *n.* the act of grasping and shaking a person's hand, as when being introduced or agreeing on a deal.

hand·some ('hændsəm) *adj.* **1.** (of a man) good-looking, esp. in having regular, pleasing, and well-defined features. **2.** (of a woman) fine-looking in a dignified way. **3.** well-proportioned, stately, or comely: *a handsome room.* **4.** liberal or ample: *a handsome allowance.* **5.** gracious or generous: *a handsome action.* [C15 *handsom* easily handled; compare Dutch *handzaam;* see HAND, -SOME[1]] —**'hand·some·ly** *adv.* —**'hand·some·ness** *n.*

hand·spike ('hænd,spaɪk) *n.* a bar or length of pipe used as a lever.

hand·spring ('hænd,sprɪŋ) *n.* a gymnastic feat in which a person starts from a standing position and leaps forwards or backwards into a handstand and then onto his feet.

hand·stand ('hænd,stænd) *n.* the act or instance of supporting the body on the hands alone in an upside down position.

hand·stroke ('hænd,strəʊk) *n. Bell-ringing.* the downward movement of the bell rope as the bell swings around allowing the ringer to grasp and pull it.

hand-to-hand *adj., adv.* at close quarters: *they fought hand-to-hand.*

hand-to-mouth *adj., adv.* with barely enough money or food to satisfy immediate needs: *a hand-to-mouth existence.*

hand·writ·ing ('hænd,raɪtɪŋ) *n.* **1.** writing by hand rather than by typing or printing. **2.** a person's characteristic writing style: *that signature is in my handwriting.*

hand·writ·ten ('hænd,rɪtᵊn) *adj.* written by hand; not printed or typed.

hand·y ('hændɪ) *adj.* **hand·i·er, hand·i·est. 1.** conveniently or easily within reach. **2.** easy to manoeuvre, handle, or use: *a handy tool.* **3.** skilful with one's hands. —**'hand·i·ness** *n.*

Han·dy ('hændɪ) *n.* **W(illiam) C(hristopher).** 1873–1958, U.S. blues composer, who wrote *St. Louis Blues.*

hand·y·man ('hændɪ,mæn) *n., pl.* **·men. 1.** a man employed to do various tasks. **2.** a man skilled in odd jobs, etc.

hang (hæŋ) *vb.* **hangs, hang·ing, hung. 1.** to fasten or be fastened from above, esp. by a cord, chain, etc.; suspend: *the picture hung on the wall; to hang laundry.* **2.** to place or be placed in position as by a hinge so as to allow free movement around or at the place of suspension: *to hang a door.* **3.** (*intr.;* sometimes foll. by *over*) to be suspended or poised; hover: *a pall of smoke hung over the city.* **4.** (*intr.;* sometimes foll. by *over*) to be imminent; threaten. **5.** (*intr.*) to be or remain doubtful or unresolved (esp. in the phrase **hang in the balance**). **6.** (*past tense and past participle* **hanged**) to suspend or be suspended by the neck until dead. **7.** (*tr.*) to fasten, fix, or attach in position or at an appropriate angle: *to hang a scythe to its handle.* **8.** (*tr.*) to decorate, furnish, or cover with something suspended or fastened: *to hang a wall with tapestry.* **9.** (*tr.*) to fasten to or suspend from a wall: *to hang wallpaper.* **10.** to exhibit (a picture or pictures) by (a particular painter, printmaker, etc.) or (of a picture or a painter, etc.) to be exhibited in an art gallery, etc. **11.** to fall or droop or allow to fall or droop: *to hang one's head in shame.* **12.** (of cloth, clothing, etc.) to drape, fall, or flow, esp. in a specified manner: *her skirt hangs well.* **13.** (*tr.*) to suspend (game such as pheasant) so that it becomes slightly decomposed and therefore more tender and tasty. **14.** (of a jury) to prevent or be prevented from reaching a verdict. **15.** (*past tense and past participle* **hanged**) *Slang.* to damn or be damned: used in mild curses or interjections: *I'll be hanged before I'll go out in that storm.* **16.** (*intr.*) to pass slowly (esp. in the phrase **time hangs heavily**). **17. hang fire.** to procrastinate or delay. See also **fire** (sense 19). ~*n.* **18.** the way in which something hangs. **19.** (*usually used with a negative*) *Slang.* a damn: *I don't care a hang for what you say.* **20. get the hang of.** *Informal.* **a.** to understand the technique of doing something. **b.** to perceive the meaning or significance of. ~See also **hang about, hang back, hang behind, hang in, hang on, hang out, hang together, hang up.** [Old English *hangian;* related to Old Norse *hanga,* Old High German *hangēn*]

hang a·bout *or* **a·round** *vb.* (*intr.*) **1.** to waste time; loiter. **2.** (*adv.,* foll. by *with*) to frequent the company (of someone).

hang·ar ('hæŋə) *n.* a large workshop or building for storing and maintaining aircraft. [C19: from French: shed, perhaps from Medieval Latin *angārium* shed used as a smithy, of obscure origin]

hang back *vb.* (*intr., adv.;* often foll. by *from*) to be reluctant to go forward or carry on (with some activity).

hang be·hind *vb.* (*intr., adv.*) to remain in a place after others have left; linger.

hang·bird ('hæŋ,bɜːd) *n. U.S.* any bird, esp. the Baltimore oriole, that builds a hanging nest.

Hang·chow *or* **Hang-chou** ('hæŋ'tʃaʊ) *n.* a port in E China, capital of Chekiang province, on **Hangchow Bay** (an inlet of the East China Sea), at the foot of the Eye of Heaven Mountains: regarded by Marco Polo as the finest city in the world; seat of two universities (1927, 1959). Pop.: 960 000 (1970 est.).

hang·dog ('hæŋ,dɒg) *adj.* **1.** downcast, furtive, or guilty in appearance or manner. ~*n.* **2.** a furtive or sneaky person.

hang·er ('hæŋə) *n.* **1. a.** any support, such as a hook, strap, peg, or loop, on or by which something may be hung. **b.** See **coat hanger. 2. a.** a person who hangs something. **b.** (*in combination*): *paperhanger.* **3.** a bracket designed to attach one part of a mechanical structure to another, such as the one that attaches the spring shackle of a motor car to the chassis. **4.** a type of dagger worn on a sword belt.

hang·er-on *n., pl.* **hang·ers-on.** a sycophantic follower or dependant, esp. one hoping for personal gain.

hang-glid·er *n.* an unpowered aircraft consisting of a large cloth wing stretched over a light framework from which the pilot hangs in a harness, using a horizontal bar to control the flight. —**'hang-glid·ing** *n.*

hang in *vb.* (*intr., prep.*) *U.S. slang.* to persist: *just hang in there for a bit longer.*

hang·ing ('hæŋɪŋ) *n.* **1. a.** the putting of a person to death by suspending the body by the neck from a noose. **b.** (*as modifier*): *a hanging offence.* **2.** (*often pl.*) a decorative textile such as a tapestry or drapery hung on a wall or over a window. **3.** the act of a person or thing that hangs. ~*adj.* **4.** not supported from below; suspended. **5.** undecided; still under discussion. **6.** inclining or projecting downwards; overhanging. **7.** situated on a steep slope or in a high place. **8.** (*prenominal*) given to issuing harsh sentences, esp. death sentences: *a hanging judge.*

Hang·ing Gar·dens of Bab·y·lon *n.* (in ancient Babylon) gardens, probably planted on terraces of a ziggurat: one of the Seven Wonders of the World.

hang·ing val·ley *n. Geography.* a tributary valley entering a main valley at a much higher level because of overdeepening of the main valley, esp. by glacial erosion.

hang·ing wall *n.* the rocks on the upper side of an inclined fault plane or mineral vein. Compare **footwall.**

hang·man ('hæŋmən) *n., pl.* **·men.** an official who carries out a sentence of hanging on condemned criminals.

hang·nail ('hæŋ,neɪl) *n.* a piece of skin torn away from, but still attached to, the base or side of a fingernail. [C17: from Old English *angnægl,* from *enge* tight + *nægl* NAIL; influenced by HANG]

hang on *vb.* (*intr.*) **1.** (*adv.*) to continue or persist in an activity, esp. with effort or difficulty: *hang on at your present job until you can get another.* **2.** (*adv.*) to cling, grasp, or hold: *she hangs on to her mother's arm.* **3.** (*prep.*) to be conditioned or contingent on; depend on: *everything hangs on this business deal.* **4.** (*prep.*) Also: **hang onto, hang upon.** to listen attentively to: *she hung on his every word.* **5.** (*adv.*) *Informal.* to wait or remain: *hang on for a few minutes.*

hang out *vb.* (*adv.*) **1.** to suspend, be suspended, or lean, esp. from an opening, as for display or airing: *to hang out the washing.* **2.** (*intr.*) *Informal.* to live at or frequent a place: *the police know where the thieves hang out.* **3.** *Slang.* to relax completely in an unassuming way (esp. in the phrase **let it all hang out**). **4.** (*intr.*) *U.S. informal.* to act or speak freely, in an open, cooperative, or indiscreet manner. ~*n.* **hang-out. 5.** *Informal.* a place where one lives or that one frequently visits.

hang·o·ver ('hæŋ,əʊvə) *n.* **1.** the delayed aftereffects of drinking too much alcohol in a relatively short period of time, characterized by headache and sometimes nausea and dizziness. **2.** a person or thing left over from or influenced by a past age.

hang to·geth·er *vb.* (*intr., adv.*) **1.** to be cohesive or united. **2.** to be consistent: *your statements don't quite hang together.*

hang up *vb.* (*adv.*) **1.** (*tr.*) to put on a hook, hanger, etc.: *please hang up your coat.* **2.** to replace (a telephone receiver) on its cradle at the end of a conversation, often breaking a conversation off abruptly. **3.** (*tr.; usually passive;* usually foll. by *on*) *Informal.* to cause to have an emotional or psychological preoccupation or problem: *he's really hung up on his mother.* ~*n.* **hang-up.** *Informal.* **4.** an emotional or psychological preoccupation or problem. **5.** a persistent cause of annoyance.

hank (hæŋk) *n.* **1.** a loop, coil, or skein, as of rope, wool, or yarn. **2.** *Nautical.* a ringlike fitting that can be opened to admit a stay for attaching the luff of a sail. **3.** a unit of measurement of cloth, yarn, etc., such as a length of 840 yards (767 m) of cotton or 560 yards (512 m) of worsted yarn. ~*vb.* **4.** (*tr.*) *Nautical.* to attach (a sail) to a stay by hanks. [C13: of Scandinavian origin; compare Old Norse *hanka* to coil, Swedish *hank* string]

hank+er ('hæŋkə) *vb.* (foll. by *for, after,* or an infinitive) to have a yearning (for something or to do something). [C17: probably from Dutch dialect *hankeren*] —'**hank+er+er** *n.*

Han+kow *or* **Han-k'ou** ('hæn'kaʊ) *n.* a former city in SE China, in SE Hupeh at the confluence of the Han and Yangtze Rivers: one of the Han Cities; merged with Hanyang and Wuchang in 1950 to form the conurbation of Wuhan.

hank·y *or* **hank·ie** ('hæŋkɪ) *n., pl.* **hank·ies.** *Informal.* short for **handkerchief.**

hank·y-pank·y ('hæŋkɪ'pæŋkɪ) *n. Informal.* **1.** dubious or suspicious behaviour. **2.** foolish behaviour or talk. **3.** illicit sexual relations. [C19: variant of HOCUS POCUS]

Han·nah ('hænə) *n. Old Testament.* the woman who gave birth to Samuel (I Samuel 1–2).

Han·ni·bal ('hænɪbəl) *n.* 247–182 B.C., Carthaginian general; son of Hamilcar Barca. He commanded the Carthaginian army in the Second Punic War (218–201). After capturing Sagunto in Spain, he invaded Italy (218), crossing the Alps with an army of about 40 000 men and defeating the Romans at Trasimene (217) and Cannae (216). In 203 he was recalled to defend Carthage and was defeated by Scipio at Zama (202). He was later forced into exile and committed suicide to avoid capture.

Han+no+ver (*German* ha'no:fər) *n.* a city in N West Germany, capital of Lower Saxony: capital of the kingdom of Hannover (1815–66); situated on the Mittelland canal. Pop.: 505 106 (1974 est.). English spelling: **Hanover.**

Ha+noi (hæ'nɔɪ) *n.* the capital of Vietnam, on the Red River: became capital of Tonkin in 1802, of French Indochina in 1887, of Vietnam in 1945, and of North Vietnam (1954–75); university (1917); industrial centre. Pop.: 1 443 500 (1976 est.).

Han·o+ver[1] ('hænəʊvə) *n.* the English spelling of **Hannover.**

Han·o+ver[2] ('hænəʊvə) *n.* **1.** a princely house of Germany (1692–1815), the head of which succeeded to the British throne as George I in 1714. **2.** the royal house of Britain (1714–1901).

Han·o·ve·ri·an (ˌhænə'vɪərɪən) *adj.* **1.** of, relating to, or situated in Hannover. **2.** of or relating to the princely house of Hanover or to the monarchs of England or their reigns from 1714 to 1901. ~*n.* **3.** a member or supporter of the house of Hanover.

Han·rat·ty (hæn'rætɪ) *n.* **James.** 1936–62, Englishman executed, despite conflicting evidence, for a murder on the A6 road. Subsequent public concern played a major part in the abolition of capital punishment in Britain.

Han+sard ('hænsɑ:d) *n.* **1.** the official verbatim report of the proceedings of the British Parliament. **2.** a similar report kept by other legislative bodies. [C19: named after L. *Hansard* (1752–1828) and his descendants, who compiled the reports until 1889]

Hanse (hæns) *or* **Han+sa** ('hænsə, -zə) *n.* **1.** a medieval guild of merchants. **2.** a fee paid by the new members of a medieval trading guild. **3. a.** another name for the **Hanseatic League. b.** (*as modifier*): *a Hanse town.* [C12: of Germanic origin; compare Old High German *hansa,* Old English *hōs* troop]

Han+se·at+ic (ˌhænsɪ'ætɪk) *adj.* **1.** of or relating to the Hanseatic League. ~*n.* **2.** a member of the Hanseatic League.

Han+se·at+ic League *n.* a commercial association of towns in N Germany formed in the mid-14th century to protect and control trade. It was at its most powerful in the 15th century. Also called: **Hansa, Hanse.**

han+sel ('hænsəl) *n., vb.* a variant spelling of **handsel.**

Han+sen's dis+ease ('hænsənz) *n. Pathol.* another name for **leprosy.** [C20: named after G. H. *Hansen* (1841–1912), Norwegian physician]

han+som ('hænsəm) *n.* (*sometimes cap.*) a two-wheeled one-horse carriage with a fixed hood. The driver sits on a high outside seat at the rear. Also called: **hansom cab.** [C19: short for *hansom cab,* named after its designer J. A. *Hansom* (1803–82)]

Hants. (hænts) *abbrev. for* Hampshire.

Ha+nuk+kah, Ha+nu+kah, Cha+nu+kah, *or* **Cha+nuk+kah** ('hɑ:nəkə, -nʊˌkɑ:; *Hebrew* xanu'ka) *n.* the eight-day Jewish festival of lights beginning on the 25th of Kislev and commemorating the rededication of the temple by Judas Maccabaeus in 165 B.C. Also called: **Feast of Dedication.** [from Hebrew: a dedication]

Han·u·man (ˌhʌnʊ'mɑ:n) *n.* **1.** another word for **entellus** (the monkey). **2.** the monkey chief of Hindu mythology and devoted helper of Rama. [from Hindi *Hanumān,* from Sanskrit *hanumant* having (conspicuous) jaws, from *hanu* jaw]

Han+yang *or* **Han-yang** ('hæn'jæŋ) *n.* a former city in SE China, in SE Hupeh at the confluence of the Han and Yangtze Rivers: one of the Han Cities; merged with Hankow and Wuchang in 1950 to form the conurbation of Wuhan.

hap (hæp) *n. Archaic.* **1.** luck; chance. **2.** an occurrence. ~*vb.* **haps, hap+ping, happed. 3.** (*intr.*) an archaic word for **happen.** [C13: from Old Norse *happ* good luck; related to Old English *gehæplic* convenient, Old Slavonic *kobŭ* fate]

ha+pax le+go+me·non ('hæpæks lə'gɒmɪˌnɒn) *n., pl.* **ha+pax le+go+men·a** (lə'gɒmɪnə). another term for **nonce word.** [Greek: thing said only once]

ha'+pen·ny ('heɪpnɪ) *n., pl.* **·nies.** *Brit.* a variant spelling of **halfpenny.**

hap+haz+ard (hæp'hæzəd) *adv., adj.* **1.** at random. ~*adj.* **2.** careless; slipshod. ~*n.* **3.** *Rare.* chance. —**hap+'haz+ard+ly** *adv.* —**hap+'haz+ard+ness** *n.*

Haph+ta+rah (hɑ:f'taʊrə; *Hebrew* hafta'ra) *n., pl.* **+ta+roth** (-'taʊraʊt; *Hebrew* -ta'rɔt) *or* **+ta+rahs.** a variant spelling of **Haftarah.**

hap+less ('hæplɪs) *adj.* unfortunate; wretched. —'**hap+less+ly** *adv.* —'**hap+less+ness** *n.*

hap+lite ('hæplaɪt) *n.* a variant spelling of **aplite.** —**hap+lit+ic** (hæp'lɪtɪk) *adj.*

hap·lo- *or before a vowel* **hapl-** *combining form.* single or simple: *haplology; haplosis.* [from Greek *haplous* simple]

hap+log+ra+phy (hæp'lɒgrəfɪ) *n., pl.* **+phies.** the accidental omission of a letter or syllable in writing, as in spelling *endodontics* as *endontics.* [C19: from Greek, from *haplous* single + -GRAPHY]

hap+loid ('hæplɔɪd) *Biology.* ~*adj. also* **hap+loi+dic. 1.** (esp. of gametes) having a single set of unpaired chromosomes. ~*n.* **2.** a haploid cell or organism. Compare **diploid.** [C20: from Greek *haploeidēs* single, from *haplous* single]

hap+lol+o·gy (hæp'lɒlədʒɪ) *n.* omission of a repeated occurrence of a sound or syllable in fluent speech, as for example in the pronunciation of *library* as ('laɪbrɪ). —**hap+lo+log+ic** (ˌhæplə'lɒdʒɪk) *adj.*

hap+lo+sis (hæp'ləʊsɪs) *n. Biology.* the production of a haploid number of chromosomes during meiosis.

hap+ly ('hæplɪ) *adv.* (*sentence modifier*) an archaic word for **perhaps.**

ha'+p'orth ('heɪpəθ) *n. Brit.* a variant spelling of **halfpennyworth.**

hap+pen ('hæpən) *vb.* **1.** (*intr.*) (of an event in time) to come about or take place; occur. **2.** (*intr.;* foll. by *to*) (of some unforeseen circumstance or event, esp. death), to fall to the lot (of); be a source of good or bad fortune (to): *if anything happens to me it'll be your fault.* **3.** (*tr.*) to chance (to be or do something): *I happen to know him.* **4.** (*tr.; takes a clause as object*) to be the case, esp. if by chance, that: *it happens that I know him.* ~*adv., sentence substitute. Northern Brit. dialect.* **5. a.** another word for **perhaps. b.** (*as sentence modifier*): *happen I'll see thee tomorrow.* [C14: see HAP, -EN[1]]
Usage. See at **occur.**

hap+pen by, past, a·long, *or* **in** *vb.* (*intr., adv.*), *Informal, chiefly U.S.* to appear, arrive, or come casually or by chance.

hap+pen+ing ('hæpənɪŋ, 'hæpnɪŋ) *n.* **1.** an occurrence; event. **2.** an improvised or spontaneous display or performance consisting of bizarre and haphazard events.

hap+pen on *or* **up·on** *vb.* (*intr.; prep.*) to find by chance: *I happened upon a pound note lying in the street.*

hap+pen+stance ('hæpənˌstæns) *n. U.S.* **1.** chance. **2.** a chance occurrence.

hap+py ('hæpɪ) *adj.* **+pi+er, +pi+est. 1.** feeling, showing, or expressing joy; pleased. **2.** causing joy or gladness. **3.** fortunate; lucky: *the happy position of not having to work.* **4.** aptly expressed; appropriate: *a happy turn of phrase.* **5.** (*postpositive*) *Informal.* slightly intoxicated. **6. happy event.** *Informal.* the birth of a child. **7. happy medium.** a course or state that avoids extremes. **8. happy release.** liberation, esp. by death, from an unpleasant condition. ~*interj.* **9.** (*in combination*): *happy birthday; happy Christmas.* ~See also **trigger-happy.** [C14: see HAP, -Y[1]] —'**hap+pi+ly** *adv.* —'**hap+pi+ness** *n.*

hap·py-go-luck·y *adj.* carefree or easygoing.

hap+py hunt+ing ground *n.* (in American Indian legend) the paradise to which a person passes after death.

Haps·burg ('hæpsˌbɜ:g) *n.* a German princely family founded by Albert, count of Hapsburg (1153). From 1440 to 1806, the Hapsburgs wore the imperial crown of the Holy Roman Empire almost uninterruptedly. They also provided rulers for Austria, Spain, Hungary, Bohemia, etc. The line continued as the royal house of **Hapsburg-Lorraine,** ruling in Austria (1806–48) and Austria-Hungary (1848–1918). German name: **Habsburg.**

hap+ten ('hæptən) *or* **hap+tene** ('hæpti:n) *n. Immunol.* an incomplete antigen that can stimulate antibody production only when complexed to a particular protein. [C20: from German, from Greek *haptein* to fasten]

hap+ter+on ('hæptərɒn) *n.* a cell or group of cells that occurs in certain plants, esp. seaweeds, and attaches the plant to its substratum. [C20: from Greek *haptein* to make fast]

hap+tic ('hæptɪk) *adj.* relating to or based on the sense of touch. [C19: from Greek, from *haptein* to touch]

hap+to+trop+ism (ˌhæptəʊ'trəʊpɪzəm) *n.* another name for **thigmotropism.**

ha+ra+ki+ri (ˌhærə'kɪrɪ) *or* **ha+ri+ka+ri** (ˌhærɪ'kɑ:rɪ) *n.* (in Japan) ritual suicide by disembowelment with a sword when disgraced or under sentence of death. Also called: **seppuku.** [C19: from Japanese, from *hara* belly + *kiri* cut]

Har·ald I ('hærəld) *n.* called *Harald Fairhair.* ?850–933, first king of Norway: his rule caused emigration to the British Isles.

ha+ram+bee (ˌhɑ:rɑ:m'beɪ) *n.* **1.** a work chant used on the E African coast. **2.** a rallying cry used in Kenya. ~*interj.* **3.** a cry of harambee. [Swahili: pull together]

ha+rangue (hə'ræŋ) *vb.* **1.** to address (a person or crowd) in an angry, vehement, or forcefully persuasive way. ~*n.* **2.** a loud, forceful, or angry speech. [C15: from Old French, from Old Italian *aringa* public speech, probably of Germanic origin; related to Medieval Latin *harenga;* see HARRY, RING[1]] —**ha+'rangu+er** *n.*

Ha+rap+pa (hə'ræpə) *n.* an ancient city in the Punjab in NW Pakistan: one of the centres of the Indus civilization that flourished from 2500 to 1700 B.C.; probably destroyed by Indo-European invaders. —**Ha+'rap+pan** *adj., n.*

Ha+rar *or* **Har+rar** ('hɑ:rə) *n.* a city in E Ethiopia: former capital of the Muslim state of Adal. Pop.: 45 840 (1971 est.).

har+ass ('hærəs) *vb.* (*tr.*) to trouble, torment, or confuse by continual persistent attacks, questions, etc. [C17: from French *harasser,* variant of Old French *harer* to set a dog on, of Germanic origin; compare Old High German *harēn* to cry out] —'**har·ass·er** *n.* —'**har·ass·ing·ly** *adv.* —'**har·ass·ment** *n.*

Har·bin (hɑːˈbiːn, -ˈbɪn) *n.* a city in NE China, capital of Heilungkiang province on the Sungari River: founded by the Russians in 1897; centre of tsarist activities after the October Revolution in Russia (1917). Pop.: 1 670 000 (1970 est.). Also called: **Ha-erh-pin.**

har·bin·ger (ˈhɑːbɪndʒə) *n.* **1.** a person or thing that announces or indicates the approach of something; forerunner. **2.** *Obsolete.* a person sent in advance of a royal party or army to obtain lodgings for them. ~*vb.* **3.** (*tr.*) to announce the approach or arrival of. [C12: from Old French *herbergere,* from *herberge* lodging, from Old Saxon *heriberga;* compare Old High German *heriberga* army shelter; see HARRY, BOROUGH]

har·bour *or U.S.* **har·bor** (ˈhɑːbə) *n.* **1.** a sheltered port. **2.** a place of refuge or safety. ~*vb.* **3.** (*tr.*) to give shelter to: *to harbour a criminal.* **4.** (*tr.*) to maintain secretly: *to harbour a grudge.* **5.** to shelter (a vessel) in a harbour or (of a vessel) to seek shelter. [Old English *herebeorg,* from *here* troop, army + *beorg* shelter; related to Old High German *heriberga* hostelry, Old Norse *herbergi*] —'**har·bour·er** *or U.S.* '**har·bor·er** *n.* —'**har·bour·less** *or U.S.* '**har·bor·less** *adj.*

har·bour·age *or U.S.* **har·bor·age** (ˈhɑːbərɪdʒ) *n.* shelter or refuge, as for a ship, or a place providing shelter.

har·bour mas·ter *n.* an official in charge of a harbour.

har·bour seal *n.* a common earless seal, *Phoca vitulina,* that is greyish-black with paler markings: occurs off the coasts of North America, N Europe, and NE Asia.

hard (hɑːd) *adj.* **1.** firm or rigid; not easily dented, crushed, or pierced. **2.** toughened by or as if by physical labour; not soft or smooth: *hard hands.* **3.** difficult to do or accomplish; arduous: *a hard task.* **4.** difficult to understand or perceive: *a hard question.* **5.** showing or requiring considerable physical or mental energy, effort, or application: *hard work; a hard drinker.* **6.** stern, cold, or intractable: *a hard judge.* **7.** exacting; demanding: *a hard master.* **8.** harsh; cruel: *a hard fate.* **9.** inflicting pain, sorrow, distress, or hardship: *hard times.* **10.** tough or adamant: *a hard man.* **11.** forceful or violent: *a hard knock.* **12.** cool or uncompromising: *we took a long hard look at our profit factor.* **13.** indisputable; real: *hard facts.* **14.** *Chem.* (of water) impairing the formation of a lather by soap. See **hardness** (sense 3). **15.** practical, shrewd, or calculating: *he is a hard man in business.* **16.** too harsh to be pleasant: *hard light.* **17. a.** (of cash, money, etc.) in coin rather than paper. **b.** (of currency) high and stable in exchange value and backed by bullion. **c.** (of credit) difficult to obtain; tight. **18.** (of alcoholic drink) being a spirit rather than a wine, beer, etc.: *the hard stuff.* **19.** (of a drug such as heroin, morphine, or cocaine) highly addictive. Compare **soft** (sense 18). **20.** *Physics.* (of radiation, such as gamma rays and x-rays) having high energy and the ability to penetrate solids. **21.** *Chiefly U.S.* (of goods) durable. **22.** short for **hard-core. 23.** *Phonetics.* **a.** an older word for **fortis. b.** (not in modern technical usage) denoting the consonants *c* and *g* in English when they are pronounced as velar stops (k, g). **c.** (of consonants in the Slavonic languages) not palatalized. **24. a.** being heavily fortified and protected. **b.** (of nuclear armament) located underground. **25.** *Brit. informal.* incorrigible or disreputable (esp. in the phrase **a hard case**). **26.** (of bread, etc.) stale and old. **27. a hard nut to crack. a.** a person not easily persuaded or won over. **b.** a thing not easily understood. **28. hard by.** near; close by. **29. hard of hearing.** deaf or partly deaf. **30. hard up.** *Informal.* **a.** in need of money; poor. **b.** (foll. by *for*) in great need (of): *hard up for suggestions.* **31. put the hard word on (someone).** *Austral. informal.* to ask or demand something from (a person). ~*adv.* **32.** with great energy, force, or vigour: *the team always played hard.* **33.** as far as possible; all the way: *hard left.* **34.** with application; earnestly or intently: *she thought hard about the formula.* **35.** with great intensity, force, or violence: *his son's death hit him hard.* **36.** (foll. by *on, upon, by,* or *after*) close; near: *hard on his heels.* **37.** (foll. by *at*) assiduously; devotedly. **38. a.** with effort or difficulty: *their victory was hard won.* **b.** (*in combination*): *hard-earned.* **39.** slowly and reluctantly: *prejudice dies hard.* **40. go hard with.** to cause pain or difficulty to (someone): *it will go hard with you if you don't tell the truth.* **41. hard at it.** working hard. **42. hard put (to it).** scarcely having the capacity (to do something): *he's hard put to get to work by 9:30.* ~*n.* **43.** any colorant that produces a harsh coarse appearance. **44.** *Brit.* a roadway across a foreshore. **45.** *Slang.* hard labour. **46.** *Taboo slang.* an erection of the penis (esp. in the phrase **get** or **have a hard on**). [Old English *heard;* related to Old Norse *harthr,* Old Frisian *herd,* Old High German *herti,* Gothic *hardus* hard, Greek *kratus* strong]

hard and fast *adj.* (**hard-and-fast** *when prenominal*). (of rules, etc.) invariable or strict.

hard·back (ˈhɑːdˌbæk) *n.* **1.** a book or edition with covers of cloth, cardboard, or leather. ~*adj.* **2.** Also: **casebound, hard·bound** (ˈhɑːdˌbaʊnd), **hard·cov·er** (ˈhɑːdˌkʌvə). of or denoting a hardback or the publication of hardbacks.

hard·bake (ˈhɑːdˌbeɪk) *n.* almond toffee.

hard-bit·ten *adj.* tough and realistic.

hard·board (ˈhɑːdˌbɔːd) *n.* a thin stiff sheet made of compressed sawdust and woodchips bound together with plastic adhesive or resin under heat and pressure.

hard-boiled *adj.* **1.** (of an egg) boiled until the yolk and white are solid. **2.** *Informal.* **a.** tough, realistic. **b.** cynical.

hard cheese *interj., n. Brit. slang.* bad luck.

hard ci·der *n. U.S.* fermented apple juice. Compare **sweet cider.**

hard coal *n.* another name for **anthracite.** Compare **soft coal.**

hard cop·y *n.* computer output that can be read by the eye, as contrasted with machine-readable output such as magnetic tape.

hard core *n.* **1.** the members of a group or movement who form an intransigent nucleus resisting change. **2.** material, such as broken bricks, stones, etc., used to form a foundation for a road, paving, building, etc. ~*adj.* **hard-core. 3.** (of pornography) describing or depicting sexual acts in explicit detail. **4.** completely and enduringly established in a belief, etc.: *hard-core Communists.*

hard court *n.* a tennis court made of asphalt, concrete, etc. See also **grass court.**

Har·de·ca·nute (ˈhɑːdɪkəˌnjuːt) *n.* a variant of **Harthacanute.**

hard-edge *adj.* of, relating to, or denoting a style of painting in which vividly coloured subjects are clearly delineated.

hard·en[1] (ˈhɑːdᵊn) *vb.* **1.** to make or become hard or harder; freeze, stiffen, or set. **2.** to make or become more hardy, tough, or unfeeling. **3.** to make or become stronger or firmer: *they hardened defences.* **4.** to make or become more resolute or set: *hardened in his resolve.* **5.** (*intr.*) *Commerce.* **a.** (of prices, a market, etc.) to cease to fluctuate. **b.** (of price) to rise higher.

hard·en[2] (ˈhɑːdᵊn) *n.* a rough fabric made from hards.

Har·den·berg (*German* ˈhardᵊnˌbɛrk) *n.* **Frie·drich von** (ˈfriːdrɪç fɔn). the original name of **Novalis.**

hard·ened (ˈhɑːdᵊnd) *adj.* **1.** rigidly set, as in a mode of behaviour. **2.** toughened, as by custom; seasoned.

hard·en·er (ˈhɑːdᵊnə) *n.* **1.** a person or thing that hardens. **2.** a substance added to paint or varnish to increase durability. **3.** an ingredient of certain adhesives that accelerates or promotes setting.

hard·en·ing (ˈhɑːdᵊnɪŋ) *n.* **1.** the act or process of becoming or making hard. **2.** a substance added to another substance or material to make it harder.

hard·en·ing of the ar·ter·ies *n.* a nontechnical name for **arteriosclerosis.**

hard·en off *vb.* (*adv.*) to accustom (a cultivated plant) or (of such a plant) to become accustomed to outdoor conditions by repeated exposure.

hard·en up *vb.* (*intr.*) *Nautical.* to tighten the sheets of a sailing vessel so as to prevent luffing.

hard·hack (ˈhɑːdˌhæk) *n.* a woody North American rosaceous plant, *Spiraea tomentosa,* with downy leaves and tapering clusters of small pink or white flowers. Also called: **steeplebush.**

hard hat *n.* **1.** a hat made of a hard material for protection, worn esp. by construction workers. **2.** *Informal, chiefly U.S.* a construction worker. ~*adj.* **hard-hat. 3.** *Informal.* characteristic of the presumed conservative attitudes and prejudices typified by construction workers.

hard-head·ed *adj.* **1.** tough, realistic, or shrewd; not moved by sentiment. **2.** *Chiefly U.S.* stubborn; obstinate. —ˌ**hard-ˈhead·ed·ly** *adv.* —ˌ**hard-ˈhead·ed·ness** *n.*

hard·heads (ˈhɑːdˌhɛdz) *n.* (*functioning as sing.*) a thistle-like plant, *Centaurea nigra,* native to Europe and introduced into North America and New Zealand, that has reddish-purple flower heads: family *Compositae* (composites). Also called: **knapweed.** See also **centaury** (sense 2).

hard·heart·ed (ˌhɑːdˈhɑːtɪd) *adj.* unkind or intolerant. —ˌ**hard·ˈheart·ed·ly** *adv.* —ˌ**hard·ˈheart·ed·ness** *n.*

hard-hit *adj.* seriously affected or hurt: *hard-hit by taxation.*

Har·di·ca·nute (ˈhɑːdɪkəˌnjuːt) *n.* a variant of **Harthacanute.**

Har·die (ˈhɑːdɪ) *n.* **(James) Keir** (kɪə). 1856–1915, Scottish labour leader and politician; the first parliamentary leader of the Labour Party.

har·di·hood (ˈhɑːdɪˌhʊd) *n.* courage, daring, or audacity.

har·di·ly (ˈhɑːdɪlɪ) *adv.* in a hardy manner; toughly or boldly.

har·di·ness (ˈhɑːdɪnɪs) *n.* the condition or quality of being hardy, robust, or bold.

Har·ding (ˈhɑːdɪŋ) *n.* **War·ren G(amaliel).** 1865–1923, 29th president of the U.S. (1921–23).

hard la·bour *n. Criminal law.* (formerly) the penalty of compulsory physical labour imposed in addition to a sentence of imprisonment: abolished in England in 1948.

hard land·ing *n.* a landing by a rocket or spacecraft in which the vehicle is destroyed on impact. Compare **soft landing.**

hard line *n.* an uncompromising course or policy. —ˌ**hard·ˈlin·er** *n.*

hard lines *interj., n. Brit. informal.* bad luck. Also: **hard cheese.**

hard·ly (ˈhɑːdlɪ) *adv.* **1.** scarcely; barely: *we hardly knew the family.* **2.** just; only just: *he could hardly hold the cup.* **3.** *Often used ironically.* almost or probably not or not at all: *he will hardly incriminate himself.* **4.** with difficulty or effort. **5.** *Rare.* harshly or cruelly.

Usage. Since *hardly, scarcely,* and *barely* already have negative force, it is redundant to use another negative in the same clause: *he had hardly had* (not *he hadn't hardly had*) *time to think; there was scarcely any* (not *scarcely no*) *bread left.*

hard-mouthed *adj.* **1.** (of a horse) not responding satisfactorily to a pull on the bit. **2.** stubborn; obstinate.

hard·ness (ˈhɑːdnɪs) *n.* **1.** the quality or condition of being hard. **2.** one of several measures of resistance to indentation, deformation, or abrasion. See **Mohs scale, Brinell number. 3.** the quality of water that causes it to impair the lathering of soap: caused by the presence of certain calcium salts. **Temporary hardness** can be removed by boiling whereas **permanent hardness** cannot.

hard-nosed *adj. U.S. slang.* tough, shrewd, and practical.
hard pal·ate *n.* the anterior bony portion of the roof of the mouth, extending backwards to the soft palate.
hard·pan ('hɑːdˌpæn) *n.* a hard impervious layer of clay below the soil, resistant to drainage and root growth.
hard paste *n.* **a.** porcelain made with kaolin and petuntse, of Chinese origin and made in Europe from the early 18th century. **b.** (*as modifier*): *hard-paste porcelain.*
hard-pressed *adj.* **1.** in difficulties: *the swimmer was hard-pressed.* **2.** subject to severe competition. **3.** subject to severe attack. **4.** closely pursued.
hard rock *n. Music.* a rhythmically simple and usually highly amplified style of rock-and-roll.
hard rub·ber *n.* a hard fairly inelastic material made by vulcanizing natural rubber. See **vulcanite.**
hards (hɑːdz) *or* **hurds** *pl. n.* coarse fibres and other refuse from flax and hemp. [Old English *heordan* (plural); related to Middle Dutch *hēde,* Greek *keskeon* tow]
hard sauce *n.* butter and sugar creamed together with rum or brandy and served with rich puddings.
hard sell *n. Chiefly U.S.* an aggressive insistent technique of selling or advertising. Compare **soft sell.**
hard-shell *adj. also* **hard-shelled. 1.** *Zoology.* having a shell or carapace that is thick, heavy, or hard. **2.** *U.S.* strictly orthodox. ~*n.* **3.** another name for the **quahog.**
hard-shell clam *n.* another name for the **quahog.**
hard-shell crab *n.* a crab, esp. of the edible species *Cancer pagurus,* that has not recently moulted and therefore has a hard shell. Compare **soft-shell crab.**
hard·ship ('hɑːdʃɪp) *n.* **1.** conditions of life difficult to endure. **2.** something that causes suffering or privation.
hard shoul·der *n. Brit.* a surfaced verge running along the edge of a motorway for emergency stops.
hard-spun *adj.* (of yarn) spun with a firm close twist.
hard·tack ('hɑːdˌtæk) *n.* a kind of hard saltless biscuit, formerly eaten esp. by sailors as a staple aboard ship. Also called: **pilot biscuit, ship's biscuit, sea biscuit.**
hard·top ('hɑːdˌtɒp) *n.* **1.** a car equipped with a metal or plastic roof that is sometimes detachable. **2.** the detachable hard roof of some sports cars.
hard·ware ('hɑːdˌwɛə) *n.* **1.** metal tools, implements, etc., esp. cutlery or cooking utensils. **2.** *Computer technol.* the physical equipment used in a computer system, such as the central processing unit, peripheral devices, and memory. Compare **software. 3.** mechanical equipment, components, etc. **4.** heavy military equipment, such as tanks and missiles or their parts. **5.** *Informal.* a gun or guns collectively.
hard-wear·ing *adj.* resilient, durable, and tough.
hard wheat *n.* a type of wheat with hard kernels, yielding a strong flour and used for bread, macaroni, etc.
hard·wood ('hɑːdˌwʊd) *n.* **1.** the wood of any of numerous broad-leaved dicotyledonous trees, such as oak, beech, ash, etc., as distinguished from the wood of a conifer. **2.** any tree from which this wood is obtained. ~Compare **softwood.**
hard-work·ing *adj.* (of a person) industrious; diligent.
har·dy[1] ('hɑːdɪ) *adj.* **·di·er, ·di·est. 1.** having or demanding a tough constitution; robust. **2.** bold; courageous. **3.** foolhardy; rash. **4.** (of plants) able to live out of doors throughout the winter. [C13: from Old French *hardi* bold, past participle of *hardir* to become bold, of Germanic origin; compare Old English *hierdan* to HARDEN, Old Norse *hertha,* Old High German *herten*]
har·dy[2] ('hɑːdɪ) *n., pl.* **·dies.** any blacksmith's tool made with a square shank so that it can be lodged in a square hole in an anvil. [C19: probably from HARD]
Har·dy ('hɑːdɪ) *n.* **Thom·as.** 1840–1928, English novelist and poet. Most of his novels are set in his native Dorset (described as Wessex) and include *Far from the Madding Crowd* (1874), *The Return of the Native* (1878), *The Mayor of Casterbridge* (1886), *Tess of the d'Urbervilles* (1891), and *Jude the Obscure* (1895), after which his work consisted chiefly of verse.
hare (hɛə) *n., pl.* **hares** *or* **hare. 1.** any solitary leporid mammal of the genus *Lepus,* such as *L. europaeus* (**European hare**). Hares are larger than rabbits, having longer ears and legs, and live in shallow nests (forms). **2. start a hare.** to raise a topic for conversation. **3. run with the hare and hunt with the hounds.** to be on good terms with both sides. ~*vb.* **4.** (*intr.;* often foll. by *off, after,* etc.) *Brit. informal.* to go or run fast or wildly. [Old English *hara;* related to Old Norse *heri,* Old High German *haso,* Swedish *hare,* Sanskrit *śaśá*] —**'hare·ˌlike** *adj.*
hare and hounds *n.* (*functioning as sing.*) a game in which certain players (**hares**) run across country scattering pieces of paper that the other players (**hounds**) follow in an attempt to catch the hares.
hare·bell ('hɛəˌbɛl) *n.* a N temperate campanulaceous plant, *Campanula rotundifolia,* having slender stems and leaves, and bell-shaped blue flowers. Also called (in Scotland): **bluebell.**
hare·brained *or* **hair·brained** ('hɛəˌbreɪnd) *adj.* rash, foolish, or badly thought out: *harebrained schemes.*
hare·lip ('hɛəˌlɪp) *n.* a congenital cleft or fissure in the midline of the upper lip, often occurring with cleft palate. —**'hare·ˌlipped** *adj.*
har·em ('hɛərəm, hɑː'riːm) *or* **har·eem** (hɑː'riːm) *n.* **1.** the part of an Oriental house reserved strictly for wives, concubines, etc. **2.** a Muslim's wives and concubines collectively. **3.** a group of female animals of the same species that are the mates of a single male. [C17: from Arabic *harīm* forbidden (place)]
hare's-foot *n.* a papilionaceous annual plant, *Trifolium arvense,* that grows on sandy soils in Europe and NW Asia and has downy heads of white or pink flowers. Also called: **hare's-foot clover.**
Har·gei·sa (hɑː'geɪsə) *n.* a city in the NW Somali Republic: former capital of British Somaliland (1941–60); trading centre for nomadic herders. Pop.: 50 000 (1972 est.).
Har·greaves ('hɑːgriːvz) *n.* **James.** died 1778, English inventor of the spinning jenny.
har·i·cot ('hærɪkəʊ) *n.* **1.** a variety of French bean with light-coloured edible seeds, which can be dried and stored. **2.** another name for **French bean. 3.** the seed or pod of any of these plants, eaten as a vegetable. [C17: from French, perhaps from Nahuatl *ayecotli*]
Ha·ri·jan ('hʌrɪdʒən) *n.* a member of certain classes in India, formerly considered inferior and untouchable. See **scheduled castes.** [Hindi, literally: man of God (so called by Mahatma Gandhi), from *Hari* god + *jan* man]
ha·ri·ka·ri (ˌhærɪ'kɑːrɪ) *n.* a variant spelling of **harakiri.**
Ha·rin·gey ('hærɪŋˌgeɪ) *n.* a borough of N Greater London. Pop.: 228 200 (1976 est.).
hark (hɑːk) *vb.* (*intr.; usually imperative*) to listen; pay attention. [Old English *heorcnian* to HEARKEN; related to Old Frisian *herkia,* Old High German *hōrechen;* see HEAR]
hark back *vb.* (*intr., adv.*) to return to an earlier subject, point, or position, as in speech or thought.
hark·en ('hɑːkən) *vb.* a variant spelling (esp. U.S.) of **hearken.** —**'hark·en·er** *n.*
harl (hɑːl) *n. Angling.* a variant of **herl.**
Har·lem ('hɑːləm) *n.* a district of New York City, in NE Manhattan: now largely a Black ghetto.
har·le·quin ('hɑːlɪkwɪn) *n.* **1.** (*sometimes cap.*) *Theatre.* a stock comic character originating in the commedia dell'arte; the foppish lover of Columbine in the English harlequinade. He is usually represented in diamond-patterned multicoloured tights, wearing a black mask. **2.** a clown or buffoon. ~*adj.* **3.** varied in colour or decoration. **4.** comic, ludicrous, etc. [C16: from Old French *Herlequin, Hellequin* leader of band of demon horsemen, perhaps from Middle English *Herle king* (unattested) King Herle, mythical being identified with Woden]
har·le·quin·ade (ˌhɑːlɪkwɪ'neɪd) *n.* **1.** (*sometimes cap.*) *Theatre.* a play or part of a pantomime in which harlequin has a leading role. **2.** buffoonery.
har·le·quin bug *n.* a brightly coloured heteropterous insect, *Murgantia histrionica,* of the U.S. and Central America: a pest of cabbages and related plants: family *Pentatomidae.*
har·le·quin duck *n.* a northern sea duck, *Histrionicus histrionicus,* the male of which has a blue and red plumage with black and white markings.
Har·ley ('hɑːlɪ) *n.* **Rob·ert,** 1st Earl of Oxford. 1661–1724, British statesman; head of the government (1710–14), negotiating the treaty of Utrecht (1713).
Har·ley Street *n.* a street in central London famous for its large number of medical specialists' consulting rooms.
har·lot ('hɑːlət) *n.* **1.** a prostitute or promiscuous woman. Related adj.: **meretricious.** ~*adj.* **2.** *Archaic.* of or like a harlot. [C13: from Old French *herlot* rascal, of obscure origin] —**'har·lot·ry** *n.*
Har·low[1] ('hɑːləʊ) *n.* a town in SE England, in W Essex: designated a new town in 1947, with a planned population of 80 000. Pop.: 77 684 (1971).
Har·low[2] ('hɑːləʊ) **Jean,** former name *Harlean Carpenter.* 1911–37, U.S. film actress, whose films include *Hell's Angel's* (1930), *Blonde Bombshell* (1933), and *Saratoga* (1937).
harm (hɑːm) *n.* **1.** physical or mental injury or damage. **2.** moral evil or wrongdoing. ~*vb.* **3.** (*tr.*) to injure physically, morally, or mentally. [Old English *hearm;* related to Old Norse *harmr* grief, Old High German *harm* injury, Old Slavonic *sramŭ* disgrace] —**'harm·er** *n.*
har·mat·tan (hɑː'mætᵊn) *n.* a dry dusty wind from the Sahara blowing towards the W African coast, esp. from November to March. [C17: from Twi *haramata,* perhaps from Arabic *harām* forbidden thing; see HAREM]
harm·ful ('hɑːmfʊl) *adj.* causing or tending to cause harm; injurious. —**'harm·ful·ly** *adv.* —**'harm·ful·ness** *n.*
harm·less ('hɑːmlɪs) *adj.* not causing or tending to cause harm. —**'harm·less·ly** *adv.* —**'harm·less·ness** *n.*
har·mon·ic (hɑː'mɒnɪk) *adj.* **1.** of, involving, producing, or characterized by harmony; harmonious. **2.** *Music.* of, relating to, or belonging to harmony. **3.** *Maths.* **a.** capable of expression in the form of sine and cosine functions. **b.** of or relating to numbers whose reciprocals form an arithmetic progression. **4.** *Physics.* of or concerned with an oscillation that has a frequency that is an integral multiple of a fundamental frequency. **5.** *Physics.* of or concerned with harmonics. ~*n.* **6.** *Physics, music.* a component of a periodic quantity, such as a musical tone, with a frequency that is an integral multiple of the fundamental frequency. The **first harmonic** is the fundamental, the **second harmonic** (twice the fundamental frequency) is the **first overtone,** the **third harmonic** (three times the fundamental frequency) is the **second overtone,** etc. **7.** *Music.* (*not in technical use*) overtone: in this case, the first overtone is the first harmonic, etc. [C16: from Latin *harmonicus* relating to HARMONY] —**har·'mon·i·cal·ly** *adv.*
har·mon·i·ca (hɑː'mɒnɪkə) *n.* **1.** a small wind instrument of the reed organ family in which reeds of graduated lengths set into a metal plate enclosed in a narrow oblong box are made to vibrate by blowing and suction. **2.** See **glass harmonica.** [C18: from Latin *harmonicus* relating to HARMONY]
har·mon·ic a·nal·y·sis *n.* **1.** the representation of a periodic function by means of the summation and integration of simple

trigonometric functions. **2.** the study of this means of representation.

har+mon+ic mean *n.* the reciprocal of the arithmetic mean of the reciprocals of a set of specified numbers: the harmonic mean of 2, 3, and 4 is $3/(\frac{1}{2}+\frac{1}{3}+\frac{1}{4}) = \frac{36}{13}$.

har+mon+ic mi+nor scale *n. Music.* a minor scale modified from the state of being natural by the sharpening of the seventh degree. See **minor.** Compare **melodic minor scale.**

har+mon+ic mo+tion *n.* a periodic motion in which the displacement is symmetrical about a point or a periodic motion that is composed of such motions. See also **simple harmonic motion.**

har+mon+ic pro+gres+sion *n.* a sequence of numbers whose reciprocals form an arithmetic progression, as $1, \frac{1}{2}, \frac{1}{3}, \ldots$.

har+mon+ics (hɑːˈmɒnɪks) *n.* **1.** (*functioning as sing.*) the science of musical sounds and their acoustic properties. **2.** (*functioning as pl.*) the overtones of a fundamental note, as produced by lightly touching the string of a stringed instrument at one of its node points while playing. See **harmonic** (sense 6).

har+mon+ic se+ries *n.* **1.** *Maths.* a series whose terms are in harmonic progression, as in $1+\frac{1}{4}+\frac{1}{7}+\frac{1}{10}+\ldots$. **2.** *Music, acoustics.* the series of tones with frequencies strictly related to one another and to the fundamental tone, as obtained by touching lightly the node points of a string while playing it. Its most important application is in the playing of brass instruments.

har+mo+ni+ous (hɑːˈməʊnɪəs) *adj.* **1.** (esp. of colours or sounds) fitting together well. **2.** having agreement or consensus. **3.** tuneful, consonant, or melodious. —**har+ˈmo+ni+ous+ly** *adv.*

har+mo+nist (ˈhɑːmənɪst) *n.* **1.** a person skilled in the art and techniques of harmony. **2.** a person who combines and collates parallel narratives. —**ˌhar+mo+ˈnis+tic** *adj.* —**ˌhar+mo+ˈnis+ti+cal+ly** *adv.*

har+mo+ni+um (hɑːˈməʊnɪəm) *n.* a musical keyboard instrument of the reed organ family, in which air from pedal-operated bellows causes the reeds to vibrate. [C19: from French, from *harmonie* HARMONY]

har+mo+nize *or* **har+mo+nise** (ˈhɑːməˌnaɪz) *vb.* **1.** to make or become harmonious. **2.** (*tr.*) *Music.* to provide a harmony for (a melody, tune, etc.). **3.** (*intr.*) to sing in harmony, as with other singers. **4.** to collate parallel narratives. —**ˈhar+mo+ˌniz+a+ble** *or* **ˈhar+mo+ˌnis+a+ble** *adj.* —**ˌhar+mo+ni+ˈza+tion** *or* **ˌhar+mo+ni+ˈsa+tion** *n.* —**ˈhar+mo+ˌniz+er** *or* **ˈhar+mo+ˌnis+er** *n.*

har+mo+ny (ˈhɑːmənɪ) *n., pl.* **+nies. 1.** agreement in action, opinion, feeling, etc.; accord. **2.** order or congruity of parts to their whole or to one another. **3.** agreeable sounds. **4.** *Music.* **a.** any combination of notes sounded simultaneously. **b.** the vertically represented structure of a piece of music. Compare **melody** (sense 1b.), **rhythm** (sense 1). **c.** the art or science concerned with the structure and combinations of chords. **5.** a collation of the material of parallel narratives, esp. of the four Gospels. [C14: from Latin *harmonia* concord of sounds, from Greek: harmony, from *harmos* a joint]

har+mo+tome (ˈhɑːməˌtəʊm) *n.* a mineral of the zeolite group consisting of hydrated aluminium barium silicate in the form of monoclinic twinned crystals. [C19: from French, from Greek *harmos* a joint + *tomē* a slice, from *temnein* to cut]

Harms·worth (ˈhɑːmzwɜːθ) *n.* **1. Al·fred Charles Wil·liam.** See (Viscount) **Northcliffe. 2. Har·old Syd·ney.** See (1st Viscount) **Rothermere.**

har+ness (ˈhɑːnɪs) *n.* **1.** an arrangement of leather straps buckled or looped together, fitted to a draught animal in order that the animal can be attached to and pull a cart. **2.** something resembling this, esp. for attaching something to the body: *a parachute harness.* **3.** *Weaving.* the part of a loom that raises and lowers the warp threads, creating the shed. **4.** *Archaic.* armour collectively. **5. in harness.** at one's routine work. ~*vb.* (*tr.*) **6.** to put harness on (a horse). **7.** (usually foll. by *to*) to attach (a draught animal) by means of harness to (a cart, etc.). **8.** to control so as to employ the energy or potential power of: *to harness the atom.* **9.** to equip or clothe with armour. [C13: from Old French *harneis* baggage, probably from Old Norse *hernest* (unattested) provisions, from *herr* army + *nest* provisions] —**ˈhar+ness+er** *n.* —**ˈhar+ness+less** *adj.* —**ˈhar·ness-ˌlike** *adj.*

har+nessed an+te+lope *n.* any of various antelopes with vertical white stripes on the back, esp. the bushbuck.

har+ness hitch *n.* a knot forming a loop with no free ends.

har+ness race *n. Horse racing.* a trotting or pacing race for standardbred horses driven in sulkies and harnessed in a special way to cause them to use the correct gait.

Har+ney Peak (ˈhɑːnɪ) *n.* a mountain in SW South Dakota: the highest peak in the Black Hills. Height: 2207 m (7242 ft.).

Har·old I (ˈhærəld) *n.* surname *Harefoot.* died 1040, king of England (1037–40); son of Canute.

Har·old II *n.* ?1022–66, king of England (1066); son of Earl Godwin and successor of Edward the Confessor. His claim to the throne was disputed by William the Conqueror, who defeated him at the Battle of Hastings (1066).

harp (hɑːp) *n.* **1.** a large triangular plucked stringed instrument consisting of a soundboard connected to an upright pillar by means of a curved crossbar from which the strings extend downwards. The strings are tuned diatonically and may be raised in pitch either one or two semitones by the use of pedals (**double-action harp**). Basic key: B major; range: nearly seven octaves. **2.** something resembling this, esp. in shape. **3.** an informal name (esp. in pop music) for **harmonica.** ~*vb.* **4.** (*intr.*) to play the harp. **5.** (*tr.*) *Archaic.* to speak; utter; express. **6.** (*intr.;* foll. by *on* or *upon*) to speak or write in a persistent and tedious manner. [Old English *hearpe;* related to Old Norse *harpa,* Old High German *harfa,* Latin *corbis* basket, Russian *korobit* to warp] —**ˈharp+er** *or* **ˈharp+ist** *n.*

Har+per's Fer+ry (ˈhɑːpəz) *n.* a village in NE West Virginia, at the confluence of the Potomac and Shenandoah Rivers: site of an arsenal seized by John Brown (1859).

harp+ings (ˈhɑːpɪŋz) *or* **harp+ins** (ˈhɑːpɪnz) *pl. n.* **1.** *Nautical.* wooden members used for strengthening the bow of a vessel. **2.** *Shipbuilding.* wooden supports used in construction. [C17: perhaps related to French *harpe* cramp iron]

har+poon (hɑːˈpuːn) *n.* **1. a.** a barbed missile attached to a long cord and hurled or fired from a gun when hunting whales, etc. **b.** (*as modifier*): *a harpoon gun.* ~*vb.* **2.** (*tr.*) to spear with or as if with a harpoon. [C17: probably from Dutch *harpoen,* from Old French *harpon* clasp, from *harper* to seize, perhaps of Scandinavian origin] —**har+ˈpoon+er** *or* **ˌhar+poon+ˈeer** *n.* —**har·ˈpoon-ˌlike** *adj.*

harp seal *n.* a brownish-grey earless seal, *Pagophilus groenlandicus,* of the North Atlantic and Arctic Oceans.

harp+si+chord (ˈhɑːpsɪˌkɔːd) *n.* a horizontally strung stringed keyboard instrument, triangular in shape, consisting usually of two manuals controlling various sets of strings plucked by plectra mounted on pivoted jacks. Some harpsichords have a pedal keyboard and stops by which the tone colour may be varied. [C17: from New Latin *harpichordium,* from Late Latin *harpa* HARP + Latin *chorda* CHORD[1]] —**ˈharp+si+ˌchord+ist** *n.*

har+py (ˈhɑːpɪ) *n., pl.* **+pies.** a cruel grasping person. [C16: from Latin *Harpyia* from Greek *Harpuiai* the Harpies, literally: snatchers, from *harpazein* to seize]

Har+py (ˈhɑːpɪ) *n., pl.* **+pies.** *Greek myth.* a ravenous creature with a woman's head and trunk and a bird's wings and claws.

har+py ea+gle *n.* a very large tropical American eagle, *Harpia harpyja,* with a black-and-white plumage and a head crest.

har+que+bus (ˈhɑːkwɪbəs) *n., pl.* **+bus·es.** a variant spelling of **arquebus.**

har+que+bu+sier (ˌhɑːkwɪbəˈsɪə) *n.* (formerly) a soldier armed with an arquebus. Also called: **arquebusier.**

Har+rar (ˈhɑːrə) *n.* a variant spelling of **Harar.**

har+ri+dan (ˈhærɪdᵊn) *n.* a scolding old woman; nag. [C17: of uncertain origin; perhaps related to French *haridelle,* literally: broken-down horse; of obscure origin]

har+ri+er[1] (ˈhærɪə) *n.* **1.** a person or thing that harries. **2.** any diurnal bird of prey of the genus *Circus,* having broad wings and long legs and tail and typically preying on small terrestrial animals: family *Accipitridae* (hawks, etc.). See also **marsh harrier, Montagu's harrier.**

har+ri+er[2] (ˈhærɪə) *n.* **1.** a smallish breed of hound used originally for hare-hunting. **2.** a cross-country runner. [C16: from HARE + -ER[1]; influenced by HARRIER[1]]

Har·ri·man (ˈhærɪmən) *n.* **W(illiam) A·ver·ell.** born 1891, U.S. diplomat: negotiated the Nuclear Test Ban Treaty with the Soviet Union (1963); governor of New York (1955–58).

Har+ris[1] (ˈhærɪs) *n.* the S part of the island of Lewis with Harris, in the Outer Hebrides. Pop.: 2879 (1971). Area: 500 sq. km (193 sq. miles).

Har·ris[2] (ˈhærɪs) *n.* **1. Frank.** 1856–1931, British writer and journalist; his books include his autobiography *My Life and Loves* (1923–27) and *Contemporary Portraits* (1915–30). **2. Jo·el Chand·ler.** 1848-1908, U.S. writer; creator of Uncle Remus. **3. Roy.** 1898-1979, U.S. composer, esp. of orchestral and choral music incorporating American folk tunes.

Har+ris+burg (ˈhærɪsˌbɜːg) *n.* a city in S Pennsylvania, on the Susquehanna River: the state capital. Pop.: 68 061 (1970).

Har·ri·son (ˈhærɪsᵊn) *n.* **1. Ben·ja·min.** 1833–1901, 23rd president of the U.S. (1889–93). **2. George.** born 1943, English rock guitarist and vocalist: member of the Beatles (1962–70). His solo albums include *All Things must pass* (1970). **3. Wil·liam Hen·ry,** grandfather of Benjamin Harrison. 1773–1841, 9th president of the U.S. (1841).

Har+ris Tweed *n. Trademark.* a loose-woven tweed made in the Outer Hebrides, esp. Lewis and Harris.

Har+ro+gate (ˈhærəgɪt) *n.* a town in N England, in North Yorkshire: a spa. Pop.: 62 290 (1971).

Har+ro+vi·an (həˈrəʊvɪən) *n.* **1.** a person educated at Harrow. ~*adj.* **2.** of or concerning Harrow. [C19: from New Latin *Harrōvia* HARROW + -AN]

har+row[1] (ˈhærəʊ) *n.* **1.** any of various implements used to level the ground, stir the soil, break up clods, destroy weeds, etc., in soil. ~*vb.* **2.** (*tr.*) to draw a harrow over (land). **3.** (*intr.*) (of soil) to become broken up through harrowing. **4.** (*tr.*) to distress; vex. [C13: of Scandinavian origin; compare Danish *harv,* Swedish *harf;* related to Middle Dutch *harke* rake] —**ˈhar+row+er** *n.* —**ˈhar+row+ing+ly** *adv.*

har+row[2] (ˈhærəʊ) *vb.* (*tr.*) *Archaic.* **1.** to plunder or ravish. **2.** (of Christ) to descend into (hell) to rescue righteous souls. [C13: variant of Old English *hergian* to HARRY] —**ˈhar+row+ment** *n.*

Har+row (ˈhærəʊ) *n.* **1.** a borough of NW Greater London. Pop.: 200 200 (1976 est.). **2.** an English boys' public school founded in 1571 at **Harrow-on-the-Hill,** a part of this borough. Related adj.: **Harrovian.**

har+rumph (həˈrʌmf) *vb.* (*intr.*) *Chiefly U.S.* to clear or make the noise of clearing the throat.

har+ry (ˈhærɪ) *vb.* **+ries, +ry+ing, +ried. 1.** (*tr.*) to harass; worry. **2.** to ravage (a town, etc.), esp. in war. [Old English *hergian;* related to *here* army, Old Norse *herja* to lay waste, Old High German *heriōn*]

harsh (hɑːʃ) *adj.* **1.** rough or grating to the senses. **2.** stern, severe, or cruel. [C16: probably of Scandinavian origin;

compare Middle Low German *harsch,* Norwegian *harsk* rancid] —'**harsh·ly** *adv.* —'**harsh·ness** *n.*

hars·let ('hɑːzlɪt, 'hɑːs-) *n.* a variant spelling of **haslet.**

hart (hɑːt) *n., pl.* **harts** *or* **hart.** the male of the deer, esp. the red deer aged five years or more. [Old English *heorot;* related to Old Norse *hjörtr,* Old High German *hiruz* hart, Latin *cervus* stag, Lithuanian *kárve* cow; see HORN]

Hart (hɑːt) *n.* **Lo·renz.** 1895–1943, U.S. lyricist: collaborated with Richard Rodgers in writing musicals.

har·tal (hɑː'tɑːl) *n.* (in India) the act of closing shops or suspending work, esp. in political protest. [C20: from Hindi *hartāl,* from *hāt* shop (from Sanskrit *hatta*) + *tālā* bolt for a door (from Sanskrit: latch)]

Harte (hɑːt) *n.* **(Francis) Bret.** 1836–1902, U.S. poet and short-story writer, noted for his sketches of Californian gold miners, such as *The Luck of Roaring Camp* (1868).

har·te·beest ('hɑːtɪˌbiːst) *or* **hart·beest** ('hɑːtˌbiːst) *n.* **1.** either of two large African antelopes, *Alcelaphus buselaphus* or *A. lichtensteini,* having an elongated muzzle, lyre-shaped horns, and a fawn-coloured coat. **2.** any similar and related animal, such as *Damaliscus hunteri* (**Hunter's hartebeest**). [C18: via Afrikaans from Dutch; see HART, BEAST]

Hart·ford ('hɑːtfəd) *n.* a port in central Connecticut, on the Connecticut River: the state capital. Pop.: 148 526 (1973 est.).

Har·tha·ca·nute ('hɑːθəkəˌnjuːt), **Har·de·ca·nute,** *or* **Har·di·ca·nute** *n.* ?1019–42, king of Denmark (1035–42) and of England (1040–42); son of Canute.

Har·tle·pool ('hɑːtlɪˌpuːl) *n.* a port in NE England, in Cleveland on the North Sea: greatly enlarged in 1967 by its amalgamation with West Hartlepool; shipbuilding and fishing. Pop.: 96 898 (1971).

Hart·ley ('hɑːtlɪ) *n.* **Da·vid.** 1705–57, English philosopher and physician. In *Observations of Man* (1749) he introduced the theory of psychological associationism.

Hart·nell ('hɑːtnᵊl) *n.* **Nor·man.** 1901-79, English couturier.

harts·horn ('hɑːtsˌhɔːn) *n.* an obsolete name for **sal volatile** (sense 2). [Old English *heortes horn* hart's horn (formerly a chief source of ammonia)]

hart's-tongue *n.* an evergreen Eurasian fern, *Phyllitis scolopendrium,* with narrow undivided fronds bearing rows of sori: family *Polypodiaceae.*

har·um-scar·um ('hɛərəm'skɛərəm) *adj., adv.* **1.** in a reckless way or of a reckless nature. ~*n.* **2.** a person who is impetuous or rash. [C17: perhaps from *hare* (in obsolete sense: harass) + *scare,* variant of STARE; compare HELTER-SKELTER]

Ha·run al-Ra·shid (hæ'ruːn 'æl ræ'ʃiːd) *n.* ?763–809 A.D., Abbasid caliph of Islam (786–809), whose court at Baghdad was idealized in the *Arabian Nights.*

ha·rus·pex (hə'rʌspɛks) *n., pl.* **ha·rus·pi·ces** (hə'rʌspɪˌsiːz). (in ancient Rome) a priest who practised divination, esp. by examining the entrails of animals. [C16: from Latin, probably from *hīra* gut + *specere* to look] —**ha·rus·pi·cal** (hə'rʌspɪkᵊl) *adj.* —**ha·rus·pi·cy** (hə'rʌspɪsɪ) *n.*

Har·vard clas·si·fi·ca·tion ('hɑːvəd) *n.* a classification of stars based on the characteristic spectral absorption lines and bands of the chemical elements present. See **spectral type.** [C20: named after the observatory at *Harvard,* Massachusetts, where it was prepared and published as part of *The Henry Draper Catalogue* (1924)]

har·vest ('hɑːvɪst) *n.* **1.** the gathering of a ripened crop. **2.** the crop itself or the yield from it in a single growing season. **3.** the season for gathering crops. **4.** the product of an effort, action, etc.: *a harvest of love.* ~*vb.* **5.** to gather or reap (a ripened crop) from (the place where it has been growing). **6.** (*tr.*) to receive or reap (benefits, consequences, etc.). [Old English *hærfest;* related to Old Norse *harfr* harrow, Old High German *herbist* autumn, Latin *carpere* to pluck, Greek *karpos* fruit, Sanskrit *kṛpāna* shears] —'**har·vest·ing** *n.* —'**har·vest·less** *adj.*

har·vest·er ('hɑːvɪstə) *n.* **1.** a person who harvests. **2.** a harvesting machine, esp. a combine harvester.

har·vest home *n.* **1.** the bringing in of the harvest. **2.** *Chiefly Brit.* a harvest supper.

har·vest·man ('hɑːvɪstmən) *n., pl.* **·men. 1.** a person engaged in harvesting. **2.** Also called (U.S.): **daddy-longlegs.** any arachnid of the order *Opiliones* (or *Phalangida*), having a small rounded body and very long thin legs.

har·vest mite *or* **tick** *n.* the bright red parasitic larva of any of various free-living mites of the genus *Trombicula* and related genera, which causes intense itching of human skin.

har·vest moon *n.* the full moon occurring nearest to the autumnal equinox.

har·vest mouse *n.* **1.** a very small reddish-brown Eurasian mouse, *Micromys minutus,* inhabiting cornfields, hedgerows, etc., and feeding on grain and seeds: family *Muridae.* **2. American harvest mouse.** any small greyish mouse of the American genus *Reithrodontomys:* family *Cricetidae.*

Har·vey ('hɑːvɪ) *n.* **Wil·liam.** 1578–1657, English physician who discovered the mechanism of blood circulation.

Har·wich ('hærɪtʃ) *n.* a port in SE England, in NE Essex on the North Sea. Pop.: 14 892 (1971).

Har·ya·na (hər'jɑːnə) *n.* a state of NE India, formed in 1966 from the Hindi-speaking parts of the state of Punjab. Capital: Chandigarh (shared with Punjab). Pop.: 10 036 808 (1971). Area: 44 506 sq. km (17 182 sq. miles).

Harz *or* **Harz Moun·tains** (hɑːts) *pl. n.* a range of wooded hills in central Germany, between the Rivers Weser and Elbe: source of many legends. Highest peak: Brocken, 1142 m (3746 ft.).

has (hæz) *vb.* (used with *he, she, it,* or a singular noun) a form of the present tense (indicative mood) of **have.**

Ha·sa ('hɑːsə) *n.* See **Al Hasa.**

has-been *n. Informal.* a person or thing that is no longer popular, successful, effective, etc.

Has·dru·bal ('hæzdrubᵊl) *n.* died 207 B.C., Carthaginian general: commanded the Carthaginian army in Spain (218–211); joined his brother Hannibal in Italy and was killed at the Metaurus.

Ha·šek (*Czech* 'haʃɛk) *n.* **Ja·ro·slav** ('jarɔslaf). 1883–1923, Czech novelist and short-story writer; author of *The Good Soldier Schweik.*

hash[1] (hæʃ) *n.* **1.** a dish of diced cooked meat, vegetables, etc., reheated in a sauce. **2.** something mixed up. **3.** a reuse or rework of old material. **4. make a hash of.** *Informal.* **a.** to mix or mess up. **b.** to defeat or destroy. **5. settle** (*or* **fix**) **one's hash.** *U.S. informal.* **a.** to subdue or silence someone. **b.** to get even with someone. ~*vb.* (*tr.*) **6.** to chop into small pieces. **7.** to mix or mess up. [C17: from Old French *hacher* to chop up, from *hache* HATCHET]

hash[2] (hæʃ) *n. Slang.* short for **hashish.**

Hash·e·mite King·dom of Jor·dan ('hæʃɪˌmaɪt) *n.* the official name of **Jordan.**

hash house *n. U.S. slang.* a cheap café or restaurant.

hash·ish ('hæʃiːʃ, -ɪʃ) *or* **hash·eesh** *n.* **1.** a purified resinous extract of the dried flower tops of the female hemp plant, used as a hallucinogenic. See also **cannabis. 2.** any hallucinogenic substance prepared from this resin. [C16: from Arabic *hashīsh* hemp, dried herbage]

Has·i·dim, Has·si·dim, Chas·i·dim, *or* **Chas·si·dim** ('hæsɪˌdiːm, -dɪm; *Hebrew* xasi'dim) *pl. n., sing.* **Has·id, Has·sid, Chas·id,** *or* **Chas·sid** ('hæsɪd; *Hebrew* xa'sid). **1.** a sect of Jewish mystics founded in Poland about 1750, characterized by religious zeal and a spirit of prayer, joy, and charity. **2.** a Jewish sect of the 2nd century B.C., formed to combat Hellenistic influences. —**Ha·sid·ic, Has·sid·ic, Cha·sid·ic,** *or* **Chas·sid·ic** (hə'sɪdɪk) *adj.* —'**Has·id·ism,** '**Has·sid·ism,** '**Chas·id·ism,** *or* '**Chas·sid·ism** *n.*

hask (hæsk, hʌsk) *Northern Brit. and north Midland English dialect.* ~*adj.* **1.** (esp. of a cough) dry or hoarse. ~*n.* **2.** a cough, usually of animals. [a dialect variant of *harsk,* an earlier form of HARSH]

has·let ('hæzlɪt) *or* **hars·let** *n.* a loaf of cooked minced pig's offal, eaten cold. [C14: from Old French *hastelet* piece of spit roasted meat, from *haste* spit, of Germanic origin; compare Old High German *harsta* frying pan]

has·n't ('hæzᵊnt) *contraction of* has not.

hasp (hɑːsp) *n.* **1.** a metal fastening consisting of a hinged strap with a slot that fits over a staple and is secured by a pin, bolt, or padlock. ~*vb.* **2.** (*tr.*) to secure (a door, window, etc.) with a hasp. [Old English *hæpse;* related to Old Norse *hespa,* Old High German *haspa* hasp, Dutch *haspel* reel, Sanskrit *capa* bow]

Has·san II (hæ'sɑːn, 'hæsᵊn) *n.* born 1929, king of Morocco since 1961.

Has·selt (*Flemish* 'hɑsəlt; *French* a'sɛlt) *n.* a market town in E Belgium, capital of Limbourg province. Pop.: 39 663 (1970).

has·sle ('hæsᵊl) *Informal.* ~*n.* **1.** a quarrel or fight. **2.** a great deal of trouble. ~*vb.* **3.** to quarrel or struggle with (someone). [C20: of unknown origin]

has·sock ('hæsək) *n.* **1.** a firm upholstered cushion used for kneeling on, esp. in church. **2.** a thick clump of grass. [Old English *hassuc* matted grass]

hast (hæst) *vb. Archaic or dialect.* (used with the pronoun *thou* or its relative equivalent) a singular form of the present tense (indicative mood) of **have.**

has·tate ('hæsteɪt) *adj.* (of a leaf) having a pointed tip and two outward-pointing lobes at the base. [C18: from Latin *hastātus* with a spear, from *hasta* spear]

haste (heɪst) *n.* **1.** speed, esp. in an action; swiftness; rapidity. **2.** the act of hurrying in a careless or rash manner. **3.** a necessity for hurrying; urgency. **4. make haste.** to hurry; rush. ~*vb.* **5.** a poetic word for **hasten.** [C14: from Old French *haste,* of Germanic origin; compare Old Norse *heifst* hate, Old English *hæst* strife, Old High German *heisti* powerful] —'**haste·ful** *adj.* —'**haste·ful·ly** *adv.*

has·ten ('heɪsᵊn) *vb.* **1.** (*may take an infinitive*) to hurry or cause to hurry; rush. **2.** (*tr.*) to be anxious (to say something): *I hasten to add that we are just good friends.* —'**has·ten·er** *n.*

Hast·ings[1] ('heɪstɪŋz) *n.* **1.** a port in SE England, in East Sussex on the English Channel: near the site of the **Battle of Hastings** (1066), in which William the Conqueror defeated King Harold; chief of the Cinque Ports. Pop.: 72 169 (1971). **2.** a town in New Zealand, on E North Island: centre of a rich agricultural and fruit-growing region. Pop.: 29 753 (1971).

Has·tings[2] ('heɪstɪŋz) *n.* **War·ren.** 1732–1818, British administrator in India; first governor general of Bengal (1773–85). He implemented important reforms but was impeached by parliament (1788) on charges of corruption; acquitted in 1795.

has·ty ('heɪstɪ) *adj.* **·ti·er, ·ti·est. 1.** rapid; swift; quick. **2.** excessively or rashly quick. **3.** short-tempered. **4.** showing irritation or anger: *hasty words.* —'**hast·i·ly** *adv.* —'**hast·i·ness** *n.*

has·ty pud·ding *n.* **1.** *Brit.* a simple pudding made from milk thickened with tapioca, semolina, etc., and sweetened. **2.** *U.S.* a mush of cornmeal, served with treacle sugar.

hat (hæt) *n.* **1. a.** any of various head coverings, esp. one with a brim and a shaped crown. **b.** (*in combination*): *hatrack.* **2.** *Informal.* a role or capacity. **3. at the drop of a hat.** immediately. **4. bad hat.** *Informal, chiefly Brit.* a bad or immoral person. **5. eat one's hat.** *Slang.* to be shocked or proved wrong if a certain event or result happens: *I'll eat my hat if this book comes out late.* **6. hat in hand.** humbly or servilely. **7. keep (something) under one's hat.** to keep (something) secret. **8. my hat.** (*interj.*) *Brit. informal.* **a.** my word! my goodness! **b.** nonsense! **9. old hat.** something stale or old-fashioned. **10. out of a hat. a.** as if by magic. **b.** at random. **11. pass** (*or* **send**) **the hat round.** to collect money, as for a cause. **12. take off one's hat to.** to admire or congratulate. **13. talk through one's hat. a.** to talk foolishly. **b.** to deceive or bluff. **14. throw** (*or* **toss**) **one's hat in the ring.** to enter into competition, esp. for political office. ~*vb.* **hats, hat·ting, hat·ted. 15.** (*tr.*) to supply (a person, etc.) with a hat or put a hat on (someone). [Old English *hætt;* related to Old Norse *höttr* cap, Latin *cassis* helmet; see HOOD[1]] —**'hat·less** *adj.* —**'hat·,like** *adj.*

hat·band ('hæt,bænd) *n.* a band or ribbon around the base of the crown of a hat.

hat·box ('hæt,bɒks) *n.* a box or case for a hat or hats.

hatch[1] (hætʃ) *vb.* **1.** to cause (the young of various animals, esp. birds) to emerge from the egg or (of young birds, etc.) to emerge from the egg. **2.** to cause (eggs) to break and release the fully developed young or (of eggs) to break and release the young animal within. **3.** (*tr.*) to contrive or devise (a scheme, plot, etc.). ~*n.* **4.** the act or process of hatching. **5.** a group of newly hatched animals. [C13: of Germanic origin; compare Middle High German *hecken* to mate (used of birds), Swedish *häcka* to hatch, Danish *hække*] —**'hatch·a·ble** *adj.* —**'hatch·er** *n.*

hatch[2] (hætʃ) *n.* **1.** a covering for a hatchway. **2.** short for **hatchway. 3.** Also called: **serving hatch.** an opening in a wall separating a kitchen from a dining area. **4.** the lower half of a divided door. **5.** a sluice or sliding gate in a dam, dyke, or weir. **6. down the hatch.** *Slang.* (used as a toast) drink up! **7. under hatches. a.** below decks. **b.** out of sight. **c.** brought low; dead. [Old English *hæcc;* related to Middle High German *heck,* Dutch *hek* gate]

hatch[3] (hætʃ) *vb. Drawing, engraving, etc.* to mark (a figure, shade, etc.) with fine parallel or crossed lines to indicate shading. Compare **hachure.** [C15: from Old French *hacher* to chop, from *hache* HATCHET] —**'hatch·ing** *n.*

hatch·back ('hætʃ,bæk) *n.* **1. a.** a sloping rear end of a car having a single door that is lifted to open. **b.** (*as modifier*): *a hatchback model.* **2.** a car having such a rear end.

hatch·el ('hætʃəl) *vb.* **·els, ·el·ling, ·elled** *or U.S.* **·els, ·el·ing, ·eled.** *n.* another word for **heckle** (senses 2, 3). [C13 *hechele,* of Germanic origin; related to Old High German *hāko* hook, Middle Dutch *hekele* HACKLE[1]] —**'hatch·el·ler** *n.*

hatch·er·y ('hætʃərɪ) *n., pl.* **·er·ies.** a place where eggs are hatched under artificial conditions.

hatch·et ('hætʃɪt) *n.* **1.** a short axe used for chopping wood, etc. **2.** a tomahawk. **3.** (*modifier*) of narrow dimensions and sharp features: *a hatchet face.* **4. bury the hatchet.** to make peace. [C14: from Old French *hachette,* from *hache* axe, of Germanic origin; compare Old High German *happa* knife] —**'hatch·et·,like** *adj.*

hatch·et job *n. Informal, chiefly U.S.* a malicious or devastating verbal or written attack.

hatch·et man *n. Informal, chiefly U.S.* **1.** a person carrying out unpleasant assignments for an employer or superior. **2.** *U.S.* a hired murderer. **3.** *U.S.* a severe or malicious critic.

hatch·ment ('hætʃmənt) *n. Heraldry.* a diamond-shaped tablet displaying the coat of arms of a dead person. Also called: **achievement.** [C16: changed from ACHIEVEMENT]

hatch·way ('hætʃ,weɪ) *n.* **1.** an opening in the deck of a vessel to provide access below. **2.** a similar opening in a wall, floor, ceiling, or roof, usually fitted with a lid or door. ~Often shortened to **hatch.**

hate (heɪt) *vb.* **1.** to dislike (something) intensely; detest. **2.** (*intr.*) to be unwilling (to be or do something). ~*n.* **3.** intense dislike. **4.** *Informal.* a person or thing that is hated (esp. in the phrase **pet hate**). [Old English *hatian;* related to Old Norse *hata,* Old Saxon *hatōn,* Old High German *hazzēn*] —**'hate·a·ble** *or* **'hat·a·ble** *adj.*

hate·ful ('heɪtfʊl) *adj.* **1.** causing or deserving hate; loathsome; detestable. **2.** *Archaic.* full of or showing hate. —**'hate·ful·ly** *adv.* —**'hate·ful·ness** *n.*

Hat·field ('hæt,fi:ld) *n.* a market town in S central England, in Hertfordshire, with a new town of the same name built on the outskirts. Pop.: Hatfield rural district, 44 927 (1971); Hatfield new town, 25 211 (1971).

hath (hæθ) *vb. Archaic or dialect* (used with the pronouns *he, she,* or *it* or a singular noun) a form of the present tense (indicative mood) of **have.**

Hath·a·way ('hæθə,weɪ) *n.* **Anne.** ?1557–1623, wife of William Shakespeare.

Hath·or ('hæθɔ:) *n.* (in ancient Egyptian religion) the mother of Horus and goddess of creation. —**Ha·thor·ic** (hæ'θɔ:rɪk -'θɒr-) *adj.*

hat·pin ('hæt,pɪn) *n.* a sturdy pin used to secure a woman's hat to her hair, often having a decorative head.

ha·tred ('heɪtrɪd) *n.* a feeling of intense dislike; enmity.

Hat·shep·sut (hæt'ʃɛpsu:t) *or* **Hat·shep·set** *n.* queen of Egypt of the 18th dynasty (?1512–1482 B.C.). She built a great mortuary temple at Deir el Bahri near Thebes.

hat stand *or esp. U.S.* **hat tree** *n.* a frame or pole equipped with hooks or arms for hanging up hats, coats, etc.

hat·ter ('hætə) *n.* **1.** a person who makes and sells hats. **2.** *Austral. informal.* a man, esp. a miner, who prefers to live and work alone, often considered eccentric. **3. mad as a hatter.** crazily eccentric.

Hat·ter·as ('hætərəs) *n.* **Cape.** a promontory off the E coast of North Carolina, on **Hatteras Island,** which is situated between Pamlico Sound and the Atlantic: known as the "Graveyard of the Atlantic" for its danger to shipping.

hat trick *n.* **1.** *Cricket.* the achievement of a bowler in taking three wickets with three successive balls. **2.** any achievement of three successive points, victories, etc.

hau·ber·geon ('hɔ:bədʒən) *n.* a variant of **habergeon.**

hau·berk ('hɔ:bɜ:k) *n.* a long coat of mail, often sleeveless. [C13: from Old French *hauberc,* of Germanic origin; compare Old High German *halsberc,* Old English *healsbeorg,* from *heals* neck + *beorg* protection, shelter]

haugh (hɒx) *n. Northern English dialect and Scot.* level ground forming part of a river valley. [Old English *healh* corner of land; see HOLLOW]

Haugh·ey ('hɔ:hɪ) *n.* **Charles James.** born 1925, Irish politician; prime minister of the Republic of Ireland (1979-81; 1982).

haugh·ty ('hɔ:tɪ) *adj.* **·ti·er, ·ti·est. 1.** having or showing arrogance. **2.** *Archaic.* noble or exalted. [C16: from Old French *haut,* literally: lofty, from Latin *altus* high] —**'haugh·ti·ly** *adv.* —**'haugh·ti·ness** *n.*

haul (hɔ:l) *vb.* **1.** to drag or draw (something) with effort. **2.** (*tr.*) to transport, as in a lorry. **3.** *Nautical.* to alter the course of (a vessel), esp. so as to sail closer to the wind. **4.** (*tr.*) *Nautical.* to draw or hoist (a vessel) out of the water onto land or a dock for repair, storage, etc. **5.** (*intr.*) *Nautical.* (of the wind) to blow from a direction nearer the bow. Compare **veer**[1] (sense 3b.). **6.** (*intr.*) to change one's opinion or action. ~*n.* **7.** the act of dragging with effort. **8.** (esp. of fish) the amount caught at a single time. **9.** something that is hauled. **10.** a distance of hauling: *a three-mile haul.* **11. in** (or **over**) **the long haul. a.** in a future time. **b.** over a lengthy period of time. [C16: from Old French *haler,* of Germanic origin; see HALE[2]] —**'haul·er** *or* **'haul·i·er** *n.*

haul·age ('hɔ:lɪdʒ) *n.* **1.** the act or labour of hauling. **2.** a rate or charge levied for the transportation of goods, esp. by rail.

haulm *or* **halm** (hɔ:m) *n.* **1.** the stems or stalks of beans, peas, potatoes, grasses, etc., collectively, as used for thatching, bedding, etc. **2.** a single stem of such a plant. [Old English *healm;* related to Old Norse *halmr,* Old High German *halm* stem, straw, Latin *culmus* stalk, Greek *kalamos* reed, Old Slavonic *slama* straw]

haul off *vb.* (*intr., adv.*) **1.** (foll. by *and*) *U.S. Informal.* to draw back in preparation (esp. to strike or fight): *I hauled off and slugged him.* **2.** *Nautical.* to alter the course of a vessel so as to avoid an obstruction, shallow waters, etc.

haul up *vb.* (*adv.*) **1.** (*tr.*) *Informal.* to call to account or criticize. **2.** *Nautical.* to sail (a vessel) closer to the wind.

haunch (hɔ:ntʃ) *n.* **1.** the human hip or fleshy hindquarter of an animal, esp. a horse or similar quadruped. **2.** the leg and loin of an animal, used for food: *a haunch of venison.* **3.** Also called: **hance.** *Architect.* the part of an arch between the impost and the apex. [C13: from Old French *hanche;* related to Spanish, Italian *anca,* of Germanic origin; compare Low German *hanke*] —**haunched** *adj.*

haunch bone *n.* a nontechnical name for the **ilium** or **hipbone.**

haunt (hɔ:nt) *vb.* **1.** to visit (a person or place) in the form of a ghost. **2.** (*tr.*) to intrude upon or recur to (the memory, thoughts, etc.): *he was haunted by the fear of insanity.* **3.** to visit (a place) frequently. **4.** to associate with (someone) frequently. ~*n.* **5.** (*often pl.*) a place visited frequently: *an old haunt of hers.* **6.** a place to which animals habitually resort for food, drink, shelter, etc. [C13: from Old French *hanter,* of Germanic origin; compare Old Norse *heimta* to bring home, Old English *hāmettan* to give a home to; see HOME]

haunt·ed ('hɔ:ntɪd) *adj.* **1.** frequented or visited by ghosts. **2.** (*postpositive*) obsessed or worried.

haunt·ing ('hɔ:ntɪŋ) *adj.* **1.** (of memories) poignant or persistent. **2.** poignantly sentimental; enchantingly or eerily evocative. —**'haunt·ing·ly** *adv.*

Haupt·mann (*German* 'hauptman) *n.* **Ger·hart** ('ge:rhart). 1862–1946, German naturalist, dramatist, novelist, and poet. His works include the historical drama *The Weavers* (1892): Nobel prize for literature 1912.

Hau·ra·ki Gulf (haʊ'rækɪ) *n.* an inlet of the Pacific in New Zealand, on the N coast of North Island.

Hau·sa ('haʊsə) *n.* **1.** (*pl.* **·sas** *or* **·sa**) a member of a Negroid people of W Africa, living chiefly in N Nigeria. **2.** the language of this people: the chief member of the Chadic subfamily of the Afro-Asiatic family of languages. It is widely used as a trading language throughout W Africa and the S Sahara.

haus·frau ('haʊs,fraʊ) *n.* a German housewife. [German, from *Haus* HOUSE + *Frau* woman, wife]

haus·tel·lum (hɔ:'stɛləm) *n., pl.* **·la** (-lə). the tip of the proboscis of a housefly or similar insect, specialized for sucking food. [C19: New Latin, diminutive of Latin *haustrum* device for drawing water, from *haurīre* to draw up; see EXHAUST]

haus·to·ri·um (hɔ:'stɔ:rɪəm) *n., pl.* **·ri·a** (-rɪə). the organ of a parasitic plant that penetrates the host tissues and absorbs food and water from them. [C19: from New Latin, from Late Latin *haustor* a water-drawer; see HAUSTELLUM] —**haus·'to·ri·al** *adj.*

haut·boy ('əʊbɔɪ) *n.* **1.** Also called: **haut·bois strawberry, hau·bois.** a strawberry, *Fragaria moschata,* of central Europe and Asia, with large fruit. **2.** an archaic word for **oboe.** [C16: from French *hautbois,* from *haut* high + *bois* wood, of Germanic origin; see BUSH[1]]

haute cou+ture *French.* (ot ku'ty:r) *n.* high fashion. [literally: high dressmaking]
haute cui+sine *French.* (ot kwi'zin) *n.* high-class cooking. [literally: high cookery]
haute é·cole *French.* (ot e'kɔl) *n.* the classical art of riding. [literally: high school]
Haute-Ga·ronne (*French* ot ga'rɔn) *n.* a department of SW France, in Midi-Pyrénées region. Capital: Toulouse. Pop.: 793 569 (1975). Area: 6367 sq. km (2483 sq. miles).
Haute-Loire (*French* ot 'lwa:r) *n.* a department of S central France, in Auvergne region. Capital: Le Puy. Pop.: 214 269 (1975). Area: 5001 sq. km (1950 sq. miles).
Haute-Marne (*French* ot 'marn) *n.* a department of NE France, in Champagne-Ardenne region. Capital: Chaumont. Pop.: 221 437 (1975). Area: 6257 sq. km (2440 sq. miles).
Haute-Nor·man+die (*French* ot nɔrmã'di) *n.* a region of NW France, on the English Channel: generally fertile and flat.
Hautes-Alpes (*French* ot 'zalp) *n.* a department of SE France in Provence-Côte-d'Azur region. Capital: Gap. Pop.: 102 694 (1975). Area: 5643 sq. km (2201 sq. miles).
Haute-Saône (*French* ot 'so:n) *n.* a department of E France, in Franche-Comté region. Capital: Vesoul. Pop.: 229 357 (1975). Area: 5375 sq. km (2096 sq. miles).
Haute-Sa·voie (*French* ot sa'vwa) *n.* a department of E France, in Rhône-Alpes region. Capital: Annecy. Pop.: 458 855 (1975). Area: 4958 sq. km (1934 sq. miles).
Hautes-Py·ré·nées (*French* ot pire'ne) *n.* a department of SW France, in Midi-Pyrénées region. Capital: Tarbes. Pop.: 234 112 (1975). Area: 4534 sq. km (1768 sq. miles).
hau+teur (əʊ'tɜ:) *n.* pride; haughtiness. [C17: from French, from *haut* high; see HAUGHTY]
Haute-Vienne (*French* ot 'vjɛn) *n.* a department of W central France, in Limousin region. Capital: Limoges. Pop.: 359 365 (1975). Area: 5555 sq. km (2166 sq. miles).
haut monde *French.* (o 'mɔ̃d) *n.* high society. [literally: high world]
Haut-Rhin (*French* o 'rɛ̃) *n.* a department of E France in Alsace region. Capital: Colmar. Pop.: 647 209 (1975). Area: 3566 sq. km (1377 sq. miles).
Hauts-de-Seine (*French* o də 'sɛn) *n.* a department of N central France, in Ile de France region just west of Paris: formed in 1964. Capital: Nanterre. Pop.: 1 448 020 (1975). Area: 175 sq. km (68 sq. miles).
Ha+van·a (hə'vænə) *n.* the capital of Cuba, a port in the northwest on the Gulf of Mexico: the largest city in the West Indies; founded in 1514 as San Cristóbal de la Habana by Diego Velásquez. Pop.: 1 755 360 (1970). Spanish name: **Habana.**
Ha+van·a ci+gar *n.* any of various cigars manufactured in Cuba, known esp. for their high quality. Also: **Havana.**
Hav+ant ('hævᵊnt) *n.* a market town in S England, in SE Hampshire. Pop. (with Waterloo): 108 999 (1971).
have (hæv) *vb.* **has, hav+ing, had.** (*mainly tr.*) **1.** to be in material possession of; own: *he has two cars.* **2.** to possess as a characteristic quality or attribute: *he has dark hair.* **3.** to receive, take, or obtain: *she had a present from him; have a look.* **4.** to hold or entertain in the mind: *to have an idea.* **5.** to possess a knowledge or understanding of: *I have no German.* **6.** to experience or undergo: *to have a shock.* **7.** to be infected with or suffer from: *to have a cold.* **8.** to gain control of or advantage over: *you have me on that point.* **9.** (*usually passive*) *Slang.* to cheat or outwit: *he was had by that dishonest salesman.* **10.** (foll. by *on*) to exhibit (mercy, compassion, etc., towards): *have mercy on us, Lord.* **11.** to engage or take part in: *to have a conversation.* **12.** to arrange, carry out, or hold: *to have a party.* **13.** to cause, compel, or require to (be, do, or be done): *have my shoes mended.* **14.** (takes an infinitive with *to*) used as an auxiliary to express compulsion or necessity: *I had to run quickly to escape him.* **15.** to eat, drink, or partake of: *to have a good meal.* **16.** *Taboo slang.* to have sexual intercourse with: *he had her on the sofa.* **17.** (*used with a negative*) to tolerate or allow: *I won't have all this noise.* **18.** to declare, state, or assert: *rumour has it that they will marry.* **19.** to put or place: *I'll have the sofa in this room.* **20.** to receive as a guest: *to have three people to stay.* **21.** to beget or bear (offspring): *she had three children.* **22.** (*takes a past participle*) used as an auxiliary to form compound tenses expressing completed action: *I have gone; I shall have gone; I would have gone; I had gone.* **23. had better** *or* **best.** ought to: used to express compulsion, obligation, etc.: *you had better go.* **24. had rather** *or* **sooner.** to consider or find preferable that: *I had rather you left at once.* **25. have done.** See **done** (sense 3). **26. have had it.** *Informal.* **a.** to be exhausted, defeated, or killed. **b.** to have lost one's last chance. **c.** to become unfashionable. **27. have it.** to win a victory. **28. have it away** (*or* **off**). *Taboo, Brit. slang.* to have sexual intercourse. **29. have it coming.** *Informal.* to be about to receive or to merit punishment or retribution. **30. have it in for.** *Informal.* to wish or intend harm towards. **31. have it so good.** to have so many benefits, esp. material benefits. **32. have to do with. a.** to have dealings or associate with: *I have nothing to do with her.* **b.** to be of relevance to: *this has nothing to do with you.* **33. I have it.** *Informal.* I know the answer. **34. let (someone) have it.** *Slang.* to launch or deliver an attack on, esp. to discharge a firearm at (someone). **35. not having any.** (foll. by *of*) *Informal.* refusing to take part or be involved (in). ~*n.* **36.** (*usually pl.*) *Informal.* a person or group of people in possession of wealth, security, etc.: *the haves and the have-nots.* [Old English *habban;* related to Old Norse *hafa,* Old Saxon *hebbian,* Old High German *habēn,* Latin *habēre*]
have at *vb.* (*intr., prep.*) *Archaic.* to make an opening attack on, esp. in fencing.
have in *vb.* (*tr., adv.*) **1.** to ask (a person) to give a service: *we must have the electrician in to mend the fire.* **2.** to invite to one's home.
Ha+vel (*German* 'ha:fᵊl) *n.* a river in East Germany, flowing south to Berlin, then west and north to join the River Elbe. Length: about 362 km (225 miles).
have+lock ('hævlɒk) *n.* a cover for a service cap with a flap extending over the back of the neck to protect the head and neck from the sun. [C19: named after Sir H. *Havelock* (1795–1857), English general in India]
ha+ven ('heɪvᵊn) *n.* **1.** a port, harbour, or other sheltered place for shipping. **2.** a place of safety or sanctuary; shelter. ~*vb.* **3.** (*tr.*) to secure or shelter in or as if in a haven. [Old English *hæfen,* from Old Norse *höfn;* related to Middle Dutch *havene,* Old Irish *cuan* to bend] —**'ha+ven+less** *adj.*
have-not *n.* (*usually pl.*) a person or group of people in possession of relatively little material wealth.
have·n't ('hævᵊnt) *contraction of* **have not.**
have on *vb.* (*tr.*) **1.** (*usually adv.*) to wear. **2.** (*usually adv.*) to have (a meeting or engagement) arranged as a commitment: *what does your boss have on this afternoon?* **3.** (*adv.*) to trick or tease (a person). **4.** (*prep.*) to have available (information or evidence, esp. when incriminating) about (a person): *the police had nothing on him, so they let him go.*
have out *vb.* (*tr., adv.*) **1.** to settle (a matter) or come to (a final decision), esp. by fighting or by frank discussion (often in the phrase **have it out**). **2.** to have extracted or removed: *I had two teeth out this morning.*
ha+ver ('heɪvə) *vb.* (*intr.*) *Brit.* **1.** to dither. **2.** *Scot. and northern English dialect.* to babble. ~*n.* **3.** (*usually pl.*) *Scot.* nonsense. [C18: of unknown origin]
Ha+ver+ing ('heɪvərɪŋ) *n.* a borough of NE Greater London, formed in 1965 from Romford and Hornchurch (both previously in Essex). Pop.: 239 200 (1976 est.).
hav+er+sack ('hævəˌsæk) *n.* a canvas bag for provisions or equipment, carried on the back or shoulder. [C18: from French *havresac,* from German *Habersack* oat bag, from Old High German *habaro* oats + *Sack* SACK[1]]
Ha+ver+sian ca+nal (hæ'vɜ:ʃən) *n. Histology.* any of the channels that form a network in bone and contain blood vessels and nerves. [C19: named after C. *Havers* (died 1702), English anatomist who discovered them]
hav+er+sine ('hævəˌsaɪn) *n.* half the value of the versed sine. [C19: combination of *half* + *versed* + *sine*[1]]
have up *vb.* (*tr., adv.; usually passive*) to cause to appear for trial: *he was had up for breaking and entering.*
hav+il+dar ('hævɪlˌdɑ:) *n.* a noncommissioned officer in the Indian army, equivalent in rank to sergeant. [C17: from Hindi, from Persian *hawāldār* one in charge]
hav+oc ('hævək) *n.* **1.** destruction; devastation; ruin. **2.** *Informal.* confusion; chaos. **3. cry havoc.** *Archaic.* to give the signal for pillage and destruction. **4. play havoc.** (often foll. by *with*) to cause a great deal of damage, distress, or confusion (to). ~*vb.* **+ocs, +ock+ing, +ocked. 5.** (*tr.*) *Archaic.* to lay waste. [C15: from Old French *havot* pillage, probably of Germanic origin] —**'hav+ock+er** *n.*
Ha+vre ('hɑ:vrə; *French* 'ɑ:vr) *n.* See **Le Havre.**
haw[1] (hɔ:) *n.* **1.** the round or oval fruit (a pome) of the hawthorn, usually red or yellow, containing one to five seeds. **2.** another name for **hawthorn.** [Old English *haga,* identical with *haga* HEDGE; related to Old Norse *hagi* pasture]
haw[2] (hɔ:) *n., interj.* **1.** an inarticulate utterance, as of hesitation, embarrassment, etc.; hem. ~*vb.* **2.** (*intr.*) to make this sound. **3. hem** (*or* **hum**) **and haw.** See **hem**[2] (sense 3). [C17: of imitative origin]
haw[3] (hɔ:) *n. Archaic.* a yard or close. [of unknown origin]
haw[4] (hɔ:) *n.* the nictitating membrane of a horse or other domestic animal. [C15: of unknown origin]
Ha+wai·i (hə'waɪɪ) *n.* a state of the U.S. in the central Pacific, consisting of over 20 volcanic islands and atolls, including Hawaii, Maui, Oahu, Kauai, and Molokai: discovered by Captain Cook in 1778; annexed by the U.S. in 1898; naval base at Pearl Harbor attacked by the Japanese in 1941, a major cause of U.S. entry into World War II; became a state in 1959. Capital: Honolulu. Pop.: 865 000 (1975 est.). Area: 16 640 sq. km (6425 sq. miles). Former name: **Sandwich Islands.**
Ha+wai+ian (hə'waɪən) *adj.* **1.** of or relating to Hawaii, its people, or their language. ~*n.* **2.** a native or inhabitant of Hawaii, esp. one descended from Melanesian or Tahitian immigrants. **3.** a language of Hawaii belonging to the Malayo-Polynesian family.
Ha+wai+ian gui+tar *n.* a ukulele with an unfretted neck, on which a characteristic glissando can be obtained with a steel bar.
Hawes Wa+ter (hɔ:z) *n.* a lake in NW England, in the Lake District: provides part of Manchester's water supply; extended by damming from 4 km (2.5 miles) to 6 km (4 miles).
haw+finch ('hɔ:ˌfɪntʃ) *n.* an uncommon European finch, *Coccothraustes coccothraustes,* having a very stout bill and brown plumage with black-and-white wings.
Haw·haw ('hɔ:ˌhɔ:) *n.* **Lord.** See (William) **Joyce.**
Haw+ick ('hɔ:ɪk) *n.* a town in SE Scotland, in the S central Borders region: knitwear industry. Pop.: 16 286 (1971).
hawk[1] (hɔ:k) *n.* **1.** any of various diurnal birds of prey of the family *Accipitridae,* such as the goshawk and Cooper's hawk, typically having short rounded wings and a long tail. **2.** *U.S.*

any of various other falconiform birds, including the falcons but not the eagles or vultures. **3.** a person who advocates or supports war or warlike policies. Compare **dove**[1] (sense 3). **4.** a ruthless or rapacious person. ~*vb.* **5.** (*intr.*) to hunt with falcons, hawks, etc. **6.** (*intr.*) (of falcons or hawks) to fly in quest of prey. **7.** to pursue or attack on the wing, as a hawk. [Old English *hafoc;* related to Old Norse *haukr,* Old Frisian *havek,* Old High German *habuh,* Polish *kobuz*] —**'hawk+ish** *adj.* —**'hawk+,like** *adj.*

hawk[2] (hɔ:k) *vb.* **1.** to offer (goods) for sale, as in the street. **2.** (*tr.; often foll. by about*) to spread (news, gossip, etc.). [C16: back formation from HAWKER[1]]

hawk[3] (hɔ:k) *vb.* **1.** (*intr.*) to clear (the throat) noisily. **2.** (*tr.*) to force (phlegm, etc.) up from the throat. **3.** *Brit.* a slang word for **spit**[1]. ~*n.* **4.** a noisy clearing of the throat. [C16: of imitative origin; see HAW[2]]

hawk[4] (hɔ:k) *n.* a small square board with a handle underneath, used for carrying wet plaster or mortar. Also called: **mortar board.** [of unknown origin]

hawk+bill ('hɔ:k,bɪl) *n.* another name for **hawksbill turtle.**

hawk+er[1] ('hɔ:kə) *n.* a person who travels from place to place selling goods. [C16: probably from Middle Low German *hōker,* from *hōken* to peddle; see HUCKSTER]

hawk+er[2] ('hɔ:kə) *n.* a person who hunts with hawks, falcons, etc. [Old English *hafecere;* see HAWK[1], -ER[1]]

hawk-eyed *adj.* **1.** having extremely keen sight. **2.** vigilant, watchful, or observant.

hawk+ing ('hɔ:kɪŋ) *n.* another name for **falconry.**

Haw·kins ('hɔ:kɪnz) *n.* **1. Cole·man.** 1904–69, U.S. pioneer of the tenor saxophone for jazz. **2.** Sir **John.** 1532–95, English naval commander and slave trader, treasurer of the navy (1577–89); commander of a squadron in the fleet that defeated the Spanish Armada (1588).

hawk moth *n.* any of various moths of the family *Sphingidae,* having long narrow wings and powerful flight, with the ability to hover over flowers when feeding from the nectar. Also called: **sphinx moth, hummingbird moth.** See also **death's-head moth.**

hawk owl *n.* a hawklike northern owl, *Surnia ulula,* with a long slender tail and brownish speckled plumage.

hawk's-beard *n.* any plant of the genus *Crepis,* having a ring of fine hairs surrounding the fruit and clusters of small dandelion-like flowers: family *Compositae* (composites).

hawks+bill tur+tle *or* **hawks+bill** ('hɔ:ks,bɪl) *n.* a small tropical turtle, *Eretmochelys imbricata,* with a hooked beaklike mouth: a source of tortoiseshell: family *Chelonidae.* Also called: **tortoiseshell turtle.**

hawk's-eye *n.* a dark blue variety of the mineral crocidolite: a semiprecious gemstone.

hawk+weed ('hɔ:k,wi:d) *n.* any typically hairy plant of the genus *Hieracium,* with clusters of dandelion-like flowers: family *Compositae* (composites).

Ha+worth ('haʊəθ) *n.* a village in N England, in West Yorkshire: home of Charlotte, Emily, and Anne Brontë.

hawse (hɔ:z) *Nautical.* ~*n.* **1.** the part of the bows of a vessel where the hawseholes are. **2.** short for **hawsehole** or **hawsepipe. 3.** the distance from the bow of an anchored vessel to the anchor. **4.** the arrangement of port and starboard anchor ropes when a vessel is riding on both anchors. ~*vb.* **5.** (*intr.*) (of a vessel) to pitch violently when at anchor. [C14: from earlier *halse,* probably from Old Norse *háls;* related to Old English *heals* neck]

hawse+hole ('hɔ:z,həʊl) *n. Nautical.* one of the holes in the upper part of the bows of a vessel through which the anchor ropes pass. Often shortened to **hawse.**

hawse+pipe ('hɔ:z,paɪp) *n. Nautical.* a strong metal pipe through which an anchor rope passes. Often shortened to **hawse.**

haws+er ('hɔ:zə) *n. Nautical.* a large heavy rope. [C14: from Anglo-French *hauceour,* from Old French *haucier* to hoist, ultimately from Latin *altus* high]

haws+er bend *n.* a knot for tying two ropes together.

haws·er-laid *adj.* (of a rope) made up of three ropes laid in a left-handed direction, each of which consists of three left-handed strands laid right-handed.

haw+thorn ('hɔ:,θɔ:n) *n.* any of various thorny trees or shrubs of the N temperate rosaceous genus *Crataegus,* esp. *C. oxyacantha,* having white or pink flowers and reddish fruits (haws). Also called (in Britain): **may, may tree, mayflower.** [Old English *haguthorn* from *haga* hedge + *thorn* thorn; related to Old Norse *hagthorn,* Middle High German *hagendorn,* Dutch *haagdoorn*]

Haw·thorne ('hɔ:,θɔ:n) *n.* **Na·than·iel.** 1804–64, U.S. novelist and short-story writer: his works include the novels *The Scarlet Letter* (1850) and *The House of Seven Gables* (1851) and the children's stories *Tanglewood Tales* (1853).

hay[1] (heɪ) *n.* **1. a.** grass, clover, etc., cut and dried as fodder. **b.** (*in combination*): *a hayfield; a hayloft.* **2. hit the hay.** *Slang.* to go to bed. **3. make hay of.** to throw into confusion. **4. make hay while the sun shines.** *Informal.* to take full advantage of an opportunity. **5. roll in the hay.** *Informal.* sexual intercourse or heavy petting. ~*vb.* **6.** to cut, dry, and store (grass, etc.) as fodder. **7.** (*tr.*) to feed with hay. [Old English *hieg;* related to Old Norse *hey,* Gothic *hawi,* Old Frisian *hē,* Old High German *houwi;* see HEW]

hay[2] *or* **hey** (heɪ) *n.* **1.** a circular figure in country dancing. **2.** a former country dance in which the dancers wove in and out of a circle. [C16: of uncertain origin]

hay+box ('heɪ,bɒks) *n.* an airtight box full of hay used for cooking by retained heat.

hay+cock ('heɪ,kɒk) *n.* a small cone-shaped pile of hay left in the field until dry enough to carry to the rick or barn.

Hay·dn ('haɪdᵊn) *n.* **1. (Franz) Jo·seph** ('jo:zɛf). 1732–1809, Austrian composer, who played a major part in establishing the classical forms of the symphony and the string quartet. His other works include the oratorios *The Creation* (1796–98) and *The Seasons* (1798–1801). **2.** his brother, **Jo·hann Mich·a·el** (*German* 'jo:han 'mɪça,e:l). 1737–1806, Austrian composer, esp. of Church music.

hay fe+ver *n.* an allergic reaction to pollen, dust, etc., characterized by sneezing, runny nose, and watery eyes due to inflammation of the mucous membranes of the eyes and nose. Technical name: **pollinosis.**

hay+fork ('heɪ,fɔ:k) *n.* a long-handled fork with two long curved prongs, used for moving or turning hay; pitchfork.

hay+mak·er ('heɪ,meɪkə) *n.* **1.** a person who helps to cut, turn, toss, spread, or carry hay. **2.** Also called: **hay conditioner.** either of two machines, one designed to crush stems of hay, the other to break and bend them, in order to cause more rapid and even drying. **3.** *Boxing slang.* a wild swinging punch. —**'hay+,mak·ing** *adj., n.*

hay+mow ('heɪ,maʊ) *n.* **1.** a part of a barn where hay is stored. **2.** a quantity of hay stored in a barn or loft.

hay+rack ('heɪ,ræk) *n.* **1.** a rack for holding hay for feeding to animals. **2.** a rack fixed to a cart or wagon to increase the quantity of hay or straw that it can carry.

hay+seed ('heɪ,si:d) *n.* **1.** seeds or fragments of grass or straw. **2.** *U.S. informal, derogatory.* a yokel.

hay+stack ('heɪ,stæk) *or* **hay+rick** *n.* a large pile of hay, esp. one built in the open air and covered with thatch.

hay+ward ('heɪ,wɔ:d) *n. Brit. obsolete.* a parish officer in charge of enclosures and fences.

hay+wire ('heɪ,waɪə) *adj.* (*postpositive*) *Informal.* **1.** (of things) not functioning properly; disorganized (esp. in the phrase **go haywire**). **2.** (of people) erratic or crazy. [C20: alluding to the disorderly tangle of wire removed from bales of hay]

ha+zan, haz+zan, *or* ***cha+zan*** *Hebrew.* (xa'zan; *English* 'hɑ:zᵊn) *n., pl.* ***+za+nim*** (-za'nim). the cantor in a Jewish synagogue. [from Late Hebrew *hazzān*]

haz+ard ('hæzəd) *n.* **1.** exposure or vulnerability to injury, loss, evil, etc. **2. at hazard.** at risk; in danger. **3.** a thing likely to cause injury, etc. **4.** *Golf.* an obstacle such as a bunker, a sand pit, etc. **5.** chance; accident (esp. in the phrase **by hazard**). **6.** a gambling game played with two dice. **7.** *Real tennis.* **a.** the receiver's side of the court. **b.** one of the winning openings. **8.** *Billiards.* a scoring stroke made either when a ball other than the striker's is pocketed (**winning hazard**) or the striker's cue ball itself (**losing hazard**). ~*vb.* (*tr.*) **9.** to chance or risk. **10.** to venture (an opinion, guess, etc.). **11.** to expose to danger. [C13: from Old French *hasard,* from Arabic *az-zahr* the die] —**'haz+ard+a·ble** *adj.* —**'haz·ard-,free** *adj.*

haz+ard+ous ('hæzədəs) *adj.* **1.** involving great risk. **2.** depending on chance. —**'haz+ard+ous+ly** *adv.* —**'haz+ard+ous+ness** *n.*

haz+ard warn+ing de+vice *n.* an appliance fitted to a motor vehicle that operates a simultaneous flashing of all the direction indicators, used when the vehicle is stationary to indicate that the vehicle is temporarily obstructing traffic.

haze[1] (heɪz) *n.* **1.** *Meteorol.* **a.** reduced visibility in the air as a result of condensed water vapour, dust, etc., in the atmosphere. **b.** the moisture or dust causing this. **2.** obscurity of perception, feeling, etc. ~*vb.* **3.** (when *intr.,* often foll. by *over*) to make or become hazy. [C18: back-formation from HAZY]

haze[2] (heɪz) *vb.* (*tr.*) **1.** *Chiefly U.S.* to subject (fellow students) to ridicule or abuse. **2.** *Nautical.* to harass with humiliating tasks. [C17: of uncertain origin] —**'haz+er** *n.*

ha+zel ('heɪzᵊl) *n.* **1.** Also called: **cob.** any of several shrubs of the N temperate genus *Corylus,* esp. *C. avellana,* having oval serrated leaves and edible rounded brown nuts: family *Corylaceae.* **2.** the wood of any of these trees. **3.** short for **hazelnut. 4. a.** a light yellowish-brown colour. **b.** (*as adj.*)*: hazel eyes.* [Old English *hæsel;* related to Old Norse *hasl,* Old High German *hasala,* Latin *corylus,* Old Irish *coll*]

ha·zel+hen ('heɪzᵊl,hɛn) *n.* a European woodland gallinaceous bird, *Tetrastes bonasia,* with a speckled brown plumage and slightly crested crown: family *Tetraonidae* (grouse).

ha·zel+nut ('heɪzᵊl,nʌt) *n.* the nut of a hazel shrub, having a smooth shiny hard shell. Also called: **filbert** or (in Britain) **cobnut, cob.**

Haz·litt ('hæzlɪt) *n.* **Wil·liam.** 1778–1830, English critic and essayist: works include *Characters of Shakespeare's Plays* (1817), *Table Talk* (1821), and *The Plain Speaker* (1826).

ha·zy ('heɪzɪ) *adj.* **+zi+er, +zi+est. 1.** characterized by reduced visibility; misty. **2.** indistinct; vague. [C17: of unknown origin] —**'ha+zi+ly** *adv.* —**'ha+zi+ness** *n.*

haz+zan *Hebrew.* (xa'zan; *English* 'hɑ:zᵊn) *n., pl.* ***+za+nim*** (-za'nim). a variant spelling of ***hazan.***

Hb *symbol for* haemoglobin.

HB (on Brit. pencils) *symbol for* hard-black: denoting a medium-hard lead. Compare **H** (sense 5), **B** (sense 8).

H-beam *n.* a rolled steel joist or girder with a cross section in the form of a capital letter *H.* Compare **I-beam.**

H.B.M. (in Britain) *abbrev. for* His (*or* Her) Britannic Majesty.

H-bomb *n.* short for **hydrogen bomb.**

H.C. *abbrev. for:* **1.** Holy Communion. **2.** (in Britain) House of Commons.

H.C.F. *or* **h.c.f.** *abbrev. for* highest common factor.

hd. *abbrev. for:* **1.** hand. **2.** head.
hdbk. *abbrev. for* handbook.
hdqrs. *abbrev. for* headquarters.
he[1] (hi:; *unstressed* i:) *pron.* (*subjective*) **1.** refers to a male person or animal: *he looks interesting; he's a fine stallion.* **2.** refers to an indefinite antecedent such as *one, whoever,* or *anybody: everybody can do as he likes in this country.* **3.** refers to a person or animal of unknown or unspecified sex: *a member of the party may vote as he sees fit.* ~*n.* **4. a.** a male person or animal. **b.** (*in combination*): *he-goat.* [Old English *hē;* related to Old Saxon *hie,* Old High German *her* he, Old Slavonic *sī* this, Latin *cis* on this side]
he[2] (heɪ; *Hebrew* he) *n.* the fifth letter of the Hebrew alphabet (ה), transliterated as *h.* [from Hebrew]
he[3] (hi:; heɪ) *interj.* an expression of amusement or derision. Also: **he-he!** or **hee-hee!**
He *the chemical symbol for* helium.
HE *or* **H.E.** *abbrev. for:* **1.** high explosive. **2.** His Eminence. **3.** His (*or* Her) Excellency.
head (hɛd) *n.* **1.** the upper or front part of the body in vertebrates, including man, that contains and protects the brain, eyes, mouth, and nose and ears when present. Related adj.: **cephalic. 2.** the corresponding part of an invertebrate animal. **3.** something resembling a head in form or function, such as the top of a tool. **4. a.** the person commanding most authority within a group, organization, etc. **b.** (*as modifier*): *head buyer.* **c.** (*in combination*): *headwaiter.* **5.** the position of leadership or command: *at the head of his class.* **6. a.** the most forward part of a thing; a part that juts out; front: *the head of a queue.* **b.** (*as modifier*): *head point.* **7.** the highest part of a thing; upper end: *the head of the pass.* **8.** the froth on the top of a glass of beer. **9.** aptitude, intelligence, and emotions (esp. in the phrases **above** or **over one's head, have a head for, keep one's head, lose one's head,** etc.): *she has a good head for figures; a wise old head.* **10.** (*pl.* **head**) a person or animal considered as a unit: *the show was two pounds per head; six hundred head of cattle.* **11.** the head considered as a measure of length or height: *he's a head taller than his mother.* **12.** *Botany.* **a.** a dense inflorescence such as that of the daisy and other composite plants. **b.** any other compact terminal part of a plant, such as the leaves of a cabbage or lettuce. **13.** a culmination or crisis (esp. in the phrase **bring** or **come to a head). 14.** the pus-filled tip or central part of a pimple, boil, etc. **15.** the head considered as the part of the body on which hair grows densely: *a fine head of hair.* **16.** the source or origin of a river or stream. **17.** (*cap. when part of name*) a headland or promontory, esp. a high one. **18.** the obverse of a coin, usually bearing a portrait of the head or a full figure of a monarch, deity, etc. Compare **tail. 19.** a main point or division of an argument, discourse, etc. **20.** (*often pl.*) the headline at the top of a newspaper article or the heading of a section within an article. **21.** *Nautical.* **a.** the front part of a ship or boat. **b.** (in sailing ships) the upper corner or edge of a sail. **c.** the top of any spar or derrick. **d.** any vertical timber cut to shape. **e.** (*often pl.*) a slang word for **lavatory. 22.** *Grammar.* **a.** the word in a phrase that determines how the phrase operates syntactically: *the head of the phrase "two men walking abreast" is the noun "men".* **b.** (*as modifier*): *a head noun.* **23.** the taut membrane of a drum, tambourine, etc. **24. a.** the height of the surface of liquid above a specific point, esp. when considered or used as a measure of the pressure at that point: *a head of four feet.* **b.** any pressure: *a head of steam in the boiler.* **25.** *Slang.* **a.** a person who regularly takes drugs, esp. LSD or cannabis. **b.** (*in combination*): *an acid-head.* **c.** (*as modifier*): *a head shop.* **26.** *Mining.* a road driven into the coal face. **27. a.** the terminal point of a route. **b.** (*in combination*): *railhead.* **28.** a device on a turning or boring machine, such as a lathe, that is equipped with one or more cutting tools held to the work by this device. **29.** See **cylinder head. 30.** an electromagnet that can read, write, or erase information on a magnetic medium such as a magnetic tape, disk, or drum, used in computers, tape recorders, etc. **31.** *Informal.* short for **headmaster. 32. a.** the head of a horse considered as a narrow margin in the outcome of a race (in the phrase **win by a head). b.** any narrow margin of victory (in the phrase **(win) by a head). 33.** *Informal.* short for **headache. 34.** *Curling.* the stones lying in the house after all 16 have been played. **35. against the head.** *Rugby.* from the opposing side's put-in to the scrum. **36. bite** *or* **snap someone's head off.** *Informal.* to speak sharply and angrily to someone. **37. bring** *or* **come to a head. a.** to bring or be brought to a crisis: *matters came to a head.* **b.** (of a boil) to cause to be or be about to burst. **38. get it into one's head.** to come to believe (an idea, esp. a whimsical one): *he got it into his head that the earth was flat.* **39. give head.** *U.S. slang, taboo.* to perform fellatio. **40. give someone** (*or* **something) his head. a.** to allow a person greater freedom or responsibility. **b.** to allow a horse to gallop by lengthening the reins. **41. go to one's head. a.** to make one dizzy or confused, as might an alcoholic drink. **b.** to make one conceited: *his success has gone to his head.* **42. head and shoulders above.** greatly superior to. **43. head over heels. a.** turning a complete somersault. **b.** completely; utterly (esp. in the phrase **head over heels in love). 44. hold up one's head.** to be unashamed. **45. keep one's head.** to remain calm. **46. keep one's head above water.** to manage to survive a difficult experience. **47. make head.** to make progress. **48. not make head nor tail of.** *Informal.* to fail to understand (a problem, etc.): *he couldn't make head nor tail of the case.* **49. off** (*or* **out of) one's head.** *Slang.* insane or delirious. **50. off the top of one's head.** without previous thought; impromptu. **51. on one's (own) head.** at a person's (own) risk or responsibility. **52. one's head off.** *Slang.* loudly or excessively: *the baby cried its head off.* **53. over someone's head. a.** without a person in the obvious position being considered, esp. for promotion: *the graduate was promoted over the heads of several of his seniors.* **b.** without consulting a person in the obvious position but referring to a higher authority: *in making his complaint he went straight to the director, over the head of his immediate boss.* **c.** beyond a person's comprehension. **54. put (our, their,** *etc.*) **heads together.** *Informal.* to consult together. **55. take it into one's head.** to conceive a notion, desire, or wish (to do something). **56. turn someone's head.** to make someone vain, conceited, etc. ~*vb.* **57.** (*tr.*) to be at the front or top of: *to head the field.* **58.** (*tr.;* often foll. by *up*) to be in the commanding or most important position. **59.** (often foll. by *for*) to go or cause to go (towards): *where are you heading?* **60.** to turn or steer (a vessel) as specified: *to head into the wind.* **61.** *Soccer.* to propel (the ball) by striking it with the head. **62.** (*tr.*) to provide with a head or heading: *to head a letter.* **63.** (*tr.*) to cut the head off (something): *to head celery.* **64.** (*intr.*) to form a head, as a boil or plant. **65.** (*intr.;* often foll. by *in*) (of streams, rivers, etc.) to originate or rise in. **66. head them.** *Austral.* to play two-up. ~See also **head for, head off, heads.** [Old English *hēafod;* related to Old Norse *haufuth,* Old Frisian *hāved,* Old Saxon *hōbid,* Old High German *houbit*] —**'head,like** *adj.*
head+ache ('hɛd,eɪk) *n.* **1.** pain in the head, caused by dilation of cerebral arteries, muscle contraction, insufficient oxygen in the cerebral blood, reaction to drugs, etc. Technical name: **cephalalgia. 2.** *Informal.* any cause of worry, difficulty, or annoyance. —**'head,ach·y** *adj.*
head ar+range+ment *n. Jazz.* a spontaneous orchestration.
head+band ('hɛd,bænd) *n.* **1.** a ribbon or band worn around the head. **2.** a narrow cloth band attached to the top of the spine of a book for protection or decoration.
head+board ('hɛd,bɔ:d) *n.* a vertical board or terminal at the head of a bed.
head butt *n.* a wrestling attack in which a wrestler uses his head to butt his opponent.
head+cheese ('hɛd,tʃi:z) *n.* the U.S. name for **brawn** (sense 3).
head col+lar *n.* another word (esp. Brit.) for **headstall.**
head+dress ('hɛd,drɛs) *n.* any head covering, esp. an ornate one or one denoting a rank or occupation.
head+ed ('hɛdɪd) *adj.* **1. a.** having a head or heads. **b.** (*in combination*): *two-headed; bullet-headed.* **2.** having a heading: *headed notepaper.* **3.** (*in combination*) having a mind or intellect as specified: *thickheaded.*
head+er ('hɛdə) *n.* **1.** a machine that trims the heads from castings, forgings, etc., or one that forms heads, as in wire, to make nails. **2.** a person who operates such a machine. **3.** Also called: **header tank.** a reservoir, tank, or hopper that maintains a gravity feed or a static fluid pressure in an apparatus. 4. a brick or stone laid across a wall so that its end is flush with the outer surface. Compare **stretcher** (sense 5). **5.** the action of striking a ball with the head. **6.** *Informal.* a headlong fall or dive. **7.** *Brit. dialect.* a mentally unbalanced person.
head+fast ('hɛdfɑ:st) *n.* a mooring rope at the bows of a ship. [C16: from HEAD (in the sense: front) + *fast* a mooring rope, from Middle English *fest,* from Old Norse *festr;* related to FAST[1]]
head+first ('hɛd'fɜ:st) *adj., adv.* **1.** with the head foremost; headlong: *he fell headfirst.* ~*adv.* **2.** rashly or carelessly.
head for *vb.* (*prep.*) **1.** to go or cause to go (towards). **2.** to be destined for: *to head for trouble.*
head gate *n.* **1.** a gate that is used to control the flow of water at the upper end of a lock. Compare **tail gate. 2.** another name for **floodgate** (sense 1).
head+gear ('hɛd,gɪə) *n.* **1.** any head covering, esp. a hat. **2.** any part of a horse's harness that is worn on the head. **3.** the hoisting mechanism at the pithead of a mine.
head-hunt·ing *n.* **1.** the practice among certain peoples of removing the heads of slain enemies and preserving them as trophies. **2.** *U.S. slang.* the destruction or neutralization of political opponents. —**'head-,hunt·er** *n.*
head+ing ('hɛdɪŋ) *n.* **1.** a title for a page, paragraph, chapter, etc. **2.** a main division, as of a lecture, speech, essay, etc. **3.** *Mining.* **a.** a horizontal tunnel. **b.** the end of such a tunnel. **4.** the angle between the direction of an aircraft and a specified meridian, often due north. **5.** the compass direction parallel to the keel of a vessel. **6.** the act of heading. **7.** anything that serves as a head.
head+land *n.* **1.** ('hɛdlənd). a narrow area of land jutting out into a sea, lake, etc. **2.** ('hɛd,lænd). a strip of land along the edge of an arable field left unploughed to allow space for machines.
head+less ('hɛdlɪs) *adj.* **1.** without a head. **2.** without a leader. **3.** foolish or stupid. **4.** *Prosody.* another word for **catalectic.**
head+light ('hɛd,laɪt) *or* **head+lamp** *n.* a powerful light, equipped with a reflector and attached to the front of a motor vehicle, locomotive, etc. See also **quartz-iodine lamp.**
head+line ('hɛd,laɪn) *n.* **1.** Also called: **head, heading. a.** a phrase at the top of a newspaper or magazine article indicating the subject of the article, usually in larger and heavier type. **b.** a line at the top of a page indicating the title, page number, etc. **2. hit the headlines.** to become prominent in the news. ~*vb.* **3.** (*tr.*) to furnish (a story or page) with a headline.
head+lin+er ('hɛd,laɪnə) *n. U.S. slang.* **1.** a person whose name appears in the headlines. **2.** a prominent person.
head-load *African.* ~*n.* **1.** baggage or goods arranged so as

to be carried on the heads of African porters. ~*vb.* **2.** (*tr.*) to convey or carry (goods) on the head.

head·lock ('hɛd,lɒk) *n.* a wrestling hold in which a wrestler locks his opponent's head between the crook of his elbow and the side of his body.

head·long ('hɛd,lɒŋ) *adv., adj.* **1.** with the head foremost; headfirst. **2.** with great haste. ~*adj.* **3.** *Archaic.* (of slopes, etc.) very steep; precipitous.

head·man ('hɛdmən) *n., pl.* ·**men.** **1.** *Anthropol.* a chief or leader. **2.** a foreman or overseer.

head·mas·ter (,hɛd'mɑːstə) *or* (*fem.*) **head·mis·tress** *n.* the principal of a school. —,**head·'mas·ter·,ship** *or* (*fem.*) ,**head·'mis·tress·,ship** *n.*

head mon·ey *n.* **1.** a reward paid for the capture or slaying of a fugitive, outlaw, etc. **2.** an archaic term for **poll tax.**

head·most ('hɛd,məʊst) *adj.* a less common word for **foremost.**

head off *vb.* (*tr., adv.*) **1.** to intercept and force to change direction: *to head off the stampede.* **2.** to prevent or forestall (something that is likely to happen).

head of the riv·er *n.* **a.** any of various annual rowing regattas held on particular rivers. **b.** the boat or team winning such a regatta: *Eton are head of the river again this year.*

head-on *adv., adj.* **1.** with the front or fronts foremost: *a head-on collision.* **2.** with directness or without compromise: *in his usual head-on fashion.*

head·phones ('hɛd,fəʊnz) *pl. n.* an electrical device consisting of two earphones held in position by a flexible metallic strap passing over the head. Informal name: **cans.**

head·piece ('hɛd,piːs) *n.* **1.** *Printing.* a decorative band at the top of a page, chapter, etc. **2.** any covering for the head, esp. a helmet. **3.** *Archaic.* the intellect. **4.** a less common word for **crownpiece** (sense 2).

head·pin ('hɛd,pɪn) *n.* *Tenpin bowling.* another word for **kingpin.**

head·quar·ters (,hɛd'kwɔːtəz) *pl. n.* (*sometimes functioning as sing.*) **1.** any centre or building from which operations are directed, as in the military, the police, etc. **2.** a military formation comprising the commander, his staff, and supporting echelons. ~Abbrev.: **HQ, H.Q., h.q.**

head·race ('hɛd,reɪs) *n.* a channel that carries water to a waterwheel, turbine, etc. Compare **tailrace.**

head·rail ('hɛd,reɪl) *n.* *Billiards, etc.* the end of the table from which play is started, nearest the baulkline.

head·reach ('hɛd,riːtʃ) *Nautical.* ~*n.* **1.** the distance made to windward while tacking. ~*vb.* **2.** (*tr.*) to gain distance over (another boat) when tacking.

head·rest ('hɛd,rɛst) *n.* a support for the head, as on a dentist's chair or car seat.

head·room ('hɛd,rʊm, -,ruːm) *or* **head·way** *n.* the height of a bridge, room, etc.; clearance.

heads (hɛdz) *interj., adv.* *Informal.* with the obverse side of a coin uppermost, esp. if it has a head on it: used as a call before tossing a coin. Compare **tails.**

head·sail ('hɛd,seɪl; *Nautical* 'hɛdsəl) *n.* any sail set forward of the foremast.

head·scarf ('hɛd,skɑːf) *n.* a scarf for the head, often worn tied under the chin.

head sea *n.* a sea in which the waves run directly against the course of a ship.

head·set ('hɛd,sɛt) *n.* a pair of headphones, esp. with a microphone attached.

head·ship ('hɛd,ʃɪp) *n.* **1.** the position or state of being a leader; command; leadership. **2.** *Education, Brit.* the position of headmaster or headmistress of a school.

head·shrink·er ('hɛd,ʃrɪŋkə) *n.* **1.** a slang name for **psychiatrist.** Often shortened to **shrink.** **2.** a headhunter who shrinks the heads of his victims.

heads·man ('hɛdzmən) *n., pl.* ·**men.** (formerly) an executioner who beheaded condemned persons.

head·spring ('hɛd,sprɪŋ) *n.* **1.** a spring that is the source of a stream. **2.** a spring using the head as a lever from a position lying on the ground. **3.** *Rare.* a source.

head·square ('hɛd,skwɛə) *n.* a scarf worn on the head.

head·stall ('hɛd,stɔːl) *n.* the part of a bridle that fits round a horse's head. Also called (esp. Brit.): **head collar.**

head·stand ('hɛd,stænd) *n.* the act or an instance of balancing on the head, usually with the hands as support.

head start *n.* an initial advantage in a competitive situation. [originally referring to a horse's having its head in front of others at the start of a race]

head·stock ('hɛd,stɒk) *n.* the part of a machine that supports and transmits the drive to the chuck. Compare **tailstock.**

head·stone ('hɛd,stəʊn) *n.* **1.** a memorial stone at the head of a grave. **2.** *Architect.* another name for **keystone.**

head·stream ('hɛd,striːm) *n.* a stream that is the source or a source of a river.

head·strong ('hɛd,strɒŋ) *adj.* **1.** self-willed; obstinate. **2.** (of an action) heedless; rash. —'**head·,strong·ly** *adv.* —'**head·,strong·ness** *n.*

head voice *or* **reg·is·ter** *n.* the high register of the human voice, in which the vibrations of sung notes are felt in the head.

head wait·er *n.* a waiter who supervises the activities of other waiters and arranges the seating of guests.

head·ward ('hɛdwəd) *adj.* **1.** (of river erosion) cutting backwards or upstream above the original source, which recedes. ~*adv.* **2.** a variant of **headwards.**

head·wards ('hɛdwədz) *or* **head·ward** *adv.* backwards beyond the original source: *a river erodes headwards.*

head·wa·ters ('hɛd,wɔːtəz) *pl. n.* the tributary streams of a river in the area in which it rises; headstreams.

head·way ('hɛd,weɪ) *n.* **1.** motion in a forward direction: *the vessel made no headway.* **2.** progress or rate of progress: *he made no headway with the problem.* **3.** another name for **headroom.** **4.** the distance or time between consecutive trains, buses, etc., on the same route.

head·wind ('hɛd,wɪnd) *n.* a wind blowing directly against the course of an aircraft or ship. Compare **tailwind.**

head·word ('hɛd,wɜːd) *n.* a key word placed at the beginning of a line, paragraph, etc., as in a dictionary entry.

head·work ('hɛd,wɜːk) *n.* **1.** mental work. **2.** the ornamentation of the keystone of an arch. —'**head·,work·er** *n.*

head·y ('hɛdɪ) *adj.* **head·i·er, head·i·est.** **1.** (of alcoholic drink) intoxicating. **2.** strongly affecting the mind or senses; extremely exciting. **3.** rash; impetuous. —'**head·i·ly** *adv.* —'**head·i·ness** *n.*

heal (hiːl) *vb.* **1.** to restore or be restored to health. **2.** (*intr.;* often foll. by *over* or *up*) (of a wound, burn, etc.) to repair by natural processes, as by scar formation. **3.** (*tr.*) **a.** to treat (a wound, etc.) by assisting in its natural repair. **b.** to cure (a disease or disorder). **4.** to restore or be restored to friendly relations, harmony, etc. [Old English *hǣlan;* related to Old Norse *heila,* Gothic *hailjan,* Old High German *heilen;* see HALE[1], WHOLE] —'**heal·a·ble** *adj.* —'**heal·er** *n.* —'**heal·ing·ly** *adv.*

heal-all *n.* another name for **selfheal.**

Hea·ley ('hiːlɪ) *n.* **Den·is (Winston).** born 1917, English Labour politician; Chancellor of the Exchequer 1974-79.

health (hɛlθ) *n.* **1.** the state of being bodily and mentally vigorous and free from disease. **2.** the general condition of body and mind: *in poor health.* **3.** the condition of any unit, society, etc.: *the economic health of a nation.* **4.** a toast to a person, wishing him or her good health, happiness, etc. **5.** (*modifier*) of or relating to food or other goods reputed to be beneficial to the health: *health food; a health store.* **6.** (*modifier*) of or relating to health, esp. to the administration of health: *a health committee; health resort; health service.* ~*interj.* **7.** an exclamation wishing someone good health as part of a toast (in the phrases **your health, good health,** etc.). [Old English *hǣlth;* related to *hāl* HALE[1]]

health cen·tre *n.* the surgery and offices of a group medical practice.

health·ful ('hɛlθfʊl) *adj.* a less common word for **healthy** (senses 1-3). —'**health·ful·ly** *adv.* —'**health·ful·ness** *n.*

health phys·ics *n.* (*functioning as sing.*) the branch of physics concerned with the health and safety of people in medical, scientific, and industrial work, esp. with protection from the biological effects of ionizing radiation.

health salts *pl. n.* magnesium sulphate or similar salts taken as a mild laxative.

health vis·i·tor *n.* *Brit.* a nurse who visits and helps the old and the sick in their homes.

health·y ('hɛlθɪ) *adj.* **health·i·er, health·i·est.** **1.** enjoying good health. **2.** functioning well or being sound: *the company's finances are not very healthy.* **3.** conducive to health; salutary. **4.** indicating soundness of body or mind: *a healthy appetite.* **5.** *Informal.* considerable in size or amount: *a healthy sum.* —'**health·i·ly** *adv.* —'**health·i·ness** *n.*

heap (hiːp) *n.* **1.** a collection of articles or mass of material gathered together in one place. **2.** (*often pl.;* usually foll. by *of*) *Informal.* a large number or quantity. **3.** *Informal.* a place or thing that is very old, untidy, unreliable, etc.: *the car was a heap.* ~*adv.* **4.** **heaps.** (intensifier): *he said he was feeling heaps better.* ~*vb.* **5.** (often foll. by *up* or *together*) to collect or be collected into or as if into a heap or pile: *to heap up wealth.* **6.** (*tr.;* often foll. by *with, on,* or *upon*) to load or supply (with) abundantly: *to heap with riches.* [Old English *hēap;* related to Old Frisian *hāp,* Old Saxon *hōp,* Old High German *houf*] —'**heap·er** *n.*

heap·ing ('hiːpɪŋ) *adj.* *U.S.* (of a spoonful, etc.) heaped.

hear (hɪə) *vb.* **hears, hear·ing, heard.** **1.** (*tr.*) to perceive (a sound) with the sense of hearing. **2.** (*tr.; may take a clause as object*) to listen to: *did you hear what I said?* **3.** (when *intr.,* sometimes foll. by *of* or *about;* when *tr., may take a clause as object*) to be informed (of); receive information (about): *to hear of his success; have you heard?* **4.** *Law.* to give a hearing to (a case). **5.** (when *intr.,* usually foll. by *of* and used with a negative) to listen (to) with favour, assent, etc.: *she wouldn't hear of it.* **6.** (*intr.;* foll. by *from*) to receive a letter, news, etc. (from). **7.** **hear! hear!** (*interj.*) an exclamation used to show approval of something said. **8.** **hear tell (of).** *Dialect.* to be told (about); learn (of). [Old English *hieran;* related to Old Norse *heyra,* Gothic *hausjan,* Old High German *hōren,* Greek *akouein*] —'**hear·a·ble** *adj.* —'**hear·er** *n.*

hear·ing ('hɪərɪŋ) *n.* **1.** the faculty or sense by which sound is perceived. **2.** an opportunity to be listened to. **3.** the range within which sound can be heard; earshot. **4.** the investigation of a matter by a court of law, esp. the preliminary inquiry into an indictable crime by magistrates. **5.** a formal or official trial of an action or lawsuit.

hear·ing aid *n.* a device for assisting the hearing of partially deaf persons, typically consisting of a small battery-powered electronic amplifier with microphone and earphone, worn by a deaf person in or behind the ear.

heark·en *or U.S.* (*sometimes*) **hark·en** ('hɑːkən) *vb.* *Archaic.* to listen to (something). —'**heark·en·er** *n.*

hear out *vb.* (*tr., adv.*) to listen in regard to every detail and give a proper or full hearing to.

hear·say ('hɪəˌseɪ) *n.* gossip; rumour.
hear·say ev·i·dence *n. Law.* evidence based on what has been reported to a witness by others rather than what he has himself observed or experienced (not generally admissible as evidence).
hearse (hɜːs) *n.* a vehicle, such as a car or carriage, used to carry a coffin to the grave. [C14: from Old French *herce,* from Latin *hirpex* harrow]
Hearst (hɜːst) *n.* **Wil·liam Ran·dolph.** 1863–1951, U.S. newspaper publisher, whose newspapers were noted for their sensationalism.
heart (hɑːt) *n.* **1.** the hollow muscular organ in vertebrates whose contractions propel the blood through the circulatory system. In mammals it consists of a right and left atrium and a right and left ventricle. Related adj.: **cardiac. 2.** the corresponding organ or part in invertebrates. **3.** this organ considered as the seat of life and emotions, esp. love. **4.** emotional mood or disposition: *a happy heart; a change of heart.* **5.** tenderness or pity: *you have no heart.* **6.** courage or spirit; bravery. **7.** the inmost or most central part of a thing: *the heart of the city.* **8.** the most important or vital part: *the heart of the matter.* **9.** the part nearest the heart of a person; breast: *she held him to her heart.* **10.** a dearly loved person: usually used as a term of address: *dearest heart.* **11.** a conventionalized representation of the heart, having two rounded lobes at the top meeting in a point at the bottom. **12. a.** a red heart-shaped symbol on a playing card. **b.** a card with one or more of these symbols or (*when pl.*) the suit of cards so marked. **13.** a fertile condition in land, conducive to vigorous growth in crops or herbage (esp. in the phrase **in good heart**). **14. after one's own heart.** appealing to one's own disposition, taste, or tendencies. **15. at heart.** in reality or fundamentally. **16. break one's** (*or* **someone's**) **heart.** to grieve (or cause to grieve) very deeply, esp. through love. **17. by heart.** by committing to memory. **18. cross my heart (and hope to die)!** I promise! **19. eat one's heart out.** to grieve inconsolably. **20. from (the bottom of) one's heart.** very sincerely or deeply. **21. have a heart!** be kind or merciful. **22. have one's heart in it.** (*usually used with a negative*) to have enthusiasm for something. **23. have one's heart in one's boots.** to be depressed or down-hearted. **24. have one's heart in one's mouth** (*or* **throat**). to be full of apprehension, excitement, or fear. **25. have one's heart in the right place. a.** to be kind, thoughtful, or generous. **b.** to mean well. **26. have the heart.** (*usually used with a negative*) to have the necessary will, callousness, etc., (to do something): *I didn't have the heart to tell him.* **27. heart and soul.** absolutely; completely. **28. heart of hearts.** the depths of one's conscience or emotions. **29. heart of oak.** a brave person. **30. in one's heart.** secretly; fundamentally. **31. lose heart.** to become despondent or disillusioned (over something). **32. lose one's heart to.** to fall in love with. **33. near** *or* **close to one's heart.** cherished or important. **34. set one's heart on.** to have as one's ambition to obtain; covet. **35. take heart.** to become encouraged. **36. take to heart.** to take seriously or be upset about. **37. to one's heart's content.** as much as one wishes. **38. wear one's heart on one's sleeve.** to show one's feelings openly. **39. with all one's** (*or* **one's whole**) **heart.** very willingly. ~*vb.* **40.** an archaic word for **hearten.** [Old English *heorte;* related to Old Norse *hjarta,* Gothic *hairtō,* Old High German *herza,* Latin *cor,* Greek *kardia,* Old Irish *cride*]
heart·ache ('hɑːtˌeɪk) *n.* intense anguish or mental suffering.
heart at·tack *n.* any sudden severe instance of abnormal heart functioning, esp. coronary thrombosis.
heart·beat ('hɑːtˌbiːt) *n.* one complete pulsation of the heart. See **diastole, systole.**
heart block *n.* impaired conduction or blocking of the impulse that regulates the heartbeat, resulting in a lack of coordination between the beating of the atria and the ventricles. Also called: **Adams-Stokes syndrome, atrioventricular block.**
heart·break ('hɑːtˌbreɪk) *n.* intense and overwhelming grief, esp. through disappointment in love. —**'heart·ˌbreak·er** *n.*
heart·break·ing ('hɑːtˌbreɪkɪŋ) *adj.* extremely sad, disappointing, or pitiful. —**'heart·ˌbreak·ing·ly** *adv.*
heart·bro·ken ('hɑːtˌbrəʊkən) *adj.* suffering from intense grief. —**'heart·ˌbro·ken·ly** *adv.* —**'heart·ˌbro·ken·ness** *n.*
heart·burn ('hɑːtˌbɜːn) *n.* a burning sensation beneath the breastbone caused by irritation of the oesophagus, as from regurgitation of the contents of the stomach. Technical names: **cardialgia, pyrosis.**
heart cher·ry *n.* a heart-shaped variety of sweet cherry.
-heart·ed *adj.* having a heart or disposition as specified: *good-hearted; cold-hearted; great-hearted; heavy-hearted.*
heart·en ('hɑːtᵊn) *vb.* to make or become cheerful. —**'heart·en·ing·ly** *adv.*
heart fail·ure *n.* **1.** a condition in which the heart is unable to pump an adequate amount of blood to the tissues, usually resulting in breathlessness, swollen ankles, etc. **2.** sudden and permanent cessation of the heartbeat, resulting in death.
heart·felt ('hɑːtˌfɛlt) *adj.* sincerely and strongly felt.
hearth (hɑːθ) *n.* **1. a.** the floor of a fireplace, esp. one that extends outwards into the room. **b.** (*as modifier*): *hearth rug.* **2.** this part of a fireplace as a symbol of the home, etc. **3.** the bottom part of a metallurgical furnace in which the molten metal is produced or contained. [Old English *heorth;* related to Old High German *herd* hearth, Latin *carbō* charcoal]
hearth·stone ('hɑːθˌstəʊn) *n.* **1.** a stone that forms a hearth. **2.** a less common word for **hearth** (sense 1). **3.** soft stone used to clean and whiten floors, steps, etc.
heart·i·ly ('hɑːtɪlɪ) *adv.* **1.** thoroughly or vigorously: *to eat heartily.* **2.** in a sincere manner: *he congratulated me heartily.*
heart·land ('hɑːtˌlænd) *n.* the central region of a country or continent.
heart·less ('hɑːtlɪs) *adj.* unkind or cruel; hard-hearted. —**'heart·less·ly** *adv.* —**'heart·less·ness** *n.*
heart-lung ma·chine *n.* a machine used to maintain the circulation and oxygenation of the blood during heart surgery.
heart mur·mur *n.* an abnormal sound heard through a stethoscope over the region of the heart.
heart-rend·ing *adj.* causing great mental pain and sorrow. —**'heart-ˌrend·ing·ly** *adv.*
hearts (hɑːts) *n.* (*functioning as sing.*) a card game in which players must avoid winning tricks containing hearts or the queen of spades. Also called: **Black Maria.**
heart-search·ing *n.* examination of one's feelings or conscience.
hearts·ease *or* **heart's-ease** ('hɑːtsˌiːz) *n.* **1.** another name for the **wild pansy. 2.** peace of mind.
heart·sick ('hɑːtˌsɪk) *adj.* deeply dejected or despondent. —**'heart·ˌsick·ness** *n.*
heart·some ('hɑːtsəm) *adj. Northern Brit. dialect.* **1.** cheering or encouraging: *heartsome news.* **2.** gay; cheerful. —**'heart·some·ly** *adv.* —**'heart·some·ness** *n.*
heart start·er *n. Austral. slang.* the first drink of the day.
heart·strings ('hɑːtˌstrɪŋz) *pl. n. Often facetious.* deep emotions or feelings. [C15: originally referring to the tendons supposed to support the heart]
heart-throb *n.* **1.** *Brit.* an object of infatuation. **2.** a heart beat.
heart-to-heart *adj.* **1.** (esp. of a conversation or discussion) concerned with personal problems or intimate feelings. ~*n.* **2.** an intimate conversation or discussion.
heart ur·chin *n.* any echinoderm of the genus *Echinocardium,* having a heart-shaped body enclosed in a rigid spiny test: class *Echinoidea* (sea urchins).
heart-warm·ing *adj.* **1.** pleasing; gratifying. **2.** emotionally moving.
heart-whole *adj. Rare.* **1.** not in love. **2.** sincere. **3.** stout-hearted. —**ˌheart-'whole·ness** *n.*
heart·wood ('hɑːtˌwʊd) *n.* the central core of dark hard wood in tree trunks, consisting of nonfunctioning xylem tissue that has become blocked with resins, tannins, and oils. Compare **sapwood.**
heart·worm ('hɑːtˌwɜːm) *n.* a parasitic nematode worm, *Dirofilaria immitis,* that lives in the heart and bloodstream of vertebrates.
heart·y ('hɑːtɪ) *adj.* **heart·i·er, heart·i·est. 1.** warm and unreserved in manner or behaviour. **2.** vigorous and enthusiastic: *a hearty slap on the back.* **3.** sincere and heartfelt: *hearty dislike.* **4.** healthy and strong (esp. in the phrase **hale and hearty**). **5.** substantial and nourishing. ~*n. Informal.* **6.** a comrade, esp. a sailor. **7.** a vigorous sporting man: *a rugby hearty.* —**'heart·i·ness** *n.*
heat (hiːt) *n.* **1.** a form of energy that is transferred by a difference in temperature: it is equal to the total kinetic energy of the atoms or molecules of a system. Related adjs.: **thermal, calorific. 2.** the sensation caused in the body by heat energy; warmth. **3.** the state or quality of being hot. **4.** hot weather: *the heat of summer.* **5.** intensity of feeling; passion: *the heat of rage.* **6.** the most intense or active part: *the heat of the battle.* **7.** a period or condition of sexual excitement in female mammals that occurs at oestrus. **8.** *Sport.* **a.** a preliminary eliminating contest in a competition. **b.** a single section of a contest. **9.** *Slang.* police activity after a crime: *the heat is off.* **10. in the heat of the moment.** without pausing to think. **11. turn on the heat.** *Informal.* to increase the intensity of activity, coercion, etc. ~*vb.* **12.** to make or become hot or warm. **13.** to make or become excited or intense. [Old English *hǣtu;* related to *hāt* HOT, Old Frisian *hēte* heat, Old High German *heizī*] —**'heat·less** *adj.*
heat bar·ri·er *n.* another name for **thermal barrier.**
heat ca·pac·i·ty *n.* the heat required to raise the temperature of a substance by unit temperature interval under specified conditions. Symbol: C_p (for constant pressure) or C_v (for constant volume).
heat con·tent *n.* another name for **enthalpy.**
heat death *n. Thermodynamics.* the condition of any closed system when its total entropy is a maximum and it has no available energy. If the universe is a closed system it should eventually reach this state.
heat·ed ('hiːtɪd) *adj.* **1.** made hot; warmed. **2.** impassioned or highly emotional. —**'heat·ed·ly** *adv.* —**'heat·ed·ness** *n.*
heat en·gine *n.* an engine that converts heat into mechanical energy.
heat·er ('hiːtə) *n.* **1.** any device for supplying heat, such as a hot-air blower, radiator, convector, etc. **2.** *U.S. slang.* a pistol. **3.** *Electronics.* a conductor carrying a current that indirectly heats the cathode in some types of valve.
heat ex·chang·er *n.* a device for transferring heat from one fluid to another without allowing them to mix.
heat ex·haus·tion *n.* a condition resulting from exposure to intense heat, characterized by dizziness, abdominal cramp, and prostration. Also called: **heat prostration.** Compare **heat-stroke.**
heath (hiːθ) *n.* **1.** *Brit.* a large open area, usually with sandy soil and scrubby vegetation, esp. heather. **2.** Also called: **heather.** any low-growing evergreen ericaceous shrub of the Old World genus *Erica* and related genera, having small bell-shaped typi-

cally pink or purple flowers. **3.** any of several nonericaceous heathlike plants, such as sea heath. **4.** *Austral.* any of various heathlike plants of the genus *Epacris.* [Old English *hǣth;* related to Old Norse *heithr* field, Old High German *heida* heather] —'**heath**,**like** *adj.* —'**heath·y** *adj.*

Heath (hiːθ) *n.* **Ed·ward** (**Richard George**). born 1916, British statesman; leader of the Conservative Party (1965–75); prime minister 1970–74.

heath·ber·ry ('hiːθˌbɛrɪ) *n., pl.* **·ries.** any of various plants that have berry-like fruits and grow on heaths, such as the bilberry and crowberry.

heath cock *n.* another name for **blackcock.**

hea·then ('hiːðən) *n., pl.* **·thens** *or* **·then. 1.** a person who does not acknowledge the God of Christianity, Judaism, or Islam; pagan. **2.** an uncivilized or barbaric person. **3. the.** (*functioning as pl.*) heathens collectively. ~*adj.* **4.** irreligious; pagan. **5.** unenlightened; uncivilized. **6.** of or relating to heathen peoples or their practices or beliefs. [Old English *hǣthen;* related to Old Norse *heithinn,* Old Frisian *hēthin,* Old High German *heidan*] —'**hea·then·ism** *or* '**hea·then·ry** *n.* —'**hea·then·ness** *n.*

hea·then·dom ('hiːðəndəm) *n.* heathen lands, peoples, or beliefs.

hea·then·ish ('hiːðənɪʃ) *adj.* of, relating to, or resembling a heathen or heathen culture. —'**hea·then·ish·ly** *adv.* —'**hea·then·ish·ness** *n.*

hea·then·ize *or* **hea·then·ise** ('hiːðəˌnaɪz) *vb.* **1.** to render or become heathen, or bring or come under heathen influence. **2.** (*intr.*) to engage in heathen practices.

heath·er ('hɛðə) *n.* **1.** Also called: **ling, heath.** a low-growing evergreen Eurasian ericaceous shrub, *Calluna vulgaris,* that grows in dense masses on open ground and has clusters of small bell-shaped typically pinkish-purple flowers. **2.** any of certain similar plants. **3.** a purplish-red to pinkish-purple colour. ~*adj.* **4.** of a heather colour. **5.** of or relating to interwoven yarns of mixed colours: *heather mixture.* [C14: originally Scottish and Northern English, probably from HEATH] —'**heath·ered** *adj.* —'**heath·er·y** *adj.*

heath·fowl ('hiːθˌfaʊl) *n.* (in British game laws) an archaic name for the **black grouse.** Compare **moorfowl.**

heath grass *or* **heath·er grass** *n.* a perennial European grass, *Sieglingia decumbens,* with flat hairless leaves.

heath hen *n.* **1.** another name for **greyhen. 2.** a recently extinct variety of the prairie chicken.

Heath Rob·in·son (hiːθ 'rɒbɪnsən) *adj.* (of a mechanical device) absurdly complicated in design and having a simple function. [C20: named after William *Heath Robinson* (1872–1944), English cartoonist who drew such contrivances]

heath wren *n.* either of two ground-nesting warblers of southern Australia, *Hylacola pyrrhopygia* or *H. cauta,* noted for their song and their powers of mimicry.

heat·ing el·e·ment *n.* a coil or other arrangement of wire in which heat is produced by an electric current.

heat-is·land *n. Meteorol.* the mass of air over a large city, characteristically having a slightly higher average temperature than that of the surrounding air.

heat light·ning *n.* flashes of light seen near the horizon, esp. on hot evenings: reflections of more distant lightning.

heat pros·tra·tion *n.* another name for **heat exhaustion.**

heat pump *n.* a device for extracting heat from a substance that is at a slightly higher temperature than its surroundings, and delivering it to a factory, etc., at a much higher temperature.

heat rash *n.* a nontechnical name for **miliaria.**

heat seek·er *n.* a type of missile that is guided onto its target by the infrared radiation emitted by the target.

heat shield *n.* a coating or barrier for shielding from excessive heat, such as that experienced by a spacecraft on re-entry into the earth's atmosphere.

heat sink *n.* **1.** a metal plate specially designed to conduct and radiate heat from an electrical component, such as a rectifier. **2.** a layer of material placed within the outer skin of high-speed aircraft to absorb heat.

heat·stroke ('hiːtˌstrəʊk) *n.* a condition resulting from prolonged exposure to intense heat, characterized by high fever and in severe cases convulsions and coma. See **sunstroke.**

heat-treat *vb.* (*tr.*) to apply heat to (a metal or alloy) in one or more temperature cycles to give it desirable properties. —'**heat-**ˌ**treat·ment** *n.*

heat wave *n.* **1.** a continuous spell of abnormally hot weather. **2.** an extensive slow-moving air mass at a relatively high temperature.

heaume (həʊm) *n.* (in the 12th and 13th centuries) a large helmet reaching and supported by the shoulders. [C16: from Old French *helme;* see HELMET]

heave (hiːv) *vb.* **heaves, heav·ing, heaved** *or* **hove. 1.** (*tr.*) to lift or move with a great effort. **2.** (*tr.*) to throw (something heavy) with effort. **3.** to utter (sounds, sighs, etc.) or breathe noisily or unhappily: *to heave a sigh.* **4.** to rise and fall or cause to rise and fall heavily. **5.** (*past tense and past participle* **hove**) *Nautical.* **a.** to move or cause to move in a specified way, direction, or position: *to heave in sight.* **b.** (*intr.*) (of a vessel) to pitch or roll. **6.** (*tr.*) to displace (rock strata, mineral veins, etc.) in a horizontal direction. **7.** (*intr.*) to retch. ~*n.* **8.** the act or an instance of heaving. **9.** a fling. **10.** a horizontal displacement of rock strata at a fault. [Old English *hebban;* related to Old Norse *hefja,* Old Saxon *hebbian,* Old High German *heffen* to raise, Latin *capere* to take, Sanskrit *kapatī* two hands full] —'**heav·er** *n.*

heave down *vb.* (*intr., adv.*) *Naut.* to turn a vessel on its side for cleaning.

heave-ho *interj.* **1.** a sailors' cry, as when hoisting anchor. ~*n.* **2.** *Informal.* dismissal, as from employment.

heav·en ('hɛvən) *n.* **1.** (*sometimes cap.*) *Christianity.* **a.** the abode of God and the angels. **b.** a place or state of communion with God after death. Compare **hell. 2.** (*usually pl.*) the sky, firmament or space surrounding the earth. **3.** (in any of various mythologies) a place, such as Elysium or Valhalla, to which those who have died in the gods' favour are brought to dwell in happiness. **4.** a place or state of joy and happiness. **5.** (*sing.* or *pl.; sometimes cap.*) God or the gods, used in exclamatory phrases of surprise, exasperation, etc.: *for heaven's sake; heavens above.* **6. in seventh heaven.** ecstatically happy. **7. move heaven and earth.** to do everything possible (to achieve something). [Old English *heofon;* related to Old Saxon *heban*]

heav·en·ly ('hɛvənlɪ) *adj.* **1.** *Informal.* alluring, wonderful, or sublime. **2.** of or occurring in space: *a heavenly body.* **3.** divine; holy. —'**heav·en·li·ness** *n.*

heav·en-sent *adj.* providential; fortunate: *a heaven-sent opportunity.*

heav·en·ward ('hɛvənwəd) *adj.* **1.** directed towards heaven or the sky. ~*adv.* **2.** a variant of **heavenwards.**

heav·en·wards ('hɛvənwədz) *or* **heav·en·ward** *adv.* towards heaven or the sky.

heaves (hiːvz) *n.* **1.** Also called: **broken wind.** a chronic respiratory disorder of animals of the horse family, of unknown cause. **2. the heaves.** *Slang.* an attack of vomiting or retching.

heave to *vb.* (*adv.*) to stop (a vessel) or (of a vessel) to stop, as by trimming the sails, etc. Also: **lay to.**

heav·i·er-than-air *adj.* **1.** having a density greater than that of air. **2.** of or relating to an aircraft that does not depend on buoyancy for support but gains lift from aerodynamic forces.

Heav·i·side ('hɛvɪˌsaɪd) *n.* **Ol·i·ver.** 1850–1925, English physicist. Independently of Kennelly, he predicted (1902) the existence of an ionized gaseous layer in the upper atmosphere (the **Heaviside layer**); he also contributed to telegraphy.

Heav·i·side lay·er *n.* another name for **E region** (of the ionosphere). [C20: named after O. HEAVISIDE]

heav·y ('hɛvɪ) *adj.* **heav·i·er, heav·i·est. 1.** of comparatively great weight: *a heavy stone.* **2.** having a relatively high density: *lead is a heavy metal.* **3.** great in yield, quality, or quantity: *heavy rain; heavy traffic.* **4.** great or considerable: *heavy emphasis.* **5.** hard to bear, accomplish, or fulfil: *heavy demands.* **6.** sad or dejected in spirit or mood: *heavy at heart.* **7.** coarse or broad: *a heavy line; heavy features.* **8.** (of soil) having a high clay content; cloggy. **9.** solid or fat: *heavy legs.* **10.** (of an industry) engaged in the large-scale complex manufacture of capital goods or extraction of raw materials. Compare **light**² (sense 19). **11.** serious; grave. **12.** *Military.* **a.** armed or equipped with large weapons, armour, etc. **b.** (of guns, etc.) of a large and powerful type. **13.** (of a syllable) having stress or accentuation. Compare **light**² (sense 21). **14.** dull and uninteresting: *a heavy style.* **15.** prodigious: *a heavy drinker.* **16.** (of cakes, bread, etc.) insufficiently leavened. **17.** deep and loud: *a heavy thud.* **18.** (of music, literature, etc.). **a.** dramatic and powerful; grandiose. **b.** not immediately comprehensible or appealing. **19.** *Slang.* **a.** unpleasant or tedious. **b.** wonderful. **c.** (of rock music) having a powerful beat; hard. **20.** weighted; burdened: *heavy with child.* **21.** clumsy and slow: *heavy going.* **22.** permeating: *a heavy smell.* **23.** cloudy or overcast, esp. threatening rain: *heavy skies.* **24.** not easily digestible: *a heavy meal.* **25.** (of an element or compound) being or containing an isotope with greater atomic weight than that of the naturally occurring element: *heavy hydrogen; heavy water.* **26.** *Horse racing.* (of the going on a racecourse) soft and muddy. ~*n., pl.* **heav·ies. 27. a.** a villainous role. **b.** an actor who plays such a part. **28.** *Military.* **a.** a large fleet unit, esp. an aircraft carrier or battleship. **b.** a large calibre or weighty piece of artillery. **29.** *Informal.* a heavyweight boxer, wrestler, etc. **30.** *Scot.* strong bitter beer. [Old English *hefig;* related to *hebban* to HEAVE, Old High German *hebīg*] —'**heav·i·ly** *adv.* —'**heav·i·ness** *n.*

heav·y-du·ty *n.* (*modifier*) **1.** made to withstand hard wear, bad weather, etc.: *heavy-duty uniforms.* **2.** subject to high import or export taxes.

heav·y earth *n.* another name for **barium oxide.**

heav·y-foot·ed *adj.* having a heavy or clumsy tread.

heav·y-hand·ed *adj.* **1.** clumsy. **2.** harsh and oppressive. —ˌ**heav·y-'hand·ed·ly** *adv.* —ˌ**heav·y-'hand·ed·ness** *n.*

heav·y-heart·ed *adj.* sad; melancholy.

heav·y hy·dro·gen *n.* another name for **deuterium.**

heav·y met·al *n. Military.* large guns or shot.

heav·y oil *n.* a hydrocarbon mixture, heavier than water, distilled from coal tar.

heav·y spar *n.* another name for **barytes.**

heav·y wa·ter *n.* water whose molecules contain deuterium atoms rather than hydrogen atoms. Formula: D_2O. Also called: **deuterium oxide.**

heav·y·weight ('hɛvɪˌweɪt) *n.* **1.** a person or thing that is heavier than average. **2. a.** a professional boxer weighing more than 175 pounds (79 kg). **b.** an amateur boxer weighing more than 81 kg (179 pounds). **c.** (*as modifier*): *the world heavyweight championship.* **3.** a wrestler in a similar weight category (usually over 214 pounds (97 kg)). **4.** *Informal.* an important or highly influential person.

Heb. *or* **Hebr.** *abbrev. for:* **1.** Hebrew (language). **2.** *Bible.* Hebrews.

Heb·bel (*German* 'hɛbəl) *n.* **Chris·tian Frie·drich** ('krɪstjan 'fri:driç). 1813–63, German dramatist and lyric poet, whose historical works were influenced by Hegel; his major plays are *Maria Magdalena* (1844), *Herodes und Marianne* (1850), and the trilogy *Die Nibelungen* (1862).

heb+do+mad ('hɛbdə,mæd) *n.* **1.** *Obsolete.* the number seven or a group of seven. **2.** a rare word for **week.** [C16: from Greek, from *hebdomos* seventh, from *heptas* seven]

heb+dom·a+dal (hɛb'dɒmədᵊl) *or* **heb+dom·a+da+ry** (hɛb'dɒmədərɪ, -drɪ) *adj.* a rare word for **weekly.** —**heb+'dom·a+dal+ly** *adv.*

Heb+dom·a+dal Coun+cil *n.* the governing council or senate of Oxford University.

He·be ('hi:bɪ) *n. Greek myth.* the goddess of youth and spring, daughter of Zeus and Hera and wife of Hercules.

he+be+phre+ni·a (,hi:bɪ'fri:nɪə) *n.* a form of pubertal schizophrenia, characterized by hallucinations, delusions, foolish behaviour, and senseless laughter. [C20: New Latin, from Greek *hēbē* youth + *-phrenia* mental disorder, from *phrēn* mind] —**he+be+phren+ic** (,hi:bɪ'frɛnɪk) *adj.*

Hé·bert (*French* e'bɛ:r) *n.* **Jacques Re·né** (ʒɑ:k rə'ne). 1755–94, French journalist and revolutionary: a leader of the sansculottes during the French Revolution. He was guillotined under Robespierre.

heb+e·tate ('hɛbɪ,teɪt) *adj.* **1.** (of plant parts) having a blunt or soft point. ~*vb.* **2.** *Rare.* to make or become blunted. [C16: from Latin *hebetāre* to make blunt, from *hebes* blunt] —,**heb+e·'ta·tion** *n.* —**'heb+e·,ta+tive** *adj.*

he+bet+ic (hɪ'bɛtɪk) *adj.* of or relating to puberty. [C19: from Greek *hēbētikos* youthful, from *hēbē* youth]

heb+e·tude ('hɛbɪ,tju:d) *n. Rare.* mental dullness or lethargy. [C17: from Late Latin *hebetūdō*, from Latin *hebes* blunt] —,**heb+e·'tu+di+nous** *adj.*

He+bra+ic (hɪ'breɪɪk), **He+bra·i+cal,** *or* **He+brew** *adj.* of, relating to, or characteristic of the Hebrews or their language or culture. —**He+'bra·i+cal+ly** *adv.*

He+bra+ism ('hi:breɪ,ɪzəm) *n.* **1.** a custom, linguistic usage, or other feature peculiar to or borrowed from the Hebrews, their language, or their culture. **2.** Hebrew customs, attitudes, and tenets collectively.

He+bra+ist ('hi:breɪɪst) *n.* a person who studies the Hebrew language and culture. —,**He+bra+'is+tic** *or* ,**He+bra+'is+ti+cal** *adj.* —,**He+bra+'is+ti+cal+ly** *adv.*

He+bra+ize *or* **He+bra+ise** ('hi:breɪ,aɪz) *vb.* to become or cause to become Hebrew or Hebraic. —,**He+bra·i+'za+tion** *or* ,**He+bra·i+'sa+tion** *n.* —**'He+bra+,iz+er** *or* **'He+bra+,is+er** *n.*

He+brew ('hi:bru:) *n.* **1.** a member of an ancient Semitic people claiming descent from Abraham; an Israelite. **2.** the ancient language of the Hebrews, revived as the official language of Israel. It belongs to the Canaanitic branch of the Semitic subfamily of the Afro-Asiatic family of languages. ~*adj.* **3.** of or relating to the Hebrews or their language. [C13: from Old French *Ebreu,* from Latin *Hebraeus,* from Greek *Hebraios,* from Aramaic *'ibhray,* from Hebrew *'ibhrī* one from beyond (the river)]

He+brew cal+en+dar *n.* another term for the **Jewish calendar.**

He+brews ('hi:bru:z) *n.* (*functioning as sing.*) a book of the New Testament.

Heb+ri+des ('hɛbrɪ,di:z) *n.* **the.** a group of over 500 islands off the W coast of Scotland: separated by the North Minch, Little Minch, and the Sea of the Hebrides; the chief islands are Skye, Rhum, Jura, Islay, Tiree, Coll, and Eigg (**Inner Hebrides**), and Harris and Lewis, North and South Uist, Benbecula, and Barra (**Outer Hebrides**). Also called: **Western Isles.** —,**Heb+ri+'de·an** *or* **He+brid+i·an** (hɛ'brɪdɪən) *adj., n.*

Heb+ron ('hɛbrɒn, 'hi:-) *n.* a city on the West Bank of the Jordan: famous for the Haram, which includes the cenotaphs of Abraham and Sarah, Isaac and Rebecca, and Jacob and Leah. Pop.: 43 000 (1967). Arabic name: **El Khalil.**

Hec·a+te *or* **Hek·a+te** ('hɛkətɪ) *n. Greek myth.* a goddess of the underworld.

hec·a+tomb ('hɛkə,təʊm, -,tu:m) *n.* **1.** (in ancient Greece or Rome) any great public sacrifice and feast, originally one in which 100 oxen were sacrificed. **2.** a great sacrifice. [C16: from Latin *hecatombē,* from Greek *hekatombē,* from *hekaton* hundred + *bous* ox]

heck[1] (hɛk) *interj.* a mild exclamation of surprise, irritation, etc. [C19: euphemistic for *hell*]

heck[2] (hɛk) *n. Northern Brit. dialect.* a frame for obstructing the passage of fish in a river. [C14: variant of HATCH[2]]

heck+el+phone ('hɛkəl,fəʊn) *n. Music.* a type of bass oboe. [C20: named after W. *Heckel* (1856–1909), German inventor]

heck+le ('hɛkᵊl) *vb.* **1.** to interrupt (a public speaker, performer, etc.) by comments, questions, or taunts. **2.** (*tr.*) Also: **hackle, hatchel.** to comb (hemp or flax). ~*n.* **3.** an instrument for combing flax or hemp. [C15: Northern and East Anglian form of HACKLE[1]] —**'heck+ler** *n.*

hec+tare ('hɛktɑ:) *n.* one hundred ares. 1 hectare is equivalent to 10 000 square metres or 2.471 acres. Symbol: ha [C19: from French; see HECTO-, ARE]

hec+tic ('hɛktɪk) *adj.* **1.** characterized by extreme activity or excitement. **2.** associated with, peculiar to, or symptomatic of tuberculosis (esp. in the phrases **hectic fever, hectic flush**). ~*n.* **3.** a hectic fever or flush. **4.** *Rare.* a person who is consumptive or who experiences a hectic fever or flush. [C14: from Late Latin *hecticus,* from Greek *hektikos* habitual, from *hexis* state, from *ekhein* to have] —**'hec+ti+cal+ly** *adv.*

hec·to- *or before a vowel* **hect-** *prefix.* denoting 100: *hectogram.* Symbol: h [via French from Greek *hekaton* hundred]

hec+to+cot·y+lus (,hɛktəʊ'kɒtɪləs) *n., pl.* **+li** (-,laɪ). a tentacle in certain male cephalopod molluscs, such as the octopus, that is specialized for transferring spermatozoa to the female. [C19: New Latin, from HECTO- + Greek *kotulē* cup]

hec+to+gram *or* **hec+to+gramme** ('hɛktəʊ,græm) *n.* one hundred grams. 1 hectogram is equivalent to 3.527 ounces. Symbol: hg

hec+to+graph ('hɛktəʊ,grɑ:f, -,græf) *n.* **1.** Also called: **copygraph.** a process for copying type or manuscript from a glycerin-coated gelatin master to which the original has been transferred. **2.** a machine using this process. —**hec+to+graph+ic** (,hɛktəʊ'græfɪk) *adj.* —,**hec+to+'graph·i+cal+ly** *adv.* —**hec+tog+ra+phy** (hɛk'tɒgrəfɪ) *n.*

hec+tor ('hɛktə) *vb.* **1.** to bully or torment by teasing. ~*n.* **2.** a blustering bully. [C17: after HECTOR (the son of Priam), in the sense: a bully]

Hec·tor ('hɛktə) *n. Classical myth.* a son of King Priam of Troy, who was killed by Achilles.

Hec·u·ba ('hɛkjʊbə) *n. Classical myth.* the wife of King Priam of Troy, and mother of Hector and Paris.

he'd (hi:d; *unstressed* i:d, hɪd, ɪd) *contraction of* he had *or* he would.

hed+dle ('hɛdᵊl) *n.* one of a set of frames of vertical wires on a loom, each wire having an eye through which a warp thread can be passed. [Old English *hefeld* chain; related to Old Norse *hafald,* Middle Low German *hevelte*]

he+der *or* ***che+der*** *Hebrew.* ('xɛdɛr; *English* 'heɪdə) *n., pl.* ***ha+da+rim*** (xada'ri:m). a school where Jewish children are taught Hebrew, the Bible, etc. [literally: room]

hedge (hɛdʒ) *n.* **1.** a row of shrubs or bushes forming a boundary to a field, garden, etc. **2.** a barrier or protection against something. **3.** the act or a method of reducing the risk of financial loss on an investment, bet, etc. **4.** a cautious or evasive statement. ~*vb.* **5.** (*tr.*) to enclose or separate with or as if with a hedge. **6.** (*tr.*) to hinder, obstruct, or restrict. **7.** (*intr.*) to evade decision or action, esp. by making noncommittal statements. **8.** (*tr.*) to guard against the risk of loss in (a bet, the paying out of a win, etc.), esp. by laying bets with other bookmakers. **9.** (*intr.*) to protect against financial loss through future price fluctuations, as by investing in futures. [Old English *hecg;* related to Old High German *heckia,* Middle Dutch *hegge;* see HAW[1]] —**'hedg+er** *n.* —**'hedg·y** *adj.*

hedge gar+lic *n.* another name for **garlic mustard.**

hedge+hog ('hɛdʒ,hɒg) *n.* **1.** any small nocturnal Old World mammal of the genus *Erinaceus,* such as *E. europaeus,* and related genera, having a protective covering of spines on the back: family *Erinaceidae,* order *Insectivora* (insectivores). **2.** any other insectivores of the family *Erinaceidae,* such as the moon rat. **3.** *U.S.* any of various other spiny animals, esp. the porcupine.

hedge+hop ('hɛdʒ,hɒp) *vb.* **+hops, +hop+ping, +hopped.** (*intr.*) (of an aircraft) to fly close to the ground, as in crop spraying. —**'hedge+,hop+per** *n.* —**'hedge+,hop+ping** *n., adj.*

hedge hys+sop *n.* any of several North American scrophulariaceous plants of the genus *Gratiola,* esp. *G. aurea,* having small yellow or white flowers.

hedge+row ('hɛdʒ,rəʊ) *n.* a hedge of shrubs or low trees growing along a bank, esp. one bordering a field or lane.

hedge spar+row *n.* a small brownish European songbird, *Prunella modularis:* family *Prunellidae* (accentors). Also called: **dunnock.**

He+djaz (hi:'dʒæz) *n.* a variant spelling of **Hejaz.**

he+don+ics (hi:'dɒnɪks) *n.* (*functioning as sing.*) **1.** the branch of psychology concerned with the study of pleasant and unpleasant sensations. **2.** (in philosophy) the study of pleasure, esp. in its relation to duty.

he+don+ism ('hi:dᵊ,nɪzəm, 'hɛd-) *n.* **1.** *Ethics.* **a.** the doctrine that the pursuit of pleasure is the highest good. **b.** the pursuit of pleasure as a matter of principle. **2.** indulgence in sensual pleasures. [C19: from Greek *hēdonē* pleasure] —**he+'don+ic** *or* ,**he+don+'is+tic** *adj.* —**'he+don+ist** *n.*

-he·dron *n. combining form.* indicating a geometric solid having a specified number of faces or surfaces: *tetrahedron.* [from Greek *-edron* -sided, from *hedra* seat, base] —**-he·dral** *adj. combining form.*

hee·bie-jee·bies ('hi:bɪ'dʒi:bɪz) *pl. n.* **the.** *Slang.* apprehension and nervousness. [C20: coined by W. De Beck (1890–1942), American cartoonist]

heed (hi:d) *n.* **1.** close and careful attention; notice (often in the phrases **give, pay,** *or* **take heed**). ~*vb.* **2.** to pay close attention to (someone or something). [Old English *hēdan;* related to Old Saxon *hōdian,* Old High German *huoten*] —**'heed+er** *n.* —**'heed+ful** *adj.* —**'heed+ful+ly** *adv.* —**'heed+ful+ness** *n.*

heed+less ('hi:dlɪs) *adj.* taking little or no notice; careless or thoughtless. —**'heed+less+ly** *adv.* —**'heed+less+ness** *n.*

hee+haw ('hi:,hɔ:) *interj.* an imitation or representation of the braying sound of a donkey.

heel[1] (hi:l) *n.* **1.** the back part of the human foot from the instep to the lower part of the ankle. Compare **calcaneus. 2.** the corresponding part in other vertebrates. **3.** the part of a shoe, stocking, etc., designed to fit the heel. **4.** the outer part of a shoe underneath the heel. **5.** the part of the palm of a glove nearest the wrist. **6.** the lower, end, or back section of something: *the heel of a loaf.* **7.** *Horticulture.* the small part of the parent plant that remains attached to a young shoot cut for propagation and that ensures more successful rooting. **8.** *Nautical.* **a.** the bottom of a mast. **b.** the after end of a ship's keel. **9.** the back part of a golf club head where it bends to join the shaft. **10.** *Rugby.* possession of the ball as obtained from a scrum (esp. in the phrase **get the heel**). **11.** *Slang.* a contemptible person. **12. at** (*or* **on**) **one's heels.** just behind or following closely. **13. cool** (*or* **kick**) **one's heels.** to be kept waiting, esp. deliberately. **14. down at heel. a.** shabby or worn. **b.** slovenly or careless. **15. rock back on one's heels.** *Informal.* to astonish or be astonished. **16. take to one's heels.** to run off. **17. to heel.** disciplined or under control, as a dog walking by a person's heel. ~*vb.* **18.** (*tr.*) to repair or replace the heel of (shoes, etc.). **19.** to perform (a dance) with the heels. **20.** (*tr.*) *Golf.* to strike (the ball) with the heel of the club. **21.** *Rugby.* to kick (the ball) backwards using the sole and heel of the boot. **22.** to follow at the heels of (a person). **23.** (*tr.*) to arm (a gamecock) with spurs. [Old English *hēla;* related to Old Norse *hǣll,* Old Frisian *hêl*] —**'heel+less** *adj.*

heel[2] (hi:l) *vb.* **1.** (of a vessel) to lean over; list. ~*n.* **2.** inclined position from the vertical: *the boat is at ten degrees of heel.* [Old English *hieldan;* related to Old Norse *hallr* inclined, Old High German *helden* to bow]

heel-and-toe *adj.* **1.** of or denoting a style of walking in which the heel of the front foot touches the ground before the toes of the rear one leave it. ~*vb.* **2.** (*intr.*) (esp. in motor racing) to use the heel and toe of the same foot to operate the brake and accelerator.

heel+ball ('hi:l,bɔ:l) *n.* **a.** a black waxy substance used by shoemakers to blacken the edges of heels and soles. **b.** a similar substance used to take rubbings, esp. brass rubbings.

heel bar *n.* a small shop or a counter in a department store where shoes are mended while the customer waits.

heel bone *n.* the nontechnical name for **calcaneus.**

heeled (hi:ld) *adj.* **1. a.** having a heel or heels. **b.** (*in combination*): *high-heeled.* **2. well-heeled.** wealthy.

heel+er ('hi:lə) *n.* **1.** *U.S.* See **ward heeler. 2.** a person or thing that heels. **3.** *Austral.* a dog that herds cattle, etc., by biting at their heels.

heel in *vb.* (*tr., adv.*) to insert (cuttings, shoots, etc.) into the soil before planting to keep them moist.

heel+piece ('hi:l,pi:s) *n.* the piece of a shoe, stocking, etc., designed to fit the heel.

heel+post ('hi:l,pəust) *n.* a post for carrying the hinges of a door or gate.

heel+tap ('hi:l,tæp) *n.* **1.** Also called: **lift.** a layer of leather, etc., in the heel of a shoe. **2.** a small amount of alcoholic drink left at the bottom of a glass after drinking.

Hee·nan ('hi:nən) *n.* **John Car·mel.** 1905–75, Irish cardinal; archbishop of Westminster (1963–75).

Heer+len ('hɪələn; *Dutch* 'he:rlə) *n.* a city in the SE Netherlands, in Limburg province: industrial centre of a coal-mining region. Pop.: 73 849 (1973 est.).

heft (hɛft) *vb.* (*tr.*) *Informal.* **1.** to assess the weight of (something) by lifting. **2.** to lift. ~*n.* **3.** weight. **4.** *U.S.* the main part. [C19: probably from HEAVE, by analogy with *thieve, theft, cleave, cleft*] —**'heft+er** *n.*

heft·y ('hɛftɪ) *adj.* **heft·i·er, heft·i·est.** *Informal.* **1.** big and strong. **2.** characterized by vigour or force: *a hefty blow.* **3.** large, bulky, or heavy. —**'heft·i+ly** *adv.* —**'heft·i+ness** *n.*

He·gel ('heɪgᵊl) *n.* **Ge·org Wil·helm Frie·drich** ('ge:ɔrk 'vɪlhɛlm 'fri:drɪç). 1770–1831, German philosopher, who created a fundamentally influential system of thought. His view of man's mind as the highest expression of the Absolute is expounded in *The Phenomonology of Mind* (1807) and he developed his concept of dialectic in *Science of Logic* (1812–16). —**He+ge·li·an** (hɪ'geɪlɪən, heɪ'gi:-) *adj.* —**He+'ge·li·an+,ism** *n.*

He+ge·li·an di·a+lec+tic *n. Philosophy.* an interpretive method in which the contradiction between a proposition (thesis) and its antithesis is resolved at a higher level of truth (synthesis).

he+gem·o·ny (hɪ'gɛmənɪ) *n., pl.* **+nies.** ascendancy or domination of one power or state within a league, confederation, etc., or of one social class over others. [C16: from Greek *hēgemonia* authority, from *hēgemōn* leader, from *hēgeisthai* to lead] —**heg+e·mon+ic** (,hɛgə'mɒnɪk) *adj.*

Heg·i+ra *or* **Hej·i+ra** ('hɛdʒɪrə) *n.* **1.** the flight of Mohammed from Mecca to Medina in 622 A.D.; the starting point of the Muslim era. **2.** the Muslim era itself. See also **A.H. 3.** (*often not cap.*) an escape or flight. [C16: from Medieval Latin, from Arabic *hijrah* flight]

he+gu+men (hɪ'gju:mɛn) *or* **he+gu+me·nos** (hɪ'gju:mɪ,nəus) *n.* the head of a monastery of the Eastern Church. [C16: from Medieval Latin *hēgūmenus,* from Late Greek *hēgoumenos* leader, from Greek *hēgeisthai* to lead]

heh (heɪ) *interj.* an exclamation of surprise or inquiry.

Hei·deg·ger (*German* 'haɪdɛgər) *n.* **Mar·tin** ('marti:n). 1889–1976, German existentialist philosopher: he expounded his ontological system in *Being and Time* (1927).

Hei+del+berg ('haɪdᵊl,bɜ:g; *German* 'haɪdᵊl,bɛrk) *n.* a city in SW West Germany, in NW Baden-Württemberg on the River Neckar: capital of the Palatinate from the 13th century until 1719; famous castle (begun in the 12th century) and university (1386), the oldest in Germany. Pop.: 120 925 (1974 est.).

Hei+del+berg man *n.* a type of primitive man, *Homo heidelbergensis,* occurring in Europe in the middle Palaeolithic age, known only from a single fossil lower jaw. [C20: referring to the site where remains were found, at Mauer, near *Heidelberg,* Germany (1907)]

Hei+duc ('haɪdʊk) *n.* a variant spelling of **Haiduk.**

heif+er ('hɛfə) *n.* a young cow. [Old English *heahfore;* related to Greek *poris* calf; see HIGH]

Hei+fetz ('haɪfɪts) *n.* **Ja·scha** ('jæʃə). born 1901, U.S. violinist, born in Russia.

heigh-ho ('heɪ'həu) *interj.* an exclamation of weariness, disappointment, surprise, or happiness.

height (haɪt) *n.* **1.** the vertical distance from the bottom or lowest part of something to the top or apex. **2.** the vertical distance of an object or place above the ground or above sea level; altitude. **3.** relatively great altitude or distance from the bottom to the top. **4.** the topmost point; summit. **5.** *Astronomy.* the angular distance of a celestial body above the horizon. **6.** the period of greatest activity or intensity: *the height of the battle.* **7.** an extreme example of its kind: *the height of rudeness.* **8.** (*often pl.*) an area of high ground. **9.** (*often pl.*) the state of being far above the ground: *I don't like heights.* **10.** (*often pl.*) a position of influence, fame, or power. [Old English *hīehthu;* related to Old Norse *hǣthe,* Gothic *hauhitha,* Old High German *hōhida;* see HIGH]

height+en ('haɪtᵊn) *vb.* **1.** to make or become high or higher. **2.** to make or become more extreme or intense. —**'height+en+er** *n.*

height of land *n. U.S.* a watershed.

height-to-pa·per *n.* the overall height of printing plates and type, standardized as 0.9175 inch (Brit.) and 0.9186 inch (U.S.).

Heil+bronn (*German* haɪl'brɔn) *n.* a city in SW West Germany, in N Baden-Württemberg on the River Neckar. Pop.: 105 767 (1974 est.).

Hei+lung+kiang ('heɪ'lʊŋ'kjæŋ, -kaɪ'æŋ) *n.* a province of NE China, in Manchuria: coal-mining, with placer gold in some rivers. Capital: Harbin. Pop.: 25 000 000 (1967–71 est.). Area: 464 000 sq. km (179 000 sq. miles).

Heim+dall, Heim+dal ('heɪm,dɑ:l), *or* **Heim+dallr** ('heɪm,dɑ:lə) *n. Norse myth.* the god of light and the dawn, and the guardian of the rainbow bridge Bifrost.

Hei·ne (*German* 'haɪnə) *n.* **Hein·rich** ('haɪnrɪç). 1797–1856, German poet and essayist, whose chief poetic work is *Das Buch der Lieder* (1827). Many of his poems have been set to music, notably by Schubert and Schumann.

hei+nous ('heɪnəs, 'hi:-) *adj.* evil; atrocious. [C14: from Old French *haineus,* from *haine* hatred, from *hair* to hate, of Germanic origin; see HATE] —**'hei+nous+ly** *adv.* —**'hei+nous+ness** *n.*

heir (ɛə) *n.* **1.** *Civil law.* the person legally succeeding to all property of a deceased person, irrespective of whether such person died testate or intestate, and upon whom devolves as well as the rights the duties and liabilities attached to the estate. **2.** any person or thing that carries on some tradition, circumstance, etc., from a forerunner. **3.** an archaic word for **offspring.** [C13: from Old French, from Latin *hērēs;* related to Greek *khēros* bereaved] —**'heir+less** *adj.*

heir ap+par+ent *n., pl.* **heirs ap+par+ent.** *Property law.* a person whose right to succeed to certain property cannot be defeated, provided such person survives his ancestor. Compare **heir presumptive.**

heir-at-law *n., pl.* **heirs-at-law.** *Property law.* the person entitled to succeed to the real property of a person who dies intestate.

heir+dom ('ɛədəm) *n. Property law.* succession by right of blood; inheritance.

heir+ess ('ɛərɪs) *n.* **1.** a woman who inherits or expects to inherit great wealth. **2.** *Property law.* a female heir.

heir+loom ('ɛə,lu:m) *n.* **1.** an object that has been in a family for generations. **2.** *Property law.* an item of personal property inherited by special custom or in accordance with the terms of a will. [C15: from HEIR + *lome* tool; see LOOM[1]]

heir pre+sump+tive *n. Property law.* a person who expects to succeed to an estate but whose right may be defeated by the birth of one nearer in blood to the ancestor. Compare **heir apparent.**

heir+ship ('ɛəʃɪp) *n. Law.* **1.** the state or condition of being an heir. **2.** the right to inherit; inheritance.

Hei·sen·berg ('haɪzᵊn,bɜ:g; *German* ,haɪzᵊn,bɛrk) *n.* **Wer·ner Karl** ('vɛrnər 'karl). 1901–76, German physicist. He contributed to quantum mechanics and formulated the uncertainty principle (1927): Nobel prize for physics 1932.

Hei·sen·berg un+cer+tain+ty prin+ci+ple *n.* a more formal name for **uncertainty principle.**

heist (haɪst) *Slang, chiefly U.S.* ~*n.* **1.** a robbery. ~*vb.* **2.** (*tr.*) to steal or burgle. [variant of HOIST] —**'heist+er** *n.*

hei+ti+ki (heɪ'ti:ki:) *n. N.Z.* a Maori neck ornament of greenstone. [C19: from Maori, from *hei* to hang + TIKI]

Heit·ler (*German* 'haɪtlər) *n.* **Wal·ter** ('valtər), 1904–81, German physicist, noted for his work on chemical bonds.

He+jaz, He+djaz, *or* **Hi+jaz** (hi:'dʒæz) *n.* a provincial area of W Saudi Arabia, along the Red Sea and the Gulf of Aqaba: formerly an independent kingdom; united with Nejd in 1932 to form Saudi Arabia. Capital: Mecca. Pop.: about 2 000 000 (1970 est.). Area: about 348 600 sq. km (134 600 sq. miles).

Hej·i+ra ('hɛdʒɪrə) *n.* a variant spelling of **Hegira.**

Hek·a+te ('hɛkətɪ) *n.* a variant spelling of **Hecate.**

Hek+la ('hɛklə) *n.* a volcano in SW Iceland: several craters, with the last eruption in 1970. Height: 1491 m (4892 ft.).

Hel (hɛl) *or* **Hel·a** ('hɛlɑ:) *n. Norse Myth.* **1.** the goddess of the dead. **2.** the underworld realm of the dead.

held (hɛld) *vb.* the past tense or past participle of **hold**[1].

Hel+den+te+nor *German.* ('hɛldᵊnte,no:r) *n., pl.* **+te+nö+re** (-te'nø:rə). a tenor with a powerful voice suited to singing heroic roles, esp. in Wagner. [literally: hero tenor]

Hel·en ('hɛlɪn) *n. Greek myth.* the beautiful daughter of Zeus and Leda, whose abduction by Paris from her husband Menelaus caused the Trojan War.

Hel+e·na ('hɛlənə) *n.* a city in W Montana: the state capital. Pop.: 22 730 (1970).

Hel+go+land ('hɛlgo,lant) *n.* the German name for **Heligoland.**

he·li·a·cal ris·ing (hɪˈlaɪəkəl) *n.* **1.** the rising of a celestial object at the same time as the rising of the sun. **2.** the date at which such a celestial object first becomes visible in the dawn sky. [C17: from Late Latin *hēliacus* relating to the sun, from Greek *hēliakos,* from *hēlios* the sun]

he·li·an·thus (ˌhiːlɪˈænθəs) *n., pl.* **·thus·es.** any plant of the genus *Helianthus,* such as the sunflower and Jerusalem artichoke, typically having large yellow daisy-like flowers with yellow, brown, or purple centres: family *Compositae* (composites). [C18: New Latin, from Greek *hēlios* sun + *anthos* flower]

hel·i·cal (ˈhɛlɪkəl) *adj.* of or shaped like a helix; spiral. —**ˈhel·i·cal·ly** *adv.*

hel·i·cal gear *n.* a gearwheel having the tooth form generated on a helical path about the axis of the wheel.

hel·i·ces (ˈhɛlɪˌsiːz) *n.* a plural of **helix.**

hel·i·chry·sum (ˌhɛlɪˈkraɪzəm) *n.* any plant of the widely cultivated genus *Helichrysum,* whose flowers retain their shape and colour when dried: family *Compositae* (composites). [C16: from Latin, from Greek *helikhrusos,* from *helix* spiral + *khrusos* gold]

hel·i·cline (ˈhɛlɪˌklaɪn) *n. Architect.* a spiral-shaped ramp. [from HELICO- + -CLINE]

hel·i·co- *or before a vowel* **hel·ic-** *combining form.* spiral or helical: *helicograph.*

hel·i·co·graph (ˈhɛlɪkəʊˌgrɑːf, -ˌgræf) *n.* an instrument for drawing spiral curves.

hel·i·coid (ˈhɛlɪˌkɔɪd) *adj. also* **hel·i·coi·dal. 1.** *Biology.* shaped like a spiral: *a helicoid shell.* ~*n.* **2.** *Geom.* any surface resembling that of a screw thread. —**ˌhel·iˈcoi·dal·ly** *adv.*

hel·i·con (ˈhɛlɪkən) *n.* a bass tuba made to coil over the shoulder of a band musician. [C19: probably from HELICON, associated with Greek *helix* spiral]

Hel·i·con (ˈhɛlɪkən) *n.* a mountain in Greece, in Boeotia: location of the springs of Hippocrene and Aganippe, believed by the Ancient Greeks to be the source of poetic inspiration and the home of the Muses. Height: 1749 m (5738 ft.). Modern Greek name: **Elikón.**

hel·i·cop·ter (ˈhɛlɪˌkɒptə) *n.* an aircraft without wings that is capable of moving vertically and hovering, obtaining its lift from the rotation of overhead blades. See also **autogiro.** [C19: from French *hélicoptère;* see HELICO- + -PTER]

hel·i·cop·ter gun·ship *n.* a heavily armed helicopter used for ground attack rather than aerial combat.

Hel·i·go·land (ˈhɛlɪgəʊˌlænd) *n.* a small island in the North Sea, one of the North Frisian Islands, separated from the coast of NW West Germany by **Heligoland Bight:** administratively part of the West German state of Schleswig-Holstein: a large island in early medieval times, now eroded to an area of about 150 hectares (380 acres); ceded by Britain to Germany in 1890 in exchange for Zanzibar. German name: **Helgoland.**

he·li·o- *or before a vowel* **he·li-** *combining form.* indicating the sun: *heliocentric; heliolithic.* [from Greek, from *hēlios* sun]

he·li·o·cen·tric (ˌhiːlɪəʊˈsɛntrɪk) *adj.* **1.** having the sun at its centre. **2.** measured from or in relation to the centre of the sun. —**ˌhe·li·o·ˈcen·tri·cal·ly** *adv.* —**he·li·o·cen·tric·i·ty** (ˌhiːlɪəʊsɛnˈtrɪsɪtɪ) *or* **he·li·o·cen·tri·cism** (ˌhiːlɪəʊˈsɛntrɪˌsɪzəm) *n.*

he·li·o·cen·tric par·al·lax *n.* See **parallax** (sense 2).

He·li·o·chrome (ˈhiːlɪəʊˌkrəʊm) *n. Trademark.* a photograph that reproduces the natural colours of the subject. —**ˌhe·li·o·ˈchro·mic** *adj.*

He·li·o·gab·a·lus (ˌhiːlɪəʊˈgæbələs) *or* **El·a·gab·a·lus** *n.* original name *Varius Avitus Bassianus.* ?204–222 A.D., Roman emperor (218–222). His reign was notorious for debauchery and extravagance.

he·li·o·graph (ˈhiːlɪəʊˌgrɑːf, -ˌgræf) *n.* **1.** an instrument used for sending messages (**heliograms**) by means of flashes of light. **2.** a device used to photograph the sun. —**he·li·og·ra·pher** (ˌhiːlɪˈɒgrəfə) *n.* —**he·li·o·graph·ic** (ˌhiːlɪəʊˈgræfɪk) *or* **ˌhe·li·o·ˈgraph·i·cal** *adj.* —**ˌhe·li·ˈog·ra·phy** *n.*

he·li·o·gra·vure (ˌhiːlɪəʊgrəˈvjʊə) *n. Printing.* a former name for **photogravure.**

he·li·ol·a·try (ˌhiːlɪˈɒlətrɪ) *n.* worship of the sun. —**ˌhe·li·ˈol·a·ter** *n.* —**ˌhe·li·ˈol·a·trous** *adj.*

he·li·o·lith·ic (ˌhiːlɪəʊˈlɪθɪk) *adj.* of or relating to a civilization characterized by sun worship and megaliths.

he·li·om·e·ter (ˌhiːlɪˈɒmɪtə) *n.* a refracting telescope having a split objective lens that is used to determine very small angular distances between celestial bodies. —**he·li·o·met·ric** (ˌhiːlɪəʊˈmɛtrɪk) *or* **ˌhe·li·o·ˈmet·ri·cal** *adj.* —**ˌhe·li·o·ˈmet·ri·cal·ly** *adv.* —**ˌhe·li·ˈom·e·try** *n.*

He·li·op·o·lis (ˌhiːlɪˈɒpəlɪs) *n.* **1.** (in ancient Egypt) a city near the apex of the Nile delta: a centre of sun worship. Ancient Egyptian name: **On. 2.** the Ancient Greek name for **Baalbek.**

He·li·os (ˈhiːlɪˌɒs) *n. Greek myth.* the god of the sun, who drove his chariot daily across the sky. Roman counterpart: **Sol.**

he·li·o·stat (ˈhiːlɪəʊˌstæt) *n.* an astronomical instrument used to reflect the light of the sun in a constant direction. —**ˌhe·li·o·ˈstat·ic** *adj.*

he·li·o·tax·is (ˌhiːlɪəʊˈtæksɪs) *n.* movement of an entire organism in response to the stimulus of sunlight. —**he·li·o·tac·tic** (ˌhiːlɪəʊˈtæktɪk) *adj.*

he·li·o·ther·a·py (ˌhiːlɪəʊˈθɛrəpɪ) *n.* the therapeutic use of sunlight.

he·li·o·trope (ˈhiːlɪəˌtrəʊp, ˈhɛljə-) *n.* **1.** any boraginaceous plant of the genus *Heliotropium,* esp. the South American *H. arborescens,* cultivated for its small fragrant purple flowers. **2. garden heliotrope.** a widely cultivated valerian, *Valeriana officinalis,* with clusters of small pink, purple, or white flowers. **3.** any of various plants that turn towards the sun. **4. a.** a bluish-violet to purple colour. **b.** (*as adj.*): *a heliotrope dress.* **5.** an instrument used in geodetic surveying employing the sun's rays reflected by a mirror as a signal for the sighting of stations over long distances. **6.** another name for **bloodstone.** [C17: from Latin *hēliotropium,* from Greek *hēliotropion,* from *hēlios* sun + *trepein* to turn]

he·li·ot·ro·pin (ˌhiːlɪˈɒtrəpɪn) *n.* another term for **piperonal.**

he·li·ot·ro·pism (ˌhiːlɪˈɒtrəˌpɪzəm) *n.* the growth of a plant in response to the stimulus of sunlight. —**he·li·o·trop·ic** (ˌhiːlɪəʊˈtrɒpɪk) *adj.* —**ˌhe·li·o·ˈtrop·i·cal·ly** *adv.*

he·li·o·type (ˈhiːlɪəʊˌtaɪp) *n.* **1.** a printing process in which an impression is taken in ink from a gelatin surface that has been exposed under a negative and prepared for printing. Also called: **heliotypy. 2.** the gelatin plate produced by such a process. **3.** a print produced from such a plate. —**he·li·o·typ·ic** (ˌhiːlɪəʊˈtɪpɪk) *adj.*

he·li·o·zo·an (ˌhiːlɪəʊˈzəʊən) *n.* any protozoan of the mostly freshwater order *Heliozoa,* typically having a siliceous shell and stiff radiating pseudopodia: class *Sarcodina* (amoeba, etc.).

hel·i·port (ˈhɛlɪˌpɔːt) *n.* an airport for helicopters. [C20: from HELI(COPTER) + PORT[1]]

he·li·um (ˈhiːlɪəm) *n.* a very light nonflammable colourless odourless element that is an inert gas, occurring in certain natural gases: used in balloons and in cryogenic research. Symbol: He; atomic no.: 2; atomic wt.: 4.0026; density: 0.178 kg/m^3; melting pt.: –272.2°C; boiling pt.: –268.6°C. See also **alpha particle.** [C19: New Latin, from HELIO- + -IUM; named from its having first been detected in the solar spectrum]

he·lix (ˈhiːlɪks) *n., pl.* **hel·i·ces** (ˈhɛlɪˌsiːz) *or* **he·lix·es. 1.** a curve that lies on a cylinder or cone, at a constant angle to the line segments making up the surface; spiral. **2.** a spiral shape or form. **3.** the incurving fold that forms the margin of the external ear. **4.** another name for **volute** (sense 2). **5.** any terrestrial gastropod mollusc of the genus *Helix,* which includes the garden snail (*H. aspersa*). [C16: from Latin, from Greek: spiral; probably related to Greek *helissein* to twist]

hell (hɛl) *n.* **1.** *Christianity.* (*sometimes cap.*) **a.** the place or state of eternal punishment of the wicked after death, with Satan as its ruler. **b.** forces of evil regarded as residing there. **2.** (*sometimes cap.*) (in various religions and cultures) the abode of the spirits of the dead. See also **Hel, Hades, Sheol. 3.** pain, extreme difficulty, etc. **4.** *Informal.* a cause of such difficulty or suffering: *war is hell.* **5.** *U.S.* high spirits or mischievousness: *there's hell in that boy.* **6.** *Printing.* another name for **hellbox. 7.** a box used by a tailor for discarded material. **8.** *Now rare.* a gambling house, booth, etc. **9. as hell.** (intensifier): *tired as hell.* **10. for the hell of it.** *Informal.* for the fun of it. **11. give someone hell.** *Informal.* **a.** to give someone a severe reprimand or punishment. **b.** to be a source of annoyance or torment to someone. **12. hell of a** *or* **helluva.** *Informal.* (intensifier): *a hell of a good performance.* **13. hell for leather.** at great speed. **14. (come) hell or high water.** *Informal.* whatever difficulties may arise. **15. hell to pay.** *Informal.* serious consequences, as of a foolish action. **16. like hell.** *Informal.* **a.** (*adv.*) (intensifier): *he works like hell.* **b.** an expression of strong disagreement with a previous statement, request, order, etc. **17. raise hell.** *Informal.* **a.** to create a noisy disturbance, as in fun. **b.** to react strongly and unfavourably. **18. the hell.** *Informal.* **a.** (intensifier): used in such phrases as **what the hell, who the hell,** etc. **b.** an expression of strong disagreement or disfavour: *the hell I will.* See **like hell.** ~*interj.* **19.** *Informal.* an exclamation of anger, annoyance, surprise, etc. (Also in exclamations such as **hell's bells, hell's teeth,** etc.). [Old English *hell;* related to *helan* to cover, Old Norse *hel,* Gothic *halja* hell, Old High German *hella*]

he'll (hiːl; *unstressed* iːl, hɪl, ɪl) *contraction of* he will *or* he shall.

Hel·lad·ic (hɛˈlædɪk) *adj.* of, characteristic of, or related to the Bronze Age civilization that flourished about 2900 to 1100 B.C. on the Greek mainland and islands.

Hel·las (ˈhɛləs) *n.* transliteration of the Ancient Greek name for **Greece.**

hell·bend·er (ˈhɛlˌbɛndə) *n.* a very large dark grey aquatic salamander, *Cryptobranchus alleganiensis,* with internal gills: inhabits rivers in E and central U.S.: family *Cryptobranchidae.*

hell·bent (ˌhɛlˈbɛnt) *adj.* (*postpositive* and foll. by *on*) *Informal.* strongly or rashly intent.

hell·box (ˈhɛlˌbɒks) *n.* a receptacle used by printers for broken or unneeded type.

hell·cat (ˈhɛlˌkæt) *n.* a spiteful fierce-tempered woman.

hell·div·er (ˈhɛlˌdaɪvə) *n. U.S. informal.* a small greyish-brown North American grebe, *Podilymbus podiceps,* with a small bill. Also called: **pied-billed grebe, dabchick.**

Hel·le (ˈhɛlɪ) *n. Greek myth.* a daughter of King Athamas, who was borne away with her brother Phrixus on the golden winged ram. She fell from its back and was drowned in the Hellespont. See also **Phrixus, Golden Fleece.**

hel·le·bore (ˈhɛlɪˌbɔː) *n.* **1.** any plant of the Eurasian ranunculaceous genus *Helleborus,* esp. *H. niger* (black hellebore), typically having showy flowers and poisonous parts. See also **Christmas rose. 2.** any of various liliaceous plants of the N temperate genus *Veratrum,* esp. *V. album,* which have greenish flowers and yield alkaloids used in the treatment of heart disease. [C14: from Greek *helleboros,* of uncertain origin]

hel·le·bor·ine (ˌhɛlɪˈbɔːriːn) *n.* any of various N temperate orchids of the genera *Cephalanthera* and *Epipactis.* [C16:

ultimately from Greek *helleborinē* a plant resembling hellebore]

Hel·len ('hɛlɪn) *n.* (in Greek legend) a Thessalian king and eponymous ancestor of the Hellenes.

Hel+lene ('hɛliːn) *or* **Hel+le+ni·an** (hɛ'liːnɪən) *n.* another name for a **Greek.**

Hel+len+ic (hɛ'lɛnɪk, -'liː-) *adj.* **1.** of or relating to the ancient or modern Greeks or their language. **2.** of or relating to ancient Greece or the Greeks of the classical period (776–323 B.C.). **3.** another word for **Greek.** ~*n.* **4.** a branch of the Indo-European family of languages consisting of Greek in its various ancient and modern dialects. —**Hel+'len·i+cal+ly** *adv.*

Hel+len+ism ('hɛlɪ,nɪzəm) *n.* **1.** the principles, ideals, and pursuits associated with classical Greek civilization. **2.** the spirit or national character of the Greeks. **3.** conformity to, imitation of, or devotion to the culture of ancient Greece. **4.** Also called: **Hellenisticism.** the cosmopolitan civilization of the Hellenistic world.

Hel+len+ist ('hɛlɪnɪst) *n.* **1.** Also called: **Hellenizer.** (in the Hellenistic world) a non-Greek, esp. a Jew, who adopted Greek culture. **2.** a specialist or devotee of the Greek civilization or language.

Hel+len+is+tic (,hɛlɪ'nɪstɪk) *or* **Hel+len+is+ti+cal** *adj.* **1.** characteristic of or relating to Greek civilization in the Mediterranean world, esp. from the death of Alexander the Great (323 B.C.) to the defeat of Antony and Cleopatra (30 B.C.). **2.** of or relating to the Greeks or to Hellenism. —,**Hel+len+'is+ti+cal+ly** *adv.*

Hel+len+ize *or* **Hel+len+ise** ('hɛlɪ,naɪz) *vb.* to make or become like the ancient Greeks. —,**Hel+len·i+'za+tion** *or* ,**Hel+len·i+'sa+tion** *n.* —**'Hel+len+,iz+er** *or* **'Hel+len+,is+er** *n.*

hel+ler[1] ('hɛlə) *n., pl.* **+ler. 1.** any of various old German or Austrian coins of low denomination. **2.** another word for **haler.** [from German, after *Hall,* town in Swabia where the coins were minted]

hel+ler[2] ('hɛlə) *n.* another word for **hellion.**

hell+er·y ('hɛlərɪ) *n. Canadian slang.* wild or mischievous behaviour.

Hel+les ('hɛlɪs) *n.* **Cape.** a cape in NW Turkey, at the S end of the Gallipoli Peninsula.

Hel+les+pont ('hɛlɪ,spɒnt) *n.* the ancient name for the **Dardanelles.**

hell+fire ('hɛl,faɪə) *n.* **1.** the torment and punishment of hell, envisaged as eternal fire. **2.** (*modifier*) characterizing sermons or preachers that emphasize this aspect of Christian belief.

hell+gram+mite ('hɛlgrə,maɪt) *n. U.S.* the larva of the dobsonfly, about 10 cm long with biting mouthparts: used as bait for bass. Also called: **dobson.** [C19: of unknown origin]

hell+hole ('hɛl,həʊl) *n.* an unpleasant or evil place.

hell+hound ('hɛl,haʊnd) *n.* **1.** a hound of hell. **2.** a fiend.

hel+lion ('hɛljən) *n. Informal.* a rough or rowdy person, esp. a child; troublemaker. Also called: **heller.** [C19: probably from dialect *hallion* rogue, of unknown origin]

hell+ish ('hɛlɪʃ) *adj.* **1.** of or resembling hell. **2.** wicked; cruel. **3.** *Informal.* very difficult or unpleasant. ~*adv.* **4.** *Brit. informal.* (intensifier): *a hellish good idea.* —**'hell+ish+ly** *adv.* —**'hell+ish+ness** *n.*

hel+lo, hal+lo, *or* **hul+lo** (hɛ'ləʊ, hə-; 'hɛləʊ) *sentence substitute.* **1.** an expression of greeting used on meeting a person or at the start of a telephone call. **2.** a call used to attract attention. **3.** an expression of surprise. ~*n., pl.* **+los. 4.** the act of saying or calling "hello". [C19: see HALLO]

Hell's An+gel *n.* a member of a motorcycle gang of a kind originating in the U.S. in the 1950s, who typically dress in denim and Nazi-style paraphernalia and are noted for their initiation rites, lawless behaviour, etc.

hell+uv·a ('hɛləvə) *adv., adj. Informal.* (intensifier): *a helluva difficult job; he's a helluva guy.*

helm[1] (hɛlm) *n.* **1.** *Nautical.* **a.** the wheel, tiller, or entire apparatus by which a vessel is steered. **b.** the position of the helm: that is, on the side of the keel opposite from that of the rudder. **2.** a position of leadership or control (esp. in the phrase **at the helm**). ~*vb.* **3.** (*tr.*) to direct or steer. [Old English *helma;* related to Old Norse *hjalm* rudder, Old High German *halmo*] —**'helm+less** *adj.* —**'helms+man** *n.*

helm[2] (hɛlm) *n.* **1.** an archaic or poetic word for **helmet.** ~*vb.* **2.** (*tr.*) *Archaic or poetic.* to supply with a helmet. [Old English *helm;* related to *helan* to cover, Old Norse *hjalmr,* Gothic *hilms,* Old High German *helm* helmet, Sanskrit *śarman* protection]

Hel+mand ('hɛlmənd) *n.* a river in S Asia, rising in E Afghanistan and flowing generally southwest to a marshy lake, Hamun Helmand, on the border with Iran. Length: 1400 km (870 miles).

hel+met ('hɛlmɪt) *n.* **1.** a piece of protective or defensive armour for the head worn by soldiers, policemen, firemen, divers, etc. See also **crash helmet, pith helmet. 2.** *Biology.* a part or structure resembling a helmet, esp. the upper part of the calyx of certain flowers. [C15: from Old French, diminutive of *helme,* of Germanic origin; see HELM[2]] —**'hel+met+ed** *adj.* —**'hel·met-,like** *adj.*

Helm·holtz (*German* 'hɛlm,hɔlts) *n.* Baron **Her·mann Lu·dwig Fer·di·nand von** ('hɛrman 'luːtvɪç 'fɛrdi,nant fɔn). 1821–94, German physiologist, physicist, and mathematician: helped to found the theory of the conservation of energy; invented the ophthalmoscope (1850); and investigated the mechanics of sight and sound.

Helm·holtz func+tion *n.* a thermodynamic property of a system equal to the difference between its internal energy and the product of its temperature and its entropy. Symbol: *A* or *F* Also called: **Helmholtz free energy.** [named after Baron Hermann Ludwig Ferdinand von HELMHOLTZ]

hel+minth ('hɛlmɪnθ) *n.* any parasitic worm, esp. a nematode or fluke. [C19: from Greek *helmins* parasitic worm] —**hel+min+thoid** ('hɛlmɪn,θɔɪd, hɛl'mɪnθɔɪd) *adj.*

hel+min+thi·a+sis (,hɛlmɪn'θaɪəsɪs) *n.* infestation of the body with parasitic worms. [C19: from New Latin, from Greek *helminthian* to be infested with worms]

hel+min+thic (hɛl'mɪnθɪk) *adj.* **1.** of, relating to, or caused by parasitic worms. ~*n., adj.* **2.** another word for **vermifuge.**

hel+min+thol+o·gy (,hɛlmɪn'θɒlədʒɪ) *n.* the study of parasitic worms. —**hel+min+tho+log·i+cal** (,hɛlmɪnθə'lɒdʒɪkəl) *adj.* —,**hel+min+'thol+o+gist** *n.*

Hel·mont (*Flemish* 'hɛlmɔnt) *n.* **Jean Bap·tiste van** (ʒɑ̃ ba'tist vɑn). 1577–1644, Flemish chemist and physician. He was the first to distinguish gases and claimed to have coined the word *gas.*

Hé·lo·ïse ('ɛləʊ,iːz; *French* elɔ'iːz) *n.* ?1101–64, pupil, mistress, and wife of Abelard.

Hel·ot ('hɛlət, 'hiː-) *n.* **1.** (in ancient Greece, esp. Sparta) a member of the class of unfree men above slaves owned by the state. **2.** (*usually not cap.*) a serf or slave. [C16: from Latin *Hēlotēs,* from Greek *Heilōtes,* alleged to have meant originally: inhabitants of Helos, who, after its conquest, were serfs of the Spartans]

hel+ot+ism ('hɛlə,tɪzəm, 'hiː-) *n.* **1.** the condition or quality of being a Helot. **2.** a sociopolitical system in which a class, minority, nation, etc., is held in a state of subjection. **3.** *Zoology.* another name for **dulosis.** ~Also (for senses 1, 2): **helotage.**

hel+ot+ry ('hɛlətrɪ, 'hiː-) *n.* **1.** serfdom or slavery. **2.** serfs or slaves as a class.

help (hɛlp) *vb.* **1.** to assist or aid (someone to do something), esp. by sharing the work, cost, or burden of something: *he helped his friend to escape; she helped him climb out of the boat.* **2.** to alleviate the burden of (someone else) by giving assistance. **3.** (*tr.*) to assist (a person) to go in a specified direction: *help the old lady up from the chair.* **4.** to promote or contribute to: *to help the relief operations.* **5.** to cause improvement in (a situation, person, etc.): *crying won't help.* **6.** (*tr.; preceded by can, could,* etc.; *usually used with a negative*) **a.** to avoid or refrain from: *we can't help wondering who he is.* **b.** (usually foll. by *it*) to prevent or be responsible for: *I can't help it if it rains.* **7.** to alleviate (an illness, etc.). **8.** (*tr.*) to serve (a customer): *can I help you, madam?* **9.** (*tr.;* foll. by *to*) **a.** to serve (someone with food, etc.) (usually in the phrase **help oneself**): *may I help you to some more vegetables? help yourself to peas.* **b.** to provide (oneself with) without permission: *he's been helping himself to money out of the petty cash.* **10. cannot help but.** to be unable to do anything else except: *I cannot help but laugh.* **11. help a person on** *or* **off with.** to assist a person in the putting on or removal of (clothes). **12. so help me. a.** on my honour. **b.** no matter what: *so help me, I'll get revenge.* ~*n.* **13.** the act of helping, or being helped, or a person or thing that helps: *she's a great help.* **14.** a helping. **15. a.** a person hired for a job; employee, esp. a farm worker or domestic servant. **b.** (*functioning as sing.*) several employees collectively. **16.** a means of remedy: *there's no help for it.* ~*interj.* **17.** used to ask for assistance. [Old English *helpan;* related to Old Norse *hjalpa,* Gothic *hilpan,* Old High German *helfan*] —**'help+a·ble** *adj.* —**'help+er** *n.*

help+ful ('hɛlpfʊl) *adj.* serving a useful function; giving help. —**'help+ful+ly** *adv.* —**'help+ful+ness** *n.*

help+ing ('hɛlpɪŋ) *n.* a single portion of food taken at a meal.

help+ing hand *n.* assistance: *many people lent a helping hand in making arrangements for the party.*

help+less ('hɛlplɪs) *adj.* **1.** unable to manage independently. **2.** made powerless or weak: *they were helpless from so much giggling.* **3.** without help. —**'help+less+ly** *adv.* —**'help+less+ness** *n.*

Help·mann ('hɛlpmən) *n.* Sir **Rob·ert.** born 1909, Australian ballet dancer and choreographer: his ballets include *Miracle in the Gorbals* (1944), *Display* (1965), and *Yugen* (1965).

help+mate ('hɛlp,meɪt) *n.* a companion and helper, esp. a wife.

help+meet ('hɛlp,miːt) *n.* a less common word for **helpmate.** [C17: from the phrase *an helpe meet* (suitable) *for him* Genesis 2:18]

help out *vb.* (*adv.*) **1.** to assist or aid (someone), esp. by sharing the burden. **2.** to share the burden or cost of something with (another person).

Hel+sing+borg (*Swedish* ,hɛlsiŋ'bɔrj) *n.* a variant spelling of **Hälsingborg.**

Hel+sing+ør (*Danish* ,hɛlseŋ'øːr) *n.* a port in NE Denmark, in NE Zealand: site of Kronborg Castle (16th century), famous as the scene of Shakespeare's *Hamlet.* Pop.: 37 560 (1970). English name: **Elsinore.**

Hel+sin+ki ('hɛlsɪŋkɪ, hɛl'sɪŋ-) *n.* the capital of Finland, a port in the south on the Gulf of Finland: founded by Gustavus I of Sweden in 1550; replaced Turku as capital in 1812, while under Russian rule; university. Pop.: 510 614 (1973 est.). Swedish name: **Hel+sing+fors** (,hɛlsɪŋ'fɔrs).

hel·ter-skel·ter ('hɛltə'skɛltə) *adj.* **1.** haphazard or carelessly hurried. ~*adv.* **2.** in a helter-skelter manner. ~*n.* **3.** *Brit.* a high spiral slide, as at a fairground. **4.** disorder or haste. [C16: probably of imitative origin]

helve (hɛlv) *n.* **1.** the handle of a hand tool such as an axe or pick. ~*vb.* **2.** (*tr.*) to fit a helve to (a tool). [Old English *hielfe;* related to Old Saxon *hëlvi,* Old High German *halb,* Lithuanian *kìlpa* stirrup; see HALTER]

Hel+vel+lyn (hɛl'vɛlɪn) *n.* a mountain in NW England, in the Lake District. Height: 950 m (3118 ft.).

Hel+ve+tia (hɛl'viːʃə) *n.* **1.** the Latin name for Switzerland. **2.** a Roman province in central Europe (1st century B.C. to the 5th century A.D.), corresponding to part of S Germany and parts of W and N Switzerland.

Hel+ve+tian (hɛl'viːʃən) *adj.* **1.** of or relating to the Helvetii. **2.** another word for **Swiss.** ~*n.* **3.** a native or citizen of Switzerland. **4.** a member of the Helvetii.

Hel+vet+ic (hɛl'vɛtɪk) *adj.* **1.** Helvetian or Swiss. **2.** of or relating to the Helvetic Confessions or to Swiss Protestantism. ~*n.* **3.** a Swiss Protestant or reformed Calvinist who subscribes to one of the two **Helvetic Confessions** (of faith) formulated in 1536 and 1566.

Hel+ve·ti·i (hɛl'viːʃɪˌaɪ) *pl. n.* a Celtic tribe from SW Germany who settled in Helvetia from about 200 B.C.

Hel·vé·ti·us (hɛl'viːʃɪəs; *French* ɛlve'sjys) *n.* **Claude A·dri·en** (kloːd adri'ɛ̃). 1715–71, French philosopher. In his chief work *De l'Esprit* (1758), he asserted that the mainspring of human action is self-interest and that differences in human intellects are due only to differences in education.

hem[1] (hɛm) *n.* **1.** an edge to a piece of cloth, made by folding the raw edge under and stitching it down. **2.** short for **hemline.** ~*vb.* **hems, hem+ming, hemmed.** (*tr.*) **3.** to provide with a hem. **4.** (usually foll. by *in, around,* or *about*) to enclose or confine. [Old English *hemm;* related to Old Frisian *hemme* enclosed land] —**'hem+mer** *n.*

hem[2] (hɛm) *n., interj.* **1.** a representation of the sound of clearing the throat, used to gain attention, express hesitation, etc. ~*vb.* **hems, hem+ming, hemmed. 2.** (*intr.*) to utter this sound. **3. hem** (*or* **hum**) **and haw.** to hesitate in speaking or in making a decision.

hem- *combining form.* a U.S. variant of **haemo-** before a vowel.

he·ma- *combining form.* a U.S. variant of **haemo-.**

he-man *n., pl.* **-men.** *Informal.* a strongly built muscular man.

he·ma·to- *or before a vowel* **he·mat-** *combining form.* U.S. variants of **haemato-.**

Hem+el Hemp+stead ('hɛməl 'hɛmstɪd) *n.* a town in SE England, in W Hertfordshire: designated a new town in 1947. Pop.: 69 371 (1971).

hem+el·y+tron (hɛ'mɛlɪˌtrɒn) *or* **hem·i+el·y+tron** *n., pl.* **+tra** (-trə). the forewing of plant bugs and related insects, having a thickened base and a membranous apex. [C19: from New Latin *hemielytron,* from HEMI- + Greek *elutron* a covering] —**hem+'el·y+tral** *or* **ˌhem·i+'el·y+tral** *adj.*

hem+er·a+lo+pi·a (ˌhɛmərə'ləʊpɪə) *n.* inability to see clearly in bright light. Nontechnical name: **day blindness.** Compare **nyctalopia.** [C18: New Latin, from Greek *hēmeralōps,* from *hēmera* day + *alaos* blind + *ōps* eye] —**hem+er·a+lop+ic** (ˌhɛmərə'lɒpɪk) *adj.*

hem·i- *prefix.* half: *hemicycle; hemisphere.* Compare **demi-** (sense 1), **semi-** (sense 1). [from Latin, from Greek *hēmi-*]

-he·mi·a *n. combining form.* U.S. variant of **-aemia.**

hem·i+al+gi·a (ˌhɛmɪ'ældʒɪə) *n.* pain limited to one side of the body.

hem·i+an+ops+i·a (ˌhɛmɪæn'ɒpsɪə) *n.* loss of one half of the field of vision in both eyes. Also: **hem·i+an+o+pi·a** (ˌhɛmɪæn'əʊpɪə). [C19: from HEMI- + AN- + Greek *opsis* sight]

hem·i+cel+lu+lose (ˌhɛmɪ'sɛljʊˌləʊz) *n.* any of a group of plant polysaccharides that occur chiefly in the cell wall.

hem·i+chor+date (ˌhɛmɪ'kɔːˌdeɪt) *n.* **1.** any small wormlike marine animal of the subphylum *Hemichordata* (or *Hemichorda*), having numerous gill slits in the pharynx: phylum *Chordata* (chordates). ~*adj.* **2.** of, relating to, or belonging to the subphylum *Hemichordata.* ~See also **acorn worm.**

hem·i+cy+cle ('hɛmɪˌsaɪkᵊl) *n.* **1.** a semicircular structure, room, arena, wall, etc. **2.** a rare word for **semicircle.** —**hem·i+cy+clic** (ˌhɛmɪ'saɪklɪk, -'sɪk-) *adj.*

hem·i+dem·i+sem·i+qua·ver (ˌhɛmɪˌdɛmɪ'sɛmɪˌkweɪvə) *n.* *Music.* a note having the time value of one sixty-fourth of a semibreve. Usual U.S. name: **sixty-fourth note.**

hem·i+el·y+tron (ˌhɛmɪ'ɛlɪˌtrɒn) *n., pl.* **+tra** (-trə). a variant spelling of **hemelytron.** —**ˌhem·i+'el·y+tral** *adj.*

hem·i+he+dral (ˌhɛmɪ'hiːdrəl) *adj.* (of a crystal) exhibiting only half the number of planes necessary for complete symmetry.

hem·i+hy+drate (ˌhɛmɪ'haɪdreɪt) *n.* *Chem.* a hydrate in which there are two molecules of substance to every molecule of water. —**ˌhem·i+'hy+drat+ed** *adj.*

hem·i+mor+phic (ˌhɛmɪ'mɔːfɪk) *adj.* (of a crystal) having different forms at each end of an axis. —**ˌhem·i+'mor+phism** *or* **'hem·i+ˌmor+phy** *n.*

hem·i+mor+phite (ˌhɛmɪ'mɔːfaɪt) *n.* a white mineral consisting of hydrated zinc silicate in orthorhombic crystalline form: a common ore of zinc. Formula: $Zn_4Si_2O_7(OH)_2.H_2O$. Former names: **calamine** (U.S.), **smithsonite** (Brit.).

Hem·ing·way ('hɛmɪŋˌweɪ) *n.* **Er·nest.** 1899–1961, U.S. novelist and short-story writer. His novels include *The Sun Also Rises* (1926), *A Farewell to Arms* (1929), *For Whom the Bell Tolls* (1940), and *The Old Man and the Sea* (1952): Nobel prize for literature 1954.

hem·i·o+la (ˌhɛmɪ'əʊlə) *or* **hem·i·o·li·a** *n.* *Music.* a rhythmical device involving the superimposition of, for example, two notes in the time of three. Also called: **sesquialtera.** [New Latin, from Greek *hēmiolia* ratio of one to one and a half, from HEMI- + (*h*)*olos* whole] —**hem·i+ol+ic** (ˌhɛmɪ'ɒlɪk) *adj.*

hem·i+par·a+site (ˌhɛmɪ'pærɪˌsaɪt) *or* **sem·i+par·a+site** *n.* **1.** a parasitic plant, such as mistletoe, that carries out photosynthesis but also obtains food from its host. **2.** an organism that can live independently or parasitically.

hem·i+ple·gi·a (ˌhɛmɪ'pliːdʒɪə) *n.* paralysis of one side of the body, usually as the result of injury to the brain. Compare **paraplegia, quadriplegia.** —**ˌhem·i+'ple+gic** *adj.*

hem·i+pode ('hɛmɪˌpəʊd) *or* **hem·i+pod** ('hɛmɪˌpɒd) *n.* another name for **button quail.**

he+mip+ter+an (hɪ'mɪptərən) *or* **he+mip+ter+on** (hɪ'mɪptəˌrɒn) *n.* any hemipterous insect. [C19: from HEMI- + Greek *pteron* wing]

he+mip+ter+ous (hɪ'mɪptərəs) *or* **he+mip+ter+an** *adj.* of, relating to, or belonging to the *Hemiptera,* a large order of insects having sucking or piercing mouthparts specialized as a beak (rostrum). The group is divided into the suborders *Homoptera* (aphids, cicadas, etc.) and *Heteroptera* (water bugs, bedbugs, etc.).

hem·i+sphere ('hɛmɪˌsfɪə) *n.* **1.** one half of a sphere. **2. a.** half of the terrestrial globe, divided into **northern** and **southern hemispheres** by the equator or into **eastern** and **western hemispheres** by some meridians, usually 0° and 180°. **b.** a map or projection of one of the hemispheres. **3.** either of the two halves of the celestial sphere that lie north or south of the celestial equator. **4.** *Anatomy.* short for **cerebral hemisphere.** —**hem·i+spher+ic** (ˌhɛmɪ'sfɛrɪk) *or* **ˌhem·i+'spher·i+cal** *adj.*

hem·i+spher+oid (ˌhɛmɪ'sfɪərɔɪd) *n.* half of a spheroid. —**ˌhem·i+spher+'oi+dal** *adj.*

hem·i+stich ('hɛmɪˌstɪk) *n.* *Prosody.* a half line of verse.

hem·i+ter+pene (ˌhɛmɪ'tɜːpiːn) *n.* any of a class of simple unsaturated hydrocarbons, such as isoprene, having the formula C_5H_8.

hem·i+trope ('hɛmɪˌtrəʊp) *n.* *Chem.* another name for **twin** (sense 3). —**hem·i+trop+ic** (ˌhɛmɪ'trɒpɪk) *adj.* —**ˌhem·i+'tro+pism** *or* **he+mit+ro+py** (hiː'mɪtrəpɪ) *n.*

hem+line ('hɛmˌlaɪn) *n.* the level to which the hem of a skirt or dress hangs; hem: *knee-length hemlines.*

hem+lock ('hɛmˌlɒk) *n.* **1.** an umbelliferous poisonous Eurasian plant, *Conium maculatum,* having finely divided leaves, spotted stems, and small white flowers. U.S. name: **poison hemlock.** See also **water hemlock. 2.** a poisonous drug derived from this plant. **3.** Also called: **hemlock spruce.** any coniferous tree of the genus *Tsuga,* of North America and E Asia, having short flat needles: family *Pinaceae.* See also **western hemlock. 4.** the wood of any of these trees, used for lumber and as a source of wood pulp. [Old English *hymlic;* perhaps related to *hymele* hop plant, Middle Low German *homele,* Old Norwegian *humli,* Old Slavonic *chŭmelĭ*]

hem+mer ('hɛmə) *n.* an attachment on a sewing machine for hemming.

he·mo- *combining form.* U.S. variant of **haemo-.**

hemp (hɛmp) *n.* **1.** Also called: **cannabis, marijuana.** an annual strong-smelling Asian moraceous plant, *Cannabis sativa,* having tough fibres, deeply lobed leaves, and small greenish flowers. See also **Indian hemp. 2.** the fibre of this plant, used to make canvas, rope, etc. **3.** any of several narcotic drugs obtained from some varieties of this plant, esp. from Indian hemp. See **bhang, cannabis, hashish, marijuana.** ~See also **bowstring hemp.** [Old English *hænep;* related to Old Norse *hampr,* Old High German *hanaf,* Greek *kannabis,* Dutch *hennep*] —**'hemp+en** *or* **'hemp+ˌlike** *adj.*

hemp ag+ri+mo+ny *n.* a Eurasian plant, *Eupatorium cannabinum,* with small clusters of reddish flowers: family *Compositae* (composites).

hemp net+tle *n.* **1.** a hairy weedy plant, *Galeopsis tetrahit,* of northern regions, having helmet-shaped pink, purple, and white flowers and toothed leaves: family *Labiatae* (labiates). **2.** any of various other plants of the genus *Galeopsis.*

hem+stitch ('hɛmˌstɪtʃ) *n.* **1.** a decorative edging stitch, usually for a hem, in which the cross threads are stitched in groups. ~*vb.* **2.** to decorate (a hem, etc.) with hemstitches. —**'hem+ˌstitch·er** *n.*

hen (hɛn) *n.* **1.** the female of any bird, esp. the adult female of the domestic fowl. **2.** the female of certain other animals, such as the lobster. **3.** *Informal.* a woman regarded as gossipy or foolish. **4.** *Scot. dialect.* a term of affectionate address, used to women and girls. [Old English *henn;* related to Old High German *henna,* Old Frisian *henne*]

hen-and-chick·ens *n., pl.* **hens-and-chick·ens.** (*functioning as sing. or pl.*) any of several plants, such as the houseleek and ground ivy, that produce many offsets or runners.

hen+bane ('hɛnˌbeɪn) *n.* a poisonous solanaceous Mediterranean plant, *Hyoscyamus niger,* with sticky hairy leaves and funnel-shaped greenish flowers: yields the drug hyoscyamine.

hen+bit ('hɛnˌbɪt) *n.* a plant, *Lamium amplexicaule,* that is native to Europe and has toothed opposite leaves and small dark red flowers: family *Labiatae* (labiates).

hence (hɛns) **1.** *sentence connector.* for this reason; following from this; therefore. ~*adv.* **2.** from this time: *a year hence.* **3.** *Archaic.* **a.** from here or from this world; away. **b.** from this origin or source. ~*interj.* **4.** *Archaic.* begone! away! [Old English *hionane;* related to Old High German *hinana* away from here, Old Irish *cen* on this side]

hence+forth ('hɛns'fɔːθ), **hence+for·wards,** *or* **hence+for·ward** *adv.* from this time forward; from now on.

hench+man ('hɛntʃmən) *n., pl.* **+men. 1.** a faithful attendant or supporter. **2.** *Archaic.* a squire; page. [C14 *hengestman,* from Old English *hengest* stallion + MAN; related to Old Norse *hestr* horse, Old High German *hengist* gelding]

hen+coop ('hɛnˌkuːp) *n.* a cage for poultry.

hen·dec·a- *combining form.* eleven: *hendecagon; hendeca-*

hedron; *hendecasyllable.* [from Greek *hendeka,* from *hen,* neuter of *heis* one + *deka* ten]

hen·dec·a·gon (hɛnˈdɛkəgən) *n.* a polygon having 11 sides. —**hen·de·cag·o·nal** (ˌhɛndɪˈkægənᵊl) *adj.*

hen·dec·a·he·dron (ˌhɛndɛkəˈhɛdrən, -ˈhiːdrən) *n., pl.* **·drons** *or* **·dra** (-drə). a solid figure having 11 plane faces. See also **polyhedron.**

hen·dec·a·syl·la·ble (ˈhɛndɛkəˌsɪləbᵊl) *n. Prosody.* a verse line of 11 syllables. [C18: via Latin from Greek *hendekasullabos*] —**hen·dec·a·syl·lab·ic** (hɛnˌdɛkəsɪˈlæbɪk) *adj.*

hen·di·a·dys (hɛnˈdaɪədɪs) *n.* a rhetorical device by which two nouns joined by a conjunction, usually *and,* are used instead of a noun and a modifier, as in *to run with fear and haste* instead of *to run with fearful haste.* [C16: from Medieval Latin, changed from Greek phrase *hen dia duoin,* literally: one through two]

Hen·drix (ˈhɛndrɪks) *n.* **Jim·i.** original name *James Marshall Hendrix.* 1942–70, U.S. rock guitarist and vocalist, noted for his outrageous stage performances and his heavy, loud, acid-rock style.

hen·e·quen, hen·e·quin, *or* **hen·i·quen** (ˈhɛnɪkɪn) *n.* **1.** an agave plant, *Agave fourcroydes,* that is native of Yucatán. **2.** the fibre of this plant, used in making rope, twine, and coarse fabrics. [C19: from American Spanish *henequén,* probably of Taino origin]

henge (hɛndʒ) *n.* a circular area, often containing a circle of stones or sometimes wooden posts, dating from the Neolithic and Bronze Ages. [back formation from STONEHENGE]

Heng·e·lo (*Dutch* ˈhɛŋəloː) *n.* a city in the E Netherlands, in Overijssel province on the Twente Canal: industrial centre, esp. for textiles. Pop.: 72 062 (1973 est.).

Hen·gist (ˈhɛŋgɪst) *n.* died ?488 A.D., a leader, with his brother Horsa, of the first Jutish settlers in Britain; he is thought to have conquered Kent (?455).

Heng-yang (ˈhɛŋˈjæŋ) *n.* a city in SE central China, in Hunan province on the Siang River. Pop.: 235 000 (1953).

hen har·ri·er *n.* a common harrier, *Circus cyaneus,* that flies over fields and marshes and nests in marshes and open land. U.S. names: **marsh hawk, marsh harrier.**

hen·house (ˈhɛnˌhaʊs) *n.* a coop for hens.

He·nie (ˈhɛnɪ) *n.* **Son·ja** (ˈsɔnjə). 1912–69, Norwegian figure-skater.

Hen·ley-on-Thames (ˈhɛnlɪ) *n.* a town in S England, in SE Oxfordshire on the River Thames: a riverside resort with an annual regatta. Pop.: 11 402 (1971). Often shortened to **Henley.**

hen·na (ˈhɛnə) *n.* **1.** a lythraceous shrub or tree, *Lawsonia inermis,* of Asia and N Africa, with white or reddish fragrant flowers. **2.** a reddish dye obtained from the powdered leaves of this plant, used as a cosmetic and industrial dye. **3.** a reddish-brown or brown colour. ~*vb.* **4.** (*tr.*) to dye with henna. ~Archaic name (for senses 1, 2): **camphire.** [C16: from Arabic *hinnā'* alcanna]

hen·ner·y (ˈhɛnərɪ) *n., pl.* **·ner·ies.** a place or farm for keeping poultry.

hen·o·the·ism (ˈhɛnəʊθiːˌɪzəm) *n.* the worship of one deity (of several) as the special god of one's family, clan, or tribe. [C19: from Greek *heis* one + *theos* god] —**ˈhen·o·the·ist** *n.* —**ˌhen·o·the·ˈis·tic** *adj.*

hen par·ty *n. Informal.* a party at which only women are present. Compare **stag party.**

hen·peck (ˈhɛnˌpɛk) *vb.* (*tr.*) (of a woman) to harass or torment (a man, esp. her husband) by persistent nagging. —**ˈhen·ˌpecked** *adj.*

Hen·ri·et·ta Ma·ri·a (ˌhɛnrɪˈɛtə məˈriːə) *n.* 1609–69, queen of England (1625–49), the wife of Charles I; daughter of Henry IV of France. Her Roman Catholicism contributed to the unpopularity of the crown in the period leading to the Civil War.

hen run *n.* an enclosure for hens, esp. one made of chicken wire.

hen·ry (ˈhɛnrɪ) *n., pl.* **·ry, ·ries,** *or* **·rys.** the derived SI unit of electric inductance; the inductance of a closed circuit in which an emf of 1 volt is produced when the current varies uniformly at the rate of 1 ampere per second. Symbol: H [C19: named after Joseph HENRY]

Hen·ry (ˈhɛnrɪ) *n.* **1. Jo·seph.** 1797–1878, U.S. physicist. He discovered the principle of electromagnetic induction independently of Faraday and constructed the first electromagnetic motor (1829). He also discovered self-induction and the oscillatory nature of electric discharges (1842). **2. O.** See **O. Henry. 3. Pat·rick.** 1736–99, American statesman and orator, a leading opponent of British rule during the War of American Independence.

Hen·ry I *n.* 1068–1135, king of England (1100–35) and duke of Normandy (1106–35); son of William the Conqueror: crowned in the absence of his elder brother, Robert II, duke of Normandy; conquered Normandy (1106).

Hen·ry II *n.* **1.** 1133–89, first Plantagenet king of England (1154–89): extended his Anglo-French domains and instituted judicial and financial reforms. His attempts to control the church were opposed by Becket. **2.** 1519–59, king of France (1547–59); husband of Catherine de' Medici. He recovered Calais from the English (1558) and suppressed the Huguenots.

Hen·ry III *n.* **1.** 1207–72, king of England (1216–72); son of John. His incompetent rule provoked the Baron's War (1264–65), during which he was captured by Simon de Montfort. **2.** 1551–89, king of France (1574–89). He plotted the massacre of Huguenots on St. Bartholomew's Day (1572) with his mother Catherine de' Medici, thus exacerbating the religious wars in France.

Hen·ry IV *n.* **1.** 1050–1106, Holy Roman Emperor (1084–1105) and king of Germany (1056–1105). He was excommunicated by Pope Gregory VII, whom he deposed (1084). **2.** surnamed *Bolingbroke.* 1367–1413, first Lancastrian king of England (1399–1413); son of John of Gaunt: deposed Richard II (1399) and suppressed rebellions led by Owen Glendower and Sir Henry Percy. **3.** known as *Henry of Navarre.* 1553–1610, first Bourbon king of France (1589–1610). He obtained toleration for the Huguenots with the Edict of Nantes (1598) and restored prosperity to France following the religious wars (1562–98).

Hen·ry V *n.* 1387–1422, king of England (1413–22); son of Henry IV. He defeated the French at the Battle of Agincourt (1415), conquered Normandy (1419), and was recognized as heir to the French throne (1420).

Hen·ry VI *n.* 1421–71, last Lancastrian king of England (1422–61; 1470–71); son of Henry V. He suffered periods of insanity, which led to the loss by 1453 of all his possessions in France except Calais and to the Wars of the Roses (1455–85). He was deposed by Edward IV (1461) but was briefly restored to the throne (1470).

Hen·ry VII *n.* 1457–1509, first Tudor king of England (1485–1509). He came to the throne (1485) after defeating Richard III at the Battle of Bosworth Field, ending the Wars of the Roses. Royal power and the prosperity of the country greatly increased during his reign.

Hen·ry VIII *n.* 1491–1547, king of England (1509–47); second son of Henry VII. His divorce from Catherine of Aragon and marriage to Anne Boleyn (1533) precipitated the Act of Supremacy, making Henry supreme head of the Church in England. Anne Boleyn was executed (1536) and Henry subsequently married Jane Seymour, Anne of Cleves, Catherine Howard, and Catherine Parr. His reign is also noted for the fame of his succession of advisers, Wolsey, Thomas More, and Thomas Cromwell.

Hen·ry's law *n. Chem.* the principle that the amount of a gas dissolved at equilibrium in a given quantity of a liquid is proportional to the pressure of the gas in contact with the liquid. [C19: named after William *Henry* (1774–1836), English chemist]

Hen·ry·son (ˈhɛnrɪsᵊn) *n.* **Rob·ert.** ?1430–?1506, Scottish poet. His works include *Testament of Cresseid* (1593), a sequel to Chaucer's *Troilus and Cressida,* and the pastoral dialogue *Robene and Makyne.*

Hen·ry the Nav·i·ga·tor *n.* 1394–1460, prince of Portugal, noted for his patronage of Portuguese voyages of exploration of the W coast of Africa.

Hens·lowe (ˈhɛnzləʊ) *n.* **Phil·ip.** died 1616, English theatre manager, noted also for his diary.

hent (hɛnt) *Archaic.* ~*vb.* **1.** (*tr.*) to seize; grasp. ~*n.* **2.** anything that has been grasped, esp. by the mind. [Old English *hentan* to pursue; related to *huntian* to HUNT]

Hen·ze (*German* ˈhɛntsə) *n.* **Hans Wer·ner** (hans ˈvɛrnə). born 1926, West German composer, whose works, in many styles, include the operas *The Stag King* (1956), *The Bassarids* (1974), and *The Tedious Way to the Place of Natasha Ungeheuer* (1970) and the oratorio *The Raft of the Medusa* (1968).

hep (hɛp) *adj.* **hep·per, hep·pest.** *Slang.* an earlier word for **hip⁴.**

hep·a·rin (ˈhɛpərɪn) *n.* a polysaccharide, containing sulphate groups, present in most body tissues: an anticoagulant used in the treatment of thrombosis. [C20: from Greek *hēpar* the liver + -IN] —**ˈhep·a·rin·ˌoid** *adj.*

he·pat·ic (hɪˈpætɪk) *adj.* **1.** of or relating to the liver. **2.** *Botany.* of or relating to the liverworts. **3.** having the colour of liver. ~*n.* **4.** any of various drugs for use in treating diseases of the liver. **5.** a less common name for a **liverwort.** [C15: from Latin *hēpaticus,* from Greek *hēpar* liver]

he·pat·i·ca (hɪˈpætɪkə) *n.* any ranunculaceous woodland plant of the N temperate genus *Hepatica,* having three-lobed leaves and white, mauve, or pink flowers. [C16: from Medieval Latin: liverwort, from Latin *hēpaticus* of the liver]

hep·a·ti·tis (ˌhɛpəˈtaɪtɪs) *n.* inflammation of the liver. See also **infectious hepatitis, serum hepatitis.**

hep·a·to- *or before a vowel* **hep·at-** *combining form.* denoting the liver: *hepatitis.* [from Greek *hēpat-, hēpar*]

Hep·burn (ˈhɛpˌbɜːn) *n.* **Kath·a·rine.** born 1909, U.S. film actress, whose films include *The Philadelphia Story* (1940), *Adam's Rib* (1949), *The African Queen* (1951), and *The Lion in Winter* (1968).

hep·cat (ˈhɛpˌkæt) *n. Obsolete slang.* a person who is hep, esp. a player or admirer of jazz and swing in the 1940s.

He·phaes·tus (hɪˈfiːstəs) *or* **He·phais·tos** (hɪˈfaɪstɒs) *n. Greek myth.* the lame god of fire and metal-working. Roman counterpart: **Vulcan.**

Hep·ple·white (ˈhɛpᵊlˌwaɪt) *adj.* a style of ornamental and carved 18th-century English furniture, of which oval or shield-shaped open chairbacks are characteristic. [C18: named after George *Hepplewhite* (died 1786), English cabinetmaker]

hep·ta- *or before a vowel* **hept-** *combining form.* seven: *heptameter.* [from Greek]

hep·tad (ˈhɛptæd) *n.* **1.** a group or series of seven. **2.** the number or sum of seven. **3.** an atom or element with a valency of seven. [C17: from Greek *heptas* seven]

hep·ta·de·ca·no·ic ac·id (ˌhɛptəˌdɛkəˈnəʊɪk) *n.* a colourless crystalline water-insoluble carboxylic acid used in organic synthesis. Formula: $CH_3(CH_2)_{15}COOH$. Also called: **margaric acid.**

hep·ta·gon ('hɛptəgən) *n.* a polygon having seven sides. —**hep·tag·o·nal** (hɛp'tægənᵊl) *adj.*

hep·ta·he·dron (ˌhɛptə'hiːdrən) *n.* a solid figure having seven plane faces. See also **polyhedron.** —ˌ**hep·ta·'he·dral** *adj.*

hep·tam·er·ous (hɛp'tæmərəs) *adj.* (esp. of plant parts such as petals or sepals) arranged in groups of seven.

hep·tam·e·ter (hɛp'tæmɪtə) *n. Prosody.* a verse line of seven metrical feet. —**hep·ta·met·ri·cal** (ˌhɛptə'mɛtrɪkᵊl) *adj.*

hep·tane ('hɛpteɪn) *n.* an alkane existing in eight isomeric forms, esp. the isomer with a straight chain of carbon atoms (*n*-heptane), which is found in petroleum and used as an anaesthetic. Formula: $CH_3(CH_2)_5CH_3$(*n*-). [C19: from HEPTA- + -ANE, so called because it has seven carbon atoms]

hep·tan·gu·lar (hɛp'tæŋgjʊlə) *adj.* having seven angles.

hep·tar·chy ('hɛptɑːkɪ) *n., pl.* **-chies.** **1.** government by seven rulers. **2.** a state divided into seven regions each under its own ruler. **3. a.** the seven kingdoms into which Anglo-Saxon England is thought to have been divided from about the 7th to the 9th centuries A.D.: Kent, East Anglia, Essex, Sussex, Wessex, Mercia, and Northumbria. **b.** the period when this grouping existed. —**'hep·tarch** *n.* —**hep·'tar·chic** *or* **hep·'tar·chal** *adj.*

hep·ta·stich ('hɛptəˌstɪk) *n. Prosody.* a poem, strophe, or stanza that consists of seven lines.

Hep·ta·teuch ('hɛptəˌtjuːk) *n.* the first seven books of the Old Testament. [C17: from Late Latin *Heptateuchos*, from Greek HEPTA- + *teukhos* book]

hep·tav·a·lent (hɛp'tævələnt, ˌhɛptə'veɪlənt) *adj. Chem.* having a valency of seven. Also: **septivalent.**

hep·tose ('hɛptəʊs, -təʊz) *n.* any monosaccharide that has seven carbon atoms per molecule.

Hep·worth ('hɛpwəθ) *n.* Dame **Bar·ba·ra.** 1903–75, English sculptress of abstract works.

her (hɜː; *unstressed* hə, ə) *pron.* (*objective*) **1.** refers to a female person or animal: *he loves her; they sold her a bag; something odd about her; lucky her!* **2.** refers to things personified as feminine or traditionally to ships and nations. **3.** *Chiefly U.S.* a dialect word for **herself** when used as an indirect object: *she needs to get her a better job.* ~*determiner.* **4.** of, belonging to, or associated with her: *her silly ideas; her hair; her smoking annoys me.* [Old English *hire*, genitive and dative of *hēo* SHE, feminine of *hē* HE¹; related to Old High German *ira*, Gothic *izōs*, Middle Dutch *hare*]
Usage. See at **me.**

her. *abbrev. for:* **1.** heraldic. **2.** heraldry.

He·ra *or* **He·re** ('hɪərə) *n. Greek myth.* the queen of the Olympian gods and sister and wife of Zeus. Roman counterpart: **Juno.**

Her·a·cle·a (ˌhɛrə'kliːə) *n.* any of several ancient Greek colonies. The most famous is the S Italian site where Pyrrhus of Epirus defeated the Romans (280 B.C.).

Her·a·cles *or* **Her·a·kles** ('hɛrəˌkliːz) *n.* the usual name (in Greek) for **Hercules.** —ˌ**Her·a·'cle·an** *or* ˌ**Her·a·'kle·an** *adj.*

Her·a·clid *or* **Her·a·klid** ('hɛrəklɪd) *n., pl.* **Her·a·cli·dae** *or* **Her·a·kli·dae** (ˌhɛrə'klaɪdiː). any person claiming descent from Hercules, esp. one of the Dorian aristocrats of Sparta. —**Her·a·cli·dan** *or* **Her·a·kli·dan** (ˌhɛrə'klaɪdᵊn) *adj.*

Her·a·cli·tus (ˌhɛrə'klaɪtəs) *n.* ?535–?475 B.C., Greek philosopher, who held that fire is the primordial substance of the universe and that all things are in perpetual flux.

He·ra·klei·on *or* **He·ra·kli·on** (*Greek* i'rakliɔn) *n.* variants of **Iráklion.**

her·ald ('hɛrəld) *n.* **1. a.** a person who announces important news. **b.** (*as modifier*): *herald angels.* **2.** *Often literary.* a forerunner; harbinger. **3.** the intermediate rank of heraldic officer, between king-of-arms and pursuivant. **4.** (in the Middle Ages) an official at a tournament. ~*vb.* (*tr.*) **5.** to announce publicly. **6.** to precede or usher in. [C14: from Old French *herault*, of Germanic origin; compare Old English *here* war; see WIELD]

he·ral·dic (hɛ'rældɪk) *adj.* **1.** of or relating to heraldry. **2.** of or relating to heralds. —**he·'ral·di·cal·ly** *adv.*

her·ald·ry ('hɛrəldrɪ) *n., pl.* **-ries.** **1.** the occupation or study concerned with the classification of armorial bearings, the allocation of rights to bear arms, the tracing of genealogies, etc. **2.** the duties and pursuit of a herald. **3.** armorial bearings, insignia, devices, etc. **4.** heraldic symbols or symbolism. **5.** the show and ceremony of heraldry. —**'her·ald·ist** *n.*

her·alds' col·lege *n.* another name for **college of arms.**

He·rat (hɛ'ræt) *n.* a city in NW Afghanistan, on the Hari Rud River: on the site of several ancient cities; at its height as a cultural centre in the 15th century. Pop.: 108 750 (1973 est.).

Hé·rault (*French* e'ro) *n.* a department of S France, in Languedoc region. Capital: Montpellier. Pop.: 658 858 (1975). Area: 6224 sq. km (2427 sq. miles).

herb (hɜːb; *U.S.* ɜːrb) *n.* **1.** a seed-bearing plant whose aerial parts do not persist above ground at the end of the growing season; herbaceous plant. **2. a.** any of various usually aromatic plants, such as parsley, rue, and rosemary, that are used in cookery and medicine. **b.** (*as modifier*): *a herb garden.* [C13: from Old French *herbe*, from Latin *herba* grass, green plants] —**'herb·ˌlike** *adj.*

her·ba·ceous (hɜː'beɪʃəs) *adj.* **1.** designating or relating to plants or plant parts that are fleshy as opposed to woody: *a herbaceous plant.* **2.** (of petals and sepals) green and leaflike. **3.** of or relating to herbs. —**her·'ba·ceous·ly** *adv.*

her·ba·ceous bor·der *n.* a flower bed that primarily contains perennials rather than annuals.

herb·age ('hɜːbɪdʒ) *n.* **1.** herbaceous plants collectively, esp. the edible parts on which cattle, sheep, etc., graze. **2.** the vegetation of pasture land; pasturage.

herb·al ('hɜːbᵊl) *adj.* **1.** of or relating to herbs. ~*n.* **2.** a book describing and listing the properties of plants.

herb·al·ist ('hɜːbᵊlɪst) *n.* **1.** a person who grows, collects, sells, or specializes in the use of herbs, esp. medicinal herbs. **2.** (formerly) a descriptive botanist.

her·bar·i·um (hɜː'bɛərɪəm) *n., pl.* **-i·ums** *or* **-i·a** (-ɪə). **1.** a collection of dried plants that are mounted and classified systematically. **2.** a building, room, etc., in which such a collection is kept. —**her·'bar·i·al** *adj.*

herb ben·net *n.* a Eurasian and N African rosaceous plant, *Geum urbanum*, with yellow flowers. Also called: **wood avens, bennet.** [from Old French *herbe benoite*, literally: blessed herb, from Medieval Latin *herba benedicta*]

herb Chris·to·pher *n., pl.* **herbs Chris·to·pher.** another name for **baneberry.** [C16: named after St. *Christopher*]

Her·bert ('hɜːbət) *n.* **George.** 1593–1633, English Metaphysical poet. His chief work is *The Temple: Sacred Poems and Private Ejaculations* (1633).

herb Ge·rard *n., pl.* **herbs Ge·rard.** another name for **goutweed.** [C16: named after St. *Gerard* (feast day April 23), who was invoked by those suffering from gout]

herb·i·cide ('hɜːbɪˌsaɪd) *n.* a chemical that destroys plants, esp. one used to control weeds. —ˌ**her·bi·'cid·al** *adj.*

her·bi·vore ('hɜːbɪˌvɔː) *n.* an animal that feeds on grass and other plants. [C19: from New Latin *herbivora* grass-eaters] —**her·biv·o·rous** (hɜː'bɪvərəs) *adj.* —**her·'biv·o·rous·ly** *adv.* —**her·'biv·o·rous·ness** *n.*

herb of grace *n.* an archaic name for **rue** (the plant).

herb Par·is *n., pl.* **herbs Par·is.** a Eurasian woodland plant, *Paris quadrifolia*, with a whorl of four leaves and a solitary yellow flower: formerly used medicinally: family *Trilliaceae*. [C16: from Medieval Latin *herba paris*, literally: herb of a pair: so called because the four leaves on the stalk look like a true lovers' knot; associated in folk etymology with *Paris*, France]

herb Rob·ert *n., pl.* **herbs Rob·ert.** a low-growing N temperate geraniaceous plant, *Geranium robertianum*, with strongly scented divided leaves and small purplish flowers. [C13: from Medieval Latin *herba Roberti* herb of Robert, probably named after St. *Robert*, 11th-century French ecclesiastic]

herb·y ('hɜːbɪ) *adj.* **herb·i·er, herb·i·est.** **1.** abounding in herbs. **2.** of or relating to medicinal or culinary herbs.

Her·ce·go·vi·na (*Serbo-Croatian* 'hɛrtsɛˌgɔvina) *n.* a variant spelling of **Herzegovina.**

Her·cu·la·ne·um (ˌhɜːkjʊ'leɪnɪəm) *n.* an ancient city in SW Italy, of marked Greek character, on the S slope of Vesuvius: buried along with Pompeii by an eruption of the volcano (79 A.D.). Excavation has uncovered well preserved streets, houses, etc.

her·cu·le·an (ˌhɜːkjʊ'liːən) *adj.* **1.** requiring tremendous effort, strength, etc.: *a herculean task.* **2.** (*sometimes cap.*) resembling Hercules in strength, courage, etc.

Her·cu·les¹ ('hɜːkjʊˌliːz), **Her·a·cles,** *or* **Her·a·kles** *n.* **1.** Also called: **Alcides.** *Classical myth.* a hero noted for his great strength, courage, and for the performance of twelve immense labours. **2.** a man of outstanding strength or size. —ˌ**Her·cu·'le·an,** ˌ**Her·a·'cle·an,** *or* ˌ**Her·a·'kle·an** *adj.*

Her·cu·les² ('hɜːkjʊˌliːz) *n., Latin genitive* **Her·cu·le·is** (ˌhɜːkjʊ'liːɪs) **1.** a large constellation in the N hemisphere lying between Lyra and Corona Borealis. **2.** a conspicuous crater in the NW quadrant of the moon, about 70 kilometres in diameter.

her·cu·les bee·tle *n.* a very large tropical American scarabaeid beetle, *Dynastes hercules:* the male has two large anterior curved horns.

Her·cu·les'-club *n.* **1.** a prickly North American araliaceous shrub, *Aralia spinosa*, with medicinal bark and leaves. **2.** a prickly North American rutaceous tree, *Zanthoxylum clava-herculis*, with medicinal bark and berries.

Her·cyn·i·an (hɜː'sɪnɪən) *adj.* denoting a period of mountain building in Europe in the late Palaeozoic. [C16: from Latin *Hercynia silva* the Hercynian forest (i.e., the wooded mountains of central Germany, esp. the Erzgebirge)]

herd (hɜːd) *n.* **1.** a large group of mammals living and feeding together, esp. a group of cattle, sheep, etc. **2.** *Often disparaging.* a large group of people. **3. the.** *Derogatory.* the large mass of ordinary people. **4. a.** *Archaic or dialect.* a man or boy who tends livestock. **b.** (*in combination*): *goatherd; swineherd.* ~*vb.* **5.** to collect or be collected into or as if into a herd. **6.** (*tr.*) to drive forward in a large group. **7.** (*tr.*) to look after (livestock). [Old English *heord;* related to Old Norse *hjörth*, Gothic *hairda*, Old High German *herta*, Greek *kórthus* troop]

herd-book *n.* a book containing the pedigrees of breeds of pigs, cattle, etc.

herd·er ('hɜːdə) *n. Chiefly U.S.* a person who cares for or drives herds of cattle or flocks of sheep, esp. on an open range. Brit. equivalent: **herdsman.**

Her·der (*German* 'hɛrdər) *n.* **Jo·hann Gott·fried von** ('joːhan 'gɔtfriːt fɔn). 1744–1803, German philosopher, critic, and poet, the leading figure in the *Sturm und Drang* movement in German literature. His chief work is *Outlines of a Philosophy of the History of Man* (1784–91).

her·dic ('hɜːdɪk) *n. U.S.* a small horse-drawn carriage with a rear entrance and side seats. [C19: named after P. *Herdic*, 19th-century American inventor]

herd in+stinct *n. Psychol.* the inborn tendency to associate with others and follow the group's behaviour.

herds+man ('hɜːdzmən) *n., pl.* **+men.** *Chiefly Brit.* a person who breeds, rears, or cares for cattle or (rarely) other livestock in the herd. U.S. equivalent: **herder.**

Herd+wick ('hɜːdwɪk) *n.* a hardy breed of coarse-woolled sheep from NW England. [C19: from obsolete *herdwick* pasture, sheep farm (see HERD (sense 4), WICK[2]); the breed is thought to have originated on the herdwicks of Furness Abbey]

here (hɪə) *adv.* **1.** in, at, or to this place, point, case, or respect: *we come here every summer; here, the policemen have no guns; here comes Roy.* **2. here and there.** at several places in or throughout an area. **3. here goes.** an exclamation indicating that the speaker is about to perform an action. **4. here's to.** a formula used in proposing a toast to someone or something. **5. here we go again.** an event or process is about to repeat itself. **6. neither here nor there.** of no relevance or importance. **7. this here.** See **this** (senses 1–3). [Old English *hēr;* related to Old Norse *hēr,* Old High German *hiar,* Old Saxon *hīr*]

here+a·bouts ('hɪərəˌbaʊts) *or* **here+a·bout** *adv.* in this region or neighbourhood; near this place.

here+af·ter (ˌhɪər'ɑːftə) *adv.* **1.** *Formal or law.* in a subsequent part of this document, matter, case, etc. **2.** a less common word for **henceforth. 3.** at some time in the future. **4.** in a future life after death. ~*n.* (usually preceded by *the*) **5.** life after death. **6.** the future.

here+at (ˌhɪər'æt) *adv. Archaic.* because of this.

here+by (ˌhɪə'baɪ) *adv.* **1.** (used in official statements, proclamations, etc.) by means of or as a result of this. **2.** *Archaic.* nearby.

he+re·des (hɪ'riːdiːz) *n.* the plural of **heres.**

he+red·i·ta·ble (hɪ'rɛdɪtəbᵊl) *adj.* a less common word for **heritable.** —**he+ˌred·i+ta·'bil+i·ty** *n.* —**he+'red·i+ta·bly** *adv.*

her+e·dit·a+ment (ˌhɛrɪ'dɪtəmənt) *n. Property law.* **1.** any kind of property capable of being inherited. **2.** property that before 1926 passed to an heir if not otherwise disposed of by will.

he+red·i·tar·i+an·ism (həˌrɛdɪ'tɛərɪəˌnɪzəm) *n. Psychol.* a school of thought that emphasizes the influence of heredity in the determination of human behaviour. Compare **environmentalism.**

he+red·i·tar·y (hɪ'rɛdɪtərɪ, -trɪ) *adj.* **1.** of, relating to, or denoting factors that can be transmitted genetically from one generation to another. **2.** *Law.* **a.** descending or capable of descending to succeeding generations by inheritance. **b.** transmitted or transmissible according to established rules of descent. **3.** derived from one's ancestors; traditional: *hereditary feuds.* —**he+'red·i+tar·i+ly** *adv.* —**he+'red·i·tar·i·ness** *n.*

he+red·i·tist (hə'rɛdɪˌtɪst) *n.* any person who places the role of heredity above that of the environment as the determining factor in human or animal behaviour.

he+red·i·ty (hɪ'rɛdɪtɪ) *n., pl.* **·ties. 1.** the transmission from one generation to another of genetic factors that determine individual characteristics: responsible for the resemblances between parents and offspring. **2.** the sum total of the inherited factors or their characteristics in an organism. [C16: from Old French *heredite,* from Latin *hērēditās* inheritance; see HEIR]

Her+e·ford ('hɛrɪfəd) *n.* **1.** a city in W England, in Hereford and Worcester county on the River Wye: trading centre for agricultural produce. Pop.: 46 503 (1971). **2.** a hardy breed of beef cattle characterized by a red body, red and white head, and white markings.

Her+e·ford and Worces+ter *n.* a county of the W Midlands of England, formed in 1974 from the two former separate counties minus a small area of NW Worcestershire. Administrative centre: Worcester. Pop.: 594 200 (1976 est.). Area: 3965 sq. km (1531 sq. miles).

Her+e·ford+shire ('hɛrɪfədˌʃɪə, -ʃə) *n.* a former county of W England, since 1974 part of Hereford and Worcester: drained chiefly by the River Wye: important agriculturally (esp. for fruit and cattle).

here+in (ˌhɪər'ɪn) *adv.* **1.** *Formal or law.* in or into this place, thing, document, etc. **2.** *Rare.* in this respect, circumstance, etc.

here+in+af·ter (ˌhɪərɪn'ɑːftə) *adv. Formal or law.* in a subsequent part or from this point on in this document, statement, etc.

here+in+be·fore (ˌhɪərɪnbɪ'fɔː) *adv. Formal or law.* in a previous part of or previously in this document, statement, etc.

here+in·to (ˌhɪər'ɪntuː) *adv. Formal or law.* into this place, circumstance, etc.

here+of (ˌhɪər'ɒv) *adv. Formal or law.* of or concerning this.

here+on (ˌhɪər'ɒn) *adv.* an archaic word for **hereupon.**

He+re·ro (hə'rɛəˌrəʊ, 'hɛərəˌrəʊ) *n.* **1.** (*pl.* **+ro** *or* **+ros**) a member of a formerly rich cattle-keeping Negroid people of southern Africa, living chiefly in central Namibia. **2.** the language of this people, belonging to the Bantu group of the Niger-Congo family.

he+res *or* **hae+res** ('hɪəriːz) *n., pl.* **he+re·des** *or* **hae+re·des** (hɪ'riːdiːz). *Civil law.* an heir. [from Latin]

he+re·si+arch (hɪ'riːzɪˌɑːk) *n.* the leader or originator of a heretical movement or sect.

her+e·sy ('hɛrəsɪ) *n., pl.* **·sies. 1. a.** an opinion or doctrine contrary to the orthodox tenets of a religious body or church. **b.** the act of maintaining such an opinion or doctrine. **2.** any opinion or belief that is or is thought to be contrary to official or established theory. **3.** belief in or adherence to unorthodox opinion. [C13: from Old French *eresie,* from Late Latin *haeresis,* from Latin: sect, from Greek *hairesis* a choosing, from *hairein* to choose]

her+e·tic ('hɛrətɪk) *n.* **1.** *Now chiefly R.C. Church.* a person who maintains beliefs contrary to the established teachings of his Church. **2.** a person who holds unorthodox opinions in any field. —**he+ret·i·cal** (hɪ'rɛtɪkᵊl) *adj.* —**he+'ret·i·cal+ly** *adv.*

here+to (ˌhɪə'tuː) *adv.* **1.** *Formal or law.* to this place, thing, matter, document, etc. **2.** an obsolete word for **hitherto.**

here+to+fore (ˌhɪətʊ'fɔː) *adv.* **1.** *Formal or law.* until now; before this time. ~*adj.* **2.** *Obsolete.* previous; former. ~*n.* **3.** (preceded by *the*) *Archaic.* the past.

here+un·der (ˌhɪər'ʌndə) *adv. Formal or law.* **1.** (in documents, etc.) below this; subsequently; hereafter. **2.** under the terms or authority of this.

here+un·to (ˌhɪərʌn'tuː) *adv.* an archaic word for **hereto** (sense 1).

here+up·on (ˌhɪərə'pɒn) *adv.* **1.** following immediately after this; at this stage. **2.** *Formal or law.* upon this thing, point, subject, etc.

He·re·ward ('hɛrɪwəd) *n.* called *Hereward the Wake.* 11th-century Anglo-Saxon rebel, who defended the Isle of Ely against William the Conqueror (1070–71): a subject of many legends.

here+with (ˌhɪə'wɪð, -'wɪθ) *adv.* **1.** *Rare or formal.* together with this: *we send you herewith your statement of account.* **2.** a less common word for **hereby** (sense 1).

her·i·ot ('hɛrɪət) *n.* (in medieval England) a death duty paid by villeins and free tenants to their lord, often consisting of the dead man's best beast or chattel. [Old English *heregeatwa,* from *here* army + *geatwa* equipment]

He+ri+sau (*German* 'heːrizaʊ) *n.* a town in NE Switzerland, capital of Appenzell Outer Rhodes demicanton. Pop.: 14 597 (1970).

her+it·a·ble ('hɛrɪtəbᵊl) *adj.* **1.** capable of being inherited; inheritable. **2.** *Chiefly law.* capable of inheriting. [C14: from Old French, from *heriter* to INHERIT] —**ˌher+it+a·'bil+i·ty** *n.* —**'her+it·a·bly** *adv.*

her+it+age ('hɛrɪtɪdʒ) *n.* **1.** something inherited at birth, such as personal characteristics, status, and possessions. **2.** anything that has been transmitted from the past or handed down by tradition. **3.** something that is reserved for a particular person or group or the outcome of an action, way of life, etc.: *the sea was their heritage; the heritage of violence.* **4.** *Law.* any property, esp. land, that by law has descended or may descend to an heir. **5.** *Bible.* **a.** the Israelites regarded as belonging inalienably to God. **b.** the land of Canaan regarded as God's gift to the Israelites. [C13: from Old French; see HEIR]

her·i·tor ('hɛrɪtə) *n. Archaic or law.* a person who inherits; inheritor. —**her·i·tress** ('hɛrɪtrɪs) *or* **'her·i·trix** *fem. n.*

herl (hɜːl) *or* **harl** *n. Angling.* **1.** the barb or barbs of a feather, used to dress fishing flies. **2.** an artificial fly dressed with such barbs. [C15: from Middle Low German *herle,* of obscure origin]

herm (hɜːm) *or* **her+ma** *n., pl.* **herms, her+mae** ('hɜːmiː), *or* **her+mai** ('hɜːmaɪ) (in ancient Greece) a stone head of Hermes surmounting a square stone pillar. [C16: from Latin *herma,* from Greek *hermēs* HERMES]

Her+mann+stadt ('hɛrmanˌʃtat) *n.* the German name for **Sibiu.**

her+maph+ro·dite (hɜː'mæfrəˌdaɪt) *n.* **1.** *Biology.* an individual animal or flower that has both male and female reproductive organs. **2.** a person having both male and female sexual characteristics and genital tissues. **3.** a person or thing in which two opposite forces or qualities are combined. ~*adj.* **4.** having the characteristics of an hermaphrodite. [C15: from Latin *hermaphrodītus,* from Greek, after HERMAPHRODITUS] —**her+ˌmaph+ro+'dit·ic** *or* **her+ˌmaph+ro+'dit·i·cal** *adj.* —**her+ˌmaph+ro+'dit·i·cal+ly** *adv.* —**her+'maph+ro+dit+ˌism** *n.*

her+maph+ro+dite brig *n.* a sailing vessel with two masts, rigged square on the foremast and fore-and-aft on the aftermast. Also called: **brigantine.**

Her·maph·ro·di·tus (hɜːˌmæfrə'daɪtəs) *n. Greek myth.* a son of Hermes and Aphrodite who merged with the nymph Salmacis to form one body.

her·me·neu+tic (ˌhɜːmɪ'njuːtɪk) *or* **her+me·neu+ti·cal** *adj.* **1.** of or relating to the interpretation of Scripture; using or relating to hermeneutics. **2.** interpretive. —**ˌher+me·'neu+ti·cal+ly** *adv.* —**ˌher+me·'neu+tist** *n.*

her+me·neu+tics (ˌhɜːmɪ'njuːtɪks) *n.* (*functioning as sing.*) **1.** the science of interpretation, esp. of Scripture. **2.** the branch of theology that deals with the principles and methodology of exegesis. [C18: from Greek *hermēneutikos* expert in interpretation, from *hermēneuein* to interpret, from *hermēneus* interpreter, of uncertain origin]

Her·mes[1] ('hɜːmiːz) *n. Greek myth.* the messenger and herald of the gods; the divinity of commerce, cunning, theft, travellers, and rascals. He was represented as wearing winged sandals. Roman counterpart: **Mercury.**

Her+mes[2] ('hɜːmiːz) *n.* a small asteroid that passes within 353 000 kilometres of the earth.

Her·mes Tris·me·gis·tus (ˌtrɪsmə'dʒɪstəs) *n.* a Greek name for the Egyptian god Thoth, credited with various works on mysticism and magic. [Greek: Hermes thrice-greatest]

her+met+ic (hɜː'mɛtɪk) *or* **her+met·i·cal** *adj.* sealed so as to be airtight. [C17: from Medieval Latin *hermēticus* belonging to HERMES TRISMEGISTUS, traditionally the inventor of a magic seal] —**her+'met·i·cal+ly** *adv.*

Her+met+ic (hɜː'mɛtɪk) *adj.* **1.** of or relating to Hermes Trismegistus or the writings and teachings ascribed to him. **2.** of or relating to ancient science, esp. alchemy.

her+mit ('hɜːmɪt) *n.* **1.** one of the early Christian recluses. **2.** any person living in solitude. [C13: from Old French *hermite,* from Late Latin *erēmīta,* from Greek *erēmitēs* living in the desert, from *erēmia* desert, from *erēmos* lonely] —**her+'mit+ic** *or* **her+'mit·i+cal** *adj.* —**her+'mit·i+cal·ly** *adv.* —**'her·mit-ˌlike** *adj.*

her+mit+age ('hɜːmɪtɪdʒ) *n.* **1.** the abode of a hermit. **2.** any place where a person may live in seclusion; retreat.

Her+mi+tage[1] ('hɜːmɪtɪdʒ) *n.* **the.** an art museum in Leningrad, originally a palace built by Catherine the Great.

Her+mit+age[2] ('hɜːmɪtɪdʒ) *n.* a full-bodied red or white wine from the Rhône valley at Tain-l'Ermitage, in SE France.

her+mit crab *n.* any small soft-bodied decapod crustacean of the genus *Pagurus* and related genera, living in and carrying about the empty shells of whelks or similar molluscs.

Her+mit+i·an con+ju+gate (hɜː'mɪtɪən) *n. Maths.* a matrix that is the transpose of the matrix of the complex conjugates of the entries of a given matrix. Also called: **adjoint.** [C19: after Charles *Hermite* (1822–1901), French mathematician]

Her+mit+i·an ma+trix *n. Maths.* a matrix whose transpose is equal to the matrix of the complex conjugates of its entries. [C20: after Charles *Hermite* (1822–1901), French mathematician]

Her+mon ('hɜːmən) *n.* **Mount.** a mountain on the border between Lebanon and SW Syria, in the Anti-Lebanon Range: represented the NE limits of Israeli conquests under Moses and Joshua. Height: 2830 m (9286 ft.).

Her+mo+si+llo (*Spanish* ˌermo'siʎo) *n.* a city in NW Mexico, capital of Sonora state, on the Sonora River: university (1938); winter resort and commercial centre for an agricultural and mining region. Pop.: 247 887 (1975 est.).

Her+mou+po+lis (hɜː'muːpəlɪs) *n.* a port in Greece, capital of Cyclades department, on the E coast of Syros Island. Pop.: 13 502 (1971).

hern (hɜːn) *n.* an archaic or dialect word for **heron.**

Her+ne (*German* 'hɛrnə) *n.* an industrial city in W West Germany, in North Rhine-Westphalia, in the Ruhr on the Rhine-Herne Canal. Pop.: 102 229 (1974 est.).

her+ni·a ('hɜːnɪə) *n., pl.* **+ni·as** *or* **+ni·ae** (-nɪˌiː). the projection of an organ or part through the lining of the cavity in which it is normally situated, esp. the protrusion of intestine through the front wall of the abdominal cavity. It is caused by muscular strain, injury, etc. Also called: **rupture.** [C14: from Latin] —**'her+ni·al** *adj.* —**'her+ni+ˌat+ed** *adj.*

her+ni+or+rha+phy (ˌhɜːnɪ'ɒrəfɪ) *n., pl.* **+phies.** surgical repair of a hernia by means of a suturing operation.

he·ro ('hɪərəʊ) *n., pl.* **·roes. 1.** a man distinguished by exceptional courage, nobility, fortitude, etc. **2.** a man who is idealized for possessing superior qualities in any field. **3.** *Classical myth.* a being of extraordinary strength and courage, often the offspring of a mortal and a god, who is celebrated for his exploits. **4.** the principal male character in a novel, play, etc. [C14: from Latin *hērōs,* from Greek]

He·ro[1] ('hɪərəʊ) *n. Greek myth.* a priestess of Aphrodite, who killed herself when her lover Leander drowned while swimming the Hellespont to visit her.

He·ro[2] ('hɪərəʊ) *or* **He+ron** *n.* 1st century A.D. Greek mathematician and inventor.

Her·od ('hɛrəd) *n.* called *the Great.* ?73–4 B.C., king of Judaea (37–4). The latter part of his reign was notable for his cruelty and he ordered the Massacre of the Innocents.

Her·od A·grip·pa I *n.* 10 B.C.–44 A.D., king of Judaea (41–44), grandson of Herod (the Great). A friend of Caligula and Claudius, he imprisoned Saint Peter and executed Saint James.

Her·od Ant·i·pas ('æntɪˌpæs) *n.* died ?40 A.D., tetrarch of Galilee and Peraea (4 B.C.–40 A.D.); son of Herod the Great. At the instigation of his wife Herodias, he ordered the execution of John the Baptist.

He·ro·di·as (hɛ'rəʊdɪˌæs) *n.* ?14 B.C. –?40 A.D., niece and wife of Herod Antipas and mother of Salome, whom she persuaded to ask for the head of John the Baptist. Her ambition led to the banishment of her husband.

He·rod·o·tus (hɪ'rɒdətəs) *n.* called *the Father of History.* ?485–?425 B.C., Greek historian, famous for his *History* dealing with the causes and events of the wars between the Greeks and the Persians (490–479).

he+ro+ic (hɪ'rəʊɪk) *or* **he+ro·i+cal** *adj.* **1.** of, like, or befitting a hero. **2.** courageous but desperate. **3.** relating to or treating of heroes and their deeds. **4.** of, relating to, or resembling the heroes of classical mythology. **5.** (of language, manner, etc.) extravagant. **6.** *Prosody.* of, relating to, or resembling heroic verse. **7.** (of the arts, esp. sculpture) larger than life-size; smaller than colossal. —**he+'ro·i·cal+ly** *adv.* —**he+'ro·i·cal+ness** *or* **he+'ro+ic+ness** *n.*

he+ro+ic age *n.* the period in an ancient culture, when legendary heroes are said to have lived.

he+ro+ic coup+let *n. Prosody.* a verse form consisting of two rhyming lines in iambic pentameter.

he+ro+ics (hɪ'rəʊɪks) *pl. n.* **1.** *Prosody.* short for **heroic verse. 2.** extravagant or melodramatic language, behaviour, etc.

he+ro+ic stan+za *n. Poetry.* a quatrain having the rhyme scheme a b a b.

he+ro+ic ten+or *n.* a tenor with a dramatic voice.

he+ro+ic verse *n. Prosody.* a type of verse suitable for epic or heroic subjects, such as the classical hexameter, the French Alexandrine, or the English iambic pentameter.

her·o+in ('hɛrəʊɪn) *n.* a white odourless bitter-tasting crystalline powder derived from morphine: a highly addictive narcotic. Formula: $C_{17}H_{17}NO(C_2H_3O_2)_2$. Also called: **diacetylmorphine.** [C19: coined in German as a trademark, probably from HERO, referring to its aggrandizing effect on the personality]

her·o+ine ('hɛrəʊɪn) *n.* **1.** a woman possessing heroic qualities. **2.** a woman idealized for possessing superior qualities. **3.** the main female character in a novel, play, film, etc.

her·o+ism ('hɛrəʊˌɪzəm) *n.* the state or quality of being a hero.

her+on ('hɛrən) *n.* any of various wading birds of the genera *Butorides, Ardea,* etc., having a long neck, slim body, and a plumage that is commonly grey or white: family *Ardeidae,* order *Ciconiiformes.* [C14: from Old French *hairon,* of Germanic origin; compare Old High German *heigaro,* Old Norse *hegri*]

He+ron ('hɪərɒn) *n.* a variant of **Hero**[2].

her+on+ry ('hɛrənrɪ) *n., pl.* **+ries.** a colony of breeding herons.

He·roph·i·lus (hɪə'rɒfɪləs) *n.* died ?280 B.C., Greek anatomist in Alexandria. He was the first to distinguish sensory from motor nerves.

he·ro wor+ship *n.* **1.** admiration for heroes or idealized persons. **2.** worship by the ancient Greeks and Romans of heroes. ~*vb.* **he·ro-wor·ship, ·ships, ·ship+ping, ·shipped** *or U.S.* **·ships, ·ship+ing, ·shiped. 3.** (*tr.*) to feel admiration or adulation for. —**'he·ro-ˌwor·ship+per** *n.*

herp., herpet., *or* **herpetol.** *abbrev. for* herpetology.

her+pes ('hɜːpiːz) *n.* any of several inflammatory diseases of the skin, esp. herpes simplex, characterized by formation of small watery blisters. [C17: via Latin from Greek: a creeping, from *herpein* to creep] —**her+pet+ic** (hɜː'pɛtɪk) *adj.*

her+pes la+bi+al+is (ˌleɪbɪ'ælɪs) *n.* a technical name for **cold sore.** [New Latin: herpes of the lip]

her+pes sim+plex ('sɪmplɛks) *n.* an acute viral disease characterized by formation of clusters of watery blisters, esp. on the margins of the lips and nostrils or on the genitals. [New Latin: simple herpes]

her+pes zos+ter ('zɒstə) *n.* a technical name for **shingles.** [New Latin: girdle herpes, from HERPES + Greek *zōstēr* girdle]

her+pe+tol+o+gy (ˌhɜːpɪ'tɒlədʒɪ) *n.* the study of reptiles and amphibians. [C19: from Greek *herpeton* creeping animal, from *herpein* to creep] —**her+pe+to+log+ic** (ˌhɜːpɪtə'lɒdʒɪk) *or* **ˌher+pe+to+'log+i·cal** *adj.* —**ˌher+pe+to+'log·i·cal+ly** *adv.* —**ˌher+pe+'tol+o+gist** *n.*

Herr (*German* hɛr) *n., pl.* **Her+ren** ('hɛrən). a German man: used before a name as a title equivalent to *Mr.* [German, from Old High German *herro* lord]

Her+ren+volk *German.* ('hɛrənˌfɔlk) *n.* See **master race.**

Her+rick ('hɛrɪk) *n.* **Rob·ert.** 1591–1674, English poet. His chief work is the *Hesperides* (1648), a collection of short, delicate, sacred, and pastoral lyrics.

her+ring ('hɛrɪŋ) *n., pl.* **+rings** *or* **+ring.** any marine soft-finned teleost fish of the family *Clupeidae,* esp. *Clupea harengus,* an important food fish of northern seas, having an elongated body covered, except in the head region, with large fragile silvery scales. [Old English *hǣring;* related to Old High German *hāring,* Old Frisian *hēring,* Dutch *haring*]

her+ring+bone ('hɛrɪŋˌbəʊn) *n.* **1. a.** a pattern used in textiles, brickwork, etc., consisting of two or more rows of short parallel strokes slanting in alternate directions to form a series of parallel Vs or zigzags. **b.** (*as modifier*): *a herringbone pattern.* **2.** *Skiing.* a method of ascending a slope by walking with the skis pointing outwards and one's weight on the inside edges. ~*vb.* **3.** to decorate (textiles, brickwork, etc.) with herringbone. **4.** (*intr.*) *Skiing.* to ascend a slope in herringbone fashion.

her+ring+bone bond *n.* a type of bricklaying in which the bricks are laid on the slant to form a herringbone pattern.

her+ring+bone gear *n.* a gearwheel having two sets of helical teeth, one set inclined at an acute angle to the other so that V-shaped teeth are formed. Also called: **double-helical gear.**

her+ring gull *n.* a common gull, *Larus argentatus,* that has a white plumage with black-tipped wings and pink legs.

Her+riot (*French* ɛ'rjo) *n.* **É·douard** (e'dwaːr). 1872–1957, French Radical statesman and writer; premier (1924–25; 1932).

hers (hɜːz) *pron.* **1.** something or someone belonging to or associated with her: *hers is the nicest dress; that cat is hers.* **2. of hers.** belonging to or associated with her. [C14: see HER, -S[1]]

Her+schel ('hɜːʃəl) *n.* **1.** Sir **John Fred·er·ick Wil·liam.** 1792–1871, English astronomer. He discovered and catalogued over 525 nebulae and star clusters. **2.** his father, Sir **Wil·liam.** original name *Friedrich Wilhelm Herschel.* 1738–1822, English astronomer, born in Germany. He constructed a reflecting telescope, which led to his discovery of the planet Uranus (1781), two of its satellites, and two of the satellites of Saturn. He also discovered the motions of binary stars.

her+self (hə'sɛlf) *pron.* **1. a.** the reflexive form of *she* or *her.* **b.** (intensifier): *the queen herself signed the letter.* **2.** (*preceded by a copula*) her normal or usual self: *she looks herself again after the operation.*

Usage. See at **myself.**

Herst+mon+ceux *or* **Hurst+mon+ceux** ('hɜːstmənˌsuː, -ˌsəʊ) *n.* a village in S England, in E Sussex north of Eastbourne: 15th-century castle, site of the Royal Observatory, which was transferred from Greenwich between 1948 and 1958.

Hert+ford ('hɑːtfəd) *n.* a town in SE England, administrative centre of Hertfordshire. Pop.: 20 379 (1971).

Hert+ford+shire ('hɑːtfədˌʃɪə, -ʃə) *n.* a county of S England, bordering on Greater London in the south: mainly low-lying, with the Chiltern Hills in the northwest; largely agricultural; expanding light industries, esp. in the new towns. Administrative centre: Hertford. Pop.: 937 300 (1976 est.). Area: 1634 sq. km (631 sq. miles).

Her+to+gen+bosch, 's (*Dutch* ˌshɛrto:xən'bɔs) *n.* See **'s Hertogenbosch.**

hertz (hɜ:ts) *n., pl.* **hertz.** the derived SI unit of frequency; the frequency of a periodic phenomenon that has a periodic time of 1 second; 1 cycle per second. Symbol: Hz [C20: named after Heinrich Rudolph HERTZ]

Hertz (hɜ:ts; *German* hɛrts) *n.* **1. Gus·tav** ('gʊstaf). 1887–1975, German atomic physicist. He provided evidence for the quantum theory by his research with Franck on the effects produced by bombarding atoms with electrons: they shared the Nobel prize for physics (1925). **2. Hein·rich Ru·dolph** ('haɪnrɪç 'ru:dɔlf). 1857–94, German physicist. He was the first to produce electromagnetic waves artificially. —**'Hertz+i·an** *adj.*

Hertz+i·an wave *n.* an electromagnetic wave with a frequency in the range from about 3×10^{10} hertz to about 1.5×10^{5} hertz. [C19: named after H. R. HERTZ]

Hert·zog ('hɜ:tsɒg) *n.* **James Bar·ry Mun·nik.** 1866–1942, South African statesman; prime minister (1924–39): founded the Nationalist Party (1913), advocating complete South African independence from Britain; opposed South African participation in World Wars I and II.

Hertz·sprung-Rus·sell di·a·gram ('hɜ:tssprʌŋ 'rʌsᵊl) *n.* a graph in which the spectral types of stars are plotted against their absolute magnitudes. Stars fall into different groupings in different parts of the graph. See also **main sequence.** [C20: named after Ejnar *Hertzsprung* (1873–1967), Danish astronomer, and Henry N. *Russell* (1877–1957), U.S. astronomer]

Her·ze·go·vi·na (ˌhɜ:tsəgəʊ'vi:nə) *or* **Her·ce·go·vi·na** (*Serbo-Croatian* 'hɛrtsɛˌgɔvina) *n.* a region of W central Yugoslavia: originally under Austro-Hungarian rule; became part of the province of Bosnia and Herzegovina (1878), which became a constituent republic of Yugoslavia in 1946.

Her·zl (*German* 'hɛrtsᵊl) *n.* **The·o·dor** ('te:oˌdo:r). 1860–1904, Austrian writer, born in Hungary; founder of the Zionist movement. In *The Jewish State* (1896), he advocated resettlement of the Jews in a state of their own.

Her·zog (*German* 'hɛrtsɔk) *n.* **Wer·ner** ('vɛrnə). born 1942, West German film director. His films include *Signs of Life* (1967), *Fata Morgana* (1970), *Aguirre, Wrath of God* (1973), and *The Enigma of Kaspar Hauser* (1974).

he's (hi:z) *contraction of* he is *or* he has.

Hesh+van *or* **Chesh+van** *Hebrew.* (xɛʃ'van) *n.* the second month of the civil year and the eighth of the ecclesiastical year in the Jewish calendar, falling approximately in October and November. [from Hebrew *marheshwān*]

Hes·i·od ('hɛsɪˌɒd) *n.* 8th-century B.C. Greek poet and the earliest author of didactic verse. His two complete extant works are the *Works and Days,* dealing with the agricultural seasons, and the *Theogony,* concerning the origin of the world and the genealogies of the gods. —ˌ**Hes·i+'od+ic** *adj.*

He·si·o·ne (hɪ'saɪəˌnɪ) *n. Greek myth.* daughter of King Laomedon, rescued by Hercules from a sea monster.

hes·i+tant ('hɛzɪtᵊnt) *adj.* wavering, hesitating, or irresolute. —**'hes·i+tant+ly** *adv.*

hes·i+tate ('hɛzɪˌteɪt) *vb.* (*intr.*) **1.** to hold back or be slow in acting; be uncertain. **2.** to be unwilling or reluctant (to do something). **3.** to stammer or pause in speaking. [C17: from Latin *haesitāre,* from *haerēre* to cling to] —**hes·i+tan+cy** ('hɛzɪtᵊnsɪ) *or* ˌ**hes·i+'ta+tion** *n.* —**'hes·i+ˌtat+er** *or* **'hes·i+ˌta+tor** *n.* —**'hes·i+ˌtat+ing+ly** *adv.* —**'hes·i+ˌta+tive** *adj.*

Hes+per·i·a (hɛ'spɪərɪə) *n.* a poetic name used by the ancient Greeks for Italy and by the Romans for Spain or beyond. [Latin, from Greek: land of the west, from *hesperos* western]

Hes+pe+ri·an (hɛ'spɪərɪən) *adj.* **1.** *Poetic.* western. **2.** of or relating to the Hesperides. ~*n.* **3.** a native or inhabitant of a western land.

Hes·per·i·des (hɛ'spɛrɪˌdi:z) *pl. n. Greek myth.* **1.** the daughters of Hesperus, nymphs who kept watch with a dragon over the garden of the golden apples in the Islands of the Blessed. **2.** (*functioning as sing.*) the gardens themselves. **3.** another name for the **Islands of the Blessed.** —**Hes+per+id+i·an** (ˌhɛspə'rɪdɪən) *or* ˌ**Hes+per+'id+e·an** *adj.*

hes+per+i+din (hɛ'spɛrɪdɪn) *n.* a glycoside extracted from orange peel or other citrus fruits and used to treat capillary fragility. [C19: from New Latin HESPERIDIUM + -IN]

hes+per+id+i·um (ˌhɛspə'rɪdɪəm) *n. Botany.* the fruit of citrus plants, in which the flesh consists of fluid-filled hairs and is protected by a tough rind. [C19: New Latin; alluding to the fruit in the garden of the HESPERIDES]

Hes+per+us ('hɛspərəs) *n.* an evening star, esp. Venus. [from Latin, from Greek *Hesperos,* from *hesperos* western]

Hess (hɛs) *n.* **1.** Dame **My·ra.** 1890–1965, English pianist. **2. Vic·tor Fran·cis.** 1883–1964, U.S. physicist, born in Austria: pioneered the investigation of cosmic rays: shared the Nobel prize for physics (1936). **3. (Walther Richard) Ru·dolf** ('ru:dɔlf). born 1894, German Nazi leader. He made a secret flight to Scotland (1941) to negotiate peace with Britain but was held as a prisoner of war; later sentenced to life imprisonment at the Nuremberg trials (1946).

Hesse[1] (hɛs) *n.* a state of E central West Germany, formed in 1945 from the former Prussian province of Hesse-Nassau and part of the former state of Hesse. Capital: Wiesbaden. Pop.: 5 381 705 (1970). Area: 21 111 sq. km (8151 sq. miles). German name: **Hes+sen** ('hɛsᵊn).

Hes·se[2] (hɛs; *German* 'hɛsə) *n.* **Her·mann** ('hɛrman). 1877–1962, German novelist, short-story writer, and poet. His novels include *Der Steppenwolf* (1927) and *Das Glasperlenspiel* (1943): Nobel prize for literature 1946.

Hesse-Nas·sau *n.* a former province of Prussia, now part of the state of Hesse, West Germany.

hes+si·an ('hɛsɪən) *n.* a coarse jute fabric similar to sacking, used for bags, upholstery, etc. [C18: from HESSE[1] + -IAN]

Hes+si·an ('hɛsɪən) *n.* **1.** a native or inhabitant of Hesse. **2. a.** a Hessian soldier in any of the mercenary units of the British Army in the War of American Independence or the Napoleonic Wars. **b.** *U.S.* any German mercenary in the British Army during the War of American Independence. **3.** *Chiefly U.S.* a mercenary or ruffian. ~*adj.* **4.** of or relating to Hesse or its inhabitants.

Hes+si·an boots *pl. n.* men's high boots with tassels around the top, fashionable in England in the early 19th century.

Hes+si·an fly *n.* a small dipterous fly, *Mayetiola destructor,* whose larvae damage wheat, barley, and rye: family *Cecidomyidae* (gall midges). [C18: so called because it was thought to have been introduced into America by Hessian soldiers]

hes+site ('hɛsaɪt) *n.* a black or grey metallic mineral consisting of silver telluride in cubic crystalline form. Formula: Ag_2Te. [C19: from German *Hessit;* named after Henry *Hess,* 19th-century chemist of Swiss origin who worked in Russia; see -ITE[1]]

hes+so+nite ('hɛsəˌnaɪt) *n.* an orange-brown variety of grossularite garnet. Also called: **essonite, cinnamon stone.** [C19: from French, from Greek *hēssōn* less, inferior + -ITE[1]; so called because it is less hard than genuine hyacinth]

hest (hɛst) *n.* an archaic word for **behest.** [Old English *hæs;* related to *hātan* to promise, command]

Hes·ti·a ('hɛstɪə) *n. Greek myth.* the goddess of the hearth. Roman counterpart: **Vesta.**

Hes·y·chast ('hɛsɪˌkæst) *n. Greek Orthodox Church.* a member of a school of mysticism developed by the monks of Mount Athos in the 14th century. [C18: from Medieval Latin *hesychasta* mystic, from Greek *hēsukhastēs,* from *hēsukhazein* to be tranquil, from *hēsukhos* quiet] —ˌ**Hes·y+'chast+ic** *adj.*

het (hɛt) *vb. Archaic or dialect.* a past tense or past participle of **heat.** ~See also **het up.**

he+tae+ra (hɪ'tɪərə) *or* **he+tai+ra** (hɪ'taɪrə) *n., pl.* **+tae+rae** (-'tɪəri:) *or* **+tai+rai** (-'taɪraɪ). (esp. in ancient Greece) a female prostitute, esp. an educated courtesan. [C19: from Greek *hetaira* concubine] —**he+'tae+ric** *or* **he+'tai+ric** *adj.*

he+tae+rism (hɪ'tɪərɪzəm) *or* **he+tai+rism** (hɪ'taɪrɪzəm) *n.* **1.** the state of being a concubine. **2.** *Sociol., anthropol.* a social system attributed to some primitive societies, in which women are communally shared. —**he+'tae+rist** *or* **he+'tai+rist** *n.* —ˌ**he+tae+'ris+tic** *or* ˌ**he+tai+'ris+tic** *adj.*

het·er·o- *combining form.* other, another, or different: *heterodyne; heterophony; heterosexual.* Compare **homo-.** [from Greek *heteros* other]

het·er·o+cer+cal (ˌhɛtərəʊ'sɜ:kᵊl) *adj. Ichthyol.* of or possessing a tail in which the vertebral column turns upwards and extends into the upper, usually larger, lobe, as in sharks. Compare **homocercal.** [C19: from HETERO- + Greek *kerkos* tail]

het·er·o+chro+mat+ic (ˌhɛtərəʊkrəʊ'mætɪk) *adj.* **1.** of or involving many different colours. **2.** *Physics.* consisting of or concerned with different frequencies or wavelengths. —ˌ**het·er·o+'chro+ma+tism** *n.*

het·er·o+chro+ma+tin (ˌhɛtərəʊ'krəʊmətɪn) *n.* the part of a chromosome that stains strongly with basic dyes in the interphase of cell division and has little genetic activity. Compare **euchromatin.**

het·er·o+chro+mo+some (ˌhɛtərəʊ'krəʊməˌsəʊm) *n.* an atypical chromosome, esp. a sex chromosome.

het·er·o+chro+mous (ˌhɛtərəʊ'krəʊməs) *adj.* (esp. of plant parts) of different colours: *the heterochromous florets of a daisy flower.*

het·er·o+clite ('hɛtərəˌklaɪt) *adj. also* **het·er·o+clit+ic** (ˌhɛtərə'klɪtɪk). **1.** (esp. of the form of a word) irregular or unusual. ~*n.* **2.** an irregularly formed word. [C16: from Late Latin *heteroclitus* declining irregularly, from Greek *heteroklitos,* from HETERO- + *klinein* to bend, inflect]

het·er·o+cy+clic (ˌhɛtərəʊ'saɪklɪk, -'sɪk-) *adj.* (of an organic compound) containing a closed ring of atoms, at least one of which is not a carbon atom. Compare **homocyclic.**

het·er·o+dac+tyl (ˌhɛtərəʊ'dæktɪl) *adj.* **1.** (of the feet of certain birds) having the first and second toes directed backwards and the third and fourth forwards. ~*n.* **2.** a bird with heterodactyl feet. ~Compare **zygodactyl.**

het·er·o+dont ('hɛtərəˌdɒnt) *adj.* (of most mammals) having teeth of different types. Compare **homodont.**

het·er·o+dox ('hɛtərəʊˌdɒks) *adj.* **1.** at variance with established, orthodox, or accepted doctrines or beliefs. **2.** holding unorthodox doctrines or opinions. [C17: from Greek *heterodoxos* holding another opinion, from HETERO- + *doxa* opinion] —**'het·er·o+ˌdox·y** *n.*

het·er·o+dyne ('hɛtərəʊˌdaɪn) *vb.* **1.** *Electronics.* to mix (two alternating signals, esp. radio signals) to produce two signals having frequencies corresponding to the sum and the difference of the original frequencies. See also **superheterodyne receiver.** ~*adj.* **2.** produced by, operating by, or involved in heterodyning two signals.

het+er+oe·cious (ˌhɛtə'ri:ʃəs) *adj.* (of parasites, esp. rust fungi) undergoing different stages of the life cycle on different host species. Compare **autoecious.** [from HETERO- + *-oecious,* from Greek *oikia* house] —ˌ**het+er+'oe·cism** *n.*

het·er·o+gam+ete (ˌhɛtərəʊgæ'mi:t) *n.* a gamete that differs in size and form from the one with which it unites in fertilization. Compare **isogamete.**

het+er+og·a+my (ˌhɛtəˈrɒgəmɪ) *n.* **1.** a type of sexual reproduction in which the gametes differ in both size and form. Compare **isogamy. 2.** a condition in which different types of reproduction occur in successive generations of an organism. **3.** the presence of both male and female flowers in one inflorescence. Compare **homogamy** (sense 1). —ˌ**het·er·ˈog·a·mous** *adj.*

het·er·o+ge·ne·ous (ˌhɛtərəʊˈdʒiːnɪəs) *adj.* **1.** composed of unrelated or differing parts or elements. **2.** not of the same kind or type. **3.** *Chem.* of, composed of, or concerned with two or more different phases. Compare **homogeneous.** [C17: from Medieval Latin *heterogeneus,* from Greek *heterogenēs,* from HETERO- + *genos* sort] —**het·er·o+ge·ne·i·ty** (ˌhɛtərəʊdʒɪˈniːɪtɪ) *or* ˌ**het·er·o+ˈge·ne·ous+ness** *n.* —ˌ**het·er·o+ˈge·ne·ous+ly** *adv.*

het·er·o+gen+e·sis (ˌhɛtərəʊˈdʒɛnɪsɪs) *n.* another name for **alternation of generations** or **abiogenesis.** —**het·er·o+ge·net+ic** (ˌhɛtərəʊdʒɪˈnɛtɪk) *or* ˌ**het·er·o+ˈgen+ic** *adj.* —ˌ**het·er·o+ge·ˈnet·i·cal+ly** *adv.*

het·er·o+gen+ous (ˌhɛtəˈrɒdʒɪnəs) *adj. Biology, med.* not originating within the body; of foreign origin: *a heterogenous skin graft.* Compare **autogenous.**

het·er·og·o·ny (ˌhɛtəˈrɒgənɪ) *n.* **1.** *Biology.* the alternation of parthenogenetic and sexual generations in rotifers and similar animals. **2.** the condition in plants, such as the primrose, of having flowers that differ from each other in the length of their stamens and styles. Compare **homogony.** —ˌ**het+er+ˈog·o+nous** *adj.* —ˌ**het+er+ˈog·o·nous+ly** *adv.*

het·er·o+graft (ˈhɛtərəʊˌgrɑːft) *n.* a tissue graft obtained from a donor of a different species from the recipient.

het+er+og+ra+phy (ˌhɛtəˈrɒgrəfɪ) *n.* **1.** the phenomenon of different letters or sequences of letters representing the same sound in different words, as for example *-ight* and *-ite* in *blight* and *bite.* **2.** any writing system in which this phenomenon occurs. —**het·er·o+graph+ic** (ˌhɛtərəʊˈgræfɪk) *or* ˌ**het·er·o+ˈgraph·i·cal** *adj.*

het+er+og·y+nous (ˌhɛtəˈrɒdʒɪnəs) *adj.* (of ants, bees, etc.) having two types of female, one fertile and the other infertile.

het·er·o+lec·i·thal (ˌhɛtərəʊˈlɛsɪθəl) *adj.* (of the eggs of birds) having an unequally distributed yolk. Compare **isolecithal.** [C19: HETERO- + Greek *lekithos* egg yolk]

het+er+ol·o+gous (ˌhɛtəˈrɒləgəs) *adj.* **1.** *Pathol.* of, relating to, or designating cells or tissues not normally present in a particular part of the body. **2.** (esp. of parts of an organism or of different organisms) differing in structure or origin. —ˌ**het+er+ˈol·o+gy** *n.*

het+er+ol·y+sis (ˌhɛtəˈrɒlɪsɪs) *n.* **1.** the dissolution of the cells of one organism by the lysins of another. Compare **autolysis. 2.** Also called: **heterolytic fission.** *Chem.* the dissociation of a molecule into two ions with opposite charges. Compare **homolysis.** —**het·er·o+lyt+ic** (ˌhɛtərəʊˈlɪtɪk) *adj.*

het+er+om+er+ous (ˌhɛtəˈrɒmərəs) *adj. Biology.* having or consisting of parts that differ, esp. in number.

het·er·o+mor+phic (ˌhɛtərəʊˈmɔːfɪk) *or* **het·er·o+mor+phous** *adj. Biology.* **1.** differing from the normal form in size, shape, and function. **2.** (of pairs of homologous chromosomes) differing from each other in size or form. **3.** (esp. of insects) having different forms at different stages of the life cycle. —ˌ**het·er·o+ˈmor+phism** *or* ˌ**het·er·o+ˈmor+phy** *n.*

het+er+on·o+mous (ˌhɛtəˈrɒnɪməs) *adj.* **1.** subject to an external law, rule, or authority. Compare **autonomous. 2.** (of the parts of an organism) differing in the manner of growth, development, or specialization. —ˌ**het+er+ˈon·o+mous+ly** *adv.* —ˌ**het+er+ˈon·o·my** *n.*

het·er·o+nym (ˈhɛtərəʊˌnɪm) *n.* one of two or more words pronounced differently but spelt alike: *the two English words spelt "bow" are heteronyms.* Compare **homograph.** [C17: from Late Greek *heteronumos,* from Greek HETERO- + *onoma* name] —**het+er+on·y·mous** (ˌhɛtəˈrɒnɪməs) *adj.* —ˌ**het+er+ˈon·y·mous+ly** *adv.*

Het·er·o+ou·si·an (ˌhɛtərəʊˈuːsɪən, -ˈaʊsɪən) *n.* **1.** a Christian who maintains that God the Father and God the Son are different in substance. ~*adj.* **2.** of or relating to this belief. [C17: from Late Greek *heteroousios,* from Greek HETERO- + *ousia* nature]

het+er+oph·o+ny (ˌhɛtəˈrɒfənɪ) *n.* the simultaneous performance of different versions of the same melody by different voices or instruments.

het·er·o+phyl+lous (ˌhɛtərəʊˈfɪləs, ˌhɛtəˈrɒfɪləs) *adj.* (of plants such as arrowhead) having more than one type of leaf on the same plant. Also: **anisophyllous.** —ˈ**het·er·o+ˌphyl+ly** *n.*

het·er·o+phyte (ˈhɛtərəʊˌfaɪt) *n.* any plant that lives as a parasite or saprophyte.

het·er·o+plas+ty (ˈhɛtərəʊˌplæstɪ) *n., pl.* **+ties.** the surgical transplantation of tissue obtained from another person or animal. —ˌ**het·er·o+ˈplas+tic** *adj.*

het·er·o+po+lar (ˌhɛtərəʊˈpəʊlə) *adj.* a less common word for **polar** (sense 5a). —**het·er·o+po+lar·i·ty** (ˌhɛtərəʊpəʊˈlærɪtɪ) *n.*

het+er+op+ter+ous (ˌhɛtəˈrɒptərəs) *or* **het+er+op+ter+an** *adj.* of, relating to, or belonging to the *Heteroptera,* a suborder of hemipterous insects, including bedbugs, water bugs, etc., in which the forewings are membranous but have leathery tips. Compare **homopterous.** [C19: from New Latin *Heteroptera,* from HETERO- + Greek *pteron* wing]

het·er·o+sce·das+tic·i·ty (ˌhɛtərəʊskədæsˈtɪsɪtɪ) *n. Statistics.* the condition occurring when all possible values that a variable may take do not have constant variance. Compare **homoscedasticity.** [C20: from HETERO- + *scedasticity,* from Greek *skedasis* a scattering, dispersion]

het·er·o+sex·u·al (ˌhɛtərəʊˈsɛksjʊəl) *n.* **1.** a person who is sexually attracted to the opposite sex. ~*adj.* **2.** of or relating to heterosexuality. ~Compare **homosexual.**

het·er·o+sex·u·al+i·ty (ˌhɛtərəʊˌsɛksjʊˈælɪtɪ) *n.* sexual attraction to or sexual relations with a person or persons of the opposite sex. Compare **homosexuality.**

het·er·o+sis (ˌhɛtəˈrəʊsɪs) *n. Biology.* another name for **hybrid vigour.** [C19: from Late Greek: alteration, from Greek *heteroioun* to alter, from *heteros* other, different]

het+er+os+po+rous (ˌhɛtəˈrɒspərəs) *adj.* (of seed plants and some ferns) producing megaspores and microspores. Compare **homosporous.** —ˌ**het+er+ˈos+po+ry** *n.*

het·er·o+sty+ly (ˈhɛtərəˌstaɪlɪ) *n.* the condition in certain plants, such as primroses, of having styles of different lengths, each type of style in flowers on different plants, which ensures cross-pollination. [C20: from Greek, from *heteros* different + *stylos* pillar] —ˌ**het·er·o+ˈsty+lous** *adj.*

het·er·o+tax+is (ˌhɛtərəʊˈtæksɪs), **het·er·o+tax·y,** *or* **het·er·o+tax·i·a** *n.* an abnormal or asymmetrical arrangement of parts, as of the organs of the body or the constituents of a rock. —ˌ**het·er·o+ˈtac+tic,** ˌ**het·er·o+ˈtac+tous,** *or* ˌ**het·er·o+ˈtax+ic** *adj.*

het·er·o+thal+lic (ˌhɛtərəʊˈθælɪk) *adj.* **1.** (of some algae and fungi) having male and female reproductive organs on different thalli. **2.** (of some fungi) having sexual reproduction that occurs only between two self-sterile mycelia. ~Compare **homothallic.** [C20: from HETERO- + Greek *thallos* green shoot, young twig]

het·er·o+to+pi·a (ˌhɛtərəʊˈtəʊpɪə) *or* **het+er+ot·o+py** (ˌhɛtəˈrɒtəpɪ) *n.* abnormal displacement of a bodily organ or part. [C19: from New Latin, from HETERO- + Greek *topos* place] —ˌ**het·er·o+ˈtop+ic** *or* ˌ**het+er+ˈot·o+pous** *adj.*

het·er·o+troph+ic (ˌhɛtərəʊˈtrɒfɪk) *adj.* (of animals and some plants) using complex organic compounds to manufacture their own organic constituents. Compare **autotrophic.** [C20: from HETERO- + Greek *trophikos* concerning food, from *trophē* nourishment]

het·er·o+typ+ic (ˌhɛtərəʊˈtɪpɪk) *or* **het·er·o+typ·i+cal** *adj.* denoting or relating to the first nuclear division of meiosis, in which the chromosome number is halved. Compare **homeotypic.**

het·er·o+zy+gote (ˌhɛtərəʊˈzaɪgəʊt, -ˈzɪgəʊt) *n.* an animal or plant that is heterozygous; a hybrid. Compare **homozygote.** —ˌ**het·er·o+zy+ˈgo+sis** *n.*

het·er·o+zy+gous (ˌhɛtərəʊˈzaɪgəs) *adj. Genetics.* (of an organism) having dissimilar alleles for any one gene: *heterozygous for eye colour.* Compare **homozygous.**

heth *or* **cheth** (hɛt; *Hebrew* xɛt) *n.* the eighth letter of the Hebrew alphabet (ח), transliterated as *ḥ* and pronounced as a pharyngeal fricative. [from Hebrew]

het+man (ˈhɛtmən) *n., pl.* **+mans.** another word for **ataman.** [C18: from Polish, from German *Hauptmann* headman]

het up *adj.* angry; excited: *don't get het up.*

heu+land+ite (ˈhjuːlənˌdaɪt) *n.* a white, grey, red, or brown zeolite mineral that consists essentially of hydrated calcium aluminium silicate in the form of elongated tabular crystals. Formula: $Ca_2(Al_4Si_{14})O_{36}.12H_2O$. [C19: named after H. *Heuland,* 19th-century English mineral collector; see -ITE[1]]

heu+ris+tic (hjʊəˈrɪstɪk) *adj.* **1.** helping to learn; guiding in discovery or investigation. **2.** (of a method of teaching) allowing pupils to learn things for themselves. **3.** *Maths., science.* using or obtained by reasoning from past experience since no algorithm exists or is relevant: *a heuristic solution.* ~*n.* **4.** *(pl.)* the science of heuristic procedure. [C19: from New Latin *heuristicus,* from Greek *heuriskein* to discover] —**heu+ˈris+ti+cal+ly** *adv.*

He·ve·lius (*German* heˈveːljʊs) *n.* **Jo·han·nes** (joˈhanəs). 1611–87, German astronomer, who published one of the first detailed maps of the lunar surface.

He·ve·sy (*Hungarian* ˈhɛvɛʃi) *n.* **Ge·org von** (ˈgeːɔrg fɔn). 1885–1966, Hungarian chemist. He worked on radioactive tracing and, with D. Coster, discovered the element hafnium (1923): Nobel prize for chemistry 1943.

hew (hjuː) *vb.* **hews, hew+ing, hewed, hewed** *or* **hewn. 1.** to strike (something, esp. wood) with cutting blows, as with an axe. **2.** *(tr.;* often foll. by *out)* to shape or carve from a substance. **3.** *(tr.;* often foll. by *away, down, from, off,* etc.) to sever from a larger or another portion. **4.** *(intr.;* often foll. by *to) U.S.* to conform (to a code, principle, etc.). [Old English *hēawan;* related to Old Norse *heggva,* Old Saxon *hāwa,* Old High German *houwan,* Latin *cūdere* to beat] —ˈ**hew+er** *n.*

H.E.W. *U.S. abbrev. for:* Department of Health, Education, and Welfare.

hex (hɛks) *U.S. dialect.* ~*vb.* **1.** *(tr.)* to bewitch. ~*n.* **2.** an evil spell or symbol of bad luck. **3.** a witch. [C19: via Pennsylvania Dutch from German *Hexe* witch, from Middle High German *hecse,* perhaps from Old High German *hagzissa;* see HAG[1]] —ˈ**hex+er** *n.*

hex. *abbrev. for* hexadecimal.

hex·a- *or before a vowel* **hex-** *combining form.* six: *hexachord; hexameter.* [from Greek, from *hex* SIX]

hex·a+chlo·ro+cy·clo+hex+ane (ˌhɛksəˌklɔːrəˌsaɪkləʊˈhɛkseɪn) *n.* a white or yellowish powder existing in many isomeric forms. A mixture of isomers, including lindane, is used as an insecticide. Formula: $C_6H_6Cl_6$.

hex·a+chlo·ro+eth·ane (ˌhɛksəˌklɔːrəʊˈɛθeɪn) *or* **hex·a+chlor+eth·ane** *n.* a colourless crystalline insoluble compound with a camphor-like odour: used in pyrotechnics and explosives. Formula: C_2Cl_6.

hex·a+chlo·ro+phene (ˌhɛksəˈklɔːrəfiːn) *n.* an insoluble almost odourless white bactericidal substance used in antiseptic soaps, deodorants, etc. Formula: $(C_6HCl_3OH)_2CH_2$.

hex·a·chord ('hɛksəˌkɔːd) *n.* (in medieval musical theory) any of three diatonic scales based upon C, F, and G, each consisting of six notes, from which solmization was developed.

hex·a·co·sa·no·ic ac·id (ˌhɛksəkəusə'nəuɪk) *n.* a white insoluble odourless wax present in beeswax, carnauba, and Chinese wax. Formula: $CH_3(CH_2)_{24}COOH$. Also called: **cerotic acid.**

hex·ad ('hɛksæd) *n.* **1.** a group or series of six. **2.** the number or sum of six. [C17: from Greek *hexas*, from *hex* six] —**hex·'ad·ic** *adj.*

hex·a·de·cane ('hɛksədɪˌkeɪn, ˌhɛksə'dɛkeɪn) *n.* another name for **cetane.** [C19: from HEXA- + DECA- + -ANE]

hex·a·dec·i·mal no·ta·tion *or* **hex·a·dec·i·mal** (ˌhɛksə'dɛsɪməl) *n.* a number system having a base 16; used in computing, one hexadecimal digit being equivalent to a group of four bits.

hex·a·em·er·on (ˌhɛksə'ɛmərɒn) *or* **hex·a·hem·er·on** *n.* **a.** the period of six days in which God created the world. **b.** the account of the Creation in Genesis 1. [C16: via Late Latin from Greek, from *hexaēmeros* (adj.) of six days, from HEXA- + *hēmera* day] —ˌ**hex·a·'em·er·ic** *or* ˌ**hex·a·'hem·er·ic** *adj.*

hex·a·gon ('hɛksəgən) *n.* a polygon having six sides.

hex·ag·o·nal (hɛk'sægənᵊl) *adj.* **1.** having six sides and six angles. **2.** of or relating to a hexagon. **3.** *Crystallog.* relating or belonging to the crystal system characterized by three equal coplanar axes inclined at 60° to each other and a fourth longer or shorter axis at right angles to their plane. See also **trigonal.** —**hex·'ag·o·nal·ly** *adv.*

hex·a·gram ('hɛksəˌgræm) *n.* **1.** a star-shaped figure formed by extending the sides of a regular hexagon to meet at six points. **2.** a group of six broken or unbroken lines which may be combined into 64 different patterns, as used in the *I Ching.* —ˌ**hex·a·'gram·moid** *adj., n.*

hex·a·he·dron (ˌhɛksə'hiːdrən) *n.* a solid figure having six plane faces. A **regular hexahedron** (cube) has square faces. See also **polyhedron.** —ˌ**hex·a·'he·dral** *adj.*

hex·a·hy·drate (ˌhɛksə'haɪdreɪt) *n.* a hydrate, such as magnesium chloride, $MgCl_2.6H_2O$, with six molecules of water per molecule of substance. —ˌ**hex·a·'hy·drat·ed** *adj.*

hex·am·er·ous (hɛk'sæmərəs) *or* **hex·am·e·ral** *adj.* (esp. of the parts of a plant) arranged in groups of six. —**hex·'am·er·ism** *n.*

hex·am·e·ter (hɛk'sæmɪtə) *n. Prosody.* **1.** a verse line consisting of six metrical feet. **2.** (in Greek and Latin epic poetry) a verse line of six metrical feet, of which the first four are usually dactyls or spondees, the fifth a dactyl, and the sixth a spondee or trochee. —**hex·a·met·ric** (ˌhɛksə'mɛtrɪk), **hex·'am·e·tral,** *or* ˌ**hex·a·'met·ri·cal** *adj.*

hex·a·meth·yl·ene·tet·ra·mine (ˌhɛksəˌmɛθɪliːn'tɛtrəˌmiːn) *n.* a colourless crystalline organic compound used as a urinary antiseptic. Formula: $C_6H_{12}N_4$. Also called: **hexamine, methenamine.**

hex·ane ('hɛkseɪn) *n.* a liquid alkane existing in five isomeric forms that are found in petroleum and used as solvents, esp. the isomer with a straight chain of carbon atoms (*n*-hexane). Formula: $CH_3(CH_2)_4CH_3$ (*n*-). [C19: from HEXA- + -ANE]

hex·an·gu·lar (hɛk'sæŋgjulə) *adj.* having six angles.

hex·a·no·ic ac·id (ˌhɛksə'nəuɪk) *n.* an insoluble oily carboxylic acid found in coconut and palm oils and in milk. Formula: $C_5H_{11}COOH$. [C20: from HEXANE + *-oic*]

hex·a·pla ('hɛksəplə) *n.* an edition of the Old Testament compiled by Origen, containing six versions of the text. [C17: from Greek *hexaploos* sixfold] —**'hex·a·plar, hex·a·plar·ic** (ˌhɛksə'plærɪk), *or* **hex·a·plar·i·an** (ˌhɛksə'plɛərɪən) *adj.*

hex·a·pod ('hɛksəˌpɒd) *n.* any arthropod of the class *Hexapoda* (or *Insecta*); an insect.

hex·ap·o·dy (hɛk'sæpədɪ) *n., pl.* **·dies.** *Prosody.* a verse measure consisting of six metrical feet. —**hex·a·pod·ic** (ˌhɛksə'pɒdɪk) *adj.*

hex·a·stich ('hɛksəˌstɪk) *or* **hex·as·ti·chon** (hɛk'sæstɪˌkɒn) *n. Prosody.* a poem, stanza, or strophe that consists of six lines. —ˌ**hex·a·'stich·ic** *adj.*

hex·a·style ('hɛksəˌstaɪl) *Architect.* ~*n.* **1.** a portico or façade with six columns. ~*adj.* **2.** having six columns.

Hex·a·teuch ('hɛksəˌtjuːk) *n.* the first six books of the Old Testament. [C19: from HEXA- + Greek *teukhos* a book] —**'Hex·a·ˌteu·chal.** *adj.*

hex·a·va·lent (hɛk'sævələnt, ˌhɛksə'veɪlənt) *adj. Chem.* having a valency of six. Also: **sexivalent.**

hex·one ('hɛksəun) *n.* another name for **methyl isobutyl ketone.**

hex·o·san ('hɛksəˌsæn) *n.* any of a group of polysaccharides that yield hexose on hydrolysis.

hex·ose ('hɛksəus, -əuz) *n.* a monosaccharide, such as glucose, that contains six carbon atoms per molecule.

hex·yl ('hɛksɪl) *n.* (*modifier*) of, consisting of, or containing the group of atoms C_6H_{13}, esp. the isomeric form of this group, $CH_3(CH_2)_4CH_2$-: *a hexyl group or radical.*

hex·yl·res·or·cin·ol (ˌhɛksɪlrɪ'zɔːsɪˌnɒl) *n.* a yellowish-white crystalline phenol that has a fatty odour and sharp taste; 2,4-dihydroxy-1-hexylbenzene: used for treating bacterial infections of the urinary tract. Formula: $C_{12}H_{18}O_2$.

hey (heɪ) *interj.* **1.** an expression indicating surprise, dismay, discovery, etc., or calling for another's attention. **2. hey presto.** an exclamation used by conjurors to herald the climax of a trick. [C13: compare Old French *hay*, German *hei*, Swedish *hej*]

hey·day ('heɪˌdeɪ) *n.* the time of most power, popularity, vigour, etc.; prime. [C16: probably based on HEY]

Hey·duck ('haɪdʊk) *n.* a variant spelling of **Haiduk.**

Hey·er·dahl (*Norwegian* 'hɛjərdaːl) *n.* **Thor** (tɔː). born 1914, Norwegian anthropologist. In 1947 he demonstrated that the Polynesians could originally have been migrants from South America, by sailing from Peru to the Pacific Islands of Tuamotu in the *Kon-Tiki*, a raft made of balsa wood.

Hey·sham ('heɪʃəm) *n.* a port in NW England, in NW Lancashire. Pop. (with Morecambe): 41 863 (1971).

Hey·wood[1] ('heɪˌwʊd) *n.* a town in NW England, in Greater Manchester near Bury. Pop.: 30 418 (1971).

Hey·wood[2] ('heɪˌwʊd) *n.* **1. John.** ?1497–?1580, English dramatist, noted for his comic interludes. **2. Thom·as.** ?1574–1641, English dramatist, noted esp. for his domestic drama *A Woman Killed with Kindness* (1607).

Hez·e·ki·ah (ˌhɛzə'kaɪə) *n.* ?715–?687 B.C. a king of Judah, noted for his religious reforms (II Kings 18–19). Douay spelling: **E·ze·chi·as.** [from Hebrew *hizqīyyāhū* God has strengthened]

Hf *the chemical symbol for* hafnium.

HF, H.F., hf, *or* **h.f.** *abbrev. for* high frequency.

hf. *abbrev. for* half.

hg *abbrev. for* hectogram.

Hg *the chemical symbol for* mercury. [from New Latin *hydrargyrum*]

HG *or* **H.G.** *abbrev. for:* **1.** High German. **2.** His (*or* Her) Grace. **3.** (in Britain) Home Guard.

hgt. *abbrev. for* height.

HGV (in Britain) *abbrev. for* heavy goods vehicle.

H.H. *abbrev. for:* **1.** His (*or* Her) Highness. **2.** His Holiness (title of the Pope).

HH (on pencils) *abbrev. for:* double hard.

hhd *or* **hhd.** *abbrev. for* hogshead.

H-hour *n. Military.* the specific hour at which any operation commences. Also called: **zero hour.**

hi (haɪ) *sentence substitute. Chiefly U.S.* an informal word for **hello:** sometimes used to attract attention. [C20: probably shortened from the phrase *how are you*]

H.I. *abbrev. for* Hawaiian Islands.

Hi·a·le·ah (ˌhaɪə'liːə) *n.* a city in SE Florida, near Miami: racetrack. Pop.: 120 809 (1973 est.).

hi·a·tus (haɪ'eɪtəs) *n., pl.* **·tus·es** *or* **·tus. 1.** (esp. in manuscripts) a break or gap where something is missing. **2.** a break or interruption in continuity. **3.** a break between adjacent vowels in the pronunciation of a word. **4.** *Anatomy.* a natural opening or aperture; foramen. **5.** *Anatomy.* a less common word for **vulva.** [C16: from Latin: gap, cleft, aperture, from *hiāre* to gape, yawn] —**hi·'a·tal** *adj.*

hi·a·tus her·ni·a *or* **hi·a·tal her·ni·a** *n.* protrusion of part of the stomach through the diaphragm at the oesophageal opening.

Hi·a·wa·tha (ˌhaɪə'wɒθə) *n.* a 16th-century Onondaga Indian chief: credited with the organization of the Five Nations.

hi·ba·chi (hɪ'bɑːtʃɪ) *n.* a portable brazier for heating and cooking food. [from Japanese, from *hi* fire + *bachi* bowl]

hi·ber·nac·u·lum (ˌhaɪbə'nækjʊləm) *or* **hi·ber·nac·le** ('haɪbəˌnækᵊl) *n., pl.* **·u·la** (-jʊlə) *or* **·les.** *Rare.* **1.** the winter quarters of a hibernating animal. **2.** the protective case or covering of a plant bud or animal. [C17: from Latin: winter residence; see HIBERNATE]

hi·ber·nal (haɪ'bɜːnᵊl) *adj.* of or occurring in winter. [C17: from Latin *hībernālis*, from *hiems* winter]

hi·ber·nate ('haɪbəˌneɪt) *vb.* (*intr.*) **1.** (of some mammals, reptiles, and amphibians) to pass the winter in a dormant condition with metabolism slowed down. Compare **aestivate. 2.** to cease from activity. [C19: from Latin *hībernāre* to spend the winter, from *hībernus* of winter, from *hiems* winter] —ˌ**hi·ber·'na·tion** *n.* —**'hi·ber·ˌna·tor** *n.*

Hi·ber·ni·a (haɪ'bɜːnɪə) *n.* the Roman name for **Ireland:** used poetically in later times. —**Hi·'ber·ni·an** *adj., n.*

Hi·ber·ni·cism (haɪ'bɜːnɪˌsɪzəm) *or* **Hi·ber·ni·an·ism** (haɪ'bɜːnɪəˌnɪzəm) *n.* an Irish expression, idiom, trait, custom, etc.

hi·bis·cus (haɪ'bɪskəs) *n., pl.* **·cus·es.** any plant of the chiefly tropical and subtropical malvaceous genus *Hibiscus*, esp. *H. rosa-sinensis*, cultivated for its large brightly coloured flowers. [C18: from Latin, from Greek *hibiskos* marsh mallow]

hic (hɪk) *interj.* a representation of the sound of a hiccup.

hic·cup ('hɪkʌp) *n.* **1.** a spasm of the diaphragm producing a sudden breathing in of air followed by a closing of the glottis, resulting in a characteristic sharp sound. Technical name: **singultus. 2.** the state or condition of having such spasms. **3.** *Informal.* a minor difficulty or problem. ~*vb.* **·cups, ·cup·ing, ·cuped** *or* **·cups, ·cup·ping, ·cupped. 4.** (*intr.*) to make a hiccup or hiccups. **5.** (*tr.*) to utter with a hiccup or hiccups. ~Also: **hiccough.** [C16: of imitative origin]

hic ja·cet *Latin.* (hɪk 'jækɛt) (on gravestones, etc.) here lies.

hick (hɪk) *Informal, chiefly U.S.* ~*n.* **a.** a country person; bumpkin. **b.** (*as modifier*): *hick ideas.* [C16: after *Hick*, familiar form of *Richard*]

hick·ey ('hɪkɪ) *n. U.S. informal.* **1.** an object or gadget: used as a substitutive name when the correct name is unknown, forgotten etc.; doohickey. **2.** a mark on the skin. [C20: of unknown origin]

Hick·ok ('hɪkɒk) *n.* **James But·ler,** known as *Wild Bill Hickok.* 1837–76, U.S. frontiersman and marshal.

hick·o·ry ('hɪkərɪ) *n., pl.* **·ries. 1.** any juglandaceous tree of the chiefly North American genus *Carya*, having nuts with edible kernels and hard smooth shells. See also **pignut** (sense 1), **bitternut** (sense 1), **shagbark. 2.** the hard tough wood of any of these trees. **3.** the nut of any of these trees. **4.** a switch or cane made of hickory wood. [C17: from earlier *pohickery*, from Algonquian *pawcohiccora* food made from ground hickory nuts]

hid (hɪd) *vb.* the past tense of **hide**[1].

hi·dal·go (hɪˈdælgəʊ; *Spanish* iˈðalɣo) *n., pl.* **·gos** (-gəʊz; *Spanish* -ɣos). a member of the lower nobility in Spain. [C16: from Spanish, from Old Spanish *fijo dalgo* nobleman, from Latin *filius* son + *dē* of + *aliquid* something]

Hi·dal·go (hɪˈdælgəʊ; *Spanish* iˈðalɣo) *n.* a state of central Mexico: consists of a high plateau, with the Sierra Madre Oriental in the north and east; ancient remains of Teltec culture (at Tula); rich mineral resources. Capital: Pachuca. Pop.: 1 193 845 (1970). Area: 20 987 sq. km (8103 sq. miles).

hid·den (ˈhɪdᵊn) *vb.* **1.** the past participle of **hide**[1]. ~*adj.* **2.** concealed or obscured: *a hidden cave; a hidden meaning.* —**ˈhid·den·ly** *adv.* —**ˈhid·den·ness** *n.*

hid·den·ite (ˈhɪdəˌnaɪt) *n.* a green transparent variety of the mineral spodumene, used as a gemstone. [C19: named after W. E. *Hidden* (1853–1918), American mineralogist who discovered it]

hide[1] (haɪd) *vb.* **hides, hid·ing, hid, hid·den** *or* **hid. 1.** to put or keep (oneself or an object) in a secret place; conceal (oneself or an object) from view or discovery: *to hide a pencil; to hide from the police.* **2.** (*tr.*) to conceal or obscure: *the clouds hid the sun.* **3.** (*tr.*) to keep secret. **4.** (*tr.*) to turn (one's head, eyes, etc.) away. ~*n.* **5.** *Brit.* a place of concealment, usually disguised to appear as part of the natural environment, used by hunters, birdwatchers, etc. U.S. equivalent: **blind.** [Old English *hȳdan;* related to Old Frisian *hēda,* Middle Low German *hüden,* Greek *keuthein*] —**ˈhid·a·ble** *adj.* —**ˈhid·er** *n.*

hide[2] (haɪd) *n.* **1.** the skin of an animal, esp. the tough thick skin of a large mammal, either tanned or raw. **2.** *Informal.* the human skin. ~*vb.* **hides, hid·ing, hid·ed. 3.** (*tr.*) *Informal.* to flog. [Old English *hȳd;* related to Old Norse *hūth,* Old Frisian *hēd,* Old High German *hūt,* Latin *cutis* skin, Greek *kutos;* see CUTICLE] —**ˈhide·less** *adj.*

hide[3] (haɪd) *n.* an obsolete Brit. unit of land measure, varying in magnitude from about 60 to 120 acres. [Old English *hīgid;* related to *hīw* family, household, Latin *cīvis* citizen]

hide-and-seek *or U.S.* **hide-and-go-seek** *n.* a game in which one player covers his eyes and waits while the others hide, and then tries to find them.

hide·a·way (ˈhaɪdəˌweɪ) *n.* a hiding place or secluded spot.

hide·bound (ˈhaɪdˌbaʊnd) *adj.* **1.** restricted by petty rules, a conservative attitude, etc. **2.** (of cattle, etc.) having the skin closely attached to the flesh as a result of poor feeding. **3.** (of trees) having a very tight bark that impairs growth.

hid·e·ous (ˈhɪdɪəs) *adj.* **1.** extremely ugly; repulsive: *a hideous person.* **2.** terrifying and horrific. [C13: from Old French *hisdos,* from *hisde* fear; of uncertain origin] —**ˈhid·e·ous·ly** *adv.* —**ˈhid·e·ous·ness** *or* **hid·e·os·i·ty** (ˌhɪdɪˈɒsɪtɪ) *n.*

hide-out *n.* **1.** a hiding place, esp. a remote place used by outlaws, etc.; hideaway. ~*vb.* **hide out. 2.** to remain deliberately concealed, esp. for a prolonged period of time.

Hi·de·yo·shi To·yo·to·mi (ˌhiːdɛˈjɔːʃɪ ˌtɔːjɔːˈtɔːmɪ) *n.* 1536–98, Japanese military dictator (1582–98). He unified all Japan under one rule (1590).

hid·ing[1] (ˈhaɪdɪŋ) *n.* **1.** the state of concealment (esp. in the phrase **in hiding**). **2. hiding place.** a place of concealment.

hid·ing[2] (ˈhaɪdɪŋ) *n. Informal.* a flogging; beating.

hi·dro·sis (hɪˈdrəʊsɪs) *n.* **1.** a technical word for **perspiration** or **sweat. 2.** any skin disease affecting the sweat glands. Also called: **hy·per·hi·dro·sis** (ˌhaɪpəhɪˈdrəʊsɪs, -haɪˈdrəʊsɪs). [C18: via New Latin from Greek: sweating, from *hidrōs* sweat] —**hi·drot·ic** (hɪˈdrɒtɪk) *adj.*

hid·y-hole *or* **hid·ey-hole** *n. Informal.* a hiding place.

hie (haɪ) *vb.* **hies, hie·ing** *or* **hy·ing, hied.** *Archaic or poetic.* to hurry; hasten; speed. [Old English *hīgian* to strive]

hie·land (ˈhiːlənd) *adj. Scot. dialect.* easily tricked; gullible. [a variant of HIGHLAND, alluding to the supposed gullibility of Highlanders in towns or cities]

hi·e·mal (ˈhaɪəməl) *adj.* a less common word for **hibernal.** [C16: from Latin *hiems* winter; see HIBERNATE]

hi·er·a·co·sphinx (ˌhaɪəˈreɪkəʊˌsfɪŋks) *n., pl.* **·sphinx·es** *or* **·sphin·ges** (-ˌsfɪndʒiːz). (in ancient Egyptian art) a hawk-headed sphinx. [C18: from Greek *hierax* hawk + SPHINX]

hi·er·arch (ˈhaɪəˌrɑːk) *n.* **1.** *Ecclesiast.* **a.** a person in a position of high priestly authority. **b.** a person holding high rank in a religious hierarchy. **2.** a person at a high level in a hierarchy. —**ˌhi·er·ˈar·chal** *adj.*

hi·er·ar·chy (ˈhaɪəˌrɑːkɪ) *n., pl.* **·chies. 1.** a system of persons or things arranged in a graded order. **2.** a body of persons in holy orders organized into graded ranks. **3.** the collective body of those so organized. **4.** a series of ordered groupings within a system, such as the arrangement of plants and animals into classes, orders, families, etc. **5.** government by an organized priesthood. [C14: from Medieval Latin *hierarchia,* from Late Greek *hierarkhia,* from *hierarkhēs* high priest; see HIERO-, -ARCHY] —**ˌhi·er·ˈar·chi·cal** *or* **ˌhi·er·ˈar·chic** *adj.* —**ˌhi·er·ˈar·chi·cal·ly** *adv.* —**ˈhi·er·ˌarch·ism** *n.*

hi·er·at·ic (ˌhaɪəˈrætɪk) *adj. also* **hi·er·at·i·cal. 1.** of or relating to priests. **2.** of or relating to a cursive form of hieroglyphics used by priests in ancient Egypt. **3.** of or relating to styles in art that adhere to certain fixed types or methods, as in ancient Egypt. ~*n.* **4.** the hieratic script of ancient Egypt. [C17: from Latin *hierāticus,* from Greek *hieratikos,* from *hiereus* a priest, from *hieros* holy] —**ˌhi·er·ˈat·i·cal·ly** *adv.*

hi·er·o- *or before a vowel* **hi·er-** *combining form.* holy or divine: *hierocracy; hierarchy.* [from Greek, from *hieros*]

hi·er·oc·ra·cy (ˌhaɪəˈrɒkrəsɪ) *n., pl.* **·cies.** government by priests or ecclesiastics. —**hi·er·o·crat·ic** (ˌhaɪərəˈkrætɪk) *or* **ˌhi·er·o·ˈcrat·i·cal** *adj.*

hi·er·o·dule (ˈhaɪərəˌdjuːl) *n.* (in ancient Greece) a temple slave, esp. a sacral prostitute. [C19: from Greek *hierodoulos,* from HIERO- + *doulos* slave] —**ˌhi·er·o·ˈdu·lic** *adj.*

hi·er·o·glyph·ic (ˌhaɪərəˈglɪfɪk) *adj. also* **hi·er·o·glyph·i·cal. 1.** of or relating to a form of writing using picture symbols, esp. as used in ancient Egypt. **2.** written with hieroglyphic symbols. **3.** difficult to read or decipher. ~*n. also* **hi·er·o·glyph. 4.** a picture or symbol representing an object, concept, or sound. **5.** a symbol or picture that is difficult to read or decipher. [C16: from Late Latin *hieroglyphicus,* from Greek *hierogluphikos,* from HIERO- + *gluphē* carving, from *gluphein* to carve] —**ˌhi·er·o·ˈglyph·i·cal·ly** *adv.* —**hi·er·o·glyph·ist** (ˌhaɪərəˈglɪfɪst, ˌhaɪəˈrɒg-) *n.*

hi·er·o·glyph·ics (ˌhaɪərəˈglɪfɪks) *n.* (*functioning as sing.*) **1.** a form of writing, esp. as used in ancient Egypt, in which pictures or symbols are used to represent objects, concepts, or sounds. **2.** difficult or undecipherable writing.

hi·er·o·gram (ˈhaɪərəˌgræm) *n.* a sacred symbol.

hi·er·ol·o·gy (ˌhaɪəˈrɒlədʒɪ) *n., pl.* **·gies. 1. a.** sacred literature. **2.** a biography of a saint. —**hi·er·o·log·ic** (ˌhaɪərəˈlɒdʒɪk) *or* **ˌhi·er·o·ˈlog·i·cal** *adj.* —**ˌhi·er·ˈol·o·gist** *n.*

Hi·er·on·y·mus (ˌhaɪəˈrɒnɪməs) *n.* **Eu·se·bi·us** (juːˈsiːbɪəs). the Latin name of (Saint) **Jerome.** —**Hi·er·o·nym·ic** (ˌhaɪərəˈnɪmɪk) *or* **ˌHi·er·o·ˈnym·i·an** *adj.*

hi·er·o·phant (ˈhaɪərəˌfænt) *n.* **1.** (in ancient Greece) an official high priest of religious mysteries, esp. those of Eleusis. **2.** a person who interprets and explains esoteric mysteries. [C17: from Late Latin *hierophanta,* from Greek *hierophantēs,* from HIERO- + *phainein* to reveal] —**ˌhi·er·o·ˈphant·ic** *adj.* —**ˌhi·er·o·ˈphan·ti·cal·ly** *adv.*

hi·fa·lu·tin (ˌhaɪfəˈluːtɪn) *adj.* a variant spelling of **highfalutin.**

hi-fi (ˈhaɪˈfaɪ) *n. Informal.* **1. a.** short for **high fidelity. b.** (*as modifier*): *hi-fi equipment.* **2.** a set of high-quality sound-reproducing equipment.

hig·gle (ˈhɪgᵊl) *vb.* a less common word for **haggle.**

hig·gle·dy-pig·gle·dy (ˈhɪgᵊldɪˈpɪgᵊldɪ) *Informal.* ~*adj., adv.* **1.** in a jumble. ~*n.* **2.** a muddle.

high (haɪ) *adj.* **1.** being a relatively great distance from top to bottom; tall: *a high building.* **2.** situated at or extending to a relatively great distance above the ground or above sea level: *a high plateau.* **3. a.** (*postpositive*) being a specified distance from top to bottom: *three feet high.* **b.** (*in combination*): *a seven-foot-high wall.* **4.** extending from an elevation: *a high dive.* **5.** (*in combination*) coming up to a specified level: *knee-high.* **6.** being at its peak or point of culmination: *high noon.* **7.** of greater than average height: *a high collar.* **8.** greater than normal in degree, intensity, or amount: *high prices; a high temperature; a high wind.* **9.** of large or relatively large numerical value: *high frequency; high voltage; high mileage.* **10.** (of sound) acute in pitch; having a high frequency. **11.** (of latitudes) situated relatively far north or south from the equator. **12.** (of meat) slightly decomposed or tainted, regarded as enhancing the flavour of game. **13.** of great eminence; very important: *the high priestess.* **14.** exalted in style or character; elevated: *high drama.* **15.** expressing or feeling contempt or arrogance: *high words.* **16.** elated; cheerful: *high spirits.* **17.** *Informal.* being in a state of altered consciousness, characterized esp. by euphoria and often induced by the use of alcohol, narcotics, etc. **18.** luxurious or extravagant: *high life.* **19.** advanced in complexity or development: *high finance.* **20.** (of a gear) providing a relatively great forward speed for a given engine speed. Compare **low**[1] (sense 19). **21.** *Phonetics.* of, relating to, or denoting a vowel whose articulation is produced by raising the back of the tongue towards the soft palate or the blade towards the hard palate, such as for the *ee* in English *see* or *oo* in English *moon.* Compare **low**[1] (sense 18). **22.** (*cap. when part of name*) formal and elaborate in style: *High Mass.* **23.** (*usually cap.*) of or relating to the High Church. **24.** remote, esp. in time. **25.** *Cards.* **a.** having a relatively great value in a suit. **b.** able to win a trick. **26. high and dry.** stranded; helpless; destitute. **27. high and low.** in all places; everywhere. **28. high and mighty.** *Informal.* arrogant. **29. high opinion.** a favourable opinion. ~*adv.* **30.** at or to a height: *he jumped high.* **31.** in a high manner. **32.** *Nautical.* close to the wind with sails full. ~*n.* **33.** a high place or level. **34.** *Informal.* a state of altered consciousness, often induced by alcohol, narcotics, etc. **35.** another word for **anticyclone. 36.** short for **high school. 37.** (*cap*) (esp. in Oxford) the High Street. **38. on high. a.** at a height. **b.** in heaven. [Old English *hēah;* related to Old Norse *hār,* Gothic *hauhs,* Old High German *hōh* high, Lithuanian *kaũkas* bump, Russian *kúčča* heap, Sanskrit *kuča* bosom]

high al·tar *n.* the principal altar of a church.

high·ball (ˈhaɪˌbɔːl) *n. U.S.* a long iced drink consisting of a spirit base with water, soda water, etc.

high·bind·er (ˈhaɪˌbaɪndə) *n. U.S. informal.* **1.** a gangster. **2.** a corrupt politician. **3.** (formerly) a member of a Chinese-American secret society that engaged in blackmail, murder, etc. [C19: named after the *High-binders,* a New York city gang]

high·born (ˈhaɪˌbɔːn) *adj.* of noble or aristocratic birth.

high·boy (ˈhaɪˌbɔɪ) *n. U.S.* a tall chest of drawers in two sections, the lower section being a lowboy. Brit. equivalent: **tallboy.**

high·brow (ˈhaɪˌbraʊ) *Often disparaging.* ~*n.* **1.** a person of scholarly and erudite tastes. ~*adj. also* **high·browed. 2.** appealing to highbrows: *highbrow literature.*

high camp *n.* a sophisticated form of **camp** (the style).

high·chair ('haɪˌtʃɛə) *n.* a long-legged chair for a child, esp. one with a table-like tray used at meal times.

High Church *n.* **1.** the party or movement within the Church of England stressing continuity with Catholic Christendom, the authority of bishops, and the importance of sacraments, rituals, and ceremonies. Compare **Broad Church, Low Church.** ~*adj.* **High-Church. 2.** of or relating to this party or movement. —'**High-'Church·man** *n.*

high-class *adj.* **1.** of very good quality; superior: *a high-class grocer.* **2.** belonging to, associated with, or exhibiting the characteristics of an upper social class: *a high-class lady; a high-class prostitute.*

high-col·oured *adj.* (of the complexion) deep red or purplish; florid.

high com·e·dy *n.* comedy set largely among cultured and articulate people and featuring witty dialogue. Compare **low comedy.** —**high co·me·di·an** *n.*

high com·mand *n.* the commander-in-chief and senior officers of a nation's armed forces.

high com·mis·sion·er *n.* **1.** the senior diplomatic representative sent by one Commonwealth country to another instead of an ambassador. **2.** the head of an international commission. **3.** the chief officer in a colony or other dependency.

High Court of Jus·tice *n.* (in England) one of the two divisions of the Supreme Court of Judicature. See also **Court of Appeal.**

High Court of Jus·ti·ci·ar·y *n.* the senior criminal court in Scotland, to which all cases of murder and rape and all cases involving heavy penalties are referred.

high day *n.* a day of celebration; festival (esp. in the phrase **high days and holidays**).

high·er crit·i·cism *n.* the use of scientific techniques of literary criticism to establish the sources of the books of the Bible. Compare **lower criticism.**

high·er ed·u·ca·tion *n.* education and training at colleges, universities, polytechnics, etc.

high·er math·e·mat·ics *n.* mathematics, including number theory and topology, that is more abstract than normal arithmetic, algebra, geometry, and trigonometry.

high·er-up *n. Informal.* a person of higher rank or in a superior position.

high·est com·mon fac·tor *n.* the largest number or quantity that is a factor of each member of a group of numbers or quantities. Abbrev.: **H.C.F., h.c.f.** Also called: **greatest common divisor.**

high ex·plo·sive *n.* an extremely powerful chemical explosive, such as TNT or gelignite.

high·fa·lu·tin, hi·fa·lu·tin (ˌhaɪfə'luːtɪn) *or* **high·fa·lu·ting** *adj. Informal.* pompous or pretentious. [C19: from HIGH + *-falutin,* perhaps variant of *fluting,* from FLUTE]

high fash·ion *n.* another name for **haute couture.**

high fi·del·i·ty *n.* **a.** the reproduction of sound using electronic equipment that gives faithful reproduction with little or no distortion. **b.** (*as modifier*): *a high-fidelity amplifier.* Often shortened to **hi-fi.**

high-fli·er *or* **high-fly·er** *n.* **1.** a person who is extreme in aims, ambition, etc. **2.** a person of great ability, esp. in a career. —'**high-ˌfly·ing** *n.*

high-flown *adj.* extravagant or pretentious in conception or intention: *high-flown ideas.*

high fre·quen·cy *n.* a radio-frequency band or radio frequency lying between 30 and 3 megahertz. Abbrev.: **HF**

High Ger·man *n.* **1.** the standard German language, historically developed from the form of West Germanic spoken in S Germany. Abbrev.: **HG** See also **German, Low German. 2.** any of the German dialects of S Germany, Austria, or Switzerland.

high-hand·ed *adj.* tactlessly overbearing and inconsiderate. —ˌ**high-'hand·ed·ly** *adv.* —ˌ**high-'hand·ed·ness** *n.*

high hat *n.* another name for **top hat.**

high-hat *Informal, chiefly U.S.* ~*adj.* **1.** snobbish and arrogant. ~*vb.* **-hats, -hat·ting, -hat·ted. 2.** to treat in a snobbish or offhand way. ~*n.* **3.** a snobbish person.

high·jack ('haɪˌdʒæk) *vb.* a less common spelling of **hijack.** —'**high·ˌjack·er** *n.*

high jinks *or* **hi·jinks** ('haɪˌdʒɪŋks) *n.* lively enjoyment.

high jump *n.* **1. a.** (usually preceded by *the*) an athletic event in which a competitor has to jump over a high bar set between two vertical supports. **b.** (*as modifier*): *high-jump techniques.* **2. the high jump.** *Brit. informal.* a severe reprimand or punishment. —**high jump·er** *n.* —**high jump·ing** *n.*

high-key *adj.* (of a photograph, painting, etc.) having a predominance of light grey tones or light colours. Compare **low-key** (sense 2).

high-keyed *adj.* **1.** having a high pitch; shrill. **2.** *U.S.* highly strung. **3.** bright in colour.

high·land ('haɪlənd) *n.* **1.** relatively high ground. **2.** (*modifier*) of or relating to a highland. —'**high·land·er** *n.*

High·land ('haɪlənd) *n.* (*modifier*) of, relating to, or denoting the Highlands of Scotland.

High·land cat·tle *n.* a breed of cattle with shaggy hair, usually reddish-brown in colour, and long horns.

High·land·er ('haɪləndə) *n.* **1.** a native of the Highlands of Scotland. **2.** a member of a Scottish Highland regiment.

High·land fling *n.* a vigorous Scottish reel.

High·land Re·gion *n.* a local government region in N Scotland, formed in 1975 from Caithness, Sutherland, Nairnshire, and most of Inverness-shire and Ross and Cromarty except for the Outer Hebrides. Administrative centre: Inverness. Pop.: 186 460 (1976 est.). Area: 25 149 sq. km (9710 sq. miles).

High·lands ('haɪləndz) *n.* **the. 1.** a mountainous region of N Scotland, north of the Grampians: sometimes includes the Inner Hebrides and Bute; distinguished by Gaelic culture. **2.** (*often not cap.*) the highland region of any country.

high-lev·el lan·guage *n.* a computer programming language that is closer to human language or mathematical notation than to machine language. Compare **low-level language.**

high·life ('haɪˌlaɪf) *n.* **a.** a style of music combining West African elements with U.S. jazz forms, found esp. in the cities of West Africa. **b.** (*as modifier*): *a highlife band.*

high·light ('haɪˌlaɪt) *n.* **1.** an area of the lightest tone in a painting, drawing, photograph, etc. **2.** the most exciting or memorable part of an event or period of time. **3.** (*often pl.*) a bleached blond streak in the hair. ~*vb.* (*tr.*) **4.** *Painting, drawing, photography, etc.* to mark (any brightly illuminated or prominent part of a form or figure) with light tone. **5.** to bring notice or emphasis to. **6.** to be the highlight of. **7.** to produce blond streaks in (the hair) by bleaching.

high·ly ('haɪlɪ) *adv.* **1.** (intensifier): *highly pleased; highly disappointed.* **2.** with great approbation or favour: *we spoke highly of it.* **3.** in a high position: *placed highly in class.* **4.** at or for a high price or cost.

high·ly strung *or U.S.* **high-strung** *adj.* tense and easily upset; excitable; nervous.

High Mass *n.* a solemn and elaborate sung Mass. Compare **Low Mass.**

high-mind·ed *adj.* **1.** having or characterized by high moral principles. **2.** *Archaic.* arrogant; haughty. —ˌ**high-'mind·ed·ly** *adv.* —ˌ**high-'mind·ed·ness** *n.*

high-muck-a-muck *n.* a conceited or haughty person. [C19: from Chinook Jargon *hiu muckamuck,* literally: plenty (of) food]

high·ness ('haɪnɪs) *n.* the condition of being high or lofty.

High·ness ('haɪnɪs) *n.* (preceded by *Your, His,* or *Her*) a title used to address or refer to a royal person.

high-oc·tane *adj.* (of petrol) having a high octane number.

high-pass fil·ter *n. Electronics.* a filter that transmits all frequencies above a specified value, substantially attenuating frequencies below this value. Compare **low-pass filter, band-pass filter.**

high-pitched *adj.* **1.** pitched high in volume or tone. See **high** (sense 10). **2.** (of a roof) having steeply sloping sides. **3.** (of an argument, style, etc.) lofty or intense.

high place *n. Old Testament.* a hilltop, used as a place of idolatrous worship.

high plac·es *pl. n.* positions and offices of influence and importance: *a scandal in high places.*

high point *n.* a moment or occasion of great intensity, interest, happiness, etc.: *the award marked a high point in his life.*

high-pow·ered *adj.* **1.** (of an optical instrument or lens) having a high magnification: *a high-powered telescope.* **2.** dynamic and energetic; highly capable.

high-pres·sure *adj.* **1.** having, using, involving, or designed to withstand a pressure above normal pressure: *a high-pressure gas; a high-pressure cylinder.* **2.** *Informal.* (of selling) persuasive in an aggressive and persistent manner.

high priest *n.* **1.** *Judaism.* the priest of highest rank who alone was permitted to enter the holy of holies of the tabernacle and Temple. **2.** *Mormon Church.* a priest of the order of Melchizedek priesthood. **3.** the head of a group or cult. —**high priest·hood** *n.*

high re·lief *n.* relief in which forms and figures stand out from the background to half or more than half of their natural depth. Also called: **alto-relievo.**

High Re·nais·sance *n.* **a. the.** the period from about the 1490s to the 1520s in painting, sculpture, and architecture in Europe, esp. in Italy, when the Renaissance ideals were considered to have been attained through the mastery of Leonardo, Michelangelo, and Raphael. **b.** (*as modifier*): *High Renaissance art.*

high-rise *adj.* (*prenominal*) of or relating to a building that has many storeys, esp. one used for flats or offices: *a high-rise block.* Compare **low-rise.**

high·road ('haɪˌrəʊd) *n.* **1.** a main road; highway. **2.** (usually preceded by *the*) the sure way: *the highroad to fame.*

high school *n.* **1.** *Brit.* another term for **grammar school. 2.** *U.S.* a secondary school from grade 7 to grade 12.

high seas *pl. n.* (*sometimes sing.*) the open seas of the world, outside the jurisdiction of any one nation.

high sea·son *n.* the most popular time of year at a holiday resort, etc.

high-sound·ing *adj.* another term for **high-flown.**

high-speed *adj. Photog.* **1.** employing or requiring a very short exposure time: *high-speed film.* **2.** recording or making exposures at a rate usually exceeding 50 and up to several million frames per second. **3.** working, moving, or operating at a high speed.

high-speed steel *n.* any of various steels that retain their hardness at high temperatures and are thus suitable for making tools used on lathes and other high-speed machines.

high-spir·it·ed *adj.* vivacious, bold, or lively. —ˌ**high-'spir·it·ed·ly** *adv.* —ˌ**high-'spir·it·ed·ness** *n.*

high spot *n. Informal.* Another word for **highlight** (sense 2).

high-step·per *n.* a horse trained to lift its feet high off the ground when walking or trotting.

High Street *n.* (*often not cap.*; usually preceded by *the*) *Brit.* the main street of a town, usually where the principal shops are situated.

hight (haɪt) *vb.* (*tr.; used only as a past tense in the passive or as a past participle*) *Archaic and poetic.* to name; call: *a maid* *hight Mary.* [Old English *heht,* from *hatan* to call; related to Old Norse *heita,* Old Frisian *hēta,* Old High German *heizzan*]

high ta·ble *n.* (*sometimes cap.*) the table, sometimes elevated, in the dining hall of a school, college, etc., at which the principal teachers, fellows, etc., sit.

high·tail ('haɪˌteɪl) *vb.* (*intr.*) *Informal, chiefly U.S.* to go or move in a great hurry. Also: **hightail it.**

High Tat·ra *n.* See **Tatra Mountains.**

high tea *n. Brit.* a substantial early evening meal consisting of sandwiches or a cooked snack, cakes, etc., and usually accompanied by tea.

high-ten·sion *n.* (*modifier*) subjected to, carrying, or capable of operating at a relatively high voltage: *a high-tension wire.* Abbrev.: **HT**

high tide *n.* **1. a.** the tide at its highest level. **b.** the time at which it reaches this. **2.** a culminating point.

high time *Informal.* ~*adv.* **1.** the latest possible time; a time that is almost too late: *it's high time you mended this shelf.* ~*n.* **2.** Also: **high old time.** an enjoyable and exciting time.

high-toned *adj.* **1.** high in tone. **2.** *U.S. informal.* affectedly superior.

high trea·son *n.* an act of treason directly affecting a sovereign or state.

high-up *n. Informal.* a person who holds an important or influential position.

High·veld ('haɪˌfɛlt, -ˌvɛlt) *n.* **the.** the high-altitude grassland region of the Transvaal, South Africa.

high wa·ter *n.* **1.** another name for **high tide** (sense 1). **2.** the state of any stretch of water at its highest level, as during a flood. ~Abbrev.: **HW**

high-wa·ter mark *n.* **1. a.** the level reached by sea water at high tide or by other stretches of water in flood. **b.** the mark indicating this level. **2.** the highest point.

high·way ('haɪˌweɪ) *n.* **1.** *Now chiefly U.S. except in legal contexts.* a main road, esp. one that connects towns or cities. **2.** a main route for any form of transport. **3.** a direct path or course.

High·way Code *n.* (in Britain) a booklet compiled by the Department of Transport for the guidance of users of public roads.

high·way·man ('haɪˌweɪmən) *n., pl.* **·men.** (formerly) a robber, usually on horseback, who held up travellers.

high·way rob·ber·y *n. Informal.* blatant overcharging.

high wire *n.* a tightrope stretched high in the air for balancing acts.

High Wy·combe ('wɪkəm) *n.* a town in S central England, in S Buckinghamshire: furniture industry. Pop.: 59 298 (1971).

H.I.H. *abbrev. for* His (*or* Her) Imperial Highness.

hi·jack *or* **high·jack** ('haɪˌdʒæk) *vb.* **1.** (*tr.*) to seize, divert, or appropriate (a vehicle or the goods it carries) while in transit: *to hijack an aircraft.* **2.** to rob (a person or vehicle) by force: *to hijack a traveller.* ~*n.* **3.** the act or an instance of hijacking. [C20: of unknown origin] —**'hi·ˌjack·er** *or* **'high·ˌjack·er** *n.*

Hi·jaz (hiː'dʒæz) *n.* a variant spelling of **Hejaz.**

hike (haɪk) *vb.* **1.** (*intr.*) to walk a long way, usually for pleasure or exercise, esp. in the country. **2.** (usually foll. by *up*) to pull or be pulled; hitch. ~*n.* **3.** a long walk. [C18: of uncertain origin] —**'hik·er** *n.*

hike out *vb.* (*intr., adv.*) *Naut.* the U.S. term for **sit out** (sense 3).

hi·lar·i·ous (hɪ'lɛərɪəs) *adj.* very funny or merry. [C19: from Latin *hilaris* glad, from Greek *hilaros*] —**hi·'lar·i·ous·ly** *adv.* —**hi·'lar·i·ous·ness** *n.*

hi·lar·i·ty (hɪ'lærɪtɪ) *n.* mirth and merriment; cheerfulness.

Hil·a·ry of Poi·tiers ('hɪlərɪ) *n.* **Saint.** ?315–?367 A.D., French bishop, an opponent of Arianism. Feast day: Jan. 13.

Hil·a·ry term *n.* the spring term at Oxford University and some other educational establishments. [C16: named after Saint HILARY of Poitiers]

Hil·bert ('hɪlbɛrt) *n.* **Da·vid.** 1862–1943, German mathematician, who made outstanding contributions to the theories of number fields and invariants and to geometry.

Hil·de·brand ('hɪldəˌbrænd) *n.* the monastic name of **Gregory VII.** —**ˌHil·de·'bran·di·an** *adj., n.* —**'Hil·de·ˌbrand·ine** *adj.*

Hil·des·heim (*German* 'hɪldəsˌhaɪm) *n.* a city in N West Germany, in Lower Saxony: a member of the Hanseatic League. Pop.: 93 400 (1970).

hill (hɪl) *n.* **1. a.** a conspicuous and often rounded natural elevation of the earth's surface, less high or craggy than a mountain. **b.** (*in combination*): *a hillside; a hilltop.* **2. a.** a heap or mound made by a person or animal. **b.** (*in combination*): *a dunghill.* **3.** an incline; slope. **4. hill and dale.** (of gramophone records) having or relating to vertical groove undulations. **5. over the hill.** *Slang.* **a.** beyond one's prime. **b.** *Military.* absent without leave or deserting. ~*vb.* (*tr.*) **6.** to form into a hill or mound. **7.** to cover or surround with a mound or heap of earth. [Old English *hyll;* related to Old Frisian *holla* head, Latin *collis* hill, Low German *hull* hill] —**'hill·er** *n.* —**'hill·y** *adj.*

Hill (hɪl) *n.* **1. Ar·chi·bald Viv·i·an.** 1886–1977, English biochemist, noted for his research into heat loss in muscle contraction: shared the Nobel prize for physiology (1922). **2. Oc·ta·vi·a.** 1838–1912, English housing reformer; a founder of the National Trust. **3.** Sir **Row·land.** 1795–1879, English originator of the penny postage.

Hil·la ('hɪlə) *n.* a market town in central Iraq, on a branch of the Euphrates: built partly of bricks from the nearby site of Babylon. Pop.: 84 704 (1965). Also: **Al Hillah.**

Hil·la·ry ('hɪlərɪ) *n.* Sir **Ed·mund.** born 1919, New Zealand explorer and mountaineer. He and his Sherpa guide, Tenzing Norgay, were the first to reach the summit of Mount Everest (1953).

hill·bil·ly ('hɪlˌbɪlɪ) *n., pl.* **·lies. 1.** *Usually disparaging.* an unsophisticated person, esp. from the mountainous areas in the southeastern U.S. **2.** another name for **country and western.** [from HILL + *Billy* (the nickname)]

hill climb *n.* a competition in which motor vehicles attempt singly to ascend a steep slope as far as possible.

Hil·lel ('hɪlɛl, -ləl) *n.* ?60 B.C.–?9 A.D., rabbi, born in Babylonia; president of the Sanhedrin. He was the first to formulate principles of biblical interpretation.

Hil·le·ry ('hɪlərɪ) *n.* **Pat·rick John.** born 1923, Irish statesman; president of the Republic of Ireland since 1976.

hill·fort ('hɪlˌfɔːt) *n. Archaeol.* a hilltop fortified with ramparts and ditches, dating from the second millennium B.C.

Hil·li·ard ('hɪlɪəd) *n.* **Nich·o·las.** 1537–1619, English miniaturist, esp. of portraits.

Hil·ling·don ('hɪlɪŋdən) *n.* a residential borough of W Greater London. Pop.: 230 800 (1976 est.).

hill my·na *n.* a starling, *Gracula religiosa,* of S and SE Asia: a popular cage bird because of its ability to talk. Also called: **Indian grackle.**

hill·ock ('hɪlək) *n.* a small hill or mound. [C14 *hilloc*] —**'hill·ocked** *or* **'hill·ock·y** *adj.*

hills (hɪlz) *pl. n.* **1. the.** a hilly and often remote region. **2. as old as the hills.** very old.

hill sta·tion *n.* (in northern India, etc.) a settlement or resort at a high altitude.

hilt (hɪlt) *n.* **1.** the handle or shaft of a sword, dagger, etc. **2. to the hilt.** to the full. ~*vb.* **3.** (*tr.*) to supply with a hilt. [Old English; related to Old Norse *hjalt,* Old Saxon *helta* oar handle, Old High German *helza*]

hi·lum ('haɪləm) *n., pl.* **·la** (-lə). **1.** *Botany.* **a.** a scar on the surface of a seed marking its point of attachment to the seed stalk (funicle). **b.** the nucleus of a starch grain. **2.** a rare word for **hilus.** [C17: from Latin: trifle; see NIHIL]

hi·lus ('haɪləs) *n.* a deep fissure or depression on the surface of a bodily organ around the point of entrance or exit of vessels, nerves, or ducts. [C19: via New Latin from Latin: a trifle] —**'hi·lar** *adj.*

Hil·ver·sum ('hɪlvəsəm; *Dutch* 'hɪlvərsym) *n.* a city in the central Netherlands, in North Holland province: Dutch radio and television centre. Pop.: 96 841 (1973 est.).

him (hɪm; *unstressed* ɪm) *pron.* (*objective*) **1.** refers to a male person or animal: *they needed him; she baked him a cake; not him again!* **2.** *Chiefly U.S.* a dialect word for **himself** when used as an indirect object: *he ought to find him a wife.* [Old English *him,* dative of *hē* HE[1]]

Usage. See at **me.**

HIM *or* **H.I.M.** *abbrev. for* His (*or* Her) Imperial Majesty.

Hi·ma·chal Pra·desh (hɪ'mɑːtʃəl prɑː'dɛʃ) *n.* a state of N India, in the W Himalayas: rises to about 6700 m (22 000 ft.) and is densely forested. Capital: Simla. Pop.: 3 460 434 (1971). Area: 55 658 sq. km (21 707 sq. miles).

Him·a·la·yas (ˌhɪmə'leɪəz, hɪ'mɑːljəz) *pl. n.* **the.** a vast mountain system in S Asia, extending 2400 km (1500 miles) from Kashmir (west) to Assam (east), between the valleys of the Rivers Indus and Brahmaputra: covers most of Nepal, Sikkim, Bhutan, and the S edge of Tibet; the highest range in the world, with several peaks over 7500 m (25 000 ft.). Highest peak: Mount Everest, 8848 m (29 028 ft.).

hi·mat·i·on (hɪ'mætɪˌɒn) *n., pl.* **·i·a** (-ɪə). (in ancient Greece) a cloak draped around the body. [C19: from Greek: a little garment, from *heima* dress, from *hennunai* to clothe]

Hi·me·ji ('hiːmɛˌdʒiː) *n.* a city in central Japan, on W Honshu: cotton textile centre. Pop.: 431 691 (1974 est.).

Himm·ler (*German* 'hɪmlər) *n.* **Hein·rich** ('haɪnrɪç). 1900–45, German Nazi leader, head of the SS and the Gestapo (1936–45); committed suicide.

Hims (hɪmz) *n.* a former name of **Homs.**

him·self (hɪm'sɛlf; *medially often* ɪm'sɛlf) *pron.* **1. a.** the reflexive form of *he* or *him.* **b.** (intensifier): *the king himself waved to me.* **2.** (*preceded by a copula*) his normal or usual self: *he seems himself once more.* [Old English *him selfum,* dative singular of *hē self;* see HE[1], SELF]

Usage. See at **myself.**

Him·yar·ite ('hɪmjəˌraɪt) *n.* **1.** a member of an ancient people of SW Arabia, sometimes regarded as including the Sabeans. ~*adj.* **2.** of or relating to this people or their culture. [C19: named after *Himyar* legendary king in ancient Yemen]

Him·yar·it·ic (ˌhɪmjə'rɪtɪk) *n.* **1.** the extinct language of the Himyarites, belonging to the SE Semitic subfamily of the Afro-Asiatic family. ~*adj.* **2.** of, relating to, or using this language.

hin (hɪn) *n.* a Hebrew unit of capacity equal to about 12 pints or 3.5 litres. [from Late Latin, from Greek, from Hebrew *hīn,* from Egyptian *hnw*]

Hi·na·ya·na (ˌhiːnə'jɑːnə) *n.* **a.** any of various early forms of Buddhism. **b.** (*as modifier*): *Hinayana Buddhism.* [from Sanskrit *hīnayāna,* from *hīna* lesser + *yāna* vehicle] —**ˌHi·na·'ya·nist** *n.* —**ˌHi·na·ya·'nis·tic** *adj.*

Hinck·ley ('hɪŋklɪ) *n.* a town in central England, in Leicestershire. Pop.: 47 982 (1971).

hind[1] (haɪnd) *adj.* **hind·er, hind·most** *or* **hin·der·most.** (*prenominal*) (esp. of parts of the body) situated at the back or rear: *a hind leg.* [Old English *hindan* at the back, related to German *hinten;* see BEHIND, HINDER[2]]

hind[2] (haɪnd) *n., pl.* **hinds** *or* **hind. 1.** the female of the deer, esp. the red deer when aged three years or more. **2.** any of several marine serranid fishes of the genus *Epinephelus,* closely related and similar to the groupers. [Old English *hind;* related to Old High German *hinta,* Greek *kemas* young deer, Lithuanian *szmúlas* hornless]

hind³ (haɪnd) *n.* (formerly) **1.** a simple peasant. **2.** (in N Britain) a skilled farm worker. **3.** a steward. [Old English *hīne,* from *hīgna,* genitive plural of *hīgan* servants]

Hind. *abbrev. for:* **1.** Hindi. **2.** Hindu. **3.** Hindustan. **4.** Hindustani.

hind·brain ('haɪndˌbreɪn) *n.* the nontechnical name for **rhombencephalon.**

Hin·de·mith (*German* 'hɪndəˌmɪt) *n.* **Paul** (paʊl). 1895–1963, German composer and musical theorist, who opposed the twelve-tone technique. His works include the song cycle *Das Marienleben* (1923) and the opera *Mathis der Maler* (1938).

Hin·den·burg¹ ('hɪndənˌbʊrk) *n.* the German name for **Zabrze.**

Hin·den·burg² ('hɪndənˌbɜːg; *German* 'hɪndənˌbʊrk) *n.* **Paul von Be·neck·en·dorff und von** ('paʊl fɔn bɛnəkənˌdɔrf ʊnt fɔn). 1847–1934, German field marshal and statesman; president (1925–34). During World War I he directed German strategy together with Ludendorff (1916–18).

Hin·den·burg line *n.* a line of strong fortifications built by the German army near the Franco-Belgian border in 1916–17. [C20: named after P. von HINDENBURG]

hin·der¹ ('hɪndə) *vb.* **1.** to be or get in the way of (someone or something); hamper. **2.** (*tr.*) to prevent. [Old English *hindrian;* related to Old Norse *hindra,* Old High German *hintarōn*] —'**hin·der·er** *n.* —'**hin·der·ing·ly** *adv.*

hind·er² ('haɪndə) *adj.* (*prenominal*) situated at or further towards the back or rear; posterior. [Old English; related to Old Norse *hindri* latter, Gothic *hindar* beyond, Old High German *hintar* behind]

hind·gut ('haɪndˌgʌt) *n.* **1.** the part of the vertebrate digestive tract comprising the colon and rectum. **2.** the posterior part of the digestive tract of arthropods. ~See also **foregut, midgut.**

Hin·di ('hɪndɪ) *n.* **1.** a language or group of dialects of N central India. It belongs to the Indic branch of the Indo-European family and is closely related to Urdu. See also **Hindustani. 2.** a formal literary dialect of this language, the official language of India, usually written in Nagari script. **3.** a person whose native language is Hindi. [C18: from Hindi *hindī,* from *Hind* India, from Old Persian *Hindu* the river Indus]

hind·most ('haɪndˌməʊst) *or* **hin·der·most** ('hɪndəˌməʊst) *adj.* furthest back; last.

Hin·doo ('hɪnduː, hɪn'duː) *n, pl.* **·doos,** *adj.* an older spelling of **Hindu.** —**Hin·doo·ism** ('hɪndʊˌɪzəm) *n.*

hind·quar·ter ('haɪndˌkwɔːtə) *n.* **1.** one of the two back quarters of a carcass of beef, lamb, etc. **2.** (*pl.*) the rear, esp. of a four-legged animal.

hin·drance ('hɪndrəns) *n.* **1.** an obstruction or snag; impediment. **2.** the act of hindering; prevention.

hind·sight ('haɪndˌsaɪt) *n.* **1.** the ability to understand, after something has happened, what should have been done or what caused the event. **2.** a firearm's rear sight.

Hin·du *or* **Hin·doo** ('hɪnduː, hɪn'duː) *n., pl.* **·dus** *or* **·doos. 1.** a person who adheres to Hinduism. **2.** an inhabitant or native of Hindustan or India, esp. one adhering to Hinduism. ~*adj.* **3.** relating to Hinduism, Hindus, or India. [C17: from Persian *Hindū,* from *Hind* India; see HINDI]

Hin·du·ism *or* **Hin·doo·ism** ('hɪndʊˌɪzəm) *n.* the complex of beliefs, values, and customs comprising the dominant religion of India, characterized by the worship of many gods, including Brahma as supreme being, a caste system, belief in reincarnation, etc.

Hin·du Kush (kʊʃ, kuːʃ) *pl. n.* a mountain range in central Asia, extending about 800 km (500 miles) east from the Koh-i-Baba Mountains of central Afghanistan to the Pamirs. Highest peak: Tirich Mir, 7590 m (25 230 ft.).

Hin·du·stan (ˌhɪndʊ'stɑːn) *or* **Hin·do·stan** *n.* **1.** the land of the Hindus, esp. India north of the Deccan and excluding Bengal. **2.** the general area around the Ganges where Hindi is the predominant language. **3.** the areas of India where Hinduism predominates, as contrasted with those areas where Islam predominates.

Hin·du·sta·ni, Hin·doo·sta·ni (ˌhɪndʊ'stɑːnɪ), *or* **Hin·do·sta·ni** *n.* **1.** the dialect of Hindi spoken in Delhi: used as a lingua franca throughout India. **2.** a group of languages or dialects consisting of all spoken forms of Hindi and Urdu considered together. ~*adj.* **3.** of or relating to these languages or Hindustan.

Hines (haɪnz) *n.* **Earl,** known as *Earl Fatha Hines.* born 1905, U.S. jazz pianist and conductor.

hinge (hɪndʒ) *n.* **1.** a device for holding together two parts such that one can swing relative to the other, typically having two interlocking metal leaves held by a pin about which they pivot. **2.** *Anatomy.* a type of joint, such as the knee joint, that moves only backwards and forwards; a joint that functions in only one plane. Technical name: **ginglymus. 3.** something on which events, opinions, etc., turn. **4.** Also called: **mount.** *Philately.* a small thin transparent strip of gummed paper for affixing a stamp to a page. ~*vb.* **5.** (*tr.*) to attach or fit a hinge to (something). **6.** (*intr.;* usually foll. by *on* or *upon*) to depend (on). **7.** (*intr.*) to hang or turn on or as if on a hinge. [C13: probably of Germanic origin; compare Middle Dutch *henge;* see HANG] —'**hinge·less** *adj.* —'**hinge·ˌlike** *adj.* —'**hing·er** *n.*

hin·ny¹ ('hɪnɪ) *n., pl.* **·nies.** the sterile hybrid offspring of a male horse and a female donkey or ass. Compare **mule**¹ (sense 1).

hin·ny² ('hɪnɪ) *vb.* **·nies, ·ny·ing, ·nied.** a less common word for **whinny.**

hin·ny³ ('hɪnɪ) *n. Northern English dialect.* a term of endearment, esp. for a woman or child. [variant of HONEY]

Hin·shel·wood ('hɪnʃəlˌwʊd) *n.* Sir **Cy·ril Nor·man.** 1897–1967, English chemist, who shared the Nobel prize for chemistry (1956) for the study of reaction kinetics.

hint (hɪnt) *n.* **1.** a suggestion or implication given in an indirect or subtle manner: *he dropped a hint.* **2.** a helpful piece of advice or practical suggestion. **3.** a small amount; trace. ~*vb.* **4.** (when *intr.,* often foll. by *at;* when *tr., takes a clause as object*) to suggest or imply indirectly. [C17: of uncertain origin] —'**hint·er** *n.*

hin·ter·land ('hɪntəˌlænd) *n.* **1.** land lying behind something, esp. a coast or the shore of a river. **2.** remote or undeveloped areas of a country. **3.** an area located near and dependent on a large city, esp. a port. [C19: from German, from *hinter* behind + *land* LAND; see HINDER²]

hip¹ *n.* **1.** (*often pl.*) either side of the body below the waist and above the thigh, overlying the lateral part of the pelvis and its articulation with the thighbones. **2.** another name for **pelvis** (sense 1). **3.** short for **hip joint. 4.** the angle formed where two sloping sides of a roof meet or where a sloping side meets a sloping end. [Old English *hype;* related to Old High German *huf,* Gothic *hups,* Dutch *heup*] —'**hip·less** *adj.* —'**hip·ˌlike** *adj.*

hip² (hɪp) *n.* the berry-like brightly coloured fruit of a rose plant: a swollen receptacle, rich in vitamin C, containing several small hairy achenes. Also called: **rosehip.** [Old English *héopa;* related to Old Saxon *hiopo,* Old High German *hiufo,* Dutch *joop,* Norwegian dialect *hjūpa*]

hip³ (hɪp) *interj.* an exclamation used to introduce cheers (in the phrase **hip, hip, hurrah**). [C18: of unknown origin]

hip⁴ (hɪp) *or* **hep** (hɛp) *adj.* **hip·per, hip·pest** *or* **hep·per, hep·pest.** *Slang.* **1.** aware of or following the latest trends in music, ideas, fashion, etc. **2.** (*often postpositive;* foll. by *to*) informed (about). [variant of earlier *hep*]

hip bath *n.* a portable bath in which the bather sits.

hip·bone ('hɪpˌbəʊn) *n.* the nontechnical name for **innominate bone.**

hip flask *n.* a small metal flask for spirits, etc., often carried in a hip pocket.

hip-hug·gers *pl. n. Chiefly U.S.* trousers that begin at the hips instead of the waist. Usual Brit. word: **hipsters.**

hip joint *n.* the ball-and-socket joint that connects each leg to the trunk of the body, in which the head of the femur articulates with the socket (acetabulum) of the pelvis.

hip·parch ('hɪpɑːk) *n.* (in ancient Greece) a cavalry commander. [C17: from Greek *hippos* horse + -ARCH]

Hip·par·chus¹ (hɪ'pɑːkəs) *n.* **1.** 2nd-century B.C. Greek astronomer. He discovered the precession of the equinoxes, calculated the length of the solar year, and developed trigonometry. **2.** died 514 B.C., tyrant of Athens (527–514).

Hip·par·chus² (hɪ'pɑːkəs) *n.* a large crater in the SW quadrant of the moon, about 130 kilometres in diameter.

hip·pe·as·trum (hɪpɪ'æstrəm) *n.* any plant of the South American amaryllidaceous genus *Hippeastrum:* cultivated for their large funnel-shaped typically red flowers. [C19: New Latin, from Greek *hippeus* knight + *astron* star]

hipped¹ (hɪpt) *adj.* **1. a.** having a hip or hips. **b.** (*in combination*): *broad-hipped; low-hipped.* **2.** (esp. of cows, sheep, reindeer, elk, etc.) having an injury to the hip, such as a dislocation of the bones. **3.** *Architect.* having a hip or hips. See also **hipped roof.**

hipped² (hɪpt) *adj.* (*often postpositive;* foll. by *on*) *U.S. slang.* very enthusiastic (about). [C20: from HIP⁴]

hipped roof *n.* a roof having sloping ends and sides.

hip·pie *or* **hip·py** ('hɪpɪ) *n., pl.* **·pies. a.** (esp. during the 1960s) a person whose behaviour, dress, use of drugs, etc., implied a rejection of conventional values. **b.** (*as modifier*): *hippie language.* [C20: see HIP⁴]

hip·po ('hɪpəʊ) *n., pl.* **·pos.** *Informal.* short for **hippopotamus.**

hip·po·cam·pus (ˌhɪpəʊ'kæmpəs) *n., pl.* **·pi** (-paɪ). **1.** a mythological sea creature with the forelegs of a horse and the tail of a fish. **2.** a structure in the floor of the lateral ventricle of the brain, which in cross section has the shape of a sea horse. [C16: from Latin, from Greek *hippos* horse + *kampos* a sea monster] —ˌ**hip·po'cam·pal** *adj.*

hip pock·et *n.* a pocket at the back of a pair of trousers.

hip·po·cras ('hɪpəʊˌkræs) *n.* an old English drink of wine flavoured with spices. [C14 *ypocras,* from Old French: HIPPOCRATES, probably referring to a filter called *Hippocrates' sleeve*]

Hip·poc·ra·tes (hɪ'pɒkrəˌtiːz) *n.* ?460–?377 B.C., Greek physician, commonly regarded as the father of medicine. —ˌ**Hip·po'crat·ic** *or* ˌ**Hip·po'crat·i·cal** *adj.*

Hip·po·crat·ic oath *n.* an oath taken by a doctor to observe a code of medical ethics derived from that of Hippocrates.

Hip·po·crene ('hɪpəʊˌkriːn, ˌhɪpəʊ'kriːnɪ) *n.* a spring on Mount Helicon in Greece, said to engender poetic inspiration. [C17: via Latin from Greek *hippos* horse + *krēnē* spring] —ˌ**Hip·po'cre·ni·an** *adj.*

hip·po·drome ('hɪpəˌdrəʊm) *n.* **1.** a music hall, variety theatre, or circus. **2.** (in ancient Greece or Rome) an open-air course for horse and chariot races. [C16: from Latin *hippodromos,* from Greek *hippos* horse + *dromos* a race]

hip·po·griff *or* **hip·po·gryph** ('hɪpəʊˌgrɪf) *n.* a monster of Greek mythology with a griffin's head, wings, and claws and a

horse's body. [C17: from Italian *ippogrifo,* from *ippo-* horse (from Greek *hippos*) + *grifo* GRIFFIN[1]]
Hip·pol·y·ta (hɪˈpɒlɪtə) *or* **Hip·pol·y·te** (hɪˈpɒlɪˌtiː) *n. Greek myth.* a queen of the Amazons, slain by Hercules in battle for her belt, which he obtained as his ninth labour.
Hip·pol·y·tus (hɪˈpɒlɪtəs) *n. Greek myth.* a son of Theseus, killed after his stepmother Phaedra falsely accused him of raping her. —**Hip+ˈpol·y+tan** *adj.*
Hip·pom·e·nes (hɪˈpɒmɪˌniːz) *n. Greek myth.* the husband, in some traditions, of Atalanta.
hip·po+pot·a+mus (ˌhɪpəˈpɒtəməs) *n., pl.* **+mus·es** *or* **+mi** (-ˌmaɪ). **1.** a very large massive gregarious artiodactyl mammal, *Hippopotamus amphibius,* living in or around the rivers of tropical Africa: family *Hippopotamidae.* It has short legs and a thick skin sparsely covered with hair. **2. pigmy hippopotamus.** a related but smaller animal, *Choeropsis liberiensis.* [C16: from Latin, from Greek *hippopotamos* river horse, from *hippos* horse + *potamos* river]
Hip+po Re+gi·us (ˈhɪpəʊ ˈriːdʒɪəs) *n.* an ancient Numidian city, adjoining present-day Annaba, Algeria. Often shortened to **Hippo.**
hip+py[1] (ˈhɪpɪ) *adj.* **+pi+er, +pi+est.** *Informal.* (esp. of a woman) having large hips.
hip+py[2] (ˈhɪpɪ) *n., pl.* **+pies.** a variant spelling of **hippie.**
hip roof *n.* a roof having sloping ends and sides.
hip+ster (ˈhɪpstə) *n.* **1.** *Slang, now rare.* **a.** a person who follows fashion. **b.** an outmoded word for **hippie. 2.** (*modifier*) (of trousers) cut so that the top encircles the hips.
hip+sters (ˈhɪpstəz) *pl. n. Brit.* trousers cut so that the top encircles the hips. Usual U.S. word: **hip-huggers.**
hi+ra+ga+na (ˌhɪərəˈgɑːnə) *n.* one of the Japanese systems of syllabic writing based on Chinese cursive ideograms. The more widely used of the two current systems, it is employed in newspapers and general literature. Compare **katakana.** [from Japanese: flat kana]
Hi+ram (ˈhaɪərəm) *n.* 10th-century B.C. king of Tyre, who supplied Solomon with materials and craftsmen for the building of the Temple (II Samuel 5:11; I Kings 5:1–18).
hir+cine (ˈhɜːsaɪn, -sɪn) *adj.* **1.** *Archaic.* of or like a goat, esp. in smell. **2.** *Literary.* lustful; lascivious. [C17: from Latin *hircīnus,* from *hircus* goat]
hire (ˈhaɪə) *vb.* (*tr.*) **1.** to acquire the temporary use of (a thing) or the services of (a person) in exchange for payment. **2.** (often foll. by *out*) to provide (something) or the services of (oneself or others) for an agreed payment, usually for an agreed period. **3.** (*tr.;* foll. by *out*) *Chiefly Brit.* to pay independent contractors for (work to be done). ~*n.* **4. a.** the act of hiring or the state of being hired. **b.** (*as modifier*)*: a hire car.* **5. a.** the price paid or payable for a person's services or the temporary use of something. **b.** (*as modifier*)*: the hire charge.* **6. for** *or* **on hire.** available for service or temporary use in exchange for payment. [Old English *hӯrian;* related to Old Frisian *hēra* to lease, Middle Dutch *hūren*] —**ˈhir+a·ble** *or* **ˈhire+a·ble** *adj.* —**ˈhir+er** *n.*
hire+ling (ˈhaɪəlɪŋ) *n. Derogatory.* a person who works only for money, esp. one paid to do something unpleasant. [Old English *hӯrling;* related to Dutch *huurling;* see HIRE, -LING[1]]
hire-pur·chase *n. Brit.* **a.** a system for purchasing merchandise, such as cars or furniture, in which the buyer takes possession of the merchandise on payment of a deposit and completes the purchase by paying a series of regular instalments while the seller retains ownership until the final instalment is paid. **b.** (*as modifier*)*: hire-purchase legislation.* Abbrev.: **H.P., h.p.** U.S. equivalent: **instalment buying.**
hi·ri Mo·tu (ˈhɪərɪ ˈməʊtuː) *n.* another name for **Motu** (the language).
Hi·ro·hi·to (ˌhɪərəʊˈhiːtəʊ) *n.* born 1901, emperor of Japan since 1926. In 1946 he became a constitutional monarch.
Hi·ro·shi·ge (ˌhɪərəʊˈʃiːgeɪ) *n.* **An·do** (ˈɑːndəʊ). 1797–1858, Japanese artist, esp. of colour wood-block prints.
Hi+ro+shi+ma (ˌhɪrɒˈʃiːmə, hɪˈrɒʃɪmə) *n.* a port in SW Japan, on SW Honshu on the delta of the Ota River: largely destroyed on August 6, 1945, by the first atomic bomb to be used in warfare, dropped by the U.S., which killed over 75 000 of its inhabitants. Pop.: 761 240 (1974 est.).
hir+sute (ˈhɜːsjuːt) *adj.* **1.** covered with hair. **2.** (of plants or their parts) covered with long but not stiff hairs. **3.** *Informal.* (of a person) having long, thick, or untrimmed hair. [C17: from Latin *hirsūtus* shaggy; related to Latin *horrēre* to bristle, *hirtus* hairy; see HORRID] —**ˈhir+sute+ness** *n.*
hir·u·din (hɪˈruːdɪn) *n. Med.* an anticoagulant extracted from the mouth glands of leeches. [C20: from Latin *hirudin-, hirudo* leech + -IN]
hi+run+dine (hɪˈrʌndɪn, -daɪn) *adj.* **1.** of or resembling a swallow. **2.** belonging to the bird family *Hirundinidae,* which includes swallows and martins. [C19: from Late Latin *hirundineus,* from Latin *hirundō* a swallow]
his (hɪz; *unstressed* ɪz) *determiner.* **1. a.** of, belonging to, or associated with him: *his own fault; his knee; I don't like his being out so late.* **b.** (*as pronoun*)*: his is on the left; that book is his.* **2. his and hers.** (of paired objects) for a man and woman respectively. ~*pron.* **3. of his.** belonging to or associated with him. [Old English *his,* genitive of *hē* HE[1] and of *hit* IT]
His+pan·i·a (hɪˈspænɪə) *n.* the Iberian peninsula in the Roman world.
His+pan+ic (hɪˈspænɪk) *adj.* relating to, characteristic of, or derived from Spain or the Spanish.
His+pan·i·cism (hɪˈspænɪˌsɪzəm) *n.* a word or expression borrowed from Spanish or modelled on the form of a Spanish word or expression.
His+pan·i·cize *or* **His+pan·i·cise** (hɪˈspænɪˌsaɪz) *vb.* (*tr.*) to make Spanish, as in custom or culture; bring under Spanish control or influence. —**His+ˈpan·i+ˌcist** *n.* —**His+ˌpan·i·ci+ˈza+tion** *or* **His+ˌpan·i+ci+ˈsa+tion** *n.*
His+pan·io+la (ˌhɪspənˈjəʊlə; *Spanish* ˌispaˈɲola) *n.* the second largest island in the West Indies, in the Greater Antilles: divided politically into Haiti and the Dominican Republic; discovered in 1492 by Christopher Columbus, who named it La Isla Española. Area: 18 703 sq. km (29 418 sq. miles). Former name: **Santo Domingo.**
his+pid (ˈhɪspɪd) *adj. Biology.* covered with stiff hairs or bristles. [C17: from Latin *hispidus* bristly] —**his+ˈpid+i+ty** *n.*
hiss (hɪs) *n.* **1.** a voiceless fricative sound like that of a prolonged *s.* **2.** such a sound uttered as an exclamation of derision, contempt, etc., esp. by an audience or crowd. **3.** *Electronics.* receiver noise with a continuous spectrum, caused by thermal agitation, shot noise, etc. ~*interj.* **4.** an exclamation of derision or disapproval. ~*vb.* **5.** (*intr.*) to produce or utter a hiss. **6.** (*tr.*) to express with a hiss, usually to indicate derision or anger. **7.** (*tr.*) to show derision or anger towards (a speaker, performer, etc.) by hissing. [C14: of imitative origin] —**ˈhiss+er** *n.*
hist (hɪst) *interj.* an exclamation used to attract attention or as a warning to be silent.
hist. *abbrev. for:* **1.** histology. **2.** historical. **3.** history.
his+tam·i+nase (hɪˈstæmɪˌneɪs) *n.* an enzyme, occurring in the digestive system, that inactivates histamine by removal of its amino group. Also called: **diamine oxidase.**
his+ta+mine (ˈhɪstəˌmiːn, -mɪn) *n.* an amine formed from histidine and released by the body tissues in allergic reactions, causing irritation. It also stimulates gastric secretions, dilates blood vessels, and contracts smooth muscle. Formula: $C_5H_9N_3$. See also **antihistamine.** [C20: from HIST(IDINE) + -AMINE] —**his+ta+min+ic** (ˌhɪstəˈmɪnɪk) *adj.*
his+ti+dine (ˈhɪstɪˌdiːn, -dɪn) *n.* a sweet-tasting crystalline amino acid that occurs in most proteins: a precursor of histamine. Formula: $C_3H_3N_2CH_2CH(NH_2)COOH$.
his+ti·o+cyte (ˈhɪstɪəˌsaɪt) *n. Physiol.* a macrophage that occurs in connective tissue. [from Greek *histion* a little web, from *histos* web + -CYTE] —**his+ti·o+cyt+ic** (ˌhɪstɪəˈsɪtɪk) *adj.*
his+to- *or before a vowel* **hist-** *combining form.* indicating animal or plant tissue: *histology; histamine.* [from Greek, from *histos* web]
his+to+chem+is+try (ˌhɪstəʊˈkɛmɪstrɪ) *n.* the chemistry of tissues, such as liver and bone, often studied with the aid of a microscope. —ˌ**his+to+ˈchem·i+cal** *adj.*
his+to+gen (ˈhɪstəˌdʒɛn) *n.* any of several distinct regions in a plant that differentiate to produce new tissue.
his+to+gen+e·sis (ˌhɪstəʊˈdʒɛnɪsɪs) *or* **his+tog+e+ny** (hɪˈstɒdʒənɪ) *n.* the formation of tissues and organs from undifferentiated cells. —**his+to+ge·net+ic** (ˌhɪstəʊdʒəˈnɛtɪk) *or* ˌ**his+to+ˈgen+ic** *adj.* —ˌ**his+to+ge·ˈnet·i·cal+ly** *or* ˌ**his+to+ˈgen·i+cal+ly** *adv.*
his+to+gram (ˈhɪstəˌgræm) *n.* a figure that represents a frequency distribution, consisting of contiguous rectangles whose width is in proportion to the class interval under consideration and whose height is the associated frequency. [C20: from HISTO(RY) + -GRAM]
his+toid (ˈhɪstɔɪd) *adj.* (esp. of a tumour) **1.** resembling normal tissue. **2.** composed of one kind of tissue.
his+tol·o·gy (hɪˈstɒlədʒɪ) *n.* **1.** the study, esp. the microscopic study, of the tissues of an animal or plant. **2.** the structure of a tissue or organ. —**his+to+log·i+cal** (ˌhɪstəˈlɒdʒɪkᵊl) *or* ˌ**his+to+ˈlog·ic** *adj.* —ˌ**his+to+ˈlog·i·cal+ly** *adv.* —**his+ˈtol·o·gist** *n.*
his+tol·y·sis (hɪˈstɒlɪsɪs) *n.* the disintegration of organic tissues. —**his+to+lyt+ic** (ˌhɪstəˈlɪtɪk) *adj.* —ˌ**his+to+ˈlyt·i+cal+ly** *adv.*
his+tone (ˈhɪstəʊn) *n.* any of a group of simple water-soluble strongly basic proteins present in cell nuclei in association with nucleic acids.
his+to+pa+thol+o·gy (ˌhɪstəʊpəˈθɒlədʒɪ) *n.* the study of the microscopic structure of diseased tissues. —**his+to+path·o+log·i·cal** (ˌhɪstəʊˌpæθəˈlɒdʒɪkᵊl) *adj.*
his+to+plas+mo+sis (ˌhɪstəʊplæzˈməʊsɪs) *n.* a severe fungal disease of the lungs caused by *Histoplasma capsulatum.*
his+to+ri·an (hɪˈstɔːrɪən) *n.* a person who writes or studies history, esp. one who is an authority on it.
his+to+ri+at+ed (hɪˈstɔːrɪˌeɪtɪd) *adj.* decorated with flowers or animals. Also: **storiated.** [C19: from Medieval Latin *historiāre* to tell a story in pictures, from Latin *historia* story]
his+tor+ic (hɪˈstɒrɪk) *adj.* **1.** famous or likely to become famous in history; significant. **2.** a less common word for **historical** (senses 1–5). **3.** Also: **secondary.** *Linguistics.* (of Latin, Greek, or Sanskrit verb tenses) referring to past time.
Usage. In careful usage, a distinction is made between *historic* (important, significant) and *historical* (pertaining to history): *a historic decision; a historical perspective.*
his+tor·i·cal (hɪˈstɒrɪkᵊl) *adj.* **1.** belonging to or typical of the study of history: *historical methods.* **2.** concerned with or treating of events of the past: *historical accounts.* **3.** based on or constituting factual material as distinct from legend or supposition. **4.** based on or inspired by history: *a historical novel.* **5.** occurring or prominent in history. **6.** a less common word for **historic** (sense 1). —**his+ˈtor·i·cal+ly** *adv.* —**his+ˈtor·i·cal+ness** *n.*
Usage. See at **historic.**
his+tor·i·cal lin+guis+tics *n.* the study of language as it

changes in the course of time, with a view either to discovering general principles of linguistic change or to establishing the correct genealogical classification of particular languages. Also called: **diachronic linguistics.** Compare **descriptive linguistics.**

his+tor·i+cal ma+te·ri+al+ism *n.* the part of Marxist theory maintaining that social structures derive from economic structures and that these are transformed as a result of class struggles, each ruling class producing another, which will overcome and destroy it, the final phase being the emergence of a communist society.

his+tor·i+cal meth+od *n.* a means of learning about something by considering its origins and development.

his+tor·i+cal pres+ent *n.* the present tense used to narrate past events, usually employed in English for special effect or in informal use, as in *a week ago I'm walking down the street and I see this accident.*

his+tor·i+cal school *n.* **1.** a group of 19th century German economists who maintained that modern economies evolved from historical institutions. **2.** the school of jurists maintaining that laws are based on social and historical circumstances rather than made by a sovereign power.

his+tor+ic e·pis+co+pate *n. Eccles.* the derivation of the episcopate of a Church in historic succession from the apostles.

his+tor·i+cism (hɪ'stɒrɪ,sɪzəm) *n.* **1.** the belief that natural laws govern historical events. **2.** the theory that social and cultural phenomena are historically determined and that each period in history has its own values, inapplicable to other periods. **3.** excessive emphasis on history, historicism, past styles, etc. —**his+'tor·i+cist** *n., adj.*

his+to+ric+i·ty (,hɪstə'rɪsɪtɪ) *n.* historical authenticity.

his+to+ri+og+ra+pher (hɪ,stɔ:rɪ'ɒgrəfə) *n.* **1.** a historian, esp. one concerned with historical method and the writings of other historians. **2.** a historian employed to write the history of a group or public institution.

his+to+ri+og+ra+phy (,hɪstɔ:rɪ'ɒgrəfɪ) *n.* **1.** the writing of history. **2.** the study of the development of historical method, historical research, and writing. **3.** any body of historical literature. —**his+to+ri+o+graph+ic** (hɪ,stɔ:rɪə'græfɪk) *adj.*

his+to+ry ('hɪstərɪ, 'hɪstrɪ) *n., pl.* **+ries. 1. a.** a record or account, often chronological in approach, of past events, developments, etc. **b.** (*as modifier*): *a history book; a history play.* **2.** all that is preserved or remembered of the past, esp. in written form. **3.** the discipline of recording and interpreting past events involving human beings. **4.** past events, esp. when considered as an aggregate. **5.** an event in the past, esp. one that has been forgotten or reduced in importance: *their quarrel was just history.* **6.** the past, background, previous experiences, etc., of a thing or person: *the house had a strange history.* **7.** a play that depicts or is based on historical events. **8.** a narrative relating the events of a character's life: *the history of Joseph Andrews.* ~Abbrev. (for senses 1,2,3): **hist.** [C15: from Latin *historia,* from Greek: enquiry, from *historein* to narrate, from *histōr* judge]

his+tri+on+ic (,hɪstrɪ'ɒnɪk) *or* **his+tri+on·i+cal** *adj.* **1.** excessively dramatic, insincere, or artificial: *histrionic gestures.* **2.** *Now rare.* dramatic. ~*n.* **3.** (*pl.*) melodramatic displays of temperament. **4.** *Rare.* (*pl., functioning as sing.*) dramatics. [C17: from Late Latin *histriōnicus* of a player, from *histriō* actor] —**,his+tri+'on·i+cal+ly** *adv.*

hit (hɪt) *vb.* **hits, hit+ting, hit.** (*mainly tr.*) **1.** (*also intr.*) to deal (a blow or stroke) to (a person or thing); strike: *the man hit the child.* **2.** to come into violent contact with: *the car hit the tree.* **3.** to reach or strike with a missile, thrown object, etc.: *to hit a target.* **4.** to make or cause to make forceful contact; knock or bump: *I hit my arm on the table.* **5.** to propel or cause to move by striking: *to hit a ball.* **6.** *Cricket.* to score (runs). **7.** to affect (a person, place, or thing) suddenly or adversely: *his illness hit his wife very hard.* **8.** to achieve or reach: *to hit the jackpot; unemployment hit a new high.* **9.** to experience or encounter: *I've hit a slight snag here.* **10.** *U.S. slang.* to murder (a rival criminal) in fulfilment of an underworld contract or vendetta. **11.** to accord or suit (esp. in the phrase **hit one's fancy**). **12.** to guess correctly or find out by accident: *you have hit the answer.* **13.** *Informal.* to set out on (a road, path, etc.): *let's hit the road.* **14.** *Informal.* to arrive or appear in: *he will hit town tomorrow night.* **15.** *Informal, chiefly U.S.* to demand or request from: *he hit me for a pound.* **16.** *Slang, chiefly U.S.* to drink an excessive amount of (alcohol): *to hit the bottle.* **17. hit it.** *Music, slang.* start playing. **18. hit the sack** (*or* **hay**). *Slang.* to go to bed. ~*n.* **19.** an impact or collision. **20.** a shot, blow, etc., that reaches its object. **21.** an apt, witty, or telling remark. **22.** *Informal.* **a.** a person or thing that gains wide appeal: *she's a hit with everyone.* **b.** (*as modifier*): *a hit record.* **23.** *Informal.* a stroke of luck. **24.** *U.S. slang.* a murder carried out as the result of an underworld vendetta or rivalry. **25.** *Slang.* a successful injection of heroin. **26. make** (*or* **score**) **a hit with.** *Informal.* to make a favourable impression on. ~See also **hit off, hit on, hit out.** [Old English *hittan,* from Old Norse *hitta*]

hit-and-run *adj.* (*prenominal*) **1. a.** involved in or denoting a motor-vehicle accident in which the driver leaves the scene without stopping to give assistance, inform the police, etc. **b.** (*as n.*): *a hit-and-run.* **2.** (of an attack, raid, etc.) relying on surprise allied to a rapid departure from the scene of operations for the desired effect: *hit-and-run tactics.* **3.** *Baseball.* denoting a play in which a base runner begins to run as the pitcher throws the ball to the batter.

hitch (hɪtʃ) *vb.* **1.** to fasten or become fastened with a knot or tie, esp. temporarily. **2.** (often foll. by *up*) to connect (a horse, team, etc.); harness. **3.** (*tr.;* often foll. by *up*) to pull up (the trousers, a skirt, etc.) with a quick jerk. **4.** (*intr.*) *Chiefly U.S.* to move in a halting manner: *to hitch along.* **5.** to entangle or become entangled: *the thread was hitched on the reel.* **6.** (*tr.; passive*) *Informal.* to marry (esp. in the phrase **get hitched**). **7.** *Informal.* to obtain (a ride or rides) by hitchhiking. ~*n.* **8.** an impediment or obstacle, esp. one that is temporary or minor: *a hitch in the proceedings.* **9.** a knot for fastening a rope to posts, other ropes, etc., that can be undone by pulling against the direction of the strain that holds it. **10.** a sudden jerk; tug; pull: *he gave it a hitch and it came loose.* **11.** *Chiefly U.S.* a hobbling gait: *to walk with a hitch.* **12.** a device used for fastening. **13.** *Informal.* a ride obtained by hitchhiking. **14.** *U.S. slang.* a period of time spent in prison, in the army, etc. [C15: of uncertain origin] —**'hitch+er** *n.*

Hitch·cock ('hɪtʃkɒk) *n.* Sir **Al·fred (Joseph).** 1889-1980, English film director, noted for his mastery in creating suspense. His films include *The Thirty-Nine Steps* (1935), *Rebecca* (1940), *Psycho* (1960), and *The Birds* (1963).

hitch+hike ('hɪtʃ,haɪk) *vb.* (*intr.*) to travel by obtaining free lifts in motor vehicles. —**'hitch+,hik·er** *n.*

hitch+ing post *n.* a post or rail to which the reins of a horse, etc., are tied.

hith+er ('hɪðə) *adv.* **1.** Also (archaic): **hith·er+ward, hith·er+wards.** to or towards this place (esp. in the phrase **come hither**). **2. hither and thither.** this way and that, as in a state of confusion. ~*adj.* **3.** *Archaic or dialect.* (of a side or part, esp. of a hill or valley) nearer; closer. [Old English *hider;* related to Old Norse *hethra* here, Gothic *hidrē,* Latin *citrā* on this side, *citrō*]

hith·er+most ('hɪðə,məʊst) *adj. Now rare.* nearest to this place or in this direction.

hith·er+to ('hɪðə'tu:) *adv.* **1.** until this time: *hitherto, there have been no problems.* **2.** *Archaic.* to this place or point.

Hit·ler ('hɪtlə) *n.* **1. A·dolf** ('a:dɒlf). 1889–1945, German dictator, born in Austria. After becoming president of the National Socialist German Workers' Party (Nazi party), he attempted to overthrow the government of Bavaria (1923). While in prison he wrote *Mein Kampf,* expressing his philosophy of the superiority of the Aryan race and the inferiority of the Jews. He was appointed chancellor of Germany (1933), transforming it from a democratic republic into the totalitarian Third Reich, of which he became Führer in 1934. He established concentration camps to exterminate the Jews, rearmed the Rhineland (1936), annexed Austria (1938) and Czechoslovakia and invaded Poland (1939), which precipitated World War II. He committed suicide. **2.** a person who displays dictatorial characteristics.

Hit+ler+ism ('hɪtlə,rɪzəm) *n.* the policies, principles, and methods of the Nazi party as developed by Adolf Hitler.

hit man *n. Chiefly U.S.* a hired assassin, esp. one employed by gangsters.

hit off *vb.* **1.** (*tr., adv.*) to represent or mimic accurately. **2. hit it off.** *Informal.* to have a good relationship with.

hit on *vb.* (*prep.*) **1.** (*tr.*) to strike. **2.** (*intr.*) Also: **hit upon.** to discover unexpectedly or guess correctly.

hit or miss *adj.* (**hit-or-miss** *when prenominal*) *Informal.* random; casual; haphazard: *his judgment is rather hit or miss; a hit-or-miss system.* Also: **hit and miss.**

hit out *vb.* (*intr., adv.;* often foll. by *at*) **1.** to direct a blow. **2.** to make a verbal attack (upon someone).

hit+ter ('hɪtə) *n.* **1.** *Informal.* a boxer who has a hard punch rather than skill or finesse. **2.** a person who hits something.

Hit+tite ('hɪtaɪt) *n.* **1.** a member of an ancient people of Anatolia, who built a great empire in N Syria and Asia Minor in the second millennium B.C. **2.** the extinct language of this people, deciphered from cuneiform inscriptions found at Boğazköy and elsewhere. It is clearly related to the Indo-European family of languages, although the precise relationship is disputed. ~*adj.* **3.** of or relating to this people, their civilization, or their language.

hive (haɪv) *n.* **1.** a structure in which social bees live and rear their young. **2.** a colony of social bees. **3.** a place showing signs of great industry (esp. in the phrase **a hive of activity**). **4.** a teeming crowd; multitude. **5.** an object in the form of a hive. ~*vb.* **6.** to cause (bees) to collect or (of bees) to collect inside a hive. **7.** to live or cause to live in or as if in a hive. **8.** (*tr.*) (of bees) to store (honey, pollen, etc.) in the hive. **9.** (*tr.;* often foll. by *up* or *away*) to store, esp. for future use: *he used to hive away a small sum every week.* [Old English *hӯf;* related to Westphalian *hüwe,* Old Norse *hūfr* ship's hull, Latin *cūpa* barrel, Greek *kupē,* Sanskrit *kūpa* cave] —**'hive+,like** *adj.*

hive bee *n.* another name for a **honeybee.**

hive dross *n.* another name for **propolis.**

hive off *vb.* (*adv.*) **1.** to transfer or be transferred from a larger group or unit. **2.** (*usually tr.*) to transfer (profitable activities of a nationalized industry) back to private ownership.

hives (haɪvz) *n. Pathol.* a nontechnical name for **urticaria.** [C16: of uncertain origin]

H.J. (on gravestones, etc.) *abbrev. for* hic jacet. [Latin: here lies]

H.J.S. (on gravestones, etc.) *abbrev. for* hic jacet sepultus. [Latin: here lies buried]

HK *international car registration for* Hong Kong.

HKJ *international car registration for* (Hashemite Kingdom of) Jordan.

hl *abbrev. for* hectolitre.

H.L. (in Britain) *abbrev. for* House of Lords.

hm *abbrev. for* hectometre.

H.M. *abbrev. for:* **1.** His (*or* Her) Majesty. **2.** headmaster; headmistress.

h'm (*spelling pron.* hmmm) *interj.* used to indicate hesitation, doubt, assent, pleasure, etc.

H.M.A.S. *abbrev. for* His (*or* Her) Majesty's Australian Ship.

H.M.I. (in Britain) *abbrev. for* Her Majesty's Inspector; a government official who examines and supervises schools.

H.M.S. *abbrev. for:* **1.** His (*or* Her) Majesty's Service. **2.** His (*or* Her) Majesty's Ship.

H.M.S.O. (in Britain) *abbrev. for* His (*or* Her) Majesty's Stationery Office.

H.N.C. (in Britain) *abbrev. for* Higher National Certificate; a qualification recognized by many national technical and professional institutions.

H.N.D. (in Britain) *abbrev. for* Higher National Diploma; a qualification in technical subjects equivalent to an ordinary degree.

ho (həʊ) *interj.* **1.** Also: **ho-ho.** an imitation or representation of the sound of a deep laugh. **2.** an exclamation used to attract attention, announce a destination, etc.: *what ho! land ho! westward ho!* [C13: of imitative origin; compare Old Norse *hó,* Old French *ho!* halt!]

Ho *the chemical symbol for* holmium.

HO *or* **H.O.** *abbrev. for:* **1.** head office. **2.** *Brit. government.* Home Office.

ho. *abbrev. for* house.

ho+ac+tzin (həʊ'æktsɪn) *n.* a variant spelling of **hoatzin.**

Hoad (həʊd) *n.* **Lew(is) A.,** born 1934, Australian tennis player.

hoar (hɔː) *n.* **1.** short for **hoarfrost.** ~*adj.* **2.** *Rare.* covered with hoarfrost. **3.** *Archaic.* a poetic variant of **hoary.** [Old English *hār,* related to Old Norse *hārr,* Old High German *hēr,* Old Slavonic *sěrŭ* grey]

hoard (hɔːd) *n.* **1.** an accumulated store hidden away for future use. **2.** a cache of ancient coins, treasure, etc. ~*vb.* **3.** to gather or accumulate (a hoard). [Old English *hord;* related to Old Norse *hodd,* Gothic *huzd,* German *Hort,* Swedish *hydda* hut] —**'hoard+er** *n.*

hoard+ing ('hɔːdɪŋ) *n.* a large board used for displaying advertising posters, as by a road. Also called (esp. U.S.): **billboard.** [C19: from C15 *hoard* fence, from Old French *hourd* palisade, of Germanic origin, related to Gothic *haurds,* Old Norse *hurth* door]

hoar+frost ('hɔːˌfrɒst) *n.* a deposit of needle-like ice crystals formed on the ground by direct condensation at temperatures below freezing point. Also called: **white frost.**

hoar+hound ('hɔːˌhaʊnd) *n.* a variant spelling of **horehound.**

hoarse (hɔːs) *adj.* **1.** gratingly harsh or raucous in tone. **2.** low, harsh, and lacking in intensity: *a hoarse whisper.* **3.** having a husky voice, as through illness, shouting, etc. [C14: of Scandinavian origin; related to Old Norse *hās,* Old Saxon *hēs*] —**'hoarse+ly** *adv.* —**'hoarse+ness** *n.*

hoars+en ('hɔːs^{ə}n) *vb.* to make or become hoarse.

hoar·y ('hɔːrɪ) *adj.* **hoar·i+er, hoar·i+est. 1.** having grey or white hair. **2.** white or whitish-grey in colour. **3.** ancient or venerable. —**'hoar·i+ly** *adv.* —**'hoar·i+ness** *n.*

hoar·y cress *n.* a perennial cruciferous Mediterranean plant, *Cardaria* (or *Lepidium*) *draba,* with small white flowers: a widespread troublesome weed.

hoatch+ing ('həʊtʃɪŋ) *adj. Scot.* infested; swarming: *this food's hoatching with flies.* [of unknown origin]

ho+at+zin (həʊ'ætsɪn) *or* **ho+act+zin** *n.* a unique South American gallinaceous bird, *Opisthocomus hoazin,* with a brownish plumage, a very small crested head, and clawed wing digits in the young: family *Opisthocomidae.* [C17: from American Spanish, from Nahuatl *uatzin* pheasant]

hoax (həʊks) *n.* **1.** a deception, esp. a practical joke. ~*vb.* **2.** (*tr.*) to deceive or play a joke on (someone). [C18: probably from HOCUS] —**'hoax+er** *n.*

hob[1] (hɒb) *n.* **1.** a shelf beside an open fire, for keeping kettles, etc., hot. **2.** a steel pattern used in forming a mould or die in cold metal. **3.** a hard steel rotating cutting tool used in machines for cutting gears. ~*vb.* **hobs, hob+bing, hobbed. 4.** (*tr.*) to cut or form with a hob. [C16: variant of obsolete *hubbe,* of unknown origin; perhaps related to HUB]

hob[2] (hɒb) *n.* **1.** a hobgoblin or elf. **2. raise** *or* **play hob.** *Informal.* to cause mischief or disturbance. [C14: variant of *Rob,* short for *Robin* or *Robert*] —**'hob+ˌlike** *adj.*

Ho+bart ('həʊbɑːt) *n.* a port in Australia, capital of the island state of Tasmania on the estuary of the Derwent: excellent natural harbour; University of Tasmania (1890). Pop.: 164 010 (1975 est.).

Hob·be·ma ('hɒbɪmə; *Dutch* 'hɔbəˌmaː) *n.* **Mein·dert** ('maɪndərt). 1638–1709, Dutch painter of peaceful landscapes, usually including a watermill.

Hobbes (hɒbz) *n.* **Thom·as.** 1588–1679, English political philosopher. His greatest work is the *Leviathan* (1651), which contains his exposition of absolute sovereignty. —**'Hobbes+i·an** *n., adj.*

Hob+bism ('hɒbɪzəm) *n.* the mechanistic political philosophy of Hobbes, which stresses the necessity for a powerful sovereign to control human beings. —**'Hob+bist** *n.*

hob+ble ('hɒb^{ə}l) *vb.* **1.** (*intr.*) to walk with a lame awkward movement. **2.** (*tr.*) to fetter the legs of (a horse) in order to restrict movement. **3.** to progress unevenly or with difficulty. ~*n.* **4.** a strap, rope, etc., used to hobble a horse. **5.** a limping gait. **6.** *Brit. dialect.* a difficult or embarrassing situation. ~Also (for senses 2, 4): **hopple.** [C14: probably from Low German; compare Flemish *hoppelen,* Middle Dutch *hobbelen* to stammer] —**'hob+bler** *n.*

hob·ble+de·hoy (ˌhɒb^{ə}ldɪ'hɔɪ) *n. Archaic or dialect.* a clumsy or bad-mannered youth. [C16: from earlier *hobbard de hoy,* of uncertain origin]

hob+ble skirt *n.* a long skirt, popular between 1910 and 1914, cut so narrow at the ankles that it hindered walking.

Hobbs (hɒbz) *n.* Sir **John Ber·ry,** known as *Jack Hobbs.* 1882–1963, English cricketer: scored 197 centuries.

hob+by[1] ('hɒbɪ) *n., pl.* **+bies. 1.** an activity pursued in spare time for pleasure or relaxation. **2.** *Archaic or dialect.* a small horse or pony. **3.** short for **hobbyhorse** (sense 1). **4.** an early form of bicycle, without pedals. [C14 *hobyn,* probably variant of proper name *Robin;* compare DOBBIN] —**'hob+by+ist** *n.*

hob+by[2] ('hɒbɪ) *n., pl.* **+bies.** any of several small Old World falcons, esp. the European *Falco subbuteo,* formerly used in falconry. [C15: from Old French *hobet,* from *hobe* falcon; probably related to Middle Dutch *hobbelen* to roll, turn]

hob·by+horse ('hɒbɪˌhɔːs) *n.* **1.** a toy consisting of a stick with a figure of a horse's head at one end. **2.** another word for **rocking horse. 3.** a figure of a horse attached to a performer's waist in a pantomime, morris dance, etc. **4.** a favourite topic or obsessive fixed idea (esp. in the phrase **on one's hobbyhorse).** ~*vb.* **5.** (*intr.*) *Nautical.* (of a vessel) to pitch violently. [C16: from HOBBY[1], originally a small horse, hence sense 3; then generalized to apply to any pastime]

hob+gob·lin (hɒb'gɒblɪn) *n.* **1.** an evil or mischievous goblin. **2.** bogy. [C16: from HOB[2] + GOBLIN]

hob+nail ('hɒbˌneɪl) *n.* **a.** a short nail with a large head for protecting the soles of heavy footwear. **b.** (*as modifier*): *hobnail boots.* [C16: from HOB[1] (in the archaic sense: peg) + NAIL] —**'hob+ˌnailed** *adj.*

hob+nob ('hɒbˌnɒb) *vb.* **+nobs, +nob+bing, +nobbed.** (*intr.;* often foll. by *with*) **1.** to socialize or talk informally. **2.** *Obsolete.* to drink (with). [C18: from *hob or nob* to drink to one another in turns, hence, to be familiar, ultimately from Old English *habban* to HAVE + *nabban* not to have]

ho·bo ('həʊbəʊ) *n., pl.* **·bos** *or* **·boes.** *Chiefly U.S.* **1.** a tramp; vagrant. **2.** a migratory worker, esp. an unskilled labourer. [C19 (U.S.): origin unknown] —**'ho·bo+ism** *n.*

Ho+bo+ken ('həʊbəʊkən) *n.* a city in N Belgium, in Antwerp province, on the River Scheldt. Pop.: 33 693 (1970).

hob·son-job·son (ˌhɒbs^{ə}n'dʒɒbs^{ə}n) *n.* another word for **folk etymology.** [C19: Anglo-Indian folk-etymological variant of Arabic *yā Hasan! yā Husayn!* O Hasan! O Husain! (ritual lament for the grandsons of Mohammed); influenced by the surnames *Hobson* and *Jobson*]

Hob·son's choice *n.* the choice of taking what is offered or nothing at all. [C16: named after Thomas *Hobson* (1544–1631), English liveryman who gave his customers no choice but had them take the nearest horse]

Hoch+hei+mer ('hɒkˌhaɪmə; *German* 'hoːxˌhaɪmər) *n.* a German white wine from the area around Hochheim near Mainz. Also called: **Hochheim.**

Hoch·huth (*German* 'hoːxhuːt) *n.* **Rolf** (rɔlf). born 1931, Swiss dramatist. His best-known works are the controversial documentary drama *The Representative* (1963), on the papacy's attitude to the Jews in World War II, and *Soldiers* (1967).

Ho Chi Minh ('həʊ 'tʃiː 'mɪn) *n.* original name *Nguyen That Tan.* 1890–1969, Vietnamese statesman; president of North Vietnam (1954–69). He headed the Vietminh (1941), which won independence for Vietnam from the French (1954).

Ho Chi Minh Cit·y *n.* a port in S Vietnam, 97 km (60 miles) from the South China Sea, on the Saigon River: captured by the French in 1859; merged with adjoining Cholon in 1932; capital of the former Republic of Vietnam (South Vietnam) from 1954 to 1976; university (1917); U.S. headquarters during the Vietnam War. Pop.: 3 460 500 (1976 est.). Former name (until 1976): **Saigon.**

hock[1] (hɒk) *n.* **1.** the joint at the tarsus of a horse or similar animal, pointing backwards and corresponding to the human ankle. **2.** the corresponding joint in domestic fowl. ~*vb.* **3.** another word for **hamstring.** [C16: short for *hockshin,* from Old English *hōhsinu* heel sinew]

hock[2] (hɒk) *n.* **1.** any of several white wines from the German Rhine. **2.** (*not in technical usage*) any dry white wine. [C17: short for obsolete *hockamore* HOCHHEIMER]

hock[3] (hɒk) *Informal, chiefly U.S.* ~*vb.* **1.** (*tr.*) to pawn or pledge. ~*n.* **2.** the state of being in pawn (esp. in the phrase **in hock**). **3. in hock. a.** in prison. **b.** in debt. [C19: from Dutch *hok* prison, debt] —**'hock+er** *n.*

hock+ey ('hɒkɪ) *n.* **1.** Also called (esp. U.S.): **field hockey. a.** a game played on a field by two opposing teams of 11 players each, who try to hit a ball into their opponents' goal using long sticks curved at the end. **b.** (*as modifier*): *hockey stick; hockey ball.* **2.** See **ice hockey.** [C19: from earlier *hawkey,* of unknown origin]

Hock·ney ('hɒknɪ) *n.* **Da·vid.** born 1937, English painter, best known for his etchings, such as those to Cavafy's poems (1966), naturalistic portraits such as *Mr. and Mrs. Clark and Percy* (1971), and for paintings of water, swimmers, and swimming pools.

Hock+tide ('hɒkˌtaɪd) *n. Brit. hist.* a former festival celebrated on the second Monday and Tuesday after Easter. [C15: from *hock-, hoke-* (of unknown origin) + TIDE[1]]

ho+cus ('həʊkəs) *vb.* **+cus·es, +cus+ing, +cused** *or* **+cus·es, +cus+sing, +cussed.** (*tr.*) *Now rare.* **1.** to take in; trick. **2.** to stupefy, esp. with a drug. **3.** to add a drug to (a drink).

ho·cus-po·cus ('həʊkəs'pəʊkəs) *n.* **1.** trickery or chicanery. **2.** mystifying jargon. **3.** an incantation used by conjurers or magicians when performing tricks. **4.** conjuring skill or practice. ~*vb.* **·cus·es, ·cus·ing, ·cused** *or* **·cus·es, ·cus·sing, ·cussed. 5.** to deceive or trick (someone). [C17: perhaps a dog-Latin formation invented by jugglers]

hod (hɒd) *n.* **1.** an open wooden box attached to a pole, for carrying bricks, mortar, etc. **2.** a tall narrow coal scuttle. [C14: perhaps alteration of C13 dialect *hot,* from Old French *hotte* pannier, creel, probably from Germanic]

hod car+ri+er *n.* a labourer who carries the materials in a hod for a mason, etc. Also called: **hodman.**

hod+den ('hɒdᵊn) *or* **hod+din** ('hɒdɪn) *n.* a coarse homespun cloth produced in Scotland: **hodden grey** is made by mixing black and white wools. [C18: Scottish, of obscure origin]

Ho+dei+da (hɒ'deɪdə) *n.* the chief port of Yemen, on the Red Sea. Pop.: 90 000 (1970 est.).

hodge+podge ('hɒdʒˌpɒdʒ) *n.* a variant spelling (esp. U.S.) of **hotchpotch.**

Hodg·kin ('hɒdʒkɪn) *n.* **1. Al·an Lloyd.** born 1914, English physiologist. With A. F. Huxley, he explained the conduction of nervous impulses in terms of the physical and chemical changes involved: shared the Nobel prize for medicine and physiology (1963). **2. Dor·o·thy Crow·foot.** born 1910, English chemist and crystallographer, who determined the three-dimensional structure of insulin: Nobel prize for chemistry 1964.

Hodg·kin's dis+ease *n.* a malignant disease characterized by enlargement of the lymph nodes, spleen, and liver. Also called: **lymphoadenoma, lymphogranulomatosis.** [C19: named after Thomas *Hodgkin* (1798–1866), London physician, who first described it]

hod+man ('hɒdmən) *n., pl.* **+men.** *Brit.* another name for a **hod carrier.**

ho+dom+e·ter (hɒ'dɒmɪtə) *n. U.S.* another name for **odometer.** —**ho+'dom+e·try** *n.*

hod·o+scope ('hɒdəˌskəʊp) *n. Physics.* any device for tracing the path of a charged particle, esp. a particle found in cosmic rays. [from Greek *hodos* way, path + -SCOPE]

hoe (həʊ) *n.* **1.** any of several kinds of long-handled hand implement equipped with a light blade and used to till the soil, eradicate weeds, etc. ~*vb.* **hoes, hoe+ing, hoed. 2.** to dig, scrape, weed, or till (surface soil) with or as if with a hoe. [C14: via Old French *houe* from Germanic: compare Old High German *houwā, houwan* to HEW, German *Haue* hoe] —**'ho·er** *n.* —**'hoe+ˌlike** *adj.*

hoe+down ('həʊˌdaʊn) *n. U.S.* **1.** a boisterous square dance. **2.** a party at which hoedowns are danced.

hoe in *vb. (intr., adv.) Austral. informal.* to eat food heartily.

hoe in·to *vb. (intr., prep.) Austral. informal.* to eat (food) heartily.

Hoek van Hol+land ('hu:k fɑn 'hɔlɑnt) *n.* the Dutch name for the **Hook of Holland.**

Ho+fei ('həʊ'feɪ) *n.* a city in SE China, capital of Anhwei province: administrative and commercial centre in a rice and cotton growing region. Pop.: 630 000 (1970 est.).

Hof·manns·thal (*German* 'ho:fmansˌta:l) *n.* **Hu·go von** ('hu:go fɔn). 1874–1929, Austrian lyric poet and dramatist, noted as the librettist for Richard Strauss' operas, esp. *Der Rosenkavalier* (1911), *Elektra* (1909), and *Ariadne auf Naxos* (1912).

Ho+fuf (hʊ'fu:f) *n.* another name for **Al Hufuf.**

hog (hɒg) *n.* **1.** a domesticated pig, esp. a castrated male weighing more than 102 kg. **2.** *U.S.* any artiodactyl mammal of the family *Suidae;* pig. **3.** Also: **hog+get** ('hɒgɪt), **hogg.** *Brit. dialect.* a sheep up to the age of one year that has yet to be sheared. **4.** *Informal.* a selfish, greedy or slovenly person. **5.** *Nautical.* a stiff brush, for scraping a vessel's bottom. **6.** *Nautical.* the amount or extent to which a vessel is hogged. Compare **sag** (sense 6). **7.** another word for **camber** (def. 4). **8. go the whole hog.** *Slang.* to do something thoroughly or unreservedly. ~*vb.* **hogs, hog+ging, hogged. 9.** *Slang.* to take more than one's share of. **10.** *(tr.)* to arch (the back) like a hog. **11.** *(tr.)* to cut (the mane) of (a horse) very short. [Old English *hogg,* from Celtic; compare Cornish *hoch*] —**'hog+ger** *n.* —**'hog+ˌlike** *adj.*

ho+gan ('həʊgən) *n.* a wooden dwelling covered with earth, typical of the Navaho Indians. [from Navaho]

Ho+garth ('həʊgɑ:θ) *n.* **Wil·liam.** 1697–1764, English engraver and painter. He is noted particularly for his series of engravings satirizing the vices and affectations of his age, such as *A Rake's Progress* (1735) and *Marriage à la Mode* (1745). —**Ho+'garth+i+an** *adj.*

hog+back ('hɒgˌbæk) *n.* **1.** Also called: **hog's back.** a narrow ridge with sides that consist of steeply inclined rock strata. **2.** *Archaeol.* a Saxon or Scandinavian tomb with sloping sides.

hog badg+er *n.* a SE Asian badger, *Arctonyx collaris,* with a piglike mobile snout. Also called: **sand badger.**

hog chol·e·ra *n.* the U.S. term for **swine fever.**

hog+fish ('hɒgˌfɪʃ) *n., pl.* **+fish** *or* **+fish·es. 1.** a wrasse, *Lachnolaimus maximus,* that occurs in the Atlantic off the SE coast of North America. The head of the male resembles a pig's snout. **2.** another name for **pigfish** (sense 1).

Hogg (hɒg) *n.* **James,** called *the Ettrick Shepherd.* 1770–1835, Scottish poet. His works include the volume of poems *The Queen's Wake* (1813).

hogged (hɒgd) *adj. Nautical.* (of a vessel) having a keel that droops at both ends. Compare **sag** (sense 6).

hog+gish ('hɒgɪʃ) *adj.* selfish, gluttonous, or dirty. —**'hog+gish+ly** *adv.* —**'hog+gish+ness** *n.*

Hog+ma+nay (ˌhɒgmə'neɪ) *n. (sometimes not cap.)* **a.** New Year's Eve in Scotland. **b.** *(as modifier): a Hogmanay party.* See also **first-foot.** [C17: Scottish and Northern English, of uncertain origin]

hog+nosed skunk ('hɒgˌnəʊzd) *n.* any of several American skunks of the genus *Conepatus,* esp. *C. leuconotus,* having a broad snoutlike nose.

hog+nose snake ('hɒgˌnəʊz) *n.* any North American non-venomous colubrid snake of the genus *Heterodon,* having a trowel-shaped snout and inflating the body when alarmed. Also called: **puff adder.**

hog+nut ('hɒgˌnʌt) *n.* another name for **pignut** (sense 1).

hog pea+nut *n.* a North American leguminous climbing plant, *Amphicarpa bracteata,* having fleshy curved one-seeded pods, which ripen in or on the ground.

hog's fen+nel *n.* any of several Eurasian umbelliferous marsh plants of the genus *Peucedanum,* esp. *P. officinale,* having clusters of small whitish flowers.

hogs+head ('hɒgzˌhɛd) *n.* **1.** a unit of capacity, used esp. for alcoholic beverages. It has several values, being 54 imperial gallons in the case of beer and 52.5 imperial gallons in the case of wine. **2.** a large cask used for shipment of wines and spirits. [C14: of obscure origin]

hog+tie ('hɒgˌtaɪ) *vb.* **+ties, +ty+ing, +tied.** *(tr.) Chiefly U.S.* **1.** to tie together the legs or the arms and legs of. **2.** to impede, hamper, or thwart.

Hogue (*French* ɔg) *n.* See **La Hogue.**

hog+wash ('hɒgˌwɒʃ) *n.* **1.** nonsense. **2.** pigswill.

hog+weed ('hɒgˌwi:d) *n.* any of several coarse weedy plants, esp. cow parsnip.

Ho+hen+lin+den (*German* ˌho:ən'lɪndᵊn) *n.* a village in S West Germany, in Bavaria east of Munich: scene of the defeat of the Austrians by the French during the Napoleonic Wars (1800).

Ho·hen·lo·he ('həʊənˌləʊə; *German* ˌho:ən'lo:ə) *n.* **Chlod·wig** ('klo:tvɪç), Prince of Hohenlohe-Schillingsfürst. 1819–1901, Prussian statesman; chancellor of the German empire (1894–1900).

Ho·hen·stau·fen ('həʊənˌʃtaʊfən *German* ˌho:ən'ʃtaufᵊn) *n.* a German princely family that provided rulers of Germany (1138–1208, 1215–54), Sicily (1194–1268), and the Holy Roman Empire (1138–1254).

Ho·hen·zol·lern ('həʊənˌzɒlən; *German* ˌho:ən'tsɔlərn) *n.* a German noble family the younger (Franconian) branch of which provided rulers of Brandenburg (1417–1701) and Prussia (1701–1918). The last kings of Prussia (1871–1918) were also emperors of Germany.

hoick (hɔɪk) *vb.* to rise or raise abruptly and sharply: *to hoick an aircraft.* [C20: of unknown origin]

hoicks (hɔɪks) *interj.* a cry used to encourage hounds to hunt. Also: **yoicks.**

hoi+den ('hɔɪdᵊn) *n., adj., vb.* a variant spelling of **hoyden.** —**'hoi+den+ish** *adj.* —**'hoi+den+ish+ness** *n.*

hoi pol+loi ('hɔɪ pə'lɔɪ) *n.* **the.** *Often derogatory.* the masses; common people. [Greek, literally: the many]

hoist (hɔɪst) *vb.* **1.** *(tr.)* to raise or lift up, esp. by mechanical means. **2. hoist with one's own petard.** See **petard** (sense 2). ~*n.* **3.** any apparatus or device for hoisting. **4.** the act of hoisting. **5.** *Nautical.* **a.** the amidships height of a sail bent to the yard with which it is hoisted. Compare **drop** (sense 13). **b.** the difference between the set and lowered positions of this yard. **6.** *Nautical.* the length of the luff of a fore-and-aft sail. **7.** *Nautical.* a group of signal flags. **8.** the inner edge of a flag next to the staff. Compare **fly**[1] (sense 25a). [C16: variant of *hoise,* probably from Low German; compare Dutch *hijschen,* German *hissen*] —**'hoist+er** *n.*

hoi·ty-toi·ty (ˌhɔɪtɪ'tɔɪtɪ) *adj. Informal.* arrogant or haughty. [C17: rhyming compound based on C16 *hoit* to romp, of obscure origin]

hoke (həʊk) *vb. (tr.;* usually foll. by *up)* to overplay (a part, etc.). [C20: perhaps from HOKUM]

ho+key co+key ('həʊkɪ 'kəʊkɪ) *n.* a Cockney song with a traditional dance routine to match the words.

ho·key-po·key (ˌhəʊkɪ'pəʊkɪ) *n.* another word for **hocus-pocus** (senses 1, 2).

Hok+kai+do (hɒ'kaɪdəʊ) *n.* the second largest and northernmost of the four main islands of Japan, separated from Honshu by the Tsugaru Strait and from the island of Sakhalin, Soviet Union, by La Pérouse Strait: constitutes an autonomous administrative division. Capital: Sapporo. Pop.: 5 184 287 (1970). Area: 78 508 sq. km (30 312 sq. miles).

hok+ku ('hɒku:) *n., pl.* **+ku.** *Prosody.* another word for **haiku.** [from Japanese, from *hok* beginning + *ku* hemistich]

ho+kum ('həʊkəm) *n. U.S. slang.* **1.** claptrap; bunk. **2.** obvious or hackneyed material of a sentimental nature in a play, film, etc. [C20: probably a blend of HOCUS-POCUS and BUNKUM]

Ho·ku·sai ('həʊkuˌsaɪ, ˌhəʊkʊ'saɪ) *n.* **Kat·su·shi·ka** (ˌkætsu:'ʃi:kɑ). 1760–1849, Japanese artist, noted for the draughtsmanship of his colour wood-block prints, which influenced the impressionists.

hol- *combining form.* variant of **holo-** before a vowel.

Hol+arc+tic (hɒ'lɑ:ktɪk) *adj.* of or denoting a zoogeographical region consisting of the Palaearctic and Nearctic regions. [C19: from HOLO- + ARCTIC]

Hol·bein (*German* 'hɔlbaɪn) *n.* **1. Hans** (hans), called *the Elder.* 1465–1524, German painter. **2.** his son, **Hans,** called *the Younger.* 1497–1543, German painter and engraver; court painter to Henry VIII of England (1536–43). He is noted particularly for his portraits, such as those of Erasmus (1524; 1532) and Sir Thomas More (1526).

hold[1] (həʊld) *vb.* **holds, hold+ing, held. 1.** to have or keep (an object) with or within the hands, arms, etc.; clasp. **2.** *(tr.)* to support or bear: *to hold a drowning man's head above water.* **3.** to maintain or be maintained in a specified state or condition: *to hold one's emotions in check; hold firm.* **4.** (*tr.*) to set aside or reserve: *they will hold our tickets until tomorrow.* **5.** (when *intr., usually used in commands*) to restrain or be restrained from motion, action, departure, etc.: *hold that man until the police come.* **6.** (*intr.*) to remain fast or unbroken: *that cable won't hold much longer.* **7.** (*intr.*) (of the weather) to remain dry and bright: *how long will the weather hold?* **8.** (*tr.*) to keep the attention of: *her singing held the audience.* **9.** (*tr.*) to engage in or carry on: *to hold a meeting.* **10.** (*tr.*) to have the ownership, possession, etc., of: *he holds a law degree from London; who's holding the ace of spades?* **11.** (*tr.*) to have the use of or responsibility for: *to hold the office of director.* **12.** (*tr.*) to have the space or capacity for: *the carton will hold only eight books.* **13.** (*tr.*) to be able to control the outward effects of drinking beer, spirits, etc.: *he can hold his drink well.* **14.** (often foll. by *to* or *by*) to remain or cause to remain committed to: *hold him to his promise; he held by his views in spite of opposition.* **15.** (*tr.; takes a clause as object*) to claim: *he holds that the theory is incorrect.* **16.** (*intr.*) to remain relevant, valid, or true: *the old philosophies don't hold nowadays.* **17.** (*tr.*) to keep in the mind: *to hold affection for someone.* **18.** (*tr.*) to regard or consider in a specified manner: *I hold him very dear.* **19.** (*tr.*) to guard or defend successfully: *hold the fort against the attack.* **20.** (*intr.*) to continue to go: *hold on one's way.* **21.** (sometimes foll. by *on*) *Music.* to sustain the sound of (a note) throughout its specified duration: *to hold on a semibreve for its full value.* **22.** (*tr.*) *Computer technol.* to retain (data) in a storage device after copying onto another storage device or onto another location in the same device. Compare **clear** (sense 49). **23. hold (good) for.** to apply or be relevant to: *the same rules hold for everyone.* **24. hold it! a.** stop! wait! **b.** stay in the same position! as when being photographed. **25. hold one's head high.** to conduct oneself in an arrogant and bold manner. **26. hold one's own. a.** to maintain one's position: *the fort held its own against several assaults.* **b.** to be sufficiently competent: *she can't hold her own in the top class.* **27. hold one's peace** *or* **tongue.** *Informal.* to be silent. **28. hold water.** to stand up to scrutiny or examination. **29. there is no holding him.** he is so spirited or resolute that he cannot be restrained. ~*n.* **30.** the act or method of holding fast or grasping, as with the hands. **31.** something to hold onto, as for support or control. **32.** an object or device that holds fast or grips something else so as to hold it fast. **33.** controlling force or influence: *she has a hold on him.* **34.** a short delay or pause. **35.** a prison or a cell in a prison. **36.** *Wrestling.* a way of seizing one's opponent: *a wrist hold.* **37.** *Music.* a pause or fermata. **38. a.** a tenure or holding, esp. of land. **b.** (*in combination*): *leasehold; freehold; copyhold.* **39.** a container. **40.** *Archaic.* a fortified place. **41. get hold of. a.** to obtain. **b.** to come into contact with. **42. no holds barred.** all limitations removed. ~See also **hold back, hold down, hold forth, hold in, hold off, hold on, hold out, hold over, hold together, hold-up, hold with.** [Old English *healdan;* related to Old Norse *halla,* Gothic *haldan,* German *halten*] —**'hold·a·ble** *adj.*

hold² (həʊld) *n.* the space in a ship or aircraft for storing cargo. [C16: variant of HOLE]

hold·all ('həʊldˌɔːl) *n. Brit.* a large strong bag or basket. Usual U.S. name: **carryall.**

hold back *vb.* (*adv.*) **1.** to restrain or be restrained. **2.** (*tr.*) to withhold: *he held back part of the payment.* ~*n.* **hold·back. 3.** a strap of the harness joining the breeching to the shaft, so that the horse can hold back the vehicle. **4.** something that restrains or hinders.

hold down *vb.* (*tr., adv.*) **1.** to restrain or control. **2.** *Informal.* to manage to retain or keep possession of: *to hold down two jobs at once.*

hold·en ('həʊldən) *vb. Archaic or dialect.* a past participle of **hold**¹.

hold·er ('həʊldə) *n.* **1.** a person or thing that holds. **2. a.** a person, such as an owner, who has possession or control of something. **b.** (*in combination*): *householder.* **3.** *Law.* a person who has possession of a bill of exchange, cheque, or promissory note that he is legally entitled to enforce. —**'hold·er·ˌship** *n.*

Höl·der·lin (*German* 'hœldərliːn) *n.* **Frie·drich** ('friːdrɪç). 1770–1843, German lyric poet, whose works include the poems *Menon's Lament for Diotima* and *Bread and Wine* and the novel *Hyperion* (1797–99).

hold·fast ('həʊldˌfɑːst) *n.* **1. a.** the act of gripping strongly. **b.** such a grip. **2.** any device used to secure an object, such as a hook, clamp, etc. **3.** the organ of attachment of a seaweed or related plant.

hold forth *vb.* (*adv.*) **1.** (*intr.*) to speak for a long time or in public. **2.** (*tr.*) to offer (an attraction or enticement).

hold in *vb.* (*tr., adv.*) **1.** to curb, control, or keep in check. **2.** to conceal or restrain (feelings).

hold·ing ('həʊldɪŋ) *n.* **1.** land held under a lease and used for agriculture or similar purposes. **2.** (*often pl.*) property to which the holder has legal title, such as land, stocks, shares, and other investments. **3.** *Sport.* the obstruction of an opponent with the hands or arms, esp. in boxing.

hold·ing com·pa·ny *n.* a company with controlling shareholdings in one or more other companies.

hold·ing pad·dock *n. Austral.* a paddock in which cattle or sheep are kept temporarily, as before shearing, etc.

hold·ing pat·tern *n.* the oval or circular path of an aircraft flying around an airport awaiting permission to land.

hold off *vb.* (*adv.*) **1.** (*tr.*) to keep apart or at a distance. **2.** (*intr.;* often foll. by *from*) to refrain (from doing something): *he held off buying the house until prices fell slightly.*

hold on *Informal.* ~*vb.* (*intr., adv.*) **1.** to maintain a firm grasp: *she held on with all her strength.* **2.** to continue or persist. **3.** (foll. by *to*) to keep or retain: *hold on to those stamps as they'll soon be valuable.* **4.** to keep a telephone line open. ~*interj.* **5.** stop! wait!

hold out *vb.* (*adv.*) **1.** (*tr.*) to offer or present. **2.** (*intr.*) to last or endure. **3.** (*intr.*) to continue to resist or stand firm, as a city under siege or a person refusing to succumb to persuasion. **4.** *Chiefly U.S.* to withhold (something due or expected). **5. hold out for.** *Informal.* to wait patiently or uncompromisingly for (the fulfilment of one's demands). **6. hold out on.** *Informal.* to delay in or keep from telling (a person) some new or important information.

hold o·ver *vb.* (*tr., mainly adv.*) **1.** to defer consideration of or action on. **2.** to postpone for a further period. **3.** to prolong (a note, chord, etc.) from one bar to the next. **4.** (*prep.*) to intimidate (a person) with (a threat). ~*n.* **hold·o·ver.** *U.S. informal.* **5.** an elected official who continues in office after his term has expired. **6.** a performer or performance continuing beyond the original engagement.

hold to·geth·er *vb.* (*adv.*) **1.** to cohere or remain or cause to cohere or remain in one piece: *your old coat holds together very well.* **2.** to stay or cause to stay united: *the children held the family together.*

hold-up *n.* **1.** a robbery, esp. an armed one. **2.** a delay; stoppage. **3.** *U.S.* an excessive charge; extortion. ~*vb.* **hold up.** (*adv.*) **4.** (*tr.*) to delay; hinder: *we were held up by traffic.* **5.** (*tr.*) to keep from falling; support. **6.** (*tr.*) to stop forcibly or waylay in order to rob, esp. using a weapon. **7.** (*tr.*) to exhibit or present: *he held up his achievements for our admiration.* **8.** (*intr.*) to survive or last: *how are your shoes holding up?* **9.** *Bridge.* to refrain from playing a high card, so delaying the establishment of (a suit).

hold with *vb.* (*intr., prep.*) to support; approve of.

hole (həʊl) *n.* **1.** an area hollowed out in a solid. **2.** an opening made in or through something. **3.** an animal's hiding place or burrow. **4.** *Informal.* an unattractive place, such as a town or a dwelling. **5.** *Informal.* a cell or dungeon. **6.** *U.S. informal.* a small anchorage. **7.** a fault: *he picked holes in my argument.* **8.** *Slang.* a difficult and embarrassing situation. **9.** the cavity in various games into which the ball must be thrust. **10.** (on a golf course) **a.** the cup on each of the greens. **b.** each of the divisions of a course (usually 18) represented by the distance between the tee and a green. **c.** the score made in striking the ball from the tee into the hole. **11.** *Physics.* **a.** a vacancy in a normally filled band of electron energies that behaves as a carrier of charge and is mathematically equivalent to a positron. **b.** (*as modifier*): *hole current.* **12. hole in the wall.** *Informal.* a small dingy place, esp. one difficult to find. **13. in the hole. a.** in debt. **b.** (of a card, the **hole card,** in stud poker) dealt face down in the first round. **14. make a hole in.** to consume or use a great amount of (food, drink, money, etc.): *to make a hole in a bottle of brandy.* ~*vb.* **15.** to make a hole or holes in (something). **16.** (when *intr.,* often foll. by *out*) *Golf.* to hit (the ball) into the hole. [Old English *hol;* related to Gothic *hulundi,* German *Höhle,* Old Norse *hylr* pool, Latin *caulis* hollow stem; see HOLLOW] —**'hole·y** *adj.*

hole-and-cor·ner *adj.* (*usually prenominal*) *Informal.* furtive or secretive.

hole in one *Golf.* ~*n.* **1.** a shot from the tee that finishes in the hole. Compare **birdie.** ~*vb.* **2.** (*intr.*) to score a hole in one. ~Also (esp. U.S.): **ace.**

hole in the heart *n.* a defect of the heart in which there is an abnormal opening in any of the walls dividing the four heart chambers.

hole up *vb.* (*intr., adv.*) *Chiefly U.S.* **1.** (of an animal) to hibernate, esp. in a cave. **2.** to hide or remain secluded. **3.** to score a hole in one.

Hol·guín (*Spanish* ol'ɣin) *n.* a city in NE Cuba, in Oriente province: trading centre. Pop.: 131 656 (1970).

hol·i·day ('hɒlɪˌdeɪ, -dɪ) *n.* **1.** (*often pl.*) *Chiefly Brit.* **a.** a period in which a break is taken from work or studies for rest, travel, or recreation. U.S. word: **vacation. b.** (*as modifier*): *a holiday mood.* **2.** a day on which work is suspended by law or custom, such as a religious festival, bank holiday, etc. Related adj.: **ferial. 3.** any of several festivals commemorating major events in Israelite or Jewish history or days connected with such festivals. ~*vb.* **4.** (*intr.*) *Chiefly Brit.* to spend a holiday. [Old English *hāligdæg,* literally: holy day]

Hol·i·day ('hɒlɪdeɪ) *n.* **Bil·lie.** original name *Eleanora Fagen;* known as *Lady Day.* 1915-59, U.S. jazz singer.

hol·i·day camp *n. Brit.* a place, esp. one at the seaside, providing accommodation, recreational facilities, etc., for holiday-makers.

hol·i·day-mak·er *n. Brit.* a person who goes on holiday. U.S. equivalents: **vacationer, vacationist.**

hol·i·er-than-thou *adj.* (*usually prenominal*) annoyingly self-righteous or smug: *a holier-than-thou attitude.*

ho·li·ly ('həʊlɪlɪ) *adv.* in a holy, devout, or sacred manner.

ho·li·ness ('həʊlɪnɪs) *n.* the state or quality of being holy.

Ho·li·ness ('həʊlɪnɪs) *n.* (preceded by *his* or *your*) a title once given to all bishops, but now reserved for the pope.

Hol·in·shed ('hɒlɪnˌʃɛd) *or* **Hol·ing·shed** *n.* **Raph·a·el.** died ?1580, English chronicler. His *Chronicles of England, Scotland, and Ireland* (1577) provided material for Shakespeare's historical and legendary plays.

ho·lism ('həʊlɪzəm) *n. Philosophy.* the idea that the whole is greater than the sum of its parts. [C20: from HOLO- + -ISM] —**ho+'lis+tic** *adj.* —**ho+'lis+ti+cal+ly** *adv.*

Hol+kar State (hɒl'kɑː) *n.* a former state of central India, ruled by the Holkar dynasty of Maratha rulers of Indore (18th century until 1947).

hol+land ('hɒlənd) *n.* a coarse linen cloth, used esp. for furnishing. [C15: after HOLLAND[1], where it was made]

Hol+land[1] ('hɒlənd) *n.* **1.** another name for the **Netherlands. 2.** a county of the Holy Roman Empire, corresponding to the present-day North and South Holland provinces of the Netherlands. **3. Parts of.** an area in E England constituting a former administrative division of Lincolnshire.

Hol·land[2] ('hɒlənd) *n.* Sir **Sid·ney George.** 1893–1961, New Zealand statesman; prime minister of New Zealand (1949–57).

hol+lan+daise sauce (ˌhɒlən'deɪz, 'hɒlənˌdeɪz) *n.* a rich sauce of egg yolks, butter, vinegar, etc., served esp. with fish. [C19: from French *sauce hollandaise* Dutch sauce]

Hol+land+er ('hɒləndə) *n.* another name for a **Dutchman.**

Hol+lan+di·a (hɒ'lændɪə) *n.* a former name of **Djajapura.**

Hol+lands ('hɒləndz) *n.* Dutch gin, often sold in stone bottles. [C18: from Dutch *hollandsch genever*]

hol+ler ('hɒlə) *Informal.* ~*vb.* **1.** to shout or yell (something). ~*n.* **2.** a shout; call. [variant of C16 *hollow,* from *holla,* from French *holà* stop! (literally: ho there!)]

Hol·li·ger (*German* 'hɔlɪgə) *n.* Heinz ('haɪnts). born 1939, West German oboist.

hol+lo ('hɒləʊ) *or* **hol+la** ('hɒlə) *n., pl.* **+los** *or* **+las.** *interj.* **1.** a cry for attention, or of encouragement. ~*vb.* **2.** (*intr.*) to shout. [C16: from French *holà* ho there!]

hol+low ('hɒləʊ) *adj.* **1.** having a hole, cavity, or space within; not solid. **2.** having a sunken area; concave. **3.** recessed or deeply set: *hollow eyes.* **4.** (of sounds) as if resounding in a hollow place. **5.** without substance or validity. **6.** hungry or empty. **7.** insincere; cynical. **8. a hollow leg** *or* **hollow legs.** the capacity to eat a lot without getting fat. **9. beat (someone) hollow.** *Brit. informal.* to defeat thoroughly and convincingly. ~*n.* **10.** a cavity, opening, or space in or within something. **11.** a depression or dip in the land. ~*vb.* (often foll. by *out,* usually when *tr.*) **12.** to make or become hollow. **13.** to form (a hole, cavity, etc.) or (of a hole, etc.) to be formed. [C12: from *holu,* inflected form of Old English *holh* cave; related to Old Norse *holr,* German *hohl;* see HOLE] —**'hol+low+ly** *adv.* —**'hol+low+ness** *n.*

hol·low-back *n. Pathol.* the nontechnical name for **lordosis.** Compare **hunchback.**

hol+ly ('hɒlɪ) *n., pl.* **+lies. 1.** any tree or shrub of the genus *Ilex,* such as the Eurasian *I. aquifolium,* having bright red berries and shiny evergreen leaves with prickly edges. **2.** branches of any of these trees, used for Christmas decorations. **3. holly oak.** another name for **holm oak.** ~See also **sea holly.** [Old English *holegn;* related to Old Norse *hulfr,* Old High German *hulis,* German *Hulst,* Old Slavonic *kolja* prick]

Hol·ly ('hɒlɪ) *n.* **Bud·dy.** original name *Charles Hardin Holley.* 1936–59, U.S. rock-and-roll singer, guitarist, and songwriter. His hits (all 1956–59) include *That'll be the Day, Maybe Baby, Peggy Sue, Oh Boy, Think it over,* and *It doesn't matter any more.*

hol+ly+hock ('hɒlɪˌhɒk) *n.* a tall widely cultivated malvaceous plant, *Althaea rosea,* with stout hairy stems and spikes of white, yellow, red, or purple flowers. Also called (U.S.): **rose mallow.** [C16: from HOLY + *hock,* from Old English *hoc* mallow]

Hol+ly+wood ('hɒlɪːˌwʊd) *n.* **1.** a NW suburb of Los Angeles, California: centre of the American film industry. **2. a.** the American film industry. **b.** (*as modifier*): *a Hollywood star.*

holm[1] (həʊm) *n. Dialect, chiefly northwestern English.* **1.** an island in a river or lake. **2.** low flat land near a river. [Old English *holm* sea, island; related to Old Saxon *holm* hill, Old Norse *holmr* island, Latin *culmen* tip]

holm[2] (həʊm) *n.* **1.** short for **holm oak. 2.** *Chiefly Brit.* a dialect word for **holly.** [C14: variant of obsolete *holin,* from Old English *holegn* HOLLY]

Holmes (həʊmz) *n.* **1. Ol·i·ver Wen·dell.** 1809–94, U.S. author, esp. of humorous essays, such as *The Autocrat of the Breakfast Table* (1858) and its sequels. **2.** his son, **Ol·i·ver Wen·dell.** 1841–1935, U.S. jurist, noted for his liberal judgments.

hol+mic ('hɒlmɪk) *adj.* of or containing holmium.

hol+mi·um ('hɒlmɪəm) *n.* a malleable silver-white metallic element of the lanthanide series. Symbol: Ho; atomic no.: 67; atomic wt.: 164.93; valency: 3; relative density: 8.80; melting pt.: 1461°C; boiling pt.: 2600°C (approx.). [C19: from New Latin *Holmia* Stockholm]

holm oak *n.* an evergreen Mediterranean oak tree, *Quercus ilex,* with prickly leaves resembling holly. Also called: **holm, holly oak, ilex.**

hol·o- *or before a vowel* **hol-** *combining form.* whole or wholly: *holograph; holotype; Holarctic.* [from Greek *holos*]

hol·o+blas+tic (ˌhɒlə'blæstɪk) *adj. Embryol.* of or showing cleavage of the entire zygote into blastomeres, as in eggs with little yolk. Compare **meroblastic.** —ˌ**hol·o+'blas+ti+cal+ly** *adv.*

Hol·o+caine ('hɒləˌkeɪn) *n.* a trademark for **phenacaine.**

hol·o+caust ('hɒləˌkɔːst) *n.* **1.** great destruction or loss of life or the source of such destruction, esp. fire. **2.** a rare word for **burnt offering.** [C13: from Late Latin *holocaustum* whole burnt offering, from Greek *holokauston,* from HOLO- + *kaustos,* from *kaiein* to burn] —ˌ**hol·o+'caus+tal** *or* ˌ**hol·o+'caus+tic** *adj.*

Hol·o+cene ('hɒləˌsiːn) *adj.* **1.** of, denoting, or formed in the second and most recent epoch of the Quaternary period, which began 10 000 years ago at the end of the Pleistocene. ~*n.* **2. the.** the Holocene epoch or rock series. ~Also: **Recent.**

hol·o+crine ('hɒləkrɪn) *adj.* (of the secretion of glands) characterized by disintegration of the entire glandular cell in releasing its product, as in sebaceous glands. Compare **merocrine, apocrine.** [C20: from HOLO- + Greek *krinein* to separate, decide]

hol·o+en+zyme (ˌhɒləʊ'ɛnzaɪm) *n.* an active enzyme consisting of a protein component (apoenzyme) and its coenzyme.

Hol·o·fer·nes (ˌhɒlə'fɜːniːz, hə'lɒfəˌniːz) *n.* the Assyrian general, who was killed by the biblical heroine Judith.

hol·o+graph ('hɒləˌgræf, -ˌgrɑːf) *n.* **a.** a book or document handwritten by its author; original manuscript; autograph. **b.** (*as modifier*): *a holograph document.*

ho+log+ra+phy (hɒ'lɒgrəfɪ) *n.* the science or practice of producing a photographic record (**hologram**) by illuminating the object with coherent light and, without using lenses, exposing a film to light reflected from this object and to a direct beam of the coherent light. When interference patterns on the film are illuminated by the coherent light a three-dimensional image is produced. —**hol·o+graph+ic** (ˌhɒlə'græfɪk) *adj.* —ˌ**hol·o+'graph+i+cal+ly** *adv.*

hol·o+he+dral (ˌhɒlə'hiːdrəl) *adj.* (of a crystal) exhibiting all the planes required for the symmetry of the crystal system. —ˌ**hol·o+'he+drism** *n.*

hol·o+mor+phic (ˌhɒlə'mɔːfɪk) *adj. Maths.* another word for **analytic** (sense 6).

hol·o+phras+tic (ˌhɒlə'fræstɪk) *adj.* **1.** denoting the stage in a child's acquisition of syntax when most utterances are single words. **2.** (of languages) tending to express in one word what would be expressed in several words in other languages; polysynthetic. [C19: from HOLO- + Greek *phrastikos* expressive, from *phrazein* to express]

hol·o+phyt+ic (ˌhɒlə'fɪtɪk) *adj.* (of plants) capable of synthesizing their food from inorganic molecules, esp. by photosynthesis. —**hol·o+phyte** ('hɒləˌfaɪt) *n.*

hol·o+plank+ton (ˌhɒlə'plæŋktən) *n.* organisms, such as diatoms and algae, that spend all stages of their life cycle as plankton. Compare **meroplankton.**

hol·o+thu+ri+an (ˌhɒlə'θjʊərɪən) *n.* **1.** any echinoderm of the class *Holothuroidea,* including the sea cucumbers, having a leathery elongated body with a ring of tentacles around the mouth. ~*adj.* **2.** of, relating to, or belonging to the *Holothuroidea.* [C19: from New Latin *Holothūria* name of type genus, from Latin: water polyp, from Greek *holothourion,* of obscure origin]

hol·o+type ('hɒləˌtaɪp) *n. Biology.* another name for **type specimen.** —**hol·o+typ+ic** (ˌhɒlə'tɪpɪk) *adj.*

hol·o+zo+ic (ˌhɒlə'zəʊɪk) *adj.* (of animals) obtaining nourishment by feeding on plants or other animals.

holp (həʊlp) *vb. Archaic or dialect.* a past tense of **help.**

hol+pen ('həʊlpən) *vb. Archaic.* a past participle of **help.**

hols (hɒlz) *pl. n. Brit. school slang.* holidays.

Holst (həʊlst) *n.* **Gus·tav (Theodore).** 1874–1934, English composer. His works include operas, choral music, and orchestral music such as the suite *The Planets* (1917).

Hol+stein[1] ('həʊlstaɪn) *n.* the usual U.S. name for **Friesian** (the cattle).

Hol+stein[2] (*German* 'hɔlʃtaɪn) *n.* a region of N West Germany, in S Schleswig-Holstein: in early times a German duchy of Saxony; became a duchy of Denmark in 1474; finally incorporated into Prussia in 1866.

hol+ster ('həʊlstə) *n.* a sheathlike leather case for a pistol, attached to a belt or saddle. [C17: via Dutch *holster* from Germanic; compare Old Norse *hulstr* sheath, Old English *heolstor* darkness, Gothic *hulistr* cover] —**'hol+stered** *adj.*

holt (həʊlt) *n. Archaic or poetic.* a wood or wooded hill. [Old English *holt;* related to Old Norse *holt,* Old High German *holz,* Old Slavonic *kladū* log, Greek *klados* twig]

Holt (həʊlt) *n.* **Har·old Ed·ward.** 1908–67, Australian statesman; prime minister (1966–67); believed drowned.

ho·lus-bo·lus ('həʊləs'bəʊləs) *adv. Informal.* all at once. [C19: pseudo-Latin based on *whole bolus;* see BOLUS]

ho·ly ('həʊlɪ) *adj.* **+li·er, +li+est. 1.** of, relating to, or associated with God or a deity; sacred. **2.** endowed or invested with extreme purity or sublimity. **3.** devout, godly, or virtuous. **4. holier-than-thou.** offensively sanctimonious or self-righteous: *a holier-than-thou attitude.* **5. holy terror.** a difficult or frightening person. ~*n., pl.* **·lies. 6. a.** a sacred place. **b. the holy.** (*functioning as pl.*) persons or things invested with holiness. [Old English *hālig, hǣlig;* related to Old Saxon *hēlag,* Gothic *hailags,* German *heilig;* see HALLOW]

Ho·ly Al+li+ance *n.* **1.** a document advocating government according to Christian principles that was signed in 1815 by the rulers of Russia, Prussia, and Austria. **2.** the informal alliance that resulted from this agreement.

Ho·ly Bi+ble *n.* another name for the **Bible.**

Ho·ly Cit·y *n.* **the. 1.** Jerusalem, esp. when regarded as the focal point of the religions of Judaism, Christianity, or Islam. **2.** *Christianity.* heaven regarded as the perfect counterpart of Jerusalem. **3.** any city regarded as especially sacred by a particular religion.

Ho·ly Com+mun+ion *n.* **1.** the celebration of the Eucharist. **2.** the consecrated elements of the Eucharist. ~Often shortened to **Communion.**

ho·ly day *n.* a day on which a religious festival is observed.

ho·ly day of ob+li+ga·tion *n.* a major feastday of the Roman Catholic Church on which Catholics are bound to attend Mass and refrain from servile work.

Ho·ly Fam·i+ly *n.* **the.** *Christianity.* the infant Jesus, Mary, and St. Joseph.
Ho·ly Fa+ther *n. R.C. Church.* a title of the pope.
Ho·ly Ghost *or* **Spir+it** *n. Christianity.* the third person of the Trinity.
Ho·ly Grail *n.* (in medieval legend) the bowl used by Jesus at the Last Supper. It was brought to Britain by Joseph of Arimathea, where it became the quest of many knights. Also called: **Grail, Sangraal.** [C14: *grail* from Old French *graal,* from Medieval Latin *gradālis* bowl, of unknown origin]
Hol·y+head ('hɒlɪ,hɛd) *n.* **1.** an island off the NW coast of Anglesey: part of the county of Gwynedd. Area: about 62 sq. km (24 sq. miles). **2.** the chief town of this island, a port on the N coast. Pop.: 10 608 (1971).
Ho·ly In+no+cents' Day *n.* Dec. 28, a day commemorating the massacre of male children at Bethlehem by Herod's order (Matthew 2:16); Childermas.
Ho·ly Is+land *n.* an island off the NE coast of Northumberland, linked to the mainland by road but accessible only at low water: site of a monastery founded by St. Aidan in 635. Also called: **Lindisfarne.**
Ho·ly Joe *n. Informal.* **1.** a minister or chaplain. **2.** any sanctimonious or self-righteous person.
Ho·ly Land *n.* **the.** another name for **Palestine** (sense 1).
Ho·ly·oake ('həʊlɪ,əʊk) *n.* Sir **Keith Jack·a** ('dʒækə). born 1904, New Zealand politician; prime minister (1957; 1960–72); governor general (1977-80).
Ho·ly Of+fice *n. R.C. Church.* a congregation established in 1542 as the final court of appeal in heresy trials; it now deals with matters of doctrine.
ho·ly of ho·lies *n.* **1.** any place of special sanctity. **2.** the innermost compartment of the Jewish tabernacle, and later of the Temple, where the Ark was enshrined.
ho·ly or+ders *n.* **1.** the sacrament or rite whereby a person is admitted to the Christian ministry. **2.** the grades of the Christian ministry. **3.** the rank or status of an ordained Christian minister.
ho·ly place *n.* **1.** the outer chamber of a Jewish sanctuary. **2.** a place of pilgrimage.
Ho·ly Roll+er *n. Derogatory.* a member of a sect that expresses religious fervour in an ecstatic or frenzied way.
Ho·ly Ro+man Em+pire *n.* the complex of European territories under the rule of the Frankish or German king who bore the title of Roman emperor, beginning with the coronation of Charlemagne in 800 A.D. The last emperor, Francis II, relinquished his crown in 1806.
ho·ly rood *n.* **1.** a cross or crucifix, esp. one placed upon the rood screen in a church. **2.** (*often cap.*) the cross on which Christ was crucified.
Ho·ly Sat+ur+day *n.* the Saturday before Easter Sunday.
Ho·ly Scrip+ture *n.* another term for the **Scriptures.**
Ho·ly See *n. R.C. Church.* **1.** the see of the pope as bishop of Rome and head of the Church. **2.** the Roman curia.
Ho·ly Sep+ul+chre *n. New Testament.* the tomb in which the body of Christ was laid after the Crucifixion.
Ho·ly Spir+it *n.* another name for the **Holy Ghost.**
ho·ly+stone ('həʊlɪ,stəʊn) *n.* **1.** a soft sandstone used for scrubbing the decks of a vessel. ~*vb.* **2.** (*tr.*) to scrub (a vessel's decks) with a holystone. [C19: perhaps so named from its being used in a kneeling position]
ho·ly syn+od *n.* the governing body of any of the Orthodox Churches.
Ho·ly Thurs+day *n. R.C. Church.* **1.** another name for **Maundy Thursday.** **2.** a rare name for **Ascension Day.**
ho·ly+tide ('həʊlɪ,taɪd) *n. Archaic.* a season of special religious observances or one regarded as especially holy.
ho·ly wa+ter *n.* water that has been blessed by a priest for use in symbolic rituals of purification.
Ho·ly Week *n.* the week preceding Easter Sunday.
Ho·ly Writ *n.* another term for the **Scriptures.**
Ho·ly Year *n. R.C. Church.* a period of remission from sin, esp. one granted every 25 years.
hom (hɒm) *or* **hom·a** ('hɒmə) *n.* **1.** a sacred plant of the Parsees and ancient Persians. **2.** a drink made from this plant. [from Persian, from Avestan *haoma*]
hom+age ('hɒmɪdʒ) *n.* **1.** a public show of respect or honour towards someone or something (esp. in the phrases **pay** or **do homage to**). **2.** (in feudal society) **a.** the act of respect and allegiance made by a vassal to his lord. See also **fealty. b.** something done in acknowledgment of vassalage. ~*vb. Archaic or poetic.* **3.** (*tr.*) to render homage to. [C13: from Old French, from *home* man, from Latin *homo*]
hom+bre[1] ('ɒmbreɪ, -brɪ) *n. Western U.S.* a slang word for **man.**
hom+bre[2] ('hɒmbə) *n.* a variant spelling of **ombre.**
hom+burg ('hɒmbɜ:g) *n.* a man's hat of soft felt with a dented crown and a stiff upturned brim. [C20: named after *Homburg,* in West Germany, town where it was originally made]
home (həʊm) *n.* **1.** the place or a place where one lives: *have you no home to go to?* **2.** a house or other dwelling. **3.** a family or other group living in a house or other place. **4.** a person's country, city, etc., esp. viewed as a birthplace, a residence during one's early years, or a place dear to one. **5.** the environment or habitat of a person or animal. **6.** the place where something is invented, founded, or developed: *the U.S. is the home of baseball.* **7. a.** a building or organization set up to care for orphans, the aged, etc **b.** an informal name for a mental home. **8.** *Sport.* one's own ground: *the match is at home.* **9.a.** the objective towards which a player strives in certain sports. **b.** an area where a player is safe from attack. **10.** *Lacrosse.* **a.** one of two positions of play nearest the opponents' goal. **b.** a player assigned to such a position: *inside home.* **11.** *Baseball.* another name for **home plate.** **12. a home from home.** a place other than one's own home where one can be at ease. **13. at home. a.** in one's own home or country. **b.** at ease, as if at one's own home. **c.** giving an informal party at one's own home. **d.** *Brit.* such a party. **14. at home in, on,** *or* **with.** familiar or conversant with. **15. home and dry.** *Brit. slang.* definitely safe or successful: *we will not be home and dry until the votes have been counted.* Austral. equivalent: **home and hosed.** **16. near home.** concerning one deeply. ~*adj.* (*usually prenominal*) **17.** of, relating to, or involving one's home, country, etc.; domestic. **18.** effective or deadly: *a home thrust.* **19.** *Sport.* relating to one's own ground: *a home game.* **20.** *U.S.* central; principal: *the company's home office.* ~*adv.* **21.** to or at home: *I'll be home tomorrow.* **22.** to or on the point. **23.** to the fullest extent: *hammer the nail home.* **24.** (of nautical gear) into or in the best or proper position: *the boom is home.* **25. bring home to. a.** to make clear to. **b.** to place the blame on. **26. come home.** *Nautical.* (of an anchor) to fail to hold. **27. come home to.** to be made absolutely clear to. **28. to write home about.** to be of particular interest: *the film was nothing to write home about.* ~*vb.* **29.** (*intr.*) (of birds and other animals) to return home accurately from a distance. **30.** (often foll. by *on* or *onto*) to direct or be directed onto a point or target, esp. by automatic navigational aids. **31.** to send or go home. **32.** to furnish with or have a home. **33.** (*intr.;* often foll. by *in* or *in on*) to be directed towards a goal, target, etc. [Old English *hām;* related to Old Norse *heimr,* Gothic *haims,* Old High German *heim,* Dutch *heem,* Greek *kōmi* village] —**'home+less** *adj., n.* —**'home+less+ness** *n.* —**'home+,like** *adj.*
Home (hju:m) *n.* **Al·ex·an·der,** Baron Home of the Hirsel; title of Sir *Alec Douglas-Home,* formerly 14th Earl of Home. born 1903, British Conservative statesman: he renounced his earldom to become prime minister of Great Britain and Northern Ireland (1963–64); foreign secretary (1970–74).
home+bred ('həʊm,brɛd) *adj.* **1.** raised or bred at home. **2.** lacking sophistication or cultivation; crude.
home-brew *n.* a beer or other alcoholic drink brewed at home rather than commercially. —**'home-'brewed** *adj.*
home+com·ing ('həʊm,kʌmɪŋ) *n.* the act of coming home.
Home Coun+ties *pl. n.* the counties surrounding London.
home e·co+nom+ics *n.* the study of diet, budgeting, child care, and other subjects concerned with running a home. —**home e·con·o+mist** *n.*
home-grown *adj.* (esp. of fruit and vegetables) produced in one's own country, district, estate, or garden.
Home Guard *n.* a volunteer part-time military force recruited for the defence of the United Kingdom in World War II.
home+land ('həʊm,lænd) *n.* **1.** the country in which one lives or was born. **2.** the official name for a **Bantustan.**
home+ly ('həʊmlɪ) *adj.* **+li+er, +li+est.** **1.** characteristic of or suited to the ordinary home; unpretentious. **2.** (of a person) **a.** *Brit.* warm and domesticated in manner or appearance. **b.** *Chiefly U.S.* plain or ugly. —**'home+li+ness** *n.*
home-made *adj.* **1.** (esp. of cakes, jam, and other foods) made at home or on the premises, esp. of high-quality ingredients. **2.** crudely fashioned.
home+mak·er ('həʊm,meɪkə) *n. U.S.* **1.** a person, esp. a housewife, who manages a home. **2.** a social worker who manages a household during the incapacity of the housewife. —**'home+,mak·ing** *n., adj.*
hom·e·o-, hom·oe·o-, *or* **hom·oi·o-** *combining form.* like or similar: *homeomorphism.* [from Latin *homoeo-,* from Greek *homoio-,* from *homos* same]
Home Of+fice *n. Brit. government.* the national department responsible for the maintenance of law and order, immigration control, and all other domestic affairs not specifically assigned to another department.
ho·me·o+mor+phism *or* **ho·moe·o+mor+phism** (,həʊmɪə'mɔ:fɪzəm) *n.* **1.** the property, shown by certain chemical compounds, of having the same crystal form but different chemical composition. **2.** *Maths.* a one-to-one correspondence, continuous in both directions, between the points of two geometric figures or between two topological spaces. —**,ho·me·o+'mor+phic, ,ho·me·o+'mor+phous** *or* **,ho·moe·o+'mor+phic, ,ho·moe·o+'mor+phous** *adj.*
ho·me·op+a+thy *or* **ho·moe·op·a·thy** (,həʊmɪ'ɒpəθɪ) *n.* a method of treating disease by the use of small amounts of a drug that, in healthy persons, produces symptoms similar to those of the disease being treated. Compare **allopathy.** —**ho·me·o+path+ic** *or* **ho·moe·o+path+ic** (,həʊmɪə'pæθɪk) *adj.* —**,ho·me·o+'path·i·cal+ly** *or* **,ho·moe·o+'path·i·cal·ly** *adv.* —**ho·me·op·a·thist** *or* **ho·moe·op·a·thist** (,həʊmi:'ɒpəθɪst) *n.*
ho·me·o+sta+sis *or* **ho·moe·o+sta+sis** (,həʊmɪəʊ'steɪsɪs) *n.* **1.** the maintenance of metabolic equilibrium within an animal by a tendency to compensate for disrupting changes. **2.** the maintenance of equilibrium within a social group, person, etc. —**ho·me·o+stat+ic** *or* **ho·moe·o+stat+ic** (,həʊmɪəʊ'stætɪk) *adj.*
ho·me·o+typ+ic (,həʊmɪəʊ'tɪpɪk), **ho·me·o+typ·i·cal** *or* **ho·moe·o+typ+ic, ho·moe·o+typ·i·cal** *adj.* denoting or relating to the second nuclear division of meiosis, which resembles mitosis. Compare **heterotypic.**
home plate *n. Baseball.* a flat often five-sided piece of hard rubber or other material that serves to define the area over which the pitcher must throw the ball for a strike and that a base runner must safely reach on his way from third base to score a run. Also called: **plate, home, home base.**

hom+er[1] ('həʊmə) *n.* **1.** another word for **homing pigeon. 2.** *U.S.* an informal word for **home run.**

ho+mer[2] ('həʊmə) *n.* a Hebrew unit of capacity equal to 10 ephahs in dry measure or 10 baths in liquid measure. [C16: from Hebrew *hōmer*]

Ho·mer ('həʊmə) *n.* circa 800 B.C., Greek poet to whom are attributed the *Iliad* and the *Odyssey*. Almost nothing is known of him, but it is thought that he was born on the island of Chios and was blind.

home range *n. Ecology.* the area in which an animal normally ranges.

Ho+mer+ic (həʊ'mɛrɪk) *or* **Ho·me·ri·an** (həʊ'mɪərɪən) *adj.* **1.** of, relating to, or resembling Homer or his poems. **2.** imposing or heroic. **3.** of or relating to the archaic form of Greek used by Homer. See **Epic.** —**Ho+'mer·i·cal+ly** *adv.*

Ho+mer+ic laugh+ter *n.* loud unrestrained laughter, as that of the gods.

home rule *n.* **1.** self-government, esp. in domestic affairs. **2.** *U.S. government.* the partial autonomy of cities and (in some states) counties, under which they manage their own affairs, with their own charters, etc., within the limits set by the state constitution and laws. **3.** the partial autonomy sometimes granted to a national minority or a colony.

Home Rule *n.* self-government for Ireland: the goal of the Irish Nationalists from about 1870 to 1920.

home run *n. Baseball.* a hit, usually out of the playing area, that no fielder can reach in time to prevent the batter from scoring.

Home Sec+re+tar·y *n. Brit. government.* short for **Secretary of State for the Home Department;** the head of the Home Office.

home+sick ('həʊmˌsɪk) *adj.* depressed or melancholy at being away from home and family. —**'home+ˌsick+ness** *n.*

home+spun ('həʊmˌspʌn) *adj.* **1.** having plain or unsophisticated character. **2.** woven or spun at home. ~*n.* **3.** cloth made at home or made of yarn spun at home. **4.** a cloth resembling this but made on a power loom.

home+stead ('həʊmˌstɛd, -stɪd) *n.* **1.** a house or estate and the adjoining land, buildings, etc., esp. a farm. **2.** (in the U.S.) a house and adjoining land designated by the owner as his fixed residence and exempt under the homestead laws from seizure and forced sale for debts. **3.** *Austral.* (on a sheep or cattle station) the owner's or manager's residence.

Home+stead Act *n.* an act passed by the U.S. Congress in 1862 making available to settlers 160-acre tracts of public land for cultivation and improvement.

home+stead+er ('həʊmˌstɛdə) *n.* **1.** a person owning a homestead. **2.** *U.S.* a person who acquires or possesses land under a homestead law.

home+stead law *n.* (in the U.S.) any of various laws conferring certain privileges on owners of homesteads.

home stretch *n.* **1.** *Horse racing.* the section of a racecourse forming the approach to the finish. **2.** the final stage of an undertaking or journey.

home teach+er *n. Brit.* a teacher who educates ill or disabled children in their homes.

home truth *n.* (*often pl.*) an unpleasant fact told to a person about himself.

home+ward ('həʊmwəd) *adj.* **1.** directed or going home. **2.** (of a ship, part of a voyage, etc.) returning to the home port. ~*adv.* *also* **home+wards. 3.** towards home.

home+work ('həʊm,wɜːk) *n.* **1.** school work done out of lessons, esp. at home. **2.** any preparatory study.

home·y ('həʊmɪ) *adj.* **hom·i·er, hom·i+est.** a variant spelling of **homy.** —**'home·y+ness** *n.*

hom·i·ci·dal (ˌhɒmɪ'saɪdᵊl) *adj.* **1.** of, involving, or characterized by homicide. **2.** likely to commit homicide: *a homicidal maniac.* —ˌ**hom·i·'ci·dal+ly** *adv.*

hom·i·cide ('hɒmɪˌsaɪd) *n.* **1.** the killing of a human being by another person. **2.** a person who kills another. [C14: from Old French, from Latin *homo* man + *caedere* to slay]

hom·i+let+ic (ˌhɒmɪ'lɛtɪk) *or* **hom·i·let·i·cal** *adj.* **1.** of or relating to a homily or sermon. **2.** of, relating to, or characteristic of homiletics. —ˌ**hom·i·'let·i·cal+ly** *adv.*

hom·i+let+ics (ˌhɒmɪ'lɛtɪks) *n.* (*functioning as sing.*) the art of preaching or writing sermons. [C17: from Greek *homilētikos* cordial, from *homilein* to converse with; see HOMILY]

hom·i·ly ('hɒmɪlɪ) *n., pl.* **+lies. 1.** a sermon or discourse on a moral or religious topic. **2.** moralizing talk or writing. [C14: from Church Latin *homīlia,* from Greek: discourse, from *homilein* to converse with, from *homilos* crowd, from *homou* together + *ilē* crowd] —**'hom·i·list** *n.*

hom+ing ('həʊmɪŋ) *n.* (*modifier*) **1.** *Zoology.* relating to the ability to return home after travelling great distances: *homing instinct.* **2.** (of an aircraft, missile, etc.) capable of guiding itself onto a target or to a specified point.

hom+ing guid+ance *n.* a method of missile guidance in which internal equipment enables it to steer itself onto the target, as by sensing the target's heat radiation.

hom+ing pi+geon *n.* any breed of pigeon developed for its homing instinct, used for carrying messages or for racing. Also called: **homer.**

hom·i+nid ('hɒmɪnɪd) *n.* **1.** any primate of the family *Hominidae,* which includes modern man (*Homo sapiens*) and the extinct precursors of man. ~*adj.* **2.** of, relating to, or belonging to the *Hominidae.* [C19: via New Latin from Latin *homo* man + -ID[2]]

hom·i+noid ('hɒmɪˌnɔɪd) *adj.* **1.** of or like man; manlike. **2.** of, relating to, or belonging to the primate superfamily *Hominoidea,* which includes the anthropoid apes and man. ~*n.* **3.** a hominoid animal. [C20: from Latin *homin-, homo* man + -OID]

hom·i·ny ('hɒmɪnɪ) *n. Chiefly U.S.* coarsely ground maize prepared as a food by boiling in milk or water. [C17: probably of Algonquian origin]

hom·i·ny grits *pl. n. U.S.* finely ground hominy. Often shortened to **grits.**

ho·mo ('həʊməʊ) *n., pl.* **·mos.** *Informal.* short for **homosexual.**

Ho·mo ('həʊməʊ) *n.* any primate of the hominid genus *Homo,* including modern man (see **Homo sapiens**) and several extinct species of primitive man. [Latin: man]

ho·mo- *combining form.* being the same or like: *homologous; homosexual.* Compare **hetero-.** [via Latin from Greek, from *homos* same]

ho·mo+cen+tric (ˌhəʊməʊ'sɛntrɪk, ˌhɒm-) *adj.* having the same centre; concentric. —ˌ**ho·mo+'cen+tri+cal+ly** *adv.*

ho·mo+cer+cal (ˌhəʊməʊ'sɜːkᵊl, ˌhɒm-) *adj. Ichthyol.* of or possessing a symmetrical tail that extends beyond the end of the vertebral column, as in most bony fishes. Compare **heterocercal.** [C19: from HOMO- + Greek *kerkos* tail]

ho·mo+chro+mat+ic (ˌhəʊməʊkrəʊ'mætɪk, ˌhɒm-) *adj.* a less common word for **monochromatic** (sense 1). —**ho·mo+chro+ma+tism** (ˌhəʊməʊ'krəʊməˌtɪzəm, ˌhɒm-) *n.*

ho·mo·chro·mous (ˌhəʊmə'krəʊməs, ˌhɒm-) *adj.* (esp. of plant parts) of only one colour.

ho·mo+cy+clic (ˌhəʊməʊ'saɪklɪk, -'sɪk-, ˌhɒm-) *adj.* (of an organic compound) containing a closed ring of atoms of the same kind, esp. carbon atoms. Compare **heterocyclic.**

ho·mo·dont ('həʊməˌdɒnt) *adj.* (of most nonmammalian vertebrates) having teeth that are all of the same type. Compare **heterodont.** [C19: from HOMO- + -ODONT]

hom·oe·o- *combining form.* variant of **homeo-.**

ho·mo+e·rot·i·cism (ˌhəʊməʊɪ'rɒtɪˌsɪzəm) *or* **ho·mo+er·o+tism** (ˌhəʊməʊ'ɛrəˌtɪzəm) *n.* eroticism centred on or aroused by persons of one's own sex. —ˌ**ho·mo+e·'rot+ic** *adj.*

ho+mog·a+my (hɒ'mɒgəmɪ) *n.* **1.** a condition in which all the flowers of an inflorescence are either of the same sex or hermaphrodite. Compare **heterogamy** (sense 3). **2.** the maturation of the anthers and stigmas of a flower at the same time, ensuring self-pollination. Compare **dichogamy.** —**ho+'mog·a+mous** *adj.*

ho+mog+e·nate (hə'mɒdʒɪnɪt, -ˌneɪt) *n.* a substance produced by homogenizing. [C20: from HOMOGENIZE + -ATE[1]]

ho·mo·ge·ne·ous (ˌhəʊmə'dʒiːnɪəs, ˌhɒm-) *adj.* **1.** composed of similar or identical parts or elements. **2.** of uniform nature. **3.** similar in kind or nature. **4.** having a constant property, such as density, throughout. **5.** *Maths.* **a.** (of a polynomial) containing terms of the same degree with respect to all the variables, as in $x^2 + 2xy + y^2$. **b.** (of a function) containing a set of variables such that when each is multiplied by a constant, this constant can be eliminated without altering the value of the function, as in $\cos x/y + x/y$. **c.** (of an equation) containing a homogeneous function made equal to 0. **6.** *Chem.* of, composed of, or concerned with a single phase. Compare **heterogeneous.** ~Also (for senses 1–4): **homogenous.** —**ho·mo+ge·ne·i·ty** (ˌhəʊməʊdʒɪ'niːɪtɪ, ˌhɒm-) *n.* —ˌ**ho·mo+'ge·ne·ous+ly** *adv.* —ˌ**ho·mo+'ge·ne·ous·ness** *n.*

ho+mog+e·nize *or* **ho+mog+e·nise** (hɒ'mɒdʒɪˌnaɪz) *vb.* **1.** (*tr.*) to break up the fat globules in (milk or cream) so that they are evenly distributed. **2.** to make or become homogeneous. —**ho+ˌmog+e·ni·'za+tion** *or* **ho+ˌmog+e·ni+'sa+tion** *n.* —**ho+'mog+e·ˌniz+er** *or* **ho+'mog+e·ˌnis+er** *n.*

ho+mog+e·nous (hə'mɒdʒɪnəs) *adj.* **1.** another word for **homogeneous** (senses 1–4). **2.** of, relating to, or exhibiting homogeny.

ho+mog+e·ny (hɒ'mɒdʒɪnɪ) *n. Biology.* similarity in structure of individuals or parts because of common ancestry. [C19: from Greek *homogeneia* community of origin, from *homogenēs* of the same kind]

ho+mog·o·ny (hɒ'mɒgənɪ) *n.* the condition in a plant of having stamens and styles of the same length in all the flowers. Compare **heterogony** (sense 2). —**ho+'mog·o·nous** *adj.* —**ho+'mog·o·nous+ly** *adv.*

ho·mo+graft ('hɒməˌgrɑːft) *n.* a tissue graft obtained from an organism of the same species as the recipient.

hom·o·graph ('hɒməˌgræf, -ˌgrɑːf) *n.* one of a group of words spelt in the same way but having different meanings. Compare **heteronym.** —ˌ**hom·o+'graph+ic** *adj.*

hom·oi·o- *combining form.* variant of **homeo-.**

ho+moi·o·ther+mic (həʊˌmɔɪə'θɜːmɪk) *or* **ho+mo+ther+mal** *adj.* (of birds and mammals) having a constant body temperature, usually higher than the temperature of the surroundings; warm-blooded. Compare **poikilothermal.**

Ho+moi+ou+si·an (ˌhəʊmɔɪ'uːsɪən, -'aʊ-) *n.* **1.** a Christian who believes that the Son is of like (and not identical) substance with the Father. Compare **Homoousian.** ~*adj.* **2.** of or relating to the Homoiousians. [C18: from Late Greek *homoiousios* of like substance, from Greek *homoio-* like + *ousia* nature] —ˌ**Ho+moi+'ou+si+an+ism** *n.*

ho+mol·o+gate (hɒ'mɒləˌgeɪt) *vb.* (*tr.*) **1.** *Law, chiefly Scot.* to approve or ratify (a deed or contract, esp. one that is defective). **2.** *Law.* to confirm (a proceeding, etc.). **3.** to recognize (a particular type of car or car component) as a production model or component rather than a prototype, as in making it eligible for a motor race. [C17: from Medieval Latin *homologāre* to agree, from Greek *homologein* to approve, from *homologos* agreeing, from HOMO- + *legein* to speak] —**ho+ˌmol·o+'ga+tion** *n.*

ho+mol·o·gize *or* **ho+mol·o·gise** (hɒ'mɒləˌdʒaɪz) *vb.* to be, show to be, or make homologous. —**ho+'mol·o+,giz+er** *or* **ho+'mol·o+,gis+er** *n.*

ho+mol·o+gous (həʊ'mɒləgəs, hɒ-), **ho·mo+log·i+cal** (ˌhəʊmə'lɒdʒɪkᵊl, ˌhɒm-), *or* **ho·mo+log+ic** *adj.* **1.** having a related or similar position, structure, etc. **2.** *Chem.* (of a series of organic compounds) having similar characteristics and structure but differing by a number of CH_2 groups. **3.** *Med.* **a.** (of two or more tissues) identical in structure. **b.** (of a vaccine) prepared from the infecting microorganism. **4.** *Biology.* (of organs and parts) having the same evolutionary origin but different functions: *the wing of a bat and the paddle of a whale are homologous.* Compare **analogous** (sense 2). **5.** *Maths.* (of elements) playing a similar role in distinct figures or functions. —**ˌho·mo+'log·i+cal+ly** *adv.*

ho+mol·o+gous chro+mo+somes *pl. n.* two chromosomes, one of paternal origin, the other of maternal origin, that are identical in appearance and pair during meiosis.

ho+mol·o+graph+ic (həʊˌmɒlə'græfɪk) *or* **ho+mal·o+graph+ic** *adj. Cartography.* another term for **equal-area.**

hom·o+logue *or U.S. (sometimes)* **hom·o+log** ('hɒməˌlɒg) *n.* **1.** *Biology.* a homologous part or organ. **2.** *Chem.* any homologous compound.

ho+mol+o·gy (həʊ'mɒlədʒɪ) *n., pl.* **·gies. 1.** the condition of being homologous. **2.** *Chem.* the similarities in chemical behaviour shown by members of a homologous series. **3.** *Maths.* a classification of geometric figures according to their geometric properties. [C17: from Greek *homologia* agreement, from *homologos* agreeing; see HOMOLOGATE]

ho+mol·o+sine pro+jec+tion (hɒ'mɒləˌsaɪn) *n.* a map projection of the world on which the oceans are distorted to allow for greater accuracy in representing the continents, combining the sinusoidal and equal-area projections. [C20: from HOMOLOGRAPHIC + SINE[1]]

ho+mol·y+sis (hɒ'mɒlɪsɪs) *n.* the dissociation of a molecule into two neutral fragments. Also called: **homolytic fission.** Compare **heterolysis** (sense 2). —**ho·mo+lyt+ic** (ˌhəʊməʊ'lɪtɪk, ˌhɒm-) *adj.*

ho·mo+mor+phism (ˌhəʊməʊ'mɔːfɪzəm, ˌhɒm-) *or* **ho·mo+mor+phy** *n. Biology.* similarity in form, as of the flowers of a plant. —**ˌho·mo+'mor+phic** *or* **ˌho·mo+'mor+phous** *adj.*

hom·o+nym ('hɒmənɪm) *n.* **1.** one of a group of words pronounced or spelt in the same way but having different meanings. Compare **homograph, homophone. 2.** a person with the same name as another. **3.** *Biology.* a specific or generic name that has been used for two or more different organisms. [C17: from Latin *homōnymum,* from Greek *homōnumon,* from *homōnumos* of the same name; see HOMO-, -ONYM] —**ˌhom·o+'nym+ic** *or* **ho+'mon·y+mous** *adj.* —**ˌhom·o+'nym·i·ty** *or* **ho+'mon·y+my** *n.*

Ho·mo+ou+si·an (ˌhəʊmɒ'uːsɪən, -'aʊ-, ˌhɒm-) *n.* **1.** a Christian who believes that the Son is of the same substance as the Father. Compare **Homoiousian.** ~*adj.* **2.** of or relating to the Homoousians. [C16: from Late Greek *homoousios* of the same substance, from Greek HOMO- + *ousia* nature] —**ˌHo·mo+'ou+si+an+ism** *n.*

ho·mo+phile ('həʊməˌfaɪl, 'hɒm-) *n.* a rare word for **homosexual.**

hom·o+phone ('hɒməˌfəʊn) *n.* **1.** one of a group of words pronounced in the same way but differing in meaning or spelling or both, as for example *bear* and *bare.* **2.** a written letter or combination of letters that represents the same speech sound as another: *"ph" is a homophone of "f" in English.*

hom·o+phon+ic (ˌhɒmə'fɒnɪk) *adj.* **1.** of or relating to homophony. **2.** of or relating to music in which the parts move together rather than independently. —**ˌhom·o·'phon·i·cal+ly** *adv.*

ho+moph·o+nous (hɒ'mɒfənəs) *adj.* of, relating to, or denoting a homophone.

ho+moph·o+ny (hɒ'mɒfənɪ) *n.* **1.** the linguistic phenomenon whereby words of different origins become identical in pronunciation. **2.** part music composed in a homophonic style.

ho+moph·y+ly (hɒ'mɒfəlɪ) *n.* resemblance due to common ancestry. [C19: from Greek, from HOMO- + PHYLUM] —**ho·mo+phyl+lic** (ˌhəʊmə'fɪlɪk, ˌhɒm-) *adj.*

ho·mo+plas+tic (ˌhəʊməʊ'plæstɪk, ˌhɒm-) *adj.* **1.** (of a tissue graft) derived from an individual of the same species as the recipient. **2.** another word for **analogous** (sense 2). —**ˌho·mo+'plas+ti+cal+ly** *adv.* —**ho·mo+ˌplas+ty** *n.* —**ho·mo+pla+sy** ('həʊməʊˌpleɪsɪ, 'hɒm-) *n.*

ho·mo+po+lar (ˌhəʊməʊ'pəʊlə) *adj. Chem.* of uniform charge; not ionic; covalent: *a homopolar bond.* —**ho·mo+po+lar+i·ty** (ˌhəʊməʊpəʊ'lærɪtɪ, ˌhɒm-) *n.*

ho+mop+ter+ous (həʊ'mɒptərəs) *or* **ho+mop+ter+an** *adj.* of, relating to, or belonging to the *Homoptera,* a suborder of hemipterous insects, including cicadas, aphids, and scale insects, having wings of a uniform texture held over the back at rest. Compare **heteropterous.** [C19: from Greek *homopteros,* from HOMO- + *pteron* wing]

ho+mor+gan+ic (ˌhəʊmɔː'gænɪk, ˌhɒm-) *adj. Phonetics.* (of a consonant) articulated at the same point in the vocal tract as a consonant in a different class. Thus *ŋ* is the homorganic nasal of *k.*

Ho·mo sa+pi+ens ('sæpɪˌɛnz) *n.* the specific name of modern man; the only extant species of the genus *Homo.* This species also includes extinct types of primitive man such as Cro-Magnon man. See also **man** (sense 5). [New Latin, from Latin *homo* man + *sapiens* wise]

ho·mo+sce·das+tic+i·ty (ˌhəʊməʊskɪdæs'tɪsɪtɪ, ˌhɒm-) *n. Statistics.* the condition occurring when all possible values that a variable may take have constant variance. Compare **heteroscedasticity.** [C20: from HOMO- + *scedasticity,* from Greek *skedasis* a scattering, dispersion]

ho·mo+sex+u·al (ˌhəʊməʊ'sɛksjʊəl, ˌhɒm-) *n.* **1.** a person who is sexually attracted to members of the same sex. ~*adj.* **2.** of or relating to homosexuals or homosexuality. **3.** of or relating to the same sex. ~Compare **heterosexual.**

ho·mo+sex+u·al+i·ty (ˌhəʊməʊˌsɛksjʊ'ælɪtɪ, ˌhɒm-) *n.* sexual attraction to or sexual relations with members of the same sex. Compare **heterosexuality.**

ho+mos+po+rous (hɒ'mɒspərəs, ˌhəʊməʊ'spɔːrəs) *adj.* (of some ferns) producing spores of one kind only, which develop into hermaphrodite gametophytes. Compare **heterosporous.** —**ho+mos+po+ry** (həʊ'mɒspərɪ) *n.*

ho·mo+tax+is (ˌhəʊməʊ'tæksɪs, ˌhɒm-) *n.* similarity of composition and arrangement in rock strata of different ages or in different regions. —**ˌho·mo+'tax+ic** *or* **ˌho·mo+'tax+i·al** *adj.* —**ˌho·mo+'tax·i·al+ly** *adv.*

ho·mo+thal+lic (ˌhəʊməʊ'θælɪk) *adj.* (of some algae and fungi) having both male and female reproductive organs on the same thallus, which is self-fertilizing. Compare **heterothallic.** —**ˌho·mo+'thal+lism** *n.*

ho·mo+ther+mal (ˌhəʊməʊ'θɜːməl, ˌhɒm-) *adj.* another word for **homoiothermic.**

ho·mo+zy+gote (ˌhəʊməʊ'zaɪgəʊt, -'zɪg-, ˌhɒm-) *n.* an animal or plant that is homozygous and breeds true to type. Compare **heterozygote.** —**ˌho·mo+zy+'go+sis** *n.* —**ho·mo+zy+got+ic** (ˌhəʊməʊzaɪ'gɒtɪk, -zɪ-, ˌhɒm-) *adj.*

ho·mo+zy+gous (ˌhəʊməʊ'zaɪgəs, -'zɪg, ˌhɒm-) *adj. Genetics.* (of an organism) having identical alleles for any one gene: *these two fruit flies are homozygous for red eye colour.* Compare **heterozygous.** —**ˌho·mo+'zy+gous+ly** *adv.*

Homs (hɒms) *or* **Hums** (hʊms) *n.* a city in W Syria, near the Orontes River: important in Roman times as the capital of Phoenicia-Lebanesia. Pop.: 215 423 (1970). Ancient name: **Emesa.** Former name: **Hims.**

ho+mun+cu+lus (hɒ'mʌŋkjʊləs) *n., pl.* **+li** (-ˌlaɪ). **1.** a miniature man; midget. **2.** (in early biological theory) a fully-formed miniature human being existing in a spermatozoon or egg. ~Also called: **ho+mun+cule** (həʊ'mʌŋkjuːl). [C17: from Latin, diminutive of *homo* man] —**ho+'mun+cu+lar** *adj.*

hom·y *or esp. U.S.* **home·y** ('həʊmɪ) *adj.* **hom·i+er, hom·i+est.** like a home, esp. in comfort or informality; cosy. —**'hom·i+ness** *or esp. U.S.* **'home·y+ness** *n.*

hon *or* **hon.** *abbrev. for:* **1.** honorary. **2.** honourable.

Hon *or* **Hon.** *abbrev. for* Honourable (title).

ho+nan ('həʊ'næn) *n.* (*sometimes cap.*) a silk fabric of rough weave.

Ho+nan ('həʊ'næn) *n.* a province of N central China: the chief centre of early Chinese culture; mainly agricultural (the largest wheat-producing province in China). Capital: Chengchow. Pop.: 50 000 000 (1967–71 est.). Area: 167 000 sq. km (65 000 sq. miles).

Hond. *abbrev. for* Honduras.

Hon+do ('hɒndəʊ) *n.* another name for **Honshu.**

Hon+du+ras (hɒn'djʊərəs) *n.* **1.** a republic in Central America: an early centre of Mayan civilization; colonized by the Spanish from 1524 onwards; gained independence in 1821. Official language: Spanish; English is also widely spoken. Religion: Roman Catholic. Currency: lempira. Capital: Tegucigalpa. Pop.: 2 653 857 (1974). Area: 112 088 sq. km (43 277 sq. miles). **2. Gulf of.** an inlet of the Caribbean, on the coasts of Honduras, Guatemala, and Belize. —**Hon+'du+ran** *adj., n.*

hone[1] (həʊn) *n.* **1.** a fine whetstone, esp. for sharpening razors. **2.** a tool consisting of a number of fine abrasive slips held in a machine head, rotated and reciprocated to impart a smooth finish to cylinder bores, etc. ~*vb.* **3.** (*tr.*) to sharpen or polish with or as if with a hone. [Old English *hān* stone; related to Old Norse *hein*]

hone[2] (həʊn) *vb.* (*intr.*) *Dialect.* **1.** (often foll. by *for* or *after*) to yearn or pine. **2.** to moan or grieve. [C17: from Old French *hogner* to growl, probably of Germanic origin; compare Old High German *hōnen* to revile]

Ho+neck·er (*German* 'hoːnɛkər) *n.* **E·rich** ('eːrɪç). born 1912, East German statesman; head of state of East Germany since 1976.

Hon·eg·ger ('hɒnɪgə; *French* ɔnɛ'gɛːr) *n.* **Ar·thur** (ar'tyːr). 1892–1955, French composer, one of Les Six. His works include the oratorios *King David* (1921) and *Joan of Arc at the Stake* (1935), and *Pacific 231* (1924) for orchestra.

hon+est ('ɒnɪst) *adj.* **1.** not given to lying, cheating, stealing, etc.; trustworthy. **2.** not false or misleading; genuine. **3.** just or fair: *honest wages.* **4.** characterized by sincerity and candour: *an honest appraisal.* **5.** without pretensions or artificial traits: *honest farmers.* **6.** *Archaic.* (of a woman) respectable. **7. honest broker.** a mediator in disputes, esp. international ones. **8. make an honest woman of.** to marry (a woman, esp. one who is pregnant) to prevent scandal. **9. honest Injun.** (*interj.*) *School slang.* genuinely, really. **10. honest to God** (*or* **goodness**). **a.** (*adj.*) completely authentic. **b.** (*interj.*) an expression of affirmation or surprise. [C13: from Old French *honeste,* from Latin *honestus* distinguished, from *honōs* HONOUR] —**'hon+est+ness** *n.*

hon+est+ly ('ɒnɪstlɪ) *adv.* **1.** in an honest manner. **2.** (intensifier): *I honestly don't believe it.* ~*interj.* **3.** an expression of disgust, surprise, etc.

hon+es+ty ('ɒnɪstɪ) *n., pl.* **+ties. 1.** the condition of being honest. **2.** sincerity or fairness. **3.** *Archaic.* virtue or respect. **4.** a purple-flowered SE European cruciferous plant, *Lunaria annua,* cultivated for its flattened silvery pods, which are used for indoor decoration. Also called: **moonwort, satinpod.**

hone+wort ('həʊnˌwɜːt) *n.* **1.** a European umbelliferous plant,

Trinia glauca, with clusters of small white flowers. **2.** any of several similar and related plants. [C17: apparently from obsolete dialect *hone* a swelling, of obscure origin; the plant was believed to relieve swellings]

hon+ey ('hʌnɪ) *n.* **1.** a sweet viscid substance made by bees from nectar and stored in their nests or hives as food. It is spread on bread or used as a sweetening agent. **2.** any similar sweet substance, esp. the nectar of flowers. **3.** anything that is sweet or delightful. **4.** (*often cap.*) *Chiefly U.S.* a term of endearment. **5.** *Informal, chiefly U.S.* something considered to be very good of its kind: *a honey of a car.* **6.** (*modifier*) of, concerned with, or resembling honey. ~*vb.* **hon+eys, hon+ey+ing, hon+eyed** *or* **hon+ied. 7.** (*tr.*) to sweeten with or as if with honey. **8.** (often foll. by *up*) to talk to (someone) in a fond or flattering way. [Old English *huneg;* related to Old Norse *hunang,* Old Saxon *hanig,* German *Honig,* Greek *knēkos* yellowish, Sanskrit *kánaka-* gold] —**'hon·ey-,like** *adj.*

hon+ey badg+er *n.* another name for **ratel.**

hon+ey bear *n.* another name for **kinkajou** (sense 1) or **sun bear.**

hon·ey+bee ('hʌnɪ,bi:) *n.* any of various social honey-producing bees of the genus *Apis,* esp. *A. mellifera,* which has been widely domesticated as a source of honey and beeswax. Also called: **hive bee.**

hon·ey+bunch ('hʌnɪ,bʌntʃ) *or* **hon·ey+bun** *n. Informal, chiefly U.S.* honey; darling: a term of endearment.

hon+ey buz+zard *n.* a common European bird of prey, *Pernis apivorus,* having broad wings and a typically dull brown plumage with white-streaked underparts: family *Accipitridae* (hawks, buzzards, etc.).

hon·ey+comb ('hʌnɪ,kəʊm) *n.* **1.** a waxy structure, constructed by bees in a hive, that consists of adjacent hexagonal cells in which honey is stored, eggs are laid, and larvae develop. **2.** something resembling this in structure or appearance. **3.** *Zoology.* another name for **reticulum** (sense 2). ~*vb.* (*tr.*) **4.** to pierce or fill with holes, cavities, etc. **5.** to permeate: *honeycombed with spies.*

hon·ey+comb moth *n.* another name for the **wax moth.**

hon+ey creep+er *n.* **1.** any small tropical American songbird of the genus *Dacnis* and related genera, closely related to the tanagers and buntings, having a slender downward-curving bill and feeding on nectar. **2.** any bird of the family *Drepanididae* of Hawaii.

hon·ey+dew ('hʌnɪ,dju:) *n.* **1.** a sugary substance excreted by aphids and similar insects. **2.** a similar substance exuded by certain plants. **3.** short for **honeydew melon.** —**'hon·ey+,dewed** *adj.*

hon·ey+dew mel+on *n.* a variety of muskmelon with a smooth greenish-white rind and sweet greenish flesh.

hon·ey-eat·er ('hʌnɪ,i:tə) *n.* any small arboreal songbird of the Australasian family *Meliphagidae,* having a downward-curving bill and a brushlike tongue specialized for extracting nectar from flowers.

hon+eyed *or* **hon+ied** ('hʌnɪd) *adj. Poetic.* **1.** flattering or soothing. **2.** made sweet or agreeable: *honeyed words.* **3.** of, full of, or resembling honey. —**'hon+eyed·ly** *or* **'hon+ied+ly** *adv.*

hon+ey fun+gus *n.* an edible agaricaceous mushroom, *Armillaria mellea,* with a brown scaly cap: grows on dead trees, etc.

hon+ey guide *n.* any small bird of the family *Indicatoridae,* inhabiting tropical forests of Africa and Asia and feeding on beeswax, honey, and insects: order *Piciformes* (woodpeckers, etc.).

hon+ey lo+cust *n.* **1.** a thorny mimosaceous tree, *Gleditsia triacanthos* of E North America, that has long pods containing a sweet-tasting pulp. **2.** another name for **mesquite.**

hon+ey mes+quite *n.* another name for **mesquite.**

hon·ey+moon ('hʌnɪ,mu:n) *n.* **1. a.** a holiday taken by a newly married couple. **b.** (*as modifier*): *a honeymoon cottage.* **2.** a holiday considered to resemble a honeymoon: *a second honeymoon.* **3.** *Chiefly U.S.* the early, usually calm period of a relationship, such as a political or business one. ~*vb.* **4.** (*intr.*) to take a honeymoon. [C16: traditionally explained as an allusion to the feelings of married couples as changing with the phases of the moon] —**'hon·ey+,moon+er** *n.*

hon+ey mouse *or* **pha+lan+ger** *n.* a small agile Australian marsupial, *Tarsipes spenserae,* having dark-striped pale brown fur, a long prehensile tail, and a very long snout and tongue with which it feeds on honey, pollen, and insects: family *Phalangeridae.* Also called: **honeysucker.**

hon+ey plant *n.* any of various plants that are particularly useful in providing bees with nectar.

hon·ey+suck·er ('hʌnɪ,sʌkə) *n.* **1.** any bird, esp. a honey-eater, that feeds on nectar. **2.** another name for **honey mouse.**

hon·ey+suck·le ('hʌnɪ,sʌkᵊl) *n.* **1.** any temperate caprifoliaceous shrub or vine of the genus *Lonicera:* cultivated for their fragrant white, yellow, or pink tubular flowers. **2.** any of several similar plants. **3.** any of various Australian trees or shrubs of the genus *Banksia,* having flowers in dense spikes: family *Proteaceae.* [Old English *hunigsūce,* from HONEY + SUCK; see SUCKLE] —**'hon·ey+,suck·led** *adj.*

hon·ey+suck·le or+na+ment *n. Arts.* another term for **anthemion.**

honey-sweet *adj.* sweet or endearing.

hong (hɒŋ) *n.* **1.** (in China) a factory, warehouse, etc. **2.** (formerly, in Canton) a foreign commercial establishment. [C18: from Chinese (Cantonese dialect)]

Hong Kong ('hɒŋ'kɒŋ) *n.* **1.** a British Crown Colony on the coast of S China: consists of Hong Kong Island, leased by China to Britain in 1842, Kowloon Peninsula, Stonecutters Island, the New Territories (mainland), and over 230 small islands; important entrepôt trade and manufacturing centre, esp. for textiles and other consumer goods; university (1912). Capital: Victoria. Pop.: 4 077 400 (1972 est.). Area: 1046 sq. km (404 sq. miles). **2.** an island in the British Colony of Hong Kong, south of Kowloon Peninsula: contains the colonial capital, Victoria. Pop.: 996 183 (1971). Area: 75 sq. km (29 sq. miles).

Ho+ni·a+ra (,həʊnɪ'ɑ:rə) *n.* the capital of the Solomon Islands, on NW Guadalcanal Island. Pop.: 15 300 (1972 est.).

hon+ied ('hʌnɪd) *adj.* a variant spelling of **honeyed.** —**'hon+ied+ly** *adv.*

ho·ni soit qui mal y pense *French.* (ɔni 'swa ki mal i 'pã:s) shamed be he who thinks evil of it: the motto of the Order of the Garter.

Hon·i+ton ('hɒnɪtᵊn) *or* **Hon·i+ton lace** *n.* a type of lace with a floral sprig pattern. [C19: named after *Honiton,* Devon, where it was first made]

honk (hɒŋk) *n.* **1.** a representation of the sound made by a goose. **2.** any sound resembling this. ~*vb.* **3.** to make or cause (something) to make such a sound. **4.** (*intr.*) *Brit.* a slang word for **vomit.** —**'honk+er** *n.*

honk·y ('hɒnkɪ) *n., pl.* **honk·ies.** *Derogatory slang, chiefly U.S.* a white man or white men collectively. [C20: of unknown origin]

honk·y-tonk ('hɒŋkɪ,tɒŋk) *n.* **1.** *U.S. slang.* **a.** a cheap disreputable nightclub, bar, etc. **b.** (*as modifier*): *a honky-tonk district.* **2. a.** a style of ragtime piano-playing, esp. on a tinny-sounding piano. **b.** (*as modifier*): *honky-tonk music.* [C19: rhyming compound based on HONK]

Hon·o+lu+lu (,hɒnə'lu:lu:) *n.* a port in Hawaii, on S Oahu Island: the state capital. Pop.: 324 871 (1970).

hon+or ('ɒnə) *n., vb.* the U.S. spelling of **honour.**

hon·o+rar+i·um (,ɒnə'rɛərɪəm) *n., pl.* **+i·ums** *or* **·i·a** (-ɪə). a fee paid for a nominally free service. [C17: from Latin: something presented on being admitted to a post of HONOUR]

hon+or·ar·y ('ɒnərərɪ, 'ɒnrərɪ) *adj.* (*usually prenominal*) **1.** (esp. of a position, title, etc.). **a.** held or given only as an honour, without the normal privileges or duties: *an honorary degree.* **b.** (of a secretary, treasurer, etc.) unpaid. **2.** having such a position or title. **3.** depending on honour rather than legal agreement.

hon+or+if+ic (,ɒnə'rɪfɪk) *adj.* **1.** showing or conferring honour or respect. **2. a.** (of a pronoun, verb inflection, etc.) indicating the speaker's respect for the addressee or his acknowledgment of inferior status. **b.** (*as n.*): *a Japanese honorific.* —**,hon+or+'if·i·cal+ly** *adv.*

hon+our *or* *U.S.* **hon+or** ('ɒnə) *n.* **1.** personal integrity; allegiance to moral principles. **2.** fame or glory. **3.** (*often pl.*) great respect, regard, esteem, etc., or an outward sign of this. **4.** (*often pl.*) high or noble rank. **5.** a privilege or pleasure: *it is an honour to serve you.* **6.** a woman's virtue or chastity. **7. a.** *Bridge, poker, etc.* any of the top five cards in a suit or any of the four aces at no trumps. **b.** *Whist.* any of the top four cards. **8.** *Golf.* the right to tee off first. **9. do honour to. a.** to pay homage to. **b.** to be a credit to. **10. do the honours. a.** to serve as host or hostess. **b.** to perform a social act, such as carving meat, proposing a toast, etc. **11. honour bright.** *Brit. school slang.* an exclamation pledging honour. **12. in honour bound.** under a moral obligation. **13. in honour of.** out of respect for. **14. on** (*or* **upon**) **one's honour.** on the pledge of one's word or good name. ~*vb.* (*tr.*) **15.** to hold in respect or esteem. **16.** to show courteous behaviour towards. **17.** to worship. **18.** to confer a distinction upon. **19.** to accept and then pay when due (a cheque, draft, etc.). **20.** to bow or curtsy to (one's dancing partner). [C12: from Old French *onor,* from Latin *honor* esteem] —**'hon+our+er** *or* *U.S.* **'hon+or+er** *n.* —**'hon+our+less** *or* *U.S.* **'hon+or+less** *adj.*

Hon+our ('ɒnə) *n.* (preceded by *Your, His,* or *Her*) **a.** a title used to or of certain judges. **b.** (in Ireland) a form of address in general use.

hon+our+a·ble *or* *U.S.* **hon+or+a·ble** ('ɒnərəbᵊl) *adj.* **1.** possessing or characterized by high principles: *honourable intentions.* **2.** worthy of or entitled to honour or esteem. **3.** consistent with or bestowing honour. —**'hon+our+a·ble+ness** *or* *U.S.* **'hon+or+a·ble+ness** *n.* —**'hon+our+a·bly** *or* *U.S.* **'hon+or+a·bly** *adv.*

Hon+our+a·ble *or* *U.S.* **Hon+or+a·ble** ('ɒnərəbᵊl, 'ɒnrəbᵊl) *adj.* (*prenominal*) **the.** a title of respect placed before a name: employed before the names of various officials in the English-speaking world, as a courtesy title in Britain for the children of viscounts and barons and the younger sons of earls, and in Parliament by one member speaking of another. Abbrev.: **Hon.**

hon+our+a·ble dis+charge *n.* See **discharge** (sense 15).

Hon+our Mod+er+a+tions *pl. n.* (at Oxford University) the first public examination, in which candidates are placed into one of three classes of honours. Sometimes shortened to **Moderations** or **Mods.**

hon+ours *or* *U.S.* **hon+ors** ('ɒnəz) *pl. n.* **1.** observances of respect. **2.** (*often cap.*) *Brit.* **a.** (in a university degree or degree course) a rank of the highest academic standard. **b.** (*as modifier*): *an honours degree.* Abbrev.: **Hons.** Compare **general** (sense 9), **pass** (sense 34). **3.** a high mark awarded for an examination; distinction. **4. last** (*or* **funeral**) **honours.** observances of respect at a funeral. **5. military honours.** marks of respect paid by or to soldiers, etc.

hon+our school *n.* (at Oxford University) one of the courses of study leading to an honours degree.

hon+ours list *n. Brit.* a list of those who have had or are having an honour, esp. a peerage or membership of an order of chivalry, conferred on them.

hon·ours of war *pl. n. Military.* the honours granted by the victorious to the defeated, esp. as of marching out with all arms and flags flying.

Hon. Sec. *abbrev. for:* Honorary Secretary.

Hon·shu ('hɒnʃuː) *n.* the largest of the four main islands of Japan, between the Pacific and the Sea of Japan; regarded as the Japanese mainland; includes a number of offshore islands and contains most of the main cities. Pop.: 82 559 580 (1970). Area: 230 448 sq. km (88 976 sq. miles). Also called: **Hondo.**

hoo (huː) *pron. West Yorkshire and south Lancashire dialect.* she. [from Old English *heo*]

hooch *or* **hootch** (huːtʃ) *n. U.S. slang.* alcoholic drink, esp. illicitly distilled spirits. [C20: shortened from Tlingit *Hootchinoo,* name of a tribe that distilled a type of liquor]

Hooch *or* **Hoogh** (huːtʃ; *Dutch* hoːx) *n.* **(Pie·ter de** ('piːtər də). 1629–?1684, Dutch genre painter, noted esp. for his light effects.

hood[1] (hʊd) *n.* **1.** a loose head covering either attached to a cloak or coat or made as a separate garment. **2.** something resembling this in shape or use. **3.** the U.S. name for **bonnet** (of a car). **4.** the folding roof of a convertible car. **5.** a hoodlike garment worn over an academic gown, indicating its wearer's degree and university. **6.** *Falconry.* a close-fitting cover, placed over the head and eyes of a falcon to keep it quiet when not hunting. **7.** *Biology.* a structure or marking, such as the fold of skin on the head of a cobra, that covers or appears to cover the head or some similar part. ~*vb.* **8.** *(tr.)* to cover or provide with or as if with a hood. [Old English *hōd;* related to Old High German *huot* hat, Middle Dutch *hoet,* Latin *cassis* helmet; see HAT] —'**hood·less** *adj.* —'**hood·,like** *adj.*

hood[2] (hʊd) *n. U.S. slang.* short for **hoodlum** (gangster).

Hood (hʊd) *n.* **1. Rob·in.** See **Robin Hood. 2. Thom·as.** 1799–1845, English poet and humorist: his work includes protest poetry, such as *The Song of the Shirt* (1843) and *The Bridge of Sighs* (1844).

-hood *suffix forming nouns.* **1.** indicating state or condition of being: *manhood.* **2.** indicating a body of persons: *knighthood; priesthood.* [Old English *-hād*]

hood·ed ('hʊdɪd) *adj.* covered with, having, or shaped like a hood.

hood·ed crow *n.* a subspecies of the carrion crow, *Corvus corone cornix,* that has a grey body and black head, wings, and tail. Also called (Scot.): **hood·ie** ('hʊdɪ), **hoodie crow.**

hood·ed seal *n.* a large greyish earless seal, *Cystophora cristata,* of the N Atlantic and Arctic Oceans, having an inflatable hoodlike sac over the nasal region. Also called: **bladdernose.**

hood·lum ('huːdləm) *n. Chiefly U.S.* **1.** a petty gangster or ruffian. **2.** a lawless youth. [C19: perhaps from Southern German dialect *Haderlump* ragged good-for-nothing] —'**hood·lum·ism** *n.*

hood·man-blind *n. Brit., archaic.* blind man's buff.

hood mould *n.* another name for **dripstone** (sense 2).

hoo·doo ('huːduː) *n., pl.* **·doos. 1.** a variant of **voodoo. 2.** *Informal.* a person or thing that brings bad luck. **3.** *Informal.* bad luck. **4.** (in the western U.S.) a strangely shaped column of rock. ~*vb.* **·doos, ·doo·ing, ·dooed. 5.** *(tr.) Informal.* to bring bad luck to. —'**hoo·doo·ism** *n.*

hood·wink ('hʊd,wɪŋk) *vb. (tr.)* **1.** to dupe; trick. **2.** *Obsolete.* to cover or hide. [C16: originally, to cover the eyes with a hood, blindfold] —'**hood·,wink·er** *n.*

hoo·ey ('huːɪ) *n., interj. Slang.* nonsense; rubbish. [C20: of unknown origin]

hoof (huːf) *n., pl.* **hooves** *or* **hoofs. 1. a.** the horny covering of the end of the foot in the horse, deer, and all other ungulate mammals. **b.** *(in combination): a hoofbeat.* Related adj.: **ungular. 2.** the foot of an ungulate mammal. **3.** a hoofed animal. **4.** *Facetious.* a person's foot. **5. on the hoof.** (of livestock) alive. ~*vb.* **6.** *(tr.)* to kick or trample with the hoofs. **7. hoof it.** *Slang.* **a.** to walk. **b.** *(intr.)* to dance. [Old English *hōf;* related to Old Norse *hōfr,* Old High German *huof* (German *Huf*), Sanskrit *saphás*] —'**hoof·less** *adj.* —'**hoof·,like** *adj.*

hoof·bound ('huːf,baʊnd) *adj. Vet. science.* (of a horse) having dry contracted hooves, with resultant pain and lameness.

hoofed (huːft) *adj.* **a.** having a hoof or hoofs. **b.** *(in combination): four-hoofed; cloven-hoofed.*

Hoogh (*Dutch* hoːx) *n.* See (Pieter de) **Hooch.**

Hoogh·ly ('huːglɪ) *n.* a river in NE India, in West Bengal: the westernmost and commercially most important channel by which the River Ganges enters the Bay of Bengal. Length: 232 km (144 miles).

hoo-ha ('huː,hɑː) *n.* a noisy commotion or fuss. [C20: of unknown origin]

hook (hʊk) *n.* **1.** a piece of material, usually metal, curved or bent and used to suspend, catch, hold, or pull something. **2.** short for **fish-hook. 3.** a trap or snare. **4.** something resembling a hook in design or use. **5. a.** a sharp bend or angle in a geological formation, esp. a river. **b.** a sharply curved spit of land. **6.** *Boxing.* a short swinging blow delivered from the side with the elbow bent. **7.** *Cricket.* a shot in which the ball is hit square on the leg side with the bat held horizontally. **8.** *Golf.* a shot that causes the ball to go to the player's left. **9.** *Surfing.* the top of a breaking wave. **10.** Also called: **hookcheck.** *Ice hockey.* the act of hooking an opposing player. **11.** a hook-shaped stroke used in writing or printing, such as a serif or (in writing) any part of a letter extending above or below the line. **12.** *Music.* a stroke added to the stem of a written or printed note to indicate time values shorter than a crotchet. **13.** another name for a **sickle. 14.** a nautical word for **anchor. 15. by hook or (by) crook.** by any means. **16. get the hook.** *U.S. slang.* to be dismissed from employment. **17. hook, line, and sinker.** *Informal.* completely: *he fell for it hook, line, and sinker.* **18. off the hook.** *Slang.* **a.** out of danger; free from obligation or guilt. **b.** (of a telephone receiver) not on the support. **19. on one's own hook.** *Slang, chiefly U.S.* on one's own initiative. **20. on the hook.** *Slang.* **a.** waiting. **b.** in a dangerous or difficult situation. **21. sling one's hook.** *Brit. slang.* to leave. ~*vb.* **22.** (often foll. by *up*) to fasten or be fastened with or as if with a hook or hooks. **23.** *(tr.)* to catch (something, such as a fish) on a hook. **24.** to curve like or into the shape of a hook. **25.** *(tr.)* (of bulls, elks, etc.) to catch or gore with the horns. **26.** *(tr.)* to make (a rug) by hooking yarn through a stiff fabric backing with a special instrument. **27.** *(tr.;* often foll. by *down)* to cut (grass or herbage) with a sickle: *to hook down weeds.* **28.** *Boxing.* to hit (an opponent) with a hook. **29.** *Ice hockey.* to impede (an opposing player) by catching hold of him with the stick. **30.** *Golf.* to play (a ball) with a hook. **31.** *Rugby.* to obtain and pass (the ball) backwards from a scrum to a member of one's team, using the feet. **32.** *Cricket.* to play (a ball) with a hook. **33.** *(tr.) Informal.* to trick. **34.** *(tr.)* a slang word for **steal. 35. hook it.** *Slang.* to run or go quickly away. ~See also **hook-up.** [Old English *hōc;* related to Middle Dutch *hōk,* Old Norse *haki*] —'**hook·less** *adj.* —'**hook·,like** *adj.*

hook·ah *or* **hook·a** ('hʊkə) *n.* an oriental pipe for smoking marijuana, tobacco, etc., consisting of one or more long flexible stems connected to a container of water or other liquid through which smoke is drawn and cooled. Also called: **hubble-bubble, kalian, narghile, water pipe.** [C18: from Arabic *huqqah*]

hook and eye *n.* a fastening for clothes consisting of a small hook hooked onto a small metal or thread loop.

Hooke (hʊk) *n.* **Rob·ert.** 1635–1703, English physicist, chemist, and inventor. He formulated Hooke's law (1678), built the first Gregorian telescope and invented a balance spring for watches.

hooked (hʊkt) *adj.* **1.** bent like a hook. **2.** having a hook or hooks. **3.** caught or trapped. **4.** a slang word for **married. 5.** *Slang.* addicted to a drug. **6.** (often foll. by *on*) obsessed (with). —**hook·ed·ness** ('hʊkɪdnɪs) *n.*

hook·er[1] ('hʊkə) *n.* a commercial fishing boat using hooks and lines instead of nets. [C17: from Dutch *hoeker*]

hook·er[2] ('hʊkə) *n.* **1.** a person or thing that hooks. **2.** *U.S. slang.* **a.** a draught of alcoholic drink, esp. of spirits. **b.** a prostitute. **3.** *Rugby.* the central forward in the front row of a scrum whose main job is to hook the ball.

Hook·er ('hʊkə) *n.* **Rich·ard.** 1554–1600, English theologian, who influenced Anglican theology with *The Laws of Ecclesiastical Polity* (1593–97).

Hooke's law *n.* the principle that the stress imposed on a solid is directly proportional to the strain produced, within the elastic limit. [C18: named after R. HOOKE]

hook·nose ('hʊk,nəʊz) *n.* a nose with a pronounced outward curve; aquiline nose. —'**hook·,nosed** *adj.*

Hook of Hol·land *n.* **the. 1.** a cape on the SW coast of the Netherlands, in south Holland province. **2.** a port on this cape. ~Dutch name: **Hoek van Holland.**

hook-up *n.* **1.** the contact of an aircraft in flight with the refuelling hose of a tanker aircraft. **2.** an alliance or relationship, esp. an unlikely one, between people, countries, etc. **3.** the linking of broadcasting equipment or stations to transmit a special programme. ~*vb.* **hook up** *(adv.).* **4.** to connect (two or more people or things). **5.** (often foll. by *with*) *Slang.* to get married (to).

hook·worm ('hʊk,wɜːm) *n.* any parasitic blood-sucking nematode worm of the family *Ancylostomatidae,* esp. *Ancylostoma duodenale* or *Necator americanus,* both of which cause disease. They have hooked mouthparts and enter their hosts by boring through the skin.

hook·worm dis·ease *n.* the nontechnical name for **ancylostomiasis.**

hook·y *or* **hook·ey** ('hʊkɪ) *n. Informal, chiefly U.S.* truancy, usually from school (esp. in the phrase **play hooky).** [C20: perhaps from *hook it* to escape]

hoo·li·gan ('huːlɪgən) *n. Slang.* a rough lawless young person. [C19: perhaps variant of *Houlihan,* Irish surname] —'**hoo·li·gan·ism** *n.*

hoop[1] (huːp) *n.* **1.** a rigid circular band of metal or wood. **2.** something resembling this. **3. a.** a band of iron that holds the staves of a barrel or cask together. **b.** *(as modifier): hoop iron.* **4.** a child's toy shaped like a hoop and rolled on the ground or whirled around the body. **5.** *Croquet.* any of the iron arches through which the ball is driven. **6. a.** a light curved frame to spread out a skirt. **b.** *(as modifier): a hoop skirt; a hoop petticoat.* **7.** *Basketball.* the round metal frame to which the net is attached to form the basket. **8.** a large ring with paper stretched over it through which performers or animals jump. **9.** *Jewellery.* **a.** an earring consisting of one or more circles of metal, plastic, etc. **b.** the part of a finger ring through which the finger fits. **10. go through the hoop.** to be subjected to an ordeal. ~*vb.* **11.** *(tr.)* to surround with or as if with a hoop. [Old English *hōp;* related to Dutch *hoep,* Old Norse *hōp* bay, Lithuanian *kabē* hook] —**hooped** *adj.* —'**hoop·,like** *adj.*

hoop[2] (huːp) *n., vb.* a variant spelling of **whoop.**

hoop·er ('huːpə) *n.* a rare word for **cooper.**

hoop·la ('huːplɑː) *n.* **1.** *Brit.* a fairground game in which a player tries to throw a hoop over an object and so win it. **2.** *U.S. slang.* noise; bustle. **3.** *U.S. slang.* nonsense; ballyhoo. [C20: see WHOOP, LA[2]]

hoo+poe ('huːpuː) *n.* an Old World bird, *Upupa epops,* having a pinkish-brown plumage with black-and-white wings and an erectile crest: family *Upupidae,* order *Coraciiformes* (kingfishers, etc.). [C17: from earlier *hoopoop,* of imitative origin; compare Latin *upupa*]

hoop pine *n. Austral.* a fast-growing timber tree, *Araucaria cunninghamii,* having rough bark with hoop-like cracks around the trunk and branches: family *Araucariaceae.*

hoop snake *n.* any of various North American snakes, such as the mud snake (*Farancia abacura*), that were formerly thought to hold the tail in the mouth and roll along like a hoop.

hoo+ray (huː'reɪ) *or* **hoo+rah** (huː'rɑː) *interj., n., vb.* **1.** variant spellings of **hurrah.** ~*interj.* **2.** Also: **hoo+roo** (huː'ruː). *Austral.* goodbye; cheerio.

hoose+gow *or* **hoos+gow** ('huːsgaʊ) *n. U.S.* a slang word for **jail.** [C20: from Mexican Spanish *jusgado* prison, from Spanish: court of justice, from *juzgar* to judge, from Latin *judicāre,* from *judex* a JUDGE; compare JUG]

hoot[1] (huːt) *n.* **1.** the mournful wavering cry of some owls. **2.** a similar sound, such as that of a train whistle. **3.** a jeer of derision. **4.** *Brit. informal.* an amusing person or thing. **5. not give a hoot.** not to care at all. ~*vb.* **6.** (often foll. by *at*) to jeer or yell (something) contemptuously (at someone). **7.** (*tr.*) to drive (political speakers, actors on stage, etc.) off or away by hooting. **8.** (*intr.*) to make a hoot. **9.** (*intr.*) *Brit.* to blow a horn. [C13 *hoten,* of imitative origin]

hoot[2] (huːt, uːt) *or* **hoots** (huːts, uːts) *interj.* an exclamation of impatience or dissatisfaction: a supposed Scotticism. [C17: of unknown origin]

hoot[3] (huːt) *n. Austral., N.Z.* a slang word for **money.** [from Maori *utu* price]

hoot+en+an+ny ('huːtᵊnˌænɪ) *or* **hoot+nan+ny** ('huːtˌnænɪ) *n., pl.* **+nies.** *U.S.* **1.** an informal performance by folk singers. **2.** something the name of which is unspecified or forgotten. [C20: of unknown origin]

hoot+er ('huːtə) *n. Chiefly Brit.* **1.** a person or thing that hoots, esp. a car horn. **2.** *Slang.* a nose.

hoot owl *n.* any owl that utters a hooting cry, as distinct from a screech owl.

Hoo+ver[1] ('huːvə) *n.* **1.** *Trademark.* a type of vacuum cleaner. ~*vb.* (*usually not cap.*) **2.** to vacuum-clean (a carpet, etc.).

Hoo·ver[2] ('huːvə) *n.* **Her·bert (Clark).** 1874–1964, U.S. statesman; 31st president of the U.S. (1929–33). He organized relief for Europe during and after World War I, but as president he lost favour after his failure to alleviate the effects of the Depression.

Hoo+ver Dam *n.* a dam in the western U.S., on the Colorado River on the border between Nevada and Arizona; forms Lake Mead. Height: 222 m (727 ft.). Length: 354 m (1180 ft.). Former name (1933–47): **Boulder Dam.**

hooves (huːvz) *n.* a plural of **hoof.**

hop[1] (hɒp) *vb.* **hops, hop+ping, hopped. 1.** (*intr.*) to make a jump forwards or upwards, esp. on one foot. **2.** (*intr.*) (esp. of frogs, birds, rabbits, etc.) to move forwards in short jumps. **3.** (*tr.*) to jump over: *he hopped the hedge.* **4.** (*intr.*) *Informal.* to move or proceed quickly (in, on, out of, etc.): *hop on a bus.* **5.** (*tr.*) *Informal.* to cross (an ocean) in an aircraft: *they hopped the Atlantic in seven hours.* **6.** (*tr.*) *U.S. informal.* to travel by means of (an aircraft, bus, etc.): *he hopped a train to Chicago.* **7.** *U.S.* to bounce or cause to bounce: *he hopped the flat stone over the lake's surface.* **8.** (*intr.*) *U.S. informal.* to begin intense activity, esp. work. **9.** (*intr.*) another word for **limp**[1]. **10. hop it** (*or* **off**). *Brit. slang.* to go away. ~*n.* **11.** the act or an instance of hopping. **12.** *Informal.* a dance, esp. one at which popular music is played: *we're all going to the school hop tonight.* **13.** *Informal.* a trip, esp. in an aircraft. **14.** *U.S.* a bounce, as of a ball. **15. on the hop.** *Informal.* **a.** active or busy. **b.** *Brit.* unawares or unprepared: *the new ruling caught me on the hop.* [Old English *hoppian;* related to Old Norse *hoppa* to hop, Middle Low German *hupfen*]

hop[2] (hɒp) *n.* **1.** any climbing plant of the N temperate genus *Humulus,* esp. *H. lupulus,* which has green conelike female flowers and clusters of small male flowers: family *Cannabiaceae* (or *Cannabidaceae*). See also **hops. 2. hop garden.** a field of hops. **3.** *Slang.* opium or any other narcotic drug. ~See also **hop up.** [C15: from Middle Dutch *hoppe;* related to Old High German *hopfo,* Norwegian *hupp* tassel]

hop clo+ver *n.* the U.S. name for **hop trefoil.**

hope (həʊp) *n.* **1.** (*sometimes pl.*) a feeling of desire for something and confidence in the possibility of its fulfilment: *his hope for peace was justified; their hopes were dashed.* **2.** a reasonable ground for this feeling: *there is still hope.* **3.** a person or thing that gives cause for hope. **4.** a thing, situation, or event that is desired: *my hope is that prices will fall.* **5. not a hope** *or* **some hope.** used ironically to express little confidence that expectations will be fulfilled. ~*vb.* **6.** (*tr.; takes a clause as object or an infinitive*) to desire (something) with some possibility of fulfilment: *we hope you can come; I hope to tell you.* **7.** (*intr.;* often foll. by *for*) to have a wish (for a future event, situation, etc.). **8.** (*tr.; takes a clause as object*) to trust, expect, or believe: *we hope that this is satisfactory.* [Old English *hopa;* related to Old Frisian *hope,* Dutch *hoop,* Middle High German *hoffe*] —**'hop+er** *n.*

Hope (həʊp) *n.* **1. An·tho·ny,** pen name of *Sir Anthony Hope Hawkins.* 1863–1933, English novelist; author of *The Prisoner of Zenda* (1894). **2. Bob.** born 1904, U.S. comedian and comic actor, born in England. His films include *Road to Morocco* (1942), *The Paleface* (1947), and *How to Commit Marriage* (1969).

hope chest *n.* the U.S. name for **bottom drawer.**

hope+ful ('həʊpfʊl) *adj.* **1.** having or expressing hope. **2.** giving or inspiring hope; promising. ~*n.* **3.** a person considered to be on the brink of success (esp. in the phrase **a young hopeful**). —**'hope+ful+ness** *n.*

hope+ful+ly ('həʊpfʊlɪ) *adv.* **1.** in a hopeful manner. **2.** *Informal.* it is hoped: *hopefully they will be married soon.*

Ho+peh *or* **Ho+pei** ('həʊ'peɪ) *n.* a province of NE China, on the Gulf of Chihli: important for the production of winter wheat, cotton, and coal. Capital: Shihchiachuang. Pop.: 43 000 000 (1967–71 est.). Area: 202 700 sq. km (79 053 sq. miles).

hope+less ('həʊplɪs) *adj.* **1.** having or offering no hope. **2.** impossible to analyse or solve. **3.** unable to learn, function, etc. **4.** *Informal.* without skill or ability. —**'hope+less+ly** *adv.* —**'hope+less+ness** *n.*

hop+head ('hɒpˌhɛd) *n. Slang, chiefly U.S.* a heroin or opium addict. [C20: from obsolete slang *hop* opium; see HOP[2]]

Ho·pi ('həʊpɪ) *n.* **1.** (*pl.* **·pis** *or* **·pi**) a member of a North American Indian people of NE Arizona. **2.** the language of this people, belonging to the Shoshonean subfamily of the Uto-Aztecan family. [from Hopi *Hópi* peaceful]

hop in+to *vb.* (*intr., prep.*) *Austral. slang.* **1.** to attack (a person). **2.** to start or set about (a task).

Hop·kins ('hɒpkɪnz) *n.* **1.** Sir **Fred·er·ick Gow·land** ('gaʊlənd). 1861–1947, English biochemist, who pioneered research into what came to be called vitamins: shared the Nobel prize for medicine 1929. **2. Ger·ard Man·ley.** 1844–89, English poet and Jesuit priest, who experimented with sprung rhythm in his highly original poetry.

hop+lite ('hɒplaɪt) *n.* (in ancient Greece) a heavily armed infantryman. [C18: from Greek *hoplitēs,* from *hoplon* weapon, from *hepein* to prepare] —**hop+lit+ic** (hɒp'lɪtɪk) *adj.*

hop+lol+o·gy (hɒp'lɒlədʒɪ) *n.* the study of weapons or armour. [C19: from Greek, from *hoplon,* weapon + -LOGY] —**hop+'lol+o+gist** *n.*

hop+per ('hɒpə) *n.* **1.** a person or thing that hops. **2.** a funnel-shaped chamber or reservoir from which solid materials can be discharged under gravity into a receptacle below, esp. for feeding fuel to a furnace, loading a railway truck with grain, etc. **3.** a machine used for picking hops; a hop-picker. **4.** any of various long-legged hopping insects, esp. the grasshopper, leaf hopper, and immature locust. **5.** Also called: **hoppercar.** an open-topped railway truck for bulk transport of loose minerals, etc., unloaded through doors on the underside. **6.** *Computer technol.* a device for holding punched cards and feeding them to a card punch or card reader.

hop-pick·er *n.* a person employed or a machine used to pick hops.

hop+ping ('hɒpɪŋ) *n.* **1.** the action of a person or animal that hops. **2.** *Tyneside dialect.* a fair, esp. (**the Hoppings**) an annual fair in Newcastle. ~*adj.* **3. hopping mad.** in a terrible rage.

hop+ple ('hɒpᵊl) *vb., n.* a less common word for **hobble** (senses 2, 4). —**'hop+pler** *n.*

Hop·pus foot ('hɒpəs) *n.* a unit of volume equal to 1.27 cubic feet, applied to timber in the round, the cross-sectional area being taken as the square of one quarter of the circumference. [C20: named after Edward *Hoppus,* 18th-century English surveyor]

hops (hɒps) *pl. n.* the dried ripe flowers, esp. the female flowers, of the hop plant, used to give a bitter taste to beer.

hop+sack ('hɒpˌsæk) *n.* **1.** a roughly woven fabric of wool, cotton, etc., used for clothing. **2.** Also called: **hopsacking.** a coarse fabric used for bags, etc., made generally of hemp or jute.

hop+scotch ('hɒpˌskɒtʃ) *n.* a children's game in which a player throws a small stone or other object to land in one of a pattern of squares marked on the ground and then hops over to it to pick it up. [C19: HOP[1] + SCOTCH]

hop, step, and jump *n.* **1.** an older term for **triple jump. 2.** Also called: **hop, skip, and jump.** a short distance: *the shops are only a hop, step, and jump from our house.*

hop up *vb.* (*tr., adv.*) **1.** to make intoxicated, esp. by narcotics. **2.** to invigorate, excite, etc. **3.** *U.S. slang.* another term for **hot up** (sense 2). ~*n.* **hop-up. 4.** a drug, chemical, etc., intended to hop up a person or thing.

hor. *abbrev. for:* **1.** horizon. **2.** horizontal.

ho+ra ('hɔːrə) *n.* a traditional Israeli or Rumanian circle dance. [from Modern Hebrew *hōrāh,* from Rumanian *horă,* from Turkish]

Hor·ace ('hɒrɪs) *n.* Latin name *Quintus Horatius Flaccus.* 65–8 B.C., Roman poet and satirist: his verse includes the lyrics in the *Epodes* and the *Odes,* the *Epistles* and *Satires,* and the *Ars Poetica.*

Ho·rae ('hɔːriː) *pl. n. Classical myth.* the goddesses of the seasons. Also called: **the Hours.** [Latin: hours]

ho+ral ('hɔːrəl) *adj.* a less common word for **hourly.** [C18: from Late Latin *hōrālis* of an HOUR]

ho+ra+ry ('hɔːrərɪ) *adj. Archaic.* **1.** relating to the hours. **2.** hourly. [C17: from Medieval Latin *hōrārius;* see HOUR]

Ho+ra+tian (hə'reɪʃən) *adj.* of, relating to, or characteristic of Horace or his poetry.

Ho+ra+tian ode *n.* an ode of several stanzas, each of the same metrical pattern. Also called: **Sapphic ode.**

Ho·ra·ti·us Co·cles (hɒ'reɪʃɪəs 'kəʊkliːz) *n.* a legendary Roman hero of the 6th century B.C., who defended a bridge over the Tiber against Lars Porsena.

horde (hɔːd) *n.* **1.** a vast crowd; throng; mob. **2.** a local group of people in a nomadic society. **3.** a nomadic group of people, esp. an Asiatic group. **4.** a large moving mass of animals, esp. insects. ~*vb.* **5.** (*intr.*) to form, move in, or live in a horde.

[C16: from Polish *horda*, from Turkish *ordū* camp; compare URDU]

hor·de·in (ˈhɔːdiːɪn) *n.* a simple protein, rich in proline, that occurs in barley. [C19: from French *hordéine*, from Latin *hordeum* barley + French *-ine* -IN]

Ho·reb (ˈhɔːrɛb) *n. Bible.* a mountain, probably Mount Sinai.

hore·hound *or* **hoar·hound** (ˈhɔːˌhaʊnd) *n.* **1.** Also called: **white horehound.** a downy perennial herbaceous Old World plant, *Marrubium vulgare*, with small white flowers that contain a bitter juice formerly used as a cough medicine and flavouring: family *Labiatae* (labiates). See also **black horehound. 2. water horehound.** another name for **bugleweed** (sense 1). [Old English *hārhūne*, from *hār* grey + *hūne* horehound, of obscure origin]

ho·ri·zon (həˈraɪzᵊn) *n.* **1.** Also called: **visible horizon, apparent horizon.** the apparent line that divides the earth and the sky. **2.** *Astronomy.* **a.** Also called: **sensible horizon.** the circular intersection with the celestial sphere of the plane tangential to the earth at the position of the observer. **b.** Also called: **celestial horizon.** the great circle on the celestial sphere, the plane of which passes through the centre of the earth and is parallel to the sensible horizon. **3.** the range or limit of scope, interest, knowledge, etc. **4.** a layer of rock within a stratum that has a particular composition, esp. of fossils, by which the stratum may be dated. **5.** a layer in a soil profile having particular characteristics. See **A horizon, B horizon, C horizon.** [C14: from Latin, from Greek *horizōn kuklos* limiting circle, from *horizein* to limit, from *horos* limit] **—ho·ˈri·zon·less** *adj.*

hor·i·zon·tal (ˌhɒrɪˈzɒntᵊl) *adj.* **1.** parallel to the plane of the horizon; level; flat. Compare **vertical** (sense 1). **2.** of or relating to the horizon. **3.** measured or contained in a plane parallel to that of the horizon. **4.** applied uniformly or equally to all members of a group. **5.** *Economics.* relating to identical stages of commercial activity: *horizontal integration.* ~*n.* **6.** a horizontal plane, position, line, etc. **—ˌhor·i·ˈzon·tal·ness** *or* **ˌhor·i·zon·ˈtal·i·ty** *n.* **—ˌhor·i·ˈzon·tal·ly** *adv.*

hor·i·zon·tal bar *n. Gymnastics.* a raised bar on which swinging and vaulting exercises are performed. Also called: **high bar.**

hor·i·zon·tal sta·bi·liz·er *n.* the U.S. name for **tailplane.**

hor·i·zon·tal un·ion *n.* another name (esp. U.S.) for **craft union.**

hor·me (ˈhɔːmɪ) *n.* (in the psychology of C. G. Jung) fundamental vital energy. [C20: from Greek *hormē* impulse] **—ˈhor·mic** *adj.*

hor·mone (ˈhɔːməʊn) *n.* **1.** a chemical substance produced in an endocrine gland and transported in the blood to a certain tissue, on which it exerts a specific effect. **2.** an organic compound produced by a plant that is essential for growth. **3.** any synthetic substance having the same effects. [C20: from Greek *hormōn*, from *horman* to stir up, urge on, from *hormē* impulse, assault] **—hor·ˈmo·nal** *adj.*

Hor·muz (ˈhɔːmʌz) *or* **Or·muz** *n.* an island off the SE coast of Iran, in the **Strait of Hormuz**: ruins of the ancient city of Hormuz, a major trading centre in the Middle Ages. Area: about 41 sq. km (16 sq. miles).

horn (hɔːn) *n.* **1.** either of a pair of permanent outgrowths on the heads of cattle, antelopes, sheep, etc., consisting of a central bony core covered with layers of keratin. Related adj.: **corneous. 2.** the outgrowth from the nasal bone of a rhinoceros, consisting of a mass of fused hairs. **3.** any hornlike projection or process, such as the eyestalk of a snail. **4.** the antler of a deer. **5. a.** the constituent substance, mainly keratin, of horns, hoofs, etc. **b.** (*in combination*): *horn-rimmed spectacles.* **6.** a container or device made from this substance or an artificial substitute: *a shoe horn; a drinking horn.* **7.** an object or part resembling a horn in shape, such as the points at either end of a crescent, the point of an anvil, the pommel of a saddle, or a cornucopia. **8.** a primitive musical wind instrument made from the horn of an animal. **9.** any musical instrument consisting of a pipe or tube of brass fitted with a mouthpiece, with or without valves. See **hunting horn, French horn, cor anglais. 10.** *Jazz slang.* any wind instrument. **11. a.** a device for producing a warning or signalling noise. **b.** (*in combination*): *a foghorn.* **12.** (*usually pl.*) the hornlike projection attributed to certain devils, deities, etc. **13.** (*usually pl.*) the imaginary hornlike parts formerly supposed to appear on the forehead of a cuckold. **14.** Also called: **horn balance.** an extension of an aircraft control surface that projects in front of the hinge providing aerodynamic assistance in moving the control. **15. a.** Also called: **acoustic horn, exponential horn.** a hollow conical device coupled to the diaphragm of a gramophone to control the direction and quality of the sound. **b.** a similar device attached to an electrical loudspeaker, esp. in a public address system. **c.** Also called: **horn antenna.** a microwave aerial, formed by flaring out the end of a waveguide. **16.** *Geology.* another name for **pyramidal peak. 17.** a stretch of land or water shaped like a horn. **18.** *Brit. taboo slang.* an erection of the penis. **19.** *Bible.* a symbol of power, victory, or success: *in my name shall his horn be exalted.* **20. blow one's own horn.** *U.S.* to boast about oneself; brag. Brit. equivalent: **blow one's own trumpet. 21. draw** (*or* **pull**) **in one's horns. a.** to suppress or control one's feelings, esp. of anger, enthusiasm, or passion. **b.** to withdraw a previous statement. **22. on the horns of a dilemma.** in a situation involving a choice between two equally unpalatable alternatives. ~*vb.* (*tr.*) **23.** to provide with a horn or horns. **24.** to gore or butt with a horn. ~See also **horn in.** [Old English; related to Old Norse *horn*, Gothic *haurn*, Latin *cornu* horn] **—ˈhorn·less** *adj.* **—ˈhorn·ˌlike** *adj.*

Horn (hɔːn) *n.* **Cape.** See **Cape Horn.**

horn·beam (ˈhɔːnˌbiːm) *n.* **1.** any tree of the betulaceous genus *Carpinus*, such as *C. betulus* of Europe and Asia, having smooth grey bark and hard white wood. **2.** the wood of any of these trees. ~Also called: **ironwood.** [C16: from HORN + BEAM, referring to its tough wood]

horn·bill (ˈhɔːnˌbɪl) *n.* any bird of the family *Bucerotidae* of tropical Africa and Asia, having a very large bill with a basal bony protuberance: order *Coraciiformes* (kingfishers, etc.).

horn·blende (ˈhɔːnˌblɛnd) *n.* a mineral of the amphibole group consisting of the aluminium silicates of calcium, sodium, magnesium, and iron: varies in colour from green to black. Formula: $CaNa(Mg,Fe)_4(Al,Fe,Ti)_3Si_6O_{22}(OH)_2$. **—horn·ˈblen·dic** *adj.*

horn·book (ˈhɔːnˌbʊk) *n.* **1.** a page bearing a religious text or the alphabet, held in a frame with a thin window of flattened cattle horn over it. **2.** any elementary primer.

horned (hɔːnd) *adj.* having a horn, horns, or hornlike parts. **—horn·ed·ness** (ˈhɔːnɪdnɪs) *n.*

horned owl *n.* any large owl of the genus *Bubo*, having prominent ear tufts: family *Strigidae*.

horned pop·py *n.* any of several Eurasian papaveraceous plants of the genera *Glaucium* and *Roemeria*, having large brightly coloured flowers and long curved seed capsules.

horned pout *n.* a North American catfish, *Ameiurus* (or *Ictalurus*) *nebulosus*, with a sharp spine on the dorsal and pectoral fins and eight long barbels around the mouth: family *Ameiuridae*. Also called: **brown bullhead.**

horned toad *or* **liz·ard** *n.* any small insectivorous burrowing lizard of the genus *Phrynosoma*, inhabiting desert regions of America, having a flattened toadlike body covered with spines: family *Iguanidae* (iguanas).

horned vi·per *n.* a venomous snake, *Cerastes cornutus*, that occurs in desert regions of N Africa and SW Asia and has a small horny spine above each eye: family *Viperidae* (vipers). Also called: **sand viper.**

hor·net (ˈhɔːnɪt) *n.* **1.** any of various large social wasps of the family *Vespidae*, esp. *Vespa crabro* of Europe, that can inflict a severe sting. **2. hornet's nest.** a strongly unfavourable reaction (often in the phrase **stir up a hornet's nest**). [Old English *hyrnetu*; related to Old Saxon *hornut*, Old High German *hornuz*]

horn·fels (ˈhɔːnfɛlz) *n.* a hard compact fine-grained metamorphic rock formed by the action of heat on clay rocks. Also called: **hornstone.** [German: literally, horn rock]

horn in *vb.* (*intr., adv.*; often foll. by *on*) to interrupt or intrude: *don't horn in on our conversation.*

Horn of Af·ri·ca *n.* a region of NE Africa, comprising Somalia and adjacent territories.

horn of plen·ty *n.* another term for **cornucopia.**

horn·pipe (ˈhɔːnˌpaɪp) *n.* **1.** an obsolete reed instrument with a mouthpiece made of horn. **2.** an old British solo dance to a hornpipe accompaniment, traditionally performed by sailors. **3.** a piece of music for such a dance.

horn sil·ver *n.* another name for **cerargyrite.**

horn·stone (ˈhɔːnˌstəʊn) *n.* another name for **chert** or **hornfels.** [C17: translation of German *Hornstein*; so called from its appearance]

horns·wog·gle (ˈhɔːnzˌwɒgᵊl) *vb.* (*tr.*) *Slang.* to cheat or trick; bamboozle. [C19: of unknown origin]

horn·tail (ˈhɔːnˌteɪl) *n.* any of various large wasplike insects of the hymenopterous family *Siricidae*, the females of which have a strong stout ovipositor and lay their eggs in the wood of felled trees. Also called: **wood wasp.**

horn·wort (ˈhɔːnˌwɜːt) *n.* any aquatic plant of the genus *Ceratophyllum*, forming submerged branching masses in ponds and slow-flowing streams: family *Ceratophyllaceae*.

horn·y (ˈhɔːnɪ) *adj.* **horn·i·er, horn·i·est. 1.** of, like, or hard as horn. **2.** having a horn or horns. **3.** *Slang.* aroused sexually. **—ˈhorn·i·ly** *adv.* **—ˈhorn·i·ness** *n.*

horol. *abbrev. for* horology.

hor·o·loge (ˈhɒrəˌlɒdʒ) *n.* a rare word for **timepiece.** [C14: from Latin *hōrologium*, from Greek *hōrologion*, from *hōra* HOUR + *-logos* from *legein* to tell]

ho·rol·o·gist (hɒˈrɒlədʒɪst) *or* **ho·rol·o·ger** *n.* a person skilled in horology, esp. an expert maker of timepieces.

hor·o·lo·gi·um (ˌhɒrəˈləʊdʒɪəm) *n., pl.* **·gi·a** (-dʒɪə). a clock-tower. [C17: from Latin; see HOROLOGE]

Hor·o·lo·gi·um (ˌhɒrəˈləʊdʒɪəm) *n., Latin genitive* **Hor·o·lo·gi·i** (ˌhɒrəˈləʊdʒɪaɪ). a faint constellation in the S hemisphere lying near Eridanus and Hydrus.

ho·rol·o·gy (hɒˈrɒlədʒɪ) *n.* the art or science of making timepieces or of measuring time. **—hor·o·log·ic** (ˌhɒrəˈlɒdʒɪk) *or* **ˌhor·o·ˈlog·i·cal** *adj.*

hor·o·scope (ˈhɒrəˌskəʊp) *n.* **1.** the prediction of a person's future based on a comparison of the zodiacal data for the time of birth with the data from the period under consideration. **2.** the configuration of the planets, the sun, and the moon in the sky at a particular moment. **3.** Also called: **chart.** a diagram showing the positions of the planets, sun, moon, etc., at a particular time and place. [Old English *horoscopus*, from Latin, from Greek *hōroskopos* ascendant birth sign, from *hōra* HOUR + -SCOPE] **—hor·o·scop·ic** (ˌhɒrəˈskɒpɪk) *adj.*

ho·ros·co·py (hɒˈrɒskəpɪ) *n., pl.* **·pies.** the casting and interpretation of horoscopes.

Hor·o·witz (ˈhɒrəvɪts) *n.* **Vlad·i·mir.** born 1904, Russian virtuoso pianist, in the U.S. since 1928.

hor·ren·dous (hɒˈrɛndəs) *adj.* another word for **horrific.** [C17: from Latin *horrendus* fearful, from *horrēre* to bristle, shudder, tremble; see HORROR] **—hor·ˈren·dous·ly** *adv.*

hor·ri·ble ('hɒrəbᵊl) *adj.* **1.** causing horror; dreadful. **2.** disagreeable; unpleasant. **3.** *Informal.* cruel or unkind. [C14: via Old French from Latin *horribilis,* from *horrēre* to tremble] —'**hor·ri·ble·ness** *n.*

hor·ri·bly ('hɒrɪblɪ) *adv.* **1.** in a horrible manner. **2.** (intensifier): *I'm horribly bored.*

hor·rid ('hɒrɪd) *adj.* **1.** disagreeable; unpleasant: *a horrid meal.* **2.** repulsive or frightening. **3.** *Informal.* unkind. [C16 (in the sense: bristling, shaggy): from Latin *horridus* prickly, rough, from *horrēre* to bristle] —'**hor·rid·ly** *adv.* —'**hor·rid·ness** *n.*

hor·rif·ic (hɒ'rɪfɪk, hə-) *adj.* provoking horror; horrible. —**hor·'rif·i·cal·ly** *adv.*

hor·ri·fy ('hɒrɪˌfaɪ) *vb.* **·fies, ·fy·ing, ·fied.** (*tr.*) **1.** to cause feelings of horror; terrify; frighten. **2.** to dismay or shock greatly. —ˌ**hor·ri·fi·'ca·tion** *n.* —'**hor·ri·ˌfy·ing·ly** *adv.*

hor·rip·i·la·tion (hɒˌrɪpɪ'leɪʃən) *n. Physiol.* **1.** a technical name for **goose flesh. 2.** the erection of any short bodily hairs. [C17: from Late Latin *horripilātiō* a bristling, from Latin *horrēre* to stand on end + *pilus* hair]

hor·ror ('hɒrə) *n.* **1.** extreme fear; terror; dread. **2.** intense loathing; hatred. **3.** (*often pl.*) a thing or person causing fear, loathing, etc. **4.** (*modifier*) having a frightening subject, esp. a supernatural one: *a horror film.* [C14: from Latin: a trembling with fear; compare HIRSUTE]

hor·rors ('hɒrəz) *pl. n.* **1.** *Slang.* a fit of depression or anxiety. **2.** *Informal.* See **delirium tremens.** ~*interj.* **3.** an expression of dismay, sometimes facetious.

hor·ror-struck *or* **hor·ror-strick·en** *adj.* shocked; horrified.

Hor·sa ('hɔːsə) *n.* died ?455 A.D., leader, with his brother Hengist, of the first Jutish settlers in Britain. See also **Hengist.**

hors con·cours *French.* (ɔr kɔ̃'kuːr) *adj.* (*postpositive*), *adv.* **1.** (of an artist, exhibitor, etc.) excluded from competing. **2.** without equal; unrivalled. [literally: out of the competition]

hors de com·bat *French.* (ɔr də kɔ̃'ba) *adj.* (*postpositive*), *adv.* disabled or injured. [literally: out of (the) fight]

hors d'oeu·vre (ɔː 'dɜːvr; *French* ɔr 'dœːvr) *n., pl.* **hors d'oeu·vre** *or* **hors d'oeu·vres** ('dɜːvr; *French* 'dœːvr). an additional dish served as an appetizer, usually before the main meal. [C18: from French, literally: outside the work, not part of the main course]

horse (hɔːs) *n.* **1.** a domesticated perissodactyl mammal, *Equus caballus,* used for draught work and riding: family *Equidae.* Related adj.: **equine. 2.** the adult male of this species; stallion. **3. wild horse. a.** a horse (*Equus caballus*) that has become feral. **b.** another name for **Przewalski's horse. 4. a.** any other member of the family *Equidae,* such as the zebra or ass. **b.** (*as modifier): the horse family.* **5.** (*functioning as pl.*) horsemen, esp. cavalry: *a regiment of horse.* **6.** Also called: **buck.** *Gymnastics.* a padded apparatus on legs, used for vaulting, etc. **7.** a narrow board supported by a pair of legs at each end, used as a frame for sawing or as a trestle, barrier, etc. **8.** a contrivance on which a person may ride and exercise. **9.** a slang word for **heroin. 10.** *Mining.* a mass of rock within a vein of ore. **11.** *Nautical.* a rod, rope, or cable, fixed at the ends, along which something may slide by means of a thimble, shackle, or other fitting; traveller. **12.** *Chess.* an informal name for **knight. 13.** *Informal.* short for **horsepower. 14.** (*modifier*) drawn by a horse or horses: *a horse cart.* **15. be** (*or* **get**) **on one's high horse.** *Informal.* to act disdainfully aloof. **16. flog** *or* **beat a dead horse.** *Chiefly Brit.* **a.** to harp on some long discarded subject. **b.** to pursue the solution of a problem long realized to be insoluble. **17. hold one's horses.** to hold back; restrain oneself. **18. a horse of another** *or* **different colour.** a completely different topic, argument, etc. **19. the horse's mouth.** the most reliable source. **20. to horse!** an order to mount horses. ~*vb.* **21.** (*tr.*) to provide with a horse or horses. **22.** to put or be put on horseback. **23.** (*tr.*) to move (something heavy) into position by sheer physical strength. [Old English *hors;* related to Old Frisian *hors,* Old High German *hros,* Old Norse *hross*] —'**horse·less** *adj.* —'**horse·ˌlike** *adj.*

horse a·round *or* **a·bout** *vb.* (*intr., adv.*) *Informal.* to indulge in horseplay.

horse·back ('hɔːsˌbæk) *n.* **a.** a horse's back (esp. in the phrase **on horseback**). **b.** *Chiefly U.S.* (*as modifier*): *horseback riding.*

horse bean *n.* another name for **broad bean.**

horse·box ('hɔːsˌbɒks) *n. Brit.* a van or trailer used for carrying horses.

horse brass *n.* a decorative brass ornament, usually circular, originally attached to a horse's harness.

horse chest·nut *n.* **1.** any of several trees of the genus *Aesculus,* esp. the Eurasian *A. hippocastanum,* having palmate leaves, erect clusters of white, pink, or red flowers, and brown shiny inedible nuts enclosed in a spiky bur: family *Hippocastanaceae.* **2.** Also called: **conker.** the nut of this tree. [C16: so called from its having been used in the treatment of respiratory disease in horses]

horse·flesh ('hɔːsˌflɛʃ) *n.* **1.** horses collectively. **2.** the flesh of a horse, esp. edible horse meat.

horse·fly ('hɔːsˌflaɪ) *n., pl.* **·flies.** any large stout-bodied dipterous fly of the family *Tabanidae,* the females of which suck the blood of mammals, esp. horses, cattle, and man. Also called: **gadfly, cleg.**

horse gen·tian *n.* any caprifoliaceous plant of the genus *Triosteum,* of Asia and North America, having small purplish-brown flowers. Also called: **feverwort.**

Horse Guards *n.* the cavalry regiment that, together with the Life Guards, comprises the cavalry part of the British sovereign's Household Brigade, with headquarters in Whitehall, London.

horse·hair ('hɔːsˌhɛə) *n.* **a.** hair taken chiefly from the tail or mane of a horse, used in upholstery and for fabric, etc. **b.** (*as modifier): a horsehair mattress.*

horse·hair worm *n.* another name for **hairworm** (sense 2).

horse·hide ('hɔːsˌhaɪd) *n.* **1.** the hide of a horse. **2.** leather made from this hide. **3.** (*modifier*) made of horsehide.

horse lat·i·tudes *pl. n. Nautical.* the latitudes near 30°N or 30°S at sea, characterized by baffling winds, calms, and high barometric pressure. [C18: referring either to the high mortality of horses on board ship in these latitudes or to *dead horse* (nautical slang: advance pay), which sailors expected to work off by this stage of a voyage]

horse laugh *n.* a coarse, mocking, or raucous laugh; guffaw.

horse·leech ('hɔːsˌliːtʃ) *n.* **1.** any of several large carnivorous freshwater leeches of the genus *Haemopis,* esp. *H. sanguisuga.* **2.** an archaic name for a **veterinary surgeon.**

horse macke·rel *n.* **1.** Also called: **scad.** a mackerel-like carangid fish, *Trachurus trachurus,* of European Atlantic waters, with a row of bony scales along the lateral line. Sometimes called (U.S.): **saurel. 2.** any of various large tunnies or related fishes.

horse·man ('hɔːsmən) *n., pl.* **·men. 1.** a person who is skilled in riding or horsemanship. **2.** a person who rides a horse. —'**horse·ˌwom·an** *fem. n.*

horse·man·ship ('hɔːsmənˌʃɪp) *n.* **1.** the art of riding on horseback. **2.** skill in riding horses.

horse ma·rine *n. U.S.* **1.** (formerly) a mounted marine or cavalryman serving in a ship. **2.** someone out of place; misfit.

horse·mint ('hɔːsˌmɪnt) *n.* **1.** a hairy European mint plant, *Mentha longifolia,* with small mauve flowers: family *Labiatae* (labiates). **2.** any of several similar and related plants, such as *Monarda punctata* of North America.

horse mush·room *n.* a large edible agaricaceous field mushroom, *Agaricus arvensis,* with a white cap and greyish gills.

horse net·tle *n.* a weedy solanceous North American plant, *Solanum carolinense,* with yellow prickles, white or blue flowers, and yellow berries.

Hor·sens (*Danish* 'hɔrsəns) *n.* a port in Denmark, in E Jutland at the head of **Horsens Fjord.** Pop.: 41 895 (1970).

horse op·er·a *n. Informal.* another term for **Western** (sense 4).

horse pis·tol *n.* a large holstered pistol formerly carried by horsemen.

horse·play ('hɔːsˌpleɪ) *n.* rough, boisterous, or rowdy play.

horse·pow·er ('hɔːsˌpaʊə) *n.* **1.** an fps unit of power, equal to 550 foot-pounds per second (equivalent to 745.7 watts). **2.** a U.S. standard unit of power, equal to 746 watts. ~Abbrevs.: **HP, H.P., h.p., hp.**

horse·pow·er-hour *n.* an fps unit of work or energy equal to the work done by 1 horsepower in 1 hour. 1 horsepower-hour is equivalent to 2.686×10^6 joules.

horse·rad·ish ('hɔːsˌrædɪʃ) *n.* **1.** a coarse Eurasian cruciferous plant, *Armoracia rusticana,* cultivated for its thick white pungent root. **2.** the root of this plant, which is ground and combined with vinegar, etc., to make a sauce.

horse sense *n.* another term for **common sense.**

horse·shit ('hɔːsˌʃɪt) *n. Taboo slang.* rubbish; nonsense.

horse·shoe ('hɔːsˌʃuː) *n.* **1.** a piece of iron shaped like a U with the ends curving inwards that is nailed to the underside of the hoof of a horse to protect the soft part of the foot from hard surfaces: commonly thought to be a token of good luck. **2.** an object of similar shape. ~*vb.* **·shoes, ·shoe·ing, ·shoed. 3.** (*tr.*) to fit with a horseshoe; shoe.

horse·shoe arch *n.* an arch formed in the shape of a horseshoe, esp. as used in Moorish architecture.

horse·shoe bat *n.* any of numerous large-eared Old World insectivorous bats, mostly of the genus *Rhinolophus,* with a fleshy growth around the nostrils, used in echo location: family *Rhinolophidae.*

horse·shoe crab *n.* any marine chelicerate arthropod of the genus *Limulus,* of North America and Asia, having a rounded heavily armoured body with a long pointed tail: class *Merostomata.* Also called: **king crab.**

horse·shoes ('hɔːsˌʃuːz) *n.* a game in which the players try to throw horseshoes so that they encircle a stake in the ground some distance away.

horse·tail ('hɔːsˌteɪl) *n.* **1.** any pteridophyte plant of the genus *Equisetum* and order *Equisetales,* having jointed stems with whorls of small dark toothlike leaves. **2.** a stylized horse's tail formerly used as the emblem of a pasha, the number of tails increasing with rank.

horse·weed ('hɔːsˌwiːd) *n.* the U.S. name for **Canadian fleabane** (see **fleabane** (sense 3)).

horse·whip ('hɔːsˌwɪp) *n.* **1.** a whip, usually with a long thong, used for managing horses. ~*vb.* **·whips, ·whip·ping, ·whipped. 2.** (*tr.*) to flog with such a whip. —'**horse·ˌwhip·per** *n.*

horst (hɔːst) *n.* a ridge of land that has been forced upwards between two faults. [C20: from German: thicket]

hors·y *or* **hors·ey** ('hɔːsɪ) *adj.* **hors·i·er, hors·i·est. 1.** of or relating to horses: *a horsy smell.* **2.** dealing with or devoted to horses. **3.** like a horse: *a horsy face.* —'**hors·i·ly** *adv.* —'**hors·i·ness** *n.*

hort. *abbrev. for:* **1.** horticultural. **2.** horticulture.

Hor·ta (*Portuguese* 'ɔrtə) *n.* a port in the Azores, on the SE coast of Fayal Island.

hor·ta·to·ry ('hɔːtətərɪ, -trɪ) *or* **hor·ta·tive** ('hɔːtətɪv) *adj.*

tending to exhort; encouraging. [C16: from Late Latin *hortātōrius,* from Latin *hortārī* to EXHORT] —**'hor·ta·to·ri·ly** *or* **'hor·ta·tive·ly** *adv.*

Hor·tense (*French* ɔr'tã:s) *n.* See (Eugénie Hortense de) **Beauharnais.**

Hor·thy (*Hungarian* 'horti) *n.* **Mik·lós** ('miklo:ʃ), full name *Horthy de Nagybánya.* 1868–1957, Hungarian admiral: suppressed Kun's Communist republic (1919); regent of Hungary (1920–44).

hor·ti·cul·ture ('hɔ:tɪˌkʌltʃə) *n.* the art or science of cultivating gardens. [C17: from Latin *hortus* garden + CULTURE, on the model of AGRICULTURE] —ˌ**hor·ti·'cul·tur·al** *adj.* —ˌ**hor·ti·'cul·tur·al·ly** *adv.* —ˌ**hor·ti·'cul·tur·ist** *n.*

hor·tus sic·cus ('hɔ:təs 'sɪkəs) *n.* a less common name for **herbarium.** [C17: Latin, literally: dry garden]

Ho·rus ('hɔ:rəs) *n.* a solar god of Egyptian mythology, usually depicted with a falcon's head. [via Late Latin from Greek *Hōros,* from Egyptian *Hur* hawk]

Hos. *Bible. abbrev. for* Hosea.

ho·san·na (həʊ'zænə) *interj.* **1.** an exclamation of praise, esp. one to God. ~*n.* **2.** the act of crying "hosanna". [Old English *osanna,* via Late Latin from Greek, from Hebrew *hōshi 'āh nnā* save now, we pray]

hose[1] (həʊz) *n.* **1.** a flexible pipe, for conveying a liquid or gas. ~*vb.* **2.** (sometimes foll. by *down*) to wash, water, or sprinkle (a person or thing) with or as if with a hose. [C15: later use of HOSE[2]]

hose[2] (həʊz) *n., pl.* **hose** *or* **hos·en. 1.** stockings, socks, and tights collectively. **2.** *History.* a man's garment covering the legs and reaching up to the waist; worn with a doublet. **3. half-hose.** socks. [Old English *hosa;* related to Old High German *hosa,* Dutch *hoos,* Old Norse *hosa*]

Ho·se·a (həʊ'zɪə) *n. Old Testament.* **1.** a Hebrew prophet of the 8th century B.C. **2.** the book containing his oracles.

ho·si·er ('həʊzɪə) *n.* a person who sells stockings, etc.

ho·si·er·y ('həʊzɪərɪ) *n.* stockings, socks, and knitted under-clothing collectively.

hosp. *abbrev. for* hospital.

hos·pice ('hɒspɪs) *or* **hos·pit·i·um** (hɒ'spɪtɪəm) *n., pl.* **hos·pic·es** *or* **hos·pit·i·a** (hɒ'spɪtɪə). *Archaic.* a place of shelter for travellers, esp. one kept by a monastic order. [C19: from French, from Latin *hospitium* hospitality, from *hospes* guest, HOST[1]]

hos·pi·ta·ble ('hɒspɪtəbᵊl, hɒ'spɪt-) *adj.* **1.** welcoming to guests or strangers. **2.** fond of entertaining. **3.** receptive: *hospitable to new ideas.* [C16: from Medieval Latin *hospitāre* to receive as a guest, from Latin *hospes* guest, HOST[1]] —**'hos·pi·ta·ble·ness** *n.* —**'hos·pi·ta·bly** *adv.*

hos·pi·tal ('hɒspɪtᵊl) *n.* **1.** an institution for the medical, surgical, obstetric, or psychiatric care and treatment of patients. **2.** (*modifier*) having the function of a hospital: *a hospital ship.* **3.** a repair shop for something specified: *a dolls' hospital.* **4.** *Archaic.* a charitable home, hospice, or school. [C13: from Medieval Latin *hospitāle* hospice, from Latin *hospitālis* relating to a guest, from *hospes, hospit-* guest, HOST[1]]

hos·pi·tal cor·ner *n.* a corner of a made-up bed in which the bedclothes have been neatly and securely folded, esp. as in hospitals.

Hos·pi·ta·let (*Spanish* ˌospita'let) *n.* a city in NE Spain, a SW suburb of Barcelona. Pop.: 241 978 (1970).

hos·pi·tal·i·ty (ˌhɒspɪ'tælɪtɪ) *n., pl.* **·ties. 1.** kindness in welcoming strangers or guests. **2.** receptiveness.

hos·pi·tal·i·za·tion *or* **hos·pi·tal·i·sa·tion** (ˌhɒspɪtəlaɪ'zeɪʃən) *n.* **1.** the act or an instance of being hospitalized. **2.** the duration of a stay in a hospital.

hos·pi·tal·ize *or* **hos·pi·tal·ise** ('hɒspɪtəˌlaɪz) *vb.* (*tr.*) to admit or send (a person) into a hospital.

hos·pi·tal·ler *or U.S.* **hos·pi·tal·er** ('hɒspɪtələ) *n.* a person, esp. a member of certain religious orders, dedicated to hospital work, ambulance services, etc. [C14: from Old French *hospitalier,* from Medieval Latin *hospitālārius,* from *hospitāle* hospice; see HOSPITAL]

Hos·pi·tal·ler *or U.S.* **Hos·pi·tal·er** ('hɒspɪtələ) *n.* a member of the order of the Knights Hospitallers.

hos·po·dar ('hɒspəˌdɑ:) *n.* (formerly) the governor or prince of Moldavia or Wallachia under Ottoman rule. [C17: via Rumanian from Ukrainian, from *hospod'* lord; related to Russian *gospodin* courtesy title, Old Slavonic *gospodĭ* lord]

host[1] (həʊst) *n.* **1.** a person who receives or entertains guests, esp. in his own home. **2.** the compere of a show or television programme. **3.** *Biology.* **a.** an animal or plant that nourishes and supports a parasite. **b.** an animal, esp. an embryo, into which tissue is experimentally grafted. **4.** the owner or manager of an inn. ~*vb.* **5.** to be the host of (a party, programme, etc.): *to host one's own show.* **6.** (*tr.*) *U.S. informal.* to leave (a restaurant) without paying the bill. [C13: from French *hoste,* from Latin *hospes* guest, foreigner, from *hostis* enemy]

host[2] (həʊst) *n.* **1.** a great number; multitude. **2.** an archaic word for **army.** [C13: from Old French *hoste,* from Latin *hostis* stranger, enemy]

Host (həʊst) *n.* the bread consecrated in the Eucharist. [C14: from Old French *oiste,* from Latin *hostia* victim]

hos·ta ('hɒstə) *n.* any plant of the liliaceous genus *Hosta,* of China and Japan: cultivated esp. for their ornamental foliage. [C19: New Latin, named after N. T. *Host* (1761–1834), Austrian physician]

hos·tage ('hɒstɪdʒ) *n.* **1.** a person given to or held by a person, organization, etc., as a security or pledge. **2.** the state of being held as a hostage. **3.** any security or pledge. [C13: from Old French, from *hoste* guest, HOST[1]]

hos·tel ('hɒstᵊl) *n.* **1.** a building providing overnight accommodation, as for young travellers, etc. See also **youth hostel. 2.** *Brit.* a supervised lodging house for nurses, workers, etc. **3.** *Archaic.* another word for **hostelry.** [C13: from Old French, from Medieval Latin *hospitāle* hospice; see HOSPITAL]

hos·tel·ler *or U.S.* **hos·tel·er** ('hɒstələ) *n.* **1.** a person who stays at youth hostels. **2.** an archaic word for **innkeeper.**

hos·tel·ling *or U.S.* **hos·tel·ing** ('hɒstəlɪŋ) *n.* the practice of staying at youth hostels when travelling.

hos·tel·ry ('hɒstəlrɪ) *n., pl.* **·ries.** *Archaic.* an inn.

hos·tel school *n.* (in N Canada) a government boarding school for Indian and Eskimo students.

host·ess ('həʊstɪs) *n.* **1.** a woman acting as host. **2.** a woman who receives and entertains patrons of a club, restaurant, etc. **3.** See **air hostess.**

host·ie ('həʊstɪ) *n. Austral. informal.* short for **air hostess.**

hos·tile ('hɒstaɪl) *adj.* **1.** antagonistic; opposed. **2.** of or relating to an enemy. **3.** unfriendly. [C16: from Latin *hostīlis,* from *hostis* enemy] —**'hos·tile·ly** *adv.*

hos·tile wit·ness *n.* a witness who gives evidence against the party calling him.

hos·til·i·ty (hɒ'stɪlɪtɪ) *n., pl.* **·ties. 1.** enmity or antagonism. **2.** an act expressing enmity or opposition. **3.** (*pl.*) fighting; warfare.

host·ler ('ɒslə) *n.* another name (esp. Brit.) for **ostler.**

hot (hɒt) *adj.* **hot·ter, hot·test. 1.** having a relatively high temperature. **2.** having a temperature higher than desirable. **3.** causing or having a sensation of bodily heat. **4.** causing a burning sensation on the tongue: *hot mustard; a hot curry.* **5.** expressing or feeling intense emotion, such as embarrassment, anger, or lust. **6.** intense or vehement: *a hot argument.* **7.** recent; fresh; new: *a hot trial; hot from the press.* **8.** *Ball games.* (of a ball) thrown or struck hard, and so difficult to respond to. **9.** much favoured or approved: *a hot tip; a hot favourite.* **10.** *Informal.* having a dangerously high level of radioactivity: *a hot laboratory.* **11.** *Slang.* (of goods or money) stolen, smuggled, or otherwise illegally obtained. **12.** *Slang.* (of people) being sought by the police. **13.** (of a colour) intense; striking: *hot pink.* **14.** close or following closely: *hot on the scent.* **15.** *Informal.* at a dangerously high electric potential: *a hot terminal.* **16.** *Physics.* having an energy level higher than that of the ground state: *a hot atom.* **17.** *Slang.* impressive or good of its kind (esp. in the phrase **not so hot**). **18.** *Jazz slang.* arousing great excitement or enthusiasm by inspired improvisation, strong rhythms, etc. **19.** *Informal.* dangerous or unpleasant (esp. in the phrase **make it hot for someone**). **20.** (in various searching or guessing games) very near the answer or object to be found. **21.** *Metallurgy.* (of a process) at a sufficiently high temperature for metal to be in a soft workable state. **22.** *Austral. informal.* (of a price, charge, etc.) excessive. **23. give it (to someone) hot.** to punish or thrash (someone). **24. hot under the collar.** *Informal.* aroused with anger, annoyance, etc. **25. in hot water.** *Informal.* in trouble, esp. with those in authority. ~*adv.* **26.** in a hot manner; hotly. [Old English *hāt;* related to Old High German *heiz,* Old Norse *heitr,* Gothic *heito* fever] —**'hot·ly** *adv.* —**'hot·ness** *n.*

hot air *n. Informal.* empty and usually boastful talk.

hot-air bal·loon *n.* a lighter-than-air craft in which air heated by a flame is trapped in a large fabric bag.

hot·bed ('hɒtˌbɛd) *n.* **1.** a glass-covered bed of soil, usually heated by fermenting material, used for propagating plants, forcing early vegetables, etc. **2.** a place offering ideal conditions for the growth of an idea, activity, etc., esp. one considered bad: *a hotbed of insurrection.*

hot-blood·ed *adj.* **1.** passionate or excitable. **2.** (of a horse) being of thoroughbred stock. —ˌ**hot-'blood·ed·ness** *n.*

hotch·pot ('hɒtʃˌpɒt) *n. Property law.* the collecting of property so that it may be redistributed in equal shares, esp. on the intestacy of a parent who has given property to his children in his lifetime. [C14: from Old French *hochepot,* from *hocher* to shake, of Germanic origin + POT[1]]

hotch·potch ('hɒtʃˌpɒtʃ) *or esp. U.S.* **hodge·podge** *n.* **1.** a jumbled mixture. **2.** a thick soup or stew made from meat and vegetables. [C15: variant of HOTCHPOT]

hot cock·les *n.* a children's game in which one blindfolded player has to guess which other player has hit him.

hot cross bun *n.* a yeast bun with currants and sometimes candied peel, marked with a cross and traditionally eaten on Good Friday.

hot dog *n.* a sausage, esp. a frankfurter, usually served hot in a long roll split lengthways.

hot-dog *vb.* to perform a series of manoeuvres in skiing, skateboarding, etc., esp. in a showy manner. [C20: from U.S. *hot dog!,* exclamation of pleasure, approval, etc.]

ho·tel (həʊ'tɛl) *n.* **1.** a commercially run establishment providing lodging and usually meals for guests. **2.** *Austral.* a public house. [C17: from French *hôtel,* from Old French *hostel;* see HOSTEL]

ho·tel·ier (hɒ'tɛljeɪ) *n.* an owner or manager of one or more hotels.

hot·foot ('hɒtˌfʊt) *adj.* **1.** with all possible speed; quickly. ~*vb.* **2.** to move quickly.

hot-gos·pel·ler *n. Informal.* a revivalist preacher with a highly enthusiastic style of addressing his audience.

hot·head ('hɒtˌhɛd) *n.* an excitable or fiery person.

hot-head·ed *adj.* impetuous, rash, or hot-tempered. —ˌ**hot-'head·ed·ly** *adv.* —ˌ**hot-'head·ed·ness** *n.*

hot·house ('hɒt,haʊs) *n.* **1. a.** a greenhouse in which the temperature is maintained at a fixed level above that of the surroundings. **b.** (*as modifier*): *a hothouse plant.* **2.** (*modifier*) *Informal, often disparaging.* sensitive or delicate.

Ho·tien *or* **Ho-t'ien** ('həʊ'tjɛn) *n.* **1.** an oasis in W China, in the Takla Makan desert of central Sinkiang province, around the seasonal Hotien (Khotan) River. **2.** the chief town of this oasis, situated at the foot of the Kunlun Mountains. Pop.: about 50 000 (1950 est.). Also called: **Khotan.**

hot line *n.* a direct telephone, teletype, or other communications link between heads of government, etc., for emergency use.

hot met·al *n.* **a.** metallic type cast into shape in the molten state. **b.** (*as modifier*): *hot-metal printing.*

hot mon·ey *n.* capital that is transferred from one commercial centre to another seeking the highest interest rates or the best opportunity for short-term gain.

hot pants *pl. n.* **1.** very brief skin-tight shorts, worn by young women. **2.** *Taboo slang.* a feeling of sexual arousal: *he has hot pants for her.*

hot pep·per *n.* **1.** any of several varieties of the pepper *Capsicum frutescens,* esp. chilli pepper. **2.** the pungent usually small fruit of any of these plants.

hot·plate ('hɒt,pleɪt) *n.* **1.** an electrically heated plate on a cooker. **2.** a portable device, heated electrically or by spirit lamps, etc., on which food can be kept warm.

hot·pot ('hɒt,pɒt) *n. Brit.* a baked stew or casserole made with meat or fish and covered with a layer of potatoes.

hot po·ta·to *n. Informal.* a difficult situation or problem.

hot-press *n.* **1.** a machine for applying a combination of heat and pressure to give a smooth surface to paper, to express oil from it, etc. ~*vb.* **2.** (*tr.*) to subject (paper, cloth, etc.) to heat and pressure to give it a smooth surface or extract oil.

hot rod *n.* a car with an engine that has been radically modified to produce increased power.

hot seat *n.* **1.** *Informal.* a precarious, difficult, or dangerous position. **2.** *U.S.* a slang term for **electric chair.**

hot spot *n.* **1.** an area of potential violence or political unrest. **2.** a lively nightclub or other place of entertainment. **3. a.** any local area of high temperature in a part of an engine, etc. **b.** part of the inlet manifold of a paraffin engine that is heated by exhaust gases to vaporize the fuel.

hot spring *n.* a natural spring of mineral water at a temperature of 21°C (70°F) or above, found in areas of volcanic activity. Also called: **thermal spring.**

hot·spur ('hɒt,spɜː) *n.* an impetuous or fiery person. [C15: from *Hotspur,* nickname of Sir Henry PERCY]

Hot·spur ('hɒt,spɜː) *n.* **Har·ry.** nickname of (Sir Henry) **Percy.**

hot stuff *n. Informal.* **1.** a person, object, etc., considered important, attractive, sexually exciting, etc. **2.** a pornographic or erotic book, play, film, etc.

Hot·ten·tot ('hɒtᵊn,tɒt) *n.* **1.** (*pl.* **·tot** *or* **·tots**) a member of a race of people of southern Africa, of low stature and a dark yellowish-brown complexion, who formerly occupied the region near the Cape of Good Hope and are now almost extinct. **2.** any of the languages of this people, belonging to the Khoisan family. [C17: from Afrikaans, of uncertain origin]

hot·tie ('hɒtɪ) *n. Austral. informal.* a hot water bottle.

hot·tish *adj.* fairly hot.

hot up *vb.* (*adv.*) *Informal.* **1.** to make or become more exciting, active, or intense: *the chase was hotting up.* **2.** (*tr.*) Also: **soup up** or (esp. U.S.) **hop up.** to modify (a car or motorcycle engine) in order to increase its power.

hot-wa·ter bot·tle *n.* a receptacle, esp. one made of rubber, designed to be filled with hot water, used for warming a bed or parts of the body.

Hou·dan ('huːdæn) *n.* a breed of light domestic fowl originally from France, with a distinctive full crest. [C19: named after *Houdan,* village near Paris where the breed originated]

Hou·di·ni (huː'diːnɪ) *n.* **Har·ry.** original name *Ehrich Weiss.* 1874–1926, U.S. magician and escapologist.

Hou·don (*French* u'dɔ̃) *n.* **Jean An·toine** (ʒɑ̃ ɑ̃'twan). 1741–1828, French neoclassical portrait sculptor.

hough (hɒk) *Brit.* ~*n.* **1.** another word for **hock**[1]. ~*vb.* (*tr.*) **2.** to hamstring (cattle, horses, etc.). [C14: from Old English *hōh* heel]

Hough·ton-le-Spring ('haʊtᵊn lə 'sprɪŋ) *n.* a town in N England, in S Tyneside: coal-mining. Pop.: 32 666 (1971).

hou·mous *or* **hou·mus** ('huːməs) *n.* a creamy dip originating in the Middle East, made from tahina, chickpeas, etc. [from Arabic]

hound[1] (haʊnd) *n.* **1. a.** any of several breeds of dog used for hunting. **b.** (*in combination*): *an otterhound; a deerhound.* **2. the hounds.** a pack of foxhounds, etc. **3.** a dog, esp. one regarded as annoying. **4.** a despicable person. **5.** (in hare and hounds) a runner who pursues a hare. **6.** *Slang, chiefly U.S.* an enthusiast: *an autograph hound.* **7. ride to hounds** *or* **follow the hounds.** to take part in a fox hunt with hounds. ~*vb.* (*tr.*) **8.** to pursue or chase relentlessly. **9.** to urge on. [Old English *hund;* related to Old High German *hunt,* Old Norse *hundr,* Gothic *hunds*] —**'hound·er** *n.*

hound[2] (haʊnd) *n.* **1.** either of a pair of horizontal bars that reinforce the running gear of a horse-drawn vehicle. **2.** *Nautical.* either of a pair of fore-and-aft braces that serve as supports for a topmast. [C15: of Scandinavian origin; related to Old Norse *hūnn* knob, cube]

hound's-tongue *n.* any boraginaceous weedy plant of the genus *Cynoglossum,* esp. the Eurasian *C. officinale,* which has small reddish-purple flowers and spiny fruits. Also called: **dog's-tongue.** [Old English *hundestunge,* translation of Latin *cynoglōssos,* from Greek *kunoglōssos,* from *kuōn* dog + *glōssa* tongue; referring to the shape of its leaves]

hound's-tooth check *n.* a pattern of broken or jagged checks, esp. one printed on or woven into cloth. Also called: **dog's-tooth check, dogtooth check.**

Houns·low ('haʊnzləʊ) *n.* a borough of Greater London, on the River Thames: site of London's first civil airport (1919). Pop.: 199 100 (1976 est.).

Hou·phou·et-Boi·gny (*French* ufwɛ bwa'ɲi) *n.* **Fé·lix** (fe'liks). born 1905, Ivory Coast statesman; president of the Republic of the Ivory Coast since 1960.

hour (aʊə) *n.* **1.** a period of time equal to 3600 seconds; 1/24th of a calendar day. Related adjs.: **horal, horary. 2.** any of the points on the face of a timepiece that indicate intervals of 60 minutes. **3. the hour.** an exact number of complete hours: *the bus leaves on the hour.* **4.** the time of day as indicated by a watch, clock, etc. **5.** the period of time allowed for or used for something: *the lunch hour; the hour of prayer.* **6.** a special moment or period: *our finest hour.* **7. the hour.** the present time: *the man of the hour.* **8.** the distance covered in an hour: *we live an hour from the city.* **9.** *Astronomy.* an angular measurement of right ascension equal to 15° or a 24th part of the celestial equator. **10. one's hour. a.** a time of success, fame, etc. **b.** Also: **one's last hour.** the time of one's death: *his hour had come.* [C13: from Old French *hore,* from Latin *hōra,* from Greek: season]

hour an·gle *n.* the angular distance along the celestial equator from the meridian of the observer to the hour circle of a particular celestial body.

hour cir·cle *n.* a great circle on the celestial sphere passing through the celestial poles and a specified point, such as a star.

hour·glass ('aʊə,glɑːs) *n.* **1.** a device consisting of two transparent chambers linked by a narrow channel, containing a quantity of sand that takes a specified time to trickle to one chamber from the other. **2.** (*modifier*) well-proportioned with a small waist: *an hourglass figure.*

hour hand *n.* the pointer on a timepiece that indicates the hour. Compare **minute hand, second hand.**

hou·ri ('hʊərɪ) *n., pl.* **·ris. 1.** (in Muslim belief) any of the nymphs of Paradise. **2.** any alluring woman. [C18: from French, from Persian *hūrī,* from Arabic *hūr,* plural of *haurā'* woman with dark eyes]

hour·long *adj., adv.* lasting an hour.

hour·ly ('aʊəlɪ) *adj.* **1.** of, occurring, or done every hour. **2.** done in or measured by the hour: *we are paid an hourly rate.* **3.** continual or frequent. ~*adv.* **4.** every hour. **5.** at any moment or time.

hours (aʊəz) *pl. n.* **1.** a period regularly or customarily appointed for work, business, etc. **2.** one's times of rising and going to bed (esp. in the phrases **keep regular, irregular,** or **late hours**). **3. the small hours.** the hours just after midnight. **4. till all hours.** until very late. **5.** an indefinite period of time. **6.** Also called (in the Roman Catholic Church): **canonical hours. a.** the seven times of the day laid down for the recitation of the prayers of the divine office. **b.** the prayers recited at these times.

Hours (aʊəz) *pl. n.* another word for the **Horae.**

house *n.* (haʊs), *pl.* **hous·es** ('haʊzɪz). **1. a.** a building used as a home; dwelling. **b.** (*as modifier*): *house dog.* **2.** the people present in a house, esp. its usual occupants. **3. a.** a building used for some specific purpose. **b.** (*in combination*): *a schoolhouse.* **4.** (*often cap.*) a family line including ancestors and relatives, esp. a noble one: *the House of York.* **5. a.** a commercial company; firm: *a publishing house.* **b.** (*as modifier*): *house style; a house journal.* **6.** an official deliberative or legislative body, such as one chamber of a bicameral legislature. **7.** a quorum in such a body (esp. in the phrase **make a house**). **8.** a dwelling for a religious community. **9.** *Astrology.* any of the 12 divisions of the zodiac. See also **planet** (sense 3). **10. a.** any of several divisions, esp. residential, of a large school. **b.** (*as modifier*): *house spirit.* **11. a.** a hotel, restaurant, bar, inn, club, etc., or the management of such an establishment: *drinks on the house.* **b.** (*as modifier*): *house rules.* **12.** the audience in a theatre or cinema. **13.** an informal word for **brothel. 14.** a hall in which an official deliberative or legislative body meets. **15.** See **full house. 16.** *Curling.* the 12-foot target circle around the tee. **17.** *Nautical.* any structure or shelter on the weather deck of a vessel. **18. bring the house down.** *Theatre.* to win great applause. **19. house and home.** an emphatic form of **home. 20. like a house on fire.** *Informal.* very well, quickly, or intensely. **21. open house.** free hospitality. **22. put one's house in order.** to settle or organize one's affairs. **23. safe as houses.** *Brit.* very secure. ~*vb.* (haʊz). **24.** (*tr.*) to provide with or serve as accommodation. **25.** to give or receive shelter or lodging. **26.** (*tr.*) to contain or cover, esp. in order to protect. **27.** (*tr.*) to fit (a piece of wood) into a mortise, joint, etc. **28.** (*tr.*) *Nautical.* **a.** to secure or stow. **b.** to secure (a topmast). **c.** to secure and stow (an anchor). [Old English *hūs;* related to Old High German *hūs,* Gothic *gudhūs* temple, Old Norse *hūs* house] —**'house·less** *adj.*

House (haʊs) **the.** *n.* **1.** See **House of Commons. 2.** *Brit. informal.* the Stock Exchange.

house a·gent *n. Brit.* another name for **estate agent.**

house ar·rest *n.* confinement to one's own home.

house·boat ('haʊs,bəʊt) *n.* a stationary boat or barge used as a home.

house·bound ('haʊs,baʊnd) *adj.* unable to leave one's house because of illness, injury, etc.

house·boy ('haʊs,bɔɪ) *n.* a male domestic servant.

house·break·ing ('haʊsˌbreɪkɪŋ) *n. Criminal law.* the act of entering a building as a trespasser for an unlawful purpose. Assimilated with burglary, 1968. —**'house·ˌbreak·er** *n.*
house-bro·ken *adj.* another word for **house-trained.**
house·carl ('haʊsˌkɑːl) *n.* (in medieval Europe) a household warrior of Danish kings and noblemen. [Old English *hūscarl,* from Old Norse *hūskarl* manservant, from *hūs* HOUSE + *karl* man; see CHURL]
house·coat ('haʊsˌkəʊt) *n.* a woman's loose robelike informal garment.
house-craft *n.* skill in domestic management.
house fac·tor *n.* a Scottish term for **estate agent.**
house·fath·er ('haʊsˌfɑːðə) *n.* a man in charge of the welfare of a particular group of children in an institution such as a children's home or approved school. —**'house·ˌmoth·er** *fem. n.*
house·fly ('haʊsˌflaɪ) *n., pl.* **·flies.** a common dipterous fly, *Musca domestica,* that frequents human habitations, spreads disease, and lays its eggs in carrion, decaying vegetables, etc.: family *Muscidae.*
house guest *n.* a guest at a house, esp. one who stays for a comparatively long time.
house·hold ('haʊsˌhəʊld) *n.* **1.** the people living together in one house collectively. **2.** (*modifier*) of, relating to, or used in the running of a household; domestic: *household management.*
house·hold·er ('haʊsˌhəʊldə) *n.* a person who owns or rents a house. —**'house·ˌhold·er·ˌship** *n.*
house·hold gods *pl. n.* **1.** (in ancient Rome) deities of the home; lares and penates. **2.** *Brit. informal.* the essentials of domestic life.
house·hold name *or* **word** *n.* a person or thing that is very well known.
house·hold troops *pl. n.* the infantry and cavalry regiments that carry out escort and guard duties for a head of state.
house·keep·er ('haʊsˌkiːpə) *n.* a person, esp. a woman, employed to run a household.
house·keep·ing ('haʊsˌkiːpɪŋ) *n.* **1.** the running of a household. **2.** money allotted for housekeeping.
hou·sel ('haʊzᵊl) *n.* **1.** a medieval name for **Eucharist.** ~*vb.* **·sels, ·sel·ling, ·selled** *or U.S.* **·sels, ·sel·ing, ·seled. 2.** (*tr.*) to give the Eucharist to (someone). [Old English *hūsl;* related to Gothic *hunsl* sacrifice, Old Norse *hūsl*]
house·leek ('haʊsˌliːk) *n.* any Old World crassulaceous plant of the genus *Sempervivum,* esp. *S. tectorum,* which has a rosette of succulent leaves and pinkish flowers: grows on walls. Also called: **hen-and-chickens.**
house lights *pl. n.* the lights in the auditorium of a theatre, cinema, etc.
house·line ('haʊsˌlaɪn) *n. Nautical.* tarred marline. Also called: **housing.**
house·maid ('haʊsˌmeɪd) *n.* a girl or woman employed to do housework, esp. one who is resident in the household.
house·maid's knee *n.* inflammation and swelling of the bursa in front of the kneecap, caused esp. by constant kneeling on a hard surface. Technical name: **prepatellar bursitis.**
house·man ('haʊsmən) *n., pl.* **·men.** *Med.* a junior doctor who is a member of the medical staff of a hospital. U.S. equivalent: **intern.**
house mar·tin *n.* a Eurasian swallow, *Delichon urbica,* with a slightly forked tail and a white and bluish-black plumage.
house·mas·ter ('haʊsˌmɑːstə) *n.* a teacher, esp. in a boarding school, responsible for the pupils in his house. —**house·mis·tress** ('haʊsˌmɪstrɪs) *fem. n.*
house mouse *n.* any of various greyish mice of the Old World genus *Mus,* esp. *M. musculus,* a common household pest in most parts of the world: family *Muridae.*
House of As·sem·bly *n.* a legislative assembly or the lower chamber of such an assembly, esp. in various British colonies and countries of the Commonwealth.
house of cards *n.* an unstable situation, plan, etc.
House of Com·mons *n.* (in Britain, Canada, etc.) the lower chamber of Parliament.
house of cor·rec·tion *n.* (formerly) a place of confinement for persons convicted of minor offences.
house of God *n.* a church, temple, or chapel.
house of ill re·pute *or* **ill fame** *n.* a euphemistic name for **brothel.**
House of Keys *n.* the lower chamber of the legislature of the Isle of Man.
House of Lords *n.* (in Britain) the upper chamber of Parliament, composed of the peers of the realm.
House of Rep·re·sen·ta·tives *n.* **1.** (in the U.S.) the lower chamber of Congress. **2.** (in Australia) the lower chamber of Parliament. **3.** the sole chamber of New Zealand's Parliament: formerly the lower chamber. **4.** (in the U.S.) the lower chamber in many state legislatures.
House of the Peo·ple *n.* another name for **Lok Sabha.**
house or·gan *n.* a periodical published by an organization for its employees or clients.
house par·ty *n.* **1.** a party, usually in a country house, at which guests are invited to stay for several days. **2.** the guests who are invited.
house phy·si·cian *or* **doc·tor** *n.* a physician who lives in a hospital or other institution where he is employed. Compare **resident** (sense 6).
house plant *n.* a plant that can be grown indoors.
house-proud *adj.* proud of the appearance, cleanliness, etc., of one's house, sometimes excessively so.
house·room ('haʊsˌrʊm, -ˌruːm) *n.* **1.** room for storage or lodging. **2. give (something) houseroom.** (*used with a negative*) to have or keep (something) in one's house: *I wouldn't give that vase houseroom.*
Hous·es of Par·lia·ment *n.* (in Britain) **1.** the building in which the House of Commons and the House of Lords assemble. **2.** these two chambers considered together.
house spar·row *n.* a small Eurasian weaverbird, *Passer domesticus,* now established in North America and Australia. It has a brown streaked plumage with grey underparts. Also called (U.S.): **English sparrow.**
house·top ('haʊsˌtɒp) *n.* **1.** the roof of a house. **2. proclaim from the housetops.** to announce (something) publicly.
house-train *vb.* (*tr.*) *Brit.* to train (pets) to urinate and defecate outside the house or in a special place.
House Un-A·mer·i·can Ac·tiv·i·ties Com·mit·tee *n.* the former name of the **Internal Security Committee** of the U.S. House of Representatives: notorious for its anti-Communist investigations in the late 1940s and 1950s. Acronym: **HUAC.**
house-warm·ing *n.* **a.** a party given after moving into a new home. **b.** (*as modifier*): *a house-warming party.*
house·wife ('haʊsˌwaɪf) *n. pl.* **·wives. 1.** a married woman who keeps house, usually without having a full-time job. **2.** ('hʌzɪf) Also called: **hussy, huswife.** *Chiefly Brit.* a small sewing kit issued to soldiers. —**house·wif·er·y** ('haʊsˌwɪfərɪ, -ˌwɪfrɪ) *n.*
house·wife·ly ('haʊsˌwaɪflɪ) *adj.* prudent and neat; domestic: *housewifely virtues.* —**'house·ˌwife·li·ness** *n.*
house·work ('haʊsˌwɜːk) *n.* the work of running a home, such as cleaning, cooking, etc. —**'house·ˌwork·er** *n.*
hous·ey-hous·ey ('haʊzɪ'haʊzɪ) *n.* another name for **bingo** or **lotto.** [C20: so called from the cry of "house!" shouted by the winner of a game, probably from FULL HOUSE]
hous·ing[1] ('haʊzɪŋ) *n.* **1. a.** houses or dwellings collectively. **b.** (*as modifier*): *a housing problem.* **2.** the act of providing with accommodation. **3.** a hole, recess, groove, or slot made in one wooden member to receive another. **4.** a part designed to shelter, cover, contain, or support a component, such as a bearing, or a mechanism, such as a pump or wheel: *a bearing housing; a motor housing; a wheel housing.* **5.** another word for **houseline.**
hous·ing[2] ('haʊzɪŋ) *n.* (*often pl.*) *Archaic.* another word for **trappings** (sense 2). [C14: from Old French *houce* covering, of Germanic origin]
hous·ing es·tate *n.* a planned area of housing, often with its own shops and other amenities.
hous·ing scheme *n.* a local-authority housing plan. Often shortened to **scheme.**
Hous·man ('haʊsmən) *n.* **A(lfred) E(dward).** 1859–1936, English poet and classical scholar, author of *A Shropshire Lad* (1896) and *Last Poems* (1922).
Hou·ston ('hjuːstən) *n.* an inland port in SE Texas, linked by the **Houston Ship Canal** to the Gulf of Mexico and the Gulf Intracoastal Waterway: capital of the Republic of Texas (1837–39; 1842–45); site of the Manned Spacecraft Center (1964). Pop.: 1 320 018 (1973 est.).
hous·to·ni·a (huː'stəʊnɪə) *n.* any small North American rubiaceous plant of the genus *Houstonia,* having blue, white or purple flowers. [C19: named after Dr. William *Houston* (died 1733), Scottish botanist]
hout·ing ('haʊtɪŋ) *n.* a European whitefish, *Coregonus oxyrhynchus,* that lives in salt water but spawns in freshwater lakes: a valued food fish. [C19: from Dutch, from Middle Dutch *houtic,* of uncertain origin]
hove (həʊv) *vb. Chiefly nautical.* a past tense or past participle of **heave.**
Hove (həʊv) *n.* a town and resort in S England, in East Sussex adjoining Brighton. Pop.: 72 659 (1971).
hov·el ('hʌvᵊl, 'hɒv-) *n.* **1.** a ramshackle dwelling place. **2.** an open shed for livestock, carts, etc. **3.** the conical building enclosing a kiln. ~*vb.* **·els, ·el·ling, ·elled** *or U.S.* **·els, ·el·ing, ·eled. 4.** to shelter or be sheltered in a hovel. [C15: of unknown origin]
hov·er ('hɒvə) *vb.* (*intr.*) **1.** to remain suspended in one place. **2.** (of certain birds, esp. hawks) to remain in one place in the air by rapidly beating the wings. **3.** to linger uncertainly in a nervous or solicitous way. **4.** to be in a state of indecision. *she was hovering between the two suitors.* ~*n.* **5.** the act of hovering. [C14 *hoveren,* variant of *hoven,* of obscure origin] —**'hov·er·er** *n.* —**'hov·er·ing·ly** *adv.*
hov·er·craft ('hɒvəˌkrɑːft) *n.* a vehicle that is able to travel across both land and water on a cushion of air. The cushion is produced by fans or a peripheral ring of nozzles.
hov·er fly *n.* any dipterous fly of the family *Syrphidae,* with a typically hovering flight, esp. *Syrphus ribesii,* which mimics a wasp.
hov·er·port ('hɒvəˌpɔːt) *n.* a port for hovercraft.
hov·er·train ('hɒvəˌtreɪn) *n.* a train that moves over a concrete track and is supported while in motion by a cushion of air supplied by powerful fans.
how[1] (haʊ) *adv.* **1.** in what way? in what manner? by what means?: *how did it happen?* Also used in indirect questions: *tell me how he did it.* **2.** to what extent?: *how tall is he?* **3.** how good? how well? what...like?: *how did she sing? how was the holiday?* **4. how about?** used to suggest something: *how about asking her? how about a cup of tea?* **5. how are you?** what is your state of health? **6. how come?** *Informal.* what is the reason (that)?: *how come you told him?* **7. how's that for...? a.** is this satisfactory as regards...: *how's that for size?* **b.** an exclamation used to draw attention to a quality, deed, etc.: *how*

is that for endurance? **8. how's that? a.** what is your opinion? **b.** *Cricket.* (an appeal to the umpire) is the batsman out? **9. how now?** *or* **how so?** *Archaic.* what is the meaning of this? **10.** Also: **as how.** *Not standard.* that: *he told me as how the shop was closed.* **11.** in whatever way: *do it how you wish.* **12. and how!** (intensifier) very much so!. **13. here's how!** (as a toast) good health! ~ *n.* **14.** the way a thing is done: *the how of it.* [Old English *hu;* related to Old Frisian *hū,* Old High German *hweo*]

how[2] (haʊ) *interj.* a greeting supposed to be or have been used by American Indians and often used humorously. [C19: of Siouan origin; related to Dakota *háo*]

How·ard ('haʊəd) *n.* **1. Cath·er·ine.** ?1521–42, fifth wife of Henry VIII of England; beheaded. **2. Charles,** Lord Howard of Effingham and 1st Earl of Nottingham. 1536–1624, Lord High Admiral of England (1585–1618). He commanded the fleet that defeated the Spanish Armada (1588). **3.** Sir **Eb·e·ne·zer.** 1850–1928, English town planner, who introduced garden cities. **4. Hen·ry.** See (Earl of) **Surrey. 5. John.** 1726–90, English prison reformer.

how+be+it (haʊ'biːɪt) *Archaic.* ~ **1.** *sentence connector.* however. ~*conj.* **2.** (*subordinating*) though; although.

how+dah ('haʊdə) *n.* a seat for riding on an elephant's back, esp. one with a canopy. [C18: from Hindi *haudah,* from Arabic *haudaj* load carried by elephant or camel]

how do you do *interj.* **1.** Also: **how do?, how d'ye do?** a formal greeting said by people who are being introduced to each other or are meeting for the first time. ~*n.* **how-do-you-do. 2.** *Informal.* a difficult situation.

how+dy ('haʊdɪ) *interj. Chiefly U.S.* an informal word for **hello.** [C16: from the phrase *how d'ye do*]

Howe (haʊ) *n.* **1. E·li·as.** 1819–67, U.S. inventor of the sewing machine (1846). **2. Geof·frey.** born 1926, British politician; Chancellor of the Exchequer since 1979. **3. Rich·ard,** 4th Viscount Howe. 1726-99, British admiral: served (1776-78) in the War of American Independence and commanded the Channel fleet against France, winning the Battle of the Glorious First of June (1794). **4.** his brother, **Wil·liam,** 5th Viscount Howe. 1729-1814, British general; commander in chief (1776-78) of British forces in the War of American Independence.

how·e'er (haʊ'ɛə) *sentence connector, adv.* a poetic contraction of **however.**

how+ev·er (haʊ'ɛvə) **1.** *sentence connector.* still; nevertheless. **2.** *sentence connector.* on the other hand; yet. ~*adv.* **3.** by whatever means; in whatever manner. **4.** (*used with adjectives expressing or admitting of quantity or degree*) no matter how: *however long it takes, finish it.* **5.** an emphatic form of **how**[1] (sense 1).

howf (haʊf, həʊf) *n. Scot.* a public house. [C16: of uncertain origin]

how+itz+er ('haʊɪtsə) *n.* a cannon having a short or medium barrel with a low muzzle velocity and a steep angle of fire. [C16: from Dutch *houwitser,* from German *Haubitze,* from Czech *houfnice* stone-sling]

howl (haʊl) *n.* **1.** a long plaintive cry or wail characteristic of a wolf or hound. **2.** a similar cry of pain or sorrow. **3.** *Slang.* **a.** a person or thing that is very funny. **b.** a prolonged outburst of laughter. **4.** *Electronics.* an unwanted prolonged high-pitched sound produced by a sound-producing system as a result of feedback. ~*vb.* **5.** to express in a howl or utter such cries. **6.** (*intr.*) (of the wind, etc.) to make a wailing noise. **7.** (*intr.*) *Informal.* to shout or laugh. [C14 *houlen;* related to Middle High German *hiuweln,* Middle Dutch *hūlen,* Danish *hyle*]

How+land Is+land ('haʊlənd) *n.* a small island in the central Pacific, near the equator northwest of Phoenix Island: U.S. airfield. Area: 2.6 sq. km (1 sq. mile).

howl down *vb.* (*tr., adv.*) to prevent (a speaker) from being heard by shouting disapprovingly.

howl+er ('haʊlə) *n.* **1.** Also called: **howler monkey.** any large New World monkey of the genus *Alouatta,* inhabiting tropical forests in South America and having a loud howling cry. **2.** *Informal.* a glaring mistake. **3.** *Brit.* a device that produces a loud tone in a telephone receiver to attract attention when the receiver is incorrectly replaced. **4.** one that howls.

how+let ('haʊlɪt) *n. Archaic, poetic.* another word for **owl.** [C15: diminutive of *howle* OWL]

howl+ing ('haʊlɪŋ) *adj.* (*prenominal*) *Informal.* (intensifier): *a howling success; a howling error.* —'**howl+ing+ly** *adv.*

How+rah ('haʊrə) *n.* an industrial city in E India, in West Bengal on the Hooghly River opposite Calcutta. Pop.: 737 877 (1971).

how+so+ev·er (ˌhaʊsəʊ'ɛvə) *sentence connector, adv.* a less common word for **however.**

how+tow+die (haʊ'taʊdɪ) *n.* a Scottish dish of boiled chicken with poached eggs and spinach. [from Scottish]

Hox·ha (*Albanian* 'hodʒa) *n.* **En·ver** ('emver). born 1908, Albanian statesman: founded the Albanian Communist Party in 1941 and has been its first secretary since 1954.

hoy[1] (hɔɪ) *n. Nautical.* **1.** a freight barge. **2.** a coastal fishing and trading vessel, usually sloop-rigged, used during the 17th and 18th centuries. [C15: from Middle Dutch *hoei*]

hoy[2] (hɔɪ) *interj.* a cry used to attract attention or drive animals. [C14: variant of HEY]

hoy·a ('hɔɪə) *n.* any plant of the asclepiadaceous genus *Hoya,* of E Asia and Australia, esp. the waxplant. [C19: named after Thomas *Hoy* (died 1821), English gardener]

hoy+den *or* **hoi+den** ('hɔɪdᵊn) *n.* a wild boisterous girl; tomboy. [C16: perhaps from Middle Dutch *heidijn* heathen] —'**hoy+den+ish** *or* '**hoi+den+ish** *adj.* —'**hoy+den+ish+ness** *or* '**hoi+den+ish+ness** *n.*

Hoy+lake ('hɔɪˌleɪk) *n.* a town and resort in NW England, in Merseyside on the Irish Sea. Pop.: 32 196 (1971).

Hoyle[1] (hɔɪl) *n.* an authoritative book of rules for card games. [after Sir Edmund *Hoyle,* 18th-century English authority on games, its compiler]

Hoyle[2] (hɔɪl) *n.* Sir **Fred.** born 1915, English astronomer and writer: his books include *The Nature of the Universe* (1950) and *Frontiers of Astronomy* (1955), and science-fiction writings.

H.P. *abbrev. for:* **1.** *Brit.* hire purchase. **2.** Also: **hp** horsepower. **3.** high pressure. **4.** (in Britain) Houses of Parliament. ~Also (for senses 1–3): **h.p.**

H.Q. *or* **h.q.** *abbrev. for* headquarters.

hr. *or* **hr** *abbrev. for* hour.

H.R. *abbrev. for:* **1.** *Brit.* Home Rule. **2.** *U.S.* House of Representatives.

Hra+dec Krá+lo+vé (*Czech* 'hradɛts 'kraːlɔveː) *n.* a town in NW Czechoslovakia, on the Elbe River. Pop.: 68 160 (1968 est.). German name: **Königgrätz.**

H.R.E. *abbrev. for* Holy Roman Emperor *or* Empire.

H.R.H. *abbrev. for* His (*or* Her) Royal Highness.

Hr·vat·ska ('hrvaːtskaː) *n.* the Serbo-Croatian name for **Croatia.**

h.s. *abbrev. for* hoc sensu. [Latin: in this sense]

H.S. (in Britain) *abbrev. for* Home Secretary.

H.S.H. *abbrev. for* His (*or* Her) Serene Highness.

Hsi (ʃiː) *n.* a variant spelling of **Si.**

Hsia-men ('ʃjɑː'mɛn) *n.* a transliteration of the modern Chinese name for **Amoy.**

Hsian (ʃjɑːn) *n.* a variant spelling of **Sian.**

Hsiang (ʃjɑːŋ) *n.* a variant spelling of **Siang.**

Hsin-hai-lien ('ʃɪn 'haɪ 'ljɛn) *n.* a variant spelling of **Sinhailien.**

Hsi+ning ('ʃiː'nɪŋ) *n.* a variant spelling of **Sining.**

Hsin+king ('ʃɪn'kɪŋ) *n.* the former name (1932–45) of **Changchun.**

H.S.M. *abbrev. for* His (*or* Her) Serene Majesty.

Hsüan T'ung ('ʃwɑːn 'tʊŋ) *n.* the title as emperor of China of (Henry) **Pu-yi.**

Hsü-chou ('ʃuː'tʃaʊ) *n.* a variant spelling of **Süchou.**

HT *Physics. abbrev. for* high tension.

ht. *abbrev. for* height.

Hts. (in place names) *abbrev. for* Heights.

Huai-nan ('hwaɪ'næn) *n.* a city in E China, in Anhwei province north of Hofei. Pop.: 600 000 (1970 est.).

Hua Kuo-feng ('hwɑː kwəʊ 'fɛŋ) *n.* born 1922, Chinese Communist statesman; prime minister of China (1976-80).

Huam+bo (*Portuguese* 'wambu) *n.* a town in central Angola: designated by the Portuguese as the future capital of the country. Pop.: 61 885 (1970). Former name (1928–73): **Nova Lisboa.**

Huang Hua (hwæŋ hwɑː) *n.* born 1913, Chinese Communist statesman; minister for foreign affairs since 1976.

Huás·car (*Spanish* 'waskar) *n.* died 1533, Inca ruler (1525–33): murdered by his half brother Atahualpa.

Huas+ca+rán (*Spanish* ˌwaska'ran) *or* **Huas+cán** (*Spanish* was'kan) *n.* an extinct volcano in W Peru, in the Peruvian Andes: the highest peak in Peru; avalanche in 1962 destroyed village and killed over 3000 people. Height: 6768 m (22 205 ft.).

hub (hʌb) *n.* **1.** the central portion of a wheel, propeller, fan, etc., through which the axle passes. **2.** the focal point. [C17: probably variant of HOB[1]]

Hub·ble ('hʌbᵊl) *n.* **Ed·win Pow·ell.** 1889–1953, U.S. astronomer, noted for his investigations of nebulae and the recession of the galaxies.

hub·ble-bub·ble ('hʌbᵊl'bʌbᵊl) *n.* **1.** another name for **hookah. 2.** hubbub; turmoil. **3.** a bubbling or gargling sound. [C17: rhyming jingle based on BUBBLE]

Hub·ble con+stant *n.* the ratio of the recessional velocity of a galaxy to its distance, the recessional velocity being determined from its red shift. It is equal to approximately 0.12 m $s^{-1}parsec^{-1}$. [C20: named after E. P. HUBBLE]

hub+bub ('hʌbʌb) *n.* **1.** a confused noise of many voices. **2.** uproar. [C16: probably from Irish *hooboobbes;* compare Scottish Gaelic *ubub!* an exclamation of contempt]

hub+by ('hʌbɪ) *n., pl.* **+bies.** an informal word for **husband.** [C17: by shortening and altering]

hub+cap ('hʌbˌkæp) *n.* a metal cap fitting onto the hub of a wheel, esp. a stainless steel or chromium-plated one.

Hub+li ('huːblɪ) *n.* a city in W India, in NW Mysore: incorporated with Dharwar in 1961; educational and trading centre. Pop. (with Dharwar): 379 116 (1971).

hu+bris ('hjuːbrɪs) *or* **hy+bris** *n.* **1.** pride or arrogance. **2.** (in Greek tragedy) an excess of ambition, pride, etc., ultimately causing the transgressor's ruin. [C19: from Greek] —**hu+'bris+tic** *or* **hy+'bris+tic** *adj.*

huck·a·back ('hʌkəˌbæk) *n.* a coarse absorbent linen or cotton fabric used for towels and informal shirts, etc. Also: **huck** (hʌk). [C17: of unknown origin]

huck+le ('hʌkᵊl) *n. Rare.* **1.** the hip or haunch. **2.** a projecting or humped part. [C16: diminutive of Middle English *huck* hip, haunch; perhaps related to Old Norse *hūka* to squat]

huck·le+ber·ry ('hʌkᵊlˌbɛrɪ) *n., pl.* **·ries. 1.** any American ericaceous shrub of the genus *Gaylussacia,* having edible dark blue berries with large seeds. **2.** the fruit of any of these shrubs. **3.** another name for **blueberry. 4.** a Brit. name for

whortleberry (sense 1). [C17: probably a variant of *hurtleberry*, of unknown origin]
huck·le·bone ('hʌkᵊl,bəʊn) *n. Archaic.* **1.** the anklebone; talus. **2.** the hipbone; innominate bone.
huck+ster ('hʌkstə) *n.* **1.** a person who uses aggressive or questionable methods of selling. **2.** *Now rare.* a person who sells small articles or fruit in the street. **3.** *U.S.* a person who writes for radio or television advertisements. *~vb.* **4.** (*tr.*) to peddle. **5.** (*tr.*) to sell or advertise aggressively or questionably. **6.** to haggle over. [C12: perhaps from Middle Dutch *hoekster*, from *hoeken* to carry on the back] —**'huck+ster+ism** *n.*
Hud+ders+field ('hʌdəz,fi:ld) *n.* a town in N England, in West Yorkshire on the River Colne: textile industry. Pop.: 130 964 (1971).
hud+dle ('hʌdᵊl) *n.* **1.** a heaped or crowded mass of people or things. **2.** *Informal.* a private or impromptu conference (esp. in the phrase **go into a huddle**). *~vb.* **3.** to crowd or cause to crowd or nestle closely together. **4.** (often foll. by *up*) to draw or hunch (oneself), as through cold. **5.** (*intr.*) *Informal.* to meet and confer privately. **6.** (*tr.*) *Chiefly Brit.* to do (something) in a careless way. **7.** (*tr.*) *Rare.* to put on (clothes) hurriedly. [C16: of uncertain origin; compare Middle English *hoderen* to wrap up] —**'hud+dler** *n.*
Hud·dle·ston ('hʌdᵊlstən) *n.* **Tre·vor.** born 1913, English prelate; suffragan bishop of Stepney (1968–78) and bishop of Mauritius since 1978.
hu+di+bras+tic (,hju:dɪ'bræstɪk) *adj.* mock-heroic in style. [C18: after *Hudibras*, poem (1663–68) by Samuel Butler]
Hud·son ('hʌdsən) *n.* **1. Hen·ry.** died 1611, English navigator: he explored the Hudson River (1609) and Hudson Bay (1610), where his crew mutinied and cast him adrift to die. **2. W(illiam) H(enry).** 1841–1922, English naturalist and novelist, born in Argentina, noted esp. for his romance *Green Mansions* (1904) and the autobiographical *Far Away and Long Ago* (1918).
Hud+son Bay *n.* an inland sea in NE Canada: linked with the Atlantic by **Hudson Strait;** the S extension forms James Bay; discovered in 1610 by Henry Hudson. Area (excluding James Bay): 647 500 sq. km (250 000 sq. miles).
Hud+son Riv+er *n.* a river in E New York State, flowing generally south into Upper New York Bay: linked to the Great Lakes, the St. Lawrence Seaway, and Lake Champlain by the New York State Barge Canal and the canalized Mohawk River. Length: 492 km (306 miles).
Hud+son's Bay Com+pa+ny *n.* an English company chartered in 1670 to trade in all parts of North America drained by rivers flowing into Hudson Bay.
Hud+son seal *n.* muskrat fur that has been dressed and dyed to resemble sealskin.
hue (hju:) *n.* **1.** the attribute of colour that enables an observer to classify it as red, green, blue, purple, etc., and excludes white, black, and shades of grey. See also **colour. 2.** a shade of a colour. **3.** aspect; complexion: *a different hue on matters.* [Old English *hīw* beauty; related to Old Norse *hȳ* fine hair, Gothic *hiwi* form]
Hué (*French* we) *n.* a port in central Vietnam, on the delta of the **Hué River** near the South China Sea: former capital of the kingdom of Annam, of French Indochina (1883–1946), and of Central Vietnam (1946–54). Pop.: 199 893 (1971).
hue and cry *n.* **1.** (formerly) the pursuit of a suspected criminal with loud cries in order to raise the alarm. **2.** any loud public outcry. [C16: from Anglo-French *hu et cri*, from Old French *hue* outcry, from *huer* to shout, from *hu!* shout of warning + *cri* CRY]
hued (hju:d) *adj. Archaic or poetic.* **a.** having a hue or colour as specified. **b.** (*in combination*): *rosy-hued dawn.*
Huel+va (*Spanish* 'welβa) *n.* a port in SW Spain, between the estuaries of the Odiel and Tinto Rivers: exports copper and other ores. Pop.: 96 689 (1970). Latin name: **Onuba.**
Hues+ca (*Spanish* 'weska) *n.* a city in NE Spain: Roman town, site of Quintus Sertorius' school (76 B.C.); 15th-century cathedral and ancient palace of Aragonese kings. Pop.: 33 185 (1970). Latin name: **Osca.**
huff (hʌf) *n.* **1.** a passing mood of anger or pique (esp. in the phrase **in a huff**). *~vb.* **2.** to make or become angry or resentful. **3.** (*intr.*) to blow or puff heavily. **4.** Also: **blow.** *Draughts.* to remove (an opponent's draught) from the board for failure to make a capture. **5.** (*tr.*) *Obsolete.* to bully. [C16: of imitative origin; compare PUFF] —**'huff+ish** *or* **'huff·y** *adj.* —**'huff·i+ness** *or* **'huff+ish+ness** *n.*
Hu+fuf (hʊ'fu:f) *n.* See **Al Hufuf.**
hug (hʌg) *vb.* **hugs, hug+ging, hugged.** (*mainly tr.*) **1.** (*also intr.*) to clasp (another person or thing) tightly or (of two people) to cling close together; embrace. **2.** to keep close to a shore, kerb, etc. **3.** to cling to (beliefs, etc.); cherish. **4.** to congratulate (oneself); be delighted with (oneself). *~n.* **5.** a tight or fond embrace. [C16: probably of Scandinavian origin; related to Old Norse *hugga* to comfort, Old English *hogian* to take care of] —**'hug+ga·ble** *adj.* —**'hug+ger** *n.*
huge (hju:dʒ) *adj.* extremely large in size, amount, or scope. Archaic form: **hugeous.** [C13: from Old French *ahuge*, of uncertain origin] —**'huge+ness** *n.*
huge+ly ('hju:dʒlɪ) *adv.* very much; enormously.
hug+ger+mug+ger ('hʌgə,mʌgə) *n.* **1.** confusion. **2.** *Rare.* secrecy. *~adj., adv. Archaic.* **3.** with secrecy. **4.** in confusion. *~vb. Obsolete.* **5.** (*tr.*) to keep secret. **6.** (*intr.*) to act secretly. [C16: of uncertain origin]
Hugh Ca·pet ('hju: 'kæpɪt, 'keɪpɪt) *n.* See (**Hugh**) **Capet.**
Hughes (hju:z) *n.* **1. How·ard.** 1905–76, U.S. industrialist, aviator, and film producer. He became a total recluse during the last years of his life. **2. Rich·ard (Arthur Warren).** 1900–76, English novelist. He wrote *A High Wind in Jamaica* (1929), *In Hazard* (1938), and *The Fox in the Attic* (1961). **3. Ted.** born 1930, English poet: his works include *The Hawk in the Rain* (1957) and *Crow* (1970). **4. Thom·as.** 1822–96, English novelist; author of *Tom Brown's Schooldays* (1857). **5. Wil·liam Mor·ris.** 1864–1952, Australian statesman, born in England; prime minister of Australia (1915–23).
Hugh·ie ('hju:ɪ) *n. Austral. informal.* the god of rain (esp. in the phrase **send her down, Hughie!**).
hug-me-tight *n.* a woman's knitted jacket.
Hu·go ('hju:gəʊ; *French* y'go) *n.* **Vic·tor (Marie)** (vik'tɔ:r). 1802–85, French poet, novelist, and dramatist; leader of the romantic movement in France. His works include the volumes of verse *Les Feuilles d'automne* (1831) and *Les Contemplations* (1856), the novels *Notre-Dame de Paris* (1831) and *Les Misérables* (1862), and the plays *Hernani* (1830) and *Ruy Blas* (1838).
Hu+gue·not ('hju:gə,nəʊ, -,nɒt) *n.* **1.** a French Calvinist, esp. of the 16th or 17th centuries. *~adj.* **2.** designating the French Protestant Church. [C16: from French, from Genevan dialect *eyguenot* one who opposed annexation by Savoy, ultimately from Swiss German *Eidgenoss* confederate; influenced by *Hugues*, surname of 16th-century Genevan burgomaster] —**,Hu+gue·'not+ic** *adj.* —**'Hu+gue·,not+ism** *n.*
huh (*spelling pron.* hʌ) *interj.* an exclamation of derision, bewilderment, enquiry, etc.
Hu+he+hot (,hu:hɪ'hɒt ,hu:ɪ-) *or* **Hu-ho-hao-t'e** (,hu:həʊ haʊ'teɪ) *n.* a town in N China, capital of Inner Mongolia Autonomous Region (since 1954) and former capital of Suiyüan province; Inner Mongolia University (1957). Pop.: 320 000 (1958 est.).
hu·la ('hu:lə) *or* **hu·la-hu·la** *n.* a Hawaiian dance performed by a woman.
Hu·la-Hoop *n. Trademark.* a light hoop that is whirled around the body by movements of the waist and hips.
hu·la skirt *n.* a skirt made of long grass attached to a waistband and worn by hula dancers.
hulk (hʌlk) *n.* **1.** the body of an abandoned vessel. **2.** *Disparaging.* a large or unwieldy vessel. **3.** *Disparaging.* a large ungainly person or thing. **4.** (*often pl.*) the frame or hull of a ship, used as a storehouse, etc., or (esp. in 19th-century Britain) as a prison. *~vb.* **5.** (*intr.*) *Brit. informal.* to move clumsily. **6.** (*intr.*; often foll. by *up*) to rise massively. [Old English *hulc*, from Medieval Latin *hulca*, from Greek *holkas* barge, from *helkein* to tow]
hulk+ing ('hʌlkɪŋ) *adj.* big and ungainly. Also: **hulky.**
hull (hʌl) *n.* **1.** the main body of a vessel, tank, flying boat, etc. **2.** the persistent calyx at the base of a strawberry, raspberry, or similar fruit. **3.** the outer casing of a missile, rocket, etc. *~vb.* **4.** to remove the hulls from (fruit). **5.** (*tr.*) to pierce the hull of (a vessel, tank, etc.). [Old English *hulu*; related to Old High German *helawa*, Old English *helan* to hide] —**'hull+er** *n.* —**'hull-less** *adj.*
Hull[1] (hʌl) *n.* **1.** a port in NE England, administrative centre of Humberside: the largest fishing port in Britain; university (1929). Pop.: 285 472 (1971). Official name: **Kingston upon Hull. 2.** a city in SE Canada, in SW Quebec on the River Ottawa: a centre of the timber trade and associated industries. Pop.: 63 580 (1971).
Hull[2] (hʌl) *n.* **Cor·dell.** 1871–1955, U.S. statesman; secretary of state (1933–44). He helped to found the U.N.: Nobel peace prize 1945.
hul+la+ba+loo *or* **hul+la+bal+loo** (,hʌləbə'lu:) *n., pl.* **+loos.** loud confused noise, esp. of protest; commotion. [C18: perhaps from interjection HALLO + Scottish *baloo* lullaby]
hull down *adj.* **1.** (of a ship) having its hull concealed by the horizon. **2.** (of a tank) having only its turret visible.
hul+lo (hʌ'ləʊ) *sentence substitute, n.* a variant spelling of **hello.**
Hul·me (hju:m) *n.* **T(homas) E(rnest).** 1883–1917, English literary critic and poet; a proponent of imagism.
hum (hʌm) *vb.* **hums, hum+ming, hummed. 1.** (*intr.*) to make a low continuous vibrating sound like that of a prolonged *m.* **2.** (*intr.*) (of a person) to sing with the lips closed. **3.** (*intr.*) to utter an indistinct sound, as in hesitation; hem. **4.** (*intr.*) *Slang.* to be in a state of feverish activity. **5.** (*intr.*) *Slang.* to smell unpleasant. **6.** (*intr.*; often foll. by *for*) *Austral., informal.* to borrow or scrounge. **7. hum and haw.** See **hem**[2] (sense 3). *~n.* **8.** a low continuous murmuring sound. **9.** *Electronics.* an undesired low-frequency noise in the output of an amplifier or receiver, esp. one caused by the power supply. *~interj., n.* **10.** an indistinct sound of hesitation, embarrassment, etc.; hem. [C14: of imitative origin; compare Dutch *hommelen*, Old High German *humbal* bumblebee] —**'hum+mer** *n.*
hu+man (hju:mən) *adj.* **1.** of, characterizing, or relating to man and mankind: *human nature.* **2.** consisting of people: *the human race; a human chain.* **3.** having the attributes of man as opposed to animals, divine beings, or machines: *human failings.* **4. a.** kind or considerate. **b.** natural. *~n.* **5.** a human being; person. [C14: from Latin *hūmānus*; related to Latin *homō* man] —**'hu+man-,like** *adj.* —**'hu+man+ness** *n.*
hu+man be+ing *n.* a member of any of the races of *Homo sapiens*; person; man, woman, or child.
hu+mane (hju:'meɪn) *adj.* **1.** characterized by kindness, mercy, sympathy, etc. **2.** inflicting as little pain as possible: *a humane killing.* **3.** civilizing or liberal (esp. in the phrases **humane studies, humane education**). [C16: variant of HUMAN] —**hu+'mane+ly** *adv.* —**hu+'mane+ness** *n.*

hu·mane so·ci·e·ty *n.* an organization for promotion of humane ideals, esp. in dealing with animals.

hu·man in·ter·est *n.* (in a newspaper story, news broadcasting, etc.) reference to individuals and their emotions.

hu·man·ism ('hju:mə,nɪzəm) *n.* **1.** a school of philosophy that believes in human effort and ingenuity rather than religion. **2.** (*often cap.*) a cultural movement of the Renaissance, based on classical studies. **3.** interest in the welfare of people. —'**hu·man·ist** *n.* —,**hu·man·'ist·ic** *adj.*

hu·man·i·tar·i·an (hju:,mænɪ'tɛərɪən) *adj.* **1.** having the interests of mankind at heart. **2.** of or relating to ethical or theological humanitarianism. ~*n.* **3.** a philanthropist. **4.** an adherent of humanitarianism.

hu·man·i·tar·i·an·ism (hju:,mænɪ'tɛərɪə,nɪzəm) *n.* **1.** humanitarian principles. **2.** *Ethics.* **a.** the doctrine that man's duty is to strive to promote the welfare of mankind. **b.** the doctrine that man can achieve perfection through his own resources. **3.** *Theol.* the belief that Jesus Christ was only a mortal man. —**hu·,man·i·'tar·i·an·ist** *n.*

hu·man·i·ty (hju:'mænɪtɪ) *n., pl.* **·ties. 1.** the human race. **2.** the quality of being human. **3.** kindness or mercy. **4.** (*pl.*) (usually preceded by *the*) the study of literature, philosophy, and the arts. **5.** the study of Ancient Greek and Roman language, literature, etc.

hu·man·ize *or* **hu·man·ise** ('hju:mə,naɪz) *vb.* **1.** to make or become human. **2.** to make or become humane. —,**hu·man·i·'za·tion** *or* ,**hu·man·i·'sa·tion** *n.* —'**hu·man·,iz·er** *or* '**hu·man·,is·er** *n.*

hu·man·kind (,hju:mən'kaɪnd) *n.* the human race; humanity.

hu·man·ly ('hju:mənlɪ) *adv.* **1.** by human powers or means. **2.** in a human or humane manner.

hu·man na·ture *n.* **1.** the qualities common to humanity. **2.** *Sociol.* the unique elements that form a basic part of human life and distinguish it from other animal life.

hu·man·oid ('hju:mə,nɔɪd) *adj.* **1.** like a human being in appearance. ~*n.* **2.** a being with human rather than anthropoid characteristics. **3.** (in science fiction) a robot or creature resembling a human being.

hu·man rights *pl. n.* the rights of individuals to liberty, justice, etc.

Hum·ber ('hʌmbə) *n.* an estuary in NE England, into which flow the Rivers Ouse and Trent: flows east into the North Sea; navigable for large ocean-going ships as far as Hull. Length: 64 km (40 miles).

Hum·ber·side ('hʌmbə,saɪd) *n.* a county of N England around the Humber estuary, formed in 1974 from parts of the East Riding of Yorkshire and N Lincolnshire. Administrative centre: Hull. Pop.: 848 600 (1976 est.). Area: 3595 sq. km (1388 sq. miles).

hum·ble ('hʌmbᵊl) *adj.* **1.** conscious of one's failings. **2.** unpretentious; lowly: *a humble cottage; my humble opinion.* **3.** deferential or servile. ~*vb.* (*tr.*) **4.** to cause to become humble; humiliate. **5.** to lower in status. [C13: from Old French, from Latin *humilis* low, from *humus* the ground] —'**hum·ble·ness** *n.* —'**hum·bler** *n.* —'**hum·bling·ly** *adv.* —'**hum·bly** *adv.*

hum·ble·bee ('hʌmbᵊl,bi:) *n.* another name for the **bumblebee.** [C15: related to Middle Dutch *hommel* bumblebee, Old High German *humbal;* see HUM]

hum·ble pie *n.* **1.** (formerly) a pie made from the heart, entrails, etc., of a deer. **2. eat humble pie.** to behave or be forced to behave humbly; be humiliated. [C17: earlier *an umble pie,* by mistaken word division from *a numble pie,* from *numbles* offal of a deer, from Old French *nombles,* ultimately from Latin *lumbulus* a little loin, from *lumbus* loin]

Hum·boldt ('hʌmbəʊlt; *German* 'hʊmbɔlt) *n.* **1.** Baron (**Friedrich Heinrich**) **Al·ex·an·der von** (,alɛk'sandər fɔn). 1769–1859, German scientist, who made important scientific explorations in Central and South America (1799–1804). In *Kosmos* (1845–62), he provided a comprehensive description of the physical universe. **2.** his brother, Baron (**Karl**) **Wil·helm von** ('vɪlhɛlm fɔn). 1767–1835, German philologist and educational reformer.

Hum·boldt Cur·rent *n.* a cold ocean current of the S Pacific, flowing north along the coasts of Chile and Peru. Also called: **Peru Current.**

hum·bug ('hʌm,bʌg) *n.* **1.** a person or thing that tricks or deceives. **2.** nonsense; rubbish. **3.** *Brit.* a hard boiled sweet, usually flavoured with peppermint and often having a striped pattern. ~*vb.* **·bugs, ·bug·ging, ·bugged. 4.** to cheat or deceive (someone). [C18: of unknown origin] —'**hum·,bug·ger** *n.* —'**hum·,bug·ger·y** *n.*

hum·ding·er ('hʌm,dɪŋə) *n. Slang.* an excellent person or thing: *a humdinger of a party.* [C20: of unknown origin]

hum·drum ('hʌm,drʌm) *adj.* **1.** ordinary; dull. ~*n.* **2.** a monotonous routine, task, or person. [C16: rhyming compound, probably based on HUM] —'**hum·,drum·ness** *n.*

Hume (hju:m) *n.* **1.** (**George**) **Ba·sil.** born 1923, English Roman Catholic Benedictine monk and cardinal; archbishop of Westminster since 1976. **2. Da·vid.** 1711–76, Scottish empiricist philosopher, economist, and historian, whose sceptic philosophy restricted human knowledge to that which can be perceived by the senses. His works include *A Treatise of Human Nature* (1740), *An Enquiry concerning the Principles of Morals* (1751), *Political Discourses* (1752), and *History of England* (1754–62). —'**Hum·ism** *n.*

hu·mec·tant (hju:'mɛktənt) *adj.* **1.** producing moisture. ~*n.* **2.** a substance added to another substance to keep it moist. [C17: from Latin *ūmectāre* to wet, from *ūmēre* to be moist, from *ūmor* moisture; see HUMOUR]

hu·mer·al ('hju:mərəl) *adj.* **1.** *Anatomy.* of or relating to the humerus. **2.** of or near the shoulder.

hu·mer·al veil *n. R.C. Church.* a silk shawl worn by a priest at High Mass, etc. Often shortened to **veil.**

hu·mer·us ('hju:mərəs) *n., pl.* **·mer·i** (-mə,raɪ). **1.** the bone that extends from the shoulder to the elbow. **2.** the corresponding bone in other vertebrates. [C17: from Latin *umerus;* related to Gothic *ams* shoulder, Greek *ōmos*]

hu·mic ('hju:mɪk) *adj.* of, relating to, or derived from humus: *humic acids.* [C19: from Latin *humus* ground + -IC]

hu·mid ('hju:mɪd) *adj.* moist; damp: *a humid day.* [C16: from Latin *ūmidus,* from *ūmēre* to be wet; see HUMECTANT, HUMOUR] —'**hu·mid·ly** *adv.* —'**hu·mid·ness** *n.*

hu·mid·i·fi·er (hju:'mɪdɪ,faɪə) *n.* a device for increasing or controlling the water vapour in a room, building, etc.

hu·mid·i·fy (hju:'mɪdɪ,faɪ) *vb.* **·fies, ·fy·ing, ·fied.** (*tr.*) to make (air, etc.) humid or damp. —**hu·,mid·i·fi·'ca·tion** *n.*

hu·mid·i·stat (hju:'mɪdɪ,stæt) *n.* a device for maintaining constant humidity. Also called: **hygrostat.**

hu·mid·i·ty (hju:'mɪdɪtɪ) *n.* **1.** the state of being humid; dampness. **2.** a measure of the amount of moisture in the air. See **relative humidity, absolute humidity.**

hu·mi·dor ('hju:mɪ,dɔ:) *n.* a humid place or container for storing cigars, tobacco, etc.

hu·mil·i·ate (hju:'mɪlɪ,eɪt) *vb.* (*tr.*) to lower or hurt the dignity or pride of. [C16: from Late Latin *humiliāre,* from Latin *humilis* HUMBLE] —**hu·'mil·i·,at·ing·ly** *adv.* —**hu·,mil·i·'a·tion** *n.* —**hu·mil·ia·tive** (hju:'mɪljətɪv) *adj.* —**hu·'mil·i·,a·tor** *n.* —**hu·'mil·i·a·to·ry** *adj.*

hu·mil·i·ty (hju:'mɪlɪtɪ) *n., pl.* **·ties.** the state or quality of being humble.

hum·mel ('hʌmᵊl) *adj. Scot.* **1.** (of cattle) hornless. **2.** (of grain) awnless. [C15: of Germanic origin; compare Low German *hummel* hornless animal]

hum·ming·bird ('hʌmɪŋ,bɜ:d) *n.* any very small American bird of the family *Trochilidae,* having a brilliant iridescent plumage, long slender bill, and wings specialized for very powerful vibrating flight: order *Apodiformes.*

hum·ming·bird moth *n. U.S.* another name for the **hawk moth.**

hum·ming top *n.* a top that hums as it spins.

hum·mock ('hʌmək) *n.* **1.** a hillock; knoll. **2.** a ridge or mound of ice in an ice field. **3.** Also: **hammock.** *Chiefly southern U.S.* a wooded area lying above the level of an adjacent marsh. [C16: of uncertain origin; compare HUMP, HAMMOCK] —'**hum·mock·y** *adj.*

hu·mor·al ('hju:mərəl) *adj. Obsolete.* of or relating to the four bodily fluids (humours).

hu·mor·esque (,hju:mə'rɛsk) *n.* a short lively piece of music. [C19: from German *Humoreske,* ultimately from English HUMOUR]

hu·mor·ist ('hju:mərɪst) *n.* a person who acts, speaks, or writes in a humorous way. —,**hu·mor·'is·tic** *adj.*

hu·mor·ous ('hju:mərəs) *adj.* **1.** funny; comical; amusing. **2.** displaying or creating humour. **3.** *Archaic.* another word for **capricious.** —'**hu·mor·ous·ly** *adv.* —'**hu·mor·ous·ness** *n.*

hu·mour *or U.S.* **hu·mor** ('hju:mə) *n.* **1.** the quality of being funny. **2.** Also called: **sense of humour.** the ability to appreciate or express that which is humorous. **3.** situations, speech, or writings that are thought to be humorous. **4. a.** a state of mind; temper; mood. **b.** (*in combination*): *ill humour; good humour.* **5.** temperament or disposition. **6.** a caprice or whim. **7.** Also called: **cardinal humour.** any of various fluids in the body, esp. the aqueous humour and vitreous humour. **8.** *Archaic.* any of the four bodily fluids (blood, phlegm, choler or yellow bile, melancholy or black bile) formerly thought to determine emotional and physical disposition. **9. out of humour.** in a bad mood. ~*vb.* (*tr.*) **10.** to attempt to gratify; indulge: *he humoured the boy's whims.* **11.** adapt oneself to: *to humour someone's fantasies.* [C14: from Latin: liquid; related to Latin *ūmēre* to be wet, Old Norse *vökr* moist, Greek *hugros* wet] —'**hu·mour·ful** *or U.S.* '**hu·mor·ful** *adj.* —'**hu·mour·less** *or U.S.* '**hu·mor·less** *adj.* —'**hu·mour·less·ness** *or U.S.* '**hu·mor·less·ness** *n.*

hu·mour·some *or U.S.* **hu·mor·some** ('hju:məsəm) *adj.* **1.** capricious; fanciful. **2.** inclined to humour (someone).

hump (hʌmp) *n.* **1.** a rounded protuberance or projection, as of earth, sand, etc. **2.** *Pathol.* a rounded deformity of the back in persons with kyphosis, consisting of a convex spinal curvature. **3.** a rounded protuberance on the back of a camel or related animal. **4. the hump.** *Brit. informal.* a fit of depression or sulking (esp. in the phrase **it gives me the hump**). **5. over the hump.** past the largest or most difficult portion of work, time, etc. ~*vb.* **6.** to form or become a hump; hunch; arch. **7.** (*tr.*) *Brit. slang.* to carry or heave. **8.** *Taboo slang.* to have sexual intercourse with (someone). **9. hump one's swag.** *Austral. informal.* (of a tramp) to carry one's belongings from place to place on one's back. [C18: probably from earlier HUMPBACKED] —'**hump·,like** *adj.*

hump·back ('hʌmp,bæk) *n.* **1.** another word for **hunchback. 2.** Also called: **humpback whale.** a large whalebone whale, *Megaptera novaeangliae,* closely related and similar to the rorquals but with a humped back and long flippers: family *Balaenopteridae.* **3.** a Pacific salmon, *Oncorhynchus gorbuscha,* the male of which has a humped back and hooked jaws. **4.** Also: **humpback bridge.** *Brit.* a road bridge having a sharp incline and decline and usually a narrow roadway. [C17:

alteration of earlier *crumpbacked,* perhaps influenced by HUNCHBACK; perhaps related to Dutch *homp* lump] —'**hump·ˌbacked** *adj.*

Hum·per·dinck (*German* 'hʊmpərˌdɪŋk) *n.* **En·gel·bert** ('ɛŋəl-bɛrt). 1854–1921, German composer, esp. of operas, including *Hansel and Gretel* (1893).

humph (*spelling pron.* hʌmf) *interj.* an exclamation of annoyance, indecision, dissatisfaction, etc.

Humph·rey ('hʌmfrɪ) *n.* **1. Duke.** See (Humphrey, Duke of) **Gloucester. 2. Hu·bert Ho·ra·ti·o.** 1911–78, vice-president of the U.S. under President Johnson (1965–69).

Hum·phreys Peak *n.* a mountain in N central Arizona, in the San Francisco Peaks: the highest peak in the state. Height: 3862 m (12 670 ft.).

hump·ty ('hʌmptɪ) *n. Brit.* a low padded seat; pouffe. [C20: from *humpty* hunchbacked, perhaps influenced by *Humpty Dumpty* (nursery rhyme)]

hump·ty dump·ty ('hʌmptɪ 'dʌmptɪ) *n. Chiefly Brit.* **1.** a short fat person. **2.** a person or thing that once overthrown or broken cannot be restored or mended. [C18: after the nursery rhyme *Humpty Dumpty*]

hump·y[1] ('hʌmpɪ) *adj.* **hump·i·er, hump·i·est. 1.** full of humps. **2.** *Brit. informal.* angry or gloomy. —'**hump·i·ness** *n.*

hump·y[2] ('hʌmpɪ) *n., pl.* **hump·ies.** *Austral.* a primitive hut. [C19: from a native Australian language]

Hums (hʊms) *n.* a variant spelling of **Homs.**

hum tone *n.* a note produced by a bell when struck, lying an octave or (in many English bells) a sixth or seventh below the strike tone. Also (esp. Brit.): **hum note.**

hu·mus ('hju:məs) *n.* a dark brown or black colloidal mass of partially decomposed organic matter in the soil. It improves the fertility and water retention of the soil and is therefore important for plant growth. [C18: from Latin: soil, earth]

Hun (hʌn) *n.* **1.** a member of any of several Asiatic nomadic peoples speaking Mongoloid or Turkic languages who dominated much of Asia and E Europe from before 300 B.C., invading the Roman Empire in the 4th and 5th centuries A.D. **2.** *Informal.* a derogatory name for a **German. 3.** *Informal.* a vandal. [Old English *Hūnas,* from Late Latin *Hūnī,* from Turkish *Hun-yū*] —'**Hun·ˌlike** *adj.*

Hu·nan ('hu:'næn) *n.* a province of S China, between the Yangtze River and the Nan Ling Mountains: drained chiefly by the Hsiang and Yüan Rivers; valuable mineral resources. Capital: Changsha. Pop.: 38 000 000 (1967–71 est.). Area: 210 500 sq. km (82 095 sq. miles).

hunch (hʌntʃ) *n.* **1.** an intuitive guess or feeling. **2.** another word for **hump. 3.** a lump or large piece. ~*vb.* **4.** to bend or draw (oneself or a part of the body) up or together. **5.** (*intr.;* usually foll. by *up*) to sit in a hunched position. [C16: of unknown origin]

hunch·back ('hʌntʃˌbæk) *n.* **1.** a person having an abnormal convex curvature of the thoracic spine. **2.** such a curvature. ~Also called: **humpback.** See **kyphosis.** Compare **hollow-back.** [C18: from earlier *hunchbacked, huckbacked* hump-backed, influenced by *bunchbacked,* from *bunch* (in obsolete sense of *hump*) + BACKED] —'**hunch·ˌbacked** *adj.*

hun·dred ('hʌndrəd) *n., pl.* **·dreds** *or* **·dred. 1.** the cardinal number that is the product of ten and ten; five score. See also **number** (sense 1). **2.** a numeral, 100, C, etc., representing this number. **3.** (*often pl.*) a large but unspecified number, amount, or quantity: *there will be hundreds of people there.* **4. the hundreds. a.** the numbers 100 to 109: *the temperature was in the hundreds.* **b.** the numbers 100 to 199: *his score went into the hundreds.* **c.** the numbers 100 to 999: *the price was in the hundreds.* **5.** (*pl.*) the 100 years of a specified century: *in the sixteen hundreds.* **6.** something representing, represented by, or consisting of 100 units. **7.** *Maths.* the position containing a digit representing that number followed by two zeros: *in 4376, 3 is in the hundred's place.* **8.** an ancient division of a county in England, Ireland, and parts of the U.S. ~*determiner.* **9. a.** amounting to or approximately a hundred: *a hundred reasons for that.* **b.** (*as pronoun*): *the hundred I chose.* **10.** amounting to 100 times a particular scientific quantity: *a hundred volts.* Related prefix: **hecto-.** [Old English; related to Old Frisian *hunderd,* Old Norse *hundrath,* German *hundert,* Gothic *hund,* Latin *centum,* Greek *hekaton*]

hun·dred days *pl. n. French history.* the period between Napoleon Bonaparte's arrival in Paris from Elba on March 20, 1815, and his abdication on June 29, 1815.

hund·red-per·cent·er *n. U.S.* an extreme or unjustified nationalist. —'**hund·red-per·'cent·ism** *n.*

hun·dreds and thou·sands *pl. n.* tiny beads of brightly coloured sugar, used in decorating cakes, sweets, etc.

hun·dredth ('hʌndrədθ) *adj.* **1.** (*usually prenominal*) **a.** being the ordinal number of 100 in numbering or counting order, position, time, etc. **b.** (*as n.*): *the hundredth in line.* ~*n.* **2. a.** one of 100 approximately equal parts of something. **b.** (*as modifier*): *a hundredth part.* **3.** one of 100 equal divisions of a particular scientific quantity. Related prefix: **centi-:** *centimetre.* **4.** the fraction equal to one divided by 100 (1/100).

hun·dred·weight ('hʌndrədˌweɪt) *n., pl.* **·weights** *or* **·weight. 1.** Also called: **long hundredweight.** *Brit.* a unit of weight equal to 112 pounds or 50.802 35 kilograms. **2.** Also called: **short hundredweight.** *U.S.* a unit of weight equal to 100 pounds or 45.359 24 kilograms. **3.** Also called: **metric hundredweight.** a metric unit of weight equal to 50 kilograms. ~Abbrev. (for senses 1, 2): **cwt**

Hun·dred Years' War *n.* the series of wars fought intermittently between England and France from 1337–1453.

hung (hʌŋ) *vb.* **1.** the past tense or past participle of **hang** (except in the sense of *to execute* or in the idiom *I'll be hanged*). ~*adj.* **2.** (of a legislative assembly) not having a party with a working majority: *a hung parliament.* **3. hung over.** *Informal.* suffering from the effects of a hangover. **4. hung up.** *Slang.* **a.** impeded by some difficulty or delay. **b.** in a state of confusion; emotionally disturbed. **5. hung up on.** *Slang, chiefly U.S.* obsessively or exclusively interested in: *he's hung up on modern art these days.*

Hung. *abbrev. for:* **1.** Hungarian. **2.** Hungary.

Hun·gar·i·an (hʌŋ'gɛərɪən) *n.* **1.** the official language of Hungary, also spoken in Rumania and elsewhere, belonging to the Finno-Ugric family and most closely related to the Ostyak and Vogul languages of NW Siberia. **2.** a native, inhabitant, or citizen of Hungary. **3.** a Hungarian-speaking person who is not a citizen of Hungary. ~*adj.* **4.** of or relating to Hungary, its people, or their language. ~Compare **Magyar.**

Hun·gar·i·an gou·lash *n.* the full name of **goulash.**

Hun·ga·ry ('hʌŋgərɪ) *n.* a republic in central Europe: Magyars first unified under Saint Stephen, the first Hungarian king (1001–38); taken by the Hapsburgs from the Turks at the end of the 17th century; gained autonomy with the establishment of the dual monarchy of Austria-Hungary (1867) and became a republic in 1918; passed under Communist control in 1949; a popular rising in 1956 was suppressed by Soviet troops. It consists chiefly of the Middle Danube basin and plains. Language: Hungarian. Currency: forint. Capital: Budapest. Pop.: 10 478 000 (1974 est.). Area: 93 030 sq. km (35 919 sq. miles). Hungarian name: **Magyarország.**

hun·ger ('hʌŋgə) *n.* **1.** a feeling of pain, emptiness, or weakness induced by lack of food. **2.** an appetite, desire, need, or craving: *hunger for a woman.* ~*vb.* **3.** to have or cause to have a need or craving for food. **4.** (*intr.;* usually foll. by *for* or *after*) to have a great appetite or desire (for). [Old English; related to Old High German *hungar,* Old Norse *hungr,* Gothic *hūhrus*]

hun·ger march *n.* a procession of protest or demonstration by the unemployed.

hun·ger strike *n.* a voluntary fast undertaken, usually by a prisoner, as a means of protest. —**hun·ger strik·er** *n.*

hung ju·ry *n.* a jury so divided in opinion that it cannot agree on a verdict.

Hung·nam (ˌhʊŋ'næm) *n.* a port in E North Korea, on the Sea of Japan southeast of Hamhung. Pop.: 150 000 (1973 est.).

hun·gry ('hʌŋgrɪ) *adj.* **·gri·er, ·gri·est. 1.** desiring food. **2.** experiencing pain, weakness, or nausea through lack of food. **3.** (*postpositive;* foll. by *for*) having a craving, desire, or need (for). **4.** expressing or appearing to express greed, craving, or desire. **5.** lacking fertility; poor. —'**hun·gri·ly** *or* '**hun·ger·ing·ly** *adv.* —'**hun·gri·ness** *n.*

hunk (hʌŋk) *n.* **1.** a large piece. **2.** Also: **hunk of a man.** *Slang, chiefly U.S.* a sexually attractive man. [C19: probably related to Flemish *hunke;* compare Dutch *homp* lump]

hunk·ers ('hʌŋkəz) *pl. n. Scot. and northern English dialect.* haunches.

hunks (hʌŋks) *n.* (*functioning as sing.*) *Rare.* **1.** a crotchety old person. **2.** a miserly person. [C17: of unknown origin]

hunk·y-do·ry (ˌhʌŋkɪ'dɔ:rɪ) *adj. Informal, chiefly U.S.* very satisfactory; fine. [C20: of uncertain origin]

Hun·nish ('hʌnɪʃ) *adj.* **1.** of, relating to, or characteristic of the Huns. **2.** barbarously destructive; vandalistic. —'**Hun·nish·ly** *adv.* —'**Hun·nish·ness** *n.*

hunt (hʌnt) *vb.* **1.** to seek out and kill or capture (game or wild animals) for food or sport. **2.** (*intr.;* often foll. by *for*) to look (for); search (for): *to hunt for a book; to hunt up a friend.* **3.** (*tr.*) to use (hounds, horses, etc.) in the pursuit of wild animals, game, etc.: *to hunt a pack of hounds.* **4.** (*tr.*) to search or draw (country) to hunt wild animals, game, etc.: *to hunt the parkland.* **5.** (*tr.;* often foll. by *down*) to track or chase diligently, esp. so as to capture: *to hunt down a criminal.* **6.** (*tr.; usually passive*) to persecute; hound. **7.** (*intr.*) (of a gauge indicator, engine speed, etc.) to oscillate about a mean value or position. **8.** (*intr.*) (of an aircraft, rocket, etc.) to oscillate about a flight path. ~*n.* **9.** the act or an instance of hunting. **10.** chase or search, esp. of animals or game. **11.** the area of a hunt. **12.** a party or institution organized for the pursuit of wild animals or game, esp. for sport. **13.** the participants in or members of such a party or institution. ~See also **hunt down, hunt up.** [Old English *huntian;* related to Old English *hentan,* Old Norse *henda* to grasp] —'**hunt·ed·ly** *adv.*

Hunt (hʌnt) *n.* **1. James.** born 1947, English motor-racing driver: world champion 1976. **2. (James Henry) Leigh.** 1784–1859, English poet and essayist: a founder of *The Examiner* (1808) in which he promoted the work of Keats and Shelley. **3. (William) Hol·man.** 1827–1910, English painter; a founder of the Pre-Raphaelite Brotherhood (1848).

hunt down *vb.* (*adv.*) **1.** (*tr.*) to pursue successfully by diligent searching and chasing: *they finally hunted down the killer in Mexico.* **2.** (*intr.*) (of a bell) to be rung progressively later during a set of changes.

hunt·ed ('hʌntɪd) *adj.* harassed and worn: *he has a hunted look.*

hunt·er ('hʌntə) *n.* **1.** a person or animal that seeks out and kills or captures game. Fem. equivalent: **hunt·ress** ('hʌntrɪs). **2. a.** a person who looks diligently for something. **b.** (*in combination*): *a fortune-hunter.* **3.** a specially bred horse used in hunting, usually characterized by strength and stamina. **4.** a specially bred dog used to hunt game. **5.** a watch with a hinged metal lid or case (**hunting case**) to protect the crystal. Also called: **hunting watch.** See also **half-hunter.**

hun·ter's moon *n.* the full moon following the harvest moon.

hunt·ing ('hʌntɪŋ) *n.* **a.** the pursuit and killing or capture of game and wild animals, regarded as a sport. **b.** (*as modifier*): *hunting boots; hunting lodge.*

hunt·ing cat *or* **leo·pard** *n.* another name for **cheetah.**

Hun·ting·don[1] ('hʌntɪŋdən) *n.* a town in E central England, in Cambridgeshire: birthplace of Oliver Cromwell. Pop.: 16 540 (1971).

Hun·ting·don[2] ('hʌntɪŋdən) *n.* **Se·li·na,** Countess of Huntingdon. 1707–91, English religious leader, who founded a Calvinistic Methodist sect.

Hun·ting·don·shire ('hʌntɪŋdən,ʃɪə, -ʃə) *n.* (until 1974) a former county of E England, now part of Cambridgeshire.

hunt·ing ground *n.* **1.** the area of a hunt. **2.** Also called: **happy hunting ground.** any place containing a supply of what is wanted or in which a search is conducted: *some resorts are a happy hunting ground for souvenirs.*

hunt·ing horn *n.* **1.** a long straight metal tube with a flared end and a cylindrical bore, used in giving signals in hunting. See **horn** (sense 9). **2.** an obsolete brass instrument from which the modern French horn was developed.

hunt·ing knife *n.* a knife used for flaying and cutting up game and sometimes for killing it.

hunt·ing spi·der *n.* another name for **wolf spider.**

hunts·man ('hʌntsmən) *n., pl.* **·men. 1.** a person who hunts. **2.** a person who looks after and trains hounds, beagles, etc., and manages them during a hunt.

hunts·man's-cup *n. U.S.* any of various pitcher plants of the genus *Sarracenia,* whose leaves are modified to form tubular pitchers.

Hunts·ville ('hʌntsvɪl) *n.* a city in NE Alabama: space-flight and guided-missile research centre. Pop.: 137 750 (1973 est.).

hunt the slip·per *n.* a children's game in which the players look for a hidden slipper or other object, such as a thimble (**hunt the thimble**).

hunt up *vb.* (*adv.*) **1.** (*tr.*) to search for, esp. successfully: *I couldn't hunt up a copy of it anywhere.* **2.** (*intr.*) (of a bell) to be rung progressively earlier during a set of changes.

Hun·ya·di (*Hungarian* 'hunjɔdi) *n.* **Já·nos** ('ja:noʃ). ?1387–1456, Hungarian general, who led Hungarian resistance to the Turks, defeating them notably at Belgrade (1456).

Hu·on pine ('hju:ɒn) *n.* a taxaceous tree, *Dacrydium franklinii,* of Australasia, SE Asia, and Chile, with scalelike leaves and cup-shaped berry-like fruits. [named after the *Huon* River, Tasmania]

Hu·peh *or* **Hu·pei** ('hu:'peɪ) *n.* a province of central China: largely low-lying, with many lakes. Capital: Wuhan. Pop.: 38 000 000 (1967–71 est.). Area: 187 500 sq. km (72 394 sq. miles).

hup·pah *or* **chup·pah** ('hʊpə) *Judaism.* ~*n.* **1.** the canopy under which a marriage is performed. **2.** the wedding ceremony as distinct from the celebration. [Hebrew]

hur·dle ('hɜ:dᵊl) *n.* **1. a.** *Athletics.* one of a number of light barriers over which runners leap in certain events. **b.** a low barrier used in certain horse races. **2.** an obstacle to be overcome: *the next hurdle in his career.* **3.** a light framework of interlaced osiers, wattle, etc., used as a temporary fence. **4.** *Brit.* a sledge on which criminals were dragged to their executions. ~*vb.* **5.** to jump (a hurdle, etc.), as in racing. **6.** (*tr.*) to surround with hurdles. **7.** (*tr.*) to overcome. [Old English *hyrdel;* related to Gothic *haurds* door, Old Norse *hurth* door, Old High German *hurd,* Latin *crātis,* Greek *kurtos* basket] —**'hur·dler** *n.*

hurds (hɜ:dz) *pl. n.* another word for **hards.**

hur·dy-gur·dy ('hɜ:dɪ'gɜ:dɪ) *n., pl.* **·dies. 1.** any mechanical musical instrument, such as a barrel organ. **2.** a medieval instrument shaped like a viol in which a rosined wheel rotated by a handle sounds the strings. [C18: rhyming compound, probably of imitative origin]

hurl (hɜ:l) *vb.* **1.** (*tr.*) to throw or propel with great force. **2.** (*tr.*) to utter with force; yell: *to hurl insults.* ~*n.* **3.** the act or an instance of hurling. [C13: probably of imitative origin] —**'hurl·er** *n.*

hur·ley ('hɜ:lɪ) *n.* **1.** *Chiefly Brit.* another word for **hurling** (the game). **2.** Also called: **hurley stick.** the stick used in playing hurling.

hurl·ing ('hɜ:lɪŋ) *n.* a traditional Irish game resembling hockey and lacrosse, played with sticks and a ball between two teams of 15 players each.

hurl·y-burl·y ('hɜ:lɪ'bɜ:lɪ) *n., pl.* **hurl·y-burl·ies. 1.** confusion or commotion. ~*adj.* **2.** turbulent. [C16: from earlier *hurling and burling,* rhyming phrase based on *hurling* in obsolete sense of uproar]

Hu·ron ('hjʊərən) *n.* **1. Lake.** a lake in North America, between the U.S. and Canada: the second largest of the Great Lakes. Area: 59 570 sq. km (23 000 sq. miles). **2.** (*pl.* **·rons** *or* **·ron**) a member of a North American Indian people or confederacy formerly living along the St. Lawrence River and in the region east of Lake Huron. **3.** the language of this people, belonging to the Iroquoian family.

hur·rah (hʊ'rɑ:), **hoo·ray** (hu:'reɪ), *or* **hoo·rah** (hu:'rɑ:) *interj., n.* **1.** a cheer of joy, victory, etc. ~*vb.* **2.** to shout "hurrah". [C17: probably from German *hurra;* compare HUZZAH]

hur·ri·cane ('hʌrɪkᵊn, -keɪn) *n.* **1.** a severe, often destructive storm, esp. a tropical cyclone. **2. a.** a wind of force 12 or above on the Beaufort scale. **b.** (*as modifier*): *a wind of hurricane force.* **3.** anything acting like such a wind. [C16: from Spanish *huracán,* from Taino *hurakán,* from *hura* wind]

hur·ri·cane deck *n.* a ship's deck that is covered by a light deck as a sunshade.

hur·ri·cane lamp *n.* a paraffin lamp, with a glass covering to prevent the flame from being blown out. Also called: **storm lantern.**

hur·ried ('hʌrɪd) *adj.* performed with great or excessive haste: *a hurried visit.* —**'hur·ried·ly** *adv.* —**'hur·ried·ness** *n.*

hur·ry ('hʌrɪ) *vb.* **·ries, ·ry·ing, ·ried. 1.** (*intr.;* often foll. by *up*) to hasten (to do something); rush. **2.** (*tr.;* often foll. by *along*) to speed up the completion, progress, etc., of. ~*n., pl.* **·ries. 3.** haste. **4.** urgency or eagerness. **5. in a hurry.** *Informal.* **a.** easily: *you won't beat him in a hurry.* **b.** willingly: *we won't go there again in a hurry.* [C16 *horyen,* probably of imitative origin; compare Middle High German *hurren;* see SCURRY] —**'hur·ry·ing·ly** *adv.*

hurst (hɜ:st) *n. Archaic.* **1.** a wood. **2.** a sandbank. [Old English *hyrst;* related to Old High German *hurst*]

Hurst·mon·ceux ('hɜ:stmən,su:, -,səʊ) *n.* a variant spelling of **Herstmonceux.**

hurt (hɜ:t) *vb.* **hurts, hurt·ing, hurt. 1.** to cause physical, moral, or mental injury to (someone or something). **2.** to produce a painful sensation in (someone): *the bruise hurts.* **3.** (*intr.*) *Informal.* to feel pain. ~*n.* **4.** physical, moral, or mental pain or suffering. **5.** a wound, cut, or sore. **6.** damage or injury; harm. [C12 *hurten* to hit, from Old French *hurter* to knock against, probably of Germanic origin; compare Old Norse *hrūtr* ram, Middle High German *hurt* a collision] —**'hurt·er** *n.*

hur·ter ('hɜ:tə) *n.* an object or part that gives protection, such as a concrete block that protects a building from traffic or the shoulder of an axle against which the hub strikes. [C14 *hurtour,* from Old French *hurtoir* something that knocks or strikes, from *hurter* to HURT]

hurt·ful ('hɜ:tfʊl) *adj.* causing distress or injury: *to say hurtful things.* —**'hurt·ful·ly** *adv.* —**'hurt·ful·ness** *n.*

hur·tle ('hɜ:tᵊl) *vb.* **1.** to project or be projected very quickly, noisily, or violently. **2.** (*intr.*) *Rare.* to collide or crash. [C13 *hurtlen,* from *hurten* to strike; see HURT]

Hus (*Czech* hus) *n.* **Jan** (jan). the Czech name of (John) **Huss.**

Hu·sain (hʊ'seɪn, -'saɪn) *n.* **1.** ?629–680 A.D., Islamic caliph, the son of Ali and Fatima and the grandson of Mohammed. **2.** a variant spelling of **Hussein.**

Hu·sák (*Czech* 'husa:k) *n.* **Gus·tav** ('gustaf). born 1913, Czechoslovak statesman; first secretary of the Communist Party since 1969; president since 1975.

hus·band ('hʌzbənd) *n.* **1.** a woman's partner in marriage. **2.** *Archaic.* **a.** a manager of an estate. **b.** a frugal person. ~*vb.* **3.** to manage or use (resources, finances, etc.) thriftily. **4.** *Archaic.* **a.** (*tr.*) to find a husband for. **b.** (of a woman) to marry (a man). **5.** (*tr.*) *Obsolete.* to till (the soil). [Old English *hūsbonda* from Old Norse *hūsbōndi,* from *hūs* house + *bōndi* one who has a household, from *bōa* to dwell] —**'hus·band·er** *n.* —**'hus·band·less** *adj.*

hus·band·man ('hʌzbəndmən) *n., pl.* **·men.** *Archaic.* a farmer.

hus·band·ry ('hʌzbəndrɪ) *n.* **1.** farming, esp. when regarded as a science, skill, or art. **2.** management of affairs and resources.

Hu·sein ibn-A·li (hʊ'seɪn 'ɪbᵊn 'ɑ:lɪ, 'ælɪ, hʊ'saɪn) *n.* 1856–1931, first king of Hejaz (1916–24). Advised by T. E. Lawrence, he took part in the Arab revolt against the Turks (1916–18); forced to abdicate by ibn-Saud.

hush[1] (hʌʃ) *vb.* **1.** to make or become silent; quieten. **2.** to soothe or be soothed. ~*n.* **3.** stillness; silence. **4.** an act of hushing. ~*interj.* **5.** a plea or demand for silence. [C16: probably from earlier *husht* quiet!, the *-t* being thought to indicate a past participle]

hush[2] (hʌʃ) *Mining, northern Brit.* ~*vb.* (*tr.*) **1.** to run water over the ground to erode (surface soil), revealing the underlying strata and any valuable minerals present. **2.** to wash (an ore) by removing particles of earth with rushing water. ~*n.* **3.** a gush of water, esp. when artificially produced. [C18: of imitative origin]

hush·a·by ('hʌʃə,baɪ) *interj.* **1.** used in quietening a baby or child to sleep. ~*n.* **2.** a lullaby. [C18: from HUSH[1] + *by,* as in BYE-BYE]

hush-hush *adj. Informal.* (esp. of official work, documents, etc.) secret; confidential.

hush mon·ey *n. Slang.* money given to a person, such as an accomplice, to ensure that something is kept secret.

hush up *vb.* (*tr., adv.*) to suppress information or rumours about.

husk (hʌsk) *n.* **1.** the external green or membranous covering of certain fruits and seeds. **2.** any worthless outer covering. ~*vb.* **3.** (*tr.*) to remove the husk from. [C14: probably based on Middle Dutch *huusken* little house, from *hūs* house; related to Old English *hosu* husk, *hūs* HOUSE] —**'husk·er** *n.* —**'husk·,like** *adj.*

husk·y[1] ('hʌskɪ) *adj.* **husk·i·er, husk·i·est. 1.** (of a voice, utterance, etc.) slightly hoarse or rasping. **2.** of, like, or containing husks. **3.** *Informal.* big, strong, and well-built. [C19: probably from HUSK, from the toughness of a corn husk] —**'husk·i·ly** *adv.* —**'husk·i·ness** *n.*

husk·y[2] ('hʌskɪ) *n., pl.* **husk·ies.** a breed of Arctic sled dog with a thick dense coat, pricked ears, and a curled tail. [C19: probably based on ESKIMO]

Huss (hʌs) *n.* **John.** Czech name *Jan Hus.* ?1372–1415, Bohemian religious reformer. Influenced by Wycliffe, he anticipated the Reformation in denouncing doctrines and abuses of the Church. His death at the stake precipitated the Hussite wars in Bohemia and Moravia.

hus·sar (hʊ'zɑ:) *n.* **1. a.** a member of any of various light cavalry regiments in European armies, renowned for their elegant dress. **b.** (*pl.; cap. when part of a name*): *the Queen's* *own Hussars.* **2.** a Hungarian horseman of the 15th century. [C15: from Hungarian *huszár* hussar, formerly freebooter, from Old Serbian *husar,* from Old Italian *corsaro* CORSAIR]

Hus·sein (hʊ'seɪn) *or* **Hu·sain** *n.* born 1935, king of Jordan since 1952.

Hus·serl (*German* 'hʊsərl) *n.* **Ed·mund** ('ɛtmʊnt). 1859–1938, German philosopher; founder of phenomenology.

Huss·ite ('hʌsaɪt) *n.* **1.** an adherent of the religious ideas of John Huss in the 14th century or a member of the movement initiated by him. ~*adj.* **2.** of or relating to John Huss, his teachings, followers, etc. —**'Huss·ism** *or* **'Huss·it·ism** *n.*

hus·sy ('hʌsɪ, -zɪ) *n., pl.* **·sies. 1.** *Contemptuous.* a shameless or promiscuous woman. **2.** *Brit. dialect.* a folder for needles, thread, etc. [C16 (in the sense: housewife): from *hussif* HOUSEWIFE]

hus·tings ('hʌstɪŋz) *n.* (*functioning as pl. or sing.*) **1.** *Brit.* (before 1872) the platform on which candidates were nominated for Parliament and from which they addressed the electors. **2.** the proceedings at a parliamentary election. **3.** political campaigning. [C11: from Old Norse *hūsthing,* from *hūs* HOUSE + *thing* assembly]

hus·tle ('hʌsᵊl) *vb.* **1.** to shove or crowd (someone) roughly. **2.** to move or cause to move hurriedly or furtively: *he hustled her out of sight.* **3.** (*tr.*) to deal with or cause to proceed hurriedly: *to hustle legislation through.* **4.** (*intr.*) *Slang.* to earn or obtain (something) forcefully. **5.** *U.S. slang.* (of procurers and prostitutes) to solicit. ~*n.* **6.** an instance of hustling. **7.** undue activity. [C17: from Dutch *husselen* to shake, from Middle Dutch *hutsen*] —**'hus·tler** *n.*

hus·tle up *vb.* (*tr.*) *Informal, chiefly U.S.* to prepare quickly.

Hus·ton ('hju:stən) *n.* **John.** born 1906, U.S. film director of *The African Queen* (1951) and *Moby Dick* (1956).

hut (hʌt) *n.* **1.** a small house or shelter, usually made of wood or metal. **2. the hut.** *Austral.* (on a sheep or cattle station) accommodation for the shearers, stockmen, etc. ~*vb.* **3.** to furnish with or live in a hut. [C17: from French *hutte,* of Germanic origin; related to Old High German *hutta* a crude dwelling]

hutch (hʌtʃ) *n.* **1.** a cage, usually of wood and wire mesh, for small animals. **2.** *Informal, derogatory.* a small house. **3.** a cart for carrying ore. **4.** a trough, esp. one used for kneading dough or (in mining) for washing ore. ~*vb.* **5.** (*tr.*) to store or keep in or as if in a hutch. [C14 *hucche,* from Old French *huche,* from Medieval Latin *hutica,* of obscure origin]

hut cir·cle *n. Archaeol.* a circle of earth or stones representing the site of a prehistoric hut.

hut·ment ('hʌtmənt) *n. Chiefly Military.* a number or group of huts.

Hu·tu ('hu:ˌtu:) *n.* **1.** (*pl.* **·tu** *or* **·tus**) a member of a Negroid people of Rwanda. **2.** the language of this people, belonging to the Bantu group of the Niger-Congo family.

Hux·ley ('hʌkslɪ) *n.* **1. Al·dous (Leonard).** 1894–1963, English novelist and essayist, noted particularly for his novel *Brave New World* (1932), depicting a scientifically controlled civilization of human robots. **2.** his brother, Sir **Ju·li·an (Sorrel).** 1887–1975, English biologist; first director-general of UNESCO (1946–48). His works include *Essays of a Biologist* (1923) and *Evolution: the Modern Synthesis* (1942). **3.** their grandfather, **Thom·as Hen·ry.** 1825–95, English biologist, the leading British exponent of Darwin's theory of evolution; his works include *Man's Place in Nature* (1863) and *Evolution and Ethics* (1893).

Hu Yao Bang (xu: jaʊ 'bɑ:ŋ) *n.* born ?1914, Chinese Communist politician; chairman of the Chinese Communist Party from 1982.

Huy·gens ('haɪgənz; *Dutch* hœjxəns) *n.* **Chris·ti·aan** ('kristi:ˌa:n). 1629–95, Dutch physicist: first formulated the wave theory of light.

Huys·mans (*French* ɥis'mɑ̃:s) *n.* **Jor·is Karl** (ʒɔ'ris karl). 1848–1907, French novelist of the Decadent school, whose works include *À rebours* (1884).

huz·zah (hə'zɑ:) *interj., n., vb.* an archaic word for **hurrah.** [C16: of unknown origin]

H.V. *or* **h.v.** *abbrev. for* high voltage.

H.W. *or* **h.w.** *abbrev. for:* **1.** high water. **2.** *Cricket.* hit wicket.

hwan (hwɑ:n, wɑ:n) *n.* another name for **won**[2] (senses 1, 2). [Korean]

Hwang Hai *or* **Huang Hai** ('wæŋ 'haɪ) *n.* the transliteration of Chinese name for the **Yellow Sea.**

Hwang Ho *or* **Huang Ho** ('wæŋ 'həʊ) *n.* transliteration of the Chinese name for the **Yellow River.**

H.W.M. *abbrev. for* high-water mark.

hw·yl ('hu:ɪl) *n.* emotional fervour, as in the recitation of poetry. [C19: Welsh]

hy·a·cinth ('haɪəsɪnθ) *n.* **1.** any liliaceous plant of the Mediterranean genus *Hyacinthus,* esp. any cultivated variety of *H. orientalis,* having a thick flower stalk bearing white, blue, or pink fragrant flowers. **2.** the flower or bulb of such a plant. **3.** any similar or related plant, such as the grape hyacinth. **4.** Also called: **jacinth.** a red or reddish-brown transparent variety of the mineral zircon, used as a gemstone **5.** *Greek myth.* a flower which sprang from the blood of the dead Hyacinthus. **6.** a colour varying from a deep purplish-blue to a medium violet. [C16: from Latin *hyacinthus,* from Greek *huakinthos*] —**hy·a·cin·thine** (ˌhaɪə'sɪnθaɪn) *adj.*

Hy·a·cin·thus (ˌhaɪə'sɪnθəs) *n. Greek myth.* a youth beloved of Apollo and inadvertently killed by him. At the spot where the youth died, Apollo caused a flower to grow.

Hy·a·des[1] ('haɪəˌdi:z) *or* **Hy·ads** ('haɪædz) *pl. n.* an open cluster of stars in the constellation Taurus. Compare **Pleiades**[2]. [C16: via Latin from Greek *huades,* perhaps from *huein* to rain]

Hy·a·des[2] ('haɪəˌdi:z) *pl. n. Greek myth.* seven nymphs, daughters of Atlas, whom Zeus placed among the stars after death.

hy·ae·na (haɪ'i:nə) *n.* a variant spelling of **hyena.** —**hy·'ae·nic** *adj.*

hy·a·lin ('haɪəlɪn) *n.* glassy translucent substance, such as occurs in certain degenerative skin conditions or in hyaline cartilage.

hy·a·line ('haɪəlɪn) *adj.* **1.** *Biology.* clear and translucent, with no fibres or granules. **2.** *Archaic.* transparent. ~*n.* **3.** *Archaic.* a glassy transparent surface. [C17: from Late Latin *hyalinus,* from Greek *hualinos* of glass, from *hualos* glass]

hy·a·line car·ti·lage *n.* a common type of cartilage with a translucent matrix containing little fibrous tissue.

hy·a·lite ('haɪəˌlaɪt) *n.* a clear and colourless variety of opal in globular form.

hy·a·lo- *or before a vowel* **hy·al-** *combining form.* of, relating to, or resembling glass: *hyaloplasm.* [from Greek *hualos* glass]

hy·a·loid ('haɪəˌlɔɪd) *adj. Anatomy, zoology.* clear and transparent; glassy; hyaline. [C19: from Greek *hualoeidēs*]

hy·a·loid mem·brane *n.* the delicate transparent membrane enclosing the vitreous humour of the eye.

hy·al·o·plasm ('haɪələʊˌplæzəm) *n.* the clear nongranular constituent of cell cytoplasm. —ˌ**hy·a·lo·'plas·mic** *adj.*

hy·a·lu·ron·ic ac·id (ˌhaɪəlʊ'rɒnɪk) *n.* a viscous polysaccharide with important lubricating properties, present, for example, in the synovial fluid in joints. [C20: HYALO- + Greek *ouron* urine + -IC] —ˌ**hy·a·lu·'ron·ic** *adj.*

hy·a·lu·ron·i·dase (ˌhaɪəlʊ'rɒnɪˌdeɪs, -ˌdeɪz) *n.* an enzyme that breaks down hyaluronic acid, thus decreasing the viscosity of the medium containing the acid. [C20: HYALO- + Greek *ouron* urine + ID[3] + -ASE]

hy·brid ('haɪbrɪd) *n.* **1.** an animal or plant resulting from a cross between genetically unlike individuals. Hybrids between different species are usually sterile. **2.** anything of mixed ancestry. **3.** a word, part of which is derived from one language and part from another, such as *monolingual,* which has a prefix of Greek origin and a root of Latin origin. ~*adj.* **4.** denoting or being a hybrid; of mixed origin. **5.** *Physics.* (of an electromagnetic wave) having components of both electric and magnetic field vectors in the direction of propagation. **6.** *Electronics.* **a.** (of a circuit) consisting of transistors and valves. **b.** (of an integrated circuit) consisting of one or more fully integrated circuits and other components, attached to a ceramic substrate. Compare **monolithic** (sense 3). [C17: from Latin *hibrida* offspring of a mixed union (human or animal)] —**'hy·brid·ism** *n.* —**hy·'brid·i·ty** *n.*

hy·brid com·put·er *n.* a computer combining some of the advantages of both analog and digital computers. A continuously varying analog input is converted into discrete values for fast digital processing.

hy·brid·ize *or* **hy·brid·ise** ('haɪbrɪˌdaɪz) *vb.* to produce or cause to produce hybrids; crossbreed. —**'hy·brid·ˌiz·a·ble** *or* **'hy·brid·ˌis·a·ble** *adj.* —ˌ**hy·brid·i·'za·tion** *or* ˌ**hy·brid·i·'sa·tion** *n.* —**'hy·brid·ˌiz·er** *or* **'hy·brid·ˌis·er** *n.*

hy·brid vig·our *n. Biology.* the increased size, strength, etc., of a hybrid as compared to either of its parents. Also called: **heterosis.**

hy·bris ('haɪbrɪs) *n.* a variant spelling of **hubris.** —**hy·'bris·tic** *adj.*

hy·dan·to·in (haɪ'dæntəʊɪn) *n.* a colourless odourless crystalline compound present in beet molasses: used in the manufacture of pharmaceuticals and synthetic resins. Formula: $C_3H_4N_2O_2$. [C20: from HYD(ROGEN + ALL)ANTOIN]

hy·da·thode ('haɪdəˌθəʊd) *n.* a pore in plants, esp. on the leaves, specialized for excreting water. [C19: from Greek, from *hudor* water + *hodos* way]

hy·da·tid ('haɪdətɪd) *n.* **1.** a large bladder containing encysted larvae of the tapeworm *Echinococcus:* causes serious disease in man. **2.** a sterile fluid-filled cyst produced in man and animals during infestation by *Echinococcus* larval forms. ~Also called: **hydatid cyst.** [C17: from Greek *hudatis* watery vesicle, from *hudōr, hudat-* water]

Hyde[1] (haɪd) *n.* a town in NW England, in E Greater Manchester. Pop.: 37 075 (1971).

Hyde[2] (haɪd) *n.* **1. Doug·las.** 1860–1949, Irish statesman and author; first president of Eire (1938–45). **2. Ed·ward.** See (1st Earl of) **Clarendon.**

Hyde Park *n.* a park in W central London: popular for open-air meetings.

Hy·der·a·bad ('haɪdərəˌbɑ:d, -ˌbæd, 'haɪdrə-) *n.* **1.** a city in S central India, capital of Andhra Pradesh state and capital of former Hyderabad state; university (1918). Pop.: 1 607 396 (1971). **2.** a former state of S India: divided in 1956 between the states of Andhra Pradesh, Mysore, and Maharashtra. **3.** a city in SW Pakistan, on the River Indus: seat of the University of Sind (1947). Pop.: 628 310 (1972).

Hy·der A·li *or* **Hai·dar A·li** ('haɪdər 'ɑ:li) *n.* 1722–82, Indian ruler of Mysore (1766–82), who waged two wars against the British in India (1767–69; 1780–82).

hyd·no·car·pate (ˌhɪdnəʊ'kɑ:peɪt) *n.* any salt or ester of hydnocarpic acid.

hyd·no·car·pic ac·id (ˌhɪdnəʊ'kɑ:pɪk) *n.* a cyclic fatty acid occurring in the form of its glycerides in chaulmoogra oil. Formula: $C_{16}H_{28}O_2$. [C20: from Greek *hudnon* truffle + *karpos* fruit + -IC]

hydr- *combining form.* variant of **hydro-** before a vowel.

hy·dra ('haɪdrə) *n., pl.* **·dras** *or* **·drae** (-dri:). **1.** any solitary freshwater hydroid coelenterate of the genus *Hydra,* in which the body is a slender polyp with tentacles around the mouth. **2.** a persistent trouble or evil: *the hydra of the Irish problem.* [C16: from Latin, from Greek *hudra* water serpent; compare OTTER]

Hy·dra[1] ('haɪdrə) *n. Greek myth.* a monster with nine heads, each of which, when struck off, was replaced by two new ones.

Hy·dra[2] ('haɪdrə) *n., Latin genitive* **Hy·drae** ('haɪdri:). a very long faint constellation lying mainly in the S hemisphere and extending from near Virgo to Cancer.

hy·drac·id (haɪ'dræsɪd) *n.* an acid, such as hydrochloric acid, that does not contain oxygen.

hy·dran·gea (haɪ'dreɪndʒə) *n.* any shrub or tree of the Asian and American genus *Hydrangea,* cultivated for their large clusters of white, pink, or blue flowers: family *Hydrangeaceae.* [C18: from New Latin, from Greek *hudōr* water + *angeion* vessel: probably from the cup-shaped fruit]

hy·drant ('haɪdrənt) *n.* an outlet from a water main, usually consisting of an upright pipe with a valve attached, from which water can be tapped for fighting fires, etc. See also **fire hydrant.** [C19: from HYDRO- + -ANT]

hy·dranth ('haɪdrænθ) *n.* a polyp in a colony of hydrozoan coelenterates that is specialized for feeding rather than reproduction. [C19: from HYDRA + Greek *anthos* flower]

hy·drar·gy·rum (haɪ'drɑ:dʒɪrəm) *n.* an obsolete name for **mercury** (sense 1). [C16: from New Latin, from Latin *hydrargyrus* from Greek *hydrarguros,* from HYDRO- + *arguros* silver] —**hy·drar·gy·ric** (ˌhaɪdrɑ:'dʒɪərɪk) *adj.*

hy·dras·tine (haɪ'dræsti:n, -tɪn) *n.* a white poisonous alkaloid extracted from the roots of the goldenseal: has been used in medicine (in the form of one of its water-soluble salts) to contract the uterus and arrest haemorrhage. Formula: $C_{21}H_{21}NO_6$. [C19: from HYDRAST(IS) + -INE[2]]

hy·dras·ti·nine (haɪ'dræstɪˌni:n) *n.* a colourless crystalline water-soluble compound whose pharmacological action resembles that of hydrastine. Formula: $C_{11}H_{13}NO_3$.

hy·dras·tis (haɪ'dræstɪs) *n.* any ranunculaceous plant of the genus *Hydrastis,* of Japan and E North America, such as goldenseal, having showy foliage and ornamental red fruits. [C18: New Latin, from Greek HYDRO- + *-astis,* of unknown origin]

hy·drate ('haɪdreɪt) *n.* **1.** a chemical compound containing water that is chemically combined with a substance and can usually be expelled without changing the constitution of the substance. **2.** a chemical compound that can dissociate reversibly into water and another compound. For example sulphuric acid (H_2SO_4) dissociates into sulphur trioxide (SO_3) and water (H_2O). **3.** (*not in technical usage*) a chemical compound, such as a carbohydrate, that contains hydrogen and oxygen atoms in the ratio two to one. ~*vb.* **4.** to undergo or cause to undergo treatment or impregnation with water. —**hy·'dra·tion** *n.* —**'hy·dra·tor** *n.*

hy·drat·ed ('haɪdreɪtɪd) *adj.* (of a compound) chemically bonded to water molecules.

hy·drau·lic (haɪ'drɒlɪk) *adj.* **1.** operated by pressure transmitted through a pipe by a liquid, such as water or oil. **2.** of, concerned with, or employing liquids in motion. **3.** of or concerned with hydraulics. **4.** hardening under water: *hydraulic cement.* [C17: from Latin *hydraulicus* of a water organ, from Greek *hudraulikos,* from *hudraulos* water organ, from HYDRO- + *aulos* pipe, reed instrument] —**hy·'drau·li·cal·ly** *adv.*

hy·drau·lic brake *n.* a type of brake, used in motor vehicles, in which the braking force is transmitted from the brake pedal to the brakes by a compressed liquid.

hy·drau·lic press *n.* a press that utilizes liquid pressure to enable a small force applied to a small piston to produce a large force on a larger piston. The small piston moves through a proportionately greater distance than the larger.

hy·drau·lic ram *n.* **1.** the larger or working piston of a hydraulic press. **2.** a form of water pump utilizing the kinetic energy of running water to provide static pressure to raise water to a reservoir higher than the source.

hy·drau·lics (haɪ'drɒlɪks) *n.* (*functioning as sing.*) another name for **fluid mechanics.**

hy·drau·lic sus·pen·sion *n.* a system of motor-vehicle suspension using hydraulic members, often with hydraulic compensation between front and rear systems (**hydroelastic suspension**).

hy·dra·zine ('haɪdrəˌzi:n, -zɪn) *n.* a colourless basic liquid made from sodium hypochlorite and ammonia: a strong reducing agent, used chiefly as a rocket fuel. Formula: N_2H_4. [C19: from HYDRO- + AZO- + -INE[2]]

hy·dra·zo·ic ac·id (ˌhaɪdrə'zəʊɪk) *n.* a colourless highly explosive liquid. Formula: HN_3. See also **azide.**

hy·dri·a ('haɪdrɪə) *n.* (in ancient Greece and Rome) a large water jar. [C19: from Latin, from Greek *hudria,* from *hudōr* water]

hy·dric ('haɪdrɪk) *adj.* **1.** of or containing hydrogen. **2.** containing or using moisture.

hy·dride ('haɪdraɪd) *n.* any compound of hydrogen with another element, including ionic compounds such as sodium hydride (NaH), covalent compounds such as borane (B_2H_6), and the transition metal hydrides formed when certain metals, such as palladium, absorb hydrogen.

hy·dri·od·ic ac·id (ˌhaɪdrɪ'ɒdɪk) *n.* the colourless or pale yellow aqueous solution of hydrogen iodide: a strong acid. [C19: from HYDRO- + IODIC]

hy·dro[1] ('haɪdrəʊ) *n., pl.* **-dros.** *Brit.* a hotel or resort, often near a spa, offering facilities for hydropathic treatment.

hy·dro[2] ('haɪdrəʊ) *adj.* **1.** short for **hydroelectric.** ~*n.* **2.** a Canadian name for **electricity.**

hy·dro- *or before a vowel* **hydr-** *combining form.* **1.** indicating or denoting water, liquid, or fluid: *hydrolysis; hydrodynamics.* **2.** indicating the presence of hydrogen in a chemical compound: *hydrochloric acid.* **3.** indicating a hydroid: *hydrozoan.* [from Greek *hudōr* water]

hy·dro·bro·mic ac·id (ˌhaɪdrəʊ'brəʊmɪk) *n.* the colourless or faintly yellow aqueous solution of hydrogen bromide: a strong acid.

hy·dro·car·bon (ˌhaɪdrəʊ'kɑ:bᵊn) *n.* any organic compound containing only carbon and hydrogen, such as the alkanes, alkenes, alkynes, terpenes, and arenes.

hy·dro·cele ('haɪdrəʊˌsi:l) *n.* an abnormal collection of fluid in any saclike space, esp. around the testicles.

hy·dro·cel·lu·lose (ˌhaɪdrəʊ'sɛljʊˌləʊs, -ˌləʊz) *n.* a gelatinous material consisting of hydrated cellulose, made by treating cellulose with water, acids, or alkalis: used in making paper, viscose rayon, and mercerized cotton.

hy·dro·ceph·a·lus (ˌhaɪdrəʊ'sɛfələs) *or* **hy·dro·ceph·a·ly** (ˌhaɪdrəʊ'sɛfəlɪ) *n.* accumulation of cerebrospinal fluid within the ventricles of the brain because its normal outlet has been blocked by congenital malformation or disease. In infancy it usually results in great enlargement of the head. Nontechnical name: **water on the brain.** —**hy·dro·ce·phal·ic** (ˌhaɪdrəʊsɛ'fælɪk), ˌ**hy·dro·'ceph·a·loid,** *or* ˌ**hy·dro·'ceph·a·lous** *adj.*

hy·dro·chlo·ric ac·id (ˌhaɪdrə'klɒrɪk) *n.* the colourless or slightly yellow aqueous solution of hydrogen chloride: a strong acid used in many industrial and laboratory processes. Formerly called: **muriatic acid.**

hy·dro·chlo·ride (ˌhaɪdrə'klɔ:raɪd) *n.* a quaternary salt formed by the addition of hydrochloric acid to an organic base, such as aniline hydrochloride, $[C_6H_5NH_3]^+Cl^-$.

hy·dro·cor·al (ˌhaɪdrə'kɒrəl) *or* **hy·dro·cor·al·line** *n.* any hydrozoan coelenterate of the order *Milleporina* (or *Hydrocorallinae*), which includes the millepores. [C20: from HYDRO- + CORAL]

hy·dro·cor·ti·sone (ˌhaɪdrəʊ'kɔ:tɪˌzəʊn) *n.* the principal glucocorticoid secreted by the adrenal cortex; 17-hydroxycorticosterone. The synthesized form is used mainly in treating rheumatic, allergic, and inflammatory disorders. Formula: $C_{21}H_{30}O_5$. Also called: **cortisol.**

hy·dro·cy·an·ic ac·id (ˌhaɪdrəʊsaɪ'ænɪk) *n.* another name for **hydrogen cyanide,** esp. when in aqueous solution.

hy·dro·dy·nam·ic (ˌhaɪdrəʊdaɪ'næmɪk, -dɪ-) *or* **hy·dro·dy·nam·i·cal** *adj.* **1.** of or concerned with the mechanical properties of fluids. **2.** of or concerned with hydrodynamics. —ˌ**hy·dro·dy·'nam·i·cal·ly** *adv.*

hy·dro·dy·nam·ics (ˌhaɪdrəʊdaɪ'næmɪks, -dɪ-) *n.* **1.** (*functioning as sing.*) the branch of science concerned with the mechanical properties of fluids, esp. liquids. Also called: **hydromechanics.** See also **hydrokinetics, hydrostatics. 2.** another name for **hydrokinetics.**

hy·dro·e·lec·tric (ˌhaɪdrəʊɪ'lɛktrɪk) *adj.* **1.** generated by the pressure of falling water: *hydroelectric power.* **2.** of or concerned with the generation of electricity by water pressure: *a hydroelectric scheme.* —**hy·dro·e·lec·tric·i·ty** (ˌhaɪdrəʊɪlɛk'trɪsɪtɪ:, -ˌi:lɛk-) *n.*

hy·dro·flu·or·ic ac·id (ˌhaɪdrəʊflu:'ɒrɪk) *n.* the colourless aqueous solution of hydrogen fluoride: a strong acid that attacks glass.

hy·dro·foil ('haɪdrəˌfɔɪl) *n.* **1.** a fast light vessel the hull of which is raised out of the water on one or more pairs of fixed vanes. **2.** any of these vanes.

hy·dro·gen ('haɪdrɪdʒən) *n.* **a.** a flammable colourless gas that is the lightest and most abundant element in the universe. It occurs mainly in water and in most organic compounds and is used in the production of ammonia and other chemicals, in the hydrogenation of fats and oils, and in welding. Symbol: H; atomic no.: 1; atomic wt.: 1.007 97; valency: 1; density: 0.0899 kg/m^3; melting pt.: –259.14°C; boiling pt.: –252.5°C. See also **deuterium, tritium. b.** (*as modifier*): *hydrogen bomb.* [C18: from French *hydrogène,* from HYDRO- + -GEN; so called because its combustion produces water]

hy·dro·gen·ate ('haɪdrədʒɪˌneɪt, haɪ'drɒdʒɪˌneɪt), **hy·dro·gen·ize,** *or* **hy·dro·gen·ise** ('haɪdrədʒɪˌnaɪz, haɪ'drɒdʒɪˌnaɪz) *vb.* to undergo or cause to undergo a reaction with hydrogen: *to hydrogenate ethylene.* —ˌ**hy·dro·gen·'a·tion,** ˌ**hy·dro·gen·i·'za·tion,** *or* ˌ**hy·dro·gen·i·'sa·tion** *n.* —**'hy·dro·gen·ˌa·tor** *n.*

hy·dro·gen bomb *n.* a type of bomb in which energy is released by fusion of hydrogen nuclei to give helium nuclei. The energy required to initiate the fusion is provided by an atom bomb, which is surrounded by a hydrogen-containing substance such as lithium deuteride. Also called: **H-bomb.** See also **fusion bomb.**

hy·dro·gen bond *n.* a weak chemical bond between an electronegative atom, such as fluorine, oxygen, or nitrogen, and a hydrogen atom bound to another electronegative atom. Hydrogen bonds are responsible for the properties of water and many biological molecules.

hy·dro·gen bro·mide *n.* **1.** a colourless pungent gas used in organic synthesis. Formula: HBr. **2.** an aqueous solution of hydrogen bromide; hydrobromic acid.

hy·dro·gen car·bon·ate *n.* another name for **bicarbonate.**

hy·dro·gen chlo·ride *n.* **1.** a colourless pungent corrosive gas obtained by the action of sulphuric acid on sodium chloride: used in making vinyl chloride and other organic chemicals.

Formula: HCl. **2.** an aqueous solution of hydrogen chloride; hydrochloric acid.

hy·dro+gen cy·a+nide *n.* a colourless poisonous liquid with a faint odour of bitter almonds, usually made by a catalysed reaction between ammonia, oxygen, and methane. It forms prussic acid in aqueous solution and is used for making plastics and dyes and as a war gas. Formula: HCN. Also called: **hydrocyanic acid.**

hy·dro+gen fluo+ride *n.* **1.** a colourless poisonous corrosive gas or liquid made by reaction between calcium fluoride and sulphuric acid: used as a fluorinating agent and catalyst. Formula: HF. **2.** an aqueous solution of hydrogen fluoride; hydrofluoric acid.

hy·dro+gen i·o·dide *n.* **1.** a colourless poisonous corrosive gas obtained by a catalysed reaction between hydrogen and iodine vapour: used in making iodides. Formula: HI. **2.** an aqueous solution of this gas; hydriodic acid.

hy·dro+gen i·on *n.* **1.** an ionized hydrogen atom, occurring in plasmas and in aqueous solutions of acids, in which it is solvated by one or more water molecules; proton. Formula: H^+ **2.** an ionized hydrogen molecule; hydrogen molecular ion. Formula: H_2^+

hy·dro+gen+ize *or* **hy·dro+gen+ise** ('haɪdrədʒɪˌnaɪz, haɪ'drɒdʒɪˌnaɪz) *vb.* variants of **hydrogenate.** —ˌ**hy·dro+gen·i+'za+tion** *or* ˌ**hy·dro+gen·i+'sa+tion** *n.*

hy·dro+gen+ol·y+sis (ˌhaɪdrəʊdʒɪ'nɒlɪsɪs) *n.* a chemical reaction in which a compound is decomposed by hydrogen.

hy+drog+e·nous (hɪ'drɒdʒɪnəs) *adj.* of or containing hydrogen.

hy·dro+gen per+ox+ide *n.* a colourless oily unstable liquid, usually used in aqueous solution. It is a strong oxidizing agent used as a bleach for textiles, wood pulp, hair, etc., and as an oxidizer in rocket fuels. Formula: H_2O_2.

hy·dro+gen sul+phate *n.* another name for **bisulphate.**

hy·dro+gen sul+phide *n.* a colourless poisonous soluble flammable gas with an odour of rotten eggs: used as a reagent in chemical analysis. Formula: H_2S. Also called: **sulphuretted hydrogen.**

hy·dro+gen sul+phite *n.* another name for **bisulphite.**

hy·dro+gen tar+trate *n.* another name for **bitartrate.**

hy·dro+graph ('haɪdrəˌgrɑːf, -ˌgræf) *n.* a graph showing the seasonal variation in the level, velocity, or discharge of a body of water.

hy+drog+ra+phy (haɪ'drɒgrəfɪ) *n.* **1.** the study, surveying, and mapping of the oceans, seas, and rivers. Compare **hydrology. 2.** the oceans, seas, and rivers as represented on a chart. —**hy+'drog+ra+pher** *n.* —**hy·dro+graph+ic** (ˌhaɪdrə'græfɪk) *or* ˌ**hy·dro+'graph·i+cal** *adj.* —ˌ**hy·dro+'graph·i+cal+ly** *adv.*

hy+droid ('haɪdrɔɪd) *adj.* **1.** of or relating to the *Hydroida*, an order of colonial hydrozoan coelenterates that have the polyp phase dominant. **2.** (of coelenterate colonies or individuals) having or consisting of hydra-like polyps. ~*n.* **3.** a hydroid colony or individual.

hy·dro+ki+net+ic (ˌhaɪdrəʊkɪ'nɛtɪk, -kaɪ-) *or* **hy·dro+ki+net·i+cal** *adj.* **1.** of or concerned with fluids that are in motion. **2.** of or concerned with hydrokinetics.

hy·dro+ki+net+ics (ˌhaɪdrəʊkɪ'nɛtɪks, -kaɪ-) *n.* (*functioning as sing.*) the branch of science concerned with the mechanical behaviour and properties of fluids in motion, esp. of liquids. Also called: **hydrodynamics.**

hy·dro+log+ic cy+cle *n.* another name for **water cycle.**

hy+drol+o·gy (haɪ'drɒlədʒɪ) *n.* the study of the distribution, conservation, use, etc., of the water of the earth and its atmosphere. —**hy·dro+log+ic** (ˌhaɪdrə'lɒdʒɪk) *or* ˌ**hy·dro+'log·i+cal** *adj.* —ˌ**hy·dro+'log·i+cal+ly** *adv.* —**hy+'drol·o+gist** *n.*

hy+drol·y+sate (haɪ'drɒlɪˌseɪt) *n.* a substance or mixture produced by hydrolysis. [C20: from HYDROLYSIS + -ATE[1]]

hy·dro+lyse *or U.S.* **hy·dro+lyze** ('haɪdrəˌlaɪz) *vb.* to subject to or undergo hydrolysis. —**'hy·dro+ˌlys·a·ble** *or U.S.* **'hy·dro+ˌlyz+a·ble** *adj.* —ˌ**hy·dro+ly+'sa+tion** *or U.S.* ˌ**hy·dro+ly+'za+tion** *n.* —**'hy·dro+ˌlys+er** *or U.S.* **'hy·dro+ˌlyz+er** *n.*

hy+drol·y+sis (haɪ'drɒlɪsɪs) *n.* a chemical reaction in which a compound reacts with water to produce other compounds.

hy·dro+lyte ('haɪdrəˌlaɪt) *n.* a substance subjected to hydrolysis.

hy·dro+lyt+ic (ˌhaɪdrə'lɪtɪk) *adj.* of, concerned with, producing, or produced by hydrolysis.

hy·dro+mag+net+ics (ˌhaɪdrəʊmæg'nɛtɪks) *n.* another name for **magnetohydrodynamics.**

hy·dro+man+cy ('haɪdrəʊˌmænsɪ) *n.* divination by water. —**'hy·dro+ˌmanc+er** *n.* —ˌ**hy·dro+'man+tic** *adj.*

hy·dro+me·chan+ics (ˌhaɪdrəʊmɪ'kænɪks) *n.* another name for **hydrodynamics.** —ˌ**hy·dro+me·'chan·i+cal** *adj.*

hy·dro+me·du+sa (ˌhaɪdrəʊmɪ'djuːsə) *n., pl.* **+sas** *or* **+sae** (-siː). the medusa form of hydrozoan coelenterates. —ˌ**hy·dro+me·'du+san** *adj.*

hy·dro+mel ('haɪdrəʊˌmɛl) *n. Archaic.* another word for **mead** (the drink). [C15: from Latin, from Greek *hudromeli*, from HYDRO- + *meli* honey]

hy·dro+met+al+lur+gy (ˌhaɪdrəʊ'mɛtᵊˌlɜːdʒɪ, -mɛ'tælədʒɪ) *n.* a technique for the recovery of a metal from an aqueous medium in which the metal or the gangue is preferentially dissolved. —ˌ**hy·dro+ˌmet+al+'lur+gi+cal** *adj.*

hy·dro+me·te·or (ˌhaɪdrəʊ'miːtɪə) *n.* any weather condition produced by water in the atmosphere, such as rain or snow. —ˌ**hy·dro+ˌme·te·or·o+'log·i+cal** *adj.* —ˌ**hy·dro+ˌme·te·or+'ol+o·gy** *n.*

hy+drom+e·ter (haɪ'drɒmɪtə) *n.* an instrument for measuring the relative density of a liquid, usually consisting of a sealed graduated tube with a weighted bulb on one end, the relative density being indicated by the length of the unsubmerged stem. —**hy·dro+met+ric** (ˌhaɪdrəʊ'mɛtrɪk) *or* ˌ**hy·dro+'met+ri+cal** *adj.* —ˌ**hy·dro+'met+ri+cal+ly** *adv.* —**hy+'drom+e+try** *n.*

hy·dro+naut ('haɪdrəʊˌnɔːt) *n. U.S. Navy.* a person trained to operate deep submergence vessels. [C20: from Greek, from HYDRO- + -*naut*, as in *aeronaut, astronaut*]

hy·dro+ni·um i·on (haɪ'drəʊnɪəm) *n. Chem.* another name for **hydroxonium ion.** [C20: from HYDRO- + (AMM)ONIUM]

hy+drop·a+thy (haɪ'drɒpəθɪ) *n.* a pseudoscientific method of treating disease by the use of large quantities of water both internally and externally. Also called: **water cure.** Compare **hydrotherapy.** —**hy·dro+path+ic** (ˌhaɪdrəʊ'pæθɪk) *or* ˌ**hy·dro+'path·i+cal** *adj.* —**hy+'drop·a+thist** *or* **'hy·dro+ˌpath** *n.*

hy·dro+phane ('haɪdrəʊˌfeɪn) *n.* a white partially opaque variety of opal that becomes translucent in water. —**hy+droph·a+nous** (haɪ'drɒfənəs) *adj.*

hy·dro+phil+ic (ˌhaɪdrəʊ'fɪlɪk) *adj. Chem.* tending to dissolve in, mix with, or be wetted by water: *a hydrophilic colloid.* Compare **hydrophobic.** —**'hy·dro+ˌphile** *n.*

hy+droph·i+lous (haɪ'drɒfɪləs) *adj. Botany.* growing in or pollinated by water. —**hy+'droph·i+ly** *n.*

hy·dro+pho+bia (ˌhaɪdrə'fəʊbɪə) *n.* **1.** another name for **rabies. 2.** a fear of drinking fluids, esp. that of a person with rabies, because of painful spasms when trying to swallow. Compare **aquaphobia.**

hy·dro+pho+bic (ˌhaɪdrə'fəʊbɪk) *adj.* **1.** of or relating to hydrophobia. **2.** *Chem.* tending not to dissolve in, mix with, or be wetted by water: *a hydrophobic colloid.* Compare **hydrophilic.**

hy·dro+phone ('haɪdrəˌfəʊn) *n.* an electroacoustic transducer that converts sound or ultrasonic waves travelling through water into electrical oscillations.

hy·dro+phyte ('haɪdrəʊˌfaɪt) *n.* a plant that grows only in water or very moist soil. —**hy·dro+phyt+ic** (ˌhaɪdrəʊ'fɪtɪk) *adj.*

hy·dro+plane ('haɪdrəʊˌpleɪn) *n.* **1.** a motorboat equipped with hydrofoils or with a shaped bottom that raises its hull out of the water at high speeds. **2.** an attachment to an aircraft to enable it to glide along the surface of water. **3.** another name (esp. U.S.) for a **seaplane. 4.** a horizontal vane on the hull of a submarine for controlling its vertical motion. ~*vb.* **5.** (*intr.*) (of a boat) to rise out of the water in the manner of a hydroplane.

hy·dro+pon+ics (ˌhaɪdrəʊ'pɒnɪks) *n.* (*functioning as sing.*) a method of cultivating plants by growing them in gravel, etc., through which water containing dissolved inorganic nutrient salts is pumped. Also called: **aquiculture.** [C20: from HYDRO- + (GEO)PONICS] —ˌ**hy·dro+'pon+ic** *adj.* —ˌ**hy·dro+'pon·i+cal+ly** *adv.*

hy·dro+pow+er ('haɪdrəʊˌpaʊə) *n.* hydroelectric power.

hy·dro+qui+none (ˌhaɪdrəʊkwɪ'nəʊn) *or* **hy·dro+quin+ol** (ˌhaɪdrəʊ'kwɪnɒl) *n.* a white crystalline soluble phenol used as a photographic developer; 1,4-dihydroxybenzene. Formula: $C_6H_4(OH)_2$. Also called: **quinol.**

hy·dro+scope ('haɪdrəˌskəʊp) *n.* any instrument for making observations of underwater objects. —**hy·dro+scop+ic** (ˌhaɪdrə'skɒpɪk) *or* ˌ**hy·dro+'scop·i+cal** *adj.*

hy·dro+ski ('haɪdrəʊˌskiː) *n.* a hydrofoil used on some seaplanes to provide extra lift when taking off.

hy·dro+sol ('haɪdrəˌsɒl) *n. Chem.* a sol that has water as its liquid phase.

hy·dro+some ('haɪdrəˌsəʊm) *or* **hy·dro+so+ma** (ˌhaɪdrə'səʊmə) *n. Zoology.* the body of a colonial hydrozoan. [C19: from *hydro-*, from HYDRA + -SOME[3]]

hy·dro+sphere ('haɪdrəˌsfɪə) *n.* the watery part of the earth's surface, including oceans, lakes, water vapour in the atmosphere, etc. —ˌ**hy·dro+'spher+ic** *adj.*

hy·dro+stat ('haɪdrəʊˌstæt) *n.* a device that detects the presence of water as a prevention against drying out, overflow, etc., esp. one used as a warning in a steam boiler.

hy·dro+stat+ic (ˌhaɪdrəʊ'stætɪk) *or* **hy·dro+stat·i+cal** *adj.* **1.** of or concerned with fluids that are not in motion: *hydrostatic pressure.* **2.** of or concerned with hydrostatics. —ˌ**hy·dro+'stat·i+cal+ly** *adv.*

hy·dro+stat+ic bal+ance *n.* a balance for finding the weight of an object submerged in water in order to determine the upthrust on it and thus determine its relative density.

hy·dro+stat+ics (ˌhaɪdrəʊ'stætɪks) *n.* (*functioning as sing.*) the branch of science concerned with the mechanical properties and behaviour of fluids that are not in motion. See also **hydrodynamics.**

hy·dro+sul+phate (ˌhaɪdrəʊ'sʌlfeɪt) *n.* any quaternary acid salt formed by addition of an organic base to sulphuric acid, such as aniline hydrosulphate, $C_6H_5NH_3HSO_4$.

hy·dro+sul+phide (ˌhaɪdrəʊ'sʌlfaɪd) *n.* any salt derived from hydrogen sulphide by replacing one of its hydrogen atoms with a metal atom. Technical name: **hydrogen sulphide.**

hy·dro+sul+phite (ˌhaɪdrəʊ'sʌlfaɪt) *n.* another name (not in technical usage) for **dithionite.** [C20: from HYDROSULPH(UROUS) + -ITE[2]]

hy·dro+sul+phur+ous acid (ˌhaɪdrəʊ'sʌlfərəs) *n.* another name (not in technical usage) for **dithionous acid.**

hy·dro+tax+is (ˌhaɪdrəʊ'taksɪs) *n.* the directional movement of an organism or cell in response to the stimulus of water. —ˌ**hy·dro+'tac+tic** *adj.*

hy·dro+ther·a+peu+tics (ˌhaɪdrəʊˌθɛrə'pjuːtɪks) *n.* (*functioning as sing.*) the branch of medical science concerned with hydrotherapy. —ˌ**hy·dro+ˌther·a+'peu+tic** *adj.*

hy·dro+ther·a+py (ˌhaɪdrəʊ'θɛrəpɪ) *n. Med.* the treatment of certain diseases by the external application of water, as for mobilizing stiff joints or strengthening weakened muscles.

Also called: **water cure.** Compare **hydropathy.** —**hy·dro+ther·a+pic** (ˌhaɪdrəʊθɪˈræpɪk) *adj.* —ˌ**hy·dro+ˈther·a+pist** *n.*

hy·dro+ther+mal (ˌhaɪdrəʊˈθɜːməl) *adj.* of or relating to the action of water under conditions of high temperature, esp. in forming rocks and minerals. —ˌ**hy·dro+ˈther+mal+ly** *adv.*

hy·dro+tho+rax (ˌhaɪdrəʊˈθɔːræks) *n. Pathol.* an accumulation of fluid in one or both pleural cavities, often resulting from disease of the heart or kidneys. —**hy·dro+tho+rac+ic** (ˌhaɪdrəʊθɔːˈræsɪk) *adj.*

hy+drot+ro+pism (haɪˈdrɒtrəˌpɪzəm) *n.* the directional growth of plants in response to the stimulus of water. —**hy·dro+trop+ic** (ˌhaɪdrəʊˈtrɒpɪk) *adj.* —ˌ**hy·dro+ˈtrop·i+cal+ly** *adv.*

hy+drous (ˈhaɪdrəs) *adj.* **1.** containing water. **2.** (of a chemical compound) combined with water molecules: *hydrous copper sulphate,* $CuSO_4.5H_2O$.

hy+drox+ide (haɪˈdrɒksaɪd) *n.* **1.** a base or alkali containing the ion OH^-. **2.** any compound containing an -OH group.

hy+drox+o·ni·um i·on (ˌhaɪdrɒkˈsəʊnɪəm) *n.* a positive ion, H_3O^+, formed by the attachment of a proton to a water molecule: occurs in solutions of acids and behaves like a hydrogen ion. Also called: **hydronium ion.**

hy+drox·y (haɪˈdrɒksɪ) *adj.* (of a chemical compound) containing one or more hydroxyl groups. [C19: HYDRO- + OXY(GEN)]

hy·drox·y- *combining form.* (in chemical compounds) indicating the presence of one or more hydroxyl groups or ions. [from HYDRO- + OXY(GEN)]

hy+drox·y ac·id *n.* **1.** any acid, such as sulphuric acid, containing hydroxyl groups in its molecules. **2.** any of a class of carboxylic acids that contain both a hydroxyl group and a carboxyl group in their molecules.

hy+drox·yl (haɪˈdrɒksɪl) *n.* (*modifier*) of, consisting of, or containing the monovalent group -OH or the ion OH^-: *a hydroxyl group or radical.* —ˌ**hy+drox+ˈyl+ic** *adj.*

hy+drox+yl·a+mine (haɪˌdrɒksɪləˈmiːn, -ˈæmɪn, -ˈsaɪləˌmiːn) *n.* a colourless crystalline compound that explodes when heated: a reducing agent. Formula: NH_2OH.

hy+drox·y+pro+line (haɪˌdrɒksɪˈprəʊliːn, -lɪn) *n.* an amino acid occurring in some proteins, esp. collagen. Formula: $(OH)C_4H_7N(COOH)$.

hy·dro+zo·an (ˌhaɪdrəʊˈzəʊən) *n.* **1.** any colonial or solitary coelenterate of the class *Hydrozoa,* which includes the hydra, Portuguese man-of-war, and the sertularians. ~*adj.* **2.** of, relating to, or belonging to the *Hydrozoa.*

Hy+drus (ˈhaɪdrəs) *n., Latin genitive* **Hy+dri** (ˈhaɪdraɪ). a constellation near the S celestial pole lying close to Eridanus and Tucana and containing part of the Small Magellanic cloud. [C17: from Latin, from Greek *hudros* water serpent, from *hudōr* water]

hy+e·na *or* **hy+ae·na** (haɪˈiːnə) *n.* any of several long-legged carnivorous doglike mammals of the genera *Hyaena* and *Crocuta,* such as *C. crocuta* (**spotted** *or* **laughing hyena**), of Africa and S Asia: family *Hyaenidae,* order *Carnivora* (carnivores). [C16: from Medieval Latin, from Latin *hyaena,* from Greek *huaina,* from *hus* hog] —**hy+ˈe·nic** *or* **hy+ˈae·nic** *adj.*

hy+e·tal (ˈhaɪɪtᵊl) *adj.* of or relating to rain, rainfall, or rainy regions. [C19: from Greek *huetos* rain + -AL[1]]

hy+et·o·graph (ˈhaɪɪtəˌgrɑːf, -ˌgræf) *n.* **1.** a chart showing the distribution of rainfall of a particular area, usually throughout a year. **2.** a self-recording rain gauge.

hy+e·tog+ra+phy (ˌhaɪɪˈtɒgrəfɪ) *n.* the study of the distribution and recording of rainfall. —**hy+e·to+graph+ic** (ˌhaɪɪtəˈgræfɪk) *or* ˌ**hy+e·to+ˈgraph·i+cal** *adj.* —ˌ**hy+e·to+ˈgraph·i+cal+ly** *adv.*

Hy·ge·ia (haɪˈdʒiːə) *n.* the Greek goddess of health. —**Hy+ˈge·ian** *adj.*

hy+giene (ˈhaɪdʒiːn) *n.* **1.** Also called: **hygienics.** the science concerned with the maintenance of health. **2.** clean or healthy practices or thinking: *personal hygiene.* [C18: from New Latin *hygiēna,* from Greek *hugieinē,* from *hugieinos* healthful, from *hugiēs* healthy]

hy+gien+ic (haɪˈdʒiːnɪk) *adj.* promoting health or cleanliness; sanitary. —**hy+ˈgien·i+cal+ly** *adv.*

hy+gien+ics (haɪˈdʒiːnɪks) *n.* (*functioning as sing.*) another word for **hygiene** (sense 1).

hy+gien+ist (ˈhaɪdʒiːnɪst), **hy+ge·ist,** *or* **hy+gie·ist** (ˈhaɪdʒiːɪst) *n.* a person skilled in the practice of hygiene. See also **dental hygienist.**

hy+gris+tor (haɪˈgrɪstə) *n.* an electronic component the resistance of which varies with humidity. [C20: from HYGRO- + (RES)ISTOR]

hy·gro- *or before a vowel* **hygr-** *combining form.* indicating moisture: *hygrometer.* [from Greek *hugros* wet]

hy·gro+graph (ˈhaɪgrəˌgrɑːf, -ˌgræf) *n.* an automatic hygrometer that produces a graphic record of the humidity of the air.

hy+grom+e·ter (haɪˈgrɒmɪtə) *n.* any of various instruments for measuring humidity. —**hy·gro+met+ric** (ˌhaɪgrəˈmɛtrɪk) *adj.* —ˌ**hy·gro+ˈmet+ri+cal·ly** *adv.* —**hy+ˈgrom+e·try** *n.*

hy·gro+phi+lous (haɪˈgrɒfɪləs) *adj.* (of a plant) growing in moist places. —**hy·gro+phile** (ˈhaɪgrəʊˌfaɪl) *n.*

hy·gro+scope (ˈhaɪgrəˌskəʊp) *n.* any device that indicates the humidity of the air without necessarily measuring it.

hy·gro+scop+ic (ˌhaɪgrəˈskɒpɪk) *adj.* (of a substance) tending to absorb water from the air. —ˌ**hy·gro+ˈscop·i+cal+ly** *adv.* —**hy·gro+sco+pic+i·ty** (ˌhaɪgrəskəʊˈpɪsɪtɪ) *n.*

hy·gro+stat (ˈhaɪgrəˌstæt) *n.* another name for **humidistat.**

hy+ing (ˈhaɪɪŋ) *vb.* the present participle of **hie.**

Hyk+sos (ˈhɪksɒs) *n., pl.* **+sos.** a member of a nomadic Asian people, probably Semites, who controlled Egypt from 1720 B.C. until 1560 B.C. [from Greek *Huksōs* name of ruling dynasty in Egypt, from Egyptian *hq's'sw* ruler of the lands of the nomads]

hy·la (ˈhaɪlə) *n.* any tree frog of the genus *Hyla,* such as *H. leucophyllata* (**white-spotted hyla**) of tropical America. [C19: from New Latin, from Greek *hulē* forest, wood]

hy·lo- *or before a vowel* **hyl-** *combining form.* **1.** indicating matter (as distinguished from spirit): *hylozoism.* **2.** indicating wood: *hylophagous.* [from Greek *hulē* wood]

hy·lo+morph+ism (ˌhaɪləˈmɔːfɪzəm) *n.* the philosophical doctrine that identifies matter with the first cause of the universe.

hy+loph·a+gous (haɪˈlɒfəgəs) *adj.* (esp. of insects) feeding on wood. [C19: from Greek *hulophagos,* from *hulē* wood + *phagein* to devour]

hy·lo+the·ism (ˌhaɪləˈθiːɪzəm) *n.* the doctrine that God is identical to matter.

hy+lo+zo+ism (ˌhaɪləˈzəʊɪzəm) *n.* the philosophical doctrine that life is one of the properties of matter. [C17: HYLO- + Greek *zōē* life] —ˌ**hy+lo+ˈzo+ic** *adj.* —ˌ**hy+lo+ˈzo+ist** *n.* —ˌ**hy+lo+zo+ˈis+tic** *adj.* —ˌ**hy+lo+zo+ˈis+ti+cal+ly** *adv.*

hy+men (ˈhaɪmɛn) *n. Anatomy.* a fold of mucous membrane that partly covers the entrance to the vagina and is usually ruptured when sexual intercourse takes place for the first time. [C17: from Greek: membrane] —ˈ**hy+men+al** *adj.*

Hy·men (ˈhaɪmɛn) *n.* the Greek and Roman god of marriage.

hy+me·ne·al (ˌhaɪmɛˈniːəl) *adj.* **1.** *Chiefly poetic.* of or relating to marriage. ~*n.* **2.** a wedding song or poem.

hy+me·ni·um (haɪˈmiːnɪəm) *n., pl.* **+ni·a** (-nɪə) *or* **+ni·ums.** (in basidiomycetous and ascomycetous fungi) a layer of cells some of which produce the spores.

hy+me·nop+ter+an (ˌhaɪmɪˈnɒptərən) *or* **hy+me·nop+ter+on** *n., pl.* **+ter+ans, +ter·a** (-tərə), *or* **+ter+ons.** any hymenopterous insect.

hy+men+op+ter+ous (ˌhaɪmɪˈnɒptərəs) *or* **hy+men+op+ter+an** *adj.* of, relating to, or belonging to the *Hymenoptera,* an order of insects, including bees, wasps, ants, and sawflies, having two pairs of membranous wings and an ovipositor specialized for stinging, sawing, or piercing. [C19: from Greek *humenopteros* membrane wing; see HYMEN, -PTEROUS]

Hy+met+tus (haɪˈmɛtəs) *n.* a mountain in SE Greece, in Attica east of Athens: famous for its marble and for honey. Height: 1032 m (3386 ft.). Modern Greek name: **Imittós.** —**Hy+ˈmet+ti·an** *or* **Hy+ˈmet+tic** *adj.*

hymn (hɪm) *n.* **1.** a Christian song of praise sung to God or a saint. **2.** a similar song praising other gods, a nation, etc. ~*vb.* **3.** to express (praises, thanks, etc.) by singing hymns. [C13: from Latin *hymnus,* from Greek *humnos*] —**hym+nic** (ˈhɪmnɪk) *adj.* —ˈ**hymn+ˌlike** *adj.*

hym+nal (ˈhɪmnᵊl) *n.* **1.** a book of hymns. ~*adj.* **2.** of, relating to, or characteristic of hymns.

hymn book *n.* a book containing the words and music of hymns.

hym+nist (ˈhɪmnɪst), **hym+no+dist** (ˈhɪmnədɪst), *or* **hym+nog+ra+pher** (hɪmˈnɒgrəfə) *n.* a person who composes hymns.

hym+no+dy (ˈhɪmnədɪ) *n.* **1.** the composition or singing of hymns. **2.** hymns collectively. ~Also called: **hymnology.** [C18: from Medieval Latin *hymnōdia,* from Greek *humnōidia,* from *humnōidein* to chant a hymn, from HYMN + *aeidein* to sing] —**hym+nod+i+cal** (hɪmˈnɒdɪkᵊl) *adj.*

hym+nol+o·gy (hɪmˈnɒlədʒɪ) *n.* **1.** the study of hymn composition. **2.** another word for **hymnody.** —**hym+no+log+ic** (ˌhɪmnəˈlɒdʒɪk) *or* ˌ**hym+no+ˈlog·i+cal** *adj.* —**hym+ˈnol+o·gist** *n.*

hy+oid (ˈhaɪɔɪd) *adj. also* **hy·oi+dal** *or* **hy·oi+de·an. 1.** of or relating to the hyoid bone. ~*n. also*: **hyoid bone. 2.** the horseshoe-shaped bone that lies at the base of the tongue and above the thyroid cartilage. **3.** a corresponding bone or group of bones in other vertebrates. [C19: from New Latin *hyoïdes,* from Greek *huoeidēs* having the shape of the letter UPSILON, from *hu* upsilon + -OID]

hy+os+cine (ˈhaɪəˌsiːn) *n.* another name for **scopolamine.** [C19: from HYOSC(YAMUS) + -INE[2]]

hy+os+cy·a+mine (ˌhaɪəˈsaɪəˌmiːn, -mɪn) *n.* a poisonous alkaloid occurring in henbane and related plants: an optically active isomer of atropine, used in medicine in a similar way. Formula: $C_{17}H_{23}NO_3$.

hy+os+cy·a+mus (ˌhaɪəˈsaɪəməs) *n.* any plant of the solanaceous genus *Hyoscyamus,* of Europe, Asia, and N Africa, including henbane. [C18: from New Latin, from Greek *huoskuamos,* from *hus* pig + *kuamos* bean; the plant was thought to be poisonous to pigs]

hyp. *abbrev. for:* **1.** hypotenuse. **2.** hypothesis. **3.** hypothetical.

hyp- *prefix.* a variant of **hypo-** before a vowel: *hypabyssal.*

hyp+a·byss+al (ˌhɪpəˈbɪsᵊl) *adj.* (of igneous rocks) derived from magma that has solidified close to the surface of the earth in the form of dykes, sills, etc.

hyp+aes+the+si·a *or U.S.* **hyp+es+the+si·a** (ˌhɪpiːsˈθiːzɪə, ˌhaɪ-) *n. Pathol.* a reduced sensibility to touch. —**hyp+aes+the+sic** *or U.S.* **hyp+es+the+sic** (ˌhɪpiːsˈθiːsɪk, ˌhaɪ-) *adj.*

hy+pae+thral *or U.S.* **hy+pe+thral** (hɪˈpiːθrəl, haɪ-) *adj.* (esp. of a classical temple) having no roof. [C18: from Latin *hypaethrus* uncovered, from Greek *hupaithros,* from HYPO- + *aithros* clear sky]

hy+pal+la+ge (haɪˈpæləˌdʒiː) *n. Rhetoric.* a figure of speech in which the natural relations of two words in a statement are interchanged, as in *the fire spread the wind.* [C16: via Late Latin from Greek *hupallagē* interchange, from HYPO- + *allassein* to exchange]

hy+pan+thi·um (haɪˈpænθɪəm) *n., pl.* **+thi·a** (-θɪə). *Botany.* the cup-shaped or flat receptacle of perigynous flowers. [C19: from New Latin, from HYPO- + Greek *anthion* a little flower, from *anthos* flower] —**hy·'pan·thi·al** *adj.*

hype[1] (haɪp) *Slang.* ~*n.* **1.** a hypodermic needle or injection. **2.** a drug addict. ~*vb.* (*intr.*; usually foll. by *up*) to inject oneself with a drug. [C20: shortened from HYPODERMIC]

hype[2] (haɪp) *Slang.* ~*n.* **1.** a deception, racket, or publicity stunt. **2.** a person who gives short change. ~*vb.* **3.** (*tr.*) to short-change (someone). [C20: of unknown origin]

hyped up *adj. Slang.* stimulated or excited by or as if by the effect of a stimulating drug.

hy·per- *prefix.* **1.** above, over, or in excess: *hypercritical.* **2.** (in medicine) denoting an abnormal excess: *hyperacidity.* **3.** indicating that a chemical compound contains a greater than usual amount of an element: *hyperoxide.* [from Greek *huper* over]

hy·per·a·cid·i·ty (ˌhaɪpərəˈsɪdɪtɪ) *n.* excess acidity of the gastrointestinal tract, esp. the stomach, producing a burning sensation. —ˌ**hy·per·'ac·id** *adj.*

hy·per·ac·tive (ˌhaɪpərˈæktɪv) *adj.* abnormally active. —ˌ**hy·per·'ac·tion** *n.* —ˌ**hy·per·ac·'tiv·i·ty** *n.*

hy·per·ae·mi·a *or U.S.* **hy·per·e·mi·a** (ˌhaɪpərˈiːmɪə) *n. Pathol.* an excessive amount of blood in an organ or part. —ˌ**hy·per·'ae·mic** *or U.S.* ˌ**hy·per·'e·mic** *adj.*

hy·per·aes·the·si·a *or U.S.* **hy·per·es·the·si·a** (ˌhaɪpəriːsˈθiːzɪə) *n. Pathol.* increased sensitivity of any of the sense organs, esp. of the skin to cold, heat, pain, etc. —**hy·per·aes·thet·ic** *or U.S.* **hy·per·es·thet·ic** (ˌhaɪpəriːsˈθɛtɪk) *adj.*

hy·per·bar·ic (ˌhaɪpəˈbærɪk) *adj.* of, concerned with, or operating at pressures higher than normal.

hy·per·ba·ton (haɪˈpɜːbəˌtɒn) *n. Rhetoric.* a figure of speech in which the normal order of words is reversed, as in *cheese I love.* [C16: via Latin from Greek, literally: an overstepping, from HYPER- + *bainein* to step]

hy·per·bo·la (haɪˈpɜːbələ) *n., pl.* **·las** *or* **·le** (-ˌliː). a conic section formed by a plane that cuts both bases of a cone; it consists of two branches asymptotic to two intersecting fixed lines and has two foci. Standard equation: $x^2/a^2 - y^2/b^2 = 1$ where $2a$ is the distance between the two intersections with the x-axis and $b = a\sqrt{(e^2 - 1)}$, where e is the eccentricity. [C17: from Greek *huperbolē*, literally: excess, extravagance, from HYPER- + *ballein* to throw]

hy·per·bo·le (haɪˈpɜːbəlɪ) *n.* a deliberate exaggeration used for effect: *he embraced her a thousand times.* [C16: from Greek: from HYPER- + *bolē* a throw, from *ballein* to throw] —**hy·'per·bo·lism** *n.*

hy·per·bol·ic (ˌhaɪpəˈbɒlɪk) *or* **hy·per·bol·i·cal** *adj.* **1.** of or relating to a hyperbola. **2.** *Rhetoric.* of or relating to a hyperbole. —ˌ**hy·per·'bol·i·cal·ly** *adv.*

hy·per·bol·ic func·tion *n.* any of a group of functions of an angle expressed as a relationship between the distances of a point on a hyperbola to the origin and to the coordinate axes. The group includes sinh (**hyperbolic sine**), cosh (**hyperbolic cosine**), tanh (**hyperbolic tangent**), sech (**hyperbolic secant**), cosech (**hyperbolic cosecant**), and coth (**hyperbolic cotangent**).

hy·per·bo·lize *or* **hy·per·bo·lise** (haɪˈpɜːbəˌlaɪz) *vb.* to express (something) by means of hyperbole.

hy·per·bo·loid (haɪˈpɜːbəˌlɔɪd) *n.* a geometric surface consisting of one sheet, or of two sheets separated by a finite distance, whose sections parallel to the three coordinate planes are hyperbolas or ellipses. Equations: $x^2/a^2 + y^2/b^2 - z^2/c^2 = 1$ (one sheet) or $x^2/a^2 - y^2/b^2 - z^2/c^2 = 1$ (two sheets) where a, b, and c are constants.

Hy·per·bo·re·an (ˌhaɪpəˈbɔːrɪən) *n.* **1.** *Greek myth.* one of a people believed to have lived beyond the North Wind in a sunny land. **2.** an inhabitant of the extreme north. ~*adj.* **3.** (*sometimes not cap.*) of or relating to the extreme north. **4.** of or relating to the Hyperboreans. [C16: from Latin *hyperboreus*, from Greek *huperboreos*, from HYPER- + *Boreas* the north wind]

hy·per·cat·a·lec·tic (ˌhaɪpəˌkætəˈlɛktɪk) *adj. Prosody.* (of a line of verse) having extra syllables after the last foot.

hy·per·cor·rect (ˌhaɪpəkəˈrɛkt) *adj.* **1.** excessively correct or fastidious. **2.** resulting from or characterized by hypercorrection. —ˌ**hy·per·cor·'rect·ness** *n.*

hy·per·cor·rec·tion (ˌhaɪpəkəˈrɛkʃən) *n.* a mistaken correction made through a desire to avoid nonstandard pronunciation or grammar: *"Between you and I" is a frequent hypercorrection for "Between you and me".*

hy·per·crit·i·cal (ˌhaɪpəˈkrɪtɪkəl) *adj.* excessively or severely critical; carping; captious. —ˌ**hy·per·'crit·ic** *n.* —ˌ**hy·per·'crit·i·cal·ly** *adv.* —ˌ**hy·per·'crit·i·ˌcism** *n.*

hy·per·du·li·a (ˌhaɪpədjʊˈlɪə) *n. R.C. Church.* special veneration accorded to the Virgin Mary. Compare **dulia, latria.** [C16: from Latin HYPER- + Medieval Latin *dulia* service] —ˌ**hy·per·'du·lic** *or* ˌ**hy·per·'du·li·cal** *adj.*

hy·per·e·mi·a (ˌhaɪpərˈiːmɪə) *n. Pathol.* the usual U.S. spelling of **hyperaemia.** —ˌ**hy·per·'e·mic** *adj.*

hy·per·es·the·si·a (ˌhaɪpəriːsˈθiːzɪə) *n. Pathol.* the usual U.S. spelling of **hyperaesthesia.** —ˌ**hy·per·es·'thet·ic** *adj.*

hy·per·eu·tec·tic (ˌhaɪpəjuːˈtɛktɪk) *or* **hy·per·eu·tec·toid** *adj.* (of a mixture or alloy with two components) containing more of the minor component than a eutectic mixture. Compare **hypoeutectic.**

hy·per·ex·ten·sion (ˌhaɪpərɪkˈstɛnʃən) *n.* extension of an arm or leg beyond its normal limits.

hy·per·fine struc·ture (ˈhaɪpəˌfaɪn) *n.* the splitting of a spectral line of an atom or molecule into two or more closely spaced components as a result of interaction of the electrons with the magnetic moments of the nuclei or with external fields. Compare **fine structure.** See also **Stark, Zeeman effect.**

hy·per·fo·cal dis·tance (ˌhaɪpəˈfəʊkəl) *n.* the distance from a camera lens to the point beyond which all objects appear sharp and clearly defined.

hy·per·gly·cae·mi·a *or U.S.* **hy·per·gly·ce·mi·a** (ˌhaɪpəglaɪˈsiːmɪə) *n. Pathol.* an abnormally large amount of sugar in the blood. [C20: from HYPER + GLYCO + -AEMIA] —ˌ**hy·per·gly·'cae·mic** *or U.S.* ˌ**hy·per·gly·'ce·mic** *adj.*

hy·per·gol·ic (ˌhaɪpəˈgɒlɪk) *adj.* (of a rocket fuel) able to ignite spontaneously on contact with an oxidizer. [C20: from German *Hypergol* (perhaps from HYP(ER-) + ERG + -OL[2]) + -IC]

hy·per·i·cum (haɪˈpɛrɪkəm) *n.* any herbaceous plant or shrub of the temperate genus *Hypericum*: family *Hypericaceae.* See **rose of Sharon** (sense 1), **Saint John's wort.** [C16: via Latin from Greek *hupereikon*, from HYPER - + *ereikē* heath]

hy·per·in·su·lin·ism (ˌhaɪpəˈɪnsjʊlɪˌnɪzəm) *n. Pathol.* an excessive amount of insulin in the blood, producing hypoglycaemia, caused by oversecretion of insulin by the pancreas or overdosage of insulin in treating diabetes. See **insulin reaction.**

Hy·pe·ri·on[1] (haɪˈpɪərɪən) *n. Greek myth.* a Titan, son of Uranus and Gaea, father of Helios (sun), Selene (moon), and Eos (dawn).

Hy·pe·ri·on[2] (haɪˈpɪərɪən) *n.* one of the smallest of the ten satellites of the planet Saturn.

hy·per·ker·a·to·sis (ˌhaɪpəˌkɛrəˈtəʊsɪs) *n. Pathol.* overgrowth and thickening of the outer layer of the skin. —**hy·per·ker·a·tot·ic** (ˌhaɪpəˌkɛrəˈtɒtɪk) *adj.*

hy·per·ki·ne·si·a (ˌhaɪpəkɪˈniːzɪə, -kaɪ-) *or* **hy·per·ki·ne·sis** (ˌhaɪpəkɪˈniːsɪs, -kaɪ-) *n. Pathol.* excessive movement, as in a muscle spasm. [C20: from HYPER- + *-kinesia* from Greek *kinēsis* movement, from *kinein* to move] —**hy·per·ki·net·ic** (ˌhaɪpəkɪˈnɛtɪk, -kaɪ-) *adj.*

hy·per·mar·ket (ˈhaɪpəˌmɑːkɪt) *n. Brit.* a huge self-service store, usually built on the outskirts of a town. [C20: translation of French *hypermarché*]

hy·per·me·ter (haɪˈpɜːmɪtə) *n. Prosody.* a verse line containing one or more additional syllables. —**hy·per·met·ric** (ˌhaɪpəˈmɛtrɪk) *or* ˌ**hy·per·'met·ri·cal** *adj.*

hy·per·me·tro·pi·a (ˌhaɪpəmɪˈtrəʊpɪə) *or* **hy·per·met·ro·py** (ˌhaɪpəˈmɛtrəpɪ) *n. Pathol.* variants of **hyperopia.** [C19: from Greek *hupermetros* beyond measure (from HYPER- + *metron* measure) + -OPIA] —**hy·per·me·trop·ic** (ˌhaɪpəmɪˈtrɒpɪk) *or* ˌ**hy·per·me·'trop·i·cal** *adj.*

hy·perm·ne·si·a (ˌhaɪpəmˈniːzɪə) *n. Psychol.* an unusually good ability to remember, found in some mental disorders and hypnosis. [C20: New Latin, from HYPER + *-mnesia*, formed on the model of AMNESIA]

hy·per·on (ˈhaɪpəˌrɒn) *n. Physics.* any baryon that is not a nucleon. [C20: from HYPER- + -ON]

hy·per·o·pi·a (ˌhaɪpəˈrəʊpɪə) *n.* inability to see near objects clearly because the images received by the eye are focused behind the retina; long-sightedness. Also called: **hypermetropia, hypermetropy.** Compare **myopia, presbyopia.** —**hy·per·op·ic** (ˌhaɪpəˈrɒpɪk) *adj.*

hy·per·os·to·sis (ˌhaɪpərɒˈstəʊsɪs) *n., pl.* **·ses** (-siːz). *Pathol.* **1.** an abnormal proliferation of bony tissue. **2.** a bony growth arising from the root of a tooth or from the surface of a bone. —**hy·per·os·tot·ic** (ˌhaɪpərɒˈstɒtɪk) *adj.*

hy·per·phys·i·cal (ˌhaɪpəˈfɪzɪkəl) *adj.* beyond the physical; supernatural or immaterial. —ˌ**hy·per·'phys·i·cal·ly** *adv.*

hy·per·pi·tu·i·ta·rism (ˌhaɪpəpɪˈtjuːɪtəˌrɪzəm) *n. Pathol.* overactivity of the pituitary gland, sometimes resulting in acromegaly or gigantism. —ˌ**hy·per·pi·'tu·i·tar·y** *adj.*

hy·per·plane (ˈhaɪpəˌpleɪn) *n. Maths.* a higher dimensional analogue of a plane in three dimensions.

hy·per·plas·i·a (ˌhaɪpəˈpleɪzɪə) *n.* enlargement of a bodily organ or part resulting from an increase in the total number of cells. Compare **hypertrophy.** —**hy·per·plas·tic** (ˌhaɪpəˈplæstɪk) *adj.*

hy·per·ploid (ˈhaɪpəˌplɔɪd) *adj. Biology.* having or relating to a chromosome number that slightly exceeds an exact multiple of the haploid number. —ˈ**hy·per·ˌploid·y** *n.*

hy·perp·noe·a *or U.S.* **hy·perp·ne·a** (ˌhaɪpəpˈniːə, ˌhaɪpəˈniːə) *n.* an increase in the breathing rate or in the depth of breathing, as after strenuous exercise. [C20: from New Latin, from HYPER- + Greek *pnoia* breath, from *pnein* to breathe]

hy·per·py·rex·i·a (ˌhaɪpəpaɪˈrɛksɪə) *n. Pathol.* an extremely high fever, with a temperature of 41°C (106°F) or above. Also called: **hyperthermia, hyperthermy.** —**hy·per·py·ret·ic** (ˌhaɪpəpaɪˈrɛtɪk) *or* ˌ**hy·per·py·'rex·i·al** *adj.*

hy·per·sen·si·tive (ˌhaɪpəˈsɛnsɪtɪv) *adj.* **1.** having unduly vulnerable feelings. **2.** abnormally sensitive to an allergen, a drug, or other agent. —ˌ**hy·per·'sen·si·tive·ness** *or* ˌ**hy·per·ˌsen·si·'tiv·i·ty** *n.*

ˌ**hy·per·'ac·tive** *adj.*
ˌ**hy·per·a·'cute** *adj.*
ˌ**hy·per·'civ·i·ˌlized** *or* ˌ**hy·per·'civ·i·ˌlised** *adj.*
ˌ**hy·per·'clas·si·cal** *adj.*
ˌ**hy·per·'con·fi·dence** *n.*
ˌ**hy·per·con·'form·i·ty** *n.*
ˌ**hy·per·'con·scious** *adj.*
ˌ**hy·per·con·'serv·a·tive** *adj.*
ˌ**hy·per·'el·e·gance** *n.*
ˌ**hy·per·e·'mo·tion·al** *adj.*
ˌ**hy·per·ˌen·er·'get·ic** *adj.*
ˌ**hy·per·en·'thu·si·asm** *n.*
ˌ**hy·per·ex·'cite·ment** *n.*
ˌ**hy·per·'func·tion·al** *adj.*
ˌ**hy·per·ˌin·tel·'lec·tu·al** *adj.*
ˌ**hy·per·in·'tel·li·gence** *n.*
ˌ**hy·per·'log·i·cal** *adj.*
ˌ**hy·per·'mod·est** *adj.*
ˌ**hy·per·'nor·mal** *adj.*

hy·per·sen·si·tize *or* **hy·per·sen·si·tise** (ˌhaɪpəˈsɛnsɪˌtaɪz) *vb.* (*tr.*) to treat (a photographic emulsion), usually after manufacture and shortly before exposure, to increase its speed. —**ˌhy·per·ˌsen·si·ti·ˈza·tion** *or* **ˌhy·per·ˌsen·si·ti·ˈsa·tion** *n.*

hy·per·son·ic (ˌhaɪpəˈsɒnɪk) *adj.* concerned with or having a velocity of at least five times that of sound in the same medium under the same conditions. —**ˌhy·per·ˈson·ics** *n.*

hy·per·space (ˌhaɪpəˈspeɪs) *n. Maths.* space having more than three dimensions: often used to describe a four-dimensional environment. —**hy·per·spa·tial** (ˌhaɪpəˈspeɪʃəl) *adj.*

hy·per·sthene (ˈhaɪpəˌsθiːn) *n.* a green, brown, or black pyroxene mineral consisting of magnesium iron silicate in orthorhombic crystalline form. Formula: $(Mg,Fe)_2Si_2O_6$. [C19: from HYPER- + Greek *sthenos* strength] —**hy·per·sthen·ic** (ˌhaɪpəˈsθɛnɪk) *adj.*

hy·per·ten·sion (ˌhaɪpəˈtɛnʃən) *n. Pathol.* abnormally high blood pressure. —**hy·per·ten·sive** (ˌhaɪpəˈtɛnsɪv) *adj., n.*

hy·per·ther·mi·a (ˌhaɪpəˈθɜːmɪə) *or* **hy·per·ther·my** (ˌhaɪpəˈθɜːmɪ) *n. Pathol.* variants of **hyperpyrexia.** —**ˌhy·per·ˈther·mal** *adj.*

hy·per·thy·roid·ism (ˌhaɪpəˈθaɪrɔɪˌdɪzəm) *n.* overproduction of thyroid hormone by the thyroid gland, causing nervousness, insomnia, sweating, palpitation, and sensitivity to heat. Also called: **thyrotoxicosis.** See **exophthalmic goitre.** —**ˌhy·per·ˈthy·roid** *adj., n.*

hy·per·ton·ic (ˌhaɪpəˈtɒnɪk) *adj.* **1.** (esp. of muscle) being in a state of abnormally high tension. **2.** (of a solution) having a higher osmotic pressure than that of a specified solution. Compare **hypotonic, isotonic.** —**hy·per·to·nic·i·ty** (ˌhaɪpətəʊˈnɪsɪtɪ) *n.*

hy·per·tro·phy (haɪˈpɜːtrəfɪ) *n., pl.* **·phies. 1.** enlargement of an organ or part resulting from an increase in the size of the cells. Compare **atrophy, hyperplasia.** ~*vb.* **·phies, ·phy·ing, ·phied. 2.** to undergo or cause to undergo this condition. —**hy·per·troph·ic** (ˌhaɪpəˈtrɒfɪk) *adj.*

hy·per·ven·ti·la·tion (ˌhaɪpəˌvɛntɪˈleɪʃən) *n.* an increase in the depth, duration, and rate of breathing, sometimes resulting in cramp and dizziness.

hy·per·vit·a·mi·no·sis (ˌhaɪpəˌvɪtəmɪˈnəʊsɪs, -vaɪ-) *n. Pathol.* the condition resulting from the chronic excessive intake of vitamins.

hyp·es·the·si·a (ˌhɪpiːsˈθiːzɪə, ˌhaɪ-) *n.* the usual U.S. spelling of **hypaesthesia.** —**hyp·es·the·sic** (ˌhɪpiːsˈθiːsɪk, ˌhaɪ-) *adj.*

hy·pe·thral (hɪˈpiːθrəl, haɪ-) *adj.* the usual U.S. spelling of **hypaethral.**

hy·pha (ˈhaɪfə) *n., pl.* **·phae** (-fiː). any of the filaments that constitute the body (mycelium) of a fungus. [C19: from New Latin, from Greek *huphē* web] —**ˈhy·phal** *adj.*

hy·phen (ˈhaɪfᵊn) *n.* **1.** the punctuation mark (-), used to separate the parts of some compound words, to link the words of a phrase, and between syllables of a word split between two consecutive lines of writing or printing. ~*vb.* **2.** (*tr.*) another word for **hyphenate.** [C17: from Late Latin (meaning: the combining of two words), from Greek *huphen* (adv.) together, from HYPO- + *heis* one]

hy·phen·ate (ˈhaɪfᵊˌneɪt) *or* **hy·phen** *vb.* (*tr.*) to separate (syllables, words, etc.) with a hyphen. —**ˌhy·phen·ˈa·tion** *n.*

hy·phen·at·ed (ˈhaɪfᵊˌneɪtɪd) *adj.* **1.** containing or linked with a hyphen. **2.** having a nationality denoted by a hyphenated word: *Anglo-Irish.*

hyp·na·gog·ic *or* **hyp·no·gog·ic** (ˌhɪpnəˈgɒdʒɪk) *adj. Psychol.* of or relating to the state just before one is fully asleep. See also: **hypnopompic.** [C19: from French *hypnagogique;* see HYPNO-, -AGOGIC]

hyp·na·gog·ic im·age *n. Psychol.* an image experienced by a person just before falling asleep, which often resembles a hallucination.

hyp·no- *or before a vowel* **hypn-** *combining form.* **1.** indicating sleep: *hypnophobia.* **2.** relating to hypnosis: *hypnotherapy.* [from Greek *hupnos* sleep]

hyp·no·a·nal·y·sis (ˌhɪpnəʊəˈnælɪsɪs) *n. Psychol.* psychoanalysis conducted on a hypnotized person. —**hyp·no·an·a·lyt·ic** (ˌhɪpnəʊˌænəˈlɪtɪk) *adj.*

hyp·no·gen·e·sis (ˌhɪpnəʊˈdʒɛnɪsɪs) *n. Psychol.* the induction of sleep or hypnosis. —**hyp·no·ge·net·ic** (ˌhɪpnəʊdʒɪˈnɛtɪk) *adj.* —**ˌhyp·no·geˈnet·i·cal·ly** *adv.*

hyp·noid (ˈhɪpˌnɔɪd) *or* **hyp·noi·dal** (hɪpˈnɔɪdᵊl) *adj. Psychol.* of or relating to a state resembling sleep or hypnosis.

hyp·nol·o·gy (hɪpˈnɒlədʒɪ) *n. Psychol.* the study of sleep and hypnosis. —**hyp·no·log·ic** (ˌhɪpnəˈlɒdʒɪk) *or* **ˌhyp·no·ˈlog·i·cal** *adj.* —**hyp·ˈnol·o·gist** *n.*

hyp·no·pae·di·a (ˌhɪpnəʊˈpiːdɪə) *n.* the learning of lessons heard during sleep. [C20: from HYPNO- + Greek *paideia* education]

hyp·no·pom·pic (ˌhɪpnəʊˈpɒmpɪk) *adj. Psychol.* relating to the state existing between sleep and full waking, characterized by the persistence of dreamlike imagery. See also **hypnagogic.** [C20: from HYPNO- + Greek *pompē* a sending forth, escort + -IC; see POMP]

Hyp·nos (ˈhɪpnɒs) *n. Greek myth.* the god of sleep. Roman counterpart: **Somnus.** Compare **Morpheus.** [Greek: sleep]

hyp·no·sis (hɪpˈnəʊsɪs) *n., pl.* **·ses** (-siːz). an artificially induced state of semiconsciousness characterized by an increased suggestibility to the words of the hypnotist: used clinically to reveal unconscious memories, etc. See also **autohypnosis.**

hyp·no·ther·a·py (ˌhɪpnəʊˈθɛrəpɪ) *n.* the use of hypnosis in the treatment of physical or mental disorders.

hyp·not·ic (hɪpˈnɒtɪk) *adj.* **1.** of, relating to, or producing hypnosis or sleep. **2.** (of a person) susceptible to hypnotism. ~*n.* **3.** a drug or agent that induces sleep. **4.** a person susceptible to hypnosis. [C17: from Late Latin *hypnōticus,* from Greek *hupnōtikos,* from *hupnoun* to put to sleep, from *hupnos* sleep] —**hyp·ˈnot·i·cal·ly** *adv.*

hyp·no·tism (ˈhɪpnəˌtɪzəm) *n.* **1.** the scientific study and practice of hypnosis. **2.** the process of inducing hypnosis.

hyp·no·tist (ˈhɪpnətɪst) *n.* a person skilled in the theory and practice of hypnosis.

hyp·no·tize *or* **hyp·no·tise** (ˈhɪpnəˌtaɪz) *vb.* (*tr.*) **1.** to induce hypnosis in (a person). **2.** to charm or beguile; fascinate. —**ˈhyp·no·ˌtiz·a·ble** *or* **ˈhyp·no·ˌtis·a·ble** *adj.* —**ˌhyp·no·ˌtiz·a·ˈbil·i·ty** *or* **ˌhyp·no·ˌtis·a·ˈbil·i·ty** *n.* —**ˌhyp·no·ti·ˈza·tion** *or* **ˌhyp·no·ti·ˈsa·tion** *n.* —**ˈhyp·no·ˌtiz·er** *or* **ˈhyp·no·ˌtis·er** *n.*

hy·po[1] (ˈhaɪpəʊ) *n.* another name for **sodium thiosulphate,** esp. when used as a fixer in photographic developing. [C19: shortened from HYPOSULPHITE]

hy·po[2] (ˈhaɪpəʊ) *n., pl.* **·pos.** *Informal.* short for **hypodermic syringe.**

hy·po- *or before a vowel* **hyp-** *prefix.* **1.** under, beneath, or below: *hypodermic.* **2.** lower; at a lower point: *hypogastrium.* **3.** less than: *hypoploid.* **4.** (in medicine) denoting a deficiency or an abnormally low level: *hypothyroid.* **5.** incomplete or partial: *hypoplasia.* **6.** indicating that a chemical compound contains an element in a lower oxidation state than usual: *hypochlorous acid.* [from Greek, from *hupo* under]

Hy·po- *prefix.* indicating a plagal mode in music: *Hypodorian.* [from Greek: beneath (it lies a fourth below the corresponding authentic mode)]

hy·po·a·cid·i·ty (ˌhaɪpəʊəˈsɪdɪtɪ) *n. Med.* abnormally low acidity, as of the contents of the stomach.

hy·po·blast (ˈhaɪpəˌblæst) *n.* **1.** Also called: **endoblast.** *Embryol.* the inner layer of an embryo at an early stage of development that becomes the endoderm at gastrulation. **2.** a less common name for **endoderm.** —**ˌhy·po·ˈblas·tic** *adj.*

hy·po·caust (ˈhaɪpəˌkɔːst) *n.* an ancient Roman heating system in which hot air circulated under the floor and between double walls. [C17: from Latin *hypocaustum,* from Greek *hupokauston* room heated from below, from *hupokaiein* to light a fire beneath, from HYPO- + *kaiein* to burn]

hy·po·cen·tre (ˈhaɪpəʊˌsɛntə) *n.* the point on the ground immediately below the centre of explosion of a nuclear bomb. Also called: **ground zero.**

hy·po·chlor·ite (ˌhaɪpəˈklɔːraɪt) *n.* any salt or ester of hypochlorous acid.

hy·po·chlor·ous ac·id (ˌhaɪpəˈklɔːrəs) *n.* an unstable acid known only in solution and in the form of its salts, formed when chlorine dissolves in water: a strong oxidizing and bleaching agent. Formula: HOCl.

hy·po·chon·dri·a (ˌhaɪpəˈkɒndrɪə) *n.* chronic abnormal anxiety concerning the state of one's health, even in the absence of any evidence of disease on medical examination. Also called: **hy·po·chon·dri·a·sis** (ˌhaɪpəʊkɒnˈdraɪəsɪs). [C18: from Late Latin: the abdomen, supposedly the seat of melancholy, from Greek *hupokhondria,* from *hupokhondrios* of the upper abdomen, from HYPO- + *khondros* cartilage]

hy·po·chon·dri·ac (ˌhaɪpəˈkɒndrɪˌæk) *n.* **1.** a person suffering from hypochondria. ~*adj. also* **hy·po·chon·dri·a·cal** (ˌhaɪpəʊkɒnˈdraɪəkᵊl). **2.** relating to or suffering from hypochondria. **3.** *Anatomy.* of or relating to the hypochondrium. —**ˌhy·po·chon·ˈdri·a·cal·ly** *adv.*

hy·po·chon·dri·um (ˌhaɪpəˈkɒndrɪəm) *n., pl.* **·dri·a** (-drɪə). *Anatomy.* the upper region of the abdomen on each side of the epigastrium, just below the lowest ribs. [C17: from New Latin, from Greek *hupokhondrion;* see HYPOCHONDRIA]

hy·poc·o·rism (haɪˈpɒkəˌrɪzəm) *n.* **1.** a pet name, esp. one using a diminutive affix: *"Sally" is a hypocorism for "Sarah".* **2.** another word for **euphemism** (sense 1). [C19: from Greek *hupokorisma,* from *hupokorizesthai* to use pet names, from *hypo-* beneath + *korizesthai,* from *korē* girl, *koros* boy] —**hy·po·co·ris·tic** (ˌhaɪpəkɔːˈrɪstɪk) *adj.* —**ˌhy·po·co·ˈris·ti·cal·ly** *adv.*

hy·po·cot·yl (ˌhaɪpəˈkɒtɪl) *n.* the part of an embryo plant between the cotyledons and the radicle. [C19: from HYPO- + COTYL(EDON)] —**ˌhy·po·ˈcot·y·lous** *adj.*

hy·poc·ri·sy (hɪˈpɒkrəsɪ) *n., pl.* **·sies. 1.** the practice of professing standards, beliefs, etc., contrary to one's real character or behaviour, esp. the pretence of virtue or piety. **2.** an act or instance of this.

hyp·o·crite (ˈhɪpəkrɪt) *n.* a person who pretends to be what he is not. [C13: from Old French *ipocrite,* via Late Latin, from Greek *hupokritēs* one who plays a part, from *hupokrinein* to feign, from *krinein* to judge] —**ˌhyp·o·ˈcrit·i·cal** *adj.* —**ˌhyp·o·ˈcrit·i·cal·ly** *adv.*

hy·po·cy·cloid (ˌhaɪpəˈsaɪklɔɪd) *n.* a curve described by a point on the circumference of a circle as the circle rolls around the inside of a fixed coplanar circle. Compare **epicycloid, cycloid** (sense 4). —**ˌhy·po·cy·ˈcloi·dal** *adj.*

hy·po·derm (ˈhaɪpəˌdɜːm) *n.* a variant spelling of **hypodermis.** —**ˌhy·po·ˈder·mal** *adj.*

hy·po·der·mic (ˌhaɪpəˈdɜːmɪk) *adj.* **1.** of or relating to the region of the skin beneath the epidermis. **2.** injected beneath

ˌhy·per·ˈor·tho·ˌdox *adj.*
ˌhy·per·ˈpur·ist *n.*
ˌhy·per·ro·ˈman·tic *adj.*
ˌhy·per·ˌsen·ti·ˈmen·tal *adj.*
ˌhy·per·so·ˈphis·ti·ˌcat·ed *adj.*
ˌhy·per·ˈtech·ni·cal *adj.*
ˌhy·per·ˈtox·ic *adj.*
ˌhy·per·ˈvig·i·lant *adj.*

the skin. —*n.* **3.** a hypodermic syringe or needle. **4.** a hypodermic injection. —ˌ**hy·po·'der·mi·cal·ly** *adv.*

hy·po·der·mic sy·ringe *n. Med.* a type of syringe consisting of a hollow cylinder, usually of glass or plastic, a tightly fitting piston, and a hollow needle (**hypodermic needle**), used for withdrawing blood samples, injecting medicine, etc.

hy·po·der·mis (ˌhaɪpəˈdɜːmɪs) *or* **hy·po·derm** *n.* **1.** *Botany.* a layer of thick-walled supportive or water-storing cells beneath the epidermis in some plants. **2.** *Zoology.* the epidermis of arthropods, annelids, etc., which secretes and is covered by a cuticle. [C19: from HYPO- + EPIDERMIS]

Hy·po·do·ri·an (ˌhaɪpəˈdɔːrɪən) *adj. Music.* denoting a plagal mode represented by the ascending diatonic scale from A to A. Compare **Dorian** (sense 3). See **Hypo-.**

hy·po·eu·tec·tic (ˌhaɪpəʊjuːˈtɛktɪk) *or* **hy·po·eu·tec·toid** *adj.* (of a mixture or alloy with two components) containing less of the minor component than a eutectic mixture. Compare **hypereutectic.**

hy·po·gas·tri·um (ˌhaɪpəˈgæstrɪəm) *n., pl.* **·tri·a** (-trɪə). *Anatomy.* the lower front central region of the abdomen, below the navel. [C17: from New Latin, from Greek *hupogastrion,* from HYPO- + *gastrion,* diminutive of *gastēr* stomach] —ˌ**hy·po·'gas·tric** *adj.*

hy·po·ge·al (ˌhaɪpəˈdʒiːəl) *or* **hy·po·ge·ous** *adj.* **1.** occurring or living below the surface of the ground. **2.** *Botany.* of or relating to seed germination in which the cotyledons remain below the ground, because of the growth of the epicotyl. [C19: from Latin *hypogēus,* from Greek *hupogeios,* from HYPO- + *gē* earth]

hy·po·gene (ˈhaɪpəˌdʒiːn) *adj.* formed, taking place, or originating beneath the surface of the earth. Compare **epigene.** —**hy·po·gen·ic** (ˌhaɪpəˈdʒɛnɪk) *adj.*

hy·pog·e·nous (haɪˈpɒdʒɪnəs) *adj. Botany.* produced or growing on the undersurface, esp. (of fern spores) growing on the undersurface of the leaves.

hy·po·ge·ous (ˌhaɪpəˈdʒiːəs) *adj.* another word for **hypogeal.**

hy·po·ge·um (ˌhaɪpəˈdʒiːəm) *n., pl.* **·ge·a** (-ˈdʒiːə). an underground vault, esp. one used for burials. [C18: from Latin, from Greek *hupogeion;* see HYPOGEAL]

hy·po·glos·sal (ˌhaɪpəˈglɒsᵊl) *adj.* **1.** situated beneath the tongue. —*n.* **2.** short for **hypoglossal nerve.**

hy·po·glos·sal nerve *n.* the twelfth cranial nerve, which supplies the muscles of the tongue.

hy·po·gly·cae·mi·a *or U.S.* **hy·po·gly·ce·mi·a** (ˌhaɪpəʊglaɪˈsiːmɪə) *n. Pathol.* an abnormally small amount of sugar in the blood. —ˌ**hy·po·gly·'cae·mic** *or U.S.* ˌ**hy·po·'gly·ce·mic** *adj.*

hy·pog·na·thous (haɪˈpɒgnəθəs) *adj.* **1.** having a lower jaw that protrudes beyond the upper jaw. **2.** (of insects) having downturned mouthparts. —**hy·'pog·na·thism** *n.*

hy·pog·y·nous (haɪˈpɒdʒɪnəs) *adj.* **1.** (of a flower) having the gynoecium situated above the other floral parts, as in the buttercup. **2.** of or relating to the parts of a flower arranged in this way. —**hy·'pog·y·ny** *n.*

hy·poid gear (ˈhaɪpɔɪd) *n.* a gear having a tooth form generated by a hypocycloidal curve; used extensively in motor vehicle transmissions to withstand a high surface loading. [C20: *hypoid,* shortened from HYPOCYCLOID]

hy·po·lim·ni·on (ˌhaɪpəʊˈlɪmnɪən) *n.* the lower and colder layer of water in a lake. [C20: from HYPO- + Greek *limnion,* diminutive of *limnē* lake]

Hy·po·lyd·i·an (ˌhaɪpəˈlɪdɪən) *adj. Music.* denoting a plagal mode represented by the diatonic scale from D to D. Compare **Lydian** (sense 2). See **Hypo-.**

hy·po·ma·ni·a (ˌhaɪpəʊˈmeɪnɪə) *n. Psychiatry.* a mild form of mania, characterized by excitability and overactivity. —**hy·po·man·ic** (ˌhaɪpəʊˈmænɪk) *adj.*

hy·po·nas·ty (ˈhaɪpəˌnæstɪ) *n.* increased growth of the upper surface of a plant part, resulting in an upward bending of the part. Compare **epinasty.** —ˌ**hy·po·'nas·tic** *adj.* —ˌ**hy·po·'nas·ti·cal·ly** *adv.*

hy·po·ni·trite (ˌhaɪpəˈnaɪtraɪt) *n.* any salt or ester of hyponitrous acid.

hy·po·ni·trous ac·id (ˌhaɪpəˈnaɪtrəs) *n.* a white soluble unstable crystalline acid: an oxidizing and reducing agent. Formula: $H_2N_2O_2$.

hy·po·phos·phate (ˌhaɪpəˈfɒsfeɪt) *n.* any salt or ester of hypophosphoric acid.

hy·po·phos·phite (ˌhaɪpəˈfɒsfaɪt) *n.* any salt of hypophosphorous acid.

hy·po·phos·phor·ic ac·id (ˌhaɪpəfɒsˈfɒrɪk) *n.* a crystalline odourless deliquescent solid: a tetrabasic acid produced by the slow oxidation of phosphorus in moist air. Formula: $H_4P_2O_6$.

hy·po·phos·phor·ous ac·id (ˌhaɪpəˈfɒsfərəs) *n.* a colourless or yellowish oily liquid or white deliquescent solid: a monobasic acid and a reducing agent. Formula: H_3PO_2.

hy·poph·y·ge (haɪˈpɒfɪdʒɪ) *n. Architect.* another name for **apophyge.**

hy·poph·y·sis (haɪˈpɒfɪsɪs) *n., pl.* **·ses** (-ˌsiːz). the technical name for **pituitary gland.** [C18: from Greek: outgrowth, from HYPO- + *phuein* to grow] —**hy·po·phys·e·al** *or* **hy·po·phys·i·al** (ˌhaɪpəˈfɪzɪəl, haɪˌpɒfɪˈsɪəl) *adj.*

hy·po·pi·tu·i·ta·rism (ˌhaɪpəpɪˈtjuːɪtəˌrɪzəm) *n. Pathol.* underactivity of the pituitary gland. —ˌ**hy·po·pi·'tu·i·tar·y** *adj.*

hy·po·plas·i·a (ˌhaɪpəʊˈpleɪzɪə) *or* **hy·po·plas·ty** (ˈhaɪpəʊˌplæstɪ) *n. Pathol.* incomplete development of an organ or part. —**hy·po·plas·tic** (ˌhaɪpəʊˈplæstɪk) *adj.*

hy·po·ploid (ˈhaɪpəˌplɔɪd) *adj.* having or designating a chromosome number that is slightly less than a multiple of the haploid number. —ˈ**hy·po·ˌploid·y** *n.*

hy·pop·noe·a *or U.S.* **hy·pop·ne·a** (haɪˈpɒpnɪə, ˌhaɪpəˈniːə) *n. Pathol.* abnormally shallow breathing, usually accompanied by a decrease in the breathing rate. [C20: New Latin, from HYPO- + Greek *pnoia* breath, from *pnein* to breathe]

hy·po·sen·si·tize *or* **hy·po·sen·si·tise** (ˌhaɪpəʊˈsɛnsɪˌtaɪz) *vb.* (*tr.*) to desensitize; render less sensitive. —ˌ**hy·po·ˌsen·si·ti·'za·tion** *or* ˌ**hy·po·ˌsen·si·ti·'sa·tion** *n.*

hy·pos·ta·sis (haɪˈpɒstəsɪs) *n., pl.* **·ses** (-ˌsiːz). **1.** *Metaphysics.* the essential nature of anything as opposed to its attributes. **2.** *Christianity.* **a.** any of the three persons of the Godhead, together constituting the Trinity. **b.** the one person of Christ in which the divine and human natures are united. **3.** the accumulation of blood in an organ or part as the result of poor circulation. **4.** another name for **epistasis** (sense 3). [C16: from Late Latin: substance, from Greek *hupostasis* foundation, from *huphistasthai* to stand under, from HYPO- + *histanai* to cause to stand] —**hy·po·stat·ic** (ˌhaɪpəˈstætɪk) *or* ˌ**hy·po·'stat·i·cal** *adj.* —ˌ**hy·po·'stat·i·cal·ly** *adv.*

hy·pos·ta·size *or* **hy·pos·ta·sise** (haɪˈpɒstəˌsaɪz) *vb.* another word for **hypostatize.** —**hy·ˌpos·ta·si·'za·tion** *or* **hy·ˌpos·ta·si·'sa·tion** *n.*

hy·pos·ta·tize *or* **hy·pos·ta·tise** (haɪˈpɒstəˌtaɪz) *vb.* (*tr.*) **1.** to regard or treat as real. **2.** to embody or personify. —**hy·ˌpos·ta·ti·'za·tion** *or* **hy·ˌpos·ta·ti·'sa·tion** *n.*

hy·pos·the·ni·a (ˌhaɪpɒsˈθiːnɪə) *n. Pathol.* a weakened condition; lack of strength. —**hy·pos·then·ic** (ˌhaɪpɒsˈθɛnɪk) *adj.*

hy·po·style (ˈhaɪpəʊˌstaɪl) *adj.* **1.** having a roof supported by columns. —*n.* **2.** a building constructed in this way.

hy·po·sul·phite (ˌhaɪpəˈsʌlfaɪt) *n.* **1.** another name for **sodium thiosulphate,** esp. when used as a photographic fixer. Often shortened to **hypo. 2.** another name for **dithionite.**

hy·po·sul·phur·ous ac·id (ˌhaɪpəˈsʌlfərəs) *n.* another name for **dithionous acid.**

hy·po·tax·is (ˌhaɪpəʊˈtæksɪs) *n. Grammar.* the subordination of one clause to another by a conjunction. Compare **parataxis.** —**hy·po·tac·tic** (ˌhaɪpəʊˈtæktɪk) *adj.*

hy·po·ten·sion (ˌhaɪpəʊˈtɛnʃən) *n. Pathol.* abnormally low blood pressure. —**hy·po·ten·sive** (ˌhaɪpəʊˈtɛnsɪv) *adj.*

hy·pot·e·nuse (haɪˈpɒtɪˌnjuːz) *n.* the side in a right-angled triangle that is opposite the right angle. Abbrev.: **hyp.** [C16: from Latin *hypotēnūsa,* from Greek *hupoteinousa grammē* subtending line, from *hupoteinein* to subtend, from HYPO- + *teinein* to stretch]

hypoth. *abbrev. for:* **1.** hypothesis. **2.** hypothetical.

hy·po·thal·a·mus (ˌhaɪpəˈθæləməs) *n., pl.* **·mi** (-ˌmaɪ). a neural control centre at the base of the brain, concerned with hunger, thirst, satiety, and other autonomic functions. —**hy·po·tha·lam·ic** (ˌhaɪpəʊθəˈlæmɪk) *adj.*

hy·poth·ec (haɪˈpɒθɪk) *n. Roman and Scot. law.* a charge on property in favour of a creditor. [C16: from Late Latin *hypotheca* a security, from Greek *hupothēkē* deposit, pledge, from *hupotithenai* to deposit as a security, place under, from HYPO- + *tithenai* to place]

hy·poth·e·cate (haɪˈpɒθɪˌkeɪt) *vb.* (*tr.*) *Law.* to pledge (personal property or a ship) as security for a debt without transferring possession or title. —**hy·ˌpoth·e·'ca·tion** *n.* —**hy·'poth·e·ˌca·tor** *n.*

hy·po·ther·mal (ˌhaɪpəʊˈθɜːməl) *adj.* **1.** of, relating to, or characterized by hypothermia. **2.** (of rocks and minerals) formed at great depth under conditions of high temperature.

hy·po·ther·mi·a (ˌhaɪpəʊˈθɜːmɪə) *n.* **1.** *Pathol.* an abnormally low body temperature, as induced in the elderly by exposure to cold weather. **2.** *Med.* the intentional reduction of normal body temperature, as by ice packs, to reduce the patient's metabolic rate: performed esp. in heart and brain surgery.

hy·poth·e·sis (haɪˈpɒθɪsɪs) *n., pl.* **·ses** (-ˌsiːz). **1.** a suggested explanation for a group of facts or phenomena, either accepted as a basis for further verification (**working hypothesis**) or accepted as likely to be true. Compare **theory** (sense 4). **2.** an assumption used in an argument; a supposition. **3.** *Logic.* an unproved theory. [C16: from Greek, from *hupotithenai* to propose, suppose, literally: put under; see HYPO-, THESIS] —**hy·'poth·e·sist** *n.*

hy·poth·e·size *or* **hy·poth·e·sise** (haɪˈpɒθɪˌsaɪz) *vb.* to form or assume as a hypothesis. —**hy·'poth·e·ˌsiz·er** *or* **hy·'poth·e·ˌsis·er** *n.*

hy·po·thet·i·cal (ˌhaɪpəˈθɛtɪkᵊl) *or* **hy·po·thet·ic** *adj.* **1.** having the nature of a hypothesis. **2.** assumed or thought to exist. **3.** *Logic.* another word for **conditional** (sense 4). **4.** existing only as an idea or concept: *a time machine is a hypothetical device.* —ˌ**hy·po·'thet·i·cal·ly** *adv.*

hy·po·thet·i·cal im·per·a·tive *n.* (in the ethical system of Kant) a principle of conduct governed by necessity rather than morality. Compare **categorical imperative.**

hy·po·thy·roid·ism (ˌhaɪpəʊˈθaɪrɔɪˌdɪzəm) *n. Pathol.* **1.** insufficient production of thyroid hormones by the thyroid gland. **2.** any disorder, such as cretinism or myxoedema, resulting from this. —ˌ**hy·po·'thy·roid** *n., adj.*

hy·po·ton·ic (ˌhaɪpəˈtɒnɪk) *adj.* **1.** *Pathol.* (of muscles) lacking normal tone or tension. **2.** (of a solution) having a lower osmotic pressure than that of a specified solution. Compare **hypertonic, isotonic.** —**hy·po·to·nic·i·ty** (ˌhaɪpətəˈnɪsɪtɪ) *n.*

hy·po·xan·thine (ˌhaɪpəˈzænθiːn, -θɪn) *n.* a white or colourless crystalline compound that is a breakdown product of nucleoproteins. Formula: $C_5H_4N_4O$.

hy·pox·i·a (haɪˈpɒksɪə) *n.* deficiency in the amount of oxygen delivered to the body tissues. [C20: from HYPO- + OXY- + -IA] —**hy·pox·ic** (haɪˈpɒksɪk) *adj.*

hyp·so- *or before a vowel* **hyps-** *combining form.* indicating height: *hypsometry.* [from Greek *huspos*]

hyp·sog·ra·phy (hɪpˈsɒgrəfɪ) *n.* **1.** the scientific study and mapping of the earth's topography above sea level. **2.** topography or relief, or a map showing this. **3.** another name for **hypsometry.** —**hyp·so·graph·ic** (ˌhɪpsəˈgræfɪk) *or* ˌ**hyp·so·ˈgraph·i·cal** *adj.*

hyp·som·e·ter (hɪpˈsɒmɪtə) *n.* **1.** an instrument for measuring altitudes by determining the boiling point of water at a given altitude. **2.** any instrument used to calculate the heights of trees by triangulation.

hyp·som·e·try (hɪpˈsɒmɪtrɪ) *n.* (in mapping) the establishment of height above sea level. Also called: **hypsography.** —**hyp·so·met·ric** (ˌhɪpsəˈmɛtrɪk) *or* ˌ**hyp·so·ˈmet·ri·cal** *adj.* —ˌ**hyp·so·ˈmet·ri·cal·ly** *adv.* —**hyp·ˈsom·e·trist** *n.*

hy·ra·coid (ˈhaɪrəˌkɔɪd) *adj.* **1.** of, relating to, or belonging to the mammalian order *Hyracoidea,* which contains the hyraxes. ~*n.* **2.** a hyrax. —ˌ**hy·ra·ˈcoi·de·an** *adj., n.*

hy·rax (ˈhaɪræks) *n., pl.* **hy·rax·es** *or* **hy·ra·ces** (ˈhaɪrəˌsiːz). any agile herbivorous mammal of the family *Procaviidae* and order *Hyracoidea,* of Africa and SW Asia, such as *Procavia capensis* (**rock hyrax**). They resemble rodents but have feet with hooflike toes. Also called: **dassie.** [C19: from New Latin, from Greek *hurax* shrewmouse]

Hyr·ca·ni·a (hɜːˈkeɪnɪə) *n.* an ancient district of Asia, southeast of the Caspian Sea. —**Hyr·ˈca·ni·an** *adj.*

hy·son (ˈhaɪsᵊn) *n.* a Chinese green tea, the early crop of which is known as **young hyson** and the inferior leaves as **hyson skin.** [C18: from Chinese (Cantonese) *hei-ch'un* bright spring]

hys·sop (ˈhɪsəp) *n.* **1.** a widely cultivated Asian plant, *Hyssopus officinalis,* with spikes of small blue flowers and aromatic leaves, used as a condiment and in perfumery and folk medicine: family *Labiatae* (labiates). **2.** any of several similar or related plants such as the hedge hyssop. **3.** a Biblical plant, used for sprinkling in the ritual practices of the Hebrews. [Old English *ysope,* from Latin *hyssōpus,* from Greek *hussōpos,* of Semitic origin; compare Hebrew *ēzōv*]

hys·ter·ec·to·mize *or* **hys·ter·ec·to·mise** (ˌhɪstəˈrɛktəˌmaɪz) *vb.* (*tr.*) to perform a hysterectomy on (someone).

hys·ter·ec·to·my (ˌhɪstəˈrɛktəmɪ) *n., pl.* **·mies.** surgical removal of the uterus.

hys·te·re·sis (ˌhɪstəˈriːsɪs) *n. Physics.* the lag in a variable property of a system with respect to the effect producing it as this effect varies, esp. the phenomenon in which the magnetic induction of a ferromagnetic material lags behind the changing external field. —**hys·ter·et·ic** (ˌhɪstəˈrɛtɪk) *adj.* —ˌ**hys·ter·ˈet·i·cal·ly** *adv.*

hys·te·re·sis loop *n.* a closed curve showing the variation of the magnetic induction of a ferromagnetic material with the external magnetic field producing it, when this field is changed through a complete cycle.

hys·te·ri·a (hɪˈstɪərɪə) *n.* **1.** a mental disorder characterized by emotional outbursts, susceptibility to autosuggestion, and, often, physical symptoms such as paralysis. **2.** any frenzied emotional state, esp. of laughter or crying. [C19: from New Latin, from Latin *hystericus* HYSTERIC]

hys·ter·ic (hɪˈstɛrɪk) *n.* **1.** a hysterical person. ~*adj.* **2.** hysterical. [C17: from Latin *hystericus* literally: of the womb, from Greek *husterikos,* from *hustera* the womb; from the belief that hysteria in women originated in disorders of the womb]

hys·ter·i·cal (hɪˈstɛrɪkᵊl) *or* **hys·ter·ic** *adj.* **1.** of or suggesting hysteria: *hysterical cries.* **2.** suffering from hysteria. **3.** *Informal.* wildly funny. —**hys·ˈter·i·cal·ly** *adv.*

hys·ter·ics (hɪˈstɛrɪks) *n.* **1.** an attack of hysteria. **2.** *Informal.* wild uncontrollable bursts of laughter.

hys·ter·o- *or before a vowel* **hys·ter-** *combining form.* **1.** indicating the uterus: *hysterotomy.* **2.** hysteria: *hysterogenic.* [from Greek *hustera* womb]

hys·ter·o·gen·ic (ˌhɪstərəˈdʒɛnɪk) *adj.* inducing hysteria. [C20: from HYSTERIA + -GENIC] —**hys·ter·og·e·ny** (ˌhɪstəˈrɒdʒənɪ) *n.*

hys·ter·oid (ˈhɪstəˌrɔɪd) *or* **hys·ter·oi·dal** *adj.* resembling hysteria.

hys·ter·on prot·er·on (ˈhɪstəˌrɒn ˈprɒtəˌrɒn) *n.* **1.** *Logic.* a fallacious argument in which the proposition to be proved is assumed as a premiss. **2.** *Rhetoric.* a figure of speech in which the normal order of two sentences, clauses, etc., is reversed: *bred and born* (*for born and bred*). [C16: from Late Latin, from Greek *husteron proteron* the latter (placed as) former]

hys·ter·ot·o·my (ˌhɪstəˈrɒtəmɪ) *n., pl.* **·mies.** surgical incision into the uterus.

hys·tri·co·morph (hɪˈstraɪkəʊˌmɔːf) *n.* **1.** any rodent of the suborder *Hystricomorpha,* which includes porcupines, cavies, agoutis, and chinchillas. ~*adj.* **2.** Also: **hys·tri·co·mor·phic** (hɪˌstraɪkəʊˈmɔːfɪk). of, relating to, or belonging to the *Hystricomorpha.* [C19: from Latin *hystrix* porcupine, from Greek *hustrix*]

Hz *abbrev. for* hertz.

I

i *or* **I** (aɪ) *n., pl.* **i's, I's,** *or* **Is. 1.** the ninth letter and third vowel of the modern English alphabet. **2.** any of several speech sounds represented by this letter, in English as in *bite* or *hit.* **3. a.** something shaped like an I. **b.** (*in combination*): *an I-beam.* **4. dot one's i's and cross one's t's.** to pay meticulous attention to detail.

i *symbol for* the imaginary number $\sqrt{-1}$.

I (aɪ) *pron.* (*subjective*) refers to the speaker or writer. [C12: reduced form of Old English *ic;* compare Old Saxon *ik,* Old High German *ih,* Sanskrit *ahám*]

I *symbol for:* **1.** *Chem.* iodine. **2.** *Physics.* current. **3.** *Physics.* isospin. ~ **4.** *the Roman numeral for* one. See **Roman numerals.** ~ **5.** *international car registration for* Italy.

i. *abbrev. for:* **1.** *Grammar.* intransitive. **2.** *Dentistry.* incisor. **3.** *Banking.* interest.

I. *abbrev. for:* **1.** Independence. **2.** Independent. **3.** Institute. **4.** International. **5.** Island *or* Isle.

i- *prefix.* variant of **y-.**

-i *suffix forming adjectives.* of or relating to a region or people, esp. of the Middle East: *Iraqi; Bangladeshi.* [from an adjectival suffix in Semitic and in Indo-Iranian languages]

-i- *connective vowel.* used between elements in a compound word: *cuneiform, coniferous.* Compare **-o-.** [from Latin, stem vowel of nouns and adjectives in combination]

Ia. *abbrev. for* Iowa.

-i·a *suffix forming nouns.* **1.** occurring in place names: *Albania; Columbia.* **2.** occurring in names of diseases and pathological disorders: *pneumonia; aphasia.* **3.** occurring in words denoting condition or quality: *utopia.* **4.** occurring in names of botanical genera: *acacia; poinsettia.* **5.** occurring in names of zoological classes: *Reptilia.* **6.** occurring in collective nouns borrowed from Latin: *marginalia; memorabilia; regalia.* [(for senses 1–4) New Latin, from Latin and Greek, suffix of feminine nouns; (for senses 5–6) from Latin, neuter plural suffix]

IAEA *abbrev. for* International Atomic Energy Agency.

I.A.F. *abbrev. for* Indian Air Force.

-i·al *suffix forming adjectives.* of; relating to; connected with: *managerial.* [from Latin *-iālis,* adj. suffix; compare -AL[1]]

i·amb ('aɪæm, 'aɪæmb) *or* **i·am·bus** (aɪ'æmbəs) *n., pl.* **i·ambs, i·am·bi** (aɪ'æmbaɪ), *or* **i·am·bus·es.** *Prosody.* **1.** a metrical foot consisting of two syllables, a short one followed by a long one (˘¯). **2.** a line of verse of such feet. [C19 *iamb,* from C16 *iambus,* from Latin, from Greek *iambos*]

i·am·bic (aɪ'æmbɪk) *Prosody.* ~*adj.* **1.** of, relating to, consisting of, or using an iamb or iambs. **2.** (in Greek literature) denoting a type of satirical verse written in iambs. ~*n.* **3.** a metrical foot, line, or stanza of verse consisting of iambs. **4.** a type of ancient Greek satirical verse written in iambs. —**i'am·bi·cal·ly** *adv.*

-i·an *suffix.* variant of **-an:** *Etonian; Johnsonian.* [from Latin *-iānus*]

-i·a·na *suffix forming nouns.* a variant of **-ana.**

I·ap·e·tus (aɪ'æpɪtəs) *n.* one of the ten satellites of Saturn.

IAS *Aeronautics. abbrev. for* indicated air speed.

Iaşi (*Rumanian* 'jaʃj) *n.* a city in NE Rumania: capital of Moldavia (1565–1859); university (1860). Pop.: 210 388 (1974 est.). German name: **Jassy.**

-i·a·sis *or* **-a·sis** *n. combining form.* (in medicine) indicating a diseased condition: *psoriasis.* Compare **-osis** (sense 2). [from New Latin, from Greek, suffix of action]

IATA (aɪ'ɑ:tə, i:'ɑ:tə) *n. acronym for* International Air Transport Association.

i·at·ric (aɪ'ætrɪk) *or* **i·at·ri·cal** *adj.* relating to medicine or physicians; medical. [C19: from Greek *iatrikos* of healing, from *iasthai* to heal]

-i·at·rics *n. combining form.* indicating medical care or treatment: *paediatrics.* Compare **-iatry.** [from IATRIC]

i·at·ro·gen·ic (aɪˌætrəʊ'dʒɛnɪk) *adj. Med.* (of an illness or symptoms) induced in a patient as the result of a physician's words or action. —**i·at·ro·ge·nic·i·ty** (aɪˌætrəʊdʒɪ'nɪsɪtɪ) *n.*

-i·a·try *n. combining form.* indicating healing or medical treatment: *psychiatry.* Compare **-iatrics.** [from New Latin *-iatria,* from Greek *iatreia* the healing art, from *iatros* healer, physician] —**-i·at·ric** *adj. combining form.*

ib. See **ibid.**

I.B.A. (in Britain) *abbrev. for* Independent Broadcasting Authority.

I·ba·dan (ɪ'bædᵊn) *n.* a city in SW Nigeria, capital of Oyo state: the largest town in West Africa; university (1948). Pop.: 847 000 (1975 est.).

I·ba·gué (*Spanish* iβa'ɣe) *n.* a city in W central Colombia. Pop.: 176 223 (1973).

I·bá·ñez (*Spanish* i'βaɲeθ) *n.* See (Vicente) **Blasco Ibáñez.**

Ib·ar·ru·ri (*Spanish* i'βaruri) *n.* **Do·lo·res.** real name of La **Pasionaria.**

I-beam *n.* a rolled steel joist or a girder with a cross section in the form of a capital letter *I.* Compare **H-beam.**

I·be·ri·a (aɪ'bɪərɪə) *n.* **1.** the Iberian Peninsula. **2.** an ancient region south of the Caucasus corresponding approximately to the present-day Georgian SSR.

I·be·ri·an (aɪ'bɪərɪən) *n.* **1.** a member of a group of ancient Caucasoid peoples who inhabited the Iberian Peninsula in preclassical and classical times. See also **Celtiberian. 2.** a native or inhabitant of the Iberian Peninsula; a Spaniard or Portuguese. **3.** a native or inhabitant of ancient Iberia in the Caucasus. ~*adj.* **4.** denoting or relating to the pre-Roman peoples of the Iberian Peninsula or of Caucasian Iberia. **5.** of or relating to the Iberian Peninsula, its inhabitants, or any of their languages.

I·be·ri·an Pen·in·su·la *n.* a peninsula of SW Europe, occupied by Spain and Portugal.

I·be·ro- ('aɪbərəʊ) *combining form.* indicating Iberia or Iberian: *Ibero-Caucasian.*

I·bert (*French* i'bɛ:r) *n.* **Jacques (François Antoine)** (ʒɑ:k). 1890–1962, French composer.

i·bex ('aɪbɛks) *n., pl.* **i·bex·es, ib·i·ces** ('ɪbɪˌsi:z, 'aɪ-), *or* **i·bex.** any of three wild goats, *Capra ibex, C. caucasica,* or *C. pyrenaica,* of mountainous regions of Europe, Asia, and North Africa, having large backward-curving horns. [C17: from Latin: chamois]

I·bib·i·o (ɪ'bɪbɪəʊ) *n.* **1.** (*pl.* **·os** *or* **·o**) a member of a Negroid people of SE Nigeria, living esp. in and around Calabar. **2.** the language or group of dialects spoken by this people, variously classified as belonging to the Benue-Congo or the Kwa branch of the Niger-Congo family.

ibid. *or* **ib.** (in annotations, bibliographies, etc., when referring to a book, article, chapter, or page previously cited) *abbrev. for* ibidem. [Latin: in the same place]

i·bis ('aɪbɪs) *n. pl.* **i·bis·es** *or* **i·bis.** any of various wading birds of the family *Threskiornithidae,* such as *Threskiornis aethiopica* (**sacred ibis**), that occur in warm regions and have a long thin down-curved bill: order *Ciconiiformes* (herons, storks, etc.). Compare **wood ibis.** [C14: via Latin from Greek, from Egyptian *hby*]

I·bi·za *or* **I·vi·za** (*Spanish* i'βiθa) *n.* **1.** a Spanish island in the W Mediterranean, one of the Balearic Islands: hilly, with a rugged coast; tourism. Pop.: 42 456 (1970). Area: 541 sq. km (209 sq. miles). **2.** the capital of Ibiza, a port on the south of the island. Pop.: 15 642 (1970).

-i·ble *suffix forming adjectives.* variant of **-able.** —**-i·bly** *suffix forming adverbs.* —**-i·bil·i·ty** *suffix forming nouns.*

ibn-Ba·tu·ta ('ɪbᵊn bɑ:'tu:tɑ:) *n.* 1304–?68, Arab traveller, who wrote the *Rihlah,* an account of his travels (1325–54) in Africa and Asia.

ibn-Rushd ('ɪbᵊn 'rʊʃt) *n.* the Arabic name of **Averroës.**

ibn-Saud ('ɪbᵊn 'saʊd) *n.* **Ab·dul-A·ziz** (æb'dʊl æ'zi:z). 1880–1953, king of Saudi Arabia (1932–53).

ibn-Si·na ('ɪbᵊn 'si:nə) *n.* the Arabic name of **Avicenna.**

I·bo *or* **Ig·bo** ('i:bəʊ) *n.* **1.** (*pl.* **·bos** *or* **·bo**) a member of a Negroid people of W Africa, living chiefly in S Nigeria. **2.** the language of this people, belonging to the Kwa branch of the Niger-Congo family: one of the chief literary and cultural languages of S Nigeria.

Ib·ra·him Pa·sha (ˌɪbrə'hi:m 'pɑ:ʃə) *n.* 1789–1848, Albanian general; son of Mehemet Ali, whom he succeeded as viceroy of Egypt (1848).

I.B.R.D. *abbrev. for* International Bank for Reconstruction and Development (the World Bank).

Ib·sen ('ɪbsən) *n.* **Hen·rik** ('hɛnrɪk). 1828–1906, Norwegian dramatist and poet. After his early verse plays *Brand* (1866) and *Peer Gynt* (1867), he began the series of social dramas in prose, including *A Doll's House* (1879), *Ghosts* (1881), and *The Wild Duck* (1886), which have had a profound influence on modern drama. His later plays, such as *Hedda Gabler* (1890) and *The Master Builder* (1892), are more symbolic.

i/c *abbrev. for* in charge (of).

IC *abbrev. for:* **1.** (in transformational grammar) immediate constituent. **2.** *Electronics.* integrated circuit.

I.C. *Astrology. abbrev. for* Imum Coeli: the lowest point on the ecliptic below the horizon, lying directly opposite the Midheaven.

-ic *suffix forming adjectives.* **1.** of, relating to, or resembling: *allergic; Germanic; periodic.* See also **-ical. 2.** (in chemistry) indicating that an element is chemically combined in the higher of two possible valence states: *ferric; stannic.* Compare **-ous** (sense 2). [from Latin *-icus* or Greek *-ikos; -ic* also occurs in nouns that represent a substantive use of adjectives (*magic*) and in nouns borrowed directly from Latin or Greek (*critic, music*)]

I·çá ('i:sɑ:; *Portuguese* i'sa) *n.* the Brazilian part of the **Putumayo River.**

I.C.A. *abbrev. for:* **1.** (in Britain) Institute of Contemporary Arts. **2.** International Cooperation Administration.

-i·cal *suffix forming adjectives.* variant of **-ic,** but in some words having a less literal application than corresponding adjectives ending in *-ic: economical; fanatical.* [from Latin *-icālis*] —**-i·cal·ly** *suffix forming adverbs.*

I.C.A.O. *abbrev. for* International Civil Aviation Organization.

I·car·i·a (aɪ'kɛərɪə, ɪ-) *n.* a Greek island in the Aegean Sea, in the Southern Sporades group. Area: 256 sq. km (99 sq. miles). Modern Greek name: **Ikaría.** Also called: **Nikaria.**

I·car·i·an[1] (aɪ'kɛərɪən, ɪ-) *adj.* of or relating to Icarus.

I·car·i·an[2] (aɪ'kɛərɪən, ɪ-) *adj.* **1.** of or relating to Icaria or its inhabitants. ~*n.* **2.** an inhabitant of Icaria.

I·car·i·an Sea *n.* the part of the Aegean Sea between the islands of Patmos and Leros and the coast of Asia Minor, where, according to legend, Icarus fell into the sea.

Ic·a·rus ('ɪkərəs, 'aɪ-) *n. Greek myth.* the son of Daedalus with whom he escaped from Crete, flying with wings made of wax and feathers. Heedless of his father's warning he flew too near the sun, causing the wax to melt, and fell into the Aegean and drowned.

ICBM *abbrev. for* intercontinental ballistic missile.

ice (aɪs) *n.* **1.** water in the solid state, formed by freezing liquid water. Related adj.: **glacial. 2.** the field of play in ice hockey. **3. break the ice. a.** to relieve shyness, etc., esp. between strangers. **b.** to be the first of a group to do something. **4.** See **ice cream. 5. cut no ice.** *Informal.* to fail to make an impression. **6. on ice.** in abeyance; pending. **7. on thin ice.** unsafe or unsafely; vulnerable or vulnerably. ~*vb.* **8.** (often foll. by *up, over,* etc.) to form or cause to form ice; freeze. **9.** (*tr.*) to mix with ice or chill (a drink, etc.). **10.** (*tr.*) to cover (a cake, etc.) with icing. [Old English *īs;* compare Old High German *īs,* Old Norse *īss*] —'**ice·less** *adj.* —'**ice·,like** *adj.*

I.C.E. (in Britain) *abbrev. for* Institution of Civil Engineers.

Ice. *abbrev. for* Iceland(ic).

ice age *n.* another name for **glacial period.**

ice axe *n.* a light axe used by mountaineers for cutting footholds in ice.

ice bag *n.* **1.** a waterproof bag used as an ice pack. **2.** a strong bag, usually made of canvas and equipped with two handles, used for carrying blocks of ice.

ice·berg ('aɪsbɜːg) *n.* **1.** a large mass of ice floating in the sea, esp. a mass that has broken off a polar glacier. **2. tip of the iceberg.** the small visible part of something, esp. a problem or difficulty, that is much larger. **3.** *Slang, chiefly U.S.* a person considered to have a cold or reserved manner. **4.** *Austral. informal.* a person who swims or surfs frequently in winter or takes cold showers. [C18: probably part translation of Middle Dutch *ijsberg* ice mountain; compare Norwegian *isberg*]

ice·blink ('aɪs,blɪŋk) *n.* **1.** Also called: **blink.** a yellowish-white reflected glare in the sky over an ice field. **2.** a coastal ice cliff.

ice·boat ('aɪs,bəʊt) *n.* another name for **icebreaker** (sense 1) or **ice yacht.**

ice·bound ('aɪs,baʊnd) *adj.* covered or made immobile by ice; frozen in: *an icebound ship.*

ice·box ('aɪs,bɒks) *n.* **1.** a compartment in a refrigerator for storing or making ice. **2.** an insulated cabinet packed with ice for storing food.

ice·break·er ('aɪs,breɪkə) *n.* **1.** Also called: **iceboat.** a vessel with a reinforced bow for breaking up the ice in bodies of water to keep channels open for navigation. **2.** any tool or device for breaking ice into smaller pieces.

ice·cap ('aɪs,kæp) *n.* a thick mass of glacial ice and snow that permanently covers an area of land, such as either of the polar regions or the peak of a mountain.

ice cream *n.* a kind of sweetened frozen liquid, properly made from cream and egg yolks but often made from milk or a custard base, flavoured in various ways.

ice-cream cone *or* **cor·net** *n.* **1.** a conical edible wafer for holding ice cream. **2.** such a cone containing ice cream.

ice-cream so·da *n. Chiefly U.S.* ice cream served in a tall glass of carbonated water and a little milk, usually flavoured in various ways.

iced (aɪst) *adj.* **1.** covered, coated, or chilled with ice. **2.** covered with icing: *iced cakes.*

ice·fall ('aɪs,fɔːl) *n.* a very steep part of a glacier that has deep crevasses and resembles a frozen waterfall.

ice field *n.* **1.** a very large flat expanse of ice floating in the sea; large ice floe. **2.** a large mass of ice permanently covering an extensive area of land.

ice fish *n.* any percoid fish of the family *Chaenichthyidae,* of Antarctic seas, having a semitransparent scaleless body.

ice floe *n.* a sheet of ice, of variable size, floating in the sea. See also **ice field** (sense 1).

ice foot *n.* a narrow belt of ice permanently attached to the coast in polar regions.

ice hock·ey *n.* a game played on ice by two opposing teams of six players each, who wear skates and try to propel a flat puck into their opponents' goal with long sticks having an offset flat blade at the end.

ice house *n.* a building for storing ice.

I·çel (iː'tʃɛl) *n.* another name for **Mersin.**

Icel. *abbrev. for* Iceland(ic).

Ice·land ('aɪslənd) *n.* an island republic in the N Atlantic, regarded as part of Europe: settled by Norsemen, who established a legislative assembly in 930; under Danish rule (1380–1918); gained independence in 1918 and became a republic in 1944; contains large areas of glaciers, snowfields, and lava beds with many volcanoes and hot springs (the chief source of domestic heat); inhabited chiefly along the SW coast. The economy is based largely on fishing. Language: Icelandic. Religion: mostly Lutheran. Currency: krona. Capital: Reykjavik. Pop.: 218 000 (1975 est.). Area: 102 828 sq. km (39 702 sq. miles).

Ice·land·er ('aɪs,lændə, 'aɪsləndə) *n.* a native, citizen, or inhabitant of Iceland.

Ice·land·ic (aɪs'lændɪk) *adj.* **1.** of, relating to, or characteristic of Iceland, its people, or their language. ~*n.* **2.** the official language of Iceland, belonging to the North Germanic branch of the Indo-European family. See also **Old Icelandic.**

Ice·land moss *n.* a lichen, *Cetraria islandica,* of arctic regions and N Europe, with brownish edible fronds.

Ice·land pop·py *n.* any of various widely cultivated arctic poppies, esp. *Papaver nudicaule,* with white or yellow nodding flowers.

Ice·land spar *n.* a pure transparent variety of calcite with double-refracting crystals used in making polarizing microscopes.

ice lol·ly *n. Brit. informal.* an ice cream or water ice on a stick. Also called: **lolly.** U.S. equivalent (trademark): **Popsicle.**

ice ma·chine *n.* a machine that automatically produces ice for use in drinks, etc.

ice nee·dle *n. Meteorol.* one of many needle-like ice crystals that form cirrus clouds in clear cold weather.

I·ce·ni (aɪ'siːnaɪ) *n.* an ancient British tribe that rebelled against the Romans in 61 A.D. under Queen Boadicea.

ice pack *n.* **1.** a bag or folded cloth containing ice, applied to a part of the body, esp. the head, to cool, reduce swelling, etc. **2.** another name for **pack ice. 3.** a sachet containing a gel that can be frozen or heated and that retains its temperature for an extended period of time, used esp. in cool bags.

ice pick *n.* a pointed tool, used for breaking ice.

ice plant *n.* a low-growing plant, *Mesembryanthemum* (or *Cryophytum*) *crystallinum,* of southern Africa, with fleshy leaves covered with icelike hairs and pink or white rayed flowers: family *Aizoaceae.*

ice point *n.* the temperature at which a mixture of ice and water are in equilibrium at a pressure of one atmosphere. It is 0° on the Celsius scale and 32° on the Fahrenheit scale. Compare **steam point.**

ice sheet *n.* a thick layer of ice covering a large area of land for a long time, esp. the layer that covered much of the N hemisphere during the last glacial period.

ice shelf *n.* a thick mass of ice that is permanently attached to the land but projects into and floats on the sea.

ice show *n.* any entertainment performed by ice-skaters.

ice skate *n.* **1.** a boot having a steel blade fitted to the sole to enable the wearer to glide swiftly over ice. **2.** the steel blade on such a boot or shoe. ~*vb.* **ice-skate. 3.** (*intr.*) to glide swiftly over ice on ice skates. —'**ice-,skat·er** *n.*

ice wa·ter *n.* **1.** water formed from ice. **2.** *U.S.* drinking water cooled by refrigeration or the addition of ice.

ice yacht *n.* a sailing craft having a cross-shaped frame with runners for travelling over ice. Also called: **iceboat.**

ICFTU *abbrev. for* International Confederation of Free Trade Unions.

I·chang *or* **I-ch'ang** ('iː'tʃæŋ) *n.* a port in S central China, in Hupeh province on the Yangtze River 1600 km (1000 miles) from the East China Sea: head of navigation of the Yangtze. Pop.: 50 000–100 000 (1953 est.).

I.Chem.E. *abbrev. for* Institution of Chemical Engineers.

I Ching ('iː 'tʃɪŋ) *n.* an ancient Chinese book of divination and a source of Confucian and Taoist philosophy. Answers to questions and advice may be obtained by referring to the text accompanying one of 64 hexagrams, selected at random. Also called: **Book of Changes.**

I·chi·no·mi·ya (,iːtʃɪ'nəʊmɪə) *n.* a town in Japan, on SE Honshu island: textile industry. Pop.: 235 130 (1974 est.).

ich·neu·mon (ɪk'njuːmən) *n.* a mongoose, *Herpestes ichneumon,* of Africa and S Europe, having greyish-brown speckled fur. [C16: via Latin from Greek, literally: tracker, hunter, from *ikhneuein* to track, from *ikhnos* a footprint; so named from the animal's alleged ability to locate the eggs of crocodiles]

ich·neu·mon fly *or* **wasp** *n.* any hymenopterous insect of the family *Ichneumonidae,* whose larvae are parasitic in caterpillars and other insect larvae.

ich·nite ('ɪknaɪt) *or* **ich·no·lite** ('ɪknə,laɪt) *n.* a fossilized footprint. [C19: from Greek *ikhnos* footprint, track + -ITE[1]]

ich·nog·ra·phy (ɪk'nɒgrəfɪ) *n.* **1.** the art of drawing ground plans. **2.** the ground plan of a building, factory, etc. [C16: from Latin *ichnographia,* from Greek *ikhnographia,* from *ikhnos* trace, track] —**ich·no·graph·ic** (,ɪknə'græfɪk) *or* **,ich·no·'graph·i·cal** *adj.* —**,ich·no·'graph·i·cal·ly** *adv.*

ich·nol·o·gy (ɪk'nɒlədʒɪ) *n.* the study of fossil footprints. [C19: from Greek *ikhnos* footprint, track] —**ich·no·log·i·cal** (,ɪknə'lɒdʒɪk°l) *adj.*

i·chor ('aɪkɔː) *n.* **1.** *Greek myth.* the fluid said to flow in the veins of the gods. **2.** *Pathol.* a foul-smelling watery discharge from a wound or ulcer. [C17: from Greek *ikhōr,* of obscure origin] —'**i·chor·ous** *adj.*

ich·thy·ic ('ɪkθɪɪk) *adj.* of, relating to, or characteristic of fishes. [C19: from Greek, from *ikhthus* fish]

ich·thy·o- *or before a vowel* **ich·thy-** *combining form.* indicating or relating to fishes: *ichthyology.* [from Latin, from Greek *ikhthus* fish]

ich·thy·oid ('ɪkθɪ,ɔɪd) *adj. also* **ich·thy·oi·dal. 1.** resembling a fish. ~*n.* **2.** a fishlike vertebrate.

ichthyol. *or* **ichth.** *abbrev. for* ichthyology.

ich·thy·o·lite ('ɪkθɪə,laɪt) *n. Rare.* any fossil fish. —**ich·thy·o·lit·ic** (,ɪkθɪə'lɪtɪk) *adj.*

ich·thy·ol·o·gy (,ɪkθɪ'ɒlədʒɪ) *n.* the study of the physiology, history, economic importance, etc., of fishes. —**ich·thy·o·log·**

ic (ˌɪkθɪəˈlɒdʒɪk) *or* **ˌich·thy·o·ˈlog·i·cal** *adj.* —**ˌich·thy·o·ˈlog·i·cal·ly** *adv.* —**ˌich·thy·ˈol·o·gist** *n.*

ich·thy·oph·a·gous (ˌɪkθɪˈɒfəgəs) *adj.* feeding on fish. —**ich·thy·oph·a·gy** (ˌɪkθɪˈɒfədʒɪ) *n.*

ich·thy·or·nis (ˌɪkθɪˈɔːnɪs) *n.* an extinct Cretaceous sea bird of the genus *Ichthyornis,* thought to have resembled a tern. [C19: New Latin, from ICHTHY- + Greek *ornis* bird]

ich·thy·o·saur (ˈɪkθɪəˌsɔː) *or* **ich·thy·o·saur·us** (ˌɪkθɪəˈsɔːrəs) *n., pl.* **-saurs, -saur·us·es,** *or* **-sau·ri** (-ˈsɔːraɪ). any extinct marine Mesozoic reptile of the order *Ichthyosauria,* which had a porpoise-like body with dorsal and tail fins and paddle-like limbs. See also **plesiosaur.**

ich·thy·o·sis (ˌɪkθɪˈəʊsɪs) *n.* a congenital disease in which the skin is coarse, dry, and scaly. Also called: **xeroderma.** Nontechnical name: **fishskin disease.** —**ich·thy·ot·ic** (ˌɪkθɪˈɒtɪk) *adj.*

-i·cian *suffix forming nouns.* indicating a person skilled or involved in a subject or activity: *physician; beautician.* [from French *-icien;* see -IC, -IAN]

i·ci·cle (ˈaɪsɪkᵊl) *n.* a hanging spike of ice formed by the freezing of dripping water. [C14: from ICE + *ickel,* from Old English *gicel* icicle, related to Old Norse *jökull* large piece of ice, glacier] —**ˈi·ci·cled** *adj.*

i·ci·ly (ˈaɪsɪlɪ) *adv.* in an icy or reserved manner.

i·ci·ness (ˈaɪsɪnɪs) *n.* **1.** the condition of being icy or very cold. **2.** a manner that is cold or reserved; aloofness.

ic·ing (ˈaɪsɪŋ) *n.* **1.** Also called (esp. U.S.): **frosting.** a sugar preparation, variously flavoured and coloured, for coating and decorating cakes, biscuits, etc. **2.** the formation of ice, as on a ship or aircraft, due to the freezing of moisture in the atmosphere.

ic·ing sug·ar *n. Brit.* a very finely ground sugar used for icings, confections, etc. U.S. term: **confectioners' sugar.**

ICJ *abbrev. for* International Court of Justice.

i·con *or* **i·kon** (ˈaɪkɒn) *n.* **1.** a representation of Christ, the Virgin Mary, or a saint, esp. one painted in oil on a wooden panel, depicted in a traditional Byzantine style and venerated in the Eastern Church. **2.** an image, picture, representation, etc. **3.** a symbol resembling or analogous to the thing it represents. [C16: from Latin, from Greek *eikōn* image, from *eikenai* to be like]

i·con·ic (aɪˈkɒnɪk) *or* **i·con·i·cal** *adj.* **1.** relating to, resembling, or having the character of an icon. **2.** (of memorial sculptures, esp. those depicting athletes of ancient Greece) having a fixed conventional style.

i·con·ic mem·o·ry *n. Psychol.* the temporary persistence of visual impressions after the stimulus has been removed.

I·co·ni·um (aɪˈkəʊnɪəm) *n.* the ancient name for **Konya.**

i·con·o- *or before a vowel* **i·con-** *combining form.* indicating an image or likeness: *iconology.* [from Greek: ICON]

i·con·o·clasm (aɪˈkɒnəˌklæzəm) *n.* the acts or beliefs of an iconoclast.

i·con·o·clast (aɪˈkɒnəˌklæst) *n.* **1.** a person who attacks established or traditional concepts, principles, laws, etc. **2. a.** a destroyer of religious images or sacred objects. **b.** an adherent of the heretical movement within the Greek Orthodox Church from 725 to 842 A.D., which aimed at the destruction of icons and religious images. —**i·ˌcon·o·ˈclas·tic** *adj.* —**i·ˌcon·o·ˈclas·ti·cal·ly** *adv.*

i·co·nog·ra·phy (ˌaɪkɒˈnɒgrəfɪ) *n., pl.* **-phies. 1. a.** the symbols used in a work of art or art movement. **b.** the conventional significance attached to such symbols. **2.** a collection of pictures of a particular subject, such as Christ. **3.** the representation of the subjects of icons or portraits, esp. on coins. —**ˌi·co·ˈnog·ra·pher** *n.* —**i·con·o·graph·ic** (aɪˌkɒnəˈgræfɪk) *or* **i·ˌcon·o·ˈgraph·i·cal** *adj.*

i·co·nol·a·try (ˌaɪkɒˈnɒlətrɪ) *n.* the worship or adoration of icons as idols. —**ˌi·co·ˈnol·a·ter** *n.* —**ˌi·co·ˈnol·a·trous** *adj.*

i·co·nol·o·gy (ˌaɪkɒˈnɒlədʒɪ) *n.* **1.** the study or field of art history concerning icons. **2.** icons collectively. **3.** the symbolic representation or symbolism of icons. —**i·con·o·log·i·cal** (aɪˌkɒnəˈlɒdʒɪkᵊl) *adj.* —**ˌi·co·ˈnol·o·gist** *n.*

i·con·o·mat·ic (aɪˌkɒnəˈmætɪk) *adj.* employing pictures to represent not objects themselves but the sound of their names. [C19: from Greek, from *eikon* image + *onoma* name] —**i·con·o·mat·i·cism** (aɪˌkɒnəˈmætɪˌsɪzəm) *n.*

i·con·o·scope (aɪˈkɒnəˌskəʊp) *n.* a television camera tube in which an electron beam scans a photoemissive surface, converting an optical image into electrical pulses.

i·co·nos·ta·sis (ˌaɪkəʊˈnɒstəsɪs) *or* **i·con·o·stas** (aɪˈkɒnəˌstæs) *n., pl.* **i·co·nos·ta·ses** (ˌaɪkəʊˈnɒstəˌsiːz) *or* **i·con·o·stas·es.** *Eastern Church.* a screen with doors and icons set in tiers, which separates the bema (sanctuary) from the nave. [C19: Church Latin, from Late Greek *eikonostasion* shrine, literally: area where images are placed, from ICONO- + *histanai* to stand]

i·co·sa·he·dron (ˌaɪkəsəˈhiːdrən) *n., pl.* **-drons** *or* **-dra** (-drə). a solid figure having 20 faces. The faces of a **regular icosahedron** are equilateral triangles. [C16: from Greek *eikosaedron,* from *eikosi* twenty + *-edron* -HEDRON] —**ˌi·co·sa·ˈhe·dral** *adj.*

-ics *suffix forming nouns; functioning as sing.* **1.** indicating a science, art, or matters relating to a particular subject: *aeronautics; politics.* **2.** indicating certain activities or practices: *acrobatics.* [plural of *-ic,* representing Latin *-ica,* from Greek *-ika,* as in *mathēmatika* mathematics]

I.C.S. *abbrev. for* Indian Civil Service.

ICSH *abbrev. for* interstitial-cell-stimulating hormone.

ic·ter·us (ˈɪktərəs) *n.* **1.** *Pathol.* another name for **jaundice. 2.** a yellowing of plant leaves, caused by excessive cold or moisture. [C18: from Latin: yellow bird, the sight of which reputedly cured jaundice, from Greek *ikteros*] —**ic·ter·ic** (ɪkˈtɛrɪk) *adj.*

Ic·ti·nus (ɪkˈtaɪnəs) *n.* 5th century B.C. Greek architect, who designed the Parthenon with Callicrates.

ic·tus (ˈɪktəs) *n., pl.* **-tus·es** *or* **-tus. 1.** *Prosody.* metrical or rhythmical stress in verse feet, as contrasted with the stress accent on words. **2.** *Med.* a sudden attack or stroke. [C18: from Latin *icere* to strike] —**ˈic·tal** *adj.*

i·cy (ˈaɪsɪ) *adj.* **i·ci·er, i·ci·est. 1.** made of, covered with, or containing ice. **2.** resembling ice. **3.** freezing or very cold. **4.** cold or reserved in manner; aloof.

i·cy pole *n.* the Australian name for an **ice lolly.**

id (ɪd) *n. Psychoanal.* the mass of primitive instincts and energies in the unconscious mind that, modified by the ego and the superego, underlies all psychic activity. [C20: New Latin, from Latin: it; used to render German *Es*]

ID *abbrev. for* identification.

I.D. *abbrev. for:* **1.** Also: **i.d.** inside diameter. **2.** Intelligence Department.

id. *abbrev. for* idem.

I'd (aɪd) *contraction of* I had *or* I would.

-id[1] *suffix forming nouns* (usually pl.). indicating the names of meteor showers that appear to radiate from a specified constellation: *Orionids* (from Orion). [from Latin *-id-, -is,* from Greek, feminine suffix of origin]

-id[2] *suffix forming nouns and adjectives.* indicating members of a zoological family: *cyprinid.* [from New Latin *-idae* or *-ida,* from Greek *-idēs* suffix indicating offspring]

-id[3] *suffix forming nouns.* variant of **-ide.**

I·da (ˈaɪdə) *n.* **Mount. 1.** a mountain in central Crete: the highest on the island; in ancient times associated with the worship of Zeus. Height: 2456 m (8057 ft.). Modern Greek name: **Idhi. 2.** a mountain in NW Turkey, southeast of the site of ancient Troy. Height: 1767 m (5797 ft.). Turkish name: **Kaz Daği.**

I.D.A. *abbrev. for* International Development Association.

-i·dae *suffix forming nouns.* indicating names of zoological families: *Felidae; Hominidae.* [New Latin, from Latin, from Greek *-idai,* suffix indicating offspring]

I·da·ho (ˈaɪdəˌhəʊ) *n.* a state of the northwestern U.S.: consists chiefly of ranges of the Rocky Mountains, with the Snake River basin in the south; important for agriculture (**Idaho potatoes**), livestock, and silver-mining. Capital: Boise. Pop.: 713 008 (1970). Area: 216 413 sq. km (83 557 sq. miles). Abbrevs.: **Id., Ida.,** or (with zip code) **ID** —**ˈI·da·ˌho·an** *adj., n.*

IDB *Chiefly S. African. abbrev. for* illicit diamond buying.

ID card *n.* a card or document that serves to identify a person, or to prove his age, membership, etc.

ide (aɪd) *n.* another name for the **silver orfe.** [C19: from New Latin *idus,* from Swedish *id*]

-ide *or* **-id** *suffix forming nouns.* **1.** (*added to the combining form of the nonmetallic or electronegative elements*) indicating a binary compound: *sodium chloride.* **2.** indicating an organic compound derived from another: *acetanilide.* **3.** indicating one of a class of compounds or elements: *peptide; lanthanide.* [from German *-id,* from French *oxide* OXIDE, based on the suffix of *acide* ACID]

i·de·a (aɪˈdɪə) *n.* **1.** the product of mental activity whereby the mind consciously conceives a thought; conception. **2.** an impression established in the mind by something perceived; notion. **3.** a belief or viewpoint; opinion: *he has an idea that what he's doing is right.* **4.** a scheme, intention, plan, etc.: *here's my idea for the sales campaign.* **5.** a vague notion or indication; inkling: *he had no idea of what life would be like in Africa.* **6.** significance or purpose: *the idea of the game is to discover the murderer.* **7.** *Philosophy.* an immediate object of thought or perception. **8.** *Music.* a thematic phrase or figure; motif. **9.** *Obsolete.* a mental image. **10. get ideas.** to become ambitious, restless, etc. **11. not one's idea of.** not what one regards as (hard work, a holiday, etc.). **12. that's an idea.** that is worth considering. **13. the very idea!** that is preposterous, unreasonable, etc. [C16: via Late Latin from Greek: model, pattern, notion, from *idein* to see] —**i·ˈde·a·less** *adj.*

I·de·a (aɪˈdɪə) *n.* (in the philosophy of Plato) the universal essence or archetype of any class of things or concepts.

i·de·al (aɪˈdɪəl) *n.* **1.** a conception of something that is perfect, esp. that which one seeks to attain. **2.** a person or thing considered to represent perfection: *he's her ideal.* **3.** something existing only as an idea. **4.** a pattern or model, esp. of ethical behaviour. ~*adj.* **5.** conforming to an ideal. **6.** of, involving, or existing in the form of an idea. **7.** *Philosophy.* **a.** of or relating to a highly desirable and possible state of affairs. **b.** of or relating to idealism. —**i·de·al·i·ty** (ˌaɪdɪˈælɪtɪ) *n.* —**i·ˈde·al·ly** *adv.* —**i·ˈde·al·ness** *n.*

i·de·al el·e·ment *n.* any element added to a mathematical theory in order to eliminate special cases. The ideal element $i = \sqrt{-1}$ allows all algebraic equations to be solved and the point at infinity (**ideal point**) ensures that any two lines in projective geometry intersect.

i·de·al gas *n.* a hypothetical gas composed of spheres of negligible volume moving at random and undergoing perfectly elastic collisions with the walls of their container and with each other. Also called: **perfect gas.**

i·de·al·ism (aɪˈdɪəˌlɪzəm) *n.* **1.** belief in or pursuance of ideals. **2.** the tendency to represent things in their ideal forms, rather than as they are. **3.** *Philosophy.* the doctrine that thought or the mind is the only reality and that external objects consist merely of ideas. Compare **materialism, phenomenalism, real-**

ism. —**i·'de·al·ist** *n.* —**i·ˌde·al·'is·tic** *adj.* —**i·ˌde·al·'is·ti·cal·ly** *adv.*

i·de·al·ize *or* **i·de·al·ise** (aɪ'dɪəˌlaɪz) *vb.* **1.** to consider or represent (something) as ideal. **2.** (*tr.*) to portray as ideal; glorify. **3.** (*intr.*) to form an ideal or ideals. —**i·ˌde·al·i·'za·tion** *or* **i·ˌde·al·i·'sa·tion** *n.* —**i·'de·al·ˌiz·er** *or* **i·'de·al·ˌis·er** *n.*

i·de·ate *vb.* (aɪ'diːeɪt). **1.** to imagine or conceive (something); form an idea of (something). ~*n.* (aɪ'diːɪt, -eɪt). **2.** another word for **ideatum.** —**ˌi·de·'a·tion** *n.* —**ˌi·de·'a·tion·al** *adj.* —**ˌi·de·'a·tion·al·ly** *adv.* —**i·de·a·tive** (aɪ'diːətɪv, 'aɪdɪˌeɪ-) *adj.*

i·de·a·tum (ˌaɪdɪ'eɪtəm) *n., pl.* **·a·ta** (-'eɪtə). *Philosophy.* the objective reality with which human ideas are supposed to correspond. [C18: New Latin, from Latin: IDEA]

i·dée fixe *French.* (ide 'fiks) *n., pl.* ***i·dées fixes*** (ide 'fiks). a fixed idea; obsession.

i·dée re·çue *French.* (ide rə'sy) *n., pl.* **i·dées re·çues** (ide rə'sy). a generally held opinion or concept. [literally: received idea]

i·dem *Latin.* ('aɪdɛm, 'ɪdɛm) *pron., adj.* the same: used to refer to an article, chapter, etc., previously cited.

i·dem·po·tent ('aɪdəmˌpəʊtənt, 'ɪd-) *adj. Maths.* (of a matrix, transformation, etc.) not changed in value following multiplication by itself. [C20: from Latin *idem* same + POTENT]

i·den·tic (aɪ'dɛntɪk) *adj.* **1.** *Diplomacy.* (esp. of opinions expressed by two or more governments) having the same wording or intention regarding another power: *identic notes.* **2.** an obsolete word for **identical.**

i·den·ti·cal (aɪ'dɛntɪkᵊl) *adj.* **1.** being the same. **2.** exactly alike, equal, or agreeing. **3.** designating either or both of a pair of twins of the same sex who developed from a single fertilized ovum that split into two. Compare **fraternal** (sense 3). —**i·'den·ti·cal·ly** *adv.* —**i·'den·ti·cal·ness** *n.*

i·den·ti·cal prop·o·si·tion *n. Logic.* a proposition in which the subject and predicate have the same content and extent, as in *that which is not alive is dead.*

i·den·ti·fi·ca·tion (aɪˌdɛntɪfɪ'keɪʃən) *n.* **1.** the act of identifying or the state of being identified. **2. a.** something that identifies a person or thing. **b.** (*as modifier*): *an identification card.* **3.** *Psychol.* **a.** the process of recognizing specific objects as the result of remembering. **b.** the process by which one incorporates aspects of another person's personality. **c.** the transferring of a response from one situation to another because the two bear similar features. See also **generalization** (sense 3).

i·den·ti·fi·ca·tion pa·rade *n.* a group of persons including one suspected of having committed a crime assembled for the purpose of discovering whether a witness can identify the suspect.

i·den·ti·fy (aɪ'dɛntɪˌfaɪ) *vb.* **·fies, ·fy·ing, ·fied.** (*mainly tr.*) **1.** to prove or recognize as being a certain person or thing; determine the identity of. **2.** to consider as the same or equivalent. **3.** (*also intr.;* often foll. by *with*) to consider (oneself) as similar to another. **4.** to determine the taxonomic classification of (a plant or animal). **5.** (*intr.;* usually foll. by *with*) *Psychol.* to engage in identification. —**i·'den·ti·ˌfi·a·ble** *adj.* —**i·'den·ti·ˌfi·a·ble·ness** *n.* —**i·'den·ti·ˌfi·er** *n.*

I·den·ti·kit (aɪ'dɛntɪˌkɪt) *n. Trademark.* **a.** a set of transparencies of various typical facial characteristics that can be superimposed on one another to build up, on the basis of a description, a picture of a person sought by the police. **b.** (*as modifier*): *an Identikit picture.*

i·den·ti·ty (aɪ'dɛntɪtɪ) *n., pl.* **·ties. 1. a.** the state of having unique identifying characteristics held by no other person or thing. **b.** (*as modifier*): *an identity card.* **2.** the individual characteristics by which a person or thing is recognized. **3.** the state of being the same in nature, quality, etc.: *they were linked by the identity of their tastes.* **4.** *Maths.* **a.** an equation that is valid for all values of its variables, as in $(x - y)(x + y) = x^2 - y^2$. Often denoted by the symbol ≡ **b.** Also called: **identity element.** a member of a set that when operating on another member, *x*, produces that member *x*: the identity for multiplication of numbers is 1 since $x.1 = 1.x = x$. See also **inverse** (sense 2b.). **5.** *Austral. informal.* a well-known person, esp. in a specified locality; figure: *a Barwidgee identity.* [C16: from Late Latin *identitās,* from Latin *idem* the same]

id·e·o- *combining form.* of or indicating idea or ideas: *ideology.* [from French *idéo-,* from Greek *idea* IDEA]

id·e·o·gram ('ɪdɪəʊˌgræm) *or* **id·e·o·graph** ('ɪdɪəʊˌgrɑːf, -ˌgræf) *n.* **1.** a sign or symbol, used in such writing systems as those of China or Japan, that directly represents a concept, idea, or thing rather than a word or set of words for it. **2.** any graphic sign or symbol, such as %, @, &, etc.

id·e·og·ra·phy (ˌɪdɪ'ɒgrəfɪ) *n.* the use of ideograms to communicate ideas.

i·de·ol·o·gist (ˌaɪdɪ'ɒlədʒɪst) *or* **i·de·o·logue** ('aɪdɪəˌlɒg) *n.* **1.** a person who supports a particular ideology, esp. a political theorist. **2.** a person who studies an ideology or ideologies. **3.** a theorist or visionary.

i·de·ol·o·gy (ˌaɪdɪ'ɒlədʒɪ) *n., pl.* **·gies. 1.** a body of ideas that reflects the beliefs and interests of a nation, political system, etc. **2.** *Philosophy.* an idea or set of ideas that is false, misleading, or held for the wrong reasons but is believed with such conviction as to be irrefutable. **3.** speculation that is imaginary or visionary. **4.** the study of the nature and origin of ideas. —**i·de·o·log·i·cal** (ˌaɪdɪə'lɒdʒɪkᵊl) *or* **ˌi·de·o·'log·ic** *adj.* —**ˌi·de·o·'log·i·cal·ly** *adv.*

i·de·o·mo·tor (ˌaɪdɪə'məʊtə) *adj. Physiol.* designating automatic muscular movements stimulated by ideas, as in absent-minded acts.

ides (aɪdz) *n.* (*functioning as sing.*) (in the Roman calendar) the 15th day in March, May, July, and October and the 13th day of each other month. See also **calends, nones.** [C15: from Old French, from Latin *īdūs* (plural), of uncertain origin]

id est *Latin.* (ɪd ɛst) the full form of **i.e.**

Í·dhi ('iðɪ) *n.* a transliteration of the Modern Greek name for Mount **Ida** (in Crete).

id·i·o- *combining form.* indicating peculiarity, isolation, or that which pertains to an individual person or thing: *idiolect.* [from Greek *idios* private, separate]

id·i·o·blast ('ɪdɪəʊˌblæst) *n.* a plant cell that differs from those around it in the same tissue. —**ˌid·i·o·'blas·tic** *adj.*

id·i·o·cy ('ɪdɪəsɪ) *n., pl.* **·cies. 1.** (*not in technical usage*) severe mental retardation. **2.** foolishness or senselessness; stupidity. **3.** a foolish act or remark.

id·i·o·graph·ic (ˌɪdɪəʊ'græfɪk) *adj. Psychol.* of or relating to the study of individuals. Compare **nomothetic.**

id·i·o·lect ('ɪdɪəˌlɛkt) *n.* the variety or form of a language used by an individual. —**ˌid·i·o·'lect·al** *or* **ˌid·i·o·'lect·ic** *adj.*

id·i·om ('ɪdɪəm) *n.* **1.** a group of words whose meaning cannot be predicted from the meanings of the constituent words, as for example (*It was raining*) *cats and dogs.* **2.** linguistic usage that is grammatical and natural to native speakers of a language. **3.** the characteristic vocabulary or usage of a specific human group or subject. **4.** the characteristic artistic style of an individual, school, period, etc. [C16: from Latin *idiōma* peculiarity of language, from Greek; see IDIO-] —**id·i·o·mat·ic** (ˌɪdɪə'mætɪk) *or* **ˌid·i·o·'mat·i·cal** *adj.* —**ˌid·i·o·'mat·i·cal·ly** *adv.* —**ˌid·i·o·'mat·i·cal·ness** *n.*

id·i·o·mor·phic (ˌɪdɪəʊ'mɔːfɪk) *adj.* (of minerals) occurring naturally in the form of well-developed crystals. —**ˌid·i·o·'mor·phi·cal·ly** *adv.* —**ˌid·i·o·'mor·phism** *n.*

id·i·op·a·thy (ˌɪdɪ'ɒpəθɪ) *n., pl.* **·thies.** any disease of unknown cause. —**id·i·o·path·ic** (ˌɪdɪəʊ'pæθɪk) *adj.*

id·i·o·phone ('ɪdɪəˌfəʊn) *n. Music.* a percussion instrument, such as a cymbal or xylophone, made of naturally sonorous material. —**id·i·o·phon·ic** (ˌɪdɪə'fɒnɪk) *adj.*

id·i·o·plasm ('ɪdɪəʊˌplæzəm) *n.* another name for **germ plasm.** —**ˌid·i·o·'plas·mic** *or* **id·i·o·plas·mat·ic** (ˌɪdɪəʊplæz'mætɪk) *adj.*

id·i·o·syn·cra·sy (ˌɪdɪəʊ'sɪŋkrəsɪ) *n., pl.* **·sies. 1.** a tendency, type of behaviour, mannerism, etc., of a specific person; quirk. **2.** the composite physical or psychological make-up of a specific person. **3.** an abnormal reaction of an individual to specific foods, drugs, or other agents. [C17: from Greek *idiosunkrasia,* from IDIO- + *sunkrasis* mixture, temperament, from *sun-* SYN- + *kerannunai* to mingle] —**id·i·o·syn·crat·ic** (ˌɪdɪəsɪŋ'krætɪk) *adj.* —**ˌid·i·o·syn·'crat·i·cal·ly** *adv.*

id·i·ot ('ɪdɪət) *n.* **1.** a person with severe mental retardation. **2.** a foolish or senseless person. [C13: from Latin *idiōta* ignorant person, from Greek *idiōtēs* private person, one who lacks professional knowledge, ignoramus; see IDIO-]

id·i·ot board *n.* a slang name for **autocue.**

id·i·ot·ic (ˌɪdɪ'ɒtɪk) *adj.* of or resembling an idiot; foolish; senseless. —**ˌid·i·'ot·i·cal·ly** *adv.* —**ˌid·i·'ot·i·cal·ness** *n.*

id·i·ot·ism ('ɪdɪəˌtɪzəm) *n.* **1.** an archaic word for **idiocy. 2.** an obsolete word for **idiom.**

i·dle ('aɪdᵊl) *adj.* **1.** unemployed or unoccupied; inactive. **2.** not operating or being used. **3.** not wanting to work; lazy. **4.** (*usually prenominal*) frivolous or trivial: *idle pleasures.* **5.** ineffective or powerless; fruitless; vain. **6.** without basis; unfounded. ~*vb.* **7.** (when *tr.*, often foll. by *away*) to waste or pass (time) fruitlessly or inactively: *he idled the hours away.* **8.** (*intr.*) to loiter or move aimlessly. **9.** (*intr.*) (of a shaft, etc.) to turn without doing useful work. **10.** (*intr.*) Also (Brit.): **tick over.** (of an engine) to run at low speed with the transmission disengaged. **11.** (*tr.*) *U.S.* to cause to be inactive or unemployed. [Old English *īdel;* compare Old High German *ītal* empty, vain] —**'i·dle·ness** *n.* —**'i·dly** *adv.*

i·dle pul·ley *or* **i·dler pul·ley** *n.* a freely rotating pulley used to control the tension or direction of a belt. Also called: **idler.**

i·dler ('aɪdlə) *n.* **1.** a person who idles. **2.** another name for **idle pulley** or **idle wheel. 3.** *Nautical.* a ship's crew member, such as a carpenter, sailmaker, etc., whose duties do not include standing regular watches.

i·dle wheel *n.* a gearwheel interposed between two others to transmit torque without changing the direction of rotation or the velocity ratio. Also called: **idler.**

I.D.N. *abbrev. for* in Dei nomine. Also: **I.N.D.** [Latin: in the name of God]

I·do ('iːdəʊ) *n.* an artificial language; a modification of Esperanto. [C20: Ido: offspring, from Greek *-id* daughter of]

i·do·crase ('aɪdəˌkreɪs, 'ɪd-) *n.* another name for **vesuvianite.** [C19: from French, from Greek *eidos* form + *krasis* a mingling]

i·dol ('aɪdᵊl) *n.* **1.** a material object, esp. a carved image, that is worshipped as a god. **2.** *Christianity, Judaism.* any being (other than the one God) to which divine honour is paid. **3.** a person who is revered, admired, or highly loved. [C13: from Late Latin *īdōlum,* from Latin: image, from Greek *eidōlon,* from *eidos* shape, form]

i·dol·a·trize *or* **i·dol·a·trise** (aɪ'dɒləˌtraɪz) *vb.* **1.** (*tr.*) a less common word for **idolize. 2.** (*intr.*) to indulge in the worship of idols. —**i·'dol·a·ˌtriz·er** *or* **i·'dol·a·ˌtris·er** *n.*

i·dol·a·try (aɪ'dɒlətrɪ) *n.* **1.** the worship of idols. **2.** great devotion or reverence. —**i·'dol·a·ter** *n. or* **i·'dol·a·tress** *fem. n.* —**i·'dol·a·trous** *adj.* —**i·'dol·a·trous·ly** *adv.* —**i·'dol·a·trous·ness** *n.*

i·dol·ize *or* **i·dol·ise** ('aɪdəˌlaɪz) *vb.* **1.** (*tr.*) to admire or revere greatly. **2.** (*tr.*) to worship as an idol. **3.** (*intr.*) to worship idols. —**'i·dol·ism, ˌi·dol·i·'za·tion** *or* **ˌi·dol·i·'sa·tion** *n.* —**'i·dol·ist, 'i·dol·ˌiz·er** *or* **'i·dol·ˌis·er** *n.*

i·do+lum (ɪ'dəʊləm) *n.* **1.** a mental picture; idea. **2.** a false idea; fallacy. [C17: from Latin: IDOL]

I·dom+e·neus (aɪ'dɒmɪˌnjuːs) *n. Greek myth.* a king of Crete who fought on the Greek side in the Trojan War.

I·dun ('iːdʊn) *or* **I·thunn** *n. Norse myth.* the goddess of spring who guarded the apples that kept the gods eternally young; wife of Bragi.

id·yll *or U.S. (sometimes)* **id·yl** ('ɪdɪl) *n.* **1.** a poem or prose work describing an idealized rural life, pastoral scenes, etc. **2.** any simple narrative or descriptive piece in poetry or prose. **3.** a charming or picturesque scene or event. **4.** a piece of music with a calm or pastoral character. [C17: from Latin *īdyllium*, from Greek *eidullion*, from *eidos* shape, (literary) form]

i·dyl+lic (ɪ'dɪlɪk, aɪ-) *adj.* **1.** of or relating to an idyll. **2.** charming; picturesque. —**i·'dyl+li+cal+ly** *adv.*

i·dyl+list *or U.S.* **i·dyl+ist** ('ɪdɪlɪst) *n.* a writer of idylls.

IE *or* **I.E.** *abbrev. for* Indo-European (languages).

i.e. *abbrev. for* id est. [Latin: that is (to say); in other words]

-ie *suffix forming nouns.* variant of **-y**[2].

I.E.E. *abbrev. for* Institution of Electrical Engineers.

Ie·per ('iːpər) *n.* the Flemish name for **Ypres.**

-ier *suffix forming nouns.* variant of **-eer:** *brigadier.* [from Old English *-ere* -ER[1] or (in some words) from Old French *-ier*, from Latin *-ārius* -ARY]

I·e·ya·su (ˌiːjɛ'jɑːsuː) *n.* a variant spelling of (Tokugawa) **Iyeuasu.**

if (ɪf) *conj. (subordinating)* **1.** in case that, or on condition that: *if you try hard it might work; if he were poor, would you marry him?* **2.** used to introduce an indirect question. In this sense, *if* approaches the meaning of *whether.* **3.** even though: *an attractive if awkward girl.* **4. a.** used to introduce expressions of desire, with *only: if I had only known.* **b.** used to introduce exclamations of surprise, dismay, etc.: *if this doesn't top everything!* **5. as if.** as it would be if; as though: *he treats me as if I were junior to him.* ~*n.* **6.** an uncertainty or doubt: *the big if is whether our plan will work at all.* **7.** a condition or stipulation: *I won't have any ifs or buts.* [Old English *gif*; related to Old Saxon *ef* if, Old High German *iba* whether, if]

IF, I.F., *or* **i.f.** *Electronics. abbrev. for* intermediate frequency.

IFC *abbrev. for* International Finance Corporation.

I·fe ('iːfɪ) *n.* a town in W central Nigeria: one of the largest and oldest Yoruba towns; university (1961); centre of the cocoa trade. Pop.: 176 000 (1975 est.).

If·ni (*Spanish* 'ifni) *n.* a former Spanish province in S Morocco, on the Atlantic: returned to Morocco in 1969.

I.F.S. *abbrev. for* Irish Free State (now called Republic of Ireland).

-i·fy *suffix forming verbs.* variant of **-fy:** *intensify.* —**-i·fi·ca·tion** *suffix forming nouns.*

IG *or* **I.G.** *abbrev. for:* **1.** Indo-Germanic (languages). **2.** Inspector General.

Ig·bo ('iːbəʊ) *n., pl.* **+bo** *or* **+bos.** a variant spelling of **Ibo.**

Ig+dra+sil ('ɪgdrəsɪl) *n.* a variant spelling of **Yggdrasil.**

IGFET ('ɪgfɛt) *n.* insulated-gate field-effect transistor; a type of field-effect transistor having one or more semiconductor gate electrodes. Compare **JUGFET.**

ig+loo *or* **ig·lu** ('ɪgluː) *n., pl.* **+loos** *or* **·lus. 1.** a dome-shaped Eskimo house, usually built of blocks of solid snow. **2.** a hollow made by a seal in the snow over its breathing hole in the ice. [C19: from Eskimo *igdlu* house]

I.G.M. *Chess. abbrev. for* International Grandmaster.

ign. *abbrev. for:* **1.** ignites. **2.** ignition. **3.** ignotus. [Latin: unknown]

Ig·na·ti·us (ɪg'neɪʃɪəs) *n.* **Saint,** surnamed *Theophorus.* died ?110 A.D., bishop of Antioch. His seven letters, written on his way to his martyrdom in Rome, give valuable insight into the early Christian Church. Feast day: Feb. 1.

Ig·na·ti·us Loy·o·la (lɔɪ'əʊlə) *n.* **Saint.** 1491–1556, Spanish ecclesiastic. He founded the Society of Jesus (1534) and was its first general (1541–56). His *Spiritual Exercises* (1548) remains the basic manual for the training of Jesuits. Feast day: July 31.

ig+ne+ous ('ɪgnɪəs) *adj.* **1.** (of rocks) derived from magma or lava that has solidified on or below the earth's surface. Compare **sedimentary, metamorphic. 2.** of or relating to fire. [C17: from Latin *igneus* fiery, from *ignis* fire]

ig+nes+cent (ɪg'nɛsᵊnt) *adj.* **1.** giving off sparks when struck, as a flint. **2.** capable of bursting into flame. ~*n.* **3.** an ignescent substance. [C19: from Latin *ignescere* to become inflamed]

ig+nis fat+u·us ('ɪgnɪs 'fætjʊəs) *n., pl.* **ig+nes fat·u·i** ('ɪgniːz 'fætjʊˌaɪ). another name for **will-o'-the-wisp.** [C16: from Medieval Latin, literally: foolish fire]

ig+nite (ɪg'naɪt) *vb.* **1.** to catch fire or set fire to; burn or cause to burn. **2.** *(tr.) Chem.* to heat strongly. [C17: from Latin *ignīre* to set alight, from *ignis* fire] —**ig+'nit+a·ble** *or* **ig+'nit+i·ble** *adj.* —**ig+ˌnit+a·'bil+i·ty** *or* **ig+ˌnit+i·'bil+i·ty** *n.*

ig+nit+er (ɪg'naɪtə) *n.* **1.** a person or thing that ignites. **2.** a fuse to fire explosive charges. **3.** an electrical device for lighting a gas turbine. **4.** a subsidiary electrode in an ignitron.

ig+ni+tion (ɪg'nɪʃən) *n.* **1.** the act or process of initiating combustion. **2.** the process of igniting the fuel in an internal-combustion engine. **3.** (usually preceded by *the*) the devices used to ignite the fuel in an internal-combustion engine.

ig+ni+tion key *n.* the key used in a motor vehicle to turn the switch that connects the battery to the ignition system and other electrical devices.

ig+ni+tron (ɪg'naɪtrɒn, 'ɪgnɪˌtrɒn) *n.* a mercury-arc rectifier controlled by a subsidiary electrode, the igniter, partially immersed in a mercury cathode. A current passed between igniter and cathode forms a hot spot sufficient to strike an arc between cathode and anode. [C20: from IGNITER + ELECTRON]

ig+no+ble (ɪg'nəʊbᵊl) *adj.* **1.** dishonourable; base; despicable. **2.** of low birth or origins; humble; common. **3.** of low quality; inferior. **4.** *Falconry.* **a.** designating short-winged hawks that capture their quarry by swiftness and adroitness of flight. Compare **noble. b.** designating quarry which is inferior or unworthy of pursuit by a particular species of hawk or falcon. [C16: from Latin *ignōbilis*, from IN-[1] + Old Latin *gnōbilis* NOBLE] —**ˌig+no+'bil+i·ty** *or* **ig+'no+ble+ness** *n.* —**ig+'no+bly** *adv.*

ig+no+min·y ('ɪgnəˌmɪnɪ) *n., pl.* **+min·ies. 1.** disgrace or public shame; dishonour. **2.** a cause of disgrace; a shameful act. [C16: from Latin *ignōminia* disgrace, from *ig-* (see IN-[2]) + *nōmen* name, reputation] —**ˌig+no+'min·i+ous** *adj.* —**ˌig+no+'min·i+ous+ly** *adv.* —**ˌig+no+'min·i·ous+ness** *n.*

ig+no+ra+mus (ˌɪgnə'reɪməs) *n., pl.* **+mus·es.** an ignorant person; fool. [C16: from legal Latin, literally: we have no knowledge of, from Latin *ignōrāre* to be ignorant of; see IGNORE; modern usage originated from the use of *Ignoramus* as the name of an unlettered lawyer in a play by G. Ruggle, 17th-century English dramatist]

ig+no+rance ('ɪgnərəns) *n.* lack of knowledge, information, or education; the state of being ignorant.

ig+no+rant ('ɪgnərənt) *adj.* **1.** lacking in knowledge or education; unenlightened. **2.** *(postpositive;* often foll. by *of)* lacking in awareness or knowledge (of): *ignorant of the law.* **3.** resulting from or showing lack of knowledge or awareness: *an ignorant remark.* —**'ig+no+rant+ly** *adv.*

ig+no+ra+ti+o e·len+chi (ˌɪgnə'reɪʃɪəʊ ɪ'lɛŋkaɪ) *n. Logic.* the fallacy of supposing that an argument proves or disproves a proposition at issue when in fact it only establishes an irrelevant conclusion. [Latin: an ignoring of proof, translating Greek *elenchou agnoia*]

ig+nore (ɪg'nɔː) *vb. (tr.)* to fail or refuse to notice; disregard. [C17: from Latin *ignōrāre* not to know, from *ignārus* ignorant of, from *i-* IN-[1] + *gnārus* knowing; related to Latin *noscere* to know] —**ig+'nor+a·ble** *adj.* —**ig+'nor+er** *n.*

ig+no+tum per ig+no+ti+us *Latin.* (ɪg'nəʊtʊm pɜː ɪg'nəʊtɪʊs) *n.* an explanation that is obscurer than the thing to be explained. [literally: the unknown by means of the more unknown]

Ig·o·rot (ˌɪgə'rəʊt, ˌiːgə-) *or* **Ig+or+ro+te** (ˌɪgə'rəʊtɪ, ˌiːgə-) *n., pl.* **+rot, +rots** *or* **+ro+te, +ro+tes.** a member of a Negrito people of the mountains of N Luzon in the Philippines: noted as early exponents of mining.

I·graine (ɪ'greɪn) *or* **Y·gerne** *n.* the mother of King Arthur.

I·gua+çú *or* **I·guas+sú** (*Portuguese* ˌigwa'su) *n.* a river in SE South America, rising in S Brazil and flowing west to join the Paraná River, forming part of the border between Brazil and Argentina. Length: 1200 km (745 miles).

I·gua+çú Falls *n.* a waterfall on the border between Brazil and Argentina, on the Iguaçú River: divided into hundreds of separate falls by forested rocky islands. Width: about 4 km (2.5 miles). Height: 82 m (269 ft.).

i·gua+na (ɪ'gwɑːnə) *n.* **1.** either of two large tropical American arboreal herbivorous lizards of the genus *Iguana*, esp. *I. iguana* **(common iguana)**, having a greyish-green body with a row of spines along the back: family *Iguanidae.* **2.** Also called: **i·gua+nid** (ɪ'gwɑːnɪd). any other lizard of the tropical American family *Iguanidae.* [C16: from Spanish, from Arawak *iwana*] —**i·'gua+ni·an** *n., adj.*

i·guan·o·don (ɪ'gwɑːnəˌdɒn) *n.* a massive herbivorous long-tailed bipedal dinosaur of the genus *Iguanodon*, common in Europe and N Africa in Jurassic and Cretaceous times: suborder *Ornithopoda* (ornithopods). [C19: New Latin, from IGUANA + Greek *odōn* tooth]

I.G.Y. *abbrev. for* International Geophysical Year.

ih+ram (ɪ'rɑːm) *n.* the customary white robes worn by Muslim pilgrims to Mecca, symbolizing a sacred or consecrated state. [C18: from Arabic *ihrām*, from *harama* he forbade]

IHS the first three letters of the name Jesus in Greek (ΙΗΣΟΥΣ), often used as a Christian emblem.

IJs+sel ('aɪsᵊl; *Dutch* 'ɛjsəl) *n.* a river in the central Netherlands: a distributary of the Rhine, flowing north to the IJsselmeer. Length: 116 km (72 miles).

IJs+sel+meer *or* **Ys+sel+meer** (*Dutch* ˌɛjsəl'meːr) *n.* a shallow lake in the NW Netherlands; formed from the S part of the Zuider Zee by the construction of the **IJsselmeer Dam** in 1932; salt water gradually replaced by fresh water from the IJssel River; fisheries (formerly marine fish, now esp. eels). Area: (before reclamation) 3690 sq. km (1425 sq. miles). Estimated final area by 1980: 1243 sq. km (480 sq. miles). English name: **Ijssel Lake.**

i·kan ('iːkan) *n.* (in Malaysia) fish: used esp. in names of cooked dishes: *assam ikan.* [from Malay]

I·ka·rí·a (ˌika'ria) *n.* a transliteration of the modern Greek name for **Icaria.**

i·ke·ba·na (ˌiːkə'bɑːnə) *n.* the Japanese decorative art of flower arrangement.

I·ke+ja (ɪ'keɪjə) *n.* a town in SW Nigeria, capital of Lagos state: residential and industrial suburb of Lagos. Pop.: 11 500 (1973 est.).

Ikh·na·ton (ɪk'nɑːtən) *n.* a variant spelling of **Akhenaten.**

i·kon ('aɪkɒn) *n.* a variant spelling of **icon.**

IL *international car registration for* Israel.

il- *prefix.* variant of **in-**[1] and **in-**[2] before *l.*

i·lang-i·lang ('iːlæŋ 'iːlæŋ) *n.* a variant spelling of **ylang-ylang.**

-ile *suffix forming adjectives and nouns.* indicating capability, liability, or a relationship with something: *agile; fragile; juvenile.* [via French from Latin or directly from Latin *-ilis*]

ILEA (ˌɪlɪə) *or* **I.L.E.A.** *abbrev. for* Inner London Education Authority.

il+e·ac (ˈɪlɪˌæk) *or* **il+e·al** *adj.* **1.** *Anatomy.* of or relating to the ileum. **2.** *Pathol.* of or relating to ileus.

Île-de-France (*French* il də ˈfrɑ̃:s) *n.* **1.** a region of N France, in the Paris Basin: part of the duchy of France in the 10th century. **2.** a former name (1715–1810) for **Mauritius.**

Île du Dia+ble (il dy ˈdjabl) *n.* the French name for **Devil's Island.**

il+e·i+tis (ˌɪlɪˈaɪtɪs) *n.* inflammation of the ileum.

il·e·o- *or before a vowel* **il·e-** *combining form.* indicating the ileum: *ileostomy.*

il+e·os+to+my (ˌɪlɪˈɒstəmɪ) *n., pl.* **+mies.** the surgical formation of a permanent opening through the abdominal wall into the ileum.

Îles Co+mores (il kɔˈmɔ:r) *n.* the French name for the **Comoro Islands.**

Îles du Sa+lut (il dy saˈly) *n.* the French name for the **Safety Islands.**

I·le·sha (ɪˈleɪʃə) *n.* a town in W Nigeria. Pop.: 224 000 (1975 est.).

Îles sous le Vent (il su lə ˈvɑ̃) *n.* the French name for the **Leeward Islands** (sense 3).

il+e·um (ˈɪlɪəm) *n.* **1.** the part of the small intestine between the jejunum and the caecum. **2.** the corresponding part in insects. [C17: New Latin, from Latin *īlium, īleum* flank, groin, of obscure origin]

il+e·us (ˈɪlɪəs) *n.* obstruction of the intestine, esp. the ileum, by mechanical occlusion or as the result of distention of the bowel following loss of muscular action. [C18: from Latin *īleos* severe colic, from Greek *eileos* a rolling, twisting, from *eilein* to roll]

i·lex (ˈaɪlɛks) *n.* **1.** any of various trees or shrubs of the widely distributed genus *Ilex*, such as the holly and inkberry: family *Aquifoliaceae.* **2.** another name for the **holm oak.** [C16: from Latin]

Il·i·a (ˈɪlɪə) *n.* (in Roman legend) the daughter of Aeneas and Lavinia, who, according to some traditions, was the mother of Romulus and Remus. See also **Rhea Silvia.**

I·li·a (iˈlia) *n.* a transliteration of the modern Greek name for **Elia**[1].

il·i·ac (ˈɪlɪˌæk) *adj. Anatomy.* of or relating to the ilium.

Il·i·ad (ˈɪlɪəd) *n.* a Greek epic poem describing the siege of Troy, attributed to Homer and probably composed before 700 B.C. —**Il·i·ad·ic** (ˌɪlɪˈædɪk) *adj.*

Il·i+am+na (ˌɪlɪˈæmnə) *n.* **1.** a lake in SW Alaska: the largest lake in Alaska. Length: about 130 km (80 miles). Width: 40 km (25 miles). **2.** a volcano in SW Alaska, northwest of Iliamna Lake. Height: 3076 m (10 092 ft.).

I·li·gan (ɪˈli:gən) *n.* a city in the Philippines, a port on the N coast of Mindanao. Pop.: 129 454 (1975 est.).

Il·i·on (ˈɪlɪən) *n.* a transliteration of the Greek name for ancient **Troy.**

il+i·um (ˈɪlɪəm) *n., pl.* **·i·a** (-ɪə). the uppermost and widest of the three sections of the hipbone.

Il+i·um (ˈɪlɪəm) *n.* the Latin name for ancient **Troy.**

ilk (ɪlk) *n.* **1.** a type; class; sort (esp. in the phrase **of that, his, her,** etc., **ilk**): *people of that ilk should not be allowed here.* **2. of that ilk.** *Scot.* of the place of the same name: used to indicate that the person named is proprietor or laird of the place named: *Moncrieff of that ilk.* [Old English *ilca* the same family, same kind; related to Gothic *is* he, Latin *is*, Old English *gelīc* like]

Usage. Although the use of *ilk* in the sense of sense 1 is often condemned as being the result of a misunderstanding of the original Scottish expression *of that ilk*, it is nevertheless well established and generally acceptable.

Il+kes+ton (ˈɪlkɪstən) *n.* a town in N central England, in SE Derbyshire. Pop.: 34 123 (1971).

Il+kley (ˈɪlklɪ) *n.* a town in N England, in West Yorkshire: nearby is **Ilkley Moor** (to the south). Pop.: 21 828 (1971).

ill (ɪl) *adj.* **worse, worst. 1.** (*usually postpositive*) not in good health; sick. **2.** characterized by or intending evil, harm, etc.; hostile: *ill deeds.* **3.** causing or resulting in pain, harm, adversity, etc.: *ill effects.* **4.** ascribing or imputing evil to something referred to: *ill repute.* **5.** promising an unfavourable outcome; unpropitious: *an ill omen.* **6.** harsh; lacking kindness: *ill will.* **7.** not up to an acceptable standard; faulty: *ill manners.* **8. ill at ease.** unable to relax; uncomfortable. ~*n.* **9.** evil or harm: *to wish a person ill.* **10.** a mild disease. **11.** misfortune; trouble. ~*adv.* **12.** badly: *the title ill befits him.* **13.** with difficulty; hardly: *he can ill afford the money.* [C11 (in the sense: evil): from Old Norse *illr* bad]

ill. *abbrev. for:* **1.** illustrated. **2.** illustration.

Ill. *abbrev. for* Illinois.

I'll (aɪl) *contraction of* I will *or* I shall.

ill-ad·vised *adj.* **1.** acting without reasonable care or thought: *you would be ill-advised to sell your house now.* **2.** badly thought out; not or insufficiently considered: *an ill-advised plan of action.* —ˌ**ill-ad·ˈvis·ed·ly** *adv.*

ill-af·fect·ed *adj.* (often foll. by *towards*) not well disposed; disaffected.

I·llam+pu (*Spanish* iˈʎampu) *n.* one of the two peaks of Mount **Sorata.**

ill-as·sort·ed *adj.* badly matched; incompatible.

il+la·tion (ɪˈleɪʃən) *n.* a rare word for **inference.** [C16: from Late Latin *illātiō* a bringing in, from Latin *illātus* brought in, from *inferre* to bring in, from IN-[2] + *ferre* to bear, carry]

il+la·tive (ɪˈleɪtɪv) *adj.* **1.** of or relating to illation; inferential. **2.** *Grammar.* denoting a word or morpheme used to signal inference, for example *so* or *therefore.* **3.** (in the grammar of Finnish and other languages) denoting a case of nouns expressing a relation of motion or direction, usually translated by the English prepositions *into* or *towards.* Compare **elative.** ~*n.* **4.** *Grammar.* **a.** the illative case. **b.** an illative word or speech element. [C16: from Late Latin *illātīvus* inferring, concluding] —**il+ˈla·tive+ly** *adv.*

Il+la+war+ra (ˌɪləˈwɒrə) *n.* **1.** a coastal district of E Australia, in S New South Wales. **2.** an Australian breed of shorthorn dairy cattle noted for its high milk yield and ability to survive on poor pastures.

ill-be·haved *adj.* poorly behaved; lacking good manners.

ill-bred *adj.* badly brought up; lacking good manners. —ˌ**ill-ˈbreed·ing** *n.*

ill-con·sid·ered *adj.* done without due consideration; not thought out: *an ill-considered decision.*

ill-de·fined *adj.* badly defined; having no clear outline.

ill-dis·posed *adj.* (often foll. by *towards*) not kindly disposed.

Ille-et-Vi·laine (*French* il e viˈlɛn) *n.* a department of NW France, in E Brittany. Capital: Rennes. Pop.: 719 320 (1975). Area: 6992 sq. km (2727 sq. miles).

il+le·gal (ɪˈli:gᵊl) *adj.* **1.** forbidden by law; unlawful; illicit. **2.** unauthorized or prohibited by a code of official or accepted rules. —**il+ˈle·gal+ly** *adv.* —ˌ**il+le·ˈgal+i·ty** *n.*

il+le·gal+ize *or* **il+le·gal+ise** (ɪˈli:gəˌlaɪz) *vb.* (*tr.*) to make illegal. —**il+ˌle·gal·i·ˈza·tion** *or* **il+ˌle·gal·i·ˈsa·tion** *n.*

il+leg·i·ble (ɪˈlɛdʒɪbᵊl) *adj.* unable to be read or deciphered. —**il+ˌleg+i·ˈbil·i·ty** *or* **il+ˈleg+i·ble+ness** *n.* —**il+ˈleg+i·bly** *adv.*

il+le·git·i·mate (ˌɪlɪˈdʒɪtɪmɪt) *adj.* **1.** born of parents who were not married to each other at the time of birth; bastard. **2.** forbidden by law; illegal; unlawful. **3.** contrary to logic; incorrectly reasoned. ~*n.* **4.** an illegitimate person; bastard. —ˌ**il+le·ˈgit·i+ma·cy** *or* ˌ**il+le·ˈgit·i·mate+ness** *n.* —ˌ**il+le·ˈgit·i+mate+ly** *adv.*

ill-fat·ed *adj.* doomed or unlucky: *an ill-fated marriage.*

ill-fa·voured *or U.S.* **ill-fa·vored** *adj. Rare.* **1.** unattractive or repulsive in appearance; ugly. **2.** offensive, disagreeable, or objectionable. —ˌ**ill-ˈfa·voured+ly** *or U.S.* ˌ**ill-ˈfa·vored+ly** *adv.* —ˌ**ill-ˈfa·voured+ness** *or U.S.* ˌ**ill-ˈfa·vored+ness** *n.*

ill feel+ing *n.* hostile feeling; animosity.

ill-found·ed *adj.* not founded on true or reliable premisses; unsubstantiated: *an ill-founded rumour.*

ill-got·ten *adj.* obtained dishonestly or illegally (esp. in the phrase **ill-gotten gains**).

ill hu+mour *n.* a disagreeable or sullen mood; bad temper. —ˌ**ill-ˈhu·moured** *adj.* —ˌ**ill-ˈhu·moured+ly** *adv.*

il+lib+er+al (ɪˈlɪbərəl) *adj.* **1.** narrow-minded; prejudiced; bigoted; intolerant. **2.** not generous; mean. **3.** lacking in culture or refinement. —**il+ˌlib+er+ˈal+i·ty, il+ˈlib+er+al+ness,** *or* **il+ˈlib+er+al+ism** *n.* —**il+ˈlib+er+al+ly** *adv.*

Il·lich (ˈɪlɪtʃ) *n.* **I·van.** born 1926, U.S. teacher and writer, born in Austria: his books include *Deschooling Society* (1971) and *Medical Nemesis* (1975).

il+lic+it (ɪˈlɪsɪt) *adj.* **1.** another word for **illegal. 2.** not allowed or approved by common custom, rule, or standard: *illicit sexual relations.* —**il+ˈlic+it+ly** *adv.* —**il+ˈlic+it+ness** *n.*

I·lli+ma+ni (*Spanish* ˌijiˈmani) *n.* a mountain in W Bolivia, in the Andes near La Paz. Height: 6882 m (22 580 ft.).

il+lim+it+a·ble (ɪˈlɪmɪtəbᵊl) *adj.* limitless; boundless. —**il+ˌlim+it+a·ˈbil·i·ty** *or* **il+ˈlim+it+a·ble+ness** *n.* —**il+ˈlim+it+a·bly** *adv.*

il+lin+i·um (ɪˈlɪnɪəm) *n. Chem.* the former name for **promethium.** [C20: New Latin, from ILLINOIS + -IUM]

Il+li+nois (ˌɪlɪˈnɔɪ) *n.* **1.** a state of the N central U.S., in the Midwest: consists of level prairie crossed by the Illinois and Kaskaskia Rivers; mainly agricultural. Capital: Springfield. Pop.: 11 113 976 (1970). Area: 144 858 sq. km (55 930 sq. miles). Abbrevs.: **Ill.** or (with zip code) **IL 2.** a river in Illinois, flowing SW to the Mississippi. Length: 439 km (273 miles). —**Il+li+nois+an** (ˌɪlɪˈnɔɪən), **Il+li+noi·an** (ˌɪlɪˈnɔɪən), *or* **Il+li+nois+i·an** (ˌɪlɪˈnɔɪzɪən) *n., adj.*

il+liq+uid (ɪˈlɪkwɪd) *adj.* **1.** (of an asset) not easily convertible into cash. **2.** (of an enterprise, organization, etc.) deficient in liquid assets.

il+lit+er+ate (ɪˈlɪtərɪt) *adj.* **1.** unable to read and write. **2.** violating accepted standards in reading and writing: *an illiterate scrawl.* **3.** uneducated, ignorant, or uncultured: *scientifically illiterate.* ~*n.* **4.** an illiterate person. —**il+ˈlit+er·a·cy** *or* **il+ˈlit+er+ate+ness** *n.* —**il+ˈlit+er+ate+ly** *adv.*

ill-judged *adj.* rash; ill-advised.

ill-man+nered *adj.* having bad manners; rude; impolite. —ˌ**ill-ˈman+nered+ly** *adv.*

ill-na+tured *adj.* naturally unpleasant and mean. —ˌ**ill-ˈna+tured+ly** *adv.* —ˌ**ill-ˈna+tured+ness** *n.*

ill+ness (ˈɪlnɪs) *n.* **1.** a disease or indisposition; sickness. **2.** a state of ill health. **3.** *Obsolete.* wickedness.

il+loc·u+tion (ˌɪləˈkju:ʃən) *n. Philosophy.* an act performed by a speaker by virtue of uttering certain words, as for example the acts of promising or of threatening. See also **performative.** Compare **perlocution.** [C20: from IL- + LOCUTION] —ˌ**il+loˈcu+tion+ar·y** *adj.*

il+log·i·cal (ɪˈlɒdʒɪkᵊl) *adj.* **1.** characterized by lack of logic; senseless or unreasonable. **2.** disregarding logical principles. —**il+log·i·cal+i·ty** (ɪˌlɒdʒɪˈkælɪtɪ) *or* **il+ˈlog·i·cal+ness** *n.* —**il+ˈlog·i·cal+ly** *adv.*

ill-o·mened *adj.* doomed to be unlucky; ill-fated.

ill-sort·ed *adj.* badly arranged or matched; ill-assorted.
ill-starred *adj.* unlucky; unfortunate; ill-fated.
ill tem+per *n.* bad temper; irritability. —**ˌill-'tem·pered** *adj.* —**ˌill-'tem·pered+ly** *adv.*
ill-timed *adj.* occurring at or planned for an unsuitable time.
ill-treat *vb.* (*tr.*) to behave cruelly or harshly towards; misuse; maltreat. —**ˌill-'treat·ment** *n.*
il+lude (ɪ'lu:d) *vb. Literary.* to trick or deceive. [C15: from Latin *illūdere* to sport with, from *lūdus* game]
il+lume (ɪ'lu:m) *vb.* (*tr.*) a poetic word for **illuminate.** [C17: shortened from ILLUMINE]
il+lu+mi+nance (ɪ'lu:mɪnəns) *n.* the luminous flux incident on unit area of a surface. It is measured in lux. Symbol: E_v Sometimes called: **illumination.** Compare **irradiance.**
il+lu+mi+nant (ɪ'lu:mɪnənt) *n.* **1.** something that provides or gives off light. ~*adj.* **2.** giving off light; illuminating.
il+lu+mi+nate *vb.* (ɪ'lu:mɪˌneɪt). **1.** (*tr.*) to throw light in or into; light up: *to illuminate a room.* **2.** (*tr.*) to make easily understood; clarify. **3.** to adorn, decorate, or be decorated with lights. **4.** (*tr.*) to decorate (a letter, page, etc.) by the application of colours, gold, or silver. **5.** (*intr.*) to become lighted up. ~*adj.* (ɪ'lu:mɪnɪt, -ˌneɪt). **6.** *Archaic.* made clear or bright with light; illuminated. ~*n.* (ɪ'lu:mɪnɪt, -ˌneɪt). **7.** a person who has or claims to have special enlightenment. [C16: from Latin *illūmināre* to light up, from *lūmen* light] —**il+'lu+mi+ˌnat+ing+ly** *adv.* —**il+'lu+mi+na+tive** *adj.* —**il+'lu+mi+ˌna+tor** *n.*
il+lu+mi+na+ti (ɪˌlu:mɪ'nɑ:ti:) *pl. n., sing.* **+to** (-təʊ). a group of persons claiming exceptional enlightenment on some subject, esp. religion. [C16: from Latin, literally: the enlightened ones, from *illūmināre* to ILLUMINATE]
Il+lu+mi+na+ti (ɪˌlu:mɪ'nɑ:ti:) *pl. n., sing.* **+to** (-təʊ). **1.** any of several groups of illuminati, esp. in 18th-century France. **2.** a group of religious enthusiasts of 16th-century Spain who were persecuted by the Inquisition. **3.** a masonic sect founded in Bavaria in 1778 claiming that the illuminating grace of Christ resided in it alone. **4.** a rare name for the Rosicrucians.
il+lu+mi+na+tion (ɪˌlu:mɪ'neɪʃən) *n.* **1.** the act of illuminating or the state of being illuminated. **2.** a source of light. **3.** (*often pl.*) *Chiefly Brit.* a light or lights, esp. coloured lights, used as decoration in streets, parks, etc. **4.** spiritual or intellectual enlightenment; insight or understanding. **5.** the act of making understood; clarification. **6.** decoration in colours, gold, or silver used on some manuscripts or printed works. **7.** *Physics.* another name (not in technical usage) for **illuminance.** —**il+ˌlu+mi+'na+tion+al** *adj.*
il+lu+mine (ɪ'lu:mɪn) *vb.* a literary word for **illuminate.** [C14: from Latin *illūmināre* to make light; see ILLUMINATE] —**il+'lu+mi+na·ble** *adj.*
il+lu+mi+nism (ɪ'lu:mɪˌnɪzəm) *n.* **1.** belief in and advocation of special enlightenment. **2.** the tenets and principles of the Illuminati or of any of several religious or political movements initiated by them. —**il+'lu+mi+nist** *n.*
ill-use *vb.* ('ɪl'ju:z). **1.** to use badly or cruelly; abuse; maltreat. ~*n.* ('ɪl'ju:s), *also* **ill-us·age. 2.** harsh or cruel treatment; abuse.
il+lu+sion (ɪ'lu:ʒən) *n.* **1.** a false appearance or deceptive impression of reality: *the mirror gives an illusion of depth.* **2.** a false or misleading perception or belief; delusion: *he has the illusion that he is really clever.* **3.** *Psychol.* a perception that is not true to reality, having been altered subjectively in some way in the mind of the perceiver. See also **hallucination. 4.** a very fine gauze or tulle used for trimmings, veils, etc. [C14: from Latin *illūsiō* deceit, from *illūdere;* see ILLUDE] —**il+'lu+sion+ar·y** *or* **il+'lu+sion+al** *adj.* —**il+'lu+sioned** *adj.*
il+lu+sion+ism (ɪ'lu:ʒəˌnɪzəm) *n.* **1.** *Philosophy.* the doctrine that the external world exists only in illusory sense perceptions. **2.** the use of highly illusory effects in art or decoration, esp. the use of perspective in painting to create an impression of three-dimensional reality.
il+lu+sion+ist (ɪ'lu:ʒənɪst) *n.* **1.** a person given to illusions; visionary; dreamer. **2.** *Philosophy.* a person who believes in illusionism. **3.** an artist who practises illusionism. **4.** a conjuror; magician. —**il+ˌlu+sion+'is+tic** *adj.*
il+lu+so·ry (ɪ'lu:sərɪ) *or* **il+lu+sive** (ɪ'lu:sɪv) *adj.* producing, produced by, or based on illusion; deceptive or unreal. —**il+'lu+so+ri+ly** *or* **il+'lu+sive+ly** *adv.* —**il+'lu+so+ri+ness** *or* **il+'lu+sive+ness** *n.*
illust. *or* **illus.** *abbrev. for:* **1.** illustrated. **2.** illustration.
il+lus+trate ('ɪləˌstreɪt) *vb.* **1.** to clarify or explain by use of examples, analogy, etc. **2.** (*tr.*) to be an example or demonstration of. **3.** (*tr.*) to explain or decorate (a book, text, etc.) with pictures. **4.** (*tr.*) an archaic word for **enlighten.** [C16: from Latin *illustrāre* to make light, explain, from *lustrāre* to purify, brighten; see LUSTRUM] —**'il+lus+ˌtrat+a·ble** *adj.* —**'il+lus+ˌtra+tive** *adj.* —**'il+lus+ˌtra+tive+ly** *adv.* —**'il+lus+ˌtra+tor** *n.*
il+lus+tra+tion (ˌɪlə'streɪʃən) *n.* **1.** pictorial matter used to explain or decorate a text. **2.** an example or demonstration: *an illustration of his ability.* **3.** the act of illustrating or the state of being illustrated. —**ˌil+lus+'tra+tion+al** *adj.*
il+lus+tri+ous (ɪ'lʌstrɪəs) *adj.* **1.** of great renown; famous and distinguished. **2.** glorious or great: *illustrious deeds.* **3.** *Obsolete.* shining. [C16: from Latin *illustris* bright, distinguished, famous, from *illustrāre* to make light; see ILLUSTRATE] —**il+'lus+tri+ous+ly** *adv.* —**il+'lus+tri+ous+ness** *n.*
il+lu+vi+a+tion (ɪˌlu:vɪ'eɪʃən) *n.* the process by which a material (**illuvium**), which includes colloids and mineral salts, is washed down from one layer of soil to a lower layer. [C20: from Latin *illuviēs* dirt, mud, from IL- + *-luviēs,* from *lavere* to wash] —**il+'lu+vi·al** *adj.*
ill will *n.* hostile feeling; enmity; antagonism.
Il+lyr·i·a (ɪ'lɪərɪə) *n.* an ancient region of uncertain boundaries on the E shore of the Adriatic Sea, including parts of present-day Yugoslavia and Albania.
Il+lyr+i·an (ɪ'lɪərɪən) *n.* **1.** a member of the group of related Indo-European peoples who occupied Illyria from the late third millennium to the early first millennium B.C. **2.** the extinct and almost unrecorded language of these peoples: of uncertain relationship within the Indo-European family, but thought by some to be the ancestor of modern Albanian. ~*adj.* **3.** of, characteristic of, or relating to Illyria, its people, or their language.
Il+lyr·i+cum (ɪ'lɪərɪkəm) *n.* a Roman province founded after 168 B.C., based on the coastal area of Illyria.
Il+men ('ɪlmən) *n.* **Lake.** a lake in the NW Soviet Union, in the Novgorod Region: drains through the Volkhov River into Lake Ladoga. Area: between 780 sq. km (300 sq. miles) and 2200 sq. km (850 sq. miles), according to the season.
il+men+ite ('ɪlmɪˌnaɪt) *n.* a weakly magnetic black mineral consisting essentially of an iron titanium oxide in hexagonal crystalline form, occurring in metamorphic and plutonic rocks: a source of titanium and titanium dioxide. Formula: $FeTiO_3$. [C19: from *Ilmen,* mountain range in the southern Urals, Russia, + -ITE[1]]
I.L.O. *abbrev. for* International Labour Organisation.
I·lo·i+lo (ˌi:ləʊ'i:ləʊ) *n.* a port in the W central Philippines, on SE Panay Island. Pop.: 247 956 (1975 est.).
I·lor+in (ɪ'lɒrɪn) *n.* a city in W Nigeria, capital of Kwara state: agricultural trade centre. Pop.: 282 000 (1975 est.).
ILS *Aeronautics. abbrev. for* instrument landing system.
I.M. *abbrev. for:* **1.** Also: **i.m.** intramuscular. **2.** *Chess.* International Master.
I'm (aɪm) *n. contraction of* I am.
im- *prefix.* variant of **in-**[1] and **in-**[2] before *b, m,* and *p.*
im+age ('ɪmɪdʒ) *n.* **1.** a representation or likeness of a person or thing, esp. in sculpture. **2.** an optically formed reproduction of an object, such as one formed by a lens or mirror. **3.** a person or thing that resembles another closely; double or copy. **4.** a mental representation or picture; idea produced by the imagination. **5.** the personality presented to the public by a person: *a criminal charge is not good for a politician's image.* **6.** the pattern of light that is focused onto the retina of the eye. **7.** *Psychol.* the mental experience of something that is not immediately present to the senses, often involving memory. See also **imagery, body image, hypnagogic image. 8.** a personification of a specified quality; epitome: *the image of good breeding.* **9.** a mental picture or association of ideas evoked in a literary work, esp. in poetry. **10.** *Maths.* (of a point) the value of a function, f(*x*), corresponding to the point *x.* **11.** an obsolete word for **apparition.** ~*vb.* (*tr.*) *Rare.* **12.** to picture in the mind; imagine. **13.** to make or reflect an image of. **14.** to portray or describe. **15.** to be an example or epitome of; typify. [C13: from Old French *imagene,* from Latin *imāgō* copy, representation; related to Latin *imitārī* to IMITATE] —**'im+age+a·ble** *adj.* —**'im+age+less** *adj.*
im+age con+vert+er *or* **tube** *n.* a device for producing a visual image formed by electromagnetic radiation, esp. x-rays or infrared radiation.
im+age in+ten+si+fi+er *n.* a device used in fluoroscopy containing a screen from which electrons are released by an x-ray beam. The electrons are focused onto a fluorescent screen to form a smaller brighter image than would have been produced by the x-ray beam.
im+age or+thi+con *n.* a television camera tube in which electrons, emitted from a photoemissive surface in proportion to the intensity of the incident light, are focused onto the target causing secondary emission of electrons. Sometimes shortened to **orthicon.**
im+age+ry ('ɪmɪdʒrɪ, -dʒərɪ) *n., pl.* **+ries. 1.** descriptive language in a literary work, esp. that appealing to the senses. **2.** images collectively. **3.** *Psychol.* **a.** the materials or general processes of the imagination. **b.** the characteristic kind of mental images formed by a particular individual. See also **image** (sense 7), **imagination** (sense 1)
im+ag·i+nal (ɪ'mædʒɪnəl) *adj.* **1.** of, relating to, or resembling an imago. **2.** of or relating to an image.
im+ag·i+nar·y (ɪ'mædʒɪnərɪ, -dʒɪnrɪ) *adj.* **1.** existing in the imagination; unreal; illusory. **2.** *Maths.* involving or containing imaginary numbers. The imaginary part of a complex number, *z,* is usually written Imz. —**im+'ag·i+nar+i+ly** *adv.* —**im+'ag·i+nar+i+ness** *n.*
im+ag·i+nar·y num+ber *n.* any complex number of the form $a + bi$, where *b* is not zero and $i = \sqrt{-1}$.
im+ag·i+nar·y part *n.* the coefficient *b* in a complex number $a + ib$, where $i = \sqrt{-1}$.
im+ag·i+na+tion (ɪˌmædʒɪ'neɪʃən) *n.* **1.** the faculty or action of producing mental images of what is not present or has not been experienced. **2.** mental creative ability. **3.** the ability to deal resourcefully with unexpected or unusual problems, circumstances, etc. **4.** (in romantic literary criticism, esp. that of S. T. Coleridge) a creative act of perception that joins passive and active elements in thinking and imposes unity on the poetic material. Compare **fancy** (sense 9). —**im+ˌag·i+'na+tion+al** *adj.*
im+ag·i+na+tive (ɪ'mædʒɪnətɪv) *adj.* **1.** produced by or indicative of a vivid or creative imagination: *an imaginative story.* **2.**

having a vivid imagination. —**im+'ag·i+na+tive+ly** *adv.* —**im+'ag·i+na+tive+ness** *n.*

im+ag+ine (ɪ'mædʒɪn) *vb.* **1.** (when *tr., may take a clause as object*) to form a mental image of. **2.** (when *tr., may take a clause as object*) to think, believe, or guess. **3.** (*tr.; takes a clause as object*) to suppose; assume: *I imagine he'll come.* **4.** an archaic word for **plot**[1]. [C14: from Latin *imāginārī* to fancy, picture mentally, from *imāgō* likeness; see IMAGE] —**im+'ag·i+na·ble** *adj.* —**im+'ag·i+na·bly** *adv.* —**im+'ag+in+er** *n.*

im+ag+ism ('ɪmɪˌdʒɪzəm) *n.* a poetic movement in England and America between 1912 and 1917, initiated chiefly by Ezra Pound, advocating the use of ordinary speech and the precise presentation of images. —**'im+ag+ist** *n., adj.* —**ˌim+ag+'is+tic** *adj.* —**ˌim+ag+'is+ti+cal+ly** *adv.*

i·ma+go (ɪ'meɪgəʊ) *n., pl.* **i·ma+goes** *or* **i·ma+gi+nes** (ɪ'mædʒəˌni:z). **1.** an adult sexually mature insect produced after metamorphosis. **2.** *Psychoanal.* an idealized image of another person, usually a parent, acquired in childhood and carried in the unconscious in later life. [C18: New Latin, from Latin: likeness; see IMAGE]

i·mam (ɪ'mɑ:m) *or* **i·maum** (ɪ'mɑ:m, ɪ'mɔ:m) *n. Islam.* **1.** a leader of congregational prayer in a mosque. **2.** a caliph, as leader of a Muslim community. **3.** an honorific title applied to eminent doctors of Islam, such as the founders of the orthodox schools. **4.** any of a succession of either seven or twelve religious leaders of the Shiites, regarded by their followers as divinely inspired. [C17: from Arabic: leader, from *amma* he guided]

i·mam+ate (ɪ'mɑ:meɪt) *n. Islam.* **1.** the region or territory governed by an imam. **2.** the office, rank, or period of office of an imam.

I.Mar.E. *abbrev. for* Institute of Marine Engineers.

i·ma+ret (ɪ'mɑ:rɛt) *n.* (in Turkey) a hospice for pilgrims or travellers. [C17: from Turkish, from Arabic *'imārah* hospice, building, from *amara* he built]

im+bal+ance (ɪm'bæləns) *n.* a lack of balance, as in emphasis, proportion, etc.: *the political imbalance of the programme.*

im+be·cile ('ɪmbɪˌsi:l, -ˌsaɪl) *n.* **1.** *Psychol.* a person of very low intelligence (I.Q. of 25 to 50), usually capable only of guarding himself against danger and of performing simple mechanical tasks under supervision. **2.** *Informal.* an extremely stupid person; dolt. ~*adj. also* **im+be·cil+ic** (ˌɪmbɪ'sɪlɪk). **3.** of or like an imbecile; mentally deficient; feeble-minded. **4.** stupid or senseless: *an imbecile thing to do.* [C16: from Latin *imbēcillus* feeble (physically or mentally)] —**'im+be·ˌcile+ly** *or* **ˌim+be·'cil+ic+al·ly** *adv.* —**ˌim+be·'cil+i·ty** *n.*

im+bed (ɪm'bɛd) *vb.* **+beds, +bed+ding, +bed+ded.** a less common spelling of **embed.** —**im+'bed+ment** *n.*

im+bibe (ɪm'baɪb) *vb.* **1.** to drink (esp. alcoholic drinks). **2.** *Literary.* to take in or assimilate (ideas, facts, etc.): *to imbibe the spirit of the Renaissance.* **3.** (*tr.*) to take in as if by drinking: *to imbibe fresh air.* **4.** to absorb or cause to absorb liquid or moisture; assimilate or saturate. [C14: from Latin *imbibere,* from *bibere* to drink] —**im+'bib+er** *n.*

im+bi+bi+tion (ˌɪmbɪ'bɪʃən) *n.* **1.** *Chem.* the absorption or adsorption of a liquid by a gel or solid. **2.** *Photog.* the absorption of dyes by gelatin, used in some colour printing processes. **3.** *Obsolete.* the act of imbibing.

im+bri+cate *adj.* ('ɪmbrɪkɪt, -ˌkeɪt), *also* **im+bri+cat+ed. 1.** *Architect.* relating to or having tiles, shingles, or slates that overlap. **2.** *Botany.* (of leaves, scales, etc.) overlapping each other. ~*vb.* ('ɪmbrɪˌkeɪt). **3.** (*tr.*) to decorate with a repeating pattern resembling scales or overlapping tiles. [C17: from Latin *imbricāre* to cover with overlapping tiles, from *imbrex* pantile] —**'im+bri+cate+ly** *adv.* —**ˌim+bri+'ca+tion** *n.*

im+bro+gli·o (ɪm'brəʊlɪˌəʊ) *n., pl.* **+gli·os. 1.** a confused or perplexing political or interpersonal situation. **2.** *Obsolete.* a confused heap; jumble. [C18: from Italian, from *imbrogliare* to confuse, EMBROIL]

Im+bros ('ɪmbrəs) *n.* a Turkish island in the NE Aegean Sea, west of the Gallipoli Peninsula: occupied by Greece (1912–14) and Britain (1914–23). Area: 280 sq. km (108 sq. miles). Turkish name: **Imroz.**

im+brue *or* **em+brue** (ɪm'bru:) *vb.* **+brues, +bru+ing, +brued.** (*tr.*) *Rare.* **1.** to stain, esp. with blood. **2.** to permeate or impregnate. [C15: from Old French *embreuver,* from Latin *imbibere* IMBIBE] —**im+'brue+ment** *or* **em+'brue+ment** *n.*

im+bue (ɪm'bju:) *vb.* **+bues, +bu+ing, +bued.** (*tr.;* usually foll. by *with*) **1.** to instil or inspire (with ideals, principles, etc.): *his sermons were imbued with the spirit of the Reformation.* **2.** *Rare.* to soak, esp. with moisture, dye, etc. [C16: from Latin *imbuere* to stain, accustom] —**im+'bue+ment** *n.*

I. Mech. E. *abbrev. for* Institution of Mechanical Engineers.

IMF *abbrev. for* International Monetary Fund.

im+id+az+ole (ˌɪmɪd'æzəʊl, -ɪdə'zəʊl) *n.* **1.** Also called: **glyoxaline, iminazole.** a white crystalline basic heterocyclic compound; 1,3-diazole. Formula: $C_3H_4N_2$. **2.** any substituted derivative of this compound. [C19: from IMIDE + AZOLE]

im+ide ('ɪmaɪd) *n.* any of a class of organic compounds whose molecules contain the divalent group -CONHCO-. [C19: alteration of AMIDE] —**im+id+ic** (ɪ'mɪdɪk) *adj.*

i·mine (ɪ'mi:n, 'ɪmi:n) *n.* any of a class of organic compounds in which a nitrogen atom is bound to one hydrogen atom and to two alkyl or aryl groups. They contain the divalent group NH. [C19: alteration of AMINE]

I. Min. E. *abbrev. for* Institution of Mining Engineers.

i·mi+no·u+re·a (ɪˌmi:nəʊjʊə'rɪə) *n.* another name for **guanidine.**

imit. *abbrev. for:* **1.** imitation. **2.** imitative.

im·i+tate ('ɪmɪˌteɪt) *vb.* (*tr.*) **1.** to try to follow the manner, style, character, etc., of or take as a model: *many writers imitated the language of Shakespeare.* **2.** to pretend to be or to impersonate, esp. for humour; mimic. **3.** to make a copy or reproduction of; duplicate; counterfeit. **4.** to make or be like; resemble or simulate: *her achievements in politics imitated her earlier successes in business.* [C16: from Latin *imitārī;* see IMAGE] —**im·i·ta·ble** ('ɪmɪtəb°l) *adj.* —**ˌim·i·ta·'bil+i·ty** *or* **'im·i·ta·ble+ness** *n.* —**'im·i+ˌta+tor** *n.*

im·i+ta+tion (ˌɪmɪ'teɪʃən) *n.* **1.** the act, practice, or art of imitating; mimicry. **2.** an instance or product of imitating, such as a copy of the manner of a person; impression. **3. a.** a copy or reproduction of a genuine article; counterfeit. **b.** (*as modifier*): *imitation jewellery.* **4.** (in contrapuntal or polyphonic music) the repetition of a phrase or figure in one part after its appearance in another, as in a fugue. **5.** a literary composition that adapts the style of an older work to the writer's own purposes. —**ˌim·i+'ta+tion+al** *adj.*

im·i+ta+tive ('ɪmɪtətɪv) *adj.* **1.** imitating or tending to imitate or copy. **2.** characterized by imitation. **3.** copying or reproducing the features of an original, esp. in an inferior manner: *imitative painting.* **4.** another word for **onomatopoeic.** —**'im·i+ta+tive+ly** *adv.* —**'im·i+ta+tive+ness** *n.*

I·mit+tós (ˌimi'tɔs) *n.* a transliteration of the modern Greek name for **Hymettus.**

im+mac·u+late (ɪ'mækjʊlɪt) *adj.* **1.** completely clean; extremely tidy: *his clothes were immaculate.* **2.** completely flawless, etc.: *an immaculate rendering of the symphony.* **3.** morally pure; free from sin or corruption. **4.** *Biology.* of only one colour, with no spots or markings. [C15: from Latin *immaculātus,* from IM- (not) + *macula* blemish] —**im+'mac·u+la+cy** *or* **im+'mac·u+late+ness** *n.* —**im+'mac·u+late+ly** *adv.*

Im+mac·u+late Con+cep+tion *n. Theol., R.C. Church.* the doctrine that the Virgin Mary was conceived without any stain of original sin.

im+ma+nent ('ɪmənənt) *adj.* **1.** existing, operating, or remaining within; inherent. **2.** *Philosophy.* (of a mental act) occurring entirely within the mind. Compare **transeunt. 3.** (of God) present throughout the universe. [C16: from Latin *immanēre* to remain in, from IM- (in) + *manēre* to stay] —**'im+ma+nence** *or* **'im+ma+nen+cy** *n.* —**'im+ma+nent+ly** *adv.*

im+ma+nent+ism ('ɪmənənˌtɪzəm) *n.* belief in the immanence of God. —**'im+ma+nent+ist** *n.*

Im+man·u·el *or* **Em+man·u·el** (ɪ'mænjʊəl) *n. Bible.* the child whose birth was foretold by Isaiah (Isaiah 7:14) and who in Christian tradition is identified with Jesus. [from Hebrew *'immānū'el,* literally: God with us]

im+ma·te·ri·al (ˌɪmə'tɪərɪəl) *adj.* **1.** of no real importance; inconsequential. **2.** not formed of matter; incorporeal; spiritual. —**ˌim+ma+ˌte·ri+'al+i·ty** *or* **ˌim+ma+'te·ri+al+ness** *n.* —**ˌim+ma+'te·ri+al+ly** *adv.*

im+ma·te·ri·al+ism (ˌɪmə'tɪərɪəˌlɪzəm) *n. Philosophy.* **1.** the doctrine that the material world exists only in the mind. **2.** the doctrine that only immaterial substances or spiritual beings exist. —**ˌim+ma+'te·ri+al+ist** *n.*

im+ma·te·ri·al+ize *or* **im+ma·te·ri·al+ise** (ˌɪmə'tɪərɪəˌlaɪz) *vb.* (*tr.*) to make immaterial.

im+ma+ture (ˌɪmə'tjʊə, -'tʃʊə) *adj.* **1.** not fully grown or developed. **2.** deficient in maturity; lacking wisdom, insight, emotional stability, etc. **3.** *Geography.* a less common term for **youthful** (sense 4). —**ˌim+ma+'tu+ri+ty** *or* **ˌim+ma+'ture+ness** *n.* —**ˌim+ma+'ture+ly** *adv.*

im+meas+ur+a·ble (ɪ'mɛʒərəb°l) *adj.* incapable of being measured, esp. by virtue of great size; limitless. —**im+ˌmeas+ur+a·'bil+i·ty** *or* **im+'meas+ur+a·ble+ness** *n.* —**im+'meas+ur+a·bly** *adv.*

im+me·di·ate (ɪ'mi:dɪət) *adj.* (*usually prenominal*) **1.** taking place or accomplished without delay: *an immediate reaction.* **2.** closest or most direct in effect or relationship: *the immediate cause of his downfall.* **3.** having no intervening medium; direct in effect: *an immediate influence.* **4.** contiguous in space, time, or relationship: *our immediate neighbour.* **5.** *Philosophy.* of or relating to an object or concept that is directly known or intuited. [C16: from Medieval Latin *immediātus,* from Latin IM- (not) + *mediāre* to be in the middle; see MEDIATE] —**im+'me·di·a·cy** *or* **im+'me·di·ate+ness** *n.*

im+me·di·ate an+nu+i·ty *n.* an annuity that starts less than a year after its purchase. Compare **deferred annuity.**

im+me·di·ate con+stit·u+ent *n.* a constituent of a linguistic construction at the first step in an analysis; for example, the immediate constituents of a sentence are the subject and the predicate.

im+me·di·ate+ly (ɪ'mi:dɪətlɪ) *adv.* **1.** without delay or intervention; at once; instantly: *it happened immediately.* **2.** very closely or directly: *this immediately concerns you.* **3.** near or close by: *he's somewhere immediately in this area.* ~*conj.* **4.** (*subordinating*) *Chiefly Brit.* at the same time as; as soon as: *immediately he opened the door, there was a gust of wind.*

im+med·i+ca·ble (ɪ'mɛdɪkəb°l) *adj.* (of wounds) unresponsive to treatment. —**im+'med·i+ca·ble+ness** *n.* —**im+'med·i+ca·bly** *adv.*

Im·mel·mann turn *or* **Im·mel·mann** ('ɪməlˌmɑ:n, -mən) *n.* an aircraft manoeuvre used to gain height while reversing the direction of flight. It consists of a half loop followed by a half roll. [C20: named after Max *Immelmann* (1890–1916), German aviator]

im+me·mo·ri·al (ˌɪmɪ'mɔ:rɪəl) *adj.* originating in the distant past; ancient (postpositive in the phrase **time immemorial**). [C17: from Medieval Latin *immemoriālis,* from Latin IM- (not) + *memoria* MEMORY] —**ˌim+me+'mo+ri+al+ly** *adv.*

im+mense (ɪ'mɛns) *adj.* **1.** unusually large; huge; vast. **2.**

without limits; immeasurable. 3. *Informal.* very good; excellent. [C15: from Latin *immensus*, literally: unmeasured, from IM- (not) + *mensus* measured, from *mētīrī* to measure] —**im'mense·ly** *adv.* —**im'mense·ness** *n.*

im·men·si·ty (ɪ'mɛnsɪtɪ) *n., pl.* **·ties.** 1. the state or quality of being immense; vastness; enormity. 2. enormous expanse, distance, or volume: *the immensity of space.* 3. *Informal.* a huge amount: *an immensity of wealth.*

im·men·su·ra·ble (ɪ'mɛnʃərəbᵊl) *adj.* a less common word for **immeasurable.**

im·merge (ɪ'mɜːdʒ) *vb.* an archaic word for **immerse.** [C17: from Latin *immergere* to IMMERSE] —**im'mer·gence** *n.*

im·merse (ɪ'mɜːs) *vb.* (*tr.*) 1. (often foll. by *in*) to plunge or dip into liquid. 2. (*often passive*; often foll. by *in*) to involve deeply; engross: *to immerse oneself in a problem.* 3. to baptize by immersion. [C17: from Latin *immergere*, from IM- (in) + *mergere* to dip] —**im'mers·i·ble** *adj.*

im·mersed (ɪ'mɜːst) *adj.* 1. sunk or submerged. 2. (of plants) growing completely submerged in water. 3. (of a plant or animal organ) embedded in another organ or part.

im·mer·sion (ɪ'mɜːʃən) *n.* 1. a form of baptism in which part or the whole of a person's body is submerged in the water. 2. Also called: **ingress.** *Astronomy.* the disappearance of a celestial body prior to an eclipse or occultation. 3. the act of immersing or state of being immersed.

im·mer·sion heat·er *n.* an electrical device, usually thermostatically controlled, for heating the liquid in which it is immersed.

im·mer·sion·ism (ɪ'mɜːʃəˌnɪzəm) *n.* the doctrine that immersion is the only true and valid form of Christian baptism. —**im'mer·sion·ist** *n.*

im·mesh (ɪ'mɛʃ) *vb.* a variant spelling of **enmesh.**

im·me·thod·i·cal (ˌɪmɪ'θɒdɪkᵊl) *adj.* lacking in method or planning; disorganized. —**ˌim·me'thod·i·cal·ly** *adv.* —**ˌim·me'thod·i·cal·ness** *n.*

im·mi·grant ('ɪmɪgrənt) *n.* 1. a. a person who immigrates. Compare **emigrant.** b. (*as modifier*): *an immigrant community.* 2. *Brit.* a person who has been settled in a country of which he is not a native for less than ten years. 3. an animal or plant that lives or grows in a region to which it has recently migrated.

im·mi·grate ('ɪmɪˌgreɪt) *vb.* 1. (*intr.*) to come to a place or country of which one is not a native in order to settle there. Compare **emigrate.** 2. (*intr.*) (of an animal or plant) to migrate to a new geographical area. 3. (*tr.*) to introduce or bring in as an immigrant. [C17: from Latin *immigrāre* to go into, from IM- + *migrāre* to move] —**ˌim·mi'gra·tion** *n.* —**ˌim·mi'gra·tion·al** *or* **'im·mi·ˌgra·to·ry** *adj.* —**'im·mi·ˌgra·tor** *n.*

im·mi·nent ('ɪmɪnənt) *adj.* 1. liable to happen soon; impending. 2. *Obsolete.* jutting out or overhanging. [C16: from Latin *imminēre* to project over, from IM- (in) + *-minēre* to project; related to *mons* mountain] —**'im·mi·nence** *or* **'im·mi·nent·ness** *n.* —**'im·mi·nent·ly** *adv.*

Im·ming·ham ('ɪmɪŋəm) *n.* a port in N England, in Humberside: docks opened in 1912, principally for the exporting of coal; now handles chiefly bulk materials, esp. imported iron ore. Pop.: 10 259 (1971).

im·min·gle (ɪ'mɪŋgᵊl) *vb. Archaic.* to blend or mix together; intermingle.

im·mis·ci·ble (ɪ'mɪsɪbᵊl) *adj.* (of two or more liquids) incapable of being mixed to form a homogeneous substance: *oil and water are immiscible.* —**im·ˌmis·ci'bil·i·ty** *n.* —**im'mis·ci·bly** *adv.*

im·mit·i·ga·ble (ɪ'mɪtɪgəbᵊl) *adj. Rare.* unable to be mitigated; relentless; unappeasable. —**im'mit·i·ga·bly** *adv.* —**im·ˌmit·i·ga'bil·i·ty** *n.*

im·mix (ɪ'mɪks) *vb.* (*tr.*) *Archaic.* to mix in; commix. —**im'mix·ture** *n.*

im·mo·bile (ɪ'məʊbaɪl) *adj.* 1. not moving; motionless. 2. not able to move or be moved; fixed. —**im·mo·bil·i·ty** (ˌɪməʊ'bɪlɪtɪ) *n.*

im·mo·bil·ism (ɪ'məʊbɪˌlɪzəm) *n.* a strongly reactionary political policy.

im·mo·bi·lize *or* **im·mo·bi·lise** (ɪ'məʊbɪˌlaɪz) *vb.* (*tr.*) 1. to make or become immobile: *to immobilize a car.* 2. *Finance.* a. to remove (specie) from circulation and hold it as a reserve. b. to convert (circulating capital) into fixed capital. —**im·ˌmo·bi·li'za·tion** *or* **im·ˌmo·bi·li'sa·tion** *n.* —**im'mo·bi·ˌliz·er** *or* **im'mo·bi·ˌlis·er** *n.*

im·mo·der·ate (ɪ'mɒdərɪt, ɪ'mɒdrɪt) *adj.* 1. lacking in moderation; excessive: *immoderate demands.* 2. *Obsolete.* venial; intemperate: *immoderate habits.* —**im'mod·er·ate·ly** *adv.* —**im·ˌmod·er'a·tion** *or* **im'mod·er·ate·ness** *n.*

im·mod·est (ɪ'mɒdɪst) *adj.* 1. indecent, esp. with regard to sexual propriety; improper. 2. bold, impudent, or shameless. —**im'mod·est·ly** *adv.* —**im'mod·es·ty** *n.*

im·mo·late ('ɪməʊˌleɪt) *vb.* (*tr.*) 1. to kill or offer as a sacrifice. 2. *Literary.* to sacrifice (something highly valued). [C16: from Latin *immolāre* to sprinkle an offering with sacrificial meal, sacrifice, from IM- (in) + *mola* spelt grain; see MILL[1]] —**ˌim·mo'la·tion** *n.* —**'im·mo·ˌla·tor** *n.*

im·mor·al (ɪ'mɒrəl) *adj.* 1. transgressing accepted moral rules; corrupt. 2. sexually dissolute; profligate or promiscuous. 3. unscrupulous or unethical: *immoral trading.* 4. tending to corrupt or resulting from corruption: *an immoral film; immoral earnings.* —**im'mor·al·ly** *adv.*

im·mor·al·ist (ɪ'mɒrəlɪst) *n.* a person who advocates or practises immorality.

im·mo·ral·i·ty (ˌɪmə'rælɪtɪ) *n., pl.* **·ties.** 1. the quality, character, or state of being immoral. 2. immoral behaviour, esp. in sexual matters; licentiousness; profligacy or promiscuity. 3. an immoral act.

im·mor·tal (ɪ'mɔːtᵊl) *adj.* 1. not subject to death or decay; having perpetual life. 2. having everlasting fame; remembered throughout time. 3. everlasting; perpetual; constant. 4. of or relating to immortal beings or concepts. ~*n.* 5. an immortal being. 6. (*often pl.*) a person who is remembered enduringly, esp. an author: *Dante is one of the immortals.* —**ˌim·mor'tal·i·ty** *n.* —**im'mor·tal·ly** *adv.*

im·mor·tal·ize *or* **im·mor·tal·ise** (ɪ'mɔːtəˌlaɪz) *vb.* (*tr.*) 1. to give everlasting fame to, as by treating in a literary work: *Macbeth was immortalized by Shakespeare.* 2. to give immortality to. —**im·ˌmor·tal·i'za·tion** *or* **im·ˌmor·tal·i'sa·tion** *n.* —**im'mor·tal·ˌiz·er** *or* **im'mor·tal·ˌis·er** *n.*

Im·mor·tals (ɪ'mɔːtᵊlz) *pl. n.* 1. (*sometimes not cap.*) the gods of ancient Greece and Rome. 2. (in ancient Persia) the royal bodyguard or a larger elite unit of 10 000 men. 3. the members of the French Academy.

im·mor·telle (ˌɪmɔː'tɛl) *n.* any of various plants, mostly of the family *Compositae* (composites), that retain their colour when dried, esp. *Xeranthemum annuum.* Also called: **everlasting, everlasting flower.** [C19: from French (*fleur*) *immortelle* everlasting (flower)]

im·mo·tile (ɪ'məʊtaɪl) *adj.* (esp. of living organisms or their parts) not motile. —**im·mo·til·i·ty** (ˌɪməʊ'tɪlɪtɪ) *n.*

im·mov·a·ble *or* **im·move·a·ble** (ɪ'muːvəbᵊl) *adj.* 1. unable to move or be moved; fixed; immobile. 2. unable to be diverted from one's intentions; steadfast. 3. unaffected by feeling; impassive. 4. unchanging; unalterable. 5. (of feasts, holidays, etc.) occurring on the same date every year. 6. *Law.* a. (of property) not liable to be removed; fixed. b. of or relating to immoveables. Compare **movable.** —**im·ˌmov·a'bil·i·ty**, **im·ˌmove·a'bil·i·ty** *or* **im'mov·a·ble·ness**, **im'move·a·ble·ness** *n.* —**im'mov·a·bly** *or* **im'move·a·bly** *adv.*

im·move·a·bles (ɪ'muːvəbᵊlz) *pl. n.* (in most foreign legal systems) real property. Compare **moveables.**

im·mune (ɪ'mjuːn) *adj.* 1. protected against a specific disease by inoculation or as the result of innate or acquired resistance. 2. relating to or conferring immunity: *an immune body* (see **antibody**). 3. (*usually postpositive*; foll. by *to*) unsusceptible (to) or secure (against): *immune to inflation.* 4. exempt from obligation, penalty, etc. ~*n.* 5. an immune person or animal. [C15: from Latin *immūnis* exempt from a public service, from IM- (not) + *mūnus* duty]

im·mu·ni·ty (ɪ'mjuːnɪtɪ) *n., pl.* **·ties.** 1. the ability of an organism to resist disease, as by producing its own antibodies or as a result of inoculation. 2. freedom from obligation or duty, esp. exemption from tax, duty, legal liability, etc. 3. any special privilege granting immunity. 4. the exemption of ecclesiastical persons or property from various civil obligations or liabilities.

im·mu·nize *or* **im·mu·nise** ('ɪmjʊˌnaɪz) *vb.* to make immune, esp. by inoculation. —**ˌim·mu·ni'za·tion** *or* **ˌim·mu·ni'sa·tion** *n.* —**'im·mu·ˌniz·er** *or* **'im·mu·ˌnis·er** *n.*

im·mu·no- *or before a vowel* **im·mun-** *combining form.* indicating immunity or immune: *immunology.*

im·mu·no·as·say (ˌɪmjʊnəʊ'æseɪ) *n. Immunol.* a technique of identifying a substance, esp. a protein, through its action as an antigen.

im·mu·no·chem·is·try (ˌɪmjʊnəʊ'kɛmɪstrɪ) *n.* the study of the chemical reactions of immunity.

im·mu·no·ge·net·ics (ˌɪmjʊnəʊdʒɪ'nɛtɪks) *n.* (*functioning as sing.*) the study of the relationship between immunity and genetics. —**ˌim·mu·no·ge'net·ic** *or* **ˌim·mu·no·ge'net·i·cal** *adj.*

im·mu·no·gen·ic (ˌɪmjʊnəʊ'dʒɛnɪk) *adj.* causing or producing immunity. —**ˌim·mu·no'gen·i·cal·ly** *adv.*

im·mu·no·glob·u·lin (ˌɪmjʊnəʊ'glɒbjʊlɪn) *n.* any of five classes of proteins, all of which show antibody activity. The most abundant ones are **immunoglobulin G (IgG)** and **immunoglobulin A (IgA).**

im·mu·nol·o·gy (ˌɪmjʊ'nɒlədʒɪ) *n.* the branch of biological science concerned with the study of immunity. —**im·mu·no·log·ic** (ˌɪmjʊnə'lɒdʒɪk) *or* **ˌim·mu·no'log·i·cal** *adj.* —**ˌim·mu·no'log·i·cal·ly** *adv.* —**ˌim·mu'nol·o·gist** *n.*

im·mu·no·re·ac·tion (ɪˌmjuːnəʊrɪ'ækʃən) *n.* the reaction between an antigen and its antibody.

im·mu·no·ther·a·py (ˌɪmjʊnəʊ'θɛrəpɪ) *n. Med.* the treatment of disease by stimulating the body's production of antibodies.

im·mure (ɪ'mjʊə) *vb.* (*tr.*) 1. *Archaic or literary.* to enclose within or as if within walls; imprison. 2. to shut (oneself) away from society. 3. *Obsolete.* to build into or enclose within a wall. 4. *Archaic.* to surround or fortify with walls. [C16: from Medieval Latin *immūrāre*, from Latin IM- (in) + *mūrus* a wall] —**im'mure·ment** *n.*

im·mu·ta·ble (ɪ'mjuːtəbᵊl) *adj.* unchanging through time; unalterable; ageless: *immutable laws.* —**im·ˌmu·ta'bil·i·ty** *or* **im'mu·ta·ble·ness** *n.* —**im'mu·ta·bly** *adv.*

I·mo ('iːməʊ) *n.* a state of SE Nigeria, formed in 1976 from part of East-Central State. Capital: Owerri. Pop.: 5 000 000 (1976 est.). Area: 8720 sq. km (3366 sq. miles).

imp (ɪmp) *n.* 1. a small demon or devil; mischievous sprite. 2. a mischievous child. ~*vb.* 3. (*tr.*) *Falconry.* to insert (new feathers) into the stumps of broken feathers in order to repair the wing of a hawk or falcon. [Old English *impa* bud, graft, hence offspring, child, from *impian* to graft, ultimately from Greek *emphutos* implanted, from *emphuein*, to implant, from *phuein* to plant]

imp. *abbrev. for:* 1. imperative. 2. imperfect. 3. imperial. 4.

impersonal. **5.** import. **6.** important. **7.** importer. **8.** imprimatur.

Imp. *abbrev. for:* **1.** Imperator. [Latin: Emperor] **2.** Imperatrix. [Latin: Empress] **3.** Imperial.

im+pact *n.* (ˈɪmpækt). **1.** the act of one body, object, etc., striking another; collision. **2.** the force with which one thing hits another or with which two objects collide. **3.** the impression made by an idea, cultural movement, social group, etc.: *the impact of the Renaissance on Medieval Europe.* ~*vb.* (ɪmˈpækt). **4.** to drive or press (an object) firmly into (another object, thing, etc.) or (of two objects) to be driven or pressed firmly together. [C18: from Latin *impactus* pushed against, fastened on, from *impingere* to thrust at, from *pangere* to drive in] —**im+ˈpac+tion** *n.*

im+pact+ed (ɪmˈpæktɪd) *adj.* **1.** (of a tooth) unable to erupt, esp. because of being wedged against another tooth below the gum. **2.** (of a fracture) having the jagged broken ends wedged into each other.

im+pair (ɪmˈpɛə) *vb.* (*tr.*) to reduce or weaken in strength, quality, etc.: *his hearing was impaired by an accident.* [C14: from Old French *empeirer* to make worse, from Late Latin *pējorāre,* from Latin *pejor* worse; see PEJORATIVE] —**im+ˈpair+a·ble** *adj.* —**im+ˈpair+er** *n.* —**im+ˈpair+ment** *n.*

im+pa+la (ɪmˈpɑːlə) *n., pl.* **+las** *or* **+la.** an antelope, *Aepyceros melampus,* of southern and eastern Africa, having lyre-shaped horns and able to move with enormous leaps when disturbed. [from Zulu]

im+pale *or* **em+pale** (ɪmˈpeɪl) *vb.* (*tr.*) **1.** (often foll. by *on, upon,* or *with*) to pierce with a sharp instrument: *they impaled his severed head on a spear.* **2.** *Archaic.* to enclose with pales or fencing; fence in. **3.** *Heraldry.* to charge (a shield) with two coats of arms placed side by side. [C16: from Medieval Latin *impālāre,* from Latin IM- (in) + *pālus* PALE[2]] —**im+ˈpale+ment** *or* **em+ˈpale+ment** *n.* —**im+ˈpal+er** *or* **em+ˈpal+er** *n.*

im+pal+pa·ble (ɪmˈpælpəbᵊl) *adj.* **1.** imperceptible, esp. to the touch: *impalpable shadows.* **2.** difficult to understand; abstruse. —**im+ˌpal+pa·ˈbil+i·ty** *n.* —**im+ˈpal+pa·bly** *adv.*

im+pa+na+tion (ˌɪmpæˈneɪʃən) *n. Christianity.* the embodiment of Christ in the consecrated bread and wine of the Eucharist. [C16: from Medieval Latin *impanātiō,* from *impanātus* embodied in bread, from Latin IM- (in) + *panis* bread]

im+pan+el (ɪmˈpænᵊl) *vb.* **+els, +el+ling, +elled** *or U.S.* **+els, +el+ing, +eled.** a variant spelling (esp. U.S.) of **empanel.** —**im+ˈpan+el+ment** *n.*

im+par·a+dise (ɪmˈpærədaɪs) *vb.* (*tr.*) **1.** to make blissfully happy; enrapture. **2.** to make into or like paradise.

im+par·i+pin+nate (ˌɪmpærɪˈpɪneɪt, -ˈpɪnɪt) *adj.* (of pinnate leaves) having a terminal unpaired leaflet. Compare **paripinnate.**

im+par·i+syl+la+bic (ɪmˌpærɪsɪˈlæbɪk) *adj.* (of a noun or verb in inflected languages) having inflected forms with different numbers of syllables. Compare **parisyllabic.**

im+par+i·ty (ɪmˈpærɪtɪ) *n., pl.* **·ties.** a less common word for **disparity** (sense 1). [C16: from Late Latin *imparitās,* from Latin *impar* unequal]

im+part (ɪmˈpɑːt) *vb.* (*tr.*) **1.** to communicate (information, etc.); relate. **2.** to give or bestow (something, esp. an abstract quality): *to impart wisdom.* [C15: from Old French *impartir,* from Latin *impertīre,* from IM- (in) + *partīre* to share, from *pars* part] —**im+ˈpart+a·ble** *adj.* —**ˌim+par+ˈta·tion** *or* **im+ˈpart·ment** *n.* —**im+ˈpart+er** *n.*

im+par·tial (ɪmˈpɑːʃəl) *adj.* not prejudiced towards or against any particular side or party; fair; unbiased. —**im+ˌpar+ti+ˈal+i·ty** *or* **im+ˈpar·tial+ness** *n.* —**im+ˈpar·tial+ly** *adv.*

im+part+i·ble (ɪmˈpɑːtəbᵊl) *adj.* **1.** *Law.* (of land, an estate, etc.) incapable of partition; indivisible. **2.** capable of being imparted. —**im+ˌpart+i·ˈbil+i·ty** *n.* —**im+ˈpart+i·bly** *adv.*

im+pass+a·ble (ɪmˈpɑːsəbᵊl) *adj.* (of terrain, roads, etc.) not able to be travelled through or over. —**im+ˌpass+a·ˈbil+i·ty** *or* **im+ˈpass+a·ble+ness** *n.* —**im+ˈpass+a·bly** *adv.*

im+passe (ɪmˈpɑːs) *n.* a situation in which progress is blocked; an insurmountable difficulty; stalemate; deadlock. [C19: from French; see IM-, PASS]

im+pas+si·ble (ɪmˈpæsəbᵊl) *adj. Rare.* **1.** not susceptible to pain or injury. **2.** impassive or unmoved. —**im+ˌpas+si·ˈbil+i·ty** *or* **im+ˈpas+si·ble+ness** *n.* —**im+ˈpas·si·bly** *adv.*

im+pas+sion (ɪmˈpæʃən) *vb.* (*tr.*) to arouse the passions of; inflame.

im+pas+sioned (ɪmˈpæʃənd) *adj.* filled with passion; fiery; inflamed: *an impassioned appeal.* —**im+ˈpas+sioned+ly** *adv.* —**im+ˈpas+sioned+ness** *n.*

im+pas+sive (ɪmˈpæsɪv) *adj.* **1.** not revealing or affected by emotion; reserved. **2.** calm; serene; imperturbable. **3.** *Rare.* unconscious or insensible. —**im+ˈpas+sive+ly** *adv.* —**im+ˈpas+sive+ness** *or* **im+pas+siv+i·ty** (ˌɪmpæˈsɪvɪtɪ) *n.*

im+paste (ɪmˈpeɪst) *vb.* (*tr.*) to apply paint thickly to. [C16: from Italian *impastare,* from *pasta* PASTE[1]] —**im+pas+ta+tion** (ˌɪmpæsˈteɪʃən) *n.*

im+pas+to (ɪmˈpæstəʊ) *n.* **1.** paint applied thickly, so that brush and palette knife marks are evident. **2.** the technique of applying paint in this way. [C18: from Italian, from *impastare;* see IMPASTE]

im+pa+tience (ɪmˈpeɪʃəns) *n.* **1.** lack of patience; intolerance of or irritability with anything that impedes or delays. **2.** restless desire for change and excitement.

im+pa+ti+ens (ɪmˈpeɪʃɪˌɛnz) *n., pl.* **+ens.** any balsaminaceous plant of the genus *Impatiens,* such as balsam, touch-me-not, and policeman's helmet. [C18: New Latin from Latin: impatient; from the fact that the ripe pods burst open when touched]

im+pa+tient (ɪmˈpeɪʃənt) *adj.* **1.** lacking patience; easily irritated at delay, opposition, etc. **2.** exhibiting lack of patience: *an impatient retort.* **3.** (*postpositive;* foll. by *of*) intolerant (of) or indignant (at): *impatient of indecision.* **4.** (*postpositive;* often foll. by *for*) restlessly eager (for something or to do something). —**im+ˈpa+tient+ly** *adv.*

im+peach (ɪmˈpiːtʃ) *vb.* (*tr.*) **1.** *Criminal law.* to bring a charge or accusation against. **2.** *Brit. criminal law.* to accuse of a crime, esp. of treason or some other offence against the state. **3.** *Chiefly U.S.* to charge (a public official) with an offence committed in office. **4.** to challenge or question (a person's honesty, integrity, etc.). [C14: from Old French *empeechier,* from Late Latin *impedicāre* to entangle, catch, from Latin IM- (in) + *pedica* a fetter, from *pēs* foot] —**im+ˈpeach+er** *n.*

im+peach+a·ble (ɪmˈpiːtʃəbᵊl) *adj.* **1.** capable of being impeached or accused. **2.** (of an offence) making a person liable to impeachment. —**im+ˌpeach+a·ˈbil+i·ty** *n.*

im+peach+ment (ɪmˈpiːtʃmənt) *n.* **1.** *Rare.* (in England) committal by the House of Commons, esp. of a minister of the Crown, for trial by the House of Lords. The last instance occurred in 1805. **2.** (in the U.S.) a proceeding brought against a federal government official. **3.** an accusation or charge. **4.** *Obsolete.* discredit; reproach.

im+pearl (ɪmˈpɜːl) *vb.* (*tr.*) *Archaic or poetic.* **1.** to adorn with pearls. **2.** to form into pearl-like shapes or drops.

im+pec+ca·ble (ɪmˈpɛkəbᵊl) *adj.* **1.** without flaw or error; faultless: *an impeccable record.* **2.** *Rare.* incapable of sinning. [C16: from Late Latin *impeccābilis* sinless, from Latin IM- (not) + *peccāre* to sin] —**im+ˌpec+ca·ˈbil+i·ty** *n.* —**im+ˈpec+ca·bly** *adv.*

im+pec+cant (ɪmˈpɛkənt) *adj.* not sinning; free from sin. [C18: from IM- (not) + Latin *peccant-,* from *peccāre* to sin] —**im+ˈpec+can+cy** *n.*

im+pe·cu+ni+ous (ˌɪmpɪˈkjuːnɪəs) *adj.* without money; penniless. [C16: from IM- (not) + *-pecunious,* from Latin *pecūniōsus* wealthy, from *pecūnia* money] —**ˌim+pe·ˈcu+ni+ous+ly** *adv.* —**ˌim+pe·ˈcu+ni+ous+ness** *or* **im+pe·cu+ni+os+i·ty** (ˌɪmpɪkjuːnɪˈɒsɪtɪ) *n.*

im+ped+ance (ɪmˈpiːdᵊns) *n.* **1.** a measure of the opposition to the flow of an alternating current equal to the square root of the sum of the squares of the resistance and the reactance, expressed in ohms. Symbol: ***Z*** **2.** a component that offers impedance. **3.** Also called: **acoustic impedance.** the ratio of the sound pressure in a medium to the rate of alternating flow of the medium through a specified surface due to the sound wave. Symbol: Z_a **4.** Also called: **mechanical impedance.** the ratio of the mechanical force, acting in the direction of motion, to the velocity of the resulting vibration. Symbol: Z_m

im+pede (ɪmˈpiːd) *vb.* (*tr.*) to restrict or retard in action, progress, etc.; hinder; obstruct. [C17: from Latin *impedīre* to hinder, literally: shackle the feet, from *pēs* foot] —**im+ˈped+er** *n.* —**im+ˈped+ing+ly** *adv.*

im+ped·i+ment (ɪmˈpɛdɪmənt) *n.* **1.** a hindrance or obstruction. **2.** a physical defect, esp. one of speech, such as a stammer. **3.** (*pl.* **+ments** *or* **+men+ta** (-ˈmɛntə)) *Law.* an obstruction to the making of a contract, esp. a contract of marriage by reason of closeness of blood or affinity. —**im+ˌped·i+ˈmen+tal** *or* **im+ˌped·i+ˈmen+tar·y** *adj.*

im+ped·i+men+ta (ɪmˌpɛdɪˈmɛntə) *pl. n.* **1.** the baggage and equipment carried by an army. **2.** any objects or circumstances that impede progress. **3.** a plural of **impediment** (sense 3). [C16: from Latin, plural of *impedīmentum* hindrance; see IMPEDE]

im+pel (ɪmˈpɛl) *vb.* **+pels, +pel+ling, +pelled.** (*tr.*) **1.** to urge or force (a person) to an action; constrain or motivate. **2.** to push, drive, or force into motion. [C15: from Latin *impellere* to push against, drive forward, from IM- (in) + *pellere* to drive, push, strike] —**im+ˈpel+lent** *n., adj.*

im+pel+ler (ɪmˈpɛlə) *n.* **1.** the vaned rotating disc of a centrifugal pump, compressor, etc. **2.** a compressor or centrifugal pump having such an impeller.

im+pend (ɪmˈpɛnd) *vb.* (*intr.*) **1.** (esp. of something threatening) to be about to happen; be imminent. **2.** (foll. by *over*) *Rare.* to be suspended; hang. [C16: from Latin *impendēre* to overhang, from *pendēre* to hang] —**im+ˈpend+ence** *or* **im+ˈpend+en+cy** *n.* —**im+ˈpend+ing** *adj.*

im+pen+e·tra·ble (ɪmˈpɛnɪtrəbᵊl) *adj.* **1.** incapable of being pierced through or penetrated: *an impenetrable forest.* **2.** incapable of being understood; incomprehensible: *impenetrable jargon.* **3.** incapable of being seen through: *impenetrable gloom.* **4.** not susceptible to ideas, influence, etc.: *impenetrable ignorance.* **5.** *Physics.* (of a body) incapable of occupying the same space as another body. —**im+ˌpen+e·tra·ˈbil+i·ty** *n.* —**im+ˈpen+e·tra·ble+ness** *n.* —**im+ˈpen+e·tra·bly** *adv.*

im+pen·i+tent (ɪmˈpɛnɪtənt) *adj.* not sorry or penitent; unrepentant. —**im+ˈpen·i+tence, im+ˈpen·i+ten+cy,** *or* **im+ˈpen·i+tent+ness** *n.* —**im+ˈpen·i+tent+ly** *adv.*

im+pen+nate (ɪmˈpɛneɪt) *adj. Rare.* (of birds) lacking true functional wings or feathers.

imper. *abbrev. for* imperative.

im+per·a+tive (ɪmˈpɛrətɪv) *adj.* **1.** extremely urgent or important; essential. **2.** peremptory or authoritative: *an imperative tone of voice.* **3.** Also: **im+per·a·ti+val** (ɪmˌpɛrəˈtaɪvᵊl). *Grammar.* denoting a mood of verbs used in giving orders, making requests, etc. In English the verb root without any inflections is the usual form, as for example *leave* in *Leave me alone.* ~*n.* **4.** something that is urgent or essential. **5.** an order or command. **6.** *Grammar.* **a.** the imperative mood. **b.** a verb in this mood. [C16: from Late Latin *imperātīvus,* from Latin *imperāre* to command] —**im+'per·a+tive+ly** *adv.* —**im+'per·a+tive+ness** *n.*

im+pe·ra+tor (ˌɪmpəˈrɑːtɔː) *n.* **1. a.** (in imperial Rome) a title of the emperor. **b.** (in republican Rome) a temporary title of honour bestowed upon a victorious general. **2.** a less common word for **emperor.** [C16: from Latin: commander, from *imperāre* to command] —**im+per·a+to+ri·al** (ɪmˌpɛrəˈtɔːrɪəl) *adj.* —**im+ˌper·a+'to+ri+al+ly** *adv.* —**ˌim+pe·'ra+tor+ˌship** *n.*

im+per+cep+ti·ble (ˌɪmpəˈsɛptɪbəl) *adj.* too slight, subtle, gradual, etc., to be perceived. —**ˌim+per+ˌcep+ti·'bil+i·ty** *or* **ˌim+per+'cep+ti·ble+ness** *n.* —**ˌim+per+'cep+ti·bly** *adv.*

im+per+cep+tive (ˌɪmpəˈsɛptɪv) *adj., also* **im+per+cip·i+ent** (ˌɪmpəˈsɪpɪənt). lacking in perception; obtuse. —**ˌim+per+'cep+tion** *n.* —**ˌim+per+'cep+tive+ly** *adv.* —**ˌim+per+cep+'tiv+i·ty, ˌim+per+'cep+tive+ness,** *or* **ˌim+per+'cip·i+ence** *n.*

imperf. *abbrev. for:* **1.** imperfect. **2.** (of stamps) imperforate.

im+per+fect (ɪmˈpɜːfɪkt) *adj.* **1.** exhibiting or characterized by faults, mistakes, etc.; defective. **2.** not fully complete or finished; incomplete; deficient. **3.** (of flowers) lacking functional stamens or pistils. **4.** *Grammar.* denoting a tense of verbs used most commonly in describing continuous or repeated past actions or events, as for example *was walking* as opposed to *walked.* **5.** *Law.* (of a trust, obligation, etc.) lacking some necessary formality to make effective or binding; incomplete; legally unenforceable. See also **executory** (sense 1). **6.** *Music.* **a.** (of a cadence) proceeding to the dominant from the tonic, subdominant, or any chord other than the dominant. **b.** of or relating to all intervals other than the fourth, fifth, and octave. Compare **perfect** (sense 9). ~*n.* **7.** *Grammar.* **a.** the imperfect tense. **b.** a verb in this tense. —**im+'per+fect+ly** *adv.* —**im+'per+fect+ness** *n.*

im+per+fect com+pe·ti+tion *n. Economics.* the market situation that exists when one or more of the necessary conditions for perfect competition do not hold.

im+per+fec+tion (ˌɪmpəˈfɛkʃən) *n.* **1.** the condition or quality of being imperfect. **2.** a fault or defect.

im+per+fec+tive (ˌɪmpəˈfɛktɪv) *Grammar.* ~*adj.* **1.** denoting an aspect of the verb in some languages, including English, used to indicate that the action is in progress without regard to its completion. Compare **perfective.** ~*n.* **2. a.** the imperfective aspect of a verb. **b.** a verb in this aspect. —**ˌim+per+'fec+tive+ly** *adv.*

im+per+fo+rate (ɪmˈpɜːfərɪt, -ˌreɪt) *adj.* **1.** not perforated. **2.** (of a postage stamp) not provided with perforation or any other means of separation. Abbrev.: **imperf.** Compare **perforate. 3.** (of a bodily part, such as the anus) without the normal opening. —**im+ˌper+fo+'ra+tion** *n.*

im+pe·ri·al (ɪmˈpɪərɪəl) *adj.* **1.** of or relating to an empire, emperor, or empress. **2.** characteristic of or befitting an emperor; majestic; commanding. **3.** characteristic of or exercising supreme authority; imperious. **4.** (esp. of products and commodities) of a superior size or quality. **5.** (*usually prenominal*) (of weights, measures, etc.) conforming to standards or definitions legally established in Great Britain: *an imperial gallon.* ~*n.* **6.** any of various book sizes, esp. 7½ by 11 inches **(imperial octavo)** or (chiefly Brit.) 11 by 15 inches **(imperial quarto). 7.** a size of writing or printing paper, 23 by 31 inches (U.S.) or 22 by 30 inches (Brit.). **8.** (formerly) a Russian gold coin originally worth ten roubles. **9.** *U.S.* **a.** the top of a carriage, such as a diligence. **b.** a luggage case carried there. **10.** *Architect.* a dome that has a point at the top. **11.** a small tufted beard popularized by the emperor Napoleon III. **12.** a member of an imperial family, esp. an emperor or empress. [C14: from Late Latin *imperiālis,* from Latin *imperium* command, authority, empire] —**im+'pe·ri+al+ly** *adv.* —**im+'pe·ri+al+ness** *n.*

Im+pe·ri·al (ɪmˈpɪərɪəl) *adj.* **1.** (*sometimes not cap.*) of or relating to a specified empire, such as the British Empire. ~*n.* **2.** a supporter or soldier of the Holy Roman Empire.

im+pe·ri·al gal+lon *n.* a formal name for **gallon** (sense 1).

im+pe·ri+al+ism (ɪmˈpɪərɪəˌlɪzəm) *n.* **1.** the policy or practice of extending a state's rule over other territories. **2.** an instance or policy of aggressive behaviour by one state against another. **3.** the extension or attempted extension of authority, influence, power, etc., by any person, country, institution, etc.: *cultural imperialism.* **4.** a system of imperial government or rule by an emperor. **5.** the spirit, character, authority, etc., of an empire. **6.** advocacy of or support for any form of imperialism. —**im+'pe·ri+al+ist** *adj., n.* —**im+ˌpe·ri+al+'is+tic** *adj.* —**im+ˌpe·ri+al+'is+ti+cal+ly** *adv.*

im+per+il (ɪmˈpɛrɪl) *vb.* (*tr.*) to place in danger or jeopardy; endanger. —**im+'per+il+ment** *n.*

im+pe·ri+ous (ɪmˈpɪərɪəs) *adj.* **1.** domineering; arrogant; overbearing. **2.** *Rare.* urgent; imperative. [C16: from Latin *imperiōsus* from *imperium* command, power] —**im+'pe·ri+ous+ly** *adv.* —**im+'pe·ri+ous+ness** *n.*

im+per+ish·a·ble (ɪmˈpɛrɪʃəbəl) *adj.* **1.** not subject to decay or deterioration: *imperishable goods.* **2.** not likely to be forgotten: *imperishable truths.* —**im+ˌper+ish+a·'bil+i·ty** *or* **im+'per+ish+a·ble+ness** *n.* —**im+'per+ish+a·bly** *adv.*

im+pe·ri·um (ɪmˈpɪərɪəm) *n., pl.* **·ri·a** (-rɪə). **1.** (in ancient Rome) the supreme power, held esp. by consuls and emperors, to command and administer in military, judicial, and civil affairs. **2.** the right to command; supreme power. **3.** a less common word for **empire.** [C17: from Latin: command, empire, from *imperāre* to command; see EMPEROR]

im+per+ma+nent (ɪmˈpɜːmənənt) *adj.* not permanent; fleeting; transitory. —**im+'per+ma+nence** *or* **im+'per+ma+nen+cy** *n.* —**im+'per+ma+nent+ly** *adv.*

im+per+me·a·ble (ɪmˈpɜːmɪəbəl) *adj.* (of a substance) not allowing the passage of a fluid through interstices; not permeable. —**im+ˌper+me·a·'bil+i·ty** *or* **im+'per+me·a·ble+ness** *n.* —**im+'per+me·a·bly** *adv.*

im+per+mis+si·ble (ˌɪmpəˈmɪsɪbəl) *adj.* not permissible; not allowed. —**ˌim+per+ˌmis+si·'bil+i·ty** *n.* —**ˌim+per+'mis+si·bly** *adv.*

impers. *abbrev. for* impersonal.

im+per+script+i·ble (ˌɪmpəˈskrɪptɪbəl) *adj.* not supported by written authority. [C19: from IM- (not) + Latin *perscribere* to write down]

im+per+son+al (ɪmˈpɜːsənəl) *adj.* **1.** without reference to any individual person; objective: *an impersonal assessment.* **2.** devoid of human warmth or sympathy; cold: *an impersonal manner.* **3.** not having human characteristics: *an impersonal God.* **4.** *Grammar.* (of a verb) having no logical subject. Usually in English the pronoun *it* is used in such cases as a grammatical subject, as for example in *It is raining.* **5.** *Grammar.* (of a pronoun) not denoting a person. —**im+ˌper+son+'al+i·ty** *n.* —**im+'per+son+al+ly** *adv.*

im+per+son+al+ize *or* **im+per+son+al+ise** (ɪmˈpɜːsənəˌlaɪz) *vb.* (*tr.*) to make impersonal, esp. to rid of such human characteristics as sympathy, warmth, etc.; dehumanize. —**im+ˌper+son+al·i+'za+tion** *or* **im+ˌper+son+al·i+'sa+tion** *n.*

im+per+son+ate (ɪmˈpɜːsəˌneɪt) *vb.* (*tr.*) **1.** to pretend to be (another person). **2.** to imitate the character, mannerisms, etc., of (another person). **3.** *Rare.* to play the part or character of. **4.** an archaic word for **personify.** —**im+ˌper+son·'a+tion** *n.* —**im+'per+son·ˌa+tor** *n.*

im+per+ti+nence (ɪmˈpɜːtɪnəns) *or* **im+per+ti+nen+cy** *n.* **1.** disrespectful behaviour or language; rudeness; insolence. **2.** an impertinent act, gesture, etc. **3.** *Rare.* lack of pertinence; irrelevance; inappropriateness.

im+per+ti+nent (ɪmˈpɜːtɪnənt) *adj.* **1.** rude; insolent; impudent. **2.** irrelevant or inappropriate. [C14: from Latin *impertinēns* not belonging, from Latin IM- (not) + *pertinēre* to be relevant; see PERTAIN] —**im+'per+ti+nent+ly** *adv.*

im+per+turb+a·ble (ˌɪmpɜːˈtɜːbəbəl) *adj.* not easily perturbed; calm; unruffled. —**ˌim+per+ˌturb+a·'bil+i·ty** *or* **ˌim+per+'turb+a·ble+ness** *n.* —**ˌim+per+'turb+a·bly** *adv.* —**im+per+tur+ba+tion** (ˌɪmpɜːtɜːˈbeɪʃən) *n.*

im+per+vi+ous (ɪmˈpɜːvɪəs) *or* **im+per+vi+a·ble** *adj.* **1.** not able to be penetrated, as by water, light, etc.; impermeable. **2.** (*often postpositive;* foll. by *to*) not able to be influenced (by) or not receptive (to): *impervious to argument.* —**im+'per+vi+ous+ly** *adv.* —**im+'per+vi+ous+ness** *n.*

im+pe·ti+go (ˌɪmpɪˈtaɪgəʊ) *n.* a contagious bacterial skin disease characterized by the formation of pustules that develop into yellowish crusty sores. [C16: from Latin: scabby eruption, from *impetere* to assail; see IMPETUS; for form, compare VERTIGO] —**im+pe+tig·i+nous** (ˌɪmpɪˈtɪdʒɪnəs) *adj.*

im+pe+trate (ˈɪmpɪˌtreɪt) *vb.* (*tr.*) *Theol.* **1.** to supplicate or entreat for, esp. by prayer. **2.** to obtain by prayer. [C16: from Latin *impetrāre* to procure by entreaty, from *-petrāre,* from *patrāre* to bring to pass, of uncertain origin; perhaps related to Latin *pater* a father] —**ˌim+pe·'tra+tion** *n.* —**'im+pe+tra+tive** *adj.* —**'im+pe·ˌtra+tor** *n.*

im+pet·u+ous (ɪmˈpɛtjʊəs) *adj.* **1.** liable to act without consideration; rash; impulsive. **2.** resulting from or characterized by rashness or haste. **3.** *Poetic.* moving with great force or violence; rushing: *the impetuous stream hurtled down the valley.* [C14: from Late Latin *impetuōsus* violent; see IMPETUS] —**im+'pet·u+ous+ly** *adv.* —**im+'pet·u+ous+ness** *or* **im+pet·u+os+i·ty** (ɪmˌpɛtjʊˈɒsɪtɪ) *n.*

im+pe+tus (ˈɪmpɪtəs) *n., pl.* **·tus·es. 1.** an impelling movement or force; incentive or impulse; stimulus. **2.** *Physics.* the force that sets a body in motion or that tends to resist changes in a body's motion. [C17: from Latin: attack, from *impetere* to assail, from IM- (in) + *petere* to make for, seek out]

impf. *or* **imperf.** *abbrev. for* imperfect.

imp. gal. *or* **imp. gall.** *abbrev. for* imperial gallon.

Im+phal (ɪmˈfɑːl, ˈɪmfəl) *n.* a city in NE India, capital of Manipur Territory, on the Manipur River: formerly the seat of the Manipur kings. Pop.: 100 366 (1971).

im+pi (ˈɪmpɪ) *n., pl.* **·pi** *or* **·pies.** a group of Bantu warriors. [C19: from Zulu]

im+pi·e+ty (ɪmˈpaɪɪtɪ) *n., pl.* **·ties. 1.** lack of reverence or proper respect for a god. **2.** any lack of proper respect. **3.** an impious act.

im+pinge (ɪmˈpɪndʒ) *vb.* **1.** (*intr.;* usually foll. by *on* or *upon*) to encroach or infringe; trespass: *to impinge on someone's time.* **2.** (*intr.;* usually foll. by *on, against,* or *upon*) to collide (with); strike. [C16: from Latin *impingere* to drive at, dash against, from *pangere* to fasten, drive in] —**im+'pinge+ment** *n.* —**im+'ping+er** *n.*

im+pinge+ment at+tack *n. Metallurgy.* a form of corrosion of metals caused by erosion of the oxide layer by a moving fluid in which there are suspended particles or air bubbles.

im+pi+ous (ˈɪmpɪəs) *adj.* **1.** lacking piety or reverence for a god; ungodly. **2.** lacking respect; undutiful. —**'im+pi+ous+ly** *adv.* —**'im+pi+ous+ness** *n.*

imp+ish (ˈɪmpɪʃ) *adj.* of or resembling an imp; mischievous. —**'imp+ish+ly** *adv.* —**'imp+ish+ness** *n.*

im+plac+a·ble (ɪmˈplækəbəl) *adj.* **1.** incapable of being placated or pacified; unappeasable. **2.** inflexible; intractable. —**im+ˌplac+a·'bil+i·ty** *or* **im+'plac+a·ble+ness** *n.* —**im+'plac+a·bly** *adv.*

im+pla+cen+tal (ˌɪmpləˈsɛntəl) *adj.* another word for **aplacental.**

im+plant *vb.* (ɪmˈplɑːnt). (*tr.*) **1.** to establish firmly; inculcate; instil: *to implant sound moral principles.* **2.** to plant or embed;

infix; entrench. **3.** *Surgery.* **a.** to graft (a tissue, etc.) into the body. **b.** to insert (a radioactive substance, hormone, etc.) into the tissues. ~*n.* ('ɪmˌplɑːnt). **4.** anything implanted, esp. surgically, such as a tissue graft. —**im+'plant+er** *n.*

im+plan+ta+tion (ˌɪmplɑːn'teɪʃən) *n.* **1.** the act of implanting or the state of being implanted. **2.** the attachment of the blastocyst of a mammalian embryo to the wall of the uterus of the mother.

im+plau+si+ble (ɪm'plɔːzəbᵊl) *adj.* not plausible; provoking disbelief; unlikely. —**im+ˌplau+si·'bil+i·ty** *or* **im+'plau+si·ble+ness** *n.* —**im+'plau+si·bly** *adv.*

im+plead (ɪm'pliːd) *vb.* (*tr.*) *Law, rare.* **1. a.** to sue or prosecute. **b.** to bring an action against. **2.** to accuse. [C13: from Anglo-French *empleder;* see IM-, PLEAD] —**im+'plead+a·ble** *adj.* —**im+'plead+er** *n.*

im+ple+ment *n.* ('ɪmplɪmənt). **1.** a piece of equipment; tool or utensil: *gardening implements.* **2.** something used to achieve a purpose; agent. ~*vb.* ('ɪmplɪˌmɛnt). (*tr.*) **3.** to carry out; put into action; perform: *to implement a plan.* **4.** *Rare.* to supply with tools. **5.** *Archaic.* to complete, satisfy, or fulfil. [C17: from Late Latin *implēmentum,* literally: a filling up, from Latin *implēre* to fill up, satisfy, fulfil] —**ˌim+ple+'men+tal** *adj.* —**ˌim+ple+men+'ta+tion** *n.* —**'im+ple+ˌment+er** *or* **'im+ple+ˌmen+tor** *n.*

im+pli+cate ('ɪmplɪˌkeɪt) *vb.* (*tr.*) **1.** to show to be involved, esp. in a crime. **2.** to involve as a necessary inference; imply: *his protest implicated censure by the authorities.* **3.** to affect intimately: *this news implicates my decision.* **4.** *Rare.* to intertwine or entangle. [C16: from Latin *implicāre* to involve, from IM- + *plicāre* to fold] —**im+plic·a+tive** (ɪm'plɪkətɪv) *adj.* —**im+'plic·a+tive+ly** *adv.*

im+pli+ca+tion (ˌɪmplɪ'keɪʃən) *n.* **1.** the act of implicating or the state of being implicated. **2.** something that is implied; suggestion: *the implication of your silence is that you're bored.* **3.** *Logic.* a relation between two propositions, such that the second can be logically deduced from the first. —**ˌim+pli+'ca+tion+al** *adj.*

im+plic+it (ɪm'plɪsɪt) *adj.* **1.** not explicit; implied; indirect: *there was implicit criticism in his voice.* **2.** absolute and unreserved; unquestioning: *you have implicit trust in him.* **3.** (*when postpositive,* foll. by *in*) contained or inherent: *to bring out the anger implicit in the argument.* **4.** *Maths.* (of a function) having an equation of the form $f(x,y) = 0$, in which y cannot be directly expressed in terms of x, as in $xy + x^2 + y^3x^2 = 0$. Compare **explicit** (sense 3). **5.** *Obsolete.* intertwined. [C16: from Latin *implicitus,* variant of *implicātus* interwoven; see IMPLICATE] —**im+'plic+it+ly** *adv.* —**im+'plic+it+ness** *or* **im+'plic+i·ty** *n.*

im+plied (ɪm'plaɪd) *adj.* hinted at or suggested; not directly expressed: *an implied criticism.* —**im+'plied+ly** *adv.*

im+plode (ɪm'pləʊd) *vb.* **1.** to collapse or cause to collapse inwards in a violent manner as a result of external pressure: *the vacu..m flask imploded.* **2.** (*tr.*) to pronounce (a consonant) with or by implosion. ~Compare **explode.** [C19: from IM- + (EX)PLODE]

im+plore (ɪm'plɔː) *vb.* (*tr.*) **1.** to beg or ask (someone) earnestly (to do something); plead with; beseech. **2.** to ask earnestly or piteously for; supplicate; beg: *to implore someone's mercy.* [C16: from Latin *implōrāre,* from IM- + *plōrāre* to bewail] —**ˌim+plo+'ra+tion** *n.* —**im+'plo+ra+to·ry** *adj.* —**im+'plor+er** *n.* —**im+'plor+ing+ly** *adv.*

im+plo+sion (ɪm'pləʊʒən) *n.* **1.** the act or process of imploding: *the implosion of a light bulb.* **2.** *Phonetics.* the suction or inhalation of breath employed in the pronunciation of an ingressive consonant.

im+plo+sive (ɪm'pləʊsɪv) *adj.* **1.** pronounced by or with implosion. ~*n.* **2.** an implosive consonant. —**im+'plo+sive+ly** *adv.*

im+ply (ɪm'plaɪ) *vb.* **+plies, +ply+ing, +plied.** (*tr.; may take a clause as object*) **1.** to express or indicate by a hint; suggest: *what are you implying by that remark?* **2.** to suggest or involve as a necessary consequence or connotation. **3.** *Obsolete.* to entangle or enfold. [C14: from Old French *emplier,* from Latin *implicāre* to involve; see IMPLICATE]
Usage. See at **infer.**

im+pol+der (ɪm'pəʊldə) *or* **em+pol+der** *vb.* to make into a polder; reclaim (land) from the sea. [C19: from Dutch *inpolderen,* see IN-², POLDER]

im+pol·i+cy (ɪm'pɒlɪsɪ) *n., pl.* **+cies.** the act or an instance of being unjudicious or impolitic.

im+po+lite (ˌɪmpə'laɪt) *adj.* discourteous; rude; uncivil. —**ˌim+po+'lite+ly** *adv.* —**ˌim+po+'lite+ness** *n.*

im+pol·i+tic (ɪm'pɒlɪtɪk) *adj.* not politic or expedient; unwise. —**im+'pol·i+tic+ly** *adv.* —**im+'pol·i+tic+ness** *n.*

im+pon+de·ra+bil·i·a (ɪmˌpɒndərə'bɪlɪə) *pl. n.* imponderables. [C20: New Latin]

im+pon+der+a+ble (ɪm'pɒndərəbᵊl, -drəbᵊl) *adj.* **1.** unable to be weighed or assessed. ~*n.* **2.** something difficult or impossible to assess. —**im+ˌpon+der+a·'bil+i·ty** *or* **im+'pon+der+a·ble+ness** *n.* —**im+'pon+der+a·bly** *adv.*

im+po+nent (ɪm'pəʊnənt) *n.* a person who imposes a duty, etc.

im+port *vb.* (ɪm'pɔːt, 'ɪmpɔːt). **1.** to buy or bring in (goods or services) from a foreign country. Compare **export. 2.** (*tr.*) to bring in from an outside source: *to import foreign words into the language.* **3.** *Rare.* to signify or be significant; mean; convey: *to import doom.* ~*n.* ('ɪmpɔːt). **4.** (*often pl.*) **a.** goods (**visible imports**) or services (**invisible imports**) that are bought from foreign countries. **b.** (*as modifier*): *an import licence.* **5.** significance or importance: *a man of great import.* **6.** meaning or signification. **7.** *Canadian slang.* a sportsman who is not native to the area where he plays. [C15: from Latin *importāre* to carry in, from IM- + *portāre* to carry] —**im+'port+a·ble** *adj.* —**im+ˌport+a·'bil+i·ty** *n.* —**im+'port+er** *n.*

im+por+tance (ɪm'pɔːtᵊns) *n.* **1.** the state of being important; significance. **2.** social status; standing; esteem: *a man of importance.* **3.** *Obsolete.* **a.** meaning or signification. **b.** an important matter. **c.** importunity.

im+por+tant (ɪm'pɔːtᵊnt) *adj.* **1.** of great significance or value; outstanding: *Voltaire is an important writer.* **2.** of social significance; notable; eminent; esteemed: *an important man in the town.* **3.** (*when postpositive,* usually foll. by *to*) specially relevant or of great concern (to); valued highly (by): *your wishes are important to me.* **4.** an obsolete word for **importunate.** [C16: from Old Italian *importante,* from Medieval Latin *importāre* to signify, be of consequence, from Latin: to carry in; see IMPORT] —**im+'por+tant+ly** *adv.*

im+por+ta+tion (ˌɪmpɔː'teɪʃən) *n.* **1.** the act, business, or process of importing goods or services. **2.** an imported product or service.

im+por+tu+nate (ɪm'pɔːtjʊnɪt) *adj.* **1.** persistent or demanding; insistent. **2.** *Rare.* troublesome; annoying. —**im+'por+tu+nate+ly** *adv.* —**im+'por+tu+nate+ness** *n.*

im+por+tune (ɪm'pɔːtjuːn) *vb.* (*tr.*) **1.** to harass with persistent requests; demand of (someone) insistently. **2.** to beg for persistently; request with insistence. **3.** *Obsolete.* **a.** to anger or annoy. **b.** to force; impel. [C16: from Latin *importūnus* tiresome, from *im-* IN-¹ + *-portūnus* as in *opportūnus* OPPORTUNE] —**im+'por+tune+ly** *adv.* —**im+'por+tun+er** *n.* —**ˌim+por+'tu+ni·ty** *or* **im+'por+tu+na+cy** *n.*

im+pose (ɪm'pəʊz) *vb.* (usually foll. by *on* or *upon*) **1.** (*tr.*) to establish as something to be obeyed or complied with; enforce: *to impose a tax on the people.* **2.** to force (oneself, one's presence, etc.) on another or others; obtrude. **3.** (*intr.*) to take advantage, as of a person or quality: *to impose on someone's kindness.* **4.** (*tr.*) *Printing.* to arrange (pages, type, etc.) for locking into a chase so that after printing and folding the pages will be in the correct order. **5.** (*tr.*) to pass off deceptively; foist: *to impose a hoax on someone.* **6.** (*tr.*) (of a bishop or priest) to lay (the hands) on the head of a candidate for certain sacraments. [C15: from Old French *imposer,* from Latin *impōnere* to place upon, from *pōnere* to place, set] —**im+'pos+a·ble** *adj.* —**im+'pos+er** *n.*

im+pos+ing (ɪm'pəʊzɪŋ) *adj.* grand or impressive: *an imposing building.* —**im+'pos+ing+ly** *adv.* —**im+'pos+ing+ness** *n.*

im+pos+ing stone *or* **ta+ble** *n. Printing.* a flat hard surface upon which pages are imposed.

im+po+si+tion (ˌɪmpə'zɪʃən) *n.* **1.** the act of imposing. **2.** something that is imposed, esp. (in Britain) a task set as a school punishment. **3.** the arrangement of pages for printing so that the finished work will have its pages in the correct order.

im+pos+si+bil+i+ty (ɪmˌpɒsə'bɪlɪtɪ, ˌɪmpɒs-) *n., pl.* **·ties. 1.** the state or quality of being impossible. **2.** something that is impossible.

im+pos+si+ble (ɪm'pɒsəbᵊl) *adj.* **1.** incapable of being done, undertaken, or experienced. **2.** incapable of occurring or happening. **3.** absurd or inconceivable; unreasonable: *it's impossible to think of him as a bishop.* **4.** *Informal.* intolerable; outrageous: *those children are impossible.* —**im+'pos+si·ble+ness** *n.* —**im+'pos+si·bly** *adv.*

im+post¹ ('ɪmpəʊst) *n.* **1.** a tax, esp. a customs duty. **2.** *Horse racing.* the specific weight that a particular horse must carry in a handicap race. ~*vb.* **3.** (*tr.*) *U.S.* to classify (imported goods) according to the duty payable on them. [C16: from Medieval Latin *impostus* tax, from Latin *impositus* imposed; see IMPOSE] —**'im+post+er** *n.*

im+post² ('ɪmpəʊst) *n. Architect.* a member at the top of a wall, pier, or column that supports an arch, esp. one that has a projecting moulding. [C17: from French *imposte,* from Latin *impositus* placed upon; see IMPOSE]

im+pos+tor *or* **im+post+er** (ɪm'pɒstə) *n.* a person who deceives others, esp. by assuming a false identity; charlatan. [C16: from Late Latin: deceiver; see IMPOSE]

im+pos+tume (ɪm'pɒstjuːm) *or* **im+pos+thume** (ɪm'pɒsθuːm) *n.* an archaic word for **abscess.** [C15: from Old French *empostume,* from Late Latin *apostēma,* from Greek, literally: separation (of pus), from *aphistanai* to remove, from *histanai* to stand]

im+pos+ture (ɪm'pɒstʃə) *n.* the act or an instance of deceiving others, esp. by assuming a false identity. [C16: from French, from Late Latin *impostūra,* from Latin *impōnere;* see IMPOSE] —**im+pos+trous** (ɪm'pɒstrəs), **im+pos+tor+ous** (ɪm'pɒstərəs), *or* **im+'pos+tur+ous** *adj.*

im+po+tent ('ɪmpətənt) *adj.* **1.** (*when postpositive, often takes an infinitive*) lacking sufficient strength; powerless. **2.** (esp. of males) unable to perform sexual intercourse. **3.** *Obsolete.* lacking self-control; unrestrained. —**'im+po+tence, 'im+po+ten+cy,** *or* **'im+po+tent+ness** *n.* —**'im+po+tent+ly** *adv.*

im+pound (ɪm'paʊnd) *vb.* (*tr.*) **1.** to confine (stray animals, illegally parked cars, etc.) in a pound. **2. a.** to seize (chattels, etc.) by legal right. **b.** to take possession of (a document, evidence, etc.) and hold in legal custody. **3.** to collect (water) in a reservoir or dam, as for irrigation. **4.** to seize or appropriate. —**im+'pound+a·ble** *adj.* —**im+'pound+age** *or* **im+'pound+ment** *n.* —**im+'pound+er** *n.*

im+pov+er+ish *or* **em+pov+er+ish** (ɪm'pɒvərɪʃ) *vb.* (*tr.*) **1.** to make poor or diminish the quality of: *to impoverish society by cutting the grant to the arts.* **2.** to deprive (soil, etc.) of fertility. [C15: from Old French *empovrir,* from *povre* POOR] —**im+'pov+er+ish+er** *or* **em+'pov+er+ish+er** *n.* —**im+'pov+er+ish+ment** *or* **em+'pov+er+ish+ment** *n.*

im·pow·er (ɪm'paʊə) *vb.* a less common spelling of **empower.**

im·prac·ti·ca·ble (ɪm'præktɪkəbᵊl) *adj.* **1.** incapable of being put into practice or accomplished; not feasible. **2.** unsuitable for a desired use; unfit. **3.** an archaic word for **intractable.** —**im·ˌprac·ti·ca·'bil·i·ty** *or* **im·'prac·ti·ca·ble·ness** *n.* —**im·'prac·ti·ca·bly** *adv.*

im·prac·ti·cal (ɪm'præktɪkᵊl) *adj.* **1.** not practical or workable: *an impractical solution.* **2.** not given to practical matters or gifted with practical skills: *he is intelligent but too impractical for commercial work.* —**im·ˌprac·ti·'cal·i·ty** *or* **im·'prac·ti·cal·ness** *n.* —**im·'prac·ti·cal·ly** *adv.*

im·pre·cate ('ɪmprɪˌkeɪt) *vb.* **1.** (*intr.*) to swear, curse, or blaspheme. **2.** (*tr.*) to invoke or bring down (evil, a curse, etc.): *to imprecate disaster on the ship.* **3.** (*tr.*) to put a curse on. [C17: from Latin *imprecārī* to invoke, from *im-* IN-² + *precārī* to PRAY] —**'im·pre·ˌca·to·ry** *adj.*

im·pre·ca·tion (ˌɪmprɪ'keɪʃən) *n.* **1.** the act of imprecating. **2.** a malediction; curse.

im·pre·cise (ˌɪmprɪ'saɪs) *adj.* not precise; inexact or inaccurate. —**ˌim·pre·'cise·ly** *adv.* —**im·pre·ci·sion** (ˌɪmprɪ'sɪʒən) *or* **ˌim·pre·'cise·ness** *n.*

im·preg·na·ble¹ (ɪm'prɛgnəbᵊl) *adj.* **1.** unable to be broken into or taken by force: *an impregnable castle.* **2.** unable to be shaken or overcome: *impregnable self-confidence.* **3.** incapable of being refuted: *an impregnable argument.* [C15 *imprenable,* from Old French, from IM- (not) + *prenable* able to be taken, from *prendre* to take] —**im·ˌpreg·na·'bil·i·ty** *or* **im·'preg·na·ble·ness** *n.* —**im·'preg·na·bly** *adv.*

im·preg·na·ble² (ɪm'prɛgnəbᵊl) *or* **im·preg·na·ta·ble** (ˌɪmprɛg'neɪtəbᵊl) *adj.* able to be impregnated; fertile.

im·preg·nate *vb.* ('ɪmprɛgˌneɪt). (*tr.*) **1.** to saturate, soak, or infuse: *to impregnate a cloth with detergent.* **2.** to imbue or permeate; pervade. **3.** to cause to conceive; make pregnant. **4.** to fertilize (an ovum). **5.** to make (land, soil, etc.) fruitful. ~*adj.* (ɪm'prɛgnɪt, -neɪt). **6.** pregnant or fertilized. [C17: from Late Latin *impraegnāre* to make pregnant, from Latin *im-* IN-² + *praegnans* PREGNANT] —**ˌim·preg·'na·tion** *n.* —**im·'preg·na·tor** *n.*

im·pre·sa (ɪm'preɪzə) *or* **im·prese** (ɪm'pri:z) *n.* an emblem or device, usually a motto, as on a coat of arms. [C16: from Italian, literally: undertaking, hence deed of chivalry, motto, from *imprendere* to undertake; see EMPRISE]

im·pre·sa·ri·o (ˌɪmprə'sɑ:rɪˌəʊ) *n., pl.* **·sa·ri·os. 1.** a producer or sponsor of public entertainments, esp. musical or theatrical ones. **2.** the director or manager of an opera, ballet, or other performing company. [C18: from Italian, literally: one who undertakes; see IMPRESA]

im·pre·scrip·ti·ble (ˌɪmprɪ'skrɪptəbᵊl) *adj. Law.* immune or exempt from prescription. —**ˌim·pre·ˌscrip·ti·'bil·i·ty** *n.* —**ˌim·pre·'scrip·ti·bly** *adv.*

im·press¹ *vb.* (ɪm'prɛs). (*tr.*) **1.** to make an impression on; have a strong, lasting, or favourable effect on: *I am impressed by your work.* **2.** to produce (an imprint, etc.) by pressure in or on (something): *to impress a seal in wax; to impress wax with a seal.* **3.** (often foll. by *on*) to stress (something to a person); urge; emphasize: *to impress the danger of a situation on someone.* **4.** to exert pressure on; press. **5.** *Electronics.* to apply (a voltage) to a circuit or device. ~*n.* ('ɪmprɛs). **6.** the act or an instance of impressing. **7.** a mark, imprint, or effect produced by impressing. [C14: from Latin *imprimere* to press into, imprint, from *premere* to PRESS¹] —**im·'press·er** *n.* —**im·'press·i·ble** *adj.*

im·press² *vb.* (ɪm'prɛs). **1.** to commandeer or coerce (men or things) into government service; press-gang. ~*n.* ('ɪmprɛs). **2.** the act of commandeering or coercing into government service; impressment. [C16: see *im-* IN-², PRESS²]

im·pres·sion (ɪm'prɛʃən) *n.* **1.** an effect produced in the mind by a stimulus; sensation: *he gave the impression of wanting to help.* **2.** an imprint or mark produced by pressing: *he left the impression of his finger in the mud.* **3.** a vague idea, consciousness, or belief: *I had the impression we had met before.* **4.** a strong, favourable, or remarkable effect: *he made an impression on the managers.* **5.** the act of impressing or the state of being impressed. **6.** *Printing.* **a.** the act, process, or result of printing from type, plates, etc. **b.** one of a number of printings of a publication printed from the same setting of type with no or few alterations. Compare **edition** (sense 2). **c.** the total number of copies of a publication printed at one time. **7.** *Dentistry.* an imprint of the teeth and gums, esp. in wax or plaster, for use in preparing crowns, inlays, or dentures. **8.** an imitation or impersonation: *he did a funny impression of the politician.* —**im·'pres·sion·al** *adj.* —**im·'pres·sion·al·ly** *adv.*

im·pres·sion·a·ble (ɪm'prɛʃənəbᵊl, -'prɛʃnə-) *adj.* easily influenced or characterized by susceptibility to influence; *an impressionable child; an impressionable age.* —**im·ˌpres·sion·a·'bil·i·ty** *or* **im·'pres·sion·a·ble·ness** *n.*

im·pres·sion·ism (ɪm'prɛʃəˌnɪzəm) *n.* **1.** (*often cap.*) a movement in French painting, developed in the 1870s chiefly by Monet, Renoir, Pissarro, and Sisley, having the aim of objectively recording experience by a system of fleeting impressions, esp. of natural light effects. **2.** the technique in art, literature, or music of conveying experience by capturing fleeting impressions of reality or of mood.

im·pres·sion·ist (ɪm'prɛʃənɪst) *n.* **1.** (*usually cap.*) any of the French painters of the late 19th century who were exponents of impressionism. **2.** (*sometimes cap.*) any artist, composer, or writer who uses impressionism. **3.** an entertainer who impersonates famous people. ~*adj.* **4.** (*often cap.*) denoting, of, or relating to impressionism or the exponents of this style. —**im·ˌpres·sion·'is·tic** *adj.*

im·pres·sive (ɪm'prɛsɪv) *adj.* capable of impressing, esp. by size, magnificence, etc.; awe-inspiring; commanding. —**im·'pres·sive·ly** *adv.* —**im·'pres·sive·ness** *n.*

im·press·ment (ɪm'prɛsmənt) *n.* the commandeering or conscription of things or men into government service.

im·pres·sure (ɪm'prɛʃə) *n.* an archaic word for **impression.** [C17: see IMPRESS¹, -URE; formed on the model of PRESSURE]

im·prest (ɪm'prest) *n.* **1.** *Chiefly Brit.* an advance from government funds for the performance of some public business or service. **2.** *Chiefly U.S.* money advanced regularly to a military unit to cover incidental or unexpected expenditure; contingency account. **3.** *Brit.* (formerly) an advance payment of income to a sailor or soldier. [C16: probably from Italian *imprestare* to lend, from Latin *in-* towards + *praestāre* to pay, from *praestō* at hand; see PRESTO]

im·pri·ma·tur (ˌɪmprɪ'meɪtə, -'mɑ:-) *n.* **1.** *R.C. Church.* a licence granted by a bishop certifying the Church's approval of a book to be published. **2.** sanction, authority, or approval, esp. for something to be printed. [C17: New Latin, literally: let it be printed]

im·pri·mis (ɪm'praɪmɪs) *adv. Archaic.* in the first place. [C15: from Latin phrase *in prīmīs,* literally: among the first things]

im·print *n.* ('ɪmprɪnt). **1.** a mark or impression produced by pressure, printing, or stamping. **2.** a characteristic mark or indication; stamp: *the imprint of great sadness on his face.* **3.** the publisher's name and address, usually with the date of publication, in a book, pamphlet, etc. **4.** the printer's name and address on any printed matter. ~*vb.* (ɪm'prɪnt). **5.** to produce (a mark, impression, etc.) on (a surface) by pressure, printing, or stamping: *to imprint a seal on wax; to imprint wax with a seal.* **6.** to establish firmly; impress; stamp: *to imprint the details on one's mind.* —**im·'print·er** *n.*

im·print·ing (ɪm'prɪntɪŋ) *n.* the development in young animals of recognition of and attraction to members of their own species.

im·pris·on (ɪm'prɪzən) *vb.* (*tr.*) to confine in or as if in prison. —**im·'pris·on·er** *n.* —**im·'pris·on·ment** *n.*

im·prob·a·ble (ɪm'prɒbəbᵊl) *adj.* not likely or probable; doubtful; unlikely. —**im·ˌprob·a·'bil·i·ty** *or* **im·'prob·a·ble·ness** *n.* —**im·'prob·a·bly** *adv.*

im·pro·bi·ty (ɪm'prəʊbɪtɪ) *n., pl.* **·ties.** dishonesty, wickedness, or unscrupulousness.

im·promp·tu (ɪm'prɒmptju:) *adj.* **1.** unrehearsed; spontaneous; extempore. **2.** produced or done without care or planning; improvised. ~*adv.* **3.** in a spontaneous or improvised way: *he spoke impromptu.* ~*n.* **4.** something that is impromptu. **5.** a short piece of instrumental music, sometimes improvisatory in character. [C17: from French, from Latin *in promptū* in readiness, from *promptus* (adj.) ready, PROMPT]

im·prop·er (ɪm'prɒpə) *adj.* **1.** lacking propriety; not seemly or fitting. **2.** unsuitable for a certain use or occasion; inappropriate: *an improper use for a tool.* **3.** irregular or abnormal. —**im·'prop·er·ly** *adv.* —**im·'prop·er·ness** *n.*

im·prop·er frac·tion *n.* a fraction in which the numerator has a greater absolute value or degree than the denominator, as 7/6 or $(x^2 + 3)/(x + 1)$.

im·prop·er in·te·gral *n.* a definite integral having one or both limits infinite or having an integrand that becomes infinite within the limits of integration.

im·pro·pri·ate *vb.* (ɪm'prəʊprɪˌeɪt). **1.** (*tr.*) to transfer (property, rights, etc.) from the Church into lay hands. ~*adj.* (ɪm'prəʊprɪɪt, -ˌeɪt). **2.** transferred in this way. [C16: from Medieval Latin *impropriāre* to make one's own, from Latin *im-* IN-² + *propriāre* to APPROPRIATE] —**im·ˌpro·pri·'a·tion** *n.* —**im·'pro·pri·ˌa·tor** *n.*

im·pro·pri·e·ty (ˌɪmprə'praɪɪtɪ) *n., pl.* **·ties. 1.** lack of propriety; indecency; indecorum. **2.** an improper act or use. **3.** the state of being improper.

im·prove (ɪm'pru:v) *vb.* **1.** to make or become better in quality; ameliorate. **2.** (*tr.*) to make (buildings, land, etc.) more valuable by additions or betterment. **3.** (*intr.;* usually foll. by *on* or *upon*) to achieve a better standard or quality in comparison (with): *to improve on last year's crop.* ~*n.* **4. on the improve.** *Austral.* improving. [C16: from Anglo-French *emprouer* to turn to profit, from *en prou* into profit, from *prou* profit, from Late Latin *prōde* beneficial, from Latin *prōdesse* to be advantageous, from PRO-¹ + *esse* to be] —**im·'prov·a·ble** *adj.* —**im·ˌprov·a·'bil·i·ty** *or* **im·'prov·a·ble·ness** *n.* —**im·'prov·a·bly** *adv.* —**im·'prov·er** *n.* —**im·'prov·ing·ly** *adv.*

im·prove·ment (ɪm'pru:vmənt) *n.* **1.** the act of improving or the state of being improved. **2.** something that improves, esp. an addition or alteration.

im·prov·i·dent (ɪm'prɒvɪdənt) *adj.* **1.** not provident; thriftless, imprudent, or prodigal. **2.** heedless or incautious; rash. —**im·'prov·i·dence** *n.* —**im·'prov·i·dent·ly** *adv.*

im·prov·i·sa·tion (ˌɪmprəvaɪ'zeɪʃən) *n.* **1.** the act or an instance of improvising. **2.** a product of improvising; something improvised. —**ˌim·pro·vi·'sa·tion·al** *adj.*

im·pro·vise ('ɪmprəˌvaɪz) *vb.* **1.** to perform or make quickly from materials and sources available, without previous planning. **2.** to perform (a poem, play, piece of music, etc.), composing as one goes along. [C19: from French, from Italian *improvvisare,* from Latin *imprōvīsus* unforeseen, from IM- (not) + *prōvīsus,* from *prōvidēre* to foresee; see PROVIDE] —**'im·pro·ˌvis·er** *n.*

im·pru·dent (ɪm'pru:dᵊnt) *adj.* not prudent; rash, heedless, or indiscreet. —**im·'pru·dence** *n.* —**im·'pru·dent·ly** *adv.*

im·pu·dence ('ɪmpjʊdəns) *or* **im·pu·den·cy** *n.* **1.** the quality of being impudent. **2.** an impudent act or statement. [C14:

from Latin *impudēns* shameless, from IM- (not) + *pudēns* modest; see PUDENCY]
im·pu·dent ('ɪmpjʊdənt) *adj.* **1.** mischievous, impertinent, or disrespectful. **2.** an obsolete word for **immodest.** —'**im·pu·dent·ly** *adv.* —'**im·pu·dent·ness** *n.*
im·pu·dic·i·ty (ˌɪmpjʊ'dɪsɪtɪ) *n. Rare.* immodesty. [C16: from Old French *impudicite,* from Latin *impudīcus* shameless, from IN-[1] + *pudīcus* modest, virtuous]
im·pugn (ɪm'pjuːn) *vb.* (*tr.*) to challenge or attack as false; assail; criticize. [C14: from Old French *impugner,* from Latin *impugnāre* to fight against, attack, from IM- + *pugnāre* to fight] —**im·'pugn·a·ble** *adj.* —**im·pug·na·tion** (ˌɪmpʌg'neɪʃən) *or* **im·'pugn·ment** *n.* —**im·'pugn·er** *n.*
im·pu·is·sant (ɪm'pjuːɪsᵊnt, ɪm'pwiː-) *adj.* powerless, ineffectual, feeble, or impotent. [C17: from French: powerless] —**im·'pu·is·sance** *n.*
im·pulse ('ɪmpʌls) *n.* **1.** an impelling force or motion; thrust; impetus. **2.** a sudden desire, whim, or inclination: *I bought it on an impulse.* **3.** an instinctive drive; urge. **4.** tendency; current; trend. **5.** *Physics.* **a.** the product of the average magnitude of a force acting on a body and the time for which it acts. **b.** the change in the momentum of a body as a result of a force acting upon it. **6.** *Physiol.* See **nerve impulse. 7.** *Electronics.* a less common word for **pulse**[1] (sense 2). **8. on impulse.** spontaneously or impulsively. [C17: from Latin *impulsus* a pushing against, incitement, from *impellere* to strike against; see IMPEL]
im·pulse buy·ing *n.* the buying of retail merchandise prompted by a whim on seeing the product displayed. —**im·pulse buy·er** *n.*
im·pulse tur·bine *n.* a turbine in which the expansion of the fluid is completed in a static nozzle, the torque being produced by the change in momentum of the fluid impinging on curved rotor blades. Compare **reaction turbine.**
im·pul·sion (ɪm'pʌlʃən) *n.* **1.** the act of impelling or the state of being impelled. **2.** motion produced by an impulse; propulsion. **3.** a driving force; compulsion.
im·pul·sive (ɪm'pʌlsɪv) *adj.* **1.** characterized by actions based on sudden desires, whims, or inclinations rather than careful thought: *an impulsive man.* **2.** based on emotional impulses or whims; spontaneous: *an impulsive kiss.* **3.** forceful, inciting, or impelling. **4.** (of physical forces) acting for a short time; not continuous. —**im·'pul·sive·ly** *adv.* —**im·'pul·sive·ness** *n.*
im·pu·ni·ty (ɪm'pjuːnɪtɪ) *n., pl.* **·ties. 1.** exemption or immunity from punishment or recrimination. **2.** exemption or immunity from unpleasant consequences: *a successful career marked by impunity from early mistakes.* **3. with impunity. a.** with no unpleasant consequences. **b.** with no care or heed for such consequences. [C16: from Latin *impūnitās* freedom from punishment, from *impūnis* unpunished, from IM- (not) + *poena* punishment]
im·pure (ɪm'pjʊə) *adj.* **1.** not pure; combined with something else; tainted or sullied. **2.** (in certain religions) **a.** (of persons) ritually unclean and as such debarred from certain religious ceremonies. **b.** (of foodstuffs, vessels, etc.) debarred from certain religious uses. **3.** (of a colour) mixed with another colour or with black or white. **4.** of more than one origin or style, as of architecture or other design. —**im·'pure·ly** *adv.* —**im·'pure·ness** *n.*
im·pu·ri·ty (ɪm'pjʊərɪtɪ) *n., pl.* **·ties. 1.** the quality of being impure. **2.** an impure thing, constituent, or element: *impurities in the water.* **3.** *Electronics.* a small quantity of an element added to a pure semiconductor crystal to control its electrical conductivity. See also **acceptor** (sense 2), **donor** (sense 5).
im·put·a·ble (ɪm'pjuːtəbᵊl) *adj.* capable of being imputed; attributable; ascribable. —**im·ˌput·a·'bil·i·ty** *or* **im·'put·a·ble·ness** *n.* —**im·'put·a·bly** *adv.*
im·pute (ɪm'pjuːt) *vb.* (*tr.*) **1.** to attribute or ascribe (something dishonest or dishonourable, esp. a criminal offence) to a person. **2.** to attribute to a source or cause: *I impute your success to nepotism.* [C14: from Latin *imputāre,* from IM- + *putāre* to think, calculate] —ˌ**im·pu·'ta·tion** *n.* —**im·'pu·ta·tive** *adj.* —**im·'put·er** *n.*
impv. *abbrev. for* imperative.
Im·roz (im'rɔz) *n.* the Turkish name for **Imbros.**
I.M.S. *abbrev. for* Indian Medical Service.
I.Mun.E. *abbrev. for* Institution of Municipal Engineers.
in (ɪn) *prep.* **1.** inside; within: *no smoking in the auditorium.* **2.** at a place where there is: *lying in the shade; walking in the rain.* **3.** indicating a state, situation, or condition: *in a deep sleep; standing in silence.* **4.** before or when (a period of time) has elapsed: *come back in one year.* **5.** using (a language, etc.) as a means of communication: *written in code.* **6.** concerned or involved with, esp. as an occupation: *in journalism.* **7.** while or by performing the action of; as a consequence of or by means of: *in crossing the street he was run over.* **8.** used to indicate goal or purpose: *in honour of the president.* **9.** (used of certain animals) about to give birth to; pregnant with (specified offspring): *in foal; in calf.* **10.** a variant of **into:** *she fell in the water; he tore the paper in two.* **11. have it in one.** (often foll. by an infinitive) to have the ability (to do something). **12. in it.** *Austral. informal.* joining in; taking part. **13. in that** *or* **in so far as.** (*conj.*) because or to the extent that; inasmuch as: *I regret my remark in that it upset you.* **14. nothing, very little, quite a bit, etc., in it.** no, a great, etc., difference or interval between two things. ~*adv.* (*particle*) **15.** in or into a particular place; inward or indoors: *come in; bring him in.* **16.** so as to achieve office, power, or authority: *the Conservatives got in at the last election.* **17.** so as to enclose: *block in; cover in a hole.* **18.** (in certain games) so as to take one's turn or one's team's turn at a certain aspect of the play; taking one's innings: *you have to get the other side out before you go in.* **19.** *Brit.* (of a fire) alight: *do you keep the fire in all night?* **20.** (*in combination*) indicating an activity or gathering, esp. one organized to protest against something: *teach-in; work-in.* **21. in at.** present at (the beginning, end, etc.). **22. in between.** between. **23. in for.** about to be affected by (something, esp. something unpleasant): *you're in for a shock.* **24. in on.** acquainted with or sharing in: *I was in on all his plans.* **25. in with.** associated with; friendly with; regarded highly by. **26. have (got) it in for.** to be seeking to give vent to a grievance against (someone). ~*adj.* **27.** (*stressed*) fashionable; modish: *the in thing to do.* ~*n.* **28. ins and outs.** intricacies or complications; details: *the ins and outs of a computer system.* [Old English; compare Old High German *in,* Welsh *yn,* Old Norse *ī,* Latin *in,* Greek *en*]
In *the chemical symbol for* indium.
in. *abbrev. for* inch(es).
in-[1], **il-, im-,** *or* **ir-** *prefix.* not; non-: *incredible; insincere; illegal; imperfect; irregular.* Compare **un-.** [from Latin *in-;* related to *ne-, nōn* not]
in-[2], **il-, im-,** *or* **ir-** *prefix.* **1.** in; into; towards; within; on: *infiltrate; immigrate.* **2.** having an intensive or causative function: *inflame; imperil.* [from IN (prep., adv.)]
-in *suffix forming nouns.* **1.** indicating a neutral organic compound, including proteins, glucosides, and glycerides: *insulin; digitoxin; tripalmitin.* **2.** indicating an enzyme in certain nonsystematic names: *pepsin.* **3.** indicating a pharmaceutical substance: *penicillin; riboflavin; aspirin.* **4.** indicating a chemical substance in certain nonsystematic names: *coumarin.* [from New Latin *-ina;* compare -INE[2]]
in·a·bil·i·ty (ˌɪnə'bɪlɪtɪ) *n.* lack of ability or means; incapacity.
in ab·sen·ti·a *Latin.* (ɪn æb'sɛntɪə) *adv.* in the absence of (someone indicated): *he was condemned in absentia.*
in·ac·ces·si·ble (ˌɪnæk'sɛsəbᵊl) *adj.* not accessible; unapproachable. —ˌ**in·ac·ˌces·si·'bil·i·ty** *or* ˌ**in·ac·'ces·si·ble·ness** *n.* —ˌ**in·ac·'ces·si·bly** *adv.*
in·ac·cu·ra·cy (ɪn'ækjʊrəsɪ) *n., pl.* **·cies. 1.** lack of accuracy; imprecision. **2.** an error, mistake, or slip.
in·ac·cu·rate (ɪn'ækjʊrɪt) *adj.* not accurate; imprecise, inexact, or erroneous. —**in·'ac·cu·rate·ly** *adv.* —**in·'ac·cu·rate·ness** *n.*
in·ac·tion (ɪn'ækʃən) *n.* lack of action; idleness; inertia.
in·ac·ti·vate (ɪn'æktɪˌveɪt) *vb.* (*tr.*) to render inactive. —**in·ˌac·ti·'va·tion** *n.*
in·ac·tive (ɪn'æktɪv) *adj.* **1.** idle or inert; not active. **2.** sluggish, passive, or indolent. **3.** *Military.* of or relating to persons or equipment not in active service. **4.** *Chem.* (of a substance) having little or no reactivity. **5.** (of an element, isotope, etc.) having little or no radioactivity. —**in·'ac·tive·ly** *adv.* —ˌ**in·ac·'tiv·i·ty** *or* **in·'ac·tive·ness** *n.*
in·ad·e·quate (ɪn'ædɪkwɪt) *adj.* **1.** not adequate; insufficient. **2.** not capable or competent; lacking. —**in·'ad·e·qua·cy** *n.* —**in·'ad·e·quate·ly** *adv.*
in·ad·mis·si·ble (ˌɪnəd'mɪsəbᵊl) *adj.* not admissible or allowable. —ˌ**in·ad·ˌmis·si·'bil·i·ty** *n.* —ˌ**in·ad·'mis·si·bly** *adv.*
in·ad·vert·ence (ˌɪnəd'vɜːtᵊns) *or* **in·ad·vert·en·cy** *n.* **1.** lack of attention; heedlessness. **2.** an instance or an effect of being inadvertent; oversight; slip.
in·ad·vert·ent (ˌɪnəd'vɜːtᵊnt) *adj.* **1.** failing to act carefully or considerately; inattentive. **2.** resulting from heedless action; unintentional. —ˌ**in·ad·'vert·ent·ly** *adv.*
in·ad·vis·a·ble (ˌɪnəd'vaɪzəbᵊl) *adj.* **1.** not advisable; not recommended. **2.** unwise; imprudent. —ˌ**in·ad·ˌvis·a·'bil·i·ty** *or* ˌ**in·ad·'vis·a·ble·ness** *n.* —ˌ**in·ad·'vis·a·bly** *adv.*
-i·nae *suffix forming plural proper nouns.* occurring in names of zoological subfamilies: *Felinae.* [New Latin, from Latin, feminine plural of *-inus* -INE[1]]
in ae·ter·num *Latin.* (ɪn iː'tɜːnəm) *n.* forever; eternally.
in·al·ien·a·ble (ɪn'eɪljənəbᵊl) *adj.* not able to be transferred to another; not alienable: *the inalienable rights of the citizen.* —**in·ˌal·ien·a·'bil·i·ty** *or* **in·'al·ien·a·ble·ness** *n.* —**in·'al·ien·a·bly** *adv.*
in·al·ter·a·ble (ɪn'ɔːltərəbᵊl) *adj.* not alterable; unalterable. —**in·ˌal·ter·a·'bil·i·ty** *or* **in·'al·ter·a·ble·ness** *n.* —**in·'al·ter·a·bly** *adv.*
in·am·o·ra·ta (ɪnˌæmə'rɑːtə, ˌɪnæmə-) *or* (*masc.*) **in·am·o·ra·to** (ɪnˌæmə'rɑːtəʊ, ˌɪnæmə-) *n., pl.* **·tas** *or* (*masc.*) **·tos.** a person with whom one is in love; lover. [C17: from Italian *innamorata, innamorato,* from *innamorare* to cause to fall in love, from *amore* love, from Latin *amor*]
in-and-in *adj.* (of breeding) carried out repeatedly among closely related individuals of the same species to eliminate or intensify certain characteristics.
in·ane (ɪ'neɪn) *adj.* **1.** senseless, unimaginative, or empty; unintelligent: *inane remarks.* ~*n.* **2.** *Archaic.* something empty or vacant, esp. the void of space. [C17: from Latin *inānis* empty] —**in·'ane·ly** *adv.*
in·an·i·mate (ɪn'ænɪmɪt) *adj.* **1.** lacking the qualities or features of living beings; not animate: *inanimate objects.* **2.** lacking any sign of life or consciousness; appearing dead. **3.** lacking vitality; spiritless; dull. —**in·'an·i·mate·ly** *adv.* —**in·'an·i·mate·ness** *or* **in·an·i·ma·tion** (ɪnˌænɪ'meɪʃən) *n.*
in·a·ni·tion (ˌɪnə'nɪʃən) *n.* **1.** exhaustion resulting from lack of food. **2.** mental, social, or spiritual weakness or lassitude. [C14: from Late Latin *inānītio* emptiness, from Latin *inānis* empty; see INANE]
in·an·i·ty (ɪ'nænɪtɪ) *n., pl.* **·ties. 1.** lack of intelligence or imagination; senselessness; silliness. **2.** a senseless action, remark, etc. **3.** an archaic word for **emptiness.**

in+ap+pel+la·ble (ˌɪnəˈpɛləbᵊl) *adj.* incapable of being appealed against, as a court decision; unchallengeable. [C19: from IN-[1] + Latin *appellāre* to APPEAL]

in+ap+pe+tence (ɪnˈæpɪtəns) *or* **in+ap+pe+ten+cy** *n. Rare.* lack of appetite or desire. —**in+ˈap+pe+tent** *adj.*

in+ap+pli+ca·ble (ɪnˈæplɪkəbᵊl, ˌɪnəˈplɪk-) *adj.* not applicable or suitable; irrelevant. —**in+ˌap+pli+ca·ˈbil+i·ty** *or* **in+ˈap+pli+ca·ble+ness** *n.* —**in+ˈap+pli+ca·bly** *adv.*

in+ap+po+site (ɪnˈæpəzɪt) *adj.* not appropriate or pertinent; unsuitable. —**in+ˈap+po+site+ly** *adv.* —**in+ˈap+po+site+ness** *n.*

in+ap+pre+cia·ble (ˌɪnəˈpriːʃəbᵊl) *adj.* **1.** incapable of being appreciated. **2.** imperceptible; negligible. —**ˌin+ap+ˈpre+cia·bly** *adv.*

in+ap+pre+cia+tive (ˌɪnəˈpriːʃətɪv) *adj.* lacking appreciation; unappreciative. —**ˌin+ap+ˈpre+cia+tive+ly** *adv.* —**ˌin+ap+ˌpre+ci+ˈa·tion** *or* **ˌin+ap+ˈpre+cia+tive+ness** *n.*

in+ap+pre+hen+sive (ˌɪnæprɪˈhɛnsɪv) *adj.* **1.** not perceiving or feeling fear or anxiety; untroubled. **2.** *Rare.* unable to understand; imperceptive. —**ˌin+ap+pre+ˈhen+sive+ly** *adv.* —**ˌin+ap+pre+ˈhen+sive+ness** *n.*

in+ap+proach+a·ble (ˌɪnəˈprəʊtʃəbᵊl) *adj.* not accessible; unapproachable; unfriendly. —**ˌin+ap+ˌproach+a·ˈbil+i·ty** *adv.* —**ˌin+ap+ˈproach+a·bly** *adv.*

in+ap+pro+pri+ate (ˌɪnəˈprəʊprɪɪt) *adj.* not fitting or appropriate; unsuitable or untimely. —**ˌin+ap+ˈpro+pri+ate+ly** *adv.* —**ˌin+ap+ˈpro+pri+ate+ness** *n.*

in+apt (ɪnˈæpt) *adj.* **1.** not apt or fitting; inappropriate. **2.** lacking skill; inept. —**in+ˈap+ti+ˌtude** *or* **in+ˈapt+ness** *n.* —**in+ˈapt+ly** *adv.*

in+arch (ɪnˈɑːtʃ) *vb.* (*tr.*) to graft (a plant) by uniting stock and scion while both are still growing independently.

in+ar+tic·u+late (ˌɪnɑːˈtɪkjʊlɪt) *adj.* **1.** unable to express oneself fluently or clearly; incoherent. **2.** (of speech, language, etc.) unclear or incomprehensible; unintelligible: *inarticulate grunts.* **3.** unable to speak; dumb. **4.** unable to be expressed; unvoiced: *inarticulate suffering.* **5.** *Biology.* having no joints, segments, or articulation. —**ˌin+ar+ˈtic·u+late+ly** *adv.* —**ˌin+ar+ˈtic·u+late+ness** *n.*

in+ar+ti+fi+cial (ˌɪnɑːtɪˈfɪʃəl) *adj. Archaic.* **1.** not artificial; real; natural. **2.** inartistic. —**ˌin+ar+ti+ˈfi+cial+ly** *adv.*

in+ar+tis+tic (ˌɪnɑːˈtɪstɪk) *adj.* lacking in artistic skill, appreciation, etc.; Philistine. —**ˌin+ar+ˈtis+ti+cal+ly** *adv.*

in+as+much as (ˌɪnəzˈmʌtʃ) *conj.* (*subordinating*) **1.** in view of the fact that; seeing that; since. **2.** to the extent or degree that; insofar as.

in+at+ten+tive (ˌɪnəˈtɛntɪv) *adj.* not paying attention; heedless; negligent. —**ˌin+at+ˈten+tion** *or* **ˌin+at+ˈten+tive+ness** *n.* —**ˌin+at+ˈten+tive+ly** *adv.*

in+au·di·ble (ɪnˈɔːdəbᵊl) *adj.* not loud enough to be heard; not audible. —**in+ˌau·di·ˈbil+i·ty** *or* **in+ˈau·di·ble+ness** *n.* —**in+ˈau·di·bly** *adv.*

in+au·gu+ral (ɪnˈɔːgjʊrəl) *adj.* **1.** characterizing or relating to an inauguration. ~*n.* **2.** a speech made at an inauguration, esp. by a president of the U.S.

in+au·gu+rate (ɪnˈɔːgjʊˌreɪt) *vb.* (*tr.*) **1.** to commence officially or formally; initiate. **2.** to place in office formally and ceremonially; induct. **3.** to open ceremonially; dedicate formally: *to inaugurate a factory.* [C17: from Latin *inaugurāre,* literally: to take omens, practise augury, hence to install in office after taking auguries; see IN-[2], AUGUR] —**in+ˌau·gu+ˈra+tion** *n.* —**in+ˈau·gu+ˌra+tor** *n.* —**in+au·gu+ra+to+ry** (ɪnˈɔːgjʊrətərɪ, -trɪ) *adj.*

In+au·gu+ra+tion Day *n.* the day on which the inauguration of a president of the U.S. takes place, Jan. 20.

in+aus+pi+cious (ˌɪnɔːˈspɪʃəs) *adj.* not auspicious; unlucky; —**ˌin+aus+ˈpi+cious+ly** *adv.* —**ˌin+aus+ˈpi+cious+ness** *n.*

inbd. *abbrev. for* inboard (on an aircraft, boat, etc.).

in+be·ing (ˈɪnˌbiːɪŋ) *n.* **1.** existence in something else; inherence. **2.** basic and inward nature; essence.

in+board (ˈɪnˌbɔːd) *adj.* **1.** (esp. of a boat's motor or engine) situated within the hull. Compare **outboard** (sense 1). **2.** situated between the wing tip of an aircraft and its fuselage: *an inboard engine.* ~*adv.* **3.** towards the centre line of or within a vessel, aircraft, etc.

in-bond shop *n. Caribbean.* a duty-free shop.

in+born (ˈɪnˈbɔːn) *adj.* existing from birth; congenital; innate.

in+bound (ˈɪnˌbaʊnd) *adj.* coming in; inward bound: *an inbound ship.*

in+breathe (ɪnˈbriːð) *vb.* (*tr.*) *Rare.* to infuse or imbue.

in+bred (ˈɪnˈbrɛd) *adj.* **1.** produced as a result of inbreeding. **2.** deeply ingrained; innate: *inbred good manners.*

in+breed (ˈɪnˈbriːd) *vb.* **+breeds, +breed+ing, +bred. 1.** to breed from unions between closely related individuals, esp. over several generations. **2.** (*tr.*) to develop within; engender. —**ˈin+ˈbreed+ing** *n., adj.*

in-built *adj.* built-in, integral.

inc. *abbrev. for:* **1.** included. **2.** including. **3.** inclusive. **4.** income. **5.** incomplete. **6.** increase.

Inc. *or* **inc.** (esp. after the names of U.S. business organizations) *abbrev. for* incorporated. Brit. equivalent: **Ltd.**

In·ca (ˈɪŋkə) *n., pl.* **·ca** *or* **·cas. 1.** a member of a South American Indian people whose great empire centred on Peru lasted from about 1100 A.D. to the Spanish conquest in the early 1530s and is famed for its complex culture. **2.** the ruler or king of this empire or any member of his family. **3.** the language of the Incas. See also **Quechua.** [C16: from Spanish, from Quechua *inka* king]

in+cal+cu+la·ble (ɪnˈkælkjʊləbᵊl) *adj.* beyond calculation; unable to be predicted or determined. —**in+ˌcal+cu+la·ˈbil+i·ty** *or* **in+ˈcal+cu+la·ble+ness** *n.* —**in+ˈcal+cu+la·bly** *adv.*

in+ca+les+cent (ˌɪnkəˈlɛsᵊnt) *adj. Chem.* increasing in temperature. [C17: from Latin *incalescere,* from IN-[2] + *calescere* to grow warm, from *calēre* to be warm] —**ˌin+ca+ˈles+cence** *n.*

in cam+er·a (ɪn ˈkæmərə) *adv., adj.* **1.** in a private or secret session; not in public. **2.** *Law.* **a.** in the privacy of a judge's chambers. **b.** in a court not open to the public. [Latin: in the chamber]

in+can+desce (ˌɪnkænˈdɛs) *vb.* (*intr.*) to exhibit incandescence.

in+can+des+cence (ˌɪnkænˈdɛsəns) *or* **in+can+des+cen+cy** *n.* **1.** the emission of light by a body as a consequence of raising its temperature. Compare **luminescence. 2.** the light produced by raising the temperature of a body.

in+can+des+cent (ˌɪnkænˈdɛsᵊnt) *adj.* emitting light as a result of being heated to a high temperature; red-hot or white-hot. [C18: from Latin *incandescere* to become hot, glow, from IN-[2] + *candescere* to grow bright, from *candēre* to be white; see CANDID] —**ˌin+can+ˈdes+cent+ly** *adv.*

in+can+des+cent lamp *n.* a source of light that contains a heated solid, such as an electrically heated filament.

in+can+ta+tion (ˌɪnkænˈteɪʃən) *n.* **1.** ritual recitation of magic words or sounds. **2.** the formulaic words or sounds used; a magic spell. [C14: from Late Latin *incantātiō* an enchanting, from *incantāre* to repeat magic formulas, from Latin, from IN-[2] + *cantāre* to sing; see ENCHANT] —**ˌin+can+ˈta+tion+al** *or* **in+ˈcan+ta+to·ry** *adj.*

in+ca+pa·ble (ɪnˈkeɪpəbᵊl) *adj.* **1.** (when *postpositive,* often foll. by *of*) not capable (of); lacking the ability (to). **2.** powerless or helpless, as through injury or intoxication. **3.** (*postpositive;* foll. by *of*) not susceptible (to); not admitting (of): *a problem incapable of solution.* —**in+ˌca+pa·ˈbil+i·ty** *or* **in+ˈca+pa·ble+ness** *n.* —**in+ˈca+pa·bly** *adv.*

in+ca+pac·i+tate (ˌɪnkəˈpæsɪˌteɪt) *vb.* (*tr.*) **1.** to deprive of power, strength, or capacity; disable. **2.** to deprive of legal capacity or eligibility. —**ˌin+ca+ˌpac·i+ˈta+tion** *n.*

in+ca+pac+i·ty (ˌɪnkəˈpæsɪtɪ) *n., pl.* **·ties. 1.** lack of power, strength, or capacity; inability. **2.** *Law.* **a.** legal disqualification or ineligibility. **b.** a circumstance causing this.

In+cap·a+ri+na (ɪnˌkæpəˈriːnə) *n.* a cheap high-protein food made of cottonseed, sorghum flours, maize, yeast, etc., used, esp. in Latin America, to prevent protein-deficiency diseases. [C20: from *Institute of Nutrition in Central America and Panama* + FARINA]

in+cap+su+late (ɪnˈkæpsjʊˌleɪt) *vb.* a less common spelling of **encapsulate.** —**in+ˌcap+su+ˈla+tion** *n.*

in-car *adj.* provided within a car: *in-car entertainment.*

in+car+cer+ate *vb.* (ɪnˈkɑːsəˌreɪt). **1.** (*tr.*) to confine or imprison. ~*adj.* (ɪnˈkɑːsərɪt, -ˌreɪt). **2.** *Rare.* imprisoned. [C16: from Medieval Latin *incarcerāre,* from Latin IN-[2] + *carcer* prison] —**in+ˌcar+cer+ˈa+tion** *n.* —**in+ˈcar+cer·ˌa+tor** *n.*

in+car+di+nate (ɪnˈkɑːdɪˌneɪt) *vb.* (*tr.*) *R.C. Church.* to transfer (a cleric) to the jurisdiction of a new bishop. [C17: from Late Latin *incardināre,* from IN-[2] + *cardinālis* CARDINAL]

in+car+di+na+tion (ɪnˌkɑːdɪˈneɪʃən) *n.* **1.** the official acceptance by one diocese of a clergyman from another diocese. **2.** the promotion of a clergyman to the status of a cardinal.

in+car+na+dine (ɪnˈkɑːnəˌdaɪn) *Archaic or literary.* ~*vb.* **1.** (*tr.*) to tinge or stain with red. ~*adj.* **2.** of a pinkish or reddish colour similar to that of flesh or blood. [C16: from French *incarnadin* flesh-coloured, from Italian, from Late Latin *incarnātus* made flesh, INCARNATE]

in+car+nate *adj.* (ɪnˈkɑːnɪt, -neɪt). (*usually immediately postpositive*) **1.** possessing bodily form, esp. the human form: *a devil incarnate.* **2.** personified or typified: *stupidity incarnate.* **3.** (esp. of plant parts) flesh-coloured or pink. ~*vb.* (ɪnˈkɑːneɪt). (*tr.*) **4.** to give a bodily or concrete form to. **5.** to be representative or typical of. [C14: from Late Latin *incarnāre* to make flesh, from Latin IN-[2] + *carō* flesh]

in+car+na+tion (ˌɪnkɑːˈneɪʃən) *n.* **1.** the act of manifesting or state of being manifested in bodily form, esp. human form. **2.** a bodily form assumed by a god, etc. **3.** a person or thing that typifies or represents some quality, idea, etc.: *the weasel is the incarnation of ferocity.*

In+car+na+tion (ˌɪnkɑːˈneɪʃən) *n. Christian theol.* the assuming of a human body by the Son of God.

in+case (ɪnˈkeɪs) *vb.* a variant spelling of **encase.** —**in+ˈcase+ment** *n.*

in+cau+tious (ɪnˈkɔːʃəs) *adj.* not careful or cautious. —**in+ˈcau+tious+ly** *adv.* —**in+ˈcau+tious+ness** *or* **in+ˈcau+tion** *n.*

in+cen+di·a+rism (ɪnˈsɛndɪəˌrɪzəm) *n.* **1.** the act or practice of illegal burning; arson. **2.** (esp. formerly) the creation of civil strife or violence for political reasons.

in+cen+di+ar·y (ɪnˈsɛndɪərɪ) *adj.* **1.** of or relating to the illegal burning of property, goods, etc. **2.** tending to create strife, violence, etc.; inflammatory. **3.** (of a substance) capable of catching fire, causing fires, or burning readily. ~*n., pl.* **+ar·ies. 4.** a person who illegally sets fire to property, goods, etc.; arsonist. **5.** (esp. formerly) a person who stirs up civil strife, violence, etc., for political reasons; agitator. **6.** Also called: **incendiary bomb.** a bomb that is designed to start fires. **7.** an incendiary substance, such as phosphorus. [C17: from Latin *incendiārius* setting alight, from *incendium* fire, from *incendere* to kindle]

in+cense[1] (ˈɪnsɛns) *n.* **1.** any of various aromatic substances burnt for their fragrant odour, esp. in religious ceremonies. **2.** the odour or smoke so produced. **3.** any pleasant fragrant odour; aroma. **4.** *Rare.* homage or adulation. ~*vb.* **5.** to burn incense in honour of (a deity). **6.** (*tr.*) to perfume or fumigate with incense. [C13: from Old French *encens,* from Church Latin *incensum,* from Latin *incendere* to kindle] —ˌ**in+cen+'sa+tion** *n.*

in+cense[2] (ɪn'sɛns) *vb.* (*tr.*) to enrage greatly. [C15: from Latin *incensus* set on fire, from *incendere* to kindle] —**in+'cense+ment** *n.*

in+cen+so+ry ('ɪnsɛnsərɪ) *n., pl.* **+ries.** a less common name for a **censer.** [C17: from Medieval Latin *incensorium*]

in+cen+tive (ɪn'sɛntɪv) *n.* **1.** a motivating influence; stimulus. **2. a.** an additional payment made to employees as a means of increasing production. **b.** (*as modifier*): *an incentive scheme.* ~*adj.* **3.** serving to incite to action. [C15: from Late Latin *incentīvus* (adj.), from Latin: striking up, setting the tune, from *incinere* to sing, from IN-[2] + *canere* to sing] —**in+'cen+tive+ly** *adv.*

in+cept (ɪn'sɛpt) *vb.* (*tr.*) **1.** (of organisms) to ingest (food). **2.** *Brit.* (formerly) to take a master's or doctor's degree at a university. [C19: from Latin *inceptus* begun, attempted, from *incipere* to begin, take in hand, from IN-[2] + *capere* to take] —**in+'cep+tor** *n.*

in+cep+tion (ɪn'sɛpʃən) *n.* the beginning, as of a project or undertaking.

in+cep+tive (ɪn'sɛptɪv) *adj.* **1.** beginning; incipient; initial. **2.** Also called: **inchoative.** *Grammar.* denoting an aspect of verbs in some languages used to indicate the beginning of an action. ~*n.* **3.** *Grammar.* **a.** the inceptive aspect of verbs. **b.** a verb in this aspect. —**in+'cep+tive+ly** *adv.*

in+cer+ti+tude (ɪn'sɜːtɪˌtjuːd) *n.* **1.** uncertainty; doubt. **2.** a state of mental or emotional insecurity.

in+ces+sant (ɪn'sɛsᵊnt) *adj.* not ceasing; continual. [C16: from Late Latin *incessāns,* from Latin IN-[1] + *cessāre* to CEASE] —**in+'ces+san+cy** *or* **in+'ces+sant+ness** *n.* —**in+'ces+sant+ly** *adv.*

in+cest ('ɪnsɛst) *n.* sexual intercourse between two persons commonly regarded as too closely related to marry. [C13: from Latin *incestus* incest (from adj.: impure, defiled), from IN-[1] + *castus* CHASTE]

in+ces+tu+ous (ɪn'sɛstjʊəs) *adj.* **1.** relating to or involving incest: *an incestuous union.* **2.** guilty of incest. **3.** *Obsolete.* resulting from incest: *an incestuous bastard.* **4.** resembling incest in excessive or claustrophobic intimacy. —**in+'ces+tu+ous+ly** *adv.* —**in+'ces+tu+ous+ness** *n.*

inch[1] (ɪntʃ) *n.* **1.** a unit of length equal to one twelfth of a foot or 0.0254 metre. **2.** *Meteorol.* **a.** an amount of precipitation that would cover a surface with water one inch deep: *five inches of rain fell in January.* **b.** a unit of pressure equal to a mercury column one inch high in a barometer. **3.** a very small distance, degree, or amount. **4. every inch.** in every way; completely: *he was every inch an aristocrat.* **5. inch by inch.** gradually; little by little. **6. within an inch of.** very close to. ~*vb.* **7.** to move or be moved very slowly or in very small steps: *the car inched forward.* [Old English *ynce,* from Latin *uncia* twelfth part; see OUNCE]

inch[2] (ɪntʃ) *n. Scot. and Irish.* a small island. [C15: from Gaelic *innis* island; compare Welsh *ynys*]

inch+meal ('ɪntʃˌmiːl) *adv.* gradually; inch by inch or little by little. [C16: from INCH[1] + -MEAL; compare PIECEMEAL]

in+cho+ate *adj.* (ɪn'kəʊeɪt, -'kəʊɪt). **1.** just beginning; incipient. **2.** undeveloped; immature; rudimentary. ~*vb.* (ɪn'kəʊeɪt). (*tr.*) **3.** to begin. [C16: from Latin *incohāre* to make a beginning, literally: to hitch up, from IN-[2] + *cohum* yokestrap] —**in+'cho+ate+ly** *adv.* —**in+'cho+ate+ness** *n.* —ˌ**in+cho+'a+tion** *n.* —**in+cho+a+tive** (ɪn'kəʊətɪv) *adj.*

In+chon *or* **In+cheon** ('ɪn'tʃɒn) *n.* a port in W South Korea, on the Yellow Sea: the chief port for Seoul. Pop.: 797 140 (1975). Former name: **Chemulpo.**

inch+worm ('ɪntʃˌwɜːm) *n.* another name for a **measuring worm.**

in+ci+dence ('ɪnsɪdəns) *n.* **1.** degree, extent, or frequency of occurrence; amount: *a high incidence of death from pneumonia.* **2.** the act or manner of impinging on or affecting by proximity or influence. **3.** *Physics.* the arrival of a beam of light or particles at a surface. See also **angle of incidence. 4.** *Geom.* the partial coincidence of two configurations, such as a point that lies on a circle.

in+ci+dent ('ɪnsɪdənt) *n.* **1.** a distinct or definite occurrence; event. **2.** a minor, subsidiary, or related event or action. **3.** a relatively insignificant event that might have serious consequences, esp. in international politics. **4.** a public disturbance: *the police had reports of an incident outside a pub.* ~*adj.* **5.** (*postpositive;* foll. by *to*) related (to) or dependent (on). **6.** (when *postpositive,* often foll. by *to*) having a subsidiary or minor relationship (with). **7.** (esp. of a beam of light or particles) arriving at or striking a surface: *incident electrons.* [C15: from Medieval Latin *incidens* an event, from Latin *incidere,* literally: to fall into, hence befall, happen, from IN-[2] + *cadere* to fall]

in+ci+den+tal (ˌɪnsɪ'dɛntᵊl) *adj.* **1.** happening in connection with or resulting from something more important; casual or fortuitous. **2.** (*postpositive;* foll. by *to*) found in connection (with); related (to). **3.** (*postpositive;* foll. by *upon*) caused (by). **4.** occasional or minor: *incidental expenses.* ~*n.* **5.** (*often pl.*) an incidental or minor expense, event, or action. —ˌ**in+ci+'den+tal+ness** *n.*

in+ci+den+tal+ly (ˌɪnsɪ'dɛntəlɪ) *adv.* **1.** as a subordinate or chance occurrence. **2.** (*sentence modifier*) by the way.

in+ci+den+tal mu+sic *n.* background music for a film, etc.

in+cin+er+ate (ɪn'sɪnəˌreɪt) *vb.* to burn up completely; reduce to ashes. [C16: from Medieval Latin *incinerāre,* from Latin IN-[2] + *cinis* ashes] —**in+ˌcin+er+'a+tion** *n.*

in+cin+er+a+tor (ɪn'sɪnəˌreɪtə) *n.* a furnace or apparatus for incinerating something, esp. refuse.

in+cip·i+ent (ɪn'sɪpɪənt) *adj.* just starting to be or happen; beginning. [C17: from Latin *incipiēns,* from *incipere* to begin, take in hand, from IN-[2] + *capere* to take] —**in+'cip·i+ence** *or* **in+'cip·i+en+cy** *n.* —**in+'cip·i+ent+ly** *adv.*

in+ci+pit ('ɪnkɪpɪt) *Latin.* here begins: used as an introductory word at the beginning of some medieval manuscripts.

in+cise (ɪn'saɪz) *vb.* (*tr.*) to produce (lines, a design, etc.) by cutting into the surface of (something) with a sharp tool. [C16: from Latin *incīdere* to cut into, from IN-[2] + *caedere* to cut]

in+cised (ɪn'saɪzd) *adj.* **1.** cut into or engraved: *an incised surface.* **2.** made by cutting or engraving: *an incised design.* **3.** (of a wound) cleanly cut, as with a surgical knife. **4.** having margins that are sharply and deeply indented: *an incised leaf.*

in+ci+sion (ɪn'sɪʒən) *n.* **1.** the act of incising. **2.** a cut, gash, or notch. **3.** a cut made with a knife during a surgical operation. **4.** any indentation in an incised leaf. **5.** *Rare.* incisiveness.

in+ci+sive (ɪn'saɪsɪv) *adj.* **1.** keen, penetrating, or acute. **2.** biting or sarcastic; mordant: *an incisive remark.* **3.** having a sharp cutting edge: *incisive teeth.* —**in+'ci+sive+ly** *adv.* —**in+'ci+sive+ness** *n.*

in+ci+sor (ɪn'saɪzə) *n.* a chisel-edged tooth at the front of the mouth. In man there are four in each jaw.

in+ci+sure (ɪn'saɪʒə) *n. Anatomy.* an incision or notch in an organ or part. —**in+'ci+sur+al** *adj.*

in+cite (ɪn'saɪt) *vb.* (*tr.*) to stir up or provoke to action. [C15: from Latin *incitāre,* from IN-[2] + *citāre* to excite] —ˌ**in+ci+'ta+tion** *n.* —**in+'cite+ment** *n.* —**in+'cit+er** *n.* —**in+'cit+ing+ly** *adv.*

in+ci+vil+i·ty (ɪnsɪ'vɪlɪtɪ) *n., pl.* **·ties. 1.** lack of civility or courtesy; rudeness. **2.** an impolite or uncivil act or remark.

incl. *abbrev. for:* **1.** including. **2.** inclusive.

in+clem+ent (ɪn'klɛmənt) *adj.* **1.** (of weather) stormy, severe, or tempestuous. **2.** harsh, severe, or merciless. —**in+'clem+en+cy** *or* **in+'clem+ent+ness** *n.* —**in+'clem+ent+ly** *adv.*

in+clin+a+ble (ɪn'klaɪnəbᵊl) *adj.* **1.** (*postpositive;* usually foll. by *to*) having an inclination or tendency (to); disposed (to). **2.** capable of being inclined.

in+cli+na+tion (ˌɪnklɪ'neɪʃən) *n.* **1.** (often foll. by *for, to, towards,* or an infinitive) a particular disposition, esp. a liking or preference; tendency: *I've no inclination for such dull work.* **2.** the degree of deviation from a particular plane, esp. a horizontal or vertical plane. **3.** a sloping or slanting surface; incline. **4.** the act of inclining or the state of being inclined. **5.** *Maths.* **a.** the angle between a line on a graph and the positive limb of the *x*-axis. **b.** the smaller dihedral angle between one plane and another. **6.** *Astronomy.* the angle between the plane of the orbit of a planet or comet and another plane, usually that of the ecliptic. **7.** *Physics.* another name for **dip** (sense 29). —ˌ**in+cli+'na+tion+al** *adj.*

in+cline *vb.* (ɪn'klaɪn). **1.** to deviate or cause to deviate from a particular plane, esp. a vertical or horizontal plane; slope or slant. **2.** (when *tr.,* may take an infinitive) to be disposed or cause to be disposed (towards some attitude or to do something): *he inclines towards levity; that does not incline me to think that you are right.* **3.** to bend or lower (part of the body, esp. the head), as in a bow or in order to listen. **4. incline one's ear.** to listen favourably (to). ~*n.* ('ɪnklaɪn, ɪn'klaɪn). **5.** an inclined surface or slope; gradient. **6.** short for **inclined railway.** [C13: from Latin *inclīnāre* to cause to lean, from *clīnāre* to bend; see LEAN[1]] —**in+'clin+er** *n.*

in+clined (ɪn'klaɪnd) *adj.* **1.** (*postpositive;* often foll. by *to*) having a disposition; tending. **2.** sloping or slanting.

in+clined plane *n.* a plane whose angle to the horizontal is less than a right angle.

in+clined rail+way *n. Chiefly U.S.* a cable railway used on particularly steep inclines unsuitable for normal adhesion locomotives.

in+cli+nom·e+ter (ˌɪnklɪ'nɒmɪtə) *n.* **1.** an aircraft instrument for indicating the angle that an aircraft makes with the horizontal. **2.** another name for **dip circle.**

in+close (ɪn'kləʊz) *vb.* a less common spelling of **enclose.** —**in+'clos+a+ble** *adj.* —**in+'clos+er** *n.* —**in+'clos+ure** *n.*

in+clude (ɪn'kluːd) *vb.* (*tr.*) **1.** to have as contents or part of the contents; be made up of or contain. **2.** to add as part of something else; put in as part of a set, group, or category. **3.** to contain as a secondary or minor ingredient or element. [C15 (in the sense: to enclose): from Latin *inclūdere* to enclose, from IN-[2] + *claudere* to close] —**in+'clud+a+ble** *or* **in+'clud+i+ble** *adj.*

in+clud+ed (ɪn'kluːdɪd) *adj.* (of the stamens or pistils of a flower) not protruding beyond the corolla. —**in+'clud+ed+ness** *n.*

in+clude out *vb.* (*tr., adv.*) to exclude: *you can include me out of that deal.*

in+clu+sion (ɪn'kluːʒən) *n.* **1.** the act of including or the state of being included. **2.** something included. **3.** *Geology.* a solid fragment, liquid globule, or pocket of gas enclosed in a mineral or rock. **4.** *Maths.* a relationship between two sets that is only valid when the members of one set are all members of the other.

in+clu+sion bod+y *n. Pathol.* any of the small particles found in cells infected with certain viruses.

in+clu+sive (ɪn'kluːsɪv) *adj.* **1.** (*postpositive;* foll. by *of*) considered together (with): *capital inclusive of profit.* **2.** (*postpositive*) including the limits specified: *Monday to Friday inclusive is five days.* **3.** comprehensive. **4.** *Logic.* (of a disjunction) true if at least one of its component propositions is true. Compare **exclusive** (sense 10). —**in+ˈclu+sive+ly** *adv.* —**in+ˈclu+sive+ness** *n.*

in+clu+sive or *n. Logic.* the connective that gives the value *true* to a disjunction if either or both of the disjuncts are true. Also called: **inclusive disjunction.** Compare **exclusive or.**

in+co+er+ci·ble (ˌɪnkəʊˈɜːsəbᵊl) *adj.* **1.** unable to be coerced or compelled. **2.** (of a gas) not capable of being liquefied by pressure alone.

incog. *abbrev. for* incognito.

in+cog·i+ta·ble (ɪnˈkɒdʒɪtəbᵊl) *adj. Rare.* not to be contemplated; unthinkable. —**in+ˌcog·i+ta·ˈbil+i·ty** *n.*

in+cog·i+tant (ɪnˈkɒdʒɪtənt) *adj. Rare.* thoughtless. [C17: from Latin *incōgitāns,* from IN-[1] + *cōgitāre* to think]

in+cog+ni+to (ˌɪnkɒgˈniːtəʊ) *or (fem.)* **in+cog+ni+ta** *adv., adj.* (*postpositive*) **1.** under an assumed name or appearance; in disguise. ~*n., pl.* **+tos** *or (fem.)* **+tas. 2.** a person who is incognito. **3.** the assumed name or disguise of such a person. [C17: from Italian, from Latin *incognitus* unknown, from IN-[1] + *cognitus* known]

in+cog+ni+zant (ɪnˈkɒgnɪzənt) *adj.* (*when postpositive,* often foll. by *of*) unaware (of). —**in+ˈcog+ni+zance** *n.*

in+co+her+ent (ˌɪnkəʊˈhɪərənt) *adj.* **1.** lacking in clarity or organization; disordered. **2.** unable to express oneself clearly; inarticulate. —**ˌin+co+ˈher+ence, ˌin+co+ˈher+en+cy,** *or* **ˌin+co+ˈher+ent+ness** *n.* —**ˌin+co+ˈher+ent+ly** *adv.*

in+com+bus+ti·ble (ˌɪnkəmˈbʌstəbᵊl) *adj.* **1.** not capable of being burnt; fireproof. ~*n.* **2.** an incombustible object or material. —**ˌin+com+ˌbus+ti·ˈbil+i·ty** *or* **ˌin+com+ˈbus+ti·ble+ness** *n.* —**ˌin+com+ˈbus+ti·bly** *adv.*

in+come (ˈɪnkʌm, ˈɪnkəm) *n.* **1.** the amount of monetary or other returns, either earned or unearned, accruing over a given period of time. **2.** receipts; revenue. **3.** *Rare.* an inflow or influx. [C13 (in the sense: arrival, entrance): from Old English *incumen* a coming in]

in+come bond *n.* a bond that pays interest at a rate in direct proportion to the issuer's earnings.

in+come group *n.* a group in a given population having incomes within a certain range.

in+come tax *n.* a personal tax, usually progressive, levied on annual income subject to certain deductions.

in+com+ing (ˈɪnˌkʌmɪŋ) *adj.* **1.** coming in; entering. **2.** about to come into office; succeeding. **3.** (of interest, dividends, etc.) being received; accruing. ~*n.* **4.** the act of coming in; entrance. **5.** (*usually pl.*) income or revenue.

in+com+men+su+ra·ble (ˌɪnkəˈmɛnʃərəbᵊl) *adj.* **1.** incapable of being judged, measured, or considered comparatively. **2.** (*postpositive;* foll. by *with*) not in accordance; incommensurate. **3.** *Maths.* **a.** not having a common factor other than 1, such as 2 and $\sqrt{-5}$. **b.** not having units of the same dimension. **c.** unrelated to another measurement by integral multiples. ~*n.* **4.** something incommensurable. —**ˌin+com+ˌmen+su+ra·ˈbil+i·ty** *or* **ˌin+com+ˈmen+su+ra·ble+ness** *n.* —**ˌin+com+ˈmen+su+ra·bly** *adv.*

in+com+men+su+rate (ˌɪnkəˈmɛnʃərɪt) *adj.* **1.** (*when postpositive,* often foll. by *with*) not commensurate; disproportionate. **2.** incommensurable. —**ˌin+com+ˈmen+su+rate+ly** *adv.* —**ˌin+com+ˈmen+su+rate+ness** *n.*

in+com+mode (ˌɪnkəˈməʊd) *vb.* (*tr.*) to bother, disturb, or inconvenience. [C16: from Latin *incommodāre* to be troublesome, from *incommodus* inconvenient, from IN-[1] + *commodus* convenient; see COMMODE]

in+com+mo+di+ous (ˌɪnkəˈməʊdɪəs) *adj.* **1.** insufficiently spacious; cramped. **2.** troublesome or inconvenient. —**ˌin+com+ˈmo+di+ous+ly** *adv.* —**ˌin+com+ˈmo+di+ous+ness** *n.*

in+com+mod+i·ty (ˌɪnkəˈmɒdɪtɪ) *n., pl.* **·ties.** a less common word for **inconvenience.**

in+com+mu+ni+ca·ble (ˌɪnkəˈmjuːnɪkəbᵊl) *adj.* **1.** incapable of being communicated. **2.** an obsolete word for **incommunicative.** —**ˌin+com+ˌmu+ni+ca·ˈbil+i·ty** *or* **ˌin+com+ˈmu+ni+ca·ble+ness** *n.* —**ˌin+com+ˈmu+ni+ca·bly** *adv.*

in+com+mu+ni+ca+do (ˌɪnkəˌmjuːnɪˈkɑːdəʊ) *adv., adj.* (*postpositive*) deprived of communication with other people, as while in solitary confinement. [C19: from Spanish *incomunicado,* from *incomunicar* to deprive of communication; see IN-[1], COMMUNICATE]

in+com+mu+ni+ca+tive (ˌɪnkəˈmjuːnɪkətɪv) *adj.* tending not to communicate with others; taciturn. —**ˌin+com+ˈmu+ni+ca+tive+ly** *adv.* —**ˌin+com+ˈmu+ni+ca+tive+ness** *n.*

in+com+mut+a·ble (ˌɪnkəˈmjuːtəbᵊl) *adj.* incapable of being commuted; unalterable. —**ˌin+com+ˌmut+a·ˈbil+i·ty** *or* **ˌin+com+ˈmut+a·ble+ness** *n.* —**ˌin+com+ˈmut+a·bly** *adv.*

in+com+pa+ra·ble (ɪnˈkɒmpərəbᵊl, -prəbᵊl) *adj.* **1.** beyond or above comparison; matchless; unequalled. **2.** lacking a basis for comparison; not having qualities or features that can be compared. —**in+ˌcom+pa+ra·ˈbil+i·ty** *or* **in+ˈcom+pa+ra·ble+ness** *n.* —**in+ˈcom+pa+ra·bly** *adv.*

in+com+pat+i·ble (ˌɪnkəmˈpætəbᵊl) *adj.* **1.** incapable of living or existing together in peace or harmony; conflicting or antagonistic. **2.** opposed in nature or quality; inconsistent. **3.** (of an office, position, etc.) only able to be held by one person at a time. **4.** *Med.* (esp. of two drugs or two types of blood) incapable of being combined or used together; antagonistic. **5.** *Logic.* (of two propositions) unable to be both true at the same time. **6.** (of plants) **a.** not capable of forming successful grafts. **b.** incapable of self-fertilization. **7.** *Maths.* another word for **inconsistent** (sense 4). ~*n.* **8.** (*often pl.*) a person or thing that is incompatible with another. —**ˌin+com+ˌpat+i·ˈbil+i·ty** *or* **ˌin+com+ˈpat+i·ble+ness** *n.* —**ˌin+com+ˈpat+i·bly** *adv.*

in+com+pe+tent (ɪnˈkɒmpɪtənt) *adj.* **1.** not possessing the necessary ability, skill, etc. to do or carry out a task; incapable. **2.** marked by lack of ability, skill, etc. **3.** *Law.* not legally qualified: *an incompetent witness.* **4.** (of rock strata, folds, etc.) yielding readily to pressure so as to undergo structural deformation. ~*n.* **5.** an incompetent person. —**in+ˈcom+pe+tence** *or* **in+ˈcom+pe+ten+cy** *n.* —**in+ˈcom+pe+tent+ly** *adv.*

in+com+plete (ˌɪnkəmˈpliːt) *adj.* **1.** not complete or finished. **2.** not completely developed; imperfect. **3.** *Logic.* meaningless unless used in a specific context. —**ˌin+com+ˈplete+ly** *adv.* —**ˌin+com+ˈplete+ness** *or* **ˌin+com+ˈple+tion** *n.*

in+com+pli+ant (ˌɪnkəmˈplaɪənt) *adj.* not compliant; unyielding or inflexible. —**ˌin+com+ˈpli+ance** *or* **ˌin+com+ˈpli+an+cy** *n.* —**ˌin+com+ˈpli+ant+ly** *adv.*

in+com+pre+hen+si·ble (ˌɪnkɒmprɪˈhɛnsəbᵊl, ɪnˌkɒm-) *adj.* **1.** incapable of being understood; unintelligible. **2.** *Archaic.* limitless; boundless. —**ˌin+com+pre+ˌhen+si·ˈbil+i·ty** *or* **ˌin+com+pre+ˈhen+si·ble+ness** *n.* —**ˌin+com+pre+ˈhen+si·bly** *adv.*

in+com+pre+hen+sion (ˌɪnkɒmprɪˈhɛnʃən, ɪnˌkɒm-) *n.* inability or failure to comprehend; lack of understanding.

in+com+pre+hen+sive (ˌɪnkɒmprɪˈhɛnsɪv, ɪnˌkɒm-) *adj.* not comprehensive; limited in range or scope. —**ˌin+com+pre+ˈhen+sive+ly** *adv.* —**ˌin+com+pre+ˈhen+sive+ness** *n.*

in+com+press+i·ble (ˌɪnkəmˈprɛsəbᵊl) *adj.* incapable of being compressed or condensed. —**ˌin+com+ˌpress+i·ˈbil+i·ty** *or* **ˌin+com+ˈpress+i·ble+ness** *n.* —**ˌin+com+ˈpress+i·bly** *adv.*

in+com+put+a·ble (ˌɪnkəmˈpjuːtəbᵊl) *adj.* incapable of being computed; incalculable. —**ˌin+com+ˌput+a·ˈbil+i·ty** *n.* —**ˌin+com+ˈput+a·bly** *adv.*

in+con+ceiv+a·ble (ˌɪnkənˈsiːvəbᵊl) *adj.* incapable of being conceived, imagined, or considered. —**ˌin+con+ˌceiv+a·ˈbil+i·ty** *or* **ˌin+con+ˈceiv+a·ble+ness** *n.* —**ˌin+con+ˈceiv+a·bly** *adv.*

in+con+clu+sive (ˌɪnkənˈkluːsɪv) *adj.* **1.** not conclusive or decisive; not finally settled; indeterminate. —**ˌin+con+ˈclu+sive+ly** *adv.* —**ˌin+con+ˈclu+sive+ness** *n.*

in+con+den+sa·ble *or* **in+con+den+si·ble** (ˌɪnkənˈdɛnsəbᵊl) *adj.* incapable of being condensed. —**ˌin+con+ˌden+sa·ˈbil+i·ty** *or* **ˌin+con+ˌden+si·ˈbil+i·ty** *n.*

in+con+dite (ɪnˈkɒndɪt, -daɪt) *adj. Rare.* **1.** poorly constructed or composed. **2.** rough or crude. —**in+ˈcon+dite+ly** *adv.*

in+con+form+i·ty (ˌɪnkənˈfɔːmɪtɪ) *n.* lack of conformity; irregularity.

in+con+gru+i·ty (ˌɪnkɒŋˈgruːɪtɪ) *n., pl.* **·ties. 1.** something incongruous. **2.** the state or quality of being incongruous.

in+con+gru+ous (ɪnˈkɒŋgrʊəs) *or* **in+con+gru+ent** *adj.* **1.** (when *postpositive,* foll. by *with* or *to*) incompatible with (what is suitable); inappropriate. **2.** containing disparate or discordant elements or parts. —**in+ˈcon+gru+ous+ly** *or* **in+ˈcon+gru+ent+ly** *adv.* —**in+ˈcon+gru+ous+ness** *or* **in+ˈcon+gru+ence** *n.*

in+con+sec·u+tive (ˌɪnkənˈsɛkjʊtɪv) *adj.* not consecutive; not in sequence. —**ˌin+con+ˈsec·u+tive+ly** *adv.* —**ˌin+con+ˈsec·u+tive+ness** *n.*

in+con+se·quen+tial (ˌɪnkɒnsɪˈkwɛnʃəl, ɪnˌkɒn-) *or* **in+con+se·quent** (ɪnˈkɒnsɪkwənt) *adj.* **1.** not following logically as a consequence. **2.** trivial or insignificant. **3.** not in a logical sequence; haphazard. —**ˌin+con+se·ˌquen+ti·ˈal+i·ty, ˌin+con+se·ˈquen+tial+ness, in+ˈcon+se·quence,** *or* **in+ˈcon+se·quent+ness** *n.* —**ˌin+con+se·ˈquen+tial+ly** *or* **in+ˈcon+se·quent+ly** *adv.*

in+con+sid+er+a·ble (ˌɪnkənˈsɪdərəbᵊl) *adj.* **1.** relatively small. **2.** not worthy of consideration; insignificant. —**ˌin+con+ˈsid+er+a·ble+ness** *n.* —**ˌin+con+ˈsid+er+a·bly** *adv.*

in+con+sid+er+ate (ˌɪnkənˈsɪdərɪt) *adj.* **1.** lacking in care or thought for others; heedless; thoughtless. **2.** *Rare.* insufficiently considered. —**ˌin+con+ˈsid+er+ate+ly** *adv.* —**ˌin+con+ˈsid+er+ate+ness** *or* **ˌin+con+ˌsid+er+ˈa+tion** *n.*

in+con+sist+en+cy (ˌɪnkənˈsɪstənsɪ) *n., pl.* **+cies. 1.** lack of consistency or agreement; incompatibility. **2.** an inconsistent feature or quality.

in+con+sist+ent (ˌɪnkənˈsɪstənt) *adj.* **1.** lacking in consistency, agreement, or compatibility; at variance. **2.** containing contradictory elements. **3.** irregular or fickle in behaviour or mood. **4.** Also: **incompatible.** *Maths.* (of two or more equations) not having one common set of values of the variables: $x + 2y = 5$ and $x + 2y = 6$ are inconsistent. **5.** *Logic.* (of a set of axioms) leading to at least one proposition that can be shown to be true by one axiom and false by another. —**ˌin+con+ˈsist+ent+ly** *adv.*

in+con+sol+a·ble (ˌɪnkənˈsəʊləbᵊl) *adj.* incapable of being consoled or comforted; disconsolate. —**ˌin+con+ˌsol+a·ˈbil+i·ty** *or* **ˌin+con+ˈsol+a·ble+ness** *n.* —**ˌin+con+ˈsol+a·bly** *adv.*

in+con+so+nant (ɪnˈkɒnsənənt) *adj.* lacking in harmony or compatibility; discordant. —**in+ˈcon+so+nance** *n.* —**in+ˈcon+so+nant+ly** *adv.*

in+con+spic·u+ous (ˌɪnkənˈspɪkjʊəs) *adj.* not easily noticed or seen; not prominent or striking. —**ˌin+con+ˈspic·u+ous+ly** *adv.* —**ˌin+con+ˈspic·u+ous+ness** *n.*

in+con+stant (ɪnˈkɒnstənt) *adj.* **1.** not constant; variable. **2.** fickle. —**in+ˈcon+stan+cy** *n.* —**in+ˈcon+stant+ly** *adv.*

in+con+sum+a·ble (ˌɪnkənˈsjuːməbᵊl) *adj.* **1.** incapable of being consumed or used up. **2.** *Economics.* providing an economic service without being consumed, as currency. —**ˌin+con+ˈsum+a·bly** *adv.*

in+con+test+a·ble (ˌɪnkənˈtɛstəbᵊl) *adj.* incapable of being contested or disputed. —**ˌin+con+ˌtest+a·ˈbil+i·ty** *or* **ˌin+con+ˈtest+a·ble+ness** *n.* —**ˌin+con+ˈtest+a·bly** *adv.*

in+con+ti+nent[1] (ɪnˈkɒntɪnənt) *adj.* **1.** lacking in restraint or control, esp. sexually. **2.** relating to or exhibiting involuntary urination or defecation. **3.** (foll. by *of*) having little or no control (over). **4.** unrestrained; uncontrolled. [C14: from Old

French, from Latin *incontinens,* from IN-[1] + *continere* to hold, restrain] —**in+'con+ti+nence** *or* **in+'con+ti+nen+cy** *n.* —**in+'con+ti+nent+ly** *adv.*

in+con+ti+nent[2] (ɪn'kɒntɪnənt) *adv.* an obsolete word for **immediately.** [C15: from Late Latin *in continentī tempore,* literally: in continuous time, that is, with no interval]

in+con+trol+la+ble (ˌɪnkən'trəʊləbᵊl) *adj.* a less common word for **uncontrollable.** —ˌ**in+con+'trol+la+bly** *adv.*

in+con+tro+vert+i+ble (ˌɪnkɒntrə'vɜːtəbᵊl, ɪnˌkɒn-) *adj.* incapable of being contradicted or disputed; undeniable. —ˌ**in+con+tro+ˌvert+i+'bil+i+ty** *or* ˌ**in+con+tro+'vert+i+ble+ness** *n.* —ˌ**in+con+tro+'vert+i+bly** *adv.*

in+con+ven+ience (ˌɪnkən'viːnjəns, -'viːnɪəns) *n.* **1.** the state or quality of being inconvenient. **2.** something inconvenient; a hindrance, trouble, or difficulty. ~*vb.* **3.** (*tr.*) to cause inconvenience to; trouble or harass.

in+con+ven+ient (ˌɪnkən'viːnjənt, -'viːnɪənt) *adj.* not convenient; troublesome, awkward, or difficult. —ˌ**in+con+'ven+ient+ly** *adv.*

in+con+vert+i+ble (ˌɪnkən'vɜːtəbᵊl) *adj.* **1.** incapable of being converted or changed. **2.** (of paper currency) **a.** not redeemable for gold or silver specie. **b.** not exchangeable for another currency. —ˌ**in+con+ˌvert+i+'bil+i+ty** *or* ˌ**in+con+'vert+i+ble+ness** *n.* —ˌ**in+con+'vert+i+bly** *adv.*

in+con+vin+ci+ble (ˌɪnkən'vɪnsəbᵊl) *adj.* refusing or not able to be convinced. —ˌ**in+con+ˌvin+ci+'bil+i+ty** *or* ˌ**in+con+'vin+ci+ble+ness** *n.* —ˌ**in+con+'vin+ci+bly** *adv.*

in+co+or+di+nate (ˌɪnkəʊ'ɔːdɪnɪt) *adj.* **1.** not coordinate; unequal in rank, order, or importance. **2.** uncoordinated.

in+co+or+di+na+tion (ˌɪnkəʊˌɔːdɪ'neɪʃən) *n.* **1.** lack of coordination or organization. **2.** *Pathol.* a lack of muscular control when making a voluntary movement.

incorp. *or* **incor.** *abbrev. for* incorporated.

in+cor+po+ra+ble (ɪn'kɔːpərəbᵊl) *adj.* capable of being incorporated or included.

in+cor+po+rate[1] *vb.* (ɪn'kɔːpəˌreɪt). **1.** to include or be included as a part or member of a united whole. **2.** to form or cause to form a united whole or mass; merge or blend. **3.** to form (individuals, an unincorporated enterprise, etc.) into a corporation or other organization with a separate legal identity from that of its owners or members. ~*adj.* (ɪn'kɔːpərɪt, -prɪt). **4.** combined into a whole; incorporated. **5.** formed into or constituted as a corporation. [C14 (in the sense: put into the body of something else): from Late Latin *incorporāre* to embody, from Latin IN-[2] + *corpus* body] —**in+'cor+po+ra+tive** *adj.* —**in+ˌcor+po+'ra+tion** *n.*

in+cor+po+rate[2] (ɪn'kɔːpərɪt, -prɪt) *adj.* an archaic word for **incorporeal.** [C16: from Late Latin *incorporātus,* from Latin IN-[1] + *corporātus* furnished with a body]

in+cor+po+rat+ed (ɪn'kɔːpəˌreɪtɪd) *adj.* **1.** united or combined into a whole. **2.** organized as a legal corporation, esp. in commerce. Abbrev.: **Inc.** *or* **inc.** —**in+'cor+po+ˌrat+ed+ness** *n.*

in+cor+po+rat+ing (ɪn'kɔːpəˌreɪtɪŋ) *adj. Linguistics.* another word for **polysynthetic.**

in+cor+po+ra+tor (ɪn'kɔːpəˌreɪtə) *n.* **1.** a person who incorporates. **2.** *U.S. commerce.* **a.** any of the signatories of a certificate of incorporation. **b.** any of the original members of a corporation.

in+cor+po+re+al (ˌɪnkɔː'pɔːrɪəl) *adj.* **1.** without material form, body, or substance. **2.** spiritual or metaphysical. **3.** *Law.* having no material existence but existing by reason of its annexation of something material, such as an easement, touchline, copyright, etc.: *an incorporeal hereditament.* —ˌ**in+cor+'po+re+al+ly** *adv.* —**in+cor+po+re+i+ty** (ɪnˌkɔːpə'riːɪtɪ) *or* ˌ**in+cor+po+re+'al+i+ty** *n.*

in+cor+rect (ˌɪnkə'rɛkt) *adj.* **1.** false; wrong: *an incorrect calculation.* **2.** not fitting or proper: *incorrect behaviour.* —ˌ**in+cor+'rect+ly** *adv.* —ˌ**in+cor+'rect+ness** *n.*

in+cor+ri+gi+ble (ɪn'kɒrɪdʒəbᵊl) *adj.* **1.** beyond correction, reform, or alteration. **2.** firmly rooted; ineradicable. ~*n.* **3.** a person or animal that is incorrigible. —**in+ˌcor+ri+gi+'bil+i+ty** *or* **in+'cor+ri+gi+ble+ness** *n.* —**in+'cor+ri+gi+bly** *adv.*

in+cor+rupt (ˌɪnkə'rʌpt) *adj.* **1.** free from corruption; pure. **2.** free from decay; fresh or untainted. **3.** (of a manuscript, text, etc.) relatively free from error or alteration. —ˌ**in+cor+'rupt+ly** *adv.* —ˌ**in+cor+'rup+tion** *or* ˌ**in+cor+'rupt+ness** *n.*

in+cor+rupt+i+ble (ˌɪnkə'rʌptəbᵊl) *adj.* **1.** incapable of being corrupted; honest; just. **2.** not subject to decay or decomposition. —ˌ**in+cor+ˌrupt+i+'bil+i+ty** *or* ˌ**in+cor+'rupt+i+ble+ness** *n.* —ˌ**in+cor+'rupt+i+bly** *adv.*

incr. *abbrev. for:* **1.** increase. **2.** increased. **3.** increasing.

in+cras+sate *adj.* (ɪn'kræsɪt, -eɪt), *also* **in+cras+sat+ed. 1.** *Biology.* thickened or swollen: *incrassate cell walls.* **2.** *Obsolete.* fattened or swollen. ~*vb.* (ɪn'kræseɪt). **3.** *Obsolete.* to make or become thicker. [C17: from Late Latin *incrassāre,* from Latin *crassus* thick, dense] —ˌ**in+cras+'sa+tion** *n.*

in+crease *vb.* (ɪn'kriːs). **1.** to make or become greater in size, degree, frequency, etc.; grow or expand. ~*n.* ('ɪnkriːs). **2.** the act of increasing; augmentation. **3.** the amount by which something increases. **4. on the increase.** increasing, esp. becoming more frequent. [C14: from Old French *encreistre,* from Latin *incrēscere,* from IN-[2] *crēscere* to grow] —**in+'creas+a+ble** *adj.* —**in+creas+ed+ly** (ɪn'kriːsɪdlɪ) *or* **in+'creas+ing+ly** *adv.* —**in+'creas+er** *n.*

in+cre+ate (ˌɪnkrɪ'eɪt, 'ɪnkrɪˌeɪt) *adj. Archaic, poetic.* (esp. of gods) never having been created. —ˌ**in+cre+'ate+ly** *adv.*

in+cred+i+ble (ɪn'krɛdəbᵊl) *adj.* **1.** beyond belief or understanding; unbelievable. **2.** *Informal.* marvellous; amazing. —**in+ˌcred+i+'bil+i+ty** *or* **in+'cred+i+ble+ness** *n.* —**in+'cred+i+bly** *adv.*

in+cre+du+li+ty (ˌɪnkrɪ'djuːlɪtɪ) *n.* lack of belief; scepticism.

in+cred+u+lous (ɪn'krɛdʒʊləs) *adj.* (often foll. by *of*) not prepared or willing to believe (something); unbelieving. —**in+'cred+u+lous+ly** *adv.* —**in+'cred+u+lous+ness** *n.*

in+cre+ment ('ɪnkrɪmənt) *n.* **1.** an increase or addition, esp. one of a series. **2.** the act of increasing; augmentation. **3.** *Maths.* a small positive or negative change in a variable or function. Symbol: Δ, as in Δx or Δf. [C15: from Latin *incrēmentum* growth, INCREASE] —**in+cre+men+tal** (ˌɪnkrɪ'mɛntᵊl) *adj.*

in+cre+men+tal plot+ter *n.* a device that plots graphs on paper from computer-generated instructions. See also **microfilm plotter.**

in+cre+men+tal re+cord+er *n. Computer technol.* a device for recording data as it is generated, usually on paper tape or magnetic tape, and feeding it into a computer.

in+cres+cent (ɪn'krɛsᵊnt) *adj.* (esp. of the moon) increasing in size; waxing. [C16: from Latin *incrēscēns*]

in+cre+tion (ɪn'kriːʃən) *n. Physiol.* **1.** direct secretion into the bloodstream, esp. of a hormone from an endocrine gland. **2.** the substance so secreted. [C20: from IN-[2] + (SE)CRETION] —**in+'cre+tion+ar+y** *or* **in+cre+to+ry** ('ɪnkrɪtərɪ, -trɪ) *adj.*

in+crim+i+nate (ɪn'krɪmɪˌneɪt) *vb.* (*tr.*) **1.** to imply or suggest the guilt or error of (someone). **2.** to charge with a crime or fault. [C18: from Late Latin *incrīmināre* to accuse, from Latin *crīmen* accusation; see CRIME] —**in+ˌcrim+i+'na+tion** *n.* —**in+'crim+i+ˌna+tor** *n.* —**in+'crim+i+na+to+ry** *adj.*

in+cross ('ɪnkrɒs) *n.* **1.** a plant or animal produced by continued inbreeding. ~*vb.* **2.** to inbreed or produce by inbreeding.

in+crust (ɪn'krʌst) *vb.* a variant spelling of **encrust.** —**in+'crust+ant** *n., adj.* —ˌ**in+crus+'ta+tion** *n.*

in+cu+bate ('ɪnkjʊˌbeɪt) *vb.* **1.** (of birds) to supply (eggs) with heat for their development, esp. by sitting on them. **2.** to cause (eggs, embryos, bacteria, etc.) to develop, esp. in an incubator or culture medium. **3.** (*intr.*) (of eggs, embryos, bacteria, etc.) to develop in favourable conditions, esp. in an incubator. **4.** (*intr.*) (of disease germs) to remain inactive in an animal or human before causing disease. **5.** to develop or cause to develop gradually; foment or be fomented. [C18: from Latin *incubāre* to lie upon, hatch, from IN-[2] + *cubāre* to lie down] —ˌ**in+cu+'ba+tion** *n.* —ˌ**in+cu+'ba+tion+al** *adj.* —'**in+cu+ˌba+tive** *or* '**in+cu+ˌba+to+ry** *adj.*

in+cu+ba+tion pe+ri+od *n. Med.* the time between exposure to an infectious disease and the appearance of the first signs or symptoms. Sometimes shortened to **incubation.**

in+cu+ba+tor ('ɪnkjʊˌbeɪtə) *n.* **1.** *Med.* an enclosed transparent boxlike apparatus for housing prematurely born babies under optimum conditions until they are strong enough to survive in the normal environment. **2.** a container kept at a constant temperature in which birds' eggs can be artificially hatched or bacterial cultures grown. **3.** a person, animal, or thing that incubates.

in+cu+bus ('ɪnkjʊbəs) *n., pl.* **+bi** (-ˌbaɪ) *or* **+bus+es. 1.** a demon believed in folklore to lie upon sleeping persons, esp. to have sexual intercourse with sleeping women. Compare **succubus. 2.** something that oppresses, worries, or disturbs greatly, esp. a nightmare or obsession. [C14: from Late Latin, from *incubāre* to lie upon; see INCUBATE]

in+cu+des (ɪn'kjuːdiːz) *n.* the plural of **incus.**

in+cul+cate ('ɪnkʌlˌkeɪt, ɪn'kʌlkeɪt) *vb.* (*tr.*) to instil by forceful or insistent repetition. [C16: from Latin *inculcāre* to tread upon, ram down, from IN-[2] + *calcāre* to trample, from *calx* heel] —ˌ**in+cul+'ca+tion** *n.* —'**in+cul+ˌca+tor** *n.*

in+cul+pa+ble (ɪn'kʌlpəbᵊl) *adj.* incapable of being blamed or accused; guiltless. —**in+ˌcul+pa+'bil+i+ty** *or* **in+'cul+pa+ble+ness** *n.* —**in+'cul+pa+bly** *adv.*

in+cul+pate ('ɪnkʌlˌpeɪt, ɪn'kʌlpeɪt) *vb.* (*tr.*) to incriminate; cause blame to be imputed to. [C18: from Late Latin *inculpāre,* from Latin *culpāre* to blame, from *culpa* fault, blame] —ˌ**in+cul+'pa+tion** *n.* —**in+cul+pa+tive** (ɪn'kʌlpətɪv) *or* **in+cul+pa+to+ry** (ɪn'kʌlpətərɪ, -trɪ) *adj.*

in+cult (ɪn'kʌlt) *adj. Rare.* **1.** (of land) uncultivated; untilled; naturally wild. **2.** lacking refinement and culture. [C16: from Latin *incultus,* from IN-[1] + *colere* to till]

in+cum+ben+cy (ɪn'kʌmbənsɪ) *n., pl.* **+cies. 1.** the state or quality of being incumbent. **2.** the office, duty, or tenure of an incumbent.

in+cum+bent (ɪn'kʌmbənt) *adj.* **1.** *Formal.* (often *postpositive* and foll. by *on* or *upon* and an infinitive) morally binding or necessary; obligatory: *it is incumbent on me to attend.* **2.** (usually *postpositive* and foll. by *on*) resting or lying (on). ~*n.* **3.** a person who holds an office, esp. a clergyman holding a benefice. [C16: from Latin *incumbere* to lie upon, devote one's attention to, from IN-[2] + *-cumbere,* related to Latin *cubāre* to lie down] —**in+'cum+bent+ly** *adv.*

in+cum+ber (ɪn'kʌmbə) *vb.* a less common spelling of **encumber.** —**in+'cum+ber+ing+ly** *adv.* —**in+'cum+brance** *n.*

in+cu+nab+u+la (ˌɪnkjʊ'næbjʊlə) *pl. n., sing.* **+lum** (-ləm). **1.** any book printed before 1500. **2.** the infancy or earliest stages of something; beginnings. [C19: from Latin, originally: swaddling clothes, hence beginnings, from IN-[2] + *cūnābula* cradle] —ˌ**in+cu+'nab+u+lar** *adj.*

in+cur (ɪn'kɜː) *vb.* **+curs, +cur+ring, +curred.** (*tr.*) **1.** to make oneself subject to (something undesirable); bring upon oneself. **2.** to run into or encounter. [C16: from Latin *incurrere* to run into, from *currere* to run] —**in+'cur+ra+ble** *adj.*

in+cur+a+ble (ɪn'kjʊərəbᵊl) *adj.* **1.** (esp. of a disease) not curable; unresponsive to treatment. ~*n.* **2.** a person having an incurable disease. —in,cur·a·'bil·i·ty *or* in'cur·a·ble·ness *n.* —in'cur·a·bly *adv.*

in·cu·ri·ous (ɪn'kjʊərɪəs) *adj.* not curious; indifferent or uninterested. —in,cu·ri·os·i·ty (ɪn,kjʊərɪ'ɒsɪtɪ) *or* in'cu·ri·ous·ness *n.* —in'cu·ri·ous·ly *adv.*

in·cur·rence (ɪn'kʌrəns) *n.* the act or state of incurring.

in·cur·rent (ɪn'kʌrənt) *adj.* **1.** (of anatomical ducts, tubes, channels, etc.) having an inward flow. **2.** flowing or running in an inward direction. [C16: from Latin *incurrēns* running into; see INCUR]

in·cur·sion (ɪn'kɜːʃən) *n.* **1.** a sudden invasion, attack, or raid. **2.** the act of running or leaking into; penetration. [C15: from Latin *incursiō* onset, attack, from *incurrere* to run into; see INCUR] —in·cur·sive (ɪn'kɜːsɪv) *adj.*

in·cur·vate *vb.* ('ɪnkɜː,veɪt), *also* **in·curve** (ɪn'kɜːv). **1.** to curve or cause to curve inwards. ~*adj.* (ɪn'kɜːvɪt, -veɪt). **2.** curved inwards. [C16: from Latin *incurvāre* (*vb.*)] —,in·cur'va·tion *n.* —in·cur·va·ture (ɪn'kɜːvətʃə) *n.*

in·cus ('ɪŋkəs) *n., pl.* **in·cu·des** (ɪn'kjuːdiːz). the central of the three small bones in the middle ear of mammals. Nontechnical name: **anvil.** Compare **malleus, stapes.** [C17: from Latin: anvil, from *incūdere* to forge] —in·cu·date ('ɪŋkjʊ,deɪt) *or* in·cu·dal ('ɪŋkjʊdᵊl) *adj.*

in·cuse (ɪn'kjuːz) *n.* **1.** a design stamped or hammered onto a coin. ~*vb.* **2.** to impress (a design) in a coin or to impress (a coin) with a design by hammering or stamping. ~*adj.* **3.** stamped or hammered onto a coin. [C19: from Latin *incūsus* hammered; see INCUS]

Ind (ɪnd) *n.* **1.** a poetic name for **India.** **2.** an obsolete name for the **Indies.**

IND *international car registration for* India.

ind. *abbrev. for:* **1.** independence. **2.** independent. **3.** index. **4.** indicative. **5.** indirect. **6.** industrial. **7.** industry.

Ind. *abbrev. for:* **1.** Independent. **2.** India. **3.** Indian. **4.** Indiana. **5.** Indies.

I.N.D. *abbrev. for* in nomine Dei. Also **I.D.N.** [Latin: in the name of God]

in·da·ba (ɪn'dɑːbə) *n.* **1.** *Anthropol., history.* (among Bantu peoples of southern Africa) a meeting to discuss a serious topic. **2.** *S. African informal.* a matter of concern or for discussion. [C19: from Zulu: topic]

in·da·mine ('ɪndə,miːn, -mɪn) *n.* **1.** Also called: **phenylene blue.** an organic base used in the production of the dye safranine. Formula: $NH_2C_6H_4N{:}C_6H_4{:}NH$ **2.** any of a class of organic bases with a similar structure to this compound. Their salts are unstable blue and green dyes. [C20: from INDIGO + AMINE]

in·debt·ed (ɪn'dɛtɪd) *adj.* (*postpositive*) **1.** owing gratitude for help, favours, etc; obligated. **2.** owing money.

in·debt·ed·ness (ɪn'dɛtɪdnɪs) *n.* **1.** the state of being indebted. **2.** the total of a person's debts.

in·de·cen·cy (ɪn'diːsənsɪ) *n., pl.* **·cies.** **1.** the state or quality of being indecent. **2.** an indecent act, etc.

in·de·cent (ɪn'diːsᵊnt) *adj.* **1.** offensive to standards of decency, esp. in sexual matters. **2.** unseemly or improper (esp. in the phrase **indecent haste**). —in'de·cent·ly *adv.*

in·de·cent as·sault *n.* the act of taking indecent liberties with a person without his or her consent.

in·de·cent ex·po·sure *n.* the offence of indecently exposing parts of one's body in public, esp. the genitals.

in·de·cid·u·ous (,ɪndɪ'sɪdjʊəs) *adj.* **1.** (of leaves) not deciduous. **2.** another word for **evergreen** (sense 1).

in·de·ci·pher·a·ble (,ɪndɪ'saɪfərəbᵊl, -frəbᵊl) *adj.* not decipherable; illegible. —,in·de,ci·pher·a·'bil·i·ty *or* ,in·de'ci·pher·a·ble·ness *n.* —,in·de'ci·pher·a·bly *adv.*

in·de·ci·sive (,ɪndɪ'saɪsɪv) *adj.* **1.** (of a person) vacillating; irresolute. **2.** not decisive or conclusive. —,in·de'ci·sion *or* ,in·de'ci·sive·ness *n.* —,in·de'ci·sive·ly *adv.*

in·de·clin·a·ble (,ɪndɪ'klaɪnəbᵊl) *adj.* (of a noun or pronoun) having only one form; not declined for case or number. —,in·de'clin·a·ble·ness *n.* —,in·de'clin·a·bly *adv.*

in·dec·o·rous (ɪn'dɛkərəs) *adj.* improper or ungraceful; unseemly. —in'dec·o·rous·ly *adv.* —in'dec·o·rous·ness *n.*

in·de·co·rum (,ɪndɪ'kɔːrəm) *n.* indecorous behaviour or speech; unseemliness.

in·deed (ɪn'diːd) **1.** (*sentence connector*) certainly; actually: *indeed, it may never happen.* ~*adv.* **2.** (intensifier): *that is indeed amazing.* **3.** or rather; what is more: *a comfortable, indeed wealthy family.* ~*interj.* **4.** an expression of doubt, surprise, etc.

indef. *abbrev. for* indefinite.

in·de·fat·i·ga·ble (,ɪndɪ'fætɪgəbᵊl) *adj.* unable to be tired out; unflagging. [C16: from Latin *indēfatīgābilis*, from IN-¹ + *dēfatīgāre*, from *fatīgāre* to tire] —,in·de,fat·i·ga·'bil·i·ty *or* ,in·de'fat·i·ga·ble·ness *n.* —,in·de'fat·i·ga·bly *adv.*

in·de·fea·si·ble (,ɪndɪ'fiːzəbᵊl) *adj. Law.* not liable to be annulled or forfeited. —,in·de,fea·si·'bil·i·ty *or* ,in·de'fea·si·ble·ness *n.* —,in·de'fea·si·bly *adv.*

in·de·fect·i·ble (,ɪndɪ'fɛktɪbᵊl) *adj.* **1.** not subject to decay or failure. **2.** flawless. —,in·de,fect·i·'bil·i·ty *n.* —,in·de'fect·i·bly *adv.*

in·de·fen·si·ble (,ɪndɪ'fɛnsəbᵊl) *adj.* **1.** not justifiable or excusable. **2.** capable of being disagreed with; untenable. **3.** incapable of defence against attack. —,in·de,fen·si·'bil·i·ty *or* ,in·de'fen·si·ble·ness *n.* —,in·de'fen·si·bly *adv.*

in·de·fin·a·ble (,ɪndɪ'faɪnəbᵊl) *adj.* incapable of being defined or analysed: *there was an indefinable sense of terror.* —,in·de'fin·a·ble·ness *n.* —,in·de'fin·a·bly *adv.*

in·def·i·nite (ɪn'dɛfɪnɪt) *adj.* **1.** not certain or determined; unsettled. **2.** without exact limits; indeterminate: *an indefinite number.* **3.** vague, evasive, or unclear. **4.** Also: **indeterminate.** *Botany.* **a.** too numerous to count: *indefinite stamens.* **b.** capable of continued growth at the tip of the stem, which does not terminate in a flower: *an indefinite inflorescence.* —in'def·i·nite·ly *adv.* —in'def·i·nite·ness *n.*

in·def·i·nite ar·ti·cle *n. Grammar.* a determiner that expresses nonspecificity of reference, such as *a, an,* or *some.* Compare **definite article.**

in·def·i·nite in·te·gral *n.* any function, symbolized as $\int f(x)dx$, whose derivative gives the function $f(x)$.

in·def·i·nite pro·noun *n. Grammar.* a pronoun having no specific referent, such as *someone, anybody,* or *nothing.*

in·de·his·cent (,ɪndɪ'hɪsᵊnt) *adj.* (of fruits, etc.) not dehiscent; not opening to release seeds, etc. —,in·de'his·cence *n.*

in·del·i·ble (ɪn'dɛlɪbᵊl) *adj.* incapable of being erased or obliterated. [C16: from Latin *indēlēbilis* indestructible, from IN-¹ + *delēre* to destroy] —in,del·i·bil·i·ty *or* in'del·i·ble·ness *n.* —in'del·i·bly *adv.*

in·del·i·cate (ɪn'dɛlɪkɪt) *adj.* **1.** coarse, crude, or rough. **2.** offensive, embarrassing, or tasteless. —in'del·i·ca·cy *or* in'del·i·cate·ness *n.* —in'del·i·cate·ly *adv.*

in·dem·ni·fy (ɪn'dɛmnɪ,faɪ) *vb.* **·fies, ·fy·ing, ·fied.** (*tr.*) **1.** to secure against future loss, damage, or liability; give security for; insure. **2.** to compensate for loss, injury, expense, etc.; reimburse. —in,dem·ni·fi'ca·tion *n.* —in'dem·ni,fi·er *n.*

in·dem·ni·ty (ɪn'dɛmnɪtɪ) *n., pl.* **·ties.** **1.** compensation for loss or damage; reimbursement; **2.** protection or insurance against future loss or damage. **3.** legal exemption from penalties or liabilities incurred through one's acts or defaults. **4. act of indemnity.** an act of Parliament granting exemption to public officers from technical penalties that they may have been compelled to incur. [C15: from Late Latin *indemnitās*, from *indemnis* uninjured, from Latin IN-¹ + *damnum* damage]

in·de·mon·stra·ble (,ɪndɪ'mɒnstrəbᵊl) *adj.* incapable of being demonstrated or proved. —,in·de,mon·stra·'bil·i·ty *n.* —,in·de'mon·stra·bly *adv.*

in·dene ('ɪndiːn) *n.* a colourless liquid hydrocarbon extracted from petroleum and coal tar and used in making synthetic resins. Formula: C_9H_8. [C20: from INDOLE + -ENE]

in·dent[1] *vb.* (ɪn'dɛnt). (*mainly tr.*) **1.** to place (written or printed matter, etc.) in from the margin, as at the beginning of a paragraph. **2.** to cut or tear (a document, esp. a contract or deed in duplicate) so that the irregular lines may be matched to confirm its authenticity. **3.** *Chiefly Brit.* (in foreign trade) to place an order for (foreign goods), usually through an agent. **4.** (when *intr.*, foll. by *for, on,* or *upon*) *Chiefly Brit.* to make an order on (a source or supply) or for (something). **5.** to notch (an edge, border, etc.); make jagged. **6.** to bind (an apprentice, etc.) by indenture. ~*n.* ('ɪn,dɛnt). **7.** *Chiefly Brit.* (in foreign trade) an order for foreign merchandise, esp. one placed with an agent. **8.** *Chiefly Brit.* an official order for goods. **9.** (in the late 18th-century U.S.) a certificate issued by federal and state governments for the principal or interest due on the public debt. **10.** another word for **indenture. 11.** another word for **indentation** (sense 4). [C14: from Old French *endenter*, from EN-¹ + *dent* tooth, from Latin *dēns*] —in'dent·er *or* in'den·tor *n.*

in·dent[2] *vb.* (ɪn'dɛnt). **1.** (*tr.*) to make a dent or depression in. ~*n.* ('ɪn,dɛnt). **2.** a dent or depression. [C15: from IN-² + DENT¹]

in·den·ta·tion (,ɪndɛn'teɪʃən) *n.* **1.** a hollowed, notched, or cut place, as on an edge or on a coastline. **2.** a series of hollows, notches, or cuts. **3.** the act of indenting or the condition of being indented. **4.** Also called: **indention, indent.** the leaving of space or the amount of space left between a margin and the start of an indented line.

in·den·tion (ɪn'dɛnʃən) *n.* another word for **indentation** (sense 4).

in·den·ture (ɪn'dɛntʃə) *n.* **1.** any deed, contract, or sealed agreement between two or more parties. **2.** (formerly) a deed drawn up in duplicate, each part having correspondingly indented edges for identification and security. **3.** (*often pl.*) a contract between an apprentice and his master. **4.** a formal or official list or certificate authenticated for use as a voucher, etc. **5.** a less common word for **indentation.** ~*vb.* **6.** (*intr.*) to enter into an agreement by indenture. **7.** (*tr.*) to bind (an apprentice, servant, etc.) by indenture. **8.** (*tr.*) *Obsolete.* to indent or wrinkle. —in'den·ture,ship *n.*

in·de·pend·ence (,ɪndɪ'pɛndəns) *n.* the state or quality of being independent. Also: **independency.**

In·de·pend·ence (,ɪndɪ'pɛndəns) *n.* a city in W Missouri, near Kansas City: starting point for the Santa Fe, Oregon, and California Trails (1831–44). Pop.: 114 272 (1973 est.).

In·de·pend·ence Day *n.* the official name for the **Fourth of July.**

in·de·pend·en·cy (,ɪndɪ'pɛndənsɪ) *n., pl.* **·cies.** **1.** a territory or state free from the control of any other power. **2.** another word for **independence.**

In·de·pend·en·cy (,ɪndɪ'pɛndənsɪ) *n.* (esp. in the Congregational Church) the principle upholding the independence of each local church or congregation.

in·de·pend·ent (,ɪndɪ'pɛndənt) *adj.* **1.** free from control in action, judgment, etc.; autonomous. **2.** not dependent on anything else for function, validity, etc.; separate: *two independent units make up this sofa.* **3.** not reliant on the support, esp. financial support, of others. **4.** capable of acting for oneself or on one's own: *a very independent little girl.* **5.** providing a large unearned sum towards one's support (esp. in the phrases **independent income, independent means**). **6.** living on an unearned income. **7.** *Maths.* (of a system of equations) not all satisfied by the same set of values for the variables. See also **independent variable. 8.** *Statistics.* (of two or more variables) distributed so that the value taken by one variable will have no effect on that taken by another or others. **9.** *Logic.* (of two or more propositions) unrelated. *~n.* **10.** an independent person or thing. **11.** a person who is not affiliated to or who acts independently of a political party. —ˌ**in+de+'pen+dent+ly** *adv.*

In+de+pend+ent (ˌɪndɪ'pɛndənt) *Ecclesiast.* *~n.* **1.** (in England) a member of the Congregational Church. *~adj.* **2.** of or relating to Independency.

in+de+pend+ent clause *n. Grammar.* a main or coordinate clause. Compare **dependent clause.**

in+de+pend+ent school *n.* (in Britain) a school that is neither financed nor controlled by the government or local authorities.

in+de+pend+ent var+i+a+ble *n.* a variable in a mathematical equation or statement whose value determines that of the dependent variable: in $y = f(x)$, x is the independent variable. Also called: **argument.**

in+de+scrib+a+ble (ˌɪndɪ'skraɪbəbᵊl) *adj.* beyond description; too intense, extreme, etc., for words. —ˌ**in+de+ˌscrib+a+'bil+i+ty** *or* ˌ**in+de+'scrib+a+ble+ness** *n.* —ˌ**in+de+'scrib+a+bly** *adv.*

in+de+struct+i+ble (ˌɪndɪ'strʌktəbᵊl) *adj.* incapable of being destroyed; very durable. —ˌ**in+de+ˌstruct+i+'bil+i+ty** *or* ˌ**in+de+'struct+i+ble+ness** *n.* —ˌ**in+de+'struct+i+bly** *adv.*

in+de+ter+mi+na+ble (ˌɪndɪ'tɜːmɪnəbᵊl) *adj.* **1.** incapable of being ascertained. **2.** incapable of being settled. —ˌ**in+de+'ter+mi+na+ble+ness** *n.* —ˌ**in+de+'ter+mi+na+bly** *adv.*

in+de+ter+mi+na+cy prin+ci+ple *n.* another name for **uncertainty principle.**

in+de+ter+mi+nate (ˌɪndɪ'tɜːmɪnɪt) *adj.* **1.** uncertain in extent, amount, or nature. **2.** not definite; inconclusive: *an indeterminate reply.* **3.** unable to be predicted, calculated, or deduced. **4.** *Physics, etc.* (of an effect) not obeying the law of causality; noncausal. **5.** *Maths.* **a.** having no numerical meaning, as 0.00 and 0/0. **b.** (of an equation) having more than one variable and an unlimited number of solutions. **6.** *Botany.* another word for **indefinite** (sense 4). **7.** (of a structure, framework, etc.) comprising forces that cannot be fully analysed, esp. by vector analysis. —ˌ**in+de+'ter+mi+na+cy,** ˌ**in+de+ˌter+mi+'na+tion,** *or* ˌ**in+de+'ter+mi+nate+ness** *n.* —ˌ**in+de+'ter+mi+nate+ly** *adv.*

in+de+ter+min+ate sen+tence *n. Law.* a prison sentence the length of which depends on the prisoner's conduct.

in+de+ter+min+ism (ˌɪndɪ'tɜːmɪˌnɪzəm) *n.* the philosophical doctrine that behaviour is not entirely determined by motives. —ˌ**in+de+'ter+min+ist** *n., adj.* —ˌ**in+de+ˌter+min+'is+tic** *adj.*

in+dex ('ɪndɛks) *n., pl.* **+dex+es** *or* **+di+ces** (-dɪˌsiːz). **1.** an alphabetical list of persons, places, subjects, etc., mentioned in the text of a printed work, usually at the back, and indicating where in the work they are referred to. **2.** See **thumb index. 3.** *Library science.* a systematic list of book titles or author's names, giving cross-references and the location of each book; catalogue. **4.** an indication, sign, or token. **5.** a pointer, needle, or other indicator, as on an instrument. **6.** *Maths.* **a.** another name for **exponent** (sense 4). **b.** a number or variable placed as a superscript to the left of a radical sign indicating by its value the root to be extracted, as in $\sqrt[3]{8} = 2$. **c.** a subscript or superscript to the right of a variable to show that the variable should be considered over a range of specified values: x_i *for the index* $i = 3$ *includes* x_1, x_2, *and* x_3. **7.** a numerical scale by means of which variables, such as levels of the cost of living, can be compared with each other or with some base number. **8.** a number or ratio indicating a specific characteristic, property, etc.: *refractive index.* **9.** Also called: **fist.** a printer's mark (☛) used to indicate notes, paragraphs, etc. **10.** *Obsolete.* a table of contents or preface. *~vb. (tr.)* **11.** to put an index in (a book). **12.** to enter (a word, item, etc.) in an index. **13.** to point out; indicate. [C16: from Latin: pointer, hence forefinger, title, index, from *indicāre* to disclose, show; see INDICATE] —**'in+dex+er** *n.* —**in+'dex+i+cal** *adj.* —**'in+dex+less** *adj.*

in+dex+a+tion (ˌɪndɛk'seɪʃən) or **in+dex-link+ing** *n.* the act of making wages, interest rates, etc., index-linked.

in+dex fin+ger *n.* the finger next to the thumb. Also called: **forefinger.**

In+dex Li+bro+rum Pro+hib+i+to+rum *Latin.* ('ɪndɛks laɪ'brɔːrʊm prəʊˌhɪbɪ'tɔːrʊm) *n. R.C. Church.* (formerly) an official list of proscribed books. Often called: **the Index.** [C17, literally: list of forbidden books]

in+dex-linked *adj.* (of wages, interest rates, etc.) directly related to the cost-of-living index and rising accordingly.

in+dex num+ber *n. Statistics.* a statistic indicating the relative change occurring in each successive period of time in the price, volume, or value of a commodity or in a general economic variable, such as the price level, national income, or gross output, with reference to a previous base period conventionally given the number 100.

in+dex of re+frac+tion *n.* another name for **refractive index.**

In+di+a ('ɪndɪə) *n.* a republic in S Asia: history dates from the Indus Valley civilization (3rd millenium B.C.); came under British supremacy in 1763 and passed to the British Crown in 1858; nationalist movement arose under Gandhi (1869–1948); Indian subcontinent divided into Pakistan (Muslim) and India (Hindu) in 1947; became a republic within the Commonwealth in 1950. It consists chiefly of the Himalayas, rising over 7500 m (25 000 ft.) in the extreme north, the Ganges plain in the north, the Thar Desert in the northwest, the Chota Nagpur plateau in the northeast, and the Deccan Plateau in the south. Official and administrative languages: Hindi and English; each state has its own language. Religion: Hindu majority. Currency: rupee. Capital: New Delhi. Pop.: 548 154 569 (1971). Area: 3 268 100 sq. km (1 261 813 sq. miles). Hindi name: **Bharat.**

In+di+a+man ('ɪndɪəmən) *n., pl.* **+men.** (formerly) a large merchant ship engaged in trade with India.

In+di+an ('ɪndɪən) *n.* **1.** a native, citizen, or inhabitant of the Republic of India. **2.** an American Indian. **3.** (*not in scholarly usage*) any of the languages of the American Indians. *~adj.* **4.** of, relating to, or characteristic of India, its inhabitants, or any of their languages. **5.** of, relating to, or characteristic of the American Indians or any of their languages.

In+di+an+a (ˌɪndɪ'ænə) *n.* a state of the N central U.S., in the Midwest: consists of an undulating plain, with sand dunes and lakes in the north and limestone caves in the south. Capital: Indianapolis. Pop.: 5 193 669 (1970). Area: 93 491 sq. km (36 097 sq. miles). Abbrevs.: **Ind.** or (with zip code) **IN** —ˌ**In+di+'an+i+an** *adj., n.*

In+di+an a+gent *n.* an official who represents the U.S. or Canadian government to a group of American Indians.

In+di+an+ap+o+lis (ˌɪndɪə'næpəlɪs) *n.* a city in central Indiana: the state capital. Pop.: 738 657 (1973 est.).

In+di+an bread *n.* another name for **corn bread.**

In+di+an chol+er+a *n.* another name for **cholera.**

In+di+an club *n.* a bottle-shaped club, usually used in pairs by gymnasts, jugglers, etc.

In+di+an corn *n.* another name for **maize** (sense 1).

In+di+an Des+ert *n.* another name for the **Thar Desert.**

In+di+an Em+pire *n.* British India and the Indian states under indirect British control, which gained independence as India and Pakistan in 1947.

In+di+an file *n.* another term for **single file.**

In+di+an giv+er *n. U.S. informal.* a person who asks for the return of a present he has given. —**In+di+an giv+ing** *n.*

In+di+an hemp *n.* **1.** another name for **hemp,** esp. the variety *Cannabis indica,* from which several narcotic drugs are obtained. **2.** Also called: **dogbane.** a perennial American apocynaceous plant, *Apocynum cannabinum,* whose fibre was formerly used by the Indians to make rope.

In+di+an ink *or esp. U.S.* **In+di+a ink** *n.* **1.** a black pigment made from a mixture of lampblack and a binding agent such as gelatin or glue: usually formed into solid cakes and sticks. **2.** a black liquid ink made from this pigment.

In+di+an liq+uo+rice *n.* a woody leguminous tropical Asian climbing plant, *Abrus precatorius,* with scarlet black-spotted poisonous seeds, used as beads, and roots used as a substitute for liquorice. Also called: **jequirity.**

In+di+an list *n. Informal.* (in Canada) a list of persons to whom spirits may not be sold. Also called: **interdict list.**

In+di+an mal+low *n.* a tall malvaceous weedy North American plant, *Abutilon theophrasti,* with small yellow flowers and large velvety leaves.

In+di+an meal *n.* another name for **corn meal.**

In+di+an mil+let *n.* another name for **durra.**

In+di+an mul+ber+ry *n.* a small rubiaceous tree, *Morinda citrifolia,* of SE Asia and Australasia, with rounded yellow fruits: yields red and yellow dyes.

In+di+an Mu+ti+ny *n.* a revolt of Indian troops (1857–59) that led to the transfer of the administration of India from the East India Company to the British Crown.

In+di+an Na+tion+al Con+gress *n.* the official name for **Congress** (the political party).

In+di+an O+cean *n.* an ocean bordered by Africa in the west, Asia in the north, and Australia in the east and merging with the Antarctic Ocean in the south. Average depth: 3900 m (13 000 ft.). Greatest depth (off the Sunda Islands): 7450 m (24 442 ft.). Area: about 73 556 000 sq. km (28 400 000 sq. miles).

In+di+an pipe *n.* a white or pinkish saprophytic woodland plant, *Monotropa uniflora,* of the N hemisphere, with a solitary nodding flower resembling a pipe: family *Monotropaceae.*

In+di+an red *n.* **1.** a red pigment containing ferric oxide, used in paints and cosmetics and produced by oxidizing iron salts. **2.** a type of red soil containing ferric oxide, found in S Asia and used as a pigment and metal polish.

In+di+an re+serve *or* **res+er+va+tion** *n.* See **reservation** (sense 4).

In+di+an rice *n.* **1.** an annual erect aquatic North American grass, *Zizania aquatica,* with edible purplish-black grain. **2.** the grain of this plant. ~Also called: **wild rice.**

In+di+an rope-trick *n.* the supposed Indian feat of climbing an unsupported rope.

In+di+an States and A+gen+cies *n.* another name for the **Native States.**

In+di+an sum+mer *n.* a period of unusually warm weather, esp. in the autumn.

In+di+an sweat+er *n.* another name for **Cowichan sweater.**

In+di+an Ter+ri+to+ry *n.* the territory established in the early 19th century in present-day Oklahoma, where Indians were forced to settle by the U.S. government. The last remnant was integrated into the new state of Oklahoma in 1907.

In+di+an to+bac+co *n.* a poisonous North American campanulaceous plant, *Lobelia inflata,* with small pale blue flowers and rounded inflated seed capsules.

In+di+an wres+tling *n.* **1.** a contest in which two people sit facing each other each with one elbow resting on a table, clasp hands, and each tries to force the other's arm flat onto the table while keeping his own elbow touching the table. **2.** any of various similar contests.

In+di+a pa+per *n.* **1.** a thin soft opaque printing paper made in the Orient. **2.** another name (not in technical usage) for **bible paper.**

In+di·a print *n.* a colourful cotton fabric, with a block-printed pattern, made in India.

In+di·a rub+ber *n.* another name for **rubber**[1] (sense 1).

In+dic ('ɪndɪk) *adj.* **1.** denoting, belonging to, or relating to a branch of Indo-European consisting of the Indo-European languages of India, including Sanskrit, Hindi and Urdu, Punjabi, Gujerati, Bengali, and Sinhalese. ~*n.* **2.** this group of languages. ~Also: **Indo-Aryan.**

indic. *abbrev. for:* **1.** indicating. **2.** indicative. **3.** indicator.

in+di+can ('ɪndɪkən) *n.* a compound secreted in the urine, usually in the form of its potassium salt; indoxylsulphuric acid. Formula: $C_8H_6NOSO_2OH$. [C19: from Latin *indicum* INDIGO + -AN]

in+di+cant ('ɪndɪkənt) *n.* something that indicates.

in+di+cate ('ɪndɪˌkeɪt) *vb.* (*tr.*) **1.** (*may take a clause as object*) to be or give a sign or symptom of; imply: *cold hands indicate a warm heart.* **2.** to point out or show. **3.** (*may take a clause as object*) to state briefly; suggest: *he indicated what his feelings were.* **4.** (of instruments) to show a reading of: *the speedometer indicated 50 miles per hour.* **5.** (*usually passive*) to recommend or require: *surgery seems to be indicated for this patient.* [C17: from Latin *indicāre* to point out, from IN-[2] + *dicāre* to proclaim; compare INDEX] —**'in+di+ˌcat+a·ble** *adj.* —**in+dic·a+to·ry** (ɪn'dɪkətərɪ, -trɪ) *adj.*

in+di+ca+tion (ˌɪndɪ'keɪʃən) *n.* **1.** something that serves to indicate or suggest; sign: *an indication of foul play.* **2.** the degree or quantity represented on a measuring instrument or device. **3.** the action of indicating. **4.** something that is indicated as advisable, necessary, or expedient.

in+dic·a+tive (ɪn'dɪkətɪv) *adj.* **1.** (*usually postpositive;* foll. by *of*) serving as a sign; suggestive: *indicative of trouble ahead.* **2.** *Grammar.* denoting a mood of verbs used chiefly to make statements. Compare **subjunctive** (sense 1). ~*n.* **3.** *Grammar.* **a.** the indicative mood. **b.** a verb in the indicative mood. ~Abbrev.: **indic.** —**in+'dic·a·tive+ly** *adv.*

in+di+ca+tor ('ɪndɪˌkeɪtə) *n.* **1.** a device to attract attention, such as the pointer of a gauge or a warning lamp. **2.** an instrument that displays certain operating conditions in a machine, such as a gauge showing temperature, speed, pressure, etc. **3.** Also called: **blinkers.** a device for indicating that a motor vehicle is about to turn left or right, esp. two pairs of lights that flash when operated or a pair of trafficators. **4.** Also called: **dial gauge.** a delicate measuring instrument used to determine small differences in the height of mechanical components. It consists of a spring-loaded plunger that operates a pointer moving over a circular scale. **5.** *Chem.* **a.** a substance used in titrations to indicate the completion of a chemical reaction, usually by a change of colour. **b.** a substance, such as litmus, that indicates the presence of an acid or alkali. **6.** *Ecology.* a plant species that thrives only under particular conditions of soil composition, etc., and therefore indicates these conditions where it is found.

in+di+ca+tor di·a+gram *n.* a graphical or other representation of the cyclic variations of pressure and volume within the cylinder of a reciprocating engine obtained by using an indicator.

in+di+ces ('ɪndɪˌsi:z) *n.* a plural of **index.**

in+di+ci·a (ɪn'dɪʃɪə) *pl. n., sing.* **+ci·um** (-ʃɪəm). distinguishing markings or signs; indications. [C17: from Latin, plural of *indicium* a notice, from INDEX] —**in+'di+ci·al** *adj.*

in+dict (ɪn'daɪt) *vb.* (*tr.*) to charge (a person) with crime, esp. formally in writing; accuse. [C14: alteration of *enditen* to INDITE] —**ˌin+dict·'ee** *n.* —**in+'dict+er** *or* **in+'dic+tor** *n.*

in+dict+a·ble (ɪn'daɪtəbᵊl) *adj. Criminal law.* **1.** (of a person) liable to be indicted. **2.** (of a crime, etc.) that makes a person liable to be indicted. —**in+'dict+a·bly** *adv.*

in+dic+tion (ɪn'dɪkʃən) *n.* (in the Roman Empire and later in various medieval kingdoms) **1.** a recurring fiscal period of 15 years, often used as a unit for dating events. **2.** a particular year in this period or the number assigned it. **3.** (from the reign of Constantine the Great) **a.** a valuation of property made every 15 years as a basis for taxation. **b.** the tax based on this valuation. [C14: from Latin *indictiō* declaration, announcement of a tax; see INDITE] —**in+'dic+tion+al** *adj.*

in+dict+ment (ɪn'daɪtmənt) *n. Criminal law.* **1.** a formal written charge of crime formerly referred to and presented on oath by a grand jury. **2.** any formal accusation of crime. **3.** *Scot.* a charge of crime brought at the instance of the Lord Advocate. **4.** the act of indicting or the state of being indicted.

In+dies ('ɪndɪz) *n.* **the. 1.** the territories of S and SE Asia included in the East Indies, India, and Indochina. **2.** See **East Indies. 3.** See **West Indies.**

in+dif+fer+ence (ɪn'dɪfrəns, -fərəns) *n.* **1.** the fact or state of being indifferent; lack of care or concern. **2.** lack of quality; mediocrity. **3.** lack of importance; insignificance.

in+dif+fer+ent (ɪn'dɪfrənt, -fərənt) *adj.* **1.** (often foll. by *to*) showing no care or concern; uninterested: *he was indifferent to my pleas.* **2.** unimportant; immaterial. **3. a.** of only average or moderate size, extent, quality, etc. **b.** not at all good; poor. **4.** showing or having no preferences; impartial. **5.** *Biology.* **a.** (of cells or tissues) not differentiated or specialized. **b.** (of a species) occurring in two or more different communities. [C14: from Latin *indifferēns* making no distinction] —**in+'dif+fer+ent+ly** *adv.*

in+dif+fer+ent+ism (ɪn'dɪfrənˌtɪzəm, -fərən-) *n.* systematic indifference, esp. in matters of religion. —**in+'dif·fer+ent+ist** *n.*

in+di+gene ('ɪndɪˌdʒi:n) *or* **in+di+gen** ('ɪndɪdʒən) *n.* an indigenous person, animal, or thing; native.

in+dig+e+nous (ɪn'dɪdʒɪnəs) *adj.* (when *postpositive,* foll. by *to*) **1.** originating or occurring naturally (in a country, region, etc.); native. **2.** innate (to); inherent (in). [C17: from Latin *indigenus,* from *indigena* indigene, from *indi-* in + *gignere* to beget] —**in+'dig+e+nous+ly** *adv.* —**in+'dig+e+nous+ness** *or* **in+di+gen+i·ty** (ˌɪndɪ'dʒɛnɪtɪ) *n.*

in+di+gent ('ɪndɪdʒənt) *adj.* **1.** so poor as to lack even necessities; very needy. **2.** (usually foll. by *of*) *Archaic.* lacking (in) or destitute (of). ~*n.* **3.** an impoverished person. [C14: from Latin *indigēre* to need, from *egēre* to lack] —**'in+di+gence** *n.* —**'in+di+gent+ly** *adv.*

in+di+gest+ed (ˌɪndɪ'dʒɛstɪd) *adj. Archaic.* undigested.

in+di+gest+i·ble (ˌɪndɪ'dʒɛstəbᵊl) *adj.* **1.** incapable of being digested or difficult to digest. **2.** difficult to understand or absorb mentally: *an indigestible book.* —**ˌin+di+ˌgest+i·'bil+i·ty** *or* **ˌin+di+'gest+i·ble+ness** *n.* —**ˌin+di+'gest+i·bly** *adv.*

in+di+ges+tion (ˌɪndɪ'dʒɛstʃən) *n.* difficulty in digesting food, accompanied by abdominal pain, heartburn, and belching. Technical name: **dyspepsia.**

in+di+ges+tive (ˌɪndɪ'dʒɛstɪv) *adj.* relating to or suffering from indigestion; dyspeptic.

in+dign (ɪn'daɪn) *adj. Obsolete or poetic.* **1.** undeserving; unworthy. **2.** unseemly; disgraceful. **3.** not deserved. [C15: from Old French *indigne,* from Latin *indignus* unworthy, from IN-[1] + *dignus* worthy; see DIGNITY]

in+dig+nant (ɪn'dɪgnənt) *adj.* feeling or showing indignation. [C16: from Latin *indignārī* to be displeased with] —**in+'dig+nant+ly** *adv.*

in+dig+na+tion (ˌɪndɪg'neɪʃən) *n.* anger or scorn aroused by something felt to be unfair, unworthy, or wrong.

in+dig+ni·ty (ɪn'dɪgnɪtɪ) *n., pl.* **·ties. 1.** injury to one's self-esteem or dignity; humiliation. **2.** *Obsolete.* disgrace or disgraceful character or conduct.

in+di+go ('ɪndɪˌgəʊ) *n., pl.* **+gos** *or* **+goes. 1.** Also called: **indigotin.** a blue vat dye originally obtained from plants but now made synthetically. **2.** any of various tropical plants of the leguminous genus *Indigofera,* such as the anil, that yield this dye. Compare **wild indigo. 3. a.** any of a group of colours that have the same blue-violet hue; a spectral colour. **b.** (*as adj.*): *an indigo carpet.* [C16: from Spanish *indico,* via Latin from Greek *Indikos* of India] —**in+di+got+ic** (ˌɪndɪ'gɒtɪk) *adj.*

in+di+go blue *n., adj.* (**indigo-blue** *when prenominal*). the full name for **indigo** (the colour and the dye).

in+di+go bunt+ing, bird, *or* **finch** *n.* a North American bunting, *Passerina cyanea,* the male of which is bright blue and the female brown.

in+di+goid ('ɪndɪˌgɔɪd) *adj.* **1.** of, concerned with, or resembling indigo or its blue colour. ~*n.* **2.** any of a number of synthetic dyes or pigments related in chemical structure to indigo.

in+di+go snake *n.* a dark-blue nonvenomous North American colubrid snake, *Drymarchon corais couperi.*

in+dig·o+tin (ɪn'dɪgətɪn, ˌɪndɪ'gəʊ-) *n.* another name for **indigo** (the dye). [C19: from INDIGO + -IN]

in+di+rect (ˌɪndɪ'rɛkt) *adj.* **1.** deviating from a direct course or line; roundabout; circuitous. **2.** not coming as a direct effect or consequence; secondary: *indirect benefits.* **3.** not straightforward, open, or fair; devious or evasive: *an indirect insult.* **4.** (of a title or an inheritance) not inherited in an unbroken line of succession from father to son. **5.** *Maths.* (of a proof) using the denial of a hypothesis to be proved to demonstrate a contradiction. Compare **direct** (sense 16b). —**ˌin+di+'rect+ly** *adv.* —**ˌin+di+'rect+ness** *n.*

in+di+rec+tion (ˌɪndɪ'rɛkʃən) *n.* **1.** indirect procedure, courses, or methods. **2.** lack of direction or purpose; aimlessness. **3.** indirect dealing; deceit.

in+di+rect light+ing *n.* reflected or diffused light from a concealed source.

in+di+rect ob+ject *n. Grammar.* a noun, pronoun, or noun phrase indicating the recipient or beneficiary of the action of a verb and its direct object, as *John* in the sentence *I bought John a newspaper.* Compare **direct object.**

in+di+rect ques+tion *n.* a question reported in indirect speech, as in *She asked why you came.* Compare **direct question.**

in+di+rect speech *or esp. U.S.* **in+di+rect dis+course** *n.* the reporting of something said or written by conveying what was meant rather than repeating the exact words, as in the sentence *He asked me whether I would go* as opposed to *He asked me, "Will you go?"* Also called: **reported speech.**

in+di+rect tax *n.* a tax levied on goods or services rather than on individuals or companies. Compare **direct tax.**

in+dis+cern+i·ble (ˌɪndɪ'sɜ:nəbᵊl) *adj.* **1.** incapable of being discerned. **2.** scarcely discernible or perceptible. —**ˌin+dis+'cern+i·ble+ness** *n.* —**ˌin+dis+'cern+i·bly** *adv.*

in+dis+ci+pline (ɪn'dɪsɪplɪn) *n.* lack of discipline.

in+dis+creet (ˌɪndɪ'skri:t) *adj.* not discreet; imprudent or tactless. —**ˌin+dis+'creet+ly** *adv.* —**ˌin+dis+'creet+ness** *n.*

in+dis+crete (ˌɪndɪ'skri:t) *adj.* not divisible or divided into parts. —**ˌin+dis+'crete+ly** *adv.* —**ˌin+dis+'crete+ness** *n.*

in+dis+cre+tion (ˌɪndɪ'skrɛʃən) *n.* **1.** the characteristic or state of being indiscreet. **2.** an indiscreet act, remark, etc. —**ˌin+dis+'cre+tion+ar·y** *adj.*

in+dis+crim·i+nate (ˌɪndɪ'skrɪmɪnɪt) *adj.* **1.** lacking discrimination or careful choice; random or promiscuous. **2.** jumbled; confused. —**ˌin+dis+'crim·i+nate+ly** *adv.* —**ˌin+dis+'crim·i+nate+ness** *n.* —**ˌin+dis+ˌcrim·i+'na+tion** *n.*

in+dis+pen+sa·ble (ˌɪndɪ'spɛnsəbᵊl) *adj.* **1.** absolutely necessary; essential. **2.** not to be disregarded or escaped: *an* *indispensable role.* ~*n.* **3.** an indispensable person or thing. —ˌ**in+dis+ˌpen+sa·'bil+i·ty** *or* ˌ**in+dis+'pen+sa·ble+ness** *n.* —ˌ**in+dis+'pen+sa·bly** *adv.*

in+dis+pose (ˌɪndɪ'spəʊz) *vb.* (*tr.*) **1.** to make unwilling or opposed; disincline. **2.** to cause to feel ill. **3.** to make unfit (for something or to do something).

in+dis+posed (ˌɪndɪ'spəʊzd) *adj.* **1.** sick or ill. **2.** disinclined. [C15: from Latin *indispositus* disordered] —**in+dis+po+si+tion** (ˌɪndɪspə'zɪʃən) *n.*

in+dis+put+a·ble (ˌɪndɪ'spju:təbᵊl) *adj.* beyond doubt; not open to question. —ˌ**in+dis+ˌput+a·'bil+i·ty** *or* ˌ**in+dis+'put+a·ble+ness** *n.* —ˌ**in+dis+'put+a·bly** *adv.*

in+dis+sol+u·ble (ˌɪndɪ'sɒljʊbᵊl) *adj.* incapable of being dissolved or broken; permanent. —ˌ**in+dis+ˌsol+u·'bil+i·ty** *or* ˌ**in+dis+'sol+u·ble+ness** *n.* —ˌ**in+dis+'sol+u·bly** *adv.*

in+dis+tinct (ˌɪndɪ'stɪŋkt) *adj.* incapable of being clearly distinguished, as by the eyes, ears, or mind; not distinct. —ˌ**in+dis+'tinct+ly** *adv.* —ˌ**in+dis+'tinct+ness** *n.*

in+dis+tinc+tive (ˌɪndɪ'stɪŋktɪv) *adj.* **1.** without distinctive qualities. **2.** unable to make distinctions; undiscriminating. —ˌ**in+dis+'tinc+tive+ly** *adv.* —ˌ**in+dis+'tinc+tive+ness** *n.*

in+dis+tin+guish+a·ble (ˌɪndɪ'stɪŋgwɪʃəbᵊl) *adj.* **1.** (*often postpositive;* foll. by *from*) identical or very similar (to): *twins indistinguishable from one another.* **2.** not easily perceptible; indiscernible. —ˌ**in+dis+ˌtin+guish+a·'bil+i·ty** *or* ˌ**in+dis+'tin+guish+a·ble+ness** *n.* —ˌ**in+dis+'tin+guish+a·bly** *adv.*

in+dite (ɪn'daɪt) *vb.* (*tr.*) **1.** *Archaic.* to write. **2.** *Obsolete.* to dictate. [C14: from Old French *enditer,* from Latin *indīcere* to declare, from IN-[2] + *dīcere* to say] —**in+'dite+ment** *n.* —**in+'dit+er** *n.*

in+di·um ('ɪndɪəm) *n.* a rare soft silvery metallic element associated with zinc ores: used in alloys, electronics, and electroplating. Symbol: In; atomic no.: 49; atomic wt.: 114.82; valency: 1, 2, or 3; relative density: 7.31; melting pt.: 156.61°C; boiling pt.: 2000°C (approx.). [C19: New Latin, from INDIGO + -IUM]

indiv. *or* **individ.** *abbrev. for* individual.

in+di+vert+i·ble (ˌɪndɪ'vɜ:tɪbᵊl) *adj.* incapable of being diverted or turned aside. —ˌ**in+di+'vert+i·bly** *adv.*

in+di+vid·u·al (ˌɪndɪ'vɪdjʊəl) *adj.* **1.** of, relating to, characteristic of, or meant for a single person or thing. **2.** separate or distinct, esp. from others of its kind; particular: *please mark the individual pages.* **3.** characterized by unusual and striking qualities; distinctive. **4.** *Obsolete.* indivisible; inseparable. ~*n.* **5.** a single person, esp. when regarded as distinct from others. **6.** *Biology.* **a.** a single animal or plant, esp. as distinct from a species. **b.** a single member of a compound organism or colony. [C15: from Medieval Latin *indīviduālis,* from Latin *indīviduus* indivisible, from IN-[1] + *dīviduus* divisible, from *dīvidere* to DIVIDE] —ˌ**in+di+'vid+u·al+ly** *adv.*

Usage. In careful speech and writing, the noun *individual* is not loosely used as a synonym of *person,* although it is appropriate in that sense when a single person is being considered in contrast to a group, as in *in mass democracy the rights of the individual must be protected.*

in+di+vid·u·al+ism (ˌɪndɪ'vɪdjʊəˌlɪzəm) *n.* **1.** the action or principle of asserting one's independence and individuality; egoism. **2.** an individual quirk or peculiarity. **3.** another word for **laissez faire** (sense 1). **4.** *Philosophy.* the doctrine that only individual things exist.

in+di+vid·u·al+ist (ˌɪndɪ'vɪdjʊəlɪst) *n.* **1.** a person who shows independence and individuality in his behaviour, opinions, or actions. **2.** an advocate of individualism. —ˌ**in+di+ˌvid·u·al+'is+tic** *adj.* —ˌ**in+di+ˌvid·u+al+'is+ti+cal+ly** *adv.*

in+di+vid·u·al+i·ty (ˌɪndɪˌvɪdjʊ'ælɪtɪ) *n., pl.* **·ties. 1.** distinctive or unique character or personality: *a work of great individuality.* **2.** the qualities that distinguish one person or thing from another; identity. **3.** the state or quality of being a separate entity; discreteness. **4.** *Archaic.* indivisibility; inseparability.

in+di+vid·u·al+ize *or* **in+di+vid·u·al+ise** (ˌɪndɪ'vɪdjʊəˌlaɪz) *vb.* (*tr.*) **1.** to make or mark as individual or distinctive in character. **2.** to consider or treat individually; particularize. **3.** to make or modify so as to meet the special requirements of a person. —ˌ**in+di+ˌvid·u·al·i·'za+tion** *or* ˌ**in+di+ˌvid·u·al·i·'sa+tion** *n.* —ˌ**in+di+'vid·u·al+ˌiz+er** *or* ˌ**in+di+'vid·u·al+ˌis+er** *n.*

in+di+vid·u·ate (ˌɪndɪ'vɪdjʊˌeɪt) *vb.* (*tr.*) **1.** to give individuality or an individual form to. **2.** to distinguish from others of the same species or group; individualize. —ˌ**in+di+ˌvid·u+'a·tion** *n.* —ˌ**in+di+'vid+u·ˌa+tor** *n.*

in+di+vis+i·ble (ˌɪndɪ'vɪzəbᵊl) *adj.* **1.** unable to be divided. **2.** *Maths.* leaving a remainder when divided by a given number: *8 is indivisible by 3.* —ˌ**in+di+ˌvis+i·'bil+i·ty** *or* ˌ**in+di+'vis+i·ble+ness** *n.* —ˌ**in+di+'vis+i·bly** *adv.*

In·do- ('ɪndəʊ-) *combining form.* denoting India or Indian: *Indo-European.*

In·do-Ar·y·an *adj.* **1.** another word for **Indic** (sense 1). ~*n.* **2.** another name for **Indic** (sense 2). **3.** a native speaker of an Indo-Aryan language.

In·do+chi·na *or* **In·do-Chi·na** ('ɪndəʊ'tʃaɪnə) **1.** Also called: **Farther India.** a peninsula in SE Asia, between India and China: consists of Burma, Thailand, Laos, Cambodia, Vietnam, and Malaya. **2.** the former French colonial possessions of Cochin China, Annam, Tonkin, Laos, and Cambodia. —'**In·do+chi·'nese** *or* '**In·do-Chi·'nese** *adj., n.*

in+do+cile (ɪn'dəʊsaɪl) *adj.* difficult to discipline or instruct. —**in+do+cil·i·ty** (ˌɪndəʊ'sɪlɪtɪ) *n.*

in+doc+tri+nate (ɪn'dɒktrɪˌneɪt) *vb.* (*tr.*) **1.** to teach (a person or group of people) systematically to accept doctrines, esp. uncritically. **2.** *Rare.* to impart learning to; instruct. —**in+ˌdoc+tri+'na+tion** *n.* —**in+'doc+tri+ˌna+tor** *n.*

In·do-Eu·ro·pe·an *adj.* **1.** denoting, belonging to, or relating to a family of languages that includes English and many other culturally and politically important languages of the world: characteristically marked by inflection showing gender, number, and case. **2.** denoting or relating to the hypothetical parent language of this family, primitive Indo-European. **3.** denoting, belonging to, or relating to any of the peoples speaking these languages. ~*n.* **4.** the Indo-European family of languages. **5.** Also called: **primitive Indo-European, Proto-Indo-European.** the reconstructed hypothetical parent language of this family. **6.** a member of the prehistoric people who spoke this language. **7.** a descendant of this people or a native speaker of an Indo-European language.

In·do-Ger·man·ic *adj., n. Obsolete.* another term for **Indo-European.**

In·do-Hit·tite *n.* the Indo-European family of languages: used by scholars who regard Hittite not as a branch of Indo-European but as a related language.

In·do-I·ra·ni·an *adj.* **1.** of or relating to the Indic and Iranian branches of the Indo-European family of languages. ~*n.* **2.** this group of languages, sometimes considered as forming a single branch of Indo-European.

in+dole ('ɪndəʊl) *or* **in+dol** ('ɪndəʊl, -dɒl) *n.* a white or yellowish crystalline heterocyclic compound extracted from coal tar and used in perfumery, medicine, and as a flavouring agent; 1-benzopyrrole. Formula: C_8H_7N. [C19: from IND(IGO) + -OLE]

in+dole+a·ce·tic ac·id (ˌɪndəʊlə'si:tɪk, -'setɪk) *n.* an auxin that causes elongation of the cells of plant stems. Formula: $C_{10}H_9NO_2$. Abbrev.: **IAA.**

in+dole+bu+tyr+ic ac·id (ˌɪndəʊlbju:'tɪrɪk) *n.* a synthetic auxin used for stimulating plant growth and root formation. Formula: $C_8H_6N(CH_2)_3COOH$.

in+do+lent ('ɪndələnt) *adj.* **1.** disliking work or effort; lazy; idle. **2.** *Pathol.* causing little pain: *an indolent tumour.* **3.** (esp. of a painless ulcer) slow to heal. [C17: from Latin *indolēns* not feeling pain, from IN-[1] + *dolēns,* from *dolēre* to grieve, cause distress] —'**in+do+lence** *n.* —'**in+do+lent+ly** *adv.*

In+dol·o·gist (ɪn'dɒlədʒɪst) *n.* a student of Indian literature, history, philosophy, etc. —**In+'dol+o·gy** *n.*

in+do+meth·a+cin (ˌɪndəʊ'meθəsɪn) *n.* a drug administered orally to relieve pain, fever, and inflammation, esp. in rheumatoid arthritis. Formula: $C_{19}H_{16}ClNO_4$. [C20: from INDOLE + METH- + ACETIC ACID + -IN]

in+dom·i·ta·ble (ɪn'dɒmɪtəbᵊl) *adj.* (of courage, pride, etc.) difficult or impossible to defeat or subdue. [C17: from Late Latin *indomitābilis,* from Latin *indomitus* untamable, from IN-[1] + *domitus* subdued, from *domāre* to tame] —**in+ˌdom·i·ta·'bil+i·ty** *or* **in+'dom·i·ta·ble+ness** *n.* —**in+'dom·i·ta·bly** *adv.*

In·do+ne·si·a (ˌɪndəʊ'ni:zɪə) *n.* a republic in SE Asia, in the Malay Archipelago, consisting of the main islands of Sumatra, Java, Bali, Celebes (Sulawesi), Lombok, Sumbawa, Flores, the Moluccas, Timor, part of Borneo (Kalimantan), West Irian, and over 3000 small islands in the Indian and Pacific Oceans: became the Dutch East Indies in 1798; declared independence in 1945; became a republic in 1950. Official language: Bahasa Indonesia. Religion: mostly Muslim. Currency: rupiah. Capital: Djakarta. Pop.: 119 232 499 (1971). Area: 1 907 568 sq. km (736 512 sq. miles). Former name (1798–1945): **Dutch East Indies.**

In+do+ne·si·an (ˌɪndəʊ'ni:zɪən) *adj.* **1.** of or relating to Indonesia, its people, or their language. ~*n.* **2.** a native or inhabitant of Indonesia. **3.** another name for **Bahasa Indonesia. 4.** a branch of the Malayo-Polynesian family of languages that includes Malay, Tagalog, and Malagasy.

in+door ('ɪnˌdɔ:) *adj.* (*prenominal*) of, situated in, or appropriate to the inside of a house or other building: *an indoor tennis court; indoor amusements.*

in+doors (ˌɪn'dɔ:z) *adv., adj.* (*postpositive*) inside or into a house or other building.

In·do-Pa·cif·ic *adj.* **1.** of or relating to the region of the Indian and W Pacific Oceans off the coast of SE Asia. ~*n.* **2.** a hypothetical phylum or superphylum of languages that would consist of Malayo-Polynesian, Mon-Khmer, certain Indian languages, Papuan, and the Australian aboriginal languages. See also **Austro-Asiatic.**

in+do+phe·nol (ˌɪndəʊ'fi:nɒl) *n.* **1.** a derivative of quinonimine. Formula: $HOC_6H_4NC_6H_4O$. **2.** any of a class of derivatives of this compound, esp. one of the blue or green dyes that are used for wool and cotton.

In+dore (ɪn'dɔ:) *n.* **1.** a city in central India, in W Madhya Pradesh. Pop.: 543 381 (1971). **2.** a former state of central India: became part of Madhya Bharat in 1948, which in turn became part of Madhya Pradesh in 1956.

in+dorse (ɪn'dɔ:s) *vb.* a variant spelling of **endorse.** —**in+'dors+a·ble** *adj.* —**in+'dorse+ment** *n.* —**in+'dors+er** *or* **in+'dor+sor** *n.*

in+dor+see (ˌɪndɔ:'si:, ɪn'dɔ:si:) *n.* a variant spelling of **endorsee.**

in+dox+yl (ɪn'dɒksɪl) *n.* a yellow water-soluble crystalline compound occurring in woad as its glucoside and in urine as its ester. Formula: C_8H_7NO. See also **indican.** [C19: from INDO- + HYDROXYL]

In·dra ('ɪndrə) *n. Hinduism.* the most celebrated god of the Rig-Veda, governing the weather and dispensing rain.

in+draught *or U.S.* **in+draft** ('ɪnˌdrɑ:ft) *n.* **1.** the act of drawing or pulling in. **2.** an inward flow, esp. of air.

in·drawn (ˌɪnˈdrɔːn) *adj.* **1.** drawn or pulled in. **2.** inward looking or introspective.

In·dre (*French* ɛ̃ːdr) *n.* a department of central France in the Centre region. Capital: Châteauroux. Pop.: 256 147 (1975). Area: 6906 sq. km (2693 sq. miles).

In·dre-et-Loire (*French* ɛ̃ːdr e ˈlwaːr) *n.* a department of W central France in the Centre region: contains many famous châteaux along the Loire. Capital: Tours. Pop.: 486 884 (1975). Area: 6158 sq. km (2402 sq. miles).

in·dris (ˈɪndrɪs) *or* **in·dri** (ˈɪndrɪ) *n.* **1.** a large Madagascan arboreal lemuroid primate, *Indri indri,* with thick silky fur patterned in black, white, and fawn: family *Indriidae.* **2. woolly indris.** a related nocturnal Madagascan animal, *Avahi laniger,* with thick grey-brown fur and a long tail. [C19: from French: lemur, from Malagasy *indry!* look! mistaken for the animal's name]

in·du·bi·ta·ble (ɪnˈdjuːbɪtəbᵊl) *adj.* incapable of being doubted; unquestionable. [C18: from Latin *indubitābilis,* from IN-[1] + *dubitāre* to doubt] —**in·ˌdu·bi·ta·ˈbil·i·ty** *or* **in·ˈdu·bi·ta·ble·ness** *n.* —**in·ˈdu·bi·ta·bly** *adv.*

induc. *abbrev. for* induction.

in·duce (ɪnˈdjuːs) *vb.* (*tr.*) **1.** (often foll. by an infinitive) to persuade or use influence on. **2.** to cause or bring about. **3.** *Med.* to initiate or hasten (labour), as by administering a drug to stimulate uterine contractions. **4.** *Logic.* to assert or establish (a general proposition, hypothesis, etc.) by induction. **5.** to produce (an electromotive force or electrical current) by induction. **6.** to transmit (magnetism) by induction. [C14: from Latin *indūcere* to lead in, from *dūcere* to lead] —**in·ˈduc·er** *n.* —**in·ˈduc·i·ble** *adj.*

in·duced drag *n.* the former name for **trailing vortex drag.**

in·duce·ment (ɪnˈdjuːsmənt) *n.* **1.** the act of inducing. **2.** a means of inducing; persuasion; incentive. **3.** *Law.* (in pleading) the introductory part that leads up to and explains the matter in dispute.

in·duct (ɪnˈdʌkt) *vb.* (*tr.*) **1.** to bring in formally or install in an office, place, etc.; invest. **2.** (foll. by *to* or *into*) to initiate in knowledge (of). **3.** *U.S.* to enlist for military service; conscript. **4.** *Physics.* another word for **induce** (senses 5, 6). [C14: from Latin *inductus* led in, past participle of *indūcere* to introduce; see INDUCE]

in·duct·ance (ɪnˈdʌktəns) *n.* **1.** Also called: **induction.** the property of an electric circuit as a result of which an electromotive force is created by a change of current in the same circuit (see **self-inductance**) or in a neighbouring circuit (see **mutual inductance**). It is usually measured in henries. Symbol: *L* **2.** Also called: **inductor.** a component, such as a coil, in an electrical circuit, the main function of which is to produce inductance.

in·duc·tee (ˌɪndʌkˈtiː) *n. U.S.* a military conscript.

in·duc·tile (ɪnˈdʌktaɪl) *adj.* not ductile, pliant, or yielding. —ˌ**in·duc·ˈtil·i·ty** *n.*

in·duc·tion (ɪnˈdʌkʃən) *n.* **1.** the act of inducting or state of being inducted. **2.** the act of inducing. **3.** *Logic.* **a.** a process of reasoning, used esp. in science, by which a general conclusion is drawn from a set of premisses, based mainly on experience or experimental evidence. The conclusion contains more information than the premisses, taken as a whole, but can be disproved by a further premiss. **b.** a conclusion reached by this process of reasoning. Compare **deduction** (sense 3). **4.** the process by which electrical or magnetic properties are transferred, without physical contact, from one circuit or body to another. See also **inductance. 5.** *Biology.* the effect of one tissue, esp. an embryonic tissue, on the development of an adjacent tissue. **6.** *Maths.* a method of proving a proposition $P(n)$, containing an arbitrary integer n, by showing first that the proposition is true for $n = 1$, secondly, that for any value $n = k$, $P(k)$ implies $P(k + 1)$, and thus thirdly every proposition, $P(1)$, $P(2)$, $P(3)$, etc., is true, since $P(2) = P(1 + 1)$, etc. **7.** a formal introduction or entry into an office or position. **8.** *U.S.* the formal enlistment of a civilian into military service. **9.** an archaic word for **preface.** —**in·ˈduc·tion·al** *adj.*

in·duc·tion coil *n.* a transformer for producing a high voltage from a low voltage. It consists of a cylindrical primary winding of few turns, a concentric secondary winding of many turns, and often a common soft-iron core. Sometimes shortened to **coil.**

in·duc·tion hard·en·ing *n.* a process in which the outer surface of a metal component is rapidly heated by means of induced eddy currents. After rapid cooling the resulting phase transformations produce a hard wear-resistant skin.

in·duc·tion heat·ing *n.* the heating of a conducting material as a result of the electric currents induced in it by an externally applied alternating magnetic field.

in·duc·tion mo·tor *n.* a type of brushless electric motor in which an alternating supply fed to the windings of the stator creates a magnetic field that induces a current in the windings of the rotor. Rotation of the rotor results from the interaction of the magnetic field created by the rotor current with the field of the stator.

in·duc·tive (ɪnˈdʌktɪv) *adj.* **1.** relating to, involving, or operated by electrical or magnetic induction: *an inductive reactance.* **2.** *Logic, maths.* of, relating to, or using induction: *inductive reasoning.* **3.** serving to induce or cause. **4.** a rare word for **introductory. 5.** *Biology.* producing a reaction within an organism, esp. induction in embryonic tissue. —**in·ˈduc·tive·ly** *adv.* —**in·ˈduc·tive·ness** *n.*

in·duc·tor (ɪnˈdʌktə) *n.* **1.** a person or thing that inducts. **2.** another name for an **inductance** (sense 2).

in·due (ɪnˈdjuː) *vb.* **·dues, ·du·ing, ·dued.** a variant spelling of **endue.**

in·dulge (ɪnˈdʌldʒ) *vb.* **1.** (when *intr.,* often foll. by *in*) to yield to or gratify (a whim or desire for): *to indulge a desire for new clothes; to indulge in new clothes.* **2.** (*tr.*) to yield to the wishes of; pamper: *to indulge a child.* **3.** (*tr.*) *Commerce.* to allow (a debtor) an extension of time for payment of (a bill, etc.). **4.** (*intr.*) *Informal.* to take alcoholic drink, esp. to excess. [C17: from Latin *indulgēre* to concede, from *-dulgēre,* probably related to Greek *dolikhos* long, Gothic *tulgus* firm] —**in·ˈdulg·er** *n.* —**in·ˈdulg·ing·ly** *adv.*

in·dul·gence (ɪnˈdʌldʒəns) *n.* **1.** the act of indulging or state of being indulgent. **2.** a pleasure, habit, etc., indulged in; extravagance: *fur coats are an indulgence.* **3.** liberal or tolerant treatment. **4.** something granted as a favour or privilege. **5.** *R.C. Church.* a remission of the temporal punishment for sin after its guilt has been forgiven. **6.** *Commerce.* an extension of time granted as a favour for payment of a debt or as fulfilment of some other obligation. **7.** Also called: **Declaration of Indulgence.** a royal grant during the reigns of Charles II and James II of England giving Nonconformists and Roman Catholics a measure of religious freedom. ~*vb.* (*tr.*) **8.** *R.C. Church.* to designate as providing indulgence: *indulgenced prayers.*

in·dul·gent (ɪnˈdʌldʒənt) *adj.* showing or characterized by indulgence. —**in·ˈdul·gent·ly** *adv.*

in·du·line (ˈɪndjʊˌlaɪn) *or* **in·du·lin** (ˈɪndjʊlɪn) *n.* any of a class of blue dyes obtained from aniline and aminoazobenzene. [C19: from INDO- + -ULE + -INE[2]]

in·dult (ɪnˈdʌlt) *n. R.C. Church.* a faculty granted by the Holy See allowing a specific deviation from the Church's common law. [C16: from Church Latin *indultum* a privilege, from Latin *indulgēre* to INDULGE]

in·du·na (ɪnˈduːnə) *n.* (in South Africa) a Black African overseer in a factory, mine, etc. [C20: from Zulu *nduna* an official]

in·du·pli·cate (ɪnˈdjuːplɪkɪt, -ˌkeɪt) *or* **in·du·pli·cat·ed** *adj.* (of the parts of a bud) bent or folded inwards with the edges touching but not overlapping. —**in·ˌdu·pli·ˈca·tion** *n.*

in·du·rate *Rare.* ~*vb.* (ˈɪndjʊˌreɪt). **1.** to make or become hard or callous. **2.** to make or become hardy. ~*adj.* (ˈɪndjʊrɪt). **3.** hardened, callous, or unfeeling. [C16: from Latin *indūrāre* to make hard; see ENDURE] —ˌ**in·du·ˈra·tion** *n.* —ˈ**in·du·ˌra·tive** *adj.*

In·dus[1] (ˈɪndəs) *n.* a faint constellation in the S hemisphere lying between Telescopium and Tucano.

In·dus[2] (ˈɪndəs) *n.* a river in S Asia, rising in SW Tibet in the Kailas Range of the Himalayas and flowing northwest through Kashmir, then southwest across Pakistan to the Arabian Sea: important throughout history, esp. for the Indus Civilization (about 3000 to 1500 B.C.), and for irrigation. Length: about 2900 km (1800 miles).

in·du·si·um (ɪnˈdjuːzɪəm) *n., pl.* **·si·a** (-zɪə). **1.** a membranous outgrowth on the undersurface of fern leaves that covers and protects the developing spores. **2.** an enveloping membrane, such as the amnion. [C18: New Latin, from Latin: tunic, from *induere* to put on] —**in·ˈdu·si·al** *adj.*

in·dus·tri·al (ɪnˈdʌstrɪəl) *adj.* **1.** of, relating to, derived from, or characteristic of industry. **2.** employed in industry: *the industrial work force.* **3.** relating to or concerned with workers in industry: *industrial conditions.* **4.** used in industry: *industrial chemicals.* —**in·ˈdus·tri·al·ly** *adv.*

in·dus·tri·al ac·tion *n. Brit.* any action, such as a strike or go-slow, taken by employees in industry to protest against working conditions.

in·dus·tri·al ar·chae·ol·o·gy *n.* the study of past industrial machines, works, etc. —**in·dus·tri·al ar·chae·ol·o·gist** *n.*

in·dus·tri·al de·sign *n.* the art or practice of designing any object for manufacture. —**in·dus·tri·al de·sign·er** *n.*

in·dus·tri·al es·tate *n. Brit.* an area of land planned for industry and business. U.S. equivalent: **industrial park.**

in·dus·tri·al·ism (ɪnˈdʌstrɪəˌlɪzəm) *n.* an organization of society characterized by large-scale mechanized manufacturing industry rather than trade, farming, etc.

in·dus·tri·al·ist (ɪnˈdʌstrɪəlɪst) *n.* a person who has a substantial interest in the ownership or control of industrial enterprise.

in·dus·tri·al·ize *or* **in·dus·tri·al·ise** (ɪnˈdʌstrɪəˌlaɪz) *vb.* **1.** (*tr.*) to develop industry on an extensive scale in (a country, region, etc.). **2.** (*intr.*) (of a country, region, etc.) to undergo the development of industry on an extensive scale. —**in·ˌdus·tri·al·i·ˈza·tion** *or* **in·ˌdus·tri·al·i·ˈsa·tion** *n.*

in·dus·tri·al re·la·tions *n.* **1.** (*functioning as pl.*) relations between the employers and employees in an industrial enterprise. **2.** (*functioning as sing.*) the management of such relations.

In·dus·tri·al Rev·o·lu·tion *n.* **the.** the transformation in the 18th and 19th centuries of first Britain and then other W European countries and the U.S. into industrial nations.

in·dus·tri·als (ɪnˈdʌstrɪəlz) *pl. n.* stocks, shares, and bonds of industrial enterprises.

in·dus·tri·al un·ion *n.* a labour organization in which all workers in a given industry are eligible for membership. Compare **craft union.**

In·dus·tri·al Work·ers of the World *n.* **the.** an international revolutionary federation of industrial unions founded in Chicago in 1905: banned in the U.S. in 1949. Abbrev.: **I.W.W.** See also **Wobbly.**

in·dus·tri·ous (ɪnˈdʌstrɪəs) *adj.* **1.** hard-working, diligent, or assiduous. **2.** an obsolete word for **skilful.** —**in·ˈdus·tri·ous·ly** *adv.* —**in·ˈdus·tri·ous·ness** *n.*

in·dus·try (ˈɪndəstrɪ) *n., pl.* **·tries. 1.** organized economic activity concerned with manufacture, extraction and processing of raw materials, or construction. **2.** a branch of commercial enterprise concerned with the output of a specified product or service: *the steel industry.* **3. a.** industrial ownership and management interests collectively, as contrasted with labour interests. **b.** manufacturing enterprise collectively, as opposed to agriculture. **4.** diligence; assiduity. [C15: from Latin *industria* diligence, from *industrius* active, of uncertain origin]

in·dwell (ɪn'dwɛl) *vb.* **·dwells, ·dwell·ing, ·dwelt. 1.** (*tr.*) (of a spirit, principle, etc.) to inhabit; suffuse. **2.** (*intr.*) to dwell; exist. —**in'dwell·er** *n.*

In·dy, d' (*French* dɛ̃'di) *n.* **Vin·cent** (vɛ̃'sɑ̃). 1851–1931, French composer.

-ine[1] *suffix forming adjectives.* **1.** of, relating to, or belonging to: *saturnine.* **2.** consisting of or resembling: *crystalline.* [from Latin *-īnus,* from Greek *-inos*]

-ine[2] *suffix forming nouns.* **1.** indicating a halogen: *chlorine.* **2.** indicating a nitrogenous organic compound, including amino acids, alkaloids, and certain other bases: *alanine; nicotine; purine.* **3.** Also: **-in.** indicating a chemical substance in certain nonsystematic names: *glycerine.* **4.** indicating a mixture of hydrocarbons: *benzine.* **5.** an obsolete equivalent of **-yne.** [via French from Latin *-ina* (from *-inus*) and Greek *-inē*]

in·earth (ɪn'ɜːθ) *vb.* (*tr.*) a poetic word for **bury.**

in·e·bri·ant (ɪn'iːbrɪənt) *adj.* **1.** causing intoxication, esp. drunkenness. ~*n.* **2.** something that inebriates.

in·e·bri·ate *vb.* (ɪn'iːbrɪˌeɪt). (*tr.*) **1.** to make drunk; intoxicate. **2.** to arouse emotionally; make excited. ~*n.* (ɪn'iːbrɪɪt). **3.** a person who is drunk, esp. habitually. ~*adj.* (ɪn'iːbrɪɪt), *also* **in·e·bri·at·ed. 4.** drunk, esp. habitually. [C15: from Latin *inēbriāre,* from IN-[2] + *ēbriāre* to intoxicate, from *ēbrius* drunk] —**in,e·bri'a·tion** *n.* —**in·e·bri·e·ty** (ˌɪnɪ'braɪɪtɪ) *n.*

in·ed·i·ble (ɪn'ɛdɪbᵊl) *adj.* not fit to be eaten; uneatable. —**in,ed·i'bil·i·ty** *n.*

in·ed·it·ed (ɪn'ɛdɪtɪd) *adj.* **1.** not edited. **2.** not published.

in·ed·u·ca·ble (ɪn'ɛdjʊkəbᵊl) *adj.* incapable of being educated, esp. on account of mental retardation. —**in,ed·u·ca'bil·i·ty** *n.*

in·ef·fa·ble (ɪn'ɛfəbᵊl) *adj.* **1.** too great or intense to be expressed in words; unutterable. **2.** too sacred to be uttered. **3.** indescribable; indefinable. [C15: from Latin *ineffābilis* unutterable, from IN-[1] + *effābilis,* from *effārī* to utter, from *fārī* to speak] —**in,ef·fa'bil·i·ty** *or* **in'ef·fa·ble·ness** *n.* —**in'ef·fa·bly** *adv.*

in·ef·face·a·ble (ˌɪnɪ'feɪsəbᵊl) *adj.* incapable of being effaced; indelible. —**,in·ef,face·a'bil·i·ty** *n.* —**,in·ef'face·a·bly** *adv.*

in·ef·fec·tive (ˌɪnɪ'fɛktɪv) *adj.* **1.** having no effect. **2.** incompetent or inefficient. —**,in·ef'fec·tive·ly** *adv.* —**,in·ef'fec·tive·ness** *n.*

in·ef·fec·tu·al (ˌɪnɪ'fɛktʃʊəl) *adj.* **1.** having no effect or an inadequate effect. **2.** lacking in power or forcefulness; impotent: *an ineffectual ruler.* —**,in·ef,fec·tu'al·i·ty** *or* **,in·ef'fec·tu·al·ness** *n.* —**,in·ef'fec·tu·al·ly** *adv.*

in·ef·fi·ca·cious (ˌɪnɛfɪ'keɪʃəs) *adj.* failing to produce the desired effect. —**,in·ef·fi'ca·cious·ly** *adv.* —**in·ef·fi·ca·cy** (ɪn'ɛfɪkəsɪ), **,in·ef·fi'ca·cious·ness,** *or* **in·ef·fi·cac·i·ty** (ˌɪnɛfɪ'kæsɪtɪ) *n.*

in·ef·fi·cient (ˌɪnɪ'fɪʃənt) *adj.* **1.** unable to perform a task or function to the best advantage; wasteful or incompetent. **2.** unable to produce the desired result. —**,in·ef'fi·cien·cy** *n.* —**,in·ef'fi·cient·ly** *adv.*

in·e·las·tic (ˌɪnɪ'læstɪk) *adj.* not elastic; not resilient. —**in·e'las·tic·al·ly** *adv.* —**in·e·las·tic·i·ty** (ˌɪnɪlæs'tɪsɪtɪ) *n.*

in·el·e·gant (ɪn'ɛlɪgənt) *adj.* **1.** lacking in elegance or refinement; unpolished or graceless. **2.** coarse or crude. —**in'el·e·gance** *or* **in'el·e·gan·cy** *n.* —**in'el·e·gant·ly** *adv.*

in·el·i·gi·ble (ɪn'ɛlɪdʒəbᵊl) *adj.* **1.** (often foll. by *for* or an infinitive) not fit or qualified: *ineligible for a grant; ineligible to vote.* ~*n.* **2.** an ineligible person. —**in,el·i·gi'bil·i·ty** *or* **in'el·i·gi·ble·ness** *n.* —**in'el·i·gi·bly** *adv.*

in·el·o·quent (ɪn'ɛləkwənt) *adj.* lacking eloquence or fluency of expression. —**in'el·o·quence** *n.* —**in'el·o·quent·ly** *adv.*

in·e·luc·ta·ble (ˌɪnɪ'lʌktəbᵊl) *adj.* (esp. of fate) incapable of being avoided; inescapable. [C17: from Latin *inēluctābilis,* from IN-[1] + *ēluctārī* to escape, from *luctārī* to struggle] —**,in·e,luc·ta'bil·i·ty** *n.* —**,in·e'luc·ta·bly** *adv.*

in·e·lud·i·ble (ˌɪnɪ'luːdəbᵊl) *adj.* a rare word for **inescapable.** —**,in·e,lud·i'bil·i·ty** *n.* —**,in·e'lud·i·bly** *adv.*

in·ept (ɪn'ɛpt) *adj.* **1.** not suitable, appropriate, or fitting; out of place. **2.** awkward, clumsy, or incompetent. —**in'ept·i,tude** *n.* —**in'ept·ly** *adv.* —**in'ept·ness** *n.*

in·eq·ua·ble (ɪn'ɛkwəbᵊl) *adj.* uneven; not uniform.

in·e·qual·i·ty (ˌɪnɪ'kwɒlɪtɪ) *n., pl.* **·ties. 1.** the state or quality of being unequal; disparity. **2.** an instance of disparity. **3.** lack of smoothness or regularity. **4.** social or economic disparity. **5.** *Maths.* **a.** a statement indicating that the value of one quantity or expression is not equal to another, as in $x \neq y$: x may be greater than y, denoted by $x > y$, or less than y, denoted by $x < y$. **b.** the relation of being unequal.

in·eq·ui·ta·ble (ɪn'ɛkwɪtəbᵊl) *adj.* not equitable; unjust or unfair. —**in'eq·ui·ta·ble·ness** *n.* —**in'eq·ui·ta·bly** *adv.*

in·eq·ui·ty (ɪn'ɛkwɪtɪ) *n., pl.* **·ties. 1.** lack of equity; injustice; unfairness. **2.** an unjust or unfair act, sentence, etc.

in·e·rad·i·ca·ble (ˌɪnɪ'rædɪkəbᵊl) *adj.* not able to be removed or rooted out; inextirpable: *an ineradicable disease.* —**,in·e'rad·i·ca·ble·ness** *n.* —**,in·e'rad·i·ca·bly** *adv.*

in·er·ra·ble (ɪn'ɛrəbᵊl) *or* **in·er·rant** (ɪn'ɛrənt) *adj.* less common words for **infallible.** —**in,er·ra'bil·i·ty, in'er·ra·ble·ness,** *or* **in'er·ran·cy** *n.* —**in'er·ra·bly** *adv.*

in·ert (ɪn'ɜːt) *adj.* **1.** having no inherent ability to move or to resist motion. **2.** inactive, lazy, or sluggish. **3.** having only a limited ability to react chemically; unreactive. [C17: from Latin *iners* unskilled, from IN-[1] + *ars* skill; see ART[1]] —**in'ert·ly** *adv.* —**in'ert·ness** *n.*

in·ert gas *n.* any of the unreactive gaseous elements helium, neon, argon, krypton, xenon, and radon. Also called: **noble gas, rare gas, argonon.**

in·er·tia (ɪn'ɜːʃə, -ʃɪə) *n.* **1.** the state of being inert; inactivity. **2.** *Physics.* **a.** the tendency of a body to preserve its state of rest or uniform motion unless acted upon by an external force. **b.** an analogous property of other physical quantities that resist change: *thermal inertia.* —**in'er·tial** *adj.*

in·er·tial guid·ance *or* **nav·i·ga·tion** *n.* a method of controlling the flight path of a missile by instruments contained within it. Velocities or distances covered, computed from the acceleration measured by these instruments, are compared with stored data and used to control the speed and direction of the missile. Compare **celestial guidance, terrestrial guidance.**

in·er·tial mass *n.* the mass of a body as determined by its momentum, as opposed to gravitational mass. The acceleration of a falling body is inversely proportional to its inertial mass but directly proportional to its gravitational mass: as all falling bodies have the same constant acceleration the two types of mass must be equal.

in·er·tial sys·tem *n.* a frame of reference within which bodies are not accelerated unless acted upon by external forces. Also called: **inertial reference frame.**

in·er·tia-reel seat-belt *n.* a type of car seat-belt in which the belt is free to unwind from a metal drum except when the drum locks as a result of rapid deceleration.

in·er·tia sell·ing *n.* (in Britain) the practice of sending unrequested goods to householders followed by a bill for the price of the goods if they do not return them.

in·es·cap·a·ble (ˌɪnɪ'skeɪpəbᵊl) *adj.* incapable of being escaped or avoided. —**,in·es'cap·a·bly** *adv.*

in·es·cutch·eon (ˌɪnɪ'skʌtʃən) *n. Heraldry.* a small shield-shaped charge in the centre of a shield.

in es·se (ɪn 'ɛsɪ) *adj.* actually existing. Compare **in posse.** [Latin, literally: in being]

in·es·sen·tial (ˌɪnɪ'sɛnʃəl) *adj.* **1.** not necessary. ~*n.* **2.** anything that is not essential. —**,in·es,sen·ti'al·i·ty** *n.*

in·es·sive (ɪn'ɛsɪv) *adj.* **1.** (in the grammar of Finnish and related languages) denoting a case of nouns, etc., used when indicating the location of the referent. ~*n.* **2.** the inessive case. [C20: from Latin *inesse* to be in]

in·es·ti·ma·ble (ɪn'ɛstɪməbᵊl) *adj.* **1.** not able to be estimated; immeasurable. **2.** of immeasurable value. —**in,es·ti·ma'bil·i·ty** *or* **in'es·ti·ma·ble·ness** *n.* —**in'es·ti·ma·bly** *adv.*

in·ev·i·ta·ble (ɪn'ɛvɪtəbᵊl) *adj.* **1.** unavoidable. **2.** sure to happen; certain. ~*n.* **3.** (often preceded by *the*) something that is unavoidable. [C15: from Latin *inēvītābilis,* from IN-[1] + *ēvītābilis,* from *ēvītāre* to shun, from *vītāre* to avoid] —**in,ev·i·ta'bil·i·ty** *or* **in'ev·i·ta·ble·ness** *n.* —**in'ev·i·ta·bly** *adv.*

in·ex·act (ˌɪnɪg'zækt) *adj.* not exact or accurate —**,in·ex'act·i,tude** *or* **,in·ex'act·ness** *n.* —**,in·ex'act·ly** *adv.*

in·ex·cus·a·ble (ˌɪnɪk'skjuːzəbᵊl) *adj.* not able to be excused or justified. —**,in·ex,cus·a'bil·i·ty** *or* **,in·ex'cus·a·ble·ness** *n.* —**,in·ex'cus·a·bly** *adv.*

in·ex·haust·i·ble (ˌɪnɪg'zɔːstəbᵊl) *adj.* **1.** incapable of being used up; endless: *inexhaustible patience.* **2.** incapable or apparently incapable of becoming tired; tireless. —**,in·ex,haust·i'bil·i·ty** *or* **,in·ex'haust·i·ble·ness** *n.* —**,in·ex'haust·i·bly** *adv.*

in·ex·ist·ent (ˌɪnɪg'zɪstənt) *adj.* a rare word for **nonexistent.** —**,in·ex'ist·ence** *or* **,in·ex'ist·en·cy** *n.*

in·ex·o·ra·ble (ɪn'ɛksərəbᵊl) *adj.* **1.** not able to be moved by entreaty or persuasion. **2.** relentless. [C16: from Latin *inexōrābilis,* from IN-[1] + *exōrābilis,* from *exōrāre* to prevail upon, from *ōrāre* to pray] —**in,ex·o·ra'bil·i·ty** *or* **in'ex·o·ra·ble·ness** *n.* —**in'ex·o·ra·bly** *adv.*

in·ex·pe·di·ent (ˌɪnɪk'spiːdɪənt) *adj.* not suitable, advisable, or judicious. —**,in·ex'pe·di·ence** *or* **,in·ex'pe·di·en·cy** *n.* —**,in·ex'pe·di·ent·ly** *adv.*

in·ex·pen·sive (ˌɪnɪk'spɛnsɪv) *adj.* not expensive; cheap. —**,in·ex'pen·sive·ly** *adv.* —**,in·ex'pen·sive·ness** *n.*

in·ex·pe·ri·ence (ˌɪnɪk'spɪərɪəns) *n.* lack of experience or of the knowledge and understanding derived from experience. —**,in·ex'pe·ri·enced** *adj.*

in·ex·pert (ɪn'ɛkspɜːt) *adj.* not expert; unskilled or unskilful; inept. —**in'ex·pert·ly** *adv.* —**in'ex·pert·ness** *n.*

in·ex·pi·a·ble (ɪn'ɛkspɪəbᵊl) *adj.* **1.** incapable of being expiated; unpardonable. **2.** *Archaic.* implacable. —**in'ex·pi·a·ble·ness** *n.* —**in'ex·pi·a·bly** *adv.*

in·ex·pli·ca·ble (ˌɪnɪk'splɪkəbᵊl) *or* **in·ex·plain·a·ble** *adj.* not capable of explanation; unexplainable. —**,in·ex·pli·ca'bil·i·ty, ,in·ex'pli·ca·ble·ness** *or* **,in·ex,plain·a'bil·i·ty, ,in·ex'plain·a·ble·ness** *n.* —**,in·ex'pli·ca·bly** *or* **,in·ex'plain·a·bly** *adv.*

in·ex·plic·it (ˌɪnɪk'splɪsɪt) *adj.* not explicit, clear, or precise; vague. —**,in·ex'plic·it·ly** *adv.* —**,in·ex'plic·it·ness** *n.*

in·ex·press·i·ble (ˌɪnɪk'sprɛsəbᵊl) *adj.* too great, etc., to be expressed or uttered; indescribable. —**,in·ex,press·i'bil·i·ty** *or* **,in·ex'press·i·ble·ness** *n.* —**,in·ex'press·i·bly** *adv.*

in·ex·pres·sive (ˌɪnɪk'sprɛsɪv) *adj.* **1.** lacking in expression: *an inexpressive face.* **2.** an archaic word for **inexpressible.** —**,in·ex'pres·sive·ly** *adv.* —**,in·ex'pres·sive·ness** *n.*

in+ex+pug+na·ble (ˌɪnɪk'spʌgnəbᵊl) *adj.* a rare word for **impregnable.** —ˌ**in+ex+**ˌ**pug+na·'bil+i·ty** *or* ˌ**in+ex+'pug+na·ble+ness** *n.* —ˌ**in+ex+'pug+na·bly** *adv.*

in+ex+pung+i·ble (ˌɪnɪks'pʌndʒɪbᵊl) *adj.* incapable of being expunged.

in+ex+ten+si·ble (ˌɪnɪk'stɛnsəbᵊl) *adj.* not capable of extension. —ˌ**in+ex+**ˌ**ten+si·'bil+i·ty** *n.*

in ex+ten+so *Latin.* (ɪn ɪk'stɛnsəʊ) *adv.* at full length.

in+ex+tin+guish+a·ble (ˌɪnɪk'stɪŋgwɪʃəbᵊl) *adj.* not able to be extinguished, quenched, or put to an end. —ˌ**in+ex+'tin+guish+a·ble+ness** *n.* —ˌ**in+ex+'tin+guish+a·bly** *adv.*

in+ex+tir+pa·ble (ˌɪnɪk'stɜːpəbᵊl) *adj.* not able to be extirpated; ineradicable. —ˌ**in+ex+'tir+pa·ble+ness** *n.*

in ex+tre+mis *Latin.* (ɪn ɪk'striːmɪs) *adv.* **1.** in extremity; in dire straits. **2.** at the point of death. [literally: in the furthest reaches]

in+ex+tri+ca·ble (ˌɪnɛks'trɪkəbᵊl) *adj.* **1.** not able to be escaped from: *an inextricable dilemma.* **2.** not able to be disentangled, etc.: *an inextricable knot.* **3.** extremely involved or intricate. —ˌ**in+ex+tri+ca·'bil+i·ty** *or* ˌ**in+ex+'tri+ca·ble+ness** *n.* —ˌ**in+ex+'tri+ca·bly** *adv.*

inf. *abbrev. for:* **1.** inferior. **2.** infinitive. **3.** influence. **4.** information. **5.** infra. [Latin: below; after; later]

Inf. *or* **inf.** *abbrev. for* infantry.

in+fal+li·bil+ism (ɪn'fælɪbᵊˌlɪzəm) *n. R.C. Church.* the principle of papal infallibility. —**in+'fal+li·bil+ist.** *n.*

in+fal+li·ble (ɪn'fæləbᵊl) *adj.* **1.** not fallible; not liable to error. **2.** not liable to failure; certain; sure: *an infallible cure.* **3.** completely dependable or trustworthy. *~n.* **4.** a person or thing that is incapable of error or failure. —**in+**ˌ**fal+li·'bil+i·ty** *or* **in+'fal+li·ble+ness** *n.* —**in+'fal+li·bly** *adv.*

in+fam+ize *or* **in+fam+ise** ('ɪnfəˌmaɪz) *vb.* (*tr.*) to make infamous.

in+fa+mous ('ɪnfəməs) *adj.* **1.** having a bad reputation; notorious. **2.** causing or deserving a bad reputation; shocking: *infamous conduct.* **3.** *Criminal law.* (formerly) **a.** (of a person) deprived of certain rights of citizenship on conviction of certain offences. **b.** (of a crime or punishment) entailing such deprivation. —**'in+fa+mous+ly** *adv.* —**'in+fa+mous+ness** *n.*

in+fa+my ('ɪnfəmɪ) *n., pl.* **+mies.** **1.** the state or condition of being infamous. **2.** an infamous act or event. [C15: from Latin *infāmis* of evil repute, from IN-[1] + *fāma* FAME]

in+fan+cy ('ɪnfənsɪ) *n., pl.* **+cies.** **1.** the state or period of being an infant; childhood. **2.** an early stage of growth or development. **3.** infants collectively. **4.** the period of life prior to attaining legal majority (reached at 21 under common law, at 18 by statute); minority nonage.

in+fant ('ɪnfənt) *n.* **1.** a child at the earliest stage of its life; baby. **2.** *Law.* another word for **minor** (sense 10). **3.** *Brit.* a young schoolchild, usually under the age of seven. **4.** a person who is beginning or inexperienced in an activity. **5.** (*modifier*) **a.** of or relating to young children or infancy. **b.** designed or intended for young children. *~adj.* **6.** in an early stage of development; nascent: *an infant science or industry.* **7.** *Law.* of or relating to the legal status of infancy. [C14: from Latin *infāns,* literally: speechless, from IN-[1] + *fārī* to speak] —**'in+fant+**ˌ**hood** *n.*

in+fan+ta (ɪn'fæntə) *n.* **1.** (formerly) a daughter of a king of Spain or Portugal. **2.** the wife of an infante. [C17: from Spanish or Portuguese, feminine of INFANTE]

in+fan+te (ɪn'fæntɪ) *n.* (formerly) a son of a king of Spain or Portugal, esp. one not heir to the throne. [C16: from Spanish or Portuguese, literally: INFANT]

in+fan+ti+cide (ɪn'fæntɪˌsaɪd) *n.* **1.** the killing of an infant. **2.** the practice of killing newborn infants, still prevalent in some primitive tribes. **3.** a person who kills an infant. —**in+**ˌ**fan+ti+'cid+al** *adj.*

in+fan+tile ('ɪnfənˌtaɪl) *adj.* **1.** like a child in action or behaviour; childishly immature; puerile. **2.** of, relating to, or characteristic of infants or infancy. **3.** in an early stage of development. —**in+fan+til+i·ty** (ˌɪnfən'tɪlɪtɪ) *n.*

in+fan+tile pa+ral·y+sis *n.* another name for **poliomyelitis.**

in+fan+ti+lism (ɪn'fæntɪˌlɪzəm) *n.* **1.** *Psychol.* **a.** a condition in which an older child or adult is mentally or physically undeveloped. **b.** isolated instances of infantile behaviour in mature persons. **2.** childish speech; baby talk.

in+fant prod·i·gy *n.* an exceptionally talented child.

in+fan+try ('ɪnfəntrɪ) *n., pl.* **+tries.** **a.** soldiers or units of soldiers who fight on foot with small arms. **b.** (*as modifier*): *an infantry unit.* [C16: from Italian *infanteria,* from *infante* boy, foot soldiers; see INFANT]

in+fan+try+man ('ɪnfəntrɪmən) *n., pl.* **+men.** a soldier belonging to the infantry.

in+fant school *n. Brit.* a school for children aged between 5 and 7. Compare **junior school.**

in+farct (ɪn'fɑːkt) *n.* a localized area of dead tissue (necrosis) resulting from obstruction of the blood supply to that part, esp. by an embolus. Also called: **infarction.** [C19: via New Latin from Latin *infarctus* stuffed into, from *farcīre* to stuff] —**in+'farct+ed** *adj.*

in+farc+tion (ɪn'fɑːkʃən) *n.* **1.** the formation or development of an infarct. **2.** another word for **infarct.**

in+fare ('ɪnˌfɛə) *n. Dialect, chiefly northern Brit.* a reception given on entering a new house or after a wedding. [Old English *innfær,* from *inn* in + *faran* to go; see FARE]

in+fat·u+ate *vb.* (ɪn'fætjʊˌeɪt). (*tr.*) **1.** to inspire or fill with foolish, shallow, or extravagant passion. **2.** to cause to act foolishly. *~adj.* (ɪn'fætjʊɪt, -ˌeɪt). **3.** an archaic word for **infatuated.** *~n.* (ɪn'fætjʊɪt, -ˌeɪt). **4.** *Literary.* a person who is infatuated. [C16: from Latin *infatuāre,* from IN-[2] + *fatuus* FATUOUS]

in+fat·u+at+ed (ɪn'fætjʊˌeɪtɪd) *adj.* (often foll. by *with*) possessed by a foolish or extravagant passion, esp. for another person. —**in+'fat·u+**ˌ**at+ed+ly** *adv.*

in+fat+u·a·tion (ɪnˌfætjʊ'eɪʃən) *n.* **1.** the act of infatuating or state of being infatuated. **2.** foolish or extravagant passion. **3.** an object of foolish or extravagant passion.

in+fea+si·ble (ɪn'fiːzəbᵊl) *adj.* a less common word for **impracticable.** —**in+**ˌ**fea+si·'bil+i·ty** *or* **in+'fea+si·ble+ness** *n.*

in+fect (ɪn'fɛkt) *vb.* (*mainly tr.*) **1.** to cause infection in; contaminate (an organism, wound, etc.) with pathogenic microorganisms. **2.** (*also intr.*) to affect or become affected with a communicable disease. **3.** to taint, pollute, or contaminate. **4.** to affect, esp. adversely, as if by contagion. **5.** *Chiefly international law.* to taint with crime or illegality; expose to penalty or subject to forfeiture. *~adj.* **6.** *Archaic.* contaminated or polluted with or as if with a disease; infected. [C14: from Latin *inficere* to dip into, stain, from *facere* to make] —**in+'fec+tor** *or* **in+'fect+er** *n.*

in+fec+tion (ɪn'fɛkʃən) *n.* **1.** invasion of the body by pathogenic microorganisms. **2.** the resulting condition in the tissues. **3.** an infectious disease. **4.** the act of infecting or state of being infected. **5.** an agent or influence that infects. **6.** persuasion or corruption, as by ideas, perverse influences, etc.

in+fec+tious (ɪn'fɛkʃəs) *adj.* **1.** (of a disease) capable of being transmitted. Compare **contagious.** **2.** (of a disease) caused by microorganisms, such as bacteria, viruses, or protozoa. **3.** causing or transmitting infection. **4.** tending or apt to spread, as from one person to another: *infectious mirth.* **5.** *International law.* **a.** tainting or capable of tainting with illegality. **b.** rendering liable to seizure or forfeiture. —**in+'fec+tious+ly** *adv.* —**in+'fec+tious+ness** *n.*

in+fec+tious hep·a+ti+tis *n.* an acute infectious viral disease characterized by inflammation and enlargement of the liver, fever, and jaundice and transmitted by ingesting contaminated food or drink. See also **hepatitis.**

in+fec+tious mon·o+nu+cle·o+sis *n.* an acute infectious disease, probably caused by a virus, characterized by fever, sore throat, swollen and painful lymph nodes, and abnormal lymphocytes in the blood. Also called: **glandular fever.**

in+fec+tive (ɪn'fɛktɪv) *adj.* **1.** capable of causing infection. **2.** a less common word for **infectious.** —**in+'fec+tive+ly** *adv.* —**in+'fec+tive+ness** *or* ˌ**in+fec+'tiv+i·ty** *n.*

in+fe+cund (ɪn'fiːkənd) *adj.* a less common word for **infertile.** —**in+fe+cun+di·ty** (ˌɪnfɪ'kʌndɪtɪ) *n.*

in+fe+lic·i·tous (ˌɪnfɪ'lɪsɪtəs) *adj.* **1.** not felicitous; unfortunate. **2.** inappropriate or unsuitable. —ˌ**in+fe+'lic·i·tous+ly** *adv.*

in+fe+lic+i·ty (ˌɪnfɪ'lɪsɪtɪ) *n., pl.* **·ties.** **1.** the state or quality of being unhappy or unfortunate. **2.** an instance of bad luck or mischance; misfortune. **3.** something, esp. a remark or expression, that is inapt or inappropriate.

in+fer (ɪn'fɜː) *vb.* **+fers, +fer+ring, +ferred.** (when *tr., may take a clause as object*) **1.** to conclude (a state of affairs, supposition, etc.) by reasoning from evidence; deduce. **2.** (*tr.*) to have or lead to as a necessary or logical consequence; indicate. **3.** (*tr.*) to hint or imply. [C16: from Latin *inferre* to bring into, from *ferre* to bear, carry] —**in+'fer+a·ble, in+'fer+i·ble, in+'fer+ra·ble,** *or* **in+'fer+ri·ble** *adj.* —**in+'fer+a·bly** *adv.* —**in+'fer+rer** *n.*

Usage. The use of *infer* in the sense of *imply* often occurs in both speech and writing but is avoided by all careful speakers and writers of English.

in+fer+ence ('ɪnfərəns, -frəns) *n.* **1.** *Logic.* a process of reasoning in which a conclusion is obtained in some way from certain facts or premisses. See also **deduction** (sense 3), **induction** (sense 3). **2.** the act or process of inferring. **3.** an inferred conclusion, deduction, etc.

in+fer+en+tial (ˌɪnfə'rɛnʃəl) *adj.* of, relating to, or derived from inference. —ˌ**in+fer+'en+tial+ly** *adv.*

in+fe+ri+or (ɪn'fɪərɪə) *adj.* **1.** lower in value or quality. **2.** lower in rank, position, or status; subordinate. **3.** not of the best; mediocre; commonplace. **4.** lower in position; situated beneath. **5.** (of a plant ovary) enclosed by and fused with the receptacle so that it is situated below the other floral parts. **6.** *Astronomy.* **a.** orbiting or occurring between the sun and the earth: *an inferior planet; inferior conjunction.* **b.** lying below the horizon. **7.** *Printing.* (of a character) printed at the foot of an ordinary character, as the 2 in H_2O. *~n.* **8.** an inferior person. **9.** *Printing.* an inferior character. [C15: from Latin: lower, from *inferus* low] —**in+fe+ri+or+i·ty** (ɪnˌfɪərɪ'ɒrɪtɪ) *n.* —**in+'fe+ri+or+ly** *adv.*

in+fe+ri+or court *n.* **1.** a court of limited jurisdiction. **2.** any court other than the Supreme Court of Judicature.

in+fe+ri+or+i·ty com+plex *n. Psychiatry.* a disorder arising from the conflict between the desire to be noticed and the fear of being humiliated, characterized by aggressiveness or withdrawal into oneself.

in+fe+ri+or plan+et *n.* either of the planets Mercury and Venus, whose orbits lie inside that of the earth.

in+fer+nal (ɪn'fɜːnᵊl) *adj.* **1.** of or relating to an underworld of the dead. **2.** deserving hell or befitting its occupants; diabolic; fiendish. **3.** *Informal.* irritating; confounded. [C14: from Late Latin *infernālis,* from *infernus* hell, from Latin (adj.): lower, hellish; related to Latin *inferus* low] —ˌ**in+fer+'nal+i·ty** *n.* —**in+'fer+nal+ly** *adv.*

in+fer+nal ma+chine *n. Archaic.* a usually disguised explosive device or booby trap.

in+fer+no (ɪn'fɜːnəʊ) *n., pl.* **+nos.** **1.** (*sometimes cap.; usually* preceded by *the*) hell; the infernal region. **2.** any place or state resembling hell, esp. a conflagration. [C19: from Italian, from Late Latin *infernus* hell]

in+fer+tile (ɪn'fɜːtaɪl) *adj.* **1.** not capable of producing offspring; sterile. **2.** (of land) not productive; barren. —**in+'fer+tile+ly** *adv.* —**in+fer+til+i+ty** (ˌɪnfə'tɪlɪtɪ) *n.*

in+fest (ɪn'fɛst) *vb.* (*tr.*) **1.** to inhabit or overrun in dangerously or unpleasantly large numbers. **2.** (of parasites such as lice) to invade and live on or in (a host). [C15: from Latin *infestāre* to molest, from *infestus* hostile] —**ˌin+fes+'ta+tion** *n.* —**in+'fest+er** *n.*

in+feu+da+tion (ˌɪnfjʊ'deɪʃən) *n.* **1.** (in feudal society) **a.** the act of putting a vassal in possession of a fief. **b.** the deed conferring such possession. **c.** the consequent relationship of lord and vassal. **2.** the granting of tithes to laymen.

in+fib+u+late (ɪn'fɪbjʊˌleɪt) *vb.* (*tr.*) *Rare.* to enclose (esp. the genitals, to prevent sexual intercourse) with a clasp. [C17: from Latin *infībulāre*, from IN-² + *fibula* clasp, FIBULA] —**in+ˌfib+u+'lation** *n.*

in+fi+del ('ɪnfɪdᵊl) *n.* **1.** a person who has no religious belief; unbeliever. ~*adj.* **2.** rejecting a specific religion, esp. Christianity or Islam. **3.** of, characteristic of, or relating to unbelievers or unbelief. [C15: from Medieval Latin *infidēlis*, from Latin (adj.): unfaithful, from IN-¹ + *fidēlis* faithful; see FEAL]

in+fi+del+i+ty (ˌɪnfɪ'dɛlɪtɪ) *n., pl.* **+ties. 1.** lack of faith or constancy, esp. sexual faithfulness. **2.** lack of religious faith; disbelief. **3.** an act or instance of disloyalty.

in+field ('ɪnˌfiːld) *n.* **1.** *Cricket.* the area of the field near the pitch. Compare **outfield. 2.** *Baseball.* **a.** the area of the playing field enclosed by the base lines and extending beyond them towards the outfield. **b.** the positions of the first baseman, second baseman, shortstop, third baseman, and sometimes the pitcher, collectively. Compare **outfield. 3.** *Agriculture.* **a.** the part of a farm nearest to the farm buildings. **b.** land from which crops are regularly taken.

in+field+er ('ɪnˌfiːldə) *or* **in+fields+man** ('ɪnfiːldzmən) *n.* a player positioned in the infield.

in+fight+ing ('ɪnˌfaɪtɪŋ) *n.* **1.** *Boxing.* combat at close quarters in which proper blows are inhibited and the fighters try to wear down each other's strength. **2.** intense competition, esp. between members of the same organization, esp. when kept secret from outsiders. —**'in+ˌfight+er** *n.*

in+fill ('ɪnfɪl) *or* **in+fil+ling** ('ɪnfɪlɪŋ) *n.* **1.** the act of filling or closing gaps, etc., in something, such as a row of buildings. **2.** material used to fill a cavity, gap, hole, etc.

in+fil+trate ('ɪnfɪlˌtreɪt) *vb.* **1.** to undergo or cause to undergo the process in which a fluid passes into the pores or interstices of a solid; permeate. **2.** *Military.* to pass undetected through (an enemy-held line or position). **3.** to gain or cause to gain entrance or access surreptitiously: *they infiltrated the party structure.* ~*n.* **4.** something that infiltrates. **5.** *Pathol.* any substance that passes into and accumulates within cells, tissues, or organs. [C18: from IN-² + FILTRATE] —**ˌin+fil+'tra+tion** *n.* —**'in+fil+ˌtra+tive** *adj.* —**'in+fil+ˌtra+tor** *n.*

infin. *abbrev. for* infinitive.

in+fi+nite ('ɪnfɪnɪt) *adj.* **1. a.** having no limits or boundaries in time, space, extent, or magnitude. **b.** (*as collective n.* preceded by *the*): *the infinite.* **2.** extremely or immeasurably great or numerous: *infinite wealth.* **3.** all-embracing, absolute, or total: *God's infinite wisdom.* **4.** *Maths.* **a.** having an unlimited or uncountable number of digits, factors, terms, members, etc.: *an infinite series.* **b.** (of a set) able to be put in a one-to-one correspondence with part of itself. **c.** (of an integral) having infinity as one or both limits of integration. Compare **finite** (sense 2). —**'in+fi+nite+ly** *adv.* —**'in+fi+nite+ness** *n.*

in+fin+i+tes+i+mal (ˌɪnfɪnɪ'tɛsɪməl) *adj.* **1.** infinitely or immeasurably small. **2.** *Maths.* of, relating to, or involving a small change in the value of a variable that approaches zero as a limit. ~*n.* **3.** *Maths.* an infinitesimal quantity. —**ˌin+fin+i+'tes+i+mal+ly** *adv.*

in+fin+i+tes+i+mal cal+cu+lus *n.* another name for **calculus** (sense 1).

in+fin+i+tive (ɪn'fɪnɪtɪv) *n. Grammar.* a form of the verb not inflected for grammatical categories such as tense and person and used without an overt subject. In English, the infinitive usually consists of the word *to* followed by the verb. —**in+fin+i+ti+val** (ˌɪnfɪnɪ'taɪvᵊl) *adj.* —**in+'fin+i+tive+ly** *or* **ˌin+fin+i+'ti+val+ly** *adv.*

in+fin+i+tive mark+er *n. Grammar.* a word or affix occurring with the verb stem in the infinitive, such as *to* in *to make.*

in+fin+i+tude (ɪn'fɪnɪˌtjuːd) *n.* **1.** the state or quality of being infinite. **2.** an infinite extent, quantity, degree, etc.

in+fin+i+ty (ɪn'fɪnɪtɪ) *n., pl.* **+ties. 1.** the state or quality of being infinite. **2.** endless time, space, or quantity. **3.** an infinitely or indefinitely great number or amount. **4.** *Optics, photog.* a point that is far enough away from a lens, mirror, etc., for the light emitted by it to fall in parallel rays on the surface of the lens, etc. **5.** *Physics.* a dimension or quantity of sufficient size to be unaffected by finite variations. **6.** *Maths.* **a.** the concept of a value greater than any finite numerical value. **b.** the reciprocal of zero. **c.** the limit of an infinite sequence of numbers. **7.** (in Euclidian geometry) a distant hypothetical point at which two parallel lines are assumed to meet. ~Symbol (for senses 4–7): ∞

in+firm (ɪn'fɜːm) *adj.* **1.** weak in health or body, esp. from old age. **2.** lacking moral certainty; indecisive or irresolute. **3.** not stable, sound, or secure: *an infirm structure; an infirm claim.* **4.** *Law.* (of a law, custom, etc.) lacking legal force; invalid. —**in+'firm+ly** *adv.* —**in+'firm+ness** *n.*

in+fir+ma+ry (ɪn'fɜːmərɪ) *n., pl.* **+ries.** a place for the treatment of the sick or injured; dispensary; hospital.

in+fir+mi+ty (ɪn'fɜːmɪtɪ) *n., pl.* **+ties. 1.** the state or quality of being infirm. **2.** physical weakness or debility; frailty. **3.** a moral flaw or failing.

in+fix *vb.* (ɪn'fɪks, 'ɪnˌfɪks). **1.** (*tr.*) to fix firmly in. **2.** (*tr.*) to instil or inculcate. **3.** *Grammar.* to insert (an affix) or (of an affix) to be inserted into the middle of a word. ~*n.* ('ɪnˌfɪks). **4.** *Grammar.* an affix inserted into the middle of a word. —**ˌin+fix+'a+tion** *or* **in+fix+ion** (ɪn'fɪkʃən) *n.*

infl. *abbrev. for:* **1.** influence. **2.** influenced.

in fla+gran+te de+lic+to (ɪn flə'græntɪ dɪ'lɪktəʊ) *adv.* See **flagrante delicto.**

in+flame (ɪn'fleɪm) *vb.* **1.** to arouse or become aroused to violent emotion. **2.** (*tr.*) to increase or intensify; aggravate. **3.** to produce inflammation in (a tissue, organ, or part) or (of a tissue, etc.) to become inflamed. **4.** to set or be set on fire; kindle. **5.** (*tr.*) to cause to redden. —**in+'flam+er** *n.* —**in+'flam+ing+ly** *adv.*

in+flam+ma+ble (ɪn'flæməbᵊl) *adj.* **1.** liable to catch fire; flammable. **2.** readily aroused to anger or passion. ~*n.* **3.** something that is liable to catch fire. —**in+ˌflam+ma+'bil+i+ty** *or* **in+'flam+ma+ble+ness** *n.* —**in+'flam+ma+bly** *adv.*

Usage. See at **flammable.**

in+flam+ma+tion (ˌɪnflə'meɪʃən) *n.* **1.** the reaction of living tissue to injury or infection, characterized by heat, redness, swelling, and pain. **2.** the act of inflaming or the state of being inflamed.

in+flam+ma+to+ry (ɪn'flæmətərɪ, -trɪ) *adj.* **1.** characterized by or caused by inflammation. **2.** tending to arouse violence, strong emotion, etc. —**in+'flam+ma+to+ri+ly** *adv.*

in+flat+a+ble (ɪn'fleɪtəbᵊl) *n.* **1.** any of various large air-filled objects made of strong plastic or rubber, used for children to play on at fairs, carnivals, etc. ~*adj.* **2.** capable of being inflated.

in+flate (ɪn'fleɪt) *vb.* **1.** to expand or cause to expand by filling with gas or air. **2.** (*tr.*) to cause to increase excessively; puff up; swell: *to inflate one's opinion of oneself.* **3.** (*tr.*) to cause inflation of (prices, money, etc.). **4.** (*tr.*) to raise in spirits; elate. **5.** (*intr.*) to undergo economic inflation. [C16: from Latin *inflāre* to blow into, from *flāre* to blow] —**in+'flat+ed+ly** *adv.* —**in+'flat+ed+ness** *n.* —**in+'flat+er** *or* **in+'fla+tor** *n.*

in+fla+tion (ɪn'fleɪʃən) *n.* **1.** the act of inflating or state of being inflated. **2.** *Economics.* a progressive increase in the general level of prices brought about by an expansion in demand or the money supply **(demand-pull inflation)** or by autonomous increases in costs **(cost-push inflation)**. Compare **deflation. 3.** *Informal.* the rate of increase of prices.

in+fla+tion+ar+y (ɪn'fleɪʃənərɪ) *adj.* of, relating to, causing, or characterized by inflation: *inflationary wage claims.*

in+fla+tion+ar+y spi+ral *n.* a continuous rise in prices caused by and causing higher incomes.

in+fla+tion+ism (ɪn'fleɪʃəˌnɪzəm) *n.* the advocacy or policy of inflation through expansion of the supply of money and credit. —**in+'fla+tion+ist** *n., adj.*

in+flect (ɪn'flɛkt) *vb.* **1.** *Grammar.* to change (the form of a word) or (of a word) to change in form by inflection. **2.** (*tr.*) to change (the voice) in tone or pitch; modulate. **3.** (*tr.*) to cause to deviate from a straight or normal line or course; bend. [C15: from Latin *inflectere* to curve round, alter, from *flectere* to bend] —**in+'flect+ed+ness** *n.* —**in+'flec+tive** *adj.* —**in+'flec+tor** *n.*

in+flec+tion *or* **in+flex+ion** (ɪn'flɛkʃən) *n.* **1.** modulation of the voice. **2.** *Grammar.* a change in the form of a word, usually modification or affixation, signalling change in such grammatical functions as tense, voice, mood, person, gender, number, or case. **3.** an angle or bend. **4.** the act of inflecting or the state of being inflected. **5.** *Maths.* a change in curvature from concave to convex or vice versa. See also **point of inflection.** —**in+'flec+tion+al** *or* **in+'flex+ion+al** *adj.* —**in+'flec+tion+al+ly** *or* **in+'flex+ion+al+ly** *adv.* —**in+'flec+tion+less** *or* **in+'flex+ion+less** *adj.*

in+flexed (ɪn'flɛkst) *adj. Biology.* curved or bent inwards and downwards towards the axis: *inflexed leaves.*

in+flex+i+ble (ɪn'flɛksəbᵊl) *adj.* **1.** not flexible; rigid; stiff. **2.** obstinate; unyielding. **3.** without variation; unalterable; fixed. [C14: from Latin *inflexibilis*; see INFLECT] —**in+ˌflex+i+'bil+i+ty** *or* **in+'flex+i+ble+ness** *n.* —**in+'flex+i+bly** *adv.*

in+flict (ɪn'flɪkt) *vb.* (*tr.*) **1.** (often foll. by *on* or *upon*) to impose (something unwelcome, such as pain, oneself, etc.). **2.** *Rare.* to cause to suffer; afflict (with). **3.** to deal out (blows, lashes, etc.). [C16: from Latin *inflīgere* to strike (something) against, dash against, from *flīgere* to strike] —**in+'flic+ta+ble** *adj.* —**in+'flict+er** *or* **in+'flic+tor** *n.* —**in+'flic+tion** *n.* —**in+'flic+tive** *adj.*

in-flight *adj.* provided during flight in an aircraft: *in-flight meals.*

in+flo+res+cence (ˌɪnflɔː'rɛsəns) *n.* **1.** the part of a plant that consists of the flower-bearing stalks. **2.** the arrangement of the flowers on the stalks. **3.** the process of flowering; blossoming. [C16: from New Latin *inflōrescentia*, from Late Latin *inflōrescere* to blossom, from *flōrescere* to bloom] —**ˌin+flo+'res+cent** *adj.*

in+flow ('ɪnˌfləʊ) *n.* **1.** something, such as a liquid or gas, that flows in. **2.** the amount or rate of flowing in. **3.** Also called: **inflowing.** the act of flowing in; influx.

in+flu+ence ('ɪnfluəns) *n.* **1.** an effect of one person or thing on another. **2.** the power of a person or thing to have such an effect. **3.** power or sway resulting from ability, wealth, position, etc. **4.** a person or thing having influence. **5.** *Astrology.* an ethereal fluid or occult power regarded as emanating from the stars and affecting a person's actions, future, etc. **6. under the influence.** *Informal.* drunk. ~*vb.* (*tr.*) **7.** to persuade or induce. **8.** to have an effect upon (actions, events, etc.); affect. [C14: from Medieval Latin *influentia* emanation of power from the stars, from Latin *influere* to flow into, from *fluere* to flow] —**'in·flu·ence·a·ble** *adj.* —**'in·flu·enc·er** *n.*

in·flu·ent ('ɪnflʊənt) *adj. also* **in·flow·ing. 1.** flowing in. ~*n.* **2.** something flowing in, esp. a tributary. **3.** *Ecology.* an organism that has a major effect on the nature of its community.

in·flu·en·tial (ˌɪnflʊ'ɛnʃəl) *adj.* having or exerting influence. —ˌ**in·flu·'en·tial·ly** *adv.*

in·flu·en·za (ˌɪnflʊ'ɛnzə) *n.* a highly contagious and often epidemic viral disease characterized by fever, prostration, muscular aches and pains, and inflammation of the respiratory passages. Also called: **grippe.** Informal name: **flu.** [C18: from Italian, literally: INFLUENCE, hence, incursion, epidemic (first applied to influenza in 1743)] —ˌ**in·flu·'en·zal** *adj.*

in·flux ('ɪnˌflʌks) *n.* **1.** the arrival or entry of many people or things. **2.** the act of flowing in; inflow. **3.** the mouth of a stream or river. [C17: from Late Latin *influxus;* see INFLUENCE]

in·fo ('ɪnfəʊ) *n. Informal.* short for **information.**

in·fold (ɪn'fəʊld) *vb.* (*tr.*) a variant spelling of **enfold.** —**in·'fold·er** *n.* —**in·'fold·ment** *n.*

in·form[1] (ɪn'fɔːm) *vb.* **1.** (*tr.;* often foll. by *of* or *about*) to give information to; tell. **2.** (*tr.;* often foll. by *of* or *about*) to make conversant (with). **3.** (*intr.;* often foll. by *against* or *on*) to give information regarding criminals, as to the police, etc. **4.** to give form to. **5.** to impart some essential or formative characteristic to. **6.** (*tr.*) to animate or inspire. **7.** (*tr.*) *Obsolete.* **a.** to train or educate. **b.** to report. [C14: from Latin *infōrmāre* to give form to, describe, from *fōrmāre* to FORM] —**in·'form·a·ble** *adj.* —**in·form·ed·ly** (ɪn'fɔːmɪdlɪ) *adv.* —**in·'form·ing·ly** *adv.*

in·form[2] (ɪn'fɔːm) *adj. Archaic.* without shape; unformed. [C16: from Latin *informis* from IN-[1] + *forma* shape]

in·for·mal (ɪn'fɔːməl) *adj.* **1.** not of a formal, official, or stiffly conventional nature: *an informal luncheon.* **2.** appropriate to everyday life or use: *informal clothes.* **3.** denoting or characterized by idiom, vocabulary, etc., appropriate to everyday conversational language rather than to formal written language. **4.** denoting a second-person pronoun in some languages used when the addressee is regarded as a friend or social inferior: *In French the pronoun "tu" is informal, while "vous" is formal.* —**in·'for·mal·ly** *adv.*

in·for·mal·i·ty (ˌɪnfɔː'mælɪtɪ) *n., pl.* **·ties. 1.** the condition or quality of being informal. **2.** an informal act.

in·for·mal vote *n. Austral.* an invalid vote or ballot.

in·form·ant (ɪn'fɔːmənt) *n.* **1.** a person who gives information about a thing, a subject being studied, etc.

in·for·ma·tion (ˌɪnfə'meɪʃən) *n.* **1.** knowledge acquired through experience or study. **2.** knowledge of specific and timely events or situations; news. **3.** the act of informing or the condition of being informed. **4. a.** an office, agency, etc., providing information. **b.** (*as modifier*): *information service.* **5. a.** a charge or complaint made before justices of the peace, usually on oath, to institute summary criminal proceedings. **b.** a complaint filed on behalf of the Crown, usually by the attorney general. **6.** *Computer technol.* **a.** the results derived from the processing of data according to programmed instructions. **b.** another word for **data** (sense 2). —ˌ**in·for·'ma·tion·al** *adj.*

in·for·ma·tion re·triev·al *n.* the branch of computer science concerned with the classification and storage of large quantities of information and the automatic retrieval of a particular item of this information when required.

in·for·ma·tion sci·ence *n.* the science of the collection, evaluation, organization, and dissemination of information, often employing computers.

in·for·ma·tion the·o·ry *n.* a collection of mathematical theories, based on statistics, concerned with methods of coding, transmitting, storing, retrieving, and decoding information.

in·form·a·tive (ɪn'fɔːmətɪv) *or* **in·form·a·to·ry** *adj.* providing information; instructive. —**in·'for·ma·tive·ly** *adv.* —**in·'for·ma·tive·ness** *n.*

in·formed (ɪn'fɔːmd) *adj.* having much knowledge or education; learned or cultured.

in·form·er (ɪn'fɔːmə) *n.* **1.** a person who informs against someone, esp. a criminal. **2.** a person who provides information: *he was the President's financial informer.*

in·fra *Latin.* ('ɪnfrə) *adv.* (esp. in textual annotation) below; further on.

in·fra- *prefix.* below; beneath; after: *infrasonic; infralapsarian.* [from Latin *infrā*]

in·fra·cos·tal (ˌɪnfrə'kɒstəl) *adj. Anatomy.* situated beneath the ribs.

in·fract (ɪn'frækt) *vb.* (*tr.*) to violate or break (a law, agreement, etc.). [C18: from Latin *infractus* broken off, from *infringere;* see INFRINGE] —**in·'frac·tion** *n.* —**in·'frac·tor** *n.*

in·fra dig ('ɪnfrə 'dɪg) *adj.* (*postpositive*) *Informal.* beneath one's dignity. [C19: from Latin phrase *infrā dignitātem*]

in·fra·lap·sar·i·an (ˌɪnfrəlæp'sɛərɪən) *n. Theol., chiefly Calvinist.* a person who believes that only after the Fall did God decree who was predestined to salvation and who was not. Compare **supralapsarian.** [C18: from INFRA- + *lapsarian* (see SUPRALAPSARIAN)] —ˌ**in·fra·lap·'sar·i·an·ism** *n.*

in·fran·gi·ble (ɪn'frændʒɪbəl) *adj.* **1.** incapable of being broken. **2.** not capable of being violated or infringed. [C16: from Late Latin *infrangibilis,* from Latin IN-[1] + *frangere* to break] —**in**ˌ**fran·gi·'bil·i·ty** *or* **in·'fran·gi·ble·ness** *n.* —**in·'fran·gi·bly** *adv.*

in·fra·red (ˌɪnfrə'rɛd) *n.* **1.** the part of the electromagnetic spectrum with a longer wavelength than light but a shorter wavelength than radio waves; radiation with wavelength between 0.8 micrometres and 1 millimetre. ~*adj.* **2.** of, relating to, or consisting of radiation lying within the infrared: *infrared radiation.*

in·fra·son·ic (ˌɪnfrə'sɒnɪk) *adj.* (of an oscillation, vibration, or pressure wave) having a frequency below that of sound.

in·fra·struc·ture ('ɪnfrəˌstrʌktʃə) *n.* **1.** the basic structure of an organization, system, etc. **2.** the stock of fixed capital equipment in a country, including factories, roads, schools, etc., considered as a determinant of economic growth.

in·fre·quent (ɪn'friːkwənt) *adj.* **1.** rarely happening or present; only occasional. —**in·'fre·quen·cy** *or* **in·'fre·quence** *n.* —**in·'fre·quent·ly** *adv.*

in·fringe (ɪn'frɪndʒ) *vb.* **1.** (*tr.*) to violate or break (a law, agreement, etc.). **2.** (*intr.;* foll. by *on* or *upon*) to encroach or trespass. [C16: from Latin *infringere* to break off, from *frangere* to break] —**in·'fringe·ment** *n.* —**in·'fring·er** *n.*

in·fu·lae ('ɪnfjʊliː) *pl. n., sing.* **·la** (-lə). the two ribbons hanging from the back of a bishop's mitre. [C17: from Latin, plural of *infula,* woollen fillet worn on forehead by ancient Romans during religious rites]

in·fun·dib·u·li·form (ˌɪnfʌn'dɪbjʊlɪˌfɔːm) *adj.* (of plant parts) shaped like a funnel.

in·fun·dib·u·lum (ˌɪnfʌn'dɪbjʊləm) *n., pl.* **·la** (-lə). *Anatomy.* any funnel-shaped part, esp. the stalk connecting the pituitary gland to the base of the brain. [C18: from Latin: funnel, from *infundere* to INFUSE] —ˌ**in·fun·'dib·u·lar** *or* ˌ**in·fun·'dib·u·late** *adj.*

in·fur·i·ate *vb.* (ɪn'fjʊərɪˌeɪt). **1.** (*tr.*) to anger; annoy. ~*adj.* (ɪn'fjʊərɪɪt). **2.** *Archaic.* furious; infuriated. [C17: from Medieval Latin *infuriāre* (*vb.*); see IN-[2], FURY] —**in·'fur·i·ate·ly** *adv.* —**in·'fur·i·at·ing·ly** *adv.* —**in**ˌ**fur·i·'a·tion** *n.*

in·fus·cate (ɪn'fʌskeɪt) *or* **in·fus·cat·ed** *adj.* (esp. of the wings of an insect) tinged with brown. [C17: from Latin *infuscāre* to darken, from *fuscus* dark]

in·fuse (ɪn'fjuːz) *vb.* **1.** (*tr.;* often foll. by *into*) to instil or inculcate. **2.** (*tr.;* foll. by *with*) to inspire; emotionally charge. **3.** to soak or be soaked in order to extract flavour or other properties. **4.** *Rare.* (foll. by *into*) to pour. [C15: from Latin *infundere* to pour into] —**in·'fus·er** *n.*

in·fus·er (ɪn'fjuːzə) *n.* any device used to make an infusion, esp. a tea maker.

in·fu·si·ble[1] (ɪn'fjuːzəbəl) *adj.* not fusible; not easily melted; having a high melting point. [C16: from IN-[1] + FUSIBLE] —**in**ˌ**fu·si·'bil·i·ty** *or* **in·'fu·si·ble·ness** *n.*

in·fu·si·ble[2] (ɪn'fjuːzəbəl) *adj.* capable of being infused. [C17: from INFUSE + -IBLE] —**in**ˌ**fu·si·'bil·i·ty** *or* **in·'fu·si·ble·ness** *n.*

in·fu·sion (ɪn'fjuːʒən) *n.* **1.** the act of infusing. **2.** something infused. **3.** an extract obtained by soaking. **4.** *Med.* introduction of a liquid, such as a saline solution, into a vein. —**in·fu·sive** (ɪn'fjuːsɪv) *adj.*

in·fu·sion·ism (ɪn'fjuːʒəˌnɪzəm) *n. Theol.* the doctrine that at the birth of each individual a pre-existing soul is implanted in his body, to remain there for the duration of his earthly life. —**in·'fu·sion·ist** *n., adj.*

in·fu·so·ri·al earth (ˌɪnfjʊ'zɔːrɪəl) *n.* another name for **diatomaceous earth.** See **diatomite.**

in·fu·so·ri·an (ˌɪnfjʊ'zɔːrɪən) *n. Obsolete.* **1.** any of the microscopic organisms, such as protozoans and rotifers, found in infusions of organic material. **2.** any member of the subclass *Ciliata* (see **ciliate** (sense 3)). ~*adj.* **3.** of or relating to infusorians. [C18: from New Latin *Infusoria* former class name; see INFUSE] —ˌ**in·fu·'so·ri·al** *adj.*

-ing[1] *suffix forming nouns.* **1.** (*from verbs*) the action of, process of, result of, or something connected with the verb: *coming; meeting; a wedding; winnings.* **2.** (*from other nouns*) something used in, consisting of, involving, etc.: *tubing; soldiering.* **3.** (*from other parts of speech*): *an outing.* [Old English *-ing, -ung*]

-ing[2] *suffix.* **1.** forming the present participle of verbs: *walking; believing.* **2.** forming participial adjectives: *a growing boy; a sinking ship.* **3.** forming adjectives not derived from verbs: *swashbuckling.* [Middle English *-ing, -inde,* from Old English *-ende*]

-ing[3] *suffix forming nouns.* a person or thing having a certain quality or being of a certain kind: *sweeting; whiting.* [Old English *-ing;* related to Old Norse *-ingr*]

in·gath·er (ɪn'gæðə) *vb.* **1.** (*tr.*) to gather together or in (a harvest, etc.). —**in·'gath·er·er** *n.*

Inge (ɪŋ) *n.* **Wil·liam Ralph,** called *the Gloomy Dean.* 1860–1954, English theologian, noted for his pessimism; dean of St. Paul's Cathedral (1911–34).

in·gem·i·nate (ɪn'dʒɛmɪˌneɪt) *vb.* (*tr.*) *Rare.* to repeat; reiterate. [C16: from Latin *ingemināre* to redouble, from IN-[2] + *gemināre* to GEMINATE] —**in**ˌ**gem·i·'na·tion** *n.*

in·gen·er·ate[1] (ɪn'dʒɛnərɪt) *adj. Rare.* inherent, intrinsic, or innate. [C17: from Late Latin *ingenerātus* not generated; see IN-[1], GENERATE]

in·gen·er·ate[2] (ɪn'dʒɛnəˌreɪt) *Archaic.* ~*vb.* (*tr.*) to produce within; engender. [C16: from Latin *ingenerāre;* see IN-[2], GENERATE] —**in**ˌ**gen·er·'a·tion** *n.*

in·gen·ious (ɪn'dʒiːnjəs, -nɪəs) *adj.* **1.** possessing or done with ingenuity; skilful or clever. **2.** *Obsolete.* having great intelligence; displaying genius. [C15: from Latin *ingeniōsus,* from *ingenium* natural ability; see ENGINE] —**in'gen·ious·ly** *adv.* —**in'gen·ious·ness** *n.*

in·gé·nue (ˌænʒeɪˈnjuː; *French* ɛ̃ʒeˈny) *n.* an artless, innocent, or inexperienced girl or young woman. [C19: from French, feminine of *ingénu* INGENUOUS]

in·ge·nu·i·ty (ˌɪndʒɪˈnjuːɪtɪ) *n., pl.* **·ties. 1.** inventive talent; cleverness. **2.** an ingenious device, act, etc. **3.** *Archaic.* frankness; candour. [C16: from Latin *ingenuitās* a freeborn condition, outlook consistent with such a condition, from *ingenuus* native, freeborn (see INGENUOUS); meaning influenced by INGENIOUS]

in·gen·u·ous (ɪnˈdʒɛnjʊəs) *adj.* **1.** naive, artless, or innocent. **2.** candid; frank; straightforward. [C16: from Latin *ingenuus* freeborn, worthy of a freeman, virtuous, from IN-[2] + *-genuus,* from *gignere* to beget] —**in'gen·u·ous·ly** *adv.* —**in'gen·u·ous·ness** *n.*

in·gest (ɪnˈdʒɛst) *vb.* (*tr.*) **1.** to take (food or liquid) into the body. **2.** (of a jet engine) to suck in (an object, bird, etc.). [C17: from Latin *ingerere* to put into, from IN-[2] + *gerere* to carry; see GEST] —**in'gest·i·ble** *adj.* —**in'ges·tion** *n.* —**in'ges·tive** *adj.*

in·ges·ta (ɪnˈdʒɛstə) *pl. n.* nourishment taken into the body through the mouth.

in·gle (ˈɪŋɡəl) *n. Archaic or dialect.* a fire in a room or a fireplace. [C16: probably from Scots Gaelic *aingeal* fire]

In·gle·bor·ough (ˈɪŋɡəlbərə, -brə) *n.* a mountain in N England, in North Yorkshire: potholes. Height: 723 m (2373 ft.).

in·gle·nook (ˈɪŋɡəlˌnʊk) *n. Brit.* a corner by a fireplace; chimney corner.

in·glo·ri·ous (ɪnˈɡlɔːrɪəs) *adj.* **1.** without courage or glory; dishonourable, shameful, or disgraceful. **2.** unknown or obscure. —**in'glo·ri·ous·ly** *adv.* —**in'glo·ri·ous·ness** *n.*

in·go·ing (ˈɪnˌɡəʊɪŋ) *adj.* **1.** coming or going in; entering. ~*n.* **2.** (*often pl.*) *English law.* the sum paid by a new tenant for fixtures left behind by the outgoing tenant.

In·gol·stadt (*German* ˈɪŋɡɔlʃtat) *n.* a city in S West Germany, in Bavaria on the River Danube: oil-refining. Pop.: 70 600 (1970).

in·got (ˈɪŋɡət) *n.* **1.** a piece of cast metal obtained from a mould in a form suitable for storage, transporting, and further use. ~*vb.* **2.** (*tr.*) to shape (metal) into ingots. [C14: perhaps from IN-[2] + Old English *goten,* past participle of *geotan* to pour]

in·got i·ron *n.* a type of steel containing a small amount of carbon and very small quantities of other elements.

in·graft (ɪnˈɡrɑːft) *vb.* a variant spelling of **engraft.** —**in'graft·ment** *or* **ˌin·graf'ta·tion** *n.*

in·grain *or* **en·grain** *vb.* (ɪnˈɡreɪn). (*tr.*) **1.** to impress deeply on the mind or nature; instil. **2.** *Archaic.* to dye into the fibre of (a fabric). ~*adj.* (ˈɪnˌɡreɪn). **3.** variants of **ingrained. 4.** (of woven or knitted articles, esp. rugs and carpets) made of dyed yarn or of fibre that is dyed before being spun into yarn. ~*n.* (ˈɪnˌɡreɪn). **5. a.** a carpet made from ingrained yarn. **b.** such yarn. [C18: from the phrase *dyed in grain* dyed with kermes through the fibre]

in·grained *or* **en·grained** (ɪnˈɡreɪnd) *adj.* **1.** deeply impressed or instilled: *his fears are deeply ingrained.* **2.** (*prenominal*) complete or inveterate; utter: *an ingrained fool.* **3.** (esp. of dirt) worked into or through the fibre, grain, pores, etc. —**in·grain·ed·ly** *or* **en·grain·ed·ly** (ɪnˈɡreɪnɪdlɪ) *adv.* —**in'grain·ed·ness** *or* **en'grain·ed·ness** *n.*

in·grate (ˈɪnɡreɪt, ɪnˈɡreɪt) *Archaic.* ~*n.* **1.** an ungrateful person. ~*adj.* **2.** ungrateful. [C14: from Latin *ingrātus* (*adj.*), from IN-[1] + *grātus* GRATEFUL] —**'in·grate·ly** *adv.*

in·gra·ti·ate (ɪnˈɡreɪʃɪˌeɪt) *vb.* (*tr.; often foll. by with*) to place (oneself) purposely in the favour (of another). [C17: from Latin, from IN-[2] + *grātia* grace, favour] —**in'gra·ti·ˌat·ing** *or* **in'gra·ti·a·to·ry** *adj.* —**in'gra·ti·ˌat·ing·ly** *adv.* —**inˌgra·ti'a·tion** *n.*

in·grat·i·tude (ɪnˈɡrætɪˌtjuːd) *n.* lack of gratitude; ungratefulness; thanklessness.

in·gra·ves·cent (ˌɪnɡrəˈvɛsənt) *adj. Rare.* (esp. of a disease) becoming more severe. [C19: from Latin *ingravescere* to become heavier, from *gravescere* to grow heavy, from *gravis* heavy] —**ˌin·gra'ves·cence** *n.*

in·gre·di·ent (ɪnˈɡriːdɪənt) *n.* **1.** a component of a mixture, compound, etc., esp. in cooking. [C15: from Latin *ingrediēns* going into, from *ingredī* to enter; see INGRESS]

In·gres (*French* ˈɛ̃ːɡr) *n.* **Jean Au·guste Do·mi·nique** (ʒɑ̃ ɔɡyst dɔmiˈnik). 1780–1867, French classical painter, noted for his draughtsmanship.

in·gress (ˈɪnɡrɛs) *n.* **1.** the act of going or coming in; an entering. **2.** a way in; entrance. **3.** the right or permission to enter. **4.** *Astronomy.* another name for **immersion** (sense 2). [C15: from Latin *ingressus,* from *ingredī* to go in, from *gradī* to step, go] —**in·gres·sion** (ɪnˈɡrɛʃən) *n.*

in·gres·sive (ɪnˈɡrɛsɪv) *adj.* **1.** of or concerning ingress. **2.** (of a speech sound) pronounced with an inhalation rather than exhalation of breath. ~*n.* **3.** an ingressive speech sound, such as a Zulu click. —**in'gres·sive·ness** *n.*

in-group *n. Sociol.* a highly cohesive and relatively closed social group characterized by the preferential treatment reserved for its members and the strength of loyalty between them. Compare **out-group.**

in·grow·ing (ˈɪnˌɡrəʊɪŋ) *adj.* **1.** (esp. of a toenail) growing abnormally into the flesh. **2.** growing within or into.

in·grown (ˈɪnˌɡrəʊn, ɪnˈɡrəʊn) *adj.* **1.** (esp. of a toenail) grown abnormally into the flesh; covered by adjacent tissues. **2.** grown within; native; innate. **3.** excessively concerned with oneself, one's own particular group, etc. **4.** ingrained.

in·growth (ˈɪnˌɡrəʊθ) *n.* **1.** the act of growing inwards: *the ingrowth of a toenail.* **2.** something that grows inwards.

in·gui·nal (ˈɪŋɡwɪnəl) *adj. Anatomy.* of or relating to the groin. [C17: from Latin *inguinālis,* from *inguen* groin]

in·gulf (ɪnˈɡʌlf) *vb.* (*tr.*) a variant of **engulf.** —**in'gulf·ment** *n.*

in·gur·gi·tate (ɪnˈɡɜːdʒɪˌteɪt) *vb.* to swallow (food, etc.) with greed or in excess; gorge. [C16: from Latin *ingurgitāre* to flood, from IN-[2] + *gurges* abyss] —**inˌgur·gi'ta·tion** *n.*

In·gush (ɪŋˈɡuːʃ) *n., pl.* **·gush·es** *or* **·gush.** a member of a people of the S Soviet Union, speaking a Circassian language and chiefly inhabiting the Checheno-Ingush ASSR.

in·hab·it (ɪnˈhæbɪt) *vb.* **1.** (*tr.*) to live or dwell in; occupy. **2.** (*intr.*) *Archaic.* to abide or dwell. [C14: from Latin *inhabitāre,* from *habitāre* to dwell] —**in'hab·it·a·ble** *adj.* —**inˌhab·it·a'bil·i·ty** *n.* —**inˌhab·i'ta·tion** *n.*

in·hab·it·ant (ɪnˈhæbɪtənt) *n.* a person or animal that is a permanent resident of a particular place or region. —**in'hab·it·an·cy** *or* **in'hab·it·ance** *n.*

in·hal·ant (ɪnˈheɪlənt) *adj.* **1.** (esp. of a volatile medicinal preparation) inhaled for its soothing or therapeutic effect. **2.** inhaling. ~*n.* **3.** an inhalant medicinal preparation.

in·ha·la·tion (ˌɪnhəˈleɪʃən) *n.* **1.** the act of inhaling; breathing in of air or other vapours. **2.** an inhalant preparation.

in·ha·la·tor (ˈɪnhəˌleɪtə) *n.* a device for issuing a vapour which is breathed in to ease discomfort of or provide medication for the respiratory system.

in·hale (ɪnˈheɪl) *vb.* to draw (breath, etc.) into the lungs; breathe in. [C18: from IN-[2] + Latin *halāre* to breathe]

in·hal·er (ɪnˈheɪlə) *n.* **1.** a device for breathing in therapeutic vapours, esp. one for relieving nasal congestion. **2.** a person who inhales.

In·ham·ba·ne (ˌɪnjəmˈbɑːnə) *n.* a port in SE Mozambique on an inlet of the Mozambique Channel (**Inhambane Bay**). Pop.: 26 701 (1970).

in·har·mo·ni·ous (ˌɪnhɑːˈməʊnɪəs) *or* **in·har·mon·ic** (ˌɪnhɑːˈmɒnɪk) *adj.* **1.** lacking harmony; discordant. **2.** lacking accord or agreement. —**ˌin·har'mo·ni·ous·ly** *adv.* —**ˌin·har'mo·ni·ous·ness** *n.*

in·haul (ˈɪnˌhɔːl) *or* **in·haul·er** *n. Nautical.* a line for hauling in a sail.

in·here (ɪnˈhɪə) *vb.* (*intr.; foll. by in*) to be an inseparable part (of). [C16: from Latin *inhaerēre* to stick in, from *haerēre* to stick]

in·her·ence (ɪnˈhɪərəns, -ˈhɛr-) *or* **in·her·en·cy** *n.* **1.** the state or condition of being inherent. **2.** *Metaphysics.* the relation of attributes, elements, etc., to the subject of which they are predicated, esp. if they are its essential constituents.

in·her·ent (ɪnˈhɪərənt, -ˈhɛr-) *adj.* existing as an inseparable part; intrinsic. —**in'her·ent·ly** *adv.*

in·her·it (ɪnˈhɛrɪt) *vb.* **1.** to receive (property, a right, title, etc.) by succession or under a will. **2.** (*intr.*) to succeed as heir. **3.** (*tr.*) to possess (a characteristic) through genetic transmission. **4.** (*tr.*) to receive (a position, attitude, property, etc.) from a predecessor. [C14: from Old French *enheriter,* from Late Latin *inhērēditāre* to appoint an heir, from Latin *hērēs* HEIR] —**in'her·it·ed** *adj.* —**in'her·i·tor** *n.* —**in'her·i·tress** *or* **in'her·i·trix** *fem.n.*

in·her·it·a·ble (ɪnˈhɛrɪtəbəl) *adj.* **1.** capable of being transmitted by heredity from one generation to a later one. **2.** capable of being inherited. **3.** *Rare.* capable of inheriting; having the right to inherit. —**inˌher·it·a'bil·i·ty** *or* **in'her·it·a·ble·ness** *n.* —**in'her·it·a·bly** *adv.*

in·her·it·ance (ɪnˈhɛrɪtəns) *n.* **1.** *Law.* **a.** hereditary succession to an estate, title, etc. **b.** the right of an heir to succeed to property on the death of an ancestor. **c.** something that may legally be transmitted to an heir. **2.** the act of inheriting. **3.** something inherited; heritage. **4.** the derivation of characteristics of one generation from an earlier one by heredity. **5.** *Obsolete.* hereditary rights.

in·her·it·ance tax *n. U.S.* a state tax imposed on an inheritance according to its size and the relationship of the beneficiary to the deceased.

in·he·sion (ɪnˈhiːʒən) *n.* a less common word for **inherence** (sense 1). [C17: from Late Latin *inhaesiō,* from *inhaerēre* to INHERE]

in·hib·it (ɪnˈhɪbɪt) *vb.* (*tr.*) **1.** to restrain or hinder (an impulse, desire, etc.). **2.** to prohibit; forbid. **3.** to stop, prevent, or decrease the rate of (a chemical reaction). **4.** *Electronics.* **a.** to prevent the occurrence of (a particular signal) in a circuit. **b.** to prevent the performance of (a particular operation). [C15: from Latin *inhibēre* to restrain, from IN-[2] + *habēre* to have] —**in'hib·it·a·ble** *adj.* —**in'hib·it·er** *or* **in'hib·i·tor** *n.* —**in'hib·i·tive** *or* **in'hib·i·to·ry** *adj.*

in·hi·bi·tion (ˌɪnɪˈbɪʃən, ˌɪnhɪ-) *n.* **1.** the act of inhibiting or the condition of being inhibited. **2.** *Psychol.* **a.** a mental state or condition in which the varieties of expression and behaviour of an individual become restricted. **b.** the prevention of a response in oneself or another person. **c.** (in psychoanalytical theory) the unconscious restraining of an impulse. See also **repression. 3.** the process of stopping or retarding a chemical reaction. **4.** *Physiol.* the suppression of the function or action of an organ or part, as by stimulation of its nerve supply. **5.** *Church of England.* an episcopal order suspending an incumbent.

in·hib·i·tor (ɪnˈhɪbɪtə) *n.* **1.** Also called: **anticatalyst.** a substance that retards or stops a chemical reaction. Compare **catalyst. 2.** any impurity in a solid that prevents luminescence. **3.** an inert substance added to some rocket fuels to inhibit ignition on certain surfaces.

in·ho·mo·ge·ne·ous (ɪn͵həʊmə'dʒiːnɪəs, -͵hɒm-) *adj.* not homogeneous or uniform. —**in·ho·mo·ge·ne·i·ty** (ɪn͵həʊmədʒɪ'niːɪtɪ, -͵hɒm-) *n.*

in·hos·pi·ta·ble (ɪn'hɒspɪtəbᵊl, ͵ɪnhɒ'spɪt-) *adj.* **1.** not hospitable; unfriendly. **2.** (of a region, environment, etc.) lacking a favourable climate, terrain, etc. —**in·'hos·pi·ta·ble·ness** *n.* —**in·'hos·pi·ta·bly** *adv.*

in·hos·pi·tal·i·ty (͵ɪnhɒspɪ'tælɪtɪ, ɪn͵hɒs-) *n.* the state or attitude of being inhospitable or unwelcoming.

in-house *adj., adv.* within an organization or group: *an in-house job; the job was done in-house.*

in·hu·man (ɪn'hjuːmən) *adj.* **1.** Also: **in·hu·mane** (͵ɪnhjuː'meɪn). lacking humane feelings, such as sympathy, understanding, etc.; cruel; brutal. **2.** not human. —͵**in·hu·'mane·ly** *adv.* —**in·'hu·man·ly** *adv.* —**in·'hu·man·ness** *n.*

in·hu·man·i·ty (͵ɪnhjuː'mænɪtɪ) *n., pl.* **·ties.** **1.** lack of humane qualities. **2.** an inhumane act, decision, etc.

in·hume (ɪn'hjuːm) *vb.* (*tr.*) to inter; bury. [C17: from Latin *inhumāre,* from IN-[2] + *humus* ground] —͵**in·hu·'ma·tion** *n.* —**in·'hum·er** *n.*

in·im·i·cal (ɪ'nɪmɪkᵊl) *adj.* **1.** adverse or unfavourable. **2.** not friendly; hostile. [C17: from Late Latin *inimīcālis,* from *inimīcus, from* IN-[1] + *amīcus* friendly; see ENEMY] —**in·'im·i·cal·ly** *adv.* —**in·'im·i·cal·ness** *or* **in·**͵**im·i·'cal·i·ty** *n.*

in·im·i·ta·ble (ɪ'nɪmɪtəbᵊl) *adj.* incapable of being duplicated or imitated; unique. —**in·**͵**im·i·ta·'bil·i·ty** *or* **in·'im·i·ta·ble·ness** *n.* —**in·'im·i·ta·bly** *adv.*

in·i·on ('ɪnɪən) *n. Anatomy.* the most prominent point at the back of the head, used as a point of measurement in craniometry. [C19: from Greek: back of the head]

in·iq·ui·ty (ɪ'nɪkwɪtɪ) *n., pl.* **·ties.** **1.** lack of justice or righteousness; wickedness; injustice. **2.** a wicked act; sin. [C14: from Latin *inīquitās,* from *inīquus* unfair, from IN-[1] + *aequus* even, level; see EQUAL] —**in·'iq·ui·tous** *adj.* —**in·'iq·ui·tous·ly** *adv.* —**in·'iq·ui·tous·ness** *n.*

init. *abbrev. for:* **1.** initial. **2.** initio. [Latin: in the beginning]

in·i·tial (ɪ'nɪʃəl) *adj.* **1.** of, at, or concerning the beginning. ~*n.* **2.** the first letter of a word, esp. a person's name. **3.** *Printing.* a large sometimes highly decorated letter set at the beginning of a chapter or work. **4.** *Botany.* a cell from which tissues and organs develop by division and differentiation; a meristematic cell. ~*vb.* **·tials, ·tial·ling, ·tialled** *or U.S.* **·tials, ·tial·ing, ·tialed.** **5.** (*tr.*) to sign with one's initials, esp. to indicate approval; endorse. [C16: from Latin *initiālis* of the beginning, from *initium* beginning, literally: an entering upon, from *inīre* to go in, from IN-[2] + *īre* to go] —**in·'i·tial·er** *or* **in·'i·tial·ler** *n.* —**in·'i·tial·ly** *adv.*

in·i·tial·ize *or* **in·i·tial·ise** (ɪ'nɪʃə͵laɪz) *vb.* (*tr.*) to assign an initial value to (a variable or storage location) in a computer program. —**in·**͵**i·tial·i·'za·tion** *or* **in·**͵**i·tial·i·'sa·tion** *n.*

in·i·ti·ate *vb.* (ɪ'nɪʃɪ͵eɪt). (*tr.*) **1.** to begin or originate. **2.** to accept (new members) into an organization such as a club, through often secret ceremonies. **3.** to teach fundamentals to: *she initiated him into the ballet.* ~*adj.* (ɪ'nɪʃɪɪt, -͵eɪt). **4.** initiated; begun. ~*n.* (ɪ'nɪʃɪɪt, -͵eɪt). **5.** a person who has been initiated, esp. recently. **6.** a beginner; novice. [C17: from Latin *initiāre* (vb.), from *initium;* see INITIAL] —**in·'i·ti·**͵**a·tor** *n.* —**in·'i·ti·a·to·ry** *adj.* —**in·'i·ti·**͵**a·tress** *or* **in·'i·ti·**͵**a·trix** *fem. n.*

in·i·ti·a·tion (ɪ͵nɪʃɪ'eɪʃən) *n.* **1.** the act of initiating or the condition of being initiated. **2.** the often secret ceremony initiating new members into an organization.

in·i·ti·a·tive (ɪ'nɪʃɪətɪv, -'nɪʃətɪv) *n.* **1.** the first step or action of a matter; commencing move: *he took the initiative; a peace initiative.* **2.** the right or power to begin or initiate something: *he has the initiative.* **3.** the ability or attitude required to begin or initiate something. **4.** *Government.* **a.** the right or power to introduce legislation, etc., in a legislative body. **b.** the procedure by which citizens originate legislation, as in many American states and Switzerland. **5. on one's own initiative.** without being prompted. ~*adj.* **6.** of or concerning initiation or serving to initiate; initiatory. —**in·'i·ti·a·tive·ly** *adv.*

in·ject (ɪn'dʒɛkt) *vb.* (*tr.*) **1.** *Med.* to introduce (a fluid) into (the body of a person or animal) by means of a syringe or similar instrument. **2.** (foll. by *into*) to introduce (a new aspect or element): *to inject humour into a scene.* **3.** to interject (a comment, idea, etc.). **4.** to place (a rocket, satellite, etc.) in orbit. [C17: from *injicere* to throw in, from *jacere* to throw] —**in·'ject·a·ble** *adj.*

in·jec·tion (ɪn'dʒɛkʃən) *n.* **1.** fluid injected into the body, esp. for medicinal purposes. **2.** something injected. **3.** the act of injecting. **4. a.** the act or process of introducing fluid under pressure, such as fuel into the combustion chamber of an engine. **b.** (*as modifier*): *injection moulding.* **5.** *Maths.* a function or mapping for which $f(x) = f(y)$ only if $x = y$ and for which the image of every element of the domain is contained in the image space. See also **surjection, bijection.** —**in·'jec·tive** *adj.*

in·jec·tor (ɪn'dʒɛktə) *n.* **1.** a person or thing that injects. **2.** a device for spraying fuel into the combustion chamber of an internal-combustion engine. **3.** a device for forcing water into a steam boiler.

in·ju·di·cious (͵ɪndʒʊ'dɪʃəs) *adj.* not discreet; imprudent. —͵**in·ju·'di·cious·ly** *adv.* —͵**in·ju·'di·cious·ness** *n.*

In·jun ('ɪndʒən) *n.* **1.** *U.S.* an informal or dialect word for (American) **Indian.** **2. honest Injun.** (*interj.*) *Slang.* genuinely; really.

in·junc·tion (ɪn'dʒʌŋkʃən) *n.* **1.** *Law.* an instruction or order issued by a court to a party to an action, esp. to refrain from some act, such as causing a nuisance. **2.** a command, admonition, etc. **3.** the act of enjoining. [C16: from Late Latin *injunctiō,* from Latin *injungere* to ENJOIN] —**in·'junc·tive** *adj.* —**in·'junc·tive·ly** *adv.*

in·jure ('ɪndʒə) *vb.* (*tr.*) **1.** to cause physical or mental harm or suffering to; hurt or wound. **2.** to offend, esp. by an injustice. [C16: back formation from INJURY] —**'in·jur·a·ble** *adj.* —**'in·jured** *adj.* —**'in·jur·er** *n.*

in·ju·ri·ous (ɪn'dʒʊərɪəs) *adj.* **1.** causing damage or harm; deleterious; hurtful. **2.** abusive, slanderous, or libellous. —**in·'ju·ri·ous·ly** *adv.* —**in·'ju·ri·ous·ness** *n.*

in·ju·ry ('ɪndʒərɪ) *n., pl.* **·ries.** **1.** physical damage or hurt. **2.** a specific instance of this: *a leg injury.* **3.** harm done to a reputation. **4.** *Law.* a violation or infringement of another person's rights that causes him harm and is actionable at law. **5.** an obsolete word for **insult.** [C14: from Latin *injūria* injustice, wrong, from *injūriōsus* acting unfairly, wrongful, from IN-[1] + *jūs* right]

in·ju·ry ben·e·fit *n.* (in the British National Insurance scheme) a weekly payment to a person injured while at work, varying according to the degree of injury.

in·ju·ry time *n. Soccer.* extra playing time added on to compensate for time spent attending to injured players during the match.

in·jus·tice (ɪn'dʒʌstɪs) *n.* **1.** the condition or practice of being unjust or unfair. **2.** an unjust act.

ink (ɪŋk) *n.* **1.** a fluid or paste used for printing, writing, and drawing. **2.** a dark brown fluid ejected into the water for self-concealment by an octopus or related mollusc from a gland (**ink sac**) near the anus. ~*vb.* (*tr.*) **3.** to mark with ink. **4.** to coat (a printing surface) with ink. ~See also **ink in, ink up.** [C13: from Old French *enque,* from Late Latin *encaustum* a purplish-red ink, from Greek *enkauston* purple ink, from *enkaustos* burnt in, from *enkaiein* to burn in; see EN-[2], CAUSTIC] —**'ink·er** *n.*

ink·ber·ry ('ɪŋk͵bɛrɪ) *n., pl.* **·ries.** **1.** a North American holly tree, *Ilex glabra,* with black berry-like fruits. **2.** another name for the **pokeweed.** **3.** the fruit of either of these plants.

ink·blot ('ɪŋk͵blɒt) *n. Psychol.* an abstract patch of ink, one of ten commonly used in the Rorschach test.

ink-cap *n.* any saprophytic agaricaceous fungi of the genus *Coprinus,* whose cap disintegrates into a black inky fluid after the spores mature.

In·ker·man ('ɪŋkəmən; *Russian* inkɪr'man) *n.* a village in the SW Soviet Union, in the S Crimea east of Sevastopol: scene of a battle during the Crimean War in which English and French forces defeated the Russians (1854).

ink·horn ('ɪŋk͵hɔːn) *n.* (formerly) a small portable container for ink, usually made from horn.

ink·horn term *n.* an affectedly learned and obscure borrowing from another language, esp. Greek or Latin.

ink in *vb.* (*adv.*) **1.** (*tr.*) to use ink to go over pencil lines in (a drawing). **2.** to apply ink to (a printing surface) in preparing to print from it.

in·kle ('ɪŋkᵊl) *n.* **1.** a kind of linen tape used for trimmings. **2.** the thread or yarn from which this tape is woven. [C16: of unknown origin]

ink·ling ('ɪŋklɪŋ) *n.* a slight intimation or suggestion; suspicion. [C14: probably from *inclen* to hint at; related to Old English *inca*]

ink·stand ('ɪŋk͵stænd) *n.* a stand or tray on which are kept writing implements and containers for ink.

ink up *vb.* (*adv.*) to apply ink to (a printing machine) in preparing it for operation.

ink·well ('ɪŋk͵wɛl) *n.* a small container for pen ink, often let into the surface of a desk.

ink·y ('ɪŋkɪ) *adj.* **ink·i·er, ink·i·est.** **1.** resembling ink, esp. in colour; dark or black. **2.** of, containing, or stained with ink: *inky fingers.* —**'ink·i·ness** *n.*

in·lace (ɪn'leɪs) *vb.* (*tr.*) a variant of **enlace.**

in·laid ('ɪn͵leɪd, ɪn'leɪd) *adj.* **1.** set in the surface, as a design in wood. **2.** having such a design or inlay: *an inlaid table.*

in·land *adj.* ('ɪnlənd). **1.** of, concerning, or located in the interior of a country or region away from a sea or border. **2.** *Chiefly Brit.* operating within a country or region; domestic; not foreign. ~*n.* ('ɪn͵lænd, -lənd). **3.** the interior of a country or region. ~*adv.* ('ɪn͵lænd, -lənd). **4.** towards or into the interior of a country or region. —**'in·land·er** *n.*

in·land bill *n.* a bill of exchange that is both drawn and made payable in the same country. Compare **foreign bill.**

In·land Rev·e·nue *n.* (in Britain) a government board that administers and collects major direct taxes, such as income tax, corporation tax, and capital gains tax. Abbrev.: **I.R.** U.S. equivalent: **internal revenue.**

In·land Sea *n.* a sea in SW Japan, between the islands of Honshu, Shikoku, and Kyushu. Japanese name: **Seto Naikai.**

in-law *n.* **1.** a relative by marriage. ~*adj.* **2.** (*postpositive; in combination*) related by marriage: *a father-in-law.* [C19: back formation from *father-in-law,* etc.]

in·lay *vb.* (ɪn'leɪ), **·lays, ·lay·ing, ·laid.** (*tr.*) **1.** to decorate (an article, esp. of furniture, or a surface) by inserting pieces of wood, ivory, etc., into prepared slots in the surface. ~*n.* ('ɪn͵leɪ). **2.** *Dentistry.* a filling, made of gold, porcelain, etc., inserted into a cavity and held in position by cement. **3.** decoration made by inlaying. **4.** an inlaid article, surface, etc. —**'in·**͵**laid** *adj.* —**'in·**͵**lay·er** *n.*

in·let *n.* ('ɪn͵lɛt). **1.** a narrow inland opening of the coastline. **2.** an entrance or opening. **3.** the act of letting someone or something in. **4.** something let in or inserted. **5. a.** a passage, valve, or part through which a substance, esp. a fluid, enters a device or machine. **b.** (*as modifier*): *an inlet valve.* ~*vb.* (ɪnˈlɛt), **-lets, let-ting, -let. 6.** (*tr.*) to insert or inlay.

in·li·er (ˈɪnˌlaɪə) *n.* an outcrop of rocks that is entirely surrounded by younger rocks.

in loc. cit. (in textual annotation) *abbrev. for* in loco citato. [Latin: in the place cited]

in lo·co pa·ren·tis *Latin.* (ɪn ˈləʊkəʊ pəˈrɛntɪs) in place of a parent: said of a person acting in a parental capacity.

in·ly (ˈɪnlɪ) *adv. Poetic.* inwardly; intimately.

in·ly·ing (ˈɪnˌlaɪɪŋ) *adj.* situated within or inside.

in·mate (ˈɪnˌmeɪt) *n.* **1.** a person who is confined to an institution such as a prison or hospital. **2.** *Obsolete.* a person who lives with others in a house.

in me·di·as res *Latin.* (ɪn ˈmiːdɪˌæs ˈreɪs) in or into the middle of events or a narrative. [literally: into the midst of things, taken from a passage in Horace's *Ars Poetica*]

in mem. *abbrev. for* in memoriam.

in me·mo·ri·am (ɪn mɪˈmɔːrɪəm) in memory of; as a memorial to: used in obituaries, epitaphs, etc.

in·mesh (ɪnˈmɛʃ) *vb.* a variant of **enmesh.**

in·mi·grant (ˈɪnˌmaɪgrənt) *adj.* **1.** coming in from another area of the same country: *an inmigrant worker.* ~*n.* **2.** an inmigrant person or animal.

in·most (ˈɪnˌməʊst) *adj.* another word for **innermost.**

inn (ɪn) *n.* **1.** a pub or small hotel providing food and accommodation. **2.** (formerly, in England) a college or hall of residence for students, esp. of law, now only in the names of such institutions as the **Inns of Court.** [Old English; compare Old Norse *inni* inn, house, place of refuge] —**ˈinn·less** *adj.*

Inn (ɪn) *n.* a river in central Europe, rising in Switzerland in Graubünden and flowing northeast through Austria and Bavaria to join the River Danube at Passau: forms part of the border between Austria and West Germany. Length: 514 km (319 miles).

in·nards (ˈɪnədz) *pl. n. Informal.* **1.** the internal organs of the body, esp. the viscera. **2.** the interior parts or components of anything, esp. the working parts. [C19: colloquial variant of *inwards*]

in·nate (ɪˈneɪt, ˈɪneɪt) *adj.* **1.** existing in a person or animal from birth; congenital; inborn. **2.** being an essential part of the character of a person or thing. **3.** instinctive; not learned: *innate ideas.* **4.** *Botany.* (of anthers) joined to the filament by the base only. [C15: from Latin, from *innascī* to be born in, from *nascī* to be born] —**in·ˈnate·ly** *adv.* —**in·ˈnate·ness** *n.*

in·ner (ˈɪnə) *adj.* (*prenominal*) **1.** being or located further inside: *an inner room.* **2.** happening or occurring inside: *inner movement.* **3.** relating to the soul, mind, spirit, etc.: *inner feelings.* **4.** more profound or obscure; less apparent: *the inner meaning.* **5.** exclusive or private: *inner regions of the party.* **6.** *Chem.* (of a compound) having a cyclic structure formed or apparently formed by reaction of one functional group in a molecule with another group in the same molecule: *an inner ester.* ~*n.* **7.** Also called: **red.** *Archery.* **a.** the red innermost ring on a target. **b.** a shot which hits this ring. —**ˈin·ner·ly** *adv.* —**ˈin·ner·ness** *n.*

in·ner bar *n. Brit.* all Queen's or King's Counsel collectively.

in·ner-di·rect·ed *adj.* guided by one's own conscience and values rather than external pressures to conform. Compare **other-directed.** —**ˈin·ner-di·ˈrec·tion** *n.*

in·ner ear *n.* another name for **internal ear.**

In·ner Light *or* **Word** *n. Quakerism.* the presence and inner working of God in the soul acting as a guiding spirit that is superior even to Scripture and unites man to Christ.

in·ner man *n. or* **in·ner wom·an** *fem. n.* **1.** the mind or soul. **2.** *Jocular.* the stomach or appetite.

In·ner Mon·go·li·a *n.* an autonomous region of NE China: consists chiefly of the Mongolian plateau, with the Gobi Desert in the north and the Great Wall of China in the south. Capital: Huhehot. Pop.: 13 000 000 (1967–71 est.). Area: 1 177 500 sq. km (459 225 sq. miles).

in·ner·most (ˈɪnəˌməʊst) *adj.* **1.** being or located furthest within; central. **2.** intimate; private: *innermost beliefs.*

in·ner plan·et *n.* any of the planets Mercury, Venus, earth, and Mars, whose orbits lie inside the asteroid belt.

in·ner space *n.* **1.** the environment beneath the surface of the sea. **2.** the human mind regarded as being as unknown or as unfathomable as space.

In·ner Tem·ple *n.* (in England) one of the four legal societies in London that together form the Inns of Court.

in·ner tube *n.* an inflatable rubber tube that fits inside a pneumatic tyre casing.

in·ner·vate (ˈɪnɜːˌveɪt) *vb.* (*tr.*) **1.** to supply nerves to (a bodily organ or part). **2.** to stimulate (a bodily organ or part) with nerve impulses. —**ˌin·ner·ˈva·tion** *n.*

in·nerve (ɪˈnɜːv) *vb.* (*tr.*) to supply with nervous energy; stimulate.

in·ning (ˈɪnɪŋ) *n.* **1.** *Baseball.* a division of the game consisting of a turn at bat and a turn in the field for each side. **2.** *Archaic.* the reclamation of land from the sea. [Old English *innung* a going in, from *innian* to go in]

in·nings (ˈɪnɪŋz) *n.* **1.** (*functioning as sing.*) *Cricket.* **a.** the batting turn of a player or team. **b.** the runs scored during such a turn. **2.** (*sometimes sing.*) a period of opportunity or action. **3.** (*functioning as pl.*) land reclaimed from the sea.

In·nis·kil·ling (ˌɪnɪsˈkɪlɪŋ) *n.* a variant spelling of **Enniskillen.**

inn·keep·er (ˈɪnˌkiːpə) *n.* an owner or manager of an inn.

in·no·cence (ˈɪnəsəns) *n.* the quality or state of being innocent. Archaic word: **in·no·cen·cy** (ˈɪnəsənsɪ). [C14: from Latin *innocentia* harmlessness, from *innocēns* doing no harm, blameless, from IN-[1] + *nocēns* harming, from *nocēre* to hurt, harm; see NOXIOUS]

in·no·cent (ˈɪnəsənt) *adj.* **1.** not corrupted or tainted with evil or unpleasant emotion; sinless; pure. **2.** not guilty of a particular crime; blameless. **3.** (*postpositive;* foll. by *of*) free (of); lacking: *innocent of all knowledge of history.* **4.** harmless or innocuous: *an innocent game.* **5.** credulous, naive, or artless. **6.** simple-minded; slow-witted. ~*n.* **7.** an innocent person, esp. a young child or an ingenuous adult. **8.** a simple-minded person; simpleton. —**ˈin·no·cent·ly** *adv.*

In·no·cent II *n.* original name *Gregorio Papareschi.* died 1143, pope (1130–43). He condemned Abelard's teachings.

In·no·cent III *n.* original name *Giovanni Lotario de' Conti.* ?1161–1216, pope (1198–1216), under whom the temporal power of the papacy reached its height. He instituted the Fourth Crusade (1202) and a crusade against the Albigenses (1208), and called the fourth Lateran Council (1215).

In·no·cent IV *n.* original name *Sinibaldo de' Fieschi.* died 1254, pope (1243–54); an unrelenting enemy of Emperor Frederick II and his heirs.

in·noc·u·ous (ɪˈnɒkjʊəs) *adj.* having little or no adverse or harmful effect; harmless. [C16: from Latin *innocuus* harmless, from IN-[1] + *nocēre* to harm] —**in·ˈnoc·u·ous·ly** *adv.* —**in·ˈnoc·u·ous·ness** *or* **in·no·cu·i·ty** (ˌɪnəˈkjuːɪtɪ) *n.*

in·nom·i·nate (ɪˈnɒmɪnɪt) *adj.* **1.** having no name; nameless. **2.** a less common word for **anonymous.**

in·nom·i·nate bone *n.* either of the two bones that form the sides of the pelvis, consisting of three fused components, the ilium, ischium, and pubis. Nontechnical name: **hipbone.**

in nom·i·ne (ɪn ˈnɒmɪˌneɪ, -ˌniː) *n. Music.* any of several pieces of music of the 16th or 17th centuries for keyboard or for a consort of viols, based on a cantus firmus derived from the Vespers antiphon *Gloria tibi Trinitas.* [from Latin *in nomine Jesu* in the name of Jesus, the first words of an introit for which this type of music was originally composed]

in·no·vate (ˈɪnəˌveɪt) *vb.* to invent or begin to apply (methods, ideas, etc.). [C16: from Latin *innovāre* to renew, from IN-[2] + *novāre* to make new, from *novus* new] —**ˈin·no·ˌva·tive** *or* **ˈin·no·ˌva·to·ry** *adj.* —**ˈin·no·ˌva·tor** *n.*

in·no·va·tion (ˌɪnəˈveɪʃən) *n.* **1.** something newly introduced, such as a new method or device. **2.** the act of innovating. —**ˌin·no·ˈva·tion·al** *adj.* —**ˌin·no·ˈva·tion·ist** *n.*

in·nox·ious (ɪˈnɒkʃəs) *adj.* not noxious; harmless. —**in·ˈnox·ious·ly** *adv.* —**in·ˈnox·ious·ness** *n.*

Inns·bruck (ˈɪnzbrʊk) *n.* a city in W Austria, on the River Inn at the foot of the Brenner Pass: tourist centre. Pop.: 115 197 (1971).

Inns of Court *pl. n.* (in England) the four private unincorporated societies in London that function as a law school and have the exclusive privilege of calling candidates to the English bar. See **Lincoln's Inn, Inner Temple, Middle Temple, Gray's Inn.**

in·nu·en·do (ˌɪnjʊˈɛndəʊ) *n., pl.* **-dos** *or* **-does. 1.** an indirect or subtle reference, esp. one made maliciously or indicating criticism or disapproval; insinuation. **2.** *Law.* (in pleading) a word introducing an explanatory phrase, usually in parenthesis. **3.** *Law.* (in an action for defamation) **a.** an explanation of the construction put upon words alleged to be defamatory where the defamatory meaning is not apparent. **b.** the words thus explained. [C17: from Latin, literally: by hinting, from *innuendum,* gerund of *innuere* to convey by a nod, from IN-[2] + *nuere* to nod]

In·nu·it *or* **In·u·it** (ˈɪnjuːɪt) *n., pl.* **-it** *or* **-its.** an Eskimo of North America or Greenland, as distinguished from one from Asia or the Aleuts.

in·nu·mer·a·ble (ɪˈnjuːmərəbᵊl, ɪˈnjuːmrəbᵊl) *or* **in·nu·mer·ous** *adj.* so many as to be uncountable; extremely numerous. —**in·ˌnu·mer·a·ˈbil·i·ty** *or* **in·ˈnu·mer·a·ble·ness** *n.* —**in·ˈnu·mer·a·bly** *adv.*

in·nu·mer·ate (ɪˈnjuːmərɪt) *adj.* **1.** having neither knowledge nor understanding of mathematics or science. ~*n.* **2.** an innumerate person. —**in·ˈnu·mer·a·cy** *n.*

in·nu·tri·tion (ˌɪnjuːˈtrɪʃən) *n.* lack or absence of nutrition. Compare **malnutrition.** —**ˌin·nu·ˈtri·tious** *adj.*

in·ob·serv·ance (ˌɪnəbˈzɜːvəns) *n.* **1.** heedlessness. **2.** lack of compliance with or adherence to a law, religious duty, etc. —**ˌin·ob·ˈserv·ant** *adj.* —**ˌin·ob·ˈserv·ant·ly** *adv.*

in·oc·u·la·ble (ɪˈnɒkjʊləbᵊl) *adj.* capable of being inoculated. —**in·ˌoc·u·la·ˈbil·i·ty** *n.*

in·oc·u·late (ɪˈnɒkjʊˌleɪt) *vb.* **1.** to introduce (the causative agent of a disease) into the body of (a person or animal), in order to induce immunity. **2.** (*tr.*) to introduce (microorganisms, esp. bacteria) into (a culture medium). **3.** (*tr.*) to cause to be influenced or imbued, as with ideas or opinions. [C15: from Latin *inoculāre* to implant, from IN-[2] + *oculus* eye, bud] —**in·ˌoc·u·ˈla·tion** *n.* —**in·ˈoc·u·la·tive** *adj.* —**in·ˈoc·u·ˌla·tor** *n.*

in·oc·u·lum (ɪˈnɒkjʊləm) *or* **in·oc·u·lant** *n., pl.* **-la** (-lə) *or* **-lants.** *Med.* the substance used in giving an inoculation. [C20: New Latin; see INOCULATE]

in·o·dor·ous (ɪnˈəʊdərəs) *adj.* odourless; having no odour.

in-off *n. Billiards.* a shot that goes into a pocket after striking another ball.

in·of·fen·sive (ˌɪnəˈfɛnsɪv) *adj.* **1.** not giving offence; unobjectionable. **2.** not unpleasant, poisonous, or harmful. —**ˌin·of·ˈfen·sive·ly** *adv.* —**ˌin·of·ˈfen·sive·ness** *n.*

in·of·fi·cious (ˌɪnəˈfɪʃəs) *adj.* contrary to moral obligation, as the disinheritance of a child by his parents: *an inofficious will.* —ˌin+of+'fi+cious+ly *adv.* —ˌin+of+'fi+cious+ness *n.*

I·nö·nü ('i:nɜ:ˌnʊ, ˌɪnɜ:'nu:) *n.* **Is·met** (ɪs'mɛt, 'ɪsmɛt). 1884–1973, Turkish statesman; president of Turkey (1938–50) and prime minister (1923–37; 1961–65).

in+op+er+a·ble (ɪn'ɒpərəbᵊl, -'ɒprə-) *adj.* **1.** incapable of being implemented or operated; unworkable. **2.** *Surgery.* not suitable for operation without risk, esp. (of a malignant tumour) because metastasis has rendered surgery useless. —**in+ˌop+er+a·'bil+i·ty** *or* **in+'op+er+a·ble+ness** *n.* —**in+'op+er+a·bly** *adv.*

in+op·er·a+tive (ɪn'ɒpərətɪv, -'ɒprə-) *adj.* **1.** not operating. **2.** useless or ineffective. —**in+'op+er+a+tive+ness** *n.*

in+op+por+tune (ɪn'ɒpəˌtju:n) *adj.* not opportune; inappropriate or badly timed. —**in+'op+por+ˌtune+ly** *adv.* —**in+'op+por+ˌtune+ness** *or* **in+ˌop+por+'tun+i·ty** *n.*

in+or+di+nate (ɪn'ɔ:dɪnɪt) *adj.* **1.** exceeding normal limits; immoderate. **2.** unrestrained, as in behaviour or emotion; intemperate. **3.** irregular or disordered. [C14: from Latin *inordinātus* disordered, from IN-[1] + *ordināre* to put in order] —**in+'or+di+na+cy** *or* **in+'or+di+nate+ness** *n.* —**in+'or+di+nate+ly** *adv.*

inorg. *abbrev. for* inorganic.

in+or+gan+ic (ˌɪnɔ:'gænɪk) *adj.* **1.** not having the structure or characteristics of living organisms; not organic. **2.** relating to or denoting chemical compounds that do not contain carbon. Compare **organic. 3.** not having a system, structure, or ordered relation of parts; amorphous. **4.** not resulting from or produced by growth; artificial. **5.** *Linguistics.* denoting or relating to a sound or letter introduced into the pronunciation or spelling of a word at some point in its history. —**ˌin+or+'gan+i·cal+ly** *adv.*

in+or+gan+ic chem+is+try *n.* the branch of chemistry concerned with the elements and all their compounds except those containing carbon. Some simple carbon compounds, such as oxides, carbonates, etc., are treated as inorganic. Compare **organic chemistry.**

in+os+cu+late (ɪn'ɒskjʊˌleɪt) *vb.* **1.** *Physiol.* (of small blood vessels) to communicate by anastomosis. **2.** to unite or be united so as to be continuous; blend. **3.** to intertwine or cause to intertwine. [C17: from IN-[2] + Latin *ōsculāre* to equip with an opening, from *ōsculum*, diminutive of *ōs* mouth] —**in+ˌos+cu+'la+tion** *n.*

in·o·si·tol (ɪ'nəʊsɪˌtɒl) *n.* a cyclic alcohol, one isomer of which (*i*-inositol) is present in yeast and is a growth factor for some organisms; cyclohexanehexol. Formula: $C_6H_{12}O_6$. [C19: from Greek *in-*, *is* sinew + -OSE[2] + -ITE[1] + -OL[1]]

in·o·trop+ic (ˌɪnə'trɒpɪk, ˌaɪnə-) *adj.* affecting or controlling the contraction of muscles, esp. those of the heart: *inotropic drugs.* [C20: from Greek, from *is* (stem *in-*) tendon + -TROPIC]

in+pa+tient ('ɪnˌpeɪʃənt) *n.* a patient living in the hospital where he is being treated. Compare **outpatient.**

in per+pe+tu·um *Latin.* (ɪn pɜ:'pɛtjʊəm) for ever.

in per+so+nam (ɪn pɜ:'səʊnæm) *adj. Law.* (of a judicial act) directed against a specific person or persons. Compare **in rem.** [Latin]

in pet+to (ɪn 'pɛtəʊ) *adj. R.C. Church.* not disclosed: used of the names of cardinals designate. [Italian, literally: in the breast]

in pos+se (ɪn 'pɒsɪ) *adj.* possible; potential. Compare **in esse.** [Latin, literally: in possibility]

in pro+pri·a per+so+na *Latin.* (ɪn 'prəʊprɪə pɜ:'səʊnə) *adv. Chiefly law.* in person; personally.

in+put ('ɪnˌpʊt) *n.* **1.** the act of putting in. **2.** that which is put in. **3.** (*often pl.*) a resource required for industrial production, such as capital goods, labour services, raw materials, etc. **4.** *Electronics.* **a.** the signal or current fed into a component or circuit. **b.** the terminals, or some other point, to which the signal is applied. **5.** *Computer technol.* **a.** the data fed into a computer from a peripheral device. **b.** the devices and operations involved in transferring the data. **6.** (*modifier*) of or relating to electronic, computer, or other input: *input program.* ~*vb.* **7.** (*tr.*) to insert (data) into a computer.

in·put/out·put *n. Computer technol.* **1. a.** the equipment that controls the passage of information into or out of a computer. **b.** the operations that control this passage of information. **c.** a data-bearing medium, such as magnetic tape or paper tape. Abbrev.: I/O **2.** (*modifier*) concerned with or relating to the passage of information into or out of a computer.

in·put-out·put a·nal·y+sis *n. Economics.* an analysis of production relationships between the industries of an economy involving a study of each industry's inputs and outputs, esp. as used in social accounting.

in+qi+lab ('ɪnkɪˌlɑ:b) *n.* (in India, Pakistan, etc.) revolution (esp. in the phrase **inqilab zindabad** long live the revolution). [Urdu]

in+quest ('ɪnˌkwɛst) *n.* **1.** an inquiry into the cause of an unexplained, sudden, or violent death held by a jury before a coroner. **2.** *Informal.* any inquiry or investigation. [C13: from Medieval Latin *inquēsta*, from Latin IN-[2] + *quaesītus* investigation, from *quaerere* to examine]

in+qui+e·tude (ɪn'kwaɪɪˌtju:d) *n.* restlessness, uneasiness, or anxiety. —**in+qui+et** (ɪn'kwaɪət) *adj.* —**in+'qui+et+ly** *adv.*

in+qui+line ('ɪnkwɪˌlaɪn) *n.* **1.** an animal that lives in close association with another animal without harming it. See also **commensal** (sense 1). ~*adj.* **2.** of or living as an inquiline. [C17: from Latin *inquilīnus* lodger, from IN-[2] + *colere* to dwell] —**in+qui+lin+ism** ('ɪnkwɪlɪˌnɪzəm) *or* **in+qui+lin+i·ty** (ˌɪnkwɪ'lɪnɪtɪ) *n.* —**in+qui+li+nous** (ˌɪnkwɪ'laɪnəs) *adj.*

in+quire (ɪn'kwaɪə) *vb.* **1.** (*intr.*; often foll. by *into*) to make a search or investigation. **2.** See **enquire.** [C13: from Latin *inquīrere* from IN-[2] + *quaerere* to seek] —**in+'quir+er** *n.* —**in+'quir·y** *n.*

in+quir+ing (ɪn'kwaɪərɪŋ) *adj.* seeking or tending to seek answers, information, etc.: *an inquiring mind.* —**in+'quir+ing+ly** *adv.*

in+qui+si+tion (ˌɪnkwɪ'zɪʃən) *n.* **1.** the act of inquiring deeply or searchingly; investigation. **2.** a deep or searching inquiry, esp. a ruthless official investigation of individuals in order to suppress revolt or root out the unorthodox. **3.** an official inquiry, esp. one held by a jury before an officer of the Crown. **4.** another word for **inquest** (sense 2). [C14: from legal Latin *inquīsītiō*, from *inquīrere* to seek for; see INQUIRE] —**ˌin+qui+'si+tion+al** *adj.* —**ˌin+qui+'si+tion+ist** *n.*

In+qui+si+tion (ˌɪnkwɪ'zɪʃən) *n. History.* a judicial institution of the Roman Catholic Church (1232–1820) founded to discover and suppress heresy. See also **Spanish Inquisition.**

in+quis·i+tive (ɪn'kwɪzɪtɪv) *adj.* **1.** excessively curious, esp. about the affairs of others; prying. **2.** eager to learn; inquiring. —**in+'quis·i+tive+ly** *adv.* —**in+'quis·i+tive+ness** *n.*

in+quis·i+tor (ɪn'kwɪzɪtə) *n.* **1.** a person who inquires, esp. deeply, searchingly, or ruthlessly. **2.** (*often cap.*) an official of the ecclesiastical court of the Inquisition.

In+quis·i·tor-Gen·er·al *n., pl.* **In+quis·i·tors-Gen·er·al.** *History.* the head of the Spanish court of Inquisition.

in+quis·i+to+ri·al (ɪnˌkwɪzɪ'tɔ:rɪəl) *adj.* **1.** of, relating to, or resembling inquisition or an inquisitor. **2.** offensively curious; prying. **3.** *Law.* denoting criminal procedure in which one party is both prosecutor and judge, or in which the trial is held in secret. Compare **accusatorial** (sense 2). —**in+ˌquis·i+'to+ri+al+ly** *adv.* —**in+ˌquis·i+'to+ri+al+ness** *n.*

in re (ɪn 'reɪ) in the matter of: used esp. in bankruptcy proceedings. [C17: from Latin]

in rem (ɪn 'rɛm) *adj. Law.* (of a judicial act) directed against property rather than against a specific person. Compare **in personam.** [Latin, literally: against the matter]

in re+rum na+tu+ra *Latin.* (ɪn 'rɛərʊm næ'tʊərə) in the nature of things.

INRI *abbrev. for* Iesus Nazarenus Rex Iudaeorum (the inscription placed over Christ's head during the Crucifixion). [Latin: Jesus of Nazareth, King of the Jews]

in+road ('ɪnˌrəʊd) *n.* **1.** an invasion or hostile attack; raid or incursion. **2.** an encroachment or intrusion.

in+rush ('ɪnˌrʌʃ) *n.* a sudden usually overwhelming inward flow or rush; influx. —**'in+ˌrush·ing** *n., adj.*

INS *abbrev. for* International News Service.

ins. *abbrev. for:* **1.** inches. **2.** inspector. **3.** insulated. **4.** insulation. **5.** insurance.

in+sal·i+vate (ɪn'sælɪˌveɪt) *vb.* (*tr.*) to saturate (food) with saliva during mastication. —**in+ˌsal·i+'va+tion** *n.*

in+sa+lu+bri+ous (ˌɪnsə'lu:brɪəs) *adj.* not salubrious; unpleasant, unhealthy, or sordid. —**ˌin+sa+'lu+bri+ous+ly** *adv.* —**in+sa+lu+bri+ty** (ˌɪnsə'lu:brɪtɪ) *n.*

in+sane (ɪn'seɪn) *adj.* **1. a.** mentally deranged; crazy; of unsound mind. **b.** (*as collective n.* preceded by *the*): *the insane.* **2.** characteristic of a person of unsound mind: *an insane stare.* **3.** irresponsible; very foolish; stupid. —**in+'sane+ly** *adv.* —**in+'sane+ness** *n.*

in+san·i+tar·y (ɪn'sænɪtərɪ, -trɪ) *adj.* not sanitary; dirty or infected. —**in+'san·i+tar·i+ness** *or* **in+ˌsan·i+'ta+tion** *n.*

in+san·i+ty (ɪn'sænɪtɪ) *n., pl.* **·ties. 1.** relatively permanent disorder of the mind; state or condition of being insane. **2.** *Law.* (not in strict legal usage) a state of mind characterized by the inability to distinguish right from wrong. **3.** utter folly; stupidity.

in+sa+tia·ble (ɪn'seɪʃəbᵊl, -ʃɪə-) *or* **in+sa+ti+ate** (ɪn'seɪʃɪɪt) *adj.* not able to be satisfied or satiated; greedy or unappeasable. —**in+ˌsa+tia·'bil·i·ty, in+'sa+tia·ble+ness,** *or* **in+'sa+ti+ate+ness** *n.* —**in+'sa+tia·bly** *or* **in+'sa+ti+ate+ly** *adv.*

in+scape ('ɪnskeɪp) *n.* the essential inner nature of a person, object, etc., as expressed in literary or artistic works. [C19: from IN-[2] + *-scape*, as in LANDSCAPE; coined by Gerard Manley Hopkins]

in+scribe (ɪn'skraɪb) *vb.* (*tr.*) **1.** to make, carve, or engrave (writing, letters, a design, etc.) on (a surface such as wood, stone, or paper). **2.** to enter (a name) on a list or in a register. **3.** to sign one's name on (a book, photograph, etc.) before presentation to another person. **4.** to draw (a geometric construction such as a circle, polygon, etc.) inside another construction so that the two are in contact but do not intersect. Compare **circumscribe** (sense 3). [C16: from Latin *inscrībere*; see INSCRIPTION] —**in+'scrib+a·ble** *adj.* —**in+'scrib+a·ble+ness** *n.* —**in+'scrib+er** *n.*

in+scrip+tion (ɪn'skrɪpʃən) *n.* **1.** something inscribed, esp. words carved or engraved on a coin, tomb, etc. **2.** a signature or brief dedication in a book or on a work of art. **3.** the act of inscribing. [C14: from Latin *inscriptiō* a writing upon, from *inscrībere* to write upon, from IN-[2] + *scrībere* to write] —**in+'scrip+tion+al** *or* **in+'scrip+tive** *adj.* —**in+'scrip+tive+ly** *adv.*

in+scru+ta+ble (ɪn'skru:təbᵊl) *adj.* incomprehensible; mysterious or enigmatic. [C15: from Late Latin *inscrūtābilis*, from Latin IN-[1] + *scrūtārī* to examine] —**in+ˌscru+ta·'bil·i·ty** *or* **in+'scru+ta+ble+ness** *n.* —**in+'scru+ta·bly** *adv.*

in+sect ('ɪnsɛkt) *n.* **1.** any small air-breathing arthropod of the class *Insecta*, having a body divided into head, thorax, and abdomen, three pairs of legs, and (in most species) two pairs of wings. Insects comprise about five sixths of all known animal species, with a total of over one million named species. **2.** (loosely) any similar invertebrate, such as a spider, tick, or centipede. **3.** a contemptible, loathsome, or insignificant person. [C17: from Latin *insectum* (animal that has been) cut into, insect, from *insecāre*, from IN-² + *secāre* to cut; translation of Greek *entomon* insect] —in·'sec·te·an, in·'sec·tan, *or* in·'sec·tile *adj.* —'in·sect·,like *adj.*

in·sec·tar·i·um (ˌɪnsɛk'tɛərɪəm) *or* **in·sec·tar·y** (ɪn'sɛktərɪ) *n., pl.* ·tar·i·ums, ·tar·i·a (-'tɛərɪə), *or* ·tar·ies. a place where living insects are kept, bred, and studied.

in·sec·ti·cide (ɪn'sɛktɪˌsaɪd) *n.* a substance used to destroy insect pests. —in·ˌsec·ti·'cid·al *adj.*

in·sec·ti·vore (ɪn'sɛktɪˌvɔː) *n.* **1.** any placental mammal of the order *Insectivora*, being typically small, with simple teeth, and feeding on invertebrates. The group includes shrews, moles, and hedgehogs. **2.** any animal or plant that derives nourishment from insects.

in·sec·tiv·o·rous (ˌɪnsɛk'tɪvərəs) *adj.* **1.** feeding on or adapted for feeding on insects: *insectivorous plants.* **2.** of or relating to the order *Insectivora.*

in·sec·tiv·o·rous bat *n.* any bat of the suborder *Microchiroptera*, typically having large ears and feeding on insects. The group includes common bats (*Myotis* species), vampire bats, etc. Compare **fruit bat.**

in·se·cure (ˌɪnsɪ'kjʊə) *adj.* **1.** anxious or afraid; not confident or certain. **2.** not adequately protected: *an insecure fortress.* **3.** unstable or shaky. —ˌin·se·'cure·ly *adv.* —ˌin·se·'cure·ness *n.* —ˌin·se·'cu·ri·ty *n.*

in·sel·berg ('ɪnzəlˌbɜːg) *n.* an isolated rocky hill rising abruptly from a flat plain. [from German, from *Insel* island + *Berg* mountain]

in·sem·i·nate (ɪn'sɛmɪˌneɪt) *vb.* (*tr.*) **1.** to impregnate (a female) with semen. **2.** to introduce (ideas or attitudes) into the mind of (a person or group). [C17: from Latin *insēmināre*, from IN-² + *sēmināre* to sow, from *sēmen* seed] —in·ˌsem·i·'na·tion *n.* —in·'sem·i·ˌna·tor *n.*

in·sen·sate (ɪn'sɛnseɪt, -sɪt) *adj.* **1.** lacking sensation or consciousness. **2.** insensitive; unfeeling. **3.** foolish; senseless. —in·'sen·sate·ly *adv.* —in·'sen·sate·ness *n.*

in·sen·si·ble (ɪn'sɛnsəbəl) *adj.* **1.** lacking sensation or consciousness. **2.** (foll. by *of* or *to*) unaware (of) or indifferent (to): *insensible to suffering.* **3.** thoughtless or callous. **4.** a less common word for **imperceptible.** —in·ˌsen·si·'bil·i·ty *or* in·'sen·si·ble·ness *n.* —in·'sen·si·bly *adv.*

in·sen·si·tive (ɪn'sɛnsɪtɪv) *adj.* **1.** lacking sensitivity; unfeeling. **2.** lacking physical sensation. **3.** (*postpositive*; foll. by *to*) not sensitive (to) or affected (by): *insensitive to radiation.* —in·'sen·si·tive·ly *adv.* —in·'sen·si·tive·ness *or* in·ˌsen·si·'tiv·i·ty *n.*

in·sen·ti·ent (ɪn'sɛnʃɪənt) *adj. Rare.* lacking consciousness or senses; inanimate. —in·'sen·ti·ence *or* in·'sen·ti·en·cy *n.*

in·sep·a·ra·ble (ɪn'sɛpərəbəl, -'sɛprə-) *adj.* incapable of being separated or divided. —in·ˌsep·a·ra·'bil·i·ty *or* in·'sep·a·ra·ble·ness *n.* —in·'sep·a·ra·bly *adv.*

in·sert *vb.* (ɪn'sɜːt). (*tr.*) **1.** to put in or between; introduce. **2.** to introduce, as into text, such as a newspaper; interpolate. ~*n.* ('ɪnsɜːt). **3.** something inserted. **4. a.** a folded section placed in another for binding in with a book. **b.** a printed sheet, esp. one bearing advertising, placed loose between the leaves of a book, periodical, etc. **5.** another word for **cut-in** (sense 6). [C16: from Latin *inserere* to plant in, ingraft, from IN-² + *serere* to join] —in·'sert·a·ble *adj.* —in·'sert·er *n.*

in·sert·ed (ɪn'sɜːtɪd) *adj.* **1.** *Anatomy.* (of a muscle) attached to the bone that it moves. **2.** *Botany.* (of parts of a plant) growing from another part, as stamens from the corolla.

in·ser·tion (ɪn'sɜːʃən) *n.* **1.** the act of inserting or something that is inserted. **2.** a word, sentence, correction, etc., inserted into text, such as a newspaper. **3.** a strip of lace, embroidery, etc., between two pieces of material. **4.** *Anatomy.* the point or manner of attachment of a muscle to the bone that it moves. **5.** *Botany.* the manner or point of attachment of one part to another. —in·'ser·tion·al *adj.*

in·ses·so·ri·al (ˌɪnsɛ'sɔːrɪəl) *adj.* **1.** (of feet or claws) adapted for perching. **2.** (of birds) having insessorial feet. [C19: from New Latin *Insessōrēs* birds that perch, from Latin: perchers, from *insidēre* to sit upon, from *sedēre* to sit]

in·set *vb.* (ɪn'sɛt), ·sets, ·set·ting, ·set. **1.** (*tr.*) to set or place in or within; insert. ~*n.* ('ɪnˌsɛt). **2.** something inserted. **3.** *Printing.* **a.** a small map or diagram set within the borders of a larger one. **b.** another name for **insert** (sense 4). **4.** a piece of fabric inserted into a garment, as to shape it or for decoration. **5.** a flowing in, as of the tide. —'in·ˌset·ter *n.*

in·shore ('ɪn'ʃɔː) *adj.* **1.** in or on the water, but close to the shore: *inshore weather.* ~*adv., adj.* **2.** towards the shore from the water: *an inshore wind; we swam inshore.*

in·shrine (ɪn'ʃraɪn) *vb.* a variant of **enshrine.**

in·side *n.* ('ɪn'saɪd). **1.** the interior; inner or enclosed part or surface. **2.** the side of a path away from the road or adjacent to a wall. **3.** (*also pl.*) *Informal.* the internal organs of the body, esp. the stomach and bowels. **4. inside of.** in a period of time less than; within. **5. inside out.** with the inside facing outwards. **6. know (something) inside out.** to know thoroughly or perfectly. ~*prep.* (ˌɪn'saɪd). **7.** in or to the interior of; within or to within; on the inside of. ~*adj.* ('ɪnˌsaɪd). **8.** on or of an interior; on the inside: *an inside door.* **9.** (*prenominal*) arranged or provided by someone within an organization or building, esp. illicitly: *the raid was an inside job; inside information.* ~*adv.* (ˌɪn'saɪd). **10.** within or to within a thing or place; indoors. **11.** by nature; fundamentally: *inside, he's a good chap.* **12.** *Slang.* in or into prison.

Usage. See at **outside.**

in·side for·ward *n. Soccer.* (esp. formerly) one of two players (the **inside right** and the **inside left**) having mainly midfield and attacking roles.

in·side job *n. Informal.* a crime committed with the assistance of someone associated with the victim, such as a person employed on the premises burgled.

in·sid·er (ɪn'saɪdə) *n.* **1.** a member of a specified group. **2.** a person with access to exclusive information.

in·sid·i·ous (ɪn'sɪdɪəs) *adj.* **1.** stealthy, subtle, cunning, or treacherous. **2.** working in a subtle or apparently innocuous way, but nevertheless deadly: *an insidious illness.* [C16: from Latin *insidiōsus* cunning, from *insidiae* an ambush, from *insidēre* to sit in; see INSESSORIAL] —in·'sid·i·ous·ly *adv.* —in·'sid·i·ous·ness *n.*

in·sight ('ɪnˌsaɪt) *n.* **1.** the ability to perceive clearly or deeply; penetration. **2.** a penetrating and often sudden understanding, as of a complex situation or problem. **3.** *Psychol.* **a.** the capacity for understanding one's own or another's mental processes. **b.** the immediate understanding of the significance of an event or action. **4.** *Psychiatry.* the ability to understand one's own problems, sometimes used to distinguish between psychotic and neurotic disorders. —'in·ˌsight·ful *adj.*

in·sig·ni·a (ɪn'sɪgnɪə) *n., pl.* ·ni·as *or* ·ni·a. **1.** a badge or emblem of membership, office, or dignity. **2.** a distinguishing sign or mark. ~Also called (rare): **in·sig·ne** (ɪn'sɪgniː). [C17: from Latin: marks, badges, from *insignis* distinguished by a mark, prominent, from IN-² + *signum* mark]

in·sig·nif·i·cant (ˌɪnsɪg'nɪfɪkənt) *adj.* **1.** having little or no importance; trifling. **2.** almost or relatively meaningless. **3.** small or inadequate: *an insignificant wage.* **4.** not distinctive in character, etc. —ˌin·sig·'nif·i·cance *or* ˌin·sig·'nif·i·can·cy *n.* —ˌin·sig·'nif·i·cant·ly *adv.*

in·sin·cere (ˌɪnsɪn'sɪə) *adj.* lacking sincerity; hypocritical. —ˌin·sin·'cere·ly *adv.* —in·sin·cer·i·ty (ˌɪnsɪn'sɛrɪtɪ) *n.*

in·sin·u·ate (ɪn'sɪnjʊˌeɪt) *vb.* **1.** (*may take a clause as object*) to suggest by indirect allusion, hints, innuendo, etc. **2.** (*tr.*) to introduce subtly or deviously. **3.** (*tr.*) to cause (someone, esp. oneself) to be accepted by gradual approaches or manoeuvres. [C16: from Latin *insinuāre* to wind one's way into, from IN-² + *sinus* curve] —in·'sin·u·a·tive *or* in·'sin·u·a·to·ry *adj.* —in·'sin·u·ˌa·tor *n.*

in·sin·u·a·tion (ɪnˌsɪnjʊ'eɪʃən) *n.* **1.** an indirect or devious hint or suggestion. **2.** the act or practice of insinuating.

in·sip·id (ɪn'sɪpɪd) *adj.* **1.** lacking spirit or interest; boring. **2.** lacking taste; unpalatable. [C17: from Latin *insipidus*, from IN-¹ + *sapidus* full of flavour, SAPID] —ˌin·si·'pid·i·ty *or* in·'sip·id·ness *n.* —in·'sip·id·ly *adv.*

in·sip·i·ence (ɪn'sɪpɪəns) *n. Archaic.* lack of wisdom. [C15: from Latin *insipientia*, from IN-¹ + *sapientia* wisdom; see SAPIENT] —in·'sip·i·ent *adj.* —in·'sip·i·ent·ly *adv.*

in·sist (ɪn'sɪst) *vb.* (when *tr., takes a clause as object;* when *intr.*, usually foll. by *on* or *upon*) **1.** to make a determined demand (for): *he insisted that his rights be respected; he insisted on his rights.* **2.** to express a convinced belief (in) or assertion (of): *he insisted that she was mad; he insisted on her madness.* [C16: from Latin *insistere* to stand upon, urge, from IN-² + *sistere* to stand] —in·'sist·er *n.* —in·'sist·ing·ly *adv.*

in·sist·ent (ɪn'sɪstənt) *adj.* **1.** making continual and persistent demands. **2.** demanding notice or attention; compelling: *the insistent cry of a bird.* —in·'sist·ence *or* in·'sist·en·cy *n.* —in·'sist·ent·ly *adv.*

in si·tu *Latin.* (ɪn 'sɪtjuː) *adv., adj.* (*postpositive*) **1.** in the natural, original, or appropriate position. **2.** *Pathol.* (esp. of a cancerous growth or tumour) not seen to be spreading from a localized position.

in·snare (ɪn'snɛə) *vb.* a less common spelling of **ensnare.** —in·'snare·ment *n.* —in·'snar·er *n.*

in·so·bri·e·ty (ˌɪnsəʊ'braɪɪtɪ) *n.* lack of sobriety; intemperance.

in so far *or U.S.* **in·so·far** *adv.* (usually foll. by *as* or *that*) to the degree or extent (that).

in·so·late ('ɪnsəʊˌleɪt) *vb.* (*tr.*) to expose to sunlight, as for drying or bleaching. [C17: from Latin *insōlāre* to place in the sun, from IN-² + *sōl* sun]

in·so·la·tion (ˌɪnsəʊ'leɪʃən) *n.* **1.** the quantity of solar radiation falling upon a body or planet, esp. per unit area. **2.** exposure to the sun's rays. **3.** another name for **sunstroke.**

in·sole ('ɪnˌsəʊl) *n.* **1.** the inner sole of a shoe or boot. **2.** a loose additional inner sole used to give extra warmth or to make a shoe fit.

in·so·lent ('ɪnsələnt) *adj.* offensive, impudent, or disrespectful. [C14: from Latin *insolens* from IN-¹ + *solēre* to be accustomed] —'in·so·lence *n.* —'in·so·lent·ly *adv.*

in·sol·u·ble (ɪn'sɒljʊbəl) *adj.* **1.** incapable of being dissolved; incapable of forming a solution, esp. in water. **2.** incapable of being solved. —in·ˌsol·u·'bil·i·ty *or* in·'sol·u·ble·ness *n.* —in·'sol·u·bly *adv.*

in·solv·a·ble (ɪn'sɒlvəbəl) *adj.* another word for **insoluble** (sense 2). —in·ˌsolv·a·'bil·i·ty *n.* —in·'solv·a·bly *adv.*

in·sol·vent (ɪn'sɒlvənt) *adj.* **1.** (of a person, company, etc.) having insufficient assets to meet debts and liabilities; bankrupt. **2.** of or relating to bankrupts or bankruptcy. ~*n.* **3.** a person who is insolvent; bankrupt. —in·'sol·ven·cy *n.*

in·som·ni·a (ɪn'sɒmnɪə) *n.* chronic inability to fall asleep or to enjoy uninterrupted sleep. [C18: from Latin, from *insomnis* sleepless, from *somnus* sleep] —in·'som·ni·ous *adj.*

in·som·ni·ac (ɪn'sɒmnɪˌæk) *adj.* **1.** exhibiting or causing insomnia. ~*n.* **2.** a person experiencing insomnia.

in·so·much (ˌɪnsəʊ'mʌtʃ) *adv.* **1.** (foll. by *as* or *that*) to such an extent or degree. **2.** (foll. by *as*) because of the fact (that); inasmuch (as).

in·sou·ci·ant (ɪn'su:sɪənt) *adj.* carefree or unconcerned; lighthearted. [C19: from French, from IN-[1] + *souciant* worrying, from *soucier* to trouble, from Latin *sollicitāre*; compare SOLICITOUS] —**in'sou·ci·ance** *n.* —**in'sou·ci·ant·ly** *adv.*

insp. *abbrev. for:* **1.** inspected. **2.** inspector.

in·span (ɪn'spæn) *vb.* ·**spans,** ·**span·ning,** ·**spanned.** (*tr.*) *Chiefly S. African.* to harness (animals) to (a vehicle); yoke. [C19: from Afrikaans, from Middle Dutch *inspannen*, from *spannen* to stretch, yoke; see SPAN]

in·spect (ɪn'spɛkt) *vb.* (*tr.*) **1.** to examine closely, esp. for faults or errors. **2.** to scrutinize officially (a document, military personnel on ceremonial parade, etc.). [C17: from Latin *inspicere*, from *specere* to look] —**in'spect·a·ble** *adj.* —**in'spect·ing·ly** *adv.* —**in'spec·tion** *n.* —**in'spec·tion·al** *adj.* —**in'spec·tive** *adj.*

in·spec·tion cham·ber *n.* a more formal name for **manhole** (sense 1).

in·spec·tor (ɪn'spɛktə) *n.* **1.** a person who inspects, esp. an official who examines for compliance with regulations, standards, etc. **2.** a police officer ranking below a superintendent or chief inspector and above a sergeant. —**in'spec·to·ral** *or* **in·spec·to·ri·al** (ˌɪnspɛk'tɔ:rɪəl) *adj.* —**in'spec·tor·ˌship** *n.*

in·spec·tor·ate (ɪn'spɛktərɪt) *n.* **1.** the office, rank, or duties of an inspector. **2.** a body of inspectors. **3.** a district under an inspector.

in·spec·tor gen·er·al *n., pl.* **in·spec·tors gen·er·al.** **1.** the head of an inspectorate or inspection system; an officer with wide investigative powers. **2.** a staff officer of the military, air, or naval service with the responsibility of conducting inspections and investigations.

in·spec·tor of tax·es *n.* an official of the Inland Revenue whose work is to assess individuals' income tax liability.

in·sphere (ɪn'sfɪə) *vb.* a variant spelling of **ensphere.**

in·spi·ra·tion (ˌɪnspɪ'reɪʃən) *n.* **1.** stimulation or arousal of the mind, feelings, etc., to special or unusual activity or creativity. **2.** the state or quality of being so stimulated or aroused. **3.** someone or something that causes this state. **4.** an idea or action resulting from such a state. **5.** the act or process of inhaling; breathing in.

in·spi·ra·tion·al (ˌɪnspɪ'reɪʃənᵊl) *adj.* **1.** of, relating to, or tending to arouse inspiration; inspiring. **2.** resulting from inspiration; inspired. —ˌ**in·spi'ra·tion·al·ly** *adv.*

in·spir·a·to·ry (ɪn'spaɪərətərɪ, -trɪ) *adj.* of or relating to inhalation or the drawing in of air.

in·spire (ɪn'spaɪə) *vb.* **1.** to exert a stimulating or beneficial effect upon (a person, etc.); animate or invigorate. **2.** (*tr.; foll. by with or to; may take an infinitive*) to arouse (with a particular emotion or to a particular action); stir. **3.** (*tr.*) to prompt or instigate; give rise to: *her beauty inspired his love.* **4.** (*tr.; often passive*) to guide or arouse by divine influence or inspiration. **5.** to take or draw (air, gas, etc.) into the lungs; inhale. **6.** (*tr.*) *Archaic.* **a.** to breathe into or upon. **b.** to breathe life into. [C14 (in the sense: to breathe upon, blow into): from Latin *inspīrāre*, from *spīrāre* to breathe] —**in'spir·a·ble** *adj.* —**in'spir·a·tive** *adj.* —**in'spir·er** *n.* —**in'spir·ing·ly** *adv.*

in·spir·it (ɪn'spɪrɪt) *vb.* (*tr.*) to fill with vigour; inspire. —**in'spir·it·er** *n.* —**in'spir·it·ing·ly** *adv.* —**in'spir·it·ment** *n.*

in·spis·sate (ɪn'spɪseɪt) *vb. Archaic.* to thicken, as by evaporation. [C17: from Late Latin *inspissātus* thickened, from Latin *spissāre* to thicken, from *spissus* thick] —ˌ**in·spis'sa·tion** *n.* —'**in·spis·ˌsa·tor** *n.*

inst. *abbrev. for:* **1.** instant (this month). **2.** instantaneous. **3.** instrumental.

Inst. *abbrev. for:* **1.** Institute. **2.** Institution.

in·sta·bil·i·ty (ˌɪnstə'bɪlɪtɪ) *n., pl.* ·**ties.** **1.** lack of stability or steadiness. **2.** tendency to variable or unpredictable behaviour. **3.** *Physics.* a sudden deformation of a plasma due to a weakening of the confining field.

in·sta·ble (ɪn'steɪbᵊl) *adj.* a less common word for **unstable.**

in·stall *or* **in·stal** (ɪn'stɔ:l) *vb.* ·**stalls,** ·**stall·ing,** ·**stalled** *or* ·**stals,** ·**stal·ling,** ·**stalled.** (*tr.*) **1.** to place (machinery, equipment, etc.) in position and connect and adjust for use. **2.** to put in a position, rank, etc. **3.** to settle (a person, esp. oneself) in a position or state: *she installed herself in an armchair.* [C16: from Medieval Latin *installāre*, from IN-[2] + *stallum* STALL[1]] —**in'stall·er** *n.*

in·stall·ant (ɪn'stɔ:lənt) *n.* **a.** a person who installs another in an office, etc. **b.** (*as modifier*): *an installant bishop.*

in·stal·la·tion (ˌɪnstə'leɪʃən) *n.* **1.** the act of installing or the state of being installed. **2.** a large device, system, or piece of equipment that has been installed. **3.** a military establishment usually serving in a support role.

in·stall·ment plan *n.* the U.S. name for **hire-purchase.**

in·stal·ment[1] *or U.S.* **in·stall·ment** (ɪn'stɔ:lmənt) *n.* **1.** one of the portions, usually equal, into which a debt is divided for payment at specified intervals over a fixed period. **2.** a portion of something that is issued, broadcast, or published in parts, such as a serial in a magazine. [C18: from obsolete *estallment*, probably from Old French *estaler* to fix, hence to agree rate of payment, from *estal* something fixed, place, from Old High German *stal* STALL[1]]

in·stal·ment[2] *or U.S.* **in·stall·ment** (ɪn'stɔ:lmənt) *n.* another word for **installation** (sense 1).

in·stance ('ɪnstəns) *n.* **1.** a case or particular example. **2. for instance.** for or as an example. **3.** a specified stage in proceedings; step (in the phrases **in the first, second,** etc., **instance**). **4.** urgent request or demand (esp. in the phrase **at the instance of**). **5.** *Archaic.* motive or reason. ~*vb.* (*tr.*). **6.** to cite as an example. [C14 (in the sense: case, example): from Medieval Latin *instantia* example, (in the sense: urgency) from Latin: a being close upon, presence, from *instāns* pressing upon, urgent; see INSTANT]

in·stan·cy ('ɪnstənsɪ) *n. Rare.* **1.** the quality of being urgent or imminent. **2.** instantaneousness; immediateness.

in·stant ('ɪnstənt) *n.* **1.** a very brief time; moment. **2.** a particular moment or point in time: *at the same instant.* **3. on the instant.** immediately; without delay. ~*adj.* **4.** immediate; instantaneous. **5.** urgent or imperative. **6.** (esp. of foods) prepared or designed for preparation with very little time and effort: *instant coffee.* **7.** (*postpositive*) *Rare except when abbreviated in formal correspondence.* **a.** of the present month: *a letter of the 7th instant.* Abbrev.: **inst.** Compare **proximo, ultimo. b.** currently under consideration. ~*adv.* **8.** a poetic word for **instantly.** [C15: from Latin *instāns*, from *instāre* to be present, press closely, from IN-[2] + *stāre* to stand]

in·stan·ta·ne·ous (ˌɪnstən'teɪnɪəs) *adj.* **1.** occurring with almost no delay; immediate. **2.** happening or completed within a moment: *instantaneous death.* **3.** *Maths.* **a.** occurring at or associated with a particular instant. **b.** equal to the limit of the average value of a given variable as the time interval over which the variable is considered approaches zero: *instantaneous velocity.* —ˌ**in·stan'ta·ne·ous·ly** *adv.* —ˌ**in·stan'ta·ne·ous·ness** *or* **in·stan·ta·ne·i·ty** (ɪnˌstæntənɪ'i:ɪtɪ) *n.*

in·stan·ter (ɪn'stæntə) *adv. Law.* without delay; (in connection with pleading) the same day or within 24 hours. [C17: from Latin: urgently, from *instans* INSTANT]

in·stan·ti·ate (ɪn'stænʃɪˌeɪt) *vb.* (*tr.*) to represent by an instance. [C20: from Latin *instantia* (see INSTANCE) + -ATE[1]] —**in·ˌstan·ti'a·tion** *n.*

in·stant·ly ('ɪnstəntlɪ) *adv.* **1.** immediately; at once. **2.** *Archaic.* urgently or insistently.

in·stant re·play *n.* another name for **action replay.**

in·star ('ɪnstɑ:) *n.* the stage in the development of an insect between any two moults. [C19: New Latin from Latin: image]

in·state (ɪn'steɪt) *vb.* (*tr.*) to place in a position or office; install. —**in'state·ment** *n.*

in·stau·ra·tion (ˌɪnstɔ:'reɪʃən) *n. Rare.* restoration or renewal. [C17: from Latin *instaurātiō*, from *instaurāre* to renew] —'**in·stau·ˌra·tor** *n.*

in·stead (ɪn'stɛd) *adv.* **1.** as a replacement, substitute, or alternative. **2. instead of.** (*prep.*) in place of or as an alternative to. [C13: from phrase *in stead* in place]

in·step ('ɪnˌstɛp) *n.* **1.** the middle section of the human foot, forming the arch between the ankle and toes. **2.** the part of a shoe, stocking, etc., covering this. [C16: probably from IN-[2] + STEP]

in·sti·gate ('ɪnstɪˌgeɪt) *vb.* (*tr.*) **1.** to bring about, as by incitement or urging: *to instigate rebellion.* **2.** to urge on to some drastic or unadvisable action. [C16: from Latin *instīgāre* to stimulate, incite; compare Greek *stizein* to prick] —'**in·sti·ˌgat·ing·ly** *adv.* —ˌ**in·sti'ga·tion** *n.* —'**in·sti·ˌga·tive** *adj.* —'**in·sti·ˌga·tor** *n.*

in·stil *or* **in·still** (ɪn'stɪl) *vb.* (*tr.*) **1.** to introduce gradually; implant or infuse. **2.** *Rare.* to pour in or inject in drops. [C16: from Latin *instillāre* to pour in a drop at a time, from *stillāre* to drip] —**in'still·er** *n.* —**in'stil·ment, in'still·ment,** *or* ˌ**in·stil'la·tion** *n.*

in·stinct ('ɪnstɪŋkt) *n.* **1.** the innate capacity of an animal to respond to a given stimulus in a relatively fixed way. **2.** inborn intuitive power. **3.** a natural and apparently innate aptitude. ~*adj.* **4.** *Rare.* (*postpositive;* often foll. by *with*) **a.** animated or impelled (by). **b.** imbued or infused (with). [C15: from Latin *instinctus* roused, from *instinguere* to incite; compare INSTIGATE]

in·stinc·tive (ɪn'stɪŋktɪv) *or* **in·stinc·tu·al** *adj.* **1.** of, relating to, or resulting from instinct. **2.** conditioned so as to appear innate: *an instinctive movement in driving.* —**in'stinc·tive·ly** *or* **in'stinc·tu·al·ly** *adv.*

in·sti·tute ('ɪnstɪˌtju:t) *vb.* (*tr.*) **1.** to organize; establish. **2.** to initiate: *to institute a practice.* **3.** to establish in a position or office; induct. **4.** (followed by *in* or *into*) to install (a clergyman) in a church. ~*n.* **5.** an organization founded for particular work, such as education, promotion of the arts, or scientific research. **6.** the building where such an organization is situated. **7.** something instituted, esp. a rule, custom, or precedent. [C16: from Latin *instituere*, from *statuere* to place, stand] —'**in·sti·ˌtu·tor** *or* '**in·sti·ˌtut·er** *n.*

in·sti·tutes ('ɪnstɪˌtju:ts) *n.* an elementary textbook designed for students of law.

In·sti·tutes ('ɪnstɪˌtju:ts) *n.* **1.** an introduction to legal study in ancient Rome, compiled by order of Justinian and divided into four books forming part of the Corpus Juris Civilis. **2.** short for **Institutes of the Christian Religion,** the book by Calvin, completed in 1536 and constituting the basic statement of the Reformed faith, that repudiates papal authority and postulates the doctrines of justification by faith alone and predestination.

in·sti·tu·tion (ˌɪnstɪ'tju:ʃən) *n.* **1.** the act of instituting. **2.** an organization or establishment founded for a specific purpose, such as a hospital, church, company, or college. **3.** the building where such an organization is situated. **4.** an established custom, law, or relationship in a society or community. **5.** *Informal.* a constant feature or practice: *Jones's drink at the bar was an institution.* **6.** the appointment or admission of an incumbent to an ecclesiastical office or pastoral charge. **7.** *Theol.* the creation of a sacrament by Christ, esp. the Eucharist. —ˌ**in·sti'tu·tion·ar·y** *adj.*

in·sti·tu·tion·al (ˌɪnstɪ'tju:ʃənᵊl) *adj.* **1.** of, relating to, or characteristic of institutions. **2.** dull, routine, and uniform:

institutional meals. **3.** relating to principles or institutes, esp. of law. —ˌ**in·sti·'tu·tion·al·ly** *adv.*

in·sti·tu·tion·al·ism (ˌɪnstɪ'tjuːʃənəˌlɪzəm) *n.* the system of or belief in institutions. —ˌ**in·sti·'tu·tion·al·ist** *n.*

in·sti·tu·tion·al·ize *or* **in·sti·tu·tion·al·ise** (ˌɪnstɪ'tjuːʃənəˌlaɪz) *vb.* **1.** (*tr.; often passive*) to subject to the deleterious effects of confinement in an institution: *a mental patient who was institutionalized into boredom and apathy.* **2.** (*tr.*) to place in an institution. **3.** to make or become an institution. —ˌ**in·sti·ˌtu·tion·al·i·'za·tion** *or* ˌ**in·sti·ˌtu·tion·al·i·'sa·tion** *n.*

in·sti·tu·tive ('ɪnstɪˌtjuːtɪv) *adj.* **1.** concerned with instituting and establishing. **2.** established by custom or law. —'**in·sti·ˌtu·tive·ly** *adv.*

instr. *abbrev. for:* **1.** instructor. **2.** instrument. **3.** instrumental.

in·struct (ɪn'strʌkt) *vb.* (*tr.*) **1.** to direct to do something; order. **2.** to teach (someone) how to do (something). **3.** to furnish with information; apprise. **4.** *Law, chiefly Brit.* **a.** (esp. of a client to his solicitor or a solicitor to a barrister) to give relevant facts or information to. **b.** to authorize (a barrister or solicitor) to conduct a case on a person's behalf: *to instruct counsel.* [C15: from Latin *instruere* to construct, set in order, equip, teach, from *struere* to build] —**in·'struct·i·ble** *adj.*

in·struc·tion (ɪn'strʌkʃən) *n.* **1.** a direction; order. **2.** the process or act of imparting knowledge; teaching; education. **3.** Also called: **command.** *Computer technol.* a part of a program consisting of coded commands to the computer to perform a specified function. —**in·'struc·tion·al** *adj.*

in·struc·tions (ɪn'strʌkʃənz) *pl. n.* **1.** directions, orders, or recommended rules for guidance, use, etc. **2.** *Law.* the facts and details relating to a case given by a client to his solicitor or by a solicitor to a barrister with directions to conduct the case: *to take instructions.*

in·struc·tive (ɪn'strʌktɪv) *adj.* serving to instruct or enlighten; conveying information. —**in·'struc·tive·ly** *adv.* —**in·'struc·tive·ness** *n.*

in·struc·tor (ɪn'strʌktə) *n.* **1.** someone who instructs; teacher. **2.** *U.S.* a university teacher ranking below assistant professor. —**in·'struc·tor·ˌship** *n.* —**in·struc·tress** (ɪn'strʌktrɪs) *fem. n.*

in·stru·ment *n.* ('ɪnstrəmənt). **1.** a mechanical implement or tool, esp. one used for precision work: *surgical instrument.* **2.** *Music.* any of various contrivances or mechanisms that can be played to produce musical tones or sounds. **3.** an important factor or agency in something: *her evidence was an instrument in his arrest.* **4.** *Informal.* a person used by another to gain an end; dupe; tool. **5.** a measuring device, such as a pressure gauge or ammeter. **6. a.** a device or system for use in navigation or control, esp. of aircraft. **b.** (*as modifier*): *instrument landing.* **7.** a formal legal document. ~*vb.* ('ɪnstrəˌmɛnt). **8.** another word for **orchestrate** (sense 1). **9.** to equip with instruments. [C13: from Latin *instrūmentum* tool, equipment, from *instruere* to erect, furnish; see INSTRUCT]

in·stru·men·tal (ˌɪnstrə'mɛntᵊl) *adj.* **1.** serving as a means or influence; helpful. **2.** of, relating to, or characterized by an instrument or instruments. **3.** played by or composed for musical instruments. **4.** *Grammar.* denoting a case of nouns, etc., in certain inflected languages, indicating the instrument used in performing an action, usually translated into English using the prepositions *with* or *by means of.* ~*n.* **5.** a piece of music composed for instruments rather than for voices. **6.** *Grammar.* **a.** the instrumental case. **b.** a word or speech element in the instrumental case. —ˌ**in·stru·men·'tal·i·ty** *n.* —ˌ**in·stru·'men·tal·ly** *adv.*

in·stru·men·tal con·di·tion·ing *n. Psychol.* a method of training by repeatedly associating the performance of a response with the presentation of a reinforcement.

in·stru·men·tal·ism (ˌɪnstrə'mɛntəˌlɪzəm) *n.* a system of pragmatic philosophy holding that ideas are instruments, that they should guide our actions and can change the world, and that their value can be measured by their success.

in·stru·men·tal·ist (ˌɪnstrə'mɛntəlɪst) *n.* **1.** a person who plays a musical instrument. **2.** *Philosophy.* a person who believes in the doctrines of instrumentalism. ~*adj.* **3.** of or relating to instrumentalism.

in·stru·men·ta·tion (ˌɪnstrəmɛn'teɪʃən) *n.* **1.** the instruments specified in a musical score or arrangement. **2.** another word for **orchestration. 3.** the study of the characteristics of musical instruments. **4.** the use of instruments or tools. **5.** means; agency.

in·stru·ment fly·ing *n.* the navigation of an aircraft by the use of instruments only.

in·stru·ment land·ing *n.* an aircraft landing relying only upon instruments and ground radio devices, usually made when visibility is very poor.

in·stru·ment pan·el *or* **board** *n.* **1.** a panel on which instruments are mounted, as on a car. See also **dashboard. 2.** an array of instruments, gauges, etc., mounted to display the condition or performance of a machine.

in·sub·or·di·nate (ˌɪnsə'bɔːdɪnɪt) *adj.* **1.** not submissive to authority; disobedient or rebellious. **2.** not in a subordinate position or rank. ~*n.* **3.** an insubordinate person. —ˌ**in·sub·'or·di·nate·ly** *adv.* —ˌ**in·sub·ˌor·di·'na·tion** *n.*

in·sub·stan·tial (ˌɪnsəb'stænʃəl) *adj.* **1.** not substantial; flimsy, tenuous, or slight. **2.** imaginary; unreal. —ˌ**in·sub·ˌstan·ti·'al·i·ty** *n.* —ˌ**in·sub·'stan·tial·ly** *adv.*

in·suf·fer·a·ble (ɪn'sʌfərəbᵊl) *adj.* intolerable; unendurable. —**in·'suf·fer·a·ble·ness** *n.* —**in·'suf·fer·a·bly** *adv.*

in·suf·fi·cien·cy (ˌɪnsə'fɪʃənsɪ) *n.* **1.** Also: ˌ**in·suf·'fi·cience.** the state of being insufficient. **2.** *Pathol.* failure in the functioning of an organ, tissue, etc.: *cardiac insufficiency.*

in·suf·fi·cient (ˌɪnsə'fɪʃənt) *adj.* not sufficient; inadequate or deficient. —ˌ**in·suf·'fi·cient·ly** *adv.*

in·suf·flate ('ɪnsʌˌfleɪt) *vb.* **1.** (*tr.*) to breathe or blow (something) into (a room, area, etc.). **2.** *Med.* to blow (air, medicated powder, etc.) into the lungs or into a body cavity. **3.** (*tr.*) to breathe or blow upon (someone or something) as a ritual or sacramental act, esp. so as to symbolize the influence of the Holy Spirit. —ˌ**in·suf·'fla·tion** *n.* —'**in·suf·ˌfla·tor** *n.*

in·su·la ('ɪnsjʊlə) *n., pl.* **·lae** (-ˌliː). a pyramid-shaped area of the brain within each cerebral hemisphere beneath parts of the frontal and temporal lobes. Also called: **island of Reil.** [Latin: literally, island]

in·su·lar ('ɪnsjʊlə) *adj.* **1.** of, relating to, or resembling an island. **2.** remote, detached, or aloof. **3.** illiberal or narrow-minded. **4.** isolated or separated. ~*n.* **5.** *Rare.* an inhabitant of an island. [C17: from Late Latin *insulāris,* from Latin *insula* island, ISLE] —'**in·su·lar·ism** *or* **in·su·lar·i·ty** (ˌɪnsjʊ'lærɪtɪ) *n.* —'**in·su·lar·ly** *adv.*

in·su·late ('ɪnsjʊˌleɪt) *vb.* (*tr.*) **1.** to prevent or reduce the transmission of electricity, heat, or sound to or from (a body, device, or region) by surrounding with a nonconducting material. **2.** to isolate or detach. [C16: from Late Latin *insulātus:* made into an island]

in·su·lat·ing tape *n. Brit.* adhesive tape, impregnated with a moisture-repelling substance, used to insulate exposed electrical conductors. U.S. name: **friction tape.**

in·su·la·tion (ˌɪnsjʊ'leɪʃən) *n.* **1.** Also called: **in·sul·ant** ('ɪnsjʊlənt). material used to insulate a body, device, or region. **2.** the act or process of insulating.

in·su·la·tor ('ɪnsjʊˌleɪtə) *n.* any material or device that insulates, esp. a material with a very low electrical conductivity or thermal conductivity or something made of such a material.

in·su·lin ('ɪnsjʊlɪn) *n.* a protein hormone, secreted in the pancreas by the islets of Langerhans, that controls the concentration of glucose in the blood. Insulin deficiency results in diabetes mellitus. [C20: from New Latin *insula* islet (of the pancreas) + -IN]

in·su·lin re·ac·tion *or* **shock** *n.* the condition in a diabetic resulting from an overdose of insulin, causing a sharp drop in the blood sugar level with tremor, profuse sweating, and convulsions. See also **hyperinsulinism.**

in·sult *vb.* (ɪn'sʌlt). **1.** (*tr.*) to treat, mention, or speak to rudely; offend; affront. **2.** (*tr.*) *Obsolete.* to assault; attack. ~*n.* ('ɪnsʌlt). **3.** an offensive or contemptuous remark or action; affront; slight. **4.** a person or thing producing the effect of an affront: *some television is an insult to intelligence.* **5.** *Med.* an injury or trauma. [C16: from Latin *insultāre* to jump upon, from IN-[2] + *saltāre* to jump] —**in·'sult·er** *n.*

in·su·per·a·ble (ɪn'suːpərəbᵊl, -prəbᵊl, -'sjuː-) *adj.* incapable of being overcome; insurmountable. —**in·ˌsu·per·a·'bil·i·ty** *or* **in·'su·per·a·ble·ness** *n.* —**in·'su·per·a·bly** *adv.*

in·sup·port·a·ble (ˌɪnsə'pɔːtəbᵊl) *adj.* **1.** incapable of being endured; intolerable; insufferable. **2.** incapable of being supported or justified; indefensible. —ˌ**in·sup·'port·a·ble·ness** *n.* —ˌ**in·sup·'port·a·bly** *adv.*

in·sup·press·i·ble (ˌɪnsə'prɛsəbᵊl) *adj.* incapable of being suppressed, overcome, or muffled: *an insuppressible giggle.* —ˌ**in·sup·'press·i·bly** *adv.*

in·sur·ance (ɪn'ʃʊərəns, -'ʃɔː-) *n.* **1. a.** the act, system, or business of providing financial protection for property, life, health, etc., against specified contingencies, such as death, loss, or damage, and involving payment of regular premiums in return for a policy guaranteeing such protection. **b.** the state of having such protection. **c.** Also called: **insurance policy.** the policy providing such protection. **d.** the pecuniary amount of such protection. **e.** the premium payable in return for such protection. **f.** (*as modifier*): *insurance agent; insurance company; insurance stamp.* **2.** a means of protecting or safeguarding against risk or injury.

in·sure (ɪn'ʃʊə, -'ʃɔː) *vb.* **1.** (often foll. by *against*) to guarantee or protect (against risk, loss, etc.): *we insured against disappointment by making an early reservation.* **2.** (often foll. by *against*) to issue (a person) with an insurance policy or take out an insurance policy (on): *his house was heavily insured against fire; after all his car accidents the company refuses to insure him again.* **3.** another word (esp. U.S.) for **ensure** (senses 1, 2). ~Also (rare) (for senses 1, 2): **ensure.** —**in·'sur·a·ble** *adj.* —**in·ˌsur·a·'bil·i·ty** *n.*

in·sured (ɪn'ʃʊəd, -'ʃɔːd) *adj.* **1.** covered by insurance: *an insured risk.* ~*n.* **2.** the person, persons, or organization covered by an insurance policy.

in·sur·er (ɪn'ʃʊərə, -'ʃɔː-) *n.* **1.** a person or company offering insurance policies in return for premiums. **2.** a person or thing that insures.

in·sur·gence (ɪn'sɜːdʒəns) *n.* rebellion, uprising, or riot.

in·sur·gent (ɪn'sɜːdʒənt) *adj.* **1.** rebellious or in revolt, as against a government in power or the civil authorities. ~*n.* **2.** a person who takes part in an uprising or rebellion; insurrectionist. **3.** *International law.* a person or group that rises in revolt against an established government or authority but whose conduct does not amount to belligerency. [C18: from Latin *insurgēns* rising upon or against, from *insurgere* to rise up, from *surgere* to rise] —**in·'sur·gen·cy** *n.*

in·sur·mount·a·ble (ˌɪnsə'maʊntəbᵊl) *adj.* incapable of being overcome; insuperable. —ˌ**in·sur·ˌmount·a·'bil·i·ty** *or* ˌ**in·sur·'mount·a·ble·ness** *n.* —ˌ**in·sur·'mount·a·bly** *adv.*

in·sur·rec·tion (ˌɪnsə'rɛkʃən) *n.* the act or an instance of rebelling against a government in power or the civil authorities; insurgency. [C15: from Late Latin *insurrectiō*, from *insurgere* to rise up] —ˌ**in+sur+'rec+tion+al** *adj.* —ˌ**in+sur+'rec+tion+ar·y** *n., adj.* —ˌ**in+sur+'rec+tion+ism** *n.* —ˌ**in+sur+'rec+tion+ist** *n., adj.*

in+sus+cep+ti·ble (ˌɪnsə'sɛptəbᵊl) *adj.* (when *postpositive,* usually foll. by *to*) not capable of being affected (by); not susceptible (to). —ˌ**in+sus+ˌcep+ti·'bil+i·ty** *n.* —ˌ**in+sus+'cep+ti·bly** *adv.*

in+swing ('ɪnˌswɪŋ) *n. Cricket.* the movement of a bowled ball from off to leg through the air. Compare **outswing.** —'**in+ˌswing·er** *n.*

int. *abbrev. for:* **1.** interest. **2.** interim. **3.** interior. **4.** internal. **5.** Also: **Int.** international. **6.** interpreter.

in+tact (ɪn'tækt) *adj.* untouched or unimpaired; left complete or perfect. [C15: from Latin *intactus* not touched, from *tangere* to touch] —**in+'tact+ness** *n.*

in+tag+li·o (ɪn'tɑːlɪˌəʊ) *n., pl.* **+li·os** *or* **+li** (-ljiː). **1.** a seal, gem, etc., ornamented with a sunken or incised design, as opposed to a design in relief. Compare **cameo. 2.** the art or process of incised carving. **3.** a design, figure, or ornamentation carved, engraved, or etched into the surface of the material used. **4.** any of various printing techniques using an etched or engraved plate. The whole plate is smeared with ink, the surface wiped clean, and the ink in the recesses then transferred to the paper or other material. **5.** an incised die used to make a design in relief. [C17: from Italian, from *intagliare* to engrave, from *tagliare* to cut, from Late Latin *tāliāre;* see TAILOR] —**in+tag+li+at+ed** (ɪn'tɑːlɪˌeɪtɪd) *adj.*

in+take ('ɪnˌteɪk) *n.* **1.** a thing or a quantity taken in: *an intake of students.* **2.** the act of taking in. **3.** the opening through which fluid enters a duct or channel, esp. the air inlet of a jet engine. **4.** a ventilation shaft in a mine. **5.** a contraction or narrowing: *an intake in a garment.*

in+tan+gi·ble (ɪn'tændʒɪbᵊl) *adj.* **1.** incapable of being perceived by touch; impalpable. **2.** imprecise or unclear to the mind: *intangible ideas.* **3.** (of property or a business asset) saleable though not possessing intrinsic productive value. ~*n.* **4.** something that is intangible. —**in+ˌtan+gi·'bil+i·ty** *or* **in+'tan+gi·ble+ness** *n.* —**in+'tan+gi·bly** *adv.*

in+tar+si·a (ɪn'tɑːsɪə) *or* **tar+si·a** ('tɑːsɪə) *n.* **1.** a decorative or pictorial mosaic of inlaid wood or sometimes ivory of a style developed in the Italian Renaissance and used esp. on wooden wall panels. **2.** the art or practice of making such mosaics. [C19: changed from Italian *intarsio*]

in+te+ger ('ɪntɪdʒə) *n.* **1.** any rational number that can be expressed as the sum or difference of a finite number of units, being a member of the set ...-3, -2, -1, 0, 1, 2, 3... **2.** an individual entity or whole unit. [C16: from Latin: untouched, entire, from *tangere* to touch]

in+te+gral ('ɪntɪgrəl) *adj.* **1.** (often foll. by *to*) being an essential part (of); intrinsic (to). **2.** intact; entire. **3.** formed of constituent parts; united. **4.** *Maths.* **a.** of or involving an integral. **b.** involving or being an integer. ~*n.* **5.** *Maths.* the sum of a large number of infinitesimally small quantities, summed either between stated limits (**definite integral**) or in the absence of limits (**indefinite integral**). Symbol: ∫ **6.** a complete thing; whole. —**in+te+gral·i·ty** (ˌɪntɪ'grælɪtɪ) *n.* —'**in+te+gral+ly** *adv.*

in+te+gral cal+cu+lus *n.* the branch of calculus concerned with the determination of integrals and their application to the solution of differential equations, the determination of areas and volumes, etc. Compare **differential calculus.**

in+te+grand ('ɪntɪˌgrænd) *n.* a mathematical function to be integrated. [C19: from Latin: to be integrated]

in+te+grant ('ɪntəgrənt) *adj.* **1.** part of a whole; integral; constituent. **2.** an integrant thing or part.

in+te+grate *vb.* ('ɪntɪˌgreɪt). **1.** to make or be made into a whole; incorporate or be incorporated. **2.** (*tr.*) to designate (a school, park, etc.) for use by all races or groups; desegregate. **3.** to amalgamate or mix (a racial or religious group) with an existing community. **4.** *Maths.* to perform an integration on (a quantity, expression, etc.). ~*adj.* ('ɪntɪgrɪt). **5.** made up of parts; integrated. [C17: from Latin *integrāre;* see INTEGER] —**in+te+gra·ble** ('ɪntəgrəbᵊl) *adj.* —ˌ**in+te+gra·'bil+i·ty** *n.* —'**in+te+ˌgra+tive** *adj.*

in+te+grat+ed cir+cuit *n.* a very small electronic circuit consisting of an assembly of elements made from a chip of semiconducting material, such as crystalline silicon.

in+te+gra+tion (ˌɪntɪ'greɪʃən) *n.* **1.** the act of combining or adding parts to make a unified whole. **2.** the act of amalgamating a racial or religious group with an existing community. **3.** the combination of previously racially segregated social facilities into a nonsegregated system. **4.** *Psychol.* organization into a unified pattern, esp. of different aspects of the personality into a hierarchical system of functions. **5.** the assimilation of nutritive material by the body during the process of anabolism. **6.** *Maths.* an operation used in calculus in which the integral of a function or variable is determined; the inverse of differentiation. —ˌ**in+te+'gra+tion+ist** *n.*

in+te+gra+tor ('ɪntɪˌgreɪtə) *n.* **1.** a person or thing that integrates, esp. a mechanical instrument that determines the value of a definite integral, as the area under a curve. See also **planimeter. 2.** *Computer technol.* **a.** an arithmetic component with two input variables, *x* and *y,* whose output variable *z* is proportional to the integral of *y* with respect to *x.* **b.** an arithmetic component whose output variable is proportional to the integral of the input variable with respect to elapsed time.

in+teg+ri+ty (ɪn'tɛgrɪtɪ) *n.* **1.** adherence to moral principles; honesty. **2.** the quality of being unimpaired; soundness. **3.** unity; wholeness. [C15: from Latin *integritās;* see INTEGER]

in+teg·u+ment (ɪn'tɛgjʊmənt) *n.* any outer protective layer or covering, such as a cuticle, seed coat, rind, or shell. [C17: from Latin *integumentum,* from *tegere* to cover] —**in+ˌteg·u+'ment+al** *or* **in+ˌteg·u+'men+ta·ry** *adj.*

in+tel+lect ('ɪntɪˌlɛkt) *n.* **1.** the capacity for understanding, thinking, and reasoning, as distinct from feeling or wishing. **2.** a mind or intelligence, esp. a brilliant one: *his intellect is wasted on that job.* **3.** *Informal.* a person possessing a brilliant mind; brain. **4.** those possessing the greatest mental power: *the intellect of a nation.* [C14: from Latin *intellectus* comprehension, intellect, from *intellegere* to understand; see INTELLIGENCE] —ˌ**in+tel+'lec+tive** *adj.* —ˌ**in+tel+'lec+tive+ly** *adv.*

in+tel+lec+tion (ˌɪntɪ'lɛkʃən) *n.* **1.** mental activity; thought. **2.** an idea or thought. —ˌ**in+tel+'lec+tive** *adj.*

in+tel+lec+tu·al (ˌɪntɪ'lɛktʃʊəl) *adj.* **1.** of or relating to the intellect, as opposed to the emotions. **2.** appealing to or characteristic of people with a developed intellect: *intellectual literature.* **3.** expressing or enjoying mental activity. ~*n.* **4.** a person who enjoys mental activity and has highly developed tastes in art, literature, etc. **5.** a person who uses or works with his intellect. **6.** a highly intelligent person. —ˌ**in+tel+ˌlec+tu+'al+i·ty** *or* ˌ**in+tel+'lec+tu+al+ness** *n.* —ˌ**in+tel+'lec+tu+al+ly** *adv.*

in+tel+lec+tu+al+ism (ˌɪntɪ'lɛktʃʊəˌlɪzəm) *n.* **1.** development and exercise of the intellect. **2.** the placing of excessive value on the intellect, esp. with disregard for the emotions. **3.** *Philosophy.* the doctrine that reason is the ultimate criterion of knowledge. —ˌ**in+tel+'lec+tu+al+ist** *n., adj.* —ˌ**in+tel+ˌlec+tu+al+'is+tic** *adj.* —ˌ**in+tel+ˌlec+tu+al+'is+ti+cal+ly** *adv.*

in+tel+lec+tu+al+ize *or* **in+tel+lec+tu+al+ise** (ˌɪntɪ'lɛktʃʊəˌlaɪz) *vb.* **1.** to make or become intellectual. **2.** to treat or consider in an intellectual way; rationalize. —ˌ**in+tel+ˌlec+tu+al+i+'za+tion** *or* ˌ**in+tel+ˌlec+tu+al·i·'sa+tion** *n.* —ˌ**in+tel+'lec+tu+al+ˌiz+er** *or* ˌ**in+tel+'lec+tu+al+ˌis+er** *n.*

in+tel+li+gence (ɪn'tɛlɪdʒəns) *n.* **1.** the capacity for understanding; ability to perceive and comprehend meaning. **2.** good mental capacity: *a person of intelligence.* **3.** *Old-fashioned.* news; information. **4.** military information about enemies, spies, etc. **5.** a group or department that gathers or deals with such information. **6.** (*often cap.*) an intelligent being, esp. one that is not embodied. **7.** (*modifier*) of or relating to intelligence: *an intelligence network.* [C14: from Latin *intellegentia,* from *intellegere* to discern, comprehend, literally: choose between, from INTER- + *legere* to choose] —**in+ˌtel+li+'gen+tial** *adj.*

in+tel+li+gence quo+tient *n.* a measure of the intelligence of an individual derived from results obtained from specially designed tests. The quotient is traditionally derived by dividing an individual's mental age by his actual age and multiplying the result by 100. Abbrev.: **I.Q.**

in+tel+li+genc+er (ɪn'tɛlɪdʒənsə) *n. Archaic.* an informant or spy.

in+tel+li+gence test *n.* any of a number of tests designed to assess the stage of mental development of a person. See also **Binet-Simon scale.**

in+tel+li+gent (ɪn'tɛlɪdʒənt) *adj.* **1.** having or indicating intelligence. **2.** having high intelligence; clever. **3.** indicating high intelligence; perceptive: *an intelligent guess.* **4.** guided by intellectual rather than emotional principles; rational. **5.** (*postpositive;* foll. by *of*) *Archaic.* having knowledge or information: *they were intelligent of his whereabouts.* —**in+'tel+li+gent+ly** *adv.*

in+tel+li+gent+si·a (ɪnˌtɛlɪ'dʒɛntsɪə) *n.* (usually preceded by *the*) the educated or intellectual people in a society or community. [C20: from Russian *intelligentsiya,* from Latin *intellegentia* INTELLIGENCE]

in+tel+li+gi·ble (ɪn'tɛlɪdʒəbᵊl) *adj.* **1.** able to be understood; comprehensible. **2.** *Philosophy.* capable of being apprehended by the mind or intellect alone. [C14: from Latin *intellegibilis;* see INTELLECT] —**in+ˌtel+li+gi·'bil+i·ty** *or* **in+'tel+li+gi·ble+ness** *n.* —**in+'tel+li+gi·bly** *adv.*

In+tel+sat ('ɪntɛlˌsæt) *n.* any of four series of communications satellites operated by the International Telecommunications Satellite Consortium.

in+tem+er+ate (ɪn'tɛmərɪt) *adj. Rare.* not defiled; pure; unsullied. [C15: from Latin *intemerātus* undefiled, pure, from IN-[1] + *temerāre* to darken, violate, from *temere* rashly] —**in+'tem+er+ate+ly** *adv.* —**in+'tem+er+ate+ness** *n.*

in+tem+per+ate (ɪn'tɛmpərɪt, -prɪt) *adj.* **1.** consuming alcoholic drink habitually or to excess. **2.** indulging bodily appetites to excess; immoderate. **3.** unrestrained: *intemperate rage.* **4.** extreme or severe: *an intemperate climate.* —**in+'tem+per+ance** *or* **in+'tem+per+ate+ness** *n.* —**in+'tem+per+ate+ly** *adv.*

in+tend (ɪn'tɛnd) *vb.* **1.** (*may take a clause as object*) to propose or plan (something or to do something); have in mind; mean. **2.** (*tr.;* often foll. by *for*) to design or destine (for a certain purpose, person, etc.): *that shot was intended for the President.* **3.** (*tr.*) to mean to express or indicate: *what do his words intend?* **4.** (*intr.*) to have a purpose as specified; mean: *he intends well.* **5.** (*tr.*) *Archaic.* to direct or turn (the attention, eyes, etc.). [C14: from Latin *intendere* to stretch forth, give one's attention to, from *tendere* to stretch] —**in+'tend+er** *n.*

in+tend+ance (ɪn'tɛndəns) *n.* **1.** any of various public departments, esp. in France. **2.** a less common word for **superintendence.**

in+tend+an+cy (ɪn'tɛndənsɪ) *n.* **1.** the position or work of an intendant. **2.** intendants collectively. **3.** *History.* the district or area administered by an intendant.

in+tend+ant (ɪn'tɛndənt) *n.* **1.** *History.* a provincial or colonial official of France, Spain, or Portugal. **2.** a senior administrator in some countries, esp. in Latin America. **3.** a superintendent or manager.

in·tend·ed (ɪn'tɛndɪd) *adj.* **1.** planned or future. ~*n.* **2.** *Informal.* a person whom one is to marry; fiancé or fiancée.

in·tend·ment (ɪn'tɛndmənt) *n.* **1.** the meaning of something as fixed or understood by the law. **2.** *Obsolete.* intention, design, or purpose.

in·ten·er·ate (ɪn'tɛnəˌreɪt) *vb.* (*tr.*) *Rare.* to soften or make tender. [C16: from IN-[2] + Latin *tener* delicate, TENDER[1]] —**in·ˌten·er·'a·tion** *n.*

intens. *abbrev. for:* **1.** intensifier. **2.** intensive.

in·tense (ɪn'tɛns) *adj.* **1.** of extreme force, strength, degree, or amount: *intense heat.* **2.** characterized by deep or forceful feelings: *an intense person.* [C14: from Latin *intensus* stretched, from *intendere* to stretch out; see INTEND] —**in·'tense·ly** *adv.* —**in·'tense·ness** *n.*

in·ten·si·fi·er (ɪn'tɛnsɪˌfaɪə) *n.* **1.** a person or thing that intensifies. **2.** a word, esp. an adjective or adverb, that has little semantic content of its own but that serves to intensify the meaning of the word or phrase that it modifies: *awfully* and *up* are intensifiers in the phrases *awfully sorry* and *cluttered up.* **3.** a substance, esp. one containing silver or uranium, used to increase the density of a photographic film or plate. Compare **reducer** (sense 1).

in·ten·si·fy (ɪn'tɛnsɪˌfaɪ) *vb.* **·fies, ·fy·ing, ·fied. 1.** to make or become intense or more intense. **2.** (*tr.*) to increase the density of (a photographic film or plate). —**in·ˌten·si·fi·'ca·tion** *n.*

in·ten·sion (ɪn'tɛnʃən) *n.* **1.** *Logic.* the set of characteristics, attributes, or properties that distinguish the referent or referents of a given word: thus, the intension of *marsupial* is the set containing the characteristics *suckling its young* and *having a pouch.* Compare **extension** (sense 11). **2.** a rare word for **intensity, determination,** or **intensification.** —**in·'ten·sion·al** *adj.* —**in·'ten·sion·al·ly** *adv.*

in·ten·si·ty (ɪn'tɛnsɪtɪ) *n., pl.* **·ties. 1.** the state or quality of being intense. **2.** extreme force, degree, or amount. **3.** *Physics.* **a.** a measure of field strength or of the energy transmitted by radiation. See **radiant intensity, luminous intensity. b.** (of sound in a specified direction) the average rate of flow of sound energy, usually in watts, for one period through unit area at right angles to the specified direction. Symbol: *I*

in·ten·sive (ɪn'tɛnsɪv) *adj.* **1.** of, relating to, or characterized by intensity: *intensive training.* **2.** (*usually in combination*) using one factor of production proportionately more than others, as specified: *capital-intensive; labour-intensive.* **3.** *Agriculture.* involving or farmed using large amounts of capital or labour. Compare **extensive** (sense 3). **4.** denoting or relating to a grammatical intensifier. **5.** denoting or belonging to a class of pronouns used to emphasize a noun or personal pronoun, such as *himself* in the sentence *John himself did it.* In English, intensive pronouns are identical in form with reflexive pronouns. **6.** of or relating to intension. **7.** *Physics.* of or relating to a property, measurement, etc., that is independent of mass. Compare **extensive** (sense 4). ~*n.* **8.** an intensifier or intensive pronoun or grammatical construction. —**in·'ten·sive·ly** *adv.* —**in·'ten·sive·ness** *n.*

in·ten·sive care *n.* extensive and continual care and treatment provided for an acutely ill patient, usually in a specially designated section (**intensive care unit**) of a hospital.

in·tent (ɪn'tɛnt) *n.* **1.** something that is intended; aim; purpose; design. **2.** the act of intending. **3.** *Law.* the will or purpose with which one does an act. **4.** implicit meaning; connotation. **5. to all intents and purposes.** for all practical purposes; virtually. ~*adj.* **6.** firmly fixed; determined; concentrated: *an intent look.* **7.** (*postpositive;* usually foll. by *on* or *upon*) having the fixed intention (of); directing one's mind or energy (to): *intent on committing a crime.* [C13 (in the sense: intention): from Late Latin *intentus* aim, intent, from Latin: a stretching out; see INTEND] —**in·'tent·ly** *adv.* —**in·'tent·ness** *n.*

in·ten·tion (ɪn'tɛnʃən) *n.* **1.** a purpose or goal; aim: *it is his intention to reform.* **2.** the act of intending. **3.** *Law.* the resolve or design with which a person does or refrains from doing an act, a necessary ingredient of certain offences. **4.** *Med.* a natural healing process, as by **first intention,** in which the edges of a wound cling together with no tissue between, or by **second intention,** in which the wound edges adhere with granulation tissue. **5.** (*usually pl.*) design or purpose with respect to a proposal of marriage (esp. in the phrase **honourable intentions**). **6.** an archaic word for **meaning** or **intentness. 7.** a less common spelling of **intension** (sense 1).

in·ten·tion·al (ɪn'tɛnʃənᵊl) *adj.* **1.** performed by or expressing intention; deliberate. **2.** of or relating to intention or purpose. **3.** *Philosophy.* **a.** of or relating to appearance or phenomenal being. **b.** of or relating to the capacity of the mind to refer to different kinds of objects. —**in·ˌten·tion·'al·i·ty** *n.* —**in·'ten·tion·al·ly** *adv.*

in·ter (ɪn'tɜː) *vb.* **·ters, ·ter·ring, ·terred.** (*tr.*) to place (a body, etc.) in the earth; bury, esp. with funeral rites. [C14: from Old French *enterrer,* from Latin IN-[2] + *terra* earth]

inter. *abbrev. for* intermediate.

inter- *prefix.* **1.** between or among: *international.* **2.** together, mutually, or reciprocally: *interdependent; interchange.* [from Latin]

in·ter·act (ˌɪntər'ækt) *vb.* (*intr.*) to act on or in close relation with each other.

in·ter·ac·tion (ˌɪntər'ækʃən) *n.* **1.** a mutual or reciprocal action or influence. **2.** *Physics.* the transfer of energy between elementary particles, between a particle and a field, or between fields. See **strong interaction, electromagnetic interaction, gravitational interaction,** and **weak interaction.** —**ˌin·ter·'ac·tion·al** *adj.*

in·ter·ac·tive (ˌɪntər'æktɪv) *adj.* **1.** allowing or relating to continuous two-way transfer of information between a computer and its user. **2.** (of two or more persons, forces, etc.) acting upon or in close relation with each other; interacting. —**ˌin·ter·ac·'tiv·i·ty** *n.*

in·ter a·li·a *Latin.* ('ɪntər 'eɪlɪə) *adv.* among other things.

in·ter a·li·os *Latin.* ('ɪntər 'eɪlɪəʊs) *adv.* among other people.

in·ter·a·tom·ic (ˌɪntərə'tɒmɪk) *adj.* existing or occurring between or among atoms. Compare **intra-atomic.**

in·ter·bed·ded (ˌɪntə'bɛdɪd) *adj. Geology.* occurring between beds, esp. (of laval rock) occurring between strata of a different origin.

in·ter·brain ('ɪntəˌbreɪn) *n. Anatomy.* a nontechnical word for **diencephalon.**

in·ter·breed (ˌɪntə'briːd) *vb.* **·breeds, ·breed·ing, ·bred. 1.** to breed within a single family or strain so as to produce particular characteristics in the offspring. **2.** another term for **crossbreed** (sense 1).

in·ter·ca·lar·y (ɪn'tɜːkələrɪ) *adj.* **1.** (of a day, month, etc.) inserted in the calendar. **2.** (of a particular year) having one or more days inserted. **3.** inserted, introduced, or interpolated. [C17: from Latin *intercalārius;* see INTERCALATE] —**ˌin·ter·ca·'lar·i·ly** *adv.*

in·ter·ca·late (ɪn'tɜːkəˌleɪt) *vb.* (*tr.*) **1.** to insert (one or more days) into the calendar. **2.** to interpolate or insert. [C17: from Latin *intercalāre* to insert, proclaim that a day has been inserted, from INTER- + *calāre* to proclaim] —**in·ˌter·ca·'la·tion** *n.* —**in·'ter·ca·la·tive** *adj.*

in·ter·cede (ˌɪntə'siːd) *vb.* (*intr.*) **1.** (often foll. by *in*) to come between parties or act as mediator or advocate: *to intercede in the strike.* **2.** *Roman history.* (of a tribune or other magistrate) to interpose a veto. [C16: from Latin *intercēdere* to intervene, from INTER- + *cēdere* to move] —**ˌin·ter·'ced·er** *n.*

in·ter·cel·lu·lar (ˌɪntə'sɛljʊlə) *adj. Biology.* between or among cells: *intercellular fluid.*

in·ter·cept *vb.* (ˌɪntə'sɛpt). (*tr.*) **1.** to stop, deflect, or seize on the way from one place to another; prevent from arriving or proceeding. **2.** *Sport.* to seize or cut off (a pass) on its way from one opponent to another. **3.** *Maths.* to cut off, mark off, or bound (some part of a line, curve, plane, or surface). ~*n.* ('ɪntəˌsɛpt). **4.** *Maths.* **a.** a point at which two figures intersect. **b.** the distance from the origin to the point at which a line, curve, or surface cuts a coordinate axis. **c.** an intercepted segment. **5.** *Sport, U.S.* the act of intercepting an opponent's pass. [C16: from Latin *intercipere* to seize before arrival, from INTER- + *capere* to take] —**ˌin·ter·'cep·tion** *n.* —**ˌin·ter·'cep·tive** *adj.*

in·ter·cep·tor *or* **in·ter·cept·er** (ˌɪntə'sɛptə) *n.* **1.** a person or thing that intercepts. **2.** a fast highly manoeuvrable fighter aircraft used to intercept enemy aircraft.

in·ter·ces·sion (ˌɪntə'sɛʃən) *n.* **1.** the act or an instance of interceding. **2.** the act of interceding or offering petitionary prayer to God on behalf of others. **3.** such petitionary prayer. **4.** *Roman history.* the interposing of a veto by a tribune or other magistrate. [C16: from Latin *intercessio;* see INTERCEDE] —**ˌin·ter·'ces·sion·al** *or* **ˌin·ter·'ces·so·ry** *adj.* —**ˌin·ter·'ces·sor** *n.* —**ˌin·ter·ces·'so·ri·al** *adj.*

in·ter·change *vb.* (ˌɪntə'tʃeɪndʒ). **1.** to change places or cause to change places; alternate; exchange; switch. ~*n.* ('ɪntəˌtʃeɪndʒ). **2.** the act of interchanging; exchange or alternation. **3.** a motorway junction of interconnecting roads and bridges designed to prevent streams of traffic crossing one another. —**ˌin·ter·'change·a·ble** *adj.* —**ˌin·ter·ˌchange·a·'bil·i·ty** *or* **ˌin·ter·'change·a·ble·ness** *n.* —**ˌin·ter·'change·a·bly** *adv.*

in·ter·clav·i·cle (ˌɪntə'klævɪkᵊl) *n.* a membrane bone between and beneath the clavicles, present in some fossil amphibians, all reptiles except snakes, and monotremes. —**in·ter·cla·vic·u·lar** (ˌɪntəklə'vɪkjʊlə) *adj.*

in·ter·co·lum·ni·a·tion (ˌɪntəkəˌlʌmnɪ'eɪʃən) *n. Architect.* **1.** the horizontal distance between two adjacent columns. **2.** the system of spacing for a set of columns. [C17: from Latin *intercolumnium* space between two columns] —**ˌin·ter·co·'lum·nar** *adj.*

in·ter·com ('ɪntəˌkɒm) *n. Informal.* an internal telephone system for communicating within a building, aircraft, etc. [C20: short for INTERCOMMUNICATION]

in·ter·com·mu·ni·cate (ˌɪntəkə'mjuːnɪˌkeɪt) *vb.* (*intr.*) **1.** to communicate mutually. **2.** to interconnect, as two rooms, etc. —**ˌin·ter·com·'mu·ni·ca·ble** *adj.* —**ˌin·ter·com·ˌmu·ni·ca·'bil·i·ty** *n.* —**ˌin·ter·com·ˌmu·ni·'ca·tion** *n.* —**ˌin·ter·com·'mu·ni·ca·tive** *adj.* —**ˌin·ter·com·'mu·ni·ˌca·tor** *n.*

in·ter·com·mun·ion (ˌɪntəkə'mjuːnjən) *n.* association between Churches, involving esp. mutual reception of Holy Communion.

in·ter·con·ti·nen·tal bal·lis·tic mis·sile (ˌɪntəˌkɒntɪ'nɛntᵊl)

ˌin·ter·ˌac·a·'dem·ic *adj.*
ˌin·ter·'al·lied *adj.*
ˌin·ter·'bank *adj.*
ˌin·ter·bel·'lig·er·ent *adj.*
ˌin·ter·'blend *vb.*
ˌin·ter·'branch *adj.*
ˌin·ter·'caste *adj.*
ˌin·ter·'cit·y *adj.*
ˌin·ter·'clasp *vb.*
ˌin·ter·'class *adj.*
ˌin·ter·'club *adj.*
ˌin·ter·col·'le·gi·ate *adj.*
ˌin·ter·co·'lo·ni·al *adj.*
ˌin·ter·com·'mu·ni·ty *adj.*
ˌin·ter·'com·pa·ny *adj.*
ˌin·ter·con·'nect *vb.*

n. a missile that follows a ballistic trajectory and has the range to carry a nuclear bomb between continents. Abbrev.: **ICBM**

in·ter·cos·tal (ˌɪntəˈkɒstᵊl) *adj. Anatomy.* between the ribs: *intercostal muscles.* [C16: via New Latin from Latin INTER- + *costa* rib]

in·ter·course (ˈɪntəˌkɔːs) *n.* **1.** communication or exchange between individuals; mutual dealings. **2.** See **sexual intercourse.** [C15: from Medieval Latin *intercursus* business, from Latin *intercurrere* to run between, from *currere* to run]

in·ter·crop (ˌɪntəˈkrɒp) *n.* **1.** a crop grown between the rows of another crop. ~*vb.* **·crops, ·crop·ping, ·cropped. 2.** to grow (one crop) between the rows of (another).

in·ter·cross (ˌɪntəˈkrɒs) *vb., n.* another word for **crossbreed.**

in·ter·cur·rent (ˌɪntəˈkʌrənt) *adj.* **1.** occurring during or in between; intervening. **2.** *Pathol.* (of a disease) occurring during the course of another disease. —**ˌin·terˈcur·rence** *n.* —**ˌin·terˈcur·rent·ly** *adv.*

in·ter·cut (ˌɪntəˈkʌt) *vb.* **·cuts, ·cut·ting, ·cut.** *Films.* another word for **crosscut.**

in·ter·den·tal (ˌɪntəˈdɛntᵊl) *adj.* **1.** situated between teeth. **2.** *Phonetics.* (of a consonant) pronounced with the tip of the tongue lying between the upper and lower front teeth, as for the *th* sounds in English *thin* and *then.* —**ˌin·terˈden·tal·ly** *adv.*

in·ter·dict *n.* (ˈɪntəˌdɪkt, -ˌdaɪt). **1.** *R.C. Church.* the exclusion of a person or all persons in a particular place from certain sacraments and other benefits, although not from communion. **2.** *Civil law.* any order made by a court or official prohibiting an act. **3.** *Scot. law.* an order having the effect of an injunction. **4.** *Roman history.* **a.** an order of a praetor commanding or forbidding an act. **b.** the procedure by which this order was sought. ~*vb.* (ˌɪntəˈdɪkt, -ˈdaɪt). *(tr.)* **5.** to place under legal or ecclesiastical sanction; prohibit; forbid. **6.** *Military.* to destroy (an enemy's lines of communication) by firepower. [C13: from Latin *interdictum* prohibition, from *interdīcere* to forbid, from INTER- + *dīcere* to say] —**ˌin·terˈdic·tive** *or* **ˌin·terˈdic·to·ry** *adj.* —**ˌin·terˈdic·tive·ly** *adv.* —**ˌin·terˈdic·tor** *n.*

in·ter·dic·tion (ˌɪntəˈdɪkʃən) *n.* **1.** the act of interdicting or state of being interdicted. **2.** an interdict.

in·ter·dict list *n.* another name for **Indian list.**

in·ter·dig·i·tate (ˌɪntəˈdɪdʒɪˌteɪt) *vb. (intr.)* to interlock like the fingers of clasped hands. [C19: from INTER- + Latin *digitus* (see DIGIT) + -ATE[1]]

in·ter·dis·ci·pli·nar·y (ˌɪntəˈdɪsɪplɪnərɪ) *adj.* involving two or more academic disciplines.

in·ter·est (ˈɪntrɪst, -tərɪst) *n.* **1.** the sense of curiosity about or concern with something or someone. **2.** the power of stimulating such a sense: *to have great interest.* **3.** the quality of such stimulation. **4.** something in which one is interested; a hobby or pursuit. **5.** *(often pl.)* benefit; advantage: *in one's own interest.* **6.** *(often pl.)* **a.** a right, share, or claim, esp. in a business or property. **b.** the business, property, etc., in which a person has such concern. **7. a.** a charge for the use of credit or borrowed money. **b.** such a charge expressed as a percentage per time unit of the sum borrowed or used. **8.** *(often pl.)* a section of a community, etc., whose members have common aims: *we must not offend the landed interest.* **9. declare an interest.** to make known one's connection, esp. a prejudicial connection, with an affair. ~*vb. (tr.)* **10.** to arouse or excite the curiosity or concern of. **11.** to cause to become involved in something; concern. [C15: from Latin: it concerns, from *interesse;* from INTER- + *esse* to be]

in·ter·est·ed (ˈɪntrɪstɪd, -tərɪs-) *adj.* **1.** showing or having interest. **2.** *(usually prenominal)* personally involved or implicated: *the interested parties met to discuss the business.* —**ˈin·ter·est·ed·ly** *adv.* —**ˈin·ter·est·ed·ness** *n.*

in·ter·est·ing (ˈɪntrɪstɪŋ, -tərɪs-) *adj.* inspiring interest; absorbing. —**ˈin·ter·est·ing·ly** *adv.* —**ˈin·ter·est·ing·ness** *n.*

in·ter·face (ˈɪntəˌfeɪs) *n.* **1.** *Physical chem.* a surface that forms the boundary between two bodies, liquids, or chemical phases. **2.** a common point or boundary between two things, subjects, etc. **3.** an electrical circuit linking one device, esp. a computer, with another. —**in·ter·fa·cial** (ˌɪntəˈfeɪʃəl) *adj.* —**ˌin·terˈfa·cial·ly** *adv.*

in·ter·fac·ing (ˈɪntəˌfeɪsɪŋ) *n.* **1.** a piece of fabric sewn beneath the facing of a garment, usually at the inside of the neck, armholes, etc., to give shape and firmness. **2.** another name for **interlining.**

in·ter·fere (ˌɪntəˈfɪə) *vb. (intr.)* **1.** (often foll. by *in*) to interpose, esp. meddlesomely or unwarrantedly; intervene. **2.** (often foll. by *with*) to come between or in opposition; hinder; obstruct. **3.** (foll. by *with*) *Euphemistic.* to assault sexually. **4.** to strike one against the other, as a horse's legs. **5.** *Physics.* to cause or produce interference. [C16: from Old French *s'entreferir* to collide, from *entre-* INTER- + *ferir* to strike, from Latin *ferīre*] —**ˌin·terˈfer·er** *n.* —**ˌin·terˈfer·ing·ly** *adv.*

in·ter·fer·ence (ˌɪntəˈfɪərəns) *n.* **1.** the act or an instance of interfering. **2.** *Physics.* the process in which two or more waves of the same frequency and phase combine to form a resultant wave in which the displacement at any point is the vector sum of the displacements of the individual waves. A series of stationary nodes or antinodes, known as **interference patterns,** are formed. **3.** Also called: **radio interference.** any undesired signal that tends to interfere with the reception of radio waves. —**in·ter·fe·ren·tial** (ˌɪntəfəˈrɛnʃəl) *adj.*

in·ter·fer·om·e·ter (ˌɪntəfəˈrɒmɪtə) *n.* **1.** *Physics.* any acoustic, optical, or microwave instrument that uses interference patterns or fringes to make accurate measurements of wavelength, wave velocity, distance, etc. **2.** *Astronomy.* a radio telescope consisting of two or more radio antennas separated by a known distance and connected to the same receiver so that radio waves from a source in space undergo interference, enabling the position of the source to be accurately determined. —**in·ter·fer·o·met·ric** (ˌɪntəˌfɛrəˈmɛtrɪk) *adj.* —**ˌin·terˌfer·oˈmet·ri·cal·ly** *adv.* —**ˌin·ter·ferˈom·e·try** *n.*

in·ter·fer·on (ˌɪntəˈfɪərɒn) *n. Biochem.* a protein produced by virus-invaded cells to inhibit the replication of the virus. [C20: from INTERFERE + -ON]

in·ter·fer·tile (ˌɪntəˈfɜːtaɪl) *adj.* (of plants and animals) able to interbreed. —**ˌin·ter·ferˈtil·i·ty** *n.*

in·ter·file (ˌɪntəˈfaɪl) *vb. (tr.)* **1.** to place (one or more items) among other items in a file or arrangement. **2.** to combine (two or more sets of items) in one file or arrangement.

in·ter·flow (ˌɪntəˈfləʊ) *vb. (intr.)* to flow together; merge.

in·ter·flu·ent (ɪnˈtɜːflʊənt) *adj.* flowing together; merging. [C17: from Latin *interfluere,* from INTER- + *fluere* to flow]

in·ter·fluve (ˈɪntəˌfluːv) *n.* a ridge or area of land dividing two river valleys. [C20: back formation from *interfluvial,* from INTER- + Latin *fluvius* river] —**ˌin·terˈflu·vi·al** *adj.*

in·ter·fuse (ˌɪntəˈfjuːz) *vb.* **1.** to diffuse or mix throughout or become so diffused or mixed; intermingle. **2.** to blend or fuse or become blended or fused. —**ˌin·terˈfu·sion** *n.*

in·ter·gla·ci·al (ˌɪntəˈgleɪsɪəl) *adj.* **1.** occurring or formed between periods of glacial action. ~*n.* **2.** a period of comparatively warm climate between two glaciations, esp. of the Pleistocene epoch.

in·ter·grade *vb.* (ˌɪntəˈgreɪd). **1.** *(intr.)* (esp. of biological species, etc.) to merge one into another. ~*n.* (ˈɪntəˌgreɪd). **2.** an intermediate stage or form. —**ˌin·ter·graˈda·tion** *n.* —**ˌin·ter·graˈda·tion·al** *adj.* —**ˌin·terˈgra·di·ent** *adj.*

in·ter·im (ˈɪntərɪm) *adj.* **1.** *(prenominal)* temporary, provisional, or intervening: *interim measures to deal with the emergency.* ~*n.* **2.** (usually preceded by *the*) the intervening time; the meantime (esp. in the phrase **in the interim**). ~*adv.* **3.** *Rare.* meantime. [C16: from Latin: meanwhile]

In·ter·im (ˈɪntərɪm) *n.* any of three provisional arrangements made during the Reformation by the German emperor and Diet to regulate religious differences between Roman Catholics and Protestants.

in·te·ri·or (ɪnˈtɪərɪə) *n.* **1.** a part, surface, or region that is inside or on the inside: *the interior of Africa.* **2.** inner character or nature. **3.** a film or scene shot inside a building, studio, etc. **4.** a picture of the inside of a room or building, as in a painting or stage design. **5.** the inside of a building or room, with respect to design and decoration. ~*adj.* **6.** of, situated on, or suitable for the inside; inner. **7.** coming or acting from within; internal. **8.** of or involving a nation's domestic affairs; internal. **9.** (esp. of one's spiritual or mental life) secret or private; not observable. [C15: from Latin (adj.), comparative of *inter* within] —**inˈte·ri·or·ly** *adv.*

In·te·ri·or (ɪnˈtɪərɪə) *n.* (*in titles;* usually preceded by *the*) the domestic or internal affairs of any of certain countries: *Department of the Interior.*

in·te·ri·or an·gle *n.* **1.** an angle of a polygon contained between two adjacent sides. **2.** any of the four angles made by a transversal that lie inside the region between the two intersected lines.

in·te·ri·or dec·o·ra·tion *n.* **1.** the colours, furniture, etc., of the interior of a house, etc. **2.** Also called: **interior design.** the art or business of an interior decorator.

in·te·ri·or dec·o·ra·tor *n.* **1.** Also called: **interior designer.** a person whose profession is the planning of the decoration and furnishings of the interior of houses, etc. **2.** a person whose profession is the painting and wallpapering of houses.

in·te·ri·or·ize *or* **in·te·ri·or·ise** (ɪnˈtɪərɪəˌraɪz) *vb. (tr.)* another word for **internalize.**

in·te·ri·or mon·o·logue *n.* a literary attempt to present the mental processes of a character before they are formed into regular patterns of speech or logical sequence. See also **stream of consciousness.**

in·te·ri·or-sprung *adj.* (esp. of a mattress) containing springs.

interj. *abbrev. for* interjection.

in·ter·ja·cent (ˌɪntəˌdʒeɪsᵊnt) *adj.* located in between; intervening. [C16: from Latin *interjacēnt-,* from *interjacēre,* from INTER- + *jacēre* to lie]

in·ter·ject (ˌɪntəˈdʒɛkt) *vb. (tr.)* **1.** to interpose abruptly or sharply; interrupt with; throw in: *she interjected clever remarks.* **2.** *Archaic.* to come between; interpose. [C16: from Latin *interjicere* to place between, from *jacere* to throw] —**ˌin·terˈjec·tor** *n.*

in·ter·jec·tion (ˌɪntəˈdʒɛkʃən) *n.* **1.** a word or remark expressing emotion; exclamation. **2.** the act of interjecting. **3.** a word or phrase that is characteristically used in syntactic isolation

---

ˌin·ter·conˈnec·tion *n.*
ˌin·terˌcon·soˈnan·tal *adj.*
ˌin·terˌcon·tiˈnent·al *adj.*
ˌin·ter·conˈvert·i·ble *adj.*
ˌin·terˈcoun·ty *adj.*
ˌin·terˈcru·ral *adj.*
ˌin·ter·deˌnom·iˈna·tion·al *adj.*
ˌin·ter·deˌpartˈment·al *adj.*
ˌin·terˌde·partˈment·al·ly *adv.*
ˌin·ter·deˈpend *vb.*
ˌin·ter·deˈpend·ence *n.*
ˌin·ter·deˈpend·en·cy *n.*
ˌin·ter·deˈpend·ent *adj.*
ˌin·ter·deˈpend·ent·ly *adv.*
ˌin·terˈdig·i·tal *adj.*
ˌin·terˈdig·i·tal·ly *adv.*
ˌin·terˈfac·tion·al *adj.*
ˌin·terˈfi·bril·lar *adj.*
ˌin·terˈfi·brous *adj.*
ˌin·terˈfold *vb.*
ˌin·ter·gaˈlac·tic *adj.*
ˌin·terˌgov·ernˈmen·tal *adj.*
ˌin·terˈgroup *adj.*
ˌin·ter·iˈon·ic *adj.*

and that usually expresses sudden emotion; expletive. Abbrev.: **interj.** —ˌ**in·ter**+**'jec**+**tion**+**al,** ˌ**in·ter**+**'jec**+**to·ry,** *or* ˌ**in·ter**+**'jec**+**tur**+**al** *adj.* —ˌ**in·ter**+**'jec**+**tion**+**al**+**ly** *adv.*

in·ter+**lace** (ˌɪntə'leɪs) *vb.* **1.** to join together (patterns, fingers, etc.) by crossing, as if woven; intertwine. **2.** (*tr.*) to mingle or blend in an intricate way. **3.** (*tr.; usually foll. by with*) to change the pattern of; diversify; intersperse: *to interlace a speech with humour.* —**in·ter**+**lac**+**ed**+**ly** (ˌɪntə'leɪsɪdlɪ) *adv.* —ˌ**in·ter**+**'lace**+**ment** *n.*

in·ter+**laced scan**+**ning** *n.* a system of scanning a television picture using one or more electron beams, first along the even-numbered lines, then along the odd-numbered lines, in one complete scan.

In·ter+**la**+**ken** ('ɪntəˌlɑ:kən) *n.* a town and resort in central Switzerland, situated between Lakes Brienz and Thun on the River Aar. Pop.: 4735 (1970).

in·ter+**lam·i**+**nate** (ˌɪntə'læmɪˌneɪt) *vb.* (*tr.*) to place, stick, or insert (a sheet, layer, etc.) between (other layers). —ˌ**in·ter**+**'lam·i·nar** *adj.* —ˌ**in·ter**+ˌ**lam·i**+**'na**+**tion** *n.*

in·ter+**lap** (ˌɪntə'læp) *vb.* +**laps,** +**lap**+**ping,** +**lapped.** a less common word for **overlap.**

in·ter+**lard** (ˌɪntə'lɑ:d) *vb.* (*tr.*) **1.** to scatter thickly in or between; intersperse: *to interlard one's writing with foreign phrases.* **2.** to occur frequently in; be scattered in or through: *foreign phrases interlard his writings.*

in·ter+**lay** (ˌɪntə'leɪ) *vb.* +**lays,** +**lay**+**ing,** +**laid. 1.** (*tr.*) to insert (layers) between; interpose: *to interlay gold among the silver; to interlay the silver with gold.* ~*n.* **2.** material, such as paper, placed between a printing plate and its base, either all over in order to bring it up to type height, or in places in order to achieve the correct printing pressure all over the plate.

in·ter+**leaf** ('ɪntəˌli:f) *n., pl.* +**leaves.** a blank leaf inserted between the leaves of a book.

in·ter+**leave** (ˌɪntə'li:v) *vb.* (*tr.*) **1.** (often foll. by *with*) to intersperse (with), esp. alternately, as the illustrations in a book (with protective leaves). **2.** to provide (a book) with blank leaves for notes, etc., or to protect illustrations.

in·ter+**li**+**brar·y loan** *n.* **1.** a system by which libraries borrow publications from other libraries. **2. a.** an instance of such borrowing. **b.** a publication so borrowed.

in·ter+**line**[1] (ˌɪntə'laɪn) *or* **in·ter**+**lin**+**e·ate** (ˌɪntə'lɪnɪˌeɪt) *vb.* (*tr.*) to write or print (matter) between the lines of (a text, book, etc.). —**'in·ter**+ˌ**lin**+**ing** *or* ˌ**in·ter**+ˌ**lin·e**+**'a**+**tion** *n.*

in·ter+**line**[2] (ˌɪntə'laɪŋ) *vb.* (*tr.*) to provide (a part of a garment, such as a collar or cuff) with a second lining, esp. of stiffened material. —**'in·ter**+ˌ**lin**+**er** *n.*

in·ter+**lin**+**e·ar** (ˌɪntə'lɪnɪə) *or* **in·ter**+**lin**+**e·al** *adj.* **1.** written or printed between lines of text. **2.** written or printed with the text in different languages or versions on alternate lines. —ˌ**in·ter**+**'lin**+**e·ar**+**ly** *or* ˌ**in·ter**+**'lin**+**e·al**+**ly** *adv.*

In·ter+**lin**+**gua** (ˌɪntə'lɪŋgwə) *n.* an artificial language based on words common to English and the Romance languages. [C20: from Italian, from INTER- + *lingua* language]

in·ter+**lin**+**ing** ('ɪntəˌlaɪnɪŋ) *n.* the material used to interline parts of garments, now often made of reinforced paper.

in·ter+**lock** *vb.* (ˌɪntə'lɒk). **1.** to join or be joined firmly, as by a mutual interconnection of parts. ~*n.* ('ɪntəˌlɒk). **2.** the act of interlocking or the state of being interlocked. **3.** a device, esp. one operated electromechanically, used in a logic circuit to prevent an activity being initiated unless preceded by certain events. —**'in·ter**+ˌ**lock**+**er** *n.*

in·ter+**lock**+**ing di**+**rec**+**tor**+**ates** *pl. n.* boards of directors of different companies having sufficient members in common to ensure that the companies involved are under the same control.

in·ter+**lo**+**cu**+**tion** (ˌɪntəlɒ'kju:ʃən) *n.* conversation, discussion, or dialogue.

in·ter+**loc·u·tor** (ˌɪntə'lɒkjʊtə) *n.* **1.** a person who takes part in a conversation. **2.** Also called: **middleman.** the man in the centre of a troupe of minstrels who engages the others in talk or acts as announcer. —ˌ**in·ter**+**'loc·u·tress,** ˌ**in·ter**+**'loc·u·trice,** *or* ˌ**in·ter**+**'loc·u·trix** *fem. n.*

in·ter+**loc·u**+**to·ry** (ˌɪntə'lɒkjʊtərɪ, -trɪ) *adj.* **1.** *Law.* pronounced during the course of proceedings; provisional: *an interlocutory injunction.* **2.** interposed, as into a conversation, narrative, etc. **3.** of, relating to, or characteristic of dialogue. —ˌ**in·ter**+**'loc·u**+**to**+**ri**+**ly** *adv.*

in·ter+**lope** (ˌɪntə'ləʊp) *vb.* (*intr.*) **1.** to interfere; meddle. **2.** to intercept another's trade, esp. illegally. [C17: probably back formation from *interloper,* from INTER- + *-loper,* from Middle Dutch *loopen* to LEAP] —**'in·ter**+ˌ**lop**+**er** *n.*

in·ter+**lude** ('ɪntəˌlu:d) *n.* **1.** a period of time or different activity between longer periods, processes, or events; episode or interval. **2.** *Theatre.* a short dramatic piece played separately or as part of a longer entertainment, common in 16th-century England. **3.** a brief piece of music, dance, etc., given between the sections of another performance. [C14: from Medieval Latin *interlūdium,* from Latin INTER- + *lūdus* play]

in·ter+**lu**+**na**+**tion** (ˌɪntəlu'neɪʃən) *n.* the monthly period during which the moon is invisible. See **new moon.** —ˌ**in·ter**+**'lu**+**nar** *adj.*

in·ter+**mar**+**ry** (ˌɪntə'mærɪ) *vb.* +**ries,** +**ry**+**ing,** +**ried.** (*intr.*) **1.** to marry someone from another group, race, religion, creed, etc. **2.** to marry within one's own family, clan, group, etc. —ˌ**in·ter**+**'mar**+**riage** *n.*

in·ter+**me·di**+**ar·y** (ˌɪntə'mi:dɪərɪ) *n., pl.* +**ar·ies. 1.** a person who acts as a mediator or agent between parties. **2.** something that acts as a medium or means. **3.** an intermediate state or period. ~*adj.* **4.** acting as an intermediary. **5.** situated, acting, or coming between; intermediate.

in·ter+**me·di**+**ate** *adj.* (ˌɪntə'mi:dɪɪt). **1.** occurring or situated between two points, extremes, places, etc.; in between. **2.** *Physics.* (of a neutron) having an energy between 100 and 100 000 electronvolts. ~*n.* (ˌɪntə'mi:dɪɪt). **3.** something intermediate. **4.** a substance formed during one of the stages of a chemical process before the desired product is obtained. ~*vb.* (ˌɪntə'mi:dɪˌeɪt). **5.** (*intr.*) to act as an intermediary or mediator. [C17: from Medieval Latin *intermediāre* to intervene, from Latin INTER- + *medius* middle] —ˌ**in·ter**+**'me·di·a**+**cy** *or* ˌ**in·ter**+**'me·di**+**ate**+**ness** *n.* —ˌ**in·ter**+**'me·di**+**ate**+**ly** *adv.* —ˌ**in·ter**+**me·di**+**'a**+**tion** *n.* —ˌ**in·ter**+**'me·di**+ˌ**a**+**tor** *n.*

in·ter+**me·di**+**ate fre**+**quen**+**cy** *n. Electronics.* the frequency to which the signal carrier frequency is changed in a superheterodyne receiver and at which most of the amplification takes place.

in·ter+**me·di**+**ate host** *n.* an animal that acts as host to a parasite that has not yet become sexually mature.

in·ter+**me·di**+**ate range bal**+**lis**+**tic mis**+**sile** *n.* a missile that follows a ballistic trajectory with a medium range, normally of the order of 750–1500 miles. Abbrev.: **IRBM**

in+**ter**+**ment** (ɪn'tɜ:mənt) *n.* burial, esp. with ceremonial rites.

in·ter+**mez**+**zo** (ˌɪntə'mɛtsəʊ) *n., pl.* +**zos** *or* +**zi** (-si:). **1.** a short piece of instrumental music composed for performance between the acts or scenes of an opera, drama, etc. **2.** an instrumental piece either inserted between two longer movements in an extended composition or intended for independent performance. **3.** another name for **interlude** (sense 3). [C19: from Italian, from Late Latin *intermedium* interval; see INTERMEDIATE]

in·ter+**mi**+**gra**+**tion** (ˌɪntəmaɪ'greɪʃən) *n.* migration between two groups of people, animals, etc., resulting in an exchange of habitat.

in+**ter**+**mi**+**na**+**ble** (ɪn'tɜ:mɪnəbᵊl) *adj.* endless or seemingly endless because of monotony or tiresome length. —**in**+ˌ**ter**+**mi**+**na**+**'bil**+**i**+**ty** *or* **in**+**'ter**+**mi**+**na**+**ble**+**ness** *n.* —**in**+**'ter**+**mi**+**na**+**bly** *adv.*

in·ter+**mis**+**sion** (ˌɪntə'mɪʃən) *n.* **1.** an interval, as between parts of a film, etc. **2.** a period between events or activities; pause. **3.** the act of intermitting or the state of being intermitted. [C16: from Latin *intermissiō,* from *intermittere* to leave off, INTERMIT] —ˌ**in**+**ter**+**'mis**+**sive** *adj.*

in·ter+**mit** (ˌɪntə'mɪt) *vb.* +**mits,** +**mit**+**ting,** +**mit**+**ted.** to suspend or cause to suspend activity temporarily or at intervals. [C16: from Latin *intermittere* to leave off, from INTER- + *mittere* to send] —ˌ**in·ter**+**'mit**+**ting**+**ly** *adv.* —ˌ**in·ter**+**'mit**+**tor** *n.*

in·ter+**mit**+**tent** (ˌɪntə'mɪtᵊnt) *adj.* occurring occasionally or at regular or irregular intervals; periodic. —ˌ**in·ter**+**'mit**+**tence** *or* ˌ**in·ter**+**'mit**+**ten**+**cy** *n.* —ˌ**in·ter**+**'mit**+**tent**+**ly** *adv.*

in·ter+**mit**+**tent clau**+**di**+**ca**+**tion** *n. Pathol.* pain and cramp in the calf muscles, aggravated by walking and caused by an insufficient supply of blood.

in·ter+**mit**+**tent fe**+**ver** *n.* any fever, such as malaria characterized by intervals of periodic remission.

in·ter+**mix**+**ture** (ˌɪntə'mɪkstʃə) *n.* **1.** the act of intermixing or state of being intermixed. **2.** another word for **mixture. 3.** an additional constituent or ingredient.

in·ter+**mo**+**lec·u**+**lar** (ˌɪntəmə'lɛkjʊlə) *adj.* occurring among or between molecules.

in+**tern** *vb.* **1.** (ɪn'tɜ:n). (*tr.*) to detain or confine (foreign or enemy citizens, ships, etc.), esp. during wartime. **2.** ('ɪntɜ:n). (*intr.*) *Chiefly U.S.* to serve or train as an intern. ~*n.* ('ɪntɜ:n). **3.** another word for **internee. 4.** Also: **interne.** the approximate U.S. equivalent of a British **houseman.** ~*adj.* (ɪn'tɜ:n). **5.** an archaic word for **internal.** [C19: from Latin *internus* internal] —**'in**+**tern**+ˌ**ship** *or* **'in**+**terne**+ˌ**ship** *n.*

in+**ter**+**nal** (ɪn'tɜ:nᵊl) *adj.* **1.** of, situated on, or suitable for the inside; inner. **2.** coming or acting from within; interior. **3.** involving the spiritual or mental life; subjective. **4.** of or involving a nation's domestic as opposed to foreign affairs. **5.** (of examinations) set and marked within a school, college, or university rather than a public body. **6.** situated within, affecting, or relating to the inside of the body. ~*n.* **7.** *Euphemistic.* a medical examination of the vagina or uterus. [C16: from Medieval Latin *internālis,* from Late Latin *internus* inward] —ˌ**in**+**ter**+**'nal**+**i**+**ty** *or* **in**+**'ter**+**nal**+**ness** *n.* —**in**+**'ter**+**nal**+**ly** *adv.*

in+**ter**+**nal-com**+**bus**+**tion en**+**gine** *n.* a heat engine, such as a petrol engine or gas turbine, in which combustion occurs within the engine rather than in an external furnace.

in+**ter**+**nal ear** *n.* the part of the ear that consists of the cochlea, vestibule, and semicircular canals. Also called: **inner ear, labyrinth.**

in+**ter**+**nal en**+**er**+**gy** *n.* the thermodynamic property of a system that changes by an amount equal to the work done on the system when it suffers an adiabatic change. It is the sum of the kinetic and potential energies of its constituent atoms, molecules, etc. Symbol: *U* or *E*

in+**ter**+**nal**+**ize** *or* **in**+**ter**+**nal**+**ise** (ɪn'tɜ:nəˌlaɪz) *vb.* (*tr.*) *Psychol., sociol.* to make internal, esp. to incorporate within oneself (values, attitudes, etc.) through learning or socialization. Compare **introject.** Also: **interiorize.** —**in**+ˌ**ter**+**nal**+**i**+**'za**+**tion** *or* **in**+ˌ**ter**+**nal**+**i**+**'sa**+**tion** *n.*

ˌ**in·ter**+**'knit** *vb.,* +**knits,** +**knit**+**ting,** +**knit**+**ted** *or* +**knit.**
ˌ**in·ter**+**'li**+**brar·y** *adj.*
ˌ**in·ter**+**'link** *vb.*
ˌ**in·ter**+**'lob·u**+**lar** *adj.*
ˌ**in·ter**+**'mesh** *vb.*
ˌ**in·ter**+**me**+**'tal**+**lic** *adj.*
ˌ**in·ter**+**'min**+**gle** *vb.*
ˌ**in·ter**+**'min**+**gle**+**ment** *n.*
ˌ**in·ter**+**'mix** *vb.*
ˌ**in·ter**+**'mix**+**a**+**ble** *adj.*
ˌ**in·ter**+**'mus**+**cu**+**lar** *adj.*

in+ter+nal med·i+cine *n.* the branch of medical science concerned with the diagnosis and nonsurgical treatment of disorders of the internal structures of the body.

in+ter+nal rhyme *n. Prosody.* rhyme that occurs between words within a verse line.

in+ter+nal se+cre+tion *n. Physiol.* a secretion, esp. a hormone, that is absorbed directly into the blood.

internat. *abbrev. for* international.

in·ter+na+tion+al (ˌɪntəˈnæʃənᵊl) *adj.* **1.** of, concerning, or involving two or more nations or nationalities. **2.** established by, controlling, or legislating for several nations: *an international court; international fishing rights.* **3.** available for use by all nations: *international waters.* ~*n.* **4.** *Sport.* **a.** a contest between two national teams. **b.** a member of these teams. —ˌ**in·ter+ˌna+tion+ˈal+i·ty** *n.* —ˌ**in·ter+ˈna+tion+al+ly** *adv.*

In·ter+na+tion+al (ˌɪntəˈnæʃənᵊl) *n.* **1.** any of several international socialist organizations. See **Comintern, First International, Labour and Socialist International, Second International, Socialist International, Trotskyist International, Vienna Union. 2.** a member of any of these organizations.

In·ter+na+tion+al Bank for Re+con+struc+tion and De+vel+op+ment *n.* the official name for the **World Bank.**

in·ter+na+tion+al can+dle *n.* a former international unit of luminous intensity, originally defined in terms of a standard candle and later in terms of a pentane-burning lamp. It has now been replaced by the candela.

In·ter+na+tion+al Court of Jus+tice *n.* a court established in the Hague to settle disputes brought by members of the United Nations. See also **World Court.**

In·ter+na+tion+al Crim·i+nal Po+lice Or+gan·i·za+tion *n.* See **Interpol.**

in·ter+na+tion+al date line *n.* the line approximately following the 180° meridian from Greenwich on the east side of which the date is one day earlier than on the west. Also called: **date line.**

In·ter+na+tion+al De+vel+op+ment As+so+ci·a+tion *n.* an organization set up in 1960 to provide low-interest loans to developing countries. It is part of the World Bank Group. Abbrev: **I.D.A.**

In·ter+na+tio+nale *French.* (ɛ̃tɛrnasjɔˈnal) *n.* **the.** a revolutionary socialist hymn, first sung in 1871 in France. [C19: shortened from French *chanson internationale* international song]

In·ter+na+tion+al Fi+nance Cor+po+ra+tion *n.* an organization that invests directly in private companies and makes or guarantees loans to private investors. It is affiliated to the World Bank and is part of the World Bank Group. Abbrev.: **I.F.C.**

In·ter+na+tion+al Ge·o+phys·i+cal Year *n.* the 18-month period from July 1, 1957, to Dec. 31, 1958, during which a number of nations agreed to cooperate in a geophysical research programme. Abbrev.: **I.G.Y.**

In·ter+na+tion+al Goth+ic *n.* a style in art during the late 14th and early 15th centuries characterized by elegant stylization of illuminated manuscripts, mosaics, stained glass, etc., and by increased interest in secular themes. Major contributors were Simone Martini, Giotto, and Pisanello.

In·ter+na+tion+al Grand+mas+ter *n. Chess.* See **grandmaster** (sense 2).

in·ter+na+tion+al+ism (ˌɪntəˈnæʃənəˌlɪzəm) *n.* **1.** the ideal or practice of cooperation and understanding between nations. **2.** the state or quality of being international.

in·ter+na+tion+al+ist (ˌɪntəˈnæʃənəlɪst) *n.* **1.** an advocate of internationalism. **2.** a person versed in international law. **3.** (*cap.*) a member of an International.

in·ter+na+tion+al+ize *or* **in·ter+na+tion+al+ise** (ˌɪntəˈnæʃənəˌlaɪz) *vb.* (*tr.*) **1.** to make international. **2.** to put under international control. —ˌ**in·ter+ˌna+tion+al·i+ˈza+tion** *or* ˌ**in·ter+ˌna+tion+al·i+ˈsa+tion** *n.*

In·ter+na+tion+al La+bour Or+gan·i+sa+tion *n.* an agency of the United Nations responsible for research and recommendations in the field of labour conditions and practices: founded in 1919 in affiliation to the League of Nations. Abbrev.: **I.L.O.**

In·ter+na+tion+al Mas+ter *n. Chess.* the second highest title awarded by the F.I.D.E. to a player: won by obtaining a certain number of points during specific international chess tournaments. Often shortened to **master.** Compare **grandmaster** (sense 2).

In·ter+na+tion+al Mon+e·tar·y Fund *n.* an international financial institution organized in 1945 to promote international trade by increasing the exchange stability of the major currencies. A fund is maintained out of which member nations with temporary balance-of-payments deficits may make withdrawals. Abbrev.: **IMF**

in·ter+na+tion+al Morse code *n.* the full name for **Morse code.**

in·ter+na+tion+al nau+ti+cal mile *n.* the full name for **nautical mile** (sense 1).

In·ter+na+tion+al Pho+net+ic Al+pha+bet *n.* a series of signs and letters propagated by the Association Phonétique Internationale for the representation of human speech sounds. It is based on the Roman alphabet but supplemented by modified signs or symbols from other writing systems, and is usually employed in its revised form of 1951. Abbrev.: **IPA**

in·ter+na+tion+al pitch *n. Music.* the frequency of 435 hertz assigned to the A above middle C, widely used until 1939. See **pitch** [1] (sense 26b).

In·ter+na+tion+al Prac+ti+cal Tem+per·a+ture Scale *n.* a temperature scale adopted by international agreement in 1968 based on thermodynamic temperature and using experimental values to define 11 fixed points. The lowest is the triple point of an equilibrium mixture of orthohydrogen and parahydrogen (-259.34°C) and the highest the freezing point of gold (1064.43°C).

in·ter+na+tion+al sea and swell scale *n.* another name for the **Douglas scale.**

In·ter+na+tion+al Stand+ards Or+gan·i·za+tion *n.* an international organization for the standardization of units of measurement, technical terminology, etc. Founded in its present form in 1947, it has a secretariat in Geneva.

in+terne (ˈɪntɜːn) *n.* a variant spelling of **intern.**

in·ter+ne·cine (ˌɪntəˈniːsaɪn) *adj.* **1.** mutually destructive or ruinous; maiming both or all sides: *internecine war.* **2.** of or relating to slaughter or carnage; bloody. **3.** of or involving conflict within a group or organization. [C17: from Latin *internecīnus,* from *internecāre* to destroy, from *necāre* to kill]

in+tern·ee (ˌɪntɜːˈniː) *n.* a person who is interned, esp. an enemy citizen in wartime or a terrorism suspect.

in·ter+neu+ron (ˌɪntəˈnjʊərɒn) *n. Physiol.* any neuron that connects afferent and efferent neurons in a reflex arc. Also called: **internuncial neuron.**

in+tern+ist (ˈɪntɜːnɪst, ɪnˈtɜːnɪst) *n.* a physician who specializes in internal medicine.

in+tern+ment (ɪnˈtɜːnmənt) *n.* **a.** the act of interning or state of being interned, esp. of enemy citizens in wartime or of terrorism suspects. **b.** (*as modifier*): *an internment camp.*

in·ter+node (ˈɪntəˌnəʊd) *n.* **1.** the part of a plant stem between two nodes. **2.** the part of a nerve fibre between two nodes of Ranvier. —ˌ**in·ter+ˈnod+al** *adj.*

in+tern+ship (ˈɪntɜːnˌʃɪp) *n. U.S.* the position of being an intern or the period during which a person is an intern.

in·ter+nun+cial (ˌɪntəˈnʌnʃəl) *adj.* **1.** *Physiol.* (esp. of neurons) interconnecting. See **internode. 2.** of, relating to, or emanating from a papal internuncio.

in·ter+nun+ci·o (ˌɪntəˈnʌnʃɪˌəʊ) *n., pl.* **+ci·os. 1.** an ambassador of the pope ranking immediately below a nuncio. **2.** a messenger, agent, or go-between. [C17: from Italian *internunzio,* from Latin *internuntius,* from INTER- + *nuntius* messenger]

in·ter·o+cep+tor (ˌɪntərəʊˈsɛptə) *n. Physiol.* a sensory receptor of an internal organ. [C20: from INTER(IOR) + (RE)CEPTOR] —ˌ**in·ter·o+ˈcep+tive** *adj.*

in·ter+os+cu+late (ˌɪntərˈɒskjʊˌleɪt) *vb.* (*intr.*) *Biology.* (of two different species or groups of organisms) to share certain characteristics. —ˌ**in·ter+ˌos+cu+ˈla+tion** *n.*

in·ter+page (ˌɪntəˈpeɪdʒ) *vb.* (*tr.*) **1.** to print (matter) on intervening pages. **2.** to insert (intervening pages) into a book.

in·ter+pel+lant (ˌɪntəˈpɛlənt) *adj.* **1.** causing an interpellation. ~*n.* **2.** a deputy who interpellates.

in·ter+pel+late (ɪnˈtɜːpɛˌleɪt) *vb.* (*tr.*) *Parliamentary procedure.* (in European legislatures) to question (a member of the government) on a point of government policy, often interrupting the business of the day. [C16: from Latin *interpellāre* to disturb, from INTER- + pellere to push] —**in+ˌter+pel+ˈla+tion** *n.* —**in+ˈter+pel+ˌla+tor** *n.*

in·ter+pen+e+trate (ˌɪntəˈpɛnɪˌtreɪt) *vb.* **1.** to penetrate (something) thoroughly; pervade. **2.** to penetrate each other or one another mutually. —ˌ**in·ter+ˈpen·e·tra·ble** *adj.* —ˌ**in·ter+ˈpen+e·trant** *adj.* —ˌ**in·ter+ˌpen+e·ˈtra+tion** *n.* —ˌ**in·ter+ˈpen+e·tra+tive** *adj.* —ˌ**in·ter+ˈpen+e·tra+tive+ly** *adv.*

in·ter+phase (ˈɪntəˌfeɪz) *n. Biology.* the period between two divisions of a cell.

in·ter+phone (ˈɪntəˌfəʊn) *n.* a telephone system for linking different rooms within a building, ship, etc.

in·ter+play (ˈɪntəˌpleɪ) *n.* reciprocal and mutual action and reaction, as in circumstances, events, or personal relations.

in·ter+plead (ˌɪntəˈpliːd) *vb.* **+pleads, +plead+ing; +plead+ed, +plead** (-ˈplɛd), *or* **+pled.** (*intr.*) *Law.* to institute interpleader proceedings.

in·ter+plead+er (ˌɪntəˈpliːdə) *n. Law.* **1.** a process by which a person holding money or property claimed by two or more parties and having no interest in it himself can require the claimants to litigate with each other to determine the issue. **2.** a person who interpleads.

In·ter+pol (ˈɪntəˌpɒl) *n. acronym for* International Criminal Police Organization, an association of over 100 national police forces, devoted chiefly to fighting international crime.

in+ter+po+late (ɪnˈtɜːpəˌleɪt) *vb.* **1.** to insert or introduce (a comment, passage, etc.) into (a conversation, text, etc.). **2.** to falsify or alter (a text, manuscript, etc.) by the later addition of (material, esp. spurious or valueless passages). **3.** (*intr.*) to make additions, interruptions, or insertions. **4.** *Maths.* to estimate (a value of a function) between the values already known or determined. Compare **extrapolate** (sense 1). [C17: from Latin *interpolāre* to give a new appearance to, from INTER- + *polīre* to POLISH] —**in+ˈter+po+ˌlat+er** *or* **in+ˈter+po+ˌla+tor** *n.* —**in+ˈter+po+la+tive** *adj.*

in+ter+po+la+tion (ɪnˌtɜːpəˈleɪʃən) *n.* **1.** the act of interpolating or the state of being interpolated. **2.** something interpolated.

in·ter+pose (ˌɪntəˈpəʊz) *vb.* **1.** to put or place between or among other things. **2.** to introduce (comments, questions, etc.) into a speech or conversation; interject. **3.** to exert or use power, influence, or action in order to alter or intervene in (a situation). [C16: from Old French *interposer,* from Latin *inter-*

ˌ**in·ter+ˈnu·cle·ar** *adj.*
ˌ**in·ter+ˌo·ce·ˈan+ic** *adj.*
ˌ**in·ter+ˈof+fice** *adj.*
ˌ**in·ter+ˈos+se·ous** *adj.*
ˌ**in·ter+pa+ˈri+e·tal** *adj.*
ˌ**in·ter+ˈplait** *vb.*
ˌ**in·ter+ˈplan+e·tar·y** *adj.*
ˌ**in·ter+ˈpo+lar** *adj.*

pōnere, from INTER- + *pōnere* to put] —ˌ**in·ter·'pos·a·ble** *adj.* —ˌ**in·ter·'pos·al** *n.* —ˌ**in·ter·'pos·er** *n.*

in·ter·po·si·tion (ˌɪntəpəˈzɪʃən) *n.* **1.** something interposed. **2.** the act of interposing or the state of being interposed.

in·ter·pret (ɪnˈtɜːprɪt) *vb.* **1.** to clarify or explain the meaning of; elucidate. **2.** to construe the significance or intention of: *to interpret a smile as an invitation.* **3.** to convey or represent the spirit or meaning of (a poem, song, etc.) in performance. **4.** (*intr.*) to act as an interpreter; translate orally. [C14: from Latin *interpretārī,* from *interpres* negotiator, one who explains, from INTER- + *-pres,* probably related to *pretium* PRICE] —**in·'ter·pret·a·ble** *adj.* —**in·ˌter·pret·a·'bil·i·ty** *or* **in·'ter·pret·a·ble·ness** *n.* —**in·'ter·pret·a·bly** *adv.*

in·ter·pre·ta·tion (ɪnˌtɜːprɪˈteɪʃən) *n.* **1.** the act or process of interpreting or explaining; elucidation. **2.** the result of interpreting; an explanation. **3.** a particular view of an artistic work, esp. as expressed by stylistic individuality in its performance. —**in·ˌter·pre·'ta·tion·al** *adj.*

in·ter·pret·er (ɪnˈtɜːprɪtə) *n.* **1.** a person who translates orally from one language into another. **2.** a person who interprets the work of others. **3.** *Computer technol.* **a.** the part of a program that translates the code in which instructions are written into machine language for immediate use by the computer. **b.** a machine that interprets the holes in a punched card and prints the corresponding characters on that card. —**in·'ter·pret·er·ˌship** *n.* —**in·'ter·pre·tress** *fem. n.*

in·ter·pre·tive (ɪnˈtɜːprɪtɪv) *or* **in·ter·pre·ta·tive** (ɪnˈtɜːprɪtətɪv) *adj.* of, involving, or providing interpretation; expository. —**in·'ter·pre·ta·tive·ly** *or* **in·'ter·pre·tive·ly** *adv.*

in·ter·pre·tive se·man·tics *n.* (*functioning as sing.*) a school of semantic theory based on the doctrine that the rules that relate sentences to their meanings form an autonomous system in the mind, separate from the rules that determine what is grammatical in a language. Compare **generative semantics.**

in·ter·ra·di·al (ˌɪntəˈreɪdɪəl) *adj.* situated between two radii or rays, esp. between the radii of a sea urchin or similar animal. —ˌ**in·ter·'ra·di·al·ly** *adv.*

in·ter·reg·num (ˌɪntəˈrɛgnəm) *n., pl.* **·nums** *or* **·na** (-nə). **1.** an interval between two reigns, governments, incumbencies, etc. **2.** any period in which a state lacks a ruler, government, etc. **3.** a period of absence of some control, authority, etc. **4.** a gap in a continuity. [C16: from Latin, from INTER- + *regnum* REIGN] —ˌ**in·ter·'reg·nal** *adj.*

in·ter·re·late (ˌɪntərɪˈleɪt) *vb.* to place in or come into a mutual or reciprocal relationship. —ˌ**in·ter·re·'la·tion** *n.* —ˌ**in·ter·re·'la·tion·ˌship** *n.*

in·ter·rex (ˌɪntəˈrɛks) *n., pl.* **in·ter·re·ges** (ˌɪntəˈriːdʒiːz). a person who governs during an interregnum; provisional ruler. [C16: from Latin, from INTER- + *rēx* king]

in·ter·ro·bang *or* **in·ter·a·bang** (ɪnˈtɛrəˌbæŋ) *n.* a newly invented punctuation mark (‽), used after a sentence that is both question and exclamation. [C20: blend of *interrogation mark* + *bang,* printer's slang for exclamation mark]

interrog. *abbrev. for:* **1.** interrogate. **2.** interrogation. **3.** interrogative.

in·ter·ro·gate (ɪnˈtɛrəˌgeɪt) *vb.* to ask questions (of), esp. to question (a witness in court, spy, etc.) closely. [C15: from Latin *interrogāre* to question, examine, from *rogāre* to ask] —**in·'ter·ro·ˌgat·ing·ly** *adv.* —**in·'ter·ro·ˌga·tor** *n.*

in·ter·ro·ga·tion (ɪnˌtɛrəˈgeɪʃən) *n.* **1.** the technique, practice, or an instance of interrogating. **2.** a question or query. **3.** *Telecomm.* the transmission of one or more triggering pulses to a transponder. —**in·ˌter·ro·'ga·tion·al** *adj.*

in·ter·ro·ga·tion mark *n.* a less common term for **question mark.**

in·ter·rog·a·tive (ˌɪntəˈrɒgətɪv) *adj.* **1.** asking or having the nature of a question. **2.** denoting a form or construction used in asking a question. **3.** denoting or belonging to a class of words, such as *which* and *whom,* that are determiners, adjectives, or pronouns and serve to question which individual referent or referents are intended. Compare **demonstrative, relative.** ~*n.* **4.** an interrogative word, phrase, sentence, or construction. **5.** a question mark. —ˌ**in·ter·'rog·a·tive·ly** *adv.*

in·ter·rog·a·to·ries (ˌɪntəˈrɒgətərɪz, -trɪz) *pl. n. Law.* written questions asked by one party to a suit, to which the other party has to give written answers under oath.

in·ter·rog·a·to·ry (ˌɪntəˈrɒgətərɪ, -trɪ) *adj.* **1.** expressing or involving a question. ~*n.* **2.** a question or interrogation.

in·ter·rupt (ˌɪntəˈrʌpt) *vb.* **1.** to break the continuity of (an action, event, etc.) or hinder (a person) by intrusion. **2.** (*tr.*) to cease to perform (some action). **3.** (*tr.*) to obstruct (a view, etc.). **4.** to prevent or disturb (a conversation, discussion, etc.) by questions, interjections, or comment. ~*n.* **5.** the signal to initiate the stopping of the running of one computer program in order to run another, after which the running of the original program is usually continued. [C15: from Latin *interrumpere,* from INTER- + *rumpere* to break] —ˌ**in·ter·'rupt·i·ble** *adj.* —ˌ**in·ter·'rup·tive** *adj.* —ˌ**in·ter·'rup·tive·ly** *adv.*

in·ter·rupt·ed (ˌɪntəˈrʌptɪd) *adj.* **1.** broken, discontinued, or hindered. **2.** (of plant organs, esp. leaves) not evenly spaced along an axis. **3.** Also: **deceptive.** *Music.* (of a cadence) progressing from the dominant chord to any other, such as the subdominant or submediant. —ˌ**in·ter·'rupt·ed·ly** *adv.*

in·ter·rupt·ed screw *n.* a screw with a slot or slots cut into the thread, esp. one used in the breech of some guns permitting both engagement and release of the block by a partial turn of the screw.

in·ter·rupt·er *or* **in·ter·rup·tor** (ˌɪntəˈrʌptə) *n.* **1.** a person or thing that interrupts. **2.** an electromechanical device for opening and closing an electric circuit.

in·ter·rup·tion (ˌɪntəˈrʌpʃən) *n.* **1.** something that interrupts, such as a comment, question, or action. **2.** an interval or intermission. **3.** the act of interrupting or the state of being interrupted.

in·ter·scho·las·tic (ˌɪntəskəˈlæstɪk) *adj.* **1.** (of sports events, competitions, etc.) occurring between two or more schools. **2.** representative of various schools.

in·ter se *Latin.* (ˈɪntə ˈseɪ) *adv.* among or between themselves.

in·ter·sect (ˌɪntəˈsɛkt) *vb.* **1.** to divide, cut, or mark off by passing through or across. **2.** (esp. of roads) to cross (each other). **3.** *Maths.* (often foll. by *with*) to have one or more points in common (with another configuration). [C17: from Latin *intersecāre* to divide, from INTER + *secāre* to cut]

in·ter·sec·tion (ˌɪntəˈsɛkʃən, ˈɪntəˌsɛk-) *n.* **1.** a point at which things intersect, esp. a road junction. **2.** the act of intersecting or the state of being intersected. **3.** *Maths.* **a.** a point or set of points common to two or more geometric configurations. **b.** Also called: **product.** the elements that are common to two or more sets. Symbol: ∩, as in $A \cap B$. —ˌ**in·ter·'sec·tion·al** *adj.*

in·ter·sex (ˈɪntəˌsɛks) *n. Zoology.* an individual with characteristics intermediate between those of a male and a female. Compare **gynandromorph, hermaphrodite** (sense 1).

in·ter·sex·u·al (ˌɪntəˈsɛksjʊəl) *adj.* **1.** occurring or existing between the sexes. **2.** relating to or being an intersex. —ˌ**in·ter·ˌsex·u·'al·i·ty** *or* ˌ**in·ter·'sex·u·al·ism** *n.* —ˌ**in·ter·'sex·u·al·ly** *adv.*

in·ter·space *vb.* (ˌɪntəˈspeɪs). **1.** (*tr.*) to make or occupy a space between. ~*n.* (ˈɪntəˌspeɪs). **2.** space between or among things. —**in·ter·spa·tial** (ˌɪntəˈspeɪʃəl) *adj.* —ˌ**in·ter·'spa·tial·ly** *adv.*

in·ter·sperse (ˌɪntəˈspɜːs) *vb.* (*tr.*) to scatter or distribute among, between, or on. [C16: from Latin *interspargere,* from INTER- + *spargere* to sprinkle] —**in·ter·spers·ed·ly** (ˌɪntəˈspɜːsɪdlɪ) *adv.* —**in·ter·sper·sion** (ˌɪntəˈspɜːʃən) *or* ˌ**in·ter·'sper·sal** *n.*

in·ter·sta·di·al (ˌɪntəˈsteɪdɪəl) *adj., n.* another word for **interglacial.** [C20: from New Latin, from INTER- + *stadium* stage]

in·ter·state (ˈɪntəˌsteɪt) *adj.* **1.** between or involving two or more of the states of the U.S., Australia, etc. ~*adv.* **2.** *Austral.* to or into another state.

in·ter·stice (ɪnˈtɜːstɪs) *n.* (*usually pl.*) **1.** a minute opening or crevice between things. **2.** *Physics.* the space between adjacent atoms in a crystal lattice. [C17: from Latin *interstitium* interval, from *intersistere,* from INTER- + *sistere* to stand]

in·ter·sti·tial (ˌɪntəˈstɪʃəl) *adj.* **1.** of or relating to an interstice or interstices. **2.** *Physics.* forming or occurring in an interstice: *an interstitial atom.* **3.** *Chem.* containing interstitial atoms or ions: *an interstitial compound.* **4.** *Anatomy, zoology.* occurring in the spaces between organs, tissues, etc.: *interstitial cells.* ~*n.* **5.** *Chem.* an atom or ion situated in the interstices of a crystal lattice. —ˌ**in·ter·'sti·tial·ly** *adv.*

in·ter·sti·tial-cell-stim·u·lat·ing hor·mone *n.* another name for **luteinizing hormone.**

in·ter·strat·i·fy (ˌɪntəˈstrætɪˌfaɪ) *vb.* **·fies, ·fy·ing, ·fied.** (*tr.; usually passive*) to arrange (a series of rock strata) in alternating beds. —ˌ**in·ter·ˌstrat·i·fi·'ca·tion** *n.*

in·ter·tex·ture (ˌɪntəˈtɛkstʃə) *n.* **1.** the act or process of interweaving or the condition of having been interwoven. **2.** something that has been interwoven.

in·ter·tid·al (ˌɪntəˈtaɪdᵊl) *adj.* of or relating to the zone of the shore between the high-water mark and low-water mark.

in·ter·tri·go (ˌɪntəˈtraɪgəʊ) *n.* chafing between two moist closely opposed skin surfaces, as at the armpit. [C18: from INTER- + *-trigo,* from Latin *terere* to rub]

In·ter·trop·i·cal Con·ver·gence Zone *n. Meteorol.* the zone of converging trade winds along the equator causing rising air currents and low atmospheric pressure. Abbrev.: **I.T.C.Z.**

in·ter·twine (ˌɪntəˈtwaɪn) *vb.* to unite or be united by twisting or twining together. Also: **intertwist.** —ˌ**in·ter·'twine·ment** *n.* —ˌ**in·ter·'twin·ing·ly** *adv.*

in·ter·val (ˈɪntəvəl) *n.* **1.** the period of time marked off by or between two events, instants, etc. **2.** the distance between two points, objects, etc. **3.** a pause or interlude, as between periods of intense activity. **4.** *Brit.* a short period between parts of a play, concert, film, etc.; intermission. **5.** *Music.* the difference of pitch between two notes, either sounded simultaneously (**harmonic interval**) or in succession as in a musical part (**melodic interval**). An interval is calculated by counting the (inclusive) number of notes of the diatonic scale between the two notes: *the interval between C and G is a fifth.* **6.** the ratio of the frequencies of two sounds. **7.** *Maths.* **a.** the set containing all real numbers or points between two given numbers or points, called the endpoints. A **closed interval** includes the endpoints, but an **open interval** does not. **b.** the set of points in *n*-dimensional space where coordinates satisfy the inequalities $a_i \leq x_i \leq b_i$ (**closed interval**) or $a_i < x_i < b_i$ (**open interval**) where $a_i < b_i$. **8. at intervals. a.** occasionally or intermittently.

ˌ**in·ter·pro·'fes·sion·al** *adj.*
ˌ**in·ter·pro·'vin·cial** *adj.*
ˌ**in·ter·'ra·cial** *adj.*
ˌ**in·ter·'re·gion·al** *adj.*
ˌ**in·ter·re·'li·gious** *adj.*
ˌ**in·ter·'school** *adj.*
ˌ**in·ter·'sep·tal** *adj.*
ˌ**in·ter·so·'ci·e·tal** *adj.*
ˌ**in·ter·'spi·nal** *or* ˌ**in·ter·'spi·nous** *adj.*
ˌ**in·ter·'stel·lar** *adj.*
ˌ**in·ter·ˌter·ri·'to·ri·al** *adj.*
ˌ**in·ter·'trib·al** *adj.*
ˌ**in·ter·'trib·al·ly** *adv.*
ˌ**in·ter·'trop·i·cal** *adj.*
ˌ**in·ter·ˌu·ni·'ver·si·ty** *adj.*

b. with spaces between. [C13: from Latin *intervallum*, literally: space between two palisades, from INTER- + *vallum* palisade, rampart] —**in·ter·val·lic** (ˌɪntəˈvælɪk) *adj.*

in·ter·val train·ing *n.* a method of athletic training using alternate sprinting and jogging. Also called: **fartlek.**

in·ter·vene (ˌɪntəˈviːn) *vb. (intr.)* **1.** (often foll. by *in*) to take a decisive or intrusive role (in) in order to modify or determine events or their outcome. **2.** (foll. by *in* or *between*) to come or be (among or between). **3.** (of a period of time) to occur between events or points in time. **4.** (of an event) to disturb or hinder a course of action. **5.** *Law.* to interpose and become a party to a legal action between others esp. in order to protect one's interests. [C16: from Latin *intervenīre* to come between, from INTER- + *venīre* to come] —ˌ**in·ter·ˈven·er** *or* ˌ**in·ter·ˈve·nor** *n.* —**in·ter·ven·tion** (ˌɪntəˈvɛnʃən) *n.* —ˌ**in·ter·ˈven·tion·al** *adj.*

in·ter·ven·tion·ist (ˌɪntəˈvɛnʃənɪst) *adj.* **1.** of, relating to, or advocating intervention, esp. in the affairs of a foreign country. ~*n.* **2.** an interventionist person or state. —ˌ**in·ter·ˈven·tion·ism** *n.*

in·ter·ver·te·bral disc *n.* any of the cartilaginous discs between individual vertebrae, acting as shock absorbers.

in·ter·view (ˈɪntəˌvjuː) *n.* **1.** a conversation with or questioning of a person, usually conducted for television, radio, or a newspaper. **2.** a formal discussion, esp. one in which an employer assesses an applicant for a job. ~*vb.* **3.** to conduct an interview with (someone). [C16: from Old French *entrevue;* see INTER-, VIEW] —ˌ**in·ter·view·ˈee** *n.* —ˈ**in·ter·ˌview·er** *n.*

in·ter·vo·cal·ic (ˌɪntəvəʊˈkælɪk) *adj.* pronounced or situated between vowels. —ˌ**in·ter·vo·ˈcal·i·cal·ly** *adv.*

in·ter·weave (ˌɪntəˈwiːv) *vb.* **·weaves, ·weav·ing, ·wove** *or* **·weaved; ·wov·en, ·wove,** *or* **·weaved.** to weave, blend, or twine together; intertwine. Also: **interwork.** —ˌ**in·ter·ˈweave·ment** *n.* —ˈ**in·ter·ˌweav·er** *n.*

in·tes·tate (ɪnˈtɛsteɪt, -tɪt) *adj.* **1. a.** (of a person) not having made a will. **b.** (of property) not disposed of by will. ~*n.* **2.** a person who dies without having made a will. ~Compare **testate.** [C14: from Latin *intestātus,* from IN-[1] + *testātus,* from *testārī* to bear witness, make a will, from *testis* a witness] —**in·ˈtes·ta·cy** *n.*

in·tes·ti·nal flo·ra *n.* harmless microorganisms that inhabit the lumen of the intestinal tract.

in·tes·tine (ɪnˈtɛstɪn) *n.* (*usually pl.*) the part of the alimentary canal between the stomach and the anus. See **large intestine, small intestine.** Related adj.: **alvine.** [C16: from Latin *intestīnum* gut, from *intestīnus* internal, from *intus* within] —**in·tes·ti·nal** (ɪnˈtɛstɪnᵊl, ˌɪntɛsˈtaɪnᵊl) *adj.* —**in·ˈtes·ti·nal·ly** *adv.*

in·ti·ma (ˈɪntɪmə) *n., pl.* **·mae** (-ˌmiː). *Anatomy, zoology.* the innermost layer of an organ or part, esp. of a blood vessel. [C19: from Latin, feminine of *intimus* innermost; see INTIMATE] —ˈ**in·ti·mal** *adj.*

in·ti·ma·cy (ˈɪntɪməsɪ) *n., pl.* **·cies. 1.** close or warm friendship or understanding; personal relationship. **2.** (*often pl.*) *Euphemistic.* sexual relations.

in·ti·mate[1] (ˈɪntɪmɪt) *adj.* **1.** characterized by a close or warm personal relationship: *an intimate friend.* **2.** deeply personal, private, or secret. **3.** (often *postpositive;* foll. by *with*) *Euphemistic.* having sexual relations (with). **4. a.** (*postpositive;* foll. by *with*) having a deep or unusual knowledge (of) **b.** (of knowledge) deep; extensive. **5.** having a friendly, warm, or informal atmosphere: *an intimate nightclub.* **6.** of or relating to the essential part or nature of something; intrinsic. **7.** denoting the informal second person of verbs and pronouns in French and other languages. [C17: from Latin *intimus* very close friend, from (adj.): innermost, deepest, from *intus* within] —ˈ**in·ti·mate·ly** *adv.* —ˈ**in·ti·mate·ness** *n.*

in·ti·mate[2] (ˈɪntɪˌmeɪt) *vb. (tr.; may take a clause as object)* **1.** to hint; suggest. **2.** *Rare.* to proclaim. [C16: from Late Latin *intimāre* to proclaim, from Latin *intimus* innermost] —ˈ**in·ti·ˌmat·er** *n.* —ˌ**in·ti·ˈma·tion** *n.*

in·tim·i·date (ɪnˈtɪmɪˌdeɪt) *vb. (tr.)* **1.** to make timid or frightened, as by threats; scare. **2.** to discourage, restrain, or silence illegally or unscrupulously, as by threats or blackmail. [C17: from Medieval Latin *intimidāre,* from Latin IN-[2] + *timidus* fearful, from *timor* fear] —**in·ˌtim·i·ˈda·tion** *n.* —**in·ˈtim·i·ˌda·tor** *n.*

in·tinc·tion (ɪnˈtɪŋkʃən) *n.* the practice of dipping the Eucharistic bread into the wine at Holy Communion. [C16: from Late Latin *intinctiō* a dipping in, from Latin *intingere* to dip in, from *tingere* to dip]

in·tine (ˈɪntɪn, -tiːn, -taɪn) *n.* the inner membrane of a pollen grain or a spore. Compare **extine.** [C19: from Latin *intimus* innermost + -INE[1]]

in·tit·ule (ɪnˈtɪtjuːl) *vb. (tr.) Parliamentary procedure.* (in Britain) to entitle (an Act). [C15: from Old French *intituler,* from Latin *titulus* TITLE]

intl. *abbrev. for* international.

in·to (ˈɪntuː; *unstressed* ˈɪntə) *prep.* **1.** to the interior or inner parts of: *to look into a case.* **2.** to the middle or midst of so as to be surrounded by: *into the water; into the bushes.* **3.** against; up against: *he drove into a wall.* **4.** used to indicate the result of a transformation or change: *he changed into a monster.* **5.** *Maths.* used to indicate a dividend: *three into six is two.* **6.** *Informal.* interested in: *I'm really into Freud these days.*

in·tol·er·a·ble (ɪnˈtɒlərəbᵊl) *adj.* **1.** more than can be tolerated or endured; insufferable. **2.** *Informal.* extremely irritating or annoying. —**in·ˌtol·er·a·ˈbil·i·ty** *or* **in·ˈtol·er·a·ble·ness** *n.* —**in·ˈtol·er·a·bly** *adv.*

in·tol·er·ant (ɪnˈtɒlərənt) *adj.* **1.** lacking respect for practices and beliefs other than one's own. **2.** (*postpositive;* foll. by *of*) not able or willing to tolerate or endure: *intolerant of noise.* —**in·ˈtol·er·ance** *n.* —**in·ˈtol·er·ant·ly** *adv.*

in·to·nate (ˈɪntəʊˌneɪt) *vb. (tr.)* **1.** to pronounce or articulate (continuous connected speech) with a characteristic rise and fall of the voice. **2.** a less common word for **intone.**

in·to·na·tion (ˌɪntəʊˈneɪʃən) *n.* **1.** the sound pattern of phrases and sentences produced by pitch variation in the voice. **2.** the act or manner of intoning. **3.** an intoned, chanted, or monotonous utterance; incantation. **4.** *Music.* the opening of a piece of plainsong, sung by a soloist. **5.** *Music.* **a.** the correct or accurate pitching of intervals. **b.** the capacity to play or sing in tune. See also **just intonation.** —ˌ**in·to·ˈna·tion·al** *adj.*

in·to·na·tion pat·tern *or* **con·tour** *n. Linguistics.* a characteristic series of musical pitch levels that serves to distinguish between questions, statements, and other types of utterance in a language.

in·tone (ɪnˈtəʊn) *vb.* **1.** to utter, recite, or sing (a chant, prayer, etc.) in a monotonous or incantatory tone. **2.** to speak with a particular or characteristic intonation or tone. **3.** to sing (the opening phrase of a psalm, etc.) in plainsong. —**in·ˈton·er** *n.*

in·tor·sion (ɪnˈtɔːʃən) *n. Botany.* a spiral twisting in plant stems or other parts.

in to·to *Latin.* (ɪn ˈtəʊtəʊ) *adv.* totally; entirely; completely.

in·tox·i·cant (ɪnˈtɒksɪkənt) *n.* **1.** anything that causes intoxication. ~*adj.* **2.** causing intoxication.

in·tox·i·cate (ɪnˈtɒksɪˌkeɪt) *vb.* **1.** (*tr.*) (of an alcoholic drink) to produce in (a person) a state ranging from euphoria to stupor, usually accompanied by loss of inhibitions and control; make drunk; inebriate. **2.** (*tr.*) to stimulate, excite, or elate so as to overwhelm. **3.** (*tr.*) (of a drug, etc.) to poison. [C16: from Medieval Latin, from *intoxicāre* to poison, from Latin *toxicum* poison; see TOXIC] —**in·ˈtox·i·ca·ble** *adj.* —**in·ˈtox·i·ˌcat·ing·ly** *adv.* —**in·ˈtox·i·ˌca·tive** *adj.* —**in·ˈtox·i·ˌca·tor** *n.*

in·tox·i·ca·tion (ɪnˌtɒksɪˈkeɪʃən) *n.* **1.** drunkenness; inebriation. **2.** great elation. **3.** the act of intoxicating. **4.** poisoning.

intr. *abbrev. for* intransitive.

in·tra- *prefix.* within; inside: *intravenous.* [from Latin *intrā* on the inside, within; see INTERIOR]

in·tra-a·tom·ic (ˌɪntrəəˈtɒmɪk) *adj.* existing or occurring within an atom or atoms. Compare **interatomic.**

in·tra·car·di·ac (ˌɪntrəˈkɑːdɪˌæk) *adj.* within the heart.

in·tra·cel·lu·lar (ˌɪntrəˈsɛljʊlə) *adj. Biology.* situated or occurring inside a cell or cells. —ˌ**in·tra·ˈcel·lu·lar·ly** *adv.*

In·tra·coast·al Wa·ter·way *n.* short for **Atlantic Intracoastal Waterway.**

in·tra·cra·ni·al (ˌɪntrəˈkreɪnɪəl) *adj.* within the skull.

in·trac·ta·ble (ɪnˈtræktəbᵊl) *adj.* **1.** difficult to influence or direct: *an intractable disposition.* **2.** (of a problem, illness, etc.) difficult to solve, alleviate, or cure. **3.** difficult to shape or mould, esp. with the hands. —**in·ˌtrac·ta·ˈbil·i·ty** *or* **in·ˈtrac·ta·ble·ness** *n.* —**in·ˈtrac·ta·bly** *adv.*

in·tra·cu·ta·ne·ous (ˌɪntrəkjuːˈteɪnɪəs) *adj. Anatomy.* within the skin. Also: **intradermal.** —ˌ**in·tra·cu·ˈta·ne·ous·ly** *adv.*

in·tra·der·mal (ˌɪntrəˈdɜːməl) *or* **in·tra·der·mic** *adj. Anatomy.* other words for **intracutaneous.** —ˌ**in·tra·ˈder·mal·ly** *or* ˌ**in·tra·ˈder·mi·cal·ly** *adv.*

in·tra·dos (ɪnˈtreɪdɒs) *n., pl.* **·dos** *or* **·dos·es.** *Architect.* the inner curve or surface of an arch or vault. Compare **extrados.** [C18: from French, from INTRA- + *dos* back, from Latin *dorsum*]

in·tra·mo·lec·u·lar (ˌɪntrəməˈlɛkjʊlə) *adj.* occurring within a molecule or molecules.

in·tra·mu·ral (ˌɪntrəˈmjʊərəl) *adj.* **1.** *Education, chiefly U.S.* operating within or involving those in a single establishment. **2.** *Anatomy.* within the walls of a cavity or hollow organ. —ˌ**in·tra·ˈmu·ral·ly** *adv.*

in·tra·mus·cu·lar (ˌɪntrəˈmʌskjʊlə) *adj. Anatomy.* within a muscle: *an intramuscular injection.* Abbrev. (esp. of an injection): **I.M., i.m.** —ˌ**in·tra·ˈmus·cu·lar·ly** *adv.*

in·tra·na·tion·al (ˌɪntrəˈnæʃənᵊl) *adj.* within one nation.

intrans. *abbrev. for* intransitive.

in·tran·si·gent (ɪnˈtrænsɪdʒənt) *adj.* **1.** not willing to compromise; obstinately maintaining an attitude. ~*n., also* **in·tran·si·gent·ist. 2.** an intransigent person, esp. in politics. [C19: from Spanish *los intransigentes* the uncompromising (ones), a name adopted by certain political extremists, from IN-[1] + *transigir* to compromise, from Latin *transigere* to settle; see TRANSACT] —**in·ˈtran·si·gence** *or* **in·ˈtran·si·gen·cy** *n.* —**in·ˈtran·si·gent·ly** *adv.*

in·tran·si·tive (ɪnˈtrænsɪtɪv) *adj.* **1. a.** denoting a verb when it does not require a direct object. **b.** denoting a verb that customarily does not require a direct object. **c.** (*as n.*) a verb in either of these categories. **2.** denoting an adjective or noun that does not require any particular noun phrase as a referent. **3.** having the property that although one object is related to a second that bears the same relationship to a third, the first does not bear this relationship to the third: *"being the mother of" is an intransitive relationship.* ~Compare **transitive, pseudo-**

ˌ**in·ter·ˈur·ban** *adj.*
ˌ**in·ter·ˈvar·si·ty** *adj.*
ˌ**in·ter·ˈver·te·bral** *adj.*
ˌ**in·ter·ˈvolve** *vb.*
ˌ**in·ter·ˈwar** *adj.*
ˌ**in·ter·ˈwind** *vb.*
ˌ**in·ter·ˈwreathe** *vb.*
ˌ**in·ter·ˈwrought** *adj.*

intransitive. —**in+'tran+si+tive+ly** *adv.* —**in+,tran+si+'tiv+i+ty** *or* **in+'tran+si+tive+ness** *n.*

in·tra+nu+cle·ar (ˌɪntrəˈnjuːklɪə) *adj.* situated or occurring within a nucleus.

in·tra+state (ˌɪntrəˈsteɪt) *adj. Chiefly U.S.* of, relating to, or confined within a single state, esp. a state of the U.S.

in·tra+tel+lu+ric (ˌɪntrətəˈljʊərɪk) *adj.* (of rocks and their constituents, processes, etc.) formed or occurring below the surface of the earth.

in·tra+u·ter+ine (ˌɪntrəˈjuːtəraɪn) *adj.* within the womb.

in·tra+u·ter+ine de+vice *n.* a metal or plastic device, in the shape of a loop, coil, or ring, inserted into the uterus to prevent conception. Abbrev.: **I.U.D.**

in+trav·a+sa+tion (ɪnˌtrævəˈseɪʃən) *n.* the passage of extraneous material, such as pus, into a blood or lymph vessel. Compare **extravasation.**

in·tra+ve·nous (ˌɪntrəˈviːnəs) *adj. Anatomy.* within a vein: *an intravenous injection.* Abbrev. (esp. of an injection): **I.V., i.v.** —**ˌin·tra+'ve·nous+ly** *adv.*

in-tray *n.* a tray for incoming papers, etc., requiring attention.

in·tra+zon+al soil (ˌɪntrəˈzəʊnᵊl) *n.* a soil that has a well-developed profile determined by relief, parent material, age, etc.

in+treat (ɪnˈtriːt) *vb.* an archaic spelling of **entreat.** —**in+'treat+ing+ly** *adv.* —**in+'treat+ment** *n.*

in+trench (ɪnˈtrɛntʃ) *vb.* a less common spelling of **entrench.** —**in+'trench+er** *n.* —**in+'trench+ment** *n.*

in+trep+id (ɪnˈtrɛpɪd) *adj.* fearless; daring; bold. [C17: from Latin *intrepidus,* from IN-[1] + *trepidus* fearful, timid] —**ˌin+tre+'pid+i+ty** *or* **in+'trep+id+ness** *n.* —**in+'trep+id+ly** *adv.*

in+tri+cate (ˈɪntrɪkɪt) *adj.* **1.** difficult to understand; obscure; complex; puzzling. **2.** entangled or involved: *intricate patterns.* [C15: from Latin *intrīcāre* to entangle, perplex, from IN-[2] + *trīcae* trifles, perplexities] —**'in+tri+ca+cy** *or* **'in+tri+cate+ness** *n.* —**'in+tri+cate+ly** *adv.*

in+tri+gant *or* **in+tri+guant** (ˈɪntrɪgənt; *French* ɛ̃triˈgɑ̃) *or* (*fem.*) **in+tri+gante** *or* **in+tri+guante** (ˌɪntrɪˈgɒnt; *French* ɛ̃triˈgɑ̃ːt) *n. Archaic.* a person who intrigues; intriguer.

in+trigue *vb.* (ɪnˈtriːg), **+trigues, +trigu+ing, +trigued.** **1.** (*tr.*) to make interested or curious: *I'm intrigued by this case, Watson.* **2.** (*intr.*) to make secret plots or employ underhand methods; conspire. **3.** (*intr.;* often foll. by *with*) to carry on a clandestine love affair. ~*n.* (ɪnˈtriːg, ˈɪntriːg). **4.** the act or an instance of secret plotting, etc. **5.** a clandestine love affair. **6.** the quality of arousing interest or curiosity; beguilement. [C17: from French *intriguer,* from Italian *intrigare,* from Latin *intrīcāre;* see INTRICATE] —**in+'tri+guer** *n.* —**in+'tri+guing+ly** *adv.*

in+trin+sic (ɪnˈtrɪnsɪk) *or* **in+trin+si+cal** *adj.* **1.** of or relating to the essential nature of a thing; inherent. **2.** *Anatomy.* situated within or peculiar to a part: *intrinsic muscles.* [C15: from Late Latin *intrinsecus* from Latin, inwardly, from *intrā* within + *secus* alongside; related to *sequī* to follow] —**in+'trin+si+cal+ly** *adv.*

in+trin+sic sem+i+con+duc+tor *n.* an almost pure semiconductor to which no impurities have been added and in which the electron and hole densities are equal at thermal equilibrium. Also called: **i-type semiconductor.**

in+tro (ˈɪntrəʊ) *n., pl.* **+tros.** *Informal.* short for **introduction.**

intro. *or* **introd.** *abbrev. for:* **1.** introduction. **2.** introductory.

in·tro- *prefix.* in, into, or inward: *introvert.* [from Latin *intrō* towards the inside, inwardly, within]

in·tro+duce (ˌɪntrəˈdjuːs) *vb.* (*tr.*) **1.** (often foll. by *to*) to present (someone) by name (to another person) or (two or more people to each other). **2.** (foll. by *to*) to cause to experience for the first time: *to introduce a visitor to beer.* **3.** to present for consideration or approval, esp. before a legislative body: *to introduce a draft bill in Congress.* **4.** to bring in; establish: *to introduce decimal currency.* **5.** to present (a radio or television programme, etc.) verbally. **6.** (foll. by *with*) to start: *he introduced his talk with some music.* **7.** (often foll. by *into*) to insert or inject: *he introduced the needle into his arm.* [C16: from Latin *intrōdūcere* to bring inside, from INTRO- + *dūcere* to lead] —**ˌin·tro+'duc+er** *n.* —**ˌin·tro+'duc+i·ble** *adj.*

in·tro+duc+tion (ˌɪntrəˈdʌkʃən) *n.* **1.** the act of introducing or fact of being introduced. **2.** a presentation of one person to another or others. **3.** a means of presenting a person to another person, group, etc., such as a **letter of introduction** or reference. **4.** a preliminary part, as of a book, speech, etc. **5.** *Music.* **a.** an instrumental passage preceding the entry of a soloist, choir, etc. **b.** an opening passage in a movement or composition that precedes the main material. **6.** something that has been or is introduced, esp. something that is not native to an area, country, etc. **7.** a basic or elementary work of instruction, reference, etc.

in·tro+duc·to·ry (ˌɪntrəˈdʌktərɪ, -trɪ) *adj.* serving as an introduction; preliminary; prefatory. —**ˌin·tro+'duc+to+ri+ly** *adv.* —**ˌin·tro+'duc+to+ri+ness** *n.*

in·tro+gres+sion (ˌɪntrəˈgrɛʃən) *n.* the introduction of genes from the gene pool of one species into that of another during hybridization.

in+troit (ˈɪntrɔɪt) *n. R.C. Church, Church of England.* a short prayer said or sung as the celebrant is entering the sanctuary to celebrate Mass or Holy Communion. [C15: from Church Latin *introitus* introit, from Latin: entrance, from *introīre* to go in, from INTRO- + *īre* to go] —**in+'troi+tal** *adj.*

in·tro+ject (ˌɪntrəˈdʒɛkt) *vb. Psychol.* **1.** (*intr.*) (esp. of a child) to incorporate ideas of others, or (in fantasy) of objects. **2.** to turn (feelings for another) towards oneself. ~Compare **project.** See also **internalize.**

in·tro+jec+tion (ˌɪntrəˈdʒɛkʃən) *n. Psychol.* the act or process of introjecting. [C20: from INTRO- + (PRO)JECTION] —**ˌin·tro+'jec+tive** *adj.*

in·tro+mis+sion (ˌɪntrəˈmɪʃən) *n.* a less common word for **insertion** or **introduction.** —**ˌin·tro+'mis+sive** *adj.*

in·tro+mit (ˌɪntrəˈmɪt) *vb.* **+mits, +mit+ting, +mit+ted.** (*tr.*) *Rare.* to enter or insert or allow to enter or be inserted. [C15: from Latin *intrōmittere* to send in, from INTRO- + *mittere* to send] —**ˌin·tro+'mis+si·ble** *adj.* —**ˌin·tro+ˌmis+si·'bil+i·ty** *n.* —**ˌin·tro+'mit+tent** *adj.* —**ˌin·tro+'mit+ter** *n.*

in+trorse (ɪnˈtrɔːs) *adj. Botany.* turned inwards or towards the axis, as anthers that shed their pollen towards the centre of the flower. [C19: from Latin *introrsus,* contraction of *intrōversus,* from INTRO- + *versus* turned, from *vertere* to turn] —**in+'trorse+ly** *adv.*

in·tro+spect (ˌɪntrəˈspɛkt) *vb.* (*intr.*) to examine and analyse one's own thoughts and feelings.

in·tro+spec+tion (ˌɪntrəˈspɛkʃən) *n.* the examination of one's own thoughts, impressions, and feelings, esp. for long periods. [C17: from Latin *intrōspicere* to look within, from INTRO- + *specere* to look] —**ˌin·tro+'spec+tion+al** *or* **ˌin·tro+'spec+tive** *adj.* —**ˌin·tro+'spec+tion+ist** *n.* —**ˌin·tro+'spec+tive+ly** *adv.* —**ˌin·tro+'spec+tive+ness** *n.*

in·tro+ver+sion (ˌɪntrəˈvɜːʃən) *n.* **1.** *Psychol.* the directing of interest inwards towards one's own thoughts and feelings rather than towards the external world or making social contacts. **2.** *Pathol.* the turning inside out of a hollow organ or part. ~Compare **extroversion.** —**ˌin·tro+'ver+sive** *or* **ˌin·tro+'ver+tive** *adj.*

in·tro+vert *n.* (ˈɪntrəˌvɜːt). **1.** *Psychol.* a person prone to introversion. ~*adj.* (ˈɪntrəˌvɜːt). **2.** Also: **introverted.** characterized by introversion. ~*vb.* (ˌɪntrəˈvɜːt). **3.** (*tr.*) *Pathol.* to turn (a hollow organ or part) inside out. ~Compare **extrovert.** [C17: see INTRO-, INVERT]

in+trude (ɪnˈtruːd) *vb.* **1.** (often foll. by *into, on,* or *upon*) to put forward or interpose (oneself, one's views, something) abruptly or without invitation. **2.** *Geology.* to force or thrust (rock material, esp. molten magma) or (of rock material) to be thrust between solid rocks. [C16: from Latin *intrūdere* to thrust in, from IN-[2] + *trūdere* to thrust] —**in+'trud+er** *n.* —**in+'trud+ing+ly** *adv.*

in+tru+sion (ɪnˈtruːʒən) *n.* **1.** the act or an instance of intruding; an unwelcome visit, interjection, etc.: *an intrusion on one's privacy.* **2. a.** the movement of magma from within the earth's crust into spaces in the overlying strata to form igneous rock. **b.** any igneous rock formed in this way. **3.** *Property law.* an unlawful entry onto land by a stranger after determination of a particular estate of freehold and before the remainderman or reversioner has made entry. —**in+'tru+sion+al** *adj.*

in+tru+sive (ɪnˈtruːsɪv) *adj.* **1.** characterized by intrusion or tending to intrude. **2.** (of igneous rocks) formed by intrusion. Compare **extrusive** (sense 2). **3.** *Phonetics.* relating to or denoting a speech sound that is introduced into a word or piece of connected speech for a phonetic rather than a historical or grammatical reason, such as the (r) often pronounced between *idea* and *of* in *the idea of it.* —**in+'tru+sive+ly** *adv.* —**in+'tru+sive+ness** *n.*

in+trust (ɪnˈtrʌst) *vb.* a less common spelling of **entrust.** —**in+'trust+ment** *n.*

in+tu+bate (ˈɪntjʊˌbeɪt) *vb.* (*tr.*) *Med.* to insert a tube or cannula into (a hollow organ); cannulate. —**ˌin+tu+'ba+tion** *n.*

INTUC (ˈɪntʌk) *acronym for* Indian National Trade Union Congress.

in+tu+it (ɪnˈtjuːɪt) *vb.* to know or discover by intuition. —**in+'tu+it+a·ble** *adj.*

in+tu·i+tion (ˌɪntjʊˈɪʃən) *n.* **1.** knowledge or perception not gained by reasoning and intelligence; instinctive knowledge or insight. **2.** anything learned or perceived in this way. [C15: from Late Latin *intuitiō* a contemplation, from Latin *intuērī* to gaze upon, from *tuērī* to look at] —**ˌin+tu·'i+tion+al** *adj.* —**ˌin+tu·'i+tion+al+ly** *adv.*

in+tu·i+tion+ism (ˌɪntjʊˈɪʃəˌnɪzəm) *or* **in+tu·i+tion+al+ism** *n. Philosophy.* **1.** the doctrine that knowledge is acquired primarily by intuition. Compare **empiricism, rationalism.** **2.** the theory that general terms are used of a variety of objects in accordance with perceived similarities. Compare **nominalism, Platonism.** **3.** the theory that the solution to moral problems can be discovered by intuition. **4.** the doctrine that external objects are known to be real by intuition. —**ˌin+tu·'i+tion+ist** *or* **ˌin+tu·'i+tion+al+ist** *n.*

in+tu·i+tive (ɪnˈtjuːɪtɪv) *adj.* **1.** resulting from intuition: *an intuitive awareness.* **2.** of, characterized by, or involving intuition. **3.** *Philosophy.* (of knowledge) obtained by intuition, not empirically or discursively. Compare **dianoetic.** —**in+'tu·i+tive+ly** *adv.* —**in+'tu·i+tive+ness** *n.*

in+tu·i+tiv+ism (ɪnˈtjuːɪtɪˌvɪzəm) *n.* **1.** *Philosophy.* another word for **intuitionism.** **2.** intuitive knowledge; intuition. —**in+'tu·i+tiv+ist** *n.*

in+tu+mesce (ˌɪntjʊˈmɛs) *vb.* (*intr.*) to swell or become swollen; undergo intumescence. [C18: from Latin *intumescere,* from *tumescere* to begin to swell, from *tumēre* to swell]

in+tu+mes+cence (ˌɪntjʊˈmɛsəns) *or* **in+tu+mes+cen+cy** *n.* **1.** *Pathol.* a swelling up, as with blood or other fluid. **2.** *Pathol.* a swollen organ or part. **3.** *Chem.* the swelling of certain substances on heating, often accompanied by the escape of water vapour. —**ˌin+tu+'mes+cent** *adj.*

in+tus+sus+cept (ˌɪntəssəˈsɛpt) *vb. Pathol.* (*tr.; usually passive*) to turn or fold (an organ or part) inwards; invaginate. —**ˌin+tus+sus+'cep+tive** *adj.*

in+tus+sus+cep+tion (ˌɪntəssəˈsɛpʃən) *n.* **1.** *Pathol.* invagination of a tubular organ or part, esp. the telescoping of one section of the intestinal tract into a lower section, causing obstruction. **2.** *Biology.* growth in the surface area of a cell by the deposition of new particles between the existing particles of the cell wall. Compare **apposition** (sense 3). [C18: from Latin *intus* within + *susceptiō* a taking up]

in+twine (ɪnˈtwaɪn) *vb.* a less common spelling of **entwine.** —**in+ˈtwine+ment** *n.*

In·u·it (ˈɪnjəwət) *n.* a variant spelling of **Innuit.**

in·u·lin (ˈɪnjʊlɪn) *n.* a fructose polysaccharide present in the tubers and rhizomes of some plants. Formula: $(C_6H_{10}O_5)_n$. [C19: from Latin *inula* elecampane + -IN]

in+unc+tion (ɪnˈʌŋkʃən) *n.* **1.** the application of an ointment to the skin, esp. by rubbing. **2.** the ointment so used. **3.** the act of anointing; anointment. [C15: from Latin *inunguere* to anoint, from *unguere;* see UNCTION]

in+un+date (ˈɪnʌnˌdeɪt) *vb.* (*tr.*) **1.** to cover completely with water; overflow; flood; swamp. **2.** to overwhelm, as if with a flood: *to be inundated with requests.* [C17: from Latin *inundāre* to flood, from *unda* wave] —**ˈin+un+dant** *or* **in+ˈun+da+to·ry** *adj.* —**ˌin+un+ˈda+tion** *n.* —**ˈin+un+ˌda+tor** *n.*

in+ur+bane (ˌɪnɜːˈbeɪn) *adj. Rare.* not urbane; lacking in courtesy or polish. —**in+ur+ban+i·ty** (ˌɪnɜːˈbænɪtɪ) *n.* —**ˌin+ur+ˈbane+ly** *adv.*

in+ure *or* **en+ure** (ɪˈnjʊə) *vb.* **1.** (*tr.; often passive;* often foll. by *to*) to cause to accept or become hardened to; habituate. **2.** (*intr.*) (esp. of a law, etc.) to come into operation; take effect. [C15 *enuren* to accustom, from *ure* use, from Old French *euvre* custom, work, from Latin *opera* works, plural of *opus*] —**in+ur+ed+ness** *or* **en+ur+ed+ness** (ɪˈnjʊərɪdnɪs) *n.* —**in+ˈure+ment** *or* **en+ˈure+ment** *n.*

in+urn (ɪnˈɜːn) *vb.* (*tr.*) **1.** to place (esp. cremated ashes) in an urn. **2.** a less common word for **inter.** —**in+ˈurn+ment** *n.*

in u·t+er·o *Latin.* (ɪn ˈjuːtəˌrəʊ) *adv.* within the womb.

in+u·tile (ɪnˈjuːtaɪl) *adj. Rare.* useless; unprofitable. —**in+ˈu·tile+ly** *adv.* —**ˌin+u·ˈtil+i·ty** *n.*

inv. *abbrev. for:* **1.** invented. **2.** invention. **3.** inventor. **4.** invoice.

in va+cu·o *Latin.* (ɪn ˈvækjʊˌəʊ) *adv.* **1.** in a vacuum. **2.** in isolation; without reference to facts or evidence.

in+vade (ɪnˈveɪd) *vb.* **1.** to enter (a country, territory, etc.) by military force. **2.** (*tr.*) to occupy in large numbers; overrun; infest. **3.** (*tr.*) to trespass or encroach upon (privacy, etc.). **4.** (*tr.*) to enter and spread throughout, esp. harmfully; pervade. **5.** (of plants, esp. weeds) to become established in (a place to which they are not native). [C15: from Latin *invādere,* from *vādere* to go] —**in+ˈvad+a·ble** *adj.* —**in+ˈvad+er** *n.*

in+vag·i+nate *vb.* (ɪnˈvædʒɪˌneɪt). **1.** *Pathol.* to push one section of (a tubular organ or part) back into itself so that it becomes ensheathed; intussuscept. **2.** (*intr.*) (of the outer layer of an organism or part) to undergo invagination. ~*adj.* (ɪnˈvædʒɪnɪt, -ˌneɪt). **3.** (of an organ or part) folded back upon itself. [C19: from Medieval Latin *invāgināre,* from Latin IN-[2] + *vāgīna* sheath] —**in+ˈvag·i+na·ble** *adj.*

in+vag·i+na+tion (ɪnˌvædʒɪˈneɪʃən) *n.* **1.** *Pathol.* the process of invaginating or the condition of being invaginated; intussusception. **2.** *Pathol.* an invaginated organ or part. **3.** an infolding of the outer layer of cells of an organism or part of an organism so as to form a pocket in the surface, as in the embryonic development of a gastrula from a blastula.

in+va+lid[1] (ˈɪnvəˌliːd, -lɪd) *n.* **1. a.** a person suffering from disablement or chronic ill health. **b.** (*as modifier*): *an invalid chair.* ~*adj.* **2.** suffering from or disabled by injury, sickness, etc. ~*vb.* (*tr.*) **3.** to cause to become an invalid; disable. **4.** (usually foll. by *out; often passive*) *Chiefly Brit.* to require (a member of the armed forces) to retire from active service through wounds or illness. [C17: from Latin *invalidus* infirm, from IN-[1] + *validus* strong]

in+val+id[2] (ɪnˈvælɪd) *adj.* **1.** not valid; having no cogency or legal force. **2.** *Logic.* having a conclusion that does not necessarily follow from its premisses and that can be true if one or more premisses are false; not valid. [C16: from Medieval Latin *invalidus* without legal force; see INVALID[1]] —**in+va+lid+i·ty** (ˌɪnvəˈlɪdɪtɪ) *or* **in+ˈval+id+ness** *n.* —**in+ˈval+id+ly** *adv.*

in+val·i+date (ɪnˈvælɪˌdeɪt) *vb.* (*tr.*) **1.** to render weak or ineffective, as an argument. **2.** to take away the legal force or effectiveness of; annul, as a contract. —**in+ˌval·i+ˈda+tion** *n.* —**in+ˈval·i+ˌda+tor** *n.*

in+va+lid+ism (ˈɪnvəlɪˌdɪzəm) *n.* **1.** the state of being an invalid, esp. by reason of ill health. **2.** a state of being abnormally preoccupied with one's physical health.

in+va+lid+i·ty ben+e·fit *n.* (in the British National Insurance scheme) a weekly payment to a person who has been off work through illness for more than six months. Abbrev.: **IVB**

in+val·u+a·ble (ɪnˈvæljʊəbᵊl) *adj.* having great value that is impossible to calculate; priceless. —**in+ˈval·u+a·ble+ness** *n.* —**in+ˈval·u+a·bly** *adv.*

In+var (ɪnˈvɑː) *n. Trademark.* an alloy containing iron (63.8 per cent), nickel (36 per cent), and carbon (0.2 per cent). It has a very low coefficient of expansion and is used for the balance springs of watches, etc. [C20: shortened from INVARIABLE]

in+var·i+a·ble (ɪnˈvɛərɪəbᵊl) *adj.* **1.** not subject to alteration; unchanging. ~*n.* **2.** a mathematical quantity having an unchanging value; a constant. —**in+ˌvar·i+a·ˈbil·i·ty** *or* **in+ˈvar·i+a·ble+ness** *n.* —**in+ˈvar·i+a·bly** *adv.*

in+var·i+ant (ɪnˈvɛərɪənt) *n.* **1.** *Maths.* an entity, quantity, etc., that is unaltered by a particular transformation of coordinates: *a point in space, rather than its coordinates, is an invariant.* ~*adj.* **2.** *Maths.* (of a relationship or a property of a function, configuration, or equation) unaltered by a particular transformation of coordinates. **3.** a rare word for **invariable.** —**in+ˈvar·i+ance** *or* **in+ˈvar·i+an+cy** *n.*

in+va+sion (ɪnˈveɪʒən) *n.* **1.** the act of invading with armed forces. **2.** any encroachment or intrusion: *an invasion of rats.* **3.** the onset or advent of something harmful, esp. of a disease. **4.** the movement of plants to an area to which they are not native. —**in+va+sive** (ɪnˈveɪsɪv) *adj.*

in+vec+tive (ɪnˈvɛktɪv) *n.* **1.** vehement accusation or denunciation, esp. of a bitterly abusive or sarcastic kind.. ~*adj.* **2.** characterized by or using abusive language, bitter sarcasm, etc. [C15: from Late Latin *invectīvus* reproachful, scolding, from Latin *invectus* carried in; see INVEIGH] —**in+ˈvec+tive+ly** *adv.* —**in+ˈvec+tive+ness** *n.*

in+veigh (ɪnˈveɪ) *vb.* (*intr.;* foll. by *against*) to speak with violent or invective language; rail. [C15: from Latin *invehī,* literally: to be carried in, hence, assail physically or verbally, from IN-[2] + *vehī* to be carried, ride] —**in+ˈveigh+er** *n.*

in+vei+gle (ɪnˈviːgᵊl, -ˈveɪ-) *vb.* (*tr.;* often foll. by *into* or an infinitive) to lead (someone into a situation) or persuade (to do something) by cleverness or trickery; cajole: *to inveigle customers into spending more.* [C15: from Old French *avogler* to blind, deceive, from *avogle* blind, from Medieval Latin *ab oculis* without eyes] —**in+ˈvei+gle+ment** *n.* —**in+ˈvei+gler** *n.*

in+vent (ɪnˈvɛnt) *vb.* **1.** to create or devise (new ideas, machines, etc.). **2.** to make up (falsehoods, etc.); fabricate. [C15: from Latin *invenīre* to find, come upon, from IN-[2] + *venīre* to come] —**in+ˈvent+i·ble** *or* **in+ˈvent+a·ble** *adj.*

in+ven+tion (ɪnˈvɛnʃən) *n.* **1.** the act or process of inventing. **2.** something that is invented. **3.** *Patent law.* the discovery or production of some new or improved process or machine that is both useful and is not obvious to persons skilled in the particular field. **4.** creative power or ability; inventive skill. **5.** *Euphemistic.* a fabrication; lie. **6.** (in traditional rhetoric) one of the five steps in preparing a speech or discourse: the process of finding suitable topics on which to talk or write. **7.** *Music.* a short piece consisting of two or three parts usually in imitative counterpoint. **8.** *Sociol.* the creation of a new cultural pattern or trait. —**in+ˈven+tion+al** *adj.* —**in+ˈven+tion+less** *adj.*

in+ven+tive (ɪnˈvɛntɪv) *adj.* **1.** skilled or quick at contriving; ingenious; resourceful. **2.** characterized by inventive skill: *an inventive programme of work.* **3.** of or relating to invention. —**in+ˈven+tive+ly** *adv.* —**in+ˈven+tive+ness** *n.*

in+ven+tor (ɪnˈvɛntə) *n.* a person who invents, esp. as a profession. —**in+ˈven+tress** *fem. n.*

in+ven+to·ry (ˈɪnvəntərɪ, -trɪ) *n.* **1.** a detailed list of articles, goods, property, etc. **2.** (*often pl.*) *Accounting, chiefly U.S.* **a.** the amount or value of a firm's current assets that consist of raw materials, work in progress, and finished goods; stock. **b.** such assets individually. ~*vb.* **3.** (*tr.*) to enter (items) in an inventory; make a list of. [C16: from Medieval Latin *inventōrium;* see INVENT] —**ˈin+ven+to+ri+a·ble** *adj.* —**ˌin+ven+ˈto+ri+al** *adj.* —**ˌin+ven+ˈto+ri+al+ly** *adv.*

in+ve+rac+i·ty (ˌɪnvəˈræsɪtɪ) *n., pl.* **·ties.** *Formal or euphemistic.* **1.** lying; untruthfulness. **2.** an untruth; lie.

In+ver+car+gill (ˌɪnvəˈkɑːgɪl) *n.* a city in New Zealand, on South Island: regional trading centre for sheep and agricultural products. Pop.: 47 098 (1971).

In+ver+ness (ˌɪnvəˈnɛs) *n.* **1.** a town in NE Scotland, in the Highland region: tourism and specialized engineering. Pop.: 34 870 (1971). **2.** (until 1975) a county of N Scotland, now part of the Highland region.

in+verse (ɪnˈvɜːs, ˈɪnvɜːs) *adj.* **1.** opposite or contrary in effect, sequence, direction, etc. **2.** *Maths.* **a.** (of a relationship) containing two variables such that an increase in one results in a decrease in the other: *the volume of a gas is in inverse ratio to its pressure.* **b.** (of an element) operating on a specified member of a set to produce the identity of the set: *the additive inverse element of x is –x, the multiplicative inverse element of x is 1/x.* **3.** (*usually prenominal*) upside down; inverted: *in an inverse position.* ~*n.* **4.** *Maths.* **a.** another name for **reciprocal** (sense 6). **b.** an inverse element. [C17: from Latin *inversus,* from *invertere* to INVERT] —**in+ˈverse+ly** *adv.*

in+verse func+tion *n.* a function whose independent variable is the dependent variable of a given trigonometric or hyperbolic function: *the inverse function of* sin *x* is arcsin *y* (*also written* $\sin^{-1}y$).

in+ver+sion (ɪnˈvɜːʃən) *n.* **1.** the act of inverting or state of being inverted. **2.** something inverted, esp. a reversal of order, mutual functions, etc.: *an inversion of their previous relationship.* **3.** Also called: **anastrophe.** *Rhetoric.* the reversal of a normal order of words. **4.** *Chem.* **a.** the conversion of a dextrorotatory solution of sucrose into a laevorotatory solution of glucose and fructose by hydrolysis. **b.** any similar reaction in which the optical properties of the reactants are opposite to those of the products. **5.** *Music.* **a.** the process or result of transposing the notes of a chord (esp. a triad) such that the root, originally in the bass, is placed in an upper part. When the bass note is the third of the triad, the resulting chord is the **first inversion;** when it is the fifth, the resulting chord is the **second inversion.** See also **root position. b.** (in counterpoint) the modification of a melody or part in which all ascending intervals are replaced by corresponding descending intervals and vice versa. **c.** the modification of an interval in which the higher note becomes the lower or the lower one the higher. See **complement** (sense 8). **6.** *Pathol.* abnormal positioning of an organ or part, as in being upside down or turned inside out. **7.** *Psychiatry.* **a.** the adoption of the role or characteristics of the opposite sex. **b.** another word for **homosexuality. 8.** *Meteorol.* an abnormal condition in which the layer of air next to the earth's surface is cooler than an overlying layer. **9.** *Anatomy or phonetics.* another word for **retroflexion** (sense 2). **10.** Also called: **negation.** *Computer technol.* an operation by which each digit of a binary number is changed to the alternative digit, as *10110* to *01001.* **11.** *Genetics.* a type of chromosomal mutation in which a section of a chromosome, and hence the order of its genes, is reversed. —**in+ˈver+sive** *adj.*

in+vert *vb.* (ɪnˈvɜːt). **1.** to turn or cause to turn upside down or inside out. **2.** (*tr.*) to reverse in effect, sequence, direction, etc. **3.** (*tr.*) *Phonetics.* **a.** to turn (the tip of the tongue) up and back. **b.** to pronounce (a speech sound) by retroflexion. ~*n.* (ˈɪnvɜːt). **4.** *Psychiatry.* **a.** a person who adopts the role of the opposite sex. **b.** another word for **homosexual. 5.** *Architect.* **a.** the lower inner surface of a drain, sewer, etc. Compare **soffit** (sense 2). **b.** an arch that is concave upwards, esp. one used in foundations. [C16: from Latin *invertere,* from IN-[2] + *vertere* to turn] —**in+ˈvert+i·ble** *adj.* —**in+ˌvert+i·ˈbil+i·ty** *n.*

in+vert+ase (ɪnˈvɜːteɪz) *n.* an enzyme, occurring in the intestinal juice of animals and in yeasts, that hydrolyses sucrose to glucose and fructose. Also called: **saccharase.**

in+ver+te·brate (ɪnˈvɜːtɪbrɪt, -ˌbreɪt) *n.* **1.** any animal lacking a backbone, including all species not classified as vertebrates. ~*adj. also* **in+ver+te·bral. 2.** of, relating to, or designating invertebrates.

in+vert+ed com+ma *or* **turned com+ma** *n.* another term for **quotation mark.**

in+vert+ed mor+dent *n. Music.* a melodic ornament consisting of the rapid single or double alternation of a principal note with a note one degree higher. Also called: **upper mordent.** See also **pralltriller.**

in+vert+ed pleat *n. Dressmaking.* a box pleat reversed so that the fullness of the material is turned inwards.

in+vert+ed snob *n.* a person who scorns the conventions or attitudes of his own class or social group by attempting to identify with people of a supposedly lower class.

in+vert+er *or* **in+ver+tor** (ɪnˈvɜːtə) *n.* **1.** any device for converting a direct current into an alternating current. **2.** *Computer technol.* another name for **NOT circuit.**

in+vert sug+ar *n.* a mixture of fructose and glucose obtained by the inversion of sucrose.

in+vest (ɪnˈvɛst) *vb.* **1.** (often foll. by *in*) to lay out (money or capital in an enterprise, esp. by purchasing shares) with the expectation of profit. **2.** (*tr.;* often foll. by *in*) to devote (effort, resources, etc., to a project). **3.** (*tr.;* often foll. by *in* or *with*) *Archaic or ceremonial.* to clothe or adorn (in some garment, esp. the robes of an office): *to invest a king in the insignia of an emperor.* **4.** (*tr.;* often foll. by *in*) to install formally or ceremoniously (in an official position, rank, etc.). **5.** (*tr.;* foll. by *in* or *with*) to place (power, authority, etc., in) or provide (with power or authority): *to invest new rights in the monarchy.* **6.** (*tr.; usually passive;* foll. by *in* or *with*) to provide or endow (a person with qualities, characteristics, etc.): *he was invested with great common sense.* **7.** (*tr.;* foll. by *with*) *Usually poetic.* to cover or adorn, as if with a coat or garment: *when spring invests the trees with leaves.* **8.** (*tr.*) *Rare.* to surround with military forces; besiege. **9.** (*intr.,* foll. by *in*) *Informal.* to purchase; buy. [C16: from Medieval Latin *investīre* to clothe, from Latin, from *vestīre,* from *vestis* a garment] —**in+ˈvest+a·ble** *or* **in+ˈvest+i·ble** *adj.* —**in+ˈves+tor** *n.*

in+ves+ti+gate (ɪnˈvɛstɪˌgeɪt) *vb.* to inquire into (a situation or problem, esp. a crime or death) thoroughly; examine systematically, esp. in order to discover the truth. [C16: from Latin *investīgāre* to search after, from IN-[2] + *vestīgium* track; see VESTIGE] —**in+ˈves+ti+ga·ble** *adj.* —**in+ˈves+ti+ˌga·tive** *or* **in+ˈves+ti+ga+to·ry** *adj.*

in+ves+ti+ga·tion (ɪnˌvɛstɪˈgeɪʃən) *n.* the act or process of investigating; a careful search or examination in order to discover facts, etc. —**in+ˌves+ti+ˈga·tion+al** *adj.*

in+ves+ti+ga·tor (ɪnˈvɛstɪˌgeɪtə) *n.* a person who investigates, such as a private detective.

in+ves+ti+ture (ɪnˈvɛstɪtʃə) *n.* **1.** the act of presenting with a title or with the robes and insignia of an office or rank. **2.** (in feudal society) the formal bestowal of the possessory right to a fief or other benefice. **3.** a less common word for **investment** (sense 5). —**in+ˈves+ti+tive** *adj.*

in+vest+ment (ɪnˈvɛstmənt) *n.* **1. a.** the act of investing money. **b.** the amount invested. **c.** an enterprise, asset, etc., in which money is or can be invested. **2.** *Biology.* the outer layer or covering of an organ, part, or organism. **3.** a less common word for **investiture** (sense 1). **4.** the act of investing or state of being invested, as with an official robe, specific quality, etc. **5.** *Rare.* the act of besieging with military forces, works, etc.

in+vest+ment trust *n.* a financial enterprise that invests its subscribed capital in securities for its investors' benefit.

in+vet+er+ate (ɪnˈvɛtərɪt) *adj.* **1.** long established, esp. so as to be deep-rooted or ingrained: *an inveterate feeling of hostility.* **2.** (*prenominal*) settled or confirmed in a habit or practice, esp. a bad one; hardened: *an inveterate smoker.* **3.** *Obsolete.* full of hatred; hostile. [C16: from Latin *inveterātus* of long standing, from *inveterāre* to make old, from IN-[2] + *vetus* old] —**in+ˈvet+er·a·cy** *or* **in+ˈvet+er+ate+ness** *n.* —**in+ˈvet+er+ate+ly** *adv.*

in+vi+a·ble (ɪnˈvaɪəbᵊl) *adj.* not viable, esp. financially; not able to survive: *an inviable company.* —**in+ˌvi+a·ˈbil+i·ty** *or* **in+ˈvi+a·ble+ness** *n.* —**in+ˈvi+a·bly** *adv.*

in+vid·i·ous (ɪnˈvɪdɪəs) *adj.* **1.** incurring or tending to arouse resentment, unpopularity, etc.: *an invidious task.* **2.** (of comparisons or distinctions) unfairly or offensively discriminating. **3.** *Obsolete.* grudging; envious. [C17: from Latin *invidiōsus* full of envy, from *invidia* ENVY] —**in+ˈvid·i·ous+ly** *adv.* —**in+ˈvid·i·ous+ness** *n.*

in+vig·i+late (ɪnˈvɪdʒɪˌleɪt) *vb.* (*intr.*) **1.** *Brit.* to watch examination candidates, esp. to prevent cheating. U.S. word: **proctor. 2.** *Archaic.* to keep watch. [C16: from Latin *invigilāre* to watch over, from IN-[2] + *vigilāre* to keep watch; see VIGIL] —**in+ˌvig·i+ˈla+tion** *n.* —**in+ˈvig·i+ˌla+tor** *n.*

in+vig+or+ate (ɪnˈvɪgəˌreɪt) *vb.* (*tr.*) to give vitality and vigour to; animate; brace; refresh: *to be invigorated by fresh air.* [C17: from IN-[2] + Latin *vigor* VIGOUR] —**in+ˈvig+or+ˌat+ing+ly** *adv.* —**in+ˌvig+or·ˈa+tion** *n.* —**in+ˈvig+or·a+tive** *adj.* —**in+ˈvig+or·a+tive+ly** *adv.* —**in+ˈvig+or·ˌa+tor** *n.*

in+vin+ci·ble (ɪnˈvɪnsəbᵊl) *adj.* **1.** incapable of being defeated; unconquerable. **2.** unable to be overcome; insuperable: *invincible prejudices.* [C15: from Late Latin *invincibilis,* from Latin IN-[1] + *vincere* to conquer] —**in+ˌvin+ci·ˈbil+i·ty** *or* **in+ˈvin+ci·ble+ness** *n.* —**in+ˈvin+ci·bly** *adv.*

in vi·no ve·ri·tas *Latin.* (ɪn ˈviːnəʊ ˈvɛrɪˌtæs) in wine there is truth; people speak the truth when they are drunk.

in+vi·o·la·ble (ɪnˈvaɪələbᵊl) *adj.* that must not or cannot be transgressed, dishonoured, or broken; to be kept sacred: *an inviolable oath.* —**in+ˌvi·o+la·ˈbil+i·ty** *or* **in+ˈvi·o+la·ble+ness** *n.* —**in+ˈvi·o+la·bly** *adv.*

in+vi·o·late (ɪnˈvaɪəlɪt, -ˌleɪt) *adj.* **1.** free from violation, injury, disturbance, etc. **2.** a less common word for **inviolable.** —**in+ˈvi·o+la+cy** *or* **in+ˈvi·o+late+ness** *n.* —**in+ˈvi·o+late+ly** *adv.*

in+vis+i·ble (ɪnˈvɪzəbᵊl) *adj.* **1.** not visible; not able to be perceived by the eye: *invisible rays.* **2.** concealed from sight; hidden. **3.** not easily seen or noticed: *invisible mending.* **4.** kept hidden from public view; secret; clandestine. **5.** *Economics.* of or relating to services rather than goods in relation to the invisible balance: *invisible earnings.* ~*n.* **6.** *Economics.* an invisible item of trade; service. —**in+ˌvis+i·ˈbil+i·ty** *or* **in+ˈvis+i·ble+ness** *n.* —**in+ˈvis+i·bly** *adv.*

in+vis+i·ble bal+ance *n. Economics.* the difference in value between total exports of services plus payment of property incomes from abroad and total imports of services plus payment abroad of property incomes. Compare **balance of trade.**

in+vis+i·ble ink *n.* a liquid used for writing that does not become visible until it has been treated with chemicals, heat, ultraviolet light, etc.

in+vi+ta+tion (ˌɪnvɪˈteɪʃən) *n.* **1. a.** the act of inviting, such as an offer of entertainment or hospitality. **b.** (*as modifier*): *an invitation dance; an invitation race.* **2.** the act of enticing or attracting; allurement.

in+vi+ta+to·ry (ɪnˈvaɪtətərɪ, -trɪ) *adj.* **1.** serving as or conveying an invitation. ~*n.* **2.** any of various invitations to prayer, such as Psalm 95 in a religious service.

in+vite *vb.* (ɪnˈvaɪt). (*tr.*) **1.** to ask (a person or persons) in a friendly or polite way (to do something, attend an event, etc.): *he invited them to dinner.* **2.** to make a request for, esp. publicly or formally: *to invite applications.* **3.** to bring on or provoke; give occasion for: *you invite disaster by your actions.* **4.** to welcome or tempt. ~*n.* (ˈɪnvaɪt). **5.** an informal word for **invitation.** [C16: from Latin *invītāre* to invite, entertain, from IN-[2] + *-vītāre,* probably related to Greek *hiesthai* to be desirous of] —**in+ˈvit+er** *n.*

in+vit+ing (ɪnˈvaɪtɪŋ) *adj.* tempting; alluring; attractive. —**in+ˈvit+ing+ly** *adv.* —**in+ˈvit+ing+ness** *n.*

in vi+tro (ɪn ˈviːtrəʊ) *adv., adj.* (of biological processes or reactions) made to occur outside the body of the organism in an artificial environment. [New Latin, literally: in glass]

in vi·vo (ɪn ˈviːvəʊ) *adv., adj.* (of biological processes or experiments) occurring or carried out in the living organism. [New Latin, literally: in a living (thing)]

in+vo+cate (ˈɪnvəˌkeɪt) *vb.* an archaic word for **invoke.** —**in+voc·a+tive** (ɪnˈvɒkətɪv) *adj.* —**ˈin+vo+ˌca+tor** *n.*

in+vo+ca+tion (ˌɪnvəˈkeɪʃən) *n.* **1.** the act of invoking or calling upon some agent for assistance. **2.** a prayer asking God for help, forgiveness, etc., esp. as part of a religious service. **3.** an appeal for inspiration and guidance from a Muse or deity at the beginning of a poem. **4. a.** the act of summoning a spirit or demon from another world by ritual incantation or magic. **b.** the incantation used in this act. —**ˌin+vo+ˈca+tion+al** *adj.* —**in+voc·a·to·ry** (ɪnˈvɒkətərɪ, -trɪ) *adj.*

in+voice (ˈɪnvɔɪs) *n.* **1.** a document issued by a seller to a buyer listing the goods or services supplied and stating the sum of money due. **2.** *Rare.* a consignment of invoiced merchandise. ~*vb.* **3.** (*tr.*) **a.** to present (a customer, etc.) with an invoice. **b.** to list (merchandise sold) on an invoice. [C16: from earlier *invoyes,* from Old French *envois,* plural of *envoi* message; see ENVOY]

in+voke (ɪnˈvəʊk) *vb.* (*tr.*) **1.** to call upon (an agent, esp. God or another deity) for help, inspiration, etc. **2.** to appeal to (an outside agent or authority) for confirmation, corroboration, etc. **3.** to implore or beg (help, etc.). **4.** to summon (a spirit, demon, etc.); conjure up. [C15: from Latin *invocāre* to call upon, appeal to, from *vocāre* to call] —**in+ˈvo+ca·ble** *adj.* —**in+ˈvok+er** *n.*

in+vol·u·cel (ɪnˈvɒljʊˌsɛl) *or* **in+vol·u·cel+lum** (ɪnˌvɒljʊˈsɛləm) *n., pl.* **+cels** *or* **+cel+la** (-ˈsɛlə). a ring of bracts at the base of the florets of a compound umbel. [C19: from New Latin *involūcellum* a little cover; see INVOLUCRE] —**in+ˌvol·u·ˈcel+ate** *or* **in+ˌvol·u·ˈcel+at+ed** *adj.*

in+vo+lu+cre (ˈɪnvəˌluːkə) *or* **in+vo+lu+crum** (ˌɪnvəˈluːkrəm) *n., pl.* **+cres** *or* **+cra** (-krə). a ring of bracts at the base of an inflorescence in such plants as the *Compositae.* [C16 (in the sense: envelope): from New Latin *involucrum,* from Latin: wrapper, from *involvere* to wrap; see INVOLVE] —**ˌin+vo+ˈlu+cral** *adj.* —**ˌin+vo+ˈlu+crate** *adj.*

in+vol+un+tar·y (ɪnˈvɒləntərɪ, -trɪ) *adj.* **1.** carried out without one's conscious wishes; not voluntary; unintentional. **2.** *Physiol.* (esp. of a movement or muscle) performed or acting without conscious control. —**in+'vol+un+tar·i·ly** *adv.* —**in+'vol+un+tar·i+ness** *n.*

in+vo+lute *adj.* ('ɪnvə,luːt), *also* **in+vo+lut+ed. 1.** complex, intricate, or involved. **2.** *Botany.* (esp. of petals, leaves, etc., in bud) having margins that are rolled inwards. **3.** (of certain shells) closely coiled so that the axis is obscured. ~*n.* ('ɪnvə,luːt). **4.** *Geom.* the curve described by the free end of a thread as it is wound around another curve, the **evolute,** such that its normals are tangential to the evolute. ~*vb.* (,ɪnvə'luːt). **5.** (*intr.*) to become involute. [C17: from Latin *involūtus,* from *involvere;* see INVOLVE] —**'in+vo+,lute+ly** *adv.* —**'in+vo+,lut+ed+ly** *adv.*

in+vo+lu+tion (,ɪnvə'luːʃən) *n.* **1.** the act of involving or complicating or the state of being involved or complicated. **2.** something involved or complicated. **3.** *Zoology.* degeneration or structural deformation. **4.** *Biology.* an involute formation or structure. **5.** *Physiol.* reduction in size of an organ or part, as of the uterus following childbirth or as a result of ageing. **6.** an algebraic operation in which a number, variable, expression etc., is raised to a specified power. Compare **evolution** (sense 5). **7.** *Grammar.* an involved construction, such as one in which the subject is separated from the predicate by an additional clause. —**,in+vo+'lu+tion+al** *adj.*

in+volve (ɪn'vɒlv) *vb.* (*tr.*) **1.** to include or contain as a necessary part: *the task involves hard work.* **2.** to have an effect on; spread to: *the investigation involved many innocent people.* **3.** (*often passive;* usually foll. by *in* or *with*) to concern or associate significantly: *many people were involved in the crime.* **4.** (*often passive*) to make complicated; tangle: *the situation was further involved by her disappearance.* **5.** *Rare, often poetic.* to wrap or surround. **6.** *Archaic.* to coil up. **7.** *Maths., obsolete.* to raise to a specified power. [C14: from Latin *involvere* to roll in, surround, from IN-[2] + *volvere* to roll] —**in+'volve+ment** *n.* —**in+'volv+er** *n.*

in+volved (ɪn'vɒlvd) *adj.* **1.** complicated; difficult to comprehend: *an involved literary style.* **2.** (*usually postpositive*) concerned or implicated: *one of the men involved.* **3.** (*postpositive;* foll. by *with*) *Euphemistic.* having sexual relations: *she was involved with a number of men.*

invt. *or* **invty.** *abbrev. for* inventory.

in+vul+ner+a·ble (ɪn'vʌlnərəbᵊl, -vʌnrəbᵊl) *adj.* **1.** incapable of being wounded, hurt, damaged, etc., either physically or emotionally. **2.** incapable of being damaged or captured: *an invulnerable fortress.* —**in+,vul+ner+a·'bil+i·ty** *or* **in+'vul+ner+a·ble+ness** *n.* —**in+'vul+ner+a·bly** *adv.*

in+vul+tu·a·tion (ɪn,vʌltʃʊ'eɪʃən) *n.* the use of or the act of making images of people, animals, etc., for witchcraft. [C19: from Medieval Latin *invultuāre* to make a likeness, from IN-[2] + *vultus* likeness]

in+ward ('ɪnwəd) *adj.* **1.** going or directed towards the middle of or into something. **2.** situated within; inside. **3.** of, relating to, or existing in the mind or spirit: *inward meditation.* ~*adv.* **4.** a variant of **inwards.** ~*n.* **5.** the inward part; inside. —**'in+ward+ness** *n.*

in+ward+ly ('ɪnwədlɪ) *adv.* **1.** within the private thoughts or feelings; secretly: *inwardly troubled, he kept smiling.* **2.** not aloud: *to laugh inwardly.* **3.** with reference to the inside or inner part; internally. **4.** *Archaic.* intimately; essentially: *the most inwardly concerned of the plotters.*

in+wards *adv.* ('ɪnwədz), *also* **in+ward. 1.** towards the interior or middle of something. **2.** in, into, or towards the mind or spirit. ~*pl. n.* ('ɪnədz). **3.** a variant of **innards.**

in+weave (ɪn'wiːv) *vb.* **+weaves, +weav+ing, +wove** *or* **+weaved; +wo+ven** *or* **+weaved.** (*tr.*) to weave together into or as if into a design, fabric, etc.; interweave.

in+wrap (ɪn'ræp) *vb.* **+wraps, +wrap+ping, +wrapped.** a less common spelling of **enwrap.**

in+wrought (,ɪn'rɔːt) *adj.* **1.** worked or woven into material, esp. decoratively. **2.** *Rare.* blended with other things.

in+ya+la (ɪn'jɑːlə) *n.* another name for **nyala.**

I·o[1] ('aɪəʊ) *n. Greek myth.* a maiden loved by Zeus and turned into a white heifer by either Zeus or Hera.

I·o[2] ('aɪəʊ) *n.* the third largest of the twelve satellites of Jupiter and the second nearest to the planet.

I/O *abbrev. for* input/output.

Io·án+ni+na (*Greek* jɔ'anina) *or* **Ya+ni+na** *n.* a city in NW Greece: belonged to the Serbs (1349–1430) and then the Turks (until 1913); seat of Ali Pasha, the "Lion of Janina," from 1788 to 1822. Pop.: 40 130 (1971). Serbian name: **Janina.**

i·o·date ('aɪə,deɪt) *n.* **1.** a salt of iodic acid. ~*vb.* **2.** (*tr.*) another word for **iodize.** —**,i·o·'da+tion** *n.*

i·od+ic (aɪ'ɒdɪk) *adj.* of or containing iodine, esp. in the pentavalent state.

i·od+ic ac·id *n.* a colourless or pale yellow soluble crystalline substance that forms acidic aqueous solutions. Used as a reagent and disinfectant. Formula: HIO_3.

i·o·dide ('aɪə,daɪd) *n.* **1.** a salt of hydriodic acid, containing the iodide ion, I^-. **2.** a compound containing an iodine atom, such as methyl iodide, CH_3I.

i·o·dine ('aɪə,diːn) *n.* a bluish-black element of the halogen group that sublimates into a violet irritating gas. Its compounds are used in medicine and photography and in dyes. The radioisotope **iodine-131 (radioiodine),** with a half-life of 8 days, is used in the diagnosis and treatment of thyroid disease. Symbol: I; atomic no.: 53; atomic wt.: 126.90; valency: 1,3,5, or 7; relative density: 4.93; melting pt.: 113.5°C; boiling pt.: 184.35°C. [C19: from French *iode,* from Greek *iōdēs* rust-coloured, but taken to mean violet-coloured, through a mistaken derivation from *ion* violet]

i·o·dism ('aɪə,dɪzəm) *n.* poisoning induced by ingestion of iodine or its compounds.

i·o·dize *or* **i·o·dise** ('aɪə,daɪz) *vb.* (*tr.*) to treat or react with iodine or an iodine compound. Also: **iodate.** —**,i·o·di+'za+tion** *or* **,i·o·di+'sa+tion** *n.* —**'i·o·,diz+er** *or* **'i·o·,dis+er** *n.*

i·o·do- *or before a vowel* **i·od-** *combining form.* indicating iodine: *iodoform; iodism.*

i·o·do+form (aɪ'ɒdə,fɔːm) *n.* a yellow crystalline insoluble volatile solid with a penetrating sweet odour made by heating alcohol with iodine and an alkali: used as an antiseptic. Formula: CHI_3. Also called: **triiodomethane.**

i·o·dom+e·try (,aɪə'dɒmɪtrɪ) *n. Chem.* a procedure used in volumetric analysis for determining the quantity of substance present that contains, liberates, or reacts with iodine. —**i·o·do+met+ric** (,aɪədəʊ'mɛtrɪk) *or* **,i·o·do+'met+ri+cal** *adj.* —**,i·o·do+'met+ri+cal+ly** *adv.*

i·o·dop+sin (,aɪə'dɒpsɪn) *n.* a violet light-sensitive pigment in the cones of the retina of the eye. Also called: **visual violet.** See also **rhodopsin.**

i·o·dous (aɪ'ɒdəs) *adj.* **1.** of or containing iodine, esp. in the trivalent state. **2.** concerned with or resembling iodine.

i·o·lite ('aɪə,laɪt) *n.* another name for **cordierite.** [C19: from Greek *ion* a violet + -LITE]

I.O.M. *abbrev. for* Isle of Man.

I·o moth *n.* an American saturniid moth, *Automeris io,* bright yellow with a blue-and-pink eyelike spot on each of the hindwings. [C19: after *Io* (who was tormented by a gadfly), referring to the sting of the larva]

i·on ('aɪən, -ɒn) *n.* an electrically charged atom or group of atoms formed by the loss or gain of one or more electrons. See also **cation, anion.** [C19: from Greek, literally: going, from *ienai* to go]

-ion *suffix forming nouns.* indicating an action, process, or state: *creation; objection.* Compare **-ation, -tion.** [from Latin *-iōn-, -io*]

I·o+na (aɪ'əʊnə) *n.* an island off the W coast of Scotland, in the Inner Hebrides: site of St. Columba's monastery (founded in 563) and an important early centre of Christianity. Area: 854 ha (2112 acres).

i·on en+gine *n.* a type of rocket engine in which thrust is obtained by the electrostatic acceleration of charged positive ions. Compare **plasma engine.**

I·o·nes·co (,iːə'nɛskəʊ; *French* jɔnɛs'ko) *n.* **Eu·gène** (ø'ʒɛn). born 1912, French dramatist, born in Rumania; a leading exponent of the theatre of the absurd. His plays include *The Bald Prima Donna* (1950) and *Rhinoceros* (1960).

i·on ex+change *n.* the process in which ions are exchanged between a solution and an insoluble solid, usually a resin. It is used to soften water, to separate radioactive isotopes, and to purify certain industrial chemicals.

I·o·ni·a (aɪ'əʊnɪə) *n.* an ancient region of W central Asia Minor, including adjacent Aegean islands: colonized by Greeks in about 1100 B.C.

I·o·ni·an (aɪ'əʊnɪən) *n.* **1.** a member of a Hellenic people who settled in Attica in about 1100 B.C. and later colonized the islands and E coast of the Aegean Sea. ~*adj.* **2.** of or relating to this people or their dialect of Ancient Greek; Ionic. **3.** of or relating to Ionia. **4.** *Music.* relating to or denoting an authentic mode represented by the ascending natural diatonic scale from C to C and forming the basis of the modern major key. See also **Hypo-.**

I·o·ni·an Is+lands *pl. n.* a group of Greek islands in the Ionian Sea, consisting of Corfu, Cephalonia, Zante, Levkas, Ithaca, Cythera, and Paxos: ceded to Greece in 1864. Pop.: 184 443 (1971). Area: 2307 sq. km (891 sq. miles).

I·o·ni·an Sea *n.* the part of the Mediterranean Sea between SE Italy, E Sicily, and Greece.

i·on+ic (aɪ'ɒnɪk) *adj.* of, relating to, or occurring in the form of ions.

I·on+ic (aɪ'ɒnɪk) *adj.* **1.** of, denoting, or relating to one of the five classical orders of architecture, characterized by fluted columns and capitals with scroll-like ornaments. See also **Doric, Composite, Tuscan, Corinthian. 2.** of or relating to Ionia, its inhabitants, or their dialect of Ancient Greek. **3.** *Prosody.* of, relating to, designating, or employing Ionics in verse. ~*n.* **4.** one of four chief dialects of Ancient Greek; the dialect spoken in Ionia. Compare **Aeolic, Arcadic, Doric. 5.** (in classical prosody) a type of metrical foot having either two long followed by two short syllables (**greater Ionic**), or two short followed by two long syllables (**lesser Ionic**).

i·on+ic bond *n.* another name for **electrovalent bond.**

i·o·ni·um (aɪ'əʊnɪəm) *n. Obsolete.* a naturally occurring radioisotope of thorium with a mass number of 230. Symbol: Io. [C20: from New Latin, from ION + -IUM]

i·on·i+za+tion *or* **i·on·i+sa+tion** (,aɪənaɪ'zeɪʃən) *n.* **a.** the formation of ions as a result of a chemical reaction, heat, electrical discharge, or radiation. **b.** (*as modifier*): *ionization temperature; ionization current.*

i·on·i+za+tion cham+ber *n.* a device for detecting and measuring ionizing radiation, consisting of a tube containing a low pressure gas and two electrodes between which a high voltage is maintained. The current between the electrodes is a function of the intensity of the radiation.

i·on·i+za+tion po+ten+tial *n.* the energy required to remove an electron from an atom, molecule, or radical, measured in electronvolts. Symbol: *I* Compare **electron affinity.**

i·on+ize *or* **i·on+ise** ('aɪəˌnaɪz) *vb.* to change or become changed into ions. —**'i·on+ˌiz+a·ble** *or* **'i·on+ˌis+a·ble** *adj.*

i·on+iz+ing ra+di+a+tion *n.* electromagnetic or corpuscular radiation that is able to cause ionization.

i·o·none ('aɪəˌnəʊn) *n.* **1.** a yellowish liquid mixture of two isomers with an odour of violets, extracted from certain plants and used in perfumery. **2.** either of these two isomers. Formula: $C_{13}H_{20}O$.

i·on·o+pause (aɪ'ɒnəˌpɔːz) *n.* the transitional zone in the atmosphere between the ionosphere and the exosphere, about 644 km (400 miles) from the earth's surface.

i·on·o+sphere (aɪ'ɒnəˌsfɪə) *n.* a region of the earth's atmosphere, extending from about 60 kilometres to 1000 km above the earth's surface, in which there is a high concentration of free electrons formed as a result of ionizing radiation entering the atmosphere from space. See also **D region, E region, F region.** —**i·on·o+spher+ic** (aɪˌɒnə'sfɛrɪk) *adj.*

i·on·o+spher+ic wave *n.* another name for **sky wave.**

i·on rock+et *n.* a rocket propelled by an ion engine.

i·on+to+pho+re·sis (aɪˌɒntəʊfə'riːsɪs) *n. Biochem.* a technique for studying neurotransmitters in the brain by the application of experimental solutions to the tissues through fine glass electrodes. [C20: from Greek *iont-, ion,* from *ienai* to go + -PHORESIS]

I.O.O.F. *abbrev. for* Independent Order of Oddfellows.

i·o·ta (aɪ'əʊtə) *n.* **1.** the ninth letter in the Greek alphabet (Ι, ι), a vowel or semivowel, transliterated as *i* or *j.* **2.** (*usually used with a negative*) a very small amount; jot (esp. in the phrase **not one** *or* **an iota**). [C16: via Latin from Greek, of Semitic origin; see JOT]

i·o·ta+cism (aɪ'əʊtəˌsɪzəm) *n.* a tendency of vowels and diphthongs, esp. in Modern Greek, to acquire the pronunciation of the vowel iota (iː).

IOU *n.* a written promise or reminder to pay a debt. [C17: representing *I owe you*]

-i·ous *suffix forming adjectives from nouns.* characterized by or full of: *ambitious; religious; suspicious.* Compare **-eous.** [from Latin *-ius* and *-iōsus* full of]

I.O.W. *abbrev. for* Isle of Wight.

I·o·wa ('aɪəʊə) *n.* a state of the N central U.S., in the Midwest: consists of rolling plains crossed by many rivers, with the Missouri forming the western border and the Mississippi the eastern. Capital: Des Moines. Pop.: 2 825 041 (1970). Area: 144 887 sq. km (55 941 sq. miles). Abbrevs.: **Ia.** or (with zip code) **IA** —**I·o·wan** ('aɪəʊən) *adj.*

IPA *abbrev. for* International Phonetic Alphabet.

ip+e·cac ('ɪpɪˌkæk) *or* **ip+e·cac·u+an+ha** (ˌɪpɪˌkækjʊ'ænə) *n.* **1.** a low-growing South American rubiaceous shrub, *Cephaelis ipecacuanha.* **2.** a drug prepared from the dried roots of this plant, used as a purgative and emetic. [C18: from Portuguese *ipecacuanha,* from Tupi *ipekaaguéne,* from *ipeh* low + *kaa* leaves + *guéne* vomit]

Iph·i·ge·ni·a (ˌɪfɪdʒɪ'naɪə) *n. Greek myth.* the daughter of Agamemnon, taken by him to be sacrificed to Artemis, who saved her life and made her a priestess.

I·poh ('iːpəʊ) *n.* a city in Malaysia, capital of Perak state: tin-mining centre. Pop.: 247 689 (1970).

ip·o+moe·a (ˌɪpə'mɪə, ˌaɪ-) *n.* **1.** any tropical or subtropical convolvulaceous plant of the genus *Ipomoea,* such as the morning glory, sweet potato, and jalap, having trumpet-shaped flowers. **2.** the dried root of a Mexican species, *I. orizabensis,* which yields a cathartic resin. [C18: New Latin, from Greek *ips* worm + *homoios* like]

Ip+sam+bul (ˌɪpsæm'buːl) *n.* another name for **Abu Simbel.**

ip·se dix+it *Latin.* ('ɪpseɪ 'dɪksɪt) *n.* an arbitrary and unsupported assertion. [C16, literally: he himself said it]

ip·si+lat+er·al (ˌɪpsɪ'lætərəl) *adj.* on or affecting the same side of the body. [C20: irregularly formed from Latin *ipse* self + LATERAL]

ip+sis+si+ma ver+ba *Latin.* (ɪp'sɪsɪmə 'vɜːbə) *pl. n.* the very words; verbatim.

ip·so fac+to ('ɪpsəʊ 'fæktəʊ) *adv.* by that very fact or act: *ipso facto his guilt was apparent.* [from Latin]

ip·so ju·re ('ɪpsəʊ 'jʊərɪ) *adv.* by the law itself; by operation of law. [from Latin]

Ip+sus ('ɪpsəs) *n.* an ancient town in Asia Minor, in S Phrygia: site of a decisive battle (301 B.C.) in the Wars of the Diadochi in which Lysimachus and Seleucus defeated Antigonus and Demetrius.

Ips+wich ('ɪpswɪtʃ) *n.* a town in E England, administrative centre of Suffolk, at the head of the Orwell estuary: manufactures agricultural and industrial machinery. Pop.: 122 814 (1971).

i.q. *abbrev. for* idem quod. [Latin: the same as]

I.Q. *abbrev. for* intelligence quotient.

Iq·bal ('ɪkbal) *n.* **Mu·ham·mad** (mʊ'hæməd). 1875–1938, Indian Muslim poet, philosopher, and political leader, who advocated the establishment of separate nations for Indian Hindus and Muslims and is generally regarded as the originator of Pakistan.

I·qui+que (*Spanish* i'kike) *n.* a port in N Chile: oil refineries. Pop.: 64 340 (1970).

I·qui+tos (*Spanish* i'kitos) *n.* an inland port in NE Peru, on the Amazon 3703 km (2300 miles) from the Atlantic: head of navigation for large steamers. Pop.: 110 242 (1972).

Ir *the chemical symbol for* iridium.

IR *international car registration for* Iran.

Ir. *abbrev. for:* **1.** Ireland. **2.** Irish.

I.R. (in Britain) *abbrev. for* Inland Revenue.

ir- *prefix.* variant of **in-**[1] and **in-**[2] before *r.*

I.R.A. *abbrev. for* Irish Republican Army.

i·ra+cund ('aɪərəˌkʌnd) *adj. Rare.* easily angered. [C19: from Latin *īrācundus,* from *īra* anger] —**ˌi·ra+'cund+i·ty** *n.*

i·ra+de (ɪ'rɑːdɛ) *n.* a written edict of a Muslim rule. [C19: from Turkish: will, desire, from Arabic *irādah*]

I·rá+kli+on (*Greek* i'raklіɔn) *n.* a port in Greece, in N Crete: former capital of Crete (until 1841); ruled by Venetians (13th–17th centuries). Pop.: 78 209 (1971). Italian name: **Candia.** Also called: **Heraklion, Herakleion.**

I·ran (ɪ'rɑːn) *n.* a republic in SW Asia, between the Caspian Sea and the Persian Gulf: consists chiefly of a high central desert plateau almost completely surrounded by mountains, a semitropical fertile region along the Caspian coast, and a hot and dry area beside the Persian Gulf. Oil is the most important export. Language: Iranian. Religion: chiefly Muslim. Currency: rial. Capital: Teheran. Pop.: 25 785 210 (1966). Area: 1 647 050 sq. km (635 932 sq. miles). Former name (until 1935): **Persia.** Official name: **Islamic Republic of Iran.**

Iran. *abbrev. for* Iranian.

I·ra+ni·an (ɪ'reɪnɪən) *n.* **1.** a native, citizen, or inhabitant of Iran. **2.** a branch of the Indo-European family of languages, divided into **West Iranian** (including Old Persian, Pahlavi, modern Persian, Kurdish, Baluchi, and Tadzhiki) and **East Iranian** (including Avestan, Sogdian, Pashto, and Ossetic). **3.** the modern Persian language. ~*adj.* **4.** relating to, denoting, or characteristic of Iran, its inhabitants, or their language; Persian. **5.** belonging to or relating to the Iranian branch of Indo-European.

I·raq (ɪ'rɑːk) *n.* a republic in SW Asia, on the Persian Gulf: coextensive with ancient Mesopotamia; became a British mandate in 1920, independent in 1932, and a republic in 1958. It consists chiefly of the mountains of Kurdistan in the northeast, part of the Syrian Desert, and the lower basin of the Rivers Tigris and Euphrates. Oil is the major export. Official language: Arabic; Kurdish is also spoken. Religion: chiefly Muslim. Currency: dinar. Capital: Baghdad. Pop.: 8 047 415 (1965). Area: 438 446 sq. km (169 284 sq. miles). —**I·ra+qi** (ɪ'rɑːkɪ) *adj., n.*

i·ras+ci·ble (ɪ'ræsɪbᵊl) *adj.* **1.** easily angered; irritable. **2.** showing irritability: *an irascible action.* [C16: from Late Latin *īrascibilis,* from Latin *īra* anger] —**i·ˌras+ci·'bil+i·ty** *or* **i·'ras+ci·ble+ness** *n.* —**i·'ras+ci·bly** *adv.*

i·rate (aɪ'reɪt) *adj.* **1.** incensed with anger; furious. **2.** marked by extreme anger: *an irate letter.* [C19: from Latin *īrātus* enraged, from *īrascī* to be angry] —**i·'rate+ly** *adv.*

Ir+bid ('ɪrbɪd) *n.* a town in NW Jordan. Pop.: 125 000 (1974 est.).

Ir+bil ('ɪəbɪl) *n.* a variant spelling of **Erbil.**

IRBM *abbrev. for* intermediate range ballistic missile.

ire (aɪə) *n. Literary.* anger; wrath. [C13: from Old French, from Latin *īra*] —**'ire+ful** *adj.* —**'ire+ful+ly** *adv.* —**'ire+ful+ness** *n.* —**'ire+less** *adj.*

Ire. *abbrev. for* Ireland.

Ire+land[1] ('aɪələnd) *n.* **1.** an island off NW Europe: part of the British Isles, separated from Britain by the North Channel, the Irish Sea, and St. George's Channel; contains large areas of peat bog, with mountains that rise over 900 m (3000 ft.) in the southwest and several large lakes. It was conquered by England in the 16th and early 17th centuries and ruled as a dependency until 1801, when it was united with Great Britain until its division in 1921 into the Republic of Ireland and Northern Ireland. Latin name: **Hibernia. 2. Republic of.** Also called: **Irish Republic, Southern Ireland.** a republic in NW Europe occupying most of Ireland: established as the Irish Free State (a British dominion) in 1921 and declared a republic in 1949; joined the Common Market in 1973. Languages: English and Gaelic. Currency: Irish pound. Capital: Dublin. Pop.: 3 086 000 (1974 est.). Area: 70 282 sq. km (27 136 sq. miles). Gaelic name: **Eire.** Related adj.: **Hibernian.** ~See also **Northern Ireland.**

Ire·land[2] ('aɪələnd) *n.* **John.** 1879–1962, English composer, esp. of songs.

I·re·ne (aɪ'riːnɪ) *n. Greek myth.* the goddess of peace.

i·ren+ic, ei·ren+ic (aɪ'riːnɪk, -'rɛn-) *or* **i·ren·i·cal, ei·ren·i·cal** *adj. Chiefly theol.* tending to conciliate or promote peace. [C19: from Greek *eirēnikos,* from *eirēnē* peace] —**i·'ren·i·cal+ly** *or* **ei·'ren·i·cal+ly** *adv.*

i·re·ni+con (aɪ'riːnɪˌkɒn) *n.* a variant spelling of **eirenicon.**

i·ren+ics (aɪ'riːnɪks, -'rɛn-) *n.* (*functioning as sing.*) that branch of theology that is concerned with unity between Christian sects and denominations.

Ire·ton ('aɪətᵊn) *n.* **Hen·ry.** 1611–51, English Parliamentarian general in the Civil War; son-in-law of Oliver Cromwell. His plan for a constitutional monarchy was rejected by Charles I (1647), whose death warrant he signed; lord deputy of Ireland (1650–51).

Ir·i+an Bar+at ('ɪərɪən 'bærɑːt) *n.* the former Indonesian name for **West Irian.**

Ir·i+an Ja·ya ('dʒɑːjə) *n.* the Indonesian name for **West Irian.**

ir·i·da+ceous (ˌɪrɪ'deɪʃəs, ˌaɪ-) *adj.* of, relating to, or belonging to the *Iridaceae,* a family of monocotyledonous plants, including iris, crocus, and gladiolus, having swordlike leaves and showy flowers.

ir·i·dec+to+my (ˌɪrɪ'dɛktəmɪ, ˌaɪ-) *n., pl.* **+mies.** surgical removal of part of the iris.

ir·i·des+cent (ˌɪrɪ'dɛsᵊnt) *adj.* displaying a spectrum of colours that shimmer and change due to interference and scattering as the observer's position changes. [C18: from IRIDO- + -ESCENT] —**ˌir·i·'des+cence** *n.* —**ˌir·i·'des+cent+ly** *adv.*

i·rid·ic (aɪˈrɪdɪc, ɪˈrɪd-) *adj.* **1.** of or containing iridium, esp. in the tetravalent state. **2.** of or relating to the iris of the eye.
i·rid·i·um (aɪˈrɪdɪəm, ɪˈrɪd-) *n.* a very hard inert yellowish-white transition element that is the most corrosion-resistant metal known. It occurs in platinum ores and is used as an alloy with platinum. Symbol: Ir; atomic no.: 77; atomic wt.: 192.2; valency: 3 or 4; relative density: 22.42; melting pt.: 2410°C; boiling pt.: 4130°C. [C19: New Latin, from IRIDO- + -IUM; from its colourful appearance when dissolving in certain acids]
ir·i·do *or before a vowel* **ir·id-** *n. combining form.* **1.** denoting the iris of the eye or the genus of plants: *iridectomy; iridaceous.* **2.** denoting a rainbow: *iridescent.* [from Latin *irid-*, IRIS]
ir·i·dos·mine (ˌɪrɪˈdɒsmaɪn, ˌaɪrɪ-) *or* **ir·i·dos·mi·um** *n.* other names for **osmiridium.** [C19: from IRIDO- + OSM(IUM) + -INE[2]]
ir·i·dot·o·my (ˌɪrɪˈdɒtəmɪ, ˌaɪrɪ-) *n., pl.* **-mies.** surgical incision into the iris, esp. to create an artificial pupil.
i·ris (ˈaɪrɪs) *n., pl.* **i·ris·es** *or* **ir·i·des** (ˈaɪrɪˌdiːz, ˈɪrɪ-). **1.** the coloured muscular diaphragm that surrounds and controls the size of the pupil. **2.** Also called: **fleur-de-lis.** any plant of the iridaceous genus *Iris,* having brightly coloured flowers composed of three petals and three drooping sepals. See also **flag**[2], **orris, stinking iris. 3.** a rare or poetic word for **rainbow. 4.** something resembling a rainbow; iridescence. [C14: from Latin: rainbow, iris (flower), crystal, from Greek]
I·ris (ˈaɪrɪs) *n.* the goddess of the rainbow along which she travelled to earth as a messenger of the gods.
i·ris di·a·phragm *n.* an adjustable diaphragm that regulates the amount of light entering an optical instrument, esp. a camera. It usually consists of a number of thin metal leaves arranged so that they open out into an approximately circular aperture.
I·rish (ˈaɪrɪʃ) *adj.* **1.** of, relating to, or characteristic of Ireland, its people, their Celtic language, or their dialect of English. ~*n.* **2. the.** (*functioning as pl.*) the natives or inhabitants of Ireland. **3.** another name for **Irish Gaelic. 4.** the dialect of English spoken in Ireland.
I·rish bull *n.* a ludicrously illogical statement. See also **bull**[2].
I·rish cof·fee *n.* hot coffee mixed with whiskey and topped with double cream.
I·rish elk *n.* an extinct Eurasian giant deer of the Pleistocene genus *Megaloceros,* which had antlers up to 4 metres across.
I·rish Free State *n.* a former name for the (Republic of) **Ireland** (1922–37).
I·rish Gael·ic *n.* the Goidelic language of the Celts of Ireland, still spoken in the southwest; an official language of the Republic of Ireland since 1921.
I·rish·ism (ˈaɪrɪˌʃɪzəm) *n.* an Irish custom or idiom.
I·rish·man (ˈaɪrɪʃmən) *or (fem.)* **I·rish·wom·an** *n., pl.* **-men** *or* **-wom·en.** a native, citizen, or inhabitant of Ireland or a descendant of one.
I·rish moss *n.* another name for **carrageen.**
I·rish po·ta·to *n. Chiefly U.S.* another name for the **potato.**
I·rish Re·pub·li·can Ar·my *n.* a militant organization of Irish nationalists founded with the aim of striving for a united independent Ireland by means of guerrilla warfare. Abbrev.: **I.R.A.**
I·rish Sea *n.* an arm of the North Atlantic Ocean between Great Britain and Ireland.
I·rish set·ter *n.* a breed of setter developed in Ireland, having a red coat. Also called: **red setter.**
I·rish stew *n.* a white stew made of mutton, lamb, or beef, with potatoes, onions, etc.
I·rish ter·ri·er *n.* a breed of terrier with a wiry brown coat.
I·rish whis·key *n.* any of the whiskeys made in Ireland, usually from malt and subject to three distillations.
I·rish wolf·hound *n.* a large breed of hound with a rough thick coat.
i·ri·tis (aɪˈraɪtɪs) *n.* inflammation of the iris of the eye. —**i·rit·ic** (aɪˈrɪtɪk) *adj.*
irk (ɜːk) *vb.* (*tr.*) to irritate, vex, or annoy. [C13 *irken* to grow weary; probably related to Old Norse *yrkja* to work]
irk·some (ˈɜːksəm) *adj.* causing vexation, annoyance, or boredom; troublesome or tedious. —**ˈirk·some·ly** *adv.* —**ˈirk·some·ness** *n.*
Ir·kutsk (*Russian* irˈkutsk) *n.* a city in the S Soviet Union: situated on the Trans-Siberian railway; university (1918); one of the largest industrial centres in Siberia, esp. for heavy engineering. Pop.: 508 000 (1975 est.).
IRL *international car registration for* Republic of Ireland.
I.R.O. *abbrev. for:* **1.** (in Brit.) Inland Revenue Office. **2.** International Refugee Organization.
i·ron (ˈaɪən) *n.* **1. a.** a malleable ductile silvery-white ferromagnetic metallic element occurring principally in haematite and magnetite. It is widely used for structural and engineering purposes. See also **steel, cast iron, wrought iron, pig iron.** Symbol: Fe; atomic no.: 26; atomic wt.: 55.847; valency: 2,3,4, or 6; relative density: 7.874; melting pt.: 1535°C; boiling pt.: 2750°C. Related adjs.: **ferric, ferrous.** Related prefix: **ferro-. b.** (*as modifier*): *iron railings.* **2.** any of certain tools or implements made of iron or steel, esp. for use when hot: *a grappling iron; a soldering iron.* **3.** an appliance for pressing fabrics using dry heat or steam, esp. a small electrically heated device with a handle and a weighted flat bottom. **4.** any of various golf clubs with metal heads, numbered from 2 to 10 according to the slant of the face, used esp. for approach shots: *a No. 6 iron.* **5.** an informal word for **harpoon** (sense 1). **6.** *U.S. slang.* a splint-like support for a malformed leg. **7.** great hardness, strength, or resolve: *a will of iron.* **8.** See **shooting iron. 9. strike while the iron is hot.** to act at an opportune moment. ~*adj.* **10.** very hard, immovable, or implacable: *iron determination.* **11.** very strong; extremely robust: *an iron constitution.* **12.** cruel or unyielding *he ruled with an iron hand.* ~*vb.* **13.** to smooth (clothes or fabric) by removing (creases or wrinkles) using a heated iron; press. **14.** (*tr.*) to furnish or clothe with iron. **15.** (*tr.*) *Rare.* to place (a prisoner) in irons. ~See also **iron out, irons.** [Old English *irēn;* related to Old High German *īsan,* Old Norse *jārn;* compare Old Irish *īarn*] —**ˈi·ron·er** *n.* —**ˈi·ron·less** *adj.* —**ˈi·ron·ˌlike** *adj.*
i·ron age *n. Classical myth.* the last and worst age in the history of the world.
I·ron Age *n.* **a.** the period following the Bronze Age characterized by the extremely rapid spread of iron tools and weapons, which began in the Middle East about 1100 B.C. **b.** (*modifier*) of or relating to this period.
i·ron·bark (ˈaɪənˌbɑːk) *n.* any of several Australian eucalyptus trees that have hard rough bark.
i·ron·bound (ˈaɪənˌbaʊnd) *adj.* **1.** bound with iron. **2.** unyielding; inflexible. **3.** (of a coast) rocky; rugged.
I·ron Chan·cel·lor *n.* **the.** nickname of (Prince Otto Eduard Leopold von) **Bismarck.**
i·ron·clad *adj.* (ˌaɪənˈklæd). **1.** covered or protected with iron: *an ironclad warship.* **2.** inflexible; rigid: *an ironclad rule.* **3.** not able to be assailed or contradicted: *an ironclad argument.* ~*n.* (ˈaɪənˌklæd). **4.** a large wooden 19th-century warship with armoured plating.
I·ron Cross *n.* the highest decoration for bravery awarded to the German armed forces in wartime.
I·ron Cur·tain *n.* **1. a.** the guarded border between the countries of the Soviet bloc and the rest of Europe. **b.** (*as modifier*): *Iron Curtain countries.* **2.** (*sometimes not caps.*) any barrier that separates communities or ideologies.
I·ron Gate *or* **I·ron Gates** *n.* a gorge of the River Danube on the border between Rumania and Yugoslavia. Length: 3 km (2 miles). Rumanian name: **Porţile de Fier.**
i·ron glance *n.* another name for **haematite.**
i·ron grey *n.* **a.** a neutral or dark grey colour. **b.** (*as adj.*): *iron-grey hair.*
I·ron Guard *n.* a Rumanian fascist party that ceased to exist after World War II.
i·ron hand *n.* harsh or rigorous control; overbearing or autocratic force: *he ruled with an iron hand.*
i·ron horse *n.* **1.** *Informal, rare.* a steamdriven railway locomotive. **2.** *Archaic.* a bicycle or tricycle.
i·ron·ic (aɪˈrɒnɪk) *or* **i·ron·i·cal** *adj.* of, characterized by, or using irony. —**iˈron·i·cal·ly** *adv.* —**iˈron·i·cal·ness** *n.*
i·ron·ing (ˈaɪənɪŋ) *n.* **1.** the act of ironing washed clothes. **2.** clothes, etc., that are to be or that have been ironed.
i·ron·ing board *n.* a board, usually on legs, with a suitable covering on which to iron clothes.
i·ro·nize *or* **i·ro·nise** (ˈaɪrəˌnaɪz) *vb.* **1.** (*intr.*) to use or indulge in irony. **2.** (*tr.*) to make ironic or use ironically. —**ˈi·ro·nist** *n.*
i·ron lung *n.* an airtight metal cylinder enclosing the entire body up to the neck and providing artificial respiration when the respiratory muscles are paralysed, as by poliomyelitis.
i·ron maid·en *n.* a medieval instrument of torture, consisting of an enclosed space lined with iron spikes, into which the victim was locked.
i·ron man *n. Austral.* an event at a surf carnival in which contestants compete at swimming, surfing, running, etc.
i·ron·mas·ter (ˈaɪənˌmɑːstə) *n. Brit.* a manufacturer of iron, esp. (formerly) the owner of an ironworks.
i·ron·mon·ger (ˈaɪənˌmʌŋgə) *n. Brit.* a dealer in metal utensils, hardware, locks, etc. U.S. equivalent: **hardware dealer.** —**ˈi·ron·ˌmon·ger·y** *n.*
i·ron out *vb.* (*tr., adv.*) **1.** to smooth, using a heated iron. **2.** to put right or settle (a problem or difficulty) as a result of negotiations or discussions. **3.** *Austral. informal.* to knock (a person) out.
i·ron py·ri·tes *n.* another name for **pyrite.**
i·ron ra·tions *pl. n.* emergency food supplies, esp. for military personnel in action. See also **K ration.**
i·rons (ˈaɪənz) *pl. n.* **1.** fetters or chains (often in the phrase **in** or **into irons**). **2. in irons.** *Nautical.* (of a sailing vessel) headed directly into the wind without steerageway. **3. have several irons in the fire.** to be involved in many projects, activities, etc.
I·ron·side (ˈaɪənˌsaɪd) *n.* nickname of Edmund II of England.
i·ron·sides (ˈaɪənˌsaɪdz) *n.* **1.** a person with great stamina or resistance. **2.** an ironclad ship. **3.** (*often cap.*) (in the English Civil War) **a.** the cavalry regiment trained and commanded by Oliver Cromwell. **b.** Cromwell's entire army.
i·ron·stone (ˈaɪənˌstəʊn) *n.* **1.** any rock consisting mainly of an iron-bearing ore. **2.** Also called: **ironstone china.** a tough durable earthenware.
i·ron·ware (ˈaɪənˌwɛə) *n.* domestic articles made of iron.
i·ron·wood (ˈaɪənˌwʊd) *n.* **1.** any of various betulaceous trees, such as hornbeam, that have very hard wood. **2.** a Californian rosaceous tree, *Lyonothamnus floribundus,* with very hard wood. **3.** the wood of any of these trees.
i·ron·work (ˈaɪənˌwɜːk) *n.* **1.** work done in iron, esp. decorative work. **2.** the craft or practice of working in iron.
i·ron·work·er (ˈaɪənˌwɜːkə) *n.* **1.** a person who works in an ironworks. **2.** a person who makes articles of iron.
i·ron·works (ˈaɪənˌwɜːks) *n.* (*sometimes functioning as sing.*) a building in which iron is smelted, cast, or wrought.
i·ro·ny[1] (ˈaɪrənɪ) *n., pl.* **-nies. 1.** the humorous or mildly

sarcastic use of words to imply the opposite of what they normally mean. **2.** an instance of this, used to draw attention to some incongruity or irrationality. **3.** incongruity between what is expected to be and what actually is, or a situation or result showing such incongruity. **4.** See **dramatic irony. 5.** *Philosophy.* See **Socratic irony.**

i·ron·y[2] ('aɪənɪ) *adj.* of, resembling, or containing iron.

Ir·o+quoi+an (ˌɪrə'kwɔɪən) *n.* **1.** a family of North American Indian languages including Cherokee, Mohawk, Seneca, Oneida, and Onondaga. *~adj.* **2.** of or relating to the Iroquois, their culture, or their languages.

Ir·o+quois ('ɪrəˌkwɔɪ, -ˌkwɔɪz) *n., pl.* **+quois. 1.** a member of any of a group of North American Indian peoples formerly living between the Hudson River and the St. Lawrence and Lake Erie. See also **Five Nations, Six Nations. 2.** any of the Iroquoian languages. *~adj.* **3.** of or relating to the Iroquois, their language, or their culture.

IRQ *international car registration for* Iraq.

ir+ra+di+ance (ɪ'reɪdɪəns) *n.* the radiant flux incident on unit area of a surface. It is measured in watts per square metre. Symbol: E_e Also called: **irradiation.** Compare **illuminance.**

ir+ra+di+ant (ɪ'reɪdɪənt) *adj.* radiating light; shining brightly.

ir+ra+di+ate (ɪ'reɪdɪˌeɪt) *vb.* **1.** (*tr.*) *Physics.* to subject to or treat with light or other electromagnetic radiation or with beams of particles. **2.** (*tr.*) to make clear or bright intellectually or spiritually; illumine. **3.** a less common word for **radiate** (sense 1). **4.** (*intr.*) *Obsolete.* to become radiant. **—ir+'ra+di·a+tive** *adj.* **—ir+'ra+di·ˌa+tor** *n.*

ir+ra+di·a+tion (ɪˌreɪdɪ'eɪʃən) *n.* **1.** the act or process of irradiating or the state of being irradiated. **2.** the apparent enlargement of a brightly lit object when it is viewed against a dark background. **3.** a shaft of light; beam or ray. **4.** *Med.* **a.** the therapeutic or diagnostic use of radiation, esp. x-rays. **b.** exposure of a patient to such radiation. **5.** another name for **radiation** or **irradiance.**

ir+ra+tion+al (ɪ'ræʃənᵊl) *adj.* **1.** inconsistent with reason or logic; illogical; absurd. **2.** incapable of reasoning. **3. a.** *Maths.* (of an equation, etc.) containing one or more variables in irreducible radical form or raised to a fractional power: $\sqrt{(x^2 + 1)} = x^{5/3}$. **b.** (*as n.*): *an irrational.* **4.** *Prosody.* (in Greek or Latin verse) **a.** of or relating to a metrical irregularity, usually the occurrence of a long syllable instead of a short one. **b.** denoting a metrical foot where such an irregularity occurs. **—ir+'ra+tion+al+ly** *adv.* **—ir+'ra+tion+al+ness** *n.*

ir+ra+tion+al·i·ty (ɪˌræʃə'nælɪtɪ) *or* **ir+ra+tion+al+ism** *n.* **1.** the state or quality of being irrational. **2.** irrational thought, action, or behaviour.

ir+ra+tion+al num+ber *n.* any real number that cannot be expressed as the ratio of two integers, such as π.

Ir+ra+wad+dy (ˌɪrə'wɒdɪ) *n.* the main river in Burma, rising in the north in two headstreams and flowing south through the whole length of Burma, to enter the Andaman Sea by nine main mouths. Length: 2100 km (1300 miles).

ir+re+claim+a·ble (ˌɪrɪ'kleɪməbᵊl) *adj.* not able to be reclaimed. **—ˌir+re+ˌclaim+a·'bil+i·ty** *or* **ˌir+re+'claim+a·ble+ness** *n.* **—ˌir+re+'claim+a·bly** *adv.*

ir+rec+on+cil+a·ble (ɪ'rɛkənˌsaɪləbᵊl, ɪˌrɛkən'saɪ-) *adj.* **1.** not able to be reconciled; uncompromisingly conflicting; incompatible. *~n.* **2.** a person or thing that is implacably hostile or uncompromisingly opposed. **3.** (*usually pl.*) one of various principles, ideas, etc., that are incapable of being brought into agreement. **—ir+ˌrec+on+ˌcil+a·'bil+i·ty** *or* **ir+'rec+on+ˌcil+a·ble+ness** *n.* **—ir+'rec+on+ˌcil+a·bly** *adv.*

ir+re+cov+er+a·ble (ˌɪrɪ'kʌvərəbᵊl, -'kʌvrə-) *adj.* **1.** not able to be recovered or regained. **2.** not able to be remedied or rectified. **—ˌir+re+'cov+er+a·ble+ness** *n.* **—ˌir+re+'cov+er+a·bly** *adv.*

ir+re+cu+sa·ble (ˌɪrɪ'kju:zəbᵊl) *adj.* not able to be rejected or challenged, as evidence, etc. **—ˌir+re+'cu+sa·bly** *adv.*

ir+re+deem+a·ble (ˌɪrɪ'di:məbᵊl) *adj.* **1.** (of bonds, debentures, shares, etc.) without a date of redemption of capital; incapable of being bought back directly or paid off. **2.** (of paper money) not convertible into specie. **3.** (of a sinner, etc.) not able to be saved or reformed. **4.** (of a loss) not able to be recovered; irretrievable. **5.** not able to be improved or rectified; irreparable. **—ˌir+re+ˌdeem+a·'bil+i·ty** *or* **ˌir+re+'deem+a·ble+ness** *n.* **—ˌir+re+'deem+a·bly** *adv.*

ir+re+den+tist (ˌɪrɪ'dɛntɪst) *n.* **1.** a person who favours the acquisition of territory that once was part of his country or is considered to have been. *~adj.* **2.** of, relating to, or advocating irredentism. [C19: from Italian *irredentista,* from the phrase *Italia irredenta,* literally: Italy unredeemed, from *ir*- IN-[1] + *redento* redeemed, from Latin *redemptus* bought back; see REDEEM] **—ˌir+re+'den+tism** *n.*

Ir+re+den+tist (ˌɪrɪ'dɛntɪst) *n.* (*sometimes not cap.*) a member of an Italian association prominent in 1878 that sought to recover for Italy certain neighbouring regions (***Italia irredenta***) with a predominantly Italian population that were under foreign control.

ir+re+duc+i·ble (ˌɪrɪ'dju:sɪbᵊl) *adj.* **1.** not able to be reduced or lessened. **2.** not able to be brought to a simpler or reduced form. **3.** *Maths.* **a.** (of a polynomial) unable to be factorized into polynomials of lower degree, as $(x^2 + 1)$. **b.** (of a radical) unable to be reduced to a rational expression, as $\sqrt{(x + 1)}$. **—ˌir+re+ˌduc+i·'bil+i·ty** *or* **ˌir+re+'duc+i·ble+ness** *n.* **—ˌir+re+'duc+i·bly** *adv.*

ir+ref+ra+ga·ble (ɪ'rɛfrəgəbᵊl) *adj.* not able to be denied or refuted; indisputable. [C16: from Late Latin *irrefrāgābilis,* from Latin IR- + *refrāgārī* to resist, thwart] **—ir+ˌref+ra+ga·'bil+i·ty** *or* **ir+'ref+ra+ga·ble+ness** *n.* **—ir+'ref+ra+ga·bly** *adv.*

ir+re+fran+gi·ble (ˌɪrɪ'frændʒəbᵊl) *adj.* **1.** not to be broken or transgressed; inviolable. **2.** *Physics.* incapable of being refracted. **—ˌir+re+ˌfran+gi·'bil+i·ty** *or* **ˌir+re+'fran+gi·ble+ness** *n.* **—ˌir+re+'fran+gi·bly** *adv.*

ir+ref·u·ta·ble (ɪ'rɛfjʊtəbᵊl, ˌɪrɪ'fju:təbᵊl) *adj.* impossible to deny or disprove; incontrovertible. **—ir+ˌref·u·ta·'bil+i·ty** *or* **ir+'ref·u·ta·ble+ness** *n.* **—ir+'ref·u·ta·bly** *adv.*

irreg. *abbrev. for* irregular(ly).

ir+reg·u·lar (ɪ'rɛgjʊlə) *adj.* **1.** lacking uniformity or symmetry; uneven in shape, position, arrangement, etc. **2.** not occurring at expected or equal intervals: *an irregular pulse.* **3.** differing from the normal or accepted practice or routine. **4.** not according to established standards of behaviour; unconventional. **5.** (of the formation, inflections, or derivations of a word) not following the usual pattern of formation in a language, as English plurals ending other than in *-s* or *-es.* **6.** of or relating to guerrillas or volunteers not belonging to regular forces: *irregular troops.* **7.** (of flowers) having any of their parts, esp. petals, differing in size, shape, etc.; asymmetric. **8.** *U.S.* (of merchandise) not up to the manufacturer's standards or specifications; flawed; imperfect. *~n.* **9.** a soldier not in a regular army. **10.** (*often pl.*) *U.S.* imperfect or flawed merchandise. Compare **second** (sense 15). **—ir+'reg·u·lar+ly** *adv.*

ir+reg·u·lar+i·ty (ɪˌrɛgjʊ'lærɪtɪ) *n., pl.* **·ties. 1.** the state or quality of being irregular. **2.** something irregular, such as a bump in a smooth surface. **3.** a breach of a convention or normal procedure.

ir+rel·a·tive (ɪ'rɛlətɪv) *adj.* **1.** unrelated. **2.** a rare word for **irrelevant. —ir+'rel·a·tive+ly** *adv.* **—ir+'rel·a·tive+ness** *n.*

ir+rel·e·vant (ɪ'rɛləvənt) *adj.* not relating or pertinent to the matter at hand; not important. **—ir+'rel·e·vance** *or* **ir+'rel+e·van+cy** *n.* **—ir+'rel·e·vant+ly** *adv.*

ir+re+liev+a·ble (ˌɪrɪ'li:vəbᵊl) *adj.* not able to be relieved.

ir+re+li·gion (ˌɪrɪ'lɪdʒən) *n.* **1.** lack of religious faith. **2.** indifference or opposition to religion. **—ˌir+re+'li+gion+ist** *n.* **—ˌir+re+'li+gious** *adj.* **—ˌir+re+'li+gious+ly** *adv.* **—ˌir+re+'li+gious+ness** *n.*

ir+rem+e·a·ble (ɪ'rɛmɪəbᵊl, ɪ'ri:-) *adj. Archaic or poetic.* affording no possibility of return. [C16: from Latin *irremeābilis,* from IR- + *remeāre* to return, from RE- + *meāre* to go] **—ir+'rem+e·a·bly** *adv.*

ir+re+me·di·a·ble (ˌɪrɪ'mi:dɪəbᵊl) *adj.* not able to be remedied; incurable or irreparable. **—ˌir+re+'me·di+a·ble+ness** *n.* **—ˌir+re+'me·di·a·bly** *adv.*

ir+re+mis+si·ble (ˌɪrɪ'mɪsəbᵊl) *adj.* **1.** unpardonable; inexcusable. **2.** that must be done, as through duty or obligation. **—ˌir+re+ˌmis+si·'bil+i·ty** *or* **ˌir+re+'mis+si·ble+ness** *n.* **—ˌir+re+'mis+si·bly** *adv.*

ir+re+mov+a·ble (ˌɪrɪ'mu:vəbᵊl) *adj.* not able to be removed. **—ˌir+re+ˌmov+a·'bil+i·ty** *or* **ˌir+re+'mov+a·ble+ness** *n.* **—ˌir+re+'mov+a·bly** *adv.*

ir+rep·a·ra·ble (ɪ'rɛpərəbᵊl, ɪ'rɛprəbᵊl) *adj.* not able to be repaired or remedied; beyond repair. **—ir+ˌrep+a+ra·'bil+i·ty** *or* **ir+'rep·a+ra·ble+ness** *n.* **—ir+'rep·a+ra·bly** *adv.*

ir+re+peal+a·ble (ˌɪrɪ'pi:ləbᵊl) *adj.* not able to be repealed. **—ˌir+re+ˌpeal+a·'bil+i·ty** *or* **ˌir+re+'peal+a·ble+ness** *n.* **—ˌir+re+'peal+a·bly** *adv.*

ir+re+place+a·ble (ˌɪrɪ'pleɪsəbᵊl) *adj.* not able to be replaced: *an irreplaceable antique.* **—ˌir+re+'place+a·bly** *adv.*

ir+re+plev·i+a·ble (ˌɪrɪ'plɛvɪəbᵊl) *or* **ir+re+plev·i+sa·ble** (ˌɪrɪ'plɛvɪsəbᵊl) *adj. Law.* not able to be replevied. [C16: see *ir*- IN-[1], REPLEVIN]

ir+re+press+i·ble (ˌɪrɪ'prɛsəbᵊl) *adj.* not capable of being repressed, controlled, or restrained. **—ˌir+re+ˌpress+i·'bil+i·ty** *or* **ˌir+re+'press+i·ble+ness** *n.* **—ˌir+re+'press+i·bly** *adv.*

ir+re+proach+a·ble (ˌɪrɪ'prəʊtʃəbᵊl) *adj.* not deserving reproach; blameless. **—ˌir+re+ˌproach+a·'bil+i·ty** *or* **ˌir+re+'proach+a·ble+ness** *n.* **—ˌir+re+'proach+a·bly** *adv.*

ir+re+sist+i·ble (ˌɪrɪ'zɪstəbᵊl) *adj.* **1.** not able to be resisted or refused; overpowering: *an irresistible impulse.* **2.** very fascinating or alluring: *an irresistible woman.* **—ˌir+re+ˌsist+i·'bil+i·ty** *or* **ˌir+re+'sist+i·ble+ness** *n.* **—ˌir+re+'sist+i·bly** *adv.*

ir+res·o·lu·ble (ɪ'rɛzəljʊbᵊl) *adj.* **1.** a less common word for **insoluble. 2.** *Archaic.* not capable of being relieved. **—ir+ˌres·o+lu·'bil+i·ty** *n.* **—ir+'res·o+lu·bly** *adv.*

ir+res·o·lute (ɪ'rɛzəˌlu:t) *adj.* lacking resolution; wavering; hesitating. **—ir+'res·o+ˌlute+ly** *adv.* **—ir+'res·o+ˌlute+ness** *or* **ir+ˌres·o+'lu+tion** *n.*

ir+re+solv+a·ble (ˌɪrɪ'zɒlvəbᵊl) *adj.* **1.** not able to be resolved into parts or elements. **2.** not able to be solved; insoluble. **—ˌir+re+ˌsolv+a·'bil+i·ty** *or* **ˌir+re+'solv+a·ble+ness** *n.* **—ˌir+re+'solv+a·bly** *adv.*

ir+re+spec+tive (ˌɪrɪ'spɛktɪv) *adj.* **1. irrespective of.** (*prep.*) without taking account of; regardless of. *~adv.* **2.** *Informal.* regardless; without due consideration: *he carried on with his plan irrespective.* **—ˌir+re+'spec+tive+ly** *adv.*

ir+re+spir+a·ble (ɪ'rɛsprɪrəbᵊl, ˌɪrɪ'spaɪərəbᵊl) *adj.* not fit for breathing or incapable of being breathed.

ir+re+spon+si·ble (ˌɪrɪ'spɒnsəbᵊl) *adj.* **1.** not showing or done with due care for the consequences of one's actions or attitudes; reckless. **2.** not capable of bearing responsibility. **3.** *Archaic.* not answerable to a higher authority for one's actions. **—ˌir+re+ˌspon+si·'bil+i·ty** *or* **ˌir+re+'spon+si·ble+ness** *n.* **—ˌir+re+'spon+si·bly** *adv.*

ir+re+spon+sive (ˌɪrɪ'spɒnsɪv) *adj.* not responsive. **—ˌir+re+'spon+sive+ly** *adv.* **—ˌir+re+'spon+sive+ness** *n.*

ir+re+ten+tive (ˌɪrɪ'tɛntɪv) *adj.* not retentive. **—ˌir+re+'ten+tive+ness** *n.*

ir+re+triev+a·ble (ˌɪrɪ'tri:vəbᵊl) *adj.* not able to be retrieved, recovered, or repaired. —ˌ**ir+re+ˌtriev+a·'bil+i·ty** *or* ˌ**ir+re+'triev+a·ble+ness** *n.* —ˌ**ir+re+'triev+a·bly** *adv.*

ir+rev+er+ence (ɪ'rɛvərəns, ɪ'rɛvrəns) *n.* **1.** lack of due respect or veneration; disrespect. **2.** a disrespectful remark or act. **3.** *Rare.* disrepute; lack of reputation. —**ir+'rev+er+ent** *or* **ir+ˌrev+e·'ren+tial** *adj.* —**ir+'rev+er+ent+ly** *adv.*

ir+re+vers+i·ble (ˌɪrɪ'vɜːsəbᵊl) *adj.* **1.** not able to be reversed: *the irreversible flow of time.* **2.** not able to be revoked or repealed; irrevocable. **3.** *Chem., physics.* capable of changing or producing a change in one direction only: *an irreversible reaction.* **4.** *Thermodynamics.* (of a change, process, etc.) occurring through a number of intermediate states that are not all in thermodynamic equilibrium. —ˌ**ir+re+ˌvers+i·'bil+i·ty** *or* ˌ**ir+re+'vers+i·ble+ness** *n.* —ˌ**ir+re+'vers+i·bly** *adv.*

ir+rev+o·ca·ble (ɪ'rɛvəkəbᵊl) *adj.* not able to be revoked, changed, or undone; unalterable. —**ir+ˌrev·o·ca·'bil+i·ty** *or* **ir+'rev·o·ca·ble+ness** *n.* —**ir+'rev·o·ca·bly** *adv.*

ir+ri+gate ('ɪrɪˌgeɪt) *vb.* **1.** to supply (land) with water by means of artificial canals, ditches, etc., esp. to promote the growth of food crops. **2.** *Med.* to bathe or wash out a bodily part, cavity, or wound. **3.** (*tr.*) to make fertile, fresh, or vital by or as if by watering. [C17: from Latin *irrigāre*, from *rigāre* to moisten, conduct water] —**'ir+ri+ga·ble** *adj.* —ˌ**ir+ri+'ga+tion** *n.* —ˌ**ir+ri+'ga+tion+al** *or* **'ir+ri+ˌga+tive** *adj.* —**'ir+ri+ˌga+tor** *n.*

ir+rig·u·ous (ɪ'rɪgjʊəs) *adj. Archaic or poetic.* well-watered; watery. [C17: from Latin *irriguus* supplied with water, from *riguus* watered; see IRRIGATE]

ir+ri+ta·ble ('ɪrɪtəbᵊl) *adj.* **1.** quickly irritated; easily annoyed; peevish. **2.** (of all living organisms) capable of responding to such stimuli as heat, light, and touch. **3.** *Pathol.* abnormally sensitive. —ˌ**ir+ri+ta·'bil+i·ty** *n.* —**'ir+ri+ta·ble+ness** *n.* —**'ir+ri+ta·bly** *adv.*

ir+ri+tant ('ɪrɪtənt) *adj.* **1.** causing irritation; irritating. ~*n.* **2.** something irritant. —**'ir+ri+tan+cy** *n.*

ir+ri+tate ('ɪrɪˌteɪt) *vb.* **1.** to annoy or anger (someone). **2.** (*tr.*) *Biology.* to stimulate (an organism or part) to respond in a characteristic manner. **3.** (*tr.*) *Pathol.* to cause (a bodily organ or part) to become excessively stimulated, resulting in inflammation, tenderness, etc. [C16: from Latin *irrītāre* to provoke, exasperate] —**'ir+ri+ˌta+tor** *n.*

ir+ri+ta+tion (ˌɪrɪ'teɪʃən) *n.* **1.** something that irritates. **2.** the act of irritating or the condition of being irritated. —**'ir+ri+ˌta+tive** *adj.*

ir+rupt (ɪ'rʌpt) *vb.* (*intr.*) **1.** to enter forcibly or suddenly. **2.** (of a human or animal population) to increase suddenly in numbers. [C19: from Latin *irrumpere* to rush into, invade, from *rumpere* to break, burst] —**ir+'rup+tion** *n.*

ir+rup+tive (ɪ'rʌptɪv) *adj.* **1.** irrupting or tending to irrupt. **2.** of, involving, or causing irruption.. **3.** (of igneous rocks) intrusive. —**ir+'rup+tive+ly** *adv.*

Ir+tysh *or* **Ir+tish** (ɪə'tɪʃ) *n.* a river in central Asia, rising in China in the Altai Mountains and flowing west into the Soviet Union, then northwest into the Ob River as its chief tributary. Length: 4444 km (2760 miles).

Ir+vine ('ɜːvɪn) *n.* a town on the W coast of Scotland, in Strathclyde: designated a new town in 1966. Pop.: 23 160 (1971).

Ir·ving ('ɜːvɪŋ) *n.* **1.** Sir **Hen·ry.** original name *John Henry Brodribb.* 1838–1905, English actor and manager of the Lyceum Theatre in London (1878–1902). **2. Wash·ing·ton.** 1783–1859, U.S. essayist and short-story writer, noted for *The Sketch Book of Geoffrey Crayon* (1820), which contains the stories *Rip Van Winkle* and *The Legend of Sleepy Hollow.*

is (ɪz) *vb.* (used with *he, she, it,* and with singular nouns) a form of the present tense (indicative mood) of **be.** [Old English; compare Old Norse *es*, German *ist*, Latin *est*, Greek *esti*]

IS *international car registration for* Iceland. [Icelandic *Island*]

Is. *abbrev. for:* **1.** Also: **Isa.** *Bible.* Isaiah. **2.** Island(s) *or* Isle(s).

is- *combining form.* variant of **iso-** before a vowel: *isentropic.*

I·saac ('aɪzək) *n.* an Old Testament patriarch, the son of Abraham and Sarah and father of Jacob and Esau (Genesis 17; 21–27).

Is·a·bel+la (ˌɪzə'bɛlə) *or* **Is·a·bel** ('ɪzəˌbɛl) *n.* **a.** a greyish-yellow colour. **b.** Also: **Isabelline.** (*as modifier*): *an Isabella mohair coat.* [C17: from the name *Isabella*; original reference uncertain]

Is·a·bel·la I *n.* called *the Catholic.* 1451–1504, queen of Castile (1474–1504) and, with her husband, Ferdinand V, joint ruler of Castile and Aragon (1479–1504).

i·sa+go+ge ('aɪsəˌgəʊdʒɪ, ˌaɪsə'gəʊ-) *n.* an academic introduction to a specialized subject field or area of research. [C17: from Latin, from Greek *eisagōgē*, from *eisagein* to introduce, from *eis-* into + *agein* to lead]

i·sa+gog+ics (ˌaɪsə'gɒdʒɪks) *n.* (*usually functioning as sing.*) **1.** introductory studies, esp. in the history of the Bible. —ˌ**i·sa+'gog+ic** *adj.*

I·sai·ah (aɪ'zaɪə) *n. Old Testament.* **1.** the first of the major Hebrew prophets, who lived in the 8th century B.C. **2.** the book of his and others' prophecies.

is+al+lo+bar (aɪ'sæləˌbɑː) *n. Meteorol.* a line on a map running through places experiencing equal pressure changes.

I·sar ('iːzɑː) *n.* a river in central Europe, rising in W Austria and flowing generally northeast through S West Germany into the Danube. Length: over 260 km (160 miles).

i·sa+tin ('aɪsətɪn) *or* **i·sa+tine** ('aɪsəˌtiːn) *n.* a yellowish-red crystalline compound soluble in hot water, used for the preparation of vat dyes. Formula: $C_8H_5NO_2$. [C19: from Latin *isatis* woad + -IN] —ˌ**i·sa+'tin+ic** *adj.*

I·sau+ri·a (aɪ'sɔːrɪə) *n.* an ancient district of S central Asia Minor, chiefly on the N slopes of the W Taurus Mountains.

I.S.B.N., ISBN *abbrev. for* International Standard Book Number.

Is·car·i·ot (ɪ'skærɪət) *n.* See **Judas** (Iscariot).

is+chae+mi·a *or* **is+che+mi·a** (ɪ'skiːmɪə) *n. Pathol.* an inadequate supply of blood to an organ or part, as from an obstructed blood flow. [C19: from Greek *iskhein* to restrict, + -EMIA] —**is+chem+ic** (ɪ'skɛmɪk) *adj.*

Is+chia ('iːskjɑː, 'ɪskɪə) *n.* a volcanic island in the Tyrrhenian Sea, at the N end of the Bay of Naples. Area: 47 sq. km (18 sq. miles).

is+chi·um ('ɪskɪəm) *n., pl.* **+chi·a** (-kɪə). one of the three sections of the hipbone, situated below the ilium. [C17: from Latin: hip joint, from Greek *iskhion*] —**'is+chi·al** *adj.*

-ise *suffix forming verbs.* a variant of **-ize.**
Usage. See at **-ize.**

is+en+trop+ic (ˌaɪsɛn'trɒpɪk) *adj.* having or taking place at constant entropy.

I·sère (*French* i'zɛːr) *n.* **1.** a department of SE France, in Rhône-Alpes region. Capital: Grenoble. Pop.: 875 526 (1975). Area: 7904 sq. km (3083 sq. miles). **2.** a river in SE France, rising in the Graian Alps and flowing west and southwest to join the River Rhône near Valence. Length: 290 km (180 miles).

I·seult, Y·seult (ɪ'suːlt), *or* **I·sol·de** (ɪ'zəʊldə) *n.* (in Arthurian legend) **1.** an Irish princess wed to Mark, king of Cornwall, but in love with his knight Tristan. **2.** (in another account) the daughter of the king of Brittany, married to Tristan.

Is+fa+han (ˌɪsfə'hɑːn) *or* **Eş+fa+hān** *n.* a city in central Iran: the second largest city in the country; capital of Persia in the 11th century and from 1598 to 1722. Pop.: 605 000 (1973 est.). Ancient name: **Aspadana.**

-ish *suffix forming adjectives.* **1.** of or belonging to a nationality or group: *Scottish.* **2.** *Often derogatory.* having the manner or qualities of; resembling: *slavish; prudish; boyish.* **3.** somewhat; approximately: *yellowish; sevenish.* **4.** concerned or preoccupied with: *bookish.* [Old English *-isc*; related to German *-isch*, Greek *-iskos*]

Ish·er·wood ('ɪshəˌwʊd) *n.* **Chris·to·pher (William Bradshaw-Isherwood).** born 1904, U.S. novelist and dramatist, born in England. His works include the novel *Goodbye to Berlin* (1939) and three verse plays written in collaboration with W.H. Auden.

Ish·ma·el ('ɪʃmeɪəl) *n.* **1.** the son of Abraham and Hagar, Sarah's handmaid: the ancestor of 12 Arabian tribes (Genesis 21:8–21; 25:12–18). **2.** a bandit chieftain, who defied the Babylonian conquerors of Judah and assassinated the governor appointed by Nebuchadnezzar (II Kings 25:25; Jeremiah 40:13–41:18).

Ish+ma+el+ite ('ɪʃmeɪəˌlaɪt) *n.* **1.** a supposed descendant of Ishmael; a member of a desert people of Old Testament times. **2.** *Rare.* an outcast. —**'Ish+ma+el+ˌit+ism** *n.*

Ish+tar ('ɪʃtɑː) *n.* the principal goddess of the Babylonians and Assyrians; divinity of love, fertility, and war.

Is·i·dore of Se+ville ('ɪzɪdɔː) *n.* **Saint.** Latin name *Isidorus Hispalensis.* ?560–636 A.D., Spanish archbishop and scholar, noted for his *Etymologies*, an encyclopedia. Feast day: April 4.

i·sin+glass ('aɪzɪŋˌglɑːs) *n.* **1.** a gelatine made from the air bladders of freshwater fish, used as a clarifying agent and adhesive and for preserving eggs. **2.** another name for **mica.** [C16: from Middle Dutch *huysenblase*, literally: sturgeon bladder; influenced by English GLASS]

I·sis¹ ('aɪsɪs) *n.* the local name for the River Thames at Oxford.

I·sis² ('aɪsɪs) *n.* an ancient Egyptian fertility goddess, usually depicted as a woman with a cow's horns, between which was the disc of the sun; wife and sister of Osiris.

Is·kan·der Bey (ɪsˌkændə 'beɪ) *n.* the Turkish name of **Scanderbeg.**

Is+ken+de+run (ɪs'kɛndəˌruːn) *n.* a port in S Turkey, on the **Gulf of Iskenderun.** Pop.: 107 437 (1975). Former name: **Alexandretta.**

Isl. *abbrev. for:* **1.** Island. **2.** Isle.

Is+lam ('ɪzlɑːm) *n.* **1.** Also called: **Islamism.** the religion of Muslims, having the Koran as its sacred scripture and teaching that there is only one God and that Mohammed is his prophet; Mohammedanism. **2. a.** Muslims collectively and their civilization. **b.** the countries where the Muslim religion is predominant. [C19: from Arabic: surrender (to God), from *aslama* to surrender] —**Is+'lam+ic** *adj.*

Is+lam·a·bad (ɪz'lɑːmɑːˌbɑːd) *n.* the capital of Pakistan, in the north on the Potwar Plateau: site chosen in 1959; surrounded by the Capital Territory of Islamabad for 909 sq. km (351 sq. miles). Pop.: 77 318 (1972).

Is+lam+ize *or* **Is+lam+ise** ('ɪzləˌmaɪz) *vb.* (*tr.*) to convert or subject to the influence of Islam; Mohammedanize. —ˌ**Is+lam·i·'za+tion** *or* ˌ**Is+lam·i·'sa+tion** *n.*

is+land ('aɪlənd) *n.* **1.** a mass of land that is surrounded by water and is smaller than a continent. **2.** something resembling this: *a traffic island.* **3.** *Anatomy.* a part, structure, or group of cells distinct in constitution from its immediate surroundings. ~Related adj.: **insular.** ~*vb.* (*tr.*) *Rare.* **4.** to cause to become an island. **5.** to intersperse with islands. **6.** to place on an island; insulate; isolate. [Old English *īgland*, from *īg* island + LAND; *s* inserted through influence of ISLE] —**'is·land-ˌlike** *adj.*

is+land+er ('aɪləndə) *n.* a native or inhabitant of an island.

is+land of Reil (raɪl) *n.* another name for **insula.** [after Johann *Reil* (died 1813), German physician]

Is+lands of the Blessed *pl. n. Greek myth.* lands where the souls of heroes and good men were taken after death. Also called: **Hesperides.**

is+land u·ni+verse *n.* a former name for **galaxy.**
Is+lay ('aɪleɪ) *n.* an island off the W coast of Scotland: the southernmost of the Inner Hebrides; separated from the island of Jura by the **Sound of Islay;** ancient seat of the Lord of the Isles. Pop.: 3825 (1971). Area: 606 sq. km (234 sq. miles).
isle (aɪl) *n. Poetic except when cap. and part of place name.* an island, esp. a small one. [C13: from Old French *isle,* from Latin *insula* island]
Isle of Man *n.* See (Isle of) **Man.**
Isle of Pines *n.* See (Isle of) **Pines.**
Isle of Wight *n.* See (Isle of) **Wight.**
Isle Roy+ale ('rɔɪəl) *n.* an island in the northeast U.S., in NW Lake Superior: forms, with over 100 surrounding islands, **Isle Royale National Park.** Area: 541 sq. km (209 sq. miles).
is+let ('aɪlɪt) *n.* a small island. [C16: from Old French *islette;* see ISLE]
is+lets of Lang+er+hans *or* **is+lands of Lang+er+hans** ('læŋəˌhæns) *pl. n.* small groups of endocrine cells in the pancreas that secrete the hormones insulin and glucagon. [C19: named after Paul *Langerhans* (1847–88), German physician]
Is+ling+ton ('ɪzlɪŋtən) *n.* a borough of N Greater London. Pop.: 171 600 (1976 est.).
ism ('ɪzəm) *n. Informal, often derogatory.* an unspecified doctrine, system, or practice.
-ism *suffix forming nouns.* **1.** indicating an action, process, or result: *criticism; terrorism.* **2.** indicating a state or condition: *paganism.* **3.** indicating a doctrine, system, or body of principles and practices: *Leninism; spiritualism.* **4.** indicating behaviour or a characteristic quality: *heroism.* **5.** indicating a characteristic usage, esp. of a language: *colloquialism; Scotticism.* [from Old French *-isme,* from Latin *-ismus,* from Greek *-ismos*]
Is+ma·i+li *or* **Is·ma'·i·li** (ˌɪzmɑː'iːlɪ) *n. Islam.* **1.** the Shiah Sect, whose head is the Aga Khan. **2.** Also called: **Is+ma·i·li·an** (ˌɪzmɑːɪ'liːən). a member of this sect.
Is+mai+li·a (ˌɪzmaɪ'lɪə) *n.* a city in NE Egypt, on the Suez Canal: founded in 1863 by the former Suez Canal Company; devastated by Israeli troops in the October War (1973). Pop.: 189 700 (1974 est.).
Is·ma·il Pa·sha (ˌɪzmɑː'iːl 'pɑːʃə) *n.* 1830–95, viceroy (1863–66) and khedive (1867–79) of Egypt, who brought his country close to bankruptcy. He was forced to submit to Anglo-French financial control (1876) and to abdicate (1879).
is·n't ('ɪzᵊnt) *contraction of* is not.
ISO *abbrev. for* International Standards Organization.
I.S.O. *abbrev. for* Imperial Service Order (a Brit. decoration).
i·so- *or before a vowel* **is-** *combining form.* **1.** equal or identical: *isomagnetic.* **2.** indicating that a chemical compound is an isomer of a specified compound: *isobutane; isocyanic acid.* [from Greek *isos* equal]
i·so+ag+glu+ti+na+tion (ˌaɪsəʊəˌgluːtɪ'neɪʃən) *n.* the agglutination of red blood cells of an organism by the blood serum of another organism of the same species. —**ˌi·so+ag+'glu+ti+na+tive** *adj.*
i·so+ag+glu+ti+nin (ˌaɪsəʊə'gluːtɪnɪn) *n.* an antibody that causes agglutination of red blood cells in animals of the same species from which it was derived.
i·so+am+yl ac+e·tate (ˌaɪsəʊ'æmɪl) *n.* a colourless volatile compound used as a solvent for cellulose lacquers and as a flavouring. Formula: $(CH_3)_2CHCH_2CH_2OOCCH_3$.
i·so+an+ti+gen (ˌaɪsəʊ'æntɪdʒən) *n. Immunol.* an antigen that stimulates antibody production in different members of the same species.
i·so+bar ('aɪsəʊˌbɑː) *n.* **1.** a line on a map connecting places of equal atmospheric pressure, usually reduced to sea level for purposes of comparison, at a given time or period. **2.** *Physics.* any of two or more atoms that have the same mass number but different atomic numbers: *tin-115 and indium-115 are isobars.* Compare **isotope.** [C19: from Greek *isobarēs* of equal weight, from ISO- + *baros* weight] —**'i·so+bar+ism** *n.*
i·so+bar+ic (ˌaɪsəʊ'bærɪk) *adj.* **1.** Also: **isopiestic.** having equal atmospheric pressure. **2.** of or relating to isobars.
i·so+bath ('aɪsəʊˌbæθ) *n.* a line on a map connecting points of equal underwater depth. [C19: from Greek *isobathēs* of equal depth, from ISO- + *bathos* depth] —**ˌi·so+'bath+ic** *adj.*
i·so+cheim *or* **i·so+chime** ('aɪsəʊˌkaɪm) *n.* a line on a map connecting places with the same mean winter temperature. [C19: from ISO- + Greek *kheima* winter weather] —**ˌi·so+'chei+mal, ˌi·so+'chei+me·nal,** *or* **ˌi·so+'chi+mal** *adj.*
i·so+chor *or* **i·so+chore** ('aɪsəʊˌkɔː) *n.* a line on a graph showing the variation of the temperature of a fluid with its pressure, when the volume is kept constant. [C19: from ISO- + Greek *khōros* place, space] —**ˌi·so+'chor+ic** *adj.*
i·so+chro+mat+ic (ˌaɪsəʊkrəʊ'mætɪk) *adj.* **1. a.** having the same colour. **b.** of uniform colour. **2.** *Photog.* (of an early type of emulsion) sensitive to green light in addition to blue light but not to red light.
i·soch+ro+nal (aɪ'sɒkrənᵊl) *or* **i·soch+ro+nous** *adj.* **1.** having the same duration; equal in time. **2.** occurring at equal time intervals; having a uniform period of vibration or oscillation. [C17: from New Latin *isochronus,* from Greek *isokhronos,* from ISO- + *khronos* time] —**i·'soch+ro+nal+ly** *or* **i·'soch+ro+nous+ly** *adv.* —**i·'soch+ro+nism** *n.*
i·soch+ro+nize *or* **i·soch+ro+nise** (aɪ'sɒkrəˌnaɪz) *vb.* (*tr.*) to make isochronal.
i·soch+ro+ous (aɪ'sɒkrəʊəs) *adj.* of uniform colour.
i·so+cli+nal (ˌaɪsəʊ'klaɪnᵊl) *or* **i·so+clin+ic** (ˌaɪsəʊ'klɪnɪk) *adj.* **1.** sloping in the same direction and at the same angle. **2.** *Geology.* (of folds) having limbs that are parallel to each other. ~*n.* **3.** Also called: **isocline, isoclinal line.** an imaginary line connecting points on the earth's surface having equal angles of dip.
i·so+cline ('aɪsəʊˌklaɪn) *n.* **1.** a series of rock strata with isoclinal folds. **2.** another name for **isoclinal** (sense 3).
i·soc+ra+cy (aɪ'sɒkrəsɪ) *n., pl.* **+cies. 1.** a form of government in which all people have equal powers. **2.** equality of political power. —**i·so+crat+ic** (ˌaɪsəʊ'krætɪk) *adj.*
I·soc·ra·tes (aɪ'sɒkrəˌtiːz) *n.* 436–338 B.C., Athenian rhetorician and teacher.
i·so+cy+an+ic ac·id (ˌaɪsəʊsaɪ'ænɪk) *n.* a hypothetical acid known only in the form of its compounds. Formula: HNCO.
i·so+cy·a·nide (ˌaɪsəʊ'saɪəˌnaɪd) *n.* any salt or ester of isocyanic acid. Also called: **carbylamine.**
i·so+di·a+met+ric (ˌaɪsəʊˌdaɪə'mɛtrɪk) *adj.* **1.** having diameters of the same length. **2.** (of a crystal) having three equal axes. **3.** (of a cell or similar body) having a similar diameter in all planes.
i·so+di·a+phere (ˌaɪsəʊ'daɪəˌfɪə) *n.* one of two or more nuclides in which the difference between the number of neutrons and the number of protons is the same: *a nuclide that has emitted an alpha particle, and its decay product, are isodiapheres.*
i·so+di+mor+phism (ˌaɪsəʊdaɪ'mɔːfɪzəm) *n.* a property of a dimorphous substance such that it is isomorphous with another dimorphous substance in both its forms. —**ˌi·so+di+'mor+phous** *or* **ˌi·so+di+'mor+phic** *adj.*
i·so+dy+nam+ic (ˌaɪsəʊdaɪ'næmɪk) *adj. Physics.* **1.** having equal force or strength. **2.** of or relating to an imaginary line on the earth's surface connecting points of equal horizontal magnetic intensity.
i·so+e·lec+tric (ˌaɪsəʊɪ'lɛktrɪk) *adj.* having the same electric potential.
i·so+e·lec+tric point *n.* the pH of a substance, such as an amino acid or protein, at which it is electrically neutral.
i·so+e·lec+tron+ic (ˌaɪsəʊɪlɛk'trɒnɪk) *adj.* (of atoms, radicals, or ions) having an equal number of electrons or a similar configuration of electrons.
i·so+gam+ete (ˌaɪsəʊgæ'miːt) *n.* a gamete that is similar in size and form to the one with which it unites in fertilization. Compare **heterogamete.** —**i·so+ga+met+ic** (ˌaɪsəʊgæ'mɛtɪk) *adj.*
i·sog·a·my (aɪ'sɒgəmɪ) *n.* (in some algae and fungi) sexual fusion of gametes of similar size and form. Compare **heterogamy** (sense 1). —**i·'sog·a+mous** *adj.*
i·sog+e·nous (aɪ'sɒdʒɪnəs) *adj. Biology.* **1.** of similar origin, as parts derived from the same embryonic tissue. **2.** Also: **isogenic.** genetically uniform. —**i·'sog+e·ny** *n.*
i·so+ge·o+therm (ˌaɪsəʊ'dʒiːəʊˌθɜːm) *n.* an imaginary line below the surface of the earth connecting points of equal temperature. —**ˌi·so+ˌge·o+'ther+mal** *or* **ˌi·so+ˌge·o+'ther+mic** *adj.*
i·so+gloss ('aɪsəʊˌglɒs) *n.* a line drawn on a map around the area in which a linguistic feature is to be found, such as a particular pronunciation of a given word. —**ˌi·so+'glos+sal** *or* **ˌi·so+'glot+tic** *adj.*
i·so+gon ('aɪsəʊˌgɒn) *n.* an equiangular polygon.
i·so+gon+ic (ˌaɪsəʊ'gɒnɪk) *or* **i·sog·o+nal** (aɪ'sɒgənᵊl) *adj.* **1.** *Maths.* having, making, or involving equal angles. ~*n.* **2.** Also called: **isogonic line, isogonal line, isogone.** *Physics.* an imaginary line connecting points on the earth's surface having equal magnetic declination.
i·so+gram ('aɪsəʊˌgræm) *n.* another name for **isopleth.**
i·so+hel ('aɪsəʊˌhɛl) *n.* a line on a map connecting places with an equal period of sunshine. [C20: from ISO- + Greek *hēlios* sun]
i·so+hy+et (ˌaɪsəʊ'haɪɪt) *n.* a line on a map connecting places having equal rainfall. [C19: from ISO- + *-hyet,* from Greek *huetos* rain]
i·so+late *vb.* ('aɪsəˌleɪt) (*tr.*) **1.** to place apart; cause to be alone. **2.** *Med.* to quarantine (a person or animal) having or suspected of having a contagious disease. **3.** to obtain (a compound) in an uncombined form. **4.** to obtain pure cultures of (bacteria, esp. those causing a particular disease). **5.** *Electronics.* to prevent interaction between (circuits, components, etc.); insulate. ~*n.* ('aɪsəlɪt). **6.** an isolated person or group. [C19: back formation from *isolated,* via Italian from Latin *insulātus,* literally: made into an island; see INSULATE] —**'i·so+la·ble** *adj.* —**ˌi·so+la·'bil+i·ty** *n.* —**'i·so+ˌla+tor** *n.*
i·so+lat+ing ('aɪsəˌleɪtɪŋ) *adj. Linguistics.* another word for **analytic.**
i·so+la+tion (ˌaɪsə'leɪʃən) *n.* **1.** the act of isolating or the condition of being isolated. **2.** (of a country, party, etc.) nonparticipation in or withdrawal from international politics. **3.** *Med.* **a.** social separation of a person who has or is suspected of having a contagious disease. Compare **quarantine. b.** (*as modifier*): *an isolation hospital.* **4.** *Sociol.* a lack of contact between persons, groups, or whole societies. **5.** *Social psychol.* the failure of an individual to maintain contact with others or genuine communication where interaction with others persists. **6. in isolation.** without regard to context, similar matters, etc.
i·so+la+tion+ism (ˌaɪsə'leɪʃəˌnɪzəm) *n.* **1.** a policy of nonparticipation in or withdrawal from international affairs. **2.** an attitude favouring such a policy. —**ˌi·so+'la+tion+ist** *n., adj.*
is·o+la+tive ('aɪsəˌleɪtɪv, 'aɪsələtɪv) *adj.* **1.** (of a sound change) occurring in all linguistic environments, as the change of Middle English /iː/ to Modern English /aɪ/, as in *time.* Compare **combinative** (sense 2). **2.** of, relating to, or concerned with isolation.
I·sol·de (ɪ'zɒldə) *n.* the German name of **Iseult.**
i·so+lec·i·thal (ˌaɪsəʊ'lɛsɪθəl) *adj.* (of the ova of mammals and

certain other vertebrates) having an evenly distributed yolk. Compare **heterolecithal.**

i·so+leu+cine (ˌaɪsəʊˈlu:si:n, -sɪn) *n.* an amino acid that occurs in proteins and is essential to man. Formula: $C_2H_5CH(CH_3)CH(NH_2)COOH$.

i·so+lex (ˈaɪsəˌlɛks) *n. Linguistics.* an isogloss marking off the area in which a particular item of vocabulary is found [C20: from ISO(GLOSS) + Greek *lex(is)*word]

i·so+line (ˈaɪsəʊˌlaɪn) *n.* another term for **isopleth.**

i·sol·o·gous (aɪˈsɒləgəs) *adj.* (of two or more organic compounds) having a similar structure but containing different atoms of the same valency. [C19: from ISO- + (HOMO)LOGOUS] —**i·so+logue** (ˈaɪsəʊˌlɒg) *n.*

i·so+mag+net+ic (ˌaɪsəʊmægˈnɛtɪk) *adj.* **1.** having equal magnetic induction or force. *~n.* **2.** Also called: **isomagnetic line.** an imaginary line connecting points on the earth's surface having equal magnetic intensity.

i·so+mer (ˈaɪsəmə) *n.* **1.** *Chem.* a compound that exhibits isomerism with one or more other compounds. **2.** *Physics.* a nuclide that exhibits isomerism with one or more other nuclides. —**i·so+mer+ic** (ˌaɪsəˈmɛrɪk) *adj.*

i·som+er+ism (aɪˈsɒməˌrɪzəm) *n.* **1.** the existence of two or more compounds having the same molecular formula but a different arrangement of atoms within the molecule. See also **stereoisomerism, optical isomerism. 2.** the existence of two or more nuclides having the same atomic numbers and mass numbers but different energy states.

i·som+er+ize *or* **i·som+er+ise** (aɪˈsɒməˌraɪz) *vb. Chem.* to change or cause to change from one isomer to another. —**i·ˌsom+er·i+ˈza·tion** *or* **i·ˌsom+er·i+ˈsa·tion** *n.*

i·som+er+ous (aɪˈsɒmərəs) *adj.* **1.** having an equal number of parts or markings. **2.** (of flowers) having floral whorls with the same number of parts. Compare **anisomerous.**

i·so+met+ric (ˌaɪsəʊˈmɛtrɪk) *adj. also* **i·so+met+ri+cal. 1.** having equal dimensions or measurements. **2.** *Physiol.* of or relating to muscular contraction that does not produce shortening of the muscle. **3.** (of a crystal or system of crystallization) having three mutually perpendicular equal axes. **4.** *Crystallog.* another word for **cubic** (sense 4). **5.** *Prosody.* having or made up of regular feet. **6.** (of a method of projecting a drawing in three dimensions) having the three axes equally inclined and all lines drawn to scale. *~n.* **7.** Also called: **isometric drawing.** a drawing made in this way. **8.** Also called: **isometric line.** a line on a graph showing variations of pressure with temperature at constant volume. [C19: from Greek *isometria* (see ISO- + -METRY) + -IC] —ˌ**i·so+ˈmet+ri+cal+ly** *adv.*

i·so+met+rics (ˌaɪsəʊˈmɛtrɪks) *n.* (*functioning as sing.*) physical exercise involving isometric contraction of muscles.

i·so+me·tro+pi·a (ˌaɪsəʊmɪˈtrəʊpɪə) *n. Ophthalmol.* equal refraction of the two eyes. [from Greek *isometros* of equal measure + -OPIA]

i·som+e·try (aɪˈsɒmɪtrɪ) *n.* **1.** *Maths.* rigid motion of a plane or space such that the distance between any two points before and after this motion is unaltered. **2.** equality of height above sea level.

i·so+morph (ˈaɪsəʊˌmɔ:f) *n.* a substance or organism that exhibits isomorphism.

i·so+mor+phism (ˌaɪsəʊˈmɔ:fɪzəm) *n.* **1.** *Biology.* similarity of form, as in different generations of the same life cycle. **2.** *Chem.* the existence of two or more substances of different composition in a similar crystalline form. **3.** *Maths.* a one-to-one correspondence between the elements of two or more sets, such as those of Arabic and Roman numerals, and between the sums or products of the elements of one of these sets and those of the equivalent elements of the other set or sets. —ˌ**i·so+ˈmor+phic** *or* ˌ**i·so+ˈmor+phous** *adj.*

i·so+ni·a+zid (ˌaɪsəʊˈnaɪəzɪd) *n.* a soluble colourless crystalline compound used to treat tuberculosis. Formula: $C_6H_7N_3O$. [C20: *isoni(cotinic acid hydr)azid(e)*]

i·son·o+my (aɪˈsɒnəmɪ) *n.* **1.** the equality before the law of the citizens of a state. **2.** the equality of civil or political rights. —**i·so+nom+ic** (ˌaɪsəʊˈnɒmɪk) *or* **i·ˈson·o+mous** *adj.*

i·so+oc·tane (ˌaɪsəʊˈɒkteɪn) *n.* a colourless liquid alkane hydrocarbon produced from petroleum and used in standardizing petrol. Formula: $(CH_3)_3CCH_2CH(CH_3)_2$. See also **octane number.**

i·so+phone (ˈaɪsəˌfəʊn) *n. Linguistics.* an isogloss marking off an area in which a particular feature of pronunciation is found. [C20: from *iso-* (as in ISOGLOSS) + *-phone* (as in PHONEME, etc.)]

i·so+pi·es+tic (ˌaɪsəʊpaɪˈɛstɪk) *adj.* another word for **isobaric** (sense 1). [C19: from ISO- + Greek *piestos* compressible, from *piezein* to press] —ˌ**i·so+pi+ˈes+ti+cal+ly** *adv.*

i·so+pleth (ˈaɪsəʊˌplɛθ) *n.* a line on a map connecting places registering the same amount or ratio of some geographical or meteorological phenomenon or phenomena. Also called: **isogram, isoline.** [C20: from Greek *isoplēthēs* equal in number, from ISO- + *plēthos* multitude, great number]

i·so+pod (ˈaɪsəʊˌpɒd) *n.* **1.** any crustacean of the order *Isopoda*, including woodlice and pill bugs, in which the body is flattened dorsoventrally. *~adj.* **2.** of, relating to, or belonging to the *Isopoda*. —**i·sop·o+dan** (aɪˈsɒpədən) *or* **i·ˈsop·o+dous** *adj.*

i·so+prene (ˈaɪsəʊˌpri:n) *n.* a colourless volatile liquid with a penetrating odour: used in making synthetic rubbers. Formula: $CH_2{:}CHC(CH_3){:}CH_2$. [C20: from ISO- + PR(OPYL) + -ENE]

i·so+pro+pyl (ˌaɪsəʊˈprəʊpɪl) *n.* (*modifier*) of, consisting of, or containing the group of atoms $(CH_3)_2CH$-, derived from propane: *an isopropyl group or radical.*

i·so+rhyth+mic (ˌaɪsəˈrɪðmɪk) *adj. Music.* (of medieval motets) having a cantus firmus that is repeated according to a strict system of internal reiterated note values.

i·sos+ce·les (aɪˈsɒsɪˌli:z) *adj.* **1.** (of a triangle) having two sides of equal length. **2.** (of a trapezium) having the two nonparallel sides of equal length. [C16: from Late Latin, from Greek *isoskelēs*, from ISO- + *skelos* leg]

i·so+seis+mal (ˌaɪsəʊˈsaɪzməl) *adj.* **1.** of or relating to equal intensity of earthquake shock. *~n.* **2.** a line on a map connecting points at which earthquake shocks are of equal intensity. *~*Also: **isoseismic.**

is+os+mot+ic (ˌaɪsɒzˈmɒtɪk) *adj.* another word for **isotonic** (sense 2).

i·so+spon+dy+lous (ˌaɪsəˈspɒndᵊləs) *adj.* of, relating to, or belonging to the *Isospondyli* (or *Clupeiformes*), an order of soft-finned teleost fishes that includes the herring, salmon, trout, and pike. [C20: from ISO- + Greek *spondulos* vertebra]

i·sos+ta+sy (aɪˈsɒstəsɪ) *n.* the theoretical state of balance between different landmasses on the earth's surface, which are assumed to float on a denser underlying material so that when one mass becomes lighter, as by erosion, it rises causing compensating subsidence of a heavier mass. [C19: ISO- + *-stasy*, from Greek *stasis* a standing] —**i·so+stat+ic** (ˌaɪsəʊˈstætɪk) *adj.*

i·so+ster+ic (ˌaɪsəʊˈstɛrɪk) *adj.* (of two different molecules) having the same number of atoms and the same number and configuration of valency electrons, as carbon dioxide and nitrous oxide.

i·so+tac+tic (ˌaɪsəʊˈtæktɪk) *adj. Chem.* (of a stereospecific polymer) having identical steric configurations of the groups on each asymmetric carbon atom on the chain. Compare **syndiotactic.**

i·so+there (ˈaɪsəʊˌθɪə) *n.* a line on a map linking places with the same mean summer temperature. Compare **isocheim.** [C19: from ISO- + Greek *theros* summer] —**i·soth+er+al** (aɪˈsɒθərəl) *adj.*

i·so+therm (ˈaɪsəʊˌθɜ:m) *n.* **1.** a line on a map linking places of equal temperature. **2.** *Physics.* a curve on a graph that connects points of equal temperature. *~*Also called: **isothermal, isothermal line.**

i·so+ther+mal (ˌaɪsəʊˈθɜ:məl) *adj.* **1.** (of a process or change) taking place at constant temperature. **2.** of or relating to an isotherm. *~n.* **3.** another word for **isotherm.** —ˌ**i·so+ˈther+mal+ly** *adv.*

i·so+tone (ˈaɪsəˌtəʊn) *n.* one of two or more atoms of different atomic number that contain the same number of neutrons.

i·so+ton+ic (ˌaɪsəʊˈtɒnɪk) *adj.* **1.** *Physiol.* (of two or more muscles) having equal tension. **2.** Also: **isosmotic.** (of two solutions) having the same osmotic pressure. Compare **hypertonic, hypotonic. 3.** *Music.* of, relating to, or characterized by the equal intervals of the well-tempered scale: *isotonic tuning.* —**i·so+to+nic+i·ty** (ˌaɪsəʊtəʊˈnɪsɪtɪ) *n.*

i·so+tope (ˈaɪsəˌtəʊp) *n.* one of two or more atoms with the same atomic number that contain different numbers of neutrons. [C20: from ISO- + Greek *topos* place] —**i·so+top+ic** (ˌaɪsəˈtɒpɪk) *adj.* —ˌ**i·so+ˈtop·i+cal+ly** *adv.* —**i·sot·o+py** (aɪˈsɒtəpɪ) *n.*

i·so+tron (ˈaɪsəˌtrɒn) *n. Physics.* a device for separating small quantities of isotopes by ionizing them and separating the ions by an electric field, as in a mass spectrometer. [C20: from ISOTOPE + -TRON]

i·so+trop+ic (ˌaɪsəʊˈtrɒpɪk) *or* **i·sot+ro+pous** (aɪˈsɒtrəpəs) *adj.* **1.** having uniform physical properties in all directions. **2.** *Biology.* not having predetermined axes: *isotropic eggs.* —ˌ**i·so+ˈtrop·i+cal+ly** *adv.* —**i·ˈsot+ro+py** *n.*

I-spy *n.* a game in which one player specifies the initial letter of the name of an object that he can see, which the other players then try to guess.

Is+ra+el (ˈɪzreɪəl, -rɪəl) *n.* **1.** a republic in SW Asia, on the Mediterranean Sea: established in 1948, in the former British mandate of Palestine, as a Jewish state; sporadic border disputes with Arab neighbours, erupting into full-scale wars in 1949, 1956, 1967 (the Six Day War), and 1973. Official language: Hebrew. Religion: Judaism. Currency: Israeli pound. Capital: Jerusalem. Pop.: 3 371 000 (1975 est.). Area (after 1949 armistice): 20 700 sq. km (7993 sq. miles). After the 1967 cease-fire Israel controlled an area of 89 359 sq. km (34 493 sq. miles). **2. a.** the ancient kingdom of the 12 Hebrew tribes at the SE end of the Mediterranean. **b.** the kingdom in the N part of this region formed by the ten northern tribes of Israel in the 10th century B.C. and destroyed by the Assyrians in 721 B.C.

Is+rae+li (ɪzˈreɪlɪ) *n., pl.* **+lis** *or* **+li. 1.** a citizen or inhabitant of the state of Israel. *~adj.* **2.** of, relating to, or characteristic of the state of Israel or its inhabitants.

Is+ra·el+ite (ˈɪzrɪəˌlaɪt, -rə-) *n.* **1.** *Bible.* a member of the ethnic group claiming descent from Jacob; a Hebrew. **2.** *Bible.* a citizen of the kingdom of Israel (922 to 721 B.C.) as opposed to Judah. **3.** a member of any of various Christian sects who regard themselves as God's chosen people. **4.** an archaic word for a **Jew.**

Is+ra+fil (ˈɪzrəˌfi:l), **Is+ra+fel** (ˈɪzrəˌfɛl), *or* **Is+ra+feel** (ˈɪzrəˌfi:l) *n. Koran.* the archangel who will sound the trumpet on the Day of Judgment, heralding the end of the world.

Is·sa·char (ˈɪsəˌkɑ:) *n. Old Testament.* **1.** the fifth son of Jacob by his wife Leah (Genesis 30:17–18). **2.** the tribe descended from this patriarch. **3.** the territory of this tribe.

is+su·a·ble (ˈɪʃjuəbᵊl) *adj.* **1.** capable of issuing or being issued. **2.** *Chiefly law.* open to debate or litigation. **3.** authorized to be issued. —**ˈis+su+a·bly** *adv.*

is+su+ance ('ɪʃjuəns) *n.* the act of issuing.
is+su+ant ('ɪʃjuənt) *adj. Archaic or heraldry.* emerging or issuing.
is+sue ('ɪʃju:) *n.* **1.** the act of sending or giving out something; supply; delivery. **2.** something issued; an edition of stamps, a magazine, etc. **3.** the act of emerging; outflow; discharge. **4.** something flowing out, such as a river. **5.** a place of outflow; outlet. **6.** the descendants of a person; offspring; progeny. **7.** a topic of interest or discussion. **8.** an important subject requiring a decision. **9.** an outcome or consequence; result. **10.** *Pathol.* **a.** a suppurating sore. **b.** discharge from a wound. **11.** *Law.* the matter remaining in dispute between the parties to an action after the pleadings. **12.** the yield from or profits arising out of land or other property. **13.** *Military.* the allocation of items of government stores, such as food, clothing, and ammunition. **14.** *Library science.* **a.** the system for recording current loans. **b.** the number of books loaned in a specified period. **15.** *Obsolete.* an act, deed, or proceeding. **16. at issue. a.** under discussion. **b.** in disagreement. **17. force the issue.** to compel decision on some matter. **18. join issue. a.** to join in controversy. **b.** to submit an issue for adjudication. **19. take issue.** to disagree. ~*vb.* **+sues, +su+ing, +sued. 20.** to come forth or emerge or cause to come forth or emerge. **21.** to publish or deliver (a newspaper, magazine, etc.). **22.** (*tr.*) to make known or announce. **23.** (*intr.*) to originate or proceed. **24.** (*intr.*) to be a consequence; result. **25.** (*intr.*; foll. by *in*) to end or terminate. **26.** (*tr.*) **a.** to give out or allocate (equipment, a certificate, etc.) officially to someone. **b.** (foll. by *with*) to supply officially (with). [C13: from Old French *eissue* way out, from *eissir* to go out, from Latin *exīre*, from EX-[1] + *īre* to go] —**'is+sue+less** *adj.* —**'is+su+er** *n.*
Is+sus ('ɪsəs) *n.* an ancient town in S Asia Minor, in Cilicia north of present-day Iskenderun: scene of a battle (333 B.C.) in which Alexander the Great defeated the Persians.
Is·syk-Kul (*Russian* is'sɪk 'kulj) *n.* a lake in the SW Soviet Union, in the NE Kirghiz SSR in the Tien Shan mountains, at an altitude of 1609 m (5280 ft.): one of the largest mountain lakes in the world. Area: 6200 sq. km (2390 sq. miles).
-ist *suffix.* **1.** (*forming nouns*) a person who performs a certain action or is concerned with something specified: *motorist; soloist.* **2.** (*forming nouns*) a person who practises in a specific field: *physicist; typist.* **3.** (*forming nouns and adjectives*) a person who advocates a particular doctrine, system, etc., or relating to such a person or the doctrine advocated: *socialist.* **4.** (*forming nouns and adjectives*) a person characterized by a specified trait, tendency, etc., or relating to such a person or trait: *purist.* [via Old French from Latin *-ista, -istēs*, from Greek *-istēs*]
i·sta+na (i:'stana) *n.* (in Malaysia) a royal palace. [from Malay]
Is+tan+bul (ˌɪstæn'bu:l) *n.* a port in NW Turkey, on the western (European) shore of the Bosporus: the largest city in Turkey; founded in about 660 B.C. by Greeks; refounded by Constantine the Great in 330 A.D. as the capital of the Eastern Roman Empire; taken by the Turks in 1453 and remained capital of the Ottoman Empire until 1922; industrial centre for shipbuilding, textiles, etc. Pop.: 2 547 364 (1975). Ancient name: **Byzantium.** Former name (330–1930): **Constantinople.**
Isth. *or* **isth.** *abbrev. for* isthmus.
isth+mi·an ('ɪsθmɪən) *adj.* relating to or situated in an isthmus.
Isth+mi·an ('ɪsθmɪən) *adj.* relating to or situated in the Isthmus of Corinth or the Isthmus of Panama.
Isth+mi·an Games *n.* a Panhellenic festival celebrated every other year in ancient Corinth.
isth+mus ('ɪsməs) *n., pl.* **+mus·es** *or* **+mi** (-maɪ). **1.** a narrow strip of land connecting two relatively large land areas. **2.** *Anatomy.* **a.** a narrow band of tissue connecting two larger parts of a structure. **b.** a narrow passage connecting two cavities. [C16: from Latin, from Greek *isthmos*] —**'isth+moid** *adj.*
-is·tic *suffix forming adjectives.* equivalent to a combination of **-ist** and **-ic** but in some words having a less specific or literal application and sometimes a mildly pejorative force, as compared with corresponding adjectives ending in **-ist:** *communistic; impressionistic.* [from Latin *-isticus*, from Greek *istikos*]
is+tle ('ɪstlɪ) *or* **ix+tle** *n.* a fibre obtained from various tropical American agave and yucca trees used in making carpets, cord, etc. [C19: from Mexican Spanish *ixtle*, from Nahuatl *ichtli*]
Is+tri·a ('ɪstrɪə) *n.* a peninsula in the N Adriatic Sea: passed from Italy to Yugoslavia (except for Trieste) in 1947. —**'Is+tri·an** *n., adj.*
it (ɪt) *pron.* (*subjective or objective*) **1.** refers to a nonhuman, animal, plant, or inanimate thing, or sometimes to a small baby: *it looks dangerous; give it a bone.* **2.** refers to an unspecified or implied antecedent or to a previous or understood clause, phrase, etc.: *it is impossible; I knew it.* **3.** used to represent human life or experience either in totality or in respect of the present situation: *how's it going? I've had it; to brazen it out.* **4.** used as a formal subject (or object), referring to a following clause, phrase, or word: *it helps to know the truth; I consider it dangerous to go on.* **5.** used in the nominative as the formal grammatical subject of impersonal verbs. When *it* functions absolutely in such sentences, not referring to any previous or following clause or phrase, the context is nearly always a description of the environment or of some physical sensation: *it is raining; it hurts.* **6.** (used as complement with *be*) *Informal.* the crucial or ultimate point: *the steering failed and I thought that was it.* ~*n.* **7.** (in children's games) the player whose turn it is to try to touch another. **8.** *Informal.* **a.** sexual intercourse. **b.** sex appeal. [Old English *hit*]
It. *abbrev. for:* **1.** Italian. **2.** Italy.
i.t.a. *or* **I.T.A.** *abbrev. for* initial teaching alphabet, a partly phonetic alphabet used to teach reading.
I.T.A. (in Britain) *abbrev. for* Independent Television Authority: now superseded by the I.B.A.
it·a+col·u+mite (ˌɪtə'kɒljʊˌmaɪt) *n.* a fine-grained micaceous sandstone that occurs in thin flexible slabs. [C19: named after *Itacolumi* mountain in Brazil where it is found]
it·a+con+ic ac·id (ˌɪtə'kɒnɪk) *n.* a white colourless crystalline carboxylic acid obtained by the fermentation of carbohydrates and used in the manufacture of synthetic resins. Formula: CH_2:C(COOH)CH_2COOH.
ital. *abbrev. for* italic.
Ital. *abbrev. for:* **1.** Italian. **2.** Italy.
I·ta+lia (i'ta:lja) *n.* the Italian name for **Italy.**
I·ta+lia ir+re+den+ta *Italian.* (ˌirre'dɛnta) See **Irredentist.**
I·tal+ian (ɪ'tæljən) *n.* **1.** the official language of Italy and one of the official languages of Switzerland: the native language of approximately 60 million people. It belongs to the Romance group of the Indo-European family, and there is a considerable diversity of dialects. **2.** a native, citizen, or inhabitant of Italy, or a descendant of one. **3.** See **Italian vermouth.** ~*adj.* **4.** relating to, denoting, or characteristic of Italy, its inhabitants, or their language.
I·tal+ian+ate (ɪ'tæljənɪt, -ˌneɪt) *or* **I·tal+ian+esque** *adj.* Italian in style or character.
I·tal+ian East Af+ri+ca *n.* a former Italian territory in E Africa, formed in 1936 from the possessions of Eritrea, Italian Somaliland, and Ethiopia: taken by British forces in 1941.
I·tal+ian+ism (ɪ'tæljəˌnɪzəm) *or* **I·tal·i+cism** (ɪ'tælɪˌsɪzəm) *n.* **1.** an Italian custom or style. **2.** Italian quality or life, or the cult of either.
I·tal+ian+ize *or* **I·tal+ian+ise** (ɪ'tæljəˌnaɪz) *vb.* to make or become Italian or like an Italian person or thing. —**I·ˌtal+ian·i+'za+tion** *or* **I·ˌtal+ian·i+'sa+tion** *n.*
I·tal+ian sixth *n.* (in musical harmony) an augmented sixth chord characterized by having a major third and an augmented sixth above the root.
I·tal+ian So+ma+li+land *n.* a former Italian colony in E Africa, united with British Somaliland in 1960 to form the independent republic of Somalia.
I·tal+ian son+net *n.* another term for **Petrarchan sonnet.**
I·tal+ian ver+mouth *n.* sweet vermouth.
i·tal+ic (ɪ'tælɪk) *adj.* **1.** Also: **Italian.** of, relating to, or denoting a style of handwriting with the letters slanting to the right. **2.** a style of printing type modelled on this, chiefly used to indicate emphasis, a foreign word, etc. Compare **roman.** ~*n.* **3.** (*often pl.*) italic type or print. [C16 (after an edition of Virgil (1501) printed in Venice and dedicated to Italy): from Latin *Italicus* of Italy, from Greek *Italikos*]
I·tal+ic (ɪ'tælɪk) *n.* **1.** a branch of the Indo-European family of languages that includes many of the ancient languages of Italy, such as Venetic and the Osco-Umbrian group, Latin, which displaced them, and the Romance languages. ~*adj.* **2.** denoting, relating to, or belonging to this group of languages, esp. the extinct ones.
i·tal·i+cize *or* **i·tal·i+cise** (ɪ'tælɪˌsaɪz) *vb.* **1.** to print (textual matter) in italic type. **2.** (*tr.*) to underline (letters, words, etc.) with a single line to indicate italics. —**i·ˌtal·i·ci+'za·tion** *or* **i·ˌtal·i+ci+'sa+tion** *n.*
I·tal·o- (ɪ'tæləʊ-) *combining form.* indicating Italy or Italian: *Italophobia; Italo-German.*
It·a+ly ('ɪtəlɪ) *n.* a republic in S Europe, occupying a peninsula in the Mediterranean between the Tyrrhenian and the Adriatic Seas, with the islands of Sardinia and Sicily to the west: first united under the Romans but became fragmented into numerous political units in the Middle Ages; united kingdom proclaimed in 1861; under the dictatorship of Mussolini (1922–43); became a republic in 1946; a member of the Common Market. It is generally mountainous, with the Alps in the north and the Apennines running the length of the peninsula. Language: Italian. Religion: Roman Catholic. Currency: lira. Capital: Rome. Pop.: 55 361 000 (1974 est.). Area: 301 247 sq. km (116 312 sq. miles). Italian name: **Italia.**
itch (ɪtʃ) *n.* **1.** an irritation or tickling sensation of the skin causing a desire to scratch. **2.** a restless desire. **3.** any skin disorder, such as scabies, characterized by intense itching. ~*vb.* **4.** (*intr.*) to feel or produce an irritating or tickling sensation. **5.** (*intr.*) to have a restless desire (to do something). **6. itching palm.** a grasping nature; avarice. **7.** *Not standard.* to scratch (the skin). [Old English *gīccean* to itch, of Germanic origin] —**'itch·y** *adj.* —**'itch·i+ness** *n.*
itch mite *n.* any mite of the family *Sarcoptidae*, all of which are skin parasites, esp. *Sarcoptes scabei*, which causes scabies.
-ite[1] *suffix forming nouns.* **1.** a native or inhabitant of: *Israelite.* **2.** a follower or advocate of; a member or supporter of a group: *Luddite; labourite.* **3.** (in biology) indicating a division of a body or organ: *neurite; somite.* **4.** indicating a mineral or rock: *nephrite; peridotite.* **5.** indicating a commercial product: *vulcanite.* [via Latin *-ita* from Greek *-itēs* or directly from Greek]
-ite[2] *suffix of nouns.* indicating a salt or ester of an acid having a name ending in *-ous: a nitrite is a salt of nitrous acid.* [from French, arbitrary alteration of -ATE[1]]
i·tem *n.* ('aɪtəm). **1.** a thing or unit, esp. included in a list or collection. **2.** *Bookkeeping.* an entry in an account. **3.** a piece of information, detail, or note: *a news item.* ~*vb.* ('aɪtəm). **4.**

(*tr.*) an archaic word for **itemize.** ~*adv.* (ˈaɪtɛm). **5.** likewise; also. [C14 (adv.) from Latin: in like manner]

i·tem·ize *or* **i·tem·ise** (ˈaɪtəˌmaɪz) *vb.* (*tr.*) to put on a list or make a list of. —**ˌi·tem·iˈza·tion** *or* **ˌi·tem·iˈsa·tion** *n.* —**ˈi·tem·ˌiz·er** *or* **ˈi·tem·ˌis·er** *n.*

i·tem ve·to *n. U.S.* the power of a state governor to veto items in bills without vetoing the entire measure.

I·té·nez (iˈtenes) *n.* the Spanish name for the **Guaporé.**

it·er·ate (ˈɪtəˌreɪt) *vb.* (*tr.*) to say or do again; repeat. [C16: from Latin *iterāre,* from *iterum* again] —**ˈit·er·ant** *adj.* —**ˌit·er·ˈa·tion** *or* **ˈit·er·ance** *n.*

it·er·a·tive (ˈɪtərətɪv) *adj.* repetitious or frequent. —**ˈit·er·a·tive·ly** *adv.* —**ˈit·er·a·tive·ness** *n.*

Ith·a·ca (ˈɪθəkə) *n.* a Greek island in the Ionian Sea, the smallest of the Ionian Islands: regarded as the home of Homer's Odysseus. Area: 93 sq. km (36 sq. miles). Modern Greek name: **I·thá·ki** (iˈθaki). —**ˈIth·a·can** *n., adj.*

I·thunn (ˈiːðuːn) *n.* a variant spelling of **Idun.**

ith·y·phal·lic (ˌɪθɪˈfælɪk) *adj.* **1.** *Prosody.* (in classical verse) of or relating to the usual metre in hymns to Bacchus. **2.** of or relating to the phallus carried in the ancient festivals of Bacchus. **3.** (of sculpture and graphic art) having or showing an erect penis. ~*n.* **4.** *Prosody.* a poem in ithyphallic metre. [C17: from Late Latin, from Greek *ithuphallikos,* from *ithuphallos* erect phallus, from *ithus* straight + *phallos* PHALLUS]

i·tin·er·an·cy (ɪˈtɪnərənsɪ, aɪ-) *or* **i·tin·er·a·cy** *n.* **1.** the act of itinerating. **2.** *Chiefly Methodist Church.* the system of appointing a minister to a circuit of churches or chapels. **3.** itinerants collectively.

i·tin·er·ant (ɪˈtɪnərənt, aɪ-) *adj.* **1.** itinerating. **2.** working for a short time in various places, esp. as a casual labourer. ~*n.* **3.** an itinerant worker or other person. [C16: from Late Latin *itinerārī* to travel, from *iter* a journey] —**iˈtin·er·ant·ly** *adv.*

i·tin·er·ar·y (aɪˈtɪnərərɪ, ɪ-) *n., pl.* **·ar·ies. 1.** a plan or line of travel; route. **2.** a record of a journey. **3.** a guidebook for travellers. ~*adj.* **4.** of or relating to travel or routes of travel. **5.** a less common word for **itinerant.**

i·tin·er·ate (aɪˈtɪnəˌreɪt, ɪ-) *vb.* (*intr.*) to travel from place to place. —**iˌtin·er·ˈa·tion** *n.*

-i·tis *suffix forming nouns.* indicating inflammation of a specified part: *tonsillitis.* [New Latin, from Greek, feminine of *-itēs* belonging to; see -ITE[1]]

it'll (ˈɪtᵊl) *contraction of* it will *or* it shall.

I·to (ˈiːtəʊ) *n.* Marquis **Hi·ro·bu·mi** (ˌhɪrəˈbuːmɪ). 1841–1909, Japanese statesman; premier (1884–88; 1892–96; 1898; 1900–01). He led the movement to modernize Japan and helped to draft the Meiji constitution (1889); assassinated.

I.T.O. *abbrev. for* International Trade Organization.

-it·ol *suffix forming nouns.* indicating that certain chemical compounds are polyhydric alcohols: *inisitol; sorbitol.* [from -ITE[2] + -OL[1]]

its (ɪts) *determiner.* **a.** of, belonging to, or associated in some way with it: *its left rear wheel; I can see its logical consequence.* **b.** (*as pronoun*): *its is over there.*

it's (ɪts) *contraction of* it is.

it·self (ɪtˈsɛlf) *pron.* **1. a.** the reflexive form of **it. b.** (*intensifier*): *even the money itself won't convince me.* **2.** (*preceded by a copula*) its normal or usual self: *my cat doesn't seem itself these days.*

Usage. See at **myself.**

I.T.U. *abbrev. for* International Telecommunications Union.

ITV (in Britain) *abbrev. for* Independent Television.

-i·ty *suffix forming nouns.* indicating state or condition: *technicality.* [from Old French *-ite,* from Latin *-itās*]

i-type sem·i·con·duc·tor *n.* another name for **intrinsic semiconductor.**

I.U. *abbrev. for:* **1.** immunizing unit. **2.** international unit.

I.U.(C.)D. *abbrev. for* intra-uterine (contraceptive) device.

I·u·lus (aɪˈjuːləs) *n.* **1.** another name for **Ascanius. 2.** the son of Ascanius, founder of the Julian gens or clan.

-i·um *or sometimes* **-um** *suffix forming nouns.* **1.** indicating a metallic element: *platinum; barium.* **2.** (in chemistry) indicating groups forming positive ions: *ammonium chloride; hydroxonium ion.* **3.** indicating a biological structure: *syncytium.* [New Latin, from Latin, from Greek *-ion,* diminutive suffix]

i.v. *abbrev. for:* **1.** initial velocity. **2.** intravenous(ly).

I.V. *or* **i.v.** *abbrev. for* intravenous.

I·van III (ˈaɪvən) *n.* called *the Great.* 1440–1505, grand duke of Muscovy (1462–1505). He expanded Muscovy by conquest, defeated the Tatars (1480), and assumed the title of Ruler of all Russia (1472).

I·van IV *n.* called *the Terrible.* 1530–84, grand duke of Muscovy (1533–47) and first tsar of Russia (1547–84). He conquered Kazan (1552), Astrakhan (1556), and Siberia (1581), but was defeated by Poland in the Livonian War (1558–82) after which his rule became increasingly oppressive.

I·va·no·vo (*Russian* ɪˈvanəvə) *n.* a city in the central Soviet Union, on the Uvod River: textile centre. Pop.: 453 000 (1975 est.). Former name (1871–1932): **I·va·no·vo-Voz·ne·sensk** (vəznɪˈsjɛnsk).

IVB *abbrev. for* invalidity benefit.

-ive *suffix.* **1.** (*forming adjectives*) indicating a tendency, inclination, character, or quality: *divisive; prohibitive; festive; massive.* **2.** (*forming nouns of adjectival origin*): *detective; expletive.* [from Latin *-īvus*]

I've (aɪv) *contraction of* I have.

Ives (aɪvz) *n.* **1. Charles Ed·ward.** 1874–1954, U.S. composer, noted for his innovative use of polytonality, polyrhythms, and quarter tones. His works include *Second Piano Sonata: Concord* (1915), five symphonies, chamber music, and songs. **2. Fred·er·ick Eu·gene.** 1856–1937, U.S. inventor of halftone photography.

i·vied (ˈaɪvɪd) *adj.* covered with ivy.

I·vi·za (*Spanish* iˈβiθa) *n.* a variant spelling of **Ibiza.**

I·vo·ries (ˈaɪvərɪz, -vrɪz) *pl. n. Slang.* **1.** the keys of a piano. **2.** another word for **teeth. 3.** another word for **dice.**

i·vo·ry (ˈaɪvərɪ, -vrɪ) *n., pl.* **·ries. 1. a.** a hard smooth creamy white variety of dentine that makes up a major part of the tusks of elephants, walruses, and similar animals. **b.** (*as modifier*): *ivory ornaments.* **2.** a tusk made of ivory. **3. a.** a yellowish-white colour; cream. **b.** (*as adj.*): *ivory shoes.* **4.** a substance resembling elephant tusk. **5.** an ornament, etc., made of ivory. **6. black ivory.** *Obsolete.* Negro slaves collectively. [C13: from Old French *ivurie,* from Latin *evoreus* made of ivory, from *ebur* ivory; related to Greek *elephas* ivory, ELEPHANT] —**ˈi·vo·ry-ˌlike** *adj.*

i·vo·ry black *n.* a black pigment obtained by grinding charred scraps of ivory in oil.

I·vo·ry Coast *n.* **the.** a republic in West Africa, on the Gulf of Guinea: Portuguese trading for ivory and slaves began in the 16th century; made a French protectorate in 1842 and became independent in 1960; third largest producer of coffee in the world. Official language: French. Religion: animist majority, with Muslim and Roman Catholic minorities. Currency: franc. Capital: Abidjan. Pop.: 6 673 013 (1975). Area: 319 820 sq. km (123 483 sq. miles).

i·vo·ry gull *n.* a white gull, *Pagophila* (or *Larus*) *eburneus,* mostly confined to arctic regions.

i·vo·ry nut *n.* **1.** the seed of the ivory palm, which contains an ivory-like substance used to make buttons, etc. **2.** any similar seed from other palms. ~Also called: **vegetable ivory.**

i·vo·ry palm *n.* a low-growing South American palm tree, *Phytelephas macrocarpa,* that yields the ivory nut.

i·vo·ry tow·er (ˈtaʊə) *n.* seclusion or remoteness of attitude regarding real problems, everyday life, etc.

i·vy (ˈaɪvɪ) *n., pl.* **i·vies. 1.** any woody climbing or trailing araliaceous plant of the Old World genus *Hedera,* esp. *H. helix,* having lobed evergreen leaves and black berry-like fruits. **2.** any of various other climbing or creeping plants, such as Boston ivy, poison ivy, and ground ivy. [Old English *īfig;* related to Old High German *ebah,* perhaps to Greek *iphuon* a plant] —**ˈi·vy-ˌlike** *adj.*

I·vy League *n. U.S.* **the. a.** a group of eight universities (Brown, Columbia, Cornell, Dartmouth College, Harvard, Princeton, Pennsylvania, and Yale) that have similar academic and social prestige in the U.S. to Oxford and Cambridge in Britain. **b.** (*as modifier*): *an Ivy-League education.*

i·wis *or* **y·wis** (ɪˈwɪs) *adv.* an archaic word for **certainly.** [C12: from Old English *gewiss* certain]

I·wo (ˈiːwəʊ) *n.* a city in SW Nigeria. Pop.: 214 000 (1975 est.).

I·wo Ji·ma (ˈiːwəʊ ˈdʒiːmə) *n.* an island in the W Pacific, about 1100 km (700 miles) south of Japan: one of the Volcano Islands; scene of prolonged fighting between U.S. and Japanese forces until taken by the U.S. in 1945; returned to Japan in 1968. Area: 20 sq. km (8 sq. miles).

I.W.W. *abbrev. for* Industrial Workers of the World.

ix·i·a (ˈɪksɪə) *n.* any plant of the iridaceous genus *Ixia,* of southern Africa, having showy ornamental funnel-shaped flowers. [C18: New Latin from Greek *ixos* mistletoe, birdlime prepared from mistletoe berries]

Ix·i·on (ɪkˈsaɪən) *n. Greek myth.* a Thessalian king punished by Zeus for his love of Hera by being bound to a perpetually revolving wheel. —**Ix·i·o·ni·an** (ˌɪksɪˈəʊnɪən) *adj.*

Ix·tac·ci·huatl (ˌiːstəkˈsiːwət(ə)l) *or* **Iz·tac·ci·huatl** *n.* a dormant volcano in central Mexico, southeast of Mexico City. Height: (central peak) 5286 m (17 342 ft.).

ix·tle (ˈɪkstlɪ, ˈɪst-) *n.* a variant spelling of **istle.**

I·yar *or* **Iy·yar** *Hebrew.* (iˈjar) *n. Judaism.* the eighth month of the civil year and the second of the ecclesiastical year, falling approximately in April and May. [from Hebrew]

I·ye·ya·su *or* **I·e·ya·su** (ˌiːjeɪˈjɑːsuː) *n.* **To·ku·ga·wa** (ˌtɒkuːˈgɑːwə). 1542–1616, Japanese general and statesman; founder of the Tokugawa shogunate (1603–1867).

iz·ard (ˈɪzəd) *n.* (esp. in the Pyrenees) another name for **chamois.**

-ize *or* **-ise** *suffix forming verbs.* **1.** to cause to become, resemble, or agree with: *legalize.* **2.** to become; change into: *crystallize.* **3.** to affect in a specified way; subject to: *hypnotize.* **4.** to act according to some practice, principle, policy, etc.: *economize.* [from Old French *-iser,* from Late Latin *-izāre,* from Greek *-izein*]

Usage. In the U.S. and in Britain, *-ize* is the standard ending for many verbs, but *-ise* is equally acceptable in British English. Certain words are, however, always spelt with *-ise* in both the U.S. and in Britain: *advertise, revise.*

I·zhevsk (*Russian* iˈʒɛfsk) *n.* an industrial city in the E Soviet Union, capital of the Udmurt ASSR. Pop.: 506 000 (1975 est.).

Iz·mir (ˈɪzmɪə) *n.* a port in W Turkey, on the **Gulf of Izmir:** the third largest city in the country; university (1955). Pop.: 636 834 (1975). Former name: **Smyrna.**

Iz·mit (ɪzˈmɪt) *n.* a town in NW Turkey, on the **Gulf of Izmit.** Pop.: 165 483 (1975).

Iz·nik (ɪzˈnɪk) *n.* the modern Turkish name of **Nicaea.**

Iz·tac·ci·huatl (ˌiːstəkˈsiːwət(ə)l) *n.* a variant spelling of **Ixtaccihuatl.**

iz·zard (ˈɪzəd) *n. Archaic.* the letter *Z.* [C18: from earlier *ezed,* probably from Old French *et zède,* literally: and zed]

J

j *or* **J** (dʒeɪ) *n., pl.* **j's, J's,** *or* **Js. 1.** the tenth letter and seventh consonant of the modern English alphabet. **2.** a speech sound represented by this letter, in English usually a voiced palato-alveolar affricate, as in *jam.*

j *symbol for:* **1.** current density. **2.** *Maths.* the unit vector along the *y*-axis. **3.** the imaginary number $\sqrt{-1}$.

J *symbol for:* **1.** *Cards.* jack. **2.** joule(s). ~**3.** *international car registration for* Japan.

J. *abbrev. for:* **1.** Journal. **2.** (*pl.* **JJ.**) Judge. **3.** (*pl.* **JJ.**) Justice.

JA *international car registration for* Jamaica.

Ja. *abbrev. for* January.

J.A. *abbrev. for:* **1.** Also: **J/A** *Banking.* joint account. **2.** Judge Advocate.

jaap (jɑːp) *n. S. African.* a simpleton or country bumpkin. [from Afrikaans]

jab (dʒæb) *vb.* **jabs, jab+bing, jabbed. 1.** to poke or thrust sharply. **2.** to strike with a quick short blow or blows. ~*n.* **3.** a sharp poke or stab. **4.** a quick short blow, esp. (in boxing) a straight punch with the leading hand. **5.** *Informal.* an injection: *polio jabs.* [C19: originally Scottish variant of JOB] —**'jab+bing+ly** *adv.*

Jab+al+pur *or* **Jub+bul+pore** (ˌdʒʌbəl'pʊə) *n.* a city in central India, in central Madhya Pradesh. Pop.: 426 224 (1971).

jab+ber ('dʒæbə) *vb.* **1.** to speak or say rapidly, incoherently, and without making sense; chatter. ~*n.* **2.** such talk. [C15: of imitative origin; compare GIBBER] —**'jab+ber+er** *n.*

jab+ber+wock·y ('dʒæbəˌwɒkɪ) *n.* nonsense verse. [C19: coined by Lewis Carroll as the title of a poem in *Through the Looking Glass* (1871)]

Ja·bir ibn Hay·yan ('dʒɑːbɪə 'iːbən hɑː'jɑːn) *n.* ?721–?815. Arab alchemist, whose many works enjoyed enormous esteem among later alchemists, such as Geber.

jab·i+ru ('dʒæbɪˌruː) *n.* **1.** a large white tropical American stork, *Jabiru mycteria,* with a dark naked head and a dark bill. **2.** Also called: **black-necked stork, policeman bird.** a large Australian stork, *Xenorhyncus asiaticus,* having a white plumage, dark green back and tail, and red legs. **3.** another name for **saddlebill. 4.** (*not in ornithological usage*) another name for **wood ibis.** [C18: via Portuguese from Tupi-Guarani]

jab·o+ran+di (ˌdʒæbə'rændɪ) *n.* **1.** any of several tropical American rutaceous shrubs of the genus *Pilocarpus,* esp. *P. jaborandi.* **2.** the dried leaves of any of these plants, used to induce sweating. [C19: from Portuguese, from Tupi-Guarani *yaborandí*]

ja+bot ('ʒæbəʊ) *n.* a frill or ruffle on the breast or throat of a garment, originally to hide the closure of a shirt. [C19: from French: bird's crop, jabot; compare Old French *gave* throat]

jac·a+mar ('dʒækəˌmɑː) *n.* any bird of the tropical American family *Galbulidae,* having an iridescent plumage and feeding on insects: order *Piciformes* (woodpeckers, etc.). [C19: from French, from Tupi *jacamá-ciri*]

ja+ça+na (ˌʒɑːsə'nɑː, ˌdʒæ-) *n.* any bird of the family *Jacanidae,* of tropical and subtropical marshy regions, having long legs and very long toes that enable walking on floating plants: order *Charadriiformes.* Also called: **lily-trotter.** [C18: from Portuguese *jaçanã,* from Tupi-Guarani *jasaná*]

jac·a+ran+da (ˌdʒækə'rændə) *n.* **1.** any bignoniaceous tree of the tropical American genus *Jacaranda,* having fernlike leaves and pale purple flowers. **2.** the fragrant ornamental wood of any of these trees. **3.** any of several related or similar trees or their wood. [C18: from Portuguese, from Tupi-Guarani *yacarandá*]

ja+cinth ('dʒæsɪnθ) *n.* another name for **hyacinth** (sense 4). [C13: from Medieval Latin *jacinthus,* from Latin *hyacinthus* plant, precious stone; see HYACINTH]

jack[1] (dʒæk) *n.* **1.** a man or fellow. **2.** a sailor. **3.** the male of certain animals, esp. of the ass or donkey. **4.** a mechanical or hydraulic device for exerting a large force, esp. to raise a heavy weight such as a motor vehicle. **5.** any of several mechanical devices that replace manpower, such as a contrivance for rotating meat on a spit. **6.** one of four playing cards in a pack, one for each suit, bearing the picture of a young prince; knave. **7.** *Bowls.* a small usually white bowl at which the players aim with their own bowls. **8.** *Electrical engineering.* a socket for receiving a plug (**jack plug**). A **break jack** breaks the normal circuit when a jack plug is inserted. **9.** a flag, esp. a small flag flown at the bow of a ship indicating the ship's nationality. Compare **Union Jack. 10.** *Nautical.* either of a pair of crosstrees at the head of a topgallant mast used as standoffs for the royal shrouds. **11.** a part of the action of a harpsichord, consisting of a fork-shaped device on the end of a pivoted lever on which a plectrum is mounted. **12.** any of various tropical and subtropical carangid fishes, esp. those of the genus *Caranx,* such as *C. hippos* (**crevalle jack**). **13.** Also called: **jackstone.** one of the pieces used in the game of jacks. **14.** short for **applejack, bootjack, jackass, jack rabbit,** and **lumberjack. 15.** *U.S.* a slang word for **money. 16. every man jack.** everyone without exception. ~*adj.* **17.** *Austral. slang.* tired or fed up (esp. in the phrase **to be jack of** something). ~*vb.* **18.** (*tr.*) to lift or push (an object) with a jack. **19.** (*tr.*) Also: **jacklight.** *U.S.* to hunt (fish or game) by seeking them out or dazzling them with a flashlight. ~See also **jack in, jack up.** [C16 *jakke,* variant of *Jankin,* diminutive of *John*]

jack[2] (dʒæk) *n.* short for **jackfruit.** [C17: from Portuguese *jaca;* see JACKFRUIT]

jack[3] (dʒæk) *n.* **1.** a short sleeveless coat of armour of the Middle Ages, consisting usually of a canvas base with metal plates. **2.** *Archaic.* a drinking vessel, often of leather. [C14: from Old French *jaque,* of uncertain origin]

jack+al ('dʒækɔːl) *n.* **1.** any of several African or S Asian canine mammals of the genus *Canis,* closely related to the dog, having long legs and pointed ears and muzzle: predators and carrion-eaters. **2.** a person who does menial tasks for another. **3.** a villain, esp. a swindler. [C17: from Turkish *chakāl,* from Persian *shagāl,* from Sanskrit *srgāla*]

jack·a+napes ('dʒækəˌneɪps) *n.* **1.** a conceited impertinent person. **2.** a mischievous child. **3.** *Archaic.* a monkey. [C16: variant of *Jakken-apes,* literally: Jack of the ape, nickname of William de la Pole (1396–1450), first Duke of Suffolk, whose badge showed an ape's ball and chain]

jack+ass ('dʒækˌæs) *n.* **1.** a male donkey. **2.** a stupid person; fool. **3. laughing jackass.** another name for **kookaburra.** [C18: from JACK[1] (male) + ASS[1]]

jack bean *n.* a tropical American leguminous plant, *Canavalia ensiformis,* that has clusters of purple flowers and long pods and is grown in the southern U.S. for forage.

jack+boot ('dʒækˌbuːt) *n.* **1.** an all-leather military boot, extending up to or above the knee. **2.** arbitrary, cruel, and authoritarian rule. —**'jack+ˌboot+ed** *adj.*

jack-by-the-hedge *n.* another name for **garlic mustard.**

jack+daw ('dʒækˌdɔː) *n.* a large common Eurasian passerine bird, *Corvus monedula,* in which the plumage is black and dark grey: noted for its thieving habits: family *Corvidae* (crows). [C16: from JACK[1] + DAW]

jack+e·roo *or* **jack·a+roo** (ˌdʒækə'ruː) *n., pl.* **·roos.** *Austral. informal.* a young male management trainee on a sheep or cattle station. [C19: from JACK[1] + (KANG)AROO]

jack+et ('dʒækɪt) *n.* **1.** a short coat, esp. one that is hip-length and has a front opening and sleeves. **2.** something that resembles this or is designed to be worn around the upper part of the body: *a life jacket.* **3.** any exterior covering or casing, such as the insulating cover of a boiler. **4.** the part of the cylinder block of an internal-combustion engine that encloses the coolant. **5.** See **dust jacket. 6. a.** the skin of a baked potato. **b.** (*as modifier*): *jacket potatoes.* **7.** a toughened metal casing used in certain types of ammunition. **8.** *U.S.* a cover to protect gramophone records. Brit. name: **sleeve. 9.** *Chiefly U.S.* a folder or envelope to hold documents. ~*vb.* **10.** (*tr.*) to put a jacket on (someone or something). [C15: from Old French *jaquet* short jacket, from *jacque* peasant, from proper name *Jaques* James] —**'jack+et+ed** *adj.* —**'jack·et-ˌlike** *adj.*

jack+fish ('dʒækˌfɪʃ) *n., pl.* **+fish** *or* **+fish·es.** a popular name for **pike** (the fish), esp. when small.

Jack Frost *n.* a personification of frost or winter.

jack+fruit ('dʒækˌfruːt) *n.* **1.** a tropical Asian moraceous tree, *Artocarpus heterophyllus.* **2.** the edible fruit of this tree, which resembles breadfruit and can weigh up to 27 kilograms (60 pounds). ~Sometimes shortened to **jack.** [C19: from Portuguese *jaca,* from Malayalam *cakka*]

Jack-go-to-bed-at-noon *n.* another name for **goatsbeard** (sense 1).

jack+ham·mer ('dʒækˌhæmə) *n.* a hand-held hammer drill, driven by compressed air, for drilling rocks, etc.

jack in *vb.* (*tr., adv.*) to abandon or leave (an attempt or enterprise).

jack-in-of·fice *n.* a self-important petty official.

jack-in-the-box *n., pl.* **jack-in-the-box·es** *or* **jacks-in-the-box.** a toy consisting of a figure on a tight spring in a box, which springs out when the lid is opened.

jack-in-the-pul·pit *n.* **1.** an E North American aroid plant, *Arisaema triphyllum,* having a leaflike spathe partly arched over a clublike spadix. **2.** *Brit.* another name for **cuckoopint.**

Jack Ketch (kɛtʃ) *n. Brit. archaic.* a hangman. [C18: after *John Ketch* (died 1686), public executioner in England]

jack+knife ('dʒækˌnaɪf) *n., pl.* **+knives. 1.** a knife with the blade pivoted to fold into a recess in the handle. **2.** a type of dive in which the diver bends at the waist in midair, with his legs straight and his hands touching his feet, finally straightening out and entering the water headfirst. ~*vb.* (*intr.*) **3.** (of an articulated lorry) to go out of control in such a way that the trailer swings round at an angle to the tractor. **4.** to make a jackknife dive.

jack lad+der *n.* another name for **Jacob's ladder** (sense 2).

jack of all trades *n., pl.* **jacks of all trades.** a person who undertakes many different kinds of work.

jack-o'-lan·tern *n.* **1.** a lantern made from a hollowed pumpkin, which has holes cut in it to represent a human face. **2.** a will-o'-the-wisp or similar phenomenon.

jack pine *n.* a coniferous tree, *Pinus banksiana,* of North

America, having paired needle-like leaves and small cones that remain on the branches for many years: family *Pinaceae*.

jack plane *n.* a carpenter's plane, usually with a wooden body, used for rough planing of timber.

jack+pot ('dʒækˌpɒt) *n.* **1.** any large prize, kitty, or accumulated stake that may be won in gambling, such as a pool in poker that accumulates until the betting is opened with a pair of jacks or higher. **2. hit the jackpot.** *Slang.* **a.** to win a jackpot. **b.** to achieve great success, esp. through luck. [C20: probably from JACK[1] (playing card) + POT]

jack rab+bit *n.* any of various W North American hares, such as *Lepus townsendi* (**white-tailed jack rabbit**), having long hind legs and large ears. [C19: shortened from *jackass-rabbit,* referring to its long ears]

jack raf+ter *n.* a short rafter used in a hip roof.

jacks (dʒæks) *n.* a game in which bone or metal pieces (**jack-stones**) are thrown and then picked up in various groups between bounces or throws of a small ball. Sometimes called: **knucklebones.** [C19: shortened from *jackstones,* variant of *checkstones* pebbles]

jack+screw ('dʒækˌskru:) *n.* another name for **screw jack.**

jack+shaft ('dʒækˌʃɑ:ft) *n.* a short length of shafting that transmits power from an engine or motor to a machine.

jack+smelt ('dʒækˌsmɛlt) *n., pl.* **+smelts** *or* **+smelt.** a marine teleost food fish, *Atherinopsis californiensis,* of American coastal waters of the North Pacific: family *Atherinidae* (silver-sides).

jack+snipe ('dʒækˌsnaɪp) *n., pl.* **+snipe** *or* **+snipes. 1.** a small Eurasian short-billed snipe, *Lymnocryptes minima.* **2.** any of various similar birds, such as the pectoral sandpiper.

Jack+son[1] ('dʒæksən) *n.* a city in and state capital of Mississippi, on the Pearl River. Pop.: 163 924 (1973 est.).

Jack·son[2] ('dʒæksən) *n.* **1. An·drew.** 1767–1845, U.S. statesman, general, and lawyer; seventh president of the U.S. (1828–36). He became a national hero after successfully defending New Orleans from the British (1815). During his administration the spoils system was introduced and the national debt was fully paid off. **2. Glen·da.** born 1936, English stage and film actress. Her films include *Women in Love* (1969), *The Music Lovers* (1970), *A Triple Echo* (1972), and *The Incredible Sarah* (1976). **3. Thom·as Jon·a·than,** known as *Stonewall Jackson.* 1824–63, Confederate general in the American Civil War, noted particularly for his command at the first Battle of Bull Run (1861). —**Jack+so+ni·an** (dʒæk'səʊnɪən) *adj., n.*

Jack+son+ville ('dʒæksənˌvɪl) *n.* a port in NE Florida: the leading commercial centre of the southeast. Pop.: 548 007 (1973 est.).

jack+stay ('dʒækˌsteɪ) *n. Nautical.* **1.** a metal rod, wire rope, or wooden batten to which an edge of a sail is fastened along a yard. **2.** a support for the parrel of a yard.

jack+straws ('dʒækˌstrɔ:z) *pl. n.* another name for **spillikins.**

Jack Tar *n. Now chiefly literary.* a sailor.

Jack-the-rags *n. South Wales dialect.* a rag-and-bone man.

Jack the Rip+per *n.* an unidentified murderer who killed at least seven prostitutes in London's East End between August and November 1888.

jack up *vb.* (*adv.*) **1.** (*tr.*) to increase (prices, salaries, etc.). **2.** (*tr.*) to raise an object, such as a car, with or as with a jack. **3.** (*intr.*) *Austral. informal.* to refuse to comply; rebel, esp. collectively.

Ja·cob ('dʒeɪkəb) *n. Old Testament.* the son of Isaac, twin brother of Esau, and father of the twelve patriarchs of Israel.

Jac·o+be·an (ˌdʒækə'bɪən) *adj.* **1.** *History.* characteristic of or relating to James I of England or to the period of his rule (1603–25). **2.** of or relating to the style of furniture current at this time, characterized by the use of dark brown carved oak. **3.** denoting, relating to, or having the style of architecture used in England during this period, characterized by a combination of late Gothic and Palladian motifs. ~*n.* **4.** any writer or other person who lived in the reign of James I. [C18: from New Latin *jacobaeus,* from *Jacōbus* James]

Ja·co·bi (dʒə'kəʊbɪ; *German* ja'ko:bi) *n.* **Karl Gus·tav Ja·cob** ('karl 'gʊstaf 'ja:kɔp). 1804–51, German mathematician. Independently of N. H. Abel, he discovered elliptic functions (1829). He also made important contributions to the study of determinants and differential equations.

Ja+co+bi·an (dʒə'kəʊbɪən) *or* **Ja+co+bi·an de+ter+mi+nant** *n. Maths.* a function from *n* equations in *n* variables whose value at any point is the *n x n* determinant of the partial derivatives of those equations evaluated at that point. [named after K. G. J. JACOBI]

Jac·o+bin ('dʒækəbɪn) *n.* **1.** a member of the most radical club founded during the French Revolution, which overthrew the Girondists in 1793 and, led by Robespierre, instituted the Reign of Terror. **2.** a leftist or extreme political radical. **3.** a French Dominican friar. **4.** (*sometimes not cap.*) a variety of fancy pigeon with a hood of feathers swept up over and around the head. ~*adj.* **5.** of, characteristic of, or relating to the Jacobins or their policies. [C14: from Old French, from Medieval Latin *Jacōbīnus,* from Late Latin *Jacōbus* James; applied to the Dominicans, from the proximity of the church of *St. Jacques* (St. James) to their first convent in Paris; the political club originally met in the convent in 1789] —ˌ**Jac·o+'bin+ic** *or* ˌ**Jac·o+'bin·i+cal** *adj.* —ˌ**Jac·o+'bin·i+cal+ly** *adv.* —**'Jac·o+bin+ism** *n.*

Jac·o+bite ('dʒækəˌbaɪt) *n.* **1.** *British history.* an adherent of James II after his overthrow in 1688, or of his descendants in their attempts to regain the throne. **2. a.** a member of the Monophysite Church of Syria, which became a schismatic church in 451 A.D. **b.** *Rare.* a Monophysite Christian of the Coptic Church of Egypt. [C17: from Late Latin *Jacōbus* James + -ITE[1]] —**Jac·o+bit+ic** (ˌdʒækə'bɪtɪk) *adj.* —**'Jac·o+ˌbit+ism** *n.*

Jac·o+bite Re+bel+lion *n.* **the.** *British history.* the last Jacobite rising (1745-46) led by Charles Edward Stuart, the Young Pretender, which after initial successes was crushed at Culloden.

Ja·cob·sen (*Danish* 'jakɔbsən) *n.* **Ar·ne** ('arnə). 1902–71, Danish architect and designer. His buildings include the Town Hall at Rodovre (1955).

Ja·cob's lad+der *n.* **1.** *Old Testament.* the ladder reaching up to heaven that Jacob saw in a dream (Genesis 28:12–17). **2.** Also called: **jack ladder.** a ladder made of wooden or metal steps supported by ropes or chains. **3.** a North American polemoniaceous plant, *Polemonium caeruleum,* with blue flowers and a ladder-like arrangement of leaves. **4.** any of several similar or related plants.

Ja·cob's staff *n.* a medieval instrument for measuring heights and distances.

ja+co+bus (dʒə'kəʊbəs) *n., pl.* **+bus·es.** an English gold coin minted in the reign of James I. [C17: from Late Latin: James]

jac·o+net ('dʒækənɪt) *n.* a light cotton fabric used for clothing, bandages, etc. [C18: from Urdu *jagannāthī,* from *Jagannāthpūrī,* India, where it was originally made]

Jac+quard ('dʒækɑ:d, dʒə'kɑ:d; *French* ʒa'ka:r) *n.* **1.** Also called: **Jacquard weave.** a fabric in which the design is incorporated into the weave instead of being printed or dyed on. **2.** Also called: **Jacquard loom.** the loom that produces this fabric. [C19: named after Joseph M. *Jacquard* (1752–1834), French inventor]

Jacque+rie *French.* (ʒa'kri) *n.* the revolt of the N French peasants against the nobility in 1358. [C16: from Old French: the peasantry, from *jacque* a peasant, from *Jacques* James, from Late Latin *Jacōbus*]

jac+ta+tion (dʒæk'teɪʃən) *n.* **1.** *Rare.* the act of boasting. **2.** *Pathol.* another word for **jactitation** (sense 3). [C16: from Latin *jactātiō* bragging, from *jactāre* to flourish, from *jacere* to throw]

jac+ti+ta+tion (ˌdʒæktɪ'teɪʃən) *n.* **1.** the act of boasting. **2.** a false boast or claim that tends to harm another person, esp. a false assertion that one is married to another, formerly actionable at law. **3.** Also called: **jactation.** *Pathol.* restless tossing in bed, characteristic of severe fevers and certain mental disorders. [C17: from Medieval Latin *jactitātiō,* from Latin *jacitāre* to utter publicly, from *jactāre* to toss about; see JACTATION]

jade[1] (dʒeɪd) *n.* **1. a.** a semiprecious stone consisting of either jadeite or nephrite. It varies in colour from white to green and is used for making ornaments and jewellery. **b.** (*as modifier*): *jade ornaments.* **2.** the green colour of jade. [C18: from French, from Italian *giada,* from obsolete Spanish *piedra de ijada* colic stone (literally: stone of the flank, because it was believed to cure renal colic); *ijada,* from Vulgar Latin *īliata* (unattested) flanks, from Latin *īlia,* plural of *īlium;* see ILEUM] —**'jade+ˌlike** *adj.*

jade[2] (dʒeɪd) *n.* **1.** an old overworked horse; nag; hack. **2.** *Derogatory.* a woman considered to be ill-tempered or disreputable. ~*vb.* **3.** to exhaust or make exhausted from work or use. [C14: of unknown origin] —**'jad+ish** *adj.* —**'jad+ish+ly** *adv.* —**'jad+ish+ness** *n.*

jad+ed ('dʒeɪdɪd) *adj.* **1.** exhausted or dissipated. **2.** satiated. —**'jad+ed+ly** *adv.* —**'jad+ed+ness** *n.*

jade green *n., adj.* **a.** a colour varying from yellowish-green to bluish-green. **b.** (*as adj.*): *a jade-green carpet.*

jade+ite ('dʒeɪdaɪt) *n.* a hard green pyroxene mineral, a variety of jade, consisting of sodium aluminium silicate in monoclinic crystalline form. Formula: $NaAlSi_2O_6$.

Ja+dot+ville (*French* ʒado'vil) *n.* the former name of **Likasi.**

j'a·doube *French.* (ʒa'du:b) *interj. Chess.* an expression of an intention to touch a piece in order to adjust its placement rather than to make a move. [literally: I adjust]

jae+ger ('jeɪgə) *n.* **1.** *Military.* a marksman in certain units of the German or Austrian armies. **2.** *U.S.* any of several skuas of the genus *Stercorarius.* **3.** *Rare.* a hunter or hunter's attendant. ~Also (for senses 1, 3): **jager** or **jäger.** [C18: from German *Jäger* hunter, from *jagen* to hunt; see YACHT]

Ja·el ('dʒeɪəl) *n. Old Testament.* the woman who killed Sisera when he took refuge in her tent (Judges 4:17–21).

Ja·én (xa'en) *n.* a city in S Spain. Pop.: 78 156 (1970).

Jaf+fa ('dʒæfə, 'dʒɑ:-) *n.* **1.** a port in W Israel, on the Mediterranean: incorporated into Tel Aviv in 1950; an old Canaanite city. Biblical name: **Joppa.** Arabic name: **Yafo. 2.** a large variety of orange, having a thick skin.

Jaff+na ('dʒæfnə) *n.* a port in N Sri Lanka: for many centuries the capital of a Tamil kingdom. Pop.: 112 000 (1973 est.).

jag[1] *or* **jagg** (dʒæg) *vb.* **jags, jag+ging, jagged. 1.** (*tr.*) to cut unevenly; make jagged. ~*n., vb.* **2.** an informal word for **jab.** ~*n.* **3.** a jagged notch or projection. [C14: of unknown origin] —**'jag+less** *adj.*

jag[2] (dʒæg) *n.* **1.** *Slang.* **a.** intoxication from drugs or alcohol. **b.** a bout of drinking or drug taking. **2.** *Dialect.* a small load, as of hay, etc. [C16: perhaps from Old English *ceacga* broom]

J.A.G. *abbrev. for* Judge Advocate General.

ja·ga ('dʒaga) (in Malaysia). ~*n.* **1.** a guard; sentry. ~*vb.* **2.** (*tr.*) to guard or watch: *jaga the door.* [from Malay]

Jag+an+nath, Jag+ga+nath ('dʒʌgəˌnɑ:t, -ˌnɔ:t), *or* **Jag+an+na+tha** (ˌdʒʌgə'nɑ:thə) *n. Hinduism.* other names for **Juggernaut.**

jä+ger ('jeɪgə) *n.* See **jaeger.**

jag·ged ('dʒægɪd) *adj.* having sharp projecting notches; ragged; serrate. —'**jag·ged·ly** *adv.* —'**jag·ged·ness** *n.*

Jag·ger ('dʒægə) *n.* **Mick.** born 1943, English rock singer and songwriter: lead vocalist with the Rolling Stones, noted for the vigour and overt sexuality of his performances on stage.

jag·ger·y, jag·gar·y, *or* **jag·gher·y** ('dʒægərɪ) *n.* a coarse brown sugar made in the East Indies from the sap of the date palm. [C16: from Hindi *jāgrī*; compare Sanskrit *śárkarā* gritty substance, sugar]

jag·gy ('dʒægɪ) *adj.* ·**gi·er,** ·**gi·est.** a less common word for **jagged.**

jag·u·ar ('dʒægjʊə) *n.* a large feline mammal, *Panthera onca,* of S North America, Central America, and N South America, similar to the leopard but with a shorter tail and larger spots on its coat. [C17: from Portuguese, from Tupi *jaguara,* Guarani *yaguara*]

ja·gua·ron·di (ˌdʒægwəˈrɒndɪ) *or* **ja·gua·run·di** (ˌdʒægwəˈrʌndɪ) *n., pl.* ·**dis.** a feline mammal, *Felis yagouaroundi,* of Central and South America, with a reddish or grey coat, short legs, and a long tail. See also **eyra.** [C19: via Portuguese from Tupi]

Jah·veh ('jɑːveɪ) *or* **Jah·weh** ('jɑːweɪ) *n.* variant spellings of **Yahweh.**

Jah·vist ('jɑːvɪst) *or* **Jah·wist** ('jɑːwɪst) *n.* variant spellings of **Yahwist.**

jai (dʒæ) *n. Indian.* victory (to). [Hindi *jaya* victory]

jai a·lai ('haɪ 'laɪ, 'haɪ əˌlaɪ, ˌhaɪ əˈlaɪ) *n.* a version of pelota played by two or four players. [via Spanish from Basque, from *jai* game, festival + *alai* merry]

Jai Hind ('dʒæ 'hɪnd) victory to India: a political slogan and a form of greeting in India. [Hindi, from *jaya* victory + *Hind* India]

jail *or* **gaol** (dʒeɪl) *n.* **1.** a place for the confinement of persons convicted and sentenced to imprisonment or of persons awaiting trial to whom bail is not granted. ~*vb.* **2.** (*tr.*) to confine in prison. [C13: from Old French *jaiole* cage, from Vulgar Latin *caveola* (unattested), from Latin *cavea* enclosure; see CAGE] —'**jail·less** *or* '**gaol·less** *adj.* —'**jail-like** *or* '**gaol-like** *adj.*

jail·bird *or* **gaol·bird** ('dʒeɪlˌbɜːd) *n.* a person who is or has been confined to jail, esp. repeatedly; convict.

jail·break *or* **gaol·break** ('dʒeɪlˌbreɪk) *n.* an escape from jail.

jail de·liv·er·y *n.* **1.** forcible and illegal liberation of prisoners from jail. **2.** *English law.* (formerly) a commission issued to assize judges when they come to a circuit town authorizing them to try all prisoners and release those acquitted.

jail·er, jail·or, *or* **gaol·er** ('dʒeɪlə) *n.* a person in charge of prisoners in a jail.

jail·house ('dʒeɪlˌhaʊs) *n. Southern U.S.* a jail; prison.

Jain (dʒaɪn) *or* **Jai·na** ('dʒaɪnə) *n.* **1.** an adherent of Jainism. **2.** one of the saints believed to be the founders of Jainism. ~*adj.* **3.** of or relating to Jainism or the Jains. [C19: from Hindi *jaina* saint, literally: overcomer, from Sanskrit]

Jain·ism ('dʒaɪnɪzəm) *n.* an ancient Hindu sect, which has its own scriptures and believes that the material world is eternal, progressing endlessly in a series of vast cycles. —'**Jain·ist** *n., adj.*

Jai·pur (dʒaɪˈpʊə) *n.* a city of great beauty in N India, capital of Rajasthan state: University of Rajasthan (1947). Pop.: 615 258 (1971).

Ja·kar·ta (dʒəˈkɑːtə) *n.* a variant spelling of **Djakarta.**

jakes (dʒeɪks) *n.* **1.** an archaic slang word for **lavatory. 2.** *Southwestern English dialect.* human excrement. [C16: probably from French *Jacques* James]

jal·ap *or* **jal·op** ('dʒæləp) *n.* **1.** a Mexican convolvulaceous plant, *Exogonium* (or *Ipomoea*) *purga.* **2.** any of several similar or related plants. **3.** the dried and powdered root of any of these plants, used as a purgative. **4.** the resin obtained from any of these plants. [C17: from French, from Mexican Spanish *jalapa,* short for *purga de Jalapa* purgative of Jalapa] —**ja·lap·ic** (dʒəˈlæpɪk) *adj.*

Ja·la·pa (*Spanish* xaˈlapa) *n.* a city in E central Mexico, capital of Veracruz State, at an altitude of 1427 m (4681 ft.): resort. Pop.: 171 937 (1975 est.).

Ja·lis·co (*Spanish* xaˈlisko) *n.* a state of W Mexico, on the Pacific: crossed by the Sierra Madre; valuable mineral resources. Capital: Guadalajara. Pop.: 3 296 587 (1970). Area: 80 137 sq. km (30 941 sq. miles).

ja·lop·y *or* **ja·lop·py** (dʒəˈlɒpɪ) *n., pl.* ·**lop·ies** *or* ·**lop·pies.** *Informal.* a dilapidated old car. [C20: of unknown origin]

jal·ou·sie ('ʒæluˌziː) *n.* **1.** a window blind or shutter constructed from angled slats of wood, plastic, etc. **2.** a window made of similarly angled slats of glass. [C19: from Old French *gelosie* latticework screen, literally: JEALOUSY, perhaps because one can look through the screen without being seen]

jam[1] (dʒæm) *vb.* **jams, jam·ming, jammed. 1.** (*tr.*) to cram or wedge into or against something: *to jam paper into an incinerator.* **2.** (*tr.*) to crowd or pack: *cars jammed the roads.* **3.** to make or become stuck or locked: *the switch has jammed.* **4.** (*tr.;* often foll. by *on*) to activate suddenly (esp. in the phrase **jam on the brakes**). **5.** (*tr.*) to block; congest: *to jam the drain with rubbish.* **6.** (*tr.*) to crush, bruise, or squeeze; smash. **7.** *Radio.* to prevent the clear reception of (radio communications or radar signals) by transmitting other signals on the same frequency. **8.** (*intr.*) *Jazz slang.* to play in a jam session. ~*n.* **9.** a crowd or congestion in a confined space: *a traffic jam.* **10.** the act of jamming or the state of being jammed. **11.** *Informal.* a difficult situation; predicament: *to help a friend out of a jam.* **12.** See **jam session.** [C18: probably of imitative origin; compare CHAMP[1]] —'**jam·mer** *n.*

jam[2] (dʒæm) *n.* a preserve containing whole fruit, which has been boiled with sugar until the mixture sets. [C18: perhaps from JAM[1] (the act of squeezing)]

Jam. *abbrev. for* **1.** Jamaica. **2.** *Bible.* James.

Ja·mai·ca (dʒəˈmeɪkə) *n.* an island and state of the West Indies in the Caribbean Sea: colonized by the Spanish from 1494 onwards, large numbers of Negro slaves being imported; captured by the British in 1655 and established as a colony in 1866; gained full independence in 1962; a member of the Commonwealth. Exports: chiefly bauxite and alumina, sugar, and bananas. Language: English. Religion: Protestant majority. Currency: Jamaican dollar. Capital: Kingston. Pop.: 2 029 000 (1975 UN est.). Area: 10 992 sq. km (4244 sq. miles). —**Ja·'mai·can** *n., adj.*

Ja·mai·ca rum *n.* a highly flavoured rum produced in Jamaica.

jamb *or* **jambe** (dʒæm) *n.* **1.** a vertical side member of a door frame, window frame, or lining. **2.** a vertical inside face of an opening in a wall. [C14: from Old French *jambe* leg, jamb, from Late Latin *gamba* hoof, hock, from Greek *kampē* joint]

jam·ba·lay·a (ˌdʒʌmbəˈlaɪə) *n.* a Creole dish made of shrimps, ham, rice, onions, etc. [C19: from Louisiana French, from Provençal *jambalaia* chicken and rice stew]

jam·beau ('dʒæmbəʊ), **jam·bart** ('dʒæmbɑːt), *or* **jam·ber** ('dʒæmbə) *n., pl.* ·**beaux** (-bəʊz), ·**barts,** *or* ·**bers.** (*often pl.*) other words for **greave.** [C14: from Anglo-French, from *jambe* leg; see JAMB]

Jam·bi ('dʒɑːmbɪ) *n.* a variant spelling of **Djambi.**

jam·bo ('dʒambə) *interj.* an E African salutation. [C20: from Swahili]

jam·bo·ree (ˌdʒæmbəˈriː) *n.* **1.** a large and often international gathering of Scouts. **2.** a party or spree. [C19: of uncertain origin]

James (dʒeɪmz) *n.* **1. Hen·ry.** 1843–1916, British novelist, short-story writer, and critic, born in the U.S. Among his novels are *Washington Square* (1880), *The Portrait of a Lady* (1881), *The Spoils of Poynton* (1897), *The Wings of the Dove* (1902), *The Ambassadors* (1903), and *The Golden Bowl* (1904). **2. Jes·se (Woodson).** 1847–82, U.S. outlaw. **3. Wil·liam,** brother of Henry James. 1842–1910, U.S. philosopher and psychologist, whose theory of pragmatism is expounded in *Essays in Radical Empiricism* (1912). His other works include *The Will to Believe* (1897), *The Principles of Psychology* (1890), and *The Varieties of Religious Experience* (1902). **4.** *New Testament.* **a.** Also called: **James the Great.** one of the twelve apostles, a son of Zebedee and brother to John the apostle (Matthew 4:21). **b.** Also called: **James the brother of the Lord.** a brother or close relative of Jesus (Mark 6:3; Galatians 1:19). **c.** the book ascribed to his authorship (in full **The Epistle of James**).

James I *n.* 1566–1625, king of England and Ireland (1603–25) and, as James VI, king of Scotland (1567–1625), in succession to Elizabeth I of England and his mother, Mary Queen of Scots, respectively. He alienated Parliament by his assertion of the divine right of kings, his favourites, esp. the Duke of Buckingham, and his subservience to Spain.

James II *n.* 1633–1701, king of England, Ireland, and, as James VII, of Scotland (1685–88); son of Charles I. His pro-Catholic sympathies and arbitrary rule caused the Whigs and Tories to unite in inviting William of Orange to take the throne. James was defeated at the Boyne (1690) when he attempted to regain the throne.

James VI *n.* title as king of Scotland of **James I.**

James VII *n.* title as king of Scotland of **James II.**

James Bay *n.* the S arm of Hudson Bay, in central Canada.

James·i·an *or* **James·e·an** ('dʒeɪmzɪən) *adj.* relating to or characteristic of Henry James or his brother, William.

Jame·son ('dʒeɪmsᵊn) *n.* Sir **Le·an·der Starr.** 1853–1917, British administrator in South Africa, who led an expedition into the Transvaal in 1895 in an unsuccessful attempt to topple its Boer regime (the **Jameson Raid**); prime minister of Cape Colony (1904–08).

James·town ('dʒeɪmzˌtaʊn) *n.* a ruined village in E Virginia, on **Jamestown Island** (a peninsula in the James River): the first permanent settlement by the English in America (1607); capital of Virginia (1607–98); abandoned in 1699.

Jam·mu ('dʒʌmuː) *n.* a city in N India, winter capital of the state of Jammu and Kashmir. Pop.: 155 338 (1971).

Jam·mu and Kash·mir *n.* the official name for the part of **Kashmir** under Indian control.

jam·my ('dʒæmɪ) *adj.* ·**mi·er,** ·**mi·est.** *Brit. slang.* **1.** pleasant; desirable. **2.** lucky.

Jam·na·gar ('dʒɑːmˌnʌgə) *n.* a city in W India, in E Gujerat. Pop.: 199 709 (1971).

jam-packed *adj.* crowded, packed, or filled to capacity.

jam·pan ('dʒæmˌpæn) *n.* a type of sedan chair used in India. [C19: from Bengali *jhāmpān*]

jam ses·sion *n. Slang.* a jazz concert, esp. one in which the music is improvised. [C20: probably from JAM[1]]

Jam·shed·pur (ˌdʒʌmʃɛdˈpʊə) *n.* a city in NE India, in SE Bihar: large iron and steel works (1907–11); a major industrial centre. Pop.: 356 783 (1971).

Jam·shid *or* **Jam·shyd** (dʒæmˈʃiːd) *n. Persian myth.* a ruler of the peris who was punished for bragging that he was immortal by being changed into human form. He then became a great king of Persia. See also **peri.**

Jan. *abbrev. for* January.

Ja·ná·ček (*Czech* 'janaːtʃɛk) *n.* **Le·oš** ('lɛɔʃ). 1854–1928, Czech composer. His music is influenced by Czech folksong and speech rhythms and is remarkable for its integration of melody and language. His works include the operas *Jenufa* (1904) and *The Cunning Little Vixen* (1924), the *Glagolitic Mass* (1927), as well as orchestral and chamber music and songs.

Ja·na Sangh (ˈdʒʌnə ˈsʌŋg) *n.* a political party in India. [Hindi, literally: people's party]

Ja+na+ta (ˈdʒʌnətɑː) *n.* **1.** (in India) the general public; the people. **2.** a political party in India: founded in 1976 and came to power in 1977. [Hindi]

jane (dʒeɪn) *n. Slang, chiefly U.S.* a girl or woman.

Ja·net (*French* ʒaˈnɛ) *n.* **Pierre Ma·rie Fé·lix** (pjɛːr mari feˈliks). 1859–1947, French psychologist and neurologist, noted particularly for his work on the origins of hysteria.

jan+gle (ˈdʒæŋgᵊl) *vb.* **1.** to sound or cause to sound discordantly, harshly, or unpleasantly: *the telephone jangled.* **2.** (*tr.*) to produce a jarring effect on: *the accident jangled his nerves.* **3.** an archaic word for **wrangle.** [C13: from Old French *jangler*, of Germanic origin; compare Middle Dutch *jangelen* to whine, complain] —ˈ**jan+gler** *n.*

Ja+nic·u+lum (dʒəˈnɪkjʊləm) *n.* a hill in Rome across the River Tiber from the Seven Hills.

Ja+ni+na (ˈjaniːna) *n.* the Serbian name for **Ioánnina.**

jan+is+sar·y (ˈdʒænɪsərɪ) *or* **jan·i+zar·y** (ˈdʒænɪzərɪ) *n., pl.* **+sar·ies** *or* **+zar·ies.** an infantryman in the Turkish sovereign's personal guard, from the 14th to the early 19th century. [C16: from French *janissaire*, from Italian *giannizzero*, from Turkish *yeniçeri*, from *yeni* new + *çeri* soldiery]

jan·i+tor (ˈdʒænɪtə) *n.* **1.** *Scot.* the caretaker of a building, esp. a school. **2.** *Chiefly U.S.* a person employed to clean and maintain a building; porter. [C17: from Latin: doorkeeper, from *jānua* door, entrance, from *jānus* covered way (compare JANUS); related to Latin *īre* to go] —**jan·i+to+ri+al** (ˌdʒænɪˈtɔːrɪəl) *adj.* —ˈ**jan·i+tress** *fem. n.*

Jan May+en (ˈjæn ˈmaɪən) *n.* an island in the Arctic Ocean, between Greenland and N Norway: volcanic, with large glaciers; former site of Dutch whaling stations; annexed to Norway in 1929. Area: 373 sq. km (144 sq. miles).

Jan·sen (ˈdʒænsᵊn) *n.* **Cor·ne·lis** (kɔːˈniːlɪs). Latin name *Cornelius Jansenius.* 1585–1638, Dutch Roman Catholic theologian. In *Augustinus* (1640) he defended the teachings of St. Augustine, esp. on free will, grace, and predestination.

Jan+sen+ism (ˈdʒænsəˌnɪzəm) *n.* **1.** *R.C. Church.* the doctrine of Cornelis Jansen and his disciples, who maintained that salvation was limited to those subject to a supernatural determinism, the rest being destined to perdition. **2.** the religious movement arising from these doctrines. —ˈ**Jan+sen+ist** *n., adj.* —ˌ**Jan+sen+ˈis+tic** *or* ˌ**Jan+sen+ˈis+ti+cal** *adj.*

Jan·u·ar·y (ˈdʒænjʊərɪ) *n., pl.* **+ar·ies.** the first month of the year, consisting of 31 days. [C14: from Latin *Jānuārius*, from adj.: (month) of JANUS]

Ja·nus[1] (ˈdʒeɪnəs) *n.* the Roman god of doorways, passages, and bridges. In art he is depicted with two heads facing opposite ways. [C16: from Latin, from *jānus* archway]

Ja+nus[2] (ˈdʒeɪnəs) *n.* one of the smallest of the ten satellites of Saturn, discovered in 1966.

Ja·nus-faced *adj.* two-faced; hypocritical; deceitful.

Jap (dʒæp) *n., adj. Informal.* short for **Japanese.**

Jap. *abbrev. for* Japan(ese).

ja+pan (dʒəˈpæn) *n.* **1.** a glossy durable black lacquer originally from the Orient, used on wood, metal, etc. **2.** work decorated and varnished in the Japanese manner. **3.** a liquid used as a paint drier. ~*adj.* **4.** relating to or varnished with japan. ~*vb.* **+pans, +pan+ning, +panned. 5.** (*tr.*) to lacquer with japan or any similar varnish.

Ja+pan (dʒəˈpæn) *n.* an archipelago and empire in E Asia, extending for 3200 km (2000 miles) between the Sea of Japan and the Pacific and consisting of the main islands of Hokkaido, Honshu, Shikoku, and Kyushu and over 3000 smaller islands: feudalism abolished in 1871, followed by industrialization and expansion of territories, esp. during World Wars I and II, when most of SE Asia came under Japanese control; dogma of the emperor's divinity abolished in 1946 under a new democratic constitution; rapid economic growth has made Japan the most industrialized nation in the Far East. Language: Japanese. Religion: Buddhist and Shintoist. Currency: yen. Capital: Tokyo. Pop.: 114 150 000 (1977 est.). Area: 369 660 sq. km (142 726 sq. miles). Japanese names: **Nippon, Nihon.**

Ja+pan Cur+rent *n.* a warm ocean current flowing northeastwards off the E coast of Japan towards the North Pacific. Also called: **Kuroshio.**

Jap·a+nese (ˌdʒæpəˈniːz) *adj.* **1.** of, relating to, or characteristic of Japan, its people, or their language. ~*n.* **2.** *pl.* **+nese.** a native or inhabitant of Japan or a descendant of one. **3.** the official language of Japan: the native language of approximately 100 million people. The only language to which it is known to be related is Korean.

Jap·a+nese an+drom+e·da *n.* an ericaceous Japanese shrub, *Pieris japonica*, with drooping clusters of small bell-shaped white flowers.

Jap·a+nese bee+tle *n.* a scarabaeid beetle, *Popillia japonica*, that eats the leaves and fruits of various plants: accidentally introduced into the U.S. from Japan.

Jap·a+nese ced+ar *n.* another name for **cryptomeria.**

Jap·a+nese i·vy *n.* another name for **Virginia creeper** (sense 2).

Jap·a+nese lan+tern *n.* another name for **Chinese lantern** (sense 1).

Jap·a+nese per+sim+mon *n.* an Asian persimmon tree, *Diospyros kaki*, with red or orange edible fruit. Also called: **kaki.**

Jap·a+nese riv+er fe+ver *n.* another name for **scrub typhus.**

Jap·a+nese slip+pers *pl. n.* (in Malaysia) a type of casual sandal; flip-flop.

Jap·a+nese stran·gle+hold *n.* a wrestling hold in which an opponent's wrists are pulled to cross his arms in front of his own neck and exert pressure on his windpipe.

Jap+an wax *or* **tal+low** *n.* a yellow wax obtained from the berries of plants of the genus *Rhus.* It is used in making matches, soaps, candles, and polishes.

jape (dʒeɪp) *n.* **1.** a jest or joke. ~*vb.* **2.** to joke or jest (about). [C14: perhaps from Old French *japper* to bark, yap, of imitative origin] —ˈ**jap+er** *n.* —ˈ**jap+er·y** *n.* —ˈ**jap+ing+ly** *adv.*

Ja·pheth (ˈdʒeɪfɛθ) *n. Old Testament.* the second son of Noah, traditionally regarded as the ancestor of a number of non-Semitic nations (Genesis 10:1–5).

Ja+phet+ic (dʒeɪˈfɛtɪk) *adj.* denoting a discredited grouping of languages that postulated a relationship between Basque, Etruscan, and Georgian among others.

ja+pon·i+ca (dʒəˈpɒnɪkə) *n.* **1.** Also called: **Japanese quince.** a Japanese rosaceous shrub, *Chaenomeles japonica*, cultivated for its red flowers and yellowish fruit. **2.** another name for the **camellia.** [C19: from New Latin, feminine of *japonicus* Japanese, from *Japonia* JAPAN]

Ja+pu+rá (*Portuguese* ˌʒapuˈra) *n.* a river in NW South America, rising in SW Colombia and flowing southeast across Colombia and Brazil to join the Amazon near Tefé: known as the Caquetá in Colombia. Length: about 2800 km (1750 miles). Spanish name: **Yapurá.**

Jaques-Dal·croze (*French* ʒɑːk dalˈkroːz) *n.* **É·mile** (eˈmil). 1865–1950, Swiss composer and teacher: invented eurythmics.

jar[1] (dʒɑː) *n.* **1.** a wide-mouthed container that is usually cylindrical, made of glass or earthenware, and without handles. **2.** Also: **jar+ful.** the contents or quantity contained in a jar. **3.** *Brit. informal.* a glass of alcoholic drink, esp. beer: *to have a jar with someone.* [C16: from Old French *jarre*, from Old Provençal *jarra*, from Arabic *jarrah* large earthen vessel]

jar[2] (dʒɑː) *vb.* **jars, jar+ring, jarred. 1.** to vibrate or cause to vibrate. **2.** to make or cause to make a harsh discordant sound. **3.** (often foll. by *on*) to have a disturbing or painful effect (on the nerves, mind, etc.). **4.** (*intr.*) to disagree; clash. ~*n.* **5.** a jolt or shock. **6.** a harsh discordant sound. [C16: probably of imitative origin; compare Old English *cearran* to creak] —ˈ**jar+ring+ly** *adv.*

jar[3] (dʒɑː) *n.* **on a** (*or* **the**) **jar.** (of a door) slightly open; ajar. [C17 (in the sense: turn): from earlier *char*, from Old English *cierran* to turn; see AJAR]

jar+di+nière (ˌʒɑːdɪˈnjɛə) *n.* **1.** an ornamental pot or trough for plants. **2.** a garnish of fresh vegetables, cooked, diced, and served around a dish of meat. [C19: from French, feminine of *jardinier* gardener, from *jardin* GARDEN]

jar+gon[1] (ˈdʒɑːgən) *n.* **1.** specialized language concerned with a particular subject, culture, or profession. **2.** language characterized by pretentious syntax, vocabulary, or meaning. **3.** gibberish. **4.** another word for **pidgin.** ~*vb.* **5.** (*intr.*) to use or speak in jargon. [C14: from Old French, perhaps of imitative origin; see GARGLE]

jar+gon[2] (ˈdʒɑːgɒn) *or* **jar+goon** (dʒɑːˈguːn) *n. Mineralogy.* a golden yellow, smoky, or colourless variety of zircon. [C18: from French, from Italian *giargone*, ultimately from Persian *zargūn* of the golden colour; see ZIRCON]

jar+gon+ize *or* **jar+gon+ise** (ˈdʒɑːgəˌnaɪz) *vb.* **1.** (*tr.*) to translate into jargon. **2.** (*intr.*) to talk in jargon. —ˌ**jar+gon·i+ˈza+tion** *or* ˌ**jar+gon·i+ˈsa+tion** *n.*

jarl (jɑːl) *n. Medieval history.* a Scandinavian chieftain or noble. [C19: from Old Norse; see EARL] —ˈ**jarl+dom** *n.*

jar·o+site (ˈdʒærəˌsaɪt) *n.* a yellow to brown secondary mineral consisting of basic hydrated sulphate of iron and potassium in masses or hexagonal crystals. Formula: $KFe_3(SO_4)_2(OH)_6$. [C19: from *Barranco Jaroso*, in Almeria, Spain + -ITE[1]]

jarp (dʒɑːp) *or* **jaup** (dʒɔːp) *vb.* (*tr.*) *Northeast English dialect.* to strike or smash, esp. to break the shell of (an egg) at Easter. [from Scottish *jaup, jawp* to dash or splash like water: perhaps of imitative origin]

jar+rah (ˈdʒærə) *n.* a widely planted Australian eucalyptus tree, *Eucalyptus marginata*, that yields a valuable timber. [from a native Australian language]

Jar+row (ˈdʒærəʊ) *n.* a port in NE England, in Tyne and Wear: ruined monastery where the Venerable Bede lived and died; its unemployed marched on London in the 1930s; shipyards, iron and steel works. Pop.: 28 779 (1971).

Jar·ry (*French* ʒaˈri) *n.* **Al+fred** (alˈfrɛd). 1873–1907, French dramatist and poet, who initiated the theatre of the absurd with his play *Ubu Roi* (1896).

jar+vey *or* **jar+vie** (ˈdʒɑːvɪ) *n. Brit. informal, obsolete.* a hackney coachman. [C19: from *Jarvey*, familiar form of personal name *Jarvis*]

Jas. *Bible. abbrev. for* James.

jas+mine (ˈdʒæsmɪn, ˈdʒæz-) *n.* **1.** Also called: **jessamine.** any oleaceous shrub or climbing plant of the tropical and subtropical genus *Jasminum*, esp. *J. officinalis*: widely cultivated for their white, yellow, or red fragrant flowers, which are used in making perfume and in flavouring tea. See also **winter jasmine. 2.** any of several other shrubs with fragrant flowers, such as the Cape jasmine, yellow jasmine, and frangipani (**red jasmine**). **3.** a light to moderate yellow colour. [C16: from Old French *jasmin*, from Arabic *yāsamīn*, from Persian *yāsmīn*]

Ja·son (ˈdʒeɪsᵊn) *n. Greek myth.* the hero who led the Argonauts in quest of the Golden Fleece. He became the husband of Medea, whom he later abandoned for Glauce.

jas·pé ('dʒæspeɪ) *adj.* resembling jasper; variegated. [C19: from French, from *jasper* to marble]

jas·per ('dʒæspə) *n.* **1.** an opaque impure microcrystalline form of quartz, red, yellow, brown, or dark green in colour, used as a gemstone and for ornamental decoration. **2.** Also called: **jasper ware.** a dense hard stoneware, invented in 1775 by Wedgwood, capable of being stained throughout its substance with metallic oxides and used as background for applied classical decoration. [C14: from Old French *jaspe*, from Latin *jaspis*, from Greek *iaspis*, of Semitic origin; related to Assyrian *ashpū*, Arabic *yashb*, Hebrew *yāshpheh*]

Jas·per Na·tion·al Park *n.* a national park in SW Canada, in W Alberta in the Rockies: wildlife sanctuary. Area: 10 900 sq. km (4200 sq. miles).

Jas·pers (*German* 'jaspərs) *n.* **Karl** (karl). 1883–1969, German existentialist philosopher.

Jas·sy ('jasi) *n.* the German name for **Iaşi.**

Jat (dʒɑːt) *n., pl.* **Jat** *or* **Jats.** a member of an Indo-European people widely dispersed throughout the Punjab, Rajputana, and Uttar Pradesh.

ja·to ('dʒeɪtəʊ) *n., pl.* **·tos.** *Aeronautics.* jet-assisted takeoff. [C20: *j(et) a(ssisted) t(ake)o(ff)*]

jaun·dice ('dʒɔːndɪs) *n.* **1.** Also called: **icterus.** yellowing of the skin and whites of the eyes due to the abnormal presence of bile pigments in the blood, as in hepatitis. **2.** a mental state of bitterness, jealousy, and ill humour resulting in distorted judgment. ~*vb.* **3.** to distort (the judgment, etc.) adversely: *jealousy had jaundiced his mind.* **4.** to affect with or as if with jaundice. [C14: from Old French *jaunisse*, from *jaune* yellow, from Latin *galbinus* yellowish, from *galbus*]

jaunt (dʒɔːnt) *n.* **1.** a short pleasurable excursion; outing. ~*vb.* **2.** (*intr.*) to go on such an excursion. [C16: of unknown origin] —'**jaunt·ing·ly** *adv.*

jaunt·ing car *or* **jaun·ty car** *n.* a light two-wheeled one-horse car, formerly widely used in Ireland.

jaun·ty ('dʒɔːntɪ) *adj.* **·ti·er, ·ti·est. 1.** sprightly, self-confident, and cheerful; brisk: *a jaunty step.* **2.** smart; trim: *a jaunty hat.* [C17: from French *gentil* noble; see GENTEEL] —'**jaun·ti·ly** *adv.* —'**jaun·ti·ness** *n.*

Jau·rès (*French* ʒɔ'rɛs) *n.* **Jean Lé·on** (ʒã le'ɔ̃). 1859–1914, French politician and writer, who founded the socialist paper *l'Humanité* (1904), and united the French socialist movement into a single party (1905); assassinated.

Jav. *abbrev. for* Javanese.

Ja·va ('dʒɑːvə) *n.* an island of Indonesia, south of Borneo, from which it is separated by the **Java Sea:** politically the most important island of Indonesia; it consists chiefly of active volcanic mountains and is densely forested. It came under Dutch control in 1596 and became part of Indonesia in 1949. It is one of the most densely populated areas in the world. Capital: Djakarta. Pop. (with Madura): 76 102 486 (1971). Area: 132 174 sq. km (51 032 sq. miles). —'**Ja·van** *or* ,**Ja·va·'nese** *n., adj.*

Ja·va man *n.* a type of primitive man, *Homo erectus* (formerly called *Pithecanthropus erectus*), that lived in the middle Palaeolithic Age in Java. Also called: **Trinil man.**

Ja·va·ri *or* **Ja·va·ry** (*Portuguese* ,ʒava'ri) *n.* a river in South America, flowing northeast as part of the border between Peru and Brazil to join the Amazon. Length: about 1050 km (650 miles). Spanish name: **Yavarí.**

Ja·va spar·row *n.* a small grey-and-pink finchlike Indonesian weaverbird, *Padda oryzivora:* a popular cage bird.

jave·lin ('dʒævlɪn) *n.* **1.** a long pointed spear thrown as a weapon or in competitive field events. **2. the javelin.** the event or sport of throwing the javelin. [C16: from Old French *javeline*, variant of *javelot*, of Celtic origin]

Jav·el wa·ter *or* **Jav·elle wa·ter** ('dʒævᵊl, dʒə'vɛl) *n.* **1.** an aqueous solution containing sodium hypochlorite and some sodium chloride, used as a bleach and disinfectant. **2.** Also called: **eau de Javelle.** a similar solution made from potassium carbonate and chlorine. [C19: partial translation of French *eau de Javel*, from *Javel*, formerly a town, now part of Paris]

jaw (dʒɔː) *n.* **1.** the part of the skull of a vertebrate that frames the mouth and holds the teeth. In higher vertebrates it consists of the **upper jaw** (maxilla) fused to the cranium and the **lower jaw** (mandible). **2.** the corresponding part of an invertebrate, esp. an insect. **3.** a pair or either of a pair of hinged or sliding components of a machine or tool designed to grip an object. **4.** *Slang.* **a.** impudent talk; cheek. **b.** idle conversation; chat. **c.** moralizing talk; a lecture. ~*vb.* **5.** (*intr.*) *Slang.* **a.** to talk idly; chat; gossip. **b.** to lecture. [C14: probably from Old French *joue* cheek; related to Italian *gota* cheek] —'**jaw**,**like** *adj.*

Ja·wan (dʒə'wɑːn) *n.* (in India) **1.** a soldier. **2.** a young man. [Urdu: young man]

Ja·wa·ra ('dʒɑːwərə) *n.* Sir **Dau·da** ('dɔːdə). born 1924, president of Gambia since 1970.

jaw·bone ('dʒɔː,bəʊn) *n.* a nontechnical name for **mandible** or (less commonly) **maxilla.**

jaw·break·er ('dʒɔː,breɪkə) *n.* **1.** Also called: **jawcrusher.** a device having hinged jaws for crushing rocks and ores. **2.** *Informal.* a word that is hard to pronounce. —'**jaw**,**break·ing** *adj.* —'**jaw**,**break·ing·ly** *adv.*

jaws (dʒɔːz) *pl. n.* **1.** the narrow opening of some confined place such as a gorge. **2. the jaws.** a dangerously close position: *the jaws of death.*

Jax·ar·tes (dʒæk'sɑːtiːz) *n.* the ancient name for **Syr Darya.**

jay (dʒeɪ) *n.* **1.** any of various passerine birds of the family *Corvidae* (crows), esp. the Eurasian *Garrulus glandarius*, with a pinkish-brown body, blue-and-black wings, and a black-and-white crest. See also **blue jay. 2.** a foolish or gullible person. [C13: from Old French *jai*, from Late Latin *gāius*, perhaps from proper name *Gāius*]

Jay (dʒeɪ) *n.* **John.** 1745–1829, American statesman, jurist, and diplomat; first chief justice of the Supreme Court (1789–95). He negotiated the treaty with Great Britain (**Jay's treaty,** 1794), that settled outstanding disputes.

Jay·a·war·den·a (,dʒeɪə'wɑːdɪnə) *n.* **Ju·nius Richard.** born 1906, Sri Lanka statesman; prime minister (1977–78) and first president (since 1978) of Sri Lanka.

Jay·cee ('dʒeɪ'siː) *n. U.S.* a young person who belongs to a junior chamber of commerce. [C20: from the initials of *J(unior) C(hamber)*, short for *United States Junior Chamber of Commerce*]

jay·walk ('dʒeɪ,wɔːk) *vb.* (*intr.*) to cross or walk in a street recklessly or illegally. —'**jay**,**walk·er** *n.* —'**jay**,**walk·ing** *n.*

jazz (dʒæz) *n.* **1. a.** a kind of music of American Negro origin, characterized by syncopated rhythms, solo and group improvisation, and a variety of harmonic idioms and instrumental techniques. It exists in a number of styles. Compare **blues.** See also: **bebop, bop, Dixieland, modern jazz, New Orleans jazz, swing** (sense 26), **trad. b.** (*as modifier*): *a jazz band.* **c.** (*in combination*): *a jazzman.* **2.** *Informal.* enthusiasm or liveliness. **3.** *Slang.* rigmarole; paraphernalia: *legal papers and all that jazz.* **4.** *U.S. Negro slang, obsolete.* sexual intercourse. ~*vb.* **5.** (*intr.*) to play or dance to jazz music. **6.** *U.S. Negro slang, obsolete.* to have sexual intercourse with (a person). [C20: of unknown origin] —'**jazz·er** *n.*

jazz up *vb.* (*tr., adv.*) *Informal.* **1.** to imbue (a piece of music) with jazz qualities, esp. by improvisation or a quicker tempo. **2.** to make more lively, gaudy, or appealing.

jazz·y ('dʒæzɪ) *adj.* **jazz·i·er, jazz·i·est.** *Informal.* **1.** of, characteristic of, or resembling jazz music. **2.** gaudy or flashy: *a jazzy car.* —'**jazz·i·ly** *adv.* —'**jazz·i·ness** *n.*

J.C. *abbrev. for:* **1.** Jesus Christ. **2.** Julius Caesar. **3.** jurisconsult.

J.C.D. *abbrev. for:* **1.** Doctor of Canon Law. [Latin: *Juris Canonici Doctor*] **2.** Doctor of Civil Law. [Latin: *Juris Civilis Doctor*]

J.C.L. *Computer technol. abbrev. for* Job Control Language.

J.C.R. *abbrev. for* junior common room.

J.C.S. *abbrev. for* Joint Chiefs of Staff.

jct. *or* **jctn.** *abbrev. for* junction.

J.D. *abbrev. for:* **1.** Doctor of Laws. [Latin: *Jurum Doctor*] **2.** juvenile delinquent.

jeal·ous ('dʒɛləs) *adj.* **1.** suspicious or fearful of being displaced by a rival: *a jealous lover.* **2.** (often *postpositive* and foll. by *of*) resentful (of) or vindictive (towards), esp. through envy: *a child jealous of his brother.* **3.** (often *postpositive* and foll. by *of*) possessive and watchful in the maintenance or protection (of): *jealous of one's reputation.* **4.** characterized by or resulting from jealousy. **5.** *Obsolete except in biblical use.* demanding exclusive loyalty: *a jealous God.* **6.** an obsolete word for **zealous.** [C13: from Old French *gelos*, from Medieval Latin *zēlōsus*, from Late Latin *zēlus* emulation, jealousy, from Greek *zēlos* ZEAL] —'**jeal·ous·ly** *adv.* —'**jeal·ous·ness** *n.*

jeal·ous·y ('dʒɛləsɪ) *n., pl.* **·ous·ies.** the state or quality of being jealous.

jean (dʒiːn) *n.* a tough twill-weave cotton fabric used for hard-wearing trousers, overalls, etc. [C16: short for *jean fustian*, from *Gene* GENOA]

Jean (*French* ʒã) *n.* born 1921, grand duke of Luxembourg since 1964.

Jean de Meung (*French* ʒã də 'mœ̃) *n.* real name *Jean Clopinel.* ?1250–?1305, French poet, who continued Guillaume de Lorris' *Roman de la Rose.* His portion of the poem consists of some 18 000 lines and contains satirical attacks on women and the Church.

Jeanne d'Arc (ʒɑn 'dark) *n.* the French name of **Joan of Arc.**

Jean Paul (*French* ʒã 'pɔl) *n.* pen name of *Johann Paul Friedrich Richter.* 1763–1825, German novelist.

jeans (dʒiːnz) *pl. n.* informal trousers for casual wear, made esp. of denim or corduroy. [plural of JEAN]

Jeans (dʒiːnz) *n.* Sir **James Hop·wood.** 1877–1946, English astronomer, physicist, and mathematician, best known for his popular books on astronomy. He made important contributions to the kinetic theory of gases and the theory of stellar evolution.

jeb·el *or* **djeb·el** ('dʒɛbᵊl) *n.* a hill or mountain in an Arab country.

Jeb·el Mu·sa ('dʒɛbᵊl 'muːsə) *n.* a mountain in NW Morocco, near the Strait of Gibraltar: one of the Pillars of Hercules. Height: 850 m (2790 ft.).

Jed·da ('dʒɛdə) *n.* another name for **Jidda.**

jeep (dʒiːp) *n.* a small military road vehicle with four-wheel drive. [C20: probably from the initials *G.P.*, for *general purpose* (*vehicle*)]

jee·pers *or* **jee·pers cree·pers** ('dʒiːpəz 'kriːpəz) *interj. U.S. slang.* a mild exclamation of surprise. [C20: euphemism for *Jesus*]

Jeeps (dʒiːps) *n.* **Dick·ie.** born 1931, English Rugby Union footballer: halfback for England (1956–62) and the British Lions (1959–62).

jeer (dʒɪə) *vb.* **1.** (often foll. by *at*) to laugh or scoff (at a person or thing); mock. ~*n.* **2.** a remark or cry of derision; gibe; taunt. [C16: of unknown origin] —'**jeer·er** *n.* —'**jeer·ing·ly** *adv.*

je·fe (*Spanish* 'xefe) *n.* (in Spanish-speaking countries) a military or political leader. [Spanish, from French *chef* CHIEF]

Jef·fer·son ('dʒɛfəsᵊn) *n.* **Thom·as.** 1743–1826, U.S. statesman: secretary of state (1790–93); third president (1801–09). He was the chief drafter of the Declaration of Independence (1776), the chief opponent of the centralizing policies of the Federalists under Hamilton, and effected the Louisiana Purchase (1803). —**Jef·fer·so·ni·an** (ˌdʒɛfə'səʊnɪən) *adj., n.*

Jef·fer·son Cit·y *n.* a city in central Missouri, the state capital, on the Missouri River. Pop.: 32 407 (1970).

Jef·frey ('dʒɛfrɪ) *n.* **Fran·cis,** Lord Jeffrey. 1773–1850, Scottish judge and literary critic. As editor of the *Edinburgh Review* (1803–29), he was noted for the severity of his criticism of the romantic poets, esp. Wordsworth.

Jef·freys ('dʒɛfrɪz) *n.* **George,** 1st Baron Jeffreys of Wem. ?1645–89, English judge, notorious for his brutality at the "Bloody Assizes" (1685), where those involved in Monmouth's rebellion were tried.

je·had (dʒɪ'hæd) *n.* a variant spelling of **jihad.**

Je·hol (dʒə'hɒl) *n.* a region and former province of NE China, north of the Great Wall: divided among Hopeh, Liaoning, and Inner Mongolia in 1956. Area: 192 380 sq. km (74 278 sq. miles).

Je·hosh·a·phat (dʒɪ'hɒʃəˌfæt, -'hɒs-) *n. Old Testament.* **1.** the king of Judah (?873–?849 B.C.) (I Kings 22:41–50). **2. Valley of Jehoshaphat.** the site of Jehovah's apocalyptic judgment upon the nations (Joel 4:14).

Je·ho·vah (dʒɪ'həʊvə) *n. Old Testament.* the personal name of God, revealed to Moses on Mount Horeb (Exodus 3). [C16: from Medieval Latin, from Hebrew YHVH YAHWEH; the vowels *a, o, a* were substituted in the Masoretic Hebrew text of the Old Testament for YHVH, this name being regarded as too sacred to be pronounced; in Medieval Latin translations they were incorporated into the name as *Jehovah* (*YaHoVaH*)]

Je·ho·vah's Wit·ness *n.* a member of a Christian sect of American origin, the followers of which believe that the end of the world is near, that all other Churches and religions are false or evil, that all war is unlawful, and that the civil law must be resisted whenever it conflicts with the sect's own religious principles.

Je·ho·vist (dʒɪ'həʊvɪst) *n.* **1.** another name for the **Yahwist. 2.** a person who maintains that the name YHVH in the Hebrew text of the Old Testament was originally pronounced *Jehovah.* ~*adj.* **3.** of or relating to the Yahwist source of the Pentateuch. —**Je·'ho·vism** *n.* —**Je·ho·vis·tic** (ˌdʒi:həʊ'vɪstɪk) *adj.*

Je·hu ('dʒi:hju:) *n. Old Testament.* the successor to Ahab as king of Israel (?842–?815 B.C.); the slayer of Jezebel (II Kings 9:11–30).

je·june (dʒɪ'dʒu:n) *adj.* **1.** simple; naive; unsophisticated. **2.** insipid; dull; dry. **3.** lacking nourishment; insubstantial or barren. [C17: from Latin *jējūnus* hungry, empty] —**je·'june·ly** *adv.* —**je·'june·ness** *or* **je·'jun·i·ty** *n.*

je·ju·num (dʒɪ'dʒu:nəm) *n.* the part of the small intestine between the duodenum and the ileum. [C16: from Latin, from *jējūnus* empty; from the belief that the jejunum is empty after death] —**je·'ju·nal** *adj.*

Jek·yll and Hyde ('dʒɛkᵊl; haɪd) *n.* **a.** a person with two distinct personalities, one good, the other evil. **b.** (*as modifier*): *a Jekyll-and-Hyde personality.* [C19: after the principal character of Robert Louis Stevenson's novel *The Strange Case of Dr. Jekyll and Mr. Hyde* (1886)]

jell *or* **gel** (dʒɛl) *vb.* **jells, jell·ing, jelled** *or* **gels, gel·ling, gelled. 1.** to make or become gelatinous; congeal. **2.** to assume definite form: *his ideas have jelled.* ~*n.* **3.** *U.S.* an informal word for **jelly.** [C19: back formation from JELLY]

jel·lab·a *or* **jel·lab·ah** ('dʒɛləbə) *n.* a kind of loose cloak with a hood, worn esp. in North Africa and the Middle East.

Jel·li·coe ('dʒɛlɪˌkəʊ) *n.* **John Rush·worth,** 1st Earl Jellicoe. 1859–1935, British admiral, who commanded the Grand Fleet at the Battle of Jutland (1916), which incapacitated the German fleet for the rest of World War I.

jel·lied ('dʒɛlɪd) *adj.* **1.** congealed into jelly, esp. by cooling. **2.** containing, set in, or coated with jelly.

jel·li·fy ('dʒɛlɪˌfaɪ) *vb.* **·fies, ·fy·ing, ·fied.** to make into or become jelly. —ˌ**jel·li·fi·'ca·tion** *n.*

jell·o ('dʒɛləʊ) *n.* the usual U.S. name for **jelly**[1] (sense 1). [C20: from the trademark *Jell-O*]

jel·ly[1] ('dʒɛlɪ) *n., pl.* **·lies. 1.** a fruit-flavoured clear dessert set with gelatine. U.S. name: **jello. 2.** a preserve made from the juice of fruit boiled with sugar and used as jam. **3.** a savoury food preparation set with gelatine or with a strong gelatinous stock and having a soft elastic consistency: *calf's-foot jelly.* **4.** anything having the consistency of jelly. ~*vb.* **·lies, ·ly·ing, ·lied. 5.** to jellify. [C14: from Old French *gelee* frost, jelly, from *geler* to set hard, from Latin *gelāre,* from *gelu* frost] —'**jel·ly**ˌ**like** *adj.*

jel·ly[2] ('dʒɛlɪ) *n. Brit.* a slang name for **gelignite.**

jel·ly ba·by *n. Brit.* a small sweet made from a gelatinous substance formed to resemble a baby in shape.

jel·ly·bean ('dʒɛlɪˌbi:n) *n.* a bean-shaped candy with a brightly coloured coating around a gelatinous filling.

jel·ly·fish ('dʒɛlɪˌfɪʃ) *n., pl.* **·fish** *or* **·fish·es. 1.** any marine medusoid coelenterate of the class *Scyphozoa,* having a gelatinous umbrella-shaped body with trailing tentacles. **2.** any other medusoid coelenterate. **3.** *Informal.* a weak indecisive person.

jem·a·dar ('dʒɛməˌdɑ:) *n.* a native junior officer belonging to a locally raised regiment serving as mercenaries in India, esp. with the British Army. [C18: from Urdu *jama 'dār,* from Persian *jama 'at* body of men + *dār* having]

Je·mappes (*French* ʒə'map) *n.* a town in SW Belgium, in Hainaut province west of Mons: scene of a battle (1792) during the French Revolutionary Wars, in which the French defeated the Austrians. Pop.: 18 040 (1970).

jem·my ('dʒɛmɪ) *or U.S.* **jim·my** *n., pl.* **·mies. 1.** a short steel crowbar used, esp. by burglars, for forcing doors and windows. ~*vb.* **·mies, ·my·ing, ·mied. 2.** (*tr.*) to prise (something) open with a jemmy. [C19: from the pet name for *James*]

Je·na (*German* 'je:na) *n.* a city in S East Germany, in Thuringia: university (1558), at which Hegel and Schiller taught; site of the battle (1806) in which Napoleon Bonaparte defeated the Prussians; optical and precision instrument industry. Pop.: 94 060 (1972 est.).

je ne sais quoi *French.* (ʒən sɛ 'kwa) *n.* an indefinable quality, esp. of personality. [literally: I don't know what]

Jen·ghis Khan ('dʒɛŋgɪs 'kɑ:n) *n.* See **Genghis Khan.**

Jenkins ('dʒɛŋkɪnz) *n.* **Roy (Harris).** born 1920, British Labour politician; president of the Common Market Commission (1977-80); cofounder of Social Democratic Party (1981); leader 1982-83.

Jen·ner ('dʒɛnə) *n.* **1. Ed·ward.** 1749–1823, English physician, who discovered vaccination by showing that injections of cowpox virus produce immunity against smallpox (1796). **2.** Sir **Wil·liam.** 1815–98, English physician and pathologist, who differentiated between typhus and typhoid fevers (1849).

jen·net, gen·et, *or* **gen·net** ('dʒɛnɪt) *n.* **1.** Also called: **jenny.** a female donkey or ass. **2.** a small Spanish riding horse. [C15: from Old French *genet,* from Catalan *ginet,* horse of the type used by the *Zenete,* from Arabic *Zanātah* the Zenete, a Moorish people renowned for their horsemanship]

jen·ny ('dʒɛnɪ) *n., pl.* **·nies. 1.** a hand-operated machine for turning up the edge of a piece of sheet metal in preparation for making a joint. **2.** the female of certain animals or birds, esp. a donkey, ass, or wren. **3.** short for **spinning jenny. 4.** *Billiards, etc.* an in-off. See **long jenny, short jenny.** [C17: from the name *Jenny,* diminutive of *Jane*]

jeop·ard·ize *or* **jeop·ard·ise** ('dʒɛpəˌdaɪz) *vb.* **1.** to risk; hazard: *he jeopardized his job by being persistently unpunctual.* **2.** (*tr.*) to put in danger; imperil.

jeop·ard·y ('dʒɛpədɪ) *n.* (usually preceded by *in*) **1.** danger of injury, loss, death, etc.; risk; peril; hazard: *his health was in jeopardy.* **2.** *Law.* danger of being convicted and punished for a criminal offence. See also **double jeopardy.** [C14: from Old French *jeu parti,* literally: divided game, hence uncertain issue, from *jeu* game, from Latin *jocus* joke, game + *partir* to divide, from Latin *partīrī*]

Jeph·thah (ˌdʒɛfθə) *n. Old Testament.* a judge of Israel, who sacrificed his daughter in fulfilment of a vow (Judges 11:12–40). Douay spelling: **Jeph·te** ('dʒɛftə).

je·quir·i·ty *or* **je·quer·i·ty** (dʒɪ'kwɪrɪtɪ) *n., pl.* **·ties. 1.** other names for **Indian liquorice. 2. jequirity bean.** the seed of the Indian liquorice. [C19: from Portuguese *jequiriti,* from Tupi-Guarani *jekiriti*]

Jer. *Bible. abbrev. for* Jeremiah.

Jer·ba ('dʒɜ:bə) *n.* a variant spelling of **Djerba.**

jer·bil ('dʒɜ:bɪl) *n.* a variant spelling of **gerbil.**

jer·bo·a (dʒɜ:'bəʊə) *n.* any small nocturnal burrowing rodent of the family *Dipodidae,* inhabiting dry regions of Asia and N Africa, having pale sandy fur, large ears, and long hind legs specialized for jumping. [C17: from New Latin, from Arabic *yarbū'*]

jer·e·mi·ad (ˌdʒɛrɪ'maɪəd) *n.* a long mournful lamentation or complaint.

Jer·e·mi·ah (ˌdʒɛrɪ'maɪə) *n. Old Testament.* **1.** a major prophet of Judah from about 626 to 587 B.C. **2.** the book containing his oracles.

Je·rez (*Spanish* xe'reθ) *n.* a town in SW Spain: famous for the making of sherry. Pop.: 149 867 (1970). Official name: **Je·rez de la Fron·te·ra** (ðe la fron'tera). Former name: **Xeres.**

Jer·i·cho ('dʒɛrɪˌkəʊ) *n.* a village in Jordan near the N end of the Dead Sea, 251 m (825 ft.) below sea level: on the site of an ancient city, the first place to be taken by the Israelites under Joshua after entering the Promised Land in the 14th century B.C. (Joshua 6).

je·rid (dʒə'ri:d) *n.* a wooden javelin used in Muslim countries in military displays on horseback. Also: **jereed, jerreed.**

jerk[1] (dʒɜ:k) *vb.* **1.** to move or cause to move with an irregular or spasmodic motion. **2.** to throw, twist, pull, or push (something) abruptly or spasmodically. **3.** (*tr.;* often foll. by *out*) to utter (words, sounds, etc.) in a spasmodic, abrupt, or breathless manner. ~*n.* **4.** an abrupt or spasmodic movement. **5.** an irregular jolting motion: *the car moved with a jerk.* **6.** (*pl.*) Also called: **physical jerks.** *Brit. informal.* physical exercises. **7.** (*pl.*) *U.S.* a slang word for **chorea. 8.** *Slang, chiefly U.S.* a person regarded with contempt esp. a stupid or ignorant person. [C16: probably variant of *yerk* to pull stitches tight in making a shoe; compare Old English *gearcian* to make ready] —'**jerk·er** *n.* —'**jerk·ing·ly** *adv.*

jerk[2] (dʒɜ:k) *vb.* **1.** to preserve venison, beef, etc., by cutting into thin strips and curing by drying in the sun. ~*n.* **2.** Also called: **jerky.** jerked meat, esp. beef. [C18: back formation from *jerky,* from CHARQUI]

jer·kin ('dʒɜ:kɪn) *n.* **1.** a sleeveless and collarless short jacket worn by men or women. **2.** a man's sleeveless and collarless fitted jacket, often made of leather, worn in the 16th and 17th centuries. [C16: of unknown origin]

jerk off *vb.* (*adv. often reflexive*) *U.S. taboo slang.* to masturbate.

jerk+wa·ter ('dʒɜːk,wɔːtə) *adj. U.S. slang.* inferior and insignificant: *a jerkwater town.* [C19: originally referring to railway locomotives for which water was taken on in buckets from streams along the route]

jerk·y ('dʒɜːkɪ) *adj.* **jerk·i+er, jerk·i+est.** characterized by jerks; spasmodic. —'**jerk·i+ly** *adv.* —'**jerk·i+ness** *n.*

jer·o+bo+am (,dʒɛrə'bəʊəm) *n.* a wine bottle holding the equivalent of four normal bottles (approximately 104 ounces). Also called: **double-magnum.** [C19: humorous allusion to JEROBOAM (sense 1), described as a "mighty man of valour" (I Kings 11:28) who "made Israel to sin" (I Kings 14:16)]

Jer·o·bo·am (,dʒɛrə'bəʊəm) *n. Old Testament.* **1.** the first king of the northern kingdom of Israel (?922–?901 B.C.). **2.** king of the northern kingdom of Israel (?786–?746 B.C.).

Je·rome (dʒə'rəʊm) *n.* **1. Saint.** Latin name *Eusebius Hieronymus.* ?347–?420 A.D., Christian monk and scholar, whose outstanding work was the production of the Vulgate. Feast day: Sept. 30. **2. Je·rome K(lapka).** 1859–1927, English humorous writer; author of *Three Men in a Boat* (1889).

jer+reed (dʒə'riːd) *n.* a variant spelling of **jerid.**

jer+ry ('dʒɛrɪ) *n., pl.* **+ries. 1.** *Brit.* an informal word for **chamber pot. 2.** short for **jeroboam.**

Jer+ry ('dʒɛrɪ) *n., pl.* **+ries.** *Brit. slang.* **1.** a German, esp. a German soldier. **2.** the Germans collectively: *Jerry didn't send his bombers out last night.*

jer·ry-build *vb.* **-builds, -build·ing, -built.** (*tr.*) to build (houses, flats, etc.) badly using cheap materials. —'**jer·ry-,build·er** *n.*

jer+ry can *n.* a flat-sided can used for storing or transporting liquids, esp. motor fuel. It has a capacity of between 4.5 and 5 gallons. [C20: from *jerry,* short for JEROBOAM]

jer+sey ('dʒɜːzɪ) *n.* **1.** a knitted garment covering the upper part of the body. **2. a.** a machine-knitted slightly elastic cloth of wool, silk, nylon, etc., used for clothing. **b.** (*as modifier*): *a jersey suit.* [C16: from JERSEY, from the woollen sweaters traditionally worn by the fishermen]

Jer+sey ('dʒɜːzɪ) *n.* **1.** an island in the English Channel, the largest of the Channel Islands: forms, with two other islands, the bailiwick of Jersey; colonized from Normandy in the 11th century and still officially French-speaking; noted for market gardening, dairy farming, and tourism. Capital: St. Helier. Pop.: 72 532 (1971). Area: 116 sq. km (45 sq. miles). **2.** a breed of dairy cattle producing milk with a high butterfat content, originating from the island of Jersey.

Jer+sey Cit·y *n.* an industrial city in NE New Jersey, opposite Manhattan on a peninsula between the Hudson and Hackensack Rivers: part of the Port of New York; site of one of the greatest railway terminals in the world. Pop.: 255 030 (1973 est.).

Je+ru+sa+lem (dʒə'ruːsələm) *n.* **1.** the capital of Israel, situated in the Judaean hills: became capital of the Hebrew kingdom after its capture by David around 1000 B.C.; destroyed by Nebuchadnezzar of Babylon in 586 B.C.; taken by the Romans in 63 B.C.; devastated in 70 A.D. and 135 A.D. during the Jewish rebellions against Rome; fell to the Arabs in 637 and to the Seljuk Turks in 1071; ruled by Crusaders from 1099 to 1187 and by the Egyptians and Turks until conquered by the British (1917); centre of the British mandate of Palestine from 1920 to 1948, when the Arabs took the old city and the Jews held the new city; unified after the Six Day War (1967) under the Israelis; the holy city of Jews, Christians, and Muslims. Pop.: 344 200 (1974 est.). **2. the New Jerusalem.** *Christianity.* Heaven.

Je+ru+sa+lem ar+ti+choke *n.* **1.** a North American sunflower, *Helianthus tuberosus,* widely cultivated for its underground edible tubers. **2.** the tuber of this plant, which is cooked and eaten as a vegetable. ~See also **artichoke** (senses 1, 2). [C17: by folk etymology from Italian *girasole articiocco;* see GIRASOL]

Je+ru+sa+lem cher+ry *n.* a small South American solanaceous shrub, *Solanum pseudo-capsicum,* cultivated as a house plant for its white flowers and inedible reddish cherry-like fruit.

Je+ru+sa+lem cross *n.* a cross the equal arms of which end in a bar. Also called: **cross potent.**

Je+ru+sa+lem oak *n.* a weedy North American chenopodiaceous plant, *Chenopodium botrys,* that has lobed leaves and smells of turpentine.

Jer+vis Bay ('dʒɑːvɪs) *n.* an inlet of the Pacific in SE Australia, on the coast of S New South Wales: part of the Australian Capital Territory: site of the Royal Australian Naval College.

Jes·per·sen ('jɛspəˀn, 'dʒɛs-) *n.* (**Jens**) **Ot·to** (**Harry**). 1860–1943, Danish philologist: author of *Modern English Grammar* (1909–31).

jess (dʒɛs) *Falconry.* ~*n.* **1.** a short leather strap, one end of which is permanently attached to the leg of a hawk or falcon while the other can be attached to a leash. ~*vb.* **2.** (*tr.*) to put jesses on (a hawk or falcon). [C14: from Old French *ges,* from Latin *jactus* a throw, from *jacere* to throw] —**jessed** *adj.*

jes+sa+mine ('dʒɛsəmɪn) *n.* another name for **jasmine** (sense 1).

Jes·se ('dʒɛsɪ) *n. Old Testament.* the father of David (I Samuel 16).

Jes+sel+ton ('dʒɛsəltən) *n.* the former name of **Kota Kinabalu.**

jest (dʒɛst) *n.* **1.** something done or said for amusement; joke. **2.** a frivolous mood or attitude; playfulness; fun: *to act in jest.* **3.** a jeer or taunt. **4.** an object of derision; laughingstock; butt. ~*vb.* **5.** to act or speak in an amusing, teasing, or frivolous way; joke. **6.** to make fun of (a person or thing); scoff or mock. [C13: variant of GEST] —'**jest+ful** *adj.* —'**jest+ful+ly** *adv.*

jest+er ('dʒɛstə) *n.* a professional clown employed by a king or nobleman, esp. at courts during the Middle Ages.

Je·su ('dʒiːzjuː) *n.* a poetic name for or vocative form of **Jesus.** [C17: from Late Latin, vocative of JESUS]

Jes+u+it ('dʒɛzjʊɪt) *n.* **1.** a member of a Roman Catholic religious order (the **Society of Jesus**) founded by Ignatius Loyola in 1534 with the aims of defending the papacy and Catholicism against the Reformation and to undertake missionary work among the heathen. **2.** (*sometimes not cap.*) *Informal, offensive.* a person given to subtle and equivocating arguments; casuist. [C16: from New Latin *Jēsuita,* from Late Latin *Jēsus* + *-ita* -ITE[1]] —,**Jes·u·'it+ic** *or* ,**Jes·u·'it·i+cal** *adj.*

Jes·u+it+ism ('dʒɛzjʊɪ,tɪzəm) *or* **Jes·u+it+ry** *n.* **1.** theology or practices of the Jesuits. **2.** *Informal, offensive.* subtle and equivocating arguments; casuistry.

Je·sus ('dʒiːzəs) *n.* **1.** Also called: **Jesus Christ, Jesus of Nazareth.** ?4 B.C.–?29 A.D., founder of Christianity, born in Galilee and brought up as a Jew. He is believed by Christians to be the Son of God and to have been miraculously conceived by the Virgin Mary, wife of Joseph. With 12 disciples, he undertook two missionary journeys through Galilee, performing miracles, teaching, and proclaiming the coming of the Kingdom of God. His revolutionary Sermon on the Mount (Matthew 5–8), which preaches love, humility, and charity, the essence of his teaching, aroused the hostility of the Pharisees. After the Last Supper with his disciples, he was betrayed by Judas and crucified. He is believed by Christians to have risen from his tomb after three days, appeared to his disciples several times, and ascended to Heaven after 40 days. **2.** *Son of Sirach.* 3rd century B.C., author of the Apocryphal book of Ecclesiasticus. ~*interj. also* **Jesus wept. 3.** used to express intense surprise, dismay, etc. [via Latin from Greek *Iēsous,* from Hebrew *Yeshūa',* shortened from *Yehōshūa'* God is help, JOSHUA]

Je·sus freak *n. Informal.* a member of any of various Christian groups that combine a hippie communal way of life with zealous evangelicalism.

jet[1] (dʒɛt) *n.* **1.** a thin stream of liquid or gas forced out of a small aperture or nozzle. **2.** an outlet or nozzle for emitting such a stream. **3.** a jet-propelled aircraft. ~*vb.* **jets, jet+ting, jet+ted. 4.** to issue or cause to issue in a jet: *water jetted from the hose; he jetted them with water.* **5.** to transport or be transported by jet aircraft. [C16: from Old French *jeter* to throw, from Latin *jactāre* to toss about, frequentative of *jacere* to throw]

jet[2] (dʒɛt) *n.* **a.** a hard black variety of lignite that takes a brilliant polish and is used for jewellery, ornaments, etc. **b.** (*as modifier*): *jet earrings.* [C14: from Old French *jaiet,* from Latin *gagātēs,* from Greek *lithos gagatēs* stone of *Gagai,* a town in Lycia, Asia Minor]

JET (dʒɛt) *n. acronym for* Joint European Torus.

jet black *n.* **a.** a deep black colour. **b.** (*as adj.*): *jet-black hair.*

je·té (ʒə'teɪ) *n. Ballet.* a step in which the dancer springs from one leg and lands on the other. [French, literally: thrown, from *jeter;* see JET[1]]

jet en+gine *n.* a gas turbine, esp. one fitted to an aircraft.

Jeth·ro ('dʒɛθrəʊ) *n. Old Testament.* a Midianite priest, the father-in-law of Moses (Exodus 3:1; 4:18).

jet lag *n.* a general feeling of fatigue and other symptoms often experienced by travellers by jet aircraft who cross several time zones in relatively few hours.

jet+lin·er ('dʒɛt,laɪnə) *n.* a commercial airliner powered by jet engines.

jet pipe *n.* the duct attached to the rear of a gas turbine through which the exhaust gases are discharged, esp. one fitted to an aircraft engine.

jet plane *n.* an aircraft powered by one or more jet engines.

jet+port ('dʒɛt,pɔːt) *n.* an airport for jet planes.

jet-pro·pelled *adj.* driven by jet propulsion.

jet pro+pul+sion *n.* **1.** propulsion by means of a jet of fluid. **2.** propulsion by means of a gas turbine, esp. when the exhaust gases provide the propulsive thrust.

jet+sam *or* **jet+som** ('dʒɛtsəm) *n.* **1.** that portion of the equipment or cargo of a vessel thrown overboard to lighten her, as during a storm. Compare **flotsam, lagan. 2.** another word for **flotsam** (sense 2). [C16: shortened from JETTISON]

jet set *n.* a rich and fashionable social set the members of which travel widely for pleasure. —'**jet+,set·ter** *n.*

jet stream *n.* **1.** *Meteorol.* an extensive high-altitude airstream (about 12 000 metres high) moving east at high speeds and having an important effect on frontogenesis. **2.** the jet of exhaust gases produced by a gas turbine, rocket motor, etc.

jet+ti+son ('dʒɛtɪsˀn, -zˀn) *vb.* (*tr.*) **1.** to throw away; abandon: *to jettison old clothes.* **2.** to throw overboard. ~*n.* **3.** another word for **jetsam** (sense 1). [C15: from Old French *getaison,* ultimately from Latin *jactātiō* a tossing about; see JACTATION]

jet+ton ('dʒɛtˀn) *n.* a counter or token, esp. a chip used in such gambling games as roulette. [C18: from French *jeton,* from *jeter* to cast up (accounts); see JET[1]]

jet+ty[1] ('dʒɛtɪ) *n., pl.* **+ties.** a pier, dock, groyne, mole, or other structure extending into the water from the shore. [C15: from Old French *jetee* projecting part, literally: something thrown out, from *jeter* to throw; see JET[1]]

jet+ty[2] ('dʒɛtɪ) *adj.* of or resembling jet, esp. in colour or polish. —'**jet+ti+ness** *n.*

jeu d'es+prit (*French* ʒø dɛs'pri) *n., pl.* ***jeux d'es+prit*** (ʒø dɛs'pri). a light-hearted display of wit or cleverness, esp. in literature. [literally: play of spirit]

jeu+nesse do+rée *French.* (ʒœnɛs dɔ're) *n.* rich and fashionable young people. [literally: gilded youth]

Jev·ons ('dʒɛvənz) *n.* **Wil·liam Stan·ley.** 1835–82, English economist and logician: introduced the concept of final or marginal utility in *The Theory of Political Economy* (1871).

Jew (dʒu:) *n.* **1.** a member of the Semitic people who are notionally descended from the ancient Israelites, are spread throughout the world, and are linked by loose cultural or religious ties. **2.** a person whose religion is Judaism. **3.** a member of the ancient tribe or nation of Judah. **4.** loosely, another word for **Israeli. 5.** (*modifier*) *Offensive.* Jewish: *a Jew boy.* **6.** (*sometimes not cap.*) *Offensive.* **a.** a person who drives a hard bargain. **b.** a miserly person. **c.** *Obsolete.* a usurer. ~*vb.* **7.** (*tr.; often not cap.*) *Offensive and obsolete.* to drive a hard bargain, esp. in order to defraud. [C12: from Old French *juiu,* from Latin *jūdaeus,* from Greek *ioudaios,* from Hebrew *yehūdī,* from *jehūdāh* JUDAH]

Jew-bait·ing *n.* active persecution or harassment of Jews. —'**Jew-ˌbait·er** *n.*

jew+el ('dʒu:əl) *n.* **1.** a precious or semiprecious stone; gem. **2.** a person or thing resembling a jewel in preciousness, brilliance, etc. **3.** a gemstone, often synthetically produced, used as a bearing in a watch. **4.** a piece of jewellery. **5.** an ornamental glass boss, sometimes faceted, used in stained glass work. ~*vb.* **+els, +el+ling, +elled** *or U.S.* **+els, +el+ing, +eled. 6.** (*tr.*) to fit or decorate with a jewel or jewels. [C13: from Old French *jouel,* perhaps from *jeu* game, from Latin *jocus*] —'**jew·el-ˌlike** *adj.*

jew·el+fish ('dʒu:əlˌfɪʃ) *n., pl.* **+fish** *or* **+fish·es.** an African cichlid, *Hemichromis bimaculatus*: a beautifully coloured and popular aquarium fish.

jew+el+ler *or U.S.* **jew+el+er** ('dʒu:ələ) *n.* a person whose business is the cutting, polishing, or setting of gemstones or the making, repairing, or selling of jewellery.

jew+el+ler's rouge *n.* a finely powdered form of ferric oxide used as a metal polish. Also called: **crocus.** See also **colcothar.**

jew+el+ler·y *or U.S.* **jew+el+ry** ('dʒu:əlrɪ) *n.* **1.** objects that are worn for personal adornment, such as bracelets, rings, necklaces, etc., considered collectively. **2.** the art or business of a jeweller.

Jew+ess ('dʒu:ɪs) *n.* a Jewish girl or woman.

jew+fish ('dʒu:ˌfɪʃ) *n., pl.* **+fish** *or* **+fish·es.** any of various large dark serranid fishes, such as *Mycteroperca bonaci,* of warm or tropical seas. [C17: of uncertain origin]

Jew+ish ('dʒu:ɪʃ) *adj.* **1.** of, relating to, or characteristic of Jews. **2.** *Offensive.* miserly. ~*n.* **3.** a less common word for **Yiddish.** —'**Jew+ish+ly** *adv.* —'**Jew+ish+ness** *n.*

Jew+ish Au·ton·o·mous Re+gion *n.* an administrative division of the SE Soviet Union, in E Siberia: colonized by Jews in 1928; largely agricultural. Capital: Birobidzhan. Pop.: 172 449 (1970). Area: 36 000 sq. km (13 895 sq. miles). Also called: **Birobidzhan.**

Jew+ish cal+en+dar *n.* the lunisolar calendar used by the Jews, in which time is reckoned from 3761 B.C., regarded as the year of the Creation. It is based on a Metonic cycle of 19 years, the 3rd, 6th, 8th, 11th, 14th, 17th, and 19th being designated leap years. Each year begins in September or October and contains the following 12 or, in intercalary years, 13 months of 29 or 30 days each: Tishri, Heshvan, Kislev, Tebet, Shebat, Adar, Adar Sheni (occurring only in intercalary years), Nisan, Iyar, Sivan, Tammuz, Ab, and Elul. Also called: **Hebrew calendar.**

Jew+ry ('dʒuərɪ) *n., pl.* **+ries. 1. a.** Jews collectively. **b.** the Jewish religion or culture. **2.** a quarter of a town inhabited by Jews. **3.** *Archaic.* the land of Judaea.

jew's-ear *n.* an edible saprophytic basidiomycetous fungus, *Auricularia auricula,* that grows on wood and has a brown or flesh-coloured jelly-like saucer-shaped body: order *Tremellales.*

jew's-harp *n.* a musical instrument consisting of a small lyre-shaped metal frame held between the teeth, with a steel tongue plucked with the finger. Changes in pitch are produced by varying the size of the mouth cavities.

Jez·e·bel ('dʒɛzəˌbɛl, -bəl) *n.* **1.** *Old Testament.* the wife of Ahab, king of Israel: she fostered the worship of Baal and tried to destroy the prophets of Israel (I Kings 18:4–13); she was killed by Jehu (II Kings 9:29–37). **2.** (*sometimes not cap.*) a shameless or scheming woman.

Jez+re+el ('dʒɛzrɪəl) *n.* **Plain of.** another name for **Esdraelon.** —'**Jez+re+el+ˌite** *n.*

Jhan+si ('dʒɑ:nsɪ) *n.* a city in central India, in SW Uttar Pradesh: scene of a mutiny against the British in 1857. Pop.: 173 292 (1971).

Jhe+lum ('dʒi:ləm) *n.* a river in Pakistan and Kashmir, rising in W central Kashmir and flowing northwest through the Vale of Kashmir, then southwest into N West Punjab to join the Chenab River: important for irrigation, having the Mangla Dam (Pakistan), completed in 1967. Length: about 720 km (450 miles).

JHVH *n.* a variant spelling of **YHVH.**

-ji (-dzi:) *Indian.* a suffix placed after a person's name or title as a mark of respect. [Hindi]

jib[1] (dʒɪb) *n.* **1.** *Nautical.* any triangular sail set forward of the foremast of a vessel. **2. cut of someone's jib.** someone's manner, behaviour, style, etc. **3.** *Obsolete.* **a.** the lower lip, usually when it protrudes forwards in a grimace. **b.** the face or nose. [C17: of unknown origin]

jib[2] (dʒɪb) *vb.* **jibs, jib+bing, jibbed.** (*intr.*) *Chiefly Brit.* **1.** (often foll. by *at*) to be reluctant (to); hold back (from); balk (at). **2.** (of an animal) to stop short and refuse to go forwards: *the horse jibbed at the jump.* **3.** *Nautical.* variant of **gybe.** [C19: of unknown origin] —'**jib+ber** *n.*

jib[3] (dʒɪb) *n.* the projecting arm of a crane or the boom of a derrick, esp. one that is pivoted to enable it to be raised or lowered. [C18: probably based on GIBBET]

jib[4] (dʒɪb) *n.* (*often pl.*) *South Wales dialect.* a contortion of the face; a face: *stop making jibs.* [special use of JIB[1] (in the sense: lower lip, face)]

jib+bons ('dʒɪbənz) *pl. n. Southwest Brit. dialect.* spring onions. [from Norman French *chiboule,* variant of French *ciboule* onion, ultimately from Latin *capulla* an onion patch, from *caepa* an onion]

jib boom *n. Nautical.* a spar forming an extension of the bowsprit.

jibe[1] (dʒaɪb), **jib,** *or* **jibb** (dʒɪb) *vb., n. Nautical.* variant spellings of **gybe.**

jibe[2] (dʒaɪb) *vb.* a variant spelling of **gibe**[1]. —'**jib+er** *n.* —'**jib+ing+ly** *adv.*

jibe[3] (dʒaɪb) *vb.* (*intr.*) *Informal.* to agree; accord; harmonize. [C19: of unknown origin]

jib-head·ed *adj. Nautical.* **1.** (of a sail) pointed at the top or head. **2.** (of a sailing vessel or rig) having sails that are triangular.

Ji+bou·ti *or* **Ji+bu+ti** (dʒɪ'bu:tɪ) *n.* variant spellings of **Djibouti.**

Jid+da ('dʒɪdə) *or* **Jed+da** *n.* a port in W Saudi Arabia, in Hejaz on the Red Sea: the diplomatic capital of the country; the port of entry for Mecca, 80 km (50 miles) east. Pop.: 194 000 (1965 est.).

jif+fy ('dʒɪfɪ) *or* **jiff** *n., pl.* **jif+fies** *or* **jiffs.** *Informal.* a very short time: *wait a jiffy.* [C18: of unknown origin]

jig (dʒɪg) *n.* **1.** any of several old rustic kicking and leaping dances. **2.** a piece of music composed for or in the rhythm of this dance, usually in three-four time. **3.** a mechanical device designed to hold and locate a component during machining and to guide the cutting tool. **4.** *Angling.* any of various spinning lures that wobble when drawn through the water. **5.** Also called: **jigger.** *Mining.* a device for separating ore or coal from waste material by agitation in water. **6.** *Obsolete.* a joke or prank. ~*vb.* **jigs, jig+ging, jigged. 7.** to dance (a jig). **8.** to jerk or cause to jerk up and down rapidly. **9.** (often foll. by *up*) to fit or be fitted in a jig. **10.** (*tr.*) to drill or cut (a workpiece) in a jig. **11.** *Mining.* to separate ore or coal from waste material using a jig. **12.** (*intr.*) to produce or manufacture a jig. [C16 (originally: a dance or the music for it; applied to various modern devices because of the verbal sense: to jerk up and down rapidly): of unknown origin]

jig+ger[1] ('dʒɪgə) *n.* **1.** a person or thing that jigs. **2.** *Golf.* a club, an iron, usually No. 4. **3.** any of a number of mechanical devices having a vibratory or jerking motion. **4.** a light lifting tackle used on ships. **5.** a small glass, esp. for whisky, with a capacity of about one and a half ounces. **6.** *Mining.* another word for **jig** (sense 5). **7.** *Nautical.* short for **jiggermast. 8.** *Billiards.* another word for **bridge**[1] (sense 10). **9.** *U.S. informal.* a device or thing the name of which is unknown or temporarily forgotten. **10.** *Liverpool dialect.* an alleyway.

jig+ger[2] *or* **jig+ger flea** ('dʒɪgə) *n.* other names for the **chigoe** (sense 1).

jig+gered ('dʒɪgəd) *adj.* (*postpositive*) **1.** *Informal.* damned; blowed: *I'm jiggered if he'll get away with it.* **2.** (sometimes foll. by *up*) *Northern Brit. dialect.* tired out. [C19: probably euphemism for *buggered;* see BUGGER]

jig·ger+mast ('dʒɪgəˌmɑ:st) *n. Nautical.* any small mast on a sailing vessel, esp. the mizzenmast of a yawl. Sometimes shortened to **jigger.**

jig·ger·y-pok·er·y ('dʒɪgərɪ'pəukərɪ) *n. Informal, chiefly Brit.* dishonest or deceitful behaviour or business; trickery. [C19: from Scottish dialect *joukery-pawkery*]

jig+gle ('dʒɪgəl) *vb.* to move or cause to move up and down or to and fro with a short jerky motion: *to jiggle the door handle.* [C19: frequentative of JIG; compare JOGGLE] —'**jig+gly** *adj.*

jig+saw ('dʒɪgˌsɔ:) *n.* **1.** a mechanical saw with a fine steel blade for cutting intricate curves in sheets of material. **2.** See **jigsaw puzzle.** [C19: from JIG (to jerk up and down rapidly) + SAW[1]]

jig+saw puz+zle *n.* a puzzle in which the player has to reassemble a picture that has been mounted on a wooden or cardboard base and cut into a large number of irregularly shaped interlocking pieces.

ji+had *or* **je+had** (dʒɪ'hæd) *n.* **1.** *Islam.* a holy war against infidels undertaken by Muslims. **2.** *Rare.* a crusade in support of a cause. [C19: from Arabic *jihād* a conflict]

jill·a+roo (ˌdʒɪlə'ru:) *n. Austral. informal.* a female jackaroo.

jil+lion ('dʒɪljən) *n. Informal.* an extremely large number or amount: *jillions of pounds.* [C20: fanciful coinage based on MILLION, BILLION, etc.] —'**jil+lionth** *adj.*

Ji+lo+lo (dʒaɪ'ləuləu) *n.* a variant spelling of **Djailolo.** See **Halmahera.**

jilt (dʒɪlt) *vb.* **1.** (*tr.*) to leave or reject (a lover), esp. without previous warning: *she was jilted at the altar.* ~*n.* **2.** a woman who jilts a lover. [C17: from dialect *jillet* flighty girl, diminutive of proper name *Gill*] —'**jilt+er** *n.*

jim crow ('dʒɪm 'krəu) (*often caps.*) *U.S.* ~*n.* **1. a.** the policy or practice of segregating Negroes. **b.** (*as modifier*): *jim-crow laws.* **2. a.** a derogatory term for Negro. **b.** (*as modifier*): *a jim-crow saloon.* **3.** an implement for bending iron bars or rails. **4.** a crowbar fitted with a claw. [C19: from *Jim Crow,* name of song used as the basis of an act by Thomas Rice (1808–60), American entertainer] —'**jim-'crow·ism** *n.*

Ji·mé·nez (*Spanish* xi'meneθ) *n.* **Juan Ra·món** (xwan ra'mon). 1881–1958, Spanish lyric poet. His most famous work is *Platero y yo* (1917), a prose poem: Nobel prize for literature 1956.

Ji·mé·nez de Cis·ne·ros (*Spanish* xi'meneθ ðe θiz'neros) *n.* **Fran·cis·co** (fran'θisko). 1436–1517, Spanish cardinal and statesman; regent of Castile (1506–07) and Spain (1516–17) and grand inquisitor for Castile and León (1507–17). Also: **Xi·me·nes de Cis·ne·ros, Xi·me·nez de Cis·ne·ros.**

jim+jams ('dʒɪm,dʒæmz) *pl. n.* **1.** a slang word for **delirium tremens.** **2.** a state of nervous tension, excitement, or anxiety. [C19: whimsical formation based on JAM[1]]

jim+my ('dʒɪmɪ) *n., pl.* **+mies,** *vb.* **+mies, +my+ing, +mied.** the U.S. spelling of **jemmy.**

Jim+my ('dʒɪmɪ) *n.* an informal name for a **Scot.**

Jim+my Wood+ser (,dʒɪmɪ 'wʊdzə) *n. Austral. informal.* **1.** a man who drinks by himself. **2.** a drink taken alone.

jim+son weed ('dʒɪmsᵊn) *n.* the U.S. name for **thorn apple** (sense 1). [C17: from earlier *Jamestown weed,* from *Jamestown,* Virginia]

Jin·ghis Khan ('dʒɪŋgɪs 'kɑːn) *n.* See **Genghis Khan.**

jin+gle ('dʒɪŋgᵊl) *vb.* **1.** to ring or cause to ring lightly and repeatedly. **2.** (*intr.*) to sound in a manner suggestive of jingling: *a jingling verse.* ~*n.* **3.** a sound of metal jingling: *the jingle of the keys.* **4.** a catchy and rhythmical verse, song, etc., esp. one used in advertising. [C16: probably of imitative origin; compare Dutch *jengelen*] —'**jin+gler** *n.* —'**jin+gly** *adj.*

jin+go ('dʒɪŋgəʊ) *n., pl.* **+goes. 1.** a loud and bellicose patriot; chauvinist. **2.** jingoism. **3. by jingo.** (*interj.*) an exclamation of surprise. [C17: originally perhaps a euphemism for *Jesus;* applied to bellicose patriots after the use of *by Jingo!* in the refrain of a 19th-century music-hall song] —'**jin+go+ish** *adj.*

jin+go+ism ('dʒɪŋgəʊ,ɪzəm) *n.* the belligerent spirit or foreign policy of jingoes; chauvinism. —'**jin+go+ist** *n., adj.* —,**jin+go+'is+tic** *adj.* —,**jin+go+'is+ti+cal+ly** *adv.*

Jin+ja ('dʒɪndʒə) *n.* a town in Uganda, on the N shore of Lake Victoria. Pop.: 52 509 (1969).

jink (dʒɪŋk) *vb.* **1.** to move swiftly or jerkily or make a quick turn in order to dodge or elude. ~*n.* **2.** a jinking movement. [C18: of Scottish origin, imitative of swift movement]

jinks (dʒɪŋks) *pl. n.* boisterous or mischievous play (esp. in the phrase **high jinks**). [C18: of unknown origin]

jinn (dʒɪn) *n.* (*often functioning as sing.*) the plural of **jinni.**

Jin·nah ('dʒɪnə) *n.* **Mo·ham·med A·li.** 1876–1948, Indian Muslim statesman. He campaigned for the partition of India into separate Hindu and Muslim states, becoming first governor general of Pakistan (1947–48).

jin+ni, jin+nee, djin+ni, *or* **djin+ny** (dʒɪ'niː, 'dʒɪnɪ) *n., pl.* **jinn** *or* **djinn** (dʒɪn). a spirit in Muslim mythology who could assume human or animal form and influence man by supernatural powers. [C17: from Arabic]

jin+rik+i+sha, jin+rick+sha, jin+rick+shaw, *or* **jin+rik+sha** (dʒɪn'rɪkʃɔː, -ʃə) *n.* other names for **rickshaw.** [C19: from Japanese, from *jin* man + *riki* power + *sha* carriage]

jinx (dʒɪŋks) *n.* **1.** an unlucky or malevolent force, person, or thing. ~*vb.* **2.** (*tr.*) to be or put a jinx on. [C20: perhaps from New Latin *Jynx* genus name of the wryneck, from Greek *iunx* wryneck, the name of a bird used in magic]

ji+pi+ja+pa (,hiːpiː'hɑːpɑː) *n.* a palmlike plant, *Carludovica palmata,* of central and South America, whose fanlike leaves are bleached for making panama hats: family *Cyclanthaceae.* [American Spanish, after *Jipijapa,* Ecuador]

jis+som ('dʒɪsəm) *n. Taboo.* an informal word for **semen.** [of unknown origin]

jit+ney ('dʒɪtnɪ) *n. U.S., now rare.* **1.** a small bus that carries passengers for a low price, originally five cents. **2.** *Slang.* a nickel; five cents. [C20: of unknown origin]

jit+ter ('dʒɪtə) *Informal.* ~*vb.* **1.** (*intr.*) to be anxious or nervous. ~*n.* **2. the jitters.** nervousness and anxiety. **3.** *Electronics.* small rapid variations in a waveform arising from fluctuations in the voltage supply, mechanical vibrations, etc. [C20: of unknown origin] —'**jit+ter·y** *adj.*

jit·ter+bug ('dʒɪtə,bʌg) *n.* **1.** a fast jerky American dance, usually to a jazz accompaniment, that was popular in the 1940s. **2.** a person who dances the jitterbug. **3.** a highly nervous or excitable person. ~*vb.* **+bugs, +bug+ging, +bugged. 4.** (*intr.*) to perform such a dance.

jiu+jit+su *or* **jiu+jut+su** (dʒuː'dʒɪtsuː) *n.* variant spellings of **jujitsu.**

jive (dʒaɪv) *n.* **1.** a style of lively and jerky dance performed to jazz and, later, to rock-and-roll, popular esp. in the 1940s and 1950s. **2.** Also called: **jive talk.** a variety of American slang spoken chiefly by Blacks, esp. jazz musicians. ~*vb.* **3.** (*intr.*) to dance the jive. [C20: of unknown origin] —'**jiv+er** *n.*

JJ. *abbrev. for:* **1.** Judges. **2.** Justices.

j.n.d. *Psychol. abbrev. for* just noticeable difference.

Jnr. *abbrev. for* junior.

jo *or* **joe** (dʒəʊ) *n., pl.* **joes.** a Scot. word for **sweetheart.** [C16: alteration of JOY]

Jo·ab ('dʒəʊæb) *n. Old Testament.* the successful commander of King David's forces and the slayer of Abner and Absalom (II Samuel 2:18–23; 3:24–27; 18:14–15).

Jo·a·chim *n.* **1.** ('joːaxɪm). **Jo·seph** ('joːzɛf). 1831–1907, Hungarian violinist and composer. **2.** ('dʒəʊəkɪm). **Saint.** 1st century B.C., traditionally the father of the Virgin Mary; feast day: Aug. 16.

Joan (dʒəʊn) *n.* known as *the Fair Maid of Kent.* 1328–85, wife of Edward the Black Prince; mother of Richard II.

jo+an+nes (dʒəʊ'æniːz) *n., pl.* **+nes.** a variant spelling of **johannes.**

Joan of Arc *n.* **Saint.** known also as *the Maid of Orléans;* French name *Jeanne d'Arc.* ?1412–31, French national heroine, who led the army that relieved Orléans in the Hundred Years' War, enabling Charles VII to be crowned at Reims (1429). After being captured (1430), she was burnt at the stake as a heretic. She was canonized in 1920. Feast day: May 30.

Jo·ão Pes+so·a (*Portuguese* ʒuɜ̃u pe'soa) *n.* a port in NE Brazil, capital of Paraíba state. Pop.: 197 398 (1970). Former name (until 1930): **Paraíba.**

job (dʒɒb) *n.* **1.** an individual piece of work or task. **2.** an occupation; post of employment. **3.** an object worked on or a result produced from working. **4.** a duty or responsibility: *her job was to cook the dinner.* **5.** *Informal.* a difficult task or problem: *I had a job to contact him.* **6.** *Informal.* a damaging piece of work: *he really did a job on that.* **7.** *Informal.* a crime, esp. a robbery or burglary. **8.** an instance of jobbery. **9.** *Computer technol.* a unit of work for a computer. **10.** *Informal.* a state of affairs: *make the best of a bad job; it's a good job I saw you.* **11. on the job. a.** actively engaged in one's employment. **b.** *Brit. taboo.* engaged in sexual intercourse. **12. just the job.** exactly what was required. ~*vb.* **jobs, job+bing, jobbed. 13.** (*intr.*) to work by the piece or at casual jobs. **14.** to make a private profit out of (a public office, etc.). **15.** (*tr.;* usually foll. by *in*) **a.** to buy and sell (goods or services) as a middleman: *he jobs in government surplus.* **b.** *Brit.* to buy and sell stocks and shares as a stockjobber: *he jobs in blue chips.* **16.** (*tr.;* often foll. by *out*) to apportion (a contract, work, etc.) among several contractors, workers, etc. [C16: of uncertain origin]

Job (dʒəʊb) *n. Old Testament.* **1.** a Jewish patriarch, who maintained his faith in God in spite of the afflictions sent by God to test him. **2.** the book containing Job's pleas to God under these afflictions, attempted explanations of them by his friends, and God's reply to him. **3.** any person who withstands great suffering without despairing.

job+ber ('dʒɒbə) *n.* **1.** *Brit.* short for **stockjobber** (sense 1). **2.** a person who jobs.

job+ber·y ('dʒɒbərɪ) *n.* the practice of making private profit out of a public office; corruption or graft.

job+bing print+er *n.* one who prints mainly commercial and display work rather than books or newspapers.

Job+cen+tre ('dʒɒbsɛntə) *n. Brit.* any of a number of government offices forming a section of the Employment Service Agency, having premises situated in the main shopping area of a town in which people seeking jobs can consult displayed advertisements in informal surroundings.

Job Corps *n. U.S.* a Federal organization established in 1964 to train unemployed youths in order to make it easier for them to find work.

job+less ('dʒɒblɪs) *adj.* **1.** unemployed. ~*n.* **2. the jobless.** unemployed people collectively. —'**job+less+ness** *n.*

job lot *n.* **1.** a miscellaneous collection of articles sold as a lot. **2.** a collection of cheap or trivial items.

Job's com+fort+er *n.* a person who, while purporting to give sympathy, succeeds only in adding to distress.

Job's-tears *n.* **1.** (*functioning as sing.*) a tropical Asian grass, *Coix lacryma-jobi,* cultivated for its white beadlike modified leaves, which contain edible seeds. **2.** (*functioning as pl.*) the beadlike structures of this plant, used as rosary or ornamental beads.

Jo·cas·ta (dʒəʊ'kæstə) *n. Greek myth.* a queen of Thebes, the wife of Laius, who married Oedipus without either of them knowing he was her son.

Jo·chum (*German* 'jɔxʊm) *n.* **Eu·gen** ('ɔɪgən). born 1902, German orchestral conductor.

jock (dʒɒk) *n. Informal.* short for **jockey** or **jockstrap.**

Jock (dʒɒk) *n.* a slang word or name for a Scot.

jock+ey ('dʒɒkɪ) *n.* **1.** a person who rides horses in races, esp. as a profession or for hire. ~*vb.* **2.** (*tr.*) **a.** to ride (a horse) in a race. **b.** (*intr.*) to ride as a jockey. **3.** (often foll. by *for*) to try to obtain an advantage by manoeuvring, esp. literally in a race or metaphorically, as in a struggle for power (esp. in the phrase **jockey for position**). **4.** to trick or cheat (a person). [C16 (in the sense: lad): from name *Jock* + -EY]

jock+ey cap *n.* a cap with a long peak projecting upwards from the forehead.

Jock+ey Club *n. Brit.* the governing body that regulates and controls horse-racing both on the flat and over jumps.

jock·o ('dʒɒkəʊ) *n., pl.* **·os.** a W African name for **chimpanzee.** [C19: from French, based on Bantu *ngeko*]

jock+strap ('dʒɒk,stræp) *n.* a piece of elasticated material worn by men, esp. athletes, to support the genitals. Also called: **athletic supporter.** [C20: from slang *jock* penis + STRAP]

jo+cose (dʒə'kəʊs) *adj.* characterized by humour; merry. [C17: from Latin *jocōsus* given to jesting, from *jocus* JOKE] —**jo+'cose+ly** *adv.* —**jo+'cose+ness** *or* **jo+cos+i·ty** (dʒə'kɒsɪtɪ) *n.*

joc·u·lar ('dʒɒkjʊlə) *adj.* **1.** characterized by joking and good humour. **2.** meant lightly or humorously; facetious. [C17: from Latin *joculāris,* from *joculus* little JOKE] —**joc·u+lar·i·ty** (,dʒɒkjʊ'lærɪtɪ) *n.* —'**joc·u+lar+ly** *adv.*

joc+und ('dʒɒkənd) *adj.* of a humorous temperament; merry. [C14: from Late Latin *jocundus,* from Latin *jūcundus* pleasant, from *juvāre* to please] —**jo+cun+di·ty** (dʒəʊ'kʌndɪtɪ) *or* '**joc+und+ness** *n.* —'**joc+und+ly** *adv.*

Jodh+pur (,dʒɒd'pʊə) *n.* **1.** a former state of NW India, one of the W Rajputana states: now part of Rajasthan. **2.** a walled city in NW India, in W Rajasthan: university (1962). Pop.: 317 612 (1971). —**Jodh·pu·ri** ('dʒɒdpʊrɪ) *adj.*

Jodh·pu·ri coat *n.* a coat worn by men in India, similar to but shorter than a sherwani. [named after JODHPUR]

jodh·purs ('dʒɒdpəz) *pl. n.* **1.** riding breeches, loose-fitting around the hips and tight-fitting from the thighs to the ankles. **2.** Also called: **jodhpur boots.** ankle-length leather riding boots. [C19: from the town JODHPUR]

Jo·do ('dʒəʊˌdəʊ) *n.* a Japanese Buddhist sect teaching salvation through faith in Buddha. [from Japanese]

Jod·rell Bank ('dʒɒdrəl) *n.* an astronomical observatory in NW England, in Cheshire: radio telescope with a steerable parabolic dish, 75 m (250 ft.) in diameter.

Joe (dʒəʊ) *n. U.S. slang.* **1.** a man or fellow. **2.** a G.I.; soldier.

Joe Blow *n. Chiefly U.S. and Austral. slang.* an average or typical man.

Jo·el ('dʒəʊəl) *n. Old Testament.* **1.** a Hebrew prophet. **2.** the book containing his oracles.

joe-pye weed ('dʒəʊ'paɪ) *n. U.S.* any of several North American plants of the genus *Eupatorium*, esp. *E. purpureum*, having pale purplish clusters of flower heads lacking rays: family *Compositae* (composites). [C19: of unknown origin]

jo·ey ('dʒəʊɪ) *n. Austral. informal.* **1.** a young kangaroo. **2.** a young animal or child. [C19: from a native Australian language]

Jo·ey Hook·er ('dʒəʊɪ 'hʊkə) *n.* another name for **gallant soldier** (a plant).

Jof·fre (*French* 'ʒɔfr) *n.* **Jos·eph Jacques Cé·saire** (ʒozɛf ʒɑːk se'zɛːr). 1852–1931, French marshal. He commanded the French army (1914–16) and was largely responsible for the Allies' victory at the Marne (1914), which halted the German advance on Paris.

jog[1] (dʒɒg) *vb.* **jogs, jog·ging, jogged. 1.** (*intr.*) to run or move slowly or at a jog trot, esp. for physical exercise. **2.** (*intr.*; foll. by *on* or *along*) to continue in a plodding way. **3.** (*tr.*) to jar or nudge slightly; shake lightly. **4.** (*tr.*) to remind; stimulate: *please jog my memory.* **5.** (*tr.*) *Printing.* to even up the edges of (a stack of paper); square up. ~*n.* **6.** the act of jogging. **7.** a slight jar or nudge. **8.** a jogging motion; trot. [C14: probably variant of *shog* to shake, influenced by dialect *jot* to jolt] —'**jog·ger** *n.*

jog[2] (dʒɒg) *n. U.S.* **1.** a sharp protruding point in a surface; jag. **2.** a sudden change in course or direction. [C18: probably variant of JAG[1]]

jog·gle ('dʒɒgᵊl) *vb.* **1.** to shake or move (someone or something) with a slightly jolting motion. **2.** (*tr.*) to join or fasten (two pieces of building material) by means of a joggle. ~*n.* **3.** the act of joggling. **4.** a slight irregular shake; jolt. **5.** a joint between two pieces of building material by means of a projection on one piece that fits into a notch in the other; dowel. **6.** a shoulder designed to take the thrust of a strut or brace. [C16: frequentative of JOG[1]] —'**jog·gler** *n.*

jog·gle post *n.* a post or beam consisting of two timbers joined to each other by joggles.

Jog·ja·kar·ta (ˌdʒəʊgjɑː'kɑːtɑː, ˌdʒɒg-), **Jok·ja·kar·ta,** *or* **Djok·ja·kar·ta** (ˌdʒəʊkjɑː'kɑːtɑː, ˌdʒɒk-) *n.* a city in S Indonesia, in central Java: seat of government of Indonesia (1946–49); university (1949). Pop.: 342 267 (1971).

jog trot *n.* **1.** an easy bouncy gait, esp. of a horse, midway between a walk and a trot. **2.** a monotonous or regular way of living or doing something. ~*vb.* **jog-trot, -trots, -trot·ting, -trot·ted. 3.** (*intr.*) to move at a jog trot.

jo·han·nes (dʒəʊ'hæniːz) *or* **jo·an·nes** *n., pl.* **·nes.** a Portuguese gold coin minted in the early 18th century. [C18: after *Joannes* (King John V) of Portugal, whose name was inscribed on the coin]

Jo·han·nes·burg (dʒəʊ'hænɪsˌbɜːg) *n.* a city in South Africa, in S Transvaal: South Africa's largest city and chief industrial centre; grew with the establishment in 1886 of the gold-mining industry; University of Witwatersrand (1922). Pop.: 1 407 963 (1970).

john (dʒɒn) *n. U.S.* a slang word for **lavatory.** [C20: special use of the proper name]

John (dʒɒn) *n.* **1.** *New Testament.* **a.** the apostle John, the son of Zebedee, identified with the author of the fourth Gospel, three epistles, and the book of Revelation. **b.** the fourth Gospel. **c.** any of three epistles (in full **The First, Second,** and **Third Epistles of John**). **2.** See **John the Baptist. 3.** known as *John Lackland.* 1167–1216, king of England (1199–1216); son of Henry II. He succeeded to the throne on the death of his brother Richard I, having previously tried to usurp the throne. War with France led to the loss of most of his French possessions. After his refusal to recognize Stephen Langton as archbishop of Canterbury an interdict was imposed on England (1208–14). In 1215 he was compelled by the barons to sign the Magna Carta. **4. Au·gus·tus (Edwin).** 1878–1961, Welsh painter, esp. of portraits. **5. Bar·ry.** born 1945, British Rugby Union footballer: halfback for Wales (1966–72) and the British Lions (1968–71). **6. El·ton.** original name *Reginald Dwight.* born 1947, English rock pianist, composer, and singer. His albums include *Tumbleweed Connection* (1970), *Don't shoot me, I'm only the Piano Player* (1973), and *Goodbye Yellow Brick Road* (1973). The words of almost all his songs are by Bernie Taupin.

John I *n.* called *the Great.* 1357–1433, king of Portugal (1385–1433). He secured independence for Portugal by his victory over Castile (1385) and initiated Portuguese overseas expansion.

John III *n.* surnamed *Sobieski.* 1624–96, king of Poland (1674–96). He raised the Turkish siege of Vienna (1683).

John XXII *n.* original name *Jacques Duèse.* ?1244–1334, pope (1316–34), residing at Avignon; involved in a long conflict with the Holy Roman Emperor Louis IV and opposed the Franciscan Spirituals.

John XXIII *n.* original name *Angelo Giuseppe Roncalli.* 1881–1963, pope (1958–63). He promoted ecumenicalism and world peace and summoned the second Vatican Council (1962–65).

John Bar·ley·corn *n. Usually humorous.* the personification of alcoholic drink, esp. of malt spirits.

John Birch So·ci·e·ty *n. U.S. politics.* a fanatical right-wing association organized along semisecret lines to fight Communism. [C20: named after *John Birch* (died 1945), American USAF captain]

John Bull *n.* **1.** a personification of England or the English people. **2.** a typical Englishman. [C18: name of a character intended to be representative of the English nation in *The History of John Bull* (1712) by John Arbuthnot] —**John Bull·ish** *adj.* —**John Bull·ish·ness** *n.* —**John Bull·ism** *n.*

John Chrys·os·tom ('krɪsəstəm) *n.* **Saint.** ?345–407 A.D., Greek bishop and theologian; one of the Fathers of the Greek Church, noted for his eloquence. Feast day: Jan. 27.

John Doe *n.* See **Doe.**

John Do·ry ('dɔːrɪ) *n.* a European dory (the fish), *Zeus faber,* having a deep compressed body, spiny dorsal fins, and massive mobile jaws. [C18: from proper name *John* + DORY[2]; on the model of DOE]

John Han·cock *n. U.S. informal.* a person's signature: *put your John Hancock on this form.* [after *John* HANCOCK, from his clear and legible signature on the American Declaration of Independence]

john·ny ('dʒɒnɪ) *n., pl.* **·nies.** *Brit.* **1.** (*often cap.*) *Informal.* a man or boy; chap. **2.** a slang word for **condom.**

john·ny cake *n. Austral.* a thin cake of flour and water paste cooked in the ashes of a fire or in a pan.

John·ny Ca·nuck ('dʒɒnɪ kə'nʌk) *n. Canadian.* **1.** an informal name for a **Canadian. 2.** a personification of Canada.

John·ny-jump-up *n. U.S.* any of several violaceous plants, esp. the wild pansy. [C19: so called from its quick growth]

John·ny Reb *n. U.S. informal.* (in the American Civil War) a Confederate soldier. [C19: from REBEL (n.)]

John of Aus·tri·a *n.* called *Don John.* 1547–78, Spanish general: defeated the Turks at Lepanto (1571).

John of Da·mas·cus *n.* **Saint.** ?675–749 A.D., Syrian theologian, who defended image worship against the iconoclasts. Feast day: March 27.

John of Gaunt (gɔːnt) *n.* Duke of Lancaster. 1340–99, son of Edward III: virtual ruler of England during the last years of his father's reign and during Richard II's minority. [*Gaunt,* variant of GHENT, where he was born]

John of Ley·den ('laɪdᵊn) *n.* original name *Jan Bockelson.* ?1509–36, Dutch Anabaptist leader. He established a theocracy in Münster (1534) but was tortured to death after the city was recaptured (1535) by its prince bishop.

John of Salis·bur·y *n.* died 1180, English ecclesiastic and scholar; bishop of Chartres (1176–80). He supported Thomas à Becket against Henry II.

John of the Cross *n.* **Saint.** original name *Juan de Yepis y Alvarez.* 1542–91, Spanish Carmelite monk, poet, and mystic. He founded the Discalced Carmelites with Saint Teresa (1568). Feast day: Nov. 24.

John o'Groats (ə'grəʊts) *n.* a village at the northeasternmost tip of the Scottish mainland: considered to be the northernmost point of the mainland of Great Britain although Dunnet Head, slightly to the west, lies further north. See also **Land's End.**

John Paul I *n.* original name *Albino Luciani.* 1912–78, pope (1978) whose brief 33-day reign was characterized by a simpler less pompous papal style and anticipated an emphasis on pastoral rather than administrative priorities.

John Paul II *n.* original name *Karol Wojtyla.* born 1920, pope since 1978, born in Poland: the first non-Italian to be elected since 1522.

John·son ('dʒɒnsᵊn) *n.* **1. A·my.** 1903–41, English flier, who made several record flights, including those to Australia (1930) and to Cape Town and back (1936). **2. An·drew.** 1808–75, U.S. Democrat statesman; 17th president of the U.S. (1865–69). His lenience towards the South after the American Civil War led to strong opposition from radical Republicans, who tried to impeach him. **3. Jack.** 1878–1946, U.S. boxer; world heavyweight champion (1908–15). **4. Lyn·don Baines,** known as *LBJ.* 1908–73, U.S. Democrat statesman; 36th president of the U.S. (1963–69). His administration carried the Civil Rights Acts of 1964 and 1965, but he lost popularity by increasing U.S. involvement in the Vietnam war. **5. Rob·ert.** ?1898–1937, U.S. blues singer and guitarist. **6. Sam·u·el,** known as *Dr. Johnson.* 1709–84, English lexicographer, critic, and conversationalist, whose greatest works are his *Dictionary* (1755), his edition of Shakespeare (1765), and his *Lives of the Most Eminent English Poets* (1779–81). His fame, however, rests as much on Boswell's biography of him as on his literary output.

John·son grass *n.* a persistent perennial Mediterranean grass, *Sorghum halepense,* cultivated for hay and pasture in the U.S. where it also grows as a weed. See also **sorghum.** [C19: named after William *Johnson* (died 1859), American agriculturalist who introduced it]

John·so·ni·an (dʒɒn'səʊnɪən) *adj.* of, relating to, or characteristic of Samuel Johnson, his works, or his style of writing.

John the Bap·tist *n. New Testament.* the son of Zacharias and Elizabeth and the cousin and forerunner of Jesus, whom he baptized. He was beheaded by Herod (Matthew 14:1–2).

Jo+hore (dʒəʊˈhɔː) *n.* a state of Malaysia, on the S Malay Peninsula: mostly forested, with large swamps; bauxite- and iron-mining. Capital: Johore Bahru. Pop.: 1 271 794 (1970). Area: 18 984 sq. km (7330 sq. miles).

Jo+hore Bah+ru (dʒəʊˈhɔː ˈbɑːruː) *n.* a city in S Malaysia, capital of Johore state: important trading centre, situated at the sole crossing point of **Johore Strait** (between Malaya and Singapore Island). Pop.: 135 936 (1970).

joie de vi+vre *French.* (ʒwad ˈvivr) *n.* joy of living; enjoyment of life; ebullience.

join (dʒɔɪn) *vb.* **1.** to come or bring together; connect. **2.** to become a member of (a club, organization, etc.). **3.** (*intr.; often foll. by with*) to become associated or allied. **4.** (*intr.; usually foll. by in*) to take part. **5.** (*tr.*) to meet (someone) as a companion. **6.** (*tr.*) to become part of; take a place in or with. **7.** (*tr.*) to unite (two people) in marriage. **8.** (*tr.*) *Geom.* to connect with a straight line or a curve. **9.** (*tr.*) an informal word for **adjoin. 10. join battle.** to engage in conflict or competition. **11. join duty.** *Indian.* to report for work after a period of leave or a strike. **12. join hands. a.** to hold one's own hands together. **b.** (of two people) to hold each other's hands. **c.** (usually foll. by *with*) to work together in an enterprise or task. ~*n.* **13.** a joint; seam. **14.** the act of joining. **15.** *Maths.* another name for **union** (sense 9). ~See **join up.** [C13: from Old French *joindre* from Latin *jungere* to yoke] —ˈ**join+a·ble** *adj.*

join+der (ˈdʒɔɪndə) *n.* **1.** the act of joining, esp. in legal contexts. **2.** *Law.* **a.** (in pleading) the stage at which the parties join issue (**joinder of issue**). **b.** the joining of two or more persons as coplaintiffs or codefendants (**joinder of parties**). **c.** the joining of two or more causes in one suit. [C17: from French *joindre* to JOIN]

join+er (ˈdʒɔɪnə) *n.* **1.** *Chiefly Brit.* a person trained and skilled in making finished woodwork, such as windows, doors, and stairs. **2.** a person or thing that joins. **3.** *Informal.* a person who joins many clubs, causes, etc.

join+er·y (ˈdʒɔɪnərɪ) *n.* **1.** the skill or craft of a joiner. **2.** work made by a joiner.

joint (dʒɔɪnt) *n.* **1.** a junction of two or more parts or objects. **2.** the part or space between two such junctions. **3.** *Anatomy.* the junction between two or more bones, usually formed of connective tissue and cartilage. **4.** the point of connection between movable parts in invertebrates, esp. insects and other arthropods. **5.** the part of a plant stem from which a branch or leaf grows. **6.** one of the parts into which a carcass of meat is cut by the butcher, esp. for roasting. **7.** *Geology.* a crack in a rock along which no displacement has occurred. **8.** *Slang.* **a.** a disreputable establishment, such as a bar or nightclub. **b.** *Often facetious.* a dwelling or meeting place. **9.** *Slang.* a marijuana cigarette. **10. out of joint. a.** dislocated. **b.** out of order or disorganized. ~*adj.* **11.** shared by or belonging to two or more: *joint property.* **12.** created by combined effort. **13.** sharing with others or with one another: *joint rulers.* **14.** *Law.* (of persons) combined in ownership or obligation; regarded as a single entity in law. ~*vb.* (*tr.*) **15.** to provide with or fasten by a joint or joints. **16.** to plane the edge of (a board, etc.) into the correct shape for a joint. **17.** to cut or divide (meat, fowl, etc.) into joints or at a joint. —ˈ**joint+ly** *adv.*

joint ac+count *n.* a bank account registered in the name of two or more persons, any of whom may make deposits and withdrawals.

joint den+si·ty func+tion *n. Statistics.* a function of two or more random variables from which can be obtained a single probability that all the variables in the function will take specified values or fall within specified intervals.

joint+ed (ˈdʒɔɪntɪd) *adj.* **1. a.** having a joint or joints. **b.** (*in combination*): *large-jointed.* **2.** (of a plant stem or similar part) marked with constrictions, at which the stem breaks into separate portions. —ˈ**joint+ed+ly** *adv.* —ˈ**joint+ed+ness** *n.*

joint+er (ˈdʒɔɪntə) *n.* **1.** a tool for pointing mortar joints, as in brickwork. **2.** Also called: **jointing plane.** a long plane for shaping the edges of planks so that they can be fitted together. **3.** a person or thing that makes joints.

joint res+o+lu+tion *n. U.S.* a resolution passed by both houses of a bicameral legislature, signed by the chief executive and legally binding.

joint+ress (ˈdʒɔɪntrɪs) *n. Law.* a woman entitled to a jointure.

joint stock *n.* capital funds held in common and usually divided into shares between the owners.

joint-stock com+pa+ny *n.* **1.** *Brit.* a business enterprise characterized by its separate legal existence and the sharing of ownership between shareholders, whose liability is limited. **2.** *U.S.* a business enterprise whose owners are issued shares of transferable stock but do not enjoy limited liability.

join+ture (ˈdʒɔɪntʃə) *n.* **1.** *Law.* **a.** provision made by a husband for his wife by settling property upon her at marriage for her use after his death. **b.** the property so settled. **2.** *Obsolete.* the act of joining or the condition of being joined. [C14: from Old French, from Latin *junctūra* a joining]

joint+worm (ˈdʒɔɪntˌwɜːm) *n. U.S.* the larva of chalcid flies of the genus *Harmolita*, esp. *H. tritici*, which form galls on the stems of cereal plants.

join up *vb.* (*adv.*) **1.** (*intr.*) to become a member of a military or other organization; enlist. **2.** (often foll. by *with*) to unite or connect.

Join·ville (*French* ʒwɛ̃ˈvil) *n.* **Jean de** (ˈʒɑ̃ də). ?1224–1317, French chronicler, noted for his *Histoire de Saint Louis* (1309).

joist (dʒɔɪst) *n.* **1.** a beam made of timber, steel, or reinforced concrete, used in the construction of floors, roofs, etc. See also **rolled-steel joist.** ~*vb.* **2.** (*tr.*) to construct (a floor, roof, etc.) with joists. [C14: from Old French *giste* beam supporting a bridge, from Vulgar Latin *jacitum* (unattested) support, from *jacēre* to lie]

joke (dʒəʊk) *n.* **1.** a humorous anecdote. **2.** something that is said or done for fun; prank. **3.** a ridiculous or humorous circumstance. **4.** a person or thing inspiring ridicule or amusement; butt. **5.** a matter to be joked about or ignored. **6. no joke.** something very serious. ~*vb.* **7.** (*intr.*) to tell jokes. **8.** (*intr.*) to speak or act facetiously or in fun. **9.** to make fun of (someone); tease. [C17: from Latin *jocus* a jest] —ˈ**jok+ey** *or* ˈ**jok·y** *adj.* —ˈ**jok+ing+ly** *adv.*

jok+er (ˈdʒəʊkə) *n.* **1.** a person who jokes, esp. in an obnoxious manner. **2.** *Slang.* a man; fellow. **3.** an extra playing card in a pack, which in many card games can substitute for or rank above any other card. **4.** *Chiefly U.S.* a clause or phrase inserted in a legislative bill in order to make the bill inoperative or to alter its apparent effect.

Jok+ja+kar+ta (ˌdʒəʊkjɑːˈkɑːtɑː, ˌdʒɒk-) *n.* a variant spelling of **Jogjakarta.**

Jo·liot-Cu·rie (*French* ʒɔljo kyˈri) *n.* **Jean-Fré·dé·ric** (ʒɑ̃ fredeˈrik), 1900–58, and his wife, **I·rène** (iˈrɛn), 1897–1956, French physicists: shared the Nobel prize for chemistry in 1935 for discovering artificial radioactivity.

jol+li+fi+ca+tion (ˌdʒɒlɪfɪˈkeɪʃən) *n.* a merry festivity.

jol+li+fy (ˈdʒɒlɪˌfaɪ) *vb.* **+fies, +fy+ing, +fied.** to be or cause to be jolly.

jol+li·ties (ˈdʒɒlɪtɪz) *pl. n. Brit.* a party or celebration.

jol+li·ty (ˈdʒɒlɪtɪ) *n., pl.* **·ties.** the condition of being jolly.

jol+ly (ˈdʒɒlɪ) *adj.* **+li+er, +li+est. 1.** full of good humour; jovial. **2.** having or provoking gaiety and merrymaking; festive. **3.** greatly enjoyable; pleasing. ~*adv.* **4.** *Brit.* (intensifier): *you're jolly nice.* ~*vb.* **+lies, +ly+ing, +lied.** (*tr.*) *Informal.* **5.** (often foll. by *up* or *along*) to try to make or keep (someone) cheerful. **6.** to make good-natured fun of. [C14: from Old French *jolif,* probably from Old Norse *jōl* YULE] —ˈ**jol+li+ness** *n.*

jol+ly boat *n.* **1.** a small boat used as a utility tender for a vessel. **2.** a small sailing boat used for pleasure. [C18: *jolly* probably from Danish *jolle* YAWL[1]]

Jol+ly Rog+er *n.* the traditional pirate flag, consisting of a white skull and crossbones on a black field.

Jo·lo (həʊˈləʊ) *n.* an island in the SW Philippines: the main island of the Sulu Archipelago. Pop.: 249 860 (1970). Area: 893 sq. km (345 sq. miles).

Jol·son (ˈdʒəʊlsən) *n.* **Al,** original name *Asa Yoelson.* 1886–1950, U.S. singer and film actor; star of the first talking picture *The Jazz Singer* (1927).

jolt (dʒəʊlt) *vb.* (*tr.*) **1.** to bump against with a jarring blow; jostle. **2.** to move in a jolting manner. **3.** to surprise or shock. ~*n.* **4.** a sudden jar or blow. **5.** an emotional shock. [C16: probably blend of dialect *jot* to jerk and dialect *joll* to bump] —ˈ**jolt+er** *n.* —ˈ**jolt+ing+ly** *adv.* —ˈ**jolt·y** *adj.*

Jon. *Bible. abbrev. for* Jonah.

Jo·nah (ˈdʒəʊnə) *or* **Jo·nas** (ˈdʒəʊnəs) *n.* **1.** *Old Testament.* **a.** a Hebrew prophet who, having been thrown overboard from a ship in which he was fleeing from God, was swallowed by a whale and vomited onto dry land. **b.** the book in which his adventures are recounted. **2.** a person believed to bring bad luck to those around him; a jinx. —ˌ**Jo+nah+**ˈ**esque** *adj.*

Jon·a+than[1] (ˈdʒɒnəθən) *n.* a variety of red apple that ripens in early autumn. [C19: named after *Jonathan* Hasbrouk (died 1846), American jurist]

Jon·a·than[2] (ˈdʒɒnəθən) *n. Old Testament.* the son of Saul and David's close friend, who was killed in battle (I Samuel 31; II Samuel 1:19–26).

Jones (dʒəʊnz) *n.* **1. Dan·iel.** 1881–1967, English phonetician. **2. Da·vid.** 1895–1974, English painter, poet, and novelist: his highly original literary works include *In Parenthesis* (1937), a novel of World War I, and the religious poem *The Anathemata* (1952). **3. In·i·go** (ˈɪnɪgəʊ). 1573–1652, English architect and theatrical designer, who introduced Palladianism to England. His buildings include the Banqueting Hall of Whitehall. He also designed the settings for court masques, being the first to use the proscenium arch and movable scenery in England. **4. James Lar·kin,** called *Jack.* born 1913, English trades union leader; general secretary of the Transport and General Workers' Union (1969–78). **5. John Paul.** 1747–92, American naval commander in the War of Independence. **6. Rob·ert Tyre,** known as *Bobby Jones.* 1902–71, U.S. golfer.

jon+gleur (*French* ʒɔ̃ˈglœːr) *n.* (in medieval France) an itinerant minstrel. [C18: from Old French *jogleour,* from Latin *joculātor* joker, jester; see JUGGLE]

Jön+kö+ping (*Swedish* ˈjœntʃøːpiŋ) *n.* a city in S Sweden, on the S shore of Lake Vättern: scene of the conclusion of peace between Sweden and Denmark in 1809. Pop.: 108 195 (1974 est.).

jon+nock (ˈdʒɒnək) *or* **jan+nock** (ˈdʒænək) *Brit. dialect.* ~*adj.* **1.** (*usually postpositive*) genuine; real. ~*adv.* **2.** honestly; truly; genuinely. [of uncertain origin]

jon+quil (ˈdʒɒŋkwɪl) *n.* a Eurasian amaryllidaceous plant, *Narcissus jonquilla* with long fragrant yellow or white short-tubed flowers. [C17: from French *jonquille,* from Spanish *junquillo,* diminutive of *junco* reed; see JUNCO]

Jon·son (ˈdʒɒnsᵊn) *n.* **Ben.** 1572–1637, English dramatist and poet, who developed the "comedy of humours", in which each character is used to satirize one particular humour or temperament. His plays include *Volpone* (1606), *The Alchemist* (1610), and *Bartholomew Fair* (1614), and he also wrote court masques.

jook (dʒʊk) *or* **chook** *Caribbean informal.* ~*vb.* **1.** (*tr.*) to poke or puncture (the skin). ~*n.* **2.** a jab or the resulting wound. [C20: of uncertain origin]

Jop·lin ('dʒɒplɪn) *n.* **1. Jan·is.** 1943–70, U.S. rock singer, noted for her hoarse and passionate style. Her albums include *Cheap Thrills* (1968), *I got dem Ol'Kozmic Blues again Mama* (1969), and *Pearl* (1970). **2. Scott.** 1868–1917, U.S. pianist: creator of ragtime.

Jop+pa ('dʒɒpə) *n.* the biblical name of **Jaffa,** the port from which Jonah embarked (Jonah 1:3).

Jor·daens (*Flemish* jɔr'da:ns) *n.* **Ja·cob** ('ja:kɔp). 1593–1678, Flemish painter, noted for his naturalistic depiction of peasant scenes.

Jor+dan ('dʒɔ:dᵊn) *n.* **1.** a kingdom in SW Asia: coextensive with the biblical Moab, Gilead, and Edom; made a League of Nations mandate and emirate under British control in 1922 and became an independent kingdom in 1946; territories west of the River Jordan and the Jordanian part of Jerusalem were occupied by Israel after the war of 1967. It contains part of the Great Rift Valley and consists mostly of desert. Language: Arabic. Religion: mostly Sunni Muslim. Currency: dinar. Capital: Amman. Pop.: 2 618 000 (1974 est.). Area: 89 185 sq. km (34 434 sq. miles). Official name: **Hashemite Kingdom of Jordan.** Former name (1922–49): **Trans-Jordan. 2.** the chief and only perennial river of Israel and Jordan, rising in several headstreams in Syria and Lebanon, and flowing south through the Sea of Galilee to the Dead Sea: occupies the N end of the Great Rift Valley system and lies mostly below sea level. Length: over 320 km (200 miles). —**Jor+da+ni·an** (dʒɔ:'deɪnɪən) *adj., n.*

Jor+dan al+mond *n.* **1.** a large variety of Spanish almond used in confectionery. **2.** a sugar-coated almond. [C15: by folk etymology from earlier *jardyne almaund,* literally: garden almond, from Old French *jardin* GARDEN]

jo+rum ('dʒɔ:rəm) *n.* a large drinking bowl or vessel or its contents: *a jorum of punch.* [C18: probably named after *Jorum,* who brought vessels of silver, gold, and brass to King David (II Samuel 8:10)]

Jos (dʒɒs) *n.* a city in central Nigeria, capital of Plateau state on the **Jos Plateau:** major centre of the tin-mining industry. Pop.: 90 402 (1963).

jo+seph ('dʒəʊzɪf) *n.* a woman's floor-length riding coat with a small cape, worn esp. in the 18th century.

Jo·seph ('dʒəʊzɪf) *n.* **1.** *Old Testament.* **a.** the eleventh son of Jacob and one of the 12 patriarchs of Israel (Genesis 30:2–24). **b.** either or both of two tribes descended from his sons Ephraim and Manasseh. **2.** *New Testament.* the husband of Mary the mother of Jesus (Matthew 1:16–25).

Jo·seph II *n.* 1741–90, Holy Roman emperor (1765–90); son of Francis I. He ruled Austria jointly with his mother, Maria Theresa, until her death (1780). He reorganized taxation, abolished serfdom, curtailed the feudal power of the nobles, and asserted his independence from the pope.

Jo+seph Bo+na+parte Gulf *n.* an inlet of the Timor Sea in N Australia. Width: 360 km (225 miles).

Jo·se·phine ('dʒəʊzəˌfi:n) *n.* **the Em+press,** previous name *Joséphine de Beauharnais;* original name *Marie Joséphine Tascher de la Pagerie.* 1763–1814, empress of France as wife of Napoleon Bonaparte (1796–1809).

Jo·seph of Ar·i·ma+the·a (ˌærɪmə'θi:ə) *n. New Testament.* a wealthy member of the Sanhedrin, who obtained the body of Jesus after the Crucifixion and laid it in his own tomb (Matthew 27:57–60).

Jo·se·phus (dʒəʊ'si:fəs) *n.* **Fla·vi·us** ('fleɪvɪəs). original name *Joseph ben Matthias.* ?37–?100 A.D., Jewish historian and general; author of *History of the Jewish War* and *Antiquities of the Jews.*

josh (dʒɒʃ) *U.S. slang.* ~*vb.* **1.** to tease (someone) in a bantering way. ~*n.* **2.** a teasing or bantering joke. [C19: perhaps from JOKE, influenced by BOSH[1]] —**'josh+er** *n.*

Josh. *Bible. abbrev. for* Joshua.

Josh·u·a ('dʒɒʃʊə) *n. Old Testament.* **1.** Moses' successor, who led the Israelites in the conquest of Canaan. **2.** the book recounting his deeds. Douay spelling: **Jos·u·e** ('dʒɒsjui:).

Josh·u·a tree *n.* a treelike desert yucca plant, *Yucca brevifolia,* of the southwestern U.S., with sword-shaped leaves and greenish-white flowers. [named after the prophet *Joshua,* alluding to the extended branches of the tree]

Jo·si·ah (dʒəʊ'saɪə) *n.* died ?609 B.C., king of Judah (?640–?609). After the discovery of a book of law (probably Deuteronomy) in the Temple he began a programme of religious reform. Douay spelling: **Jo·si·as** (dʒəʊ'saɪəs).

Jos+quin des Prés (*French* ʒɔskɛ̃ de 'pre) *n.* See **des Prés.**

joss (dʒɒs) *n.* a Chinese deity worshipped in the form of an idol. [C18: from pidgin English, from Portuguese *deos* god, from Latin *deus*]

joss house *n.* a Chinese temple or shrine where an idol or idols are worshipped.

joss stick *n.* a stick of dried perfumed paste, giving off a fragrant odour when burnt as incense.

jos+tle ('dʒɒsᵊl) *or* **jus+tle** ('dʒʌsᵊl) *vb.* **1.** to bump or push (someone) roughly. **2.** to come or bring into contact. **3.** to force (one's way) by pushing. ~*n.* **4.** the act of jostling. **5.** a rough bump or push. [C14: see JOUST] —**'jos+tle+ment** *or* **'jus+tle+ment** *n.* —**'jos+tler** *or* **'jus+tler** *n.*

jot (dʒɒt) *vb.* **jots, jot+ting, jot+ted. 1.** (*tr.;* usually foll. by *down*) to write a brief note of. ~*n.* **2.** (*used with a negative*) a little bit (in phrases such as **not to care** (*or* **give**) **a jot**) [C16: from Latin *jota,* from Greek *iōta,* of Semitic origin; see IOTA]

jo·ta (*Spanish* 'xota) *n.* a Spanish dance with castanets in fast triple time, usually to a guitar and voice accompaniment. [Spanish, probably modification of Old Spanish *sota,* from *sotar* to dance, from Latin *saltāre*]

jot+ter ('dʒɒtə) *n.* a small notebook.

jot+ting ('dʒɒtɪŋ) *n.* something jotted down.

Jo·tun *or* **Jo·tunn** ('jɔ:tʊn) *n. Norse myth.* any of a race of giants. [from Old Norse *jötunn* giant; related to EAT]

Jo+tun+heim *or* **Jo+tunn+heim** ('jɔ:tʊnˌheɪm) *n. Norse myth.* the home of the giants in the northeast of Asgard. [from Old Norse, from *jötunn* giant + *heimr* world, HOME]

joual (ʒwɑ:l) *n.* nonstandard Canadian French dialect, esp. as associated with ill-educated speakers. [from the pronunciation in this dialect of French *cheval* horse]

joule (dʒu:l) *n.* the derived SI unit of work or energy; the work done when the point of application of a force of 1 newton is displaced through a distance of 1 metre in the direction of the force. 1 joule is equivalent to 1 watt-second, 10^7 ergs, 0.2390 calories, or 0.738 foot-pound. Symbol: J [C19: named after J. P. JOULE]

Joule (dʒu:l) *n.* **James Pres·cott.** 1818–89, English physicist, who evaluated the mechanical equivalent of heat and contributed to the study of heat and electricity.

Joule's law *n.* **1.** *Physics.* the principle that the heat produced by an electric current is equal to the product of the resistance of the conductor, the square of the current, and the time for which it flows. **2.** *Thermodynamics.* the principle that at constant temperature the internal energy of an ideal gas is independent of volume. Real gases change their internal energy with volume as a result of intermolecular forces. [C19: named after J. P. JOULE]

Joule-Thom·son ef+fect *n.* a fall in temperature of a gas when it expands without doing external work, usually demonstrated by passing the gas through a small hole. It is caused by work being done against the intermolecular forces in the gas. Also called: **Joule-Kel·vin ef+fect.** [C20: named after J. P. JOULE and Sir William Thomson, 1st Baron KELVIN]

jounce (dʒaʊns) *vb.* **1.** to shake or jolt or cause to shake or jolt; bounce. ~*n.* **2.** a jolting movement; shake; bump. [C15: probably a blend of dialect *joll* to bump + BOUNCE]

jour. *abbrev. for:* **1.** journal. **2.** journalist. **3.** journeyman.

jour+nal ('dʒɜ:nᵊl) *n.* **1.** a newspaper or periodical. **2.** a book in which a daily record of happenings, etc., is kept. **3.** an official record of the proceedings of a legislative body. **4.** *Bookkeeping.* **a.** one of several books in which transactions are initially recorded to facilitate subsequent entry in the ledger. **b.** another name for **daybook. 5.** the part of a shaft or axle in contact with or enclosed by a bearing. **6.** a plain cylindrical bearing to support a shaft or axle. [C14: from Old French: daily, from Latin *diurnālis;* see DIURNAL]

jour+nal box *n. Machinery.* a case enclosing or supporting a journal, often used as a means of retaining the lubricant.

jour+nal+ese (ˌdʒɜ:nᵊ'li:z) *n. Derogatory.* a superficial style of writing regarded as typical of newspapers, etc.

jour+nal+ism ('dʒɜ:nᵊˌlɪzəm) *n.* **1.** the profession or practice of reporting about, photographing, or editing news stories for one of the mass media. **2.** newspapers and magazines collectively; the press. **3.** the material published in a newspaper, etc.: *this is badly written journalism.* **4.** news reports presented factually without analysis.

jour+nal+ist ('dʒɜ:nᵊlɪst) *n.* **1.** a person whose occupation is journalism. **2.** a person who keeps a journal.

jour+nal+is+tic (ˌdʒɜ:nᵊ'lɪstɪk) *adj.* of, relating to, or characteristic of journalism or journalists. —**ˌjour+nal+'is+ti+cal+ly** *adv.*

jour+nal+ize *or* **jour+nal+ise** ('dʒɜ:nᵊˌlaɪz) *vb.* to record (daily events) in a journal. —**ˌjour+nal·i+'za+tion** *or* **ˌjour+nal·i·'sa+tion** *n.* —**'jour+nal+ˌiz+er** *or* **'jour+nal+ˌis+er** *n.*

jour+ney ('dʒɜ:nɪ) *n.* **1.** a travelling from one place to another; trip or voyage. **2. a.** the distance travelled in a journey. **b.** the time taken to make a journey. ~*vb.* **3.** (*intr.*) to make a journey. [C13: from Old French *journee* a day, a day's travelling, from Latin *diurnum* day's portion; see DIURNAL] —**'jour+ney+er** *n.*

jour·ney+man ('dʒɜ:nɪmən) *n., pl.* **+men. 1.** a craftsman, artisan, etc., who is qualified to work at his trade in the employment of another. **2.** a competent workman. **3.** (formerly) a worker hired on a daily wage. [C15: from JOURNEY (in obsolete sense: a day's work) + MAN]

jour·ney+work ('dʒɜ:nɪˌwɜ:k) *n. Rare.* **1.** necessary, routine, and menial work. **2.** the work of a journeyman.

journ·o ('dʒɜ:nəʊ) *n., pl.* **journ·os.** *Austral. slang.* a journalist.

joust (dʒaʊst) *History.* ~*n.* **1.** a combat between two mounted knights tilting against each other with lances. A tournament consisting of a series of such engagements. ~*vb.* **2.** (*intr.;* often foll. by *against* or *with*) to encounter or engage in such a tournament: *he jousted with five opponents.* [C13: from Old French *jouste,* from *jouster* to fight on horseback, from Vulgar Latin *juxtāre* (unattested) to come together, from Latin *juxtā* close] —**'joust+er** *n.*

j'ou+vert ('ʒu:vɛət) *n. Chiefly Caribbean.* the eve of Mardi gras; the Monday morning on which the festivities begin. [from French *jour ouvert* the day having been opened]

Jove (dʒəʊv) *n.* **1.** another name for **Jupiter**[1]. **2. by Jove.** an exclamation of surprise or excitement. [C14: from Old Latin *Jovis* Jupiter]

jo+vi·al ('dʒəʊvɪəl) *adj.* having or expressing convivial humour; jolly. [C16: from Latin *joviālis* of (the planet) Jupiter, considered by astrologers to foster good humour] —**ˌjo+vi+'al+i·ty** *or* **'jo+vi+al+ness** *n.* —**'jo+vi+al+ly** *adv.*

Jo+vi·an[1] ('dʒəʊvɪən) *adj.* **1.** of or relating to the god Jove (Jupiter). **2.** of, occurring on, or relating to the planet Jupiter. [C16: from Old Latin *Jovis* Jupiter]

Jo·vi·an[2] ('dʒəʊvɪən) *n.* full name *Flavius Claudius Jovianus.* ?331–364 A.D., Roman emperor (363–64): he made peace with Persia, relinquishing Roman provinces beyond the Tigris, and restored privileges to the Christians.

Jo·wett ('dʒaʊɪt) *n.* **Ben·ja·min.** 1817–93, English classical scholar and educator: translated the works of Plato.

jowl[1] (dʒaʊl) *n.* **1.** the jaw, esp. the lower one. **2.** (*often pl.*) a cheek, esp. a prominent one. **3. cheek by jowl.** See **cheek** (sense 7). [Old English *ceafl* jaw; related to Middle High German *kivel,* Old Norse *kjaptr*] **—jowled** *adj.*

jowl[2] (dʒaʊl) *n.* **1.** fatty flesh hanging from the lower jaw. **2.** a similar fleshy part in animals, such as the wattle of a fowl or the dewlap of a bull. [Old English *ceole* throat; compare Old High German *kela*]

joy (dʒɔɪ) *n.* **1.** a deep feeling or condition of happiness or contentment. **2.** something causing such a feeling; a source of happiness. **3.** an outward show of pleasure or delight; rejoicing. **4.** *Brit. informal.* success; luck: *I went to the bank for a loan, but got no joy.* ~*vb.* **5.** (*intr.*) to feel joy. **6.** (*tr.*) *Obsolete.* to make joyful; gladden. [C13: from Old French *joie,* from Latin *gaudium* joy, from *gaudēre* to be glad]

joy+ance ('dʒɔɪəns) *n. Archaic.* a joyous feeling or festivity.

Joyce (dʒɔɪs) *n.* **1. James (Augustine Aloysius).** 1882–1941, Irish novelist and short-story writer. He profoundly influenced the development of the modern novel by his use of complex narrative techniques, esp. stream of consciousness and parody, and of compound and coined words. His works include the novels *Ulysses* (1922) and *Finnegans Wake* (1939) and the short stories *Dubliners* (1914). **2. Wil·liam,** known as *Lord Haw-Haw.* 1906-46, British broadcaster of Nazi propaganda to Britain, who was executed for treason. **—Joyc+e·an** ('dʒɔɪsɪən) *n., adj.*

joy+ful ('dʒɔɪfʊl) *adj.* **1.** full of joy; elated. **2.** expressing or producing joy: *a joyful look; a joyful occasion.* **—'joy+ful+ly** *adv.* **—'joy+ful+ness** *n.*

joy+less ('dʒɔɪlɪs) *adj.* having or producing no joy or pleasure. **—'joy+less+ly** *adv.* **—'joy+less+ness** *n.*

joy+ous ('dʒɔɪəs) *adj.* **1.** having a happy nature or mood. **2.** joyful. **—'joy+ous+ly** *adv.* **—'joy+ous+ness** *n.*

joy+pop ('dʒɔɪˌpɒp) *vb.* **+pops, +pop+ping, +popped.** (*intr.*) *Slang.* to take addictive drugs occasionally without becoming addicted.

joy ride *Informal.* ~*n.* **1.** an enjoyable ride taken in a car, esp. in a stolen car driven recklessly. ~*vb.* **joy-ride, -rides, -rid·ing, -rode, -rid·den. 2.** (*intr.*) to take such a ride. **—'joy+ˌrid·er** *n.*

joy stick *n. Informal.* the control stick of an aircraft.

J.P. *abbrev. for* Justice of the Peace.

Jr. *or* **jr.** *abbrev. for* junior.

J.S.D. *abbrev. for* Doctor of Juristic Science.

jt. *abbrev. for* joint.

Juan Car·los I (*Spanish* xwan 'karlos) *n.* born 1938, king of Spain since 1975. He was nominated by Franco as the latter's successor and as the first king of the restored Spanish monarchy that was to follow Franco's death.

Ju·an de Fu·ca ('dʒu:ən dɪ 'fju:kə; *Spanish* 'xwan de 'fuka) *n.* **Strait of.** a strait between Vancouver Island (Canada) and NW Washington (U.S.). Length: about 129 km (80 miles). Width: about 24 km (15 miles).

Ju·an Fer+nán+dez Is+lands ('dʒu:ən fə'nændɛz; *Spanish* 'xwan fer'nandes) *pl. n.* a group of three islands in the S Pacific Ocean, administered by Chile: volcanic and wooded. Area: about 180 sq. km (70 sq. miles).

Juan·to·re·na (*Spanish* xwanto'rena) *n.* **Al·ber·to** (al'βerto). born 1951, Cuban runner: won the 400 metres and the 800 metres in the 1976 Olympic Games.

Juá+rez[1] ('xwares) *n.* short for **Ciudad Juárez.**

Juá·rez[2] (*Spanish* 'xwares) *n.* **Be·ni·to Pa·blo** (be'nito 'paβlo). 1806–72, Mexican statesman. As president (1861–65; 1867–72) he thwarted Napoleon III's attempt to impose an empire under Maximilian and introduced many reforms.

ju·ba ('dʒu:bə) *n.* a lively Negro dance developed in the southern U.S. [C19: of Zulu origin]

Ju·ba ('dʒu:bə) *n.* a river in NE Africa, rising in S central Ethiopia and flowing south across the Somali Republic to the Indian Ocean: the chief river of the Somali Republic. Length: about 1660 km (1030 miles).

Ju+bal ('dʒu:bᵊl) *n. Old Testament.* the alleged inventor of musical instruments (Genesis 4:21).

jub+bah ('dʒʊbə) *n.* a long loose outer garment with wide sleeves, worn by Muslim men and women, esp. in India. [C16: from Arabic]

Jub+bul+pore (ˌdʒʌbᵊl'pʊə) *n.* a variant spelling of **Jabalpur.**

ju·be[1] ('dʒu:bɪ) *n.* **1.** a gallery or loft over the rood screen in a church or cathedral. **2.** another name for **rood screen.** [C18: from French *jubé,* from opening words of Medieval Latin prayer *Jube, Domine, benedicere* Bid, Lord, a blessing; probably from the deacon's standing by the rood screen or in the rood loft to pronounce this prayer]

jube[2] (dʒu:b) *n. Austral. informal.* any jelly-like sweet. [C20: shortened from JUJUBE]

ju+bi+lant ('dʒu:bɪlənt) *adj.* feeling or expressing great joy. [C17: from Latin *jūbilāns* shouting for joy, from *jūbilāre* to give a joyful cry, from *jūbilum* a shout, wild cry] **—'ju+bi+lance** *or* **'ju+bi+lan+cy** *n.* **—'ju+bi+lant+ly** *adv.*

ju+bi+late ('dʒu:bɪˌleɪt) *vb.* (*intr.*) **1.** to have or express great joy; rejoice. **2.** to celebrate a jubilee. [C17: from Latin *jūbilāre* to raise a shout of joy; see JUBILANT]

Ju+bi+la+te (ˌdʒu:bɪ'lɑ:tɪ) *n.* **1.** *R.C. Church, Church of England.* the 100th psalm used as a canticle in the liturgy. **2.** a musical setting of this psalm. [from the opening word (*Jubilate* make a joyful noise) of the Vulgate version]

ju+bi+la+tion (ˌdʒu:bɪ'leɪʃən) *n.* **1.** the act of rejoicing; exultation. **2.** a celebration or joyful occasion.

ju+bi+lee ('dʒu:bɪˌli:, ˌdʒu:bɪ'li:) *n.* **1.** a time or season for rejoicing. **2.** a special anniversary, esp. a 25th or 50th one. **3.** *R.C. Church.* a specially appointed period, now ordinarily every 25th year, in which special indulgences are granted. **4.** *Old Testament.* a year that was to be observed every 50th year, during which Hebrew slaves were to be liberated, alienated property was to be restored, etc. **5.** a less common word for **jubilation.** [C14: from Old French *jubile,* from Late Latin *jubilaeus,* from Late Greek *iōbēlaios,* from Hebrew *yōbhēl* ram's horn, used for the proclamation of the year of jubilee; influenced by Latin *jūbilāre* to shout for joy]

Jud. *Bible. abbrev. for:* **1.** Also: **Judg.** Judges. **2.** Judith.

J.U.D. *abbrev. for* Doctor of Canon and Civil Law. [Latin *Juris Utriusque Doctor*]

Ju+dae·a *or* **Ju+de·a** (dʒu:'dɪə) *n.* the S division of ancient Palestine, succeeding the kingdom of Judah: a Roman province during the time of Christ. **—Ju+'dae·an** *or* **Ju+'de·an** *adj., n.*

Ju·dae·o- *or U.S.* **Ju·de·o-** (dʒu:'deɪəʊ-, dʒu:'di:əʊ-) *combining form.* relating to Judaism: *Judaeo-Christian.*

Ju·dae·o-Ger·man *n.* another name for **Yiddish.**

Ju·dae·o-Span·ish *n.* another name for **Ladino.**

Ju·dah ('dʒu:də) *n. Old Testament.* **1.** the fourth son of Jacob, one of whose descendants was to be the Messiah (Genesis 29:35; 49:8–12). **2.** the tribe descended from him. **3.** the tribal territory of his descendants which became the nucleus of David's kingdom and, after the kingdom had been divided into Israel and Judah, the southern kingdom of Judah, with Jerusalem as its centre. Douay spelling: **Ju·da.**

Ju·dah ha-Na·si (hɑ:nɑ:'si:) *n.* ?135–?220 A.D., rabbi and patriarch of the Sanhedrin, who compiled the Mishnah.

Ju+da+ic (dʒu:'deɪɪk) *or* **Ju+da·i+cal** *adj.* **1.** of or relating to the Jews or Judaism. **2.** a less common word for **Jewish.** **—Ju+'da·i+cal+ly** *adv.*

Ju·da·i·ca (dʒu:'deɪɪkə) *pl. n.* the literature, customs, culture, etc., of the Jews, esp. as presented in books or articles. [Latin, literally: Jewish matters]

Ju+da+ism ('dʒu:deɪˌɪzəm) *n.* **1.** the religion of the Jews, based on the Old Testament and the Talmud and having as its central point a belief in the one God as transcendent creator of all things and the source of all righteousness. **2.** the religious and cultural traditions, customs, attitudes, and way of life of the Jews. **3.** the Jews collectively. **—'Ju+da+ist** *n.* **—ˌJu+da+'is+tic** *adj.*

Ju+da+ize *or* **Ju+da+ise** ('dʒu:deɪˌaɪz) *vb.* **1.** to conform or bring into conformity with Judaism. **2.** (*tr.*) to convert to Judaism. **3.** (*tr.*) to imbue with Jewish principles. **—ˌJu+da·i+'za+tion** *or* **ˌJu+da·i+'sa+tion** *n.* **—'Ju+da+ˌiz+er** *or* **'Ju+daˌis+er** *n.*

ju+das ('dʒu:dəs) *n.* (*sometimes cap.*) a peephole or a very small window in a door. Also called: **judas window, judas hole.** [C19: after *Judas Iscariot*]

Ju·das ('dʒu:dəs) *n.* **1.** *New Testament.* the apostle who betrayed Jesus to his enemies for 30 pieces of silver (Luke 22:3–6, 47–48). Full name: **Judas Iscariot. 2.** a person who betrays a friend; traitor. **3.** a brother or relative of James and also of Jesus (Matthew 13:55). This figure, Thaddaeus, and Jude were probably identical. ~*adj.* **4.** denoting an animal or bird used to lure others of its kind or lead them to slaughter.

Ju·das Mac·ca·bae·us (ˌmækə'bi:əs) *n.* Jewish leader, whose revolt (166–161 B.C.) against the Seleucid kingdom of Antiochus IV (Epiphanes) enabled him to recapture Jerusalem and rededicate the Temple.

Ju+das tree *n.* small Eurasian leguminous tree, *Cercis siliquastrum,* with pinkish-purple flowers that bloom before the leaves appear: popularly thought to be the tree on which Judas hanged himself. See also **redbud.**

jud+der ('dʒʌdə) *Informal, chiefly Brit.* ~*vb.* **1.** (*intr.*) to shake or vibrate. ~*n.* **2.** abnormal vibration in a mechanical system, esp. due to grabbing between friction surfaces, as in the clutch of a motor vehicle. **3.** a juddering motion. [probably blend of JAR[2] + SHUDDER]

Jude (dʒu:d) *n.* **1.** a book of the New Testament (in full **The Epistle of Jude**). **2.** Also called: **Judas.** the author of this, stated to be the brother of James (Jude 1) and almost certainly identical with Thaddaeus (Matthew 10:2–4).

Ju+de·a (dʒu:'dɪə) *n.* a variant spelling of **Judaea.**

Ju+dez+mo (dʒʊ'dɛzməʊ) *n.* another name for **Ladino.** [from Ladino: Jewish]

judge (dʒʌdʒ) *n.* **1.** a public official with authority to hear cases in a court of law and pronounce judgment upon them. Compare **magistrate, justice** (senses 5, 6). **2.** a person who is appointed to determine the result of contests or competitions. **3.** a person qualified to comment critically: *a good judge of antiques.* **4.** a leader of the peoples of Israel from Joshua's death to the accession of Saul. ~*vb.* **5.** to hear and decide upon (a case at law). **6.** (*tr.*) to pass judgment on; sentence. **7.** (*when tr., may take a clause as object or an infinitive*) to decide or deem (something) after inquiry or deliberation. **8.** to determine the result of (a contest or competition). **9.** to appraise (something) critically. **10.** (*tr.; takes a clause as object*) to believe something to be the case; suspect. [C14: from Old French *jugier,* from Latin *jūdicāre* to pass judgment, from *jūdex* a judge] **—'judge+**

a·ble *adj.* —**'judge+less** *adj.* —**'judge+,like** *adj.* —**'judg+er** *n.* —**'judg+ing+ly** *adv.*

judge ad+vo+cate *n., pl.* **judge ad+vo+cates.** an officer who superintends proceedings at a military court martial.

judge ad+vo+cate gen+er+al *n., pl.* **judge ad+vo+cates gen+er+al** *or* **judge ad+vo+cate gen+er+als.** the civil adviser to the Crown on matters relating to courts martial and on military law generally.

judge-made *adj.* based on a judge's interpretation or decision (esp. in the phrase **judge-made law**).

Judg·es ('dʒʌdʒɪz) *n.* the book of the Old Testament recounting the history of Israel under the warrior champions and national leaders known as judges.

judge+ship ('dʒʌdʒ,ʃɪp) *n.* the position, office, or function of a judge.

judg·es' rules *pl. n.* (in English law) a set of rules, not legally binding, governing the behaviour of police towards suspects, as in administering a caution to a person under arrest.

judg+ment *or* **judge+ment** ('dʒʌdʒmənt) *n.* **1.** the faculty of being able to make critical distinctions and achieve a balanced viewpoint; discernment. **2. a.** the verdict pronounced by a court of law. **b.** an obligation arising as a result of such a verdict, such as a debt. **c.** the document recording such a verdict. **d.** (*as modifier*): *a judgment debtor.* **3.** the formal decision of one or more judges at a contest or competition. **4.** a particular decision or opinion formed in a case in dispute or doubt. **5.** an estimation: *a good judgment of distance.* **6.** criticism or censure. **7.** *Logic.* **a.** the act of establishing a relation between two or more terms, esp. as an affirmation or denial. **b.** the expression of such a relation. **8. against one's better judgment.** contrary to a more appropriate or preferred course of action. **9. sit in judgment. a.** to preside as judge. **b.** to assume the position of critic. —**judg+men+tal** *or* **judge+men+tal** (dʒʌdʒ'mɛntᵊl) *adj.*

Judg+ment ('dʒʌdʒmənt) *n.* **1.** the estimate by God of the ultimate worthiness or unworthiness of the individual (the **Particular Judgment**) or of all mankind (the **General Judgment** or **Last Judgment**). **2.** God's subsequent decision determining the final destinies of all individuals.

Judg+ment Day *n.* the occasion of the Last (or General) Judgment by God at the end of the world. Also called: **Day of Judgment.** See **Last Judgment.**

ju+di+ca·ble ('dʒu:dɪkəbᵊl) *adj.* capable of being judged, esp. in a court of law.

ju+di+ca+tive ('dʒu:dɪkətɪv) *adj.* **1.** having the function of trying causes. **2.** competent to judge and pass sentence.

ju+di+ca+tor ('dʒu:dɪ,keɪtə) *n.* a person who acts as a judge.

ju+di+ca+to·ry ('dʒu:dɪ,keɪtərɪ) *adj.* **1.** of or relating to the administration of justice. ~*n.* **2.** a court of law. **3.** the administration of justice. —**,ju+di+ca+'to+ri·al** *adj.*

ju+di+ca+ture ('dʒu:dɪkətʃə) *n.* **1.** the administration of justice. **2.** the office, function, or power of a judge. **3.** the extent of authority of a court or judge. **4.** a body of judges or persons exercising judicial authority; judiciary. **5.** a court of justice or such courts collectively.

ju+di+cial (dʒu:'dɪʃəl) *adj.* **1.** of or relating to the administration of justice. **2.** of or relating to judgment in a court of law or to a judge exercising this function. **3.** inclined to pass judgment; discriminating. **4.** allowed or enforced by a court of law: *a decree of judicial separation.* **5.** having qualities appropriate to a judge. **6.** giving or seeking judgment, esp. determining or seeking determination of a contested issue. [C14: from Latin *jūdiciālis* belonging to the law courts, from *jūdicium* judgment, from *jūdex* a judge] —**ju+'di+cial+ly** *adv.*

Ju+di+cial Com+mit+tee of the Priv·y Coun+cil *n.* the highest appellate court for Britain's dependencies and for some dominions of the Commonwealth.

ju+di+cial sep·a+ra+tion *n. Family law.* a decree prohibiting a man and wife from cohabiting but not dissolving the marriage. See also **a mensa et thoro.** Compare **divorce.**

ju+di+ci+ar·y (dʒu:'dɪʃɪərɪ, -'dɪʃərɪ) *adj.* **1.** of or relating to courts of law, judgment, or judges. ~*n., pl.* **+ar·ies. 2.** the branch of the central authority in a state concerned with the administration of justice. Compare **executive** (sense 2), **legislature. 3.** the system of courts in a country. **4.** the judges collectively; bench.

ju+di+cious (dʒu:'dɪʃəs) *adj.* having or proceeding from good judgment. —**ju+'di+cious+ly** *adv.* —**ju+'di+cious+ness** *n.*

Ju·dith ('dʒu:dɪθ) *n.* **1.** the heroine of one of the books of the Apocrypha, who saved her native town by decapitating Holofernes. **2.** the book recounting this episode.

ju·do ('dʒu:dəʊ) *n.* **a.** the modern sport derived from jujitsu, in which the object is to throw, hold to the ground, or otherwise force an opponent to submit, using the minimum of physical effort. **b.** (*as modifier*): *a judo throw.* [Japanese, from *jū* gentleness + *dō* art] —**'ju+do+ist** *n.*

ju+do+gi (dʒʊ'dəʊgɪ) *n.* a white two-piece cotton costume worn during judo contests. [from Japanese]

ju+do+ka ('dʒu:dəʊ,kɑ:) *n.* a competitor or expert in judo. [Japanese; see JUDO]

Ju·dy ('dʒu:dɪ) *n., pl.* **-dies. 1.** the wife of Punch in the children's puppet show *Punch and Judy.* See **Punch. 2.** (*often not cap.*) *Brit. slang.* a girl; young woman.

jug (dʒʌg) *n.* **1.** a vessel for holding or pouring liquids, usually having a handle and a spout or lip. U.S. equivalent: **pitcher. 2.** *Austral.* such a vessel used as a kettle: *an electric jug.* **3.** *U.S.* a large vessel with a narrow mouth. **4.** Also called: **jug+ful.** the amount of liquid held by a jug. **5.** *Brit. informal.* a glass of alcoholic drink, esp. beer. **6.** a slang word for **jail.** ~*vb.* **jugs, jug+ging, jugged. 7.** to stew or boil (meat, esp. hare) in an earthenware container. **8.** (*tr.*) *Slang.* to put in jail. [C16: probably from *Jug,* nickname from girl's name *Joan*]

ju+gal ('dʒu:gᵊl) *adj.* **1.** of or relating to the zygomatic bone. ~*n.* **2.** Also called: **jugal bone.** other names for **zygomatic bone.** [C16: from Latin *jugālis* of a yoke, from *jugum* a yoke]

ju+gate ('dʒu:geɪt, -gɪt) *adj.* (esp. of compound leaves) having parts arranged in pairs. [C19: from New Latin *jugātus* (unattested), from Latin *jugum* a yoke]

jug band *n.* a small group playing folk or jazz music, using empty jugs that are played by blowing across their openings to produce bass notes.

Ju+gend+stil *German.* ('ju:gᵊnt,ʃti:l) *n.* another name for **art nouveau.** [from *Jugend* literally: youth, name of illustrated periodical that first appeared in 1896, + *Stil* STYLE]

JUGFET ('dʒʌgfɛt) *n. acronym for* junction-gate field-effect transistor; a type of field-effect transistor in which the semiconductor gate region or regions form one or more p-n junctions with the conduction channel. Compare **IGFET.**

jugged hare *n.* a stew of hare cooked in an earthenware pot or casserole.

jug+ger+naut ('dʒʌgə,nɔ:t) *n.* **1.** any terrible force, esp. one that destroys or that demands complete self-sacrifice. **2.** *Brit.* a very large lorry for transporting goods by road, esp. one that travels throughout Europe.

Jug+ger+naut ('dʒʌgə,nɔ:t) *n. Hinduism.* **1.** a crude idol of Krishna worshipped at Puri and throughout Orissa and Bengal. At an annual festival the idol is wheeled through the town on a gigantic chariot and devotees are supposed to have formerly thrown themselves under the wheels in the hope of going straight to paradise. **2.** a form of Krishna miraculously raised by Brahma from the state of a crude idol to that of a living god. [C17: from Hindi *Jagannath,* from Sanskrit *Jagannātha* lord of the world (that is, Vishnu, chief of the Hindu gods), from *jagat* world + *nātha* lord]

jug+gins ('dʒʌgɪnz) *n. Brit. informal.* a silly fellow. [C19: special use of the surname *Juggins*]

jug+gle ('dʒʌgᵊl) *vb.* **1.** to throw and catch (several objects) continuously so that most are in the air all the time, as an entertainment. **2.** to arrange or manipulate (facts, figures, etc.) so as to give a false or misleading picture. **3.** (*tr.*) to keep (several activities) in progress, esp. with difficulty. ~*n.* **4.** an act of juggling. [C14: from Old French *jogler* to perform as a jester, from Latin *joculārī* to jest, from *jocus* a jest] —**'jug+gler·y** *n.*

jug+gler ('dʒʌglə) *n.* **1.** a person who juggles, esp. a professional entertainer. **2.** a person who fraudulently manipulates facts or figures.

ju+glan+da+ceous (,dʒu:glæn'deɪʃəs) *adj.* of, relating to, or belonging to the *Juglandaceae,* a family of trees that includes walnut and hickory. [C19: via New Latin from Latin *juglans* walnut, from *ju-,* shortened from *Jovi-* of Jupiter + *glans* acorn]

Ju+go+sla+vi·a (,ju:gəʊ'slɑ:vɪə) *n.* a variant spelling of **Yugoslavia.** —**'Ju+go+,slav** *or* **,Ju+go+'sla+vi·an** *adj., n.*

jug·u+lar ('dʒʌgjʊlə) *adj.* **1.** of, relating to, or situated near the throat or neck. **2.** of, having, or denoting pelvic fins situated in front of the pectoral fins: *a jugular fish.* ~*n.* **3.** short for **jugular vein.** [C16: from Late Latin *jugulāris,* from Latin *jugulum* throat]

jug·u+lar vein *n.* any of three large veins of the neck that return blood to the heart from the head and face.

jug·u+late ('dʒʌgjʊ,leɪt) *vb.* (*tr.*) *Rare.* to check (a disease) by extreme measures or remedies. [C17 (in the obsolete sense: kill by cutting the throat of): from Latin *jugulāre,* from *jugulum* throat, from *jugum* yoke] —**,jug·u+'la+tion** *n.*

ju+gum ('dʒu:gəm) *n.* **1.** a small process at the base of each forewing in certain insects by which the forewings are united to the hindwings during flight. **2.** *Botany.* a pair of opposite leaflets. [C19: from Latin, literally: YOKE]

Ju·gur·tha (dʒu:'gɜ:θə) *n.* died 104 B.C., king of Numidia (?112–104), who waged war against the Romans (the **Jugurthine War,** 112–105) and was defeated and executed.

juice (dʒu:s) *n.* **1.** any liquid that occurs naturally in or is secreted by plant or animal tissue: *the juice of an orange; digestive juices.* **2.** *Informal.* **a.** fuel for an engine, esp. petrol. **b.** electricity. **c.** alcoholic drink. **3. a.** vigour or vitality. **b.** essence or fundamental nature. [C13: from Old French *jus,* from Latin] —**'juice+less** *adj.*

juice ex+trac+tor *n.* a kitchen appliance, usually operated by electricity, for extracting juice from fruits and vegetables. U.S. equivalent: **juicer.**

juice up *vb.* (*tr., adv.*) **1.** *U.S. slang.* to make lively: *to juice up a party.* **2.** (*often passive*) to cause to be drunk: *he got juiced up on Scotch last night.*

juic·y ('dʒu:sɪ) *adj.* **juic·i+er, juic·i+est. 1.** full of juice. **2.** provocatively interesting; spicy: *juicy gossip.* **3.** *Slang.* voluptuous or seductive: *she's a juicy bit.* **4.** *Chiefly U.S.* profitable: *a juicy contract.* —**'juic·i+ly** *adv.* —**'juic·i+ness** *n.*

Juiz de Fo·ra (*Portuguese* 'ʒwiz di 'fɔra) *n.* a city in SE Brazil, in Minas Gerais state on the Rio de Janeiro–Belo Horizonte railway: textiles. Pop.: 218 832 (1970).

ju+jit+su, ju+jut+su, *or* **jiu+jut+su** (dʒu:'dʒɪtsu:) *n.* the traditional Japanese system of unarmed self-defence perfected by the samurai. See also **judo.** [C19: from Japanese, from *jū* gentleness + *jutsu* art]

ju·ju ('dʒu:dʒu:) *n.* **1.** an object superstitiously revered by certain West African peoples and used as a charm or fetish. **2.** the power associated with a juju. **3.** a taboo effected by a juju. **4.** any process in which a mystery is exploited to confuse people. [C19: probably from Hausa *djudju* evil spirit, fetish] —'**ju+ju+ism** *n.* —'**ju+ju+ist** *n.*

ju+jube ('dʒu:dʒu:b) *n.* **1.** any of several Old World spiny rhamnaceous trees of the genus *Ziziphus*, esp. *Z. jujuba*, that have small yellowish flowers and dark red edible fruits. See also **Christ's-thorn. 2.** the fruit of any of these trees. **3.** a chewy sweet made of flavoured gelatine and sometimes medicated to soothe sore throats. ~Also called (for senses 1, 2): **Chinese date.** [C14: from Medieval Latin *jujuba*, modification of Latin *zīzyphum*, from Greek *zizuphon*]

juke+box ('dʒu:kˌbɒks) *n.* an automatic gramophone, usually in a large case, in which records may be selected by inserting coins and pressing appropriate buttons. [C20: from Gullah *juke* bawdy (as in *juke house* brothel) + BOX[1]]

Jul. *abbrev. for* July.

ju+lep ('dʒu:lɪp) *n.* **1.** a sweet drink, variously prepared and sometimes medicated. **2.** *Chiefly U.S.* short for **mint julep.** [C14: from Old French, from Arabic *julāb*, from Persian *gulāb* rose water, from *gul* rose + *āb* water]

Jul·ian[1] ('dʒu:ljən, -lɪən) *n.* called *the Apostate;* Latin name *Flavius Claudius Julianus.* 331–363 A.D., Roman emperor (361–363), who attempted to revive paganism in the Roman empire while remaining tolerant to Christians and Jews.

Jul+ian[2] ('dʒu:ljən, -lɪən) *adj.* **1.** of or relating to Julius Caesar. **2.** denoting or relating to the Julian calendar.

Ju·li·an·a (ˌdʒu:lɪ'ɑ:nə; *Dutch* ˌjy:li:'a:na:) *n.* full name *Juliana Louise Emma Marie Wilhelmina.* born 1909, queen of the Netherlands 1948–80.

Jul+ian Alps *pl. n.* a mountain range in NW Yugoslavia, in Slovenia: an E range of the Alps.

Jul+ian cal+en+dar *n.* the calendar introduced by Julius Caesar in 46 B.C., identical to the present calendar in all but two aspects: the beginning of the year was not fixed on Jan. 1 and leap years occurred every fourth year and in every centenary year. Compare **Gregorian calendar.**

ju+li+enne (ˌdʒu:lɪ'ɛn) *adj.* **1.** (of vegetables) cut into thin shreds. ~*n.* **2.** a clear consommé to which a mixture of such vegetables has been added.

Ju+li+et cap ('dʒu:lɪɪt) *n.* a close-fitting decorative cap, worn esp. by brides. [C20: after the heroine of Shakespeare's *Romeo and Juliet*]

Jul·ius II (ˌdʒu:ljəs, -lɪəs) *n.* original name *Guiliano della Rovere.* 1443–1513, pope (1503–13). He completed the restoration of the Papal States to the Church, began the building of St. Peter's, Rome (1506), and patronized Michelangelo, Raphael, and Bramante.

Jul·ius Cae·sar *n.* See **Caesar.**

Jul+lun+dur ('dʒʌləndə) *n.* a city in NW India, in central Punjab. Pop.: 296 106 (1971).

Ju·ly (dʒu:'laɪ, dʒə-, dʒʊ-) *n., pl.* **·lies.** the seventh month of the year, consisting of 31 days. [C13: from Anglo-French *julie*, from Latin *Jūlius*, after Gaius *Julius* CAESAR, in whose honour it was named]

Ju+ma+da (dʒʊ'mɑ:də) *n.* either the fifth or the sixth month of the Muslim year, known respectively as **Jumada I** and **Jumada II.** [Arabic]

jum+ble ('dʒʌmbᵊl) *vb.* **1.** to mingle (objects, papers, etc.) in a state of disorder. **2.** (*tr.; usually passive*) to remember in a confused form; muddle. ~*n.* **3.** a disordered mass, state, etc. **4.** Also called: **jumbal.** a small thin cake, variously flavoured. **5.** articles donated for a jumble sale. [C16: of uncertain origin] —'**jum+bler** *n.* —'**jum+bling+ly** *adv.* —'**jum+bly** *adj.*

jum+ble sale *n.* a sale of miscellaneous articles, usually cheap and predominantly secondhand, in aid of charity. U.S. equivalent: **rummage sale.**

jum+bo ('dʒʌmbəʊ) *n., pl.* **+bos. 1.** *Informal.* **a.** a very large person or thing. **b.** (*as modifier*): *a jumbo box of detergent.* **2.** See **jumbo jet.** [C19: after the name of a famous elephant exhibited by P. T. Barnum, from Swahili *jumbe* chief]

jum+bo jet *n. Informal.* a type of large jet-propelled airliner.

jum+buck ('dʒʌmˌbʌk) *n. Austral.* an informal word for **sheep.** [C19: from a native Australian language]

Jum+na ('dʒʌmnə) *n.* a river in N India, rising in Uttar Pradesh in the Himalayas and flowing south and southeast to join the Ganges just below Allahabad (a confluence held sacred by Hindus). Length: 1385 km (860 miles).

jump (dʒʌmp) *vb.* **1.** (*intr.*) to leap or spring clear of the ground or other surface by using the muscles in the legs and feet. **2.** (*tr.*) to leap over or clear (an obstacle): *to jump a gap.* **3.** (*tr.*) to cause to leap over an obstacle: *to jump a horse over a hedge.* **4.** to move or proceed hastily (into, onto, out of, etc.): *she jumped into a taxi and was off.* **5.** (*tr.*) *Informal.* to board so as to travel illegally on: *he jumped the train as it was leaving.* **6.** (*intr.*) to parachute from an aircraft. **7.** (*intr.*) to jerk or start, as with astonishment, surprise, etc.: *she jumped when she heard the explosion.* **8.** to rise or cause to rise suddenly or abruptly. **9.** to pass or skip over (intervening objects or matter): *she jumped a few lines and then continued reading.* **10.** (*intr.*) to change from one thing to another, esp. from one subject to another. **11.** (*tr.*) to drill by means of a jumper. **12.** (*intr.*) (of a film) **a.** to have sections of a continuous sequence omitted, as through faulty cutting. **b.** to flicker, as through faulty alignment of the film. **13.** (*tr.*) *U.S.* to promote in rank, esp. unexpectedly or to a higher rank than expected. **14.** (*tr.*) to start (a car) using jump leads. **15.** *Draughts.* to capture (an opponent's piece) by moving one of one's own pieces over it to an unoccupied square. **16.** (*intr.*) *Bridge.* to bid in response to one's partner at a higher level than is necessary, to indicate a strong hand. **17.** (*tr.*) to come off (a track, rail, etc.): *the locomotive jumped the rails.* **18.** (*intr.*) (of the stylus of a record player) to be jerked out of the groove. **19.** (*intr.*) *Slang.* to be lively: *the party was jumping when I arrived.* **20.** (*tr.*) *Informal.* to attack without warning: *thieves jumped the old man as he walked through the park.* **21.** (*tr.*) *Informal.* (of a driver or a motor vehicle) to pass through (a red traffic light) or move away from (traffic lights) before they change to green. **22.** (*tr.*) *Brit. slang.* (of a man) to have sexual intercourse with. **23. jump bail.** to forfeit one's bail by failing to appear in court, esp. by absconding. **24. jump down someone's throat.** *Informal.* to address someone sharply; scold. **25. jump ship.** to desert, esp. to leave a ship in which one is legally bound to serve. **26. jump the queue.** *Informal.* to obtain prior consideration or some other advantage out of turn or unfairly. **27. jump to it.** *Informal.* to begin something quickly and efficiently. ~*n.* **28.** an act or instance of jumping. **29.** a space, distance, or obstacle to be jumped or that has been jumped. **30.** a descent by parachute from an aircraft. **31.** *Sport.* any of several contests involving a jump: *the high jump.* **32.** a sudden rise: *the jump in prices last month.* **33.** a sudden or abrupt transition. **34.** a sudden jerk or involuntary muscular spasm, esp. as a reaction of surprise. **35.** a step or degree: *one jump ahead.* **36.** *Draughts.* a move that captures an opponent's piece by jumping over it. **37.** *Films.* **a.** a break in continuity in the normal sequence of shots. **b.** (*as modifier*): *a jump cut.* **38.** *Computer technol.* another name for **branch** (sense 7). **39.** *Brit. slang.* an act of sexual intercourse. **40. on the jump.** *Informal, chiefly U.S.* **a.** in a hurry. **b.** busy and energetic. ~See also **jump at, jump-off, jump on, jump-up.** [C16: probably of imitative origin; compare Swedish *gumpa* to jump] —'**jump+a·ble** *adj.* —'**jump+ing+ly** *adv.*

jump at *vb.* (*intr., prep.*) to be glad to accept: *I would jump at the chance of going.*

jump ball *n. Basketball.* a ball thrown high by the referee between two opposing players to put it in play, as after a stoppage in which no foul or violation was committed.

jump bid *n. Bridge.* a bid by the responder at a higher level than is necessary.

jumped-up *adj. Informal.* suddenly risen in significance, esp. when appearing arrogant.

jump+er[1] ('dʒʌmpə) *n.* **1.** *Chiefly Brit.* a sweater or pullover. **2.** the U.S. term for **pinafore dress.** [C19: from obsolete *jump* man's loose jacket, variant of *jupe*, from Old French, from Arabic *jubbah* long cloth coat]

jump+er[2] ('dʒʌmpə) *n.* **1.** a boring tool that works by repeated impact, such as a steel bit in a hammer drill used in boring rock. **2.** Also called: **jumper cable, jumper lead.** a short length of wire used to make a connection, usually temporarily, between terminals or to bypass a component. **3.** a type of sled with a high crosspiece. **4.** a person or animal that jumps.

jump+ing bean *n.* a seed of any of several Mexican euphorbiaceous plants, esp. species of *Sebastiania*, that contains a moth caterpillar whose movements cause it to jerk about.

jump+ing jack *n.* **1.** a firework having a long narrow tube filled with gunpowder, folded like an accordion so that when lit it burns with small explosions causing it to jump along the ground. **2.** a toy figure of a man with jointed limbs that can be moved by pulling attached strings.

jump+ing mouse *n.* any long-tailed small mouselike rodent of the family *Zapodidae*, of North America, E Asia, and N and E Europe, having long hind legs specialized for leaping.

jump·ing-off place *or* **point** *n.* **1.** a starting point, as in an enterprise. **2.** a final or extreme condition. **3.** *U.S.* a very remote spot.

jump jet *n. Informal.* a fixed-wing jet aircraft that is capable of landing and taking off vertically.

jump leads (li:dz) *pl. n.* two heavy cables fitted with crocodile clips used to start a motor vehicle with a discharged battery by connecting the battery to an external battery. U.S. name: **jumper cables.**

jump-off *n.* **1.** an extra round in a showjumping contest when two or more horses are equal first, the fastest round deciding the winner. ~*vb.* **jump off. 2.** (*intr., adv.*) to begin or engage in a jump-off.

jump on *vb.* (*intr., prep.*) *Informal.* to berate or reprimand.

jump seat *n.* **1.** a folding seat on the flight deck of some aircraft for an additional crew member. **2.** *Brit.* a folding seat in a motor vehicle such as in a London taxi.

jump shot *n. Basketball.* a shot at the basket made by a player releasing the ball at the highest point of a leap.

jump-start *vb.* **1.** to start the engine of (a car) by pushing or rolling it and then engaging the gears or (of a car) to start in this way. ~*n.* **2.** the act of starting a car in this way. ~Also called (in Brit.): **bump-start.**

jump suit *n.* a one-piece garment of combined trousers and jacket or shirt.

jump-up *n.* **1.** (in the Caribbean) an occasion of mass dancing and merrymaking, as in a carnival. ~*vb.* **jump up.** (*intr., adv.*) **2.** to stand up quickly and suddenly. **3.** (in the Caribbean) to take part in a jump-up.

jump·y ('dʒʌmpɪ) *adj.* **jump·i+er, jump·i+est. 1.** nervous or apprehensive. **2.** moving jerkily or fitfully. —'**jump·i+ly** *adv.* —'**jump·i+ness** *n.*

Jun. *abbrev. for:* **1.** June. **2.** Also: **jun.** junior.

junc. *abbrev. for* junction.

jun+ca+ceous (dʒʌŋ'keɪʃəs) *adj.* of, relating to, or belonging to the *Juncaceae*, a family of grasslike plants with small brown flowers: includes the rushes and woodrushes. Compare **cyperaceous.** [C19: via New Latin from Latin *juncus* a rush]

jun·co ('dʒʌŋkəʊ) *n., pl.* **·cos.** any North American buntings of the genus *Junco,* having a greyish plumage with white outer tail feathers. [C18: from Spanish: a rush, a marsh bird, from Latin *juncus* rush]

junc·tion ('dʒʌŋkʃən) *n.* **1.** a place where several routes or lines meet, link, or cross each other: *a railway junction.* **2.** *Electronics.* **a.** a contact between two different metals or other materials: *a thermocouple junction.* **b.** a transition region between regions of differing electrical properties in a semiconductor: *a p-n junction.* **3.** a connection between two or more conductors or sections of transmission lines. **4.** the act of joining or the state of being joined. [C18: from Latin *junctiō* a joining, from *junctus* joined, from *jungere* to join] —**'junc·tion·al** *adj.*

junc·tion box *n.* an earthed enclosure within which wires or cables can be safely connected.

junc·tion tran·sis·tor *n.* a bipolar transistor consisting of two p-n junctions combined to form either an n-p-n or a p-n-p transistor, having the three electrodes, the emitter, base, and collector.

junc·ture ('dʒʌŋktʃə) *n.* **1.** a point in time, esp. a critical one (often in the phrase **at this juncture**). **2.** *Linguistics.* **a.** a pause in speech or a feature of pronunciation that introduces, accompanies, or replaces a pause. **b.** the set of phonological features signalling a division between words, such as those that distinguish *a name* from *an aim.* **3.** a less common word for **junction.**

Jun·dia·í (*Portuguese* ˌʒundja'i) *n.* an industrial city in SE Brazil, in São Paulo state. Pop.: 145 785 (1970).

June (dʒuːn) *n.* the sixth month of the year, consisting of 30 days. [Old English *iunius,* from Latin *junius,* probably from *Junius* name of Roman gens]

Ju·neau ('juːnəʊ) *n.* a port in SE Alaska: state capital. Pop.: 6050 (1970).

June·ber·ry ('dʒuːnˌbɛrɪ) *n., pl.* **·ries.** another name for **serviceberry** (senses 1, 2).

June bug *or* **bee·tle** *n.* any of various large brown North American scarabaeid beetles that are common in late spring and early summer, esp. any of the genus *Polyphylla.* Also called: **May beetle, May bug.**

Jung (jʊŋ) *n.* **Carl Gus·tav** (karl 'gʊstaf). 1875–1961, Swiss psychologist. His criticism of Freud's emphasis on the sexual instinct ended their early collaboration. He went on to found analytic psychology, developing the concepts of the collective unconscious and its archetypes and of the extrovert and introvert as the two main psychological types.

Jung·frau (*German* 'jʊŋˌfraʊ) *n.* a mountain in S Switzerland, in the Bernese Alps south of Interlaken. Height: 4158 m (13 642 ft.).

Jung·i·an ('jʊŋɪən) *adj.* of, following, or relating to C. G. Jung, his system of psychoanalysis, or to analytic psychology.

jun·gle ('dʒʌŋgᵊl) *n.* **1.** an equatorial forest area with luxuriant vegetation, often almost impenetrable. **2.** any dense or tangled thicket or growth. **3.** a place of intense competition or ruthless struggle for survival: *the concrete jungle.* **4.** *U.S. slang.* (esp. in the Depression) a gathering place for the unemployed, etc. [C18: from Hindi *jangal,* from Sanskrit *jāngala* wilderness] —**'jun·gly** *adj.*

jun·gle fe·ver *n.* a serious malarial fever occurring in the East Indies.

jun·gle fowl *n.* **1.** any small gallinaceous bird of the genus *Gallus,* of S and SE Asia, the males of which have an arched tail and a combed and wattled head: family *Phasianidae* (pheasants). *G. gallus* (**red jungle fowl**) is thought to be the ancestor of the domestic fowl. **2.** *Austral.* any of several megapodes, esp. *Megapodius freycinet.*

jun·gle juice *n.* **1.** a slang name for alcoholic liquor, esp. home-made liquor. **2.** *Austral.* a slang name for **kerosene.**

jun·ior ('dʒuːnjə) *adj.* **1.** lower in rank or length of service; subordinate. **2.** younger in years: *junior citizens.* **3.** of or relating to youth or childhood: *junior pastimes.* **4.** *Brit.* of or relating to schoolchildren between the ages of 7 and 11 approximately. **5.** *U.S.* of, relating to, or designating the third year of a four-year course at college or high school. ~*n.* **6.** *Law.* (in England) any barrister below the rank of Queen's Counsel. **7.** a junior person. **8.** *Brit.* a junior schoolchild. **9.** *U.S.* a junior student. [C17: from Latin: younger, from *juvenis* young]

Jun·ior ('dʒuːnjə) *adj. Chiefly U.S.* being the younger: usually used after a name to distinguish the son from the father with the same first name or names: *Charles Parker, Junior.* Abbrev.: **Jnr., Jr., Jun., Junr.**

jun·ior col·lege *n. U.S.* **1.** an educational establishment providing a two-year course that either terminates with an associate degree or is the equivalent of the freshman and sophomore years of a four-year undergraduate course. **2.** the junior section of a college or university.

jun·ior com·mon room *n.* (in certain universities and colleges) a common room for the use of students. Compare **senior common room, middle common room.**

jun·ior light·weight *n.* **a.** a professional boxer weighing 126–130 pounds (57–59 kg). **b.** (*as modifier*): *a junior-lightweight bout.*

jun·ior mid·dle·weight *n.* **a.** a professional boxer weighing 147–154 pounds (66.5–70 kg). **b.** (*as modifier*): *the junior-middleweight championship.* Compare **light middleweight.**

jun·ior school *n. Brit.* a school for children aged between 7 and 11: Compare **infant school.**

jun·ior wel·ter·weight *n.* **a.** a professional boxer weighing 135–140 pounds (61–63.5 kg). **b.** (*as modifier*): *a junior-welterweight fight.* Compare **light welterweight.**

ju·ni·per ('dʒuːnɪpə) *n.* **1.** any coniferous shrub or small tree of the genus *Juniperus,* of the N hemisphere, having purple berry-like cones. The cones of *J. communis* (**common** or **dwarf juniper**) are used as a flavouring in making gin. See also **red cedar** (sense 1). **2.** any of various similar trees, grown mainly as ornamentals. **3.** *Old Testament.* one of the trees used in the building of Solomon's temple (I Kings 6:15, 34) and for shipbuilding (Ezekiel 27:5). [C14: from Latin *jūniperus,* of obscure origin]

Jun·ius ('dʒuːnjəs) *n.* pen name of the anonymous author of a series of letters (1769–72) attacking the ministries of George III of England: now generally believed to have been written by Sir Philip Francis (1740–1818), a clerk in the War Office.

junk[1] (dʒʌŋk) *n.* **1.** discarded or secondhand objects, etc., collectively. **2.** *Informal.* nonsense; rubbish: *the play was absolute junk.* **3.** *Slang.* any narcotic drug, esp. heroin. ~*vb.* **4.** (*tr.*) *Informal, chiefly U.S.* to discard as junk; scrap. [C15: *jonke* old useless rope]

junk[2] (dʒʌŋk) *n.* a sailing vessel used in Chinese waters and characterized by a very high poop, flat bottom, and square sails supported by battens. [C17: from Portuguese *junco,* from Javanese *jon;* related to Dutch *jonk*]

Jun·ker ('jʊŋkə) *n.* **1.** *History.* any of the aristocratic landowners of Prussia who were devoted to maintaining their identity and extensive social and political privileges. **2.** an arrogant, narrow-minded, and tyrannical German army officer or official. **3.** (formerly) a young German nobleman. [C16: from German, from Old High German *junchērro* young lord, from *junc* young + *hērro* master, lord] —**'Jun·ker·dom** *n.* —**'Jun·ker·ism** *n.*

jun·ket ('dʒʌŋkɪt) *n.* **1.** a sweet dessert made of flavoured milk set to a curd with rennet. **2.** a feast. **3.** *U.S.* an excursion, esp. one made for pleasure at public expense by a public official or committee. ~*vb.* **4.** to have or entertain with a feast. **5.** (*intr.*) *U.S.* (of a public official, committee, etc.) to go on a junket. [C14 (in the sense: rush basket, hence custard served on rushes): from Old French (dialect) *jonquette,* from *jonc* rush, from Latin *juncus* reed] —**'jun·ket·er, 'jun·ket·ter,** *or* **ˌjun·ke·'teer** *n.*

junk·ie *or* **junk·y** ('dʒʌŋkɪ) *n., pl.* **junk·ies.** an informal word for **drug addict,** esp. one who injects heroin into himself.

junk·man ('dʒʌŋkˌmæn) *n., pl.* **·men.** the U.S. term for **rag-and-bone man.**

junk shop *n.* **1.** a shop selling miscellaneous secondhand goods. **2.** *Derogatory.* a shop selling antiques.

junk·yard ('dʒʌŋkˌjɑːd) *n.* a place where junk is stored or collected for sale.

Ju·no[1] ('dʒuːnəʊ) *n.* **1.** (in Roman tradition) the queen of the Olympian gods. Greek counterpart: **Hera. 2.** a woman of stately bearing and regal beauty.

Ju·no[2] ('dʒuːnəʊ) *n. Astronomy.* the fourth largest known asteroid (approximate diameter 240 kilometres) and one of the four brightest.

Ju·no·esque (ˌdʒuːnəʊ'ɛsk) *adj.* having stately bearing and regal beauty like the goddess Juno.

Junr. *or* **junr.** *abbrev. for* junior.

jun·ta ('dʒʊntə, 'dʒʌn-; *U.S.* 'hʊntə) *n.* **1.** a group of military officers holding the power in a country, esp. after a coup d'état. **2.** Also called: **junto.** a small group of men; cabal, faction, or clique. **3.** a legislative or executive council in some parts of Latin America. [C17: from Spanish: council, from Latin *junctus* joined, from *jungere* to JOIN]

jun·to ('dʒʊntəʊ, 'dʒʌn-) *n., pl.* **·tos.** a cabal, faction, or clique; junta. [C17: variant of JUNTA]

Ju·pi·ter[1] ('dʒuːpɪtə) *n.* (in Roman tradition) the king and ruler of the Olympian gods. Greek counterpart: **Zeus.**

Ju·pi·ter[2] ('dʒuːpɪtə) *n.* the largest of the planets and the fifth from the sun. It has 12 satellites and is surrounded by a system of swirling cloud belts at a temperature of about −130°C. Mean distance from sun: 778 million km; period of revolution around sun: 11.86 years; period of axial rotation: 9.83 hours; diameter and mass: 11.2 and 317.9 times that of earth respectively.

ju·pon ('ʒuːpɒn) *n.* a short close-fitting sleeveless padded garment, used in the late 14th and early 15th centuries with armour. Also called: **gipon.** [C15: from Old French, from Old French *jupe;* see JUMPER[1]]

ju·ra ('dʒʊərə) *n.* the plural of **jus.**

Ju·ra ('dʒʊərə) *n.* **1.** a department of W France, in Franche-Comté region. Capital: Lons-le-Saunier. Pop.: 247 370 (1975). Area: 5055 sq. km (1971 sq. miles). **2.** an island off the W coast of Scotland, in the Inner Hebrides, separated from the mainland by the **Sound of Jura.** Pop.: (with Colonsay) 343 (1971). Area: 381 sq. km (147 sq. miles). **3.** a mountain range in W central Europe, between the Rivers Rhine and Rhône: mostly in E France, extending into W Switzerland. **4.** a range of mountains in the NE quadrant of the moon lying on the N border of the Mare Imbrium.

ju·ral ('dʒʊərəl) *adj.* **1.** of or relating to law or to the administration of justice. **2.** of or relating to rights and obligations. [C17: from Latin *iūs* law + -AL[1]] —**'ju·ral·ly** *adv.*

Ju·ras·sic (dʒʊ'ræsɪk) *adj.* **1.** of, denoting, or formed in the second period of the Mesozoic era, between the Triassic and Cretaceous periods, lasting for 45 million years during which dinosaurs and ammonites flourished. ~*n.* **2. the.** the Jurassic period or rock system. [C19: from French *jurassique*, after the JURA (Mountains)]

ju·rat ('dʒʊəræt) *n.* **1.** *Law.* a statement at the foot of an affidavit, naming the parties, stating when, where, and before whom it was sworn, etc. **2.** (in England) a municipal officer of the Cinque Ports, having a similar position to that of an alderman. **3.** (in France and the Channel Islands) a magistrate. [C16: from Medieval Latin *jūrātus* one who has been sworn, from Latin *jūrāre* to swear]

ju·ra·to·ry ('dʒʊərətərɪ, -trɪ) *adj. Law.* of, relating to, or expressed in an oath.

Jur. D. *abbrev. for* Doctor of Law. [Latin: *Juris Doctor*]

ju·rel (huː'rɛl) *n.* any of several carangid food fishes of the genus *Caranx*, of warm American Atlantic waters. [C18: from Spanish, from Catalan *sorell*, from Late Latin *saurus* horse mackerel, from Greek *sauros* lizard]

ju·rid·i·cal (dʒʊ'rɪdɪkᵊl) *or* **ju·rid·ic** *adj.* of or relating to law, to the administration of justice, or to the office or function of a judge; legal. [C16: from Latin *jūridicus*, from *iūs* law + *dicere* to say] —**ju·'rid·i·cal·ly** *adv.*

ju·rid·i·cal days *pl. n. Law.* days on which the courts are in session. Compare **dies non.**

ju·ris·con·sult (ˌdʒʊərɪs'kɒnsʌlt) *n.* **1.** a person qualified to advise on legal matters. **2.** a master of jurisprudence. [C17: from Latin *jūris consultus;* see JUS, CONSULT]

ju·ris·dic·tion (ˌdʒʊərɪs'dɪkʃən) *n.* **1.** the right or power to administer justice and to apply laws. **2.** the exercise or extent of such right or power. **3.** power or authority in general. [C13: from Latin *jūrisdictiō* administration of justice; see JUS, DICTION] —**ˌju·ris·'dic·tion·al** *adj.* —**ˌju·ris·'dic·tion·al·ly** *adv.* —**ˌju·ris·'dic·tive** *adj.*

jurisp. *abbrev. for* jurisprudence.

ju·ris·pru·dence (ˌdʒʊərɪs'pruːdᵊns) *n.* **1.** the science or philosophy of law. **2.** a system or body of law. **3.** a branch of law: *medical jurisprudence.* [C17: from Latin *jūris prūdentia;* see JUS, PRUDENCE] —**ju·ris·pru·den·tial** (ˌdʒʊərɪspruː'dɛnʃəl) *adj.* —**ˌju·ris·pru·'den·tial·ly** *adv.*

ju·ris·pru·dent (ˌdʒʊərɪs'pruːdᵊnt) *adj.* **1.** skilled in jurisprudence or versed in the principles of law. ~*n.* **2.** a jurisprudent person.

ju·rist ('dʒʊərɪst) *n.* **1.** a person versed in the science of law, esp. Roman or civil law. **2.** a writer on legal subjects. **3.** a student or graduate of law. **4.** (in the U.S.) a lawyer. [C15: from French *juriste*, from Medieval Latin *jūrista;* see JUS]

ju·ris·tic (dʒʊ'rɪstɪk) *or* **ju·ris·ti·cal** *adj.* **1.** of or relating to jurists. **2.** of, relating to, or characteristic of the study of law or the legal profession. —**ju·'ris·ti·cal·ly** *adv.*

ju·ris·tic act *n.* **1.** a proceeding designed to have a legal effect. **2.** an act by an individual aimed at altering, terminating, or otherwise affecting a legal right.

ju·ror ('dʒʊərə) *n.* **1.** a member of a jury. **2.** a person whose name is included on a panel from which a jury is selected. **3.** a person who takes an oath. [C14: from Anglo-French *jurour*, from Old French *jurer* to take an oath, from Latin *jūrāre*]

Ju·ruá (*Portuguese* ʒu'rwa) *n.* a river in South America, rising in E central Peru and flowing northeast across NW Brazil to join the Amazon. Length: 1900 km (1200 miles).

ju·ry[1] ('dʒʊərɪ) *n., pl.* **·ries.** **1.** a group of twelve people sworn to deliver a true verdict according to the evidence upon a case presented in a court of law. See also **grand jury, petit jury. 2.** a body of persons appointed to judge a competition and award prizes. [C14: from Old French *juree*, from *jurer* to swear; see JUROR]

ju·ry[2] ('dʒʊərɪ) *adj. Chiefly nautical.* (in combination) makeshift: *jury-rigged.* [C17: of unknown origin]

ju·ry box *n.* an enclosure where the jury sit in court.

ju·ry·man ('dʒʊərɪmən) *n., pl.* **·men.** a member of a jury.

ju·ry pro·cess *n.* the writ used to summon jurors.

ju·ry-rigged *adj. Chiefly nautical.* set up in a makeshift manner, usually as a result of the loss of regular gear.

jus (dʒʌs) *n., pl.* **ju·ra** ('dʒʊərə). *Law.* **1.** a right, power, or authority. **2.** law in the abstract or as a system, as distinguished from specific enactments. [Latin: law]

jus. *or* **just.** *abbrev. for* justice.

jus ca·no·ni·cum ('dʒʌs kə'nɒnɪkəm) *n.* canon law. [from Latin]

jus ci·vi·le ('dʒʌs sɪ'viːlɪ) *n.* **1.** the civil law of the Roman state. **2.** the body of law derived from the principles of this law. Compare **jus gentium, jus naturale.** [from Latin]

jus di·vi·num ('dʒʌs dɪ'viːnəm) *n.* divine law. [from Latin]

jus gen·ti·um ('dʒʌs 'dʒɛntɪəm) *n. Roman law.* those rules of law common to all nations. [from Latin]

jus na·tu·ra·le ('dʒʌs ˌnætjʊ'reɪlɪ) *n. Roman law.* **1.** (originally) a system of law based on fundamental ideas of right and wrong; natural law. **2.** (in later usage) another term for **jus gentium.** [from Latin]

jus san·gui·nis ('dʒʌs 'sæŋgwɪnɪs) *n. Law.* the principle that a person's nationality at birth is the same as that of his natural parents. Compare **jus soli.** [Latin, literally: law of blood]

jus·sive ('dʒʌsɪv) *adj. Grammar.* another word for **imperative** (sense 3). [C19: from Latin *jūssus* ordered, from *jubēre* to command]

jus so·li ('dʒʌs 'səʊlaɪ) *n. Law.* the principle that a person's nationality at birth is determined by the territory within which he was born. Compare **jus sanguinis.** [from Latin, literally: law of soil]

just *adj.* (dʒʌst). **1. a.** fair or impartial in action or judgment. **b.** (*as n.*): *the just.* **2.** conforming to high moral standards; honest. **3.** consistent with justice: *a just action.* **4.** rightly applied or given; deserved: *a just reward.* **5.** legally valid; lawful: *a just inheritance.* **6.** well-founded; reasonable: *just criticism.* **7.** correct, accurate, or true: *a just account.* ~*adv.* (dʒʌst; *unstressed* dʒəst). **8.** used with forms of *have* to indicate an action performed in the very recent past: *I have just closed the door.* **9.** at this very instant: *he's just coming in to land.* **10.** no more than; merely; only: *just an ordinary car.* **11.** exactly; precisely: *that's just what I mean.* **12.** by a small margin; barely: *he just got there in time.* **13.** (intensifier): *it's just wonderful to see you.* **14. just about. a.** at the point of starting (to do something). **b.** very nearly; almost: *I've just about had enough.* **15. just a moment, second,** *or* **minute.** an expression requesting the hearer to wait or pause for a brief period of time. **16. just so. a.** an expression of complete agreement or of unwillingness to dissent. **b.** conforming precisely to a required standard. [C14: from Latin *jūstus* righteous, from *jūs* justice] —**'just·ly** *adv.* —**'just·ness** *n.*

jus·tice ('dʒʌstɪs) *n.* **1.** the quality or fact of being just. **2.** *Ethics.* the moral principle that determines the fairness of actions, etc. **3.** the administration of law according to prescribed and accepted principles. **4.** conformity to the law; legal validity. **5.** a judge of the Supreme Court of Judicature. **6.** short for **justice of the peace. 7.** good reason (esp. in the phrase **with justice**): *he was disgusted by their behaviour, and with justice.* **8. do justice to. a.** to show to full advantage: *the picture did justice to her beauty.* **b.** to show full appreciation of by action: *he did justice to the meal.* **c.** to treat or judge fairly. **9. do oneself justice.** to make full use of one's abilities. **10. bring to justice.** to capture, try, and usually punish (a criminal, outlaw, etc.). [C12: from Old French, from Latin *jūstitia*, from *justus* JUST]

jus·tice court *n.* an inferior court presided over by a justice of the peace.

jus·tice of the peace *n.* a lay magistrate, appointed by the crown or acting *ex officio*, whose function is to preserve the peace in his area, try summarily such cases as are within his jurisdiction, and perform miscellaneous administrative duties.

jus·tice·ship ('dʒʌstɪsˌʃɪp) *n.* the rank or office of a justice.

jus·ti·ci·a·ble (dʒʌ'stɪʃɪəbᵊl) *adj.* **1.** capable of being determined by a court of law. **2.** liable to be brought before a court for trial; subject to jurisdiction. —**jus·ˌti·ci·a·'bil·i·ty** *n.*

jus·ti·ci·ar (dʒʌ'stɪʃɪˌɑː) *n. English legal history.* the chief political and legal officer from the time of William I to that of Henry III, who deputized for the king in his absence and presided over the kings' courts. Also called: **justiciary.** —**jus·'ti·ci·ar·ˌship** *n.*

jus·ti·ci·ar·y (dʒʌ'stɪʃɪərɪ) *adj.* **1.** of or relating to the administration of justice. ~*n., pl.* **·ar·ies. 2.** an officer or administrator of justice; judge. **3.** another word for **justiciar.**

jus·ti·fi·a·ble ('dʒʌstɪˌfaɪəbᵊl) *adj.* capable of being justified; understandable. —**ˌjus·ti·ˌfi·a·'bil·i·ty** *or* **'jus·ti·ˌfi·a·ble·ness** *n.* —**'jus·ti·ˌfi·a·bly** *adv.*

jus·ti·fi·a·ble hom·i·cide *n.* lawful killing, as in the execution of a death sentence.

jus·ti·fi·ca·tion (ˌdʒʌstɪfɪ'keɪʃən) *n.* **1.** reasonable grounds for complaint, defence, etc. **2.** the act of justifying; proof, vindication, or exculpation. **3.** *Theol.* **a.** the act of justifying. **b.** the process of being justified or the condition of having been justified.

jus·ti·fi·ca·to·ry ('dʒʌstɪfɪˌkeɪtərɪ, -trɪ) *or* **jus·ti·fi·ca·tive** ('dʒʌstɪfɪˌkeɪtɪv) *adj.* serving as justification or capable of justifying; vindicatory.

jus·ti·fy ('dʒʌstɪˌfaɪ) *vb.* **·fies, ·fy·ing, ·fied.** (*mainly tr.*) **1.** (*often passive*) to prove or see to be just or valid; vindicate: *he was certainly justified in taking the money.* **2.** to show to be reasonable; warrant or substantiate: *his behaviour justifies our suspicion.* **3.** to declare or show to be free from blame or guilt; absolve. **4.** *Law.* **a.** to show good reason in court for (some action taken). **b.** to show adequate grounds for doing (that with which a person is charged): *to justify a libel.* **5.** (*also intr.*) *Printing.* to adjust the spaces between words in (a line of type) so that it is of the required length or (of a line of type) to fit exactly. **6. a.** *Protestant theol.* to account or declare righteous by the imputation of Christ's merits to the sinner. **b.** *R.C. theol.* to change from sinfulness to righteousness by the transforming effects of grace. **7.** (*also intr.*) *Law.* to prove (a person) to have sufficient means to act as surety, etc., or (of a person) to qualify to provide bail or surety. [C14: from Old French *justifier*, from Latin *justificāre*, from *jūstus* JUST + *facere* to make] —**'jus·ti·ˌfi·er** *n.* —**'jus·ti·ˌfy·ing·ly** *adv.*

Jus·tin·i·an I (dʒʌ'stɪnɪən) *n.* called *the Great;* Latin name *Flavius Anicius Justinianus.* 483–565 A.D., Byzantine emperor (527–565). He recovered North Africa, SE Spain, and Italy, largely owing to the brilliance of generals such as Belisarius. He sponsored the Justinian Code.

Jus·tin·i·an Code *n.* the codification of Roman law made by order of Justinian I. See **Corpus Juris Civilis.**

Jus·tin Mar·tyr ('dʒʌstɪn) *n.* **Saint.** ?100–?165 A.D., Christian apologist and philosopher. Feast day: April 14.

just in·to·na·tion *n.* a form of tuning employing the pitch intervals of the untempered natural scale, sometimes employed in the playing of the violin, cello, etc.

jus·tle ('dʒʌsᵊl) *vb.* a less common word for **jostle.** —**'jus·tle·ment** *n.* —**'jus·tler** *n.*

just no·tice·a·ble dif·fer·ence *n. Psychol.* the smallest detectable difference between two stimuli. Abbrev.: **j.n.d.**

jut (dʒʌt) *vb.* **juts, jut·ting, jut·ted. 1.** (*intr.;* often foll. by *out*) to stick out or overhang beyond the surface or main part; protrude or project. ~*n.* **2.** something that juts out. [C16: variant of JET[1]] —**'jut·ting·ly** *adv.*

jute (dʒu:t) *n.* **1.** either of two Old World tropical yellow-flowered herbaceous plants, *Corchorus capsularis* or *C. olitorius,* cultivated for their strong fibre: family *Tiliaceae.* **2.** this fibre, used in making sacks, rope, etc. [C18: from Bengali *jhuto,* from Sanskrit *jūta* braid of hair, matted hair]

Jute (dʒu:t) *n.* a member of one of various Germanic tribes, some of whom invaded England in the 6th century A.D., settling in Kent.

Jut+ish ('dʒu:tɪʃ) *adj.* **1.** of or relating to the Jutes. ~*n.* **2.** another name for **Kentish.**

Jut+land ('dʒʌtlənd) *n.* a peninsula of N Europe: forms the continental portion of Denmark and geographically includes the N part of the West German province of Schleswig-Holstein, while politically it includes only the mainland of Denmark and the islands north of Limfjorden; an indecisive naval battle was fought off its NW coast in 1916 between the British and German fleets. Danish name: **Jylland.** —**'Jut+land+er** *n.*

ju+ve•nal ('dʒu:vɪnᵊl) *adj. Ornithol.* a variant spelling (esp. U.S.) of **juvenile** (sense 4).

Ju•ve•nal ('dʒu:vɪnᵊl) *n.* Latin name *Decimus Junius Juvenalis.* ?60–?140 A.D., Roman satirist. In his 16 verse satires, he denounced the vices of imperial Rome.

ju+ve•nes+cence (ˌdʒu:vɪ'nɛsəns) *n.* **1.** youth or immaturity. **2.** the act or process of growing from childhood to youth. **3.** restoration of youth; rejuvenation.

ju+ve•nes+cent (ˌdʒu:vɪ'nɛsᵊnt) *adj.* becoming or being young or youthful. [C19: from Latin *juvenēscere* to grow up, regain strength, from *juvenis* youthful]

ju+ve•nile ('dʒu:vɪˌnaɪl) *adj.* **1.** young, youthful, or immature. **2.** suitable or designed for young people: *juvenile pastimes.* **3.** (of animals or plants) not yet fully mature. **4.** of or denoting young birds that have developed their first plumage of adult feathers. ~*n.* **5.** a juvenile person, animal, or plant. **6.** an actor who performs youthful roles. **7.** a book intended for young readers. [C17: from Latin *juvenīlis* youthful, from *juvenis* young] —**'ju+ve•ˌnile+ly** *adv.* —**'ju+ve•ˌnile+ness** *n.*

ju+ve•nile court *n.* a court that deals with juvenile offenders and children beyond parental control or in need of care.

ju+ve•nile de+lin+quen+cy *n.* antisocial or criminal conduct by juvenile delinquents.

ju+ve•nile de+lin+quent *n.* a child or young person guilty of some offence, act of vandalism, or antisocial behaviour or whose conduct is beyond parental control and who may be brought before a juvenile court.

ju+ve•nile hor+mone *n.* a hormone, secreted by insects from a pair of glands behind the brain, that promotes the growth of larval characteristics and inhibits metamorphosis.

ju+ve•nil•i•a (ˌdʒu:vɪ'nɪlɪə) *pl. n.* works of art, literature, or music produced in youth or adolescence, before the artist, author, or composer has formed a mature style. [C17: from Latin, literally: youthful things; see JUVENILE]

ju+ve•nil+i•ty (ˌdʒu:vɪ'nɪlɪtɪ) *n., pl.* **•ties. 1.** the quality or condition of being juvenile, esp. of being immature. **2.** (*often pl.*) a juvenile act or manner. **3.** juveniles collectively.

jux+ta+pose (ˌdʒʌkstə'pəʊz) *vb.* (*tr.*) to place close together or side by side. [C19: back formation from *juxtaposition,* from Latin *juxta* next to + POSITION] —**ˌjux+ta+po+'si+tion** *n.* —**ˌjux+ta+po+'si+tion+al** *adj.*

J.W.V. *abbrev. for* Jewish War Veterans.

Jyl+land ('jylan) *n.* the Danish name for **Jutland.**

K

k *or* **K** (keɪ) *n., pl.* **k's, K's,** *or* **Ks. 1.** the 11th letter and 8th consonant of the modern English alphabet. **2.** a speech sound represented by this letter, usually a voiceless velar stop, as in *kitten.*

k *symbol for:* **1.** kilo(s). **2.** *Maths.* the unit vector along the *z*-axis.

K *symbol for:* **1.** kelvin(s). **2.** *Chess.* king. **3.** *Chem.* potassium. [from New Latin *kalium*] **4.** *Physics.* kaon. **5.** one thousand. [from KILO-] **6.** *Computer technol.* a unit of 1024 words, bytes, or bits.

K. *or* **k.** *abbrev. for:* **1.** (*not cap.*) karat. **2.** king. **3.** *Currency.* **a.** kip. **b.** kopeck. **c.** krona. **d.** krone. **4.** knight. **5.** (*cap.*) Köchel: indicating the serial number in the catalogue (1862) of the works of Mozart made by Ludwig von Köchel, 1800–77.

K2 *n.* a mountain in N India, in N Kashmir in the Karakoram Range: the second highest mountain in the world. Height: 8610 m (28 250 ft.). Also called: **Godwin Austen, Dapsang.**

ka (kɑː) *n.* (in ancient Egypt) an attendant spirit supposedly dwelling as a vital force in a man or statue. [from Egyptian]

Kaa+ba *or* **Caa+ba** (ˈkɑːbə) *n.* a cube-shaped building in Mecca, the most sacred Muslim pilgrim shrine, into which is built the black stone believed to have been given by Gabriel to Abraham. Muslims turn in its direction when praying. [from Arabic *ka'bah,* from *ka'b* cube]

kab (kæb) *n.* a variant spelling of **cab**[2].

ka+ba+ka (kaˈbaka) *n.* any of the former rulers of the Baganda people of S Uganda. [C19: from Luganda]

Ka+ba+le·ga Falls (ˌkɑːbəˈleɪgə) *pl. n.* rapids on the lower Victoria Nile, about 35 km (22 miles) east of Lake Albert, where the Nile drops 120 m (400 ft.).

ka+ba+ra+go+ya (kəˌbɑːrəˈgəʊjə) *n.* a very large monitor lizard, *Varanus salvator,* of SE Asia: it grows to a length of three metres. Also called: **Malayan monitor.** [perhaps Tagalog]

Ka+bar·di·no-Bal·kar Au·ton·o+mous So+vi+et So+cial+ist Re+pub+lic (ˌkæbəˈdiːnəʊˌbælkə) *n.* an administrative division of the S Soviet Union, on the N side of the Caucasus Mountains. Capital: Nalchik. Pop.: 588 203 (1970). Area: 12 500 sq. km (4825 sq. miles).

kab+ba+la *or* **ka+ba+la** (kəˈbɑːlə) *n.* variant spellings of **cabbala.** —**kab+ba+lism** *or* **kab·a+lism** (ˈkæbəˌlɪzəm) *n.* —**ˈkab+ba+list** *or* **ˈkab·a+list** *n.* —**ˌkab+ba+ˈlis+tic** *or* **ˌkab·a+ˈlis+tic** *adj.*

ka+bob (kəˈbɒb) *n.* another name for **kebab.**

ka+bu+ki (kəˈbuːkɪ) *n.* a form of Japanese drama based on popular legends and characterized by elaborate costumes, stylized acting, and the use of male actors for all roles. See also **No**[1]. [Japanese, from *kabu* music and dancing + *ki* art]

Ka+bul (kəˈbʊl, ˈkɔːbᵊl) *n.* **1.** the capital of Afghanistan, in the northeast of the country at an altitude of 1800 m (5900 ft.) on the **Kabul River:** over 3000 years old, with a strategic position commanding passes through the Hindu Kush and main routes to the Khyber Pass; destroyed and rebuilt many times; capital of the Mogul Empire from 1504 until 1738 and of Afghanistan from 1773; university (1932). Pop.: 318 094 (1971 est.). **2.** a river in Afghanistan and Pakistan, rising in the Hindu Kush and flowing east into the Indus at Attock, Pakistan. Length: 700 km (435 miles).

Ka+byle (kəˈbaɪl) *n.* **1.** (*pl.* **+byles** *or* **+byle**) a member of a Berber people inhabiting the E Atlas Mountains in Tunisia and Algeria. **2.** the dialect of Berber spoken by this people. [C19: from Arabic *qabā'il,* plural of *qabīlah* tribe]

ka+chang pu+teh (ˈkatʃaŋ puːˈteɪ) *n.* (in Malaysia) roasted or fried nuts or beans. [from Malay, literally: white beans]

ka+chi+na (kəˈtʃiːnə) *n.* any of the supernatural beings believed by the Hopi Indians to be the ancestors of living humans. [from Hopi *qačina* supernatural]

Ká·dár (ˈkɑːdɑːr) *n.* **Já·nos** (ˈjɑːnɒʃ). born 1912, Hungarian statesman; Communist prime minister of Hungary (1956–58; 1961–65) and first secretary of the Communist Party since 1965.

Kad+dish (ˈkædɪʃ) *n., pl.* **Kad+di+shim** (kæˈdɪʃɪm). **1.** an ancient Jewish liturgical prayer consisting of a doxology of three to six verses. **2.** a form of this prayer used on the anniversary of a death and during the eleven-month period of mourning after a death. [C17: from Aramaic *qaddīsh* holy]

ka·di (ˈkɑːdɪ, ˈkeɪdɪ) *n., pl.* **·dis.** a variant spelling of **cadi.**

Ka+di+yev+ka (*Russian* ˈkadijɪfkə) *n.* a city in the S Soviet Union, in the E Ukrainian SSR in the Donbass: coal-mining centre. Pop.: 141 000 (1975 est.).

Ka+du+na (kəˈduːnə) *n.* **1.** a state of N Nigeria. Capital: Kaduna. Pop.: 4 098 305 (1976 est.). Area: 68 989 sq. km (26 631 sq. miles). Former name (until 1976): **North-Central State. 2.** a city in N central Nigeria, capital of Kaduna state on the **Kaduna River** (a principal tributary of the Niger). Pop.: 202 000 (1975 est.).

Kaf+fir *or* **Kaf+ir** (ˈkæfə) *n., pl.* **+firs, +fir** *or* **+irs, +ir. 1.** *Offensive.* **a.** (in southern Africa) any Black African. **b.** (*as modifier*): *Kaffir farming.* **2.** a former name for the **Xhosa** language. **3.** *Offensive.* (among Muslims) a non-Muslim or infidel. [C19: from Arabic *kāfir* infidel, from *kafara* to deny, refuse to believe]

kaf+fir beer *n. S. African.* beer made from sorghum (kaffir corn) or millet.

kaf+fir corn *or U.S.* (*sometimes*) **kaf+ir corn** *n.* a Southern African variety of sorghum, cultivated in dry regions for its grain and as fodder. Sometimes shortened to **kaffir** or (U.S.) **kafir.**

Kaf+firs (ˈkæfəz) *pl. n. Stock Exchange.* South African mining shares.

Kaf+frar·i·a (kæˈfrɛərɪə) *n.* a former region of South Africa, in E Cape Province: inhabited chiefly by the Kaffirs; British Kaffraria was a crown colony established in 1853 in the southwest of the region and annexed to Cape Colony in 1865. —**Kaf+ˈfrar+i·an** *adj., n.*

Kaf+ir (ˈkæfə) *n., pl.* **+irs** *or* **+ir. 1.** another name for the **Nuri. 2.** a variant spelling of **Kaffir.** [C19: from Arabic; see KAFFIR]

Ka+fi+ri+stan (ˌkæfɪrɪˈstɑːn) *n.* the former name of **Nuristan.**

Kaf·ka (ˈkæfkə; *Czech* ˈkafka) *n.* **Franz** (frants). 1883–1924, Czech novelist writing in German. In his two main novels *The Trial* (1925) and *The Castle* (1926), published posthumously against his wishes, he portrays man's fear, isolation, and bewilderment in a nightmarish dehumanized world. —**Kaf·ka+esque** (ˌkæfkəˈɛsk) *adj.*

kaf+tan *or* **caf+tan** (ˈkæftæn, -ˌtɑːn) *n.* **1.** a long coatlike garment, usually worn with a belt and made of rich fabric, worn in the East. **2.** an imitation of this, worn, esp. by women, in the West, consisting of a loose dress with long wide sleeves. [C16: from Turkish *qaftān*]

Ka+ge·ra (kæˈgɛrə) *n.* a river in E Africa, rising in headstreams on the border between Tanzania and Rwanda and flowing east to Lake Victoria: the most remote headstream of the Nile and largest tributary of Lake Victoria. Length: about 480 km (300 miles).

Ka+go+shi+ma (ˌkɑːgɔːˈʃiːmə) *n.* a port in SW Japan, on S Kyushu. Pop.: 443 966 (1974 est.).

ka·gu (ˈkɑːguː) *n.* a crested nocturnal bird, *Rhynochetos jubatus,* with a red bill and greyish plumage: occurs only in New Caledonia and is nearly extinct: family *Rhynochetidae,* order *Gruiformes* (cranes, rails, etc.). [native name in New Caledonia]

Kahn (kɑːn) *n.* **Her·man.** born 1922, U.S. mathematician and futurologist; director since 1961 of the Hudson Institute.

kai+ak (ˈkaɪæk) *n.* a variant spelling of **kayak.**

Kai+e·teur Falls (ˌkaɪəˈtʊə) *pl. n.* a waterfall in Guyana, on the Potaro River. Height: 226 m (741 ft.). Width: about 107 m (350 ft.).

kaif (kaɪf) *n.* a variant spelling of **kif.**

Kai+feng (ˈkaɪˈfɛŋ) *n.* a city in E China, in N Honan on the Yellow River: one of the oldest cities in China and its capital (as Pien-liang) from 907 to 1126. Pop.: 450 000 (1970 est.).

kail (keɪl) *n.* a variant spelling of **kale.**

kail+yard (ˈkeɪlˌjɑːd) *n.* a variant spelling of **kaleyard.**

kain (keɪn) *n. History.* a variant spelling of **cain.**

kai+nite (ˈkaɪnaɪt) *n.* a white mineral consisting of potassium chloride and magnesium sulphate: a fertilizer and source of potassium salts. Formula: $KCl.MgSO_4.3H_2O$. [C19: from German *Kainit,* from Greek *kainos* new + -ITE[1]]

kai+no+gen+e·sis (ˌkaɪnəʊˈdʒɛnɪsɪs) *n.* another name for **caenogenesis.** —**kai+no+ge+net+ic** (ˌkaɪnəʊdʒəˈnɛtɪk) *adj.* —**ˌkai+no+ge·ˈnet+i·cal+ly** *adv.*

Kair+ouan (*French* kɛˈrwã), **Kair+wan,** *or* **Qair+wan** (kaɪəˈwɑːn) *n.* a city in NE Tunisia: one of the holy cities of Islam; pilgrimage and trading centre. Pop.: 82 229 (1969).

Kai+ser[1] (ˈkaɪzə) *n.* (*sometimes not cap.*) *History.* **1.** either German emperor, esp. Wilhelm II (1888–1918). **2.** *Obsolete.* any Austro-Hungarian emperor. [C16: from German, ultimately from Latin *Caesar* emperor, from the cognomen of Gaius Julius CAESAR] —**ˈkai+ser+dom** *or* **ˈkai+ser+ism** *n.*

Kai·ser[2] (*German* ˈkaɪzər) *n.* **Ge·org** (ˈgeːɔrk). 1878–1945, German expressionist dramatist.

Kai+sers+lau+tern (*German* ˌkaɪzərsˈlautərn) *n.* a city in West Germany, in S Rhineland-Palatinate. Pop.: 102 450 (1974 est.).

ka·ka (ˈkɑːkə) *n.* a green New Zealand parrot, *Nestor meridionalis,* with a long compressed bill. [C18: from Maori, perhaps imitative of its call]

ka+ka+po (ˈkɑːkəˌpəʊ) *n., pl.* **+pos.** a ground-living nocturnal parrot, *Strigops habroptilus,* of New Zealand, resembling an owl. [C19: from Maori, literally: night kaka]

ka+ke·mo+no (ˌkækɪˈməʊnəʊ) *n., pl.* **+nos.** a Japanese paper or silk wall hanging, usually long and narrow, with a picture or inscription on it and a roller at the bottom. [C19: from Japanese, from *kake* hanging + *mono* thing]

ka·ki (ˈkɑːkɪ) *n., pl.* **+kis.** another name for **Japanese persimmon.** [Japanese]

ka·la-a·zar (ˌkɑːləəˈzɑː) *n.* a tropical infectious disease caused by the protozoan *Leishmania donovani* in the liver, spleen, etc., characterized by fever and weight loss; visceral leishmaniasis.

Ka+la+ha+ri (ˌkæləˈhɑːrɪ) *n.* **the.** an extensive arid plateau of

South Africa, South West Africa, and Botswana: inhabited by Bushmen. Also called: **Kalahari Desert.**

Kal·a·ma·zoo (ˌkæləmə'zuː) *n.* a city in SW Michigan, midway between Detroit and Chicago. Pop.: 85 555 (1970).

Ka·lat *or* **Khe·lat** (kə'lɑːt) *n.* a division of SW Pakistan, in S Baluchistan: formerly a princely state ruled by the Khan of Kalat, which joined Pakistan in 1948. Capital: Kalat. Pop.: 156 480 (1961). Area: 65 610 sq. km (25 332 sq. miles).

kale *or* **kail** (keɪl) *n.* **1.** a cultivated variety of cabbage, *Brassica oleracea acephala,* with crinkled leaves: used as a potherb. See also **collard. 2.** *Scot.* a cabbage. **3.** *U.S. slang.* money. ~Compare (for senses 1, 2) **sea kale.** [Old English *cāl;* see COLE]

ka·lei·do·scope (kə'laɪdəˌskəʊp) *n.* **1.** an optical toy for producing symmetrical patterns by multiple reflections in inclined mirrors enclosed in a tube. Loose pieces of coloured glass, paper, etc., are placed in the tube between the mirrors and as this is turned, changing patterns are formed. **2.** any complex pattern of frequently changing shapes and colours. **3.** a complicated set of circumstances. [C19: from Greek *kalos* beautiful + *eidos* form + -SCOPE] **—ka·lei·do·scop·ic** (kəˌlaɪdə'skɒpɪk) *adj.* **—ka·ˌlei·do·'scop·i·cal·ly** *adv.*

kal·ends ('kælɪndz) *pl. n.* a variant spelling of **calends.**

Ka·le·va·la (ˌkɑːlə'vɑːlə; *Finnish* 'kɑlɛˌvɑlɑ) *n.* *Finnish legend.* **1.** the land of the hero Kaleva, who performed legendary exploits. **2.** the Finnish national epic in which these exploits are recounted, compiled by Elias Lönnrot from folk poetry in 1835 to 1849. [Finnish, from *kaleva* of a hero + *-la* dwelling place, home]

kale·yard *or* **kail·yard** ('keɪlˌjɑːd) *n.* *Scot.* a vegetable garden. [C19, literally: cabbage garden]

kale·yard school *n.* a group of writers who depicted the sentimental and homely aspects of life in the Scottish Lowlands from about 1880 to 1914. The best known contributor to the school was J. M. Barrie.

Kal·gan ('kɑːl'gɑːn) *n.* a former name of **Changchiakow.**

Kal·goor·lie (kæl'gʊəlɪ) *n.* a city in Western Australia, adjoining the town of Boulder: a centre of the Coolgardie gold rushes of the early 1890s; declining gold resources superseded by the discovery of nickel ore in 1966. Pop.: 20 784 (including Boulder) (1971).

kal·i ('kælɪ, 'keɪ-) *n.* another name for **saltwort** (sense 1).

Ka·li ('kɑːlɪ) *n.* the Hindu goddess of destruction, consort of Siva. Her cult was characterized by savagery and cannibalism.

kal·ian (kæl'jɑːn) *n.* another name for **hookah.** [C19: from Persian, from Arabic *qalyān*]

Ka·li·da·sa (ˌkælɪ'dɑːsə) *n.* ?5th century A.D., Indian dramatist and poet, noted for his romantic verse drama *Sakuntala.*

ka·lif ('keɪlɪf, 'kæl-) *n.* a variant spelling of **caliph.**

Ka·li·man·tan (ˌkælɪ'mæntən) *n.* the Indonesian name for Borneo: applied to the Indonesian part of the island only, excluding the Malaysian states of Sabah and Sarawak and the sultanate of Brunei. Pop.: 5 152 166 (1971).

Ka·li·nin[1] (*Russian* ka'linin) *n.* a city in the central Soviet Union, at the confluence of the Volga and Tversta Rivers: chief port of the upper Volga, linked by canal with Moscow. Pop.: 389 000 (1975 est.). Former name (until 1932): **Tver.**

Ka·li·nin[2] (*Russian* ka'linin) *n.* **Mi·kha·il I·va·no·vich** (mixa'il i'vanəvitʃ). 1875–1946, Soviet statesman: titular head of state (1919–46); a founder of *Pravda* (1912).

Ka·li·nin·grad (*Russian* kəlinin'grat) *n.* a port in the W Soviet Union, on the Pregolya River: severely damaged in World War II as the chief German naval base on the Baltic; ceded to the Soviet Union in 1945 and is now its chief Baltic naval base. Pop.: 338 000 (1975 est.). Former name (until 1946): **Königsberg.**

Ka·lisz (*Polish* 'kalijʃ) *n.* a town in central Poland, on an island in the Prosna River: textile industry. Pop.: 83 600 (1972 est.). Ancient name: **Calissia.**

Ka·li·yu·ga (ˌkɑːlɪ'juːgə) *n.* (in Hindu mythology) the fourth (present) age of the world, characterized by total decadence.

Kal·mar (*Swedish* 'kalmar) *n.* a port in SE Sweden, partly on the mainland and partly on a small island in the **Sound of Kalmar,** opposite Öland: scene of the signing of the Union of Kalmar, which united Sweden, Denmark, and Norway into a single monarchy (1397–1523). Pop.: 52 774 (1970).

kal·mi·a ('kælmɪə) *n.* any evergreen ericaceous shrub of the North American genus *Kalmia,* having showy clusters of white or pink flowers. See also: **mountain laurel.** [C18: named after Peter *Kalm* (1715–79), Swedish botanist and pupil of Linnaeus]

Kal·muck ('kælmʌk) *or* **Kal·myk** ('kælmɪk) *n.* **1.** (*pl.* **·mucks, ·muck** *or* **·myks, ·myk**) a member of a Mongoloid people of Buddhist tradition, who migrated from NE China in the 17th century. **2.** the language of this people, belonging to the Mongolic branch of the Altaic family.

Kal·muck Au·ton·o·mous So·vi·et So·cial·ist Re·pub·lic *n.* an administrative division of the S Soviet Union, on the Caspian Sea: became subject to Russia in 1646. Capital: Elista. Pop.: 267 993 (1970). Area: 75 900 sq. km (29 300 sq. miles). Also called: **Kalmyk Autonomous Soviet Socialist Republic.**

ka·long ('kɑːlɒŋ) *n.* any fruit bat of the genus *Pteropus;* a flying fox. [Javanese]

kal·pa ('kælpə) *n.* (in Hindu cosmology) a period in which the universe experiences a cycle of creation and destruction. [C18: Sanskrit]

kal·pak ('kælpæk) *n.* a variant spelling of **calpac.**

kal·so·mine ('kælsəˌmaɪn, -mɪn) *n.* a variant spelling of **calcimine.**

Ka·lu·ga (*Russian* ka'lugə) *n.* a city in the central Soviet Union, on the Oka River. Pop.: 247 000 (1975 est.).

Ka·ma[1] (*Russian* 'kamə) *n.* a river in the E Soviet Union, rising in the Ural Mountains and flowing to the River Volga, of which it is the largest tributary. Length: 2030 km (1260 miles).

Ka·ma[2] ('kɑːmə) *n.* the Hindu god of love. [from Sanskrit]

kam·a·cite ('kæməˌsaɪt) *n.* an alloy of iron and nickel, occurring in meteorites. [C19: from (obsolete) German *Kamacit,* from Greek *kamax* shaft, pole + -ITE[1]]

Kam·a·ku·ra (ˌkɑːmə'kʊərə) *n.* a city in central Japan, on S Honshu: famous for its Great Buddha (Daibutsu), a 13th-century bronze, 15 m (49 ft.) high. Pop.: 163 117 (1974 est.).

ka·ma·la (kə'mɑːlə, 'kæmələ) *n.* **1.** an East Indian euphorbiaceous tree, *Mallotus philippinensis.* **2.** a powder obtained from the seed capsules of this tree, used as a dye and formerly as a worm powder. [C19: from Sanskrit, probably of Dravidian origin; compare Kanarese *kōmale*]

Ka·ma·su·tra (ˌkɑːmə'suːtrə) *n.* **the.** an ancient Hindu text on erotic pleasure and other topics. [Sanskrit: book on love, from *kāma* love + *sūtra* thread]

Kam·chat·ka (*Russian* kam'tʃatkə) *n.* a peninsula in the E Soviet Union, between the Sea of Okhotsk and the Bering Sea. Length: about 1200 km (750 miles). **—Kam·'chat·kan** *adj., n.*

kame (keɪm) *n.* an irregular mound or ridge of gravel, sand, etc., deposited by water derived from melting glaciers. [C19: Scottish and northern English variant of COMB]

Ka·mensk-U·ral·ski (*Russian* 'kamɪnsk u'ralskɪj) *n.* an industrial city in the W Soviet Union. Pop.: 181 000 (1975 est.).

Ka·me·rad *German.* (ˌkamə'raːt; *English* 'kæməˌrɑːd) *n.* a shout of surrender, used by German soldiers. [German: COMRADE]

Ka·me·run (ˌkamə'ruːn) *n.* the German name for **Cameroon.**

Ka·met ('kɑːmɛt, 'kʌmeɪt) *n.* a mountain in N India, in Uttar Pradesh in the Himalayas. Height: 7756 m (25 447 ft.).

ka·mi ('kɑːmɪ) *n., pl.* **·mi.** a divine being or spiritual force in Shinto. [C18: from Japanese: god, lord]

ka·mi·ka·ze (ˌkæmɪ'kɑːzɪ) *n.* (*often cap.*) **1.** (in World War II) **a.** one of a group of Japanese pilots who performed suicidal missions by crashing their aircraft, loaded with explosives, into an enemy target, esp. a ship. **b.** (*as modifier*): *a kamikaze attack.* **2.** an aircraft used for such a mission. [C20: from Japanese, from *kami* divine + *kaze* wind]

Kam·pa·la (kæm'pɑːlə) *n.* the capital and largest city of Uganda, in Buganda province on Lake Victoria: Makerere University (1961). Pop.: 330 700 (1969).

kam·pong ('kæmpɒŋ, kæm'pɒŋ) *n.* (in Malaysia) a village. Also called: **compound.** [C19: from Malay]

Kam·pu·che·a (ˌkæmpʊ'tʃɪə) *n.* the official name (since 1976) of **Cambodia.**

kam·seen (kæm'siːn) *or* **kam·sin** ('kæmsɪn) *n.* a variant spelling of **khamsin.**

ka·na ('kɑːnə) *n.* the Japanese syllabary, which consists of two written varieties. See **hiragana, katakana.** [C18: from Japanese, literally: false letters; compare KANJI, which are regarded as real letters]

Ka·nak·a (kə'nækə, 'kænəkə) *n.* **1.** (esp. in Hawaii) a native Hawaiian. **2.** (*often not cap.*) any native of the South Pacific islands, esp. (formerly) one abducted to work in Australia. [C19: from Hawaiian: man, human being]

kan·a·my·cin (ˌkænə'maɪsɪn) *n.* an antibiotic obtained from the soil bacterium *Streptomyces kanamyceticus,* used in the treatment of various infections, esp. those caused by Gram-negative bacteria. Formula: $C_{18}H_{36}N_4O_{11}$. [C20: from New Latin *kanamyceticus*]

Ka·nan·ga (kə'næŋgə) *n.* a city in SW Zaïre: a commercial centre on the railway from Lubumbashi to Port Francqui. Pop.: 601 239 (1974 est.). Former name (until 1966): **Luluabourg.**

Ka·na·ra *or* **Ca·na·ra** (kə'nɑːrə) *n.* a region of SW India, in Karnataka on the Deccan Plateau and the W Coast. Area: about 155 000 sq. km (60 000 sq. miles).

Ka·na·rese *or* **Ca·na·rese** (ˌkænə'riːz) *n.* **1.** (*pl.* **·rese**) a member of a people of S India living chiefly in Kanara. **2.** the language of this people; Kannada.

Kan·a·za·wa (ˌkænə'zɑːwə) *n.* a port in central Japan, on W Honshu: textile and porcelain industries. Pop.: 383 451 (1974 est.).

Kan·chen·jun·ga (ˌkæntʃən'dʒʌŋgə) *n.* a variant spelling of **Kangchenjunga.**

Kan·chi·pu·ram (kɑːn'tʃiːpərəm) *n.* a city in SE India, in Tamil Nadu: a sacred Hindu town known as "the Benares of the South"; textile industries. Pop.: 110 657 (1971).

Kan·da·har (ˌkændə'hɑː) *n.* a city in S Afghanistan: an important trading centre, built by Ahmad Shah Durrani (1724–73) as his capital on the site of several former cities. Pop.: 140 024 (1973 est.).

Kan·din·sky (*Russian* kan'dinskij) *n.* **Va·si·li** (va'silij). 1866–1944, Russian expressionist painter and theorist, regarded as the first to develop an entirely abstract style: a founder of *der Blaue Reiter.*

Kan·dy ('kændɪ) *n.* a city in central Sri Lanka: capital of the kingdom of Kandy from 1480 until 1815, when occupied by the British; sacred Buddhist temple; University of Sri Lanka. Pop.: 94 000 (1971).

kan·ga *or* **khan·ga** ('kɑːŋgɑː) *n.* a piece of gaily decorated thin cotton cloth used as a garment by women in E Africa. [from Swahili]

kan·ga·roo (ˌkæŋgə'ruː) *n., pl.* **·roos. 1.** any large herbivorous marsupial of the genus *Macropus* and related genera, of Australia and New Guinea, having large powerful hind legs, used for leaping, and a long thick tail: family *Macropodidae*. See also **rat kangaroo, tree kangaroo.** ~*vb.* **2.** *Informal.* (of a car) to move forward or to cause (a car) to move forward with short sudden jerks, as a result of improper use of the clutch. [C18: probably from a native Australian language] —ˌ**kan·ga·ˈroo-ˌlike** *adj.*

kan+ga+roo clos+ure *n. Parliamentary procedure.* a form of closure in which the chairman or speaker selects certain amendments for discussion and excludes others. Compare **guillotine** (sense 4).

kan+ga+roo court *n.* an irregular court, esp. one set up by prisoners in a jail or by trade unionists.

kan+ga+roo grass *n.* a tall widespread Australian grass, *Themeda australis,* which is highly palatable to cattle and is used for fodder.

Kan+ga+roo Is+land *n.* an island in the Indian Ocean, off South Australia. Area: 4350 sq. km (1680 sq. miles).

kan+ga+roo paw *n.* any plant of the Australian genus *Anigozanthos,* having green-and-red hairy flowers: family *Haemodoraceae.*

kan+ga+roo rat *n.* **1.** any small leaping rodent of the genus *Dipodomys,* related to the squirrels and inhabiting desert regions of North America, having a stocky body and very long hind legs and tails: family *Heteromyidae.* **2.** Also called: **kangaroo mouse.** any of several leaping murine rodents of the Australian genus *Notomys.*

Kang+chen+jun+ga, Kan+chen+jun+ga (ˌkæntʃənˈdʒʌŋgə), *or* **Kin+chin+jun+ga** *n.* a mountain on the border between Nepal and Sikkim, in the Himalayas: the third highest mountain in the world. Height: 8600 m (28 216 ft.).

K'ang-te (ˈkæŋ ˈteɪ) *n.* title as emperor of Manchukuo of (Henry) **Pu-yi.**

Ka+Ngwa+ne (ˌkɑːᵊŋˈgwɑːneɪ) *n.* a Bantustan in South Africa, in E Transvaal. Capital: Schoemansdal. Former name: **Swazi Territory.**

kan+ji (ˈkændʒɪ, ˈkɑːn-) *n., pl.* **+ji** *or* **+jis.** a Japanese syllabary derived from Chinese orthography. [Japanese, from Chinese *hantzû,* from *han* Chinese + *tsû* word, character]

Kan+na+da (ˈkɑːnədə, ˈkæn-) *n.* a language of S India belonging to the Dravidian family of languages: the state language of Karnataka, also spoken in Madras and Maharashtra. Also called: **Kanarese.**

Ka·no (ˈkɑːnəʊ, ˈkeɪnəʊ) *n.* **1.** a state of N Nigeria: consists of wooded savanna in the south and scrub vegetation in the north. Capital: Kano. Pop.: 5 774 842 (1976 est.). Area: 42 593 sq. km (16 442 sq. miles). **2.** a city in N Nigeria, capital of Kano state: transport and market centre. Pop.: 399 000 (1975 est.).

Kan+pur (kɑːnˈpʊə) *n.* an industrial city in NE India, in S Uttar Pradesh on the River Ganges: scene of the massacre by Nana Sahib of British soldiers and European families in 1857. Pop.: 1 154 388 (1971). Former name: **Cawnpore.**

Kans. *abbrev. for* Kansas.

Kan+sas (ˈkænzəs) *n.* a state of the central U.S.: consists of undulating prairie, drained chiefly by the Arkansas, Kansas, and the Missouri Rivers; mainly agricultural. Capital: Topeka. Pop.: 2 249 071 (1970). Area: 211 828 sq. km (81 787 sq. miles). Abbrevs.: **Kan., Kans.,** or (with zip code) **KS**

Kan+sas Cit·y *n.* **1.** a city in W Missouri, at the confluence of the Missouri and Kansas Rivers: important centre of livestock and meat-packing industry. Pop.: 487 799 (1973 est.). **2.** a city in NE Kansas, adjacent to Kansas City, Missouri. Pop.: 172 994 (1973 est.).

Kan+su (ˈkænˈsuː) *n.* a province of NW China, between Tibet and Inner Mongolia: mountainous, with desert regions; forms a corridor, the old Silk Road, much used in early and medieval times for trade with Turkistan, India, and Persia. Capital: Lanchow. Pop.: 18 000 000 (1976 est.). Area: 355 100 sq. km (137 100 sq. miles).

Kant (kænt; *German* kant) *n.* **Im·man·u·el** (iˈmaːnʊˌeːl). 1724–1804, German idealist philosopher. He sought to determine the limits of man's knowledge in *Critique of Pure Reason* (1781) and propounded his system of ethics as guided by the categorical imperative in *Critique of Practical Reason* (1788). —**ˈKant+i·an** (ˈkæntɪən) *adj., n.* —**ˈKant·i·an+ism** *or* **ˈKant+ism** *n.*

kan+tar (kænˈtɑː) *n.* a unit of weight used in E Mediterranean countries, equivalent to 100 pounds or 45 kilograms but varying from place to place. [C16: from Arabic *qinṭār,* from Late Greek *kentēnarion* weight of a hundred pounds, from Late Latin *centēnārium,* from *centum* hundred]

KANU (ˈkɑːnuː) *n. acronym for* Kenya African National Union.

kan+zu (ˈkænzʊ) *n.* a long garment, usually white, with long sleeves, worn by E African men. [C20: from Swahili]

Kao+hsiung *or* **Kao-hsiung** (ˈkaʊˈʃjʊŋ) *n.* a port in SW Taiwan, on the South China Sea: the chief port of the island. Pop.: 884 000 (1972 est.). Japanese name: **Takao.**

Ka·o+lack (ˈkɑːəʊˌlæk, ˈkaʊlæk) *n.* a port in SW Senegal, on the Saloum River. Pop.: 95 000 (1970 est.).

ka·o+li+ang (ˌkeɪəʊlɪˈæŋ) *n.* any of various E Asian varieties of the sorghum *Sorghum vulgare.* [from Chinese *kao* tall + *liang* grain]

ka·o+lin *or* **ka·o+line** (ˈkeɪəlɪn) *n.* a fine white clay used for the manufacture of hard-paste porcelain and bone china and in medicine as a poultice and gastrointestinal absorbent. Also called: **china clay, china stone.** [C18: from French, from Chinese *Kaoling* Chinese mountain where supplies for Europe were first obtained, from *kao* high + *ling* hill] —ˌ**ka·o·ˈlin+ic** *adj.*

ka·o+lin+ite (ˈkeɪəlɪˌnaɪt) *n.* a white or grey clay mineral consisting of hydrated aluminium silicate in triclinic crystalline form, the main constituent of kaolin. Formula: $Al_2Si_2O_5(OH)_4$.

ka·on (ˈkeɪɒn) *n.* a meson that has a positive or negative charge and a rest mass of about 996 electron masses, or no charge and a rest mass of 964 electron masses. Also called: **K-meson.** [C20: *ka* representing the letter *k* + (MES)ON]

ka+pell+meis+ter (kæˈpɛlˌmaɪstə) *n., pl.* **+ter.** a person in charge of an orchestra, esp. the private orchestra of an 18th century German prince. See also **maestro di cappella.** [German, from *Kapelle* chapel + *Meister* MASTER]

Kap+fen+berg (*German* ˈkapfᵊnˌbɛrk) *n.* an industrial town in E Austria, in Styria. Pop.: 26 001 (1971).

kaph (kɔːf, kɑːf; *Hebrew* kaf) *n.* the 11th letter of the Hebrew alphabet (כ or, at the end of a word, ך) transliterated as *k* or, when final, *kh.* [Hebrew, literally: palm of the hand]

ka+pok (ˈkeɪpɒk) *n.* a silky fibre obtained from the hairs covering the seeds of a tropical bombacaceous tree, *Ceiba pentandra* (**kapok tree** or **silk-cotton tree**): used for stuffing pillows, etc., and for sound insulation. Also called: **silk cotton.** [C18: from Malay]

kap+pa (ˈkæpə) *n.* the tenth letter in the Greek alphabet (Κ, κ), a consonant, transliterated as *c* or *k.* [*Greek, of Semitic origin*]

ka+put (kæˈpʊt) *adj.* (*postpositive*) *Informal.* ruined, broken, or not functioning. [C20: from German *kaputt* done for, from French *être capot* to have made no tricks (literally: to be hoodwinked), from *capot* hooded cloak]

kar·a·bi+ner (ˌkærəˈbiːnə) *n. Mountaineering.* a metal clip with a spring for attaching to a piton or joining two ropes. Also called: **snap ring.** [shortened from German *Karabinerhaken,* literally: carbine hook, that is, one used to attach carbines to a belt]

Ka·ra·chai-Cher·kess Au·ton·o·mous Re+gion (kərʌˈtʃaɪ tʃɛəˈkɛs) *n.* an administrative division of the S Soviet Union, on the N side of the Caucasus Mountains. Capital: Cherkessk. Pop.: 344 651 (1970). Area: 14 100 sq. km (5440 sq. miles). Also: **Ka+ra+cha·ye·vo-Cher·kess Autonomous Region** (kərʌˈtʃaɪevəʊ tʃɛəˈkɛs).

Ka+ra+chi (kəˈrɑːtʃɪ) *n.* a port in S Pakistan, on the Arabian Sea: capital of Pakistan (1947–60); university (1950); chief port, commercial, and industrial centre. Pop.: 3 498 634 (1972).

Ka+ra+fu+to (ˌkɑːrɑːˈfuːtɔ) *n.* transliteration of the Japanese name for **Sakhalin.**

Ka+ra+gan+da (*Russian* kərəganˈda) *n.* a city in the SW Soviet Union, in the W Kazakh SSR: a major coal-mining and industrial centre. Pop.: 564 000 (1975 est.).

Kar·a+ite (ˈkɛərəˌaɪt) *n.* **1.** a member of a Jewish sect originating in the 8th century A.D., which rejected the Talmud, favoured strict adherence to and a literal interpretation of the Bible, and attempted to deduce a code of life from it. ~*adj.* **2.** of, relating to, or designating the Karaite sect. [C18: from Hebrew *qārāīm* members of the sect, scripturalists, from *qārā* to read]

Ka·ra·jan (*German* ˈkarajan) *n.* **Her·bert von** (ˈhɛrbɛrt fɔn). born 1908, Austrian conductor.

Ka·ra-Kal·pak (kəˈrɑː kəlˈpɑːk) *n.* **1.** (*pl.* **·paks** *or* **·pak**) a member of a Mongoloid people of Soviet central Asia. **2.** the language of this people, belonging to the Turkic branch of the Altaic family.

Ka·ra-Kal·pak Au·ton·o+mous So+vi+et So+cial+ist Re+pub+lic *n.* an administrative division of the S Soviet Union, in the Uzbek SSR, on the Aral Sea: came under Russian rule by stages from 1873 onwards. Capital: Nukus. Pop.: 702 264 (1970). Area: 165 600 sq. km (63 900 sq. miles). Also called: **Ka·ra-Kal·pa·ki·a** (kəˈrɑː kəlˈpɑːkɪə), **Ka·ra-Kal·pa·ki·stan** (kəˈrɑː kəlˌpɑːkɪˈstæn, -ˈstɑːn).

Ka+ra+ko+ram *or* **Ka+ra+ko+rum** (ˌkærəˈkɔːrəm) *n.* a mountain system in N Kashmir, extending for about 480 km (300 miles) from northwest to southeast: contains the second highest peak in the world (K2); crossed by several high passes, notably the **Karakoram Pass,** 5575 m (18 290 ft.).

Ka+ra+ko+rum (ˌkærəˈkɔːrəm) *n.* a ruined city in the Mongolian People's Republic: founded in 1220 by Ghenghis Khan; destroyed by Kublai Khan when his brother rebelled against him, after Kublai Khan had moved his capital to Peking.

kar·a+kul *or* **car·a+cul** (ˈkærəkᵊl) *n.* **1.** a breed of sheep of central Asia having coarse black, grey, or brown hair: the lambs have soft curled usually black hair. **2.** the fur prepared from these lambs. ~See also **Persian lamb.** [C19: from Russian, from the name of a region in Bokhara where the sheep originated]

Ka·ra Kum (*Russian* kaˈra ˈkum) *n.* a desert in the SW Soviet Union, covering most of the Turkmen SSR: extensive areas now irrigated. Area: about 300 000 sq. km (120 000 sq. miles).

Ka·ra·man·lis (*Greek* karamanˈlis) *n.* **Kon·stan·ti·nos** (kɔnstanˈtinɔs). born 1907, Greek statesman; prime minister of Greece (1955-58; 1958-61; 1961-63; 1974-80).

Ka·ra Sea (ˈkɑːrə) *n.* a shallow arm of the Arctic Ocean off the N coast of the Soviet Union: ice-free for about three months of the year.

kar+at (ˈkærət) *n.* the usual U.S. spelling of **carat** (sense 2).

ka+ra+te (kəˈrɑːtɪ) *n.* a traditional Japanese system of unarmed combat, employing smashes, chops, kicks, etc., made with the hands, feet, elbows, or legs. [Japanese, literally: empty hand, from *kara* empty + *te* hand]

Kar+ba+la (ˈkɑːbələ) *or* **Ker+be+la** *n.* a town in central Iraq: the chief holy city of Iraq and centre of Shiah Muslim pilgrimage. Pop.: 107 500 (1970 est.).

Ka+re·li·a (kəˈriːlɪə; *Russian* kaˈreljə) *n.* a region of NE Europe, formerly in Finland but annexed in several stages by the Soviet Union: corresponds roughly to the Karelian ASSR.

Ka+re·li·an (kə'ri:lıən) *adj.* **1.** of or relating to Karelia, its people, or their language. ~*n.* **2.** a native or inhabitant of Karelia. **3.** the dialect of Finnish spoken in Karelia.

Ka+re·li·an Au·ton·o+mous So+vi+et So+cial+ist Re+pub+lic *n.* an administrative division of the NW Soviet Union between the White Sea and Lakes Onega and Ladoga. Capital: Petrozavodsk. Pop.: 713 451 (1970). Area: 172 400 sq. km (66 560 sq. miles).

Ka+re·li·an Isth+mus *n.* a strip of land between the Gulf of Finland and Lake Ladoga: annexed by the Soviet Union after the Russo-Finnish War (1939–40).

Ka+ren (kə'rɛn) *n.* **1.** (*pl.* **+rens** *or* **+ren**) a member of a Thai people of Burma. **2.** the language of this people, probably related to Thai and belonging to the Sino-Tibetan family.

Ka+ri+ba (kə'ri:bə) *n.* **Lake.** a lake on the Zambia-Rhodesia border, created by the building of the Kariba Dam across the Zambezi for hydroelectric power. Length: 282 km (175 miles).

Karl-Marx-Stadt (*German* 'karl 'marks 'ʃtat) *n.* a city in S East Germany, at the foot of the Erz Mountains: a textile centre; engineering works. Pop.: 304 055 (1975 est.). Former name (until 1953): **Chemnitz.**

Kar·loff ('kɑ:lɒf) *n.* **Bo·ris.** stage name of *William Pratt.* 1887–1969, English film actor, famous for his roles in horror films, esp. *Frankenstein* (1931).

Kar+lo+vy Va·ry (*Czech* 'karlɔvi 'vari) *n.* a city in W Czechoslovakia, at the confluence of the Tepla and Ohře Rivers: warm mineral springs. Pop.: 43 708 (1970). German name: **Karlsbad.**

Karls+bad ('karls,ba:t) *n.* the German name for **Karlovy Vary.**

Karls+ruh·e (*German* 'karls,ru:ə) *n.* a city in West Germany, in Baden-Württemberg: capital of the former Baden state; now the seat of justice of West Germany. Pop.: 261 250 (1974 est.).

kar+ma ('kɑ:mə) *n.* **1.** *Hinduism, Buddhism.* the principle of retributive justice determining a person's state of life and the state of his reincarnations as the effect of his past deeds. **2.** *Theosophy.* the doctrine of inevitable consequence. **3.** destiny or fate. [C19: from Sanskrit: action, effect, from *karoti* **he** does] —'**kar+mic** *adj.*

Kar+nak ('kɑ:næk) *n.* a village in E Egypt, on the Nile: site of the N part of the ruins of ancient Thebes.

Kar+na+tak·a (kə'nɑ:təkə) *n.* a state of S India, on the Arabian Sea: consists of a narrow coastal plain rising to the South Deccan plateau; mainly agricultural. Capital: Bangalore. Pop.: 29 299 014 (1971). Area: 192 204 sq. km (74 210 sq. miles). Former name (1956–73): **Mysore.**

Kar+na+tak mu+sic *n.* the classical music of South India.

Kärn+ten ('kɛrntᵊn) *n.* the German name for **Carinthia.**

ka+roo *or* **kar+roo** (kə'ru:) *n., pl.* **+roos.** a dry tableland of southern Africa, with semidesert vegetation. [C18: from Afrikaans *karo,* perhaps from Hottentot *garo* desert]

Ka+roo *or* **Kar+roo** (kə'ru:) *n., pl.* **+roos. 1.** any of several high arid plateaus in South Africa, esp. the **Great (Central) Karoo** and the **Little Karoo** in S Cape Province. The High Veld, north of the Great Karoo, is sometimes called the **Northern Karoo. 2.** a period or rock system in southern Africa equivalent to the period or system extending from the Upper Carboniferous to the Lower Jurassic: divided into **Lower** and **Upper Karoo.** ~*adj.* **3.** of, denoting, or formed in the Karoo period. [C18: from Afrikaans *karo,* probably from Hottentot *garo* desert]

ka+ross (kə'rɒs) *n.* a garment of skins worn by indigenous peoples in southern Africa. [C18: from Afrikaans *karos,* perhaps from Dutch *kuras,* from French *cuirasse* CUIRASS]

Kar·pov (*Russian* 'karpəf) *n.* **A·na·to·ly** (ana'tɔlij). born 1951, Soviet chess player: world champion since 1975.

kar+ri ('kɑ:rı) *n.* **1.** an Australian eucalyptus tree, *Eucalyptus diversifolia.* **2.** the durable wood of this tree, used for construction, etc. [from a native Australian language]

karst (kɑ:st) *n.* (*modifier*) denoting the characteristic scenery of a limestone region, including underground streams, gorges, etc. [C19: German, from *Karst,* limestone plateau near Trieste] —'**karst+ic** *adj.*

kart (kɑ:t) *n.* a light low-framed vehicle with small wheels and engine used for recreational racing **(karting).** Also called: **go-cart, go-kart.**

kar·y·o- *or* **car·y·o-** *combining form.* indicating the nucleus of a cell: *karyogamy.* [from New Latin, from Greek *karuon* kernel, nut]

kar·y+og·a·my (,kærı'ɒgəmı) *n. Biology.* the fusion of two gametic nuclei during fertilization. —**kar·y·o+gam+ic** (,kærıə'gæmık) *adj.*

kar·y·o+ki+ne·sis (,kærıəʊkı'ni:sıs, -kaı-) *n.* another name for **mitosis.** —**kar·y·o·ki+net+ic** (,kærıəʊkı'nɛtık, -kaı-) *adj.*

kar·y·o+lymph ('kærıəʊ,lımf) *n.* the liquid portion of the nucleus of a cell.

kar·y+ol·y+sis (,kærı'ɒlısıs) *n. Cytology.* the disintegration of a cell nucleus, which occurs on death of the cell. [C20: from Greek, from *karyon* a nut + -LYSIS] —**kar·y·o+lyt+ic** (,kærıə'lıtık) *adj.*

kar·y·o+plasm ('kærıəʊ,plæzəm) *n.* another name for **nucleoplasm.** —,**kar·y·o+'plas+mic** *adj.*

kar·y·o+some ('kærıəʊ,səʊm) *n.* **1.** any of the dense aggregates of chromatin in the nucleus of a cell: thought to be thickened segments of chromosomes. **2.** the nucleus of a cell.

kar·y·o+tin (,kærı'əʊtın) *n.* a less common word for **chromatin.** [from KARYO- + (CHROMA)TIN]

kar·y·o+type ('kærıə,taıp) *n.* the appearance of the chromosomes in a somatic cell of an individual or species, with reference to their number, size, shape, etc. —**kar·y·o+typ+ic** (,kærıə'tıpık) *or* ,**kar·y·o+'typ·i+cal** *adj.*

Ka+sai (kɑ:'saı) *n.* a river in southwestern Africa, rising in central Angola and flowing east then north as part of the border between Angola and Zaïre, continuing northwest through Zaïre to the River Congo. Length: 2154 km (1338 miles).

kas+bah *or* **cas+bah** ('kæzbɑ:) (*sometimes cap.*) ~*n.* **1.** the citadel of any of various North African cities. **2.** the quarter in which a kasbah is located. Compare **medina.**

ka+sha ('kɑ:ʃə) *n.* a dish originating in Eastern Europe, consisting of boiled or baked buckwheat. [from Russian]

ka+sher ('kɑ:ʃə) *n.* a variant spelling of **kosher.**

Kash+gar ('kɑ:ʃ'gɑ:) *n.* an oasis city in W China, in W Sinkiang-Uigur AR. Pop.: 100 000 (1958 est.). Chinese names: **Shufu, Sufu.**

kash+mir ('kæʃmıə) *n.* a variant spelling of **cashmere.**

Kash+mir (kæʃ'mıə) *n.* a region of SW central Asia: from the 16th century ruled by the Moguls, Afghanis, Sikhs, and British successively; since 1947 disputed between India and Pakistan; 84 000 sq. km (33 000 sq. miles) in the northwest are held by Pakistan and known as Azad Kashmir (Free Kashmir); the remainder was in 1956 officially incorporated into India as the state of Jammu and Kashmir; traversed by the Himalaya and Karakoram mountain ranges and the Rivers Jhelum and Indus; a fruit-growing and cattle-grazing region, with a woollen industry. Capitals: (Azad Kashmir) Muzaffarabad; (Jammu and Kashmir) Srinagar (summer), Jammu (winter).

Kash+mir goat *n.* a Himalayan breed of goat having an undercoat of silky wool from which cashmere wool is obtained.

Kash+mir·i (kæʃ'mıərı) *adj.* **1.** of or relating to Kashmir, its people, or their language. ~*n.* **2.** (*pl.* **+mir·is** *or* **+mir·i**) a member of the people of Kashmir. **3.** the state language of Kashmir, belonging to the Dardic group of the Indo-European family of languages. —**Kash+'mir·i·an** *adj., n.*

kash+ruth* or *kash+rut *Hebrew.* (kaʃ'ru:t) *n.* **1.** the condition of being kosher. **2.** the Jewish dietary laws. [literally: appropriateness, fitness]

Kas+sa ('kɔʃʃɔ) *n.* the Hungarian name for **Košice.**

Kas+sa+la (kə'sɑ:lə) *n.* a city in the E Sudan: founded as a fort by the Egyptians in 1834. Pop.: 106 602 (1973).

Kas+sel *or* **Cas+sel** (*German* 'kasᵊl) *n.* a city in E West Germany, in Hesse: capital of Westphalia (1807–13) and of the Prussian province of Hesse-Nassau (1866–1945). Pop.: 212 575 (1974 est.).

Ka+strop-Rau·xel (*German* 'kastrɔp 'raʊksᵊl) *n.* a variant spelling of **Castrop-Rauxel.**

kat *or* **khat** (kæt, kɑ:t) *n.* a white-flowered evergreen shrub, *Catha edulis,* of Africa and Arabia, whose leaves have narcotic properties and are chewed or prepared as a drink. [C19: from Arabic *qāt*]

kat·a- *prefix.* variant of **cata-.**

ka+tab·a+sis (kə'tæbəsıs) *n., pl.* **+ses** (-,si:z). **1.** the retreat of the Greek mercenaries of Cyrus the Younger, after his death at Cunaxa, from the Euphrates to the Black Sea in 401–400 B.C. under the leadership of Xenophon: recounted in his *Anabasis.* Compare **anabasis. 2.** *Literary.* a retreat. [C19: from Greek: a going down, from *katabainein* to go down]

kat·a+bat+ic (,kætə'bætık) *adj.* (of winds) blowing downhill through having become denser with cooling, esp. at night when heat is lost from the earth's surface. Compare **anabatic.**

ka+tab·o+lism (kə'tæbə,lızəm) *n.* a variant spelling of **catabolism.** —**kat·a+bol+ic** (,kætə'bɒlık) *adj.* —,**kat·a+'bol·i+cal+ly** *adv.*

ka+ta+ka+na (,kɑ:tə'kɑ:nə) *n.* one of the two systems of syllabic writing employed for the representation of Japanese, based on Chinese ideograms. It is used mainly for scientific articles and official documents. [Japanese, from *kata* side + KANA]

Ka+tan+ga (kə'tæŋgə) *n.* the former name (until 1972) of **Shaba.**

Ka+tar (kæ'tɑ:) *n.* a variant spelling of **Qatar.**

Ka+thak ('kʌtək) *n.* a form of Indian classical dancing that tells a story. [Bengali: narrator, from Sanskrit *kathayati* he tells]

Ka+tha+re·vu+sa *or* **Ka+tha+re·vou+sa** (,kɑ:θə'rɛvə,sɑ:) *n.* a literary style of Modern Greek, derived from the Attic dialect of Ancient Greek and including many archaic features. Compare **Demotic.**

ka+thar+sis (kə'θɑ:sıs) *n.* a less common spelling of **catharsis.** —**ka+'thar+tic** *adj.*

Ka+thi·a+war (,kætıə'wɑ:) *n.* a large peninsula of W India, in Gujerat between the Gulf of Kutch and the Gulf of Cambay. Area: about 60 690 sq. km (23 430 sq. miles).

Kat+mai ('kætmaı) *n.* **Mount.** a volcano in SW Alaska, in the Aleutian Range: erupted in 1912 forming the Valley of Ten Thousand Smokes, a region with numerous fumaroles; established as **Katmai National Monument,** 10 917 sq. km (4215 sq. miles), in 1918. Height: 2100 m (7000 ft.). Depth of crater: 1130 m (3700 ft.). Width of crater: about 4 km (2.5 miles).

Kat+man+du *or* **Kath+man+du** (,kætmæn'du:) *n.* the capital of Nepal, in the east at the confluence of the Baghmati and Vishnumati Rivers. Pop.: 353 756 (1971).

Ka+to+wi+ce (*Polish* ,katɔ'vitsɛ) *n.* an industrial city in S Poland. Pop.: 320 400 (1974 est.). Former name (1953–56): **Stalinogrod.**

Kat+rine ('kætrın) *n.* **Loch.** a lake in central Scotland, east of Loch Lomond: noted for its associations with Sir Walter Scott's *Lady of the Lake.* Length: about 13 km (8 miles).

Kat+si·na (kæt'si:nə) *n.* a city in N Nigeria in Kaduna state: a major intellectual and cultural centre of the Hausa people (16th–18th centuries). Pop.: 109 424 (1971 est.).

Kat+te+gat *or* **Cat+te+gat** ('kætɪ,gæt) *n.* a strait between Denmark and Sweden: linked by the Sound, the Great Belt, and the Little Belt with the Baltic Sea and by the Skagerrak with the North Sea.

ka+ty+did ('keɪtɪ,dɪd) *n.* any typically green long-horned grasshopper of the genus *Microcentrum* and related genera, living among the foliage of trees in North America. [C18: of imitative origin]

kat+zen+jam+mer ('kætsən,dʒæmə) *n. Chiefly U.S.* **1.** a confused uproar. **2.** a hangover. [German, from *Katzen* cats + *jammer* misery]

Ka+u+a·i (kɑː'wɑːiː) *n.* a volcanic island in NW Hawaii, northwest of Oahu. Chief town: Lihue. Pop.: 29 524 (1970). Area: 1433 sq. km (553 sq. miles).

Kau+nas ('kaʊnəs) *n.* a city in the W Soviet Union, in the S central Lithuanian SSR at the confluence of the Neman and Viliya Rivers: ceded by Poland to Russia in 1795; became the provisional capital of Lithuania (1920–40); incorporated into the Soviet Union in 1944; university (1922). Pop.: 344 000 (1975 est.). Russian name: **Kovno.**

Ka·un·da (kɑː'ʊndə) *n.* **Ken·neth (David).** born 1924, Zambian statesman. He led his country into independence and became its first president (1964).

kau+ri *or* **kau+ry** ('kaʊrɪ) *n., pl.* **+ris** *or* **+ries. 1.** a New Zealand coniferous tree, *Agathis australis*, with oval leaves and round cones, cultivated for wood and resin: family *Araucariaceae*. **2.** the wood or resin of this tree. [C19: from Maori *kawri*]

ka.va ('kɑːvə) *n.* **1.** a Polynesian shrub, *Piper methysticum*: family *Piperaceae*. **2.** an alcoholic drink prepared from the aromatic roots of this shrub. [C18: from Polynesian (Tongan): bitter]

Ka+vál+la (kə'vælə; *Greek* ka'vala) *n.* a port in E Greece, in Macedonia on the **Bay of Kavälla**: an important Macedonian fortress of the Byzantine empire; ceded to Greece by Turkey after the Balkan War (1912–13). Pop.: 46 887 (1971). Ancient name: **Neapolis.**

Ka+ver·i ('kɔːvərɪ) *n.* a variant spelling of **Cauvery.**

Ka+wa+sa+ki (,kɑːwə'sɑːkɪ) *n.* a port in central Japan, on SE Honshu, between Tokyo and Yokohama: heavy industries. Pop.: 1 020 000 (1975).

Kay (keɪ) *n.* **Sir.** (in Arthurian legend) the braggart foster brother and steward of King Arthur.

kay+ak *or* **kai+ak** ('kaɪæk) *n.* a small light canoe-like boat used by Eskimos, consisting of a light frame covered with watertight animal skins. [C18: from Eskimo (Greenland dialect)]

kay·o *or* **KO** ('keɪ'əʊ) *n., vb. Boxing, slang.* another term for **knockout** or **knock out.** [C20: from the initial letters of *knock out*]

Kay+se·ri (,kaɪsɛ'riː; *Turkish* 'kɑjseri) *n.* a city in central Turkey: trading centre since ancient times as the chief city of Cappadocia. Pop.: 207 037 (1975). Ancient name: **Caesarea Mazaca.**

ka+za+chok (,kɑːzə'tʃɒk) *n.* a Russian folk dance in which the performer executes high kicks from a squatting position. [Russian]

Ka+zakh *or* **Ka+zak** (kə'zɑːk, kɑː-) *n.* **1.** (*pl.* **+zakhs** *or* **+zaks**) a member of a traditionally Muslim Mongoloid people of the Kazakh SSR. **2.** the language of this people, belonging to the Turkic branch of the Altaic family.

Ka+zakh So+vi+et So+cial+ist Re+pub+lic *n.* an administrative division of the S central Soviet Union, on the Caspian Sea. Capital: Alma-Ata. Pop.: 12 849 573 (1970). Area: 2 715 100 sq. km (1 048 030 sq. miles). Also: **Kazak Soviet Socialist Republic, Ka+zakh+stan,** *or* **Ka+zak+stan** (,kɑːzɑːk'stæn, -'stɑːn).

Ka+zan[1] (kə'zæn, -'zɑːn; *Russian* ka'zanj) *n.* a city in the E Soviet Union, capital of the Tatar ASSR on the River Volga: capital of an independent khanate in the 15th century; university (1804); a major industrial centre. Pop.: 946 000 (1975 est.).

Ka·zan[2] (kə'zɑːn) *n.* **E·lia** ('iːljə). born 1909, U.S. stage and film director and writer, born in Turkey. His films include *Gentleman's Agreement* (1947), *On the Waterfront* (1954), and *East of Eden* (1955).

Ka+zan Ret+to (kɑː'zɑːn 'rɛtəʊ) *n.* transliteration of the Japanese name for the **Volcano Islands.**

Ka·zan·tza·kis (*Greek* kazan'dzakis) *n.* **Ni·kos** ('nikɔs). 1885–1957, Greek novelist, poet, and dramatist, noted particularly for his novel *Zorba the Greek* (1946) and his epic poem *The Odyssey* (1938).

Kaz+bek (kɑːz'bɛk) *n.* **Mount.** an extinct volcano in the S Soviet Union, in the N Georgian SSR in the central Caucasus Mountains. Height: 5047 m (16 558 ft.).

Kaz Daği ('kɑz 'dɑj) *n.* the Turkish name for (Mount) **Ida** (sense 2).

ka+zoo (kə'zuː) *n., pl.* **+zoos.** a cigar-shaped musical instrument of metal or plastic with a membranous diaphragm of thin paper that vibrates with a nasal sound when the player hums into it. [C20: probably imitative of the sound produced]

kb *abbrev. for* kilobar.

KB *Chess. symbol for* king's bishop.

K.B. (in Britain) *abbrev. for:* **1.** King's Bench. **2.** Knight Bachelor.

K.B.E. *abbrev. for* Knight (Commander of the Order) of the British Empire.

KBP *Chess. symbol for* king's bishop's pawn.

kc *abbrev. for* kilocycle.

K.C. (in Britain) *abbrev. for* King's Counsel.

kcal *abbrev. for* kilocalorie.

K.C.B. *abbrev. for* Knight Commander of the Bath (a Brit. title).

K.C.M.G. *abbrev. for* Knight Commander of St. Michael and St. George (a Brit. title).

Kčs. *abbrev. for* koruna. [Czech *koruna československá*]

K.C.V.O. *abbrev. for* Knight Commander of the Royal Victorian Order (a Brit. title).

K.D. *or* **k.d.** *Commerce. abbrev. for* knocked down: indicating furniture, machinery, etc., in separate parts.

K.E. *abbrev. for* kinetic energy.

ke·a ('keɪə) *n.* a large New Zealand parrot, *Nestor notabilis*, with brownish-green plumage. [C19: from Maori, imitative of its call]

Ké·a ('kɛa) *n.* transliteration of the Modern Greek name for **Keos.**

Kean (kiːn) *n.* **Ed·mund.** 1789–1833, English actor, noted for his Shakespearian roles.

Kea·ton ('kiːtᵊn) *n.* **Bust·er,** original name *Joseph Francis Keaton.* 1895–1966, U.S. film comedian who starred in silent films such as *The Navigator* (1924), *The General* (1926), and *Steamboat Bill Junior* (1927).

Keats (kiːts) *n.* **John.** 1795–1821, English poet. His finest poetry is contained in *Lamia and other Poems* (1820), which includes *The Eve of St. Agnes, Hyperion,* and the odes *On a Grecian Urn, To a Nightingale, To Autumn,* and *To Psyche.*

ke+bab (kə'bæb) *n.* a dish consisting of small pieces of meat, tomatoes, onions, etc., threaded onto skewers and grilled, generally over charcoal. Also called: **shish kebab, kabob, cabob.** [C17: via Urdu from Arabic *kabāb* roast meat]

Ke·ble ('kiːbᵊl) *n.* **John.** 1792–1866, English clergyman. His sermon on national apostasy (1833) is considered to have inspired the Oxford Movement.

keck[1] (kɛk) *vb. (intr.) Chiefly U.S.* **1.** to retch or feel nausea. **2.** to feel or express disgust. [C17: of imitative origin]

keck[2] (kɛk) *n.* another name for **cow parsnip** and **cow parsley.** [C17: from KEX, which was mistaken as a plural (as if *kecks*)]

Kecs+ke+mét (*Hungarian* 'kɛtʃkɛmeːt) *n.* a city in central Hungary: vineyards and fruit farms. Pop.: 77 000 (1970).

ked (kɛd) *n.* See **sheep ked.**

Ked+ah ('kɛdə) *n.* a state of NW Malaysia: under Thai control until it came under the British in 1909; the chief exports are rice, tin, and rubber. Capital: Alor Star. Pop.: 952 421 (1970). Area: 9425 sq. km (3639 sq. miles).

ked+dah ('kɛdə) *n.* a variant spelling of **kheda.**

kedge (kɛdʒ) *Nautical.* ~*vb.* **1.** to draw (a vessel) along by hauling in on the cable of a light anchor that has been dropped at some distance from it, or (of a vessel) to be drawn in this fashion. ~*n.* **2.** a light anchor, used esp. for kedging. [C15: from *caggen* to fasten]

ked+ger+ee (,kɛdʒə'riː) *n. Chiefly Brit.* a dish consisting of rice, cooked flaked fish, and hard-boiled eggs. [C17: from Hindi *khicarī*, from Sanskrit *khiccā*, of obscure origin]

Ke+di+ri (kɪ'dɪərɪ) *n.* a city in Indonesia, in E Java: commercial centre. Pop.: 178 865 (1971).

Ked+ron ('kɛdrɒn) *or* **Ki+dron** *n. Bible.* a ravine under the eastern wall of Jerusalem.

keef (kiːf) *n.* a variant spelling of **kif.**

Kee·gan ('kiːgən) *n.* **Ke·vin.** born 1951, English footballer: a striker, he played for Liverpool (1971–77), Hamburg (from 1977), and England (from 1972).

keek (kiːk) *n., vb.* a Scot. word for **peep**[1]. [C18: probably from Middle Dutch *kīken* to look]

keel[1] (kiːl) *n.* **1.** one of the main longitudinal structural members of a vessel to which the frames are fastened and that may extend into the water to provide lateral stability. **2. on an even keel.** well-balanced; steady. **3.** any structure corresponding to or resembling the keel of a ship, such as the central member along the bottom of an aircraft fuselage. **4.** *Biology.* a ridgelike part; carina. **5.** a poetic word for **ship.** ~*vb.* **6.** See **keel over.** [C14: from Old Norse *kjölr*; related to Middle Dutch *kiel*, KEEL[2]] —**'keel-less** *adj.*

keel[2] (kiːl) *n. Northern Brit. dialect.* **1.** a flat-bottomed vessel, esp. one used for carrying coal. **2.** a measure of coal equal to about 21 tons. [C14 *kele*, from Middle Dutch *kiel*; compare Old English *cēol* ship]

keel[3] (kiːl) *n.* **1.** red ochre stain used for marking sheep, timber, etc. ~*vb.* **2.** to mark with this stain. [Old English *cēlan*, from *cōl* COOL]

keel[4] (kiːl) *vb.* an archaic word for **cool** (esp. in the phrase **keel the pot**). [C15: probably from Scottish Gaelic *cīl*]

keel[5] (kiːl) *n.* a fatal disease of young ducks, characterized by intestinal bleeding. [C19: from KEEL[1]; see KEEL OVER]

keel arch *n.* another name for **ogee arch.**

keel+boat ('kiːl,bəʊt) *n.* a river boat with a shallow draught and a keel, used for freight and moved by towing, punting, or rowing.

keel+haul ('kiːl,hɔːl) *vb. (tr.)* **1.** to drag (a person) by a rope from one side of a vessel to the other through the water under the keel. **2.** to rebuke harshly. [C17: from Dutch *kielhalen*; see KEEL[1], HAUL]

Keel+ing Is+lands ('kiːlɪŋ) *pl. n.* another name for the **Cocos Islands.**

keel o·ver *vb. (adv.)* **1.** to turn upside down; capsize. **2.** *(intr.) Informal.* to collapse suddenly.

keel+son ('kɛlsən, 'kiːl-) *or* **kel+son** ('kɛlsən) *n.* a longitudinal beam fastened to the keel of a vessel for strength and stiffness. [C17: probably from Low German *kielswin*, keel swine, ultimately of Scandinavian origin]

Kee+lung ('kiː'lʊŋ) *n.* another name for **Chilung.**

keen[1] (kiːn) *adj.* **1.** eager or enthusiastic. **2.** (*postpositive;* foll. by *on*) fond (of); devoted (to): *keen on a girl; keen on golf.* **3.** intellectually acute: *a keen wit.* **4.** (of sight, smell, hearing, etc.) capable of recognizing fine distinctions. **5.** having a sharp cutting edge or point. **6.** extremely cold and penetrating: *a keen wind.* **7.** intense or strong: *a keen desire.* **8.** *Chiefly Brit.* extremely competitive: *keen prices.* **9.** *Slang, chiefly U.S.* very good. [Old English *cēne;* related to Old High German *kuoni* brave, Old Norse *koenn* wise; see CAN[1], KNOW] —**ˈkeen+ly** *adv.* —**ˈkeen+ness** *n.*

keen[2] (kiːn) *vb.* **1.** to lament the dead. ~*n.* **2.** a dirge or lament for the dead. [C19: from Irish Gaelic *caoine,* from Old Irish *coīnim* I wail] —**ˈkeen+er** *n.*

keep (kiːp) *vb.* **keeps, keep+ing, kept. 1.** (*tr.*) to have or retain possession of. **2.** (*tr.*) to have temporary possession or charge of: *keep my watch for me during the game.* **3.** (*tr.*) to store in a customary place: *I keep my books in the desk.* **4.** to remain or cause to remain in a specified state or condition: *keep the dog quiet; keep ready.* **5.** to continue or cause to continue: *keep the beat; keep in step.* **6.** (*tr.*) to have or take charge or care of: *keep the shop for me till I return.* **7.** (*tr.*) to look after or maintain for use, pleasure, etc.: *to keep chickens; keep two cars.* **8.** (*tr.*) to provide for the upkeep or livelihood of. **9.** (*tr.*) to support financially, esp. in return for sexual favours: *he keeps a mistress in the country.* **10.** to confine or detain or be confined or detained. **11.** to withhold or reserve or admit of withholding or reserving: *your news will keep till later.* **12.** (*tr.*) to refrain from divulging or violating: *to keep a secret; keep one's word.* **13.** to preserve or admit of preservation. **14.** (*tr.;* sometimes foll. by *up*) to observe with due rites or ceremonies: *to keep Christmas.* **15.** (*tr.*) to maintain by writing regular records in: *to keep a diary.* **16.** (when *intr.,* foll. by *in, on, to,* etc.) to stay in, on, or at (a place or position): *please keep your seats; keep to the path.* **17.** (*tr.*) to associate with (esp. in the phrase **keep bad company**). **18.** (*tr.*) to maintain in existence: *to keep court in the palace.* **19.** (*tr.*) *Chiefly Brit.* to have habitually in stock: *this shop keeps all kinds of wool.* **20. how are you keeping?** how are you? **21. keep tabs on** (*or* **track of**). *Informal.* to continue to be informed about. **22. keep time.** See **time** (sense 42). **23. keep wicket.** to play as wicketkeeper in the game of cricket. **24. you can keep it.** *Informal.* I have no interest in what you are offering. ~*n.* **25.** living or support: *he must work for his keep.* **26.** charge or care: *the dog is in your keep while I am away.* **27.** Also called: **dungeon, donjon.** the main tower within the walls of a medieval castle or fortress. **28. for keeps.** *Informal.* **a.** completely; permanently. **b.** for the winner or possessor to keep permanently. [Old English *cēpan* to observe; compare Old Saxon *kapōn* to look, Old Norse *kōpa* to stare]

keep at *vb.* (*prep.*) **1.** (*intr.*) to persevere with or persist in. **2.** (*tr.*) to constrain (a person) to continue doing (a task).

keep a·way *vb.* (*adv.;* often foll. by *from*) **1.** to refrain or prevent from coming (near). **2.** to stop using, touching, etc.

keep back *vb.* (*adv.;* often foll. by *from*) **1.** (*tr.*) to refuse to reveal or disclose. **2.** to prevent, be prevented, or refrain from advancing, entering, etc.

keep down *vb.* (*adv., mainly tr.*) **1.** to repress; hold in submission. **2.** to restrain or control: *he had difficulty keeping his anger down.* **3.** to cause not to increase or rise: *prices were kept down for six months.* **4.** (*intr.*) not to show oneself to one's opponents; lie low. **5.** to cause (food) to stay in the stomach; not vomit.

keep+er (ˈkiːpə) *n.* **1.** a person in charge of animals, esp. in a zoo. **2.** a person in charge of a museum, collection, or section of a museum. **3.** a person in charge of other people, such as a warder in a jail. **4.** See **goalkeeper, wicketkeeper, gamekeeper. 5.** a person who keeps something. **6.** a device, such as a clip, for keeping something in place. **7.** a soft-iron or steel bar placed across the poles of a permanent magnet to close the magnetic circuit when it is not in use. —**ˈkeep+er+less** *adj.* —**ˈkeep+er+ˌship** *n.*

keep+er ring *n.* another name for **guard ring.**

keep from *vb.* (*prep.*) **1.** (foll. by a gerund) to prevent or restrain (oneself or another); refrain or cause to refrain. **2.** (*tr.*) to preserve or protect.

keep in *vb.* (*mainly adv.*) **1.** (*intr.; also prep.*) to stay indoors. **2.** (*tr.*) to restrain (an emotion); repress. **3.** (*tr.*) to detain (a schoolchild) after hours as a punishment. **4.** (of a fire) to stay alight or cause (a fire) to stay alight. **5.** (*tr., prep.*) to allow a constant supply of: *her prize money kept her in new clothes for a year.* **6. keep in with.** to maintain good relations with.

keep+ing (ˈkiːpɪŋ) *n.* **1.** conformity or harmony (esp. in the phrases **in** *or* **out of keeping**). **2.** charge or care: *valuables in the keeping of a bank.*

keep+net (ˈkiːpˌnɛt) *n.* a cylindrical net strung on wire hoops and sealed at one end, suspended in water by anglers to keep alive the fish they have caught.

keep off *vb.* **1.** to stay or cause to stay at a distance (from). **2.** (*prep.*) not to eat or drink or prevent from eating or drinking. **3.** (*prep.*) to avoid or cause to avoid (a topic). **4.** (*intr., adv.*) not to start: *the rain kept off all day.*

keep on *vb.* (*adv.*) **1.** to continue or persist in (doing something): *keep on running.* **2.** (*tr.*) to continue to wear. **3.** (*tr.*) to continue to employ: *the firm kept on only ten men.* **4.** (*intr.;* foll. by *about*) to persist in talking (about). **5.** (*intr.;* foll. by *at*) to nag (a person).

keep out *vb.* (*adv.*) **1.** to remain or cause to remain outside. **2. keep out of. a.** to remain or cause to remain unexposed to: *keep out of the sun.* **b.** to avoid or cause to avoid: *the boss is in an angry mood, so keep out of his way.*

keep+sake (ˈkiːpˌseɪk) *n.* a gift that evokes memories of a person or event with which it is associated.

keep to *vb.* (*prep.*) **1.** to adhere to or stand by or cause to adhere to or stand by: *to keep to a promise.* **2.** to confine or be confined to. **3. keep to oneself. a.** (*intr.*) to avoid the society of others. **b.** (*tr.*) to refrain from sharing or disclosing. **4. keep oneself to oneself.** to avoid the society of others.

keep un·der *vb.* **1.** to remain or cause to remain below (a surface). **2.** (*tr.*) to cause to remain unconscious. **3.** (*tr., adv.*) to hold in submission.

keep up *vb.* (*adv.*) **1.** (*tr.*) to maintain (prices, one's morale) at the present level. **2.** (*intr.*) to maintain a pace or rate set by another. **3.** (*intr.;* often foll. by *with*) to remain informed: *to keep up with technological developments.* **4.** (*tr.*) to maintain in good condition. **5.** (*tr.*) to hinder (a person) from going to bed at night: *the excitement kept the children up well past their bedtime.* **6. keep it up.** to continue a good performance. **7. keep one's chin up.** to maintain one's courage or cheerfulness. **8. keep up with.** to remain in contact, esp. by letter. **9. keep up with (the Joneses).** *Informal.* to compete with (one's neighbours) in material possessions, etc.

kees+hond (ˈkeɪsˌhɒnd, ˈkiːs-) *n., pl.* **+honds** *or* **+hond·en** (-ˌhɒndᵊn). a breed of dog of the Spitz type with a shaggy greyish coat and tightly curled tail, originating in Holland. [C20: from Dutch, probably from *Kees* nickname for *Cornelis* Cornelius, from Latin + *hond* HOUND]

Kee+wa+tin (kiːˈwɒtɪn) *n.* an administrative district of the Northwest Territories of Canada stretching from the district of Mackenzie to Hudson Bay: mostly tundra. Pop.: 3403 (1971). Area: 590 930 sq. km (228 160 sq. miles).

kef (kɛf) *n.* a variant spelling of **kif.**

kef+fi+yeh (kɛˈfiːjə) *n.* a cotton headdress worn by Arabs. [C19: from Arabic, perhaps from Late Latin *cofea* COIF]

keg (kɛg) *n.* **1.** a small barrel with a capacity of between five and ten gallons. **2.** *Brit.* **a.** an aluminium container in which beer is transported and stored. **b.** the beer kept in a keg. [C17: variant of Middle English *kag,* of Scandinavian origin; related to Old Norse *kaggi* cask]

keg+ler (ˈkɛglə) *or* **keg+e·ler** *n. Informal, chiefly U.S.* a participant in a game of tenpin bowling. [from German, from *Kegel* pin, from Old High German *kegil* peg]

Keigh+ley (ˈkiːθlɪ) *n.* a town in N England, in West Yorkshire on the River Aire: textile industry. Pop.: 55 263 (1971).

Kei+jo (ˌkeɪˈdʒəʊ) *n.* transliteration of the Japanese name for **Seoul.**

keis+ter *or* **kees+ter** (ˈkiːstə) *n. Slang, chiefly U.S.* **1.** the rump; buttocks. **2.** a suitcase, trunk, or box. [C20: of uncertain origin]

Kei·tel (ˈkaɪtᵊl) *n.* **Wil·helm** (ˈvɪlhɛlm). 1882–1946, German field marshal; chief of the supreme command of the armed forces (1938–45). He was convicted at the Nuremberg trials and executed.

keit+lo·a (ˈkaɪtləʊə, ˈkeɪt-) *n.* a southern African variety of the black two-horned rhinoceros, *Diceros bicornis.* [C19: from Tswana *khetlwa*]

Kek·ko·nen (*Finnish* ˈkɛkkɔnɛn) *n.* **Ur·ho** (ˈurhɔ). born 1900, Finnish statesman; president 1956–82.

Ke·ku·lé for+mu+la (ˈkɛkjʊˌleɪ) *n.* a representation of the benzene molecule as six carbon atoms at the corners of a regular hexagon with alternate double and single bonds joining them and with one hydrogen atom bound to each carbon atom. See **benzene ring.** [C19: named after F. A. *Kekulé* von Stradonitz (1829–96), German chemist]

Ke+lan+tan (kɛˈlæntən, kɪˌlænˈtæn) *n.* a state of NE Malaysia: under Thai control until it came under the British in 1909; produces rice and rubber. Capital: Kota Bharu. Pop.: 684 312 (1970). Area: 14 930 sq. km (5765 sq. miles).

Kel·ler (ˈkɛlə) *n.* **Hel·en (Adams).** 1880–1968, U.S. author and lecturer. Blind and deaf from infancy, she was taught to read, write, and speak and became noted for her work for the handicapped.

Kell·y (ˈkɛlɪ) *n.* **Ned.** 1855–80, Australian horse and cattle thief and bushranger, active in Victoria: captured by the police and hanged.

ke+loid *or* **che+loid** (ˈkiːlɔɪd) *n. Pathol.* a hard smooth pinkish raised growth of scar tissue at the site of an injury, tending to occur more frequently in dark-skinned races. [C19: from Greek *khēlē* claw] —**ke+ˈloi+dal** *or* **che+ˈloi+dal** *adj.*

kelp (kɛlp) *n.* **1.** any large brown seaweed, esp. any species of *Laminaria.* **2.** the ash of such seaweed, used as a source of iodine and potash. [C14: of unknown origin]

kel+pie[1] *or* **kel+py** (ˈkɛlpɪ) *n., pl.* **+pies.** a breed of sheepdog with pointed ears, originally from Australia. [C18: of unknown origin]

kel+pie[2] (ˈkɛlpɪ) *n.* (in Scottish folklore) a water spirit in the form of a horse that drowned its riders. [C18: probably related to Scottish Gaelic *cailpeach* heifer, of obscure origin]

kel+son (ˈkɛlsən) *n.* a variant spelling of **keelson.**

kelt (kɛlt) *n.* a salmon that has recently spawned and is usually in poor condition. [C14: of unknown origin]

Kelt (kɛlt) *n.* a variant spelling of **Celt.** —**ˈKelt+ic** *adj.* —**ˈKelt·i·cal+ly** *adv.* —**ˈKelt·i·cism** *n.* —**ˈKelt·i·cist** *or* **ˈKelt+ist** *n.*

kel+ter (ˈkɛltə) *or esp. U.S.* **kil+ter** *n.* order or condition (esp. in the phrases **in good kelter, out of kelter**). [C17: of unknown origin]

kel+vin (ˈkɛlvɪn) *n.* the basic SI unit of thermodynamic temperature; the fraction 1/273.16 of the thermodynamic temperature of the triple point of water. Symbol: K

Kel·vin ('kɛlvɪn) *n.* **Wil·liam Thom·son,** 1st Baron Kelvin. 1824–1907, British physicist, noted for his work in thermodynamics, inventing the Kelvin scale, and in electricity, pioneering undersea telegraphy.

Kel·vin scale *n.* a scale of temperature in which the degree is equal to that on the Celsius scale and the zero value is -273.15°C. It has now been replaced by the International Practical Temperature Scale of 1968. Also called: **absolute scale.** Compare **Rankine scale.**

Ke·mal A·ta·türk (kɛ'mɑ:l 'ætəˌtɜ:k) *n.* See **Atatürk.** —**Ke'mal·ism** *n.* —**Ke'mal·ist** *n., adj.*

Kem·ble ('kɛmbᵊl) *n.* **1. Fran·ces Anne,** known as *Fanny.* 1809–93, English actress, in the U.S. from 1832. **2.** her uncle, **John Phil·ip.** 1757–1823, English actor and theatrical manager.

Ke·me·ro·vo (*Russian* 'kjemɪrəvə) *n.* a city in the S Soviet Union: a major coal-mining centre of the Kuznetsk Basin, with important chemical plants. Pop.: 435 000 (1975 est.). Former name (until 1932): **Shcheglovsk.**

Kem·pe (*German* 'kɛmpə) *n.* **Ru·dolf** ('ru:dɔlf). 1910–76, German orchestral conductor, noted esp. for his interpretations of Wagner.

Kem·pis ('kɛmpɪs) *n.* **Thom·as à.** ?1380–1471, German Augustinian monk, generally regarded as the author of the devotional work *The Imitation of Christ.*

kempt (kɛmpt) *adj.* (of hair) tidy; combed. See also **unkempt.** [C20: back formation from *unkempt;* originally past participle of dialect *kemb* to COMB]

ken (kɛn) *n.* **1.** range of knowledge or perception (esp. in the phrase **beyond** *or* **in one's ken**). ~*vb.* **kens, ken·ning, kenned** *or* **kent. 2.** (*tr.*) *Northern Brit. dialect.* to know. **3.** *Northern Brit. dialect.* to understand; perceive. **4.** (*tr.*) *Archaic.* to see. [Old English *cennan;* related to Old Norse *kenna* to perceive, Old High German *kennen* to make known; see CAN[1]]

ke·naf (kə'næf) *n.* another name for **ambary.** [from Persian]

Ken·dal ('kɛndᵊl) *n.* a town in NW England, in Cumbria: a gateway town to the Lake District, with an ancient woollen industry. Pop.: 21 572 (1971).

Ken·dal green *n.* **1.** a green woollen cloth, formerly worn by foresters. **2.** the colour of this cloth, produced by a dye obtained from the woad plant. [C14: from *Kendal,* where it originated]

ken·do ('kɛndəʊ) *n.* a Japanese form of fencing employing wooden staves, usually of bamboo. [from Japanese]

Ken·il·worth ('kɛnɪlˌwɜ:θ) *n.* a town in central England, in Warwickshire: ruined 12th-century castle, subject of Sir Walter Scott's novel *Kenilworth.* Pop.: 20 121 (1971).

Ké·ni·tra (*French* keni'tra) *n.* another name for **Mina Hassan Tani.**

Ken·ne·dy[1] ('kɛnɪdɪ) *n.* **Cape.** a former name (1963–73) of **Cape Canaveral.**

Ken·ne·dy[2] ('kɛnɪdɪ) *n.* **1. Ed·ward Moore.** born 1932, U.S. Democrat politician; senator since 1962. **2.** his brother, **John Fitz·ger·ald.** 1917–63, U.S. Democrat statesman; 35th president of the U.S. (1961–63), the first Roman Catholic and the youngest man ever to be president. He demanded the withdrawal of Soviet missiles from Cuba (1962) and prepared civil rights reforms; assassinated. **3.** his brother, **Rob·ert Fran·cis.** 1925–68, U.S. Democrat statesman; attorney general (1961–64) and senator for New York (1965–68); assassinated.

ken·nel[1] ('kɛnᵊl) *n.* **1.** a hutlike shelter for a dog. U.S. name: **doghouse. 2.** (*usually pl.*) an establishment where dogs are bred, trained, boarded, etc. **3.** the lair of a fox or other animal. **4.** a ramshackle house; hovel. **5.** a pack of hounds. ~*vb.* **·nels, ·nel·ling, ·nelled** *or U.S.* **·nels, ·nel·ing, ·neled. 6.** to put or go into a kennel; keep or stay in a kennel. [C14: from Old French *chenil,* from Vulgar Latin *canīle* (unattested), from Latin *canis* dog]

ken·nel[2] ('kɛnᵊl) *n.* *Archaic.* an open sewer or street gutter. [C16: variant of *cannel* CHANNEL[1]]

Ken·nel·ly ('kɛnəlɪ) *n.* **Ar·thur Ed·win.** 1861–1939, U.S. electrical engineer: independently of Heaviside, he predicted the existence of an ionized layer in the upper atmosphere, known as the Kennelly-Heaviside layer or E region.

Ken·nel·ly-Heav·i·side lay·er *n.* See **E region.**

ken·ning ('kɛnɪŋ) *n.* a conventional metaphoric name for something, esp. in Old Norse and Old English poetry, such as Old English *bānhūs* (bone house) for "body." [C14: from Old Norse, from *kenna;* see KEN]

Ken·ny meth·od *or* **treat·ment** *n.* a method of treating poliomyelitis by applying hot moist packs to the affected muscles alternated by passive and later active movement of the muscles. [C20: named after Sister Elizabeth *Kenny,* 1886–1952, Australian nurse who developed it]

ke·no, kee·no, ki·no, *or* **qui·no** ('ki:no) *n.* *U.S.* a game of chance similar to bingo. [C19: of unknown origin]

ke·no·gen·e·sis (ˌki:nəʊ'dʒɛnɪsɪs) *n.* a secondary U.S. spelling of **caenogenesis.** —**ke·no·ge·net·ic** (ˌki:nəʊdʒə'nɛtɪc) *adj.* —ˌ**ke·no·ge·'net·i·cal·ly** *adv.*

ke·no·sis (kɪ'nəʊsɪs) *n.* *Christianity.* Christ's voluntary renunciation of certain divine attributes, in order to identify himself with mankind (Philippians 2:6–7). [C19: from Greek: an emptying, from *kenoun* to empty from *kenos* empty] —**ke·not·ic** (kɪ'nɒtɪk) *adj., n.*

Ken·sing·ton and Chel·sea ('kɛnzɪŋtən) *n.* a borough of Greater London, on the River Thames: **Kensington Palace** (17th century) and gardens. Pop.: 161 400 (1976 est.).

ken·speck·le ('kɛnˌspɛkᵊl) *adj.* *Scot.* easily seen or recognized. [C18: from dialect *kenspeck,* of Scandinavian origin; compare Old Norse *kennispecki* power of recognition; related to KEN]

kent (kɛnt) *vb.* a past tense or past participle of **ken.**

Kent[1] (kɛnt) *n.* a county of SE England, on the English Channel: the first part of Great Britain to be colonized by the Romans; one of the seven kingdoms of Anglo-Saxon England until absorbed by Wessex in the 9th century A.D. Apart from the Downs it is mostly low-lying and agricultural, specializing in fruit and hops. There is a small coalfield on the S coast. Administrative centre: Maidstone. Pop.: 1 448 100 (1976 est.). Area: 4237 sq. km (1636 sq. miles).

Kent[2] (kɛnt) *n.* **Wil·liam.** ?1685–1748, English painter, architect, and landscape gardener.

ken·te ('kɛntɪ) *n.* **1.** Also called: **kente cloth.** a brightly coloured handwoven cloth of Ghana, usually with some gold thread. **2.** the toga made of this cloth. [from a Ghanaian language, possibly Akan]

Kent·ish ('kɛntɪʃ) *adj.* **1.** of or relating to Kent. ~*n.* **2.** Also called: **Jutish.** the dialect of Old and Middle English spoken in Kent. See also **Anglian, West Saxon.**

kent·ledge ('kɛntlɪdʒ) *n.* *Nautical.* scrap metal used as ballast in a vessel. [C17: perhaps from Old French *quintelage* ballast, from *quintal* hundredweight, ultimately from Arabic *qinṭār;* see KANTAR]

Ken·tuck·y (kɛn'tʌkɪ) *n.* **1.** a state of the S central U.S.: consists of an undulating plain in the west, the Bluegrass region in the centre, the Tennessee and Ohio River basins in the southwest, and the Appalachians in the east. Capital: Frankfort. Pop.: 3 219 311 (1970). Area: 102 693 sq. km (39 650 sq. miles). Abbrevs.: **Ken., Ky.** or (with zip code) **KY 2.** a river in central Kentucky, rising in the Cumberland Mountains and flowing northwest to the Ohio River. Length: 417 km (259 miles). —**Ken'tuck·i·an** *adj., n.*

Ken·tuck·y blue·grass *n.* a Eurasian grass, *Poa pratensis,* grown for forage and naturalized throughout North America.

Ken·tuck·y cof·fee tree *n.* a North American leguminous tree, *Gymnocladus dioica,* whose seeds, in brown curved pulpy pods, were formerly used as a coffee substitute.

Ken·tuck·y Der·by *n.* a race for three-year-old horses run annually since 1875 at Louisville, Kentucky.

Ken·ya ('kɛnjə, 'ki:njə) *n.* **1.** a republic in E Africa, on the Indian Ocean: became a British protectorate in 1895 and a colony in 1920; gained independence in 1963 and is a member of the Commonwealth. Coffee constitutes about a third of the total exports. Official languages: English and Swahili. Religions: animist and Christian. Currency: shilling. Capital: Nairobi. Pop.: 10 942 705 (1969). Area: 582 647 sq. km (224 960 sq. miles). **2. Mount.** an extinct volcano in central Kenya: the second highest mountain in Africa; girth at 2400 m (8000 ft.) is about 150 km (95 miles). The regions above 3200 m (10 500 ft.) constitute **Mount Kenya National Park.** Height: 5200 m (17 058 ft.). —**'Ken·yan** *adj., n.*

Ken·yat·ta (kɛn'jætə) *n.* **Jo·mo** ('dʒəʊməʊ). ?1891–1978, Kenyan statesman: imprisoned as a leader of the Mau Mau revolt (1953–59); elected president of the Kenya African National Union (1961); prime minister of independent Kenya (1963) and president (1964–78).

Ke·os ('keɪɒs) *n.* an island in the Aegean Sea, in the NW Cyclades. Pop.: 4347 (1971). Area: 174 sq. km (67 sq. miles). Italian name: **Zea.** Modern Greek name: **Kéa.**

kep (kɛp) *vb.* (*tr.*) *Northern Brit. dialect.* to catch. [from KEEP (in obsolete sense: to put oneself in the way of)]

Ke·phal·li·ní·a (ˌkɛfali'nia; *English* ˌkɛfə'li:nɪə) *n.* transliteration of the modern Greek name for **Cephalonia.**

kep·i ('keɪpi:) *n., pl.* **kep·is.** a military cap with a circular top and a horizontal peak. [C19: from French *képi,* from German (Swiss dialect) *käppi* a little cap, from *kappe* CAP]

Kep·ler[1] ('kɛplə) *n.* **Jo·han** ('jo:han). 1571–1630, German astronomer. As discoverer of Kepler's laws of planetary motion he is regarded as one of the founders of modern astronomy.

Kep·ler[2] ('kɛplə) *n.* a small crater in the NE quadrant of the moon, about 35 kilometres in diameter.

Kep·ler's laws *pl. n.* three laws of planetary motion published by Kepler between 1609 and 1619. The first states that the orbit of a planet describes an ellipse with the sun at one focus. The second states that, during one orbit, the straight line joining the sun and a planet sweeps out equal areas in equal times. The third states that the squares of the periods of any two planets are proportional to the cubes of their mean distances from the sun.

kept (kɛpt) *vb.* **1.** the past tense or past participle of **keep. 2. kept woman.** *Censorious.* a woman maintained by a man as his mistress.

Ker·a·la ('kɛrələ, kə'rɑ:lə) *n.* a state of SW India, on the Arabian Sea: formed in 1956, it includes the former state of Travancore-Cochin; has the highest population density of any Indian state. Capital: Trivandrum. Pop.: 21 347 375 (1971). Area: 38 855 sq. km (15 153 sq. miles).

ke·ram·ic (kɪ'ræmɪk) *adj.* a rare spelling of **ceramic.**

ke·ram·ics (kɪ'ræmɪks) *n.* a rare spelling of **ceramics.**

ker·a·tin ('kɛrətɪn) *or* **cer·a·tin** *n.* a fibrous sulphur-containing protein that occurs in the outer layer of the skin and in hair, nails, feathers, hooves, etc.

ke·rat·in·ize *or* **ke·rat·in·ise** (kɪ'rætɪˌnaɪz, 'kɛrətɪ-) *vb.* to become or cause to become impregnated with keratin. —**keˌrat·in·i'za·tion** *or* **keˌrat·in·i'sa·tion** *n.*

ker·a·ti·tis (ˌkɛrə'taɪtɪs) *n.* inflammation of the cornea.

ker·a·to- *or before a vowel* **ker·at-** *combining form.* indicating horn or a horny substance: *keratin; keratogenous.* [from Greek *kerat-, keras* horn]

ker·a+tog+e·nous (ˌkɛrəˈtɒdʒɪnəs) *adj.* developing or causing the growth of horny tissue.

ker·a+toid (ˈkɛrəˌtɔɪd) *adj.* resembling horn or keratin; horny.

ker·a+to+plas+ty (ˈkɛrətəʊˌplæstɪ) *n., pl.* **+ties.** plastic surgery of the cornea, esp. involving corneal grafting. —ˌ**ker·a+to+ˈplas+tic** *adj.*

ker·a+tose (ˈkɛrəˌtəʊs, -ˌtəʊz) *adj.* (esp. of certain sponges) having a horny skeleton.

ker·a+to+sis (ˌkɛrəˈtəʊsɪs) *n. Pathol.* **1.** any skin condition marked by a horny growth, such as a wart. **2.** a horny growth.

kerb *or U.S.* **curb** (kɜːb) *n.* **1.** a line of stone or concrete forming an edge between a pavement and a roadway. ~*vb.* **2.** (*tr.*) to provide with or enclose with a kerb. [C17: from Old French *courbe* bent, from Latin *curvus;* see CURVE]

ker+ba+ya (ˈkɛrbaja) *n.* a blouse worn by Malay women. [from Malay]

kerb drill *n.* a pedestrian's procedure for crossing a road safely, esp. as taught to children.

Ker+be+la (ˈkɜːbələ) *n.* a variant spelling of **Karbala.**

kerb+ing *or U.S.* **curb+ing** (ˈkɜːbɪŋ) *n.* **1.** material used for a kerb. **2.** a less common word for **kerb.**

kerb mar+ket *n. Stock Exchange.* **1.** an after-hours street market. **2.** a street market dealing in unquoted securities.

kerb+stone *or U.S.* **curb+stone** (ˈkɜːbˌstəʊn) *n.* one of a series of stones that form a kerb.

kerb weight *n.* the weight of a motor car without occupants, luggage, etc.

Kerch (*Russian* ˈkjertʃ) *n.* a port in the SW Soviet Union, in the Ukrainian SSR on the **Kerch Peninsula** and the **Strait of Kerch** (linking the Black Sea with the Sea of Azov): founded as a Greek colony in the 6th century B.C.; ceded to Russia in 1774; iron-mining and fishing. Pop.: 149 000 (1975 est.).

ker+chief (ˈkɜːtʃɪf) *n.* a piece of cloth worn tied over the head or around the neck. [C13: from Old French *cuevrechef,* from *covrir* to COVER + *chef* head; see CHIEF] —**ˈker+chiefed** *adj.*

Ke·ren·ski *or* **Ke·ren·sky** (kəˈrɛnskɪ; *Russian* ˈkjerɪnskij) *n.* **A·le·ksan·dr Fyo·do·ro·vich** (alɪˈksandr ˈfjɔdərəvitʃ). 1881–1970, Russian liberal revolutionary leader; prime minister (July–October 1917): overthrown by the Bolsheviks.

kerf (kɜːf) *n.* the cut made by a saw, axe, etc. [Old English *cyrf* a cutting; related to Old English *ceorfan* to CARVE]

ker+fuf+fle, car+fuf+fle, *or* **kur+fuf+fle** (kəˈfʌfᵊl) *n.* **1.** *Informal, chiefly Brit.* commotion; disorder; agitation. ~*vb.* **2.** (*tr.*) *Scot.* to put into disorder or disarray; ruffle or disarrange. [from Scottish *curfuffle, carfuffle,* from Scottish Gaelic *car* twist, turn + *fuffle* to disarrange]

Ker+gue+len (ˈkɜːgɪlɪn) *n.* an archipelago in the S Indian Ocean: consists of one large volcanic island (Kerguelen or Desolation Island) and 300 small islands; part of the French Southern and Antarctic Territories.

Kerk+ra+de (*Dutch* ˈkɛrkraːdə) *n.* a town in the SE Netherlands, in Limburg: one of the oldest coal-mining centres in Europe. Pop.: 47 301 (1973 est.).

Kér+ky+ra (ˈkɛrkira) *n.* transliteration of the Modern Greek name for **Corfu.**

Ker+man (kəˈmɑːn) *n.* a city in SE Iran: carpet-making centre. Pop.: 100 000 (1972 est.).

Ker+man+shah (ˌkɜːmænˈʃɑː) *n.* a city in W Iran, in the valley of the Qareh Su: oil refinery. Pop.: 249 000 (1973 est.).

ker+mes (ˈkɜːmɪz) *n.* **1.** the dried bodies of female scale insects of the genus *Kermes,* esp. *K. ilices* of Europe and W Asia, used as a red dyestuff. **2.** a small evergreen Eurasian oak tree, *Quercus coccifera:* the host plant of kermes scale insects. [C16: from French *kermès,* from Arabic *qirmiz,* from Sanskrit *krmija-* red dye, literally: produced by a worm, from *krmi* worm + *ja-* produced]

ker+mis (ˈkɜːmɪs) *or* **kir+mess** *n.* **1.** (in Belgium and the Netherlands, esp. formerly) an annual country festival or carnival. **2.** *U.S.* a similar event, esp. one held to collect money for charity. [C16: from Middle Dutch *kercmisse,* from *kerc* church + *misse* MASS; originally a festival held to celebrate the dedication of a church]

kern[1] *or* **kerne** (kɜːn) *n.* **1.** the part of the character on a piece of printer's type that projects beyond the body. ~*vb.* **2.** (*tr.*) to furnish (a typeface) with a kern. [C17: from French *carne* corner of type, projecting angle, ultimately from Latin *cardō* hinge]

kern[2] (kɜːn) *n.* **1.** a lightly armed foot soldier in medieval Ireland or Scotland. **2.** a troop of such soldiers. **3.** *Archaic.* a loutish peasant. [C14: from Middle Irish *cethern* band of foot soldiers, from *cath* battle]

kern[3] (kɜːn) *n. Engineering.* the central area of a wall, column, etc., through which all compressive forces pass.

Kern (kɜːn) *n.* **Je·rome (David).** 1885–1945, U.S. composer of musical comedies, esp. *Show Boat* (1927).

ker+nel (ˈkɜːnᵊl) *n.* **1.** the edible seed of a nut or fruit within the shell or stone. **2.** the grain of a cereal, esp. wheat, consisting of the seed in a hard husk. **3.** the central or essential part of something. ~*vb.* **+nels, +nel+ling, +nelled** *or U.S.* **+nels, +nel+ing, +neled. 4.** (*intr.*) *Rare.* to form kernels. [Old English *cyrnel* a little seed, from *corn* seed; see CORN] —**ˈker+nel-less** *adj.*

ker+nite (ˈkɜːnaɪt) *n.* a light soft colourless or white mineral consisting of a hydrated sodium borate in monoclinic crystalline form: an important source of borax and other boron compounds. Formula: $Na_2B_4O_7.4H_2O$. [C20: from *Kern* County, California, where it was found + -ITE[1]]

Ker·o (ˈkɛrəʊ) *n. Austral.* See **kerosene.**

ker·o+sene *or* **ker·o+sine** (ˈkɛrəˌsiːn) *n.* another name for **paraffin,** (esp. U.S.) except when used as a fuel for jet aircraft. [C19: from Greek *kēros* wax + -ENE]

Ke·rou·ac (ˈkɛrʊˌæk) *n.* **Jack,** original name *Jean-Louis Lefris de Kérouac.* 1922–69, U.S. novelist and poet of the beat generation. His works include *On the Road* (1957) and *Big Sur* (1962).

Kerr (kɜː) *n.* Sir **John Robert.** born 1914, Australian public servant. As governor general of Australia (1974–77), he dismissed the Labour prime minister Gough Whitlam (1975) amid great controversy.

Kerr ef+fect (kɜː) *n.* **1.** Also called: **electro-optical effect.** the production of double refraction in certain transparent substances by the application of a strong electric field. **2.** Also called: **magneto-optical effect.** a slight elliptical polarization of plane polarized light when reflected from one of the poles of a strong magnet. [C19: named after John *Kerr* (1824–1907), Scottish physicist]

Ker+ry[1] (ˈkɛrɪ) *n.* a county of SW Ireland, in W Munster province: mostly mountainous (including the highest peaks in Ireland), with a deeply indented coast and many offshore islands. County town: Tralee. Pop.: 112 772 (1971). Area: 4701 sq. km (1815 sq. miles).

Ker+ry[2] (ˈkɛrɪ) *n., pl.* **+ries.** a small black breed of dairy cattle, originally from Ireland. [C19: named after County *Kerry,* Ireland]

Ker+ry blue ter+ri+er *n.* a breed of terrier with a thick wavy grey coat.

ker+sey (ˈkɜːzɪ) *n.* **1.** a smooth woollen cloth used for overcoats, etc. **2.** a twilled woollen cloth with a cotton warp. [C14: probably from *Kersey,* village in Suffolk]

ker+sey+mere (ˈkɜːzɪˌmɪə) *n.* a fine soft woollen cloth of twill weave. [C18: from KERSEY + (CASSI)MERE]

Kes·sel·ring (ˈkɛsᵊlrɪŋ) *n.* **Al·bert** (ˈalbɛrt). 1885–1960, German field marshal. He commanded the Luftwaffe attacks on France, Britain, and North Africa (1939–45) and on the western front (1945).

Kes+te+ven (ˈkɛstɪvᵊn) *n.* **Parts of.** an area in E England constituting a former administrative division of Lincolnshire.

kes+trel (ˈkɛstrəl) *n.* any of several small falcons, esp. the European *Falco tinnunculus,* that tend to hover against the wind and feed on small mammals on the ground. [C15: changed from Old French *cresserele,* from *cressele* rattle, from Vulgar Latin *crepicella* (unattested), from Latin *crepitāre* to crackle, from *crepāre* to rustle]

Kes+wick (ˈkɛzɪk) *n.* a market town in NW England, in the Lake District: tourist centre. Pop.: 5169 (1971).

ketch (kɛtʃ) *n.* a two-masted sailing vessel, fore-and-aft rigged, with a tall mainmast and a mizzen stepped forward of the rudderpost. Compare **yawl**[1] (def. 1). [C15 *cache,* probably from *cacchen* to hunt; see CATCH]

ketch+up (ˈkɛtʃəp), **catch+up,** *or* **cat+sup** *n.* any of various piquant sauces containing vinegar: *tomato ketchup.* [C18: from Chinese (Amoy) *kōetsiap* brine of pickled fish, from *kōe* seafood + *tsiap* sauce]

ke+tene (ˈkiːtiːn, ˈket-) *n.* a colourless irritating toxic gas used as an acetylating agent in organic synthesis. Formula: CH_2:CO. Also called: **ethonone.**

ke·to- *or before a vowel* **ket-** *combining form.* indicating that a chemical compound is a ketone or is derived from a ketone: *ketose; ketoxine.*

ke·to·e·nol tau+tom+er+ism (ˈkiːtəʊˈiːnɒl) *n. Chem.* tautomerism in which the tautomers are an enol and a keto form. The change occurs by transfer of a hydrogen atom within the molecule.

ke·to form (ˌkiːtou) *n.* the form of tautomeric compounds when they are ketones rather than enols. See **keto-enol tautomerism.**

ke+tone (ˈkiːtəʊn) *n.* any of a class of compounds with the general formula R′COR, where R and R′are usually alkyl or aryl groups. See also **acetone.** [C19: from German *Keton,* from *Aketon* ACETONE] —**ke+ton+ic** (kɪˈtɒnɪk) *adj.*

ke+tone bod·y *n. Biochem.* any of three compounds (acetoacetic acid, 3-hydroxybutanoic acid, and acetone) produced when fatty acids are broken down in the liver to provide a source of energy. Excess ketone bodies are present in the blood and urine of people unable to use glucose as an energy source, as in diabetes and starvation. Also called: **acetone body.**

ke+tone group *n. Chem.* the functional group of ketones: a carbonyl group attached to the carbon atoms of two other organic groups.

ke+to+nu+ri·a (ˌkiːtəʊˈnjʊərɪə) *n. Pathol.* the presence of ketone bodies in the urine.

ke+tose (ˈkiːtəʊz) *n.* any monosaccharide that contains a ketone group.

ke+to+sis (kɪˈtəʊsɪs) *n. Pathol.* the condition resulting from excess production of ketone bodies.

ke+tox+ime (kiːˈtɒksiːm) *n.* an oxime formed by reaction between hydroxylamine and a ketone.

Ket+ter+ing (ˈkɛtərɪŋ) *n.* a town in central England, in Northamptonshire: footwear industry. Pop.: 42 628 (1971).

ket+tle (ˈkɛtᵊl) *n.* **1.** a metal container with a handle and spout for boiling water. **2.** any of various metal containers for heating liquids, cooking fish, etc. **3.** an open-topped refractory-lined steel vessel in which metals with low melting points are refined. **4.** short for **kettle hole.** [C13: from Old Norse *ketill;* related to Old English *cietel* kettle, Old High German *kezzil;* all ultimately from Latin *catillus* a little pot, from *catīnus* pot]

ket·tle·drum ('kɛtᵊl,drʌm) *n. Music.* a percussion instrument of definite pitch consisting of a hollow hemisphere covered with a skin or membrane, supported on a tripod. The pitch may be adjusted by means of screws, which alter the tension of the skin. —'**ket·tle,drum·mer** *n.*

ket+tle hole *n.* a round hollow formed by the melting of a mass of buried ice. Often shortened to **kettle.**

ket+tle of fish *n.* an awkward situation; mess (often used ironically in the phrase **a pretty** or **fine kettle of fish**).

kev+el ('kɛvᵊl) *n. Nautical.* a strong bitt or bollard for securing heavy hawsers. [C14: from Old Northern French *keville,* from Latin *clāvicula* a little key, from *clāvis* key]

Kew (kju:) *n.* part of the Greater London borough of Richmond-upon-Thames, on the River Thames: famous for **Kew Gardens** (the Royal Botanic Gardens), established in 1759 and given to the nation in 1841.

kew+pie doll ('kju:pɪ) *n. U.S.* **1.** any brightly coloured doll, commonly given as a prize at carnivals. **2.** (*caps.*) *Trademark.* a doll having rosy cheeks and a curl of hair on its head. [C20: *kewpie,* perhaps from *Cupid*]

kex (kɛks) *n.* **1.** any of several large hollow-stemmed umbelliferous plants, such as cow parsnip and chervil. **2.** the dried stalks of any of these plants. [C14: of obscure origin]

key[1] (ki:) *n.* **1.** a metal instrument, usually of a specifically contoured shape, that is made to fit a lock and, when rotated, operates the lock's mechanism. **2.** any instrument that is rotated to operate a valve, clock winding mechanism, etc. **3.** a small metal peg or wedge inserted into keyways. **4.** any of a set of levers operating a typewriter, computer, etc. **5.** any of the visible parts of the lever mechanism of a musical keyboard instrument that when depressed set in motion the action that causes the instrument to sound. **6. a.** Also called: **tonality.** any of the 24 major and minor diatonic scales considered as a corpus of notes upon which a piece of music draws for its tonal framework. **b.** the main tonal centre in an extended composition: *a symphony in the key of F major.* **c.** the tonic of a major or minor scale. **d.** See **tuning key. 7.** something that is crucial in providing an explanation or interpretation: *the key to adult behaviour lies in childhood.* **8.** a means of achieving a desired end: *the key to happiness.* **9.** a means of access or control: *Gibraltar is the key to the Mediterranean.* **10.** a list of explanations of symbols, codes, etc. **11.** a text that explains or gives information about a work of literature, art, or music. **12.** Also called: **key move.** the correct initial move in the solution of a set problem. **13.** *Biology.* a systematic list of taxonomic characteristics, used to identify animals or plants. **14.** *Photog., painting.* the dominant tonal value and colour intensity of a picture. See also **low-key** (sense 2), **high-key. 15.** *Electrical engineering.* **a.** a hand-operated device for opening or closing a circuit or for switching circuits. **b.** a hand-operated switch for transmitting coded signals, esp. Morse code. **16.** the grooving or scratching of a surface or the application of a rough coat of plaster, etc., to provide a bond for a subsequent finish. **17.** pitch: *he spoke in a low key.* **18.** a characteristic mood or style: *a poem in a melancholic key.* **19.** level of intensity: *she worked herself up to a high key.* **20.** *Railways.* a wooden wedge placed between a rail and a chair to keep the rail firmly in place. **21.** a wedge for tightening a joint or for splitting stone or timber. **22.** short for **keystone** (sense 1). **23.** *Botany.* any dry winged fruit, esp. that of the ash. **24.** (*modifier*) of great importance: *a key issue.* **25.** (*modifier*) *Photog.* determining the tonal value of a photograph: *flesh colour is an important key tone.* ~*vb.* (*tr.*) **26.** (foll. by *to*) to harmonize (with): *to key one's actions to the prevailing mood.* **27.** to adjust or fasten with a key or some similar device. **28.** to provide with a key or keys. **29.** (often foll. by *up*) to locate the position of (a piece of copy, artwork, etc.) on a layout by the use of symbols. **30.** to include a distinguishing device in (an advertisement, etc.), so that responses to it can be identified. **31.** to provide a keystone for (an arch). ~See also **key up.** [Old English *cǣg;* related to Old Frisian *kēi,* Middle Low German *keie* spear] —'**key+less** *adj.*

key[2] (ki:) *n.* a variant spelling of **cay.**

key+board ('ki:,bɔ:d) *n.* **1. a.** a complete set of keys, usually hand-operated, as on a piano, organ, typewriter, or typesetting machine. **b.** (*as modifier*): *a keyboard instrument.* ~*vb.* **2.** (*tr.*) to set (a text) in type, onto magnetic tape, or into some other medium by using a keyboard machine.

key+hole ('ki:,həʊl) *n.* **1.** an aperture in a door or a lock case through which a key may be passed to engage the lock mechanism. **2. a.** any small aperture resembling a keyhole in shape or function. **b.** (*as modifier*): *keyhole surgery.*

key mon+ey *n.* a fee payment required from a new tenant of a house or flat before he moves in.

Keynes (keɪnz) *n.* **John May·nard,** 1st Baron Keynes. 1883–1946, English economist. In *The General Theory of Employment, Interest and Money* (1936) he advocated the use of government fiscal and monetary policy to adjust demand and maintain full employment without inflation (**Keynesianism**). He helped to found the International Monetary Fund and the World Bank. —'**Keynes·i+an** *adj., n.*

key+note ('ki:,nəʊt) *n.* **1. a.** a central or determining principle in a speech, literary work, etc. **b.** (*as modifier*): *a keynote speech.* **2.** the note upon which a scale or key is based; tonic. ~*vb.* (*tr.*) **3.** to deliver a keynote address to (a political convention, etc.). **4.** to outline (political issues, policy, etc.) in or as in a keynote address.

key punch *n.* **1.** Also called: **card punch.** a device having a keyboard that is operated manually to transfer data onto punched cards, paper tape, etc. ~*vb.* **key-punch. 2.** to transfer (data) onto punched cards, paper tape, etc., by using a key punch.

key sig+na+ture *n. Music.* a group of sharps or flats appearing at the beginning of each stave line to indicate the key in which a piece, section, etc., is to be performed.

key+stone ('ki:,stəʊn) *n.* **1.** Also called: **headstone, quoin.** the central stone at the top of an arch or the top stone of a dome or vault. **2.** something that is necessary to connect or support a number of other related things.

key+stroke ('ki:,strəʊk) *n.* a single operation of the mechanism of a typewriter or keyboard-operated typesetting machine by the action of a key.

key up *vb.* (*tr., adv.*) to raise the intensity, excitement, tension, etc., of.

key+way ('ki:,weɪ) *n.* a longitudinal slot cut into a component to accept a key that engages with a similar slot on a mating component to prevent relative motion of the two components.

key word *n.* **1.** a word used as a key to a code. **2.** any significant word or thing, esp. a word used to describe the contents of a document.

kg *or* **kg.** *abbrev. for:* **1.** kilogram. **2.** keg.

K.G. *abbrev. for* Knight of the Order of the Garter (a Brit. title).

K.G.B. *abbrev.* the Soviet secret police since 1954. [from Russian *Komitet Gosudarstvennoi Bezopasnosti* State Security Committee]

Kha+ba+rovsk (*Russian* xə'barəfsk) *n.* a port in the E Soviet Union, on the Amur River: the administrative centre of the whole Soviet Far Eastern territory until 1938; a major industrial centre. Pop.: 500 000 (1975 est.).

Kha·cha·tur·i·an (,kɑ:tʃə'tʊərɪən; *Russian* xətʃətur'jan) *n.* **Ar·am Il·ich** ('arəm il'jitʃ). 1903–78, Russian composer. His works, which often incorporate Armenian folk tunes, include a piano concerto and the ballet *Gayaneh* (1942).

khad+dar ('kɑ:də) *or* **kha+di** ('kɑ:dɪ) *n.* a cotton cloth of plain weave, produced in India. [from Hindi *khādar*]

Kha+kass Au·ton·o+mous Re+gion (kə'kæs) *n.* an administrative division of the S central Soviet Union, in the Krasnoyarsk Territory of the RSFSR: formed in 1930. Capital: Abakan. Pop.: 445 824 (1970). Area: 61 900 sq. km (23 855 sq. miles).

kha+ki ('kɑ:kɪ) *n., pl.* **+kis. 1. a.** a dull yellowish-brown colour. **b.** (*as adj.*): *a khaki background.* **2. a.** a hard-wearing fabric of this colour, used esp. for military uniforms. **b.** (*as modifier*): *a khaki jacket.* [C19: from Urdu, from Persian: dusty, from *khāk* dust]

Kha·lid ibn Ab·dul Az·iz ('kɑ:lɪd 'ɪbᵊn 'æbdʊl ɑ'zi:z) *n.* 1913–82, king and President of the Council of Ministers of Saudi Arabia 1975–82.

kha+lif ('keɪlɪf, 'kæl-) *n.* a variant spelling of **caliph.**

Khal+kha ('kælkə) *n.* the dialect of Mongolian that is the official language of the Mongolian People's Republic.

Khal+ki+di+ki (,xalkiði'ki) *n.* transliteration of the Modern Greek name for **Chalcidice.**

Khal+kís (xal'kis) *n.* transliteration of the Modern Greek name for **Chalcis.**

Kha·ma ('kɑ:mə) *n.* Sir **Se·ret·se** (sə'rɛtsɪ). 1921-80, Botswana statesman; first president of Botswana (1966-80).

kham+sin ('kæmsɪn, kæm'si:n), **kam+seen,** *or* **kam+sin** *n.* a hot southerly wind blowing from about March to May, esp. in Egypt. [C17: from Arabic, literally: fifty]

khan[1] (kɑ:n) *n.* **1. a.** (formerly) a title borne by medieval Chinese emperors and Mongol and Turkic rulers: usually added to a name: *Kublai Khan.* **b.** such a ruler. **2.** a title of respect borne by important personages in Afghanistan and central Asia. [C14: from Old French *caan,* from Medieval Latin *caanus,* from Turkish *khān,* contraction of *khāqān* ruler]

khan[2] (kɑ:n) *n.* an inn in Turkey, certain Arab countries, etc.; caravanserai. [C14: via Arabic from Persian]

khan+ate ('kɑ:neɪt, 'kæn-) *n.* **1.** the territory ruled by a khan. **2.** the position or rank of a khan.

khan+ga ('kæŋgə) *n.* a variant spelling of **kanga.**

Kha+nia (xa'nja) *n.* transliteration of the Modern Greek name for **Canea.**

kha+rif (kə'ri:f) *n.* (in Pakistan, India, etc.) a crop that is harvested at the beginning of winter. Compare **rabi.** [Urdu, ultimately from Arabic *kharafa* to gather]

Khar+kov (*Russian* 'xarjkəf) *n.* a city in the S Soviet Union, in the E Ukrainian SSR: capital of the Ukrainian SSR (1917–34); university (1805). Pop.: 1 357 000 (1975 est.).

Khar+toum *or* **Khar+tum** (kɑ:'tu:m) *n.* the capital of the Sudan, at the junction of the Blue and the White Nile: with adjoining Khartoum North and Omdurman, the largest conurbation in the country destroyed by the Mahdists in 1885 when General Gordon was killed; seat of the Anglo-Egyptian government of the Sudan until 1954, then capital of the new republic. Pop.: 261 840 (1971 est.).

khat (kæt, kɑ:t) *n.* a variant spelling of **kat.**

kha+yal (kə'jɑ:l) *n.* a kind of Indian classical vocal music. [Urdu: literally: thought, imagination]

Khay·yám (kaɪ'am) *n.* **O·mar.** See **Omar Khayyám.**

khed·a, khed+ah, *or* **ked+dah** ('kɛdə) *n.* (in India, Burma, etc.) an enclosure into which wild elephants are driven to be captured. [from Hindi]

khe+dive (kɪ'di:v) *n.* the viceroy of Egypt under Ottoman suzerainty (1867–1914). [C19: from French *khédive,* from Turkish *hidiv,* from Persian *khidīw* prince] —**khe+'di+val** *or* **khe+'di+vi+al** *adj.* —**khe+'di+vate** *or* **khe+'di+vi+ate** *n.*

Khe+lat (kə'lɑ:t) *n.* a variant spelling of **Kalat.**

Kher·son (*Russian* xɪr'sɔn) *n.* a port in the SW Soviet Union, in the S Ukrainian SSR on the Dnieper River near the Black Sea: shipyards. Pop.: 307 000 (1975 est.).

Khieu (kjuː) *n.* **Sam·phan** ('sæmfæn). born 1932, Cambodian Communist statesman; president of Cambodia 1976–79.

Khin·gan Moun·tains ('ʃɪŋ'ɑːn) *pl. n.* a mountain system of NE China, in W Manchuria. Highest peak: 2034 m (6673 ft.).

Khi·os ('çiɔs) *n.* transliteration of the Modern Greek name for **Chios.**

Khir·bet Qum·ran ('kɪəbɛt 'kʊmrɑːn) *n.* an archaeological site in NW Jordan, near the NW shore of the Dead Sea: includes the caves where the Dead Sea Scrolls were found.

Khi·va (*Russian* xi'va) *n.* a former khanate of W Asia, on the Amu Darya River: divided between the Uzbek and Turkmen SSRs in 1924.

Khmer (kmɛə, kmɜː) *n.* **1.** a member of a people of Cambodia, noted for a civilization that flourished from about 800 A.D. to about 1370, remarkable for its architecture. **2.** the language of this people, belonging to the Mon-Khmer family: the official language of Cambodia. ~*adj.* **3.** of or relating to this people or their language. —'**Khmer·i·an** *adj.*

Khmer Re·pub·lic *n.* the former official name (1970–76) of **Cambodia.**

Khmer Rouge ('ruːʒ) *n.* the Cambodian communist party, ruled (1975-79) after seizing power in a civil war.

Khoi·khoi ('kɔɪkɔɪ) *n.* a group of the Khoisan languages, spoken mostly by Hottentots.

Khoi·san ('kɔɪsɑːn, kɔɪ'sɑːn) *n.* **1.** a family of languages, divided into the Khoikhoi and San subfamilies, spoken in southern Africa by the Hottentots and Bushmen and by two small groups in Tanzania. A characteristic phonological feature of these languages is the use of suction stops (clicks). ~*adj.* **2.** denoting, relating to, or belonging to this family of languages.

Kho·mei·ni ('xɒmeɪ'niː) *n.* **Ru·hol·la** ('rʊhɒ'lɑː). known as *Ayatollah Khomeini.* born 1901, Muslim religious leader; deposed shah of Iran and instituted an Islamic republic.

Khrush·chev (kruːs'tʃɒf, 'krʊstʃɒf; *Russian* xru'ʃtʃɔf) *n.* **Ni·ki·ta Ser·ge·ye·vich** (ni'kitə sɪr'gjejɪvitʃ). 1894–1971, Soviet statesman; premier of the Soviet Union (1958–64). On Stalin's death he became first secretary of the Soviet Communist Party (1953–64) and initiated a destalinization policy (1956). As premier, he pursued a policy of peaceful coexistence with the West, but alienated Communist China. He was removed from office in 1964.

Khu·fu ('kuːfuː) *n.* the original name of **Cheops.**

Khul·na ('kʊlnɑː) *n.* a city in S Bangladesh. Pop.: 437 304 (1974).

khus·khus ('kʊskʊs) *n.* an aromatic perennial Indian grass, *Vetiveria zizanioides* (or *Andropogon squarrosus*), whose roots are woven into mats, fans, and baskets. [Hindi]

Khy·ber Pass ('kaɪbə) *n.* a narrow pass over the Safed Koh Range between Afghanistan and Pakistan, over which came the Persian, Greek, Tatar, Mogul, and Afghan invasions of India; scene of bitter fighting between the British and Afghans (1838–42, 1878–80). Length: about 53 km (33 miles). Highest point: 1072 m (3518 ft.).

kHz *abbrev. for* kilohertz.

ki·aat ('kiɑːt) *n.* **1.** a tropical African leguminous tree, *Pterocarpus angolensis.* **2.** the wood of this tree, used for furniture, floors, etc. [from Afrikaans, probably from a Bantu language]

ki·ang (kɪ'æŋ) *n.* a variety of the wild ass, *Equus hemionus,* that occurs in Tibet and surrounding regions. Compare **onager.** [C19: from Tibetan *rkyan*]

Kiang·si ('kjæŋ'siː) *n.* a province of SE central China, in the basins of the Kan River and the Po-yang Lake: mineral resources include coal and tungsten. Capital: Nanchang. Pop.: 28 000 000 (1976 est.). Area: 164 800 sq. km (64 300 sq. miles).

Kiang·su ('kjæŋ'suː) *n.* a province of E China, on the Yellow Sea: consists mostly of the marshy delta of the Yangtze River, with some of China's largest cities and most densely populated areas. Capital: Nanking. Pop.: 55 000 000 (1976 est.). Area: 102 200 sq. km (39 860 sq. miles).

Kiao·chow ('kjaʊ'tʃaʊ) *n.* a territory of NE China, in SE Shantung province, surrounding **Kiaochow Bay** (an inlet of the Yellow Sea): leased to Germany from 1898 to 1914. Area: about 520 sq. km (200 sq. miles).

kib·ble[1] ('kɪbᵊl) *n. Brit.* a bucket used in wells or in mining for hoisting. [C17: from German *kübel;* related to Old English *cyfel,* ultimately from Medieval Latin *cuppa* CUP]

kib·ble[2] ('kɪbᵊl) *vb. (tr.)* to grind into small pieces. [C18: of unknown origin]

kib·butz (kɪ'bʊts) *n., pl.* **kib·but·zim** (ˌkɪbʊt'siːm). a collective agricultural settlement in modern Israel, owned and administered communally by its members and on which children are reared collectively. [C20: from Modern Hebrew *qibbūs:* gathering, from Hebrew *qibbūtz*]

kibe (kaɪb) *n.* a chilblain, esp. an ulcerated one on the heel. [C14: probably from Welsh *cibi,* of obscure origin]

ki·bit·ka (kɪ'bɪtkə) *n.* **1.** (in Russia) a covered sledge or wagon. **2.** a felt tent used among the Tatars of central Asia. **3.** a Tatar family. [C18: Russian, from Tatar *kibits*]

kib·itz ('kɪbɪts) *vb. (intr.) U.S. informal.* to interfere or offer unwanted advice, esp. as a spectator at a card game. [C20: from Yiddish *kibitzen,* from German *kiebitzen* to be an onlooker, from *Kiebitz* busybody, literally: plover] —'**kib·itz·er** *n.*

kib·lah *or* **kib·la** ('kɪblɑː) *n. Islam.* the direction of Mecca, to which Muslims turn in prayer, indicated in mosques by a niche (mihrab) in the wall. [C18: from Arabic *qiblah* that which is placed opposite; related to *qabala* to be opposite]

ki·bosh ('kaɪˌbɒʃ) *Slang.* ~*n.* **1. put the kibosh on.** to put a stop to; prevent from continuing; halt. ~*vb.* **2.** *(tr.) Rare.* to put a stop to. [C19: of unknown origin]

kick (kɪk) *vb.* **1.** *(tr.)* to drive or impel with the foot. **2.** *(tr.)* to hit with the foot or feet. **3.** *(intr.)* to strike out or thrash about with the feet, as in fighting or swimming. **4.** *(intr.)* to raise a leg high, as in dancing. **5.** (of a gun, etc.) to recoil or strike in recoiling when fired. **6.** *(tr.) Rugby.* **a.** to make (a conversion or a drop goal) by means of a kick. **b.** to score (a goal) by means of a kicked conversion. **7.** *(tr.) Soccer.* to score (a goal) by a kick. **8.** *(intr.) Cricket.* (of a ball) to rear up sharply. **9.** *(intr.;* sometimes foll. by *against) Informal.* to object or resist. **10.** *(intr.) Informal.* to be active and in good health (esp. in the phrase **alive and kicking**). **11.** *Informal.* to change gear in a car, esp. a racing car: *he kicked into third and passed the bigger car.* **12.** *(tr.) Informal.* to free oneself of (an addiction, etc.): *to kick heroin; to kick the habit.* **13. kick against the pricks. a.** to act against one's own conscience. **b.** to resist the inevitable. **14. kick one's heels.** to be idle or be kept waiting. **15. kick over the traces.** See **trace**[2] (sense 3). **16. kick the bucket.** *Slang.* to die. **17. kick up one's heels.** *Informal.* to enjoy oneself without inhibition. ~*n.* **18.** a thrust or blow with the foot. **19.** any of certain rhythmic leg movements used in swimming. **20.** the recoil of a gun or other firearm. **21.** *Informal.* stimulating or exciting quality or effect (esp. in the phrases **get a kick out of, for kicks**). **22.** *Informal.* the sudden stimulating or intoxicating effect of strong alcoholic drink or certain drugs. **23.** *Informal.* power or force. **24.** *Slang.* a temporary enthusiasm: *he's on a new kick every week.* **25. kick in the pants.** *Slang.* **a.** a reprimand. **b.** a setback. **26. kick in the teeth.** *Slang.* a humiliating rebuff. [C14 *kiken,* perhaps of Scandinavian origin] —'**kick·a·ble** *adj.*

kick a·bout *or* **a·round** *vb. (mainly adv.) Informal.* **1.** *(tr.)* to treat harshly. **2.** *(tr.)* to discuss (ideas, etc.) informally. **3.** *(intr.)* to wander aimlessly. **4.** *(intr.)* to lie neglected or forgotten. **5.** *(intr.; also prep.)* to be present in (some place).

kick·back ('kɪkˌbæk) *n.* **1.** a strong reaction. **2.** *U.S.* part of an income paid to a person having influence over the size or payment of the income, esp. by some illegal arrangement. ~*vb.* **kick back.** *(adv.)* **3.** *(intr.)* to have a strong reaction. **4.** *(intr.)* (esp. of a gun) to recoil. **5.** *U.S.* to pay a kickback to (someone).

kick·down ('kɪkˌdaʊn) *n.* a method of changing gear in a car with automatic transmission, by fully depressing the accelerator.

kick·er ('kɪkə) *n.* **1.** a person or thing that kicks. **2.** *Sport.* a player in a rugby or occasionally a soccer team whose task is to attempt to kick conversions, penalty goals, etc. **3.** *U.S. slang.* a hidden and disadvantageous factor, such as a clause in a contract. **4.** *Informal.* any light outboard motor for propelling a boat.

kick off *vb. (intr., adv.)* **1.** to start play in a game of football by kicking the ball from the centre of the field. **2.** *Informal.* to commence (a discussion, job, etc.). ~*n.* **kick·off. 3. a.** a place kick from the centre of the field in a game of football. **b.** the time at which the first such kick is due to take place: *kickoff is at 2:30 p.m.* **4.** *Informal.* **a.** the beginning of something. **b. for a kickoff.** to begin with.

kick out *vb. (adv.)* **1.** *(tr.) Informal.* to eject or dismiss. **2.** *(intr.)* to turn a skateboard or surfboard into the air, as in surfing over a wave, by shifting weight to the back of the board with the foot. ~*n.* **kick-out. 3.** an act or instance of kicking out.

kick pleat *n.* a back pleat at the hem of a straight skirt to allow the wearer greater ease in walking.

kick·shaw ('kɪkˌʃɔː) *or* **kick·shaws** *n.* **1.** a valueless trinket. **2.** *Archaic.* a small elaborate or exotic delicacy. [C16: back formation from *kickshaws,* by folk etymology from French *quelque chose* something]

kick·sort·er ('kɪkˌsɔːtə) *n. Physics.* a multichannel pulse-height analyser used esp. to distinguish between isotopes by sorting their characteristic pulses (kicks).

kick·stand ('kɪkˌstænd) *n.* a short metal bar attached to and pivoting on the bottom of the frame of a motorcycle or bicycle, which when kicked into a vertical position holds the stationary vehicle upright.

kick-start ('kɪkˌstɑːt) *vb.* to start an engine, esp. of a motorcycle, by means of a pedal that is kicked downwards. —'**kick-ˌstart·er** *n.*

kick·tail ('kɪkˌteɪl) *n.* the slightly turned-up part of the back of a skateboard, designed to make manoeuvres easier.

kick turn *n.* **1.** *Skiing.* a standing turn performed by swivelling each ski separately through 180°. **2.** *Skateboarding.* a manoeuvre in which the front wheels are lifted off the ground by the rider changing his weight distribution, to alter the direction of forward movement.

kick up *vb. (adv.) Informal.* to cause (trouble, a fuss, etc.).

kick up·stairs *vb. (tr., adv.) Informal.* to promote to a nominally higher but effectively powerless position.

kid[1] (kɪd) *n.* **1.** the young of a goat or of a related animal, such as an antelope. **2. a.** soft smooth leather made from the hide of a kid. **3.** *Informal.* **a.** a young person; child. **b.** *(modifier)* younger or being still a child: *kid brother; kid sister.* **4. our kid.** *Liverpool dialect.* one's younger brother or sister. ~*vb.* **kids, kid·ding, kid·ded. 5.** (of a goat) to give birth to (young). [C12: of Scandinavian origin; compare Old Norse *kith,* Shetland Islands *kidi* lamb] —'**kid·dish·ness** *n.* —'**kid·ˌlike** *adj.*

kid[2] (kɪd) *Informal.* ~*vb.* **kids, kid·ding, kid·ded. 1.** *(tr.)* to tease or deceive. **2.** (*intr.*) to behave or speak deceptively for fun. [C19: probably from KID[1]] —'**kid·der** *n.* —'**kid·ding·ly** *adv.*

kid[3] (kɪd) *n.* a small wooden tub. [C18: probably variant of KIT[1] (in the sense: barrel)]

Kid (kɪd) *n.* **Thom·as.** a variant spelling of (Thomas) **Kyd.**

Kidd (kɪd) *n.* **Wil·liam,** known as *Captain Kidd.* 1645–1701, Scottish privateer, pirate, and murderer; hanged.

Kid·der·min·ster ('kɪdəˌmɪnstə) *n.* **1.** a town in W central England, in NE Hereford and Worcester on the River Stour: carpet industry. Pop.: 47 255 (1971). **2.** a type of ingrain reversible carpet originally made at Kidderminster.

kid·dle ('kɪdᵊl) *n.* *Brit., archaic.* a device, esp. a barrier constructed of nets and stakes, for catching fish in a river or in the sea. [C13: from Anglo-French, from Old French *quidel,* of obscure origin]

Kid·dush ('kɪdəʃ; *Hebrew* ki'duʃ) *n.* *Judaism.* a traditional blessing recited over bread or a cup of wine on the Sabbath or a festival. [from Hebrew *qiddūsh* sanctification]

kid·dy *or* **kid·die** ('kɪdɪ) *n., pl.* **·dies.** *Informal.* an affectionate word for **child.**

kid glove *n.* **1.** a glove made of kidskin. **2. handle with kid gloves.** to treat with great tact or caution. ~*adj.* **kid·glove. 3.** overdelicate or overrefined. **4.** diplomatic; tactful: *a kidglove approach.*

kid·nap ('kɪdnæp) *vb.* **·naps, ·nap·ping, ·napped** *or U.S.* **·naps, ·nap·ing, ·naped.** (*tr.*) to carry off and hold (a person), usually for ransom. [C17: KID[1] + obsolete *nap* to steal; see NAB] —'**kid·nap·per** *n.*

kid·ney ('kɪdnɪ) *n.* **1.** either of two bean-shaped organs at the back of the abdominal cavity in man, one on each side of the spinal column. They maintain water and electrolyte balance and filter waste products from the blood, which are excreted as urine. Related adj.: **renal. 2.** the corresponding organ in other animals. **3.** the kidneys of certain animals used as food. **4.** class, type, or disposition (esp. in the phrases **of the same** or **a different kidney**). [C14: of uncertain origin] —'**kidn·ey-like** *adj.*

kid·ney bean *n.* **1.** any of certain bean plants having kidney-shaped seeds, esp. the French bean and scarlet runner. **2.** the seed of any of these beans.

kid·ney mach·ine *n.* another name for **artificial kidney.** See **haemodialysis.**

kid·ney stone *n.* *Pathol.* a hard mass formed in the kidney, usually composed of oxalates, phosphates, and carbonates. Also called: **renal calculus.**

kid·ney vetch *n.* a silky papilionaceous perennial plant, *Anthyllis vulneraria,* of Europe and N Africa, with yellow or orange flowers. Also called: **ladies' fingers.**

Ki·dron ('kiːdrən) *n.* a variant spelling of **Kedron.**

kid·skin ('kɪdˌskɪn) *n.* a soft smooth leather made from the hide of a young goat. Often shortened to **kid.**

kids' stuff *n.* **1.** something considered fit only for children. **2.** something considered simple or easy.

kief (kiːf) *n.* a variant spelling of **kif.**

Kiel (kiːl) *n.* a port in N West Germany, capital of Schleswig-Holstein state, on the **Kiel Canal** (connecting the North Sea with the Baltic): joined the Hanseatic League in 1284; became part of Denmark in 1773 and passed to Prussia in 1866; an important naval base in World Wars I and II; shipbuilding and engineering industries. Pop.: 265 587 (1974 est.).

Kiel·ce (*Polish* 'kjɛltsɛ) *n.* an industrial city in S Poland. Pop.: 142 000 (1974 est.).

kier (kɪə) *n.* a vat in which cloth is bleached. [C16: from Old Norse *ker* tub; related to Old High German *kar*]

Kier·ke·gaard ('kɪəkəˌgɑːd; *Danish* 'kirgəˌɔːr) *n.* **Søren Aa·bye** ('sœːrən 'ɔːby). 1813–55, Danish philosopher and theologian. He rejected organized Christianity and anticipated the existentialists in emphasizing man's moral responsibility and freedom of choice. His works include *Either/Or* (1843), *The Concept of Dread* (1844), and *The Sickness unto Death* (1849). —ˌ**Kier·ke·'gaard·i·an** *adj.*

kie·sel·guhr ('kiːzᵊlˌgʊə) *n.* an unconsolidated form of **diatomite.** [C19: from German *Kieselgur,* from *Kiesel* flint, pebble + *Gur* loose earthy deposit]

kie·ser·ite ('kiːzəˌraɪt) *n.* a white mineral consisting of hydrated magnesium sulphate. Formula: $MgSO_4.H_2O$. [C19: named after Dietrich G. *Kieser* (died 1862), German physician; see -ITE[1]]

Ki·ev ('kiːɛf; *Russian* 'kijɪf) *n.* a city in the SW Soviet Union, capital of the Ukrainian SSR, on the Dnieper River: formed the first Russian state by the late 9th century; university (1834). Pop.: 1 947 000 (1975 est.).

kif (kɪf, kiːf), **kaif, keef, kef,** *or* **kief** *n.* **1.** another name for **marijuana. 2.** any drug or agent that when smoked is capable of producing a euphoric condition. **3.** the euphoric condition produced by smoking marijuana. [C20: from Arabic *kayf* pleasure]

Ki·ga·li (kɪ'gɑːlɪ) *n.* the capital of Rwanda, in the central part. Pop.: 54 403 (1970 est.).

kike (kaɪk) *n.* *U.S. slang.* an offensive word for **Jew.** [C20: probably variant of *kiki,* reduplication of *-ki,* common name-ending among Jews from Slavic countries]

Ki·klá·dhes (ki'klaðɛs) *n.* transliteration of the modern Greek name for **Cyclades.**

ki·koi ('kiːkɔɪ) *n.* (in E Africa) **a.** a piece of cotton cloth with coloured bands, worn wrapped around the body. **b.** (*as modifier*): *kikoi material.* [C20: from Swahili]

kik·u·mon ('kɪkuːˌmɒn) *n.* the chrysanthemum emblem of the imperial family of Japan. [Japanese]

Ki·ku·yu (kɪ'kuːjuː) *n.* **1.** (*pl.* **·yus** *or* **·yu**) a member of a Negroid people of E Africa, living chiefly in Kenya on the high foothills around Mount Kenya. **2.** the language of this people, belonging to the Bantu group of the Niger-Congo family.

Ki·la·u·e·a (ˌkiːlɑːuː'eɪə) *n.* a crater on the E side of Mauna Loa volcano, on SE Hawaii Island: the world's largest active crater. Height: 1247 m (4090 ft.). Width: 3 km (2 miles).

Kil·dare (kɪl'dɛə) *n.* a county of E Ireland, in Leinster province: mostly low-lying and fertile. County town: Naas. Pop.: 71 977 (1971). Area: 1694 sq. km (654 sq. miles).

kil·der·kin ('kɪldəkɪn) *n.* an obsolete unit of capacity equal to approximately 18 Imperial gallons. [C14: from Middle Dutch *kindekijn,* from *kintal* hundredweight, from Medieval Latin *quintale;* see KENTLEDGE]

Kil·i·man·ja·ro (ˌkɪlɪmən'dʒɑːrəʊ) *n.* a volcanic massif in N Tanzania: the highest peak in Africa; extends from east to west for 80 km (50 miles). Height: 5895 m (19 340 ft.).

Kil·ken·ny (kɪl'kɛnɪ) *n.* **1.** a county of SE Ireland, in Leinster province: mostly agricultural. County town: Kilkenny. Pop.: 61 473 (1971). Area: 2062 sq. km (796 sq. miles). **2.** a market town in SE Ireland, county town of Co. Kilkenny: capital of the ancient kingdom of Ossory. Pop.: 12 351 (1971).

kill[1] (kɪl) *vb.* (*mainly tr.*) **1.** (*also intr.;* when *tr.,* sometimes foll. by *off*) to cause the death of (a person or animal). **2.** to put an end to; destroy: *to kill someone's interest.* **3.** to make (time) pass quickly, esp. while waiting for something. **4.** to deaden (sound). **5.** *Informal.* to tire out; exhaust: *the effort killed him.* **6.** *Informal.* to cause to suffer pain or discomfort: *my shoes are killing me.* **7.** *Informal.* to cancel, cut, or delete: *to kill three lines of text.* **8.** *Informal.* to quash, defeat, or veto: *the bill was killed in the House of Lords.* **9.** *Informal.* to switch off; stop: *to kill a motor.* **10.** (*also intr.*) *Informal.* to overcome with attraction, laughter, surprise, etc.: *she was dressed to kill; his gags kill me.* **11.** *Slang.* to consume (alcoholic drink) entirely: *he killed three bottles of rum.* **12.** *Tennis, squash, etc.* to hit (a ball) so hard or so accurately that the opponent cannot return it. **13.** *Soccer.* to bring (a moving ball) under control; trap. **14. kill oneself.** *Informal.* to overexert oneself: *don't kill yourself.* **15. kill two birds with one stone.** to achieve two results with one action. ~*n.* **16.** the act of causing death, esp. at the end of a hunt, bullfight, etc. **17.** the animal or animals killed during a hunt. **18.** the destruction of a battleship, tank, etc. **19. in at the kill.** present at the end or climax of some undertaking. [C13 *cullen;* perhaps related to Old English *cwellan* to kill; compare German (Westphalian dialect) *küllen;* see QUELL]

kill[2] (kɪl) *n.* *U.S.* a channel, stream, or river (chiefly as part of place names). [C17: from Middle Dutch *kille;* compare Old Norse *kíll* small bay, creek]

Kil·lar·ney (kɪ'lɑːnɪ) *n.* a town in SW Ireland, in Co. Kerry: a tourist centre near the **Lakes of Killarney.** Pop.: 7150 (1971).

kill·deer ('kɪlˌdɪə) *n., pl.* **·deer** *or* **·deers.** a large brown-and-white North American plover, *Charadrius vociferus,* with two black breast bands and a noisy cry. [C18: of imitative origin]

kill·er ('kɪlə) *n.* **1. a.** a person or animal that kills, esp. habitually. **b.** (*as modifier*): *a killer shark.* **2.** another name for **slaughterman.**

kill·er whale *n.* a ferocious black-and-white toothed whale, *Orcinus orca,* with a large erect dorsal fin, most common in cold seas: family *Delphinidae.* Also called: **killer, grampus, orc.**

kil·lick ('kɪlɪk) *or* **kil·lock** ('kɪlək) *n.* *Nautical.* a small anchor, esp. one made of a heavy stone. [C17: of unknown origin]

Kil·lie·cran·kie (ˌkɪlɪ'kræŋkɪ) *n.* a pass in central Scotland, in the Grampians: scene of a battle (1689) in which the Jacobites defeated William III's forces but lost their leader, Viscount Dundee.

kil·li·fish ('kɪlɪˌfɪʃ) *n., pl.* **·fish** *or* **·fish·es.** any of various chiefly American minnow-like cyprinodont fishes of the genus *Fundulus* and related genera, of fresh and brackish waters: used as aquarium fishes, to control mosquitoes, and as anglers' bait. [C19: see KILL[2], FISH]

kil·li·ki·nick (ˌkɪlɪkɪ'nɪk) *n.* a variant spelling of **kinnikinnick.**

kill·ing ('kɪlɪŋ) *Informal.* ~*adj.* **1.** very tiring; exhausting: *a killing pace.* **2.** extremely funny; hilarious. ~*n.* **3.** a sudden stroke of success, as in speculations on the stock market (esp. in the phrase **make a killing**). —'**kill·ing·ly** *adv.*

kill-joy *n.* a person who spoils other people's pleasure.

kill-time *n.* **a.** an occupation that passes the time. **b.** (*as modifier*): *kill-time pursuits.*

Kil·mar·nock (kɪl'mɑːnək) *n.* a town in SW Scotland, in SW Strathclyde region: associations with Robert Burns; engineering and textile industries; whisky blending. Pop.: 48 785 (1971).

kiln (kɪln) *n.* **1.** a large oven for burning, drying, or processing something, such as porcelain or bricks. ~*vb.* **2.** (*tr.*) to fire or process in a kiln. [Old English *cylen,* from Late Latin *culīna* kitchen, from Latin *coquere* to COOK]

ki·lo ('kiːləʊ) *n., pl.* **·los.** short for **kilogram** *or* **kilometre.**

kil·o- *prefix.* **1.** denoting 10^3 (1000): *kilometre.* Symbol: k **2.** (in computer technology) denoting 2^{10} (1024): *kilobyte.* [from French, from Greek *khilioi* thousand]

kil·o·cal·o·rie ('kɪləʊˌkælərɪ) *n.* another name for **Calorie.**

kil·o·cy·cle ('kɪləʊˌsaɪkᵊl) *n.* short for kilocycle per second: a former unit of frequency equal to 1 kilohertz.

kil·o·gram *or* **kil·o·gramme** ('kɪləʊˌgræm) *n.* **1.** one thousand grams. **2.** the basic SI unit of mass, equal to the mass of the international prototype held by the *Bureau International des Poids et Mesures.* One kilogram is equivalent to 2.204 62 pounds. Symbol: kg

kil·o·gram cal·o·rie *n.* another name for **Calorie.**

kil·o+hertz ('kɪləʊˌhɜːts) *n.* one thousand hertz; one thousand cycles per second. Symbol: kHz

kil·o·me·tre *or U.S.* **kil·o+me·ter** ('kɪləˌmiːtə, kɪ'lɒmɪtə) *n.* one thousand metres, equal to 0.621 371 miles. Symbol: km —**kil·o·met+ric** (ˌkɪləʊ'mɛtrɪk) *or* ˌ**kil·o+'met+ri+cal** *adj.*

kil·o+ton ('kɪləʊˌtʌn) *n.* **1.** one thousand tons. **2.** an explosive power, esp. of a nuclear weapon, equal to the power of 1000 tons of TNT.

kil·o+volt ('kɪləʊˌvəʊlt) *n.* one thousand volts. Symbol: kV

kil·o+watt ('kɪləʊˌwɒt) *n.* one thousand watts. Symbol: kW

kil·o·watt-hour *n.* a unit of energy equal to the work done by a power of 1000 watts in one hour. Symbol: kW-hr

kilt (kɪlt) *n.* **1.** a knee-length pleated skirt, esp. one in plaid, as worn by men in the Scottish Highlands. ~*vb.* (*tr.*) **2.** to tuck (the skirt) up around one's body. **3.** to put pleats in (cloth, a skirt, etc.). [C18: of Scandinavian origin; compare Danish *kilte* to tuck up, Old Swedish *kilta* lap] —**'kilt+ed** *adj.* —**'kilt+ˌlike** *adj.*

kil+ter ('kɪltə) *n.* a variant spelling (esp. U.S.) of **kelter.** [C17: origin unknown]

Ki+lung ('kiː'lʊŋ) *n.* another name for **Chilung.**

Kim+ber+ley ('kɪmbəlɪ) *n.* **1.** a city in central South Africa, in N Cape Province: besieged (1899–1900) for 126 days during the Boer War; diamond-mining and -marketing centre, with heavy engineering works. Pop.: 103 789 (1970). **2.** Also called: **The Kimberleys.** a plateau region of NW Australia, in N Western Australia: consists of rugged mountains surrounded by grassland. Area: about 360 000 sq. km (140 000 sq. miles).

kim+ber+lite ('kɪmbəˌlaɪt) *n.* a type of peridotite that occurs in South Africa and often contains diamonds. [C19: from KIMBERLEY + -ITE[1]]

Kim Il Sung ('kɪm ɪl 'sʊŋ). *n.* born 1912, North Korean statesman and marshal; prime minister (1948–72) and president (since 1972) of North Korea.

ki+mo+no (kɪ'məʊnəʊ) *n., pl.* **+nos. 1.** a loose sashed ankle-length garment with wide sleeves, worn in Japan. **2.** any garment copied from this. [C19: from Japanese: clothing, from *ki* to wear + *mono* thing] —**ki+'mo+noed** *adj.*

kin (kɪn) *n.* **1.** a person's relatives collectively; kindred. **2.** a class or group with similar characteristics. **3.** See **next of kin.** ~*adj.* **4.** (*postpositive*) related by blood. **5.** a less common word for **akin.** [Old English *cyn;* related to Old Norse *kyn* family, Old High German *kind* child, Latin *genus* kind]

-kin *suffix forming nouns.* small: *lambkin.* [from Middle Dutch, of West Germanic origin; compare German *-chen*]

ki·na ('kiːnə) *n.* the standard monetary unit of Papua New Guinea, divided into 100 toeas. [from a Papuan language]

Kin·a·ba+lu (ˌkɪnəbə'luː) *n.* a mountain in Malaysia, on N Borneo in central Sabah: the highest peak in Borneo. Height: 4125 m (13 533 ft.).

kin+aes+the+si·a (ˌkɪniːs'θiːzɪə, ˌkaɪn-), **kin+aes+the+sis** *or U.S.* **kin+es+the+si·a, kin+es+the+sis** *n.* the sensation by which bodily position, weight, muscle tension, and movement are perceived. Also called: **muscle sense.** [C19: from New Latin, from Greek *kinein* to move + AESTHESIA] —**kin+aes+thet+ic** *or U.S.* **kin+es+thet+ic** (ˌkɪnɛs'θɛtɪk, ˌkaɪn-) *adj.*

ki+nase ('kaɪneɪz, 'kɪn-) *n.* a biochemical agent, such as a metal ion or a protein, that can convert an inactive zymogen to an enzyme. [C20: from KIN(ETIC) + -ASE]

Kin+car+dine (kɪn'kɑːdɪn) *n.* (until 1975) a county of E Scotland, now part of Grampian region.

Kin+chin+jun+ga (ˌkɪntʃɪn'dʒʌŋgə) *n.* a variant spelling of **Kangchenjunga.**

kin+cob ('kɪŋkɒb) *n.* a fine silk fabric embroidered with threads of gold or silver, of a kind made in India. [C18: from Urdu *kimkhāb*]

kind[1] (kaɪnd) *adj.* **1.** having a friendly or generous nature or attitude. **2.** helpful to others or to another: *a kind deed.* **3.** considerate or humane. **4.** cordial; courteous (esp. in the phrase **kind regards**). **5.** pleasant; agreeable; mild: *a kind climate.* **6.** *Informal.* beneficial or not harmful: *a detergent that is kind to the hands.* **7.** *Archaic.* loving. [Old English *gecynde* natural, native; see KIND[2]]

kind[2] (kaɪnd) *n.* **1.** a class or group having characteristics in common; sort; type: *two of a kind; what kind of creature?* **2.** an instance or example of a class or group, esp. a rudimentary one: *heating of a kind.* **3.** essential nature or character: *the difference is one of kind rather than degree.* **4.** *Archaic.* gender or sex. **5.** *Archaic.* nature; the natural order. **6. in kind. a.** (of payment) in goods or produce rather than in money. **b.** with something of the same sort: *to return an insult in kind.* **7. kind of.** (*adv.*) *Informal.* somewhat; rather: *kind of tired.* [Old English *gecynd* nature; compare Old English *cyn* KIN, Gothic *kuni* race, Old High German *kikunt,* Latin *gens*]

Usage. Careful users of English avoid the mixture of plural and singular constructions frequently used informally with *kind,* as in *those kind* (instead of *kinds*) *of buildings seem badly designed.*

kin+der+gar+ten ('kɪndəˌgɑːtᵊn) *n.* a class or small school for young children, usually between the ages of four and six to prepare them for primary education. In Australia, often shortened to **kinder.** [C19: from German, literally: children's garden] —**'kin+der+ˌgar+ten+er** *n.*

kind-heart·ed *adj.* characterized by kindness; sympathetic. —ˌ**kind-'heart·ed·ly** *adv.* —ˌ**kind-'heart·ed·ness** *n.*

kin+dle ('kɪndᵊl) *vb.* **1.** to set alight or start to burn. **2.** to arouse or be aroused: *the project kindled his interest.* **3.** to make or become bright. [C12: from Old Norse *kynda,* influenced by Old Norse *kyndill* candle] —**'kin+dler** *n.*

kind+less ('kaɪndlɪs) *adj. Archaic.* **1.** heartless. **2.** against nature; unnatural. —**'kind+less+ly** *adv.*

kin+dling ('kɪndlɪŋ) *n.* material for starting a fire, such as dry wood, straw, etc.

kind+ly ('kaɪndlɪ) *adj.* **+li+er, +li+est. 1.** having a sympathetic or warm-hearted nature. **2.** motivated by warm and sympathetic feelings: *a kindly act.* **3.** pleasant, mild, or agreeable: *a kindly climate.* **4.** *Archaic.* natural; normal. ~*adv.* **5.** in a considerate or humane way. **6.** with tolerance or forbearance: *he kindly forgave my rudeness.* **7.** cordially; pleasantly: *he greeted us kindly.* **8.** please (often used to express impatience or formality): *will you kindly behave yourself!* **9.** *Archaic.* in accordance with nature; appropriately. **10. take kindly.** to react favourably. —**'kind+li+ness** *n.*

kind+ness ('kaɪndnɪs) *n.* **1.** the practice or quality of being kind. **2.** a kind, considerate, or helpful act.

kin+dred ('kɪndrɪd) *adj.* **1.** having similar or common qualities, origin, etc. **2.** related by blood or marriage. **3. kindred spirit.** a person with whom one has something in common. ~*n.* **4.** relationship by blood. **5.** similarity in character. **6.** a person's relatives collectively. [C12 *kinred,* from KIN + *-red,* from Old English *rǣden* rule, from *rǣdan* to rule] —**'kin+dred+ness** *or* **'kin+dred+ˌship** *n.*

kine (kaɪn) *n.* (*functioning as pl.*) an archaic word for **cows** or **cattle.** [Old English *cȳna* of cows, from *cū* COW[1]]

kin+e·mat+ics (ˌkɪnɪ'mætɪks, ˌkaɪ-) *n.* (*functioning as sing.*) the study of the motion of bodies without reference to mass or force. Compare **dynamics** (sense 1). [C19: from Greek *kinēma* movement; see CINEMA, -ICS] —ˌ**kin+e·'mat+ic** *adj.* —ˌ**kin+e·'mat·i·cal+ly** *adv.*

kin+e·mat+ic vis+cos+i·ty *n.* a measure of the resistance to flow of a fluid, equal to its absolute viscosity divided by its density. Symbol: ν

kin+e·mat·o·graph (ˌkɪnɪ'mætəˌgrɑːf, ˌkaɪnɪ-) *n.* a variant spelling of **cinematograph.** —**kin+e·ma+tog+ra+pher** (ˌkɪnəmə'tɒgrəfə) *n.* —**kin+e·mat·o·graph+ic** (ˌkɪnɪˌmætə'græfɪk, ˌkaɪnɪ-) *adj.* —ˌ**kin+e·ma+'tog+ra+phy** *n.*

ki+ne·sics (kɪ'niːsɪks) *n.* (*functioning as sing.*) the study of the role of body movements, such as winking, shrugging, etc., in communication.

ki+ne·si·ol·o·gy (kɪˌniːsɪ'ɒlədʒɪ) *n.* the study of the mechanics and anatomy of human muscles.

kin+es+the+si·a (ˌkɪniːs'θiːzɪə, ˌkaɪn-) *or* **kin+es+the+sis** *n.* the usual U.S. spelling of **kinaesthesia.** —**kin+es+thet+ic** (ˌkɪnɛs'θɛtɪk, ˌkaɪn-) *adj.*

ki+net+ic (kɪ'nɛtɪk, kaɪ-) *adj.* relating to, characterized by, or caused by motion. [C19: from Greek *kinētikos,* from *kinein* to move] —**ki+'net·i·cal+ly** *adv.*

ki+net+ic art *n.* art, esp. sculpture, that moves or has moving parts.

ki+net+ic en+er+gy *n.* the energy of motion of a body or system. It is equal to the product of half its mass and the square of its velocity and is measured in joules (SI units), electronvolts, etc. Symbol: E_k, *I,* or *K* Abbrev.: **K.E.**

ki+net+ics (kɪ'nɛtɪks, kaɪ-) *n.* (*functioning as sing.*) **1.** another name for **dynamics** (sense 2). **2.** the branch of mechanics, including both dynamics and kinematics, concerned with the study of bodies in motion. **3.** the branch of dynamics that excludes the study of bodies at rest. **4.** the branch of chemistry concerned with the rates of chemical reactions.

ki+net+ic the·o+ry (of gas·es) *n.* **the.** a theory of gases postulating that they consist of particles of negligible size moving at random and undergoing elastic collisions.

ki+net·o+plast (kɪ'nɛtəˌplæst, -'niː-, -ˌplɑːst) *n.* a small granular cell body close to the nucleus in some flagellate protozoans. Also called: **ki+net·o+nu+cle+us** (kɪˌnɛtəʊ'njuːklɪəs). [C20: from Greek; see KINETIC, -PLAST]

kin+folk ('kɪnˌfəʊk) *pl. n. Chiefly U.S.* another word for **kinsfolk.**

king (kɪŋ) *n.* **1.** a male sovereign prince who is the official ruler of an independent state; monarch. Related adjs.: **royal, regal, monarchical. 2. a.** a ruler or chief: *king of the fairies.* **b.** (*in combination*): *the pirate king.* **3. a.** a person, animal, or thing considered as the best or most important of its kind. **b.** (*as modifier*): *a king bull.* **4.** any of four playing cards in a pack, one for each suit, bearing the picture of a king. **5.** the most important chess piece, although theoretically the weakest, being able to move only one square at a time in any direction. See also **check** (sense 30), **checkmate. 6.** *Draughts.* a piece that has moved entirely across the board and has been crowned, after which it may move backwards as well as forwards. **7. king of kings. a.** God. **b.** a title of any of various oriental monarchs. ~*vb.* (*tr.*) to make (someone) a king. **8. king it.** to act in a superior fashion. [Old English *cyning;* related to Old High German *kunig* king, Danish *konge*] —**'king+ˌhood** *n.* —**'king+less** *adj.* —**'king+ˌlike** *adj.*

King (kɪŋ) *n.* **1. Bil·lie Jean** (*née Moffitt*). born 1943, U.S. tennis player: Wimbledon champion 1966–68, 1972–73, and 1975; U.S. champion 1967, 1971–72, and 1974. **2. Mar·tin Lu·ther.** 1929–68, U.S. Baptist minister and civil rights leader. He advocated nonviolence in his campaigns against the segregation of Negroes in the South: assassinated: Nobel peace prize 1964. **3. Ri·ley,** called *B*(*lues*) *B*(*oy*) *King.* born 1925, U.S. blues singer and guitarist. **4. Wil·liam Ly·on Mac·ken·zie.** 1874–1950, Canadian Liberal statesman; prime minister (1921–26; 1926–30; 1935–48).

king+bird ('kɪŋˌbɜːd) *n.* any of several large American flycatchers of the genus *Tyrannus,* esp. *T. tyrannus* (**eastern kingbird** *or* **bee martin**).

king·bolt ('kɪŋˌbəʊlt) *or* **king rod** *n.* **a.** the pivot bolt that connects the body of a horse-drawn carriage to the front axle and provides the steering joint. **b.** a similar bolt placed between a railway carriage and the bogies.

King Charles span·iel *n.* a toy breed of spaniel with very long ears and a wavy coat. [C17: named after Charles II of England, who popularized the breed]

king co·bra *n.* a very large venomous tropical Asian elapid snake, *Ophiophagus hannah,* that feeds on snakes and other reptiles and extends its neck into a hood when alarmed. Also called: **hamadryad.**

king crab *n.* another name for the **horseshoe crab.**

king·craft ('kɪŋˌkrɑːft) *n. Archaic.* the art of ruling as a king, esp. by diplomacy and cunning.

king·cup ('kɪŋˌkʌp) *n. Brit.* any of several yellow-flowered ranunculaceous plants, esp. the marsh marigold.

king·dom ('kɪŋdəm) *n.* **1.** a territory, state, people, or community ruled or reigned over by a king or queen. **2.** any of the three groups into which natural objects may be divided: the animal, plant, and mineral kingdoms. **3.** *Theol.* the eternal sovereignty of God. **4.** an area of activity, esp. mental activity, considered as being the province of something specified: *the kingdom of the mind.* —'**king·dom·less** *adj.*

king·dom come *n.* **1.** the next world; life after death. **2.** *Informal.* the end of the world (esp. in the phrase **until kingdom come**). **3.** *Informal.* unconsciousness or death.

king·fish ('kɪŋˌfɪʃ) *n., pl.* **·fish** *or* **·fish·es. 1.** any marine sciaenid food and game fish of the genus *Menticirrhus,* occurring in warm American Atlantic coastal waters. **2.** another name for **opah** (the fish). **3.** any of various other large food fishes, esp. the Spanish mackerel.

king·fish·er ('kɪŋˌfɪʃə) *n.* any coraciiform bird of the family *Alcedinidae,* esp. the Eurasian *Alcedo atthis,* which has a greenish-blue and orange plumage. Kingfishers have a large head, short tail, and long sharp bill and tend to live near open water and feed on fish. [C15: originally *king's fisher*]

king-hit *Austral. informal.* ~*n.* **1.** a knockout blow, esp. an unfair one. ~*vb.* to deliver a knockout blow.

King James Ver·sion *or* **Bi·ble** *n.* **the.** another name for the **Authorized Version.**

king·let ('kɪŋlɪt) *n.* **1.** *Often derogatory.* the king of a small or insignificant territory. **2.** *U.S.* any of various small warblers of the genus *Regulus,* having a black-edged yellow crown: family *Muscicapidae.*

king·ly ('kɪŋlɪ) *adj.* **1.** appropriate to a king; majestic. **2.** royal. ~*adv.* **3.** *Poetic or archaic.* in a manner appropriate to a king. —'**king·li·ness** *n.*

king·mak·er ('kɪŋˌmeɪkə) *n.* a person who has control over appointments to positions of authority.

king-of-arms *n., pl.* **kings-of-arms. 1.** the highest rank of heraldic officer. **2.** a person holding this rank.

king of the cas·tle *n. Chiefly Brit.* **1.** a children's game in which each child attempts to stand alone on a mound, sandcastle, etc., by pushing other children off it. **2.** *Informal.* a person who is in a commanding or superior position.

king of the her·rings *n.* another name for **oarfish** or **rabbitfish** (sense 1).

king·pin ('kɪŋˌpɪn) *n.* **1.** Also called (Brit.): **swivel pin.** a pivot pin that provides a steering joint in a motor vehicle by securing the stub axle to the axle beam. **2.** *Tenpin bowling.* the front pin in the triangular arrangement of the ten pins. **3.** *Informal.* the most important person in an organization. **4.** (in ninepins) the central pin in the diamond pattern of the nine pins. **5.** *Informal.* the crucial or most important feature of a theory, argument, etc.

king post *n.* a vertical post connecting the apex of a triangular roof truss to the tie beam. Also called: **joggle post.** Compare **queen post.**

king prawn *n. Austral.* any of several large prawns of the genus *Penaeus,* which are fished commercially in Australian waters.

Kings (kɪŋz) *n. Old Testament.* (in versions based on the Hebrew, including the Authorized Version) either of the two books called **I** and **II Kings,** recounting the histories of the kings of Judah and Israel.

king salm·on *n.* another name for **Chinook salmon.**

King's Bench *n.* (when the sovereign is male) another name for **Queen's Bench.**

King's Coun·sel *n.* (when the sovereign is male) another name for **Queen's Counsel.**

King's Eng·lish *n.* (esp. when the British sovereign is male) standard Southern British English.

king's ev·i·dence *n.* (when the sovereign is male) another name for **queen's evidence** (esp. in the phrase **turn king's evidence**).

king's e·vil *n.* **the.** *Pathol.* a former name for **scrofula.** [C14: from the belief that the king's touch would heal scrofula]

king's high·way *n.* (in Britain, esp. when the sovereign is male) any public road or right of way.

king·ship ('kɪŋʃɪp) *n.* **1.** the position or authority of a king. **2.** the skill or practice of ruling as a king.

king-size *or* **king-sized** *adj.* larger or longer than a standard size.

Kings·ley ('kɪŋzlɪ) *n.* **Charles.** 1819–75, English clergyman and author. His works include the historical romances *Westward Ho!* (1855) and *Hereward the Wake* (1866) and the children's story *The Water Babies* (1863).

King's Lynn ('kɪŋz 'lɪn) *n.* a market town in E England, in Norfolk on the estuary of the Great Ouse near the Wash: a leading port in the Middle Ages. Pop.: 30 102 (1971). Also called: **Lynn, Lynn Regis.**

king snake *n.* any nonvenomous North American colubrid snake of the genus *Lampropeltis,* feeding on other snakes, small mammals, etc.

king's peace *n.* **1.** (in early medieval England) the protection secured by the king for particular people or places. **2.** (in medieval England) the general peace secured to the entire realm by the law administered in the king's name.

King's proc·tor *n.* (in England when the sovereign is male) an official empowered to intervene in divorce and certain other cases when it is alleged that facts are being suppressed.

King's Reg·u·la·tions *pl. n.* (in Britain and the Commonwealth when the sovereign is male) the code of conduct for members of the armed forces that deals with discipline, aspects of military law, etc.

King's Scout *n.* (in Britain and the Commonwealth when the sovereign is male) another name for **Queen's Scout.** U.S. equivalent: **Eagle Scout.**

king's shil·ling *or, when the sovereign was female,* **queen's shil·ling** *n.* **1.** (until 1879) a shilling paid to new recruits to the British army. **2. take the king's** (*or* **queen's**) **shilling.** *Brit. archaic.* to enlist in the army.

King's speech *n.* (in Britain and the dominions of the Commonwealth when the sovereign is male) another name for the **speech from the throne.**

King·ston ('kɪŋstən) *n.* **1.** the capital and chief port of Jamaica, on the SE coast: University of the West Indies. Pop.: 117 400 (1970). **2.** a port in SE Canada, in SE Ontario: the chief naval base of Lake Ontario and a large industrial centre; university (1841). Pop.: 59 047 (1971). **3.** short for **Kingston upon Thames.**

Kings·ton up·on Hull *n.* the official name of **Hull**[1].

King·ston up·on Thames *n.* a borough of SW Greater London, on the River Thames: formed in 1965 by the amalgamation of several former boroughs of Surrey. Pop.: 135 600 (1976 est.).

Kings·town ('kɪŋzˌtaʊn) *n.* a port in the West Indies, in the Windward Islands, capital of St. Vincent. Pop.: 23 645 (1970).

King·wa·na (kɪŋ'wɑːnə) *n.* a language of Zaïre in W Africa, closely related to Swahili and used as a lingua franca.

king·wood ('kɪŋˌwʊd) *n.* **1.** the hard fine-grained violet-tinted wood of a Brazilian leguminous tree, *Dalbergia cearensis,* used in cabinetwork. **2.** the tree yielding this wood.

ki·nin ('kaɪnɪn) *n.* any of a group of polypeptides in the blood that cause dilation of the blood vessels and make smooth muscles contract. [C20: from Greek *kin(ēma)* motion + -IN]

kink (kɪŋk) *n.* **1.** a sharp twist or bend in a wire, rope, hair, etc., esp. one caused when it is pulled tight. **2.** a crick in the neck or similar muscular spasm. **3.** a flaw or minor difficulty in some undertaking or project. **4.** a flaw or idiosyncrasy of personality; quirk. **5.** *Brit. informal.* a sexual deviation. **6.** *U.S.* a clever or unusual idea. [C17: from Dutch: a curl in a rope; compare Middle Low German *kinke* kink, Old Norse *kinka* to nod]

kin·ka·jou ('kɪŋkəˌdʒuː) *n.* **1.** Also called: **honey bear, potto.** an arboreal fruit-eating mammal, *Potos flavus,* of Central and South America, with a long prehensile tail: family *Procyonidae* (raccoons) order *Carnivora* (carnivores). **2.** another name for **potto** (sense 1). [C18: from French *quincajou,* from Algonquian; related to Ojibwa *gwīngwâage* wolverine]

kink·y ('kɪŋkɪ) *adj.* **kink·i·er, kink·i·est. 1.** *Slang.* given to unusual, abnormal, or deviant sexual practices. **2.** *Slang.* exhibiting unusual idiosyncrasies of personality; quirky; eccentric. **3.** *Slang.* attractive or provocative in a bizarre way: *kinky clothes.* **4.** tangled or tightly looped, as a wire or rope. **5.** tightly curled, as hair. —'**kink·i·ly** *adv.* —'**kink·i·ness** *n.*

kin·ni·kin·nick, kin·ni·ki·nic (ˌkɪnɪkɪ'nɪk), *or* **kil·li·ki·nick** *n.* **1.** the dried leaves and bark of certain plants, sometimes with tobacco added, formerly smoked by some North American Indians. **2.** any of the plants used for such a preparation, such as the sumach *Rhus glabra.* [C18: from Algonquian, literally: that which is mixed; related to Natick *kinukkinuk* mixture]

ki·no ('kiːnəʊ) *n.* a dark red resin obtained from various tropical plants, esp. an Indian leguminous tree, *Pterocarpus marsupium,* used as an astringent and in tanning. Also called: **kino gum.** [C18: of West African origin; related to Mandingo *keno*]

Kin·ross (kɪn'rɒs) *n.* (until 1975) a county of E central Scotland, now part of Tayside region.

Kin·sey ('kɪnzɪ) *n.* **Al·fred Charles.** 1894–1956, U.S. zoologist, who directed a survey of human sexual behaviour.

kins·folk ('kɪnzˌfəʊk) *pl. n.* one's family or relatives.

Kin·sha·sa (kɪn'ʃɑːzə, -'ʃɑːsə) *n.* the capital of Zaïre, on the River Congo opposite Brazzaville: became capital of the Belgian Congo in 1929 and of the new republic of Zaïre in 1960; university (1954). Pop.: 2 008 352 (1974 est.). Former name (until 1966): **Léopoldville.**

kin·ship ('kɪnʃɪp) *n.* **1.** blood relationship. **2.** the state of having common characteristics or a common origin.

kins·man ('kɪnzmən) *n., pl.* **·men. 1.** a blood relation or a relation by marriage. **2.** a member of the same race, tribe, or ethnic stock. —'**kins·ˌwom·an** *fem. n.*

ki·osk ('kiːɒsk) *n.* **1.** a small sometimes movable booth from which cigarettes, newspapers, light refreshments, etc., are sold. **2.** *Chiefly Brit.* a telephone box. **3.** *Chiefly U.S.* a thick post on which advertisements are posted. **4.** (in Turkey, Iran, etc., esp. formerly) a light open-sided pavilion. [C17: from

French *kiosque* bandstand, from Turkish *kösk*, from Persian *kūshk* pavilion]

kip[1] (kɪp) *Brit. slang.* ~*n.* **1.** sleep or slumber: *to get some kip.* **2.** a bed or lodging. **3.** *Obsolete.* a brothel. ~*vb.* **kips, kip·ping, kipped.** (*intr.*) **4.** to sleep or take a nap. **5.** (foll. by *down*) to prepare for sleep. [C18: of uncertain origin; apparently related to Danish *kippe* common alehouse]

kip[2] (kɪp) *or* **kip·skin** *n.* the hide of a young animal, esp. a calf or lamb. [C16: from Middle Dutch *kipp;* related to Middle Low German *kip,* Old Norse *kippa* bundle]

kip[3] (kɪp) *n.* a unit of weight equal to one thousand pounds. [C20: from KI(LO) + P(OUND)]

kip[4] (kɪp) *n.* the standard monetary unit of Laos, divided into 100 at. [from Thai]

kip[5] (kɪp) *n. Austral.* a small board used to spin the coins in two-up. [C19: from KEP]

Kip·ling (ˈkɪplɪŋ) *n.* **(Joseph) Rud·yard** (ˈrʌdjəd). 1865–1936, English poet, short-story writer, and novelist, born in India. His works include *Barrack-Room Ballads* (1892), the two *Jungle Books* (1894, 1895), *Stalky and Co.* (1899), *Kim* (1901), and the *Just So Stories* (1902): Nobel prize for literature 1907.

kip·per[1] (ˈkɪpə) *n.* **1.** a fish, esp. a herring, that has been cleaned, salted, and smoked. **2.** a male salmon during the spawning season. **3.** *Austral. derogatory slang.* an Englishman. ~*vb.* **4.** (*tr.*) to cure (herrings, etc.) by salting and smoking. [Old English *cypera,* perhaps from *coper* COPPER; referring to its colour]

kip·per[2] (ˈkɪpə) *n.* an Australian Aborigine youth who has completed an initiation rite. [from a native Australian language]

Kipp's ap·pa·rat·us (kɪps) *n.* a laboratory apparatus for producing a gas, usually hydrogen sulphide, by the action of a liquid on a solid without heating. [C19: named after Petrus Jacobus *Kipp* (1808–84), Dutch chemist]

Kirch·hoff (*German* ˈkɪrçhɔf) *n.* **Gus·tav Rob·ert** (ˈgʊstaf ˈroːbɛrt). 1824–87, German physicist. With Bunsen he developed the method of spectrum analysis that led to their discovery of caesium (1860) and rubidium (1861): also worked on electrical networks.

Kirch·hoff's laws *n.* two laws describing the flow of currents in electric circuits. The first states that the algebraic sum of all the electric currents meeting at any point in a circuit is zero. The second states that in a closed loop of a circuit the algebraic sum of the products of the resistances and the currents flowing through them is equal to the algebraic sum of all the electromotive forces acting in the loop.

Kir·ghiz *or* **Kir·giz** (ˈkɜːgɪz) *n.* **1.** (*pl.* **·ghiz** or **·giz**) a member of a Mongoloid people of the Soviet Union, inhabiting a vast area of central Siberia. **2.** the language of this people, belonging to the Turkic branch of the Altaic family.

Kir·ghiz So·vi·et So·cial·ist Re·pub·lic *n.* an administrative division of the S central Soviet Union: annexed by Russia in 1864. Capital: Frunze. Pop.: 2 932 805 (1970). Area: 198 500 sq. km (76 460 sq. miles). Also: **Kirgiz Soviet Socialist Republic** *or* **Kir·ghi·zi·a, Kir·gi·zi·a** (kɜːˈgɪzɪə).

Kir·ghiz Steppe *n.* a vast steppe region of the SW Soviet Union, in the central Kazakh SSR. Also called: (the) **Steppes.**

Kir·i·bati (ˈkɪrɪbæf) *n.* the official name (since 1979) of the **Gilbert Islands.**

kir·i·gami (ˌkɪrɪˈgɑːmɪ) *n.* **1.** the art, originally Japanese, of folding and cutting paper into decorative shapes. Compare **origami.** [C20: from Japanese]

Ki·rin (ˈkiːˈrɪn) *n.* **1.** a province of NE China, in central Manchuria. Capital: Changchun. Pop.: 23 000 000 (1976 est.). Area: 187 000 sq. km (72 930 sq. miles). **2.** Also called: **Chi-lin** (ˈtʃiːˈlɪn). a river port in NE China, in N central Kirin province on the Sungari River. Pop.: 720 000 (1970 est.).

kirk (kɜːk) *n.* **1.** a Scot. word for **church. 2.** a Scottish church. [C12: from Old Norse *kirkja,* from Old English *cirice* CHURCH]

Kirk[1] (kɜːk) *n.* **the.** *Informal.* the Presbyterian Church of Scotland.

Kirk[2] (kɜːk) *n.* **Nor·man.** 1923–74, prime minister of New Zealand (1972–74).

Kirk·by (ˈkɜːbɪ) *n.* a town in NW England, in N Merseyside. Pop.: 59 759 (1971).

Kirk·cal·dy (kɜːˈkɔːdɪ) *n.* a port in E Scotland, in SE Fife on the Firth of Forth. Pop.: 50 338 (1971).

Kirk·cud·bright (kɜːˈkuːbrɪ) *n.* (until 1975) a county of SW Scotland, now part of Dumfries and Galloway region.

kirk·man (ˈkɜːkmən) *n., pl.* **·men.** *Scot.* **1.** a member or strong upholder of the Kirk. **2.** a churchman; clergyman.

Kirk·pat·rick (kɜːkˈpætrɪk) *n.* **Mount.** a mountain in Antarctica, in S Victoria Land in the Queen Alexandra Range. Height: 4554 m (14 942 ft.).

kirk ses·sion *n.* the lowest court of the Presbyterian church.

Kir·kuk (kɜːˈkʊk, ˈkɜːkʊk) *n.* a city in NE Iraq: centre of a rich oilfield with pipelines to the Mediterranean. Pop.: 175 303 (1965).

Kirk·wall (ˈkɜːkˌwɔːl) *n.* a town in NE Scotland, administrative centre of the island authority of Orkney, on the N coast of Mainland: cathedral built by Norsemen (begun in 1137). Pop.: 4618 (1971).

Kir·man (kɪəˈmɑːn) *n.* a Persian carpet or rug. [named after KERMAN, Iran]

Ki·rov[1] (*Russian* ˈkirəf) *n.* a city in the W Soviet Union, on the Vyatka River: an early trading centre; engineering industries. Pop.: 371 000 (1975 est.). Former name (1780–1934): **Vyatka.**

Ki·rov[2] (*Russian* ˈkirəf) *n.* **Ser·gei Mi·ro·no·vich** (sirˈgjej miˈrɔnəvitʃ). 1888–1934, Soviet politician; one of Stalin's chief aides. His assassination was the starting point for Stalin's purge of the Communist Party (1934–38).

Ki·ro·va·bad (*Russian* kirəvaˈbat) *n.* a city in the S Soviet Union, in the NW Azerbaijan SSR: annexed by the Russians in 1804; centre of a cotton-growing region. Pop.: 207 000 (1975 est.). Former names: **Gandzha** (until 1813 and 1920–35), **Yelisavetpol** (1813–1920).

Ki·ro·vo·grad (*Russian* kirəvaˈgrat) *n.* a city in the SW Soviet Union, in the S central Ukrainian SSR on the Ingul River: manufacturing centre of a rich agricultural area. Pop.: 218 000 (1975 est.). Former names: **Yelisavetgrad** (until 1924), **Zinoviyevsk** (1924–36).

Kirsch (kɪəʃ) *or* **Kirsch·was·ser** (ˈkɪəʃˌvɑːsə) *n.* a brandy distilled from cherries, made chiefly in the Black Forest in Germany and in the Jura and Vosges districts of France. [German *Kirschwasser:* cherry water]

kir·tle (ˈkɜːtᵊl) *n. Archaic.* **1.** a woman's skirt or dress. **2.** a man's coat. [Old English *cyrtel,* probably from *cyrtan* to shorten, ultimately from Latin *curtus* cut short]

Ki·ru·na (*Swedish* ˈkiːrʊna) *n.* a town in N Sweden: iron-mining centre. Pop.: 30 534 (1970).

Ki·run·di (kɪˈrʊndɪ) *n.* the official language of Burundi, belonging to the Bantu group of the Niger-Congo family and closely related to Rwanda.

Kis·an·ga·ni (ˌkɪsæŋˈgɑːnɪ) *n.* a city in N Zaïre, at the head of navigation of the River Congo below Stanley Falls: Université Libre du Congo (1963). Pop.: 310 705 (1974 est.). Former name (until 1966): **Stanleyville.**

kish (kɪʃ) *n. Metallurgy.* graphite formed on the surface of molten iron that contains a large amount of carbon. [C19: perhaps changed from German *Kies* gravel; related to Old High German *kisil* pebble]

Ki·shi·nev (*Russian* kiʃɪˈnjɔf) *n.* a city in the SW Soviet Union, capital of the Moldavian SSR on the Byk River: manufacturing centre of a rich agricultural region; university (1945). Pop.: 452 000 (1975 est.). Rumanian name: **Chişinău.**

kish·ke (ˈkɪʃkə) *n.* a beef or fowl intestine or skin stuffed with flour, onion, etc., and boiled and roasted. [Yiddish: gut, probably from Russian *kishka*]

Kis·lev *Hebrew.* (kiˈslev) *n. Judaism.* the ninth month of the civil year and the third of the ecclesiastical year in the Jewish calendar, falling approximately in November and December. [from Hebrew *kislēw,* from Akkadian *kistimu*]

Kis·ma·yu (kɪsˈmɑːjuː) *n.* another name for **Chisimaio.**

kis·met (ˈkɪzmɛt, ˈkɪs-) *n.* **1.** *Islam.* the will of Allah. **2.** fate or destiny. [C19: from Turkish, from Persian *qismat,* from Arabic, *qasama* he divided]

kiss (kɪs) *vb.* **1.** (*tr.*) to touch with the lips or press the lips against as an expression of love, greeting, respect, etc. **2.** (*intr.*) to join lips with another person in an act of love or desire. **3.** to touch (each other) lightly: *their hands kissed.* ~*n.* **4.** the act of kissing; a caress with the lips. **5.** a light touch. [Old English *cyssan,* from *coss;* compare Old High German *kussen,* Old Norse *kyssa*] —**ˈkiss·a·ble** *adj.*

kiss curl *n. Brit.* a circular curl of hair pressed flat against the cheek or forehead. U.S. term: **spit curl.**

kis·sel (ˈkɪsᵊl) *n.* a Russian dessert of sweetened fruit purée thickened with arrowroot. [from Russian *kisel*]

kiss·er (ˈkɪsə) *n.* **1.** a person who kisses, esp. in a way specified. **2.** a slang word for **mouth** or **face.**

kiss·ing bug *n.* a North American assassin bug, *Melanolestes picipes,* with a painful bite, usually attacking the lips or cheeks of man.

Kis·sin·ger (ˈkɪsɪndʒə) *n.* **Hen·ry.** born 1923, U.S. academic and diplomat, born in Germany; assistant to President Nixon for national security affairs (1968–73); Secretary of State (1973–76): shared the Nobel Peace Prize 1972.

kiss·ing gate *n.* a gate set in a U- or V-shaped enclosure, allowing only one person to pass through at a time.

kiss of death *n.* an act or relationship, that has fatal or disastrous consequences. [from Judas' kiss that betrayed Jesus in the garden of Gethsemane (Mark 14:44–45)]

kiss off *Slang, chiefly U.S.* ~*vb.* **1.** (*tr., adv.*) to ignore or dismiss rudely and abruptly. ~*n.* **kiss-off. 2.** a rude and abrupt dismissal.

kiss of life *n.* **the.** *Informal.* mouth-to-mouth resuscitation in which a person blows gently into the victim's mouth, allowing the lungs to deflate after each blow.

kist[1] (kɪst) *n. Scot. and northern Brit. dialect.* a large chest or coffer. [C14: from Old Norse *kista;* see CHEST]

kist[2] (kɪst) *n. Archaeol.* a variant spelling of **cist**[2].

kist[3] (kɪst) *n. S. African.* a large wooden chest in which linen is stored, esp. one used to store a bride's trousseau. [from Afrikaans, from Dutch: CHEST]

Kist·na (ˈkɪstnə) *n.* another name for the (River) **Krishna.**

Ki·su·mu (kɪˈsuːmuː) *n.* a port in W Kenya, in Nyanza province on the NE shore of Lake Victoria: fishing and trading centre. Pop.: 30 700 (1969).

kit[1] (kɪt) *n.* **1.** a set of tools, supplies, construction materials, etc., for use together or for a purpose: *a first-aid kit; a model aircraft kit.* **2.** the case or container for such a set. **3.** clothing and other personal effects, esp. those of a traveller or soldier: *safari kit; battle kit.* **4. the whole kit** *or* **kit and caboodle.** *Informal.* everything or everybody. ~See also **kit out.** [C14: from Middle Dutch *kitte* tankard]

kit[2] (kɪt) *n.* a kind of small violin, now obsolete, used esp. by dancing masters in the 17th–18th centuries. [C16: of unknown origin]

kit[3] (kɪt) *n.* an informal or diminutive name for **kitten.** [C16: by shortening]

Ki+ta+kyu+shu (ˌki:tə'kju:ʃu:) *n.* a port in Japan, on N Kyushu: formed in 1963 by the amalgamation of the cities of Wakamatsu, Yahata, Tobata, Kokura, and Moji; one of Japan's largest industrial centres. Pop.: 1 060 000 (1975).

kit+bag ('kɪtˌbæg) *n.* a canvas or other bag for a serviceman's kit.

kitch+en ('kɪtʃɪn) *n.* **a.** a room or part of a building equipped for preparing and cooking food. **b.** (*as modifier*): *a kitchen table.* [Old English *cycene,* ultimately from Late Latin *coquīna,* from Latin *coquere* to COOK; see KILN]

Kitch·e·ner[1] ('kɪtʃɪnə) *n.* an industrial town in SE Canada, in S Ontario: founded in 1806 as Dutch Sand Hills, it was renamed Berlin in 1830 and Kitchener in 1916. Pop.: 111 804 (1971).

Kitch·e·ner[2] ('kɪtʃɪnə) *n.* **Ho·ra·ti·o Her·bert,** 1st Earl Kitchener of Khartoum. 1850–1916, British field marshal. As head of the Egyptian army (1892–98), he expelled the Mahdi from the Sudan (1898), occupying Khartoum; he also commanded British forces (1900–02) in the Boer War and (1902–09) in India. He conducted the mobilization of the British army for World War I as war minister (1914–16).

kitch+en+ette *or* **kitch+en+et** (ˌkɪtʃɪ'nɛt) *n.* a small kitchen or part of another room equipped for use as a kitchen.

kitch+en gar+den *n.* a garden where vegetables and sometimes also fruit are grown. —**kitch+en gar+den+er** *n.*

kitch+en kaf+fir *n.* a derogatory term for **Fanagalo.**

kitch+en mid+den *n. Archaeology.* the site of a large mound of domestic refuse marking a prehistoric settlement: usually including bones, potsherds, seashells, etc.

kitch+en po+lice *pl. n. U.S.* soldiers who have been detailed to work in the kitchen, esp. as a punishment. *Abbrev:* K.P.

kitch+en sink *n.* **1.** a sink in a kitchen for washing dishes, vegetables, etc. **2. everything except the kitchen sink.** everything that can be conceived of. **3.** (*modifier*) denoting a type of drama or painting of the 1950s depicting the sordid aspects of domestic reality.

kitch+en tea *n. Austral.* a party held before a wedding to which female guests bring items of kitchen equipment as wedding presents.

kitch·en+ware ('kɪtʃɪnˌwɛə) *n.* pots and pans, knives, forks, spoons, and other utensils used in the kitchen.

kite (kaɪt) *n.* **1.** a light frame covered with a thin material flown in the wind at the end of a length of string. **2.** *Brit. slang.* an aeroplane. **3.** (*pl.*) *Nautical.* any of various light sails set in addition to the working sails of a vessel. **4.** any diurnal bird of prey of the genera *Milvus, Elanus,* etc., typically having a long forked tail and long broad wings and usually preying on small mammals and insects: family *Accipitridae* (hawks, etc.). **5.** *Archaic.* a person who preys on others. **6.** *Commerce.* a negotiable paper drawn without any actual transaction or assets and designed to obtain money on credit, give an impression of affluence, etc. ~*vb.* **7.** to issue (fictitious papers) to obtain credit or money. **8.** (*tr.*) *U.S.* to write (a cheque) in anticipation of sufficient funds to cover it. **9.** (*intr.*) to soar and glide. [Old English *cȳta;* related to Middle High German *küze* owl, Old Norse *kȳta* to quarrel] —**'kit+er** *n.*

kite fight+ing *n.* (in Malaysia) a game in which one player attempts to cut the string of his opponent's kite with the string of his own. See also **glass string.**

Kite mark *n. Brit.* the official mark of quality and reliability, in the form of a kite, on articles approved by the British Standards Institution.

ki+ten+ge (ki:'tɛŋgɛ) *n. E African.* **a.** a thick cotton cloth measuring 114 × 213 cm (45 × 84 inches), used in making garments. **b.** (*as modifier*): *a kitenge dress.* [C20: from Swahili]

kit fox *n.* another name for **swift fox.**

kith (kɪθ) *n.* one's friends and acquaintances (esp. in the phrase **kith and kin**). [Old English *cȳthth,* from *cūth;* see UNCOUTH]

kith·a+ra ('kɪθərə) *n.* a variant spelling of **cithara.**

Kí+thi+ra ('kiθira) *n.* transliteration of the Modern Greek name for **Cythera.**

kit out *or* **up** *vb.* **kits, kit+ting, kit+ted.** (*tr., adv.*) *Chiefly Brit.* to provide with or acquire (a kit of personal effects and necessities).

kitsch (kɪtʃ) *n.* **a.** tawdry, vulgarized, or pretentious art, literature, etc., usually with popular or sentimental appeal. **b.** (*as modifier*): *a kitsch plaster bust of Beethoven.* [C20: from German: rubbish]

kit+ten ('kɪtᵊn) *n.* **1.** a young cat. **2. have kittens.** Also: **have a canary.** *Brit. informal.* to react with disapproval, anxiety, etc.: *she had kittens when she got the bill.* U.S. equivalent: **have a cow.** ~*vb.* **3.** (of cats) to give birth to (young). [C14: from Old Northern French *caton,* from CAT; probably influenced by Middle English *kiteling*] —**'kit·ten-ˌlike** *adj.*

kit+ten+ish ('kɪtᵊnɪʃ) *adj.* **1.** like a kitten; lively. **2.** (of a woman) flirtatious, esp. coyly flirtatious. —**'kit+ten+ish+ly** *adv.* —**'kit+ten+ish+ness** *n.*

kit+ti+wake ('kɪtɪˌweɪk) *n.* either of two oceanic gulls of the genus *Rissa,* esp. *R. tridactyla,* having a white plumage with pale grey black-tipped wings and a square-cut tail. [C17: of imitative origin]

kit+tle ('kɪtᵊl) *Scot.* ~*adj.* **1.** capricious and unpredictable. ~*vb.* **2.** to be troublesome or puzzling to (someone). **3.** to tickle. [C16: probably from Old Norse *kitla* to TICKLE]

kit+ty[1] ('kɪtɪ) *n., pl.* **+ties.** a diminutive or affectionate name for a **kitten** or **cat.** [C18: see KIT[3]]

kit+ty[2] ('kɪtɪ) *n., pl.* **+ties. 1.** the pool of bets in certain gambling games. **2.** any shared fund of money, etc. **3.** (in bowls) the jack. [C19: see KIT[1]]

Kit+ty Hawk *n.* a village in NE North Carolina, near Kill Devil Hill, where the Wright brothers made the first aeroplane flight in the U.S. (1903).

Kit+we ('kɪtweɪ) *n.* a city in N Zambia: commercial centre of the Copper Belt. Pop.: 199 798 (1969).

Kiu+shu ('kju:ʃu:) *n.* a variant spelling of **Kyushu.**

ki·va ('ki:və) *n.* a large underground or partly underground room in a Pueblo Indian village, used chiefly for religious ceremonies. [from Hopi]

Ki·vu ('ki:vu:) *n.* **Lake.** a lake in central Africa, between Zaïre and Rwanda at an altitude of 1460 m (4790 ft.). Area: 2698 sq. km (1042 sq. miles). Depth: (maximum) 475 m (1558 ft.).

Ki+wa+nis (kɪ'wɑ:nɪs) *n.* a North American organization of men's clubs founded in 1915 to promote community service. [C20: alleged to be from an American Indian language: to make oneself known] —**Ki+'wan+i·an** *n.*

ki·wi ('ki:wɪ) *n., pl.* **·wis. 1.** any nocturnal flightless New Zealand bird of the genus *Apteryx,* having a long beak, stout legs, and weakly barbed feathers: order *Apterygiformes* (see **ratite**). **2.** Also called: **Chinese gooseberry.** an Asian climbing plant, *Actinidia chinensis,* with fuzzy edible fruit: family *Actinidiaceae.* **3.** *Slang.* a New Zealander. [C19: from Maori, of imitative origin]

Ki+zil Ir+mak (kɪ'zɪl ɪə'mɑ:k) *n.* a river in Turkey, rising in the Kizil Dag and flowing southwest, northwest, and northeast to the Black Sea: the longest river in Asia Minor. Length: about 1150 km (715 miles). Ancient name: **Halys.**

K.K.K. *abbrev. for* Ku Klux Klan.

KKt *Chess. symbol for* king's knight.

KKtP *Chess. symbol for* king's knight's pawn.

kl. *abbrev. for* kilolitre.

Kla+gen+furt (*German* 'kla:gᵊnˌfʊrt) *n.* a city in S Austria, capital of Carinthia province: tourist centre. Pop.: 74 326 (1971).

Klai+pe+da (*Russian* 'klajpɪdə) *n.* a port in the W Soviet Union, in the Lithuanian SSR on the Baltic: shipbuilding. Pop.: 164 000 (1975 est.). German name: **Memel.**

Klan (klæn) *n.* (usually preceded by *the*) short for **Ku Klux Klan.** —**'Klan+ism** *n.*

klang+far+be ('klɑ:ŋˌfɑ:bə) *n.* (*often cap.*) instrumental timbre or tone colour. [German: tone colour]

Klans+man ('klænzmən) *n., pl.* **+men.** a member of the Ku Klux Klan.

Klau+sen+burg ('klaʊzᵊnˌbʊrk) *n.* the German name for **Cluj.**

klax+on *or* **clax+on** ('klæksᵊn) *n.* a type of loud horn formerly used on motor vehicles. [C20: former trademark, from the name of the manufacturing company]

Klé·ber (*French* kle'bɛ:r) *n.* **Jean Bap·tiste** (ʒɑ̃ ba'tist). 1753–1800, French general, who succeeded Napoleon as commander in Egypt (1799); assassinated.

Klebs-Löf·fler ba·cil+lus ('klɛbz 'lʌflə; *German* 'kle:ps 'lœflər) *n.* a rodlike Gram-positive bacterium, *Corynebacterium diphtheriae,* that causes diphtheria: family *Corynebacteriaceae.* [C19: named after Edwin *Klebs* (1834–1913) and Friedrich A. J. *Löffler* (1852–1915), German bacteriologists]

Klee (*German* kle:) *n.* **Paul** (paʊl). 1879–1940, Swiss painter and etcher. A founder member of *der Blaue Reiter,* he subsequently evolved an intensely personal style of unusual fantasy and wit.

Kleen+ex ('kli:nɛks) *n., pl.* **+ex** *or* **+ex·es.** *Trademark.* a kind of soft paper tissue, used esp. as a handkerchief.

Klein bot·tle (klaɪn) *n. Maths.* a one-sided surface having no edges that encloses a three-dimensional space and is formed by inserting the smaller end of an open tapered tube through the surface of the tube and making this end contiguous with the other end. [named after Felix *Klein* (1849–1925) German mathematician]

Kleist (klaɪst) *n.* **(Bernd) Hein·rich (Wilhelm) von** ('haɪnrɪç fɔn). 1777–1811, German dramatist, poet, and short-story writer. His plays include *The Broken Pitcher* (1808), *Penthesilea* (1808), and *The Prince of Homburg* (published 1821).

Klem·pe·rer ('klɛmpərə) *n.* **Ot·to.** 1885–1973, orchestral conductor, born in Germany. He was best known for his interpretations of Beethoven.

klepht (klɛft) *n.* any of the Greeks who fled to the mountains after the 15th-century Turkish conquest of Greece and survived as brigands into the 19th century. [C19: from Modern Greek *klephtēs,* from Greek *kleptēs* thief] —**'kleph+tic** *adj.*

klep+to+ma+ni·a *or* **clep+to+ma+ni·a** (ˌklɛptəʊ'meɪnɪə) *n. Psychol.* a strong impulse to steal, esp. when there is no obvious motivation. [C19: *klepto-* from Greek *kleptēs* thief, from *kleptein* to steal + -MANIA] —**klep+to+'ma+ni+ˌac** *or* **ˌclep+to+'ma+ni+ac** *n.*

klieg light (kli:g) *n.* an intense carbon-arc light used for illumination in producing films. [C20: named after John H. *Kliegl* (1869–1959) and his brother Anton (1872–1927), German-born American inventors in the field of lighting]

Klimt (klɪmt) *n.* **Gus·tav** ('gʊstaf). 1862–1918, Austrian painter. He founded the Vienna Sezession (1897), a group of painters influenced by art nouveau.

Kline (klaɪn) *n.* **Franz** (frænts). 1910–62, U.S. abstract expressionist painter. His works are characterized by heavy black strokes on a white or grey background.

klip+spring+er ('klɪpˌsprɪŋə) *n.* a small agile antelope, *Oreotragus oreotragus,* inhabiting rocky regions of Africa south of the Sahara. [C18: from Afrikaans, from Dutch *klip* rock (see CLIFF) + *springer,* from *springen* to SPRING]

Klon+dike ('klɒndaɪk) *n.* **1.** a region of NW Canada, in the Yukon in the basin of the Klondike River: site of rich gold deposits, discovered in 1896 but largely exhausted by 1910. Area: about 2100 sq. km (800 sq. miles). **2.** a river in NW Canada, rising in the Yukon and flowing west to the Yukon River. Length: about 145 km (90 miles).

klong (klɒŋ) *n.* a type of canal in Thailand. [from Thai]

kloof (klu:f) *n.* a mountain pass or gorge in southern Africa. [C18: from Afrikaans, from Middle Dutch *clove* a cleft; see CLEAVE[1]]

klootch+man ('klu:tʃmən) *n., pl.* **+mans** *or* **+men.** *Northwestern Canadian.* an Indian woman; squaw. Also called: **klootch, klooch.** [C19: from Chinook jargon, from Nootka *hlotssma* woman, wife]

Klop·stock (*German* 'klɔpˌʃtɔk) *n.* **Frie·drich Gott·lieb** ('fri:drɪç 'gɔtli:p). 1724–1803, German poet, noted for his religious epic *Der Messias* (1748–73) and for his odes.

klutz (klʌts) *n. U.S. slang.* a clumsy or stupid person. [from German *Klotz* dolt; compare CLOT] —**'klutz·y** *adj.*

klys+tron ('klɪstrɒn, 'klaɪ-) *n.* an electron tube for the amplification or generation of microwaves by means of velocity modulation. [C20: *klys-*, from Greek *klus-*, *kluzein* to wash over, break over + -TRON]

km *or* **km.** *abbrev. for* kilometre.

k-me·son *n.* another name for **kaon.**

kn. *abbrev. for:* **1.** *Nautical.* knot. **2.** krona. **3.** krone.

KN *Chess. symbol for* king's knight.

knack (næk) *n.* **1.** a skilful, ingenious, or resourceful way of doing something. **2.** a particular talent or aptitude, esp. an intuitive one. [C14: probably variant of *knak* sharp knock, rap, of imitative origin]

knack+er ('nækə) *Brit.* ~*n.* **1.** a person who buys up old horses for slaughter. **2.** a person who buys up old buildings and breaks them up for scrap. **3.** (*usually pl.*) *Slang.* another word for **testicle.** ~*vb.* **4.** (*tr.; usually passive*) *Slang.* to exhaust; tire. [C16: probably from *nacker* saddler, probably of Scandinavian origin; compare Old Norse *hnakkur* saddle] —**'knack+er+y** *n.*

knack+wurst *or* **knock+wurst** ('nɒkˌwɜ:st) *n.* a short fat highly seasoned sausage. [German, from *knacken* to make a cracking sound + *Wurst* sausage]

knag (næg) *n.* **1.** a knot in wood. **2.** a wooden peg. [C15: perhaps from Low German *knagge*]

knap[1] (næp) *n. Dialect.* the crest of a hill. [Old English *cnæpp* top; compare Old Norse *knappr* knob]

knap[2] (næp) *vb.* **knaps, knap+ping, knapped.** (*tr.*) *Brit. dialect.* to hit, hammer, or chip. [C15 (in the sense: to strike with a sharp sound): of imitative origin; compare Dutch *knappen* to crack] —**'knap+per** *n.*

knap+sack ('næpˌsæk) *n.* a canvas or leather bag carried strapped on the back or shoulder. [C17: from Low German *knappsack*, probably from *knappen* to bite, snap + *sack* bag; related to Dutch *knapzak;* see SACK[1]]

knap+weed ('næpˌwi:d) *n.* any of several plants of the genus *Centaurea*, having purplish thistle-like flowers: family *Compositae* (composites). See also **centaury** (sense 2), **hardheads.** [C15 *knopwed;* see KNOP, WEED[1]]

knar (nɑ:) *n.* a variant of **knur.** [C14: *knarre* rough stone, knot on a tree; related to Low German *knarre*] —**knarred** *or* **'knar+ry** *adj.*

knave (neɪv) *n.* **1.** *Archaic.* a dishonest man; rogue. **2.** another word for **jack** (the playing card). **3.** *Obsolete.* a male servant. [Old English *cnafa;* related to Old High German *knabo* boy] —**'knav+ish** *adj.* —**'knav+ish+ly** *adv.* —**'knav+ish+ness** *n.*

knav+er+y ('neɪvərɪ) *n., pl.* **+er+ies. 1.** a deceitful or dishonest act. **2.** dishonest conduct; trickery.

knaw+el ('nɔ:əl) *n.* any of several Old World caryophyllaceous plants of the genus *Scleranthus*, having heads of minute petalless flowers. [C16: from German *Knauel*, literally: ball of yarn, from Old High German *kliuwa* ball]

knead (ni:d) *vb.* (*tr.*) **1.** to work and press (a soft substance, such as bread dough) into a uniform mixture with the hands. **2.** to squeeze, massage, or press with the hands. **3.** to make by kneading. [Old English *cnedan;* related to Old Saxon *knedan*, Old Norse *knotha*] —**'knead+er** *n.*

knee (ni:) *n.* **1.** the joint of the human leg connecting the tibia and fibula with the femur and protected in front by the patella. **2. a.** the area surrounding and above this joint. **b.** (*modifier*) reaching or covering the knee: *knee breeches; knee socks.* **3.** a corresponding or similar part in other vertebrates. **4.** the part of a garment that covers the knee. **5.** anything resembling a knee in action, such as a device pivoted to allow one member angular movement in relation to another. **6.** anything resembling a knee in shape, such as an angular bend in a pipe. **7.** any of the hollow rounded protuberances that project upwards from the roots of the swamp cypress: thought to aid respiration in waterlogged soil. **8. bend** *or* **bow the knee.** to kneel or submit. **9. bring someone to his knees.** to force someone into submission. ~*vb.* **knees, knee+ing, kneed. 10.** (*tr.*) to strike, nudge, or push with the knee. [Old English *cnēow;* compare Old High German *kneo*, Old Norse *knē*, Latin *genu*]

knee+cap ('ni:ˌkæp) *n.* **1.** *Anatomy.* a nontechnical name for **patella. 2.** another word for **poleyn.** ~*vb.* **+caps, +cap+ping, +capped.** (*tr.*) **3.** (esp. of certain terrorist groups) to shoot (a person) in the kneecap, esp. as an act of retaliation.

knee-deep *adj.* **1.** so deep as to reach or cover the knees: *knee-deep mud.* **2.** (*postpositive;* often foll. by *in*) **a.** sunk or covered to the knees: *knee-deep in sand.* **b.** immersed; deeply involved: *knee-deep in work.*

knee drop *n.* a wrestling attack in which a wrestler lifts his opponent and drops him onto his bent knee.

knee-high *adj.* **1.** another word for **knee-deep** (sense 1). **2.** as high as the knee: *a knee-high child.*

knee+hole ('ni:ˌhəʊl) *n.* **a.** a space for the knees, esp. under a desk. **b.** (*as modifier*): *a kneehole desk.*

knee jerk *n. Physiol.* an outward reflex kick of the lower leg caused by a sharp tap on the tendon just below the patella. Also called: **patellar reflex.**

kneel (ni:l) *vb.* **kneels, kneel+ing, knelt** *or* **kneeled. 1.** (*intr.*) to rest, fall, or support oneself on one's knees. ~*n.* **2.** the act or position of kneeling. [Old English *cnēowlian;* see KNEE] —**'kneel+er** *n.*

knee-length *adj.* reaching to the knee; *a knee-length skirt; knee-length boots.*

knee+pad ('ni:ˌpæd) *n.* any of several types of protective covering for the knees. Also called: **kneecap.**

knee+pan ('ni:ˌpæn) *n. Anatomy.* another word for **patella.**

knell (nɛl) *n.* **1.** the sound of a bell rung to announce a death or a funeral. **2.** something that precipitates or indicates death or destruction. ~*vb.* **3.** (*intr.*) to ring a knell. **4.** (*tr.*) to proclaim or announce by or as if by a tolling bell. [Old English *cnyll;* related to Middle High German *knüllen* to strike, Dutch *knallen* to bang]

Knel·ler ('nɛlə) *n.* Sir **God·frey.** ?1646–1723, portrait painter at the English court, born in Germany.

knelt (nɛlt) *vb.* a past tense or past participle of **kneel.**

Knes+set *or* **Knes+seth** ('knɛsɪt) *n.* the unicameral parliament of Israel. [Hebrew, literally: gathering]

knew (nju:) *vb.* the past tense of **know.**

Knick·er·bock·er ('nɪkəˌbɒkə) *n. U.S.* **1.** a descendant of the original Dutch settlers of New York. **2.** an inhabitant of New York. [C19: named after Diedrich *Knickerbocker*, fictitious Dutchman alleged to be the author of Washington Irving's *History of New York* (1809)]

knick+er+bock+ers ('nɪkəˌbɒkəz) *pl. n.* baggy breeches fastened with a band at the knee or above the ankle. Also called: **knickers.** [C19: regarded as the traditional wear of the Dutch settlers in America; see KNICKERBOCKER]

knick+ers ('nɪkəz) *pl. n.* **1.** any pants for women, esp. baggy wool or silk ones held up by elastic. **2.** a variant of **knickerbockers.** [C19: contraction of KNICKERBOCKERS]

knick+knack *or* **nick+nack** ('nɪkˌnæk) *n.* **1.** a cheap ornament; trinket. **2.** an ornamental article of furniture, dress, etc. [C17: by reduplication from *knack*, in obsolete sense: toy] —**ˌknick+'knack+er+y** *or* **ˌnick'nack+er+y** *n.*

knick+point *or esp. U.S.* **nick+point** ('nɪkˌpɔɪnt) *n.* a break in the slope of a river profile caused by renewed erosion by a rejuvenated river. [C20: partial translation of German *knickpunkt*, from *knicken* to bend + *Punkt* POINT]

knife (naɪf) *n., pl.* **knives** (naɪvz). **1.** a cutting instrument consisting of a sharp-edged often pointed blade of metal fitted into a handle or onto a machine. **2.** a similar instrument used as a weapon. **3. have one's knife into someone.** to have a grudge against or victimize someone. **4. under the knife.** undergoing a surgical operation. ~*vb.* (*tr.*) **5.** to cut, stab, or kill with a knife. **6.** to betray, injure, or depose in an underhand way. [Old English *cnīf;* related to Old Norse *knīfr*, Middle Low German *knīf*] —**'knife+ˌlike** *adj.* —**'knif+er** *n.*

knife edge *n.* **1.** the sharp cutting edge of a knife. **2.** any sharp edge. **3.** a sharp-edged wedge of hard material on which the beam of a balance pivots or about which a pendulum is suspended. **4.** a critical point in the development of a situation, process of making a decision, etc.

knife grind+er *n.* a person who makes and sharpens knives, esp. an itinerant one.

knife pleat *n.* a single pleat turned in one direction.

knife-point *n.* **1.** the tip of a knife blade. **2. at knife-point.** under threat of being stabbed.

knife+rest ('naɪfˌrɛst) *n.* a support on which a carving knife or carving fork is placed at the table.

knife switch *n.* an electric switch in which a flat metal blade, hinged at one end, is pushed between fixed contacts.

knight (naɪt) *n.* **1.** (in medieval Europe) **a.** (originally) a person who served his lord as a mounted and heavily armed soldier. **b.** (later) a gentleman invested by a king or other lord with the military and social standing of this rank. **2.** (in modern times) a person invested by a sovereign with a nonhereditary rank and dignity usually in recognition of personal services, achievements, etc. A British knight bears the title *Sir* placed before his name: *Sir Winston Churchill.* **3.** a chess piece, usually shaped like a horse's head, that moves either two squares horizontally and one square vertically or one square horizontally and two squares vertically. **4.** a champion of a lady or of a cause or principle. **5.** a member of the Roman class of the equites. ~*vb.* **6.** (*tr.*) to make (a person) a knight; dub. [Old English *cniht* servant; related to Old High German *kneht* boy]

knight bach+e·lor *n., pl.* **knights bach+e·lors** *or* **knights bach+e·lor.** another name for a **bachelor** (sense 3).

knight ban+ner+et *n., pl.* **knights ban+ner+ets.** another name for a **banneret.**

knight er+rant *n., pl.* **knights er+rant.** (esp. in medieval romance) a knight who wanders in search of deeds of courage, chivalry, etc.

knight er+rant+ry *n.* **1.** the practices of a knight errant. **2.** quixotic behaviour or practices.

knight+head ('naɪt,hɛd) *n. Nautical.* either of a pair of vertical supports for each side of the bowsprit. [C18: originally decorated with carvings of knights' heads]
knight+hood ('naɪthʊd) *n.* **1.** the order, dignity, or rank of a knight. **2.** the qualities of a knight; knightliness. **3.** knights collectively.
knight+ly ('naɪtlɪ) *adj.* of, relating to, resembling, or befitting a knight. —**'knight+li+ness** *n.*
knight mar+shal *n.* another name for **marshal** (sense 5).
knight of the road *n. Brit. informal or facetious.* a lorry driver.
Knights Hos+pi+tal+lers *n.* **1.** Also called: **Knights of St. John of Jerusalem.** a military religious order founded about the time of the first crusade (1096–99) among European crusaders. It took its name from a hospital and hostel in Jerusalem. Full name: **Knights of the Hospital of St. John of Jerusalem. 2.** See **Hospitaller.**
Knights of the Round Ta+ble *n.* (in Arthurian legend) an order of knights created by King Arthur.
Knight Tem+plar *n., pl.* **Knights Tem+plars** *or* **Knights Tem+plar.** another term for **Templar.**
knish (knɪʃ) *n.* a piece of dough stuffed with potato, meat, or some other filling and baked or fried. [Yiddish, from Russian *knysh* cake; compare Polish *knysz*]
knit (nɪt) *vb.* **knits, knit+ting, knit+ted** *or* **knit. 1.** to make (a garment, etc.) by looping and entwining (yarn, esp. wool) by hand by means of long eyeless needles (**knitting needles**) or by machine (**knitting machine**). **2.** to join or be joined together closely. **3.** to draw (the brows) together or (of the brows) to come together, as in frowning or concentrating. ~*n.* **4. a.** a fabric or garment made by knitting. **b.** (*in combination*): *a heavy knit.* [Old English *cnyttan* to tie in; related to Middle Low German *knütten* to knot together; see KNOT[1]] —**'knit+ta·ble** *adj.* —**'knit+ter** *n.*
knit+ting ('nɪtɪŋ) *n.* **a.** knitted work or the process of producing it. **b.** (*as modifier*): *a knitting machine.*
knit+wear ('nɪt,wɛə) *n.* knitted clothes, esp. sweaters.
knives (naɪvz) *n.* the plural of **knife.**
knob (nɒb) *n.* **1.** a rounded projection from a surface, such as a lump on a tree trunk. **2.** a handle of a door, drawer, etc., esp. one that is rounded. **3.** a round hill or knoll or morainic ridge. **4.** *Brit. taboo.* a slang word for **penis. 5. and the same to you with (brass) knobs on.** *Brit. informal.* the same to you but even more so. ~*vb.* **knobs, knob+bing, knobbed. 6.** (*tr.*) to supply or ornament with knobs. **7.** (*intr.*) to form into a knob; bulge. [C14: from Middle Low German *knobbe* knot in wood; see KNOP] —**'knob+by** *adj.* —**'knob+,like** *adj.*
knob+ker+rie ('nɒb,kɛrɪ) *or* **knob+stick** *n.* a stick with a round knob at the end, used as a club or missile by South African tribesmen. [C19: from Afrikaans *knopkierie,* from *knop* knob, from Middle Dutch *cnoppe* + *kierie* stick, from Hottentot *kīrri*]
knock (nɒk) *vb.* **1.** (*tr.*) to give a blow or push to; strike. **2.** (*intr.*) to rap sharply with the knuckles, a hard object, etc., esp. to capture attention: *to knock at the door.* **3.** (*tr.*) to make or force by striking: *to knock a hole in the wall.* **4.** (*intr.;* usually foll. by *against*) to collide (with). **5.** (*tr.*) to bring into a certain condition by hitting or pushing: *to knock someone unconscious.* **6.** (*tr.*) *Informal.* to criticize adversely; belittle: *to knock someone's work.* **7.** (*intr.*) Also **pink.** (of an internal-combustion engine) to emit a characteristic metallic noise as a result of faulty combustion. **8.** (*intr.*) (of a bearing, esp. one in an engine) to emit a regular characteristic sound as a result of wear. **9.** *Brit. slang.* to have sexual intercourse with (a person). **10. knock (a person) into the middle of next week.** *Informal.* to hit (a person) with a very heavy blow. **11. knock one's head against.** to encounter (adverse facts or circumstances) in a forceful manner. **12. knock on the head. a.** to daze or kill (a person) by striking on the head. **b.** to effectively prevent the further development of (a plan). **13. take the knock.** *Slang.* to suffer financially. ~*n.* **14. a.** a blow, push, or rap: *he gave the table a knock.* **b.** the sound so caused. **15.** the sound of knocking in an engine or bearing. [Old English *cnocian,* of imitative origin; related to Old Norse *knoka* to hit]
knock a+bout *or* **a+round** *vb.* **1.** (*intr., adv.*) to wander about aimlessly. **2.** (*intr., prep.*) to travel about, esp. as resulting in varied or exotic experience: *he's knocked about the world a bit.* **3.** (*intr., adv.;* foll. by *with*) to associate: *to knock about with a gang.* **4.** (*tr., adv.*) to treat brutally: *he knocks his wife about.* **5.** (*tr., adv.*) to consider or discuss informally: *to knock an idea about.* ~*n.* **knock+a+bout. 6.** a sailing vessel, usually sloop-rigged, without a bowsprit and with a single jib.
knock back *vb.* (*tr., adv.*) *Informal.* **1.** to drink, esp. quickly. **2.** to cost: *how much did the car knock you back?* ~*n.* **knock+back. 3.** *Prison slang.* failure to obtain parole. **4.** *Slang.* a refusal or rejection.
knock down *vb.* (*tr., adv.*) **1.** to strike to the ground with a blow, as in boxing. **2.** (in auctions) to declare (an article) sold, as by striking a blow with a gavel. **3.** to demolish. **4.** to dismantle, for ease of transport. **5.** *Informal.* to reduce (a price, etc.). ~*adj.* **knock+down.** (*prenominal*) **6.** overwhelming; powerful: *a knockdown blow.* **7.** *Chiefly Brit.* cheap: *I got the table at a knockdown price.* **8.** easily dismantled: *knockdown furniture.* ~*n.* **knock+down. 9.** *Informal, U.S. and Austral.* an introduction: *will you give me a knockdown to her?*
knock+er ('nɒkə) *n.* **1.** an object, usually ornamental and made of metal, attached to a door by a hinge and used for knocking. **2.** (*usually pl.*) *Slang.* a female breast. **3.** a person or thing that knocks. **4. on the knocker.** *Austral. informal.* promptly; at once: *you pay on the knocker here.*
knock·ing-shop *n. Brit.* a slang word for **brothel.**
knock-knee *n.* a condition in which the legs are bent inwards causing the knees to touch when standing. Technical name: **genu valgum.** —**'knock-,kneed** *adj.*
knock off *vb.* (*mainly adv.*) **1.** (*intr., also prep.*) *Informal.* to finish work: *we knocked off an hour early.* **2.** (*tr.*) *Informal.* to make or do hastily or easily: *to knock off a novel in a week.* **3.** (*tr.; also prep.*) *Informal.* to reduce the price of (an article) by (a stated amount). **4.** (*tr.*) *Slang.* to kill. **5.** (*tr.*) *Slang.* to rob or steal: *to knock off a bank; to knock off a watch.* **6.** (*tr.*) *Slang.* to stop doing something, used as a command: *knock it off!* **7.** (*tr.*) *Slang.* to have sexual intercourse with (a woman).
knock-on *Rugby.* ~*n.* **1.** the infringement of playing the ball forward with the hand or arm. ~*vb.* **knock on** (*adv.*). **2.** to play (the ball) forward with the hand or arm.
knock+out ('nɒk,aʊt) *n.* **1.** the act of rendering unconscious. **2.** a blow that renders an opponent unconscious. **3. a.** a competition in which competitors are eliminated progressively. **b.** (*as modifier*): *a knockout contest.* **4.** a series of absurd invented games, esp. obstacle races, involving physical effort or skill. **5.** *Informal.* a person or thing that is overwhelmingly impressive or attractive: *she's a knockout.* ~*vb.* **knock out.** (*tr., adv.*) **6.** to render unconscious, esp. by a blow. **7.** *Boxing.* to defeat (an opponent) by a knockout. **8.** to destroy, damage, or injure badly. **9.** to eliminate, esp. in a knockout competition. **10.** *Informal.* to overwhelm or amaze, esp. with admiration or favourable reaction: *I was knocked out by that new song.* **11.** to remove the ashes from (one's pipe) by tapping. **12. knock the bottom out of.** *Informal.* to invalidate (an argument).
knock+out drops *pl. n. Slang.* a drug secretly put into someone's drink to cause stupefaction. See also **Mickey Finn.**
knock up *vb.* (*adv., mainly tr.*) **1.** Also: **knock together.** *Informal.* to assemble quickly; improvise: *to knock up a set of shelves.* **2.** *Brit. informal.* to waken; rouse: *to knock someone up early.* **3.** *Slang.* to make pregnant. **4.** *Brit. informal.* to exhaust: *the heavy work knocked him up.* **5.** *Cricket.* to score (runs). **6.** (*intr.*) *Tennis, squash, etc.* to practise or hit the ball about informally, esp. before a match. ~*n.* **knock-up. 7.** a practice session at tennis, squash, or a similar game.
knock+wurst ('nɒk,wɜːst) *n.* another word for **knackwurst.**
knoll[1] (nəʊl) *n.* a small rounded hill. [Old English *cnoll;* compare Old Norse *knollr* hilltop] —**'knoll·y** *adj.*
knoll[2] (nəʊl) *n., vb.* an archaic or dialect word for **knell.** —**'knoll+er** *n.*
knop (nɒp) *n. Archaic.* a knob, esp. an ornamental one. [C14: from Germanic; compare Middle Dutch *cnoppe* bud, Old High German *knopf*]
Knos+sos *or* **Cnos+sus** ('nɒsəs, 'knɒs-) *n.* a ruined city in N central Crete: remains of the Minoan Bronze Age civilization.
knot[1] (nɒt) *n.* **1.** any of various fastenings formed by looping and tying a piece of rope, cord, etc., in upon itself, to another piece of rope, or to another object. **2.** a prescribed method of tying a particular knot. **3.** a decorative bow or fastening, as of ribbon or braid. **4.** a small closely knit group. **5.** a tie or bond: *the marriage knot.* **6.** a difficult problem. **7.** a protuberance or lump of plant tissues, such as that occurring on the trunks of certain trees. **8. a.** *Pathol.* a lump of vessels or fibres formed in a part, as in a muscle. **b.** *Anatomy.* a protuberance on an organ or part. **9.** a unit of speed used by nautical vessels and aircraft, being one nautical mile (about 1.15 statute miles or 1.85 km) per hour. **10.** one of a number of equally spaced knots on a log line used to indicate the speed of a ship in nautical miles per hour. **11.** another term (not in technical use) for **nautical mile. 12. at a rate of knots.** very fast. **13. tie (someone) in knots.** to completely perplex or confuse (someone). ~*vb.* **knots, knot+ting, knot+ted. 14.** (*tr.*) to tie or fasten in a knot. **15.** to form or cause to form into a knot. **16.** (*tr.*) to ravel or entangle or become ravelled or entangled. [Old English *cnotta;* related to Old High German *knoto,* Old Norse *knūtr*] —**'knot+ter** *n.* —**'knot+less** *adj.* —**'knot+,like** *adj.*
knot[2] (nɒt) *n.* a small northern sandpiper, *Calidris canutus,* with a short bill and grey plumage. [C15: of unknown origin]
knot gar+den *n.* (esp. formerly) a formal garden of intricate design.
knot+grass ('nɒt,grɑːs) *n.* **1.** Also called: **allseed.** a polygonaceous weedy plant, *Polygonum aviculare,* whose small green flowers produce numerous seeds. **2.** any of several related plants.
knot+hole ('nɒt,həʊl) *n.* a hole in a piece of wood where a knot has been.
knot+ted ('nɒtɪd) *adj.* **1.** (of wood, rope, etc.) having knots. **2. get knotted!** *Brit. slang.* used as a response to express disapproval or rejection.
knot+ting ('nɒtɪŋ) *n.* a sealer applied over knots in new wood before priming to prevent resin from exuding.
knot+ty ('nɒtɪ) *adj.* **knot+ti+er, knot+ti+est. 1.** (of wood, rope, etc.) full of or characterized by knots. **2.** extremely difficult or intricate. —**'knot+ti+ly** *adv.* —**'knot+ti+ness** *n.*
knot+weed ('nɒt,wiːd) *n.* any of several polygonaceous plants of the genus *Polygonum,* having small flowers and jointed stems.
knot+work ('nɒt,wɜːk) *n.* ornamentation consisting of a mass of intertwined and knotted cords.
knout (naʊt) *n.* a stout whip used formerly in Russia as an instrument of punishment. [C17: from Russian *knut,* of Scandinavian origin; compare Old Norse *knūtr* knot]
know (nəʊ) *vb.* **knows, know+ing, knew, known.** (*mainly tr.*) **1.** (*also intr.; may take a clause as object*) to be or feel certain of the truth or accuracy of (a fact, etc.). **2.** to be acquainted or

familiar with: *she's known him five years.* **3.** to have a familiarity or grasp of, as through study or experience. *he knows French.* **4.** (*also intr.; may take a clause as object*) to understand, have knowledge of, or perceive (facts, etc.): *he knows the answer now.* **5.** (foll. by *how*) to be sure or aware of (how to be or do something). **6.** to experience, esp. deeply: *to know poverty.* **7.** to be intelligent, informed, or sensible enough (to do something): *she knew not to go home yet.* **8.** (*may take a clause as object*) to be able to distinguish or discriminate. **9.** *Archaic.* to have sexual intercourse with. **10. I know what.** I have an idea. **11. know what's what.** to know how one thing or things in general work. **12. you know.** *Informal.* a parenthetical filler phrase used to make a pause in speaking or add slight emphasis to a statement. **13. you never know.** things are uncertain. ~*n.* **14. in the know.** *Informal.* aware or informed. [Old English *gecnāwan;* related to Old Norse *knā* I can, Latin *noscere* to come to know] —'**know+a·ble** *adj.* —'**know+er** *n.*

know-all *n. Informal, disparaging.* a person who pretends or appears to know a great deal.

know-how *n. Informal.* **1.** ingenuity, aptitude, or skill; knack. **2.** commercial and saleable knowledge of how to do a particular thing; experience.

know+ing ('nəʊɪŋ) *adj.* **1.** suggesting secret information or knowledge. **2.** wise, shrewd, or clever. **3.** deliberate; intentional. ~*n.* **there is no knowing.** one cannot tell. —'**know+ing+ly** *adv.* —'**know+ing+ness** *n.*

knowl+edge ('nɒlɪdʒ) *n.* **1.** the facts, feelings or experiences known by a person or group of people. **2.** the state of knowing. **3.** awareness, consciousness, or familiarity gained by experience or learning. **4.** erudition or informed learning. **5.** specific information about a subject. **6.** sexual intercourse (obsolete except in the legal phrase **carnal knowledge**). **7. come to one's knowledge.** to become known to one. **8. to my (his, etc.) knowledge. a.** as I understand it. **b.** as I know.

knowl+edge+a·ble *or* **knowl+edg+a·ble** ('nɒlɪdʒəbᵊl) *adj.* possessing or indicating much knowledge. —'**knowl+edge+a·ble+ness** *n.* —'**knowl+edge+a·bly** *adv.*

known (nəʊn) *vb.* **1.** the past participle of **know.** ~*adj.* **2.** specified and identified: *a known criminal.* ~*n.* **3.** a fact known.

known quan+ti·ty *n.* a mathematical quantity representing a given value.

Knox (nɒks) *n.* **John.** ?1505–72, Scottish theologian and historian. In exile during the reign of Mary I of England (1553–58), he returned to Scotland in 1559 and established the Presbyterian Church of Scotland (1560). His chief historical work was the *History of the Reformation in Scotland* (1586).

Knox+ville ('nɒksvɪl) *n.* an industrial city in E Tennessee, on the Tennessee River: state capital (1796–1812; 1817–19). Pop.: 182 276 (1973 est.).

KNP *Chess. symbol for* king's knight's pawn.

Knt. *abbrev. for* Knight.

knuck+le ('nʌkᵊl) *n.* **1.** a joint of a finger, esp. that connecting a finger to the hand. **2.** a joint of veal, pork, etc., consisting of the part of the leg below the knee joint, often used in making stews or stock. **3.** the cylindrical portion of a hinge through which the pin passes. **4.** an angle joint between two members of a structure. **5. near the knuckle.** *Informal.* approaching indecency. ~*vb.* **6.** (*tr.*) to rub or press with the knuckles. **7.** (*intr.*) to keep the knuckles on the ground while shooting a marble. [C14: related to Middle High German *knöchel,* Middle Low German *knoke* bone, Dutch *knok*] —'**knuck+ly** *adj.*

knuck·le+bone ('nʌkᵊl,bəʊn) *n.* any bone forming part of a knuckle or knuckle joint.

knuck·le+bones ('nʌkᵊl,bəʊnz) *n.* a less common name for **jacks** (the game).

knuck+le down *vb.* (*intr., adv.*) *Informal.* to apply oneself diligently: *to knuckle down to some work.*

knuck·le-dust·er *n.* (*often pl.*) a metal bar fitted over the knuckles, often with holes for the fingers, for inflicting injury by a blow with the fist.

knuck·le+head ('nʌkᵊl,hɛd) *n. Informal.* fool; idiot. —'**knuck·le+,head·ed** *adj.*

knuck+le joint *n.* **1.** any of the joints of the fingers. **2.** *Mechanical engineering.* a hinged joint between two rods, often a ball and socket joint.

knuck+le un+der *vb.* (*intr., adv.*) to give way under pressure or authority; yield.

knur, knurr (nɜː), *or* **knar** *n.* a knot or protuberance in a tree trunk or in wood. [C16 *knor;* related to Middle High German *knorre* knot; compare KNAR]

knurl *or* **nurl** (nɜːl) *vb.* (*tr.*) **1.** to impress with a series of fine ridges or serrations. ~*n.* **2.** a small ridge, esp. one of a series providing a rough surface that can be gripped. [C17: probably from KNUR, influenced by GNARL]

knurl·y ('nɜːlɪ) *adj.* **knurl·i+er, knurl·i+est.** a rare word for **gnarled.**

Knut (kə'njuːt) *n.* a variant spelling of **Canute.**

KO, or K.O., *or* **k.o.** ('keɪ'əʊ) *vb.* **KO's, KO'ing, KO'd; K.O.'s, K.O.'ing, K.O.'d; k.o.'s, k.o.'ing, k.o.'d,** *n., pl.* **KO's, K.O.'s,** *or* **k.o.'s.** a slang term for **knock out** or **knockout.**

ko·a ('kəʊə) *n.* **1.** a Hawaiian mimosaceous tree, *Acacia koa,* yielding a hard wood. **2.** the reddish wood of this tree, used esp. for furniture. [C19: from Hawaiian]

ko·a+la *or* **ko·a+la bear** (kəʊ'ɑːlə) *n.* a slow-moving Australian arboreal marsupial, *Phascolarctus cinereus,* having dense greyish fur and feeding on eucalyptus leaves and bark. Also called (in Australia): **native bear.**

ko·an ('kəʊæn) *n.* (in Zen Buddhism) a problem or riddle that admits no logical solution. [from Japanese]

kob (kɒb) *n.* any African antelope of the genus *Kobus*: similar to waterbucks. [C20: from a Niger-Congo language; compare Wolof *koba,* Fulani *kōba*]

Ko+ba+rid ('kəʊbə,riːd; *Serbo-Croatian* 'kɔba,rid) *n.* a village in NW Yugoslavia, in Slovenia on the Isonzo River: part of Italy until 1947; scene of the defeat of the Italians by Austro-German forces (1917). Italian name: **Caporetto.**

Ko·be ('kəʊbɪ) *n.* a port in S Japan, on S Honshu on Osaka Bay: formed in 1889 by the amalgamation of Hyogo and Kobe; a major industrial complex, producing ships, steel, and rubber goods. Pop.: 1 360 000 (1975).

Kø+ben+havn (,købən'haʊn) *n.* the Danish name for **Copenhagen.**

Ko+blenz *or* **Co+blenz** (*German* 'koːblɛnts) *n.* a city in West Germany, in the Rhineland-Palatinate at the confluence of the Rivers Moselle and Rhine: ruled by the archbishop-electors of Trier from 1018 until occupied by the French in 1794; passed to Prussia in 1815, becoming capital of the Rhine Province (1824–1945) and of the Rhineland-Palatinate (1946–50); wine trade centre. Pop.: 119 476 (1974 est.). Latin name: **Confluentes.**

kob+old ('kɒbəʊld) *n. German myth.* **1.** a mischievous household sprite. **2.** a spirit that haunts subterranean places, such as mines. [C19: from German; see COBALT]

Koch (*German* kɔx) *n.* **Ro·bert** ('roːbɛrt). 1843–1910, German bacteriologist, who isolated the anthrax bacillus (1876), the tubercle bacillus (1882), and the cholera bacillus (1883): Nobel prize for physiology and medicine 1905.

Köch+el ('kœçᵊl) *n.* See **K.**

Ko+chi (kəʊ'tʃiː) *n.* a port in SW Japan, on central Shikoku on Urado Bay. Pop.: 274 609 (1974 est.).

Ko·dá·ly (*Hungarian* 'kodaːj) *n.* **Zol·tán** ('zoltaːn). 1882–1967, Hungarian composer. His works were often inspired by native folk songs and include the comic opera *Háry János* (1926) and *Psalmus Hungaricus* (1923) for chorus and orchestra.

Ko+di+ak ('kəʊdɪ,æk) *n.* an island in S Alaska, in the Gulf of Alaska: site of the first European settlement in Alaska, made by Russians in 1784. Pop.: 9409 (1970). Area: 8974 sq. km (3465 sq. miles).

Ko+di+ak bear *or* **Ko+di+ak** *n.* a large variety of the brown bear, *Ursus arctos,* inhabiting Alaskan islands, esp. Kodiak.

Ko+dok ('kəʊdɒk) *n.* the modern name for **Fashoda.**

ko·el ('kəʊəl) *n.* any of several parasitic cuckoos of the genus *Eudynamys,* esp. *E. scolopacea,* of S and SE Asia and Australia. [C19: from Hindi, from Sanskrit *kokila*]

Koes·tler ('kɜːstlə) *n.* **Ar·thur.** 1905–83, British writer born in Hungary. Of his early antitotalitarian novels *Darkness at Noon* (1940) is outstanding. His later works, *The Sleepwalkers* (1959), *The Act of Creation* (1964), and *The Ghost in the Machine* (1967) reflect his interest in science, philosophy, and psychology.

kof+ta ('kɒftə) *n.* an Indian dish of seasoned minced meat shaped into small balls and cooked. [Urdu]

koft+gar ('kɒftgɑː) *n.* (in India) a person skilled in the art of inlaying steel with gold (**koftgari**). [C19: Urdu]

Ko·fu ('kəʊfuː) *n.* a city in central Japan, on S Honshu: hot springs. Pop.: 193 406 (1974 est.).

Ko+hel+eth (kəʊ'hɛlɪθ) *n. Old Testament.* Ecclesiastes or its author, supposedly Solomon. [from Hebrew *qōheleth*]

Ko+hi+ma ('kəʊhɪ,mɑː) *n.* a city in NE India, capital of Nagaland, near the Burmese border: centre of fierce fighting in World War II, when it was surrounded by the Japanese but not captured (1944). Pop.: 21 545 (1971).

Koh·i·noor, Koh·i·nor, *or* **Koh·i·nur** ('kəʊɪ,nʊə) *n.* a very large oval Indian diamond, part of the British crown jewels since 1849, weighing 108.8 carats. [C19: from Persian *Kōh-i-nūr,* literally: mountain of light, from *kōh* mountain + Arabic *nūr* light]

kohl (kəʊl) *n.* a cosmetic powder used originally esp. in Moslem and Asian countries to darken the area around the eyes. It is usually powdered antimony sulphide. [C18: from Arabic *kohl*; see ALCOHOL]

Kohl (kəʊl) *n.* **Hel·mut** ('hɛlmuːt). born 1930, German politician; chancellor of West Germany from 1982.

Köh·ler (*German* 'køːlər) *n.* **Wolf·gang** ('vɔlfgaŋ). 1887–1967, German psychologist, a leading exponent of gestalt psychology.

kohl+ra+bi (kəʊl'rɑːbɪ) *n., pl.* **+bies.** a cultivated variety of cabbage, *Brassica oleracea caulorapa* (or *gongylodes*), whose thickened stem is eaten as a vegetable. Also called: **turnip cabbage.** [C19: from German, from Italian *cavoli rape* (pl.), from *cavolo* cabbage (from Latin *caulis*) + *rapa* turnip (from Latin); influenced by German *Kohl* cabbage]

Ko+hou+tek (kə'huːtɛk) *n.* a comet of almost parabolic orbit that reached its closest approach to the sun in Dec. 1973. [C20: named after Luboš *Kohoutek,* Czech astronomer working in Germany who discovered it in March, 1973]

koi+ne ('kɔɪniː) *n.* a common language among speakers of different languages; lingua franca. [from Greek *koinē dialektos* common language]

Koi+ne ('kɔɪniː) *n.* (*sometimes not cap.*) **the.** the Ancient Greek dialect that was the lingua franca of the empire of Alexander the Great and was widely used throughout the E Mediterranean area in Roman times.

ko+kan·ee (kəʊ'kænɪ) *n.* a landlocked salmon, *Oncorhynchus nerka kennerlyi,* of lakes in W North America: a variety of sockeye. [probably from *Kokanee* Creek, in SE British Columbia]

ko+ko+beh ('kʌkʌbɛ) *adj.* (of certain fruit) having a rough skin: *kokobeh breadfruit.* [from Twi: leprosy]

Ko·ko Nor ('kəʊ'kəʊ 'nɔː) *or* **Ku·ku Nor** *n.* a lake in W China, in Tsinghai province in the NE Tibetan Highlands at an altitude of about 3000 m (10 000 ft.): the largest lake in China. Area: about 4100 sq. km (1600 sq. miles). Chinese name: **Tsinghai.**

Ko·kosch·ka (*German* ko'kɔʃka, 'kɔkɔʃka) *n.* **Os·kar** ('ɔskar). 1886–1980, Austrian expressionist painter and dramatist, noted for his landscapes and portraits.

Ko+ku+ra (ˌkəʊkə'rɑː) *n.* a former city in SW Japan, on N Kyushu: merged with adjacent townships in 1963 to form the new city of **Kitakyushu.**

ko·la ('kəʊlə) *n.* a variant spelling of **cola**[1].

ko·la nut *n.* a variant spelling of **cola nut.**

Ko·la Pen+in+su+la ('kəʊlə) *n.* a peninsula of the NW Soviet Union, between the Barents and White Seas: forms most of the Murmansk Region of the RSFSR. Area: about 130 000 sq. km (50 000 sq. miles).

Ko+lar Gold Fields (kəʊ'lɑː) *n.* a city in S India, in SE Karnataka: a major gold-mining centre since 1881. Pop.: 118 861 (1971).

Kol+ding (*Danish* 'kɔleŋ) *n.* a port in Denmark, in E Jutland at the head of **Kolding Fjord** (an inlet of the Little Belt). Pop.: 40 176 (1970).

Kol+ha+pur (ˌkəʊlhɑː'pʊə) *n.* a city in W India, in S Maharashtra: university (1963). Pop.: 259 050 (1971).

ko+lin+sky (kə'lɪnskɪ) *n., pl.* **+skies. 1.** any of various Asian minks, esp. *Mustela sibirica* of Siberia. **2.** the rich tawny fur of this animal. [C19: from Russian *kolinski* of KOLA]

kol+khoz, kol+khos (kɒl'hɔːz; *Russian* kal'xɔs), *or* **kol+koz** (kɒl'kɔːz) *n.* a Russian collective farm. [C20: from Russian, short for *kollektivnoe khozyaistvo* collective farm]

Koll·witz (*German* 'kɔlvɪts) *n.* **Kä·the** ('kɛːtə). 1867–1945, German lithographer and sculptress.

Kol+mar ('kɔlmar) *n.* the German name for **Colmar.**

Köln (kœln) *n.* the German name for **Cologne.**

Kol Ni+dre (kɔːl 'nɪdreɪ; *Hebrew* kol niː'dre) *n. Judaism.* the opening prayer recited on the eve of Yom Kippur, containing an annulment of all one's vows of the preceding year. [Aramaic *kōl nidhrē* all the vows; the prayer's opening words]

ko+lo ('kəʊləʊ) *n., pl.* **·los. 1.** a Serbian folk dance in which a circle of people dance slowly around one or more dancers in the centre. **2.** a piece of music composed for or in the rhythm of this dance. [Serbo-Croatian, from Old Slavonic: wheel; related to Old English *hwēol* WHEEL]

Ko+lom+na (*Russian* ka'lɔmnə) *n.* a city in the W central Soviet Union, at the confluence of the Moskva and Oka Rivers: railway engineering centre. Pop.: 144 000 (1975 est.).

Ko+lozs+vár ('koloʒˌvaːr) *n.* the Hungarian name for **Cluj.**

Ko+ly+ma (*Russian* kəlɪ'ma) *n.* a river in the NE Soviet Union, rising in the Kolyma Mountains north of the Sea of Okhotsk and flowing generally north to the East Siberian Sea. Length: 2600 km (1615 miles).

Ko+ly+ma Range *n.* a mountain range in the NE Soviet Union, in NE Siberia, extending about 1100 km (700 miles) between the Kolyma River and the Sea of Okhotsk. Highest peak: 1862 m (6109 ft.).

Ko+ma+ti (kə'mɑːtɪ, 'kəʊmətɪ) *n.* a river in southern Africa, rising in South Africa in SE Transvaal and flowing east through Swaziland and Mozambique to the Indian Ocean at Delagoa Bay. Length: about 800 km (500 miles).

ko+mat+ik ('kəʊmætɪk) *n.* a sledge having wooden runners and crossbars bound with rawhide, used by Eskimos. [C20: from Eskimo (Labrador)]

Ko+mi ('kəʊmɪ) *n.* **1.** (*pl.* **·mi** or **·mis**) a member of a Finnish people living chiefly in the Komi ASSR, in the NW Urals. **2.** the Finno-Ugric language of this people; Zyrian.

Ko+mi Au·ton·o·mous So+vi+et So+cial+ist Re+pub+lic *n.* an administrative division of the NW Soviet Union: annexed by the princes of Moscow in the 14th century. Capital: Syktyvkar. Pop.: 964 802 (1970). Area: 415 900 sq. km (160 540 sq. miles).

Kom+mu+narsk (*Russian* kəmu'narsk) *n.* a city in the SW Soviet Union, in the E Ukrainian SSR. Pop.: 129 000 (1975 est.).

Kom+mu+niz+ma Peak (*Russian* kəmu'njizmə) *n.* a mountain in the SE Tadzhik SSR in the Pamirs: the highest mountain in the Soviet Union. Height: 7495 m (24 590 ft.). Former name: **Stalin Peak.**

Ko+mo+do drag+on *or* **liz+ard** (kə'məʊdəʊ) *n.* the largest monitor lizard, *Varanus komodoensis,* of Komodo and other East Indian islands: grows to a length of 3 metres (about 10 feet) and a weight of 135 kilograms (about 300 lbs.).

Kom+so+mol (ˌkɒmsə'mɒl, 'kɒmsəˌmɒl; *Russian* kəmsa'mɔl) *n.* the youth association of the Soviet Union for 14- to 26-year-olds. [C20: from Russian, from *Kom(munisticheski) So(yuz) Mol(odezhi)* Communist Union of Youth]

Kom+so+molsk (*Russian* kəmsa'mɔljsk) *n.* an industrial city in the E Soviet Union, in the S Khabarovsk Territory on the Amur River: built by members of the Komsomol in 1932. Pop.: 240 000 (1975 est.).

Ko+na+kry *or* **Ko+na+kri** (*French* kɔna'kri) *n.* variant spellings of **Conakry.**

kon+do ('kɒndəʊ) *n., pl.* **+dos.** (in Uganda) a thief or armed robber. [C20: from Luganda]

Kon+go ('kɒŋgəʊ) *n.* **1.** (*pl.* **+gos** *or* **+go**) a member of a Negroid people of Africa living in the tropical forests of Zaïre, the Congo Republic, and Angola. **2.** the language of this people, belonging to the Bantu group of the Niger-Congo family.

kon+go+ni (kɒŋ'gəʊnɪ) *n.* an E African hartebeest, *Alcelaphus buselaphus.* See **hartebeest** (sense 1). [Swahili]

Kö+nig+grätz (ˌkøːnɪç'grɛːts) *n.* the German name for **Hradec Králové.**

Kö+nigs+berg ('kɜːnɪgzˌbɜːg; *German* 'køːnɪçsˌbɛrk) *n.* the former name (until 1946) of **Kaliningrad.**

Kö+nigs+hüt+te ('køːnɪçsˌhytɛ) *n.* the German name for **Chorzów.**

ko+ni+ol+o·gy *or* **co+ni+ol+o·gy** (ˌkəʊnɪ'ɒlədʒɪ) *n.* the study of atmospheric dust and its effects. [C20: from Greek *konia* dust + -LOGY]

Kon+stanz ('kɔnstants) *n.* the German name for **Constance.**

Kon+ya *or* **Kon·ia** ('kɔːnjɑː) *n.* a city in SW central Turkey: in ancient times a Phrygian city and capital of Lycaonia. Pop.: 246 727 (1975). Ancient name: **Iconium.**

koo+doo ('kuːduː) *n.* a variant spelling of **kudu.**

kook (kuːk) *n. U.S. informal.* an eccentric, crazy, or foolish person. [C20: probably from CUCKOO]

kook·a+bur+ra ('kʊkəˌbʌrə) *n.* a large arboreal Australian kingfisher, *Dacelo novaeguineae* (or *gigas*), with a cackling cry. Also called: **laughing jackass.** [C19: from a native Australian language]

kook·y *or* **kook·ie** ('kuːkɪ) *adj.* **kook·i+er, kook·i+est.** *U.S. informal.* crazy, eccentric, or foolish.

Koo+ning ('kuːnɪŋ) *n.* **Wil·lem de** ('wɪləm də). born 1904, U.S. abstract expressionist painter, born in Holland.

Koo+te+nay *or* **Koo+te+nai** ('kuːtᵊniː, 'kuːtneɪ) *n.* a river in W North America, rising in SE British Columbia and flowing south into NW Montana, then north into Idaho before re-entering British Columbia, broadening into **Kootenay Lake,** then flowing to the Columbia River. Length: 655 km (407 miles).

kop (kɒp) *n.* a prominent isolated hill or mountain in southern Africa. See **inselberg.** [from Afrikaans: head, hence high part; compare German *Kopf* head; see COP[2]]

ko+peck, ko+pek, *or* **co+peck** ('kəʊpɛk) *n.* a Soviet monetary unit worth one hundredth of a rouble. [Russian *kopeika,* from *kopye* lance; so called because of the representation of Tsar Ivan IV on the coin with a lance in his hand]

Ko+peisk *or* **Ko+peysk** (*Russian* ka'pjejsk) *n.* a city in the W central Soviet Union, in Chelyabinsk Region: lignite-mining. Pop.: 156 000 (1975 est.). Former name: **Ko·pi** ('kɔpi).

koph *or* **qoph** (kɒf) *n.* the 19th letter in the Hebrew alphabet (ק) transliterated as *q,* and pronounced as a velar or uvular. [from Hebrew *qoph;* see QOPH]

kop+je *or* **kop+pie** ('kɒpɪ) *n.* a small kop. [C19: from Afrikaans *koppie,* from Dutch *kopje,* literally: a little head, from *kop* head; see KOP]

kop+pa ('kɒpə) *n.* a consonantal letter in the Greek alphabet pronounced like kappa (Κ) with the point of articulation further back in the throat. It became obsolete in classical (Attic) Greek orthography, but was passed on to the Romans who incorporated it into their alphabet as *Q.* [Greek, of Semitic origin]

kor (kɔː) *n.* another name for **homer**[2]. [Hebrew *kōr* measure]

Ko+ran (kɔː'rɑːn) *n.* the sacred book of Islam, believed by Muslims to be the infallible word of God dictated to Mohammed through the medium of the angel Gabriel. Also: **Qur'an.** [C17: from Arabic *qur'ān* reading, book; related to *qara'a* to read, recite] —**Ko+'ran+ic** *adj.*

Kor·but (*Russian* 'kɔrbut) *n.* **Ol·ga** ('ɔlgə). born 1955, Soviet gymnast: noted for her highly individualistic style, which greatly increased the popularity of the sport, esp. following her performance in the 1972 Olympic Games.

Kor+çë (*Albanian* 'kortʃə) *n.* a market town in SE Albania. Pop.: 47 300 (1970 est.).

Korch·noi ('kɔːtʃˌnɔɪ) *n.* **Vic·tor.** born 1931, Soviet chess player: Soviet champion 1960, 1962, and 1964.

Kor+do+fan (ˌkɔːdəʊ'fæn) *n.* a province of the central Sudan: consists of a plateau with rugged uplands (the Nuba Mountains). Capital: El Obeid. Pop.: 2 010 289 (1973). Area: 380 548 sq. km (146 930 sq. miles).

Kor+do+fan+i·an (ˌkɔːdə'feɪnɪən) *n.* **1.** a group of languages spoken in the Kordofan and Nuba Hills of the S Sudan: classed as an independent family, probably distantly related to Niger-Congo. ~*adj.* **2.** denoting, relating to, or belonging to this group of languages. **3.** of or relating to Kordofan.

Ko+re·a (kə'riːə) *n.* a former country in E Asia, occupying the peninsula between the Sea of Japan and the Yellow Sea: an isolated vassal of Manchu China for three centuries until the opening of ports to Japanese trade in 1876; gained independence in 1895; annexed to Japan in 1910 and divided in 1945 into two occupation zones (Russian in the north, American in the south), which became North Korea and South Korea in 1948. Korean name for North Korea: *Choson;* for South Korea: *Hanguk.* Japanese name (1910–45): **Chosen.**

Ko+re·an (kə'riːən) *adj.* **1.** of or relating to Korea, its people, or their language. ~*n.* **2.** a native or inhabitant of Korea. **3.** the official language of North and South Korea.

Ko+re·an War *n.* the war (1950–53) fought between North Korea, aided by Communist China, and South Korea, supported by the U.S. and other members of the UN.

Ko+re·a Strait *n.* a strait between South Korea and SW Japan, linking the Sea of Japan with the East China Sea.

korf+ball ('kɔːfˌbɔːl) *n.* a game similar to basketball, in which each team consists of six men and six women. [C20: from Dutch *korfbal* basketball]

Kó+rin+thos ('korinθɔs) *n.* transliteration of the Modern Greek name for **Corinth.**

kor+ma ('kɔːmə) *n.* any of a variety of Indian dishes consisting of meat or vegetables braised with water, stock, yoghurt, or cream. [from Urdu]

Kort+rijk ('kɔrtrɛjk) *n.* the Flemish name for **Courtrai.**

ko+ru+na (kɒ'ruːnə) *n.* the standard monetary unit of Czechoslovakia, divided into 100 halers. [Czech, from Latin *corōna* crown, wreath; see CROWN]

Kor·zyb·ski (kɔː'zɪbskɪ) *n.* **Al·fred (Habdank Skarbek).** 1879–1950, U.S. originator of the theory and study of general semantics, born in Poland.

kos (kəʊs) *n., pl.* **kos.** an Indian unit of distance having different values in different localities. It is usually between 1 and 3 miles or 1 and 5 kilometres. Also called: **coss.**

Kos *or* **Cos** (kɒs) *n.* an island in the SE Aegean Sea, in the Greek Dodecanese Islands: separated from SW Turkey by the **Kos Channel;** settled in ancient times by Dorians and became famous for literature and medicine. Pop.: 17 939 (1971). Area: 282 sq. km (109 sq. miles).

Kos+ci+us+ko[1] (ˌkɒsɪ'ʌskəʊ) *n.* **Mount.** a mountain in Australia, in SE New South Wales in the Australian Alps: the highest peak in Australia. Height: 2230 m (7316 ft.).

Kos·ci·us·ko[2] (ˌkɒsɪ'ʌskəʊ) *n.* **Thad·de·us,** Polish name *Tadeusz Kósciuszko.* 1746–1817, Polish general: fought for the colonists in the War of American Independence and led an unsuccessful revolt against the partitioning of Poland (1794).

ko+sher ('kəʊʃə) *or* **ka+sher** ('kɑːʃə) *adj.* **1.** *Judaism.* prepared according to or conforming to Jewish dietary laws. **2.** *Informal.* **a.** genuine or authentic. **b.** legitimate or proper. ~*n.* **3.** kosher food. [C19: from Yiddish, from Hebrew *kāshēr* right, proper]

Ko+ši+ce (*Czech* 'kɔʃitsɛ) *n.* a city in SE Czechoslovakia: passed from Hungary to Czechoslovakia in 1920. Pop.: 166 240 (1974 est.). Hungarian name: **Kassa.**

Ko·so·vo-Me·to·hi+ja (*Serbo-Croatian* 'kɔsɔvɔ mɛ'tɔhija) *n.* an autonomous region in S central Yugoslavia, in SW Serbia: created in 1946 from parts of Serbia and Montenegro; mainly a plateau. Capital: **Priština.** Pop.: 1 242 272 (1971). Area: 10 350 sq. km (4000 sq. miles).

Kos·suth (*Hungarian* 'koʃuːt) *n.* **La·jos** ('lɔjoʃ). 1802–94, Hungarian statesman. He led the revolution against Austria (1848) and was provisional governor (1849), but he fled when the revolt was suppressed (1849).

Ko+stro+ma (*Russian* kəstra'ma) *n.* a city in the W central Soviet Union, on the River Volga: fought over bitterly by Novgorod, Tver, and Moscow, until annexed by Moscow in 1329; textile centre. Pop.: 244 000 (1975 est.).

Ko·sy·gin (*Russian* ka'sɪgin) *n.* **A·le·ksei Ni·ko·la·ye·vich** (alɪ'ksjej nika'lajɪvitʃ). 1904–80, Soviet statesman; premier of the Soviet Union (1964–80).

Ko·ta *or* **Ko+tah** ('kəʊtə) *n.* a city in NW India, in Rajasthan on the Chambal River: textile industry. Pop.: 212 991 (1971).

Ko+ta+ba+ru ('kəʊtə'bɑːruː) *n.* a former name of **Djajapura.**

Ko·ta Bha+ru *or* **Bah+ru** ('kəʊtə 'bɑːruː) *n.* a port in Malaysia, on the SE Malay Peninsula: capital of Kelantan state on the delta of the Kelantan River. Pop.: 55 052 (1970).

Ko·ta Kin·a·ba·lu ('kəʊtə ˌkɪnəbə'luː) *n.* a port in Malaysia, capital of Sabah state on the South China Sea: exports timber and rubber. Pop.: 41 830 (1970). Former name: **Jesselton.**

ko·to ('kəʊtəʊ) *n., pl.* **·tos.** a Japanese stringed instrument, consisting of a rectangular wooden body over which are stretched silk strings, which are plucked with plectra or a nail-like device. [Japanese]

kou+li+bia+ca *or* **cou+li+bia+ca** (ˌkəʊlɪ'bjɑːkə) *n.* a Russian baked dish consisting of flaked fish mixed with semolina encased in pastry. [from Russian]

kou+mis ('kuːmɪs) *n.* a variant spelling of **kumiss.**

Kov+no ('kɔvnə) *n.* transliteration of the Russian name for **Kaunas.**

Kov+rov (*Russian* kav'rɔf) *n.* a city in the W central Soviet Union, on the Klyazma River: textiles and heavy engineering. Pop.: 135 000 (1975 est.).

Ko+weit (kəʊ'weɪt) *n.* a variant spelling of **Kuwait.**

kow+hai ('kəʊaɪ) *n.* *N.Z.* a small leguminous tree, *Sophora tetraptera,* of New Zealand and Chile, with clusters of yellow flowers. [C19: from Maori]

Kow+loon ('kaʊ'luːn) *n.* **1.** a peninsula of SE China, opposite Hong Kong Island: part of the British colony of Hong Kong. Area: 10 sq. km (3.75 sq. miles). **2.** a port in Hong Kong, on Kowloon Peninsula. Pop.: 716 272 (1971).

kow+tow ('kaʊtaʊ) *vb.* (*intr.*) **1.** to touch the forehead to the ground as a sign of respect or deference: a former Chinese custom. **2.** (often foll. by *to*) to be servile or obsequious (towards). ~*n.* **3.** the act of kowtowing. [C19: from Chinese (Mandarin) *k'o t'ou,* from *k'o* to strike, knock + *t'ou* head] —**'kow+tow+er** *n.*

Ko+zhi+kode (ˌkəʊʒɪ'kəʊd) *n.* a port in SW India, in W Kerala on the Malabar coast: important European trading post (1511–1765): formerly calico-manufacturing. Pop.: 333 979 (1971). Former name: **Calicut.**

KP *Chess. symbol. for* king's pawn.

K.P. *U.S. military. abbrev. for* kitchen police.

Kr *the chemical symbol for* krypton.

KR *Chess. symbol for* king's rook.

kr. *abbrev. for:* **1.** krona. **2.** krone.

Kra (krɑː) *n.* **Isthmus of.** an isthmus of SW Thailand, between the Bay of Bengal and the Gulf of Siam: the narrowest part of the Malay Peninsula. Width: about 56 km (35 miles).

kraal *or* **craal** (krɑːl) *S. African.* ~*n.* **1.** a hut village in southern Africa, esp. one surrounded by a stockade. **2.** an enclosure for livestock. ~*adj.* **3.** denoting or relating to the tribal aspects of the Black African way of life. ~*vb.* **4.** (*tr.*) to enclose (cattle, etc.) in a kraal. [C18: from Afrikaans, from Portuguese *curral* pen; see CORRAL]

Krafft-E·bing (*German* 'kraft 'ɛbɪŋ) *n.* **Ri·chard** ('rɪçart), Baron von Krafft-Ebing. 1840–1902, German neurologist and psychiatrist; author of *Psychopathia Sexualis* (1886).

kraft (krɑːft) *n.* strong wrapping paper, made from pulp processed with a sulphate solution. [German; force]

Kra+gu+je+vac (*Serbo-Croatian* 'kragujɛvats) *n.* a town in E central Yugoslavia, in Serbia; capital of Serbia (1818–39); automobile industry. Pop.: 71 180 (1971).

krait (kraɪt) *n.* any nonaggressive brightly coloured venomous elapid snake of the genus *Bungarus,* of S and SE Asia. [C19: from Hindi *karait,* of obscure origin]

Kra+ka+to+a (ˌkrɑːkə'təʊə, ˌkrækə'təʊə) *or* **Kra+ka+tau** (ˌkrɑːkə'taʊ, ˌkrækə'taʊ) *n.* a volcanic island in Indonesia, in the Sunda Strait between Java and Sumatra: partially destroyed by its eruption in 1883, the greatest in recorded history. Further eruptions 44 years later formed a new island, **Anak Krakatau** ("Child of Krakatau"). Also called: **Rakata.**

Kra+kau ('kraːkaʊ) *n.* the German name for **Cracow.**

kra+ken ('krɑːkən) *n.* a legendary sea monster of gigantic size believed to dwell off the coast of Norway. [C18: from Norwegian, of obscure origin]

Kra+ków ('krakuf) *n.* the Polish name for **Cracow.**

Kra+ma+torsk (*Russian* krəma'tɔrsk) *n.* a city in the SW Soviet Union, in the E Ukrainian SSR: a major industrial centre of the Donets Basin. Pop.: 165 000 (1975 est.).

kra+me+ri·a (krə'mɪərɪə) *n.* another name for **rhatany** (plant or drug). [C18: New Latin, named (by Linnaeus) after J. G. H. *Kramer,* an Austrian botanist]

Kra+nj ('krɑːnjə) *n.* the Slovene name for **Carniola.**

krans (krɑːns) *n.* *S. African.* a sheer rock face; precipice. [C18: from Afrikaans]

Kras+no+dar (*Russian* krəsna'dar) *n.* an industrial city in the SW Soviet Union, on the Kuban River. Pop.: 532 000 (1975 est.).

Kras+no+yarsk (*Russian* krəsna'jarsk) *n.* a city in the E central Soviet Union, on the Yenisei River: the country's largest hydroelectric power station is nearby. Pop.: 748 000 (1975 est.).

K ra+tion *n.* a small package containing emergency rations used by U.S. forces in the field in World War II. [C20: *K,* from the initial of the surname of Ancel *Keys* (born 1904), American physiologist who instigated it]

Kraut (kraʊt) *n., adj.* *Slang.* a derogatory word for **German.** [from German (*sauer*)*kraut,* literally: (pickled) cabbage]

Krebs (krɛbz) *n.* Sir **Hans A·dolf.** 1900–81, British biochemist, born in Germany, who shared a Nobel prize for physiology (1953) for the discovery of the Krebs cycle.

Krebs cy+cle *n.* a stage of tissue respiration: a series of biochemical reactions occurring in mitochondria in the presence of oxygen by which acetate, derived from the break down of foodstuffs, is converted to carbon dioxide and water, with the release of energy. Also called: **citric acid cycle.** [C20: named after H. A. KREBS]

Kre+feld ('kreɪfɛld; *German* 'kreːˌfɛlt) *n.* a city in West Germany, in W North Rhine-Westphalia: textile industries. Pop.: 221 240 (1974 est.).

Kreis·ky (*German* 'kraɪski) *n.* **Bru·no** ('bruːno). born 1911, Austrian statesman; federal chancellor of Austria since 1970.

Kreis·ler (*German* 'kraɪslər) *n.* **Fritz** (frɪts). 1875–1962, U.S. violinist, born in Austria.

Kre+men+chug (*Russian* krɪmɪn'tʃuk) *n.* an industrial city in the SW Soviet Union, in the E central Ukrainian SSR on the Dnieper River. Pop.: 175 000 (1975 est.).

krem+lin ('krɛmlɪn) *n.* the citadel of any Russian city. [C17: from obsolete German *Kremelin,* from Russian *kreml'*]

Krem+lin ('krɛmlɪn) *n.* **1.** the 12th-century citadel in Moscow, containing the former Imperial Palace, three Cathedrals, and the offices of the Soviet government. **2.** the central government of the Soviet Union.

Krems (*German* krɛms) *n.* a town in NE Austria, capital of Lower Austria on the River Danube. Pop.: 21 912 (1971).

krep+lach ('krɛplɑːk, -lɑːx) *pl. n.* small filled dough casings usually served in soup. [C20: from Yiddish]

kreut+zer *or* **kreu+zer** ('krɔɪtsə) *n.* any of various former copper and silver coins of Germany or Austria. [C16: from German *Kreuzer,* from *Kreuz* cross, from Latin *crux;* referring to the cross originally stamped upon such coins]

krieg+spiel ('kriːgˌspiːl) *n.* (*sometimes cap.*) another word for **war game.** [C19: from German *Kriegsspiel*]

Kriem·hild ('kriːmhɪlt) *or* **Kriem·hil·de** ('kriːmˌhɪldə) *n.* (in the *Nibelungenlied*) the wife of Siegfried. She corresponds to Gudrun in Norse mythology.

krill (krɪl) *n., pl.* **krill.** any small shrimplike marine crustacean of the order *Euphausiacea:* the principal food of whalebone whales. [C20: from Norwegian *kril* young fish]

krim+mer *or* **crim+mer** ('krɪmə) *n.* a tightly curled light grey fur obtained from the skins of lambs from the Crimean region. [C20: from German, from *Krim* CRIMEA]

Kri·o ('kriːəʊ) *n.* **1.** the English-based creole widely used as a lingua franca in Sierra Leone. Its principal language of admixture is Yoruba. **2.** (*pl.* **·os**) a native speaker of Krio. **3.** (*modifier*) of or relating to the Krio language or Krios: *Krio poetry.* [alteration of CREOLE]

kris (krɪs) *n.* a Malayan and Indonesian stabbing or slashing knife with a scalloped edge. Also called: **crease, creese.** [C16: from Malay *kris*]

Krish+na[1] ('krɪʃnə) *n.* a river in S India, rising in the Western Ghats and flowing generally southeast to the Bay of Bengal. Length: 1300 km (800 miles). Also called: **Kistna.**

Krish+na[2] ('krɪʃnə) *n. Hinduism.* the most celebrated of the Hindu deities, whose life story is told in the *Mahabharata*. [via Hindi from Sanskrit, literally: dark, black] —**'Krish·na·ism** *n.*

Krish·na Men·on ('kri:ʃnə 'mɛnən) *n.* **Ven·ga·lil Krish·nan** ('vɛŋgəlɪl 'kri:ʃnən). See (Vengalil Krishnan Krishna) **Menon.**

Kriss Krin+gle (ˌkrɪs 'krɪŋgᵊl) *n. U.S.* another name for **Santa Claus.** [changed from German *Christkindl* little Christ child, from CHRIST + *Kindl*, from *Kind* child]

Kris+tian+sand *or* **Chris+tian+sand** ('krɪstʃənˌsænd; *Norwegian* ˌkristian'san) *n.* a port in S Norway, on the Skagerrak: shipbuilding. Pop.: 56 914 (1970).

Kris+tian+stad ('krɪstʃənˌstɑ:d; *Swedish* kri'ʃansta:d) *n.* a town in S Sweden: founded in 1614 as a Danish fortress, it was finally acquired by Sweden in 1678. Pop.: 55 403 (1970).

Kri+ti ('kriti) *n.* transliteration of the Modern Greek name for **Crete.**

Kri+voy Rog (*Russian* kri'vɔj 'rɔk) *n.* a city in the SW Soviet Union, in the SE Ukrainian SSR: founded in the 17th century by Cossacks; iron-mining centre; iron and steel works. Pop.: 628 000 (1975 est.).

kro+mes+ky (krə'mɛskɪ) *n.* a croquette consisting of a piece of bacon wrapped round minced meat or fish. [C19: from Russian *kromochka*, diminutive of *kroma* slice of bread]

kró+na ('krəʊnə) *n., pl.* **+nur** (nə). **1.** the standard monetary unit of Iceland, divided into 100 aurar. **2.** the standard monetary unit of Sweden, divided into 100 ore.

kro+ne[1] ('krəʊnə) *n., pl.* **+ner** (-nə). **1.** the standard monetary unit of Denmark and its dependencies, divided into 100 ore. **2.** the standard monetary unit of Norway, divided into 100 ore. [C19: from Danish or Norwegian, from Middle Low German *krōne*, ultimately from Latin *corōna* CROWN]

kro+ne[2] ('krəʊnə) *n., pl.* **+nen** (-nən). **1.** a former German gold coin worth ten marks. **2.** a former Austrian monetary unit. [C19: from German, literally: crown; see KRONE[1]]

Kro+nos ('krəʊnɒs) *n.* a variant spelling of **Cronus.**

Kron+stadt *n.* **1.** (*Russian* kran'ʃtat). a port in the NW Soviet Union, on Kotlin island in the Gulf of Finland: naval base. Pop.: 175 264 (1969 est.). **2.** ('kro:nˌʃtat). the German name for **Braşov.**

kroon (kru:n) *n., pl.* **kroons** *or* **kroon·i** ('kru:nɪ). the monetary unit of Estonia before 1940. [Estonian *kron*, from German *krone* KRONE[2]]

Kro·pot·kin (*Russian* kra'pɔtkin) *n.* Prince **Pe·ter,** Russian name *Pyotr Alexeyevich.* 1842–1921, Russian anarchist: his books include *Mutual Aid* (1902) and *Modern Science and Anarchism* (1903).

KRP *Chess. abbrev. for* king's rook's pawn.

Kru·ger ('kru:gə) *n.* **Ste·pha·nus Jo·han·nes Paul·us** ('stɛfənʊs jəʊ'hænɪs 'pɔ:lʊ), known as *Oom Paul.* 1825–1904, Boer statesman; president of the Transvaal (1883–1900). His opposition to Cecil Rhodes and his denial of civil rights to the Uitlanders led to the Boer War (1899–1902).

Kru+ger Na+tion+al Park *n.* a wildlife sanctuary in NE South Africa, in E Transvaal: the world's largest game reserve. Area: over 21 700 sq. km (8400 sq. miles).

Kru+gers+dorp ('kru:gəzˌdɔ:p) *n.* a city in NE South Africa, in S Transvaal on the Witwatersrand, at an altitude of 1722 m (5650 ft.): a gold, manganese, and uranium mining centre. Pop.: 96 514 (1970).

krul+ler ('krʌlə) *n.* a variant spelling of **cruller.**

krumm+horn ('krʌmˌhɔ:n) *n.* a variant spelling of **crumhorn.**

Krupp (krʊp, krʌp) *n.* a German family of steel and armaments manufacturers, including **Alfred,** 1812–87, his son **Friedrich Alfred,** 1854–1902, and the latter's son-in-law, **Gustav Krupp von Bohlen und Halbach,** 1870–1950.

Kruš+ne Ho·ry ('krʊʃnɛ 'hɔrɪ) *n.* the Czech name for the **Erzgebirge.**

Krym *or* **Krim** (krɪm) *n.* transliteration of the Russian name for **Crimea.**

kryp+ton ('krɪptɒn) *n.* an inert gaseous element occurring in trace amounts in air and used in fluorescent lights and lasers. Symbol: Kr; atomic no.: 36; atomic wt.: 83.80; density: 3.733 kg/m^3; melting pt.: −169°C; boiling pt.: −151.7°C. [C19: from Greek, from *kruptos* hidden; see CRYPT]

Kshat+ri+ya ('kʃætrɪə) *n.* a member of the second of the four main Hindu castes, the warrior caste. [C18: from Sanskrit, from *kshatra* rule]

K. St. J. *abbrev. for* Knight of the Order of St. John.

Kt *Chess. abbrev. for* knight. Also: **N**

kt. *abbrev. for:* **1.** karat. **2.** *Nautical.* knot.

Kt. *or* **Knt.** *abbrev. for* knight.

K.T. *abbrev. for:* **1.** Knight of the Order of the Thistle (a Brit. title). **2.** Knight Templar.

Kua+la Lum+pur ('kwɑ:lə 'lʊmpʊə, -pə) *n.* the capital of Malaysia, in the SW Malay Peninsula: became capital of the Federated Malay States in 1895, and of Malaysia in 1963; capital of Selangor state from 1880 to 1973, when it was made a federal territory. Pop.: 451 728 (1970).

Ku+ban (*Russian* ku'banj) *n.* a river in the S central Soviet Union, rising in the Caucasus Mountains and flowing north and northwest to the Sea of Azov. Length: 906 km (563 miles).

Ku·be·lik (*Czech* 'kubɛli:k) *n.* **Raph·a·el** ('ra:faɛl). born 1914, Czech conductor and composer.

Ku·blai Khan ('ku:blaɪ 'kɑ:n) *n.* grandson of Genghis Khan. ?1216–94, Mongol emperor of China. He completed his grandfather's conquest of China by overthrowing the Sung dynasty (1279) and founded the Yüan dynasty (1279–1368).

Ku·brick ('kju:brɪk) *n.* **Stan·ley.** born 1928, U.S. film director and producer. He directed *Paths of Glory* (1958), *Lolita* (1962), *2001: A Space Odyssey* (1969), and *A Clockwork Orange* (1971).

Kuch Bi+har ('ku:tʃ bɪ'hɑ:) *n.* a variant spelling of **Cooch Behar.**

ku+chen ('ku:xən) *n.* a breadlike cake containing apple, nuts, and sugar, originating from Germany. [German: CAKE]

Ku+ching ('ku:tʃɪŋ) *n.* a port in E Malaysia, capital of Sarawak state, on the Sarawak River 24 km (15 miles) from its mouth. Pop.: 63 491 (1970).

ku+dos ('kju:dɒs) *n.* (*functioning as sing.*) acclaim, glory, or prestige. [C18: from Greek]

ku·du *or* **koo+doo** ('ku:du:) *n.* either of two spiral-horned antelopes, *Tragelaphus strepsiceros* (**greater kudu**) or *T. imberbis* (**lesser kudu**), which inhabit the bush of Africa. [C18: from Afrikaans *koedoe*, probably from Xhosa *iqudu*]

kud+zu ('kʊdzu:) *n.* a hairy leguminous climbing plant, *Pueraria thunbergiana*, of China and Japan, with trifoliate leaves and purple fragrant flowers. [from Japanese *kuzu*]

ku·eh ('kɔeɪ) *n.* (*functioning as sing. or pl.*) (in Malaysia) any cake of Malay, Chinese, or Indian origin. [from Malay]

Kuen+lun ('kʊn'lʊn) *n.* a variant spelling of **Kunlun.**

Ku+fic *or* **Cu+fic** ('ku:fɪk, 'kju:-) *adj.* **1.** of, relating to, or denoting an early form of the Arabic alphabet employed in making copies of the Koran. ~*n.* **2.** the script formed by the letters of this alphabet.

Kui+by+shev *or* **Kuy+by+shev** (*Russian* 'kujbɪʃəf) *n.* a port in the SW central Soviet Union, on the River Volga: centre of an important industrial complex; oil refining. Pop.: 1 164 000 (1975 est.). Former name (until 1935): **Samara.**

Ku Klux Klan ('ku: 'klʌks 'klæn) *n.* **1.** a secret organization of white Southerners formed after the U.S. Civil War to fight Black emancipation and Northern domination. **2.** a secret organization of White Protestant Americans, mainly in the South who use violence against Blacks, Jews, and other minority groups. [C19: *Ku Klux*, probably based on Greek *kuklos* CIRCLE + *Klan* CLAN] —**Ku Klux+er** *or* **Ku Klux Klan+ner** *n.* —**Ku Klux+ism** *n.*

kuk+ri ('kʊkrɪ) *n.* a knife with a curved blade that broadens towards the point, esp. as used by Gurkhas. [from Hindi]

Ku·ku Nor ('ku:'ku: 'nɔ:) *n.* a variant spelling of **Koko Nor.**

ku·la ('ku:lə) *n.* a ceremonial gift exchange practised among a group of islanders in the W Pacific, used to establish relations between islands. [of Melanesian origin]

ku+lak ('ku:læk) *n.* (in Russia after 1906) a member of the class of peasants who became proprietors of their own farms. After the October Revolution the kulaks opposed collectivization of land, but in 1929 Stalin initiated their liquidation. [C19: from Russian fist, hence, tight-fisted person; related to Turkish *kol* arm]

Kul+tur (kʊl'tʊə) *n.* (often used ironically) German civilization, esp. as characterized by authoritarianism and earnestness. [German, from Latin *cultūra* CULTURE]

Kul+tur+kampf (kʊl'tʊəˌkæmpf, 'kʊltə-) *n.* the struggle of the Prussian state against the Roman Catholic Church (1872–87), which took the form of laws designed to bring education, marriage, etc., under the control of the state. [German: culture struggle]

Ku+lun ('ku:'lu:n) *n.* the Chinese name for **Ulan Bator.**

Kum (kʊm) *n.* a variant spelling of **Qum.**

Ku+ma+mo+to (ˌkʊmə'məʊtəʊ) *n.* a city in SW Japan, on W central Kyushu: Kumamoto Medical University (1949). Pop.: 467 296 (1974 est.).

Ku+mas·i (ku:'mæsɪ) *n.* a city in S Ghana: seat of Ashanti kings since 1663; university (1961); market town for a cocoa-producing region. Pop.: 260 286 (1970).

kum+ba+loi (ˌkʊmbə'lɔɪ) *pl. n.* another name for **worry beads.** [C20: Modern Greek]

ku+miss, kou+miss, kou+mis, *or* **kou+myss** ('ku:mɪs) *n.* a drink made from fermented mare's or other milk, drunk by certain Asian tribes, esp. in Russia or used for dietetic and medicinal purposes. [C17: from Russian *kumys*, from Kazan Tatar *kumyz*]

küm+mel ('kʊməl; *German* 'kyməl) *n.* a German liqueur flavoured with aniseed and cumin. [C19: from German *Kümmel*, from Old High German *kumil*, probably variant of *kumin* CUMIN]

kum+mer+bund ('kʌməˌbʌnd) *n.* a variant spelling of **cummerbund.**

kum+quat *or* **cum+quat** ('kʌmkwɒt) *n.* **1.** any of several small Chinese trees of the rutaceous genus *Fortunella.* **2.** the small round orange fruit of such a tree, with a sweet rind, used in preserves and confections. [C17: from Chinese (Cantonese) *kam kwat*, representing Mandarin Chinese *chin chü* golden orange]

Kun (ku:n) *n.* **Bé·la** ('be:lɔ). 1886–?1937, Hungarian Communist leader, president of the short-lived Communist republic in Hungary (1919). He was forced into exile and died in a Stalinist purge.

kung fu ('kʌŋ 'fu:) *n.* a Chinese martial art combining principles of karate and judo. [from Chinese: martial art]

K'ung Fu-tse ('kʊŋ 'fu: 'tseɪ) *n.* the Chinese name of **Confucius.**

Kun+gur *or* **Qun+gur** ('kʊngʊə) *n.* a mountain in China, in W Sinkiang: the highest peak in the Pamirs. Height: 7719 m (25 236 ft.).

Kun·lun, Kuen·lun, *or* **Kwen·lun** ('kʊn'lʊn) *n.* a mountain range in China, between the Tibetan plateau and the Tarim Basin, extending over 1600 km (1000 miles) east from the Pamirs: the largest mountain system of Asia. Highest peak: Ulugh Muztagh, 7723 m (25 338 ft.).

Kun·ming *or* **K'un-ming** ('kʊn'mɪŋ) *n.* a city in SW China, capital of Yünnan province, near Lake Tien: important during World War II as a Chinese military centre, American air base, and transport terminus for the Burma Road; Yünnan University (1934). Pop.: 1 100 000 (1970 est.).

kunz·ite ('kʊntsaɪt) *n.* a lilac-coloured transparent variety of the mineral spodumene: a gemstone. [C20: named after George F. *Kunz* (1856–1932), American gem expert]

Kuo·min·tang ('kwəʊ'mɪn'tæŋ) *n.* the political party founded by Sun Yat-sen in 1911 and dominant in China from 1928 until 1949 under the leadership of Chiang Kai-shek. Since then it has been the official ruling party of Taiwan. [C20: from Chinese (Mandarin): National People's Party, from *kuo* nation + *min* people + *tang* party]

Kuo·pi·o (*Finnish* 'kwɔpjɔ) *n.* a city in S central Finland. Pop.: 64 169 (1970).

Ku·ra (kʊ'rɑː) *n.* a river in W Asia, rising in NE Turkey and flowing into the Soviet Union across the Georgian and Azerbaijan SSRs to the Caspian Sea. Length: 1515 km (941 miles).

kur·cha·to·vi·um (ˌkɜːtʃə'təʊvɪəm) *n.* another name for **rutherfordium,** esp. as used in the Soviet Union. [C20: from Russian, named after I. V. *Kurchatov* (1903–60), Soviet physicist]

Kurd (kɜːd) *n.* a member of a largely nomadic Turkic people living chiefly in E Turkey, N Iraq, and W Iran.

Kurd·ish ('kɜːdɪʃ) *n.* **1.** the language of the Kurds, belonging to the West Iranian branch of the Indo-European family. ~*adj.* **2.** of or relating to the Kurds or their language.

Kur·di·stan, Kur·de·stan, *or* **Kor·de·stan** (ˌkɜːdɪ'stɑːn) *n.* a large plateau and mountain region of E Turkey, N Iraq, NW Iran, and the Armenian SSR of the Soviet Union. Area: over 29 000 sq. km (74 000 sq. miles).

Ku·re (kuː'reɪ) *n.* a port in SW Japan, on SW Honshu: a naval base; shipyards. Pop.: 241 931 (1974 est.).

Kur·gan (*Russian* kur'gan) *n.* a city in the W central Soviet Union, on the Tobol River: industrial centre for an agricultural region. Pop.: 287 000 (1975 est.).

Ku·ril Is·lands *or* **Ku·rile Is·lands** (kʊ'riːl) *pl. n.* a chain of 56 volcanic islands off the NE coast of Asia, extending for 1200 km (750 miles) from the S tip of the Kamchatka Peninsula to NE Hokkaido. Area: 14 990 sq. km (6020 sq. miles). Japanese name: **Chishima.**

Kur·land ('kʊələnd) *n.* a variant spelling of **Courland.**

Ku·ro·sa·wa (ˌkʊərə'sɑːwə) *n.* **A·ki·ra** (ə'kɪərə). born 1910, Japanese film director. His works, include *Rashomon* (1950), *The Seven Samurai* (1954), and *Red Beard* (1965).

Ku·ro·shi·o (kə'rəʊʃɪˌəʊ) *n.* another name for **Japan Current.**

kur·ra·jong *or* **cur·ra·jong** ('kʌrəˌdʒɒŋ) *n.* any of various Australian trees or shrubs, esp. *Brachychiton populneum,* a sterculiaceous tree that yields a tough durable fibre. [C19: from a native Australian language]

kur·saal ('kɜːzᵊl) *n.* **1.** a public room at a health resort. **2.** an amusement park at a seaside or other resort. [from German, literally: cure room]

Kursk (*Russian* kursk) *n.* a city in the W central Soviet Union: industrial centre of an agricultural region. Pop.: 351 000 (1975 est.).

kur·to·sis (kə'təʊsɪs) *n. Statistics.* the sharpness of a peak on a curve of a density function, esp. in comparison with that of a normal density with the same variance. [from Greek: curvature, from *kurtos* arched]

ku·rus (kʊ'ruːʃ) *n., pl.* **·rus.** another word for **piastre** (sense 2b). [from Turkish]

Kur·ze·me ('kʊrzɛmɛ) *n.* the Latvian name for **Courland.**

Kush (kʌʃ, kʊʃ) *n.* a variant spelling of **Cush.**

Kus·ko·kwim ('kʌskəˌkwɪm) *n.* a river in SW Alaska, rising in the Alaska Range and flowing generally southwest to **Kuskokwim Bay,** an inlet of the Bering Sea. Length: about 970 km (600 miles).

Ku·ta·i·si (*Russian* kuta'isi) *n.* an industrial city in the SW Soviet Union, in the W Georgian SSR on the Rioni River: one of the oldest towns of the Caucasus. Pop.: 173 000 (1975 est.).

Kutch *or* **Cutch** (kʌtʃ) *n.* **1.** a former state of W India, on the **Gulf of Kutch** (an inlet of the Arabian Sea: part of Gujarat state since 1960. **2. Rann of.** an extensive salt waste in W central India, and S Pakistan: consists of the Great Rann in the north and the Little Rann in the southeast; seasonal alternation between marsh and desert; some salt works. In 1968 an international tribunal awarded about 10 per cent of the border area to Pakistan. Area: 23 000 sq. km (9000 sq. miles).

Ku·tu·zov (*Russian* ku'tuzəf) *n.* Prince **Mi·kha·il Il·a·ri·o·no·vich** (mixa'il ilərіa'nɔvitʃ). 1745–1813, Russian field marshal, who harried the French army under Napoleon throughout their retreat from Moscow (1812–13).

Ku·wait (kʊ'weɪt) *n.* **1.** a state on the NW coast of the Persian Gulf: came under British protection in 1899 and gained independence in 1961; mainly desert. The economy is dependent on oil. Official language: Arabic. Religion: mostly Muslim. Currency: dinar. Capital: Kuwait. Pop.: 994 837 (1975). Area: 24 280 sq. km (9375 sq. miles). **2.** the capital of Kuwait: a port on the Persian Gulf. Pop.: 80 405 (1970). **—Ku·'wai·ti** *adj., n.*

Kuz·netsk Ba·sin (*Russian* kuz'njɛtsk) *or* **Kuz·bass** (*Russian* kuz'bas) *n.* a region of the Soviet Union, in the Kemerovo Region of W Siberia: the richest coalfield in the country, with reserves of iron ore. Chief industrial centre: Novokuznetsk. Area: about 69 900 sq. km (27 000 sq. miles).

kV *abbrev. for* kilovolt.

K.V. *abbrev. for* Köchel Verzeichnis. See **K.** (sense 5). [German, literally: Köchel catalogue]

Kva·løy (*Norwegian* 'kva:lœj) *n.* two islands in the Arctic Ocean, off the N coast of Norway: **North Kvaløy,** 329 sq. km (127 sq. miles), and **South Kvaløy,** 735 sq. km (284 sq. miles).

kvass, kvas, *or* **quass** (kvɑːs) *n.* an alcoholic drink of low strength made in the Soviet Union and E Europe from cereals and stale bread. [C16: from Russian *kvas;* related to Old Slavic *kvasĭ* yeast, Latin *cāseus* cheese]

kW *or* **kw** *abbrev. for* kilowatt.

Kwa (kwɑː) *n.* **1.** a group of languages, now generally regarded as a branch of the Niger-Congo family, spoken in an area of W Africa extending from the Ivory Coast to E Nigeria and including Akan, Ewe, Yoruba, and Ibo. ~*adj.* **2.** relating to or belonging to this group of languages.

kwa·cha ('kwɑːtʃɑː) *n.* **1.** the standard monetary unit of Zambia, divided into 100 ngwee. **2.** the standard monetary unit of Malawi. [from native word in Zambia]

Kwa·ja·lein ('kwɑːdʒəˌleɪn) *n.* an atoll in the W Pacific, in the W Marshall Islands, in the central part of the Ralik Chain. Length: about 125 km (78 miles).

Kwa·ki·u·tl (ˌkwɑːkɪ'uːtᵊl) *n.* **1.** (*pl.* **·u·tl** *or* **·u·tls**) a member of a North American Indian people of N Vancouver Island and the adjacent mainland. **2.** the language of this people, belonging to the Wakashan family.

Kwang·chow ('kwæŋ'tʃaʊ) *n.* the Chinese name for **Canton.**

Kwang·chow·an ('kwæŋ'tʃaʊ'wɑːn) *n.* a territory of SE China, in SW Kwantung province: leased to France as part of French Indochina from 1898 to 1945. Area: 842 sq. km (325 sq. miles).

Kwang·ju ('kwæŋ'dʒuː) *n.* a city in SW South Korea: an important military base during the Korean War; cotton textile industry. Pop.: 606 503 (1975).

Kwang·si-Chuang Au·ton·o·mous Re·gion ('kwæŋ'siː-'tʃwæŋ) *n.* an administrative division of S China: the least developed of Chinese regions. Capital: Nanning. Pop.: 24 000 000 (1967–71 est.). Area: 220 400 sq. km (85 956 sq. miles).

Kwang·tung ('kwæŋ'tʊŋ) *n.* a province of SE China, on the South China Sea: includes the Luichow Peninsula and Hainan Island, with densely populated river valleys; the only truly tropical climate in China, and the only remaining foreign enclaves (Macao and Hong Kong). Capital: Canton. Pop.: 43 000 000 (1967–71 est.). Area: 231 400 sq. km (90 246 sq. miles).

Kwan·tung Leased Ter·ri·to·ry *n.* a strategic territory of NE China, at the S tip of the Liaotung Peninsula of Manchuria: leased forcibly by Russia in 1898; taken over by Japan in 1905; occupied by the Soviet Union in 1945 and subsequently returned to China on the condition of shared administration; made part of Liaoning province by China in 1954. Area: about 3400 sq. km (1300 sq. miles). Also: **Kuan-tung.**

kwan·za ('kwænzə) *n.* the monetary unit of Angola. [from a Bantu language]

Kwa·ra ('kwɑːrə) *n.* a state of W Nigeria: mainly wooded savanna. Capital: Ilorin. Pop.: 2 399 365 (1976 est.). Area: 73 400 sq. km (28 334 sq. miles).

kwash·i·or·kor (ˌkwæʃɪ'ɔːkə) *n.* severe malnutrition of infants and young children, esp. soon after weaning, resulting from dietary deficiency of protein. [C20: from native word in Ghana]

Kwa·zu·lu (kwɑː'zuːlʊ) *n.* a Bantustan in South Africa, in Natal: consists of ten separate territories. Capital: Ulundi. Pop.: 2 134 951 (1970).

Kwei·chow *or* **Kuei·chou** ('kweɪ'tʃaʊ) *n.* a province of SW China, between the Yangtze and Hsi Rivers: a high plateau. Capital: Kweiyang. Pop.: 24 000 000 (1976 est.). Area: 174 000 sq. km (69 278 sq. miles).

Kwei·lin *or* **Kuei-lin** ('kweɪ'lɪn) *n.* a city in S China, in Kwangsi-Chuang AR on the Li River: noted for the unusual caves and formations of the surrounding karst scenery; trade and manufacturing centre. Pop.: 170 000 (1958 est.).

Kwei·sui ('kweɪ'sweɪ) *n.* the former name of **Huhehot.**

Kwei·yang *or* **Kuei-yang** ('kweɪ'jæŋ) *n.* a city in S China, capital of Kweichow province: reached by rail in 1959, with subsequent industrial growth. Pop.: 660 000 (1970 est.).

kwe·la ('kweɪlə, 'kwɛlə) *n.* a type of beat music popular among the Bantu communities of South Africa. [C20: said to be from Zulu or Xhosa: jump up]

kWh, kwh, *or* **kw-h** *abbrev. for* kilowatt-hour.

KWIC (kwɪk) *n. acronym for* keyword in context (esp. in the phrase **KWIC index**).

KWOC (kwɒk) *n. acronym for* keyword out of context.

KWT *international car registration for* Kuwait.

Ky (kiː) *n.* **Ngu·yen Kao** (ᵊŋ'guːjɛn 'kaʊ). born 1930, premier of South Vietnam (1965–67); vice president (1967–69).

Ky. *abbrev. for* Kentucky.

ky·a·nite ('kaɪəˌnaɪt) *n.* a variant spelling of **cyanite.** **—ky·a·nit·ic** (ˌkaɪə'nɪtɪk) *adj.*

ky·an·ize *or* **ky·an·ise** ('kaɪəˌnaɪz) *vb.* (*tr.*) to treat (timber) with corrosive sublimate to make it resistant to decay. [C19: after J. H. *Kyan* (died 1850), English inventor of the process] **—ˌky·an·i·'za·tion** *or* **ˌky·an·i·'sa·tion** *n.*

ky·at (kɪ'ɑːt) *n.* the standard monetary unit of Burma, divided into 100 pyas. [from Burmese]

Kyd *or* **Kid** (kɪd) *n.* **Thom·as.** 1558–94, English dramatist, noted for his revenge play *The Spanish Tragedy* (1586).

kyle (kaɪl) *n. Scot.* (esp. in place names) a narrow strait or channel: *Kyle of Lochalsh.* [C16: from Gaelic *caol,* from *caol* narrow]

ky·lin (ˈkiːˈlɪn) *n.* (in Chinese art) a mythical animal of composite form. [C19: from Chinese *ch'i-lin,* literally: male-female]

ky·lix *or* **cy·lix** (ˈkaɪlɪks, ˈkɪl-) *n., pl.* **·li·kes** (-lɪˌkiːz). a shallow two-handled drinking vessel used in ancient Greece. [C19: from Greek *kulix* cup; compare CHALICE]

ky·loe (ˌkaɪləʊ) *n.* a breed of small long-horned long-haired beef cattle from NW Scotland. [C19: of uncertain origin]

ky·mo·graph (ˈkaɪməˌgrɑːf, -ˌgræf) *or* **cy·mo·graph** *n.* **1.** *Med.* a rotatable drum for holding paper on which a tracking stylus continuously records variations in blood pressure, respiratory movements, etc. **2.** *Phonetics.* this device as applied to the measurement of variations in the muscular action of the articulatory organs. **3.** an instrument for recording the angular oscillations of an aircraft in flight. —ˌ**ky·mo·ˈgraph·ic** *or* ˌ**cy·mo·ˈgraph·ic** *adj.*

Kym·ric (ˈkɪmrɪk) *n., adj.* a variant spelling of **Cymric.**

Kym·ry (ˈkɪmrɪ) *pl. n.* a variant spelling of **Cymry.**

Kyn·e·wulf (ˈkɪnəˌwʊlf) *n.* a variant spelling of **Cynewulf.**

Kyong·song (ˈkjɔːŋˈsɔːŋ) *n.* another name for **Seoul.**

Kyo·to *or* **Kio·to** (kɪˈəʊtəʊ, ˈkjəʊ-) *n.* a city in central Japan, on S Honshu: the capital of Japan from 794 to 1868; cultural centre famous for Chinese classical music, with two universities (1875, 1897). Pop.: 1 460 000 (1975).

ky·pho·sis (kaɪˈfəʊsɪs) *n. Pathol.* backward curvature of the thoracic spine, of congenital origin or resulting from injury or disease; hunchback. See also **Pott's disease.** Compare **lordosis, scoliosis.** [C19: from New Latin, from Greek *kuphōsis,* from *kuphos* humpbacked] —**ky·phot·ic** (kaɪˈfɒtɪk) *adj.*

Kyp·ri·a·nou (ˌkɪprɪˈɑːnuː) *n.* **Spy·ros** (ˈspɪərɒs). born 1932, Cypriot statesman; president of Cyprus since 1977.

Kyr·i·e e·lei·son (ˈkɪrɪɪ əˈleɪsᵊn) *n.* **1.** a formal invocation used in the liturgies of the Roman Catholic, Greek Orthodox, and Anglican Churches. **2.** a musical setting of this. Often shortened to **Kyrie.** [C14: via Late Latin from Late Greek *kurie, eleēson* Lord, have mercy]

Ky·the·ra (ˈkɪθɪrə) *n.* a variant spelling of **Cythera.**

kyu (kjuː) *n. Judo.* **1.** one of the six student grades for inexperienced competitors. **2.** a student in the kyu grades. ~Compare **dan**[2]. [from Japanese]

Kyu·shu *or* **Kiu·shu** (ˈkjuːʃuː) *n.* an island of SW Japan: the southernmost of Japan's four main islands, with over 300 surrounding small islands; contains the country's main coalfield. Chief cities: Fukuoka and Nagasaki. Pop.: 12 496 433 (1970). Area: 35 659 sq. km (13 768 sq. miles).

Ky·zyl Kum (*Russian* kɪˈzɪl ˈkum) *n.* a desert in the SW Soviet Union, in the Kazakh and Uzbek SSRs.

L

l *or* **L** (ɛl) *n., pl.* **l's, L's,** *or* **Ls. 1.** the 12th letter and ninth consonant of the modern English alphabet. **2.** a speech sound represented by this letter, usually a lateral, as in *label.* **3. a.** something shaped like an L. **b.** (*in combination*): *an L-shaped room.*

L *symbol for:* **1.** ell (unit). **2.** lambert(s). **3.** large. **4.** Latin. **5.** (on British motor vehicles) learner driver. **6.** *Physics.* length. **7.** Usually written: **£.** pound. [Latin *libra*]. **8.** longitude. **9.** *Electronics.* inductor (in circuit diagrams). **10.** *Physics.* **a.** latent heat. **b.** self inductance. **11.** *Chem.* the Avogadro constant. **12.** *the Roman numeral for* 50. See **Roman numerals.** ~**13.** *international car registration for* Luxembourg.

L. *or* **l.** *abbrev. for:* **1.** lake. **2.** latitude. **3.** law. **4.** leaf. **5.** league. **6.** left. **7.** length. **8.** liber. [Latin: book] **9.** (*pl.* **LL.** *or* **ll.**) line. **10.** link. **11.** lire. **12.** litre(s). **13.** low.

L. *abbrev. for:* **1.** *Politics.* Liberal. **2.** *Currency.* **a.** lempira. **b.** len. **c.** lev. **3.** (in titles) Licentiate. **4.** Linnaeus. **5.** (fraternal) Lodge.

la[1] (lɑː) *n. Music.* an alternative spelling of **Lah.**

la[2] (lɔː) *interj.* an exclamation of surprise or emphasis. [Old English *lā* LO]

La *the chemical symbol for* lanthanum.

La. *abbrev. for* Louisiana.

L.A. *abbrev. for:* **1.** Legislative Assembly. **2.** Library Association. **3.** local agent. **4.** Los Angeles.

laa+ger *or* **la+ger** (ˈlɑːgə) *n.* **1.** (in Africa) a camp, esp. one defended by a circular formation of wagons. **2.** *Military.* a place where armoured vehicles are parked. ~*vb.* **3.** to form (wagons) into a laager. **4.** (*tr.*) to park (armoured vehicles) in a laager. [C19: from Afrikaans *lager,* via German from Old High German *legar* bed, lair]

Laa+land (*Danish* ˈlɔlan) *n.* a variant spelling of **Lolland.**

lab (læb) *n. Informal.* short for **laboratory.**

lab. *abbrev. for:* **1.** laboratory. **2.** labour.

Lab. *abbrev. for:* **1.** *Politics.* Labour. **2.** Labrador.

La·ban (ˈleɪbᵊn) *n. Old Testament.* the father-in-law of Jacob, father of Leah and Rachel (Genesis 29:16).

lab·a+rum (ˈlæbərəm) *n., pl.* **+ra** (-rə). **1.** a standard or banner carried in Christian religious processions. **2.** the military standard bearing a Christian monogram used by Constantine the Great. [C17: from Late Latin, of obscure origin]

lab+da+num (ˈlæbdənəm) *or* **la+da+num** (ˈlædənəm) *n.* a dark resinous juice obtained from various rockroses of the genus *Cistus,* used in perfumery and in the manufacture of fumigants and medicinal plasters. [C16: Latin, from Greek *ladanon,* from *lēdon* rockrose, from Semitic]

La·be (ˈlabɛ) *n.* the Czech name for the (River) **Elbe.**

lab+e·fac+tion (ˌlæbɪˈfækʃən) *or* **lab+e·fac+ta+tion** (ˌlæbɪfækˈteɪʃən) *n. Rare.* deterioration; weakening. [C17: from Late Latin *labefactiō,* from Latin *labefacere* shake, from *lābī* to fall + *facere* to make]

la+bel (ˈleɪbᵊl) *n.* **1.** a piece of paper, card, or other material attached to an object to identify it or give instructions or details concerning its ownership, use, nature, destination, etc.; tag. **2.** a brief descriptive phrase or term given to a person, group, school of thought, etc.: *the label "Romantic" is applied to many different kinds of poetry.* **3.** a word or phrase heading a piece of text to indicate or summarize its contents. **4.** a trademark or company or brand name on certain goods, esp. on gramophone records. **5.** another name for **dripstone** (sense 2). **6.** *Heraldry.* a charge consisting of a horizontal line across the chief of a shield with three or more pendants: the charge of an eldest son. **7.** *Computer technol.* a set of characters by which a file is identified by the central processing unit. **8.** *Chem.* a radioactive element used in a compound to trace the mechanism of a chemical reaction. ~*vb.* **+bels, +bel+ling, +belled** *or U.S.* **+bels, +bel+ing, +beled.** (*tr.*) **9.** to fasten a label to. **10.** to mark with a label. **11.** to describe or classify in a word or phrase: *to label someone a liar.* **12.** to make (one or more atoms in a compound) radioactive, for use in determining the mechanism of a reaction. [C14: from Old French, from Germanic; compare Old High German *lappa* rag] —**ˈla+bel+ler** *n.*

la+bel+lum (ləˈbɛləm) *n., pl.* **+la** (-lə). **1.** the part of the corolla of certain plants, esp. orchids, that forms a distinct, often lobed, lip. **2.** a lobe at the tip of the proboscis of a fly. [C19: New Latin, diminutive of Latin *labrum* lip] —**la+ˈbel+loid** *adj.*

la·bi·a (ˈleɪbɪə) *n.* the plural of **labium.**

la·bi·al (ˈleɪbɪəl) *adj.* **1.** of, relating to, or near lips or labia. **2.** *Music.* producing sounds by the action of an air stream over a narrow liplike fissure, as in a flue pipe of an organ. **3.** *Phonetics.* relating to a speech sound whose articulation involves movement or use of the lips: *a labial click.* ~*n.* **4.** Also called: **labial pipe.** *Music.* an organ pipe with a liplike fissure. **5.** *Phonetics.* a speech sound such as English *p* or *m,* whose articulation involves movement or use of the lips. [C16: from Medieval Latin *labiālis,* from Latin *labium* lip] —**ˌla+bi+ˈal+i·ty** *n.* —**ˈla+bi·al+ly** *adv.*

la+bi·al+ize *or* **la+bi·al+ise** (ˈleɪbɪəˌlaɪz) *vb.* (*tr.*) *Phonetics.* to pronounce with articulation involving rounded lips, such as for (k) before a close back vowel (uː) as in English *cool.* —**ˈla+bi+al+ˌism, ˌla+bi·al·i+ˈza+tion,** *or* **ˌla+bi+al·i+ˈsa+tion** *n.*

la+bi·a ma+jo+ra (məˈdʒɔːrə) *pl. n.* the two elongated outer folds of skin in human females surrounding the vaginal orifice. [C18: New Latin: greater lips]

la+bi·a mi+no+ra (mɪˈnɔːrə) *pl. n.* the two small inner folds of skin in human females forming the margins of the vaginal orifice. [C18: New Latin: smaller lips]

la+bi+ate (ˈleɪbɪˌeɪt, -ɪt) *n.* **1.** any plants of the family *Labiatae,* having square stems, aromatic leaves, and a two-lipped corolla: includes mint, thyme, sage, rosemary, etc. ~*adj.* **2.** of, relating to, or belonging to the family *Labiatae.* [C18: from New Latin *labiātus,* from Latin *labium* lip]

La·biche (*French* laˈbiʃ) *n.* **Eu·gène Ma·rin** (øʒɛn maˈrɛ̃). 1815–88, French dramatist, noted for his farces of middle-class life, which include *Le Chapeau de paille d'Italie* (1851) and *Le Voyage de Monsieur Perrichon* (1860).

la+bile (ˈleɪbɪl) *adj.* **1.** *Chem.* (of a compound) prone to chemical change. **2.** liable to change or move. [C15: via Late Latin *lābilis,* from Latin *lābī* to slide, slip] —**la+bil+i·ty** (ləˈbɪlɪtɪ) *n.*

la·bi·o- *or before a vowel* **la·bi-** *combining form.* relating to or formed by the lips and (another organ or part): *labiodental.* [from Latin *labium* lip]

la+bi·o+den+tal (ˌleɪbɪəʊˈdɛntᵊl) *Phonetics.* ~*adj.* **1.** pronounced by bringing the bottom lip into contact or near contact with the upper teeth, as for the fricative (f) in English *fat, puff.* ~*n.* **2.** a labiodental consonant.

la+bi·o+na+sal (ˌleɪbɪəʊˈneɪzᵊl) *Phonetics.* ~*adj.* **1.** pronounced by making a complete closure of the air passage at the lips and lowering the soft palate allowing air to escape through the nasal cavity. ~*n.* **2.** a labionasal consonant, such as *m.*

la+bi·o+ve·lar (ˌleɪbɪəʊˈviːlə) *Phonetics.* ~*adj.* **1.** relating to or denoting a speech sound pronounced with simultaneous articulation at the soft palate and the lips. ~*n.* **2.** a labiovelar speech sound, such as some pronunciations of the consonant spelt *q* in English.

la+bi·um (ˈleɪbɪəm) *n., pl.* **+bi·a** (-bɪə). **1.** a lip or liplike structure. **2.** any one of the four lip-shaped folds of the female vulva. See **labia majora, labia minora. 3.** the fused pair of appendages forming the lower lip of insects. **4.** the lower lip of the corolla of labiate flowers. [C16: from Latin: lip]

lab+lab (ˈlæbˌlæb) *n.* **1.** a twining leguminous plant, *Dolichos lablab* (or *Lablab niger*), of tropical Africa. **2.** the edible pod or bean of this plant. [from Arabic]

la+bor (ˈleɪbə) *vb., n.* the U.S. spelling of **labour.**

la+bor·a+to·ry (ləˈbɒrətərɪ, -trɪ; *U.S.* ˈlæbrəˌtɔːrɪ) *n., pl.* **·ries. 1. a.** a building or room equipped for conducting scientific research or for teaching practical science. **b.** (*as modifier*): *laboratory equipment.* **2.** a place where chemicals or medicines are manufactured. ~Often shortened to **lab.** See also **language laboratory.** [C17: from Medieval Latin *labōrātōrium* workshop, from Latin *labōrāre* to LABOUR]

la+bo+ri+ous (ləˈbɔːrɪəs) *adj.* **1.** involving great exertion or long effort. **2.** given to working hard. **3.** (of literary style, etc.) not fluent. —**la+ˈbo+ri+ous+ly** *adv.* —**la+ˈbo+ri+ous+ness** *n.*

La+bor Par+ty *n.* one of the two chief political parties of Australia, generally supporting the interests of organized labour.

la+bor un+ion *n.* the U.S. name for **trade union.**

la+bour *or U.S.* **la+bor** (ˈleɪbə) *n.* **1.** productive work, esp. physical toil done for wages. **2. a.** the people, class, or workers involved in this, esp. as opposed to management, capital, etc. **b.** (*as modifier*): *a labour dispute; labour relations.* **3. a.** difficult or arduous work or effort. **b.** (*in combination*): *labour-saving.* **4.** a particular job or task, esp. of a difficult nature. **5. a.** the pain or effort of childbirth or the time during which this takes place. **b.** (*as modifier*): *labour pains.* ~*vb.* **6.** (*intr.*) to perform labour; work. **7.** (*intr.;* foll. by *for,* etc.) to strive or work hard (for something). **8.** (*intr.;* usually foll. by *under*) to be burdened (by) or be at a disadvantage (because of): *to labour under a misapprehension.* **9.** (*intr.*) to make one's way with difficulty. **10.** (*tr.*) to deal with or treat too persistently: *to labour a point.* **11.** (*intr.*) (of a woman) to be in labour. **12.** (*intr.*) (of a ship) to pitch and toss. [C13: via Old French from Latin *labor;* perhaps related to *lābī* to fall] —**ˈla+bour+ing+ly** *or U.S.* **ˈla+bor+ing+ly** *adv.*

La+bour and So+cial+ist In+ter+na+tion+al *n.* **the.** an international association of socialist parties formed in Hamburg in 1923: destroyed by World War II. Also called: **Second International.**

la+bour camp *n.* **1.** a penal colony involving forced labour. **2.** a camp for migratory labourers.

La+bour Day *n.* a public holiday in many countries in honour of labour, usually held on May 1.

la+boured *or U.S.* **la+bored** (ˈleɪbəd) *adj.* **1.** (of breathing) performed with difficulty. **2.** showing effort. —**ˈla+boured+ly** *or U.S.* **ˈla+bored+ly** *adv.* —**ˈla+boured+ness** *or U.S.* **ˈla+bored+ness** *n.*

la+bour+er or *U.S.* **la+bor+er** ('leɪbərə) *n.* a person engaged in physical work, esp. of an unskilled kind.
la+bour ex+change *n. Brit.* a former name for the **Employment Service Agency.**
la+bour+ism or *U.S.* **la+bor+ism** ('leɪbəˌrɪzəm) *n.* **1.** the dominance of the working classes. **2.** a political, social, or economic system that favours such dominance. **3.** support for workers' rights.
la+bour+ist or *U.S.* **la+bor+ist** ('leɪbərɪst) *n.* **1.** a person who supports workers' rights. **2.** a supporter of labourism.
La+bour+ite ('leɪbəˌraɪt) *n.* an adherent of the Labour Party.
La+bour Par+ty *n.* **1.** a British political party, formed in 1900 as an amalgam of various trade unions and socialist groups, generally supporting the interests of organized labour and advocating nationalization, social welfare, etc. **2.** any similar party in any of various other countries.
Lab+ra+dor ('læbrəˌdɔː) *n.* **1.** Also called: **Labrador-Ungava.** a large peninsula of NE Canada, on the Atlantic, the Gulf of St. Lawrence, Hudson Strait, and Hudson Bay: contains most of the province of Quebec and the mainland part of Newfoundland; geologically part of the Canadian Shield. Area: 1 619 000 sq. km (625 000 sq. miles). **2.** Also called: **Coast of Labrador.** a region of NE Canada, on the Atlantic and consisting of the mainland part of Newfoundland province. **3.** (*often not cap.*) short for **Labrador retriever.**
Lab+ra+dor Cur+rent *n.* a cold ocean current flowing southwards off the coast of Labrador and meeting the warm Gulf Stream, causing dense fogs off Newfoundland.
lab+ra+dor+ite (ˌlæbrəˈdɔːraɪt) *n.* a blue, green, or reddish-brown feldspar mineral of the plagioclase series: used as a decorative stone. Formula: $CaAl_2Si_2O_8.NaAlSi_3O_8$. [C18: named after LABRADOR, where it was found; see -ITE[1]]
Lab+ra+dor re+triev+er *n.* a variety of retriever with a short black or golden-brown coat. Often shortened to **Labrador.**
Lab+ra+dor tea *n.* **1.** either of two arctic evergreen ericaceous shrubs, *Ledum groenlandicum* or *L. palustre* var. *decumbens.* **2.** (in Canada) an infusion brewed from the leaves of either of these plants.
la+bret ('leɪbrɛt) *n.* a piece of bone, shell, etc.; inserted into the lip as an ornament by certain peoples. [C19: from Latin *labrum* lip]
lab+roid ('læbrɔɪd, 'leɪ-) or **lab+rid** ('læbrɪd) *n.* **1.** any percoid fish of the family *Labridae* (wrasses). ~*adj.* **2.** of or relating to the *Labridae.* [C19: from New Latin *Labroidea,* from Latin *lābrus* a fish, from *labrum* lip]
la+brum ('leɪbrəm, 'læb-) *n., pl.* **+bra** (-brə). a lip or liplike part, such as the cuticular plate forming the upper lip of insects. [C19: New Latin, from Latin]
La Bru·yère (*French* la bryˈjɛːr) *n.* **Jean de** (ʒɑ̃ də). 1645–96, French moralist, noted for his *Caractères* (1688), satirical character studies, including portraits of contemporary public figures.
La+bu·an (ləˈbuːən) *n.* an island in Malaysia, off the NW coast of Borneo: part of the Straits settlements until 1946, when transferred to North Borneo. Chief town: Victoria. Area: 98 sq. km (38 sq. miles).
la+bur+num (ləˈbɜːnəm) *n.* any papilionaceous tree or shrub of the Eurasian genus *Laburnum,* having clusters of yellow drooping flowers: all parts of the plant are poisonous. [C16: New Latin, from Latin]
lab·y+rinth ('læbərɪnθ) *n.* **1.** a mazelike network of tunnels, chambers, or paths, either natural or man-made. Compare **maze** (sense 1). **2.** any complex or confusing system of streets, passages, etc. **3.** a complex or intricate situation. **4. a.** any system of interconnecting cavities, esp. those comprising the internal ear. **b.** another name for **internal ear. 5.** *Electronics.* an enclosure behind a high-performance loudspeaker, consisting of a series of air chambers designed to absorb unwanted sound waves. [C16: via Latin from Greek *laburinthos,* of obscure origin]
Lab·y+rinth ('læbərɪnθ) *n. Greek myth.* a huge maze constructed for King Minos in Crete by Daedalus to contain the Minotaur.
lab·y+rinth fish *n.* any tropical freshwater spiny-finned fish of the family *Anabantidae* of SE Asia and Africa, having a lunglike respiratory organ. See also **anabantid.**
lab·y+rin+thine (ˌlæbəˈrɪnθaɪn), **lab·y+rin+thi·an** (ˌlæbəˈrɪnθɪən), or **lab·y+rin+thic** (ˌlæbəˈrɪnθɪk) *adj.* **1.** of or relating to a labyrinth. **2.** resembling a labyrinth in complexity. —ˌ**lab·y+ˈrin+thi+cal+ly** *adv.*
lab·y+rinth·o·dont (ˌlæbɪˈrɪnθəˌdɒnt) *n.* any primitive amphibians of the order *Labyrinthodontia,* of late Devonian to Triassic times, having teeth with much-folded dentine. [C19: from Greek *laburinthos* LABYRINTH + -ODONT]
lac[1] (læk) *n.* a resinous substance secreted by certain lac insects, used in the manufacture of shellac. [C16: from Dutch *lak* or French *laque,* from Hindi *lākh* resin, ultimately from Sanskrit *lākshā*]
lac[2] (lɑːk) *n.* a variant spelling of **lakh.**
L.A.C. *Brit. abbrev. for* leading aircraftman.
Lac+ca+dive, Mi+ni+coy, and A·min+di+vi Is+lands ('lækədɪv, 'mɪnɪˌkɔɪ, ˌʌmənˈdiːviː) *pl. n.* the former name (until 1973) of the **Lakshadweep Islands.**
lac+co+lith ('lækəlɪθ) or **lac+co+lite** ('lækəˌlaɪt) *n.* a dome of igneous rock between two layers of older sedimentary rock: formed by the intrusion of magma, forcing the overlying strata into a dome. [C19: from Greek *lakkos* cistern + -LITH] —ˌ**lac+co+ˈlith+ic** or **lac+co+lit+ic** (ˌlækəˈlɪtɪk) *adj.*
lace (leɪs) *n.* **1.** a delicate decorative fabric made from cotton, silk, etc., woven in an open web of different symmetrical patterns and figures. **2.** a cord or string drawn through holes or eyelets or around hooks to fasten a shoe or garment. **3.** ornamental braid often used on military uniforms, etc. **4.** a dash of spirits added to a beverage. ~*vb.* **5.** to fasten (shoes, etc.) with a lace. **6.** (*tr.*) to draw (a cord or thread) through holes, eyes, etc., as when tying shoes. **7.** (*tr.*) to compress the waist of (someone), as with a corset. **8.** (*tr.*) to add a dash of spirits to (a beverage). **9.** (*tr.; usually passive* and foll. by *with*) to streak or mark with lines or colours: *the sky was laced with red.* **10.** (*tr.*) to intertwine; interlace. **11.** (*tr.*) *Informal.* to give a sound beating to. [C13 *las,* from Old French *laz,* from Latin *laqueus* noose] —**ˈlace+ˌlike** *adj.* —**ˈlac+er** *n.*
Lac+e·dae+mon (ˌlæsɪˈdiːmən) *n.* another name for **Sparta** or **Laconia.**
Lac+e·dae+mo·ni·an (ˌlæsɪdɪˈməʊnɪən) *adj., n.* another word for **Spartan.**
lace in·to *vb.* (*intr., prep*) to attack violently, either verbally or physically.
lac+er+ant ('læsərənt) *adj.* painfully distressing; harrowing.
lac+er+ate *vb.* ('læsəˌreɪt). (*tr.*) **1.** to tear (the flesh, etc.) jaggedly. **2.** to hurt or harrow (the feelings, etc.). ~*adj.* ('læsəˌreɪt, -rɪt). **3.** having edges that are jagged or torn; lacerated: *lacerate leaves.* [C16: from Latin *lacerāre* to tear, from *lacer* mangled] —**ˈlac+er+a·ble** *adj.* —ˌ**lac+er+a·ˈbil+i·ty** *n.* —ˌ**lac+er·ˈa+tion** *n.* —**ˈlac·er·a+tive** *adj.*
La+cer+ta (ləˈsɜːtə) *n., Latin genitive* **La+cer+tae** (ləˈsɜːtiː). a small faint constellation in the N hemisphere, part of which is crossed by the Milky Way, lying between Cygnus and Andromeda. [Latin: lizard]
lac+er+til·i·an (ˌlæsəˈtɪlɪən) *n. also* **la+cer+tian** (ləˈsɜːʃən). **1.** any reptile of the suborder *Lacertilia* (lizards). ~*adj.* **2.** of, relating to, or belonging to the *Lacertilia.* [C19: New Latin, from Latin *lacerta* lizard]
lace up *vb.* **1.** (*tr., adv.*) to tighten or fasten (clothes or footwear) with laces. ~*adj.* **lace-up. 2.** (of footwear) to be fastened with laces. ~*n.* **3.** a lace-up shoe or boot.
lace+wing ('leɪsˌwɪŋ) *n.* any of various neuropterous insects, esp. any of the families *Chrysopidae* (**green lacewings**) and *Hemerobiidae* (**brown lacewings**), having lacy wings and preying on aphids and similar pests.
lach+es ('lætʃɪz) *n. Law.* negligence or unreasonable delay in pursuing a legal remedy. [C14 *lachesse,* via Old French *lasche* slack, from Latin *laxus* LAX]
Lach·e·sis ('lækɪsɪs) *n. Greek myth.* one of the three Fates. [via Latin from Greek, from *lakhesis* destiny, from *lakhein* to befall by lot]
Lach+lan ('lɒklən) *n.* a river in SE Australia, rising in central New South Wales and flowing northwest then southwest to the Murrumbidgee River. Length: about 1450km (900 miles). [named after *Lachlan* Macquarie, governor of New South Wales (1809–21)]
lach+ry+ma Chris+ti ('lækrəmə 'krɪstɪ) *n.* a red or white wine from the bay of Naples in S Italy. [C17: from Latin: Christ's tear]
lach+ry+mal ('lækrɪməl) *adj.* a variant spelling of **lacrimal.**
lach+ry+ma+tor ('lækrɪˌmeɪtə) *n.* a variant spelling of **lacrimator.**
lach+ry+ma+to·ry ('lækrɪmətərɪ, -trɪ) *n., pl.* **·ries. 1.** a small vessel found in ancient tombs, formerly thought to hold the tears of mourners. ~*adj.* **2.** a variant spelling of **lacrimatory.**
lach+ry+mose ('lækrɪˌməʊs, -ˌməʊz) *adj.* **1.** given to weeping; tearful. **2.** mournful; sad. —**ˈlach+ry+ˌmose+ly** *adv.* —**lach+ry+mos+i·ty** (ˌlækrɪˈmɒsɪtɪ) *n.*
lac+ing ('leɪsɪŋ) *n.* **1.** *Chiefly Brit.* a course of bricks, stone, etc., for strengthening a rubble or flint wall. **2.** another word for **lace** (senses 2-4). **3.** *Informal.* a severe beating (esp. in the phrase **give someone a lacing**).
la+cin·i+ate (ləˈsɪnɪˌeɪt, -ɪt) or **la+cin·i+at+ed** *adj.* **1.** *Biology.* jagged: *a laciniate leaf.* **2.** having a fringe. [C17: from Latin *lacinia* flap] —**la+ˌcin·i·ˈa+tion** *n.*
lac in+sect (læk) *n.* any of various homopterous insects of the family *Lacciferidae,* esp. *Laccifer lacca* of India, the females of which secrete lac.
lack (læk) *n.* **1.** an insufficiency, shortage, or absence of something required or desired. **2.** something that is required but is absent or in short supply. ~*vb.* **3.** (when *intr.;* often foll. by *in* or *for*) to be deficient (in) or have need (of): *to lack purpose.* [C12: related to Middle Dutch *laken* to be wanting]
lack·a·dai+si+cal (ˌlækəˈdeɪzɪkəl) *adj.* **1.** lacking vitality and purpose. **2.** lazy or idle, esp. in a dreamy way. [C18: from earlier *lackadaisy,* extended form of LACKADAY] —ˌ**lack·a+ˈdai+si+cal+ly** *adv.* —ˌ**lack·a·ˈdai+si+cal+ness** *n.*
lack·a·day ('lækəˌdeɪ) *interj. Archaic.* another word for **alas.** [C17: from *alack the day*]
lack+er ('lækə) *n.* a variant spelling of **lacquer.**
lack+ey ('lækɪ) *n.* **1.** a servile follower; hanger-on. **2.** a liveried male servant or valet. **3.** a person who is treated like a servant. ~*vb.* **4.** (when *intr.,* often foll. by *for*) to act as a lackey (to). ~Also (rare): **lac+quey.** [C16: via French *laquais,* from Old French, perhaps from Catalan *lacayo, alacayo;* perhaps related to ALCALDE]
lack+lus·tre or *U.S.* **lack+lus·ter** ('lækˌlʌstə) *adj.* lacking force, brilliance, or vitality.
La·clos (*French* laˈklo) *n.* **Pierre Cho·der·los de** (pjɛːr ʃɔdɛrˈlo də). 1741–1803, French soldier and writer, noted for his novel in epistolary form *Les Liaisons dangereuses* (1782).
La+co+ni·a (ləˈkəʊnɪə) *n.* an ancient country of S Greece, in the SE Peloponnese, of which Sparta was the capital: corresponds

to the present-day department of Lakonia. —**La·'co·ni·an** *n., adj.*
la·con·ic (lə'kɒnɪk) *or* **la·con·i·cal** *adj.* (of a person's speech) using few words; terse. [C16: via Latin from Greek *Lakōnikos*, from *Lakōn* Laconian, Spartan; referring to the Spartans' terseness of speech] —**la·'con·i·cal·ly** *adv.*
lac·o·nism ('lækəˌnɪzəm) *or* **la·con·i·cism** (lə'kɒnɪˌsɪzəm) *n. Rare.* **1.** economy of expression. **2.** a terse saying.
La Co·ru·ña (*Spanish* la ko'ruɲa) *n.* a port in NW Spain, on the Atlantic: point of departure for the Spanish Armada (1588); site of the defeat of the French by the English under Sir John Moore in the Peninsular War (1809). Pop.: 189 654 (1970). English name: **Corunna.**
lac·quer ('lækə) *n.* **1.** a hard glossy coating made by dissolving cellulose derivatives or natural resins in a volatile solvent. **2.** a black resinous substance, obtained from certain trees, used to give a hard glossy finish to wooden furniture. **3. lacquer tree.** Also called: **varnish tree.** an E Asian anacardiaceous tree, *Rhus verniciflua*, whose stem yields a toxic exudation from which black lacquer is obtained. **4.** Also called: **hair lacquer.** a mixture of shellac and alcohol for spraying onto the hair to hold a style in place. 5. *Art.* decorative objects coated with such lacquer, often inlaid. [C16: from obsolete French *lacre* sealing wax, from Portuguese *laca* LAC[1]] —**'lac·quer·er** *n.*
lac·ri·mal, lach·ry·mal, *or* **lac·ry·mal** ('lækrɪməl) *adj.* of or relating to tears or to the glands that secrete tears.
lac·ri·mal duct *n.* a short tube in the inner corner of the eyelid through which tears drain into the nose. Nontechnical name: **tear duct.**
lac·ri·mal gland *n.* the compound gland that secretes tears and lubricates the surface of the eye and the conjunctiva of the eyelid.
lac·ri·ma·tion (ˌlækrɪ'meɪʃən) *n.* the secretion of tears.
lac·ri·ma·tor, lach·ry·ma·tor, *or* **lac·ry·ma·tor** ('lækrɪˌmeɪtə) *n.* a substance causing an increase in the flow of tears. See **tear gas.**
lac·ri·ma·to·ry, lach·ry·ma·to·ry, *or* **lac·ry·ma·to·ry** ('lækrɪmətərɪ, -trɪ) *adj.* of, causing, or producing tears.
la·crosse (lə'krɒs) *n.* a ball game invented by American Indians, now played by two teams who try to propel a ball into each other's goal by means of long-handled rackets (crosses). [C19: Canadian French: the hooked stick]
lac·tal·bu·min (læk'tælbjumɪn) *n.* a protein occurring in milk that contains all the amino acids essential to man. See also **caseinogen.** [C19: from LACTO- + ALBUMIN]
lac·tam ('læktæm) *n. Chem.* any of a group of inner amides, derived from amino acids, having the characteristic group -CONH-. [C20: from LACT(ONE) + AM(IDE)]
lac·ta·ry ('læktərɪ) *adj. Rare.* of or relating to milk. [C17: from Latin *lactārius*, from *lact-*, *lac* milk]
lac·tase ('lækteɪs, -teɪz) *n.* any of a group of enzymes that hydrolyse lactose to glucose and galactose. [C20: from LACTO- + -ASE]
lac·tate[1] ('lækteɪt) *n.* an ester or salt of lactic acid. [C18: from LACTO- + -ATE[1]]
lac·tate[2] ('lækteɪt) *vb.* (*intr.*) (of mammals) to produce or secrete milk.
lac·ta·tion (læk'teɪʃən) *n.* **1.** the secretion of milk from the mammary glands after parturition. **2.** the period during which milk is secreted. —**lac·'ta·tion·al** *adj.* —**lac·'ta·tion·al·ly** *adv.*
lac·te·al ('læktɪəl) *adj.* **1.** of, relating to, or resembling milk. **2.** (of lymphatic vessels) conveying or containing chyle. ~*n.* **3.** any of the lymphatic vessels conveying chyle from the small intestine to the thoracic duct. [C17: from Latin *lacteus* of milk, from *lac* milk] —**'lac·te·al·ly** *adv.*
lac·tes·cent (læk'tɛsᵊnt) *adj.* **1.** (of plants and certain insects) secreting a milky fluid. **2.** milky or becoming milky. [C18: from Latin *lactescēns*, from *lactescēre* to become milky, from *lact-*, *lac* milk] —**lac·'tes·cence** *n.*
lac·tic ('læktɪk) *adj.* relating to or derived from milk. [C18: from Latin *lact-*, *lac* milk]
lac·tic ac·id *n.* a colourless syrupy carboxylic acid found in sour milk and many fruits and used as a preservative for foodstuffs and for making pharmaceuticals and adhesives. Formula: $CH_3CH(OH)COOH$.
lac·tif·er·ous (læk'tɪfərəs) *adj.* **1.** producing, conveying, or secreting milk or a milky fluid: *lactiferous ducts.* **2.** *Botany.* another word for **laticiferous.** [C17: from Latin *lactifer*, from *lact-*, *lac* milk] —**lac·'tif·er·ous·ness** *n.*
lac·to- *or before a vowel* **lact-** *combining form.* indicating milk: *lactobacillus.* [from Latin *lact-*, *lac* milk]
lac·to·ba·cil·lus (ˌlæktəʊbə'sɪləs) *n., pl.* **-li** (-laɪ). any Gram-positive rod-shaped bacterium of the genus *Lactobacillus*, which ferments carbohydrates: family *Lactobacillaceae.*
lac·to·fla·vin (ˌlæktəʊ'fleɪvɪn) *n.* a less common name for **riboflavin.**
lac·to·gen·ic (ˌlæktə'dʒɛnɪk) *adj.* inducing lactation: *lactogenic hormone.* See also **prolactin.**
lac·tom·e·ter (læk'tɒmɪtə) *n.* a hydrometer used to measure the relative density of milk and thus determine its quality. Also called: **galactometer.**
lac·tone ('læktəʊn) *n.* any of a class of organic compounds formed from hydroxy acids and containing the group -C(CO)OC-, where the carbon atoms are part of a ring. —**lac·ton·ic** (læk'tɒnɪk) *adj.*
lac·to·pro·tein (ˌlæktəʊ'prəʊtiːn) *n.* any protein, such as lactalbumin or caseinogen, that is present in milk.
lac·to·scope ('læktəˌskəʊp) *n.* an instrument for measuring the amount of cream in milk.
lac·tose ('læktəʊs, -təʊz) *n.* a white crystalline disaccharide occurring in milk and used in the manufacture of pharmaceuticals and baby foods. Formula: $C_{12}H_{22}O_{11}$. Also called: **milk sugar.**
La Cum·bre (lə 'kuːmbreɪ) *n.* another name for the **Uspallata Pass.**
la·cu·na (lə'kjuːnə) *n., pl.* **-nae** (-niː) *or* **-nas. 1.** a gap or space, esp. in a book or manuscript. **2.** *Biology.* a cavity or depression, such as any of the spaces in the matrix of bone. **3.** another name for **coffer** (sense 3). [C17: from Latin *lacūna* pool, cavity, from *lacus* lake] —**la·'cu·nose, la·'cu·nal,** *or* **la·'cu·nar·y** *adj.* —**lac·u·nos·i·ty** (ˌlækjʊ'nɒsɪtɪ) *n.*
la·cu·nar (lə'kjuːnə) *n., pl.* **la·cu·nars** *or* **la·cu·nar·i·a** (ˌlækjʊ'nɛərɪə). **1.** Also called: **lequear.** a ceiling, soffit, or vault having coffers. **2.** another name for **coffer** (sense 3). ~*adj.* **3.** of, relating to, or containing a lacuna or lacunas. [C17: from Latin *lacūnar* panelled ceiling, from *lacūna* cavity; see LACUNA]
la·cus·trine (lə'kʌstraɪn) *adj.* **1.** of or relating to lakes. **2.** living or growing in or on the shores of a lake. [C19: from Italian *lacustre*, from Latin *lacus* lake]
L.A.C.W. *Brit. abbrev. for* leading aircraftwoman.
lac·y ('leɪsɪ) *adj.* **lac·i·er, lac·i·est.** made of or resembling lace. —**'lac·i·ly** *adv.* —**'lac·i·ness** *n.*
lad (læd) *n.* **1.** a boy or young man. **2.** *Informal.* a familiar form of address for any male. **3.** *Brit.* a boy or man who looks after horses. [C13 *ladde*; perhaps of Scandinavian origin]
la·da·num ('lædənəm) *n.* another name for **labdanum.**
lad·der ('lædə) *n.* **1.** a portable framework of wood, metal, rope, etc., in the form of two long parallel members connected by several parallel rungs or steps fixed to them at right angles, for climbing up or down. **2.** any hierarchy conceived of as having a series of ascending stages, levels, etc: *the social ladder.* **3. a.** anything resembling a ladder. **b.** (*as modifier*): *ladder stitch.* **4.** Also called: **run.** *Chiefly Brit.* a line of connected stitches that have come undone in knitted material, esp. stockings. **5.** See **ladder tournament.** ~*vb.* **6.** *Chiefly Brit.* to cause a line of interconnected stitches in (stockings, etc.) to undo, as by snagging, or (of a stocking) to come undone in this way. [Old English *hlǣder*; related to Old High German *leitara*]
lad·der back *n.* a type of chair in which the back is constructed of horizontal slats between two uprights.
lad·der tourn·a·ment *n.* Also called: **ladder.** a tournament in a sport or game in which each contestant in a list attempts to defeat and displace the contestant above him.
lad·die ('lædɪ) *n. Chiefly Scot.* a familiar term for a male, esp. a young man; lad.
lade (leɪd) *vb.* **lades, lad·ing, lad·ed, lad·en** *or* **lad·ed. 1.** to put cargo or freight on board (a ship, etc.) or (of a ship, etc.) to take on cargo or freight. **2.** (*tr.; usually passive* and foll. by *with*) to burden or oppress. **3.** (*tr.; usually passive* and foll. by *with*) to fill or load. **4.** to remove (liquid) with or as if with a ladle. [Old English *hladen* to load; related to Dutch *laden*] —**'lad·er** *n.*
lad·en ('leɪdᵊn) **1.** a past participle of **lade.** ~*adj.* **2.** weighed down with a load; loaded. **3.** encumbered; burdened.
la-di-da, lah-di-dah, *or* **la-de-da** (ˌlɑːdiː'dɑː) *adj.* **1.** *Informal.* affecting exaggeratedly genteel manners or speech. ~*n.* **2.** a la-di-da person. [C19: mockingly imitative of affected speech]
la·dies *or* **la·dies' room** *n.* (*functioning as sing.*) *Informal.* a women's public lavatory.
la·dies' fin·gers *n.* (*functioning as sing. or pl.*) another name for **kidney vetch.**
la·dies' gal·ler·y *n.* (in Britain) a gallery in the old House of Commons set aside for women spectators.
la·dies' man *or* **la·dy's man** *n.* a man who is fond of, attentive to, and successful with women.
la·dies-tress·es *n.* a variant spelling of **lady's-tresses.**
La·din (læ'diːn) *n.* a Rhaetian dialect spoken in parts of South Tyrol. Compare **Friulian, Romansch.** [C19: from Italian *ladino*, from Latin *latinus* Latin]
lad·ing ('leɪdɪŋ) *n.* a load; cargo; freight.
la·di·no (lə'diːnəʊ) *n., pl.* **-nos.** an Italian variety of white clover grown as a forage crop in North America. [C20: perhaps from Italian *ladino* (see LADIN), referring to a person or thing from the Italian-speaking area of Switzerland, where the clover is grown]
La·di·no (lə'diːnəʊ) *n.* Also called: **Judaeo-Spanish, Judezmo.** a language of Sephardic Jews, based on Spanish with some Hebrew elements and usually written in Hebrew characters. [from Spanish: Latin]
Lad·is·laus I ('lædɪsˌlɔːs) *or* **Lad·is·las** ('lædɪsˌlæs) *n.* **Saint.** 1040–95, king of Hungary (1077–95). He extended his country's boundaries and suppressed paganism. Feast day: June 27.
la·dle ('leɪdᵊl) *n.* **1.** a long-handled spoon having a deep bowl for serving or transferring liquids: *a soup ladle.* **2.** a large bucket-shaped container for transferring molten metal. ~*vb.* **3.** (*tr.*; often foll. by *out*) to lift or serve out with or as if with a ladle. [Old English *hlædel*, from *hladan* to draw out] —**'la·dle·ˌful** *n.* —**'la·dler** *n.*
la·dle out *vb.* (*tr., adv.*) *Informal.* to distribute (money, gifts, etc.) generously.
La·do·ga (*Russian* 'ladəgə) *n.* **Lake.** a lake in the NW Soviet Union, in the N Leningrad Region and the SW Karelian ASSR: the largest lake in Europe; drains through the River Neva into the Gulf of Finland. Area: about 18 000 sq. km (7000 sq.

miles). Russian name: **La·dozh·sko·ye O·ze·ro** ('ladəʃskəjə 'ɔzɪrə).

La·drone Is·lands (lə'drəʊn) *pl. n.* the former name (1521–1668) of the **Mariana Islands.**

lad's love *n.* another name for **southernwood.**

la·dy ('leɪdɪ) *n., pl.* **·dies. 1.** a woman regarded as having the characteristics of a good family and high social position; female counterpart of **gentleman** (sense 1). **2. a.** a polite name for a woman. **b.** (*as modifier*): *a lady doctor.* **3.** an informal name for **wife. 4. lady of the house.** the female head of the household. **5.** *History.* a woman with proprietary rights and authority, as over a manor. Compare **lord** (sense 3). [Old English *hlǣfdīge, from hlāf* bread + *dīge* kneader, related to *dāh* dough]

La·dy ('leɪdɪ) *n., pl.* **·dies. 1.** (in Britain) a title of honour borne by various classes of women of the peerage. **2. my lady.** a term of address to holders of the title Lady, used esp. by servants. **3. Our Lady.** a title of the Virgin Mary. **4.** *Archaic.* an allegorical prefix for the personifications of certain qualities: *Lady Luck.* **5.** *Chiefly Brit.* the term of address by which certain positions of respect are prefaced when held by women: *Lady Chairman.*

la·dy·bird ('leɪdɪˌbɜːd) *n.* any of various small brightly coloured beetles of the family *Coccinellidae,* such as *Adalia bipunctata* **(two-spotted ladybird),** which has red elytra marked with black spots. Usual U.S. name: **ladybug.**

la·dy boun·ti·ful *n.* an ostentatiously charitable woman. [after a character in George Farquhar's play *The Beaux' Stratagem* (1707)]

La·dy Chap·el *n.* a chapel within a church or cathedral, dedicated to the Virgin Mary.

La·dy Day *n.* **1.** Also called: **Annunciation Day.** March 25, the feast of the Annunciation of the Virgin Mary; one of the four quarter days in England, Wales, and Ireland.

la·dy·fin·ger ('leɪdɪˌfɪŋgə) *or* **la·dy's·fin·ger** *n.* a small finger-shaped sponge cake.

la·dy·fy *or* **la·di·fy** ('leɪdɪˌfaɪ) *vb.* **·fies, ·fy·ing, ·fied.** (*tr.*) to make a lady of (someone).

la·dy-in-wait·ing *n., pl.* **la·dies-in-wait·ing.** a lady of a royal household who attends a queen or princess.

la·dy-kill·er *n. Informal.* a man who is irresistibly fascinating to women. **—'la·dy-ˌkill·ing** *n., adj.*

la·dy·like ('leɪdɪˌlaɪk) *adj.* **1.** like or befitting a lady. **2.** *Derogatory.* (of a man) effeminate. **—'la·dy·ˌlike·ness** *n.*

la·dy·love ('leɪdɪˌlʌv) *n. Now rare.* a beloved woman.

la·dy may·or·ess *n. Brit.* the wife of a lord mayor.

La·dy of the Lake *n.* (in Arthurian legend) another name for **Vivian.**

la·dy's bed·straw *n.* a Eurasian rubiaceous plant, *Galium verum,* with clusters of small yellow flowers.

la·dy's fin·ger *n.* another name for **bhindi.**

La·dy·ship ('leɪdɪˌʃɪp) *n.* (preceded by *your* or *her*) a title used to address or refer to any peeress except a duchess.

la·dy's maid *n.* a maid who assists a woman in dressing.

la·dy's man *n.* a variant spelling of **ladies' man.**

la·dy's man·tle *n.* any of various rosaceous plants of the N temperate genus *Alchemilla,* having small green flowers.

La·dy·smith ('leɪdɪˌsmɪθ) *n.* a city in E South Africa, in W Natal: besieged by Boers for four months (1899–1900) during the Boer War. Pop.: 37 700 (1970).

la·dy·snow ('leɪdɪˌsnəʊ) *n.* a slang word for **cocaine.**

la·dy's-slip·per *n.* any of various orchids of the Eurasian genus *Cypripedium,* esp. *C. calceolus,* having reddish or purple flowers. See also **moccasin flower, cypripedium.**

la·dy's-smock *n.* a N temperate cruciferous plant, *Cardamine pratensis,* with white or rose-pink flowers. Also called: **cuckooflower.**

la·dy's-thumb *n.* the usual U.S. name for **red shank** (the plant).

la·dy's-tress·es *or* **la·dies'-tress·es** *n.* (*functioning as sing. or pl.*) any of various orchids of the genus *Spiranthes,* having spikes of small white fragrant flowers.

La·ën·nec (*French* laɛ'nɛk) *n.* **Re·né Thé·o·phile Hya·cinthe** (rəne teɔfil ja'sɛ̃:t). 1781–1826, French physician, who invented the stethoscope.

La·er·tes (leɪ'ɜːtiːz) *n. Greek myth.* the father of Odysseus.

lae·vo- *or U.S.* **le·vo-** *combining form.* **1.** on or towards the left: *laevorotatory.* **2.** (in chemistry) denoting a laevorotatory compound: *laevulose.* [from Latin *laevus* left]

lae·vo·gy·rate (ˌliːvəʊ'dʒaɪreɪt) *adj.* another word for **laevorotatory.**

lae·vo·ro·ta·tion (ˌliːvəʊrəʊ'teɪʃən) *n.* **1.** a rotation to the left. **2.** an anticlockwise rotation of the plane of polarization of plane-polarized light as a result of its passage through a crystal, liquid, or solution. ~Compare **dextrorotation.**

lae·vo·ro·ta·to·ry (ˌliːvəʊ'rəʊtətərɪ, -trɪ) *or* **lae·vo·ro·ta·ry** *adj.* of, having, or causing laevorotation. Also: **laevogyrate.**

laev·u·lin ('lɛvjʊlɪn) *n.* a polysaccharide occurring in the tubers of certain helianthus plants. [C19: from LAEVULOSE + -IN]

laev·u·lose ('lɛvjʊˌləʊs, -ˌləʊz) *n.* another name for **fructose.** [C19: from LAEVO- + -ULE + -OSE²]

La·fa·yette *or* **La Fa·yette** (*French* lafa'jɛt) *n.* **1. Ma·rie Jo·seph Paul Yves Roch Gil·bert du Mo·tier** (mari ʒozɛf pɔl iːv rɔk ʒilbɛːr dy mɔ'tje), Marquis de Lafayette. 1757–1834, French general and statesman. He fought on the side of the colonists in the War of American Independence and, as commander of the National Guard (1789–91; 1830), he played a leading part in the French Revolution and the revolution of 1830. **2. Ma·rie-Made·leine** (mari ma'dlɛn), Comtesse de Lafayette. 1634–93, French novelist, noted for her historical romance *La Princesse de Clèves* (1678).

La Fon·taine (*French* la fɔ̃'tɛn) *n.* **Jean de** (ʒɑ̃ də). 1621–95, French poet, famous for his *Fables* (1668–94).

La·forgue (*French* la'fɔrg) *n.* **Jules** (ʒyl). 1860–87, French symbolist poet. An originator of free verse, his influence on modern poetry was considerable.

lag¹ (læg) *vb.* **lags, lag·ging, lagged.** (*intr.*) **1.** (often foll. by *behind*) to hang (back) or fall (behind) in movement, progress, development, etc. **2.** to fall away in strength or intensity. **3.** to determine an order of play in certain games, as by rolling marbles towards a line or, in billiards, hitting cue balls up the table against the top cushion in an attempt to bring them back close to the headrail. ~*n.* **4.** the act or state of slowing down or falling behind. **5.** the interval of time between two events, esp. between an action and its effect. **6.** an act of lagging in a game, such as billiards. [C16: of obscure origin]

lag² (læg) *Slang.* ~*n.* **1.** a convict or ex-convict (esp. in the phrase **old lag**). **2.** a term of imprisonment. ~*vb.* **lags, lag·ging, lagged. 3.** (*tr.*) to arrest or put in prison. [C19: of unknown origin]

lag³ (læg) *vb.* **lags, lag·ging, lagged. 1.** (*tr.*) to cover (a pipe, cylinder, etc.) with lagging to prevent loss of heat. ~*n.* **2.** the insulating casing of a steam cylinder, boiler, etc.; lagging. **3.** a stave or lath. [C17: of Scandinavian origin; related to Swedish *lagg* stave]

lag·an ('lægᵊn) *or* **li·gan** ('laɪgᵊn) *n.* goods or wreckage on the sea bed, sometimes attached to a buoy to permit recovery. Compare **flotsam, jetsam.** [C16: from Old French *lagan,* probably of Germanic origin; compare Old Norse *lögn* dragnet]

Lag b'O·mer *Hebrew.* (lag bə'ɔmɛr; *English* læg 'bəʊmə) *n.* a Jewish holiday celebrated on the 18th day of Iyar. [Hebrew, literally: 33rd (day) of the Omer]

la·ge·na (lə'dʒiːnə) *n.* **1.** a bottle with a narrow neck. **2.** an outgrowth of the sacculus in the ear of fishes and amphibians, thought to be homologous to the cochlea of mammals. [C19: Latin, a flask, from Greek *lagēnos*]

la·ger¹ ('lɑːgə) *n.* a light-bodied effervescent beer, stored for varying periods before use. [C19: from German *Lagerbier* beer for storing, from *Lager* storehouse]

la·ger² ('lɑːgə) *n.* a variant spelling of **laager.**

La·ger·kvist (*Swedish* 'lɑːgərkvist) *n.* **Pär (Fabian)** (pæːr). 1891–1974, Swedish novelist and dramatist. His works include the novels *The Dwarf* (1944) and *Barabbas* (1950): Nobel prize for literature 1951.

La·ger·löf (*Swedish* 'lɑːgərˌløːv) *n.* **Sel·ma** ('sɛlma). 1858–1940, Swedish novelist, noted esp. for her children's classic *The Wonderful Adventures of Nils* (1906–07): Nobel prize for literature 1909.

lag·gard ('lægəd) *n.* **1.** a person who lags behind. **2.** a dawdler or straggler. ~*adj.* **3.** *Rare.* sluggish, slow, or dawdling. **—'lag·gard·ly** *adv.* **—'lag·gard·ness** *n.*

lag·ging ('lægɪŋ) *n.* **1.** insulating material wrapped around pipes, boilers, etc., or laid in a roof loft, to prevent loss of heat. **2.** the act or process of applying lagging. **3.** a wooden frame used to support an arch during construction.

la·gniappe *or* **la·gnappe** (læn'jæp, 'lænjæp) *n. Southern U.S. dialect.* a small gift, esp. one given to a customer who makes a purchase. [C19: Louisiana French, from American Spanish *la ñapa,* from Quechua *yápa* addition]

lag·o·morph ('lægəʊˌmɔːf) *n.* any placental mammal of the order *Lagomorpha,* having two pairs of upper incisors specialized for gnawing: includes pikas, rabbits, and hares. [C19: via New Latin from Greek *lagōs* hare; see -MORPH] **—ˌlag·o·'mor·phic** *or* **ˌlag·o·'mor·phous** *adj.*

la·goon *or* **la·gune** (lə'guːn) *n.* **1.** a body of water cut off from the open sea by coral reefs or sand bars. **2.** any small body of water, esp. one adjoining a larger one. [C17: from Italian *laguna,* from Latin *lacūna* pool; see LACUNA]

La·goon Is·lands *pl. n.* a former name of **Tuvala.**

La·gos ('leɪgɒs) *n.* **1.** the chief port and commercial capital of Nigeria, on the Bight of Benin: first settled in the sixteenth century; a slave market until the nineteenth century; ceded to Britain (1861); capital of Nigeria; university (1962). Pop.: 1 060 848 (1975 est.). **2.** a state of SW Nigeria. Capital: Ikeja. Pop.: 1 000 000 (1976 est.). Area: 14 712 sq. km (5679 sq. miles).

La·grange (*French* la'grɑ̃:ʒ) *n.* Comte **Jo·seph Louis** (ʒozɛf 'lwi). 1736–1813, French mathematician and astronomer, noted particularly for his work on harmonics, mechanics, and the calculus of variations.

La Gran·ja (*Spanish* la 'graŋxa) *n.* another name for **San Ildefonso.**

lag screw *n.* a woodscrew with a square head. [from LAG³; the screw was originally used to fasten barrel staves]

Lag·ting *or* **Lag·thing** ('lɑːgtɪŋ) *n.* the upper chamber of the Norwegian parliament. See also **Storting, Odelsting.** [Norwegian, from *lag* law + *ting* parliament]

La Guai·ra *or* **La Guay·ra** (*Spanish* la 'gwaɪra) *n.* the chief seaport of Venezuela, on the Caribbean. Pop.: 20 344 (1971).

La Guar·di·a (lə'gwɑːdɪə) *n.* **Fi·o·rel·lo H(enry)** (ˌfɪə'rɛləʊ). 1882–1947, U.S. politician. As mayor of New York (1933–45), he organized slum-clearance and labour safeguard schemes and suppressed racketeering.

lah (lɑː) *n. Music.* (in tonic solfa) the sixth note of any major scale; submediant. [C14: see GAMUT]

lah-di-dah (ˌlɑːdiː'dɑː) *adj., n. Informal.* a variant spelling of **la-di-da.**

Lahn·da ('lɑːndə) *n.* a language or group of dialects of Pakistan, belonging to the Indic branch of the Indo-European family and closely related to Punjabi.

La Hogue (*French* la 'ɔg) *n.* a roadstead off the NW coast of France: scene of the defeat of the French by the Dutch and English fleet (1692).

La+hore (lə'hɔː) *n.* **1.** a city in NE Pakistan: capital of the former province of West Pakistan (1955–70); University of the Punjab (1882). Pop.: 2 165 372 (1972). **2.** a variety of large domestic fancy pigeon having a black-and-white plumage.

Lah+ti (*Finnish* 'lahti) *n.* a town in S Finland: site of the main Finnish radio and television stations; furniture industry. Pop.: 88 844 (1970).

Lai+bach ('laɪbax) *n.* the German name for **Ljubljana.**

la·ic ('leɪɪk) *adj. also* **la·i·cal. 1.** of or involving the laity; secular. ~*n.* **2.** a rare word for **layman.** [C15: from Late Latin *lāicus* LAY[3]] —**'la·i+cal+ly** *adv.* —**'la·i·cism** *n.*

la·i·cize *or* **la·i·cise** ('leɪɪˌsaɪz) *vb.* (*tr.*) to withdraw clerical or ecclesiastical character or status from (an institution, building, etc.). —**ˌla·i·ci·'za+tion** *or* **ˌla·i·ci·'sa+tion** *n.*

laid (leɪd) *vb.* the past tense or past participle of **lay**[1].

laid pa+per *n.* paper with a regular mesh impressed upon it by the dandy roller on a paper-making machine. Compare **wove paper.**

laik (leɪk) *vb. Northern English dialect.* **1.** (when *intr.*, often foll. by *about*) to play (a game, etc.). **2.** (*intr.*) to be on holiday, esp. to take a day off work. **3.** (*intr.*) to be unemployed. [C14: *leiken*, from Old Norse *leika;* related to Old English *lacan* to manoeuvre; compare LARK[2]]

lain (leɪn) *vb.* the past participle of **lie**[2].

Laing (læŋ) *n.* **R(onald) D(avid).** born 1927, Scottish psychiatrist; his best known books include *The Divided Self* (1960), *The Politics of Experience and the Bird of Paradise* (1967), and *Knots* (1970).

lair (lɛə) *n.* **1.** the resting place of a wild animal. **2.** *Informal.* a place of seclusion or hiding. ~*vb.* **3.** (*intr.*) (esp. of a wild animal) to retreat to or rest in a lair. **4.** (*tr.*) to drive or place (an animal) in a lair. [Old English *leger;* related to LIE[2] and Old High German *leger* bed]

laird (lɛəd) *n. Scot.* a landowner, esp. of a large estate. [C15: Scottish variant of LORD]

lair·y ('lɛərɪ) *adj.* **lair·i·er, lair·i·est.** *Austral. slang.* gaudy or flashy. [C20: from LEERY]

lais+sez al+ler *or* ***lais+ser al+ler*** *French.* (lɛse a'le) *n.* lack of constraint; freedom. [literally: let go]

lais+sez faire *or* ***lais+ser faire*** *French.* (lɛse 'fɛːr; *English* ˌlɛseɪ 'fɛə) *n.* **1. a.** Also called: **individualism.** the doctrine of unrestricted freedom in commerce, esp. for private interests. **b.** (*as modifier*): *a laissez-faire economy.* **2.** indifference or noninterference, esp. in the affairs of others. [French, literally: let (them) act] —**ˌlais·sez-'faire·ism** *or* **ˌlais·ser-'faire·ism** *n.*

lais+sez pas+ser *or* ***lais+ser pas+ser*** *French.* (lɛse pa'se) *n.* a document granting unrestricted access or movement to its holder. [literally: let pass]

la+i·ty ('leɪɪtɪ) *n.* **1.** laymen, as distinguished from clergymen. **2.** all people not of a specific occupation. [C16: from LAY[3]]

La·ius ('laɪəs) *n. Greek myth.* a king of Thebes, killed by his son Oedipus, who did not know of their relationship.

lake[1] (leɪk) *n.* **1.** an expanse of water entirely surrounded by land and unconnected to the sea except by rivers or streams. Related adj.: **lacustrine. 2.** anything resembling this. [C13 *lac*, via Old French from Latin *lacus* basin]

lake[2] (leɪk) *n.* **1.** a bright pigment used in textile dyeing and printing inks, produced by the combination of an organic colouring matter with an inorganic compound, usually a metallic salt, oxide, or hydroxide. See also **mordant. 2.** a red dye obtained by combining a metallic compound with cochineal. [C17: variant of LAC[1]]

Lake Dis+trict *n.* a region of lakes and mountains in NW England, in Cumbria: includes England's largest lake (Windermere) and highest mountain (Scafell Pike); national park; literary associations (the Lake Poets); tourist region. Also called: **Lakeland.**

lake dwell+ing *n.* a dwelling, esp. in prehistoric villages, constructed on platforms supported by wooden piles driven into the bottom of a lake. —**lake dwell+er** *n.*

lake her+ring *n.* **1.** a whitefish, *Coregonus artedi*, of deep North American lakes. **2.** another name for **powan.**

Lake+land ('leɪkˌlænd) *n.* **1.** another name for the **Lake District.** ~*adj.* **2.** of or relating to the Lake District.

Lake+land ter+ri+er *n.* a wire-haired breed of terrier, originally from the Lake District and used for hunting.

Lake of the Woods *n.* a lake in N central North America, mostly in SW Ontario (Canada): fed chiefly by the Rainy River; drains into Lake Winnipeg by the Winnipeg River; many islands; tourist region. Area: 3846 sq. km (1485 sq. miles).

Lake Po·ets *pl. n.* the English poets Wordsworth, Coleridge, and Southey, who lived in and drew inspiration from the Lake District at the beginning of the 19th century.

lak+er ('leɪkə) *n.* a cargo vessel used on lakes.

Lake Suc+cess *n.* a village in SE New York State, on W Long Island: headquarters of the United Nations Security Council from 1946 to 1951. Pop.: 3254 (1970).

lakh *or* **lac** (lɑːk) *n.* (in India) the number 100 000, esp. when referring to this sum of rupees. [C17: from Hindi *lākh*, ultimately from Sanskrit *lakshā* a sign]

lak+sa ('læksa) *n.* (in Malaysia) a dish of Chinese origin consisting of rice noodles served in curry or hot soup. [from Malay: ten thousand]

Lak+shad+weep Is+lands (læk'ʃædwiːp) *pl. n.* a group of 26 coral islands and reefs in the Arabian Sea, off the SW coast of India: a union territory of India since 1956. Administrative centre: Kavaratti Island. Pop.: 31 810 (1971). Area: 28 sq. km (11 sq. miles). Former name (until 1973): **Laccadive, Minicoy and Amindivi Islands.**

lak·y ('leɪkɪ) *adj.* **lak·i·er, lak·i·est.** of the reddish colour of the pigment lake.

La·la ('lɑːlɑː) *n.* a title or form of address, equivalent to *Mr.*, used in India. [Hindi]

la+lang ('lɑːlɑːŋ) *n.* a coarse weedy Malaysian grass, *Imperata arundinacea.* [Malay]

la+la+pa+loo+za (ˌlɒləpə'luːzə) *n.* a variant spelling of **lollapalooza.**

-la·li·a *combining form.* indicating a speech defect or abnormality: *coprolalia; echolalia.* [New Latin, from Greek *lalia* chatter, from *lalein* to babble]

La Lí+ne·a (*Spanish* la 'linea) *n.* a town in SW Spain, on the Bay of Gibraltar. Pop.: 52 127 (1970). Official name: **La Lí+ne·a de la Con+cep+ción** (ðe la ˌkonθep'θjon).

Lal+lans ('lælənz) *or* **Lal+lan** ('lælən) *n.* **1.** a dialect of English spoken and written in the Lowlands of Scotland, still used as a literary language. **2.** (*modifier*) of or relating to the Lowlands of Scotland or their dialect. [Scottish variant of LOWLANDS]

lal+la+tion (læ'leɪʃən) *n. Phonetics.* a defect of speech consisting of the pronunciation of (r) as (l). [C17: from Latin *lallāre* to sing lullaby, of imitative origin]

lal+ly+gag ('lælɪˌgæg) *vb.* **+gags, +gag+ging, +gagged.** (*intr.*) *U.S.* to loiter aimlessly. [C20: of unknown origin]

lam[1] (læm) *vb.* **lams, lam+ming, lammed.** *Slang.* **1.** (*tr.*) to thrash or beat. **2.** (*intr.;* usually foll. by *into* or *out*) to make a sweeping stroke or blow. [C16: from Scandinavian; related to Old Norse *lemja*]

lam[2] (læm) *U.S. slang.* ~*n.* **1.** a sudden flight or escape, esp. to avoid arrest. **2. on the lam.** making an escape. **3. take it on the lam.** to escape or flee, esp. from the police. ~*vb.* **lams, lam+ming, lammed. 4.** (*intr.*) to escape or flee. [C19: perhaps from LAM[1]; (hence, to be off)]

lam. *abbrev. for* laminated.

Lam. *Bible. abbrev. for* Lamentations.

la·ma ('lɑːmə) *n.* a priest or monk of Lamaism. [C17: from Tibetan *blama*]

La+ma+ism ('lɑːməˌɪzəm) *n.* the Mahayana form of Buddhism of Tibet and Mongolia. See also **Dalai Lama.** —**'La+ma+ist** *n., adj.* —**ˌLa+ma+'is+tic** *adj.*

La Man+cha (*Spanish* la 'mantʃa) *n.* a plateau of central Spain, between the mountains of Toledo and the hills of Cuenca: traditionally associated with episodes in *Don Quixote.* Average height: 600 m (2000 ft.).

La Manche (*French* la 'mɑ̃ːʃ) *n.* See **Manche** (sense 2).

La·marck (*French* la'mark) *n.* **Jean Bap·tiste Pierre An·toine de Mo·net** (ʒã batist pjɛːr ãtwan də mɔ'nɛ), Chevalier de Lamarck. 1744–1829, French naturalist. He outlined his theory of organic evolution (Lamarckism) in *Philosophie zoologique* (1809).

La+marck+i·an (lɑː'mɑːkɪən) *adj.* **1.** of or relating to Lamarck. ~*n.* **2.** a supporter of Lamarckism.

La+marck+ism (lɑː'mɑːkɪzəm) *n.* the theory of organic evolution proposed by Lamarck, based on the principle that characteristics of an organism modified during its lifetime are inheritable. See also **acquired characteristic, Neo-Lamarckism.**

La·mar·tine (*French* lamar'tin) *n.* **Al·phonse Ma·rie Louis de Prat de** (alfɔ̃ːs mari lwi də 'pra də). 1790–1869, French romantic poet, historian, and statesman: his works include *Méditations poétiques* (1820) and *Histoire des Girondins* (1847).

la+ma+ser·y ('lɑːməsərɪ) *n., pl.* **+ser·ies.** a monastery of lamas. [C19: from French *lamaserie*, from LAMA + French *-serie*, from Persian *serāī* palace]

lamb (læm) *n.* **1.** the young of a sheep. **2.** the meat of a young sheep. **3.** a person, esp. a child, who is innocent, meek, good, etc. **4.** a person easily deceived. **5. like a lamb to the slaughter. a.** without resistance. **b.** innocently. ~*vb.* **6.** (*intr.*) (of a ewe) to give birth. ~See also **lamb down.** [Old English *lamb*, from Germanic; compare German *Lamm*, Old High German and Old Norse *lamb*] —**'lamb+ˌlike** *adj.*

Lamb[1] (læm) *n.* **the.** a title given to Christ in the New Testament.

Lamb[2] (læm) *n.* **1. Charles,** pen name *Elia.* 1775–1834, English essayist and critic. He collaborated with his sister Mary on *Tales from Shakespeare* (1807). His other works include *Specimens of English Dramatic Poets* (1808) and the largely autobiographical essays collected in *Essays of Elia* (1823; 1833). **2. Wil·liam.** See (2nd Viscount) **Melbourne. 3. Wil·lis Eu·gene.** born 1913, U.S. physicist. He detected the small difference in energy between two states of the hydrogen atom (**Lamb shift**). Nobel prize for physics 1955.

Lam+ba+ré+né (*French* lãbare'ne) *n.* a town in W Gabon on the Ogooué River: site of the hospital built by Albert Schweitzer, who died and was buried here (1965). Pop.: 35 322 (1972).

lam+baste (læm'beɪst) *or* **lam+bast** *vb.* (*tr.*) *Slang.* **1.** to beat or whip severely. **2.** to reprimand or scold. [C17: perhaps from LAM[1] + BASTE[3]]

lamb+da ('læmdə) *n.* the 11th letter of the Greek alphabet (Λ, λ), a consonant transliterated as *l.* [C14: from Greek, from Semitic; related to LAMED]

lamb+da+cism ('læmdəˌsɪzəm) *n. Phonetics.* **1.** excessive use or idiosyncratic pronunciation of *l.* **2.** another word for **lallation.** [C17: from Late Latin *labdacismus*, from Greek]

lamb+doid ('læmdɔɪd) *or* **lamb+doi·dal** *adj.* **1.** having the shape of the Greek letter lambda. **2.** of or denoting the suture near the back of the skull between the occipital and parietal bones. [C16: via French from Greek *lambdoeidēs*]

lamb down *vb.* (*tr., adv.*) *Austral. informal.* to persuade (someone) to spend all his money.

lam+bent ('læmbənt) *adj.* **1.** (esp. of a flame) flickering softly over a surface. **2.** glowing with soft radiance. **3.** (of wit or humour) light or brilliant. [C17: from the present participle of Latin *lambere* to lick] —**'lam+ben+cy** *n.* —**'lam+bent+ly** *adv.*

lam+bert ('læmbət) *n.* the cgs unit of illumination, equal to 1 lumen per square centimetre. Symbol: L [named after J. H. *Lambert* (1728–77), German mathematician and physicist]

Lam·bert ('læmbət) *n.* **Con·stant.** 1905–51, English composer and conductor. His works include much ballet music and *The Rio Grande* (1929), a work for chorus, orchestra, and piano, using jazz idioms.

Lam+beth ('læmbəθ) *n.* **1.** a borough of S Greater London, on the Thames: contains **Lambeth Palace** (the London residence of the Archbishop of Canterbury). Pop.: 290 300 (1976 est.). **2.** the Archbishop of Canterbury in his official capacity.

Lam+beth Con+fer+ence *n.* the decennial conference of Anglican bishops, begun in 1867. See also **Lambeth Quadrilateral.**

Lam+beth Quad+ri+lat+er+al *n.* the four essentials agreed upon at the Lambeth Conference of 1888 for a United Christian Church, namely, the Holy Scriptures, the Apostles' Creed, the sacraments of baptism and Holy Communion, and the historic episcopate.

Lam+beth walk *n. Chiefly Brit.* a line dance popular in the 1930s.

lamb+kin ('læmkɪn) *or* **lamb·ie** *n.* **1.** a small or young lamb. **2.** a term of affection for a small endearing child.

Lamb of God *n.* a title given to Christ in the New Testament, probably with reference to his sacrificial death.

lam+bre+quin ('læmbrɪkɪn, 'læmbə-) *n.* **1.** an ornamental hanging covering the edge of a shelf or the upper part of a window or door. **2. a.** a border pattern giving a draped effect, used on ceramics, etc. **b.** (*as modifier*): *a lambrequin pattern.* **3.** (*often pl.*) a scarf worn over a helmet. **4.** *Heraldry.* another name for **mantling.** [C18: from French, from Dutch *lamperkin* (unattested), diminutive of *lamper* veil]

lamb+skin ('læm,skɪn) *n.* **1.** the skin of a lamb, esp. with the wool still on. **2. a.** a material or garment prepared from this skin. **b.** (*as modifier*): *a lambskin coat.* **3.** a cotton or woollen fabric resembling this skin.

lamb's let+tuce *n.* another name for **corn salad.**

lamb's-quar·ters *n., pl.* **lamb's-quar·ters.** a U.S. name for **fat hen.**

lamb's tails *pl. n.* the pendulous catkins of the hazel tree.

LAMDA *abbrev. for* London Academy of Music and Dramatic Art.

lame[1] (leɪm) *adj.* **1.** disabled or crippled in the legs or feet. **2.** painful or weak: *a lame back.* **3.** not effective or enthusiastic: *a lame try.* **4.** *U.S. slang.* conventional or uninspiring. ~*vb.* **5.** (*tr.*) to make lame. [Old English *lama;* related to Old Norse *lami,* German *lahm*] —**'lame+ly** *adv.* —**'lame+ness** *n.*

lame[2] (leɪm) *n.* one of the overlapping metal plates used in armour after about 1330; splint. [C16: via Old French from Latin *lāmina* a thin plate, LAMINA]

la·mé ('lɑːmeɪ) *n.* **a.** a fabric of silk, cotton, or wool interwoven with threads of metal. **b.** (*as modifier*): *a gold lamé gown.* [from French, from Old French *lame* gold or silver thread, thin plate, from Latin *lāmina* thin plate]

lame+brain ('leɪm,breɪn) *n. Informal.* a stupid or slow-witted person.

la+med ('lɑːmɪd; *Hebrew* 'lamed) *n.* the 12th letter in the Hebrew alphabet (ל), transliterated as *l.* Also: **lamedh.** [from Hebrew, literally: ox goad (from its shape)]

lame duck *n. Informal.* **1.** a person or thing that is disabled or ineffectual. **2.** *Stock Exchange.* a speculator who cannot discharge his liabilities. **3.** *U.S.* **a.** an elected official or body of officials remaining in office in the interval between the election and inauguration of a successor. **b.** (*as modifier*): *a lame-duck president.* **4.** (*modifier*) *U.S.* designating a term of office after which the officeholder will not run for re-election.

la+mel+la (lə'mɛlə) *n., pl.* **+lae** (-liː) *or* **+las. 1.** a thin layer, plate, or membrane, esp. any of the calcified layers of which bone is formed. **2.** *Botany.* **a.** any of the spore-bearing gills of a mushroom. **b.** any of the membranes in a chloroplast. **c.** Also called: **middle lamella.** a layer of pectin cementing together adjacent cells. **3.** one of a number of timber, metal, or concrete members connected along a pattern of intersecting diagonal lines to form a framed vaulted roof structure. **4.** any thin sheet of material or thin layer in a fluid. [C17: New Latin, from Latin, diminutive of *lāmina* thin plate] —**la+'mel+lar, lam+el+late** ('læmɪ,leɪt, -lɪt; lə'mɛleɪt, -lɪt), *or* **la+mel+lose** (lə'mɛləʊs, 'læmɪ,ləʊs) *adj.* —**la+'mel+lar+ly** *or* **'lam+el+late+ly** *adv.* —**'lam+el+,lat+ed** *adj.* —**,lam+el+'la+tion** *n.* —**lam+el+los+i+ty** (,læmə'lɒsɪtɪ) *n.*

la·mel·li- *combining form.* indicating lamella or lamellae: *lamellibranch.*

la+mel+li+branch (lə'mɛlɪ,bræŋk) *n., adj.* another word for **bivalve** (senses 1, 2). [C19: from New Latin *lamellibranchia* plate-gilled (animals); see LAMELLA, BRANCHIA] —**la+,mel+li+'bran+chi+ate** *adj., n.*

la+mel+li+corn (lə'mɛlɪ,kɔːn) *n.* **1.** any beetle of the superfamily *Lamellicornia,* having flattened terminal plates to the antennae: includes the scarabs and stag beetles. ~*adj.* **2.** of, relating to, or belonging to the *Lamellicornia.* **3.** designating antennae with platelike terminal segments. [C19: from New Latin *Lamellicornia* plate-horned (animals)]

la+mel+li+form (lə'mɛlɪ,fɔːm) *adj.* shaped like a lamella; platelike: *lamelliform antennae.*

la+mel+li+ros+tral (lə,mɛlɪ'rɒstrəl) *or* **la+mel+li+ros+trate** (lə,mɛlɪ'rɒstreɪt) *adj.* (of ducks, geese, etc.) having a bill fringed with thin plates on the inner edge for straining water from food. [C19: from New Latin *lāmellirostris,* from LAMELLA + *rostrum* beak]

la+ment (lə'mɛnt) *vb.* **1.** to feel or express sorrow, remorse, or regret (for or over). ~*n.* **2.** an expression of sorrow. **3.** a poem or song in which a death is lamented. [C16: from Latin *lāmentum*] —**la+'ment+er** *n.* —**la+'ment+ing+ly** *adv.*

lam+en+ta·ble ('læməntəbᵊl) *adj.* **1.** wretched, deplorable, or distressing. **2.** an archaic word for **mournful.** —**'lam+en+ta·ble+ness** *n.* —**'lam+en+ta·bly** *adv.*

la+men+ta+tion (,læmɛn'teɪʃən) *n.* **1.** a lament; expression of sorrow. **2.** the act of lamenting.

Lam+en+ta+tions (,læmɛn'teɪʃənz) *n.* **1.** a book of the Old Testament, traditionally ascribed to the prophet Jeremiah, lamenting the destruction of Jerusalem. **2.** a musical setting of these poems.

la+ment+ed (lə'mɛntɪd) *adj.* grieved for or regretted (often in the phrase **late lamented**): *our late lamented employer.* —**la+'ment+ed+ly** *adv.*

la+mi·a ('leɪmɪə) *n., pl.* **+mi·as** *or* **+mi·ae** (-mɪ,iː). **1.** *Classical myth.* one of a class of female monsters depicted with a snake's body and a woman's head and breasts. **2.** a vampire or sorceress. [C14: via Latin from Greek *Lamia*]

lam·i+na ('læmɪnə) *n., pl.* **+nae** (-,niː) *or* **+nas. 1.** a thin plate, esp. of bone or mineral. **2.** *Botany.* the flat blade of a leaf, petal, or thallus. [C17: New Latin, from Latin: thin plate] —**'lam·i+nar** *or* **lam·i+nose** ('læmɪ,nəʊs, -,nəʊz) *adj.*

lam·i+nar flow *n.* nonturbulent motion of a fluid in which parallel layers have different relative velocities. Compare **turbulent flow.** See also **streamline flow.**

lam·i+nar·i·a (,læmɪ'nɛərɪə) *n.* any brown seaweeds of the genus *Laminaria,* having large fluted leathery fronds. [C19: genus name formed from Latin *lamina* plate]

lam·i+nate *vb.* ('læmɪ,neɪt). **1.** (*tr.*) to make (material in sheet form) by bonding together two or more thin sheets. **2.** to split or be split into thin sheets. **3.** (*tr.*) to beat, form, or press (material, esp. metal) into thin sheets. **4.** (*tr.*) to cover or overlay with a thin sheet of material. ~*n.* ('læmɪ,neɪt, -nɪt). **5.** a material made by bonding together two or more sheets. ~*adj.* ('læmɪ,neɪt, -nɪt). **6.** having or composed of lamina; laminated. [C17: from New Latin *lāminātus* plated] —**lam·i+na·ble** ('læmɪnəbᵊl) *adj.* —**'lam·i+,na+tor** *n.*

lam·i+na+tion (,læmɪ'neɪʃən) *n.* **1.** the act of laminating or the state of being laminated. **2.** a layered structure. **3.** a layer; lamina.

lam+ing+ton ('læmɪŋtən) *n. Austral.* a cube of sponge cake coated in chocolate and dried coconut. [C20 (in the earlier sense: a homburg hat): named after Baron *Lamington,* governor of Queensland (1896–1901)]

lam·i+ni+tis (,læmɪ'naɪtɪs) *n.* inflammation of the laminated tissue structure to which the hoof of a horse is attached. Also called: **founder.** [C19: from New Latin, from LAMINA + -ITIS]

Lam+mas ('læməs) *n.* **1.** *R.C. Church.* Aug. 1, held as a feast, commemorating St. Peter's miraculous deliverance from prison. **2.** Also called: **Lammas Day.** the same day formerly observed in England as a harvest festival. In Scotland Lammas is a quarter day. [Old English *hlāfmæsse,* loaf mass]

Lam·mas+tide ('læməs,taɪd) *n. Archaic.* the season of Lammas.

lam+mer+gei+er *or* **lam+mer+gey+er** ('læmə,gaɪə) *n.* a rare vulture, *Gypaetus barbatus,* of S Europe, Africa, and Asia, with dark wings, a pale breast, and black feathers around the bill: family *Accipitridae* (hawks). Also called: **bearded vulture.** [C19: from German *Lämmergeier,* from *Lämmer* lambs + *Geier* vulture]

lamp (læmp) *n.* **1. a.** any of a number of devices that produce illumination: *an electric lamp; a gas lamp; an oil lamp.* **b.** (*in combination*): *lampshade.* **2.** a device for holding one or more electric light bulbs: *a table lamp.* **3.** a vessel in which a liquid fuel is burned to supply illumination. **4.** any of a variety of devices that produce radiation, esp. for therapeutic purposes: *an ultraviolet lamp.* [C13 *lampe,* via Old French from Latin *lampas,* from Greek, from *lampein* to shine]

lam+pas[1] ('læmpəs) *or* **lam+pers** ('læmpəz) *n.* a swelling of the mucous membrane of the hard palate of horses. [C16: from Old French; origin obscure]

lam+pas[2] ('læmpəs) *n.* an ornate damask-like cloth of cotton or silk and cotton, used in upholstery. [C14 (a kind of crepe): probably from Middle Dutch *lampers*]

lamp+black ('læmp,blæk) *n.* a finely divided form of almost pure carbon produced by the incomplete combustion of organic compounds, such as natural gas, used in making carbon electrodes and dynamo brushes and as a pigment.

lamp chim+ney *n.* a glass tube that surrounds the wick in an oil lamp.

Lam+pe·du+sa (,læmpɪ'djuːzə) *n.* an island in the Mediterranean, between Malta and Tunisia. Area: about 21 sq. km (8 sq. miles).

lam+per eel ('læmpə) *n.* another name for **lamprey.** [C19 *lamper,* variant of LAMPREY]

lam+pern ('læmpən) *n.* a migratory European lamprey, *Lampetra fluviatilis,* that spawns in rivers. Also called: **river lamprey.** [C14 *laumprun,* from Old French, from *lampreie* LAMPREY]

lam+pi·on ('læmpɪən) *n.* an oil-burning lamp. [C19: from French via Italian *lampione,* from Old French *lampe* LAMP]

lamp+light·er ('læmp,laɪtə) *n.* **1.** (formerly) a person who lit and extinguished street lamps, esp. gas ones. **2.** *Chiefly U.S.* any of various devices used to light lamps.

lam+poon (læm'puːn) *n.* **1.** a satire in prose or verse ridiculing a person, literary work, etc. ~*vb.* **2.** (*tr.*) to attack or satirize in a lampoon. [C17: from French *lampon,* perhaps from *lampons* let us drink (frequently used as a refrain in poems)] —**lam+'poon+er** *or* **lam+'poon+ist** *n.* —**lam+'poon+er·y** *n.*

lamp+post ('læmp,pəʊst) *n.* a post supporting a lamp, esp. in a street.

lam+prey ('læmprɪ) *n.* any eel-like cyclostome vertebrate of the family *Petromyzonidae,* having a round sucking mouth for clinging to and feeding on the blood of other animals. Also called: **lamper eel.** See also **sea lamprey.** [C13: from Old French *lamproie,* from Late Latin *lamprēda;* origin obscure]

lam+pro+phyre ('læmprə,faɪə) *n.* any of a group of basic igneous rocks consisting of feldspar and ferromagnesian minerals, esp. biotite: occurring as dykes and minor intrusions. [from Greek *lampros* bright + *-phyre,* from PORPHYRY]

lamp shell *n.* another name for a **brachiopod.** [C19: from its likeness in shape to an ancient Roman oil lamp]

lamp stan+dard *n.* a tall metal or concrete post supporting a street lamp.

la+na·i (lɑː'nɑːɪ, lə'naɪ) *n.* a Hawaiian word for **veranda.**

La+na·i (lɑː'nɑːɪ, lə'naɪ) *n.* an island in central Hawaii, west of Maui Island. Pop.: 2204 (1970). Area: 363 sq. km. (140 sq. miles).

Lan+ark ('lænək) *n.* (until 1975) a county of S Scotland, now part of Strathclyde region.

la+nate ('leɪneɪt) *or* **la+nose** ('leɪnəʊs, -nəʊz) *adj. Biology.* having or consisting of a woolly covering of hairs. [C18: from Latin *lānātus,* from *lāna* wool]

Lan+ca+shire ('læŋkə,ʃɪə, -ʃə) *n.* **1.** a county of NW England, on the Irish Sea: became a county palatine in 1351 and a duchy attached to the Crown; much reduced in size after the 1974 boundary changes, losing the Furness district to Cumbria and much of the south to Greater Manchester, Merseyside, and Cheshire. It was traditionally a cotton textiles manufacturing region. Administrative centre: Preston. Pop.: 1 375 500 (1976 est.). Area: 3004 sq. km (1160 sq. miles). Abbrev.: **Lancs. 2.** a mild whitish-coloured cheese with a crumbly texture.

Lan·cas·ter[1] ('læŋkəstə, 'læŋ,kæstə) *n.* the English royal house that reigned from 1399 to 1461.

Lan+cas+ter[2] ('læŋkəstə) *n.* a city in NW England, former county town of Lancashire, on the River Lune: castle (built on the site of a Roman camp); university (1964). Pop.: 49 525 (1971).

Lan+cas+tri·an (læŋ'kæstrɪən) *n.* **1.** a native or resident of Lancashire or Lancaster. **2.** an adherent of the house of Lancaster in the Wars of the Roses. Compare **Yorkist.** ~*adj.* **3.** of or relating to Lancashire or Lancaster. **4.** of or relating to the house of Lancaster.

lance (lɑːns) *n.* **1.** a long weapon with a pointed head used by horsemen to unhorse or injure an opponent. **2.** a similar weapon used for hunting, whaling, etc. **3.** *Surgery.* another name for **lancet. 4.** short for **sand lance** (another name for **sand eel**). **5. break a lance (with).** to engage in argument (with someone). ~*vb.* **6.** (*tr.*) to pierce (an abscess or boil) with a lancet to drain off pus. [C13 *launce,* from Old French *lance,* from Latin *lancea*]

lance cor+po+ral *n.* a noncommissioned officer of the lowest rank in the British Army.

lance+jack ('lɑːns,dʒæk) *n. Brit. military slang.* a lance corporal.

lance+let ('lɑːnslɪt) *n.* any of several marine animals of the genus *Amphioxus,* esp. *A. lanceolatus,* that are closely related to the vertebrates: subphylum *Cephalochordata* (cephalochordates). Also called: **amphioxus.** [C19: referring to the slender shape]

Lance·lot ('lɑːnslət) *n.* (in Arthurian legend) one of the Knights of the Round Table; the lover of Queen Guinevere.

lan+ce·o+late ('lɑːnsɪə,leɪt, -lɪt) *adj.* narrow and tapering to a point at each end: *lanceolate leaves.* [C18: from Late Latin *lanceolātus,* from *lanceola* small LANCE]

lanc+er ('lɑːnsə) *n.* **1.** (formerly) a cavalryman armed with a lance. **2. a.** a member of a regiment retaining such a title. **b.** (*pl.; cap. when part of a name*): *the 21st Lancers.*

lance rest *n.* a hinged bracket on the breastplate of a medieval horseman on which the lance was rested.

lan+cers ('lɑːnsəz) *or* **lan+ciers** (læn'sɪəz) *n.* (*functioning as sing.*) **1.** a quadrille for eight or sixteen couples. **2.** a piece of music composed for this dance.

lance ser+geant *n.* a corporal acting as a sergeant, usually on a temporary basis and without additional pay.

lan+cet ('lɑːnsɪt) *n.* **1.** Also called: **lance.** a pointed surgical knife with two sharp edges. **2.** short for **lancet arch** or **lancet window.** [C15 *lancette,* from Old French: small LANCE]

lan+cet arch *n.* a narrow acutely pointed arch having two centres of equal radii. Sometimes shortened to **lancet.** Also called: **acute arch, Gothic arch, pointed arch, ogive.**

lan+cet+ed ('lɑːnsɪtɪd) *adj. Architect.* having one or more lancet arches or windows.

lan+cet fish *n.* either of two deep-sea teleost fishes, *Alepisaurus ferox* or *A. borealis,* having a long body with a long sail-like dorsal fin: family *Alepisauridae.*

lan+cet win+dow *n.* a narrow window having a lancet arch. Sometimes shortened to **lancet.**

lance+wood ('lɑːns,wʊd) *n.* **1.** any of various tropical trees, esp. *Oxandra lanceolata,* yielding a tough elastic wood: family *Annonaceae.* **2.** the wood of any of these trees.

Lan+chow *or* **Lan-chou** ('læn'tʃaʊ) *n.* a city in N China, capital of Kansu province, on the Yellow River: situated on the main route between China and the West. Pop.: 1 450 000 (1970 est.).

lan+cin+ate ('lɑːnsɪ,neɪt) *adj.* (esp. of pain) sharp or cutting. [C17: from Latin *lancinātus* pierced, rent; related to *lacer* mangled] —**,lan+ci+'na+tion** *n.*

Lancs. *abbrev. for* Lancashire.

land (lænd) *n.* **1.** the solid part of the surface of the earth as distinct from seas, lakes, etc. Related adj.: **terrestrial. 2. a.** ground, esp. with reference to its use, quality, etc. **b.** (*in combination*): *land-grabber.* **3.** rural or agricultural areas as contrasted with urban ones. **4.** farming as an occupation or way of life. **5.** *Law.* **a.** any tract of ground capable of being owned as property, together with any buildings on it, extending above and below the surface. **b.** any hereditament, tenement, or other interest; realty. **6. a.** a country, region, or area. **b.** the people of a country, etc. **7.** a realm, sphere, or domain. **8.** *Economics.* the factor of production consisting of all natural resources. **9.** the unindented part of a grooved surface, esp. one of the ridges inside a rifle bore. **10. how the land lies.** the prevailing conditions or state of affairs. ~*vb.* **11.** to transfer (something) or go from a ship or boat to the shore: *land the cargo.* **12.** (*intr.*) to come to or touch shore. **13.** to come down or bring (something) down to earth after a flight or jump. **14.** to come or bring to some point, condition, or state. **15.** (*tr.*) *Angling.* to retrieve (a hooked fish) from the water. **16.** (*tr.*) *Informal.* to win or obtain: *to land a job.* **17.** (*tr.*) *Informal.* to deliver (a blow). ~See also **land up, land with.** [Old English; compare Old Norse, Gothic *land,* Old High German *lant*] —**'land+less** *adj.* —**'land+less+ness** *n.*

Land (lænd) *n.* **Ed·win Her·bert.** born 1909, U.S. inventor of the Polaroid Land camera.

land a·gent *n.* **1.** a person who administers a landed estate and its tenancies. **2.** a person who acts as an agent for the sale of land. —**land a·gen+cy** *n.*

land+am+mann ('lændəmən) *n.* (*sometimes cap.*) the chairman of the governing council in any of several Swiss cantons. [C18: Swiss German, from *Land* country + *Ammann,* from *Amt* office + *Mann* MAN]

lan+dau ('lændɔː) *n.* a four-wheeled horse-drawn carriage with two folding hoods that meet over the middle of the passenger compartment. [C18: named after *Landau,* (a town in Bavaria) where it was first made]

Lan·dau (*Russian* lan'daʊ) *n.* **Lev Da·vi·do·vich** (ljɛf da'vidəvitʃ). 1908–68, Soviet physicist, noted for his researches on quantum theory and his work on the theories of solids and liquids: Nobel prize for physics 1962.

lan+dau+let *or* **lan+dau+lette** (,lændɔː'lɛt) *n.* **1.** a small landau. **2.** *U.S.* an early type of car with a folding hood over the passenger seats and an open driver's seat.

land bank *n.* a bank that issues banknotes on the security of property.

land bridge *n.* (in zoogeography) a connecting tract of land between two continents, enabling animals to pass from one continent to the other.

land crab *n.* any of various crabs, esp. of the tropical family *Gecarcinidae,* that are adapted to a partly terrestrial life.

land+ed ('lændɪd) *adj.* **1.** owning land: *landed gentry.* **2.** consisting of or including land: *a landed estate.*

Landes (*French* lɑ̃ːd) *n.* **1.** a department of SW France, in Aquitaine region. Capital: Mont-de-Marsan. Pop.: 298 585 (1975). Area: 9364 sq. km (3652 sq. miles). **2.** a region of SW France, on the Bay of Biscay: occupies most of the Landes department and parts of Gironde and Lot-et-Garonne; consists chiefly of the most extensive forest in France. Area: 14 000 sq. km (5400 sq. miles).

Lan+des+haupt+mann ('lɑːndɪs,haʊptmən) *n.* the head of government in an Austrian state. [C20: from German, from *Land* country + *Hauptmann* leader]

land+fall ('lænd,fɔːl) *n.* **1.** the act of sighting or nearing land, esp. from the sea. **2.** the land sighted or neared.

land forc·es *pl. n.* armed forces serving on land.

land+form ('lænd,fɔːm) *n. Geology.* any feature of the earth's surface, such as valleys and mountains.

land grant *U.S.* ~*n.* **1.** a grant of public land to a college, railway, etc. **2.** (*modifier*) designating a state university established with such a grant.

land+grave ('lænd,greɪv) *n. German history.* **1.** (from the 13th century to 1806) a count who ruled over a specified territory. **2.** (after 1806) the title of any of various sovereign princes in central Germany. [C16: via German, from Middle High German *lantgrāve,* from *lant* land + *grāve* count]

land+gra+vi+ate (lænd'greɪvɪɪt, -,eɪt) *or* **land+gra+vate** ('lændgrə,veɪt) *n.* the domain or position of a landgrave or landgravine.

land+gra+vine ('lændgrə,viːn) *n.* **1.** the wife or widow of a landgrave. **2.** a woman who held the rank of landgrave.

land-hold·er *n. Chiefly U.S.* a person who owns or occupies land. —**'land-,hold·ing** *adj., n.*

land+ing ('lændɪŋ) *n.* **1. a.** the act of coming to land, esp. after a sea voyage. **b.** (*as modifier*): *landing place.* **2.** a place of disembarkation. **3.** the floor area at the top of a flight of stairs or between two flights of stairs.

land+ing beam *n.* a radio beam transmitted from a landing field to enable aircraft to make an instrument landing.

land+ing craft *n. Military.* any small vessel designed for the landing of troops and equipment on beaches.

land+ing field *n.* an area of land on which aircraft land and from which they take off.

land·ing gear *n.* the usual U.S. name for **undercarriage** (sense 1).
land·ing net *n. Angling.* a loose long-handled net on a triangular frame for lifting hooked fish from the water.
land·ing stage *n.* a platform used for landing goods and passengers from a vessel.
land·ing strip *n.* another name for **airstrip.**
land·la·dy ('lænd,leɪdɪ) *n., pl.* **·dies. 1.** a woman who owns and leases property. **2.** a landlord's wife. **3.** a woman who owns or runs a lodging house, inn, etc.
länd·ler (*German* 'lɛntlər) *n.* **1.** an Austrian country dance in which couples spin and clap. **2.** a piece of music composed for or in the rhythm of this dance, in three-four time. [German, from dialect *Landl* Upper Austria]
land line *n.* a telegraphic wire or cable laid over land.
land·locked ('lænd,lɒkt) *adj.* **1.** (esp. of lakes) completely surrounded by land. **2.** (esp. of certain salmon) living in fresh water that is permanently isolated from the sea.
land·lop·er ('lænd,ləʊpə) *n. Scot.* a vagabond or vagrant. [C16: from Dutch, from LAND + *loopen* to run, LEAP]
land·lord ('lænd,lɔːd) *n.* **1.** a man who owns and leases property. **2.** a man who owns or runs a lodging house, inn, etc. **3.** *Brit. archaic.* the lord of an estate.
land·lord·ism ('lændlɔː,dɪzəm) *n.* the system by which land under private ownership is rented for a fixed sum to tenants.
land·lub·ber ('lænd,lʌbə) *n. Nautical.* any person having no experience at sea. [C18: LAND + LUBBER]
land·mark ('lænd,mɑːk) *n.* **1.** a prominent or well-known object in or feature of a particular landscape. **2.** an important or unique decision, event, fact, discovery, etc. **3.** a boundary marker or signpost.
land·mass ('lænd,mæs) *n.* a large continuous area of land, as opposed to seas or islands.
land mine *n. Military.* an explosive charge placed in the ground, usually detonated by stepping or driving on it.
land of·fice *n. U.S.* an office that administers the sale of public land.
land-of·fice busi·ness *n. U.S. informal.* a booming or thriving business.
land of milk and hon·ey *n.* **1.** the land of natural fertility promised to the Israelites by God. **2.** any fertile land, state, etc.
land of Nod *n.* **1.** *Old Testament.* a region to the east of Eden to which Cain went after he had killed Abel (Genesis 4:14). **2.** an imaginary land of sleep.
Land of the Mid·night Sun *n.* **1.** any land north of the Arctic Circle, which has continuous daylight throughout the short summer: includes N parts of Norway, Sweden, and Finland, and the extreme NW Soviet Union. **2.** an informal name for **Lapland.**
Lan·dor ('lændɔː) *n.* **Wal·ter Sav·age.** 1775–1864, English poet, noted also for his prose works, including *Imaginary Conversations* (1824–29).
land·own·er ('lænd,əʊnə) *n.* a person who owns land. —**'land·,own·er·,ship** *n.* —**'land·,own·ing** *n., adj.*
Lan·dow·ska (*Polish* lan'dɔfska) *n.* **Wan·da** ('vanda). 1877–1959, U.S. harpsichordist, born in Poland.
land-poor *adj.* owning much unprofitable land and lacking the money to maintain its fertility or improve it.
land·race ('lænd,reɪs) *n. Chiefly Brit.* a white lop-eared breed of pork pig. [from Danish, literally: land race]
land rail *n.* another name for **corncrake.**
land re·form *n.* the redistributing of large agricultural holdings among the landless.
lands (lændz) *pl. n.* **1.** holdings in land. **2.** *S. African.* the part of a farm on which crops are grown.
land·scape ('lænd,skeɪp) *n.* **1.** an extensive area of scenery as viewed from a single aspect: *slagheaps dominated the landscape.* **2.** a painting, drawing, photograph, etc., depicting natural scenery. **3. a.** the genre including such pictures. **b.** (*as modifier*): *landscape painter.* ~*vb.* **4.** (*tr.*) to improve the natural features of (a garden, park, etc.), as by creating contoured features and planting trees. **5.** (*intr.*) to work as a landscape gardener. [C16 *landskip* (originally a term in painting), from Middle Dutch *lantscap* region; related to Old English *landscipe* tract of land, Old High German *lantscaf* region]
land·scape gar·den·ing *n.* the art of laying out grounds in imitation of natural scenery. Also called: **landscape architecture.** —**land·scape gar·den·er** *n.*
land·scap·ist ('lænd,skeɪpɪst) *n.* a painter of landscapes.
Land·seer ('lænsɪə) *n.* Sir **Ed·win Hen·ry.** 1802–73, English painter, noted for his studies of animals.
Land's End *n.* a granite headland in SW England, on the SW coast of Cornwall: the westernmost point of England.
land·shark ('lænd,ʃɑːk) *n. Informal.* a person who makes inordinate profits by buying and selling land.
Lands·hut (*German* 'lants,huːt) *n.* a city in SE West Germany, in Bavaria: Trausnitz castle (13th century); manufacturing centre for machinery and chemicals. Pop.: 52 400 (1970).
land·side ('lænd,saɪd) *n.* the part of a plough that slides along the face of the furrow wall on the opposite side to the mouldboard.
lands·knecht ('læntskə,nɛkt) *n.* a mercenary foot soldier in late 15th-, 16th-, and 17th-century Europe, esp. a German pikeman. [German, literally: landknight]
land·slide ('lænd,slaɪd) *n.* **1.** Also called: **landslip. a.** the sliding of a large mass of rock material, soil, etc., down the side of a mountain or cliff. **b.** the material dislodged in this way. **2. a.** an overwhelming electoral victory. **b.** (*as modifier*): *a landslide win.*
Lands·mål ('lɑːntsmɔːl) *n.* another name for **Nynorsk.**
lands·man[1] ('lændzmən) *n., pl.* **·men. 1.** a person who works or lives on land, as distinguished from a seaman. **2.** a person with no experience at sea.
lands·man[2] ('lændzmən) *n., pl.* **·men.** a Jewish compatriot from the same district, etc., as another. [from Yiddish]
Land·sturm *German.* ('lant,ʃturm) *n.* (in German-speaking countries) **1.** a reserve force; militia. **2.** a general levy in wartime. [C19: literally: landstorm; originally a summons to arms by means of storm-warning bells]
Land·tag ('lɑːnt,tɑːk) *n.* **1.** the legislative assembly of each state in present-day West Germany and Austria. **2.** the estates of principalities in medieval and modern Germany. **3.** the assembly of numerous states in 19th-century Germany. [C16: German: land assembly]
land tax *n.* (formerly) a tax payable annually by virtue of ownership of land, abolished in Britain in 1963.
land up *vb.* (*adv., usually intr.*) to arrive or cause to arrive at a final point: *after a summer in Europe, he suddenly landed up at home.*
land·wait·er ('lænd,weɪtə) *n.* an officer of the Custom House.
land·ward ('lændwəd) *adj.* **1.** lying, facing, or moving towards land. **2.** in the direction of the land. ~*adv.* **3.** a variant of **landwards.**
land·wards ('lændwədz) *or* **land·ward** *adv.* towards land.
Land·wehr *German.* ('lantveːr) *n.* (in German-speaking countries) the army reserve. [C19: land defence]
land with *vb.* (*tr., prep.*) to give or present to, so as to put in difficulties: *why did you land me with this extra work?*
lane[1] (leɪn) *n.* **1. a.** a narrow road or way between buildings, hedges, fences, etc. **b.** (*cap. as part of a street name*): *Drury Lane.* **2.** any narrow well-defined track or course, as for lines of traffic in a road, or for ships or aircraft. **3.** one of the parallel strips into which a running track or swimming bath is divided for races. **4.** the long strip of wooden flooring down which balls are bowled in a bowling alley. [Old English *lane, lanu,* of Germanic origin; related to Middle Dutch *lāne* lane]
lane[2] (leɪn) *adj. Scot. dialect.* lone or alone.
Lan·franc ('lænfræŋk) *n.* ?1005–89, Italian ecclesiastic and scholar; archbishop of Canterbury (1070–89) and adviser to William the Conqueror. He instituted many reforms in the English Church.
lang (læŋ) *adj.* a Scot. word for **long.**
Lang (læŋ) *n.* **1. Cos·mo Gor·don,** 1st Baron Lang of Lambeth. 1864–1945, British churchman; archbishop of Canterbury (1928–42). **2. Fritz.** 1890–1976, Austrian film director, later in the U.S., most notable for his silent films, such as *Metropolis* (1926), *M* (1931), and *The Testament of Dr. Mabuse* (1932).
lang. *abbrev. for* language.
Lang·land ('læŋlənd) *or* **Lang·ley** *n.* **Wil·liam.** ?1332–?1400, English poet. The allegorical religious poem in alliterative verse, *The Vision of William concerning Piers the Plowman,* is attributed to him.
lang·lauf ('lɑːŋ,laʊf) *n.* cross-country skiing. [German, literally: long run] —**lang·läuf·er** ('lɑːŋ,lɔɪfə) *n.*
Lang·ley ('læŋlɪ) *n.* **1. Ed·mund of.** See (1st Duke of) **York. 2. Sam·u·el Pier·pont,** 1834–1906, U.S. astronomer and physicist: invented the bolometer (1878) and pioneered the construction of heavier-than-air flying machines. **3. Wil·liam.** See **Langland.**
Lang·muir ('læŋmjʊə) *n.* **Ir·ving.** 1881–1957, U.S. chemist. He developed the gas-filled tungsten lamp and the atomic hydrogen welding process: Nobel prize for chemistry 1932.
Lan·go·bard ('læŋgə,bɑːd) *n.* a less common name for a **Lombard.** [C18: from Late Latin *Langobardicus* Lombard]
Lan·go·bar·dic (,læŋgə'bɑːdɪk) *n.* **1.** the language of the ancient Lombards: a dialect of Old High German. ~*adj.* **2.** of or relating to the Lombards or their language.
lan·gouste ('lɒŋguːst, lɒŋ'guːst) *n.* another name for the **spiny lobster.** [French, from Old Provençal *langosta,* perhaps from Latin *lōcusta* lobster, locust]
lan·grage ('læŋgrɪdʒ), **lan·grel** ('læŋgrəl), *or* **lan·gridge** *n.* shot consisting of scrap iron packed into a case, formerly used in naval warfare. [C18: of unknown origin]
Langres Pla·teau (*French* 'lɑːgr) *n.* a calcareous plateau of E France north of Dijon between the Seine and the Saône, reaching over 580 m (1900 ft.): forms a watershed between rivers flowing to the Mediterranean and to the English Channel.
lang·syne (,læŋ'saɪn) *Scot.* ~*adv.* **1.** long ago; long since. ~*n.* **2.** times long past, esp. those fondly remembered. See also **auld lang syne.** [C16: Scottish: long since]
Lang·ton ('læŋtən) *n.* **Ste·phen.** ?1150–1228, English cardinal; archbishop of Canterbury (1213–28). He was consecrated archbishop by Pope Innocent III in 1207 but was kept out of his see by King John until 1213. He was partly responsible for the Magna Carta (1215).
Lang·try ('læŋtrɪ) *n.* **Lil·lie,** known as *the Jersey Lily.* 1852–1929, English actress, noted for her beauty and for her friendship with Edward VII.
lan·guage ('læŋgwɪdʒ) *n.* **1.** a system for the expression of thoughts, feelings, etc., by the use of spoken sounds or conventional symbols. **2.** the faculty for the use of such systems, which is a distinguishing characteristic of man as compared with other animals. **3.** the language of a particular nation or people: *the French language.* **4.** any other systematic or nonsystematic means of communicating, such as gesture or animal sounds: *the language of love.* **5.** the specialized vocabulary used by a particular group: *medical language.* **6.** a particular manner or style of verbal expression: *your language*

is disgusting. **7.** *Computer technol.* See **programming language. 8.** *Linguistics.* another word for **langue. 9. speak the same language.** to communicate with understanding because of common background, values, etc. [C13: from Old French *langage,* ultimately from Latin *lingua* tongue]

lan·guage la·bor·a·to·ry *n.* a room equipped with tape recorders, etc., for learning foreign languages.

langue (lɑːŋg) *n. Linguistics.* language considered as an abstract system or a social institution, being the common possession of a speech community. Compare **parole.** [C19: from French: language]

langue de chat (ˈlɑːŋ də ˈʃɑː) *n.* **1.** a flat sweet finger-shaped biscuit. **2.** a piece of chocolate having the same shape. [French: cat's tongue]

langue d'oc *French.* (lãg ˈdɔk) *n.* the group of medieval French dialects spoken in S France: often regarded as including Provençal. Compare ***langue d'oïl.*** [literally: language of *oc* (form for the Provençal *yes*), ultimately from Latin *hoc* this]

Langue·doc (*French* lãgˈdɔk) *n.* **1.** a former province of S France, lying between the foothills of the Pyrenees and the River Rhone: formed around the countship of Toulouse in the 13th century; important production of bulk wines. **2.** a wine from this region.

Langue·doc-Rous·sil·lon (*French* lãgdɔk rusiˈjɔ̃) *n.* a region of S France, on the Gulf of Lions: consists of the departments of Lozère, Gard, Hérault, Aude, and Pyrénées-Orientales; mainly mountainous with a coastal plain.

langue d'oïl *French.* (lãg dɔˈil) *n.* the group of medieval French dialects spoken in France north of the Loire; the medieval basis of modern French. [literally: language of *oïl* (the northern form for *yes*), ultimately from Latin *hoc ille* (*fecit*) this he (did)]

lan·guet (ˈlæŋgwɛt) *n. Rare.* anything resembling a tongue in shape or function. [C15: from Old French *languette,* diminutive of *langue* tongue]

lan·guid (ˈlæŋgwɪd) *adj.* **1.** without energy or spirit. **2.** without interest or enthusiasm. **3.** sluggish; inactive. [C16: from Latin *languidus,* from *languēre* to languish] **—ˈlan·guid·ly** *adv.* **—ˈlan·guid·ness** *n.*

lan·guish (ˈlæŋgwɪʃ) *vb.* (*intr.*) **1.** to lose or diminish in strength or energy. **2.** (often foll. by *for*) to be listless with desire; pine. **3.** to suffer deprivation, hardship, or neglect: *to languish in prison.* **4.** to put on a tender, nostalgic, or melancholic expression. [C14 *languishen,* from Old French *languiss-,* stem of *languir,* ultimately from Latin *languēre*] **—ˈlan·guish·er** *n.* **—ˈlan·guish·ment** *n.*

lan·guor (ˈlæŋgə) *n.* **1.** physical or mental laziness or weariness. **2.** a feeling of dreaminess and relaxation. **3.** oppressive silence or stillness. [C14 *langour,* via Old French from Latin *languor,* from *languēre* to languish; the modern spelling is directly from Latin]

lan·guor·ous (ˈlæŋgərəs) *adj.* **1.** characterized by or producing languor. **2.** another word for **languid. —ˈlan·guor·ous·ly** *adv.* **—ˈlan·guor·ous·ness** *n.*

lan·gur (lʌŋˈgʊə) *n.* any of various agile arboreal Old World monkeys of the genus *Presbytis* and related genera, of S and SE Asia having a slender body, long tail and hands, and long hair surrounding the face. [Hindi, perhaps related to Sanskrit *lāngūla* tailed]

lan·iard (ˈlænjəd) *n.* a variant spelling of **lanyard.**

la·ni·ar·y (ˈlænɪərɪ) *adj.* **1.** (esp. of canine teeth) adapted for tearing. **~*n., pl.* ·ar·ies. 2.** a tooth adapted for tearing. [C19: from Latin *lanius* butcher, from *laniāre* to tear]

la·nif·er·ous (ləˈnɪfərəs) *or* **la·nig·er·ous** (ləˈnɪdʒərəs) *adj. Biology.* bearing wool or fleecy hairs resembling wool. [C17: from Latin *lānifer,* from *lāna* wool]

lank (læŋk) *adj.* **1.** long and limp. **2.** thin or gaunt. [Old English *hlanc* loose] **—ˈlank·ly** *adv.* **—ˈlank·ness** *n.*

Lan·kes·ter (ˈlæŋkɪstə) *n.* Sir **Ed·win Ray.** 1847–1929, English zoologist, noted particularly for his work in embryology and protozoology.

lank·y (ˈlæŋkɪ) *adj.* **lank·i·er, lank·i·est.** tall, thin, and loose-jointed. **—ˈlank·i·ly** *adv.* **—ˈlank·i·ness** *n.*

lan·ner (ˈlænə) *n.* **1.** a large falcon, *Falco biarmicus,* of Mediterranean regions, N Africa, and S Asia. **2.** *Falconry.* the female of this falcon. Compare **lanneret.** [C15: from Old French (*faucon*) *lanier* cowardly (falcon), from Latin *lanārius* wool worker, coward; referring to its sluggish flight and timid nature]

lan·ner·et (ˈlænəˌrɛt) *n.* the male or tercel of the lanner falcon. [C15: diminutive of LANNER]

lan·o·lin (ˈlænəlɪn) *or* **lan·o·line** (ˈlænəlɪn, -ˌliːn) *n.* a yellowish viscous substance extracted from wool, consisting of a mixture of esters of fatty acids: used in some ointments. Also called: **wool fat.** [C19: via German from Latin *lāna* wool + *oleum* oil; see -IN] **—lan·o·lat·ed** (ˈlænəˌleɪtɪd) *adj.*

la·nose (ˈleɪnəʊs, -nəʊz) *adj.* another word for **lanate.** [C19: from Latin *lānosus*] **—la·nos·i·ty** (leɪˈnɒsɪtɪ) *n.*

Lan·sing (ˈlænsɪŋ) *n.* a city in S Michigan, on the Grand River: the state capital. Pop.: 129 186 (1973 est.).

lans·que·net (ˈlænskəˌnɛt) *n.* **1.** a gambling game of chance. **2.** an archaic spelling of **landsknecht.** [from French]

lan·ta·na (lænˈteɪnə, -ˈtɑː-) *n.* any verbenaceous shrub or herbaceous plant of the tropical American genus *Lantana,* having spikes of yellow or orange flowers. [C18: New Latin, from Italian dialect *lantana* wayfaring tree]

lan·tern (ˈlæntən) *n.* **1.** a light with a transparent or translucent protective case. **2.** a structure on top of a dome or roof having openings or windows to admit light or air. **3.** the upper part of a lighthouse that houses the light. **4.** *Photog.* short for **magic lantern.** [C13: from Latin *lanterna,* from Greek *lamptēr* lamp, from *lampein* to shine]

lan·tern fish *n.* any small deep-sea teleost fish of the family *Myctophidae,* having a series of luminescent spots along the body.

lan·tern fly *n.* any of various tropical insects of the homopterous family *Fulgoridae,* many species of which have a snoutlike process formerly thought to emit light.

lan·tern jaw *n.* (when *pl.,* refers to upper and lower jaw; when *sing.* usually to lower jaw) a long hollow jaw that gives the face a drawn appearance. **—ˈlan·tern-ˌjawed** *adj.*

lan·tern pin·ion *or* **wheel** *n.* a type of gearwheel, now used only in clocks, consisting of two parallel circular discs connected by a number of pins running parallel to the axis.

lan·tern slide *n. Rare.* a photographic slide for projection, used originally in a magic lantern.

lan·tha·nide (ˈlænθəˌnaɪd) *or* **lan·tha·non** (ˈlænθəˌnɒn) *n.* any element of the lanthanide series. Also called: **rare earth, rare-earth element.** [C19: from LANTHANUM + -IDE]

lan·tha·nide se·ries *n.* a class of 15 chemically related elements with atomic numbers from 57 (lanthanum) to 71 (lutecium).

lan·tha·num (ˈlænθənəm) *n.* a silvery-white ductile metallic element of the lanthanide series, occurring principally in bastnaesite and monazite: used in pyrophoric alloys, electronic devices, and in glass manufacture. Symbol: La; atomic no.: 57; atomic wt.: 138.91; valency: 3; relative density: 6.17; melting pt.: 920°C; boiling pt.: 3454°C. [C19: New Latin, from Greek *lanthanein* to lie unseen]

lant·horn (ˈlæntˌhɔːn, ˈlæntən) *n.* an archaic word for **lantern.**

la·nu·go (ləˈnjuːgəʊ) *n., pl.* **·gos.** a layer of fine hairs, esp. the covering of the human fetus before birth. [C17: from Latin: down, from *lāna* wool] **—la·nu·gi·nous** (ləˈnjuːdʒɪnəs) *or* **la·ˈnu·gi·ˌnose** *adj.* **—la·ˈnu·gi·nous·ness** *n.*

La·nús (*Spanish* laˈnus) *n.* a city in E Argentina: a S suburb of Buenos Aires. Pop.: 449 824 (1970).

lan·yard *or* **lan·iard** (ˈlænjəd) *n.* **1.** a cord, esp. one worn around the neck, to hold a whistle, knife, etc. **2.** a cord with an attached hook used in firing certain types of cannon. **3.** *Nautical.* a line rove through deadeyes for extending or tightening standing rigging. [C15 *lanyer,* from French *lanière,* from *lasne* strap, probably of Germanic origin]

Lao (laʊ) *or* **Lao·ti·an** (ˈlaʊʃɪən) *n.* **1.** (*pl.* **Lao, Laos,** *or* **Lao·ti·ans**) a member of a Buddhist people of Laos and NE Thailand, related to the Thais. **2.** the language of this people, belonging to the Sino-Tibetan family and closely related to Thai. **~*adj.* 3.** of or relating to this people or their language or to Laos.

LAO *international car registration for* Laos.

La·oag (lɑːˈwɑːg) *n.* a city in the N Philippines, on NW Luzon: trade centre for an agricultural region. Pop.: 61 727 (1970).

La·oc·o·on (leɪˈɒkəʊˌɒn) *n. Greek myth.* a priest of Apollo at Troy who warned the Trojans against the wooden horse left by the Greeks; killed with his twin sons by two sea serpents.

La·od·i·ce·a (ˌleɪəʊdɪˈsɪə) *n.* the ancient name of several Greek cities in W Asia, notably of **Latakia.**

la·od·i·ce·an (ˌleɪəʊdɪˈsɪən) *adj.* **1.** lukewarm and indifferent, esp. in religious matters. **~*n.* 2.** a person having a lukewarm attitude towards religious matters. [C17: referring to the early Christians of Laodicea (Revelation 3:14–16)]

Laoigh·is (ˈleɪɪʃ) *n.* a county of central Ireland, in Leinster province: formerly boggy but largely reclaimed for agriculture. County town: Portlaoise. Pop.: 45 259 (1971). Area: 1719 sq. km (664 sq. miles). Also called: **Leix.** Former name: **Queen's County.**

La·om·e·don (leɪˈɒmɪˌdɒn) *n. Greek myth.* the founder and ruler of Troy, who cheated Apollo and Poseidon of their wage for constructing the city's walls; the father of Priam.

Laos (laʊz, laʊs) *n.* a republic in SE Asia: first united as the kingdom of Lan Xang ("million elephants") in 1353, after being a province of the Khmer Empire for about four centuries; made part of French Indochina in 1893 and gained independence in 1949; became a republic in 1975. It is generally forested and mountainous, with the Mekong River running almost the whole length of the W border. Official language: Lao. Currency: kip. Capital: Vientiane. Pop.: 3 181 000 (1973). Area: 236 000 sq. km (91 000 sq. miles). Official name: **People's Democratic Republic of Laos. —Lao·ti·an** (ˈlaʊʃɪən) *adj., n.*

Lao·tze (ˈlaʊˈtzeɪ) *or* **Lao·tzu** (ˈlaʊˈtsuː) *n.* ?604–?531 B.C., Chinese philosopher, traditionally regarded as the founder of Taoism and the author of the *Tao-te Ching.*

lap[1] (læp) *n.* **1.** the area formed by the upper surface of the thighs of a seated person. **2.** Also called: **lap·ful.** the amount held in one's lap. **3.** a protected place or environment: *in the lap of luxury.* **4.** any of various hollow or depressed areas, such as a hollow in the land. **5.** the part of one's clothing that covers the lap. **6. drop in someone's lap.** give someone the responsibility of. **7. in the lap of the gods.** beyond human control and power. [Old English *læppa* flap; see LOBE, LAPPET, LOP[2]]

lap[2] (læp) *n.* **1.** one circuit of a racecourse or track. **2.** a stage or part of a journey, race, etc. **3. a.** an overlapping part or projection. **b.** the extent of overlap. **4.** the length of material needed to go around an object. **5.** a rotating disc coated with fine abrasive for polishing gemstones. **6.** any device for bedding mechanical components together using a fine abrasive to polish the mating surfaces. **7.** *Metallurgy.* a defect in rolled metals caused by the folding of a fin onto the surface. **8.** a sheet or band of fibres, such as cotton, prepared for further processing.

~*vb.* **laps, lap+ping, lapped. 9.** (*tr.*) to wrap or fold (around or over): *he lapped a bandage around his wrist.* **10.** (*tr.*) to enclose or envelop in: *he lapped his wrist in a bandage.* **11.** to place or lie partly or completely over or project beyond. **12.** (*tr.; usually passive*) to envelop or surround with comfort, love, etc.: *lapped in luxury.* **13.** (*intr.*) to be folded. **14.** (*tr.*) to overtake (an opponent) in a race so as to be one or more circuits ahead. **15.** (*tr.*) to polish or cut (a workpiece, gemstone, etc.) with a fine abrasive, esp. to hone (mating metal parts) against each other with an abrasive. **16.** to form (fibres) into a sheet or band. [C13 (in the sense: to wrap): probably from LAP[1]] —**'lap+per** *n.*

lap[3] (læp) *vb.* **laps, lap+ping, lapped. 1.** (of small waves) to wash against (a shore, boat, etc.), usually with light splashing sounds. **2.** (often foll. by *up*) (esp. of animals) to scoop (a liquid) into the mouth with the tongue. ~*n.* **3.** the act or sound of lapping. **4.** a thin food for dogs or other animals. ~See also **lap up.** [Old English *lapian;* related to Old High German *laffan,* Latin *lambere,* Greek *laptein*] —**'lap+per** *n.*

La Pal+ma (*Spanish* la 'palma) *n.* an island in the N Atlantic, in the NW Canary Islands: administratively part of Spain. Chief town: Santa Cruz de la Palma. Pop.: 73 749 (1970). Area: 725 sq. km (280 sq. miles).

lap·a+rot+o·my (ˌlæpə'rɒtəmɪ) *n., pl.* **·mies. 1.** surgical incision through the abdominal wall, esp. to investigate the cause of an abdominal disorder. **2.** surgical incision into the loin. [C19: from Greek *laparos* soft + -TOMY]

La Paz (læ 'pæz; *Spanish* la 'pas) *n.* a city in W Bolivia, at an altitude of 3600 m (12 000 ft.): seat of government since 1898 (though Sucre is still the official capital); the country's largest city; founded in 1548 by the Spaniards; University (1830). Pop.: 660 700 (1975 est.).

lap+board ('læpˌbɔːd) *n.* a flat board that can be used on the lap as a makeshift table or desk.

lap-chart *n. Motor racing.* a log of every lap covered by each car in a race, showing the exact position throughout.

lap dis+solve *n. Films.* the transposing from one picture to another by reducing one picture in brightness and amplitude while increasing the other until it replaces the first.

lap dog *n.* **1.** a pet dog small and docile enough to be cuddled in the lap. **2.** *Informal.* a person who attaches himself to someone in admiration or infatuation.

la+pel (lə'pɛl) *n.* the continuation of the turned or folded back collar on a suit coat, jacket, etc. [C18: from LAP[1]] —**la+'pelled** *adj.*

lap·i·dar·y ('læpɪdərɪ) *n., pl.* **+dar·ies. 1.** a person whose business is to cut, polish, set, or deal in gemstones. ~*adj.* **2.** of or relating to gemstones or the work of a lapidary. **3.** Also **lap·i+dar+i·an** (ˌlæpɪ'dɛərɪən). engraved, cut, or inscribed in a stone or gemstone. **4.** of sufficiently high quality to be engraved on a stone: *a lapidary inscription.* [C14: from Latin *lapidārius,* from *lapid-, lapis* stone] —**ˌlap·i+'dar+i·an** *adj.*

lap·i+date ('læpɪˌdeɪt) *vb.* (*tr.*) *Literary.* **1.** to pelt with stones. **2.** to kill by stoning. [C17: from Latin *lapidāre,* from *lapis* stone] —**ˌlap·i+'da+tion** *n.*

la+pid·i+fy (lə'pɪdɪˌfaɪ) *vb.* **+fies, +fy+ing, +fied.** to change into stone. [C17: from French *lapidifier,* from Medieval Latin *lapidificāre,* ultimately from Latin *lapis* stone] —**la+ˌpid·i+fi+'ca+tion** *n.*

la+pil+lus (lə'pɪləs) *n., pl.* **+li** (-laɪ). a small piece of lava thrown from a volcano. [C18: Latin: little stone]

lap+is laz·u+li *or* **laz·u+li** ('læpɪs) *n.* **1.** a brilliant blue variety of the mineral lazurite, used as a gemstone. **2.** the deep blue colour of lapis lazuli. ~Also: **lapis.** [C14: from Latin *lapis* stone + Medieval Latin *lazulī,* from *lazulum,* from Arabic *lāzaward,* from Persian *lāzhuward,* of obscure origin]

Lap+ith ('læpɪθ) *n., pl.* **Lap·i+thae** ('læpɪˌθiː) *or* **Lap+iths.** *Greek myth.* a member of a people in Thessaly who at the wedding of their king, Pirithoüs, fought the drunken centaurs.

lap joint *n.* a joint made by placing one member over another and fastening them together. Also called: **lapped joint.** —**'lap-ˌjoint·ed** *adj.*

La·place (*French* la'plas) *n.* **Pierre Si·mon** (pjɛːr si'mɔ̃), Marquis de Laplace. 1749–1827, French mathematician, physicist, and astronomer. He formulated the nebular hypothesis (1796). He also developed the theory of probability.

La+place op+er+a+tor *n. Maths.* the operator $\partial^2/\partial x^2 + \partial^2/\partial y^2 + \partial^2/\partial z^2$, used in differential analysis. Symbol: ∇^2 Also: **La+pla+ci·an** (lə'pleɪʃɪən).

Lap+land ('læpˌlænd) *n.* an extensive region of N Europe, mainly within the Arctic Circle: consists of the N parts of Norway, Sweden, Finland, and the Kola Peninsula of the extreme NW Soviet Union. Also called: **Land of the Midnight Sun.** —**'Lap+ˌland+er** *n.*

La Pla+ta (*Spanish* la 'plata) *n.* a port in E Argentina, near the Río de la Plata estuary: founded in 1882 and modelled on Washington, D.C.; university (1897). Pop.: 506 287 (1970).

lap of hon+our *n.* a ceremonial circuit of a racing track, etc., by the winner of a race.

Lapp (læp) *n.* **1.** a member of a nomadic people living chiefly in N Scandinavia and the Kola Peninsula of the Soviet Union. **2.** the language of this people, belonging to the Finno-Ugric family. ~*adj.* **3.** of or relating to this people or their language. —**'Lapp+ish** *adj.,n.*

lap+pet ('læpɪt) *n.* **1.** a small hanging flap or piece of lace, etc., such as one dangling from a headdress. **2.** *Zoology.* a lobelike hanging structure, such as the wattle on a bird's head. [C16: from LAP[1] + -ET] —**'lap+pet+ed** *adj.*

lapse (læps) *n.* **1.** a drop in standard of an isolated or temporary nature: *a lapse of justice.* **2.** a break in occurrence, usage, etc.: *a lapse of five weeks between letters.* **3.** a gradual decline or a drop to a lower degree, condition, or state: *a lapse from high office.* **4.** a moral fall. **5.** *Law.* the termination of some right, interest, or privilege, as by neglecting to exercise it or through failure of some contingency. **6.** *Insurance.* the termination of coverage following a failure to pay the premiums. ~*vb.* (*intr.*) **7.** to drop in standard or fail to maintain a norm. **8.** to decline gradually or fall in status, condition, etc. **9.** to be discontinued, esp. through negligence or other failure. **10.** (usually foll. by *into*) to drift or slide (into a condition): *to lapse into sleep.* **11.** (often foll. by *from*) to turn away (from beliefs or norms). **12.** *Law.* (of a devise or bequest) to become void, as on the beneficiary's predeceasing the testator. **13.** (of time) to slip away. [C15: from Latin *lāpsus* error, from *lābī* to glide] —**'laps+a·ble** *or* **'laps+i·ble** *adj.* —**'laps+er** *n.*

lapse rate *n.* the rate of change of any meteorological factor with altitude, esp. atmospheric temperature, which usually decreases at a rate of 0.6°C per 100 metres (**environmental lapse rate**). Unsaturated air loses about 1°C per 100 m (**dry adiabatic lapse rate**), whereas saturated air loses an average 0.5°C per 100 m (**saturated adiabatic lapse rate**).

lap+strake ('læpˌstreɪk) *or* **lap+streak** ('læpˌstriːk) *Nautical.* ~*adj.* **1.** another term for **clinker-built.** ~*n.* **2.** a clinker-built boat. [C18: from LAP[2] + STRAKE]

lap+sus ('læpsəs) *n., pl.* **+sus.** *Formal.* a lapse or error. [from Latin: LAPSE]

Lap+tev Sea ('læptɪf) *n.* a shallow arm of the Arctic Ocean, along the N coast of the Soviet Union between the Taimyr Peninsular and the New Siberian Islands. Former name: **Nordenskjöld Sea.**

lap up *vb.* (*tr., adv.*) *Informal.* **1.** to eat or drink. **2.** to relish or delight in: *he laps up old horror films.* **3.** to believe or accept uncritically: *he laps up tall stories.*

lap+wing ('læpˌwɪŋ) *n.* any of several plovers of the genus *Vanellus,* esp. *V. vanellus,* typically having a crested head, wattles, and spurs. Also called: **green plover, pewit, peewit.** [C17: altered form of Old English *hlēapewince,* plover, from *hlēapan* to LEAP + *wincian* to jerk, WINK[1]]

lar (lɑː) *n.* the singular of **lares.** See **lares and penates.**

lar+board ('lɑːbəd) *n., adj. Nautical.* a former word for **port**[2]. [C14 *laddeborde* (changed to *larboard* by association with *starboard*), from *laden* to load + *borde* BOARD]

lar+ce·ny ('lɑːsɪnɪ) *n., pl.* **·nies.** *Law.* (formerly) a technical word for **theft.** [C15: from Old French *larcin,* from Latin *lātrocinium* robbery, from *latrō* robber] —**'lar+ce·nist** *or* **'lar+ce·ner** *n.* —**'lar+ce·nous** *adj.* —**'lar+ce·nous+ly** *adv.*

larch (lɑːtʃ) *n.* **1.** any coniferous tree of the genus *Larix,* having deciduous needle-like leaves and egg-shaped cones: family *Pinaceae.* **2.** the wood of any of these trees. [C16: from German *Lärche,* ultimately from Latin *larix*]

lard (lɑːd) *n.* **1.** the rendered fat from a pig, esp. from the abdomen, used in cooking. **2.** *Informal.* excess fat on a person's body. ~*vb.* (*tr.*) **3.** to prepare (lean meat, poultry, etc.) by inserting small strips of bacon or fat before cooking. **4.** to cover or smear (foods) with lard. **5.** to add extra material to (speech or writing); embellish. [C15: via Old French from Latin *lāridum* bacon fat] —**'lard+ˌlike** *adj.* —**'lard·y** *adj.*

lar+der ('lɑːdə) *n.* a room or cupboard, used as a store for food. [C14: from Old French *lardier,* from LARD]

lar+der bee+tle *n.* a small blackish beetle, *Dermestes lardarius,* feeding on hides, bacon, etc.: family *Dermestidae.*

lar+don ('lɑːdᵊn) *or* **lar+doon** (lɑː'duːn) *n.* a strip of fat used in larding meat. [C15: from Old French, from LARD]

lard pig *n.* a large type of pig used principally for lard.

lard·y cake ('lɑːdɪ) *n. Brit.* a rich sweet cake made of bread dough, lard, sugar, and dried fruit.

lar·es and pe+na+tes ('lɛəriːz, 'lɑː-) *pl. n.* **1.** *Roman myth.* **a.** household gods. **b.** statues of these gods kept in the home. **2.** the valued possessions of a household.

large (lɑːdʒ) *adj.* **1.** having a relatively great size, quantity, extent, etc.; big. **2.** of wide or broad scope, capacity, or range; comprehensive: *a large effect.* **3.** having or showing great breadth of understanding: *a large heart.* **4.** *Nautical.* (of the wind) blowing from a favourable direction. **5.** *Rare.* overblown; pretentious. **6.** generous. **7.** *Obsolete.* (of manners and speech) gross; rude. ~*n.* **8. at large. a.** (esp. of a dangerous criminal or wild animal) free; not confined. **b.** roaming freely, as in a foreign country. **c.** as a whole; in general. **d.** in full detail; exhaustively. **e.** *U.S.* representing or assigned to a state, district, or nation: *an ambassador at large.* **9. in (the) large.** as a totality or on a broad scale. ~*adv.* **10.** *Nautical.* with the wind blowing from a favourable direction. **11. by and large. a.** (*sentence modifier*) generally; as a rule: *by and large, the man is the breadwinner.* **b.** *Nautical.* towards and away from the wind. **12. loom large.** to be very prominent or important. [C12 (originally: generous): via Old French from Latin *largus* ample, abundant] —**'large+ness** *n.*

large cal·o+rie *n.* another name for **Calorie.**

large-hand·ed *adj.* generous; profuse.

large-heart·ed *adj.* kind; sympathetic. Also: **large-souled.**

large in+tes+tine *n.* the part of the alimentary canal consisting of the caecum, colon, and rectum. It extracts moisture from food residues, which are later excreted as faeces. Compare **small intestine.**

large+ly ('lɑːdʒlɪ) *adv.* **1.** principally; to a great extent. **2.** on a large scale or in a large manner.

large-mind·ed *adj.* generous or liberal in attitudes. —**ˌlarge-'mind·ed+ly** *adv.* —**ˌlarge-'mind·ed+ness** *n.*

large·mouth bass ('lɑːdʒˌmaʊθ 'bæs) *n.* a common North American freshwater black bass, *Micropterus salmoides*: a popular game fish.
larg·en ('lɑːdʒən) *vb.* (*tr.*) another word for **enlarge.**
large-scale *adj.* **1.** wide-ranging or extensive. **2.** (of maps and models) constructed or drawn to a big scale.
lar·gess *or* **lar·gesse** (lɑː'dʒɛs) *n.* **1.** the generous bestowal of gifts, favours, or money. **2.** the things so bestowed. **3.** generosity of spirit or attitude. [C13: from Old French, from LARGE]
lar·ghet·to (lɑː'gɛtəʊ) *Music.* ~*adj., adv.* **1.** to be performed moderately slowly. ~*n., pl.* **·tos. 2.** a piece or passage to be performed in this way. [Italian: diminutive of LARGO]
larg·ish ('lɑːdʒɪʃ) *adj.* fairly large.
lar·go ('lɑːgəʊ) *Music.* ~*adj., adv.* **1.** to be performed slowly and broadly. ~*n., pl.* **·gos. 2.** a piece or passage to be performed in this way. [C17: from Italian, from Latin *largus* LARGE]
lar·i·at ('lærɪət) *n. U.S.* **1.** another word for **lasso. 2.** a rope for tethering animals. [C19: from Spanish *la reata* the RIATA]
lar·ine ('læraɪn, -rɪn) *adj.* **1.** of, relating to, or resembling a gull. **2.** of, relating to, or belonging to the suborder *Lari*, which contains the gulls, terns, skuas, and skimmers. [C20: via New Latin from *Larus* genus name, from Greek *laros* a kind of gull]
La·ri·sa *or* **La·ris·sa** (lə'rɪsə; *Greek* 'larisa) *n.* a city in E Greece, in E Thessaly: fortified by Justinian; annexed to Greece in 1881. Pop.: 72 760 (1971).
lark[1] (lɑːk) *n.* **1.** any brown songbird of the predominantly Old World family *Alaudidae*, esp. the skylark: noted for their singing. **2.** short for **titlark** or **meadowlark. 3.** (*often cap.*) any of various slender but powerful fancy pigeons, such as the **Coburg Lark. 4. up with the lark.** *adv.* up early in the morning. [Old English *lāwerce, lǣwerce*, of Germanic origin; related to German *Lerche*, Icelandic *lǣvirki*]
lark[2] (lɑːk) *Informal.* ~*n.* **1.** a carefree adventure or frolic. **2.** a harmless piece of mischief. **3. what a lark!** how amusing! ~*vb.* **4.** (*intr.*; often foll. by *about*) to have a good time by frolicking. **5.** (*intr.*) to play a prank. [C19: originally slang, perhaps related to LAIK] —**'lark·er** *n.* —**'lark·ish·ness** *n.* —**'lark·some** *adj.*
Lar·kin ('lɑːkɪn) *n.* **Phil·ip.** born 1922, English poet: his verse collections include *The Less Deceived* (1955) and *The Whitsun Weddings* (1964).
lark·spur ('lɑːkˌspɜː) *n.* any of various ranunculaceous plants of the genus *Delphinium*, with spikes of blue, pink, or white irregular spurred flowers. [C16: LARK[1] + SPUR]
Lar·mor pre·ces·sion ('lɑːmɔː) *n.* precession of the orbit of an electron in an atom that is subjected to a magnetic field. [C20: named after Sir Joseph *Larmor* (1857–1942), British physicist]
larn (lɑːn) *vb. Not standard.* **1.** *Facetious.* to learn. **2.** (*tr.*) to teach (someone) a lesson: *that'll larn you!* [C18: from a dialect form of LEARN]
lar·nax ('lɑːnæks) *n. Archaeol.* a coffin made of terracotta. [from Greek; perhaps related to Late Greek *narnax* chest]
La Roche·fou·cauld (*French* la rɔʃfu'ko) *n.* **Fran·çois** (frã'swa), Duc de La Rochefoucauld. 1613–80, French writer. His best-known work is *Réflexions ou sentences et maximes morales* (1665), a collection of epigrammatic and cynical observations on human nature.
La Ro·chelle (*French* la rɔ'ʃɛl) *n.* a port in W France, on the Bay of Biscay: a Huguenot stronghold until its submission through famine to Richelieu's forces after a long siege (1627–28). Pop.: 81 884 (1975).
La·rousse (*French* la'rus) *n.* **Pierre A·tha·nase** (pjɛːr ata'nɑːz). 1817–75, French grammarian, lexicographer, and encyclopedist. He edited and helped to compile the *Grand Dictionnaire universel du XIX siècle* (1866–76).
lar·ri·gan ('lærɪgən) *n.* a knee-high oiled leather moccasin boot worn by trappers, etc. [C19: of unknown origin]
lar·ri·kin ('lærɪkɪn) *n. Austral. slang.* **a.** a hooligan. **b.** (*as modifier*): *a larrikin bloke.* [C19: from English dialect: a mischievous youth]
lar·rup ('lærəp) *vb.* (*tr.*) *Brit. dialect.* to beat or flog. [C19: of unknown origin] —**'lar·rup·er** *n.*
lar·um ('lærəm) *n.* an archaic word for **alarm.**
lar·va ('lɑːvə) *n., pl.* **·vae** (-viː). an immature free-living form of many animals that develops into a different adult form by metamorphosis. [C18: (C17 in the original Latin sense: ghost): New Latin] —**'lar·val** *adj.*
lar·vi·cide ('lɑːvɪˌsaɪd) *n.* a chemical used for killing larvae. —**ˌlar·vi·'cid·al** *adj.*
Lar·wood ('lɑːwʊd) *n.* **Har·old.** born 1904, English cricketer. An outstanding fast bowler, he played 21 times for England between 1926 and 1932.
lar·yn·ge·al (ˌlærɪn'dʒiːəl, lə'rɪndʒɪəl) *or* **la·ryn·gal** (lə'rɪŋgᵊl) *adj.* **1.** of or relating to the larynx. **2.** *Phonetics.* articulated at the larynx; glottal. [C18: from New Latin *laryngeus* of the LARYNX] —**la·ryn·'ge·al·ly** *adv.*
lar·yn·gi·tis (ˌlærɪn'dʒaɪtɪs) *n.* inflammation of the larynx. —**lar·yn·git·ic** (ˌlærɪn'dʒɪtɪk) *adj.*
la·ryn·go- *or before a vowel* **la·ryng-** *combining form.* indicating the larynx: *laryngoscope.*
lar·yn·gol·o·gy (ˌlærɪŋ'gɒlədʒɪ) *n.* the branch of medicine concerned with the larynx and its diseases. —**la·ryn·go·log·i·cal** (ləˌrɪŋgə'lɒdʒɪkᵊl) *or* **laˌryn·go·'log·ic** *adj.* —**laˌryn·go·'log·i·cal·ly** *adv.* —**ˌlar·yn·'gol·o·gist** *n.*
la·ryn·go·scope (lə'rɪŋgəˌskəʊp) *n.* a medical instrument for examining the larynx. —**la·ryn·go·scop·ic** (ləˌrɪŋgə'skɒpɪk) *adj.* —**laˌryn·go·'scop·i·cal·ly** *adv.* —**lar·yn·gos·co·pist** (ˌlærɪŋ'gɒskəpɪst) *n.* —**ˌlar·yn·'gos·co·py** *n.*
lar·yn·got·o·my (ˌlærɪŋ'gɒtəmɪ) *n., pl.* **·mies.** surgical incision into the larynx.
lar·ynx ('lærɪŋks) *n., pl.* **la·ryn·ges** (lə'rɪndʒiːz) *or* **lar·ynx·es.** a cartilaginous and muscular hollow organ forming part of the air passage to the lungs: in higher vertebrates it contains the vocal cords. [C16: from New Latin *larynx*, from Greek *larunx*]
la·sa·gne *or* **la·sa·gna** (lə'zænjə, -'sæn-) *n.* **1.** a form of pasta consisting of wide flat sheets. **2.** any of several dishes made from layers of lasagne and meat, cheese, etc. [from Italian *lasagna*, from Latin *lasanum* cooking pot]
La Salle[1] (lə 'sæl) *n.* a city in SE Canada, in Quebec: a S suburb of Montreal. Pop.: 72 912 (1971).
La Salle[2] (*French* la 'sal) *n.* Sieur **Ro·bert Ca·ve·lier de** (rɔbɛːr kavə'lje də). 1643–87, French explorer and fur trader in North America; founder of Louisiana (1682).
las·car ('læskə) *or* **lash·kar** ('læʃkə) *n.* a sailor from the East Indies. [C17: from Urdu *lashkar* soldier, from Persian: the army]
Las·caux (*French* las'ko) *n.* site of a cave in SW France, in the Dordogne: contains Palaeolithic wall drawings and paintings.
las·civ·i·ous (lə'sɪvɪəs) *adj.* **1.** lustful; lecherous. **2.** exciting sexual desire. [C15: from Late Latin *lascīviōsus*, from Latin *lascīvia* wantonness, from *lascīvus*] —**las·'civ·i·ous·ly** *adv.* —**las·'civ·i·ous·ness** *n.*
lase (leɪz) *vb.* (*intr.*) (of a substance, such as carbon dioxide or ruby) to be capable of acting as a laser.
la·ser ('leɪzə) *n.* **1.** Also called: **optical maser.** a device for converting light of mixed frequencies into an intense narrow monochromatic beam of coherent light. It consists of a ruby rod, gas-filled tube, etc., illuminated by a flash lamp to excite its atoms. Light emitted by these atoms is reflected backwards and forwards along the tube and stimulates further emission. **2.** any similar device for producing a beam of any electromagnetic radiation, such as infrared or microwave radiation. See also **maser.** [C20: from *l*ight *a*mplification by *s*timulated *e*mission of *r*adiation]
lash[1] (læʃ) *n.* **1.** a sharp cutting blow from a whip or other flexible object: *twenty lashes was his punishment.* **2.** the flexible end or ends of a whip. **3.** a cutting or hurtful blow to the feelings, as one caused by ridicule or scolding. **4.** a forceful beating or impact, as of wind, rain, or waves against something. **5. have a lash (at).** *Austral. informal.* to make an attempt at or take part in (something). **6.** See **eyelash.** ~*vb.* (*tr.*) **7.** to hit (a person or thing) sharply with a whip, rope, etc., esp. as a former punishment. **8.** (of wind, waves, etc.) to beat forcefully against. **9.** to attack with words, ridicule, etc. **10.** to flick or wave sharply to and fro: *the restless panther lashed his tail.* **11.** to urge or drive with or as if with a whip: *to lash the audience into a violent mood.* [C14: perhaps imitative] —**'lash·er** *n.* —**'lash·ing·ly** *adv.*
lash[2] (læʃ) *vb.* (*tr.*) to bind or secure with rope, string, etc. [C15: from Old French *lachier*, ultimately from Latin *laqueāre* to ensnare, from *laqueus* noose] —**'lash·er** *n.*
-lashed *adj.* having eyelashes as specified: *long-lashed.*
lash·ing[1] ('læʃɪŋ) *n.* **1.** a whipping; flogging. **2.** a scolding. **3.** (*pl.*; usually foll. by *of*) *Brit. informal.* large amounts; lots.
lash·ing[2] ('læʃɪŋ) *n.* rope, cord, etc., used for binding or securing.
Lash·i·o ('læʃɪˌəʊ) *n.* a town in NE central Burma: starting point of the Burma Road to Chungking, China.
Lash·kar ('lʌʃkə) *n.* a former city in N India, in Madhya Pradesh: capital of the former states of Gwalior and Madhya Bharat; now part of the city of Gwalior.
lash out *vb.* (*intr., adv.*) **1.** to burst into or resort to verbal or physical attack. **2.** *Informal.* to be extravagant, as in spending.
lash-up ('læʃˌʌp) *n.* **a.** Also called: **hook-up.** a temporary connection of equipment for experimental or emergency use. **b.** (*as modifier*): *lash-up equipment.*
Las·ker ('læskə) *n.* **E·man·u·el.** 1868–1941, German chess player: world champion (1894–1921).
las·ket ('læskɪt) *n.* a loop at the foot of a sail onto which an extra sail may be fastened. [C18: perhaps an alteration of French *lacet* LATCHET, through the influence of GASKET]
Las·ki ('læskɪ) *n.* **Har·old Jo·seph.** 1893–1950, English political scientist and socialist leader.
Las Pal·mas (*Spanish* las 'palmas) *n.* a port in the central Canary Islands, on NE Grand Canary: a major fuelling port on the main shipping route between Europe and South America. Pop.: 287 038 (1970).
La Spe·zia (*Italian* la 'spettsja) *n.* a port in NW Italy, in Liguria, on the **Gulf of Spezia:** the chief naval base in Italy. Pop.: 122 284 (1975 est.).
lass (læs) *n.* a girl or young woman. [C13: origin uncertain]
Las·sa ('lɑːsə) *n.* a variant spelling of **Lhasa.**
Las·sa fe·ver *n.* a serious viral disease of Central West Africa, characterized by high fever and muscular pains.
Las·salle (*German* la'sal) *n.* **Fer·di·nand** ('fɛrdiˌnant). 1825–64, German socialist and writer: a founder of the first German workers' political party (1863), which later became the Social Democratic Party.
Las·sen Peak ('læsᵊn) *n.* a volcano in S California, in the S Cascade Range: the only active volcano in the U.S. outside Alaska and Hawaii. An area of 416 sq. km (161 sq. miles) was established as **Lassen Volcanic National Park** in 1916. Height: 3187 m (10 457 ft.).
las·sie ('læsɪ) *n. Informal.* a little lass; girl.
las·si·tude ('læsɪˌtjuːd) *n.* physical or mental weariness. [C16: from Latin *lassitūdō*, from *lassus* tired]
las·so ('læsəʊ, læ'suː) *n., pl.* **·sos** *or* **·soes. 1.** a long rope or

thong with a running noose at one end, used (esp. in America) for roping horses, cattle, etc.; lariat. ~*vb.* **+sos** *or* **+soes; +so+ing, +soed. 2.** (*tr.*) to catch with or as if with a lasso. [C19: from Spanish *lazo,* ultimately from Latin *laqueus* noose] —**'las+so+er** *n.*

Las·sus ('læsəs) *n.* **Ro·land de.** Italian name *Orlando di Lasso.* ?1532–94, Flemish composer, noted for his mastery in both sacred and secular music.

last[1] (lɑːst) *adj.* (*often prenominal*) **1.** being, happening, or coming at the end or after all others: *the last horse in the race.* **2.** being or occurring just before the present; most recent: *last Thursday.* **3. last but not least.** coming last in order but nevertheless important. **4. last but one.** next to last. **5.** only remaining: *one's last cigarette.* **6.** most extreme; utmost. **7.** least suitable, appropriate, or likely: *he was the last person I would have chosen.* **8.** (esp. relating to the end of a person's life or of the world) **a.** final or ultimate: *last rites.* **b.** (*cap.*): *the Last Judgment.* **9.** (*postpositive*) *Liverpool dialect.* inferior, unpleasant, or contemptible: *this ale is last.* ~*adv.* **10.** after all others; at or in the end: *he came last.* **11. a.** most recently: *he was last seen in the mountains.* **b.** (*in combination*): *last-mentioned.* **12.** (*sentence modifier*) as the last or latest item. ~*n.* **13. the last. a.** a person or thing that is last. **b.** the final moment; end. **14.** one's last moments before death. **15.** the last thing a person can do (esp. in the phrase **breathe one's last**). **16.** the final appearance, mention, or occurrence: *we've seen the last of him.* **17. at last.** in the end; finally. **18. at long last.** finally, after difficulty, delay, or irritation. ~See also **last out.** [Middle English *laste,* variant of Old English *latest, lætest,* superlative of LATE]

last[2] (lɑːst) *vb.* **1.** (when *intr.,* often foll. by *for*) to remain in being (for a length of time); continue: *his hatred lasted for several years.* **2.** to be sufficient for the needs of (a person) for (a length of time): *it will last us until Friday.* **3.** (when *intr.,* often foll. by *for*) to remain fresh, uninjured, or unaltered (for a certain time or duration): *he lasted for three hours underground.* [Old English *lǣstan;* related to Gothic *laistjan* to follow] —**'last+er** *n.*

last[3] (lɑːst) *n.* **1.** the wooden or metal form on which a shoe or boot is fashioned or repaired. ~*vb.* **2.** (*tr.*) to fit (a shoe or boot) on a last. [Old English *lǣste,* from *lāst* footprint; related to Old Norse *leistr* foot, Gothic *laists*] —**'last+er** *n.*

last[4] (lɑːst) *n.* a unit of weight or capacity having various values in different places and for different commodities. Commonly used values are 2 tons, 2000 pounds, 80 bushels, or 640 gallons. [Old English *hlæst* load; related to *hladan* to LADE]

last-cy·clic *adj. Transformational grammar.* denoting rules that apply only to main clauses. Compare **cyclic** (sense 6), **post-cyclic.**

last-ditch *n.* (*modifier*) made or done as a last desperate attempt or effort in the face of opposition.

last+ing ('lɑːstɪŋ) *adj.* **1.** permanent or enduring. ~*n.* **2.** a strong durable closely woven fabric used for shoe uppers, etc. —**'last+ing+ly** *adv.* —**'last+ing+ness** *n.*

Last Judg+ment *n.* **the.** the occasion, after the resurrection of the dead at the end of the world, when, according to biblical tradition, God will decree the final destinies of all men according to the good and evil in their earthly lives. Also called: **the Last Day, Doomsday, Judgment Day.**

last+ly ('lɑːstlɪ) *adv.* **1.** at the end or at the last point. ~*sentence connector.* **2.** in the end; finally: *lastly, he put on his jacket.*

last-min·ute *n.* (*modifier*) given or done at the latest possible time: *last-minute preparations.*

last out *vb.* (*intr., adv.*) **1.** to be sufficient for one's needs: *how long will our supplies last out?* **2.** to endure or survive: *some old people don't last out the winter.*

last post *n.* (in the British military services) **1.** a bugle call that orders men to retire for sleep. **2.** a similar call sounded at military funerals.

last quar+ter *n.* one of the four principal phases of the moon, occurring between full moon and new moon, when half the lighted surface is visible. Compare **first quarter.**

last rites *pl. n. Christianity.* religious rites prescribed for those close to death.

last straw *n.* **the.** the final irritation or problem that stretches one's endurance or patience beyond the limit. [from the proverb, "It is the last straw that breaks the camel's back"]

Last Sup+per *n.* **the.** the meal eaten by Christ with his disciples on the night before his Crucifixion, during which he is believed to have instituted the Eucharist. Also called: the **Lord's Supper.**

last thing *adv.* as the final action, esp. before retiring to bed at night.

Las Ve+gas (læs 'veɪgəs) *n.* a city in SE Nevada: famous for luxury hotels and casinos. Pop.: 144 333 (1973 est.).

lat (læt) *n., pl.* **lats, la·tu** ('lætuː), *or* **la·ti** ('lætiː). the monetary unit of Latvia before 1940.

lat. *abbrev. for* latitude.

Lat. *abbrev. for* Latin.

Lat·a·ki·a *or* **Lat·ta·ki·a** (ˌlætə'kiːə) *n.* the chief port of Syria, in the northwest: tobacco industry. Pop.: 125 716 (1970). Latin name: **Laodicea ad Mare.**

latch (lætʃ) *n.* **1.** a fastening for a gate or door that consists of a bar that may be slid or lowered into a groove, hole, etc. **2.** a spring-loaded door lock that can be opened by a key from outside. **3.** Also called: **latch circuit.** *Electronics.* a logic circuit that transfers the input states to the output states when signalled. ~*vb.* **4.** to fasten, fit, or be fitted with or as if with a latch. [Old English *læccan* to seize, of Germanic origin; related to Greek *lazesthai*]

latch+et ('lætʃɪt) *n. Archaic.* a shoe fastening, such as a thong or lace. [C14: from Old French *lachet,* from *las* LACE]

latch+key ('lætʃˌkiː) *n.* **1.** a key for an outside door or gate, esp. one that lifts a latch. **2. a.** a supposed freedom from restrictions. **b.** (*as modifier*): *a latchkey existence.*

latch+key child *n.* a child who has to let himself in at home on returning from school, as his parents are out at work.

latch on *vb.* (*intr., adv.;* often foll. by *to*) **1.** to attach oneself (to): *to latch on to new ideas.* **2.** to understand. **3.** *U.S.* to obtain; get.

latch+string ('lætʃˌstrɪŋ) *n.* a length of string fastened to a latch and passed through a hole in the door so that it can be opened from the other side.

late (leɪt) *adj.* **1.** occurring or arriving after the correct or expected time: *the train was late.* **2.** (*prenominal*) occurring, scheduled for, or being at a relatively advanced time: *a late marriage.* **3.** (*prenominal*) towards or near the end: *the late evening.* **4.** at an advanced time in the evening or at night: *it was late.* **5.** (*prenominal*) occurring or being just previous to the present time: *his late remarks on industry.* **6.** (*prenominal*) having died, esp. recently: *my late grandfather.* **7.** (*prenominal*) just preceding the present or existing person or thing; former: *the late manager of this firm.* **8. of late.** recently; lately. ~*adv.* **9.** after the correct or expected time: *he arrived late.* **10.** at a relatively advanced age: *she married late.* **11.** recently; lately: *as late as yesterday he was selling books.* **12. late hours.** rising and going to bed later than is usual. **13. late in the day. a.** at a late or advanced stage. **b.** too late. [Old English *læt;* related to Old Norse *latr,* Gothic *lats*] —**'late+ness** *n.*

late+com·er ('leɪtˌkʌmə) *n.* a person or thing that comes late.

lat+ed ('leɪtɪd) *adj.* an archaic word for **belated.**

la+teen (lə'tiːn) *adj. Nautical.* denoting a rig with a triangular sail (**lateen sail**) bent to a yard hoisted to the head of a low mast, used esp. in the Mediterranean. [C18: from French *voile latine* Latin sail]

la·teen+rigged *adj. Nautical.* rigged with a lateen sail.

Late Greek *n.* the Greek language from about the 3rd to the 8th centuries A.D. Compare **Medieval Greek, Koine.**

Late Lat+in *n.* the form of written Latin used from the 3rd to the 7th centuries A.D. See also **Biblical Latin.**

late+ly ('leɪtlɪ) *adv.* in recent times; of late.

la+ten+cy pe+ri+od *n. Psychoanal.* a period, from the age of about five to puberty, when sexual interest is diminished.

La Tène (læ 'tɛn) *adj.* of or relating to a Celtic culture in Europe from about the 5th to the 1st centuries B.C., characterized by a distinctive type of curvilinear decoration. See also **Hallstatt.** [C20: from *La Tène,* a part of Lake Neuchâtel, Switzerland, where remains of this culture were first discovered]

la+tent ('leɪtᵊnt) *adj.* **1.** potential but not obvious or explicit. **2.** (of buds, spores, etc.) dormant. **3.** *Pathol.* (esp. of an infectious disease) not yet revealed or manifest. **4.** *Psychoanal.* relating to that part of a dream expressive of repressed desires. [C17: from Latin *latēnt-,* from *latens* present participle of *latēre* to lie hidden] —**'la+ten+cy** *n.* —**'la+tent+ly** *adv.*

la+tent heat *n.* (*no longer in technical usage*) the heat evolved or liberated when a substance changes phase without any change in its temperature.

la+tent im+age *n. Photog.* the invisible image produced by the action of light, etc., on silver halide crystals suspended in the emulsion of a photographic material. It becomes visible after development.

la+tent learn+ing *n. Psychol.* learning that occurs covertly while the organism is involved in other activities.

la+tent pe+ri+od *n.* **1.** the incubation period of an infectious disease, before symptoms appear. **2.** *Physiol., psychol.* the interval between a stimulus and its response.

lat+er ('leɪtə) *adj., adv.* **1.** the comparative of **late.** ~*adv.* **2.** afterwards; subsequently. **3. see you later.** *Informal.* an expression of farewell. **4. sooner or later.** eventually.

lat+er+al ('lætərəl) *adj.* **1.** of or relating to the side or sides: *a lateral blow.* **2.** *Phonetics.* (of a speech sound like *l*) pronounced with the tip of the tongue touching the centre of the alveolar ridge, leaving space on one or both sides for the passage of the airstream. ~*n.* **3.** a lateral object, part, passage, or movement. **4.** *Phonetics.* a lateral speech sound. [C17: from Latin *laterālis,* from *latus* side] —**'lat+er+al+ly** *adv.*

lat+er+al line sys+tem *n.* a system of sensory organs in fishes and aquatic amphibians consisting of a series of cells on the head and along the sides of the body that detect pressure changes and vibrations.

lat+er+al think+ing *n.* a way of solving problems by rejecting traditional methods and employing unorthodox and apparently illogical means.

Lat+er+an ('lætərən) *n.* **the. 1.** Also called: **Lateran palace.** a palace in Rome, formerly the official residence of the popes. **2.** any of five ecumenical councils held in this palace between 1123 and 1512. **3.** the basilica of Saint John Lateran, the cathedral church of Rome. [from Latin: the district is named after the ancient Roman family *Plautii Laterani*]

lat+er+ite ('lætəˌraɪt) *n.* any of a group of deposits consisting of residual insoluble deposits of ferric and aluminium oxides: formed by weathering of rocks in tropical regions. [C19: from Latin *later* brick, tile] —**lat+er+it+ic** (ˌlætə'rɪtɪk) *adj.*

lat+er·o·ver+sion (ˌlætərəʊ'vɜːʃən) *n.* abnormal lateral displacement of a bodily organ or part, esp. of the uterus. [C20: from LATERAL + *-version,* from Latin *versiō* a turning]

lat+est ('leɪtɪst) *adj., adv.* **1.** the superlative of **late.** ~*adj.* **2.**

most recent, modern, or new: *the latest fashions.* ~*n.* **3. at the latest.** no later than the time specified. **4. the latest.** *Informal.* the most recent fashion or development.

la+tex ('leɪtɛks) *n., pl.* **la+tex·es** *or* **lat·i+ces** ('lætɪˌsiːz). **1.** a whitish milky fluid containing protein, starch, alkaloids, etc., that is produced by many plants. Latex from the rubber tree is used in the manufacture of rubber. **2.** a suspension of synthetic rubber or plastic in water, used in the manufacture of synthetic rubber products, etc. [C19: New Latin, from Latin: liquid, fluid]

lath (lɑːθ) *n., pl.* **laths** (lɑːðz, lɑːθs). **1.** one of several thin narrow strips of wood used to provide a supporting framework for plaster, tiles, etc. **2.** expanded sheet metal, wire mesh, etc., used to provide backing for plaster or rendering. **3.** any thin strip of wood. ~*vb.* **4.** (*tr.*) to attach laths to (a ceiling, roof, floor, etc.). [Old English *lætt;* related to Dutch *lat,* Old High German *latta*] —**'lath+,like** *adj.*

lathe[1] (leɪð) *n.* **1.** a machine for shaping, boring, facing, or cutting a screw thread in metal, wood, etc., in which the workpiece is turned about a horizontal axis against a fixed tool. ~*vb.* **2.** (*tr.*) to shape, bore, or cut a screw thread in or on (a workpiece) on a lathe. [perhaps C15 *lath* a support, of Scandinavian origin; compare Old Danish *lad* lathe, Old English *hlæd* heap]

lathe[2] (leɪð) *n. Brit. history.* any of the former administrative divisions of Kent.

lath+er ('lɑːðə) *n.* **1.** foam or froth formed by the action of soap or a detergent in water. **2.** foam formed by other liquid, such as the saliva of a horse. **3.** *Informal.* a state of agitation or excitement. ~*vb.* **4.** to coat or become coated with lather. **5.** (*intr.*) to form a lather. **6.** (*tr.*) *Informal.* to beat; flog. [Old English *lēathor* soap; related to Old Norse *lauthr* foam] —**'lath+er·y** *adj.*

la+thi ('lɑːtɪ) *n.* a long heavy wooden stick used as a weapon in India, esp. by the police. [Hindi]

lath·y ('lɑːθɪ) *adj.* **lath·i+er, lath·i+est.** resembling a lath, esp. in being tall and thin.

lat·i+ces ('lætɪˌsiːz) *n.* a plural of **latex.**

lat·i+cif+er+ous (ˌlætɪ'sɪfərəs) *adj. Botany.* containing or yielding latex: *laticiferous tissue.* Also: **lactiferous.** [C19: from New Latin *latic-* LATEX + -FEROUS]

lat·i+fun+di·um (ˌlætɪ'fʌndɪəm) *n., pl.* **+di·a** (-dɪə). a large agricultural estate, esp. one worked by slaves in ancient Rome. [C17: from Latin *lātus* broad + *fundus* farm, estate]

Lat·i·mer ('lætəmə) *n.* **Hugh.** ?1485–1555, English Protestant bishop: burnt at the stake for heresy under Mary I.

lat·i+me·ri·a (ˌlætɪ'mɪərɪə) *n.* any coelacanth fish of the genus *Latimeria.* [C20: named after Marjorie Courtenay-*Latimer* (born 1902), South African museum curator]

Lat+in ('lætɪn) *n.* **1.** the language of ancient Rome and the Roman Empire and of the educated in medieval Europe, which achieved its classical form during the 1st century B.C. Having originally been the language of Latium, belonging to the Italic branch of the Indo-European family, it later formed the basis of the Romance group. See **Late Latin, Low Latin, Medieval Latin, New Latin, Old Latin.** See also **Romance. 2.** a member of any of those peoples whose languages are derived from Latin. **3.** an inhabitant of ancient Latium. ~*adj.* **4.** of or relating to the Latin language, the ancient Latins, or Latium. **5.** characteristic of or relating to those peoples whose languages are derived from Latin. **6.** of or relating to, the Roman Catholic Church. **7.** denoting or relating to the Roman alphabet. [Old English *latin* and *læden* Latin, language, from Latin *Latīnus* of Latium]

La+ti+na (*Italian* la'tiːna) *n.* a city in W central Italy, in Lazio: built as a planned town in 1932 on reclaimed land of the Pontine Marshes. Pop.: 78 227 (1971). Former name (until 1947): **Littoria.**

Lat+in al+pha+bet *n.* another term for **Roman alphabet.**

Lat+in A·mer·i+ca *n.* those areas of America whose official languages are Spanish and Portuguese, derived from Latin: South America, Central America, Mexico, and certain islands in the Caribbean. —**Lat+in A·mer·i+can** *n., adj.*

Lat+in+ate ('lætɪˌneɪt) *adj.* (of writing vocabulary, etc.) imitative of or derived from Latin.

Lat+in Church *n.* the Roman Catholic Church.

Lat+in cross *n.* a cross the lowest arm of which is longer than the other three.

Lat+in+ism ('lætɪˌnɪzəm) *n.* a word, idiom, or phrase borrowed from Latin.

Lat+in+ist ('lætɪnɪst) *n.* a person who studies or is proficient in Latin.

La+tin+i+ty (lə'tɪnɪtɪ) *n.* **1.** facility in the use of Latin. **2.** Latin style, esp. in literature.

Lat+in+ize *or* **Lat+in+ise** ('lætɪˌnaɪz) *vb.* (*tr.*) **1.** to translate into Latin or Latinisms. **2.** to transliterate into the Latin alphabet. **3.** to cause to acquire Latin style or customs. **4.** to bring Roman Catholic influence to bear upon (the form of religious ceremonies, etc.). —**ˌLat+in·i+'za+tion** *or* **ˌLat+in·i+'sa+tion** *n.* —**'Lat+in+ˌiz+er** *or* **'Lat+in+ˌis+er** *n.*

La+ti+no (læ'tiːnəʊ) *n., pl.,* **+nos.** *U.S. informal.* an inhabitant of the U.S. who is of Latin American origin.

Lat+in Quar+ter *n.* an area of Paris, on the S bank of the River Seine: contains the city's main educational establishments; centre for students and artists.

Lat+in square *n.* (in statistical analysis) one of a set of square arrays of *n* rows and columns built up from *n* different symbols so that no symbol occurs more than once in any row or column.

lat+ish ('leɪtɪʃ) *adj.* rather late.

lat·i+tude ('lætɪˌtjuːd) *n.* **1. a.** an angular distance in degrees north or south of the equator (latitude 0°), equal to the angle subtended at the centre of the globe by the meridian between the equator and the point in question. **b.** (*often pl.*) a region considered with regard to its distance from the equator. See **longitude** (sense 1). **2.** scope for freedom of action, thought, etc.; freedom from restriction: *his parents gave him a great deal of latitude.* **3.** *Photog.* the range of exposure over which a photographic emulsion gives an acceptable negative. **4.** *Astronomy.* See **celestial latitude.** [C14: from Latin *lātitūdō,* from *lātus* broad] —**ˌlat·i+'tu+di+nal** *adj.* —**ˌlat·i+'tu+di+nal+ly** *adv.*

lat·i+tu+di+nar+i+an (ˌlætɪˌtjuːdɪ'nɛərɪən) *adj.* **1.** permitting or marked by freedom of attitude or behaviour, esp. in religious matters. **2.** (*sometimes cap.*) of or relating to a school of thought within the Church of England in the 17th century. ~*n.* **3.** a person with latitudinarian views. [C17: from Latin *lātitūdō* breadth, LATITUDE, influenced in form by TRINITARIAN] —**ˌlat·i+ˌtu+di+'nar·i+an+ism** *n.*

La+ti·um ('leɪʃɪəm) *n.* a region of W central Italy, on the Tyrrhenian Sea: less extensive ancient territory inhabited by the Latin people from the 10th century B.C. until dominated by Rome (4th century B.C.); includes the plain of the lower Tiber, the reclaimed Pontine Marshes, and Campagna. Capital: Rome. Pop.: 4 702 093 (1971). Area: 17 203 sq. km (6709 sq. miles). Italian name: **Lazio.**

La·to·na (lə'təʊnə) *n.* the Roman name of **Leto.**

La·tour (*French* la'tuːr) *n.* **Mau·rice Quen·tin de** (mɔris kɑ̃'tɛ̃ də) 1704–88, French pastellist noted for the vivacity of his portraits.

La Tour (*French* la 'tuːr) *n.* **Georges de** (ʒɔrʒ də). ?1593–1652, French painter, esp. of candlelit religious scenes.

La Trappe (*French* la 'trap) *n.* a monastery in NW France, in the village of Soligny-la-Trappe northeast of Alençon: founded in about 1140, site of the Trappist reform of Cistercian order in 1664.

la+tri·a (lə'traɪə) *n. R.C. Church, theol.* the adoration that may be offered to God alone. [C16: via Latin from Greek *latreia* worship]

la+trine (lə'triːn) *n.* a lavatory, as in a barracks, camp, etc. [C17: from French, from Latin *lātrīna,* shortened form of *lavātrīna* bath, from *lavāre* to wash]

-la·try *n. combining form.* indicating worship of or excessive veneration of: *idolatry; Mariolatry.* [from Greek *-latria,* from *latreia* worship] —**-la·trous** *adj.*

lat+ten ('lætᵊn) *n.* metal or alloy, esp. brass, made in thin sheets. [C14: from Old French *laton,* of unknown origin]

lat+ter ('lætə) *adj.* (*prenominal*) **1. a.** denoting the second or second mentioned of two: distinguished from *former.* **b.** (*as n.; functioning as sing. or pl.*): *the latter is not important.* **2.** near or nearer the end: *the latter part of a film.* **3.** more advanced in time or sequence; later.

Usage. In careful usage, *latter* is used when only two items are in question: *he gave the money to Christopher and not to John, the latter being less in need of it. Last-named* is used to refer to the last-named of three or more items.

lat·ter-day *adj.* present-day; modern.

Lat·ter-day Saint *n.* a more formal name for a **Mormon.**

lat+ter+ly ('lætəlɪ) *adv.* recently; lately.

lat·ter+most ('lætəˌməʊst) *adj.* a less common word for **last**[1].

lat+tice ('lætɪs) *n.* **1.** Also called: **latticework.** an open framework of strips of wood, metal, etc., arranged to form an ornamental pattern. **2. a.** a gate, screen, etc., formed of such a framework. **b.** (*as modifier*): *a lattice window.* **3.** something, such as a decorative or heraldic device, resembling such a framework. **4.** an array of objects or points in a periodic pattern in two or three dimensions, esp. an array of atoms, ions, etc., in a crystal or an array of points indicating their positions in space. See also **Bravais lattice.** ~*vb.* **5.** to make, adorn, or supply with a lattice or lattices. [C14: from Old French *lattis,* from *latte* LATH] —**'lat+ticed** *adj.*

la+tus rec+tum ('lɑːtəs 'rɛktəm) *n., pl.* **lat+er·a rec+ta** ('lætərə 'rɛktə). *Geom.* a chord that passes through the focus of a conic and is perpendicular to the major axis. [C18: New Latin: straight side]

Lat+vi·a ('lætvɪə) *n.* the unofficial name of **Latvian Soviet Socialist Republic.**

Lat+vi·an ('lætvɪən) *adj.* **1.** of, relating to, or characteristic of Latvia, its people, or their language. ~*n.* **2.** Also called: **Lettish.** an official language of the Latvian SSR, along with Russian: closely related to Lithuanian and belonging to the Baltic branch of the Indo-European family. **3.** a native or inhabitant of Latvia.

Lat+vi·an So+vi+et So+cial+ist Re+pub+lic *n.* an administrative division of the W Soviet Union, on the Gulf of Riga and the Baltic Sea. Capital: Riga. Pop.: 2 364 127 (1970). Area: 63 700 sq. km (25 590 sq. miles).

laud (lɔːd) *Literary.* ~*vb.* **1.** (*tr.*) to praise or glorify. ~*n.* **2.** praise or glorification. [C14: vb. from Latin *laudāre;* n. from *laudēs,* pl. of Latin *laus* praise] —**'laud+er** *n.*

Laud (lɔːd) *n.* **Wil·liam.** 1573–1645, English prelate; archbishop of Canterbury (1633–45). His persecution of Puritans and his High Church policies in England and Scotland were a cause of the Civil War; he was impeached by the Long Parliament (1640) and executed.

Lau·da (*German* 'laʊda) *n.* **Ni·ki** ('nɪki). born 1949, Austrian motor-racing driver.

laud+a·ble ('lɔːdəbᵊl) *adj.* deserving or worthy of praise; admirable; commendable. —**'laud+a·ble+ness** *or* **ˌlaud+a·'bil+i·ty** *n.* —**'laud+a·bly** *adv.*

lau+da+num ('lɔːdᵊnəm) *n.* **1.** a tincture of opium. **2.** (formerly) any medicine of which opium was the main ingredient. [C16: New Latin, name chosen by Paracelsus for a preparation probably containing opium, perhaps based on LABDANUM]

lau+da+tion (lɔː'deɪʃən) *n.* a formal word for **praise.**

laud·a+to·ry ('lɔːdətərɪ, -trɪ) *or* **laud·a+tive** *adj.* expressing or containing praise; eulogistic.

Lau·der ('lɔːdə) *n.* Sir **Har·ry.** original surname *MacLennan.* 1870–1950, Scottish ballad singer and music hall comedian.

Laud+i·an ('lɔːdɪən) *adj. Church of England.* of or relating to the High-Church standards set up for the Church of England by Archbishop Laud.

lauds (lɔːdz) *n.* (*functioning as sing. or pl.*) *Chiefly R.C. Church.* the traditional morning prayer of the Western Church, constituting with matins the first of the seven canonical hours. [C14: see LAUD]

Lau·e (*German* 'laʊə) *n.* **Max The·o·dor Fe·lix von** (maks 'teːoˌdoːr 'feːlɪks fɔn). 1879–1960, German physicist. He pioneered the technique of measuring the wavelengths of x-rays by their diffraction by crystals and contributed to the theory of relativity: Nobel prize for physics 1914.

laugh (lɑːf) *vb.* **1.** (*intr.*) to express or manifest emotion, esp. mirth or amusement, typically by expelling air from the lungs in short bursts to produce an inarticulate voiced noise, with the mouth open. **2.** (*intr.*) (esp. of certain mammals or birds) to make a noise resembling a laugh. **3.** (*tr.*) to utter or express with laughter: *he laughed his derision at the play.* **4.** (*tr.*) to bring or force (someone, esp. oneself) into a certain condition by laughter: *he laughed himself sick.* **5.** (*intr.;* foll. by *at*) to make fun (of); jeer (at). **6.** (intr.; foll. by *over*) to read or discuss something with laughter. **7. don't make me laugh.** *Informal.* I don't believe you for a moment. **8. laugh in a person's face.** to show open contempt or defiance towards a person. **9. laugh like a drain.** *Informal.* to laugh loudly and coarsely. **10. laugh up one's sleeve.** to laugh or have grounds for amusement, self-satisfaction, etc., secretly. **11. laugh on the other side of one's face.** to show sudden disappointment or shame after appearing cheerful or confident: *you'll laugh on the other side of your face when you see how bad your work is.* **12. be laughing.** *Informal.* to be in a favourable situation. ~*n.* **13.** the act or an instance of laughing. **14.** a manner of laughter. **15.** *Informal.* a person or thing that causes laughter: *that holiday was a laugh.* **16. the last laugh.** the final success in an argument, situation, etc., after previous defeat. [Old English *læhan, hliehhen;* related to Gothic *hlahjan,* Dutch *lachen*] —**'laugh+er** *n.* —**'laugh+ing+ly** *adv.*

laugh+a·ble ('lɑːfəbᵊl) *adj.* **1.** producing scorn; ludicrous: *he offered me a laughable sum for the picture.* **2.** arousing laughter. —**'laugh+a·ble+ness** *n.* —**'laugh+a·bly** *adv.*

laugh a·way *vb.* (*tr., adv.*) **1.** to dismiss or dispel (something unpleasant) by laughter. **2.** to make (time) pass pleasantly by jesting.

laugh down *vb.* (*tr., adv.*) to silence by laughing contemptuously.

laugh+ing gas *n.* another name for **nitrous oxide.**

laugh+ing hy+e·na *n.* another name for the **spotted hyena** (see **hyena**).

laugh+ing jack·ass *n.* another name for the **kookaburra.**

laugh+ing stock *n.* an object of humiliating ridicule: *his mistakes have made him a laughing stock.*

laugh off *vb.* (*tr., adv.*) to treat or dismiss lightly, esp. with stoicism: *he laughed off his injuries.*

laugh+ter ('lɑːftə) *n.* **1.** the action of or noise produced by laughing. **2.** the experience or manifestation of mirth, amusement, scorn, or joy. [Old English *hleahtor;* related to Old Norse *hlātr*]

Laugh·ton ('lɔːtᵊn) *n.* **Charles.** 1899–1962, U.S. actor, born in England: noted esp. for his films of the 1930s, such as *Mutiny on the Bounty* (1935) and the unfinished *I Claudius* (1937).

launce (lɑːns) *n.* another name for the **sand eel.**

Laun+ces·ton ('lɔːnsəstən) *n.* a city in Australia, the chief port of the island state of Tasmania on the Tamar River, 64 km (40 miles) from Bass Strait. Pop.: 62 181 (1971).

launch[1] (lɔːntʃ) *vb.* **1.** to move (a vessel) into the water. **2.** to move (a newly built vessel) into the water for the first time. **3.** (*tr.*) to start off or set in motion: *to launch a scheme.* **4.** (*tr.*) to propel with force. **5.** to involve (oneself) totally and enthusiastically: *to launch oneself into work.* **6.** (*tr.*) to set (a missile, spacecraft, etc.) into motion. **7.** (*tr.*) to catapult (an aircraft), as from the deck of an aircraft carrier. **8.** (*intr.;* foll. by *into*) to start talking or writing (about): *he launched into a story.* **9.** (*intr.;* usually foll. by *out*) to start (out) on a fresh course. **10.** (*intr.;* usually foll. by *out*) *Informal.* to pay (out) a lot of money. ~*n.* **11.** an act or instance of launching. [C14: from Anglo-French *lancher,* from Late Latin *lanceāre* to use a lance, hence, to set in motion. See LANCE]

launch[2] (lɔːntʃ) *n.* **1.** a motor driven boat used chiefly as a transport boat. **2.** the largest of the boats of a man-of-war. [C17: via Spanish *lancha* and Portuguese from Malay *lancharan* boat, from *lanchar* speed]

launch com+plex *n.* an installation for the construction and launching of spacecraft, artificial satellites, or rockets.

launch+er ('lɔːntʃə) *n.* any installation, vehicle, or other device for launching rockets, missiles, or other projectiles.

launch+ing pad *or* **launch pad** *n.* a platform in a launch complex from which a spacecraft, rocket, etc., is launched.

launch+ing shoe *or* **launch shoe** *n.* an attachment to an aircraft from which a missile is launched.

launch ve+hi+cle *or* **launch+ing ve+hi+cle** *n.* **1.** a rocket, without its payload, used to launch a spacecraft. **2.** another name for **booster** (sense 2).

launch win+dow *n.* the limited period during which a spacecraft can be launched on a particular mission.

laun+der ('lɔːndə) *vb.* **1.** to wash and often also to iron (clothes, linen, etc.). ~*n.* **2.** a water trough, esp. one used for washing ore in mining. [C14 (n., meaning: a person who washes linen): changed from *lavender* washerwoman, from Old French *lavandiere,* ultimately from Latin *lavāre* to wash] —**'laun+der+er** *n.*

Laun+der+ette (ˌlɔːndə'rɛt, lɔːn'drɛt) *or U.S.* **Laun+dro+mat** ('lɔːndrəˌmæt) *n. Trademark.* a commercial establishment where clothes can be washed and dried, using coin-operated machines.

laun+dress ('lɔːndrɪs) *n.* a woman who launders clothes, sheets, etc., for a living.

laun+dry ('lɔːndrɪ) *n., pl.* **+dries. 1.** a place where clothes are washed and ironed. **2.** the clothes or linen washed and ironed. **3.** the act of laundering. [C16: changed from C14 *lavendry;* see LAUNDER]

laun·dry+man ('lɔːndrɪmən) *or* (*fem.*) **laun·dry+wom·an** *n., pl.* **+men** *or* **+wom·en. 1.** a person who collects or delivers laundry. **2.** a person who works in a laundry.

lau+ra+ceous (lɔː'reɪʃəs) *adj.* of, relating to, or belonging to the *Lauraceae,* a family of aromatic trees and shrubs having leathery leaves: includes the laurels and avocado.

Laur·a+sia (lɔː'reɪʃə) *n.* a hypothetical mass of land in the N hemisphere in the Palaeozoic era that later separated to form the northern continents. [C20: from New Latin *Laur(entia)* (referring to the ancient N American land mass, from *Laurentian* strata of the Canadian Shield) + (*Eur*)*asia*]

lau+re·ate ('lɔːrɪɪt) *adj.* (*usually immediately postpositive*) **1.** *Literary.* crowned with laurel leaves as a sign of honour. **2.** *Archaic.* made of laurel. ~*n.* **3.** short for **poet laureate. 4.** *Rare.* a person honoured with the laurel crown or wreath. [C14: from Latin *laureātus,* from *laurea* LAUREL] —**'lau+re·ate+ˌship** *n.* —**lau+re·a·tion** (ˌlɔːrɪ'eɪʃən) *n.*

lau+rel ('lɒrəl) *n.* **1.** Also called: **bay, bay laurel, sweet bay, true laurel.** a small Mediterranean lauraceous evergreen tree, *Laurus nobilis,* with glossy aromatic leaves, used for flavouring in cooking, and small blackish berries. **2.** a similar and related tree, *Laurus canariensis,* of the Canary Islands and Azores. **3.** short for **cherry laurel** or **mountain laurel. 4. spurge laurel.** a European thymelaeaceous evergreen shrub, *Daphne laureola,* with glossy leaves and small green flowers. **5. spotted** or **Japan laurel.** an evergreen cornaceous shrub, *Aucuba japonica,* of S and SE Asia, the female of which has yellow-spotted leaves. **6.** (*pl.*) a wreath of true laurel, worn on the head as an emblem of victory or honour in classical times. **7.** (*pl.*) honour, distinction, or fame. **8. look to one's laurels.** to be on guard against one's rivals. **9. rest on one's laurels.** to be satisfied with distinction won by past achievements. ~*vb.* **+rels, +rel+ling, +relled** *or U.S.* **+rels, +rel+ing, +reled. 10.** (*tr.*) to crown with laurels. [C13 *lorer,* from old French *lorier* laurel tree, ultimately from Latin *laurus*]

Lau·rel and Har·dy ('lɒrəl; 'hɑːdɪ) *n.* a team of U.S. film comedians, **Stan Laurel,** 1890–1965, the thin one, and his partner, **Oliver Hardy,** 1892–1957, the fat one.

Lau+ren+tian (lɔː'rɛnʃən) *adj.* **1.** Also: **Lawrentian.** of or resembling the style of D. H. or T. E. Lawrence. **2.** of, relating to, or situated near the St. Lawrence River.

Lau+ren+tian Moun+tains (lɔː'rɛnʃən) *pl. n.* a range of low mountains in E Canada, in Quebec between the St. Lawrence River and Hudson Bay. Highest point: 1191 m (3905 ft.). Also: **Lau+ren+tides** ('lɔːrənˌtaɪdz).

Lau+ren+tian Shield *n.* another name for the **Canadian Shield.** Also: **Laurentian Plateau.**

lau+ric ac·id ('lɔːrɪk, 'lɒ-) *n.* another name for **dodecanoic acid.** [C19: from Latin *laurus* laurel; from its occurrence in the berries of the laurel (*Laurus nobilis*)]

Lau·ri·er ('lɒrɪə) *n.* Sir **Wil·frid.** 1841–1919, Canadian Liberal statesman; the first French-Canadian prime minister (1896–1911).

lau+rus+ti+nus (ˌlɔːrə'staɪnəs) *n.* a Mediterranean caprifoliaceous shrub, *Viburnum tinus,* with glossy evergreen leaves and white or pink fragrant flowers. [C17: from New Latin, from Latin *laurus* laurel]

lau+ryl al+co+hol ('lɔːrɪl, 'lɒ-) *n.* a water-insoluble crystalline solid used in the manufacture of detergents; 1-dodecanol. Formula: $CH_3(CH_2)_{10}CH_2OH$. [C20: from LAUR(IC ACID) + -YL]

Lau+sanne (ləʊ'zæn; *French* lo'zan) *n.* a city in W Switzerland, capital of Vaud canton, on Lake Geneva; cultural and commercial centre; university (1537). Pop.: 135 200 (1975 est.).

Lau+trec (*French* lo'trɛk) *n.* See (Henri de) **Toulouse-Lautrec.**

lav (læv) *n. Brit. informal.* short for **lavatory.**

la·va ('lɑːvə) *n.* magma emanating from volcanoes and other vents. Any extrusive igneous rock formed by the cooling and solidification of lava. [C18: from Italian (Neapolitan dialect), from Latin *lavāre* to wash]

la+va+bo (lə'veɪbəʊ) *n., pl.* **+boes** *or* **+bos.** *Chiefly R.C. Church.* **1. a.** the ritual washing of the celebrant's hands after the offertory at Mass. **b.** (*as modifier*): *lavabo basin; lavabo towel.* **2.** another name for **washbasin. 3.** a trough for washing in a convent or monastery. [C19: from Latin: I shall wash, the opening of Psalm 26:6]

lav+age ('lævɪdʒ, læ'vɑːʒ) *n. Med.* the washing out of a hollow organ by flushing with water. [C19: via French, from Latin *lavāre* to wash]

La·val[1] (lə'væl) *n.* a city in SE Canada, in Quebec: a NW suburb of Montreal. Pop.: 228 010 (1971).

La·val[2] (*French* la'val) *n.* **Pierre** (pjɛ:r). 1883–1945, French statesman. He was premier of France (1931–32; 1935–36) and premier of the Vichy government (1942–44). He was executed for collaboration with Germany.

la·va-la·va *n.* a draped skirtlike garment of printed cotton or calico worn by Polynesians. [Samoan]

la+va+tion (læ'veɪʃən) *n. Formal or literary.* the act or process of washing. [C17: from Latin *lavātio,* from *lavāre* to wash] —**la+'va+tion+al** *adj.*

lav·a+to·ry ('lævətərɪ, -trɪ) *n., pl.* **-ries. 1.** Also called: **toilet, water closet, W.C. a.** a sanitary installation for receiving and disposing of urine and faeces, consisting of a bowl fitted with a water-flushing device and connected to a drain. **b.** a room containing such an installation. **2.** the washing place in a convent or monastic establishment. [C14: from Late Latin *lavātōrium,* from Latin *lavāre* to wash]

lav·a+to·ry pa+per *n. Brit.* another name for **toilet paper.**

lave (leɪv) *vb.* an archaic word for **wash.** [Old English *lafian,* perhaps from Latin *lavāre* to wash]

lav+en+der ('lævəndə) *n.* **1.** any of various perennial shrubs or herbaceous plants of the genus *Lavandula,* esp. *L. vera,* cultivated for its mauve or blue flowers and as the source of a fragrant oil (**oil of lavender**): family *Labiatae* (labiates). See also **spike lavender.** Compare **sea lavender. 2.** the dried parts of *L. vera,* used to perfume clothes. **3. a.** a pale or light bluish-purple to a very pale violet colour. **b.** (*as adj.*): *lavender socks.* **4.** perfume scented with lavender. [C13: *lavendre,* via French from Medieval Latin *lavendula,* of obscure origin]

la+ver[1] ('leɪvə) *n.* **1.** *Old Testament.* a large basin of water used by the priests for ritual ablutions. **2.** the font or the water of baptism. [C14: from Old French *laveoir,* from Late Latin *lavātōrium* washing place]

la+ver[2] ('lɑ:və) *n.* any of several seaweeds of the genus *Porphyra* and related genera, with edible fronds: family *Rhodophyceae* (red algae). [C16: from Latin]

La·ver ('leɪvə) *n.* **Rod(ney).** born 1938, Australian tennis player: Wimbledon champion 1968, 1969; U.S. champion 1969.

la+ver bread ('lɑ:və) *n.* laver seaweed fried as a breakfast food; popular in Wales.

lav+er+ock ('lævərək) *n.* a northern Brit. dialect word for **skylark** (bird). [Old English *lǣwerce* LARK[1]]

lav+ish ('lævɪʃ) *adj.* **1.** prolific, abundant, or profuse. **2.** generous; unstinting; liberal. **3.** extravagant; prodigal; wasteful: *lavish expenditure.* ~*vb.* **4.** (*tr.*) to give, expend, or apply abundantly, generously, or in profusion. [C15: adj. use of *lavas* profusion, from Old French *lavasse* torrent, from Latin *lavāre* to wash] —**'lav+ish+er** *n.* —**'lav+ish+ly** *adv.* —**'lav+ish+ment** *n.* —**'lav+ish+ness** *n.*

La·voi·sier (*French* lavwa'zje) *n.* **An·toine Lau·rent** (ɑ̃twan lɔ'rɑ̃). 1743–94, French chemist; one of the founders of modern chemistry. He disproved the phlogiston theory, named oxygen, and discovered its importance in respiration and combustion.

la+vol+ta (lə'vɒltə) *n.* another word for **volta.** [C16: from Italian *la volta* the turn; see VOLTA]

law (lɔ:) *n.* **1.** a rule or set of rules legally or constitutionally instituted in order to punish those who offend the conventions of society. **2. a.** a rule or body of rules made by the legislature. See **statute law. b.** a rule or body of rules made by a municipal or other authority. See **bylaw. 3. a.** the condition and control enforced by such rules. **b.** (*in combination*): *lawcourt.* **4.** a rule of conduct: *a law of etiquette.* **5.** one of a set of rules governing a particular field of activity: *the laws of tennis.* **6. the law. a.** the legal or judicial system. **b.** the profession or practice of law. **c.** *Informal.* the police or a policeman. **7.** a binding force or statement: *his word is law.* **8.** Also called: **law of nature.** a generalization based on a recurring fact or event. **9.** the science or knowledge of law; jurisprudence. **10.** the principles originating and formerly applied only in courts of common law. Compare **equity** (sense 3). **11.** a general principle, formula, or rule describing a phenomenon in mathematics, science, philosophy, etc.: *the laws of thermodynamics.* **12.** (*often cap.;* preceded by *the*) **a.** short for **Law of Moses. b.** another word for **Torah. 13. a law unto itself (oneself, etc.)** a person or thing that is outside established laws. **14. go to law.** to resort to legal proceedings on some matter. **15. lay down the law.** to speak in an authoritative or dogmatic manner. **16. take the law into one's own hands.** to ignore or bypass the law when redressing a grievance. ~Related adjs.: **judicial, juridical, legal.** [Old English *lagu,* from Scandinavian; compare Icelandic *lög* (pl.) things laid down, law]

Law (lɔ:) *n.* **1. An·drew Bon·ar** ('bɒnə). 1858–1923, British Conservative statesman, born in Canada; prime minister (1922–23). **2. John.** 1671–1729, Scottish financier. He founded the first bank in France (1716) and the Mississippi Scheme for the development of Louisiana (1717), which collapsed due to excessive speculation.

law-a·bid·ing *adj.* adhering more or less strictly to the laws: *a law-abiding citizen.* —**'law-a·,bid·ing+ness** *n.*

law a·gent *n.* (in Scotland) a solicitor holding a certificate from the Law Society of Scotland and thereby entitled to appear for a client in any Sheriff Court.

law+break·er ('lɔ:,breɪkə) *n.* **1.** a person who breaks the law. **2.** *Informal.* something that does not conform with legal standards or requirements. —**'law+,break·ing** *n., adj.*

law cen+tre *n. Brit.* an independent service financed by a local authority, which provides free legal advice and information to the general public.

Lawes (lɔ:z) *n.* **1. Hen·ry.** 1596–1662, English composer, noted for his music for Milton's masque *Comus* (1634) and for his settings of some of Robert Herrick's poems. **2.** his brother, **Wil·liam.** 1602–45, English composer, noted for his harmonically experimental instrumental music.

Law French *n.* a set of Anglo-Norman terms used in English laws and law books.

law+ful ('lɔ:fʊl) *adj.* allowed, recognized, or sanctioned by law; legal. —**'law+ful+ly** *adv.* —**'law+ful+ness** *n.*

law+giv·er ('lɔ:,gɪvə) *n.* **1.** the giver of a code of laws. **2.** Also called: **lawmaker.** a maker of laws. —**'law+,giv·ing** *n., adj.*

lawks (lɔ:ks) *interj. Brit.* an expression of surprise or dismay. [C18: variant of *Lord!,* probably influenced in form by ALACK]

law+less ('lɔ:lɪs) *adj.* **1.** without law. **2.** disobedient to the law. **3.** contrary to or heedless of the law. **4.** uncontrolled; unbridled: *lawless rage.* —**'law+less+ly** *adv.* —**'law+less+ness** *n.*

Law Lords *pl. n.* members of the House of Lords who sit as the highest court of appeal, although in theory the full House of Lords has this role.

law+man ('lɔ:mən) *n., pl.* **+men.** *Chiefly U.S.* an officer of the law, such as a policeman or sheriff.

law mer+chant *n. Mercantile law.* the body of rules and principles determining the rights and obligations of the parties to commercial transactions; commercial law.

lawn[1] (lɔ:n) *n.* **1.** a flat and usually level area of mown and cultivated grass. **2.** an archaic or dialect word for **glade.** [C16: changed form of C14 *launde,* from Old French *lande,* of Celtic origin; compare Breton *lann* heath; related to LAND] —**'lawn·y** *adj.*

lawn[2] (lɔ:n) *n.* a fine linen or cotton fabric, used for clothing. [C15: probably from *Laon,* a town in France where linen was made] —**'lawn·y** *adj.*

lawn mow+er *n.* a hand-operated or power-operated machine with rotary blades for cutting grass on lawns.

lawn ten+nis *n.* **1.** tennis played on a grass court. **2.** the formal name for **tennis.**

Law of Mo·ses *n.* **1.** the body of laws contained in the first five books of the Old Testament, traditionally ascribed to Moses. **2.** *Judaism.* the first five books of the Old Testament; Pentateuch.

law of na+tions *n.* another term for **international law.**

law of ther+mo+dy+nam+ics *n.* **1.** any of three principles governing the relationships between different forms of energy. The **first law of thermodynamics** (law of conservation of energy) states that the change in the internal energy of a system is equal to the sum of the heat added to the system and the work done on it. The **second law of thermodynamics** states that heat cannot be transferred from a colder to a hotter body within a system without net changes occurring in other bodies within that system; in any irreversible process, entropy always increases. The **third law of thermodynamics** (Nernst heat theorem) states that it is impossible to reduce the temperature of a system to absolute zero in a finite number of steps. **2.** Sometimes called: the **zeroth law of thermodynamics.** the principle that if two bodies are each in thermal equilibrium with a third body then the first two bodies are in thermal equilibrium with each other.

Law·rence ('lɒrəns) *n.* **1. D(avid) H(erbert).** 1885–1930, English novelist, poet, and short-story writer. Many of his works deal with the destructiveness of modern industrial society, contrasted with the beauty of nature and instinct, esp. the sexual impulse. His novels include *Sons and Lovers* (1913), *The Rainbow* (1915), *Women in Love* (1920), and *Lady Chatterley's Lover* (1928). **2. Er·nest Or·lan·do.** 1901–58, U.S. physicist who invented the cyclotron (1931): Nobel prize for physics 1939. **3. Ger·trude.** 1898–1952, English actress, noted esp. for her roles in comedies such as Noël Coward's *Private Lives* (1930). **4.** Sir **Thom·as.** 1769–1830, English portrait painter. **5. T(homas) E(dward),** known as *Lawrence of Arabia.* 1888–1935, British soldier and writer. He took a major part in the Arab revolt against the Turks (1916–18), proving himself an outstanding guerrilla leader. He described his experiences in *The Seven Pillars of Wisdom* (1926).

law+ren+ci·um (lɒ'rɛnsɪəm, lɔ:-) *n.* a transuranic element artificially produced from californium. Symbol: Lr; atomic no.: 103; half-life of most stable isotope, ^{256}Lr: 35 seconds; valency: 3. [C20: named after Ernest O. LAWRENCE]

Law+ren+tian (lɔ:'rɛnʃən) *adj.* relating to or characteristic of D.H. Lawrence.

Law So+ci+e·ty *n.* (in England or Scotland) the professional body of solicitors, established in 1825 and entrusted with the registration of solicitors (requiring the passing of certain examinations) and the regulation of professional conduct.

law sta+tion+er *n.* **1.** a stationer selling articles used by lawyers. **2.** *Brit.* a person who makes handwritten copies of legal documents.

law+suit ('lɔ:,su:t, -,sju:t) *n.* a proceeding in a court of law brought by one party against another, esp. a civil action.

law term. *n.* **1.** an expression or word used in law. **2.** any of various periods of time appointed for the sitting of lawcourts.

law+yer ('lɔ:jə, 'lɔɪə) *n.* **1.** a member of the legal profession, esp. a solicitor. See also **advocate, barrister, solicitor. 2.** a popular name for **burbot** (a fish). [C14: from LAW]

lax (læks) *adj.* **1.** lacking firmness; not strict. **2.** lacking precision or definition. **3.** not taut. **4.** *Phonetics.* (of a speech sound) pronounced with little muscular effort and consequently having relatively imprecise accuracy of articulation and little temporal duration. In English the vowel *i* in *bit* is lax. **5.** (of flower clusters) having loosely arranged parts. [C14 (originally used with reference to the bowels): from Latin *laxus* loose] —'**lax+ly** *adv.* —'**lax+i·ty** *or* '**lax+ness** *n.*

lax·a+tion (læk'seɪʃən) *n.* **1.** the act of making lax or the state of being lax. **2.** *Physiol.* another word for **defecation.** [C14: from Latin *laxātio,* from *laxāre* to slacken]

lax·a+tive ('læksətɪv) *n.* **1.** an agent stimulating evacuation of faeces. ~*adj.* **2.** stimulating evacuation of faeces. [C14 (originally: relaxing): from Medieval Latin *laxātīvus,* from Latin *laxāre* to loosen]

lay[1] (leɪ) *vb.* **lays, lay+ing, laid.** (*mainly tr.*) **1.** to put in a low or horizontal position; cause to lie: *to lay a cover on a bed.* **2.** to place, put, or be in a particular state or position: *he laid his finger on his lips.* **3.** (*intr.*) *Dialect or not standard.* to be in a horizontal position; lie: *he often lays in bed all the morning.* **4.** (sometimes foll. by *down*) to establish as a basis: *to lay a foundation for discussion.* **5.** to place or dispose in the proper position: *to lay a carpet.* **6.** to arrange (a table) for eating a meal. **7.** to prepare for lighting by placing fuel in the grate, etc.: *lay the fire.* **8.** (*also intr.*) (of birds, esp. the domestic hen) to produce (eggs). **9.** to present or put forward: *he laid his case before the magistrate.* **10.** to impute or attribute: *all the blame was laid on him.* **11.** to arrange, devise, or prepare: *to lay a trap.* **12.** to place, set, or locate: *the scene is laid in London.* **13.** to apply on or as if on a surface: *to lay a coat of paint.* **14.** to impose as a penalty or burden: *to lay a fine.* **15.** to make (a bet) with (someone): *I lay you five to one on Prince.* **16.** to cause to settle: *to lay the dust.* **17.** to allay; suppress: *to lay a rumour.* **18.** to bring down forcefully: *to lay a whip on someone's back.* **19.** *Taboo slang.* to have sexual intercourse with. **20.** to press down or make smooth: *to lay the nap of cloth.* **21.** to arrange and twist together (strands) in order to form (a rope, cable, etc.). **22.** *Military.* to apply settings of elevation and training to (a weapon) prior to firing. **23.** (foll. by *on*) *Hunting.* to put (hounds or other dogs) onto a scent. **24.** another word for **inlay. 25.** (*intr.;* often foll. by *to* or *out*) *Dialect or informal.* to plan, scheme, or devise. **26.** (*intr.*) *Nautical.* to move or go, esp. into a specified position or direction: *to lay close to the wind.* **27. lay aboard.** *Nautical.* (formerly) to move alongside a warship to board it. **28. lay a course. a.** *Nautical.* to sail on a planned course without tacking. **b.** to plan an action. **29. lay bare.** to reveal or explain: *he laid bare his plans.* **30. lay hands on.** See **hands** (sense 12). **31. lay hold of.** to seize or grasp. **32. lay oneself open.** to make oneself vulnerable (to criticism, attack, etc.). **33. lay open.** to reveal or disclose. **34. lay siege to.** to besiege (a city, etc.). ~*n.* **35.** the manner or position in which something lies or is placed. **36.** *Taboo slang.* **a.** an act of sexual intercourse. **b.** a sexual partner. **37.** a portion of the catch or the profits from a whaling or fishing expedition. **38.** the amount or direction of hoist in the strands of a rope. ~See also **layabout, lay aside, lay away, lay-by, lay down, lay in, lay into, lay off, lay on, lay out, lay over, lay to, lay up.** [Old English *lecgan;* related to Gothic *lagjan,* Old Norse *leggja*]

Usage. In careful English, the verb *lay* is used with an object and *lie* without one: *the soldier laid down his arms; the book was lying on the table.* In informal English, *lay* is frequently used for *lie: the book was laying on the table.* All careful writers observe the distinction even in informal contexts.

lay[2] (leɪ) *vb.* the past tense of **lie**[2].

lay[3] (leɪ) *adj.* **1.** of, involving, or belonging to people who are not clergymen. **2.** nonprofessional; amateur. [C14: from Old French *lai,* from Late Latin *lāicus,* ultimately from Greek *laos* people]

lay[4] (leɪ) *n.* **1.** a ballad or short narrative poem, esp. one intended to be sung. **2.** a song or melody. [C13: from Old French *lai,* perhaps of Germanic origin]

lay+a·bout ('leɪə,baʊt) *n.* **1.** a lazy person; loafer. ~*vb.* **lay about. 2.** (*prep., usually intr. or reflexive*) *Old-fashioned.* to hit out with violent and repeated blows in all directions.

Lay·a·mon ('laɪəmən) *or* **Law·man** ('lɔːmən) *n.* 12th-century English poet and priest; author of the *Brut,* a chronicle providing the earliest version of the Arthurian story in English.

lay an·a+lyst *n.* a person without medical qualifications who practises psychoanalysis.

Layard (lɛəd) *n.* Sir **Aus·ten Hen·ry.** 1817–94, English archaeologist, noted for his excavations at Nineveh.

lay a·side *vb.* (*tr., adv.*) **1.** to abandon or reject. **2.** to store or reserve for future use.

lay a·way *vb.* (*tr., adv.*) **1.** to store or reserve for future use. **2.** to reserve (merchandise) for future delivery, while payments are being made.

lay broth+er *n.* a man who has taken the vows of a religious order but is not ordained and not bound to divine office.

lay-by *n.* **1.** *Brit.* a place for drivers to stop at the side of a main road. **2.** *Nautical.* an anchorage in a narrow waterway, away from the channel. **3.** a small railway siding where rolling stock may be stored or parked. **4.** *Chiefly Austral.* a system of payment whereby a buyer pays a deposit on an article, which is reserved for him until he has paid the full price. ~*vb.* **lay by** (*adv.*) **5.** (*tr.*) to set aside or save for future needs. **6.** Also: **lay to.** to cause (a sailing vessel) to stop in open water or (of a sailing vessel) to stop.

lay days *pl. n.* **1.** *Commerce.* the number of days permitted for the loading or unloading of a ship without payment of demurrage. **2.** *Nautical.* the time during which a ship is kept from sailing because of loading, bad weather, etc.

lay down *vb.* (*tr., adv.*) **1.** to place on the ground, etc. **2.** to relinquish or discard: *to lay down one's life.* **3.** to formulate (a rule, principle, etc.). **4.** to build or begin to build: *the railway was laid down as far as Chester.* **5.** to record (plans) on paper. **6.** to convert (land) into pasture. **7.** to store or stock: *to lay down wine.* **8.** *Informal.* to wager or bet.

lay+er ('leɪə) *n.* **1.** a thickness of some homogeneous substance, such as a stratum or a coating on a surface. **2.** a laying hen. **3.** *Horticulture.* **a.** a shoot or branch rooted during layering. **b.** a plant produced as a result of layering. ~*vb.* **4.** to form or make a layer of (something). **5.** to take root or cause to take root by layering. [C14 *leyer, legger,* from LAY[1] + -ER[1]]

lay+er cake *n.* a cake made in layers with a filling.

lay+er+ing ('leɪərɪŋ) *n.* *Horticulture.* a method of propagation that induces a shoot or branch to take root while it is still attached to the parent plant.

lay+ette (leɪ'ɛt) *n.* a complete set of articles, including clothing, bedclothes, and other accessories, for a newborn baby. [C19: from French, from Old French, from *laie,* from Middle Dutch *laege* box]

lay fig+ure *n.* **1.** an artist's jointed dummy, used in place of a live model, esp. for studying effects of drapery. **2.** a person considered to be subservient or unimportant. [C18: from obsolete *layman,* from Dutch *leeman,* literally: joint-man]

lay in *vb.* (*tr., adv.*) to accumulate and store: *we must lay in food for the party.*

lay+ing on of hands *n.* (in Christian ordination, confirmation, faith healing, etc.) the act of laying hands on a person's head to confer spiritual blessing.

lay in·to *vb.* (*intr., prep.*) **1.** to attack forcefully. **2.** to berate severely.

lay+man ('leɪmən) *or* (*fem.*) **lay+wom·an** *n., pl.* **+men** *or* **+wom·en. 1.** a person who is not a clergyman. **2.** a person who does not have specialized or professional knowledge of a subject: *science for the layman.*

lay off *vb.* **1.** (*tr., adv.*) to dismiss from employment, esp. temporarily: *the firm had to lay off 100 men.* **2.** (*intr.*) *Informal.* to leave (a person, thing, or activity) alone: *lay off me, will you!* **3.** (*tr., adv.*) to mark off the boundaries of. **4.** (*tr., adv.*) *Soccer.* to pass or deflect (the ball) to a teammate, esp. one in a more advantageous position. **5.** *Gambling.* another term for **hedge** (sense 8). ~*n.* **lay-off. 6.** the act of dismissing employees. **7.** a period of imposed unemployment.

lay on *vb.* (*tr., adv.*) **1.** to provide or supply: *to lay on entertainment.* **2.** *Brit.* to install: *to lay on electricity.* **3. lay it on.** *Slang.* **a.** to exaggerate, esp. when flattering. **b.** to charge an exorbitant price. **c.** to punish or strike harshly.

lay out *vb.* (*tr., adv.*) **1.** to arrange or spread out. **2.** to prepare (a corpse) for burial. **3.** to plan or contrive. **4.** *Informal.* to spend (money), esp. lavishly. **5.** *Informal.* to knock unconscious. **6.** *Informal.* to exert (oneself) or put (oneself) to an effort: *he laid himself out to please us.* ~*n.* **lay+out. 7.** the act of laying out. **8.** something laid out. **9.** the arrangement of written material, photographs, or other artwork on an advertisement or page in a book, newspaper, etc. **10.** a preliminary plan indicating this. **11.** a drawing showing the relative disposition of parts in a machine, etc. **12.** the formation of cards on the table in various games, esp. in patience. **13.** *Informal, chiefly U.S.* a residence or establishment, esp. a large one.

lay o·ver *U.S.* ~*vb.* (*adv.*) **1.** (*tr.*) to postpone for future action. **2.** (*intr.*) to make a temporary stop in a journey. ~*n.* **lay+o·ver. 3.** a break in a journey, esp. in waiting for a connection.

lay read+er *n.* **1.** *Church of England.* a person licensed by a bishop to conduct religious services other than the Eucharist. **2.** *R.C. Church.* a layman chosen from among the congregation to read the epistle at Mass and sometimes other prayers.

lay+shaft ('leɪ,ʃɑːft) *n.* an auxiliary shaft in a gearbox, running parallel to the main shaft, to and from which drive is transferred to enable varying ratios to be obtained.

lay to *vb.* (*intr. adv.*) *Nautical.* **1.** to bring a vessel into a haven. **2.** another term for **heave to.**

lay up *vb.* (*tr., adv.*) **1.** to store or reserve for future use. **2.** (*usually passive*) *Informal.* to incapacitate or confine through illness.

laz+ar ('læzə) *n.* an archaic word for **leper.** [C14: via Old French and Medieval Latin, after LAZARUS] —'**laz·ar-,like** *adj.*

laz·a+ret+to (,læzə'rɛtəʊ), **laz·a+ret,** *or* **laz·a+rette** (,læzə'rɛt) *n., pl.* **+ret+tos, +rets,** *or* **+rettes. 1.** Also called: **glory hole.** *Nautical.* a small locker at the stern of a boat or a storeroom between decks of a ship. **2.** Also called: **lazar house, pesthouse.** (formerly) a hospital for persons with infectious diseases, esp. leprosy. [C16: Italian, from *lazzaro* LAZAR]

Laz·a·rus ('læzərəs) *n.* *New Testament.* **1.** the brother of Mary and Martha, whom Jesus restored to life (John 11–12). **2.** the beggar who lay at the gate of the rich man Dives in Jesus' parable (Luke 16:19–31).

laze (leɪz) *vb.* **1.** (*intr.*) to be indolent or lazy. **2.** (*tr.;* often foll. by *away*) to spend (time) in indolence. ~*n.* **3.** the act or an instance of idling. [C16: back formation from LAZY]

La+zio ('lattsjo) *n.* the Italian name for **Latium.**

laz·u+li ('læzjʊ,laɪ) *n.* short for **lapis lazuli.**

laz·u+lite ('læzjʊ,laɪt) *n.* a blue mineral, consisting of hydrated magnesium iron phosphate, occurring in metamorphic rocks. Formula: $(Mg,Fe)Al_2(PO_4)_2(OH)_2$. [C19: from Medieval Latin *lāzulum* azure, LAPIS LAZULI]

laz·u+rite ('læzjʊ,raɪt) *n.* a rare blue mineral consisting of a sodium aluminium silicate and sulphide: used as the gemstone lapis lazuli. Formula: $Na_{4-5}Al_3Si_3O_{12}S$. [C19: from Medieval Latin *lāzur* LAPIS LAZULI]

la·zy ('leɪzɪ) *adj.* **+zi+er, +zi+est. 1.** not inclined to work or exertion. **2.** conducive to or causing indolence. **3.** moving in a languid or sluggish manner: *a lazy river.* **4.** (of a brand letter or mark on livestock) shown as lying on its side. [C16: origin uncertain] —**'la·zi·ly** *adv.* —**'la·zi·ness** *n.*

la·zy·bones ('leɪzɪˌbəʊnz) *n. Informal.* a lazy person.

la·zy dai·sy stitch *n.* an embroidery stitch consisting of a long chain stitch, usually used in making flower patterns.

la·zy Su·san *n. Chiefly U.S.* a revolving tray, often divided into sections, for holding condiments, etc.

la·zy tongs *pl. n.* a set of tongs with a framework of hinged crossed rods that allows objects to be gripped at a distance.

lb *or* **lb.** *abbrev. for* pound (weight). [Latin: *libra*]

LB *international car registration for* Liberia.

l.b. *Cricket. abbrev. for* leg bye.

l.b.w. *Cricket. abbrev. for* leg before wicket.

l.c. *abbrev. for:* **1.** left centre (of a stage, etc.). **2.** loco citato. [Latin: in the place cited] **3.** *Printing.* lower case.

L.C. (in the U.S.) *abbrev. for* Library of Congress.

L/C, l/c, *or* **l.c.** *abbrev. for* letter of credit.

L.C.C. *abbrev. for* London County Council (now superseded by the Greater London Council).

l.c.d., lcd, L.C.D., *or* **LCD** *abbrev. for* lowest common denominator.

L.C.J. *Brit. abbrev. for* Lord Chief Justice.

L.C.L. *or* **l.c.l.** *Commerce. abbrev. for* less than carload lot.

l.c.m. *or* **L.C.M.** *abbrev. for* lowest common multiple.

L/Cpl. *abbrev. for* lance corporal.

LD *abbrev. for:* **1.** lethal dose. **2.** Also: **L.D.** Low Dutch.

ld. *abbrev. for:* **1.** *Printing.* lead. **2.** load.

Ld. *abbrev. for* Lord (title).

L-D con·vert·er *n. Metallurgy.* a vessel in which steel is made from pig iron by blowing oxygen into the molten metal through a water-cooled tube. [C20: L(inz)-D(onawitz), from the Austrian towns of *Linz* and *Donawitz,* where the process was first used successfully]

Ldg. *abbrev. for* leading: *leading seaman.*

L-do·pa (ɛl'dəʊpə) *n.* a substance occurring naturally in the body and used to treat Parkinson's disease. Formula: $C_9H_{11}NO_4$. [C20: from *L-d(ihydr)o(xy)p(henyl)a(lanine)*]

L.D.S. *abbrev. for:* **1.** Latter-day Saints. **2.** laus Deo semper. [Latin: praise be to God for ever] **3.** Also **LDS** (in Britain) Licentiate in Dental Surgery.

lea[1] (li:) *n.* **1.** *Poetic.* a meadow or field. **2.** land that has been sown with grass seed. [Old English *lēah;* related to German dialect *loh* thicket]

lea[2] (li:) *n.* **1.** a unit for measuring lengths of yarn, usually taken as 80 yards for wool, 120 yards for cotton and silk, and 300 yards for linen. **2.** a measure of yarn expressed as the length per unit weight, usually the number of leas per pound. [C14: of uncertain origin]

LEA (in Britain) *abbrev. for* Local Education Authority.

lea. *abbrev. for:* **1.** league. **2.** leather.

leach[1] (li:tʃ) *vb.* **1.** to remove or be removed from a substance by a percolating liquid. **2.** to lose or cause to lose soluble substances by the action of a percolating liquid. **3.** another word for **percolate** (senses 1, 2). ~*n.* **4.** the act or process of leaching. **5.** a substance that is leached or the constituents removed by leaching. **6.** a porous vessel for leaching. [C17: variant of obsolete *letch* to wet, perhaps from Old English *leccan* to water; related to LEAK] —**'leach·er** *n.*

leach[2] (li:tʃ) *n.* a variant spelling of **leech**[2].

Lea·cock ('li:kɒk) *n.* **Ste·phen But·ler.** 1869–1944, Canadian humorist and economist: his comic works include *Literary Lapses* (1910) and *Frenzied Fiction* (1917).

lead[1] (li:d) *vb.* **leads, lead·ing, led. 1.** to show the way to (an individual or a group) by going with or ahead: *lead the party into the garden.* **2.** to guide or be guided by holding, pulling, etc.: *he led the horse by its reins.* **3.** (*tr.*) to cause to act, feel, think, or behave in a certain way; induce; influence: *he led me to believe that he would go.* **4.** (*tr.*) to phrase a question to (a witness) that tends to suggest the desired answer. **5.** (when *intr.,* foll. by *to*) (of a road, route, etc.) to serve as the means of reaching a place. **6.** (*tr.*) to go ahead so as to indicate (esp. in the phrase **lead the way**). **7.** to guide, control, or direct: *to lead an army.* **8.** (*tr.*) to direct the course of or conduct (water, a rope or wire, etc.) along or as if along a channel. **9.** to initiate the action of (something); have the principal part in (something): *to lead a discussion.* **10.** to go at the head of or have the top position in (something): *he leads his class in geography.* **11.** (*intr.;* foll. by *with*) to have as the first or principal item: *the newpaper led with the royal birth.* **12.** *Music.* **a.** *Brit.* to play first violin in (an orchestra). **b.** (*intr.*) (of an instrument or voice) to be assigned an important entry in a piece of music. **13.** to direct and guide (one's partner) in a dance. **14.** (*tr.*) **a.** to pass or spend: *I lead a miserable life.* **b.** to cause to pass a life of a particular kind: *to lead a person a dog's life.* **15.** (*intr.;* foll. by *to*) to tend (to) or result (in): *this will only lead to misery.* **16.** to initiate a round of cards by putting down (the first card) or to have the right to do this: *she led a diamond.* **17.** (*tr.*) to aim at a point in front of (a moving target) in shooting, etc., in order to allow for the time of flight. **18.** (*intr.*) *Boxing.* to make an offensive blow, esp. as one's main attacking punch: *southpaws lead with their right.* **19. lead astray.** to mislead so as to cause error or wrongdoing. **20. lead by the nose.** *Informal.* to dominate or impose one's will on, esp. imperceptibly. ~*n.* **21. a.** the first, foremost, or most prominent place. **b.** (*as modifier*): *lead singer.* **22.** example, precedence, or leadership: *the class followed the teacher's lead.* **23.** an advance or advantage held over others: *the runner had a lead of twenty yards.* **24.** anything that guides or directs; indication; clue. **25.** another name for **leash. 26.** the act or prerogative of playing the first card in a round of cards or the card so played. **27.** the principal role in a play, film, etc., or the person playing such a role. **28. a.** the principal news story in a newspaper: *the scandal was the lead in the papers.* **b.** the opening paragraph of a news story. **c.** (*as modifier*): *lead story.* **29.** *Music.* an important entry assigned to one part usually at the beginning of a movement or section. **30.** a wire, cable, or other conductor for making an electrical connection. **31.** *Boxing.* **a.** one's habitual attacking punch. **b.** a blow made with this. **32.** *Nautical.* the direction in which a rope runs. **33.** a deposit of metal or ore; lode. **34.** the firing of a gun, missile, etc., ahead of a moving target to correct for the time of flight of the projectile. ~See also **lead off, lead on, lead up to.** [Old English *lǣdan;* related to *līthan* to travel, Old High German *līdan* to go]

lead[2] (lɛd) *n.* **1.** a heavy toxic bluish-white metallic element that is highly malleable: occurs principally as galena and used in alloys, accumulators, cable sheaths, paints, and as a radiation shield. Symbol: Pb; atomic no.: 82; atomic wt.: 207.2; valency: 2 or 4; relative density: 11.35; melting pt.: 327.5°C; boiling pt.: 1740°C. Related adjs.: **plumbic, plumbous. 2.** a lead weight suspended on a line used to take soundings of the depth of water. **3.** lead weights or shot, as used in cartridges, fishing lines, etc. **4.** a thin grooved strip of lead for holding small panes of glass or pieces of stained glass. **5.** (*pl.*) **a.** thin sheets or strips of lead used as a roof covering. **b.** a flat or low-pitched roof covered with such sheets. **6.** Also called: **leading.** *Printing.* a thin strip of type metal used for spacing between lines. Compare **reglet** (sense 2). **7. a.** graphite or a mixture containing graphite, clay, etc., used for drawing. **b.** a thin stick of this material, esp. the core of a pencil. **8.** (*modifier*) of, consisting of, relating to, or containing lead. ~*vb.* (*tr.*) **9.** to fill or treat with lead. **10.** to surround, cover, or secure with lead or leads. **11.** *Printing.* to space (type) by use of leads. [Old English; related to Dutch *lood,* German *Lot*] —**'lead·less** *adj.* —**'lead·y** *adj.*

lead ac·e·tate (lɛd) *n.* a white crystalline toxic solid used in dyeing cotton and in making varnishes and enamels. Formula: $Pb(CH_3CO)_2$. Also called: **sugar of lead.**

lead ar·se·nate (lɛd) *n.* a white insoluble toxic crystalline powder used as an insecticide and fungicide. Formula: $Pb_3(AsO_4)_2$.

Lead·bel·ly ('lɛdˌbɛlɪ) *n.* stage name of *Huddie Ledbetter.* 1888–1949, U.S. blues singer and guitarist.

lead col·ic (lɛd) *n.* a symptom of lead poisoning characterized by intense abdominal pain. Also called: **painter's colic.**

lead·en ('lɛdᵊn) *adj.* **1.** heavy and inert. **2.** laboured or sluggish: *leaden steps.* **3.** gloomy, spiritless, or lifeless. **4.** made partly or wholly of lead. **5.** of a dull greyish colour: *a leaden sky.* —**'lead·en·ly** *adv.* —**'lead·en·ness** *n.*

lead·er ('li:də) *n.* **1.** a person who rules, guides, or inspires others; head. **2.** *Music.* **a.** Also called (esp. U.S.): **concertmaster.** the principal first violinist of an orchestra, who plays solo parts, and acts as the conductor's deputy and spokesman for the orchestra. **b.** *U.S.* a conductor or director of an orchestra or chorus. **3.** the leading horse or dog in a team. **4.** *Chiefly U.S.* an article offered at a sufficiently low price to attract customers. See also **loss leader. 5.** a statistic or index that gives an advance indication of the state of the economy. **6.** *Chiefly Brit.* the leading editorial in a newspaper. Usual U.S. term: **leading article. 7.** *Angling.* another word for **trace**[2] (sense 2). **8.** *Nautical.* another term for **fairlead. 9.** a strip of blank film or tape used to facilitate threading a projector, developing machine, etc., and to aid identification. **10.** (*pl.*) *Printing.* rows of dots or hyphens used to guide the reader's eye across a page, as in a table of contents. **11.** *Botany.* any of the long slender shoots that grow from the stem or branch of a tree: usually removed during pruning. **12.** *Brit.* a member of the Government having primary authority in initiating legislative business (esp. in the phrases **Leader of the House of Commons** and **Leader of the House of Lords**). **13.** the senior barrister, usually a Queen's Counsel, in charge of the conduct of a case. Compare **junior** (sense 6). —**'lead·er·less** *adj.* —**'lead·er·ˌship** *n.*

lead glass (lɛd) *n.* glass that contains lead oxide as a flux.

lead-in ('li:dˌɪn) *n.* **1. a.** an introduction to a subject. **b.** (*as modifier*): *a lead-in announcement.* **2.** the connection between a radio transmitter, receiver, etc., and the aerial or transmission line.

lead·ing[1] ('li:dɪŋ) *adj.* **1.** capable of guiding, directing, or influencing. **2.** (*prenominal*) principal or primary. **3.** in the first position: *the leading car in the procession.* **4.** *Maths.* (of a coefficient) associated with the term of highest degree in a polynomial containing one variable: *in* $5x^2 + 2x + 3$, *5 is the leading coefficient.* —**'lead·ing·ly** *adv.*

lead·ing[2] ('lɛdɪŋ) *n. Printing.* another name for **lead**[2] (sense 6).

lead·ing air·craft·man ('li:dɪŋ) *n. Brit. airforce.* the rank above aircraftman. —**lead·ing air·craft·wom·an** *fem. n.*

lead·ing ar·ti·cle ('li:dɪŋ) *n. Journalism.* the usual U.S. term for **leader** (sense 6).

lead·ing edge ('li:dɪŋ) *n.* the forward edge of a propeller blade or aerofoil. Compare **trailing edge.**

lead·ing light ('li:dɪŋ) *n.* **1.** *Informal.* an important or outstanding person, esp. in an organization or cause. **2.** *Nautical.* a less common term for **range light.**

lead·ing man ('li:dɪŋ) *n.* a man who plays the main part in a film, play, etc. —**lead·ing la·dy** *fem. n.*

lead·ing note ('li:dɪŋ) *n. Music.* **1.** another word for **subtonic. 2.** (esp. in cadences) a note, usually the subtonic of a scale, that tends most naturally to resolve to the note lying one semitone above it.

lead·ing ques·tion ('li:dɪŋ) *n.* a question phrased in a manner that tends to suggest the desired answer, such as *What do you think of the horrible effects of pollution?*

lead·ing reins *or U.S.* **lead·ing strings** ('li:dɪŋ) *pl. n.* **1.** straps or a harness and strap used to assist and control a child who is learning to walk. **2.** excessive guidance or restraint.

lead line (lɛd) *n. Nautical.* a length of line for swinging a lead, marked at various points to indicate multiples of fathoms.

lead mon·ox·ide (lɛd) *n.* a poisonous insoluble oxide of lead existing in red and yellow forms: used in making glass, glazes, and cements, and as a pigment. Formula: PbO. Also called: **litharge, plumbous oxide.**

lead off (li:d) *vb.* (*adv.*) **1.** to initiate the action of (something); begin. ~*n.* **lead-off. 2.** an initial move or action. **3.** a person or thing that begins something.

lead on (li:d) *vb.* (*tr., adv.*) to lure or entice, esp. into trouble or wrongdoing.

lead pen·cil (lɛd) *n.* a pencil in which the writing material is a thin stick of a graphite compound.

lead poi·son·ing (lɛd) *n.* **1.** Also called: **plumbism, saturnism.** acute or chronic poisoning by lead or its salts, characterized by abdominal pain, vomiting, convulsions, and coma. **2.** *U.S. slang.* death or injury resulting from being shot with bullets.

lead screw (li:d) *n.* a threaded rod that drives the tool carriage in a lathe when screw cutting, etc.

leads·man ('lɛdzmən) *n., pl.* **·men.** *Nautical.* a sailor who takes soundings with a lead line.

lead tet·ra·e·thyl (lɛd) *n.* another name for **tetraethyl lead.**

lead time (li:d) *n.* **1.** *Manufacturing, chiefly U.S.* the time between the design of a product and its production. **2.** *Commerce.* the time from the placing of an order to the delivery of the goods.

lead up to *vb.* (*intr., adv. + prep.*) **1.** to act as a preliminary or introduction to. **2.** to approach (a topic) gradually or cautiously.

lead·wort ('lɛd,wɜ:t) *n.* any shrub of the plumbaginaceous genus *Plumbago,* of tropical and subtropical regions, with red, blue, or white flowers.

leaf (li:f) *n., pl.* **leaves** (li:vz). **1.** the main organ of photosynthesis and transpiration in higher plants, usually consisting of a flat green blade attached to the stem directly or by a stalk. **2.** foliage collectively. **3. in leaf.** (of shrubs, trees, etc.) having a full complement of foliage leaves. **4.** one of the sheets of paper in a book. **5.** a hinged, sliding, or detachable part, such as an extension to a table. **6.** metal in the form of a very thin flexible sheet: *gold leaf.* **7.** a foil or thin strip of metal in a composite material; lamina. **8.** short for **leaf spring. 9.** the inner or outer wall of a cavity wall. **10.** a crop that is harvested in the form of leaves. **11.** a metal strip forming one of the laminations in a leaf spring. **12.** a slang word for **marijuana. 13. take a leaf out of** (*or* **from**) **someone's book.** to imitate someone, esp. in one particular course of action. **14. turn over a new leaf.** to change or resolve to improve one's behaviour. ~*vb.* **15.** (when *intr.,* usually foll. by *through*) to turn (through pages, sheets, etc.) cursorily. **16.** (*intr.*) (of plants) to produce leaves. [Old English; related to Gothic *laufs,* Icelandic *lauf*] —**'leaf·less** *adj.* —**'leaf·less·ness** *n.* —**'leaf·,like** *adj.*

leaf·age ('li:fɪdʒ) *n.* a less common word for **foliage.**

leaf beet *n.* another name for **chard.**

leaf-climb·er *n.* a plant that climbs by using leaves specialized as tendrils.

leaf·cut·ter ant ('li:f,kʌtə) *n.* any of various South American ants of the genus *Atta* that cut pieces of leaves and use them as fertilizer for the fungus on which they feed.

leaf·cut·ter bee *n.* any of various solitary bees of the genus *Megachile* that nest in soil or rotten wood, constructing the cells in which they lay their eggs from pieces of leaf.

leaf fat *n.* the dense fat that accumulates in layers around the kidneys of certain animals, esp. pigs.

leaf-hop·per *n.* any homopterous insect of the family *Cicadellidae,* including various pests of crops.

leaf in·sect *n.* any of various mostly tropical Asian insects of the genus *Phyllium* and related genera, having a flattened leaflike body: order *Phasmida.* See also **stick insect.**

leaf-lard *n.* lard prepared from the leaf fat of a pig.

leaf·let ('li:flɪt) *n.* **1.** a printed and usually folded sheet of paper for distribution, esp. for advertising. **2.** any of the subdivisions of a compound leaf such as a fern leaf. **3.** any small leaf or leaflike part.

leaf min·er *n.* **1.** any of various insect larvae that bore into and feed on leaf tissue, esp. the larva of dipterous flies of the genus *Philophylla* (family *Trypetidae*) and the caterpillar of moths of the family *Gracillariidae.* **2.** the adult insect of any of these larvae.

leaf mon·key *n.* another name for **langur.**

leaf mould *n.* **1.** a nitrogen-rich material consisting of decayed leaves, etc., used as a fertilizer. **2.** any of various fungus diseases affecting the leaves of certain plants.

leaf spot *n.* any of various plant diseases, usually caused by fungi: characterized by dark lesions on the leaves.

leaf spring *n.* **1.** one of a number of metal strips bracketed together in length to form a compound spring. **2.** the compound spring so formed.

leaf·stalk ('li:f,stɔ:k) *n.* the stalk attaching a leaf to a stem or branch. Technical name: **petiole.**

leaf·y ('li:fɪ) *adj.* **leaf·i·er, leaf·i·est. 1.** covered with or having leaves. **2.** resembling a leaf or leaves. —**'leaf·i·ness** *n.*

league[1] (li:g) *n.* **1.** an association or union of persons, nations, etc., formed to promote the interests of its members. **2.** an association of sporting clubs that organizes matches between member teams of a similar standard. **3.** a class, category, or level: *he is not in the same league.* **4. in league (with).** working or planning together with. **5.** (*modifier*) of, involving, or belonging to a league: *a league game; a league table.* ~*vb.* **leagues, leagu·ing, leagued. 6.** to form or be formed into a league. [C15: from Old French *ligue,* from Italian *liga,* ultimately from Latin *ligāre* to bind]

league[2] (li:g) *n.* an obsolete unit of distance of varying length. It is commonly equal to 3 miles. [C14 *leuge,* from Late Latin *leuga, leuca,* of Celtic origin]

League of Na·tions *n.* an international association of states founded in 1920 with the aim of preserving world peace: dissolved in 1946.

lea·guer[1] ('li:gə) *n. Archaic.* **1.** an encampment, esp. of besiegers. **2.** the siege itself. [C16: from Dutch *leger* siege; related to LAIR]

leagu·er[2] ('li:gə) *n. Chiefly U.S.* a member of a league.

Leah ('lɪə) *n. Old Testament.* the first wife of Jacob and elder sister of Rachel, his second wife (Genesis 29).

leak (li:k) *n.* **1. a.** a crack, hole, etc., that allows the accidental escape or entrance of fluid, light, etc. **b.** such escaping or entering fluid, light, etc. **2. spring a leak.** to develop a leak. **3.** something resembling this in effect: *a leak in the defence system.* **4.** the loss of current from an electrical conductor because of faulty insulation, etc. **5.** a disclosure, often unintentional, of secret information. **6.** the act or an instance of leaking. **7.** a slang word for **urination.** ~*vb.* **8.** to enter or escape or allow to enter or escape through a crack, hole, etc. **9.** (when *intr.,* often foll. by *out*) to disclose (secret information), often unintentionally, or (of secret information) to be disclosed. **10.** (*intr.*) a slang word for **urinate.** [C15: from Scandinavian; compare Old Norse *leka* to drip] —**'leak·er** *n.*

leak·age ('li:kɪdʒ) *n.* **1.** the act or an instance of leaking. **2.** something that escapes or enters by a leak. **3.** *Commerce.* an allowance made for partial loss (of stock, etc.) due to leaking. **4.** *Physics.* **a.** an undesired flow of electric current, neutrons, etc., **b.** (*as modifier*): *leakage current.*

Lea·key ('li:kɪ) *n.* **1. Lou·is Sey·mour Baz·ett** ('bæzɪt). 1903–72, English anthropologist and archaeologist. He discovered fossil remains of manlike apes in E Africa. **2.** his son **Rich·ard.** born 1944, anthropologist, who discovered the remains of primitive man over 2 million years old in E Africa.

leak·y ('li:kɪ) *adj.* **leak·i·er, leak·i·est.** leaking or tending to leak. —**'leak·i·ness** *n.*

leal (li:l) *adj. Archaic or Scot.* loyal; faithful. [C13: from Old French *leial,* from Latin *lēgālis* LEGAL; related to LOYAL] —**'leal·ly** *adv.* —**le·al·ty** ('li:əltɪ) *n.*

Leam·ing·ton Spa ('lɛmɪŋtən) *n.* a town in central England, in central Warwickshire: saline springs. Pop.: 44 989 (1971). Official name: **Royal Leamington Spa.**

lean[1] (li:n) *vb.* **leans, lean·ing; leant** *or* **leaned. 1.** (foll. by *against, on,* or *upon*) to rest or cause to rest against a support. **2.** to incline or cause to incline from a vertical position. **3.** (*intr.;* foll. by *to* or *towards*) to have or express a tendency or leaning. **4.** (*intr.;* foll. by *on* or *upon*) to depend for advice, support, etc. **5. lean over backwards.** *Informal.* to do more than is expected. ~*n.* **6.** the condition of inclining from a vertical position. [Old English *hleonian, hlinian;* related to Old High German *hlinēn,* Latin *clīnāre* to INCLINE]

lean[2] (li:n) *adj.* **1.** not fat or full. **2.** (of meat) having little or no fat. **3.** not rich, abundant, or satisfying. **4.** (of a mixture of fuel and air) containing insufficient fuel and too much air: *a lean mixture.* **5.** (of printer's type) having a thin appearance. **6.** (of a paint) containing relatively little oil. **7.** (of an ore) not having a high mineral content. ~*n.* **8.** the part of meat that contains little or no fat. [Old English *hlæne,* of Germanic origin] —**'lean·ly** *adv.* —**'lean·ness** *n.*

Le·an·der (lɪ'ændə) *n.* (in Greek legend) a youth of Abydos, who drowned in the Hellespont in a storm on one of his nightly visits to Hero, his beloved. See also **Hero**[1].

lean·ing ('li:nɪŋ) *n.* a tendency or inclination.

leant (lɛnt) *vb.* a past tense or past participle of **lean**[1].

lean-to *n., pl.* **-tos. 1.** a roof that has a single slope with its upper edge adjoining a wall or building. **2.** a shed or outbuilding with such a roof.

leap (li:p) *vb.* **leaps, leap·ing; leapt** *or* **leaped. 1.** (*intr.*) to jump suddenly from one place to another. **2.** (*intr.;* often foll. by *at*) to move or react quickly. **3.** (*tr.*) to jump over. **4.** to come into prominence rapidly: *the thought leapt into his mind.* **5.** (*tr.*) to cause (an animal, esp. a horse) to jump a barrier. ~*n.* **6.** the act of jumping. **7.** a spot from which a leap was or may be made. **8.** the distance of a leap. **9.** an abrupt change or increase. **10.** Also called (U.S.): **skip.** *Music.* a relatively large melodic interval, esp. in a solo part. **11. a leap in the dark.** an action performed without knowledge of the consequences. **12. by leaps and bounds.** extremely fast. [Old English *hlēapan;* related to Gothic *hlaupan,* German *laufen*] —**'leap·er** *n.*

leap·frog ('li:p,frɒg) *n.* **1.** a children's game in which each player in turn leaps over the others' bent backs, leaning on them with the hands and spreading the legs wide. ~*vb.* **·frogs, ·frog·ging, ·frogged. 2. a.** (*intr.*) to play leapfrog. **b.** (*tr.*) to leap in this way over (something). **3.** to advance or cause to advance by jumps or stages.

leapt (lɛpt, li:pt) *vb.* a past tense or past participle of **leap.**

leap year *n.* a calendar year of 366 days, February 29 (**leap day**) being the additional day, that occurs every four years (those whose number is divisible by four). It offsets the difference between the length of the solar year (365.2422 days) and the calendar year of 365 days.

Lear (lɪə) *n.* **Ed·ward.** 1812–88, English humorist and painter, noted for his illustrated nonsense poems and limericks.

learn (lɜːn) *vb.* **learns, learn·ing; learnt** *or* **learned** (lɜːnd). **1.** (when *tr., may take a clause as object*) to gain knowledge of (something) or acquire skill in (some art or practice). **2.** (*tr.*) to commit to memory. **3.** (*tr.*) to gain by experience, example, etc. **4.** (*intr.; often foll. by of or about*) to become informed; know. **5.** *Not standard.* to teach. [Old English *leornian;* related to Old High German *lirnen*] —**'learn·a·ble** *adj.* —**'learn·er** *n.*

learn·ed ('lɜːnɪd) *adj.* **1.** having great knowledge or erudition. **2.** involving or characterized by scholarship. **3.** (*prenominal*) a title applied in referring to a member of the legal profession, esp. to a barrister: *my learned friend.* —**'learn·ed·ly** *adv.* —**'learn·ed·ness** *n.*

learn·ing ('lɜːnɪŋ) *n.* **1.** knowledge gained by study; instruction or scholarship. **2.** the act of gaining knowledge. **3.** *Psychol.* any relatively permanent change in behaviour that occurs as a direct result of experience.

learnt (lɜːnt) *vb.* a past tense or the past participle of **learn.**

lease[1] (liːs) *n.* **1.** a contract by which property is conveyed to a person for a specified period, usually for rent. **2.** the instrument by which such property is conveyed. **3.** the period of time for which it is conveyed. **4.** a prospect of renewed health, happiness, etc.: *a new lease of life.* ~*vb.* (*tr.*) **5.** to grant possession of (land, buildings, etc.) by lease. **6.** to take a lease of (property); hold under a lease. [C15: via Anglo-French from Old French *lais* (n.), from *laissier* to let go, from Latin *laxāre* to loosen] —**'leas·a·ble** *adj.* —**'leas·er** *n.*

lease[2] (liːz) *n. Dialect.* open pasture or common. [Old English *lǣs;* perhaps related to Old Norse *lāth* property]

lease·back ('liːsˌbæk) *n.* a property transaction in which the buyer leases the property to the seller.

lease·hold ('liːsˌhəʊld) *n.* **1.** land or property held under a lease. **2.** the tenure by which such property is held. **3.** (*modifier*) held under a lease.

lease·hold·er ('liːsˌhəʊldə) *n.* **1.** a person in possession of leasehold property. **2.** a tenant under a lease.

leash (liːʃ) *n.* **1.** a line or rope used to walk or control a dog or other animal; lead. **2.** something resembling this in function: *he kept a tight leash on his emotions.* **3.** *Hunting.* three of the same kind of animal, usually hounds, foxes, or hares. **4.** **straining at the leash.** eagerly impatient to begin something. ~*vb.* **5.** (*tr.*) to control or secure by or as if by a leash. [C13: from Old French *laisse,* from *laissier* to loose (hence, to let a dog run on a leash), ultimately from Latin *laxus* LAX]

least (liːst) *determiner.* **1. a. the.** the superlative of **little:** *you have the least talent of anyone.* **b.** (*as pronoun; functioning as sing.*): *least isn't necessarily worst.* **2. at least. a.** if nothing else: *you should at least try.* **b.** at the least. **3. at the least.** Also: **at least.** at the minimum: *at the least you should earn a hundred pounds.* **4. in the least.** (*usually used with a negative*) in the slightest degree; at all: *I don't mind in the least.* ~*adv.* **5. the least.** superlative of **little:** *they travel the least of all.* ~*adj.* **6.** of very little importance or rank. [Old English *lǣst,* superlative of *lǣssa* LESS]

least com·mon de·nom·i·na·tor *n.* another name for **lowest common denominator.**

least com·mon mul·ti·ple *n.* another name for **lowest common multiple.**

least squares *n.* a method for determining the best value of an unknown quantity relating one or more sets of observations or measurements, esp. to find a curve that best fits a set of data. It states that the sum of the squares of the deviations of the experimentally determined value from its optimum value should be a minimum.

least·ways ('liːstˌweɪz) *or U.S.* **least·wise** *adv. Informal.* at least; anyway; at any rate.

leat (liːt) *n. Brit.* a trench or ditch that conveys water to a mill wheel. [Old English *-gelǣt* (as in *wætergelǣt* water channel), from LET[1]]

leath·er ('lɛðə) *n.* **1. a.** a material consisting of the skin of an animal made smooth and flexible by tanning, removing the hair, etc. **b.** (*as modifier*): *leather goods.* **2.** something, such as a garment, made of leather. **3.** the flap of a dog's ear. ~*vb.* (*tr.*) **4.** to cover with leather. **5.** to whip with or as if with a leather strap. [Old English *lether-* (in compound words); related to Old High German *leder,* Old Norse *lethr-*]

leath·er·back ('lɛðəˌbæk) *n.* a large turtle, *Dermochelys coriacea,* of warm and tropical seas, having a ridged leathery carapace: family *Dermochelidae.* Also called (in Britain): **leathery turtle.**

Leath·er·ette (ˌlɛðə'rɛt) *n. Trademark.* an imitation leather made from paper, cloth, etc.

leath·er·head ('lɛðəˌhɛd) *n.* another name for **friarbird.**

Leath·er·head ('lɛðəˌhɛd) *n.* a town in S England, in Surrey. Pop.: 40 112 (1971).

leath·er·jack·et ('lɛðəˌdʒækɪt) *n.* **1.** any of various tropical carangid fishes of the genera *Oligoplites* and *Scomberoides,* having a leathery skin. **2.** any of various brightly coloured tropical triggerfishes of the genus *Monacanthus* and related genera. **3.** the greyish-brown tough-skinned larva of certain craneflies, esp. of the genus *Tipula,* which destroy the roots of grasses, etc.

leath·ern ('lɛðən) *adj. Archaic.* made of or resembling leather.

leath·er·neck ('lɛðəˌnɛk) *n. Slang.* a member of the U.S. Marine Corps.

leath·er·wood ('lɛðəˌwʊd) *n.* **1.** Also called: **wicopy.** a North American thymelaeaceous shrub, *Dirca palustris,* with pale yellow flowers and tough flexible branches. **2.** any of various Australian shrubs of the family *Cunoniaceae.*

leath·er·y ('lɛðərɪ) *adj.* having the appearance or texture of leather, esp. in toughness. —**'leath·er·i·ness** *n.*

leave[1] (liːv) *vb.* **leaves, leav·ing, left.** (*mainly tr.*) **1.** (*also intr.*) to go or depart (from a person or place). **2.** to cause to remain behind, often by mistake, in a place: *he often leaves his keys in his coat.* **3.** to cause to be or remain in a specified state: *paying the bill left him penniless.* **4.** to renounce or abandon: *to leave a political movement.* **5.** to refrain from consuming or doing something: *the things we have left undone.* **6.** to result in; cause: *childhood problems often leave emotional scars.* **7.** to allow to be or remain subject to another person or thing: *leave the past to look after itself.* **8.** to entrust or commit: *leave the shopping to her.* **9.** to submit in place of one's personal appearance: *will you leave your name and address?* **10.** to pass in a specified direction: *flying out of the country, we left the cliffs on our left.* **11.** to be survived by (members of one's family): *he leaves a wife and two children.* **12.** to bequeath: *he left his investments to his children.* **13.** (*tr.*) to have as a remainder: *37 –14 leaves 23.* **14.** *Not standard.* to permit; let. **15. leave be.** *Informal.* to leave undisturbed. **16. leave go** *or* **hold of.** *Not standard.* to stop holding. **17. leave it at that.** *Informal.* to take a matter no further. **18. leave much to be desired.** to be very unsatisfactory. **19. leave (someone) alone. a.** to refrain from persecuting, bothering, etc. **b.** to permit to stay or be alone. **20. leave someone to himself.** not to control or direct someone. [Old English *lǣfan;* related to *belīfan* to be left as a remainder] —**'leav·er** *n.*

leave[2] (liːv) *n.* **1.** permission to do something: *he was granted leave to speak.* **2. by or with your leave.** with your permission. **3.** permission to be absent, as from a place of work or duty: *leave of absence.* **4.** the duration of such absence: *ten days' leave.* **5.** a farewell or departure (esp. in the phrase **take (one's) leave). 6. on leave.** officially excused from work or duty. **7. take leave (of).** to say farewell (to). **8. take leave of one's senses.** to go mad. [Old English *lēaf;* related to *alȳfan* to permit, Middle High German *loube* permission]

leave[3] (liːv) *vb.* **leaves, leav·ing, leaved.** (*intr.*) to produce or grow leaves.

leave be·hind *vb.* (*tr.*) **1.** (*adv.*) to forget or neglect to bring or take. **2.** to cause to remain as a result or sign of something: *the storm left a trail of damage behind.* **3.** to pass: *once the wind came up, we soon left the land behind us.*

leaved (liːvd) *adj.* **a.** having a leaf or leaves; leafed. **b.** (*in combination*): *a five-leaved stem.*

leav·en ('lɛvᵊn) *n.* also **leav·en·ing. 1.** any substance that produces fermentation in dough or batter, such as yeast, and causes it to rise. **2.** a piece of such a substance kept to ferment a new batch of dough. **3.** an agency or influence that produces a gradual change. ~*vb.* (*tr.*) **4.** to cause fermentation in (dough or batter). **5.** to pervade, causing a gradual change. [C14: via Old French ultimately from Latin *levāmen* relief, (hence, raising agent, leaven), from *levāre* to raise]

Leav·en·worth ('lɛvᵊnˌwɜːθ, -wəθ) *n.* a city in NE Kansas, on the Missouri River: the state's oldest city, founded in 1854 by proslavery settlers from Missouri. Pop.: 25 147 (1970).

leave off *vb.* **1.** (*intr.*) to stop; cease. **2.** (*tr., adv.*) to stop wearing or using.

leave out *vb.* (*tr., adv.*) **1.** to cause to remain in the open: *you can leave your car out tonight.* **2.** to omit or exclude.

leaves (liːvz) *n.* the plural of **leaf.**

leave-tak·ing *n.* the act of departing; a farewell.

leav·ings ('liːvɪŋz) *pl. n.* something remaining, such as food on a plate, residue, refuse, etc.

Lea·vis ('liːvɪs) *n.* **F(rank) R(aymond).** 1895–1978, English literary critic. He edited *Scrutiny* (1932–53) and his books include *The Great Tradition* (1948) and *The Common Pursuit* (1952).

Leb·a·non ('lɛbənən) *n.* (sometimes preceded by *the*) a republic in W Asia, on the Mediterranean: an important centre of the Phoenician civilization in the third millennium B.C.; part of the Ottoman Empire from 1516 until 1919; gained independence in 1941 (effective by 1945). Official language: Arabic; French and English are also widely spoken. Religion: Muslim and Christian. Currency: Lebanese pound. Capital: Beirut. Pop.: 2 784 000 (1974 UN est.). Area: 10 400 sq. km (4015 sq. miles). —**Leb·a·nese** (ˌlɛbə'niːz) *adj., n.*

Leb·a·non Moun·tains *pl. n.* a mountain range in central Lebanon, extending across the whole country parallel with the Mediterranean coast. Highest peak: 3104 m (10 184 ft.). Arabic name: **Jeb·el Li·ban** ('dʒɛbᵊl 'liːbɑːn).

leb·en ('lɛbᵊn) *n.* a semiliquid food made from curdled milk in N Africa and the Levant. [C17: from Arabic *laban*]

Le·bens·raum ('leɪbənzˌraʊm) *n.* territory claimed by a nation or state on the grounds that it is necessary for survival or growth. [German: literally, living space]

leb·ku·chen ('leɪbˌkuːkən) *n. pl.* **·chen.** a biscuit, originating from Germany, usually containing honey, spices, etc. [German: literally, loaf cake]

Le·blanc (*French* lə'blɑ̃) *n.* **Ni·co·las** (nikɔ'lɑ). ?1742–1806, French chemist, who invented a process for the manufacture of soda from common salt.

Le·bow·a (lə'bəʊə) *n.* a Bantustan in South Africa, in N Transvaal: consists of three separate territories with several smaller exclaves.

Le·brun (*French* lə'brœ̃) *n.* **1. Al·bert** (al'bɛːr). 1871–1950, French statesman; president (1932–40). **2.** Also: **Le Brun. Charles** (ʃarl). 1619–90, French historical painter. He was court painter to Louis XIV and executed much of the decoration of the palace of Versailles.

Le Car·ré (lə ˈkæreɪ) *n.* **John.** pen name of *David John Cornwell.* born 1931, English novelist, esp. of spy thrillers such as *The Spy who came in from the Cold* (1963), *Tinker, Tailor, Soldier, Spy* (1974), and *The Honourable Schoolboy* (1977).

Lec·ce (*Italian* ˈlettʃe) *n.* a walled city in SE Italy, in Puglia: Greek and Roman remains. Pop.: 82 175 (1971).

lech *or* **letch** (lɛtʃ) *Informal.* ~*vb.* **1.** (*intr.;* usually foll. by *after*) to behave lecherously (towards); lust (after). ~*n.* **2.** a lecherous act or indulgence. [C19: back formation from LECHER]

Lech (lɛk; *German* lɛç) *n.* a river in central Europe, rising in SW Austria and flowing generally north through S West Germany to the River Danube. Length: 285 km (177 miles).

Le Cha·te·lier's prin·ci·ple (lə ʃæˈtɛljeɪz) *n. Chem.* the principle that if a system in chemical equilibrium is subjected to a disturbance it tends to change in a way that opposes this disturbance. [C19: named after H. L. *Le Chatelier* (1850–1936), French chemist]

lech·er (ˈlɛtʃə) *n.* a promiscuous or lewd man. [C12: from Old French *lecheor* lecher, from *lechier* to lick, of Germanic origin; compare Old High German *leccōn* to lick]

lech·er·ous (ˈlɛtʃərəs) *adj.* characterized by or inciting lechery. —**ˈlech·er·ous·ly** *adv.*

lech·er·y (ˈlɛtʃərɪ) *n., pl.* **·er·ies.** unrestrained and promiscuous sexuality.

lec·i·thin (ˈlɛsɪθɪn) *n. Biochem.* any of a group of yellow-brown phospholipids that are found in many plant and animal tissues, esp. egg yolk: used in making candles, cosmetics, and inks. [C19: from Greek *lekithos* egg yolk]

le·cith·i·nase (ləˈsɪθɪˌneɪs) *n.* any of a group of enzymes that remove the fatty-acid residue from lecithins: present in the venom of many snakes.

Leck·y (ˈlɛkɪ) *n.* **Wil·liam Ed·ward Hart·pole** (ˈhɑːtˌpəʊl). 1838–1903, Irish historian; author of *The History of England in the 18th Century* (1878–90).

Le·conte de Lisle (*French* ləkõt də ˈlil) *n.* **Charles Ma·rie Re·né** (ʃarl mari rəˈne). 1818–94, French Parnassian poet.

Le Cor·bu·sier (*French* lə kɔrbyˈzje) *n.* pseudonym of *Charles Édouard Jeanneret.* 1887–1965, French architect and town planner, born in Switzerland. He is noted for his use of reinforced concrete and for his modular system, which used units of a standard size. His works include Unité d'Habitation at Marseilles (1946–52) and the city of Chandigarh, India (1954).

Le Creu·sot (*French* lə krøˈzo) *n.* a town in E central France: metal and machinery industries. Pop.: 33 480 (1975).

lect. *abbrev. for:* **1.** lecture. **2.** lecturer.

lec·tern (ˈlɛktən) *n.* **1.** a reading desk or support in a church. **2.** any similar desk or support. [C14: from Old French *lettrun,* from Late Latin *lectrum,* ultimately from *legere* to read]

lec·tion (ˈlɛkʃən) *n.* a variant reading of a passage in a particular copy or edition of a text. [C16: from Latin *lectio* a reading, from *legere* to read, select]

lec·tion·ar·y (ˈlɛkʃənərɪ) *n., pl.* **·ar·ies.** a book containing readings appointed to be read at divine services. [C15: from Church Latin *lectiōnārium,* from *lectio* LECTION]

lec·tor (ˈlɛktɔː) *n.* **1.** a lecturer or reader in certain universities. **2.** *R.C. Church.* **a.** a person appointed to read lessons at certain services. **b.** (in convents or monastic establishments) a member of the community appointed to read aloud during meals. [C15: from Latin, from *legere* to read] —**lec·tor·ate** (ˈlɛktərɪt) *or* **ˈlec·tor·ˌship** *n.*

lec·ture (ˈlɛktʃə) *n.* **1.** a discourse on a particular subject given or read to an audience. **2.** the text of such a discourse. **3.** a method of teaching by formal discourse. **4.** a lengthy reprimand or scolding. ~*vb.* **5.** to give or read a lecture (to an audience or class). **6.** (*tr.*) to reprimand at length. [C14: from Medieval Latin *lectūra* reading, from *legere* to read]

lec·tur·er (ˈlɛktʃərə) *n.* **1.** a person who lectures. **2.** a teacher in higher education without professorial status.

lec·ture·ship (ˈlɛktʃəˌʃɪp) *n.* **1.** the office or position of lecturer. **2.** an endowment financing a series of lectures.

lec·y·thus (ˈlɛsɪθəs) *n., pl.* **·thi** (-ˌθaɪ). (in ancient Greece) a vase with a narrow neck. [from Greek *lēkuthos*]

led (lɛd) *vb.* the past tense or past participle of **lead.**

LED *Electronics. abbrev. for* light-emitting diode.

Le·da (ˈliːdə) *n. Greek myth.* a queen of Sparta who was the mother of Helen and Pollux by Zeus, who visited her in the form of a swan.

le·der·ho·sen (ˈleɪdəˌhəʊzᵊn) *pl. n.* leather shorts with H-shaped braces, worn by men in Austria, Bavaria, etc. [German: leather trousers]

ledge (lɛdʒ) *n.* **1.** a narrow horizontal surface resembling a shelf and projecting from a wall, window, etc. **2.** a layer of rock that contains an ore; vein. **3.** a ridge of rock that lies beneath the surface of the sea. **4.** a narrow shelflike rock projection on a cliff or mountain. [C14 *legge,* perhaps from *leggen* to LAY[1]] —**ˈledg·y** *or* **ledged** *adj.*

ledg·er (ˈlɛdʒə) *n.* **1.** *Book-keeping.* the principal book in which the commercial transactions of a company are recorded. **2.** a flat horizontal slab of stone. **3.** a horizontal scaffold pole fixed to two upright poles for supporting the outer ends of putlogs. **4.** *Angling.* **a.** a wire trace that allows the weight to rest on the bottom and the bait to float freely. **b.** (*as modifier*): *ledger tackle.* ~*vb.* **5.** (*intr.*) *Angling.* to fish using a ledger. [C15 *legger* book retained in a specific place, probably from *leggen* to LAY[1]]

ledg·er board *n.* **1.** a timber board forming the top rail of a fence or balustrade. **2.** Also called: **ribbon strip.** a timber board fixed horizontally to studding to support floor joists.

ledg·er line *n.* **1.** *Music.* a short line placed above or below the staff to accommodate notes representing pitches above or below the staff. **2.** *Angling.* a line using ledger tackle.

Led Zep·pe·lin *n.* English rock group (formed 1968): comprising Jimmy Page (born 1944; guitar), John Paul Jones (born *John Baldwin,* 1946; bass guitar, keyboards), Robert Plant (born 1948; vocals), and John Bonham (1949-80; drums).

lee (liː) *n.* **1.** a sheltered part or side; the side away from the direction from which the wind is blowing. **2. by the lee.** *Nautical.* so that the wind is blowing on the wrong side of the sail. **3. under the lee.** *Nautical.* towards the lee. ~*adj.* **4.** (*prenominal*) *Nautical.* on, at, or towards the side or part away from the wind: *on a lee shore.* Compare **weather** (sense 5). [Old English *hlēow* shelter; related to Old Norse *hle*]

Lee[1] (liː) *n.* a river in SW Ireland, flowing east into Cork Harbour. Length: about 80 km (50 miles).

Lee[2] (liː) *n.* **1. Kuan Yew** (ˈkwɑːn ˈjuː). born 1923, Singapore statesman; prime minister since 1959. **2. Rich·ard Hen·ry.** 1732–94, American Revolutionary statesman, who moved the resolution in favour of American independence (1776). **3. Rob·ert E(dward).** 1807–70, American general; commander-in-chief of the Confederate armies in the Civil War. **4. T(sung)-D(ao).** born 1926, U.S. physicist, born in China. With Yang he disproved the principle that parity is always conserved and shared the Nobel prize for physics in 1957.

lee·board (ˈliːˌbɔːd) *n. Nautical.* one of a pair of large adjustable paddle-like boards that may be lowered along the lee side to reduce sideways drift or leeway.

leech[1] (liːtʃ) *n.* **1.** any annelid worm of the class *Hirudinea,* which have a sucker at each end of the body and feed on the blood or tissues of other animals. See also **horseleech, medicinal leech. 2.** a person who clings to or preys on another person. **3. a.** an archaic word for **physician. b.** (*in combination*): *leechcraft.* **4. cling like a leech.** to cling or adhere persistently to something. ~*vb.* (*tr.*) **5.** to use leeches to suck the blood of (a person), as a method of medical treatment. **6.** *Archaic.* to cure or heal. [Old English *lǣce, lȳce;* related to Middle Dutch *lieke*] —**ˈleech·ˌlike** *adj.*

leech[2] *or* **leach** (liːtʃ) *n. Nautical.* the after edge of a fore-and-aft sail or either of the vertical edges of a squaresail. [C15: of Germanic origin; compare Dutch *lijk*]

Leeds (liːdz) *n.* a city in N England, in West Yorkshire on the River Aire: linked with Liverpool and Goole by canals; a chief centre of the clothing industry; university (1904). Pop.: 494 971 (1971).

leek (liːk) *n.* **1.** Also called: **scallion.** an alliaceous plant, *Allium porrum,* with a slender white bulb, cylindrical stem, and broad flat overlapping leaves: used in cooking. **2.** any of several related species, such as *A. ampeloprasum* (wild leek). **3.** the national emblem of Wales. [Old English *lēac;* related to Old Norse *laukr,* Old High German *louh*]

leer (lɪə) *vb.* **1.** (*intr.*) to give an oblique, sneering, or suggestive look or grin. ~*n.* **2.** such a look. [C16: perhaps verbal use of obsolete *leer* cheek, from Old English *hlēor*] —**ˈleer·ing·ly** *adv.*

leer·y *or* **lear·y** (ˈlɪərɪ) *adj.* **leer·i·er, leer·i·est** *or* **lear·i·er, lear·i·est. 1.** *Now chiefly dialect.* knowing or sly. **2.** *Slang.* (foll. by *of*) suspicious or wary. [C18: perhaps from obsolete sense (to look askance) of LEER] —**ˈleer·i·ness** *or* **ˈlear·i·ness** *n.*

lees (liːz) *pl. n.* the sediment from an alcoholic drink. [C14: plural of obsolete *lee,* from Old French, probably from Celtic; compare Irish *lige* bed]

leet[1] (liːt) *n. English history.* **1.** Also called: **court-leet.** a special kind of manorial court that some lords were entitled to hold. **2.** the jurisdiction of this court. [C15: from Anglo-French, of unknown origin]

leet[2] (liːt) *n. Scot.* a list of candidates for an office. [C15: perhaps from Anglo-French *litte,* variant of LIST[1]]

Leeu·war·den (*Dutch* ˈleːˌwardə) *n.* a city in the N Netherlands, capital of Friesland province. Pop.: 86 339 (1973 est.).

Leeu·wen·hoek (ˈleɪvᵊnˌhuːk, *Dutch* ˈleːwənˌhuːk) *n.* **An·ton van** (ˈɑntɔn vɑn). 1632–1723, Dutch microscopist, whose microscopes enabled him to give the first accurate description of blood corpuscles, spermatozoa, and microbes.

lee·ward (ˈliːwəd; *nautical* ˈluːəd) *Chiefly nautical.* ~*adj.* **1.** of, in, or moving to the quarter towards which the wind blows. ~*n.* **2.** the point or quarter towards which the wind blows. **3.** the side towards the lee. ~*adv.* **4.** towards the lee. ~Compare **windward.**

Lee·ward Is·lands (ˈliːwəd) *pl. n.* **1.** a group of islands in the West Indies, in the N Lesser Antilles between Puerto Rico and Martinique. **2.** a former British colony in the E West Indies (1871–1956), consisting of Antigua, Barbuda, Redonda, St. Kitts, Nevis, Anguilla, Montserrat, and the British Virgin Islands. **3.** a group of islands in the S Pacific, in French Polynesia in the W Society Archipelago: Huahiné, Raiatéa, Tahaa, Bora-Bora, and Maupiti. Pop.: 15 718 (1970). French name: **Îles sous le Vent.**

lee·way (ˈliːˌweɪ) *n.* **1.** room for free movement within limits, as in action or expenditure. **2.** sideways drift of a boat or aircraft.

left[1] (lɛft) *adj.* **1.** (*usually prenominal*) of, or designating, the side of something or someone that faces west when the front is turned towards the north. **2.** (*usually prenominal*) worn on a left hand, foot, etc. **3.** (*sometimes cap.*) of or relating to the political or intellectual left. **4.** (*sometimes cap.*) radical or progressive, esp. as compared to less radical or progressive groups, persons, etc. *~adv.* **5.** on or in the direction of the left. *~n.* **6.** a left side, direction, position, area, or part. Related adjs.: **sinister, sinistral.** **7.** (*often cap.*) the supporters or advocates of varying degrees of social, political, or economic change, reform, or revolution designed to promote the greater freedom, power, welfare, or comfort of the common people. **8.** **to the left.** radical in the methods, principles, etc., employed in striving to achieve such change. **9.** *Boxing.* **a.** a blow with the left hand. **b.** the left hand. [Old English *left* idle, weak, variant of *lyft-* (in *lyftādl* palsy, literally: left-disease); related to Middle Dutch *lucht* left]

left[2] (lɛft) *vb.* the past tense or past participle of **leave.**

Left Bank *n.* a district of Paris, on the S bank of the River Seine; frequented by artists, students, etc.

left-foot·er *n. Informal.* (esp. in Ireland) a Roman Catholic. [C20: from the Northern Irish saying that farm workers in Eire use the left foot to push a spade when digging]

left-hand *adj.* (*prenominal*) **1.** of, relating to, located on, or moving towards the left: *this car is left-hand drive; a left-hand bend.* **2.** for use by the left hand; left-handed.

left-hand·ed *adj.* **1.** using the left hand with greater ease than the right. **2.** performed with the left hand. **3.** designed or adapted for use by the left hand. **4.** worn on the left hand. **5.** awkward or clumsy. **6.** ironically ambiguous: *a left-handed compliment.* **7.** turning from right to left; anticlockwise. **8.** *Law.* another term for **morganatic.** *~adv.* **9.** with the left hand. —ˌ**left-ˈhand·ed·ly** *adv.* —ˌ**left-ˈhand·ed·ness** *n.*

left-hand·er *n.* **1.** a blow with the left hand. **2.** a left-handed person.

left+ist (ˈlɛftɪst) *adj.* **1.** of, tending towards, or relating to the political left or its principles. *~n.* **2.** a person who supports or belongs to the political left. —ˈ**left+ism** *n.*

left-lug·gage of+fice *n. Brit.* a place at a railway station, airport, etc., where luggage may be left for a small charge with an attendant for safekeeping. U.S. name: **checkroom.**

left+o·ver (ˈlɛftˌəʊvə) *n.* **1.** (*often pl.*) an unused portion or remnant, as of material or of cooked food. *~adj.* **2.** left as an unused portion or remnant.

left+ward (ˈlɛftwəd) *adj.* **1.** on or towards the left. *~adv.* **2.** a variant of **leftwards.**

left+wards (ˈlɛftwədz) *or* **left+ward** *adv.* towards or on the left.

left wing *n.* **1.** (*often cap.*) the leftist faction of an assembly, party, group, etc.; the radical or progressive wing. **2.** the units of an army situated on the left of a battle position. **3.** *Sports.* **a.** the left-hand side of the field of play from the point of view of either team facing its opponents' goal. **b.** a player positioned in this area in certain games. *~adj.* **left-wing.** **4.** of, belonging to, or relating to the political left wing. —ˌ**left-ˈwing·er** *n.*

left·y (ˈlɛftɪ) *n., pl.* **left·ies.** *Informal.* **1.** a left-winger. **2.** *Chiefly U.S.* a left-handed person.

leg (lɛg) *n.* **1. a.** either of the two lower limbs, including the bones and fleshy covering of the femur, tibia, fibula, and patella. **b.** (*as modifier*): *leg guard; leg rest.* **2.** any similar or analogous structure in animals that is used for locomotion or support. **3.** this part of an animal, esp. the thigh, used for food: *leg of lamb.* **4.** something similar to a leg in appearance or function, such as one of the four supporting members of a chair. **5.** a branch, limb, or part of a forked or jointed object. **6.** the part of a garment that covers the leg. **7.** a section or part of a journey or course. **8.** a single stage, lap, length, etc., in a relay race. **9.** either the opposite or adjacent side of a right-angled triangle. **10.** *Nautical.* **a.** the distance travelled without tacking. **b.** (in yacht racing) the course between any two marks. **11.** one of a series of games, matches, or parts of games. **12.** *Cricket.* **a.** the side of the field to the left of and behind a right-handed batsman as he faces the bowler. **b.** (*as modifier*): *a leg slip; leg stump.* **13. a leg up.** help to another person in climbing up a wall, etc., by pushing upwards. **14. not have a leg to stand on.** *Informal.* to have no reasonable or logical basis for an opinion or argument. **15. on his, its, etc., last legs.** (of a person or thing) worn out; exhausted. **16. pull someone's leg.** *Informal.* to tease, fool, or make fun of someone. **17. shake a leg.** *Slang.* to hurry up: usually used in the imperative. **18. show a leg.** *Informal.* to get up in the morning. **19. stretch one's legs.** to stand up or walk around, esp. after sitting for some time. *~vb.* **legs, leg+ging, legged.** **20.** (*tr.*) *Obsolete.* to propel (a canal boat) through a tunnel by lying on one's back and walking one's feet along the tunnel roof. **21. leg it.** *Informal.* to walk, run, or hurry. [C13: from Old Norse *leggr,* of obscure origin] —ˈ**leg+less** *adj.* —ˈ**leg+ˌlike** *adj.*

leg. *abbrev. for:* **1.** legal. **2.** legate. **3.** legato. **4.** legislation. **5.** legislative. **6.** legislature.

leg·a·cy (ˈlɛgəsɪ) *n., pl.* **+cies.** **1.** a gift by will, esp. of money or personal property. **2.** something handed down or received from an ancestor or predecessor. [C14 (meaning: office of a legate), C15 (meaning: bequest): from Medieval Latin *lēgātia* commission; see LEGATE]

le+gal (ˈliːgᵊl) *adj.* **1.** established by or founded upon law; lawful. **2.** of or relating to law. **3.** recognized, enforceable, or having a remedy at law rather than in equity. **4.** relating to or characteristic of the profession of law. [C16: from Latin *lēgālis,* from *lēx* law] —ˈ**le+gal+ly** *adv.*

le+gal aid *n.* financial assistance available to persons unable to meet the full cost of legal proceedings.

le+gal cap *n. U.S.* ruled writing paper, about 8 by 13½ inches with the fold at the top, for use by lawyers.

le+gal+ese (ˌliːgəˈliːz) *n.* the conventional language in which legal documents, etc., are written.

le+gal hol·i+day *n. U.S.* any of several weekdays which are observed as national holidays. Brit. equivalent: **bank holiday.**

le+gal+ism (ˈliːgəˌlɪzəm) *n.* strict adherence to the law, esp. the stressing of the letter of the law rather than its spirit. —ˈ**le+gal+ist** *n., adj.* —ˌ**le+gal+ˈis+tic** *adj.* —ˌ**le+gal+ˈis+ti+cal+ly** *adv.*

le+gal+i+ty (lɪˈgælɪtɪ) *n., pl.* **·ties.** **1.** the state or quality of being legal or lawful. **2.** adherence to legal principles.

le+gal+ize *or* **le+gal+ise** (ˈliːgəˌlaɪz) *vb.* (*tr.*) **1.** to make lawful or legal. **2.** to confirm or validate (something previously unlawful). —ˌ**le+gal+i+ˈza+tion** *or* ˌ**le+gal+i+ˈsa+tion** *n.*

le+gal med·i+cine *n.* another name for **forensic medicine.**

le+gal sep·a+ra+tion *n.* another term (esp. U.S.) for **judicial separation.**

le+gal ten+der *n.* currency in specified denominations that a creditor must by law accept in redemption of a debt.

Le+gas+pi (lɛˈgæspɪ) *n.* a port in the Philippines, on SE Luzon on the Gulf of Albay. Pop.: 84 090 (1970).

leg+ate (ˈlɛgɪt) *n.* **1.** a messenger, envoy, or delegate. **2.** *R.C. Church.* an emissary to a foreign state representing the Pope. [Old English, via Old French from Latin *lēgātus* deputy, from *lēgāre* to delegate; related to *lēx* law] —ˈ**leg+ate+ˌship** *n.* —**leg·a·tine** (ˈlɛgəˌtaɪn) *adj.*

leg·a·tee (ˌlɛgəˈtiː) *n.* a person to whom a legacy is bequeathed. Compare **devisee.**

le+ga·tion (lɪˈgeɪʃən) *n.* **1.** a diplomatic mission headed by a minister. **2.** the official residence and office of a diplomatic minister. **3.** the act of sending forth a diplomatic envoy. **4.** the mission or business of a diplomatic envoy. **5.** the rank or office of a legate. [C15: from Latin *lēgātiō,* from *lēgātus* LEGATE] —**le+ˈga·tion+ar·y** *adj.*

le+ga+to (lɪˈgɑːtəʊ) *Music.* *adj., adv.* **1.** to be performed smoothly and connectedly. *~n., pl.* **+tos.** **2. a.** a style of playing in which no perceptible gaps are left between notes. **b.** (*as modifier*): *a legato passage.* [C19: from Italian, literally: bound]

leg·a·tor (ˌlɛgəˈtɔː) *n.* a person who gives a legacy or makes a bequest. [C17: from Latin, from *lēgāre* to bequeath; see LEGATE] —ˌ**leg·a·ˈto·ri·al** *adj.*

leg be+fore wick+et *n. Cricket.* a manner of dismissal on the grounds that a batsman has been struck on the leg by a bowled ball that otherwise would have hit the wicket. Abbrev.: **l.b.w.**

leg break *n. Cricket.* a bowled ball that spins from leg to off on pitching.

leg bye *n. Cricket.* a run scored after the ball has hit the batsman's leg or some other part of his body, except his hand, without touching the bat. Abbrev.: **l.b.**

leg+end (ˈlɛdʒənd) *n.* **1.** a popular story handed down from earlier times whose truth has not been ascertained. **2.** a group of such stories: *the Arthurian legend.* **3.** a modern story that has taken on the characteristics of a traditional legendary tale. **4.** a person whose fame or notoriety makes him a source of exaggerated or romanticized tales or exploits. **5.** an inscription or title, as on a coin or beneath a coat of arms. **6.** explanatory matter accompanying a table, map, chart, etc. **7. a.** a story of the life of a saint. **b.** a collection of such stories. [C14 (in the sense: a saint's life or a collection of saints' lives): from Medieval Latin *legenda* passages to be read, from Latin *legere* to read] —ˈ**leg+end+ry** *n.*

leg+end+ar·y (ˈlɛdʒəndərɪ, -drɪ) *adj.* **1.** of or relating to legend. **2.** celebrated or described in a legend or legends. **3.** very famous or notorious.

Le·gen·dre (*French* ləˈʒɑ̃ːdr) *n.* **A·dri·en Ma·rie** (adriɛ̃ maˈri). 1752–1833, French mathematician, noted for his work on the theory of numbers, the theory of elliptical functions, and the method of least squares.

Lé·ger (*French* leˈʒe) *n.* **Fer·nand** (fɛrˈnɑ̃). 1881–1955, French cubist painter, influenced by industrial technology.

leg+er+de·main (ˌlɛdʒədəˈmeɪn) *n.* **1.** another name for **sleight of hand.** **2.** cunning deception or trickery. [C15: from Old French: light of hand] —ˌ**leg+er+de·ˈmain+ist** *n.*

leg+er line (ˈlɛdʒə) *n.* a variant spelling of **ledger line.**

le+ges (ˈliːdʒiːz) *n.* the plural of **lex.**

leg+ged (ˈlɛgɪd, lɛgd) *adj.* **a.** having a leg or legs. **b.** (*in combination*): *three-legged; long-legged.*

leg+gings (ˈlɛgɪŋz) *pl. n.* an extra outer covering for the lower legs. —ˈ**leg+ginged** *adj.*

leg+gy (ˈlɛgɪ) *adj.* **+gi+er, +gi+est.** **1.** having unusually long legs. **2.** *Informal.* (of a woman) having long and shapely legs. **3.** (of a plant) having an unusually long and weak stem. —ˈ**leg+gi+ness** *n.*

Leg+horn *n.* **1.** (ˈlɛgˌhɔːn). the English name for **Livorno.** **2.** (lɛˈgɔːn). a breed of domestic fowl laying white eggs.

leg+horn (ˈlɛgˌhɔːn) *n.* **1.** a type of Italian wheat straw that is woven into hats. **2.** any hat made from this straw when plaited. [C19: named after LEGHORN (Livorno)]

leg+i·ble (ˈlɛdʒəbᵊl) *adj.* **1.** (of handwriting, print, etc.) able to be read or deciphered. **2.** able to be discovered; discernible. [C14: from Late Latin *legibilis,* from Latin *legere* to read] —ˌ**leg+i+ˈbil+i·ty** *or* ˈ**leg+i+ble+ness** *n.* —ˈ**leg+i·bly** *adv.*

le+gion (ˈliːdʒən) *n.* **1.** a military unit of the ancient Roman army made up of infantry with supporting cavalry, numbering some three to six thousand men. **2.** any large military force: *the French Foreign Legion.* **3.** (*usually cap.*) an association of ex-servicemen: *the British Legion.* **4.** (*often pl.*) any very large number, esp. of people. *~adj.* **5.** (*usually postpositive*) very large or numerous. [C13: from Old French, from Latin *legio,* from *legere* to choose]

le+gion+ar·y (ˈliːdʒənərɪ) *adj.* **1.** of or relating to a legion. *~n., pl.* **+ar·ies.** **2.** a soldier belonging to a legion.

le·gion·ar·y ant *n.* another name for the **army ant.**

le·gion·naire (ˌliːdʒəˈnɛə) *n.* (*often cap.*) a member of certain military forces or associations, such as the French Foreign Legion or the British Legion.

Le·gion of Hon·our *n.* an order for civil or military merit instituted by Napoleon in France in 1802. French name: **Lé·gion d'Hon·neur** (leʒjɔ̃ dɔˈnœːr).

legis. *abbrev. for:* **1.** legislation. **2.** legislative. **3.** legislature.

leg·is·late (ˈlɛdʒɪsˌleɪt) *vb.* **1.** (*intr.*) to make or pass laws. **2.** (*tr.*) to bring into effect by legislation. [C18: back formation from LEGISLATOR]

leg·is·la·tion (ˌlɛdʒɪsˈleɪʃən) *n.* **1.** the act or process of making laws; enactment. **2.** the laws so made.

leg·is·la·tive (ˈlɛdʒɪslətɪv) *adj.* **1.** of or relating to legislation. **2.** having the power or function of legislating: *a legislative assembly.* **3.** of or relating to a legislature. ~*n.* **4.** *Rare.* another word for **legislature.** —**ˈleg·is·la·tive·ly** *adv.*

leg·is·la·tive as·sem·bly *n.* (*often cap.*) **1.** the bicameral legislature in 28 states of the U.S. **2.** the unicameral legislature in most Canadian provinces. **3.** the lower chamber of the bicameral state legislatures in several other Commonwealth countries, such as Australia. **4.** any assembly with legislative powers.

leg·is·la·tive coun·cil *n.* (*often cap.*) **1.** the upper chamber of certain bicameral legislatures, such as those of the Indian and Australian states. **2.** the unicameral legislature of certain colonies or dependent territories. **3.** (in the U.S.) a committee composed of members of both chambers of a state legislature, that meets to discuss problems, construct a legislative programme, etc.

leg·is·la·tor (ˈlɛdʒɪsˌleɪtə) *n.* **1.** a person concerned with the making or enactment of laws. **2.** a member of a legislature. [C17: from Latin *lēgis lātor,* from *lēx* law + *lātor* from *lātus,* past participle of *ferre* to bring] —**ˈleg·is·ˌla·tor·ˌship** *n.* —**ˈleg·is·ˌla·tress** *fem. n.*

leg·is·la·to·ri·al (ˌlɛdʒɪsləˈtɔːrɪəl) *adj.* of or relating to a legislator or legislature.

leg·is·la·ture (ˈlɛdʒɪsˌleɪtʃə) *n.* a body of persons vested with power to make, amend, and repeal laws. Compare **executive, judiciary.**

le·gist (ˈliːdʒɪst) *n.* a person versed in the law. [C15: from Medieval Latin *lēgista,* from *lēx* law]

le·git (ləˈdʒɪt) *Slang.* ~*adj.* **1.** short for **legitimate.** ~*n.* **2.** legitimate or professionally respectable drama.

le·git·i·mate *adj.* (lɪˈdʒɪtɪmɪt). **1.** born in lawful wedlock; enjoying full filial rights. **2.** conforming to established standards of usage, behaviour, etc. **3.** based on correct or acceptable principles of reasoning. **4.** reasonable, sensible, or valid: *a legitimate question.* **5.** authorized, sanctioned by, or in accordance with law. **6.** of, relating to, or ruling by hereditary right: *a legitimate monarch.* **7.** of or relating to serious drama as distinct from films, television, vaudeville, etc.: *the legitimate theatre.* ~*vb.* (lɪˈdʒɪtɪˌmeɪt). **8.** (*tr.*) to make, pronounce, or show to be legitimate. [C15: from Medieval Latin *lēgitimātus* made legal, from *lēx* law] —**le·ˈgit·i·ma·cy** *or* **le·ˈgit·i·mate·ness** *n.* —**le·ˈgit·i·mate·ly** *adv.* —**le·ˌgit·i·ˈma·tion** *n.*

le·git·i·ma·tize, le·git·i·ma·tise (lɪˈdʒɪtɪməˌtaɪz) *or* **le·git·i·mize, le·git·i·mise** (lɪˈdʒɪtɪˌmaɪz) *vb.* (*tr.*) to make legitimate; legalize. —**le·ˌgit·i·ma·ti·ˈza·tion, le·ˌgit·i·ma·ti·ˈsa·tion** *or* **le·ˌgit·i·mi·ˈza·tion, le·ˌgit·i·mi·ˈsa·tion** *n.*

le·git·i·mist (lɪˈdʒɪtɪmɪst) *n.* **1.** a monarchist who supports the rule of a legitimate dynasty or of its senior branch. **2.** (formerly) a supporter of the elder line of the Bourbon family in France. **3.** a supporter of legitimate authority. ~*adj.* also **le·git·i·mis·tic. 4.** of or relating to legitimists. —**le·ˈgit·i·mism** *n.*

leg·man (ˈlɛgmən) *n., pl.* **·men.** *Chiefly U.S.* **1.** a newsman who reports on news stories from the scene of action or original source. **2.** *Informal.* a person employed to run errands, collect information, etc., outside an office.

Leg·ni·ca (*Polish* lɛgˈnitsa) *n.* an industrial town in SW Poland. Pop.: 77 900 (1972 est.). German name: **Liegnitz.**

leg-of-mut·ton *or* **leg-o'-mut·ton** *n.* (*modifier*) (of a sail, sleeve, etc.) tapering sharply or having a triangular profile.

leg-pull *n. Brit. informal.* a practical joke or mild deception.

leg·room (ˈlɛgˌruːm) *n.* room to move one's legs comfortably, as in a car.

leg·ume (ˈlɛgjuːm, lɪˈgjuːm) *n.* **1.** the long dry dehiscent fruit produced by leguminous plants; a pod. **2.** any table vegetable of the superfamily *Leguminosae,* esp. beans or peas. **3.** any leguminous plant. [C17: from French *légume,* from Latin *legūmen* bean, from *legere* to pick (a crop)]

le·gu·min (lɪˈgjuːmɪn) *n.* a protein obtained mainly from the seeds of leguminous plants. [C19: from LEGUME]

le·gu·mi·nous (lɪˈgjuːmɪnəs) *adj.* of, relating to, or belonging to the *Leguminosae* (or *Fabaceae*), a superfamily of flowering plants having pods (or legumes) as fruits and root nodules enabling storage of nitrogen-rich material: includes mimosaceous, caesalpiniaceous, and papilionaceous plants. [C17: from Latin *legūmen;* see LEGUME]

leg·work (ˈlɛgˌwɜːk) *n. Informal.* work that involves travelling on foot or as if on foot.

Le·hár (ˈleɪhɑː, lɪˈhɑː) *n.* **Franz** (frants). 1870–1948, Hungarian composer of operettas, esp. *The Merry Widow* (1905).

Le Ha·vre (lə ˈhɑːvrə; *French* lə ˈɑːvr) *n.* a port in N France, on the English Channel at the mouth of the River Seine: transatlantic trade; oil refining. Pop.: 219 583 (1975).

Leh·mann (ˈleɪmən) *n.* **1. Lil·li** (ˈlɪlɪ). 1848–1929, German soprano. **2. Lot·te** (ˈlɒtə). 1888–1976, U.S. soprano, born in Germany.

Lehm·bruck (*German* ˈleːmˌbrʊk) *n.* **Wil·helm** (ˈvɪlhɛlm). 1881–1919, German sculptor and graphic artist.

lehr (lɪə) *n.* a long tunnel-shaped oven used for annealing glass. [from German: pattern, model]

lei[1] (leɪ) *n.* (in Hawaii) a garland of flowers, worn around the neck. [from Hawaiian]

lei[2] (leɪ) *n.* the plural of **leu.**

Leib·nitz *or* **Leib·niz** (ˈlaɪbnɪts) *n.* Baron **Gott·fried Wil·helm von** (ˈgɔtfriːt ˈvɪlhɛlm fɔn). 1646–1716, German rationalist philosopher and mathematician. He conceived of the universe as a hierarchy of independent units or monads, synchronized by preestablished harmony. His works include *Théodicée* (1710) and *Monadologia* (1714). He also devised a system of calculus, independently of Newton. —**Leib·ˈnitz·i·an** *adj.*

Leib·nitz Moun·tains (ˈlaɪbnɪts) *pl. n.* a mountain range on the SW limb of the moon, containing the highest peaks (10 000 metres) on the moon.

Leices·ter[1] (ˈlɛstə) *n.* **1.** a city in central England, administrative centre of Leicestershire, on the River Soar: Roman remains and a ruined Norman castle; university (1918); light engineering, hosiery, and footwear industries. Pop.: 283 549 (1971). **2.** short for **Leicestershire. 3.** a breed of sheep with long wool, originally from Leicestershire. **4.** a fairly mild dark orange whole-milk cheese, similar to Cheddar but looser and more moist.

Leices·ter[2] (ˈlɛstə) *n.* **Earl of.** title of *Robert Dudley.* ?1532–88, English courtier; favourite of Elizabeth I. He led an unsuccessful expedition to the Netherlands (1585–87).

Leices·ter·shire (ˈlɛstəˌʃɪə, -ʃə) *n.* a county of central England, including (since 1974) the former county of Rutland: largely agricultural. Administrative centre: Leicester. Pop.: 837 900 (1976 est.). Area: 2548 sq. km (984 sq. miles). Shortened form: **Leicester.** Abbrev.: **Leics.**

Leich·hardt (ˈlaɪkˌhɑːt; *German* ˈlaɪçˈhart) *n.* **Fried·rich Wil·helm Lud·wig** (ˈfriːdrɪç ˈvɪlhɛlm ˈluːtvɪç).1813-48, Australian explorer, born in Prussia. He disappeared during an attempt to cross Australia from East to West.

Leics. *abbrev. for* Leicestershire.

Lei·den *or* **Ley·den** (ˈlaɪdᵊn; *Dutch* ˈlɛɪdə) *n.* a city in the W Netherlands, in South Holland province: residence of the Pilgrim Fathers for 11 years before they sailed for America in 1620; university (1575). Pop.: 98 060 (1973 est.).

Leif Er·ic·son (ˈliːf ˈɛrɪksən) *n.* See **Ericson.**

Leigh (liː) *n.* a town in NW England, in Greater Manchester: engineering industries. Pop.: 46 117 (1971).

Lein·ster (ˈlɛnstə) *n.* a province of E and SE Ireland: it consists of the counties of Carlow, Dublin, Kildare, Kilkenny, Laoighis, Longford, Louth, Meath, Offaly, Westmeath, Wexford, and Wicklow. Pop.: 1 498 196 (1971). Area: 19 632 sq. km (7580 sq. miles).

Leip·zig (ˈlaɪpsɪg; *German* ˈlaɪptsɪç) *n.* a city in S East Germany: famous fairs, begun about 1170; publishing and music centre; university (1409); scene of a decisive defeat for Napoleon Bonaparte in 1813. Pop.: 568 877 (1975 est.).

Lei·ri·a (*Portuguese* ləjˈriə) *n.* a city in central Portugal: site of the first printing press in Portugal (1466). Pop.: 83 258 (1970).

leish·ma·ni·a (liːʃˈmeɪnɪə) *n.* any parasitic flagellate protozoan of the genus *Leishmania:* occurs in man and animals and causes certain skin diseases. [C20: New Latin, named after Sir W.B. *Leishman* (1865–1926), Scottish bacteriologist]

leish·man·i·a·sis (ˌliːʃməˈnaɪəsɪs) *or* **leish·ma·ni·o·sis** (liːʃˌmeɪnɪˈəʊsɪs, -ˌmæn-) *n.* any disease, such as kala-azar, caused by protozoa of the genus *Leishmania.*

leis·ter (ˈliːstə) *n.* **1.** a spear with three or more prongs for spearing fish, esp. salmon. ~*vb.* **2.** (*tr.*) to spear (a fish) with a leister. [C16: from Scandinavian; related to Old Norse *ljōstr,* from *ljōsta* to stab]

lei·sure (ˈlɛʒə; *U. S. also* ˈliːʒər) *n.* **1. a.** time or opportunity for ease, relaxation, etc. **b.** (*as modifier*): *leisure activities.* **2.** ease or leisureliness. **3. at leisure. a.** having free time for ease, relaxation, etc. **b.** not occupied or engaged. **c.** without hurrying. **4. at one's leisure.** when one has free time. [C14: from Old French *leisir;* ultimately from Latin *licēre* to be allowed] —**ˈlei·sure·less** *adj.*

lei·sured (ˈlɛʒəd) *adj.* **1.** (*usually prenominal*) having much leisure, as through unearned wealth: *the leisured classes.* **2.** unhurried or relaxed: *in a leisured manner.*

lei·sure·ly (ˈlɛʒəlɪ) *adj.* **1.** unhurried; relaxed. ~*adv.* **2.** without haste; in a relaxed way. —**ˈlei·sure·li·ness** *n.*

Leith (liːθ) *n.* a port in SE Scotland, on the Firth of Forth: part of Edinburgh since 1920.

leit·mo·tiv *or* **leit·mo·tif** (ˈlaɪtməʊˌtiːf) *n.* **1.** *Music.* a recurring short melodic phrase or theme used, esp. in Wagnerian music dramas, to suggest a character, thing, etc. **2.** an often repeated word, phrase, image, or theme in a literary work. [C19: from German: leading motif]

Lei·trim (ˈliːtrɪm) *n.* a county of N Ireland in Connaught province, on Donegal Bay: agricultural. County town: Carrick-on-Shannon. Pop.: 28 360 (1971). Area: 1525 sq. km (589 sq. miles).

Leix (liːʃ) *n.* another name for **Laoighis.**

lek (lɛk) *n.* the standard monetary unit of Albania, divided into 100 qintars. [from Albanian]

lek·ker (ˈlɛkə) *adj. S. African slang.* pleasing, enjoyable, or likeable. [from Afrikaans, from Dutch]

Le·ly (ˈliːlɪ) *n.* Sir **Pe·ter.** Dutch name *Pieter van der Faes.* 1618–80, Dutch portrait painter in England.

L.E.M. (lɛm) *n. acronym for* lunar excursion module.

lem·an ('lɛmən, 'li:-) *n. Archaic.* **1.** a beloved; sweetheart. **2.** a lover or mistress. [C13 *lemman, leofman,* from *leof* dear, LIEF + MAN]

Lé·man (le'mã) *n.* **Lac.** the French name for Lake **Geneva.**

Le Mans (*French* lə 'mã) *n.* a city in NW France: scene of the first experiments in motoring and flying; annual motor race. Pop.: 155 245 (1975).

Lem·berg ('lɛm,bɛrk) *n.* the German name for **Lvov.**

lem·ma[1] ('lɛmə) *n., pl.* **·mas** *or* **·ma·ta** (-mətə). **1.** a subsidiary proposition, assumed to be valid, that is used in the proof of another proposition. **2.** an argument or theme, esp. when used as the subject or title of a composition. [C16 (meaning: proposition), C17 (meaning: title, theme): via Latin from Greek: premiss, from *lambanein* to take (for granted)]

lem·ma[2] ('lɛmə) *n., pl.* **·mas** *or* **·ma·ta** (-mətə). the outer of two bracts surrounding each floret of a grass inflorescence. [C19: from Greek: rind, from *lepein* to peel]

lem·ming ('lɛmɪŋ) *n.* any of various volelike rodents of the genus *Lemmus* and related genera, of northern and arctic regions of Europe, Asia, and North America: family *Cricetidae.* [C17: from Norwegian; related to Latin *latrāre* to bark]

lem·nis·cate ('lɛmnɪskɪt) *n.* a closed plane curve consisting of two symmetrical loops meeting at a node. Equation: $(x^2 + y^2)^2 = a^2(x^2 - y^2)$, where a is the greatest distance from the curve to the origin.

lem·nis·cus (lɛm'nɪskəs) *n., pl.* **·nis·ci** (-'nɪsaɪ, -'nɪski:). *Anatomy.* a technical name for **fillet** (sense 9). [C19: New Latin, from Latin, from Greek *lēmniskos* ribbon]

Lem·nos ('lɛmnɒs) *or* **Lím·nos** *n.* a Greek island in the N Aegean Sea: famous for its medicinal earth **(Lemnian seal).** Chief town: Kastron. Pop.: 17 789 (1971). Area: 477 sq. km (184 sq. miles). —**Lem·ni·an** ('lɛmnɪən) *adj., n.*

lem·on ('lɛmən) *n.* **1.** a small Asian evergreen tree, *Citrus limon,* widely cultivated in warm and tropical regions, having pale green glossy leaves and edible fruits. Related adjs.: **citric, citrine, citrous. 2. a.** the yellow oval fruit of this tree, having juicy acidic flesh rich in vitamin C. **b.** (*as modifier*): *a lemon jelly.* **3.** Also called: **lemon yellow. a.** a greenish-yellow or strong yellow colour. **b.** (*as adj.*): *lemon wallpaper.* **4.** a distinctive tart flavour made from or in imitation of the lemon. **5.** *Slang.* a person or thing considered to be useless or defective. [C14: from Medieval Latin *lemōn-,* from Arabic *laymūn*] —'**lem·on·ish** *adj.* —'**lem·on-,like** *adj.*

lem·on·ade (,lɛmə'neɪd) *n.* a drink made from lemon juice, sugar, and water or from carbonated water, citric acid, etc.

lem·on balm *n.* the full name of **balm** (sense 5).

lem·on cheese *or* **curd** *n.* a soft paste made from lemons, sugar, eggs, and butter, used as a spread or filling.

lem·on drop *n.* a lemon-flavoured boiled sweet.

lem·on ge·ra·ni·um *n.* a cultivated geraniaceous plant, *Pelargonium limoneum,* with lemon-scented leaves.

lemon grass *n.* a perennial grass, *Cymbopogon citratus,* with a large flower spike: grown in tropical regions as the source of an aromatic oil **(lemon grass oil).**

lem·on sole *n.* a European flatfish, *Microstomus kitt,* with a variegated brown body: highly valued as a food fish: family *Pleuronectidae.*

lem·on squash *n. Brit.* a drink made from a sweetened lemon concentrate and water.

lem·on squeez·er *n.* any of various devices for extracting the juice from citrus fruit.

lem·on ver·be·na *n.* a tropical American verbenaceous shrub, *Lippia citriodora,* with slender lemon-scented leaves yielding an oil used in perfumery.

lem·on·y ('lɛmənɪ) *adj.* **1.** having or resembling the taste or colour of a lemon. **2.** *Austral. slang.* angry or irritable.

lem·pi·ra (lɛm'pɪərə) *n.* the standard monetary unit of Honduras, divided into 100 centavos. [American Spanish, after *Lempira,* Indian chief who opposed the Spanish]

le·mur ('li:mə) *n.* **1.** any Madagascan prosimian primate of the family *Lemuridae,* such as *Lemur catta* (the **ring-tailed lemur**). They are typically arboreal, having foxy faces and long tails. **2.** any similar or closely related animal, such as a loris or indris. [C18: New Latin, adapted from Latin *lemurēs* ghosts; so named by Linnaeus for its ghost-like face and nocturnal habits] —'**le·mur-,like** *adj.*

lem·u·res ('lɛmjʊ,ri:z) *pl. n. Roman myth.* the spirits of the dead. [Latin: see LEMUR]

lem·u·roid ('lɛmjʊ,rɔɪd) *or* **lem·u·rine** ('lɛmjʊ,raɪn, -rɪn) *adj.* **1.** of, relating to, or belonging to the superfamily *Lemuroidea,* which includes the lemurs and indrises. **2.** resembling or closely related to a lemur. ~*n.* **3.** an animal that resembles or is closely related to a lemur.

Le·na (*Russian* 'ljɛnə; *English* 'li:nə) *n.* a river in the E Soviet Union, rising in S Siberia and flowing generally north through the Yakutsk SSR to the Laptev Sea by an extensive delta: the longest river in the Soviet Union. Length: 4271 km (2653 miles).

lend (lɛnd) *vb.* **lends, lend·ing, lent. 1.** (*tr.*) to permit the use of (something) with the expectation of return of the same or an equivalent. **2.** to provide (money) temporarily, often at interest. **3.** (*intr.*) to provide loans, esp. as a profession. **4.** (*tr.*) to impart or contribute (something, esp. some abstract quality): *her presence lent beauty.* **5.** (*tr.*) to provide, esp. in order to assist or support: *he lent his skill to the company.* **6. lend an ear.** to listen. **7. lend oneself** *or* **itself.** to possess the right characteristics or qualities for: *the novel lends itself to serialization.* [C15 *lende* (originally the past tense), from Old English *lǣnan,* from *lǣn* LOAN; related to Icelandic *lāna,* Old High German *lēhanōn*] —'**lend·er** *n.*

Usage. Although the use of *loan* as a verb equivalent to *lend* is widespread, it is avoided by careful speakers and writers except when referring to the formal lending of money: *the bank loaned him the money.*

lend·ing li·brar·y *n.* **1.** Also called (esp. U.S.): **circulating library.** the department of a public library providing books for use outside the building. **2.** a small commercial library.

lend-lease *n.* (during World War II) the system organized by the U.S. in 1941 by which equipment and services were provided for those countries fighting Germany.

Leng·len (*French* lã'glã) *n.* **Su·zanne** (sy'zan). 1899–1938, French tennis player: Wimbledon champion (1919-25).

length (lɛŋkθ, lɛŋθ) *n.* **1.** the linear extent or measurement of something from end to end, usually being the longest dimension or, for something fixed, the longest horizontal dimension. **2.** the extent of something from beginning to end, measured in some more or less regular units or intervals: *the book was 600 pages in length.* **3.** a specified distance, esp. between two positions or locations: *the length of a race.* **4.** a period of time, as between specified limits or moments. **5.** something of a specified, average, or known size or extent measured in one dimension, often used as a unit of measurement: *a length of cloth.* **6.** a piece or section of something narrow and long: *a length of tubing.* **7.** the quality, state, or fact of being long rather than short. **8.** (*usually pl.*) the amount of trouble taken in pursuing or achieving something (esp. in the phrase **to great lengths**). **9.** (*often pl.*) the extreme or limit of action (in phrases such as **to any length(s), to what length(s) would someone go,** etc.). **10.** *Prosody, phonetics.* the metrical quantity or temporal duration of a vowel or syllable. **11.** the distance from one end of a rectangular swimming bath to the other. Compare **width** (sense 4). **12.** *Prosody.* the quality of a vowel, whether stressed or unstressed, that distinguishes it from another vowel of similar articulatory characteristics. Thus (i:) in English *beat* is of greater length than (ɪ) in English *bit.* **13.** *Cricket.* the distance from the batsman at which the ball pitches. **14.** *Bridge.* a holding of four or more cards in a suit. **15. at length. a.** in depth; fully. **b.** eventually. [Old English *lengthu;* related to Middle Dutch *lengede,* Old Norse *lengd*]

length·en ('lɛŋkθən, 'lɛŋθən) *vb.* to make or become longer. —'**length·en·er** *n.*

length·man ('lɛŋkθmən, 'lɛŋθ-) *n., pl.* **·men.** *Brit.* a person whose job it is to maintain a particular length of road or railway line.

length·ways ('lɛŋkθ,weɪz, 'lɛŋθ-) *or U.S.* **length·wise** *adv., adj.* in, according to, or along the direction of length.

length·y ('lɛŋkθɪ, 'lɛŋθɪ) *adj.* **length·i·er, length·i·est.** of relatively great or tiresome extent or duration. —'**length·i·ly** *adv.* —'**length·i·ness** *n.*

le·ni·ent ('li:nɪənt) *adj.* **1.** showing or characterized by mercy or tolerance. **2.** *Archaic.* caressing or soothing. [C17: from Latin *lēnīre* to soothe, from *lēnis* soft] —'**le·ni·en·cy** *or* '**le·ni·ence** *n.* —'**le·ni·ent·ly** *adv.*

Len·in ('lɛnɪn) *n.* **Vla·di·mir Il·yich** (vla'dimir ilj'jitʃ), original surname *Ulyanov.* 1870–1924, Russian statesman and Marxist theoretician; first premier of the Soviet Union. He formed the Bolsheviks (1903) and led them in the October Revolution (1917), which established the Soviet Government. He adopted the New Economic Policy (1921) after the Civil War had led to the virtual collapse of the Russian economy, formed the Comintern (1919), and was the originator of the guiding doctrine of the Soviet Union, Marxism-Leninism.

Le·ni·na·bad (*Russian* lɪnina'bat) *n.* a town in the S central Soviet Union, in the Tadzhik SSR on the Syr Darya River: one of the oldest towns in central Asia; textile industries. Pop.: 118 000 (1975 est.). Former name (until 1936): **Khojent.**

Le·ni·na·kan (*Russian* lɪnina'kan) *n.* a city in the SW Soviet Union, in the NW Armenian SSR: textile centre. Pop.: 184 000 (1975 est.). Former name (1840–1924): **Aleksandropol.**

Le·nin·grad ('lɛnɪn,græd; *Russian* lɪnin'grat) *n.* a city and port in the NW Soviet Union, on the Gulf of Finland at the mouth of the Neva River: founded by Peter the Great in 1703 and built on low-lying marshes subject to frequent flooding; capital of Russia from 1712 to 1918; a cultural and educational centre, with a university (1819); a major industrial centre, with engineering, shipbuilding, chemical, textile, and printing industries. Pop.: 3 512 974 (1970). Former names: **Saint Petersburg** (1703–1914), **Petrograd** (1914–24).

Len·in·ism ('lɛnɪ,nɪzəm) *n.* **1.** the political and economic theories of Lenin. **2.** another name for **Marxism-Leninism.** —'**Len·in·ist** *or* '**Len·in·ite** *n., adj.*

Len·in Peak *n.* a mountain in the S central Soviet Union, in the NE Tadzhik SSR; the highest peak in the Trans Alai Range and the second highest in the Soviet Union. Height: 7134 m (23 406 ft.).

le·nis ('li:nɪs) *Phonetics.* ~*adj.* **1.** (of a consonant) articulated with weak muscular tension. ~*n., pl.* **le·nes** ('li:ni:z). **2.** a consonant, such as English *b* or *v,* pronounced with weak muscular force. ~Compare **fortis.** [C19: from Latin: gentle]

len·i·tive ('lɛnɪtɪv) *adj.* **1.** soothing or alleviating pain or distress. ~*n.* **2.** a lenitive drug. [C16: from Medieval Latin *lēnītīvus,* from Latin *lēnīre* to soothe]

len·i·ty ('lɛnɪtɪ) *n., pl.* **·ties.** the state or quality of being lenient. [C16: from Latin *lēnitās* gentleness, from *lēnis* soft]

Len·non ('lɛnən) *n.* **John.** 1940-80, English rock guitarist, vocalist, and songwriter: member of the Beatles (1962-70); also made several recordings with his wife Yoko Ono.

le·no ('li:nəʊ) *n., pl.* **·nos. 1.** (in textiles) a weave in which the warp yarns are twisted together in pairs between the weft or filling yarns. **2.** a fabric of this weave. [C19: probably from French *linon* lawn, from *lin* flax, from Latin *līnum*. See LINEN]

lens (lɛnz) *n.* **1.** a piece of glass or other transparent material, used to converge or diverge transmitted light and form optical images. **2.** Also called: **compound lens.** a combination of such lenses for forming images or concentrating a beam of light. **3.** a device that diverges or converges a beam of electromagnetic radiation, sound, or particles. See **electron lens. 4.** *Anatomy.* See **crystalline lens.** [C17: from Latin *lēns* lentil, referring to the similarity of a lens to the shape of a lentil]

lent (lɛnt) *vb.* the past tense or past participle of **lend.**

Lent (lɛnt) *n.* **1.** *Christianity.* the period of forty weekdays lasting from Ash Wednesday to Holy Saturday, observed as a time of penance and fasting commemorating Jesus' fasting in the wilderness. **2.** (*modifier*) falling within or associated with the season before Easter: *Lent observance.* **3.** (*pl.*) (at Cambridge University) Lent term boat races. [Old English *lencten, lengten* spring, literally: lengthening (of hours of daylight)]

len+ta+men+te (ˌlɛntə'mɛntɪ) *adv. Music.* to be played slowly. [C18: Italian, from LENTO]

len+ten ('lɛntən) *adj.* **1.** (*often cap.*) of or relating to Lent. **2.** *Archaic or literary.* spare, plain, or meagre: *lenten fare.* **3.** *Archaic.* cold, austere, or sombre: *a lenten lover.*

len+tic ('lɛntɪk) *adj. Ecology.* of, relating to, or inhabiting still water: *a lentic fauna.* Compare **lotic.** [C20: from Latin *lentus* slow]

len+ti+cel ('lɛntɪˌsɛl) *n.* any of numerous pores in the stem of a woody plant allowing exchange of gases between the plant and the exterior. [C19: from New Latin *lenticella,* from Latin *lenticula* diminutive of *lēns* LENTIL] —**len+ti+cel+late** (ˌlɛntɪ'sɛlɪt) *adj.*

len+tic·u·lar (lɛn'tɪkjʊlə) *or* **len+ti+form** ('lɛntɪˌfɔ:m) *adj.* **1.** Also: **len+toid** ('lɛntɔɪd). shaped like a biconvex lens. **2.** of or concerned with a lens or lenses. **3.** shaped like a lentil seed. [C17: from Latin *lenticulāris* like a LENTIL]

len+ti+go (lɛn'taɪgəʊ) *n., pl.* **len+tig·i·nes** (lɛn'tɪdʒɪˌni:z). a technical name for a **freckle.** [C14: from Latin, from *lēns* LENTIL] —**len+'tig·i·nous** *or* **len+'tig·i·nose** *adj.*

len+til ('lɛntɪl) *n.* **1.** a small annual leguminous plant, *Lens culinaris,* of the Mediterranean region and W Asia, having edible brownish convex seeds. **2.** any of the seeds of this plant, which are cooked and eaten as a vegetable, in soups, etc. [C13: from Old French *lentille,* from Latin *lenticula,* diminutive of *lēns* lentil]

len+tis+si+mo (lɛn'tɪsɪˌməʊ) *adj., adv. Music.* to be played very slowly. [Italian, superlative of *lento* slow]

lent lil·y *n.* another name for the **daffodil.**

len+to ('lɛntəʊ) *Music.* ~*adj., adv.* **1.** to be performed slowly. ~*n., pl.* **+tos. 2.** a movement or passage performed in this way. [C18: Italian, from Latin *lentus* slow]

Lent term *n.* the spring term at Cambridge University and some other educational establishments.

Lenz's law ('lɛntsɪz) *n. Physics.* the principle that the direction of the current induced in a circuit by a changing magnetic field is such that the magnetic field produced by this current will oppose the original field. [C19: named after H. F. E. *Lenz* (1804–65), German physicist]

Le·o¹ ('li:əʊ) *n.* a name for a lion, used in children's tales, fables, etc. [from Latin: lion]

Le·o² ('li:əʊ) *n., Latin genitive* **Le·o+nis** (li:'əʊnɪs). **1.** *Astronomy.* a zodiacal constellation in the N hemisphere, lying between Cancer and Virgo on the ecliptic, that contains the star Regulus and the radiant of the Leonid meteor shower. **2.** *Astrology.* **a.** Also called: the **Lion.** the fifth sign of the zodiac, symbol ♌, having a fixed fire classification and ruled by the sun. The sun is in this sign between about July 23 and Aug. 22. **b.** a person born during a period when the sun is in this sign. ~*adj.* **3.** *Astrology.* born under or characteristic of Leo. ~Also (for senses 2b, 3): **Le·o+ni·an** (li:'əʊnɪən).

Le·o I ('li:əʊ) *n.* **Saint,** called *the Great.* ?390–461 A.D., pope (440–461). He extended the authority of the papacy in the West and persuaded Attila not to attack Rome (452). Feast day: April 11.

Le·o III *n.* **Saint.** ?750–816 A.D., pope (795–816). He crowned Charlemagne emperor of the Romans (800). Feast day: June 12.

Le·o X *n.* original name *Giovanni de' Medici.* 1475–1521, pope (1513–21): noted for his patronage of Renaissance art and learning; excommunicated Luther (1521).

Le·o XIII *n.* original name *Gioacchino Pecci.* 1810–1903, pope (1878–1903). His many important encyclicals include *Rerum novarum* (1891) on the need for Catholic action on social problems.

Le·o+ben (*German* le'o:bən) *n.* a city in E central Austria, in Styria on the Mur River: lignite-mining. Pop.: 35 153 (1971).

Le·o Mi+nor *n.* a small faint constellation in the N hemisphere lying near Leo and Ursa Major.

Le·ón (*Spanish* le'on) *n.* **1.** a region and former kingdom of NW Spain, which united with Castile in 1230. **2.** a city of NW Spain: capital of the kingdom of León (10th century). Pop.: 105 235 (1970). **3.** a city in central Mexico, in W Guanajuato state: commercial centre of a rich agricultural region. Pop.: 496 598 (1970). Official name **Le·ón de los Al+da+mas** (ðe los 'aldamas). **4.** a city in W Nicaragua: one of the oldest towns of Central America, founded in 1524; capital of Nicaragua until 1855; university (1812). Pop.: 197 271 (1970 est.).

Le·o·nar·do da Vin·ci (ˌli:ə'nɑ:dəʊ də 'vɪntʃɪ) *n.* 1452–1519, Italian painter, sculptor, architect, and engineer: the most versatile talent of the Italian Renaissance. His most famous paintings include *The Virgin of the Rocks* (1483–85), the *Mona Lisa* (or *La Gioconda,* 1503), and the *Last Supper* (?1495–97). His numerous drawings, combining scientific precision in observation with intense imaginative power, reflect the breadth of his interests, which ranged over biology, physiology, hydraulics, and aeronautics. He invented the first armoured tank and foresaw the invention of aircraft and submarines. —**Le·o+nar+desque** (ˌli:ənɑ:'dɛsk) *adj.*

Le·on·ca·val·lo (*Italian* ˌleoŋka'vallo) *n.* **Rug·gie·ro** (rud'dʒɛ:ro). 1858–1919, Italian composer of operas, notably *I Pagliacci* (1892).

le·o+ne (li:'əʊnɪ) *n.* the standard monetary unit of Sierra Leone, divided into 100 cents. [C20: from SIERRA LEONE]

Le·o+nid ('li:ənɪd) *n., pl.* **Le·o+nids** *or* **Le+on+i+des** (lɪ'ɒnɪˌdi:z). any member of a meteor shower occurring annually between Nov. 12 and 17 and appearing to radiate from the constellation Leo. [C19: from New Latin *Leōnidēs,* from *leō* lion]

Le·on·i·das (lɪ'ɒnɪˌdæs) *n.* died 480 B.C., king of Sparta (?490–480), hero of the Battle of Thermopylae, in which he was killed by the Persians under Xerxes.

le·o+nine ('li:əˌnaɪn) *adj.* of, characteristic of, or resembling a lion. [C14: from Latin *leōnīnus,* from *leō* lion]

Le·o+nine ('li:əˌnaɪn) *adj.* **1.** connected with one of the popes called Leo: an epithet applied to **a.** a district of Rome on the right bank of the Tiber fortified by Pope Leo IV (**Leonine City**). **b.** certain prayers in the Mass prescribed by Leo XIII. ~*n.* **2. Leonine verse. a.** a type of medieval hexameter or elegiac verse having internal rhyme. **b.** a type of English verse with internal rhyme.

leop+ard ('lɛpəd) *n.* **1.** Also called: **panther.** a large feline mammal, *Panthera pardus,* of forests of Africa and Asia, usually having a tawny yellow coat with black rosette-like spots. **2.** any of several similar felines, such as the snow leopard and cheetah. **3. clouded leopard.** a feline, *Neofelis nebulosa,* of SE Asia and Indonesia with a yellowish-brown coat marked with darker spots and blotches. **4.** *Heraldry.* a stylized leopard, painted as a lion with the face turned towards the front. **5.** the pelt of a leopard. [C13: from Old French *lepart,* from Late Latin *leōpardus,* from Late Greek *leópardos,* from *leōn* lion + *pardos* PARD (the leopard was thought to be the result of cross-breeding)] —**'leop+ard+ess** *fem. n.*

Le·o·par·di (*Italian* ˌleo'pardi) *n.* Count **Gia·co·mo** ('dʒa:komo). 1798–1837, Italian poet and philosopher, noted esp. for his lyrics, collected in *I Canti* (1831).

leop+ard lil·y *n.* a North American lily plant, *Lilium pardalinum,* cultivated for its large orange-red flowers, with brown-spotted petals and long stamens.

leop+ard moth *n.* a nocturnal European moth, *Zeuzera pyrina,* having white wings and body, both marked with black spots: family *Cossidae.*

leop·ard's-bane *n.* any of several Eurasian perennial plants of the genus *Doronicum,* esp. *D. plantagineum,* having clusters of yellow flowers: family *Compositae* (composites).

Le·o·pold I ('lɪəˌpəʊld) *n.* **1.** 1640–1705, Holy Roman Emperor (1658–1705). His reign was marked by wars with Louis XIV of France and with the Turks. **2.** 1790–1865, first king of the Belgians (1831–65).

Le·o·pold II *n.* **1.** 1747–92, Holy Roman Emperor (1790–92). He formed an alliance with Prussia against France (1792) after the downfall of his brother-in-law Louis XVI. **2.** 1835–1909, king of the Belgians (1865–1909); son of Leopold I. He financed Stanley's explorations in Africa, becoming first sovereign of the Congo Free State (1885).

Le·o·pold III *n.* born 1901, king of the Belgians (1934–51); son of Albert I. His surrender to the Nazis (1940) forced his eventual abdication in favour of his son, Baudouin.

Lé·o+pold+ville ('lɪəpəʊldˌvɪl; *French* leɔpɔl'vil) *n.* the former name (until 1966) of **Kinshasa.**

le·o+tard ('lɪəˌtɑ:d) *n.* a tight-fitting garment covering the body from the shoulders down to the thighs and worn by acrobats, ballet dancers, etc. [C19: named after Jules *Léotard,* French acrobat]

Le+pan+to *n.* **1.** ('lɛ:panto). the Italian name for **Návpaktos. 2.** (lɪ'pæntəʊ). **Gulf of.** another name for the (Gulf of) **Corinth.**

Le+pa+ya (lɪ'pɑ:jə) *n.* a variant spelling of **Liepāja.**

lep+er ('lɛpə) *n.* **1.** a person who has leprosy. **2.** a person who is ignored or despised. [C14: via Late Latin from Greek *lepra,* noun use of *lepros* scaly, from *lepein* to peel]

lep·i·do- *or before a vowel* **lep·id-** *combining form.* scale or scaly: *lepidopterous.* [from Greek *lepis* scale; see LEPER]

le+pid·o+lite (lɪ'pɪdəˌlaɪt, 'lɛpɪdəˌlaɪt) *n.* a lilac, pink, or greyish mica consisting of a hydrous silicate of lithium, potassium, aluminium, and fluorine, containing rubidium as an impurity: a source of lithium and rubidium. Formula: $K_2Li_3Al_4Si_7O_{21}(OH,F)_3$.

lep·i·dop+ter·an (ˌlɛpɪ'dɒptərən) *n., pl.* **+ter+ans** *or* **+ter·a** (-tərə), *also* **lep·i·dop+ter·on. 1.** any of numerous insects of the order *Lepidoptera,* typically having two pairs of wings covered with fragile scales, mouthparts specialized as a suctorial proboscis, and caterpillars as larvae: comprises the butterflies and moths. ~*adj. also* **lep·i·dop+ter+ous. 2.** of, relating to, or belonging to the order *Lepidoptera.*

lep·i·dop+ter+ist (ˌlɛpɪ'dɒptərɪst) *n.* a person who studies or collects moths and butterflies.

lep·i+do+si+ren (ˌlɛpɪdəʊ'saɪərən) *n.* a South American lungfish,

Lepidosiren paradoxa, having an eel-shaped body and whiplike paired fins.

lep·i·dote ('lɛpɪˌdəʊt) *adj. Biology.* covered with scaly leaves or spots. [C19: via New Latin *lepidōtus*, from Greek, from *lepis* scale]

Lep·i·dus ('lɛpɪdəs) *n.* **Mar·cus Ae·mil·i·us** ('mɑːkəs iː'mɪlɪəs). died ?13 B.C., Roman statesman: formed the Second Triumvirate with Octavian (later Augustus) and Mark Antony.

Le·pon·tine Alps (lɪ'pɒntaɪn) *pl. n.* a range of the S central Alps, in S Switzerland and N Italy. Highest peak: Monte Leone, 3553 m (11 657 ft.).

lep·o·rid ('lɛpərɪd) *adj.* **1.** of, relating to, or belonging to the *Leporidae*, a family of lagomorph mammals having long ears and limbs and a short tail: includes rabbits and hares. ~*n.* **2.** any animal belonging to the family *Leporidae*. [C19: from Latin *lepus* hare]

lep·o·rine ('lɛpəˌraɪn) *adj.* of, relating to, or resembling a hare. [C17: from Latin *leporīnus*, from *lepus* hare]

lep·re·chaun ('lɛprəˌkɔːn) *n.* (in Irish folklore) a mischievous elf, often believed to have a treasure hoard. [C17: from Irish Gaelic *leipreachān*, from Middle Irish *lūchorpān*, from *lū* small + *corp* body, from Latin *corpus* body]

lep·ro·sar·i·um (ˌlɛprə'sɛərɪəm) *n., pl.* **·i·a** (-ɪə). a hospital or other centre for the treatment or care of lepers. [C20: from Medieval Latin: see LEPER]

lep·rose ('lɛprəʊs, -rəʊz) *adj. Biology.* having or denoting a whitish scurfy surface.

lep·ro·sy ('lɛprəsɪ) *n. Pathol.* a chronic infectious disease occurring mainly in tropical and subtropical regions, characterized by the formation of painful inflamed nodules beneath the skin and disfigurement and wasting of affected parts, caused by the bacillus *Mycobacterium leprae*. Also called: **Hansen's disease.** [C16: from LEPROUS + -Y[3]]

lep·rous ('lɛprəs) *adj.* **1.** having leprosy. **2.** relating to or resembling leprosy. **3.** *Biology.* a less common word for **leprose.** [C13: from Old French, from Late Latin *leprosus*, from *lepra* LEPER] —**'lep·rous·ly** *adv.* —**'lep·rous·ness** *n.*

-lep·sy *or sometimes* **-lep·si·a** *n. combining form.* indicating a seizure or attack: *catalepsy.* [from New Latin *-lepsia*, from Greek, from *lēpsis* a seizure, from *lambanein* to seize] —**-lep·tic** *adj. combining form.*

lep·to- *or before a vowel* **lept-** *combining form.* fine, slender, or slight: *leptosome.* [from Greek *leptos* thin, literally: peeled, from *lepein* to peel]

lep·to·ceph·a·lus (ˌlɛptəʊ'sɛfələs) *n., pl.* **·li** (-ˌlaɪ). the slender transparent oceanic larva of eels of the genus *Anguilla* that migrates from its hatching ground near the West Indies to European freshwater habitats.

lep·ton[1] ('lɛptɒn) *n., pl.* **·ta** (-tə). **1.** a Greek monetary unit worth one hundredth of a drachma. **2.** a small coin of ancient Greece. [from Greek *lepton* (*nomisma*) small (coin)]

lep·ton[2] ('lɛptɒn) *n. Physics.* any of a group of elementary particles and their antiparticles, such as an electron, muon, or neutrino, that participate in weak interactions and have a half-integral spin. [C20: from LEPTO- + -ON] —**lep'ton·ic** *adj.*

lep·ton num·ber *n. Physics.* a quantum number describing the behaviour of elementary particles, equal to the number of leptons present minus the number of antileptons. It is thought to be conserved in all processes. Symbol: *l*

lep·to·phyl·lous (ˌlɛptəʊ'fɪləs) *adj.* (of plants) having long slender leaves.

lep·tor·rhine ('lɛptərɪn) *adj.* another word for **catarrhine** (sense 2).

lep·to·some ('lɛptəˌsəʊm) *n.* a person with a small bodily frame and a slender physique. —ˌ**lep·to'so·mic** *or* **lep·to·so·mat·ic** (ˌlɛptəʊsə'mætɪk) *adj.*

lep·to·spi·ro·sis (ˌlɛptəʊspaɪ'rəʊsɪs) *n.* any of several infectious diseases caused by spirochaete bacteria of the genus *Leptospira*, transmitted to man by animals and characterized by jaundice, meningitis, and kidney failure. [C20: from New Latin *Leptospira* (LEPTO- + Greek *speira* coil + -OSIS)]

lep·to·tene ('lɛptəʊˌtiːn) *n.* the first stage of the prophase of meiosis during which the nuclear material becomes resolved into slender single-stranded chromosomes. [C20: from LEPTO- + *-tene*, from Greek *tainia* band, filament]

Lep·us ('lɛpəs, 'liː-) *n., Latin genitive* **Lep·or·is** ('lɛpərɪs). a small constellation in the S hemisphere lying between Orion and Columba. [New Latin, from Latin: hare]

le·quear (lə'kwɪə) *n.* another name for **lacunar** (sense 1).

Lé·ri·da (*Spanish* 'leriða) *n.* a city in NE Spain, in Catalonia: commercial centre of an agricultural region. Pop.: 90 884 (1970).

Ler·mon·tov (*Russian* 'ljɛrməntəf) *n.* **Mi·kha·il Yu·rie·vich** (mixa'il 'jurjɪvɪtʃ). 1814–41, Russian novelist and poet: noted esp. for the novel *A Hero of Our Time* (1840).

Ler·wick ('lɜːwɪk) *n.* a town in N Scotland, administrative centre of the island authority of Shetland, on the island of Mainland: the most northerly town in the British Isles; knitwear, oil refining. Pop.: 6107 (1971).

Le Sage *or* **Le·sage** (*French* lə 'saːʒ) *n.* **A·lain-Re·né** (alɛ̃ rə'ne). 1668–1747, French novelist and dramatist, author of the picaresque novel *Gil Blas* (1715–35).

les·bi·an ('lɛzbɪən) *n.* **1.** a female homosexual. ~*adj.* **2.** of or characteristic of lesbians. [C19: from the homosexuality attributed to Sappho] —**'les·bi·an·ism** *n.*

Les·bi·an ('lɛzbɪən) *n.* **1.** a native or inhabitant of Lesbos. **2.** the Aeolic dialect of Ancient Greek spoken in Lesbos. ~*adj.* **3.** of or relating to Lesbos. **4.** of or relating to the poetry of Lesbos, esp. that of Sappho.

Les·bos ('lɛzbɒs) *n.* an island in the E Aegean, off the NW coast of Turkey: a centre of lyric poetry, led by Alcaeus and Sappho (6th century B.C.); annexed to Greece in 1913. Chief town: Mytilene. Pop.: 114 802 (1971). Area: 1630 sq. km (630 sq. miles). Modern Greek name: **Lésvos.** Former name: **Mytilene.**

Les Cayes (leɪ 'keɪ; *French* le 'kaj) *n.* a port in SW Haiti, on the S Tiburon Peninsula. Pop.: 14 000 (1971 est.). Also: **Cayes.**

lese-maj·es·ty ('liːz'mædʒɪstɪ) *n.* **1.** any of various offences committed against the sovereign power in a state; treason. **2.** an attack on authority or position. [C16: from French *lèse majesté*, from Latin *laesa mājestās* wounded majesty]

le·sion ('liːʒən) *n.* **1.** any structural change in a bodily part resulting from injury or disease. **2.** an injury or wound. [C15: via Old French from Late Latin *laesiō* injury, from Latin *laedere* to hurt]

Le·so·tho (lɪ'suːtʊ, lə'səʊtəʊ) *n.* a kingdom in southern Africa, forming an enclave in the Republic of South Africa: annexed to British Cape Colony in 1871; made a protectorate in 1884; gained independence in 1966; a member of the Commonwealth. It is generally mountainous, with temperate grasslands throughout. Languages: Sesotho and English. Religion: Christian majority. Currency: rand. Capital: Maseru. Pop.: 935 000 (1971 est.). Area: 30 344 sq. km (11 716 sq. miles). Former name (1884–1966): **Basutoland.**

less (lɛs) *determiner.* **1. a.** the comparative of **little** (sense 1): *less sugar; less spirit than before.* **b.** (*as pronoun; functioning as sing. or pl.*): *she has less than she needs; the less you eat, the less you want.* **2.** (usually preceded by *no*) lower in rank or importance: *no less a man than the president; St. James the Less.* **3. no less.** *Informal.* used to indicate surprise or admiration, often sarcastic, at the preceding statement: *she says she's been to Italy, no less.* **4. less of.** to a smaller extent or degree: *we see less of John these days; less of a success than I'd hoped.* ~*adv.* **5.** the comparative of *a little: she walks less than she should; less quickly; less beautiful.* **6. much** *or* **still less.** used to reinforce a negative: *we don't like it, still less enjoy it.* **7. think less of.** to have a lower opinion of. ~*prep.* **8.** subtracting; minus: *three weeks less a day.* [Old English *lǣssa* (adj.), *lǣs* (adv., n.)]

Usage. *Less* should not be confused with *fewer. Less* means less in quantity: *there is less water than before. Fewer* means smaller in number: *there are fewer people than before.*

-less *suffix forming adjectives.* **1.** without; lacking: *speechless.* **2.** not able to (do something) or not able to be (done, performed, etc.): *countless.* [Old English *-lās*, from *lēas* lacking]

les·see (lɛ'siː) *n.* a person to whom a lease is granted; a tenant under a lease. [C15: via Anglo-French from Old French *lessé*, from *lesser* to LEASE] —**les'see·ship** *n.*

less·en ('lɛsᵊn) *vb.* **1.** to make or become less. **2.** (*tr.*) to make little of.

Les·seps ('lɛsəps; *French* lɛ'sɛps) *n.* Vicomte **Fer·di·nand Ma·rie de** (fɛrdinɑ̃ ma'ri də). 1805–94, French diplomat: directed the construction of the Suez Canal (1859–69).

less·er ('lɛsə) *adj.* not as great in quantity, size, or worth.

Less·er An·til·les *pl. n.* **the.** a group of islands in the West Indies, including the Leeward Islands, the Windward Islands, Barbados, and the Netherlands Antilles. Also called: **Caribees.**

less·er cel·an·dine *n.* a Eurasian ranunculaceous plant, *Ranunculus ficaria*, having yellow flowers and heart-shaped leaves. Also called: **pilewort.** Compare **greater celandine.**

less·er pan·da *n.* See **panda** (sense 2).

Less·er Sun·da Is·lands *pl. n.* another name for **Nusa Tenggara.**

Les·sing ('lɛsɪŋ) *n.* **1. Dor·is (May).** born 1919, English novelist and short-story writer, brought up in Rhodesia: her novels include *The Golden Notebook* (1962). **2. Gott·hold E·phra·im** ('gɔthɔlt 'eːfraɪm). 1729–81, German dramatist and critic. His plays include *Miss Sara Sampson* (1755), the first German domestic tragedy, and *Nathan der Weise* (1779). He is noted for his criticism of French classical dramatists, and for his treatise on aesthetics *Laokoon* (1766).

les·son ('lɛsᵊn) *n.* **1. a.** a unit, or single period of instruction in a subject; class: *an hour-long music lesson.* **b.** the content of such a unit. **2.** material assigned for individual study. **3.** something from which useful knowledge or principles can be learned; example. **4.** the principles, knowledge, etc., gained. **5.** a reprimand or punishment intended to correct. **6.** a portion of Scripture appointed to be read at divine service. ~*vb.* **7.** (*tr.*) *Rare.* to censure or punish. [C13: from Old French *leçon*, from Latin *lēctiō*, from *legere* to read]

les·sor ('lɛsɔː, lɛ'sɔː) *n.* a person who grants a lease of property.

lest (lɛst) *conj.* (*subordinating; takes a subjunctive vb.*) *Archaic.* **1.** so as to prevent any possibility that: *keep down lest anyone see us.* **2.** (*after verbs or phrases expressing fear, worry, anxiety, etc.*) for fear that; in case: *he was alarmed lest she should find out.* [Old English *the lǣste*, earlier *thȳ lǣs the*, literally: whereby less that]

Lés·vos ('lɛzvɔs) *n.* transliteration of the Modern Greek name for **Lesbos.**

let[1] (lɛt) *vb.* **lets, let·ting, let.** (*tr.*; usually takes an infinitive without *to* or an implied infinitive) **1.** to permit; allow: *she lets him roam around.* **2.** (*imperative or dependent imperative*) **a.** used as an auxiliary to express a request, proposal, or command, or to convey a warning or threat: *let's get on; just let me catch you here again!* **b.** (in mathematical or philosophical discourse) used as an auxiliary to express an assumption or hypothesis: *let "a" equal "b".* **c.** used as an auxiliary to express resigned acceptance of the inevitable: *let the worst happen.* **3. a.** to allow the occupation of (accommodation) in return for rent. **b.** to assign (a contract for work). **4.** to allow or cause the movement of (something) in a specified direction: *to let air out of a tyre.* **5. let alone.** (*conj.*) much less; not to mention: *I can't afford wine, let alone champagne.* **6. let alone** *or* **be.** to leave (something) undisturbed or unchanged: *let the poor cat alone.* **7. let go.** See **go**[1] (sense 55). **8. let loose.** to set free. ~See also **let down, let in, let into, let off, let on, let out, let through, let up.** [Old English *lǣtan* to permit; related to Gothic *lētan,* German *lassen*]

let[2] (lɛt) *n.* **1.** an impediment or obstruction (esp. in the phrase **without let or hindrance**). **2.** *Tennis, squash, etc.* **a.** a minor infringement or obstruction of the ball, requiring a point to be replayed. **b.** the point so replayed. ~*vb.* **lets, let·ting, let·ted** *or* **let. 3.** (*tr.*) *Archaic.* to hinder; impede. [Old English *lettan* to hinder, from *læt* LATE; related to Old Norse *letja*]

-let *suffix forming nouns.* **1.** small or lesser: *booklet; starlet.* **2.** an ornament worn on a specified part of the body: *anklet.* [from Old French *-elet,* from Latin *-āle,* neuter of adj. suffix *-ālis* or from Latin *-ellus,* diminutive suffix]

letch (lɛtʃ) *vb., n.* a variant spelling of **lech.** [C18: perhaps back formation from LECHER]

Letch·worth (ˈlɛtʃwəθ, -ˌwɜːθ) *n.* a town in SE England, in N Hertfordshire: the first garden city in Great Britain (founded in 1903). Pop.: 30 884 (1971).

let down *vb.* (*tr., mainly adv.*) **1.** (*also prep.*) to lower. **2.** to fail to fulfil the expectations of (a person); disappoint. **3.** to undo, shorten, and resew (the hem) so as to lengthen (a dress, skirt, etc.). **4.** to untie (long hair that is bound up) and allow to fall loose. **5.** to deflate: *to let down a tyre.* ~*n.* **let·down. 6.** a disappointment. **7.** the gliding descent of an aircraft in preparation for landing.

le·thal (ˈliːθəl) *adj.* **1.** able to cause or causing death. **2.** of or suggestive of death. [C16: from Latin *lēthālis,* from *lētum* death] —**le·thal·i·ty** (liːˈθælɪtɪ) *n.* —**ˈle·thal·ly** *adv.*

le·thal dose *n.* the amount of a drug or other agent that if administered to an animal or human will prove fatal. Abbrev.: **LD.**

leth·ar·gy (ˈlɛθədʒɪ) *n., pl.* **·gies. 1.** sluggishness, slowness, or dullness. **2.** an abnormal lack of energy, esp. as the result of a disease. [C14: from Late Latin *lēthargia,* from Greek *lēthargos* drowsy, from *lēthē* forgetfulness] —**le·thar·gic** (lɪˈθɑːdʒɪk) *or* **le·ˈthar·gi·cal** *adj.* —**le·ˈthar·gi·cal·ly** *adv.*

Leth·bridge (ˈlɛθbrɪdʒ) *n.* a city in Canada, in S Alberta: coal-mining. Pop.: 41 217 (1971).

Le·the (ˈliːθɪ) *n.* **1.** *Greek myth.* a river in Hades that caused forgetfulness in those who drank its waters. **2.** forgetfulness. [C16: via Latin from Greek, from *lēthē* oblivion] —**Le·the·an** (lɪˈθiːən) *adj.*

let in *vb.* (*tr., adv.*) **1.** to allow to enter. **2. let in for.** to involve (oneself or another) in (something more than is expected): *he let himself in for a lot of extra work.* **3. let in on.** to allow (someone) to know about or participate in.

let in·to *vb.* (*tr., prep*) **1.** to allow to enter. **2.** to put into the surface of: *to let a pipe into the wall.* **3.** to allow (someone) to share (a secret).

Le·to (ˈliːtəʊ) *n.* the mother by Zeus of Apollo and Artemis. Roman name **Latona.**

let off *vb.* (*tr., mainly adv.*) **1.** (*also prep.*) to allow to disembark or leave. **2.** to explode or fire (a bomb, gun, etc.). **3.** (*also prep.*) to excuse from (work or other responsibilities): *I'll let you off for a week.* **4.** *Informal.* to allow to get away without the expected punishment, work, etc. **5.** to let (accommodation) in portions. **6.** to release (liquid, air, etc.). **7. let off** (*or* **blow off**) **steam.** *Informal.* **a.** to give vent to pent-up emotions. **b.** to use up excess energy, as by hard exercise. **8. let (someone) off with.** to give (a light punishment) to (someone).

let on *vb.* (*adv.;* when *tr., takes a clause as object*) **1.** to allow (something, such as a secret) to be known; reveal: *he never let on that he was married.* **2.** (*tr.*) to pretend.

let out *vb.* (*adv., mainly tr.*) **1.** to give vent to; emit: *to let out a howl.* **2.** to allow to go or run free; release. **3.** (*may take a clause as object*) to reveal (a secret). **4.** to make available to tenants, hirers, or contractors. **5.** to permit to flow out: *to let air out of the tyres.* **6.** to make (a garment) larger, as by unpicking (the seams) and sewing nearer the outer edge. ~*n.* **let-out. 7.** a chance to escape.

let's (lɛts) *contraction of* let us: used to express a suggestion, command, etc., by the speaker to himself and his hearers.

Lett (lɛt) *n.* another name for a **Latvian.**

let·ter (ˈlɛtə) *n.* **1.** any of a set of conventional symbols used in writing or printing a language, each symbol being associated with a group of phonetic values in the language; character of the alphabet. **2.** a written or printed communication addressed to a person, company, etc., usually sent by post in an envelope. **3.** (often preceded by *the*) the strict legalistic or pedantic interpretation of the meaning of an agreement, document, etc.; exact wording as distinct from actual intention (esp. in the phrase **the letter of the law**). Compare **spirit**[1] (sense 10). **4.** *Printing, archaic.* a style of typeface: *a fancy letter.* **5. to the letter. a.** following the literal interpretation or wording exactly. **b.** attending to every detail. ~*vb.* **6.** to write or mark letters on (a sign, etc.), esp. by hand. **7.** (*tr.*) to set down or print using letters. ~See also **letters.** [C13: from Old French *lettre,* from Latin *littera* letter of the alphabet] —**ˈlet·ter·er** *n.*

let·ter bomb *n.* a thin explosive device inside an envelope, detonated when the envelope is opened.

let·ter box *n. Chiefly Brit.* **a.** a private box into which letters, etc., are delivered. **b.** a public box into which letters, etc., are put for collection and delivery.

let·ter card *n.* a card, usually one on which the postage is prepaid, that is sealed by being folded in half so that its gummed edges come into contact with each other.

let·tered (ˈlɛtəd) *adj.* **1.** well educated in literature, the arts, etc. **2.** literate. **3.** of or characterized by learning or culture. **4.** printed or marked with letters.

let·ter·head (ˈlɛtəˌhɛd) *n.* a sheet of paper printed with one's address, name, etc., for writing a letter on.

let·ter-high *adj.* another term for **type-high.**

let·ter·ing (ˈlɛtərɪŋ) *n.* **1.** the act, art, or technique of inscribing letters on to something. **2.** the letters so inscribed.

let·ter of ad·vice *n.* a commercial letter giving a specific notification, such as the consignment of goods.

let·ter of cred·it *n.* **1.** a letter issued by a bank entitling the bearer to draw funds up to a specified maximum from that bank or its agencies. **2.** a letter addressed by a bank instructing the addressee to allow the person named to draw a specified sum on the credit of the addressor bank.

let·ter of in·tro·duc·tion *n.* a letter given by one person to another, introducing him formally to a person or organization.

let·ter of marque *or* **let·ters of marque** *n.* **1.** a licence granted by a state to a private citizen to arm a ship and seize merchant vessels of another nation. **2.** a similar licence issued by a nation allowing a private citizen to seize goods or citizens of another nation. ~Also called: **letter of marque and reprisal.**

let·ter-per·fect *adj.* another term (esp. in the U.S.) for **word-perfect.**

let·ter·press (ˈlɛtəˌprɛs) *n.* **1. a.** a method of printing in which ink is transferred from raised surfaces to paper by pressure; relief printing. **b.** matter so printed. **2.** text matter as distinct from illustrations.

let·ters (ˈlɛtəz) *n.* **1.** literary knowledge, ability, or learning: *a man of letters.* **2.** literary culture in general. **3.** an official title, degree, etc., indicated by an abbreviation: *letters after one's name.*

let·ter·set (ˈlɛtəˌsɛt) *n.* a method of rotary printing in which ink is transferred from raised surfaces to paper via a rubber-covered cylinder. [C20: from LETTER(PRESS) + (OFF)SET]

let·ters of ad·min·is·tra·tion *n. Law.* a formal document nominating a specified person to take over, administer, and dispose of an estate when there is no executor to carry out the testator's will.

let·ters of cre·dence *or* **let·ters cre·den·tial** *n.* a formal document accrediting a diplomatic officer to a foreign court or government.

let·ters pat·ent *n.* See **patent** (sense 1).

let·ter tel·e·gram *n.* a telegram sent abroad that is cheaper than an ordinary cable but can take up to 24 hours to arrive. Abbrev.: **LT.**

let through *vb.* (*tr.*) to allow to pass (through): *the invalid was let through to the front of the queue.*

Let·tish (ˈlɛtɪʃ) *n., adj.* another word for **Latvian.**

let·tre de ca·chet *French.* (lɛtr də kaˈʃɛ) *n., pl.* ***let·tres de ca·chet*** (lɛtr də kaˈʃɛ). *French history.* a letter under the sovereign's seal, often authorizing imprisonment without trial.

let·tuce (ˈlɛtɪs) *n.* **1.** any of various plants of the genus *Lactuca,* esp. *L. sativa,* which is cultivated in many varieties for its large edible leaves: family *Compositae* (composites). **2.** the leaves of any of these varieties, which are eaten in salads. **3.** any of various plants that resemble true lettuce, such as lamb's lettuce and sea lettuce. [C13: probably from Old French *laitues,* pl. of *laitue,* from Latin *lactūca,* from *lac-* milk, because of its milky juice]

let up *vb.* (*intr., adv.*) **1.** to diminish, slacken, or stop. **2.** (foll. by *on*) *Informal.* to be less harsh (towards someone). ~*n.* **let-up. 3.** *Informal.* a lessening or abatement.

le·u (ˈleɪuː) *n., pl.* **lei** (leɪ). the standard monetary unit of Rumania, divided into 100 bani. [from Rumanian: lion]

Leu·cas (ˈluːkəs) *n.* a variant spelling of **Leukas.**

leu·cine (ˈluːsiːn) *or* **leu·cin** (ˈluːsɪn) *n.* a white crystalline amino acid found in many proteins and essential to man. Formula: $(CH_3)_2CHCH_2CH(NH_2)COOH$.

Leu·cip·pus (luːˈsɪpəs) *n.* 5th-century B.C. Greek philosopher who originated the atomist theory of matter, developed by his disciple, Democritus.

leu·cite (ˈluːsaɪt) *n.* a grey or white mineral consisting of potassium aluminium silicate: a source of potash for fertilizers and of aluminium. Formula: $KAlSi_2O_6$. —**leu·cit·ic** (luːˈsɪtɪk) *adj.*

leu·co-, leu·ko- *or before a vowel* **leuc-, leuk-** *combining form.* white or lacking colour: *leucocyte; leucorrhoea; leukaemia.* [from Greek *leukos* white]

leu·co base (ˈluːkəʊ) *n.* a colourless compound formed by reducing a dye so that the original dye can be regenerated by oxidation.

leu·co·crat·ic (ˌluːkəˈkrætɪk) *adj.* (of igneous rocks) light-coloured because of a low content of ferromagnesian minerals.

leu·co·cyte *or esp. U.S.* **leu·ko·cyte** (ˈluːkəˌsaɪt) *n.* any of the various large unpigmented cells in the blood of vertebrates. Also called: **white blood cell, white (blood) corpuscle.** See also **lymphocyte, granulocyte, monocyte.** —**leu·co·cyt·ic** *or esp. U.S.* **leu·ko·cyt·ic** (ˌluːkəˈsɪtɪk) *adj.*

leu·co·cy·to·sis *or esp. U.S.* **leu·ko·cy·to·sis** (ˌluːkəʊsaɪˈtəʊsɪs) *n.* a gross increase in the number of white blood cells in the blood, usually as a response to an infection. —**leu·co·cy·tot·ic** *or esp. U.S.* **leu·ko·cy·tot·ic** (ˌluːkəʊsaɪˈtɒtɪk) *adj.*

leu·co·der·ma *or esp. U.S.* **leu·ko·der·ma** (ˌluːkəʊˈdɜːmə) *n.* any area of skin that is white from congenital (see **albinism**) or acquired absence or loss of melanin pigmentation. Also called:

vitiligo. —ˌleu+co+ˈder·mal, ˌleu+co+ˈder+mic *or esp. U.S.* ˌleu+ko+ˈder+mal, ˌleu+ko+ˈder+mic *adj.*

leu+co+ma (luːˈkəʊmə) *n. Pathol.* a white opaque scar of the cornea.

leu+co+maine (ˈluːkəˌmeɪn) *n. Biochem.* any of a group of toxic amines produced during animal metabolism. [C20: from LEUCO- + *-maine,* as in *ptomaine*]

leu+co+pe·ni·a *or esp. U.S.* **leu+ko+pe·ni·a** (ˌluːkəʊˈpiːnɪə) *n. Pathol.* an abnormal reduction in the number of white blood cells in the blood, characteristic of certain diseases. [C19: from LEUCO- + Greek *penia* poverty] —ˌ**leu+co+ˈpe·nic** *or esp. U.S.* ˌ**leu+ko+ˈpe·nic** *adj.*

leu+co+plast (ˈluːkəˌplæst) *or* **leu+co+plas+tid** *n.* any of the small colourless bodies occurring in the cytoplasm of plant cells and used for storing food material, esp. starch.

leu+co+poi+e·sis *or esp. U.S.* **leu+ko+poi+e·sis** (ˌluːkəʊpɔɪˈiːsɪs) *n. Physiol.* formation of leucocytes in the body. Also called: **leucocytopoiesis.** —**leu+co+poi+et+ic** *or esp. U.S.* **leu+ko+poi+et+ic** (ˌluːkəʊpɔɪˈɛtɪk) *adj.*

leu+cor+rhoe·a *or esp. U.S.* **leu+kor+rhe·a** (ˌluːkəˈriːə) *n. Pathol.* a white or yellowish discharge of mucous material from the vagina, often an indication of infection. —ˌ**leu+cor+ˈrhoe·al** *or esp. U.S.* ˌ**leu+kor+ˈrhe·al** *adj.*

leu+cot+o·my (luːˈkɒtəmɪ) *n.* the surgical operation of cutting some of the nerve fibres within the brain for treating intractable mental disorders. See also **lobotomy.**

Leuc+tra (ˈluːktrə) *n.* an ancient town in Greece southwest of Thebes in Boeotia: site of a victory of Thebes over Sparta (371 B.C.), which marked the end of Spartan military supremacy in Greece.

leu+kae+mi·a *or esp. U.S.* **leu+ke+mi·a** (luːˈkiːmɪə) *n.* an acute or chronic disease characterized by a gross proliferation of leucocytes, which crowd into the bone marrow, spleen, lymph nodes, etc., and suppress the blood-forming apparatus.

Leu+kas (ˈluːkəs) *n.* another name for **Levkás.**

leu·ko- *combining form.* variant of **leuco-.**

Leu+ven (ˈløːvə) *n.* the Flemish name for **Louvain.**

lev (lɛf) *n., pl.* **lev·a** (ˈlɛvə). the standard monetary unit of Bulgaria, divided into 100 stotinki. [from Bulgarian: lion]

Lev. *Bible. abbrev. for* Leviticus.

Le+val+loi+si·an (ˌlɛvəˈlɔɪzɪən) *or* **Le+val+lois** (ləˈvælwɑː) *adj.* of or relating to a Lower Palaeolithic culture in W Europe, characterized by a method of flaking flint tools so that one side of the core is flat and the other domed.

le+vant[1] (lɪˈvænt) *n.* a type of leather made from the skins of goats, sheep, or seals, having a pattern of irregular creases. [C19: shortened from *Levant morocco* (type of leather)]

le+vant[2] (lɪˈvænt) *vb.* (*intr.*) *Brit.* to bolt or abscond, esp. to avoid paying debts. [C18: perhaps from slang use of LEVANT]

Le+vant (lɪˈvænt) *n.* **the.** a former name for the area of the E Mediterranean now occupied by Lebanon, Syria, and Israel. [C15: from Old French, from the present participle of *lever* to raise (referring to the rising of the sun in the east), from Latin *levāre*]

le+vant+er[1] (lɪˈvæntə) *n.* (*sometimes cap.*) **1.** an easterly wind in the W Mediterranean area, esp. in the late summer. **2.** an inhabitant of the Levant.

le+vant+er[2] (lɪˈvæntə) *n. Brit.* a person who bolts or absconds.

le+van+tine (ˈlɛvənˌtaɪn) *n.* a cloth of twilled silk.

Le+van+tine (ˈlɛvənˌtaɪn) *adj.* **1.** of or relating to the Levant. ~*n.* **2.** (esp. formerly) an inhabitant of the Levant.

le+va+tor (lɪˈveɪtə, -tɔː) *n.* **1.** *Anatomy.* any of various muscles that raise a part of the body. **2.** *Surgery.* an instrument for elevating a part or structure. [C17: New Latin, from Latin *levāre* to raise]

lev·ee[1] (ˈlɛvɪ) *n.* **1.** an embankment alongside a river constructed to prevent flooding. **2.** an embankment that surrounds a field that is to be irrigated. **3.** a landing place on a river; quay. [C18: from French, from Medieval Latin *levāta,* from Latin *levāre* to raise]

lev·ee[2] (ˈlɛvɪ, ˈlɛveɪ) *n.* **1.** a formal reception held by a sovereign just after rising from bed. **2.** (in Britain) a public court reception for men, held in the early afternoon. [C17: from French, variant of *lever,* a rising, from Latin *levāre* to raise]

lev+el (ˈlɛvᵊl) *adj.* **1.** on a horizontal plane. **2.** having a surface of completely equal height. **3.** being of the same height as something else. **4.** (of quantities to be measured, as in recipes) even with the top of the cup, spoon, etc. **5.** equal to or even with (something or someone else). **6.** not having or showing inconsistency or irregularities. **7.** Also: **level-headed.** even-tempered; steady. **8. one's level best.** the best one can do. ~*vb.* **+els, +el+ling, +elled** *or U.S.* **+els, +el+ing, +eled. 9.** (*tr.; sometimes foll. by off*) to make (a surface) horizontal, level, or even. **10.** to make (two or more people or things) equal, as in position or status. **11.** (*tr.*) to raze to the ground. **12.** (*tr.*) to knock (a person) down by or as if by a blow. **13.** (*tr.*) to direct (a gaze, criticism, etc.) emphatically at someone. **14.** (*intr.; often foll. by with*) *Informal.* to be straightforward and frank. **15.** (*intr.; foll. by off or out*) to manoeuvre an aircraft into a horizontal flight path after a dive, climb, or glide. **16.** (often foll. by *at*) to aim (a weapon) horizontally. **17.** *Surveying.* to determine the elevation of a section of (land), sighting through a levelling instrument to a staff at successive pairs or points. ~*n.* **18.** a horizontal datum line or plane. **19.** a device, such as a spirit level, for determining whether a surface is horizontal. **20.** a surveying instrument consisting basically of a telescope with a spirit level attached, used for measuring relative heights of land. See **Abney level, Dumpy level. 21.** a reading of the difference in elevation of two points taken with such an instrument. **22.** position or status in a scale of values. **23.** amount or degree of progress; stage. **24.** a specified vertical position; altitude. **25.** a horizontal line or plane with respect to which measurement of elevation is based: *sea level.* **26.** a flat even surface or area of land. **27.** a horizontal passage or drift in a mine. **28.** any of the successive layers of material that have been deposited with the passage of time to build up and raise the height of the land surface. **29.** *Physics.* the ratio of the magnitude of a physical quantity to an arbitrary magnitude: *sound-pressure level.* **30. do one's level best.** to try very hard. **31. find one's level.** to find one's most suitable place socially, professionally, etc. **32. on a level.** on the same horizontal plane as another. **33. on the level.** *Informal.* sincere or genuine. [C14: from Old French *livel,* from Vulgar Latin *lībellum* (unattested), from Latin *lībella,* diminutive of *lībra* scales] —**ˈlev+el+ly** *adv.* —**ˈlev+el+ness** *n.*

lev+el cross+ing *n. Brit.* a point at which a railway and a road cross, esp. one with barriers that close the road when a train is scheduled to pass. U.S. name: **grade crossing.**

lev·el-head·ed *adj.* even-tempered, balanced, and reliable; steady. —ˌ**lev·el-ˈhead·ed+ly** *adv.* —ˌ**lev·el-ˈhead·ed+ness** *n.*

lev+el+ler *or U.S.* **lev+el+er** (ˈlɛvələ) *n.* **1.** a person or thing that levels. **2.** a person who works for the abolition of inequalities.

Lev+el+ler (ˈlɛvələ) *n. English history.* a member of a radical group on the Parliamentarian side during the Civil War that advocated republicanism, freedom of worship, etc.

lev+el+ling screw *n.* a screw, often one of three, for adjusting the level of an apparatus.

lev+el peg+ging *Brit. informal.* ~*n.* **1.** equality between two contestants. ~*adj.* **2.** (of two contestants) equal.

Le+ven (ˈliːvᵊn) *n.* **Loch. 1.** a lake in E central Scotland: one of the shallowest of Scottish lochs, with seven islands, on one of which Mary Queen of Scots was imprisoned (1567–8). Length: 6 km (3·7miles). Width: 4 km (2·5miles). **2.** a sea loch in W Scotland, extending for about 14 km (9 miles) east from Loch Linnhe.

lev+er (ˈliːvə) *n.* **1.** a rigid bar pivoted about a fulcrum, used to transfer a force to a load and usually to provide a mechanical advantage. **2.** any of a number of mechanical devices employing this principle. **3.** a means of exerting pressure in order to accomplish something; strategic aid. ~*vb.* **4.** to prise or move (an object) with a lever. [C13: from Old French *leveour,* from *lever* to raise, from Latin *levāre* from *levis* light] —**ˈlev·er-ˌlike** *adj.*

lev+er+age (ˈliːvərɪdʒ, -vrɪdʒ) *n.* **1.** the action of a lever. **2.** the mechanical advantage gained by employing a lever. **3.** power to accomplish something; strategic advantage.

lev+er+et (ˈlɛvərɪt, -vrɪt) *n.* a young hare, esp. one less than one year old. [C15: from Norman French *levrete,* diminutive of *levre,* from Latin *lepus* hare]

Le·ver·hulme (ˈliːvəˌhjuːm) *n.* **Wil·liam Hes·keth,** 1st Viscount. 1851-1925, English soap manufacturer and philanthropist, who founded (1881) the model industrial town Port Sunlight.

Le+ver+ku+sen (*German* ˈleːvərˌkuːzᵊn) *n.* a town in West Germany, in North Rhine-Westphalia on the Rhine: chemical industries. Pop.: 109 520 (1974 est.).

Le·ver·ri·er (*French* ləvɛˈrje) *n.* **Ur·bain Jean Jo·seph** (yrbɛ̃ ʒɑ̃ ʒoˈzɛf). 1811–77, French astronomer: calculated the existence and position of the planet Neptune.

Le·vi (ˈliːvaɪ) *n.* **1.** *Old Testament.* **a.** the third son of Jacob and Leah and the ancestor of the tribe of Levi (Genesis 29:34). **b.** the priestly tribe descended from this patriarch (Numbers 18:21–24). **2.** *New Testament.* another name for **Matthew** (the apostle).

lev·i·a·ble (ˈlɛvɪəbᵊl) *adj.* **1.** (of taxes, etc.) liable to be levied. **2.** (of goods, etc.) liable to bear a levy; taxable.

le+vi·a+than (lɪˈvaɪəθən) *n.* **1.** *Bible.* a monstrous beast, esp. a sea monster. **2.** any huge or powerful thing. [C14: from Late Latin, ultimately from Hebrew *liwyāthān,* of obscure origin]

lev·i+gate (ˈlɛvɪˌgeɪt) *vb. Chem.* **1.** (*tr.*) to grind into a fine powder or a smooth paste. **2.** to form or cause to form a homogeneous mixture, as in the production of gels. **3.** (*tr.*) to suspend (fine particles) by grinding in a liquid, esp. as a method of separating fine from coarse particles. ~*adj.* **4.** *Botany.* having a smooth polished surface; glabrous. [C17: from Latin *lēvigāre,* from *lēvis* smooth] —ˌ**lev·i·ˈga+tion** *n.* —**ˈlev·i+ˌga+tor** *n.*

lev+in (ˈlɛvɪn) *n.* an archaic word for **lightning.** [C13: probably from Scandinavian; compare Danish *lygnild*]

lev·i+rate (ˈlɛvɪrɪt) *n.* the practice, required by Old Testament law, of marrying the widow of one's brother. [C18: from Latin *lēvir* a husband's brother] —**lev·i+rat+ic** (ˌlɛvɪˈrætɪk) *or* ˌ**lev·i+ˈrat·i+cal** *adj.*

Le+vis (ˈliːvaɪz) *pl. n. Trademark.* jeans, usually blue and made of denim.

Lé·vi-Strauss (ˈlɛvɪ ˈstraʊs; *French* levi ˈstroːs) *n.* **Claude** (kloːd). born 1908, French anthropologist, leading exponent of structuralism. His books include *The Elementary Structures of Kinship* (1969), *Totemism* (1962), *The Savage Mind* (1966), and *Mythologies* (1964–71).

Levit. *Bible. abbrev. for* Leviticus.

lev·i+tate (ˈlɛvɪˌteɪt) *vb.* **1.** to rise or cause to rise and float in the air, usually attributed to supernatural intervention. **2.** (*tr.*) *Med.* to support (a patient) on a cushion of air in the treatment of severe burns. [C17: from Latin *levis* light + *-tate,* as in *gravitate*] —ˌ**lev·i·ˈta+tion** *n.* —**ˈlev·i+ˌta+tor** *n.*

Le+vite (ˈliːvaɪt) *n.* **1.** *Old Testament.* a member of the priestly tribe of Levi. **2.** *Judaism.* a member of the body of assistants to the priests of the Temple.

Le+vit·i·cal (lɪ'vɪtɪkᵊl) *or* **Le+vit+ic** *adj.* **1.** of or relating to the Levites. **2.** of or relating to the book of Leviticus. —**Le+'vit·i+cal+ly** *adv.*

Le+vit·i·cus (lɪ'vɪtɪkəs) *n. Old Testament.* the third book of the Old Testament, containing Levitical law and ritual precepts.

lev+i·ty ('lɛvɪtɪ) *n., pl.* **·ties. 1.** inappropriate lack of seriousness. **2.** fickleness or instability. **3.** *Archaic.* lightness in weight. [C16: from Latin *levitās* lightness, from *levis* light]

Lev+kás (lɛf'kæs) *or* **Leu+kas** *n.* a Greek island in the Ionian Sea, in the Ionian Islands. Pop.: 24 581 (1971). Area: 295 sq. km (114 sq. miles). Italian name: **Santa Maura.**

le·vo- *combining form.* U.S. variant of **laevo-.** [from Latin *laevus* left, on the left]

lev·y ('lɛvɪ) *vb.* **lev·ies, lev·y+ing, lev·ied.** (*tr.*) **1.** to impose and collect (a tax, tariff, fine, etc.). **2.** to conscript troops for service. **3.** to seize or attach (property) in accordance with the judgment of a court. ~*n., pl.* **lev·ies. 4. a.** the act of imposing and collecting a tax, tariff, etc. **b.** the money so raised. **5. a.** the conscription of troops for service. **b.** a person conscripted in this way. [C15: from Old French *levée* a raising, from *lever,* from Latin *levāre* to raise] —**'lev·i·er** *n.*

lev·y en masse ('lɛvɪ ɒn 'mæs) *n.* the conscription of the civilian population in large numbers in the face of impending invasion. Also: **lev·ée en masse** (*French* ləve ɑ̃ 'mas).

lewd (lu:d) *adj.* **1.** characterized by or intended to excite crude sexual desire; obscene. **2.** *Obsolete.* **a.** wicked. **b.** ignorant. [C14: from Old English *lǣwde* lay, ignorant; see LAY[3]] —**'lewd+ly** *adv.* —**'lewd+ness** *n.*

Lew+es ('lu:ɪs) *n.* a market town in S England, administrative centre of East Sussex, on the River Ouse: site of a battle (1264) in which Henry III was defeated by Simon de Montfort. Pop.: 14 015 (1971).

lew+is ('lu:ɪs) *or* **lew+is+son** *n.* a lifting device for heavy stone blocks consisting of a number of pieces of metal fitting into a dovetailed recess cut into the stone. [C18: perhaps from the name of the inventor]

Lew+is[1] ('lu:ɪs) *n.* the N part of the island of Lewis with Harris, in the Outer Hebrides. Pop.: 20 309 (1971). Area: 1634 sq. km (631 sq. miles).

Lew·is[2] ('lu:ɪs) *n.* **1.** See (Cecil) **Day Lewis. 2. C(live) S(taples).** 1898–1963, English novelist, critic, and Christian apologist, noted for his critical work, *Allegory of Love* (1936), his theological study, *The Screwtape Letters* (1942), and for his children's books. **3. (Harry) Sin·clair.** 1885–1951, U.S. novelist. He satirized the complacency and philistinism of American small-town life, esp. in *Main Street* (1920) and *Babbitt* (1922): Nobel prize for literature 1930. **4. Mat·thew Greg·o·ry,** known as *Monk Lewis.* 1775–1818, English novelist and dramatist, noted for his Gothic horror story *The Monk* (1796). **5. Mer·i·weth·er.** 1774–1807, American explorer who, with William Clark, led an overland expedition from St. Louis to the Pacific Ocean (1804–06). **6. (Percy) Wynd·ham.** 1884–1957, British painter, novelist, and critic, born in the U.S. A founder of vorticism, his writings include *Time and Western Man* (1927), *The Apes of God* (1930), and the trilogy *The Human Age* (1928–55).

Lew·is ac·id *n.* a substance capable of accepting a pair of electrons from a base to form a covalent bond. Compare **Lewis base.** [C20: named after G. N. *Lewis* (1875–1946), U.S. chemist]

Lew·is base *n.* a substance capable of donating a pair of electrons to an acid to form a covalent bond. Compare **Lewis acid.** [C20: named after G. N. *Lewis;* see LEWIS ACID]

Lew·is gun *n.* a light air-cooled gas-operated machine gun used in World War I. [C20: named after I. N. *Lewis* (1858–1931), U.S. soldier]

Lew·i·sham ('lu:ɪʃəm) *n.* a borough of S Greater London, on the River Thames. Pop.: 237 300 (1976 est.).

lew+is+ite ('lu:ɪ,saɪt) *n.* a colourless oily poisonous liquid with an odour resembling that of geraniums, having a powerful vesicant action and used as a war gas; 1-chloro-2-dichloroarsinoethene. Formula: $ClCH:CHAsCl_2$. [C20: named after W. L. *Lewis* (1878–1943), American chemist]

Lew+is with Har+ris *or* **Lew+is and Har+ris** *n.* an island in the Outer Hebrides, separated from the NW coast of Scotland by the Minch: consists of Lewis in the north and Harris in the south; many lakes and peat moors; economy based chiefly on the Harris tweed industry, with some fishing. Chief town: Stornoway. Pop.: 23 188 (1971). Area: 2134 sq. km (824 sq. miles).

lex (lɛks) *n., pl.* **leg·es** ('li:dʒi:z). **1.** a system or body of laws. **2.** a particular specified law.

lex. *abbrev. for* lexicon.

lex+eme ('lɛksi:m) *n. Linguistics.* a minimal unit, such as a word or stem, in the vocabulary of a language, as opposed to a basic grammatical unit (morpheme) or a basic semantic unit (sememe). [C20: from LEX(ICON) + -EME]

lex·i·cal ('lɛksɪkᵊl) *adj.* **1.** of or relating to items of vocabulary in a language. **2.** of or relating to a lexicon. —**lex·i·cal+i·ty** (,lɛksɪ'kælɪtɪ) *n.* —**'lex·i·cal+ly** *adv.*

lex·i·cal in·ser·tion *n. Generative grammar.* the process in which actual morphemes of a language are substituted either for semantic material or for place-fillers in the course of a derivation of a sentence.

lex·i·cal mean+ing *n.* the meaning of a word in relation to the physical world or to abstract concepts, without reference to any sentence in which the word may occur. Compare **grammatical meaning, content word.**

lexicog. *abbrev. for:* **1.** lexicographical. **2.** lexicography.

lex·i·cog+ra+phy (,lɛksɪ'kɒgrəfɪ) *n.* the process or profession of writing or compiling dictionaries. —,**lex·i·'cog+ra+pher** *n.* —**lex·i·co·graph·ic** (,lɛksɪkə'græfɪk) *or* ,**lex·i·co·'graph·i·cal** *adj.* —,**lex·i·co·'graph·i·cal+ly** *adv.*

lex·i·col·o·gy (,lɛksɪ'kɒlədʒɪ) *n.* the study of the overall structure and history of the vocabulary of a language. —**lex·i·co·log·i·cal** (,lɛksɪkə'lɒdʒɪkᵊl) *adj.* —,**lex·i·co·'log·i·cal+ly** *adv.* —,**lex·i·'col·o·gist** *n.*

lex·i·con ('lɛksɪkən) *n.* **1.** a dictionary, esp. one of an ancient language such as Greek or Hebrew. **2.** a list of terms relating to a particular subject. **3.** *Linguistics.* the set of all the morphemes of a language. [C17: New Latin, from Greek *lexikon* n. use of *lexikos* relating to words, from Greek *lexis* word, from *legein* to speak]

lex·i·co+sta+tis+tics (,lɛksɪkəʊstə'tɪstɪks) *n.* the statistical study of the vocabulary of a language, with special attention to the historical links with other languages. See also **glottochronology.**

lex·i·gra+phy (lɛk'sɪgrəfɪ) *n.* a system of writing in which each word is represented by a sign. [C19: from Greek *lexis* word + -GRAPHY]

Lex+ing+ton ('lɛksɪŋtən) *n.* **1.** a city in NE central Kentucky, in the Bluegrass region: major centre for horse-breeding. Pop.: 184 603 (1973 est.). **2.** a city in Massachusetts, northwest of Boston: site of the first action (1775) of the War of American Independence. Pop.: 31 886 (1970).

lex+is ('lɛksɪs) *n.* the totality of vocabulary items in a language, including all forms having lexical meaning or grammatical function. [C20: from Greek *lexis* word]

lex lo·ci ('ləʊsaɪ, -ki:) *n.* the law of the place. [from Latin]

lex non scrip+ta (nɒn 'skrɪptə) *n.* the unwritten law; common law. [from Latin]

lex scrip+ta *n.* the written law; statute law. [from Latin]

lex ta+li·o+nis (,tælɪ'əʊnɪs) *n.* the law of revenge or retaliation. [C16: New Latin]

ley (li:, laɪ) *n.* **1.** grassland. **2.** a line joining two prominent points in the landscape, thought to be the line of a prehistoric track. Also called: **ley line.** [variant of LEA[1]]

Ley+den[1] ('laɪdᵊn; *Dutch* 'lɛɪdə) *n.* a variant spelling of **Leiden.**

Ley·den[2] ('laɪdᵊn) *n.* See **Lucas van Leyden.**

Ley+den jar *n. Physics.* an early type of capacitor consisting of a glass jar with the lower part of the inside and outside coated with tin foil. [C18: first made in Leiden]

Ley+te ('leɪteɪ) *n.* an island in the central Philippines, in the Visayan Islands. Chief town: Tacloban. Pop.: 1 362 051 (1970). Area: 7215 sq. km (2786 sq. miles).

Ley+te Gulf *n.* an inlet of the Pacific in the E Philippines, east of Leyte and south of Samar: scene of a battle (1944) during World War II, in which the Americans defeated the Japanese.

l.f. *Printing. abbrev. for* light face.

L.F. *Radio. abbrev. for* low frequency.

LG *or* **L.G.** *abbrev. for* Low German.

lg. *or* **lge.** *abbrev. for* large.

lgth. *abbrev. for* length.

LH *abbrev. for* luteinizing hormone.

l.h. *or* **L.H.** *abbrev. for* left hand.

Lha+sa *or* **Las+sa** ('lɑ:sə) *n.* a city in SW China, capital of Tibet AR, at an altitude of 3606 m (11 830 ft.): for centuries the sacred city of Lamaism and residence of the Dalai Lamas from the 17th century until 1950; known as the Forbidden City because it was closed to Westerners until the beginning of the 20th century; annexed by China in 1951 and revolted in 1959, when the Dalai Lama fled. Pop.: 85 000 (1960 est.).

l.h.d. *abbrev. for* left-hand drive.

li (li:) *n.* a Chinese unit of length, approximately equal to 590 yards. [from Chinese]

Li *the chemical symbol for* lithium.

L.I. *abbrev. for:* **1.** Long Island. **2.** Light Infantry.

li·a·bil·i·ties (,laɪə'bɪlɪtɪz) *pl. n. Accounting.* business obligations incurred but not discharged and entered as claims on the assets shown on the balance sheet. Compare **assets** (sense 1).

li·a·bil·i·ty (,laɪə'bɪlɪtɪ) *n., pl.* **·ties. 1.** the state of being liable. **2.** a financial obligation. **3.** a hindrance or disadvantage. **4.** likelihood or probability.

li·a+ble ('laɪəbᵊl) *adj.* (*postpositive*) **1.** legally obliged or responsible; answerable. **2.** susceptible or exposed; subject. **3.** probable, likely, or capable: *it's liable to happen soon.* [C15: perhaps via Anglo-French, from Old French *lier* to bind, from Latin *ligāre*] —**'li·a+ble+ness** *n.*

Usage. Careful users of English take *liable* to mean *responsible for* and *subject to* in sentences such as *he was liable for his employees' accidents* and *he was liable to accidents.* The use of *liable* in the sense of *likely* is avoided: *he was likely* (not *liable*) *to have accidents.*

li+aise (lɪ'eɪz) *vb.* (*intr.;* usually foll. by *with*) to communicate and maintain contact (with). [C20: back formation from LIAISON]

li·ai·son (lɪ'eɪzɒn) *n.* **1.** communication and contact between groups or units. **2.** a secretive or adulterous sexual relationship. **3.** the relationship between military units necessary to ensure unity of purpose. **4.** (in the phonology of several languages, esp. French) the pronunciation of a normally silent consonant at the end of a word immediately before another word commencing with a vowel, in such a way that the consonant is taken over as the initial sound of the following word. Liaison is seen between French *ils* (i:l) and *ont* (ɔ̃), to give *ils ont* (i:l'zɔ̃). **5.** any thickening for soups, sauces, etc., such as egg yolks or cream. **6.** (*modifier*) of or relating to liaison between groups or units: *a liaison officer.* [C17: via French from Old French, from *lier* to bind, from Latin *ligāre*]

Liá·kou·ra ('ljakura) *n.* transliteration of the Modern Greek name for (Mount) **Parnassus.**

li·a·na (lɪ'ɑːnə) *or* **li·ane** (lɪ'ɑːn) *n.* any of various woody climbing plants of tropical forests. [C19: changed from earlier *liane* (through influence of French *lier* to bind), from French, of obscure origin] —**li·'a·noid** *adj.*

Liao (ljaʊ) *n.* a river in NE China, rising in SE Inner Mongolia and flowing northeast then southwest to the Gulf of Liaotung. Length: about 1100 km (700 miles).

Liao·ning ('ljaʊ'nɪŋ) *n.* a province of NE China, in S Manchuria. Capital: Shen-yang. Pop.: 28 000 000 (1967–71 est.). Area: 150 000 sq. km (58 500 sq. miles).

Liao·tung ('ljaʊ'tʊŋ) *n.* **1.** a peninsula of NE China, in S Manchuria extending south into the Yellow Sea: forms the S part of Liaoning province. **2. Gulf of.** the N part of the Gulf of Chihli, west of the peninsula of Liaotung.

Liao·yang ('ljaʊ'jæŋ) *n.* a city in NE China, in S Manchuria, in Liaoning province: a regional capital in the early dynasties. Pop.: 169 000 (1958 est.).

li·ar ('laɪə) *n.* a person who has lied or lies repeatedly.

li·ard (lɪ'ɑːd) *n.* a former small coin of various European countries. [C16: after G. *Liard*, French minter]

Li·ard ('liːɑːd, liː'ɑːd, -'ɑː) *n.* a river in W Canada, rising in the SE Yukon and flowing east and then northwest to the Mackenzie River. Length: 885 km (550 miles).

Li·as ('laɪəs) *n.* the lowest series of rocks of the Jurassic system. [C15 (referring to a kind of limestone), C19 (geological sense) from Old French *liois*, perhaps from *lie* lees, dregs, so called from its appearance] —**Li·as·sic** (laɪ'æsɪk) *adj.*

lib (lɪb) *n. Informal.* short for **liberation:** used in the names of movements agitating for the emancipation or social equality of particular groups, such as *women's lib* and *gay lib.*

lib. *abbrev. for:* **1.** liber. [Latin: book] **2.** librarian. **3.** library.

Lib. *abbrev. for* Liberal.

li·ba·tion (laɪ'beɪʃən) *n.* **1. a.** the pouring out of wine, etc., in honour of a deity. **b.** the liquid so poured out. **2.** *Usually facetious.* an alcoholic drink. [C14: from Latin *lībātiō*, from *lībāre* to pour an offering of drink] —**li·'ba·tion·al** *or* **li·'ba·tion·ar·y** *adj.*

Li·bau ('liːbaʊ) *n.* the German name for **Liepāja.**

Li·ba·va (lɪ'bavə) *n.* transliteration of the Russian name for **Liepāja.**

Lib·by ('lɪbɪ) *n.* **Wil·lard Frank.** born 1908, U.S. chemist, who devised the technique of radiocarbon dating: Nobel prize for chemistry 1960.

li·bec·ci·o (lɪ'bɛtʃɪəʊ) *or* **li·bec·chi·o** (lɪ'bɛkɪəʊ) *n.* a strong westerly or southwesterly wind blowing onto the W coast of Corsica. [Italian, via Latin, from Greek *libs*]

li·bel ('laɪbᵊl) *n.* **1.** *Law.* **a.** the publication of defamatory matter in permanent form, as by a written or printed statement, picture, etc. **b.** the act of publishing such matter. **2.** any defamatory or unflattering representation or statement. **3.** *Ecclesiastical law.* a plaintiff's written statement of claim. ~*vb.* **·bels, ·bel·ling, ·belled** *or U.S.* **·bels, ·bel·ing, ·beled.** (*tr.*) **4.** *Law.* to make or publish a defamatory statement or representation about (a person). **5.** to misrepresent injuriously. **6.** *Ecclesiastical law.* to bring an action against (a person) in the ecclesiastical courts. [C13 (in the sense: written statement), hence C14 legal sense: a plaintiff's statement, via Old French from Latin *libellus* a little book, from *liber* a book] —**'li·bel·ler** *or* **'li·bel·ist** *n.* —**'li·bel·lous** *or* **'li·bel·ous** *adj.*

li·bel·lant *or U.S.* **li·bel·ant** ('laɪbᵊlənt) *n.* **1.** a party who brings an action in the ecclesiastical courts by presenting a libel. **2.** a person who publishes a libel.

li·bel·lee *or U.S.* **li·bel·ee** (ˌlaɪbᵊ'liː) *n.* a person against whom a libel has been filed in an ecclesiastical court.

li·ber ('laɪbə) *n.* a rare name for **phloem.** [C18: from Latin, in original sense: tree bark]

lib·er·al ('lɪbərəl, 'lɪbrəl) *adj.* **1.** relating to or having social and political views that favour progress and reform. **2.** relating to or having policies or views advocating individual freedom. **3.** giving and generous in temperament or behaviour. **4.** tolerant of other people. **5.** abundant; lavish: *a liberal helping of cream.* **6.** not strict; free: *a liberal translation.* **7.** of or relating to an education that aims to develop general cultural interests and intellectual ability. ~*n.* **8.** a person who has liberal ideas or opinions. [C14: from Latin *līberālis* of freedom, from *līber* free] —**'lib·er·al·ly** *adv.* —**'lib·er·al·ness** *n.*

Lib·er·al ('lɪbərəl, 'lɪbrəl) *n.* **1.** a member or supporter of a Liberal Party. ~*adj.* **2.** of or relating to a Liberal Party.

lib·er·al arts *pl. n.* the fine arts, humanities, sociology, languages, and literature. Often shortened to **arts.**

lib·er·al·ism ('lɪbərəˌlɪzəm, 'lɪbrə-) *n.* **1.** liberal opinions, practices, or politics. **2.** a movement in modern Protestantism that rejects biblical authority. —**'lib·er·al·ist** *n., adj.* —**ˌlib·er·al·'is·tic** *adj.*

lib·er·al·i·ty (ˌlɪbə'rælɪtɪ) *n., pl.* **·ties. 1.** generosity; bounty. **2.** the quality or condition of being liberal.

lib·er·al·ize *or* **lib·er·al·ise** ('lɪbərəˌlaɪz, 'lɪbrə-) *vb.* to make or become liberal. —**ˌlib·er·al·i·'za·tion** *or* **ˌlib·er·al·i·'sa·tion** *n.* —**'lib·er·alˌiz·er** *or* **'lib·er·alˌis·er** *n.*

Lib·er·al Par·ty *n.* **1.** the third largest political party in Britain; successor to the Whigs and a major party in the 19th and early 20th centuries. **2.** one of the major political parties in Australia, a conservative party, generally opposed to the Labor Party. **3.** any other party supporting liberal policies.

lib·er·al stud·ies *n.* (*functioning as sing.*) *Brit.* a supplementary arts course for those specializing in scientific, technical, or professional studies.

Lib·er·al Un·ion·ist *n.* a Liberal who opposed Gladstone's policy of Irish Home Rule in 1886 and after. —**Lib·er·al Un·ion·ism** *n.*

lib·er·ate ('lɪbəˌreɪt) *vb.* (*tr.*) **1.** to give liberty to; make free. **2.** to release (something, esp. a gas) from chemical combination during a chemical reaction. **3.** to release from occupation or subjugation by a foreign power. —**ˌlib·er·'a·tion** *n.* —**'lib·er·ˌa·tor** *n.* —**'lib·er·ˌa·tress** *fem. n.*

Li·be·rec (*Czech* 'libɛrɛts) *n.* a city in NW Czechoslovakia, on the Neisse River: a centre of the German Sudeten movement in 1938. Pop.: 72 752 (1970). German name: **Reichenberg.**

Li·be·ri·a (laɪ'bɪərɪə) *n.* a republic in W Africa, on the Atlantic: originated in 1822 as a home for freed Afro-American slaves, with land purchased by the American Colonization Society; republic declared in 1847; exports are predominantly rubber and iron ore. Official language: English. Religion: mostly animist. Currency: U.S. dollar. Capital: Monrovia. Pop.: 1 708 000 (1975 UN est.). Area: 111 400 sq. km (43 000 sq. miles). —**Li·'be·ri·an** *adj., n.*

lib·er·tar·i·an (ˌlɪbə'tɛərɪən) *n.* **1.** a believer in freedom of thought, expression, etc. **2.** a believer in the doctrine of free will. ~*adj.* **3.** of, relating to, or characteristic of a libertarian. [C18: from LIBERTY] —**ˌlib·er·'tar·i·an·ism** *n.*

li·ber·ti·cide (lɪ'bɜːtɪˌsaɪd) *n.* **1.** a destroyer of freedom. **2.** the destruction of freedom. —**liˌber·ti·'cid·al** *adj.*

lib·er·tine ('lɪbəˌtiːn, -ˌtaɪn) *n.* **1.** a morally dissolute person. ~*adj.* **2.** morally dissolute. [C14 (in the sense: freedman, dissolute person): from Latin *lībertīnus* freedman, from *lībertus* freed, from *līber* free] —**'lib·erˌtin·age** *or* **'lib·er·tinˌism** *n.*

lib·er·ty ('lɪbətɪ) *n., pl.* **·ties. 1.** the power of choosing, thinking, and acting for oneself; freedom from control or restriction. **2.** the right or privilege of access to a particular place; freedom. **3.** (*often pl.*) a social action regarded as being familiar, forward, or improper. **4.** (*often pl.*) an action that is unauthorized or unwarranted in the circumstances: *he took liberties with the translation.* **5. a.** authorized leave granted to a sailor. **b.** (*as modifier*): *liberty man; liberty boat.* **6. at liberty.** free, unoccupied, or unrestricted. **7. take liberties (with).** to be overfamiliar or overpresumptuous. **8. take the liberty (of** *or* **to).** to venture or presume (to do something). [C14: from Old French *liberté*, from Latin *lībertās*, from *līber* free]

lib·er·ty bod·ice *n.* a sleeveless vest-like undergarment made from thick cotton and covering the upper part of the body, formerly worn esp. by young children.

lib·er·ty cap *n.* a cap of soft felt worn as a symbol of liberty, esp. during the French Revolution, from the practice in ancient Rome of giving a freed slave such a cap.

lib·er·ty hall *n. Informal.* a place or condition of complete liberty.

lib·er·ty horse *n.* (in a circus) a riderless horse that performs movements to verbal commands.

Lib·er·ty Is·land *n.* a small island in upper New York Bay: site of the Statue of Liberty. Area: 5 hectares (12 acres). Former name (until 1956): **Bedloe's Island.**

lib·er·ty ship *n.* a supply ship of World War II.

Li·bia ('liːbja) *n.* the Italian name for **Libya.**

li·bid·i·nous (lɪ'bɪdɪnəs) *adj.* **1.** characterized by excessive sexual desire. **2.** of or relating to the libido. —**li·'bid·i·nous·ly** *adv.* —**li·'bid·i·nous·ness** *n.*

li·bi·do (lɪ'biːdəʊ) *n., pl.* **·dos. 1.** *Psychoanal.* psychic energy emanating from the id. **2.** sexual urge or desire. [C20 (in psychoanalysis): from Latin: desire] —**li·bid·i·nal** (lɪ'bɪdɪnᵊl) *adj.* —**li·'bid·i·nal·ly** *adv.*

li·bra ('laɪbrə) *n., pl.* **·brae** (-briː). an ancient Roman unit of weight corresponding to 1 pound, but equal to about 12 ounces. [C14: from Latin, literally: scales]

Li·bra ('liːbrə) *n., Latin genitive* **Li·brae** ('liːbriː). **1.** *Astronomy.* a small faint zodiacal constellation in the S hemisphere, lying between Virgo and Scorpius on the ecliptic. **2.** *Astrology.* **a.** Also called: the **Scales,** the **Balance.** the seventh sign of the zodiac, symbol ♎, having a cardinal air classification and ruled by the planet Venus. The sun is in this sign between about Sept. 23 and Oct. 22. **b.** a person born under this sign. ~*adj.* **3.** *Astrology.* born under or characteristic of Libra. ~Also (for senses 2b., 3): **Lib·ran** ('lɪbrən).

li·brar·i·an (laɪ'brɛərɪən) *n.* a person in charge of a library.

li·brar·i·an·ship (laɪ'brɛərɪənˌʃɪp, laɪ-) *n.* the professional administration of library resources and services. Now often called **library science.**

li·brar·y ('laɪbrərɪ) *n., pl.* **·brar·ies. 1.** a room or set of rooms where books and other literary materials are kept. **2.** a collection of literary materials, films, tapes, gramophone records, etc., kept for reference or borrowing. **3.** the building or institution that houses such a collection: *a public library.* **4.** a set of books published as a series, often in a similar format. **5.** *Computer technol.* a collection of standard programs and subroutines for immediate use, usually stored on disk or some other storage device. [C14: from Old French *librairie*, from Medieval Latin *librāris*, n. use of Latin *librārius* relating to books, from *liber* book]

li·brar·y e·di·tion *n.* an edition of a book having a superior quality of paper, binding, etc.

li·brar·y sci·ence *n.* the study of the theory and practice of library administration, bibliographic skills, and information retrieval. Also called (esp. Brit.): **librarianship.**

li+brate ('laɪbreɪt) *vb.* (*intr.*) **1.** to oscillate or waver. **2.** to hover or be balanced. [C17: from Latin *librātus,* from *librāre* to balance] —**li+bra+to+ry** ('laɪbrətərɪ, -trɪ) *adj.*

li+bra+tion (laɪ'breɪʃən) *n.* **1.** the act or an instance of oscillating. **2.** a real or apparent oscillation of the moon enabling approximately nine per cent of the surface facing away from earth to be seen. —**li+'bra+tion+al** *adj.*

li+bret+tist (lɪ'brɛtɪst) *n.* the author of a libretto.

li+bret+to (lɪ'brɛtəʊ) *n., pl.* **+tos** *or* **+ti** (-tiː). a text written for and set to music in an opera, etc. [C18: from Italian, diminutive of *libro* book]

Li+bre·ville (*French* librə'vil) *n.* the capital of Gabon, in the west on the estuary of the Gabon River: founded as a French trading post in 1843 and expanded with the settlement of freed slaves in 1848. Pop.: 167 394 (1972).

li+bri+form ('laɪbrɪˌfɔːm) *adj.* (of a fibre of woody tissue) elongated and having a pitted thickened cell wall.

Lib·y·a ('lɪbɪə) *n.* a republic in N Africa, on the Mediterranean: became an Italian colony in 1912; divided after World War II into Tripolitania and Cyrenaica (under British administration) and Fezzan (under French); gained independence in 1951; monarchy overthrown by a military junta in 1969. It consists almost wholly of desert and is a major exporter of oil. Language: Arabic. Religion: mostly Sunni Muslim. Currency: Libyan pound. Capital: Tripoli. Pop.: 2 257 037 (1973). Area: 1 760 000 sq. km (680 000 sq. miles). Official name: **The Popular Socialist Libyan Arab Jamahiriya.**

Lib·y+an ('lɪbɪən) *adj.* **1.** of or relating to Libya, its people, or its language. ~*n.* **2.** a native or inhabitant of Libya. **3.** the extinct Hamitic language of ancient Libya.

Lib·y+an Des+ert *n.* a desert in N Africa, in E Libya, W Egypt, and the NW Sudan: the NE part of the Sahara.

lice (laɪs) *n.* the plural of **louse.**

li+cence *or U.S.* **li+cense** ('laɪsəns) *n.* **1.** a certificate, tag, document, etc., giving official permission to do something. **2.** formal permission or exemption. **3.** liberty of action or thought; freedom. **4.** intentional disregard of or deviation from conventional rules to achieve a certain effect: *poetic licence.* **5.** excessive freedom. **6.** licentiousness. [C14: via Old French and Medieval Latin *licentia* permission, from Latin: freedom, from *licet* it is allowed]

li+cense ('laɪsəns) *vb.* (*tr.*) **1.** to grant or give a licence for (something, such as the sale of alcohol). **2.** to give permission to or for. —**'li+cens+a·ble** *adj.* —**'li+cens+er** *or* **'li+cen+sor** *n.*

li+cen+see (ˌlaɪsən'siː) *n.* a person who holds a licence, esp. one to sell alcoholic drink.

li+cense plate *n.* the U.S. term for **numberplate.**

li+cen+ti+ate (laɪ'sɛnʃɪɪt) *n.* **1.** a person who holds a licence to practise a certain profession or teach a certain skill or subject. **2.** a higher degree awarded by certain universities. **3.** a person who holds this degree. **4.** *Chiefly Presbyterian Church.* a person holding a licence to preach. [C15: from Medieval Latin *licentiātus,* from *licentiāre* to permit] —**li+'cen+ti+ate+ˌship** *n.* —**li+ˌcen+ti·'a+tion** *n.*

li+cen+tious (laɪ'sɛnʃəs) *adj.* **1.** sexually unrestrained or promiscuous. **2.** *Now rare.* showing disregard for convention. [C16: from Latin *licentiōsus* capricious, from *licentia* LICENCE] —**li+'cen+tious+ly** *adv.* —**li+'cen+tious+ness** *n.*

li+chee (ˌlaɪ'tʃiː) *n.* a variant spelling of **litchi.**

li+chen ('laɪkən, 'lɪtʃən) *n.* **1.** any plant of the division *Lichenes,* which are formed by the symbiotic association of a fungus and an alga and occur as crusty patches or bushy growths on tree trunks, bare ground, etc. **2.** *Pathol.* any of various eruptive disorders of the skin. [C17: via Latin from Greek *leikhēn,* from *leikhein* to lick] —**'li·chen-ˌlike** *adj.* —**'li+chen+ˌoid** *adj.* —**'li+chen+ous** *or* **'li+chen+ˌose** *adj.*

li+chen+in ('laɪkənɪn) *n.* a complex polysaccharide occurring in certain species of mosses.

li+chen+ol+o·gy (ˌlaɪkə'nɒlədʒɪ, ˌlɪ-) *n.* the study of the structure, physiology, and ecology of lichens.

Lich+field ('lɪtʃˌfiːld) *n.* a city in central England, in SE Staffordshire: cathedral with three spires (13th-14th century); birthplace of Samuel Johnson, during whose lifetime the **Lichfield Group** (a literary circle) flourished. Pop.: 22 672 (1971).

lich gate *or* **lych gate** (lɪtʃ) *n.* a roofed gate to a churchyard, formerly used during funerals as a temporary shelter for the bier. [C15: *lich,* from Old English *līc* corpse]

li+chi (ˌlaɪ'tʃiː) *n.* a variant spelling of **litchi.**

Lich·ten·stein ('lɪktənˌstaɪn) *n.* **Roy.** born 1923, U.S. pop artist.

lic+it ('lɪsɪt) *adj.* a less common word for **lawful.** [C15: from Latin *licitus* permitted, from *licēre* to be permitted] —**'lic+it+ly** *adv.* —**'lic+it+ness** *n.*

lick (lɪk) *vb.* **1.** (*tr.*) to pass the tongue over, esp. in order to taste or consume. **2.** to flicker or move lightly over or round (something): *the flames licked around the door.* **3.** (*tr.*) *Informal.* **a.** to defeat or vanquish. **b.** to flog or thrash. **c.** to be or do much better than. **4. lick into shape.** to put into a satisfactory condition. **5. lick one's lips.** to anticipate or recall something with pleasure. **6. lick one's wounds.** to retire after a defeat or setback in order to husband one's resources. **7. lick the boots of.** See **boot**[1] (sense 11). ~*n.* **8.** an instance of passing the tongue over something. **9.** a small amount: *a lick of paint.* **10.** a block of compressed salt or chemical matter provided for domestic animals to lick for medicinal purposes. **11.** a place to which animals go to lick exposed natural deposits of salt. **12.** *Informal.* a hit; blow. **13.** an informal word for **speed. 14. a lick and a promise.** something hastily done, esp. a hurried wash. [Old English *liccian;* related to Old High German *leckon,* Latin *lingere,* Greek *leikhein*] —**'lick+er** *n.*

lick+er+ish *or* **liq+uor+ish** ('lɪkərɪʃ) *adj. Archaic.* **1.** lecherous or lustful. **2.** greedy; gluttonous. **3.** appetizing or tempting. [C16: changed from C13 *lickerous,* via Norman French from Old French *lechereus* lecherous; see LECHER] —**'lick+er+ish+ly** *or* **'liq+uor+ish+ly** *adv.* —**'lick+er+ish+ness** *or* **'liq+uor+ish+ness** *n.*

lick·et·y-split ('lɪkɪtɪ'splɪt) *adv. U.S. slang.* very quickly; speedily. [C19: from LICK + SPLIT]

lick+ing ('lɪkɪŋ) *n. Informal.* **1.** a beating. **2.** a defeat.

lick+spit+tle ('lɪkˌspɪtᵊl) *n.* a flattering or servile person.

lic·o+rice ('lɪkərɪs) *n.* the usual U.S. spelling of **liquorice.**

lic+tor ('lɪktə) *n.* one of a group of ancient Roman officials, usually bearing fasces, who attended magistrates, etc. [C16 *lictor,* C14 *littour,* from Latin *ligāre* to bind]

lid (lɪd) *n.* **1.** a cover, usually removable or hinged, for a receptacle: *a saucepan lid; a desk lid.* **2.** short for **eyelid. 3.** *Botany.* another name for **operculum** (sense 2). **4. dip one's lid.** *Austral. informal.* to raise one's hat as a greeting, etc. **5. flip one's lid.** *Slang.* to become crazy or angry. **6. put the lid on.** *Informal.* **a.** *Brit.* to be the final blow to. **b.** to curb, prevent, or discourage. **7. take the lid off.** *Informal.* to make startling or spectacular revelations about. [Old English *hlid;* related to Old Friesian *hlid,* Old High German *hlit* cover] —**'lid+ded** *adj.*

Lid·dell Hart ('lɪdᵊl 'hɑːt) *n.* Sir **Ba·sil Hen·ry.** 1895–1970, English military strategist and historian: he advocated the development of mechanized warfare in World War II.

Li+di+ce (*Czech* 'lidjitsɛ) *n.* a mining village in Czechoslovakia, in W central Bohemia: destroyed by the Germans in 1942 in reprisal for the assassination of Reinhard Heydrich; rebuilt as a national memorial.

lid+less ('lɪdlɪs) *adj.* **1.** having no lid or top. **2.** (of animals) having no eyelids. **3.** *Archaic.* vigilant and watchful.

li·do ('liːdəʊ) *n., pl.* **·dos.** *Brit.* a public place of recreation, including a pool for swimming or water sports. [C20: after the *Lido,* island bathing beach near Venice, from Latin *litus* shore]

li+do+caine ('laɪdəˌkeɪn) *n.* the U.S. name for **lignocaine.** [C20: from *acetanilid* + *-caine* as in *cocaine*]

lie[1] (laɪ) *vb.* **lies, ly+ing, lied. 1.** (*intr.*) to speak untruthfully with intent to mislead or deceive. **2.** (*intr.*) to convey a false impression or practise deception: *the camera does not lie.* ~*n.* **3.** an untrue or deceptive statement deliberately used to mislead. **4.** something that is deliberately intended to deceive. **5. give the lie to. a.** to disprove. **b.** to accuse of lying. ~Related adj.: **mendacious.** [Old English *lyge* (n.), *lēogan* (vb.); related to Old High German *liogan,* Gothic *liugan*]

lie[2] (laɪ) *vb.* **lies, ly+ing, lay, lain.** (*intr.*) **1.** (often foll. by *down*) to place oneself or be in a prostrate position, horizontal to the ground. **2.** to be situated, esp. on a horizontal surface: *the pencil is lying on the desk; India lies to the south of Russia.* **3.** to be buried: *here lies Jane Brown.* **4.** (*copula*) to be and remain (in a particular state or condition): *to lie dormant.* **5.** to stretch or extend: *the city lies before us.* **6.** (usually foll. by *on* or *upon*) to rest or weigh: *my sins lie heavily on my mind.* **7.** (usually foll. by *in*) to exist or consist inherently: *strength lies in unity.* **8.** (foll. by *with*) **a.** to be or rest (with): *the ultimate decision lies with you.* **b.** *Archaic.* to have sexual intercourse (with). **9.** (of an action, claim, appeal, etc.) to subsist; be maintainable or admissible. **10.** *Archaic.* to stay temporarily. **11. lie low. a.** to keep or be concealed or quiet. **b.** to wait for a favourable opportunity. ~*n.* **12.** the manner, place, or style in which something is situated. **13.** the hiding place or lair of an animal. **14.** *Golf.* **a.** the position of the ball after a shot: *a bad lie.* **b.** the angle made by the shaft of the club before the upswing. **15. lie of the land. a.** the topography of the land. **b.** the way in which a situation is developing or people are behaving. ~See also **lie down, lie in, lie to, lie up.** [Old English *licgan* akin to Old High German *ligen* to lie, Latin *lectus* bed]

Usage. See at **lay.**

Lie (liː) *n.* **Tryg·ve Halv·dan** ('trygvə 'halðan). 1896–1968, Norwegian statesman; first secretary-general of the United Nations (1946–52).

Lieb+frau+milch ('liːbfraʊˌmɪlk; *German* 'liːpfraʊˌmɪlç) *or* **Lieb+frau+en+milch** (*German* liːp'fraʊənˌmɪlç) *n.* a white table wine from the Rhine vineyards. [German: from *Liebfrau* the Virgin Mary + *Milch* milk; after *Liebfrauenstift* convent in Worms where the wine was originally made]

Lie·big (*German* 'liːbɪç) *n.* **Jus·tus** ('jʊstʊs), Baron von Liebig. 1803–73, German chemist, who founded agricultural chemistry. He also contributed to organic chemistry, esp. to the concept of radicals, and he discovered chloroform.

Lieb·knecht (*German* 'liːpknɛçt) *n.* **1. Karl** (karl). 1871–1919, German socialist leader: with Rosa Luxemburg he led an unsuccessful Communist revolt (1919) and was assassinated. **2.** his father, **Wil·helm** ('vɪlhɛlm). 1826–1900, German socialist leader and journalist, a founder (1869) of what was to become (1891) the German Social Democratic Party.

Liech+ten+stein ('lɪktənˌstaɪn; *German* 'lɪçtᵊnˌʃtaɪn) *n.* a small mountainous principality in central Europe on the Rhine: formed in 1719 by the uniting of the lordships of Schellenburg and Vaduz, which had been purchased by the Austrian family of Liechtenstein; customs union formed with Switzerland in 1924. Language: German. Religion: mostly Roman Catholic. Currency: Swiss franc. Capital: Vaduz. Pop.: 24 000 (1974 est.). Area: 160 sq. km (62 sq. miles).

lied (liːd; *German* liːt) *n., pl.* **lied+er** ('liːdə; *German* 'liːdər). *Music.* any of various musical settings for solo voice and piano of a romantic or lyrical poem, for which composers such as

Schubert, Schumann, and Wolf are famous. [from German: song]

lie de·tec·tor *n. Informal.* a polygraph used esp. by a police interrogator to detect false or devious answers to questions, a sudden change in one or more involuntary physiological responses being considered a manifestation of guilt, fear, etc. See **polygraph** (sense 1).

lie down *vb. (intr., adv.)* **1.** to place oneself or be in a prostrate position in order to rest or sleep. **2.** to accept without protest or opposition (esp. in the phrases **lie down under, take something lying down**). *~n.* **lie-down. 3.** a rest.

lief (li:f) *adv.* **1.** *Now rare.* gladly; willingly: *I'd as lief go today as tomorrow.* *~adj.* **2.** *Archaic.* **a.** ready; glad. **b.** dear; beloved. [Old English *leof;* related to *lufu* love]

liege (li:dʒ) *adj.* **1.** (of a lord) owed feudal allegiance (esp. in the phrase **liege lord**). **2.** (of a vassal or servant) owing feudal allegiance: *a liege subject.* **3.** of or relating to the relationship or bond between liege lord and liegeman: *liege homage.* **4.** faithful; loyal. *~n.* **5.** a liege lord. **6.** a liegeman or true subject. [C13: from Old French *lige,* from Medieval Latin *lēticus,* from *lētus, laetus* serf, of Germanic origin]

Li·ège (lɪˈeɪʒ; *French* ljɛ:ʒ) *n.* **1.** a province of E Belgium: formerly a principality of the Holy Roman Empire, much larger than the present-day province. Pop.: 1 019 266 (1975 est.). Area: 3877 sq. km (1497 sq. miles). **2.** a city in E Belgium, capital of Liège province: the largest French-speaking city in Belgium; river port and industrial centre. Pop.: 144 875 (1971 est.). *~*Flemish name: **Luik.**

liege·man (ˈli:dʒˌmæn) *n., pl.* **·men. 1.** (formerly) the subject of a sovereign or feudal lord; vassal. **2.** a loyal follower.

Lieg·nitz (ˈli:gnɪts) *n.* the German name for **Legnica.**

lie in *vb. (intr., adv.)* **1.** to remain in bed late in the morning. **2.** to be confined in childbirth. *~n.* **lie-in. 3.** a long stay in bed in the morning.

lien (lɪən, ˈli:ən) *n. Law.* a right to retain possession of another's property pending discharge of a debt. [C16: via Old French from Latin *ligāmen* bond, from *ligāre* to bind]

li·en·al (ˈlaɪənᵊl) *adj.* of or relating to the spleen. [C19: from Latin *lien* SPLEEN]

li·en·ter·y (ˈlaɪəntərɪ, -trɪ) *n. Pathol.* the passage of undigested food in the faeces. [C16: from French, from Medieval Latin, from Greek *leienteria,* from *leios* smooth + *enteron* intestine] —ˌ**li·en·ˈter·ic** *adj.*

Lie·pā·ja *or* **Le·pa·ya** (lɪˈpɑ:jə) *n.* a port in the W Soviet Union, in the W Latvian SSR on the Baltic Sea: a naval and industrial centre, with a fishing fleet. Pop.: 100 000 (1975 est.). Russian name: **Libava.** German name: **Libau.**

li·erne (lɪˈɜ:n) *n. Architect.* a short secondary rib that connects the intersections of the primary ribs, esp. as used in Gothic vaulting. [C19: from French, perhaps related to *lier* to bind]

Lies·tal (*German* ˈli:sta:l) *n.* a city in NW Switzerland, capital of Basel-Land demicanton. Pop.: 12 500 (1970).

lie to *vb. (intr., adv.) Nautical.* (of a vessel) to be hove to with little or no swinging.

Li·e·tu·va (lɪəˈtu:və) *n.* the Lithuanian name for **Lithuanian Soviet Socialist Republic.**

lieu (lju:, lu:) *n.* stead; place (esp. in the phrases **in lieu, in lieu of**). [C13: from Old French, ultimately from Latin *locus* place]

lie up *vb. (intr., adv.)* **1.** to go into or stay in one's room or bed, as through illness. **2.** to be out of commission or use: *my car has been lying up for months.*

Lieut. *abbrev. for* lieutenant. Also: **Lt.**

lieu·ten·ant (lɛfˈtɛnənt; in the Navy, ləˈtɛnənt; *U.S.* lu:ˈtɛnənt) *n.* **1.** a military officer holding commissioned rank immediately junior to a captain. **2.** a naval officer holding commissioned rank immediately junior to a lieutenant commander. **3.** *U.S.* an officer in a police or fire department ranking immediately junior to a captain. **4.** a person who holds an office in subordination to or in place of a superior. [C14: from Old French, literally: place-holding] —**lieu·ˈten·an·cy** *n.*

lieu·ten·ant colo·nel *n.* an officer holding commissioned rank immediately junior to a colonel in certain armies, air forces, and marine corps.

lieu·ten·ant com·man·der *n.* an officer holding commissioned rank in certain navies immediately junior to a commander.

lieu·ten·ant gen·er·al *n.* an officer holding commissioned rank in certain armies, air forces, and marine corps immediately junior to a general.

lieu·ten·ant gov·er·nor *n.* **1.** a deputy governor. **2.** (in the U.S.) an elected official who acts as deputy to a state governor and succeeds him if he dies. **3.** (in Canada) the representative of the Crown in a province: appointed by the federal government.

life (laɪf) *n., pl.* **lives** (laɪvz). **1.** the state or quality that distinguishes living beings or organisms from dead ones and from inorganic matter, characterized chiefly by metabolism, growth, and the ability to reproduce and respond to stimuli. Related adj.: **animate. 2.** the period between birth and death. **3.** a living person or being: *to save a life.* **4.** the time between birth and the present time. **5. a.** the remainder or extent of one's life. **b.** (*as modifier*)*: a life sentence; life membership; life subscription; life work.* **6.** the amount of time that something is active or functioning: *the life of a battery.* **7.** a present condition, state, or mode of existence: *my life is very dull here.* **8. a.** a biography. **b.** (*as modifier*)*: a life story.* **9. a.** a characteristic state or mode of existence: *town life.* **b.** (*as modifier*)*: life style.* **10.** the sum or course of human events and activities. **11.** liveliness or high spirits: *full of life.* **12.** a source of strength, animation, or vitality: *he was the life of the show.* **13.** all living things, taken as a whole: *there is no life on Mars; plant life.* **14.** sparkle, as of wines. **15.** strong or high flavour, as of fresh food. **16.** (*modifier*) *Arts.* drawn or taken from a living model: *life drawing; a life mask.* **17.** *Physics.* another name for **lifetime. 18.** (in certain games) one of a number of opportunities of participation. **19. as large as life.** *Informal.* real and living. **20. larger than life.** in an exaggerated form. **21. come to life. a.** to become animate or conscious. **b.** to be realistically portrayed or represented. **22. for dear life.** *Informal.* urgently or with extreme vigour or desperation. **23. for the life of me (him, her,** etc.) though trying desperately. **24. go for your life.** *Austral. informal.* an expression of encouragement. **25. a matter of life and death.** a matter of extreme urgency. **26. not on your life.** *Informal.* certainly not. **27. the life of Riley.** *Informal.* an easy life. **28. to the life.** (of a copy or image) resembling the original exactly. **29. to save (one's) life.** *Informal.* in spite of all considerations or attempts: *he couldn't play football to save his life.* **30. the time of one's life.** a memorably enjoyable time. **31. true to life.** faithful to reality. [Old English *līf;* related to Old High German *lib,* Old Norse *līf* life, body]

life as·sur·ance *n.* a form of insurance providing for the payment of a specified sum to a named beneficiary on the death of the policyholder. Also called: **life insurance.**

life belt *n.* a ring filled with buoyant material or air, used to keep a person afloat when in danger of drowning.

life·blood (ˈlaɪfˌblʌd) *n.* **1.** the blood, considered as vital to sustain life. **2.** the essential or animating force.

life·boat (ˈlaɪfˌbəʊt) *n.* a boat, propelled by oars or a motor, used for rescuing people at sea, escaping from a sinking ship, etc.

life buoy *n.* any of various kinds of buoyant devices for keeping people afloat in an emergency.

life cy·cle *n.* the series of changes occurring in an animal or plant between one development stage and the identical stage in the next generation.

life es·tate *n.* property that may be held only for the extent of the holder's lifetime.

life ex·pec·tan·cy *n.* the statistically determined average number of years of life remaining after a specified age. Also called: **expectation of life.**

life·guard (ˈlaɪfˌgɑ:d) *n.* a person present at a beach or pool to guard people against the risk of drowning. Also called: **life-saver.**

Life Guards *n.* (*in Britain*) a cavalry regiment forming part of the Household Brigade, who wear scarlet jackets and white plumes in their helmets.

life his·to·ry *n.* **1.** the series of changes undergone by an organism between fertilization of the egg and death. **2.** the series of events that make up a person's life.

life in·stinct *n. Psychoanal.* the instinct for reproduction and self-preservation.

life in·ter·est *n.* interest (esp. from property) that is payable to a person during his life but ceases with his death.

life jack·et *n.* an inflatable sleeveless jacket worn to keep a person afloat when in danger of drowning.

life·less (ˈlaɪflɪs) *adj.* **1.** without life; inanimate; dead. **2.** not sustaining living organisms. **3.** having no vitality or animation. **4.** unconscious. —**ˈlife·less·ly** *adv.* —**ˈlife·less·ness** *n.*

life·like (ˈlaɪfˌlaɪk) *adj.* closely resembling or representing life. —**ˈlife·ˌlike·ness** *n.*

life·line (ˈlaɪfˌlaɪn) *n.* **1.** a line thrown or fired aboard a vessel for hauling in a hawser for a breeches buoy. **2.** any rope or line attached to a vessel or trailed from it for the safety of passengers, crew, swimmers, etc. **3.** a line by which a deep-sea diver is raised or lowered. **4.** a vital line of access or communication.

life·long (ˈlaɪfˌlɒŋ) *adj.* lasting for or as if for a lifetime.

life mask *n.* a cast taken from the face of a living person, usually using plaster of Paris.

life peer *n. Brit.* a peer whose title lapses at his death.

life pre·serv·er *n.* **1.** *Brit.* a club or bludgeon, esp. one kept for self-defence. **2.** *U.S.* a life belt or life jacket.

lif·er (ˈlaɪfə) *n. Informal.* a prisoner sentenced to life imprisonment.

life raft *n.* a raft for emergency use at sea.

life-sav·er *n.* **1.** the saver of a person's life. **2.** another name for **lifeguard. 3.** *Informal.* a person or thing that gives help in time of need. —**ˈlife-ˌsav·ing** *adj., n.*

life sci·ence *n.* any one of the branches of science concerned with the structure and behaviour of living organisms, such as biology, botany, zoology, physiology, or biochemistry. Compare **physical science.** See also **social science.**

life-size *or* **life-sized** *adj.* representing actual size.

life space *n. Psychol.* a spatial representation of all the forces that control a person's behaviour.

life span *n.* the period of time during which a human being, animal, machine, etc., may be expected to live or function under normal conditions.

life style *n.* the particular attitudes, beliefs, habits, or behaviour associated with an individual or group.

life-sup·port sys·tem *n.* all the equipment collectively required to sustain human life in an unnatural environment, such as in space or below the sea.

life ta·ble *n.* another name for **mortality table.**

life·time (ˈlaɪfˌtaɪm) *n.* **1. a.** the length of time a person or animal is alive. **b.** (*as modifier*)*: a lifetime supply.* **2.** the length of time that something functions, is useful, etc.. **3.** *Physics.* the average time of existence of an unstable or reactive entity, such as a nucleus or elementary particle, etc.; mean life.

Lif+fey ('lɪfɪ) *n.* a river in E Ireland, rising in the Wicklow Mountains and flowing west, then northeast through Dublin into Dublin Bay. Length: 80 km (50 miles).

lift (lɪft) *vb.* **1.** to rise or cause to rise upwards from the ground or another support to a higher place: *to lift a sack.* **2.** to move or cause to move upwards: *to lift one's eyes.* **3.** (*tr.*) to take hold of in order to carry or remove: *to lift something down from a shelf.* **4.** (*tr.*) to raise in status, spirituality, estimation, etc.: *his position lifted him from the common crowd.* **5.** (*tr.*) to revoke or rescind: *to lift tax restrictions.* **6.** to make or become audible or louder: *to lift one's voice in song.* **7.** (*tr.*) to take (plants or underground crops) out of the ground for transplanting or harvesting. **8.** (*intr.*) to disappear by lifting or as if by lifting: *the fog lifted.* **9.** to transport in a vehicle. **10.** (*tr.*) *Informal.* to take unlawfully or dishonourably; steal. **11.** (*tr.*) to perform a face-lift on. **12.** (*tr.*) *U.S.* to pay off (a mortgage, etc.). ~*n.* **13.** the act or an instance of lifting. **14.** the power or force available or used for lifting. **15. a.** *Brit.* a platform, compartment, or cage raised or lowered in a vertical shaft to transport persons or goods in a building. U.S. word: **elevator. b.** See **chair lift, ski lift. 16.** the distance or degree to which something is lifted. **17.** a ride in a car or other vehicle. **18.** a rise in the height of the ground. **19.** an elevation of the spirits or temperament. **20.** the force required to lift an object. **21.** a layer of the heel of a shoe, etc., or a detachable pad inside the shoe to give the wearer added height. **22.** aid; help. **23.** *Mining.* **a.** the thickness of ore extracted in one operation. **b.** a set of pumps used in a mine. **24. a.** the component of the aerodynamic forces acting on an aerofoil, etc., at right angles to the airflow and opposing gravity. **b.** the upward force exerted by the gas in a balloon, airship, etc. **25.** See **airlift** (sense 1). [C13: from Scandinavian; related to Old Norse *lypta,* Old English *lyft* sky; compare LOFT] —**'lift+a·ble** *adj.* —**'lift+er** *n.*

lift+boy ('lɪft,bɔɪ) *or* **lift+man** *n., pl.* **+boys** *or* **+men.** a person who operates a lift, esp. in large public or commercial buildings and hotels.

lift+ing bod·y *n.* a wingless aircraft or spacecraft that derives its aerodynamic lift from the shape of its body.

lift+off ('lɪft,ɒf) *n.* **1.** the initial movement or ascent of a rocket from its launching pad. **2.** the instant at which this occurs. ~*vb.* **lift off. 3.** (*intr., adv.*) (of a rocket) to leave its launching pad.

lift pump *n.* a pump that raises a fluid to a higher level. It usually consists of a piston and vertical cylinder with flap or ball valves in both piston and cylinder base. Compare: **force pump.**

lig·a·ment ('lɪgəmənt) *n.* **1.** *Anatomy.* any one of the bands or sheets of tough fibrous connective tissue that restrict movement in joints, connect various bones or cartilages, support muscles, etc. **2.** any physical or abstract connection or bond. [C14: from Medieval Latin *ligāmentum,* from Latin (in the sense: bandage), from *ligāre* to bind]

lig·a+men+tous (,lɪgə'mɛntəs), **lig·a+men+tal,** *or* **lig·a+men+ta+ry** *adj.* relating to or shaped like a ligament.

li+gan ('laɪgən) *n.* a variant spelling of **lagan.**

lig+and ('lɪgənd, 'laɪ-) *n. Chem.* an atom, molecule, radical, or ion forming a complex with a central atom. [C20: from Latin *ligandum,* gerund of *ligāre* to bind]

li+gate ('laɪgeɪt) *vb.* (*tr.*) to tie up or constrict (something) with a ligature. [C16: from Latin *ligātus,* from *ligāre* to bind] —**li+'ga+tion** *n.* —**lig·a·tive** ('lɪgətɪv) *adj.*

lig·a·ture ('lɪgətʃə, -,tʃʊə) *n.* **1.** the act of binding or tying up. **2.** something used to bind. **3.** a link, bond, or tie. **4.** *Surgery.* a thread or wire for tying around a vessel, duct, etc., as for constricting the flow of blood to a part. **5.** *Printing.* a character of two or more joined letters, such as fi, fl, ffi, ffl, usually cast on the same piece of type. **6.** *Music.* **a.** a slur or the group of notes connected by it. **b.** (in plainsong notation) a symbol indicating two or more notes grouped together. ~*vb.* **7.** (*tr.*) to bind with a ligature; ligate. [C14: from Late Latin *ligātūra,* ultimately from Latin *ligāre* to bind]

li+ger ('laɪgə) *n.* the hybrid offspring of a female tiger and a male lion.

Li·ge·ti (*Hungarian* 'ligɛti) *n.* **György** (djørdj). born 1923, Hungarian composer, resident in Vienna. His works, noted for their experimentalism, include *Atmospheres* (1961) for orchestra, *Volumina* (1962) for organ, and a requiem mass (1965).

light[1] (laɪt) *n.* **1.** the medium of illumination that makes sight possible. **2.** Also called: **visible radiation.** electromagnetic radiation that is capable of causing a visual sensation and has wavelengths from about 380 to about 780 nanometres. **3.** (*not in technical usage*) electromagnetic radiation that has a wavelength outside this range, esp. ultraviolet radiation: *ultraviolet light.* **4.** the sensation experienced when electromagnetic radiation within the visible spectrum falls on the retina of the eye. **5.** anything that illuminates, such as a lamp or candle. **6.** See **traffic light. 7.** a particular quality or type of light: *a good light for reading.* **8. a.** illumination from the sun during the day; daylight. **b.** the time this appears; daybreak; dawn. **9.** anything that allows the entrance of light, such as a window or compartment of a window. **10.** the condition of being visible or known (esp. in the phrases **bring** *or* **come to light**). **11.** an aspect or view: *he saw it in a different light.* **12.** mental understanding or spiritual insight. **13.** a person considered to be an authority or leader. **14.** brightness of countenance, esp. a sparkle in the eyes. **15. a.** the act of igniting or kindling something, such as a cigarette. **b.** something that ignites or kindles, esp. in a specified manner, such as a spark or flame. **c.** something used for igniting or kindling, such as a match. **16.** See **lighthouse. 17. a.** the effect of illumination on objects or scenes, as created in a picture. **b.** an area of brightness in a picture, as opposed to shade. **18.** a poetic or archaic word for **eyesight. 19.** the answer to a clue in a crossword. **20. in (the) light of.** in view of; taking into account; considering. **21. out like a light.** quickly asleep or unconscious. **22. see the light (of day). a.** to come into being. **b.** to come to public notice. **c.** to acquire insight, esp. concerning something one has previously opposed. **23. shed** (*or* **throw**) **light on.** to clarify or supply additional information on. **24. stand in a person's light. a.** to stand so as to obscure a person's vision. **b.** to impede a person's progress or success. **25. strike a light. a.** (*vb.*) to ignite something, esp. a match, by friction. **b.** (*interj.*) *Brit.* an exclamation of surprise. ~*adj.* **26.** full of light; well-lighted. **27.** (of a colour) reflecting or transmitting a large amount of light: *light yellow.* Compare **medium** (sense 2), **dark** (sense 2). **28.** *Phonetics.* relating to or denoting an (l) pronounced with front vowel resonance; clear: *the French "l" is much lighter than that of English.* Compare **dark** (sense 9). ~*vb.* **lights, light+ing, light+ed** *or* **lit. 29.** to ignite or cause to ignite. **30.** (often foll. by *up*) to illuminate or cause to illuminate. **31.** to make or become cheerful or animated. **32.** (*tr.*) to guide or lead by light. ~See also **light up.** [Old English *lēoht;* related to Old High German *lioht,* Gothic *liuhath,* Latin *lux*] —**'light+ish** *adj.* —**'light+less** *adj.*

light[2] (laɪt) *adj.* **1.** not heavy; weighing relatively little. **2.** having relatively low density: *magnesium is a light metal.* **3.** lacking sufficient weight; not agreeing with standard or official weights. **4.** not great in degree, intensity, or number: *light rain; a light eater.* **5.** without burdens, difficulties, or problems; easily borne or done: *a light heart; light work.* **6.** graceful, agile, or deft: *light fingers.* **7.** not bulky or clumsy. **8.** not serious or profound; entertaining: *light verse.* **9.** without importance or consequence; insignificant: *no light matter.* **10.** frivolous or capricious. **11.** loose in morals. **12.** dizzy or unclear: *a light head.* **13.** (of bread, cake, etc.) spongy or well leavened. **14.** easily digested: *a light meal.* **15.** relatively low in alcoholic content: *a light wine.* **16.** (of a soil) having a crumbly texture. **17.** (of a vessel, lorry, etc.) **a.** designed to carry light loads. **b.** not loaded. **18.** carrying light arms or equipment: *light infantry.* **19.** (of an industry) engaged in the production of small consumer goods using light machinery. Compare **heavy** (sense 10). **20.** *Bridge.* **a.** (of a bid) made on insufficient values. **b.** (of a player) having failed to take sufficient tricks to make his contract. **21.** *Phonetics, prosody.* (of a syllable, vowel, etc.) unaccented or weakly stressed; short. Compare **heavy** (sense 13). See **light**[1] (sense 28). **22.** *Phonetics.* the least of three levels of stress in an utterance, in such languages as English. **23. light on.** *Austral. informal.* lacking a sufficient quantity of (something). **24. make light of.** to treat as insignificant or trifling. ~*adv.* **25.** a less common word for **lightly. 26.** with little equipment, baggage, etc.: *to travel light.* ~*vb.* **lights, light+ing, light+ed** *or* **lit.** (*intr.*) **27.** (esp. of birds) to settle or land after flight. **28.** to get down from a horse, vehicle, etc. **29.** (foll. by *on* or *upon*) to come upon unexpectedly. **30.** to strike or fall on: *the choice lighted on me.* ~See also **light into, light out.** [Old English *lēoht;* related to Dutch *licht,* Gothic *leihts*] —**'light+ish** *adj.* —**'light+ly** *adv.* —**'light+ness** *n.*

Light (laɪt) *n.* **1.** God regarded as a source of illuminating grace and strength. **2.** *Quakerism.* short for **Inner Light.**

light air *n.* very light air movement of force one on the Beaufort scale.

light breeze *n.* a very light wind of force two on the Beaufort scale.

light bulb *n.* a glass bulb containing a gas, such as argon or nitrogen, at low pressure and enclosing a thin metal filament that emits light when an electric current is passed through it. Sometimes shortened to **bulb.**

light+en[1] ('laɪtᵊn) *vb.* **1.** to become or make light. **2.** (*intr.*) to shine; glow. **3.** (*intr.*) (of lightning) to flash. **4.** (*tr.*) *Archaic.* to cause to flash. **5.** (*tr.*) an archaic word for **enlighten.**

light+en[2] ('laɪtᵊn) *vb.* **1.** to make or become less heavy. **2.** to make or become less burdensome or oppressive; mitigate. **3.** to make or become more cheerful or lively.

light en+gine *n.* a railway locomotive in motion without drawing any carriages or wagons. U.S. equivalent: **wildcat.**

light+er[1] ('laɪtə) *n.* **1.** a small portable device for providing a naked flame or red-hot filament to light cigarettes, etc. **2.** a person or thing that ignites something.

light+er[2] ('laɪtə) *n.* a flat-bottomed barge used for transporting cargo, esp. in loading or unloading a ship. [C15: probably from Middle Dutch; compare C16 Dutch *lichter*]

light+er+age ('laɪtərɪdʒ) *n.* **1.** the conveyance or loading and unloading of cargo by means of a lighter. **2.** the charge for this service.

light+er than air *adj.* (**lighter-than-air** *when prenominal*). **1.** having a lower density than that of air. **2.** of or relating to an aircraft, such as a balloon or airship, that depends on buoyancy for support in the air.

light face *n.* **1.** *Printing.* a weight of type characterized by light thin lines. Compare **bold face.** ~*adj. also* **light-faced. 2.** (of type) having this weight.

light-fast *adj.* (of a dye or dyed article) unaffected by light.

light-fin·gered *adj.* having nimble or agile fingers, esp. for thieving or picking pockets. —**,light-'fin·gered+ness** *n.*

light fly+weight *n.* **a.** an amateur boxer weighing not more than 48 kg (106 pounds). **b.** (*as modifier*): *a light-flyweight fight.*

light-foot·ed *adj.* having a light or nimble tread. —ˌ**light-'foot·ed·ly** *adv.* —ˌ**light-'foot·ed·ness** *n.*

light-head·ed *adj.* **1.** frivolous in disposition or behaviour. **2.** giddy; feeling faint or slightly delirious. —ˌ**light-'head·ed·ly** *adv.* —ˌ**light-'head·ed·ness** *n.*

light-heart·ed *adj.* cheerful or carefree in mood or disposition. —ˌ**light-'heart·ed·ly** *adv.* —ˌ**light-'heart·ed·ness** *n.*

light heav·y·weight *n.* **1.** Also (in Brit.): **cruiserweight. a.** a professional boxer weighing 160–175 pounds (72.5–79.5 kg). **b.** an amateur boxer weighing 75–81 kg (165–179 pounds). **c.** (*as modifier*): *a light-heavyweight bout.* **2.** a wrestler in a similar weight category (usually 192–214 pounds (87–97 kg)).

light horse *n.* lightly armed and highly mobile cavalry. —ˌ**light-'horse·man** *n.*

light·house ('laɪtˌhaʊs) *n.* a fixed structure in the form of a tower equipped with a light visible to mariners for warning them of obstructions, for marking harbour entrances, etc.

light·ing ('laɪtɪŋ) *n.* **1.** the act or quality of illumination or ignition. **2.** the apparatus for supplying artificial light effects to a stage, film, or television set. **3.** the distribution of light on an object or figure, as in painting, photography, etc.

light·ing-up time *n.* the time when vehicles are required by law to have their lights switched on.

light in·to *vb.* (*intr., prep.*) *Informal.* to assail physically or verbally.

light me·ter *n.* another name for **exposure meter.**

light mid·dle·weight *n.* **a.** an amateur boxer weighing 67–71 kg (148–157). **b.** (*as modifier*): *a light-middleweight bout.* Compare **junior middleweight.**

light mu·sic *n.* music for popular entertainment.

light·ness ('laɪtnɪs) *n.* the attribute of an object or colour that enables an observer to judge the extent to which the object or colour reflects or transmits incident light. See also **colour.**

light·ning ('laɪtnɪŋ) *n.* **1.** a flash of light in the sky, occurring during a thunderstorm and caused by a discharge of electricity, either between clouds or between a cloud and the earth. **2.** (*modifier*) fast and sudden: *a lightning raid.* [C14: variant of *lightening*]

light·ning ar·rest·er *n.* a device that protects electrical equipment, such as an aerial, from an excessive voltage resulting from a lightning discharge or other accidental electric surge, by discharging it to earth.

light·ning bug *n. U.S.* another name for the **firefly.**

light·ning con·duc·tor *or* **rod** *n.* a metal strip terminating in a series of sharp points, attached to the highest part of a building, etc., to provide a safe path to earth for lightning discharges.

light op·er·a *n.* another term for **operetta.**

light out *vb.* (*intr., adv.*) *Informal.* to depart quickly, as if being chased.

light pen *n. Computer technol.* a penlike photoelectric device capable of making lines or marks on the screen of a visual display unit.

light re·ac·tion *n. Botany.* the stage of photosynthesis during which light energy is absorbed by chlorophyll and transformed into chemical energy stored in ATP. Compare **dark reaction.**

lights[1] (laɪts) *pl. n.* a person's ideas, knowledge, or understanding: *he did it according to his lights.*

lights[2] (laɪts) *pl. n.* the lungs, esp. of sheep, bullocks, and pigs, used for feeding pets and occasionally in human food. [C13: plural noun use of LIGHT[2], referring to the light weight of the lungs]

light·ship ('laɪtˌʃɪp) *n.* a ship equipped as a lighthouse and moored where a fixed structure would prove impracticable.

light show *n.* a kaleidoscopic display of moving lights, etc., projected onto a screen, esp. during pop concerts.

light·some[1] ('laɪtsəm) *adj. Archaic or poetic.* **1.** lighthearted or gay. **2.** airy or buoyant. **3.** not serious; frivolous. —'**light·some·ly** *adv.* —'**light·some·ness** *n.*

light·some[2] ('laɪtsəm) *adj. Archaic or poetic.* **1.** producing or reflecting light. **2.** full of or flooded with light.

lights out *n.* **1.** the time when those resident at an institution, such as soldiers in barracks or children at a boarding school, are expected to retire to bed. **2.** a fanfare or other signal indicating or signifying this.

light up *vb.* (*adv.*) **1.** to light a cigarette, pipe, etc. **2.** to illuminate or cause to illuminate. **3.** to make or become cheerful or animated.

light·weight ('laɪtˌweɪt) *adj.* **1.** of a relatively light weight. **2.** not serious; trivial. ~*n.* **3.** a person or animal of a relatively light weight. **4. a.** a professional boxer weighing 130–135 pounds (59–61 kg). **b.** an amateur boxer weighing 57–60 kg (126–132 pounds). **c.** (*as modifier*): *the lightweight contender.* **5.** a wrestler in a similar weight category (usually 115–126 pounds (52–57 kg)). **6.** *Informal.* an incompetent and unimportant person.

light wel·ter·weight *n.* **a.** an amateur boxer weighing 60–63.5 kg (132–140 pounds). **b.** (*as modifier*): *the light welterweight champion.* Compare **junior welterweight.**

light year *n.* a unit of distance used in astronomy, equal to the distance travelled by light in one mean solar year, i.e. 9.4607×10^{15} metres or 5.8784×10^{12} miles.

lign·al·oes (laɪ'næləʊz, lɪg-) *n.* (*functioning as sing.*) another name for **eaglewood** (sense 2). [C14 *ligne aloes,* from Medieval Latin *lignum aloēs* wood of the aloe]

lig·ne·ous ('lɪgnɪəs) *adj.* of or resembling wood. [C17: from Latin *ligneus,* from *lignum* wood]

lig·ni-, lig·no-, *or before a vowel* **lign-** *combining form.* indicating wood: *lignocellulose.* [from Latin *lignum* wood]

lig·ni·form ('lɪgnɪˌfɔːm) *adj.* having the appearance of wood.

lig·ni·fy ('lɪgnɪˌfaɪ) *vb.* **·fies, ·fy·ing, ·fied.** *Botany.* to make or become woody as a result of the deposition of lignin in the cell walls. —ˌ**lig·ni·fi·'ca·tion** *n.*

lig·nin ('lɪgnɪn) *n.* a complex polymer occurring in certain plant cell walls making the plant rigid.

lig·nite ('lɪgnaɪt) *n.* a brown carbonaceous sedimentary rock with woody texture that consists of accumulated layers of partially decomposed vegetation deposited in the late Cretaceous period: used as a fuel. Fixed carbon content: 46–60 per cent; calorific value: 1.28×10^7 to 1.93×10^7 J/kg (5500 to 8300 Btu/lb). Also called: **brown coal.** —**lig·nit·ic** (lɪg'nɪtɪk) *adj.*

lig·no·caine ('lɪgnəˌkeɪn) *n.* a powerful local anaesthetic administered by injection, or topically to mucous membranes. Formula: $C_{14}H_{22}N_2O.HCl.H_2O$. U.S. name: **lidocaine.**

lig·no·cel·lu·lose (ˌlɪgnəʊ'sɛljʊˌləʊs, -ˌləʊz) *n.* a compound of lignin and cellulose that occurs in the walls of xylem cells in woody tissue.

lig·num vi·tae ('lɪgnəm 'vaɪtɪ) *n.* **1.** either of two zygophyllaceous tropical American trees, *Guaiacum officinale* or *G. sanctum,* having blue or purple flowers. **2.** the heavy resinous wood of either of these trees, which is used in machine bearings, casters, etc.: formerly thought to have medicinal properties. ~See also **guaiacum.** [New Latin, from Late Latin, literally: wood of life]

lig·ro·in ('lɪgrəʊɪn) *n.* a volatile fraction of petroleum containing aliphatic hydrocarbons of the paraffin series. It has an approximate boiling point range of 70°–130°C and is used as a solvent. [origin unknown]

lig·u·la ('lɪgjʊlə) *n., pl.* **·lae** (-ˌliː) *or* **·las. 1.** *Entomol.* the terminal part of the labium of an insect consisting of paired lobes. **2.** a variant spelling of **ligule.** [C18: New Latin; see LIGULE] —'**lig·u·lar** *adj.* —'**lig·u·ˌloid** *adj.*

lig·u·late ('lɪgjʊlɪt, -ˌleɪt) *adj.* **1.** having the shape of a strap. **2.** *Biology.* of, relating to, or having a ligule or ligula.

lig·ule ('lɪgjuːl) *or* **lig·u·la** *n.* **1.** a strap-shaped membranous outgrowth at the junction between the leaf blade and sheath in many grasses. **2.** a strap-shaped corolla, such as that of the ray flower in the daisy. [C19: via French, from Latin *ligula* strap, variant of *lingula,* from *lingua* tongue]

lig·ure ('lɪgjʊə) *n. Old Testament.* any of the 12 precious stones used in the breastplates of high priests. [C14: from Late Latin *ligūrius,* from Late Greek *ligurion*]

Li·gu·ri·a (lɪ'gjʊərɪə) *n.* a region of NW Italy, on the **Ligurian Sea** (an arm of the Mediterranean): the third smallest of the regions of Italy. Pop.: 1 848 539 (1971). Area: 5410 sq. km (2089 sq. miles). —**Li·'gu·ri·an** *adj., n.*

lik·a·ble *or* **like·a·ble** ('laɪkəbᵊl) *adj.* easy to like; pleasing. —'**lik·a·ble·ness** *or* '**like·a·ble·ness** *n.*

Li·ka·si (lɪ'kɑːsɪ) *n.* a city in S Zaïre, in Shaba province: a centre of copper and cobalt production. Pop.: 146 394 (1969 est.). Former name: **Jadotville.**

like[1] (laɪk) *adj.* **1.** (*prenominal*) similar; resembling. ~*prep.* **2.** similar to; similarly to; in the manner of: *acting like a maniac; he's so like his father.* **3.** used correlatively to express similarity in certain proverbs: *like mother, like daughter.* **4.** such as: *there are lots of ways you might amuse yourself—like taking a long walk, for instance.* ~*adv.* **5.** a dialect word for **likely. 6.** *Not standard.* as it were: often used as a parenthetic filler: *there was this policeman just staring at us, like.* ~*conj.* **7.** *Not standard.* as though; as if: *you look like you've just seen a ghost.* **8.** in the same way as; in the same way that: *she doesn't dance like you do.* ~*n.* **9. the like.** similar things: *dogs, foxes, and the like.* **10. the likes** (*or* **like**) **of.** people or things similar to (someone or something specified): *we don't want the likes of you around here.* [shortened from Old English *gelīc;* compare Old Norse *glīkr* and *līkr* like]

like[2] (laɪk) *vb.* **1.** (*tr.*) to find (something) enjoyable or agreeable or find it enjoyable or agreeable (to do something): *he likes boxing; he likes to hear music.* **2.** (*tr.*) to be fond of. **3.** (*tr.*) to prefer or wish (to do something): *we would like you to go.* **4.** (*tr.*) to feel towards; consider; regard: *how did she like it?* **5.** (*intr.*) to feel disposed or inclined; choose; wish. **6.** (*tr.*) *Archaic.* to please; agree with: *it likes me not to go.* ~*n.* **7.** (*usually pl.*) a favourable feeling, desire, preference, etc. (esp. in the phrase **likes and dislikes**). [Old English *līcian;* related to Old Norse *līka,* Dutch *lijken*]

-like *suffix forming adjectives.* **1.** resembling or similar to: *lifelike; springlike.* **2.** having the characteristics of: *childlike; ladylike.* [from LIKE[1] (prep.)]

like·li·hood ('laɪklɪˌhʊd) *or* **like·li·ness** *n.* **1.** the condition of being likely or probable; probability. **2.** something that is probable.

like·ly ('laɪklɪ) *adj.* **1.** (usually foll. by an infinitive) tending or inclined; apt: *likely to rain.* **2.** probable: *a likely result.* **3.** believable or feasible; plausible. **4.** appropriate for a purpose or activity. **5.** having good possibilities of success: *a likely candidate.* **6.** *Dialect, chiefly U.S.* attractive, agreeable, or enjoyable: *her likely ways won her many friends.* ~*adv.* **7.** probably or presumably. [C14: from Old Norse *līkligr*]

like-mind·ed *adj.* agreeing in opinions, goals, etc. —ˌ**like-'mind·ed·ly** *adv.* —ˌ**like-'mind·ed·ness** *n.*

lik·en ('laɪkən) *vb.* (*tr.*) to see or represent as the same or similar; compare. [C14: from LIKE[1] (adj.)]

like·ness ('laɪknɪs) *n.* **1.** the condition of being alike; similarity. **2.** a painted, carved, moulded, or graphic image of a person or thing. **3.** an imitative appearance; semblance.

like·wise ('laɪk,waɪz) *adv.* **1.** in addition; moreover; also. **2.** in like manner; similarly.

lik·ing ('laɪkɪŋ) *n.* **1.** the feeling of a person who likes; fondness. **2.** a preference, inclination, or pleasure.

li·ku·ta (li:'ku:tɑ:) *n., pl.* **ma·ku·ta** (mɑ:'ku:tɑ:). a coin of Zaïre worth one hundredth of a zaire. [C20: from Congolese]

li·lac ('laɪlək) *n.* **1.** Also called: **syringa.** any of various Eurasian oleaceous shrubs or small trees of the genus *Syringa,* esp. *S. vulgaris* (**common lilac**) which has large sprays of purple or white fragrant flowers. **2. French lilac.** another name for **goat's-rue** (sense 1). **3. a.** a light or moderate purple colour, sometimes with a bluish or reddish tinge. **b.** (*as adj.*): *a lilac carpet.* [C17: via French from Spanish, from Arabic *līlak,* changed from Persian *nīlak* bluish, from *nīl* blue]

Lil·burne ('lɪl,bɜ:n) *n.* **John.** ?1614–57, English Puritan pamphleteer and leader of the Levellers, a radical group prominent during the Civil War.

lil·i·a·ceous (,lɪlɪ'eɪʃəs) *adj.* of, relating to, or belonging to the *Liliaceae,* a family of plants having showy flowers and a bulb or bulblike organ: includes the lily, tulip, bluebell, and onion. [C18: from Late Latin *līliāceus,* from *līlium* lily]

Li·lien·thal (*German* 'li:ljən,ta:l) *n.* **Ot·to** ('ɔto). 1848–96, German aeronautical engineer, a pioneer of glider design.

Lil·ith ('lɪlɪθ) *n.* **1.** (in the Old Testament and in Jewish folklore) a female demon, who attacks children. **2.** (in Talmudic literature) Adam's first wife. **3.** a witch notorious in medieval demonology.

Li·li·u·o·ka·la·ni (li:,li:uəʊkɑ:'lɑ:ni:) *n.* **Lyd·i·a Ka·me·ke·ha** (,kɑ:meɪ'keɪhɑ:). 1838–1917, queen and last sovereign of the Hawaiian Islands (1891–93).

Lille (*French* lil) *n.* an industrial city in N France: the medieval capital of Flanders; forms with Roubaix and Tourcoing one of the largest conurbations in France. Pop.: 177 218 (1975).

Lil·le Bælt ('lilə 'bɛld) *n.* the Danish name for the **Little Belt.**

Lil·li·pu·ti·an (,lɪlɪ'pju:ʃɪən) *n.* **1.** a tiny person or being. ~*adj.* **2.** tiny; very small. **3.** petty or trivial. [C18: from *Lilliput,* an imaginary country of tiny inhabitants in Swift's *Gulliver's Travels*]

lil·ly-pil·ly ('lɪlɪ,pɪlɪ) *n. Austral.* a tall myrtaceous tree, *Eugenia smithii,* having dark green leaves, spikes of feathery flowers, and white to purplish edible berries.

Li·lo ('laɪ,ləʊ) *n., pl.* **·los.** *Trademark.* a type of inflatable plastic or rubber mattress.

Li·long·we (lɪ'lɒŋwɪ) *n.* the capital of Malawi, in the central part west of Lake Malawi. Pop.: 24 000 (1974 est.).

lilt (lɪlt) *n.* **1.** (in music) a jaunty rhythm. **2.** a buoyant motion. ~*vb.* (*intr.*) **3.** (of a melody) to have a lilt. **4.** to move in a buoyant manner. [C14 *lulten,* origin obscure]

lil·y ('lɪlɪ) *n., pl.* **lil·ies. 1.** any liliaceous perennial plant of the N temperate genus *Lilium,* such as the Turk's-cap lily and tiger lily, having scaly bulbs and showy typically pendulous flowers. **2.** the bulb or flower of any of these plants. **3.** any of various similar or related plants, such as the water lily, plantain lily, and day lily. [Old English, from Latin *līlium;* related to Greek *leirion* lily] —**'lil·y-,like** *adj.*

lil·y i·ron *n.* a harpoon, the head of which is detachable. [C19: from the shape of its shaft, which resembles lily leaves]

lil·y-liv·ered *adj.* cowardly; timid.

lil·y of the val·ley *n., pl.* **lil·ies of the val·ley.** a small liliaceous plant, *Convallaria majalis,* of Eurasia and North America cultivated as a garden plant, having two long oval leaves and spikes of white bell-shaped flowers.

lil·y pad *n.* any of the floating leaves of a water lily.

lil·y-trot·ter *n.* another name for **jacana.**

lil·y-white *adj.* **1.** of a pure white: *lily-white skin.* **2.** *Informal.* pure; irreproachable. **3.** *U.S. informal.* **a.** discriminating against Negroes: *a lily-white club.* **b.** racially segregated.

Li·ma ('li:mə) *n.* the capital of Peru, near the Pacific coast on the Rímac River: the centre of Spanish colonization in South America; university founded in 1551 (the oldest in South America); an industrial centre with a port at nearby Callao. Pop.: 2 833 609 (1972).

li·ma bean ('laɪmə) *n.* **1.** any of several varieties of the bean plant, *Phaseolus lunatus* (or *P. limensis*), native to tropical America but cultivated in the U.S. for its flat pods containing pale green edible seeds. **2.** the seed of such a plant. ~See also **butter bean.** [C19: named after *Lima,* Peru]

lim·a·cine ('lɪmə,saɪn, -sɪn, 'laɪ-) *adj.* of, relating to, or resembling slugs, esp. those of the genus *Limax.* [C19: from New Latin, from Latin *līmax,* from *līmus* mud]

li·ma·çon ('lɪmə,sɒn) *n.* a heart-shaped curve generated by a point lying on a line at a fixed distance from the intersection of the line with a fixed circle, the line rotating about a point on the circumference of the circle. [French, literally: snail (so named by Pascal)]

Li·mas·sol ('lɪmə,sɒl) *n.* a port in S Cyprus: trading centre. Pop.: 51 500 (1970). Ancient name: **Lemessus.**

limb[1] (lɪm) *n.* **1.** an arm or leg, or the analogous part on an animal, such as a wing. **2.** any of the main branches of a tree. **3.** a branching or projecting section or member; extension. **4.** a person or thing considered to be a member, part, or agent of a larger group or thing. **5. out on a limb. a.** in a precarious or questionable position. **b.** *Brit.* isolated, esp. because of unpopular opinions. ~*vb.* **6.** (*tr.*) a rare word for **dismember.** [Old English *lim;* related to Old Norse *limr*] —**limbed** *adj.* —**'limb·less** *adj.*

limb[2] (lɪm) *n.* **1.** the edge of the apparent disc of the sun, a moon, or a planet. **2.** a graduated arc attached to instruments, such as the sextant, used for measuring angles. **3.** *Botany.* **a.** the expanded upper part of a bell-shaped corolla. **b.** the expanded part of a leaf, petal, or sepal. **4.** either of the two halves of a bow. [C15: from Latin *limbus* edge]

lim·bate ('lɪmbeɪt) *adj. Biology.* having an edge or border of a different colour from the rest: *limbate flowers.* [C19: from Late Latin *limbātus* bordered, from LIMBUS]

limbed (lɪmd) *adj.* **a.** having limbs. **b.** (*in combination*): *short-limbed; strong-limbed.*

lim·ber[1] ('lɪmbə) *adj.* **1.** capable of being easily bent or flexed; pliant. **2.** able to move or bend freely; agile. [C16: origin uncertain] —**'lim·ber·ly** *adv.* —**'lim·ber·ness** *n.*

lim·ber[2] ('lɪmbə) *n.* **1.** part of a gun carriage, consisting of an axle, pole, and two wheels, that is attached to the rear of an item of equipment, esp. field artillery. ~*vb.* **2.** (usually foll. by *up*) to attach the limber (to a gun, etc.). [C15 *lymour* shaft of a gun carriage, origin uncertain]

lim·ber[3] ('lɪmbə) *n.* (*often pl.*) *Nautical.* (in the bilge of a vessel) a fore-and-aft channel through a series of holes in the frames (**limber holes**) where water collects and can be pumped out. [C17: probably changed from French *lumière* hole (literally: light)]

lim·ber up *vb.* (*adv.*) **1.** (*intr.*) (esp. in sports) to exercise in order to be limber and agile. **2.** (*tr.*) to make flexible.

lim·bic sys·tem ('lɪmbɪk) *n.* the part of the brain bordering on the corpus callosum: concerned with basic emotion, hunger, and sex. [C19 *limbic,* from French *limbique,* from *limbe* limbus, from New Latin *limbus,* from Latin: border]

lim·bo[1] ('lɪmbəʊ) *n., pl.* **·bos. 1.** (*often cap.*) *Christianity.* the supposed abode of infants dying without baptism and the just who died before Christ. **2.** an imaginary place for lost, forgotten, or unwanted persons or things. **3.** an unknown intermediate place or condition between two extremes: *in limbo.* **4.** a prison or confinement. [C14: from Medieval Latin *in limbo* on the border (of hell)]

lim·bo[2] ('lɪmbəʊ) *n., pl.* **·bos.** a West Indian dance in which dancers pass, while leaning backwards, under a bar. [C20: origin uncertain]

Lim·bourg (lɛ̃'bu:r) *n.* the French name for **Limburg** (sense 3).

Lim·burg ('lɪmbɜ:g; *Dutch* 'lɪmbyrx) *n.* **1.** a medieval duchy of W Europe: divided between the Netherlands and Belgium in 1839. **2.** a province of the SE Netherlands: contains a coalfield and industrial centres. Capital: Maastricht. Pop.: 1 030 200 (1973 est.). Area: 2253 sq. km (809 sq. miles). **3.** a province of NE Belgium: contains the industrial regions of the Kempen coalfield. Capital: Hassett. Pop.: 685 576 (1975 est.). Area: 2422 sq. km (935 sq. miles). French name: **Limbourg.**

Lim·burg·er ('lɪmbɜ:gə) *n.* a semihard white cheese of very strong smell and flavour. Also called: **Limburg cheese.**

lim·bus ('lɪmbəs) *n., pl.* **·bi** (-baɪ). *Anatomy.* the edge or border of any of various structures or parts. [C15: from Latin: edge] —**'lim·bic** *adj.*

lime[1] (laɪm) *n.* **1.** short for **quicklime, birdlime, slaked lime. 2.** *Agriculture.* any of certain calcium compounds, esp. calcium hydroxide, spread as a dressing on lime-deficient land. ~*vb.* (*tr.*) **3.** to spread (twigs, etc.) with birdlime. **4.** to spread a calcium compound upon (land) to improve plant growth. **5.** to catch (animals, esp. birds) with or as if with birdlime. **6.** to whitewash or cover (a wall, ceiling, etc.) with a mixture of lime and water (**limewash**). [Old English *līm;* related to Icelandic *līm* glue, Latin *līmus* slime]

lime[2] (laɪm) *n.* **1.** a small Asian citrus tree, *Citrus aurantifolia,* with stiff sharp spines and small round or oval greenish fruits. **2. a.** the fruit of this tree, having acid fleshy pulp rich in vitamin C. **b.** (*as modifier*): *lime juice.* ~*adj.* **3.** having the flavour of lime fruit. [C17: from French, from Provençal, from Arabic *līmah*]

lime[3] (laɪm) *n.* a European linden tree, *Tilia europaea,* planted in many varieties for ornament. [C17: changed from obsolete *line,* from Old English *lind* LINDEN]

lime[4] (laɪm) *vb.* (*intr.*) *Caribbean slang.* (of young people) to sit or stand around on the pavement. [of unknown origin]

lime·ade (,laɪm'eɪd) *n.* a drink made from sweetened lime juice and plain or carbonated water.

lime burn·er *n.* a person whose job it is to burn limestone to make lime.

lime green *n., adj.* **a.** a moderate greenish-yellow colour. **b.** (*as adj.*): *a lime-green dress.*

lime·kiln ('laɪm,kɪln) *n.* a kiln in which calcium carbonate is calcined to produce quicklime.

lime·light ('laɪm,laɪt) *n.* **1. the.** a position of public attention or notice (esp. in the phrase **in the limelight**). **2. a.** a type of lamp, formerly used in stage lighting, in which light is produced by heating lime to white heat. **b.** Also called **calcium light.** brilliant white light produced in this way. —**'lime·,light·er** *n.*

li·men ('laɪmɛn) *n., pl.* **li·mens** *or* **lim·i·na** ('lɪmɪnə). *Psychol.* another term for **threshold** (sense 4). [C19: from Latin]

lime pit *n.* (in tanning) a pit containing lime in which hides are placed to remove the hair.

lim·er·ick ('lɪmərɪk) *n.* a form of comic verse consisting of five anapaestic lines of which the first, second, and fifth have three metrical feet and rhyme together and the third and fourth have two metrical feet and rhyme together. [C19: allegedly from *will you come up to Limerick?,* a refrain sung between nonsense verses at a party]

Lim·er·ick ('lɪmərɪk) *n.* **1.** a county of SW Ireland, in N Munster province: consists chiefly of an undulating plain with rich pasture and mountains in the south. County town:

Limerick. Pop.: 140 459 (1971). Area: 2686 sq. km (1037 sq. miles). **2.** a port in SW Ireland, county town of Limerick, at the head of the Shannon estuary. Pop.: 57 161 (1971).

li+mes ('laɪmiːz) *n., pl.* **lim·i+tes** ('lɪmɪˌtiːz). the fortified boundary of the Roman Empire. [from Latin]

lime+stone ('laɪmˌstəʊn) *n.* a sedimentary rock consisting mainly of calcium carbonate, deposited as the calcareous remains of marine animals or chemically precipitated from the sea: used as a building stone and in the manufacture of cement, lime, etc.

lime+wa·ter ('laɪmˌwɔːtə) *n.* **1.** a clear colourless solution of calcium hydroxide in water, sometimes used in medicine as an antacid. **2.** water that contains dissolved lime or calcium salts, esp. calcium carbonate or calcium sulphate.

lim+ey ('laɪmɪ) *U.S. slang.* ~*n.* **1.** a British person. **2.** a British sailor or ship. ~*adj.* **3.** British. [abbreviated from C19 *lime-juicer,* because British sailors were required to drink lime juice as a protection against scurvy]

li+mic·o+line (laɪ'mɪkəˌlaɪn, -lɪn) *adj.* of, relating to, or belonging to the *Charadrii,* a suborder of birds containing the plovers, sandpipers, snipes, oystercatchers, avocets, etc. [C19: from New Latin *Limicolae* former name of order, from Latin *līmus* mud + *colere* to inhabit]

li+mic·o+lous (laɪ'mɪkələs) *adj.* (of certain animals) living in mud or muddy regions.

lim·i+nal ('lɪmɪnᵊl) *adj. Psychol.* relating to the point (or threshold) beyond which a sensation becomes too faint to be experienced. [C19: from Latin *līmen* threshold]

lim+it ('lɪmɪt) *n.* **1.** (*sometimes pl.*) the ultimate extent, degree, or amount of something: *the limit of endurance.* **2.** (*often pl.*) the boundary or edge of a specific area: *the city limits.* **3.** (*often pl.*) the area of premises within specific boundaries. **4.** the largest quantity or amount allowed. **5.** *Maths.* **a.** a value to which a function f(x) approaches as closely as desired as the independent variable approaches a specified value (x = a) or approaches infinity. **b.** a value to which a sequence a_n approaches arbitrarily close as n approaches infinity. **c.** the limit of a sequence of partial sums of a convergent infinite series: *the limit of* $1 + \frac{1}{2} + \frac{1}{4} + \frac{1}{8} + \ldots$ *is* 2. **6.** *Maths.* one of the two specified values between which a definite integral is evaluated. **7. the limit.** *Informal.* a person or thing that is intolerably exasperating. **8. off limits.** forbidden to military personnel without special permission to enter. **9. within limits.** to a certain or limited extent: *I approve of it within limits.* ~*vb.* (*tr.*) **10.** to restrict or confine, as to area, extent, time, etc. **11.** *Law.* to agree, fix, or assign specifically. [C14: from Latin *līmes* boundary] —**'lim+it+a·ble** *adj.* —**'lim+it+a·ble+ness** *n.* —**'lim+it+er** *n.* —**'lim+it+less** *adj.* —**'lim+it+less+ly** *adv.* —**'lim+it+less+ness** *n.*

lim·i+tar·i·an (ˌlɪmɪ'tɛərɪən) *n. Christianity.* a person who regards salvation as limited to only a part of mankind.

lim·i+tar·y ('lɪmɪtərɪ, -trɪ) *adj.* **1.** of, involving, or serving as a limit. **2.** restricted or limited.

lim·i+ta+tion (ˌlɪmɪ'teɪʃən) *n.* **1.** something that limits a quality or achievement. **2.** the act of limiting or the condition of being limited. **3.** *Law.* a certain period of time, legally defined, within which an action, claim, etc., must be commenced. **4.** *Property law.* a restriction upon the duration or extent of an estate.

lim+it+ed ('lɪmɪtɪd) *adj.* **1.** having a limit; restricted; confined. **2.** without fullness or scope; narrow. **3.** (of governing powers, sovereignty, etc.) restricted or checked, by or as if by a constitution, laws, or an assembly: *limited government.* **4.** *U.S.* (of a train) stopping only at certain stations and having only a set number of cars for passengers. **5.** *Chiefly Brit.* (of a business enterprise) owned by shareholders whose liability for the enterprise's debts is restricted. ~*n.* **6.** *U.S.* a limited train, bus, etc. —**'lim+it+ed+ly** *adv.* —**'lim+it+ed+ness** *n.*

lim+it+ed com+pa+ny *n. Brit.* a company whose owners enjoy limited liability for the company's debts and losses.

lim+it+ed e·di+tion *n.* an edition of a book that is limited to a specified number of copies.

lim+it+ed li·a·bil+i·ty *n. Brit.* liability restricted to the unpaid portion (if any) of the par value of the shares of a limited company. It is a feature of share ownership.

lim+it+ed mon+ar+chy *n.* another term for **constitutional monarchy.**

lim+it+er *n.* an electronic circuit that produces an output signal whose positive or negative amplitude, or both, is limited to some predetermined value above which the peaks become flattened. Also called: **clipper.**

lim+it man *n.* (in a handicap sport or game) the competitor with the maximum handicap.

lim+it point *n. Maths.* a point in a topological space such that there is at least one other point of the space in every neighbourhood of the given point: 0 *is the limit point of the sequence* $1, \frac{1}{2}, \frac{1}{3}, \frac{1}{4}, \ldots$ Also called: **accumulation point.**

lim·i+trophe ('lɪmɪˌtrəʊf) *adj.* (of a country or region) on or near a frontier. [C19: via French from Late Latin *limitrophus,* from *limit-* LIMIT + Greek *-trophus* supporting; originally referring to borderland that supported frontier troops]

limn (lɪm) *vb.* (*tr.*) **1.** to represent in drawing or painting. **2.** *Archaic.* to describe in words. **3.** an obsolete word for **illuminate.** [C15: from Old French *enluminer* to illumine (a manuscript) from Latin *inlūmināre* to brighten, from *lūmen* light] —**lim+ner** ('lɪmnə) *n.*

lim+net+ic (lɪm'nɛtɪk) *adj.* of, relating to, or inhabiting the open water of lakes down to the depth of light penetration: *the limnetic zone.* [C20: from Greek *limnē* pool]

lim+nol+o·gy (lɪm'nɒlədʒɪ) *n.* the study of bodies of fresh water with reference to their plant and animal life, physical properties, geographical features, etc. [C20: from Greek *limnē* lake] —**lim+no+log·i·cal** (ˌlɪmnə'lɒdʒɪkᵊl) *or* ˌ**lim+no+'log·ic** *adj.* —ˌ**lim+no+'log·i·cal+ly** *adv.* —**lim+'nol·o+gist** *n.*

Lím+nos ('limnɔs) *n.* transliteration of the Modern Greek name of **Lemnos.**

Li+moges (lɪ'məʊʒ; *French* li'mɔːʒ) *n.* a city in S central France, on the Vienne River: a centre of the porcelain industry since the 18th century. Pop.: 147 442 (1975).

lim·o+nene ('lɪməˌniːn) *n.* a liquid optically active terpene with a lemon-like odour, found in lemon, orange, peppermint, and other essential oils and used as a wetting agent and in the manufacture of resins. Formula: $C_{10}H_{16}$. [C19: from New Latin *limonum* lemon]

li+mo+nite ('laɪməˌnaɪt) *n.* a common brown, black, or yellow amorphous secondary mineral that consists of hydrated ferric oxides and is a source of iron. Formula: $FeO(OH).nH_2O$. [C19: probably from Greek *leimōn,* translation of earlier German name, *Wiesenerz* meadow ore] —**li+mo+nit+ic** (ˌlaɪmə'nɪtɪk) *adj.*

Li+mou+sin (*French* limu'zɛ̃) *n.* a region and former province of W central France, in the W part of the Massif Central.

lim+ou+sine ('lɪməˌziːn, ˌlɪmə'ziːn) *n.* **1.** any large and luxurious car, esp. one that has a glass division between the driver and passengers. **2.** a former type of car in which the roof covering the rear seats projects over the driver's compartment. [C20: from French, literally: cloak (originally one worn by shepherds in *Limousin*), hence later applied to the car]

limp[1] (lɪmp) *vb.* (*intr.*) **1.** to walk with an uneven step, esp. with a weak or injured leg. **2.** to advance in a labouring or faltering manner. ~*n.* **3.** an uneven walk or progress. [C16: probably a back formation from obsolete *limphalt* lame, from Old English *lempheal*t; related to Middle High German *limpfen* to limp] —**'limp+er** *n.* —**'limp+ing+ly** *adv.*

limp[2] (lɪmp) *adj.* **1.** not firm or stiff. **2.** not energetic or vital. **3.** (of the binding of a book) not stiffened with boards. [C18: probably of Scandinavian origin; related to Icelandic *limpa* looseness] —**'limp+ly** *adv.* —**'limp+ness** *n.*

lim+pet ('lɪmpɪt) *n.* **1.** any of numerous marine gastropods, such as *Patella vulgata* (**common limpet**) and *Fissurella* (or *Diodora*) *apertura* (**keyhole limpet**), that have a conical shell and are found clinging to rocks. **2.** any of various similar freshwater gastropods, such as *Ancylus fluviatilis* (**river limpet**). **3.** (*modifier*) relating to or denoting certain weapons that are attached to their targets by magnetic or adhesive properties and resist removal: *limpet mines.* [Old English *lempedu,* from Latin *lepas,* from Greek]

lim+pid ('lɪmpɪd) *adj.* **1.** clear or transparent. **2.** (esp. of writings, style, etc.) free from obscurity. **3.** calm; peaceful. [C17: from French *limpide,* from Latin *limpidus* clear] —**lim+'pid+i·ty** *or* **'lim+pid+ness** *n.* —**'lim+pid+ly** *adv.*

limp+kin ('lɪmpkɪn) *n.* a rail-like wading bird, *Aramus guarauna,* of tropical American marshes, having dark brown plumage with white markings and a wailing cry: order *Gruiformes* (cranes, rails, etc.). Also called: **courlan.** [C19: named from its awkward gait]

Lim+po+po (lɪm'pəʊpəʊ) *n.* a river in SE Africa, rising in South Africa in S Transvaal and flowing northeast, then southeast as the border between South Africa and Rhodesia and through Mozambique to the Indian Ocean. Length: 1770 km (1100 miles). Also called (esp. in its upper course): **Crocodile River.**

lim+u+lus ('lɪmjʊləs) *n., pl.* **+li** (-ˌlaɪ). any horseshoe crab of the genus *Limulus,* esp. *L. polyphemus.* [C19: from New Latin (name of genus), from Latin *līmus* sidelong]

lim·y[1] ('laɪmɪ) *adj.* **lim·i·er, lim·i+est.** of, like, or smeared with birdlime. —**'lim·i·ness** *n.*

lim·y[2] ('laɪmɪ) *adj.* **lim·i·er, lim·i+est.** of or tasting of lime (the fruit).

lin. *abbrev. for:* **1.** lineal. **2.** linear.

lin+ac ('lɪnæk) *n.* short for **linear accelerator.**

Lin·a·cre ('lɪnəkə) *n.* **Thom·as.** ?1460–1524, English humanist and physician: founded the Royal College of Physicians (1518).

lin+age *or* **line+age** ('laɪnɪdʒ) *n.* **1.** the number of lines in a piece of written or printed matter. **2.** payment for written material calculated according to the number of lines. **3.** a less common word for **alignment.**

lin+al·o·ol (lɪ'nælәʊˌɒl, 'lɪnəˌluːl) *or* **lin+al·ol** ('lɪnəˌlɒl) *n.* an optically active colourless fragrant liquid found in many essential oils and used in perfumery. Formula: $C_{10}H_{18}O$. [from LIGNALOES + -OL[1]]

Li+na+res (*Spanish* li'nares) *n.* a city in S Spain: site of Scipio Africanus' defeat of the Carthaginians (208 B.C.); lead mines. Pop.: 50 516 (1970).

linch+pin ('lɪntʃˌpɪn) *n.* **1.** a pin placed transversely through an axle to keep a wheel in position. **2.** a person or thing regarded as an essential or coordinating element: *the linchpin of the company.* [C14 *lynspin,* from Old English *lynis*]

Lin+coln[1] ('lɪŋkən) *n.* **1.** a city in E central England, administrative centre of Lincolnshire: an important ecclesiastical and commercial centre in the Middle Ages; Roman ruins, a castle (founded by William the Conqueror) and a famous cathedral (begun in 1086). Pop.: 74 207 (1971). Latin name: **Lindum. 2.** a city in SE Nebraska: state capital; University of Nebraska (1869). Pop.: 163 440 (1973 est.). **3.** short for **Lincolnshire. 4.** a breed of long-woolled sheep, originally from Lincolnshire.

Lin·coln[2] ('lɪŋkən) *n.* **A·bra·ham.** 1809–65, U.S. Republican statesman; 16th president of the U.S. His fame rests on his success in saving the Union in the Civil War (1861–65) and on his emancipation of slaves (1863); assassinated by Booth.

Lin+coln green *n., adj.* **1. a.** a yellowish-green or brownish-green colour. **b.** (*as adj.*)*: a Lincoln-green suit.* **2.** a cloth of this colour. [C16: so named after a green fabric formerly made at Lincoln]

Lin+coln+shire ('lɪŋkən,ʃɪə, -ʃə) *n.* a county of E England, on the North Sea and the Wash: mostly low-lying and fertile, with fenland around the Wash and hills (the **Lincoln Wolds**) in the east; one of the main agricultural counties of Great Britain. Administrative centre: Lincoln. Pop.: 524 500 (1976 est.). Area: 58 848 sq. km (2272 sq. miles). Abbrev.: **Lincs.**

Lin·coln's Inn *n.* one of the four legal societies in London which together form the Inns of Court.

lin+crus+ta (lɪn'krʌstə) *n.* a type of wallpaper having a hard embossed surface. [C19: from Latin *linum* flax + *crusta* rind]

Lincs. (lɪŋks) *abbrev. for* Lincolnshire.

linc+tus ('lɪŋktəs) *n., pl.* **+tus·es.** a syrupy medicinal preparation, taken to relieve coughs and sore throats. [C17 (in the sense: medicine to be licked with the tongue): from Latin, past participle of *lingere* to lick]

Lind (lɪnd) *n.* **Jen·ny.** Swedish name *Johanna Maria Lind Goldschmidt.* 1820–87, Swedish coloratura soprano.

lin+dane ('lɪndeɪn) *n.* a white poisonous crystalline powder with a slight musty odour: used as an insecticide, weed killer, and, in low concentrations, in treating scabies; 1,2,3,4,5,6-hexachlorocyclohexane. Formula: $C_6H_6Cl_6$. [C20: named after T. van der *Linden,* Dutch chemist]

Lind·bergh ('lɪndbɜːg, 'lɪnbɜːg) *n.* **Charles Au·gus·tus.** 1902–74, U.S. aviator, who made the first solo nonstop flight across the Atlantic (1927).

lin+den ('lɪndən) *n.* any of various tiliaceous deciduous trees of the N temperate genus *Tilia,* having heart-shaped leaves and small fragrant yellowish flowers: cultivated for timber and as shade trees. See also **lime**[3]**, basswood.** [C16: n. use of obsolete adj. *linden,* from Old English *linde* lime tree]

Lind+es+nes ('lɪndɪs,nɛs) *n.* a cape at the S tip of Norway, projecting into the North Sea. Also called: (the) **Naze.**

Lin+dis+farne ('lɪndɪs,fɑːn) *n.* another name for **Holy Island.**

Lind+sey ('lɪndzɪ) *n.* **Parts of.** an area in E England constituting a former administrative division of Lincolnshire.

Lind·wall ('lɪnd,wɔːl) *n.* **Ray(mond Russell).** born 1921, Australian cricketer. A fast bowler, he played for Australia 61 times between 1946 and 1958.

line[1] (laɪn) *n.* **1.** a narrow continuous mark, as one made by a pencil, pen, or brush across a surface. **2.** such a mark cut into or raised from a surface. **3.** a thin indented mark or wrinkle. **4.** a straight or curved continuous trace having no breadth that is produced by a moving point. **5.** *Maths.* **a.** any straight one-dimensional geometrical element whose identity is determined by two points. A **line segment** lies between any two points on a line. **b.** a set of points (x, y) that satisfies the equation $y = mx + c$, where m is the gradient and c is the intercept with the y-axis. **6.** a border or boundary: *the county line.* **7.** *Sport.* **a.** a white or coloured band indicating a boundary or division on a field, track, etc. **b.** a mark or imaginary mark at which a race begins or ends. **8.** *American football.* **a.** See **line of scrimmage. b.** the players arranged in a row on either side of the line of scrimmage at the start of each play. **9.** a specified point of change or limit: *the dividing line between sanity and madness.* **10. a.** the edge or contour of a shape, as in sculpture or architecture, or a mark on a painting, drawing, etc., defining or suggesting this. **b.** the sum or type of such contours or marks, characteristic of a style or design: *the line of a draughtsman; the line of a building.* **11.** anything long, flexible, and thin, such as a wire or string: *a washing line; a fishing line.* **12.** a telephone connection: *a direct line to New York.* **13. a.** a conducting wire, cable, or circuit for making connections between pieces of electrical apparatus, such as a cable for electric-power transmission, telecommunications, etc. **b.** (*as modifier*)*: the line voltage.* **14.** a system of travel or transportation, esp. over agreed routes: *a shipping line.* **15.** a company operating such a system. **16.** a route between two points on a railway. **17.** *Chiefly Brit.* **a.** a railway track, including the roadbed, sleepers, etc. **b.** one of the rails of such a track. **18.** a course or direction of movement or advance: *the line of flight of a bullet.* **19.** a course or method of action, behaviour, etc.: *take a new line with him.* **20.** a policy or prescribed course of action or way of thinking (often in the phrases **bring** *or* **come into line**). **21.** a field of study, interest, occupation, trade, or profession: *this book is in your line.* **22.** alignment; true (esp. in the phrases **in line, out of line**). **23.** one kind of product or article: *a nice line in hats.* **24.** a row of persons or things: *a line of cakes on the conveyor belt.* **25.** a chronological or ancestral series, esp. of people: *a line of prime ministers.* **26.** a row of words printed or written across a page or column. **27.** a unit of verse consisting of the number of feet appropriate to the metre being used and written or printed with the words in a single row. **28.** a short letter; note: *just a line to say thank you.* **29.** a piece of useful information or hint about something: *give me a line on his work.* **30.** one of a number of narrow horizontal bands forming a television picture. **31.** a narrow band in an electromagnetic spectrum, resulting from a transition in an atom of a gas. **32.** *Music.* **a.** any of the five horizontal marks that make up the stave. Compare **space** (sense 9). **b.** the musical part or melody notated on one such set. **c.** a discernible shape formed by sequences of notes or musical sounds: *a meandering melodic line.* **d.** (in polyphonic music) a set of staves that are held together with a bracket or brace. **33.** the horizontal line on a bridge score sheet that divides game points (**below the line**) from premium (bonus) points (**above the line**). **34.** a unit of magnetic flux equal to 1 maxwell. **35.** a defensive or fortified position, esp. one that marks the most forward position in war or a national boundary: *the front line.* **36. line ahead** *or* **line abreast.** a formation adopted by a naval unit for manoeuvring. **37.** a formation adopted by a body or a number of military units when drawn up abreast. **38.** the combatant forces of certain armies and navies, excluding supporting arms. **39.** *Fencing.* one of four divisions of the target on a fencer's body, considered as areas to which specific attacks are made. **40.** the scent left by a fox. **41. a.** the equator (esp. in the phrase **crossing the line**). **b.** any circle or arc on the terrestrial or celestial sphere. **42.** the amount of insurance written by an underwriter for a particular risk. **43.** the U.S. word for **queue. 44. all along the line. a.** at every stage in a series. **b.** in every detail. **45. draw the line (at).** to reasonably object (to) or set a limit (on): *her father draws the line at her coming in after midnight.* **46. get a line on.** *Informal.* to obtain information about. **47. hold the line. a.** to keep a telephone line open. **b.** *Football.* to prevent the opponents from taking the ball forward. **c.** (of soldiers) to keep formation, as when under fire. **48. in line for.** in the running for; a candidate for: *he's in line for a directorship.* **49. in line with.** conforming to. **50. in the line of duty.** as a necessary and usually undesired part of the performance of one's responsibilities. **51. lay** *or* **put on the line. a.** to pay money. **b.** to speak frankly and directly. **c.** to risk (one's career, reputation, etc.) on something. **52. shoot a line.** to try to create a false image, as by boasting or bragging. **53. toe the line.** to conform to expected standards, attitudes, etc. *~vb.* **54.** (*tr.*) to mark with a line or lines. **55.** (*tr.*) to draw or represent with a line or lines. **56.** (*tr.*) to be or put as a border to: *tulips lined the lawns.* **57.** to place in or form a row, series, or alignment. ~See also **lines, line-up.** [C13: partly from Old French *ligne,* ultimately from *līnea,* n. use of *līneus* flaxen, from *līnum* flax; partly from Old English *līn,* ultimately also from Latin *līnum* flax] **—'lin+a·ble** *or* **'line+a·ble** *adj.* **—'line+,like** *adj.* **—'lin·y** *or* **'lin+ey** *adj.*

line[2] (laɪn) *vb.* (*tr.*) **1.** to attach an inside covering to (a garment, curtain, etc.), as for protection, to hide the seaming, or so that it should hang well. **2.** to cover or fit the inside of: *to line the walls with books.* **3.** to fill plentifully: *a purse lined with money.* **4.** to reinforce the back of (a book) with fabric, paper, etc. [C14: ultimately from Latin *līnum* flax, since linings were often made of linen]

lin+e·age[1] ('lɪnɪɪdʒ) *n.* **1.** direct descent from an ancestor, esp. a line of descendants from one ancestor. **2.** a less common word for **derivation.** [C14: from Old French *lignage,* ultimately from Latin *līnea* LINE[1]]

line+age[2] ('laɪnɪdʒ) *n.* a variant spelling of **linage.**

lin+e·al ('lɪnɪəl) *adj.* **1.** being in a direct line of descent from an ancestor. **2.** of, involving, or derived from direct descent. **3.** a less common word for **linear.** [C14: via Old French from Late Latin *līneālis,* from Latin *līnea* LINE[1]] **—'lin+e·al+ly** *adv.*

lin·e·a+ment ('lɪnɪəmənt) *n.* (*often pl.*) **1.** a facial outline or feature. **2.** a distinctive characteristic or feature. [C15: from Latin: line, from *līneāre* to draw a line] **—lin·e·a+men+tal** (,lɪnɪə'mɛntᵊl) *adj.*

lin+e·ar ('lɪnɪə) *adj.* **1.** of, in, along, or relating to a line. **2.** of or relating to length. **3.** resembling, represented by, or consisting of a line or lines. **4.** having one dimension. **5.** designating a style in the arts, esp. painting, that obtains its effects through line rather than colour or light and in which the edges of forms and planes are sharply defined. Compare **painterly. 6.** *Maths.* of or relating to the first degree: *a linear equation.* **7.** narrow and having parallel edges: *a linear leaf.* **8.** *Electronics.* **a.** Also: **analogue.** (of a circuit, etc.) having an output that is directly proportional to input: *linear amplifier.* Compare **digital** (sense 5). **b.** having components arranged in a line. [C17: from Latin *līneāris* of or by means of lines] **—lin+e·ar+i·ty** (,lɪnɪ'ærɪtɪ) *n.* **—'lin+e·ar+ly** *adv.*

Lin+e·ar A *n.* a hitherto undeciphered script, partly syllabic and partly ideographic, found on tablets and pottery in Crete and dating mainly from the 15th century B.C.

lin+e·ar ac+cel+er·a+tor *n.* an accelerator in which charged particles are accelerated along a linear path by potential differences applied to a number of electrodes along their path. Sometimes shortened to **linac.**

Lin+e·ar B *n.* an ancient system of writing, apparently a modified form of Linear A, found on clay tablets and jars of the second millennium B.C. The earliest excavated examples, dating from about 1400, came from Knossos, in Crete, but all the later finds are at Pylos and Mycenae on the Greek mainland, dating from the 14th–12th centuries. The script is generally accepted as being an early representation of Mycenaean Greek.

lin+e·ar e·qua+tion *n.* a polynomial equation of the first degree, such as $x + y = 7$.

lin+e·ar meas+ure *n.* a unit or system of units for the measurement of length. Also called: **long measure.**

lin+e·ar mo+tor *n.* a form of electric motor in which the stator and the rotor are linear and parallel. It can be used to drive a train, one part of the motor being in the locomotive, the other in the track.

lin+e·ar per+spec+tive *n.* the branch of perspective in which the apparent size and shape of objects and their position with respect to foreground and background are established by actual or suggested lines converging on the horizon.

lin+e·ar pro+gram+ming *n. Maths.* a technique used in economics, etc., for determining the maximum or minimum of a linear function of non-negative variables subject to constraints expressed as linear equalities or inequalities.

lin+e·ate ('lɪnɪɪt, -,eɪt) *or* **lin+e·at+ed** *adj.* marked with lines; streaked. [C17: from Latin *līneātus* drawn with lines]

lin·e·a·tion (ˌlɪnɪ'eɪʃən) *n.* **1.** the act of marking with lines. **2.** an arrangement of or division into lines. **3.** an outline or contour. **4.** any linear arrangement involving rocks or minerals, such as a series of parallel rock strata.
line block *n.* a letterpress printing block made by a photo-engraving process without the use of a screen.
line breed·ing *n.* selective inbreeding that produces individuals possessing one or more of the favourable characteristics of their common ancestor.
line·cast·er ('laɪnˌkɑːstə) *n.* a printing machine that casts metal type in lines.
line draw·ing *n.* a drawing made with lines only, gradations in tone being provided by the spacing and thickness of the lines.
line-en·grav·ing *n.* **1.** the art or process of hand-engraving in intaglio and copper plate. **2.** a plate so engraved. **3.** a print taken from such a plate. —**'line-en·ˌgrav·er** *n.*
Line Is·lands *pl. n.* a group of coral islands in the central Pacific, including Fanning, Washington, and Christmas Islands: part of the Gilbert Islands, with Palmyra and Jarvis administered by the U.S.
line·man ('laɪnmən) *n., pl.* **·men. 1.** another name for **platelayer. 2.** a person who does the chaining, taping, or marking of points for a surveyor. **3.** *Austral.* the member of a beach life-saving team who controls the line used to help drowning swimmers and surfers. **4.** *American football.* a member of a line.
lin·en ('lɪnɪn) *n.* **1. a.** a hard-wearing fabric woven from the spun fibres of flax. **b.** (*as modifier*): *a linen tablecloth.* **2.** yarn or thread spun from flax fibre. **3.** clothes, sheets, tablecloths, etc., made from linen cloth or from a substitute such as cotton. **4.** See **linen paper.** [Old English *linnen*, ultimately from Latin *līnum* flax, LINE²]
lin·en pa·per *n.* paper made from flax fibres or having a similar texture.
line of bat·tle *n.* a formation adopted by a military or naval force when preparing for action.
line of cred·it *n. U.S.* another name for **credit line.**
line of fire *n.* the flight path of a missile discharged or to be discharged from a firearm.
line of force *n.* a line in a field of force, such as an electric or magnetic field, for which the tangent at any point is the direction of the force at that point.
line of scrim·mage *n. American football.* an imaginary line, parallel to the goal lines, on which the ball is placed at the start of each play and on either side of which the teams line up.
line of sight *n.* **1.** the straight line along which an observer looks or a beam of radiation travels. **2.** *Ophthalmol.* another term for **line of vision.**
line of vi·sion *n. Ophthalmol.* a straight line extending from the fovea centralis of the eye to an object on which the eye is focused. Also called: **line of sight.**
lin·e·o·late ('lɪnɪəˌleɪt) *or* **lin·e·o·lat·ed** *adj. Biology.* marked with very fine parallel lines. [C19: from Latin *līneola*, diminutive of *līnea* LINE¹]
line-out *n. Rugby Union.* the method of restarting play when the ball goes into touch, the forwards forming two parallel lines at right angles to the touchline and jumping for the ball when it is thrown in.
line print·er *n.* an electromechanical device that prints a line of characters at a time rather than a character at a time, at speeds from about 200 to 3000 lines per minute: used in printing and in computer systems.
lin·er¹ ('laɪnə) *n.* **1.** a passenger ship or aircraft, esp. one that is part of a commercial fleet. **2.** See **freightliner. 3.** Also called: **eye liner.** a cosmetic used to outline the eyes, consisting of a liquid or cake mixed with water and applied by brush or a grease pencil. **4.** a person or thing that uses lines, esp. in drawing or copying.
lin·er² ('laɪnə) *n.* **1.** a material used as a lining. **2.** a person who supplies or fits linings.
lines (laɪnz) *pl. n.* **1.** general appearance or outline: *a car with fine lines.* **2.** a plan of procedure or construction: *built on traditional lines.* **3. a.** the spoken words of a theatrical presentation. **b.** the words of a particular role: *he forgot his lines.* **4.** *Informal, chiefly Brit.* a marriage certificate: *marriage lines.* **5.** luck, fate, or fortune (esp. in the phrase **hard lines**). **6. a.** rows of buildings, temporary stabling, etc., in a military camp: *transport lines.* **b.** a defensive position, row of trenches, or other fortification: *we broke through the enemy lines.* **7. a.** a school punishment of writing the same sentence or phrase out a specified number of times. **b.** the phrases or sentences so written out: *a hundred lines.* **8. read between the lines.** to understand or find an implicit meaning in addition to the obvious one.
lines·man ('laɪnzmən) *n., pl.* **·men. 1.** an official who helps the referee or umpire in various sports, esp. by indicating when the ball has gone out of play. **2.** *Chiefly Brit.* a person who installs, maintains, or repairs telephone or electric-power lines. U.S. name: **lineman.**
line squall *n.* a squall or series of squalls along a cold front.
line-up *n.* **1.** a row or arrangement of people or things assembled for a particular purpose: *the line-up for the football match.* **2.** the members of such a row or arrangement. ~*vb.* **line up.** (*adv.*) **3.** to form, put into, or organize a line-up. **4.** (*tr.*) to produce, organize, and assemble: *they lined up some questions.* **5.** (*tr.*) to align.
ling¹ (lɪŋ) *n., pl.* **ling** *or* **lings. 1.** any of several gadoid food fishes of the northern coastal genus *Molva*, esp. *M. molva*, having an elongated body with long fins. **2.** another name for **burbot** (a fish). [C13: probably from Low German; related to LONG¹]
ling² (lɪŋ) *n.* another name for **heather** (sense 1). [C14: from Old Norse *lyng*] —**'ling·y** *adj.*
ling. *abbrev. for* linguistics.
-ling¹ *suffix forming nouns.* **1.** *Often disparaging.* a person or thing belonging to or associated with the group, activity, or quality specified: *nestling; underling.* **2.** used as a diminutive: *duckling.* [Old English *-ling*, of Germanic origin; related to Icelandic *-lingr*, Gothic *-lings*]
-ling² *suffix forming adverbs.* in a specified condition, manner, or direction: *darkling; sideling.* [Old English *-ling*, adverbial suffix]
lin·gam ('lɪŋgəm) *or* **lin·ga** ('lɪŋgə) *n.* **1.** (in Sanskrit grammar) the masculine gender. **2. a.** the Hindu phallic image of the god Siva. **b.** the penis. [C18: from Sanskrit]
Lin·ga·yen Gulf ('lɪŋgɑː'jɛn) *n.* a large inlet of the South China Sea in the Philippines, on the NW coast of Luzon.
ling·cod ('lɪŋˌkɒd) *n., pl.* **·cod** *or* **·cods.** any scorpaenoid food fish of the family *Ophiodontidae*, esp. *Ophiodon elongatus*, of the North Pacific Ocean.
lin·ger ('lɪŋgə) *vb.* (*mainly intr.*) **1.** to delay or prolong departure. **2.** to go in a slow or leisurely manner; saunter. **3.** to remain just alive for some time prior to death. **4.** to persist or continue, esp. in the mind. **5.** to be slow to act; dither; procrastinate. [C13 (northern dialect) *lengeren* to dwell, from *lengen* to prolong, from Old English *lengan* related to Old Norse *lengja;* see LONG¹] —**'lin·ger·er** *n.* —**'lin·ger·ing·ly** *adv.*
lin·ge·rie ('lɒnʒərɪ) *n.* **1.** women's underwear and nightwear. **2.** *Archaic.* linen goods collectively. [C19: from French, from *linge*, from Latin *līneus* linen, from *līnum* flax]
lin·go ('lɪŋgəʊ) *n., pl.* **·goes.** *Informal.* any foreign or unfamiliar language, jargon, etc. [C17: perhaps from LINGUA FRANCA; compare Portuguese *lingoa* tongue]
lin·gua ('lɪŋgwə) *n., pl.* **·guae** (-gwiː). *Anatomy.* **1.** the technical name for **tongue. 2.** any tongue-like structure. [C17: Latin]
lin·gua fran·ca ('fræŋkə) *n., pl.* **lin·gua fran·cas** *or* **lin·guae fran·cae** ('frænsiː). **1.** a language used for communication among people of different mother tongues. **2.** a hybrid language containing elements from several different languages used in this way. **3.** any system of communication providing mutual understanding. [C17: Italian, literally: Frankish tongue]
Lin·gua Fran·ca *n.* a particular lingua franca spoken from the time of the Crusades to the 18th century in the ports of the Mediterranean, based on Italian, Spanish, French, Arabic, Greek, and Turkish.
lin·gual ('lɪŋgwəl) *adj.* **1.** *Anatomy.* of or relating to the tongue or a part or structure resembling a tongue. **2. a.** *Rare.* of or relating to language or languages. **b.** (*in combination*): *polylingual.* **3.** articulated with the tongue. ~*n.* **4.** a lingual consonant, such as Scots (r). —**'lin·gual·ly** *adv.*
lin·gui·form ('lɪŋgwɪˌfɔːm) *adj.* shaped like a tongue.
lin·gui·ni (lɪŋ'gwiːnɪ) *n.* a kind of pasta in the shape of thin flat strands. [from Italian: small tongues]
lin·guist ('lɪŋgwɪst) *n.* **1.** a person who has the capacity to learn and speak foreign languages. **2.** a person who studies linguistics. **3.** *West African, esp. Ghanaian.* the spokesman for a chief. [C16: from Latin *lingua* tongue]
lin·guis·tic (lɪŋ'gwɪstɪk) *adj.* **1.** of or relating to language. **2.** of or relating to linguistics. —**lin·'guis·ti·cal·ly** *adv.*
lin·guis·tic at·las *n.* an atlas showing the distribution of distinctive linguistic features of languages or dialects.
lin·guis·tic bor·row·ing *n.* another name for **loan word.**
lin·guis·tic ge·og·ra·phy *n.* the study of the distribution of dialectal speech elements. —**lin·guis·tic ge·og·ra·pher** *n.*
lin·guis·tics (lɪŋ'gwɪstɪks) *n.* (*functioning as sing.*) the scientific study of language. See also **historical linguistics, descriptive linguistics.**
lin·gu·late ('lɪŋgjʊˌleɪt) *or* **lin·gu·lat·ed** *adj.* shaped like a tongue: *a lingulate leaf.* [C19: from Latin *lingulātus*]
lin·hay ('lɪnɪ) *n. Brit. dialect.* a farm building with an open front. [C17: of unknown origin]
lin·i·ment ('lɪnɪmənt) *n.* a medicated liquid, usually containing alcohol, camphor, and an oil, applied to the skin to relieve pain, stiffness, etc. [C15: from Late Latin *linīmentum*, from *linere* to smear, anoint]
li·nin ('laɪnɪn) *n.* the network of viscous material in the nucleus of a cell that connects the chromatin granules. [C19: from Latin *līnum* flax + -IN]
lin·ing ('laɪnɪŋ) *n.* **1. a.** material used to line a garment, curtain, etc. **b.** (*as modifier*): *lining satin.* **2.** a material, such as mull or brown paper, used to strengthen the back of a book. **3.** any material used as an interior covering.
link¹ (lɪŋk) *n.* **1.** any of the separate rings, loops, or pieces that connect or make up a chain. **2.** something that resembles such a ring, loop, or piece. **3.** a road connection, as between two main routes. **4.** a connecting part or episode. **5.** a connecting piece in a mechanism, often having pivoted ends. **6.** Also called: **radio link.** a system of transmitters and receivers that connect two locations by means of radio and television signals. **7.** a unit of length equal to one hundredth of a chain. 1 link of a Gunter's chain is equal to 7.92 inches, and of an engineer's chain to 1 foot. ~*vb.* **8.** (often foll. by *up*) to connect or be connected with or as if with links. **9.** (*tr.*) to connect by association, etc. [C14: from Scandinavian; compare Old Norse *hlekkr* link] —**'link·a·ble** *adj.*
link² (lɪŋk) *n.* (formerly) a torch used to light dark streets. [C16: perhaps from Latin *lychnus*, from Greek *lukhnos* lamp]

link+age ('lɪŋkɪdʒ) *n.* **1.** the act of linking or the state of being linked. **2.** a system of interconnected levers or rods for transmitting or regulating the motion of a mechanism. **3.** *Electronics.* the product of the total number of lines of magnetic flux and the number of turns in a coil or circuit through which they pass. **4.** *Genetics.* the occurrence of two genes close together on the same chromosome so that they are unlikely to be separated during crossing over and tend to be inherited as a single unit.

link+boy ('lɪŋk,bɔɪ) *or* **link+man** *n., pl.* **+boys** *or* **+men.** (formerly) a boy who carried a torch for pedestrians in dark streets.

link+man ('lɪnkmən) *n., pl.* **+men. 1.** a presenter of a television or radio programme, esp. a sports transmission, consisting of a number of outside broadcasts from different locations. **2.** another word for **linkboy.**

link mo·tion *n.* a mechanism controlling the valves of a steam engine, consisting of a slotted link terminating in a pair of eccentrics.

Lin+kö+ping (*Swedish* 'lint,çø:piŋ) *n.* a city in S Sweden: a political and ecclesiastical centre in the Middle Ages; engineering industry. Pop.: 108 034 (1974 est.).

links (lɪŋks) *pl. n.* **1.** short for **golf links.** See **golf course. 2.** *Chiefly Scot.* undulating sandy ground near the shore. [Old English *hlincas* plural of *hlinc* ridge]

Link train+er *n. Trademark.* a ground-training device for training pilots and aircrew in the use of flight instruments. Compare **flight simulator.**

link+work ('lɪŋk,wɜ:k) *n.* **1.** something made up of links. **2.** a mechanism consisting of a series of links to impart or control motion; linkage.

Lin+lith+gow (lɪn'lɪθgəʊ) *n.* **1.** a town in SE Scotland, in Lothian region: ruined palace, residence of Scottish kings and birthplace of Mary Queen of Scots. Pop.: 5685 (1971). **2.** the former name of **West Lothian.**

linn (lɪn) *n. Chiefly Scot.* **1.** a waterfall or a pool at the foot of it. **2.** a ravine or precipice. [C16: probably from a confusion of two words, Scottish Gaelic *linne* pool and Old English *hlynn* torrent]

Lin+nae·us (lɪ'ni:əs, -'neɪ-) *n.* **Car·o·lus** ('kærələs), original name *Carl von Linné.* 1707–78, Swedish botanist, who established the binomial system of biological nomenclature that forms the basis of modern classification.

Lin+ne·an *or* **Lin+nae·an** (lɪ'ni:ən, -'neɪ-) *adj.* **1.** of or relating to Linnaeus. **2.** relating to the system of classification of plants and animals using binomial nomenclature.

lin+net ('lɪnɪt) *n.* **1.** a brownish Old World finch, *Acanthis cannabina*: the male has a red breast and forehead. **2.** Also called: **house finch.** a similar and related North American bird, *Carpodacus mexicanus.* [C16: from Old French *linotte,* ultimately from Latin *līnum* flax (because the bird feeds on flaxseeds)]

Lin+nhe ('lɪnɪ) *n.* **Loch.** a sea loch of W Scotland, at the SW end of the Great Glen. Length: about 32 km (20 miles).

li+no ('laɪnəʊ) *n.* short for **linoleum.**

li+no+cut ('laɪnəʊ,kʌt) *n.* **1.** a design cut in relief on a block of linoleum. **2.** a print made from such a block.

li+no+le·ate (lɪ'nəʊlɪ,eɪt) *n.* an ester or salt of linoleic acid.

lin·o+le·ic ac·id (,lɪnəʊ'li:ɪk) *n.* a colourless oily essential fatty acid found in many natural oils, such as linseed: used in the manufacture of soaps, emulsifiers, and driers. Formula: $C_{18}H_{32}O_2$. [C19: from Latin *linum* flax + OLEIC ACID; so named because it is found in linseed oil]

lin·o+len+ic ac·id (,lɪnəʊ'lɛnɪk, -'li:-) *n.* a colourless unsaturated essential fatty acid found in drying oils, such as linseed oil, and used in making paints and synthetic resins; 9,12,15-octadecatrienoic acid. Formula: $C_{18}H_{30}O_2$.

li+no+le·um (lɪ'nəʊlɪəm) *n.* a sheet material made of hessian, jute, etc., coated under pressure and heat with a mixture of powdered cork, linseed oil, rosin, and pigment, used as a floor covering. Often shortened to **lino.** [C19: from Latin *līnum* flax + *oleum* oil]

li·no tile *n.* a tile made of linoleum or a similar substance, used as a floor covering.

Li+no+type ('laɪnəʊ,taɪp) *n.* **1.** *Trademark.* a typesetting machine, operated by a keyboard, that casts an entire line on one solid slug of metal. **2.** type produced by such a machine.

Lin Pi·ao ('lɪn 'pjaʊ) *n.* 1908–71, Chinese Communist general and statesman. He became minister of defence (1959) and second in rank to Mao Tse-tung (1966). He fell from grace and is reported to have died in an air crash while attempting to flee to the Soviet Union.

lin+sang ('lɪnsæŋ) *n.* any of several forest-dwelling viverrine mammals, *Poiana richardsoni* of W Africa or either of the two species of *Prionodon* of S Asia: closely related to the genets, having a very long tail and a spotted or banded coat of thick fur. [C19: Malay]

lin+seed ('lɪn,si:d) *n.* another name for **flaxseed.** [Old English *līnsǣd,* from *līn* flax + *sǣd* seed]

lin+seed oil *n.* a yellow oil extracted from seeds of the flax plant. It has great drying qualities and is used in making oil paints, printer's ink, linoleum, etc.

lin·sey-wool·sey ('lɪnzɪ'wʊlzɪ) *n.* a thin rough fabric of linen warp and coarse wool or cotton filling. [C15: probably from *Lindsey,* Suffolk village where the fabric was first made + WOOL (with rhyming suffix *-sey*)]

lin+stock ('lɪn,stɒk) *n.* a long staff holding a lighted match, formerly used to fire a cannon. [C16: from Dutch *lontstok,* from *lont* match + *stok* stick]

lint (lɪnt) *n.* **1.** an absorbent cotton or linen fabric with the nap raised on one side, used to dress wounds, etc. **2.** shreds of fibre, yarn, etc. **3.** *Chiefly U.S.* staple fibre for making cotton yarn. [C14: probably from Latin *linteus* made of linen, from *līnum* flax] —**'lint·y** *adj.*

lin+tel ('lɪntᵊl) *n.* a horizontal beam, as over a door or window. [C14: via Old French probably from Late Latin *līmitāris* (unattested) of the boundary, influenced in meaning by *līminaris* of the threshold]

lint+er ('lɪntə) *n.* **1.** a machine for stripping the short fibres of ginned cotton seeds. **2.** (*pl.*) the fibres so removed.

lint+white ('lɪnt,waɪt) *n. Archaic or poetic, chiefly Scot.* the linnet. [Old English *līnetwige,* probably from *līn* flax + *-twige,* perhaps related to Old High German *zwigon* to pluck]

Linz (lɪnts) *n.* a port in N Austria, capital of Upper Austria, on the River Danube: cultural centre; steel works. Pop.: 202 874 (1971). Latin name: **Lentia.**

li·on ('laɪən) *n.* **1.** a large gregarious predatory feline mammal, *Panthera leo,* of open country in parts of Africa and India, having a tawny yellow coat and, in the male, a shaggy mane. Related adj.: **leonine. 2.** a conventionalized lion, the principal beast used as an emblem in heraldry. It has become the national emblem of Great Britain. **3.** a courageous, strong, or bellicose person. **4.** a celebrity or idol who attracts much publicity and a large following. **5. beard the lion in his den.** to approach a feared or influential person, esp. in order to ask a favour. **6. the lion's share.** the largest portion. [Old English *līo, lēo* (Middle English *lioun,* from Anglo-French *liun*), both from Latin *leo,* Greek *leōn*]

Li·on ('laɪən) *n.* **the.** the constellation Leo, the fifth sign of the zodiac.

li+on+ess ('laɪənɪs) *n.* a female lion.

li·on+fish ('laɪən,fɪʃ) *n., pl.* **+fish** *or* **+fish·es.** any of various scorpion fishes of the tropical Pacific genus *Pterois,* having a striped body and elongated spiny fins.

li·on-heart·ed *adj.* very brave; courageous. —**'li·on-,heart·ed+ly** *adv.* —**'li·on-,heart·ed+ness** *n.*

li+on+ize *or* **li+on+ise** ('laɪə,naɪz) *vb.* (*tr.*) to treat as or make into a celebrity. —**,li+on·i+'za+tion** *or* **,li+on·i+'sa+tion** *n.* —**'li+on+,iz+er** *or* **'li+on+,is+er** *n.*

Li·ons ('laɪənz) *n.* **Gulf of.** a wide bay of the Mediterranean off the S coast of France, between the Spanish border and Toulon. French name: **Golfe du Lion** (gɔlf dy 'ljɔ̃).

lip (lɪp) *n.* **1.** *Anatomy.* **a.** either of the two fleshy folds surrounding the mouth, playing an important role in the production of speech sounds, retaining food in the mouth, etc. Related adj.: **labial. b.** (*as modifier*): *lip salve.* **2.** the corresponding part in animals, esp. mammals. **3.** any structure resembling a lip, such as the rim of a crater, the margin of a gastropod shell, etc. **4.** a nontechnical word for **labium** and **labellum** (sense 1). **5.** *Slang.* impudent talk or backchat. **6.** the embouchure and control in the lips needed to blow wind and brass instruments. **7. bite one's lip. a.** to stifle one's feelings. **b.** to be annoyed or irritated. **8. button one's lip.** *Slang, chiefly U.S.* to stop talking: often imperative. **9. keep a stiff upper lip.** to show courage or composure. **10. smack one's lips.** to anticipate or recall something with glee or relish. ~*vb.* **lips, lip+ping, lipped. 11.** (*tr.*) to touch with the lip or lips. **12.** (*tr.*) to form or be a lip or lips for. **13.** (*tr.*) *Rare.* to murmur or whisper. **14.** (*intr.*) to use the lips in playing a wind instrument. [Old English *lippa;* related to Old High German *leffur,* Norwegian *lepe,* Latin *labium*] —**'lip+less** *adj.* —**'lip+,like** *adj.*

lip- *combining form.* variant of **lipo-** before a vowel.

Lip·a+ri Is+lands ('lɪpərɪ) *pl. n.* a group of volcanic islands under Italian administration off the N coast of Sicily: remains that form a continuous record from Neolithic times. Chief town: Lipari. Pop.: 10 037 (1971). Area: 114 sq. km (44 sq. miles). Also called: **Aeolian Islands.** Italian name: **I·so+le E·o+lie** ('i:zole e'ɔ:lje).

li+pase ('laɪpeɪs, 'lɪpeɪs) *n.* any of a group of fat-digesting enzymes produced in the stomach, pancreas, and liver and also occurring widely in the seeds of plants. [C19: from Greek *lipos* fat + -ASE]

Lip·chitz ('lɪpʃɪts) *n.* **Jacques** (ʒɑ:k). 1891–1973, U.S. sculptor, born in Lithuania: he pioneered cubist sculpture.

Li+petsk (*Russian* 'lipitsk) *n.* a city in the central Soviet Union, on the Voronezh River: steel works. Pop.: 351 000 (1975 est.).

li+pid *or* **li+pide** ('laɪpɪd, 'lɪpɪd) *n. Biochem.* any of a large group of organic compounds that are esters of fatty acids (**simple lipids,** such as fats and waxes) or closely related substances (**compound lipids,** such as phospholipids): usually insoluble in water but soluble in alcohol and other organic solvents. They are important structural materials in living organisms. Former name: **lipoid.** [C20: from French *lipide,* from Greek *lipos* fat]

Li Po *or* **Li T'ai-po** ('li: 'taɪ 'pəʊ) *n.* ?700–762 A.D., Chinese poet. His lyrics deal mostly with wine, nature, and women and are remarkable for their imagery.

lip·o- *or before a vowel* **lip-** *combining form.* fat or fatty: *lipoprotein.* [from Greek *lipos* fat]

li+pog+ra+phy (lɪ'pɒgrəfɪ) *n.* the accidental omission of words or letters in writing. [C19: from Greek *lip-,* stem of *leipein* to omit + -GRAPHY]

lip+oid ('lɪpɔɪd, 'laɪ-) *adj. also* **lip+oi+dal. 1.** resembling fat; fatty. ~*n.* **2.** a fatlike substance, such as wax. **3.** *Biochem.* a former name for **lipid.**

li+pol·y+sis (lɪ'pɒlɪsɪs) *n. Chem.* the hydrolysis of fats resulting in the production of carboxylic acids and glycerol. —**lip·o+lyt+ic** (,lɪpəʊ'lɪtɪk) *adj.*

li+po+ma (lɪ'pəʊmə) *n., pl.* **+mas** *or* **+ma+ta** (-mətə). *Pathol.* a tumour composed of fatty tissue. [C19: New Latin] —**li+pom·a·tous** (lɪ'pɒmətəs) *adj.*

lip·o·phil+ic (ˌlɪpəʊ'fɪlɪk) *or* **lip·o·trop+ic** (ˌlɪpəʊ'trɒpɪk, 'laɪ-) *adj. Chem.* having an affinity for lipids.

lip·o·pro+tein (ˌlɪpəʊ'prəʊti:n, 'laɪ-) *n.* any of a group of proteins to which a lipid molecule is attached.

Lip+pe ('lɪpə) *n.* **1.** a former state of NW Germany: now part of the West German state of North Rhine-Westphalia. **2.** a river in N West Germany, flowing west to the Rhine. Length: about 240 km (150 miles).

-lipped *adj.* having a lip or lips as specified: *tight-lipped.*

Lip+pi (*Italian* 'lippi) *n.* **1. Fi·lip·pi·no** (ˌfilip'pi:no). ?1457–1504, Italian painter of the Florentine school. **2.** his father, **Fra Fi·lip·po** (fra fi'lippo). ?1406–69, Italian painter of the Florentine school, noted particularly for his frescoes at Prato Cathedral (1452–64).

lip+pie ('lɪpɪ) *n. Austral. informal.* lipstick.

Lip+pi·zan+er (ˌlɪpɪt'sɑ:nə) *n.* a breed of riding and carriage horse used by the Spanish Riding School in Vienna and nearly always grey in colour. [German, after *Lippiza,* Yugoslavia, where these horses were bred]

Lipp·mann('lɪpmən; *French* lip'man) *n.* **Ga·bri·el** (gabri'ɛl). 1845–1921, French physicist. He devised the earliest process of colour photography: Nobel prize for physics 1908.

lip+py ('lɪpɪ) *adj.* **+pi+er, +pi+est.** *U.S. slang.* insolent or cheeky.

lip-read ('lɪpˌri:d) *vb.* **-reads, -read·ing, -read** (-'rɛd). to interpret (words) by lip-reading.

lip-read·ing *n.* a method used by the deaf to comprehend spoken words by interpreting movements of the speaker's lips. Also called: **speech-reading.** —**'lip-ˌread·er** *n.*

lip serv+ice *n.* insincere tribute or respect.

lip+stick ('lɪpˌstɪk) *n.* a cosmetic for colouring the lips, usually in the form of a stick.

liq. *abbrev. for:* **1.** liquid. **2.** liquor.

li+quate ('laɪkweɪt) *vb.* (*tr.;* often foll. by *out*) to separate one component of (an alloy, impure metal, or ore) by heating so that the more fusible part melts. [C17: from Latin *liquāre* to dissolve] —**li+'qua·tion** *n.*

liq+ue+fa+cient (ˌlɪkwɪ'feɪʃənt) *n.* **1.** a substance that liquefies or causes liquefaction. ~*adj.* **2.** becoming or causing to become liquid. [C19: from Latin *liquefacere* to make LIQUID]

liq+ue+fied pe·tro+le·um gas *n.* propane or butane liquefied under pressure. See also **bottled gas.**

liq+ue+fy *or* **liq+ui+fy** ('lɪkwɪˌfaɪ) *vb.* **+fies, +fy+ing, +fied.** (esp. of a gas) to become or cause to become liquid. [C15: via Old French from Latin *liquefacere* to make liquid] —**liq+ue+fac+tion** *or* **liq+ui+fac+tion** (ˌlɪkwɪ'fækʃən) *n.* —**ˌliq+ue+'fac+tive** *or* **ˌliq+ui+'fac+tive** *adj.* —**'liq+ue+ˌfi+a·ble** *or* **'liq+ui+ˌfi+a·ble** *adj.* —**'liq+ue+ˌfi+er** *or* **'liq+ui+ˌfi+er** *n.*

li+quesce (lɪ'kwɛs) *vb.* (*intr.*) to become liquid.

li+ques+cent (lɪ'kwɛsᵊnt) *adj.* (of a solid or gas) becoming or tending to become liquid. [C18: from Latin *liquescere*] —**li+'ques+cence** *or* **li+'ques+cen+cy** *n.*

li+queur (lɪ'kjʊə; *French* li'kœ:r) *n.* **1. a.** any of several highly flavoured sweetened spirits such as kirsch or cointreau, intended to be drunk after a meal. **b.** (*as modifier*): *liqueur glass.* **2.** a small hollow chocolate sweet containing liqueur. [C18: from French; see LIQUOR]

liq+uid ('lɪkwɪd) *n.* **1.** a substance in a physical state in which the force of attraction between its molecules or atoms is only sufficient to hold them in a state of aggregation so that the substance can easily change its shape but cannot be expanded or compressed. Compare **gas** (sense 1), **solid** (sense 1). **2.** a substance that is a liquid at room temperature and atmospheric pressure. **3.** *Phonetics.* a frictionless continuant, esp. (l) or (r). ~*adj.* **4.** of, concerned with, or being a liquid or having the characteristic state of liquids: *liquid wax.* **5.** shining, transparent, or brilliant. **6.** flowing, fluent, or smooth. **7.** (of assets) in the form of money or easily convertible into money. [C14: via Old French from Latin *liquidus,* from *liquēre* to be fluid] —**'liq+uid+ly** *adv.*

liq+uid air *n.* air that has been liquefied by cooling. It is a pale blue and consists mainly of liquid oxygen (boiling pt.: -182.9°C) and liquid nitrogen (boiling pt.: -195.7°C): used in the production of pure oxygen, nitrogen, and the inert gases, and as a refrigerant.

liq+uid+am+bar (ˌlɪkwɪd'æmbə) *n.* **1.** any deciduous tree of the hamamelidaceous genus *Liquidambar,* of Asia and North and Central America, with star-shaped leaves, and exuding a yellow aromatic balsam. See also **sweet gum. 2.** the balsam of this tree, used in medicine. See also **storax** (sense 3). [C16: New Latin, from Latin *liquidus* liquid + Medieval Latin *ambar* AMBER]

liq+ui+date ('lɪkwɪˌdeɪt) *vb.* **1. a.** to settle or pay off (a debt, claim, etc.). **b.** to determine by litigation or agreement the amount of (damages, indebtedness, etc.). **2. a.** to terminate the operations of (a commercial firm, bankrupt estate, etc.) by assessment of liabilities and appropriation of assets for their settlement. **b.** (of a commercial firm, etc.) to terminate operations in this manner. **3.** (*tr.*) to convert (assets) into cash. **4.** (*tr.*) to eliminate or kill.

liq+ui+da+tion (ˌlɪkwɪ'deɪʃən) *n.* **1. a.** the process of terminating the affairs of a business firm, etc., by realizing its assets to discharge its liabilities. **b.** the state of a business firm, etc., having its affairs so terminated (esp. in the phrase **to go into liquidation**). **2.** destruction; elimination.

liq+ui+da+tor ('lɪkwɪˌdeɪtə) *n.* a person assigned to supervise the liquidation of a business concern and whose legal authorization, rights, and duties differ according to whether the liquidation is compulsory or voluntary.

liq+uid crys+tal *n.* a liquid that has some crystalline characteristics, such as the presence of different optical properties in different directions; a substance in a mesomorphic state. See also **smectic, nematic.**

liq+uid crys+tal dis+play *n.* a display of numbers, esp. in an electronic calculator, using liquid-crystal cells that change their reflectivity when an electric field is applied to them.

liq+uid fire *n.* inflammable petroleum or other liquid used as a weapon of war in flamethrowers, etc.

liq+uid glass *n.* another name for **water glass.**

li+quid+i·ty (lɪ'kwɪdɪtɪ) *n.* **1.** the possession of sufficient liquid assets to discharge current liabilities. **2.** the state or quality of being liquid.

li+quid+i·ty pref+er+ence *n. Economics.* the Keynesian demand function for holding money, consisting of three component motives: transactions, precaution, and speculation.

li+quid+i·ty ra+ti·o *n.* the ratio of total liquid assets to total deposits, which commercial banks maintain by custom. Also called: **liquid assets ratio.**

liq+uid+ize *or* **liq+uid+ise** ('lɪkwɪˌdaɪz) *vb.* **1.** to make or become liquid; liquefy. **2.** (*tr.*) to pulverize (food) in a liquidizer so as to produce a fluid.

liq+uid+iz+er *or* **liq+uid+is+er** ('lɪkwɪˌdaɪzə) *n.* a kitchen appliance with blades for cutting and puréeing vegetables, blending liquids, etc. Also called: **blender.**

liq+uid meas+ure *n.* a unit or system of units for measuring volumes of liquids or their containers.

liq+uid ox·y+gen *n.* the clear pale blue liquid state of oxygen produced by liquefying air and allowing the nitrogen to evaporate: used in rocket fuels. Also called: **lox.**

liq+uid par+af+fin *n.* a colourless almost tasteless oily liquid obtained by petroleum distillation and used as a laxative. Also called (esp. U.S.): **mineral oil.**

liq+ui+fy ('lɪkwɪˌfaɪ) *vb.* **+fies, +fy+ing, +fied.** a variant spelling of **liquefy.**

liq+uor ('lɪkə) *n.* **1.** any alcoholic drink, esp. spirits, or such drinks collectively. **2.** any liquid substance, esp. that in which food has been cooked. **3.** *Pharmacol.* a solution of a pure substance in water. **4.** *Brewing.* warm water added to malt to form wort. **5. in liquor.** drunk; intoxicated. ~*vb.* **6.** *Brewing.* to steep (malt) in warm water to form wort; mash. [C13: via Old French from Latin, from *liquēre* to be liquid]

liq·uo+rice *or U.S.* **lic·o+rice** ('lɪkərɪs, -ərɪʃ) *n.* **1.** a perennial Mediterranean leguminous shrub, *Glycyrrhiza glabra,* having spikes of pale blue flowers and flat red-brown pods. **2.** the dried root of this plant, used as a laxative and in confectionery. **3.** a sweet having a liquorice flavour. [C13: via Anglo-Norman and Old French from Late Latin *liquirītia,* from Latin *glycyrrhīza,* from Greek *glukurrhiza,* from *glukus* sweet + *rhiza* root]

liq+uor+ish ('lɪkərɪʃ) *adj.* **1.** a variant spelling of **lickerish. 2.** *Brit.* a variant of **liquorice.** —**'liq+uor+ish+ly** *adv.* —**'liq+uor+ish+ness** *n.*

liq+uor up *vb.* (*adv.*) *U.S. slang.* to become or cause to become drunk.

li·ra ('lɪərə; *Italian* 'li:ra) *n., pl.* **li·re** ('lɪərɪ; *Italian* 'li:re) *or* **li·ras. 1.** the standard monetary unit of Italy and San Marino. **2.** Also called: **pound.** the standard monetary unit of Turkey, divided into 100 piastres. [Italian, from Latin *libra* pound]

lir·i·o+den+dron (ˌlɪrɪəʊ'dɛndrən) *n., pl.* **+drons** *or* **+dra** (-drə). either of the two deciduous trees of the magnoliaceous genus *Liriodendron,* the tulip tree of North America or *L. chinense* of China. [C18: New Latin, from Greek *leiron* lily + *dendron* tree]

lir·i·pipe ('lɪrɪˌpaɪp) *or* **lir·i·poop** ('lɪrɪˌpu:p) *n.* the tip of a graduate's hood. [C14: Medieval Latin *liripipium,* origin obscure]

Lis+bon ('lɪzbən) *n.* the capital and chief port of Portugal, in the southwest on the Tagus estuary: became capital in 1256; subject to earthquakes and severely damaged in 1755; university (1911). Pop.: 774 500 (1974 est.). Portuguese name: **Lis+bo·a** (liʒ'boə).

Li+sieux (*French* li'zjø) *n.* a town in NW France: Roman Catholic pilgrimage centre, for its shrine of St. Thérèse, who lived there. Pop.: 26 674 (1975).

lisle (laɪl) *n.* **a.** a strong fine cotton thread or fabric. **b.** (*as modifier*): *lisle stockings.* [C19: named after *Lisle* (now Lille), town in France where this type of thread was originally manufactured]

lisp (lɪsp) *n.* **1.** the articulation of *s* and *z* like or nearly like the *th* sounds in English *thin* and *then* respectively. **2.** the habit or speech defect of pronouncing *s* and *z* in this manner. **3.** the sound of a lisp in pronunciation. ~*vb.* **4.** to use a lisp in the pronunciation of (speech). **5.** to speak or pronounce imperfectly or haltingly. [Old English *āwlispian,* from *wlisp* lisping (adj.), of imitative origin; related to Old High German *lispen*] —**'lisp+er** *n.* —**'lisp+ing+ly** *adv.*

lis pen+dens (lɪs 'pɛndɛnz) *n.* **1.** a suit pending in a court that concerns the title to land. **2.** a notice filed to warn interested persons of such a suit. [Latin: pending lawsuit]

Lis+sa+jous fig+ure ('li:səˌʒu:, ˌli:sə'ʒu:) *n.* a curve traced out by a point that undergoes two simple harmonic motions in mutually perpendicular directions. The shape of these curves is characteristic of the relative phases and frequencies of the motion; they are used to determine the frequencies and phases of alternating voltages. [C19: named after Jules A. *Lissajous* (1822–80), French physicist]

lis+som *or* **lis+some** ('lɪsəm) *adj.* **1.** supple in the limbs or body; lithe; flexible. **2.** agile; nimble. [C19: variant of LITHESOME] —**'lis+som+ly** *or* **'lis+some+ly** *adv.* —**'lis+som+ness** *or* **'lis+some+ness** *n.*

list[1] (lɪst) *n.* **1.** an item-by-item record of names or things, usually written or printed one under the other. **2. be on the danger list.** *Informal.* to be in a critical medical or physical condition. ~*vb.* **3.** (*tr.*) to make a list of. **4.** (*tr.*) to include in a list. **5.** (*tr.*) *Stock Exchange.* to obtain an official quotation for (a security) so that it may be traded on the recognized market. **6.** an archaic word for **enlist.** [C17: from French, ultimately related to LIST[2]; compare Italian *lista* list of names (earlier: border, strip, as of paper), Old High German *līsta* border] —**'list+a·ble** *adj.*

list[2] (lɪst) *n.* **1.** a border or edging strip, esp. of cloth. **2.** a less common word for **selvage. 3.** a strip of bark, sapwood, etc., trimmed from a board or plank. **4.** another word for **fillet** (sense 4). **5.** a strip, band, ridge or furrow. **6.** *Agriculture.* a ridge in ploughed land formed by throwing two furrows together. ~*vb.* (*tr.*) **7.** to border with or as if with a list or lists. **8.** *Agriculture.* to plough (land) so as to form lists. **9.** to cut a list from (a board, plank, etc.). [Old English *līst*; related to Old High German *līsta*]

list[3] (lɪst) *vb.* **1.** (esp. of ships) to lean over or cause to lean over to one side. ~*n.* **2.** the act or an instance of leaning to one side. [C17: origin unknown]

list[4] (lɪst) *Archaic.* ~*vb.* **1.** to be pleasing to (a person). **2.** (*tr.*) to desire or choose. ~*n.* **3.** a liking or desire. [Old English *lystan*; related to Old High German *lusten* and Gothic *lūston* to desire]

list[5] (lɪst) *vb.* an archaic or poetic word for **listen.** [Old English *hlystan*; related to Old Norse *hlusta*]

list+ed build+ing *n.* (in Britain) a building officially recognized as having special historical or architectural interest and therefore protected from demolition or alteration.

lis+tel ('lɪstᵊl) *n.* another name for **fillet** (sense 6). [C16: via French from Italian *listello*, diminutive of *lista* band, LIST[2]]

lis+ten ('lɪsᵊn) *vb.* (*intr.*) **1.** to concentrate on hearing something. **2.** to take heed; pay attention: *I told you many times but you wouldn't listen.* [Old English *hlysnan*; related to Old High German *lūstrēn*] —**'lis+ten+er** *n.*

lis+ten in *vb.* (*intr., adv.*; often foll. by *to*) **1.** to listen to the radio. **2.** to intercept radio communications. **3.** to listen but not contribute (to a discussion), esp. surreptitiously.

lis+ten+ing post *n.* **1.** *Military.* a forward position set up to obtain early warning of enemy movement. **2.** any strategic position or place for obtaining information about another country or area.

lis+ter ('lɪstə) *n. U.S., agriculture.* a plough with a double mouldboard designed to throw soil to either side of a central furrow. Also called: **lister plough, middlebreaker, middle buster.** [C19: from LIST[2]]

Lis·ter ('lɪstə) *n.* **Jo·seph,** 1st Baron Lister. 1827–1912, English surgeon, who introduced the use of antiseptics.

Lis+ter+ism ('lɪstəˌrɪzəm) *n. Surgery.* the use of or theory of using antiseptic techniques.

list+ing ('lɪstɪŋ) *n.* a list or an entry in a list.

list+less ('lɪstlɪs) *adj.* lacking vigour or energy. [C15: from *list* desire + -LESS] —**'list+less+ly** *adv.* —**'list+less+ness** *n.*

list price *n.* the selling price of merchandise as quoted in a catalogue or advertisement.

lists (lɪsts) *pl. n.* **1.** *History.* **a.** the enclosed field of combat at a tournament. **b.** the barriers enclosing the field at a tournament. **2.** any arena or scene of conflict, controversy, etc. **3. enter the lists.** to engage in a conflict, controversy, etc. [C14: plural of LIST[2] (border, boundary)]

Liszt (lɪst) *n.* **Franz** (frants). 1811–86, Hungarian composer and pianist. The greatest piano virtuoso of the 19th century, he originated the symphonic poem, pioneered the one-movement sonata form, and developed new harmonic combinations. His works include the symphonies *Faust* (1861) and *Dante* (1867), piano compositions and transcriptions, songs, and church music.

lit[1] (lɪt) *vb.* **1.** a past tense or past participle of **light**[1]. **2.** an alternative past tense or past participle of **light**[2].

lit[2] (lɪt) *or* **li+tas** ('li:tɑ:s) *n., pl.* **lits, li+tai** ('li:teɪ), *or* **li·tu** ('li:tu:). the monetary unit of Lithuania before 1940.

lit. *abbrev. for:* **1.** literal(ly). **2.** literary. **3.** literature.

Li T'ai-po ('li: 'taɪ 'pəʊ) *n.* See **Li Po.**

lit·a·ny ('lɪtənɪ) *n., pl.* **+nies. 1.** *Christianity.* **a.** a form of prayer consisting of a series of invocations, each followed by an unvarying response. **b. the Litany.** the general supplication in this form included in the Book of Common Prayer. **2.** any long or tedious speech or recital. [C13: via Old French from Medieval Latin *litania*, from Late Greek *litaneia* prayer, ultimately from Greek *litē* entreaty]

li+tchi, li+chee, li+chi, *or* **ly+chee** (ˌlaɪ'tʃi:) *n.* **1.** a Chinese sapindaceous tree, *Litchi chinensis*, cultivated for its round edible fruits. **2.** the fruit of this tree, which has whitish juicy pulp and is usually eaten dried or as a preserve. **3. litchi nut.** the dried fruit of this tree. [C16: from Cantonese *lai chi*]

-lite *n. combining form.* (in names of minerals) stone: *chrysolite.* Compare **-lith.** [from French *-lite* or *-lithe*, from Greek *lithos* stone]

li+ter ('li:tə) *n.* the U.S. spelling of **litre.**

lit+er·a+cy ('lɪtərəsɪ) *n.* **1.** the ability to read and write. **2.** the ability to use language proficiently.

lit+e·rae hu·ma·ni·o·res ('lɪtəˌri: hju:ˌmænɪ'ɔ:ri:z) *n.* (at Oxford University) the faculty concerned with Greek and Latin literature, ancient history, and philosophy; classics. [Latin, literally: the more humane letters]

lit+er+al ('lɪtərəl) *adj.* **1.** in exact accordance with or limited to the primary or explicit meaning of a word or text. **2.** word for word. **3.** dull, factual, or prosaic. **4.** consisting of, concerning, or indicated by letters. **5.** true; actual. **6.** *Maths.* containing or using coefficients and constants represented by letters: *$ax^2 + b$ is a literal expression.* Compare **numerical** (sense 3a.). ~*n.* **7.** Also called: **literal error.** a misprint or misspelling in a text. [C14: from Late Latin *litterālis* concerning letters, from Latin *littera* LETTER] —**'lit+er+al+ness** *or* **lit+er+al+i·ty** (ˌlɪtə'rælɪtɪ) *n.*

lit+er+al+ism ('lɪtərəˌlɪzəm) *n.* **1.** the disposition to take words and statements in their literal sense. **2.** literal or realistic portrayal in art or literature. —**'lit+er+al+ist** *n.* —**ˌlit+er+al+'is+tic** *adj.* —**ˌlit+er+al+'is+ti+cal+ly** *adv.*

lit+er+al+ly ('lɪtərəlɪ) *adv.* **1.** in a literal manner. **2.** (intensifier): *there were literally thousands of people.*

lit+er+ar·y ('lɪtərərɪ, 'lɪtrərɪ) *adj.* **1.** of, relating to, concerned with, or characteristic of literature or scholarly writing: *a literary discussion; a literary style.* **2.** versed in or knowledgeable about literature: *a literary man.* **3.** (of a word) formal; not colloquial. [C17: from Latin *litterārius* concerning reading and writing. See LETTER] —**'lit+er+ar·i+ly** *adv.* —**'lit+er+ar·i+ness** *n.*

lit+er+ar·y a·gent *n.* a person who manages the business affairs of an author. —**lit+er+ar·y a·gen+cy** *n.*

lit+er+ate ('lɪtərɪt) *adj.* **1.** able to read and write. **2.** educated; learned. **3.** used to words rather than numbers as a means of expression. Compare **numerate.** ~*n.* **4.** a literate person. [C15: from Latin *litterātus* learned. See LETTER] —**'lit+er+ate+ly** *adv.*

lit+e·ra+ti (ˌlɪtə'rɑ:ti:) *pl. n.* literary or scholarly people. [C17: from Latin]

lit+e·ra+tim (ˌlɪtə'rɑ:tɪm) *adv.* letter for letter. [C17: from Medieval Latin, from Latin *littera* LETTER]

lit+er·a+tion (ˌlɪtə'reɪʃən) *n.* the use of letters to represent sounds or words.

lit+er·a+tor ('lɪtəˌreɪtə) *n.* another word for **littérateur.** [C18: from Latin, from *littera* letter]

lit+er·a+ture ('lɪtərɪtʃə, 'lɪtrɪ-) *n.* **1.** written material such as poetry, novels, essays, etc. **2.** the body of written work of a particular culture or people: *Scandinavian literature.* **3.** written or printed matter of a particular type or genre: *scientific literature; the literature of the violin.* **4.** the art or profession of a writer. **5.** *Obsolete.* learning. [C14: from Latin *litterātūra* writing; see LETTER]

lith. *abbrev. for:* **1.** lithograph. **2.** lithography.

Lith. *abbrev. for* Lithuania(n).

-lith *n. combining form.* indicating stone or rock: *megalith.* Compare **-lite.** [from Greek *lithos* stone]

lith+arge ('lɪθɑ:dʒ) *n.* another name for **lead monoxide.** [C14: via Old French from Latin *lithargyrus*, from Greek, from *lithos* stone + *arguros* silver]

lithe (laɪð) *adj.* flexible or supple. [Old English (in the sense: gentle; C15: supple); related to Old High German *lindi* soft, Latin *lentus* slow] —**'lithe+ly** *adv.* —**'lithe+ness** *n.*

lithe+some ('laɪðsəm) *adj.* a less common word for **lissom.**

lith·i·a ('lɪθɪə) *n.* **1.** another name for **lithium oxide. 2.** lithium present in mineral waters as lithium salts. [C19: New Latin, ultimately from Greek *lithos* stone]

li+thi·a+sis (lɪ'θaɪəsɪs) *n. Pathol.* the formation of a calculus. [C17: New Latin; see LITHO-, -IASIS]

lith·i·a wa+ter *n.* a natural or artificial mineral water that contains lithium salts.

lith+ic ('lɪθɪk) *adj.* **1.** of, relating to, or composed of stone: *a lithic sandstone.* **2.** *Pathol.* of or relating to a calculus or calculi, esp. one in the urinary bladder. **3.** of or containing lithium. [C18: from Greek *lithikos* stony]

-lith·ic *adj. combining form.* (in anthropology) relating to the use of stone implements in a specified cultural period: *Neolithic.* [from Greek *lithikos*, from *lithos* stone]

lith+i·um ('lɪθɪəm) *n.* a soft silvery element of the alkali metal series: the lightest known metal, used as an alloy hardener, as a reducing agent, and in batteries. Symbol: Li; atomic no.: 3; atomic wt.: 6.941; valency: 1; relative density: 0.534; melting pt.: 179°C; boiling pt.: 1317°C. [C19: New Latin, from LITHO- + -IUM]

lith+i·um ox+ide *n.* a white crystalline compound. It absorbs carbon dioxide and water vapour.

li+tho ('laɪθəʊ) *n., pl.* **+thos,** *adj., adv.* short for **lithography, lithograph, lithographic,** or **lithographically.**

litho. *or* **lithog.** *abbrev. for:* **1.** lithograph. **2.** lithography.

lith·o- *or before a vowel* **lith-** *combining form.* stone: *lithograph.* [from Latin, from Greek, from *lithos* stone]

lith·o+graph ('lɪθəˌgrɑ:f) *n.* **1.** a print made by lithography. ~*vb.* **2.** (*tr.*) to reproduce (pictures, text, etc.) by lithography. —**lith·o+graph+ic** (ˌlɪθə'græfɪk) *or* **ˌlith·o+'graph·i·cal** *adj.* —**ˌlith·o+'graph·i+cal+ly** *adv.*

li+thog+ra+phy (lɪ'θɒgrəfɪ) *n.* a method of printing from a metal or stone surface on which the printing areas are not raised but made ink-receptive as opposed to ink-repellent. [C18: from New Latin *lithographia, from* LITHO- + -GRAPHY] —**li+'thog+ra+pher** *n.*

lith+oid ('lɪθɔɪd) *or* **li+thoi+dal** (lɪ'θɔɪdᵊl) *adj.* resembling stone or rock. [C19: from Greek *lithoeidēs*, from *lithos* stone]

lithol. *abbrev. for* lithology.

li+thol·o·gy (lɪ'θɒlədʒɪ) *n.* **1.** the physical characteristics of a rock, including colour, composition, and texture. **2.** the study of rocks. —**lith·o·log·ic** (ˌlɪθəˈlɒdʒɪk) *or* **ˌlith·o·ˈlog·i·cal** *adj.* —**ˌlith·o·ˈlog·i·cal·ly** *adv.* —**li·ˈthol·o·gist** *n.*

lith·o·marge (ˈlɪθəˌmɑːdʒ) *n.* a smooth compact type of kaolin: white or reddish and often mottled. [C18: from New Latin *lithomarga* from LITHO- + Latin *marga* marl]

lith·o·me·te·or (ˌlɪθəˈmiːtɪə) *n.* a mass of solid particles, such as dust, sand, etc., suspended in the atmosphere.

lith·o·phyte (ˈlɪθəˌfaɪt) *n.* **1.** a plant that grows on rocky or stony ground. **2.** an organism, such as a coral, that is partly composed of stony material. —**lith·o·phyt·ic** (ˌlɪθəˈfɪtɪk) *adj.*

lith·o·pone (ˈlɪθəˌpəʊn) *n.* a white pigment consisting of a mixture of zinc sulphide, zinc oxide, and barium sulphate. [C20: from LITHO- + Greek *ponos* work]

lith·o·sol (ˈlɪθəˌsɒl) *n. Chiefly U.S.* a type of azonal soil consisting chiefly of unweathered or partly weathered rock fragments, usually found on steep slopes. [C20: from LITHO- + Latin *solum* soil]

lith·o·sphere (ˈlɪθəˌsfɪə) *n.* **1.** the rigid outer layer of the earth's crust, consisting of rocks and superficial deposits of soil, drift, etc. See also **asthenosphere. 2.** the earth's crust.

li·thot·o·my (lɪˈθɒtəmɪ) *n., pl.* **·mies.** the surgical removal of a calculus, esp. one in the urinary bladder. [C18: via Late Latin from Greek, from LITHO- + -TOMY] —**lith·o·tom·ic** (ˌlɪθəˈtɒmɪk) *or* **ˌlith·o·ˈtom·i·cal** *adj.* —**li·ˈthot·o·mist** *n.*

li·thot·ri·ty (lɪˈθɒtrɪtɪ) *n., pl.* **·ties.** *Surgery.* the crushing of a calculus in the bladder so that it can be expelled by urinating. [C19: from LITHO- + Latin *trītus,* from *terere* to crush]

Lith·u·a·ni·an (ˌlɪθjuˈeɪnɪən) *adj.* **1.** of, relating to, or characteristic of Lithuania, its people, or their language. ~*n.* **2.** an official language of the Lithuanian SSR, along with Russian: belonging to the Baltic branch of the Indo-European family. **3.** a native or inhabitant of Lithuania.

Lith·u·a·ni·an So·vi·et So·cial·ist Re·pub·lic *n.* an administrative division of the W Soviet Union, on the Baltic Sea: a grand duchy in medieval times. Capital: Vilnius. Pop.: 3 128 236 (1970). Area: 65 200 sq. km (25 174 sq. miles). Also called: **Lithuania.** Lithuanian name: **Lietuva.**

lit·i·ga·ble (ˈlɪtɪgəbᵊl) *adj. Law.* that may be the subject of litigation.

lit·i·gant (ˈlɪtɪgənt) *n.* **1.** a party to a lawsuit. ~*adj.* **2.** engaged in litigation.

lit·i·gate (ˈlɪtɪˌgeɪt) *vb.* **1.** to bring or contest (a claim, action, etc.) in a lawsuit. **2.** (*intr.*) to engage in legal proceedings. [C17: from Latin *lītigāre,* from *līt-,* stem of *līs* lawsuit + *agere* to carry on] —**ˈlit·iˌga·tor** *n.*

lit·i·ga·tion (ˌlɪtɪˈgeɪʃən) *n.* **1.** the act or process of bringing or contesting a lawsuit. **2.** a judicial proceeding or contest.

li·ti·gious (lɪˈtɪdʒəs) *adj.* **1.** excessively ready to go to law. **2.** of or relating to litigation. **3.** inclined to dispute or disagree. [C14: from Latin *lītigiōsus* quarrelsome, from *lītigium* strife] —**li·ˈti·gious·ly** *adv.* —**li·ˈti·gious·ness** *n.*

lit·mus (ˈlɪtməs) *n.* a soluble powder obtained from certain lichens. It turns red under acid conditions and blue under basic conditions and is used as an indicator. [C16: perhaps from Scandinavian; compare Old Norse *litmosi,* from *litr* dye + *mosi* moss]

li·to·tes (ˈlaɪtəʊˌtiːz) *n., pl.* **·tes.** understatement for rhetorical effect, esp. when achieved by using negation with a term in place of using an antonym of that term, as in "She was not a little upset" for "She was extremely upset". [C17: from Greek, from *litos* small]

li·tre *or U.S.* **li·ter** (ˈliːtə) *n.* **1.** one cubic decimetre. **2.** formerly, the volume occupied by 1 kilogram of pure water at 4°C and 760 millimetres of mercury. This is equivalent to 1.000 028 cubic decimetres or about 1.76 pints. [C19: from French, from Medieval Latin *litra,* from Greek: a unit of weight]

Litt.B. *or* **Lit.B.** *abbrev. for* Bachelor of Letters *or* Bachelor of Literature. [Latin: *Litterarum Baccalaureus*]

Litt.D. *or* **Lit.D.** *abbrev. for* Doctor of Letters *or* Doctor of Literature. [Latin: *Litterarum Doctor*]

lit·ter (ˈlɪtə) *n.* **1. a.** small refuse or waste materials carelessly dropped, esp. in public places. **b.** (*as modifier*): *litter bin.* **2.** a disordered or untidy condition or a collection of objects in this condition. **3.** a group of offspring produced at one birth by a mammal such as a sow. **4.** a layer of partly decomposed leaves, twigs, etc., on the ground in a wood or forest. **5.** straw, hay, or similar material used as bedding, protection, etc., by animals or plants. **6.** a means of conveying people, esp. sick or wounded people, consisting of a light bed or seat held between parallel sticks. ~*vb.* **7.** to make (a place) untidy by strewing (refuse). **8.** to scatter (objects, etc.) about or (of objects) to lie around or upon (anything) in an untidy fashion. **9.** (of pigs, cats, etc.) to give birth to (offspring). **10.** (*tr.*) to provide (an animal or plant) with straw or hay for bedding, protection, etc. [C13 (in the sense: bed): via Anglo-French, ultimately from Latin *lectus* bed]

lit·té·ra·teur (ˌlɪtərəˈtɜː; *French* literaˈtœːr) *n.* an author, esp. a professional writer. [C19: from French from Latin *litterātor* a grammarian]

lit·ter lout *or U.S.* **lit·ter·bug** (ˈlɪtəˌbʌg) *n. Slang.* a person who tends to drop refuse in public places.

lit·tle (ˈlɪtᵊl) *determiner.* **1.** (often preceded by *a*) **a.** a small quantity, extent, or duration of: *the little hope there is left; very little milk.* **b.** (*as pronoun*): *save a little for me.* **2.** not much: *little damage was done.* **3. make little of.** to regard or treat as insignificant; dismiss. **4. not a little. a.** very. **b.** a lot. **5. quite a little.** a considerable amount. **6. think little of.** to have a low opinion of. ~*adj.* **7.** of small or less than average size. **8.** young: *a little boy; our little ones.* **9.** endearingly familiar; dear: *my husband's little ways.* **10.** contemptible, mean, or disagreeable: *your filthy little mind.* **11.** (of a region or district) resembling another country or town in miniature: *little Venice.* **12. little game.** a person's secret intention or business: *so that's his little game!* **13. no little.** considerable. ~*adv.* **14.** (usually preceded by *a*) in a small amount; to a small extent or degree; not a lot: *to laugh a little.* **15.** (*used preceding a verb*) not at all, or hardly: *he little realized his fate.* **16.** not much or often: *we go there very little now.* **17. little by little.** by small degrees. ~See also **less, lesser, least, littler, littlest.** [Old English *lȳtel;* related to *lȳr* few, Old High German *luzzil*]

Lit·tle A·mer·i·ca *n.* the chief U.S. base in the Antarctic, on the Ross Ice Shelf: first established by Richard Byrd (1928); used for polar exploration.

Lit·tle Bear *n.* **the.** the English name for **Ursa Minor.**

Lit·tle Belt *n.* a strait in Denmark, between Jutland and Fyn Island, linking the Kattegat with the Baltic. Length: about 48 km (30 miles). Width: up to 29 km (18 miles). Danish name: **Lille Bælt.**

Lit·tle Big·horn *n.* a river in the W central U.S., rising in N Wyoming and flowing north to the Bighorn River. Its banks were the scene of the defeat (1876) and killing of General Custer and his command by Indians.

Lit·tle Cor·po·ral *n.* **the.** a nickname of Napoleon Bonaparte.

Lit·tle Di·o·mede *n.* the smaller of the two Diomede Islands in the Bering Strait: administered by the U.S. Area: about 10 sq. km (4 sq. miles).

Lit·tle Dip·per *n.* **the.** a U.S. name for **Ursa Minor.**

Lit·tle Dog *n.* **the.** the English name for **Canis Minor.**

lit·tle end *n.* **1.** *Brit.* the smaller end of a connecting rod in an internal-combustion engine or reciprocating pump. Compare: **big end. 2.** *Brit.* the bearing surface between the smaller end of a connecting rod and the gudgeon pin.

lit·tle grebe *n.* a small brownish European diving bird, *Podiceps ruficollis,* frequenting lakes, family *Podicipitidae* (grebes).

lit·tle hours *pl. n. R.C. Church.* the canonical hours of prime, terce, sext, and nones in the divine office.

Lit·tle John *n.* one of Robin Hood's companions, noted for his great size and strength.

lit·tle mag·a·zine *n.* a literary magazine that features experimental or other writing of interest to a limited number of readers.

lit·tle man *n.* **1.** a man of no importance or significance. **2.** *Brit.* a tradesman or artisan operating on a small scale.

lit·tle of·fice *n. R.C. Church.* a series of psalms and prayers similar to the divine office but shorter.

lit·tle owl *n.* a small Old World owl, *Athene noctua,* having a speckled brown plumage and flattish head.

lit·tle peo·ple *or* **folk** *pl. n. Folklore.* small supernatural beings, such as elves, pixies, or leprechauns.

lit·tler (ˈlɪtlə) *determiner. Not standard.* the comparative of **little.**

Lit·tle Rock *n.* a city in central Arkansas, on the Arkansas River: state capital. Pop.: 142 065 (1973 est.).

Lit·tle Rus·sia *n.* a region of the SW Soviet Union, consisting chiefly of the Ukrainian SSR.

Lit·tle Rus·sian *n., adj.* a former word for **Ukrainian.**

lit·tle slam *n. Bridge, etc.* the winning of all tricks except one by one side, or the contract to do so. Also called: **small slam.**

lit·tlest (ˈlɪtlɪst) *determiner. Not standard.* the superlative of **little.**

Lit·tle St. Ber·nard Pass *n.* a pass over the Savoy Alps, between Bourg-Saint-Maurice, France, and La Thuile, Italy: 11th-century hospice. Height: 2187 m (7177 ft.).

lit·tle the·a·tre *n. Theatre, chiefly U.S.* experimental or avant-garde drama originating from a theatrical movement of the 1920s.

lit·tle wom·an *n.* **the.** *Brit., old fashioned.* a facetious term for **wife.**

lit·to·ral (ˈlɪtərəl) *adj.* **1.** of or relating to the shore of a sea, lake, or ocean. **2.** *Biology.* inhabiting the shore of a sea or lake or the shallow waters near the shore: *littoral fauna.* ~*n.* **3.** a coastal or shore region. [C17: from Late Latin *littorālis,* from *lītorālis,* from *lītus* shore]

Lit·to·ria (*Italian* litˈtɔːrja) *n.* the former name (until 1947) of **Latina.**

lit up *adj. Slang.* drunk.

li·tur·gi·cal (lɪˈtɜːdʒɪkᵊl) *or* **li·tur·gic** *adj.* **1.** of or relating to public worship. **2.** of or relating to the liturgy. —**li·ˈtur·gi·cal·ly** *adv.*

li·tur·gics (lɪˈtɜːdʒɪks) *n.* (*functioning as sing.*) the study of liturgies. Also called: **li·tur·gi·ol·o·gy** (lɪˌtɜːdʒɪˈɒlədʒɪ).

lit·ur·gist (ˈlɪtədʒɪst) *n.* a student or composer of liturgical forms. —**ˈlit·ur·gism** *n.* —**ˌlit·ur·ˈgis·tic** *adj.*

lit·ur·gy (ˈlɪtədʒɪ) *n., pl.* **·gies. 1.** the forms of public services officially prescribed by a Church. **2.** (*often cap.*) Also called: **Divine Liturgy.** *Chiefly Eastern Churches.* the Eucharistic celebration. **3.** a particular order or form of public service laid down by a Church. [C16: via Medieval Latin, from Greek *leitourgia,* from *leitourgos* minister, from *leit-* people + *ergon* work]

Liu Shao-ch'i (ˈljuː ˈʃaʊˈtʃiː) *n.* 1898–1974, Chinese Communist statesman; chairman of the People's Republic of China (1959–68); deposed during the Cultural Revolution.

liv·a·ble *or* **live·a·ble** (ˈlɪvəbᵊl) *adj.* **1.** (of a room, house, etc.) suitable for living in. **2.** worth living; tolerable. **3.** (foll. by *with*) pleasant to live (with). —**ˈliv·a·ble·ness, ˈlive·a·ble·ness** *or* **ˌliv·a·ˈbil·i·ty, ˌlive·a·ˈbil·i·ty** *n.*

live[1] (lɪv) *vb.* (*mainly intr.*). **1.** to show the characteristics of life; be alive. **2.** to remain alive or in existence. **3.** to exist in a specified way: *to live poorly.* **4.** (usually foll. by *in* or *at*) to reside or dwell: *to live in London.* **5.** (often foll. by *on*) to continue or last: *the pain still lives in her memory.* **6.** (usually foll. by *by*) to order one's life (according to a certain philosophy, religion, etc.). **7.** (foll. by *on, upon,* or *by*) to support one's style of life; subsist: *to live by writing.* **8.** (foll. by *with*) to endure the effects (of a crime, mistake, etc.). **9.** (foll. by *through*) to experience and survive: *he lived through the war.* **10.** (*tr.*) to pass or spend (one's life, etc.). **11.** to enjoy life to the full: *he knows how to live.* **12.** (*tr.*) to put into practice in one's daily life; express: *he lives religion every day.* **13. live and let live.** to refrain from interfering in others' lives; to be tolerant. **14. where one lives.** *U.S. informal.* in one's sensitive or defenceless position. [Old English *libban, lifian;* related to Old High German *libēn,* Old Norse *lifa*] ~See also **live down, live in, live together, live up.**

live[2] (laɪv) *adj.* **1.** (*prenominal*) showing the characteristics of life. **2.** (*usually prenominal*) of, relating to, or abounding in life: *the live weight of an animal.* **3.** (*usually prenominal*) of current interest; controversial: *a live issue.* **4.** actual: *a real live cowboy.* **5.** *Informal.* full of life and energy. **6.** (of a coal, ember, etc.) glowing or burning. **7.** (esp. of a volcano) not extinct. **8.** loaded or capable of exploding: *a live bomb.* **9.** *Radio, television, etc.* transmitted or present at the time of performance, rather than being a recording: *a live show.* **10.** connected to a source of electric power: *a live circuit.* **11.** (esp. of a colour or tone) brilliant or splendid. **12.** *Sport.* (of a ball) in play. **13.** (of rocks, ores, etc.) not quarried or mined; native. **14.** being in a state of motion or transmitting power; positively connected to a driving member. **15.** *Printing.* **a.** (of copy) not yet having been set into type. **b.** (of type that has been set) still in use. [C16: from *on live* ALIVE]

live-bear·er *n.* a fish, esp. a cyprinodont, that gives birth to living young.

live cen·tre (laɪv) *n.* a conically pointed rod mounted in the headstock of a lathe that locates and turns with the workpiece. Compare **dead centre** (sense 2).

-lived (-lɪvd) *adj.* having or having had a life as specified: *short-lived.*

live down (lɪv) *vb.* (*tr., adv.*) to withstand the effects of (a crime, mistake, etc.) by waiting until others forget or forgive it.

live in *or* **out** (lɪv) *vb.* (*intr., adv.*) (of an employee) to dwell at (or away from) one's place of employment.

live·li·hood ('laɪvlɪˌhʊd) *n.* occupation or employment.

live load (laɪv) *n.* a variable weight on a structure, such as moving traffic on a bridge. Also called: **superload.** Compare **dead load.**

live·long ('lɪvˌlɒŋ) *adj. Chiefly poetic.* **1.** (of time) long or seemingly long, esp. in a tedious way (esp. in the phrase **all the livelong day**). **2.** whole; entire. ~*n.* **3.** *Brit.* another name for **orpine.**

live·ly ('laɪvlɪ) *adj.* **·li·er, ·li·est. 1.** full of life or vigour. **2.** vivacious or animated, esp. when in company. **3.** busy; eventful. **4.** characterized by mental or emotional intensity; vivid. **5.** having a striking effect on the mind or senses. **6.** refreshing or invigorating: *a lively breeze.* **7.** springy or bouncy or encouraging springiness: *a lively ball.* **8.** (of a boat or ship) readily responsive to the helm. ~*adv. also* **'live·li·ly. 9.** in a brisk or lively manner: *step lively.* **10. look lively.** (*interj.*) make haste. —**'live·li·ness** *n.*

liv·en ('laɪvᵊn) *vb.* (usually foll. by *up*) to make or become lively; enliven. —**'liv·en·er** *n.*

live oak (laɪv) *n.* a hard-wooded evergreen oak, *Quercus virginianus,* of S North America: used for shipbuilding.

liv·er[1] ('lɪvə) *n.* **1.** a multilobed highly vascular reddish-brown glandular organ occupying most of the upper right part of the human abdominal cavity immediately below the diaphragm. It secretes bile, stores glycogen, and detoxifies certain poisons. Related adj.: **hepatic. 2.** the corresponding organ in animals. **3.** the liver of certain animals used as food. **4.** a reddish-brown colour, sometimes with a greyish tinge. [Old English *lifer;* related to Old High German *lebrav,* Old Norse *lefr,* Greek *liparos* fat] —**'liv·er·less** *adj.*

liv·er[2] ('lɪvə) *n.* a person who lives in a specified way: *a fast liver.*

liv·er ex·tract *n.* an extract of raw mammalian liver containing a high concentration of vitamin B_{12}: sometimes used to treat pernicious anaemia.

liv·er fluke *n.* any of various parasitic flatworms, esp. *Fasciola hepatica,* that inhabit the bile ducts of sheep, cattle, etc., and have a complex life cycle: class *Digenea.* See also **trematode.**

liv·er·ied ('lɪvərɪd) *adj.* (esp. of servants or footmen) wearing livery.

liv·er·ish ('lɪvərɪʃ) *adj.* **1.** *Informal.* having a disorder of the liver. **2.** disagreeable; peevish. —**'liv·er·ish·ness** *n.*

liv·er of sul·phur *n.* a mixture of potassium sulphides used as a fungicide and insecticide and in the treatment of skin diseases.

Liv·er·pool[1] ('lɪvəˌpu:l) *n.* a city in NW England, administrative centre of Merseyside, on the Mersey estuary: second largest seaport in Great Britain; developed chiefly in the 17th century with the industrialization of S Lancashire; university (1881). Pop.: 606 834 (1971).

Liv·er·pool[2] ('lɪvəˌpu:l) *n.* **Rob·ert Banks Jen·kin·son,** 2nd Earl of Liverpool. 1770–1828, British Tory statesman; prime minister (1812–27). His government was noted for its repressive policies until about 1822, when more liberal measures were introduced by such men as Peel and Canning.

Liv·er·pud·li·an (ˌlɪvə'pʌdlɪən) *n.* **1.** a native or inhabitant of Liverpool. ~*adj.* **2.** of or relating to Liverpool. [C19: from LIVERPOOL, with humorous alteration of *pool* to *puddle*]

liv·er salts *pl. n.* a preparation of mineral salts used to treat indigestion.

liv·er sau·sage *or esp. U.S.* **liv·er·wurst** ('lɪvəˌwɜ:st) *n.* a sausage made of or containing liver.

liv·er·wort ('lɪvəˌwɜ:t) *n.* any bryophyte plant of the class *Hepaticae,* growing in wet places and resembling green seaweeds or leafy mosses. See also **scale moss.** [late Old English *liferwyrt*]

liv·er·y[1] ('lɪvərɪ) *n., pl.* **·er·ies. 1.** the identifying uniform, badge, etc., of a member of a guild or one of the servants of a feudal lord. **2.** a uniform worn by some menservants and chauffeurs. **3.** an individual or group that wears such a uniform. **4.** distinctive dress or outward appearance. **5. a.** the stabling, keeping, or hiring out of horses for money. **b.** (*as modifier*): *a livery horse.* **6. at livery.** being kept in a livery stable. **7.** *Legal history.* an ancient method of conveying freehold land. [C14: via Anglo-French from Old French *livrée* allocation, from *livrer* to hand over, from Latin *līberāre* to set free]

liv·er·y[2] ('lɪvərɪ) *adj.* **1.** of or resembling liver. **2.** another word for **liverish.**

liv·er·y com·pa·ny *n. Brit.* one of the chartered companies of the City of London originating from the craft guilds.

liv·er·y·man ('lɪvərɪmən) *n., pl.* **·men. 1.** *Brit.* a member of a livery company. **2.** a worker in a livery stable.

liv·er·y sta·ble *n.* a stable where horses are accommodated and from which they may be hired out.

lives (laɪvz) *n.* the plural of **life.**

live steam (laɪv) *n.* steam supplied directly from a boiler at full pressure, before it has performed any work.

live·stock ('laɪvˌstɒk) *n.* (*functioning as sing. or pl.*) cattle, horses, poultry, and similar animals kept for domestic use but not as pets, esp. on a farm or ranch.

live to·geth·er (lɪv) *vb.* (*intr., adv.*) (esp. of an unmarried couple) to dwell in the same house or flat; cohabit. Also: **live with.**

live trap (laɪv) *n.* **1.** a box constructed to trap an animal without injuring it. ~*vb.* **live·trap, ·traps, ·trap·ping, ·trapped. 2.** (*tr.*) to catch (an animal) in such a box.

live up (lɪv) *vb.* **1.** (*intr., adv.;* foll. by *to*) to fulfil (an expectation, obligation, principle, etc.). **2. live it up.** *Informal.* to enjoy oneself, esp. flamboyantly.

live·ware ('laɪvˌwɛə) *n.* the programmers, systems analysts, operating staff, and other personnel working in a computer system. Compare **hardware** (sense 2), **software.**

live wire (laɪv) *n.* **1.** *Slang.* an energetic or enterprising person. **2.** a wire carrying an electric current.

liv·id ('lɪvɪd) *adj.* **1.** (of the skin) discoloured, as from a bruise or contusion. **2.** of a greyish tinge or colour: *livid pink.* **3.** *Informal.* angry or furious. [C17: via French from Latin *līvidus,* from *līvēre* to be black and blue] —**'liv·id·ly** *adv.* —**'liv·id·ness** *or* **li·'vid·i·ty** *n.*

liv·ing ('lɪvɪŋ) *adj.* **1. a.** possessing life; not dead. **b.** (*as collective n.* preceded by *the*): *the living.* **2.** having the characteristics of life (used esp. to distinguish organisms from nonliving matter). **3.** currently in use or valid: *living language.* **4.** seeming to be real: *a living image.* **5.** (of animals or plants) existing in the present age; extant. Compare **extinct** (sense 1). **6.** *Geology.* another word for **live**[2] (sense 13). **7.** presented by actors before a live audience: *living theatre.* **8.** (*prenominal*) (intensifier): *the living daylights.* ~*n.* **9.** the condition of being alive. **10.** the manner in which one conducts his or her life: *fast living.* **11.** the means, esp. the financial means, whereby one lives. **12.** *Church of England.* another term for **benefice. 13.** (*modifier*) of, involving, or characteristic of everyday life: *living area.* **14.** (*modifier*) of or involving those now alive (esp. in the phrase **living memory**).

liv·ing death *n.* a life or lengthy experience of constant misery.

liv·ing fos·sil *n.* an animal or plant, such as the coelacanth and ginkgo, belonging to a group most of whose members are extinct.

liv·ing pic·ture *n.* another term for **tableau vivant.**

liv·ing room *n.* a room in a private house or flat used for relaxation and entertainment of guests.

Liv·ing·ston ('lɪvɪŋstən) *n.* a town in SE Scotland, in W Lothian: founded as a new town in 1962. Pop.: 8500 (1969).

Liv·ing·stone ('lɪvɪŋstən) *n.* **Da·vid.** 1813–73, Scottish missionary and explorer in Africa. After working as a missionary in Botswana, he led a series of expeditions, discovering Lake Ngami (1849), the Zambezi River (1851), the Victoria Falls (1855), and Lake Malawi (1859). In 1866 he set out to search for the source of the Nile and was found in dire straits and rescued (1871) by the journalist H. M. Stanley.

liv·ing wage *n.* a wage adequate to permit a man and his family to live in reasonable comfort.

Li·vo·ni·a (lɪ'vəʊnɪə) *n.* **1.** a former Russian province on the Baltic, north of Lithuania: became Russian in 1721; divided between Estonia and Latvia in 1918. **2.** a city in SE Michigan, west of Detroit. Pop.: 114 922 (1973 est.). —**Li·'vo·ni·an** *adj., n.*

Li·vor·no (*Italian* li'vorno) *n.* a port in W central Italy, in Tuscany on the Ligurian Sea: shipyards; oil-refining. Pop.: 177 649 (1975 est.). English name: **Leghorn.**

li·vrai·son (*French* livrɛ'zɔ̃) *n. Rare.* one of the numbers of a book published in parts. [literally: delivery (of goods)]

li·vre ('li:vrə; *French* 'livr) *n.* a former French unit of money of account, equal to 1 pound of silver. [C16: via Old French from Latin *lībra* the Roman pound]

Liv·y ('lɪvɪ) *n.* Latin name *Titus Livius.* 59 B.C.–17 A.D., Roman historian, famous for his history of Rome in 142 books of which only 35 survive.

lix+iv·i+ate (lɪk'sɪvɪˌeɪt) *vb.* (*tr.*) *Chem.* a less common word for **leach**[1] (senses 1, 2). [C17: from LIXIVIUM]

lix+iv+i·um (lɪk'sɪvɪəm) *n., pl.* **+i·ums** *or* **·i·a** (-ɪə). **1.** the alkaline solution obtained by leaching wood ash with water; lye. **2.** any solution obtained by leaching. [C17: from Late Latin, from *lix* lye]

liz+ard ('lɪzəd) *n.* **1.** any reptile of the suborder *Lacertilia* (or *Sauria*), esp. those of the family *Lacertidae* (Old World lizards), typically having an elongated body, four limbs, and a long tail: includes the geckos, iguanas, chameleons, monitors, and slow worms. **2. a.** leather made from the skin of such an animal. **b.** (*as modifier*): *a lizard handbag.* [C14: via Old French from Latin *lacerta*]

Liz+ard ('lɪzəd) *n.* **the.** a promontory in SW England, in SW Cornwall: the southernmost point in Great Britain. Also called: **Lizard Head, Lizard Peninsula.**

liz+ard fish *n.* any small teleost fish of the family *Synodontidae*, having a slender body and a lizard-like head and living at the bottom of warm seas.

L.J. *Brit. abbrev. for* Lord Justice.

Lju+blja+na (lu:'bljɑ:nə) *n.* a city in NW Yugoslavia, capital of Slovenia: capital of Illyria (1816–49); became part of Yugoslavia in 1918; university (1595). Pop.: 173 853 (1971). German name: **Laibach.**

L.L. *abbrev. for:* **1.** Late Latin. **2.** Low Latin. **3.** Lord Lieutenant.

ll. *abbrev. for* lines (of written matter).

lla+ma ('lɑ:mə) *n.* **1.** a domesticated South American cud-chewing mammal, *Lama glama* (or *L. peruana*), that is used as a beast of burden and is valued for its hair, flesh, and hide: family *Camelidae* (camels). **2.** the cloth made from the wool of this animal. **3.** any other animal of the genus *Lama.* See **alpaca, guanaco.** [C17: via Spanish from Quechua]

Llan+daff ('lændəf, -dæf) *or* **Llan+daf** (*Welsh* hlan'dav) *n.* a town in SE Wales, in South Glamorgan: a suburb of Cardiff; the oldest bishopric in Wales (6th century).

Llan+dud+no (læn'dɪdnəu; *Welsh* hlan'dɪdnɔ) *n.* a town and resort in NW Wales, in NE Gwynedd on the Irish Sea. Pop.: 19 009 (1971).

Llan+ell·i *or* **Llan+ell·y** (θlæ'nɛθlɪ; *Welsh* hla'nɛhli:) *n.* an industrial town in S Wales, in S Dyfed on an inlet of Carmarthen Bay. Pop.: 26 320 (1971).

Llan+fair+pwll+gwyn+gyll (*Welsh* hlanˌvaɪrpuhl'gwɪngɪhl), **Llan+fair+pwll,** *or* **Llan+fair P. G.** *n.* a village in NW Wales, in SE Anglesey: reputed to be the longest place name in Great Britain when unabbreviated; means: St. Mary's Church in the hollow of the white hazel near the rapid whirlpool of Llandysilio of the red cave. Full name: **Llan+fair+pwll+gwyn+gyll+go+ger+y+chwyrn+dro+bwll+llan+ty+si+lio+go+go+goch** (*Welsh* hlan-'vaɪrpuhl'gwɪngɪhlgə'gɛrəxwɪrn'drɔbuhl'hlantə'sɪljɔ'gɔgɔ'gɔx).

Llan+go+llen (*Welsh* hlan'gɔhlɛn) *n.* a town in NE Wales, in Clwyd on the River Dee: International Musical Eisteddfod held annually since 1946. Pop.: 3108 (1971).

lla+no ('lɑ:nəu; *Spanish* 'ʎano) *n., pl.* **+nos** (-nəuz; *Spanish* -nos). an extensive grassy treeless plain, esp. in South America. [C17: Spanish, from Latin *plānum* level ground]

Lla+no Es+ta+ca+do ('lɑ:nəu ˌɛstə'kɑ:dəu) *n.* the S part of the Great Plains of the U.S., extending over W Texas and E New Mexico: oil and natural gas resources. Chief towns: Lubbock and Amarillo. Area: 83 700 sq. km (30 000 sq. miles). Also called: **Staked Plain.**

LL.B. *abbrev. for* Bachelor of Laws. [Latin: *Legum Baccalaureus*]

LL.D. *abbrev. for* Doctor of Laws. [Latin: *Legum Doctor*]

Llew·el·lyn (lu:'ɛlɪn) *n.* Colonel **Har·ry.** born 1911, Welsh show-jumping rider: on Foxhunter, he was a member of the British team that won the gold medal at the 1952 Olympic Games.

Lleyn Pen+in+su+la (*Welsh* hli:n) *n.* a peninsula in NW Wales between Cardigan Bay and Caernarvon Bay.

LL.M. *abbrev. for* Master of Laws. [Latin: *Legum Magister*]

Lloyd (lɔɪd) *n.* **1. Har·old (Clayton).** 1893–1971, U.S. comic film actor. **2. Ma·rie.** stage name of *Matilda Alice Victoria Wood.* 1870–1922, English music-hall comedienne.

Lloyd George *n.* **Da·vid,** 1st Earl Lloyd George of Dwyfor. 1863–1945, British Liberal statesman: prime minister (1916–22). As chancellor of the exchequer (1908–15) he introduced old age pensions (1908), a radical budget (1909), and an insurance scheme (1911).

Lloyd's (lɔɪdz) *n.* an association of London underwriters, set up in the late 17th century. Originally concerned exclusively with marine insurance and a shipping information service, it now subscribes a variety of insurance policies and publishes a daily list (**Lloyd's List**) of shipping data and news. [C17: named after Edward *Lloyd* (died ?1726) at whose coffee house in London the underwriters originally carried on their business]

lm *abbrev. for* lumen.

ln *abbrev. for* (natural) logarithm.

lo (ləu) *interj.* Look! See! (now often in the phrase **lo and behold**). [Old English *lā*]

loach (ləutʃ) *n.* any carp-like freshwater cyprinoid fish of the family *Cobitidae*, of Eurasia and Africa, having a long narrow body with barbels around the mouth. [C14: from Old French *loche*, of obscure origin]

load (ləud) *n.* **1.** something to be borne or conveyed; weight. **2. a.** the usual amount borne or conveyed. **b.** (*in combination*): *a carload.* **3.** something that weighs down, oppresses, or burdens: *that's a load off my mind.* **4.** a single charge of a firearm. **5.** the weight that is carried by a structure. See also **dead load, live load. 6.** *Electrical engineering, electronics.* **a.** a device that receives or dissipates the power from an amplifier, oscillator, generator, or some other source of signals. **b.** the power delivered by a machine, generator, circuit, etc. **7.** the weight of a component in a mechanism or structure. **8.** the resistance overcome by an engine or motor when it is driving a machine, etc. **9.** an external force applied to a component or mechanism. **10. a load of.** *Informal.* a quantity of: *a load of nonsense.* **11. get a load of.** *Informal.* pay attention to. **12. have a load on.** *U.S. slang.* to be intoxicated. **13. shoot one's load.** *Taboo slang.* (of a man) to ejaculate at orgasm. ~*vb.* (*mainly tr.*) **14.** (*also intr.*) to place or receive (cargo, goods, etc.) upon (a ship, lorry, etc.). **15.** to burden or oppress. **16.** to cause to be prejudicial: *to load a question.* **17.** (*also intr.*) to put an ammunition charge into (a firearm). **18.** *Photog.* to position (a film, cartridge, or plate) in (a camera). **19.** to weight or bias (a roulette wheel, dice, etc.). **20.** *Insurance.* to increase (a premium) to cover expenses, etc. **21.** to draw power from (an electrical device, such as a generator). **22.** to add material of high atomic number to (concrete) to increase its effectiveness as a radiation shield. **23.** to increase the power output of (an electric circuit). **24.** to increase the work required from (an engine or motor). **25.** to apply force to (a mechanism or component). **26.** *Computer technol.* to transfer (a program) to a memory. **27. load the dice. a.** to add weights to dice in order to bias them. **b.** to arrange to have a favourable or unfavourable position. [Old English *lād* course; in meaning, influenced by LADE; related to LEAD[1]]

load dis+place+ment *n. Nautical.* the total weight of a cargo vessel loaded so that its waterline reaches the summer load line.

load+ed ('ləudɪd) *adj.* **1.** carrying a load. **2.** (of dice, a roulette wheel, etc.) weighted or otherwise biased. **3.** (of a question or statement) containing a hidden trap or implication. **4.** charged with ammunition. **5.** *Slang.* wealthy. **6.** (*postpositive*) *Slang, chiefly U.S.* **a.** drunk. **b.** drugged; influenced by drugs.

load+er ('ləudə) *n.* **1.** a person who loads a gun or other firearm. **2.** (*in combination*) designating a firearm or machine loaded in a particular way: *breech-loader; top-loader.*

load fac+tor *n.* **1.** the ratio of the average electric load to the peak load over a period of time. **2.** *Aeronautics.* **a.** the ratio of a given external load to the weight of an aircraft. **b.** the actual payload carried by an aircraft as a percentage of its maximum payload.

load+ing ('ləudɪŋ) *n.* **1.** a load or burden; weight. **2.** the addition of an inductance to electrical equipment, such as a transmission line or aerial, to improve its performance. See **loading coil. 3.** an addition to an insurance premium to cover expenses, provide a safer profit margin, etc. **4.** the ratio of the gross weight of an aircraft to its engine power (**power loading**), wing area (**wing loading**), or some other parameter. **5.** *Psychol.* the correlation of a factor, such as a personality trait, with a performance score derived from a psychological test. **6.** material, such as china clay or size, added to paper, textiles, or similar materials to produce a smooth surface, increase weight, etc. **7.** *Chiefly Austral.* a payment made in addition to a basic wage or salary to reward special skills, compensate for unfavourable conditions, etc.

load+ing coil *n.* an inductance coil inserted at regular intervals and in series with the conductors of a transmission line in order to improve its characteristics.

load line *n. Nautical.* a pattern of lines painted on the hull of a ship, usually near the bow, indicating the various levels that the waterline should reach if the ship is properly loaded under given circumstances.

loads (ləudz) *Informal.* ~*pl. n.* **1.** (often foll. by *of*) a lot: *loads to eat.* ~*adv.* **2.** (intensifier): *loads better; thanks loads.*

load shed+ding *n.* the act or practice of temporarily reducing the supply of electricity to an area to avoid overloading the generators.

load+star ('ləudˌstɑ:) *n.* a variant spelling of **lodestar.**

load+stone ('ləudˌstəun) *n.* a variant spelling of **lodestone.**

loaf[1] (ləuf) *n., pl.* **loaves** (ləuvz). **1.** a shaped mass of baked bread. **2.** any shaped or moulded mass of food, such as sugar, cooked meat, etc. **3.** *Slang.* the head; sense: *use your loaf!* [Old English *hlāf*; related to Old High German *hleib* bread, Old Norse *hleifr*, Latin *libum* cake]

loaf[2] (ləuf) *vb.* **1.** (*intr.*) to loiter or lounge around in an idle way. **2.** (*tr.*; foll. by *away*) to spend (time) idly: *he loafed away his life.* [C19: perhaps back formation from LOAFER]

loaf+er ('ləufə) *n.* **1.** a person who avoids work; idler. **2.** *Chiefly U.S.* a moccasin-like shoe for casual wear. [C19: perhaps from German *Landläufer* vagabond]

loam (ləum) *n.* **1.** rich soil consisting of a mixture of sand, clay, and decaying organic material. **2.** a paste of clay and sand used for making moulds in a foundry, plastering walls, etc. ~*vb.* **3.** (*tr.*) to cover, treat, or fill with loam. [Old English *lām*; related to Old Swedish *lēmo* clay, Old High German *leimo*] —**'loam·y** *adj.* —**'loam·i·ness** *n.*

loan (ləun) *n.* **1.** the act of lending: *the loan of a car.* **2. a.** property lent, esp. money lent at interest for a period of time. **b.** (*as modifier*): *loan holder.* **3.** the adoption by speakers of one language of a form current in another language. **4.** short for **loan word. 5. on loan. a.** lent out; borrowed. **b.** (esp. of personnel) transferred from a regular post to a temporary one

elsewhere. ~*vb.* **6.** to lend (something, esp. money). [C13 *loon, lan,* from Old Norse *lān;* related to Old English *lǣn* loan; compare German *Lehen* fief, *Lohn* wages] —'**loan·a·ble** *adj.* —'**loan·er** *n.*
Usage. See at **lend.**

loan col·lec·tion *n.* a number of works of art lent by their owners for a temporary public exhibition.

Lo·an·da (ləʊ'ændə) *n.* a variant spelling of **Luanda.**

loan·ing ('ləʊnɪŋ) *n. Northern Brit. dialect.* **1.** a lane. **2.** a place where cows are milked. [C14 *lonnying, lonying,* from *loan* lane, from Old English *lone,* variant of LANE]

loan shark *n. Informal, chiefly U.S.* a person who lends funds at illegal or exorbitant rates of interest.

loan trans·la·tion *n.* the adoption by one language of a phrase or compound word whose components are literal translations of the components of a corresponding phrase or compound in a foreign language: *English "superman" from German "Übermensch."* Also called: **calque.**

loan word *n.* a word adopted, often with some modification of its form, from one language into another.

loath *or* **loth** (ləʊθ) *adj.* **1.** (usually foll. by *to*) reluctant or unwilling. **2. nothing loath.** willing. [Old English *lāth* (in the sense: hostile); related to Old Norse *leithr*] —'**loath·ness** *or* '**loth·ness** *n.*

loathe (ləʊð) *vb.* (*tr.*) to feel strong hatred or disgust for. [Old English *lāthiān,* from LOATH] —'**loath·er** *n.*

loath·ing ('ləʊðɪŋ) *n.* abhorrence; disgust. —'**loath·ing·ly** *adv.*

loath·ly[1] ('ləʊθlɪ) *adv.* with reluctance; unwillingly.

loath·ly[2] ('ləʊðlɪ) *adj.* an archaic word for **loathsome.**

loath·some ('ləʊðsəm) *adj.* causing loathing; abhorrent. —'**loath·some·ly** *adv.* —'**loath·some·ness** *n.*

loaves (ləʊvz) *n.* the plural of **loaf**[1].

lob[1] (lɒb) *Sport.* ~*n.* **1.** a ball struck in a high arc. **2.** *Cricket.* a ball bowled in a slow high arc. ~*vb.* **lobs, lob·bing, lobbed. 3.** to hit or kick a ball in a high arc. **4.** *Informal.* to throw. [C14: probably of Low German origin, originally in the sense: something dangling; compare Middle Low German *lobbe* hanging lower lip, Old English *loppe* spider]

lob[2] (lɒb) *n.* short for **lobworm.** [C17 (in the sense: pendulous object): related to LOB[1]]

Lo·ba·chev·sky (*Russian* ləba'tʃɛfskij) *n.* **Ni·ko·lai I·va·no·vich** (nika'laj i'vanəvitʃ). 1793–1856, Russian mathematician; a founder of non-Euclidean geometry.

lo·bar ('ləʊbə) *adj.* of, relating to, or affecting a lobe.

lo·bate ('ləʊbeɪt) *or* **lo·bat·ed** *adj.* **1.** having or resembling lobes. **2.** (of birds) having separate toes that are each fringed with a weblike lobe. —'**lo·bate·ly** *adv.*

lob·by ('lɒbɪ) *n., pl.* **·bies. 1.** a room or corridor used as an entrance hall, vestibule, etc. **2.** *Chiefly Brit.* a hall in a legislative building used for meetings between the legislators and members of the public. **3.** Also called: **division lobby.** *Chiefly Brit.* one of two corridors in a legislative building in which members vote. **4.** a group of persons who attempt to influence legislators on behalf of a particular interest. ~*vb.* **·bies, ·by·ing, ·bied. 5.** to attempt to influence (legislators, etc.) in the formulation of policy. **6.** (*intr.*) to act in the manner of a lobbyist. **7.** (*tr.*) to apply pressure or influence for the passage of (a bill, etc.). [C16: from Medieval Latin *lobia* portico, from Old High German *lauba* arbor, from *laub* leaf] —'**lob·by·er** *n.*

lob·by·ist ('lɒbɪɪst) *n. Chiefly U.S.* a person employed by a particular interest to lobby. —'**lob·by,ism** *n.*

lobe (ləʊb) *n.* **1.** any rounded projection forming part of a larger structure. **2.** any of the subdivisions of a bodily organ or part, delineated by shape or connective tissue. **3.** short for **ear lobe. 4.** any of the loops that form part of the graphic representation of the radiation pattern of a transmitting aerial. Compare **radiation pattern. 5.** any of the parts, not entirely separate from each other, into which a flattened plant part, such as a leaf, is divided. [C16: from Late Latin *lobus,* from Greek *lobos* lobe of the ear or of the liver]

lo·bec·to·my (ləʊ'bɛktəmɪ) *n., pl.* **·mies.** surgical removal of a lobe from any organ or gland in the body.

lo·be·li·a (ləʊ'bi:lɪə) *n.* any plant of the genus *Lobelia,* having red, blue, white, or yellow five-lobed flowers with the three lower lobes forming a lip: family *Lobeliaceae.* [C18: from New Latin, named after Matthias de Lobel (1538–1616), Flemish botanist]

lo·be·line ('ləʊbə,li:n) *n.* a crystalline alkaloid extracted from the seeds of the Indian tobacco plant, used as a smoking deterrent and respiratory stimulant. [C19: from LOBELIA]

Lo·ben·gu·la (,ləʊbən'gju:lə) *n.* ?1836–94, last Matabele king (1870–93); his kingdom was destroyed by the British.

Lo·bi·to (*Portuguese* lu'βitu) *n.* the chief port in Angola, in the west on **Lobito Bay:** terminus of the railway through Benguela to Mozambique. Pop.: 59 528 (1970).

lob·lol·ly ('lɒb,lɒlɪ) *n., pl.* **·lies. 1.** a southern U.S. pine tree, *Pinus taeda,* with bright red-brown bark, green needle-like leaves, and reddish-brown cones. **2.** *Nautical or dialect.* a thick gruel. **3.** *U.S. dialect,* a mire; mudhole. [C16: perhaps from dialect *lob* to boil + obsolete dialect *lolly* thick soup]

lob·lol·ly boy *or* **man** *n. Brit., naval.* (formerly) a boy or man acting as a medical orderly on board ship. [C18: from LOBLOLLY sense 2, applied to a ship's doctor's medicines]

lo·bo ('ləʊbəʊ) *n., pl.* **·bos.** *Western U.S.* another name for **timber wolf.** [Spanish, from Latin *lupus* wolf]

lo·bo·la *or* **lo·bo·lo** (lɔ:'bɔ:lə, lə'bəʊ-) *n.* (in southern Africa) an African custom by which a bridegroom's family makes a payment in cattle or cash to the bride's family shortly before the marriage. [from Zulu]

lo·bot·o·my (ləʊ'bɒtəmɪ) *n., pl.* **·mies. 1.** surgical incision into a lobe of any organ. **2.** Also called: **prefrontal leucotomy.** surgical interruption of one or more nerve tracts in the frontal lobe of the brain: used in the treatment of intractable mental disorders. [C20: from LOBE + -TOMY]

lob·scouse ('lɒb,skaʊs) *n.* a sailor's stew of meat, vegetables, and hardtack. [C18: perhaps from dialect *lob* to boil + *scouse,* broth; compare LOBLOLLY]

lob·ster ('lɒbstə) *n., pl.* **·sters** *or* **·ster. 1.** any of several large marine decapod crustaceans of the genus *Homarus,* esp. *H. vulgaris,* occurring on rocky shores and having the first pair of limbs modified as large pincers. **2.** any of several similar crustaceans, esp. the spiny lobster. **3.** the flesh of any of these crustaceans, eaten as a delicacy. [Old English *loppestre,* from *loppe* spider]

lob·ster New·burg ('nju:bɜ:g) *n.* lobster cooked in a rich cream sauce flavoured with sherry.

lob·ster pot *or* **trap** *n.* a round basket or trap made of open slats used to catch lobsters.

lob·ster ther·mi·dor ('θɜ:mɪ,dɔ:) *n.* a dish of cooked lobster, replaced in its shell with a creamy cheese sauce.

lob·ule ('lɒbju:l) *n.* a small lobe or a subdivision of a lobe. [C17: from New Latin *lobulus,* from Late Latin *lobus* LOBE] —**lob·u·lar** ('lɒbjʊlə), **lob·u·late** ('lɒbjʊlɪt), '**lob·u·,lat·ed,** *or* '**lob·u·lose** *adj.* —,**lob·u·'la·tion** *n.*

lob·worm ('lɒb,wɜ:m) *n.* **1.** another name for **lugworm.** Sometimes shortened to **lob. 2.** a large earthworm used as bait in fishing. [C17: from obsolete *lob* lump + WORM]

lo·cal ('ləʊkᵊl) *adj.* **1.** characteristic of or associated with a particular locality or area. **2.** of, concerned with, or relating to a particular place or point in space. **3.** *Med.* of, affecting, or confined to a limited area or part. Compare **general** (sense 10), **systemic** (sense 2). **4.** (of a train, bus, etc.) stopping at all stations or stops. ~*n.* **5.** a train, bus, etc., that stops at all stations or stops. **6.** an inhabitant of a specified locality. **7.** *Brit. informal.* a pub close to one's home or place of work. **8.** *Med.* short for **local anaesthetic. 9.** *U.S.* an item of local interest in a newspaper. **10.** *U.S.* a local or regional branch of an association. [C15: via Old French from Late Latin *locālis,* from Latin *locus* place, LOCUS] —'**lo·cal·ness** *n.*

lo·cal an·aes·thet·ic *n. Med.* a drug that produces local anaesthesia. Often shortened to **local.** See **anaesthesia** (sense 2).

lo·cal au·thor·i·ty *n. Brit.* the governing body of a county, district, etc. U.S. equivalent: **local government.**

lo·cal col·our *n.* the characteristic features or atmosphere of a place or time.

lo·cale (ləʊ'kɑ:l) *n.* a place or area, esp. with reference to events connected with it. [C18: from French *local* (n. use of adj.); see LOCAL]

lo·cal ex·am·i·na·tions *pl. n.* any of various examinations, such as the G.C.E., set by university boards and conducted in local centres, schools, etc.

lo·cal gov·ern·ment *n.* **1.** government of the affairs of counties, towns, etc., by locally elected political bodies. **2.** the U.S. equivalent of **local authority.**

lo·cal·ism ('ləʊkə,lɪzəm) *n.* **1.** a pronunciation, phrase, etc., peculiar to a particular locality. **2.** another word for **provincialism.** —'**lo·cal·ist** *n.* —,**lo·cal·'is·tic** *adj.*

lo·cal·i·ty (ləʊ'kælɪtɪ) *n., pl.* **·ties. 1.** a neighbourhood or area. **2.** the site or scene of an event. **3.** the fact or condition of having a location or position in space.

lo·cal·ize *or* **lo·cal·ise** ('ləʊkə,laɪz) *vb.* **1.** to make or become local in attitude, behaviour, etc. **2.** (*tr.*) to restrict or confine (something) to a particular area or part. **3.** (*tr.*) to assign or ascribe to a particular region. —'**lo·cal·,iz·a·ble** *or* '**lo·cal·,is·a·ble** *adj.* —,**lo·cal·i·'za·tion** *or* ,**lo·cal·i·'sa·tion** *n.* —'**lo·cal·,iz·er** *or* '**lo·cal·,is·er** *n.*

lo·cal·ly ('ləʊkəlɪ) *adv.* within a particular area or place.

lo·cal op·tion *n.* (esp. in the U.S. and Scotland) the privilege of a municipality, county, etc., to determine by referendum whether a particular activity shall be permitted there.

lo·cal os·cil·la·tor *n. Electronics.* **a.** the oscillator in a superheterodyne receiver whose output frequency is mixed with the incoming modulated radio-frequency carrier signal to produce the required intermediate frequency. **b.** an oscillator in any similar device, such as a frequency discriminator.

lo·cal time *n.* the time in a particular region or area expressed with reference to the meridian passing through it.

Lo·car·no (*Italian* lo'karno) *n.* a town in S Switzerland, in Ticino canton at the N end of Lake Maggiore: tourist resort. Pop.: 14 143 (1970).

lo·cate (ləʊ'keɪt) *vb.* **1.** (*tr.*) to discover the position, situation, or whereabouts of; find. **2.** (*tr.; often passive*) to situate or place: *located on the edge of the city.* **3.** (*intr.*) *U.S.* to become established or settled. —**lo·'cat·a·ble** *adj.* —**lo·'cat·er** *n.*

lo·ca·tion (ləʊ'keɪʃən) *n.* **1.** a site or position; situation. **2.** the act or process of locating or the state of being located. **3.** a place outside a studio where filming is done: *shot on location.* **4.** (in South Africa) **a.** a Black African or Coloured township, usually located near a small town. See also **township** (sense 3). **b.** a Black African tribal reserve in the E Cape Province. **5.** *Computer technol.* a position in a memory capable of holding a unit of information, such as a word, and identified by its address. **6.** *Roman and Scot. law.* the letting out on hire of a chattel or of personal services.

loc·a·tive ('lɒkətɪv) *Grammar.* ~*adj.* **1.** (of a word or phrase) indicating place or direction. **2.** denoting a case of nouns, etc., that refers to the place at which the action described by the verb occurs. ~*n.* **3. a.** the locative case. **b.** a word or speech element in this case. [C19: LOCATE + -IVE, on the model of *vocative*]

loc. cit. (in textual annotation) *abbrev. for* loco citato. [Latin: in the place cited]

loch (lɒk, lɒx) *n.* **1.** a Scot. word for **lake. 2.** a long narrow bay or arm of the sea in Scotland. [C14: from Gaelic]

loch·i·a ('lɒkɪə) *n.* a vaginal discharge of cellular debris, mucus, and blood following childbirth. [C17: New Latin from Greek *lokhia*, from *lokhios*, from *lokhos* childbirth] —**'loch·i·al** *adj.*

lo·ci ('ləʊsaɪ) *n.* a plural of **locus.**

lock[1] (lɒk) *n.* **1.** a device fitted to a gate, door, drawer, lid, etc., to keep it firmly closed and often to prevent access by unauthorized persons. **2.** a similar device attached to a machine, vehicle, etc., to prevent use by unauthorized persons: *a steering lock.* **3. a.** a section of a canal or river that may be closed off by gates to control the water level and the raising and lowering of vessels that pass through it. **b.** (*as modifier*): *a lock gate.* **4.** the jamming, fastening, or locking together of parts. **5.** *Brit.* the extent to which a vehicle's front wheels will turn: *this car has a good lock.* **6.** a mechanism that detonates the charge of a gun. **7. lock, stock, and barrel.** completely; entirely. **8.** any wrestling hold in which a wrestler seizes a part of his opponent's body and twists it or otherwise exerts pressure upon it. **9.** Also called: **lock forward.** *Rugby.* **a.** the player at the back of a scrum who holds the forwards in the second row together. **b.** this position. **10.** a gas bubble in a hydraulic system or a liquid bubble in a pneumatic system that stops or interferes with the fluid flow in a pipe, capillary, etc.: *an air lock.* ~*vb.* **11.** to fasten (a door, gate, etc.) or (of a door, etc.) to become fastened with a lock, bolt, etc., so as to prevent entry or exit. **12.** (*tr.*) to secure (a building) by locking all doors, windows, etc. **13.** to fix or become fixed together securely or inextricably. **14.** to become or cause to become rigid or immovable: *the front wheels of the car locked.* **15.** (when *tr., often passive*) to clasp or entangle (someone or each other) in a struggle or embrace. **16.** (*tr.*) to furnish (a canal) with locks. **17.** (*tr.*) to move (a vessel) through a system of locks. **18. lock horns.** (esp. of two equally matched opponents) to become engaged in argument or battle. **19. lock the stable door after the horse has bolted** *or* **been stolen.** to take precautions after harm has been done. ~See also **lock on to, lock out, lock up.** [Old English *loc*; related to Old Norse *lok*] —**'lock·a·ble** *adj.*

lock[2] (lɒk) *n.* **1.** a strand, curl, or cluster of hair. **2.** a tuft or wisp of wool, cotton, etc. **3.** (*pl.*) *Chiefly literary.* hair, esp. when curly or fine. [Old English *loc*; related to Old Frisian *lok*, Old Norse *lokkr* lock of wool]

lock·age ('lɒkɪdʒ) *n.* **1.** a system of locks in a canal. **2.** passage through a lock or the fee charged for such passage.

Locke (lɒk) *n.* **1. John.** 1632–1704, English philosopher, who discussed the concept of empiricism in his *Essay Concerning Human Understanding* (1690). He influenced political thought, esp. in France and America, with his *Two Treatises on Government* (1690), in which he sanctioned the right to revolt. **2. Mat·thew.** ?1630–77, English composer, esp. of works for the stage.

lock·er ('lɒkə) *n.* **1. a.** a small compartment or drawer that may be locked, as one of several in a gymnasium, etc., for clothes and valuables. **b.** (*as modifier*): *a locker room.* **2.** a person or thing that locks. **3.** *U.S.* a refrigerated compartment for keeping frozen foods, esp. one rented in an establishment.

lock·et ('lɒkɪt) *n.* a small ornamental case, usually on a necklace or chain, that holds a picture, keepsake, etc. [C17: from French *loquet* latch, diminutive of *loc* LOCK[1]]

lock·jaw ('lɒk,dʒɔː) *n. Pathol.* a nontechnical name for **trismus** and (often) **tetanus.**

lock·nut ('lɒk,nʌt) *n.* **1.** a supplementary nut screwed down upon a primary nut to prevent it from shaking loose. **2.** a threaded nut having a feature, such as a nylon insert, to prevent it from shaking loose.

lock on to *vb.* (*intr., adv.* + *prep.*) (of a radar beam) to automatically follow (a target).

lock out *vb.* (*tr., adv.*) **1.** to prevent from entering by locking a door. **2.** to prevent (employees) from working during an industrial dispute, as by closing a factory. ~*n.* **lock·out. 3.** the closing of a place of employment by an employer, in order to bring pressure on employees to agree to terms.

lock·smith ('lɒk,smɪθ) *n.* a person who makes or repairs locks. —**'lock·,smith·er·y** *or* **'lock·,smith·ing** *n.*

lock step *n.* a method of marching in step such that the men follow one another as closely as possible.

lock stitch *n.* a sewing-machine stitch in which the top thread interlocks with the bobbin thread.

lock up *vb.* (*adv.*) **1.** (*tr.*) Also: **lock in, lock away.** to imprison or confine. **2.** to lock or secure the doors, windows, etc., of (a building). **3.** (*tr.*) to keep or store securely: *secrets locked up in history.* **4.** (*tr.*) to invest (funds) so that conversion into cash is difficult. **5.** *Printing.* to secure (type, etc.) in a chase or in the bed of the printing machine by tightening the quoins. ~*n.* **lock·up. 6.** the action or time of locking up. **7.** a jail or block of cells. **8.** *Brit.* a small shop with no attached quarters for the owner or shopkeeper. **9.** *Brit.* a garage or storage place separate from the main premises. **10.** *Printing.* the pages of type held in a chase by the positioning of quoins.

Lock·yer ('lɒkjə) *n.* Sir **Jo·seph Nor·man.** 1836–1920, English astronomer: a pioneer in solar spectroscopy, he was the first to observe helium in the sun's atmosphere (1868).

lo·co[1] ('ləʊkəʊ) *n. Informal.* short for **locomotive.**

lo·co[2] ('ləʊkəʊ) *adj.* **1.** *Slang. Chiefly U.S.* insane. **2.** (of an animal) affected with loco disease. ~*n., pl.* **·cos. 3.** *U.S.* short for **locoweed.** ~*vb.* (*tr.*) **4.** to poison with locoweed. **5.** *U.S. slang.* to make insane. [C19: via Mexican Spanish from Spanish: crazy]

lo·co dis·ease *or* **poi·son·ing** *n.* a disease of cattle, sheep, and horses characterized by paralysis and faulty vision, caused by ingestion of locoweed.

lo·co·ism ('ləʊkəʊ,ɪzəm) *n.* another word for **loco disease.**

lo·co·man ('ləʊkəʊmən) *n., pl.* **·men.** *Brit. informal.* a railwayman, esp. an engine-driver.

lo·co·mo·tion (,ləʊkə'məʊʃən) *n.* the act, fact, ability, or power of moving. [C17: from Latin *locō* from a place, ablative of *locus* place + MOTION]

lo·co·mo·tive (,ləʊkə'məʊtɪv) *n.* **1. a.** Also called: **locomotive engine.** a self-propelled engine driven by steam, electricity, or diesel power and used for drawing trains along railway tracks. **b.** (*as modifier*): *a locomotive shed; a locomotive works.* ~*adj.* **2.** of or relating to locomotion. **3.** moving or able to move, as by self-propulsion. —**,lo·co·'mo·tive·ly** *adv.* —**,lo·co·'mo·tive·ness** *n.*

lo·co·mo·tor (,ləʊkə'məʊtə) *adj.* of or relating to locomotion. [C19: from Latin *locō* from a place, ablative of *locus* place + MOTOR (mover)]

lo·co·mo·tor a·tax·i·a *n. Pathol.* another name for **tabes dorsalis.**

lo·co·weed ('ləʊkəʊ,wiːd) *n.* any of several perennial leguminous plants of the genera *Oxytropis* and *Astragalus* of W North America that cause loco disease in horses, cattle, and sheep.

Lo·cris *or* **Lo·kris** ('ləʊkrɪs, 'lɒk-) *n.* an ancient region of central Greece. —**'Lo·cri·an** *or* **'Lo·kri·an** *adj., n.*

loc·u·lar ('lɒkjʊlə) *or* **loc·u·late** ('lɒkjʊ,leɪt, -lɪt) *adj. Biology.* divided into compartments by septa: *the locular ovary of a plant.* [C19: from New Latin *loculāris* kept in boxes] —**,loc·u·'la·tion** *n.*

loc·ule ('lɒkjuːl) *or* **loc·u·lus** ('lɒkjʊləs) *n., pl.* **loc·ules** *or* **loc·u·li** ('lɒkjʊ,laɪ). **1.** *Botany.* any of the chambers of an ovary or anther. **2.** *Biology.* any small cavity or chamber. [C19: New Latin, from Latin: compartment, from *locus* place]

lo·cum te·nens ('ləʊkəm 'tiːnɛnz) *n., pl.* **lo·cum te·nen·tes** (tə'nɛntiːz). *Chiefly Brit.* a person who stands in temporarily for another member of the same profession, esp. for a physician, chemist, or clergyman. Often shortened to **locum.** [C17: Medieval Latin: (someone) holding the place (of another)]

lo·cus ('ləʊkəs) *n., pl.* **lo·ci** ('ləʊsaɪ). **1.** (in many legal phrases) a place or area, esp. the place where something occurred. **2.** *Maths.* a set of points or lines whose location satisfies or is determined by one or more specified conditions: *the locus of points equidistant from a given point is a circle.* **3.** *Genetics.* the position of a particular gene on a chromosome. [C18: Latin]

lo·cus clas·si·cus ('klæsɪkəs) *n., pl.* **lo·ci clas·si·ci** ('klæsɪ,saɪ). an authoritative and often quoted passage from a standard work. [Latin: classical place]

lo·cus si·gil·li (sɪ'dʒɪlaɪ) *n., pl.* **lo·ci si·gil·li.** the place to which the seal is affixed on legal documents, etc. [Latin]

lo·cus stan·di ('stændaɪ) *n. Law.* the right of a party to appear and be heard before a court. [from Latin: a place for standing]

lo·cust ('ləʊkəst) *n.* **1.** any of numerous orthopterous insects of the genera *Locusta*, *Melanoplus*, etc., such as *L. migratoria*, of warm and tropical regions of the Old World, which travels in vast swarms, stripping large areas of vegetation. See also **grasshopper** (sense 1). Compare **seventeen-year locust. 2.** Also called: **locust tree, false acacia.** a North American leguminous tree, *Robinia pseudoacacia*, having prickly branches, hanging clusters of white fragrant flowers, and reddish-brown seed pods. **3.** the yellowish durable wood of this tree. **4.** any of several similar trees, such as the honey locust and carob. [C13 (the insect): from Latin *locusta* locust; applied to the tree (C17) because the pods resemble locusts] —**'lo·cust-,like** *adj.*

lo·cust bird *n.* any of various pratincoles, esp. *Glareola nordmanni* (**black-winged pratincole**), that feed on locusts.

lo·cu·tion (ləʊ'kjuːʃən) *n.* **1.** a word, phrase, or expression. **2.** manner or style of speech or expression. [C15: from Latin *locūtiō* an utterance, from *loquī* to speak]

Lod (lɒd) *n.* a town in central Israel, southeast of Tel Aviv: Israel's chief airport. Pop.: 30 500 (1972). Also called: **Lydda.**

lode (ləʊd) *n.* **1.** a deposit of valuable ore occurring between definite limits in the surrounding rock; vein. **2.** a deposit of metallic ore filling a fissure in the surrounding rock. [Old English *lād* course. Compare LOAD]

lo·den ('ləʊdᵊn) *n.* a thick, heavily fulled wool with a short pile, used for coats. [German, from Old High German *lodo* thick cloth, perhaps related to Old English *lotha* cloak]

lode·star *or* **load·star** ('ləʊd,stɑː) *n.* **1.** a star, esp. the North Star, used in navigation or astronomy as a point of reference. **2.** something that serves as a guide or model. [C14: literally, guiding star. See LODE]

lode·stone *or* **load·stone** ('ləʊd,stəʊn) *n.* **1. a.** magnetite that is naturally magnetic. **b.** a piece of this, which can be used as a magnet. **2.** a person or thing regarded as a focus of attraction. [C16: literally, guiding stone]

lodge (lɒdʒ) *n.* **1.** *Chiefly Brit.* a small house at the entrance to the grounds of a country mansion, usually occupied by a gatekeeper or gardener. **2.** a house or cabin used occasionally, as for some seasonal activity. **3.** *U.S.* a central building in a resort, camp, or park. **4.** (*cap. when part of a name*) a large house or hotel. **5.** a room for the use of porters in a university, college, etc. **6.** a local branch or chapter of certain societies. **7.** the building used as the meeting place of such a society. **8.** the dwelling place of certain animals, esp. the dome-shaped den constructed by beavers. **9.** a hut or tent of certain North American Indian peoples. **10.** (at Cambridge University) the residence of the head of a college. *~vb.* **11.** to provide or be provided with accommodation or shelter, esp. rented accommodation. **12.** to live temporarily, esp. in rented accommodation. **13.** to implant, embed, or fix or be implanted, embedded, or fixed. **14.** (*tr.*) to deposit or leave for safety, storage, etc. **15.** (*tr.*) to bring (a charge or accusation) against someone. **16.** (*tr.; often foll. by in or with*) to place (authority, power, etc.) in the control (of someone). **17.** (*intr.; often foll. by in*) *Archaic.* to exist or be present (in). **18.** (*tr.*) *Archaic.* (of wind, rain, etc.) to beat down (crops). [C15: from Old French *loge,* perhaps from Old High German *louba* porch] **—'lodge+a·ble** *adj.*

Lodge[1] (lɒdʒ) *n.* **1.** Sir **Ol·i·ver (Joseph).** 1851–1940, English physicist, who perfected the coherer. **2. Thom·as.** ?1558–1625, English writer. His romance *Rosalynde* (1590) supplied the plot for Shakespeare's *As You Like It.*

Lodge[2] (lɒdʒ) *n.* **the.** the official Canberra residence of the Australian Prime Minister.

lodg+er ('lɒdʒə) *n.* a person who pays rent in return for accommodation in someone else's house.

lodg+ing ('lɒdʒɪŋ) *n.* **1.** a temporary residence. **2.** (*sometimes pl.*) sleeping accommodation. **3.** (*sometimes pl.*) (at Oxford University) the residence of the head of a college.

lodg+ing house *n.* a private home providing accommodation and meals for lodgers.

lodg+ings ('lɒdʒɪŋz) *pl. n.* a rented room or rooms in which to live, esp. in another person's house.

lodg+ing turn *n.* a period of work or duty, esp. among railway workers, which involves sleeping away from home.

lodg+ment *or* **lodge+ment** ('lɒdʒmənt) *n.* **1.** the act of lodging or the state of being lodged. **2.** a blockage or accumulation. **3.** a small area gained and held in enemy territory.

Lo·di (*Italian* 'lɔ:di) *n.* a town in N Italy, in Lombardy: scene of Napoleon's defeat of the Austrians in 1796. Pop.: 44 422 (1971).

lod·i+cule ('lɒdɪˌkju:l) *n.* any of two or three minute scales at the base of the ovary in grass flowers that represent the corolla. [C19: from Latin *lōdīcula* diminutive of *lōdix* blanket]

Łódź (*Polish* wutʃ) *n.* a city in central Poland: the country's second largest city; major centre of the textile industry; university (1945). Pop.: 784 000 (1974 est.).

Loeb (lɜ:b; *German* lø:p) *n.* **Jacques** (ʒɑ:k). 1859–1924, U.S. physiologist, born in Germany, noted esp. for his pioneering work on artificial parthenogenesis.

lo+ess ('ləʊɪs; *German* lœs) *n.* a light-coloured fine-grained accumulation of clay and silt particles that have been deposited by the wind. [C19: from German *Löss,* from Swiss German dialect *lösch* loose] **—lo+ess+i·al** (ləʊ'ɛsɪəl) *or* **lo+'ess+al** *adj.*

Loe·we *or* **Lö·we** (*German* 'lø:və) *n.* **(Johann) Karl (Gottfried)** (karl). 1796–1869, German composer, esp. of songs, such as *Der Erlkönig* (1818).

Loe·wi ('ləʊɪ) *n.* **Ot·to.** 1873–1961, U.S. pharmacologist, born in Germany. He shared a Nobel prize for medicine (1936) with Dale for their work on the chemical transmission of nerve impulses.

Lo+fo+ten and Ves+ter+å+len (*Norwegian* 'lu:futən; 'vɛstərˌɔ:lən) *pl. n.* a group of islands off the NW coast of Norway, within the Arctic Circle. Largest island: Hinny. Pop.: 56 066 (1970). Area: about 5130 sq. km (1980 sq. miles).

loft (lɒft) *n.* **1.** the space inside a roof. **2.** a gallery, esp. one for the choir in a church. **3.** a room over a stable used to store hay. **4.** *U.S.* an upper storey of a warehouse or factory. **5.** a raised house or coop in which pigeons are kept. **6.** *Sport.* **a.** (in golf) the angle from the vertical made by the club face to give elevation to a ball. **b.** elevation imparted to a ball. **c.** a lofting stroke or shot. *~vb.* (*tr.*) **7.** *Sport.* to strike or kick (a ball) high in the air. **8.** to store or place in a loft. **9.** *Golf.* to slant (the face of a golf club). **10.** to lay out a full-scale working drawing of (the lines of a vessel's hull). [Late Old English, from Old Norse *lopt* air, ceiling; compare Old Danish and Old High German *loft* (German *Luft* air)]

loft+er ('lɒftə) *n. Golf.* a club; an iron with a wide-angled face for lofting. Also called: **lofting iron.**

loft·y ('lɒftɪ) *adj.* **loft·i·er, loft·i·est. 1.** of majestic or imposing height. **2.** exalted or noble in character or nature. **3.** haughty or supercilious. **4.** elevated, eminent, or superior. **—'loft·i+ly** *adv.* **—'loft·i·ness** *n.*

log[1] (lɒg) *n.* **1. a.** a section of the trunk or a main branch of a tree, when stripped of branches. **b.** (*modifier*) constructed out of logs: *a log cabin.* **2. a.** a detailed record of a voyage of a ship or aircraft. **b.** a record of the hours flown by pilots and aircrews. **c.** a book in which these records are made; logbook. **3.** a written record of information about transmissions kept by radio stations, amateur radio operators, etc. **4. a.** a device consisting of a float with an attached line, formerly used to measure the speed of a ship. **b. heave the log.** to determine a ship's speed with such a device. **5.** *Austral.* a claim for better pay and conditions presented by a trade union to an employer. **6. like a log.** without stirring or being disturbed (in the phrase **sleep like a log**). *~vb.* **logs, log+ging, logged. 7.** (*tr.*) to fell the trees of (a forest, area, etc.) for timber. **8.** (*tr.*) to saw logs from (trees). **9.** (*intr.*) to work at the felling of timber. **10.** (*tr.*) to enter (a distance, event, etc.) in a logbook or log. **11.** (*tr.*) to record the punishment received by (a sailor) in a logbook. **12.** (*tr.*) to travel (a specified distance or time) or move at (a specified speed). [C14: origin obscure]

log[2] (lɒg) *n.* short for **logarithm.**

-log *combining form.* U.S. variant of **-logue.**

lo+gan ('ləʊgən) *n. Canadian.* another name for **bogan** (a backwater).

Lo+gan ('ləʊgən) *n.* **Mount.** a mountain in NW Canada, in SW Yukon in the St. Elias Range: the highest peak in Canada and the second highest in North America. Height: 6050 m (19 850 ft.).

lo·gan+ber·ry ('ləʊgənbərɪ, -brɪ) *n., pl.* **·ries. 1.** a trailing prickly hybrid rosaceous plant, *Rubus loganobaccus,* cultivated for its edible fruit. **2. a.** the purplish-red acid fruit of this plant. **b.** (*as modifier*): *loganberry pie.* [C19: named after James H. *Logan* (1841–1928), American judge and horticulturist who first grew it (1881)]

lo+ga+ni·a+ceous (ləʊˌgeɪnɪ'eɪʃəs) *adj.* of, relating to, or belonging to the *Loganiaceae,* a tropical and subtropical family of plants that includes nux vomica, pinkroot, and gelsemium. [C19: from New Latin *Logania,* named after James *Logan* (1674–1751) Irish-American botanist]

log·a+oe·dic (ˌlɒgə'i:dɪk) (in classical prosody) *~adj.* **1.** of or relating to verse in which mixed metres are combined within a single line to give the effect of prose. *~n.* **2.** a line or verse of this kind. [C19: via Late Latin from Greek *logaoidikos,* from *logos* speech + *aoidē* poetry]

log·a+rithm ('lɒgəˌrɪðəm) *n.* the exponent indicating the power to which a fixed number, the base, must be raised to obtain a given number or variable. It is used esp. to simplify multiplication and division: *if* $a^x = M$, then the logarithm of M to the base *a* ($\log_a M$) is *x.* Often shortened to **log** See also **common logarithm, natural logarithm.** [C17: from New Latin *logarithmus,* coined 1614 by John NAPIER, from Greek, *logos* ratio, reckoning + *arithmos* number]

log·a+rith+mic (ˌlɒgə'rɪðmɪk) *or* **log·a+rith+mi+cal** *adj.* **1.** of, relating to, using, or containing logarithms of a number or variable. **2.** consisting of, relating to, or using points or lines whose distances from a fixed point or line are proportional to the logarithms of numbers. *~*Abbrev.: **log. —ˌlog·a+'rith+mi+cal+ly** *adv.*

log·a+rith+mic func+tion *n.* **a.** the mathematical function $y = \log x$. **b.** a function that can be expressed in terms of this function.

log+book ('lɒgˌbʊk) *n.* **1.** a book containing the official record of trips made by a ship or aircraft; log. **2.** *Brit.* (formerly) a document listing the registration, manufacture, identity of ownership, etc., of a motor vehicle.

log chip *n. Nautical.* the chip of a chip log.

loge (ləʊʒ) *n.* **1.** a small enclosure or box in a theatre or opera house. **2.** the upper section in a theatre or cinema. [C18: French; see LODGE]

log+ger ('lɒgə) *n.* **1.** another word for **lumberjack. 2.** a tractor or crane for handling logs.

log+ger+head ('lɒgəˌhɛd) *n.* **1.** Also called: **loggerhead turtle.** a large headed turtle, *Caretta caretta,* occurring in most seas: family *Chelonidae.* **2. loggerhead shrike.** a North American shrike, *Lanius ludovicianus,* having a grey head and body, black-and-white wings and tail, and black facial stripe. **3.** a tool consisting of a large metal sphere attached to a long handle, used for warming liquids, melting tar, etc. **4.** a strong round upright post in a whaleboat for belaying the line of a harpoon. **5.** *Archaic or dialect.* a blockhead; dunce. **6. at loggerheads.** engaged in dispute or confrontation. [C16: probably from dialect *logger* wooden block + HEAD] **—'log+ger+ˌhead+ed** *adj.*

log+gia ('lɒdʒə, 'lɒdʒɪə) *n., pl.* **+gias** *or* **+gie** (-dʒɛ). **1.** a covered area on the side of a building, esp. one that serves as a porch. **2.** an open balcony in a theatre. [C17: Italian, from French *loge.* See LODGE]

log+ging ('lɒgɪŋ) *n.* the work of felling, trimming, and transporting timber.

log·i·a ('lɒgɪə) *n.* **1.** a supposed collection of the sayings of Christ held to have been drawn upon by the writers of the gospels. **2.** the plural of **logion.**

log+ic ('lɒdʒɪk) *n.* **1.** the branch of philosophy concerned with analysing the patterns of reasoning by which a conclusion is drawn from a set of premisses, without reference to meaning or context. See also **formal logic, deduction** (sense 3), **induction** (sense 3). **2.** the system and principles of reasoning used in a specific field of study. **3.** a particular method of argument or reasoning. **4.** force or effectiveness in argument or dispute. **5.** reasoned thought or argument, as distinguished from irrationality. **6.** the relationship and interdependence of a series of events, facts, etc. **7. chop logic.** to use excessively subtle or involved logic or argument. See **choplogic. 8.** *Electronics, computer technol.* **a.** the principles underlying the units in a computer system that perform arithmetical and logical operations. See also **logic circuit. b.** (*as modifier*): *a logic element.* [C14: from Old French *logique* from Medieval Latin *logica* (neuter plural, treated in Medieval Latin as feminine singular), from Greek *logikos* concerning speech or reasoning]

log·i+cal ('lɒdʒɪkᵊl) *adj.* **1.** relating to, used in, or characteristic of logic. **2.** using, according to, or deduced from the principles of logic: *a logical conclusion.* **3.** capable of or characterized by clear or valid reasoning. **4.** reasonable or necessary because of facts, events, etc.: *the logical candidate.* **5.** *Computer technol.* of, performed by, used in, or relating to the logic circuits in a computer. **—ˌlog·i+'cal+i·ty** *or* **'log·i·cal+ness** *n.* **—'log·i·cal+ly** *adv.*

log·i+cal op+er+a+tion *n. Computer technol.* an operation involving the use of words representing logical functions, such as *and* or *or,* that are applied to the input signals of a particular logic circuit.

log·i·cal pos·i·tiv·ism *or* **em·pir·i·cism** *n.* a philosophical system claiming to reject metaphysical speculation and holding that the only meaningful statements are those that are analytic or can be tested empirically.

log·ic cir·cuit *n.* an electronic circuit used in computers to perform a logical operation on its two or more input signals. There are six basic circuits, the AND, NOT, NAND, OR, NOR, and exclusive OR circuits, which can be combined into more complex circuits.

lo·gi·cian (lɒˈdʒɪʃən) *n.* a person who specializes in or is skilled at logic.

log·i·cism (ˈlɒdʒɪˌsɪzəm) *n.* the philosophical theory that all of mathematics can be deduced from logic. Compare **intuitionism, formalism.**

log·i·on (ˈlɒgɪˌɒn) *n., pl.* **log·i·a** (ˈlɒgɪə). a saying of Christ regarded as authentic. See also **logia.** [C16: from Greek: a saying, oracle, from *logos* word]

lo·gis·tic[1] (lɒˈdʒɪstɪk) *n.* **1.** a system of symbolic logic. ~*adj.* **2.** *Maths.* (of a curve) having an equation of the form $y = k/(1 + e^{a+bx})$, where *b* is less than zero, and used to describe a continuously increasing function. **3.** *Rare.* of, relating to, or skilled in arithmetical calculations. [C17: via French, from Late Latin *logisticus* of calculation, from Greek *logistikos* rational, from *logos* word, reason]

lo·gis·tic[2] (lɒˈdʒɪstɪk) *or* **lo·gis·ti·cal** *adj.* of or relating to logistics. —**lo·ˈgis·ti·cal·ly** *adv.*

lo·gis·tics (lɒˈdʒɪstɪks) *n.* **1.** (*functioning as sing. or pl.*) the science of the movement and maintenance of military forces. **2.** the handling of an operation involving the movement of labour and materials, etc. [C19: from French *logistique*, from *loger* to LODGE] —**log·is·ti·cian** (ˌlɒdʒɪˈstɪʃən) *n.*

log jam *n. Chiefly U.S.* **1.** blockage caused by the crowding together of a number of logs floating in a river. **2.** a deadlock; standstill.

log·log (ˈlɒglɒg) *n.* the logarithm of a logarithm (in equations, etc.).

log·o (ˈlɒugəʊ, ˈlɒg-) *n., pl.* **·os.** short for **logotype** (sense 2).

log·o- *combining form.* indicating word or speech: *logogram.* [from Greek; see LOGOS]

log·o·gram (ˈlɒgəˌgræm) *or* **log·o·graph** (ˈlɒgəˌgrɑːf, -ˌgræf) *n.* a single symbol representing an entire morpheme, word, or phrase, as for example the symbol (%) meaning *per cent.* —**log·o·gram·mat·ic** (ˌlɒgəgrəˈmætɪk), **log·o·graph·ic** (ˌlɒgəˈgræfɪk), *or* **ˌlog·o·ˈgraph·i·cal** *adj.* —**ˌlog·o·gram·ˈmat·i·cal·ly** *or* **ˌlog·o·ˈgraph·i·cal·ly** *adv.*

lo·gog·ra·phy (lɒˈgɒgrəfɪ) *n.* **1.** the use of logotypes in printing. **2.** (formerly) a method of longhand reporting. —**lo·ˈgog·ra·pher** *n.*

log·o·griph (ˈlɒgəʊˌgrɪf) *n.* a word puzzle, esp. one based on recombination of the letters of a word. [C16: via French from Greek LOGO- + GRIPHOS puzzle] —**ˌlog·o·ˈgriph·ic** *adj.*

lo·gom·a·chy (lɒˈgɒməkɪ) *n., pl.* **·chies.** argument about words or the meaning of words. [C16: from Greek *logomakhia.* See LOGO-, -MACHY] —**lo·ˈgom·a·chist** *n.*

log·o·pae·dics *or U.S.* **log·o·pe·dics** (ˌlɒgəˈpiːdɪks) *n.* (*functioning as sing.*) another name for **speech therapy.** —**ˌlog·o·ˈpae·dic** *or U.S.* **ˌlog·o·ˈpe·dic** *adj.*

log·or·rhoe·a *or esp. U.S.* **log·or·rhe·a** (ˌlɒgəˈrɪə) *n.* excessive, uncontrollable, or incoherent talkativeness.

log·os (ˈlɒgɒs) *n. Philosophy.* reason or the rational principle expressed in words and things. [C16: from Greek: word, reason, discourse, from *legein* to speak]

Log·os (ˈlɒgɒs) *n.* the divine Word; the second person of the Trinity.

log·o·type (ˈlɒgəʊˌtaɪp) *n.* **1.** *Printing.* a piece of type with several uncombined characters cast on it. **2.** Also called: **logo.** a trademark, company emblem, or similar device. —**ˈlo·go·ˌtyp·y** *n.*

log·roll (ˈlɒgˌrəʊl) *vb. Chiefly U.S.* to use logrolling in order to procure the passage of (legislation). —**ˈlog·ˌroll·er** *n.*

log·roll·ing (ˈlɒgˌrəʊlɪŋ) *n.* **1.** *U.S.* the practice of undemocratic agreements between politicians involving mutual favours, the trading of votes, etc. **2.** another name for **birling.** See **birl**[1]. **3.** the transporting of logs, esp. by water.

Lo·gro·ño (*Spanish* loˈɣroɲo) *n.* a walled city in N Spain, on the Ebro River: trading centre of an agricultural region noted for its wine. Pop.: 84 456 (1970).

-logue *or U.S.* **-log** *n. combining form.* indicating speech or discourse of a particular kind: *travelogue; monologue.* [from French, from Greek *-logos*]

log·way (ˈlɒgˌweɪ) *n.* another name for **gangway** (sense 1).

log·wood (ˈlɒgˌwʊd) *n.* **1.** a leguminous tree, *Haematoxylon campechianum*, of the West Indies and Central America. **2.** the heavy reddish-brown wood of this tree, yielding the dye haematoxylin. See also **haematoxylon.**

lo·gy (ˈləʊgɪ) *adj.* **·gi·er, ·gi·est.** *U.S.* dull or listless. [C19: perhaps from Dutch *log* heavy] —**ˈlo·gi·ness** *n.*

-lo·gy *n. combining form.* **1.** indicating the science or study of: *musicology.* **2.** indicating writing, discourse, or body of writings: *trilogy; phraseology; martyrology.* [from Latin *-logia*, from Greek, from *logos* word; see LOGOS] —**-log·i·cal** *or* **-log·ic** *adj. combining form.* —**-lo·gist** *n. combining form.*

Lo·hen·grin (ˈləʊɪngrɪn) *n.* (in German legend) a son of Parzival and knight of the Holy Grail.

loin (lɔɪn) *n.* **1.** Also called: **lumbus.** *Anatomy.* the part of the lower back and sides between the pelvis and the ribs. Related adj.: **lumbar. 2.** a cut of meat from this part of an animal. [C14: from Old French *loigne*, perhaps from Vulgar Latin *lumbra* (unattested), from Latin *lumbus* loin]

loin·cloth (ˈlɔɪnˌklɒθ) *n.* a piece of cloth worn round the loins. Also called: **breechcloth.**

loins (lɔɪnz) *pl. n.* **1.** the hips and the inner surface of the legs where they join the trunk of the body; crotch. **2. a.** *Euphemistic.* the reproductive organs. **b.** *Chiefly literary.* the womb.

Loire (*French* lwaːr) *n.* **1.** a department of E central France, in Rhône-Alpes region. Capital: St. Étienne. Pop.: 751 598 (1975). Area: 4799 sq. km (1872 sq. miles). **2.** a river in France, rising in the Massif Central and flowing north and west in a wide curve to the Bay of Biscay: the longest river in France. Its valley is famous for its wines and châteaux. Length: 1020 km (634 miles). Ancient name: **Liger.**

Loire-At·lan·tique (*French* lwar atlɑ̃ˈtik) *n.* a department of W France, in Pays de la Loire region. Capital: Nantes. Pop.: 948 307 (1975). Area: 6980 sq. km (2722 sq. miles).

Loi·ret (*French* lwaˈrɛ) *n.* a department of central France, in Centre region. Capital: Orléans. Pop.: 502 213 (1975). Area: 6812 sq. km (2657 sq. miles).

Loir-et-Cher (*French* lwar e ˈʃɛːr) *n.* a department of N central France, in Centre region. Capital: Blois. Pop.: 289 474 (1975). Area: 6422 sq. km (2505 sq. miles).

loi·ter (ˈlɔɪtə) *vb.* (*intr.*) to stand or act aimlessly or idly. [C14: perhaps from Middle Dutch *löteren* to wobble: perhaps related to Old English *lūtian* to lurk] —**ˈloi·ter·er** *n.* —**ˈloi·ter·ing·ly** *adv.*

Lo·ki (ˈləʊkɪ) *n. Norse myth.* the god of mischief and destruction.

Lok Sa·bha (ˈləʊk ˈsʌbɑː) *n.* the lower chamber of India's Parliament. Compare **Rajya Sabha.** [Hindi, from *lok* people + *sabha* assembly]

loll (lɒl) *vb.* **1.** (*intr.*) to lie, lean, or lounge in a lazy or relaxed manner. **2.** to hang or allow to hang loosely. ~*n.* **3.** an act or instance of lolling. [C14: perhaps imitative; perhaps related to Middle Dutch *lollen* to doze] —**ˈloll·er** *n.* —**ˈloll·ing·ly** *adv.*

Lol·land *or* **Laa·land** (*Danish* ˈlɔlan) *n.* an island of Denmark in the Baltic Sea, south of Sjaelland. Pop.: 78 916 (1970). Area: 1240 sq. km (480 sq. miles).

lol·la·pa·loo·za (ˌlɒləpəˈluːzə) *or* **lal·a·pa·loo·za** *n. U.S. slang.* something excellent. [origin unknown]

Lol·lard (ˈlɒləd) *n. English history.* a follower of John Wycliffe during the 14th, 15th, and 16th centuries. [C14: from Middle Dutch; mutterer, from *lollen* to mumble (prayers)] —**ˈLol·lard·y, ˈLol·lard·ry,** *or* **ˈLol·lard·ism** *n.*

lol·li·pop (ˈlɒlɪˌpɒp) *n.* **1.** a boiled sweet or toffee stuck on a small wooden stick. **2.** *Brit.* another word for **ice lolly.** [C18: perhaps from Northern English dialect *lolly* the tongue (compare LOLL) + POP[1]]

lol·lop (ˈlɒləp) *vb.* (*intr.*) *Chiefly Brit.* **1.** to walk or run with a clumsy or relaxed bouncing movement. **2.** a less common word for **lounge.** [C18: probably from LOLL + *-op* as in GALLOP, to emphasize the contrast in meaning]

lol·ly (ˈlɒlɪ) *n., pl.* **·lies. 1.** an informal word for **lollipop. 2.** *Brit.* short for **ice lolly. 3.** *Brit.* a slang word for money. **4.** *Austral. informal.* a sweet, esp. a boiled one. **5. do the** (*or* **one's**) **lolly.** *Austral. informal.* to lose one's temper. [shortened from LOLLIPOP]

lol·ly wa·ter *n. Austral. informal.* any of various coloured soft drinks.

Lo·max (ˈləʊmæks) *n.* **Al·an.** born 1915, and his father **John A·ver·y** (ˈeɪvərɪ) (1867–1948), U.S. folklorists.

Lom·bard[1] (ˈlɒmbəd, -bɑːd, ˈlʌm-) *n.* **1.** a native or inhabitant of Lombardy. **2.** Also called: **Langobard.** a member of an ancient Germanic people who settled in N Italy after 568 A.D. ~*adj. also* **Lom·bar·dic. 3.** of or relating to Lombardy or the Lombards.

Lom·bard[2] (ˈlɒmbəd, -bɑːd, ˈlʌm-) *n.* **Pe·ter.** ?1100–?60, Italian theologian, noted for his *Sententiarum libri quatuor.*

Lom·bard Street *n.* the British financial and banking world. [C16: from a street in London once occupied by Lombard bankers]

Lom·bard·y (ˈlɒmbədɪ, ˈlʌm-) *n.* a region of N central Italy, bordering on the Alps: dominated by prosperous lordships and city-states during the Middle Ages; later ruled by Spain and then by Austria before becoming part of Italy in 1859; intensively cultivated and in parts highly industrialized. Pop.: 8 526 718 (1971). Area: 23 804 sq. km (9284 sq. miles). Italian name: **Lom·bar·di·a** (ˌlombarˈdiːa).

Lom·bard·y pop·lar *n.* an Italian poplar tree, *Populus nigra italica*, with upwardly pointing branches giving it a columnar shape.

Lom·bok (ˈlɒmbɒk) *n.* an island of Indonesia, in the Nusa Tenggara Islands east of Java: came under Dutch rule in 1894; important biologically as being transitional between Asian and Australian in flora and fauna, the line of demarcation beginning at **Lombok Strait** (a channel between Lombok and Bali, connecting the Flores Sea with the Indian Ocean). Chief town: Mataram. Pop.: 1 300 234 (1961). Area: 4730 sq. km (1826 sq. miles).

Lom·bro·si·an (lɒmˈbrəʊzɪən) *adj.* of or relating to the doctrine propounded by Lombroso that criminals are a product of hereditary and atavistic factors and can be classified as a definite abnormal type.

Lom·bro·so (*Italian* lomˈbroːso) *n.* **Ce·sa·re** (ˈtʃeːzare). 1836–1909, Italian criminologist: he postulated the existence of a criminal type.

Lo·mé (*French* lɔˈme) *n.* the capital and chief port of Togo, on the Bight of Benin. Pop.: 148 443 (1970).

lo·ment (ˈləʊmɛnt) *or* **lo·men·tum** (ləʊˈmɛntəm) *n., pl.* **·ments** *or* **·men·ta** (-ˈmɛntə). the pod of certain leguminous plants, constricted between each seed and breaking into one-seeded portions when ripe. [C19: from Latin *lomentum* bean meal] —**lo+men+ta+ceous** (ˌləʊmənˈteɪʃəs) *adj.*

Lo+mond (ˈləʊmənd) *n.* **1. Loch.** a lake in W Scotland, north of Glasgow: the largest Scottish lake. Length: about 38 km (24 miles). Width: up to 8 km (5 miles). **2.** See **Ben Lomond.**

Lon+don[1] (ˈlʌndən) *n.* **1.** the capital of the United Kingdom, a port in S England on the River Thames near its estuary on the North Sea: consists of the **City** (the financial quarter), the **West End** (the entertainment and major shopping centre), the **East End** (the industrial and dock area), and extensive suburbs. Latin name: **Londinium.** See also **City. 2. Greater.** the administrative area of London, consisting of the City of London and 32 boroughs (12 Inner London boroughs and 20 Outer London boroughs): formed in 1965 from the City, parts of Surrey, Kent, Essex, and Hertfordshire, and almost all of Middlesex. Pop.: 7 028 200 (1976 est.). Area: 1610 sq. km (628 sq. miles). **3.** a city in SE Canada, in SE Ontario on the Thames River: University of Western Ontario (1878). Pop.: 223 222 (1971). —ˈ**Lon+don+er** *n.*

Lon+don[2] (ˈlʌndən) *n.* **Jack,** pen name of *John Griffith London.* 1876–1916, U.S. novelist, short-story writer, and adventurer. His works include *Call of the Wild* (1903), *The Sea Wolf* (1904), *The Iron Heel* (1907), and the semiautobiographical *John Barleycorn* (1913).

Lon+don+der+ry (ˈlʌndənˌdɛrɪ) *or* **Der+ry** *n.* **1.** a county of Northern Ireland, on the Atlantic. County town: Londonderry. Pop.: 130 296 (1971). Area: 2108 sq. km (814 sq. miles). **2.** a port in N Northern Ireland, county town of Londonderry and second city of Northern Ireland: given to the City of London in 1613 to be colonized by Londoners; besieged by James II's forces (1688–89). Pop.: 31 437 (1971).

Lon+don pride *n.* a saxifragaceous plant, a hybrid between *Saxifraga spathularis* and *S. umbrosa,* having a basal rosette of leaves and pinkish-white flowers.

Lon+dri+na (*Portuguese* lonˈdrina) *n.* a city in S Brazil, in Paraná: centre of a coffee-growing area. Pop.: 156 670 (1970).

lone (ləʊn) *adj.* (*prenominal*) **1.** unaccompanied; solitary. **2.** single or isolated: *a lone house.* **3.** a literary word for **lonely. 4.** *Rare.* unmarried or widowed. [C14: from the mistaken division of ALONE into *a lone*] —ˈ**lone+ness** *n.*

lone hand *n.* **1.** (in card games such as euchre) an independent player or hand played without a partner. **2. play a lone hand.** to operate without assistance.

lone+ly (ˈləʊnlɪ) *adj.* **+li+er, +li+est. 1.** unhappy as a result of being without the companionship of others: *a lonely man.* **2.** causing or resulting from the state of being alone: *a lonely existence.* **3.** isolated, unfrequented, or desolate. **4.** without companions; solitary. —ˈ**lone+li+ness** *n.*

lone+ly heart *n.* a person made unhappy by being or living alone, esp. an unmarried person.

lon+er (ˈləʊnə) *n. Informal.* a person who avoids the company of others or prefers to be alone.

lone+some (ˈləʊnsəm) *adj.* **1.** *Chiefly U.S.* another word for **lonely.** ~*n.* **2. by one's lonesome.** *U.S. informal.* on one's own. —ˈ**lone+some+ly** *adv.* —ˈ**lone+some+ness** *n.*

lone wolf *n.* a person who prefers to be alone.

long[1] (lɒŋ) *adj.* **1.** having relatively great extent in space or duration in time. **2. a.** (*postpositive*) of a specified number of units in extent or duration: *three hours long.* **b.** (*in combination*): *a two-foot-long line.* **3.** having or consisting of a relatively large number of items or parts: *a long list.* **4.** having greater than the average or expected range: *a long memory.* **5.** being the longer or longest of alternatives: *the long way to the bank.* **6.** having more than the average or usual quantity, extent, or duration: *a long match.* **7.** intense or thorough (esp. in the phrase **a long look**). **8.** (of drinks) containing a large quantity of nonalcoholic beverage. **9.** *Informal.* (foll. by *on*) plentifully supplied or endowed (with): *long on good ideas.* **10.** *Phonetics.* (of a speech sound, esp. a vowel) **a.** of relatively considerable duration. **b.** classified as long, as distinguished from the quality of other vowels. **c.** (in popular usage) denoting the qualities of the five English vowels in such words as *mate, mete, mite, moat, moot,* and *mute.* **11.** from end to end; lengthwise. **12.** unlikely to win, happen, succeed, etc.: *a long chance.* **13.** *Prosody.* **a.** denoting a vowel of relatively great duration or (esp. in classical verse) followed by more than one consonant. **b.** denoting a syllable containing such a vowel. **c.** (in verse that is not quantitative) carrying the emphasis or ictus. **14.** *Finance.* having or characterized by large holdings of securities or commodities in anticipation of rising prices: *a long position.* **15.** *Cricket.* (of a fielding position) near the boundary: *long leg.* **16.** (of people) tall and slender. **17. in the long run.** ultimately; after or over a period of time. **18. long in the tooth.** *Informal.* old. ~*adv.* **19.** for a certain time or period: *how long will it last?* **20.** for or during an extensive period of time: *long into the next year.* **21.** at a distant time; quite a bit of time: *long before I met you; long ago.* **22.** *Finance.* into a position with more security or commodity holdings than are required by sale contracts and therefore dependent on rising prices for profit: *to go long.* **23. as** (*or* **so**) **long as. a.** for or during just the length of time that. **b.** inasmuch as; since. **c.** provided that; if. **24. no longer.** not any more; formerly but not now. ~*n.* **25.** a long time (esp. in the phrase **for long**). **26.** a relatively long thing, such as a signal in Morse code. **27.** a clothing size for tall people, esp. in trousers. **28.** *Phonetics.* a long vowel or syllable. **29.** *Finance.* a person with large holdings of a security or commodity in expectation of a rise in its price; bull. **30.** *Music.* a note common in medieval music but now obsolete, having the time value of two breves. **31. before long.** soon. **32. the long and the short of it.** the essential points or facts. [Old English *lang;* related to Old High German *lang,* Old Norse *langr,* Latin *longus*]

long[2] (lɒŋ) *vb.* (*intr.;* foll. by *for* or an infinitive) to have a strong desire. [Old English *langian;* related to LONG[1]]

long[3] (lɒŋ) *vb.* (*intr.*) *Archaic.* to belong, appertain, or be appropriate. [Old English *langian* to belong, from *gelang* at hand, belonging to; compare ALONG]

Long (lɒŋ) *n.* **Craw·ford Wil·liam·son.** 1815–78, U.S. surgeon. He was the first to use ether as an anaesthetic.

long. *abbrev. for* longitude.

long- *adv.* (*in combination*) for or lasting a long time: *long-awaited; long-established; long-lasting.*

lon+gan (ˈlɒŋgən) *or* **lun+gan** *n.* **1.** a sapindaceous tree, *Euphoria longan,* of tropical and subtropical Asia, with small yellowish-white flowers and small edible fruits. **2.** the fruit of this tree, which is similar to but smaller than the litchi, having white juicy pulp and a single seed. [C18: from Chinese *lung yen* dragon's eye]

long-and-short work. *n. Architect.* the alternation in masonry of vertical and horizontal blocks of stone.

lon+ga+nim+i·ty (ˌlɒŋgəˈnɪmɪtɪ) *n. Now rare.* patience or forbearance. [C15: from Late Latin *longanimitās,* from *longanimis* forbearing, from *longus* long + *animus* mind, soul] —**lon+gan+i+mous** (lɒŋˈgænəməs) *adj.*

long arm *n. Informal.* **1.** power, esp. far-reaching power: *the long arm of the law.* **2. make a long arm.** to reach out for something, as from a sitting position.

Long Beach *n.* a city in SW California, on San Pedro Bay: resort and naval base; oil-refining. Pop.: 346 793 (1973 est.).

Long+ben+ton (ˌlɒŋˈbɛntən) *n.* a town in N England, in Tyneside near Newcastle. Pop.: 48 970 (1971).

long+boat (ˈlɒŋˌbəʊt) *n.* **1.** the largest boat carried aboard a commercial sailing vessel. **2.** another term for **longship.**

long+bow (ˈlɒŋˌbəʊ) *n.* a large powerful hand-drawn bow, esp. as used in medieval England.

long+case clock (ˈlɒŋˌkeɪs) *n.* another name for **grandfather clock.**

long+cloth (ˈlɒŋˌklɒθ) *n.* **1.** a fine plain-weave cotton cloth made in long strips. **2.** *U.S.* a light soft muslin.

long-coats *pl. n.* dress-like garments formerly worn by a baby. Archaic name: **long clothes.**

long-dat·ed *adj.* (of a gilt-edged security) having more than 15 years to run before redemption. Compare **medium-dated, short-dated.**

long-day *adj.* (of certain plants) able to mature and flower only if exposed to long periods of daylight (more than 12 hours), each followed by a shorter period of darkness. Compare **short-day.**

long-dis·tance *n.* **1.** (*modifier*) covering relatively long distances: *a long-distance driver.* **2.** (*modifier*) (of telephone calls, lines, etc.) connecting points a relatively long way apart. **3.** *Chiefly U.S.* a long-distance telephone call. **4.** a long-distance telephone system or its operator. ~*adv.* **5.** by a long-distance telephone line: *he phoned long-distance.*

long-drawn-out *adj.* over-prolonged or extended.

longe (lʌndʒ, lɒndʒ) *n.* an older spelling of **lunge**[2]. [C17: via Old French from Latin *longus* LONG[1]]

long-eared owl *n.* a slender European owl, *Asio otus,* with long ear tufts: most common in coniferous forests.

Long Ea·ton (ˈiːtᵊn) *n.* a town in N central England, in SE Derbyshire. Pop.: 33 694 (1971).

lon+ge·ron (ˈlɒndʒərən) *n.* a main longitudinal structural member of an aircraft. [C20: from French: side support, ultimately from Latin *longus* LONG[1]]

lon+gev+i·ty (lɒnˈdʒɛvɪtɪ) *n.* **1.** long life. **2.** relatively long duration of employment, service, etc. [C17: from Late Latin *longaevitās,* from Latin *longaevus* long-lived, from *longus* LONG[1] + *aevum* age] —**lon+ge·vous** (lɒnˈdʒiːvəs) *adj.*

long face *n.* a disappointed, solemn, or miserable facial expression. —ˌ**long-**ˈ**faced** *adj.*

Long·fel·low (ˈlɒŋˌfɛləʊ) *n.* **Hen·ry Wads·worth.** 1807–82, U.S. poet, noted particularly for his long narrative poems *Evangeline* (1847) and *The Song of Hiawatha* (1855).

Long+ford (ˈlɒŋfəd) *n.* **1.** a county of N Ireland, in Leinster province. County town: Longford. Pop.: 28 250 (1971). Area: 1043 sq. km (403 sq. miles). **2.** a town in N Ireland, county town of Co. Longford. Pop.: 4791 (1971).

long+hand (ˈlɒŋˌhænd) *n.* a form of handwriting in which letters, words, etc., are set down in full.

long haul *n.* **1.** a journey over a long distance, esp. one involving the transport of goods. **2.** a lengthy job.

long-head·ed *adj.* astute; shrewd; sagacious. —ˌ**long-**ˈ**head·ed+ly** *adv.* —ˌ**long-**ˈ**head·ed·ness** *n.*

long hop *n. Cricket.* a short-pitched ball, which can easily be hit.

long+horn (ˈlɒŋˌhɔːn) *n.* **1.** Also called: **Texas longhorn.** a long-horned breed of beef cattle, usually red or variegated, formerly common in the southwestern U.S. **2.** a British breed of beef cattle with long curved horns.

long-horned bee+tle *n.* another name for **longicorn beetle** (see **longicorn** (sense 1)).

long house *n.* **1.** a long communal dwelling of the Iroquois and other North American Indian peoples. It often served as a council house as well. **2.** a long dwelling found in other parts of the world, such as Borneo.

long hun·dred+weight *n.* the full name for **hundredweight** (sense 1).

lon+gi+corn (ˈlɒndʒɪˌkɔːn) *n.* **1.** Also called: **longicorn beetle,**

long-horned beetle. any beetle of the family *Cerambycidae,* having a long narrow body, long legs, and long antennae. ~*adj.* **2.** *Zoology.* having or designating long antennae. [C19: from New Latin *longicornis* long-horned]

long·ing ('lɒŋɪŋ) *n.* **1.** a prolonged unfulfilled desire or need. ~*adj.* **2.** having or showing desire or need: *a longing look.* —**'long·ing·ly** *adv.* —**'long·ing·ness** *n.*

Lon·gi·nus (lɒn'dʒaɪnəs) *n.* **Di·o·ny·si·us** (ˌdaɪə'nɪsɪəs). ?2nd century A.D., supposed author of the famous Greek treatise on literary criticism, *On the Sublime.* —**Lon·gin·e·an** (lɒn'dʒɪnɪən) *adj.*

long·ish ('lɒŋɪʃ) *adj.* rather long.

Long Is·land *n.* an island in SE New York State, separated from the S shore of Connecticut by **Long Island Sound** (an arm of the Atlantic): contains the New York City boroughs of Brooklyn and Queens in the west, many resorts (notably Coney Island), and two large airports (La Guardia and the John F. Kennedy). Area: 4462 sq. km (1723 sq. miles).

lon·gi·tude ('lɒndʒɪˌtjuːd) *n.* **1.** distance in degrees east or west of the prime meridian at 0° measured by the angle between the plane of the prime meridian and that of the meridian through the point in question, or by the corresponding time difference. See **latitude** (sense 1). **2.** *Astronomy.* short for **celestial longitude.** [C14: from Latin *longitūdō* length, from *longus* LONG[1]]

lon·gi·tu·di·nal (ˌlɒndʒɪ'tjuːdɪnᵊl) *adj.* **1.** of or relating to longitude or length. **2.** placed or extended lengthways. Compare **transverse** (sense 1). —**ˌlon·gi·'tu·di·nal·ly** *adv.*

lon·gi·tu·di·nal wave *n.* a wave that is propagated in the same direction as the displacement of the transmitting medium. Compare **transverse wave.**

long jen·ny *n. Billiards.* an in-off up the cushion into a far pocket. Compare **short jenny.** [from *Jenny,* pet form of *Janet*]

long johns *pl. n. Informal.* underpants with long legs.

long jump *n.* an athletic contest in which competitors try to cover the farthest distance possible with a running jump from a fixed board or mark. U.S. equivalent: **broad jump.** —**long jump·ing** *n.*

long·leaf pine ('lɒŋˌliːf) *n.* a North American pine tree, *Pinus palustris,* with long needle-like leaves and orange-brown bark: the most important timber tree of the southeastern U.S.

long-legged ('lɒŋˌlɛgd, -ˌlɛgɪd) *adj.* **1.** having long legs. **2.** *Informal.* (of a person or animal) able to run fast.

long-lived *adj.* having long life, existence, or currency. —**ˌlong-'lived·ness** *n.*

Long March *n.* **the.** a journey of about 10 000 km (6000 miles) undertaken (1934–35) by some 100 000 Chinese Communists when they were forced out of their base in Kiangsi in SE China. They made their way to Shensi in NW China; only about 8000 survived the rigours of the journey.

long mark *n.* another name for **macron.**

long meas·ure *n.* another name for **linear measure.**

long me·tre *n.* **1.** a stanzaic form consisting of four octosyllabic lines, used esp. for hymns.

long moss *n.* another name for **Spanish moss.**

Lon·go·bard ('lɒŋgəˌbɑːd) *n., pl.* **·bards** *or* **·bar·di** (-ˌbɑːdɪ). a rare name for an ancient **Lombard.** —**ˌLon·go·'bar·di·an** *or* **ˌLon·go·'bar·dic** *adj.*

Long Par·lia·ment *n. English history.* **1.** the Parliament summoned by Charles I that assembled on Nov. 3, 1640, was expelled by Cromwell in 1653, and was finally dissolved in 1660. See also **Rump. 2.** the Cavalier Parliament of 1661–79. **3.** the Parliament called in Henry IV's reign that met from March 1 to Dec. 22, 1406.

long pig *n.* human flesh eaten by cannibals. [translation of a Maori and Polynesian term]

long-play·ing *adj.* of or relating to an LP (long-player).

long prim·er *n.* a size of printer's type, approximately equal to 10 point.

long purse *n. Informal.* wealth; riches.

long-range *adj.* **1.** of or extending into the future: *a long-range weather forecast.* **2.** (of vehicles, aircraft, etc.) capable of covering great distances without refuelling. **3.** (of weapons) made to be fired at a distant target.

longs (lɒŋz) *pl. n.* **1.** full-length trousers. **2.** long-dated gilt-edged securities.

long *s* *n.* a lower-case *s,* printed ʃ, formerly used in handwriting and printing. Also called: **long ess.**

long·ship ('lɒŋˌʃɪp) *n.* a narrow open vessel with oars and a square sail, used esp. by the Vikings during medieval times.

long·shore ('lɒŋˌʃɔː) *adj.* situated on, relating to, or along the shore. [C19: shortened form of *alongshore*]

long·shore drift *n.* the process whereby beach material is gradually shifted laterally as a result of waves meeting the shore at an oblique angle.

long·shore·man ('lɒŋˌʃɔːmən) *n., pl.* **·men.** a U.S. word for **docker**[1].

long shot *n.* **1.** a competitor, as in a race, considered to be unlikely to win. **2.** a bet against heavy odds. **3.** an undertaking, guess, or possibility with little chance of success. **4.** *Films.* a shot where the camera is or appears to be distant from the object to be photographed. **5. by a long shot.** by any means: *he still hasn't finished by a long shot.*

long-sight·ed *adj.* **1.** related to or suffering from hyperopia. **2.** able to see distant objects in focus. **3.** having foresight. —**ˌlong-'sight·ed·ly** *adv.* —**ˌlong-'sight·ed·ness** *n.*

Longs Peak *n.* a mountain in N Colorado, in the Front Range of the Rockies: the highest peak in the Rocky Mountain National Park. Height: 4344 m (14 255 ft.).

long·spur ('lɒŋˌspɜː) *n. U.S.* any of various buntings of the genera *Calcarius* and *Rhyncophanes,* all of which have a long claw on the hind toe.

long-stand·ing *adj.* existing or in effect for a long time.

long-suf·fer·ing *adj.* **1.** enduring pain, unhappiness, etc., without complaint. ~*n.* also **long-suf·fer·ance. 2.** long and patient endurance. —**ˌlong-'suf·fer·ing·ly** *adv.*

long suit *n.* **1. a.** the longest suit in a hand of cards. **b.** a holding of four or more cards of a suit. **2.** *Informal.* an outstanding advantage, personal quality, or talent.

long-tailed tit *n.* a small European songbird, *Aegithalos caudatus,* with a black, white, and pink plumage and a very long tail: family *Paridae* (tits).

long-term *adj.* **1.** lasting, staying, or extending over a long time: *long-term prospects.* **2.** *Finance.* maturing after a long period of time: *a long-term bond.*

long-term mem·o·ry *n. Psychol.* that section of the memory storage system in which experiences are stored on a semi-permanent basis. Compare **short-term memory.**

long·time ('lɒŋˌtaɪm) *adj.* of long standing.

long tin *n. Brit.* a tall long loaf of bread.

long tom *n.* **1.** a long swivel cannon formerly used in naval warfare. **2.** a long-range land gun. **3.** an army slang name for **cannon** (sense 1).

long ton *n.* the full name for **ton**[1] (sense 1).

Lon·gueuil (lɒŋ'geɪl; *French* lɔ̃'gœj) *n.* a city in SE Canada, in S Quebec: a suburb of Montreal. Pop.: 97 590 (1971).

lon·gueur (*French* lɔ̃'gœːr) *n.* a period of boredom or dullness. [literally: length]

Lon·gus ('lɒŋgəs) *n.* ?3rd century A.D., Greek author of the prose romance *Daphnis and Chloe.*

long va·ca·tion *n.* the long period of holiday in the summer during which universities, law courts, etc., are closed.

long view *n.* the consideration of events or circumstances likely to occur in the future.

long wave *n.* **a.** a radio wave with a wavelength greater than 1000 metres. **b.** (*as modifier*): *a long-wave broadcast.*

long·ways ('lɒŋˌweɪz) *or U.S.* **long·wise** *adv.* another word for **lengthways.**

long-wind·ed *adj.* **1.** tiresomely long. **2.** capable of energetic activity without becoming short of breath. —**ˌlong-'wind·ed·ly** *adv.* —**ˌlong-'wind·ed·ness** *n.*

long-wire aer·i·al *n.* a travelling-wave aerial consisting of one or more conductors, the length of which usually exceeds several wavelengths.

Long·year·byen ('lɒŋjɪəˌbjɛn) *n.* a village on West Spitsbergen island, administrative centre of the Svalbard archipelago: coal-mining.

lo·nic·er·a (lɒ'nɪsərə) *n.* See **honeysuckle.**

Lons-le-Sau·nier (*French* lɔ̃ lə so'nje) *n.* a town in E France: saline springs; manufactures sparkling wines. Pop.: 23 292 (1975).

loo[1] (luː) *n., pl.* **loos.** *Brit.* an informal word for **lavatory.** [C20: perhaps from French *lieux d'aisance* water closet]

loo[2] (luː) *n., pl.* **loos. 1.** a gambling card game. **2.** a stake used in this game. [C17: shortened form of *lanterloo,* via Dutch from French *lanterelu,* originally a meaningless word from the refrain of a popular song]

loo·by ('luːbɪ) *n., pl.* **·bies.** a foolish or stupid person. [C14: of unknown origin]

loo·fah ('luːfə) *n.* **1.** the fibrous interior of the fruit of the dishcloth gourd, which is dried, bleached, and used as a bath sponge or for scrubbing. **2.** another name for **dishcloth gourd.** ~Also (esp. U.S.): **loo·fa, luf·fa.** [C19: from New Latin *luffa,* from Arabic *lūf*]

look (lʊk) *vb.* (*mainly intr.*) **1.** (often foll. by *at*) to direct the eyes (towards): *to look at the sea.* **2.** (often foll. by *at*) to direct one's attention (towards): *let's look at the circumstances.* **3.** (often foll. by *to*) to turn one's interests or expectations (towards): *to look to the future.* **4.** (*copula*) to give the impression of being by appearance to the eye or mind; seem: *that looks interesting.* **5.** to face in a particular direction: *the house looks north.* **6.** to expect or hope (to do something): *I look to hear from you soon.* **7.** (foll. by *for*) **a.** to search or seek: *I looked for you everywhere.* **b.** to cherish the expectation (of); hope (for): *I look for success.* **8.** (foll. by *to*) **a.** to be mindful (of): *to look to the promise one has made.* **b.** to have recourse (to): *look to your swords, men!* **9.** to be a pointer or sign: *these early inventions looked towards the development of industry.* **10.** (foll. by *into*) to carry out an investigation: *to look into a mystery.* **11.** (*tr.*) to direct a look at (someone) in a specified way: *she looked her rival up and down.* **12.** (*tr.*) to accord in appearance with (something): *to look one's age.* **13. look alive** *or* **lively.** hurry up; get busy (often used in a nautical context). **14. look daggers.** See **dagger** (sense 4). **15. look here.** an expression used to attract someone's attention, add emphasis to a statement, etc. **16. look sharp** *or* **smart.** (*imperative*) to hurry up; make haste. **17. not look at.** to refuse to consider: *they won't even look at my offer of £5000.* **18. not much to look at.** unattractive; plain. ~*n.* **19.** the act or an instance of looking: *a look of despair.* **20.** a view or sight (of something): *let's have a look.* **21.** (*often pl.*) appearance to the eye or mind; aspect: *the look of innocence; I don't like the looks of this place.* ~See also **look after, look back, look down, look forward to, look-in, look on, lookout, look over, look through, look up.** [Old English *lōcian;* related to Middle Dutch *læken,* Old High German *luogen* to look out]

Usage. See at **feel.**

look af·ter *vb.* (*intr., prep.*) **1.** to take care of; be responsible

for: *she looked after the child while I was out.* **2.** to follow with the eyes: *he looked after the girl thoughtfully.*
look back *vb.* (*intr., adv.*) **1.** to cast one's mind to the past. **2.** (*usually used in negative*) to cease to make progress: *after his book was published, he never looked back.* **3.** *Chiefly Brit.* to pay another visit later.
look down *vb.* **1.** (*intr., adv.;* foll. by *on* or *upon*) to express or show contempt or disdain (for). **2. look down one's nose at.** to express disdain for.
look·er ('lʊkə) *n. Informal.* **1.** a person who looks. **2.** *Chiefly U.S.* a very attractive person, esp. a woman or girl.
look for·ward to *vb.* (*intr., adv. + prep.*) to wait or hope for, esp. with pleasure.
look-in *Informal.* ~*n.* **1.** a chance to be chosen, participate, etc. **2.** a short visit. ~*vb.* **look in. 3.** (*intr., adv.;* often foll. by *on*) to pay a short visit.
look·ing glass *n.* a mirror, esp. a ladies' dressing mirror.
look on *vb.* (*intr.*) **1.** (*adv.*) to be a spectator at an event or incident. **2.** (*prep.*) Also: **look upon.** to consider or regard: *she looked on the whole affair as a joke; he looks on his mother-in-law with disapproval.* —ˌ**look·er-'on** *n.*
look·out ('lʊkˌaʊt) *n.* **1.** the act of keeping watch against danger, etc. **2.** a person or persons instructed or employed to keep such a watch, esp. on a ship. **3.** a strategic point from which a watch is kept. **4.** *Informal.* worry or concern: *that's his lookout.* **5.** *Chiefly Brit.* outlook, chances, or view. ~*vb.* **look out.** (*adv., mainly intr.*) **6.** to heed one's behaviour; be careful: *look out for the children's health.* **7.** to be on the watch: *look out for my mother at the station.* **8.** (*tr.*) to search for and find: *I'll look out some curtains for your new house.* **9.** (foll. by *on* or *over*) to face in a particular direction: *the house looks out over the moor.*
look o·ver *vb.* **1.** (*intr., prep.*) to inspect by making a tour of (a factory, house, etc.): *we looked over the country house.* **2.** (*tr., adv.*) to examine (a document, letter, etc.): *please look the papers over quickly.*
look-see *n. U.S. slang.* a brief inspection or look.
look through *vb.* **1.** (*intr., prep.* or *tr., adv.*) to examine, esp. cursorily: *he looked through his notes before the lecture.* **2.** (*intr., prep.*) to ignore (a person) deliberately: *whenever he meets his ex-girlfriend, she looks straight through him.*
look up *vb.* (*adv.*) **1.** (*tr.*) to discover (something required to be known) by resorting to a work of reference, such as a dictionary. **2.** (*intr.*) to increase, as in quality or value: *things are looking up.* **3.** (*intr.;* foll. by *to*) to have respect (for): *I've always wanted a girlfriend I could look up to.* **4.** (*tr.*) to visit or make contact with (a person): *I'll look you up when I'm in town.*
loom[1] (lu:m) *n.* **1.** an apparatus, worked by hand or mechanically (**power loom**), for weaving yarn into a textile. **2.** the middle portion of an oar, which acts as a fulcrum swivelling in the rowlock. [C13 (meaning any kind of tool): variant of Old English *gelōma* tool; compare HEIRLOOM]
loom[2] (lu:m) *vb.* (*intr.*) **1.** to come into view indistinctly with an enlarged and often threatening aspect. **2.** (of an event) to seem ominously close. **3.** (often foll. by *over*) (of large objects) to dominate or overhang. ~*n.* **4.** a rising appearance, as of something far away. [C16: perhaps from East Frisian *lomen* to move slowly]
loom[3] (lu:m) *n. Archaic or dialect.* **1.** another name for **diver** (the bird). **2.** any of various other birds, esp. the guillemot. [C17: from Old Norse *lomr*]
loo mask *n.* a half-mask worn during the 18th century for masquerades, etc. Also called: **loup.** [C17 *loo,* from French *loup,* literally: wolf, from Latin *lupus*]
loom-state *adj.* (of a woven cotton fabric) not yet dyed.
loon[1] (lu:n) *n.* the U.S. name for **diver** (the bird). [C17: of Scandinavian origin; related to Old Norse *lōmr*]
loon[2] (lu:n) *n.* **1.** *Informal.* a simple-minded or stupid person. **2.** *Archaic.* a person of low rank or occupation (esp. in the phrase **lord and loon**). [C15: origin obscure]
loon·y, loon·ey, *or* **lun·y** ('lu:nɪ) *Slang.* ~*adj.* **loon·i·er, loon·i·est** *or* **lun·i·er, lun·i·est. 1.** lunatic; insane. **2.** foolish or ridiculous. ~*n., pl.* **loon·ies, loon·eys,** *or* **lun·ies. 3.** a foolish or insane person. —'**loon·i·ness** *or* '**lun·i·ness** *n.*
loon·y bin *n. Slang.* a mental hospital or asylum.
loop[1] (lu:p) *n.* **1.** the round or oval shape formed by a line, string, etc., that curves around to cross itself. **2.** any round or oval-shaped thing that is closed or nearly closed. **3.** an intrauterine contraceptive device in the shape of a loop. **4.** *Electronics.* **a.** a closed electric or magnetic circuit through which a signal can circulate, as in a feedback control system. **b.** short for **loop aerial. 5.** a flight manoeuvre in which an aircraft flies one complete circle in the vertical plane. **6.** Also called: **loop line.** *Chiefly Brit.* a railway branch line which leaves the main line and rejoins it after a short distance. **7.** *Maths, physics.* a closed curve on a graph: *hysteresis loop.* **8.** another name for **antinode. 9.** *Anatomy.* **a.** the most common basic pattern of the human fingerprint, formed by several sharply rising U-shaped ridges. Compare **arch**[1] (sense 4b.). **b.** a bend in a tubular structure, such as the U-shaped curve in a kidney tubule. (**Henle's loop**). **10.** *Computer technol.* a series of instructions in a program, performed repeatedly until some specified condition is satisfied. ~*vb.* **11.** (*tr.*) to make a loop in or of (a line, string, etc.). **12.** (*tr.*) to fasten or encircle with a loop or something like a loop. **13.** Also: **loop the loop.** to cause (an aircraft) to perform a loop or (of an aircraft) to perform a loop. **14.** (*intr.*) to move in loops or in a path like a loop. [C14: *loupe,* origin unknown]
loop[2] (lu:p) *n.* an archaic word for **loophole.** [C14: perhaps related to Middle Dutch *lupen* to watch, peer]
loop aer·i·al *n.* an aerial that consists of one or more coils of wire wound on a frame. Maximum radiation or reception is in the plane of the loop, the minimum occurring at right angles to it. Sometimes shortened to **loop.** Also called: **frame aerial.**
loop·er ('lu:pə) *n.* **1.** a person or thing that loops or makes loops. **2.** another name for a **measuring worm.**
loop·hole ('lu:pˌhəʊl) *n.* **1.** an ambiguity, omission, etc., as in a law, by which one can avoid a penalty or responsibility. **2.** a small gap or hole in a wall, esp. one in a fortified wall. ~*vb.* **3.** (*tr.*) to provide with loopholes.
loop knot *n.* a knot that leaves a loop extending from it.
loop·y ('lu:pɪ) *adj.* **loop·i·er, loop·i·est. 1.** full of loops; curly or twisted. **2.** *Informal.* slightly mad, crazy, or stupid.
loose (lu:s) *adj.* **1.** free or released from confinement or restraint. **2.** not close, compact, or tight in structure or arrangement. **3.** not fitted or fitting closely: *loose clothing is cooler.* **4.** not bundled, packaged, fastened, or put in a container: *loose nails.* **5.** inexact; imprecise: *a loose translation.* **6.** (of funds, cash, etc.) not allocated or locked away; readily available. **7. a.** (esp. of women) promiscuous or easy. **b.** (of attitudes, ways of life, etc.) immoral or dissolute. **8.** lacking a sense of responsibility or propriety: *loose talk.* **9. a.** (of the bowels) emptying easily, esp. excessively; lax. **b.** (of a cough) accompanied by phlegm, mucus, etc. **10.** (of a dye or dyed article) fading as a result of washing; not fast. **11.** *Informal, chiefly U.S.* very relaxed; easy. ~*n.* **12. the loose.** *Rugby.* the part of play when the forwards close round the ball in a ruck or loose scrum. See **scrum. 13. on the loose. a.** free from confinement or restraint. **b.** *Informal.* on a spree. ~*adv.* **14. a.** in a loose manner; loosely. **b.** (*in combination*): *loose-fitting.* ~*vb.* **15.** (*tr.*) to set free or release, as from confinement, restraint, or obligation. **16.** (*tr.*) to unfasten or untie. **17.** to make or become less strict, tight, firmly attached, compact, etc. **18.** (when *intr.,* often foll. by *off*) to let fly (a bullet, arrow, or other missile). [C13 (in the sense: not bound): from Old Norse *lauss* free; related to Old English *lēas* free from, -LESS] —'**loose·ly** *adv.* —'**loose·ness** *n.*
loose·box ('lu:sˌbɒks) *n.* an enclosed and covered stall with a door in which an animal can be confined.
loose change *n.* money in the form of coins suitable for small expenditures.
loose cov·er *n.* a fitted but easily removable cloth cover for a chair, sofa, etc. U.S. name: **slipcover.**
loose end *n.* **1.** a detail that is left unsettled, unexplained, or incomplete. **2. at a loose end.** *Informal.* **a.** unoccupied. **b.** not sure what to do or think.
loose-joint·ed *adj.* **1.** supple and easy in movement. **2.** loosely built; with ill-fitting joints. —ˌ**loose-'joint·ed·ness** *n.*
loose-leaf *adj.* **1.** (of a binder, album, etc.) capable of being opened to allow removal and addition of pages. ~*n.* **2.** a serial publication published in loose leaves and kept in such a binder.
loose-limbed *adj.* (of a person) having supple limbs.
loos·en ('lu:sᵊn) *vb.* **1.** to make or become less tight, fixed, etc. **2.** (often foll. by *up*) to make or become less firm, compact, or rigid. **3.** (*tr.*) to untie. **4.** (*tr.*) to let loose; set free. **5.** (often foll. by *up*) to make or become less strict, severe, etc. **6.** (*tr.*) to rid or relieve (the bowels) of constipation. [C14: from LOOSE] —'**loos·en·er** *n.*
loose or·der *n. Military.* a formation in which soldiers, units, etc., are widely separated from each other.
loose smut *n.* a disease of cereal grasses caused by smut fungi of the genus *Ustilago,* in which powdery spore masses replace the host tissue.
loose·strife ('lu:sˌstraɪf) *n.* **1.** any of various primulaceous plants of the genus *Lysimachia,* esp. the yellow-flowered *L. vulgaris* (**yellow loosestrife**). See also **moneywort. 2. purple loosestrife.** Also called: **willowherb.** a purple-flowered lythraceous marsh plant, *Lythrum salicaria.* **3.** any of several similar or related plants, such as the primulaceous plant *Naumburgia thyrsiflora* (**tufted loosestrife**). [C16: LOOSE + STRIFE, an erroneous translation of Latin *lysimachia,* as if from Greek *lusimakhos* ending strife, instead of from the name of the supposed discoverer, *Lusimakhos*]
loose-tongued *adj.* careless or irresponsible in talking.
loos·ing *or* **low·sen·ing** ('lu:sɪŋ, -zɪŋ, 'lɔɪ-) *n. Yorkshire dialect.* a celebration of one's 21st birthday.
loot (lu:t) *n.* **1.** goods stolen during pillaging, as in wartime, during riots, etc. **2.** goods, money, etc., obtained illegally. **3.** *Informal.* money or wealth. **4.** the act of looting or plundering. ~*vb.* **5.** to pillage (a city, settlement, etc.) during war or riots. **6.** to steal (money or goods), esp. during pillaging. [C19: from Hindi *lūt*] —'**loot·er** *n.*
lop[1] (lɒp) *vb.* **lops, lop·ping, lopped.** (*tr.;* usually foll. by *off*) **1.** to sever (parts) from a tree, body, etc., esp. with swift strokes. **2.** to cut out or eliminate from as excessive. ~*n.* **3.** a part or parts lopped off, as from a tree. [C15 *loppe* branches cut off; compare LOB[1]] —'**lop·per** *n.*
lop[2] (lɒp) *vb.* **lops, lop·ping, lopped. 1.** to hang or allow to hang loosely. **2.** (*intr.*) to slouch about or move awkwardly. **3.** (*intr.*) a less common word for **lope.** [C16: perhaps related to LOP[1]; compare LOB[1]]
lop[3] (lɒp) *n. Northern English dialect.* a flea. [probably from Old Norse *hloppa* (unattested) flea, from *hlaupa* to LEAP]
lope (ləʊp) *vb.* **1.** (*intr.*) (of a person) to move or run with a long swinging stride. **2.** (*intr.*) (of four-legged animals) to run with a regular bounding movement. **3.** to cause (a horse) to canter

with a long easy stride or (of a horse) to canter in this manner. ~*n.* **4.** a long steady gait or stride. [C15: from Old Norse *hlaupa* to LEAP; compare Middle Dutch *lopen* to run] —**'lop+er** *n.*

lop-eared *adj.* (of animals) having ears that droop.

Lo·pe de Ve·ga (*Spanish* 'lope ðe 'βeɣa) *n.* full name *Lope Felix de Vega Carpio.* 1562–1635, Spanish dramatist, novelist, and poet. He established the classic form of Spanish drama and was a major influence on European, esp. French, literature. Some 500 of his 1800 plays are extant.

lo·pho- *n. combining form.* indicating a crested or tufted part: *lophophore.* [from Greek *lophos* crest]

lo+pho+branch ('ləʊfəˌbræŋk) *n.* **1.** any teleost fish of the suborder *Lophobranchii,* having the gills arranged in rounded tufts: includes the pipefishes and sea horses. ~*adj.* **2.** of, relating to, or belonging to the *Lophobranchii.* —**loph·o+bran+chi+ate** (ˌləʊfə'bræŋkɪɪt, -ˌeɪt) *adj.*

lo+pho+phore ('ləʊfəˌfɔː) *n.* a circle or horseshoe of ciliated tentacles surrounding the mouth and used for the capture of food in minute sessile animals of the phyla *Brachiopoda, Phoronida,* and *Ectoprocta.* —**'lo+pho+'phor+ate** *adj.*

lop+sid·ed (ˌlɒp'saɪdɪd) *adj.* **1.** leaning or inclined to one side. **2.** greater in weight, height, or size on one side. —ˌ**lop+'sid·ed+ly** *adv.* —ˌ**lop+'sid·ed+ness** *n.*

loq. *abbrev. for* loquitur.

lo+qua+cious (lɒ'kweɪʃəs) *adj.* characterized by or showing a tendency to talk a great deal. [C17: from Latin *loquāx* from *loquī* to speak] —**lo+'qua+cious+ly** *adv.* —**lo+quac+i·ty** (lɒ'kwæsɪtɪ) *or* **lo+'qua+cious+ness** *n.*

lo+quat ('ləʊkwɒt, -kwæt) *n.* **1.** an ornamental evergreen rosaceous tree, *Eriobotrya japonica,* of China and Japan, having reddish woolly branches, white flowers, and small yellow edible plumlike fruits. **2.** the fruit of this tree. ~Also called: **Japan plum.** [C19: from Chinese (Cantonese) *lō kwat,* literally: rush orange]

lo+qui+tur *Latin.* ('lɒkwɪtə) he (or she) speaks: used, esp. formerly, as a stage direction. Usually abbreviated to **loq.**

lor (lɔː) *interj. Not standard.* an exclamation of surprise or dismay. [from LORD (*interj.*)]

lo+ran ('lɔːrən) *n.* a radio navigation system operating over long distances. Synchronized pulses are transmitted from widely spaced radio stations to aircraft or shipping, the time of arrival of the pulses being used to determine position. [C20: *lo(ng)-ra(nge) n(avigation)*]

Lor+ca[1] (*Spanish* 'lorka) *n.* a town in SE Spain, on the Guadalentín River. Pop.: 60 609 (1970).

Lor·ca[2] (*Spanish* 'lorka) *n.* **Fe·de·ri·co Gar·ci·a** (ˌfeðe'riko gar'θia). 1899–1936, Spanish poet and dramatist. His poetry, such as *Romancero gitano* (1928), shows his debt to Andalusian folk poetry. His plays include the trilogy *Bodas de sangre* (1933), *Yerma* (1935), and *La Casa de Bernarda Alba* (1936).

lord (lɔːd) *n.* **1.** a person who has power or authority over others, such as a monarch or master. **2.** a male member of the nobility, esp. in Britain. **3.** (in medieval Europe) a feudal superior, esp. the master of a manor. Compare **lady** (sense 5). **4.** a husband considered as head of the household (archaic except in the facetious phrase **lord and master**). **5.** *Astrology.* a planet having a dominating influence. **6. my lord.** a respectful form of address used to a judge, bishop, or nobleman. ~*vb.* **7.** (*tr.*) *Now rare.* to make a lord of (a person). **8.** to act in a superior manner towards (esp. in the phrase **lord it over**). [Old English *hlāford* bread keeper; see LOAF[1], WARD] —**'lord+less** *adj.* —**'lord+ˌlike** *adj.*

Lord (lɔːd) *n.* **1.** a title given to God or Jesus Christ. **2.** *Brit.* **a.** a title given to men of high birth, specifically to an earl, marquess, baron, or viscount. **b.** a courtesy title given to the younger sons of a duke or marquess. **c.** the ceremonial title of certain high officials or of a bishop or archbishop: *Lord Mayor; Lord of Appeal; Law Lord; Lord Bishop of Durham.* ~*interj.* **3.** (*sometimes not cap.*) an exclamation of dismay, surprise, etc.: *Good Lord!; Lord only knows!*

Lord Ad+vo+cate *n.* the minister of the Crown with responsibility for drafting Scottish legislation.

Lord Cham+ber+lain *n.* (in Britain) the chief official of the royal household.

Lord Chan+cel+lor *n. Brit. government.* the cabinet minister who is head of the judiciary in England and Wales and Speaker of the House of Lords.

Lord Chief Jus+tice *n.* the judge who is second only to the Lord Chancellor in the English legal hierarchy; president of one division of the High Court of Justice.

Lord High Chan+cel+lor *n.* another name for the **Lord Chancellor.**

lord+ing ('lɔːdɪŋ) *n.* **1.** *Archaic.* a gentleman; lord: used in the plural as a form of address. **2.** an obsolete word for **lordling.** [Old English *hlāfording,* from *hlāford* LORD + -ING[3], suffix indicating descent]

Lord Jus+tice of Ap+peal *n.* an ordinary judge of the Court of Appeal.

Lord Lieu+ten+ant *n.* **1.** (in Britain) the representative of the Crown in a county. **2.** (formerly) the British viceroy in Ireland.

lord+ling ('lɔːdlɪŋ) *n. Now rare.* a young lord.

lord+ly ('lɔːdlɪ) *adj.* **+li+er, +li+est. 1.** haughty; arrogant; proud. **2.** of or befitting a lord. ~*adv.* **3.** *Archaic.* in the manner of a lord. —**'lord+li+ness** *n.*

Lord May+or *n.* the mayor in the City of London and in certain other important boroughs.

Lord of Ap+peal *n. Brit.* one of several judges appointed to assist the House of Lords in hearing appeals.

Lord of Hosts *n.* Jehovah or God when regarded as having the angelic forces at his command.

Lord of Mis+rule *n.* (formerly, in England) a person appointed master of revels at a Christmas celebration.

lor+do+sis (lɔː'dəʊsɪs) *n. Pathol.* forward curvature of the lumbar spine: congenital or caused by trauma or disease. Nontechnical name: **hollow-back.** Compare **kyphosis, scoliosis.** [C18: New Latin from Greek *lordōsis,* from *lordos* bent backwards] —**lor+dot+ic** (lɔː'dɒtɪk) *adj.*

Lord Pres·i+dent of the Coun+cil *n.* (in Britain) the Cabinet minister who presides at meetings of the Privy Council.

Lord Priv·y Seal *n.* (in Britain) the senior cabinet minister without official duties.

Lord Pro+tec+tor *n.* See **Protector.**

Lord Pro+vost *n.* the provost of one of the four major Scottish burghs (Edinburgh, Glasgow, Aberdeen, and Dundee).

Lords (lɔːdz) *n.* **the.** short for **House of Lords.**

Lord's (lɔːdz) *n.* a cricket ground in N London; headquarters of the M.C.C.

lords-and-la·dies *n.* another name for **cuckoopint.**

Lord's Day *n.* **the.** the Christian Sabbath; Sunday.

lord+ship ('lɔːdʃɪp) *n.* the position or authority of a lord.

Lord+ship ('lɔːdʃɪp) *n.* (preceded by *Your* or *His*) *Brit.* a title used to address or refer to a bishop, a judge of the high court, or any peer except a duke.

Lord's Prayer *n.* **the.** the prayer taught by Jesus Christ to his disciples, as in Matthew 6:9–13, Luke 11:2–4. Also called: **Our Father, Paternoster** (esp. Latin version).

Lords Spir·i+tu+al *pl. n.* the Anglican bishops of England and Wales in their capacity as members of the House of Lords.

Lord's Sup+per *n.* **the.** another term for **Holy Communion** (I Corinthians 11:20).

Lord's ta+ble *n.* **the.** *Chiefly Protestantism.* **1.** Holy Communion. **2.** another name for **altar.**

Lords Tem+por+al *pl. n.* **the.** (in Britain) peers other than bishops in their capacity as members of the House of Lords.

lord·y ('lɔːdɪ) *interj. Chiefly U.S.* an exclamation of surprise or dismay.

lore[1] (lɔː) *n.* **1.** collective knowledge or wisdom on a particular subject, esp. of a traditional nature. **2.** knowledge or learning. **3.** *Archaic.* teaching, or something that is taught. [Old English *lār;* related to *leornian* to LEARN]

lore[2] (lɔː) *n.* **1.** the surface of the head of a bird between the eyes and the base of the bill. **2.** the corresponding area in a snake or fish. [C19: from New Latin *lōrum,* from Latin: strap]

Lo+re·lei ('lɒrəˌlaɪ) *n.* (in German legend) a siren, said to dwell on a rock at the edge of the Rhine south of Koblenz, who lures boatmen to destruction. [C19: from German *Lurlei* name of the rock; from a poem by Clemens Brentano (1778–1842)]

Lor·en (*Italian* 'lɔːren) *n.* **So·phi·a** (so'fiːa). original name *Sophia Scicolon;* born 1934, Italian film actress. Her films include *Two Women* (1961), *The Millionairess* (1961), *The Fall of the Roman Empire* (1964), *A Countess from Hong Kong* (1966), *Man of La Mancha* (1972), and *The Cassandra Crossing* (1977).

Lo·rentz (*Dutch* 'loːrənts) *n.* **Hen·drik An·toon** ('hɛndrɪk 'antoːn). 1853–1928, Dutch physicist: shared the Nobel prize for physics (1902) with Zeeman for their work on electromagnetic theory. With G. F. Fitzgerald, he formulated the theory of moving bodies, known as the Lorentz-Fitzgerald contraction.

Lo·renz (*German* 'loːrɛnts) *n.* **Kon·rad Zach·a·ri·as** ('kɔnraːt ˌtsaxa'riːas) born 1903, Austrian zoologist, who founded ethology. His works include *On Aggression* (1966): shared the Nobel prize for medicine 1973.

lor+gnette (lɔː'njɛt) *n.* a pair of spectacles or opera glasses mounted on a handle. [C19: from French, from *lorgner* to squint, from Old French *lorgne* squinting]

lor+gnon (*French* lɔr'ɲɔ̃) *n.* **1.** a monocle or pair of spectacles. **2.** another word for **lorgnette.** [C19: from French, from *lorgner;* see LORGNETTE]

lo+ri+ca (lɒ'raɪkə) *n., pl.* **+cae** (-siː, -kiː). **1.** the hard outer covering of rotifers, ciliate protozoans, and similar animals. **2.** an ancient Roman cuirass of leather or metal. [C18: from New Latin, from Latin: leather cuirass; related to *lōrum* thong] —**lor·i·cate** ('lɒrɪˌkeɪt) *or* **'lor·i+ˌcat+ed** *adj.*

Lo+rient (*French* lɔ'rjã) *n.* a port in W France, on the Bay of Biscay. Pop.: 71 923 (1975).

lor·i+keet ('lɒrɪˌkiːt, ˌlɒrɪ'kiːt) *n.* any of various small lories, such as *Glossopsitta versicolor* (**varied lorikeet**) or *Trichoglossus moluccanus* (**rainbow lorikeet**). [C18: from LORY + *-keet,* as in PARAKEET]

lor·i+mer ('lɒrɪmə) *or* **lor·i+ner** ('lɒrɪnə) *n. Brit.* (formerly). a person who made bits, spurs, and other small metal objects. [C15: from Old French, from *lorain* harness strap, ultimately from Latin *lōrum* strap]

lo+ris ('lɔːrɪs) *n., pl.* **+ris.** any of several omnivorous nocturnal slow-moving prosimian primates of the family *Lorisidae,* of S and SE Asia, esp. *Loris tardigradus* (**slow loris**) and *Nycticebus coucang* (**slender loris**), having vestigial digits and no tails. [C18: from French; of uncertain origin]

lorn (lɔːn) *adj. Poetic.* forsaken or wretched. [Old English *loren,* past participle of *-lēosan* to lose] —**'lorn+ness** *n.*

Lor+rain (*French* lɔ'rɛ̃) *n.* See **Claude Lorrain.**

Lor+raine (lɒ'reɪn; *French* lɔ'rɛn) *n.* **1.** a region and former province of E France; ceded to Germany in 1871 after the Franco-Prussian war and regained by France in 1919; rich iron-ore deposits. German name: **Lothringen. 2. Kingdom of.** an early medieval kingdom on the Meuse, Moselle, and Rhine rivers: later a duchy. **3.** a former duchy in E France, once the S half of this kingdom.

Lor·raine cross *n.* See **cross of Lorraine.**

Lor·ris (*French* lɔ'ris) *n.* See **Guillaume de Lorris.**

lor·ry ('lɒrɪ) *n., pl.* **·ries. 1.** a large motor vehicle designed to carry heavy loads, esp. one with a flat platform. U.S. name: **truck.** See also **articulated lorry. 2.** any of various vehicles with a flat load-carrying surface, esp. one designed to run on rails. [C19: perhaps related to northern British dialect *lurry* to pull, tug]

lo·ry ('lɔːrɪ) *n., pl.* **·ries.** any of various small brightly coloured parrots of Australia and Indonesia, having a brush-tipped tongue with which to feed on nectar and pollen. [C17: via Dutch from Malay *lūrī,* variant of *nūrī*]

Los An·ge·les (lɒs 'ændʒɪˌliːz) *n.* a city in SW California, on the Pacific: the third largest city in the U.S., having absorbed many adjacent townships; industrial centre and port, with several universities. Pop.: 2 746 854 (1973 est.). Abbrev.: **L.A.**

lose (luːz) *vb.* **los·es, los·ing, lost.** (*mainly tr.*) **1.** to part with or come to be without, as through theft, accident, negligence, etc. **2.** to fail to keep or maintain: *to lose one's balance.* **3.** to suffer the loss or deprivation of: *to lose a parent.* **4.** to cease to have or possess. **5.** to fail to get or make use of: *to lose a chance.* **6.** (*also intr.*) to fail to gain or win (a contest, game, etc.): *to lose the match.* **7.** to fail to see, hear, perceive, or understand: *I lost the gist of his speech.* **8.** to waste: *to lose money gambling.* **9.** to wander from so as to be unable to find: *to lose one's way.* **10.** to cause the loss of: *his delay lost him the battle.* **11.** to allow to go astray or out of sight: *we lost him in the crowd.* **12.** (*usually passive*) to absorb or engross: *he was lost in contemplation.* **13.** (*usually passive*) to cause the death or destruction of: *two men were lost in the crush.* **14.** to outdistance or elude: *he soon lost his pursuers.* **15.** (*intr.*) to decrease or depreciate in value or effectiveness: *poetry always loses in translation.* **16.** (*also intr.*) (of a timepiece) to run slow (by a specified amount): *the clock loses ten minutes every day.* **17.** (of a physician) to fail to sustain the life of (a patient). **18.** (of a woman) to fail to give birth to (a viable baby), esp. as the result of a miscarriage. **19.** *Motor racing slang.* to lose control of (the car), as on a bend: *he lost it going into Woodcote.* [Old English *losian* to perish; related to Old English *-lēosan* as in *forlēosan* to forfeit. Compare LOOSE] —'**los·a·ble** *adj.* —'**los·a·ble·ness** *n.*

lo·sel ('ləuzᵊl) *Archaic or dialect.* ~*n.* **1.** a worthless person. ~*adj.* **2.** (of a person) worthless, useless, or wasteful. [C14: from *losen,* from the past participle of LOSE]

lose out *vb.* **1.** (*intr., adv.*) to be defeated or unsuccessful. **2.** **lose out on.** *Informal.* to fail to secure or make use of: *we lost out on the sale.*

los·er ('luːzə) *n.* **1.** a person or thing that loses. **2.** *Informal.* a person or thing that seems destined to be taken advantage of, fail, etc.: *a born loser.*

Lo·sey ('ləusɪ) *n.* **Jo·seph.** born 1909, U.S. film director, in Britain since 1952. His films include *The Servant* (1963), *Accident* (1967), and *Secret Ceremony* (1968).

los·ing ('luːzɪŋ) *adj.* unprofitable; failing: *the business was a losing concern.*

los·ings ('luːzɪŋz) *pl. n.* losses, esp. money lost in gambling.

loss (lɒs) *n.* **1.** the act or an instance of losing. **2.** the disadvantage or deprivation resulting from losing: *a loss of reputation.* **3.** the person, thing, or amount lost: *a large loss.* **4.** (*pl.*) military personnel lost by death or capture. **5.** (*sometimes pl.*) the amount by which the costs of a business transaction or operation exceed its revenue. **6.** a measure of the power lost in an electrical system expressed as the ratio of or difference between the input power and the output power. **7.** *Insurance.* **a.** an occurrence of something that has been insured against, thus giving rise to a claim by a policyholder. **b.** the amount of the resulting claim. **8. at a loss. a.** unable or too perplexed (to do something). **b.** bewildered. **c.** rendered helpless (for lack of something): *at a loss for words.* **9. dead loss.** *Slang.* a useless or contemptible person, thing, etc. [C14: noun probably formed from *lost,* past participle of *losen* to perish, from Old English *lōsian* to be destroyed, from *los* destruction]

loss lead·er *n.* an article offered below cost in the hope that customers attracted by it will buy other goods.

loss ra·ti·o *n.* the ratio of the annual losses sustained to the premiums received by an insurance company.

los·sy ('lɒsɪ) *adj.* (of a dielectric material, transmission line, etc.) designed to have a high attenuation; dissipating energy: *lossy line.* [C20: from LOSS]

lost (lɒst) *adj.* **1.** unable to be found or recovered. **2.** unable to find one's way or ascertain one's whereabouts. **3.** confused, bewildered, or helpless: *he is lost in discussions of theory.* **4.** (sometimes foll. by *on*) not utilized, noticed, or taken advantage of (by): *rational arguments are lost on her.* **5.** no longer possessed or existing because of defeat, misfortune, or the passage of time: *a lost art.* **6.** destroyed physically: *the lost platoon.* **7.** (foll. by *to*) no longer available or open (to). **8.** (foll. by *to*) insensible or impervious (to a sense of shame, justice, etc.). **9.** (foll. by *in*) engrossed (in): *he was lost in his book.* **10.** morally fallen: *a lost woman.* **11.** damned: *a lost soul.* **12. get lost.** (*usually imperative*) *Informal.* go away and stay away.

lost cause *n.* a cause with no chance of success.

Lost Gen·er·a·tion *n.* (*sometimes not cap.*) **1.** the large number of talented young men killed in World War I. **2.** the generation of writers, esp. American authors such as Scott Fitzgerald and Hemingway, active after World War I.

lost tribes *pl. n.* **the.** *Old Testament.* the ten tribes deported from the N kingdom of Israel in 721 B.C. and believed never to have returned to Palestine.

lot (lɒt) *pron.* **1.** (*functioning as sing. or pl.; preceded by a*) a great number or quantity: *a lot to do; a lot of people; a lot of trouble.* ~*n.* **2.** a collection of objects, items, or people: *a nice lot of youngsters.* **3.** portion in life; destiny; fortune: *it falls to my lot to be poor.* **4.** any object, such as a straw or slip of paper, drawn from others at random to make a selection or choice (esp. in the phrase **draw** *or* **cast lots**). **5.** the use of lots in making a selection or choice (esp. in the phrase **by lot**). **6.** an assigned or apportioned share. **7.** an item or set of items for sale in an auction. **8.** *Chiefly U.S.* an area of land: *a parking lot.* **9.** *U.S.* a piece of land with fixed boundaries forming part of an administrative district. **10.** *U.S.* a film studio and the site on which it is located. **11. a bad lot.** an unpleasant or disreputable person. **12. cast** *or* **throw in one's lot with.** to join with voluntarily and share the fortunes of. **13. the lot.** the entire amount or number. ~*adv.* (preceded by *a*) *Informal.* **14.** to a considerable extent, degree, or amount; very much: *to delay a lot.* **15.** a great deal of the time or often: *to sing madrigals a lot.* ~*vb.* **lots, lot·ting, lot·ted. 16.** to draw lots for (something). **17.** (*tr.*) to divide (land, etc.) into lots. **18.** (*tr.*) another word for **allot.** [Old English *hlot;* related to Old High German *lug* portion of land, Old Norse *hlutr* lot, share]

Lot[1] (lɒt) *n.* **1.** a department of S central France, in Midi-Pyrénées region. Capital: Cahors. Pop.: 157 079 (1975). Area: 5226 sq. km (2038 sq. miles). **2.** a river in S France, rising in the Cevennes and flowing west into the Garonne River. Length: about 483 km (300 miles).

Lot[2] (lɒt) *n. Old Testament.* Abraham's nephew: he escaped the destruction of Sodom, but his wife was changed into a pillar of salt for looking back as they fled (Genesis 19).

lo·ta *or* **lo·tah** ('ləutə) *n.* a globular water container, usually of brass, used in India, Burma, etc. [C19: from Hindi *lotā*]

Lot-et-Ga·ronne (*French* lɔt e ga'rɔn) *n.* a department of SW France, in Aquitaine. Capital: Agen. Pop.: 299 157 (1975). Area: 5385 sq. km (2100 sq. miles).

loth (ləuθ) *adj.* a variant spelling of **loath.** —'**loth·ness** *n.*

Lo·thair I (ləu'θɛə) *n.* ?795–855 A.D., German king (840–43) and Holy Roman Emperor (840–55); son of Louis I.

Lo·thair II *n.* called *the Saxon.* ?1070–1137, German king (1125–37) and Holy Roman Emperor (1133–37). He was elected German king over the hereditary Hohenstaufen claimant.

Lo·thar·i·o (ləu'θɑːrɪˌəu) *n., pl.* **·os.** (*sometimes not cap.*) a rake, libertine, or seducer. [C18: after a seducer in Nicholas Rowe's tragedy *The Fair Penitent* (1703)]

Lo·thi·an Re·gion ('ləuðɪən) *n.* a local government region in SE central Scotland, formed in 1975 from East Lothian, most of Midlothian, and West Lothian. Administrative centre: Edinburgh. Pop.: 755 293 (1976 est.). Area: 1813 sq. km (700 sq. miles).

Lo·thi·ans ('ləuðɪənz) *n.* **the.** three former counties of SE central Scotland: East Lothian, West Lothian, and Midlothian.

Lo·thring·en ('loːtrɪŋən) *n.* the German name for **Lorraine.**

lo·tic ('ləutɪk) *adj. Ecology.* of, relating to, or designating natural communities living in rapidly flowing water. Compare **lentic.** [C20: from Latin *lotus,* a past participle of *lavāre* to wash]

lo·tion ('ləuʃən) *n.* a liquid preparation having a soothing, cleansing, or antiseptic action, applied to the skin, eyes, etc. [C14: via Old French from Latin *lōtiō* a washing, from *lōtus* past participle of *lavāre* to wash]

lots (lɒts) *pl. n. Informal.* **1.** (often foll. by *of*) great numbers or quantities: *lots of people; to eat lots.* ~*adv.* **2.** a great deal. **3.** (intensifier): *the journey is lots quicker by train.*

lot·ter·y ('lɒtərɪ) *n., pl.* **·ter·ies. 1.** a game of chance in which tickets are sold, one or more of which may later qualify the holder for a prize. **2.** an activity or endeavour the success of which is regarded as a matter of fate or luck. [C16: from Old French *loterie,* from Middle Dutch *loterije.* See LOT]

lot·to ('lɒtəu) *n.* a children's game in which numbered discs, counters, etc., are drawn at random and called out, while the players cover the corresponding numbers on cards, the winner being the first to cover all the numbers, a particular row, etc. Compare **bingo.** [C18: from Italian, from Old French *lot,* from Germanic. See LOT]

lo·tus *or* **lo·tos** ('ləutəs) *n.* **1.** (in Greek mythology) a fruit that induces forgetfulness and a dreamy languor in those who eat it. **2.** the plant bearing this fruit, thought to be the date, the jujube, or any of various other plants. **3.** any of several water lilies of tropical Africa and Asia, esp. the **white lotus** (*Nymphaea lotus*), which was regarded as sacred in ancient Egypt. **4.** a related plant, *Nelumbo nucifera,* which is the sacred lotus of India, China, and Tibet: family *Nelumbonaceae.* **5.** a representation of such a plant, common in Hindu, Buddhist, and ancient Egyptian carving and decorative art. **6.** any leguminous plant of the genus *Lotus,* of the Old World and North America, having yellow, pink, or white pealike flowers. [C16: via Latin from Greek *lōtos,* from Semitic; related to Hebrew *lōt* myrrh]

lo·tus-eat·er *n. Greek myth.* one of a people encountered by Odysseus in North Africa who lived in indolent forgetfulness, drugged by the fruit of the legendary lotus.

lo·tus po·si·tion *n.* a seated cross-legged position used in yoga, meditation, etc.

louche (luːʃ) *adj.* shifty or disreputable. [C19: from French, literally: squinting]

loud (laud) *adj.* **1.** (of sound) relatively great in volume: *a loud shout.* **2.** making or able to make sounds of relatively great volume: *a loud engine.* **3.** clamorous, insistent, and emphatic: *loud protests.* **4.** (of colours, designs, etc.) offensive or obtrusive to look at. **5.** characterized by noisy, vulgar, and offensive behaviour. ~*adv.* **6.** in a loud manner. **7. out loud.** *Informal.* audibly, as distinct from silently. [Old English *hlūd;* related to Old Swedish *hlūd,* German *laut*] —'**loud·ly** *adv.* —'**loud·ness** *n.*

loud·en ('laʊdᵊn) *vb.* to make or become louder.

loud-hail·er *n. Brit.* a portable loudspeaker having a built-in amplifier and microphone. U.S. name: **bullhorn.**

loud·ish ('laʊdɪʃ) *adj.* fairly loud; somewhat loud.

loud·mouth ('laʊd,maʊθ) *n. Informal.* **1.** a person who brags or talks too loudly. **2.** a person who is gossipy or tactless. —**loud·mouthed** ('laʊd,maʊðd, -,maʊθt) *adj.*

loud·speak·er (,laʊd'spiːkə) *n.* a device for converting audio-frequency signals into the equivalent sound waves by means of a vibrating conical diaphragm. Sometimes shortened to **speaker.**

loud·speak·er van *n.* a motor vehicle carrying a public address system. U.S. name: **sound truck.**

lough (lɒk, lɒx) *n.* **1.** an Irish and northern Brit. word for **lake. 2.** a long narrow bay or arm of the sea in Ireland. ~Compare **loch.** [C14: from Irish *loch* lake]

Lough·bor·ough ('lʌfbərə, -brə) *n.* a town in central England, in N Leicestershire: university (1966). Pop.: 45 863 (1971).

lou·is ('luːɪ; *French* lwi) *n., pl.* **lou·is** ('luːɪz; *French* lwi). short for **louis d'or.**

Lou·is ('luːɪs) *n.* **Joe.** original name *Joseph Louis Barrow.* 1914–81, U.S. boxer; world heavyweight champion (1937–49).

Lou·is I ('luːɪ; *French* lwi) *n.* called *the Pious* or *the Debonair.* 778–840 A.D., king of France and Holy Roman Emperor (814–40).

Lou·is II *n.* **1.** called *the German.* ?804–876 A.D., king of Germany (843–76); son of Louis I. **2. de Bour·bon.** See (Prince de) **Condé.**

Lou·is IV *n.* called *the Bavarian.* ?1287–1347, king of Germany (1314–47) and Holy Roman Emperor (1328–47).

Lou·is V *n.* called *le Fainéant.* ?967–987 A.D., last Carolingian king of France (986–87).

Lou·is IX *n.* known as *Saint Louis.* 1214–70, king of France (1226–70): led the Sixth Crusade (1248–54) and was held to ransom (1250); died at Tunis while on another crusade.

Lou·is XI *n.* 1423–83, king of France (1461–83); involved in a struggle with his vassals, esp. the duke of Burgundy, in his attempt to unite France under an absolute monarchy.

Lou·is XII *n.* 1462–1515, king of France (1498–1515), who fought a series of unsuccessful wars in Italy.

Lou·is XIII *n.* 1601–43, king of France (1610–43). His mother (Marie de Médicis) was regent until 1617; after 1624 he was influenced by his chief minister Richelieu.

Lou·is XIV *n.* called *le roi soleil* (the Sun King). 1638–1715, king of France (1643–1715); son of Louis XIII and Anne of Austria. Effective ruler from 1661, he established an absolute monarchy. His attempt to establish French supremacy in Europe, waging almost continual wars from 1667 to 1714, ultimately failed. But his reign is regarded as a golden age of French literature and art.

Lou·is XV *n.* 1710–74, king of France (1715–74); great-grandson of Louis XIV. He engaged France in a series of wars, esp. the disastrous Seven Years' War (1756–63), which undermined the solvency and authority of the crown.

Lou·is XVI *n.* 1754–93, king of France (1774–92); grandson of Louis XV. He married Marie Antoinette in 1770 and they were guillotined during the French Revolution.

Lou·is XVII *n.* 1785–95, titular king of France (1793–95) during the Revolution, after the execution of his father Louis XVI; he died in prison.

Lou·is XVIII *n.* 1755–1824, king of France (1814–24); younger brother of Louis XVI. He became titular king after the death of Louis XVII (1795) and ascended the throne at the Bourbon restoration in 1814. He was forced to flee during the Hundred Days.

Lou·is·burg *or* **Lou·is·bourg** ('luːɪs,bɜːg) *n.* a fortress in Canada, in Nova Scotia on SE Cape Breton Island: founded in 1713 by the French and strongly fortified (1720–40); captured by the British (1758) and demolished; currently being reconstructed as a historic site.

lou·is d'or (,luːɪ 'dɔː; *French* lwi 'dɔːr) *n., pl.* **lou·is d'or** (,luːɪz 'dɔː; *French* lwi 'dɔːr). **1.** a former French gold coin worth 20 francs. **2.** an old French coin minted in the reign of Louis XIII. ~Often shortened to **louis.** [C17: from French: golden louis, named after Louis XIII]

Lou·i·si·an·a (luː,iːzɪ'ænə) *n.* a state of the southern U.S., on the Gulf of Mexico: originally a French colony; bought by the U.S. in 1803 as part of the Louisiana Purchase; chiefly low-lying. Capital: Baton Rouge. Pop.: 3 643 180 (1970). Area: 116 368 sq. km (44 930 sq. miles). Abbrevs.: **La.** or (with zip code) **LA.**

Lou·i·si·an·a Pur·chase *n.* the large region of North America sold by Napoleon I to the U.S. in 1803 for 15 million dollars: consists of the W part of the Mississippi basin. Area: about 2 292 150 sq. km (885 000 sq. miles).

Lou·is Na·po·le·on *n.* the original name of **Napoleon III.**

Lou·is Phi·lippe (*French* fi'lip) *n.* known as the *Citizen King.* 1773–1850, king of the French (1830–48). His régime became excessively identified with the bourgeoisie and he was forced to abdicate by the revolution of 1848.

Lou·is Qua·torze (kə'tɔːz) *adj.* of or relating to the baroque style of furniture, decoration, and architecture of the time of Louis XIV of France and characterized by massive forms and heavy ornamentation.

Lou·is Quinze (kænz) *adj.* of or relating to the rococo style of the furniture, decoration, and architecture of the time of Louis XV of France.

Lou·is Seize (sɛz) *adj.* of or relating to the style of furniture, decoration, and architecture of the time of Louis XVI of France, belonging to the late French rococo and early neoclassicism.

Lou·is Treize (trɛz) *adj.* of or relating to the style of furniture, decoration, and architecture of the time of Louis XIII of France, with rich decorative features based on classical models.

Lou·is·ville ('luːɪ,vɪl) *n.* a port in N Kentucky, on the Ohio River: site of the annual Kentucky Derby; university (1837). Pop.: 335 696 (1973 est.).

lounge (laʊndʒ) *vb.* **1.** (*intr.;* often foll. by *about* or *around*) to sit, lie, walk, or stand in a relaxed manner. **2.** to pass (time) lazily or idly. ~*n.* **3. a.** a communal room in a hotel, ship, theatre, etc., used for waiting or relaxing in. **b.** (*as modifier*): *lounge chair.* **4.** *Chiefly Brit.* a living room in a private house. **5.** Also called: **lounge bar, saloon bar.** *Brit.* a more expensive bar in a pub or hotel. **6.** *Chiefly U.S.* **a.** an expensive bar, esp. in a hotel. **b.** short for **cocktail lounge. 7.** a sofa or couch, esp. one with a headrest and no back. **8.** the act or an instance of lounging. [C16: origin unknown] —'**loung·er** *n.*

lounge liz·ard *n. Informal.* an idle frequenter of places where rich or prominent people gather.

lounge suit *n.* the customary suit of matching jacket and trousers worn for the normal business day.

loup (luː) *n.* another name for **loo mask.** [C19: from French, from Latin *lupus* wolf]

loupe (luːp) *n.* a magnifying glass used by jewellers, horologists, etc. [C20: from French (formerly an imperfect precious stone), from Old French, of obscure origin]

loup·ing ill ('laʊpɪŋ, 'ləʊ-) *n.* a viral disease of sheep causing muscular twitching and partial paralysis: caused by the bite of an infected tick (*Ixodes ricinus*). [C18: *louping,* from C14 *loup,* Scottish variant of LEAP]

lour (laʊə) *vb.* a variant spelling of **lower**[2]. —'**lour·ing·ly** *adv.*

Lourdes (*French* lurd) *n.* a town in SW France: a leading place of pilgrimage for Roman Catholics after a peasant girl, Bernadette Soubirous, had visions of the Virgin Mary in 1858. Pop.: 18 096 (1975).

Lou·ren·ço Mar·ques (lə'rɛnsəʊ 'mɑːk, 'mɑːks; *Portuguese* lo'rẽsu 'markɪʃ) *n.* the former name (until 1976) of **Maputo.**

louse (laʊs) *n., pl.* **lice** (laɪs). **1.** any wingless bloodsucking insect of the order *Anoplura:* includes *Pediculus capitis* (**head louse**), *Pediculus corporis* (**body louse**), and the crab louse, all of which infest man. **2. biting** *or* **bird louse.** any wingless insect of the order *Mallophaga,* such as the chicken louse: external parasites of birds and mammals with biting mouthparts. **3.** any of various similar but unrelated insects, such as the plant louse and book louse. **4.** *pl.* **lous·es.** *Slang.* an unpleasant or mean person. ~*vb.* (*tr.*) **5.** to remove lice from. **6.** (foll. by *up*) *Slang.* to ruin or spoil. [Old English *lūs;* related to Old High German, Old Norse *lūs*]

louse·wort ('laʊs,wɜːt) *n.* any of various N temperate scrophulariaceous plants of the genus *Pedicularis,* having spikes of white, yellow, or mauve flowers. See also **betony** (sense 3).

lous·y ('laʊzɪ) *adj.* **lous·i·er, lous·i·est. 1.** *Slang.* very mean or unpleasant: *a lousy thing to do.* **2.** *Slang.* inferior or bad: *this is a lousy film.* **3.** infested with lice. **4.** (foll. by *with*) *Slang.* provided with an excessive amount (of): *he's lousy with money.* —'**lous·i·ly** *adv.* —'**lous·i·ness** *n.*

lout[1] (laʊt) *n.* a crude or oafish person; boor. [C16: perhaps from LOUT[2]]

lout[2] (laʊt) *vb.* (*intr.*) *Archaic.* to bow or stoop. [Old English *lūtan;* related to Old Norse *lūta*]

Louth (laʊθ) *n.* a county of NE Ireland, in Leinster province on the Irish Sea: the smallest of the counties. County town: Dundalk. Pop.: 74 951 (1971). Area: 821 sq. km (317 sq. miles).

lout·ish ('laʊtɪʃ) *adj.* characteristic of a lout; unpleasant and uncouth. —'**lout·ish·ly** *adv.* —'**lout·ish·ness** *n.*

Lou·vain (*French* lu'vɛ̃) *n.* a town in central Belgium, in Brabant province: capital of the duchy of Brabant (11th–15th centuries) and centre of the cloth trade; university (1426). Pop.: 32 189 (1970). Flemish name: **Leuven.**

lou·var ('luːvɑː) *n.* a large silvery whalelike scombroid fish, *Luvarus imperialis,* that occurs in most tropical and temperate seas and feeds on plankton: family *Luvaridae.* [from Italian (Calabrian and Sicilian dialect) *lùvaru,* perhaps from Latin *ruber* red]

lou·vre *or U.S.* **lou·ver** ('luːvə) *n.* **1. a.** any of a set of horizontal parallel slats in a door or window, sloping outwards to throw off rain and admit air. **b.** Also called: **louvre boards.** the slats together with the frame supporting them. **2.** *Architect.* a lantern or turret that allows smoke to escape. [C14: from Old French *lovier,* of obscure origin] —'**lou·vred** *or U.S.* '**lou·vered** *adj.*

Lou·vre (*French* 'luːvr) *n.* the national museum and art gallery of France, in Paris: formerly a royal palace, begun in 1546; used for its present purpose since 1793.

lou·vred *or U.S.* **lou·vered** ('luːvəd) *adj.* (of a window, door, etc.) having louvres.

lov·a·ble *or* **love·a·ble** ('lʌvəbᵊl) *adj.* attracting or deserving affection. —,**lov·a·'bil·i·ty,** ,**love·a·'bil·i·ty** *or* '**lov·a·ble·ness,** '**love·a·ble·ness** *n.* —'**lov·a·bly** *or* '**love·a·bly** *adv.*

lov·age ('lʌvɪdʒ) *n.* **1.** a European umbelliferous plant, *Levisticum officinale,* with greenish-white flowers and aromatic fruits, which are used for flavouring food. **2.** a similar and related plant, *Ligusticum scoticum,* of N Europe. [C14 *loveache,* from Old French *luvesche,* from Late Latin *levisticum,* from Latin *ligusticum,* literally: Ligurian (plant)]

lov+at ('lʌvət) *n.* a yellowish-green or bluish-green mixture, esp. in tweeds or woollens. [named after *Lovat*, Inverness-shire]

love (lʌv) *vb.* **1.** (*tr.*) to have a great attachment to and affection for. **2.** (*tr.*) to have passionate desire, longing, and feelings for. **3.** (*tr.*) to like or desire (to do something) very much. **4.** (*tr.*) to make love to. **5.** (*intr.*) to be in love. ~*n.* **6. a.** an intense emotion of affection, warmth, fondness, and regard towards a person or thing. **b.** (*as modifier*): *love song; love story.* **7.** a deep feeling of sexual attraction and desire. **8.** wholehearted liking for or pleasure in something. **9.** *Christianity.* **a.** God's benevolent attitude towards man. **b.** man's attitude of reverent devotion towards God. **10.** Also: **my love.** a beloved person: used esp. as an endearment. **11.** *Brit. informal.* a term of address, esp. but not necessarily for a person regarded as likable. **12.** (in tennis, squash, etc.) a score of zero. **13. fall in love.** to become in love. **14. for love.** without payment. **15. for love or money.** by any means. **16. for the love of.** for the sake of. **17. in love.** in a state of strong emotional attachment and usually sexual attraction. **18. make love (to). a.** to have sexual intercourse (with). **b.** *Now archaic.* to make advances (to). [Old English *lufu;* related to Old High German *luba;* compare also Latin *libēre* (originally *lubēre*) to please]

love af+fair *n.* **1.** a romantic or sexual relationship, esp. a temporary one, between two people. **2.** a great enthusiasm or liking for something: *a love affair with ballet.*

love ap+ple *n.* an archaic name for **tomato.**

love+bird ('lʌv,bɜːd) *n.* **1.** any of several small African parrots of the genus *Agapornis,* often kept as cage birds. **2.** another name for **budgerigar. 3.** *Informal.* a lover: *the lovebirds are in the garden.*

love child *n. Euphemistic.* an illegitimate child; bastard.

love feast *n.* **1.** Also called: **agape.** (among the early Christians) a religious meal eaten with others as a sign of mutual love and fellowship. **2.** a ritual meal modelled upon this.

love game *n. Tennis.* a game in which the loser has a score of zero.

love-in-a-mist *n.* an erect S European ranunculaceous plant, *Nigella damascena,* cultivated as a garden plant, having finely cut leaves and white or pale blue flowers. See also **fennelflower.**

love-in-i·dle·ness *n.* another name for the **wild pansy.**

love knot *n.* a stylized bow, usually of ribbon, symbolizing the bond between two lovers. Also called: **lover's knot.**

Love·lace ('lʌv,leɪs) *n.* **Rich·ard.** 1618–58, English Cavalier poet, noted for *To Althea from Prison* (1642) and *Lucasta* (1649).

love+less ('lʌvlɪs) *adj.* **1.** without love: *a loveless marriage.* **2.** receiving or giving no love. —**'love+less+ly** *adv.* —**'love+less+ness** *n.*

love let+ter *n.* **1.** a letter or note written by someone to his or her sweetheart or lover. **2.** (in Malaysia) a type of biscuit, made from eggs and rice flour and folded.

love-lies-bleed·ing *n.* any of several amaranthaceous plants of the genus *Amaranthus,* esp. *A. caudatus,* having drooping spikes of small red flowers.

Lov·ell ('lʌvəl) *n.* Sir **Ber·nard.** born 1913, English radio astronomer; founder (1951) and director of Jodrell Bank.

love+lock ('lʌv,lɒk) *n.* a long lock of hair worn on the forehead.

love+lorn ('lʌv,lɔːn) *adj.* miserable because of unrequited love or unhappiness in love. —**'love+,lorn+ness** *n.*

love+ly ('lʌvlɪ) *adj.* **+li+er, +li+est. 1.** very attractive or beautiful. **2.** highly pleasing or enjoyable: *a lovely time.* **3.** loving and attentive. **4.** inspiring love; lovable. ~*n.* **5.** *Slang.* a lovely woman. —**'love+li+ness** *n.*

love+mak·ing ('lʌv,meɪkɪŋ) *n.* **1.** sexual play and activity between lovers, esp. including sexual intercourse. **2.** an archaic word for **courtship.**

love match *n.* a betrothal or marriage, based on mutual love rather than any other considerations.

love nest *n.* a place suitable for or used for making love.

love po+tion *n.* any drink supposed to arouse sexual love in the one who drinks it.

lov+er ('lʌvə) *n.* **1.** a person, now esp. a man, who has an extramarital or premarital sexual relationship with another person. **2.** (*often pl.*) either of the two people involved in a love affair. **3. a.** someone who loves a specified person or thing: *a lover of music.* **b.** (*in combination*): *a music-lover; cat-lover.*

love seat *n.* a small upholstered sofa for two people.

love set *n. Tennis.* a set in which the loser has a score of zero.

love+sick ('lʌv,sɪk) *adj.* pining or languishing because of love. —**'love+,sick+ness** *n.*

lov+ey ('lʌvɪ) *n. Brit. informal.* another word for **love** (sense 11).

lov·ey-dov·ey *adj.* making an excessive or ostentatious display of affection.

lov+ing ('lʌvɪŋ) *adj.* feeling, showing, or indicating love and affection. —**'lov+ing+ly** *adv.* —**'lov+ing+ness** *n.*

lov+ing cup *n.* **1.** a large vessel, usually two-handled, out of which people drink in turn at a banquet. **2.** a similar cup awarded to the winner of a competition.

low[1] (ləʊ) *adj.* **1.** having a relatively small distance from base to top; not tall or high: *a low hill; a low building.* **2. a.** situated at a relatively short distance above the ground, sea level, the horizon, or other reference position: *low cloud.* **b.** (*in combination*): *low-lying.* **3. a.** involving or containing a relatively small amount of something: *a low supply.* **b.** (*in combination*): *low-powered.* **4. a.** having little value or quality. **b.** (*in combination*): *low-grade.* **5.** coarse or vulgar: *a low conversation.* **6. a.** inferior in culture or status. **b.** (*in combination*): *low-class.* **7.** in a physically or mentally depressed or weakened state. **8.** low-necked: *a low dress.* **9.** stricken, prostrate, or dead. **10.** with a hushed tone; quiet or soft: *a low whisper.* **11.** of relatively small price or monetary value: *low cost.* **12.** *Music.* relating to or characterized by a relatively low pitch. **13.** (of latitudes) situated not far north or south of the equator. **14.** having little or no money. **15.** overthrown or defeated. **16.** uncommunicative or secretive. **17.** abject or servile. **18.** *Phonetics.* of, relating to, or denoting a vowel whose articulation is produced by moving the back of the tongue away from the soft palate or the blade away from the hard palate, such as for the *a* in English *father.* Compare **high** (sense 20). **19.** (of a gear) providing a relatively low forward speed for a given engine speed. **20.** (*usually cap.*) of or relating to the Low Church. ~*adv.* **21.** in a low position, level, degree, intensity, etc.: *to bring someone low.* **22.** at a low pitch; deep: *to sing low.* **23.** at a low price; cheaply: *to buy low.* **24. lie low. a.** to keep or be concealed or quiet. **b.** to wait for a favourable opportunity. ~*n.* **25.** a low position, level, or degree: *an all-time low.* **26.** an area of relatively low atmospheric pressure, esp. a depression. [C12 *lāh,* from Old Norse *lāgr;* related to Old Frisian *lēch* low, Dutch *laag*] —**'low+ness** *n.*

low[2] (ləʊ) *n. also* **low+ing. 1.** the sound uttered by cattle; moo. ~*vb.* **2.** to make or express by a low or moo. [Old English *hlōwan;* related to Dutch *loeien,* Old Saxon *hlōian*]

Low (ləʊ) *n.* Sir **Da·vid.** 1891–1963, British political cartoonist, born in New Zealand: created Colonel Blimp.

low+an ('ləʊən) *n. Austral.* another name for **mallee fowl.**

Low Ar+chi+pel·a+go *n.* another name for the **Tuamotu Archipelago.**

low+born (,ləʊ'bɔːn) *or* **low+bred** (,ləʊ'brɛd) *adj. Now rare.* of ignoble or common parentage; not royal or noble.

low+boy ('ləʊ,bɔɪ) *n. U.S.* a table fitted with drawers.

low+brow ('ləʊ,braʊ) *Disparaging.* ~*n.* **1.** a person who has uncultivated or nonintellectual tastes. ~*adj. also* **low+browed. 2.** of or characteristic of such a person. —**'low+,brow+ism** *n.*

low camp *n.* an unsophisticated form of **camp** (the style).

Low Church *n.* **1.** the school of thought in the Church of England stressing evangelical beliefs and practices. Compare **Broad Church, High Church.** ~*adj.* **Low-Church. 2.** of or relating to this school. —**,Low-'Church·man** *n.*

low com+e·dy *n.* comedy characterized by slapstick and physical action. —**low co+me·di·an** *n.*

Low Coun+tries *pl. n.* the lowland region of W Europe, on the North Sea: consists of Belgium, Luxembourg, and the Netherlands.

low-down *Informal.* ~*adj.* **1.** mean, underhand, or despicable. ~*n.* **low+down. 2.** information, esp. secret or true information.

Lö·we (*German* 'løːvə) *n.* See (Karl) **Loewe.**

Low·ell ('ləʊəl) *n.* **1. A·my (Lawrence).** 1874–1925, U.S. Imagist poet and critic. **2. James Rus·sell.** 1819–91, U.S. poet, essayist, and diplomat, noted for his series of poems in Yankee dialect, *Biglow Papers* (1848; 1867). **3. Rob·ert.** 1917–77, U.S. poet. His volumes of verse include *Lord Weary's Castle* (1946), *Life Studies* (1959), and *For the Union Dead* (1964). He also wrote a trilogy of verse dramas, *The Old Glory* (1968), and a book of free translations, of European poems, *Imitations* (1961).

low+er[1] ('ləʊə) *adj.* **1.** being below one or more other things: *the lower shelf; the lower animals.* **2.** reduced in amount or value: *a lower price.* **3.** *Maths.* (of a limit or bound) less than or equal to one or more numbers or variables. **4.** (*sometimes cap.*) *Geology.* denoting the early part or division of a period, system, formation, etc.: *Lower Silurian.* ~*vb.* **5.** (*tr.*) to cause to become low or on a lower level; bring, put, or cause to move down. **6.** (*tr.*) to reduce or bring down in estimation, dignity, value, etc.: *to lower oneself.* **7.** to reduce or be reduced: *to lower one's confidence.* **8.** (*tr.*) to make quieter: *to lower the radio.* **9.** (*tr.*) to reduce the pitch of. **10.** (*tr.*) *Phonetics.* to modify the articulation of (a vowel) by bringing the tongue further away from the roof of the mouth. **11.** (*intr.*) to diminish or become less. [C12 (comparative of LOW[1]); C17 (vb.)] —**'low+er+a·ble** *adj.*

low+er[2] *or* **lour** ('laʊə) *vb.* (*intr.*) **1.** (esp. of the sky, weather, etc.) to be overcast, dark, and menacing. **2.** to scowl or frown. ~*n.* **3.** a menacing scowl or appearance. [C13 *louren* to scowl; compare German *lauern* to lurk] —**'low+er+ing+ly** *or* **'lour+ing+ly** *adv.*

Low+er Aus+tri+a *n.* a province of NE Austria: the largest Austrian province, containing most of the Vienna basin. Pop.: 1 414 876 (1971). Area: 19 170 sq. km (7476 sq. miles). German name: **Niederösterreich.**

Low+er Bur+ma *n.* the coastal region of Burma.

Low+er Cal+i+for+nia *n.* a mountainous peninsula of NW Mexico, between the Pacific and the Gulf of California: administratively divided into the states of Baja California and Baja California Sur. Spanish name: **Baja California.**

Low+er Can+a+da *n.* (from 1791 to 1841) the official name of the S region of the present-day province of Quebec. Compare **Upper Canada.**

low+er case *n.* **1.** the bottom half of a compositor's type case, in which the small letters are kept. ~*adj.* **low·er-case. 2.** of or relating to small letters. ~*vb.* **low·er-case. 3.** (*tr.*) to print with lower-case letters.

low+er cham+ber *n.* another name for a **lower house.**

low+er class *n.* **1.** the social stratum having the lowest position in the social hierarchy. Compare **middle class, upper class,**

working class. *~adj.* **low·er-class. 2.** of or relating to the lower class. **3.** inferior or vulgar.
low+er+class+man (ˌləʊəˈklɑːsmən) *n., pl.* **+men.** *U.S.* a freshman or sophomore. Also called: **underclassman.**
low+er crit·i·cism *n.* textual criticism, esp. the study of the extant manuscripts of the Scriptures in order to establish the original text. Compare **higher criticism.**
low+er deck *n.* **1.** the deck of a ship situated immediately above the hold. **2.** *Informal.* the petty officers and seamen of a ship collectively.
Low+er E·gypt *n.* one of the two main administrative districts of Egypt: consists of the Nile Delta.
low+er house *n.* one of the two houses of a bicameral legislature: usually the larger and more representative house. Also called: **lower chamber.** Compare **upper house.**
Low+er Hutt (hʌt) *n.* an industrial town in New Zealand on the S coast of North Island. Pop.: 58 561 (1971).
Low+er Lakes *n. Chiefly Canadian.* Lakes Erie and Ontario.
low+er mor+dent *n.* another term for **mordent.**
low+er+most (ˈləʊəˌməʊst) *adj.* lowest.
Low+er Pal·ae·o+lith+ic *n.* **1.** the earliest of the three sections of the Palaeolithic, beginning about 3 million years ago and ending about 70 000 B.C. with the emergence of Neanderthal man. *~adj.* **2.** of or relating to this period.
Low+er Pa+lat·i+nate *n.* another name for the **Rhine Palatinate.** See **Palatinate.**
low+er re+gions *pl. n.* (usually preceded by *the*) hell.
Low+er Sax·o·ny *n.* a state of N West Germany, on the North Sea and including the E Frisian Islands; a leading European producer of petroleum. Capital: Hanover. Pop.: 7 082 158 (1970). Area: 47 408 sq. km (18 489 sq. miles). German name: **Niedersachsen.**
low+er world *n.* **1.** the earth as opposed to heaven or the spiritual world. **2.** another name for **hell.**
low+est com+mon de+nom·i+na+tor *n.* the smallest integer or polynomial that is exactly divisible by each denominator of a set of fractions. Abbrev.: **L.C.D., l.c.d.** Also called: **least common denominator.**
low+est com+mon mul+ti+ple *n.* the smallest number or quantity that is exactly divisible by each member of a set of numbers or quantities. Abbrev.: **L.C.M., l.c.m.** Also called: **least common multiple.**
Lowes+toft (ˈləʊstɒft) *n.* a fishing port and resort in E England, in NE Suffolk on the North Sea. Pop.: 52 182 (1971).
low ex+plo+sive *n.* an explosive of relatively low power, as used in firearms.
low fre+quen+cy *n.* a radio-frequency band or a frequency lying between 300 and 30 kilohertz. Abbrev.: **LF.**
Low Ger+man *n.* a language of N Germany, spoken esp. in rural areas: more closely related to Dutch than to standard High German. Also called: **Plattdeutsch.** Abbrev.: **LG.**
low-key *or* **low-keyed** *adj.* **1.** having a low intensity or tone. **2.** (of a photograph, painting, etc.) having a predominance of dark grey tones or dark colours with few highlights. Compare **high-key.**
low+land (ˈləʊlənd) *n.* **1.** relatively low ground. **2.** (*often pl.*) a low generally flat region. *~adj.* **3.** of or relating to a lowland or lowlands. **—ˈlow+land+er** *n.*
Low+land (ˈləʊlənd) *adj.* of or relating to the Lowlands of Scotland or the dialect of English spoken there.
Low+lands (ˈləʊləndz) *n.* **the.** a low generally flat region of central Scotland, around the Forth and Clyde valleys, separating the Southern Uplands from the Highlands. **—ˈLow+land+er** *n.*
Low Lat+in *n.* any form or dialect of Latin other than the classical, such as Vulgar or Medieval Latin.
low-lev·el lan+guage *n.* a computer programming language that is closer to machine language than to human language. Compare **high-level language.**
low+ly (ˈləʊlɪ) *Now rare.* *~adj.* **+li+er, +li+est. 1.** humble or low in position, rank, status, etc. **2.** full of humility; meek. **3.** simple, unpretentious, or plain. *~adv.* **4.** in a low or lowly manner. **—ˈlow+li+ness** *n.*
Low Mass *n.* a Mass that has a simplified ceremonial form and is spoken rather than sung. Compare **High Mass.**
low-mind·ed *adj.* having a vulgar or crude mind and character. **—ˌlow-ˈmind·ed·ly** *adv.* **—ˌlow-ˈmind·ed·ness** *n.*
low-necked *adj.* (of a woman's garment) having a low neckline.
low-pass fil+ter *n. Electronics.* a filter that transmits all frequencies below a specified value, substantially attenuating frequencies above this value. Compare **high-pass filter, band-pass filter.**
low-pitched *adj.* **1.** pitched low in tone. **2.** (of a roof) having sides with a shallow slope.
low-pres·sure *adj.* **1.** having, using, or involving a pressure below normal: *a low-pressure gas.* **2.** relaxed or calm.
low pro+file *n.* a position or attitude characterized by a deliberate avoidance of prominence or publicity.
low re+lief *n.* another term for **bas-relief.**
low-rise *adj.* **1.** of or relating to a building having only a few storeys. Compare **high-rise.** *~n.* **2.** such a building.
Low·ry (ˈlaʊrɪ) *n.* **L(awrence) S(tephen).** 1887–1976, English painter, noted for his bleak northern industrial scenes, often containing primitive or stylized figures.
low-spir·it·ed *adj.* depressed, dejected, or miserable. **—ˌlow-ˈspir·it·ed·ly** *adv.* **—ˌlow-ˈspir·it·ed·ness** *n.*
Low Sun+day *n.* the Sunday after Easter.
low-ten·sion *adj.* subjected to, carrying, or capable of operating at a low voltage. Abbrev.: **LT**
low tide *n.* **1.** the tide when it is at its lowest level or the time at which it reaches this. **2.** a lowest point.
Low+veld (ˈləʊˌfɛlt, -ˌvɛlt) *n.* **the.** another name for **Bushveld.**
low wa·ter *n.* **1.** another name for **low tide** (sense 1). **2.** the state of any stretch of water at its lowest level.
low-wa·ter mark *n.* **1.** the level reached by seawater at low tide or by other stretches of water at their lowest level. **2.** the lowest point or level; nadir.
lox[1] (lɒks) *n.* a kind of smoked salmon. [C19: from Yiddish *laks,* from Middle High German *lahs* salmon]
lox[2] (lɒks) *n.* short for **liquid oxygen,** esp. when used as an oxidizer for rocket fuels.
lox·o·drom+ic (ˌlɒksəˈdrɒmɪk) *or* **lox·o·drom·i+cal** *adj.* of or relating to rhumb lines or to map projections on which rhumb lines appear straight, as on a Mercator projection. [C17: from Greek *loxos* oblique + *dromikos* relating to a course] **—ˌlox·o+ˈdrom·i·cal+ly** *adv.*
lox·o+drom+ics (ˌlɒksəˈdrɒmɪks) *or* **lox+od+ro+my** (lɒkˈsɒdrəmɪ) *n.* (*functioning as sing.*) the technique of navigating using rhumb lines.
loy+al (ˈlɔɪəl) *adj.* **1.** having or showing continuing allegiance. **2.** faithful to one's country, government, etc. **3.** of or expressing loyalty. [C16: from Old French *loial, leial,* from Latin *lēgālis* LEGAL] **—ˈloy+al+ly** *adv.* **—ˈloy+al+ness** *n.*
loy+al+ist (ˈlɔɪəlɪst) *n.* a patriotic supporter of his sovereign or government. **—ˈloy+al+ism** *n.*
Loy+al+ist (ˈlɔɪəlɪst) *n.* **1.** (in Northern Ireland) any of the Protestants wishing to retain Ulster's link with Britain. **2.** (in North America) an American colonist who supported Britain during the War of American Independence. **3.** (during the Spanish Civil War) a supporter of the republican government.
loy+al+ty (ˈlɔɪəltɪ) *n., pl.* **+ties. 1.** the state or quality of being loyal. **2.** (*often pl.*) a feeling of allegiance.
Lo+yang (ˈləʊˈjæŋ) *n.* a city in E China, in N Honan province on the Lo River near its confluence with the Yellow River: an important Buddhist centre in the 5th and 6th centuries; a commercial and industrial centre. Pop.: 580 000 (1970 est.).
Loy·o·la (lɔɪˈəʊlə) *n.* See (Saint) **Ignatius Loyola.**
loz+enge (ˈlɒzɪndʒ) *n.* **1.** Also called: **pastille, troche.** *Med.* a medicated tablet held in the mouth until it has dissolved. **2.** *Geom.* another name for **rhombus. 3.** *Heraldry.* a diamond-shaped charge. [C14: from Old French *losange* of Gaulish origin; compare Vulgar Latin *lausa* flat stone]
loz+enged (ˈlɒzɪndʒd) *adj.* decorated with lozenges.
loz+eng·y (ˈlɒzɪndʒɪ) *adj.* (*usually postpositive*) *Heraldry.* divided by diagonal lines to form a lattice.
Lo+zère (*French* lɔˈzɛːr) *n.* a department of S central France, in Languedoc-Roussillon region. Capital: Mende. Pop.: 80 234 (1975). Area: 5180 sq. km (2020 sq. miles).
Lo·zi (ˈləʊzɪ) *n.* the language of the Barotse people of Zambia, belonging to the Bantu group of the Niger-Congo family.
LP *n.* **a.** Also called: **long player.** a long-playing gramophone record: usually one 12 inches (30 cm) or 10 inches (25 cm) in diameter, designed to rotate at 33 1/3 revolutions per minute. Compare **EP. b.** (*as modifier*): *an LP sleeve.*
L/P *Printing. abbrev. for* letterpress.
L.P. *abbrev. for:* **1.** Also: **LP** (in Britain) Lord Provost. **2.** Also: **l.p.** low pressure.
LPG *or* **LP gas** *abbrev. for* liquefied petroleum gas.
L.P.S. (in Britain) *abbrev. for* Lord Privy Seal.
Lr *the chemical symbol for* lawrencium.
l.s. (on a document) the place of the seal. [from Latin *locus sigilli*]
LS *international car registration for* Lesotho.
LSD *n.* lysergic acid diethylamide; a crystalline compound prepared from lysergic acid, used in experimental medicine and taken illegally as a hallucinogenic drug. Informal name (as an illegal hallucinogen): **acid.**
L.S.D., £.s.d., *or* **l.s.d.** (in Britain, esp. formerly) *abbrev. for* libræ, solidi, denarii. [Latin: pounds, shillings, pence]
L.S.E. (often used in speech) *abbrev. for* London School of Economics.
LSI *Electronics. abbrev. for* large scale integration.
LT *abbrev. for:* **1.** low-tension. **2.** letter telegram.
Lt. *abbrev. for* Lieutenant.
l.t. *abbrev. for:* **1.** long ton. **2.** (esp. in the U.S.) local time.
Lt. Col. *abbrev. for* lieutenant colonel.
Lt. Comdr. *abbrev. for* lieutenant commander.
Ltd. *or* **ltd.** (esp. after the names of British business organizations) *abbrev. for* limited (liability). U.S. equivalent: **Inc.**
Lt. Gen. *abbrev. for* lieutenant general.
Lt. Gov. *abbrev. for* lieutenant governor.
Lu *the chemical symbol for* lutetium.
LU *Physics. abbrev. for* loudness unit.
Lu·a+la+ba (ˌluːəˈlɑːbə) *n.* a river in SE Zaïre, rising in Shaba province and flowing north as the W headstream of the River Congo. Length: about 1800 km (1100 miles).
Lu+an+da (luˈændə) *n.* the capital of Angola, a port in the west, on the Atlantic: founded in 1576, it became a centre of the slave trade to Brazil in the 17th and 18th centuries; oil refining. Pop.: 474 328 (1970). Official name: **São Paulo de Loanda.**
Lu+ang Pra+bang (luːˈæŋ prɑːˈbæŋ) *n.* a market town in N Laos, on the Mekong River: residence of the monarch of Laos (1946–75). Pop.: 25 000 (1970 est.).
lu·au (luːˈaʊ, ˈluːaʊ) *n.* **1.** a feast of Hawaiian food. **2.** a dish of

taro leaves usually prepared with coconut cream and octopus or chicken. [from Hawaiian *lu'au*]

Lu·ba ('lu:bə) *n.* **1.** (*pl.* **Lu·ba**). a member of a Negroid people of Africa living chiefly in Shaba province of Zaïre. **2.** Also called: **Tshiluba.** the language of this people, belonging to the Bantu group of the Niger-Congo family.

lub+ber ('lʌbə) *n.* **1.** a big, awkward, or stupid person. **2.** short for **landlubber.** [C14 *lobre,* probably from Scandinavian. See LOB[1]] —'**lub+ber+ly** *adj., adv.* —'**lub+ber+li+ness** *n.*

lub+ber line *n.* a mark on a ship's compass that designates the fore-and-aft axis of the vessel. Also called: **lubber's line.**

lub+ber's hole *n. Nautical.* a hole in a top or platform on a mast through which a sailor can climb.

Lub+bock ('lʌbək) *n.* a city in NW Texas: cotton market. Pop.: 153 752 (1973 est.).

Lü+beck (*German* 'ly:bɛk) *n.* a port in N West Germany, in Schleswig-Holstein: the leading member of the Hanseatic League, and a major European commercial centre until the 15th century; West Germany's chief Baltic port, with large shipyards and many industries. Pop.: 236 047 (1974 est.).

Lu+blin (*Polish* 'lublin) *n.* an industrial city in E Poland: provisional seat of the government in 1918 and 1944. Pop.: 259 000 (1974 est.).

lu+bra ('lu:brə) *n. Austral.* an Aboriginal woman. [C19: from a native Australian language]

lub+ri+cant ('lu:brɪkənt) *n.* **1.** a lubricating substance, such as oil. ~*adj.* **2.** serving to lubricate. [C19: from Latin *lūbricāns,* present participle of *lūbricāre.* See LUBRICATE]

lu+bri+cate ('lu:brɪˌkeɪt) *vb.* **1.** (*tr.*) to cover or treat with an oily or greasy substance so as to lessen friction. **2.** (*tr.*) to make greasy, slippery, or smooth. **3.** (*intr.*) to act as a lubricant. [C17: from Latin *lūbricāre,* from *lūbricus* slippery] —ˌ**lu+bri+'ca+tion** *n.* —ˌ**lu+bri+'ca+tion+al** *adj.* —'**lu+bri+ˌca+tive** *adj.*

lu+bri+ca+tor ('lu:brɪˌkeɪtə) *n.* **1.** a person or thing that lubricates. **2.** a device for applying lubricant.

lu+bric+i+ty (lu:'brɪsɪtɪ) *n.* **1.** *Formal or literary.* lewdness or salaciousness. **2.** *Rare.* smoothness or slipperiness. **3.** capacity to lubricate. [C15 (lewdness), C17 (slipperiness): from Old French *lubricité,* from Medieval Latin *lubricitās,* from Latin, from *lūbricus* slippery]

lu+bri+cous ('lu:brɪkəs) *or* **lu+bri+cious** (lu:'brɪʃəs) *adj.* **1.** *Formal or literary.* lewd, lascivious. **2.** *Rare.* oily or slippery. [C16: from Latin *lūbricus*] —'**lu+bri+cous+ly** *or* **lu+'bri+cious+ly** *adv.*

lu+bri+to+ri+um (ˌlu:brɪ'tɔ:rɪəm) *n., pl.* **+ri+a** (-rɪə). *Chiefly U.S.* a place, as in a service station, for the lubrication of motor vehicles. [C20: from LUBRICATE + *-orium,* as in *sanatorium*]

Lu+bum+ba+shi (ˌlu:bʊm'bæʃɪ) *n.* a city in S Zaïre, capital of Shaba province: founded in 1910 as a copper-mining centre; university (1955). Pop.: 403 623 (1974 est.). Former name (until 1966): **Élizabethville.**

Lu·can[1] ('lu:kən) *n.* Latin name *Marcus Annaeus Lucanus.* 39–65 A.D., Roman poet. His epic poem *Pharsalia* describes the civil war between Caesar and Pompey.

Lu+can[2] ('lu:kən) *adj.* of or relating to St. Luke or St. Luke's gospel.

Lu+ca+ni·a (lu:'keɪnɪə) *n.* the Latin name for **Basilicata.**

lu+carne (lu:'kɑ:n) *n.* a type of dormer window. [C16: from French, from Provençal *lucana,* of obscure origin]

Lu·cas van Ley·den ('lu:kəs væn 'laɪdᵊn) *n.* ?1494–1533, Dutch painter and engraver.

Luc+ca (*Italian* 'lukka) *n.* a city in NW Italy, in Tuscany: centre of a rich agricultural region, noted for the production of olive oil. Pop.: 89 944 (1971). Ancient name: **Luca.**

luce (lu:s) *n.* another name for the **pike** (the fish). [C14: from Old French *lus,* from Late Latin *lūcius* pike]

lu+cent ('lu:sᵊnt) *adj.* brilliant, shining, or translucent. [C16: from Latin *lūcēns,* present participle of *lūcēre* to shine] —'**lu+cent+ly** *adv.*

lu+cerne (lu:'sɜ:n) *n. Brit.* another name for **alfalfa.**

Lu+cerne (lu:'sɜ:n; *French* ly'sɛrn) *n.* **1.** a canton in central Switzerland, northwest of Lake Lucerne: joined the Swiss Confederacy in 1332. Pop.: 289 641 (1970). Area: 1494 sq. km (577 sq. miles). **2.** a city in central Switzerland, capital of Lucerne canton, on Lake Lucerne: tourist centre. Pop.: 69 879 (1970). **3. Lake.** a lake in central Switzerland: fed and drained chiefly by the River Reuss. Area: 115 sq. km (44 sq. miles). German name: **Vierwaldstättersee.** ~German name (for senses 1 and 2): **Luzern.**

Lu·ci·an ('lu:sɪən) *n.* 2nd century A.D., Greek writer, noted esp. for his satirical *Dialogues of the Gods* and *Dialogues of the Dead.*

lu+cid ('lu:sɪd) *adj.* **1.** readily understood; clear. **2.** shining or glowing. **3.** *Psychiatry.* of or relating to a period of normality between periods of insane or irresponsible behaviour. [C16: from Latin *lūcidus* full of light, from *lūx* light] —**lu+'cid+i+ty** *or* '**lu+cid+ness** *n.* —'**lu+cid+ly** *adv.*

lu+ci+fer ('lu:sɪfə) *n.* a friction match: originally a trade name for a match manufactured in England in the 19th century.

Lu+ci+fer ('lu:sɪfə) *n.* **1.** the leader of the rebellion of the angels: usually identified with Satan. **2.** the planet Venus when it rises as the morning star. [Old English, from Latin *Lūcifer,* light-bearer, from *lūx* light + *ferre* to bear]

lu+cif+er+in (lu:'sɪfərɪn) *n. Biochem.* a substance occurring in bioluminescent organisms, such as glow-worms and fireflies. It undergoes an enzyme-catalysed oxidation and emits light on decaying to its ground state. [C20: from Latin *lucifer* (literally: light-bearer) + -IN]

lu+cif+er+ous (lu:'sɪfərəs) *adj. Rare.* bringing or giving light.

Lu·cil·i·us (lu:'sɪlɪəs) *n.* **Gai·us** ('gaɪəs). ?180–102 B.C., Roman satirist, regarded as the originator of poetical satire.

Lu·ci·na (lu:'saɪnə) *n. Roman myth.* a title or name given to Juno as goddess of childbirth. [C14: from Latin *lūcīnus* bringing to the light, from *lūx* light]

luck (lʌk) *n.* **1.** events that are beyond control and seem subject to chance; fortune. **2.** success or good fortune. **3.** something considered to bring good luck. **4. down on one's luck.** having little or no good luck to the point of suffering hardships. **5. no such luck.** unfortunately not. **6. try one's luck.** to attempt something that is uncertain. ~*vb.* **7.** (*intr.;* foll. by *out*) *U.S. informal.* to succeed with (something). [C15: from Middle Dutch *luc;* related to Middle High German *gelücke,* late Old Norse *lukka, lykka*]

luck+less ('lʌklɪs) *adj.* having no luck; unlucky. —'**luck+less+ly** *adv.* —'**luck+less+ness** *n.*

Luck+now ('lʌknaʊ) *n.* a city in N India, capital of Uttar Pradesh: capital of Oudh (1775–1856); the British residency was beseiged (1857) during the Indian Mutiny. Pop.: 749 239 (1971).

luck·y ('lʌkɪ) *adj.* **luck·i·er, luck·i·est. 1.** having or bringing good fortune. **2.** happening by chance, esp. as desired. —'**luck·i·ly** *adv.* —'**luck·i+ness** *n.*

luck·y dip *n. Brit.* **1.** a barrel or box filled with sawdust and small prizes for which children search. **2.** *Informal.* an undertaking of uncertain outcome.

luc+ra+tive ('lu:krətɪv) *adj.* producing a profit; profitable; remunerative. [C15: from Old French *lucratif;* see LUCRE] —'**lu+cra+tive+ly** *adv.* —'**lu+cra+tive+ness** *n.*

lu+cre ('lu:kə) *n. Usually facetious.* money or wealth (esp. in the phrase **filthy lucre**). [C14: from Latin *lucrum* gain; related to Old English *lēan* reward, German *Lohn* wages]

Lu·cre·ti·a (lu:'kri:ʃɪə) *n.* (in Roman legend) a Roman woman who killed herself after being raped by a son of Tarquin the Proud.

Lu·cre·ti·us (lu:'kri:ʃɪəs) *n.* full name *Titus Lucretius Carus.* ?96–55 B.C., Roman poet and philosopher. In his didactic poem *De rerum natura,* he expounds Epicurus' atomist theory of the universe. —**Lu+'cre·ti·an** *adj.*

lu+cu+brate ('lu:kjʊˌbreɪt) *vb.* (*intr.*) to write or study, esp. at night. [C17: from Latin *lūcubrāre* to work by lamplight] —'**lu+cu+ˌbra+tor** *n.*

lu+cu+bra+tion (ˌlu:kjʊ'breɪʃən) *n.* **1.** laborious study, esp. at night. **2.** (*often pl.*) a solemn literary work.

lu+cu+lent ('lu:kjʊlənt) *adj. Rare.* **1.** easily understood; lucid. **2.** bright or shining; glowing. [C15: from Latin *lūculentus* full of light, from *lūx* light] —'**lu+cu+lent+ly** *adv.*

Lu·cul·lus (lu:'kʌləs) *n.* **Lu·ci·us Li·ci·ni·us** ('lu:sɪəs lɪ'sɪnɪəs). ?110–56 B.C., Roman general and consul, famous for his luxurious banquets. He fought Mithradates VI (74–66). —**Lu+'cul+lan, Lu+cul+le·an** (ˌlu:kʌ'li:ən), *or* ˌ**Lu+cul+'li·an** *adj.*

Lu·cy ('lu:sɪ) *n.* **Saint.** died ?303 A.D., a virgin martyred by Diocletian in Syracuse. Feast day: Dec 13.

lud (lʌd) *Brit.* ~*n.* **1.** lord (in the phrase **my lud, m'lud**): used when addressing a judge in court. ~*interj.* **2.** *Archaic.* an exclamation of dismay or surprise.

Lud+dite ('lʌdaɪt) *n. English history.* **1.** any of the textile workers opposed to mechanization who rioted and organized machine-breaking between 1811 and 1816. **2.** any opponent of industrial change or innovation. ~*adj.* **3.** of or relating to the Luddites. [C19: alleged to be named after Ned *Ludd,* an 18th-century Leicestershire workman, who destroyed industrial machinery] —'**Lud+dism** *n.*

Lu·den·dorff (*German* 'lu:dᵊnˌdɔrf) *n.* **E·rich Frie·drich Wil·helm von** ('e:rɪç 'fri:drɪç 'vɪlhɛlm fɔn). 1865–1937, German general, Hindenburg's aide in World War I.

Lü+den+scheid (*German* 'ly:dᵊnˌʃaɪt) *n.* a city in NW West Germany, in North Rhine-Westphalia: manufacturing centre for aluminium and plastics. Pop.: 79 100 (1970).

Lü+der+itz (*German* 'ly:dərɪts) *n.* a port in South West Africa: diamond-mining centre. Pop.: 6642 (1970).

Lu+dhi+a+na (ˌlʊdɪ'ɑ:nə) *n.* a city in N India, in the central Punjab: Punjab Agricultural University (1962). Pop.: 397 850 (1971).

lu+di+crous ('lu:dɪkrəs) *adj.* absurd or incongruous to the point of provoking ridicule or laughter. [C17: from *lūdicrus* done in sport, from *lūdus* game; related to *lūdere* to play] —'**lu+di+crous+ly** *adv.* —'**lu+di+crous+ness** *n.*

Lud+low[1] ('lʌdləʊ) *n. Trademark.* a machine for casting type from matrices set by hand, used esp. for headlines.

Lud+low[2] ('lʌdləʊ) *n.* a market town in W central England, in Salop: castle (11th–16th century). Pop.: 23 481 (1971).

lu+do ('lu:dəʊ) *n. Brit.* a simple board game in which players advance counters by throwing dice. [C19: from Latin: I play]

Lud+wigs+burg (*German* 'lu:tvɪçsˌbʊrk) *n.* a city in SW West Germany, in Baden-Württemberg northeast of Stuttgart: expanded in the 18th century around the palace of the dukes of Württemberg. Pop.: 78 100 (1970).

Lud+wigs+ha+fen (*German* 'lu:tvɪçsˌha:fᵊn) *n.* city in SW West Germany, in the Rhineland-Palatinate, on the Rhine: chemical industry. Pop.: 173 141 (1974 est.).

lu·es ('lu:i:z) *n., pl.* **lu·es.** *Rare.* **1.** any venereal disease. **2.** a pestilence. [C17: from New Latin, from Latin: calamity] —**lu+et+ic** (lu:'ɛtɪk) *adj.* —**lu+'et+i+cal+ly** *adv.*

luff (lʌf) *n.* **1.** *Nautical.* the leading edge of a fore-and-aft sail. ~*vb.* **2.** *Nautical.* to head (a sailing vessel) into the wind so that her sails flap. **3.** (*intr.*) *Nautical.* (of a sail) to flap when the wind is blowing equally on both sides. **4.** to move the jib of (a crane) or raise or lower the boom of (a derrick) in order to shift a load. [C13 (in the sense: steering gear): from Old French *lof,* perhaps from Middle Dutch *loef* peg of a tiller; compare Old High German *laffa* palm of hand, oar blade, Russian *lapa* paw]

luf+fa ('lʌfə) *n.* **1.** any tropical climbing plant of the cucurbitaceous genus *Luffa,* esp. the dishcloth gourd. **2.** *U.S.* another name for **loofah.**

Luft+waf+fe (*German* 'lʊft,vafə) *n.* the German Air Force. [C20: German, literally: air weapon]

lug[1] (lʌg) *vb.* **lugs, lug+ging, lugged. 1.** to carry or drag (something heavy) with great effort. **2.** (*tr.*) to introduce (an irrelevant topic) into a conversation or discussion. **3.** (*tr.*) (of a sailing vessel) to carry too much (sail) for the amount of wind blowing. ~*n.* **4.** the act or an instance of lugging. [C14: probably from Scandinavian; apparently related to Norwegian *lugge* to pull by the hair]

lug[2] (lʌg) *n.* **1.** a projecting piece by which something is connected, supported, or lifted. **2.** Also called: **tug.** a leather loop used in harness for various purposes. **3.** a box or basket for vegetables or fruit with a capacity of 28 to 40 pounds. **4.** *Brit. informal or Scot.* another word for **ear. 5.** *Slang.* a man, esp. a stupid or awkward one. [C15 (Scots dialect) *lugge* ear, perhaps related to LUG[1] (in the sense: to pull by the ear)]

lug[3] (lʌg) *n. Nautical.* short for **lugsail.**

lug[4] (lʌg) *n.* short for **lugworm.** [C16: origin uncertain]

Lu+gan+da (lu:'gændə, -'gɑ:ndə) *n.* the language of the Buganda, spoken chiefly in Uganda, belonging to the Bantu group of the Niger-Congo family.

Lu+gansk (*Russian* lu'gansk) *n.* the former name (until 1935) of **Voroshilovgrad.**

luge (lu:ʒ) *n.* a light one-man toboggan. [C20: from French]

Lu+ger ('lu:gə) *n. Trademark.* a German semiautomatic pistol.

lug+gage ('lʌgɪdʒ) *n.* suitcases, trunks, etc., containing personal belongings for a journey; baggage. [C16: perhaps from LUG[1], influenced in form by BAGGAGE]

lug+gage van *n. Brit.* a railway carriage used to transport passengers' luggage, bicycles, etc. U.S. name: **baggage car.**

lug+ger ('lʌgə) *n. Nautical.* a small working boat rigged with a lugsail. [C18: from LUGSAIL]

Lu+go (*Spanish* 'luɣo) *n.* a city in NW Spain: Roman walls; Romanesque cathedral. Pop.: 63 830 (1970). Latin name: **Lucus Augusti.**

lug+sail ('lʌgsəl) *or* **lug** (lʌg) *n. Nautical.* a four-sided sail bent and hoisted on a yard. [C17: perhaps from Middle English (now dialect) *lugge* pole, or from *lugge* ear]

lug screw *n.* a small screw without a head.

lu+gu+bri+ous (lʊ'gu:brɪəs) *adj.* excessively mournful; doleful. [C17: from Latin *lūgubris* mournful, from *lūgēre* to grieve] —**lu+'gu+bri+ous+ly** *adv.* —**lu+'gu+bri+ous+ness** *n.*

lug+worm ('lʌg,wɜ:m) *n.* any polychaete worm of the genus *Arenicola,* living in burrows on sandy shores and having tufted gills: much used as bait by fishermen. Sometimes shortened to **lug.** Also called: **lobworm.**

lug wrench *n.* a spanner with a lug or lugs projecting from its jaws to engage the component to be rotated.

Lui+chow Pen+in+su+la ('lu:'tʃaʊ) *n.* a peninsula of SE China, in SW Kwantung province, separated from Hainan Island by Hainan Strait.

Luik (lœjk) *n.* the Flemish name for **Liège.**

Lu·kács ('lu:kætʃ) *n.* **Ge·org** ('geɪɔ:k), original name *György.* 1885–1971, Hungarian Marxist philosopher and literary critic, whose works include *History and Class Consciousness* (1923), *Studies in European Realism* (1946), and *The Historical Novel* (1955).

Luke (lu:k) *n. New Testament.* **1.** the Evangelist, a fellow worker of Paul and a physician (Colossians 4:14). **2.** the third Gospel, traditionally ascribed to Luke. Related adj.: **Lucan.**

luke+warm (,lu:k'wɔ:m) *adj.* **1.** (esp. of water) moderately warm; tepid. **2.** having or expressing little enthusiasm or conviction. [C14 *luke* probably from Old English *hlēow* warm; compare German *lauwarm*] —**,luke+'warm+ly** *adv.* —**,luke+'warm+ness** *n.*

Lu+le·å (*Swedish* 'lu:lə,o:) *n.* a port in N Sweden, on the Gulf of Bothnia: industrial and shipbuilding centre; icebound in winter. Pop.: 58 946 (1970).

lull (lʌl) *vb.* **1.** to soothe (a person or animal) by soft sounds or motions (esp. in the phrase **lull to sleep**). **2.** to calm (someone or someone's fears, suspicions, etc.), esp. by deception. ~*n.* **3.** a short period of calm or diminished activity. [C14: possibly imitative of crooning sounds; related to Middle Low German *lollen* to soothe, Middle Dutch *lollen* to talk drowsily, mumble] —**'lull+ing+ly** *adv.*

lull·a·by ('lʌlə,baɪ) *n., pl.* **+bies. 1.** a quiet song to lull a child to sleep. **2.** the music for such a song. ~*vb.* **+bies, +by+ing, +bied. 3.** (*tr.*) to quiet or soothe with or as if with a lullaby. [C16: perhaps a blend of LULL + GOODBYE]

Lul·ly *n.* **1.** (*French* ly'li). **Jean Bap·tiste** (ʒɑ̃ ba'tist), Italian name *Giovanni Battista Lulli.* 1632–87, French composer, born in Italy; founder of French opera. With Philippe Quinault as librettist, he wrote operas such as *Alceste* (1674) and *Armide* (1686); as superintendent of music at the court of Louis XIV, he wrote incidental music to comedies by Molière. **2.** ('lʌli). Also: **Lull** (lul). **Ray·mond** *or* **Ra·món** (ra'mon). ?1235–1315, Spanish philosopher, mystic, and missionary. His chief works are *Ars generalis sive magna* and the Utopian novel *Blaquerna.*

lu·lu ('lu:lu:) *n. Chiefly U.S. slang.* a person or thing considered to be outstanding in size, appearance, etc. [C20: probably from the nickname for *Louise*]

Lu+lu·a+bourg (lu:'lu:ə,bʊə) *n.* the former name (until 1966) of **Kananga.**

lum+ba+go (lʌm'beɪgəʊ) *n.* pain in the lower back; backache affecting the lumbar region. [C17: from Late Latin *lumbāgo,* from Latin *lumbus* loin]

lum+bar ('lʌmbə) *adj.* of, near, or relating to the part of the body between the lowest ribs and the hipbones. [C17: from New Latin *lumbāris,* from Latin *lumbus* loin]

lum+bar punc+ture *n. Med.* insertion of a hollow needle into the lower region of the spinal cord to withdraw cerebrospinal fluid, introduce drugs, etc.

lum+ber[1] ('lʌmbə) *n.* **1.** *Chiefly U.S. and Canadian.* **a.** logs; sawn timber. **b.** (*as modifier*): *the lumber trade.* **2.** *Brit.* **a.** useless household articles that are stored away. **b.** (*as modifier*): *lumber room.* ~*vb.* **3.** (*tr.*) to pile together in a disorderly manner. **4.** (*tr.*) to fill up or encumber with useless household articles. **5.** *Chiefly U.S. and Canadian.* to convert (the trees) of (a forest) into marketable timber. **6.** (*tr.*) *Brit. informal.* to burden with something unpleasant, tedious, etc. [C17: perhaps from a noun use of LUMBER[2]] —**'lum+ber+er** *n.*

lum+ber[2] ('lʌmbə) *vb.* (*intr.*) **1.** to move or proceed in an awkward heavy manner. **2.** an obsolete word for **rumble.** [C14 *lomeren;* perhaps related to *lome* LAME, Swedish dialect *loma* to move ponderously]

lum+ber+ing[1] ('lʌmbərɪŋ) *n. Chiefly U.S. and Canadian.* the business or trade of cutting, preparing, or selling timber.

lum+ber+ing[2] ('lʌmbərɪŋ) *adj.* **1.** awkward or heavy in movement. **2.** moving with a rumbling sound. —**'lum+ber+ing+ly** *adv.* —**'lum+ber+ing+ness** *n.*

lum·ber+jack ('lʌmbə,dʒæk) *n.* (esp. in North America) a person whose work involves felling trees, transporting the timber, etc. [C19: from LUMBER[1] + JACK[1] (man)]

lum·ber+jack·et ('lʌmbə,dʒækɪt) *n.* a boldly coloured, usually checked jacket in warm cloth, as worn by lumberjacks. U.S. name: **lumberjack.**

lum·ber+yard ('lʌmbə,jɑ:d) *n.* the U.S. word for **timberyard.**

lum+bri+ca+lis (,lʌmbrɪ'keɪlɪs) *n. Anatomy.* any of the four wormlike muscles in the hand or foot. [C18: New Latin, from Latin *lumbrīcus* worm] —**lum+bri+cal** ('lʌmbrɪk^{ə}l) *adj.*

lum+bri+coid ('lʌmbrɪ,kɔɪd) *adj.* **1.** *Anatomy.* designating any part or structure resembling a worm. **2.** of, relating to, or resembling an earthworm. [C19: from New Latin *lumbricoides,* from Latin *lumbrīcus* worm]

lu+men ('lu:mɪn) *n., pl.* **+mens** *or* **+mi+na** (-mɪnə). **1.** the derived SI unit of luminous flux; the flux emitted in a solid angle of 1 steradian by a point source having a uniform intensity of 1 candela. Symbol: lm **2.** *Anatomy.* a passage, duct, or cavity in a tubular organ. **3.** a cavity within a plant cell enclosed by the cell walls. [C19: New Latin, from Latin: light, aperture] —**'lu+men+al** *or* **'lu+min+al** *adj.*

Lu·mière (*French* ly'mjɛ:r) *n.* **Au·guste Ma·rie Louis Ni·co·las** (ogyst mari lwi nikɔ'lɑ). 1862–1954, and his brother, **Louis Jean** (lwi 'ʒɑ̃), 1864–1948, French chemists and cinema pioneers, who invented a cinematograph and a process of colour photography.

lu+mi+nance ('lu:mɪnəns) *n.* **1.** a state or quality of radiating or reflecting light. **2.** a measure (in candelas per square metre) of the brightness of a point on a surface that is radiating or reflecting light. It is the luminous intensity in a given direction of a small element of surface area divided by the orthogonal projection of this area onto a plane at right angles to the direction. Symbol: *L* [C19: from Latin *lūmen* light]

lu+mi+nar·y ('lu:mɪnərɪ) *n., pl.* **+nar·ies. 1.** a person who enlightens or influences others. **2.** a famous person. **3.** *Literary.* something, such as the sun or moon, that gives off light. ~*adj.* **4.** of, involving, or characterized by light or enlightenment. [C15: via Old French, from Latin *lūmināre* lamp, from *lūmen* light]

lu+mi+nesce (,lu:mɪ'nɛs) *vb.* (*intr.*) to exhibit luminescence. [back formation from LUMINESCENT]

lu+mi+nes+cence (,lu:mɪ'nɛsəns) *n. Physics.* **a.** the emission of light at low temperatures by any process other than incandescence, such as phosphorescence or chemiluminescence. **b.** the light emitted by such a process. [C19: from Latin *lūmen* light] —**,lu+mi+'nes+cent** *adj.*

lu+mi+nos+i+ty (,lu:mɪ'nɒsɪtɪ) *n., pl.* **·ties. 1.** the condition of being luminous. **2.** something that is luminous. **3.** *Astronomy.* a measure of the amount of light emitted by a star. **4.** *Physics.* the attribute of an object or colour enabling the extent to which an object emits light to be observed. Former name: **brightness.** See also **colour.**

lu+mi+nous ('lu:mɪnəs) *adj.* **1.** radiating or reflecting light; shining; glowing: *luminous colours.* **2.** (*not in technical use*) exhibiting luminescence: *luminous paint.* **3.** full of light; well-lit. **4.** (of a physical quantity in photometry) evaluated according to the visual sensation produced in an observer rather than by absolute energy measurements: *luminous flux; luminous intensity.* Compare **radiant. 5.** easily understood; lucid; clear. **6.** enlightening or wise. [C15: from Latin *lūminōsus* full of light, from *lūmen* light] —**'lu+mi+nous+ly** *adv.* —**'lu+mi+nous+ness** *n.*

lu+mi+nous ef+fi+ca+cy *n.* **1.** the quotient of the luminous flux of a radiation and its corresponding radiant flux. Symbol: *K* **2.** the quotient of the luminous flux emitted by a source of radiation and the power it consumes. It is measured in lumens per watt. Symbol: η_v, Φ_v

lu+mi+nous ef+fi+cien+cy *n.* the efficiency of polychromatic radiation in producing a visual sensation. It is the radiant flux weighed according to the spectral luminous efficiencies of its constituent wavelengths divided by the corresponding radiant flux. Symbol: V

lu·mi·nous en·er·gy *n.* energy emitted or propagated in the form of light; the product of a luminous flux and its duration, measured in lumen seconds. Symbol: Q_v

lu·mi·nous ex·i·tance *n.* the ability of a surface to emit light expressed as the luminous flux per unit area at a specified point on the surface. Symbol: M_v

lu·mi·nous flux *n.* a measure of the rate of flow of luminous energy, evaluated according to its ability to produce a visual sensation. For a monochromatic light it is the radiant flux multiplied by the spectral luminous efficiency of the light. It is measured in lumens. Symbol: Φ_v

lu·mi·nous in·ten·si·ty *n.* a measure of the amount of light that a point source radiates in a given direction. It is expressed by the luminous flux leaving the source in that direction per unit of solid angle. Symbol: I_v

lu·mis·te·rol (luːˈmɪstəˌrɒl) *n. Biochem.* a steroid compound produced when ergosterol is exposed to ultraviolet radiation. Formula: $C_{28}H_{44}O$. [C20: from Latin *lumin-, lūmen* light + STEROL]

lum·me *or* **lum·my** (ˈlʌmɪ) *interj. Brit.* an exclamation of surprise or dismay. [C19: alteration of *Lord love me*]

lum·mox (ˈlʌməks) *n. Informal.* a clumsy or stupid person. [C19: origin unknown]

lump[1] (lʌmp) *n.* **1.** a small solid mass without definite shape. **2.** *Pathol.* any small swelling or tumour. **3.** a collection of things; aggregate. **4.** *Informal.* an awkward, heavy, or stupid person. **5. the lump.** *Brit.* **a.** self-employed workers in the building trade considered collectively, esp. with reference to tax and national insurance evasion. **b.** (*as modifier*): *lump labour.* **6.** (*modifier*) in the form of a lump or lumps: *lump sugar.* **7. a lump in one's throat.** a tight dry feeling in one's throat, usually caused by great emotion. **8. in the lump.** collectively; en masse. ~*vb.* **9.** (*tr.*; often foll. by *together*) to collect into a mass or group. **10.** (*intr.*) to grow into lumps or become lumpy. **11.** (*tr.*) to consider as a single group, often without justification. **12.** (*tr.*) to make or cause lumps in or on. **13.** (*intr.*; often foll. by *along*) to move or proceed in a heavy manner. [C13: probably related to early Dutch *lompe* piece, Scandinavian dialect *lump* block, Middle High German *lumpe* rag]

lump[2] (lʌmp) *vb.* (*tr.*) *Informal.* to tolerate or put up with; endure (in the phrase **lump it**). [C16: origin uncertain]

lump·en (ˈlʌmpᵊn) *Informal. adj.* stupid or unthinking. [from German *Lump* vagabond, influenced in meaning by *Lumpen* rag, as in LUMPENPROLETARIAT]

lum·pen·pro·le·tar·i·at (ˌlʌmpənˌprəʊlɪˈtɛərɪət) *n.* (esp. in Marxist theory) the amorphous urban social group below the proletariat, consisting of criminals, tramps, etc. [German, literally: ragged proletariat]

lum·per (ˈlʌmpə) *n. U.S.* a stevedore; docker.

lump·fish (ˈlʌmpˌfɪʃ) *n., pl.* **·fish** *or* **·fish·es. 1.** a North Atlantic scorpaenoid fish, *Cyclopterus lumpus*, having a globular body covered with tubercles, pelvic fins fused into a sucker, and an edible roe: family *Cyclopteridae.* **2.** any other fish of the family *Cyclopteridae.* ~Also called: **ˈlump·ˌsuck·er.** [C16 *lump* (now obsolete) lumpfish, from Middle Dutch *lumpe*, perhaps related to LUMP[1]]

lump·ish (ˈlʌmpɪʃ) *adj.* **1.** resembling a lump. **2.** stupid, clumsy, or heavy. —**ˈlump·ish·ly** *adv.* —**ˈlump·ish·ness** *n.*

lump sum *n.* a relatively large sum of money, paid at one time, esp. in cash.

lump·y (ˈlʌmpɪ) *adj.* **lump·i·er, lump·i·est. 1.** full of or having lumps. **2.** (esp. of the sea) rough. **3.** (of a person) heavy or bulky. —**ˈlump·i·ly** *adv.* —**ˈlump·i·ness** *n.*

lump·y jaw *n. Vet. science.* a nontechnical name for **actinomycosis.**

Lu·mum·ba (lʊˈmʊmbə) *n.* **Pa·trice** (pəˈtriːs). 1925–61, Congolese statesman; first prime minister of the Democratic Republic of the Congo (now Zaïre) (1960); assassinated.

Lu·na[1] (ˈluːnə) *n.* **1.** the alchemical name for **silver. 2.** the Roman goddess of the moon. Greek counterpart: **Selene.** [from Latin: moon]

Lu·na[2] (ˈluːnə) *or* **Lu·nik** (ˈluːnɪk) *n.* any of a series of Soviet lunar space-probes, one of which, **Luna 9**, made the first soft landing on the moon (1966).

lu·na·cy (ˈluːnəsɪ) *n., pl.* **·cies. 1.** (formerly) any severe mental illness. **2.** foolishness or a foolish act.

lu·na moth *n.* a large American saturniid moth, *Tropaea* (or *Actias*) *luna*, having light green wings with a yellow crescent-shaped marking on each forewing. [C19: so named from the markings on its wings]

lu·nar (ˈluːnə) *adj.* **1.** of or relating to the moon. **2.** occurring on, used on, or designed to land on the surface of the moon: *lunar module.* **3.** relating to, caused by, or measured by the position or orbital motion of the moon. **4.** of or containing silver. [C17: from Latin *lūnāris*, from *lūna* the moon]

lu·nar caus·tic *n.* silver nitrate fused into sticks, which were formerly used in cauterizing.

lu·nar e·clipse *n.* See under **eclipse** (sense 1).

lu·nar·i·an (luːˈnɛərɪən) *n.* **1.** an archaic word for **selenographer. 2.** *Myth.* an inhabitant of the moon.

lu·nar mod·ule *n.* the module used to carry two of the three astronauts on an Apollo spacecraft to the surface of the moon and back to the spacecraft.

lu·nar month *n.* another name for **synodic month.** See **month** (sense 6).

lu·nar year *n.* See under **year** (sense 6).

lu·nate (ˈluːneɪt) *or* **lu·nat·ed** *adj.* **1.** *Anatomy, botany.* shaped like a crescent. ~*n.* **2.** a crescent-shaped bone forming part of the wrist. [C18: from Latin *lūnātus*, crescent-shaped, from *lūnāre*, from *lūna* moon] —**ˈlu·nate·ly** *adv.*

lu·na·tic (ˈluːnətɪk) *adj.* also **lu·nat·i·cal** (luːˈnætɪkᵊl). **1.** an informal or archaic word for **insane.** ~*n.* **2.** a person who is insane. [C13 (adj.) via Old French from Late Latin *lūnāticus* crazy, moonstruck, from Latin *lūna* moon] —**luˈnat·i·cal·ly** *adv.*

lu·na·tic a·sy·lum *n.* another name, usually regarded as offensive, for **mental hospital.**

lu·na·tic fringe *n.* the members of a society or group who adopt or support views regarded as extreme or fanatical.

lu·na·tion (luːˈneɪʃən) *n.* another name for **synodic month.** See **month** (sense 6).

lunch (lʌntʃ) *n.* **1.** a meal eaten during the middle of the day. **2.** *Caribbean.* (among older people) midafternoon tea. Compare **breakfast** (sense 1), **tea** (sense 5). ~*vb.* **3.** (*intr.*) to eat lunch. **4.** (*tr.*) to provide or buy lunch for. [C16: probably short form of LUNCHEON] —**ˈlunch·er** *n.*

lunch·eon (ˈlʌntʃən) *n.* a lunch, esp. a formal one. [C16: probably variant of *nuncheon*, from Middle English *noneschench*, from *none* NOON + *schench* drink]

lunch·eon·ette (ˌlʌntʃəˈnɛt) *n. U.S.* a café or small informal restaurant where light meals and snacks are served.

lunch·eon meat *n.* a ground mixture of meat (often pork) and cereal, usually tinned.

lunch·eon vouch·er *n.* a voucher worth a specified amount issued to employees and redeemable at a restaurant for food. Abbrev.: **LV** U.S. equivalent: **meal ticket.**

lunch hour *n.* **1.** Also called: **lunch break.** a break in the middle of the working day, usually of one hour, during which lunch may be eaten. **2.** Also called: **lunch time.** the time at which lunch is usually eaten.

Lund (lʊnd) *n.* a city in SE Sweden, northeast of Malmö: founded in about 1020 by the Danish King Canute; the archbishopric for all Scandinavia in the Middle Ages; university (1668). Pop.: 55 986 (1970).

Lun·dy's Lane (ˈlʌndɪz) *n.* the site, near Niagara Falls, of a major battle (1814) in the War of 1812, in which British and Canadian forces defeated the Americans.

lune[1] (luːn) *n.* **1. a.** a section of the surface of a sphere enclosed between two semicircles that intersect at opposite points on the sphere. **b.** a crescent-shaped figure formed on a plane surface by the intersection of the arcs of two circles. **2.** something shaped like a crescent. **3.** *R.C. Church.* another word for **lunette** (sense 6). [C18: from Latin *lūna* moon]

lune[2] (luːn) *n. Falconry.* a leash for hawks or falcons. [C14 *loigne*, from Old French, from Medieval Latin *longia, longea*, from Latin *longus* LONG[1]]

Lü·ne·burg (*German* ˈlyːnəˌbʊrk) *n.* a city in N West Germany, in Lower Saxony: capital of the duchy of Brunswick-Lüneburg from 1235 to 1369; prominent Hanse town; saline springs. Pop.: 59 800 (1970).

lu·nette (luːˈnɛt) *n.* **1.** anything that is shaped like a crescent. **2.** an oval or circular opening to admit light in a dome. **3.** a semicircular panel containing a window, mural, or sculpture. **4.** a ring attached to a vehicle, into which a hook is inserted so that it can be towed. **5.** a type of fortification like a detached bastion. **6.** Also called: **lune.** *R.C. Church.* a case fitted with a bracket to hold the consecrated host. [C16: from French: crescent, from *lune* moon, from Latin *lūna*]

Lu·né·ville (*French* lyneˈvil) *n.* a city in NE France: scene of the signing of the **Peace of Lunéville** between France and Austria (1801). Pop.: 24 700 (1975).

lung (lʌŋ) *n.* **1.** either one of a pair of spongy saclike respiratory organs within the thorax of higher vertebrates, which oxygenate the blood and remove its carbon dioxide. **2.** any similar or analogous organ in other vertebrates or in invertebrates. **3. at the top of one's lungs.** in one's loudest voice; yelling. [Old English *lungen*; related to Old High German *lungun* lung. Compare LIGHTS[2]]

lun·gan (ˈlʌŋgən) *n.* another name for **longan.**

lunge[1] (lʌndʒ) *n.* **1.** *Fencing.* a thrust made by advancing the front foot and straightening the back leg, extending the sword arm forwards. **2.** a sudden forward motion. ~*vb.* **3.** (*intr.*) *Fencing.* to make a lunge. **4.** to move or cause to move with a lunge. [C18: shortened form of obsolete C17 *allonge*, from French *allonger* to stretch out (one's arm) from Late Latin *ēlongāre* to lengthen. Compare ELONGATE] —**ˈlung·er** *n.*

lunge[2] (lʌndʒ) *n.* **1.** a rope used in training or exercising a horse. ~*vb.* **2.** to exercise or train (a horse) on a lunge. [C17: from Old French *longe*, shortened from *allonge*, ultimately from Latin *longus* LONG; related to LUNGE[1]]

lung·fish (ˈlʌŋˌfɪʃ) *n., pl.* **·fish** *or* **·fish·es.** any freshwater bony fish of the subclass *Dipnoi*, having an air-breathing lung, fleshy paired fins, and an elongated body. The only living species are those of the genera *Lepidosiren* of South America, *Protopterus* of Africa, and *Neoceratodus* of Australia.

lun·gi *or* **lun·gee** (ˈlʊŋgiː) *n.* a long piece of cotton cloth worn as a loincloth, sash, or turban by Indian men or as a skirt. [C17: Hindi, from Persian]

Lung·ki *or* **Lung-chi** (ˈlʊŋˈkiː) *n.* a city in SE China, in S Fukien province on the Saikoe River. Pop.: 100 000 (1970 est.). Former name: **Changchow.**

lung·worm (ˈlʌŋˌwɜːm) *n.* **1.** any parasitic nematode worm of the family *Metastrongylidae*, occurring in the lungs of mammals, esp. *Metastrongylus apri* which infects pigs. **2.** any of certain other nematodes that are parasitic in the lungs.

lung+wort ('lʌŋˌwɜːt) *n.* **1.** any of several Eurasian plants of the boraginaceous genus *Pulmonaria*, esp. *P. officinalis*, which has spotted leaves and clusters of blue or purple flowers: formerly used to treat lung diseases. **2.** any of various boraginaceous plants of the N temperate genus *Mertensia* having drooping clusters of tubular usually blue flowers.

Lu+nik ('luːnɪk) *n.* another name for **Luna**[2].

lu+ni+so+lar (ˌluːnɪ'səʊlə) *adj.* resulting from, relating to, or based on the combined gravitational attraction of the sun and moon. [C17: from Latin *lūna* moon + SOLAR]

lu+ni+tid+al (ˌluːnɪ'taɪdᵊl) *adj.* of or relating to tidal phenomena as produced by the moon. [C19: from Latin *lūna* moon + TIDAL]

lu+ni+tid+al in+ter+val *n.* the difference in time between the moon crossing a meridian and the following high tide at that meridian.

Luns (*Dutch* lyns) *n.* **Jo·seph** ('joːzɛf) (**Marie Antoine Herbert**). born 1911, Dutch diplomat and politician; secretary general of the North Atlantic Treaty Organization since 1971.

lu+nu+la ('luːnjʊlə) *or* **lu+nule** ('luːnjuːl) *n., pl.* **+nu+lae** (-njʊˌliː) *or* **+nules.** the white crescent-shaped area at the base of the human fingernail. Nontechnical name: **half-moon.** [C16: from Latin: small moon, from *lūna*]

lu+nu+late ('luːnjʊˌleɪt) *or* **lu+nu+lat+ed** *adj.* **1.** having markings shaped like crescents: *lunulate patterns on an insect.* **2.** Also: **lunular.** shaped like a crescent.

Lu·o (lə'wəʊ, 'luːəʊ) *n.* **1.** (*pl.* **·o** *or* **·os**) a member of a cattle-herding Nilotic people living chiefly east of Lake Victoria in Kenya. **2.** the language of this people, belonging to the Nilotic group of the Nilo-Saharan family.

Lu+per+ca+li·a (ˌluːpɜː'keɪlɪə) *n., pl.* **+li·a** *or* **+li·as.** an ancient Roman festival of fertility, celebrated annually on Feb. 15. See also **Saint Valentine's Day.** [Latin, from *Lupercālis* belonging to *Lupercus*, a Roman god of the flocks] —ˌ**Lu+per+'ca+li·an** *adj.*

lu+pin *or U.S.* **lu+pine** ('luːpɪn) *n.* any papilionaceous plant of the genus *Lupinus*, of North America, Europe, and Africa, with large spikes of brightly coloured flowers and flattened pods. [C14: from Latin *lupīnus* wolfish (see LUPINE); from the belief that the plant ravenously exhausted the soil]

lu+pine ('luːpaɪn) *adj.* of, relating to, or resembling a wolf. [C17: from Latin *lupīnus*, from *lupus* wolf]

lu+pu+lin ('luːpjʊlɪn) *n.* a resinous powder extracted from the female flowers of the hop plant and used as a sedative. [C19: from New Latin *lupulus*, diminutive of *lupus* the hop plant]

lu+pus ('luːpəs) *n.* any of various ulcerative skin diseases. [C16: via Medieval Latin from Latin: wolf; said to be so called because it rapidly eats away the affected part]

Usage. In current usage the word *lupus* alone is generally understood to signify lupus vulgaris, lupus erythematosus being normally referred to in full or by the abbreviation LE.

Lu+pus ('luːpəs) *n., Latin genitive* **Lu·pi** ('luːpaɪ). a constellation in the S hemisphere lying between Centaurus and Ara.

lu+pus er·y+the+ma+to+sus (ˌɛrɪˌθiːmə'təʊsəs) *n.* either of two inflammatory diseases of the connective tissue. **Discoid lupus erythematosus** is characterized by a scaly rash over the cheeks and bridge of the nose; **disseminated** or **systemic lupus erythematosus** affects the joints, lungs, kidneys, or skin. Abbrev.: **LE, L.E.**

lu+pus vul+gar+is (vʌl'gɛərɪs) *n.* tuberculosis of the skin, esp. of the face, with the formation of raised translucent nodules. Sometimes shortened to **lupus.**

lur *or* **lure** (lʊə) *n., pl.* **lur·es** ('lʊərɪz). a large bronze musical horn found in Danish peat bogs and probably dating to the Bronze Age. [from Danish (and Swedish and Norwegian) *lur*, from Old Norse *lūthr* trumpet]

lurch[1] (lɜːtʃ) *vb.* (*intr.*) **1.** to lean or pitch suddenly to one side. **2.** to stagger or sway. ~*n.* **3.** the act or an instance of lurching. [C19: origin unknown] —**'lurch+ing+ly** *adv.*

lurch[2] (lɜːtʃ) *n.* **1. leave (someone) in the lurch.** to desert (someone) in trouble. **2.** *Cribbage.* the state of a losing player with less than 30 points at the end of a game (esp. in the phrase **in the lurch**). [C16: from French *lourche* a game similar to backgammon, apparently from *lourche* (adj.) deceived, probably of Germanic origin]

lurch[3] (lɜːtʃ) *vb.* (*intr.*) *Archaic or dialect.* to prowl or steal about suspiciously. [C15: perhaps a variant of LURK]

lurch+er ('lɜːtʃə) *n.* **1.** a person who prowls or lurks. **2.** a crossbred hunting dog, esp. one trained to hunt silently. [C16: from LURCH[3]]

lur+dan ('lɜːdᵊn) *Archaic.* ~*n.* **1.** a stupid or dull person. ~*adj.* **2.** dull or stupid. [C14: from Old French *lourdin*, Old French *lourd* heavy, from Latin *lūridus* LURID]

lure (lʊə) *vb.* (*tr.*) **1.** (sometimes foll. by *away* or *into*) to tempt or attract by the promise of some type of reward. **2.** *Falconry.* to entice (a hawk or falcon) from the air to the falconer by a lure. ~*n.* **3.** a person or thing that lures. **4.** *Angling.* any of various types of brightly-coloured artificial spinning baits, usually consisting of a plastic or metal body mounted with hooks and trimmed with feathers, etc. See **jig, plug, spoon. 5.** *Falconry.* a feathered decoy to which small pieces of meat can be attached and which is equipped with a long thong. [C14: from Old French *loirre* falconer's lure, from Germanic; related to Old English *lathian* to invite] —**'lur+er** *n.* —**'lur+ing+ly** *adv.*

Lu+rex ('lʊərɛks) *n.* **1.** *Trademark.* a thin aluminium thread coated with plastic. **2.** fabric containing such thread.

lu+rid ('lʊərɪd) *adj.* **1.** vivid in shocking detail; sensational. **2.** horrible in savagery or violence. **3.** pallid in colour; wan. **4.** glowing with an unnatural glare. [C17: from Latin *lūridus* pale yellow; probably related to *lūtum* a yellow vegetable dye] —**'lu+rid+ly** *adv.* —**'lu+rid+ness** *n.*

lurk (lɜːk) *vb.* (*intr.*) **1.** to move stealthily or be concealed, esp. for evil purposes. **2.** to be present in an unobtrusive way; go unnoticed. ~*n.* **3.** *Austral. slang.* a scheme or stratagem for success. [C13: probably frequentative of LOWER[2]; compare Middle Dutch *loeren* to lie in wait] —**'lurk+er** *n.* —**'lurk+ing+ly** *adv.*

Lu+sa+ka (luː'zɑːkə, -'sɑːkə) *n.* the capital of Zambia, in the southeast at an altitude of 1280 m (4200 ft.): became capital of Northern Rhodesia in 1932 and of Zambia in 1964; University of Zambia (1966). Pop.: 262 182 (1969).

Lu+sa+ti·a (luː'seɪʃɪə) *n.* a region of central Europe, lying between the upper reaches of the Elbe and Oder Rivers: now mostly in S East Germany, extending into SW Poland; inhabited chiefly by Sorbs.

Lu+sa+ti·an (luː'seɪʃɪən) *adj.* **1.** of or relating to Lusatia, its people, or their language. ~*n.* **2.** a native or inhabitant of Lusatia; a Sorb. **3.** the Sorbian language.

lus+cious ('lʌʃəs) *adj.* **1.** extremely pleasurable, esp. to the taste or smell. **2.** very attractive. **3.** *Archaic.* cloying. [C15 *lucius, licius*, perhaps a shortened form of DELICIOUS] —**'lus+cious+ly** *adv.* —**'lus+cious+ness** *n.*

lush[1] (lʌʃ) *adj.* **1.** (of vegetation) abounding in lavish growth. **2.** (esp. of fruits) succulent and fleshy. **3.** luxurious, elaborate, or opulent. [C15: probably from Old French *lasche* lax, lazy, from Latin *laxus* loose; perhaps related to Old English *læc*, Old Norse *lakr* weak, German *lasch* loose] —**'lush+ly** *adv.* —**'lush+ness** *n.*

lush[2] (lʌʃ) *U.S. slang.* ~*n.* **1.** a heavy drinker, esp. an alcoholic. **2.** alcoholic drink. ~*vb.* **3.** to drink (alcohol) to excess. [C19: origin unknown]

Lü-shun ('luː'ʃʊn) *n.* a port in NE China, in S Liaoning province, adjoining Lü-ta at the S end of the Liaotung peninsula: jointly held by China and the Soviet Union (1945–55). Pop. (with Lü-ta): 3 600 000 (1965 Western est.). Former name: **Port Arthur.**

Lu+si+ta+ni·a (ˌluːsɪ'teɪnɪə) *n.* an ancient region of the W Iberian Peninsula: a Roman province from 27 B.C. to the late 4th century A.D.; corresponds to most of present-day Portugal and the Spanish provinces of Salamanca and Cáceres.

lust (lʌst) *n.* **1.** a strong desire for sexual gratification. **2.** a strong desire or drive. ~*vb.* **3.** (*intr.*; often foll. by *after* or *for*) to have a lust (for). [Old English; related to Old High German *lust* desire, Old Norse *losti* sexual desire, Latin *lascīvus* playful, wanton, lustful. Compare LISTLESS]

lust+ful ('lʌstfʊl) *adj.* **1.** driven by lust. **2.** *Archaic.* vigorous or lusty. —**'lust+ful+ly** *adv.* —**'lust+ful+ness** *n.*

lus+tral ('lʌstrəl) *adj.* **1.** of or relating to the lustrum. **2.** taking place at intervals of five years; quinquennial. [C16: from Latin *lūstrālis* adj. from LUSTRUM]

lus+trate ('lʌstreɪt) *vb.* (*tr.*) to purify by means of religious rituals or ceremonies. [C17: from Latin *lūstrāre* to brighten] —**lus+'tra+tion** *n.* —**lus+tra+tive** ('lʌstrətɪv) *adj.*

lus+tre *or U.S.* **lus+ter** ('lʌstə) *n.* **1.** reflected light; sheen; gloss. **2.** radiance or brilliance of light. **3.** great splendour of accomplishment, beauty, etc. **4.** a substance used to polish or put a gloss on a surface. **5.** a vase or chandelier from which hang cut-glass drops. **6.** a drop-shaded piece of cut glass or crystal used as a decoration on a chandelier, vase, etc. **7. a.** a shiny metallic surface on some pottery and porcelain. **b.** (*as modifier*): *lustre decoration.* **8.** *Mineralogy.* the way in which light is reflected from the surface of a mineral. It is one of the properties by which minerals are defined. ~*vb.* **9.** to make, be, or become lustrous. [C16: from Old French, from Old Italian *lustro*, from Latin *lustrāre* to make bright; related to LUSTRUM] —**'lus+tre+less** *or U.S.* **'lus+ter+less** *adj.* —**'lus+trous** *adj.*

lus·tre+ware *or U.S.* **lus·ter+ware** ('lʌstəˌwɛə) *n.* pottery or porcelain ware with lustre decoration.

lus+tring ('lʌstrɪŋ) *or* **lute+string** ('luːtˌstrɪŋ) *n.* a glossy silk cloth, formerly used for clothing, upholstery, etc. [C17: from Italian *lustrino*, from *lustro* LUSTRE]

lus+trum ('lʌstrəm) *or* **lus+tre** *n., pl.* **+trums** *or* **+tra** (-trə). a period of five years. [C16: from Latin: ceremony of purification, from *lustrāre* to brighten, purify]

lust·y ('lʌstɪ) *adj.* **lust·i+er, lust·i·est. 1.** having or characterized by robust health. **2.** strong or invigorating: *a lusty brew.* —**'lust·i+ly** *adv.* —**'lust·i·ness** *n.*

lu+sus na+tu+rae ('luːsʊs næ'tʊəriː) *n.* a freak, mutant, or monster. [C17: Latin: whim of nature]

Lü-ta ('luː'tɑː) *n.* a port in NE China, in S Liaoning province, adjoining Lü-shun at the S end of the Liaotung peninsula: the chief northern port. Pop. (with Lü-shun): 3 600 000 (1965 Western est.). Former name: **Dairen.**

lu+tan+ist ('luːtənɪst) *n.* a variant spelling of **lutenist.**

lute[1] (luːt) *n.* **1.** an ancient plucked stringed instrument, consisting of a long fingerboard with gut frets and strings, and a body shaped like a sliced pear. [C14: from Old French *lut*, via Old Provençal from Arabic *al 'ūd*, literally: the wood]

lute[2] (luːt) *n.* **1.** Also called: **luting.** a mixture of cement and clay used to seal the joints between pipes, etc. ~*vb.* **2.** (*tr.*) to seal (a joint or surface) with lute. [C14: via Old French ultimately from Latin *lutum* clay]

lu+te·al ('luːtɪəl) *adj.* relating to or characterized by the development of the corpus luteum: *the luteal phase of the oestrous cycle.* [C20: from Latin *lūteus* yellow, relating to *lūtum* a yellow weed]

lu·te·in·iz·ing hor·mone ('lu:tɪɪˌnaɪzɪŋ) *n.* a gonadotropic hormone secreted by the anterior lobe of the pituitary gland. In female vertebrates it stimulates ovulation, and in mammals it also induces the conversion of the ruptured follicle into the corpus luteum. In male vertebrates it promotes maturation of the interstitial cells of the testes and stimulates androgen secretion. Abbrev.: **LH** Also called: **interstitial cell-stimulating hormone.** See also **follicle-stimulating hormone, prolactin.** [C19: from Latin *lūteum* egg yolk, from *lūteus* yellow]

lu·te·nist ('lu:tɪnɪst) *or U.S.* (*sometimes*) **lut·ist** ('lu:tɪst) *n.* a person who plays the lute. [C17: from Medieval Latin *lūtānista,* from *lūtāna,* apparently from Old French *lut* LUTE[1]]

lu·te·o·lin ('lu:tɪəlɪn) *n.* a yellow crystalline compound found, in the form of its glycoside, in many plants. Formula: $C_{15}H_{10}O_6$. [C19: via French from New Latin *reseda lūteola,* dyer's rocket, from which this substance is obtained; *lūteola* from Latin *lūteus* yellow]

lu·te·ous ('lu:tɪəs) *adj.* of a light to moderate greenish-yellow colour. [C17: from Latin *lūteus* yellow]

lute·string ('lu:tˌstrɪŋ) *n. Textiles.* a variant of **lustring.**

Lu·te·tia *or* **Lu·te·tia Pa·ris·i·o·rum** (lu:'ti:ʃə pəˌrɪzɪ'ɔ:rəm) *n.* an ancient name for **Paris** (the French city).

lu·te·ti·um *or* **lu·te·ci·um** (lʊ'ti:ʃɪəm) *n.* a silvery-white metallic element of the lanthanide series, occurring in monazite and used as a catalyst in cracking, alkylation, and polymerization. Symbol: Lu; atomic no.: 71; atomic wt.: 174.97; valency: 3; relative density: 9.835; melting pt.: 1656°C; boiling pt.: 3315°C. [C19: New Latin, from Latin *Lūtētia* ancient name of Paris, home of G. Urbain (1872–1938), French chemist, who discovered it]

Luth. *abbrev. for* Lutheran.

Lu·ther ('lu:θə) *n.* **Mar·tin.** 1483–1546, German leader of the Protestant Reformation. As professor of biblical theology at Wittenberg University from 1511, he began preaching the crucial doctrine of justification by faith rather than by works, and in 1517 he nailed 95 theses to the church door at Wittenberg, attacking Tetzel's sale of indulgences. He was excommunicated and outlawed by the Diet of Worms (1521) as a result of his refusal to recant, but he was protected in Wartburg Castle by Frederick III of Saxony (1521–22). He translated the Bible into German (1521–34) and approved Melanchthon's Augsburg Confession (1530), defining the basic tenets of Lutheranism. —**'Lu·ther·ism** *n.*

Lu·ther·an ('lu:θərən) *n.* **1.** a follower of Luther or a member of a Lutheran Church. ~*adj.* **2.** of or relating to Luther or his doctrines. **3.** of or relating to a Lutheran Church. —**'Lu·ther·an·ism** *n.*

lu·thern ('lu:θən) *n.* another name for **dormer.** [C17: probably from LUCARNE, perhaps influenced by LUTHERAN]

Lu·thu·li (lu:'tu:lɪ) *n.* Chief **Al·bert John.** 1899–1967, South African political leader. As president of the African National Congress (1952–60), he campaigned for nonviolent resistance to apartheid: Nobel peace prize 1961.

Lu·tine bell ('lu:ti:n, lu:'ti:n) *n.* a bell, taken from the ship *Lutine,* kept at Lloyd's in London and rung before important announcements, esp. the loss of a vessel.

lut·ing ('lu:tɪŋ) *n.* **1.** another name for **lute**[2] (sense 1). **2.** a strip of pastry placed around the dish to seal the lid of a pie. Also called: **luting paste.**

lut·ist ('lu:tɪst) *n.* **1.** *U.S.* another word for **lutenist. 2.** a person who makes lutes.

Lu·ton ('lu:tᵊn) *n.* a town in SE central England, in S Bedfordshire: airport; motor-vehicle industries. Pop.: 161 188 (1971).

Lu·to·slaw·ski (*Polish* luto'slavski) *n.* **Wi·told** ('vitɔlt). born 1913, Polish composer, whose works frequently juxtapose aleatoric and notated writing.

Lu·tyens ('lʌtʃəns) *n.* **1.** Sir **Ed·win.** 1869–1944, English architect, noted for his neoclassical country houses and his planning of New Delhi, India. **2.** his daughter **E·lis·a·beth.** born 1906, English composer.

Lüt·zen (*German* 'lytsᵊn) *n.* a town near Leipzig in East Germany: site of a battle (1632) in the Thirty Years' War in which the Imperialists under Wallenstein were defeated by the Swedes under Gustavus Adolphus, who died in the battle.

Lüt·zow-Holm Bay ('lʊtsəʊ 'həʊm) *n.* an inlet of the Indian Ocean on the coast of Antarctica, between Enderby Land and Queen Maud Land.

lux (lʌks) *n., pl.* **lux.** the derived SI unit of illumination equal to a luminous flux of 1 lumen per square metre. 1 lux is equivalent to 0.0929 foot-candle. Symbol: lx [C19: from Latin: light]

Lux. *abbrev. for* Luxembourg.

lux·ate ('lʌkseɪt) *vb.* (*tr.*) *Pathol.* to put (a shoulder, knee, etc.) out of joint; dislocate. [C17: from Latin *luxāre* to displace, from *luxus* dislocated; related to Greek *loxos* oblique] —**lux·'a·tion** *n.*

luxe (lʌks, lʊks; *French* lyks) *n.* See **de luxe.** [C16: from French from Latin *luxus* extravagance, LUXURY]

Lux·em·bourg ('lʌksəmˌbɜ:g; *French* lyksã'bu:r) *n.* **1.** a grand duchy in W Europe: formed the Benelux customs union with Belgium and the Netherlands in 1948 and is now a member of the Common Market. Languages: French and German. Religion: mostly Roman Catholic. Currency: (Belgian) franc. Capital: Luxembourg. Pop.: 357 000 (1975 est.). Area: 2586 sq. km (999 sq. miles). **2.** the capital of Luxembourg, on the Alzette River: an industrial centre. Pop.: 78 403 (1974 est.). **3.** a province in SE Belgium, in the Ardennes. Capital: Arlon. Pop.: 219 642 (1975 est.). Area: 4416 sq. km (1705 sq. miles).

Lux·em·burg (*German* 'lʊksᵊmˌbʊrk) *n.* **Ro·sa** ('ro:za). 1871–1919, German socialist theoretician and leader, involved with Karl Liebknecht in an unsuccessful Communist revolt (1919) and assassinated.

Lux·or ('lʌksɔ:) *n.* a town in S Egypt, on the River Nile: the southern part of the site of ancient Thebes; many ruins and tombs, notably the temple built by Amenhotep III (about 1411–1375 B.C.). Pop.: about 77 578 (1966).

lux·ul·ia·nite *or* **lux·ul·lia·nite** (lʌk'su:ljəˌnaɪt) *n.* a rare variety of granite containing tourmaline embedded in quartz and feldspar. [C19: named after *Luxulyan,* a village in Cornwall near which it was first found]

lux·u·ri·ant (lʌg'zjʊərɪənt) *adj.* **1.** rich and abundant; lush. **2.** very elaborate or ornate. **3.** extremely productive or fertile. [C16: from Latin *luxuriāns,* present participle of *luxuriāre* to abound to excess] —**lux·'u·ri·ance** *n.* —**lux·'u·ri·ant·ly** *adv.*

lux·u·ri·ate (lʌg'zjʊərɪˌeɪt) *vb.* (*intr.*) **1.** (foll. by *in*) to take voluptuous pleasure; revel. **2.** to flourish extensively or profusely. **3.** to live in a sumptuous way. [C17: from Latin *luxuriāre*] —**lux·ˌu·ri·'a·tion** *n.*

lux·u·ri·ous (lʌg'zjʊərɪəs) *adj.* **1.** characterized by luxury. **2.** enjoying or devoted to luxury. **3.** an archaic word for **lecherous.** [C14: via Old French from Latin *luxuriōsus* excessive] —**lux·'u·ri·ous·ly** *adv.* —**lux·'u·ri·ous·ness** *n.*

lux·u·ry ('lʌkʃərɪ) *n., pl.* **·ries. 1.** indulgence in and enjoyment of rich, comfortable, and sumptuous living. **2.** (*sometimes pl.*) something that is considered an indulgence rather than a necessity. **3.** (*modifier*) relating to, indicating, or supplying luxury: *a luxury liner.* [C14 (in the sense: lechery): via Old French from Latin *luxuria* excess, from *luxus* extravagance]

Lu·zern (lu'tsɛrn) *n.* the German name for **Lucerne.**

Lu·zon (lu:'zɒn) *n.* the main and largest island of the Philippines, in the N part of the archipelago, separated from the other islands by the Sibuyan Sea: important agriculturally, producing most of the country's rice, with large forests and rich mineral resources; industrial centres at Manila and Batangas. Capital: Quezon City. Pop.: 18 001 270 (1970). Area: 108 378 sq. km (41 845 sq. miles).

LV (in Britain) *abbrev. for* luncheon voucher.

lv. *abbrev. for* leave (of absence, as from military duty).

Lvov (*Russian* ljvɔf) *n.* an industrial city in the SW Soviet Union, in the W Ukrainian SSR: belonging to Poland from 1340 until 1772 and to Austria until 1918; annexed to the Soviet Union in 1945; Ukrainian cultural centre, with a university (1661). Pop.: 617 000 (1975 est.). Ukrainian name: **Lviv** (lvif). Polish name: **Lwów.** German name: **Lemberg.**

Lw *the former chemical symbol for* lawrencium (now superseded by **Lr**).

L.W. *abbrev. for:* **1.** *Radio.* long wave. **2.** low water.

l.w.l. *or* **L.W.L.** *abbrev. for* length waterline; the length of a vessel at the waterline, taken at the centre axis.

L.W.M. *or* **l.w.m.** *abbrev. for* low water mark.

Lwów (lvuf) *n.* the Polish name for **Lvov.**

lx *Physics. abbrev. for* lux.

LXX *symbol for* Septuagint.

-ly[1] *suffix forming adjectives.* **1.** having the nature or qualities of: *brotherly; godly.* **2.** occurring at certain intervals; every: *daily; yearly.* [Old English *-lic*]

-ly[2] *suffix forming adverbs.* in a certain manner; to a certain degree: *quickly; recently; chiefly.* [Old English *-lice,* from *-lic* -LY[1]]

Ly·all·pur (ˌlaɪəl'pʊə) *n.* a city in NE Pakistan: commercial and manufacturing centre of a cotton and wheat growing region; university (1961). Pop.: 822 263 (1972).

Lyau·tey (*French* ljo'tɛ) *n.* **Louis Hu·bert Gon·zalve** (lwi ybɛ:r gɔ̃'zalv). 1854–1934, French marshal and colonial administrator; resident general in Morocco (1912–25).

ly·can·thrope ('laɪkənˌθrəʊp, laɪ'kænθrəʊp) *n.* **1.** a werewolf. **2.** *Psychiatry.* a person who believes that he is a wolf. [C17: via New Latin, from Greek *lukanthrōpos,* from *lukos* wolf + *anthrōpos* man]

ly·can·thro·py (laɪ'kænθrəpɪ) *n.* **1.** the supposed magical transformation of a human being into a wolf. **2.** *Psychiatry.* a delusion in which a person believes that he is a wolf. [C16: from Greek *lukānthropía,* from *lukos* wolf + *anthrōpos* man] —**ly·can·throp·ic** (ˌlaɪkən'θrɒpɪk) *adj.*

Ly·ca·on (laɪ'keɪɒn) *n. Greek myth.* a king of Arcadia said to have offered Zeus a plate of human flesh to learn whether the god was omniscient.

Lyc·a·o·ni·a (ˌlɪkə'əʊnɪə) *n.* an ancient region of S Asia Minor, north of the Taurus Mountains; corresponds to present-day S central Turkey.

ly·cée ('li:seɪ) *n., pl.* **·cées** (-seɪz). *Chiefly French.* a secondary school. [C19: French, from Latin: LYCEUM]

ly·ce·um (laɪ'sɪəm) *n.* (now chiefly in the names of buildings) **1.** a public building for concerts, lectures, etc. **2.** *U.S.* a cultural organization responsible for presenting concerts, lectures, etc. **3.** another word for **lycée.**

Ly·ce·um (laɪ'sɪəm) *n.* **the. 1.** a school and sports ground of ancient Athens: site of Aristotle's discussions with his pupils. **2.** the Aristotelian school of philosophy. [from Greek *Lukeion,* named after a temple nearby dedicated to *Apollo Lukeios,* an epithet of unknown origin]

ly·chee (ˌlaɪ'tʃi:) *n.* a variant spelling of **litchi.**

lych gate (lɪtʃ) *n.* a variant spelling of **lich gate.**

lych·nis ('lɪknɪs) *n.* any caryophyllaceous plant of the genus *Lychnis,* having red, pink, or white five-petalled flowers. See also **ragged robin.** [C17: New Latin, via Latin, from Greek *lukhnis* a red flower; related to *lukhnos* lamp]

Ly·ci·a ('lɪsɪə) *n.* an ancient region on the coast of SW Asia Minor: a Persian, Rhodian, and Roman province.

Ly·ci·an ('lɪsɪən) *adj.* **1.** of or relating to ancient Lycia, its inhabitants, or their language. ~*n.* **2.** an inhabitant of Lycia. **3.** the extinct language of the Lycians, belonging to the Anatolian group or family.

ly+co+pod ('laɪkəˌpɒd) *n.* another name for **club moss,** esp. one of the genus *Lycopodium.*

ly+co+po+di·um (ˌlaɪkə'pəʊdɪəm) *n.* any club moss of the genus *Lycopodium,* resembling moss but having woody tissue and spore-bearing cones: family *Lycopodiaceae.* See also **ground pine** (sense 2). [C18: New Latin, from Greek, from *lukos* wolf + *pous* foot]

Ly·cur·gus (laɪ'kɜːgəs) *n.* 9th century B.C., Spartan lawgiver. He is traditionally regarded as the founder of the Spartan constitution, military institutions, and educational system.

Lyd+da ('lɪdə) *n.* another name for **Lod.**

lydd+ite ('lɪdaɪt) *n.* an explosive consisting chiefly of fused picric acid. [C19: named after *Lydd,* a town in Kent near which the first tests were made]

Lyd·gate ('lɪdˌgeɪt) *n.* **John.** ?1370–?1450, English poet and monk. His vast output includes devotional works and translations, such as that of a French version of Boccaccio's *The Fall of Princes* (1430–38).

Lyd·i·a ('lɪdɪə) *n.* an ancient region on the coast of W Asia Minor: a powerful kingdom in the century and a half before the Persian conquest (546 B.C.). Chief town: Sardis.

Lyd+i·an ('lɪdɪən) *adj.* **1.** of or relating to ancient Lydia, its inhabitants, or their language. **2.** *Music.* of or relating to an authentic mode represented by the ascending natural diatonic scale from F to F. See also **Hypo-.** Compare **Hypolydian.** ~*n.* **3.** an inhabitant of Lydia. **4.** the extinct language of the Lydians, thought to belong to the Anatolian group or family.

lye (laɪ) *n.* **1.** any solution obtained by leaching, such as the caustic solution obtained by leaching wood ash. **2.** a concentrated solution of sodium hydroxide or potassium hydroxide. [Old English *lēag;* related to Middle Dutch *lōghe,* Old Norse *laug* bath, Latin *lavāre* to wash]

Ly·ell ('laɪəl) *n.* Sir **Charles.** 1797–1875, Scottish geologist. In *Principles of Geology* (1830–33) he advanced the theory of uniformitarianism, refuting the doctrine of catastrophism.

ly+ing[1] ('laɪɪŋ) *vb.* the present participle and gerund of **lie**[1].

ly+ing[2] ('laɪɪŋ) *vb.* the present participle and gerund of **lie**[2].

ly·ing-in *n., pl.* **ly·ings-in. a.** confinement in childbirth. **b.** (*as modifier*): *a lying-in hospital.*

lyke-wake ('laɪkˌweɪk) *n. Brit.* a watch held over a dead person, often with festivities. [C16: perhaps from Old Norse; see LICH GATE, WAKE[1]]

Lyl·y ('lɪlɪ) *n.* **John.** ?1554–1606, English dramatist and novelist, noted for his two romances, *Euphues, or the Anatomy of Wit* (1578) and *Euphues and his England* (1580), written in an elaborate style. See also **euphuism.**

lyme grass (laɪm) *n.* a N temperate perennial dune grass, *Elymus arenarius,* with a creeping stem and rough bluish leaves. [C18: probably a respelling (influenced by its genus name, *Elymus*) of LIME[1], referring to its stabilizing effect (like lime in mortar)]

Lym+ing+ton ('lɪmɪŋtən) *n.* a market town in S England, in SW Hampshire on the Solent: yachting centre and holiday resort. Pop.: 35 644 (1971).

lymph (lɪmf) *n.* the almost colourless fluid, containing chiefly white blood cells, that is collected from the tissues of the body and transported in the lymphatic system. [C17: from Latin *lympha* water, from earlier *limpa* influenced in form by Greek *numphē* nymph]

lym+phad+e+ni+tis (lɪmˌfædɪ'naɪtɪs, ˌlɪmfæd-) *n.* inflammation of a lymph node. [C19: New Latin. See LYMPH, ADENITIS]

lym+phan+gi·al (lɪm'fændʒɪəl) *adj.* of or relating to a lymphatic vessel.

lym+phan+gi+tis (ˌlɪmfæn'dʒaɪtɪs) *n., pl.* **+git·i+des** (-'dʒɪtɪˌdiːz). inflammation of one or more of the lymphatic vessels. [C19: see LYMPH, ANGIO-, -ITIS] —**lym+phan+git+ic** (ˌlɪmfæn'dʒɪtɪk) *adj.*

lym+phat+ic (lɪm'fætɪk) *adj.* **1.** of, relating to, or containing lymph: *the lymphatic vessels.* **2.** of or relating to the lymphatic system. **3.** sluggish or lacking vigour. ~*n.* **4.** a lymphatic vessel. [C17 (meaning: mad): from Latin *lymphāticus.* Original meaning perhaps arose from a confusion between *nymph* and LYMPH; compare Greek *numphaleptos* frenzied] —**lym+'phat·i+cal+ly** *adv.*

lym+phat+ic sys+tem *n.* an extensive network of capillary vessels that transports the interstitial fluid of the body as lymph to the venous blood circulation.

lymph cell *n.* another name for **lymphocyte.**

lymph gland *n.* a former name for **lymph node.**

lymph node *n.* any of numerous bean-shaped masses of tissue, situated along the course of lymphatic vessels, that help to protect against infection by killing bacteria and neutralizing toxins and are the source of lymphocytes.

lym·pho- *or before a vowel* **lymph-** *combining form.* indicating lymph or the lymphatic system: *lymphogranuloma.*

lym+pho+ad+e+no+ma (ˌlɪmfəʊˌædɪ'nəʊmə) *or* **lym+pho+gran+u+lo+ma+to+sis** (ˌlɪmfəʊˌgrænjʊˌləʊmə'təʊsɪs) *n.* other names for **Hodgkin's disease.**

lym+pho+blast ('lɪmfəʊˌblɑːst) *n.* an immature lymphocyte. —**lym+pho+blas+tic** (ˌlɪmfəʊ'blæstɪk) *adj.*

lym+pho+cyte ('lɪmfəʊˌsaɪt) *n.* a type of white blood cell formed in lymphoid tissue. —**lym+pho+cyt+ic** (ˌlɪmfəʊ'sɪtɪk) *adj.*

lym+pho+cy+to+sis (ˌlɪmfəʊsaɪ'təʊsɪs) *n.* an abnormally large number of lymphocytes in the blood: often found in diseases such as glandular fever and smallpox. —**lym+pho+cy+tot+ic** (ˌlɪmfəʊsaɪ'tɒtɪk) *adj.*

lym+phoid ('lɪmfɔɪd) *adj.* of or resembling lymph or lymphatic tissue, or relating to the lymphatic system.

lym+pho+ma (lɪm'fəʊmə) *n., pl.* **+ma+ta** (-mətə) *or* **+mas.** a tumour originating in a lymph node or lymphoid tissue. —**lym+'pho+ma+ˌtoid** *adj.*

lym+pho+poi+e·sis (ˌlɪmfəʊpɔɪ'iːsɪs) *n., pl.* **·ses** (-siːz). the formation of lymphatic tissue or lymphocytes. —**lym+pho+poi+et+ic** (ˌlɪmfəʊpɔɪ'ɛtɪk) *adj.*

lyn+ce·an (lɪn'siːən) *adj.* **1.** of or resembling a lynx. **2.** *Rare.* having keen sight. [C17: probably via Latin, from Greek *Lunkeios* concerning *Lunkeos,* an Argonaut renowned for his sharpsightedness, from *lunx* lynx]

lynch (lɪntʃ) *vb.* (*tr.*) (of a mob) to kill (a person) for some supposed offence. [probably after Charles *Lynch* (1736–96), Virginia justice of the peace, who presided over extralegal trials of Tories during the American War of Independence] —**'lynch+er** *n.* —**'lynch+ing** *n.*

Lynch (lɪntʃ) *n.* **John,** known as *Jack.* born 1917, Irish statesman; prime minister of the Republic of Ireland (1966–73; 1977–79).

lynch+et ('lɪntʃɪt) *n.* a terrace or ridge formed in prehistoric or medieval times by ploughing a hillside. [Old English *hlinc* ridge]

lynch law *n.* the practice of condemning and punishing a person by mob action without a proper trial.

Lynn (lɪn) *n.* another name for **King's Lynn.** Also called: **Lynn Re+gis** ('riːdʒɪs).

lynx (lɪŋks) *n., pl.* **lynx·es** *or* **lynx. 1.** a feline mammal, *Felis lynx* (or *canadensis*), of Europe and North America, with grey-brown mottled fur, tufted ears, and a short tail. **2.** the fur of this animal. **3. bay lynx.** another name for **bobcat. 4. desert lynx.** another name for **caracal. 5.** Also called: **Polish lynx.** a large fancy pigeon from Poland, with spangled or laced markings. [C14: via Latin from Greek *lunx;* related to Old English *lox,* German *Luchs*] —**'lynx+ˌlike** *adj.*

Lynx (lɪŋks) *n., Latin genitive* **Lyn+cis** ('lɪnsɪs). a faint constellation in the N hemisphere lying between Ursa Major and Cancer.

lynx-eyed *adj.* having keen sight.

ly·o- *combining form.* indicating dispersion or dissolution: *lyophilic; lyophilize; lyophobic.* [from Greek *luein* to loose]

Lyon (*French* ljɔ̃) *n.* a city in SE central France, capital of Rhône department, at the confluence of the Rivers Rhône and Saône: the third largest city in France; a major industrial centre and river port. Pop.: 462 841 (1975). English name: **Ly+ons** ('laɪənz). Ancient name: **Lugdunum.**

Ly·on King of Arms ('laɪən) *n.* the chief herald of Scotland. Also called: **Lord Lyon.** [C14: archaic spelling of LION, referring to the figure on the royal shield]

Lyon+nais (*French* ljɔ'nɛ) *n.* a former province of E central France, on the Rivers Rhône and Saône: occupied by the present-day departments of Rhône and Loire. Chief town: Lyon.

ly+on+naise (ˌlaɪə'neɪz; *French* ljɔ'nɛːz) *adj.* (of food) cooked or garnished with onions, usually fried.

Ly+on+nesse (ˌlaɪə'nɛs) *n.* (in Arthurian legend) the mythical birthplace of Sir Tristram, situated in SW England and believed to have been submerged by the sea.

Ly·ons ('laɪənz) *n.* **Jo·seph Al·oy·sius.** 1879–1939, Australian statesman; prime minister of Australia (1931–39).

ly·o+phil+ic (ˌlaɪəʊ'fɪlɪk) *adj. Chem.* (of a colloid) having a dispersed phase with a high affinity for the continuous phase: *a lyophilic sol.* Compare **lyophobic.**

ly+oph·i+lize *or* **ly+oph·i+lise** (laɪ'ɒfɪˌlaɪz) *vb.* (*tr.*) to dry (blood, serum, tissue, etc.) by freezing in a high vacuum.

ly·o+pho+bic (ˌlaɪəʊ'fəʊbɪk) *adj. Chem.* (of a colloid) having a dispersed phase with little or no affinity for the continuous phase: *a lyophobic sol.* Compare **lyophilic.**

Ly·ra ('laɪərə) *n., Latin genitive* **Ly·rae** ('laɪəriː). a small constellation in the N hemisphere lying near Cygnus and Draco and containing the star Vega, an eclipsing binary (**Beta Lyrae**), a planetary nebula (the **Ring nebula**), and a variable star, **RR Lyrae.**

ly+rate ('laɪərɪt) *or* **ly+rat+ed** *adj.* **1.** shaped like a lyre. **2.** (of leaves) having a large terminal lobe and smaller lateral lobes. [C18: from New Latin *lyrātus,* Latin from *lyra* LYRE] —**'ly+rate+ly** *adv.*

ly·ra vi·ol *n.* a lutelike musical instrument popular in the 16th and 17th centuries: the forerunner of the mandolin.

lyre (laɪə) *n.* **1.** an ancient Greek stringed instrument consisting of a resonating tortoise shell to which a crossbar was attached by two projecting arms. It was plucked with a plectrum and used for accompanying songs. **2.** any ancient instrument of similar design. **3.** a medieval bowed instrument of the violin family. [C13: via Old French from Latin *lyra,* from Greek *lura*]

lyre+bird ('laɪəˌbɜːd) *n.* either of two pheasant-like Australian birds, *Menura superba* and *M. alberti,* constituting the family *Menuridae:* during courtship displays, the male spreads its tail into the shape of a lyre.

lyr+ic ('lɪrɪk) *adj.* **1.** (of poetry) **a.** expressing the writer's personal feelings and thoughts. **b.** having the form and manner of a song. **2.** of or relating to such poetry. **3.** (of a singing voice) having a light quality and tone. **4.** intended for singing, esp. (in classical Greece) to the accompaniment of the lyre. ~*n.* **5.** a short poem of songlike quality. **6.** (*pl.*) the words of a popular song. ~Also (for senses 1–3): **lyrical.** [C16: from

Latin *lyricus*, from Greek *lurikos*, from *lura* LYRE] —'lyr·i·cal·ly *adv.* —'lyr·i·cal·ness *n.*

lyr·i·cal ('lɪrɪkᵊl) *adj.* **1.** another word for lyric (senses 1–3). **2.** enthusiastic; effusive (esp. in the phrase **to wax lyrical**).

lyr·i·cism ('lɪrɪˌsɪzəm) *n.* **1.** the quality or style of lyric poetry. **2.** emotional or enthusiastic outpouring.

lyr·i·cist ('lɪrɪsɪst) *n.* **1.** a person who writes the words for a song, opera, or musical play. **2.** Also called: **lyrist.** a lyric poet.

lyr·ism ('lɪrɪzəm) *n.* **1.** the art or technique of playing the lyre. **2.** a less common word for **lyricism.**

lyr·ist *n.* **1.** ('laɪərɪst). a person who plays the lyre. **2.** ('lɪrɪst). another word for **lyricist** (sense 2).

lys- *combining form.* variant of **lyso-** before a vowel.

Ly·san·der (laɪ'sændə) *n.* died 395 B.C., Spartan naval commander of the Peloponnesian War.

lyse (laɪs, laɪz) *vb.* to undergo or cause to undergo lysis.

Ly·sen·ko (lɪ'sɛŋkəʊ; *Russian* lɪ'sjenkə) *n.* **Tro·fim De·ni·so·vich** (tra'fim dɪ'nisəvitʃ). 1898–1976, Russian biologist and geneticist.

Ly·sen·ko·ism (lɪ'sɛŋkəʊˌɪzəm) *n.* a form of Neo-Lamarckism advocated by Lysenko, emphasizing the importance of the inheritance of acquired characteristics.

ly·ser·gic ac·id (lɪ'sɜːdʒɪk, laɪ-) *n.* a crystalline compound with a polycyclic molecular structure: used in medical research. Formula $C_{16}H_{16}N_2O_2$. [C20: from (HYDRO)LYS(IS) + ERG(OT) + -IC]

ly·ser·gic ac·id di·eth·yl·a·mide (daɪˌɛθɪl'eɪmaɪd, -ˌiːθaɪl-) *n.* See **LSD.**

Lys·i·as ('lɪsɪˌæs) *n.* ?450–?380 B.C., Athenian orator.

Ly·sim·a·chus (laɪ'sɪməkəs) *n.* ?360–281 B.C., Macedonian general under Alexander the Great; king of Thrace (323–281); killed in battle by Seleucus I.

ly·sim·e·ter (laɪ'sɪmɪtə) *n.* an instrument for determining solubility, esp. the amount of water-soluble matter in soil. [C20: from *lysi-* (variant of LYSO-) + -METER]

ly·sin ('laɪsɪn) *n.* any of a group of antibodies or other agents that cause dissolution of cells against which they are directed.

ly·sine ('laɪsiːn, -sɪn) *n.* an essential amino acid that occurs esp. in casein and gelatin. Formula: $(NH_2)(CH_2)_4CHNH_2COOH$.

Ly·sip·pus (laɪ'sɪpəs) *n.* 4th century B.C., Greek sculptor. He introduced a new naturalism into Greek sculpture.

ly·sis ('laɪsɪs) *n., pl.* **-ses** (-siːz). **1.** the destruction or dissolution of cells by the action of a particular lysin. **2.** *Med.* the gradual reduction in severity of the symptoms of a disease. [C19: New Latin, from Greek, from *luein* to release]

-ly·sis *n. combining form.* indicating a loosening, decomposition, or breaking down: *electrolysis; paralysis.* [from Greek, from *lusis* a loosening; see LYSIS]

ly·so- *or before a vowel* **lys-** *combining form.* indicating a dissolving or loosening: *lysozyme.* [from Greek *lusis* a loosening]

Ly·sol ('laɪsɒl) *n. Trademark.* a solution containing a mixture of cresols in water, used as an antiseptic and disinfectant.

ly·so·some ('laɪsəˌsəʊm) *n.* any of numerous small particles, containing digestive enzymes, that are present in the cytoplasm of most cells. —ˌ**ly·so·'so·mal** *adj.*

ly·so·zyme ('laɪsəˌzaɪm) *n.* an enzyme occurring in tears, certain body tissues, and egg white: destroys bacteria by hydrolysing polysaccharides in their cell walls. [C20: from LYSO- + (EN)ZYME]

lys·sa ('lɪsə) *n. Pathol.* a less common word for **rabies.**

-lyte *n. combining form.* indicating a substance that can be decomposed or broken down: *electrolyte.* [from Greek *lutos* soluble, from *luein* to loose]

Lyth·am Saint Anne's ('lɪðəm sənt 'ænz) *n., usually abbreviated to* **Lyth·am St. Anne's.** a resort in NW England, in Lancashire on the Irish Sea. Pop.: 40 089 (1971).

lyth·ra·ceous (lɪ'θreɪʃəs, laɪ'θreɪ-) *adj.* of, relating to, or belonging to the *Lythraceae*, a mostly tropical American family of herbaceous plants, shrubs, and trees that includes purple loosestrife and crape myrtle. [C19: from New Latin *Lythrum* type genus, from Greek *luthron* blood, from the red flowers]

lyt·ic ('lɪtɪk) *adj.* **1.** relating to, causing, or resulting from lysis. **2.** of or relating to a lysin. [C19: Greek *lutikos* capable of loosing]

-lyt·ic *adj. combining form.* indicating a loosening or dissolving: *paralytic.* [from Greek, from *lusis*; see -LYSIS]

lyt·ta ('lɪtə) *n., pl.* **-tas** *or* **-tae** (-tiː). a rodlike mass of cartilage beneath the tongue in the dog and other carnivores. [C17: New Latin, from Greek *lussa* madness; in dogs, it was believed to be a cause of rabies]

Lyt·ton ('lɪtᵊn) *n.* **1st Baron,** title of *Edward George Earle Lytton Bulwer-Lytton.* 1803–73, English novelist, dramatist, and statesman, noted particularly for his historical romances.

Lyu·blin ('ljublɪn) *n.* transliteration of the Russian name for **Lublin.**

M

m *or* **M** (ɛm) *n., pl.* **m's, M's,** *or* **Ms. 1.** the 13th letter and tenth consonant of the modern English alphabet. **2.** a speech sound represented by this letter, usually a bilabial nasal, as in *mat.*
m *symbol for:* **1.** metre(s). **2.** mile(s). **3.** milli-. **4.** minute(s). **5.** mutual inductance.
M *symbol for:* **1.** *Printing.* em. **2.** mach. **3.** mega-. **4.** *Currency.* mark(s). **5.** million. **6.** *Astronomy.* Messier catalogue; a catalogue published in 1784, in which 103 nebulae and clusters are listed using a numerical system: *M13 is the globular cluster in Hercules.* **7.** Middle. **8.** *Physics.* modulus. **9.** (in Britain) motorway: *the M1 runs from London to Leeds.* **10.** *Logic.* the middle term of a syllogism. **11.** *Physics.* mutual inductance. **12.** *Chem.* molar. ~**13.** *the Roman numeral for* 1000. See **Roman numerals.** ~**14.** *international car registration for* Malta.
m. *abbrev. for:* **1.** *Cricket.* maiden (over). **2.** male. **3.** mare. **4.** married. **5.** masculine. **6.** medicine. **7.** medium (size). **8.** meridian. **9.** month.
M. *abbrev. for:* **1.** Majesty. **2.** Manitoba. **3.** marquis. **4.** Master. **5.** Medieval. **6.** (in titles) Member. **7.** Middle. **8.** million. **9.** Monday. **10.** (*pl.* **MM.** *or* **MM**) Also: **M** *French.* Monsieur. [French equivalent of *Mr.*] **11.** mountain.
M'- *prefix.* variant of **Mac-.**
'm *contraction of:* **1.** (*vb.*) am. **2.** (*n.*) madam: *yes'm.*
M-1 ri+fle *n.* a semiautomatic .30 calibre rifle formerly used by the U.S. Army. Also called: **Garand rifle.**
ma (mɑː) *n.* an informal word for **mother.**
MA *international car registration for* Morocco. [from French *Maroc*]
M.A. *abbrev. for:* **1.** Master of Arts. **2.** *Psychol.* mental age. **3.** Military Academy.
ma'am (mæm, mɑːm; *unstressed* məm) *n.* short for **madam:** used as a title of respect, esp. for female royalty.
maar (mɑː) *n., pl.* **maars** *or* **maar·e** ('mɑːrə). (*sometimes cap.*) a coneless volcanic crater that has been formed by a single explosion. [C19: from German]
Maa+ri+an+ha+mi+na ('mɑːriɑnˌhɑminɑ) *n.* the Finnish name for **Mariehamn.**
Maas (mɑːs) *n.* the Dutch name for the **Meuse.**
Maas+tricht *or* **Maes+tricht** ('mɑːstrɪxt; *Dutch* mɑː'strɪxt) *n.* a city in the SE Netherlands near the Belgian and German borders: capital of Limburg province, on the River Maas (Meuse); formerly a strategic fortress. Pop.: 111 615 (1974 est.).
Mab (mæb) *n.* (in English and Irish folklore) a fairy queen said to create and control men's dreams.
ma+bel·a (mɑː'bɛlə) *n. S. African.* ground kaffir corn used for making porridge. [from Zulu *amabele* kaffir corn]
Ma·buse (mə'bjuːz; *French* ma'byːz) *n.* **Jan** (jɑn). original name *Jan Gossaert.* ?1478–?1533, Flemish painter.
mac *or* **mack** (mæk) *n. Informal.* short for **mackintosh.**
Mac (mæk) *n. Chiefly U.S.* an informal term of address to a man. [C20: abstracted from MAC-, prefix of Scottish surnames]
Mac. *abbrev. for* Maccabees (books of the Apocrypha).
Mac-, Mc-, *or* **M'-** *prefix.* (in surnames of Gaelic origin) son of: *MacDonald; MacNeice.* For names beginning with this prefix, see also under **Mc-** [from Gaelic *mac* son of; compare Welsh *mab,* Cornish *mab*]
ma+ca+bre (mə'kɑːbə, -brə) *adj.* **1.** gruesome; ghastly; grim. **2.** resembling or associated with the danse macabre. [C15: from Old French *danse macabre* dance of death, probably from *macabé* relating to the Maccabees, who were associated with death because of the doctrines and prayers for the dead in II Macc. (12:43–46)] —**ma'ca+bre+ly** *adv.*
ma+ca+co (mə'kɑːkəʊ, -'keɪ-) *n., pl.* **+cos.** any of various lemurs, esp. *Lemur macaco,* the males of which are usually black and the females brown. [C18: from French *mococo,* of unknown origin]
mac+ad+am (mə'kædəm) *n.* a road surface made of compressed layers of small broken stones, esp. one that is bound together with tar or asphalt. [C19: named after John *McAdam* (1756–1836), Scottish engineer, the inventor]
mac·a+da+mi·a (ˌmækə'deɪmɪə) *n.* **1.** any tree of the Australian proteaceous genus *Macadamia,* esp. *M. ternifolia,* having clusters of small white flowers and edible nutlike seeds. **2. macadamia nut.** the seed of this tree. [C19: New Latin, named after John *Macadam* (died 1865), Australian chemist]
mac+ad+am+ize *or* **mac+ad+am+ise** (mə'kædəˌmaɪz) *vb.* (*tr.*) to construct or surface (a road) with macadam. —**mac+ˌad+am·i+'za+tion** *or* **mac+ˌad+am·i+'sa+tion** *n.* —**mac+'ad+am+ˌiz+er** *or* **mac+'ad+am+ˌis+er** *n.*
Ma+cao (mə'kaʊ) *n.* a Portuguese overseas province and city on the coast of S China, across the estuary of the Chu Chiang from Hong Kong: chief centre of European trade with China in the 18th century; attained partial autonomy in 1976; transit trade with China; tourism. Pop.: 248 636 (1970). Area: 16 sq. km (6 sq. miles). Portuguese name: **Macáu.**
Ma+ca+pá (*Portuguese* maka'pa) *n.* a town in NE Brazil, capital of the federal territory of Amapá, on the Canal do Norte of the Amazon delta. Pop.: 87 755 (1970).
ma+caque (mə'kɑːk) *n.* any of various Old World monkeys of the genus *Macaca,* inhabiting wooded or rocky regions of Asia and Africa. Typically the tail is short or absent and cheek pouches are present. [C17: from French, from Portuguese *macaco,* from Fiot (a W African language) *makaku, from kaku* monkey]
mac+a+ro+ni *or* **mac+ca+ro+ni** (ˌmækə'rəʊnɪ) *n., pl.* **+nis** *or* **+nies. 1.** pasta tubes made from wheat flour. **2.** (in 18th-century Britain) a dandy who affected foreign manners and style. [C16: from Italian (Neapolitan dialect) *maccarone,* probably from Greek *makaria* food made from barley]
mac+a+ron+ic (ˌmækə'rɒnɪk) *adj.* **1.** (of verse) characterized by a mixture of vernacular words jumbled together with Latin words or Latinized words. ~*n.* **2.** (*often pl.*) macaronic verse. [C17: from New Latin *macarōnicus,* literally: resembling macaroni (in lack of sophistication); see MACARONI] —**ˌmac·a+'ron·i+cal+ly** *adv.*
mac+a+ro+ni cheese *n.* a dish of macaroni with a cheese sauce.
mac·a+roon (ˌmækə'ruːn) *n.* a kind of sweet biscuit made of ground almonds, sugar, and egg whites. [C17: via French *macaron* from Italian *maccarone* MACARONI]
Mac·Ar·thur (mə'kɑːθə) *n.* **Doug·las.** 1880–1964, U.S. general. During World War II he became commanding general of U.S. armed forces in the Pacific (1944) and accepted the surrender of Japan, the Allied occupation of which he commanded (1945–51). He was commander in chief of United Nations forces in Korea (1950–51).
Ma+cas+sar (mə'kæsə) *n.* a variant spelling of **Makasar.**
Ma+cas+sar oil *n.* an oily preparation put on the hair to make it smooth and shiny.
Ma+cáu (mə'kaʊ) *n.* the Portuguese name for **Macao.**
Ma·cau·lay (mə'kɔːlɪ) *n.* **Thom·as Bab·ing·ton,** 1st Baron Macaulay. 1800–59, English historian, essayist, and statesman. His *History of England from the Accession of James the Second* (1848–61) is regarded as a classic of the Whig interpretation of history.
ma+caw (mə'kɔː) *n.* any large tropical American parrot of the genera *Ara* and *Anodorhynchus,* having a long tail and brilliant plumage. [C17: from Portuguese *macau,* of unknown origin]
Mac+beth (mək'bɛθ, mæk-) *n.* died 1057, king of Scotland (1040–57): succeeded Duncan, whom he killed in battle; defeated and killed by Duncan's son Malcolm III.
Macc. *abbrev. for* Maccabees (books of the Apocrypha).
Mac+ca+be·an (ˌmækə'biːən) *adj.* of or relating to the Maccabees or to Judas Maccabaeus.
Mac+ca+bees ('mækəˌbiːz) *n.* **1.** a Jewish family of patriots who freed Judaea from Seleucid oppression (168–142 B.C.). **2.** any of four books of Jewish history, including the last two of the Apocrypha.
mac+ca+boy, mac+co+boy ('mækəˌbɔɪ), *or* **mac+ca+baw** ('mækəˌbɔː) *n.* a dark rose-scented snuff. [C18: from French *macouba,* from the name of the district of Martinique where it is made]
mac+ca+ro+ni (ˌmækə'rəʊnɪ) *n., pl.* **+nis** *or* **+nies.** a variant spelling of **macaroni.**
Mac+cles+field ('mækəlzˌfiːld) *n.* a market town in NW England, in Cheshire: silk industry. Pop.: 44 240 (1971).
Mac·don·ald (mək'dɒnəld) *n.* **1. Flo·ra.** 1722–90, Scottish heroine, who helped the Young Pretender to escape to Skye after his defeat at the battle of Culloden (1746). **2.** Sir **John Al·ex·an·der.** 1815–91, Canadian statesman, born in Scotland, who was the first prime minister of the Dominion of Canada (1867–73; 1878–91).
Mac·Don·ald (mək'dɒnəld) *n.* **(James) Ram·say.** 1866–1937, British statesman, who led the first Labour Government (1924; 1929–31); he also led a coalition (1931–35), which the majority of the Labour Party refused to support.
Mac+don+nell Ranges (mək'dɒnəl) *pl. n.* a mountain system of central Australia, in S central Northern Territory, extending about 160 km (100 miles) east and west of Alice Springs. Highest peak: Mount Ziel, 1510 m (4955 ft.).
mace[1] (meɪs) *n.* **1.** a club, usually having a spiked metal head, used esp. in the Middle Ages. **2.** a ceremonial staff of office carried by certain officials. **3.** See **macebearer. 4.** an early form of billiard cue. [C13: from Old French, probably from Vulgar Latin *mattea* (unattested); apparently related to Latin *mateola* mallet]
mace[2] (meɪs) *n.* a spice made from the dried aril round the nutmeg seed. [C14: formed as a singular from Old French *macis* (wrongly assumed to be plural), from Latin *macir* an oriental spice]
Mace (meɪs) *U.S.* ~*n.* **1.** *Trademark.* a liquid causing tears and nausea, used as a spray for riot control, etc. ~*vb.* **2.** (*tr.*) (*sometimes not cap.*) to use Mace on.
mace+bear·er ('meɪsˌbɛərə) *n.* a person who carries a mace in processions or ceremonies.

Maced. *abbrev. for* Macedonia(n).
ma+ce·doine (ˌmæsɪˈdwaːn) *n.* **1.** a hot or cold mixture of diced vegetables. **2.** a mixture of fruit served in a syrup or in jelly. **3.** any mixture; medley. [C19: from French, literally: Macedonian, alluding to the mixture of nationalities in Macedonia]
Mac+e·don (ˈmæsɪˌdɒn) *or* **Mac+e·do·ni·a** *n.* a region of the S Balkans, now divided among Greece, Bulgaria, and Yugoslavia. As a kingdom in the ancient world it achieved prominence under Philip II (359–336 B.C.) and his son Alexander the Great.
Mac+e·do+ni·a (ˌmæsɪˈdəʊnɪə) *n.* **1.** a division of N Greece. Pop.: 1 890 684 (1971). Area: 34 203 sq. km (13 339 sq. miles). Modern Greek name: **Makedhonia. 2.** a constituent republic of S Yugoslavia. Capital: Skopje. Pop.: 1 647 308 (1971). Area: 25 713 sq. km (10 028 sq. miles). Serbian name: **Makedonija. 3.** a district of SW Bulgaria, now occupied by Blagoevgrad province. Area: 6465 sq. km (2496 sq. miles).
Mac+e·do+ni·an (ˌmæsɪˈdəʊnɪən) *adj.* **1.** of or relating to Macedonia, its inhabitants, or any of their languages or dialects. *~n.* **2.** a native or inhabitant of Macedonia. **3.** the language of modern Macedonia, belonging to the Slavonic branch of the Indo-European family. **4.** an extinct language spoken in ancient Macedonia.
Ma+cei·ó (maseˈjɔ) *n.* a port in NE Brazil, capital of Alagôas state, on the Atlantic. Pop.: 242 867 (1970).
mac+er (ˈmeɪsə) *n.* a macebearer, esp. (in Scotland) an official who acts as usher in a court of law. [C14: from Old French *massier,* from *masse* MACE]
mac+er+ate (ˈmæsəˌreɪt) *vb.* **1.** to soften or separate or be softened or separated as a result of soaking. **2.** to break up or cause to break up by soaking: *macerated peaches.* **3.** to become or cause to become thin. [C16: from Latin *mācerāre* to soften] **—ˈmac+er+ˌat+er** *or* **ˈmac+er·ˌa+tor** *n.* **—ˈmac+er·a·tive** *adj.* **—ˌmac+er·ˈa+tion** *n.*
Mach[1] (mæk) *n.* short for **Mach number.**
Mach[2] (*German* max) *n.* **Ernst** (ɛrnst). 1838–1916, Austrian physicist and philosopher. He devised the system of speed measurement using the Mach number. He also founded logical positivism, asserting that the validity of a scientific law is proved only after empirical testing.
mach. *abbrev. for:* **1.** machine. **2.** machinery. **3.** machinist.
Ma·cha·do (*Portuguese* maˈʃadu) *n.* **Joa·quim Ma·ri·a** (ʒwaˈkĩ maˈria). 1839–1908, Brazilian author of novels and short stories, whose novels include *Epitaph of a Small Winner* (1881) and *Dom Casmurro* (1899).
ma+chan (məˈtʃɑːn) *n.* (in India) a raised platform used in tiger hunting. [C19: from Hindi]
Ma·chel (məˈʃɛl) *n.* **Sam·o·ra (Moises)** (səˈmɔːrə). born 1933, Mozambique statesman; president of Mozambique since 1975.
ma+chet·e (məˈʃɛtɪ, -ˈtʃeɪ-) *n.* a broad heavy knife used for cutting or as a weapon, esp. in parts of Central and South America. [C16 *macheto,* from Spanish *machete,* from *macho* club, perhaps from Vulgar Latin *mattea* (unattested) club]
Mach·i·a·vel·li (ˌmækɪəˈvɛlɪ) *n.* **Nic·co·lò** (ˌnikkoˈlɔ). 1469–1527, Florentine statesman and political philosopher; secretary to the war council of the Florentine republic (1498–1512). His most famous work is *Il Principe* (*The Prince,* 1532).
Mach·i·a+vel+li·an *or* **Mach·i·a+vel+i·an** (ˌmækɪəˈvɛlɪən) *adj.* (*sometimes not cap.*) **1.** of or relating to the alleged political principles of Machiavelli; cunning, amoral, and opportunist. *~n.* **2.** a cunning, amoral, and opportunist person, esp. a politician. **—ˌMach·i·a+ˈvel+li·an+ism** *or* **ˌMach·i·a+ˈvel+lism** *n.* **—ˌMach·i·a+ˈvel+list** *adj., n.*
ma+chic·o+late (məˈtʃɪkəʊˌleɪt) *vb.* (*tr.*) to construct machicolations at the top of (a wall). [C18: from Old French *machicoller,* ultimately from Provençal *machacol,* from *macar* to crush + *col* neck]
ma+chic·o+la+tion (məˌtʃɪkəʊˈleɪʃən) *n.* **1.** (esp. in medieval castles) a projecting gallery or parapet supported on corbels having openings through which missiles could be dropped. **2.** any such opening.
mach·i+nate (ˈmækɪˌneɪt) *vb.* (*usually tr.*) to contrive, plan, or devise (schemes, plots, etc.). [C17: from Latin *māchinārī* to plan, from *māchina* MACHINE] **—ˈmach·i+ˌna+tor** *n.*
mach·i+na+tion (ˌmækɪˈneɪʃən) *n.* **1.** an intrigue, plot, or scheme. **2.** the act of devising plots or schemes.
ma+chine (məˈʃiːn) *n.* **1.** an assembly of interconnected components arranged to transmit or modify force in order to perform useful work. **2.** Also called: **simple machine.** a device for altering the magnitude or direction of a force, esp. a lever, screw, wedge, or pulley. **3.** a mechanically operated device or means of transport, such as a car, aircraft, etc. **4.** any mechanical or electrical device that automatically performs tasks or assists in performing tasks. **5.** any intricate structure or agency: *the war machine.* **6.** a mechanically efficient, rigid, or obedient person. **7.** an organized body of people that controls activities, policies, etc. **8.** (esp. in the classical theatre) a device such as a pulley to provide spectacular entrances and exits for supernatural characters. **9.** an event, etc., introduced into a literary work for special effect. *~vb.* **10.** (*tr.*) to shape, cut, or remove (excess material) from (a workpiece) using a machine tool. **11.** to use a machine to carry out a process on (something). [C16: via French from Latin *māchina* machine, engine, from Doric Greek *makhana* pulley; related to *makhos* device, contrivance] **—ma+ˈchin+a·ble** *or* **ma+ˈchine+a·ble** *adj.* **—ma+ˌchin+a·ˈbil+i·ty** *n.* **—ma+ˈchine+less** *adj.* **—ma+ˈchine-ˌlike** *adj.*
ma+chine bolt *n.* a fastening bolt with a machine-cut thread.
ma+chine gun *n.* **1. a.** a rapid-firing automatic gun, usually mounted, from which small-arms ammunition is discharged. **b.** (*as modifier*): *machine-gun fire.* *~vb.* **ma·chine-gun, -guns, -gun·ning, -gunned. 2.** (*tr.*) to shoot or fire at with a machine gun. **—ma+chine gun+ner** *n.*
ma+chine lan+guage *or* **code** *n.* instructions for the processing of data in a binary code that can be understood and executed by a computer.
ma+chine read+a·ble *adj.* (of data) in a form in which it can be fed into a computer.
ma+chin+er·y (məˈʃiːnərɪ) *n., pl.* **+er·ies. 1.** machines, machine parts, or machine systems collectively. **2.** a particular machine system or set of machines. **3.** a system similar to a machine: *the machinery of government.* **4.** literary devices used for effect in epic poetry.
ma+chine screw *n.* a fastening screw with a machine-cut thread throughout the length of its shank.
ma+chine shop *n.* a workshop in which machine tools are operated.
ma+chine tool *n.* a power-driven machine, such as a lathe, miller, or grinder, for cutting, shaping, and finishing metals or other materials. **—ma·ˈchine-ˌtooled** *adj.*
ma+chin+ist (məˈʃiːnɪst) *n.* **1.** a person who operates machines to cut or process materials. **2.** a maker or repairer of machines.
ma+chis+mo (mæˈkɪzməʊ, -ˈtʃɪz-) *n.* strong or exaggerated masculine pride or masculinity. [Mexican Spanish, from Spanish *macho* male, from Latin *masculus* MASCULINE]
Mach+me·ter (ˈmækˌmiːtə) *n.* an instrument for measuring the Mach number of an aircraft in flight.
Mach num+ber *n.* (*often not cap.*) the ratio of the speed of a body in a particular medium to the speed of sound in that medium. Mach number 1 corresponds to the speed of sound. Often shortened to **Mach.** [C19: named after Ernst MACH]
ma+chree (məˈkriː) *adj.* (*postpositive*) *Irish.* my dear: *mother machree.* [from Irish *mo croidhe,* literally: my heart]
macht+pol·i·tik (ˈmɑːxt,pɒlɪtiːk) *n.* power politics. [from German]
Ma+chu Pic+chu (ˈmɑːtʃuː ˈpiːktʃuː) *n.* a ruined Incan city in S central Peru.
mach+zor *Hebrew.* (maxˈzɔr; *English* mɑːkˈzɔː) *n., pl.* **+zo+rim** (-zɔˈriːm). a variant spelling of ***mahzor.***
Ma+ci+as N·gue+ma (məˈsiːəs ᵊŋˈgweɪmə) *n.* an island in the Gulf of Guinea, off the coast of Cameroon: part of Equatorial Guinea. Capital: Malabo. Area: 2017 sq. km (786 sq. miles). Former name (until 1973): **Fernando Po.**
mac+in+tosh (ˈmækɪnˌtɒʃ) *n.* a variant spelling of **mackintosh.**
mack[1] (mæk) *n.* **1.** *Brit. informal.* short for **mackintosh. 2.** *U.S.* short for **mackinaw.**
mack[2] (mæk) *n. Slang.* a pimp. [C19: shortened from obsolete *mackerel,* from Old French, of uncertain origin]
Mac+kay (məˈkaɪ) *n.* a port in E Australia, in Queensland: artificial harbour. Pop.: 28 416 (1971).
Mac+ken+zie[1] (məˈkɛnzɪ) *n.* **1.** an administrative district of the Northwest Territories of Canada: includes the W edge of the Canadian Shield, lowlands, and mountains. Pop.: 23 657 (1971). Area: 1 366 199 sq. km (527 490 sq. miles). **2.** a river in NW Canada, in the Northwest Territories, flowing northwest from Great Slave Lake to the Beaufort Sea: the longest river in Canada; navigable in summer. Length: 1770 km (1100 miles).
Mac·ken·zie[2] (məˈkɛnzɪ) *n.* **1.** Sir **Al·ex·an·der.** ?1755–1820, Scottish explorer and fur trader in Canada. He explored the Mackenzie River (1789) and was the first European to cross America north of Mexico (1793). **2. Al·ex·an·der.** 1822–92, Canadian statesman; first Liberal prime minister (1873–78). **3.** Sir **Comp·ton.** 1883–1972, British author. His works include *Sinister Street* (1913–14) and the comic novel *Whisky Galore* (1947). **4.** Sir **Thom·as.** 1854–1930, New Zealand statesman born in Scotland: prime minister of New Zealand (1912). **5. Wil·liam Ly·on.** 1795–1861, Canadian journalist and politician, born in Scotland. He led an unsuccessful rebellion against the oligarchic Family Compact (1837).
macke+rel (ˈmækrəl) *n., pl.* **+rel** *or* **+rels. 1.** a spiny-finned food fish, *Scomber scombrus,* occurring in northern coastal regions of the Atlantic and in the Mediterranean: family *Scombridae.* It has a deeply forked tail and a greenish-blue body marked with wavy dark bands on the back. Compare **Spanish mackerel** (sense 1). **2.** any of various other fishes of the family *Scombridae,* such as *Scomber colias* (**Spanish mackerel**) and *S. japonicus* (**Pacific mackerel**). *~*Compare **horse mackerel.** [C13: from Anglo-French, from Old French *maquerel,* of unknown origin]
macke+rel breeze *n.* a strong breeze.
macke+rel shark *n.* another name for **porbeagle.**
macke+rel sky *n.* a sky patterned with cirrocumulus or small altocumulus clouds.
Mac·ker·ras (məˈkɛrəs) *n.* **Charles.** born 1925, Australian conductor, esp. of opera; resident in England.
Mack·i·nac (ˈmækɪˌnɔː, -ˌnæk) *n.* a wooded island in N Michigan, in the **Straits of Mackinac** (a channel between the lower and upper peninsulas of Michigan): an ancient Indian burial ground; state park. Length: 5 km (3 miles).
Mack·i·naw coat (ˈmækɪˌnɔː) *n. Chiefly U.S.* a thick short double-breasted plaid coat. Also called: **mackinaw.** [C19: named after *Mackinaw,* variant of MACKINAC]
mack+in+tosh *or* **mac+in+tosh** (ˈmækɪnˌtɒʃ) *n.* **1.** a waterproof raincoat made of rubberized cloth. **2.** such cloth. **3.** any raincoat. [C19: named after Charles *Macintosh* (1760–1843), who invented it]
Mack·in·tosh (ˈmækɪnˌtɒʃ) *n.* **Charles Ren·nie.** 1868–1928, Scottish architect and artist, exponent of the Art Nouveau style; designer of the Glasgow School of Art (1896).

mack·le ('mæk°l) *or* **mac·ule** ('mækju:l) *n. Printing.* a double or blurred impression caused by shifting paper or type. [C16: via French from Latin *macula* spot, stain]

Mac·lau·rin's se·ries (mə'klɔ:rınz) *n. Maths.* an infinite sum giving the value of a function f(x) in terms of the derivatives of the function evaluated at zero: f(x) = f(0) + (f′(0)x)/1! + (f″(0)x^2)/2! + ... Also called: **Maclaurin series.**

ma·cle ('mæk°l) *n.* another name for **chiastolite** and **twin** (sense 3). [C19: via French from Latin *macula* spot, stain]

Mac·lean (mə'kleın) *n.* **Don·ald.** 1913–83, British civil servant, who spied for the Russians: fled to the Soviet Union (with Guy Burgess) in 1951.

Mac·leod (mə'klaud) *n.* **John James Rick·ard.** 1876–1935, Scottish physiologist: shared the Nobel prize for medicine (1923) with Banting for their part in discovering insulin.

Mac·ma·hon (*French* makma'ɔ̃) *n.* **Ma·rie Ed·me Pat·rice Mau·rice** (mari ɛdmə patris mɔ'ris), Comte de Macmahon. 1808–93, French military commander. He commanded the troops that suppressed the Paris Commune (1871) and was elected president of the Third Republic (1873–79).

Mac·mil·lan (mək'mılən) *n.* **(Maurice) Har·old.** born 1894, British statesman; Conservative prime minister (1957–63).

Mac·Neice (mək'ni:s) *n.* **Lou·is.** 1907–63, British poet, born in Northern Ireland. His works include the poems in *Autumn Sequel* (1954) and *Solstices* (1961) and a translation of the *Agamemnon* of Aeschylus (1936).

Ma·con ('meıkən) *n.* a city in central Georgia, on the Ocmulgee River. Pop.: 121 714 (1973 est.).

Mâ·con (*French* mɑ'kɔ̃) *n.* **1.** a city in E central France, in the Saône valley: a centre of the wine-producing region of lower Burgundy. Pop.: 40 490 (1975). **2.** a red or white wine from the Mâcon area, heavier than the other burgundies.

Mac·pher·son (mək'fɜ:s°n) *n.* **James.** 1736–96, Scottish poet and translator. He published verse, which he claimed to be translations of the legendary Gaelic poet Ossian.

Mac·quar·ie[1] (mə'kwɒrı) *n.* **Lach·lan.** 1762–1824, Australian statesman; Governor of New South Wales (1809–21), noted for his reformist policies towards ex-convicts and for his record in public works such as road-building in the colony.

Mac·quar·ie[2] (mə'kwɒrı) *n.* **1.** an Australian island in the Pacific, southeast of Tasmania: noted for its species of albatross and penguin. Area: about 168 sq. km (65 sq. miles). **2.** a river in SE Australia, in E central New South Wales, rising in the Blue Mountains and flowing northwest to the Darling. Length: about 1200 km (750 miles).

mac·ra·mé (mə'krɑ:mı) *n.* a type of ornamental work made by knotting and weaving coarse thread into a pattern. [C19: via French and Italian from Turkish *makrama* towel, from Arabic *migramah* striped cloth]

Mac·rea·dy (mə'kri:dı) *n.* **Wil·liam Charles.** 1793–1873, English actor and theatre manager.

mac·ren·ceph·a·ly (,mækrən'sɛfəlı) *or* **mac·ren·ce·pha·li·a** (,mækrənsɛ'feılıə) *n.* the condition of having an abnormally large brain.

mac·ro *or* **mac·ro in·struc·tion** ('mækrəu) *n., pl.* **·ros.** a single computer instruction that initiates a set of instructions to perform a specific task.

mac·ro- *or before a vowel* **macr-** *combining form.* **1.** large, long, or great in size or duration: *macroscopic.* **2.** (in pathology) indicating abnormal enlargement or overdevelopment: *macrocyte.* Compare **micro-** (sense 5). [from Greek *makros* large; compare Latin *macer* MEAGRE]

mac·ro·bi·ot·ics (,mækrəubaı'ɒtıks) *n.* (*functioning as sing.*) a dietary system in which foods are classified according to the principles of Yin and Yang. It advocates diets of whole grains and vegetables grown without chemical additives. —**,mac·ro·bi·'ot·ic** *adj.*

mac·ro·ceph·a·ly (,mækrəu'sɛfəlı) *or* **mac·ro·ce·pha·li·a** (,mækrəusı'feılıə) *n.* the condition of having an abnormally large head or skull. —**mac·ro·ce·phal·ic** (,mækrəusı'fælık) *or* **,mac·ro·'ceph·a·lous** *adj.*

mac·ro·cli·mate ('mækrəu,klaımıt) *n.* the prevailing climate of a large area. —**mac·ro·cli·mat·ic** (,mækrəuklaı'mætık) *adj.* —**,mac·ro·cli·'mat·i·cal·ly** *adv.*

mac·ro·cosm ('mækrə,kɒzəm) *n.* **1.** a complex structure, such as the universe or society, regarded as an entirety, as opposed to microcosms, which have a similar structure and are contained within it. **2.** any complex entity regarded as a complete system in itself. ~Compare **microcosm.** [C16: via French and Latin from Greek *makros kosmos* great world] —**,mac·ro·'cos·mic** *adj.* —**,mac·ro·'cos·mi·cal·ly** *adv.*

mac·ro·cyst ('mækrəu,sıst) *n.* **1.** an unusually large cyst. **2.** (in slime moulds) an encysted resting protoplasmic mass. (See **plasmodium** (sense 1).

mac·ro·cyte ('mækrəu,saıt) *n. Pathol.* an abnormally large red blood cell, over 10 µm in diameter. —**mac·ro·cyt·ic** (,mækrəu'sıtık) *adj.*

mac·ro·cy·to·sis (,mækrəusaı'təusıs) *n. Pathol.* the presence in the blood of macrocytes.

mac·ro·e·co·nom·ics (,mækrəu,i:kə'nɒmıks, -,ɛk-) *n.* (*functioning as sing.*) the branch of economics concerned with aggregates, such as national income, consumption, and investment. Compare **microeconomics.** —**,mac·ro·,e·co·'nom·ic** *adj.*

mac·ro·ev·o·lu·tion (,mækrəu,i:və'lu:ʃən) *n. Biology.* the evolution of large taxonomic groups such as genera and families. —**,mac·ro·,ev·o·'lu·tion·ar·y** *adj.*

mac·ro·gam·ete (,mækrəugæ'mi:t) *or* **meg·a·ga·mete** (,mɛgəgæ'mi:t) *n.* the larger and apparently female of two gametes in conjugating protozoans. Compare **microgamete.**

mac·ro·graph ('mækrəu,grɑ:f, -,græf) *n.* a photograph, drawing, etc., in which an object appears as large as or several times larger than the original. —**mac·ro·graph·ic** (,mækrəu'græfık) *adj.*

mac·ro·mol·e·cule (,mækrəu'mɒlı,kju:l) *n.* any very large molecule, such as a protein or synthetic polymer. —**mac·ro·mo·lec·u·lar** (,mækrəumə'lɛkjulə) *adj.*

mac·ron ('mækrɒn) *n.* a diacritical mark (¯) placed over a letter, used in prosody, in the orthography of some languages, and in several types of phonetic respelling systems, to represent a long vowel. [C19: from Greek *makron* something long, from *makros* long]

mac·ro·nu·cle·us (,mækrəu'nju:klıəs) *n., pl.* **·cle·i** (-klı,aı). the larger of the two nuclei in ciliated protozoans, involved in feeding and similar processes. Compare **micronucleus.**

mac·ro·nu·tri·ent (,mækrəu'nju:trıənt) *n.* any substance, such as carbon, hydrogen, or oxygen, that is required in large amounts for healthy growth and development.

mac·ro·phage ('mækrəu,feıdʒ) *n.* any large phagocytic cell occurring in the blood, lymph, and connective tissue of vertebrates. See also **histiocyte.** —**mac·ro·phag·ic** (,mækrəu'fædʒık) *adj.*

mac·ro·phys·ics (,mækrəu'fızıks) *n.* (*functioning as sing.*) the branch of physics concerned with macroscopic systems and objects.

mac·rop·ter·ous (mæ'krɒptərəs) *adj.* (of certain animals, esp. some types of ant) having large wings.

mac·ro·scop·ic (,mækrəu'skɒpık) *adj.* **1.** large enough to be visible to the naked eye. Compare **microscopic. 2.** comprehensive; concerned with large units. **3.** having astronomical dimensions. **4.** *Physics.* capable of being described by the statistical properties of a large number of parts. ~Also: **megascopic.** [C19: see MACRO-, -SCOPIC] —**,mac·ro·'scop·i·cal·ly** *or* **,meg·a·'scop·i·cal·ly** *adv.*

mac·ro·spo·ran·gi·um (,mækrəuspɔ:'rændʒıəm) *n., pl.* **·gi·a** (-dʒıə). another name for **megasporangium.**

mac·ro·spore ('mækrəu,spɔ:) *n.* another name for **megaspore.**

ma·cru·ran (mə'kruərən) *n.* **1.** any decapod crustacean of the group (formerly suborder) *Macrura,* which includes the lobsters, prawns, and crayfish. ~*adj. also* **ma·cru·rous, ma·cru·ral,** *or* **ma·cru·roid. 2.** of, relating to, or belonging to the *Macrura.* [C19: via New Latin, from Greek *makros* long + *oura* tail]

mac·u·la ('mækjulə) *or* **mac·ule** ('mækju:l) *n., pl.* **·u·lae** (-ju,li:) *or* **·ules.** *Anatomy.* **1.** a small spot or area of distinct colour, esp. the macula lutea. **2.** any small discoloured spot or blemish on the skin, such as a freckle. [C14: from Latin] —**'mac·u·lar** *adj.*

mac·u·la lu·te·a ('lu:tıə) *n., pl.* **mac·u·lae lu·te·ae** ('lu:tı,i:). a small yellowish oval-shaped spot, rich in cones, near the centre of the retina of the eye, where vision is especially sharp. See also **fovea centralis.** [New Latin, literally: yellow spot]

mac·u·late *Archaic or literary.* ~*vb.* ('mækju,leıt). **1.** (*tr.*) to spot, stain, or pollute. ~*adj.* ('mækjulıt). **2.** spotted or polluted. [C15: from Latin *maculāre* to stain]

mac·u·la·tion (,mækju'leıʃən) *n.* **1.** a pattern of spots, as on certain animals and plants. **2.** *Archaic.* the act of maculating or the state of being maculated.

mac·ule ('mækju:l) *n.* **1.** *Anatomy.* another name for **macula. 2.** *Printing.* another name for **mackle.** [C15: from Latin *macula* spot]

Ma·cum·ba *Portuguese.* (ma'kumba) *n.* a religious cult in Brazil that combines Christian and voodoo elements.

mad (mæd) *adj.* **mad·der, mad·dest. 1.** mentally deranged; insane. **2.** senseless; foolish: *a mad idea.* **3.** (often foll. by *at*) *Informal.* angry; resentful. **4.** (foll. by *about, on,* or *over;* often postpositive) wildly enthusiastic (about) or fond (of): *mad about football; football-mad.* **5.** extremely excited or confused; frantic: *a mad rush.* **6.** wildly gay; boisterous: *a mad party.* **7.** temporarily overpowered by violent reactions, emotions, etc.: *mad with grief.* **8.** (of animals) **a.** unusually ferocious: *a mad buffalo.* **b.** afflicted with rabies. **9. like mad.** *Informal.* with great energy, enthusiasm, or haste; wildly. **10. mad as a hatter.** crazy. ~*vb.* **mads, mad·ding, mad·ded. 11.** *U.S. or archaic.* to make or become mad; act or cause to act as if mad. [Old English *gemǣded,* past participle of *gemǣdan* to render insane; related to *gemād* insane, and to Old High German *gimeit* silly, crazy, Old Norse *meitha* to hurt, damage] —**'mad·dish** *adj.*

ma·da·fu (ma'dafu:) *n. E. African.* coconut milk. [C19: from Swahili]

Madag. *abbrev. for* Madagascar.

Mad·a·gas·car (,mædə'gæskə) *n.* an island republic in the Indian Ocean, off the E coast of Africa: made a French protectorate in 1895; became autonomous in 1958 and fully independent in 1960; contains unique flora and fauna. Language: Malagasy. Religions: animist and Christian. Currency: franc. Capital: Tananarive. Pop.: 7 650 000 (1971 est.). Area: 587 041 sq. km (266 657 sq. miles). Official name (since 1975): **Democratic Republic of Madagascar.** Former name (1958–75): **Malagasy Republic.** —**,Mad·a·'gas·can** *n., adj.*

mad·am ('mædəm) *n.* **1.** a polite term of address for a woman, esp. one considered to be of relatively high social status. **2.** a woman who runs a brothel. **3.** *Brit. informal.* a precocious or pompous little girl. [C13: from Old French *ma dame* my lady]

mad·ame ('mædəm; *French* ma'dam) *n., pl.* **mes·dames** ('meı,dæm; *French* me'dam). a married Frenchwoman: usually used as a title equivalent to *Mrs.,* and sometimes extended to older unmarried women to show respect. [C17: from French. See MADAM]

mad·cap ('mæd,kæp) *adj.* **1.** impulsive, reckless, or lively. ~*n.* **2.** an impulsive, reckless, or lively person.

mad·den ('mædᵊn) *vb.* to make or become mad or angry.

mad·den·ing ('mædᵊnɪŋ) *adj.* **1.** serving to send mad. **2.** *Informal.* extremely annoying; exasperating. —**'mad·den·ing·ly** *adv.* —**'mad·den·ing·ness** *n.*

mad·der ('mædə) *n.* **1.** any of several rubiaceous plants of the genus *Rubia,* esp. the Eurasian *R. tinctoria,* which has small yellow flowers and a red fleshy root. **2.** the root of this plant. **3.** a dark reddish-purple dye formerly obtained by fermentation of this root; identical to the synthetic dye, alizarin. **4.** a red lake obtained from alizarin and an inorganic base; used as a pigment in inks and paints. [Old English *mædere;* related to Middle Dutch *mēde,* Old Norse *mathra*]

mad·ding ('mædɪŋ) *adj. Archaic.* **1.** acting or behaving as if mad: *the madding crowd.* **2.** making mad; maddening. —**'mad·ding·ly** *adv.*

made (meɪd) *vb.* **1.** the past tense and past participle of **make.** ~*adj.* **2.** artificially produced. **3.** (*in combination*) produced or shaped as specified: *handmade.* **4. get** *or* **have it made.** *Slang.* to be assured of success. **5. made of money.** very rich.

made dish *n. Cooking.* a dish consisting of a number of different ingredients cooked together.

Ma·dei·ra (mə'dɪərə; *Portuguese* ma'dɛɪrə) *n.* **1.** a group of volcanic islands in the N Atlantic, west of Morocco: constitutes the Portuguese administrative district of Funchal; consists of the chief island, Madeira, Pôrto Santo, and the uninhabited Deserta and Selvagen Islands; gained partial autonomy in 1976. Capital: Funchal. Pop.: 268 700 (1970). Area: 797 sq. km (311 sq. miles). **2.** a river in W Brazil, flowing northeast to the Amazon below Manaus. Length: 3241 km (2013 miles). **3.** a rich strong fortified white wine made on Madeira.

Ma·dei·ra cake *n. Brit.* a kind of rich sponge cake.

mad·e·leine ('mædəlɪn, -,leɪn) *n.* a small fancy sponge cake usually coated with jam and coconut. [C19: perhaps after *Madeleine* Paulmier, French pastry cook]

mad·e·moi·selle (,mædmwə'zɛl: *French* madmwa'zɛl) *n., pl.* **mes·de·moi·selles** (,meɪdmwə'zɛl; *French* medmwa'zɛl). **1.** a young unmarried French girl or woman: usually used as a title equivalent to *Miss.* **2.** a French teacher or governess. [C15: French, from *ma* my + *demoiselle* DAMSEL]

made-up *adj.* **1.** invented; fictional: *a made-up story.* **2.** wearing make-up: *a well made-up woman.* **3.** put together; assembled. **4.** (of a road) surfaced with tarmac, concrete, etc.

mad·house ('mæd,haʊs) *n. Informal.* **1.** a mental hospital or asylum. **2.** a state of uproar or confusion.

Madh·ya Bha·rat ('mʌdjə 'bɑːrət) *n.* a former state of central India: part of Madhya Pradesh since 1956.

Madh·ya Pra·desh ('mʌdjə prɑː'dɛʃ) *n.* a state of central India, situated on the Deccan Plateau: the largest Indian state; rich in mineral resources, with several industrial cities. Capital: Bhopal. Pop.: 41 654 119 (1971). Area: 443 452 sq. km (171 217 sq. miles).

Ma·di·na do Bo·e (mə'diːnə dəʊ 'bəʊeɪ) *n.* the provisional capital of Guinea-Bissau (since 1974), in the eastern part of the country.

Mad·i·son[1] ('mædɪsᵊn) *n.* a city in S central Wisconsin, on an isthmus between Lakes Mendota and Monona: the state capital. Pop.: 169 749 (1973 est.).

Mad·i·son[2] ('mædɪsᵊn) *n.* **James.** 1751–1836, U.S. statesman; 4th president of the U.S. (1809–17). He helped to draft the U.S. Constitution and Bill of Rights. His presidency was dominated by the War of 1812.

Mad·i·son Av·e·nue *n.* a street in New York City: a centre of American advertising and public-relations firms and a symbol of their attitudes and methods.

mad·ly ('mædlɪ) *adv.* **1.** in an insane or foolish manner. **2.** with great speed and energy. **3.** *Informal.* extremely or excessively: *I love you madly.*

mad·man ('mædmən) *or* (*fem.*) **mad·wom·an** *n., pl.* **·men** *or* **·wom·en.** a person who is insane, esp. one who behaves violently; lunatic.

mad·ness ('mædnɪs) *n.* **1.** insanity; lunacy. **2.** extreme anger, excitement, or foolishness. **3.** a nontechnical word for **rabies.**

Ma·don·na (mə'dɒnə) *n.* **1.** *Chiefly R.C. Church.* a designation of the Virgin Mary. **2.** (*sometimes not cap.*) a picture or statue of the Virgin Mary. [C16: Italian, from *ma* my + *donna* lady]

Ma·don·na lil·y *n.* a perennial widely cultivated Mediterranean lily plant, *Lilium candidum,* with white trumpet-shaped flowers. Also called: **Annunciation lily.**

mad·ras ('mædrəs; mə'dræs, -'drɑːs) *n.* **1. a.** a strong fine cotton or silk fabric, usually with a woven stripe. **b.** (*as modifier*): *madras cotton.* **2.** something made of this, esp. a scarf.

Ma·dras (mə'drɑːs, -'dræs) *n.* **1.** a port in SE India, capital of Tamil Nadu, on the Bay of Bengal: founded in 1639 by the English East India Company as **Fort St. George;** traditional burial place of St. Thomas; university (1857). Pop.: 2 469 449 (1971). **2.** the former name (until 1968) for the state of **Tamil Nadu.**

Ma·dre de Dios (*Spanish* 'maðre ðe 'ðjos) *n.* a river in NE South America, rising in SE Peru and flowing northeast to the Beni River in N Bolivia. Length: about 965 km (600 miles).

mad·re·pore (,mædrɪ'pɔː) *n.* any coral of the genus *Madrepora,* many of which occur in tropical seas and form large coral reefs: order *Zoantharia.* [C18: via French from Italian *madrepora* mother-stone, from *madre* mother + *-pora*] —**,mad·re·'por·al, mad·re·por·ic** (,mædrɪ'pɒrɪk), **mad·re·por·it·ic** (,mædrɪpə'rɪtɪk), *or* **,mad·re·'po·ri·an** *adj.*

Ma·drid (mə'drɪd) *n.* the capital of Spain, situated centrally in New Castile: the highest European capital, at an altitude of about 700 m (2300 ft.); a Moorish fortress in the 10th century, captured by Castile in 1083 and made capital of Spain in 1561; university (1836). Pop.: 3 146 071 (1970).

mad·ri·gal ('mædrɪgᵊl) *n.* **1.** *Music.* a type of 16th- or 17th-century part song for unaccompanied voices with an amatory or pastoral text. Compare **glee. 2.** a 14th-century Italian song, related to a pastoral stanzaic verse form. [C16: from Italian, from Medieval Latin *mātricāle* primitive, apparently from Latin *mātrīcālis* of the womb, from *matrīx* womb] —**'mad·ri·gal·,esque** *adj.* —**mad·ri·gal·i·an** (,mædrɪ'gælɪən, -'geɪ-) *adj.* —**'mad·ri·gal·ist** *n.*

mad·ri·lène ('mædrɪ,lɛn, -,leɪn; *French* madri'lɛn) *n.* a cold consommé flavoured with tomato juice. [shortened from French (*consommé*) *madrilène* from Spanish *madrileño* of Madrid]

ma·dro·ña (mə'drəʊnjə), **ma·dro·ño** (mə'drəʊnjəʊ), *or* **ma·dro·ne** (mə'drəʊnə) *n., pl.* **·ñas, ·ños,** *or* **·nes.** an ericaceous North American evergreen tree or shrub, *Arbutus menziesii,* with white flowers and red berry-like fruits. See also **strawberry tree.** [C19: from Spanish]

Ma·du·ra (mə'dʊərə) *n.* an island in Indonesia, off the NE coast of Java: extensive forests and saline springs. Capital: Pamekasan. Area: 5472 sq. km (2113 sq. miles). —**Ma·du·rese** (,mædjʊ'riːz) *adj., n.*

Ma·du·rai ('mædjʊ,raɪ) *n.* a city in S India, in S Tamil Nadu: centre of Dravidian culture for over 2000 years; cotton industry. Pop.: 549 114 (1971). Former name: **Madura.**

ma·du·ro (mə'dʊərəʊ) *adj.* **1.** (of cigars) dark and strong. ~*n., pl.* **·ros. 2.** a cigar of this type. [Spanish, literally: ripe, from Latin *mātūrus* ripe, MATURE]

mad·wort ('mæd,wɜːt) *n.* **1.** a low-growing Eurasian boraginaceous plant, *Asperugo procumbens,* with small blue flowers. **2.** any of certain other plants, such as alyssum. [C16: once alleged to be a cure for madness]

Mae·an·der *or* **Me·an·der** (miː'ændə) *n.* ancient names of the river **Menderes** (sense 1).

Ma·e·ba·shi ('mɑːɛ'bɑːʃiː) *n.* a city in central Japan, on central Honshu: centre of sericulture and silk-spinning; university (1949). Pop.: 248 312 (1974 est.).

Mae·ce·nas (miː'siːnæs) *n.* **Gai·us** ('gaɪəs). ?70–8 B.C., Roman statesman; adviser to Augustus and patron of Horace and Virgil.

mael·strom ('meɪlstrəʊm) *n.* **1.** a large powerful whirlpool. **2.** any turbulent confusion. [C17: from obsolete Dutch *maelstroom,* from *malen* to grind, whirl round + *stroom* STREAM]

Mael·strom ('meɪlstrəʊm) *n.* a strong tidal current in a restricted channel in the Lofoten Islands off the NW coast of Norway.

mae·nad *or* **me·nad** ('miːnæd) *n.* **1.** *Classical myth.* a woman participant in the orgiastic rites of Dionysus; bacchante. **2.** a frenzied woman. [C16: from Latin *Maenas,* from Greek *mainas* madwoman] —**mae·'nad·ic** *adj.* —**mae·'nad·i·cal·ly** *adv.* —**'mae·nad·ism** *n.*

maes·to·so (maɪ'stəʊsəʊ) *Music.* ~*adj., adv.* **1.** to be performed majestically. ~*n.* **2.** a piece or passage directed to be played in this way. [C18, Italian: majestic, from Latin *māiestās* MAJESTY]

Maes·tricht ('mɑːstrɪxt; *Dutch* maː'strɪxt) *n.* an obsolete spelling of **Maastricht.**

maes·tro ('maɪstrəʊ) *n., pl.* **·tri** (-trɪ) *or* **·tros. 1.** a distinguished music teacher, conductor, or musician. **2.** any man regarded as the master of an art: often used as a term of address. **3.** See **maestro di cappella.** [C18, Italian: master]

maes·tro di cap·pel·la (dɪ kə'pɛlə) *n.* a person in charge of an orchestra, esp. a private one attached to the palace of a prince in Italy during the baroque period. See **kapellmeister.** [Italian: master of the chapel]

Mae·ter·linck ('meɪtə,lɪŋk; *French* mɛtɛr'lɛ̃ːk) *n.* Comte **Mau·rice** (mɔ'ris). 1862–1949, Belgian poet and dramatist, noted particularly for his symbolist plays, such as *Pelléas et Mélisande* (1892), which served as the basis for an opera by Debussy, and *L'Oiseau bleu* (1909). Nobel prize for literature 1911.

mae west (meɪ) *n. Slang.* an inflatable life jacket, esp. as issued to the U.S. armed forces for emergency use. [C20: after *Mae West,* 1892-1980, American actress, renowned for her generous bust]

Ma·e·wo (mɑː'ɛɪwəʊ) *n.* an almost uninhabited island in the New Hebrides. Also called: **Aurora.**

Maf·e·king ('mæfɪ,kɪŋ) *n.* a town in S South Africa, in NE Cape Province: besieged by the Boers for 217 days (1899–1900) during the Boer War; administrative headquarters of the British protectorate of Bechuanaland until 1965, although outside its borders. Pop.: 6900 (1970).

maf·fick ('mæfɪk) *vb.* (*intr.*) *Brit., archaic.* to celebrate extravagantly and publicly. [C20: back formation from *Mafeking,* from the rejoicings at the relief of the siege there in 1900] —**'maf·fick·er** *n.*

Ma·fi·a *or* **Maf·fi·a** ('mæfɪə) *n.* **1. the.** an international secret organization founded in Sicily, probably in opposition to tyranny. It developed into a criminal organization and in the late 19th century was carried to the U.S. by Italian immigrants. **2.** any group considered to resemble the Mafia. See also **Black Hand, Camorra, Cosa Nostra.** [C19: from

Sicilian dialect of Italian, literally hostility to the law, boldness, perhaps from Arabic *mahyah* bragging]

ma·fi·o·so (ˌmæfɪˈəʊsəʊ; *Italian* ˌmafiˈoso) *n., pl.* **-sos** *or* **-si** (*Italian* -si:). a person belonging to the Mafia.

mag (mæg) *n. Informal.* See **magazine.**

mag. *abbrev. for:* **1.** magazine. **2.** magnesium. **3.** magnetic. **4.** magnetism. **5.** magnets. **6.** magnitude.

Ma·ga·lla·nes (*Spanish* ˌmagaˈʎanes) *n.* the former name of **Punta Arenas.**

mag·a·zine (ˌmægəˈzi:n) *n.* **1.** a periodic paperback publication containing articles, fiction, photographs, etc. **2. a.** a metal case holding several cartridges used in some kinds of automatic firearms. **b.** this compartment itself. **3.** a building or compartment for storing weapons, explosives, military provisions, etc. **4.** a stock of ammunition. **5.** a device for continuously recharging a stove or boiler with solid fuel. **6.** *Photog.* another name for **cartridge** (sense 5). **7.** a rack for automatically feeding a number of slides through a projector. [C16: via French *magasin* from Italian *magazzino,* from Arabic *makhāzin,* plural of *makhzan* storehouse, from *khazana* to store away]

mag·da·len (ˈmægdəlɪn) *or* **mag·da·lene** (ˈmægdəˌli:n, ˌmægdəˈli:nɪ) *n.* **1.** *Literary.* a reformed prostitute. **2.** *Rare.* a reformatory for prostitutes. [from MARY MAGDALENE]

Mag·da·le·na (ˌmægdəˈleɪnə, -ˈli:-; *Spanish* ˌmaγðaˈlena) *n.* a river in SW Colombia, rising on the E slopes of the Andes and flowing north to the Caribbean near Barranquilla. Length: 1540 km (956 miles).

Mag·da·le·na Bay *n.* an inlet of the Pacific on the coast of NW Mexico, in Lower California.

Mag·da·lene (ˈmægdəˌli:n, ˌmægdəˈli:nɪ) *n.* See **Mary Magdalene.**

Mag·da·le·ni·an (ˌmægdəˈli:nɪən) *adj.* **1.** of or relating to the latest Palaeolithic culture in Europe, which ended about 10 000 years ago. ~*n.* **2.** the Magdalenian culture. [C19: from French *magdalénien,* after *La Madeleine,* village in Dordogne, France, near which artifacts of the culture were found]

Mag·de·burg (ˈmægdəˌbɜ:g; *German* ˈmakdəˌbʊrk) *n.* an industrial city and port in W East Germany, on the River Elbe: a leading member of the Hanseatic League, whose local laws, the **Magdeburg Laws,** were adopted by many European cities. Pop.: 276 580 (1975 est.).

mage (meɪdʒ) *n.* an archaic word for **magician.** [C14: from MAGUS]

Ma·gel·lan[1] (məˈgɛlən) *n.* **Strait of.** a strait between the mainland of S South America and Tierra del Fuego, linking the S Pacific with the S Atlantic. Length: 600 km (370 miles). Width: up to 32 km (20 miles).

Ma·gel·lan[2] (məˈgɛlən) *n.* **Fer·di·nand.** Portuguese name *Fernão de Magalhães.* ?1480–1521, Portuguese navigator in the service of Spain. He commanded an expedition of five ships that set out to sail to the East Indies via the West. He discovered the Strait of Magellan (1520), crossed the Pacific, and reached the Philippines (1521), where he was killed by natives. One of his ships reached Spain (1522) and was therefore the first to circumnavigate the world.

Mag·el·lan·ic cloud (ˌmægɪˈlænɪk) *n.* either of two small irregular galaxies, the **Large Magellanic Cloud** (Nubecula Major) and the **Small Magellanic Cloud** (Nubecula Minor), situated near the S celestial pole at a distance of 160 000 light years and classified as satellites of the Galaxy.

Ma·gen Da·vid *or* **Mo·gen Da·vid** (ˈmɔ:gən ˈdeɪvɪd) *n.* *Judaism.* another name for the **Star of David.**

ma·gen·ta (məˈdʒɛntə) *n.* **1. a.** a deep purplish red that is the complementary colour of green and, with yellow and cyan, forms a set of primary colours. **b.** (*as adj.*): *a magenta filter.* **2.** another name for **fuchsin.** [C19: named after *Magenta,* Italy, alluding to the blood shed in a battle there (1859)]

mag·gie (ˈmægɪ) *n. Austral. slang.* a magpie.

Mag·gi·o·re (ˌmædʒɪˈɔ:rɪ; *Italian* madˈdʒore) *n.* **Lake.** a lake in N Italy and S Switzerland, in the S Lepontine Alps.

mag·got (ˈmægət) *n.* **1.** the soft limbless larva of dipterous insects, esp. the housefly and blowfly, occurring in decaying organic matter. **2.** *Rare.* a fancy or whim. [C14: from earlier *mathek;* related to Old Norse *mathkr* worm, Old English *matha,* Old High German *mado* grub]

mag·got·y (ˈmægətɪ) *adj.* **1.** relating to, resembling, or ridden with maggots. **2.** *Austral. slang.* annoyed or angry.

Ma·ghreb *or* **Ma·ghrib** (ˈmʌgrəb) *n.* NW Africa, including Morocco, Algeria, Tunisia, and sometimes Libya. [from Arabic, literally: the West] —**ˈMa·ghre·bi** *or* **ˈMa·ghri·bi** *adj., n.*

ma·gi (ˈmeɪdʒaɪ) *pl. n., sing.* **·gus** (-gəs). **1.** the Zoroastrian priests of the ancient Medes and Persians. **2. the three Magi.** the wise men from the East who came to do homage to the infant Jesus (Matthew 2:1–12) and traditionally called Caspar, Melchior, and Balthazar. —**ma·gi·an** (ˈmeɪdʒɪən) *adj.*

mag·ic (ˈmædʒɪk) *n.* **1.** the art that, by use of spells, supposedly invokes supernatural powers to influence events; sorcery. **2.** the practice of this art. **3.** the practice of illusory tricks to entertain other people; conjuring. **4.** any mysterious or extraordinary quality or power: *the magic of springtime.* **5. like magic.** very quickly. ~*adj. also* **mag·i·cal. 6.** of or relating to magic: *a magic spell.* **7.** possessing or considered to possess mysterious powers: *a magic wand.* **8.** unaccountably enchanting: *magic beauty.* ~*vb.* **9.** (*tr.*) to transform or produce by or as if by magic. **10.** (*tr.;* foll. by *away*) to cause to disappear by or as if by magic. [C14: via Old French *magique,* from Greek *magikē* witchcraft, from *magos* MAGUS] —**ˈmag·i·cal** *adj.* —**ˈmag·i·cal·ly** *adv.*

mag·ic car·pet *n.* (in fairy stories) a carpet capable of transporting people through the air.

mag·ic eye *n.* another name for **electric eye.**

ma·gi·cian (məˈdʒɪʃən) *n.* **1.** another term for **conjurer. 2.** a person who practises magic. **3.** a person who has extraordinary skill, influence, or qualities.

mag·ic lan·tern *n.* an early type of slide projector. Sometimes shortened to **lantern.**

mag·ic num·ber *n. Physics.* any of the numbers 2, 8, 20, 28, 50, 82, and 126. Nuclides with these numbers of nucleons appear to have greater stability than other nuclides.

mag·ic square *n.* a square array of rows of integers arranged so that the sum of the integers is the same when taken vertically, horizontally, or diagonally.

ma·gilp (məˈgɪlp) *n. Arts.* a variant spelling of **megilp.**

Ma·gi·not line (ˈmæʒɪˌnəʊ; *French* maʒiˈno) *n.* **1.** a line of fortifications built by France to defend its border with Germany prior to World War II; it proved ineffective against the German invasion. **2.** any line of defence in which blind confidence is placed. [named after André *Maginot* (1877–1932), French minister of war when the fortifications were begun in 1929]

mag·is·te·ri·al (ˌmædʒɪˈstɪərɪəl) *adj.* **1.** commanding; authoritative. **2.** domineering; dictatorial. **3.** of or relating to a teacher or person of similar status. **4.** of or relating to a magistrate. [C17: from Late Latin *magisteriālis,* from *magister* master] —ˌ**mag·is·ˈte·ri·al·ly** *adv.* —ˌ**mag·is·ˈte·ri·al·ness** *n.*

mag·is·ter·y (ˈmædʒɪstərɪ, -trɪ) *n., pl.* **-ter·ies.** *Alchemy.* **1.** an agency or substance, such as the philosopher's stone, believed to transmute other substances. **2.** any substance capable of healing. [C16: from Medieval Latin *magisterium,* from Latin: mastery, from *magister* master]

mag·is·tra·cy (ˈmædʒɪstrəsɪ) *or* **mag·is·tra·ture** (ˈmædʒɪstrəˌtjʊə) *n., pl.* **-cies** *or* **-tures. 1.** the office or function of a magistrate. **2.** magistrates collectively. **3.** the district under the jurisdiction of a magistrate.

mag·is·tral (ˈmædʒɪstrəl) *adj.* **1.** *Pharmacol.* made up according to a special prescription. Compare **officinal. 2.** *Fortifications.* determining the location of other fortifications: *the magistral line.* ~*n.* **3.** a fortification in a determining position. [C16: from Latin *magistrālis* concerning a master, from *magister* master] —**mag·is·tral·i·ty** (ˌmædʒɪˈstrælɪtɪ) *n.* —**ˈmag·is·tral·ly** *or* **mag·is·trat·i·cal·ly** (ˌmædʒɪˈstrætɪklɪ) *adv.*

mag·is·trate (ˈmædʒɪˌstreɪt, -strɪt) *n.* **1.** a public officer concerned with the administration of law. **2.** another name for **justice of the peace.** [C17: from Latin *magistrātus,* from *magister* master] —**ˈmag·is·ˌtrate·ship** *n.*

mag·is·trates' court *n.* (in England) a court of summary jurisdiction held before two or more justices of the peace or a stipendiary magistrate to deal with minor crimes, certain civil actions, and preliminary hearings.

Mag·le·mo·si·an *or* **Mag·le·mo·se·an** (ˌmægləˈməʊzɪən) *n.* **1.** the first Mesolithic culture of N Europe, dating from 8000 B.C. to about 5000 B.C.: important for the rare wooden objects that have been preserved, such as dugout canoes. ~*adj.* **2.** designating or relating to this culture. [C20: named after the site at *Maglemose,* Denmark, where the culture was first classified]

mag·ma (ˈmægmə) *n., pl.* **-mas** *or* **-ma·ta** (-mətə). **1.** a paste or suspension consisting of a finely divided solid dispersed in a liquid. **2.** a hot viscous liquid within the earth's crust, consisting mainly of silica: it solidifies to form igneous rock. [C15, from Latin: dregs (of an ointment), from Greek: salve made by kneading, from *massein* to knead] —**mag·mat·ic** (mægˈmætɪk) *adj.* —**ˈmag·ma·tism** *n.*

Mag·na Car·ta (ˈmægnə ˈkɑ:tə) *or* **Mag·na Char·ta** *n.* *English history.* the charter granted by King John at Runnymede in 1215, recognizing the rights and privileges of the barons, church, and freemen. [Medieval Latin: great charter]

mag·na cum lau·de (ˈmægnə kʊm ˈlaʊdeɪ) *Chiefly U.S.* with great praise: the second of three designations for above-average achievement in examinations. [Latin]

Mag·na Grae·ci·a (ˈmægnə ˈgri:ʃɪə) *n.* (in the ancient world) S Italy, where numerous colonies were founded by Greek cities. [Latin: Great Greece]

mag·na·nim·i·ty (ˌmægnəˈnɪmɪtɪ) *n., pl.* **-ties.** generosity. [C14: via Old French from Latin *magnanimitās,* from *magnus* great + *animus* soul]

mag·nan·i·mous (mægˈnænɪməs) *adj.* generous and noble. [C16: from Latin *magnanimus* great-souled] —**magˈnan·i·mous·ly** *adv.* —**magˈnan·i·mous·ness** *n.*

mag·nate (ˈmægneɪt, -nɪt) *n.* **1.** a person of power and rank in any sphere, esp. in industry. **2.** *History.* a great nobleman. **3.** (formerly) a member of the upper chamber in certain European parliaments, as in Hungary. [C15: back formation from earlier *magnates* from Late Latin: great men, plural of *magnās,* from Latin *magnus* great] —**ˈmag·nate·ˌship** *n.*

mag·ne·sia (mægˈni:ʃə) *n.* another name for **magnesium oxide.** [C14: via Medieval Latin from Greek *Magnēsia,* of *Magnēs* ancient mineral-rich region] —**magˈne·sian, mag·ne·sic** (mægˈni:sɪk), *or* **magˈne·sial** *adj.*

mag·ne·site (ˈmægnɪˌsaɪt) *n.* a white, colourless, or lightly tinted mineral consisting of naturally occurring magnesium carbonate in hexagonal crystalline form: a source of magnesium and also used in the manufacture of refractory bricks. Formula: $MgCO_3$. [C19: from MAGNESIUM + -ITE[1]]

mag·ne·si·um (mægˈni:zɪəm) *n.* a light silvery-white metallic element of the alkaline earth series that burns with an intense white flame, occurring principally in magnesite, dolomite, and carnallite: used in light structural alloys, flash bulbs, flares, and fireworks. Symbol: Mg; atomic no.: 12; atomic wt.: 24.312; valency: 2; relative density: 1.738; melting pt.: 651°C; boiling pt.: 1107°C. [C19: New Latin, from MAGNESIA]

mag+ne+si·um ox+ide *n.* a white tasteless substance occurring naturally as periclase: used as an antacid and laxative and in refractory materials, such as crucibles and fire bricks. Formula: MgO. Also called: **magnesia.**

mag+net ('mægnɪt) *n.* **1.** a body that can attract certain substances, such as iron or steel, as a result of a magnetic field; a piece of ferromagnetic substance. See also **electromagnet. 2.** a person or thing that exerts a great attraction. [C15: via Latin from Greek *magnēs,* shortened from *ho Magnēs lithos* the Magnesian stone. See MAGNESIA]

mag+net+ic (mæg'nɛtɪk) *adj.* **1.** of, producing, or operated by means of magnetism. **2.** of or concerned with a magnet. **3.** of or concerned with the magnetism of the earth: *the magnetic equator.* **4.** capable of being magnetized. **5.** exerting a powerful attraction: *a magnetic personality.* **—mag+'net·i·cal+ly** *adv.*

mag+net+ic bot+tle *n.* a configuration of magnetic fields for containing the plasma in controlled thermonuclear reactions.

mag+net+ic char+ac+ter read+er *n.* a device that automatically scans and interprets characters printed with magnetic ink. It operates by the process of **magnetic character recognition.**

mag+net+ic cir+cuit *n.* a closed path described by magnetic flux, analogous to a circuit through which an electric current flows.

mag+net+ic com+pass *n.* a compass containing a magnetic needle pivoted in a horizontal plane, that indicates the direction of magnetic north at points on the earth's surface.

mag+net+ic con+stant *n.* the permeability of free space, which has the value $4\pi \times 10^{-7}$ henry per metre. Symbol: M_0 Also called: **absolute permeability.**

mag+net+ic course *n.* an aircraft's course in relation to the magnetic north. Also called: **magnetic heading.**

mag+net+ic dec+li+na+tion *n.* the angle that a compass needle makes with the direction of the geographical north pole at any given point on the earth's surface. Also called: **declination, magnetic variation.**

mag+net+ic dip *or* **in+cli+na+tion** *n.* another name for **dip** (sense 29).

mag+net+ic di+pole mo+ment *n.* a measure of the magnetic strength of a magnet or current-carrying coil, expressed as the torque produced when the magnet or coil is set with its axis perpendicular to unit magnetic field. Symbol: ***m, j*** Also called: **magnetic moment.** Compare **electromagnetic moment.**

mag+net+ic disk *n. Computer technol.* another name for **disk** (sense 2).

mag+net+ic drum *n. Computer technol.* another name for **drum**[1] (sense 8).

mag+net+ic e·qua+tor *n.* an imaginary line on the earth's surface, near the equator, at all points on which there is no magnetic dip. Also called: **aclinic line.**

mag+net+ic field *n.* a field of force surrounding a permanent magnet or a moving charged particle, in which another permanent magnet or moving charge experiences a force. Compare **electric field.**

mag+net+ic flux *n.* **1.** a measure of the strength of a magnetic field over a given area, equal to the product of the area and the magnetic flux density through it. Symbol: ϕ **2.** a magnetic field.

mag+net+ic flux den+si·ty *n.* a measure of the strength of a magnetic field at a given point, expressed by the force per unit length on a conductor carrying unit current at that point. Symbol: ***B*** Also called: **magnetic induction.**

mag+net+ic in+duc+tion *n.* another name for **magnetic flux density.**

mag+net+ic ink *n.* ink containing particles of a magnetic material used for printing characters for magnetic character recognition.

mag+net+ic lens *n.* a set of magnets, esp. electromagnets, used to focus or defocus a beam of charged particles in an electron microscope, particle accelerator, or similar device.

mag+net+ic me+rid+i·an *n.* a continuous imaginary line around the surface of the earth passing through both magnetic poles.

mag+net+ic mine *n.* a mine designed to activate when a magnetic field such as that generated by the metal of a ship's hull is detected.

mag+net+ic mo+ment *n.* short for **magnetic dipole moment** or **electromagnetic moment.**

mag+net+ic nee+dle *n.* a slender magnetized rod used in certain instruments, such as the magnetic compass, for indicating the direction of a magnetic field.

mag+net+ic north *n.* the direction in which a compass needle points, at an angle (the declination) from the direction of true (geographic) north.

mag+net+ic pick+up *n.* a type of gramophone pickup in which the stylus moves an iron core in a coil, causing a changing magnetic field that produces the current.

mag+net+ic pole *n.* **1.** either of two regions in a magnet where the magnetic induction is concentrated. **2.** either of two variable points on the earth's surface towards which a magnetic needle points, where the lines of force of the earth's magnetic field are vertical.

mag+net+ics (mæg'nɛtɪks) *n.* (*functioning as sing.*) the branch of physics concerned with magnetism.

mag+net+ic storm *n.* a sudden severe disturbance of the earth's magnetic field, caused by emission of charged particles from the sun.

mag+net+ic tape *n.* a long narrow plastic strip coated with iron oxide, used to record sound or video signals or to store information in computers. Sometimes (informally) shortened to **mag tape.**

mag+net+ic tape u·nit *or* **drive** *n.* a computer device that moves reels of magnetic tape past read-write heads so that data can be transferred to or from the computer.

mag+net+ic var·i·a+tion *n.* another name for **magnetic declination.**

mag+net+ism ('mægnɪ,tɪzəm) *n.* **1.** the property of attraction displayed by magnets. **2.** any of a class of phenomena in which a field of force is caused by a moving electric charge. See also **electromagnetism, ferromagnetism, diamagnetism, paramagnetism. 3.** the branch of physics concerned with magnetic phenomena. **4.** powerful attraction. **—'mag+net+ist** *n.*

mag+net+ite ('mægnɪ,taɪt) *n.* a black magnetizable mineral that consists of ferrous and ferric oxides in cubic crystalline form with the iron sometimes replaced by magnesium, zinc, chromium, etc. It is widely distributed in igneous and metamorphic rocks, esp. in Russia and Sweden, and is an important source of iron. Formula: $FeO.Fe_2O_3$. **—mag+net+it+ic** (,mægnɪ'tɪtɪk) *adj.*

mag+net+ize *or* **mag+net+ise** ('mægnɪ,taɪz) *vb.* (*tr.*) **1.** to make (a substance or object) magnetic. **2.** to attract strongly. **3.** an obsolete word for **mesmerize. —,mag+net+'iz+a·ble** *or* **,mag+net+'is+a·ble** *adj.* **—,mag+net·i+'za+tion** *or* **,mag+net·i+'sa+tion** *n.* **—'mag+net+,iz+er** *or* **'mag+net+,is+er** *n.*

mag+ne+to (mæg'ni:təʊ) *n., pl.* **+tos.** a small electric generator in which the magnetic field is produced by a permanent magnet, esp. one for providing the spark in an internal-combustion engine. [C19: short for *magneto-electric generator*]

mag·ne·to- *combining form.* indicating magnetism or magnetic properties: *magnetosphere.*

mag+ne+to+chem+is+try (mæg,ni:təʊ'kɛmɪstrɪ) *n.* the branch of chemistry concerned with the relationship between magnetic and chemical properties. **—mag+,ne+to+'chem·i+cal** *adj.*

mag+ne+to+e·lec+tric+i·ty (mæg,ni:təʊɪlɛk'trɪsɪti:) *n.* electricity produced by the action of magnetic fields. **—mag+,ne+to+e·'lec+tric** *or* **mag+,ne+to+e·'lec+tri+cal** *adj.*

mag+ne+to+graph (mæg'ni:təʊ,grɑ:f, -,græf) *n.* a recording magnetometer, usually used for studying variations in the earth's magnetic field.

mag+ne+to+hy+dro+dy+nam+ics (mæg,ni:təʊ,haɪdrəʊdaɪ'næmɪks) (*functioning as sing.*) ~*n.* **1.** the study of the behaviour of conducting fluids, such as liquid metals or plasmas, in magnetic fields. **2.** the generation of electricity by subjecting a plasma to a magnetic field and collecting the deflected free electrons. ~Abbrev.: **MHD. —mag+,ne+to+,hy+dro+dy'nam+ic** *adj.*

mag+ne+tom+e·ter (,mægnɪ'tɒmɪtə) *n.* any instrument for measuring the intensity or direction of a magnetic field, esp. the earth's field. **—mag+ne+to+met+ric** (,mægnɪtəʊ'mɛtrɪk) *adj.* **—,mag+ne+'tom+e·try** *n.*

mag+ne+to+mo+tive (mæg,ni:təʊ'məʊtɪv) *adj.* causing a magnetic flux.

mag+ne+to+mo+tive force *n.* the agency producing a magnetic flux, considered analogous to the electromotive force in an electric circuit; equal to the circular integral of the magnetic field strength. Symbol: *F*

mag+ne+ton ('mægnɪ,tɒn, mæg'ni:tɒn) *n.* **1.** Also called: **Bohr magneton.** a unit of magnetic moment equal to $eh/4\pi m$ where e and m are the charge and mass of an electron and h is the Planck constant. It has the value $9.274\,096 \times 10^{-24}$ joule per tesla. Symbol: β or m_B **2.** Also called: **nuclear magneton.** a similar unit equal to $\beta m/M$ where M is the mass of the proton. [C20: from MAGNET + (ELECTR)ON]

mag+ne+to+sphere (mæg'ni:təʊ,sfɪə) *n.* the region surrounding the earth in which the behaviour of charged particles is dominated by the earth's magnetic field. **—mag+ne+to+spher+ic** (mæg,ni:təʊ'sfɛrɪk) *adj.*

mag+ne+to+stric+tion (mæg,ni:təʊ'strɪkʃən) *n.* a change in dimensions of a ferromagnetic material that is subjected to a magnetic field. [C19: from MAGNETO- + CONSTRICTION] **—mag+,ne+to+'stric+tive** *adj.*

mag+ne+tron ('mægnɪ,trɒn) *n.* a two-electrode electronic valve used with an applied magnetic field to generate high-power microwave oscillations, esp. for use in radar. [C20: from MAGNET + ELECTRON]

mag+nif+ic (mæg'nɪfɪk) *or* **mag+nif·i+cal** *adj. Archaic.* magnificent, grandiose, or pompous. [C15: via Old French from Latin *magnificus* great in deeds, from *magnus* great + *facere* to do] **—mag+'nif·i+cal+ly** *adv.*

Mag+nif·i+cat (mæg'nɪfɪ,kæt) *n. Ecclesiast.* the hymn of the Virgin Mary (Luke 1:46-55), used as a canticle. [from the opening phrase in the Latin version, *Magnificat anima mea Dominum* (my soul doth magnify the Lord)]

mag+ni+fi+ca+tion (,mægnɪfɪ'keɪʃən) *n.* **1.** the act of magnifying or the state of being magnified. **2.** the degree to which something is magnified. **3.** a copy, photograph, drawing, etc., of something magnified. **4.** a measure of the ability of a lens or other optical instrument to magnify, expressed as the ratio of the size of the image to that of the object.

mag+nif·i+cence (mæg'nɪfɪsəns) *n.* the quality of being magnificent. [C14: via French from Latin *magnificentia*]

mag+nif·i+cent (mæg'nɪfɪsᵊnt) *adj.* **1.** splendid or impressive in appearance. **2.** superb or very fine. **3.** (esp. of ideas) noble or elevated. **4.** *Archaic.* great or exalted in rank or action. [C16: from Latin *magnificentior* more splendid, irregular comparative of *magnificus* great in deeds; see MAGNIFIC] —**mag+'nif·i+cent+ly** *adv.* —**mag+'nif·i+cent+ness** *n.*

mag+nif·i+co (mæg'nɪfɪˌkəʊ) *n., pl.* **+coes.** a magnate; grandee. [C16: Italian from Latin *magnificus;* see MAGNIFIC]

mag+ni+fy ('mægnɪˌfaɪ) *vb.* **+fies, +fy+ing, +fied. 1.** to increase, cause to increase, or be increased in apparent size, as through the action of a lens, microscope, etc. **2.** to exaggerate or become exaggerated in importance: *don't magnify your troubles.* **3.** (*tr.*) *Rare.* to increase in actual size. **4.** (*tr.*) *Archaic.* to glorify. [C14: via Old French from Latin *magnificāre* to praise; see MAGNIFIC] —**'mag+ni+ˌfi+er** *n.* —**'mag+ni+ˌfi+a·ble** *adj.*

mag+ni+fy+ing glass *or* **mag+ni+fi+er** *n.* a convex lens used to produce an enlarged image of an object.

mag+nil·o+quent (mæg'nɪləkwənt) *adj.* (of speech) lofty in style; grandiloquent. [C17: from Latin *magnus* great + *loquī* to speak] —**mag+'nil·o+quence** *n.* —**mag+'nil·o+quent+ly** *adv.*

Mag+ni+to+gorsk (*Russian* məgnita'gɔrsk) *n.* a city in the central Soviet Union, on the Ural River: founded in 1930 to exploit local magnetite ores; site of one of the world's largest metallurgical plants. Pop.: 388 000 (1975 est.).

mag+ni+tude ('mægnɪˌtju:d) *n.* **1.** relative importance or significance: *a problem of the first magnitude.* **2.** relative size or extent: *the magnitude of the explosion.* **3.** *Maths.* a number assigned to a quantity, such as weight, and used as a basis of comparison for the measurement of similar quantities. **4.** Also called: **apparent magnitude.** *Astronomy.* the apparent brightness of a celestial body expressed on a numerical scale on which bright stars have a low value. Values range from –27 (the sun) to +23 measured either by eye (**visual magnitude**) or by photographic methods (**photographic magnitude**). Each integral value represents a brightness 2.512 times greater than the next highest integral value. See also **absolute magnitude.** [C14: from Latin *magnitūdō* size, from *magnus* great] —**ˌmag+ni+'tu+di+nous** *adj.*

mag+no+li·a (mæg'nəʊlɪə) *n.* **1.** any tree or shrub of the magnoliaceous genus *Magnolia* of Asia and North America: cultivated for their white, pink, purple, or yellow showy flowers. **2.** the flower of any of these plants. **3. a.** a very pale pinkish-white or purplish-white colour. [C18: New Latin, named after Pierre *Magnol* (1638–1715), French botanist]

mag+no+li·a+ceous (mægˌnəʊlɪ'eɪʃəs) *adj.* of, relating to, or belonging to the *Magnoliaceae,* a family of trees and shrubs, including magnolias and the tulip tree, having large showy flowers.

mag+num ('mægnəm) *n., pl.* **+nums.** a wine bottle holding the equivalent of two normal bottles (approximately 52 fluid ounces). [C18: from Latin: a big thing, from *magnus* large]

mag+num o·pus *n.* a great work of art or literature, esp. the greatest single work of an artist. [Latin]

mag+nus hitch ('mægnəs) *n.* a knot similar to a clove hitch but having one more turn. [C19: *magnus,* of unknown origin]

Ma·gog ('meɪgɒg) *n.* See **Gog and Magog.**

ma+got (mɑ:'gəʊ, 'mægət) *n.* **1.** a Chinese or Japanese figurine in a crouching position, usually grotesque. **2.** a less common name for **Barbary ape.** [C17: from French: grotesque figure, after the Biblical giant MAGOG]

mag+pie ('mægˌpaɪ) *n.* **1.** any of various passerine birds of the genus *Pica,* esp. *P. pica,* having a black-and-white plumage, long tail, and a chattering call: family *Corvidae* (crows, etc.). **2.** any of various similar birds of the Australian family *Cracticidae.* See also **butcherbird** (sense 2). **3.** any of various other similar or related birds. **4.** (*often cap.*) a variety of domestic fancy pigeon typically having black-and-white markings. **5.** *Brit.* a person who hoards small objects. **6.** a person who chatters. **7. a.** the outmost ring but one on a target. **b.** a shot that hits this ring. [C17: from *Mag* diminutive of *Margaret,* used to signify a chatterbox + PIE[2]]

M.Agr. *abbrev. for* Master of Agriculture.

Ma·gritte (*French* ma'grit) *n.* **Re·né** (rə'ne). 1898–1967, Belgian surrealist painter. By juxtaposing incongruous objects, depicted with meticulous realism, his works create a bizarre and disturbing impression.

mag tape (mæg) *n. Informal.* short for **magnetic tape.**

mag+uey ('mægweɪ) *n.* **1.** any of various tropical American agave plants of the genera *Agave* or *Furcraea,* esp. one that yields a fibre or is used in making an alcoholic beverage. **2.** the fibre from any of these plants, used esp. for rope. [C16: Spanish, from Taino]

ma+gus ('meɪgəs) *n., pl.* **+gi** (-dʒaɪ). **1.** a Zoroastrian priest. **2.** an astrologer, sorcerer, or magician of ancient times. [C14: from Latin, from Greek *magos,* from Old Persian *magus* magician]

Ma·gus ('meɪgəs) *n.* **Si·mon.** *New Testament.* a sorcerer, who tried to buy spiritual powers from the apostles (Acts 8:9-24).

Mag+yar ('mægjɑ:) *n.* **1.** (*pl.* **+yars**) a member of the predominant ethnic group of Hungary, also found in NW Siberia. **2.** the Hungarian language. ~*adj.* **3.** of or relating to the Magyars or their language. **4.** *Sewing.* of or relating to a style of sleeve cut in one piece with the bodice.

Ma+gyar+or+szág ('mɔdjɔrˌorsa:g) *n.* the Hungarian name for **Hungary.**

Ma+ha+bha+ra+ta (məˌhɑ:'bɑ:rətə), **Ma+ha+bha+ra+tam,** *or* **Ma+ha+bha+ra+tum** (məˌhɑ:'bɑ:rətəm) *n.* an epic Sanskrit poem of India, dealing chiefly with the struggle between two rival families. It contains many separate episodes, the most notable of which is the *Bhagavad-Gita.* [Sanskrit, from *mahā* great + *bhārata* story]

Ma+hal+la el Ku+bra (mə'hɑ:lə ɛl 'ku:brə) *n.* a city in N Egypt, on the Nile delta: one of the largest diversified textile centres in Egypt. Pop.: 287 800 (1974 est.).

Ma+ha+na+di (mə'hɑ:nədɪ) *n.* a river in E India, rising in S Madhya Pradesh and flowing north, then south and east to the Bay of Bengal. Length: 885 km (550 miles).

ma+ha+ra+jah *or* **ma+ha+ra+ja** (ˌmɑ:hə'rɑ:dʒə) *n.* any of various Indian princes, esp. any of the rulers of the former native states. [C17: Hindi, from *mahā* great + RAJAH]

ma+ha+ra+ni *or* **ma+ha+ra+nee** (ˌmɑ:hə'rɑ:ni:) *n.* **1.** the wife of a maharajah. **2.** a woman holding the rank of maharajah. [C19: from Hindi, from *mahā* great + RANI]

Ma+ha+rash+tra (ˌmɑ:hɑ:'ræʃtrə) *n.* a state of W central India, formed in 1960 from the Marathi-speaking S and E parts of former Bombay state: lies mainly on the Deccan plateau; mainly agricultural. Capital: Bombay. Pop.: 50 412 235 (1971). Area: 306 345 sq. km (119 475 sq. miles).

ma+ha+ri+shi (ˌmɑ:hɑ:'ri:ʃɪ, mə'hɑ:ri:ʃɪ) *n. Hinduism.* a Hindu teacher of religious and mystical knowledge. [from Hindi, from *mahā* great + RISHI]

ma+hat+ma (mə'hɑ:tmə, -'hæt-) *n.* (*sometimes cap.*) **1.** *Hinduism.* a Brahman sage. **2.** *Theosophy.* an adept or sage. [C19: from Sanskrit *mahātman,* from *mahā* great + *ātman* soul] —**ma+'hat+ma+ism** *n.*

Ma+ha+ya+na (ˌmɑ:hə'jɑ:nə) *n.* **a.** a liberal Buddhist school of Tibet, China and Japan, whose adherents aim to disseminate Buddhist doctrines, seeking enlightenment not for themselves alone, but for all sentient beings. **b.** (*as modifier*): *Mahayana Buddhism.* [from Sanskrit, from *mahā* great + *yāna* vehicle] —**ˌMa+ha+'ya+nist** *n.*

Mah+di ('mɑ:dɪ) *n.* **1.** the title assumed by *Mohammed Ahmed,* ?1843–85, Sudanese military leader, who led a revolt against Egypt (1881) and captured Khartoum (1885). **2.** *Islam.* any of a number of Muslim messiahs expected to forcibly convert all mankind to Islam. [Arabic *mahdīy* one who is guided, from *madā* to guide aright] —**'Mah+dism** *n.* —**'Mah+dist** *n., adj.*

Ma·hé (mɑ:'heɪ) *n.* an island in the Indian Ocean, the chief island of the Seychelles. Capital: Victoria. Pop.: 31 684 (1971). Area: 147 sq. km (57 sq. miles).

ma+he+wu (ma'hewʊ, -'xe-) *n.* (in South Africa) fermented liquid mealie-meal porridge, used as a stimulant by Black Africans. [from Xhosa *amarewu*]

Ma+hi+can (mə'hi:kən) *or* **Mo+hi+can** ('məʊɪkən, məʊ'hi:kən) *n.* **1.** (*pl.* **+cans** *or* **+can**) a member of a North American Indian people formerly living along the Hudson river and east of it. **2.** the language of this people, belonging to the Algonquian family.

mah+jong *or* **mah-jongg** (ˌmɑ:'dʒɒŋ) *n.* a game of Chinese origin, usually played by four people, in which tiles bearing various designs are drawn and discarded until one player has an entire hand of winning combinations. [from Chinese, literally: sparrows]

Mah+ler ('mɑ:lə) *n.* **Gus·tav** ('gʊstaf). 1860–1911, Austrian composer and conductor, whose music links the romantic tradition of the 19th century with the music of the 20th century. His works include nine complete symphonies for large orchestras, the symphonic song cycle *Das Lied von der Erde* (1908), and the song cycle *Kindertotenlieder* (1902).

mahl+stick ('mɔ:lˌstɪk) *n.* a variant spelling of **maulstick.**

ma+hog·a+ny (mə'hɒgənɪ) *n., pl.* **+nies. 1.** any of various tropical American trees of the meliaceous genus *Swietenia,* esp. *S. mahagoni* and *S. macrophylla,* valued for their hard reddish-brown wood. **2.** any of several trees with similar wood, such as African mahogany and Philippine mahogany. **3. a.** the wood of any of these trees. See also **acajou** (sense 1). **b.** (*as modifier*): *a mahogany table.* **4.** a reddish-brown colour. [C17: origin obscure]

Ma·hom·et (mə'hɒmɪt) *n.* a variant of **Mohammed.**

Ma+hom·e·tan (mə'hɒmɪtᵊn) *n., adj.* a former word for **Muslim.** —**Ma+'hom+e·tan+ism** *n.*

ma+ho+ni·a (mə'həʊnɪə) *n.* any evergreen berberidaceous shrub of the Asian and American genus *Mahonia,* esp. *M. aquifolium:* cultivated for their ornamental spiny divided leaves and clusters of small yellow flowers. [C19: New Latin, named after Bernard *McMahon* (died 1816), American botanist]

Ma+hound (mə'haʊnd, -'hu:nd) *n.* an archaic name for **Mohammed.** [C16: from Old French *Mahun*]

ma+hout (mə'haʊt) *n.* (in India and the East Indies) an elephant driver or keeper. [C17: Hindi *mahāut,* from Sanskrit *mahāmātra* of great measure, originally a title]

Mah+rat+ta (mə'rɑ:tə) *n.* a variant spelling of **Maratha.** —**Mah+'rat+ti** *n., adj.*

Mäh+ren ('mɛ:rən) *n.* the German name for **Moravia.**

mah+seer ('mɑ:sɪə) *n.* any of various large freshwater Indian cyprinid fishes, such as *Barbus tor.* [from Hindi]

mah+zor *or* **mach+zor** *Hebrew.* (max'zɔr; *English* mɑ:k'zɔ:) *n., pl.* **+zo+rim** (-zɔ'ri:m; *English* -zə'ri:m). a Jewish prayer book containing prescribed holiday rituals. [literally: cycle]

Ma·ia ('maɪə) *n. Greek myth.* the eldest of the seven Pleiades, mother by Zeus of Hermes.

maid (meɪd) *n.* **1.** *Archaic or literary.* a young unmarried girl; maiden. **2. a.** a female servant. **b.** (*in combination*): *a housemaid.* **3.** a spinster. [C12: shortened form of MAIDEN] —**'maid+ish** *adj.* —**'maid+ish+ness** *n.*

mai+dan (mæ'dɑ:n) *n.* (in Pakistan, India, etc.) an open space used for meetings, sports, etc. [Urdu, from Arabic]

maid+en ('meɪdᵊn) *n.* **1.** *Archaic or literary.* **a.** a young unmarried girl, esp. when a virgin. **b.** (*as modifier*): *a maiden blush.* **2.** *Horse racing.* **a.** a horse that has never won a race. **b.** (*as modifier*): *a maiden race.* **3.** *Cricket.* See **maiden over. 4.** Also called: **clothes maiden.** *Northern English dialect.* a frame on which clothes are hung to dry; clothes horse. **5.** (*modifier*) of or relating to an older unmarried woman: *a maiden aunt.* **6.** (*modifier*) of or involving an initial experience or attempt: *a maiden voyage; maiden speech.* **7.** (*modifier*) (of a person or thing) untried; unused. **8.** (*modifier*) (of a place) never trodden, penetrated, or captured. [Old English *mægden;* related to Old High German *magad,* Old Norse *mogr* young man, Old Irish *mug* slave] —**'maid·en·ish** *adj.* —**'maid·en·,like** *adj.* —**'maid·en·,ship** *n.*

maid·en·hair fern *or* **maid·en·hair** ('meɪdᵊn,hɛə) *n.* any fern of the genus *Adiantum,* esp. *A. capillis-veneris,* of tropical and warm regions, having delicate fan-shaped fronds with small pale-green leaflets: family *Polypodiaceae.*

maid·en·hair tree *n.* another name for **ginkgo.**

maid·en·head ('meɪdᵊn,hɛd) *n.* **1.** a nontechnical word for the **hymen.** **2.** virginity; maidenhood. [C13: from *maiden* + *-hed,* variant of -HOOD]

Maid·en·head ('meɪdᵊn,hɛd) *n.* a town in S England, in Berkshire on the River Thames. Pop.: 45 306 (1971).

maid·en·hood ('meɪdᵊn,hʊd) *n.* **1.** the time during which a woman is a maiden or a virgin. **2.** the condition of being a maiden or virgin.

maid·en·ly ('meɪdᵊnlɪ) *adj.* of or befitting a maiden. —**'maid·en·li·ness** *n.*

maid·en name *n.* a woman's surname before marriage.

maid·en o·ver *n. Cricket.* an over in which no runs are scored.

maid·en voy·age *n. Nautical.* the first voyage of a vessel.

Maid Mar·i·an *n.* **1.** a character in morris dancing, played by a man dressed as a woman. **2.** *Legend.* the sweetheart of Robin Hood.

maid of hon·our *n.* **1.** *U.S.* the principal unmarried attendant of a bride. Compare **bridesmaid, matron of honour.** **2.** *Brit.* a small tart with an almond-flavoured filling. **3.** an unmarried lady attending a queen or princess.

Maid of Or·lé·ans *n.* **the.** another name for **Joan of Arc.**

maid·ser·vant ('meɪd,sɜːvənt) *n.* a female servant.

Maid·stone ('meɪdstən, -,stəʊn) *n.* a town in SE England, administrative centre of Kent, on the River Medway. Pop.: 70 918 (1971).

Mai·du·gu·ri (,maɪdʊ'guːrɪ) *n.* a city in NE Nigeria, capital of Bornu State; agricultural trade centre. Pop. (with Yerwa) 189 000 (1975 est.). Also called: **Yerwa-Maiduguri.**

ma·ieu·tic (meɪ'juːtɪk) *or* **ma·ieu·ti·cal** *adj. Philosophy.* of or relating to the Socratic method of eliciting knowledge by a series of questions and answers. [C17: from Greek *maieutikos* relating to midwifery (used figuratively by Socrates), from *maia* midwife]

mai·gre ('meɪgə) *adj. R.C. Church.* **1.** not containing flesh, and so permissible as food on days of religious abstinence: *maigre food.* **2.** of or designating such a day. [C17: from French: thin; see MEAGRE]

mai·hem ('meɪhɛm) *n.* a variant spelling of **mayhem.**

Mai·kop (*Russian* maj'kɔp) *n.* a city in the SW Soviet Union, capital of the Adygei AR: extensive oilfields to the southwest; mineral springs. Pop.: 125 000 (1975 est.).

mail¹ (meɪl) *n.* **1.** Also called (esp. Brit.): **post.** letters, packages, etc., that are transported and delivered by the post office. **2.** the postal system. **3.** a single collection or delivery of mail. **4.** a train, ship, or aircraft that carries mail. **5.** (*modifier*) of, involving, or used to convey mail: *a mail train.* ~*vb.* **6.** (*tr.*) *Chiefly U.S.* to send by mail. Usual Brit. word: **post.** [C13: from Old French *male* bag, probably from Old High German *malha* wallet] —**'mail·a·ble** *adj.*

mail² (meɪl) *n.* **1.** a type of flexible armour consisting of riveted metal rings or links. **2.** the hard protective shell of such animals as the turtle and lobster. ~*vb.* **3.** (*tr.*) to clothe or arm with mail: *a mailed glove.* [C14: from Old French *maille* mesh, from Latin *macula* spot] —**'mail·less** *adj.*

mail³ (meɪl) *n. Archaic, chiefly Scot.* a monetary payment, esp. of rent or taxes. [Old English *māl* terms, from Old Norse *māl* agreement]

mail·bag ('meɪl,bæg), **mail·sack,** *or U.S.* (*sometimes*) **mail·pouch** *n.* a large bag used for transporting or delivering mail.

mail·box ('meɪl,bɒks) *n.* another name (esp. U.S.) for **letter box.**

mail·coach ('meɪl,kəʊtʃ) *or U.S.* **mail·car** *n.* a railway coach specially constructed for the transportation of mail.

mail drop *n. Chiefly U.S.* a receptacle or chute for mail.

mail·er ('meɪlə) *n.* **1.** a person who addresses or mails letters, etc. **2.** *U.S.* a machine used for stamping and addressing mail.

Mai·ler ('meɪlə) *n.* **Nor·man.** born 1923, U.S. author. His works, which are frequently critical of modern American society, include the war novel *The Naked and the Dead* (1948), *The American Dream* (1965), and his account of the 1967 peace march on Washington *The Armies of the Night* (1968).

mail·ing list *n.* a register of names and addresses to which advertising matter, etc., is sent by post.

Mail·lol (*French* ma'jɔl) *n.* **A·ris·tide** (aris'tid). 1861–1944, French sculptor, esp. of monumental female nudes.

mail·lot (mæ'jəʊ) *n.* **1.** tights worn for ballet, etc. **2.** a woman's swimsuit. **3.** a jersey. [from French]

mail·man ('meɪl,mæn) *n., pl.* **·men.** *Chiefly U.S.* another name for **postman.**

mail or·der *n.* **1.** an order for merchandise sent by post. **2. a.** a system of buying and selling merchandise through the post. **b.** (*as modifier*): *a mail-order firm.*

mail·sack ('meɪl,sæk) *n.* another name for a **mailbag.**

maim (meɪm) *vb.* (*tr.*) **1.** to mutilate, cripple, or disable a part of the body of (a person or animal). **2.** to make defective. ~*n.* **3.** *Obsolete.* an injury or defect. [C14: from Old French *mahaignier* to wound, probably of Germanic origin] —**maim·ed·ness** ('meɪmɪdnɪs) *n.* —**'maim·er** *n.*

Mai·mon·i·des (maɪ'mɒnɪ,diːz) *n.* also called Rabbi *Moses ben Maimon.* 1135–1204, Jewish philosopher, physician, and jurist, born in Spain. He codified Jewish law in *Mishneh Torah* (1180). —**Mai·,mon·i·'de·an** *adj., n.*

main¹ (meɪn) *adj.* (*prenominal*) **1.** chief or principal in rank, importance, size, etc. **2.** sheer or utmost (esp. in the phrase **by main force**). **3.** *Nautical.* of, relating to, or denoting any gear, such as a stay or sail, belonging to the mainmast. **4.** *Obsolete.* significant or important. ~*n.* **5.** a principal pipe, conduit, duct, or line in a system used to distribute water, electricity, etc. **6.** (*pl.*) **a.** the main distribution network for water, gas, or electricity. **b.** (*as modifier*): *mains voltage.* **7.** the chief or most important part or consideration. **8.** great strength or force (now chiefly in the phrase **might and main**). **9.** *Literary.* the open ocean. **10.** *Archaic.* short for **Spanish Main.** **11.** *Archaic.* short for **mainland.** **12. in** (*or* **for**) **the main.** on the whole; for the most part. [C13: from Old English *mægen* strength]

main² (meɪn) *n.* **1.** a throw of the dice in dice games. **2.** a cockfighting contest. **3.** a match in archery, boxing, etc. [C16: of unknown origin]

Main (meɪn; *German* maɪn) *n.* a river in central and W West Germany, flowing west through Würzburg and Frankfurt to the Rhine. Length: about 515 km (320 miles).

main·brace ('meɪn,breɪs) *n. Nautical.* a brace attached to the main yard.

main clause *n. Grammar.* a clause that can stand alone as a sentence. Compare **subordinate clause.**

main course *n.* **1.** the principal dish of a meal. **2.** *Nautical.* a square mainsail.

main deck *n.* the uppermost sheltered deck that runs the entire length of a vessel.

Maine (meɪn) *n.* a state of the northeastern U.S., on the Atlantic: chiefly hilly, with many lakes, rivers, and forests. Capital: Augusta. Pop.: 993 663 (1970). Area: 80 082 sq. km (30 920 sq. miles). Abbrev. (with zip code): **ME**

Maine-et-Loire (*French* mɛn e 'lwaːr) *n.* a department of W France, in Pays de la Loire region. Capital: Angers. Pop.: 644 458 (1975). Area: 7218 sq. km (2815 sq. miles).

main-frame com·put·er *n.* a high-speed general-purpose computer, usually with a large store capacity, with the main storage structured in 32- or 64-bit words.

main·land ('meɪnlənd) *n.* the main part of a land mass as opposed to an island or peninsula. —**'main·land·er** *n.*

Main·land ('meɪnlənd) *n.* **1.** an island off N Scotland: the largest of the Shetland Islands. Chief town: Lerwick. Pop.: 13 150 (1971). Area: about 583 sq. km (225 sq. miles). **2.** Also called: **Pomona.** an island off N Scotland: the largest of the Orkney Islands. Chief town: Kirkwall. Pop.: 6502 (1971). Area: 492 sq. km (190 sq. miles).

main line *n.* **1.** *Railways.* **a.** the trunk route between two points, usually fed by branch lines. **b.** (*as modifier*): *a main-line station.* **2.** *U.S.* a main road. **3.** *Slang.* a main vein, into which a narcotic drug, esp. heroin, can be injected. ~*vb.* **main·line.** **4.** (*intr.*) *Slang.* to inject a drug thus. ~*adj.* **main·line.** **5.** having an important or moderate position; principal. —**'main·,lin·er** *n.*

main·ly ('meɪnlɪ) *adv.* **1.** for the most part; to the greatest extent; principally. **2.** *Obsolete.* strongly; very much.

main·mast ('meɪn,mɑːst) *n. Nautical.* the chief mast of a sailing vessel with two or more masts, being the foremast of a yawl, ketch, or dandy and the second mast from the bow of most others.

main plane *n.* **a.** one of the principal supporting surfaces of an aircraft, esp. either of the wings. **b.** both wings considered together.

main·sail ('meɪn,seɪl; *Nautical* 'meɪnsᵊl) *n. Nautical.* the largest and lowermost sail on the mainmast.

main se·quence *n. Astronomy.* **a.** a stellar grouping consisting of the vast majority of stars of population I, graphically represented on the Hertzsprung-Russell diagram as a diagonal band. **b.** (*as modifier*): *a main-sequence star.*

main·sheet ('meɪn,ʃiːt) *n. Nautical.* the line used to control the angle of the mainsail to the wind.

main·spring ('meɪn,sprɪŋ) *n.* **1.** the principal spring of a mechanism, esp. in a watch or clock. **2.** the chief cause or motive of something.

main·stay ('meɪn,steɪ) *n.* **1.** *Nautical.* the forestay that braces the mainmast. **2.** a chief support of something.

main store *n. Computer technol.* another name for **memory** (sense 7).

main·stream ('meɪn,striːm) *n.* **1. a.** the main current (of a river, cultural trend, etc.): *in the mainstream of modern literature.* **b.** (*as modifier*): *mainstream politics.* ~*adj.* **2.** of or relating to the style of jazz that lies between the traditional and the modern.

main·tain (meɪn'teɪn) *vb.* (*tr.*) **1.** to continue or retain; keep in existence. **2.** to keep in proper or good condition: *to maintain a building.* **3.** to support a style of living: *the money maintained us for a month.* **4.** (*takes a clause as object*) to state or assert: *he maintained that Talbot was wrong.* **5.** to defend against contradiction; uphold: *she maintained her innocence.* **6.** to defend against physical attack. [C13: from Old French *maintenir,* ultimately from Latin *manū tenēre* to hold in the hand] —**main·'tain·a·ble** *adj.* —**main·'tain·er** *n.*

main·tained school *n.* a school financially supported by the state.

main·te·nance ('meɪntɪnəns) *n.* **1.** the act of maintaining or the state of being maintained. **2.** a means of support; livelihood. **3.** (*modifier*) of or relating to the maintaining of buildings, machinery, etc.: *maintenance man.* **4.** *Law.* the interference in a legal action by a person having no interest in it, as by providing funds to continue the action. See also **champerty.** **5.** *Law.* a provision ordered to be made by way of periodical payments or a lump sum, as after a divorce for a spouse. [C14: from Old French; see MAINTAIN]

Mainte·non (*French* mɛ̃t'nɔ̃) *n.* **Mar·quise de,** title of *Françoise d'Aubigné.* 1635–1719, the mistress and, from about 1685, second wife of Louis XIV.

main·top ('meɪn,tɒp) *n.* a top or platform at the head of the mainmast.

main-top·mast *n. Nautical.* the mast immediately above the mainmast.

main·top·sail (,meɪn'tɒpseɪl; *Nautical* ,meɪn'tɒpsəl) *n. Nautical.* a topsail set on the mainmast.

main yard *n. Nautical.* a yard for a square mainsail.

Mainz (*German* maɪnts) *n.* a port in W West Germany, capital of the Rhineland-Palatinate, at the confluence of the Main and Rhine: an archbishopric from about 780 until 1801; important in the 15th century for the development of printing (by Johann Gutenberg). Pop.: 183 363 (1974 est.). French name: **Mayence.**

ma·iol·i·ca (mə'jɒlɪkə) *n.* a variant spelling of **majolica.**

mai·son·ette *or* **mai·son·nette** (,meɪzə'nɛt) *n.* self-contained living accommodation often occupying two floors of a larger house and having its own outside entrance. [C19: from French, diminutive of *maison* house]

Mait·land[1] ('meɪtlənd) *n.* a town in SE Australia, in E New South Wales: industrial centre of an agricultural region. Pop.: 33 200 (1975).

Mait·land[2] ('meɪtlənd) *n.* **Fred·er·ic Wil·liam.** 1850–1906, English legal historian.

maî·tre d'hô·tel (,mɛtrə dəʊ'tɛl; *French* mɛtr do'tɛl) *n., pl.* **maî·tres d'hô·tel.** **1.** a head waiter or steward. **2.** the manager or owner of a hotel. [C16: from French: master of (the) hotel]

maî·tre d'hô·tel but·ter *n.* melted butter mixed with parsley and lemon juice.

maize (meɪz) *n.* **1.** Also called: **Indian corn. a.** a tall annual grass, *Zea mays,* cultivated for its yellow edible grains, which develop on a spike. **b.** the grain of this plant, used for food, fodder, and as a source of oil. Usual U.S. name: **corn.** See also **sweet corn. 2.** a yellow colour. [C16: from Spanish *maíz,* from Taino *mahiz*]

Maj. *abbrev. for* Major.

ma·jes·tic (mə'dʒɛstɪk) *or* **ma·jes·ti·cal** *adj.* having or displaying majesty or great dignity; grand; lofty. —**ma·'jes·ti·cal·ly** *adv.*

maj·es·ty ('mædʒɪstɪ) *n.* **1.** great dignity or bearing; loftiness; grandeur. **2.** supreme power or authority. **3.** an archaic word for **royalty.** [C13: from Old French, from Latin *mājestās;* related to Latin *major,* comparative of *magnus* great]

Maj·es·ty ('mædʒɪstɪ) *n., pl.* **·ties.** (preceded by *Your, His, Her,* or *Their*) a title used to address or refer to a sovereign or the wife or widow of a sovereign.

Maj. Gen. *abbrev. for* Major General.

Maj·lis ('mædʒlɪs) *n.* **1.** the parliament of Iran. **2.** (in various N African and Middle Eastern countries) an assembly; council. [from Persian: assembly]

ma·jol·i·ca (mə'dʒɒlɪkə, mə'jɒl-) *or* **ma·iol·i·ca** *n.* a type of porous pottery glazed with bright metallic oxides that originated in Majorca and was extensively made in Italy during the Renaissance. [C16: from Italian, from Late Latin *mājorica* Majorca]

ma·jor ('meɪdʒə) *n.* **1.** *Military.* an officer immediately junior to a lieutenant colonel. **2.** a person who is superior in a group or class. **3.** (often preceded by *the*) *Music.* a major key, chord, mode, or scale. **4.** *U.S., Austral.* **a.** the principal field of study of a student at a university, etc.: *his major is sociology.* **b.** a student who is studying a particular subject as his principal field: *a sociology major.* **5.** a person who has reached the age of legal majority. **6.** *Logic.* a major term or premiss. ~*adj.* **7.** larger in extent, number, etc.: *the major part.* **8.** of greater importance or priority. **9.** very serious or significant: *a major disaster.* **10.** of, involving, or making up a majority. **11.** *Music.* **a.** (of a scale or mode) having notes separated by the interval of a whole tone, except for the third and fourth degrees, and seventh and eighth degrees, which are separated by a semitone. **b.** relating to or employing notes from the major scale: *a major key.* **c.** (*postpositive*) denoting a specified key or scale as being major: *C major.* **d.** denoting a chord or triad having a major third above the root. **e.** (in jazz) denoting a major chord with a major seventh added above the root. **12.** *Logic.* (of a term or premiss) having greater generality or scope than another term or proposition. **13.** *Chiefly U.S. and Austral.* of or relating to a student's principal field of study at a university, etc. **14.** *Brit.* the elder: used after a schoolboy's surname if he has one or more younger brothers in the same school: *Price major.* **15.** of full legal age. **16.** (*postpositive*) *Change-ringing.* of, relating to, or denoting a method rung on eight bells. ~*vb.* **17.** (*intr.;* usually foll. by *in*) *U.S., Austral.* to do one's principal study (in a particular subject): *to major in English literature.* [C15 (adj.): from Latin, comparative of *magnus* great; C17 (n., in military sense): from French, short for SERGEANT MAJOR] —**'ma·jor·ship** *n.*

ma·jor ax·is *n.* the longer or longest axis of an ellipse or ellipsoid.

Ma·jor·ca (mə'dʒɔːkə, -'jɔː-) *n.* an island in the W Mediterranean: the largest of the Balearic Islands; tourism. Capital: Palma. Pop.: 438 656 (1970). Area: 3639 sq. km (1465 sq. miles). Spanish name: **Mallorca.**

ma·jor-do·mo (,meɪdʒə'dəʊməʊ) *n., pl.* **·mos. 1.** the chief steward or butler of a great household. **2.** *Facetious.* a steward or butler. [C16: from Spanish *mayordomo,* from Medieval Latin *mājor domūs* head of the household]

ma·jor·ette (,meɪdʒə'rɛt) *n.* See **drum majorette.**

ma·jor gen·er·al *n. Military.* an officer immediately junior to a lieutenant general. —**'ma·jor-'gen·er·al·,ship** *or* **'ma·jor-'gen·er·al·cy** *n.*

ma·jor·i·ty (mə'dʒɒrɪtɪ) *n., pl.* **·ties. 1.** the greater number or part of something: *the majority of the constituents.* **2.** (in an election) the number of votes or seats by which the strongest party or candidate beats the combined opposition or the runner-up. See **relative majority, absolute majority. 3.** the largest party or group that votes together in a legislative or deliberative assembly. **4.** the time of reaching or state of having reached full legal age, when a person is held competent to manage his own affairs, exercise civil rights and duties, etc. **5.** the rank, office, or commission of major. **6.** *Euphemistic.* the dead (esp. in the phrases **join the majority, go** *or* **pass over to the majority**). **7.** *Obsolete.* the quality or state of being greater; superiority. **8.** (*modifier*) of, involving, or being a majority: *a majority decision; a majority verdict.* **9. in the majority.** forming or part of the greater number of something. [C16: from Medieval Latin *mājoritās,* from MAJOR (adj.)]

ma·jor·i·ty car·ri·er *n.* the entity responsible for carrying the greater part of the current in a semiconductor. In n-type semiconductors the majority carriers are electrons; in p-type semiconductors they are positively charged holes. Compare **minority carrier.**

ma·jor league *n. U.S.* a league of highest classification in baseball, football, hockey, etc.

Ma·jor Mitch·ell *n.* an Australian cockatoo, *Kakatoe leadbeateri,* with a white-and-pink plumage. [C19: named after *Major* (later Sir) Thomas *Mitchell* (died 1855), Australian explorer]

ma·jor or·ders *pl. n. R.C. Church.* the three higher degrees of holy orders: bishop, priest, and deacon.

ma·jor plan·et *n.* a planet of the solar system, as opposed to an asteroid (minor planet).

ma·jor prem·iss *n. Logic.* the premiss of a syllogism containing the predicate of its conclusion.

ma·jor sev·enth chord *n.* a chord much used in modern music, esp. jazz and pop, consisting of a major triad with an added major seventh above the root. Compare **minor seventh chord.** Often shortened to **major seventh.**

ma·jor suit *n. Bridge.* hearts or spades. Compare **minor suit.**

ma·jor term *n. Logic.* the predicate of the conclusion of a syllogism, also occurring as the subject or predicate in the major premiss.

Ma·jun·ga (*French* maʒœ̃'ga) *n.* a port in NW Madagascar, on Bombetoka Bay. Pop.: 43 500 (1970 est.).

ma·jus·cule ('mædʒə,skjuːl) *n.* **1.** a large letter, either capital or uncial, used in printing or writing. ~*adj.* **2.** relating to, printed, or written in such letters. Compare **minuscule.** [C18: via French from Latin *mājusculus,* diminutive of *mājor* bigger, MAJOR] —**ma·jus·cu·lar** (mə'dʒʌskjʊlə) *adj.*

Ma·ka·lu ('mʌkə,luː) *n.* a massif in NE Nepal, on the border with Tibet in the Himalayas.

Ma·kar·i·os III (mə'kɑːrɪ,ɒs) *n.* original name *Mikhail Christodoulou Mouskos.* 1913–77, Cypriot archbishop, patriarch, and statesman; first president of the republic of Cyprus (1960–74; 1974–77).

Ma·kas·ar, Ma·kas·sar, *or* **Ma·cas·sar** (mə'kæsə, -'kɑː-) *n.* a port in central Indonesia, on SW Sulawesi: an important native port before Portuguese (16th century) and Dutch (17th century) control; capital of Dutch East Indonesia (1946–49); a major Indonesian distribution and transshipment port. Pop.: 434 766 (1971). Official name: **Ujung Pandang.**

make[1] (meɪk) *vb.* **makes, mak·ing, made.** (*mainly tr.*) **1.** to bring into being by shaping, changing, or combining materials, ideas, etc.; form or fashion; create: *to make a chair from bits of wood; make a poem.* **2.** to draw up, establish, or form: *to make a decision; make one's will.* **3.** to cause to exist, bring about, or produce: *don't make a noise.* **4.** to cause, compel, or induce: *please make him go away.* **5.** to appoint or assign, as to a rank or position: *they made him chairman.* **6.** to constitute: *one swallow doesn't make a summer.* **7.** (*also intr.*) to come or cause to come into a specified state or condition: *to make merry; make someone happy.* **8.** (*copula*) to be or become through development: *he will make a good teacher.* **9.** to cause or ensure the success of: *your news has made my day.* **10.** to amount to: *twelve inches make a foot.* **11.** to serve as or be suitable for: *that piece of cloth will make a coat.* **12.** to prepare or put into a fit condition for use: *to make a bed.* **13.** to be the essential element in or part of: *charm makes a good salesman.* **14.** to carry out, effect, or do: *to make a gesture.* **15.** (*intr.;* foll. by *to, as if to,* or *as though to*) to act with the intention or with a show of doing something: *they made to go out; he made as if to hit her.* **16.** to use for a specified purpose: *I will make this town my base.* **17.** to deliver or pronounce: *to make a speech.* **18.** to judge, reckon, or give one's own opinion or information as to: *what time do you make it?* **19.** to cause to seem or represent as being: *that furniture makes the room look dark.* **20.** to earn, acquire, or win for oneself: *to make friends; make a fortune.* **21.** to engage in: *make love not war.* **22.** to traverse or cover (distance) by travelling: *we can make a hundred miles by nightfall.* **23.** to arrive in time for: *he didn't* *make the first act of the play.* **24.** *Cards.* **a.** to win a trick with (a specified card). **b.** to shuffle (the cards). **c.** *Bridge.* to fulfil (a contract) by winning the necessary number of tricks. **25.** *Cricket.* to score (runs). **26.** *Electronics.* to close (a circuit) permitting a flow of current. Compare **break** (sense 43). **27.** (*intr.*) to increase in depth: *the water in the hold was making a foot a minute.* **28.** (*intr.*) (of hay) to dry and mature. **29.** *Informal.* to gain a place or position on or in: *to make the headlines; make the first team.* **30.** *Informal, chiefly U.S.* to achieve the rank of. **31.** *Taboo slang.* to succeed in having sexual intercourse with (a girl). **32. make a book.** to take bets on a race or other contest. **33. make a day, etc., of it.** to cause an activity to last a day, etc. **34. make do.** See **do**[1] (sense 34). **35. make eyes at.** to flirt with or ogle. **36. make good. a.** to repair or provide restitution for: *he will make good the damage.* **b.** to be successful in (a plan, activity, etc.): *he made good his intention to marry.* **37. make heavy weather (of). a.** *Nautical.* to roll and pitch in heavy seas. **b.** *Informal.* to carry out with great difficulty or unnecessarily great effort. **38. make it. a.** *Informal.* to be successful in doing something. **b.** (foll. by *with*) *Taboo slang.* to have sexual intercourse. **c.** *Slang.* to inject a narcotic drug. **39. make like.** *Slang, chiefly U.S.* to imitate. **40. make love (to). a.** to have sexual intercourse (with). **b.** to engage in courtship (with). **41. make time.** See **time** (sense 45). **42. make water. a.** another term for **urinate. b.** (of a boat, hull, etc.) to let in water. ~*n.* **43.** brand, type, or style: *what make of car is that?* **44.** the manner or way in which something is made. **45.** disposition or character; make-up. **46.** the act or process of making. **47.** the amount or number made. **48.** *Bridge.* the contract to be played. **49.** *Cards.* a player's turn to shuffle. **50. on the make.** *Slang.* **a.** out for profit or conquest. **b.** in search of a sexual partner. ~See also **make away, make for, make of, make off, make out, make over, make-up, make with.** [Old English *macian;* related to Old Frisian *makia* to construct, Dutch *maken,* German *machen* to make] —**'mak·a·ble** *adj.*

make[2] (meɪk) *n. Archaic.* **1.** a peer or consort. **2.** a mate or spouse. [Old English *gemaca* mate; related to MATCH[1]] —**'make·less** *adj.*

make a·way *vb.* (*intr., adv.*) **1.** to depart in haste. **2. make away with. a.** to steal or abduct. **b.** to kill, destroy, or get rid of.

make be·lieve *vb.* **1.** to pretend or enact a fantasy: *the children made believe they were nurses and doctors.* ~*n.* **make-be·lieve. 2. a.** a fantasy, pretence, or unreality. **b.** (*as modifier*): *a make-believe world.* **3.** a person who pretends.

Mak·e·dho·ni·a (ˌmakɛðɔ'nia) *n.* transliteration of the Modern Greek name for **Macedonia** (sense 1).

make·fast ('meɪkˌfɑːst) *n.* a strong support to which a vessel is secured.

make for *vb.* (*intr., prep.*) **1.** to head towards, esp. in haste. **2.** to prepare to attack. **3.** to help to bring about: *your cooperation will make for the success of our project.*

make of *vb.* (*tr., prep.*) **1.** to interpret as the meaning of: *what do you make of this news?* **2.** to produce or construct from: *houses made of brick.* **3. make little, much, etc. of. a.** to gain little, much, etc., benefit from. **b.** to attribute little, much, etc., significance to.

make off *vb.* **1.** (*intr., adv.*) to go or run away in haste. **2. make off with.** to steal or abduct.

make out *vb.* (*adv.*) **1.** (*tr.*) to discern or perceive: *can you make out that house in the distance?* **2.** (*tr.*) to understand or comprehend: *I can't make out this letter.* **3.** (*tr.*) to write out: *he made out a cheque.* **4.** (*tr.*) to attempt to establish or prove: *he made out a case for her innocence; he made me out to be a liar.* **5.** (*intr.*) to pretend: *he made out that he could cook.* **6.** (*intr.*) to manage or fare: *how did you make out in the contest?* **7.** (*intr.;* often foll. by *with*) *Slang, chiefly U.S.* to engage in necking or petting: *Alan is making out with Jane.*

make o·ver *vb.* (*tr., adv.*) **1.** to transfer the title or possession of (property, etc.). **2.** to renovate or remodel: *she made over the dress to fit her sister.*

mak·er ('meɪkə) *n.* a person who executes a legal document, esp. one who signs a promissory note.

Mak·er ('meɪkə) *n.* **1.** a title given to **God** (as Creator). **2. (go to) meet one's Maker.** to die.

make-read·y *n. Printing.* the process of preparing the forme and the cylinder or platen packing to achieve the correct impression all over the forme.

make·shift ('meɪkˌʃɪft) *adj.* **1.** serving as a temporary or expedient means, esp. during an emergency. ~*n.* **2.** something serving in this capacity.

make-up *n.* **1.** cosmetics, such as powder, lipstick, etc., applied to the face to improve its appearance. **2. a.** the cosmetics, false hair, etc., used by an actor to highlight his features or adapt his appearance. **b.** the art or result of applying such cosmetics. **3.** the manner of arrangement of the parts or qualities of someone or something. **4.** the arrangement of type matter and illustrations on a page or in a book. **5.** mental or physical constitution. ~*vb.* **make up.** (*adv.*) **6.** (*tr.*) to form or constitute: *these arguments make up the case for the defence.* **7.** (*tr.*) to devise, construct, or compose, sometimes with the intent to deceive: *to make up a song; to make up an excuse.* **8.** (*tr.*) to supply what is lacking or deficient in; complete: *these extra people will make up our total.* **9.** (*tr.*) to put in order, arrange, or prepare: *to make up a bed.* **10.** (*intr.;* foll. by *for*) to compensate or atone (for): *his kindness now makes up for his rudeness yesterday.* **11.** to settle (differences) amicably (often in the phrase **make it up**). **12.** to apply cosmetics to (the face, etc.) to enhance one's appearance or so as to alter the appearance for a theatrical role. **13.** to assemble (type and illustrations) into (columns or pages). **14.** (*tr.*) to surface (a road) with tarmac, concrete, etc. **15.** (*tr.*) **a.** to set in order and balance (accounts). **b.** to draw up (accounting statements). **16. make up one's mind.** to make a decision (about something or to do something): *he made up his mind to take vengeance.* **17. make up to.** *Informal.* **a.** to make friendly overtures to. **b.** to flirt with.

make·weight ('meɪkˌweɪt) *n.* **1.** something put on a scale to make up a required weight. **2.** an unimportant person or thing added to make up a lack.

make with *vb.* (*intr., prep.*) *Slang, chiefly U.S.* to proceed with the doing, showing, etc., of: *make with the music.*

Ma·ke·yev·ka (*Russian* ma'kjejɪfkə) *n.* a city in the SW Soviet Union, in the SE Ukrainian SSR: coal-mining centre. Pop.: 398 000 (1975 est.).

Ma·khach·ka·la (*Russian* məxətʃka'la) *n.* a port in the S Soviet Union, capital of the Dagestan SSR, on the Caspian Sea: fishing fleet; oil refining. Pop.: 224 000 (1975 est.). Former name (until 1921): **Petrovsk.**

mak·ing ('meɪkɪŋ) *n.* **1. a.** the act of a person or thing that makes or the process of being made. **b.** (*in combination*): *watchmaking.* **2. be the making of.** to cause the success of. **3. in the making.** in the process of becoming or being made: *a politician in the making.* **4.** something made or the quantity of something made at one time. **5.** make-up; composition.

ma·kings ('meɪkɪŋz) *pl. n.* **1.** potentials, qualities, or materials: *he had the makings of a leader.* **2.** Also called: **rollings.** *U.S., Austral., and N.Z. slang.* the tobacco and cigarette paper used for rolling a cigarette. **3.** profits; earnings.

Mak·kah *or* **Mak·ah** ('mækə, -kɑː) *n.* transliteration of the Arabic name for **Mecca.**

ma·ko[1] ('mɑːkəʊ) *n., pl.* **·kos.** any shark of the genus *Isurus,* esp. *I. glauca* of Indo-Pacific and Australian seas: family *Isuridae.* [from Maori]

ma·ko[2] ('mɑːkəʊ) *n., pl.* **·kos.** a small evergreen New Zealand tree, *Aristotelia serrata:* family *Elaeocarpaceae.* [from Maori]

Ma·kur·di (mə'kɜːdɪ) *n.* a port in E central Nigeria, capital of Benue State on the Benue River: agricultural trade centre. Pop.: 67 000 (1973 est.).

ma·ku·ta (mɑː'kuːtɑː) *n.* the plural of **likuta.**

MAL *international car registration for* Malaysia.

Mal. *abbrev. for:* **1.** *Bible.* Malachi. **2.** Malay(an).

mal- *combining form.* bad or badly; wrong or wrongly; imperfect or defective: *maladjusted; malfunction.* [Old French, from Latin *malus* bad, *male* badly]

Mal·a·bar Coast *or* **Mal·a·bar** ('mæləˌbɑː) *n.* a region along the SW coast of India, extending from Goa to Cape Comorin: includes most of Kerala state.

Ma·la·bo (mə'lɑːbəʊ) *n.* the capital and chief port of Equatorial Guinea, on the Island of Macías Nguema Biyoga in the Gulf of Guinea. Pop.: 25 000 (1970 est.). Former name (until 1973): **Santa Isabel.**

ma·lac·ca *or* **ma·lac·ca cane** (mə'lækə) *n.* **1.** the stem of the rattan palm. **2.** a walking stick made from this stem.

Ma·lac·ca (mə'lækə) *n.* a state of SW West Malaysia: rubber plantations. Capital: Malacca. Pop.: 403 061 (1970). Area: 1650 sq. km (637 sq. miles).

Mal·a·chi ('mæləˌkaɪ) *n. Old Testament.* **1.** a Hebrew prophet of the fifth century B.C. **2.** the book containing his oracles. Douay spelling: **Mal·a·chi·as** (ˌmælə'kaɪəs).

mal·a·chite ('mæləˌkaɪt) *n.* a green secondary mineral consisting of hydrated basic copper carbonate in monoclinic crystalline form: a source of copper, also used for making ornaments. Formula: $Cu_2CO_3(OH)_2$. [C16: via Old French from Latin *molochītes,* from Greek *molokhitis* mallow-green stone, from *molokhē* mallow]

mal·a·co- *or before a vowel* **mal·ac-** *n. combining form.* denoting softness: *malacology; malacostracan.* [from Greek *malakos*]

mal·a·col·o·gy (ˌmælə'kɒlədʒɪ) *n.* the branch of zoology concerned with the study of molluscs. —**mal·a·co·log·i·cal** (ˌmæləkə'lɒdʒɪkəl) *adj.* —ˌ**mal·a·'col·o·gist** *n.*

mal·a·coph·yl·lous (ˌmælə'kɒfɪləs) *adj.* (of plants living in dry regions) having fleshy leaves in which water is stored.

mal·a·cop·te·ryg·i·an (ˌmæləˌkɒptə'rɪdʒɪən) *adj.* **1.** of, relating to, or belonging to the *Malacopterygii,* a group of teleost fishes, including herrings and salmon, having soft fin rays. ~*n.* **2.** any malacopterygian fish; a soft-finned fish. ~Compare **acanthopterygian.** [C19: from New Latin *Malacopterygii,* from MALACO- + Greek *pterux* wing, fin]

mal·a·cos·tra·can (ˌmælə'kɒstrəkən) *n.* **1.** any crustacean of the subclass or group *Malacostraca,* including lobsters, crabs, woodlice, sand hoppers, and opossum shrimps. ~*adj.* also **mal·a·cos·tra·cous. 2.** of, relating to, or belonging to the *Malacostraca.* [C19: from New Latin, from Greek *malakostrakos,* from MALACO- + *ostrakon* shell]

mal·ad·dress (ˌmælə'drɛs) *n.* awkwardness; tactlessness.

mal·ad·just·ed (ˌmælə'dʒʌstɪd) *adj.* **1.** *Psychol.* suffering from maladjustment. **2.** badly adjusted.

mal·ad·just·ment (ˌmælə'dʒʌstmənt) *n.* **1.** *Psychol.* a failure to meet the demands of society, such as coping with problems and social relationships: usually reflected in emotional instability. **2.** faulty or bad adjustment.

mal·ad·min·is·ter (ˌmæləd'mɪnɪstə) *vb.* (*tr.*) to administer badly, inefficiently, or dishonestly. —ˌ**mal·ad**ˌ**min·is·'tra·tion** *n.* —ˌ**mal·ad·'min·is**ˌ**tra·tor** *n.*

mal·a·droit (ˌmælə'drɔɪt) *adj.* **1.** showing or characterized by clumsiness; not dexterous. **2.** tactless and insensitive in behaviour or speech. [C17: from French, from *mal* badly + ADROIT] —ˌ**mal·a·'droit·ly** *adv.* —ˌ**mal·a·'droit·ness** *n.*

mal·a·dy ('mælədɪ) *n., pl.* **-dies.** **1.** any disease or illness. **2.** any unhealthy, morbid, or desperate condition: *a malady of the spirit.* [C13: from Old French, from Vulgar Latin *male habitus* (unattested) in poor condition, from Latin *male* badly + *habitus,* from *habēre* to have]

mal·a fi·de ('mælə 'faɪdɪ) *adj.* undertaken in bad faith. [from Latin]

Má·la·ga ('mæləgə; *Spanish* 'malaɣa) *n.* **1.** a port and resort in S Spain, in Andalusia on the Mediterranean. Pop.: 374 452 (1970). **2.** a sweet fortified dessert wine from Málaga.

Mal·a·gas·y ('mælə'gɑːzɪ) *n.* **1.** (*pl.* **-gas·y** *or* **-gas·ies**) a native or inhabitant of Madagascar. **2.** the official language of the Malagasy Republic, belonging to the Malayo-Polynesian family. *~adj.* **3.** of or relating to Madagascar, the Malagasy Republic, its people, or their language.

Mal·a·gas·y Re·pub·lic *n.* the former name (1958–75) of **Madagascar.**

ma·la·gue·ña (ˌmælə'geɪnjə) *n.* a Spanish dance similar to the fandango. [Spanish: of MÁLAGA]

ma·laise (mæ'leɪz) *n.* a feeling of unease, mild sickness, or depression. [C18: from Old French, from *mal* bad + *aise* EASE]

mal·am ('mælæm, -əm) *n.* a variant spelling of **mallam.**

mal·a·mute *or* **mal·e·mute** ('mæləˌmuːt) *n.* an Alaskan Eskimo dog. [from the name of an Eskimo tribe]

mal·an·ders, mal·lan·ders, *or* **mal·len·ders** ('mæləndəz) *n.* a disease of horses characterized by an eczematous inflammation behind the knee. [C15: via Old French from Latin *malandria* sore on the neck of a horse]

Ma·lang ('mælæŋ) *n.* a city in S Indonesia, on E Java: commercial centre. Pop.: 422 428 (1971).

mal·a·pert ('mæləˌpɜːt) *Archaic or literary.* *~adj.* **1.** saucy or impudent. *~n.* **2.** a saucy or impudent person. [C15: from Old French: unskilful (see MAL-, EXPERT); meaning in English influenced by *apert* frank, from Latin *apertus* open] **—'mal·a·ˌpert·ly** *adv.* **—'mal·a·ˌpert·ness** *n.*

mal·a·prop·ism ('mæləprɒpˌɪzəm) *or* **mal·a·prop** *n.* **1.** the unintentional misuse of a word by confusion with one of similar sound, esp. when creating a ridiculous effect, as in *I am not under the affluence of alcohol.* **2.** the habit of misusing words in this manner. [C18: after Mrs. *Malaprop* in Sheridan's play *The Rivals* (1775), a character who misused words, from MALAPROPOS] **—ˌmal·a·'prop·i·an** *adj.*

mal·ap·ro·pos (ˌmælæprə'pəʊ) *adj.* **1.** of an inappropriate or misapplied nature or kind. *~adv.* **2.** in an inappropriate way or manner. *~n.* **3.** something inopportune or inappropriate. [C17: from French *mal à propos* not to the purpose]

ma·lar ('meɪlə) *adj.* **1.** of or relating to the cheek or cheekbone. *~n.* **2.** Also called: **malar bone.** another name for **zygomatic bone.** [C18: from New Latin *mālāris,* from Latin *māla* jaw]

Mä·lar ('meɪlə) *n.* **Lake.** a lake in S Sweden, extending 121 km (75 miles) west from Stockholm, where it joins with an inlet of the Baltic Sea (the **Saltsjön**). Area: 1140 sq. km (440 sq. miles). Swedish name: **Mä·ler·en** ('melaren).

ma·lar·i·a (mə'lɛərɪə) *n.* an infectious disease characterized by recurring attacks of chills and fever, caused by the bite of an anopheles mosquito infected with any of four protozoans of the genus *Plasmodium* (*P. vivax, P. falciparum, P. malariae,* or *P. ovale*). [C18: from Italian *mala aria* bad air, from the belief that the disease was caused by the unwholesome air in swampy districts] **—ma·'lar·i·al, ma·'lar·i·an,** *or* **ma·'lar·i·ous** *adj.*

ma·lar·key *or* **ma·lar·ky** (mə'lɑːkɪ) *n. Informal.* nonsense; rubbish. [C20: of unknown origin]

mal·as·sim·i·la·tion (ˌmæləˌsɪmɪ'leɪʃən) *n. Pathol.* defective assimilation of nutrients.

mal·ate ('mæleɪt, 'meɪ-) *n.* any salt or ester of malic acid. [C18: from MALIC ACID]

Ma·la·tes·ta (*Italian* mala'tɛsta) *n.* an Italian family that ruled Rimini from the 13th to the 16th century.

Mal·a·thi·on (ˌmælə'θaɪɒn) *n. Trademark.* a yellow organophosphorus insecticide used as a dust or mist for the control of house flies and garden pests. Formula: $C_{10}H_{19}O_6PS_2$. [C20: from (DIETHYL) MAL(EATE) + THIO- + -ON]

Ma·la·tya (ˌmɑːlɑː'tjɑː) *n.* a city in E central Turkey: nearby is the ruined Roman and medieval city of Melitene (Old Malatya). Pop.: 154 505 (1975).

Ma·la·wi (mə'lɑːwɪ) *n.* **1.** a republic in E central Africa: established as a British protectorate in 1891; became independent in 1964 and a republic, within the Commonwealth, in 1966; lies along the Great Rift Valley, with Lake Malawi along the E border, the Nyika Plateau in the northwest, and the Shiré Highlands in the southeast. Languages: English and various Bantu languages. Religion: Christian, Muslim, and animist. Currency: kwacha. Capital: Lilongwe. Pop.: 4 549 000 (1971 est.). Area: 117 050 sq. km (45 193 sq. miles). Former name: **Nyasaland.** **2. Lake.** a lake in central Africa at the S end of the Great Rift Valley: the third largest lake in Africa, drained by the Shiré River into the Zambezi. Area: about 28 500 sq. km (11 000 sq. miles). Former name: **Lake Nyasa.**

Ma·lay (mə'leɪ) *n.* **1.** a member of a people living chiefly in Malaysia and Indonesia who are descendants of Mongoloid immigrants. **2.** the language of this people, belonging to the Malayo-Polynesian family. *~adj.* **3.** of or relating to the Malays or their language.

Ma·lay·a (mə'leɪə) *n.* **1. States of.** part of Malaysia, in the S Malay Peninsula, constituting West Malaysia: consists of the former Federated Malay States, the former Unfederated Malay States, and the former Straits Settlements. Capital: Kuala Lumpur. Pop.: 8 801 399 (1970). Area: 131 587 sq. km (50 806 sq. miles). **2. Federation of.** a federation of the nine Malay States of the Malay Peninsula and two of the Straits Settlements (Malacca and Penang): formed in 1948: became part of the British Commonwealth in 1957 and joined Malaysia in 1963. **—Ma·'lay·an** *adj., n.*

Mal·a·ya·lam *or* **Mal·a·ya·laam** (ˌmælɪ'ɑːləm) *n.* a language of SW India, belonging to the Dravidian family and closely related to Tamil: the state language of Kerala.

Ma·lay Ar·chi·pel·a·go *n.* a group of islands in the Indian and Pacific Oceans, between SE Asia and Australia: the largest group of islands in the world; includes over 3000 Indonesian islands, about 7000 islands of the Philippines, and, sometimes, New Guinea.

Ma·lay·o-Pol·y·ne·sian *n.* **1.** Also called: **Austronesian.** a family of languages extending from Madagascar to the central Pacific, including Malagasy, Malay, Indonesian, Tagalog, and Polynesian. See also **Austro-Asiatic.** *~adj.* **2.** of or relating to this family of languages.

Ma·lay Pen·in·su·la *n.* a peninsula of SE Asia, extending south from the Isthmus of Kra in Thailand to Cape Tanjong Piai in Malaysia: consists of SW Thailand and the states of Malaya (West Malaysia). Ancient name: **Chersonesus Aurea.**

Ma·lay·si·a (mə'leɪzɪə) *n.* a federation in SE Asia (within the Commonwealth), consisting of **West Malaysia,** on the Malay Peninsula, and **East Malaysia** (Sabah and Sarawak), occupying the N part of the island of Borneo: formed in 1963 as a federation of Malaya, Sarawak, Sabah, and Singapore (the latter seceded in 1965); densely forested and mostly mountainous. Languages: Malay and English, with various Chinese and Indian minority languages. Religion: mostly Muslim. Currency: ringgit. Capital: Kuala Lumpur. Pop.: 10 319 324 (1970). Area: 333 403 sq. km (128 727 sq. miles). **—Ma·'lay·si·an** *adj., n.*

Ma·lay States *n.* the former states of the Malay Peninsula that, together with Penang and Malacca, formed the Union of Malaya (1946) and the Federation of Malaya (1948). Perak, Selangor, Negri Sembilan, and Pahang were established as the **Federated Malay States** by the British in 1895 and Perlis, Kedah, Kelantan, and Trengannu as the **Unfederated Malay States** in 1909 (joined by Johore in 1914).

Mal·colm ('mælkəm) *n.* **George.** born 1917, English harpsichordist.

Mal·colm III ('mælkəm) *n.* died 1093, king of Scotland (1057–93). He became king after Macbeth.

Mal·colm X ('mælkəm 'ɛks) *n.* original name *Malcolm Little.* 1925–65, U.S. Negro leader: assassinated.

mal·con·tent ('mælkənˌtɛnt) *adj.* **1.** disgusted or discontented. *~n.* **2.** a person who is malcontent. [C16: from Old French]

mal de mer *French.* (mal də 'mɛːr) *n.* seasickness.

Mal·dives ('mɔːldaɪvz) *pl. n.* **Re·pub·lic of.** a republic occupying an archipelago of 1087 coral islands in the Indian Ocean, southwest of Sri Lanka: came under British protection in 1887; became independent in 1965 and a republic in 1968. Language: Divehi. Religion: Sunni Muslim. Currency: rupee. Capital: Male. Pop.: 122 673 (1972). Area: 298 sq. km. (115 sq. miles). Also called: **Maldive Islands.** **—Mal·div·i·an** (mɔːl'dɪvɪən) *or* **Mal·di·van** ('mɔːldaɪvᵊn, -dɪ-) *adj., n.*

Mal·don ('mɔːldən) *n.* a market town in SE England, in Essex; scene of a battle (991) between the East Saxons and the victorious Danes, celebrated in *The Battle of Maldon,* an Old English poem. Pop.: 13 840 (1971).

male (meɪl) *adj.* **1.** of, relating to, or designating the sex producing gametes (spermatozoa) that can fertilize female gametes (ova). **2.** of, relating to, or characteristic of a man; masculine. **3.** for or composed of men or boys: *a male choir.* **4.** (of gametes) capable of fertilizing an egg cell in sexual reproduction. **5.** (of reproductive organs, such as a testis or stamen) capable of producing male gametes. **6.** (of flowers) bearing stamens but lacking a functional pistil. **7.** *Electronics, mechanical engineering.* having a projecting part or parts that fit into a female counterpart: *a male plug.* *~n.* **8.** a male person, animal, or plant. [C14: via Old French from Latin *masculus* MASCULINE] **—'male·ness** *n.*

Ma·le ('mɑːleɪ) *n.* the capital of the Republic of the Maldives, on Male Island in the centre of the island group. Pop.: 13 610 (1970).

ma·le·ate ('mælɪˌeɪt) *n.* any salt or ester of maleic acid. [C19: from MALE(IC) + -ATE[1]]

Male·branche (*French* mal'brɑ̃ːʃ) *n.* **Ni·co·las** (nikɔ'la). 1638–1715, French philosopher. Originally a follower of Descartes, he developed the philosophy of occasionalism, esp. in *De la Recherche de la vérité* (1674).

male chau·vin·ism *n.* the belief, held or alleged to be held by certain men, that men are inherently superior to women. **—male chau·vin·ist** *n.*

male chau·vin·ist pig *n. Informal, derogatory.* a man who exhibits male chauvinism.

mal·e·dict ('mælɪdɪkt) *~vb.* **1.** (*tr.*) *Literary.* to utter a curse against. *~adj.* **2.** *Archaic.* cursed or detestable.

mal·e·dic·tion (ˌmælɪ'dɪkʃən) *n.* **1.** the utterance of a curse against someone or something. **2.** slanderous accusation or comment. [C15: from Latin *maledictiō* a reviling, from *male* ill + *dīcere* to speak] **—ˌmal·e·'dic·tive** *or* **ˌmal·e·'dic·to·ry** *adj.*

mal·e·fac·tor ('mælɪˌfæktə) *n.* a criminal; wrongdoer. [C15: via Old French from Latin, from *malefacere* to do evil] **—'mal·e·ˌfac·tion** *n.* **—'mal·e·ˌfac·tress** *fem. n.*

male fern *n.* a fern, *Dryopteris filix-mas,* having scaly stalks and pinnate fronds with kidney-shaped spore-producing bodies on the underside: family *Polypodiaceae.*

ma·lef·i·cent (mə'lɛfɪsənt) *adj.* causing or capable of producing evil or mischief; harmful or baleful. [C17: from Latin *maleficent-*, from *maleficus* wicked, prone to evil, from *malum* evil] —**ma·'lef·ic** *adj.* —**ma·'lef·i·cence** *n.*

ma·le·ic ac·id (mə'leɪɪk) *n.* a colourless soluble crystalline substance used to synthesize other compounds; *cis*-butenedioic acid. Formula: HOOCCH:CHCOOH. [C19: from French *maléique*, altered form of *malique*; see MALIC ACID]

mal·e·mute ('mælə,muːt) *n.* a variant spelling of **malamute.**

Ma·le·vich (*Russian* 'malɪvitʃ) *n.* **Ka·si·mir** (kəzi'mir). 1878–1935, Russian painter. He founded the abstract art movement known as Suprematism.

ma·lev·o·lent (mə'lɛvələnt) *adj.* **1.** wishing or appearing to wish evil to others; malicious. **2.** *Astrology.* having an evil influence. [C16: from Latin *malevolens*, from *male* ill + *volens*, present participle of *velle* to wish] —**ma·'lev·o·lence** *n.* —**ma·'lev·o·lent·ly** *adv.*

mal·fea·sance (mæl'fiːzᵊns) *n. Law.* the doing of a wrongful or illegal act, esp. by a public official. Compare **misfeasance, nonfeasance.** [C17: from Old French *mal faisant*, from *mal* evil + *faisant* doing, from *faire* to do, from Latin *facere*] —**mal·'fea·sant** *n., adj.*

mal·for·ma·tion (,mælfɔː'meɪʃən) *n.* **1.** the condition of being faulty or abnormal in form or shape. **2.** *Pathol.* a deformity in the shape or structure of a part, esp. when congenital. —**mal·'formed** *adj.*

mal·func·tion (mæl'fʌŋkʃən) *vb.* **1.** (*intr.*) to function imperfectly or irregularly or fail to function. ~*n.* **2.** failure to function or defective functioning.

mal·gré lui *French.* (malgre 'lwi) *adv.* in spite of himself.

Mal·herbe (*French* ma'lɛrb) *n.* **Fran·çois de** (frɑ̃'swa də). 1555–1628, French poet and critic. He advocated the classical ideals of clarity and concision of meaning.

Ma·li ('mɑːlɪ) *n.* a landlocked republic in West Africa: conquered by the French by 1898 and incorporated (as French Sudan) into French West Africa; became independent in 1960; settled chiefly in the basins of the Rivers Senegal and Niger in the south. Official language: French. Religion: Muslim and animist. Currency: franc. Capital: Bamako. Pop.: 5 697 000 (1975 UN est.). Area: 1 239 710 sq. km (478 652 sq. miles). Former name (1898–1959): **French Sudan.**

mal·ic ac·id ('mælɪk, 'meɪ-) *n.* a colourless crystalline compound occurring in apples and other fruits. Formula: $HOOCCH_2CH(OH)COOH$. [C18 *malic*, via French *malique* from Latin *mālum* apple]

mal·ice ('mælɪs) *n.* **1.** the desire to do harm or mischief. **2.** evil intent. **3.** *Law.* the state of mind with which an act is committed and from which the intent to do wrong may be inferred. See also **malice aforethought.** [C13: via Old French from Latin *malitia*, from *malus* evil]

mal·ice a·fore·thought *n. Criminal law.* **1.** the predetermination to do an unlawful act, esp. to kill or seriously injure. **2.** the intent with which an unlawful killing is effected, which must be proved for the crime to constitute murder. See also **murder, manslaughter.**

ma·li·cious (mə'lɪʃəs) *adj.* **1.** characterized by malice. **2.** motivated by wrongful, vicious, or mischievous purposes. —**ma·'li·cious·ly** *adv.* —**ma·'li·cious·ness** *n.*

ma·lign (mə'laɪn) *adj.* **1.** evil in influence, intention, or effect. ~*vb.* **2.** (*tr.*) to slander or defame. [C14: via Old French from Latin *malīgnus* spiteful, from *malus* evil] —**ma·'lign·er** *n.* —**ma·'lign·ly** *adv.*

ma·lig·nan·cy (mə'lɪgnənsɪ) *n., pl.* **·cies. 1.** the state or quality of being malignant. **2.** *Pathol.* a cancerous growth.

ma·lig·nant (mə'lɪgnənt) *adj.* **1.** having or showing desire to harm others. **2.** tending to cause great harm; injurious. **3.** *Pathol.* (of a tumour, etc.) uncontrollable or resistant to therapy; rapidly spreading. [C16: from Late Latin *malīgnāre* to behave spitefully, from Latin *malīgnus* MALIGN] —**ma·'lig·nant·ly** *adv.*

ma·lig·ni·ty (mə'lɪgnɪtɪ) *n., pl.* **·ties. 1.** the condition or quality of being malign, malevolent, or deadly. **2.** (*often pl.*) a malign or malicious act or feeling.

ma·li·hi·ni (,mɑːlɪ'hiːnɪ) *n., pl.* **·nis.** (in Hawaii) a foreigner or stranger. [from Hawaiian]

mal·im·print·ed (,mælɪm'prɪntɪd) *adj.* (of an animal or person) suffering from a defect in the behavioural process of imprinting, resulting in attraction to members of other species, fetishism, etc. —**,mal·im·'print·ing** *n.*

ma·lines (mə'liːn) *n.* **1.** a type of silk net used in dressmaking. **2.** another name for **Mechlin lace.** [French *Malines* (Mechelen), where this lace was traditionally made]

Ma·lines (ma'lin) *n.* the French name for **Mechelen.**

ma·lin·ger (mə'lɪŋgə) *vb.* (*intr.*) to pretend or exaggerate illness, esp. to avoid work. [C19: from French *malingre* sickly, perhaps from *mal* badly + Old French *haingre* feeble] —**ma·'lin·ger·er** *n.*

Ma·lin·ke (mə'lɪŋkɪ) *or* **Ma·nin·ke** *n.* **1.** (*pl.* **·ke** *or* **·kes**) a member of a Negroid people of W Africa, living chiefly in Guinea and Mali, noted for their use of cowry shells as currency. **2.** the language of this people, belonging to the Mande branch of the Niger-Congo family.

Ma·li·now·ski (,mælɪ'nɒfskɪ) *n.* **Bro·ni·slaw Kas·per** (brɔ'nislaf 'kaspɛr). 1884–1942, Polish anthropologist in England and the U.S., who researched into the sexual behaviour of primitive people in New Guinea and Melanesia.

mal·i·son ('mælɪzᵊn, -sᵊn) *n.* an archaic or poetic word for **curse.** [C13: via Old French from Latin *maledictiō* MALEDICTION]

mal·kin ('mɔːkɪn, 'mɔːl-, 'mæl-) *n.* **1.** an archaic or Brit. dialect name for a **cat.** Compare **grimalkin. 2.** a variant spelling of **mawkin.** [C13: diminutive of *Maud*]

mall (mɔːl, mæl) *n.* **1.** a shaded avenue, esp. one that is open to the public. **2.** *U.S., Canadian, and Austral.* a street or area lined with shops and closed to vehicles. **3.** See **pall-mall.** [C17: after *The Mall*, in St. James's Park, London. See PALL-MALL]

mal·lam *or* **mal·am** ('mælæm, -əm) *n. W. African.* **1.** (in Islamic W Africa) a man learned in Koranic studies. **2.** (in N Nigeria) a title and form of address for a learned or educated man. [C20: from Hausa]

mal·lard ('mælɑːd) *n., pl.* **·lard** *or* **·lards.** a duck, *Anas platyrhynchos*, common over most of the N hemisphere, the male of which has a dark green head and reddish-brown breast: the ancestor of all domestic breeds of duck. [C14: from Old French *mallart*, perhaps from *maslart* (unattested); see MALE, -ARD]

Mal·lar·mé (*French* malar'me) *n.* **Sté·phane** (ste'fan). 1842–1898, French symbolist poet, noted for his free verse, in which he chooses words for their evocative qualities; his works include *L'Après-midi d'un Faune* (1876), *Vers et Prose* (1893), and *Divagations* (1897).

mal·le·a·ble ('mælɪəbᵊl) *adj.* **1.** (esp. of metal) able to be worked, hammered, or shaped under pressure or blows without breaking. **2.** able to be influenced; pliable or tractable. [C14: via Old French from Medieval Latin *malleābilis*, from Latin *malleus* hammer] —**,mal·le·a·'bil·i·ty** *or* **'mal·le·a·ble·ness** *n.* —**'mal·le·a·bly** *adv.*

mal·le·a·ble i·ron *n.* **1.** Also called: **malleable cast iron.** cast iron that has been toughened by gradual heating or slow cooling. **2.** a less common name for **wrought iron.**

mal·lee ('mæliː) *n.* **1.** any of several low shrubby eucalyptus trees that flourish in desert regions of Australia. **2.** (usually preceded by *the*) *Austral.* another name for the **bush** (sense 4). **3.** See **mallee root.** [C19: native Australian name]

mal·lee fowl *n.* an Australian megapode, *Leipoa ocellata*, that allows its eggs to incubate naturally in a sandy mound.

mal·lee root *n. Austral.* the rootstock (rhizome) of a mallee tree, often used as fuel.

mal·le·muck ('mælɪ,mʌk) *n.* any of various sea birds, such as the albatross, fulmar, or shearwater. [C17: from Dutch *mallemok* from *mal* silly + *mok* gull]

mal·len·ders ('mæləndəz) *n.* a less common spelling of **malanders.**

mal·le·o·lus (mə'liːələs) *n., pl.* **·li** (-,laɪ). either of two rounded bony projections of the tibia and fibula on the side of each ankle joint. [C17: diminutive of Latin *malleus* hammer] —**mal·'le·o·lar** *adj.*

mal·let ('mælɪt) *n.* **1.** a tool resembling a hammer but having a large head of wood, copper, lead, leather, etc., used for driving chisels, beating sheet metal, etc. **2.** a long stick with a head like a hammer used to strike the ball in croquet or polo. **3.** *Chiefly U.S.* a very large powerful steam locomotive with a conventional boiler but with two separate articulated engine units. [C15: from Old French *maillet* wooden hammer, diminutive of *mail* MAUL (n.)]

mal·le·us ('mælɪəs) *n., pl.* **·le·i** (-lɪ,aɪ). the outermost and largest of the three small bones in the middle ear of mammals. Nontechnical name: **hammer.** See also **incus, stapes.** [C17: from Latin: hammer]

Ma·llor·ca (ma'ʎorka) *n.* the Spanish name for **Majorca.**

mal·low ('mæləʊ) *n.* **1.** any plant of the malvaceous genus *Malva*, esp. *M. sylvestris* of Europe, having purple, pink, or white flowers. See also **dwarf mallow, musk mallow. 2.** any of various related plants, such as the marsh mallow, rose mallow, Indian mallow, and tree mallow. [Old English *mealuwe*, from Latin *malva*; probably related to Greek *malakhē* mallow]

malm (mɑːm) *n.* **1.** a soft greyish limestone that crumbles easily. **2.** a chalky soil formed from this limestone. **3.** an artificial mixture of clay and chalk used to make bricks. [Old English *mealm-* (in compound words); related to Old Norse *malmr* ore, Gothic *malma* sand]

Mal·mé·dy (*French* malme'di) *n.* See **Eupen and Malmédy.**

Malm·ö ('mælməʊ; *Swedish* 'mal,møː) *n.* a port in S Sweden, on the Sound: part of Denmark until 1658; industrial centre. Pop.: 246 647 (1974 est.).

malm·sey ('mɑːmzɪ) *n.* a sweet Madeira wine. [C15: from Medieval Latin *Malmasia*, corruption of Greek *Monembasia*, Greek port from which the wine was shipped]

mal·nour·ished (mæl'nʌrɪʃt) *adj.* undernourished.

mal·nu·tri·tion (,mælnjuː'trɪʃən) *n.* lack of adequate nutrition resulting from insufficient food, unbalanced diet, or defective assimilation.

mal·oc·clu·sion (,mælə'kluːʒən) *n. Dentistry.* a defect in the normal position of the upper and lower teeth when the mouth is closed, as from abnormal development of the jaw. —**,mal·oc·'clud·ed** *adj.*

mal·o·dor·ous (mæl'əʊdərəs) *adj.* having a bad smell. —**mal·'o·dor·ous·ly** *adv.* —**mal·'o·dor·ous·ness** *n.*

ma·lo·nic ac·id (mə'ləʊnɪk, -'lɒn-) *n.* another name for **propanedioic acid.** [from French *malonique*, altered form of *malique*; see MALIC ACID]

mal·o·nyl·u·re·a (,mælənɪljʊ'rɪə, -'jʊərɪə, -niːl-) *n.* another name for **barbituric acid.**

Mal·o·ry ('mælərɪ) *n.* Sir **Thom·as.** 15th-century English author of *Le Morte d'Arthur* (?1470), a prose collection of Arthurian legends, translated from the French.

Mal·pi·ghi (*Italian* mal'piːgi) *n.* **Mar·cel·lo** (mar'tʃɛllo). 1628–94, Italian physiologist. A pioneer in microscopic anatomy, he identified the capillary system (1661). —**Mal+pigh+i+an** (mælˈpɪgɪən) *adj.*

mal+pigh·i·a+ceous (mælˌpɪgɪˈeɪʃəs) *adj.* of, relating to, or belonging to the *Malpighiaceae*, a family of tropical plants many of which are lianas. [C19: from New Latin *Malpighia*, after Marcello MALPIGHI]

Mal+pigh+i·an cor+pus+cle *or* **bod·y** *n. Anatomy.* an encapsulated cluster of capillaries at the end of each urine-secreting tubule of the kidney.

Mal+pigh+i·an lay+er *n. Anatomy.* the innermost layer of the epidermis.

Mal+pigh+i·an tub+ules *or* **tubes** *pl. n.* organs of excretion in insects and many other arthropods: narrow tubules opening into the anterior part of the hindgut.

mal+po+si+tion (ˌmælpəˈzɪʃən) *n.* abnormal position of a bodily part. —**mal+posed** (mælˈpəʊzd) *adj.*

mal+prac+tice (mælˈpræktɪs) *n.* **1.** immoral, illegal, or unethical professional conduct or neglect of professional duty. **2.** any instance of improper professional conduct. —**mal+prac+ti+tion+er** (ˌmælprækˈtɪʃənə) *n.*

Mal·raux (*French* malˈro) *n.* **An·dré** (ɑ̃ˈdre). 1901–76, French writer and statesman. His novels include *La Condition humaine* (1933) on the Kuomintang revolution (1927–28) and *L'Espoir* (1937) on the Spanish Civil War, in both of which events he took part. He also wrote on art, notably in *Les Voix du silence* (1951).

malt (mɔːlt) *n.* **1.** cereal grain, such as barley, that is kiln-dried after it has germinated by soaking in water. **2.** See **malt liquor.** ~*vb.* **3.** to make into or become malt. **4.** to make (something, esp. liquor) with malt. [Old English *mealt;* related to Dutch *mout,* Old Norse *malt;* see also MELT]

Mal+ta (ˈmɔːltə) *n.* a republic occupying the islands of Malta, Gozo, and Comino, in the Mediterranean south of Sicily: governed by the Knights Hospitallers from 1530 until Napoleon's conquest in 1798; taken by the British in 1800 and annexed in 1814; suffered severely in World War II; became independent in 1964 and a republic in 1974; a member of the Commonwealth. Languages: Maltese and English. Religion: Roman Catholic. Capital: Valletta. Pop.: 323 000 (1974 est.). Area: 316 sq. km (122 sq. miles).

Mal+ta fe+ver *n.* another name for **brucellosis.**

malt+ase (ˈmɔːlteɪz) *n.* an enzyme that hydrolyses maltose and similar glucosides (α-glucosides) to glucose. Also called: **α-glucosidase.**

malt+ed milk *n.* **1.** a soluble powder made from dehydrated milk and malted cereals. **2.** a drink made from this powder.

Mal+tese (mɔːlˈtiːz) *adj.* **1.** of or relating to Malta, its inhabitants, or their language. ~*n.* **2.** (*pl.* **+tese**) a native or inhabitant of Malta. **3.** the official language of Malta, a form of Arabic with borrowings from Italian, etc. **4.** a domestic fancy pigeon having long legs and a long neck.

Mal+tese cross *n.* a cross with triangular arms that taper towards the centre, sometimes having indented outer sides: formerly worn by the Knights of Malta.

Mal+tese dog *n.* a small white long-haired breed of dog.

malt ex+tract *n.* a sticky substance obtained from an infusion of malt.

mal+tha (ˈmælθə) *n.* **1.** another name for **mineral tar. 2.** any of various naturally occurring mixtures of hydrocarbons, such as ozocerite. [C15: via Latin from Greek: a mixture of wax and pitch]

Mal+thus (ˈmælθəs) *n.* **Thom·as Rob·ert.** 1766–1834, English economist. He propounded his population theory in *An Essay on the Principle of Population* (1798).

Mal+thu+si·an (mælˈθjuːzɪən) *adj.* **1.** of or relating to the theory of Malthus stating that increases in population tend to exceed increases in the means of subsistence and that therefore sexual restraint should be exercised. ~*n.* **2.** a supporter of this theory. —**Mal+ˈthu+si+an+ism** *n.*

malt+ing (ˈmɔːltɪŋ) *n.* a building in which malt is made or stored. Also called: **malt house.**

malt liq+uor *n.* any alcoholic drink brewed from malt.

malt+ose (ˈmɔːltəʊz) *n.* a disaccharide of glucose formed by the enzymic hydrolysis of starch: used in bacteriological culture media and as a nutrient in infant feeding. Formula: $C_{12}H_{22}O_{11}$.

mal+treat (mælˈtriːt) *vb.* (*tr.*) to treat badly, cruelly, or inconsiderately. [C18: from French *maltraiter*] —**mal+ˈtreat+er** *n.* —**mal+ˈtreat+ment** *n.*

malt+ster (ˈmɔːltstə) *n.* a person who makes or deals in malt.

malt·y (ˈmɔːltɪ) *adj.* **malt·i+er, malt·i+est.** of, like, or containing malt. —**ˈmalt·i+ness** *n.*

Ma+lu+ku (mɑːˈluːkuː) *n.* the Indonesian name for the **Moluccas.**

mal+va+ceous (mælˈveɪʃəs) *adj.* of, relating to, or belonging to the *Malvaceae*, a family of plants that includes mallow, cotton, okra, althaea, and abutilon. [C17: from Latin *malvāceus*, from *malva* MALLOW]

mal+va+si·a (ˌmælvəˈsɪə) *n.* **1.** another word for **malmsey. 2.** the type of grape used to make malmsey. [C19: from Italian, from Greek *Monembasia;* see MALMSEY] —ˌ**mal+va+ˈsi+an** *adj.*

Mal+vern (ˈmɔːlvən) *n.* a town and resort in W England, in Hereford and Worcester on the E slopes of the **Malvern Hills:** annual dramatic festival; mineral springs. Pop.: 29 004 (1971).

mal+ver+sa+tion (ˌmælvɜːˈseɪʃən) *n. Rare.* professional or public misconduct. [C16: from French, from *malverser* to behave badly, from Latin *male versārī*]

mal+voi+sie (ˈmælvɔɪzɪ, -və-) *n.* an amber dessert wine made in France, similar to malmsey. [C14: via Old French from Italian *Malvasia*, from Greek *Monembasia;* see MALMSEY]

mal+wa (ˈmalwa) *n.* a Ugandan drink brewed from millet. [from Rutooro, a language of W Uganda]

mam (mæm) *n. Brit. dialect.* another word for **mother.**

ma·ma (məˈmɑː) *n. Old-fashioned.* an informal word for **mother.**

ma+ma+guy (ˈmɑːməˌgaɪ) *Caribbean.* ~*vb.* **1.** (*tr.*) to deceive or tease, either in jest or by deceitful flattery. ~*n.* **2.** an instance of such deception or flattery. [from Spanish *mamar el gallo,* literally: to feed the cock]

mam+ba (ˈmæmbə) *n.* any aggressive partly arboreal tropical African venomous elapid snake of the genus *Dendroaspis*, esp. *D. angusticeps* (**green** and **black mambas**). [from Zulu *imamba*]

mam+bo (ˈmæmbəʊ) *n., pl.* **+bos. 1.** a modern Latin American dance, resembling the rumba, derived from the ritual dance of voodoo. ~*vb.* **2.** (*intr.*) to perform this dance. [American Spanish, probably from Haitian Creole: voodoo priestess]

mam+e·lon (ˈmæməlᵊn) *n.* a small rounded hillock. [C19: from French: nipple]

Mam+e·luke *or* **Mam·a+luke** (ˈmæmɪˌluːk) *n.* **1.** a member of a military class, originally of Turkish slaves, ruling in Egypt from about 1250 to 1517 and remaining powerful until the early 19th century. **2.** (in Muslim countries) a slave. [C16: via French, ultimately from Arabic *mamlūk* slave, from *malaka* to possess]

ma+mey, mam+mee, *or* **mam+mee ap+ple** (mæˈmiː) *n.* **1.** a tropical American tree, *Mammea americana,* cultivated for its large edible fruits: family *Guttiferae.* **2.** the fruit of this tree, having yellow pulp and a red skin. **3.** another name for the **marmalade tree.** [C16: from Spanish *mamey,* from Haitian]

ma+mil+la *or U.S.* **mam+mil+la** (mæˈmɪlə) *n., pl.* **+lae** (-liː). **1.** a nipple or teat. **2.** any nipple-shaped part or prominence. [C17: from Latin, diminutive of *mamma* breast] —**ˈma+mil+lar·y** *or U.S.* **ˈmam+mil+ar·y** *adj.*

ma+mil+late (ˈmæmɪˌleɪt), **ma+mil+lat+ed** *or U.S.* **mam+mil+late, mam+mil+lat+ed** *adj.* having nipples or nipple-like protuberances.

mam+ma[1] *n. Chiefly U.S.* **1.** (məˈmɑː). a variant spelling of **mama. 2.** (ˈmɑːmə). *Informal.* a buxom and voluptuous woman. [C16: reduplication of childish syllable *ma;* compare Welsh *mam,* French *maman,* Russian *mama*]

mam+ma[2] (ˈmæmə) *n., pl.* **+mae** (-miː). **1.** the milk-secreting organ of female mammals: the breast in women, the udder in cows, etc. **2.** (*functioning as pl.*) breast-shaped protuberances, esp. from the base of cumulonimbus clouds. [C17: from Latin: breast]

mam+mal (ˈmæməl) *n.* any animal of the *Mammalia,* a large class of warm-blooded vertebrates having mammary glands in the female, a thoracic diaphragm, and a four-chambered heart. The class includes the whales, carnivores, rodents, bats, primates, etc. [C19: via New Latin from Latin *mamma* breast] —**mam+ma+li·an** (mæˈmeɪlɪən) *adj., n.* —**ˈmam·mal-ˌlike** *adj.*

mam+mal+o·gy (mæˈmælədʒɪ) *n.* the branch of zoology concerned with the study of mammals. —**mam+ma+log·i·cal** (ˌmæməˈlɒdʒɪkᵊl) *adj.* —**mam+ˈmal·o·gist** *n.*

mam+ma+ry (ˈmæmərɪ) *adj.* of, relating to, or like a mamma or breast.

mam+ma+ry gland *n.* any of the milk-producing glands in mammals. In higher mammals each gland consists of a network of tubes and cavities connected to the exterior by a nipple.

mam+mee (mæˈmiː) *n.* a variant spelling of **mamey.**

mam+met (ˈmæmɪt) *n.* another word for **maumet.**

mam+mif+er+ous (mæˈmɪfərəs) *adj.* having breasts or mammae.

mam+mil+la (mæˈmɪlə) *n., pl.* **+lae** (-liː). the U.S. spelling of **mamilla.** —**ˈmam+mil+lar·y** *adj.*

mam+mil+late (ˈmæmɪˌleɪt) *or* **mam+mil+lat+ed** *adj.* the U.S. spellings of **mamillate, mamillated.**

mam+mock (ˈmæmək) *Brit. dialect.* ~*n.* **1.** a fragment. ~*vb.* **2.** (*tr.*) to tear or shred. [C16: of unknown origin]

mam+mon (ˈmæmən) *n.* **1.** riches or wealth regarded as a source of evil and corruption. **2.** avarice or greed. [C14: via Late Latin from New Testament Greek *mammōnas,* from Aramaic *māmōnā* wealth] —**ˈmam+mon+ish** *adj.* —**ˈmam+mon+ism** *n.* —**ˈmam+mon+ist** *or* **ˈmam+mon+ite** *n.* —ˌ**mam+mon+ˈis+tic** *adj.*

Mam+mon (ˈmæmən) *n. New Testament.* the personification of riches and greed in the form of a false god.

mam+moth (ˈmæməθ) *n.* **1.** any large extinct elephant of the Pleistocene genus *Mammuthus* (or *Elephas*), such as *M. primigenius* (**woolly mammoth**), having a hairy coat and long curved tusks. ~*adj.* **2.** of gigantic size or importance. [C18: from Russian *mamot,* from Tartar *mamont,* perhaps from *mamma* earth, because of a belief that the animal made burrows]

Mam+moth Cave Na+tion+al Park *n.* a national park in W central Kentucky: established in 1941 to protect a system of limestone caverns.

mam+my *or* **mam+mie** (ˈmæmɪ) *n., pl.* **+mies. 1.** a child's word for **mother. 2.** *Chiefly southern U.S.* a Negro woman employed as a nurse or servant to a white family.

mam+my wag+on *n.* a W African vehicle built on a lorry chassis, capable of carrying both passengers and goods.

Ma+mo+ré (*Spanish* ˌmamoˈre) *n.* a river in central Bolivia, flowing north to the Beni River to form the Madeira River. Length: about 1500 km (930 miles).

mam+pa+ra (mamˈpɑːrə) *n. S. African informal.* a clumsy Black African. [of unknown origin]

man (mæn) *n., pl.* **men** (mɛn). **1.** an adult male human being, as distinguished from a woman. **2.** (*modifier*) male; masculine: *a man child.* **3.** a human being regardless of sex or age, considered as a representative of mankind; a person. **4.** (*sometimes cap.*) human beings collectively; mankind: *the development of man.* **5.** Also called: **modern man. a.** a member of any of the living races of *Homo sapiens,* characterized by erect bipedal posture, a highly developed brain, and powers of articulate speech, abstract reasoning, and imagination. **b.** any extinct member of the species *Homo sapiens,* such as Cro-Magnon man. **6.** a member of any of the extinct species of the genus *Homo,* such as Java man, Heidelberg man, and Solo man. **7.** an adult male human being with qualities associated with the male, such as courage or virility: *be a man.* **8.** manly qualities or virtues: *the man in him was outraged.* **9. a.** a subordinate, servant, or employee contrasted with an employer or manager. **b.** (*in combination*): *the number of man-days required to complete a job.* **10.** (*usually pl.*) a member of the armed forces who does not hold commissioned, warrant, or noncommissioned rank (as in the phrase **officers and men**). **11.** a member of a group, team, etc. **12.** a husband, boyfriend, etc.: *man and wife.* **13.** an expression used parenthetically by hippies, etc., to indicate an informal relationship between speaker and hearer. **14.** a movable piece in various games, such as draughts. **15.** a vassal of a feudal lord. **16. as one man.** with unanimous action or response. **17. be one's own man.** to be independent or free. **18. he's your man.** he's the person needed (for a particular task, etc.). **19. man and boy.** from childhood. **20. sort out** *or* **separate the men from the boys.** to separate the experienced from the inexperienced. **21. to a man. a.** unanimously. **b.** without exception: *they were slaughtered to a man.* ~*interj.* **22.** *Informal.* an exclamation or expletive, often indicating surprise or pleasure. ~*vb.* **mans, man·ning, manned.** (*tr.*) **23.** to provide with sufficient men for operation, defence, etc.: *to man a ship.* **24.** to take one's place at or near in readiness for action. **25.** *Falconry.* to induce (a hawk or falcon) to endure the presence of and handling by man, esp. strangers. [Old English *mann;* related to Old Frisian *man,* Old High German *man,* Dutch *man,* Icelandic *mathr*] —**'man·less** *adj.*

Man[1] (mæn) *n. U.S.* **the.** (*sometimes not cap.*) **1.** *Negro slang.* a white man or white men collectively, esp. when in authority, in the police, or held in contempt. **2.** *Slang.* drug peddler.

Man[2] (mæn) *n.* **Isle of.** an island in the British Isles, in the Irish Sea between Cumbria and Northern Ireland: a Crown possession with its own parliament, the Court of Tynwald; a dependency of Norway until 1266, when it came under Scottish rule; its own language, Manx, is now extinct. Capital: Douglas. Pop.: 49 743 (1971). Area: 588 sq. km (227 sq. miles).

Man. *abbrev. for:* **1.** Manila (paper). **2.** Manitoba.

ma·na ('mɑːnə) *n. Anthropol.* **1.** (in Polynesia, etc.) a concept of a life force, believed to be seated in the head, and associated with high social status and ritual power. **2.** any power achieved by ritual means. [from Polynesian]

man a·bout town *n.* a fashionable sophisticate, esp. one in a big city.

man·a·cle ('mænəkᵊl) *n.* **1.** (*usually pl.*) a shackle, handcuff, or fetter, used to secure the hands of a prisoner, convict, etc. ~*vb.* (*tr.*) **2.** to put manacles on. **3.** to confine or constrain. [C14: via Old French from Latin *manicula,* diminutive of *manus* hand]

Ma·na·do (məˈnɑːdəʊ) *n.* a variant spelling of **Menado.**

man·age ('mænɪdʒ) *vb.* (*mainly tr.*) **1.** (*also intr.*) to be in charge (of); administer: *to manage one's affairs; to manage a shop.* **2.** to succeed in being able (to do something) despite obstacles; contrive: *did you manage to go to sleep.* **3.** to have room, time, etc., for: *can you manage dinner tomorrow?* **4.** to exercise control or domination over, often in a tactful or guileful manner. **5.** (*intr.*) to contrive to carry on despite difficulties, esp. financial ones: *he managed quite well on very little money.* **6.** to wield or handle (a weapon). **7.** *Rare.* to be frugal in the use of. ~*n.* **8.** an archaic word for **manège.** [C16: from Italian *maneggiare* to control, train (esp. horses), ultimately from Latin *manus* hand]

man·age·a·ble ('mænɪdʒəbᵊl) *adj.* able to be managed or controlled. —ˌ**man·age·a'bil·i·ty** *or* **'man·age·a·ble·ness** *n.* —**'man·age·a·bly** *adv.*

man·aged cur·ren·cy *n.* a currency that is subject to governmental control with respect to the amount in circulation and the rate of exchange with other currencies.

man·age·ment ('mænɪdʒmənt) *n.* **1.** the members of the executive or administration of an organization or business. **2.** managers or employers collectively. **3.** the technique, practice, or science of managing or controlling. **4.** the skilful or resourceful use of materials, time, etc. **5.** the specific treatment of a disease, etc.

man·age·ment ac·count·ing *n.* another name for **cost accounting.**

man·ag·er ('mænɪdʒə) *n.* **1.** a person who directs or manages an organization, industry, shop, etc. **2.** a person who controls the business affairs of an actor, entertainer, etc. **3.** a person who controls the training of a sportsman or team. **4.** a person who has a talent for managing efficiently. **5.** *Law.* a person appointed by a court to carry on a business during receivership. **6.** (in Britain) a member of either House of Parliament appointed to arrange a matter in which both Houses are concerned. —**'man·ag·er·ˌship** *n.*

man·ag·er·ess (ˌmænɪdʒəˈrɛs, 'mænɪdʒəˌrɛs) *n.* a woman who is in charge of a shop, department, canteen, etc.

man·a·ge·ri·al (ˌmænɪˈdʒɪərɪəl) *adj.* of or relating to a manager or to the functions, responsibilities, or position of management. —ˌ**man·a'ge·ri·al·ly** *adv.*

man·ag·ing ('mænɪdʒɪŋ) *adj.* having administrative control or authority: *a managing director.*

Ma·na·gua (məˈnægwə; *Spanish* maˈnaɣwa) *n.* **1.** the capital of Nicaragua, on the S shore of Lake Managua: chosen as capital in 1857; devastated by earthquakes in 1931 and 1972. Pop.: 398 514 (1971). **2. Lake.** a lake in W Nicaragua: drains into Lake Nicaragua by the Tipitapa River. Length: 61 km (38 miles). Width: about 26 km (16 miles).

man·a·kin ('mænəkɪn) *n.* **1.** any small South American passerine bird of the family *Pipridae,* having a colourful plumage, short bill, and elaborate courtship behaviour. **2.** a variant spelling of **manikin.**

Ma·na·ma (məˈnɑːmə) *n.* the capital of Bahrain, at the N end of Bahrain Island: transit port. Pop.: 88 785 (1971).

ma·ña·na *Spanish.* (maˈɲana; *English* məˈnjɑːnə) *n., adv.* **a.** tomorrow. **b.** some other and later time.

Ma·náos (*Portuguese* məˈnaʊs) *n.* a variant spelling of **Manaus.**

Ma·nas·sas (məˈnæsəs) *n.* a town in NE Virginia, west of Alexandria: site of the victory of Confederate forces in the Battles of Bull Run, or First and Second Manassas (1861; 1862), during the American Civil War. Pop.: 9164 (1970).

Ma·nas·seh (məˈnæsɪ) *n. Old Testament.* **1.** the elder son of Joseph (Genesis 41:51). **2.** the Israelite tribe descended from him. **3.** the territory of this tribe, in the upper Jordan valley. Douay spelling: **Ma·na·ses** (məˈnæsiːz).

man-at-arms *n., pl.* **men-at-arms.** a soldier, esp. a heavily armed mounted soldier in medieval times.

man·a·tee (ˌmænəˈtiː) *n.* any sirenian mammal of the genus *Trichechus,* occurring in tropical coastal waters of America, the West Indies, and Africa: family *Trichechidae.* They resemble whales and have a prehensile upper lip and a broad flattened tail. [C16: via Spanish from Carib *Manattouï*] —**'man·a·ˌtoid** *adj.*

Ma·naus *or* **Ma·náos** (*Portuguese* məˈnaʊs) *n.* a port in N Brazil, capital of Amazonas state, on the Rio Negro 19 km (12 miles) above its confluence with the Amazon: chief commercial centre of the Amazon basin. Pop.: 284 118 (1970).

Manche (*French* mɑ̃ːʃ) *n.* **1.** a department of NW France, in Basse-Normandie region. Capital: St. Lô. Pop.: 466 319 (1975). Area: 6412 sq. km (2501 sq. miles). **2. La.** the French name for the **English Channel.**

Man·ches·ter ('mæntʃɪstə) *n.* a city in NW England, linked to the Mersey estuary by the **Manchester Ship Canal:** commercial and industrial centre, esp. of the cotton and textile trades; university (1846). Pop.: 541 468 (1971). Latin name: **Mancunium.**

Man·ches·ter ter·ri·er *n.* a breed of terrier with a glossy black-and-tan coat. Also called: **black-and-tan terrier.**

man·chi·neel (ˌmæntʃɪˈniːl) *n.* a tropical American euphorbiaceous tree, *Hippomane mancinella,* having fruit and milky highly caustic poisonous sap, which causes skin blisters. [C17: via French from Spanish MANZANILLA]

Man·chu (mænˈtʃuː) *n.* **1.** (*pl.* **·chus** *or* **·chu**) a member of a Mongoloid people of Manchuria who conquered China in the 17th century, establishing an imperial dynasty that lasted until 1912. **2.** the language of this people, belonging to the Tungusic branch of the Altaic family. ~*adj.* **3.** Also: **Ching.** of or relating to the dynasty of the Manchus. [from Manchu, literally: pure]

Man·chu·kuo *or* **Man·chou·kuo** ('mænˈtʃuːˈkwəʊ) *n.* a former state of E Asia (1932–45), consisting of the three provinces of old Manchuria and Jehol.

Man·chu·ri·a (mænˈtʃʊərɪə) *n.* a region of NE China, historically the home of the Manchus, rulers of China from 1644 to 1912: includes part of the Inner Mongolian AR and the provinces of Heilungkiang, Kirin, and Liaoning. Area: about 1 300 000 sq. km (502 000 sq. miles). —**Man'chu·ri·an** *adj., n.*

man·ci·ple ('mænsɪpᵊl) *n.* a steward who buys provisions, esp. in a college, Inn of Court, or monastery. [C13: via Old French from Latin *mancipium* purchase, from *manceps* purchaser, from *manus* hand + *capere* to take]

Man·cu·ni·an (mæŋˈkjuːnɪən) *n.* **1.** a native or inhabitant of Manchester. ~*adj.* **2.** of or relating to Manchester. [from Medieval Latin *Mancunium* Manchester]

-man·cy *n. combining form.* indicating divination of a particular kind: *chiromancy.* [from Old French *-mancie,* from Latin *-mantia,* from Greek *manteia* soothsaying] —**-man·tic** *adj. combining form.*

Man·dae·an *or* **Man·de·an** (mænˈdɪən) *n.* **1.** a member of a Gnostic sect of Iraq. **2.** the form of Aramaic used by this sect. ~*adj.* **3.** of or relating to this sect. [C19: from Aramaic *mandaya* Gnostics, from *mandā* knowledge] —**Man'dae·an·ism** *or* **Man'de·an·ism** *n.*

man·da·la ('mændələ, mænˈdɑːlə) *n. Hindu and Buddhist art.* any of various designs symbolizing the universe, usually circular. [Sanskrit: circle]

Man·da·lay ('mændəˌleɪ) *n.* a city in central Burma, on the Irrawaddy River: the second largest city in the country and former capital of Burma and of Upper Burma; Buddhist religious centre. Pop.: 401 633 (1970 est.).

man·da·mus (mænˈdeɪməs) *n., pl.* **·mus·es.** *Law.* (formerly) a writ, now a prerogative order, from a superior court commanding an inferior tribunal, public official, corporation, etc., to take some specified action. [C16: Latin, literally: we command, from *mandāre* to command]

man·da·rin ('mændərɪn) *n.* **1.** (in the Chinese Empire) a member of any of the nine senior grades of the bureaucracy, entered by examinations. **2.** a high-ranking official whose powers are extensive and thought to be outside political control. **3. a.** a small citrus tree, *Citrus nobilis,* cultivated for its edible fruit. **b.** the fruit of this tree, resembling the tangerine.

[C16: from Portuguese *mandarim*, via Malay *menteri* from Sanskrit *mantrin* counsellor, from *mantra* counsel] —'**man+dar+in+ate** *n.*

Man+da+rin Chin+ese *or* **Man+da+rin** *n.* the official language of China since 1917; the form of Chinese spoken by about two thirds of the population and taught in schools throughout China. See also **Chinese, Pekingese.**

Man+da+rin col+lar *n.* a high stiff round collar.

man+da+rin duck *n.* an Asian duck, *Aix galericulata*, the male of which has a distinctive brightly coloured and patterned plumage and crest.

man+date *n.* ('mændeɪt, -dɪt). **1.** an official or authoritative instruction or command. **2.** *Politics.* the support or commission given to a government and its policies or an elected representative and his policies through an electoral victory. **3.** (*often cap.*) Also called: **mandated territory.** (formerly) any of the territories under the trusteeship of the League of Nations administered by one of its member states. **4. a.** *Roman law.* a contract by which one person commissions another to act for him gratuitously and the other accepts the commission. **b.** *Contract law.* a contract of bailment under which the party entrusted with goods undertakes to perform gratuitously some service in respect of such goods. **c.** *Scot. law.* a contract by which a person is engaged to act in the management of the affairs of another. ~*vb.* ('mændeɪt). (*tr.*) **5.** *International law.* to assign (territory) to a nation under a mandate. **6.** to delegate authority to. **7.** *Obsolete.* to give a command to. [C16: from Latin *mandātum* something commanded, from *mandāre* to command, perhaps from *manus* hand + *dāre* to give] —'**man+ˌda+tor** *n.*

man+da+to+ry ('mændətərɪ, -trɪ) *adj. also* **man+da+tar+y. 1.** having the nature or powers of a mandate. **2.** obligatory; compulsory. **3.** (of a state) having received a mandate over some territory. ~*n., pl.* **-ries. 4.** a person or state holding a mandate. —'**man+da+to+ri+ly** *adv.*

Man+de ('mɑːndeɪ) *n., pl.* **+de** *or* **+des. 1.** a group of African languages, a branch of the Niger-Congo family, spoken chiefly in Mali, Guinea, and Sierra Leone. ~*adj.* **2.** of or relating to this group of languages.

Man+de+ville ('mændəvɪl) *n.* **1. Ber+nard de.** ?1670–1733, English author, born in Holland, noted for his satire *The Fable of the Bees* (1723). **2.** Sir **John.** 14th-century English author of *The Travels of Sir John Mandeville.* The book claims to be an account of the author's journeys in the East but is largely a compilation from other works.

man+di ('mʌndɪ) *n.* (in India) a big market. [Hindi]

man+di+ble ('mændɪbᵊl) *n.* **1.** the lower jawbone in vertebrates. See **jaw** (sense 1). **2.** either of a pair of mouthparts in insects and other arthropods that are usually used for biting and crushing food. **3.** *Ornithol.* either the upper or the lower part of the bill, esp. the lower part. [C16: via Old French from Late Latin *mandibula* jaw, from *mandere* to chew] —**man+dib+u+lar** (mæn'dɪbjʊlə) *adj.* —**man+dib+u+late** (mæn'dɪbjʊlɪt, -ˌleɪt) *n., adj.*

Man+din+go (mæn'dɪŋgəʊ) *n., pl.* **+gos** *or* **+goes.** a former name for **Mande** or **Malinke.**

man+dir ('mʌndɪə) *n.* a Hindu or Jain temple. [Hindi, from Sanskrit *mandira*]

man+do+la ('mændələ) *n.* an early type of mandolin. [from Italian]

man+do+lin *or* **man+do+line** (ˌmændə'lɪn) *n.* a plucked stringed instrument related to the lute, having four pairs of strings tuned in ascending fifths stretched over a small light body with a fretted finger board. It is usually played with a plectrum, long notes being sustained by the tremelo. [C18: via French from Italian *mandolino*, diminutive of *mandora* lute, ultimately from Greek *pandoura* musical instrument with three strings] —ˌ**man+do+'lin+ist** *n.*

man+dor+la (mæn'dɔːlə) *n.* (in painting, sculpture, etc.) an almond-shaped area of light, usually surrounding the resurrected Christ or the Virgin at the Assumption. Also called: **vesica.** [from Italian, literally: almond, from Late Latin *amandula*; see ALMOND]

man+drake ('mændreɪk) *or* **man+drag+o+ra** (mæn'drægərə) *n.* **1.** a Eurasian solanaceous plant, *Mandragora officinarum*, with purplish flowers and a forked root. It was formerly thought to have magic powers and a narcotic was prepared from its root. **2.** another name for the **May apple.** [C14: probably via Middle Dutch from Latin *mandragoras* (whence Old English *mandragora*), from Greek. The form *mandrake* was probably adopted through folk etymology, because of the allegedly human appearance of the root and because *drake* (dragon) suggested magical powers]

man+drel *or* **man+dril** ('mændrəl) *n.* **1.** a spindle on which a workpiece is supported during machining operations. **2.** a shaft or arbor on which a machining tool is mounted. **3.** the driving spindle in the headstock of a lathe. **4.** *Brit.* a miner's pick. [C16: perhaps related to French *mandrin* lathe]

man+drill ('mændrɪl) *n.* an Old World monkey, *Mandrillus sphinx*, of W Africa. It has a short tail and brown hair, and the ridged muzzle, nose, and hindquarters are red and blue. [C18: from MAN + DRILL[4]]

man+du+cate ('mændjʊˌkeɪt) *vb.* (*tr.*) *Literary.* to eat or chew. [C17: from Latin *mandūcāre* to chew] —ˌ**man+du+'ca+tion** *n.* —ˌ**man+du+'ca+to+ry** *adj.*

mane (meɪn) *n.* **1.** the long coarse hair that grows from the crest of the neck in such mammals as the lion and horse. **2.** long thick human hair. [Old English *manu*; related to Old High German *mana*, Old Norse *mön*, and perhaps to Old English *mene* and Old High German *menni* necklace] —**maned** *adj.* —'**mane+less** *adj.*

man-eat+er *n.* **1.** an animal, such as a tiger, that has become accustomed to eating human flesh. **2.** any of various sharks that feed on human flesh, esp. the great white shark (*Carcharodon carcharias*). **3.** a human cannibal. **4.** *Informal.* a woman with many lovers. —'**man-ˌeat+ing** *adj.*

ma+nège *or* **ma+nege** (mæ'neɪʒ) *n.* **1.** the art of training horses and riders. Compare **dressage. 2.** a riding school. [C17: via French from Italian *maneggio*, from *maneggiare* to MANAGE]

ma+nes ('mɑːneɪz; *Latin* 'mɑːnɛs) *pl. n.* (*sometimes cap.*) (in Roman legend) **1.** the spirits of the dead, often revered as minor deities. **2.** (*functioning as sing.*) the shade of a dead person. [C14: from Latin, probably: the good ones, from Old Latin *mānus* good]

Ma+nes ('meɪniːz) *n.* See **Mani.**

Ma+net (*French* ma'nɛ) *n.* **Édouard** (e'dwaːr). 1832–83, French painter. His painting *Le Déjeuner sur l'herbe* (1863), which was condemned by the Parisian establishment, was acclaimed by the impressionists, whom he decisively influenced.

ma+neu+ver (mə'nuːvə) *n., vb.* the usual U.S. spelling of **manoeuvre.** —**ma+'neu+ver+a+ble** *adj.* —**ma+ˌneu+ver+a+'bil+i+ty** *n.* —**ma+'neu+ver+er** *n.*

man Fri+day *n.* a loyal male servant or assistant. [after the native in Daniel Defoe's novel *Robinson Crusoe* (1719)]

man+ful ('mænfʊl) *adj.* a less common word for **manly.** —'**man+ful+ly** *adv.* —'**man+ful+ness** *n.*

man+ga+bey ('mæŋgəˌbeɪ) *n.* any of several large agile arboreal Old World monkeys of the genus *Cercocebus*, of central Africa, having long limbs and tail and white upper eyelids. [C18: after the name of a region in Madagascar]

Man+ga+lore (ˌmæŋgə'lɔː) *n.* a port in S India, in Karnataka on the Malabar Coast. Pop.: 165 174 (1971).

man+ga+nate ('mæŋgəˌneɪt) *n.* a salt of manganic acid.

man+ga+nese (ˌmæŋgə'niːz) *n.* a brittle greyish-white metallic element that exists in four allotropic forms, occurring principally in pyrolusite and rhodonite: used in making steel and ferromagnetic alloys. Symbol: Mn; atomic no.: 25; atomic wt.: 54.938; valency: 1,2,3,4,6, or 7. [C17: via French from Italian *manganese*, probably altered form of Medieval Latin MAGNESIA]

man+ga+nese bronze *n.* any of various alloys containing copper (55–60 per cent), zinc (35–42 per cent), and manganese (about 3.5 per cent).

man+ga+nese steel *n.* any very hard steel containing manganese (11–14 per cent), used in dredger buckets, rock-crushers, railway points, etc.

man+gan+ic (mæn'gænɪk) *adj.* of or containing manganese in the trivalent state.

man+gan+ic ac+id *n.* a hypothetical dibasic acid known only in solution and in the form of manganate salts. Formula: H_2MnO_4.

Man+gan+in ('mæŋgənɪn) *n. Trademark.* an alloy of copper containing manganese (13–18 per cent) and nickel (1–4 per cent): it has a high electrical resistance that does not vary greatly with temperature and is used in resistors.

man+ga+nite ('mæŋgəˌnaɪt) *n.* a blackish mineral consisting of basic manganese oxide in monoclinic crystalline form: a source of manganese. Formula: MnO(OH).

man+ga+nous ('mæŋgənəs, mæn'gænəs) *adj.* of or containing manganese in the divalent state.

mange (meɪndʒ) *n.* an infectious disorder mainly affecting domestic animals, characterized by itching, formation of papules and vesicles, and loss of hair: caused by parasitic mites. [C14: from Old French *mangeue* itch, literally: eating, from *mangier* to eat]

man+gel+wur+zel ('mæŋgᵊlˌwɜːzᵊl) *or* **man+gold+wur+zel** ('mæŋgəʊldˌwɜːzᵊl) *n.* a Eurasian variety of the beet plant, *Beta vulgaris*, cultivated as a cattle food, having a large yellowish root. Often shortened to **mangel, mangold.** [C18: from German *Mangoldwurzel*, from *Mangold* beet + *Wurzel* root]

man+ger ('meɪndʒə) *n.* **1.** a trough or box in a stable, barn, etc., from which horses or cattle feed. **2.** *Nautical.* a basin-like construction in the bows of a vessel for catching water draining from an anchor rode or coming in through the hawseholes. [C14: from Old French *maingeure* food trough, from *mangier* to eat, ultimately from Latin *mandūcāre* to chew]

man+gle[1] ('mæŋgᵊl) *vb.* (*tr.*) **1.** to mutilate, disfigure, or destroy by cutting, crushing, or tearing. **2.** to ruin, spoil, or mar. [C14: from Norman French *mangler*, probably from Old French *mahaignier* to maim] —'**man+gler** *n.*

man+gle[2] ('mæŋgᵊl) *n.* **1.** a machine for pressing or drying textiles, clothes, etc., consisting of two heavy rollers between which the cloth is passed. **2.** *Chiefly Brit.* another word for **wringer.** ~*vb.* (*tr.*) **3.** to press or dry in a mangle. [C18: from Dutch *mangel*, ultimately from Late Latin *manganum.* See MANGONEL]

man+go ('mæŋgəʊ) *n., pl.* **+goes** *or* **+gos. 1.** a tropical Asian anacardiaceous evergreen tree, *Mangifera indica*, cultivated in the tropics for its fruit. **2.** the ovoid edible fruit of this tree, having a smooth rind and sweet juicy orange-yellow flesh. [C16: via Portuguese from Malay *mangā*, from Tamil *mānkāy* from *mān* mango tree + *kāy* fruit]

man+go+nel ('mæŋgəˌnɛl) *n. History.* a war engine for hurling stones. [C13: via Old French from Medieval Latin *manganellus*, ultimately from Greek *manganon*]

man+go+steen ('mæŋgəʊˌstiːn) *n.* **1.** an East Indian tree, *Garcinia mangostana*, with thick leathery leaves and edible fruit: family *Guttiferae.* **2.** the fruit of this tree, having a sweet juicy pulp and a hard skin. [C16: from Malay *mangustan*]

man+grove ('mæŋgrəʊv, 'mæn-) *n.* **1.** any tropical evergreen tree or shrub of the genus *Rhizophora,* having stiltlike intertwining aerial roots and forming dense thickets along coasts: family *Rhizophoraceae.* **2.** any of various similar trees or shrubs of the genus *Avicennia:* family *Avicenniaceae.* [C17 *mangrow* (changed through influence of *grove*), from Portuguese *mangue,* ultimately from Taino]

man+gy *or* **man+gey** ('meɪndʒɪ) *adj.* +gi+er, +gi+est. **1.** having or caused by mange: *a mangy dog.* **2.** scruffy or shabby: *a mangy carpet.* —'**man+gi+ly** *adv.* —'**man+gi+ness** *n.*

man+han·dle ('mæn,hændᵊl, ,mæn'hændᵊl) *vb.* (*tr.*) **1.** to handle or push (someone) about roughly. **2.** to move or do by manpower rather than by machinery.

Man+hat+tan (mæn'hætᵊn, mən-) *n.* **1.** an island at the N end of New York Bay, between the Hudson, East, and Harlem Rivers: administratively (with adjacent islets) a borough of New York City; a major financial, commercial, and cultural centre. Pop.: 1 539 233 (1970). Area: 47 sq. km (22 sq. miles). **2.** a mixed drink consisting of four parts whisky, one part vermouth, and a dash of bitters.

Man+hat+tan Dis+trict *n.* (during World War II) the code name for a unit of U.S. army engineers established in 1942 to produce the atomic bomb in secret.

man+hole ('mæn,həʊl) *n.* **1.** Also called: **inspection chamber.** a shaft with a removable cover that leads down to a sewer or drain. **2.** a hole, usually with a detachable cover, through which a man can enter a boiler, tank, etc.

man+hood ('mænhʊd) *n.* **1.** the state or quality of being a man or being manly. **2.** men collectively. **3.** the state of being human.

man+hood suf+frage *n.* the right of adult male citizens to vote.

man-hour *n.* a unit for measuring work in industry, equal to the work done by one man in one hour.

man+hunt ('mæn,hʌnt) *n.* an organized search, usually by police, for a wanted man or fugitive. —'**man+,hunt·er** *n.*

Ma·ni ('mɑːnɪ) *n.* ?216–?276 A.D., Persian prophet who founded Manichaeism. Also called: **Manes, Manichaeus.**

ma·ni·a ('meɪnɪə) *n.* **1.** a mental disorder characterized by great excitement and occasionally violent behaviour. See also **manic-depressive. 2.** an obsessional enthusiasm or partiality: *a mania for mushrooms.* [C14: via Late Latin from Greek: madness]

-ma·ni·a *n. combining form.* indicating extreme desire or pleasure of a specified kind or an abnormal excitement aroused by something: *kleptomania; nymphomania; pyromania.* [from MANIA] —**-ma·ni·ac** *n. and adj. combining form.*

ma+ni+ac ('meɪnɪ,æk) *n.* **1.** *Informal.* a wild disorderly person. **2.** *Informal.* a person who has a great craving or enthusiasm for something: *a football maniac.* **3.** *Psychiatry, obsolete.* a person afflicted with mania. [C17: from Late Latin *maniacus* belonging to madness, from Greek]

ma+ni+a+cal (mə'naɪəkᵊl) *or* **ma+ni+ac** *adj.* **1.** affected with or characteristic of mania. **2.** characteristic of or befitting a maniac: *maniacal laughter.* —**ma+'ni+a+cal+ly** *adv.*

man+ic ('mænɪk) *adj.* **1.** characterizing, denoting, or affected by mania. ~*n.* **2.** a person afflicted with mania. [C19: from Greek, from MANIA]

man·ic-de·pres+sive *Psychiatry.* ~*adj.* **1.** denoting a mental disorder characterized by an alternation between extreme excitement and confidence and deep depression. ~*n.* **2.** a person afflicted with this disorder. Compare **cyclothymia.**

Man·i·chae+ism *or* **Man·i·che+ism** ('mænɪkiː,ɪzəm) *n.* **1.** the system of religious doctrines, including elements of Gnosticism, Zoroastrianism, Christianity, Buddhism, etc., taught by the Persian prophet Mani about the 3rd century A.D. It was based on a supposed primordial conflict between light and darkness or goodness and evil. **2.** *Chiefly R.C. Church.* any similar heretical philosophy involving a radical dualism. [C14: from Late Latin *Manichaeus,* from Late Greek *Manikhaios* of Mani] —,**Man·i+'chae·an** *or* ,**Man·i+'che·an** *adj., n.* —'**Man·i+chee** *n.*

Man·i·chae·us *or* **Man·i·che·us** (,mænɪ'kiːəs) *n.* See **Mani.**

ma+ni+cot+ti (,mænɪ'kɒtɪ) *n.* large tubular noodles, usually stuffed with ricotta cheese and baked in a tomato sauce. [Italian: sleeves, plural of *manicotto,* diminutive of *manica* sleeve]

man·i+cure ('mænɪ,kjʊə) *n.* **1.** care of the hands and fingernails, involving shaping the nails, removing cuticles, etc. **2.** another word for **manicurist.** ~*vb.* **3.** to care for (the hands and fingernails) in this way. **4.** (*tr.*) *U.S.* to trim neatly. [C19: from French, from Latin *manus* hand + *cūra* care]

man·i+cur+ist ('mænɪ,kjʊərɪst) *n.* a person who gives manicures, esp. as a profession.

man·i+fest ('mænɪ,fɛst) *adj.* **1.** easily noticed or perceived; obvious; plain. **2.** *Psychoanal.* of or relating to apparently conscious impulses that may conceal unconscious ones. Compare **latent** (sense 4). ~*vb.* **3.** (*tr.*) to show plainly; reveal or display: *to manifest great emotion.* **4.** (*tr.*) to prove beyond doubt. **5.** (*intr.*) (of a disembodied spirit) to appear in visible form. **6.** (*tr.*) to list in a ship's manifest. ~*n.* **7.** a customs document containing particulars of a ship, its cargo, and its destination. **8.** *Chiefly U.S.* **a.** a list of cargo, passengers, etc., on an aeroplane. **b.** a list of railway trucks or their cargo. **c.** a fast freight train carrying perishables, etc. [C14: from Latin *manifestus* plain, literally: struck with the hand, from *manū* with the hand + *-festus* struck] —'**man·i+,fest+a·ble** *adj.* —'**man·i+,fest+ly** *adv.* —'**man·i+,fest+ness** *n.*

man·i+fes+ta·tion (,mænɪfɛ'steɪʃən) *n.* **1.** the act of demonstrating; display: *a manifestation of solidarity.* **2.** the state of being manifested. **3.** an indication or sign. **4.** a public demonstration of feeling. **5.** the materialization of a disembodied spirit. —,**man·i·fes+'ta·tion+al** *adj.* —**man·i+'fes+ta+tive** *adj.*

Man·i+fest Des+ti+ny *n.* (esp. in the 19th-century U.S.) the belief that the U.S. was a chosen land that had been allotted the entire North American continent by God.

man·i+fes+to (,mænɪ'fɛstəʊ) *n., pl.* +toes *or* +tos. a public declaration of intent, policy, aims, etc., as issued by a political party, government, or movement. [C17: from Italian, from *manifestare* to MANIFEST]

man·i+fold ('mænɪ,fəʊld) *adj. Formal.* **1.** of several different kinds; multiple: *manifold reasons.* **2.** having many different forms, features, or elements: *manifold breeds of dog.* ~*n.* **3.** something having many varied parts, forms, or features. **4.** a copy of a page, book, etc. **5.** a chamber or pipe with a number of inlets or outlets used to collect or distribute a fluid. In an internal-combustion engine the **inlet manifold** carries the vaporized fuel from the carburettor to the inlet ports and the **exhaust manifold** carries the exhaust gases away. **6.** *Maths.* **a.** a collection of objects or a set. **b.** a topological space having specific properties. ~*vb.* **7.** (*tr.*) to duplicate (a page, book, etc.). **8.** to make manifold; multiply. [Old English *manigfeald.* See MANY, -FOLD] —'**man·i+,fold+er** *n.* —'**man·i+,fold+ly** *adv.* —'**man·i+,fold+ness** *n.*

man·i+kin, man·a+kin, *or* **man+ni+kin** ('mænɪkɪn) *n.* **1.** a little man; dwarf or child. **2. a.** an anatomical model of the body or a part of the body, esp. for use in medical or art instruction. **b.** Also called: **phantom.** an anatomical model of a fully developed fetus, for use in teaching midwifery or obstetrics. **3.** variants of **mannequin.** [C17: from Dutch *manneken,* diminutive of MAN]

Ma+nil·a (mə'nɪlə) *n.* **1.** the chief port of the Philippines, on S Luzon on Manila Bay: capital of the republic until 1948; seat of the Far Eastern University and the University of Santo Tomas (1611). Pop.: 1 438 252 (1975 est.). **2.** a type of cigar made in this city.

Ma+nil·a Bay *n.* an almost landlocked inlet of the South China Sea in the Philippines, in W Luzon: mostly forms Manila harbour. Area: 1994 sq. km (770 sq. miles).

Ma+nil·a hemp *or* **Ma+nil+la hemp** *n.* a fibre obtained from the plant abaca, used for rope, paper, etc.

Ma+nil·a pa+per *or* **Ma+nil+la pa+per** *n.* a strong usually brown paper made from Manila hemp or similar fibres.

Ma+nil·a rope *or* **Ma+nil+la rope** *n.* rope of Manila hemp.

ma+nil+la (mə'nɪlə) *n.* an early form of currency in W Africa in the pattern of a small bracelet. [from Spanish: bracelet, diminutive of *mano* hand, from Latin *manus*]

ma+nille (mæ'nɪl) *n.* (in ombre and quadrille) the second best trump. [C17: from French, from Spanish *malilla,* diminutive of *mala* bad]

Ma+nin+ke (mə'nɪŋkə) *n., pl.* +ke *or* +kes. a variant spelling of **Malinke.**

man in the moon *n.* **1.** the moon when considered to resemble the face of a man. **2.** (in folklore and nursery rhyme) a character dwelling in the moon.

man in the street *n.* the typical or ordinary person, esp. as a hypothetical unit in statistics, etc.

man·i+oc ('mænɪ,ɒk) *or* **man·i·o·ca** (,mænɪ'əʊkə) *n.* another name for **cassava** (sense 1). [C16: from Tupi *mandioca;* earlier form *manihot* from French, from Guarani *mandio*]

man·i+ple ('mænɪpᵊl) *n.* **1.** (in ancient Rome) a unit of 120 to 200 foot soldiers. **2.** *Ecclesiast.* an ornamental band formerly worn on the left arm by the celebrant at the Eucharist. [C16: from Medieval Latin *manipulus* (the Eucharistic vestment), from Latin, literally: a handful, from *manus* hand]

ma+nip·u·lar (mə'nɪpjʊlə) *adj.* **1.** of or relating to an ancient Roman maniple. **2.** of or relating to manipulation.

ma+nip·u·late (mə'nɪpjʊ,leɪt) *vb.* **1.** (*tr.*) to handle or use, esp. with some skill, in a process or action: *to manipulate a pair of scissors.* **2.** to negotiate, control, or influence (something) cleverly or skilfully. **3.** to falsify (accounts, etc.) for one's own advantage. **4.** (in physiotherapy) to examine or treat manually, as in loosening a joint. [C19: back formation from *manipulation,* from Latin *manipulus* handful] —**ma+nip·u·la·bil+i·ty** (mə,nɪpjʊlə'bɪlɪtɪ) *n.* —**ma+'nip·u+,lat+a·ble** *or* **ma+'nip·u+la·ble** *adj.* —**ma+,nip·u+'la·tion** *n.* —**ma+'nip·u+la+tive** *adj.* —**ma+'nip·u+la+tive+ly** *adv.* —**ma+'nip·u+,la+tor** *n.* —**ma+'nip·u+la+to·ry** *adj.*

Ma+ni+pur (,mʌnɪ'pʊə) *n.* a union territory of NE India: largely densely forested mountains. Capital: Imphal. Pop.: 1 072 753 (1971). Area: 20 793 sq. km (8109 sq. miles).

Ma+ni+sa ('mɑːnɪ,sɑː) *n.* a city in W Turkey: the Byzantine seat of government (1204–1313). Pop.: 70 022 (1970).

Man·i+to+ba (,mænɪ'təʊbə) *n.* **1.** a province of W Canada: consists of prairie in the southwest, with extensive forests in the north and tundra near Hudson Bay in the northeast. Capital: Winnipeg. Pop.: 1 021 506 (1976). Area: 650 090 sq. km (251 000 sq. miles). **2. Lake.** a lake in W Canada, in S Manitoba: fed by the outflow from Lake Winnipegosis; drains into Lake Winnipeg. Area: 4706 sq. km (1817 sq. miles).

man·i+tou, man·i+tu ('mænɪ,tuː), *or* **man·i+to** ('mænɪ,təʊ) *n., pl.* +tous, +tus, +tos *or* +tou, +tu, +to. (among the Algonquian Indians) a deified spirit or force. [C17: from Algonquian; related to Ojibwa *manito* spirit]

Man·i+tou+lin Is+land (,mænɪ'tuːlɪn) *n.* an island in N Lake Huron in Ontario: the largest freshwater island in the world. Length: 129 km (80 miles). Width: up to 48 km (30 miles).

Man·i+za+les (,mænɪ'zɑːlɛs; *Spanish* ,mani'sales) *n.* a city in W

Colombia, in the Cordillera Central of the Andes at an altitude of 2100 m (7000 ft.): commercial centre of a rich coffee-growing area. Pop.: 199 904 (1973).

man jack *n. Informal.* a single individual (in the phrases **every man jack, no man jack**).

man+kind (ˌmæn'kaɪnd) *n.* **1.** human beings collectively; humanity. **2.** men collectively, as opposed to womankind.

mank·y ('mæŋkɪ) *adj.* **mank·i·er, mank·i·est.** *Central Scot. dialect.* dirty or decayed, as a building. [of unknown origin]

Man·ley ('mænlɪ) *n.* **Mi·chael Nor·man.** born 1924, Jamaican statesman; prime minister of Jamaica (1972-80).

man+like ('mænˌlaɪk) *adj.* resembling or befitting a man.

man+ly ('mænlɪ) *adj.* **+li+er, +li+est. 1.** possessing qualities, such as vigour or courage, generally regarded as appropriate to or typical of a man; masculine. **2.** characteristic of or befitting a man: *a manly sport.* ~*adv.* **3.** *Archaic.* in a manly manner. —**'man+li+ness** *n.*

man-made *adj.* made or produced by man; artificial.

Mann (*German* man) *n.* **1. Hein·rich** ('haɪnrɪç). 1871–1950, German novelist: works include *The Blue Angel* (1905) and *Man of Straw* (1918). **2.** his brother **Thom·as** ('to:mas). 1875–1955, German novelist, in the U.S. after 1937. His works deal mainly with the problem of the artist in bourgeois society and include the short story *Death in Venice* (1913) and the novels *Buddenbrooks* (1900), *The Magic Mountain* (1924), and *Doctor Faustus* (1947): Nobel prize for literature 1929.

man+na ('mænə) *n.* **1.** *Old Testament.* the miraculous food which sustained the Israelites in the wilderness (Exodus 16:14–36). **2.** any spiritual or divine nourishment. **3.** a sweet substance obtained from various plants, esp. from an ash tree, *Fraxinus ornus* (**manna** or **flowering ash**) of S Europe, used as a mild laxative. [Old English via Late Latin from Greek, from Hebrew *mān*]

Man+nar (mə'nɑ:) *n.* **Gulf of.** the part of the Indian Ocean between SE India and the island of Sri Lanka: pearl fishing.

manned (mænd) *adj.* **1.** supplied or equipped with men, esp. soldiers. **2.** (of spacecraft, etc.) having a human crew.

man+ne+quin ('mænɪkɪn) *n.* **1.** a woman who wears the clothes displayed at a fashion show; model. **2.** a life-size dummy of the human body used to fit or display clothes. **3.** *Arts.* another name for **lay figure.** [C18: via French from Dutch *manneken* MANIKIN]

man+ner ('mænə) *n.* **1.** a way of doing or being. **2.** a person's bearing and behaviour: *she had a cool manner.* **3.** the style or customary way of doing or accomplishing something: *sculpture in the Greek manner.* **4.** type or kind: *what manner of man is this?* **5.** mannered style, as in art; mannerism. **6. by all manner of means.** certainly; of course. **7. by no manner of means.** under no circumstances. **8. in a manner of speaking.** in a way; so to speak. **9. to the manner born.** naturally fitted to a specified role or activity. [C12: via Norman French from Old French *maniere,* from Vulgar Latin *manuāria* (unattested) a way of handling something, noun use of Latin *manuārius* belonging to the hand, from *manus* hand]

man+nered ('mænəd) *adj.* **1.** having idiosyncrasies or mannerisms; affected: *mannered gestures.* **2.** of or having mannerisms of style, as in art or literature. **3.** (*in combination*) having manners as specified: *ill-mannered.*

Man·ner·heim ('mænəˌhaɪm) *n.* Baron **Carl Gus·taf E·mil.** 1867–1951, Finnish soldier and statesman; president of Finland (1944–46).

man+ner+ism ('mænəˌrɪzəm) *n.* **1.** a distinctive and individual gesture or trait; idiosyncrasy. **2.** (*often cap.*) a principally Italian movement in art and architecture between the High Renaissance and Baroque periods (1520–1600) that sought to represent an ideal of beauty rather than natural images of it, using characteristic distortion and exaggeration of human proportions, perspective, etc. **3.** adherence to a distinctive or affected manner, esp. in art or literature. —**'man+ner+ist** *n.* —**ˌman+ner+'is+tic** *or* **ˌman+ner+'is+ti+cal** *adj.* —**ˌman+ner+'is+ti+cal+ly** *adv.*

man+ner+less ('mænəlɪs) *adj.* having bad manners; boorish. —**'man+ner+less+ness** *n.*

man+ner+ly ('mænəlɪ) *adj.* **1.** well-mannered; polite; courteous. ~*adv.* **2.** *Now rare.* with good manners; politely; courteously. —**'man+ner+li+ness** *n.*

man+ners ('mænəz) *pl. n.* **1.** social conduct: *he has the manners of a pig.* **2.** a socially acceptable way of behaving.

Mann+heim ('mænhaɪm; *German* 'manhaɪm) *n.* **1.** a city in SW West Germany, in Baden-Württemberg at the confluence of the Rhine and Neckar: one of Europe's largest inland harbours; a cultural and musical centre. Pop.: 325 386 (1974 est.). **2.** (*modifier*) *Music.* of or relating to the Mannheim School.

Mann+heim School *n. Music.* a group of musicians and composers connected with the court orchestra at Mannheim during the mid-18th century, who evolved the controlled orchestral crescendo as well as a largely homophonic musical style.

man+ni+kin ('mænɪkɪn) *n.* a variant spelling of **manikin.**

Man·ning ('mænɪŋ) *n.* **Hen·ry Ed·ward.** 1808–92, English churchman. Originally an Anglican, he was converted to Roman Catholicism (1851) and made archbishop of Westminster (1865) and cardinal (1875).

man+nish ('mænɪʃ) *adj.* **1.** (of a woman) having or displaying qualities regarded as typical of a man. **2.** of or resembling a man. —**'man+nish+ly** *adv.* —**'man+nish+ness** *n.*

man+ni+tol ('mænɪˌtɒl) *or* **man+nite** ('mænaɪt) *n.* a white crystalline water-soluble sweet-tasting alcohol, found in plants and used in dietetic sweets and as a dietary supplement. Formula: $C_6H_8(OH)_6$. [from MANNOSE + -ITE + -OL] —**man+nit+ic** (mə'nɪtɪk) *adj.*

man+nose ('mænəʊs, -nəʊz) *n.* a hexose sugar occurring in mannitol and many polysaccharides. Formula: $C_6H_{12}O_6$. [C20: from MANNA + -OSE[2]]

ma+noeu+vre *or U.S.* **ma+neu+ver** (mə'nu:və) *n.* **1.** a contrived, complicated, and possibly deceptive plan or action: *political manoeuvres.* **2.** a movement or action requiring dexterity and skill. **3. a.** a tactic or movement of one or a number of military or naval units. **b.** (*pl.*) tactical exercises, usually on a large scale. **4.** a planned movement of an aircraft in flight. ~*vb.* **5.** (*tr.*) to contrive or accomplish with skill or cunning. **6.** (*intr.*) to manipulate situations, etc., in order to gain some end: *to manoeuvre for the leadership.* **7.** (*intr.*) to perform a manoeuvre or manoeuvres. **8.** to move or deploy or be moved or deployed, as military units, etc. [C15: from French, from Medieval Latin *manuopera* manual work, from Latin *manū operāre* to work with the hand] —**ma+'noeu+vra·ble** *or U.S.* **ma+'neu+ver+a·ble** *adj.* —**ma+ˌnoeu+vra·'bil+i+ty** *or U.S.* **ma+ˌneu+ver+a·'bil+i+ty** *n.* —**ma+'noeu+vrer** *or U.S.* **ma+'neu+ver+er** *n.*

man of God *n.* **1.** a saint or prophet. **2.** a clergyman.

man of straw *n.* **1.** a person of little substance. **2.** Also called: **straw man.** *Chiefly U.S.* a person used as a cover for some dubious plan or enterprise; front.

man-of-war *or* **man o' war** *n., pl.* **men-of-war, men o' war. 1.** a warship. **2.** See **Portuguese man-of-war.**

man-of-war bird *or* **man-o'-war bird** *n.* another name for **frigate bird.**

Ma·no·le·te (*Spanish* ˌmano'lete) *n.* original name *Manuel Rodriguez y Sánchez.* 1917–47, Spanish bullfighter.

ma+nom+e·ter (mə'nɒmɪtə) *n.* an instrument for comparing pressures; typically a glass U-tube containing mercury, in which pressure is indicated by the difference in levels in the two arms of the tube. [C18: from French *manomètre,* from Greek *manos* sparse + *metron* measure] —**man·o+met+ric** (ˌmænəʊ'mɛtrɪk) *or* **ˌman·o+'met+ri+cal** *adj.* —**ˌman·o+'met+ri+cal+ly** *adv.* —**ma+'nom+e+try** *n.*

man+or ('mænə) *n.* **1.** (in medieval Europe) the manor house of a lord and the lands attached to it. **2.** (before 1776 in some North American colonies) a tract of land granted with rights of inheritance by royal charter. **3.** a manor house. **4.** a landed estate. **5.** *Brit. informal.* a police district. [C13: from Old French *manoir* dwelling, from *maneir* to dwell, from Latin *manēre* to remain] —**ma+no+ri+al** (mə'nɔ:rɪəl) *adj.*

man+or house *or* **seat** *n.* (esp. formerly) the house of the lord of a manor.

man+pow·er ('mænˌpaʊə) *n.* **1.** power supplied by men. **2.** a unit of power based on the rate at which a man can work; approximately 75 watts. **3.** available or suitable power: *the manpower of a battalion.*

man+qué *French.* (mɑ̃'ke; *English* 'mɒŋkeɪ) *adj.* (*postpositive*) unfulfilled; potential; would-be: *the manager is an actor manqué.* [C19: literally: having missed]

Man+re+sa (*Spanish* man'resa) *n.* a city in NE Spain: contains a cave used as the spiritual retreat of St. Ignatius Loyola. Pop.: 57 846 (1970).

man+rope ('mænˌrəʊp) *n. Nautical.* a rope railing.

man+sard ('mænsɑ:d, -səd) *n.* **1.** Also called: **mansard roof.** a roof having two slopes on both sides and both ends, the lower slopes being steeper than the upper. Compare **gambrel roof. 2.** an attic having such a roof. [C18: from French *mansarde,* after François MANSART]

Man·sart (*French* mɑ̃'sa:r) *n.* **1. Fran·çois** (frɑ̃'swa). 1598–1666, French architect, who established the classical style in French architecture. **2.** his great-nephew, **Jules Har·douin** (ʒyl ar'dwɛ̃). 1646–1708, French architect, who completed the Palace of Versailles.

manse (mæns) *n.* **1.** (in certain religious denominations) the house provided for a minister. **2.** *Archaic.* a large house. [C15: from Medieval Latin *mansus* dwelling, from the past participle of Latin *manēre* to stay]

man+ser·vant ('mænˌsɜ:vənt) *n., pl.* **men+ser·vants.** a male servant, esp. a valet.

Mans+field[1] ('mænsˌfi:ld) *n.* a town in central England, in W Nottinghamshire: coal-mining and hosiery industries. Pop.: 57 598 (1971).

Mans·field[2] ('mænsˌfi:ld) *n.* **Ka·the·rine,** pen name of *Kathleen Mansfield Beauchamp.* 1888–1923, English writer, born in New Zealand, noted for her short stories, such as those in *Bliss* (1920) and *The Garden Party* (1922).

Mans·holt (*Dutch* 'mɑnshɔlt) *n.* **Sic·co Leen·dert** ('sɪko 'le:ndərt). born 1908, Dutch economist and politician; vice president (1958–72) and president (1972–73) of the Common Market Commission. He was the author of the Mansholt Plan for the agricultural organization of the Common Market.

man+sion ('mænʃən) *n.* **1.** Also called: **mansion house.** a large and imposing house. **2.** a less common word for **manor house. 3.** *Archaic.* any residence. **4.** (*pl.*) a block of flats. **5.** *Astrology.* any of 28 divisions of the zodiac each occupied on successive days by the moon. [C14: via Old French from Latin *mansio* a remaining, from *mansus;* see MANSE]

Man+sion House *n.* **the.** the residence of the Lord Mayor of London.

man-sized *adj.* **1.** of a size appropriate for or convenient for a man. **2.** *Informal.* big; large.

man+slaugh·ter ('mænˌslɔ:tə) *n.* **1.** *Law.* the unlawful killing of one human being by another without malice aforethought.

Compare **murder.** See also **homicide, malice aforethought. 2.** (loosely) the killing of a human being.

man·sue·tude ('mænswɪˌtju:d) *n. Archaic.* gentleness or mildness. [C14: from Latin *mansuētūdō,* from *mansuētus,* past participle of *mansuēscere* to make tame by handling, from *manus* hand + *suescere* to train]

Man·sû·ra (mæn'sʊərə) *n.* See **El Mansûra.**

man·ta ('mæntə; *Spanish* 'manta) *n.* **1.** Also called: **manta ray, devilfish, devil ray.** any large ray (fish) of the family *Mobulidae,* having very wide winglike pectoral fins and feeding on plankton. **2.** a rough cotton cloth made in Spain and Spanish America. **3.** a piece of this used as a blanket or shawl. **4.** another word for **mantelet** (sense 2). [Spanish: cloak, from Vulgar Latin; see MANTLE. The manta ray is so called because it is caught in a trap resembling a blanket]

man·teau ('mæntəʊ; *French* mɑ̃'to) *n., pl.* **·teaus** (-təʊz) *or* **·teaux** (*French* -'to). a cloak or mantle. [C17: via French from Latin *mantellum* MANTLE]

Man·te·gna (*Italian* man'teɲɲa) *n.* **An·dre·a** (an'drɛːa). 1431–1506, Italian painter and engraver, noted esp. for his frescoes, such as those in the Ducal Palace, Mantua.

man·tel *or* **man·tle** ('mæntᵊl) *n.* **1.** a wooden or stone frame around the opening of a fireplace, together with its decorative facing. **2.** Also called: **mantel shelf.** a shelf above this frame. [C15: from French, variant of MANTLE]

man·tel·et ('mæntᵊˌlɛt) *or* **man·tlet** *n.* **1.** a woman's short mantle, often lace-trimmed, worn in the mid-19th century. **2.** a portable bulletproof screen or shelter. [C14: from Old French, diminutive of *mantel* MANTLE]

man·tel·let·ta (ˌmæntɪ'lɛtə) *n. R.C. Church.* a sleeveless knee-length vestment, worn by cardinals, bishops, etc. [Italian, from Old French *mantelet* or Medieval Latin *mantelletum,* diminutive of Latin *mantellum* MANTLE]

man·tel·piece ('mæntᵊlˌpi:s) *n.* **1.** Also called: **mantel shelf, chimneypiece.** a shelf above a fireplace often forming part of the mantel. **2.** another word for **mantel** (sense 1).

man·tel·tree *or* **man·tle·tree** ('mæntᵊlˌtri:) *n.* a beam made of stone or wood that forms the lintel over a fireplace.

man·tic ('mæntɪk) *adj.* **1.** of or relating to divination and prophecy. **2.** having divining or prophetic powers. [C19: from Greek *mantikos* prophetic, from *mantis* seer] **—'man·ti·cal·ly** *adv.*

-man·tic *adj. combining form.* forming adjectives corresponding to nouns ending in **-mancy:** *necromantic.*

man·til·la (mæn'tɪlə) *n.* **1.** a woman's lace or silk scarf covering the shoulders and head, often worn over a comb in the hair, esp. in Spain. **2.** a similar covering for the shoulders only. [C18: Spanish, diminutive of *manta* cloak]

Man·ti·ne·a *or* **Man·ti·nei·a** (ˌmæntɪ'neɪə) *n.* (in ancient Greece) a city in E Arcadia; site of several battles.

man·tis ('mæntɪs) *n., pl.* **·tis·es** *or* **·tes** (-ti:z). any carnivorous typically green insect of the family *Mantidae,* of warm and tropical regions, having a long body and large eyes and resting with the first pair of legs raised as if in prayer: order *Dictyoptera.* Also called: **praying mantis.** See also **cockroach.** [C17: New Latin, from Greek: prophet, alluding to its praying posture]

man·tis·sa (mæn'tɪsə) *n.* the fractional part of a common logarithm representing the digits of the associated number but not its magnitude: *the mantissa of 2.4771 is .4771.* Compare **characteristic** (sense 2a.). [C17: from Latin: something added, of Etruscan origin]

man·tis shrimp *or* **crab** *n.* any of various borrowing marine shrimplike crustaceans of the order *Stomatopoda* that have a pair of large grasping appendages: subclass *Malacostraca.* See also **squilla.**

man·tle ('mæntᵊl) *n.* **1.** *Archaic.* a loose wrap or cloak. **2.** anything that covers completely or envelops: *a mantle of snow.* **3.** a small dome-shaped or cylindrical mesh impregnated with cerium or thorium nitrates, used to increase illumination in a gas or oil lamp. **4.** Also called: **pallium.** *Zoology.* **a.** a protective layer of epidermis in molluscs that secretes a substance forming the shell. **b.** a similar structure in brachiopods. **5.** *Ornithol.* the feathers of the folded wings and back, esp. when these are of a different colour from the remaining feathers. **6.** *Geology.* the part of the earth between the crust and the core, thought to consist of a solid ultrabasic material. **7.** a less common spelling of **mantel. 8.** *Anatomy.* another word for **pallium** (sense 3). **9.** a clay mould formed around a wax model which is subsequently melted out. ~*vb.* **10.** (*tr.*) to envelop or supply with a mantle. **11.** to spread over or become spread over: *the trees were mantled with snow.* **12.** (*intr.*) *Falconry.* (of a hawk or falcon) to spread the wings and tail over food. [C13: via Old French from Latin *mantellum,* diminutive of *mantum* cloak]

man·tle rock *n.* the loose rock material, including glacial drift, soils, etc., that covers the bedrock and forms the land surface. Also called: **regolith.**

man·tling ('mæntlɪŋ) *n. Heraldry.* the drapery or scrollwork around a shield. [C16: from MANTLE]

man-to-man *adj.* characterized by directness or candour: *a man-to-man discussion.*

Man·toux test (mæn'tu:; *French* mɑ̃'tu) *n. Med.* a test for determining the presence of a tubercular infection by injecting tuberculin into the skin. [C19: named after C. *Mantoux,* French physician (1877–1956)]

Man·to·va ('mantova) *n.* the Italian name for **Mantua.**

man·tra ('mæntrə, 'mʌn-) *n.* **1.** *Hinduism.* any of those parts of the Vedic literature which consist of the metrical psalms of praise. **2.** *Hinduism, Buddhism.* any sacred word or syllable used as an object of concentration and embodying some aspect of spiritual power. [C19: from Sanskrit, literally: speech, instrument of thought, from *man* to think]

man·trap ('mænˌtræp) *n.* a snare for catching men, esp. trespassers.

man·tu·a ('mæntjʊə) *n.* a loose gown of the 17th and 18th centuries, worn open in front to show the underskirt. [C17: changed from MANTEAU, through the influence of MANTUA]

Man·tu·a ('mæntjʊə) *n.* a city in N Italy, in E Lombardy, surrounded by lakes: birthplace of Virgil. Pop.: 65 926 (1971). Italian name: **Mantova.**

man·u·al ('mænjʊəl) *adj.* **1.** of or relating to a hand or hands. **2.** operated or done by hand: *manual controls.* **3.** physical, as opposed to mental or mechanical: *manual labour.* **4.** by human labour rather than automatic or computer-aided means. **5.** of, relating to, or resembling a manual. ~*n.* **6.** a book, esp. of instructions or information: *a car manual.* **7.** *Music.* one of the keyboards played by hand on an organ. **8.** *Military.* the prescribed drill with small arms. [C15: via Old French from Latin *manuālis,* from *manus* hand] **—'man·u·al·ly** *adv.*

ma·nu·bri·um (mə'nju:brɪəm) *n., pl.* **·bri·a** (-brɪə) *or* **·bri·ums. 1.** *Anatomy.* any handle-shaped part, esp. the upper part of the sternum. **2.** *Zoology.* the tubular mouth that hangs down from the centre of a coelenterate medusa such as a jellyfish. [C17: from New Latin, from Latin: handle, from *manus* hand] **—ma·'nu·bri·al** *adj.*

manuf. *or* **manufac.** *abbrev. for:* **1.** manufacture. **2.** manufactured. **3.** manufacturer. **4.** manufacturing.

man·u·fac·to·ry (ˌmænjʊ'fæktərɪ, -trɪ) *n., pl.* **·ries.** an obsolete word for **factory.** [C17: from obsolete *manufact;* see MANUFACTURE]

man·u·fac·ture (ˌmænjʊ'fæktʃə) *vb.* **1.** to process or make (a product) from a raw material, esp. as a large-scale operation using machinery. **2.** (*tr.*) to invent or concoct: *to manufacture an excuse.* ~*n.* **3.** the production of goods, esp. by industrial processes. **4.** a manufactured product. **5.** the creation or production of anything. [C16: from obsolete *manufact* handmade, from Late Latin *manūfactus,* from Latin *manus* hand + *facere* to make] **—ˌman·u·'fac·tur·a·ble** *adj.* **—ˌman·u·'fac·tur·al** *adj.* **—ˌman·u·'fac·tur·ing** *n.*

man·u·fac·tur·er (ˌmænjʊ'fæktʃərə) *n.* a person or business concern that manufactures goods or owns a factory.

ma·nu·ka ('mɑ:nʊkə) *n.* a New Zealand myrtaceous tree, *Leptospermum sloparium,* with strong elastic wood and aromatic leaves.

Ma·nu·kau ('mɑ:nʊˌkaʊ) *n.* a city in New Zealand, on **Manukau Harbour** (an inlet of the Tasman Sea) near Auckland on NW North Island. Pop.: 127 800 (1974 est.).

man·u·mit (ˌmænjʊ'mɪt) *vb.* **·mits, ·mit·ting, ·mit·ted.** (*tr.*) to free from slavery, servitude, etc.; emancipate. [C15: from Latin *manūmittere* to release, from *manū* from one's hand + *ēmittere* to send away] **—man·u·mis·sion** (ˌmænjʊ'mɪʃən) *n.* **—ˌman·u·'mit·ter** *n.*

ma·nure (mə'njʊə) *n.* **1.** animal excreta, usually with straw, etc., used to fertilize land. **2.** *Chiefly Brit.* any material, esp. chemical fertilizer, used to fertilize land. ~*vb.* **3.** (*tr.*) to spread manure upon (fields or soil). [C14 (verb): from Anglo-French *mainoverer;* see MANOEUVRE] **—ma·'nur·er** *n.*

ma·nus ('meɪnəs) *n., pl.* **·nus. 1.** *Anatomy.* the wrist and hand. **2.** the corresponding part in other vertebrates. **3.** *Roman law.* the authority of a husband over his wife. **4.** *English law.* (formerly) an oath or the person taking an oath. [C19: Latin: hand]

man·u·script ('mænjʊˌskrɪpt) *n.* **1.** a book or other document written by hand. **2.** the original handwritten or typed version of a book, article, etc., as submitted by an author for publication. **3. a.** handwriting, as opposed to printing. **b.** (*as modifier*): *a manuscript document.* [C16: from Medieval Latin *manūscriptus,* from Latin *manus* hand + *scribere* to write]

Ma·nu·ti·us (mə'nju:ʃɪəs) *n.* See **Aldus Manutius.**

Manx (mæŋks) *adj.* **1.** of, relating to, or characteristic of the Isle of Man, its inhabitants, their language, or their dialect of English. ~*n.* **2.** an almost extinct language of the Isle of Man, belonging to the N Celtic branch of the Indo-European family and closely related to Scottish Gaelic. [C16: earlier *Maniske,* from Scandinavian, from *Mana* Isle of Man + *-iske* -ISH]

Manx cat *n.* a short-haired tailless variety of cat, believed to originate on the Isle of Man.

Manx·man ('mæŋksmən) *n., pl.* **·men.** a native or inhabitant of the Isle of Man.

Manx shear·wa·ter *n.* a European oceanic bird, *Puffinus puffinus,* with long slender wings and black-and-white plumage: family *Procellariidae* (shearwaters).

man·y ('mɛnɪ) *determiner.* **1.** (sometimes preceded by *a great* or *a good*) **a.** a large number of: *many coaches; many times.* **b.** (*as pronoun; functioning as pl.*): *many are seated already.* **2.** (foll. by *a, an,* or *another,* and a sing. noun) each of a considerable number of: *many a man.* **3.** (preceded by *as, too, that,* etc.) **a.** a great number of: *as many apples as you like; too many clouds to see.* **b.** (*as pronoun; functioning as pl.*): *I have as many as you.* ~*n.* **4. the many.** the majority of mankind, esp. the common people: *the many are kept in ignorance while the few prosper.* Compare **few** (sense 7). ~See also **more, most.** [Old English *manig;* related to Old Frisian *manich,* Middle Dutch *menech,* Old High German *manag*]

man·y·plies ('mɛnɪˌplaɪz) *n.* (*functioning as sing.*) another name for **psalterium.** [C18: from the large number of plies or folds of its membrane]

man·y-sid·ed *adj.* having many sides, aspects, etc.: *a many-sided personality.* —ˌ**man·y-ˈsid·ed·ness** *n.*

man·y-val·ued log·ic *n.* the study of logical systems in which the truth values that a proposition may have are not restricted to two, representing only truth and falsity.

man·za·nil·la (ˌmænzəˈnɪlə) *n.* a very dry pale sherry. [C19: from Spanish: camomile (referring to its bouquet)]

Man·zo·ni (*Italian* manˈdzoːni) *n.* **A·les·san·dro** (ˌalesˈsandro). 1785–1873, Italian romantic novelist and poet, famous for his historical novel *I Promessi sposi* (1825–27).

Mao·ism (ˈmaʊɪzəm) *n.* **1.** Marxism-Leninism as interpreted by Mao Tse-tung: distinguished by its theory of guerrilla warfare and its emphasis on the revolutionary potential of the peasantry. **2.** adherence to or reverence for Mao Tse-tung and his teachings. —**ˈMao·ist** *n., adj.*

Mao·ri (ˈmaʊrɪ, ˈmɑːrɪ) *n.* **1.** (*pl.* **·ris** *or* **·ri**) a member of the people living in New Zealand since before the arrival of European settlers. They are descended from Polynesian voyagers who migrated in successive waves from the 16th century onwards. **2.** the language of this people, belonging to the Malayo-Polynesian family. ~*adj.* **3.** of or relating to this people or their language. —**ˈMao·ri·ˌland** *n.*

Mao Tse-tung (ˈmaʊ tseɪˈtʊŋ) *n.* 1893–1976, Chinese Marxist theoretician and statesman. The son of a peasant farmer, he helped to found the Chinese Communist Party (1921) and established a soviet republic in SE China (1931–34). He led the retreat of Communist forces to NW China known as the Long March (1935–36), emerging as leader of the party. In opposing the Japanese in World War II, he united with the Kuomintang regime, which he then defeated in the ensuing civil war. He founded the People's Republic of China (1949) of which he was chairman until 1959. As party chairman until his death, he instigated the Cultural Revolution in 1966.

map (mæp) *n.* **1.** a diagrammatic representation of the earth's surface or part of it, showing the geographical distributions, positions, etc., of natural or artificial features such as roads, towns, relief, rainfall, etc. **2.** a diagrammatic representation of the distribution of stars or of the surface of a celestial body: a lunar map. **3.** a maplike drawing of anything. **4.** *Maths.* another name for **function** (sense 4b.). **5.** a slang word for **face** (sense 1). **6. put on the map.** to make (a town, company, etc.) well-known. ~*vb.* **maps, map·ping, mapped.** (*tr.*) **7.** to make a map of. **8.** *Maths.* to represent or transform (a function, figure, set, etc.). [C16: from Medieval Latin *mappa* (*mundi*) map (of the world), from Latin *mappa* cloth] —**ˈmap·pa·ble** *adj.*

Map (mæp) *or* **Mapes** (mæps, ˈmeɪpiːz) *n.* **Wal·ter.** ?1140–?1209, Welsh ecclesiastic and satirical writer. His chief work is the miscellany *De Nugis curialium.*

ma·ple (ˈmeɪpᵊl) *n.* **1.** any tree or shrub of the N temperate genus *Acer,* having winged seeds borne in pairs and lobed leaves: family *Aceraceae.* **2.** the hard closed-grained wood of any of these trees, used for furniture and flooring. **3.** the flavour of the sap of the sugar maple. ~See also **sugar maple, silver maple, Norway maple, sycamore.** [C14: from Old English *mapel-,* as in *mapeltrēow* maple tree]

ma·ple sug·ar *n. U.S.* sugar made from the sap of the sugar maple.

ma·ple syr·up *n. Chiefly U.S.* a very sweet syrup made from the sap of the sugar maple.

map out *vb.* (*tr., adv.*) to plan or design: *to map out a route.*

map·ping (ˈmæpɪŋ) *n. Maths.* another name for **function** (sense 4b.).

map pro·jec·tion *n.* a means of representing or a representation of the globe or celestial sphere or part of it on a flat map, using a grid of lines of latitude and longitude.

Ma·pu·to (məˈpuːtəʊ) *n.* the capital and chief port of Mozambique, in the south on Delagoa Bay: became capital in 1907; the nearest port to the Rand gold-mining and industrial region of South Africa. Pop.: 383 775 (1970). Former name (until 1975): **Lourenço Marques.**

ma·quette (mæˈkɛt) *n.* a sculptor's small preliminary model or sketch. [C20: from French, from Italian *macchietta* a little sketch, from *macchia,* from *macchiare,* from Latin *maculāre* to stain, from *macula* spot, blemish]

ma·quill·age *French.* (makiˈjaʒ) *n.* **1.** make-up; cosmetics. **2.** the application of make-up. [from *maquiller* to make up]

ma·quis (mɑːˈkiː) *n., pl.* **·quis** (-ˈkiː). **1.** shrubby mostly evergreen vegetation found in coastal regions of the Mediterranean: includes myrtles, heaths, arbutus, cork oak, and ilex. **2.** (*often cap.*) **a.** the French underground movement that fought against the German occupying forces in World War II. **b.** a member of this movement. [C20: from French, from Italian *macchia* thicket, from Latin *macula* spot]

mar (mɑː) *vb.* **mars, mar·ring, marred. 1.** (*tr.*) to cause harm to; spoil or impair. ~*n.* **2.** a disfiguring mark; blemish. [Old English *merran;* compare Old Saxon *merrian* to hinder, Old Norse *merja* to bruise] —**ˈmar·rer** *n.*

mar. *abbrev. for:* **1.** maritime. **2.** married.

Mar. *abbrev. for* March.

ma·ra (məˈrɑː) *n.* a harelike South American rodent, *Dolichotis patagonum,* inhabiting the pampas of Argentina: family *Caviidae* (cavies). [from American Spanish *mará,* perhaps of Araucanian origin]

mar·a·bou (ˈmærəˌbuː) *n.* **1.** a large black-and-white African carrion-eating stork, *Leptoptilos crumeniferus,* with a very short naked neck and a straight heavy bill. See also **adjutant bird. 2.** a down feather of this bird, used to trim garments. **3. a.** a fine white raw silk. **b.** fabric made of this. [C19: from French, from Arabic *murābit* MARABOUT, so called because the stork is considered a holy bird in Islam]

mar·a·bout (ˈmærəˌbuː) *n.* **1.** a Muslim holy man or hermit of North Africa. **2.** a shrine of the grave of a marabout. [C17: via French and Portuguese *marabuto,* from Arabic *murābit*]

ma·ra·bun·ta (ˌmærəˌbʌntə) *n. Caribbean.* **1.** any of several social wasps. **2.** *Slang.* an ill-tempered woman. [C19: perhaps of W African origin]

ma·rac·a (məˈrækə) *n.* a percussion instrument, usually one of a pair, consisting of a gourd or plastic shell filled with dried seeds, etc. It is used chiefly in Latin American music. [C20: Brazilian Portuguese, from Tupi]

Mar·a·cai·bo (ˌmærəˈkaɪbəʊ; *Spanish* ˌmaraˈkaɪβo) *n.* **1.** a port in NW Venezuela, on the channel from Lake Maracaibo to the Gulf of Venezuela: the second largest city in the country; University of Zulia (1891); major oil centre. Pop.: 651 574 (1971). **2. Lake.** a lake in NW Venezuela, linked with the Gulf of Venezuela by a dredged channel: centre of the Venezuelan and South American oil industry. Area: about 13 000 sq. km (500 sq. miles).

Mar·a·can·da (ˌmærəˈkændə) *n.* the ancient name for **Samarkand.**

Ma·ra·cay (*Spanish* ˌmaraˈkaɪ) *n.* a city in N central Venezuela: developed greatly as the headquarters of Juan Vicente Gómez during his dictatorship; textile industries. Pop.: 255 134 (1971).

mar·ag·ing steel (ˈmɑːˌreɪdʒɪŋ) *n.* a strong low-carbon steel containing nickel and small amounts of titanium, aluminium, and niobium, produced by transforming to a martensitic structure and heating at 500°C. [C20 *maraging,* from MAR(TENSITE) + AGING]

Ma·ra·jó (*Portuguese* ˌmaraˈʒɔ) *n.* an island in N Brazil, at the mouth of the Amazon. Area: 38 610 sq. km (15 444 sq. miles).

Ma·ra·nhão (*Portuguese* ˌmarəˈɲɐ̃ʊ) *n.* a state of NE Brazil, on the Atlantic: forested and humid in the northwest, with high plateaus in the east and south. Capital: São Luís. Pop.: 2 992 686 (1970). Area: 328 666 sq. km (128 179 sq. miles).

Ma·ra·ñón (*Spanish* ˌmaraˈɲon) *n.* a river in NE Peru, rising in the Andes and flowing northwest into the Ucayali River, forming the Amazon. Length: about 1450 km (900 miles).

ma·ras·ca (məˈræskə) *n.* a European cherry tree, *Prunus cerasus marasca,* with red acid-tasting fruit from which maraschino is made. [C19: from Italian, variant of *amarasca* from *amaro,* from Latin *amārus* bitter]

mar·a·schi·no (ˌmærəˈskiːnəʊ) *n.* a liqueur made from marasca cherries and flavoured with the kernels, having a taste like bitter almonds. [C18: from Italian; see MARASCA]

mar·a·schi·no cher·ry *n.* a cherry preserved in maraschino or an imitation of this liqueur, used as a garnish.

ma·ras·mus (məˈræzməs) *n. Pathol.* general emaciation and wasting, esp. of infants, thought to be associated with severe malnutrition or impaired utilization of nutrients. [C17: from New Latin, from Greek *marasmos,* from *marainein* to waste] —**ma·ˈras·mic** *adj.*

Ma·rat (*French* maˈra) *n.* **Jean Paul** (ʒɑ̃ ˈpɔl). 1743–93, French revolutionary leader and journalist. He founded the radical newspaper *L'Ami du peuple* and was elected to the National Convention (1792). He was instrumental in overthrowing the Girondists (1793); he was stabbed to death in his bath by Charlotte Corday.

Ma·ra·tha *or* **Mah·rat·ta** (məˈrɑːtə) *n.* a member of a people of India living chiefly in Maharashtra.

Ma·ra·thi *or* **Mah·rat·ti** (məˈrɑːtɪ) *adj.* **1.** of or relating to Maharashtra state in India, its people, or their language. ~*n.* **2.** the state language of Maharashtra, belonging to the Indic branch of the Indo-European family.

mar·a·thon (ˈmærəθən) *n.* **1.** a race on foot of 26 miles 385 yards (42.195 kilometres): an event in the modern Olympics. **2. a.** any long or arduous task, etc. **b.** (*as modifier*): *a marathon effort.* [referring to the feat of the messenger who ran 26 miles from Marathon to Athens to bring the news of victory in 490 B.C.]

Mar·a·thon (ˈmærəθən) *n.* a plain in Attica northeast of Athens: site of a victory of the Athenians and Plataeans over the Persians (490 B.C.).

ma·raud (məˈrɔːd) *vb.* **1.** to search (a place) for plunder. ~*n.* **2.** an archaic word for **foray.** [C18: from French *marauder* to prowl, from *maraud* vagabond] —**ma·ˈraud·er** *n.*

mar·a·ve·di (ˌmærəˈveɪdɪ) *n., pl.* **·dis.** any of various Spanish coins of copper or gold. [C15: from Spanish, from Arabic *Murābitīn* (plural of *murābit* MARABOUT), the Moorish dynasty in Córdoba, 1087–1147]

mar·ble (ˈmɑːbᵊl) *n.* **1. a.** a hard crystalline metamorphic rock resulting from the recrystallization of a limestone: takes a high polish and is used for building and sculpture. **b.** (*as modifier*): *a marble bust.* **2.** a block or work of art of marble. **3.** a small round glass or stone ball used in playing marbles. **4. make one's marble good.** *Austral. informal.* to succeed or do the right thing. **5. pass in one's marble.** *Austral. informal.* to die. ~*vb.* **6.** (*tr.*) to mottle with variegated streaks in imitation of marble. ~*adj.* **7.** cold, hard, or unresponsive. **8.** white like some kinds of marble. [C12: via Old French from Latin *marmor,* from Greek *marmaros* related to Greek *marmairein* to gleam] —**ˈmar·bled** *adj.* —**ˈmar·bler** *n.* —**ˈmar·bly** *adj.*

mar·ble cake *n.* a cake with a marbled appearance obtained by incompletely mixing dark and light batters.

mar·bles (ˈmɑːbᵊlz) *n.* **1.** (*functioning as sing.*) a game in which marbles are rolled at one another, similar to bowls. **2.** *Informal.* wits: *to lose one's marbles.*

mar·bling (ˈmɑːblɪŋ) *n.* **1.** a mottled effect or pattern resembling marble. **2.** such an effect obtained by transferring floating colours from a bath of gum solution. **3.** the streaks of fat in lean meat.

Mar·burg (ˈmɑːˌbɜːg; *German* ˈmaːrbʊrk) *n.* **1.** a city in central West Germany, in Hesse; famous for the religious debate between Luther and Zwingli in 1529; Europe's first Protestant university (1527). Pop.: 47 500 (1971). **2.** the German name for **Maribor.**

marc (mɑːk; *French* mar) *n.* **1.** the remains of grapes or other fruit that have been pressed for wine-making. **2.** a brandy distilled from these. [C17: from French, from Old French *marchier* to trample (grapes), MARCH[1]]

Marc (*German* mark) *n.* **Franz** (frants). 1880–1916, German expressionist painter; cofounder with Kandinsky of the *Blaue Reiter* group (1911). He is noted for his symbolic compositions of animals.

mar·ca·site (ˈmɑːkəˌsaɪt) *n.* **1.** a metallic pale yellow mineral consisting of iron pyrites in orthorhombic crystalline form used in jewellery. **2.** a cut and polished form of steel or any white metal used for making jewellery. [C15: from Medieval Latin *marcasīta*, from Arabic *marqashītā*, perhaps from Persian] —**mar·ca·sit·i·cal** (ˌmɑːkəˈsɪtɪkəl) *adj.*

Mar·ceau (*French* marˈso) *n.* **Mar·cel** (marˈsɛl). born 1923, French mime.

mar·cel (mɑːˈsɛl) *n.* **1.** Also called: **marcel wave.** a hair style characterized by repeated regular waves, popular in the 1920s. ~*vb.* **·cels, ·cel·ling, ·celled. 2.** (*tr.*) to make such waves in (the hair) with special hot irons. [C20: after *Marcel Grateau* (1852–1936), French hairdresser] —**mar·ˈcel·ler** *n.*

Mar·cel·lus (mɑːˈsɛləs) *n.* **Mar·cus Clau·di·us** (ˈmɑːkəs ˈklɔːdɪəs). ?268–208 B.C., Roman general and consul, who captured Syracuse (212) in the Second Punic War.

mar·ces·cent (mɑːˈsɛsənt) *adj.* (of the parts of certain plants) remaining attached to the plant when withered. [C18: from Latin *marcescere* to grow weak, from *marcēre* to wither] —**mar·ˈces·cence** *n.*

march[1] (mɑːtʃ) *vb.* **1.** (*intr.*) to walk or proceed with stately or regular steps, usually in a procession or military formation. **2.** (*tr.*) to make (a person or group) proceed: *he marched his army to the town.* **3.** (*tr.*) to traverse or cover by marching: *to march a route.* ~*n.* **4.** the act or an instance of marching. **5.** a regular stride: *a slow march.* **6.** a long or exhausting walk. **7.** advance; progression (of troops, etc.). **8.** a distance or route covered by marching. **9.** a piece of music, usually in four beats to the bar, having a strongly accented rhythm. **10. steal a march on.** to gain an advantage over, esp. by a secret or underhand enterprise. [C16: from Old French *marchier* to tread, probably of Germanic origin; compare Old English *mearcian* to MARK[1]] —**ˈmarch·er** *n.*

march[2] (mɑːtʃ) *n.* **1.** Also called: **marchland.** a frontier, border, or boundary or the land lying along it, often of disputed ownership. ~*vb.* **2.** (*intr.*; often foll. by *upon* or *with*) to share a common border (with). [C13: from Old French *marche*, from Germanic; related to MARK[1]]

March[1] (mɑːtʃ) *n.* the third month of the year, consisting of 31 days. [from Old French, from Latin *Martius* (month) of Mars]

March[2] (març) *n.* the German name for the **Morava** (sense 1).

March. *abbrev. for* Marchioness.

M.Arch. *abbrev. for* Master of Architecture.

Marche (*French* marʃ) *n.* a former province of central France.

march·er (ˈmɑːtʃə) *n.* **1.** an inhabitant of any of the Marches. **2.** (formerly) **a.** a lord governing and defending such a borderland. **b.** (*as modifier*): *the marcher lords.*

March·es (ˈmɑːtʃɪz) *n.* **the. 1.** the border area between England and Wales or Scotland, both characterized by continual feuding (13th–16th centuries). **2.** a region of central Italy. Capital: Ancona. Pop.: 1 359 063 (1971). Area: 9692 sq. km (3780 sq. miles). Italian name: **Le Mar·che** (le ˈmarke). **3.** any of various other border regions.

mar·che·sa *Italian.* (marˈkeːsa) *n., pl.* **·se** (-sɛ). (in Italy) the wife or widow of a marchese; marchioness.

mar·che·se *Italian.* (marˈkeːse) *n., pl.* **·si** (-si). (in Italy) a nobleman ranking below a prince and above a count; marquis.

Mar·chesh·van *Hebrew.* (marxɛʃˈvan) *n.* another word for **Heshvan.** [from Hebrew]

March hare *n.* a hare during its breeding season in March, noted for its wild and excitable behaviour (esp. in the phrase **mad as a March hare**).

march·ing or·ders *pl. n.* **1.** military orders, esp. to infantry, giving instructions about a march, its destination, etc. **2.** *Informal.* **a.** notice of dismissal from employment, etc. **b.** the instruction to proceed with a task. **3.** *Informal.* any dismissal, esp. one given by a girl to a boy friend.

mar·chion·ess (ˈmɑːʃənɪs, ˌmɑːʃəˈnɛs) *n.* **1.** the wife or widow of a marquis. **2.** a woman who holds the rank of marquis. [C16: from Medieval Latin *marchionissa*, feminine of *marchiō* MARQUIS]

march·land (ˈmɑːtʃˌlænd, -lənd) *n.* a less common word for **borderland.**

march·pane (ˈmɑːtʃˌpeɪn) *n.* an archaic word for **marzipan.** [C15: from French]

Mar·ci·an·o (ˌmɑːsɪˈænəʊ, -ˈɑːnəʊ) *n.* **Rock·y.** original name *Rocco Francis Marchegiano.* 1923–69, U.S. heavyweight boxer; world heavyweight champion, 1952–56.

Mar·cio·nism (ˈmɑːʃəˌnɪzəm) *n.* a Gnostic movement of the 2nd and 3rd centuries A.D. [C16: after *Marcion* of Sinope, 2nd-century Gnostic]

Mar·co·ni (mɑːˈkəʊnɪ) *n.* **Gu·gliel·mo** (guʎˈʎɛlmo). 1874–1937, Italian physicist, who developed radio telegraphy and succeeded in transmitting signals across the Atlantic (1901): Nobel prize for physics 1909.

Mar·co·ni rig *n. Nautical.* a fore-and-aft sailing boat rig with triangular sails. —**Mar·ˈco·ni-ˌrigged** *adj.*

Mar·co Po·lo (ˈmɑːkəʊ ˈpəʊləʊ) *n.* See (Marco) **Polo.**

Mar·cos (ˈmɑːkɒs) *n.* **Fer·di·nand (Edralin).** born 1917, Filipino statesman; president of the Philippines since 1965.

Mar·cus Au·re·li·us An·to·ni·nus (ˈmɑːkəs ɔːˈriːlɪəs ˌæntəˈnaɪnəs) *n.* original name *Marcus Annius Verus.* 121–180 A.D., Roman emperor (161–180) noted particularly for his *Meditations*, propounding his stoic view of life.

Mar·cu·se (mɑːˈkuːzə) *n.* **Her·bert.** 1898–1979, U.S. philosopher, born in Germany. In his later works he analysed the situation of man under monopoly capitalism and the dehumanizing effects of modern technology. His works include *Eros and Civilization* (1958) and *One Dimensional Man* (1964).

Mar del Pla·ta (*Spanish* ˈmar ðel ˈplata) *n.* a city and resort in E Argentina, on the Atlantic: fishing port. Pop.: 299 700 (1970).

Mar·di Gras (ˈmɑːdɪ ˈgrɑː) *n.* the festival of Shrove Tuesday, celebrated in some cities with great revelry. [French: fat Tuesday]

Mar·duk (ˈmɑːdʊk) *n.* the chief god of the Babylonian pantheon.

mard·y (ˈmɑːdɪ) *adj. Northern Brit. dialect.* **1.** (of a child) spoilt. **2.** irritable. [from *marred*, past participle of MAR]

mare[1] (mɛə) *n.* the adult female of a horse or zebra. [C12: from Old English, of Germanic origin; related to Old High German *mariha*, Old Norse *merr* mare]

ma·re[2] (ˈmɑːreɪ, -rɪ) *n., pl.* **ma·ri·a** (ˈmɑːrɪə) **1.** (*cap. when part of a name*) any of a large number of huge dry plains on the surface of the moon, visible as dark markings and once thought to be seas: *Mare Imbrium* (*Sea of Showers*). **2.** a similar area on the surface of Mars, such as *Mare Sirenum.* [from Latin: sea]

ma·re clau·sum (ˈmɑːreɪ ˈklaʊsʊm) *n. Law.* a sea coming under the jurisdiction of one nation and closed to all others. Compare **mare liberum.** [Latin: closed sea]

ma·re li·be·rum (ˈmɑːreɪ ˈliːbərʊm) *n. Law.* a sea open to navigation by shipping of all nations. Compare **mare clausum.** [Latin: free sea]

ma·rem·ma (məˈrɛmə) *n., pl.* **·me** (-miː). a marshy unhealthy region near the shore, esp. in Italy. [C19: from Italian, from Latin *maritima* MARITIME]

Ma·ren·go[1] (məˈrɛŋgəʊ) *adj.* (*postpositive*) browned in oil and cooked with tomatoes, mushrooms, garlic, wine, etc.: *chicken Marengo.* [C19: after a dish prepared for Napoleon after the battle of Marengo]

Ma·ren·go[2] (məˈrɛŋgəʊ; *Italian* maˈreŋgo) *n.* a village in NW Italy: site of a major battle in which Napoleon decisively defeated the Austrians (1800).

ma·re nos·trum *Latin.* (ˈmɑːreɪ ˈnɒstrʊm) *n.* the Latin name for the **Mediterranean.** [Latin: our sea]

Ma·ren·zio (*Italian* maˈrɛntsjo) *n.* **Lu·ca** (ˈluːka). 1553–99, Italian composer of madrigals.

mare's-nest *n.* **1.** a discovery imagined to be important but proving worthless. **2.** a disordered situation.

mare's-tail *n.* **1.** a wisp of trailing cirrus cloud, indicating strong winds at high levels. **2.** an erect pond plant, *Hippuris vulgaris*, with minute flowers and crowded whorls of narrow leaves: family *Hippuridaceae.*

marg (mɑːdʒ) *n. Brit. informal.* short for **margarine.**

marg. *abbrev. for* margin(al).

Mar·ga·ret (ˈmɑːgrət) *n.* **Princess.** born 1930, younger sister of Queen Elizabeth II of Great Britain and Northern Ireland.

Mar·ga·ret of An·jou (ˈmɑːgrɪt) *n.* 1430–82, queen of England. She married the mentally unstable Henry VI of England in 1445 to confirm the truce with France during the Hundred Years' War. She became a leader of the Lancastrians in the Wars of the Roses and was defeated at Tewkesbury (1471) by Edward IV.

Mar·ga·ret of Na·varre *n.* 1492–1549, queen of Navarre (1544–49) by marriage to Henry II of Navarre; sister of Francis I of France. She was a poet and a patron of humanism.

Mar·ga·ret of Va·lois *n.* 1553–1615, daughter of Henry II of France and Catherine de' Medici; queen of Navarre (1572) by marriage to Henry of Navarre. The marriage was dissolved (1599) after his accession as Henry IV of France: noted for her *Mémoires.*

mar·gar·ic (mɑːˈgærɪk) *or* **mar·gar·it·ic** *adj.* of or resembling pearl. [C19: from Greek *margaron* pearl]

mar·gar·ic ac·id *n.* another name for **heptadecanoic acid.**

mar·ga·rine (ˌmɑːdʒəˈriːn) *or* **mar·ga·rin** (ˈmɑːdʒərɪn, ˌmɑːdʒəˈriːn) *n.* a substitute for butter, prepared from vegetable and animal fats by emulsifying them with water and adding small amounts of milk, salt, vitamins, colouring matter, etc. [C19: from MARGARIC]

mar·ga·ri·ta (ˌmɑːgəˈriːtə) *n.* a mixed drink consisting of tequila and lemon juice. [C20: from the woman's name]

Mar·ga·ri·ta (ˌmɑːgəˈriːtə) *n.* an island in the Caribbean, off the NE coast of Venezuela: pearl fishing. Capital: La Asunción.

mar·ga·rite (ˈmɑːgəˌraɪt) *n.* **1.** a pink pearly micaceous mineral consisting of hydrated calcium aluminium silicate. Formula: $CaAl_4Si_2O_{10}(OH)_2$. **2.** an aggregate of minute beadlike masses occurring in some glassy igneous rocks. [C19: via German from Greek *margaron* pearl]

Mar·gate (ˈmɑːgeɪt) *n.* a town and resort in SE England, in E Kent on the Isle of Thanet. Pop.: 50 145 (1971).

Mar·gaux (*French* marˈgo) *n.* a red wine produced in the region around the village of Margaux near Bordeaux.

mar·gay (ˈmɑːˌgeɪ) *n.* a feline mammal, *Felis wiedi*, of Central and South America, having a dark-striped coat. [C18: from French, from Tupi *mbaracaiá*]

marge[1] (mɑːdʒ) *n. Brit. informal.* short for **margarine.**

marge[2] (mɑːdʒ) *n. Archaic.* a margin. [C16: from French]

mar·gin (ˈmɑːdʒɪn) *n.* **1.** an edge or rim, and the area immediately adjacent to it; border. **2.** the blank space surrounding the text on a page. **3.** a vertical line on a page, esp. one on the left-hand side, delineating this space. **4.** an additional amount or one beyond the minimum necessary: *a margin of error.* **5.** *Austral.* a payment made in addition to a basic wage, esp. for special skill or responsibility. **6.** a bound or limit. **7.** the amount by which one thing differs from another: *a large margin separated the parties.* **8.** *Commerce.* the profit on a transaction. **9.** *Economics.* the minimum return below which an enterprise becomes unprofitable. **10.** *Finance.* **a.** collateral deposited by a client with a broker as security. **b.** the excess of the value of a loan's collateral over the value of the loan. ~Also (archaic): **mar·gent** (ˈmɑːdʒənt). ~*vb.* (*tr.*) **11.** to provide with a margin; border. **12.** *Finance.* to deposit a margin upon. [C14: from Latin *margō* border; related to MARCH[2], MARK[1]]

mar·gin·al (ˈmɑːdʒɪnᵊl) *adj.* **1.** of, in, on, or constituting a margin. **2.** close to a limit, esp. a lower limit: *marginal legal ability.* **3.** *Economics.* relating to goods or services produced and sold at the margin of profitability: *marginal cost.* **4.** *Politics, chiefly Brit.* of or designating a constituency in which elections tend to be won by small margins: *a marginal seat.* **5.** designating agricultural land on the margin of cultivated zones. —**mar·gin·al·i·ty** (ˌmɑːdʒɪˈnælɪtɪ) *n.* —**ˈmar·gin·al·ly** *adv.*

mar·gi·na·li·a (ˌmɑːdʒɪˈneɪlɪə) *pl. n.* notes in the margin of a book, manuscript, or letter. [C19: New Latin, noun (neuter plural) from *marginālis* marginal]

mar·gin·ate (ˈmɑːdʒɪˌneɪt) *vb.* **1.** (*tr.*) to provide with a margin or margins. ~*adj.* **2.** *Biology.* having a margin of a distinct colour or form: *marginate leaves.* [C18: from Latin *margināre*] —ˌ**mar·gin·ˈa·tion** *n.*

mar·gra·vate (ˈmɑːgrəvɪt) *or* **mar·gra·vi·ate** (mɑːˈgreɪvɪɪt) *n.* the domain of a margrave.

mar·grave (ˈmɑːˌgreɪv) *n.* a German nobleman ranking above a count. Margraves were originally counts appointed to govern frontier provinces, but all had become princes of the Holy Roman Empire by the 12th century. [C16: from Middle Dutch *markgrave,* literally: count of the MARCH[2]]

mar·gra·vine (ˈmɑːgrəˌviːn) *n.* **1.** the wife or widow of a margrave. **2.** a woman who holds the rank of margrave. [C17: from Middle Dutch, feminine of MARGRAVE]

Marg·re·the II (*Danish* marˈgreːdə) *n.* born 1940, queen of Denmark since 1972.

mar·gue·rite (ˌmɑːgəˈriːt) *n.* **1.** a cultivated garden plant, *Chrysanthemum frutescens,* whose flower heads have white or pale yellow rays around a yellow disc: family *Compositae* (composites). **2.** any of various related plants with daisy-like flowers, esp. *C. leucanthemum.* [C19: from French: daisy, pearl, from Latin *margarīta,* from Greek *margaritēs,* from *margaron*]

Mar·hesh·van *or* ***Mar·chesh·van*** *Hebrew.* (marxɛʃˈvan) *n.* another word for ***Heshvan.***

ma·ri·a (ˈmɑːrɪə) *n.* the plural of **mare**[2].

mar·i·ach·i (ˌmɑːrɪˈɑːtʃɪ) *n.* a small ensemble of street musicians in Mexico. [C20: from Mexican Spanish]

Ma·ri·a de' Me·di·ci (*Italian* maˈriːa de ˈmeːditʃi) *n.* French name *Marie de Médicis.* 1573–1642, queen of France (1600–10) by marriage to Henry IV of France; daughter of Francesco, grand duke of Tuscany. She became regent for her son (later Louis XIII) but continued to wield power after he came of age (1614). She was finally exiled from France in 1631 after plotting to undermine Richelieu's influence at court.

ma·riage de con·ve·nance *French.* (maˈrjaʒ də kõvəˈnɑ̃ːs) *n., pl.* ***ma·riages de con·ve·nance.*** another term for **marriage of convenience.**

Mar·i·an (ˈmɛərɪən) *adj.* **1.** of or relating to the Virgin Mary. **2.** of or relating to some other Mary, such as Mary Queen of Scots or Mary I of England. ~*n.* **3.** a person who has a special devotion to the Virgin Mary. **4.** a supporter of some other Mary.

Mar·i·a·na Is·lands (ˌmærɪˈɑːnə) *pl. n.* a chain of volcanic and coral islands in the W Pacific, east of the Philippines and north of New Guinea: divided politically into Guam and the islands north of Guam, part of the United States Trust Territory of the Pacific Islands (since 1947). Pop.: 193 980 (1970). Area: 958 sq. km (370 sq. miles). Former name (1521–1668): **Ladrone Islands.**

Ma·ria·na·o (*Spanish* ˌmarjaˈnao) *n.* a city in NW Cuba, adjacent to W Havana city: the chief Cuban military base. Pop.: 229 576 (1960).

Ma·ri·anne (*French* maˈrjan) *n.* a female figure personifying the French republic after the Revolution (1789).

Ma·ri·án·ské Láz·ně (*Czech* ˈmarijaːnske ˈlaːznjɛ) *n.* a town in W Czechoslovakia: a fashionable spa in the 18th and 19th centuries. Pop.: 13 402 (1971). German name: **Marienbad.**

Ma·ri·a The·re·sa (məˈriːə təˈreɪzə) *n.* 1717–80, archduchess of Austria and queen of Hungary and Bohemia (1740–80); the daughter and heiress of Emperor Charles VI of Austria; the wife of Emperor Francis I; the mother of Emperor Joseph II. In the War of the Austrian Succession (1740–48) she was confirmed in all her possessions except Silesia, which she attempted unsuccessfully to regain in the Seven Years' War (1756–63).

Ma·ri Au·ton·o·mous So·vi·et So·cial·ist Re·pub·lic (ˈmɑːrɪ) *n.* an administrative division of the W central Soviet Union, in the middle Volga basin. Capital: Yoshkar-Ola. Pop.: 684 748 (1970). Area: 23 200 sq. km (8955 sq. miles).

Ma·ri·bor (ˈmærɪbɔː) *n.* an industrial city in N Yugoslavia, in Slovenia on the Drava River: a flourishing Hapsburg trading centre in the 13th century; resort. Pop.: 97 167 (1971). German name: **Marburg.**

mar·i·cul·ture (ˈmærɪˌkʌltʃə) *n.* the cultivation of marine plants and animals in their natural environment. [C20: from Latin *mari-, mare* sea + CULTURE]

Ma·rie An·toi·nette (*French* mari ɑ̃twaˈnɛt) *n.* 1755–93, queen of France (1774–93) by marriage to Louis XVI of France. Her opposition to reform during the Revolution contributed to the overthrow of the monarchy; guillotined.

Ma·rie Byrd Land (ˈmɑːrɪ ˈbɜːd) *n.* the former name of **Byrd Land.**

Ma·rie Ga·lante (*French* mari gaˈlɑ̃ːt) *n.* an island in the E West Indies southeast of Guadeloupe, of which it is a dependency. Chief town: Grand Bourg. Pop.: 15 867 (1967). Area: 155 sq. km (60 sq. miles).

Ma·ri·e·hamn (ˌmarɪəˈhamn) *n.* a city in SW Finland, chief port of the Åland Islands. Pop.: 8546 (1970). Finnish name: **Maarianhamina.**

Ma·rie Lou·ise (*French* mari ˈlwiːz) *n.* 1791–1847, empress of France (1811–15) as the second wife of Napoleon I; daughter of Francis I of Austria. On Napoleon's abdication (1815) she became Duchess of Parma.

Ma·ri·en·bad (ˈmærɪənˌbæd; *German* maˈriːənˌbaːt) *n.* the German name for **Mariánské Lázně.**

mar·i·gold (ˈmærɪˌgəʊld) *n.* **1.** any of various tropical American plants of the genus *Tagetes,* esp. *T. erecta,* cultivated for their yellow or orange flower heads and strongly scented foliage: family *Compositae* (composites). **2.** any of various similar or related plants, such as the marsh marigold, pot marigold, bur marigold, and fig marigold. [C14: from *Mary* (the Virgin) + GOLD]

ma·ri·ju·a·na (ˌmærɪjʊˈɑːnə) *or* **ma·ri·hua·na** (ˌmærɪˈhwɑːnə) *n.* **1.** the dried leaves and flowers of the hemp plant, used as a narcotic, esp. in the form of cigarettes. See also **cannabis. 2.** *U.S.* another name for **hemp** (the plant). [C19: from Mexican Spanish]

ma·rim·ba (məˈrɪmbə) *n.* a Latin American percussion instrument consisting of a set of hardwood plates placed over tuned metal resonators, played with soft-head hammers. [C18: of West African origin]

Mar·in (ˈmɑːrɪn) *n.* **John.** 1870–1953, U.S. painter, noted esp. for his watercolour landscapes and seascapes.

ma·ri·na (məˈriːnə) *n.* an elaborate docking facility for yachts and other pleasure boats. [C19: via Italian and Spanish from Latin: MARINE]

mar·i·nade *n.* (ˌmærɪˈneɪd). **1.** a spiced liquid mixture of oil, wine, vinegar, herbs, etc., in which meat or fish is soaked before cooking. **2.** meat or fish soaked in this liquid. ~*vb.* (ˈmærɪˌneɪd). **3.** a variant of **marinate.** [C17: from French, from Spanish *marinada,* from *marinar* to pickle in brine, MARINATE]

mar·i·nate (ˈmærɪˌneɪt) *vb.* to soak in marinade. [C17: probably from Italian *marinato,* from *marinare* to pickle, ultimately from Latin *marīnus* MARINE] —ˌ**mar·i·ˈna·tion** *n.*

Ma·rin·du·que (ˌmɑːrɪnˈduːkeɪ) *n.* an island of the central Philippines, east of Mindoro: forms, with offshore islets, a province of the Philippines. Capital: Boac. Pop.: 144 109 (1970). Area: 960 sq. km (370 sq. miles).

ma·rine (məˈriːn) *adj.* (*usually prenominal*) **1.** of, found in, or relating to the sea. **2.** of or relating to shipping, navigation, etc. **3.** of or relating to a body of seagoing troops or a government department concerned with maritime affairs: *marine corps.* **4.** used or adapted for use at sea: *a marine camera.* ~*n.* **5.** shipping and navigation in general. **6.** (*cap. when part of a name*) **a.** a member of a marine corps or similar body. **b.** the branch of the army connected with the sea. See **merchant navy. 7.** a picture of a ship, seascape, etc. **8. tell it to the marines.** *Informal.* an expression of disbelief. [C15: from Old French *marin,* from Latin *marīnus,* from *mare* sea]

ma·rine in·sur·ance *n.* insurance covering damage to or loss of ship, passengers, or cargo caused by the sea.

mar·i·ner (ˈmærɪnə) *n.* a formal or literary word for **seaman.** [C13: from Anglo-French, ultimately from Latin *marīnus* MARINE]

Mar·i·ner (ˈmærɪnə) *n.* any of a series of U.S. space probes launched between 1962 and 1971 that sent back photographs and information concerning the surface of Mars and Venus and also studied interplanetary matter.

ma·rine rail·way *n.* another term for **slipway** (sense 2).

Ma·ri·net·ti (*Italian* ˌmariˈnetti) *n.* **Fi·lip·po Tom·ma·so** (fiˈlippo tomˈmaːzo). 1876–1944, Italian poet; founder of futurism (1909).

Mar·i·ol·a·try *or* **Mar·y·ol·a·try** (ˌmɛərɪˈɒlətrɪ) *n. R.C. Church.* exaggerated veneration of the Virgin Mary. —ˌ**Mar·i·ˈol·a·ter** *or* ˌ**Mar·y·ˈol·a·ter** *n.* —ˌ**Mar·i·ˈol·a·trous** *or* ˌ**Mar·y·ˈol·a·trous** *adj.*

Mar·i·ol·o·gy *or* **Mar·y·ol·o·gy** (ˌmɛərɪˈɒlədʒɪ) *n. R.C. Church.* the study of the traditions and doctrines concerning the Virgin Mary. —ˌ**Mar·i·ˈol·o·gist** *or* ˌ**Mar·y·ˈol·o·gist** *n.*

mar·i·on·ette (ˌmærɪəˈnɛt) *n.* an articulated puppet or doll whose jointed limbs are moved by strings. [C17: from French, from *Marion,* diminutive of *Marie* Mary + -ETTE]

mar·i·po·sa (ˌmærɪˈpəʊzə, -sə) *n.* any of several liliaceous plants of the genus *Calochortus,* of the southwestern U.S. and Mexico, having brightly coloured tulip-like flowers. Also called: **mariposa lily** or **tulip.** [C19: from Spanish: butterfly; from the likeness of the blooms to butterflies]

mar·ish ('mærɪʃ) *adj. Obsolete.* marshy; swampy. [C14: from Old French *marais* MARSH]

Mar·ist ('mɛərɪst) *n.* a member of the Society of Mary, a Christian religious congregation founded in 1824. [C19: from French *Mariste,* from *Marie* Mary (the virgin)]

mar·it·age ('mærɪtɪdʒ) *n. Feudal history.* **1.** the right of a lord to choose the spouses of his wards, etc. **2.** a sum paid to a lord in lieu of his exercising this right.

Ma·ri·tain (*French* mari'tɛ̃) *n.* **Jacques** (ʒɑːk). 1882–1973, French neo-Thomist Roman Catholic philosopher.

mar·i·tal ('mærɪtᵊl) *adj.* **1.** of or relating to marriage: *marital status.* **2.** of or relating to a husband. [C17: from Latin *marītālis,* from *marītus* married (adj.), husband (n.); related to *mās* male] —'**mar·i·tal·ly** *adv.*

mar·i·time ('mærɪˌtaɪm) *adj.* **1.** of or relating to navigation, shipping, etc.; seafaring. **2.** of, relating to, near, or living near the sea. **3.** (of a climate) having small temperature differences between summer and winter; equable. [C16: from Latin *maritimus* from *mare* sea]

Mar·i·time Alps *pl. n.* a range of the W Alps in SE France and NW Italy. Highest peak: Argentera, 3316 m (10 880 ft.).

Mar·i·time Prov·inc·es *or* **Mar·i·times** *pl. n.* **the.** certain of the Canadian provinces with coasts facing the Gulf of St. Lawrence or the Atlantic: New Brunswick, Nova Scotia, Prince Edward Island, and sometimes Newfoundland.

Mar·i·tim·er ('mærɪˌtaɪmə) *n.* a native or inhabitant of the Maritime Provinces of Canada.

Ma·rit·sa (*Bulgarian* ma'ritsa) *n.* a river in S Europe, rising in S Bulgaria and flowing east into Turkey, then south from Edirne as part of the border between Turkey and Greece to the Aegean. Length: 483 km (300 miles). Turkish name: **Meriç.** Greek name: **Évros.**

Ma·ri·u·pol (*Russian* məri'upəlj) *n.* the former name (until 1948) of **Zhdanov.**

Mar·i·us ('mɛərɪəs, 'mærɪəs) *n.* **Gai·us** ('gaɪəs). ?155–86 B.C., Roman general and consul. He defeated Jugurtha, the Cimbri, and the Teutons (107–101), but his rivalry with Sulla caused civil war (88). He was exiled but returned (87) and took Rome.

Ma·ri·vaux (*French* mari'vo) *n.* **Pierre Car·let de Cham·blain de** (pjɛːr karlɛ də ʃɑ̃'blɛ̃ də). 1688–1763, French dramatist and novelist, noted particularly for his comedies, such as *Le Jeu de l'amour et du hasard* (1730) and *La Vie de Marianne* (1731–41).

mar·jo·ram ('mɑːdʒərəm) *n.* **1.** Also called: **sweet marjoram.** an aromatic Mediterranean plant, *Origanum* (or *Marjorana*) *hortensis,* with small pale purple flowers and sweet-scented leaves, for seasoning food and in salads: family *Labiatae* (labiates). **2.** Also called: **wild marjoram, pot marjoram, origan.** a similar and related European plant, *Origanum vulgare.* See also **oregano.** [C14: via Old French *majorane,* from Medieval Latin *marjorana*]

mark[1] (mɑːk) *n.* **1.** a visible impression, stain, etc., on a surface, such as a spot or scratch. **2** a sign, symbol, or other indication that distinguishes something: *an owner's mark.* **3.** a cross or other symbol made instead of a signature. **4.** a written or printed sign or symbol, as for punctuation: *a question mark.* **5.** a letter, number, or percentage used to grade academic work. **6.** a thing that indicates position or directs; marker. **7.** a desired or recognized standard: *he is not up to the mark.* **8.** an indication of some quality, feature, or prowess: *he has the mark of an athlete.* **9.** quality or importance; note: *a person of little mark.* **10.** a target or goal. **11.** impression or influence: *he left his mark on German literature.* **12.** *Slang.* a suitable victim, esp. for swindling. **13.** (*often cap.*) (in trade names) model, brand, or type: *the car is a Mark 4.* **14.** *Nautical.* one of the intervals distinctively marked on a sounding lead. Compare **deep** (sense 22). **15.** *Bowls.* another name for the **jack. 16.** (*interj.*) *Rugby.* shouted by a player on catching a forward kick, throw, or knock by an opponent, which entitles him to a free kick. **17.** *Australian Rules football.* a catch of the ball from a kick of at least 10 yards, after which a free kick is taken. **18. the mark.** *Boxing.* the middle of the stomach at or above the line made by the boxer's trunks. **19.** (in medieval England and Germany) a piece of land held in common by the free men of a community. **20.** an obsolete word for **frontier. 21.** *Statistics.* See **class mark. 22. beside the mark.** irrelevant or off the point. **23. make one's mark.** to succeed or achieve recognition. **24. on your mark** *or* **marks.** a command given to runners in a race to prepare themselves at the starting line. ~*vb.* **25.** to make or receive (a visible impression, trace, or stain) on (a surface). **26.** (*tr.*) to characterize or distinguish: *his face was marked by anger.* **27.** (often foll. by *off* or *out*) to set boundaries or limits (on): *to mark out an area for negotiation.* **28.** (*tr.*) to select, designate, or doom by or as if by a mark: *to mark someone as a criminal.* **29.** (*tr.*) to put identifying or designating labels, stamps, etc., on, esp. to indicate price: *to mark the book at one pound.* **30.** (*tr.*) to pay heed or attention to: *mark my words.* **31.** to observe; notice. **32.** to grade or evaluate (scholastic work): *she marks fairly.* **33.** *Brit., football, etc.* to stay close to (an opponent) to hamper his play. **34.** to keep (score) in some games. **35. mark time. a.** to move the feet alternately as in marching but without advancing. **b.** to act in a mechanical and routine way. **c.** to halt progress temporarily, while awaiting developments. See also **markdown, mark-up.** [Old English *mearc* mark; related to Old Norse *mörk* boundary land, Old High German *marha* boundary, Latin *margō* MARGIN]

mark[2] (mɑːk) *n.* **1.** See **deutsche mark, markka, Reichsmark, ostmark. 2.** a former monetary unit and coin in England and Scotland worth two thirds of a pound sterling. **3.** a silver coin of Germany until 1924. [Old English *marc* unit of weight of precious metal, perhaps from the marks on metal bars; apparently of Germanic origin and related to MARK[1]]

Mark (mɑːk) *n. New Testament.* **1.** one of the four Evangelists. Feast day: April 25. **2.** the second Gospel, traditionally ascribed to him.

Mark An·to·ny *n.* See (Mark) **Antony.**

mark·down ('mɑːkˌdaʊn) *n.* **1.** a price reduction. ~*vb.* **mark down. 2.** (*tr., adv.*) to reduce in price.

marked (mɑːkt) *adj.* **1.** obvious, evident, or noticeable. **2.** singled out, esp. for punishment, killing, etc.: *a marked man.* **3.** *Linguistics.* distinguished by a specific feature, as in phonology. For example, of the two phonemes /t/ and /d/, the /d/ is marked because it exhibits the feature of voice. —**mark·ed·ly** ('mɑːkɪdlɪ) *adv.* —'**mark·ed·ness** *n.*

mark·er ('mɑːkə) *n.* **1. a.** something used for distinguishing or marking. **b.** (*as modifier*): *a marker buoy.* **2.** a person or thing that marks. **3.** a person or object that keeps or shows scores in a game.

mar·ket ('mɑːkɪt) *n.* **1. a.** an event or occasion, usually held at regular intervals, at which people meet for the purpose of buying and selling merchandise. **b.** (*as modifier*): *market day.* **2.** a place, such as an open space in a town, at which a market is held. **3.** a shop that sells a particular merchandise: *an antique market.* **4. the market.** business or trade in a commodity as specified: *the sugar market.* **5.** the trading or selling opportunities provided by a particular group of people: *the foreign market.* **6.** demand for a particular product or commodity: *there is no market for furs here.* **7.** See **stock market. 8.** See **market price, market value. 9. at market.** at the current price. **10. be in the market for.** to wish to buy or acquire. **11. on the market.** available for purchase. **12. play the market. a.** to speculate on a stock exchange. **b.** to act aggressively or unscrupulously in one's own commercial interests. **13. seller's** (*or* **buyer's**) **market.** a market characterized by excess demand (or supply) and thus favourable to sellers (or buyers). ~*vb.* **14.** to offer or produce for sale. **15.** (*intr.*) to buy or deal in a market. [C12: from Latin *mercātus;* from *mercārī* to trade, from *merx* merchandise] —'**mar·ket·er** *n.*

mar·ket·a·ble ('mɑːkɪtəbᵊl) *adj.* **1.** (of commodities, assets, etc.) **a.** being in good demand; saleable. **b.** suitable for sale. **2.** of or relating to buying or selling on a market: *marketable value.* —ˌ**mar·ket·a·'bil·i·ty** *or* '**mar·ket·a·ble·ness** *n.* —'**mar·ket·a·bly** *adv.*

mar·ket gar·den *n. Chiefly Brit.* an establishment where fruit and vegetables are grown. —**mar·ket gar·den·er** *n.*

mar·ket gar·den·ing *n. Chiefly Brit.* the business of growing fruit and vegetables on a commercial scale. Also called (in the U.S.): **truck farming, trucking.**

mar·ket·ing ('mɑːkɪtɪŋ) *n.* the business of selling goods, including advertising, packaging, etc.

mar·ket mam·my *n.* a W African woman trader.

mar·ket or·der *n.* an instruction to a broker to sell or buy at the best price currently obtainable on the market.

mar·ket·place ('mɑːkɪtˌpleɪs) *n.* **1.** a place where a public market is held. **2.** any centre where ideas, opinions, etc., are exchanged. **3.** the commercial world of buying and selling.

mar·ket price *n.* the prevailing price, as determined by supply and demand, at which goods, services, etc., may be bought or sold.

mar·ket re·search *n.* the collection and analysis of data relating to the demand for a product, often undertaken before marketing it.

mar·ket town *n. Chiefly Brit.* a town that holds a market, esp. an agricultural centre in a rural area.

mar·ket val·ue *n.* the amount obtainable on the open market for the sale of property, financial assets, or goods and services. Compare **par value, book value.**

Mark·ham ('mɑːkəm) *n.* **Mount.** a mountain in Antarctica, in Victoria Land. Height: 4375 m (14 355 ft.).

mar·khor ('mɑːkɔː) *or* **mar·khoor** ('mɑːkʊə) *n., pl.* **·khors, ·khor** *or* **·khoors, ·khoor.** a large wild Himalayan goat, *Capra falconeri,* with a reddish-brown coat and large spiralled horns. [C19: from Persian, literally: snake-eater, from *mār* snake + *-khōr* eating]

mark·ing ('mɑːkɪŋ) *n.* **1.** a mark or series of marks. **2.** the arrangement of colours on an animal, plant, etc.

mark·ing ink *n.* indelible ink used for marking linen, clothes, etc.

mark·ka ('mɑːkɑː, -kə) *n., pl.* **·kaa** (-kɑː). the standard monetary unit of Finland, divided into 100 pennia. [Finnish. See MARK[2]]

Mar·ko·va (mɑː'kəʊvə) *n.* Dame **A·lic·ia.** original name *Lilian Alicia Marks.* born 1910, English ballerina.

Mar·kov chain ('mɑːkɒf) *n. Statistics.* a sequence of events the probability for each of which is dependent on the event immediately preceding it. [C20: named after Andrei *Markov* (1856–1922), Russian mathematician]

marks·man ('mɑːksmən) *n., pl.* **·men. 1.** a person skilled in shooting. **2.** a serviceman selected for his skill in shooting, esp. for a minor engagement. **3.** a qualification awarded in certain armed services for skill in shooting. —'**marks·man**ˌ**ship** *n.* —'**marks**ˌ**wom·an** *fem. n.*

mark-up *n.* **1.** a percentage or amount added to the cost of a commodity to provide the seller with a profit and to cover overheads, costs, etc. **2. a.** an increase in the price of a commodity. **b.** the amount of this increase. ~*vb.* **mark up.**

(*tr., adv.*) **3.** to add a percentage for profit, etc., to the cost of (a commodity). **4.** to increase the price of.

marl[1] (mɑːl) *n.* **1.** a fine-grained sedimentary rock consisting of clay minerals, calcite or aragonite, and silt: used as a fertilizer. ~*vb.* **2.** (*tr.*) to fertilize (land) with marl. [C14: via Old French, from Late Latin *margila*, diminutive of Latin *marga*] —**mar·la·cious** (mɑːˈleɪʃəs) *or* ˈ**marl·y** *adj.*

marl[2] (mɑːl) *vb. Nautical.* to seize (a rope) with marline, using a hitch at each turn. [C15 *marlyn* to bind; related to Dutch *marlen* to tie, Old English *mǣrels* cable]

Marl·bor·ough[1] (ˈmɑːlbərə, -brə, ˈmɔːl-) *n.* a town in S England, in Wiltshire: besieged and captured by Royalists in the Civil War (1642); site of Marlborough College, a public school founded in 1843. Pop.: 6031 (1971).

Marl·bor·ough[2] (ˈmɑːlbərə, -brə, ˈmɔːl-) *n.* **1st Duke of,** title of *John Churchill.* 1650–1722, English general; commander of British forces in the War of the Spanish Succession (1701–14), in which he won victories at Blenheim (1704), Ramillies (1706), Oudenaarde (1708), and Malplaquet (1709).

Mar·ley (ˈmɑːlɪ) *n.* **Bob.** 1945-81, Jamaican reggae singer, guitarist, and songwriter. With his group, the Wailers, his albums include *Burnin'* (1973), *Natty Dread* (1975), *Rastaman Vibration* (1976), and *Exodus* (1977).

mar·lin (ˈmɑːlɪn) *n., pl.* **·lin** *or* **·lins.** any of several large scombroid food and game fishes of the genera *Makaira, Istiompax,* and *Tetrapturus,* of warm and tropical seas, having a very long upper jaw: family *Istiophoridae.* Also called: **spearfish.**

mar·line, mar·lin (ˈmɑːlɪn), *or* **mar·ling** (ˈmɑːlɪŋ) *n. Nautical.* a light rope, usually tarred, made of two strands laid left-handed. [C15: from Dutch *marlijn,* from *marren* to tie + *lijn* line]

mar·line·spike, mar·lin·spike (ˈmɑːlɪnˌspaɪk), *or* **mar·ling·spike** (ˈmɑːlɪŋˌspaɪk) *n. Nautical.* a pointed metal tool used as a fid, spike, and for various other purposes.

mar·lite (ˈmɑːlaɪt) *or* **marl·stone** (ˈmɑːlˌstəʊn) *n.* a type of marl that contains clay and calcium carbonate and is resistant to the decomposing action of air.

Mar·lowe (ˈmɑːləʊ) *n.* **Chris·to·pher.** 1564–93, English dramatist and poet, who established blank verse as a creative form of dramatic expression. His plays include *Tamburlaine the Great* (1590), *Edward II* (?1592), and *Dr. Faustus* (1604). He was stabbed to death in a tavern brawl.

mar·ma·lade (ˈmɑːməˌleɪd) *n.* **1.** a preserve made by boiling the pulp and rind of citrus fruits, esp. oranges, with sugar. ~*adj.* **2.** (of cats) streaked orange or yellow and brown. [C16: via French from Portuguese *marmelada,* from *marmelo* quince, from Latin, from Greek *melimēlon,* from *meli* honey + *mēlon* apple]

mar·ma·lade tree *n.* a tropical American sapotaceous tree, *Calocarpum sapota,* with durable wood: its fruit is used to make preserves. Also called: **mamey.**

Mar·ma·ra *or* **Mar·mo·ra** (ˈmɑːmərə) *n.* **Sea of.** a deep inland sea in NW Turkey, linked with the Black Sea by the Bosporus and with the Aegean by the Dardanelles: separates Turkey in Europe from Turkey in Asia. Area: 11 471 sq. km (4429 sq. miles). Ancient name: **Propontis.**

mar·mite (ˈmɑːmaɪt) *n.* **1.** a large cooking pot. **2.** soup cooked in such a pot. **3.** an individual covered casserole for serving soup. [from French: pot]

Mar·mite (ˈmɑːmaɪt) *n. Brit. trademark.* a yeast and vegetable extract used as a spread, flavouring, etc.

Mar·mo·la·da (*Italian* ˌmarmoˈlada) *n.* a mountain in NE Italy: highest peak in the Dolomites. Height: 3342 m (10 965 ft.).

mar·mo·re·al (mɑːˈmɔːrɪəl) *or* **mar·mo·re·an** *adj.* of, relating to, or resembling marble: *a marmoreal complexion.* [C18: from Latin *marmoreus,* from *marmor* marble] —**mar·ˈmo·re·al·ly** *adv.*

mar·mo·set (ˈmɑːməˌzɛt) *n.* **1.** any small South American monkey of the genus *Callithrix* and related genera, having long hairy tails, clawed digits, and tufts of hair around the head and ears: family *Callithricidae.* **2. pygmy marmoset.** a related form, *Cebuella pygmaea:* the smallest monkey, inhabiting tropical forests of the Amazon. [C14: from Old French *marmouset* grotesque figure, of obscure origin]

mar·mot (ˈmɑːmət) *n.* **1.** any burrowing sciurine rodent of the genus *Marmota,* of Europe, Asia, and North America. They are heavily built, having short legs, a short furry tail, and coarse fur. **2. prairie marmot.** another name for **prairie dog.** [C17: from French *marmotte,* perhaps ultimately from Latin *mūr-* (stem of *mūs*) mouse + *montis* of the mountain]

Marne (*French* marn) *n.* **1.** a department of NE France, in Champagne-Ardenne region. Capital: Châlons-sur-Marne. Pop.: 549 485 (1975). Area: 8205 sq. km (3200 sq. miles). **2.** a river in NE France, rising on the plateau of Langres and flowing north, then west to the River Seine, north of Paris: linked by canal with the Rivers Saône, Rhine, and Aisne; scene of two unsuccessful German offensives (1914, 1918) during World War I. Length: 525 km (326 miles).

Ma·roc (maˈrɔk) *n.* the French name for **Morocco.**

mar·o·cain (ˈmærəˌkeɪn) *n.* **1.** a fabric of ribbed crepe. **2.** a garment made from this fabric.

Mar·o·nite (ˈmærəˌnaɪt) *n. Christianity.* a member of a body of Uniats of Syrian origin, now living chiefly in Lebanon. [C16: from Late Latin *Marōnīta,* after *Maro,* fifth-century Syrian monk]

ma·roon[1] (məˈruːn) *vb.* (*tr.*) **1.** to leave ashore and abandon, esp. on an island. **2.** to isolate without resources. ~*n.* **3.** a descendant of a group of runaway slaves living in the remoter areas of the West Indies or Guyana. [C17 (applied to fugitive slaves): from American Spanish *cimarrón* wild, literally: dwelling on peaks, from Spanish *cima* summit]

ma·roon[2] (məˈruːn) *n.* **1. a.** a dark red to purplish-red colour. **b.** (*as adj.*): *a maroon carpet.* **2.** an exploding firework, esp. one used as a warning signal. [C18: from French, literally: chestnut, MARRON]

mar·o·quin (ˌmærəˈkiːn; ˈmærəkɪn, -kwɪn) *n. Tanning.* morocco leather. [C16: from French: Moroccan]

Ma·ros (ˈmɔrɔʃ) *n.* the Hungarian name for the **Mureş.**

Mar·pre·late (ˈmɑːprɛlɪt) *n.* **Mar·tin,** the pen name of the anonymous author or authors of a series of satirical Puritan tracts (1588–89), attacking the bishops of the Church of England.

Marq. *abbrev. for* Marquis.

Mar·quand (mɑːˈkwɒnd) *n.* **J(ohn) P(hillips).** 1893–1960, U.S. novelist, noted for his stories featuring the Japanese detective Mr. Moto and for his satirical comedies of New England life, such as *The Late George Apley* (1937).

marque (mɑːk) *n.* **1.** a brand of product, esp. of a car. **2.** an emblem or nameplate used to identify a product, esp. a car. [from French, from *marquer* to MARK]

mar·quee (mɑːˈkiː) *n.* **1.** a large tent used for entertainment, etc. **2.** Also called: **marquise.** *Chiefly U.S.* a canopy over the entrance to a theatre, hotel, etc. [C17 (originally an officer's tent): invented singular form of MARQUISE, erroneously taken to be plural]

Mar·que·san (mɑːˈkeɪzᵊn, -sᵊn) *adj.* **1.** of or relating to the Marquesas Islands or their inhabitants. ~*n.* **2.** a native or inhabitant of the Marquesas Islands.

Mar·que·sas Islands (mɑːˈkeɪsæs) *pl. n.* a group of volcanic islands in the S Pacific, in French Polynesia. Pop.: 5593 (1971). Area: 1287 sq. km (497 sq. miles). French name: **Îles Marquises** (il marˈkiːz).

mar·quess (ˈmɑːkwɪs) *n.* **1.** (in the British Isles) a nobleman ranking between a duke and an earl. **2.** See **marquis.**

mar·quess·ate (ˈmɑːkwɪzɪt) *n.* (in the British Isles) the dignity, rank, or position of a marquess; marquisate.

mar·que·try *or* **mar·que·te·rie** (ˈmɑːkɪtrɪ) *n., pl.* **·que·tries** *or* **·que·te·ries.** a pattern of inlaid veneers of wood, brass, ivory, etc., fitted together to form a picture or design, used chiefly as ornamentation in furniture. Compare **parquetry.** [C16: from Old French, from *marqueter* to inlay, from *marque* MARK[1]]

Mar·quette (mɑːˈkɛt) *n.* **Jacques** (ʒɑːk), known as *Père Marquette.* 1637–75, French Jesuit missionary and explorer, with Louis Jolliet, of the Mississippi river.

mar·quis (ˈmɑːkwɪs, mɑːˈkiː; *French* marˈki) *n., pl.* **·quis·es** *or* **·quis.** (in various countries) a nobleman ranking above a count, corresponding to a British marquess. The title of marquis is often used in place of that of marquess. [C14: from Old French *marchis,* literally: count of the march, from *marche* MARCH[2]]

Mar·quis (ˈmɑːkwɪs) *n.* **Don(ald Robert Perry).** 1878–1937, U.S. humorist; author of *archy and mehitabel* (1927).

mar·quis·ate (ˈmɑːkwɪzɪt) *n.* **1.** the rank or dignity of a marquis. **2.** the domain of a marquis.

mar·quise (mɑːˈkiːz; *French* marˈkiːz) *n.* **1.** (in various countries) another word for **marchioness. 2. a.** a gemstone, esp. a diamond, cut in a pointed oval shape and usually faceted. **b.** a piece of jewellery, esp. a ring, set with such a stone or with an oval cluster of stones. **3.** another name for **marquee** (sense 2). [C18: from French, feminine of MARQUIS]

mar·qui·sette (ˌmɑːkɪˈzɛt, -kwɪ-) *n.* a leno-weave fabric of cotton, silk, etc. [C20: from French, diminutive of MARQUISE]

Mar·ra·kech *or* **Mar·ra·kesh** (məˈrækɛʃ, ˌmærəˈkɛʃ) *n.* a city in W central Morocco: several times capital of Morocco; tourist centre. Pop.: 332 741 (1971).

mar·ram grass (ˈmærəm) *n.* any of several grasses of the genus *Ammophila* (or *Psamma*), esp. *A. arenaria,* that grow on sandy shores and can withstand drying: often planted to stabilize sand dunes. [C17: *marram,* from Old Norse *marálmr,* from *marr* sea + *hálmr* HAULM]

Mar·ra·no (məˈrɑːnəʊ) *n., pl.* **·nos.** a Spanish or Portuguese Jew of the late Middle Ages who was converted to Christianity, esp. one forcibly converted but secretly adhering to Judaism. [from Spanish, literally: pig, with reference to the Jewish prohibition against eating pork]

mar·riage (ˈmærɪdʒ) *n.* **1.** the state or relationship of being husband and wife. **2. a.** the legal union or contract made by a man and woman to live as husband and wife. **b.** (*as modifier*): *marriage licence; marriage certificate.* **3.** the religious or legal ceremony formalizing this union; wedding. **4.** a close or intimate union, relationship, etc.: *a marriage of ideas.* **5.** (in certain card games, such as bezique, pinochle) the king and queen of the same suit. [C13: from Old French; see MARRY[1], -AGE]

mar·riage·a·ble (ˈmærɪdʒəbᵊl) *adj.* (esp. of women) suitable for marriage, usually with reference to age. —ˌ**mar·riage·a·ˈbil·i·ty** *or* ˈ**mar·riage·a·ble·ness** *n.*

mar·riage guid·ance *n.* **a.** advice given to couples who have problems in their married life. **b.** (*as modifier*): *a marriage guidance counsellor.*

mar·riage of con·ven·i·ence *n.* a marriage based on expediency rather than on love.

mar·ried (ˈmærɪd) *adj.* **1.** having a husband or wife. **2.** joined in marriage: *a married couple.* **3.** of or involving marriage or married persons. **4.** closely or intimately united. ~*n.* **5.** (*usually pl.*) a married person (esp. in the phrase **young marrieds**).

mar·ron ('mærən; *French* ma'rɔ̃) *n.* a large edible sweet chestnut. [from French, of obscure origin]

mar·rons gla·cés *French.* (marɔ̃ gla'se) *pl. n.* chestnuts cooked in syrup and glazed.

mar·row[1] ('mærəʊ) *n.* **1.** the fatty network of connective tissue that fills the cavities of bones. **2.** the vital part; essence. **3.** vitality. **4.** rich food. **5.** *Brit.* short for **vegetable marrow.** [Old English *mærg;* related to Old Frisian *merg,* Old Norse *mergr*] —'**mar·row·y** *adj.*

mar·row[2] ('mærəʊ, -rə) *n. Northeastern English dialect, chiefly Durham.* a companion, esp. a workmate. [C15 *marwe* fellow worker, perhaps of Scandinavian origin; compare Icelandic *margr* friendly]

mar·row·bone ('mærəʊˌbəʊn) *n.* **a.** a bone containing edible marrow. **b.** (*as modifier*): *marrowbone jelly.*

mar·row·bones ('mærəʊˌbəʊnz) *pl. n.* **1.** *Facetious.* the knees. **2.** a rare word for **crossbones.**

mar·row·fat ('mærəʊˌfæt) *or* **mar·row pea** *n.* **1.** any of several varieties of pea plant that have large seeds. **2.** the seed of such a plant.

mar·row squash *n. U.S.* any of several oblong squashes that have a hard smooth rind, esp. the vegetable marrow.

mar·ry[1] ('mærɪ) *vb.* **·ries, ·ry·ing, ·ried. 1.** to take (someone as one's husband or wife) in marriage. **2.** (*tr.*) to join or give in marriage. **3.** (*tr.*) to acquire (something) by marriage: *marry money.* **4.** to unite closely or intimately. **5.** (*tr.*) *Nautical.* **a.** to match up (the strands) of unlaid ropes before splicing. **b.** to seize (two ropes) together at intervals along their lengths. [C13: from Old French *marier,* from Latin *marītāre,* from *marītus* married (man), perhaps from *mās* male]

mar·ry[2] ('mærɪ) *interj. Archaic.* an exclamation of surprise, anger, etc. [C14: euphemistic for the Virgin *Mary*]

Mar·ry·at ('mærɪət) *n.* **Fred·er·ick.** 1792–1848, English novelist and naval officer; author of novels of sea life, such as *Mr. Midshipman Easy* (1836), and children's stories, such as *The Children of the New Forest* (1847).

mar·ry in·to *vb.* (*intr., prep.*) to become a member of (a family) by marriage.

mar·ry off *vb.* (*tr., adv.*) to find a husband or wife for (a person, esp. one's son or daughter).

Mars (mɑːz) *n.* **1.** Also called: the **Red Planet.** the fourth planet from the sun, having a reddish-orange surface with numerous dark patches and two white polar caps. The surface ranges in temperature from about –70°C at night to –40°C during the day. The planet has two tiny satellites, Phobos and Deimos. Mean distance from sun: 228 million km; period of revolution around sun: 686.98 days; period of axial rotation: 24.6225 hours; diameter and mass: 53.2 and 10.7 per cent that of earth respectively. See also **canal** (sense 4). **2.** the Roman god of war, the father of Romulus and Remus. Greek counterpart: **Ares. 3.** the alchemical name for **iron.**

Mar·sa·la (mɑː'sɑːlə) *n.* **1.** a port in W Sicily: landing place of Garibaldi at the start of his Sicilian campaign (1860). Pop.: 79 920 (1971). **2.** a dark sweet dessert wine made in Sicily.

Mar·seil·laise (ˌmɑːsə'leɪz; *French* marsɛ'jɛːz) *n.* **the.** the French national anthem. It was written in 1792 by C. J. Rouget de Lisle as a war song for the Rhine army of revolutionary France. [C18: from French (*chanson*) *Marseillaise* song of Marseilles (it was first sung in Paris by some natives of Marseilles)]

mar·seille (mɑː'seɪl) *or* **mar·seilles** (mɑː'seɪlz) *n.* a strong cotton fabric with a raised pattern, used for bedspreads, etc. [C18: from *Marseille quilting,* made in Marseilles]

Mar·seille (*French* mar'sɛj) *n.* a port in SE France, on the Gulf of Lions: second largest city in the country and a major port; founded in about 600 B.C. by Greeks from Phocaea; oil refining. Pop.: 914 356 (1975). Ancient name: **Massilia.** English name: **Mar·seilles** (mɑː'seɪ, -'seɪlz).

marsh (mɑːʃ) *n.* low poorly drained land that is sometimes flooded and often lies at the edge of lakes, etc. Compare **swamp** (sense 1). [Old English *merisc;* related to German *Marsch,* Dutch *marsk;* related to MERE[2]] —'**marsh·ˌlike** *adj.*

mar·shal ('mɑːʃəl) *n.* **1.** (in some armies and air forces) an officer of the highest rank. **2.** (in England) an officer, usually a junior barrister, who accompanies a judge on circuit and performs miscellaneous secretarial duties. **3.** (in the U.S.) **a.** a Federal court officer assigned to a judicial district whose functions are similar to those of a sheriff. **b.** (in some states) the chief police or fire officer. **4.** an officer who organizes or conducts ceremonies, parades, etc. **5.** Also called: **knight marshal.** (formerly in England) an officer of the royal family or court, esp. one in charge of protocol. **6.** an obsolete word for **ostler.** ~*vb.* **·shals, ·shal·ling, ·shalled** *or U.S.* **·shals, ·shal·ing, ·shaled.** (*tr.*) **7.** to arrange in order: *to marshal the facts.* **8.** to assemble and organize (troops, vehicles, etc.) prior to onward movement. **9.** to arrange (assets, mortgages, etc.) in order of priority. **10.** to guide or lead, esp. in a ceremonious way. **11.** to combine (two or more coats of arms) on one shield. [C13: from Old French *mareschal;* related to Old High German *marahscalc* groom, from *marah* horse + *scalc* servant] —'**mar·shal·cy** *or* '**mar·shal·ˌship** *n.* —'**mar·shal·ler** *or U.S.* '**mar·shal·er** *n.*

Mar·shall ('mɑːʃəl) *n.* **1. Al·fred.** 1842–1924, English economist, author of *Principles of Economics* (1890). **2. George Cat·lett.** 1880–1959, U.S. general and statesman. He was chief of staff of the U.S. army (1939–45) and, as secretary of state (1947–49), he proposed the Marshall Plan (1947), later called the European Recovery Programme: Nobel peace prize 1953. **3. John.** 1755–1835, U.S. jurist and statesman. As chief justice of the Supreme Court (1801–35), he established the principles of U.S. constitutional law. **4. Sir John Ross.** born 1912, New Zealand politician; prime minister 1972.

mar·shall·ing yard *n. Railways.* a place or depot where railway wagons are shunted and made up into trains and where engines, carriages, etc., are kept when not in use.

Mar·shall Is·lands *pl. n.* a group of 34 coral islands in the W central Pacific, in E Micronesia: administratively part of the United States Trust Territory of the Pacific Islands since 1947; consists of two parallel chains, Ralik and Ratak. Pop.: 23 166 (1971). Area: (land) 158 sq. km (61 sq. miles); (lagoon) 11 655 sq. km (4500 sq. miles).

Mar·shall Plan *n.* a programme of U.S. economic aid for the reconstruction of post-World War II Europe (1948–52). Official name: **European Recovery Programme.**

Mar·shal·sea ('mɑːʃəlˌsiː) *n.* **1.** (formerly in England) a court held before the knight marshal: abolished 1849. **2.** a prison for debtors and others, situated in Southwark, London: abolished in 1842. [C14: see MARSHAL, -CY]

marsh an·drom·e·da *n.* a low-growing pink-flowered ericaceous evergreen shrub, *Andromeda polifolia,* that grows in peaty bogs of northern regions. Also called: **moorwort.**

marsh el·der *n.* any of several North American shrubs of the genus *Iva,* growing in salt marshes: family *Compositae* (composites). Compare **elder**[2].

marsh fe·ver *n.* another name for **malaria.**

marsh gas *n.* a gas largely composed of methane produced when vegetation decomposes under water.

marsh har·ri·er *n.* **1.** a European harrier, *Circus aeruginosus,* that frequents marshy regions. **2.** a U.S. name for **hen harrier.**

marsh hawk *n.* the U.S. name for the **hen harrier.**

marsh hen *n.* any bird that frequents marshes and swamps, esp. a rail, coot, or gallinule.

marsh·land ('mɑːʃlənd) *n.* land consisting of marshes.

marsh mal·low *n.* **1.** a malvaceous plant, *Althaea officinalis,* that grows in salt marshes and has pale pink flowers. The roots yield a mucilage formerly used to make marshmallows. **2.** *U.S.* another name for **rose mallow** (sense 1).

marsh·mal·low (ˌmɑːʃ'mæləʊ) *n.* **1.** a sweet of a spongy texture containing gum arabic or gelatine, sugar, etc. **2.** a sweetened paste or confection made from the root of the marsh mallow. —ˌ**marsh·'mal·low·y** *adj.*

marsh mar·i·gold *n.* a yellow-flowered ranunculaceous plant, *Caltha palustris,* that grows in swampy places. Also called: **kingcup, May blobs,** and (U.S.) **cowslip.**

marsh tit *n.* a small European songbird, *Parus palustris,* with a black head and greyish-brown body: family *Paridae* (tits).

marsh·y ('mɑːʃɪ) *adj.* **marsh·i·er, marsh·i·est.** of, involving, or like a marsh. —'**marsh·i·ness** *n.*

Mar·sil·i·us of Pad·u·a (mɑː'sɪlɪəs) *n.* Italian name *Marsiglio dei Mainardini.* ?1290–?1343, Italian political philosopher, best known as the author of the *Defensor pacis* (1324), which upheld the power of the temporal ruler over that of the church.

mar·si·po·branch ('mɑːsɪpəʊˌbræŋk) *n., adj.* another word for **cyclostome.** [C19: from New Latin *Marsipobranchia,* from Greek *marsipos* pouch + *branchia* gills]

Mars·ton ('mɑːstən) *n.* **John.** ?1576–1634, English dramatist and satirist. His works include the revenge tragedies *Antonio and Mellida* (1602) and *Antonio's Revenge* (1602) and the satirical comedy *The Malcontent* (1604).

Mars·ton Moor *n.* a flat low-lying area in NE England, west of York: scene of a battle (1644) in which the Parliamentarians defeated the Royalists.

mar·su·pi·al (mɑː'sjuːpɪəl, -'suː-) *n.* **1.** any mammal of the order *Marsupialia,* in which the young are born in an immature state and continue development in the marsupium. The order occurs mainly in Australia and South and Central America and includes the opossums, bandicoots, koala, wombats, and kangaroos. ~*adj.* **2.** of, relating to, or belonging to the *Marsupialia.* **3.** of or relating to a marsupium. [C17: see MARSUPIUM] —**mar·su·pi·a·li·an** (mɑːˌsjuːpɪ'eɪlɪən, -ˌsuː-) *or* **mar·'su·pi·an** *n., adj.*

mar·su·pi·al mole *n.* any molelike marsupial of the family *Notoryctidae.*

mar·su·pi·al mouse *n.* any mouselike insectivorous marsupial of the subfamily *Phascogalinae:* family *Dasyuridae.*

mar·su·pi·um (mɑː'sjuːpɪəm, -'suː-) *n., pl.* **·pi·a** (-pɪə). an external pouch in most female marsupials within which the newly born offspring are suckled and complete their development. [C17: New Latin, from Latin: purse, from Greek *marsupion,* diminutive of *marsipos*]

mart (mɑːt) *n.* a market or trading centre. [C15: from Middle Dutch *mart* MARKET]

Mar·ta·ban (ˌmɑːtɑː'bɑːn) *n.* **Gulf of.** an inlet of the Bay of Bengal in Lower Burma.

mar·ta·gon *or* **mar·ta·gon lil·y** ('mɑːtəgən) *n.* a Eurasian lily plant, *Lilium martagon,* cultivated for its mottled purplish-red flowers with reflexed petals. Also called: **Turk's-cap lily.** [C15: from French, from Turkish *martağan* a type of turban]

Mar·tel (mɑː'tɛl) *n.* See **Charles Martel.**

mar·tel·la·to (ˌmɑːtə'lɑːtəʊ) *or* **mar·tel·lan·do** *n.* (in string playing) the practice of bowing the string with a succession of short sharp blows. [Italian: hammered]

Mar·tel·lo tow·er *or* **Mar·tel·lo** (mɑː'tɛləʊ) *n.* a small circular tower for coastal defence, formerly much used in Europe. [C18: after Cape *Mortella* in Corsica, where the British navy captured a tower of this type in 1794]

mar·ten ('mɑːtɪn) *n., pl.* **·tens** *or* **·ten. 1.** any of several agile arboreal musteline mammals of the genus *Martes,* of Europe, Asia, and North America, having bushy tails and golden brown to blackish fur. See also **pine marten.** **2.** the highly valued fur of these animals, esp. that of *M. americana.* ~See also **sable** (sense 1). [C15: from Middle Dutch *martren,* from Old French *(peau) martrine* skin of a marten, from *martre,* probably of Germanic origin]

mar·ten·site ('mɑːtɪnˌzaɪt) *n.* a constituent formed in steels by rapid quenching, consisting of a supersaturated solid solution of carbon in iron. It is formed by the breakdown of austenite when the rate of cooling is large enough to prevent pearlite forming. [C20: named after Adolf *Martens* (died 1914), German metallurgist] —**mar·ten·sit·ic** (ˌmɑːtɪn'zɪtɪk) *adj.*

Mar·tha ('mɑːθə) *n. New Testament.* a sister of Mary and Lazarus, who lived at Bethany and ministered to Jesus (Luke 10:38–42).

mar·tial ('mɑːʃəl) *adj.* of, relating to, or characteristic of war, soldiers, or the military life. [C14: from Latin *martiālis* of Mars] —'**mar·tial·ism** *n.* —'**mar·tial·ist** *n.* —'**mar·tial·ly** *adv.* —'**mar·tial·ness** *n.*

Mar·tial[1] ('mɑːʃəl) *adj.* of or relating to Mars.

Mar·tial[2] ('mɑːʃəl) *n.* full name *Marcus Valerius Martialis.* ?40–?104 A.D., Latin epigrammatist and poet, born in Spain.

mar·tial law *n.* the rule of law established and maintained by the military in the absence of civil law.

Mar·tian ('mɑːʃən) *adj.* **1.** of, occurring on, or relating to the planet Mars. ~*n.* **2.** an inhabitant of Mars, esp. in science fiction.

mar·tin ('mɑːtɪn) *n.* any of various swallows of the genera *Progne, Delichon, Riparia,* etc., having a square or slightly forked tail. See also **house martin.** [C15: perhaps from St. Martin, because the birds were believed to migrate at the time of Martinmas]

Mar·tin ('mɑːtɪn) *n.* **1. Frank.** 1890–1974, Swiss composer. He used a modified form of the twelve-note technique in some of his works, which include *Petite Symphonie Concertante* (1946) and the oratorio *Golgotha* (1949). **2. Saint,** called *Saint Martin of Tours.* ?316–?397 A.D., bishop of Tours (?371–?397); patron saint of France. He furthered monasticism in Gaul. Feast day: Nov. 11.

Mar·tin du Gard (*French* martɛ̃ dy 'gaːr) *n.* **Ro·ger** (rɔ'ʒe). 1881–1958, French novelist, noted for his series of novels, *Les Thibault* (1922–40): Nobel prize for literature 1937.

Mar·ti·neau ('mɑːtɪˌnəʊ) *n.* **1. Har·ri·et.** 1802–76, English author of books on political economy and of novels and children's stories. **2.** her brother, **James.** 1805–1900, English Unitarian theologian and minister.

mar·ti·net (ˌmɑːtɪ'nɛt) *n.* a person who maintains strict discipline, esp. in a military force. [C17: from French, from the name of General *Martinet,* drill-master under Louis XIV] —ˌ**mar·ti·'net·ish** *adj.* —ˌ**mar·ti·'net·ism** *n.*

mar·tin·gale ('mɑːtɪnˌgeɪl) *n.* **1.** a strap from the reins to the girth of a horse preventing it from carrying its head too high. **2.** any gambling system in which the stakes are raised, usually doubled, after each loss. **3.** Also called: **martingale boom.** *Nautical.* **a.** a chain or cable running from a bowsprit to the stern, and serving to counteract the strain of the headstays. **b.** another term for **dolphin striker.** [C16: from French, of uncertain origin]

mar·ti·ni (mɑː'tiːnɪ) *n., pl.* **·nis. 1.** (*often cap.*) *Trademark.* an Italian vermouth. **2.** a cocktail of gin and vermouth. [C19 (sense 2): perhaps from the name of the inventor]

Mar·ti·ni (*Italian* mar'tiːni) *n.* **Si·mo·ne** (si'moːne). ?1284–1344, Sienese painter.

Mar·ti·nique (ˌmɑːtɪ'niːk) *n.* an island in the E Caribbean, in the Windward Islands of the Lesser Antilles: administratively an overseas region of France. Capital: Fort-de-France. Pop.: 328 239 (1975). Area: 1090 sq. km (420 sq. miles). —ˌ**Mar·ti·'ni·can** *n., adj.*

Mar·tin·mas ('mɑːtɪnməs) *n.* the feast of St. Martin on Nov. 11; one of the four quarter days in Scotland.

Mar·ti·nů ('mɑːtɪˌnuː; *Czech* 'martjinuː) *n.* **Bo·hu·slav** ('bɔhuslaf). 1890–1959, Czech composer.

mart·let ('mɑːtlɪt) *n.* **1.** an archaic name for a **martin. 2.** *Heraldry.* a footless bird often found in coats of arms, standing for either a martin or a swallow. [C16: from French *martelet,* variant of *martinet,* diminutive of MARTIN]

mar·tyr ('mɑːtə) *n.* **1.** a person who suffers death rather than renounce his religious beliefs. **2.** a person who suffers greatly or dies for a cause, belief, etc. **3.** a person who suffers from poor health, misfortune, etc.: *he's a martyr to rheumatism.* **4.** *Facetious or derogatory.* a person who feigns suffering to gain sympathy, help, etc. ~*vb. also* **mar·tyr·ize** *or* **mar·tyr·ise.** (*tr.*) **5.** to kill as a martyr. **6.** to make a martyr of. [Old English *martir,* from Church Latin *martyr,* from Late Greek *martur-, martus* witness] —ˌ**mar·tyr·i·'za·tion** *or* ˌ**mar·tyr·i·'sa·tion** *n.*

mar·tyr·dom ('mɑːtədəm) *n.* **1.** the sufferings or death of a martyr. **2.** great suffering or torment.

mar·tyr·ol·o·gy (ˌmɑːtə'rɒlədʒɪ) *n., pl.* **·gies. 1.** an official list of martyrs. **2.** *Christianity.* the study of the lives of the martyrs. **3.** a historical account of the lives of martyrs. —**mar·tyr·o·log·i·cal** (ˌmɑːtərə'lɒdʒɪkəl) *or* ˌ**mar·tyr·o·'log·ic** *adj.* —ˌ**mar·tyr·'ol·o·gist** *n.*

mar·tyr·y ('mɑːtərɪ) *n., pl.* **·tyr·ies.** a shrine or chapel erected in honour of a martyr.

mar·vel ('mɑːvəl) *vb.* **·vels, ·vel·ling, ·velled** *or U.S.* **·vels, ·vel·ing, ·veled. 1.** (when *intr.,* often foll. by *at* or *about;* when *tr., takes a clause as object*) to be filled with surprise or wonder. ~*n.* **2.** something that causes wonder. **3.** *Archaic.* astonishment. [C13: from Old French *merveille,* from Late Latin *mīrābilia,* from Latin *mīrābilis* from *mīrārī* to wonder at] —'**mar·vel·ment** *n.*

Mar·vell ('mɑːvəl) *n.* **An·drew.** 1621–78, English poet and satirist. He is noted for his lyrical poems and verse and prose satires attacking the government after the Restoration.

mar·vel·lous *or U.S.* **mar·vel·ous** ('mɑːvələs) *adj.* **1.** causing great wonder, surprise, etc.; extraordinary. **2.** improbable or incredible. **3.** *Informal.* excellent; splendid. —'**mar·vel·lous·ly** *or U.S.* '**mar·vel·ous·ly** *adv.* —'**mar·vel·lous·ness** *or U.S.* '**mar·vel·ous·ness** *n.*

mar·vel-of-Pe·ru *n., pl.* **mar·vels-of-Pe·ru.** another name for **four-o'clock** (the plant). [first found in Peru]

Marx (mɑːks) *n.* **Karl** (karl). 1818–83, German founder of modern communism, in England from 1849. With Engels, he wrote *The Communist Manifesto* (1848). He developed his theories of the class struggle and the economics of capitalism in *Das Kapital* (1867; 1885; 1895). He was one of the founders of the International Workingmen's Association (First International) (1864).

Marx Broth·ers (mɑːks) *n.* **the.** a U.S. family of film comedians, esp. **Arthur Marx,** called *Harpo* (1893–1964), **Herbert Marx,** called *Zeppo* (born 1901), **Julius Marx,** called *Groucho* (1895–1977), and **Leonard Marx,** called *Chico* (1891–1961). Their films include *Animal Crackers* (1930), *Monkey Business* (1931), *Horsefeathers* (1932), *Duck Soup* (1933), and *A Day at the Races* (1937).

Marx·i·an ('mɑːksɪən) *adj.* of or relating to Karl Marx and his theories. —'**Marx·i·an·ism** *n.*

Marx·ism ('mɑːksɪzəm) *n.* the economic and political theory and practice originated by Karl Marx and Friedrich Engels that holds that actions and human institutions are economically determined, that the class struggle is the basic agency of historical change, and that capitalism will ultimately be superseded by communism.

Marx·ism-Len·in·ism *n.* the modification of Marxism by Lenin stressing that imperialism is the highest form of capitalism. —'**Marx·ist-'Len·in·ist** *n., adj.*

Marx·ist ('mɑːksɪst) *n.* **1.** a follower of Marxism. ~*adj.* **2.** of or relating to Marx and his teachings.

Mar·y ('mɛərɪ) *n.* **1.** *New Testament.* **a.** Also called: the **Virgin Mary.** the mother of Jesus, believed to have conceived and borne him while still a virgin; she was married to Joseph (Matthew 1:18–25). **b.** the sister of Martha and Lazarus (Luke 10:38–42; John 11:1–2). **2.** original name *Princess Mary of Teck.* 1867–1953, queen of Great Britain and Northern Ireland (1910–36) by marriage to George V. **3.** (*pl.* **·ries**) *Austral. slang.* an Aboriginal woman or girl.

Mar·y I *n.* family name *Tudor,* known as *Bloody Mary.* 1516–58, queen of England (1553–58). The daughter of Henry VIII and Catherine of Aragon, she married Philip II of Spain in 1554. She restored Roman Catholicism to England and about 300 Protestants were burnt at the stake as heretics.

Mar·y II *n.* 1662–94, queen of England, Scotland, and Ireland (1689–94), ruling jointly with her husband William III. They were offered the crown by the opposition to the arbitrary rule of her father James II.

mar·y jane *n. U.S.* a slang term for **marijuana.**

Mar·y·land ('mɛərɪˌlænd, 'mɛrɪlənd) *n.* a state of the eastern U.S., on the Atlantic: divided into two unequal parts by Chesapeake Bay: mostly low-lying, with the Alleghenies in the northwest. Capital: Annapolis. Pop.: 3 922 399 (1970). Area: 31 864 sq. km (12 303 sq. miles). Abbrevs.: **Md.** or (with zip code) **MD**

Mar·y Mag·da·lene *n. New Testament.* a woman of **Mag·da·la** ('mægdələ) in Galilee whom Jesus cured of evil spirits (Luke 8:2) and who is often identified with the sinful woman of Luke 7:36–50. In Christian tradition she is usually taken to have been a prostitute. See **magdalen.**

Mar·y Queen of Scots *n.* family name *Stuart.* 1542–87, queen of Scotland (1542–67); daughter of James V of Scotland and Mary of Guise. She was married to Francis II of France (1558–60), her cousin Lord Darnley (1565–67), and the Earl of Bothwell (1567–71), who was commonly regarded as Darnley's murderer. She was forced to abdicate in favour of her son (later James VI of Scotland) and fled to England. Imprisoned by Elizabeth I until 1587, she was beheaded for plotting against the English crown.

mar·zi·pan ('mɑːzɪˌpæn) *n.* a paste made from ground almonds, sugar, and egg whites, used to coat fruit cakes or moulded into sweets. Also called (esp. formerly): **marchpane.** [C19: via German from Italian *marzapane.* See MARCHPANE]

-mas *n. combining form.* indicating a Christian festival: *Christmas; Michaelmas.* [from MASS]

Ma·sac·cio (*Italian* ma'zattʃo) *n.* original name *Tommaso Guidi.* 1401–28, Florentine painter. He was the first to apply to painting the laws of perspective discovered by Brunelleschi. His chief work is the frescoes in the Brancacci chapel in the church of Sta. Maria del Carmine, Florence.

Ma·sai ('mɑːsaɪ, mɑː'saɪ) *n.* **1.** (*pl.* **·sais** *or* **·sai**) a member of a Nilotic people, formerly noted as warriors, living chiefly in Kenya and Tanzania. **2.** the language of this people, belonging to the Nilotic group of the Nilo-Saharan family.

Ma·san ('mɑːˌsɑːn) *n.* a port in SE South Korea, on an inlet of the Korea Strait: first opened to foreign trade in 1899. Pop.: 190 992 (1970).

Ma·sa·ryk ('mæsərɪk; *Czech* 'masarik) *n.* **1. Jan** (jan). 1886–1948, Czech statesman; foreign minister (1941–48). He died in mysterious circumstances after the Communists took control of the government. **2.** his father, **Tom·áš Gar·rigue** ('tɔmaːʃ 'garik). 1850–1937, Czech philosopher and statesman; a founder of Czechoslovakia (1918) and its first president (1918–35).

Mas·ba·te (mæs'bɑːtɪ) *n.* **1.** an island in the central Philippines, between Negros and SE Luzon: agricultural, with resources of gold, copper, and manganese. Pop.: 492 908 (1970). Area: 4045 sq. km (1562 sq. miles). **2.** the capital of this island, a port in the northeast. Pop.: 45 591 (1970).

masc. *abbrev. for* masculine.

Mas·ca·gni (*Italian* mas'kaɲɲi) *n.* **Pie·tro** ('pjɛːtro). 1863–1945, Italian composer of operas, including *Cavalleria rusticana* (1890).

mas·car·a (mæ'skɑːrə) *n.* a cosmetic substance for darkening, colouring, and thickening the eyelashes, applied with a brush or rod. [C20: from Spanish: mask]

Mas·ca·rene Is·lands (ˌmæskə'riːn) *pl. n.* a group of volcanic islands in the W Indian Ocean, east of Madagascar: consists of the islands of Réunion, Mauritius, and Rodrigues. French name: **Îles Mascareignes.**

mas·cle ('mɑːskᵊl) *n. Heraldry.* a charge consisting of a lozenge with a lozenge-shaped hole in the middle. Also called: **voided lozenge.** [C14: from Old French *macle,* perhaps from Latin *macula* spot]

mas·con ('mæskɒn) *n.* any of several lunar regions of high gravity. [C20: from MAS(S) + CON(CENTRATION)]

mas·cot ('mæskət) *n.* a person, animal, or thing considered to bring good luck. [C19: from French *mascotte,* from Provençal *mascotto* charm, from *masco* witch]

mas·cu·line ('mæskjʊlɪn) *adj.* **1.** possessing qualities or characteristics considered typical of or appropriate to a man; manly. **2.** unwomanly. **3.** *Grammar.* **a.** denoting a gender of nouns, occurring in many inflected languages, that includes all kinds of referents as well as some male animate referents. **b.** (*as n.*): *German "Weg" is a masculine.* [C14: via French from Latin *masculīnus,* from *masculus* male, from *mās* a male] —'**mas·cu·line·ly** *adv.* —ˌ**mas·cu·'lin·i·ty** *or* '**mas·cu·line·ness** *n.*

mas·cu·line end·ing *n. Prosody.* a stressed syllable at the end of a line of verse. Compare **feminine ending.**

mas·cu·line rhyme *n. Prosody.* a rhyme between stressed monosyllables or between the final stressed syllables of polysyllabic words: *book, cook; collect, direct.* Compare **feminine rhyme.**

Mase·field ('meɪsˌfiːld) *n.* **John.** 1878–1967, English poet, novelist, and critic; poet laureate (1930–67).

ma·ser ('meɪzə) *n.* a device for amplifying microwaves, working on the same principle as a laser. [C20: *m(icrowave) a(mplification by) s(timulated) e(mission of) r(adiation)*]

Ma·se·ru (mə'sɛəruː) *n.* the capital of Lesotho, in the northwest near the W border with South Africa; established as capital of Basutoland in 1869. Pop.: 16 312 (1971 est.).

mash (mæʃ) *n.* **1.** a soft pulpy mass or consistency. **2.** *Agriculture.* a feed of bran, meal, or malt mixed with water and fed to horses, cattle, or poultry. **3.** (esp. in brewing) a mixture of mashed malt grains and hot water, from which malt is extracted. **4.** *Brit.* mashed potatoes. **5.** *Northern Brit. dialect.* a brew of tea. ~*vb.* (*tr.*) **6.** to beat or crush into a mash. **7.** to steep (malt grains) in hot water in order to extract malt, esp. for making malt liquors. **8.** *Northern Brit. dialect.* to brew (tea). **9.** *Archaic.* to flirt with. [Old English *mǣsc-* (in compound words); related to Middle Low German *mēsch*] —'**mash·er** *n.*

Mash·ar·brum *or* **Mash·er·brum** ('mʌʃəˌbrʊm) *n.* a mountain in N India, in N Kashmir in the Karakoram Range of the Himalayas. Height: 7822 m (25 660 ft.).

Mash·had (mæʃ'hæd) *or* **Me·shed** *n.* a city in NE Iran: the holy city of Shi'ite Muslims; carpet manufacturing. Pop.: 592 000 (1973).

mash·ie *or* **mash·y** ('mæʃɪ) *n., pl.* **mash·ies.** *Golf.* an iron for lofting shots, usually No. 5. [C19: perhaps from French *massue* club, ultimately from Latin *mateola* mallet]

Ma·sho·na (mə'ʃəʊnə) *n., pl.* **·na** *or* **·nas.** another name for the **Shona** (sense 1).

Mas·i·nis·sa *or* **Mas·si·nis·sa** (ˌmæsə'nɪsə) *n.* ?238–?149 B.C., king of Numidia (?210–149), who fought as an ally of Rome against Carthage in the Second Punic War.

mas·jid *or* **mus·jid** ('mʌsdʒɪd) *n.* a mosque in an Arab country. [Arabic; see MOSQUE]

mask (mɑːsk) *n.* **1.** any covering for the whole or a part of the face worn for amusement, protection, disguise, etc. **2.** a fact, action, etc., that conceals something: *his talk was a mask for his ignorance.* **3.** another name for **masquerade. 4.** a likeness of a face or head, either sculpted or moulded, such as a death mask. **5.** an image of a face worn by an actor, esp. in ancient Greek and Roman drama, in order to symbolize the character being portrayed. **6.** a variant spelling of **masque. 7.** *Surgery.* a sterile gauze covering for the nose and mouth worn esp. during operations to minimize the spread of germs. **8.** *Sport.* a protective covering for the face worn for fencing, ice hockey, etc. **9.** a carving in the form of a face or head, used as an ornament. **10.** a natural land feature or artificial object which conceals troops, etc., from view. **11.** a device placed over the nose and mouth to facilitate or prevent inhalation of a gas. **12.** *Photog.* a shield of paper, paint, etc., placed over an area of unexposed photographic surface to stop light falling on it. **13.** *Electronics.* a thin sheet of material from which a pattern has been cut, placed over a semiconductor chip so that an integrated circuit can be formed on the exposed areas. **14.** *Entomol.* a large prehensile mouthpart (labium) of the dragonfly larva. **15.** the face or head of an animal, such as a fox, or the dark coloration of the face of some animals, such as Siamese cats and certain dogs. **16.** another word for **face pack. 17.** *Now rare.* a person wearing a mask. ~*vb.* **18.** to cover with or put on a mask. **19.** (*tr.*) to conceal; disguise: *to mask an odour.* **20.** (*tr.*) *Photog.* to shield a particular area of (an unexposed photographic surface) in order to prevent or reduce the action of light there. **21.** (*tr.*) to cover (cooked food, esp. meat) with a savoury sauce or glaze. [C16: from Italian *maschera,* ultimately from Arabic *maskharah* clown, from *sakhira* mockery] —'**mask·ˌlike** *adj.*

mas·ka·nonge ('mæskəˌnɒndʒ), **mas·ki·nonge** ('mæskɪˌnɒndʒ), *or* **mas·ka·longe** ('mæskəˌlɒndʒ) *n., pl.* **·nong·es, ·nonge** *or* **·long·es, ·longe.** variants of **muskellunge.**

masked (mɑːskt) *adj.* **1.** disguised or covered by or as if by a mask. **2.** *Botany.* another word for **personate**[2].

masked ball *n.* a ball at which masks are worn.

mask·er *or* **mas·quer** ('mɑːskə) *n.* a person who wears a mask or takes part in a masque.

mask·ing tape *n.* an adhesive tape used to mask and protect surfaces surrounding an area to be painted.

mas·o·chism ('mæsəˌkɪzəm) *n.* **1.** *Psychiatry.* an abnormal condition in which pleasure, esp. sexual pleasure, is derived from pain or from humiliation, domination, etc., by another person. **2.** *Psychoanal.* the directing towards oneself of any destructive tendencies. **3.** a tendency to take pleasure from one's own suffering. Compare **sadism.** [C19: named after Leopold von Sacher *Masoch* (1836–95), Austrian novelist, who described it] —'**mas·o·chist** *n.* —ˌ**mas·o·'chis·tic** *adj.* —ˌ**mas·o·'chis·ti·cal·ly** *adv.*

ma·son ('meɪsᵊn) *n.* **1.** a person skilled in building with stone. **2.** a person who dresses stone. ~*vb.* **3.** (*tr.*) to construct or strengthen with masonry. [C13: from Old French *masson,* of Frankish origin; perhaps related to Old English *macian* to make]

Ma·son ('meɪsᵊn) *n.* short for **Freemason.**

ma·son bee *n.* any bee of the family *Megachilidae* that builds a hard domelike nest of sand, clay, etc., held together with saliva.

Ma·son-Dix·on Line *or* **Ma·son and Dix·on Line** *n.* the state boundary between Maryland and Pennsylvania: surveyed between 1763 and 1767 by Charles Mason and Jeremiah Dixon; popularly regarded as the dividing line between North and South, esp. between the free and the slave states before the American Civil War.

ma·son·ic (mə'sɒnɪk) *adj.* **1.** (*often cap.*) of, characteristic of, or relating to Freemasons or Freemasonry. **2.** of or relating to masons or masonry. —**ma·'son·i·cal·ly** *adv.*

ma·son·ry ('meɪsənrɪ) *n., pl.* **·ries. 1.** the craft of a mason. **2.** work that is built by a mason; stonework or brickwork. **3.** (*often cap.*) short for **Freemasonry.**

Ma·so·ra, Ma·so·rah, Mas·so·ra, *or* **Mas·so·rah** (mə'sɔːrə) *n.* **1.** the text of the Hebrew Bible as officially revised by the Masoretes from the 6th to the 10th centuries A.D., with critical notes and commentary. **2.** the collection of these notes, etc. [C17: from Hebrew: tradition]

Mas·o·rete, Mas·so·rete ('mæsəˌriːt), *or* **Mas·o·rite** ('mæsəˌraɪt) *n.* **1.** a member of the school of rabbis that produced the Masora. **2.** a Hebrew scholar who is expert in the Masora. [C16: from Hebrew *māsōreth* MASORA]

Mas·o·ret·ic, Mas·so·ret·ic (ˌmæsə'rɛtɪk) *or* **Mas·o·ret·i·cal, Mas·so·ret·i·cal** *adj.* of or relating to the Masora, the Masoretes, or the system of textual criticism and explanation evolved by them.

Mas·qat ('mʌskət, -kæt) *n.* a transliteration of the Arabic name for **Muscat.**

masque *or* **mask** (mɑːsk) *n.* **1.** a dramatic entertainment of the 16th to 17th centuries in England, consisting of pantomime, dancing, dialogue, and song, often performed at court. **2.** the words and music written for a masque. **3.** short for **masquerade.** [C16: variant of MASK]

mas·quer·ade (ˌmæskə'reɪd) *n.* **1.** a party or other gathering to which the guests wear masks and costumes. **2.** the disguise worn at such a function. **3.** a pretence or disguise. ~*vb.* (*intr.*) **4.** to participate in a masquerade; disguise oneself. **5.** to dissemble. [C16: from Spanish *mascarada,* from *mascara* MASK] —ˌ**mas·quer·'ad·er** *n.*

mass (mæs) *n.* **1.** a large coherent body of matter without a definite shape. **2.** a collection of the component parts of something. **3.** a large amount or number, such as a great body of people. **4.** the main part or majority: *the mass of the people voted against the government's policy.* **5. in the mass.** in the main; collectively. **6.** the size of a body; bulk. **7.** *Physics.* a physical quantity expressing the amount of matter in a body. It is a measure of a body's resistance to changes in velocity (**inertial mass**) and also of the force experienced in a gravitational field (**gravitational mass**): according to the theory of relativity, inertial and gravitational masses are equal. **8.** (in painting, drawing, etc.) an area of unified colour, shade, or intensity, usually denoting a solid form or plane. **9.** *Pharmacol.* a pastelike composition of drugs from which pills are made. **10.** *Mining.* an irregular deposit of ore not occurring in veins. ~(*modifier*) **11.** done or occurring on a large scale: *mass hysteria; mass radiography.* **12.** consisting of a mass or large number, esp. of people: *a mass meeting.* ~*vb.* **13.** to form (people or things) or (of people or things) to join together into a mass: *the crowd massed outside the embassy.* ~See also **mass in.** [C14: from Old French *masse,* from Latin *massa* that which forms a lump, from Greek *maza* barley cake; perhaps related to Greek *massein* to knead] —**mass·ed·ly** ('mæsɪdlɪ, 'mæstlɪ) *adv.*

Mass (mæs, mɑːs) *n.* **1.** (in the Roman Catholic Church and certain Protestant Churches) the celebration of the Eucharist.

See also **High Mass, Low Mass. 2.** a musical setting of those parts of the Eucharistic service sung by choir or congregation. [Old English *mæsse,* from Church Latin *missa,* ultimately from Latin *mittere* to send away; perhaps derived from the concluding dismissal in the Roman Mass, *Ite, missa est,* Go, it is the dismissal]

Mass. *abbrev. for* Massachusetts.

Mas+sa (*Italian* 'massa) *n.* a town in W Italy, in NW Tuscany. Pop.: 62 922 (1971).

Mas+sa+chu+set (ˌmæsəˈtʃuːsɪt) *or* **Mas+sa+chu+setts** *n.* **1.** (*pl.* **+sets, +set,** *or* **+setts**) a member of a North American Indian people formerly living around Massachusetts Bay. **2.** the language of this people, belonging to the Algonquian family. [probably from Algonquian, literally: at the big hill]

Mas+sa+chu+setts (ˌmæsəˈtʃuːsɪts) *n.* a state of the northeastern U.S., on the Atlantic: a centre of resistance to English colonial policy during the War of American Independence; consists of a coastal plain rising to mountains in the west. Capital: Boston. Pop.: 5 689 170 (1970). Area: 20 269 sq. km (7826 sq. miles). Abbrevs.: **Mass.** or (with zip code) **MA**

Mas+sa+chu+setts Bay *n.* an inlet of the Atlantic on the E coast of Massachusetts.

mas+sa+cre (ˈmæsəkə) *n.* **1.** the wanton or savage killing of large numbers of people, as in battle. **2.** *Informal.* an overwhelming defeat, as in a game. ~*vb.* (*tr.*) **3.** to kill indiscriminately or in large numbers. **4.** *Informal.* to defeat overwhelmingly. [C16: from Old French, of unknown origin] —**mas+sa+crer** (ˈmæsəkrə) *n.*

Mas+sa+cre of the In+no+cents *n.* the slaughter of all the young male children of Bethlehem at Herod's command in an attempt to destroy Jesus (Matthew 2:16–18).

mas+sage (ˈmæsɑːʒ, -sɑːdʒ) *n.* **1.** the act of kneading, rubbing, etc., parts of the body to promote circulation, suppleness, or relaxation. ~*vb.* (*tr.*) **2.** to give a massage to. **3.** to treat (stiffness, etc.) by a massage. [C19: from French, from *masser* to rub; see MASS] —**ˈmas+sag+er** *or* **ˈmas+sag+ist** *n.*

mas+sa+sau+ga (ˌmæsəˈsɔːgə) *n.* a North American venomous snake, *Sistrurus catenatus,* that has a horny rattle at the end of the tail: family *Crotalidae* (pit vipers). [C19: named after the *Missisauga* River, Ontario, Canada, where it was first found]

Mas·sa·soit (ˈmæsəˌsɔɪt) *n.* died 1661, Wampanoag Indian chief, who negotiated peace with the Pilgrim Fathers (1621).

Mas+sa+wa *or* **Mas+sa·ua** (məˈsɑːwə) *n.* a port in N Ethiopia, on the Red Sea: capital of the Italian colony of Eritrea from 1885 until 1900. Pop.: 19 820 (1971 est.).

mass de+fect *n. Physics.* the amount by which the mass of a particular nucleus is less than the total mass of its constituent particles. See also **binding energy.**

mas+sé *or* **mas+sé shot** (ˈmæsɪ) *n. Billiards.* a stroke made by hitting the cueball off centre with the cue held nearly vertically, esp. so as to make the ball move in a curve around another ball before hitting the object ball. [C19: from French, from *masser* to hit from above with a hammer, from *masse* sledge hammer, from Old French *mace* MACE¹]

Mas·sé·na (*French* maseˈna) *n.* **An·dré** (ãˈdre), Prince d'Essling. 1758–1817, French marshal under Napoleon I.

mass-en·er·gy *n.* mass and energy considered as equivalent and interconvertible, according to the theory of relativity.

Mas+se+net (ˈmæsəˌneɪ; *French* masˈnɛ) *n.* **Jules É·mile Fré·dé·ric** (ʒyl emil fredeˈrik). 1842–1912, French composer of operas, including *Manon* (1884), *Werther* (1892), and *Thais* (1894).

mass·es (ˈmæsɪz) *pl. n.* **1.** (preceded by *the*) the body of common people. **2.** (often foll. by *of*) *Informal, chiefly Brit.* great numbers or quantities: *masses of food.*

mas+se+ter (mæˈsiːtə) *n. Anatomy.* a muscle of the cheek used in moving the jaw, esp. in chewing. [C17: from New Latin from Greek *masētēr* one who chews, from *masāsthai* to chew] —**mas+se+ter+ic** (ˌmæsɪˈtɛrɪk) *adj.*

mas+seur (mæˈsɜː) *or* (*fem.*) **mas+seuse** (mæˈsɜːz) *n.* a person who gives massages, esp. as a profession. [C19: from French *masser* to MASSAGE]

Mas·sey (ˈmæsɪ) *n.* **1. Vin·cent.** 1887–1967, Canadian statesman; first Canadian governor general of Canada (1952–59). **2. Wil·liam Fer·gu·son.** 1856–1925, New Zealand statesman, born in Ireland: prime minister of New Zealand (1912–25).

mas+si+cot (ˈmæsɪˌkɒt) *n.* a yellow earthy secondary mineral consisting of lead oxide. Formula: PbO. [C15: via French from Italian *marzacotto* ointment, perhaps from Arabic *shabb qubti* Egyptian alum]

mas+sif (ˈmæsiːf; *French* maˈsif) *n.* **1.** a mass of rock or a series of connected masses forming the peaks of a mountain range. **2.** a part of the earth's crust that is bounded by faults and may be shifted by tectonic movements. [C19: from French, noun use of *massif* MASSIVE]

Mas+sif Cen+tral (*French* masif sãˈtral) *n.* a mountainous plateau region of S central France, occupying about one sixth of the country: contains several extinct volcanic cones, notably Puy de Dôme, 1465 m (4806 ft.). Highest point: Puy de Sancy, 1886 m (6188 ft.). Area: about 85 000 sq. km (33 000 sq. miles).

mass in *vb.* (*adv.*) to fill or block in (the areas of unified colour, shade, etc.) in a painting or drawing.

Mas·sine (mɑːˈsiːn) *n.* **Lé·o·nide** (leɔˈnid). 1896-1979, U.S. ballet dancer and choreographer, born in Russia.

Mas·sin·ger (ˈmæsɪndʒə) *n.* **Phil·ip.** 1583–?1640, English dramatist, noted esp. for his comedy *A New Way to pay Old Debts* (1633).

Mas·si·nis·sa (ˌmæsɪˈnɪsə) *n.* a variant spelling of **Masinissa.**

mas+sive (ˈmæsɪv) *adj.* **1.** (of objects) large in mass; bulky, heavy, and usually solid. **2.** impressive or imposing in quality, degree, or scope: *massive grief.* **3.** relatively intensive or large; considerable: *a massive dose.* **4.** *Pathol.* affecting a large area of the body: *a massive cancer.* **5.** *Geology.* **a.** (of igneous rocks) having no stratification, cleavage, etc.; homogeneous. **b.** (of sedimentary rocks) arranged in thick poorly defined strata. **6.** *Mineralogy.* without obvious crystalline structure. [C15: from French *massif,* from *masse* MASS] —**ˈmas+sive+ly** *adv.* —**ˈmas+sive+ness** *or* **mas+ˈsiv+i+ty** *n.*

mass leave *n.* (in India) leave taken by a large number of employees at the same time, as a form of protest.

mass me+di·a *pl. n.* the means of communication that reach large numbers of people in a short time, such as television, newspapers, magazines, and radio.

mass noun *n.* a noun that refers to an extended substance rather than to each of a set of isolable objects, as, for example, *water* as opposed to *lake.* In English when used indefinitely they are characteristically preceded by *some* rather than *a* or *an;* they do not have plural forms. Compare **count noun.**

mass num+ber *n.* the total number of neutrons and protons in the nucleus of a particular atom. Symbol: *A* Also called: **nucleon number.**

mass ob+ser+va+tion *n. Chiefly Brit.* (*sometimes cap.*) the study of the social habits of people through observation, interviews, etc.

Mas+so+rete (ˈmæsəˌriːt) *n.* a variant spelling of **Masorete.**

mas+so+ther·a+py (ˌmæsəʊˈθɛrəpɪ) *n.* medical treatment by massage. [C20: from MASS(AGE) + THERAPY] —**mas+so+ther·a+peu+tic** (ˌmæsəʊˌθɛrəˈpjuːtɪk) *adj.* —**ˌmas+so+ˈther·a+pist** *n.*

mass-pro·duce *vb.* (*tr.*) to manufacture (goods) to a standardized pattern on a large scale by means of extensive mechanization and division of labour. —**ˌmass-pro·ˈduced** *adj.* —**ˌmass-pro·ˈduc+er** *n.* —**mass pro+duc+tion** *n.*

mass ra+ti·o *n.* the ratio of the mass of a fully fuelled rocket at liftoff to the mass of the rocket without fuel.

mass spec+tro+graph *n.* a mass spectrometer that produces a photographic record of the mass spectrum.

mass spec+trom+e+ter *or* **spec+tro+scope** *n.* an analytical instrument in which ions, produced from a sample, are separated by electric or magnetic fields according to their ratios of charge to mass. A record is produced (**mass spectrum**) of the types of ion present and their relative amounts.

mass·y (ˈmæsɪ) *adj.* **mass·i+er, mass·i+est.** a literary word for **massive.** —**ˈmass·i+ness** *n.*

mast¹ (mɑːst) *n.* **1.** *Nautical.* any vertical spar for supporting sails, rigging, flags, etc., above the deck of a vessel or any components of such a composite spar. **2.** any sturdy upright pole used as a support. **3.** Also called: **captain's mast.** *Nautical.* a hearing conducted by the captain of a vessel into minor offences of the crew. **4. before the mast.** *Nautical.* as an apprentice seaman. ~*vb.* **5.** (*tr.*) *Nautical.* to equip with a mast or masts. [Old English *mæst;* related to Middle Dutch *mast* and Latin *mālus* pole] —**ˈmast+less** *adj.* —**ˈmast+ˌlike** *adj.*

mast² (mɑːst) *n.* the fruit of forest trees, such as beech, oak, etc., used as food for pigs. [Old English *mæst;* related to Old High German *mast* food, and perhaps to MEAT]

mast- *combining form.* variant of **masto-** before a vowel.

mas+ta+ba *or* **mas+ta+bah** (ˈmæstəbə) *n.* a mudbrick superstructure above tombs in ancient Egypt from which the pyramid developed. [from Arabic: bench]

mast cell *n.* any of various granular basophil cells in connective tissue that are thought to produce histamine.

mas+tec+to+my (mæˈstɛktəmɪ) *n., pl.* **+mies.** the surgical removal of a breast.

-mast·ed *adj. Nautical.* having a mast or masts of a specified kind or number: *three-masted; tall-masted.*

mas+ter (ˈmɑːstə) *n.* **1.** the man in authority, such as the head of a household, the employer of servants, or the owner of slaves or animals. **2. a.** a person with exceptional skill at a certain thing: *a master of the violin.* **b.** (*as modifier*): *a master thief.* **3. a.** a person who has complete control of a situation, etc. **b.** an abstract thing regarded as having power or influence: *they regarded fate as the master of their lives.* **4. a.** a workman or craftsman fully qualified to practise his trade and to train others in it. **b.** (*as modifier*): *master carpenter.* **5. a.** an original copy, stencil, etc., from which duplicates are made. **b.** (*as modifier*): *master copy.* **6.** a player of a game, esp. chess or bridge, who has won a specified number of tournament games. **7.** the principal of some colleges. **8.** a highly regarded teacher or leader whose religion or philosophy is accepted by followers. **9.** a graduate holding a master's degree. **10.** the chief executive officer aboard a merchant ship. **11.** a person presiding over a function, organization, or institution. **12.** *Chiefly Brit.* a male teacher. **13.** an officer of the Supreme Court of Judicature subordinate to a judge. **14.** the superior person or side in a contest. **15.** a machine or device that operates to control a similar one. **16.** (*often cap.*) the heir apparent of a Scottish viscount or baron. ~(*modifier*) **17.** overall or controlling: *master plan.* **18.** designating a device or mechanism that controls others: *master switch.* **19.** main; principal: *master bedroom.* ~*vb.* (*tr.*) **20.** to become thoroughly proficient in: *to master the art of driving.* **21.** to overcome; defeat: *to master your emotions.* **22.** to rule or control as master. [Old English *magister* teacher, from Latin; related to Latin *magis* more, to a greater extent] —**ˈmas+ter+dom** *n.* —**ˈmas+ter+ˌhood** *n.* —**ˈmas+ter+less** *adj.* —**ˈmas+ter+ˌship** *n.*

Mas+ter (ˈmɑːstə) *n.* **1.** a title of address placed before the first name or surname of a boy. **2.** a respectful term of address, esp. as used by disciples when addressing or referring to a religious teacher. **3.** an archaic equivalent of **Mr.**

mas·ter-at-arms *n., pl.* **mas·ters-at-arms.** the senior rating, of Chief Petty Officer rank, in a naval unit responsible for discipline, administration, and police duties.

mas+ter build+er *n.* a person skilled in the design and construction of buildings, esp. before the foundation of the profession of architecture.

mas+ter cyl+in+der *n.* a large cylinder in a hydraulic system in which the working fluid is compressed by a piston. See also **slave cylinder.**

mas+ter+ful ('mɑːstəfʊl) *adj.* **1.** having or showing mastery. **2.** fond of playing the master; imperious. —**'mas+ter+ful+ly** *adv.* —**'mas+ter+ful+ness** *n.*

mas+ter key *n.* a key that opens all the locks of a set, the individual keys of which are not interchangeable. Also called: **pass key.**

mas+ter+ly ('mɑːstəlɪ) *adj.* of the skill befitting a master: *a masterly performance.* —**'mas+ter+li+ness** *n.*

mas·ter+mind ('mɑːstəˌmaɪnd) *vb.* **1.** (*tr.*) to plan and direct (a complex undertaking): *he masterminded the robbery.* ~*n.* **2.** a person of great intelligence or executive talent, esp. one who directs an undertaking.

Mas+ter of Arts *n.* a degree, usually postgraduate and in a nonscientific subject, or the holder of this degree. Abbrev.: **M.A.**

mas+ter of cer+e·mo+nies *n.* a person who presides over a public ceremony, formal dinner, or entertainment, introducing the events, performers, etc.

mas+ter of fox+hounds *n.* a person responsible for the maintenance of a pack of foxhounds and the associated staff, equipment, hunting arrangements, etc. Abbrev.: **MFH**

Mas+ter of Sci+ence *n.* a postgraduate degree in science, or the holder of this degree. Abbrev.: **M.Sc.**

Mas+ter of the Horse *n.* (in England) the third official of the royal household.

Mas+ter of the Queen's Mu+sic *n.* (in Britain when the sovereign is female) a court post dating from the reign of Charles I. It is an honorary title and normally held by an established English composer. Also called (when the sovereign is male): **Master of the King's Music.**

Mas+ter of the Rolls *n.* (in England) a judge of the court of appeal: the senior civil judge in the country and the Keeper of the Records at the Public Record Office.

mas+ter+piece ('mɑːstəˌpiːs) *or* **mas·ter+work** *n.* **1.** an outstanding work, achievement, or performance. **2.** the most outstanding piece of work of a creative artist, craftsman, etc. [C17: compare Dutch *meesterstuk*, German *Meisterstück*, a sample of work submitted to a guild by a craftsman in order to qualify for the rank of master]

mas+ter race *n.* a race, nation, or group, such as the Germans or Nazis as viewed by Hitler, believed to be superior to other races. German name: **Herrenvolk.**

mas+ter ser+geant *n.* a senior noncommissioned officer in the U.S. Army, Air Force, and Marine Corps and certain other military forces, ranking immediately below the most senior noncommissioned rank.

mas·ter+sing·er ('mɑːstəˌsɪŋə) *n.* an English spelling of **Meister-singer.**

mas·ter+stroke ('mɑːstəˌstrəʊk) *n.* an outstanding piece of strategy, skill, talent, etc.: *your idea is a masterstroke.*

mas·ter·y ('mɑːstərɪ) *n., pl.* **·ter·ies. 1.** full command or understanding of a subject. **2.** outstanding skill; expertise. **3.** the power of command; control. **4.** victory or superiority.

mast+head ('mɑːstˌhɛd) *n.* **1.** *Nautical.* **a.** the head of a mast. **b.** (*as modifier*): *masthead sail.* **2.** Also called: **flag.** the name of a newspaper or periodical, its proprietors, staff, etc., printed in large type at the top of the front page. ~*vb.* (*tr.*) **3.** to send (a sailor) to the masthead as a punishment. **4.** to raise (a sail) to the masthead.

mas+tic ('mæstɪk) *n.* **1.** an aromatic resin obtained from the mastic tree and used as an astringent and to make varnishes and lacquers. **2. mastic tree. a.** a small Mediterranean anacardiaceous evergreen tree, *Pistacia lentiscus*, that yields the resin mastic. **b.** any of various similar trees, such as the pepper tree. **3.** any of several sticky putty-like substances used as a filler, adhesive, or seal in wood, plaster, or masonry. **4.** a liquor flavoured with mastic gum. [C14: via Old French from Late Latin *mastichum*, from Latin from Greek *mastikhē* resin used as chewing gum; from *mastikhan* to grind the teeth]

mas+ti+cate ('mæstɪˌkeɪt) *vb.* **1.** to chew (food). **2.** to reduce (materials such as rubber) to a pulp by crushing, grinding, or kneading. [C17: from Late Latin *masticāre*, from Greek *mastikhan* to grind the teeth] —**'mas+ti+ca·ble** *adj.* —**ˌmas+ti+'ca+tion** *n.* —**'mas+ti+ˌca+tor** *n.*

mas+ti+ca+to·ry ('mæstɪkətərɪ, -trɪ) *adj.* **1.** of, relating to, or adapted to chewing. ~*n., pl.* **+tor·ies. 2.** a medicinal substance chewed to increase the secretion of saliva.

mas+tiff ('mæstɪf) *n.* an old breed of large powerful short-haired dog, usually fawn brown with a dark mask. [C14: from Old French, ultimately from Latin *mansuētus* tame; see MANSUETUDE]

mas+ti+goph·o·ran (ˌmæstɪ'gɒfərən) *n. also* **mas+ti+go+phore** ('mæstɪgəˌfɔː). **1.** any protozoan of the class *Mastigophora* (or *Flagellata*), having one or more flagella. ~*adj. also* **mas+ti+goph·o·rous. 2.** of, relating to, or belonging to the *Mastigophora*. ~Also: **flagellate.** [C19 *mastigophore* whip-bearer, from Greek *mastigophoros*, from *mastix* whip + *-phoros* -PHORE]

mas+ti+tis (mæ'staɪtɪs) *n.* inflammation of a breast or an udder.

mas·to- *or before a vowel* **mast-** *combining form.* indicating the breast, mammary glands, or something resembling a breast or nipple: *mastodon; mastoid.* [from Greek *mastos* breast]

mas+to+don ('mæstəˌdɒn) *n.* any extinct elephant-like proboscidean mammal of the genus *Mammut* (or *Mastodon*), common in Pliocene times. [C19: from New Latin, literally: breast-tooth, referring to the nipple-shaped projections on the teeth] —**ˌmas+to+'don+tic** *adj.*

mas+toid ('mæstɔɪd) *adj.* **1.** shaped like a nipple or breast. **2.** designating or relating to a nipple-like process of the temporal bone behind the ear. ~*n.* **3.** the mastoid process. **4.** *Informal.* mastoiditis.

mas+toid+ec+to+my (ˌmæstɔɪ'dɛktəmɪ) *n., pl.* **+mies.** surgical removal of the mastoid process.

mas+toid+i·tis (ˌmæstɔɪ'daɪtɪs) *n.* inflammation of the mastoid process.

mas+tur+bate ('mæstəˌbeɪt) *vb.* to stimulate the genital organs of (oneself or another) to achieve sexual pleasure. [C19: from Latin *masturbārī*, of unknown origin; formerly thought to be derived from *manus* hand + *stuprāre* to defile] —**ˌmas+tur+'ba+tion** *n.* —**'mas+tur+ˌba+tor** *n.* —**mas+tur+ba+to·ry** ('mæstəˌbeɪtərɪ) *adj.*

Ma+su+ri·a (mə'sjʊərɪə) *n.* a region of NE Poland: until 1945 part of East Prussia: includes the **Masurian Lakes,** scene of Russian defeats by the Germans (1914, 1915) during World War I. —**Ma+'su+ri·an** *adj., n.*

ma+su+ri·um (mə'sʊərɪəm) *n.* the former name for **technetium.** [C20: New Latin, after MASURIA, where it was discovered]

mat[1] (mæt) *n.* **1.** a thick flat piece of fabric used as a floor covering, a place to wipe one's shoes, etc. **2.** a smaller pad of material used to protect a surface from the heat, etc., of an object placed upon it. **3.** a large piece of thick padded material put on the floor as a surface for wrestling, judo, or gymnastic sports. **4.** any surface or mass that is densely interwoven or tangled: *a mat of grass and weeds.* **5.** the solid part of a lace design. **6.** a heavy net of cable or rope laid over a blasting site to prevent the scatter of debris. **7.** *Civil engineering.* short for **mattress** (sense 3). ~*vb.* **mats, mat+ting, mat+ted. 8.** to tangle or weave or become tangled or woven into a dense mass. **9.** (*tr.*) to cover with a mat or mats. [Old English *matte*; related to Old High German *matta*] —**'mat+less** *adj.*

mat[2] (mæt) *n.* **1.** a border of cardboard, cloth, etc., placed around a picture to act as a frame or as a contrast between picture and frame. **2.** a surface, as on metal or paint. ~*adj.* **3.** having a dull, lustreless, or roughened surface. ~*vb.* **mats, mat+ting, mat+ted.** (*tr.*) **4.** to furnish (a picture) with a mat. **5.** to give (a surface) a mat finish. ~Also (for senses 2, 3, 5): **matt.** [C17: from French, literally: dead; see CHECKMATE]

mat[3] (mæt) *n. Printing, informal.* short for **matrix** (sense 5).

mat. *abbrev. for* matinee.

Mat·a+be+le (ˌmætə'biːlɪ, -'bɛlɪ) *n.* **1.** (*pl.* **+les** *or* **+le**) a member of a formerly warlike Negroid people of southern Africa, now living in Rhodesia: driven out of the Transvaal by the Boers in 1837. **2.** the language of this people, belonging to the Bantu group of the Niger-Congo family.

Mat·a+be+le+land (ˌmætə'biːlɪˌlænd, -'bɛlɪ-) *n.* a region of W Rhodesia, between the Rivers Limpopo and Zambezi: rich gold deposits. Chief town: Bulawayo. Area: 181 605 sq. km (70 118 sq. miles).

Ma+ta+di (mə'tɑːdɪ) *n.* the chief port of Zaïre, in the west at the mouth of the River Congo. Pop.: 143 598 (1974 est.).

mat·a+dor ('mætədɔː) *n.* **1.** the principal bullfighter who is appointed to kill the bull. **2.** (in some card games such as skat) one of the highest ranking cards. **3.** a game played with dominoes in which the dots on adjacent halves must total seven. [C17: from Spanish, from *matar* to kill]

Ma·ta Ha+ri ('mɑːtə 'hɑːrɪ) *n.* original name *Margarete Gertrud Zelle.* 1876–1917, Dutch dancer in France, who was executed as a German spy in World War I.

ma·ta-ma·ta ('mata'mata) *n.* (in Malaysia) a former name for **police.** [from Malay, reduplicated plural of *mata* eye]

Mat·a+mo+ros (ˌmætə'mɔːrəs; *Spanish* ˌmata'moros) *n.* a port in NE Mexico, on the Rio Grande: scene of bitter fighting during the U.S.–Mexican War; centre of a cotton-growing area. Pop.: 172 195 (1975 est.).

Ma+tan+zas (mə'tænzəs; *Spanish* ma'tansas) *n.* a port in W central Cuba: founded in 1693 and developed into the second city of Cuba in the mid-19th century; exports chiefly sugar. Pop.: 85 400 (1970).

Mat·a+pan ('mætəˌpæn, ˌmætə'pæn) *n.* **Cape.** a cape in S Greece, at the S central tip of the Peloponnese: the southern point of the mainland of Greece. Modern Greek name: **Taínaron.**

match[1] (mætʃ) *n.* **1.** a formal game or sports event in which people, teams, etc., compete to win. **2.** a person or thing able to provide competition for another: *she's met her match in talking ability.* **3.** a person or thing that resembles, harmonizes with, or is equivalent to another in a specified respect: *that coat is a good match for your hat.* **4.** a person or thing that is an exact copy or equal of another. **5. a.** a partnership between a man and a woman, as in marriage. **b.** an arrangement for such a partnership. **6.** a person regarded as a possible partner, as in marriage. ~*vb.* (*mainly tr.*) **7.** to fit (parts) together: *to match the tongue and groove of boards.* **8.** (*also intr.*; sometimes foll. by *up*) to resemble, harmonize with, correspond to, or equal (one another or something else): *the skirt matches your shoes well.* **9.** (sometimes foll. by *with* or *against*) to compare in order to determine which is the superior: *they matched wits.* **10.** (often foll. by *to* or *with*) to adapt so as to correspond with: *to match hope with reality.* **11.** (often foll. by *with* or *against*) to arrange a competition between. **12.** to find a match for. **13.** *Electronics.* to connect (two circuits) so that their impedances are equal or are equalized by a coupling device, to produce a maximum transfer of energy. [Old English *gemæcca* spouse; related to Old High German *gimmaha* wife, Old Norse *maki* mate] —**'match·a·ble** *adj.* —**'match·er** *n.*

match[2] (mætʃ) *n.* **1.** a thin strip of wood or cardboard tipped with a chemical that ignites by friction when rubbed on a rough surface or a surface coated with a suitable chemical (see **safety match**). **2.** a length of cord or wick impregnated with a chemical so that it burns slowly. It is used to fire cannons, etc. [C14: from Old French *meiche,* perhaps from Latin *myxa* wick, from Greek *muxa* lamp nozzle]

match·board ('mætʃˌbɔːd) *n.* a long thin board with a tongue along one edge and a corresponding groove along the other, used with similar boards to line walls, ceilings, etc.

match·box ('mætʃˌbɒks) *n.* a small box for holding matches.

match·less ('mætʃlɪs) *adj.* unequalled; incomparable; peerless. —**'match·less·ly** *adv.* —**'match·less·ness** *n.*

match·lock ('mætʃˌlɒk) *n.* **1.** an obsolete type of gunlock igniting the powder by means of a slow match. **2.** a gun having such a lock.

match·mak·er[1] ('mætʃˌmeɪkə) *n.* **1.** a person who brings together suitable partners for marriage. **2.** a person who arranges competitive matches. —**'match·ˌmak·ing** *n., adj.*

match·mak·er[2] ('mætʃˌmeɪkə) *n.* a person who makes matches (for igniting). —**'match·ˌmak·ing** *n., adj.*

match·mark ('mætʃˌmɑːk) *n.* **1.** a mark made on mating components of an engine, etc., to ensure that the components are assembled in the correct relative positions. ~*vb.* **2.** (*tr.*) to stamp (an object) with matchmarks.

match play *n. Golf.* **a.** scoring according to the number of holes won and lost. **b.** (*as modifier*): *a matchplay tournament.* Compare **stroke play.** —**match play·er** *n.*

match point *n.* **1.** *Tennis, squash, etc.* the final point needed to win a match. **2.** *Bridge.* the unit used for scoring in tournaments.

match·stick ('mætʃˌstɪk) *n.* the wooden part of a match.

match·wood ('mætʃˌwʊd) *n.* **1.** wood suitable for making matches. **2.** splinters or fragments: *the bomb blew the house to matchwood.*

mate[1] (meɪt) *n.* **1.** the sexual partner of an animal. **2.** a marriage partner. **3. a.** *Informal, chiefly Brit. and Austral.* a friend, usually of the same sex: often used to any male in direct address. **b.** (*in combination*) an associate, colleague, fellow sharer, etc.: *a classmate; a flatmate.* **4.** one of a pair of matching items. **5.** *Nautical.* **a.** short for **first mate. b.** any officer below the master on a commercial ship. **c.** a warrant officer's assistant on a ship. **6.** (in some professions) an assistant: *a plumber's mate.* **7.** *Archaic.* a suitable associate. ~*vb.* **8.** to pair (a male and female animal) or (of animals) to pair for reproduction. **9.** to marry or join in marriage. **10.** (*tr.*) to join as a pair; match. [C14: from Middle Low German; related to Old English *gemetta* table-guest, from *mete* MEAT] —**'mate·less** *adj.*

mate[2] (meɪt) *n., vb. Chess.* See **checkmate.**

ma·té *or* **ma·te** ('mɑːteɪ, 'mæteɪ) *n.* **1.** an evergreen tree, *Ilex paraguariensis,* cultivated in South America for its leaves, which contain caffeine: family *Aquifoliaceae.* **2.** a stimulating milky beverage made from the dried leaves of this tree. ~Also called: **Paraguay tea, yerba, yerba maté.** [C18: from American Spanish (originally referring to the vessel in which the drink was brewed), from Quechua *máti* gourd]

mate·las·sé (mæt'læseɪ) *adj.* (in textiles) having a raised design, as quilting; embossed. [C19: from French *matelasser* to quilt, from *matelas* MATTRESS]

mate·lot, mat·lo, *or* **mat·low** ('mætləʊ) *n. Slang, chiefly Brit.* a sailor. [C20: from French]

mat·e·lote *or* **mat·e·lotte** ('mætəˌləʊt; *French* mat'lɔt) *n.* fish served with a sauce of wine, onions, seasonings, and fish stock. [C18: from French, feminine of *matelot* sailor]

ma·ter ('meɪtə) *n. Brit. public school slang.* a word for **mother:** often used facetiously. [C16: from Latin]

ma·ter do·lo·ro·sa (ˌdɒlə'rəʊsə) *n.* the Virgin Mary sorrowing for the dead Christ, esp. as depicted in art. [Latin: sorrowful mother]

ma·ter·fa·mil·i·as (ˌmeɪtəfə'mɪlɪˌæs) *n.* the mother of a family or the female head of a family. [C18: from Latin]

ma·te·ri·al (mə'tɪərɪəl) *n.* **1.** the substance of which a thing is made or composed; component or constituent matter: *raw material.* **2.** facts, etc., that a finished work may be based on or derived from: *enough material for a book.* **3.** cloth or fabric. **4.** a person who has qualities suitable for a given occupation, training, etc.: *that boy is not university material.* ~*adj.* **5.** of, relating to, or composed of physical substance; corporeal. **6.** of, relating to, or affecting economic or physical well-being: *material ease.* **7.** of or concerned with physical rather than spiritual interests. **8.** of great import or consequence: *of material benefit to the workers.* **9.** (often foll. by *to*) relevant. **10.** *Philosophy.* of or relating to matter as opposed to form. **11.** *Law.* relevant to the issue before court: applied esp. to facts or testimony of much significance: *a material witness.* [C14: via French from Late Latin *māteriālis,* from Latin *māteria* MATTER] —**ma·'te·ri·al·ness** *n.*

ma·te·ri·al·ism (mə'tɪərɪəˌlɪzəm) *n.* **1.** interest in and desire for money, possessions, etc., rather than spiritual or ethical values. **2.** *Philosophy.* the doctrine that matter is the only reality and that the mind, the emotions, etc., are merely functions of it. Compare **idealism. 3.** *Ethics.* the rejection of any religious or supernatural account of things. —**ma·'te·ri·al·ist** *n.* —**ma·ˌte·ri·al·'is·tic** *adj.* —**ma·ˌte·ri·al·'is·ti·cal·ly** *adv.*

ma·te·ri·al·i·ty (məˌtɪərɪ'ælɪtɪ) *n., pl.* **·ties. 1.** the state or quality of being physical or material. **2.** substance; matter.

ma·te·ri·al·ize *or* **ma·te·ri·al·ise** (mə'tɪərɪəˌlaɪz) *vb.* **1.** (*intr.*) to become fact; actually happen: *our hopes never materialized.* **2.** to invest or become invested with a physical shape or form. **3.** to cause (a spirit, as of a dead person) to appear in material form or (of a spirit) to appear in such form. **4.** (*intr.*) to take shape; become tangible: *after hours of discussion, the project finally began to materialize.* —**ma·ˌte·ri·al·i·'za·tion** *or* **ma·ˌte·ri·al·i·'sa·tion** *n.* —**ma·'te·ri·al·ˌiz·er** *or* **ma·'te·ri·al·ˌis·er** *n.*

ma·te·ri·al·ly (mə'tɪərɪəlɪ) *adv.* **1.** to a significant extent; considerably: *his death alters the situation materially.* **2.** with respect to material objects. **3.** *Philosophy.* with respect to substance as distinct from form.

ma·te·ri·als (mə'tɪərɪəlz) *pl. n.* the equipment necessary for a particular activity.

ma·te·ri·a med·i·ca (mə'tɪərɪə 'mɛdɪkə) *n.* **1.** the branch of medical science concerned with the study of drugs used in the treatment of disease: includes pharmacy, pharmacology, and the history and physical and chemical properties of drugs. **2.** the drugs used in the treatment of disease. [C17: from Medieval Latin: medical matter]

ma·te·ri·el *or* **ma·té·ri·el** (məˌtɪərɪ'ɛl) *n.* the materials and equipment of an organization, esp. of a military force. Compare **personnel.** [C19: from French: MATERIAL]

ma·ter·nal (mə'tɜːnəl) *adj.* **1.** of, relating to, derived from, or characteristic of a mother. **2.** related through the mother's side of the family: *his maternal uncle.* [C15: from Medieval Latin *māternālis,* from Latin *māternus,* from *māter* mother] —**ma·'ter·nal·ism** *n.* —**ma·ˌter·nal·'is·tic** *adj.* —**ma·'ter·nal·ly** *adv.*

ma·ter·ni·ty (mə'tɜːnɪtɪ) *n.* **1.** motherhood. **2.** the characteristics associated with motherhood; motherliness. **3.** (*modifier*) relating to pregnant women or women at the time of childbirth: *a maternity ward.*

ma·ter·ni·ty ben·e·fit *n.* (in the British National Insurance scheme) a payment (**maternity allowance**) made to a woman having a child, normally from 11 weeks before confinement for a period of 18 weeks, in addition to a flat-rate benefit (**maternity grant**).

mate·y ('meɪtɪ) *Brit. informal.* ~*adj.* **1.** friendly or intimate; on good terms. ~*n.* **2.** friend or fellow: usually used in direct address. —**'mate·y·ness** *or* **'mat·i·ness** *n.*

math (mæθ) *n. U.S. informal.* short for **mathematics.** Brit. equivalent: **maths**

math. *U.S. abbrev. for* mathematics.

math·e·mat·i·cal (ˌmæθə'mætɪkəl) *or* **math·e·mat·ic** *adj.* **1.** of, used in, or relating to mathematics. **2.** characterized by or using the precision of mathematics; exact. **3.** using, determined by, or in accordance with the principles of mathematics. —ˌ**math·e·'mat·i·cal·ly** *adv.*

math·e·mat·i·cal ex·pec·ta·tion *n. Statistics.* another name for **expected value.**

math·e·mat·i·cal log·ic *n.* another name for **symbolic logic.**

math·e·ma·ti·cian (ˌmæθəmə'tɪʃən) *n.* an expert or specialist in mathematics.

math·e·mat·ics (ˌmæθə'mætɪks) *n.* **1.** (*functioning as sing.*) a group of related sciences, including algebra, geometry, and calculus, concerned with the study of number, quantity, shape, and space and their interrelationships by using a specialized notation. **2.** (*functioning as sing. or pl.*) mathematical operations and processes involved in the solution of a problem or study of some scientific field. [C14 *mathematik* (n.), via Latin from Greek (adj.), from *mathēma* a science, *mathēmatikos* (adj.); related to *manthanein* to learn]

maths (mæθs) *n. Brit. informal.* short for **mathematics.** U.S. equivalent: **math**

maths. *Brit. abbrev. for* mathematics.

Ma·thu·ra ('mʌtʊərə, mʌ'θʊərə) *n.* a city in N India, in W Uttar Pradesh on the Jumna River: a place of Hindu pilgrimage, revered as the birthplace of Krishna. Pop.: 132 028 (1971). Former name: **Muttra.**

Ma·til·da[1] (məˌtɪldə) *n. Austral. informal.* **1.** a bushman's swag. **2. walk** *or* **waltz Matilda.** to travel the road carrying one's swag. [C20: from the Christian name]

Ma·til·da[2] (mə'tɪldə) *n.* called *the Empress Maud.* 1102–67, only daughter of Henry I of England and wife of Geoffrey of Anjou. After her father's death (1135) she unsuccessfully waged a civil war with Stephen for the English throne; her son succeeded as Henry II.

mat·in, mat·tin ('mætɪn), *or* **mat·in·al** *adj.* of or relating to matins. [C14: see MATINS]

mat·i·née ('mætɪˌneɪ) *n.* a daytime, esp. afternoon, performance of a play, concert, etc. [C19: from French; see MATINS]

mat·i·née coat *n.* a short coat for a baby.

mat·i·née i·dol *n.* (esp. in the 1930s and 1940s) an actor popular as a romantic figure among women.

mat·ins *or* **mat·tins** ('mætɪnz) *n.* (*functioning as sing. or pl.*) **1. a.** *Chiefly R.C. Church.* the first of the seven canonical hours of prayer, originally observed at night but now often recited with lauds at daybreak. **b.** the service of morning prayer in the Church of England. **2.** *Literary.* a morning song, esp. of birds. [C13: from Old French, ultimately from Latin *mātūtīnus* of the morning, from *Mātūta* goddess of dawn]

Ma·tisse (*French* ma'tis) *n.* **Hen·ri** (ā'ri). 1869–1954, French painter and sculptor; leader of Fauvism.

mat+lo *or* **mat+low** ('mætləʊ) *n.* variant spellings of **matelot.**

Mat+lock ('mæt,lɒk) *n.* a town in N England, on the River Derwent, administrative centre of Derbyshire: mineral springs. Pop.: 19 575 (1971).

Ma·to Gros+so *or* **Mat+to Gros+so** ('mætəʊ 'grɒsəʊ; *Portuguese* 'matu 'grosu) *n.* **1.** a high plateau of SW Brazil: forms the watershed separating the Amazon and Plata river systems. **2.** a state of W central Brazil: mostly on the Mato Grosso Plateau, with the Amazon basin to the north; valuable mineral resources. Capital: Cuiabá. Pop.: 1 597 090 (1970). Area: 1 231 549 sq. km (480 304 sq. miles).

ma+to+ke (ma'tɔkɛ) *n.* (in Uganda) the flesh of bananas; boiled and mashed as a food. [C20: from Luganda]

Ma+to+po Hills (mə'təʊpə) *or* **Ma+to+pos** *pl. n.* the granite hills south of Bulawayo, Rhodesia, where Cecil Rhodes chose to be buried.

Ma+to+zi+nhos (*Portuguese* mətu'ziɲuʃ) *n.* a port in N Portugal, on the estuary of the Leça River north of Oporto: fishing industry. Pop.: 90 554 (1970).

mat+rass *or* **mat+trass** ('mætrəs) *n. Chem., obsolete.* a long-necked glass flask, used for distillation, etc. [C17: from French, perhaps related to Latin *mētiri* to measure]

ma·tri- *combining form.* mother or motherhood: *matriarchy.* [from Latin *māter* mother]

ma+tri+arch ('meɪtrɪ,ɑːk) *n.* **1.** a woman who dominates an organization, community, etc. **2.** the female head of a tribe or family, esp. in a matriarchy. **3.** a very old or venerable woman. [C17: from MATRI- + -ARCH, by false analogy with PATRIARCH] —**'ma+tri+,ar+chal** *or* **'ma+tri+,ar+chic** *adj.* —**,ma+tri+'ar+chal+ism** *n.*

ma+tri+ar+chate ('meɪtrɪ,ɑːkɪt, -keɪt) *n. Rare.* a family or people under female domination or government.

ma+tri+ar+chy ('meɪtrɪ,ɑːkɪ) *n., pl.* **+chies. 1.** a form of social organization in which a female is head of the family or society, and descent and kinship are traced through the female line. **2.** any society dominated by women.

ma+tric (mə'trɪk) *n. Brit.* short for **matriculation** (sense 2).

ma+tri+ces ('meɪtrɪ,siːz, 'mæ-) *n.* the plural of **matrix.**

mat+ri+cide ('mætrɪ,saɪd, 'meɪ-) *n.* **1.** the act of killing one's own mother. **2.** a person who kills his mother. [C16: from Latin *mātrīcīdium* (the act), *mātrīcīda* (the agent). See MATRI-, -CIDE] —**,mat+ri+'cid+al** *adj.*

mat+ri+cli+nous (,mætrɪ'klaɪnəs), **mat+ro+cli+nous,** *or* **mat+ro+cli+nal** *adj.* (of an animal or plant) showing the characters of the female parent. Compare **patriclinous.**

ma+tric·u+late *vb.* (mə'trɪkjʊ,leɪt). **1.** to enrol or be enrolled in an institution, esp. a college or university. **2.** (*intr.*) to attain the academic standard required for a course at such an institution. ~*n.* (mə'trɪkjʊlɪt). **3.** Also called: **ma+tric·u+lant.** a person who has matriculated. [C16: from Medieval Latin *mātrīculāre* to register, from *mātrīcula,* diminutive of *matrix* list, MATRIX] —**ma+'tric·u+,la+tor** *n.*

ma+tric·u+la+tion (mə,trɪkjʊ'leɪʃən) *n.* **1.** the process of matriculating. **2.** (in Great Britain) a former school examination, now replaced by the General Certificate of Education (Ordinary Level).

mat+ri+lin+e+al (,mætrɪ'lɪnɪəl, ,meɪ-) *adj.* relating to descent or kinship through the female line. —**,mat+ri+'lin+e+al+ly** *adv.*

mat+ri+lo+cal ('mætrɪ,ləʊkᵊl, 'meɪ-) *adj.* denoting, having, or relating to a marriage pattern in which the couple live with the wife's family. —**mat+ri+lo+cal+i+ty** (,mætrɪləʊ'kælɪtɪ, ,meɪ-) *n.* —**,mat+ri+'lo+cal+ly** *adv.*

mat+ri+mo+ni+al (,mætrɪ'məʊnɪəl) *adj.* relating to marriage: *matrimonial troubles.* —**,mat+ri+'mo+ni+al+ly** *adv.*

mat+ri+mo+ny ('mætrɪmənɪ) *n., pl.* **+nies. 1.** the state or condition of being married. **2.** the ceremony or sacrament of marriage. **3. a.** a card game in which the king and queen together are a winning combination. **b.** such a combination. [C14: via Norman French from Latin *mātrimōnium* wedlock, from *māter* mother. See MATRI-, -MONY]

mat+ri+mo+ny vine *n.* any of various shrubs of the solanaceous genus *Lycium,* cultivated for their purple flowers and colourful berries. Also called: **boxthorn.**

ma+trix ('meɪtrɪks, 'mæ-) *n., pl.* **ma+tri+ces** ('meɪtrɪ,siːz, 'mæ-) *or* **ma+trix·es. 1.** a substance, situation, or environment in which something has its origin, takes form, or is enclosed. **2.** *Anatomy.* the thick tissue at the base of a nail from which a fingernail or toenail develops. **3.** the intercellular substance of bone, cartilage, connective tissue, etc. **4. a.** the rock material in which fossils, pebbles, etc., are embedded. **b.** the material in which a mineral is embedded; gangue. **5.** *Printing.* **a.** a metal mould for casting type. **b.** a papier-mâché or plastic mould impressed from the forme and used for stereotyping. Sometimes shortened to **mat. 6.** a mould used in the production of gramophone records. It is obtained by electrodeposition onto the master. **7.** a bed of perforated material placed beneath a workpiece in a press or stamping machine against which the punch operates. **8.** *Metallurgy.* **a.** the shaped cathode used in electroforming. **b.** the metal constituting the major part of an alloy. **c.** the soft metal in a plain bearing in which the hard particles of surface metal are embedded. **9.** *Maths.* a rectangular array of elements set out in rows and columns, used to facilitate the solution of problems, such as the transformation of coordinates. Usually indicated by parentheses: $\begin{pmatrix} a & b & c \\ d & e & f \end{pmatrix}$. Compare **determinant** (sense 3). **10.** *Computer technol.* a rectangular array of circuit elements usually used to generate one set of signals from another. **11.** *Obsolete.* the womb. [C16: from Latin: womb, female animal used for breeding, from *māter* mother]

mat+ro+cli+nous (,mætrə'klaɪnəs) *adj.* a variant spelling of **matriclinous.**

ma+tron ('meɪtrən) *n.* **1.** a married woman regarded as staid or dignified, esp. a middle-aged woman with children. **2.** a woman in charge of the domestic or medical arrangements in an institution. **3.** *U.S.* a wardress in a prison. **4.** *Brit.* formerly, the administrative head of the nursing staff in a hospital. [C14: via Old French from Latin *mātrōna,* from *māter* mother] —**'ma+tron+al** *adj.* —**'ma+tron+,hood** *or* **'ma+tron+,ship** *n.* —**'ma tron-,like** *adj.*

ma+tron+age ('meɪtrənɪdʒ) *n.* **1.** the state of being a matron. **2.** supervision or care by a matron. **3.** matrons collectively.

ma+tron+ly ('meɪtrənlɪ) *adj.* of, characteristic of, or suitable for a matron. —**'ma+tron+li+ness** *n.*

ma+tron of hon+our *n., pl.* **ma+trons of hon+our. 1.** a married woman serving as chief attendant to a bride. Compare **bridesmaid, maid of honour. 2.** a married woman, usually a member of the nobility, who attends a queen or princess.

mat+ro+nym+ic (,mætrəʊ'nɪmɪk) *adj., n.* a less common word for **metronymic.**

Ma+tsu (mæt'suː) *n.* an island group in Formosa Strait, off the SE coast of mainland China: belongs to Taiwan. Pop.: 17 061 (1971). Area: 44 sq. km (17 sq. miles).

Ma+tsu+ya+ma (,mætsʊ'jɑːmə) *n.* a port in SW Japan, on NW Shikoku: textile and chemical industries; Ehime University (1949). Pop.: 364 645 (1974 est.).

matt *or* **matte** (mæt) *adj., n., vb.* variant spellings of **mat²** (senses 2, 3, 5).

Matt. *Bible. abbrev. for* Matthew.

mat+ta+more ('mætə,mɔː) *n.* a subterranean storehouse or dwelling. [C17: from French, from Arabic *matmūra,* from *tamara* to store, bury]

matte (mæt) *n.* an impure fused material consisting of metal sulphides produced during the smelting of a sulphide ore. [C19: from French]

mat+ted ('mætɪd) *adj.* **1.** tangled into a thick mass: *matted hair.* **2.** covered with or formed of matting.

mat+ter ('mætə) *n.* **1.** that which makes up something, esp. a physical object; material. **2.** substance that occupies space and has mass, as distinguished from substance that is mental, spiritual, etc. **3.** substance of a specified type: *vegetable matter; reading matter.* **4.** (sometimes foll. by *of* or *for*) thing; affair; concern; question: *a matter of taste; several matters to attend to; no laughing matter.* **5.** a quantity or amount: *a matter of a few pence.* **6.** the content of written or verbal material as distinct from its style or form. **7.** (*used with a negative*) importance; consequence. **8.** *Philosophy.* **a.** (in the writings of Aristotle and the Scholastics) that which is itself formless but can receive form and become substance. **b.** that which is organized into chemical substances and living things. **c.** (in the Cartesian tradition) one of two basic modes of existence, the other being **mind. 9.** *Printing.* **a.** type set up, either standing or for use. **b.** copy to be set in type. **10.** a secretion or discharge, such as pus. **11.** *Law.* **a.** something to be proved. **b.** statements or allegations to be considered by a court. **12. for that matter.** as regards that. **13. grey matter.** *Informal.* intellectual ability. **14. no matter. a.** regardless of; irrespective of: *no matter what the excuse, you must not be late.* **b.** (*sentence substitute*) it is unimportant. **15. the matter.** wrong; the trouble: *there's nothing the matter.* ~*vb.* (*intr.*) **16.** to be of consequence or importance. **17.** to form and discharge pus. [C13 (n.), C16 (vb.): from Latin *māteria* cause, substance, esp. wood, or a substance that produces something else; related to *māter* mother]

Mat+ter+horn ('mætə,hɔːn) *n.* a mountain on the border between Italy and Switzerland, in the Pennine Alps. Height: 4477 m (14 688 ft.). French name: **Mont Cervin.** Italian name: **Mon+te Cer+vi+no** ('monte tʃer'viːno).

mat+ter of course *n.* **1.** an event or result that is natural or inevitable. ~*adj.* **mat·ter-of-course. 2.** (*usually postpositive*) occurring as a matter of course. **3.** accepting things as inevitable or natural: *a matter-of-course attitude.*

mat+ter of fact *n.* **1.** a fact that is undeniably true. **2.** *Law.* a statement of facts the truth of which the court must determine on the basis of the evidence before it: contrasted with **matter of law, matter of opinion. 3. as a matter of fact.** actually; in fact. ~*adj.* **mat·ter-of-fact. 4.** unimaginative or emotionless: *he gave a matter-of-fact account of the murder.*

mat+ter·y ('mætərɪ) *adj.* discharging pus.

Mat·thew ('mæθjuː) *n. New Testament.* **1.** Also called: **Levi.** a tax collector of Capernaum called by Christ to be one of the 12 apostles (Matthew 9:9–13; 10:3). **2.** the first Gospel, traditionally ascribed to Matthew.

Mat·thew Par·is *n.* See (Matthew) **Paris.**

Mat·thews ('mæθjuːz) *n.* Sir **Stan·ley.** born 1915, English footballer.

Mat·thew Walk·er *n.* a knot made at the end of a rope by unlaying the strands and passing them up through the loops formed in the next two strands. [C19: probably named after the man who introduced it]

Mat·thi·as (mə'θaɪəs) *n. New Testament.* the disciple chosen by lot to replace Judas as one of the 12 apostles (Acts 1:15–26).

mat+ting¹ ('mætɪŋ) *n.* **1.** a coarsely woven fabric, usually made of a natural fibre such as straw or hemp and used as a floor covering, packing material, etc. **2.** the act or process of making mats. **3.** material for mats.

mat+ting² ('mætɪŋ) *n.* **1.** another word for **mat²** (sense 1). **2.** the process of producing a mat finish.

mat+tins ('mætɪnz) *n.* a variant spelling of **matins.**

mat+tock ('mætək) *n.* a type of large pick that has one end of its blade shaped like an adze, used for loosening soil, cutting roots, etc. [Old English *mattuc,* of unknown origin; related to Latin *mateola* club, mallet]

Mat+to Gros+so ('mætəʊ 'grɒsəʊ) *n.* a variant spelling of **Mato Grosso.**

mat+toid ('mætɔɪd) *n. Rare.* a person displaying eccentric behaviour and mental characteristics that approach the psychotic. [C19: from Italian, from *matto* insane]

mat+trass ('mætrəs) *n.* a variant spelling of **matrass.**

mat+tress ('mætrɪs) *n.* **1.** a large flat pad with a strong cover, filled with straw, foam rubber, etc., and often incorporating coiled springs, used as a bed or as part of a bed. **2.** a woven mat of brushwood, poles, etc., used to protect an embankment, dyke, etc., from scour. **3.** a concrete or steel raft or slab used as a foundation or footing. Sometimes shortened to **mat. 4.** a network of reinforcing rods or expanded metal sheeting, used in reinforced concrete. **5.** *Civil engineering.* another name for **blinding** (sense 3). [C13: via Old French from Italian *materasso,* from Arabic *almatrah* place where something is thrown]

mat·u+rate ('mætjʊˌreɪt, 'mætʃʊ-) *vb.* **1.** to mature or bring to maturity. **2.** a less common word for **suppurate.** —**ma+tur·a+tive** (mæ'tjʊərətɪv, mæ'tʃʊə-) *adj.*

mat·u+ra+tion (ˌmætjʊ'reɪʃən, 'mætʃʊ-) *n.* **1.** the process of maturing or ripening. **2.** *Zoology.* the development of ova and spermatozoa from precursor cells in the ovary and testis, involving meiosis. **3.** a less common word for **suppuration.** —ˌ**mat·u+'ra+tion+al** *adj.*

ma+ture (mə'tjʊə, -'tʃʊə) *adj.* **1.** relatively advanced physically, mentally, emotionally, etc.; grown-up. **2.** (of plans, theories, etc.) fully considered; perfected. **3.** due or payable: *a mature debenture.* **4.** *Biology.* **a.** fully developed or differentiated: *a mature cell.* **b.** fully grown; adult: *a mature animal.* **5.** (of fruit, wine, cheese, etc.) ripe or fully aged. **6.** (of a river valley or land surface) in the middle stage of the cycle of erosion, characterized by meanders, maximum relief, etc. See also **youthful** (sense 4), **old** (sense 18). ~*vb.* **7.** to make or become mature. **8.** (*intr.*) (of notes, bonds, etc.) to become due for payment or repayment. [C15: from Latin *mātūrus* early, developed] —**ma+'ture+ly** *adv.* —**ma+'ture+ness** *n.*

ma+tur+i·ty (mə'tjʊərɪtɪ, -'tʃʊə-) *n.* **1.** the state or quality of being mature; full development. **2.** *Finance.* **a.** the date upon which a bill of exchange, bond, note, etc., becomes due for repayment. **b.** the state of a bill, note, etc., when due.

ma+tu+ti+nal (ˌmætjʊ'taɪnᵊl) *adj.* of, occurring in, or during the morning. [C17: from Late Latin *mātūtīnālis,* from Latin *mātūtīnus,* from *Mātūta* goddess of the dawn] —ˌ**ma+tu+'ti+nal+ly** *adv.*

mat+zo, mat+zoh ('mætsəʊ) *or* **mat+za, mat+zah** ('mætsə) *n., pl.* **mat+zos, mat+zohs, mat+zas, mat+zahs,** *or* **ma+tzoth** (*Hebrew* ma'tsɔt). a large brittle very thin biscuit of unleavened bread, traditionally eaten during the Jewish Passover. [from Yiddish *matse,* from Hebrew *massāh*]

mat+zoon (mɑːt'suːn) *or* **mad+zoon** (mɑːd'zuːn) *n.* a fermented milk product similar to yoghurt. [from Armenian *madzun*]

Mau+beuge (*French* mo'bøːʒ) *n.* an industrial town in N France, near the border with Belgium. Pop.: 35 474 (1975).

mau+by ('mɑːbɪ, 'mɔː-) *n., pl.* **+bies.** (in the E Caribbean) a bittersweet drink made from the bark of a rhamnaceous tree. [C20: of uncertain origin]

maud (mɔːd) *n.* a shawl or rug of grey wool plaid worn in Scotland. [C18: of unknown origin]

maud+lin ('mɔːdlɪn) *adj.* foolishly tearful or sentimental, as when drunk, etc. [C17: from Middle English *Maudelen* Mary Magdalene, typically portrayed as a tearful penitent] —'**maud+lin+ism** *n.* —'**maud+lin+ly** *adv.* —'**maud+lin+ness** *n.*

Maugham ('mɔːm) *n.* **W(illiam) Som·er·set.** 1874–1965, English writer. His works include the novels *Of Human Bondage* (1915) and *Cakes and Ale* (1930), short stories, and comedies.

mau+gre *or* **mau+ger** ('mɔːgə) *prep. Obsolete.* in spite of. [C13 (meaning: ill will): from Old French *maugre,* literally: bad pleasure]

Mau·i ('maʊɪ) *n.* a volcanic island in S central Hawaii: the second largest of the Hawaiian Islands. Pop.: 38 691 (1970). Area: 1885 sq. km (728 sq. miles).

maul (mɔːl) *vb.* (*tr.*) **1.** to handle clumsily; paw. **2.** to batter or lacerate. ~*n.* **3.** a heavy two-handed hammer suitable for driving piles, etc. **4.** *Rugby.* a loose scrum. [C13: from Old French *mail,* from Latin *malleus* hammer. See MALLET] —'**maul+er** *n.*

Mau+la+na (mɔː'lɑːnɑː) *n.* (in Pakistan, India, etc.) a title used for a scholar of Persian and Arabic. [Urdu, from Arabic *mawlānā*]

maul+ers ('mɔːləz) *pl. n. Brit. slang.* the hands.

Maul+main (maʊl'meɪn) *n.* a variant spelling of **Moulmein.**

maul+stick ('mɔːlˌstɪk) *or* **mahl+stick** ('mɑːlˌstɪk, 'mɔːl-) *n.* a long stick used by artists to steady the hand holding the brush. [C17: partial translation of Dutch *maalstok,* from obsolete *malen* to paint + *stok* STICK]

Mau Mau ('maʊ 'maʊ) *n., pl.* **Mau Maus** *or* **Mau Mau. 1.** a secret political society consisting chiefly of Kikuyu tribesmen that was founded in 1952 to drive European settlers from Kenya by acts of terrorism. **2.** *East African slang.* a Ugandan motorcycle policeman who directs traffic.

mau+met ('mɔːmɪt) *or* **mam+met** ('mæmɪt) *n. Obsolete.* a false god; idol. [C13: from Old French *mahomet* idol, literally: the prophet *Mohammed,* from the belief that his image was worshipped] —'**mau+met+ry** *n.*

maun, man (mɑːn, mɔːn), *or* **mun** (mʌn) *vb.* a Scot. dialect word for **must.** [C14: from Old Norse *man* must, will]

Mau+na Ke·a ('maʊnɑː 'keɪɑː) *n.* an extinct volcano in Hawaii, on N central Hawaii Island: the highest island mountain in the world. Height: 4206 m (13 796 ft.).

Mau+na Lo·a ('maʊnɑː 'ləʊɑː) *n.* an active volcano in Hawaii, on S central Hawaii Island. Height: 4171 m (13 680 ft.).

maund (mɔːnd) *n.* a unit of weight used in Asia, esp. India, having different values in different localities. A common value in India is 82 pounds or 37 kilograms. [C17: from Hindi *man,* from Sanskrit *manā*]

maun+der ('mɔːndə) *vb.* (*intr.*) to move, talk, or act aimlessly or idly. [C17: perhaps from obsolete *maunder* to beg, from Latin *mendīcāre;* see MENDICANT] —'**maun+der+er** *n.*

maun+dy ('mɔːndɪ) *n., pl.* **maun+dies.** *Christianity.* the ceremonial washing of the feet of poor persons in commemoration of Jesus' washing of his disciples' feet (John 13:4–34), re-enacted in some churches on Maundy Thursday. [C13: from Old French *mandé* something commanded, from Latin *mandatum* commandment, from the words of Christ: *Mandātum novum dō vōbīs* A new commandment give I unto you]

Maun+dy mon+ey *n.* specially minted coins given by the British sovereign to poor people on Maundy Thursday.

Maun+dy Thurs+day *n. Christianity.* the Thursday before Easter observed as a commemoration of the Last Supper.

maun+gy ('mɔːndʒɪ) *adj.* **+gi+er, +gi+est.** *West Yorkshire dialect.* (esp. of a child) sulky, bad-tempered, or peevish. [variant of MANGY, in extended sense: restless, dissatisfied]

Mau·pas·sant (*French* mopɑ'sɑ̃) *n.* **(Henri René Albert) Guy de** ('gi də). 1850–93, French writer, noted esp. for his short stories, such as *Boule de suif* (1880), *La Maison Tellier* (1881), and *Mademoiselle Fifi* (1883). His novels include *Bel Ami* (1885) and *Pierre et Jean* (1888).

Mau·per·tuis (*French* mopɛr'twi) *n.* **Pierre Louis Mo·reau de** (pjɛːr lwi mɔ'ro də). 1698–1759, French mathematician, who originated the principle of least action (or Maupertuis principle).

Mau+re+ta+ni·a (ˌmɒrɪ'teɪnɪə) *n.* an ancient region of N Africa, corresponding approximately to the N parts of modern Algeria and Morocco. —ˌ**Mau+re+'ta+ni·an** *adj., n.*

Mau·riac (*French* mɔ'rjak) *n.* **Fran·çois** (frɑ̃'swa). 1885–1970, French novelist, noted esp. for his psychological studies of the conflict between religious belief and human desire. His works include *Le Désert de l'amour* (1925), *Thérèse Desqueyroux* (1927), and *Le Noeud de vipères* (1932): Nobel prize for literature 1952.

Mau·rice ('mɒrɪs) *n.* **1.** 1521–53, duke of Saxony (1541–53) and elector of Saxony (1547–53). He was instrumental in gaining recognition of Protestantism in Germany. **2.** known as *Maurice of Nassau.* 1567–1625, prince of Orange and count of Nassau; the son of William the Silent, after whose death he led the United Provinces of the Netherlands in their struggle for independence from Spain (achieved by 1609). **3. Fred·er·ick Den·i·son.** 1805–72, English Anglican theologian and pioneer of Christian socialism.

Mau+rist ('mɔʊrɪst) *n.* a member of a congregation of French Benedictine monks founded in 1621 and noted for its scholarly work. [C19: named after *St. Maurus,* 6th-century disciple of St. Benedict]

Mau+ri+ta+ni·a (ˌmɒrɪ'teɪnɪə) *n.* a republic in NW Africa, on the Atlantic: established as a French protectorate in 1903 and a colony in 1920; gained full independence in 1960; lies mostly in the Sahara; contains rich resources of iron ore. Official languages: Arabic and French. Religion: Muslim. Currency: franc. Capital: Nouakchott. Pop.: 1 200 000 (1971 UN est.). Area: 1 085 805 sq. km (419 232 sq. miles). Official name: **Islamic Republic of Mauritania.** —ˌ**Mau+ri+'ta+ni·an** *adj., n.*

Mau+ri+tius (mə'rɪʃəs) *n.* an island and state in the Indian Ocean, east of Madagascar: originally uninhabited, it was settled by the Dutch (1638–1710) then abandoned; taken by the French in 1715 and the British in 1810; became an independent member of the Commonwealth in 1968. It is economically dependent on sugar. Official language: English; a French creole is widely spoken. Religion: mostly Hindu and Christian. Currency: rupee. Capital: Port Louis. Pop.: 851 335 (1972). Area: 1865 sq. km (720 sq. miles). Former name (1715–1810): **Île-de-France.** —**Mau+'ri+tian** *adj., n.*

Mau·rois (*French* mɔ'rwa) *n.* **An·dré** (ɑ̃'dre), pen name of *Émile Herzog.* 1885–1967, French writer, best known for his biographies, such as those of Shelley, Byron, and Proust.

Mau·ry ('mɔːrɪ) *n.* **Mat·thew Fon·taine.** 1806–73, U.S. pioneer hydrographer and oceanographer.

Mau·rya ('maʊrjə) *n.* a dynasty (*c* 321–*c* 185 B.C.) that united most of the Indian subcontinent and presided over a great flowering of Indian civilization.

Mau+ser ('maʊzə) *n. Trademark.* **1.** a high-velocity magazine rifle. **2.** a type of automatic pistol. [C19: named after P. P. von *Mauser* (1838–1914), German firearms inventor]

mau+so+le·um (ˌmɔːsə'lɪəm) *n., pl.* **+le·ums** *or* **+le·a** (-'lɪə). a large stately tomb. [C16: via Latin from Greek *mausōleion,* the tomb of *Mausolus,* king of Caria; built at Halicarnassus in the 4th century B.C.] —ˌ**mau+so+'le·an** *adj.*

mau+vais quart d'heure *French.* (move kar 'dœr) *n. Brit.* a brief unpleasant experience. [literally: (a) bad quarter of an hour]

mauve (məʊv) *n.* **1. a.** any of various pale to moderate pinkish-purple or bluish-purple colours. **b.** (*as adj.*): *a mauve flower.* **2.** Also called: **Perkin's mauve, mauveine** ('məʊvi:n, -vɪn). a reddish-purple aniline dye. [C19: from French, from Latin *malva* MALLOW]

mav·er·ick ('mævərɪk) *n.* **1.** (in U.S. cattle-raising regions) an unbranded animal, esp. a stray calf. **2. a.** a person of independent or unorthodox views. **b.** (*as modifier*): *a maverick politician.* [C19: after Samuel A. *Maverick* (1803–70), Texas rancher, who did not brand his cattle]

ma·vis ('meɪvɪs) *n.* a popular name for the **song thrush.** [C14: from Old French *mauvis* thrush; origin obscure]

ma·vour·neen *or* **ma·vour·nin** (mə'vʊəni:n) *n. Irish.* my darling. [C18: from Irish, from *mo* my + *muirnīn* love]

maw (mɔ:) *n.* **1.** the mouth, throat, crop, or stomach of an animal, esp. of a voracious animal. **2.** *Informal.* the mouth or stomach of a greedy person. [Old English *maga;* related to Middle Dutch *maghe,* Old Norse *magi*]

maw·ger ('mɔ:gə) *adj. Caribbean.* (of persons or animals) thin or lean. [from Dutch *mager* thin, MEAGRE]

maw·kin ('mɔ:kɪn) *n.* **1.** a variant spelling of **malkin. 2.** *Brit. dialect.* **a.** a slovenly woman. **b.** a scarecrow.

mawk·ish ('mɔ:kɪʃ) *adj.* **1.** falsely sentimental, esp. in a weak or maudlin way. **2.** nauseating or insipid in flavour, smell, etc. [C17: from obsolete *mawk* MAGGOT + -ISH] —**'mawk·ish·ly** *adv.* —**'mawk·ish·ness** *n.*

maw·sie ('mɔ:zɪ) *n. Northeast Scot. dialect.* a woollen jersey, cardigan, or vest. [perhaps a special use of MARSEILLE]

Maw·son ('mɔ:sən) *n.* Sir **Doug·las.** 1882–1958, Australian Antarctic explorer, born in England.

max. *abbrev. for* maximum.

max·i ('mæksɪ) *adj.* **1. a.** (of a garment) reaching the ankle. **b.** (*as n.*): *she wore a maxi.* **c.** (*in combination*): *a maxidress.* **2.** large or considerable in size for its type: *a maxi saving on fuel.* [C20: shortened from MAXIMUM]

max·il·la (mæk'sɪlə) *n., pl.* **·lae** (-li:). **1.** the upper jawbone in vertebrates. See **jaw** (sense 1) **2.** any member of one or two pairs of mouthparts in insects and other arthropods used as accessory jaws. [C17: New Latin, from Latin: jaw] —**max·il·lar** (mæk'sɪlə) *or* **max·'il·lar·y** *adj.*

max·il·li·ped (mæk'sɪlɪˌpɛd) *n.* any member of three pairs of appendages in crustaceans, behind the maxillae: specialized for feeding. [C19: *maxilli-,* from MAXILLA + -PED] —**max·ˌil·li·'ped·a·ry** *adj.*

max·im ('mæksɪm) *n.* a brief expression of a general truth, principle, or rule of conduct. [C15: via French from Medieval Latin, from *maxima,* in the phrase *maxima prōpositio* basic axiom (literally: greatest proposition); see MAXIMUM]

Max·im ('mæksɪm) *n.* Sir **Hi·ram Ste·vens.** 1840–1916, English inventor of the first automatic machine gun (1884), born in the U.S.

max·i·ma ('mæksɪmə) *n.* a plural of **maximum.**

max·i·mal ('mæksɪməl) *adj.* **1.** of, relating to, or achieving a maximum; being the greatest or best possible. **2.** *Maths.* (of a member of an ordered set) being preceded, in order, by all other members of the set. —**'max·i·mal·ly** *adv.*

max·i·mal·ist ('mæksɪməlɪst) *n.* a person who favours direct action to achieve all his goals and rejects compromise.

Max·i·mal·ist ('mæksɪməlɪst) *n.* (in early 20th-century Russia) **1.** a member of the radical faction of Social Revolutionaries that supported terrorism against the tsarist regime and advocated a short period of postrevolutionary working-class dictatorship. **2.** a less common name for a **Bolshevik.** Compare **Minimalist.** [C20: from French, a translation of Russian; see BOLSHEVIK]

Max·im gun *n.* an obsolete water-cooled machine gun having a single barrel and utilizing the recoil force of each shot to maintain automatic fire. [C19: named after Sir Hiram MAXIM]

Max·i·mil·i·an (ˌmæksɪ'mɪlɪən) *n.* full name *Ferdinand Maximilian Joseph.* 1832–67, archduke of Austria and emperor of Mexico (1864–67). After the French had partially conquered Mexico, he was offered the throne but was defeated and shot by the Mexicans under Juárez.

Max·i·mil·i·an I *n.* 1459–1519, king of Germany (1486–1519) and Holy Roman Emperor (1493–1519).

max·i·min ('mæksɪˌmɪn) *n.* **1.** *Maths.* the highest of a set of minimum values. **2.** (in games theory, etc.) the procedure of choosing the strategy that most benefits the least advantaged member of a group. Compare **minimax.** [C20: from MAXI(MUM) + MIN(IMUM)]

max·im·ize *or* **max·im·ise** ('mæksɪˌmaɪz) *vb.* **1.** (*tr.*) to make as high or great as possible; increase to a maximum: *to maximize output.* **2.** *Maths.* to find the maximum of (a function). —ˌ**max·i·mi·'za·tion,** ˌ**max·i·mi·'sa·tion,** *or* ˌ**max·i·'ma·tion** *n.* —**'max·iˌmiz·er** *or* **'max·iˌmis·er** *n.*

max·i·mum ('mæksɪməm) *n.* **1.** the greatest possible amount, degree, etc. **2.** the highest value of a variable quantity. **3.** *Maths.* **a.** a value of a function that is greater than any neighbouring value. **b.** a stationary point on a curve at which the tangent changes from a positive value on the left of this point to a negative value on the right. Compare **minimum** (sense 4). **c.** the largest number in a set. **4.** *Astronomy.* **a.** the time at which the brightness of a variable star has its greatest value. **b.** the magnitude of the star at that time. ~*adj.* **5.** of, being, or showing a maximum or maximums. ~Abbrev.: **max.** [C18: from Latin: greatest (the neuter form used as noun), from *magnus* great]

max·i·mum like·li·hood *n. Statistics.* a technique for estimation and hypothesis-testing concerned with the formulation of an estimator giving greatest likelihood to the variable's observed values.

max·i·mus ('mæksɪməs) *n. Change-ringing.* a method rung on twelve bells. [from Latin: superlative of *magnus* great]

max·i·sin·gle ('mæksɪˌsɪŋgᵊl) *n.* an EP or small LP.

ma·xixe (mə'ʃi:ʃ, mæk'si:ks, mə'ʃi:ʃeɪ) *n.* a Brazilian dance in duple time, a precursor of the tango. [from Brazilian Portuguese]

Max Mül·ler (*German* maks 'mylər) *n.* See (Friedrich Max) **Müller.**

max·well ('mækswəl) *n.* the cgs unit of magnetic flux equal to the flux through one square centimetre normal to a field of one gauss. It is equivalent to 10^{-8} weber. Abbrev.: **Mx** [C20: named after J. C. MAXWELL]

Max·well ('mækswəl) *n.* **James Clerk.** 1831–79, Scottish physicist. He made major contributions to the electromagnetic theory, developing the equations (**Maxwell equations**) upon which classical theory is based. He also contributed to the kinetic theory of gases, and colour vision.

may[1] (meɪ) *vb. past* **might.** (takes an infinitive without *to* or an implied infinitive) used as an auxiliary **1.** to indicate that permission is requested by or granted to someone: *he may go to the park tomorrow if he behaves himself.* **2.** (often foll. by *well*) to indicate possibility: *the rope may break; he may well be a spy.* **3.** to indicate ability or capacity, esp. in questions: *may I help you?* **4.** to express a strong wish: *long may she reign.* **5.** to indicate result or purpose: used only in clauses introduced by *that* or *so that: he writes so that the average reader may understand.* **6.** to express courtesy in a question: *whose child may this little girl be?* **7. be that as it may.** in spite of that: a sentence connector conceding the possible truth of a previous statement and introducing an adversative clause: *be that as it may, I still think he should come.* **8. come what may.** whatever happens. **9. that's as may be.** (foll. by a clause introduced by *but*) that may be so. [Old English *mæg,* from *magan:* compare Old High German *mag,* Old Norse *mā*]

Usage. In careful written usage, *may* is used rather than *can* when reference is made to permission rather than to capability. *He may do it* is, for this reason, more appropriate than *he can do it* when the desired sense is *he is allowed to do it.* In spoken English, however, *can* is often used where the correct use of *may* results in forms that are considered to be awkward. *Can't I?* is preferred on this ground to *mayn't I?* in speech. The difference between *may* and *might* is one of emphasis: *he might be coming* usually indicates less certainty than *he may be coming.* Similarly, *might I have it?* is felt to be more hesitant than *may I have it?*

may[2] (meɪ) *n.* an archaic word for **maiden.** [Old English *mæg;* related to Old High German *māg* kinsman, Old Norse *māgr* a relative by marriage]

may[3] *or* **may tree** (meɪ) *n.* a Brit. name for **hawthorn.** [C16: from the month of MAY]

May (meɪ) *n.* the fifth month of the year, consisting of 31 days. [from Old French, from Latin *Maius* (month) of *Maia,* Roman goddess]

ma·ya ('maɪə, 'mɑ:jə, 'mɑ:jɑ:) *Hinduism. n.* illusion, esp. the material world of the senses regarded as illusory. [C19: from Sanskrit] —**'may·yan** *adj.*

Ma·ya[1] ('maɪə; 'mɑ:jə, -jɑ:) *n.* the Hindu goddess of illusion, the personification of the power of maya. —**'Ma·yan** *adj.*

Ma·ya[2] ('maɪə) *n.* **1.** (*pl.* **·ya** *or* **·yas**) Also called: **Mayan.** a member of an American Indian people of Yucatan, Belize, and N Guatemala, having an ancient culture once characterized by outstanding achievements in architecture, astronomy, chronology, painting, and pottery. **2.** the language of this people. See also **Mayan.**

Ma·ya·güez (*Spanish* ˌmaja'ɣwes) *n.* a port in W Puerto Rico; needlework industry. Pop.: 68 872 (1970).

Ma·ya·kov·ski *or* **Ma·ya·kov·sky** (*Russian* məjɪ'kɔfskij) *n.* **Vla·di·mir Vla·di·mi·ro·vich** (vla'dimir vla'dimirəvitʃ). 1893–1930, Russian Futurist poet and dramatist. His poems include *150 000 000* (1921) and *At the Top of my Voice* (1930); his plays include *Vladimir Mayakovsky—a Tragedy* (1913) and *The Bedbug* (1929).

Ma·yan ('maɪən) *adj.* **1.** of, relating to, or characteristic of the Maya or any of their languages. ~*n.* **2.** a family of Central American Indian languages including Maya. **3.** another name for a **Maya**[2].

May ap·ple *n.* **1.** an American plant, *Podophyllum peltatum,* with edible yellowish egg-shaped fruit: family *Podophyllaceae.* **2.** the fruit of this plant.

may·be ('meɪˌbi:) *adv.* **1. a.** perhaps. **b.** (*as sentence modifier*): *maybe I'll come tomorrow.* ~ **2.** *sentence substitute.* possibly; neither yes nor no.

May bee·tle *or* **bug** *n.* another name for **cockchafer** and **June bug.**

May blobs *n.* (*functioning as sing.*) another name for **marsh marigold.**

May·day ('meɪˌdeɪ) *n.* the international radiotelephone distress signal. [C20: phonetic spelling of French *m'aider* help me]

May Day *n.* **a.** the first day of May, traditionally a celebration of the coming of spring: in some countries now observed as a holiday in honour of workers. **b.** (*as modifier*): *May-Day celebrations.*

Ma·yence (ma'jɑ̃:s) *n.* the French name for **Mainz.**

Ma·yenne (*French* ma'jɛn) *n.* a department of NW France, in

Pays de la Loire region. Capital: Laval. Pop.: 268 108 (1975). Area: 5212 sq. km (2033 sq. miles).

May·er (*German* 'maɪər) *n.* **Ju·lius Rob·ert von** ('ju:ljus 'ro:bɛrt fɔn). 1814–78, German physicist, who stated the law of conservation of energy independently of Joule (1842).

may+est ('meɪɪst) *vb.* a variant of **mayst.**

May+fair ('meɪˌfɛə) *n.* a fashionable district of west central London.

may+flow·er ('meɪˌflaʊə) *n.* **1.** any of various plants that bloom in May. **2.** *U.S.* another name for **trailing arbutus. 3.** *Brit.* another name for **hawthorn, cowslip, or marsh marigold.**

May+flow·er ('meɪˌflaʊə) *n.* **the.** the ship in which the Pilgrim Fathers sailed from Plymouth to Massachusetts in 1620.

may+fly ('meɪˌflaɪ) *n., pl.* **+flies. 1.** Also called: **dayfly.** any insect of the order *Ephemeroptera* (or *Ephemerida*). The short-lived adults, found near water, have long tail appendages and large transparent wings; the larvae are aquatic. **2.** *Angling.* an artificial fly resembling this.

may+hap ('meɪˌhæp) *adv.* an archaic word for **perhaps.** [C16: shortened from *it may hap*]

may+hem *or* **mai+hem** ('meɪhɛm) *n.* **1.** *Law.* the wilful and unlawful infliction of injury upon a person, esp. formerly the injuring or removing of a limb rendering him less capable of defending himself against attack. **2.** any violent destruction or confusion. [C15: from Anglo-French *mahem* injury, from Germanic; related to Icelandic *meitha* to hurt. See MAIM]

May+ing ('meɪɪŋ) *n.* the traditional celebration of May Day.

may·n't ('meɪənt, meɪnt) *contraction of* may not.

May·o ('meɪəʊ) *n.* a county of NW Ireland, in NW Connacht province, on the Atlantic: has many offshore islands and several large lakes. County town: Castlebar. Pop.: 109 525 (1971). Area: 5397 sq. km (2084 sq. miles).

Ma+yon (mɑ:'jɔ:n) *n.* a volcano in the Philippines, on SE Luzon: Height: 2435 m (7989 ft.).

may+on+naise (ˌmeɪə'neɪz) *n.* a thick creamy sauce made from egg yolks, oil, and vinegar or lemon juice, eaten with salads, eggs, etc. [C19: from French, perhaps from *Mahonnais* of *Mahón*, a port in Minorca]

mayor (mɛə) *n.* the chief officer of a municipal corporation in many countries. Scottish equivalent: **provost.** [C13: from Old French *maire*, from Latin *maior* greater. See MAJOR] —**'mayor+al** *adj.* —**'mayor+ˌship** *n.*

mayor+al+ty ('mɛərəltɪ) *n., pl.* **+ties.** the office or term of office of a mayor. [C14: from Old French *mairalté*]

mayor+ess ('mɛərɪs) *n.* **1.** *Chiefly Brit.* the wife of a mayor. **2.** a female mayor.

Ma+yotte (*French* ma'jɔt) *n.* an island in the Indian Ocean, northwest of Madagascar. Chief town: Dzaoudzi. Pop.: 31 930 (1966). Area: 374 sq. km (146 sq. miles).

may+pole ('meɪˌpəʊl) *n.* a tall pole fixed upright in an open space during May-Day celebrations, around which people dance holding streamers attached at its head.

May queen *n.* a girl chosen, esp. for her beauty, to preside over May-Day celebrations.

mayst (meɪst) *or* **may+est** ('meɪɪst) *vb. Archaic or dialect.* (used with the pronoun *thou* or its relative equivalent) a singular form of the present tense of **may.**

may tree *n.* a Brit. name for **hawthorn.**

may+weed ('meɪˌwi:d) *n.* **1.** Also called: **dog fennel, stinking mayweed.** a widespread Eurasian weedy plant, *Anthemis cotula*, having evil-smelling leaves and daisy-like flower heads: family *Compositae* (composites). **2. scentless mayweed.** a similar and related plant, *Tripleurospermum maritimum*, with scentless leaves. [C16: changed from Old English *mægtha* mayweed + WEED[1]]

maz+ard *or* **maz+zard** ('mæzəd) *n.* **1.** an obsolete word for the **head** or **skull. 2.** another word for **mazer.** [C17: altered from MAZER]

Maz·a·rin ('mæzərɪn; *French* maza'rɛ̃) *n.* **Jules** (ʒyl), original name *Giulio Mazarini.* 1602–61, French cardinal and statesman, born in Italy. He succeeded Richelieu (1642) as chief minister to Louis XIII and under the regency of Anne of Austria (1643–61). Despite the disturbances of the Fronde (1648–53), he strengthened the power of France in Europe.

Ma+zat·lán (*Spanish* ˌmasat'lan) *n.* a port in W Mexico, in S Sinaloa on the Pacific: situated opposite the tip of the peninsula of Lower California, for which it is the chief link with the mainland. Pop.: 154 140 (1975 est.).

Maz+da+ism *or* **Maz+de+ism** ('mæzdəˌɪzəm) *n.* another word for **Zoroastrianism.**

maze (meɪz) *n.* **1.** a complex network of paths or passages, esp. one with high hedges in a garden, designed to puzzle those walking through it. Compare **labyrinth** (sense 1). **2.** a similar system represented diagrammatically as a pattern of lines. **3.** any confusing network of streets, etc.: *a maze of paths.* **4.** a state of confusion. ~*vb.* **5.** an archaic or dialect word for **amaze.** [C13: see AMAZE] —**'maze+ˌlike** *adj.* —**'maze+ment** *n.*

ma+zer ('meɪzə), **maz+ard,** *or* **maz+zard** ('mæzəd) *n. Obsolete.* a large hardwood drinking bowl. [C12: from Old French *masere*, of Germanic origin; compare Old Norse *mösurr* maple]

ma+zu+ma (mə'zu:mə) *n. Slang, chiefly U.S.* money. [C20: from Yiddish]

ma+zur+ka *or* **ma+zour+ka** (mə'zɜ:kə) *n.* **1.** a Polish national dance in triple time. **2.** a piece of music composed for this dance. [C19: from Polish: (dance) of *Mazur* (Mazovia) province in Poland]

ma·zy ('meɪzɪ) *adj.* **+zi+er, +zi+est.** of or like a maze; perplexing or confused. —**'ma+zi+ly** *adv.* —**'ma+zi+ness** *n.*

maz+zard *or* **ma+zard** ('mæzəd) *n.* a wild sweet cherry tree, *Prunus avium*, often used as a grafting stock for cultivated cherries. [C16: perhaps related to MAZER]

Maz·zi·ni (*Italian* mat'tsi:ni) *n.* **Giu·sep·pe** (dʒu'zɛppe). 1805–72, Italian nationalist. In 1831, in exile, he established the Young Italy association in Marseille, which sought to unite Italy as a republic. In 1849 he was one of the triumvirate that ruled the short-lived Roman republic.

mb *abbrev. for* millibar.

MB *abbrev. for* maternity benefit.

M.B. *abbrev. for* Bachelor of Medicine.

M.B.A. *abbrev. for* Master of Business Administration.

Mba+ba+ne (ᵊmbɑ:'bɑ:nɪ) *n.* the capital of Swaziland, in the northwest: administrative and financial centre, with a large iron mine nearby. Pop.: 20 800 (1973 est.).

M.B.E. *abbrev. for* Member of the Order of the British Empire (a Brit. title).

Mbu+ji+ma+yi (ᵊm'bu:dʒɪˌmaɪi:) *n.* a city in S Zaïre: diamond mining. Pop.: 336 654 (1974 est.).

MC *international car registration for* Monaco.

M.C. *abbrev. for:* **1.** Master of Ceremonies. **2.** *Astrology.* Medium Coeli. [Latin: Midheaven]. **3.** (in the U.S.) Member of Congress. **4.** (in Britain) Military Cross.

Mc- *prefix.* variant of **Mac-.**

Mc·Bride (mək'braɪd) *n.* **Wil·lie John.** born 1940, Irish Rugby Union footballer. A forward, he played for Ireland (1962–75) and the British Lions (1962–74).

M.C.C. (in Britain) *abbrev. for* Marylebone Cricket Club.

Mc·Car·thy (mə'kɑ:θɪ) *n.* **1. Eu·gene Jo·seph.** born 1916, U.S. senator, a leader of the movement against the Vietnam war and a contender for the Democratic presidential nomination in 1968. **2. Jo·seph R(aymond).** 1908–57, U.S. Republican senator, who led (1950–54) the notorious investigations of alleged Communist infiltration into the U.S. government. **3. Mar·y (Therese).** born 1912, U.S. novelist and critic; her works include *The Group* (1963).

Mc·Car+thy+ism (mə'kɑ:θɪˌɪzəm) *n. Chiefly U.S.* **1.** the practice of making unsubstantiated accusations of disloyalty or Communist leanings. **2.** the use of unsupported accusations for any purpose. [C20: after Senator Joseph MCCARTHY] —**Mc·'Car+thy+ist** *n., adj.*

Mc·Cart·ney (mə'kɑ:tnɪ) *n.* **Paul.** born 1942, English rock musician and songwriter: bass guitarist and vocalist with the Beatles (1962–70); subsequently formed his own band, Wings.

Mc·Cor·mack (mə'kɔ:mæk) *n.* **John.** 1884–1945, U.S. tenor, born in Ireland.

Mc·Cor·mick (mə'kɔ:mɪk) *n.* **Cy·rus Hall.** 1809–84, U.S. inventor of the reaping machine (1831).

Mc·Coy (mə'kɔɪ) *n. Slang.* the genuine person or thing (esp. in the phrase **the real McCoy).** [C20: perhaps after Kid *McCoy*, professional name of Norman Selby (1873–1940), American boxer, who was called "the real McCoy" to distinguish him from another boxer of that name]

Mc·Cul·lers (mə'kʌləz) *n.* **Car·son.** 1917–67, U.S. writer, whose novels include *The Heart is a Lonely Hunter* (1940).

Mc·Diar·mid (mək'dɛəmɪd) *n.* **Hugh,** pen name of *Christopher Murray Grieve.* 1892–1978, Scottish poet; a founder of the Scottish Nationalist Party. His *Collected Poems* were published in 1962.

Mc·Gon·a·gall (mə'gɒnəgəl) *n.* **Wil·liam.** 1830–?1902, Scottish writer of doggerel, noted for its bathos, repetitive rhymes, poor scansion, and ludicrous effect.

M.Ch. *abbrev. for* Master of Surgery. [Latin *Magister Chirurgiae*]

Mc·Kin·ley[1] (mə'kɪnlɪ) *n.* **Mount.** a mountain in S central Alaska, in the Alaska Range: the highest peak in North America. Height: 6194 m (20 320 ft.).

Mc·Kin·ley[2] (mə'kɪnlɪ) *n.* **Wil·liam.** 1843–1901, 25th president of the U.S. (1897–1901). His administration was marked by the highest tariffs in American history and by expansionist policies. He was assassinated.

Mc·Lu·han (mə'klu:ən) *n.* **(Herbert) Mar·shall.** born 1911, Canadian author of works analysing the mass media, including *Understanding Media* (1964) and *The Medium is the Message* (1967).

Mc·Mah·on (mək'mɑ:ən) *n.* **Wil·liam.** born 1908, Australian statesman; prime minister of Australia (1971–72).

Mc·mur·do Sound (mək'mɜ:dəʊ) *n.* an inlet of the Ross Sea in Antarctica, north of Victoria Land.

Mc·Naugh·ten Rules *or* **Mc·Nagh·ten Rules** (mək'nɔ:tᵊn) *pl. n.* (in English law) a set of rules established by the case of Regina v. McNaughten (1843) by which legal proof of insanity in the commission of a crime depends upon whether or not the accused can show either that he did not know what he was doing or that he is incapable of realizing that what he was doing was wrong.

M. Com. *abbrev. for* Master of Commerce.

Mc·Queen (mə'kwi:n) *n.* **Steve.** 1932–80, U.S. film actor, noted for his portrayal of tough characters.

Md *the chemical symbol for* mendelevium.

Md. *abbrev. for* Maryland.

M.D. *abbrev. for:* **1.** Doctor of Medicine. [from Latin *Medicinae Doctor*] **2.** Medical Department. **3.** mentally deficient. **4.** Managing Director.

M.D.S. *abbrev. for* Master of Dental Surgery.

mdse. *abbrev. for* merchandise.

me[1] (mi:; *unstressed* mɪ) *pron.* (*objective*) **1.** refers to the speaker or writer: *that shocks me; he gave me the glass.* **2.** *Chiefly U.S.* a dialect word for **myself** when used as an indirect object: *I want to get me a car.* ~*n.* **3.** *Informal.* the personality of the speaker or writer or something that expresses it: *the real me comes out when I'm happy.* [Old English *mē* (dative); compare Dutch, German *mir,* Latin *mē* (accusative), *mihi* (dative)]

Usage. Although the nominative case is traditionally required after the verb *to be,* even careful speakers say *it is me* (or *him, her,* etc.) rather than *it is I* in informal contexts. The use of *me,* etc., before an *-ing* form of the verb (*he disapproved of me coming*) is common, but careful speakers and writers use the possessive form: *he disapproved of my coming.*

me[2] (mi:) *n.* a variant spelling of **mi.**

Me *chemical symbol for* the methyl group.

Me. *abbrev. for:* **1.** Maine. **2.** Maitre.

ME *or* **M.E.** *abbrev. for* Middle English.

M.E. *abbrev. for:* **1.** Marine Engineer. **2.** Mechanical Engineer. **3.** Methodist Episcopal. **4.** Mining Engineer. **5.** (in titles) Most Excellent.

me·a cul·pa *Latin.* ('meɪɑ: 'kʊlpɑ:) an acknowledgment of guilt. [literally: my fault]

mead[1] (mi:d) *n.* a wine made by fermenting a solution of honey, often with spices added. [Old English *meodu;* related to Old High German *metu,* Greek *methu,* Welsh *medd*]

mead[2] (mi:d) *n.* an archaic or poetic word for **meadow.** [Old English *mæd*]

Mead[1] (mi:d) *n.* **Lake.** a reservoir in NW Arizona and SE Nevada, formed by the Hoover Dam across the Colorado River: one of the largest man-made lakes in the world. Area: 588 sq. km (227 sq. miles).

Mead[2] (mi:d) *n.* **Mar·gar·et.** 1901–78, U.S. anthropologist. Her works include *Coming of Age in Samoa* (1928) and *Male and Female* (1949).

Meade (mi:d) *n.* **George Gor·don.** 1815–72, Union general in the American Civil War. He commanded the Army of the Potomac, defeating the Confederates at Gettysburg (1863).

mead·ow ('mɛdəʊ) *n.* **1.** an area of grassland, often used for hay or for grazing of animals. **2.** a low-lying piece of grassland, often boggy and near a river. [Old English *mædwe,* from *mæd* MEAD[2]; related to *māwan* to MOW[1]] —'**mead·ow·y** *adj.*

mead·ow fes·cue *n.* an erect Eurasian perennial grass, *Festuca pratensis,* with lustrous leaves and stem bases surrounded by dark brown sheaths.

mead·ow grass *n.* a perennial grass, *Poa pratensis,* that has erect hairless leaves and grows in meadows and similar places in N temperate regions.

mead·ow·lark ('mɛdəʊ,lɑ:k) *n.* either of two North American yellow-breasted songbirds, *Sturnella magna* (**eastern meadowlark**) or *S. neglecta* (**western meadowlark**): family *Icteridae* (American orioles).

mead·ow lil·y *n.* another name for **Canada lily.**

mead·ow mouse *n. U.S.* another name for a **vole.**

mead·ow mush·room *n.* a saprophytic agaricaceous edible fungus, *Agaricus* (or *Psalliota*) *campestris,* having a white cap with pink or brown gills on the underside.

mead·ow pip·it *n.* a common European songbird, *Anthus pratensis,* with a pale brown speckled plumage: family *Motacillidae* (pipits and wagtails).

mead·ow rue *n.* any ranunculaceous plant of the N temperate genus *Thalictrum,* esp. *T. flavum,* having clusters of small yellowish-green, white, or purple flowers.

mead·ow saf·fron *n.* another name for **autumn crocus.**

mead·ow·sweet ('mɛdəʊ,swi:t) *n.* **1.** a Eurasian rosaceous plant, *Filipendula ulmaria,* with dense heads of small fragrant cream-coloured flowers. See also **dropwort** (sense 1). **2.** any of several North American rosaceous plants of the genus *Spiraea,* having pyramid-shaped sprays of small flowers.

Meads (mi:dz) *n.* **Col·in.** born 1935, New Zealand Rugby Union footballer. A forward, he played for the All Blacks (1957–71).

mea·gre *or U.S.* **mea·ger** ('mi:gə) *adj.* **1.** deficient in amount, quality, or extent. **2.** thin or emaciated. **3.** lacking in richness or strength. [C14: from Old French *maigre,* from Latin *macer* lean, poor] —'**mea·gre·ly** *adv.*

meal[1] (mi:l) *n.* **1. a.** any of the regular occasions, such as breakfast, lunch, dinner, etc., when food is served and eaten. **b.** (*in combination*): *mealtime.* Related adj.: **prandial. 2.** the food served and eaten. **3. make a meal of.** *Informal.* to perform (a task) with unnecessarily great effort. [Old English *mæl* measure, set time, meal; related to Old High German *māl* mealtime]

meal[2] (mi:l) *n.* **1.** the edible part of a grain or pulse (excluding wheat) ground to a coarse powder, used chiefly as animal food. **2.** *Scot.* oatmeal. **3.** *U.S.* maize flour. [Old English *melu;* compare Dutch *meel,* Old High German *melo,* Old Norse *mjöl*] —'**meal·less** *adj.*

meal·ie ('mi:lɪ) *n. S. African.* an ear of maize. [C19: from Afrikaans *milie,* from Portuguese *milho,* from Latin *milium* millet]

meal·ie meal *n. S. African.* finely ground maize.

meal·ies ('mi:lɪz) *n.* a South African word for **maize.**

meal tick·et *n.* **1.** the U.S. equivalent of **luncheon voucher. 2.** *Slang.* a person, situation, etc., providing a source of livelihood or income.

meal·worm ('mi:l,wɜ:m) *n.* the larva of various beetles of the genus *Tenebrio,* esp. *T. molitor,* feeding on meal, flour, and similar stored foods: family *Tenebrionidae.*

meal·y ('mi:lɪ) *adj.* **meal·i·er, meal·i·est. 1.** resembling meal; powdery. **2.** containing or consisting of meal or grain. **3.** sprinkled or covered with meal or similar granules. **4.** (esp. of horses) spotted; mottled. **5.** pale in complexion. **6.** short for **mealy-mouthed.** —'**meal·i·ness** *n.*

meal·y bug *n.* any plant-eating homopterous insect of the genus *Pseudococcus* and related genera, coated with a powdery waxy secretion: some species are pests of citrus fruits and greenhouse plants: family *Pseudococcidae.*

meal·y-mouthed *adj.* hesitant or afraid to speak plainly; not outspoken. [C16: from MEALY (in the sense: soft, soft-spoken)] —,**meal·y-'mouth·ed·ness** *n.*

mean[1] (mi:n) *vb.* **means, mean·ing, meant.** (*mainly tr.*) **1.** (*may take a clause as object or an infinitive*) to intend to convey or express. **2.** (*may take a clause as object or an infinitive*) intend: *she didn't mean to hurt it.* **3.** (*may take a clause as object*) to say or do in all seriousness: *the boss means what he says about strikes.* **4.** (*often passive;* often foll. by *for*) to destine or design (for a certain person or purpose): *she was meant for greater things.* **5.** (*may take a clause as object*) to denote or connote; signify; represent: *examples help show exactly what a word means.* **6.** (*may take a clause as object*) to produce; cause: *the weather will mean long traffic delays.* **7.** to have the importance of: *money means nothing to him.* **8.** (*intr.*) to have the intention of behaving or acting (esp. in the phrases **mean well** *or* **mean ill**). **9. mean business.** to be serious about something, even to the point of ruthlessness. [Old English *mænan;* compare Old Saxon *mēnian* to intend, Dutch *meenen*]

mean[2] (mi:n) *adj.* **1.** *Chiefly Brit.* miserly, ungenerous, or petty. **2.** unpleasant: *in a mean mood.* **3.** despicable, ignoble, or callous: *a mean action.* **4.** poor or shabby: *mean clothing; a mean abode.* **5.** *Informal, chiefly U.S.* bad-tempered; vicious. **6.** *Informal.* ashamed: *he felt mean.* **7.** *Informal.* unwell; in low spirits. **8.** *Slang.* excellent; skilful: *he plays a mean trombone.* **9. no mean. a.** of high quality: *no mean performer.* **b.** difficult: *no mean feat.* [C12: from Old English *gemǣne* common; related to Old High German *gimeini,* Latin *communis* common, at first with no pejorative sense] —,**mean·ly** *adv.* —,**mean·ness** *n.*

mean[3] (mi:n) *n.* **1.** the middle point, state, or course between limits or extremes. **2.** moderation. **3.** *Maths.* **a.** the second and third terms of a proportion, as b and c in $a/b = c/d$. **b.** another name for **average** (sense 2). See also **geometric mean. 4.** *Statistics.* a statistic obtained by multiplying each possible value of a variable by its probability and then taking the sum or integral over the range of the variable. ~*adj.* **5.** intermediate or medium in size, quantity, etc. **6.** occurring halfway between extremes or limits; average. [C14: via Anglo-Norman from Old French *moien,* from Late Latin *mediānus* MEDIAN]

me·an·der (mɪ'ændə) *vb.* (*intr.*) **1.** to follow a winding course. **2.** to wander without definite aim or direction. ~*n.* **3.** (*often pl.*) a curve or bend, as in a river. **4.** (*often pl.*) a winding course or movement. **5.** an ornamental pattern, esp. as used in ancient Greek architecture. [C16: from Latin *maeander,* from Greek *Maiandros* the River Maeander; see MENDERES (sense 1)] —**me·'an·der·er** *n.* —**me·'an·der·ing·ly** *adv.* —**me·'an·drous** *adj.*

mean de·vi·a·tion *n. Statistics.* **1.** the difference between an observed value of a variable and its mean. **2.** Also called: **mean deviation from the mean** (or **median**), **average deviation.** a measure of dispersion derived by computing the mean of the absolute values of the differences between observed values of a variable and the variable's mean.

mean dis·tance *n.* the average of the greatest and least distances of a celestial body from its primary.

mean free path *n.* the average distance travelled by a particle, atom, etc., between collisions.

mean·ing ('mi:nɪŋ) *n.* **1.** the sense or significance of a word, sentence, symbol, etc.; import; semantic or lexical content. **2.** the purpose underlying or intended by speech, action, etc. **3.** the inner, symbolic, or true interpretation, value, or message: *the meaning of a dream.* **4.** valid content; efficacy: *a law with little or no meaning.* ~*adj.* **5.** expressive of some sense, intention, criticism, etc.: *a meaning look.* ~See also **well-meaning.**

mean·ing·ful ('mi:nɪŋfʊl) *adj.* having great meaning or validity. —'**mean·ing·ful·ly** *adv.* —'**mean·ing·ful·ness** *n.*

mean·ing·less ('mi:nɪŋlɪs) *adj.* futile or empty of meaning. —'**mean·ing·less·ly** *adv.* —'**mean·ing·less·ness** *n.*

mean life *n. Physics.* the average time of existence of an unstable or reactive entity, such as a nucleus, elementary particle, charge carrier, etc.; lifetime. It is equal to the half-life divided by 0.693 15. Symbol: τ

means (mi:nz) *n.* **1.** (*functioning as sing. or pl.*) the medium, method, or instrument used to obtain a result or achieve an end: *a means of communication.* **2.** (*functioning as pl.*) resources or income. **3.** (*functioning as pl.*) considerable wealth or income: *a man of means.* **4. by all means.** without hesitation or doubt; certainly: *come with us by all means.* **5. by means of.** with the use or help of. **6. by no manner of means.** definitely not: *he was by no manner of means a cruel man.* **7. by no** (*or* **not by any**) **means.** on no account; in no way: *by no means come!*

means of pro·duc·tion *pl. n.* (in Marxist theory) the raw materials and means of labour (tools, machines, etc.) employed in the production process.

mean so·lar day *n.* the time between two successive passages of the mean sun across the meridian at noon. It is the standard for the 24-hour day.

means test *n.* a test involving the checking of a person's income to determine whether he qualifies for financial or social aid from a government.

mean sun *n.* an imaginary sun moving along the celestial equator at a constant speed and completing its annual course in the same time as the sun takes to move round the ecliptic at a varying speed. It is used in the measurement of mean solar time.

meant (mɛnt) *vb.* the past tense or past participle of **mean**[1].

mean time *or* **mean so+lar time** *n.* the times, at a particular place, measured in terms of the passage of the mean sun, giving 24-hour days (mean solar days) throughout a year.

mean+time ('mi:n,taɪm) *n.* **1.** the intervening time or period, as between events (esp. in the phrase **in the meantime**). *~adv.* **2.** another word for **meanwhile.**

mean-tone tun+ing *n.* See **temperament** (sense 4).

mean+while ('mi:n,waɪl) *adv.* **1.** during the intervening time, period, or interval. **2.** at the same time, esp. in another place. *~n.* **3.** another word for **meantime.**

mean·y *or* **mean·ie** ('mi:nɪ) *n., pl.* **mean·ies.** *Informal.* **1.** *Chiefly Brit.* a miserly or stingy person. **2.** *Informal, chiefly U.S.* a nasty ill-tempered person.

meas. *abbrev. for* measure.

mea+sled ('mi:zəld) *adj.* (of cattle, sheep, or pigs) infested with tapeworm larvae; measly.

mea+sles ('mi:zəlz) *n.* **1.** a highly contagious viral disease common in children, characterized by fever, profuse nasal discharge of mucus, conjunctivitis, and a rash of small red spots spreading from the forehead down to the limbs. Technical names: **morbilli, rubeola.** See also **German measles. 2.** a disease of cattle, sheep, and pigs, caused by infestation with tapeworm larvae. [C14: from Middle Low German *masele* spot on the skin; influenced by Middle English *mesel* leper, from Latin *misellus,* diminutive of *miser* wretched]

mea+sly ('mi:zlɪ) *adj.* **+sli+er, +sli+est. 1.** *Informal.* meagre in quality or quantity. **2.** (of meat) measled. **3.** having or relating to measles. [C17: see MEASLES]

meas+ur+a·ble ('mɛʒərəbᵊl, 'mɛʒrə-) *adj.* able to be measured; perceptible or significant. **—,meas+ur+a·'bil+i·ty** *or* **'meas+ur+a·ble+ness** *n.* **—'meas+ur+a·bly** *adv.*

meas+ure ('mɛʒə) *n.* **1.** the extent, quantity, amount, or degree of something, as determined by measurement or calculation. **2.** a device for measuring distance, volume, etc., such as a graduated scale or container. **3.** a system of measurement: *give the size in metric measure.* **4.** a standard used in a system of measurements: *the international prototype kilogram is the measure of mass in SI units.* **5.** a specific or standard amount of something: *a measure of grain; short measure; full measure.* **6.** a basis or standard for comparison: *his work was the measure of all subsequent attempts.* **7.** reasonable or permissible limit or bounds: *we must keep it within measure.* **8.** degree or extent (often in phrases such as **in some measure, in a measure,** *etc.*): *they gave him a measure of freedom.* **9.** (*often pl.*) a particular action intended to achieve an effect: *they took measures to prevent his leaving.* **10.** a legislative bill, act, or resolution: *to bring in a measure.* **11.** *Music.* another word for **bar**[1] (sense 15a.). **12.** *Prosody.* poetic rhythm or cadence; metre. **13.** a metrical foot. **14.** *Poetic.* a melody or tune. **15.** the act of measuring; measurement. **16.** *Archaic.* a dance. **17.** *Printing.* the width of a page or column of type. **18. for good measure.** as an extra precaution or beyond requirements. **19. made to measure.** (of clothes) made to fit an individual purchaser. *~vb.* **20.** (*tr.; often foll. by up*) to determine the size, amount, etc., of by measurement. **21.** (*intr.*) to make a measurement or measurements. **22.** (*tr.*) to estimate or determine: *I measured his strength to be greater than mine.* **23.** (*tr.*) to function as a measurement of: *the ohm measures electrical resistance.* **24.** (*tr.*) to bring into competition or conflict with: *he measured his strength against that of his opponent.* **25.** (*intr.*) to be as specified in extent, amount, etc.: *the room measures six feet.* **26.** (*tr.*) to travel or move over as if measuring. **27.** (*tr.*) to adjust or choose: *he measured his approach to suit the character of his client.* **28.** (*intr.*) to allow or yield to measurement. **29. measure one's length.** to fall flat. [C13: from Old French, from Latin *mēnsūra* measure, from *mēnsus,* past participle of *mētīrī* to measure] **—'meas+ur+er** *n.*

meas+ured ('mɛʒəd) *adj.* **1.** determined by measurement. **2.** slow, stately, or leisurely. **3.** carefully considered; deliberate. **—'meas+ured+ly** *adv.* **—'meas+ured+ness** *n.*

meas+ure+less ('mɛʒəlɪs) *adj.* limitless, vast, or infinite. **—'meas+ure+less+ly** *adv.* **—'meas+ure+less+ness** *n.*

meas+ure+ment ('mɛʒəmənt) *n.* **1.** the act or process of measuring. **2.** an amount, extent, or size determined by measuring. **3.** a system of measures based on a particular standard.

meas+ure+ment ton *n.* the full name for **ton**[1] (sense 5).

meas+ure off *or* **out** *vb.* (*tr., adv.*) to determine the limits of; mark out: *to measure off an area.*

meas+ure out *vb.* (*tr., adv.*) **1.** to pour or dole out: *they measure out a pint of fluid.* **2.** to administer; mete out: *they measured out harsh punishments.*

meas+ures ('mɛʒəz) *pl. n.* rock strata that are characterized by a particular type of sediment or deposit: *coal measures.*

meas+ure up *vb.* **1.** (*adv.*) to determine the size, etc., (of) by measurement. **2. measure up to.** to fulfil (expectations, standards, etc.).

meas+ur+ing cup *n.* a graduated cup used in cooking to measure ingredients.

meas+ur+ing worm *n.* the larva of a geometrid moth: it has legs on its front and rear segments only and moves in a series of loops. Also called: **looper, inchworm.**

meat (mi:t) *n.* **1.** the flesh of mammals used as food, as distinguished from that of birds and fish. **2.** anything edible, esp. flesh with the texture of meat: *crab meat.* **3.** food, as opposed to drink. **4.** the essence or gist. **5.** an archaic word for **meal**[1]. **6. meat and drink.** a source of pleasure. [Old English *mete;* related to Old High German *maz* food, Old Saxon *meti,* Gothic *mats*] **—,meat+less** *adj.*

meat+ball ('mi:t,bɔ:l) *n.* **1.** minced beef, shaped into a ball before cooking. **2.** *U.S. slang.* a stupid or boring person.

Meath (mi:θ) *n.* a county of E Ireland, in Leinster province on the Irish Sea: formerly a kingdom much larger than the present county; livestock farming. County town: Trim. Pop.: 71 729 (1971). Area: 2338 sq. km (903 sq. miles).

me·a+tus (mɪ'eɪtəs) *n., pl.* **+tus·es** *or* **+tus.** *Anatomy.* a natural opening or channel, such as the canal leading from the outer ear to the eardrum. [C17: from Latin: passage, from *meāre* to pass]

meat·y ('mi:tɪ) *adj.* **meat·i+er, meat·i·est. 1.** of, relating to, or full of meat: *a meaty stew.* **2.** heavily built; fleshy or brawny. **3.** full of import or interest: *a meaty discussion.* **—'meat·i+ly** *adv.* **—'meat·i+ness** *n.*

mec·a+myl·a+mine (,mɛkə'mɪlə,mi:n) *n.* a drug administered orally to lower high blood pressure. Formula: $C_{11}H_{21}N.HCl$. [C20: from ME(THYL) + *cam(phane)* (a former name of bornane) + -YL + AMINE]

Mec+ca ('mɛkə) *n.* **1.** a city in W Saudi Arabia, joint capital (with Riyadh) of Saudi Arabia and capital of Hejaz: birthplace of Mohammed; the holiest city of Islam, containing the Kaaba. Pop.: 185 000 (1965 est.). Arabic name: **Makkah. 2.** (*sometimes not cap.*) a place that attracts many visitors: *Athens is a Mecca for tourists.*

Mec+ca+no (mɪ,kɑ:nəʊ) *n. Trademark.* a construction set consisting of miniature metal or plastic parts from which mechanical models can be made.

mech. *abbrev. for:* **1.** mechanical. **2.** mechanics. **3.** mechanism.

me+chan+ic (mɪ'kænɪk) *n.* **1.** a person skilled in maintaining or operating machinery, motors, etc. **2.** *Archaic.* a common labourer. [C14: from Latin *mēchanicus,* from Greek *mēkhanikos,* from *mēkhanē* MACHINE]

me+chan·i·cal (mɪ'kænɪkᵊl) *adj.* **1.** made, performed, or operated by or as if by a machine or machinery: *a mechanical process.* **2.** concerned with machines or machinery. **3.** relating to or controlled or operated by physical forces. **4.** of or concerned with mechanics. **5.** (of a gesture, etc.) automatic; lacking thought, feeling, etc. **6.** *Philosophy.* accounting for phenomena by physically determining forces. *~n.* **7.** *Printing.* another name for **camera-ready copy. —me+'chan·i+cal+ism** *n.* **—me+'chan·i+cal+ly** *adv.* **—me+'chan·i+cal+ness** *n.*

me+chan·i·cal ad+van+tage *n.* the ratio of the working force exerted by a mechanism to the applied effort.

me+chan·i·cal draw+ing *n.* a drawing to scale of a machine, machine component, architectural plan, etc., from which dimensions can be taken.

me+chan·i·cal en+gi+neer+ing *n.* the branch of engineering concerned with the design, construction, and operation of machines and machinery. **—me+chan·i·cal en+gi+neer** *n.*

me+chan·i·cal e·quiv·a+lent of heat *n. Physics.* a factor for converting units of energy into heat units. It has the value 4.1855 joules per calorie. Symbol: *J*

me+chan·i·cal in+stru+ment *n.* a musical instrument, such as a barrel organ or music box, that plays a preselected piece of music by mechanical means.

mech·a+ni+cian (,mɛkə'nɪʃən) *or* **mech·a+nist** *n.* a person skilled in making machinery and tools; technician.

me+chan+ics (mɪ'kænɪks) *n.* **1.** (*functioning as sing.*) the branch of science, divided into statics, dynamics, and kinematics, concerned with the equilibrium or motion of bodies in a particular frame of reference. See also **quantum mechanics, wave mechanics, statistical mechanics. 2.** (*functioning as sing.*) the science of designing, constructing, and operating machines. **3.** the working parts of a machine. **4.** the technical aspects of something: *the mechanics of poetic style.*

mech·a+nism ('mɛkə,nɪzəm) *n.* **1.** a system or structure of moving parts that performs some function, esp. in a machine. **2.** something resembling a machine in the arrangement and working of its parts: *the mechanism of the ear.* **3.** any form of mechanical device or any part of such a device. **4.** a process or technique, esp. of execution: *the mechanism of novel writing.* **5.** *Philosophy.* the attempt to explain phenomena in mechanical terms. Compare **dynamism, vitalism. 6.** *Psychoanal.* **a.** the ways in which psychological forces interact and operate. **b.** a structure having an influence on the behaviour of a person, such as a defence mechanism.

mech·a+nist ('mɛkənɪst) *n.* **1.** a person who accepts a mechanistic philosophy. **2.** another name for a **mechanician.**

mech·a+nis+tic (,mɛkə'nɪstɪk) *adj.* **1.** *Philosophy.* of or relating to the theory of mechanism. **2.** *Maths.* of or relating to mechanics. **—,mech·a+'nis+ti+cal+ly** *adv.*

mech·a+nize *or* **mech·a+nise** ('mɛkə,naɪz) *vb.* (*tr.*) **1.** to equip (a factory, etc.) with machinery. **2.** to make mechanical, automatic, or monotonous. **3.** to equip (an army, etc.) with motorized or armoured vehicles. **—,mech·a+ni+'za+tion** *or* **,mech·a+ni+'sa+tion** *n.* **—'mech·a+,niz+er** *or* **'mech·a+,nis+er** *n.*

mech·a+no+ther·a+py (,mɛkənəʊ'θɛrəpɪ) *n.* the treatment of disorders or injuries by means of mechanical devices, esp. devices that provide exercise for bodily parts.

Mech+e+len ('mɛxələn) *n.* a city in N Belgium, in Antwerp province: capital of the Netherlands from 1507 to 1530; formerly famous for lace-making; now has an important vegetable

market. Pop.: 65 466 (1970). French name: **Malines.** English name: **Mechlin.**
Mech·lin ('mɛklɪn) *n.* the English name for **Mechelen.**
Mech·lin lace *n.* bobbin lace made at Mechlin, characterized by patterns outlined by a heavier flat thread. Also called: **malines.**
meck (mɛk) *n. Northeastern Scot. dialect.* a small coin, formerly a halfpenny. [of obscure origin]
Meck·len·burg ('mɛklən,bɜ:g *German;* 'me:klən,burk) *n.* a region and former state of NE Germany, along the Baltic coast: divided in 1952 into the East German administrative districts of Rostock, Schwerin, and Neubrandenburg.
M. Econ. *abbrev. for* Master of Economics.
me·co·ni·um (mɪ'kəʊnɪəm) *n.* **1.** the dark green mucoid material that forms the first faeces of a newborn infant. **2.** opium or the juice from the opium poppy. [C17: from New Latin, from Latin: poppy juice (used also of infant's excrement because of similarity in colour), from Greek *mēkōneion,* from *mēkōn* poppy]
med. *abbrev. for:* **1.** medical. **2.** medicine. **3.** medieval. **4.** medium.
Med (mɛd) *n. Informal.* the Mediterranean region.
M.Ed. *abbrev. for* Master of Education.
med·al ('mɛdᵊl) *n.* **1.** a small flat piece of metal bearing an inscription or image, given as an award or commemoration of some outstanding event, etc. ~*vb.* **·als, ·al·ling, ·alled** *or U.S.* **·als, ·al·ing, ·aled. 2.** (*tr.*) to honour with a medal. [C16: from French *médaille,* probably from Italian *medaglia,* ultimately from Latin *metallum* METAL] **—me·dal·lic** (mɪ'dælɪk) *adj.*
me·dal·lion (mɪ'dæljən) *n.* **1.** a large medal. **2.** an oval or circular decorative device resembling a medal, usually bearing a portrait or relief moulding, used in architecture and textile design. [C17: from French, from Italian *medaglione,* from *medaglia* MEDAL] **—me·'dal·lion·ist** *n.*
med·al·list *or U.S.* **med·al·ist** ('mɛdᵊlɪst) *n.* **1.** a designer, maker, or collector of medals. **2.** *Chiefly sport.* a winner or recipient of a medal or medals.
Med·al of Hon·or *n.* (in the U.S.) a military decoration awarded for gallantry in the name of Congress.
med·al play *n. Golf.* another name for **stroke play.**
Me·dan ('mɛdɑ:n) *n.* a city in Indonesia, in NE Sumatra: seat of the University of North Sumatra (1952) and the Indonesian Islam University (1952). Pop.: 635 562 (1971).
Med·a·war ('mɛdəwə) *n.* Sir **Pe·ter Bri·an.** born 1915, English zoologist, who shared the Nobel prize for medicine (1960) with Sir Macfarlane Burnet for work on immunology.
med·dle ('mɛdᵊl) *vb.* **1.** (*intr.;* usually foll. by *with*) to interfere officiously or annoyingly. **2.** (*intr.;* usually foll. by *in*) to involve oneself unwarrantedly: *to meddle in someone's private affairs.* [C14: from Old French *medler,* ultimately from Latin *miscēre* to mix] **—'med·dler** *n.* **—'med·dling·ly** *adv.*
med·dle·some ('mɛdᵊlsəm) *adj.* intrusive or meddling. **—'med·dle·some·ly** *adv.* **—'med·dle·some·ness** *n.*
Mede (mi:d) *n.* a member of an Indo-European people of West Iranian speech who established an empire in SW Asia in the 7th and 6th centuries B.C. **—'Me·di·an** *n., adj.*
Me·de·a (mɪ'dɪə) *n. Greek myth.* a princess of Colchis, who assisted Jason in obtaining the Golden Fleece from her father.
Me·del·lín (*Spanish* meðe'jin) *n.* a city in W Colombia, at an altitude of 1554 m (5100 ft.): the second largest city in the country, with three universities; important coffee centre, with large textile mills. Pop.: 1 070 924 (1973).
me·di·a¹ ('mi:dɪə) *n.* **1.** a plural of **medium. 2.** *Informal.* the mass media collectively.
me·di·a² ('mɛdɪə) *n., pl.* **·di·ae** (-dɪ,i:). **1.** the middle layer of the wall of a blood or lymph vessel. **2.** one of the main veins in the wing of an insect. **3.** *Phonetics.* **a.** a consonant whose articulation lies midway between that of a voiced and breathed speech sound. **b.** a consonant pronounced with weak voice, as *c* in French *second.* [C19: from Latin *medius* middle]
Me·di·a ('mi:dɪə) *n.* an ancient country of SW Asia, south of the Caspian Sea: inhabited by the Medes; overthrew the Assyrian Empire in 612 B.C. in alliance with Babylonia; conquered by Cyrus the Great in 550 B.C.; corresponds to present-day NW Iran.
me·di·a·cy ('mi:dɪəsɪ) *n.* **1.** the quality or state of being mediate. **2.** a less common word for **mediation.**
me·di·ae·val (,mɛdɪ'i:vᵊl) *adj.* a variant spelling of **medieval.**
me·di·al ('mi:dɪəl) *adj.* **1.** of or situated in the middle. **2.** ordinary or average in size. **3.** *Maths.* relating to an average. **4.** another word for **median** (senses 1, 2, 3). **5.** *Zoology.* of or relating to a media. ~*n.* **6.** *Phonetics.* a speech sound between being fortis and lenis; media. [C16: from Late Latin *mediālis,* from *medius* middle] **—'me·di·al·ly** *adv.*
me·di·an ('mi:dɪən) *adj.* **1.** of, relating to, situated in, or directed towards the middle. **2.** *Biology.* of or relating to the plane that divides an organism or organ into symmetrical parts. **3.** *Statistics.* of or relating to the median. ~*n.* **4.** a middle point, plane, or part. **5.** *Geom.* **a.** a straight line joining one vertex of a triangle to the midpoint of the opposite side. See also **centroid. b.** a straight line joining the midpoints of the nonparallel sides of a trapezium. **6.** *Statistics.* the middle value in a frequency distribution, below and above which lie values with equal total frequencies. **7.** *Statistics.* the middle number or average of the two middle numbers in an ordered sequence of numbers: *7 is the median of both 1, 7, 31 and 2, 5, 9, 16.* **8.** the Canadian word for **central reserve.** [C16: from Latin *mediānus,* from *medius* middle] **—'me·di·an·ly** *adv.*
me·di·an strip *n.* the U.S. term for **central reserve.**
me·di·ant ('mi:dɪənt) *n. Music.* **a.** the third degree of a minor scale. **b.** (*as modifier*): *a mediant chord.* [C18: from Italian *mediante,* from Late Latin *mediāre* to be in the middle]
me·di·as·ti·num (,mi:dɪə'staɪnəm) *n., pl.* **·na** (-nə). *Anatomy.* **1.** a membrane between two parts of an organ or cavity such as the pleural tissue between the two lungs. **2.** the part of the thoracic cavity that lies between the lungs, containing the heart, trachea, etc. [C16: from medical Latin, neuter of Medieval Latin *mediastīnus* median, from Latin: low grade of servant, from *medius* mean] **—,me·di·as·'ti·nal** *adj.*
me·di·ate *vb.* ('mi:dɪ,eɪt). **1.** (*intr.;* usually foll. by *between* or *in*) to intervene (between parties or in a dispute) in order to bring about agreement. **2.** to bring about (an agreement). **3.** to bring about (an agreement) between parties in a dispute. **4.** to resolve (differences) by mediation. **5.** (*intr.*) to be in a middle or intermediate position. **6.** (*tr.*) to serve as a medium for causing (a result) or transferring (objects, information, etc.). ~*adj.* ('mi:dɪɪt). **7.** occurring as a result of or dependent upon mediation. **8.** a rare word for **intermediate.** [C16: from Late Latin *mediāre* to be in the middle] **—'me·di·ate·ly** *adv.* **—'me·di·ate·ness** *n.* **—'me·di·a·tive, 'me·di·a·to·ry,** *or* **,me·di·a·'to·ri·al** *adj.* **—'me·di,a·tor** *n.* **—,me·di·a·'to·ri·al·ly** *adv.*
me·di·a·tion (,mi:dɪ'eɪʃən) *n.* **1.** the act of mediating; intercession. **2.** *International law.* an attempt to reconcile disputed matters arising between states, esp. by the friendly intervention of a neutral power.
me·di·a·tize *or* **me·di·a·tise** ('mi:dɪə,taɪz) *vb.* (*tr.*) to annex (a state) to another state, allowing the former ruler to retain his title and some authority. [C19: from French *médiatiser;* see MEDIATE, -IZE] **—,me·di·a·ti·'za·tion** *or* **,me·di·a·ti·'sa·tion** *n.*
med·ic¹ ('mɛdɪk) *n. Informal.* a doctor, medical orderly, or medical student. [C17: from MEDICAL]
med·ic² ('mɛdɪk) *n.* the usual U.S. spelling of **medick.**
med·i·ca·ble ('mɛdɪkəbᵊl) *adj.* potentially able to be treated or cured medically. **—'med·i·ca·bly** *adv.*
Med·i·caid ('mɛdɪ,keɪd) *n. U.S.* a health assistance programme financed by federal, state, and local taxes to help pay hospital and medical costs for persons of low income. [C20: MEDIC(AL) + AID]
med·i·cal ('mɛdɪkᵊl) *adj.* **1.** of or relating to the science of medicine or to the treatment of patients by drugs, etc., as opposed to surgery. **2.** a less common word for **medicinal.** ~*n.* **3.** *Informal.* a medical examination. [C17: from Medieval Latin *medicālis,* from Latin *medicus* physician, surgeon, from *medērī* to heal] **—'med·i·cal·ly** *adv.*
med·i·cal cer·tif·i·cate *n.* **1.** a document stating the result of a satisfactory medical examination. **2.** a doctor's certificate giving evidence of a person's unfitness for work, etc.
med·i·cal ex·am·i·na·tion *n.* an examination carried out to determine the physical fitness of an applicant for a job, life insurance, etc.
med·i·cal ex·am·in·er *n.* **1.** *Chiefly U.S.* a medical expert, usually a physician, employed by a state or local government to determine the cause of sudden death in cases of suspected violence, suicide, etc. Compare **coroner. 2.** a physician who carries out medical examinations.
med·i·cal ju·ris·pru·dence *n.* another name for **forensic medicine.**
me·dic·a·ment (mɪ'dɪkəmənt, 'mɛdɪ-) *n.* a medicine or remedy. [C16: via French from Latin *medicāmentum* from *medicāre* to cure] **—med·i·ca·men·tal** (,mɛdɪkə'mɛntᵊl) *or* **,med·i·ca·'men·ta·ry** *adj.*
Med·i·care ('mɛdɪ,kɛə) *n. U.S.* a federally sponsored health insurance programme for persons of 65 or older. [C20: MEDI(CAL) + CARE]
med·i·cate ('mɛdɪ,keɪt) *vb.* (*tr.*) **1.** to cover or impregnate (a wound, etc.) with an ointment, etc. **2.** to treat (a patient) with a medicine. **3.** to add a medication to (a bandage, shampoo, etc.). [C17: from Latin *medicāre* to heal] **—'med·i·ca·tive** *adj.*
med·i·ca·tion (,mɛdɪ'keɪʃən) *n.* **1.** treatment with drugs or remedies. **2.** a drug or remedy.
Med·i·ci ('mɛdɪtʃɪ, mə'di:tʃɪ; *Italian* 'me:ditʃi) *n.* **1.** an Italian family of bankers, merchants, and rulers of Florence and Tuscany, prominent in Italian political and cultural history in the 15th, 16th, and 17th centuries, including: **2. Cathe·rine de'** (kat'ri:n de). See **Catherine de' Medici. 3. Co·si·mo I** ('kɔ:zimo), called *the Great.* 1519–74, duke of Florence and first grand duke of Tuscany (1569–74). **4. Cosimo de',** called *the Elder.* 1389–1464, Italian banker, statesman, and patron of arts, who established the political power of the family in Florence (1434). **5. Gio·van·ni de',** (dʒo'vanni de). See **Leo X. 6. Giu·lio de'** ('dʒu:ljo de). See **Clement VII. 7. Lo·ren·zo de'** (lo'rɛntso de), called *the Magnificent.* 1449–92, Italian statesman, poet, and scholar; ruler of Florence (1469–92) and first patron of Michelangelo. **8. Ma·ria de'** (ma'ri:a de). See **Maria de Medici.** ~French: **Mé·di·cis** (medi'sis). **—Med·i·ce·an** (,mɛdɪ'si:ən, -'tʃi:-) *adj.*
me·dic·i·nal (mɛ'dɪsɪnᵊl) *adj.* **1.** relating to or having therapeutic properties. ~*n.* **2.** a medicinal substance. **—me·'dic·i·nal·ly** *adv.*
me·dic·i·nal leech *n.* a large European freshwater leech, *Hirudo medicinalis,* formerly used in medical bloodletting.
med·i·cine ('mɛdɪsɪn, 'mɛdsɪn) *n.* **1.** any drug or remedy for use in treating, preventing, or alleviating the symptoms of disease. **2.** the science of preventing, diagnosing, alleviating, or curing disease. **3.** any nonsurgical branch of medical science. **4.** the practice or profession of medicine: *he's in medicine.* **5.** something regarded by primitive people as having

magical or remedial properties. **6. take one's medicine.** to accept a deserved punishment. **7. a taste** (*or* **dose**) **of one's own medicine.** an unpleasant experience in retaliation for and by similar methods to an unkind or aggressive act. [C13: via Old French from Latin *medicīna* (*ars*) (art of) healing, from *medicus* doctor, from *medērī* to heal]

med·i·cine ball *n.* a heavy ball used for physical training.

med·i·cine chest *n.* a small chest or cupboard for storing medicines, bandages, etc.

med·i·cine lodge *n.* a wooden structure used for magical and religious ceremonies among certain North American Indian peoples.

med·i·cine man *n.* (among certain peoples, esp. North American Indians) a person believed to have supernatural powers of healing; a magician or sorcerer.

med·i·cine shop *n.* (in Malaysia) a Chinese chemist's shop where traditional herbs are sold as well as modern drugs. It is not, however, a dispensary for prescribed medicines.

med·ick *or U.S.* **med·ic** ('mɛdɪk) *n.* any small papilionaceous plant of the genus *Medicago,* such as black medick or sickle medick, having yellow or purple flowers and trifoliate leaves. [C15: from Latin *mēdica,* from Greek *mēdikē* (*poa*) Median (grass), a type of clover]

med·i·co ('mɛdɪˌkəʊ) *n., pl.* **·cos.** *Informal.* a doctor or medical student. [C17: via Italian from Latin *medicus*]

med·i·co- *combining form.* medical: *medicolegal.*

me·di·e·val *or* **me·di·ae·val** (ˌmɛdɪ'iːvᵊl) *adj.* **1.** of, relating to, or in the style of the Middle Ages. **2.** *Informal.* old-fashioned; primitive. [C19: from New Latin *medium aevum* the middle age. See MEDIUM, AGE] —ˌ**me·di·'e·val·ly** *or* ˌ**me·di·'ae·val·ly** *adv.*

Me·di·e·val Greek *n.* the Greek language from the 7th century A.D. to shortly after the sacking of Constantinople in 1204. Also called: **Middle Greek, Byzantine Greek.** Compare **Koine, Late Greek, Ancient Greek.**

me·di·e·val·ism *or* **me·di·ae·val·ism** (ˌmɛdɪ'iːvəˌlɪzəm) *n.* **1.** the beliefs, life, or style of the Middle Ages or devotion to those. **2.** a belief, custom, or point of style copied or surviving from the Middle Ages.

me·di·e·val·ist *or* **me·di·ae·val·ist** (ˌmɛdɪ'iːvəlɪst) *n.* a student or devotee of the Middle Ages. —ˌ**me·di·ˌe·val·'is·tic** *or* ˌ**me·di·ˌae·val·'is·tic** *adj.*

Me·di·e·val Lat·in *n.* the Latin language as used throughout Europe in the Middle Ages. It had many local forms incorporating Latinized words from other languages.

me·di·na (mɛ'diːnə) *n.* (*sometimes cap.*) the ancient quarter of any of various North African cities. Compare **kasbah.**

Me·di·na (mɛ'diːnə) *n.* a city in W Saudi Arabia, in Hejaz province: the second most holy city of Islam (after Mecca), with the tomb of Mohammed; university (1960). Pop.: 100 000 (1965 est.). Arabic name: **Al Madinah.**

me·di·o·cre (ˌmiːdɪ'əʊkə, 'miːdɪˌəʊkə) *adj. Often derogatory.* average or ordinary in quality: *a mediocre book.* [C16: via French from Latin *mediocris* moderate, literally: halfway up the mountain, from *medius* middle + *ocris* stony mountain]

me·di·oc·ri·ty (ˌmiːdɪ'ɒkrɪtɪ, ˌmɛd-) *n., pl.* **·ties. 1.** the state or quality of being mediocre. **2.** a mediocre person or thing: *he is a mediocrity.*

Medit. *abbrev. for* Mediterranean.

med·i·tate ('mɛdɪˌteɪt) *vb.* (*intr.*) **1.** (foll. by *on* or *upon*) to think about something deeply. **2.** to reflect deeply on spiritual matters, esp. as a religious act. [C16: from Latin *meditārī* to reflect upon] —'**med·i·ˌtat·ing·ly** *adv.* —'**med·i·ta·tive** *adj.* —'**med·i·ta·tive·ly** *adv.* —'**med·i·ta·tive·ness** *n.* —'**med·i·ˌta·tor** *n.*

med·i·ta·tion (ˌmɛdɪ'teɪʃən) *n.* **1.** the act of meditating; contemplation; reflection. **2.** contemplation of spiritual matters, esp. as a religious practice.

Med·i·ter·ra·ne·an (ˌmɛdɪtə'reɪnɪən) *n.* **1.** short for the **Mediterranean Sea. 2.** a native or inhabitant of a Mediterranean country. ~*adj.* **3.** of, relating to, situated or dwelling on or near the Mediterranean Sea. **4.** denoting a postulated subdivision of the Caucasoid race, characterized by slender build and dark complexion. **5.** *Meteorol.* (of a climate) characterized by hot summers and relatively warm winters when most of the annual rainfall occurs. **6.** (*often not cap.*) *Obsolete.* situated in the middle of a land mass; inland. [C16: from Latin *mediterrāneus,* from *medius* middle + *-terrāneus,* from *terra* land, earth]

Med·i·ter·ra·ne·an fe·ver *n.* another name for **brucellosis.**

Med·i·ter·ra·ne·an Sea *n.* a large inland sea between S Europe, N Africa, and SW Asia: linked with the Atlantic by the Strait of Gibraltar, with the Red Sea by the Suez Canal, and with the Black Sea by the Dardanelles, Sea of Marmara, and Bosporus; many ancient civilizations developed around its shores. Greatest depth: 4770 m (15 900 ft.). Length: (west to east) over 3700 km (2300 miles). Greatest width: about 1368 km (850 miles). Area: (excluding the Black Sea) 2 512 300 sq. km (970 000 sq. miles). Ancient name: **Mare Internum.**

me·di·um ('miːdɪəm) *adj.* **1.** midway between extremes; average: *a medium size.* **2.** (of a colour) reflecting or transmitting a moderate amount of light: *a medium red.* Compare **light**[1] (sense 27), **dark** (sense 2). ~*n., pl.* **·di·a** (-dɪə) *or* **·di·ums. 3.** an intermediate or middle state, degree, or condition; mean: *the happy medium.* **4.** an intervening substance or agency for transmitting or producing an effect; vehicle: *air is a medium for sound.* **5.** a means or agency for communicating or diffusing information, etc., to the public: *television is a powerful medium.* **6.** a person supposedly used as a spiritual intermediary between the dead and the living. **7.** the substance in which specimens of animals and plants are preserved or displayed. **8.** *Biology.* short for **culture medium. 9.** the substance or surroundings in which an organism naturally lives or grows. **10.** *Art.* **a.** the category of a work of art, as determined by its materials and methods of production: *the medium of wood engraving.* **b.** the materials used in a work of art. **11.** any solvent in which pigments are mixed and thinned. **12.** any one of various sizes of writing or printing paper, esp. 18½ by 23½ inches or 17½ by 22 inches (**small medium**). [C16: from Latin: neuter singular of *medius* middle]

Usage. Careful writers and speakers do not use *media* as a singular noun when referring to a medium of mass communication, although this use is common: *television is a valuable medium* (not *media*) *for advertising.*

me·di·um-dat·ed *adj.* (of a gilt-edged security) having between five and fifteen years to run before redemption. Compare **long-dated, short-dated.**

me·di·um fre·quen·cy *n.* a radio-frequency band or radio frequency lying between 3000 and 300 kilohertz. Abbrev: **MF.**

me·di·um of ex·change *n.* anything acceptable as a measure of value and a standard of exchange for goods and services in a particular country, region, etc.

me·di·ums *pl. n.* medium-dated gilt-edged securities.

me·di·um wave *n.* **a.** a radio wave with a wavelength between 100 and 1000 metres. **b.** (*as modifier*): *a medium-wave broadcast.*

med·lar ('mɛdlə) *n.* **1.** a small Eurasian rosaceous tree, *Mespilus germanica.* **2.** the fruit of this tree, which resembles the crab apple and is not edible until it has begun to decay. **3.** any of several other rosaceous trees or their fruits. [C14: from Old French *medlier,* from Latin *mespilum* medlar fruit, from Greek *mespilon*]

med·ley ('mɛdlɪ) *n.* **1.** a mixture of various types or elements. **2.** a musical composition consisting of various tunes arranged as a continuous whole. **3.** Also called: **medley relay. a.** *Swimming.* a race in which a different stroke is used for each length. **b.** *Athletics.* a relay race in which each leg has a different distance. **4.** an archaic word for **melee.** ~*adj.* **5.** of, being, or relating to a mixture or variety. [C14: from Old French *medlee,* from *medler* to mix, quarrel]

Mé·doc (meɪ'dɒk, 'mɛdɒk; *French* me'dɔk) *n.* **1.** a district of SW France, on the left bank of the Gironde estuary: famous vineyards. **2.** a fine red wine from this district.

me·dul·la (mɪ'dʌlə) *n., pl.* **·las** *or* **·lae** (-liː). **1.** *Anatomy.* **a.** the innermost part of an organ or structure. **b.** short for **medulla oblongata. 2.** *Botany.* another name for **pith** (sense 4). [C17: from Latin: marrow, pith, probably from *medius* middle] —**me·'dul·lar·y** *or* **me·'dul·lar** *adj.*

me·dul·la ob·lon·ga·ta (ˌɒblɒŋ'gɑːtə) *n., pl.* **me·dul·la ob·lon·ga·tas** *or* **me·dul·lae ob·lon·ga·tae** (mɪ'dʌliː ˌɒblɒŋ'gɑːtiː). the lower stalklike section of the brain, continuous with the spinal cord, containing control centres for the heart and lungs. [C17: New Latin: oblong-shaped medulla]

me·dul·lar·y ray *n.* any of the sheets of conducting tissue that run radially through the vascular tissue of some higher plants.

me·dul·lar·y sheath *n.* **1.** *Anatomy.* a myelin layer surrounding and insulating certain nerve fibres. **2.** a layer of thick-walled cells surrounding the pith of the stems of some higher plants.

med·ul·lat·ed ('mɛdəˌleɪtɪd, mɪ'dʌl-) *adj.* **1.** *Anatomy.* encased in a myelin sheath. **2.** having a medulla.

me·du·sa (mɪ'djuːzə) *n., pl.* **·sas** *or* **·sae** (-ziː). **1.** another name for **jellyfish. 2.** one of the two forms in which a coelenterate exists. It has a jelly-like umbrella-shaped body, is free swimming, and produces gametes. Also called: **medusoid, medusan.** Compare **polyp.** [C18: from the likeness of its tentacles to the snaky locks of Medusa] —**me·'du·san** *adj.*

Me·du·sa (mɪ'djuːzə) *n. Greek myth.* a mortal woman who was transformed by Athena into one of the three Gorgons. Her appearance was so hideous that those who looked directly at her were turned to stone. Perseus eventually slew her. See also **Pegasus**[1]. —**Me·'du·san** *adj.*

me·du·soid (mɪ'djuːzɔɪd) *adj.* **1.** of, relating to, or resembling a medusa. ~*n.* **2.** another name for **medusa** (sense 2).

Med·way ('mɛdˌweɪ) *n.* a river in SE England, flowing through Kent and the **Medway towns** (Rochester, Chatham, and Gillingham) to the Thames estuary. Length: 110 km (70 miles).

mee (miː) *n.* (in Malaysia) noodles or a dish containing noodles. [from Chinese (Cantonese) *mien* noodles]

meed (miːd) *n. Archaic.* a recompense; reward. [Old English: wages; compare Old High German *mēta* pay]

meek (miːk) *adj.* **1.** patient, long-suffering, or submissive in disposition or nature; humble. **2.** spineless or spiritless; compliant. **3.** an obsolete word for **gentle.** [C12: related to Old Norse *mjūkr* amenable; compare Welsh *mwytho* to soften] —'**meek·ly** *adv.* —'**meek·ness** *n.*

meer·kat ('mɪəˌkæt) *n.* any of several South African mongooses, esp. *Suricata suricatta* (**slender-tailed meerkat** or **suricate**), which has a lemur-like face and four-toed feet. [C19: from Dutch: sea-cat]

meer·schaum ('mɪəʃəm) *n.* **1.** Also called: **sepiolite.** a white, yellowish, or pink compact earthy mineral consisting of hydrated magnesium silicate: used to make tobacco pipes and as a building stone. Formula: $Mg_2Si_3O_6(OH)_4$. **2.** a tobacco pipe having a bowl made of this mineral. [C18: German, literally: sea foam]

Mee·rut ('mɪərət) *n.* an industrial city in N India, in W Uttar Pradesh: founded as a military base by the British in 1806 and scene of the first uprising (1857) of the Indian Mutiny. Pop.: 270 993 (1971).

meet[1] (miːt) *vb.* **meets, meet+ing, met. 1.** (sometimes foll. by *up* or *with*) to come together (with), either by design or by accident; encounter: *I met him unexpectedly; we met at the station.* **2.** to come into or be in conjunction or contact with (something or each other): *the roads meet in the town; the sea meets the sky.* **3.** (*tr.*) to come to or be at the place of arrival of: *to meet a train.* **4.** to make the acquaintance of or be introduced to (someone or each other): *have you two met?* **5.** to gather in the company of (someone or each other): *the board of directors meets on Tuesday.* **6.** to come into the presence of (someone or each other) as opponents: *Joe meets Fred in the boxing match.* **7.** (*tr.*) to cope with effectively; satisfy: *to meet someone's demands.* **8.** (*tr.*) to be apparent to (esp. in the phrase **meet the eye**). **9.** (*tr.*) to return or counter: *to meet a blow with another.* **10.** to agree with (someone or each other): *we met him on the price he suggested.* **11.** (*tr.*) to experience; suffer: *he met his death in a road accident.* **12.** to occur together: *courage and kindliness met in him.* **13.** (*tr.*) *Caribbean.* to find (a person, situation, etc.) in a specified condition: *I met the door open.* ~*n.* **14.** the assembly of hounds, huntsmen, etc., prior to a hunt. **15.** a meeting, esp. a sports meeting. **16.** *U.S.* the place where the paths of two railway trains meet or cross. [Old English *mētan;* related to Old Norse *mœta,* Old Saxon *mōtian*] —**'meet+er** *n.*

meet[2] (miːt) *adj. Archaic.* proper, fitting, or correct. [C13: from variant of Old English *gemǣte;* related to Old High German *māza* suitability, Old Norse *mǣtr* valuable] —**'meet+ly** *adv.*

meet+ing ('miːtɪŋ) *n.* **1.** an act of coming together; encounter. **2.** an assembly or gathering. **3.** a conjunction or union.

meet+ing house *n.* the place in which Quakers hold their meetings for worship.

meg·a- *combining form.* **1.** denoting 10^6: *megawatt.* Symbol: M **2.** (in computer technology) denoting 2^{20} (1 048 576): *megabyte.* **3.** large or great: *megalith.* [from Greek *megas* huge, powerful]

meg·a+ceph·a+ly (ˌmɛgə'sɛfəlɪ) *or* **meg·a+lo+ceph·a+ly** *n.* the condition of having an unusually large head or cranial capacity. It can be of congenital origin or result from an abnormal overgrowth of the facial bones. Compare **microcephaly.** —**meg·a+ce·phal+ic** (ˌmɛgəsɪ'fælɪk), **ˌmeg·a+'ceph·a+lous, ˌmeg·a+lo+ce·'phal+ic,** *or* **ˌmeg·a+lo+'ceph·a+lous** *adj.*

meg·a+cy+cle ('mɛgəˌsaɪkᵊl) *n.* a former unit of frequency equal to one million cycles per second; megahertz.

meg·a+death ('mɛgəˌdɛθ) *n.* the death of a million people, esp. in a nuclear war or attack.

Me·gae·ra (mɪ'dʒɪərə) *n. Greek myth.* one of the three Furies; the others are Alecto and Tisiphone.

meg·a+ga+mete (ˌmɛgəgæ'miːt) *n.* another name for **macrogamete.**

meg·a+lith ('mɛgəlɪθ) *n.* a stone of great size, esp. one forming part of a prehistoric monument. See also **alignment** (sense 6), **circle** (sense 11). —**ˌmeg·a+'lith+ic** *adj.*

meg·a+lith+ic tomb *n.* a burial chamber constructed of large stones, either underground or covered by a mound and usually consisting of long transepted corridors (**gallery graves**) or of a distinct chamber and passage (**passage graves**). The tombs may date from the 4th millennium B.C.

meg·a·lo- *or before a vowel* **meg·al-** *combining form.* indicating greatness, or abnormal size: *megalopolis; megaloblast.* [from Greek *megas* great]

meg·a+lo+blast ('mɛgələʊˌblɑːst) *n.* an abnormally large red blood cell present in certain types of anaemia. —**meg·a+lo+blast+ic** (ˌmɛgələʊ'blæstɪk) *adj.*

meg·a+lo+blast+ic a·nae+mi·a *n.* any anaemia, esp. pernicious anaemia, characterized by the presence of megaloblasts in the blood or bone marrow.

meg·a+lo+car+di·a (ˌmɛgələʊ'kɑːdɪə) *n. Pathol.* abnormal increase in the size of the heart. Also called: **cardiomegaly.**

meg·a+lo+ceph·a+ly (ˌmɛgələʊ'sɛfəlɪ) *n.* another word for **megacephaly.**

meg·a+lo+ma+ni·a (ˌmɛgələʊ'meɪnɪə) *n.* a mental illness characterized by delusions of grandeur, power, wealth, etc. —**ˌmeg·a+lo+'ma+ni+ac** *adj., n.* —**meg·a+lo+ma+ni·a+cal** (ˌmɛgələʊmə'naɪəkᵊl) *adj.*

meg·a+lop·o+lis (ˌmɛgə'lɒpəlɪs) *n.* an urban complex, usually comprising several large towns. [C20: MEGALO- + Greek *polis* city] —**meg·a+lo+pol·i+tan** (ˌmɛgələ'pɒlɪtᵊn) *adj., n.*

meg·a+lo+saur ('mɛgələʊˌsɔː) *n.* any very large Jurassic or Cretaceous bipedal carnivorous dinosaurs of the genus *Megalosaurus,* common in Europe: suborder *Theropoda* (theropods). [C19: from New Latin *megalosaurus,* from MEGALO- + Greek *sauros* lizard] —**ˌmeg·a+lo+'sau+ri·an** *adj., n.*

meg·a+phone ('mɛgəˌfəʊn) *n.* a funnel-shaped instrument used to amplify the voice. See also **loud-hailer.** —**meg·a·phon+ic** (ˌmɛgə'fɒnɪk) *adj.* —**ˌmeg·a+'phon·i+cal+ly** *adv.*

meg·a+pode ('mɛgəˌpəʊd) *n.* any ground-living gallinaceous bird of the family *Megapodiidae,* of Australia, New Guinea, and adjacent islands. Their eggs incubate in mounds of sand, rotting vegetation, etc., by natural heat. Also called: **mound-builder.** See also **brush turkey, mallee fowl.**

Meg·a+ra ('mɛgərə) *n.* a town in E central Greece: an ancient trading city, founding many colonies in the 7th and 8th centuries B.C. Pop.: 17 260 (1971).

meg·a+ron ('mɛgəˌrɒn) *n., pl.* **+ra** (-rə). a tripartite rectangular room containing a central hearth surrounded by four pillars, found in Bronze Age Greece and Asia Minor. [from Greek, from *megas* large]

meg·a+scop+ic (ˌmɛgə'skɒpɪk) *adj.* another word for **macroscopic.**

meg·a+spo+ran+gi·um (ˌmɛgəspɔː'rændʒɪəm) *n., pl.* **+gi·a** (-dʒɪə). the structure in certain ferns in which the megaspores are formed: corresponds to the ovule in seed plants. Compare **microsporangium.**

meg·a+spore ('mɛgəˌspɔː) *n.* **1.** Also called: **macrospore.** the larger of the two types of spore produced by some ferns, which develops into the female gametophyte. Compare **microspore** (sense 1). **2.** the embryo sac of flowering plants. —**ˌmeg·a+'spor+ic** *adj.*

meg·a+spo+ro+phyll (ˌmɛgə'spɔːrəfɪl) *n.* a leaf on which the megaspores are formed: corresponds to the carpel of a flowering plant. Compare **microsporophyll.**

me+gass *or* **me+gasse** (mə'gæs) *n.* another name for **bagasse** (sense 2). [C19: of obscure origin]

meg·a+there ('mɛgəˌθɪə) *n.* any of various gigantic extinct American sloths of the genus *Megatherium* and related genera, common in late Cenozoic times. [C19: from New Latin *megathērium,* from MEGA- + *-there,* from Greek *thērion* wild beast] —**ˌmeg·a+'ther+i·an** *adj.*

meg·a+ton ('mɛgəˌtʌn) *n.* **1.** one million tons. **2.** an explosive power, esp. of a nuclear weapon, equal to the power of one million tons of TNT. —**meg·a+ton+ic** (ˌmɛgə'tɒnɪk) *adj.*

meg·a+volt ('mɛgəˌvɒlt) *n.* one million volts. Symbol: MV

meg·a+watt ('mɛgəˌwɒt) *n.* one million watts. Symbol: MW

Meg+ger ('mɛgə) *n. Trademark.* an instrument that generates a high voltage in order to test the resistance of insulation, etc.

Me+gha+la+ya (ˌmeɪgə'leɪə) *n.* a state of NE India, created in 1969 from part of Assam. Capital: Shillong. Pop.: 1 011 699 (1971). Area: 22 445 sq. km (7800 sq. miles).

Me+gid+do (mə'gɪdəʊ) *n.* an ancient town in N Palestine, strategically located on a route linking Egypt to Mesopotamia: site of many battles, including an important Egyptian victory over rebel chieftains in 1469 or 1468 B.C.

me+gil+lah (mə'gɪlə; *Hebrew* migi'la) *n., pl.* **+lahs** *or* **+loth** (*Hebrew* -'lɔt). a Hebrew scroll containing the Book of Esther. [Hebrew: scroll]

me+gilp *or* **ma+gilp** (mə'gɪlp) *n.* an oil-painting medium of linseed oil mixed with mastic varnish or turpentine. [C18: of unknown origin]

meg+ohm ('mɛgˌəʊm) *n.* one million ohms. Symbol: MΩ

me+grim ('miːgrɪm) *n. Archaic.* **1.** (*often pl.*) a caprice. **2.** a migraine. [C14: see MIGRAINE]

me+grims ('miːgrɪmz) *n.* **1.** *Now rare.* a fit of depression. **2.** a disease of horses and cattle; staggers.

Me·hem·et A·li (mɪ'hɛmɪt 'ɑːlɪ) *or* **Mo·ham·med A·li** *n.* 1769–1849, Albanian commander in the service of Turkey. He was made viceroy of Egypt (1805) and its hereditary ruler (1841), founding a dynasty that ruled until 1952.

Mei+ji ('meɪ'dʒiː) *n.* **1.** *Japanese history.* the reign of Emperor Mutsuhito (1867-1912), during which Japan began a rapid process of Westernization, industrialization, and expansion in foreign affairs. **2.** the throne name of **Mutsuhito** (ˌmuːtsu'hiːtou). 1852–1912, emperor of Japan (1867–1912). [Japanese, from Chinese *ming* enlightened + *dji* government]

Meil·hac (*French* mɛ'jak) *n.* **Hen·ri** (ɑ̃'ri). 1831–97, French dramatist, who collaborated with Halévy on opera libretti, esp. Offenbach's *La Belle Hélène* (1865) and *La Vie parisienne* (1867).

mein·y *or* **mein·ie** ('meɪnɪ) *n., pl.* **mein·ies.** *Obsolete.* **1.** a retinue or household. **2.** *Scot.* a crowd. [C13: from Old French *mesnie,* from Vulgar Latin *mansiōnāta* (unattested), from Latin *mansiō* a lodging; see MANSION]

mei·o·sis (maɪ'əʊsɪs) *n., pl.* **+ses** (-ˌsiːz). **1.** a type of cell division in which a nucleus divides into four daughter nuclei, each containing half the chromosome number of the parent nucleus: occurs in all sexually reproducing organisms in which haploid gametes or spores are produced. Compare **mitosis.** See also **prophase** (sense 2). **2.** *Rhetoric.* another word for **litotes. 3.** *Rare.* any division or splitting. [C16: via New Latin from Greek: a lessening, from *meioun* to diminish, from *meiōn* less] —**mei·ot·ic** (maɪ'ɒtɪk) *adj.* —**mei+'ot·i+cal+ly** *adv.*

Me·ir (meɪ'ɪə) *n.* **Gol·da** ('gəʊldə) 1898–1978, Israeli statesman, born in Russia; prime minister (1969–74).

Meis+sen (*German* 'maɪsᵊn) *n.* a town in SE East Germany, in Dresden district on the River Elbe: famous for its porcelain (Dresden china), begun here in 1710. Pop.: 44 111 (1972 est.).

Meis+ter+sing+er ('maɪstəˌsɪŋə) *n., pl.* **+sing+er** *or* **+sing+ers.** a member of one of the various German guilds of workers or craftsmen organized to compose and perform poetry and music. These flourished in the 15th and 16th centuries. [C19: German: master singer]

Meit·ner (*German* 'maɪtnər) *n.* **Li·se** ('liːzə). 1878–1968, Austrian nuclear physicist. With Hahn, she discovered protactinium (1918), and they demonstrated with F. Strassmann the fission of uranium.

Mé+ji+co ('mexiko) *n.* the Spanish name for **Mexico.**

Mek+ka ('mɛkə) *n.* a variant spelling of **Mecca.**

Mek+nès (mɛk'nɛs) *n.* a city in N central Morocco, in the Middle Atlas Mountains: noted for the making of carpets. Pop.: 248 369 (1971).

Me+kong (ˌmiː'kɒŋ) *n.* a river in SE Asia, rising in SW China in Tsinghai province: flows southeast forming the border between Laos and Burma, and part of the border between Laos and Thailand, then continues south across Cambodia and Vietnam to the South China Sea by an extensive delta, one of the greatest rice-growing areas in Asia. Length: about 4025 km (2500 miles).

mel (mɛl) *n. Pharmacol.* a pure form of honey used in pharmaceutical products. [from Latin]

me·la·leu·ca (ˌmɛləˈluːkə) *n.* any shrub or tree of the mostly Australian myrtaceous genus *Melaleuca,* found in sandy or swampy regions.

mel·a·mine (ˈmɛləˌmiːn) *n.* **1.** a colourless crystalline compound used in making synthetic resins; 2,4,6-triamino-1,3,5-triazine. Formula: $C_3H_6N_6$. **2.** melamine resin or a material made from this resin. [C19: from German *Melamin,* from *Melam* distillate of ammonium thiocyanate, with *-am* representing *ammonia*]

mel·a·mine res·in *n.* a thermosetting amino resin, stable to heat and light, produced from melamine and used for moulded products, adhesives, and surface coatings.

mel·an·cho·li·a (ˌmɛlənˈkəʊlɪə) *n. Psychiatry.* a mental state characterized by depression and irrational fears. —**ˌmel·an·ˈcho·li·ˌac** *adj., n.*

mel·an·chol·ic (ˌmɛlənˈkɒlɪk) *adj.* **1.** relating to or suffering from melancholy or melancholia. ~*n.* **2.** a person who suffers from melancholia. —**ˌmel·an·ˈchol·i·cal·ly** *adv.*

mel·an·chol·y (ˈmɛlənkəlɪ) *n., pl.* **·chol·ies.** **1.** a constitutional tendency to gloominess or depression. **2.** a sad thoughtful state of mind; pensiveness. **3.** *Archaic.* **a.** a gloomy character, thought to be caused by too much black bile. **b.** one of the four bodily humours; black bile. See **humour** (sense 8). ~*adj.* **4.** characterized by, causing, or expressing sadness, dejection, etc. [C14: via Old French from Late Latin *melancholia,* from Greek *melankholia,* from *melas* black + *kholē* bile] —**mel·an·chol·i·ly** (ˈmɛlənˌkɒlɪlɪ) *adv.* —**ˈmel·an·ˌchol·i·ness** *n.*

Me·lanch·thon (məˈlæŋkθən; *German* meˈlançtɔn) *n.* **Phil·ipp** (ˈfiːlɪp). original surname *Schwarzerd.* 1497–1560, German Protestant reformer. His *Loci Communes* (1521) was the first systematic presentation of Protestant theology and in the Augsburg Confession (1530) he stated the faith of the Lutheran churches. He also reformed the German educational system.

Mel·a·ne·si·a (ˌmɛləˈniːzɪə) *n.* one of the three divisions of islands in the Pacific (the others being Micronesia and Polynesia); the SW division of Oceania: includes Fiji, New Caledonia, New Hebrides, the Bismarck Archipelago, and the Louisiade, Solomon, Santa Cruz, and Loyalty Islands, which all lie northeast of Australia.

Mel·a·ne·si·an (ˌmɛləˈniːzɪən) *adj.* **1.** of or relating to Melanesia, its people, or their languages. ~*n.* **2.** a native or inhabitant of Melanesia: generally Negroid with frizzy hair and small stature. **3.** a group or branch of languages spoken in Melanesia, belonging to the Malayo-Polynesian family. **4.** See also **Neo-Melanesian.**

mé·lange *French.* (meˈlɑ̃ːʒ) *n.* a mixture; confusion. [C17: from *mêler* to mix. See MEDLEY]

me·lan·ic (məˈlænɪk) *adj.* relating to melanism or melanosis.

mel·a·nin (ˈmɛlənɪn) *n.* any of a group of black or dark brown pigments present in the hair, skin, and eyes of man and animals: produced in excess in certain skin diseases and in melanomas.

mel·a·nism (ˈmɛləˌnɪzəm) *n.* **1.** the condition in man and animals of having dark-coloured or black skin, feathers, etc. **Industrial melanism** is the occurrence of dark varieties of animals, esp. moths, in smoke-blackened industrial regions, in which they are well camouflaged. **2.** another name for **melanosis.** —**ˌmel·a·ˈnis·tic** *adj.*

mel·a·nite (ˈmɛləˌnaɪt) *n.* a black variety of andradite garnet.

mel·a·no- *or before a vowel* **mel·an-** *combining form.* black or dark: *melanin; melanism; melanocyte; melanoma.* [from Greek *melas* black]

Mel·a·noch·ro·i (ˌmɛləˈnɒkrəʊˌaɪ) *pl. n.* a postulated subdivision of the Caucasoid race, characterized by dark hair and pale complexion. [C19: New Latin (coined by T. H. Huxley), from Greek, from *melas* dark + *ōchros* pale] —**Mel·a·noch·roid** (ˌmɛləˈnɒkrɔɪd) *adj.*

mel·a·no·cyte (ˈmɛlənəʊˌsaɪt) *n. Anatomy, zoology.* a cell, usually in the epidermis, that contains melanin.

mel·a·noid (ˈmɛləˌnɔɪd) *adj.* **1.** resembling melanin; dark coloured. **2.** characterized by or resembling melanosis.

mel·a·no·ma (ˌmɛləˈnəʊmə) *n., pl.* **·mas** *or* **·ma·ta** (-mətə). *Pathol.* a tumour composed of darkly pigmented cells.

mel·a·no·sis (ˌmɛləˈnəʊsɪs) *or* **mel·a·nism** (ˈmɛləˌnɪzəm) *n. Pathol.* a skin condition characterized by excessive deposits of melanin. —**mel·a·not·ic** (ˌmɛləˈnɒtɪk) *adj.*

mel·a·nous (ˈmɛlənəs) *adj.* having a dark complexion and black hair. —**mel·a·nos·i·ty** (ˌmɛləˈnɒsɪtɪ) *n.*

mel·a·phyre (ˈmɛləˌfaɪə) *n. Geology, obsolete.* a type of weathered amygdaloidal basalt or andesite. [C19: via French from Greek *melas* black + (*por*)*phura* purple]

mel·a·to·nin (ˌmɛləˈtəʊnɪn) *n.* the hormone-like secretion of the pineal gland, causing skin colour changes in some animals and thought to be involved in reproductive function. [C20: probably from MELA(NOCYTE) + (SERO)TONIN]

Mel·ba (ˈmɛlbə) *n.* **1.** Dame **Nel·lie,** stage name of *Helen Porter Mitchell.* 1861–1931, Australian operatic soprano. **2. do a Melba.** *Austral. slang.* to make repeated farewell appearances.

Mel·ba sauce *n.* a sweet sauce made from fresh raspberries and served with peach melba, fruit sundaes, etc. [C20: named after Dame Nellie MELBA]

Mel·ba toast *n.* very thin crisp toast. [C20: named after Dame Nellie MELBA]

Mel·bourne[1] (ˈmɛlbən) *n.* a port in SE Australia, capital of Victoria, on Port Phillip Bay: the second largest city in the country; settled in 1835 and developed rapidly with the discovery of rich goldfields in 1851; three universities. Pop.: 2 661 400 (1975 est.). —**Mel·bur·ni·an** (mɛlˈbɜːnɪən) *n., adj.*

Mel·bourne[2] (ˈmɛlbən) *n.* **Wil·liam Lamb,** 2nd Viscount. 1779–1848; Whig prime minister (1834; 1835–41). He was the chief political adviser to the young Queen Victoria.

Mel·chi·or (ˈmɛlkɪˌɔː) *n.* **1.** (in Christian tradition) one of the Magi, the others being Balthazar and Caspar. **2. Lau·ritz** (ˈlaʊrɪts). 1890–1973, U.S. operatic tenor, born in Denmark.

Mel·chite (ˈmɛlkaɪt) *Eastern Churches.* ~*adj.* **1.** of or relating to the Uniat Greek Catholic Church in Syria, Egypt, and Israel. ~*n.* **2.** a member of this Church. [C17: from Church Latin *Melchīta,* from Medieval Greek *Melkhītes,* literally: royalist, from Syriac *malkā* king]

Mel·chiz·e·dek (mɛlˈkɪzəˌdɛk) *n. Old Testament.* the priest-king of Salem who blessed Abraham (Genesis 14:18-19) and was taken as a prototype of the Christian priest (Hebrews 7). Douay spelling: **Mel·chis·e·dech.**

meld[1] (mɛld) *vb.* **1.** (in some card games) to declare or lay down (cards), which then score points. ~*n.* **2.** the act of melding. **3.** a set of cards for melding. [C19: from German *melden* to announce; related to Old English *meldian*]

meld[2] (mɛld) *vb.* to blend or become blended; combine. [C20: blend of MELT + WELD[1]]

Mel·e·a·ger (ˌmɛlɪˈeɪgə) *n. Greek myth.* one of the Argonauts, slayer of the Calydonian boar.

me·lee *or* **mê·lée** (ˈmɛleɪ) *n.* a noisy riotous fight or brawl; a lively debate. [C17: from French *mêlée.* See MEDLEY]

me·li·a·ce·ous (ˌmiːlɪˈeɪʃɪəs) *adj.* of, relating to, or belonging to the *Meliaceae,* a family of tropical and subtropical trees, including mahogany, some of which yield valuable timber. [C19: from New Latin *Melia* type genus, from Greek: ash]

mel·ic (ˈmɛlɪk) *adj.* (of poetry, esp. ancient Greek lyric poems) intended to be sung. [C17: via Latin from Greek *melikos,* from *melos* song]

Mé·liès (*French* meˈljɛs) *n.* **Georges** (ʒɔrʒ). 1861–1938, French pioneer film director.

Me·lil·la (*French* meliˈja) *n.* the chief town of a Spanish enclave in Morocco, on the Mediterranean coast: founded by the Phoenicians; exports iron ore. Pop.: 79 056 (1970).

mel·i·lot (ˈmɛlɪˌlɒt) *n.* any papilionaceous plant of the Old World genus *Meliotus,* having narrow clusters of small white or yellow fragrant flowers. Also called: **sweet clover.** [C15: via Old French from Latin *melilōtos,* from Greek: sweet clover, from *meli* honey + *lōtos* LOTUS]

mel·i·nite (ˈmɛlɪˌnaɪt) *n.* a high explosive made from picric acid. [C19: via French from Greek *mēlinos* (colour) of a quince, from *mēlon* fruit, quince]

me·li·o·rate (ˈmiːlɪəˌreɪt) *vb.* a variant of **ameliorate.** —**ˈme·li·o·ra·ble** *adj.* —**me·li·o·ra·tive** (ˈmiːlɪərətɪv) *adj., n.* —**ˈme·li·o·ˌra·tor** *n.*

me·li·o·ra·tion (ˌmiːlɪəˈreɪʃən) *n.* the act or an instance of improving or the state of being improved.

me·li·o·rism (ˈmiːlɪəˌrɪzəm) *n.* the notion that the world can be improved by human effort. [C19: from Latin *melior* better] —**ˈme·li·o·rist** *adj., n.* —**ˌme·li·o·ˈris·tic** *adj.*

me·lis·ma (mɪˈlɪzmə) *n., pl.* **·ma·ta** *or* **·mas.** *Music.* an expressive vocal phrase or passage consisting of several notes sung to one syllable. [C19: from Greek: melody] —**mel·is·mat·ic** (ˌmɛlɪzˈmætɪk) *adj.*

Me·li·to·pol (*Russian* mɪlɪˈtɔpəlj) *n.* a city in the SW Soviet Union, in the SE Ukrainian SSR. Pop.: 152 000 (1975 est.).

mel·lif·er·ous (mɪˈlɪfərəs) *or* **mel·lif·ic** (mɪˈlɪfɪk) *adj.* forming or producing honey. [C17: from Latin *mellifer,* from *mel* honey + *ferre* to bear]

mel·lif·lu·ous (mɪˈlɪfluəs) *or* **mel·lif·lu·ent** *adj.* (of sounds or utterances) smooth or honeyed; sweet. [C15: from Late Latin *mellifluus* flowing with honey, from Latin *mel* honey + *fluere* to flow] —**mel·ˈlif·lu·ous·ly** *or* **mel·ˈlif·lu·ent·ly** *adv.* —**mel·ˈlif·lu·ous·ness** *or* **mel·ˈlif·lu·ence** *n.*

mel·lo·phone (ˈmɛləˌfəʊn) *n. Music.* a brass band instrument similar in tone to a French horn. [C20: from MELLOW + -PHONE]

mel·low (ˈmɛləʊ) *adj.* **1.** (esp. of fruits) full-flavoured; sweet; ripe. **2.** (esp. of wines) well-matured. **3.** (esp. of colours or sounds) soft or rich. **4.** kind-hearted, esp. through maturity or old age. **5.** genial, as through the effects of alcohol. **6.** (of soil) soft and loamy. ~*vb.* **7.** to make or become mellow; soften; mature. [C15: perhaps from Old English *meru* soft (as through ripeness)] —**ˈmel·low·ly** *adv.* —**ˈmel·low·ness** *n.*

me·lo·de·on *or* **me·lo·di·on** (mɪˈləʊdɪən) *n. Music.* **1.** a type of small accordion. **2.** a type of keyboard instrument similar to the harmonium. [C19: from German, from *Melodie* melody]

me·lod·ic (mɪˈlɒdɪk) *adj.* **1.** of or relating to melody. **2.** of or relating to a part in a piece of music. **3.** tuneful or melodious. —**me·ˈlod·i·cal·ly** *adv.*

me·lod·ic mi·nor scale *n. Music.* a minor scale modified from the natural by the sharpening of the sixth and seventh when taken in ascending order and the restoration of their original pitches when taken in descending order. See **minor** (sense 4a.). Compare **harmonic minor scale.**

me·lo·di·ous (mɪˈləʊdɪəs) *adj.* **1.** having a tune that is pleasant to the ear. **2.** of or relating to melody; melodic. —**me·ˈlo·di·ous·ly** *adv.* —**me·ˈlo·di·ous·ness** *n.*

mel·o·dist (ˈmɛlədɪst) *n.* **1.** a composer of melodies. **2.** a singer.

mel·o·dize *or* **mel·o·dise** (ˈmɛləˌdaɪz) *vb.* **1.** (*tr.*) to provide with a melody. **2.** (*tr.*) to make melodious. **3.** (*intr.*) to sing or play melodies. —**ˈmel·o·ˌdiz·er** *or* **ˈmel·o·ˌdis·er** *n.*

mel·o·dra·ma (ˈmɛləˌdrɑːmə) *n.* **1.** a play, film, etc., characterized by extravagant action and emotion. **2.** (formerly) a romantic drama characterized by sensational incident, music, and song. **3.** overdramatic emotion or behaviour. **4.** a poem or part of a play or opera spoken to a musical accompaniment. [C19: from French *mélodrame,* from Greek *melos* song + *drame* DRAMA] —**mel·o+dram·a+tist** (ˌmɛlə'dræmətɪst) *n.* —**mel·o+dra+mat+ic** (ˌmɛlədrə'mætɪk) *adj.* —ˌ**mel·o+dra+'mat·i·cal+ly** *adv.*

mel·o+dram·a+tize *or* **mel·o+dram·a+tise** (ˌmɛləʊ'dræməˌtaɪz) *vb.* (*tr.*) to make melodramatic.

mel·o+dy ('mɛlədɪ) *n., pl.* **+dies. 1.** *Music.* **a.** a succession of notes forming a distinctive sequence; tune. **b.** the horizontally represented aspect of the structure of a piece of music. Compare **harmony** (sense 4b.). **2.** sounds that are pleasant because of tone or arrangement, esp. words of poetry. [C13: from Old French, from Late Latin *melōdia,* from Greek *melōidia* singing, from *melos* song + *-ōidia,* from *aoidein* to sing]

mel+oid ('mɛlɔɪd) *n.* **1.** any long-legged beetle of the family *Meloidae,* which includes the blister beetles and oil beetles. ~*adj.* **2.** of, relating to, or belonging to the *Meloidae.* [C19: from New Latin *Meloē* name of genus]

mel+on ('mɛlən) *n.* **1.** any of several varieties of two cucurbitaceous vines (see **muskmelon, watermelon**), cultivated for their edible fruit. **2.** the fruit of any of these plants, which has a hard rind and juicy flesh. **3. cut a melon.** *U.S. slang.* to declare an abnormally high dividend to shareholders. [C14: via Old French from Late Latin *mēlo,* shortened form of *mēlopepō,* from Greek *mēlopepōn,* from *mēlon* apple + *pepōn* gourd]

Me+los ('mi:lɒs) *n.* an island in the SW Aegean Sea, in the Cyclades: of volcanic origin, with hot springs; centre of early Aegean civilization, where the Venus de Milo was found. Pop.: 8613 (1971). Area: 132 sq. km (51 sq. miles). Modern Greek name: **Mílos.**

Mel·pom·e·ne (mɛl'pɒmɪnɪ) *n. Greek myth.* the Muse of tragedy.

melt (mɛlt) *vb.* **melts, melt+ing, melt+ed; melt+ed** *or* **mol+ten. 1.** to liquefy (a solid) or (of a solid) to become liquefied, as a result of the action of heat. **2.** to become or make liquid; dissolve: *cakes that melt in the mouth.* **3.** (often foll. by *away*) to disappear; fade. **4.** (foll. by *down*) to melt (metal scrap) for reuse. **5.** (often foll. by *into*) to blend or cause to blend gradually. **6.** to make or become emotional or sentimental; soften. ~*n.* **7.** the act or process of melting. **8.** something melted or an amount melted. [Old English *meltan* to digest; related to Old Norse *melta* to malt (beer), digest, Greek *meldein* to melt] —'**melt+a·ble** *adj.* —ˌ**melt+a·'bil+i·ty** *n.* —'**melt+er** *n.* —'**melt+ing+ly** *adv.* —'**melt+ing+ness** *n.*

melt+age ('mɛltɪdʒ) *n.* the process or result of melting or the amount melted: *rapid meltage of ice.*

melt+ing point *n.* the temperature at which a solid turns into a liquid. It is equal to the freezing point.

melt+ing pot *n.* **1.** a pot in which metals or other substances are melted, esp. in order to mix them. **2.** an area in which many races, ideas, etc., are mixed.

mel+ton ('mɛltən) *n.* a heavy smooth woollen fabric with a short nap, used for coats, etc. Also called: **melton cloth.** [C19: from *Melton Mowbray,* Leicestershire, a former centre for making this cloth]

melt+wa·ter ('mɛltˌwɔ:tə) *n.* melted snow or ice.

me+lun+geon (mə'lʌndʒən) *n.* any of a dark-skinned group of people of the Appalachians in E Tennessee, of mixed Indian, White, and Negro ancestry. [C20: of unknown origin]

Mel·ville ('mɛlvɪl) *n.* **Her·man.** 1819–91, U.S. novelist and short-story writer. Among his works, *Moby Dick* (1851) and *Billy Budd* (1924) are outstanding.

Mel+ville Is+land *n.* **1.** an island in the Arctic Ocean, north of Victoria Island: administratively part of the Northwest Territories of Canada. Area: 41 865 sq. km (16 164 sq. miles). **2.** an island in the Arafura Sea, off the N central coast of Australia, separated from the mainland by Clarence Strait. Area: 6216 sq. km (2400 sq. miles).

Mel+ville Pen+in+su+la *n.* a peninsula of N Canada, in the Northwest Territories, between the Gulf of Boothia and Foxe Basin.

mem (mɛm) *n.* the 13th letter in the Hebrew alphabet (מ or, at the end of a word, ם), transliterated as *m.* [Hebrew, literally: water]

mem. *abbrev. for:* **1.** member. **2.** memoir. **3.** memorandum. **4.** memorial.

mem+ber ('mɛmbə) *n.* **1.** a person who belongs to a club, political party, etc. **2.** any individual plant or animal in a taxonomic group: *a member of the species.* **3.** any part of an animal body, such as a limb. **4.** another word for **penis. 5.** any part of a plant, such as a petal, root, etc. **6.** *Maths.* any individual object belonging to a set or logical class. **7.** a distinct part of a whole, such as a proposition in a syllogism. **8.** a component part of a building or construction. [C13: from Latin *membrum* limb, part] —'**mem+ber+less** *adj.*

Mem+ber ('mɛmbə) *n.* (*sometimes not cap.*) **1.** short for **Member of Parliament. 2.** short for **Member of Congress. 3.** a member of some other legislative body.

Mem+ber of Par+lia+ment *n.* a member of the House of Commons or similar legislative body, as in many Commonwealth countries. Abbrev.: **MP**

mem+ber+ship ('mɛmbəˌʃɪp) *n.* **1.** the members of an organization collectively. **2.** the state of being a member.

mem+brane ('mɛmbreɪn) *n.* **1.** any thin pliable sheet of material. **2.** a pliable sheetlike usually fibrous tissue that covers, lines, or connects plant and animal organs or cells. **3.** a skin of parchment forming part of a roll. [C16: from Latin *membrāna* skin covering a part of the body, from *membrum* MEMBER]

mem+brane bone *n.* any bone that develops within membranous tissue, such as the clavicle and bones of the skull, without cartilage formation. Compare **cartilage bone.**

mem+bra+nous, mem+brane+ous ('mɛmbrənəs, mɛm'breɪnəs), *or* **mem+bra+na+ceous** (ˌmɛmbrə'neɪʃəs) *adj.* of or relating to a membrane. —'**mem+bra+nous+ly** *adv.*

Me+mel ('me:məl) *n.* **1.** the German name for **Klaipeda. 2.** the lower course of the Neman River.

me+men+to (mɪ'mɛntəʊ) *n., pl.* **+tos** *or* **+toes. 1.** something that reminds one of past events; souvenir. **2.** *R.C. Church.* either of two prayers occurring during the Mass. [C15: from Latin, imperative of *meminisse* to remember]

me+men+to mo·ri ('mɔ:ri:) *n.* an object, such as a skull, intended to remind people of the inevitability of death. [C16: Latin: remember you must die]

Mem·ling ('mɛmlɪŋ) *or* **Mem·linc** ('mɛmlɪŋk) *n.* **Hans** (hɑns). ?1430–94, Flemish painter of religious works and portraits.

Mem·non ('mɛmnɒn) *n.* **1.** *Greek myth.* a king of Ethiopia, son of Eos: slain by Achilles in the Trojan War. **2.** a colossal statue of Amenhotep III at Thebes in ancient Egypt, which emitted a sound thought by the Greeks to be the voice of Memnon. —**Mem+no·ni·an** (mɛm'nəʊnɪən) *adj.*

mem·o ('mɛməʊ, 'mi:məʊ) *n., pl.* **mem·os.** short for **memorandum.**

mem+oir ('mɛmwɑ:) *n.* **1.** a biography or historical account, esp. one based on personal knowledge. **2.** an essay or monograph, as on a specialized topic. **3.** *Obsolete.* a memorandum. [C16: from French, from Latin *memoria* MEMORY] —'**mem+oir+ist** *n.*

mem+oirs ('mɛmwɑ:z) *pl. n.* **1.** a collection of reminiscences about a period, series of events, etc., written from personal experience or special sources. **2.** an autobiographical record. **3.** a collection or record, as of transactions of a society, etc.

mem·o+ra+bil·i·a (ˌmɛmərə'bɪlɪə) *pl. n., sing.* **+rab·i+le** (-'ræbɪlɪ). memorable events or things. [C17: from Latin, from *memorābilis* MEMORABLE]

mem·o+ra·ble ('mɛmərəbᵊl, 'mɛmrə-) *adj.* worth remembering or easily remembered; noteworthy. [C15: from Latin *memorābilis,* from *memorāre* to recall, from *memor* mindful] —ˌ**mem·o+ra·'bil·i·ty** *or* '**mem·o+ra·ble+ness** *n.* —'**mem·o+ra·bly** *adv.*

mem·o+ran+dum (ˌmɛmə'rændəm) *n., pl.* **+dums** *or* **+da** (-də). **1.** a written statement, record, or communication. **2.** a note of things to be remembered. **3.** an informal diplomatic communication, often unsigned: often summarising the point of view of a government. **4.** *Law.* a short written summary of the terms of a transaction. ~Often (esp. for senses 1 and 2) shortened to **memo.** [C15: from Latin: (something) to be remembered]

me+mo+ri·al (mɪ'mɔ:rɪəl) *adj.* **1.** serving to preserve the memory of the dead or a past event. **2.** of or involving memory. ~*n.* **3.** something serving as a remembrance. **4.** a written statement of facts submitted to a government, authority, etc., in conjunction with a petition. **5.** an informal diplomatic paper. [C14: from Late Latin *memoriāle* a reminder, neuter sing. of *memoriālis* belonging to remembrance] —**me+'mo+ri+al+ly** *adv.*

Me+mo+ri·al Day *n.* a holiday in the United States, May 30th in most states, commemorating the servicemen killed in all American wars.

me+mo+ri+al+ist (mɪ'mɔ:rɪəlɪst) *n.* **1.** a person who writes or presents a memorial. **2.** a writer of a memoir or memoirs.

me+mo+ri+al+ize *or* **me+mo+ri·al+ise** (mɪ'mɔ:rɪəˌlaɪz) *vb.* (*tr.*) **1.** to honour or commemorate. **2.** to present or address a memorial to. —**me+ˌmo+ri+al·i+'za+tion** *or* **me+ˌmo+ri+al·i+'sa+tion** *n.* —**me+'mo+ri+al+ˌiz+er** *or* **me+'mo+ri+al+ˌis+er** *n.*

me+mo+ri·a tech+ni+ca (mɪ'mɔ:rɪə 'tɛknɪkə) *n.* a method or device for assisting the memory. [C18: New Latin: artificial memory]

mem·o+rize *or* **mem·o+rise** ('mɛməˌraɪz) *vb.* (*tr.*) to commit to memory; learn so as to remember. —'**mem·o+ˌriz+a·ble** *or* '**mem·o+ˌris+a·ble** *adj.* —ˌ**mem·o+ri+'za+tion** *or* ˌ**mem·o+ri+'sa+tion** *n.* —'**mem·o+ˌriz+er** *or* '**mem·o+ˌris+er** *n.*

mem·o+ry ('mɛmərɪ) *n., pl.* **+ries. 1.** the ability of the brain to store and recall past sensations, thoughts, knowledge, etc.: *he can do it from memory.* **2.** the sum of everything retained by the mind. **3.** a particular recollection of an event, person, etc. **4.** the time over which recollection extends: *within his memory.* **5.** commemoration or remembrance: *in memory of our leader.* **6.** the state of being remembered, as after death. **7.** Also called: **memory bank, core store, main store, store.** a part of a computer in which information is stored for immediate use by the central processing unit. See also **virtual storage. 8.** the tendency for a material, system, etc., to show effects that depend on its past treatment or history. **9.** the ability of a material, etc., to return to a former state after a constraint has been removed. [C14: from Old French *memorie,* from Latin *memoria,* from *memor* mindful]

mem·o+ry bank *n.* another name for **data bank.**

mem·o+ry span *n. Psychol.* the capacity of short-term memory.

mem·o+ry trace *n. Psychol.* the hypothetical structural alteration in brain cells following learning. See also **engram.**

Mem+phi·an ('mɛmfɪən) *adj.* **1.** of or relating to ancient Memphis or its inhabitants. ~*n.* **2.** an inhabitant or native of ancient Memphis.

Mem+phis ('mɛmfɪs) *n.* **1.** a port in SW Tennessee, on the Mississippi River: the largest city in the state; a major cotton and timber market; Memphis State University (1909). Pop.: 658 868 (1973 est.). **2.** a ruined city in N Egypt, the ancient centre of Lower Egypt, on the Nile: administrative and artistic centre, sacred to the worship of Ptah.

Mem·phre·ma·gog (ˌmɛmfriːˈmeɪgɒg) *n.* **Lake.** a lake on the border between the U.S. and Canada, in N Vermont and S Quebec. Length: about 43 km (27 miles). Width: up to 6 km (4 miles).

mem·sa·hib (ˈmɛmˌsɑːɪb, -hɪb) *n.* (formerly in India) a term of respect used of a European married woman. [C19: from MA'AM + SAHIB]

men (mɛn) *n.* the plural of **man.**

men·ace (ˈmɛnɪs) *vb.* **1.** to threaten with violence, danger, etc. ~*n.* **2.** *Literary.* a threat or the act of threatening. **3.** something menacing; a source of danger. **4.** *Informal.* a nuisance. [C13: ultimately related to Latin *minax* threatening, from *minārī* to threaten] —**ˈmen·ac·er** *n.* —**ˈmen·ac·ing·ly** *adv.*

men·a·di·one (ˌmɛnəˈdaɪəʊn) *n.* a yellow crystalline compound used in fungicides and as an additive to animal feeds. Also called: **vitamin K_3.** Formula: $C_{11}H_8O_2$. [C20: from ME(THYL) + NA(PHTHA) + DI- + -ONE]

Me·na·do (mɛˈnɑːdəʊ) *or* **Ma·na·do** *n.* a port in NE Indonesia, on NE Sulawesi: founded by the Dutch in 1657. Pop.: 169 684 (1971).

mé·nage (meɪˈnɑːʒ; *French* meˈnaːʒ) *n.* the persons of a household. [C17: from French, from Vulgar Latin *mansiōnāticum* (unattested) household; see MANSION]

mé·nage à trois *French.* (menaːʒ a ˈtrwa) *n., pl.* ***mé·nages à trois*** (menaːʒ a ˈtrwa). a sexual arrangement involving a married couple and the lover of one of them. [literally: household of three]

me·nag·er·ie (mɪˈnædʒərɪ) *n.* **1.** a collection of wild animals kept for exhibition. **2.** the place where such animals are housed. [C18: from French: household management, which formerly included care of domestic animals. See MÉNAGE]

Men·ai Strait (ˈmɛnaɪ) *n.* a channel of the Irish Sea between the island of Anglesey and the mainland of NW Wales: famous suspension bridge (1819–26) designed by Thomas Telford and tubular bridge (1846–50) by Robert Stephenson. Length: 24 km (15 miles). Width: up to 3 km (2 miles).

Me·nam (miːˈnæm) *n.* another name for the **Chao Phraya.**

Me·nan·der (məˈnændə) *n.* ?342–?292 B.C., Greek comic dramatist. The *Dyskolos* is his only complete extant comedy but others survive in adaptations by Terence and Plautus.

men·a·qui·none (ˌmɛnəkwɪˈnəʊn) *n.* a form of vitamin K synthesized by bacteria in the intestine or in putrefying organic matter. Also called: **vitamin K_2.** [C20: from *me(thyl)-na(phtho)quinone*]

men·ar·che (mɛˈnɑːkɪ) *n.* the first occurrence of menstruation in a woman's life. [C20: New Latin, from Greek *mēn* month + *arkhē* beginning] —**men·ˈar·che·al** *or* **men·ˈar·chi·al** *adj.*

Men·ci·us (ˈmɛnʃɪəs, -ʃəs) *n.* Chinese name *Meng-tzu.* ?372–?289 B.C., Chinese philosopher, who propounded the ethical system of Confucius.

Menck·en (ˈmɛŋkən) *n.* **H(enry) L(ouis).** 1880–1956, U.S. journalist and literary critic, noted for *The American Language* (1919): editor of the *Smart Set* and the *American Mercury,* which he founded (1924).

mend (mɛnd) *vb.* **1.** (*tr.*) to repair (something broken or unserviceable). **2.** to improve or undergo improvement; reform (often in the phrase **mend one's ways**). **3.** (*intr.*) to heal or recover. **4.** (of conditions) to improve; become better. ~*n.* **5.** the act of repairing. **6.** a mended area, esp. on a garment. **7. on the mend.** becoming better, esp. in health. [C12: shortened from AMEND] —**ˈmend·a·ble** *adj.* —**ˈmend·er** *n.*

men·dac·i·ty (mɛnˈdæsɪtɪ) *n., pl.* **·ties. 1.** the tendency to be untruthful. **2.** a falsehood. [C17: from Late Latin *mendācitās,* from Latin *mendāx* untruthful] —**men·da·cious** (mɛnˈdeɪʃəs) *adj.* —**men·ˈda·cious·ly** *adv.* —**menˈda·cious·ness** *n.*

Men·del (ˈmɛndəl) *n.* **Greg·or Jo·hann** (ˈgreːgɔr ˈjoːhan). 1822–84, Austrian monk and botanist; founder of the science of genetics. He developed his theory of organic inheritance from his experiments on the hybridization of green peas. His findings were published (1865) but remained unrecognized until 1900. See **Mendel's laws.**

men·de·le·vi·um (ˌmɛndɪˈliːvɪəm) *n.* a transuranic element artificially produced by bombardment of einsteinium. Symbol: Md; atomic no.: 101; half-life of most stable isotope, ^{258}Md: 60 days (approx.). [C20: named after D. I. MENDELEYEV]

Men·de·le·yev *or* **Men·de·le·ev** (*Russian* mɪndɪˈljejɪf) *n.* **Dmi·tri I·va·no·vich** (ˈdmitrij iˈvanəvitʃ). 1834–1907, Russian chemist. He devised the first form of the periodic table of the chemical elements (1869).

Men·de·li·an (mɛnˈdiːlɪən) *adj.* of or relating to Mendel's laws.

Men·del·ism (ˈmɛndəˌlɪzəm) *or* **Men·de·li·an·ism** (mɛnˈdiːlɪəˌnɪzəm) *n.* the science of heredity based on Mendel's laws with some modifications in the light of more recent knowledge.

Men·del's laws *pl. n.* the principles of heredity proposed by Gregor Mendel. The **Law of Segregation** states that every somatic cell of an individual carries a pair of hereditary units for each character: the pairs separate during meiosis so that each gamete carries only one unit of each pair. The **Law of Independent Assortment** states that the separation of the units of each pair is not influenced by that of any other pair.

Men·dels·sohn (ˈmɛndəlsən; *German* ˈmɛndəlˌzoːn) *n.* **1. Fe·lix** (ˈfeːlɪks), full name *Jacob Ludwig Felix Mendelssohn-Bartholdy.* 1809–47, German romantic composer. His works include the overtures *A Midsummer Night's Dream* (1826) and *Fingal's Cave* (1832), five symphonies, the oratorio *Elijah* (1846), piano pieces and songs. He was instrumental in the revival of the music of J. S. Bach in the 19th century. **2.** his grandfather, **Mo·ses** (ˈmoːzəs). 1729–86, German Jewish philosopher. His best-known work is *Jerusalem* (1783), in which he defends Judaism and appeals for religious toleration.

Men·de·res (ˌmɛndɛˈrɛs) *n.* **1.** a river in SW Turkey flowing southwest, then west to the Aegean. Length: about 386 km (240 miles). Ancient name: **Maeander. 2.** a river in NW Turkey flowing west and northwest to the Dardanelles. Length: 104 km (65 miles). Ancient name: **Scamander.**

Men·dès-France (*French* mɛ̃dɛs ˈfrɑ̃ːs) *n.* **Pierre** (pjɛːr). born 1907, French statesman; prime minister (1954-55). He concluded the war in Indochina and granted independence to Tunisia.

men·di·cant (ˈmɛndɪkənt) *adj.* **1.** begging. **2.** (of a member of a religious order) dependent on alms for sustenance: *mendicant friars.* **3.** characteristic of a beggar. ~*n.* **4.** a mendicant friar. **5.** a less common word for **beggar.** [C16: from Latin *mendīcāre* to beg, from *mendīcus* beggar, from *mendus* flaw] —**ˈmen·di·can·cy** *or* **men·dic·i·ty** (mɛnˈdɪsɪtɪ) *n.*

mend·ing (ˈmɛndɪŋ) *n.* something to be mended, esp. clothes.

Men·dips (ˈmɛndɪps) *pl. n.* a range of limestone hills in SW England, in N Somerset: includes the Cheddar Gorge and numerous caves. Highest point: 325 m (1068 ft.). Also called: **Men·dip Hills.**

Men·do·za[1] (mɛnˈdəʊzə; *Spanish* menˈdoθa) *n.* a city in W central Argentina, in the foothills of the Sierra de los Paramillos: largely destroyed by an earthquake in 1861; commercial centre of an intensively cultivated irrigated region; University of Cuyo (1939). Pop.: 470 896 (1970).

Men·do·za[2] (*Spanish* menˈdoθa) *n.* **Ped·ro de** (ˈpeðro ðe). died 1537, Spanish soldier and explorer; founder of Buenos Aires (1536).

Men·e·la·us (ˌmɛnɪˈleɪəs) *n. Greek myth.* a king of Sparta and the brother of Agamemnon. He was the husband of Helen, whose abduction led to the Trojan War.

Men·e·lik II (ˈmɛnɪlɪk) *n.* 1844–1913, emperor of Abyssinia (1889–1910). He defeated the Italians at Aduwa (1896), maintaining the independence of Abyssinia in an era of European expansion in Africa.

me·ne, me·ne, tek·el, u·phar·sin (ˈmiːniː ˈmiːniː ˈtɛkəl juːˈfɑːsɪn) *n. Old Testament.* the words that appeared on the wall during Belshazzar's Feast (Daniel 5:25), interpreted by Daniel to mean that God had doomed the kingdom of Belshazzar. [Aramaic: numbered, numbered, weighed, divided]

Me·nes (ˈmiːniːz) *n.* the first king of the first dynasty of Egypt (?3100 B.C.). He is said to have united Upper and Lower Egypt and founded Memphis.

men·folk (ˈmɛnˌfəʊk) *or U.S.* (*sometimes*) **men·folks** *pl. n.* men collectively, esp. the men of a particular family.

Men·gel·berg (ˈmɛŋgəlˌbɜːg; *Dutch* ˈmɛŋəlˌbɛrx) *n.* **(Josef) Wil·lem** (ˈwɪləm). 1871–1951, Dutch orchestral conductor, noted for his performances of the music of Mahler.

Men·gis·tu Hai·le Ma·ri·am (mɛŋˈgɪstuː ˈhaɪlɪ ˈmɑːrɪəm) *n.* born 1937, Ethiopian soldier and statesman; head of state since 1977.

Meng·tze (ˈmɛŋˈtseɪ) *n.* the Chinese name of **Mencius.**

men·ha·den (mɛnˈheɪdən) *n., pl.* **·den.** a marine North American fish, *Brevoortia tyrannus:* source of fish meal, fertilizer, and oil: family *Clupeidae* (herrings, etc.). [C18: from Algonquian; probably related to Narragansett *munnawhatteaúg* fertilizer, menhaden]

men·hir (ˈmɛnhɪə) *n.* a single standing stone, often carved, dating from the middle Bronze Age in England and from the late Neolithic Age in W Europe. [C19: from Breton *men* stone + *hir* long]

me·ni·al (ˈmiːnɪəl) *adj.* **1.** consisting of or occupied with work requiring little skill, esp. domestic duties such as cleaning. **2.** of, involving, or befitting servants. **3.** servile. ~*n.* **4.** a domestic servant. **5.** a servile person. [C14: from Anglo-Norman *meignial,* from Old French *meinie* household. See MEINY] —**ˈme·ni·al·ly** *adv.*

Mé·nière's syn·drome *or* **dis·ease** (meɪnˈjɛəz) *n.* a disorder of the inner ear characterized by a ringing or buzzing in the ear, dizziness, and impaired hearing. [C19: named after Prosper *Ménière* (1799–1862), French physician]

me·nin·ges (mɪˈnɪndʒiːz) *pl. n., sing.* **me·ninx** (ˈmiːnɪŋks). the three membranes (**dura mater, arachnoid, pia mater**) that envelop the brain and spinal cord. [C17: from Greek, pl. of *meninx* membrane] —**me·nin·ge·al** (mɪˈnɪndʒɪəl) *adj.*

men·in·gi·tis (ˌmɛnɪnˈdʒaɪtɪs) *n.* inflammation of the membranes that surround the brain or spinal cord, caused by infection. —**men·in·git·ic** (ˌmɛnɪnˈdʒɪtɪk) *adj.*

me·nin·go·cele (mɛˈnɪŋgəʊˌsiːl) *n. Pathol.* protrusion of the meninges through the skull or backbone. [C19: from *meningo-* (see MENINGES) + -CELE]

me·nis·cus (mɪˈnɪskəs) *n., pl.* **·nis·ci** (-ˈnɪsaɪ) *or* **·nis·cus·es. 1.** the curved upper surface of a liquid standing in a tube, produced by the surface tension. **2.** a crescent or half-moon-shaped body or design. **3.** a crescent-shaped fibrous cartilage between the bones at certain joints, esp. at the knee. **4.** a crescent-shaped lens; a concavo-convex or convexo-concave lens. [C17: from New Latin, from Greek *mēniskos* crescent, diminutive of *mēnē* moon] —**me·ˈnis·coid** *adj.*

men·i·sper·ma·ceous (ˌmɛnɪspɜːˈmeɪʃəs) *adj.* of, relating to, or belonging to the *Menispermaceae,* a family of mainly tropical and subtropical plants, most of which are woody climbers with small flowers. [C19: from New Latin *Mēnispermum* name of genus, from Greek *mēnē* moon + *sperma* seed]

Men·non·ite ('mɛnəˌnaɪt) *n.* a member of a Protestant sect that rejects infant baptism, Church organization, and the doctrine of transubstantiation and in most cases refuses military service, public office, and the taking of oaths. [C16: from German *Mennonit,* after *Menno* Simons (1496–1561), Frisian religious leader] —'**Men·no·ˌnit·ism** *n.*

me·no ('mɛnəʊ) *adv. Music.* **1.** (esp. preceding a dynamic or tempo marking) to be played less quickly, less softly, etc. **2.** short for **meno mosso.** [from Italian, from Latin *minus* less]

me·no- *n. combining form.* menstruation: *menorrhagia.* [from Greek *mēn* month]

me·nol·o·gy (mɪ'nɒlədʒɪ) *n., pl.* **·gies. 1.** an ecclesiastical calendar of the months. **2.** *Eastern Churches.* a liturgical book containing the lives of the saints arranged by months. [C17: from New Latin *mēnologium,* from Late Greek *mēnologion,* from Greek *mēn* month + *logos* word, account]

Me·nom·i·ni *or* **Me·nom·i·nee** (mə'nɒmənɪ) *n.* **1.** (*pl.* **·ni, ·nis** *or* **·nee, ·nees**) a member of a North American Indian people formerly living between Lake Michigan and Lake Superior. **2.** the language of this people, belonging to the Algonquian family.

me·no mos·so ('mɛnəʊ 'mɒsəʊ) *adv. Music.* to be played at reduced speed. Often shortened to **meno.** [Italian: less rapid]

Men·on ('mɛnən) *n.* **Ven·ga·lil Krish·nan Krish·na** ('vɛŋgəlɪl 'kri:ʃnən 'kri:ʃnə). 1897–1974, Indian diplomat and politician, who was a close associate of Nehru and played a key role in the Indian nationalist movement.

men·o·pause ('mɛnəʊˌpɔ:z) *n.* the period during which a woman's menstrual cycle ends, normally occurring at an age of 45 to 50. Nontechnical name: **change of life.** [C19: from French, from Greek *mēn* month + *pausis* halt] —ˌ**men·o·'pau·sic** *or* ˌ**men·o·'pau·sal** *adj.*

me·no·rah (mɪ'nɔ:rə) *n. Judaism.* **1.** a seven-branched candelabrum used in ceremonies. **2.** a stand with nine lamps used during the Hanukkah festival. [from Hebrew: candlestick]

Me·nor·ca (me'norka) *n.* the Spanish name for **Minorca** (sense 1).

men·or·rha·gi·a (ˌmɛnɔ:'reɪdʒɪə) *n.* excessive bleeding during menstruation. —**men·or·rhag·ic** (ˌmɛnə'rædʒɪk) *adj.*

Me·not·ti (mə'nɒtɪ; *Italian* me'nɔtti) *n.* **Gian Car·lo** (dʒan 'karlo). born 1911, Italian composer, in the U.S. from 1928. His works include the operas *The Medium* (1946), *The Consul* (1950), and *The Saint of Bleecker Street* (1954).

Men·sa ('mɛnsə) *n., Latin genitive* **Men·sae** ('mɛnsi:). a faint constellation in the S hemisphere lying between Hydrus and Volans and containing part of the Large Magellanic Cloud.

men·sal[1] ('mɛns°l) *adj. Rare.* monthly. [C15: from Latin *mensis* month]

men·sal[2] ('mɛns°l) *adj. Rare.* relating to or used at the table. [C15: from Latin *mensālis,* from *mensa* table]

men·ses ('mɛnsi:z) *n., pl.* **men·ses. 1.** another name for **menstruation. 2.** the period of time, usually from three to five days, during which menstruation occurs. **3.** the matter discharged during menstruation. [C16: from Latin, pl. of *mensis* month]

Men·she·vik ('mɛnʃɪvɪk) *or* **Men·she·vist** *n.* a member of the moderate wing of the Russian Social Democratic Party, advocating gradual reform to achieve socialism. Compare **Bolshevik.** [C20: from Russian, literally: minority, from *menshe* less, from *malo* few] —'**Men·she·vism** *n.*

mens re·a ('mɛnz 'reɪə) *n. Law.* a criminal intention or knowledge that an act is wrong. It is assumed to be an ingredient of all criminal offences although some minor statutory offences are punishable irrespective of it. [Latin, literally: guilty mind]

men·stru·al ('mɛnstrʊəl) *adj.* of or relating to menstruation or the menses.

men·stru·ate ('mɛnstrʊˌeɪt) *vb.* (*intr.*) to undergo menstruation. [C17: from Latin *menstruāre,* from *mensis* month]

men·stru·a·tion (ˌmɛnstrʊ'eɪʃən) *n.* the approximately monthly discharge of blood and cellular debris from the uterus by nonpregnant women from puberty to the menopause. Also called: **menses.** Nontechnical name: **period.** —**men·stru·ous** ('mɛnstru:əs) *adj.*

men·stru·um ('mɛnstrʊəm) *n., pl.* **·stru·ums** *or* **·stru·a** (-strʊə). a solvent, esp. one used in the preparation of a drug. [C17 (meaning: solvent), C14 (menstrual discharge): from Medieval Latin, from Latin *mēnstruus* monthly, from *mēnsis* month; from an alchemical comparison between a base metal being transmuted into gold and the supposed action of the menses]

men·sur·a·ble ('mɛnsjʊrəb°l, -ʃə-) *adj.* a less common word for **measurable.** [C17: from Late Latin *mēnsūrābilis,* from *mēnsūra* MEASURE] —ˌ**men·sur·a·'bil·i·ty** *n.*

men·su·ral ('mɛnʃərəl) *adj.* **1.** of or involving measure. **2.** *Music.* of or relating to music in which notes have fixed values in relation to each other. [C17: from Late Latin *mēnsūrālis,* from *mēnsūra* MEASURE]

men·su·ra·tion (ˌmɛnʃə'reɪʃən) *n.* **1.** the study of the measurement of geometric magnitudes such as length. **2.** the act or process of measuring; measurement. —ˌ**men·su·'ra·tion·al** *adj.* —**men·su·ra·tive** ('mɛnʃərətɪv) *adj.*

mens·wear ('mɛnzˌwɛə) *n.* clothing for men.

-ment *suffix forming nouns, esp. from verbs.* **1.** indicating state, condition, or quality: *enjoyment.* **2.** indicating the result or product of an action: *embankment.* **3.** indicating process or action: *management.* [from French, from Latin *-mentum*]

men·tal[1] ('mɛnt°l) *adj.* **1.** of or involving the mind or an intellectual process. **2.** occurring only in the mind: *mental calculations.* **3.** affected by mental illness: *a mental patient.* **4.** concerned with care for persons with mental illness: *a mental hospital.* **5.** *Slang.* foolish. [C15: from Late Latin *mentālis,* from Latin *mēns* mind] —'**men·tal·ly** *adv.*

men·tal[2] ('mɛnt°l) *adj. Anatomy.* of or relating to the chin. Also: **genial.** [C18: from Latin *mentum* chin]

men·tal age *n. Psychol.* the mental ability of a child, expressed in years and based on a comparison of his test performance with the performance of children having the same chronological age. See also **intelligence quotient.**

men·tal block *n.* See **block** (sense 19).

men·tal cru·el·ty *n.* behaviour that causes distress to another person but that does not involve physical assault.

men·tal de·fi·cien·cy *n. Psychiatry.* a condition of low intellectual development requiring special education and employment. Also called: **mental handicap, mental retardation, mental subnormality.**

men·tal heal·ing *n.* the healing of a disorder by mental concentration or suggestion. —**men·tal heal·er** *n.*

men·tal hos·pi·tal *or* **in·sti·tu·tion** *n.* a hospital or institution for people who are mentally ill.

men·tal·ism ('mɛnt°ˌlɪzəm) *n. Philosophy.* the doctrine that mind is the fundamental reality and that objects of knowledge exist only as aspects of the subject's consciousness. —'**men·tal·ist** *n.* —ˌ**men·tal·'is·tic** *adj.* —ˌ**men·tal·'is·ti·cal·ly** *adv.*

men·tal·i·ty (mɛn'tælɪtɪ) *n., pl.* **·ties. 1.** the state or quality of mental or intellectual ability. **2.** a way of thinking; mental inclination or character: *his weird mentality.*

men·tal res·er·va·tion *n.* a tacit withholding of full assent or an unexpressed qualification made when one is taking an oath, making a statement, etc.

men·tha·ce·ous (mɛn'θeɪʃɪəs) *adj.* of, relating to, or belonging to the labiate plant genus *Mentha* (mints, etc.) the members of which have scented leaves. [from New Latin, from Latin *mentha* MINT[1]]

men·thol ('mɛnθɒl) *n.* an optically active organic compound found in peppermint oil and used as an antiseptic, in inhalants, and as an analgesic. Formula: $C_{10}H_{20}O$. [C19: from German, from Latin *mentha* MINT[1]]

men·tho·lat·ed ('mɛnθəˌleɪtɪd) *adj.* containing, treated, or impregnated with menthol.

men·tion ('mɛnʃən) *vb.* (*tr.*) **1.** to refer to or speak about briefly or incidentally. **2.** to acknowledge or honour. **3. not to mention (something).** to say nothing of (something too obvious to mention). ~*n.* **4.** a recognition or acknowledgment. **5.** a slight reference or allusion: *he only got a mention in the article; the author makes no mention of that.* **6.** the act of mentioning. [C14: via Old French from Latin *mentiō* a calling to mind, naming, from *mēns* mind] —'**men·tion·a·ble** *adj.* —'**men·tion·er** *n.*

Men·ton (mɛn'təʊn; *French* mã'tõ) *n.* a town and resort in SE France, on the Mediterranean: belonged to Monaco from the 14th century until 1848, then an independent republic until purchased by France in 1860. Pop.: 25 314 (1975).

men·tor ('mɛntɔ:) *n.* a wise or trusted adviser or guide. [C18: from MENTOR] —**men·'to·ri·al** *adj.*

Men·tor ('mɛntɔ:) *n.* the friend whom Odysseus put in charge of his household when he left for Troy. He was the adviser of the young Telemachus.

men·u ('mɛnju:) *n.* a list of dishes served at a meal or that can be ordered in a restaurant. [C19: from French *menu* small, detailed (list), from Latin *minūtus* MINUTE]

Me·nu·hin ('mɛnjʊɪn) *n.* **Ye·hu·di** (jɛ'hu:dɪ). born 1916, U.S. violinist, in England since 1959.

Men·zies ('mɛnzɪz) *n.* Sir **Rob·ert Gor·don.** 1894–1978, Australian statesman; prime minister (1939–41; 1949–66).

me·ow, mi·aou, mi·aow (mɪ'aʊ, mjaʊ), *or* **mi·aul** ('mɪaʊl, mjaʊl) *vb.* **1.** (*intr.*) (of a cat) to make a characteristic crying sound. ~*interj.* **2.** an imitation of this sound.

mep·a·crine ('mɛpəkrɪn) *n. Brit.* a drug formerly widely used to treat malaria but now largely replaced by chloroquine. Formula: $C_{23}H_{30}ClN_3O.2HCl.2H_2O$. U.S. name: **quinacrine.** [C20: from ME(THYL) + PA(LUDISM + A)CR(ID)INE]

me·per·i·dine (mə'pɛrɪˌdi:n, -dɪn) *n.* a white crystalline water-soluble drug used as an analgesic. Formula: $C_{15}H_{21}NO_2.HCl$. Also called: **meperidine hydrochloride.** [C20: from METHYL + PIPERIDINE]

Meph·i·stoph·e·les (ˌmɛfɪ'stɒfɪˌli:z) *or* **Me·phis·to** (mə'fɪstəʊ) *n.* devil in medieval mythology and the one to whom Faust sold his soul in the Faust legend. —**Meph·is·to·phe·le·an** *or* **Meph·is·to·phe·li·an** (ˌmɛfɪstə'fi:lɪən) *adj.*

me·phit·ic (mɪ'fɪtɪk) *or* **me·phit·i·cal** *adj.* **1.** poisonous; foul. **2.** foul-smelling; putrid. [C17: from Late Latin *mephīticus* pestilential. See MEPHITIS] —**me·'phit·i·cal·ly** *adv.*

me·phi·tis (mɪ'faɪtɪs) *n.* **1.** a foul or poisonous stench. **2.** a poisonous or unpleasant gas emitted from the earth. [C18: from Latin: unwholesome smell, origin obscure]

me·pro·ba·mate (mə'prəʊbəˌmeɪt, ˌmɛprəʊ'bæmeɪt) *n.* a white bitter powder used as a tranquillizer. Formula: $C_9H_{18}N_2O_4$. [ME(THYL) + PRO(PYL + CAR)BAMATE]

mer. *abbrev. for* meridian.

-mer *suffix forming nouns. Chem.* denoting a substance of a particular class: *monomer; polymer.* [from Greek *meros* part]

Me·ra·no (mə'ra:nəʊ; *Italian* me'ra:no) *n.* a town and resort in NE Italy, in the foothills of the central Alps: capital of the Tyrol (12th–15th century); under Austrian rule until 1919. Pop.: 33 235 (1971). German name: **Me·ran** (me'ra:n).

mer·bro·min (mə'brəʊmɪn) *n.* a green iridescent crystalline compound that forms a red solution in water: used in medicine as an antiseptic. Formula: $C_{20}H_8Br_2HgNa_2O_6$. See also **Mercurochrome.** [C20: blend of MERCURIC + *dibromofluorescein*]

Mer+ca ('mɛəkə) *n.* a port in the S Somali Republic on the Indian Ocean. Pop.: 56 000 (1965 est.).

mer+can+tile ('mɜːkənˌtaɪl) *adj.* **1.** of, relating to, or characteristic of trade or traders; commercial. **2.** of or relating to mercantilism. [C17: from French, from Italian, from *mercante* MERCHANT]

mer+can+tile a·gen+cy *n.* an enterprise that collects and supplies information about the financial credit standing of individuals and enterprises.

mer+can+tile pa+per *n.* another name for **commercial paper.**

mer+can+til+ism ('mɜːkəntɪˌlɪzəm) *n.* **1.** Also called: **mercantile system.** *Economics.* a theory prevalent in Europe during the 17th and 18th centuries asserting that the wealth of a nation depends on its possession of precious metals and therefore that the government of a nation must maximize the foreign trade surplus, and foster national commercial interests, a merchant marine, the establishment of colonies, etc. **2.** a rare word for **commercialism** (sense 1). —**'mer+can+ˌtil+ist** *n., adj.*

mer+cap+tan (mɜː'kæptæn) *n.* another name for **thiol.** [C19: from German, from Medieval Latin *mercurium captans,* literally: seizing quicksilver]

mer+cap+tide (mə'kæptaɪd, mɜː-) *n.* a salt of a mercaptan, containing the ion RS^-, where R is an alkyl or aryl group.

mer+cap+to- (mɜː'kæptəʊ) *combining form.* (in chemical compounds) indicating the presence of an HS- group.

mer+cap+to+pu+rine (məˌkæptə'pjʊəriːn) *n.* a drug used in the treatment of leukaemia. Formula: $C_5H_4N_4S$.

Mer·ca·tor (mɜː'keɪtə) *n.* **Ger·ar·dus** (dʒə'rɑːdəs). Latinized name of *Gerhard Kremer.* 1512–94, Flemish cartographer and mathematician.

Mer·ca·tor pro+jec+tion *n.* an orthomorphic map projection on which parallels and meridians form a rectangular grid, scale being exaggerated with increasing distance from the equator. Also called: **Mercator's projection.** [C17: named after G. MERCATOR]

mer+ce+nar·y ('mɜːsɪnərɪ, -sɪnrɪ) *adj.* **1.** influenced by greed or gain. **2.** of or relating to a mercenary or mercenaries. ~*n., pl.* **+nar·ies. 3.** a man hired to fight for a foreign army, etc. **4.** *Rare.* any person who works solely for pay. [C16: from Latin *mercēnārius,* from *mercēs* wages] —**ˌmer+ce+'nar·i·ly** *adv.* —**'mer+ce+nar·i·ness** *n.*

mer+cer ('mɜːsə) *n. Brit.* a dealer in textile fabrics and fine cloth. [C13: from Old French *mercier* dealer, from Vulgar Latin *merciārius* (unattested), from Latin *merx* goods, wares] —**'mer+cer·y** *n.*

mer+cer+ize *or* **mer+cer+ise** ('mɜːsəˌraɪz) *vb.* (*tr.*) to treat (cotton yarn) with an alkali to increase its strength and reception to dye and impart a lustrous silky appearance. [C19: named after John *Mercer* (1791–1866), English maker of textiles] —**ˌmer+cer·i·'za+tion** *or* **ˌmer+cer·i·'sa+tion** *n.*

mer+chan+dise *n.* ('mɜːtʃənˌdaɪs, -ˌdaɪz). **1.** commercial goods; commodities. ~*vb.* ('mɜːtʃənˌdaɪz). **2.** to engage in the commercial purchase and sale of (goods or services); trade. [C13: from Old French. See MERCHANT] —**'mer+chan+ˌdis+er** *n.*

mer+chant ('mɜːtʃənt) *n.* **1.** a person engaged in the purchase and sale of commodities for profit, esp. on international markets; trader. **2.** *Chiefly U.S.* a person engaged in retail trade. **3.** (esp. in historical contexts) any trader. **4.** *Derogatory.* a person dealing or involved in something undesirable: *a gossip merchant.* **5.** (*modifier*) **a.** of the merchant navy: *a merchant sailor.* **b.** of or concerned with trade: *a merchant ship.* ~*vb.* **6.** (*tr.*) to conduct trade in; deal in. [C13: from Old French, probably from Vulgar Latin *mercātāre* (unattested), from Latin *mercārī* to trade, from *merx* goods, wares] —**'mer·chant-ˌlike** *adj.*

mer+chant+a·ble ('mɜːtʃəntəbᵊl) *adj.* suitable for trading.

mer+chant bank *n. Brit.* a financial institution engaged primarily in accepting foreign bills and underwriting new security issues. —**mer+chant bank+er** *n.*

mer+chant+man ('mɜːtʃəntmən) *n., pl.* **+men.** a merchant ship.

mer+chant na·vy *or* **ma+rine** *n.* the ships or crew engaged in a nation's commercial shipping.

mer+chant prince *n.* a very wealthy merchant.

mer+chet ('mɜːtʃɪt) *n.* (in feudal England) a fine paid by a tenant, esp. a villein, to his lord for allowing the marriage of his daughter. [C13: from Anglo-French, literally: MARKET]

Mer+ci·a ('mɜːʃɪə) *n.* a kingdom and earldom of central and S England during the Anglo-Saxon period that reached its height under King Offa (757–96).

Mer+ci·an ('mɜːʃɪən) *adj.* **1.** of or relating to Mercia or the dialect spoken there. ~*n.* **2.** the dialect of Old and Middle English spoken in the Midlands of England south of the River Humber. See also **Anglian, Northumbrian.**

mer+ci+ful ('mɜːsɪfʊl) *adj.* showing or giving mercy; compassionate. —**'mer+ci+ful+ly** *adv.* —**'mer+ci+ful+ness** *n.*

mer+ci+less ('mɜːsɪlɪs) *adj.* without mercy; pitiless, cruel, or heartless. —**'mer+ci+less+ly** *adv.* —**'mer+ci+less+ness** *n.*

Mer·cou·ri (ˌmɜː'kuːrɪ) *n.* **Mel·in·a** (mə'liːnə). born 1923, Greek stage and film actress: her films include *Never on Sunday* (1960).

mer+cu+rate ('mɜːkjʊˌreɪt) *vb.* **1.** (*tr.*) to treat or mix with mercury. **2.** to undergo or cause to undergo a chemical reaction in which a mercury atom is added to a compound. —**ˌmer+cu+'ra+tion** *n.*

mer+cu+ri·al (mɜː'kjʊərɪəl) *adj.* **1.** of, like, containing, or relating to mercury. **2.** volatile; lively: *a mercurial temperament.* **3.** (*sometimes cap.*) of, like, or relating to the god or the planet Mercury. ~*n.* **4.** *Med.* any salt of mercury for use as a medicine. [C14: from Latin *mercuriālis*] —**mer+'cu+ri+al+ly** *adv.* —**mer+'cu+ri+al+ness** *or* **mer+ˌcu+ri+'al+i·ty** *n.*

mer+cu+ri+al+ism (mɜː'kjʊərɪəˌlɪzᵊm) *n.* poisoning caused by chronic ingestion of mercury.

mer+cu+ri+al+ize *or* **mer+cu+ri+al+ise** (mɜː'kjʊərɪəˌlaɪz) *vb.* (*tr.*) **1.** to make mercurial. **2.** to treat with mercury or a mercury compound. —**mer+ˌcu+ri+al·i·'za+tion** *or* **mer+ˌcu+ri+al·i·'sa+tion** *n.*

mer+cu+ric (mɜː'kjʊərɪk) *adj.* of or containing mercury in the divalent state.

mer+cu+ric chlo+ride *n.* a white poisonous soluble crystalline substance used as a pesticide, antiseptic, and preservative for wood. Formula: $HgCl_2$. Also called: **bichloride of mercury, corrosive sublimate.**

mer+cu+ric ox+ide *n.* a soluble poisonous substance existing in red and yellow powdered forms: used as pigments. Formula: HgO.

mer+cu+ric sul+phide *n.* a compound of mercury, usually existing as a black solid (**metacinnabarite**) or a red solid (**cinnabar** or **vermillion**), which is used as a pigment. Formula: HgS.

Mer+cu+ro+chrome (mə'kjʊərəˌkrəʊm) *n. Trademark.* a solution of merbromin, used as tropical antibacterial agent.

mer+cu+rous ('mɜːkjʊrəs) *n.* of or containing mercury in the monovalent state. Mercurous salts contain the divalent ion Hg_2^{2+}.

mer+cu+rous chlo+ride *n.* a white tasteless insoluble powder used as a fungicide and formerly as a medical antiseptic, cathartic, and diuretic. Formula: Hg_2Cl_2. Also called: **calomel.**

mer+cu+ry ('mɜːkjʊrɪ) *n., pl.* **+ries. 1.** Also called: **quicksilver, hydrargyrum.** a heavy silvery-white toxic liquid metallic element occurring principally in cinnabar: used in thermometers, barometers, mercury-vapour lamps, and dental amalgams. Symbol: Hg; atomic no.: 80; atomic wt.: 200.59; valency: 1 or 2; relative density: 13.546; melting pt.: –38.87°C; boiling pt.: 356.58°C. **2.** any plant of the euphorbiaceous genus *Mercurialis.* See **dog's mercury. 3.** *Archaic.* a messenger or courier. [C14: from Latin *Mercurius* messenger of Jupiter, god of commerce; related to *merx* merchandise]

Mer·cu·ry[1] ('mɜːkjərɪ) *n. Roman myth.* the messenger of the gods. Greek counterpart: **Hermes.**

Mer+cu·ry[2] ('mɜːkjərɪ) *n.* the smallest planet and the nearest to the sun. Mean distance from sun: 57.9 million km; period of revolution around sun: 88 days; period of axial rotation: 59 days; diameter and mass: 38 and 5.4 per cent that of earth respectively.

mer+cu+ry arc *n.* **a.** an electric discharge through ionized mercury vapour, producing a brilliant bluish-green light containing ultraviolet radiation. **b.** (*as modifier*): *a mercury-arc rectifier.* See also **ignitron.**

mer+cu+ry chlo+ride *n.* See **mercurous chloride, mercuric chloride.**

mer·cu·ry-va·pour lamp *n.* a lamp in which an electric discharge through a low pressure of mercury vapour is used to produce a greenish-blue light. It is used for street lighting and is also a source of ultraviolet radiation.

mer+cy ('mɜːsɪ) *n., pl.* **+cies. 1.** compassionate treatment of or attitude towards an offender, adversary, etc., who is in one's power or care; clemency; pity. **2.** the power to show mercy: *to throw oneself on someone's mercy.* **3.** a relieving or welcome occurrence or state of affairs: *his death was a mercy after weeks of pain.* **4. at the mercy of.** in the power of. [C12: from Old French, from Latin *mercēs* wages, recompense, price, from *merx* goods]

mer+cy flight *n.* an aircraft flight to bring a seriously ill or injured person to hospital from an isolated community.

mer+cy kill+ing *n.* another term for **euthanasia.**

mer+cy seat *n.* **1.** *Old Testament.* the gold platform covering the Ark of the Covenant and regarded as the throne of God where he accepted sacrifices and gave commandments (Exodus 25:17, 22). **2.** *Theol.* the throne of God.

mere[1] (mɪə) *adj. superlative* **mer+est.** being nothing more than something specified: *she is a mere child.* [C15: from Latin *merus* pure, unmixed] —**'mere+ly** *adv.*

mere[2] (mɪə) *n.* **1.** *Brit. dialect or archaic.* a lake or marsh. **2.** *Obsolete.* the sea or an inlet of it. [Old English *mere* sea, lake; related to Old Saxon *meri* sea, Old Norse *marr,* Old High German *mari;* compare Latin *mare*]

mere[3] (mɪə) *n. Archaic.* a boundary or boundary marker. [Old English *gemǣre*]

mer·e[4] ('mɛrɪ) *n.* a Maori war club or a miniature copy of one worn as an ornament. [from Maori]

-mere *n. combining form.* indicating a part or division: *blastomere.* [from Greek *meros* part, portion] —**-mer·ic** *adj. combining form.*

Mer·e·dith ('mɛrɪdɪθ) *n.* **George.** 1828–1909, English novelist and poet. His works, notable for their social satire and analysis of character, include the novels *Beauchamp's Career* (1876) and *The Egoist* (1879) and the long tragic poem *Modern Love* (1862).

me+ren+gue (mə'rɛŋgeɪ) *n.* a Caribbean dance in duple time with syncopated rhythm. [from American Spanish and Haitian Creole]

mer+e+tri+cious (ˌmɛrɪ'trɪʃəs) *adj.* **1.** superficially or garishly attractive. **2.** insincere: *meretricious praise.* **3.** *Archaic.* of, like, or relating to a prostitute. [C17: from Latin *merētrīcius,* from *merētrix* prostitute, from *merēre* to earn money] —**ˌmer+e·'tri+cious+ly** *adv.* —**ˌmer+e·'tri+cious+ness** *n.*

mer+gan+ser (mɜː'gænsə) *n., pl.* **+sers** *or* **+ser.** any of several typically crested large marine diving ducks of the genus *Mergus,* having a long slender hooked bill with serrated edges. Also called: **sawbill.** See also **goosander.** [C18: from New Latin, from Latin *mergus* waterfowl, from *mergere* to plunge + *anser* goose]

merge (mɜːdʒ) *vb.* **1.** to meet and join or cause to meet and join. **2.** to blend or cause to blend; fuse. [C17: from Latin *mergere* to plunge] —**'mer+gence** *n.*

mer+ger ('mɜːdʒə) *n.* **1.** *Commerce.* the combination of two or more companies, either by the creation of a new organization or by absorption by one of the others. Often called (Brit.): **amalgamation. 2.** *Law.* the extinguishment of an estate, interest, contract, right, offence, etc., by its absorption into a greater one. **3.** the act of merging or the state of being merged.

Mer+gui Ar·chi+pel·a+go (mɜːˈgwiː) *n.* a group of over 200 islands in the Andaman Sea, off the Tenasserim coast of S Burma: mountainous and forested.

Me+riç (məˈriːtʃ) *n.* the Turkish name for the **Maritsa.**

Mé+ri+da (*Spanish* ˈmeriða) *n.* **1.** a city in SE Mexico, capital of Yucatán state: founded in 1542 on the site of the ancient Mayan city of T'ho; centre of the henequen industry; university. Pop.: 239 222 (1975 est.). **2.** a city in W Venezuela: founded in 1558 by Spanish conquistadores; University of Los Andes (1785). Pop.: 74 214 (1971). **3.** a market town in W Spain, in Estremadura, on the Guadiana River: founded in 25 B.C.; became the capital of Lusitania and one of the chief cities of Iberia. Pop.: 40 059 (1970). Latin name: **Augusta Emerita.**

me+rid+i·an (məˈrɪdɪən) *n.* **1. a.** one of the imaginary lines joining the north and south poles at right angles to the equator, designated by degrees of longitude from 0° at Greenwich to 180°. **b.** the great circle running through both poles. See **prime meridian. 2.** *Astronomy.* **a.** the great circle on the celestial sphere passing through the north and south celestial poles and the zenith and nadir of the observer. **b.** (*as modifier*): *a meridian instrument.* **3.** Also called: **meridian section.** *Maths.* a section of a surface of revolution, such as a paraboloid, that contains the axis of revolution. **4.** the peak; zenith: *the meridian of his achievements.* **5.** *Obsolete.* noon. ~*adj.* **6.** along or relating to a meridian. **7.** of or happening at noon. **8.** relating to the peak of something. [C14: from Latin *merīdiānus* of midday, from *merīdiēs* midday, from *medius* MID[1] + *diēs* day]

me+rid+i·an cir+cle *n.* an instrument used in astronomy for determining the declination and right ascension of stars. It consists of a telescope attached to a graduated circle.

me+rid+i·o+nal (məˈrɪdɪənᵊl) *adj.* **1.** along, relating to, or resembling a meridian. **2.** characteristic of or located in the south, esp. of Europe. ~*n.* **3.** an inhabitant of the south, esp. of France. [C14: from Late Latin *merīdiōnālis* southern; see MERIDIAN; for form, compare *septentriōnālis* SEPTENTRIONAL] —**me+ˈrid·i·o+nal+ly** *adv.*

Mé·ri·mée (*French* meriˈme) *n.* **Pros·per** (prɔsˈpɛːr). 1803–70, French novelist, dramatist, and short-story writer, noted particularly for his short novels *Colomba* (1840) and *Carmen* (1845), on which Bizet's opera was based.

me+ringue (məˈræŋ) *n.* **1.** stiffly beaten egg whites mixed with sugar and baked, often as a topping for pastry, etc. **2.** a small cake or shell of this mixture, often filled with cream. [C18: from French, origin obscure]

me+ri+no (məˈriːnəʊ) *n., pl.* **+nos. 1.** a breed of sheep, originating in Spain. **2.** the long fine wool of this sheep. **3.** the yarn made from this wool, often mixed with cotton. **4. pure merino.** *Austral. informal.* **a.** an affluent and socially prominent person. **b.** (*as modifier*): *a pure merino cricketer.* ~*adj.* **5.** made from merino wool. [C18: from Spanish, origin uncertain]

Mer·i·on·eth+shire (ˌmɛrɪˈɒnɪθˌʃɪə, -ʃə) *n.* (until 1974) a county of N Wales, now part of Gwynedd.

me+ri+stem (ˈmɛrɪˌstɛm) *n.* a plant tissue responsible for growth, whose cells divide and differentiate to form the tissues and organs of the plant. Meristems occur within the stem (see **cambium**) and leaves and at the tips of stems and roots. [C19: from Greek *meristos* divided, from *merizein* to divide, from *meris* portion] —**mer·i+ste·mat+ic** (ˌmɛrɪstɪˈmætɪk) *adj.*

me+ris+tic (məˈrɪstɪk) *adj. Biology.* **1.** of or relating to the number of organs or parts in an animal or plant body: *meristic variation.* **2.** segmented: *meristic worms.*

mer+it (ˈmɛrɪt) *n.* **1.** worth or superior quality; excellence: *work of great merit.* **2.** (*often pl.*) a deserving or commendable quality or act: *judge him on his merits.* **3.** *Theol.* spiritual credit granted or received for good works. **4.** the fact or state of deserving; desert. **5.** an obsolete word for **reward.** ~*vb.* **6.** (*tr.*) to be worthy of; deserve: *he merits promotion.* [C13: via Old French from Latin *meritum* reward, desert, from *merēre* to deserve] —**ˈmer+it+ed+ly** *adv.* —**ˈmer+it+less** *n.*

mer·i+toc+ra+cy (ˌmɛrɪˈtɒkrəsɪ) *n., pl.* **+cies. 1.** rule by persons chosen not because of birth or wealth, but for their superior talents or intellect. **2.** the persons constituting such a group. **3.** a social system formed on such a basis.

mer·i+to+ri+ous (ˌmɛrɪˈtɔːrɪəs) *adj.* praiseworthy; showing merit. [C15: from Latin *meritōrius* earning money] —**ˌmer·i+ˈto+ri+ous+ly** *adv.* —**ˌmer·i+ˈto+ri+ous+ness** *n.*

mer+its (ˈmɛrɪts) *pl. n.* **1.** the actual and intrinsic rights and wrongs of an issue, esp. in a law case, as distinct from extraneous matters and technicalities. **2. on its (his, her,** etc.) **merits.** on the intrinsic qualities or virtues.

mer+it sys+tem *n. U.S.* the system of employing and promoting civil servants solely on the basis of ability rather than patronage. Compare **spoils system.**

mer+kin (ˈmɜːkɪn) *n.* **1.** an artificial hairpiece for the pudendum; a pubic wig. **2.** *Obsolete.* the pudendum itself. [C16: of unknown origin]

merle *or* **merl** (mɜːl) *n. Scot.* another name for the (European) **blackbird.** [C15: via Old French from Latin *merula*]

Mer·leau-Pon·ty (*French* mɛrlo pɔ̃ˈti) *n.* **Mau·rice** (moˈris). 1908–61, French phenomenological philosopher.

mer+lin (ˈmɜːlɪn) *n.* a small falcon, *Falco columbarius,* that has a dark plumage with a black-barred tail: used in falconry. See also **pigeon hawk.** [C14: from Old French *esmerillon,* from *esmeril,* of Germanic origin]

Mer·lin (ˈmɜːlɪn) *n.* (in Arthurian legend) a wizard and counsellor to King Arthur eternally imprisoned in a tree by a woman to whom he revealed his secret craft.

mer+lon (ˈmɜːlən) *n. Fortifications.* the solid upright section in a crenellated battlement. [C18: from French, from Italian *merlone,* from *merlo* battlement]

mer+maid (ˈmɜːˌmeɪd) *n.* an imaginary sea creature fabled to have a woman's head and upper body and a fish's tail. [C14: from *mere* lake, inlet + MAID]

mer+maid's purse *n.* another name for **sea purse.**

mer+man (ˈmɜːˌmæn) *n., pl.* **+men.** a male counterpart of the mermaid. [C17: see MERMAID]

mer·o- *combining form.* part or partial: *merocrine.* [from Greek *meros* part, share]

mer·o+blas+tic (ˌmɛrəʊˈblæstɪk) *adj. Embryol.* of or showing cleavage of only the nonyolky part of the zygote, as in birds' eggs. Compare **holoblastic.** —**ˌmer·o+ˈblas+ti+cal+ly** *adv.*

mer·o+crine (ˈmɛrəˌkraɪn, -krɪn) *adj.* (of the secretion of glands) characterized by formation of the product without undergoing disintegration. Compare **holocrine, apocrine.** [C20: from MERO- + Greek *krinein* to separate]

Mer·o·ë (ˈmɛrəʊˌiː) *n.* an ancient city in N Sudan, on the Nile; capital of a kingdom that flourished from about 700 B.C. to about 350 A.D.

mer·o+plank+ton (ˌmɛrəʊˈplæŋktən) *n.* plankton consisting of organisms at a certain stage of their life cycles, esp. larvae, the other stages not being spent as part of the plankton community. Compare **holoplankton.**

-mer·ous *adj. combining form.* (in biology) having a certain number or kind of parts: *dimerous.* [from Greek *meros* part, division]

Mer·o+vin+gi·an (ˌmɛrəʊˈvɪndʒɪən) *adj.* **1.** of or relating to a Frankish dynasty founded by Clovis I, which ruled Gaul and W Germany from about 500 to 751 A.D. ~*n.* **2.** a member or supporter of this dynasty. [C17: from French, from Medieval Latin *Merovingi* offspring of *Merovaeus,* Latin form of *Merowig,* traditional founder of the line]

mer·o+zo+ite (ˌmɛrəʊˈzəʊaɪt) *n.* any of the cells formed by fission of a schizont during the life cycle of sporozoan protozoans, such as the malaria parasite. Compare **trophozoite.**

mer+ri+ment (ˈmɛrɪmənt) *n.* gaiety, fun, or mirth.

mer+ry (ˈmɛrɪ) *adj.* **+ri+er, +ri+est. 1.** cheerful; jolly. **2.** very funny; hilarious. **3.** *Brit. informal.* slightly drunk. **4.** *Archaic.* delightful. **5. play merry hell with.** *Informal.* to disturb greatly; disrupt. [Old English *merige* agreeable] —**ˈmer+ri+ly** *adv.* —**ˈmer+ri+ness** *n.*

mer·ry-an·drew *n.* a joker, clown, or buffoon. [C17: original reference of *Andrew* unexplained]

mer+ry danc+ers *pl. n. Scot.* the aurora borealis.

mer·ry-go-round *n.* **1.** another name for **roundabout** (sense 1). **2.** a whirl of activity or events: *the merry-go-round of the fashion world.*

mer·ry+mak·ing (ˈmɛrɪˌmeɪkɪŋ) *n.* fun, revelry, or festivity. —**ˈmer·ry+ˌmak·er** *n.*

mer+ry men *pl. n. Facetious.* a person's assistants or followers. [C19: originally, the companions of a knight, outlaw, etc.]

mer·ry+thought (ˈmɛrɪˌθɔːt) *n. Brit.* a less common word for **wishbone.**

Merse (mɜːs) *n.* **the.** a fertile lowland area of SE Scotland, in the Borders region, north of the Tweed.

Mer+se+burg (*German* ˈmɛrzəˌbʊrk) *n.* a city in S East Germany, on the Saale River: residence of the dukes of Saxe-Merseburg (1656–1738); chemical industry. Pop.: 55 225 (1972 est.).

Mer+sey (ˈmɜːzɪ) *n.* a river in W England, rising in N Derbyshire and flowing northwest and west to the Irish Sea through a large estuary on which is situated the port of Liverpool. Length: about 112 km (70 miles).

Mer·sey+side (ˈmɜːzɪˌsaɪd) *n.* a metropolitan county of NW England, comprising the districts of Sefton, Liverpool, St. Helens, Knowsley, and Wirral. Administrative centre: Liverpool. Pop.: 1 578 000 (1976 est.). Area: 652 sq. km (252 sq. miles).

Mer+sey sound *n.* the characteristic pop music of the Beatles and other groups from Liverpool in the 1960s.

Mer+sin (mɛəˈsiːn) *n.* a port in S Turkey, on the Mediterranean: oil refinery. Pop.: 152 236 (1975). Also called: **Içel.**

Mer+thyr Tyd+fil (ˈmɜːθə ˈtɪdvɪl) *n.* a town in SE Wales, in Mid Glamorgan: situated on the S Wales coalfield. Pop.: 55 215 (1971).

Mer+ton (ˈmɜːtᵊn) *n.* a borough in SW Greater London. Pop.: 169 400 (1976 est.).

mes- *combining form.* variant of **meso-** before a vowel: *mesarch; mesencephalon; mesenteron.*

me+sa (ˈmeɪsə) *n.* a flat tableland with steep edges, common in the southwestern U.S. [from Spanish: table]

mé+sal+li+ance (meˈzælɪəns; *French* mezalˈjɑ̃ːs) *n.* marriage with a person of lower social status. [C18: from French: MISALLIANCE]

mes+arch (ˈmɛsɑːk) *adj. Botany.* (of a xylem strand) having the first-formed xylem surrounded by that formed later, as in fern stems. Compare **exarch[2], endarch.**

Me·sa Verde ('meɪsə 'vɜ:d) *n.* a high plateau in SW Colorado: remains of numerous prehistoric cliff dwellings, inhabited by the Pueblo Indians.

mes+cal (mɛ'skæl) *n.* **1.** Also called: **peyote.** a spineless globe-shaped cactus, *Lophophora williamsii,* of Mexico and the southwestern U.S. Its button-like tubercles (**mescal buttons**) contain mescaline and are chewed by certain Indian tribes for their hallucinogenic effects. **2.** a colourless alcoholic spirit distilled from the fermented juice of certain agave plants. [C19: from American Spanish, from Nahuatl *mexcalli* the liquor, from *metl* MAGUEY + *ixcalli* stew]

mes+ca+line *or* **mes+ca+lin** ('mɛskə,li:n, -lɪn) *n.* a hallucinogenic drug derived from mescal buttons. Formula: $C_{11}H_{17}NO_3$.

mes+dames ('meɪ,dæm; *French* me'dam) *n.* the plural of **madame.**

mes+de+moi+selles (,meɪdmwə'zɛl; *French* medmwa'zɛl) *n.* the plural of **mademoiselle.**

me+seems (mɪ'si:mz) *vb. past* **me+seemed.** (*tr.; takes a clause as object*) *Archaic.* it seems to me.

mes+em+bry+an+the·mum (mɪz,ɛmbrɪ'ænθɪməm) *n.* any plant of the genus *Mesembryanthemum:* family *Aizoaceae.* See **fig marigold, ice plant.** [C18: New Latin, from Greek *mesēmbria* noon + *anthemon flower*]

mes+en+ceph·a+lon (,mɛsɛn'sɛfə,lɒn) *n.* the part of the brain that develops from the middle portion of the embryonic neural tube. Compare **prosencephalon, rhombencephalon.** Nontechnical name: **midbrain.** —**mes+en+ce·phal+ic** (,mɛsɛnsɪ'fælɪk) *adj.*

mes+en+chyme ('mɛsɛŋ,kaɪm) *n. Embryol.* the part of the mesoderm that develops into connective tissue, cartilage, lymph, blood, etc. [C19: New Latin, from MESO- + ENCHYMA] —**mes+en+chy+mal** (mɛs'ɛŋkɪməl) *or* **mes+en+chym·a+tous** (,mɛsɛŋ'kɪmətəs) *adj.*

mes+en+ter+i+tis (mɛs,ɛntə'raɪtɪs) *n.* inflammation of the mesentery.

mes+en+ter+on (mɛs'ɛntə,rɒn) *n., pl.* **+ter·a** (-tərə). a former name for **midgut** (sense 1). —**mes+,en+ter+'on+ic** *adj.*

mes+en+ter·y ('mɛsəntərɪ, 'mɛz-) *n., pl.* **+ter·ies.** the double layer of peritoneum that is attached to the back wall of the abdominal cavity and supports most of the small intestine. [C16: from New Latin *mesenterium;* see MESO- + ENTERON] —**,mes+en+'ter+ic** *adj.*

mesh (mɛʃ) *n.* **1.** a network; net. **2.** an open space between the strands of a network. **3.** (*often pl.*) the strands surrounding these spaces. **4.** anything that ensnares, or holds like a net: *the mesh of the secret police.* **5.** the engagement of teeth on interacting gearwheels: *the gears are in mesh.* **6.** a measure of spacing of the strands of a mesh or grid, expressed as the distance between strands for coarse meshes or a number of strands per unit length for fine meshes. ~*vb.* **7.** to entangle or become entangled. **8.** (of gear teeth) to engage or cause to engage. **9.** (*intr.;* often foll. by *with*) to coordinate (with): *to mesh with a policy.* **10.** to work or cause to work in harmony. [C16: probably from Dutch *maesche;* related to Old English *masc,* Old High German *masca*] —**'mesh·y** *adj.*

Me·shach ('mi:ʃæk) *n. Old Testament.* one of Daniel's three companions who, together with Shadrach and Abednego, was miraculously saved from destruction in Nebuchadnezzar's fiery furnace (Daniel 3:12-30).

mesh con+nec+tion *n. Electrical engineering.* (in a polyphase system) an arrangement in which the end of each phase is connected to the beginning of the next, forming a ring, each junction being connected to a terminal. See also **delta connection, star connection.**

Me+shed (mɛ'ʃɛd) *n.* a variant spelling of **Mashhad.**

me+shu+ga (mɪ'ʃʊgə) *adj. Yiddish.* crazy. [from Hebrew]

me·si·al ('mi:zɪəl) *adj. Anatomy.* another word for **medial** (sense 1). [C19: from MESO- + -IAL] —**'me+si+al+ly** *adv.*

me+sic ('mi:zɪk) *adj.* **1.** of, relating to, or growing in conditions of medium water supply: *mesic plants.* **2.** of or relating to a meson. —**'mes·i+cal+ly** *adv.*

me+sit·y+lene (mɪ'sɪtɪ,li:n, 'mɛsɪtɪ,li:n) *n.* a colourless liquid that occurs in crude petroleum; 1,3,5-trimethylbenzene. Formula: $C_6H_3(CH_3)_3$. [C19: from *mesityl,* from *mesite,* from New Latin *mesita,* from Greek *mesitēs* mediator + -ENE]

mes+mer+ism ('mɛzmə,rɪzəm) *n. Psychol.* **1.** a hypnotic state induced by the operator's imposition of his will on that of the patient. **2.** an early doctrine concerning this. [C19: named after F. A. *Mesmer* (1734–1815), Austrian physician] —**mes+mer+ic** (mɛz'mɛrɪk) *adj.* —**mes+'mer·i+cal+ly** *adv.* —**'mes+mer+ist** *n.*

mes+mer+ize *or* **mes+mer+ise** ('mɛzmə,raɪz) *vb.* (*tr.*) **1.** a former word for **hypnotize. 2.** to hold (someone) as if spellbound. —**,mes+mer·i+'za+tion** *or* **,mes+mer·i+'sa+tion** *n.* —**'mes+mer+,iz+er** *or* **'mes+mer+,is+er** *n.*

mes+nal+ty ('mi:nəltɪ) *n., pl.* **+ties.** *History.* the lands of a mesne lord. [C16: from legal French, from MESNE]

mesne (mi:n) *adj. Law.* **1.** intermediate or intervening: used esp. of any assignment of property before the last: *a mesne assignment.* **2. mesne profits.** rents or profits accruing during the rightful owner's exclusion from his land. [C15: from legal French *meien* in the middle, MEAN[3]]

mesne lord *n.* (in feudal society) a lord who held land from a superior lord and kept his own tenants on it.

me·so- *or before a vowel* **mes-** *combining form.* middle or intermediate: *mesomorph.* [from Greek *misos* middle]

mes·o+ben+thos (,mɛzə'bɛnθɒs, ,mɛsə-) *n.* flora and fauna living at the bottom of seas 182 to 914 metres deep.

mes·o+blast ('mɛsəʊ,blæst) *n.* another name for **mesoderm.** —**,mes·o+'blas+tic** *adj.*

mes·o+carp ('mɛsəʊ,kɑ:p) *n.* the middle layer of the pericarp of a fruit, such as the flesh of a peach.

mes·o+ce·phal+ic (,mɛsəʊsɪ'fælɪk) *Anatomy.* ~*adj.* **1.** having a medium-sized head, esp. one with a cephalic index between 75 and 80. ~*n.* **2.** an individual with such a head. ~Compare **brachycephalic, dolichocephalic.** —**mes·o+ceph+al·y** (,mɛsəʊ'sɛfəlɪ) *n.*

mes·o+crat+ic (,mɛsə'krætɪk) *adj.* (of igneous rocks) containing 30–60 per cent of ferromagnesian minerals.

mes·o+derm ('mɛsəʊ,dɜ:m) *n.* the middle germ layer of an animal embryo, giving rise to muscle, blood, bone, connective tissue, etc. See also **ectoderm, endoderm.** —**,mes·o+'der+mal** *or* **,mes·o+'der+mic** *adj.*

mes·o+gas+tri·um (,mɛsəʊ'gæstrɪəm) *n.* the mesentery supporting the embryonic stomach. —**,mes·o+'gas+tric** *adj.*

mes·o+gle·a *or* **mes·o+gloe·a** (,mɛsəʊ'gli:ə) *n.* the gelatinous material between the outer and inner cellular layers of jellyfish and other coelenterates. [C19: New Latin, from MESO- + Greek *gloia* glue]

me+sog+na+thous (mɪ'sɒgnəθəs) *adj. Anthropol.* **1.** having slightly projecting jaws. **2.** having a medium gnathic index. —**me+'sog+na+thism** *or* **me+'sog+na+thy** *n.*

Mes·o+lith+ic (,mɛsəʊ'lɪθɪk) *n.* **1.** the period between the Palaeolithic and the Neolithic, in Europe from about 12 000 to 3000 B.C., characterized by the appearance of microliths. ~*adj.* **2.** of or relating to the Mesolithic.

Me+so+lon+ghi (,mɛsə'lɔ:ŋgɪ) *n.* a variant spelling of **Missolonghi.**

Me+so+lón+gi+on (,mɛsə'lɒŋgɪ,ɒn) *n.* transliteration of the modern Greek name for **Missolonghi.**

mes·o+morph ('mɛsəʊ,mɔ:f) *n.* a type of person having a muscular body build with a relatively prominent underlying bone structure. Compare **ectomorph, endomorph.**

mes·o+mor+phic (,mɛsəʊ'mɔ:fɪk) *adj. also* **mes·o+mor+phous. 1.** *Chem.* existing in or concerned with an intermediate state of matter between a true liquid and a true solid. See also **liquid crystal, smectic, nematic. 2.** relating to or being a mesomorph. —**,mes·o+'mor+phism** *n.* —**'mes·o+,mor+phy** *n.*

me+son ('mi:zɒn) *n.* any of a group of elementary particles, such as a pion or kaon, that has a rest mass between those of an electron and a proton, and an integral spin. They are responsible for the force between nucleons in the atomic nucleus. Former name: **mesotron.** See also **muon.** [C20: from MESO- + -ON] —**me+'son+ic** *or* **'me+sic** *adj.*

mes·o+neph+ros (,mɛsəʊ'nɛfrɒs) *n.* the middle part of the embryonic kidney in vertebrates, becoming the adult kidney in fishes and amphibians and the epididymis in reptiles, birds, and mammals. See also **pronephros, metanephros.** [C19: New Latin, from MESO- + Greek *nephros* kidney] —**,mes·o+'neph+ric** *adj.*

mes·o+pause ('mɛsəʊ,pɔ:z) *n. Meteorol.* the zone of minimum temperature between the mesosphere and the thermosphere.

mes·o+phyll ('mɛsəʊ,fɪl) *n.* the soft chlorophyll-containing tissue of a leaf between the upper and lower layers of epidermis: involved in photosynthesis. —**,mes·o+'phyl+lic** *or* **,mes·o+'phyl+lous** *adj.*

mes·o+phyte ('mɛsəʊ,faɪt) *n.* any plant that grows in surroundings receiving an average supply of water. —**mes·o+phyt+ic** (,mɛsəʊ'fɪtɪk) *adj.*

Mes·o+po+ta+mi·a (,mɛsəpə'teɪmɪə) *n.* a region of SW Asia between the lower and middle reaches of the Tigris and Euphrates rivers: site of several ancient civilizations. [Latin, from Greek *mesopotamia* (*khora*) (the land) between rivers] —**,Mes·o+po+'ta+mi·an** *n., adj.*

mes·o+sphere ('mɛsəʊ,sfɪə) *n.* the atmospheric layer lying between the stratosphere and the thermosphere, characterized by a rapid decrease in temperature with height. —**mes·o+spher+ic** (,mɛsəʊ'sfɛrɪk) *adj.*

mes·o+the·li+o+ma (,mɛzəʊ,θi:lɪ'əʊmə) *n.* a tumour of the epithelium lining the lungs, abdomen, or heart: sometimes associated with exposure to asbestos dust. [C20: from MESOTHELI(UM) + -OMA]

mes·o+the·li·um (,mɛsəʊ'θi:lɪəm) *n.* epithelium, derived from embryonic mesoderm lining body cavities. [from New Latin, from MESO- + (EPI)THELIUM] —**,mes·o+'the·li·al** *adj.*

mes·o+tho+rax (,mɛsəʊ'θɔ:ræks) *n., pl.* **+rax·es** *or* **+ra·ces** (-rə,si:z). the middle segment of the thorax of an insect, bearing the second pair of walking legs and the first pair of wings. See also **prothorax, metathorax.** —**mes·o+tho+rac+ic** (,mɛsəʊθɔ:'ræsɪk) *adj.*

mes·o+tho+ri·um (,mɛsəʊ'θɔ:rɪəm) *n. Physics, obsolete.* either of two radioactive elements. **Mesothorium I** is now called radium-228. **Mesothorium II** is now called actinium-228.

mes·o+tron ('mɛsə,trɒn) *n.* a former name for **meson.**

Mes·o+zo+ic (,mɛsəʊ'zəʊɪk) *adj.* **1.** of, denoting, or relating to an era of geological time that began 225 000 000 years ago with the Triassic period and lasted about 155 000 000 years until the end of the Cretaceous period. ~*n.* **2. the.** the Mesozoic era.

mes+quite *or* **mes+quit** (mɛ'ski:t, 'mɛski:t) *n.* any small mimosaceous tree of the genus *Prosopis,* esp. the tropical American *P. juliflora,* whose sugary pods (**mesquite beans**) are used as animal fodder. Also called: **algarroba, honey locust, honey mesquite.** [C19: from Mexican Spanish, from Nahuatl *mizquitl*]

mess (mɛs) *n.* **1.** a state of confusion or untidiness, esp. if dirty or unpleasant: *the house was in a mess.* **2.** a chaotic or troublesome state of affairs; muddle: *his life was a mess.* **3.** *Informal.* a dirty or untidy person or thing. **4.** *Archaic.* a portion of food, esp. soft or semiliquid food. **5.** a place where service personnel eat or take recreation: *an officers' mess.* **6.** a group of people, usually servicemen, who eat together. **7.** the meal so taken. **8. mess of pottage.** a material gain involving the sacrifice of a higher value. ~*vb.* **9.** (*tr.*; often foll. by *up*) to muddle or dirty. **10.** (*intr.*) to make a mess. **11.** (*intr.*) (often foll. by *with*) to interfere; meddle. **12.** (*intr.*) (often foll. by *with* or *together*) *Military.* to group together, esp. for eating. [C13: from Old French *mes* dish of food, from Late Latin *missus* course (at table), from Latin *mittere* to send forth, set out]

mess a·bout *or* **a·round** *vb.* (*adv.*) **1.** (*intr.*) to occupy oneself trivially; potter. **2.** (when *intr.*, often foll. by *with*) to interfere or meddle (with).

mes+sage ('mɛsɪdʒ) *n.* **1.** a communication, usually brief, from one person or group to another. **2.** an implicit meaning or moral, as in a work of art. **3.** a formal communiqué. **4.** an inspired communication of a prophet or religious leader. **5.** a mission; errand. **6. get the message.** *Informal.* to understand what is meant. ~*vb.* **7.** (*tr.*) to send as a message, esp. to signal (a plan, etc.). [C13: from Old French, from Vulgar Latin *missāticum* (unattested) something sent, from Latin *missus*, past participle of *mittere* to send]

mes+sage stick *n.* a stick bearing carved symbols, carried by an Australian Aborigine as identification.

Mes·sa·li·na (ˌmɛsə'li:nə) *n.* **Va·ler·i·a** (və'lɪərɪə). died 48 A.D., wife of the Roman emperor Claudius, notorious for her debauchery and cruelty.

mes+sa+line (ˌmɛsə'li:n, 'mɛsəˌli:n) *n.* a light lustrous twilled-silk fabric. [C20: from French, origin obscure]

Mes+sa·pi·an (mə'seɪpɪən) *or* **Mes+sa+pic** (mə'seɪpɪk, -'sæpɪk) *n.* a scantily recorded language of an ancient people of Calabria (the **Messapii**), thought by some to be related to ancient Illyrian.

Messeigneurs *French.* (mesɛ'ɲœ:r) *n.* plural of **Monseigneur.**

Mes+se·ne (mɛ'si:nɪ) *n.* an ancient Greek city in the SW Peloponnese: founded in 369 B.C. as the capital of Messenia.

mes+sen+ger ('mɛsɪndʒə) *n.* **1.** a person who takes messages from one person or group to another or others. **2.** a person who runs errands or is employed to run errands. **3.** a carrier of official dispatches; courier. **4.** *Nautical.* **a.** a light line used to haul in a heavy rope. **b.** an endless belt of chain, rope, or cable, used on a powered winch to take off power. **5.** *Archaic.* a herald. [C13: from Old French *messagier*, from MESSAGE]

mes+sen+ger RNA *n. Biochem.* a form of RNA, transcribed from a single strand of DNA, that carries genetic information required for protein synthesis from DNA to the ribosomes. Sometimes shortened to **m-RNA.** See also **transfer RNA, genetic code.**

Mes·se·ni·a (mə'si:nɪə) *n.* the southwestern area of the Peloponnese in S Greece.

mess hall *n.* a military dining room, usually large.

Mes·siaen (*French* mɛ'sjã) *n.* **O·li·vier** (ɔli'vje). born 1908, French composer and organist. His music is distinguished by its rhythmic intricacy and is influenced by Hindu and Greek rhythms and bird song.

Mes+si+ah (mɪ'saɪə) *n.* **1.** *Judaism.* the awaited king of the Jews, to be sent by God to free them. **2.** Jesus Christ, when regarded in this role. **3.** an exceptional liberator of a country or people. [C14: from Old French *Messie*, ultimately from Hebrew *māshīah* anointed] —**Mes+'si+ah+ˌship** *n.*

mes+si+an+ic (ˌmɛsɪ'ænɪk) *adj.* **1.** (*sometimes cap.*) *Bible.* **a.** of or relating to the Messiah, his awaited deliverance of the Jews, or the new age of peace expected to follow this. **b.** of or relating to Jesus Christ or the salvation believed to have been brought by him. **2. a.** of or relating to any popular leader promising deliverance or an ideal era of peace and prosperity. **b.** of or relating to promises of this kind or to an ideal era of this kind. —ˌ**mes+si+'an·i·cal+ly** *adv.* —**mes+si+an+ism** (mɛ'saɪənɪzm) *n.*

Mes+si+dor *French.* (mɛsi'dɔ:r) *n.* the month of harvest: the tenth month of the French revolutionary calendar, extending from June 20 to July 19. [C19: from French, from Latin *messis* harvest + Greek *dōron* gift]

mes+sieurs ('mɛsəz; *French* me'sjø) *n.* the plural of **monsieur.**

Mes+si+na (mɛ'si:nə) *n.* a port in NE Sicily, on the **Strait of Messina:** colonized by Greeks around 730 B.C.; under Spanish rule (1282–1676 and 1678–1713); university (1549). Pop.: 261 332 (1975 est.).

mess jack+et *n.* a waist-length jacket tapering to a point at the back, worn by officers in the mess for formal dinners.

mess kit *n. Military.* **1.** *Brit.* formal evening wear for officers. **2.** Also called: **mess gear.** eating utensils used esp. in the field.

mess+mate ('mɛsˌmeɪt) *n.* **1.** a person with whom one shares meals in a mess, esp. in the army. **2.** *Austral.* any of various eucalyptus trees that grow amongst other species.

Messrs. ('mɛsəz) *n.* the plural of **Mr.**

mes+suage ('mɛswɪdʒ) *n. Property law.* a dwelling house together with its outbuildings, curtilage, and the adjacent land appropriated to its use. [C14: from Norman French: household, perhaps through misspelling of Old French *mesnage* MÉNAGE]

mess·y ('mɛsɪ) *adj.* **mess·i·er, mess·i·est.** dirty, confused, or untidy. —**'mess·i+ly** *adv.* —**'mess·i+ness** *n.*

mes+tee (mɛ'sti:) *n.* a variant spelling of **mustee.**

mes+ter ('mɛstə) *n. South Yorkshire dialect.* **1.** master: used as a term of address for a man who is the head of a house. **2. bad mester.** a term for the devil, used when speaking to children.

mes+ti+zo (mɛ'sti:zəʊ, mɪ-) *n., pl.* **+zos** *or* **+zoes.** a person of mixed parentage, esp. the offspring of a Spanish American and an American Indian. [C16: from Spanish, ultimately from Latin *miscēre* to mix] —**mes+ti+za** (mɛ'sti:zə) *fem. n.*

mes+tra+nol ('mɛstrəˌnɒl, -ˌnəʊl) *n.* a synthetic oestrogen used in combination with progesterones as an oral contraceptive. Formula: $C_{21}H_{26}O_2$. [C20: from M(ETHYL) + (O)ESTR(OGEN) + (*pregn*)*an*(*e*) ($C_{21}H_{36}$) + -OL]

Meš·tro·vić (*Serbo-Croatian* 'mɛʃtrɔˌvitʃ) *n.* **I·van** ('ivan). 1883–1962, U.S. sculptor, born in Austria: his works include portraits of Sir Thomas Beecham and Pope Pius XI.

met (mɛt) *vb.* the past tense or past participle of **meet.**

met. *abbrev. for:* **1.** metaphor. **2.** metaphysics. **3.** meteorological: *the met. office weather report.* **4.** meteorology. **5.** metropolitan.

Me·ta ('meɪtə; *Spanish* 'meta) *n.* a river in Colombia, rising in the Andes and flowing northeast and east, forming part of the border between Colombia and Venezuela, to join the Orinoco River. Length: about 1000 km (620 miles).

met·a- *or sometimes before a vowel* **met-** *prefix.* **1.** indicating change, alteration, or alternation: *metabolism; metamorphosis.* **2.** transcending or going beyond: *metapsychology.* **3.** occurring or situated behind or after: *metaphase.* **4.** (*often in italics*) denoting that an organic compound contains a benzene ring with substituents in the 1,3-positions: *metadinitrobenzene; meta*-cresol. Abbrev.: *m*-. Compare **ortho-** (sense 4), **para-**[1] (sense 6). **5.** denoting an isomer, polymer, or compound related to a specified compound (often differing from similar compounds that are prefixed by *para-*): *metaldehyde.* **6.** denoting an oxyacid that is the highest hydrated form of the anhydride or a salt of such an acid: *metaphosphoric acid.* Compare **ortho-** (sense 5). [from Greek (prep.)]

met·a+bol+ic path+way *n.* any of the sequences of biochemical reactions, catalysed by enzymes, that occur in all living cells: concerned mainly with the exchange of energy and chemicals. See also **Krebs cycle.**

me+tab·o+lism (mɪ'tæbəˌlɪzəm) *n.* **1.** the sum total of the chemical processes that occur in living organisms, resulting in growth, production of energy, elimination of waste material, etc. See **anabolism, basal metabolism, catabolism. 2.** the sum total of the chemical processes affecting a particular substance in the body: *carbohydrate metabolism; iodine metabolism.* [C19: from Greek *metabolē* change, from *metaballein* to change, from META- + *ballein* to throw] —**met·a+bol+ic** (ˌmɛtə'bɒlɪk) *adj.* —ˌ**met·a+'bol·i·cal·ly** *adv.*

me+tab·o+lite (mɪ'tæbəˌlaɪt) *n.* a substance produced during or taking part in metabolism. [C19: METABOL(ISM) + -ITE[1]]

me+tab·o+lize *or* **me+tab·o·lise** (mɪ'tæbəˌlaɪz) *vb.* to produce or be produced by metabolism. —**me+'tab·o+ˌliz+a·ble** *or* **me+'tab·o+ˌlis+a·ble** *adj.*

met·a+car+pal (ˌmɛtə'kɑ:pᵊl) *Anatomy.* ~*adj.* **1.** of or relating to the metacarpus. ~*n.* **2.** a metacarpal bone.

met·a+car+pus (ˌmɛtə'kɑ:pəs) *n., pl.* **+pi** (-paɪ). **1.** the skeleton of the hand between the wrist and the fingers, consisting of five long bones. **2.** the corresponding bones in other vertebrates.

met·a+cen+tre *or U.S.* **met·a+cen+ter** ('mɛtəˌsɛntə) *n.* the intersection of a vertical line through the centre of buoyancy of a floating body at equilibrium with a vertical line through the centre of buoyancy when the body is tilted. —ˌ**met·a+'cen+tric** *adj.*

met·a+chro+mat+ic (ˌmɛtəkrəʊ'mætɪk) *adj.* **1.** (of tissues and cells stained for microscopical examination) taking a colour different from that of the dye solution. **2.** (of dyes) capable of staining tissues or cells a colour different from that of the dye solution. **3.** of or relating to metachromatism.

met·a+chro+ma+tism (ˌmɛtə'krəʊməˌtɪzəm) *n.* a change in colour, esp. when caused by a change in temperature. [C19: from META- + CHROMATO- + -ISM]

met·a+cin+nab+a+rite (ˌmɛtəsɪ'næbəˌraɪt) *n.* the black solid form of mercuric sulphide.

met·a+fe·male (ˌmɛtə'fi:meɪl) *n. Genetics.* a sterile female organism, esp. a fruit fly (*Drosophila*) that has three X chromosomes. Former name: **superfemale.**

met·a+gal+ax·y (ˌmɛtə'gæləksɪ) *n., pl.* **+ax·ies.** the total system of galaxies and intergalactic space making up the universe. —**met·a+ga+lac+tic** (ˌmɛtəgə'læktɪk) *adj.*

met+age ('mi:tɪdʒ) *n.* **1.** the official measuring of weight or contents. **2.** a charge for this. [C16: from METE[1]]

met·a+gen+e·sis (ˌmɛtə'dʒɛnɪsɪs) *n.* another name for **alternation of generations.** —**met·a+ge·net+ic** (ˌmɛtədʒɪ'nɛtɪk) *or* ˌ**met·a+'gen+ic** *adj.* —ˌ**met·a+ge·'net·i·cal+ly** *adv.*

me+tag+na+thous (mɪ'tægnəθəs) *adj.* (of the beaks of birds such as the crossbill) having crossed tips. [C19: from META- + GNATHOUS] —**me+'tag+na+ˌthism** *n.*

met+al ('mɛtᵊl) *n.* **1. a.** any of a number of chemical elements, such as iron or copper, that are often lustrous ductile solids, have acidic oxides, form positive ions, and are good conductors of heat and electricity. **b.** an alloy, such as brass or steel, containing one or more of these elements. **2.** *Printing.* type made of metal. **3.** the substance of glass in a molten state or as the finished product. **4.** short for **road metal. 5.** *Navy.* **a.** the total weight of projectiles that can be shot by a ship's guns at any one time. **b.** the total weight or number of a ship's guns. **6.** *Heraldry.* gold or silver. **7.** the basic quality of a person or thing; stuff. **8.** (*pl.*) the rails of a railway. ~*adj.* **9.** made of metal. ~*vb.* **+als, +al+ling, +alled** *or U.S.* **+als, +al+ing, +aled.** (*tr.*) **10.** to fit or cover with metal. **11.** to make or mend (a road) with **road metal.** [C13: from Latin *metallum* mine, product of a mine, from Greek *metallon*] —**'met·al·ˌlike** *adj.*

metal. *or* **metall.** *abbrev. for:* **1.** metallurgical. **2.** metallurgy.

met·a+lan+guage ('mɛtəˌlæŋgwɪdʒ) *n.* a language or system of symbols used to discuss another language or system. See also **formal language, natural language.** Compare **object language.**

me+tal+lic (mɪ'tælɪk) *adj.* **1.** of, concerned with, or consisting of metal or a metal. **2.** suggestive of a metal: *a metallic click; metallic lustre.* **3.** *Chem.* (of a metal element) existing in the free state rather than in combination: *metallic copper.* —**me+'tal+li+cal+ly** *adv.*

me+tal+lic bond *n. Chem.* the covalent bonding between atoms in metals, in which the valence electrons are free to move through the crystal.

me+tal+lic soap *n.* any one of a number of colloidal stearates, palmitates, or oleates of various metals, including aluminium, calcium, magnesium, iron, and zinc. They are used as bases for ointments, fungicides, fireproofing and waterproofing agents, and driers for paints and varnishes.

met+al+lif+er+ous (ˌmɛtᵊ'lɪfərəs) *adj.* containing a metallic element: *a metalliferous ore.* [C17: from Latin *metallifer* yielding metal, from *metallum* metal + *ferre* to bear]

met+al+line ('mɛtəˌlaɪn) *adj.* **1.** of, resembling, or relating to metals. **2.** containing metals or metal ions.

met+al+list *or U.S.* **met+al+ist** ('mɛtᵊlɪst) *n.* **1.** a person who works with metals. **2.** a person who advocates a system of currency based on a metal, such as gold or silver.

met+al+lize, met+al+lise, *or U.S.* **met+al+ize** ('mɛtəˌlaɪz) *vb.* (*tr.*) to make metallic or to coat or treat with metal. —ˌ**met+al+li+'za+tion,** ˌ**met+al+li+'sa+tion,** *or U.S.* ˌ**met+al+i+'za+tion** *n.*

met+al+lo- *n. combining form.* denoting metal: *metallography; metalloid; metallurgy.* [from Greek *metallon*]

me+tal+lo+cene (mɪ'tæləʊˌsiːn) *n. Chem.* any one of a class of organometallic sandwich compounds of the general formula $M(C_5H_5)_2$, where M is a metal atom. See **ferrocene.** [C20: from METALLO- + *-cene,* as in FERROCENE]

met+al+log+ra+phy (ˌmɛtə'lɒgrəfɪ) *n.* **1.** the branch of metallurgy concerned with the composition and structure of metals and alloys. **2.** a lithographic process using metal plates instead of stone; metal lithography. —ˌ**met+al+'log+ra+pher** *or* ˌ**met+al+'log+ra+phist** *n.* —**me+tal+lo+graph+ic** (mɪˌtælə'græfɪk) *adj.* —**me+ˌtal+lo+'graph+i+cal+ly** *adv.*

met+al+loid ('mɛtəˌlɔɪd) *n.* **1.** a nonmetallic element, such as arsenic or silicon, that has some of the properties of a metal. ~*adj. also* **met+al+loi+dal** (ˌmɛtə'lɔɪdᵊl). **2.** of or being a metalloid. **3.** resembling a metal.

met+al+lo+phone (mɛ'tæləˌfəʊn) *n.* any of various musical instruments consisting of tuned metal bars struck with a hammer, such as the glockenspiel.

met+al+lur+gy (mɛ'tælədʒɪ; *U.S.* 'mɛtᵊˌlɜːdʒɪ) *n.* the scientific study of the extraction, refining, alloying, and fabrication of metals and of their structure and properties. —ˌ**met+al+'lur+gic** *or* ˌ**met+al+'lur+gi+cal** *adj.* —ˌ**met+al+'lur+gi+cal+ly** *adv.* —**met+al+lur+gist** ('mɛtəˌlɜːdʒɪst, mɛ'tælədʒɪst) *n.*

met+al spray+ing *n.* a process in which a layer of one metal is sprayed onto another in the molten state.

met+al+work ('mɛtᵊlˌwɜːk) *n.* **1.** the craft of working in metal. **2.** work in metal or articles made from metal.

met+al+work+ing ('mɛtᵊlˌwɜːkɪŋ) *n.* the processing of metal to change its shape, size, etc., as by rolling, forging, etc., or by making metal articles. —'**met+al+ˌwork+er** *n.*

met+a+male ('mɛtəˌmeɪl) *n. Genetics.* a sterile male organism, esp. a fruit fly (*Drosophila*) that has one X chromosome and three sets of autosomes. Former name: **supermale.**

met+a+math+e+mat+ics (ˌmɛtəˌmæθɪ'mætɪks) *n.* (*functioning as sing.*) the logical analysis of the reasoning, principles, and rules that control the use and combination of mathematical symbols, numbers, etc. —ˌ**met+a+ˌmath+e+'mat+i+cal** *adj.* —ˌ**met+a+ˌmath+e+ma+'ti+cian** *n.*

met+a+mer ('mɛtəmə) *n.* any of two or more isomeric compounds exhibiting metamerism.

met+a+mere ('mɛtəˌmɪə) *n.* one of the similar body segments into which earthworms, crayfish, and similar animals are divided longitudinally. Also called: **somite.** —**me+tam+er+al** (mɪ'tæmərəl) *adj.*

met+a+mer+ic (ˌmɛtə'mɛrɪk) *adj.* **1.** divided into or consisting of metameres. See also **metamerism** (sense 1). **2.** of or concerned with metamerism. —ˌ**met+a+'mer+i+cal+ly** *adv.*

me+tam+er+ism (mɪ'tæməˌrɪzəm) *n.* **1.** Also called: **(metameric) segmentation.** the division of an animal into similar segments (metameres). In many vertebrates it is confined to the embryonic nervous and muscular systems. **2.** *Chem.* a type of isomerism in which molecular structures differ by the attachment of different groups to the same atom, as in $CH_3OC_3H_7$ and $C_2H_5OC_2H_5$.

met+a+mor+phic (ˌmɛtə'mɔːfɪk) *or* **met+a+mor+phous** *adj.* **1.** relating to or resulting from metamorphosis or metamorphism. **2.** (of rocks) altered considerably from the original structure and composition by pressure and heat. Compare **igneous, sedimentary.**

met+a+mor+phism (ˌmɛtə'mɔːfɪzəm) *n.* **1.** the process by which metamorphic rocks are formed. **2.** a variant of **metamorphosis.**

met+a+mor+phose (ˌmɛtə'mɔːfəʊz) *vb.* to undergo or cause to undergo metamorphosis or metamorphism.

met+a+mor+pho+sis (ˌmɛtə'mɔːfəsɪs) *n., pl.* **+ses** (-ˌsiːz). **1.** a complete change of physical form or substance. **2.** a complete change of character, appearance, etc. **3.** a person or thing that has undergone metamorphosis. **4.** *Zoology.* the rapid transformation of a larva into an adult that occurs in certain animals, for example the stage between tadpole and frog or between chrysalis and butterfly. [C16: via Latin from Greek: transformation, from META- + *morphē* form]

met+a+neph+ros (ˌmɛtə'nɛfrɒs) *n., pl.* **+roi** (-rɔɪ). the last-formed posterior part of the embryonic kidney in reptiles, birds, and mammals, which remains functional in the adult. See also **pronephros, mesonephros.** [C19: New Latin, from META- + Greek *nephros* kidney]

metaph. *abbrev. for:* **1.** metaphor(ical). **2.** metaphysics.

met+a+phase ('mɛtəˌfeɪz) *n.* **1.** *Biology.* the second stage of mitosis during which a body of longitudinally arranged threads (see **spindle** (sense 7)) is formed within the cell. See also **prophase, anaphase, telophase. 2.** the corresponding stage of the first division of meiosis.

met+a+phor ('mɛtəfə, -ˌfɔː) *n.* a figure of speech in which a word or phrase is applied to an object or action that it does not literally denote in order to imply a resemblance, for example *he is a lion in battle.* Compare **simile.** [C16: from Latin, from Greek *metaphora,* from *metapherein* to transfer, from META- + *pherein* to bear] —**met+a+phor+ic** (ˌmɛtə'fɒrɪk) *or* ˌ**met+a+'phor+i+cal** *adj.* —ˌ**met+a+'phor+i+cal+ly** *adv.* —ˌ**met+a+'phor+i+cal+ness** *n.*

met+a+phos+phate (ˌmɛtə'fɒsfeɪt) *n.* any salt of metaphosphoric acid.

met+a+phos+phor+ic ac+id (ˌmɛtəfɒs'fɒrɪk) *n.* a glassy deliquescent highly polymeric solid, used as a dehydrating agent. Formula: $(HPO_3)_x$. See also **polyphosphoric acid.**

met+a+phrase ('mɛtəˌfreɪz) *n.* **1.** a literal translation. Compare **paraphrase.** ~*vb.* (*tr.*) **2.** to alter or manipulate the wording of. **3.** to translate literally. [C17: from Greek *metaphrazein* to translate]

met+a+phrast ('mɛtəˌfræst) *n.* a person who metaphrases, esp. one who changes the form of a text, as by rendering verse into prose. [C17: from Medieval Greek *metaphrastēs* translator] —ˌ**met+a+'phras+tic** *or* ˌ**met+a+'phras+ti+cal** *adj.* —ˌ**met+a+'phras+ti+cal+ly** *adv.*

met+a+phys+ic (ˌmɛtə'fɪzɪk) *n.* **1.** the system of first principles and assumptions underlying an enquiry or philosophical theory. **2.** an obsolete word for **metaphysician.** ~*adj.* **3.** *Rare.* another word for **metaphysical.**

met+a+phys+i+cal (ˌmɛtə'fɪzɪkᵊl) *adj.* **1.** of or relating to metaphysics. **2.** based on abstract reasoning. **3.** abstruse or over-theoretical. **4.** incorporeal; supernatural. —ˌ**met+a+'phys+i+cal+ly** *adv.*

Met+a+phys+i+cal (ˌmɛtə'fɪzɪkᵊl) *adj.* **1.** denoting or relating to certain 17th-century poets who combined intense feeling with ingenious thought and often used elaborate imagery and conceits. Notable among them were Donne, Herbert, and Marvell. ~*n.* **2.** a poet of this group.

met+a+phys+i+cize *or* **met+a+phys+i+cise** (ˌmɛtə'fɪzɪˌsaɪz) *vb.* **1.** (*intr.*) to think, write, etc., metaphysically. **2.** (*tr.*) to treat (a subject) metaphysically.

met+a+phys+ics (ˌmɛtə'fɪzɪks) *n.* (*functioning as sing.*) **1.** the branch of philosophy that deals with first principles, esp. of being and knowing. **2.** (popularly) abstract or subtle discussion or reasoning. [C16: from Medieval Latin, from Greek *ta meta ta phusika* the things after the physics, from the arrangement of the subjects treated in the works of Aristotle] —**met+a+phy+si+cian** ('mɛtəfɪ'zɪʃən) *or* **met+a+phys+i+cist** ('mɛtə'fɪzɪsɪst) *n.*

met+a+pla+si+a (ˌmɛtə'pleɪzɪə) *n.* the transformation of one kind of tissue into a different kind.

met+a+plasm ('mɛtəˌplæzəm) *n.* the nonliving constituents, such as starch and pigment granules, of the cytoplasm of a cell. —ˌ**met+a+'plas+mic** *adj.*

met+a+pol+i+tics (ˌmɛtə'pɒlɪtɪks) *n.* political theory (often used derogatorily).

met+a+psy+chol+o+gy (ˌmɛtəsaɪ'kɒlədʒɪ) *Psychol.* ~*n.* **1.** the study of philosophical questions, such as the relation between mind and body, that go beyond the laws of experimental psychology. **2.** any attempt to state the general laws of psychology. **3.** another word for **parapsychology.** —**met+a+psy+cho+log+i+cal** (ˌmɛtəˌsaɪkə'lɒdʒɪkᵊl) *adj.*

met+a+so+ma+tism (ˌmɛtə'səʊməˌtɪzəm) *or* **met+a+so+ma+to+sis** (ˌmɛtəˌsəʊmə'təʊsɪs) *n.* change in the composition of a rock or mineral by the addition or replacement of chemicals. [C19: from New Latin; see META-, SOMATO-]

met+a+sta+ble (ˌmɛtə'steɪbᵊl) *Physics.* ~*adj.* **1.** (of a body or system) having a state of apparent equilibrium although capable of changing to a more stable state. **2.** (of an atom, molecule, ion, or atomic nucleus) existing in an excited state with a relatively long lifetime. ~*n.* **3.** a metastable atom, ion, molecule, or nucleus. —ˌ**met+a+sta+'bil+i+ty** *n.*

me+tas+ta+sis (mɪ'tæstəsɪs) *n., pl.* **+ses** (-ˌsiːz). **1.** *Pathol.* the spreading of a disease, esp. cancer cells, from one part of the body to another. **2.** a transformation or change, as in rhetoric, from one point to another. **3.** a rare word for **metabolism.** [C16: via Latin from Greek: transition] —**met+a+stat+ic** (ˌmɛtə'stætɪk) *adj.* —ˌ**met+a+'stat+i+cal+ly** *adv.*

me+tas+ta+size *or* **me+tas+ta+sise** (mɪ'tæstəˌsaɪz) *vb.* (*intr.*) *Pathol.* (esp. of cancer cells) to spread to a new site in the body via blood or lymph vessels.

met+a+tar+sal (ˌmɛtə'tɑːsᵊl) *Anatomy.* ~*adj.* **1.** of or relating to the metatarsus. ~*n.* **2.** any bone of the metatarsus.

met+a+tar+sus (ˌmɛtə'tɑːsəs) *n., pl.* **+si** (-saɪ). **1.** the skeleton of the foot between the toes and the tarsus, consisting of five long bones. **2.** the corresponding skeletal part in other vertebrates.

met+a+the+o+ry ('mɛtəˌθɪərɪ) *n.* the critical study of the nature and purpose of philosophy.

met+a+the+ri+an (ˌmɛtə'θɪərɪən) *adj.* **1.** of, relating to, or belonging to the *Metatheria,* a subclass of mammals comprising the marsupials. ~*n.* **2.** any metatherian mammal; a marsupial.

~Compare **eutherian, prototherian.** [C19: from New Latin, from META- + Greek *thērion* animal]

me·tath·e·sis (mɪ'tæθəsɪs) *n., pl.* **·ses** (-ˌsi:z). **1.** the transposition of two sounds or letters in a word or of two words in a sentence. **2.** *Chem.* another name for **double decomposition.** [C16: from Late Latin, from Greek, from *metatithenai* to transpose] —**met·a·thet·ic** (ˌmɛtə'θɛtɪk) *or* ˌ**met·a·'thet·i·cal** *adj.*

me·tath·e·size *or* **me·tath·e·sise** (mɪ'tæθɪˌsaɪz) *vb.* to change or cause to change by metathesis.

met·a·tho·rax (ˌmɛtə'θɔ:ræks) *n., pl.* **·rax·es** *or* **·ra·ces** (-rəˌsi:z). the third and last segment of an insect's thorax, which bears the third pair of walking legs and the second pair of wings. See also **prothorax, mesothorax.** —**met·a·tho·rac·ic** (ˌmɛtəθɔ:'ræsɪk) *adj.*

met·a·xy·lem (ˌmɛtə'zaɪlɛm) *n.* xylem tissue that consists of rigid thick-walled cells and occurs in parts of the plant that have finished growing. Compare **protoxylem.**

met·a·zo·an (ˌmɛtə'zəʊən) *n.* **1.** any animal of the group *Metazoa,* in which the body is composed of many cells: includes all animals except sponges and protozoans. ~*adj. also* **met·a·zo·ic. 2.** of, relating to, or belonging to the *Metazoa.* [C19: from New Latin *Metazoa;* see META-, -ZOA]

Metch·ni·koff (*French* mɛtʃni'kɔf; *Russian* 'mjetʃnikəf) *n.* **É·lie** (e'li). 1845–1916, Russian bacteriologist in France. He formulated the theory of phagocytosis and shared the Nobel prize for medicine (1908).

mete[1] (mi:t) *vb.* (*tr.*) **1.** (usually foll. by *out*) *Formal.* to distribute or allot (something, often unpleasant). ~*vb., n.* **2.** *Poetic, dialect.* to measure. [Old English *metan;* compare Old Saxon *metan,* Old Norse *meta,* German *messen* to measure]

mete[2] (mi:t) *n. Rare.* a mark, limit, or boundary (esp. in the phrase **metes and bounds**). [C15: from Old French, from Latin *mēta* goal, turning post (in race)]

met·em·pir·i·cal (ˌmɛtɛm'pɪrɪkᵊl) *or* **met·em·pir·ic** *adj.* **1.** beyond the realm of experience. **2.** of or relating to metempirics. —ˌ**met·em·'pir·i·cal·ly** *adv.*

met·em·pir·ics (ˌmɛtɛm'pɪrɪks) *n.* the branch of philosophy that deals with things existing beyond the realm of experience. —ˌ**met·em·'pir·i·cist** *n.*

me·tem·psy·cho·sis (ˌmɛtəmsaɪ'kəʊsɪs) *n., pl.* **·ses** (-si:z). **1.** the migration of a soul from one body to another. **2.** the entering of a soul after death upon a new cycle of existence in a new body either of human or animal form. [C16: via Late Latin from Greek, from *metempsukhousthai,* from META- + *-em-* in + *psukhē* soul] —ˌ**me·tem·psy·'cho·sist** *n.*

met·en·ceph·a·lon (ˌmɛtɛn'sɛfəˌlɒn) *n., pl.* **·lons** *or* **·la** (-lə). the part of the embryonic hindbrain that develops into the cerebellum and pons Varolii. —**met·en·ce·phal·ic** (ˌmɛtɛnsɪ'fælɪk) *adj.*

me·te·or ('mi:tɪə) *n.* **1.** a very small meteoroid that has entered the earth's atmosphere. Such objects have speeds approaching 70 kilometres per second. **2.** Also called: **shooting star, falling star.** the bright streak of light appearing in the sky due to the incandescence of such a body heated by friction at its surface. [C15: from Medieval Latin *meteōrum,* from Greek *meteōron* something aloft, from *meteōros* lofty, from *meta-* (intensifier) + *aeirein* to raise]

me·te·or·ic (ˌmi:tɪ'ɒrɪk) *adj.* **1.** of, formed by, or relating to meteors. **2.** like a meteor in brilliance, speed, or transience. **3.** *Rare.* of or relating to the weather; meteorological. —ˌ**me·te·'or·i·cal·ly** *adv.*

me·te·or·ite ('mi:tɪəˌraɪt) *n.* a rocklike object consisting of the remains of a meteoroid that has fallen on earth. It may be stony (see **aerolite**) or metallic (see **siderite**). —**me·te·or·it·ic** (ˌmi:tɪə'rɪtɪk) *adj.*

me·te·or·o·graph ('mi:tɪərəˌgrɑ:f, -ˌgræf) *n.* an instrument that records various meteorological conditions. —ˌ**me·te·or·o·'graph·ic** *or* ˌ**me·te·or·o·'graph·i·cal** *adj.*

me·te·or·oid ('mi:tɪəˌrɔɪd) *n.* any of the small celestial bodies that are thought to orbit the sun, possibly as the remains of comets. When they enter the earth's atmosphere, they become visible as meteors. —ˌ**me·te·or·'oid·al** *adj.*

meteorol. *or* **meteor.** *abbrev. for:* **1.** meteorological. **2.** meteorology.

me·te·or·ol·o·gy (ˌmi:tɪə'rɒlədʒɪ) *n.* the study of the earth's atmosphere, esp. of weather-forming processes and weather forecasting. —**me·te·or·o·log·i·cal** (ˌmi:tɪərə'lɒdʒɪkᵊl) *or* ˌ**me·te·or·o·'log·ic** *adj.* —ˌ**me·te·or·o·'log·i·cal·ly** *adv.* —ˌ**me·te·or·'ol·o·gist** *n.*

me·te·or show·er *n.* a transient rain of meteors, such as the Perseids, occurring at regular intervals and coming from a particular region in the sky. It is caused by the earth passing through a large number of meteoroids (a **meteor swarm**).

me·ter[1] ('mi:tə) *n.* the U.S. spelling of **metre**[1].

me·ter[2] ('mi:tə) *n.* the U.S. spelling of **metre**[2].

me·ter[3] ('mi:tə) *n.* **1.** any device that measures and records the quantity of a substance, such as gas, that has passed through it during a specified period. **2.** any device that measures and sometimes records an electrical or magnetic quantity, such as current, voltage, etc. **3.** See **parking meter.** ~*vb.* (*tr.*) **4.** to measure (a rate of flow) with a meter. **5.** to print with stamps by means of a postage meter. [C19: see METE[1]]

-me·ter *n. combining form.* **1.** indicating an instrument for measuring: *barometer.* **2.** *Prosody.* indicating a verse having a specified number of feet: *pentameter.* [from Greek *metron* measure]

me·tered mail *n.* mail franked privately, under licence, with a machine bearing special markings (**meter marks**).

me·ter maid *n. Brit. informal.* a female traffic warden.

met·es·trus (mɛt'ɛstrəs, -'i:strəs) *n.* the U.S. spelling of **metoestrus.** —**met·'es·trous** *adj.*

Meth. *abbrev. for* Methodist.

meth- *combining form.* indicating a chemical compound derived from methane or containing methyl groups: *methacrylate resin.*

meth·ac·ry·late (mɛθ'ækrɪˌleɪt) *n.* **1.** any ester of methacrylic acid. **2.** See **methacrylate resin.**

meth·ac·ry·late res·in *n.* any acrylic resin derived from methacrylic acid.

meth·a·cryl·ic ac·id (ˌmɛθə'krɪlɪk) *n.* a colourless crystalline water-soluble substance used in the manufacture of acrylic resins; 2-methylpropenoic acid. Formula: CH_2:$C(CH_3)COOH$.

meth·a·done ('mɛθəˌdəʊn) *or* **meth·a·don** ('mɛθəˌdɒn) *n.* a narcotic analgesic drug similar to morphine but less habit-forming. Formula: $C_{21}H_{27}NO$. [C20: from (DI)METH(YL) + A(MINO) + D(IPHENYL) + -ONE]

met·hae·mo·glo·bin (mɛtˌhi:mə'gləʊbɪn, mɛˌθi:mə-) *n.* a brown compound of oxygen and haemoglobin formed in the blood by the action of certain drugs.

me·thane ('mi:θeɪn) *n.* a colourless odourless flammable gas, the simplest alkane and the main constituent of natural gas: used as a fuel. Formula: CH_4. See also **marsh gas, firedamp.**

me·thane se·ries *n.* another name for the **alkane series.** See **alkane.**

meth·a·nol ('mɛθəˌnɒl) *n.* a colourless volatile poisonous liquid compound used as a solvent and fuel. Formula: CH_3OH. Also called: **methyl alcohol, wood alcohol.** [C20: from METHANE + -OL[1]]

me·theg·lin (mə'θɛglɪn) *n.* (esp. formerly) spiced or medicated mead. [C16: from Welsh *meddyglyn,* from *meddyg* healer (from Latin *medicus* MEDICAL) + *llyn* liquor]

me·the·na·mine (mɛ'θi:nəˌmi:n, -ˌmaɪn) *n.* another name for **hexamethylenetetramine.** [C20: METH- + -ENE + AMINE]

me·thinks (mɪ'θɪŋks) *vb. past* **me·thought.** (*tr.*) (*takes a clause as object*) *Archaic.* it seems to me.

me·thi·o·nine (mɛ'θaɪəˌni:n, -ˌnaɪn) *n.* an essential amino acid containing sulphur, which occurs in many proteins; 2-amino-4-(methylthio)-butanoic acid. Formula: $CH_3SCH_2CH_2CH(NH_2)COOH$. [C20: METH- + THIONINE]

meth·o ('mɛθəʊ) *n. Austral.* an informal name for **methylated spirits.**

meth·od ('mɛθəd) *n.* **1.** a way of proceeding or doing something, esp. a systematic or regular one. **2.** orderliness of thought, action, etc. **3.** (*often pl.*) the techniques or arrangement of work for a particular field or subject. **4.** *Bell-ringing.* any of several traditional sets of changes. See **major** (sense 16), **minor** (sense 8). [C16: via French from Latin *methodus,* from Greek *methodos,* literally: a going after, from *meta-* after + *hodos* way] —**'meth·od·ist** *n.*

Meth·od ('mɛθəd) *n.* (*sometimes not cap.*) **a.** a technique of acting based on the theories of Stanislavsky, in which the actor bases his role on the inner motivation of the character he plays. **b.** (*as modifier*): *a Method actor.*

me·thod·i·cal (mɪ'θɒdɪkᵊl) *or* **me·thod·ic** *adj.* characterized by method or orderliness; systematic. —**me·'thod·i·cal·ly** *adv.* —**me·'thod·i·cal·ness** *n.*

Meth·od·ism ('mɛθəˌdɪzəm) *n.* the system and practices of the Methodist church, developed by John Wesley and his followers.

Meth·od·ist ('mɛθəˌdɪst) *n.* **1.** a member of any of the Nonconformist denominations that derive from the system of faith and practice initiated by John Wesley and his followers. ~*adj. also* **Meth·od·is·tic** *or* **Meth·od·is·ti·cal. 2.** of or relating to Methodism or the Church embodying it (the **Methodist Church**). —ˌ**Meth·od·'is·ti·cal·ly** *adv.*

Meth·o·di·us (mɛ'θəʊdi:əs) *n.* **Saint,** with his younger brother Saint Cyril called *the Apostles of the Slavs.* 815–885 A.D., Greek Christian theologian sent as a missionary to the Moravians. Feast day: July 7.

meth·od·ize *or* **meth·od·ise** ('mɛθəˌdaɪz) *vb.* (*tr.*) to organize according to a method; systematize. —ˌ**meth·od·i·'za·tion** *or* ˌ**meth·od·i·'sa·tion** *n.* —**'meth·od·ˌiz·er** *or* **'meth·od·ˌis·er** *n.*

meth·od·ol·o·gy (ˌmɛθə'dɒlədʒɪ) *n., pl.* **·gies. 1.** the system of methods and principles used in a particular discipline. **2.** the branch of philosophy concerned with the science of method and procedure. —**meth·od·o·log·i·cal** (ˌmɛθədə'lɒdʒɪkᵊl) *adj.* —ˌ**meth·od·o·'log·i·cal·ly** *adv.* —ˌ**meth·od·'ol·o·gist** *n.*

meth·o·trex·ate (ˌmɛθəʊ'trɛkseɪt, ˌmi:θəʊ-) *n.* a drug used in the treatment of certain cancers. Formula: $C_{20}H_{22}N_8O_5$.

me·thought (mɪ'θɔ:t) *vb. Archaic.* the past tense of **methinks.**

meth·ox·ide (mɛθ'ɒksaɪd) *n.* a saltlike compound in which the hydrogen atom in the hydroxyl group of methanol has been replaced by a metal atom, usually an alkali metal atom as in sodium methoxide, $NaOCH_3$. Also called: **methylate.**

meths (mɛθs) *n. Chiefly Brit.* an informal name for **methylated spirits.**

Me·thu·se·lah[1] (mə'θju:zələ) *n.* a wine bottle holding the equivalent of eight normal bottles.

Me·thu·se·lah[2] (mɪ'θju:zələ) *n. Old Testament.* a patriarch supposed to have lived 969 years (Genesis 5:21–27) who has come to be regarded as a type of longevity. Douay spelling: **Ma·thu·sa·la.**

me·thyl ('mi:θaɪl, 'mɛθɪl) *n.* **1.** (*modifier*) of, consisting of, or containing the monovalent group of atoms CH_3. **2.** an organometallic compound in which methyl groups are bound directly to a metal atom. [C19: from French *méthyle,* back formation from METHYLENE] —**me·thyl·ic** (mə'θɪlɪk) *adj.*

me·thyl ac·e·tate *n.* a colourless volatile flammable liquid ester with a fragrant odour, used as a solvent, esp. in paint removers. Formula: CH_3COOCH_3.

meth·yl·al ('mɛθɪ,læl) *n.* a colourless volatile flammable liquid with an odour resembling that of chloroform, used as a solvent and in the manufacture of perfumes and adhesives. Formula: $(CH_3O)_2CH_2$. Also called: **formal.**

me·thyl al·co·hol *n.* another name for **methanol.**

me·thyl·a·mine (mi:'θaɪlə,mi:n) *n.* a colourless flammable water-soluble gas, used in the manufacture of herbicides, dyes, and drugs. Formula: CH_3NH_2.

meth·yl·ate ('mɛθɪ,leɪt) *vb.* **1.** (*tr.*) to mix with methanol. **2.** to undergo or cause to undergo a chemical reaction in which a methyl group is introduced into a molecule. ~*n.* **3.** another name for **methoxide.** —,**meth·yl·'a·tion** *n.* —'**meth·yl·,a·tor** *n.*

meth·yl·at·ed spir·its *n.* alcohol that has been denatured by the addition of methanol and pyridine and a violet dye. Also called: **metho, meths.**

me·thyl bro·mide *n.* a colourless poisonous gas or volatile liquid with an odour resembling that of chloroform, used as a solvent, and extinguishant. Formula: CH_3Br.

me·thyl chlo·ride *n.* a colourless gas with an ether-like odour, used as a refrigerant and anaesthetic. Formula: CH_3Cl.

me·thyl·do·pa (,mi:θaɪl'dəʊpə) *n.* a catecholamine drug used to treat hypertension. Formula: $C_{10}H_{13}NO_4$. [C20: from *methyl* + *d(ihydr)o(xy)p(henyl)a(lanine)*]

meth·yl·ene ('mɛθɪ,li:n) *n.* (*modifier*) of, consisting of, or containing the divalent group of atoms $=CH_2$: *a methylene group or radical.* [C19: from French *méthylène*, from Greek *methu* wine + *hulē* wood + -ENE: originally referring to a substance distilled from wood]

meth·yl·ene blue *n.* a dark-green crystalline compound forming a blue aqueous solution, used as a mild antiseptic and biological stain. Formula: $C_{16}H_{18}N_3SCl.3H_2O$. Also called: **methylthionine chloride.**

me·thyl e·thyl ke·tone *n.* another name for **butanone.**

me·thyl i·so·bu·tyl ke·tone (,aɪsəʊ'bju:taɪl, -tɪl) *n.* a colourless insoluble liquid ketone used as a solvent for organic compounds, esp. nitrocellulose; 4-methylpentan-2-one. Formula: $CH_3COC_4H_9$. Also called: **hexone.**

me·thyl meth·ac·ry·late *n.* a colourless liquid compound, used in the manufacture of certain methacrylate resins. Formula: $CH_2C(CH_3)COOCH_3$.

me·thyl·naph·tha·lene (,mi:θaɪl'næpθə,li:n) *n.* either of two isomeric derivatives of naphthalene: a liquid (1-methylnaphthalene), used in standardizing diesel fuels, or a solid (2-methylnaphthalene), an insecticide.

me·thyl·thi·o·nine chlo·ride (,mi:θaɪl'θaɪə,ni:n) *n.* another name for **methylene blue.**

met·ic ('mɛtɪk) *n.* (in ancient Greece) an alien having some rights of citizenship in the city in which he lives. [C19: from Greek *metoikos*, from META- (indicating change) + *-oikos* dwelling]

me·tic·u·lous (mɪ'tɪkjʊləs) *adj.* very precise about details, even trivial ones; painstaking. [C16 (meaning: timid): from Latin *meticulōsus* fearful, from *metus* fear] —**me·'tic·u·lous·ly** *adv.* —**me·'tic·u·lous·ness** or **me·tic·u·los·i·ty** (mɪ,tɪkjʊ'lɒsɪtɪ) *n.*

mé·ti·er ('mɛtɪeɪ) *n.* **1.** a profession or trade, esp. that to which one is well suited. **2.** a person's strong point or speciality. [C18: from French, ultimately from Latin *ministerium* service]

Mé·tis (mɛ'ti:s) or **Mé·tif** (mɛ'ti:f) *n., pl.* **·tis** (-'ti:s, -'ti:z). or **·tifs. 1.** a person of mixed parentage, esp. the offspring of a French Canadian and a North American Indian. **2.** *U.S.* a person having one eighth Negro ancestry; octoroon. [C19: from French, from Vulgar Latin *mixtīcius* (unattested) of mixed race; compare MESTIZO] —**Mé·tisse** (mɛ'ti:s) *fem. n.*

met·oes·trus (mɛt'i:strəs, -'ɛstrəs) or *U.S.* **met·es·trus** *n.* *Zoology.* the period in the oestrous cycle following oestrus, characterized by lack of sexual activity. —**met·'oes·trous** or *U.S.* **met·'es·trous** *adj.*

me·tol ('mi:tɒl) *n.* a colourless soluble organic substance used, in the form of its sulphate, as a photographic developer; *p*-methylaminophenol. See also **aminophenol.** [C20: from German, an arbitrary coinage]

Me·ton·ic cy·cle (mɪ'tɒnɪk) *n.* a cycle of 235 synodic months after which the phases of the moon recur on the same day of the month. See also **golden number.** [C17: named after *Meton*, 5th-century B.C. Athenian astronomer]

met·o·nym ('mɛtənɪm) *n.* a word used in a metonymy. For example *the bottle* is a metonym for *alcoholic drink.*

me·ton·y·my (mɪ'tɒnɪmɪ) *n., pl.* **·mies.** the substitution of a word referring to an attribute for the thing that is meant, as for example the use of *the crown* to refer to a monarch. Compare **synecdoche.** [C16: from Late Latin from Greek: a changing of name, from *meta-* (indicating change) + *onoma* name] —**met·o·nym·i·cal** (,mɛtə'nɪmɪkᵊl) or ,**met·o·'nym·ic** *adj.* —,**met·o·'nym·i·cal·ly** *adv.*

met·ope ('mɛtəʊp, 'mɛtəpɪ) *n.* *Architect.* a square space between two triglyphs in a Doric frieze. [C16: via Latin from Greek *metopē*, from *meta* between + *opē* one of the holes for the beam ends]

me·top·ic (mɪ'tɒpɪk) *adj.* of or relating to the forehead.

me·tral·gi·a (mɪ'trældʒɪə) *n.* pain in the uterus. [C20: from METRO-¹ + -ALGIA]

me·tre¹ or *U.S.* **me·ter** ('mi:tə) *n.* **1.** a metric unit of length equal to approximately 1.094 yards. **2.** the basic SI unit of length; 1 650 763.73 wavelengths in vacuum of the radiation corresponding to the transition between the levels $2p_{10}$ and $5d_5$ of krypton-86. In 1960 this definition replaced the definition based on the platinum-iridium metre bar kept in Paris. Symbol: m [C18: from French; see METRE²]

me·tre² or *U.S.* **me·ter** ('mi:tə) *n.* **1.** *Prosody.* the rhythmic arrangement of syllables in verse, usually according to the number and kind of feet in a line. **2.** *Music.* another word (esp. U.S.) for **time** (sense 22). [C14: from Latin *metrum*, from Greek *metron* measure]

me·tre-kil·o·gram-sec·ond *n.* See **mks units.**

met·ric ('mɛtrɪk) *adj.* **1.** of or relating to the metre or metric system. **2.** *Maths.* denoting or relating to a set containing pairs of points for each of which a non-negative real number $\rho(x,y)$ (the distance) can be defined, satisfying specific conditions. ~*n.* **3.** *Maths.* the function $\rho(x,y)$ satisfying the conditions of membership of such a set (a **metric space**).

met·ri·cal ('mɛtrɪkᵊl) or **met·ric** ('mɛtrɪk) *adj.* **1.** of or relating to measurement. **2.** of or in poetic metre. —'**met·ri·cal·ly** *adv.*

met·ri·cal psalm *n.* a translation of one of the psalms into rhyming strict-metre verse usually sung as a hymn.

met·ri·cate ('mɛtrɪ,keɪt) *vb.* to convert (a measuring system, instrument, etc.) from nonmetric to metric units. —**met·ri·'ca·tion** *n.*

met·ric hun·dred·weight *n.* See **hundredweight** (sense 3).

met·rics ('mɛtrɪks) *n.* (*functioning as sing.*) *Prosody.* the art of using poetic metre.

met·ric sys·tem *n.* any decimal system of units based on the metre. For scientific purposes the Système International d'Unités (SI units) is used.

met·ric ton *n.* a unit of mass equal to 1000 kilograms or 2204.6 pounds. Also called: **tonne.**

met·ri·fy ('mɛtrɪ,faɪ) *vb.* **·fies, ·fy·ing, ·fied.** (*tr.*) *Prosody.* to render into poetic metre. —'**met·ri·,fi·er** *n.*

met·rist ('mɛtrɪst) *n.* *Prosody.* a person skilled in the use of poetic metre.

me·tri·tis (mɪ'traɪtɪs) *n.* inflammation of the uterus.

met·ro ('mɛtrəʊ) or **mét·ro** *n., pl.* **·ros.** an underground railway system in certain cities, esp. in Europe, such as that in Paris. [C20: from French, short for *chemin de fer métropolitain* metropolitan railway]

met·ro-¹ or *before a vowel* **metr-** *combining form.* indicating the uterus: *metrorrhagia.* [from Greek *mētra* womb]

met·ro-² *combining form.* indicating a measure: *metronome.* [from Greek *metron* measure]

me·trol·o·gy (mɪ'trɒlədʒɪ) *n., pl.* **·gies. 1.** the science of weights and measures; the study of units of measurement. **2.** a particular system of units. [C19: from Greek *metron* measure] —**met·ro·log·i·cal** (,mɛtrəʊ'lɒdʒɪkᵊl) *adj.* —,**met·ro·'log·i·cal·ly** *adv.* —**me·'trol·o·gist** *n.*

met·ro·ni·da·zole (,mɛtrə'naɪdə,zəʊl) *n.* a pale yellow crystalline compound used to treat vaginal trichomoniasis. Formula: $C_6H_9N_3O_3$. [C20: from ME(THYL) + (NI)TRO- + *-n-* + (IM)ID(E) + AZOLE]

met·ro·nome ('mɛtrə,nəʊm) *n.* a mechanical device which indicates the exact tempo of a piece of music by producing a clicking sound from a pendulum with an adjustable period of swing. [C19: from Greek *metron* measure + *nomos* rule, law] —**met·ro·nom·ic** (,mɛtrə'nɒmɪk) *adj.*

met·ro·nym·ic (,mɛtrəʊ'nɪmɪk) or **mat·ro·nym·ic** *adj.* **1.** (of a name) derived from the name of its bearer's mother or another female ancestor. ~*n.* **2.** a metronymic name. [C19: from Greek *mētronumikos*, from *mētēr* mother + *onoma* name]

me·trop·o·lis (mɪ'trɒpəlɪs) *n., pl.* **·lis·es. 1.** the main city, esp. of a country or region; capital. **2.** a centre of activity. **3.** the chief see in an ecclesiastical province. [C16: from Late Latin from Greek: mother city or state, from *mētēr* mother + *polis* city]

met·ro·pol·i·tan (,mɛtrə'pɒlɪtən) *adj.* **1.** of or characteristic of a metropolis. **2.** constituting a city and its suburbs: *the metropolitan area.* **3.** of, relating to, or designating an ecclesiastical metropolis. **4.** of or belonging to the home territories of a country, as opposed to overseas territories: *metropolitan France.* ~*n.* **5. a.** *Eastern Churches.* the head of an ecclesiastical province, ranking between archbishop and patriarch. **b.** *Church of England.* an archbishop. **c.** *R.C. Church.* an archbishop or bishop having authority in certain matters over the dioceses in his province. —,**met·ro·'pol·i·tan·ism** *n.*

met·ro·pol·i·tan coun·ty *n.* (in England since April 1, 1974) any of the six conurbations established as units in the new local government system, with elected councils possessing powers resembling those of counties.

met·ro·pol·i·tan dis·trict *n.* (in England since April 1, 1974) any of the districts into which the new metropolitan counties are divided. Each metropolitan district has an elected council responsible for education, social services, etc. See also **district** (sense 4).

me·tror·rha·gi·a (,mi:trɔ:'reɪdʒɪə, ,mɛt-) *n.* abnormal bleeding from the uterus.

-me·try *n. combining form.* indicating the process or science of measuring: *anthropometry; geometry.* [from Old French *-metrie*, from Latin *-metria*, from Greek, from *metron* measure] —**-met·ric** *adj. combining form.*

Met·ter·nich (*German* 'mɛtərnɪç) *n.* **Kle·mens** ('kle:məns). 1773–1859, Austrian statesman. He became foreign minister (1809) and made a significant contribution to the Congress of Vienna (1815). From 1821 to 1848 he was both foreign minister and chancellor of Austria and is noted for his defence of autocracy in Europe.

met·tle ('mɛtᵊl) *n.* **1.** courage; spirit. **2.** inherent character. **3.**

on one's mettle. roused to putting forth one's best efforts. [C16: originally a spelling variant of METAL]
met+tled ('mɛtᵊld) *or* **met+tle+some** ('metᵊlsəm) *adj.* courageous or valiant.
Metz (mɛts; *French* mɛs) *n.* a city in NE France on the River Moselle: a free imperial city in the 13th century; annexed by France in 1552; part of Germany (1871–1918); centre of the Lorraine iron-mining region. Pop.: 117 199 (1975).
meu (mju:) *n.* another name for **spignel.** [C16: from Latin *mēum,* from Greek *mēon*]
Meung (*French* mœ̃) *n.* See **Jean de Meung.**
meu+nière (mən'jɛə; *French* mønjɛ:r) *adj.* (of fish) dredged with flour, fried in butter, and served with butter, lemon juice, and parsley. [French, literally: miller's wife]
Meurthe-et-Mo·selle (*French* mœrt e mo'zɛl) *n.* a department of NE France, in Lorraine region. Capital: Nancy. Pop.: 741 437 (1975). Area: 5280 sq. km (2059 sq. miles).
Meuse (mɜ:z; *French* mø:z) *n.* **1.** a department of N France, in Lorraine region: heavy fighting occurred here in World War I. Capital: Bar-le-Duc. Pop.: 214 398 (1975). Area: 6241 sq. km (2434 sq. miles). **2.** a river in W Europe, rising in NE France and flowing north across E Belgium and the S Netherlands to join the Waal River before entering the North Sea. Length: 926 km (575 miles). Dutch name: **Maas.**
MeV *abbrev. for* million electronvolts (10^6 electronvolts).
mew[1] (mju:) *vb.* **1.** (*intr.*) (esp. of a cat) to make a characteristic high-pitched cry. ~*n.* **2.** such a sound. [C14: imitative]
mew[2] (mju:) *n.* any sea gull, esp. the common gull, *Larus canus.* Also called: **mew gull, sea mew.** [Old English *mǣw;* compare Old Saxon *mēu,* Middle Dutch *mēwe*]
mew[3] (mju:) *n.* **1.** a room or cage for hawks, esp. while moulting. ~*vb.* **2.** (*tr.;* often foll. by *up*) to confine (hawks or falcons) in a shelter, etc., usually by tethering them to a perch. **3.** to confine, conceal. [C14: from Old French *mue,* from *muer* to moult, from Latin *mūtāre* to change]
mew[4] (mju:) *vb.* **1.** (*intr.*) (of hawks or falcons) to moult. **2.** (*trs.*) *Obsolete.* to shed (one's covering, clothes, etc.). [C14: from Old French *muer* to moult, from Latin *mūtāre* to change]
Me+war (mɛ'wɑ:) *n.* another name for **Udaipur** (sense 1).
mewl (mju:l) *vb.* **1.** (*intr.*) (esp. of a baby) to cry weakly; whimper (often in the phrase **mewl and puke**). ~*n.* **2.** such a cry. [C17: imitative] —'**mewl+er** *n.*
mews (mju:z) *n. Chiefly Brit.* **1.** a yard or street lined by buildings originally used as stables but now often converted into dwellings. **2.** the buildings around a mews. [C14: pl. of MEW[3], originally referring to royal stables built on the site of hawks' mews at Charing Cross in London]
MEX *international car registration for* Mexico.
Mex. *abbrev. for:* **1.** Mexican. **2.** Mexico.
Mex·i+cal·i (ˌmɛksɪ'kɑ:lɪ; *Spanish* ˌmexi'kali) *n.* a city in NW Mexico, capital of Baja California state, on the border with the U.S. adjoining Calexico, California: centre of a rich irrigated agricultural region. Pop.: 331 059 (1975 est.).
Mex·i+can hair+less *n.* a breed of small hairless dog with mottled skin.
Mex·i+can War *n.* the war fought between the U.S. and Mexico (1846–48), through which the U.S. acquired the present-day Southwest.
Mex·i+co ('mɛksɪˌkəʊ) *n.* **1.** a republic in North America, on the Gulf of Mexico and the Pacific: early Mexican history includes the Maya, Toltec, and Aztec civilizations; conquered by the Spanish between 1519 and 1525 and achieved independence in 1821; lost Texas to the U.S. in 1836 and California and New Mexico in 1848. It is generally mountainous with three ranges of the Sierra Madre (east, west, and south) and a large central plateau. Official language: Spanish. Religion: chiefly Roman Catholic. Currency: peso. Capital: Mexico City. Pop.: 48 225 238 (1970). Area: 1 967 183 sq. km (761 530 sq. miles). Official name: **United Mexican States.** Spanish name: **Méjico. 2.** a state of Mexico, on the central plateau surrounding Mexico City, which is not administratively part of the state. Capital: Toluca. Pop.: 3 833 185 (1970). Area: 21 460 sq. km (8287 sq. miles). **3. Gulf of.** an arm of the Atlantic, bordered by the U.S., Cuba, and Mexico: linked with the Atlantic by the Florida Strait and with the Caribbean by the Yucatán Channel. Area: about 160 000 sq. km (618 000 sq. miles). —**Mex·i+can** ('mɛksɪkən) *adj., n.*
Mex·i+co Cit·y *n.* the capital of Mexico, on the central plateau at an altitude of 2240 m (7350 ft.): founded as the Aztec capital (Tenochtitlán) in about 1300; conquered and rebuilt by the Spanish in 1521; forms, with its suburbs, the federal district of Mexico; the largest industrial complex in the country. Pop.: 3 025 564 (1970).
Mey·er·beer (*German* 'maɪərˌbe:r) *n.* **Gia·co·mo** ('dʒa:komo). real name *Jakob Liebmann Beer.* 1791–1864, German composer, esp. of operas, such as *Robert le diable* (1831) and *Les Huguenots* (1836).
Mey·er·hof (*German* 'maɪərˌho:f) *n.* **Ot·to (Fritz)** ('ɔto). 1884–1951, German physiologist, noted for his work on the metabolism of muscles. He shared the Nobel prize for medicine (1922).
MEZ *abbrev. for* Central European Time. [from German *Mitteleuropäische Zeit*]
mez+cal (mɛ'skæl) *n.* a variant spelling of **mescal.**
mez+ca+line ('mɛzkəˌli:n) *n.* a variant spelling of **mescaline.**
me+ze·re·on (mɛ'zɪərɪən) *n.* **1.** a Eurasian thymelaeaceous shrub, *Daphne mezereum,* with fragrant early-blooming purplish-pink flowers and small scarlet fruits. **2.** another name for **mezereum.** [C15: via Medieval Latin from Arabic *māzaryūn*]
me+ze·re·um (mɪ'zɪərɪəm) *or* **me+ze·re·on** *n.* the dried bark of certain shrubs of the genus *Daphne,* esp. mezereon, formerly used as a vesicant and to treat arthritis.
Mé+zières (*French* me'zjɛ:r) *n.* a town in NE France, on the River Meuse opposite Charleville. See **Charleville-Mézières.**
me+zu+zah (mə'zuzə, -'zu:-; *Hebrew* məzu'za) *n., pl.* **+zu+zahs** *or* **+zu+zoth** (*Hebrew* -zu'zɔt). *Judaism.* a piece of parchment inscribed with scriptural passages. It is fixed to the doorpost of a Jewish house, etc., or worn round the neck. [from Hebrew, literally: doorpost]
mez+za+nine ('mɛzəˌni:n, 'mɛtsəˌni:n) *n.* **1.** Also called: **mezzanine floor, entresol.** an intermediate storey, esp. a low one between the ground and first floor of a building. **2.** *Theatre, U.S.* the first balcony. **3.** *Theatre, Brit.* a room or floor beneath the stage. [C18: from French, from Italian, diminutive of *mezzano* middle, from Latin *mediānus* MEDIAN]
mez+za voc·e ('mɛtsə 'vəʊtʃɪ; *Italian* 'meddza 'votʃe) *adv. Music.* (in singing) softly; quietly. [Italian, literally: half voice]
mez+zo ('mɛtsəʊ) *Music.* ~*adv.* **1.** moderately; quite: *mezzo forte; mezzo piano.* ~*n., pl.* **+zos. 2.** See **mezzo-soprano.** [C19: from Italian, literally; half, from Latin *medius* middle]
mez·zo-re·lie·vo *or* **mez·zo-ri·lie·vo** (ˌmɛtsəʊrɪ'li:vəʊ) *n.* carving in which the depth of the relief is halfway between that of high relief and low relief. [Italian: half relief]
mez·zo-so·pra·no *n., pl.* **·nos. 1.** a female voice intermediate between a soprano and contralto and having a range from the A below middle C to the F an eleventh above it. Sometimes shortened to **mezzo. 2.** a singer with such a voice.
mez+zo+tint ('mɛtsəʊˌtɪnt) *n.* **1.** a method of engraving a copper plate by scraping and burnishing the roughened surface. **2.** a print made from a plate so treated. ~*vb.* **3.** (*tr.*) to engrave (a copper plate) in this fashion. [C18: from Italian *mezzotinto* half tint] —'**mez+zo+ˌtint+er** *n.*
mf *Music. abbrev. for* mezzo forte. [Italian: moderately loud]
MF *abbrev. for:* **1.** *Radio.* medium frequency. **2.** Middle French.
mfd. *abbrev. for* manufactured.
mfg. *abbrev. for* manufacturing.
MFH *Hunting. abbrev. for* Master of Foxhounds.
mfr. *abbrev. for:* **1.** manufacture. **2.** manufacturer.
mg *or* **mg.** *abbrev. for* milligram.
Mg *the chemical symbol for* magnesium.
MG *abbrev. for* machine gun.
M.G.B. *abbrev. for* Ministry of State Security; the Soviet secret police from 1946 to 1954. [from Russian *Ministerstvo gosudarstvennoi bezopasnosti*]
Mgr. *abbrev. for:* **1.** manager. **2.** Monseigneur. **3.** Monsignor.
M.H.A. (in Australia) *abbrev. for* Member of the House of Assembly.
MHD *abbrev. for* magnetohydrodynamics.
MHG *abbrev. for* Middle High German.
mho (məʊ) *n., pl.* **mhos.** the former name for **siemens.** [C19: formed by reversing the letters of OHM (first used by Lord Kelvin)]
M.H.R. (in the U.S. and Australia) *abbrev. for* Member of the House of Representatives.
MHz *abbrev. for* megahertz.
mi *or* **me** (mi:) *n. Music.* (in tonic sol-fa) the third degree of any major scale; mediant. [C16: see GAMUT]
MI *abbrev. for* Military Intelligence.
mi. *abbrev. for* mile.
MI5 *abbrev. for* Military Intelligence, section five; a former official and present-day popular name for the counterintelligence agency of the British Government.
MI6 *abbrev. for* Military Intelligence, section six; a former official and present-day popular name for the intelligence and espionage agency of the British Government.
M.I.A. *abbrev. for* Murrumbidgee Irrigation Area.
Mi+am·i (maɪ'æmɪ) *n.* a city and resort in SE Florida, on Biscayne Bay: developed chiefly after 1896, esp. with the Florida land boom of the 1920s; centre of an extensive tourist area. Pop.: 353 984 (1973 est.).
mi·a mi·a ('mi:ə'mi:ə) *n.* an Australian Aborigine's hut. [from a native Australian language]
Mi+am·i Beach *n.* a resort in SE Florida, on an island separated from Miami by Biscayne Bay. Pop.: 87 072 (1970).
mi·aou *or* **mi·aow** (mɪ'aʊ, mjaʊ) *vb., interj.* variant spellings of **meow.**
mi+as+ma (mɪ'æzmə) *n., pl.* **+ma+ta** (-mətə) *or* **+mas. 1.** an unwholesome or foreboding atmosphere. **2.** pollution in the atmosphere, esp. noxious vapours from decomposing organic matter. [C17: New Latin, from Greek: defilement, from *miainein* to defile] —**mi+'as+mal, mi+as+mat+ic** (ˌmi:əz'mætɪk), ˌ**mi·as+'mat·i·cal,** *or* **mi+'as+mic** *adj.*
mi+aul (mɪ'aʊl) *vb.* (*intr.*) another word for **meow.**
Mic. *Bible abbrev. for* Micah.
mi·ca ('maɪkə) *n.* any of a group of lustrous rock-forming minerals consisting of hydrous silicates of aluminium, potassium, etc., in monoclinic crystalline form, occurring in igneous and metamorphic rock. Because of their resistance to electricity and heat they are used as dielectrics, in heating elements, etc. Also called: **isinglass.** [C18: from Latin: grain, morsel] —**mi+ca+ceous** (maɪ'keɪʃəs) *adj.*
Mi·cah ('maɪkə) *n. Old Testament.* **1.** a Hebrew prophet of the late 8th century B.C. **2.** the book containing his prophecies. Douay spelling: **Mi·che·as** (maɪ'ki:əs).
Mi+caw+ber (mɪ'kɔ:bə) *n.* a person who idles and trusts to

fortune. [C19: after a character in Dickens' novel *David Copperfield*] —**Mi+'caw+ber+ish** *adj.* —**Mi+'caw+ber+ism** *n.*

mice (maɪs) *n.* the plural of **mouse.**

mi+celle, mi+cell (mɪ'sɛl), *or* **mi+cel+la** (mɪ'sɛlə) *n. Chem.* **a.** a charged aggregate of molecules of colloidal size in a solution. **b.** any molecular aggregate of colloidal size, such as a particle found in coal. [C19: from New Latin *micella*, diminutive of Latin *mīca* crumb] —**mi+'cel+lar** *adj.*

Mich. *abbrev. for:* **1.** Michaelmas. **2.** Michigan.

Mi·chael ('maɪkᵊl) *n. Bible.* one of the archangels.

Mich+ael+mas ('mɪkᵊlməs) *n.* Sept. 29, the feast of St. Michael the archangel; in England, Ireland, and Wales, one of the four quarter days.

Mich+ael+mas dai+sy *n. Brit.* any of various plants of the genus *Aster* that have small autumn-blooming purple, pink, or white flowers: family *Compositae* (composites).

Mich+ael+mas term *n.* the autumn term at Oxford and Cambridge Universities and some other educational establishments.

Mi·chel·an·ge·lo (ˌmaɪkᵊl'ændʒɪˌləʊ) *n.* full name *Michelangelo Buonarroti.* 1475–1564, Florentine sculptor, painter, architect, and poet; one of the outstanding figures of the Renaissance. Among his creations are the sculptures of *David* (1504) and of *Moses* which was commissioned for the tomb of Julius II, for whom he also painted the ceiling of the Sistine Chapel (1508–12). *The Last Judgment* (1533–41), also in the Sistine, includes a torturous vision of Hell and a disguised self-portrait. His other works include the design of the Laurentian Library (1523–29) and of the dome of St. Peter's, Rome.

Mi·che·loz·zo (*Italian* ˌmike'lɔttso) *n.* full name *Michelozzo di Bartolommeo.* 1396–1472, Italian architect and sculptor. His most important design was the Palazzo Riccardo for the Medici family in Florence (1444–59).

Mi·chel·son ('maɪkᵊlsᵊn) *n.* **Al·bert A·bra·ham.** 1852–1931, U.S. physicist, born in Germany: noted for his part in the Michelson-Morley experiment: Nobel prize for physics 1907.

Mi·chel·son-Mor·ley ex·per·i·ment *n.* an experiment first performed in 1887 by A. A. Michelson and E. W. Morley, in which an interferometer was used to attempt to detect a difference in the velocities of light in directions parallel and perpendicular to the earth's motion. The negative result was explained by the special theory of relativity.

mich·i+gan ('mɪʃɪgən) *n.* the U.S. name for **newmarket** (sense 2).

Mich·i+gan ('mɪʃɪgən) *n.* **1.** a state of the N central U.S., occupying two peninsulas between Lakes Superior, Huron, Michigan and Erie: generally low-lying. Capital: Lansing. Pop.: 8 875 083 (1970). Area: 147 156 sq. km (56 817 sq. miles). Abbrevs.: **Mich.** or (with zip code) **MI** **2. Lake.** a lake in the N central U.S. between Wisconsin and Michigan: the third largest of the five Great Lakes and the only one wholly in the U.S.; linked with Lake Huron by the Straits of Mackinac. Area: 58 000 sq. km (22 400 sq. miles). —**Mich·i+gan+der** (ˌmɪʃɪ'gændə) *n.* —**'Mich·i+gan+ˌite** *adj., n.*

Mi+cho·a+cán (*Spanish* ˌmitʃoa'kan) *n.* a state of SW Mexico, on the Pacific: rich mineral resources. Capital: Morelia. Pop.: 2 324 226 (1970). Area: 59 864 sq. km (23 114 sq. miles).

Mick (mɪk) *or* **Mick·ey** *n.* (*sometimes not cap.*) *Derogatory.* a slang name for an Irishman or a Roman Catholic. [C19: from the nickname for *Michael*]

mick+e·ry ('mɪkərɪ) *n. Austral.* a pool or soakage in a river bed.

mick+ey[1] *or* **mick·y** ('mɪkɪ) *n. Informal.* **take the mickey** *or* **micky out of.** to tease. [C20: of unknown origin]

mick+ey[2] *or* **mick·y** ('mɪkɪ) *n. Austral. informal.* a young bull, esp. one that is wild and unbranded.

Mick·ey Finn *n. Slang.* **a.** a drink containing a drug to make the drinker unconscious, usually formed by the combination of chloral hydrate and alcohol. It can be poisonous. **b.** the drug itself. Often shortened to **Mickey.** [C20: of unknown origin]

Mick·ey Mouse *adj.* (*sometimes not caps.*) *Slang, chiefly U.S.* **1.** (of music, esp. that of dance bands) mechanical or spiritless. **2.** ineffective; petty: *he settled for a Mickey Mouse job instead of something challenging.* [C20: from the name of a cartoon character created by Walt Disney, known for his simple-minded attitudes]

Mic·kie·wicz (*Polish* mits'kjɛvitʃ) *n.* **Ad·am** ('adam). 1798–1855, Polish poet, whose epic *Thaddeus* (1834) is regarded as a masterpiece of Polish literature.

mick+le ('mɪkᵊl) *or* **muck+le** ('mʌkᵊl) *Archaic or northern Brit. dialect.* ~*adj.* **1.** great or abundant. ~*adv.* **2.** much; greatly. ~*n.* **3.** a great amount, esp. in the proverb, *many a little makes a mickle.* [C13 *mikel*, from Old Norse *mikell*, replacing Old English *micel* MUCH]

Mic+mac ('mɪkmæk) *n.* **1.** (*pl.* **+macs** *or* **+mac**) a member of a North American Indian people formerly living in the Maritime Provinces of Canada. **2.** the language of this people, belonging to the Algonquian family.

mi+cra ('maɪkrə) *n.* a plural of **micron.**

mi·cro- *or before a vowel* **micr-** *combining form.* **1.** small or minute: *microspore.* **2.** indicating magnification or amplification: *microscope; microphone.* **3.** involving the use of a microscope: *micrography.* **4.** indicating a method or instrument for dealing with small quantities: *microelectronics; micrometer.* **5.** (in pathology) indicating abnormal smallness or underdevelopment: *microcephaly; microcyte.* Compare **macro-** (sense 2). **6.** denoting 10^{-6}: *microsecond.* Symbol: μ [from Greek *mikros* small]

mi·cro·a+nal·y+sis (ˌmaɪkrəʊə'nælɪsɪs) *n., pl.* **+ses** (-ˌsi:z). the qualitative or quantitative chemical analysis of very small amounts of substances. —**mi·cro+an·a+lyst** (ˌmaɪkrəʊ'ænəlɪst) *n.* —**mi·cro+an·a+lyt+ic** (ˌmaɪkrəʊˌænə'lɪtɪk) *or* ˌ**mi·cro+ˌan·a+'lyt·i·cal** *adj.*

mi·cro+bal+ance ('maɪkrəʊˌbæləns) *n.* a precision balance designed to weigh quantities between 10^{-6} and 10^{-9} kilogram.

mi·cro+bar·o·graph (ˌmaɪkrəʊ'bærəˌgrɑ:f, -ˌgræf) *n.* a barograph that records minute changes in atmospheric pressure.

mi+crobe ('maɪkrəʊb) *n.* any microscopic organism, esp. a disease-causing bacterium. [C19: from French, from MICRO- + Greek *bios* life] —**mi+'cro+bi·al, mi+'cro+bic,** *or* **mi+'cro+bi·an** *adj.*

mi·cro+bi+ol·o·gy (ˌmaɪkrəʊbaɪ'ɒlədʒɪ) *n.* the branch of biology involving the study of microorganisms and their effects on man. —**mi·cro+bi·o·log·i·cal** (ˌmaɪkrəʊˌbaɪə'lɒdʒɪkᵊl) *or* ˌ**mi·cro+ˌbi·o+'log+ic** *adj.* —ˌ**mi·cro+ˌbi·o+'log·i·cal+ly** *adv.* —ˌ**mi·cro+bi+'ol·o+gist** *n.*

mi·cro+ceph·a+ly (ˌmaɪkrəʊ'sɛfəlɪ) *n.* the condition of having an abnormally small head or cranial capacity. Compare **megacephaly.** —**mi·cro+ce·phal+ic** (ˌmaɪkrəʊsɪ'fælɪk) *adj., n.* —ˌ**mi·cro+'ceph·a+lous** *adj.*

mi·cro+chem+is+try (ˌmaɪkrəʊ'kɛmɪstrɪ) *n.* chemical experimentation with minute quantities of material. —ˌ**mi·cro+'chem·i·cal** *adj.*

mi·cro+cir+cuit ('maɪkrəʊˌsɜ:kɪt) *n.* a miniature electronic circuit, esp. one in which a number of circuit components are contained in one small chip of semiconducting material. See **integrated circuit.** —ˌ**mi·cro+'cir+cuit+ry** *n.*

mi·cro+cli+mate ('maɪkrəʊˌklaɪmɪt) *n. Ecology.* **1.** the atmospheric conditions affecting an individual or a small group of organisms, esp. when they differ from the climate of the rest of the community. **2.** the entire environment of an individual or small group of organisms. —**mi·cro+cli+mat+ic** (ˌmaɪkrəʊklaɪ'mætɪk) *adj.* —ˌ**mi·cro+cli+'mat·i·cal+ly** *adv.*

mi·cro+cli+ma+tol+o·gy (ˌmaɪkrəʊˌklaɪmə'tɒlədʒɪ) *n.* the study of climate on a small scale, as of a city. —**mi·cro+cli+ma+to+log+ic** (ˌmaɪkrəʊˌklaɪmətə'lɒdʒɪk) *or* ˌ**mi·cro+ˌcli+ma+to+'log·i+cal** *adj.* —ˌ**mi·cro+ˌcli+ma+'tol·o+gist** *n.*

mi·cro+cline ('maɪkrəʊˌklaɪn) *n.* a white, red, or green feldspar mineral consisting of an aluminium silicate of potassium in triclinic crystalline form: used in ceramics, as an abrasive, and as a gemstone. Formula: $KAlSi_3O_8$.

mi·cro+coc+cus (ˌmaɪkrəʊ'kɒkəs) *n., pl.* **+coc+ci** (-'kɒksaɪ). **1.** any spherical Gram-positive bacterium of the genus *Micrococcus,* causing fermentation of milk: family *Micrococcaceae.* **2.** any other bacterium of the family *Micrococcaceae.*

mi·cro+cop·y ('maɪkrəʊˌkɒpɪ) *n., pl.* **+cop·ies.** a greatly reduced photographic copy of a printed page, drawing, etc., on microfilm or microfiche. Sometimes called: **microphotograph.**

mi·cro+cosm ('maɪkrəʊˌkɒzəm) *or* **mi·cro+cos+mos** (ˌmaɪkrəʊ'kɒzmɒs) *n.* **1.** a miniature representation of something, esp. a unit, group, or place regarded as a copy of a larger one. **2.** man regarded as epitomizing the universe. ~Compare **macrocosm.** [C15: via Medieval Latin from Greek *mikros kosmos* little world] —ˌ**mi·cro+'cos+mic** *or* ˌ**mi·cro+'cos+mi+cal** *adj.*

mi·cro+cos+mic salt *n.* a white soluble solid obtained from human urine; ammonium sodium hydrogen phosphate. It is used as a flux in bead tests on metal oxides.

mi·cro+crys+tal+line (ˌmaɪkrəʊ'krɪstᵊˌlaɪn) *adj.* (of a solid) composed of microscopic crystals.

mi·cro+cyte ('maɪkrəʊˌsaɪt) *n.* an unusually small red blood cell. —**mi·cro+cyt+ic** (ˌmaɪkrəʊ'sɪtɪk) *adj.*

mi·cro+de·tec·tor (ˌmaɪkrəʊdɪ'tɛktə) *n.* any instrument for measuring small quantities or detecting small effects, esp. a sensitive galvanometer.

mi·cro+dont ('maɪkrəʊˌdɒnt) *or* **mi·cro+don+tous** (ˌmaɪkrəʊ'dɒntəs) *adj.* having unusually small teeth.

mi·cro+dot ('maɪkrəʊˌdɒt) *n.* a microcopy about the size of a pinhead, used esp. in espionage.

mi·cro+e·co·nom·ics (ˌmaɪkrəʊˌi:kə'nɒmɪks, -ˌɛkə-) *n.* the branch of economics concerned with particular commodities, firms, or individuals and the economic relationships between them. Compare **macroeconomics.** —ˌ**mi·cro+ˌe·co+'nom+ic** *adj.*

mi·cro+e·lec+tron+ics (ˌmaɪkrəʊɪlɛk'trɒnɪks) *n.* (*functioning as sing.*) the branch of electronics concerned with microcircuits. —ˌ**mi·cro+e·lec+'tron+ic** *adj.*

mi·cro+fiche ('maɪkrəʊˌfi:ʃ) *n.* a sheet of film, usually the size of a filing card, on which books, newspapers, documents, etc., can be recorded in miniaturized form. Sometimes shortened to **fiche.** See also **ultrafiche.** [C20: from French, from MICRO- + *fiche* small card, from Old French *fichier* to fix]

mi·cro+film ('maɪkrəʊˌfɪlm) *n.* **1.** a strip of film of standard width on which books, newspapers, documents, etc., can be recorded in miniaturized form. ~*vb.* **2.** to photograph (a page, document, etc.) on microfilm. See also **microfiche.**

mi·cro+film plot+ter *n. Computer technol.* a type of incremental plotter that has a film rather than a paper output.

mi·cro+gam+ete (ˌmaɪkrəʊ'gæmi:t) *n.* the smaller and apparently male of two gametes in conjugating protozoans. Compare **macrogamete.**

mi·cro+graph ('maɪkrəʊˌgræf, -ˌgrɑ:f) *n.* **1.** a photograph or drawing of an object as viewed through a microscope. **2.** an instrument or machine for producing very small writing or engraving.

mi+crog+ra+phy (maɪ'krɒgrəfɪ) *n.* **1.** the description, study, drawing, or photography of microscopic objects. **2.** the technique of using a microscope. **3.** the art or practice of writing in minute characters. —**mi+'crog+ra+pher** *n.* —**mi·cro+graph+ic** (ˌmaɪkrəʊ'græfɪk) *adj.* —ˌ**mi·cro+'graph·i·cal+ly** *adv.*

mi·cro·groove ('maɪkrəʊˌgruːv) *n.* **a.** the narrow groove in a long-playing gramophone record. **b.** (*as modifier*): *a microgroove record.*

mi·cro+hab·i+tat (ˌmaɪkrəʊ'hæbɪtæt) *n. Ecology.* the smallest part of the environment that supports a distinct flora and fauna, such as a fallen log in a forest.

mi·cro+lith ('maɪkrəʊˌlɪθ) *n. Archaeol.* a small Mesolithic flint tool which was made from a blade and formed part of hafted tools. —ˌ**mi·cro+'lith+ic** *adj.*

mi·cro+me·te·or+ite (ˌmaɪkrəʊ'miːtɪəˌraɪt) *n.* a tiny meteorite having a diameter of 10–40 micrometres, found esp. in rainwater and seawater, having entered the atmosphere as a **micrometeoroid** (extremely small meteoroid).

mi·cro+me·te·or+ol+o·gy (ˌmaɪkrəʊˌmiːtɪə'rɒlədʒɪ) *n.* the study of the layer of air immediately above the earth and of small-scale meteorological processes.

mi+crom+e·ter (maɪ'krɒmɪtə) *n.* **1.** any of various instruments or devices for the accurate measurement of distances or angles. **2.** Also called: **micrometer gauge, micrometer calliper.** a type of gauge for the accurate measurement of small distances, thicknesses, diameters, etc. The gap between its measuring faces is adjusted by a fine screw, the rotation of the screw giving a sensitive measure of the distance moved by the face. —**mi+'crom+e·try** *n.* —**mi·cro+met+ric** (ˌmaɪkrəʊ'mɛtrɪk) *or* ˌ**mi·cro+'met+ri+cal** *adj.*

mi+crom+e·ter screw *n.* a screw with a fine thread of definite pitch, such as that of a micrometer gauge.

mi·cro+min·ia+tur·i+za+tion *or* **mi·cro+min·ia+tur·i+sa+tion** (ˌmaɪkrəʊˌmɪnɪtʃəraɪ'zeɪʃən) *n.* the production and application of very small semiconductor components and the circuits and equipment in which they are used.

mi+cron ('maɪkrɒn) *n.* a unit of length equal to 10^{-6} metre. It is being replaced by the micrometre, the equivalent SI unit. [C19: New Latin, from Greek *mikros* small]

Mi·cro+ne·si·a (ˌmaɪkrəʊ'niːzɪə) *n.* one of the three divisions of islands in the Pacific (the others being Melanesia and Polynesia); the NW division of Oceania: includes the Mariana, Caroline, Marshall, and Gilbert island groups, and Nauru Island.

Mi·cro+ne·si·an (ˌmaɪkrəʊ'niːzɪən) *adj.* **1.** of or relating to Micronesia, its inhabitants, or their languages. ~*n.* **2.** a member of the people that inhabit Micronesia, more akin to the Polynesians than the Melanesians, but having Mongoloid traces. **3.** a group of languages spoken in Micronesia, belonging to the Malayo-Polynesian family.

mi·cro+nu+cle·us (ˌmaɪkrəʊ'njuːklɪəs) *n., pl.* **+cle·i** (-klɪˌaɪ) *or* **+cle·us·es.** the smaller of two nuclei in ciliated protozoans, involved in reproduction. Compare **macronucleus.**

mi·cro+nu+tri+ent (ˌmaɪkrəʊ'njuːtrɪənt) *n.* any substance, such as a vitamin, essential for healthy growth and development but required only in minute amounts.

mi·cro+or+gan+ism (ˌmaɪkrəʊ'ɔːgəˌnɪzəm) *n.* any organism, such as a bacterium, protozoan, or virus, of microscopic size.

mi·cro+pal·ae+on+tol+o·gy (ˌmaɪkrəʊˌpælɪɒn'tɒlədʒɪ) *n.* the branch of palaeontology concerned with the study of microscopic fossils. —**mi·cro+pal·ae+on+to+log·i+cal** (ˌmaɪkrəʊˌpælɪɒntə'lɒdʒɪk^əl) *or* ˌ**mi·cro+ˌpal·ae+on+to+'log+ic** *adj.* —ˌ**mi·cro+ˌpal·ae+on+'tol·o·gist** *n.*

mi·cro+par·a+site (ˌmaɪkrəʊ'pærəˌsaɪt) *n.* any parasitic microorganism. —**mi·cro+par·a+sit+ic** (ˌmaɪkrəʊˌpærə'sɪtɪk) *adj.*

mi·cro+phone ('maɪkrəˌfəʊn) *n.* a device used in sound-reproduction systems for converting sound into electrical energy, usually by means of a ribbon or diaphragm set into motion by the sound waves. The vibrations are converted into the equivalent audio-frequency electric currents. Informal name: **mike.** See also **carbon microphone.** Compare **loudspeaker.** —**mi·cro+phon+ic** (ˌmaɪkrə'fɒnɪk) *adj.*

mi·cro+pho+to+graph (ˌmaɪkrəʊ'fəʊtəˌgrɑːf, -ˌgræf) *n.* **1.** a photograph in which the image is greatly reduced and therefore requires optical enlargement for viewing purposes. **2.** a less common name for **microcopy** or **photomicrograph** (sense 1). —ˌ**mi·cro+ˌpho+to+'graph+ic** *adj.* —**mi·cro+pho+tog+ra+phy** (ˌmaɪkrəʊfə'tɒgrəfɪ) *n.*

mi·cro+phys+ics (ˌmaɪkrəʊ'fɪzɪks) *n.* (*functioning as sing.*) the branch of physics concerned with small objects and systems, such as atoms, molecules, nuclei, and elementary particles. —ˌ**mi·cro+'phys·i·cal** *adj.*

mi·cro+phyte ('maɪkrəʊˌfaɪt) *n.* any microscopic plant, esp. a parasite. —**mi·cro+phyt+ic** (ˌmaɪkrəʊ'fɪtɪk) *adj.*

mi·cro+print ('maɪkrəʊˌprɪnt) *n.* a microphotograph reproduced on paper and read by a magnifying device. It is used in order to reduce the size of large books, etc.

mi·cro+pro+ces+sor (ˌmaɪkrəʊ'prəʊsɛsə) *n. Computer technol.* a single integrated circuit performing the basic functions of the central processing unit in a small computer.

mi·cro+pyle ('maɪkrəʊˌpaɪl) *n.* **1.** a small opening in the integuments of a plant ovule through which the male gametes pass. **2.** a small pore in the shell of an insect's eggs through which the sperm passes. [C19: from MICRO- + Greek *pulē* gate] —ˌ**mi·cro+'py+lar** *adj.*

mi·cro+py+rom+e·ter (ˌmaɪkrəʊpaɪ'rɒmɪtə) *n.* a pyrometer for measuring the temperature of very small objects.

mi·cro+read+er ('maɪkrəʊˌriːdə) *n.* an apparatus that produces an enlarged image of a microphotograph.

mi·cro+scope ('maɪkrəˌskəʊp) *n.* **1.** an optical instrument that uses a lens or combination of lenses to produce a magnified image of a small, close object. Modern optical microscopes have magnifications of about 1500 to 2000. See also: **simple microscope, compound microscope, ultramicroscope. 2.** any instrument, such as the electron microscope, for producing a magnified visual image of a small object.

mi·cro+scop+ic (ˌmaɪkrə'skɒpɪk) *or* **mi·cro+scop·i·cal** *adj.* **1.** not large enough to be seen with the naked eye but visible under a microscope. Compare **macroscopic. 2.** very small; minute. **3.** of, concerned with, or using a microscope. **4.** characterized by or done with great attention to detail. —ˌ**mi·cro+'scop·i·cal+ly** *adv.*

Mi·cro+sco+pi·um (ˌmaɪkrə'skəʊpɪəm) *n., Latin genitive* **Mi·cro+sco+pi·i** (ˌmaɪkrə'skəʊpɪˌaɪ). a faint constellation in the S hemisphere lying near Sagittarius and Capricornus.

mi+cros+co+py (maɪ'krɒskəpɪ) *n.* **1.** the study, design, and manufacture of microscopes. **2.** investigation by use of a microscope. —**mi+cros+co+pist** (maɪ'krɒskəpɪst) *n.*

mi·cro+sec+ond ('maɪkrəʊˌsɛkənd) *n.* one millionth of a second. Symbol: μs

mi·cro+seism ('maɪkrəʊˌsaɪzəm) *n.* a very slight tremor of the earth's surface, thought not to be caused by an earthquake. —**mi·cro+seis+mic** (ˌmaɪkrəʊ'saɪzmɪk) *or* ˌ**mi·cro+'seis+mi+cal** *adj.*

mi·cro+some ('maɪkrəʊˌsəʊm) *n.* any of the small particles consisting of ribosomes and fragments of attached endoplasmic reticulum that can be isolated from cells by centrifugal action. —ˌ**mi·cro+'so+mal** *adj.*

mi·cro+spo+ran+gi·um (ˌmaɪkrəʊspɔː'rændʒɪəm) *n., pl.* **+gi·a** (-dʒɪə). the structure in certain ferns in which the microspores are formed: corresponds to the pollen sac in seed plants. Compare **megasporangium.**

mi·cro+spore ('maɪkrəʊˌspɔː) *n.* **1.** the smaller of two types of spore produced by some ferns, which develops into the male gametophyte. Compare **megaspore** (sense 1). **2.** the pollen grain of seed plants. —ˌ**mi·cro+'spor+ic** *or* ˌ**mi·cro+'spo+rous** *adj.*

mi·cro+spor·o+phyll (ˌmaɪkrəʊ'spɔːrəfɪl) *n.* a leaf on which the microspores are formed: corresponds to the stamen of a flowering plant. Compare **megasporophyll.**

mi·cro+stom·a+tous (ˌmaɪkrəʊ'stɒmətəs) *or* **mi+cros+to+mous** (maɪ'krɒstəməs) *adj. Anatomy.* having an unusually small mouth.

mi·cro+struc+ture ('maɪkrəʊˌstrʌktʃə) *n.* structure on a microscopic scale, esp. the structure of an alloy as observed by etching, polishing, and observation under a microscope.

mi·cro+tome ('maɪkrəʊˌtəʊm) *n.* an instrument used for cutting thin sections, esp. of biological material, for microscopical examination.

mi+crot·o+my (maɪ'krɒtəmɪ) *n., pl.* **+mies.** the cutting of sections with a microtome. —**mi·cro+tom+ic** (ˌmaɪkrəʊ'tɒmɪk) *or* ˌ**mi·cro+'tom·i·cal** *adj.* —**mi+'crot·o·mist** *n.*

mi·cro+tone ('maɪkrəʊˌtəʊn) *n.* any musical interval smaller than a semitone. —ˌ**mi·cro+'ton+al** *adj.* —ˌ**mi·cro+to+'nal·i·ty** *n.* —ˌ**mi·cro+'ton+al+ly** *adv.*

mi·cro+wave ('maɪkrəʊˌweɪv) *n.* **a.** electromagnetic radiation in the wavelength range 0.3 to 0.001 metres; used in radar, cooking, etc. **b.** (*as modifier*): *microwave generator.*

mi·cro+wave ov·en *n.* an oven in which food is cooked by microwaves.

mi·cro+wave spec+tros+co+py *n.* a type of spectroscopy in which information is obtained on the structure and chemical bonding of molecules and crystals by measurements of the wavelengths of microwaves emitted or absorbed by the sample. —**mi·cro+wave spec+tro+scope** *n.*

mi+crur·gy ('maɪkrɜːdʒɪ) *n. Biology.* the manipulation and examination of single cells under a microscope. [C20: from MICRO- + Greek *-ourgia* work]

mic+tu+rate ('mɪktjʊˌreɪt) *vb.* (*intr.*) a less common word for **urinate.** [C19: from Latin *micturīre* to desire to urinate, from *mingere* to urinate] —**mic+tu+ri+tion** (ˌmɪktjʊ'rɪʃən) *n.*

mid[1] (mɪd) *adj.* **1.** *Phonetics.* of, relating to, or denoting a vowel whose articulation lies approximately halfway between high and low, such as *e* in English *bet.* ~*n.* **2.** an archaic word for **middle.** [C12 *midre* (inflected form of *midd,* unattested); related to Old Norse *mithr,* Gothic *midjis*]

mid[2] *or* **'mid** (mɪd) *prep.* a poetic word for **amid.**

mid. *abbrev. for* middle.

Mid. *abbrev. for* Midshipman.

mid- *combining form.* indicating a middle part, point, time, or position: *midday; mid-April; mid-Victorian.* [Old English; see MIDDLE, MID[1]]

mid+air (ˌmɪd'ɛə) *n.* **a.** some point above ground level, in the air. **b.** (*as modifier*): *a midair collision of aircraft.*

Mi·das ('maɪdəs) *n.* **1.** *Greek legend.* a king of Phrygia given the power by Dionysus of turning everything he touched to gold. **2. the Midas touch.** ability to make money.

MIDAS ('maɪdəs) *n. acronym for* Missile Defence Alarm System.

mid+brain ('mɪdˌbreɪn) *n.* the nontechnical name for **mesencephalon.**

mid+day ('mɪd'deɪ) *n.* **a.** the middle of the day; noon. **b.** (*as modifier*): *a midday meal.*

Mid+del+burg ('mɪd^əlˌbɜːg; *Dutch* 'mɪdəlˌbyrx) *n.* a city in the SW Netherlands, capital of Zeeland province, on Walcheren Island: an important trading centre in the Middle Ages and member of the Hanseatic League; 12th-century abbey; market town. Pop.: 33 470 (1973 est.).

mid+den ('mɪd^ən) *n.* **1. a.** *Archaic or dialect.* a dunghill or pile of refuse. **b.** *Brit. dialect.* a dustbin. **c.** *Northern English dialect.* an earth closet. **2.** See **kitchen midden.** [C14: from Scandinavian; compare Danish *mödding* from *mög* MUCK + *dynge* pile]

mid·dle ('mɪdᵊl) *adj.* **1.** equally distant from the ends or periphery of something; central. **2.** intermediate in status, situation, etc. **3.** located between the early and late parts of a series, time sequence, etc. **4.** not extreme, esp. in size; medium. **5.** (esp. in Greek and Sanskrit grammar) denoting a voice of verbs expressing reciprocal or reflexive action. Compare **active** (sense 5), **passive** (sense 5). **6.** (*usually cap.*) (of a language) intermediate between the earliest and the modern forms: *Middle English.* ~*n.* **7.** an area or point equal in distance from the ends or periphery or in time between the early and late parts. **8.** an intermediate part or section, such as the waist. **9.** *Grammar.* the middle voice. **10.** *Logic.* See **middle term. 11.** the ground between rows of growing plants. **12.** a discursive article in a journal, placed between the leading articles and the book reviews. ~*vb.* (*tr.*) **13.** to place in the middle. **14.** *Nautical.* to fold in two. **15.** *Football.* to return (the ball) from the wing to midfield. **16.** *Cricket.* to hit (the ball) with the middle of the bat. [Old English *middel;* compare Old Frisian *middel,* Dutch *middel,* German *mittel*]

mid·dle age *n.* the period of life between youth and old age, usually (in man) considered to occur approximately between the ages of 40 and 60. —ˌ**mid·dle-'aged** *adj.*

Mid·dle Ag·es *n.* **the.** *European history.* **1.** (broadly) the period from the end of classical antiquity (or the deposition of the last W Roman emperor in 476 A.D.) to the Italian Renaissance (or the fall of Constantinople in 1453). **2.** (narrowly) the period from about 1000 A.D. to the 15th century. Compare **Dark Ages.**

Mid·dle A·mer·i·ca *n.* **1.** the territories between the U.S. and South America: Mexico, Central America, Panama, and the Greater and Lesser Antilles. **2.** the U.S. middle class, esp. those groups that are politically conservative. —**Mid·dle A·mer·i·can** *adj., n.*

Mid·dle At·lan·tic States *or* **Mid·dle States** *n.* the states of New York, Pennsylvania, and New Jersey.

mid·dle·break·er ('mɪdᵊlˌbreɪkə) *or* **mid·dle·bust·er** *n.* a type of plough that cuts a furrow with the soil heaped on each side, often used for sowing. Also called: **lister.**

mid·dle·brow ('mɪdᵊlˌbraʊ) *Disparaging.* ~*n.* **1.** a person with conventional tastes and limited cultural appreciation. ~*adj. also* **mid·dle·browed. 2.** of or appealing to middlebrows: *middlebrow culture.* —'**mid·dle·ˌbrow·ism** *n.*

mid·dle C *n. Music.* the note graphically represented on the first ledger line below the treble staff or the first ledger line above the bass staff and corresponding in pitch to an internationally standardized fundamental frequency of 261.63 hertz.

mid·dle class *n.* **1.** Also called: **bourgeoisie.** a social stratum that is not clearly defined but is positioned between the lower and upper classes. It consists of businessmen, professional people, etc., along with their families, and is marked by bourgeois values. Compare **lower class, upper class, working class.** ~*adj.* **mid·dle-class. 2.** of, relating to, or characteristic of the middle class.

mid·dle com·mon room *n.* (in certain universities and colleges) a common room for the use of postgraduate students. Compare **junior common room, senior common room.**

Mid·dle Con·go *n.* one of the four territories of former French Equatorial Africa, in W central Africa: became an autonomous member of the French Community, as the Republic of the Congo, in 1958.

mid·dle-dis·tance *adj.* **1.** *Athletics.* relating to or denoting races of a length between the sprints and the distance events, esp. the 800 metres and the 1500 metres. ~*n.* **mid·dle dis·tance. 2.** (of a painting, esp. a landscape) between the foreground and far distance.

Mid·dle Dutch *n.* the Dutch language from about 1100 to about 1500. Abbrev.: **MD.**

mid·dle ear *n.* the sound-conducting part of the ear, containing the malleus, incus, and stapes.

Mid·dle East *n.* **1.** (loosely) the area around the E Mediterranean, esp. Israel and the Arab countries from Turkey to North Africa and eastwards to Iran. **2.** (formerly) the area extending from the Tigris and Euphrates to Burma. —**Mid·dle East·ern** *adj.*

mid·dle eight *n.* the third contrasting eight-bar section of a 32-bar pop song.

Mid·dle Eng·lish *n.* the English language from about 1100 to about 1450: main dialects are Kentish, Southwestern (West Saxon), East Midland (which replaced West Saxon as the chief literary form and developed into Modern English), West Midland, and Northern (from which Scottish Lallans and other modern dialects developed). Compare **Old English, Modern English.** Abbrev.: **ME.**

mid·dle game *n. Chess.* the central phase between the opening and the endgame.

Mid·dle Greek *n.* another name for **Medieval Greek.**

Mid·dle High Ger·man *n.* High German from about 1200 to about 1500. Abbrev.: **MHG.**

Mid·dle I·rish *n.* Irish Gaelic from about 1100 to about 1500.

Mid·dle King·dom *n.* **1.** a period of Egyptian history extending from the late 11th to the 13th dynasty (?2040–?1670 B.C.). **2. a.** the former Chinese empire (from the belief that it lay at the centre of the earth). **b.** the original 18 provinces of China; China proper.

Mid·dle Low Ger·man *n.* Low German from about 1200 to about 1500. Abbrev.: **MLG.**

mid·dle·man ('mɪdᵊlˌmæn) *n., pl.* **·men. 1.** an independent trader engaged in the distribution of goods from producer to consumer. **2.** an intermediary. **3.** *Theatre.* the interlocutor in minstrel shows.

mid·dle·most ('mɪdᵊlˌməʊst) *adj.* another word for **midmost.**

mid·dle-of-the-road *adj.* not extreme, esp. in political views; moderate. —'**mid·dle-of-the-'road·er** *n.*

Mid·dle Pal·ae·o·lith·ic *n.* **1.** the period between the Lower and the Upper Palaeolithic, usually taken as equivalent to the Mousterian. ~*adj.* **2.** of or relating to this period.

mid·dle pas·sage *n.* **the.** *History.* the journey across the Atlantic Ocean from the W coast of Africa to the West Indies: the longest part of the journey of the slave ships sailing to the West Indies or the Americas.

Mid·dle Per·sian *n.* the classical form of modern Persian, spoken from about 300 A.D. to about 900. See also **Pahlavi²**.

Mid·dles·brough ('mɪdᵊlzbrə) *n.* an industrial town in NE England, on the Tees estuary, administrative centre of Cleveland. Pop.: 157 580 (1967).

mid·dle school *n. Brit.* a school for children aged between 8 or 9 and 12 or 13. Compare **first school.**

Mid·dle·sex ('mɪdᵊlˌsɛks) *n.* a former county of SE England: became mostly part of N and W Greater London in 1965.

Mid·dle States *n.* another name for the **Middle Atlantic States.**

Mid·dle Tem·ple *n.* (in England) one of the four legal societies in London which together form the Inns of Court.

mid·dle term *n. Logic.* the term that appears in both the major and minor premisses of a syllogism, but not in the conclusion. Also called: **mean, middle.**

Mid·dle·ton¹ ('mɪdᵊltən) *n.* a town in NW England, in Greater Manchester. Pop.: 53 419 (1971).

Mid·dle·ton² ('mɪdᵊltən) *n.* **Thom·as.** ?1570–1627, English dramatist. His plays include the tragedies *Women beware Women* (1621) and, in collaboration with William Rowley (?1585–?1642), *The Changeling* (1622) and the political satire *A Game at Chess* (1624).

mid·dle watch *n. Nautical.* the watch between midnight and 4 a.m.

mid·dle·weight ('mɪdᵊlˌweɪt) *n.* **1. a.** a professional boxer weighing 154–160 pounds (70–72.5 kg). **b.** an amateur boxer weighing 71–75 kg (157–165 pounds). **c.** (*as modifier*): *a middleweight contest.* **2.** a wrestler in a similar weight category (usually 172–192 pounds (78–87 kg)).

Mid·dle West *n.* another name for the **Midwest.** —**Mid·dle West·ern** *adj.* —**Mid·dle West·ern·er** *n.*

mid·dling ('mɪdlɪŋ) *adj.* **1.** mediocre in quality, size, etc.; neither good nor bad, esp. in health (often in the phrase **fair to middling**). ~*adv.* **2.** *Informal.* moderately: *middling well.* [C15 (northern English and Scottish): from MID¹ + -LING²] —'**mid·dling·ly** *adv.*

mid·dlings ('mɪdlɪŋz) *pl. n.* **1.** the poorer or coarser part of flour or other products. **2.** commodities of intermediate grade, quality, size, or price. **3.** *Chiefly U.S.* the part of a pig between the ham and shoulder.

mid·dy ('mɪdɪ) *n., pl.* **·dies. 1.** *Informal.* See **midshipman. 2.** See **middy blouse. 3.** *Austral.* a glass of beer of a specific size, most commonly half a pint.

mid·dy blouse *n.* a blouse with a sailor collar, worn by women and children, esp. formerly.

Mid·east (mɪd'iːst) *n. Chiefly U.S.* another name for **Middle East.**

mid·field (ˌmɪd'fiːld) *n. Soccer.* **a.** the general area between the two opposing defences. **b.** (*as modifier*): *a midfield player.*

Mid·gard ('mɪdgɑːd), **Mid·garth** ('mɪdgɑːð), *or* **Mith·gar·thr** ('mɪðgɑːðə) *n. Norse myth.* the dwelling place of mankind, formed from the body of the giant Ymir and linked by the bridge Bifrost to Asgard, home of the gods. [C19: from Old Norse *mithgarthr;* see MID¹, YARD²]

midge (mɪdʒ) *n.* **1.** any fragile mosquito-like dipterous insect of the family *Chironomidae,* occurring in dancing swarms, esp. near water. **2.** any similar or related insect, such as the biting midge and gall midge. **3.** a small or diminutive person or animal. [Old English *mycge;* compare Old High German *mucca,* Danish *myg*]

midg·et ('mɪdʒɪt) *n.* **1.** a dwarf whose skeleton and features are of normal proportions. **2. a.** something small of its kind. **b.** (*as modifier*): *a midget car.* [C19: see MIDGE]

Mid Gla·mor·gan *n.* a county in S Wales, formed in 1974 from parts of Breconshire, Glamorgan, and Monmouthshire. Administrative centre: Cardiff. Pop.: 540 400 (1976 est.). Area: 100 sq. km (393 sq. miles).

mid·gut ('mɪdˌgʌt) *n.* **1.** the middle part of the digestive tract of vertebrates, including the small intestine. **2.** the middle part of the digestive tract of arthropods. ~See also **foregut, hindgut.**

Mid·heav·en ('mɪd'hɛvᵊn) *n. Astrology.* **1.** the point on the ecliptic, measured in degrees, that crosses the meridian of a particular place at a particular time. On a person's birth chart it relates to the time of birth. Abbrev.: **M.C. 2.** the sign of the zodiac containing this point. [C16: initials *M.C.* represent Latin *medium caeli* middle of the sky]

mid·i ('mɪdɪ) *adj.* **a.** (of a skirt, etc.) reaching to below the knee or midcalf. **b.** (*as n.*): *she wore her new midi.*

Mi·di (*French* mi'di) *n.* **1.** the south of France. **2. Canal du.** a canal in S France, extending from the River Garonne at Toulouse to the Mediterranean at Sète and providing a link between the Mediterranean and Atlantic coasts: built between 1666 and 1681. Length: 181 km (150 miles).

Mid·i·an ('mɪdɪən) *n. Old Testament.* **1.** a son of Abraham (Genesis 25:1–2). **2.** a nomadic nation claiming descent from him. —'**Mid·i·an·ˌite** *n., adj.* —'**Mid·i·an·ˌit·ish** *adj.*

mid·i·nette (ˌmɪdɪ'nɛt; *French* midi'nɛt) *n., pl.* **·nettes** (-'nɛts; *French* -'nɛt). a Parisian seamstress or salesgirl in a clothes shop. [C20: from French, from *midi* noon + *dinette* light meal, since the girls had time for no more than a snack at midday]

Mi·di-Py·ré·nées (*French* midi pire'ne) *n.* a region of SW France: consists of N slopes of the Pyrenees in the south, a fertile lowland area in the west crossed by the River Garonne, and the edge of the Massif Central in the north and east.

mid+i·ron ('mɪd,aɪən) *n. Golf.* a club, a No. 2 iron, used for approach shots.

mid+land ('mɪdlənd) *n.* **a.** the central or inland part of a country. **b.** (*as modifier*): *a midland region.*

Mid+lands ('mɪdləndz) *n.* **the.** the central counties of England, including Warwickshire, Northamptonshire, Leicestershire, Nottinghamshire, Derbyshire, Staffordshire, the West Midlands metropolitan county, and the E part of Hereford and Worcester: characterized by manufacturing industries. —**'Mid+land+er** *n.*

Mid+lo+thi·an (mɪd'ləʊðɪən) *n.* (until 1975) a county of SE central Scotland, now part of Lothian region.

mid+most ('mɪd,məʊst) *adj., adv.* in the middle or midst.

mid+night ('mɪd,naɪt) *n.* **1. a.** the middle of the night; 12 o'clock at night. **b.** (*as modifier*): *the midnight hour.* **2. burn the midnight oil.** to work or study late into the night. —**'mid+,night+ly** *adj., adv.*

mid+night blue *n.* **a.** a very dark blue colour; bluish black. **b.** (*as adj.*): *a midnight-blue suit.*

mid+night sun *n.* the sun visible at midnight during the summer inside the Arctic and Antarctic circles.

mid-off *n. Cricket.* **1.** the fielding position on the off side closest to the bowler. **2.** a fielder in this position.

mid-on *n. Cricket.* **1.** the fielding position on the on side closest to the bowler. **2.** a fielder in this position.

mid+point ('mɪd,pɔɪnt) *n.* **1.** the point on a line that is at an equal distance from either end. **2.** a point in time halfway between the beginning and end of an event.

mid+rash ('mɪdræʃ; *Hebrew* mi'draʃ) *n., pl.* **mid+ra+shim** (mɪ'drɔʃɪm; *Hebrew* midra'ʃim). *Judaism.* **1.** commentaries on the Bible based on the Jewish methods of interpretation, and composed between 400 and 1200 A.D. **2.** a commentary on a passage of Scripture based on such methods. [C17: from Hebrew: commentary, from *darash* to search] —**mid+rash+ic** (mɪd'ræʃɪk) *adj.*

mid+rib ('mɪd,rɪb) *n.* the main vein of a leaf, running down the centre of the blade.

mid+riff ('mɪdrɪf) *n.* **1. a.** the middle part of the human body, esp. between waist and bust. **b.** (*as modifier*): *midriff bulge.* **2.** *Anatomy.* another name for the **diaphragm. 3.** the part of a woman's garment covering the midriff. **4.** *U.S.* a woman's garment which exposes the midriff. [Old English *midhrif,* from MID[1] + *hrif* belly]

mid+sec+tion ('mɪd,sɛkʃən) *n.* **1.** the middle of something. **2.** the middle region of the human body; midriff.

mid+ship ('mɪd,ʃɪp) *adj. Nautical.* **1.** in, of, or relating to the middle of a vessel. ~*n.* **2.** the middle of a vessel.

mid+ship+man ('mɪd,ʃɪpmən) *n., pl.* **+men. 1.** a probationary rank held by young naval officers under training, or an officer holding such a rank. **2.** any of several American toadfishes of the genus *Porichthys,* having small light-producing organs on the undersurface of their bodies.

mid+ships ('mɪd,ʃɪps) *adv., adj. Nautical.* See **amidships.**

midst[1] (mɪdst) *n.* **1. in the midst of.** surrounded or enveloped by; at a point during, esp. a climactic one. **2. in our midst.** among us. **3.** *Archaic.* the centre. [C14: back formation from *amiddes* AMIDST]

midst[2] (mɪdst) *prep. Poetic.* See **amidst, amid.**

mid+sum+mer ('mɪd'sʌmə) *n.* **1. a.** the middle or height of the summer. **b.** (*as modifier*): *a midsummer carnival.* **2.** another name for **summer solstice.**

Mid+sum+mer Day *or* **Mid+sum+mer's Day** *n.* June 24, the feast of St. John the Baptist; in England, Ireland, and Wales, one of the four quarter days. See also **summer solstice.**

mid+sum+mer mad+ness *n.* foolish or extravagant behaviour, supposed to occur during the summer.

mid+sum·mer-men *n.* (*functioning as sing. or pl.*) another name for **rose-root.**

mid+term ('mɪd'tɜ:m) *n.* **1.** *U.S. Politics.* **a.** the middle of a term of office, esp. of a presidential term, when congressional and local elections are held. **b.** (*as modifier*): *midterm elections.* **2. a.** the middle of the gestation period. **b.** (*as modifier*): *midterm pregnancy.* See **term** (sense 6).

mid+town ('mɪd,taʊn) *n. U.S.* the centre of a town. See also **downtown, uptown.**

mid-Vic·to·ri·an *adj.* **1.** *British history.* of or relating to the middle period of the reign of Queen Victoria (1837–1901). ~*n.* **2.** a person of the mid-Victorian era.

mid+way ('mɪd,weɪ) *adj.* **1.** in or at the middle of the distance; halfway. ~*n.* **2.** *U.S.* a place in a fair, etc., where sideshows are located. **3.** *Obsolete.* a middle place, way, etc.

Mid+way Is+lands *pl. n.* an atoll in the central Pacific, about 2100 km (1300 miles) northwest of Honolulu: annexed by the U.S. in 1867. Pop.: 2200 (1970). Area: 5 sq. km (2 sq. miles).

mid+week ('mɪd'wi:k) *n.* **a.** the middle of the week. **b.** (*as modifier*): *a midweek holiday.* —**,mid+'week+ly** *adj.*

Mid+west ('mɪd'wɛst) *or* **Mid+dle West** *n.* the N central part of the U.S.; the region consisting of the states from Ohio westwards that border on the Great Lakes, often extended to include the upper Mississippi and Missouri valleys. —**'Mid+'west+ern** *adj.* —**'Mid+'west+ern+er** *n.*

mid-wick·et *n. Cricket.* **1.** the fielding position on the on side, approximately midway between square leg and mid-on. **2.** a fielder in this position.

mid+wife ('mɪd,waɪf) *n., pl.* **+wives.** a woman skilled in aiding in the delivery of babies. [C14: from Old English *mid* with + *wif* woman]

mid+wife+ry ('mɪd,wɪfərɪ) *n.* the art or practice of a midwife.

mid+wife toad *n.* a European toad, *Alytes obstetricans,* the male of which carries the fertilized eggs on its hind legs until they hatch: family *Discoglossidae.*

mid+win+ter ('mɪd'wɪntə) *n.* **1. a.** the middle or depth of the winter. **b.** (*as modifier*): *a midwinter festival.* **2.** another name for **winter solstice.**

mid+year ('mɪd'jɪə) *n.* **a.** the middle of the year. **b.** (*as modifier*): *a midyear examination.*

mien (mi:n) *n. Literary.* a person's manner, bearing, or appearance, expressing personality or mood: *a noble mien.* [C16: probably variant of obsolete *demean* appearance; related to French *mine* aspect]

Mie+res (*Spanish* 'mjeres) *n.* a city in N Spain, south of Oviedo: steel and chemical industries; iron and coal mines. Pop.: 64 552 (1970).

Mies van der Ro+he ('mi:z væn də 'rəʊə) *n.* **Lud·wig.** 1886–1969, U.S. architect, born in Germany. He directed the Bauhaus (1929–33) and developed a rational functional style, characterized by pure geometrical design. His works include the Seagram building, New York (1958).

miff (mɪf) *Informal.* ~*vb.* **1.** to take offence or offend. ~*n.* **2.** a petulant mood. **3.** a petty quarrel. [C17: perhaps an imitative expression of bad temper]

mif+fy ('mɪfɪ) *adj.* **+fi+er, +fi+est.** *Informal.* easily upset; oversensitive. —**'mif+fi+ness** *n.*

might[1] (maɪt) *vb.* (takes an implied infinitive or an infinitive without *to*) used as an auxiliary: **1.** making the past tense or subjunctive mood of **may**[1]: *he might have come last night.* **2.** (often foll. by *well*) expressing theoretical possibility: *he might well come.* In this sense *might* looks to the future and functions as a weak form of *may.* See **may**[1] (sense 2).

Usage. See at **may.**

might[2] (maɪt) *n.* **1.** power, force, or vigour, esp. of a great or supreme kind. **2.** physical strength. **3. (with) might and main.** See **main**[1] (sense 8). [Old English *miht;* compare Old High German *maht,* Dutch *macht*]

might·i+ly ('maɪtɪlɪ) *adv.* **1.** to a great extent, amount, or degree. **2.** with might; powerfully or vigorously.

might·y ('maɪtɪ) *adj.* **might·i+er, might·i+est. 1. a.** having or indicating might; powerful or strong. **b.** (*as collective n.*): *the mighty.* **2.** very large; vast. **3.** *Informal.* very great in extent, importance, etc. ~*adv.* **4.** *Informal, chiefly U.S.* (intensifier): *he was mighty tired.* —**'might·i+ness** *n.*

mi+gnon ('mɪnjɒn; *French* mi'ɲɔ̃) *adj.* small and pretty; dainty. [C16: from French, from Old French *mignot* dainty] —**mi+gnonne** ('mɪnjɒn; *French* mi'ɲɔn) *fem. n.*

mi+gnon+ette (,mɪnjə'nɛt) *n.* **1.** any of various mainly Mediterranean plants of the resedaceous genus *Reseda,* such as *R. odorata* (**garden mignonette**), that have spikes of small greenish-white flowers with prominent anthers. **2.** a type of fine pillow lace. ~*adj.* **3.** of a greyish-green colour; reseda. [C18: from French, diminutive of MIGNON]

mi+graine ('mi:greɪn, 'maɪ-) *n.* a throbbing headache usually affecting only one side of the head and commonly accompanied by nausea and visual disturbances. [C18: (earlier form, C14 *mygrame* MEGRIM): from French, from Late Latin *hēmicrānia* pain in half of the head, from Greek *hēmikrania,* from HEMI- + *kranion* CRANIUM] —**'mi+grain+ous** *adj.*

mi+grant ('maɪgrənt) *n.* **1.** a person or animal that moves from one region, place, or country to another. **2.** an itinerant agricultural worker who travels from one district to another. **3.** *Austral.* **a.** an immigrant, esp. a recent one. **b.** (*as modifier*): *a migrant hostel.* ~*adj.* **4.** moving from one region, place, or country to another; migratory. [C17: from Latin *migrāre* to change one's abode]

mi+grate (maɪ'greɪt) *vb.* (*intr.*) **1.** to go from one region, country, or place of abode to settle in another, esp. in a foreign country. **2.** (of birds, fishes, etc.) to journey between different habitats at specific times of the year. [C17: from Latin *migrāre* to change one's abode] —**mi+'gra+tor** *n.*

mi+gra+tion (maɪ'greɪʃən) *n.* **1.** the act or an instance of migrating. **2.** a group of people, birds, etc., migrating in a body. **3.** *Chem.* a movement of atoms, ions, or molecules, such as the motion of ions in solution under the influence of electric fields. —**mi+'gra+tion+al** *adj.*

mi+gra+to+ry ('maɪgrətərɪ, -trɪ) *adj.* **1.** of, relating to, or characterized by migration. **2.** nomadic; itinerant.

mih+rab ('mi:ræb, -rəb) *n. Islam.* the niche in a mosque showing the direction of Mecca. [From Arabic]

mi+ka+do (mɪ'kɑ:dəʊ) *n., pl.* **+dos.** (*often cap.*) *Archaic.* the Japanese emperor. Compare **Tenno.** [C18: from Japanese, from *mi-* honourable + *kado* door, palace gate]

mike[1] (maɪk) *n. Informal.* short for **microphone.**

mike[2] (maɪk) *Brit. slang.* ~*vb.* (*intr.*) **1.** to idle; wait about. ~*n.* **2.** an evasion of work: *to do a mike.* [C19: origin unknown]

mil (mɪl) *n.* **1.** a unit of length equal to one thousandth of an inch. **2.** an obsolete pharmaceutical unit of volume equal to one millilitre. **3.** a unit of angular measure, used in gunnery, equal to one sixty-four-thousandth of a circumference. [C18: short for Latin *millēsimus* thousandth]

mil. *abbrev. for:* **1.** military. **2.** militia.

mi+la+dy *or* **mi+la+di** (mɪ'leɪdɪ) *n., pl.* **+dies.** (formerly) a continental title used for an English gentlewoman.

mil+age ('maɪlɪdʒ) *n.* a variant spelling of **mileage.**

Mi·lan (mɪˈlæn) *n.* a city in N Italy, in central Lombardy: Italy's second largest city and chief financial and industrial centre; a centre of the Renaissance under the Visconti and Sforza families. Pop.: 1 731 281 (1975 est.). Italian name: **Mi·la·no** (miˈlaːno).

Mil·an·ese (ˌmɪləˈniːz) *adj.* **1.** of or relating to Milan, its people, culture, etc. **2.** of a fine lightweight knitted fabric of silk, rayon, etc. ~*n., pl.* **·ese. 3.** the Italian dialect spoken in Milan. **4.** a native or inhabitant of Milan.

Mi·laz·zo (*Italian* miˈlattso) *n.* a port in NE Sicily: founded in the 8th century B.C.; scene of a battle (1860), in which Garibaldi defeated the Bourbon forces. Pop.: 27 204 (1971). Ancient name: **Mylae.**

milch (mɪltʃ) *n.* **1.** (*modifier*) (esp. of cattle) yielding milk. **2.** **milch cow.** *Informal.* a source of easy income, esp. a person. [C13: from Old English *-milce* (in compounds); related to Old English *melcan* to milk]

mild (maɪld) *adj.* **1.** (of a taste, sensation, etc.) not powerful or strong; bland: *a mild curry.* **2.** gentle or temperate in character, climate, behaviour, etc. **3.** not extreme; moderate: *a mild rebuke.* **4.** feeble; unassertive. ~*n.* **5.** *Brit.* draught beer, of darker colour than bitter and flavoured with fewer hops. **6.** **draw it mild.** speak or act moderately. [Old English *milde*; compare Old Saxon *mildi*, Old Norse *mildr*] —**ˈmild·ly** *adv.* —**ˈmild·ness** *n.*

mild·en (ˈmaɪldən) *vb.* to make or become mild or milder.

mil·dew (ˈmɪlˌdjuː) *n.* **1.** any of various diseases of plants that affect mainly the leaves and are caused by parasitic fungi. See also **downy mildew, powdery mildew. 2.** any fungus causing this kind of disease. **3.** another name for **mould**[2]. ~*vb.* **4.** to affect or become affected with mildew. [Old English *mildēaw*, from *mil-* honey (compare Latin *mel*, Greek *mēli*) + *dēaw* DEW] —**ˈmilˌdew·y** *adj.*

mild steel *n.* any of a class of strong tough steels that contain a low quantity of carbon (0.1–0.25 per cent).

mile (maɪl) *n.* **1.** Also called: **statute mile.** a unit of length used in English-speaking countries, equal to 1760 yards. 1 mile is equivalent to 1.609 34 kilometres. **2.** See **nautical mile. 3.** See **Swedish mile. 4.** any of various units of length used at different times and places, esp. the Roman mile, equivalent to 1620 yards. **5.** (*often pl.*) *Informal.* a great distance; great deal: *he missed by a mile.* **6.** a race extending over a mile. ~*adv.* **7.** **miles.** (intensifier): *he likes his new job miles better.* [Old English *mīl*, from Latin *mīlia* (*passuum*) a thousand (paces)]

mile·age or **mil·age** (ˈmaɪlɪdʒ) *n.* **1.** a distance expressed in miles. **2.** the total number of miles that a motor vehicle has travelled. **3.** allowance for travelling expenses, esp. as a fixed rate per mile. **4.** the number of miles a motor vehicle will travel on one gallon of fuel. **5.** *Informal, chiefly U.S.* use, benefit, or service provided by something: *this scheme has a lot of mileage left.*

mile·om·e·ter or **mi·lom·e·ter** (maɪˈlɒmɪtə) *n.* a device that records the number of miles that a bicycle or motor vehicle has travelled. Usual U.S. name: **odometer.**

mile·post (ˈmaɪlˌpəʊst) *n.* **1.** *Horse racing.* a marking post on a racecourse a mile before the finishing line. **2.** Also called (esp. Brit.): **milestone.** *Chiefly U.S.* a signpost that shows the distance in miles to or from a place.

mil·er (ˈmaɪlə) *n.* an athlete, horse, etc., that runs or specializes in races of one mile.

mi·les glo·ri·o·sus *Latin.* (ˈmiːleɪs ˌglɔːrɪˈəʊsʊs) *n., pl.* ***mi·li·tes glo·ri·o·si*** (ˈmiːlɪˌteɪs ˌglɔːrɪˈəʊsaɪ). a braggart soldier, esp. as a stock figure in comedy. [from the title of a comedy by Plautus]

Mi·le·si·an[1] (maɪˈliːzɪən) *adj.* **1.** of or relating to Miletus. ~*n.* **2.** an inhabitant of Miletus. [via Latin from Greek *Milēsios*]

Mi·le·si·an[2] (maɪˈliːzɪən) *Facetious. adj.* **1.** Irish. ~*n.* **2.** an Irishman. [C16: from *Milesius*, a fictitious king of Spain whose sons were supposed to have conquered Ireland]

mile·stone (ˈmaɪlˌstəʊn) *n.* **1.** a stone pillar that shows the distance in miles to or from a place. **2.** a significant event in life, history, etc.

Mi·le·tus (mɪˈliːtəs) *n.* an ancient city on the W coast of Asia Minor: a major Ionian centre of trade and learning in the ancient world.

mil·foil (ˈmɪlˌfɔɪl) *n.* **1.** another name for **yarrow. 2.** See **water milfoil.** [C13: from Old French, from Latin *milifolium*, from *mille* thousand + *folium* leaf]

Mil·ford Ha·ven (ˈmɪlfəd) *n.* a port in SW Wales, in Dyfed on **Milford Haven** (a large inlet of St. George's Channel): major oil port. Pop.: 13 745 (1971).

Mi·lhaud (*French* miˈjo) *n.* **Da·rius** (daˈrjys). 1892–1974, French composer; member of Les Six. A notable exponent of polytonality, his large output includes operas, symphonies, ballets, string quartets, and songs.

mil·i·ar·i·a (ˌmɪlɪˈɛərɪə) *n.* an acute itching eruption of the skin, caused by blockage of the sweat glands. Nontechnical names: **heat rash, prickly heat.** [C19: from New Latin, from Latin *miliārius* MILIARY]

mil·iar·y (ˈmɪljərɪ) *adj.* **1.** resembling or relating to millet seeds. **2.** (of a disease or skin eruption) characterized by small lesions resembling millet seeds: *miliary tuberculosis.* [C17: from Latin *miliārius*, from *milium* MILLET]

mil·iar·y fe·ver *n.* an acute infectious fever characterized by profuse sweating and the formation on the skin of minute fluid-filled vesicles. Nontechnical name: **sweating sickness.**

mi·lieu (ˈmiːljɜː; *French* miˈljø) *n., pl.* **·lieus** or *French* **·lieux** (-ˈljø). surroundings, location, or setting. [C19: from French, from *mi-* MID[1] + *lieu* place]

milit. *abbrev. for* military.

mil·i·tant (ˈmɪlɪtənt) *adj.* **1.** aggressive or vigorous, esp. in the support of a cause: *a militant protest.* **2.** warring; engaged in warfare. ~*n.* **3.** a militant person. [C15: from Latin *mīlitāre* to be a soldier, from *mīles* soldier] —**ˈmil·i·tan·cy** or **ˈmil·i·tant·ness** *n.* —**ˈmil·i·tant·ly** *adv.*

mil·i·ta·rism (ˈmɪlɪtəˌrɪzəm) *n.* **1.** military spirit; pursuit of military ideals. **2.** domination by the military in the formulation of policies, ideals, etc., esp. on a political level.

mil·i·ta·rist (ˈmɪlɪtərɪst) *n.* **1.** a supporter of or believer in militarism. **2.** a devotee of military history, strategy, etc. —**ˌmil·i·ta·ˈris·tic** *adj.* —**ˌmil·i·ta·ˈris·ti·cal·ly** *adv.*

mil·i·ta·rize or **mil·i·ta·rise** (ˈmɪlɪtəˌraɪz) *vb.* (*tr.*) **1.** to convert to military use. **2.** to imbue with militarism. —**ˌmil·i·ta·ri·ˈza·tion** or **ˌmil·i·ta·ri·ˈsa·tion** *n.*

mil·i·tar·y (ˈmɪlɪtərɪ, -trɪ) *adj.* **1.** of or relating to the armed forces, warlike matters, etc. **2.** of, characteristic of, or about soldiers. ~*n., pl.* **·tar·ies** or **·tar·y. 3.** (preceded by *the*) the armed services. [C16: via French from Latin *mīlitāris*, from *mīles* soldier] —**ˈmil·i·tar·i·ly** *adv.*

mil·i·tar·y a·cad·e·my *n.* a training establishment for young officer cadets entering the army.

mil·i·tar·y en·gi·neer·ing *n.* the design, construction, etc., of military fortifications and communications.

mil·i·tar·y hon·ours *pl. n.* ceremonies performed by troops in honour of royalty, at the burial of an officer, etc.

mil·i·tar·y law *n.* articles or regulations that apply to those belonging to the armed services. Compare **martial law.**

mil·i·tar·y pace *n.* the pace of a single step in marching, taken to be 30 inches for quick time (120 paces to the minute) in both the British and U.S. armies.

mil·i·tar·y po·lice *n.* a corps within an army that performs police and disciplinary duties. —**mil·i·tar·y po·lice·man** *n.*

mil·i·tate (ˈmɪlɪˌteɪt) *vb.* (*intr.*; usually foll. by *against* or *for*) (of facts, etc.) to have influence or effect: *the evidence militated against his release.* [C17: from Latin *mīlitātus*, from *mīlitāre* to be a soldier] —**ˌmil·iˈta·tion** *n.*

mi·li·tia (mɪˈlɪʃə) *n.* **1.** a body of citizen (as opposed to professional) soldiers. **2.** an organization containing men enlisted for service in emergency only. [C16: from Latin: soldiery, from *mīles* soldier]

mi·li·tia·man (mɪˈlɪʃəmən) *n., pl.* **·men.** a man serving with the militia.

mil·i·um (ˈmɪlɪəm) *n., pl.* **·i·a** (-ɪə). *Pathol.* a small whitish nodule on the skin, usually resulting from a clogged sebaceous gland. [C19: from Latin: millet]

milk (mɪlk) *n.* **1. a.** a whitish nutritious fluid produced and secreted by the mammary glands of mature female mammals and used for feeding their young until weaned. **b.** the milk of cows, goats, or other animals used by man as a food or in the production of butter, cheese, etc. **2.** any similar fluid in plants, such as the juice of a coconut. **3.** any of various milklike pharmaceutical preparations, such as milk of magnesia. **4.** **cry over spilt milk.** to lament something that cannot be altered. ~*vb.* **5.** to draw milk from the udder of (a cow, goat, or other animal). **6.** (*intr.*) (of cows, goats, or other animals) to yield milk. **7.** (*tr.*) to draw off or tap in small quantities: *to milk the petty cash.* **8.** (*tr.*) to extract as much money, help, etc., as possible from: *to milk a situation of its news value.* **9.** (*tr.*) to extract venom, sap, etc., from. [Old English *milc*; compare Old Saxon *miluk*, Old High German *miluh*, Old Norse *mjolk*]

milk-and-wa·ter *adj.* (**milk and wa·ter** *when postpositive*). weak, feeble, or insipid.

milk bar *n.* **a.** a snack bar at which milk drinks and light refreshments are served. **b.** (in Australia) a shop selling, in addition, basic provisions and other items.

milk choc·o·late *n.* chocolate that has been made with milk, having a creamy taste. Compare **plain chocolate.**

milk·er (ˈmɪlkə) *n.* **1.** a cow, goat, etc., that yields milk, esp. of a specified quality or amount: *a poor milker.* **2.** a person who milks. **3.** another name for **milking machine.**

milk fe·ver *n.* **1.** a fever that sometimes occurs shortly after childbirth, once thought to result from engorgement of the breasts with milk but now thought to be caused by infection. **2.** *Vet. science.* a disease of cows, goats, etc., occurring shortly after parturition, characterized by low blood calcium levels, paralysis, and loss of consciousness.

milk·fish (ˈmɪlkˌfɪʃ) *n., pl.* **·fish** or **·fish·es.** a large silvery tropical clupeoid food and game fish, *Chanos chanos*: family *Chanidae.*

milk float *n. Brit.* a small motor vehicle used to deliver milk to houses.

milk glass *n.* opaque white glass, originally produced in imitation of Chinese porcelain.

milk·ing ma·chine *n.* an apparatus for milking cows.

milk·ing stool *n.* a low three-legged stool.

milk leg *n.* inflammation and thrombosis of the femoral vein following childbirth, characterized by painful swelling of the leg. Also called: **white leg.** Technical name: **phlegmasia alba dolens.**

milk·maid (ˈmɪlkˌmeɪd) *n.* a girl or woman who milks cows.

milk·man (ˈmɪlkmən) *n., pl.* **·men. 1.** a man who delivers or sells milk. **2.** a man who milks cows; dairyman.

milk·o (ˈmɪlkəʊ) *n. Austral.* an informal name for **milkman.**

milk of mag·ne·sia *n.* a suspension of magnesium hydroxide in water, used as an antacid and laxative.

milk pud+ding *n. Chiefly Brit.* a hot or cold pudding made by boiling or baking milk with a grain, esp. rice.

milk punch *n.* a spiced drink made of milk and spirits.

milk run *n. Aeronautics, informal.* a routine and uneventful flight, esp. on a dangerous mission. [C20: referring to the routine daily delivery of milk]

milk shake *n.* a cold frothy drink made of milk, flavouring, and sometimes ice cream, whisked or beaten together.

milk sick+ness *n.* **1.** an acute disease characterized by weakness, vomiting, and constipation, caused by ingestion of the flesh or dairy products of cattle affected with trembles. **2.** *Vet. science.* another name for **trembles.**

milk snake *n.* a nonvenomous brown-and-grey North American colubrid snake *Lampropeltis doliata,* related to the king snakes.

milk+sop ('mɪlkˌsɒp) *n.* **1.** a feeble or ineffectual man or youth. **2.** *Brit.* a dish of bread soaked in warm milk, given esp. to infants and invalids. —**'milk+ˌsop+py** *or* **'milk+ˌsop+ping** *adj.* —**'milk+ˌsop+ism** *n.*

milk stout *n. Brit.* a rich mellow stout lacking a bitter aftertaste.

milk sug+ar *n.* another name for **lactose.**

milk this+tle *n.* another name for **sow thistle.**

milk tooth *n.* any of the first teeth to erupt; a deciduous tooth. Also called: **baby tooth.** See also **dentition.**

milk vetch *n.* any of various papilionaceous plants of the genus *Astragalus,* esp. *A. glycyphyllos,* with clusters of purple, white, or yellowish flowers: formerly reputed to increase milk production in goats.

milk+weed ('mɪlkˌwi:d) *n.* **1.** Also called: **silkweed.** any plant of the mostly North American genus *Asclepias,* having milky sap and pointed pods that split open to release tufted seeds: family *Asclepiadaceae.* **2.** any of various other plants having milky sap. **3. orange milkweed.** another name for **butterfly weed. 4.** another name for **monarch** (the butterfly).

milk+wort ('mɪlkˌwɜ:t) *n.* any of several plants of the genus *Polygala,* having small blue, pink, or white flowers with two petal-like sepals: family *Polygalaceae.* They were formerly believed to increase milk production in nursing women. See also **senega.**

milk·y ('mɪlkɪ) *adj.* **milk·i+er, milk·i+est. 1.** resembling milk, esp. in colour or cloudiness. **2.** of or containing milk. **3.** spiritless or spineless. —**'milk·i+ly** *adv.* —**'milk·i+ness** *n.*

Milk·y Way *n.* **the. 1.** the diffuse band of light stretching across the night sky that consists of millions of faint stars, nebulae, etc., and forms part of the Galaxy. **2.** another name for the **Galaxy.** [C14: translation of Latin *via lactea*]

mill[1] (mɪl) *n.* **1.** a building fitted with machinery for processing materials, manufacturing goods, etc.; factory. **2.** a machine that processes materials, manufactures goods, etc., by performing a continuous or repetitive operation, esp. one involving rotary motion, such as a machine to grind flour, pulverize solids, or press fruit. **3.** a machine that tools or polishes metal. **4.** a hard roller for impressing a design, esp. in a textile-printing machine or in a machine for printing bank notes. **5.** a system, institution, etc., that influences people or things in the manner of a factory: *going through the educational mill.* **6.** an unpleasant experience; ordeal (esp. in the phrase **go** or **be put through the mill**). **7.** a fist fight. **8. run of the mill.** ordinary or routine. ~*vb.* **9.** (*usually tr.*) to grind, press, or pulverize in or as if in a mill. **10.** (*usually tr.*) to process or produce in or with a mill. **11.** to cut or roll (metal) with or as if with a milling machine. **12.** (*tr.*) to groove or flute the edge of (a coin). **13.** (often foll. by *about* or *around*) to move about or cause to move about in a confused manner. **14.** (*usually tr.*) *Now rare.* to beat (chocolate, etc.). **15.** *Archaic slang.* to fight, esp. with the fists. [Old English *mylen* from Late Latin *molīna* a mill, from Latin *mola* mill, millstone, from *molere* to grind] —**'mill+a·ble** *adj.*

mill[2] (mɪl) *n.* a U.S. monetary unit used in calculations, etc., equal to one thousandth of a dollar. [C18: short for Latin *millēsimum* a thousandth (part)]

Mill (mɪl) *n.* **1. James.** 1773–1836, Scottish philosopher, historian, and economist. He expounded Bentham's utilitarian philosophy in *Elements of Political Economy* (1821) and *Analysis of the Phenomena of the Human Mind* (1829) and also wrote a *History of British India* (1817–18). **2.** his son **John Stu·art.** 1806–73, English philosopher and economist. He modified Bentham's utilitarian philosophy in *Utilitarianism* (1861) and in his treatise *On Liberty* (1859) he defended the rights and freedom of the individual. Other works include *A System of Logic* (1843) and *Principles of Political Economy* (1848).

Mil·lais (mɪ'leɪ) *n.* Sir **John Ev·er·ett.** 1829–96, English painter, who was a founder of the Pre-Raphaelite Brotherhood. His works include *The Order of Release* (1853) and *The Blind Girl* (1856).

mill+board ('mɪlˌbɔ:d) *n.* strong pasteboard, used esp. in book covers. [C18: changed from *milled board*]

mill+dam ('mɪlˌdæm) *n.* a dam built in a stream to raise the water level sufficiently for it to turn a mill wheel.

milled (mɪld) *adj.* **1.** (of coins, etc.) having a grooved or fluted edge. **2.** made or treated in a mill.

mille+feuille *French.* (mil'fœ:j) *n. Brit.* a small iced cake made of puff pastry filled with jam and cream. U.S. name: **napoleon.** [literally: thousand leaves]

mille+fleurs ('mi:lˌflɜ:) *n.* a design of stylized floral patterns, used in textiles, etc. [French: thousand flowers]

mil+le+nar+i·an (ˌmɪlɪ'nɛərɪən) *or* **mil+le+nar·y** *adj.* **1.** of or relating to a thousand or to a thousand years. **2.** of or relating to the millennium or millenarianism. ~*n.* **3.** an adherent of millenarianism.

mil+le+nar+i+an+ism (ˌmɪlɪ'nɛərɪəˌnɪzəm) *n.* **1.** *Christianity.* the belief in a future millennium following the Second Coming of Christ during which he will reign on earth in peace: based on Revelation 20:1–5. **2.** any belief in a future period of ideal peace and happiness.

mil+le+nar·y (mɪ'lɛnərɪ) *n., pl.* **+nar·ies. 1.** a sum or aggregate of one thousand, esp. one thousand years. **2.** another word for a **millennium.** ~*adj., n.* **3.** another word for **millenarian.** [C16: from Late Latin *millēnārius* containing a thousand, from Latin *mille* thousand]

mil+len+ni·um (mɪ'lɛnɪəm) *n., pl.* **+ni·ums** *or* **+ni·a** (-nɪə). **1. the.** *Christianity.* the period of a thousand years of Christ's awaited reign upon earth. **2.** a period or cycle of one thousand years. **3.** a time of peace and happiness, esp. in the distant future. **4.** a thousandth anniversary. [C17: from New Latin, from Latin *mille* thousand + *annus* year; for form, compare QUADRENNIUM] —**mil+'len+ni+al** *adj.* —**mil+'len+ni+al+ist** *n.* —**mil+'len+ni+al+ly** *adv.*

mil+le+pede ('mɪlɪˌpi:d) *or* **mil+le+ped** ('mɪlɪˌpɛd) *n.* variant spellings of **millipede.**

mil+le+pore ('mɪlɪˌpɔ:) *n.* any tropical colonial coral-like medusoid hydrozoan of the order *Milleporina,* esp. of the genus *Millepora,* having a calcareous skeleton. [C18: from New Latin, from Latin *mille* thousand + *porus* hole]

mil+ler ('mɪlə) *n.* **1.** a person who keeps, operates, or works in a mill, esp. a corn mill. **2.** another name for **milling machine. 3.** a person who operates a milling machine.

Mil·ler ('mɪlə) *n.* **1. Ar·thur.** born 1915, U.S. dramatist. His plays include *Death of a Salesman* (1949), *The Crucible* (1953), and *A View from the Bridge* (1955). **2. Hen·ry.** 1891-1980, U.S. novelist, author of *Tropic of Cancer* (1934) and *Tropic of Capricorn* (1938). **3. John·ny.** born 1947, U.S. professional golfer: won the U.S. Open Championship (1973) and the British Open Championship (1976).

mil+ler+ite ('mɪləˌraɪt) *n.* a yellow mineral consisting of nickel sulphide in hexagonal crystalline form: a minor ore of nickel. Formula: NiS. [C19: named after W. H. *Miller* (1801–1880), English mineralogist]

mil+ler's thumb *n.* any of several small freshwater European fishes of the genus *Cottus,* esp. *C. gobio,* having a flattened body: family *Cottidae* (bullheads, etc.). [C15: from the alleged likeness of the fish's head to a thumb]

mil+les·i+mal (mɪ'lɛsɪməl) *adj.* **1. a.** denoting a thousandth. **b.** (*as n.*): *a millesimal.* **2.** of, consisting of, or relating to a thousandth. [C18: from Latin *millēsimus*]

mil+let ('mɪlɪt) *n.* **1.** a cereal grass, *Setaria italica,* cultivated for grain and animal fodder. **2. a.** an East Indian annual grass, *Panicum miliaceum,* cultivated for grain and forage, having pale round shiny seeds. **b.** the seed of this plant. **3.** any of various similar or related grasses, such as pearl millet and Indian millet. [C14: via Old French from Latin *milium;* related to Greek *melinē* millet]

Mil·let (*French* mi'lɛ) *n.* **Jean Fran·çois** (ʒã frã'swa). 1814–75, French painter of the Barbizon school, noted for his studies of peasants at work.

mil·li- *prefix.* denoting 10^{-3}: *millimetre.* Symbol: m [from French, from Latin *mille* thousand, this meaning being maintained in words borrowed from Latin (*millipede*)]

mil+li+ard ('mɪlɪˌɑ:d, 'mɪljɑ:d) *n. Brit.* a thousand million. U.S. equivalent: **billion.** [C19: from French]

mil+liar·y ('mɪljərɪ) *adj.* relating to or marking a distance equal to an ancient Roman mile of a thousand paces. [C17: from Latin *milliārius* containing a thousand, from *mīlle* thousand]

mil+li+bar ('mɪlɪˌbɑ:) *n.* a cgs unit of atmospheric pressure equal to 10^{-3} bar, 100 newtons per square metre or 0.7500617 millimetres of mercury.

mil+lieme (mi:l'jɛm) *n.* a Tunisian monetary unit worth one thousandth of a dinar. Also called: **millime.** [from French *millième* thousandth]

Mil·li·gan ('mɪlɪgən) *n.* **Spike.** born 1918, Irish radio, stage, and film comedian. He appeared on *The Goon Show* (with Peter Sellers and Harry Secombe; BBC Radio, 1952–60) and his films include *Postman's Knock* (1962), *Adolf Hitler, My Part in his Downfall* (1972), *The Three Musketeers* (1974), and *The Last Remake of Beau Geste* (1977).

mil+li+gram *or* **mil+li+gramme** ('mɪlɪˌgræm) *n.* one thousandth of a gram. Symbol: mg [C19: from French]

Mil·li·kan ('mɪlɪkən) *n.* **Rob·ert An·drews.** 1868–1953, U.S. physicist. He isolated the electron and determined its charge (1917): Nobel prize for physics 1923.

mil+li+li+tre *or U.S.* **mil+li+li+ter** ('mɪlɪˌli:tə) *n.* one thousandth of a litre. Symbol: ml

mil+li+me·tre *or U.S.* **mil+li+me·ter** ('mɪlɪˌmi:tə) *n.* one thousandth of a metre. Symbol: mm

mil+li+mi+cron ('mɪlɪˌmaɪkrɒn) *n.* an obsolete name for a nanometre; one millionth of a millimetre.

mil+line ('mɪlˌlaɪn, mɪl'laɪn) *n.* **1.** a unit of advertising copy equal to one agate line of one column width appearing in one million copies of a publication. **2.** Also called: **milline rate.** the cost of this unit. [C20: from MILLION + LINE[1]]

mil+li+ner ('mɪlɪnə) *n.* a person who makes or sells women's hats. [C16: originally *Milaner,* a native of *Milan,* at that time famous for its fancy goods]

mil+li+ner·y ('mɪlɪnərɪ, -ɪnrɪ) *n.* **1.** hats, trimmings, etc., sold by a milliner. **2.** the business or shop of a milliner.

mill+ing ('mɪlɪŋ) *n.* **1.** the act or process of grinding, pressing, or crushing in a mill. **2.** the vertical grooves or fluting on the edge of a coin, etc. **3.** (in W North America) a method of halting a stampede of cattle by turning the leaders in a wide arc until the herd turns in upon itself in a tightening spiral.

mill·ing ma·chine *n.* a power-driven machine tool in which a horizontal arbor or vertical spindle rotates a cutting tool above a horizontal table.

mil·lion ('mɪljən) *n., pl.* **·lions** *or* **·lion. 1.** the cardinal number that is the product of 1000 multiplied by 1000. See also **number** (sense 1). **2.** a numeral, 1 000 000, 10^6, M̄, etc., representing this number. **3.** (*often pl.*) an extremely large but unspecified number, quantity, or amount: *I have millions of things to do.* ~*determiner.* **4.** (preceded by *a* or by a numeral) **a.** amounting to a million: *a million light years away.* **b.** (*as pronoun*): *I can see a million under the microscope.* ~Related prefix: **mega-. 5. gone a million.** *Austral. informal.* done for; sunk. **6. the million.** the mass of the population. [C17: via Old French from early Italian *millione*, from *mille* thousand, from Latin]

mil·lion·aire *or* **mil·lion·naire** (ˌmɪljəˈnɛə) *n.* a person whose assets are worth at least a million of the standard monetary units of his country. —**ˌmil·lion·ˈair·ess** *fem. n.*

mil·lionth ('mɪljənθ) *n.* **1. a.** one of 1 000 000 approximately equal parts of something. **b.** (*as modifier*): *a millionth part.* **2.** one of 1 000 000 equal divisions of a particular scientific quantity. Related prefix: **micro-. 3.** the fraction equal to one divided by 1 000 000. ~*adj.* **4.** (*usually prenominal*) **a.** being the ordinal number of 1 000 000 in numbering or counting order, etc. **b.** (*as n.*): *the millionth to be manufactured.*

mil·li·pede, mil·le·pede ('mɪlɪˌpi:d), *or* **mil·le·ped** ('mɪlɪˌpɛd) *n.* any terrestrial herbivorous arthropod of the class *Diplopoda*, having a cylindrical body, each segment of which bears two pairs of walking legs. See also **myriapod.** [C17: from Latin, from *mille* thousand + *pēs* foot]

mil·li·sec·ond ('mɪlɪˌsɛkənd) *n.* one thousandth of a second. Symbol: ms

mill·pond ('mɪlˌpɒnd) *n.* **1.** a pool formed by damming a stream to provide water to turn a mill wheel. **2.** any expanse of calm water: *the sea was a millpond.*

mill·race ('mɪlˌreɪs) *or* **mill·run** *n.* **1.** the current of water that turns a millwheel. **2.** the channel for this water.

mill-rind *n.* an iron support fitted across an upper millstone.

mill·run ('mɪlˌrʌn) *n.* **1.** another name for **millrace. 2.** *Mining.* **a.** the process of milling an ore or rock in order to determine the content or quality of the mineral. **b.** the mineral so examined. ~*adj.* **mill-run. 3.** *Chiefly U.S.* (of commodities) taken straight from the production line; unsorted as to quality.

Mills bomb (mɪlz) *n.* a type of high-explosive hand grenade. [C20: named after Sir William *Mills* (1856–1932), English inventor]

mill·stone ('mɪlˌstəʊn) *n.* **1.** one of a pair of heavy flat disc-shaped stones that are rotated one against the other to grind grain. **2.** a heavy burden, such as a responsibility or obligation: *his debts were a millstone round his neck.*

mill·stream ('mɪlˌstri:m) *n.* a stream of water used to turn a millwheel.

mill·wheel ('mɪlˌwi:l) *n.* a wheel, esp. a waterwheel, that drives a mill.

mill·work ('mɪlˌwɜ:k) *n.* work done in a mill.

mill·wright ('mɪlˌraɪt) *n.* a person who designs, builds, or repairs grain mills or mill machinery.

Milne (mɪln) *n.* **A(lan) A(lexander).** 1882–1956, English writer, noted for his books and verse for children, including *When We Were Very Young* (1924) and *Winnie the Pooh* (1926).

mi·lo ('maɪləʊ) *n., pl.* **·los.** any of various early-growing cultivated varieties of sorghum with heads of yellow or pinkish seeds resembling millet.

mi·lom·e·ter (maɪˈlɒmɪtə) *n.* a variant spelling of **mileometer.**

mi·lord (mɪˈlɔ:d) *n.* (formerly) a continental title used for an English gentleman. [C19: via French from English *my lord*]

Mí·los ('mi:lɔs) *n.* transliteration of the Modern Greek name for **Melos.**

milque·toast ('mɪlkˌtəʊst) *n. U.S.* a meek, submissive, or timid person. [C20: from Caspar *Milquetoast*, a cartoon character invented by H. T. Webster (1885–1952)]

mil·reis ('mɪlˌreɪs; *Portuguese* milˈrɛjʃ) *n., pl.* **·reis.** a former monetary and currency unit of Portugal and Brazil, divided into 1000 reis. [C16: from Portuguese, from *mil* thousand + *réis*, pl. of *real* royal]

Mil·stein ('mɪlstaɪn) *n.* **Na·than.** born 1904, U.S. violinist, born in Russia.

milt (mɪlt) *n.* **1.** the testis of a fish. **2.** the spermatozoa and seminal fluid produced by a fish. **3.** *Rare.* the spleen of certain animals, esp. fowls and pigs. ~*vb.* **4.** to fertilize (the roe of a female fish) with milt, esp. artificially. [Old English *milte* spleen; in the sense: fish sperm, probably from Middle Dutch *milte*]

mil·ter ('mɪltə) *n.* a male fish that is mature and ready to breed.

Mil·ti·a·des (mɪlˈtaɪəˌdi:z) *n.* ?540–?489 B.C., Athenian general, who defeated the Persians at Marathon (490).

Mil·ton ('mɪltən) *n.* **John.** 1608–74, English poet. His early works, notably *L'Allegro* and *Il Penseroso* (1632), the masque *Comus* (1634), and the elegy *Lycidas* (1637), show the influence of his Christian humanist education and his love of Italian Renaissance poetry. A staunch Parliamentarian and opponent of episcopacy, he published many pamphlets during the Civil War period, including *Areopagitica* (1644), which advocated freedom of the press. His greatest works were the epic poems *Paradise Lost* (1667; 1674), and *Paradise Regained* (1671) and the verse drama *Samson Agonistes* (1671).

Mil·ton·ic (mɪlˈtɒnɪk) *or* **Mil·to·ni·an** (mɪlˈtəʊnɪən) *adj.* characteristic of or resembling Milton's literary style, esp. in being sublime and majestic.

Mil·ton Keynes ('mɪltən 'ki:nz) *n.* a new town in N Buckinghamshire, founded in 1967. Pop.: 46 473 (1971).

Mil·ton Work count *n. Bridge.* a system of hand valuation in which aces count 4, kings 3, queens 2, and jacks 1. [C20: named after *Milton Work*, authority on auction bridge]

Mil·wau·kee (mɪlˈwɔ:ki:) *n.* a port in SE Wisconsin, on Lake Michigan: the largest city in the state; established as a trading post in the 18th century; an important industrial centre. Pop.: 690 685 (1973 est.).

mim (mɪm) *adj. Brit. dialect.* prim, modest, or demure. [C17: perhaps imitative of lip-pursing]

Mi·mas ('maɪməs, -mæs) *n.* one of the smaller of the ten satellites of the planet Saturn.

mime (maɪm) *n.* **1.** the theatrical technique of expressing an idea or mood or portraying a character entirely by gesture and bodily movement without the use of words. **2.** Also called: **mime artist.** a performer specializing in such a technique, esp. a comic actor. **3.** a dramatic presentation using such a technique. **4.** (in the classical theatre) **a.** a comic performance depending for effect largely on exaggerated gesture and physical action. **b.** an actor in such a performance. ~*vb.* **5.** to express (an idea, etc.) in actions or gestures without speech. [Old English *mīma*, from Latin *mīmus* mimic actor, from Greek *mimos* imitator] —**'mim·er** *n.*

Mim·e·o·graph ('mɪmɪəˌgræf, -ˌgrɑ:f) *n.* **1.** *Trademark.* an office machine for printing multiple copies of text or line drawings from an inked drum to which a cut stencil is fixed. **2.** a copy produced by this machine. ~*vb.* **3.** to print copies from (a prepared stencil) using this machine.

mi·me·sis (mɪˈmi:sɪs) *n.* **1.** *Art, literature.* the imitative representation of nature or human behaviour. **2. a.** any disease that shows symptoms of another disease. **b.** a condition in a hysterical patient that mimics an organic disease. **3.** *Biology.* another name for **mimicry** (sense 2). **4.** *Rhetoric.* representation of another person's alleged words in a speech. [C16: from Greek, from *mimeisthai* to imitate]

mi·met·ic (mɪˈmɛtɪk) *adj.* **1.** of, resembling, or relating to mimesis or imitation, as in art, etc. **2.** *Biology.* of or exhibiting mimicry. —**mi·'met·i·cal·ly** *adv.*

mim·e·tite ('mɪmɪˌtaɪt, 'maɪmɪ-) *n.* a rare secondary mineral consisting of a chloride and arsenate of lead in the form of white or yellowish needle-like hexagonal crystals. Formula: $Pb_5Cl(AsO_4)_3$. [C19: from German, from Greek *mimētēs* imitator (of pyromorphite)]

mim·ic ('mɪmɪk) *vb.* **·ics, ·ick·ing, ·icked.** (*tr.*) **1.** to imitate (a person, a manner, etc.), esp. for satirical effect; ape. **2.** to take on the appearance of; resemble closely: *certain flies mimic wasps.* **3.** to copy closely or in a servile manner. ~*n.* **4.** a person or an animal, such as a parrot, that is clever at mimicking. **5.** an animal that displays mimicry. ~*adj.* **6.** of, relating to, or using mimicry; imitative. **7.** simulated, make-believe, or mock. [C16: from Latin *mīmicus*, from Greek *mimikos*, from *mimos* MIME] —**'mim·ick·er** *n.*

mim·ic·ry ('mɪmɪkrɪ) *n., pl.* **·ries. 1.** the act or art of copying or imitating closely; mimicking. **2.** the resemblance shown by one animal species, esp. an insect, to another, which protects it from predators.

M.I.Min.E. *abbrev. for* Member of the Institute of Mining Engineers.

mim·i·ny-pim·i·ny (ˌmɪmɪnɪˈpɪmɪnɪ) *adj.* a variant spelling of **niminy-piminy.**

Mi·mir ('mi:mɪə) *n. Norse myth.* a giant who guarded the well of wisdom near the roots of Yggdrasil.

mi·mo·sa (mɪˈməʊsə, -zə) *n.* **1.** any tropical shrubs or trees of the Mimosaceous genus *Mimosa*, having ball-like clusters of typically yellow flowers and compound leaves that are often sensitive to touch or light. See also **sensitive plant. 2.** any similar or related tree. [C18: from New Latin, probably from Latin *mīmus* MIME, because the plant's sensitivity to touch imitates the similar reaction of animals]

mim·o·sa·ceous (ˌmɪməˈseɪʃəs, ˌmaɪmə-) *adj.* of, relating to, or belonging to the *Mimosaceae*, a family of tropical and temperate leguminous plants with tiny ball-like clusters: includes acacia, mimosa, and the fever tree.

M.I.Mun.E. *abbrev. for* Member of the Institution of Municipal Engineers.

min *symbol for* minim (liquid measure).

Min (mɪn) *n.* any of the dialects or forms of Chinese spoken in Fukien province. Also called: **Fukien.**

min. *abbrev. for:* **1.** mineralogy *or* mineralogical. **2.** minimum. **3.** mining. **4.** minute or minutes.

Min. *abbrev. for:* **1.** Minister. **2.** Ministry.

mi·na[1] ('maɪnə) *n., pl.* **·nae** (-ni:) *or* **·nas.** an ancient unit of weight and money, used in Asia Minor, equal to one sixtieth of a talent. [C16: via Latin from Greek *mnā*, of Semitic origin; related to Hebrew *māneh* mina]

mi·na[2] ('maɪnə) *n.* a variant spelling of **myna** (bird). [C18: from Hindi *mainā*]

mi·na·cious (mɪˈneɪʃəs) *adj.* threatening. [C17: from Latin *minax*, from *minārī* to threaten] —**mi·'na·cious·ly** *adv.* —**mi·nac·i·ty** (mɪˈnæsɪtɪ) *n.*

Mi·na Has·san Ta·ni ('mi:nə hɑ:ˈsɑ:n 'tɑ:nɪ) *n.* a port in NW Morocco, on the Sebou River 16 km (10 miles) from the Atlantic. Pop.: 139 206 (1971). Also called: **Kenitra.** Former name (1932–56): **Port Lyautey.**

min·a·ret (ˌmɪnəˈrɛt, 'mɪnəˌrɛt) *n.* **1.** a slender tower of a mosque having one or more balconies. **2.** any structure resembling this. [C17: from French, from Turkish, from Arabic *manārat* lamp, from *nār* fire] —ˌ**min·a·'ret·ed** *adj.*

Mi·nas Ba·sin ('maɪnəs) *n.* a bay in E Canada, in central Nova Scotia: the NE arm of the Bay of Fundy, with which it is linked by **Minas Channel.**

Mi·nas Ge·rais (*Portuguese* 'minaʒ ʒe'rajs) *n.* an inland state of E Brazil: situated on the high plateau of the Brazilian Highlands; large reserves of iron ore and manganese. Capital: Belo Horizonte. Pop.: 11 487 415 (1970). Area: 587 172 sq. km (226 707 sq. miles).

min·a·to·ry ('mɪnətərɪ, -trɪ) *or* **min·a·to·ri·al** *adj.* threatening or menacing. [C16: from Late Latin *minātōrius,* from Latin *minārī* to threaten] —'**min·a·to·ri·ly** *or* ˌ**min·a·'to·ri·al·ly** *adv.*

mince (mɪns) *vb.* **1.** (*tr.*) to chop, grind, or cut into very small pieces. **2.** (*tr.*) to soften or moderate, esp. for the sake of convention or politeness: *I didn't mince my words.* **3.** (*intr.*) to walk or speak in an affected dainty manner. ~*n.* **4.** *Chiefly Brit.* minced meat. [C14: from Old French *mincier,* from Vulgar Latin *minūtiāre* (unattested), from Late Latin *minūtia* smallness; see MINUTIAE] —'**minc·er** *n.*

mince·meat ('mɪnsˌmi:t) *n.* **1.** a mixture of dried fruit, spices, etc., used esp. for filling pies. **2.** minced meat. **3. make mincemeat of.** to defeat completely.

mince pie *n.* a small round pastry tart filled with mincemeat.

Minch (mɪntʃ) *n.* **the.** a channel of the Atlantic divided into the **North Minch,** between the mainland of Scotland and the Isle of Lewis, and the **Little Minch,** between the Isle of Skye and Harris and North Uist.

minc·ing ('mɪnsɪŋ) *adj.* (of a person) affectedly elegant in gait, manner, or speech. —'**minc·ing·ly** *adv.*

mind (maɪnd) *n.* **1.** the entity in an individual responsible for thought, feelings, and speech. **2.** intelligence or the intellect, esp. as opposed to feelings or wishes. **3.** recollection or remembrance; memory: *it comes to mind.* **4.** the faculty of original or creative thought; imagination: *it's all in the mind.* **5.** a person considered as an intellectual being: *the great minds of the past.* **6.** opinion or sentiment: *we are of the same mind; to change one's mind; to have a mind of one's own; to know one's mind.* **7.** condition, state, or manner of feeling or thought: *no peace of mind; his state of mind.* **8.** an inclination, desire, or purpose: *I have a mind to go.* **9.** attention or thoughts: *keep your mind on your work.* **10.** a sound mental state; sanity: *to lose your mind.* **11.** intelligence, as opposed to material things: *the mind of the universe.* **12.** (in Cartesian philosophy) one of two basic modes of existence, the other being matter. **13. blow someone's mind.** *Slang.* **a.** to cause someone to have a psychedelic experience. **b.** to astound or surprise someone. **14. in** *or* **of two minds.** undecided; wavering: *he was in two minds about marriage.* **15. make up one's mind.** to decide (something or to do something): *he made up his mind to go.* **16. on one's mind.** in one's thoughts. **17. piece of one's mind.** an expression of one's candid opinion, esp. a rebuke. ~*vb.* **18.** (when *tr., may take a clause as object*) to take offence at: *do you mind if I smoke? I don't mind.* **19.** to pay attention to (something); heed; notice: *to mind one's own business.* **20.** (*tr.; takes a clause as object*) to make certain; ensure: *mind you tell her.* **21.** (*tr.*) to take care of; have charge of: *to mind the shop.* **22.** (when *tr., may take a clause as object*) to be cautious or careful about (something): *mind how you go; mind your step.* **23.** (*tr.*) to obey (someone or something); heed: *mind your father!* **24.** to be concerned (about); be troubled (about): *never mind your hat; never mind about your hat; never mind.* **25. mind you.** an expression qualifying a previous statement: *Dogs are nice. Mind you, I don't like all dogs.* ~Related adj.: **mental.** ~See also **mind out.** [Old English *gemynd* mind; related to Old High German *gimunt* memory] —'**mind·er** *n.*

Min·da·nao (ˌmɪndə'naʊ) *n.* the second largest island of the Philippines, in the S part of the archipelago: mountainous and volcanic. Chief towns: Davao, Zamboanga. Pop.: 7 484 402 (1970). Area: (including offshore islands) 94 631 sq. km (36 537 sq. miles).

mind·ed ('maɪndɪd) *adj.* **1.** having a mind, inclination, intention, etc., as specified: *politically minded.* **2.** (*in combination*): *money-minded.*

Min·del ('mɪndᵊl) *n.* the second major Pleistocene glaciation of Alpine Europe. See also **Günz, Riss, Würm.** [C20: named after the River *Mindel,* in Bavaria, Germany]

mind·ful ('maɪndfʊl) *adj.* (usually *postpositive* and foll. by *of*) keeping aware; heedful: *mindful of your duties.* —'**mind·ful·ly** *adv.* —'**mind·ful·ness** *n.*

mind·less ('maɪndlɪs) *adj.* **1.** stupid or careless. **2.** requiring little or no intellectual effort: *a mindless task.* —'**mind·less·ly** *adv.* —'**mind·less·ness** *n.*

Min·do·ro (mɪn'dɔ:rəʊ) *n.* a mountainous island in the central Philippines, south of Luzon. Pop.: 472 396 (1970). Area: 9736 sq. km (3759 sq. miles).

mind out *vb.* (*intr., adv.*) *Brit.* to be careful or pay attention.

mind-read·er *n.* a person seemingly able to discern the thoughts of another. —'**mind-ˌread·ing** *n.*

mind's eye *n.* the visual memory or the imagination.

Mind·szen·ty ('mɪndsɛntɪ) *n.* **Jo·seph.** 1892–1975, Hungarian cardinal. He was sentenced to life imprisonment on a charge of treason (1949) but released during the 1956 Revolution.

mind-your-own-busi·ness *n.* a Mediterranean urticaceous plant, *Helxine soleirolii,* with small dense leaves: used for cover. Also called: **mother-of-thousands.**

mine[1] (maɪn) *pron.* **1.** something or someone belonging to or associated with me: *mine is best.* **2. of mine.** belonging to or associated with me. ~*determiner.* **3.** (*preceding a vowel*) an archaic word for **my:** *mine eyes.* [Old English *mīn;* compare Old High German, Old Norse *mīn,* Dutch *mijn*]

mine[2] (maɪn) *n.* **1.** a system of excavations made for the extraction of minerals, esp. coal, ores, or precious stones. **2.** any deposit of ore or minerals. **3.** a lucrative source or abundant supply: *she was a mine of information.* **4.** a device containing an explosive designed to destroy ships, vehicles, or personnel, usually laid beneath the ground or in water. **5.** a tunnel or sap dug to undermine a fortification, etc. **6.** a groove or tunnel made by certain insects, esp. in a leaf. ~*vb.* **7.** to dig into (the earth) for (minerals). **8.** to make (a hole, tunnel, etc.) by digging or boring. **9.** to place explosive mines in position below the surface of (the sea or land). **10.** to undermine (a fortification, etc.) by digging mines or saps. **11.** another word for **undermine.** [C13: from Old French, probably of Celtic origin; compare Irish *mein,* Welsh *mwyn* ore, mine] —'**min·a·ble** *or* '**mine·a·ble** *adj.*

mine de·tec·tor *n.* an instrument designed to detect mines. —**mine de·tec·tion** *n.*

mine·field ('maɪnˌfi:ld) *n.* an area of ground or water containing mines.

mine·lay·er ('maɪnˌleɪə) *n.* a warship or aircraft designed for the carrying and laying of mines.

min·er ('maɪnə) *n.* **1.** a person who works in a mine. **2.** Also called: **continuous miner.** a large machine for the automatic extraction of minerals, esp. coal, from a mine. **3.** any of various insects or insect larvae that bore into and feed on plant tissues. See also **leaf miner. 4.** *Austral.* any of several honeyeaters of the genus *Myzantha,* esp. *Myzantha melanocephala* (**noisy miner**), of scrub regions.

min·er·al ('mɪnərəl, 'mɪnrəl) *n.* **1.** any of a class of naturally occurring solid inorganic substances with a characteristic crystalline form and a homogeneous chemical composition. **2.** any inorganic matter. **3.** any substance obtained by mining, esp. a metal ore. **4.** (*often pl.*) *Brit.* short for **mineral water. 5.** *Brit.* a soft drink containing carbonated water and flavourings. Usual U.S. word: **soda.** ~*adj.* **6.** of, relating to, containing, or resembling minerals. [C15: from Medieval Latin *minerāle* (n.), from *minerālis* (adj.); related to *minera* mine, ore, of uncertain origin]

mineral. *abbrev. for* mineralogy *or* mineralogical.

min·er·al·ize *or* **min·er·al·ise** ('mɪnərəˌlaɪz, 'mɪnrə-) *vb.* (*tr.*) **1. a.** to impregnate (organic matter, water, etc.) with a mineral substance. **b.** to convert (such matter) into a mineral; petrify. **2.** (of gases, vapours, etc., in magma) to transform (a metal) into an ore. —ˌ**min·er·al·i·'za·tion** *or* ˌ**min·er·al·i·'sa·tion** *n.*

min·er·al·iz·er *or* **min·er·al·is·er** ('mɪnərəˌlaɪzə) *n.* **1.** any of various gases dissolved in magma that affect the crystallization of igneous rocks and the formation of minerals when the magma cools. **2.** an element, such as oxygen, that combines with a metal to form an ore.

min·er·al jel·ly *n.* another name for **petrolatum.**

min·er·al king·dom *n.* all nonliving material, esp. rocks and minerals. Compare **animal kingdom, plant kingdom.**

min·er·al·o·cor·ti·coid (ˌmɪnərələʊ'kɔ:tɪˌkɔɪd) *n.* any corticosteroid that controls electrolyte and water balance, esp. by promoting retention of sodium by the kidney tubules.

min·er·al·o·gy (ˌmɪnə'rælədʒɪ) *n.* the branch of geology concerned with the study of minerals. —**min·er·al·og·i·cal** (ˌmɪnərə'lɒdʒɪkᵊl) *or* ˌ**min·er·al·'og·ic** *adj.* —ˌ**min·er·al·'og·i·cal·ly** *adv.* —ˌ**min·er·'al·o·gist** *n.*

min·er·al oil *n.* **1.** *Brit.* any oil of mineral origin, esp. petroleum. **2.** a U.S. name for **liquid paraffin.**

min·er·al pitch *n.* another name for **asphalt.**

min·er·al spring *n.* a spring of water that contains a high proportion of dissolved mineral salts.

min·er·al tar *n.* a natural black viscous tar intermediate in properties between petroleum and asphalt. Also called: **maltha.**

min·er·al wa·ter *n.* water containing dissolved mineral salts or gases, usually having medicinal properties.

min·er·al wax *n.* another name for **ozocerite.**

min·er·al wool *n.* a fibrous material made by blowing steam or air through molten slag and used for packing and insulation. Also called: **rock wool.**

Mi·ner·va (mɪ'nɜ:və) *n.* the Roman goddess of wisdom. Greek counterpart: **Athena.**

min·e·stro·ne (ˌmɪnɪ'strəʊnɪ) *n.* a soup made from a variety of vegetables and pasta. [from Italian, from *minestrare* to serve]

mine·sweep·er ('maɪnˌswi:pə) *n.* a naval vessel equipped to detect and clear mines. —'**mine·ˌsweep·ing** *n.*

Ming (mɪŋ) *n.* **1.** the imperial dynasty of China from 1368 to 1644. ~*adj.* **2.** of or relating to Chinese porcelain produced during the Ming dynasty, characterized by the use of brilliant colours and a fine-quality body.

minge (mɪndʒ) *n. Brit. taboo slang.* **1.** the female genitals. **2.** women collectively considered as sexual objects. [C20: from Romany]

min·gle ('mɪŋgᵊl) *vb.* **1.** to mix or cause to mix. **2.** (*intr.; often foll. by with*) to come into close association. [C15: from Old English *mengan* to mix; related to Middle Dutch *mengen,* Old Frisian *mengja*] —'**min·gler** *n.*

Min·gre·li·an (mɪŋ'gri:lɪən) *or* **Min·grel** ('mɪŋgrəl) *n.* **1.** a member of a Georgian people of the Soviet Union living in the mountains northeast of the Black Sea. **2.** the language of this people, belonging to the South Caucasian family and closely related to Georgian. ~*adj.* **3.** of or relating to the Mingrelians or their language.

ming tree *n.* an artificial plant resembling a bonsai plant.
Min·gus ('mɪŋgəs) *n.* **Charles.** called *Charlie.* 1922-79, U.S. jazz double bassist, composer, and bandleader.
min·gy ('mɪndʒɪ) *adj.* **·gi·er, ·gi·est.** *Brit. informal.* miserly, stingy, or niggardly. [C20: probably a blend of MEAN² + STINGY]
Mi·nho ('miɲu) *n.* the Portuguese name for the **Miño.**
min·i ('mɪnɪ) *adj.* **1.** (of a woman's dress, skirt, etc.) very short; thigh-length. **2.** (*prenominal*) small; miniature. ~*n.* **3.** something very small of its kind, esp. a small car or a miniskirt.
min·i- *combining form.* smaller or shorter than the standard size: *minibus; miniskirt.* [C20: from MINIATURE and MINIMUM]
min·ia·ture ('mɪnɪtʃə) *n.* **1.** a model, copy, or similar representation on a very small scale. **2.** anything that is very small of its kind: *miniature terriers.* **3.** a very small painting, esp. a portrait, showing fine detail on ivory or vellum. **4.** an illuminated letter or other decoration in a manuscript. **5. in miniature.** on a small scale: *games are real life in miniature.* ~*adj.* **6.** greatly reduced in size, etc. **7.** on a small scale; minute. [C16: from Italian, from Medieval Latin *miniātūra,* from *miniāre* to paint red; (in illuminating manuscripts), from MINIUM]
min·ia·ture cam·er·a *n.* a small camera using 35 millimetre film.
min·ia·tur·ist ('mɪnɪtʃərɪst) *n.* a person who paints miniature portraits.
min·ia·tur·ize *or* **min·ia·tur·ise** ('mɪnɪtʃə,raɪz) *vb.* (*tr.*) to make or construct (something, esp. electronic equipment) on a very small scale; reduce in size. —,**min·ia·tur·i·'za·tion** *or* ,**min·ia·tur·i·'sa·tion** *n.*
min·i·bus ('mɪnɪ,bʌs) *n.* a small bus able to carry approximately ten passengers.
min·i·cab ('mɪnɪ,kæb) *n.* a small saloon car used as a taxi.
min·i·com·put·er (,mɪnɪkəm'pju:tə) *n.* a small comparatively cheap digital computer.
min·i·dress ('mɪnɪ,drɛs) *n.* a very short dress, at least four inches above the knee. Often shortened to **mini.**
Min·i·é ball ('mɪnɪ,eɪ; *French* mi'ɲe) *n.* a conical rifle bullet, used in the 19th century, manufactured with a hollow base designed to expand when fired to fit the rifling. [C19: named after Capt. C. E. *Minié* (1814–1879), French army officer who invented it]
min·i·fy ('mɪnɪ,faɪ) *vb.* **·fies, ·fy·ing, ·fied.** (*tr.*) *Rare.* to minimize or lessen the size or importance of (something). [C17: from Latin *minus* less; for form, compare MAGNIFY] —**min·i·fi·ca·tion** (,mɪnɪfɪ'keɪʃən) *n.*
min·i·kin ('mɪnɪkɪn) *n. Obsolete.* **1.** a small, dainty, or affected person or thing. ~*adj.* **2.** dainty, prim, or affected. [C16: from Dutch *minneken,* diminutive of *minne* love]
min·im ('mɪnɪm) *n.* **1.** a unit of fluid measure equal to one sixtieth of a drachm. It is approximately equal to one drop. Symbol: M, ♏ **2.** *Music.* a note having the time value of half a semibreve. Usual U.S. name: **half-note. 3.** a small or insignificant person or thing. **4.** a downward stroke in calligraphy. ~*adj.* **5.** *Rare.* very small; tiny. [C15 (in its musical meaning): from Latin *minimus* smallest]
min·i·ma ('mɪnɪmə) *n.* a plural of **minimum.**
min·i·mal ('mɪnɪməl) *adj.* of the least possible; minimum or smallest. —'**min·i·mal·ly** *adv.*
min·i·mal·ist ('mɪnɪməlɪst) *n.* a person advocating a minimal policy, style, technique, action, etc.
Min·i·mal·ist ('mɪnɪməlɪst) *n.* (in early 20th-century Russia) **1.** a member of the faction of the Social Revolutionaries that advocated immediate postrevolutionary democracy. **2.** a less common name for a **Menshevik.** ~Compare **Maximalist.**
min·i·mal pair *n. Linguistics.* a pair of speech elements in a given language differing in only one respect and thus serving to identify minimum units such as phonemes, morphemes, etc. For example, *tin* and *din* constitute a minimal pair in English.
min·i·max ('mɪnɪ,mæks) *n.* **1.** *Maths.* the lowest of a set of maximum values. **2.** (in games theory, etc.) the procedure of choosing the strategy that least benefits the most advantaged member of a group. Compare **maximin.** [C20: from MINI(MUM) + MAX(IMUM)]
min·i·mize *or* **min·i·mise** ('mɪnɪ,maɪz) *vb.* (*tr.*) **1.** to reduce to or estimate at the least possible degree or amount: *to minimize a risk.* **2.** to rank or treat at less than the true worth; belittle: *to minimize someone's achievements.* —,**min·i·mi·'za·tion** *or* ,**min·i·mi·'sa·tion** *n.* —'**min·i·,miz·er** *or* '**min·i·,mis·er** *n.*
min·i·mum ('mɪnɪməm) *n., pl.* **·mums** *or* **·ma** (-mə). **1.** the least possible amount, degree, or quantity. **2.** the least amount recorded, allowed, or reached: *the minimum in our temperature record this month was 50°.* **3.** (*modifier*) being the least possible, recorded, allowed, etc.: *minimum age.* **4.** *Maths.* a value of a function that is less than any neighbouring value. ~*adj.* **5.** of or relating to a minimum or minimums. [C17: from Latin: smallest thing, from *minimus* least]
min·i·mum lend·ing rate *n.* the minimum rate at which the Bank of England discounts approved bills. It influences all other lending and discount rates. *Abbrev.:* **MLR.**
min·i·mum wage *n.* the lowest wage that an employer is permitted to pay by law or union contract.
min·i·mus ('mɪnɪməs) *adj.* (*immediately postpositive*) *Brit.* the youngest: sometimes used after the surname of a schoolboy, having elder brothers at the same school: *Hunt minimus.*
min·ing ('maɪnɪŋ) *n.* **1.** the act, process, or industry of extracting coal, ores, etc., from the earth. **2.** *Military.* the process of laying mines.
min·ion ('mɪnjən) *n.* **1.** a favourite or dependant, esp. a servile or fawning one. **2.** a servile agent: *the minister's minions.* **3.** a size of printer's type, approximately equal to 7 point. ~*adj.* **4.** dainty, pretty, or elegant. [C16: from French *mignon,* from Old French *mignot,* of Gaulish origin]
min·i·pill ('mɪnɪ,pɪl) *n.* a low-dose oral contraceptive containing progesterone only.
min·i·skirt ('mɪnɪ,skɜ:t) *n.* a very short skirt at least four inches above the knee, introduced in the 1960s. Often shortened to **mini.** —'**min·i·,skirt·ed** *adj.*
min·is·ter ('mɪnɪstə) *n.* **1.** (esp. in Presbyterian and some Nonconformist Churches) a clergyman. **2.** a person appointed to head a government department. **3.** any diplomatic agent accredited to a foreign government or head of state. **4.** short for **minister plenipotentiary** or **envoy extraordinary and minister plenipotentiary.** See **envoy**[1] (sense 1). **5.** short for **minister resident;** a diplomat ranking after an envoy extraordinary and minister plenipotentiary. **6.** a person who attends to the needs of others, esp. in religious matters. **7.** a person who acts as the agent or servant of a person or thing. ~*vb.* **8.** (*intr.;* often foll. by *to*) to attend to the needs (of); take care (of). **9.** (*tr.*) *Archaic.* to provide; supply. [C13: via Old French from Latin: servant; related to *minus* less] —'**min·is·ter·,ship** *n.*
min·is·te·ri·al (,mɪnɪ'stɪərɪəl) *adj.* **1.** of or relating to a minister of religion or his office. **2.** of or relating to a government minister or ministry: *a ministerial act.* **3.** (*often cap.*) of or supporting the ministry or government against the opposition. **4.** *Law.* relating to or possessing delegated executive authority. **5.** *Law.* (of an office, duty, etc.) requiring the exercise of no special skill or competence. **6.** acting as an agent or cause; instrumental. —,**min·is·'te·ri·al·ly** *adv.*
min·is·te·ri·al·ist (,mɪnɪ'stɪərɪə,lɪst) *n. Brit.* a supporter of the governing ministry.
min·is·te·ri·um (,mɪnɪ'stɪərɪəm) *n., pl.* **·ri·a** (-rɪə). the body of the Lutheran ministers in a district. [C19: Latin: MINISTRY]
min·is·ter of state *n.* **1.** (in the British Parliament) a minister, usually below cabinet rank, appointed to assist a senior minister with heavy responsibilities. **2.** any government minister.
Min·is·ter of the Crown *n. Brit.* any Government minister of cabinet rank.
min·is·ter plen·i·po·ten·tiar·y *n., pl.* **min·is·ters plen·i·po·ten·tiar·y.** See **envoy**[1] (sense 1).
min·is·trant ('mɪnɪstrənt) *adj.* **1.** ministering or serving as a minister. ~*n.* **2.** a person who ministers. [C17: from Latin *ministrans,* from *ministrāre* to wait upon]
min·i·stra·tion (,mɪnɪ'streɪʃən) *n.* **1.** the act or an instance of serving or giving aid. **2.** the act or an instance of ministering religiously. [C14: from Latin *ministrātiō,* from *ministrāre* to wait upon] —**min·is·tra·tive** ('mɪnɪstrətɪv) *adj.*
min·is·try ('mɪnɪstrɪ) *n., pl.* **·tries. 1. a.** the profession or duties of a minister of religion. **b.** his performance of these duties. **2.** ministers of religion or government ministers considered collectively. **3.** the tenure of a minister. **4. a.** a government department headed by a minister. **b.** the buildings of such a department. [C14: from Latin *ministerium* service; see MINISTER]
Min·i·track ('mɪnɪ,træk) *n. Trademark.* a system for tracking the course of rockets or satellites by radio signals received at ground stations.
min·i·um ('mɪnɪəm) *n.* another name for **red lead.** [C14 (meaning: vermilion): from Latin]
min·i·ver ('mɪnɪvə) *n.* white fur, used in ceremonial costumes. [C13: from Old French *menu vair,* from *menu* small + *vair* variegated fur, VAIR]
min·i·vet ('mɪnɪvɛt) *n.* any brightly coloured tropical Asian cuckoo shrike of the genus *Pericrocotus.* [C19: of unknown origin]
mink (mɪŋk) *n.* **1.** any of several semiaquatic musteline mammals of the genus *Mustela,* of Europe, Asia, and North America, having slightly webbed feet. **2.** the highly valued fur of these animals, esp. that of the American mink (*M. vison*). **3.** a garment made of this, esp. a woman's coat or stole. [C15: from Scandinavian; compare Danish *mink,* Swedish *mänk*]
Min·kow·ski world *or* **u·ni·verse** (mɪŋ'kɒfskɪ) *n.* a four-dimensional space, not curved, in which three coordinates specify the position of a point in space and the fourth represents the time at which an event occurred at that point. [C20: named after Hermann *Minkowski* (1864–1909), Russian mathematician who postulated four-dimensional space (1908)]
min min (mɪn mɪn) *n. Austral.* will-o'-the-wisp. [from a native Australian language]
Minn. *abbrev. for* Minnesota.
Min·na ('mɪnə) *n.* a city in W central Nigeria, capital of Niger state. Pop.: 74 500 (1973 est.).
Min·ne·ap·o·lis (,mɪnɪ'æpəlɪs) *n.* a city in SE Minnesota, on the Mississippi River adjacent to St. Paul: the largest city in the state; important centre for the grain trade. Pop.: 382 423 (1973 est.).
min·ne·sing·er ('mɪnɪ,sɪŋə) *n.* one of the German lyric poets and musicians of the 12th to 14th centuries. [C19: from German: love-singer]
Min·ne·so·ta (,mɪnɪ'səʊtə) *n.* **1.** a state of the N central U.S.: chief U.S. producer of iron ore. Capital: St. Paul. Pop.: 2 216 912 (1970). Area: 122 496 sq. km (47 296 sq. miles). Abbrevs.: **Minn.** or (with zip code) **MN 2.** a river in S Minnesota, flowing southeast and northeast to the Mississippi River near St. Paul. Length: 534 km (332 miles). —,**Min·ne·'so·tan** *adj., n.*
min·now ('mɪnəʊ) *n., pl.* **·nows** *or* **·now. 1.** a small slender European freshwater cyprinid fish, *Phoxinus phoxinus.* **2.** any

other small cyprinid. **3.** a small or insignificant person. [C15: related to Old English *myne* minnow; compare Old High German *muniwa* fish]

Mi·ño (*Spanish* 'miɲo) *n.* a river in SW Europe, rising in NW Spain and flowing southwest (as part of the border between Spain and Portugal) to the Atlantic. Length: 338 km (210 miles). Portuguese name: **Minho.**

Mi+no+an (mɪ'nəʊən) *adj.* **1.** denoting the Bronze Age culture of Crete from about 3000 B.C. to about 1100 B.C. Compare **Mycenaean. 2.** of or relating to the linear writing systems used in Crete and later in mainland Greece. See **Linear A, Linear B.** ~*n.* **3.** a Cretan belonging to the Minoan culture. [C19: named after MINOS, from the excavations at his supposed palace at Knossos]

mi+nor ('maɪnə) *adj.* **1.** lesser or secondary in amount, extent, importance, or degree: *a minor poet; minor burns.* **2.** of or relating to the minority. **3.** below the age of legal majority. **4.** *Music.* **a.** (of a scale) having a semitone between the second and third and fifth and sixth degrees (**natural minor**). See also **harmonic minor, melodic minor scale. b.** (of a key) based on the minor scale. **c.** (*postpositive*) denoting a specified key based on the minor scale: *C minor.* **d.** (of an interval) reduced by a semitone from the major. **e.** (of a chord, esp. a triad) having a minor third above the root. **f.** (esp. in jazz) of or relating to a chord built upon a minor triad and containing a minor seventh: *a minor ninth.* See also **minor key, minor mode. 5.** *Logic.* (of a term or premiss) having less generality or scope than another term or proposition. **6.** *U.S. education.* of or relating to an additional secondary subject taken by a student. **7.** *Brit.* the younger or junior: sometimes used after the surname of a schoolboy if he has an older brother in the same school: *Hunt minor.* **8.** (*postpositive*) *Change-ringing.* a set of changes rung on six bells: *grandsire minor.* ~*n.* **9.** a person or thing that is lesser or secondary. **10.** a person below the age of legal majority. **11.** *U.S. education.* a subsidiary subject in which a student needs fewer credits than in his major. **12.** *Music.* a minor key, chord, mode, or scale. **13.** *Logic.* a minor term or premiss. **14.** (*cap.*) another name for **Minorite.** ~*vb.* **15.** (*intr.; usually foll. by in*) *U.S. education.* to take a minor. ~Compare **major.** [C13: from Latin: less, smaller; related to Old High German *minniro* smaller, Gothic *minniza* least, Latin *minuere* to diminish, Greek *meiōn* less]

mi+nor ax·is *n.* the shorter or shortest axis of an ellipse or ellipsoid.

Mi+nor+ca (mɪ'nɔːkə) *n.* **1.** an island in the W Mediterranean, northeast of Majorca: the second largest of the Balearic Islands. Chief town: Mahón. Pop.: 48 817 (1970). Area: 702 sq. km (271 sq. miles). Spanish name: **Menorca. 2.** a breed of light domestic fowl with glossy white, black, or blue plumage. —**Mi+'nor+can** *adj., n.*

mi+nor can+on *n. Church of England.* a clergyman who is attached to a cathedral to assist at daily services but who is not a member of the chapter.

Mi+no+rite ('maɪnə,raɪt) *n.* a member of the Franciscan Friars Minor. Also: **Minor.** [C16: from Medieval Latin *frātrēs minōrēs* lesser brethren, name adopted by St. Francis as a token of humility]

mi+nor+i·ty (maɪ'nɒrɪtɪ, mɪ-) *n., pl.* **·ties. 1.** the smaller in number of two parts, factions, or groups. **2.** a group that is different racially, politically, etc., from a larger group of which it is a part. **3. a.** the state of being a minor. **b.** the period during which a person is below legal age. Compare **majority. 4.** (*modifier*) relating to or being a minority: *a minority opinion.* [C16: from Medieval Latin *minōritās,* from Latin MINOR]

mi+nor+i·ty car+ri+er *n.* the entity responsible for carrying the lesser part of the current in a semiconductor. Compare **majority carrier.**

mi+nor key *n. Music.* a key based on notes taken from a corresponding minor scale.

mi+nor league *n.* **1.** *U.S.* any non-professional league in baseball. Compare **major league. 2.** (*modifier*) of relatively little importance: *that firm is very minor league.*

mi+nor mode *n. Music.* any arrangement of notes present in or characteristic of a minor scale or key.

mi+nor or+ders *pl. n. R.C. Church.* the four lower degrees of holy orders, namely porter, exorcist, lector, and acolyte. Compare **major orders.**

mi+nor plan+et *n.* another name for **asteroid** (sense 1).

mi+nor prem+iss *n. Logic.* the premiss of a syllogism containing the subject of its conclusion.

mi+nor sev+enth chord *n.* a chord consisting of a minor triad with an added minor seventh above the root. Compare **major seventh chord.** Often shortened to **minor seventh.**

mi+nor suit *n. Bridge.* diamonds or clubs. Compare **major suit.**

mi+nor term *n. Logic.* the subject of the conclusion of a syllogism, also occurring as the subject or predicate in the minor premiss.

Mi·nos ('maɪnɒs) *n. Greek myth.* a king of Crete for whom Daedalus built the Labyrinth to contain the Minotaur.

Min·o·taur ('mɪnə,tɔː) *n. Greek myth.* a monster with the head of a bull and the body of a man. It was kept in the Labyrinth in Crete, feeding on human flesh, until destroyed by Theseus. [C14: via Latin from Greek *Minōtauros,* from MINOS + *tauros* bull]

Minsk (mɪnsk) *n.* an industrial city in the W Soviet Union, capital of the Byelorussian SSR: educational and cultural centre, with a university (1921). Pop.: 907 104 (1970).

min+ster ('mɪnstə) *n. Brit.* any of certain cathedrals and large churches, usually originally connected to a monastery. [Old English *mynster,* probably from Vulgar Latin *monisterium* (unattested), variant of Church Latin *monastērium* MONASTERY]

min+strel ('mɪnstrəl) *n.* **1.** a medieval wandering musician who performed songs or recited poetry with instrumental accompaniment. **2.** a performer in a minstrel show. **3.** *Archaic or poetic.* any poet, musician, or singer. [C13: from Old French *menestral,* from Late Latin *ministeriālis* an official, from Latin MINISTER]

min+strel show *n.* a theatrical entertainment consisting of songs, dances, comic turns, etc., performed by a troupe of actors wearing black face make-up.

min+strel+sy ('mɪnstrəlsɪ) *n., pl.* **+sies. 1.** the art of a minstrel. **2.** the poems, music, or songs of a minstrel. **3.** a troupe of minstrels.

mint[1] (mɪnt) *n.* **1.** any N temperate plant of the genus *Mentha,* having aromatic leaves and spikes of small typically mauve flowers: family *Labiatae* (labiates). The leaves of some species are used for seasoning and flavouring. See also **peppermint, spearmint, horsemint, water mint. 2. stone mint.** another name for **dittany** (sense 2). **3.** a sweet flavoured with mint. [Old English *minte,* from Latin *mentha,* from Greek *minthē;* compare Old High German *minza*] —**'mint·y** *adj.*

mint[2] (mɪnt) *n.* **1.** a place where money is coined by governmental authority. **2.** a very large amount of money: *he made a mint in business.* **3.** (*modifier*) **in mint condition.** in perfect condition; as if new. ~*adj.* **4.** (of coins, postage stamps, etc.) in perfect condition as issued. ~*vb.* **5.** to make (coins) by stamping metal. **6.** (*tr.*) to invent (esp. phrases or words). [Old English *mynet* coin, from Latin *monēta* money, mint, from the temple of Juno *Monēta,* used as a mint in ancient Rome] —**'mint+er** *n.*

mint+age ('mɪntɪdʒ) *n.* **1.** the process of minting. **2.** money minted. **3.** a fee paid for minting a coin. **4.** an official impression stamped on a coin.

mint bush *n. Austral.* an aromatic shrub of the genus *Prostanthera* with a mintlike odour: family *Labiatae* (labiates).

mint ju+lep *n. Chiefly U.S.* a long drink consisting of bourbon whiskey, crushed ice, sugar, and sprigs of mint.

Min·toff ('mɪntɒf) *n.* **Dom(inic).** born 1916, Maltese statesman; prime minister of Malta (1955–58; since 1971).

Min+ton ('mɪntən) *n.* **a.** fine-quality porcelain ware produced in Stoke-on-Trent since 1798. **b.** (*as modifier*): *Minton plate.* [C19: named after Thomas *Minton* (1765–1836), English potter]

mint sauce *n.* a sauce made from mint leaves, sugar, and vinegar, usually served with lamb.

min·u+end ('mɪnjʊ,ɛnd) *n.* the number from which another number, the **subtrahend,** is to be subtracted. [C18: from Latin *minuendus* (*numerus*) (the number) to be diminished]

min·u+et (,mɪnjʊ'ɛt) *n.* **1.** a stately court dance of the 17th and 18th centuries in triple time. **2.** a piece of music composed for or in the rhythm of this dance, sometimes as a movement in a suite, sonata, or symphony. See also **scherzo.** [C17: from French *menuet* dainty (referring to the dance steps), from *menu* small]

mi+nus ('maɪnəs) *prep.* **1.** reduced by the subtraction of: *four minus two* (written 4 − 2). **2.** *Informal.* deprived of; lacking: *minus the trimmings, that hat would be ordinary.* ~*adj.* **3. a.** indicating or involving subtraction: *a minus sign.* **b.** Also: **negative.** having a value or designating a quantity less than zero: *a minus number.* **4.** on the negative part of a scale or coordinate axis: *a value of minus 40°C.* **5.** involving a disadvantage, harm, etc.: *a minus factor.* **6.** (*postpositive*) *Education.* slightly below the standard of a particular grade: *he received a B minus for his essay.* **7.** *Botany.* designating the strain of a fungus that can only undergo sexual reproduction with a plus strain. **8.** denoting a negative electric charge. ~*n.* **9.** short for **minus sign. 10.** a negative quantity. **11.** a disadvantage, loss, or deficit. **12.** *Informal.* something detrimental or negative. ~Mathematical symbol: −. [C15: from Latin, neuter of MINOR]

mi+nus+cule ('mɪnə,skjuːl) *n.* **1.** a lower-case letter. **2.** writing using such letters. **3.** a small cursive 7th-century style of lettering derived from the uncial. ~*adj.* **4.** relating to, printed in, or written in small letters. Compare **majuscule. 5.** very small. **6.** (of letters) lower-case. [C18: from French, from Latin (*littera*) *minuscula* very small (letter), diminutive of MINOR] —**mi+nus+cu+lar** (mɪ'nʌskjʊlə) *adj.*

mi+nus sign *n.* the symbol −, indicating subtraction or a negative quantity.

min+ute[1] ('mɪnɪt) *n.* **1.** a period of time equal to 60 seconds; one sixtieth of an hour. **2.** a unit of angular measure equal to one sixtieth of a degree. Symbol: ′. Also called: **minute of arc. 3.** any very short period of time; moment. **4.** a short note or memorandum. **5.** the distance that can be travelled in a minute: *it's only two minutes away.* **6. up to the minute** (**up-to-the-minute** *when prenominal*). very latest or newest. ~*vb.* (*tr.*) **7.** to record in minutes: *to minute a meeting.* **8.** to time in terms of minutes. [C14: from Old French from Medieval Latin *minūta,* n. use of Latin *minūtus* MINUTE[2]]

mi+nute[2] (maɪ'njuːt) *adj.* **1.** very small; diminutive; tiny. **2.** unimportant; petty. **3.** precise or detailed: *a minute examination.* [C15: from Latin *minūtus,* past participle of *minuere* to diminish] —**mi+'nute+ness** *n.*

min+ute gun *n.* a gun fired at one-minute intervals as a sign of distress or mourning.

min+ute hand *n.* the pointer on a timepiece that indicates minutes, typically the longer hand of two. Compare **hour hand, second hand.**

mi+nute+ly[1] (maɪ'njuːtlɪ) *adv.* in great detail.

min+ute+ly[2] ('mɪnɪtlɪ) *adj.* **1.** occurring every minute. ~*adv.* **2.** every minute.

Min+ute+man ('mɪnɪtˌmæn) *n., pl.* **+men. 1.** (*sometimes not cap.*) (in the War of American Independence) a colonial militiaman who promised to be ready to fight at one minute's notice. **2.** a U.S. three-stage intercontinental ballistic missile.

min+ute mark *n.* the symbol ′ used for minutes of arc and linear feet.

min+utes ('mɪnɪts) *pl. n.* an official record of the proceedings of a meeting, conference, convention, etc.

min+ute steak *n.* a small piece of steak that can be cooked quickly.

mi+nu+ti+ae (mɪ'njuːʃɪˌiː) *pl. n., sing.* **+ti·a** (-ʃɪə). small, precise, or trifling details. [C18: pl. of Late Latin *minūtia* smallness, from Latin *minūtus* MINUTE[2]]

minx (mɪŋks) *n.* a bold, flirtatious, or scheming woman. [C16: of unknown origin] —**'minx+ish** *adj.*

Min+ya ('mɪnjə) *n.* See **El Minya.**

min+yan *Hebrew.* (min'jan; *English* 'mɪnjən) *n., pl.* ***min+ya+nim*** (-ja'nim) *or* ***min+yans.*** the number of persons required by Jewish law to be present for a religious service, namely, at least ten males over thirteen years of age. [literally: number]

Mi·o+cene ('maɪəˌsiːn) *adj.* **1.** of, denoting, or formed in the fourth epoch of the Tertiary period, between the Oligocene and Pliocene epochs, which lasted for 14 million years. ~*n.* **2. the Miocene.** this epoch or rock series. [C19: from Greek *meiōn* less + -CENE]

mi+om+bo (mɪ'ɒmbəʊ) *n.* (in E Africa) a dry wooded area with sparse deciduous growth. [C19: probably from a Niger-Congo language]

mi·o+sis *or* **my·o+sis** (maɪ'əʊsɪs) *n., pl.* **+ses** (-siːz). **1.** excessive contraction of the pupil of the eye, as in response to drugs. **2.** a variant spelling of **meiosis** (sense 1). [C20: from Greek *muein* to shut the eyes + -OSIS] —**mi+ot+ic** *or* **my+ot+ic** (maɪ'ɒtɪk) *adj., n.*

Mi+que+lon ('miːkəˌlɒn; *French* mi'klɔ̃) *n.* a group of islands in the French territory of **St. Pierre and Miquelon.**

mir *Russian.* (mir) *n., pl.* ***mir·i*** ('miri). a peasant commune in prerevolutionary Russia. [literally: world]

Mir·a·beau (*French* mira'bo) *n.* **Comte de,** title of *Honoré-Gabriel Riqueti.* 1749–91, French Revolutionary politician.

mi+ra+bi+le dic+tu *Latin.* (mɪ'ræbɪleɪ 'dɪktuː) wonderful to relate; amazing to say.

Mi·ra Ce·ti ('maɪrə 'siːtaɪ) *n.* a binary star one component of which, a red supergiant, is a long-period variable with an average period of 330 days.

mi+ra+cid+i+um (ˌmaɪrə'sɪdɪəm) *n., pl.* **·i·a** (-ɪə). the flat ciliated larva of flukes that hatches from the egg and gives rise asexually to other larval forms. [C20: New Latin, via Late Latin *miracidion,* from Greek *meirax* boy, girl] —ˌ**mi+ra+'cid+i·al** *adj.*

mir·a+cle ('mɪrək^əl) *n.* **1.** a marvellous event attributed to a supernatural cause. **2.** any amazing or wonderful event. **3.** a person or thing that is a marvellous example of something: *the bridge was a miracle of engineering.* **4.** short for **miracle play. 5.** (*modifier*) being or seeming a miracle: *a miracle cure.* [C12: from Latin *mīrāculum,* from *mīrārī* to wonder at]

mir·a+cle play *n.* a medieval play based on a biblical story or the life of a saint. Compare **mystery play.**

mi+rac·u·lous (mɪ'rækjʊləs) *adj.* **1.** of, like, or caused by a miracle; marvellous. **2.** surprising. **3.** having the power to work miracles. —**mi+'rac·u·lous+ly** *adv.* —**mi+'rac·u·lous+ness** *n.*

mir·a+dor (ˌmɪrə'dɔː) *n.* a window, balcony, or turret. [C17: from Spanish, from *mirar* to look]

Mi+ra+flo+res (ˌmɪrə'flɔːrəs; *Spanish* ˌmira'flores) *n.* **Lake.** an artificial lake in the S Canal Zone of the Panama Canal.

mi+rage ('mɪrɑːʒ) *n.* **1.** an image of a distant object or sheet of water, often inverted or distorted, caused by atmospheric refraction by hot air. **2.** something illusory. [C19: from French, from (*se*) *mirer* to be reflected]

Mi+ran+da (mɪ'rændə) *n.* the smallest of the five satellites of Uranus and the nearest to the planet.

mire (maɪə) *n.* **1.** a boggy or marshy area. ~*vb.* **2.** to sink or cause to sink in a mire. **3.** (*tr.*) to make dirty or muddy. **4.** (*tr.*) to involve, esp. in difficulties, etc. [C14: from Old Norse *mýrr;* related to MOSS] —**'mir·i·ness** *n.* —**'mir·y** *adj.*

mire+poix (mɪə'pwɑː) *n.* a mixture of sautéed root vegetables used as a base for braising meat or for various sauces. [French, probably named in honour of C. P. G. F. de Lévis, Duke of *Mirepoix,* 18th-century French general]

Mir·i·am ('mɪrɪəm) *n. Old Testament.* the sister of Moses and Aaron. (Numbers 12:1–15). Douay name: **Mar·y.**

mirk (mɜːk) *n.* a variant spelling of **murk.** —**'mirk·y** *adj.* —**'mirk·i·ly** *adv.* —**'mirk·i·ness** *n.*

Mi·ró (*Spanish* mi'ro) *n.* **Joan** (xwan). born 1893, Spanish surrealist painter.

mir+ror ('mɪrə) *n.* **1.** a surface, such as polished metal or glass coated with a metal film, that reflects light without diffusion and produces an image of an object placed in front of it. **2.** such a reflecting surface mounted in a frame. **3.** any reflecting surface. **4.** a thing that reflects or depicts something else: *the press is a mirror of public opinion.* ~*vb.* **5.** (*tr.*) to reflect, represent, or depict faithfully: *he mirrors his teacher's ideals.* [C13: from Old French from *mirer* to look at, from Latin *mīrārī* to wonder at] —**'mir·ror-ˌlike** *adj.*

mir+ror carp *n.* a variety of the common carp (*Cyprinus carpio*) with reduced scales, giving a smooth shiny body surface.

mir+ror im+age *n.* **1.** an image as observed in a mirror. **2.** an object that corresponds to another object in the same way as it would correspond to its image in a mirror.

mir+ror sym+met·ry *n.* symmetry about a plane (**mirror plane**) that divides the object or system into two mutual mirror images.

mir+ror writ+ing *n.* backward writing that forms a mirror image of normal writing.

mirth (mɜːθ) *n.* laughter, gaiety, or merriment. [Old English *myrgth;* compare MERRY] —**'mirth+ful** *adj.* —**'mirth+ful+ly** *adv.* —**'mirth+ful+ness** *n.* —**'mirth+less** *adj.* —**'mirth+less+ly** *adv.* —**'mirth+less+ness** *n.*

MIRV (mɜːv) *n. acronym for* multiple independently targeted re-entry vehicle: a missile that has several warheads, each one being directed to different enemy targets.

mir+za ('mɜːzə, mɪə'zɑː) *n.* (in Iran) **1.** a title of respect placed before the surname of an official, scholar, or other distinguished man. **2.** a royal prince: used as a title after a name. [C17: from Persian: son of a lord]

mis-[1] *prefix.* **1.** wrong, bad, or erroneous; wrongly, badly, or erroneously: *misunderstanding; misfortune; misspelling; mistreat; mislead.* **2.** lack of; not: *mistrust.* [Old English *mis(se)-;* related to Middle English *mes-,* from Old French *mes-;* compare Old High German *missa-,* Old Norse *mis-*]

mis-[2] *prefix.* variant of **miso-** before a vowel.

mis+ad+ven+ture (ˌmɪsəd'vɛntʃə) *n.* **1.** an unlucky event; misfortune. **2.** *Law.* accidental death not due to crime or negligence.

mis+al+li+ance (ˌmɪsə'laɪəns) *n.* an unsuitable alliance or marriage.

mis+an+thrope ('mɪzənˌθrəʊp) *or* **mis+an+thro+pist** (mɪ'zænθrəˌpɪst) *n.* a person who dislikes or distrusts other people or mankind in general. [C17: from Greek *mīsanthrōpos,* from *misos* hatred + *anthrōpos* man] —**mis+an+throp+ic** (ˌmɪzən'θrɒpɪk) *or* ˌ**mis+an+'throp·i·cal** *adj.* —**mis+an+'throp·i·cal+ly** *adv.* —**mis+an+thro+py** (mɪ'zænθrəpɪ) *n.*

mis+ap+ply (ˌmɪsə'plaɪ) *vb.* **+plies, +ply+ing, +plied.** (*tr.*) **1.** to apply wrongly or badly. **2.** another word for **misappropriate.** —**mis+ap+pli+ca+tion** (ˌmɪsæplɪ'keɪʃən) *n.*

mis+ap+pre+hend (ˌmɪsæprɪ'hɛnd) *vb.* (*tr.*) to misunderstand. —**mis+ap+pre+hen+sion** (ˌmɪsæprɪ'hɛnʃən) *n.* —ˌ**mis+ap+pre+'hen+sive** *adj.* —ˌ**mis+ap+pre+'hen+sive+ly** *adv.* —ˌ**mis+ap+pre+'hen+sive+ness** *n.*

mis+ap+pro+pri+ate (ˌmɪsə'prəʊprɪˌeɪt) *vb.* (*tr.*) to appropriate for a wrong or dishonest use; embezzle or steal. —ˌ**mis+ap+ˌpro+pri·'a+tion** *n.*

mis+be+come (ˌmɪsbɪ'kʌm) *vb.* **+comes, +com+ing, +came.** (*tr.*) to be unbecoming to or unsuitable for.

mis+be+got+ten (ˌmɪsbɪ'gɒt^ən) *adj.* **1.** unlawfully obtained: *misbegotten gains.* **2.** badly conceived, planned, or designed: *a misbegotten scheme.* **3.** Also: **misbegot** (ˌmɪsbɪ'gɒt). *Literary and dialect.* illegitimate; bastard.

mis+be+have (ˌmɪsbɪ'heɪv) *vb.* to behave (oneself) badly. —ˌ**mis+be+'hav+er** *n.* —**mis+be+hav+iour** (ˌmɪsbɪ'heɪvjə) *n.*

mis+be+lief (ˌmɪsbɪ'liːf) *n.* a false or unorthodox belief.

misc. *abbrev. for:* **1.** miscellaneous. **2.** miscellany.

mis+cal+cu+late (ˌmɪs'kælkjʊˌleɪt) *vb.* (*tr.*) to calculate wrongly. —ˌ**mis+cal+cu+'la+tion** *n.* —ˌ**mis+'cal+cu+ˌla+tor** *n.*

mis+call (ˌmɪs'kɔːl) *vb.* (*tr.*) **1.** to call by the wrong name. **2.** *Brit. dialect.* to abuse or malign. —ˌ**mis+'call+er** *n.*

mis+car+riage (mɪs'kærɪdʒ) *n.* **1.** (mɪs'kærɪdʒ, 'mɪskær-). spontaneous expulsion of a fetus from the womb, esp. prior to the 20th week of pregnancy. **2.** an act of mismanagement or failure: *a miscarriage of justice.* **3.** *Brit.* the failure of freight to reach its destination.

mis+car+ry (mɪs'kærɪ) *vb.* **+ries, +ry+ing, +ried.** (*intr.*) **1.** to expel a fetus prematurely from the womb; abort. **2.** to fail: *all her plans miscarried.* **3.** *Brit.* (of freight, mail, etc.) to fail to reach a destination.

mis+cast (ˌmɪs'kɑːst) *vb.* **+casts, +cast+ing, +cast.** (*tr.*) **1.** to cast badly. **2.** (*often passive*) **a.** to cast (a role or the roles) in (a play, film, etc.) inappropriately: *Falstaff was certainly miscast.* **b.** to assign an inappropriate role to: *he was miscast as Othello.*

mis+ce+ge+na+tion (ˌmɪsɪdʒɪ'neɪʃən) *n.* interbreeding of races, esp. where differences of pigmentation are involved. [C19: from Latin *miscēre* to mingle + *genus* race] —**mis+ce+ge+net+ic** (ˌmɪsɪdʒɪ'nɛtɪk) *adj.*

mis+cel+la+ne+a (ˌmɪsə'leɪnɪə) *pl. n.* a collection of miscellaneous items, esp. literary works. [C16: from Latin: neut. pl. of *miscellāneus* MISCELLANEOUS]

mis+cel+la+ne+ous (ˌmɪsə'leɪnɪəs) *adj.* **1.** composed of or containing a variety of things; mixed; varied. **2.** having varied capabilities, sides, etc. [C17: from Latin *miscellāneus,* from *miscellus* mixed, from *miscēre* to mix] —ˌ**mis+cel+'la+ne+ous+ly** *adv.* —ˌ**mis+cel+'la+ne+ous+ness** *n.*

mis+cel+la+nist (mɪ'sɛlənɪst) *n.* a writer of miscellanies.

mis+cel+la+ny (mɪ'sɛlənɪ; *U.S.* 'mɪsəˌleɪnɪ) *n., pl.* **+nies.** (*some-*

ˌ**mis+a+'dapt** *vb.*
mis+'add *vb.*
ˌ**mis+ad+'dress** *vb.*
ˌ**mis+ad+ˌmin+is+'tra+tion** *n.*
ˌ**mis+a+'lign** *vb.*
ˌ**mis+a+'lign+ment** *n.*
ˌ**mis+al+'ly** *vb.,* **+lies, +ly+ing, +lied.**
ˌ**mis+ap+pel+'la+tion** *n.*
ˌ**mis+ap+'praise** *vb.*
ˌ**mis+ar+'range** *vb.*
ˌ**mis+ar+'range+ment** *n.*
ˌ**mis+as+'so+ci+ˌate** *vb.*
ˌ**mis+as+ˌso+ci+'a+tion** *n.*
mis+'cat+e+go+ˌrize *or* **mis+'cat+e+go+ˌrise** *vb.*

times pl.) a miscellaneous collection of items, esp. essays, poems, etc., by different authors in one volume. [C16: from French *miscellanées* (pl.) MISCELLANEA]

mis·chance (mɪsˈtʃɑːns) *n.* **1.** bad luck. **2.** a stroke of bad luck.

mis·chief (ˈmɪstʃɪf) *n.* **1.** wayward but not malicious behaviour, usually of children, that causes trouble, etc. **2.** a playful inclination to behave in this way or to tease or disturb. **3.** a person who indulges in or causes mischief. **4.** injury or harm caused by a person or thing. **5.** a source of trouble, difficulty, etc. *floods are a great mischief to the farmer.* [C13: from Old French *meschief* disaster, from *meschever* to meet with calamity; from *mes-* MIS-[1] + *chever* to reach an end, from *chef* end, CHIEF]

mis·chie·vous (ˈmɪstʃɪvəs) *adj.* **1.** inclined to acts of mischief. **2.** teasing; slightly malicious: *a mischievous grin.* **3.** causing or intended to cause harm: *a mischievous plot.* —**ˈmis·chie·vous·ly** *adv.* —**ˈmis·chie·vous·ness** *n.*

misch met·al (mɪʃ) *n.* an alloy of cerium and other rare earth metals, used esp. as a flint in cigarette lighters. [C20: from German *Mischmetall,* from *mischen* to mix]

mis·ci·ble (ˈmɪsɪbᵊl) *adj.* capable of mixing: *alcohol is miscible with water.* [C16: from Medieval Latin *miscibilis,* from Latin *miscēre* to mix] —**ˌmis·ci·ˈbil·i·ty** *n.*

mis·con·ceive (ˌmɪskənˈsiːv) *vb.* to fail to understand. —**ˌmis·con·ˈceiv·er** *n.*

mis·con·cep·tion (ˌmɪskənˈsɛpʃən) *n.* a false or mistaken view, opinion, or attitude.

mis·con·duct *n.* (mɪsˈkɒndʌkt). **1.** behaviour, such as adultery or professional negligence, that is regarded as immoral or unethical. ~*vb.* (ˌmɪskənˈdʌkt). (*tr.*) **2.** to conduct (oneself) in such a way. **3.** to manage (something) badly.

mis·con·struc·tion (ˌmɪskənˈstrʌkʃən) *n.* **1.** a false interpretation of evidence, facts, etc. **2.** a faulty construction, esp. in grammar.

mis·con·strue (ˌmɪskənˈstruː) *vb.* **·strues, ·stru·ing, ·strued.** (*tr.*) to interpret mistakenly.

mis·count (ˌmɪsˈkaʊnt) *vb.* **1.** to count or calculate incorrectly. ~*n.* **2.** a false count or calculation.

mis·cre·ance (ˈmɪskrɪəns) *or* **mis·cre·an·cy** *n. Archaic.* lack of religious belief or faith.

mis·cre·ant (ˈmɪskrɪənt) *n.* **1.** a wrongdoer or villain. **2.** *Archaic.* an unbeliever or heretic. ~*adj.* **3.** evil or villainous. **4.** *Archaic.* unbelieving or heretical. [C14: from Old French *mescreant* unbelieving, from *mes-* MIS-[1] + *creant,* ultimately from Latin *credere* to believe]

mis·cre·ate *vb.* (ˌmɪskrɪˈeɪt). **1.** to create (something) badly or incorrectly. ~*adj.* (ˈmɪskrɪɪt, -ˌeɪt). **2.** *Archaic.* badly or unnaturally formed or made. —**ˌmis·cre·ˈa·tion** *n.*

mis·cue (ˌmɪsˈkjuː) *n.* **1.** *Billiards, etc.* a faulty stroke in which the cue tip slips off the cue ball or misses it altogether. **2.** *Informal.* a blunder or mistake. ~*vb.* (*intr.*) **·cues, ·cu·ing, ·cued. 3.** *Billiards.* to make a miscue. **4.** *Theatre.* to fail to answer one's own cue or answer the cue of another. **5.** *Informal.* to blunder.

mis·date (mɪsˈdeɪt) *vb.* (*tr.*) to date (a letter, event, etc.) wrongly.

mis·deal (ˌmɪsˈdiːl) *vb.* **·deals, ·deal·ing, ·dealt. 1.** (*intr.*) to deal out cards incorrectly. ~*n.* **2.** a faulty deal. —**ˌmis·ˈdeal·er** *n.*

mis·deed (ˌmɪsˈdiːd) *n.* an evil or illegal action.

mis·de·mean (ˌmɪsdɪˈmiːn) *vb.* a rare word for **misbehave.**

mis·de·mean·ant (ˌmɪsdɪˈmiːnənt) *n. Criminal law.* (formerly) a person who has committed or been convicted of a misdemeanour. Compare **felon**[1].

mis·de·mean·our *or U.S.* **mis·de·mean·or** (ˌmɪsdɪˈmiːnə) *n.* **1.** *Criminal law.* (formerly) an offence generally less heinous than a felony and which until 1967 involved a different form of trial. Compare **felony. 2.** any minor offence or transgression.

mis·di·rect (ˌmɪsdɪˈrɛkt) *vb.* (*tr.*) **1.** to give (a person) wrong directions or instructions. **2.** to address (a letter, parcel, etc.) wrongly. —**ˌmis·di·ˈrec·tion** *n.*

mis·doubt (mɪsˈdaʊt) *vb.* an archaic word for **doubt** or **suspect.**

mise (miːz, maɪz) *n. Law.* **1.** the issue in the obsolete writ of right. **2.** an agreed settlement. [C15: from Old French: action of putting, from *mettre* to put]

mise en scène *French.* (miz ɑ̃ ˈsɛn) *n.* **1. a.** the arrangement of properties, scenery, etc., in a play. **b.** the objects so arranged; stage setting. **2.** the environment of an event.

Mi·se·no (*Italian* miˈzɛːno) *n.* a cape in SW Italy, on the N shore of the Bay of Naples: remains of the town of **Misenum,** a naval base constructed by Agrippa in 31 B.C.

mi·ser (ˈmaɪzə) *n.* **1.** a person who hoards money or possessions, often living miserably. **2.** selfish person. [C16: from Latin: wretched]

mis·er·a·ble (ˈmɪzərəbᵊl, ˈmɪzrə-) *adj.* **1.** unhappy or depressed; wretched. **2.** causing misery, discomfort, etc.: *a miserable life.* **3.** contemptible: *a miserable villain.* **4.** sordid or squalid: *miserable living conditions.* **5.** *Chiefly Austral.* mean; stingy. **6.** (pejorative intensifier): *you miserable wretch.* [C16: from Old French, from Latin *miserābilis* worthy of pity, from *miserārī* to pity, from *miser* wretched] —**ˈmis·er·a·ble·ness** *n.* —**ˈmis·er·a·bly** *adv.*

mi·sère (mɪˈzɛə) *n.* **1.** a call in solo whist and other card games declaring a hand that will win no tricks. **2.** a hand that will win no tricks. [C19: from French: misery]

mis·e·re·re (ˌmɪzəˈrɛərɪ, -ˈrɪərɪ) *n.* another word for **misericord** (sense 1).

Mis·e·re·re (ˌmɪzəˈrɛərɪ, -ˈrɪərɪ) *n.* the 51st psalm, the Latin version of which begins "Miserere mei, Deus" ("Have mercy on me, O God").

mis·er·i·cord *or* **mis·er·i·corde** (mɪˈzɛrɪˌkɔːd) *n.* **1.** a ledge projecting from the underside of the hinged seat of a choir stall in a church, on which the occupant can support himself while standing. **2.** *Christianity.* **a.** a relaxation of certain monastic rules for infirm or aged monks or nuns. **b.** a monastery where such relaxations can be enjoyed. **3.** a small medieval dagger used to give the death stroke to a wounded foe. [C14: from Old French, from Latin *misericordia* compassion, from *miserēre* to pity + *cor* heart]

mi·ser·ly (ˈmaɪzəlɪ) *adj.* of or resembling a miser; avaricious. —**ˈmi·ser·li·ness** *n.*

mis·er·y (ˈmɪzərɪ) *n., pl.* **·er·ies. 1.** intense unhappiness, discomfort, or suffering; wretchedness. **2.** a cause of such unhappiness, etc. **3.** squalid or poverty-stricken conditions. **4.** *Brit. informal.* a person who is habitually depressed: *he is such a misery.* **5.** *Dialect.* a pain or ailment. [C14: via Anglo-Norman from Latin *miseria,* from *miser* wretched]

mis·fea·sance (mɪsˈfiːzəns) *n. Law.* the improper performance of an act that is lawful in itself. Compare **malfeasance, nonfeasance.** [C16: from Old French *mesfaisance,* from *mesfaire* to perform misdeeds] —**mis·ˈfea·sor** *n.*

mis·file (ˌmɪsˈfaɪl) *vb.* to file (papers, etc.) wrongly.

mis·fire (ˌmɪsˈfaɪə) *vb.* (*intr.*) **1.** (of a firearm or its projectile) to fail to fire, explode, or ignite as or when expected. **2.** (of a motor engine or vehicle, etc.) to fail to fire at the appropriate time, often causing a backfire. **3.** to fail to operate or occur as intended. ~*n.* **4.** the act or an instance of misfiring.

mis·fit *n.* (ˈmɪsˌfɪt). **1.** a person not suited in behaviour or attitude to a particular social environment. **2.** something that does not fit or fits badly. ~*vb.* (ˌmɪsˈfɪt), **·fits, ·fit·ting, ·fit·ted. 3.** to fail to fit or be fitted.

mis·for·tune (mɪsˈfɔːtʃən) *n.* **1.** evil fortune; bad luck. **2.** an unfortunate or disastrous event; calamity.

mis·give (mɪsˈgɪv) *vb.* **·gives, ·giv·ing, ·gave, ·giv·en.** to make or be apprehensive or suspicious.

mis·giv·ing (mɪsˈgɪvɪŋ) *n.* (*often pl.*) a feeling of uncertainty, apprehension, or doubt. —**mis·ˈgiv·ing·ly** *adv.*

mis·gov·ern (ˌmɪsˈgʌvən) *vb.* to govern badly. —**ˌmis·ˈgov·ern·ment** —**ˌmis·ˈgov·er·nor** *n.*

mis·guide (ˌmɪsˈgaɪd) *vb.* (*tr.*) to guide or direct wrongly or badly. —**ˌmis·ˈguid·ance** *n.* —**ˌmis·ˈguid·er** *n.*

mis·guid·ed (ˌmɪsˈgaɪdɪd) *adj.* foolish or unreasonable, esp. in action or behaviour. —**ˌmis·ˈguid·ed·ly** *adv.*

mis·han·dle (ˌmɪsˈhændᵊl) *vb.* (*tr.*) to handle or treat badly or inefficiently.

mis·hap (ˈmɪshæp) *n.* **1.** an unfortunate accident. **2.** bad luck.

mis·hear (ˌmɪsˈhɪə) *vb.* **·hears, ·hear·ing, ·heard.** to fail to hear correctly.

Mi·shi·ma (ˈmɪʃɪmə) *n.* **Yu·ki·o** (ˈjuːkɪəʊ). 1925–70, Japanese novelist and short-story writer, whose works reflect a preoccupation with homosexuality and death. He committed harakiri in protest at the decline of traditional Japanese values.

mis·hit *Sport.* ~*n.* (ˈmɪsˌhɪt). **1.** a faulty shot or stroke. ~*vb.* (ˌmɪsˈhɪt), **·hits, ·hit·ting, ·hit. 2.** to hit (a ball) with a faulty stroke.

mish·mash (ˈmɪʃˌmæʃ) *n.* a confused collection or mixture; hodgepodge. [C15: reduplication of MASH]

Mish·nah *or* **Mish·na** (ˈmɪʃnə; *Hebrew* miʃˈna) *n., pl.* **Mish·na·yoth** (mɪʃˈnɑːjəʊt; *Hebrew* miʃnaˈjɔt) *Judaism.* a compilation of precepts passed down as an oral tradition and collected by Judah ha-Nasi in the late second century A.D. It forms the earlier part of the Talmud. See also **Gemara.** [C17: from Hebrew: instruction by repetition, from *shānāh* to repeat] —**Mish·na·ic** (mɪʃˈneɪɪk), **ˈMish·nic,** *or* **ˈMish·ni·cal** *adj.*

mis·in·form (ˌmɪsɪnˈfɔːm) *vb.* (*tr.*) to give incorrect information to. —**ˌmis·in·ˈform·ant** *or* **ˌmis·in·ˈform·er** *n.* —**mis·in·for·ma·tion** (ˌmɪsɪnfəˈmeɪʃən) *n.*

mis·in·ter·pret (ˌmɪsɪnˈtɜːprɪt) *vb.* (*tr.*) to interpret badly, misleadingly, or incorrectly. —**ˌmis·in·ˌter·pre·ˈta·tion** *n.* —**ˌmis·in·ˈter·pret·er** *n.*

mis·join·der (mɪsˈdʒɔɪndə) *n. Law.* the improper joining of parties as coplaintiffs or codefendants or of different causes of action in one suit. Compare **nonjoinder.**

mis·judge (ˌmɪsˈdʒʌdʒ) *vb.* to judge (a person or persons) wrongly or unfairly. —**ˌmis·ˈjudg·er** *n.* —**ˌmis·ˈjudg·ment** *or* **ˈmis·ˈjudge·ment** *n.*

Mis·kolc (*Hungarian* ˈmiʃkolts) *n.* a city in NE Hungary: the second most important industrial centre in Hungary; iron and steel industries. Pop.: 194 648 (1974 est.).

mis·lay (mɪsˈleɪ) *vb.* **·lays, ·lay·ing, ·laid.** (*tr.*) **1.** to lose (something) temporarily, esp. by forgetting where it is. **2.** to lay (something) badly. —**mis·ˈlay·er** *n.*

mis·lead (mɪsˈliːd) *vb.* **·leads, ·lead·ing, ·led.** (*tr.*) **1.** to give false or misleading information to. **2.** to lead or guide in the wrong direction. —**mis·ˈlead·er** *n.*

---

misˈchar·ac·ter·ˌize *or* **misˈchar·ac·ter·ˌise** *vb.*
misˈchoose *vb.,* **·choos·es, ·choos·ing, ·chose, ·chos·en.**
misˈclas·si·ˌfy *vb.,* **·fies, ·fy·ing, ·fied.**
ˌmis·com·pu·ˈta·tion *n.*
ˌmis·con·ˈjec·ture *vb.*
mis·ˈcop·y *vb.,* **·cop·ies, ·cop·y·ing, ·cop·ied.**
ˌmis·de·ˈfine *vb.*
mis·ˈed·u·ˌcate *vb.*
ˌmis·ed·u·ˈca·tion *n.*
ˌmis·em·ˈploy *vb.*
mis·ˈes·ti·ˌmate *vb., n.*
ˌmis·es·ti·ˈma·tion *n.*
mis·ˈgauge *vb.*
ˌmis·i·ˌden·ti·fi·ˈca·tion *n.*
ˌmis·i·ˈden·ti·ˌfy *vb.,* **·fies, ·fy·ing, ·fied.**
ˌmis·in·ˈstruct *vb.*
ˌmis·in·ˈstruc·tion *n.*
mis·ˈla·bel *vb.,* **·bels, ·bel·ling, ·belled.**

mis+lead+ing (mɪs'liːdɪŋ) *adj.* tending to confuse or mislead; deceptive. —**mis+'lead+ing+ly** *adv.*

mis+like (mɪs'laɪk) *Archaic.* ~*vb.* (*tr.*) to dislike. ~*n.* also **mis+lik+ing.** dislike or aversion. —**mis+'lik+er** *n.*

mis+man+age (ˌmɪs'mænɪdʒ) *vb.* (*tr.*) to manage badly or wrongly. —ˌ**mis+'man+age+ment** *n.* —ˌ**mis+'man+ag+er** *n.*

mis+match (ˌmɪs'mætʃ) *vb.* **1.** to match badly, esp. in marriage. ~*n.* **2.** a bad or inappropriate match.

mis+no+mer (ˌmɪs'nəʊmə) *n.* **1.** an incorrect or unsuitable name or term for a person or thing. **2.** the act of referring to a person by the wrong name. [C15: via Anglo-Norman from Old French *mesnommer* to misname, from Latin *nōmināre* to call by name]

mi+so ('miːsəʊ) *n.* a thick brown salty paste made from soya beans, used to flavour savoury dishes. [from Japanese]

mis·o- *or before a vowel* **mis-** *combining form.* indicating hatred: *misogyny.* [from Greek *misos* hatred]

mi+sog·a·my (mɪ'sɒgəmɪ, maɪ-) *n.* hatred of marriage. —**mi+'sog·a·mist** *n.*

mi+sog·y·ny (mɪ'sɒdʒɪnɪ, maɪ-) *n.* hatred of women. [C17: from Greek, from MISO- + *gunē* woman] —**mi+'sog·y+nist** *n.* —**mi+'sog·y+nous** *adj.*

mi+sol+o·gy (mɪ'sɒlədʒɪ, maɪ-) *n.* hatred of reasoning or reasoned argument. —**mi+'sol·o·gist** *n.*

mis·o+ne·ism (ˌmɪsəʊ'niːˌɪzəm, ˌmaɪ-) *n.* hatred of anything new. [C19: from Italian *misoneismo;* see MISO-, NEO-, -ISM] —ˌ**mis·o+'ne·ist** *n.* —ˌ**mis·o·ne·'is+tic** *adj.*

mis+pick+el ('mɪsˌpɪkəl) *n.* another name for **arsenopyrite.** [C17: from German]

mis+place (ˌmɪs'pleɪs) *vb.* (*tr.*) **1.** to put (something) in the wrong place, esp. to lose (something) temporarily by forgetting where it was placed; mislay. **2.** (*often passive*) to bestow (trust, confidence, affection, etc.) inadvisedly. —ˌ**mis+'place+ment** *n.*

mis+placed mod·i·fi·er *n. Grammar.* a participle intended to modify a noun but having the wrong grammatical relationship to it as for example *having left* in the sentence *Having left Europe for good, Peter's future seemed bleak indeed.* Usual U.S. name: **dangling participle.**

mis+play (ˌmɪs'pleɪ) *vb.* **1.** (*tr.*) to play badly or wrongly in games or sports: *the batsman misplayed the ball.* ~*n.* **2.** a wrong or unskilful play.

mis+plead (mɪs'pliːd) *vb.* **+pleads, +plead+ing, +plead+ed, +plead** (-'plɛd), *or* **+pled.** (*tr.*) to plead incorrectly.

mis+plead+ing (mɪs'pliːdɪŋ) *n. Law.* an error or omission in pleading.

mis+print *n.* ('mɪsˌprɪnt). **1.** an error in printing, made through damaged type, careless reading, etc. ~*vb.* (ˌmɪs'prɪnt). **2.** (*tr.*) to print (a letter) incorrectly.

mis+pri+sion[1] (mɪs'prɪʒən) *n.* **a.** a failure to inform the proper authorities of the commission of an act of treason. **b.** the deliberate concealment of the commission of a felony. [C15: via Anglo-French from Old French *mesprision* error, from *mesprendre* to mistake, from *mes-* MIS-[1] + *prendre* to take]

mis+pri+sion[2] (mɪs'prɪʒən) *n. Archaic.* **1.** contempt. **2.** failure to appreciate the value of something. [C16: from MISPRIZE]

mis+prize *or* **mis+prise** (mɪs'praɪz) *vb.* to fail to appreciate the value of; undervalue or disparage. [C15: from Old French *mesprisier,* from *mes-* MIS-[1] + *prisier* to PRIZE[2]]

mis+pro+nounce (ˌmɪsprə'naʊns) *vb.* to pronounce (a word) wrongly. —**mis+pro+nun+ci·a·tion** (ˌmɪsprəˌnʌnsɪ'eɪʃən) *n.*

mis+quote (ˌmɪs'kwəʊt) *vb.* to quote (a text, speech, etc.) inaccurately. —ˌ**mis+quo+'ta+tion** *n.*

mis+read (ˌmɪs'riːd) *vb.* **+reads, +read+ing, +read** (-'rɛd). (*tr.*) **1.** to read incorrectly. **2.** to misinterpret.

mis+re+port (ˌmɪsrɪ'pɔːt) *vb.* **1.** (*tr.*) to report falsely or inaccurately. ~*n.* **2.** an inaccurate or false report. —ˌ**mis+re+'port+er** *n.*

mis+rep+re+sent (ˌmɪsrɛprɪ'zɛnt) *vb.* (*tr.*) to represent wrongly or inaccurately. —ˌ**mis+rep+re+sen+'ta+tion** *n.* —ˌ**mis+rep+re+'sen+ta+tive** *adj.* —ˌ**mis+rep+re+'sent+er** *n.*

mis+rule (ˌmɪs'ruːl) *vb.* **1.** (*tr.*) to govern inefficiently or without humanity or justice. ~*n.* **2.** inefficient or inhumane government. **3.** disorder.

miss[1] (mɪs) *vb.* **1.** to fail to reach, hit, meet, find, or attain (some specified or implied aim, goal, target, etc.). **2.** (*tr.*) to fail to attend or be present for: *to miss a train; to miss an appointment.* **3.** (*tr.*) to fail to see, hear, understand, or perceive: *to miss a point.* **4.** (*tr.*) to lose, overlook, or fail to take advantage of: *to miss an opportunity.* **5.** (*tr.*) to leave out; omit: *to miss an entry in a list.* **6.** (*tr.*) to discover or regret the loss or absence of: *he missed his watch; she missed him.* **7.** (*tr.*) to escape or avoid (something, esp. a danger), usually narrowly: *he missed death by inches.* **8. miss the boat.** to lose an opportunity. ~*n.* **9.** a failure to reach, hit, meet, find, etc. **10. give (something) a miss.** *Informal.* to avoid (something): *give the lecture a miss; give the pudding a miss.* ~See also **miss out.** [Old English *missan* (meaning: to fail to hit); related to Old High German *missan,* Old Norse *missa*]

miss[2] (mɪs) *n. Informal or fashion trade use.* **1.** an unmarried woman or girl, esp. a schoolgirl. **2.** a garment size in young women's clothes. [C17: shortened form of MISTRESS]

Miss (mɪs) *n.* a title of an unmarried woman or girl, usually used before the surname or sometimes alone in direct address. [C17: shortened from MISTRESS]

Usage. When reference is made to two or more unmarried women with the same surname, *the Misses Smith* is more formal than *the Miss Smiths.*

Miss. *abbrev. for* Mississippi.

mis+sal ('mɪsəl) *n. R.C. Church.* a book containing the prayers, etc., of the Masses for a complete year. [C14: from Church Latin *missāle* (n.), from *missālis* concerning the MASS]

mis+sel thrush ('mɪsəl) *n.* a variant spelling of **mistle thrush.**

mis+shape (ˌmɪs'ʃeɪp) *vb.* (*tr.*) **+shapes, +shap+ing, +shaped** *or* **+shap+en. 1.** to shape badly; deform. ~*n.* **2.** something that is badly shaped.

mis+shap+en (ˌmɪs'ʃeɪpən) *adj.* badly shaped; deformed. —ˌ**mis+'shap+en+ly** *adv.* —ˌ**mis+'shap+en+ness** *n.*

mis+sile ('mɪsaɪl) *n.* **1.** any object or weapon that is thrown at a target or shot from an engine, gun, etc. **2. a.** a rocket-propelled weapon that flies either in a fixed trajectory (**ballistic missile**) or in a trajectory that can be controlled during flight (**guided missile**). **b.** (*as modifier*): *a missile carrier.* [C17: from Latin: *missilis,* from *mittere* to send]

mis+sile+ry *or* **mis+sil+ry** ('mɪsaɪlrɪ) *n.* **1.** missiles collectively. **2.** the design, operation, or study of missiles.

mis+sing ('mɪsɪŋ) *adj.* **1.** not present; absent or lost. **2.** not able to be traced and not known to be dead: *nine men were missing after the attack.*

mis+sing link *n.* **1.** (*sometimes cap.;* usually preceded by *the*) a hypothetical extinct animal or animal group, formerly thought to be intermediate between the anthropoid apes and man. **2.** any missing section or part in an otherwise complete series.

mis+sion ('mɪʃən) *n.* **1.** a specific task or duty assigned to a person or group of people: *their mission was to irrigate the desert.* **2.** a person's vocation (often in the phrase **mission in life**). **3.** a group of persons representing or working for a particular country, business, etc., in a foreign country. **4. a.** a special embassy sent to a foreign country for a specific purpose. **b.** *U.S.* a permanent legation. **5. a.** a group of people sent by a religious body, esp. a Christian church, to a foreign country to do religious and social work. **b.** the campaign undertaken by such a group. **c.** the area assigned to a particular missionary. **6.** a building or group of buildings in which missionary work is performed. **7.** the dispatch of aircraft or spacecraft to achieve a particular task. **8.** a church or chapel that has no incumbent of its own. **9.** charitable centre that offers shelter, aid, or advice to the destitute or underprivileged. **10.** (*modifier*) of or relating to an ecclesiastical mission: *a mission station.* **11.** (*modifier*) *U.S.* (of furniture) in the style of the early Spanish missions of the southwestern U.S. ~*vb.* **12.** (*tr.*) to direct a mission to or establish a mission in (a given region). [C16: from Latin *missiō,* from *mittere* to send]

mis+sion+ar·y ('mɪʃənərɪ) *n., pl.* **+ar·ies. a.** a member of a religious mission. **b.** (*as modifier*): *missionary work.*

Mis+sion+ar·y Ridge *n.* a ridge in NW Georgia and SE Tennessee: site of a battle (1863) during the Civil War.

mis+sion+er ('mɪʃənə) *n.* **1.** another name for **missionary. 2.** a person heading a parochial mission in a Christian country.

mis+sis *or* **mis+sus** ('mɪsɪz, -ɪs) *n.* (usually preceded by *the*) *Informal.* one's wife or the wife of the person addressed or referred to. [C19: spoken version of MISTRESS]

Mis+sis+sau+ga (ˌmɪsə'sɔːgə) *n.* a town in SE Ontario: a SW suburb of Toronto. Pop.: 156 070 (1971).

Mis+sis+sip+pi (ˌmɪsɪ'sɪpɪ) *n.* **1.** a state of the southeastern U.S., on the Gulf of Mexico: consists of a largely forested undulating plain, with swampy regions in the northwest and on the coast, the Mississippi River forming the W Border; cotton, rice, and oil. Capital: Jackson. Pop.: 2 216 912 (1970). Area: 122 496 sq. km (47 296 sq. miles). Abbrevs.: **Miss.** or (with zip code) **MS 2.** a river in the central U.S., rising in NW Minnesota and flowing generally south to the Gulf of Mexico through several mouths, known as the Passes: the second longest river in North America (after its tributary, the Missouri), with the third largest drainage basin in the world (after the Amazon and the Congo). Length: 3780 km (2348 miles).

Mis+sis+sip+pi·an (ˌmɪsɪ'sɪpɪən) *adj.* **1.** of or relating to the state of Mississippi or the Mississippi river. **2.** (in North America) of, denoting, or formed in the lower of two subdivisions of the Carboniferous period (see also **Pennsylvanian** (sense 2)), which lasted for 50 million years. ~*n.* **3.** an inhabitant or native of the state of Mississippi. **4. the Mississippian.** the Mississippian period or rock system equivalent to the lower Carboniferous of Europe.

mis+sive ('mɪsɪv) *n.* **1.** a formal or official letter. **2.** a formal word for **letter.** ~*adj.* **3.** *Rare.* sent or intended to be sent. [C15 : from Medieval Latin *missivus,* from *mittere* to send]

Mis+so+lon+ghi (ˌmɪsə'lɒŋgɪ) *or* **Me+so+lon+ghi** *n.* a town in W Greece, near the Gulf of Patras: famous for its defence against the Turks in 1822–23 and 1825–26 and for its association with Lord Byron, who died here in 1824. Pop.: 11 614 (1971). Modern Greek name: **Mesolóngion.**

Mis+sour·i (mɪ'zʊərɪ) *n.* **1.** a state of the central U.S.: consists of rolling prairies in the north, the Ozark Mountains in the south, and part of the Mississippi flood plain in the southeast, with the Mississippi forming the E border; chief U.S. producer of lead and barytes. Capital: Jefferson City. Pop.: 4 677 399 (1970). Area: 178 699 sq. km (68 995 sq. miles). Abbrevs.: **Mo.** or (with zip code) **MO 2.** a river in the W and central U.S.,

---

mis+'mar+riage *n.*
mis+'meas+ure *vb.*
mis+'name *vb.*
mis+'num+ber *vb.*
ˌ**mis+per+'cep+tion** *n.*
mis+'phrase *vb.*
mis+'prin+ci+pled *adj.*
ˌ**mis+pro+'por+tion** *n.*
mis+'punc+tu+ˌate *vb.*
ˌ**mis+punc+tu+'a+tion** *n.*
mis+'rec+og+ˌnize *or* **mis+'rec+og+ˌnise** *vb.*
ˌ**mis+re+'late** *vb.*
ˌ**mis+re+'la+tion** *n.*
ˌ**mis+re+'mem+ber** *vb.*
mis+'rhymed *adj.*

rising in SW Montana: flows north, east, and southeast to join the Mississippi above St. Louis; the longest river in North America; chief tributary of the Mississippi. Length: 3970 km (2466 miles). —**Mis+'sou+ri+an** *n., adj.*

miss out *vb.* (*intr., adv.;* often foll. by *on*) to fail to experience: *by leaving early you missed out on the celebrations.*

mis+spell (ˌmɪsˈspɛl) *vb.* **+spells, +spell+ing, +spelt** *or* **+spelled.** to spell (a word or words) wrongly.

mis+spell+ing (ˌmɪsˈspɛlɪŋ) *n.* a wrong spelling.

mis+spend (ˌmɪsˈspɛnd) *vb.* **+spends, +spend+ing, +spent.** to spend thoughtlessly or wastefully. —ˌ**mis+'spend+er** *n.*

mis+state (ˌmɪsˈsteɪt) *vb.* (*tr.*) to state incorrectly. —ˌ**mis+'state+ment** *n.*

mis+step (ˌmɪsˈstɛp) *n.* **1.** a false step. **2.** an error.

mis+sus (ˈmɪsɪz, -ɪs) *n.* a variant spelling of **missis.**

miss·y (ˈmɪsɪ) *n., pl.* **miss·ies.** *Informal.* an affectionate or sometimes disparaging form of address to a young girl.

mist (mɪst) *n.* **1.** a thin fog resulting from condensation in the air near the earth's surface. **2.** *Meteorol.* such an atmospheric condition with a horizontal visibility of 1–2 kilometres. **3.** a fine spray of any liquid, such as that produced by an aerosol container. **4.** *Chem.* a colloidal suspension of a liquid in a gas. **5.** condensed water vapour on a surface that blurs the surface. **6.** something that causes haziness or lack of clarity, such as a film of tears. ~*vb.* **7.** to cover or be covered with or as if with mist. [Old English; related to Middle Dutch, Swedish *mist,* Greek *omikhlē* fog]

mis+tak+a+ble *or* **mis+take+a+ble** (mɪˈsteɪkəbᵊl) *adj.* liable to be mistaken. —**mis+'tak+a+bly** *or* **mis+'take+a+bly** *adv.*

mis+take (mɪˈsteɪk) *n.* **1.** an error or blunder in action, opinion, or judgment. **2.** a misconception or misunderstanding. ~*vb.* **+takes, +tak+ing, +took, +tak+en. 3.** (*tr.*) to misunderstand; misinterpret: *she mistook his meaning.* **4.** (*tr.;* foll. by *for*) to take (for), interpret (as), or confuse (with): *she mistook his direct manner for honesty.* **5.** (*tr.*) to choose badly or incorrectly: *he mistook his path.* **6.** (*intr.*) to make a mistake in action, opinion, judgment, etc. [C13 (meaning: to do wrong, err): from Old Norse *mistaka* to take erroneously] —**mis+'tak+er** *n.* —**mis+'tak+ing+ly** *adv.*

mis+tak+en (mɪˈsteɪkən) *adj.* **1.** (*usually predicative*) wrong in opinion, judgment, etc.: *she is mistaken.* **2.** arising from error in judgment, etc.: *a mistaken viewpoint.* —**mis+'tak+en+ly** *adv.* —**mis+'tak+en+ness** *n.*

mis+tal (ˈmɪstəl) *n. Northern Brit. dialect.* a cowshed; byre. [C17: of uncertain origin]

Mis+tas+si+ni (ˌmɪstəˈsiːnɪ) *n.* **Lake.** a lake in E Canada, in N Quebec: the largest lake in the province; drains through the Rupert River into James Bay. Area: 2175 sq. km (840 sq. miles). Length: about 160 km (100 miles).

mis+ter (ˈmɪstə) (*sometimes cap.*) ~*n.* **1.** an informal form of address for a man. **2.** *Naval.* **a.** the official form of address for subordinate or senior warrant officers. **b.** the official form of address for all officers in a merchant ship, other than the captain. **c.** *U.S. Navy.* the official form of address used by the commanding officer to his officers, esp. to the more junior. **3.** *Brit.* the form of address for a surgeon. **4.** the form of address for officials holding certain positions: *mister chairman.* ~*vb.* **5.** (*tr.*) *Informal.* to call (someone) mister. [C16: variant of MASTER]

Mis+ter (ˈmɪstə) *n.* the full form of **Mr.**

Mis+ti (*Spanish* ˈmisti) *n.* See **El Misti.**

mis+ti+gris (ˈmɪstɪgriː) *n.* **1.** the joker or a blank card used as a wild card in a variety of draw poker. **2.** the variety of draw poker using this card. [C19: from French *mistigris* jack of clubs, game in which this card was wild]

mis+time (ˌmɪsˈtaɪm) *vb.* (*tr.*) to time (an action, utterance, etc.) wrongly.

mis+tle thrush *or* **mis+sel thrush** (ˈmɪsᵊl) *n.* a large European thrush, *Turdus viscivorus,* with a brown back and spotted breast, noted for feeding on mistletoe berries. [C18: from Old English *mistel* MISTLETOE]

mis+tle+toe (ˈmɪsᵊlˌtəʊ) *n.* **1.** a Eurasian evergreen shrub, *Viscum album,* with leathery leaves, yellowish flowers, and waxy white berries: grows as a partial parasite on various trees: used as a Christmas decoration: family *Loranthaceae.* **2.** any of several similar and related American plants, esp. *Phoradendron flavescens.* **3. mistletoe cactus.** an epiphytic cactus, *Rhipsalis cassytha,* that grows in tropical America. [Old English *misteltān,* from *mistel* mistletoe + *tān* twig; related to Old Norse *mistilteinn*]

mis+took (mɪˈstʊk) *vb.* the past tense of **mistake.**

mis+tral (ˈmɪstrəl, mɪˈstrɑːl) *n.* a strong cold dry wind that blows through the Rhône valley and S France to the Mediterranean coast, mainly in the winter. [C17: via French from Provençal, from Latin *magistrālis* MAGISTRAL, as in *magistrālis ventus* master wind]

Mis+tral *n.* **1.** (*French* misˈtral). **Fré·dé·ric** (fredeˈrik). 1830–1914, French Provençal poet, who led a movement to revive Provençal language and literature: shared the Nobel prize for literature (1904). **2.** (*Spanish* misˈtral). **Ga·brie·la** (gaˈβrjela), pen name of *Lucila Godoy de Alcayaga.* 1889–1957, Chilean poet, educationist and diplomatist. Her poetry includes the collection *Desolación* (1922): Nobel prize for literature 1945.

mis+treat (ˌmɪsˈtriːt) *vb.* (*tr.*) to treat badly. —ˌ**mis+'treat+ment** *n.*

mis+tress (ˈmɪstrɪs) *n.* **1.** a woman who has a continuing extramarital sexual relationship with a man. **2.** a woman in a position of authority, ownership, or control, such as the head of a household. **3.** a woman or female personification having control over something specified: *she was mistress of her own destiny.* **4.** *Chiefly Brit.* short for **schoolmistress. 5.** an archaic or dialect word for **sweetheart.** [C14: from Old French; see MASTER, -ESS]

Mis+tress (ˈmɪstrɪs) *n.* an archaic or dialect title equivalent to **Mrs.**

Mis+tress of the Robes *n. Brit.* a lady of high rank in charge of the Queen's wardrobe.

mis+tri+al (mɪsˈtraɪəl) *n.* **1.** a trial made void because of some error, such as a defect in procedure. **2.** (in the U.S.) an inconclusive trial, as when a jury cannot agree on a verdict.

mis+trust (ˌmɪsˈtrʌst) *vb.* **1.** to have doubts or suspicions about (someone or something). ~*n.* **2.** distrust. —ˌ**mis+'trust+er** *n.* —ˌ**mis+'trust+ful** *adj.* —ˌ**mis+'trust+ful+ly** *adv.* —ˌ**mis+'trust+ful+ness** *n.* —ˌ**mis+'trust+ing+ly** *adv.*

mist·y (ˈmɪstɪ) *adj.* **mist·i·er, mist·i·est. 1.** consisting of or resembling mist. **2.** obscured by or as if by mist. **3.** indistinct; blurred: *the misty past.* —**'mist·i·ly** *adv.* —**'mist·i·ness** *n.*

mis+un·der+stand (ˌmɪsʌndəˈstænd) *vb.* **+stands, +stand+ing, +stood.** to fail to understand properly.

mis+un·der+stand+ing (ˌmɪsʌndəˈstændɪŋ) *n.* **1.** a failure to understand properly. **2.** a disagreement.

mis+un·der+stood (ˌmɪsʌndəˈstʊd) *adj.* not properly or sympathetically understood: *a misunderstood work of art; misunderstood adolescent.*

mis+use *n.* (ˌmɪsˈjuːs), *also* **mis+us+age. 1.** erroneous, improper, or unorthodox use: *misuse of words.* **2.** cruel or inhumane treatment. ~*vb.* (ˌmɪsˈjuːz). (*tr.*) **3.** to use wrongly. **4.** to treat badly or harshly.

mis+us+er (ˌmɪsˈjuːzə) *n. Law.* an abuse of some right, privilege, office, etc., such as one that may lead to its forfeiture. [C17: from Old French *mesuser* (infinitive used as noun)]

M.I.T. *abbrev. for* Massachusetts Institute of Technology.

mitch *or* **mich** (mɪtʃ) *vb.* (*intr.*) *Dialect.* to play truant from school. [C13: probably from Old French *muchier, mucier* to hide, lurk]

Mitch·ell (ˈmɪtʃəl) *n.* **1. Mar·ga·ret.** 1900–49, U.S. novelist; author of *Gone with the Wind* (1936). **2. Reg·i·nald Jo·seph.** 1895–1937, English aeronautical engineer; designer of the Spitfire fighter.

mite[1] (maɪt) *n.* any of numerous small free-living or parasitic arachnids of the order *Acarina* (or *Acari*) that can occur in terrestrial or aquatic habitats. See also **harvest mite, itch mite, spider mite.** Compare **tick**[2]. [Old English *mīte;* compare Old High German *mīza* gnat, Dutch *mijt*]

mite[2] (maɪt) *n.* **1.** a very small particle, creature, or object. **2.** a very small contribution or sum of money. See also **widow's mite. 3.** a former Flemish coin of small value. **4. a mite.** (*adv.*) *Informal.* somewhat: *he's a mite foolish.* [C14: from Middle Low German, Middle Dutch *mīte;* compare MITE[1]]

mi+ter (ˈmaɪtə) *n., vb.* the usual U.S. spelling of **mitre.**

mi·ter+wort (ˈmaɪtəˌwɜːt) *n.* the U.S. spelling of **mitrewort.**

mith+er (ˈmɪðə) *n.* a Scot. word for **mother.**

Mith+gar+thr (ˈmɪðˌgɑːðə) *n.* a variant spelling of **Midgard.**

Mith+ra+ism (ˈmɪθreɪˌɪzəm) *or* **Mith+ra·i+cism** (mɪθˈreɪɪˌsɪzəm) *n.* the ancient Persian religion of Mithras. It spread to the Roman Empire during the first three centuries A.D. —**Mith+ra+ic** (mɪθˈreɪɪk) *or* ˌ**Mith+ra+'is+tic** *adj.* —**'Mith+ra+ist** *n., adj.*

Mith+ras (ˈmɪθræs) *or* **Mith+ra** (ˈmɪθrə) *n. Persian myth.* the god of light, identified with the sun, who slew a primordial bull and fertilized the world with its blood.

mith+ri+date (ˈmɪθrɪˌdeɪt) *n. Obsolete.* a substance believed to be an antidote to every poison and a cure for every disease. [C16: from Late Latin *mithradatium,* after MITHRIDATES VI, alluding to his legendary immunity to poisons]

Mith·ri·da·tes VI *or* **Mith·ra·da·tes VI** (ˌmɪθrɪˈdeɪtiːz) *n.* called *the Great.* ?132–63 B.C., king of Pontus (?120–63). He waged three wars against Rome (88–84; 83–81; 74–64) and was finally defeated by Pompey: committed suicide.

mith+ri+da+tism (ˈmɪθrɪdeɪˌtɪzəm) *n.* immunity to large doses of poison by prior ingestion of gradually increased doses. —**mith+ri+dat+ic** (ˌmɪθrɪˈdætɪk, -ˈdeɪ-) *adj.*

mit·i·cide (ˈmɪtɪˌsaɪd) *n.* any drug or agent that destroys mites. —ˌ**mit·i·'cid+al** *adj.*

mit·i·gate (ˈmɪtɪˌgeɪt) *vb.* to make or become less severe or harsh; moderate. [C15: from Latin *mītigāre,* from *mītis* mild + *agere* to make] —**mit·i·ga·ble** (ˈmɪtɪgəbᵊl) *adj.* —ˌ**mit·i·'ga+tion** *n.* —**'mit·i·ˌga+tive** *or* **'mit·i·ˌga+to+ry** *adj.* —**'mit·i·ˌga+tor** *n.*

mit·i·gat+ing cir+cum+stanc+es *pl. n.* circumstances that may be considered to lessen the culpability of an offender.

Mi+ti+li+ni (ˌmitiˈlini) *n.* transliteration of the modern Greek name for **Mytilene** (sense 1).

mi+tis (ˈmaɪtɪs, ˈmiː-) *or* **mi+tis met+al** *n.* a malleable iron, fluid enough for casting, made by adding a small amount of aluminium to wrought iron. [C19: from Latin: soft]

mi+to+chon+dri+on (ˌmaɪtəʊˈkɒndrɪən) *n., pl.* **+dri·a** (-drɪə). a small spherical or rodlike body, bounded by a double membrane, in the cytoplasm of most cells: contains enzymes responsible for energy production. Also called: **chondriosome.** [C19: New Latin, from Greek *mitos* thread + *khondrion* small grain] —ˌ**mi+to+'chon+dri+al** *adj.*

mi+to+sis (maɪˈtəʊsɪs, mɪ-) *n.* a method of cell division, in which

---

mis+'teach *vb.,* **+teach·es, +teach+ing, +taught.**
mis+'term *vb.*
mis+'ti+tle *vb.*
ˌ**mis+trans+'late** *vb.*
mis+'type *vb.*
mis+'val·ue *vb.,* **·ues, ·u·ing, +ued.**

the nucleus divides into daughter nuclei, each containing the same number of chromosomes as the parent nucleus. See **prophase, metaphase, anaphase, telophase.** Compare **meiosis** (sense 1). [C19: from New Latin, from Greek *mitos* thread] —**mi+tot+ic** (maɪˈtɒtɪk, mɪ-) *adj.* —**mi+ˈtot·i·cal+ly** *adv.*

mi+trail+leuse (ˌmɪtraɪˈɜːz) *n.* an early form of breech-loading machine gun having several parallel barrels. [C19: from French, from *mitraille* small shot, from Old French *mistraille* pieces of money, from MITE[2]]

mi+tral (ˈmaɪtrəl) *adj.* **1.** of or like a mitre. **2.** *Anatomy.* of or relating to the mitral valve.

mi+tral valve *n.* the valve between the left atrium and the left ventricle of the heart, consisting of two membranous flaps, that prevents regurgitation of blood into the atrium. Also called: **bicuspid valve.**

mi+tre *or U.S.* **mi+ter** (ˈmaɪtə) *n.* **1.** *Christianity.* the liturgical headdress of a bishop or abbot, in most western churches consisting of a tall pointed cleft cap with two bands hanging down at the back. **2.** short for **mitre joint. 3.** a bevelled surface of a mitre joint. **4.** (in sewing) a diagonal join where the hems along two sides meet at a corner of the fabric. ~*vb.* (*tr.*) **5.** to make a mitre joint between (two pieces of wood, etc.). **6.** to make a mitre in (a fabric). **7.** to confer a mitre upon: *a mitred abbot.* [C14: from Old French, from Latin *mitra,* from Greek *mitra* turban]

mi+tre block *n.* a block of wood with slots for cutting mitre joints with a saw.

mi+tre box *n.* an open-ended box with sides having narrow slots to guide a saw in cutting mitre joints.

mi+tre joint *n.* a corner joint formed between two pieces of material, esp. wood, by cutting bevels of equal angles at the ends of each piece. Sometimes shortened to **mitre.**

mi+tre square *n.* a tool with two blades that are at a fixed angle to one another, used to bevel a mitre joint.

mi·tre+wort *or U.S.* **mi·ter+wort** (ˈmaɪtəˌwɜːt) *n.* any of several Asian and North American saxifragaceous plants of the genus *Mitella,* having clusters of small white flowers and capsules resembling a bishop's mitre. Also called: **bishop's-cap.**

mitt (mɪt) *n.* **1.** any of various glove-like hand coverings, such as one that does not cover the fingers. **2.** *Baseball.* a large round thickly padded leather mitten worn by the catcher. See also **glove** (sense 2). **3.** (*often pl.*) a slang word for **hand. 4.** *Slang.* a boxing glove. [C18: shortened from MITTEN]

Mit+tel+land Ca+nal (*German* ˈmɪtəlˌlant) *n.* a canal in West Germany, linking the Rivers Rhine and Elbe. Length: 325 km (202 miles).

mit+ten (ˈmɪtən) *n.* **1.** a glove having one section for the thumb and a single section for the other fingers. Sometimes shortened to **mitt. 2.** *Slang.* a boxing glove. [C14: from Old French *mitaine,* of uncertain origin]

Mit·ter·rand (*French* miteˈrã) *n.* **Fran·çois Mau·rice Ma·rie,** (frãswa mɔris maˈri). born 1916, French politician; first secretary of the socialist party from 1971; president from 1981.

mit+ti+mus (ˈmɪtɪməs) *n., pl.* **+mus·es.** *Law.* a warrant of commitment to prison or a command to a jailer directing him to hold someone in prison. [C15: from Latin: we send, the first word of such a command]

mitz+vah (ˈmɪtsvə; *Hebrew* mitsˈva) *n., pl.* **+vahs** *or* **+voth** (*Hebrew* -ˈvɔt). *Judaism.* **1.** a commandment or precept, esp. one found in the Bible. **2.** a good deed. [from Hebrew: commandment]

mix (mɪks) *vb.* **1.** (*tr.*) to combine or blend (ingredients, liquids, objects, etc.) together into one mass. **2.** (*intr.*) to become or have the capacity to become combined, joined, etc.: *some chemicals do not mix.* **3.** (*tr.*) to form (something) by combining two or more constituents: *to mix cement.* **4.** (*tr.;* often foll. by *in* or *into*) to add as an additional part or element (to a mass or compound): *to mix flour into a batter.* **5.** (*tr.*) to do at the same time; combine: *to mix study and pleasure.* **6.** (*tr.*) to consume (drinks or foods) in close succession. **7.** to come or cause to come into association socially: *Pauline has never mixed well.* **8.** (*intr.;* often foll. by *with*) to go together; complement. **9.** (*tr.*) to crossbreed (differing strains of plants or breeds of livestock), esp. more or less at random. **10.** (*tr.*) *Electronics.* to combine (two or more signals). **11.** (*tr.*) to merge (two lengths of film) so that the effect is imperceptible. **12. mix it.** *Informal.* to cause mischief or trouble, often for a person named: *she tried to mix it for John.* ~*n.* **13.** the act or an instance of mixing. **14.** the result of mixing; mixture. **15.** a mixture of ingredients, esp. one commercially prepared for making a cake, bread, etc. **16.** *Informal.* a state of confusion, bewilderment. ~See also **mix-up.** [C15: back formation from *mixt* mixed, via Old French from Latin *mixtus,* from *miscēre* to mix] —**ˈmix+a·ble** *adj.* —**ˌmix+a·ˈbil+i·ty** *n.*

mixed (mɪkst) *adj.* **1.** formed or blended together by mixing. **2.** composed of different elements, races, sexes, etc.: *a mixed school; mixed feelings.* **3.** (of a legal action, etc.) **a.** having the nature of both a real and a personal action, such as a demand for the return of wrongfully withheld property as well as for damages to compensate for the loss. **b.** having aspects or issues determinable by different persons or bodies: *a mixed question of law and fact.* **4.** (of an inflorescence) containing cymose and racemose branches. **5.** *Maths.* **a.** (of a number) consisting of the sum of an integer and a fraction, as $5\frac{1}{2}$. **b.** (of a decimal) consisting of the sum of an integer and a decimal fraction, as 17.43. **c.** (of an algebraic expression) consisting of the sum of a polynomial and a rational fraction, such as $2x + 4x^2 + 2/3x$. —**mix+ed+ness** (ˈmɪksɪdnɪs) *n.*

mixed bag *n. Informal.* something composed of diverse elements, characteristics, people, etc.

mixed bless+ing *n.* an event, situation, etc., having both advantages and disadvantages.

mixed bud *n.* a bud containing both rudimentary flowers and foliage leaves.

mixed crys+tal *n. Chem.* a crystal consisting of a solid solution of two or more distinct compounds.

mixed doub+les *pl. n. Tennis.* a doubles game with a man and a woman as partners on each side.

mixed farm+ing *n.* combined arable and livestock farming (on **mixed farms).**

mixed grill *n.* a dish made of several kinds of grilled meats, often served with grilled tomatoes and mushrooms.

mixed lan+guage *n.* any language containing items of vocabulary or other linguistic characteristics borrowed from two or more existing languages. See also: **pidgin, creole** (sense 1), **lingua franca.**

mixed mar+riage *n.* a marriage between persons of different races or religions.

mixed met·a+phor *n.* a combination of incongruous metaphors, as *when the Nazi jackboots sing their swansong.*

mixed-up *adj.* in a state of mental confusion; perplexed.

mix+er (ˈmɪksə) *n.* **1.** a person or thing that mixes. **2.** *Informal.* **a.** a person considered in relation to his ability to mix socially. **b.** a person who creates trouble for others. **3.** a kitchen appliance, usually electrical, used for mixing foods, etc. **4.** a drink such as ginger ale, fruit juice, etc., used in preparing cocktails. **5.** *Electronics.* a device in which two or more input signals are combined to give a single output signal. **6.** short for **sound mixer.**

mix·o+lyd+i·an (ˌmɪksəʊˈlɪdɪən) *adj. Music.* of, relating to, or denoting an authentic mode represented by the ascending natural diatonic scale from G to G. See **Hypo-.** [C16: from Greek *mixoludios* half-Lydian]

Mix+tec (ˈmiːstɛk) *n.* **1.** (*pl.* **+tecs** or **+tec**) a member of an American Indian people of Mexico. **2.** the language of this people. —**Mix+ˈtec+an** *adj., n.*

mix+ture (ˈmɪkstʃə) *n.* **1.** the act of mixing or state of being mixed. **2.** something mixed; a result of mixing. **3.** *Chem.* a substance consisting of two or more substances mixed together without any chemical bonding between them. **4.** *Pharmacol.* a liquid medicine in which an insoluble compound is suspended in the liquid. **5.** *Music.* an organ stop that controls several ranks of pipes sounding the upper notes in a harmonic series. **6.** the mixture of petrol vapour and air in an internal-combustion engine.

mix-up *n.* **1.** a confused condition or situation. **2.** *Informal.* a fight. ~*vb.* **mix up.** (*tr., adv.*) **3.** to make into a mixture: *to mix up ingredients.* **4.** to confuse or confound: *Tom mixes John up with Bill.* **5.** (*often passive*) to put (someone) into a state of confusion: *I'm all mixed up.* **6.** (foll. by *in* or *with;* usually passive) to involve in (an activity or group, esp. one that is illegal): *why did you get mixed up in that drugs racket?* **7. mix it up.** *U.S. informal.* to fight.

Mi+zar (ˈmaɪzɑː) *n.* a multiple star having four components that lies in the Plough in the constellation Ursa Major and forms a visible binary with the star Alcor (period 300 years). Visual magnitude: 2.2; spectral type: A2. [from Arabic *mi'zar* cloak]

Mi·zo·gu·chi (ˌmiːtsəˈguːtʃɪ) *n.* **Ken·ji** (ˈkɛndʒɪ). 1898–1956, Japanese film director. His films include *A Paper Doll's Whisper of Spring* (1925), *Woman of Osaka* (1940), and *Ugetsu Monogatari* (1952).

Mi+zo+ram (mɪˈzɔːrəm) *n.* a union territory of NE India, created in 1972 from the former Mizo Hills District of Assam. Capital: Aijal. Pop.: 321 686 (1971). Area: about 21 230 sq. km (8280 sq. miles).

miz+zen *or* **miz+en** (ˈmɪzən) *Nautical.* ~*n.* **1.** a sail set on a mizzenmast. **2.** short for **mizzenmast.** ~*adj.* **3.** of or relating to any kind of gear used with a mizzenmast: *a mizzen staysail.* [C15: from French *misaine,* from Italian *mezzana, mezzano* middle]

miz+zen+mast *or* **miz+en+mast** (ˈmɪzənˌmɑːst; *Nautical* ˈmɪzənməst) *Nautical.* ~*n.* **1.** (on a yawl, ketch, or dandy) the after mast. **2.** (on a vessel with three or more masts) the third mast from the bow.

miz+zle[1] (ˈmɪzəl) *vb., n.* a dialect word for **drizzle.** [C15: perhaps from Low German *miseln* to drizzle; compare Dutch dialect *miezelen* to drizzle] —**ˈmiz+zly** *adj.*

miz+zle[2] (ˈmɪzəl) *vb.* (*intr.*) *Brit. slang.* to decamp. [C18: of unknown origin]

mk. *Currency. abbrev. for:* **1.** mark. **2.** markka.

Mk. *abbrev. for* mark (type of car, etc.).

MKSA sys+tem *n.* another name for **Giorgi system.**

mks u·nits *pl. n.* a metric system of units based on the metre, kilogram, and second as the units of length, mass, and time; it forms the basis of the SI units.

mkt. *abbrev. for* market.

ml *symbol for:* **1.** millilitre. **2.** mile.

M.L. *abbrev. for* Medieval Latin.

M.L.A. *abbrev. for:* **1.** Member of the Legislative Assembly. **2.** Modern Language Association (of America).

M.L.C. (in India) *abbrev. for* Member of the Legislative Council.

MLD *abbrev. for* minimum lethal dose (the smallest amount of a drug or toxic agent that will kill a laboratory animal).

MLF *abbrev. for* multilateral (nuclear) force.

M.L.G. *abbrev. for* Middle Low German.

M.Litt. (in Britain) *abbrev. for* Master of Letters. [Latin *Magister Litterarum*]

Mlle *or* **Mlle.** *pl.* **Mlles** *or* **Mlles.** the French equivalent of **Miss.** [from French *Mademoiselle*]
MLR *abbrev. for* minimum lending rate.
mm *abbrev. for* millimetre.
MM. the French equivalent of **Messrs.** [from French *Messieurs*]
m.m. *abbrev. for* mutatis mutandis.
M.M. *abbrev. for* Military Medal.
Mme *or* **Mme.** *pl.* **Mmes** *or* **Mmes.** the French equivalent of **Mrs.** [from French *Madame, Mesdames*]
m.m.f. *abbrev. for* magnetomotive force.
mmHg *abbrev. for* millimetre(s) of mercury (a unit of pressure equal to the pressure that can support a column of mercury 1 millimetre high).
M.Mus. *abbrev. for* Master of Music.
Mn *the chemical symbol for* manganese.
M.N. (in Britain) *abbrev. for* Merchant Navy.
M'Nagh·ten Rules *pl. n.* See **McNaughten Rules.**
mne+mon+ic (nɪˈmɒnɪk) *adj.* **1.** aiding or meant to aid one's memory. **2.** of or relating to memory or mnemonics. ~*n.* **3.** something, such as a verse, to assist memory. [C18: from Greek *mnēmonikos,* from *mnēmōn* mindful, from *mnasthai* to remember] —**mne+ˈmon·i·cal+ly** *adv.*
mne+mon+ics (nɪˈmɒnɪks) *n.* (*usually functioning as sing.*) **1.** the art or practice of improving or of aiding the memory. **2.** a system of rules to aid the memory.
Mne·mos·y·ne (niːˈmɒzɪˌniː, -ˈmɒs-) *n. Greek myth.* the goddess of memory and mother by Zeus of the Muses.
mo (məʊ) *n. Informal.* **1.** *Chiefly Brit.* short for **moment** (sense 1) (esp. in the phrase **half a mo**). **2.** *Austral.* short for **moustache.**
Mo *the chemical symbol for* molybdenum.
mo. *pl.* **mos.** *abbrev. for* month.
Mo. *abbrev. for* Missouri.
m.o. *or* **M.O.** *abbrev. for:* **1.** mail order. **2.** money order.
M.O. *abbrev. for* Medical Officer.
-mo *suffix forming nouns.* (in bookbinding) indicating book size by specifying the number of leaves formed by folding one sheet of paper: *12mo, twelvemo,* or *duodecimo; 16mo* or *sixteenmo.* [abstracted from DUODECIMO]
mo·a (ˈməʊə) *n.* any large flightless bird of the recently extinct order *Dinornithiformes* of New Zealand (see **ratite**). [C19: from Maori]
Mo·ab (ˈməʊæb) *n. Old Testament.* an ancient kingdom east of the Dead Sea, in what is now the SW part of Jordan: flourished mainly from the 9th to the 6th centuries B.C. —**Mo+ab+ite** (ˈmoʊəˌbait) *adj., n.*
moan (məʊn) *n.* **1.** a low prolonged mournful sound expressive of suffering or pleading. **2.** any similar mournful sound, esp. that made by the wind. **3.** *Informal.* a grumble or complaint. ~*vb.* **4.** to utter (words, etc.) in a low mournful manner. **5.** (*intr.*) to make a sound like a moan. **6.** (*usually intr.*) *Informal.* to lament (esp. in the phrase **moan and groan**). [C13: related to Old English *mǣnan* to grieve over] —**ˈmoan+er** *n.* —**ˈmoan+ful** *adj.* —**ˈmoan+ing+ly** *adv.*
moat (məʊt) *n.* **1.** a wide water-filled ditch surrounding a fortified place, such as a castle. ~*vb.* **2.** (*tr.*) to surround with or as if with a moat: *a moated grange.* [C14: from Old French *motte* mound]
mob (mɒb) *n.* **1. a.** a riotous or disorderly crowd of people; rabble. **b.** (*as modifier*): *mob law; mob violence.* **2.** *Often derogatory.* a group or class of people, animals, or things. **3.** *Often derogatory.* the masses. **4.** *Slang.* a gang of criminals. ~*vb.* **mobs, mob+bing, mobbed.** (*tr.*) **5.** to attack in a group resembling a mob. **6.** to surround, esp. in order to acclaim: *they mobbed the film star.* **7.** *U.S.* to crowd into (a building, plaza, etc.). ~See also **mobs.** [C17: shortened from Latin *mōbile vulgus* the fickle populace; see MOBILE] —**ˈmob+ber** *n.* —**ˈmob+bish** *adj.*
mob+cap (ˈmɒbˌkæp) *n.* a woman's large cotton cap with a pouched crown and usually a frill, worn esp. during the 18th century. Often shortened to **mob.** [C18: from obsolete *mob* woman, esp. a loose-living woman, + CAP]
mo+bile (ˈməʊbaɪl) *adj.* **1.** having freedom of movement; movable. **2.** changing quickly in expression: *a mobile face.* **3.** *Sociol.* (of individuals or social groups) moving within and between classes, occupations, and localities. See also **vertical mobility, horizontal mobility. 4.** (of military forces) able to move freely and quickly to any given area. **5.** (*postpositive*) *Informal.* having transport available: *are you mobile tonight?* ~*n.* **6. a.** a sculpture suspended in midair with delicately balanced parts that are set in motion by air currents. **b.** (*as modifier*): *mobile sculpture.* **7.** short for **mobile library.** [C15: via Old French from Latin *mōbilis,* from *movēre* to move] —**mo+bil+i·ty** (məʊˈbɪlɪtɪ) *n.*
Mo+bile (ˈməʊbiːl, məʊˈbiːl) *n.* a port in SW Alabama, on **Mobile Bay** (an inlet of the Gulf of Mexico): the state's only port and its first permanent settlement, made by French colonists in 1711. Pop.: 188 531 (1973 est.).
mo+bile home *n.* living quarters mounted on wheels and capable of being towed by a motor vehicle.
mo+bile li+brar·y *n.* a vehicle providing lending library facilities. U.S. equivalent: **bookmobile.**
mo+bi+lize *or* **mo+bi+lise** (ˈməʊbɪˌlaɪz) *vb.* **1.** to prepare for war or other emergency by organizing (national resources, the armed services, etc.). **2.** (*tr.*) to organize for a purpose; marshal. **3.** (*tr.*) to put into motion, circulation, or use. —**ˈmo+bi+ˌliz+a·ble** *or* **ˈmo+bi+ˌlis+a·ble** *adj.* —**ˌmo+bi+li+ˈza+tion** *or* **ˌmo+bi+li+ˈsa+tion** *n.*
Mö·bi·us strip (ˈmɜːbɪəs; *German* ˈmøːbɪʊs) *n. Maths.* a one-sided continuous surface, formed by twisting a long narrow rectangular strip of material through 180° and joining the ends. [C19: named after August *Möbius* (1790–1868), German mathematician who invented it]
mob+oc+ra+cy (mɒˈbɒkrəsɪ) *n., pl.* **+cies. 1.** rule or domination by a mob. **2.** the mob that rules. —**mob·o+crat** (ˈmɒbəˌkræt) *n.* —**ˌmob·o+ˈcrat·ic** *or* **ˌmob·o+ˈcrat·i·cal** *adj.*
mobs (mɒbz) *Austral. informal.* ~*pl. n.* **1.** (usually foll. by *of*) great numbers or quantities; lots: *mobs of people.* ~*adv.* **2.** a great deal: *mobs better.*
mob+ster (ˈmɒbstə) *n.* a U.S. slang word for **gangster.**
Mo+bu+tu[1] (məˈbuːtuː) *n.* **Lake.** the official name for Lake **Albert.**
Mo·bu·tu[2] (məˈbuːtuː) *n.* **Se·se Se·ko** (ˈsɛsɛ ˈsɛkəʊ), former name *Joseph.* born 1930, Zaïrese statesman; president of Zaïre since 1965.
Mo+çam+bi+que (musəmˈbikə) *n.* the Portuguese name for **Mozambique.**
moc+ca+sin (ˈmɒkəsɪn) *n.* **1.** a shoe of soft leather, esp. deerskin, worn by North American Indians. **2.** any soft shoe resembling this. **3.** short for **water moccasin.** [C17: from Algonquian; compare Narragansett *mocussin* shoe]
moc+ca+sin flow+er *n.* any of several North American orchids of the genus *Cypripedium* with a pink solitary flower. See also **lady's-slipper, cypripedium.**
moc+ca+sin tel+e·graph *n. Canadian informal.* the transmission of rumour or secret information; the grapevine.
mo+cha (ˈmɒkə) *n.* **1.** a strongly flavoured dark brown coffee originally imported from Arabia. **2.** a flavouring made from coffee and chocolate. **3.** a soft glove leather with a suede finish, made from goatskin or sheepskin. **4. a.** a dark brown colour. **b.** (*as adj.*): *mocha shoes.*
Mo+cha *or* **Mo+kkha** (ˈmɒkə) *n.* a port in SW Yemen, on the Red Sea: formerly important for the export of Arabian coffee. Pop.: about 5000 (1972 est.).
mo+cha stone *n.* another name for **moss agate.**
mock (mɒk) *vb.* **1.** (when *intr.*, often foll. by *at*) to behave with scorn or contempt (towards); show ridicule (for). **2.** (*tr.*) to imitate, esp. in fun; mimic. **3.** (*tr.*) to deceive, disappoint, or delude. **4.** (*tr.*) to defy or frustrate: *the team mocked the visitors' attempt to score.* ~*n.* **5.** the act of mocking. **6.** a person or thing mocked. **7.** a counterfeit; imitation. ~*adj.* (*prenominal*) **8.** sham or counterfeit. **9.** serving as an imitation or substitute, esp. for practice purposes: *a mock battle; mock finals.* ~See also **mock-up.** [C15: from Old French *mocquer*] —**ˈmock·a·ble** *adj.* —**ˈmock+er** *n.* —**ˈmock+ing+ly** *adv.*
mock+ers (ˈmɒkəz) *n. Informal.* **put the mockers on.** to ruin the chances of success of. Also (Austral.): **put the mock** (*or* **mocks**) **on.**
mock+er·y (ˈmɒkərɪ) *n., pl.* **+er·ies. 1.** ridicule, contempt, or derision. **2.** a derisive action or comment. **3.** an imitation or pretence, esp. a derisive one. **4.** a person or thing that is mocked. **5.** a person, thing, or action that is inadequate or disappointing.
mock-he·ro·ic *adj.* **1.** (of a literary work, esp. a poem) imitating the style of heroic poetry in order to satirize an unheroic subject, as in Pope's *The Rape of the Lock.* ~*n.* **2.** burlesque imitation of the heroic style or a single work in this style.
mock·ing+bird (ˈmɒkɪŋˌbɜːd) *n.* any American songbird of the family *Mimidae,* having a long tail and grey plumage: noted for their ability to mimic the song of other birds.
mock moon *n.* another name for **paraselene.**
mock or+ange *n.* **1.** Also called: **syringa.** any shrub of the genus *Philadelphus,* esp. *P. coronarius,* with white fragrant flowers resembling those of the orange: family *Philadelphaceae.* **2.** any other shrub or tree resembling the orange tree.
mock sun *n.* another name for **parhelion.**
mock tur+tle soup *n.* an imitation turtle soup made from the calf's head.
mock-up *n.* **1.** a working full-scale model of a machine, apparatus, etc., for testing, research, etc. **2.** a layout of printed matter. ~*vb.* **mock up. 3.** (*tr., adv.*) to build or make a mock-up of.
mod[1] (mɒd) *adj.* **1.** of or relating to any fashion in dress regarded as stylish, esp. that of the early 1960s in Britain. ~*n.* **2.** *Brit.* a member of a group of teenagers in the mid-1960s, noted for their clothes consciousness and opposition to the rockers. [C20: from MODERN]
mod[2] (mɒd) *n.* an annual Highland meeting with musical and literary competitions. [C19: from Gaelic *mōd* assembly, from Old Norse; related to MOOT]
M.O.D. (in Britain) *abbrev. for* Ministry of Defence.
mod. *abbrev. for:* **1.** moderate. **2.** moderato. **3.** modern.
mod+al (ˈməʊdᵊl) *adj.* **1.** of, relating to, or characteristic of mode or manner. **2.** *Grammar.* (of a verb form or auxiliary verb) expressing a distinction of mood, such as that between possibility and actuality. The modal auxiliaries in English include *can, do, may, must, need, ought, shall, should, will,* and *would.* **3.** characterized by or expressing logical modality. **4.** *Metaphysics.* of or relating to the form of a thing as opposed to its attributes, substance, etc. **5.** *Music.* of or relating to a mode. **6.** of or relating to a statistical mode. —**ˈmo+dal+ly** *adv.*
mo+dal+i·ty (məʊˈdælɪtɪ) *n., pl.* **·ties. 1.** the condition of being modal. **2.** a quality, attribute, or circumstance that denotes mode, mood, or manner. **3.** Also called: **mode.** *Logic.* the qualification by which a proposition is classified depending on whether it affirms or denies the impossibility, possibility,

contingency, or necessity of its content. **4.** any physical or electrical therapeutic method or agency. **5.** any of the five senses.

mod+al log+ic *n.* **1.** the logical study of such philosophical concepts as necessity, possibility, contingency, etc. **2.** the logical study of concepts whose formal properties resemble certain moral, epistemological, and psychological concepts. See also **alethic, deontic, epistemic, doxastic.**

mod cons *pl. n. Informal.* modern conveniences; the usual installations of a modern house, such as hot water, heating, etc.

mode (məʊd) *n.* **1.** a manner or way of doing, acting, or existing. **2.** the current fashion or style. **3.** *Music.* **a.** any of the various scales of notes within one octave, esp. any of the twelve natural diatonic scales taken in ascending order used in plainsong, folksong, and art music until 1600. **b.** (in the music of classical Greece) any of the descending diatonic scales from which the liturgical modes evolved. **c.** either of the two main scale systems in music since 1600: *major mode; minor mode.* **4.** *Logic, linguistics.* another name for **modality** (sense 3) or **mood**² (sense 2). **5.** *Philosophy.* the form in which a thing or one of the attributes of a thing manifests itself. **6.** the predominating value in a set of values as determined from statistical data or by observation. **7.** the quantitative mineral composition of an igneous rock. **8.** *Physics.* one of the possible configurations of a travelling or stationary wave. **9.** *Physics.* one of the fundamental vibrations. [C14: from Latin *modus* measure, manner]

mod+el ('mɒdᵊl) *n.* **1. a.** a representation, usually on a smaller scale, of a device, structure, etc. **b.** (*as modifier*): *a model train.* **2. a.** a standard to be imitated: *she was my model for good scholarship.* **b.** (*as modifier*): *a model wife.* **3.** a representative form, style, or pattern. **4.** a person who poses for a sculptor, painter, or photographer. **5.** a person who wears clothes to display them to prospective buyers; mannequin. **6.** a preparatory sculpture in clay, wax, etc., from which the finished work is copied. **7.** a design or style, esp. one of a series of designs of a particular product: *last year's model.* **8.** *Brit.* **a.** an original unique article of clothing. **b.** (*as modifier*): *a model coat.* **9.** a simplified representation or description of a system or complex entity, esp. one designed to facilitate calculations and predictions. ~*vb.* **+els, +el+ling, +elled** *or U.S.* **+els, +el+ing, +eled. 10.** to make a model (of something or someone). **11.** to form in clay, wax, etc.; mould. **12.** to display (clothing and accessories) as a mannequin. **13.** to plan or create according to a model or models. [C16: from Old French *modelle,* from Italian *modello,* from Latin *modulus,* diminutive of *modus* MODE] —**'mod+el+ler** *n.*

mo+dem ('məʊdɛm) *n. Computer technol.* a device for connecting two computers by a telephone line, consisting of a modulator that converts computer signals into audio signals and a corresponding demodulator. [C20: from *mo(dulator) dem(odulator)*]

Mo·de·na (*Italian* 'mɔːde,na) *n.* **1.** a city in N Italy, in Emilia-Romagna: ruled by the Este family (18th–19th century); university (1678). Pop.: 177 201 (1975 est.). Ancient name: **Mutina. 2.** (*sometimes not cap.*) a popular variety of domestic fancy pigeon originating in Modena.

mod+er+ate *adj.* ('mɒdərɪt, 'mɒdrɪt). **1.** not extreme or excessive; within due or reasonable limits: *moderate demands.* **2.** not violent; mild or temperate. **3.** of average quality or extent: *moderate success.* ~*n.* ('mɒdərɪt, 'mɒdrɪt). **4.** a person who holds moderate views, esp. in politics. ~*vb.* ('mɒdə,reɪt). **5.** to become or cause to become less extreme or violent. **6.** (when *intr.,* often foll. by *over*) to preside over a meeting, discussion, etc. **7.** *Physics.* to slow down (neutrons), esp. by using a moderator. [C14: from Latin *moderātus* observing moderation, from *moderārī* to restrain] —**'mod+er+ate+ly** *adv.* —**'mod+er+ate+ness** *n.* —**'mod+er+at+ism** *n.*

mod+er+ate breeze *n.* a wind of force four on the Beaufort scale.

mod+er+ate gale *n.* a gale of force seven on the Beaufort scale, capable of swaying trees.

mod+er·a+tion (,mɒdə'reɪʃən) *n.* **1.** the state or an instance of being moderate. **2.** the act of moderating. **3. in moderation.** within moderate or reasonable limits.

Mod+er·a+tions (,mɒdə,reɪʃənz) *pl. n.* short for **Honour Moderations.**

mod+e·ra+to ('mɒdə'rɑːtəʊ) *adv. Music.* **1.** at a moderate tempo. **2.** (preceded by a tempo marking) a direction indicating that the tempo specified is to be used with restraint: *allegro moderato.*

mod+er·a+tor ('mɒdə,reɪtə) *n.* **1.** a person or thing that moderates. **2.** *Presbyterian Church.* a minister appointed to preside over a Church court, synod, or general assembly. **3.** a presiding officer at a public or legislative assembly. **4.** a material, such as heavy water or graphite, used for slowing down neutrons in the cores of nuclear reactors so that they have more chance of inducing nuclear fission. **5.** an examiner at Oxford or Cambridge Universities in first public examinations. —**'mod+er·,a+tor+,ship** *n.*

mod+ern ('mɒdən) *adj.* **1.** of, involving, or befitting the present or a recent time; contemporary. **2.** of, relating to, or characteristic of contemporary styles or schools of art, literature, music, etc., esp. those of an experimental kind. **3.** belonging or relating to the period in history from the end of the Middle Ages to the present. ~*n.* **4.** a contemporary person. **5.** *Printing.* a type style that originated around the beginning of the 19th century, characterized chiefly by marked contrast between thick and thin strokes. Compare **old face.** [C16: from Old French, from Late Latin *modernus,* from *modō* (adv.) just recently, from *modus* MODE] —**'mod+ern+ly** *adv.* —**'mod+ern+ness** *n.*

mod+ern dance *n.* a style of free and expressive theatrical dancing not bound by the classical rules of ballet.

mo+derne (mə'dɛən) *adj. Chiefly U.S.* of or relating to the style of architecture and design, prevalent in Europe and the U.S. in the late 1920s and 1930s, typified by the use of straight lines, tubular chromed steel frames, contrasting inlaid woods, etc. Compare **Art Deco.**

Mod+ern Eng+lish *n.* the English language since about 1450, esp. any of the standard forms developed from the S East Midland dialect of Middle English. See also **English, Middle English, Old English.**

mod+ern greats *n.* (at Oxford University) the Honour School of Philosophy, Politics, and Economics.

Mod+ern Greek *n.* the Greek language since about 1453 A.D. (the fall of Byzantium). Compare **Demotic, Katharevusa.**

Mod+ern He+brew *n.* the official language of the state of Israel; a revived form of ancient Hebrew.

mod+ern+ism ('mɒdə,nɪzəm) *n.* **1.** modern tendencies, characteristics, thoughts, etc., or the support of these. **2.** something typical of contemporary life or thought. **3.** (*cap.*) *R.C. Church.* the movement at the end of the 19th and beginning of the 20th centuries that sought to adapt doctrine to the supposed requirements of modern thought. —**'mod+ern+ist** *n., adj.* —**,mod+ern+'is+tic** *adj.* —**,mod+ern+'is+ti+cal+ly** *adv.*

mo+der+ni+ty (mɒ'dɜːnɪtɪ) *n., pl.* **·ties. 1.** the quality or state of being modern. **2.** something modern.

mod+ern+ize *or* **mod+ern+ise** ('mɒdə,naɪz) *vb.* **1.** (*tr.*) to make modern in appearance or style: *to modernize a room.* **2.** (*intr.*) to adopt modern ways, ideas, etc. —**,mod+ern+i+'za+tion** *or* **,mod+ern+i+'sa+tion** *n.* —**'mod+ern+,iz+er** *or* **'mod+ern+,is+er** *n.*

mod+ern jazz *n.* any of the styles of jazz that evolved between the early 1940s and the later emergence of avant-garde jazz, characterized by a greater harmonic and rhythmic complexity than hitherto.

mod+est ('mɒdɪst) *adj.* **1.** having or expressing a humble opinion of oneself or one's accomplishments or abilities. **2.** reserved or shy: *modest behaviour.* **3.** not ostentatious or pretentious. **4.** not extreme or excessive; moderate. [C16: via Old French from Latin *modestus* moderate, from *modus* MODE] —**'mod+est+ly** *adv.*

mod+es+ty ('mɒdɪstɪ) *n., pl.* **+ties.** the quality or condition of being modest.

modge (mɒdʒ) *vb.* (*tr.*) *Midland English dialect.* to do shoddily; make a mess of. [C20: perhaps a variant of *mudge* to crush (hops)]

mod+i+cum ('mɒdɪkəm) *n.* a small amount or portion. [C15: from Latin: a little way, from *modicus* moderate]

mod·i+fi+ca+tion (,mɒdɪfɪ'keɪʃən) *n.* **1.** the act of modifying or the condition of being modified. **2.** something modified; the result of a modification. **3.** a small change or adjustment. **4.** *Grammar.* the relation between a modifier and the word or phrase that it modifies. —**'mod·i+fi+,ca+to·ry** *or* **'mod·i+fi+,ca+tive** *adj.*

mod·i+fi+er ('mɒdɪ,faɪə) *n.* **1.** Also called: **qualifier.** *Grammar.* a word or phrase that qualifies the sense of another word; for example, the noun *alarm* is a modifier of *clock* in *alarm clock* and the phrase *every day* is an adverbial modifier of *walks* in *he walks every day.* **2.** a person or thing that modifies.

Usage. Nouns are frequently used in English to modify other nouns: *police officer; chicken farm.* They should be used with restraint, however, esp. when the appropriate adjective can be used without awkwardness: *lunar research* (not *moon research*); *educational system* (not *education system*).

mod·i+fy ('mɒdɪ,faɪ) *vb.* **+fies, +fy+ing, +fied.** (*mainly tr.*) **1.** to change the structure, character, intent, etc., of. **2.** to make less extreme or uncompromising: *to modify a demand.* **3.** *Grammar.* (of a word or group of words) to bear the relation of modifier to (another word or group of words). **4.** *Linguistics.* to change (a vowel) by umlaut. **5.** (*intr.*) to be or become modified. [C14: from Old French *modifier,* from Latin *modificāre* to limit, control, from *modus* measure + *facere* to make] —**'mod·i+,fi+a·ble** *adj.* —**,mod·i+,fi+a·'bil·i·ty** *or* **'mod·i+,fi+a·ble+ness** *n.*

Mo·di·glia·ni (*Italian* ,modiʎ'ʎaːni) *n.* **A·me·de·o** (,ame'dɛːo). 1884–1920, Italian painter and sculptor, noted esp. for the elongated forms of his portraits.

mo+dil+lion (mə'dɪljən) *n. Architect.* one of a set of ornamental brackets under a cornice, esp. as used in the Corinthian order. Compare **mutule.** [C16: via French from Italian *modiglione,* probably from Vulgar Latin *mutiliō* (unattested), from Latin *mūtulus* MUTULE]

mo·di·o·lus (məʊ'daɪələs, mə-) *n., pl.* **+li** (-,laɪ). the central bony pillar of the cochlea. [C19: New Latin, from Latin: hub of a wheel, from *modus* a measure]

mod+ish ('məʊdɪʃ) *adj.* in the current fashion or style; contemporary. —**'mod+ish+ly** *adv.* —**'mod+ish+ness** *n.*

mo+diste (məʊ'diːst) *n.* a fashionable dressmaker or milliner. [C19: from French, from *mode* fashion]

Mo·dred ('məʊdrɪd) *or* **Mor·dred** ('mɔːdrɛd) *n.* (in Arthurian legend) a knight of the Round Table who rebelled against and killed his uncle King Arthur.

Mods (mɒdz) *n.* (at Oxford University) short for **Honour Moderations.**

mod·u+lar ('mɒdjʊlə) *adj.* of, consisting of, or resembling a module or modulus.

mod·u+late ('mɒdjʊ,leɪt) *vb.* **1.** (*tr.*) to change the tone, pitch, or volume of. **2.** (*tr.*) to adjust or regulate the degree of. **3.**

Music. **a.** to subject to or undergo modulation in music. **b.** (often foll. by *to*) to make or become in tune (with a pitch, key, etc.). **4.** *Physics, electronics.* to cause to vary by a process of modulation. [C16: from Latin *modulātus* in due measure, melodious, from *modulārī* to regulate, from *modus* measure] —**mod·u·la·bil·i·ty** (ˌmɒdjʊləˈbɪlɪtɪ) *n.* —**ˈmod·u·la·tive** *or* **ˈmod·u·la·to·ry** *adj.* —**ˈmod·u·ˌla·tor** *n.*

mod·u·la·tion (ˌmɒdjʊˈleɪʃən) *n.* **1.** the act of modulating or the condition of being modulated. **2.** *Music.* the transition from one key to another. **3.** *Grammar.* **a.** another word for **intonation** (sense 1). **b.** the grammatical expression of modality. **4.** *Electrical engineering.* **a.** the act or process of superimposing the amplitude, frequency, phase, etc., of a wave or signal onto another wave or signal or onto an electron beam. See also **amplitude modulation, frequency modulation, phase modulation, velocity modulation. b.** the variation of the modulated signal.

mod·ule (ˈmɒdjuːl) *n.* **1.** a standard unit of measure, esp. one used to coordinate the dimensions of buildings and components; in classical architecture, half the diameter of a column at the base of the shaft. **2.** a standard self-contained unit or item, such as an assembly of electronic components or a piece of computer hardware, that can be used in combination with other units. **3.** *Astronautics.* any of several self-contained separable units making up a spacecraft or launch vehicle, each of which has one or more specified tasks: *command module; service module.* [C16: from Latin *modulus*, diminutive of *modus* MODE]

mod·u·lus (ˈmɒdjʊləs) *n., pl.* **·li** (-ˌlaɪ). **1.** *Physics.* a coefficient expressing a specified property of a specified substance. See **bulk modulus, modulus of rigidity, Young's modulus. 2.** *Maths.* another name for the **absolute value** (sense 2) of a complex number. **3.** *Maths.* the number by which a logarithm to one base is multiplied to give the corresponding logarithm to another base. **4.** *Maths.* an integer that can be divided exactly into the difference between two other integers: *7 is a modulus of 25 and 11.* See also **congruence** (sense 2). [C16: from Latin, diminutive of *modus* measure]

mod·u·lus of e·las·tic·i·ty *n.* the ratio of the stress applied to a body or substance to the resulting strain within the elastic limit. Also called: **elastic modulus.** See also **Young's modulus, bulk modulus, modulus of rigidity.**

mod·u·lus of ri·gid·i·ty *n.* a modulus of elasticity equal to the ratio of the tangential force per unit area to the resulting angular deformation. Symbol: G

mo·dus op·e·ran·di *Latin.* (ˈməʊdəs ˌɒpəˈrændiː) *n., pl.* ***mo·di op·e·ran·di*** (ˈməʊdiː ˌɒpəˈrændiː). a method of operating.

mo·dus vi·ven·di *Latin.* (ˈmɒdəs vɪˈvɛndiː) *n., pl.* ***mo·di vi·ven·di*** (ˈmɒdiː vɪˈvɛndiː). a working arrangement between conflicting interests; practical compromise. [literally: way of living]

mo·fette (məʊˈfɛt) *n.* an opening in a region of nearly extinct volcanic activity, through which carbon dioxide, nitrogen, and other gases pass. [C19: from French, from Neapolitan Italian *mofeta;* compare dialect German *muffezen* to smell fetid]

mog (mɒg) *or* **mog·gy** *n. Brit.* a slang name for **cat.** [C20: of dialect origin, originally a pet name for a cow]

Mog·a·disc·i·o (ˌmɒgəˈdɪʃɪˌəʊ, -ˈdɪʃəʊ) *or* **Mog·a·dish·u** (ˌmɒgəˈdɪʃuː) *n.* the capital and chief port of the Somali Republic, on the Indian Ocean: founded by Arabs around the 10th century; taken by the Sultan of Zanzibar in 1871 and sold to Italy in 1905. Pop.: 230 000 (1972 est.).

Mog·a·dor (ˌmɒgəˈdɔː; *French* mɔgaˈdɔːr) *n.* the former name (until 1956) of **Essaouira.**

Mo·gen Da·vid (ˈməʊgən ˌdeɪvɪd) *n.* another name for the **Star of David.**

Mo·gi·lev (*Russian* məgiˈljɔf) *or* **Mo·hi·lev** *n.* an industrial city in the W Soviet Union, in the E Byelorussian SSR on the Dnieper River: passed to Russia in 1772 after Polish rule. Pop.: 255 000 (1975 est.).

mo·gul[1] (ˈməʊgʌl, məʊˈgʌl) *n.* **1.** an important or powerful person. **2.** a type of steam locomotive with a wheel arrangement of two leading wheels, six driving wheels, and no trailing wheels. [C18: from MOGUL]

mo·gul[2] (ˈməʊgᵊl) *n.* a mound of hard snow on a ski slope. [C20: perhaps from South German dialect *Mugl*]

Mo·gul (ˈməʊgʌl, məʊˈgʌl) *n.* **1. a.** a member of the Muslim dynasty of Indian emperors established by Baber in 1526. See **Great Mogul. 2.** a Muslim Indian, Mongol, or Mongolian. ~*adj.* **3.** of or relating to the Moguls or their empire. [C16: from Persian *mughul* Mongol]

M.O.H. (in Brit.) *abbrev. for* Medical Officer of Health.

mo·hair (ˈməʊˌhɛə) *n.* **1.** Also called: **angora.** the long soft silky hair that makes up the outer coat of the Angora goat. **2. a.** a fabric made from the yarn of this hair and cotton or wool. **b.** (*as modifier*): *a mohair suit.* [C16: variant (influenced by *hair*) of earlier *mocayare*, ultimately from Arabic *mukhayyar*, literally: choice, from *khayyara* to choose]

Moham. *abbrev. for* Mohammedan.

Mo·ham·med (məʊˈhæmɪd) *or* **Mu·ham·mad** *n.* ?570–632 A.D., the prophet and founder of Islam. He began to teach in Mecca in 610 but persecution forced him to flee with his followers to Medina in 622. After several battles, he conquered Mecca (630), establishing the principles of Islam (embodied in the Koran) over all Arabia. Other names: **Mahomet, Mahound.**

Mo·ham·med II *n.* ?1430–81, Ottoman sultan of Turkey (1451–81). He captured Constantinople (1453) and conquered large areas of the Balkans.

Mo·ham·med Ah·med (məʊˈhæmɪd ˈɑːmɛd) *n.* the original name of the **Mahdi.**

Mo·ham·med A·li *n.* See **Mehemet Ali.**

Mo·ham·med·an (məʊˈhæmɪdᵊn) *n., adj.* another word for **Muslim.**

Mo·ham·med·an·ism (məʊˈhæmɪdᵊˌnɪzəm) *n.* the Mohammedan religion; Islam. See **Islam.**

Mo·ham·med·an·ize *or* **Mo·ham·med·an·ise** (məʊˈhæmɪdᵊˌnaɪz) *vb.* (*tr.*) to convert or subject to the religious or cultural influence of Islam; Islamize.

Mo·ham·med Ri·za Pah·la·vi (məʊˈhæmɪd ˈriːzə ˈpɑːləvɪ) *n.* See **Pahlavi**[1].

Mo·ha·ve *or* **Mo·ja·ve** (məʊˈhɑːvɪ) *n.* **1.** (*pl.* **·ves** *or* **·ve**) a member of a North American Indian people formerly living along the Colorado River. **2.** the language of this people, belonging to the Yuman family.

Mo·ha·ve Des·ert *or* **Mo·ja·ve Des·ert** *n.* a desert in S California, south of the Sierra Nevada: part of the Great Basin. Area: 38 850 sq. km (15 000 sq. miles).

mo·hawk (ˈməʊhɔːk) *n. Ice skating.* a half turn from either edge of either skate to the corresponding edge of the other skate. [C19: after MOHAWK[1]]

Mo·hawk[1] (ˈməʊhɔːk) *n.* **1.** (*pl.* **·hawks** *or* **·hawk**) a member of North American Indian people formerly living along the Mohawk River; one of the Iroquois peoples. **2.** the language of this people, belonging to the Iroquoian family.

Mo·hawk[2] (ˈməʊhɔːk) *n.* a river in E central New York State, flowing south and east to the Hudson River at Cohoes: the largest tributary of the Hudson. Length: 238 km (148 miles).

Mo·hen·jo-Da·ro (məˈhɛndʒəʊ ˈdɑːrəʊ) *n.* an excavated city in SE Pakistan, southwest of Sukkur near the River Indus: flourished during the third millennium B.C.

Mo·hi·can (ˈməʊɪkən, məʊˈhiːkən) *n., pl.* **·cans** *or* **·can.** a variant spelling of **Mahican.**

Mo·ho (ˈməʊhəʊ) *n.* short for **Mohorovičić discontinuity.**

Mo·hock (ˈməʊhɒk) *n.* (in 18th-century London) one of a group of aristocratic ruffians, who attacked people in the streets at night. [C18: variant of MOHAWK]

Mo·hole (ˈməʊˌhəʊl) *n.* an abandoned research project to drill through the earth's crust down to the Mohorovičić discontinuity to obtain samples of mantle rocks. [C20: from MOHO(ROVIČIĆ) + HOLE]

Mo·holy-Nagy (ˈməʊhɔɪ ˈnɒdj) *n.* **Lasz·lo** (ˈlæzləʊ) or **La·dis·laus** (ˈlaːdɪsˌlaʊs). 1895–1946, U.S. painter and teacher, born in Hungary. He worked at the Bauhaus (1923–29).

Mo·ho·ro·vi·čić dis·con·ti·nu·i·ty (ˌməʊhəˈrəʊvɪtʃɪtʃ) *n.* a zone beneath the earth's surface where changes in seismic waves occur: represents the boundary between the earth's crust and its mantle. Often shortened to **Moho.** [C20: named after Andrija *Mohorovičić* (1857–1936), Yugoslav geologist]

Mohs scale (məʊz) *n.* a scale for expressing the hardness of solids by comparing them with ten standards ranging from talc, with a value of 0, to diamond, with a value of 10. [C19: named after Friedrich *Mohs* (1773–1839), German mineralogist]

mo·hur (ˈməʊhə) *n.* a former Indian gold coin worth 15 rupees. [C17: from Hindi]

MOI *abbrev. for* Ministry of Information (now superseded by **COI**).

moi·dore (ˈmɔɪdɔː) *n.* a former Portuguese gold coin. [C18: from Portuguese *moeda de ouro:* money of gold]

moi·e·ty (ˈmɔɪɪtɪ) *n., pl.* **·ties. 1.** a half. **2.** one of two parts or divisions of something. [C15: from Old French *moitié*, from Latin *mediētās* middle, from *medius*]

moil (mɔɪl) *Archaic or dialect.* ~*vb.* **1.** to moisten or soil or become moist, soiled, etc. **2.** (*intr.*) to toil or drudge (esp. in the phrase **toil and moil**). ~*n.* **3.** toil; drudgery. **4.** confusion; turmoil. [C14 (to moisten; later: to work hard in unpleasantly wet conditions) from Old French *moillier*, ultimately from Latin *mollis* soft] —**ˈmoil·er** *n.* —**ˈmoil·ing·ly** *adv.*

Moi·rai (ˈmɔɪraɪ) *pl. n., sing.* **Moi·ra** (ˈmɔɪrə), **the.** the Greek goddesses of fate. Roman counterparts: the **Parcae.** See **Fates.**

moire (mwɑː) *n.* a fabric, usually silk, having a watered effect. [C17: from French, earlier *mouaire*, from MOHAIR]

moi·ré (ˈmwɑːreɪ) *adj.* **1.** having a watered or wavelike pattern. ~*n.* **2.** such a pattern, impressed on fabrics by means of engraved rollers. **3.** any fabric having such a pattern; moire. [C17: from French, from *moire* MOHAIR]

moist (mɔɪst) *adj.* **1.** slightly damp or wet. **2.** saturated with or suggestive of moisture. [C14: from Old French, ultimately related to Latin *mūcidus* musty, from *mūcus* MUCUS] —**ˈmoist·ly** *adv.* —**ˈmoist·ness** *n.*

mois·ten (ˈmɔɪsᵊn) *vb.* to make or become moist. —**ˈmoist·en·er** *n.*

mois·ture (ˈmɔɪstʃə) *n.* water or other liquid diffused as vapour or condensed on or in objects. —**ˈmois·ture·less** *adj.*

mois·tur·ize *or* **mois·tur·ise** (ˈmɔɪstʃəˌraɪz) *vb.* (*tr.*) to add or restore moisture to (the air, the skin, etc.). —**ˈmoist·tur·ˌiz·er** *or* **ˈmois·tur·ˌis·er** *n.*

moi·ther (ˈmɔɪðə) *or* **moi·der** (ˈmɔɪdə) *vb. Brit. dialect.* **1.** (*tr.; usually passive*) to bother or bewilder. **2.** (*intr.*) to talk in a rambling or confused manner. [C17: of obscure origin]

Mo·ja·ve (məʊˈhɑːvɪ) *n.* a variant spelling of **Mohave.**

moke (məʊk) *n.* **1.** *Brit.* a slang name for **donkey. 2.** *Austral. slang.* an inferior type of horse. [C19: origin obscure]

Mo·kha (ˈməʊkə, ˈmɒk-) *n.* a variant spelling of **Mocha.**

Mok·po (ˌməʊkˈpəʊ) *n.* a port in SW South Korea, on the Yellow Sea. Pop.: 177 801 (1970).

mol *Chem. symbol for* mole[3].

mol. *abbrev. for:* **1.** molecular. **2.** molecule.

mo·la ('məʊlə) *n., pl.* **·la** *or* **·las.** another name for **sunfish** (sense 1). [C17: from Latin, literally: millstone]

mo·lal ('məʊləl) *adj. Chem.* of or consisting of a solution containing one mole of solute per thousand grams of solution. [C20: from MOLE[3] + -AL[1]]

mo·lal·i·ty (mɒ'lælɪtɪ) *n., pl.* **·ties.** (*not in technical usage*) a measure of concentration equal to the number of moles of solute in a thousand grams of solvent.

mo·lar[1] ('məʊlə) *n.* **1.** any of the 12 broad-faced grinding teeth in man. **2.** a corresponding tooth in other mammals. ~*adj.* **3.** of, relating to, or designating any of these teeth. **4.** used for or capable of grinding. [C16: from Latin *molāris* for grinding, from *mola* millstone]

mo·lar[2] ('məʊlə) *adj.* **1.** (of a physical quantity) per unit amount of substance: *molar volume.* **2.** (*not recommended in technical usage*) (of a solution) containing one mole of solute per litre of solution. [C19: from Latin *mōlēs* a mass]

mo·lar·i·ty (mɒ'lærɪtɪ) *n.* another name (not in technical usage) for **concentration** (sense 4).

mo·las·ses (mə'læsɪz) *n.* **1.** the thick brown uncrystallized bitter syrup obtained from sugar during refining. **2.** the U.S. name for **treacle** (sense 1). [C16: from Portuguese *melaço,* from Late Latin *mellāceum* must, from Latin *mel* honey]

mold (məʊld) *n., vb.* the U.S. spelling of **mould.** —**'mold·a·ble** *adj.* —**,mold·a·'bil·i·ty** *n.*

Mol·dau ('mɔldaʊ) *n.* **1.** the German name for **Moldavia. 2.** the German name for the **Vltava.**

Mol·da·vi·a (mɒl'deɪvɪə) *n.* **1.** a former principality of E Europe, consisting of the basins of the Rivers Prut and Dniester: in 1940 the E part (Bessarabia) was ceded to the Soviet Union and became the Moldavian SSR; the W part remains a province of Rumania. Rumanian name: **Mol·do·va** (mol'dova). German name: **Moldau. 2.** another name for the **Moldavian SSR.** —**Mol·'da·vi·an** *adj., n.*

Mol·da·vi·an So·vi·et So·cial·ist Re·pub·lic *n.* an administrative division of the SW Soviet Union, bordering on Rumania, by which it was ceded to the Soviet Union in 1940. Capital: Kishinev. Pop.: 3 568 873 (1970). Area: 33 700 sq. km (13 012 sq. miles). Also called: **Moldavia, Bessarabia.**

mol·da·vite ('mɒldə,vaɪt) *n.* natural green glass found in Bohemia, thought to be meteoritic in origin. [C19: named after MOLDAVIA]

mold·board ('məʊld,bɔ:d) *n.* the U.S. spelling of **mouldboard.**

mold·er[1] ('məʊldə) *vb.* the U.S. spelling of **moulder**[1].

mold·er[2] ('məʊldə) *n.* the U.S. spelling of **moulder**[2].

mold·ing ('məʊldɪŋ) *n.* the U.S. spelling of **moulding.**

mold·y ('məʊldɪ) *adj.* **mold·i·er, mold·i·est.** the U.S. spelling of **mouldy.** —**'mold·i·ness** *n.*

mole[1] (məʊl) *n. Pathol.* a nontechnical name for **naevus.** [Old English *māl;* related to Old High German *meil* spot]

mole[2] (məʊl) *n.* **1.** any small burrowing mammal, of the family *Talpidae,* of Europe, Asia, and North and Central America: order *Insectivora* (insectivores). They have velvety, typically dark fur and forearms specialized for digging. **2. golden mole.** any small African burrowing molelike mammal of the family *Chrysochloridae,* having copper-coloured fur: order *Insectivora* (insectivores). [C14: from Middle Dutch *mol,* of Germanic origin; compare Middle Low German *mol*]

mole[3] (məʊl) *n.* the basic SI unit of amount of substance; the amount that contains as many elementary entities as there are atoms in 0.012 kilogram of carbon-12. The entity must be specified and may be an atom, a molecule, an ion, a radical, an electron, a photon, etc. Symbol: mol [C20: from German *Mol,* short for *Molekül* MOLECULE]

mole[4] (məʊl) *n.* **1.** a breakwater. **2.** a harbour protected by a breakwater. [C16: from French *môle,* from Latin *mōlēs* mass]

mole[5] (məʊl) *n. Pathol.* a fleshy growth in the uterus formed by the degeneration of fetal tissues. [C17: medical use of Latin *mola* millstone]

Mo·lech ('məʊlɛk) *n. Old Testament.* a variant spelling of **Moloch.**

mole crick·et *n.* any subterranean orthopterous insect of the family *Gryllotalpidae,* of Europe and North America, similar and related to crickets but having the first pair of legs specialized for digging.

mo·lec·u·lar (məʊ'lɛkjʊlə, mə-) *adj.* of or relating to molecules: *molecular hydrogen.* —**mo·'lec·u·lar·ly** *adv.*

mo·lec·u·lar beam *or* **ray** *n. Physics.* a parallel beam of atoms or molecules that are at low pressure and suffer no interatomic or intermolecular collisions.

mo·lec·u·lar bi·ol·o·gy *n.* the study of the structure and function of biological molecules, esp. nucleic acids and proteins.

mo·lec·u·lar dis·til·la·tion *n.* distillation in which a substance is heated under vacuum, the condensing surface being so close to the substance that no intermolecular collisions can occur before condensation.

mo·lec·u·lar film *n.* another name for **monolayer.**

mo·lec·u·lar for·mu·la *n.* a chemical formula indicating the numbers and types of atoms in a molecule: *H_2SO_4 is the molecular formula of sulphuric acid.* Compare **empirical formula, structural formula.**

mo·lec·u·lar sieve *n. Chem.* a material that can absorb large amounts of certain compounds while not absorbing others and is thus suitable for use in separating mixtures.

mo·lec·u·lar vol·ume *n.* the volume occupied by one mole of a substance. Also called: **molar volume.**

mo·lec·u·lar weight *n.* the sum of all the atomic weights (relative atomic masses) of the atoms in a molecule; the ratio of the average mass per molecule of a specified isotopic composition of a substance to 1/12 the mass of an atom of carbon-12. Abbrev.: **mol. wt.** Also called: **relative molecular mass.**

mol·e·cule ('mɒlɪ,kju:l) *n.* **1.** the simplest unit of a chemical compound that can exist, consisting of two or more atoms held together by chemical bonds. **2.** a very small particle. [C18: via French from New Latin *mōlēcula,* diminutive of Latin *mōlēs* mass, MOLE[4]]

mole·hill ('məʊl,hɪl) *n.* **1.** the small mound of earth thrown up by a burrowing mole. **2. make a mountain out of a molehill.** to exaggerate an unimportant matter out of all proportion.

mole rat *n.* **1.** any burrowing molelike African rodent of the family *Bathyergidae.* **2.** any similar rodent, esp. any member of the genus *Spalax,* of Asia and North Africa: family *Spalacidae.* **3.** another name for **bandicoot rat** (see **bandicoot** (sense 2)).

mole·skin ('məʊl,skɪn) *n.* **1.** the dark grey dense velvety pelt of a mole, used as a fur. **2.** a hard-wearing cotton fabric of twill weave used for work clothes, etc. **3.** (*modifier*) made from moleskin: *a moleskin waistcoat.*

mole·skins ('məʊl,skɪnz) *pl. n.* clothing of moleskin.

mo·lest (mə'lɛst) *vb.* (*tr.*) **1.** to disturb or annoy by malevolent interference. **2.** to accost or attack, esp. with the intention of assaulting sexually. [C14: from Latin *molestāre* to annoy, from *molestus* troublesome, from *mōlēs* mass] —**mo·les·ta·tion** (,məʊlɛ'steɪʃən) *n.* —**mo·'lest·er** *n.*

Mo·lière (*French* mɔ'ljɛ:r) *n.* pen name of *Jean-Baptiste Poquelin,* 1622–73, French dramatist, regarded as the greatest French writer of comedy. His works include *Tartuffe* (1664), *Le Misanthrope* (1666), *L'Avare* (1668), *Le Bourgeois gentilhomme* (1670), and *Le Malade imaginaire* (1673).

Mo·li·na (*Spanish* mo'lina) *n.* See **Tirso de Molina.**

mo·line (mə'laɪn) *adj. Heraldry.* (of a cross) having arms of equal length, forked and curved back at the ends. [C16: probably from Anglo-French *moliné,* from *molin* MILL[1], referring to the arms curved back like the ends of a mill-rind]

Mo·li·se (*Italian* 'mɔli:ze) *n.* a region of S central Italy, the second smallest of the regions: separated from **Abruzzi e Molise** in 1965. Capital: Campobasso. Pop.: 319 629 (1971). Area: 4438 sq. km (1731 sq. miles).

moll (mɒl) *n. Slang.* **1.** the female accomplice of a gangster. **2.** a prostitute. [C17: from *Moll,* familiar form of *Mary*]

Mol·lah ('mɔ:lə) *n.* an older spelling of **Mullah.**

mol·les·cent (mɒ'lɛsənt) *adj. Rare.* tending to soften or become soft. [C19: from Latin *mollēscere* to grow soft, from *mollis* soft] —**mol·'les·cence** *n.*

mol·li·fy ('mɒlɪ,faɪ) *vb.* **·fies, ·fy·ing, ·fied.** (*tr.*) **1.** to pacify; soothe. **2.** to lessen the harshness or severity of. [C15: from Old French *mollifier,* via Late Latin, from Latin *mollis* soft + *facere* to make] —**'mol·li·,fi·a·ble** *adj.* —**,mol·li·fi·'ca·tion** *n.* —**'mol·li·,fi·er** *n.* —**'mol·li·,fy·ing·ly** *adv.*

mol·lusc *or U.S.* **mol·lusk** ('mɒləsk) *n.* any invertebrate of the phylum *Mollusca,* having a soft unsegmented body and often a shell, secreted by a fold of skin (the mantle). The group includes the gastropods (snails, slugs, etc.), bivalves (clams, mussels, etc.), and cephalopods (cuttlefish, octopuses, etc.). [C18: via New Latin from Latin *molluscus,* from *mollis* soft] —**mol·lus·can** *or U.S.* **mol·lus·kan** (mɒ'lʌskən) *adj., n.* —**'mol·lusc-,like** *or U.S.* **'mol·lusk-,like** *adj.*

mol·lus·coid (mɒ'lʌskɔɪd) *or* **mol·lus·coi·dal** (,mɒlʌs'kɔɪdəl) *adj.* of, relating to, or belonging to the *Molluscoidea,* a former phylum including the brachiopods and bryozoans now classified separately. [C19: via New Latin from Latin *molluscus* soft]

Moll·wei·de pro·jec·tion ('mɒl,vaɪdə) *n.* an equal-area map projection with the parallels and the central meridian being straight lines and the other meridians curved. It is often used to show world distributions of various phenomena. [C19: named after Karl B. *Mollweide* (1774–1825), German mathematician and astronomer]

mol·ly ('mɒlɪ) *n., pl.* **·lies.** any brightly coloured tropical or subtropical American freshwater cyprinodont fishes of the genus *Mollienesia.* [*C19: from New Latin Mollienesia,* from Comte F. N. *Mollien* (1758–1850), French statesman]

mol·ly·cod·dle ('mɒlɪ,kɒdəl) *vb.* **1.** (*tr.*) to treat with indulgent care; pamper. ~*n.* **2.** a pampered person. [C19: from obsolete slang *molly* an effeminate boy, from *Molly* girl's name + CODDLE] —**'mol·ly·,cod·dler** *n.*

Mol·ly Ma·guire ('mɒlɪ mə'gwaɪə) *n.* **1.** *Irish history.* a member of a secret society that terrorized law officers during the 1840s to prevent evictions. **2.** (in Pennsylvania from about 1865 to 1877) a member of a society of miners that terrorized mine owners and their agents in an effort to obtain better pay. [C19: the name refers to the female disguise adopted by members of these societies]

Mol·nár (*Hungarian* 'molna:r) *n.* **Fe·renc** ('fɛrɛnts). 1878–1952, Hungarian dramatist and novelist. His works include the play *Liliom* (1909).

mo·loch ('məʊlɒk) *n.* a spiny Australian desert-living lizard, *Moloch horridus,* that feeds on ants: family *Agamidae* (agamas). Also called: **mountain devil, spiny lizard.**

Mo·loch ('məʊlɒk) *or* **Mo·lech** ('məʊlɛk) *n. Old Testament.* a Semitic deity to whom parents sacrificed their children.

Mo·lo·ka·i (,məʊləʊ'kɑ:ɪ) *n.* an island in central Hawaii. Pop.: 5261 (1970). Area: 676 sq. km (261 sq. miles).

Mo·lo·po (mə'ləʊpəʊ) *n.* a seasonal river in South Africa, rising in N Cape Province and flowing west and southwest to the Orange river. Length: about 1000 km (600 miles).

Mol·o+tov[1] ('mɒlə,tɒf; *Russian* 'mɔlətəf) *n.* the former name (1940–62) for **Perm.**

Mol·o·tov[2] ('mɒlə,tɒf; *Russian* 'mɔlətəf) *n.* **Vya·che·slav Mi·khai·lo·vich** (vjɪtʃɪ'slaf mi'xajləvitʃ), original surname *Skriabin.* born 1890, Soviet statesman. As commissar for foreign affairs (1939–49; 1953–56) he negotiated the nonaggression pact with Nazi Germany and attended the founding conference of the United Nations and the Potsdam conference (1945).

Mol·o·tov cock+tail *n.* an elementary incendiary weapon, usually a bottle of petrol with a short delay fuse or wick; petrol bomb. [C20: named after V. M. MOLOTOV]

molt (məʊlt) *vb., n.* the usual U.S. spelling of **moult.** —**'molt+er** *n.*

mol+ten ('məʊltən) *adj.* **1.** liquefied; melted: *molten lead.* **2.** made by having been melted: *molten casts.* ~*vb.* **3.** the past participle of **melt.**

Molt·ke (*German* 'mɔltkə) *n.* **1.** Count **Hel·muth Jo·han·nes Lud·wig von** ('hɛlmu:t jo'hanəs 'lu:tvɪç fɔn). 1848–1916, German general; chief of the German general staff (1906–14). **2.** his uncle Count **Hel·muth Karl Bern·hard von** ('hɛlmu:t karl 'bɛrnhart fɔn). 1800–91, German field marshal; chief of the Prussian general staff (1858–88).

mol+to ('mɒltəʊ) *adv. Music.* (preceded or followed by a musical direction, esp. a tempo marking) very: *allegro molto; molto adagio.* [from Italian, from Latin *multum* (adv.) much]

Mo+luc+cas (məʊ'lʌkəz, mə-) *or* **Mo+luc+ca Is+lands** *pl. n.* a group of islands in the Malay Archipelago, between Sulawesi (Celebes) and New Guinea. Capital: Amboina. Area: about 74 505 sq. km (28 766 sq. miles). Indonesian name: **Maluku.** Former name: **Spice Islands.**

mol. wt. *abbrev. for* molecular weight.

mo·ly ('məʊlɪ) *n., pl.* **·lies. 1.** *Greek myth.* a magic herb given by Hermes to Odysseus to nullify the spells of Circe. **2.** a liliaceous plant, *Allium moly,* that is native to S Europe and has yellow flowers in a dense cluster. [C16: from Latin *mōly,* from Greek *mōlu*]

mo+lyb+date (mɒ'lɪbdeɪt) *n.* a salt or ester of a molybdic acid.

mo+lyb+de+nite (mɒ'lɪbdɪ,naɪt) *n.* a soft grey mineral consisting of molybdenum sulphide in hexagonal crystalline form with rhenium as an impurity: the main source of molybdenum and rhenium. Formula: MoS_2.

mo+lyb+de+nous (mɒ'lɪbdɪnəs) *adj.* of or containing molybdenum in the divalent state.

mo+lyb+de+num (mɒ'lɪbdɪnəm) *n.* a very hard ductile silvery-white metallic element occurring principally in molybdenite: used mainly in alloys, esp. to harden and strengthen steels. Symbol: Mo; atomic no.: 42; atomic wt.: 95.94; valency: 2–6; relative density: 10.22; melting pt.: 2610°C; boiling pt.: 5560°C. [C19: from New Latin, from Latin *molybdaena* galena, from Greek *molubdaina,* from *molubdos* lead]

mo+lyb+dic (mɒ'lɪbdɪk) *adj.* of or containing molybdenum in the trivalent or hexavalent state.

mo+lyb+dous (mɒ'lɪbdəs) *adj.* of or containing molybdenum, esp. in a low valence state.

mom (mɒm) *n. Chiefly U.S.* an informal word for **mother.**

Mom+ba+sa (mɒm'bæsə) *n.* a port in S Kenya, on a coral island in a bay of the Indian Ocean: the chief port for Kenya, Uganda, and NE Tanzania; became British in 1887, capital of the East African Protectorate until 1907. Pop.: 301 000 (1973 est.).

mo+ment ('məʊmənt) *n.* **1.** a short indefinite period of time: *he'll be here in a moment.* **2.** a specific instant or point in time: *at the moment he came, I was out.* **3. the moment.** the present point of time: *at the moment it's fine.* **4.** import, significance, or value: *a man of moment.* **5.** *Physics.* **a.** a tendency to produce motion, esp. rotation about a point or axis. **b.** the product of a physical quantity, such as force or mass, and its distance from a fixed reference point. See also **moment of inertia. 6.** *Statistics.* the mean of a specified power of the deviations of all the values of a variable in its frequency distribution. The power of the deviations indicates the order of the moment and the deviations may be from the origin (giving a **moment about the origin**) or from the mean (giving a **moment about the mean**). **7.** *Philosophy.* **a.** an aspect of something. **b.** an essential or constituent element of something. [C14: from Old French, from Latin *mōmentum,* from *movēre* to move]

mo+men+tar+i+ly ('məʊməntərəlɪ, -trɪlɪ) *adv.* **1.** for an instant; temporarily. **2.** from moment to moment; every instant. ~Also: **mo+ment+ly** ('məʊməntlɪ). ~*adv.* **3.** *U.S.* very soon.

mo+men+tar·y ('məʊməntərɪ, -trɪ) *adj.* **1.** lasting for only a moment; temporary. **2.** occurring or present at each moment. —**'mo+men+tar+i+ness** *n.*

mo+ment of in+er+tia *n.* the tendency of a body to resist angular acceleration, expressed as the sum of the products of the mass of each particle in the body and the square of its perpendicular distance from the axis of rotation. Symbol: *I*

mo+ment of truth *n.* **1.** a moment when a person or thing is put to the test. **2.** the point in a bullfight when the matador is about to kill the bull.

mo+men+tous (məʊ'mɛntəs) *adj.* of great significance. —**mo+'men+tous+ly** *adv.* —**mo+'men+tous+ness** *n.*

mo+men+tum (məʊ'mɛntəm) *n., pl.* **+ta** (-tə) *or* **+tums. 1.** *Physics.* the product of a body's mass and its velocity. Symbol: *p* See also **angular momentum. 2.** the impetus of a body resulting from its motion. **3.** driving power or strength. **4.** another word for **moment** (sense 7). [C17: from Latin: movement; see MOMENT]

mom+ism ('mɒmɪzəm) *n.* excessive dependence on or affection for one's mother.

Momm·sen (*German* 'mɔmzᵊn) *n.* **The·o·dor** ('te:o,do:r). 1817–1903, German historian, noted esp. for *The History of Rome* (1854–56): Nobel prize for literature 1902.

Mo·mus ('məʊməs) *n., pl.* **·mus·es** *or* **·mi** (-maɪ). *Greek myth.* **1.** the god of blame and mockery. **2.** a cavilling critic.

Mon (məʊn) *n.* **1.** (*pl.* **Mon** *or* **Mons**) a member of a people of Burma and Thailand related to the Khmer of Cambodia. **2.** the language of this people, belonging to the Mon-Khmer family. ~Also called: **Talaing.**

mon. *abbrev. for* monetary.

Mon. *abbrev. for* Monday.

mon- *combining form.* variant of **mono-** before a vowel.

mo·na ('məʊnə) *n.* a W African guenon monkey, *Cercopithecus mona,* with dark fur on the back and white or yellow underparts. [C18: from Spanish or Portuguese: monkey]

mon·a+chal ('mɒnəkᵊl) *adj.* a less common word for **monastic.** [C16: from Old French, from Church Latin *monachālis,* from *monachus* MONK] —**'mon·a+chism** *n.* —**'mon·a+chist** *adj., n.*

mon+ac·id (mɒn'æsɪd) *or* **mon+a·cid+ic** (,mɒnə'sɪdɪk) *adj.* variants of **monoacid.**

Mon·a·co ('mɒnə,kəʊ, mə'nɑ:kəʊ; *French* mɔna'ko) *n.* a principality in SW Europe, on the Mediterranean and forming an enclave in SE France: the second smallest sovereign state in the world (after the Vatican); consists of **Monaco-Ville** (the capital) on a rocky headland, **La Condamine** (a business area and port), **Monte Carlo** (the resort centre), and **Fontvieille,** a light industrial area. Language: French. Religion: Roman Catholic. Currency: franc. Pop.: 24 000 (1974 UN est.). Area: 189 hectares (476 acres). Related adj.: **Monegasque.** —**Mon·a+can** ('mɒnəkən, mə'nɑ:-) *n., adj.*

mon+ad ('mɒnæd, 'məʊ-) *n.* **1.** *pl.* **+ads** *or* **·a+des** (-ə,di:z). *Philosophy.* **a.** any fundamental singular metaphysical entity, esp. if autonomous. **b.** (in the metaphysics of Leibnitz) a simple indestructible nonspatial element regarded as the basis of all reality. **c.** (in the pantheistic philosophy of Giordano Bruno) a fundamental metaphysical unit that is spatially extended and psychically aware. **2.** a single-celled organism, esp. a flagellate protozoan. **3.** an atom, ion, or radical with a valency of one. ~Also called (for senses 1, 2): **monas.** [C17: from Late Latin *monas,* from Greek: unit, from *monos* alone] —**mo+nad+ic** (mɒ'nædɪk) *or* **mo+'nad·i·cal** *adj.* —**mo+'nad·i·cal+ly** *adv.*

mon·a+del+phous (,mɒnə'dɛlfəs) *adj.* **1.** (of stamens) having united filaments forming a tube around the style. **2.** (of flowers) having monadelphous stamens. [C19: from MONO- + -ADELPHOUS]

mon+ad+ism ('mɒnə,dɪzəm, 'məʊ-) *or* **mon+ad+ol+o·gy** (,mɒnə'dɒlədʒɪ, ,məʊ-) *n.* (esp. in the writings of Leibnitz) the philosophical doctrine that monads are the ultimate units of reality. —**,mon+ad+'is+tic** *adj.*

mo+nad+nock (mə'nædnɒk) *n.* a residual hill that consists of hard rock in an otherwise eroded area. [C19: named after Mount *Monadnock,* in New Hampshire]

Mon·a+ghan ('mɒnəhən) *n.* **1.** a county of NE Ireland, in Ulster province: many small lakes. County town: Monaghan. Pop.: 46 242 (1971). Area: 1292 sq. km (499 sq. miles). **2.** a town in NE Ireland, county town of Co. Monaghan. Pop.: 5256 (1971).

mon+al *or* **mon+aul** ('mɒnɔ:l) *n.* any of several S Asian pheasants of the genus *Lophophorus,* the males of which have a brilliantly coloured plumage. [C18: from Hindi]

Mo·na Li·sa ('məʊnə 'li:zə) *n.* a portrait of a young woman painted by Leonardo da Vinci, admired for her enigmatic smile. Also called: **La Gioconda.**

mo+nan+drous (mɒ'nændrəs) *adj.* **1.** having or preferring only one male sexual partner over a period of time. **2.** (of plants) having flowers with only one stamen. **3.** (of flowers) having only one stamen. [C19: from MONO- + -ANDROUS] —**mo+'nan+dry** *n.*

mo+nan+thous (mɒ'nænθəs) *adj.* (of certain plants) having or producing only one flower. [C19: from MONO- + Greek *anthos* flower]

Mo·na Pas+sage ('məʊnə) *n.* a strait between Puerto Rico and the Dominican Republic, linking the Atlantic with the Caribbean.

mon+arch ('mɒnək) *n.* **1.** a sovereign head of state, esp. a king, queen, or emperor, who rules usually by hereditary right. **2.** a supremely powerful or pre-eminent person or thing. **3.** Also called: **milkweed.** a large migratory butterfly, *Danaus plexippus,* that has orange-and-black wings and feeds on the milkweed plant: family *Danaidae.* [C15: from Late Latin *monarcha,* from Greek; see MONO-, -ARCH] —**mo+nar+chal** (mɒ'nɑ:kᵊl) *or* **mo+nar+chi+al** (mɒ'nɑ:kɪəl) *adj.* —**mo+'nar+chal+ly** *adv.* —**mo+'nar+chi+cal** *adj.* —**mo+'nar+chi+cal+ly** *adv.* —**'mon+ar+chism** *n.* —**'mon+ar+chist** *n., adj.* —**,mon+ar+'chis+tic** *adj.*

mon+ar+chy ('mɒnəkɪ) *n., pl.* **+chies. 1.** a form of government in which supreme authority is vested in a single and usually hereditary figure, such as a king, and whose powers can vary from those of an absolute despot to those of a figurehead. **2.** a country reigned over by a king, prince, or other monarch.

mo+nar+da (mɒ'nɑ:də) *n.* any mintlike North American plant of the genus *Monarda:* family *Labiatae* (labiates). See also **horsemint** (sense 2), **bergamot** (sense 4). [C19: from New Latin, named after N. *Monardés* (1493–1588), Spanish botanist]

mon+as ('mɒnæs, 'məʊ-) *n., pl.* **mon·a·des** ('mɒnə,di:z). another word for **monad** (senses 1, 2).

mon+as+ter·y ('mɒnəstərɪ, -strɪ) *n., pl.* **+ter·ies.** the residence of a religious community, esp. of monks, living in seclusion from secular society and bound by religious vows. [C15: from

Church Latin *monastērium,* from Late Greek *monastērion,* from Greek *monázein* to live alone, from *monos* alone] —**mon+as+te+ri·al** (ˌmɒnəˈstɪərɪəl) *adj.*

mo+nas+tic (məˈnæstɪk) *adj. also* **mo+nas+ti+cal.** **1.** of or relating to monasteries or monks, nuns, etc. **2.** resembling this sort of life; reclusive. ~*n.* **3.** a person who is committed to this way of life, esp. a monk. —**mo+ˈnas+ti+cal+ly** *adv.*

mo+nas+ti+cism (məˈnæstɪˌsɪzəm) *n.* the monastic system, movement, or way of life.

mon+a·tom+ic (ˌmɒnəˈtɒmɪk) *or* **mon·o+a·tom+ic** (ˌmɒnəʊəˈtɒmɪk) *adj. Chem.* **1.** (of an element) having or consisting of single atoms: *argon is a monatomic gas.* **2.** (of a compound or molecule) having only one atom or group that can be replaced in a chemical reaction. **3.** a less common word for **monovalent.**

mon+au·ral (mɒˈnɔːrəl) *adj.* **1.** relating to, having, or hearing with only one ear. **2.** another word for **monophonic.** —**mon+ˈau·ral+ly** *adv.*

mon+ax+i·al (mɒˈnæksɪəl) *adj.* another word for **uniaxial.**

mon·a+zite (ˈmɒnəˌzaɪt) *n.* a yellow to reddish-brown mineral consisting of a phosphate of thorium, cerium, and lanthanum in monoclinic crystalline form. [C19: from German, from Greek *monazein* to live alone, so called because of its rarity]

Mön·chen-Glad·bach (*German* ˈmœnçənˈglatbax) *n.* a city in West Germany, in W North Rhine-Westphalia: headquarters of NATO forces in N central Europe; textile industry. Pop.: 150 274 (1974 est.). Former name: **München-Gladbach.**

Monck (mʌŋk) *n.* **George.** 1st duke of Albemarle. 1608–70, English general. In the Civil War he was a Royalist until captured (1644) and persuaded to support the Commonwealth. After Cromwell's death he was instrumental in the restoration of Charles II (1660).

Monc+ton (ˈmɒŋktən) *n.* a city in E Canada, in SE New Brunswick. Pop.: 47 891 (1971).

Mon·dale (ˈmɒnˌdeɪl) *n.* **Wal·ter.** born 1928, U.S. Democratic politician; vice president of the U.S. (1977-81).

Mon+day (ˈmʌndɪ) *n.* the second day of the week; first day of the working week. [Old English *mōnandæg* moon's day, translation of Late Latin *lūnae diēs*]

Mon+day Club *n.* (in Britain) a club made up of right-wing Conservatives who originally met together for lunch on Monday: founded in 1961.

mond·i·al (ˈmɒndɪəl) *adj.* of or involving the whole world. [C20: from French, ultimately from Latin *mundus*]

Mond pro+cess (mɒnd; *German* mɔnt) *n.* a process for obtaining nickel by heating the ore in carbon monoxide to produce nickel carbonyl vapour, which is then decomposed at a higher temperature to yield the metal. [C19: named after Ludwig *Mond* (1839–1909), German chemist and industrialist]

Mon·dri·an (*Dutch* ˈmɔndriːˌaːn) *n.* **Piet** (piːt). 1872–1944, Dutch painter, noted esp. as an exponent of the abstract art movement De Stijl.

mo+ne·cious (mɒˈniːʃəs) *adj.* a variant spelling of **monoecious.** —**mo+ˈne·cious+ly** *adv.*

Mon+e·gasque (ˌmɒnəˈgæsk) *n.* **1.** a native or inhabitant of Monaco. ~*adj.* **2.** of or relating to Monaco or its inhabitants. [from French, from Provençal *mounegasc,* from *Mounegue* Monaco]

Mo·nel met+al *or* **Mo·nell met+al** (mɒˈnɛl) *n. Trademark.* any of various silvery corrosion-resistant alloys containing copper (28 per cent), nickel (67 per cent), and smaller quantities of such metals as iron, manganese, and aluminium. [C20: named after A. Monell (died 1921), president of the International Nickel Co., New York, which introduced the alloys]

mo+neme (ˈməʊniːm) *n. Linguistics.* a less common word for **morpheme.** [C20: from MONO- + -EME]

Mo·net (*French* mɔˈnɛ) *n.* **Claude** (kloːd). 1840–1926, French landscape painter; the leading exponent of impressionism. His interest in the effect of light on colour led him to paint series of pictures of the same subject at different times of day. These include *Haystacks* (1889–93), *Rouen Cathedral* (1892–94), the *Thames* (1899–1904), and *Water Lilies* (1899–1906).

mon+e·tar+ist *n.* a person who advocates regulation of the money supply as a method of controlling the economy of a country.

mon+e·tar·y (ˈmʌnɪtərɪ, -trɪ) *adj.* of or relating to money or currency. [C19: from Late Latin *monētārius,* from Latin *monēta* MONEY] —**mon+e·tar·i+ly** *adv.*

mon+e·tar·y u·nit *n.* a unit of value and money of a country, esp. the major or standard unit.

mon+e·tize *or* **mon+e·tise** (ˈmʌnɪˌtaɪz) *vb.* (*tr.*) **1.** to establish as the legal tender of a country. **2.** to give a legal value to (a coin). —ˌ**mon+e·ti+ˈza·tion** *or* ˌ**mon+e·ti+ˈsa·tion** *n.*

mon+ey (ˈmʌnɪ) *n., pl.* **+eys** *or* **·ies.** **1.** a medium of exchange that functions as legal tender. **2.** the official currency, in the form of bank notes, coins, etc., issued by a government or other authority. **3.** a particular denomination or form of currency: *silver money.* **4.** property or assets with reference to their realizable value. **5.** a pecuniary sum or income. **6.** an unspecified amount of paper currency or coins: *money to lend.* **7. for one's money.** in one's opinion. **8. in the money.** *Informal.* well-off; rich. **9. one's money's worth.** full value for the money one has paid for something. **10. put money into.** to invest money in. **11. put money on.** to place a bet on. ~Related adj.: **pecuniary.** [C13: from Old French *moneie,* from Latin *monēta* coinage; see MINT[2]]

mon·ey+bags (ˈmʌnɪˌbægz) *n. Slang.* a very rich person.

mon·ey+chang·er (ˈmʌnɪˌtʃeɪndʒə) *n.* **1.** a person engaged in the business of exchanging currencies or money. **2.** *Chiefly U.S.* a machine for dispensing coins.

mon+ey cow+ry *n.* **1.** a tropical marine gastropod, *Cypraea moneta.* **2.** the shell of this mollusc, used as money in some parts of Africa and S Asia.

mon+eyed *or* **mon+ied** (ˈmʌnɪd) *adj.* **1.** having a great deal of money; rich. **2.** arising from or characterized by money.

mon+ey+er (ˈmʌnɪə) *n.* **1.** *Archaic.* a person who coins money. **2.** an obsolete word for **banker**[1].

mon·ey-grub·bing *adj. Informal.* seeking greedily to obtain money at every opportunity. —**ˈmon·ey-ˌgrub·ber** *n.*

mon·ey+lend·er (ˈmʌnɪˌlɛndə) *n.* a person who lends money at interest as a living. —**ˈmon·ey+ˌlend·ing** *adj., n.*

mon·ey+mak·er (ˈmʌnɪˌmeɪkə) *n.* **1.** a person who is intent on accumulating money. **2.** a person or thing that is or might be profitable. —**ˈmon·ey+ˌmak·ing** *adj., n.*

mon+ey mar+ket *n. Finance.* the financial institutions dealing with short-term loans and capital and with foreign exchange. Compare **capital market.**

mon+ey of ac+count *n.* another name (esp. U.S.) for **unit of account.**

mon+ey or·der *n.* another name (esp. U.S.) for **postal order.**

mon+ey spi+der *n.* any of certain small shiny brownish spiders of the family *Linyphiidae.*

mon·ey-spin·ner *n. Informal.* an enterprise, idea, person, or thing that is a source of wealth.

mon+ey wag·es *pl. n. Economics.* wages evaluated with reference to the money paid rather than the equivalent purchasing power. Also called: **nominal wages.** Compare **real wages.**

mon·ey+wort (ˈmʌnɪˌwɜːt) *n.* a European and North American creeping primulaceous plant, *Lysimachia nummularia,* with round leaves and yellow flowers. Also called: **creeping Jennie.**

mong (mʌŋ) *n. Austral. informal.* short for **mongrel.**

mon+ger (ˈmʌŋgə) *n.* **1.** (*in combination except in archaic use*) a trader or dealer: *ironmonger.* **2.** (*in combination*) a promoter of something unpleasant: *warmonger.* [Old English *mangere,* ultimately from Latin *mangō* dealer; compare Old High German *mangari*] —**ˈmon+ger+ing** *n., adj.*

mon+go *or* **mon+goe** (ˈmɒŋgəʊ) *n., pl.* **+gos** *or* **+goes.** a Mongolian monetary unit worth one hundredth of a tugrik.

mon+gol (ˈmɒŋgəl) *n.* a person affected with mongolism.

Mon+gol (ˈmɒŋgɒl, -gəl) *n.* **1.** a native or inhabitant of Mongolia, esp. a nomad. **2.** the Mongolian language.

Mon+go·li·a (mɒŋˈgəʊlɪə) *n.* a vast region of central Asia, inhabited chiefly by Mongols: now divided into the Mongolian People's Republic, the Inner Mongolian Autonomous Region of China, and the Tuva ASSR of the Soviet Union; at its height during the 13th century under Genghis Khan.

mon+go·li·an (mɒŋˈgəʊlɪən) *adj.* of, relating to, or having mongolism.

Mon+go·li·an (mɒŋˈgəʊlɪən) *adj.* **1.** of or relating to Mongolia, its people, or their language. ~*n.* **2.** (*pl.* **·ians**) a native of Mongolia. **3.** the language of Mongolia: the chief member of the Mongolic branch of the Altaic family.

Mon+go·li·an Peo+ple's Re+pub+lic *n.* a republic in E central Asia: made a Chinese province in 1691; became autonomous in 1911 and a republic in 1924. It consists chiefly of a high plateau, with the Gobi Desert in the south, a large lake district in the northwest, and the Altai and Khangai Mountains in the west. Language: Khalkha. Currency: tugrik. Capital: Ulan Bator. Pop.: 1 197 600 (1969). Area: 1 565 000 sq. km (604 095 sq. miles). Former name (until 1924): **Outer Mongolia.**

Mon+gol+ic (mɒŋˈgɒlɪk) *n.* **1.** a branch or subfamily of the Altaic family of languages, including Mongolian, Kalmuck, and Buryat. **2.** another word for **Mongoloid.**

mon+go+lism (ˈmɒŋgəˌlɪzəm) *or* **mon+go+li·an id·i·o+cy** *n. Pathol.* a chromosomal abnormality resulting in a flat face and nose, short stubby fingers, a vertical fold of skin at the inner edge of the eye, and mental retardation. Also called: **Down's syndrome.**

mon+gol+oid (ˈmɒŋgəˌlɔɪd) *adj.* **1.** relating to or characterized by mongolism. ~*n.* **2.** a mongoloid person.

Mon+gol+oid (ˈmɒŋgəˌlɔɪd) *adj.* **1.** denoting, relating to, or belonging to one of the major racial groups of mankind, characterized by yellowish complexion, straight black hair, slanting eyes, short nose, and scanty facial hair, including most of the peoples of Asia, the Eskimos, and the North American Indians. ~*n.* **2.** a member of this group.

mon+goose (ˈmɒŋˌguːs) *n., pl.* **+goos·es.** any small predatory viverrine mammal of the genus *Herpestes* and related genera, occurring in Africa and from S Europe to SE Asia, typically having a long tail and brindled coat. [C17: from Marathi *mangūs,* of Dravidian origin]

mon+grel (ˈmʌŋgrəl) *n.* **1.** a plant or animal, esp. a dog, of mixed or unknown breeding; a crossbreed or hybrid. **2.** *Derogatory.* a person of mixed race. ~*adj.* **3.** of mixed origin, breeding, character, etc. [C15: from obsolete *mong* mixture; compare Old English *gemong* a mingling] —**ˈmon+grel+ism** *or* **ˈmon+grel+ness** *n.* —**ˈmon+grel+ly** *adj.*

mon+grel+ize *or* **mon+grel+ise** (ˈmʌŋgrəˌlaɪz) *vb.* (*tr.*) to make mixed or mongrel in breed, race, character, kind, etc. —ˌ**mon+grel·i+ˈza·tion** *or* ˌ**mon+grel·i+ˈsa·tion** *n.* —**ˈmon+grel+ˌiz+er** *or* **ˈmon+grel+ˌis+er** *n.*

'mongst (mʌŋst) *prep. Poetic.* short for **amongst.**

mon+ied (ˈmʌnɪd) *adj.* a less common spelling of **moneyed.**

mon·ies (ˈmʌnɪz) *n.* a plural of **money.**

mon·i+ker *or* **mon+ick+er** (ˈmɒnɪkə) *n. Informal.* a person's name or nickname. [C19: origin unknown]

mo+nil·i+form (mɒˈnɪlɪˌfɔːm) *adj. Biology.* shaped like a string of beads: *moniliform fungi.* [C19: from New Latin *monīliformis*, from Latin *monīle* necklace + *forma* shape]

mon·ism ('mɒnɪzəm) *n.* **1.** *Philosophy.* the doctrine that reality consists of only one basic substance or element, such as mind or matter. Compare **dualism, pluralism. 2.** *Epistemology.* the theory that the object and datum of consciousness are identical. **3.** the attempt to explain anything in terms of one principle only. —**'mon·ist** *n., adj.* —**mo·'nis·tic** *adj.* —**mo·'nis·ti·cal·ly** *adv.*

mo·ni·tion (məʊ'nɪʃən) *n.* **1.** a warning or caution; admonition. **2.** *Ecclesiast.* a formal notice from a bishop or ecclesiastical court requiring a person to refrain from committing a specific offence. [C14: via Old French from Latin *monitiō*, from *monēre* to warn]

mon·i·tor ('mɒnɪtə) *n.* **1.** a person or piece of equipment that warns, checks, controls, or keeps a continuous record of something. **2.** *Education.* **a.** a senior pupil with various supervisory duties, etc. **b.** a pupil assisting a teacher in classroom organization, etc. **3.** a television set used in a studio for viewing or checking a programme being transmitted. **4.** a device for controlling the direction of a water jet in fire fighting. **5.** any large predatory lizard of the genus *Varanus* and family *Varanidae*, inhabiting warm regions of Africa, Asia, and Australia. See also **Komodo dragon. 6.** Also called: **giant.** *Mining.* a nozzle for directing a high-pressure jet of water at the material to be excavated. **7.** (formerly) a small heavily armoured warship used for coastal assault. ~*vb.* **8.** to act as a monitor of. **9.** (*tr.*) to observe or record (the activity or performance) of (an engine or other device). **10.** (*tr.*) to check (the technical quality) of (a radio or television broadcast). [C16: from Latin, from *monēre* to advise] —**mon·i·to·ri·al** (ˌmɒnɪ'tɔːrɪəl) *adj.* —ˌ**mon·i·'to·ri·al·ly** *adv.* —**'mon·i·tor·ˌship** *n.* —**'mon·i·tress** *fem. n.*

mon·i·to·ry ('mɒnɪtərɪ, -trɪ) *adj. also* **mon·i·to·ri·al. 1.** warning or admonishing: *a monitory look.* ~*n., pl.* **·ries. 2.** *Rare.* a letter containing a monition.

monk (mʌŋk) *n.* **1.** a male member of a religious community bound by vows of poverty, chastity, and obedience. Related adj.: **monastic. 2.** (*sometimes cap.*) a fancy pigeon having a bald pate and often large feathered footings. [Old English *munuc*, from Late Latin *monachus*, from Late Greek: solitary (man), from Greek *monos* alone]

Monk (mʌŋk) *n.* **1. The·lo·ni·us (Sphere)** (θə'ləʊnɪəs). 1920–82, U.S. jazz pianist and composer. **2.** a variant spelling of (George) **Monck.**

monk·er·y ('mʌŋkərɪ) *n., pl.* **·er·ies.** *Derogatory.* **1.** monastic life or practices. **2.** a monastery or monks collectively.

mon·key ('mʌŋkɪ) *n.* **1.** any of numerous long-tailed primates excluding the prosimians (lemurs, tarsiers, etc.): comprise the families *Cercopithecidae* (see **Old World monkey**), *Cebidae* (see **New World monkey**), and *Callithricidae* (marmosets). **2.** any primate except man. **3.** a naughty or mischievous person, esp. a child. **4.** the head of a pile driver (**monkey engine**) or of some similar mechanical device. **5.** (*modifier*) *Nautical.* denoting a small light structure or piece of equipment contrived to suit an immediate purpose: *a monkey foresail; a monkey bridge.* **6.** *U.S. slang.* an addict's dependence on a drug (esp. in the phrase **have a monkey on one's back**). **7.** *Slang.* a butt of derision; someone made to look a fool (esp. in the phrase **make a monkey of**). **8.** *Slang.* (esp. in bookmaking) £500. **9.** *U.S. slang.* $500. **10.** *Austral. slang.* a sheep. ~*vb.* **11.** (*intr.; usually foll. by around, with,* etc.) to meddle, fool, or tinker. **12.** (*tr.*) *Rare.* to imitate; ape. [C16: perhaps from Low German; compare Middle Low German *Moneke* name of the ape's son in the tale of Reynard the Fox]

mon·key bread *n.* **1.** the gourdlike fruit of the baobab tree. **2. monkey bread tree.** another name for **baobab.**

mon·key busi·ness *n. Informal.* mischievous, suspect, dishonest, or meddlesome behaviour or acts.

mon·key flow·er *n.* any of various scrophulariaceous plants of the genus *Mimulus*, cultivated for their yellow or red flowers. See also **musk** (sense 3).

mon·key jack·et *n.* a short close-fitting jacket, esp. a waist-length jacket similar to a mess jacket.

mon·key nut *n. Brit.* another name for a **peanut** (sense 1).

mon·key·pot ('mʌŋkɪˌpɒt) *n.* **1.** any of various tropical trees of the genus *Lecythis*: family *Lecythidaceae.* **2.** the large urn-shaped pod of any of these trees, formerly used to catch monkeys by baiting it with sugar. **3.** a melting pot used in making flint glass.

mon·key puz·zle *n.* a South American coniferous tree, *Araucaria araucana*, having branches shaped like a candelabra and stiff sharp leaves: family *Araucariaceae.* Also called: **Chile pine.** [so called because monkeys have difficulty climbing them]

mon·key suit *n. U.S. slang.* a man's evening dress.

mon·key tricks *or U.S.* **mon·key shines** *pl. n. Informal.* mischievous behaviour or acts, such as practical jokes.

mon·key wrench *n.* a wrench with adjustable jaws.

monk·fish ('mʌŋkˌfɪʃ) *n., pl.* **·fish** *or* **·fish·es. 1.** Also called (U.S.): **goosefish.** any of various anglers of the genus *Lophius.* **2.** another name for the **angel shark.**

Mon-Khmer *n.* **1.** a family of languages spoken in Cambodia, Burma, and Assam, sometimes considered to be related to the Malayo-Polynesian family. See also **Austro-Asiatic.** ~*adj.* **2.** of or belonging to this family of languages.

monk·hood ('mʌŋkhʊd) *n.* **1.** the condition of being a monk. **2.** monks collectively.

monk·ish ('mʌŋkɪʃ) *adj.* of, relating to, or resembling a monk or monks. —**'monk·ish·ly** *adv.* —**'monk·ish·ness** *n.*

monk's cloth *n.* a heavy cotton fabric of basket weave, used mainly for bedspreads.

monks·hood ('mʌŋksˌhʊd) *n.* any of several poisonous N temperate plants of the ranunculaceous genus *Aconitum*, esp. *A. napellus*, that have hooded blue-purple flowers.

Mon·mouth[1] ('mɒnməθ) *n.* a market town in E Wales, in Gwent: Norman castle, where Henry V was born in 1387. Pop.: 6545 (1971).

Mon·mouth[2] ('mɒnməθ) *n.* **James Scott,** Duke of Monmouth. 1649–85, the illegitimate son of Charles II of England, he led a rebellion against James II in support of his own claim to the Crown; captured and beheaded.

Mon·mouth·shire ('mɒnməθˌʃɪə, -ʃə) *n.* (until 1974) a county of E Wales, now corresponding roughly to the county of Gwent: administratively part of England for three centuries (until 1830).

Mon·net (*French* mɔ'nɛ) *n.* **Jean** (ʒɑ̃). 1888-1979, French economist and public servant, regarded as founding father of the European Economic Community. He was first president (1952-55) of the European Coal and Steel Community.

mon·o ('mɒnəʊ) *adj.* **1.** short for **monophonic.** ~*n.* **2.** monophonic sound; monophony.

mon·o- *or before a vowel* **mon-** *combining form.* **1.** one; single: *monochrome; monorail.* **2.** indicating that a chemical compound contains a single specified atom or group: *monoxide.* [from Greek *monos*]

mon·o·ac·id (ˌmɒnəʊ'æsɪd), **mon·ac·id, mon·o·a·cid·ic** (ˌmɒnəʊə'sɪdɪk), *or* **mon·a·cid·ic** *adj. Chem.* (of a base) capable of reacting with only one molecule of a monobasic acid; having only one hydroxide ion per molecule.

mon·o·a·tom·ic (ˌmɒnəʊə'tɒmɪk) *adj.* a variant spelling of **monatomic.**

mon·o·ba·sic (ˌmɒnəʊ'beɪsɪk) *adj. Chem.* (of an acid, such as hydrogen chloride) having only one replaceable hydrogen atom per molecule.

mon·o·carp ('mɒnəʊˌkɑːp) *n.* a plant that is monocarpic.

mon·o·car·pel·lar·y (ˌmɒnəʊ'kɑːpɪlərɪ) *or* **mon·o·car·pous** (ˌmɒnəʊ'kɑːpəs) *adj.* **1.** (of flowers) having only one carpel. **2.** (of a plant gynoecium) consisting of one carpel.

mon·o·car·pic (ˌmɒnəʊ'kɑːpɪk) *or* **mon·o·car·pous** *adj.* (of some flowering plants) producing fruit only once before dying.

Mo·noc·er·os (mə'nɒsərəs) *n., Latin genitive* **Mo·noc·er·o·tis** (məˌnɒsə'rəʊtɪs). a faint constellation on the celestial equator crossed by the Milky Way and lying close to Orion and Canis Major. [C14: via Old French from Latin: unicorn, from Greek *monokeros* with a single horn, from MONO- + *keras* horn]

mon·o·cha·si·um (ˌmɒnəʊ'keɪzɪəm) *n., pl.* **·si·a** (-zɪə). *Botany.* a cymose inflorescence in which each branch gives rise to one other branch only, as in the forget-me-not and buttercup. Compare **dichasium.** [C19: MONO- + *-chasium* as in DICHASIUM] —ˌ**mon·o·'cha·si·al** *adj.*

mon·o·chlo·ride (ˌmɒnə'klɔːraɪd) *n.* a chloride containing one atom of chlorine per molecule.

mon·o·chord ('mɒnəʊˌkɔːd) *n.* an instrument employed in acoustic analysis or investigation, consisting usually of one string stretched over a resonator of wood. Also called: **sonometer.** [C15: from Old French, from Late Latin, from Greek *monokhordon*, from MONO- + *khordē* string]

mon·o·chro·mat (ˌmɒnəʊ'krəʊmæt) *or* **mon·o·chro·mate** (ˌmɒnəʊ'krəʊmeɪt) *n.* a person who perceives all colours as a single hue.

mon·o·chro·mat·ic (ˌmɒnəʊkrəʊ'mætɪk) *or* **mon·o·chro·ic** (ˌmɒnəʊ'krəʊɪk) *adj.* **1.** Also: **homochromatic.** (of light or other electromagnetic radiation) having only one wavelength. **2.** *Physics.* (of moving particles) having only one kinetic energy. **3.** of or relating to monochromatism. ~*n.* **4.** a person who is totally colour-blind. —ˌ**mon·o·chro·'mat·i·cal·ly** *adv.*

mon·o·chro·ma·tism (ˌmɒnəʊ'krəʊməˌtɪzəm) *n.* a visual defect in which all colours appear as variations of a single hue.

mon·o·chrome ('mɒnəˌkrəʊm) *n.* **1.** a black-and-white photograph or transparency. **2.** *Photog.* black and white. **3. a.** a painting, drawing, etc., done in a range of tones of a single colour. **b.** the technique or art of this. **4.** (*modifier*) executed in or resembling monochrome: *a monochrome print.* ~Also called (for senses 3,4): **monotint.** [C17: via Medieval Latin from Greek *monokhrōmos* of one colour] —ˌ**mon·o·'chro·mic** *or* ˌ**mon·o·'chro·mi·cal** *adj.* —**'mon·o·ˌchrom·ist** *n.*

mon·o·cle ('mɒnəkᵊl) *n.* a lens for correcting defective vision of one eye, held in position by the facial muscles. [C19: from French, from Late Latin *monoculus* one-eyed, from MONO- + *oculus* eye] —**'mon·o·cled** *adj.*

mon·o·cline ('mɒnəʊˌklaɪn) *n.* a fold in stratified rocks in which the strata are inclined in the same direction from the horizontal. [C19: from MONO- + Greek *klīnein* to lean] —ˌ**mon·o·'cli·nal** *adj., n.* —ˌ**mon·o·'cli·nal·ly** *adv.*

mon·o·clin·ic (ˌmɒnəʊ'klɪnɪk) *adj. Crystallog.* relating to or belonging to the crystal system characterized by three unequal axes, one pair of which are not at right angles to each other.

mon·o·cli·nous (ˌmɒnəʊ'klaɪnəs, 'mɒnəʊˌklaɪnəs) *adj.* (of flowering plants) having the male and female reproductive organs on the same flower. Compare **diclinous.** —**'mon·o·ˌcli·nism** *n.*

mon·o·coque ('mɒnəˌkɒk) *n.* **1.** a type of aircraft fuselage, car body, etc., in which all or most of the loads are taken by the skin. **2.** a type of racing-car design with no separate chassis and body. ~*adj.* **3.** of or relating to the design characteristic of a monocoque. [C20: from French, from MONO- + *coque* shell]

mon·o·cot·y·le·don (ˌmɒnəʊˌkɒtɪ'liːdᵊn) *n.* any flowering plant of the group *Monocotyledonae,* having a single embryonic seed leaf, leaves with parallel veins, and flowers with parts in threes: includes grasses, lilies, palms, and orchids. Often shortened to **monocot.** Compare **dicotyledon.** —ˌ**mon·o**+ˌ**cot·y**+'**le·don**+**ous** *adj.*

mo+**noc**+**ra**+**cy** (mɒ'nɒkrəsɪ) *n., pl.* +**cies.** government by one person. —**mon·o**+**crat** ('mɒnəˌkræt) *n.* —ˌ**mon·o**+'**crat**+**ic** *adj.*

mo+**noc·u**+**lar** (mɒ'nɒkjʊlə) *adj.* having or intended for the use of only one eye. [C17: from Late Latin *monoculus* one-eyed] —**mo**+'**noc·u**+**lar**+**ly** *adv.*

mon·o+**cul**+**ture** ('mɒnəʊˌkʌltʃə) *n.* the continuous growing of one type of crop.

mon·o+**cy**+**cle** ('mɒnəˌsaɪkᵊl) *n.* another name for **unicycle.**

mon·o+**cy**+**clic** (ˌmɒnəʊ'saɪklɪk) *adj.* **1.** (of a chemical compound) containing only one ring of atoms. Also: **mononuclear. 2.** (of sepals, petals, or stamens) arranged in a single whorl. **3.** another word for **annual** (sense 3).

mon·o+**cyte** ('mɒnəʊˌsaɪt) *n.* a large phagocytic leucocyte with a spherical nucleus and clear cytoplasm. —**mon·o**+**cyt**+**ic** (ˌmɒnə'sɪtɪk) *adj.* —ˌ**mon·o**+'**cy**+**toid** *adj.*

mon·o+**dra**+**ma** ('mɒnəʊˌdrɑːmə) *n.* a play or other dramatic piece for a single performer.

mon·o+**dy** ('mɒnədɪ) *n., pl.* +**dies. 1.** (in Greek tragedy) an ode sung by a single actor. **2.** any poem of lament for someone's death. **3.** *Music.* a style of composition consisting of a single vocal part, usually with accompaniment. **4.** *Chiefly U.S.* a monotonous sound. [C17: via Late Latin from Greek *monōidia,* from MONO- + *aeidein* to sing] —**mo**+**nod**+**ic** (mɒ'nɒdɪk) *or* **mo**+'**nod·i·cal** *adj.* —**mo**+'**nod·i·cal**+**ly** *adv.* —'**mon·o**+**dist** *n.*

mo+**noe·cious, mo**+**ne·cious** (mɒ'niːʃəs), *or* **mo**+**noi**+**cous** (mɒ'nɔɪkəs) *adj.* **1.** (of some flowering plants) having the male and female reproductive organs in separate flowers on the same plant. **2.** (of some animals and lower plants) hermaphrodite. ~Compare **dioecious.** [C18: from New Latin *monoecia,* from MONO- + Greek *oikos* house] —**mo**+'**noe·cious**+**ly** *or* **mo**+'**ne·cious**+**ly** *adv.*

mon·o+**fil·a**+**ment** (ˌmɒnə'fɪləmənt) *or* **mon·o**+**fil** ('mɒnəfɪl) *n.* synthetic thread or yarn composed of a single strand rather than twisted fibres.

mo+**nog·a**+**mist** (mə'nɒgəmɪst) *n.* a person who advocates or practises monogamy. —**mo**+ˌ**nog·a**+'**mis**+**tic** *adj.*

mo+**nog·a**+**my** (mɒ'nɒgəmɪ) *n.* **1.** the state or practice of having only one husband or wife over a period of time. Compare **bigamy, polygamy** (sense 1). **2.** *Zoology.* the practice of having only one mate. Compare **digamy.** [C17: via French from Late Latin *monogamia,* from Greek; see MONO- + -GAMY] —**mo**+'**nog·a**+**mous** *adj.* —**mo**+'**nog·a**+**mous**+**ly** *adv.* —**mo**+'**nog·a**+**mous**+**ness** *n.*

mon·o+**gen**+**e·sis** (ˌmɒnəʊ'dʒɛnɪsɪs) *or* **mo**+**nog**+**e·ny** (mɒ'nɒdʒɪnɪ) *n.* **1.** the hypothetical descent of all organisms from a single cell or organism. **2.** asexual reproduction in animals. **3.** the direct development of an ovum into an organism resembling the adult. **4.** the hypothetical descent of all human beings from a single pair of ancestors. ~Compare **polygenesis.**

mon·o+**ge·net**+**ic** (ˌmɒnəʊdʒɪ'nɛtɪk) *or* **mo**+**nog**+**e·nous** (mɒ'nɒdʒənəs) *adj.* **1.** of, relating to, or showing monogenesis. **2.** of or relating to animals, such as some flukes, that complete their life cycle on only one host. **3.** (of rocks and rock formations) formed from one source or by one process.

mon·o+**gen**+**ic** (ˌmɒnəʊ'dʒɛnɪk) *adj.* **1.** *Genetics.* of or relating to an inherited character difference that is controlled by one pair of genes. **2.** (of animals) producing offspring of one sex.

mon·o+**gram** ('mɒnəˌgræm) *n.* a design of one or more letters, esp. initials, embroidered on clothing, printed on stationery, etc. [C17: from Late Latin *monogramma,* from Greek; see MONO-, -GRAM] —**mon·o**+**gram**+**mat·ic** (ˌmɒnəgrə'mætɪk) *adj.*

mon·o+**graph** ('mɒnəˌgræf, -ˌgrɑːf) *n.* **1.** a paper, book, or other work concerned with a single subject or aspect of a subject. ~*vb.* (*tr.*) **2.** to write a monograph on. —**mo**+**nog**+**ra**+**pher** (mɒ'nɒgrəfə) *or* **mo**+'**nog**+**ra**+**phist** *n.* —ˌ**mon·o**+'**graph**+**ic** *adj.* —ˌ**mon·o**+'**graph**+**i·cal**+**ly** *adv.*

mo+**nog·y**+**ny** (mɒ'nɒdʒɪnɪ) *n.* the custom of having only one female sexual partner over a period of time. —**mo**+'**nog·y**+**nist** *n.* —**mo**+'**nog·y**+**nous** *adj.*

mon·o+**hull** ('mɒnəʊˌhʌl) *n.* a sailing vessel with a single hull. Compare **multihull.**

mon·o+**hy**+**brid** (ˌmɒnəʊ'haɪbrɪd) *n. Genetics.* the offspring of two individuals that differ with respect to one pair of genes.

mon·o+**hy**+**drate** (ˌmɒnəʊ'haɪdreɪt) *n.* a hydrate, such as ferrous sulphate monohydrate, $FeSO_4.H_2O$, containing one molecule of water per molecule of the compound. —ˌ**mon·o**+'**hy**+**drat**+**ed** *adj.*

mon·o+**hy**+**dric** (ˌmɒnəʊ'haɪdrɪk) *adj.* another word for **monohydroxy,** esp. when applied to alcohols.

mon·o+**hy**+**drox·y** (ˌmɒnəʊhaɪ'drɒksɪ) *adj.* (of a chemical compound) containing one hydroxyl group per molecule. Also: **monohydric.**

mo+**noi**+**cous** (mɒ'nɔɪkəs) *adj.* a variant spelling of **monoecious.** —**mo**+'**noi**+**cous**+**ly** *adv.*

mo+**nol·a**+**try** (mɒ'nɒlətrɪ) *n.* the exclusive worship of one god without excluding the existence of others. —**mo**+**nol·a**+**ter** (mɒ'nɒlətə) *or* **mo**+'**nol·a**+**trist** *n.* —**mo**+'**nol·a**+**trous** *adj.*

mon·o+**lay**+**er** ('mɒnəʊˌleɪə) *n.* a single layer of atoms or molecules adsorbed on a surface. Also called: **molecular film.**

mon·o+**lin**+**gual** (ˌmɒnəʊ'lɪŋgwəl) *adj.* knowing or expressed in only one language. Compare **bilingual, multilingual.**

mon·o+**lith** ('mɒnəlɪθ) *n.* **1.** a large block of stone or anything that resembles one in appearance, intractability, etc. **2.** a statue, obelisk, column, etc., cut from one block of stone. **3.** a large hollow foundation piece sunk as a caisson and having a number of compartments that are filled with concrete when it has reached its correct position. [C19: via French from Greek *monolithos* made from a single stone]

mon·o+**lith**+**ic** (ˌmɒnə'lɪθɪk) *adj.* **1.** of, relating to, or like a monolith. **2.** characterized by hugeness, impenetrability, or intractability: *a monolithic government.* **3.** *Electronics.* (of an integrated circuit) having all components manufactured into or on top of a single chip of silicon. Compare **hybrid** (sense 6). —ˌ**mon·o**+'**lith·i·cal**+**ly** *adv.*

mon·o+**logue** ('mɒnəˌlɒg) *n.* **1.** a long speech made by one actor in a play, film, etc., esp. when alone. **2.** a dramatic piece for a single performer. **3.** any long speech by one person, esp. when interfering with conversation. [C17: via French from Greek *monologos* speaking alone] —**mon·o**+**log**+**ic** (ˌmɒnə'lɒdʒɪk) *or* ˌ**mon·o**+'**log·i·cal** *adj.* —**mon·o**+**log**+**ist** ('mɒnəˌlɒgɪst, mə'nɒləgɪst) *n.* —**mo**+**nol**+**o·gy** (mɒ'nɒlədʒɪ) *n.*

mon·o+**ma**+**ni·a** (ˌmɒnəʊ'meɪnɪə) *n.* an excessive mental preoccupation with one thing, idea, etc. —ˌ**mon·o**+'**ma**+**ni**+ˌ**ac** *n.* —**mon·o**+**ma**+**ni·a**+**cal** (ˌmɒnəʊmə'naɪəkᵊl) *adj.*

mon·o+**mark** ('mɒnəmɑːk) *Brit. n.* a series of letters or figures to identify goods, personal articles, etc.

mon·o+**mer** ('mɒnəmə) *n. Chem.* a compound whose molecules can join together to form a polymer. —**mon·o**+**mer**+**ic** (ˌmɒnə'mɛrɪk) *adj.*

mo+**nom**+**er**+**ous** (mɒ'nɒmərəs) *adj.* (of flowers) having whorls consisting of only one member.

mon·o+**me**+**tal**+**lic** (ˌmɒnəʊmɪ'tælɪk) *adj.* **1.** (esp. of coins) consisting of one metal only. **2.** relating to monometallism.

mon·o+**met**+**al**+**lism** (ˌmɒnəʊ'mɛtᵊˌlɪzəm) *n.* **1.** the use of one metal, esp. gold or silver, as the sole standard of value and currency. **2.** the economic policies supporting a monometallic standard. —ˌ**mon·o**+'**met**+**al**+**list** *n.*

mo+**nom**+**e·ter** (mɒ'nɒmɪtə) *n. Prosody.* a line of verse consisting of one metrical foot. —**mon·o**+**met**+**ri**+**cal** (ˌmɒnəʊ'mɛtrɪkᵊl) *or* ˌ**mon·o**+'**met**+**ric** *adj.*

mo+**no**+**mi·al** (mɒ'nəʊmɪəl) *n.* **1.** *Maths.* an expression consisting of a single term, such as 5*ax.* ~*adj.* **2.** consisting of a single algebraic term. **3.** *Biology.* of, relating to, or denoting a taxonomic name that consists of a single term. [C18: MONO- + (BIN)OMIAL]

mon·o+**mo**+**lec·u**+**lar** (ˌmɒnəʊmə'lɛkjʊlə) *adj.* of, concerned with, or involving single molecules: *a monomolecular layer.*

mon·o+**mor**+**phic** (ˌmɒnəʊ'mɔːfɪk) *or* **mon·o**+**mor**+**phous** *adj.* **1.** (of an individual organism) showing little or no change in structure during the entire life history. **2.** (of a species) existing or having parts that exist in only one form. **3.** (of a chemical compound) having only one crystalline form. —ˌ**mon·o**+'**mor**+**phism** *n.*

Mo+**non**+**ga**+**he**+**la** (məˌnɒŋgə'hiːlə) *n.* a river in the northeastern U.S., flowing generally north to the Allegheny River at Pittsburgh, Pennsylvania, forming the Ohio River. Length: 206 km (128 miles).

mon·o+**nu**+**cle·ar** (ˌmɒnəʊ'njuːklɪə) *adj.* **1.** (of a cell) having only one nucleus. **2.** another word for **monocyclic.**

mon·o+**nu**+**cle·o**+**sis** (ˌmɒnəʊˌnjuːklɪ'əʊsɪs) *n.* **1.** *Pathol.* the presence of a large number of monocytes in the blood. **2.** See **infectious mononucleosis.**

mon·o+**pet**+**al**+**ous** (ˌmɒnəʊ'pɛtᵊləs) *adj.* **1.** another word for **gamopetalous. 2.** (of flowers) having only one petal.

mo+**noph·a**+**gous** (mə'nɒfəgəs) *adj.* feeding on only one type of food: *monophagous insects.* —**mo**+'**noph·a**+**gy** *n.*

mon·o+**pho**+**bi·a** (ˌmɒnəʊ'fəʊbɪə) *n.* a strong fear of being alone. —ˌ**mon·o**+'**pho**+**bic** *adj.*

mon·o+**phon**+**ic** (ˌmɒnəʊ'fɒnɪk) *adj.* **1.** Also: **monaural.** (of a system of broadcasting, recording, or reproducing sound) using only one channel between source and loudspeaker. Sometimes shortened to **mono.** Compare **stereophonic. 2.** *Music.* of or relating to a style of musical composition consisting of a single melodic line. See also **monody** (sense 3). —**mo**+**noph·o**+**ny** (mɒ'nɒfənɪ) *n.*

mon+**oph**+**thong** ('mɒnəfˌθɒŋ) *n.* a simple or pure vowel. [C17: from Greek *monophthongos,* from MONO- + *thongos* sound] —**mon**+**oph**+**thon**+**gal** (ˌmɒnəf'θɒŋgᵊl) *adj.*

mon·o+**phy**+**let**+**ic** (ˌmɒnəʊfaɪ'lɛtɪk) *adj.* **1.** relating to or characterized by descent from a single ancestral group of animals or plants. **2.** (of animals or plants) of or belonging to a single stock.

mon·o+**phyl**+**lous** (ˌmɒnəʊ'fɪləs) *adj. Botany.* having or consisting of only one leaf or leaflike part.

Mo+**noph·y**+**site** (mɒ'nɒfɪˌsaɪt) *n. Christianity.* **1.** a person who holds that there is only one nature in the person of Christ, which is primarily divine with human attributes. ~*adj.* **2.** of or relating to this belief. [C17: via Church Latin from Late Greek, from MONO- + *phusis* nature] —**Mon·o**+**phy**+**sit**+**ic** (ˌmɒnəʊfɪ'sɪtɪk) *adj.* —**Mo**+'**noph·y**+ˌ**sit**+**ism** *n.*

mon·o+**plane** ('mɒnəʊˌpleɪn) *n.* an aeroplane with only one pair of wings. Compare **biplane.**

mon·o+**ple·gi·a** (ˌmɒnəʊ'pliːdʒɪə) *n. Pathol.* paralysis limited to one limb or a single group of muscles. —**mon·o**+**ple·gic** (ˌmɒnəʊ'pliːdʒɪk) *adj.*

mon·o+**ploid** ('mɒnəˌplɔɪd) *adj., n.* a less common word for **haploid.**

mon·o+**pode** ('mɒnəˌpəʊd) *n.* **1.** a member of a legendary one-legged race of Africa. **2.** another word for **monopodium.** [C19: from Late Latin *monopodius*]

mon·o+**po·di·um** (ˌmɒnə'pəʊdɪəm) *n., pl.* +**di·a** (-dɪə). the main axis of growth in the pine tree and similar plants: the main stem, which elongates from the tip and gives rise to lateral branches. Compare **sympodium.** [C19: New Latin, from Greek *monopous,* from MONO- + *pous* foot] —ˌ**mon·o·'po·di·al** *adj.* —ˌ**mon·o·'po·di·al·ly** *adv.*

mo·nop·o·lis·tic com·pe·ti·tion *n. Economics.* the form of imperfect competition that exists when the commodity produced in the market is not homogeneous.

mo·nop·o·lize *or* **mo·nop·o·lise** (məˈnɒpəˌlaɪz) *vb.* (*tr.*) **1.** to have, control, or make use of fully, excluding others. **2.** to obtain, maintain, or exploit a monopoly of (a market, commodity, etc.). —**mo·ˌnop·o·li·'za·tion** *or* **mo·ˌnop·o·li·'sa·tion** *n.* —**mo·'nop·o·ˌliz·er** *or* **mo·'nop·o·ˌlis·er** *n.*

mo·nop·o·ly (məˈnɒpəlɪ) *n., pl.* **·lies. 1.** exclusive control of the market supply of a product or service. **2. a.** an enterprise exercising this control. **b.** the product or service so controlled. **3.** *Law.* the exclusive right or privilege granted to a person, company, etc., by the state to purchase, manufacture, use, or sell some commodity or to carry on trade in a specified country or area. **4.** exclusive control, possession, or use of something. [C16: from Late Latin, from Greek *monopōlion,* from MONO- + *pōlein* to sell] —**mo·'nop·o·lism** *n.* —**mo·'nop·o·list** *n.* —**mo·ˌnop·o·'lis·tic** *adj.* —**mo·ˌnop·o·'lis·ti·cal·ly** *adv.*

Mo·nop·o·ly (məˈnɒpəlɪ) *n. Trademark.* a board game for two to six players who throw dice to advance their tokens around a board, the object being to acquire the property on which their tokens land.

mon·o·pro·pel·lant (ˌmɒnəʊprəˈpɛlənt) *n.* a solid or liquid rocket propellant containing both the fuel and the oxidizer.

mo·nop·so·ny (məˈnɒpsənɪ) *n., pl.* **·nies.** a situation in which the entire market demand for a product or service consists of only one buyer. [C20: MONO- + Greek *opsōnia* purchase, from *opsōnein* to buy] —**mo·ˌnop·so·'nis·tic** *adj.*

mon·op·te·ros (mɒnˈɒptəˌrɒs) *or* **mon·op·te·ron** *n., pl.* **·te·roi** (-təˌrɔɪ) *or* **·te·ra** (-tərə). a circular classical building, esp. a temple, that has a single ring of columns surrounding it. [C18: Late Latin from Greek, from MONO- + *pteron* a wing] —**mon·'op·te·ral** *adj.*

mon·o·rail (ˈmɒnəʊˌreɪl) *n.* a single-track railway, often elevated and with suspended cars.

mon·o·sac·cha·ride (ˌmɒnəʊˈsækəˌraɪd, -rɪd) *n.* a simple sugar, such as glucose or fructose, that does not hydrolyse to yield other sugars.

mon·o·se·my (ˈmɒnəʊˌsiːmɪ) *n.* the fact of having only a single meaning; absence of ambiguity in a word. Compare **polysemy.** [C20: from MONO- + (POLY)SEMY]

mon·o·sep·a·lous (ˌmɒnəʊˈsɛpələs) *adj.* **1.** another word for **gamosepalous. 2.** (of flowers) having only one sepal.

mon·o·so·di·um glu·ta·mate (ˌmɒnəʊˈsəʊdɪəm ˈgluːtəˌmeɪt) *n.* a white crystalline substance, the sodium salt of glutamic acid, that has a meaty taste: used as a food additive. Formula: $NaC_5H_8O_4$. Also called: **sodium glutamate.**

mon·o·some (ˈmɒnəˌsəʊm) *n.* an unpaired chromosome, esp. an X-chromosome in an otherwise diploid cell. —**mon·o·so·mic** (ˌmɒnəʊˈsəʊmɪk) *adj.*

mon·o·sper·mous (ˌmɒnəʊˈspɜːməs) *or* **mon·o·sper·mal** *adj.* (of certain plants) producing only one seed.

mon·o·stich (ˈmɒnəˌstɪk) *n.* a poem of a single line. [C16: via Late Latin from Greek; see MONO-, STICH] —ˌ**mon·o·'stich·ic** *adj.*

mon·o·stich·ous (ˌmɒnəʊˈstaɪkəs) *adj. Botany.* (of parts) forming one row.

mon·o·stome (ˈmɒnəˌstəʊm) *or* **mo·nos·to·mous** (mɒˈnɒstəməs) *adj. Zoology, botany.* having only one mouth, pore, or similar opening.

mo·nos·tro·phe (mɒˈnɒstrəfɪ, ˈmɒnəˌstrəʊf) *n.* a poem in which all the stanzas or strophes are written in the same metre. —**mon·o·stroph·ic** (ˈmɒnəˈstrɒfɪk) *adj.*

mon·o·sty·lous (ˌmɒnəʊˈstaɪləs) *adj. Botany.* having only one style.

mon·o·syl·lab·ic (ˌmɒnəsɪˈlæbɪk) *adj.* **1.** (of a word) containing only one syllable. **2.** characterized by monosyllables; curt: *a monosyllabic answer.* —ˌ**mon·o·syl·'lab·i·cal·ly** *adv.*

mon·o·syl·la·ble (ˈmɒnəˌsɪləbᵊl) *n.* a word of one syllable, esp. one used as a sentence. —ˌ**mon·o·'syl·la·ˌbism** *n.*

mon·o·sym·met·ric (ˌmɒnəsɪˈmɛtrɪk) *or* **mon·o·sym·met·ri·cal** *adj.* **1.** *Crystallog.* variants of **monoclinic. 2.** *Biology.* variants of **zygomorphic.** —ˌ**mon·o·sym·'met·ri·cal·ly** *adv.* —**mon·o·sym·met·ry** (ˌmɒnəˈsɪmɪtrɪ) *n.*

mon·o·the·ism (ˈmɒnəʊθɪˌɪzəm) *n.* the belief or doctrine that there is only one God. —**'mon·o·ˌthe·ist** *n., adj.* —ˌ**mon·o·the·'is·tic** *adj.* —ˌ**mon·o·the·'is·ti·cal·ly** *adv.*

mon·o·tint (ˈmɒnəˌtɪnt) *n.* another word for **monochrome** (senses 3,4).

mon·o·tone (ˈmɒnəˌtəʊn) *n.* **1.** a single unvaried pitch level in speech, sound, etc. **2.** utterance, etc., without change of pitch. **3.** lack of variety in style, expression. etc. ~*adj.* **4.** unvarying or monotonous. **5.** Also: **mon·o·ton·ic** (ˌmɒnəˈtɒnɪk). *Maths.* (of a sequence or function) consistently increasing or decreasing in value.

mo·not·o·nize *or* **mo·not·o·nise** (məˈnɒtəˌnaɪz) *vb.* (*tr.*) to make monotonous.

mo·not·o·nous (məˈnɒtənəs) *adj.* **1.** dull and tedious, esp. because of repetition. **2.** unvarying in pitch or cadence. —**mo·'not·o·nous·ly** *adv.* —**mo·'not·o·nous·ness** *n.*

mo·not·o·ny (məˈnɒtənɪ) *n., pl.* **·nies. 1.** wearisome routine; dullness. **2.** lack of variety in pitch or cadence.

mon·o·treme (ˈmɒnəʊˌtriːm) *n.* any mammal of the primitive order *Monotremata,* of Australia and New Guinea: egg-laying toothless animals with a single opening (cloaca) for the passage of eggs or sperm, faeces, and urine. The group contains only the echidnas and the platypus. [C19: via New Latin from MONO- + Greek *trēma* hole] —**mon·o·tre·ma·tous** (ˌmɒnəʊˈtriːmətəs) *adj.*

mo·no·tri·chous (mɒˈnɒtrɪkəs) *or* **mon·o·trich·ic** (ˌmɒnəʊˈtrɪkɪk) *adj.* (of bacteria) having a single flagellum.

mon·o·type (ˈmɒnəˌtaɪp) *n.* **1.** a single print made from a metal or glass plate on which a picture has been painted. **2.** *Biology.* a monotypic genus or species.

Mon·o·type (ˈmɒnəˌtaɪp) *n.* **1.** *Trademark.* a typesetting machine, operated by a keyboard, in which each character is cast individually from hot metal. **2.** type produced on such a machine.

mon·o·typ·ic (ˌmɒnəʊˈtɪpɪk) *adj.* **1.** (of a genus or species) consisting of only one type of animal or plant. **2.** of or relating to a monotype.

mon·o·va·lent (ˌmɒnəʊˈveɪlənt) *adj. Chem.* Also: **univalent. a.** having a valency of one. **b.** having only one valency. —ˌ**mon·o·'va·lence** *or* ˌ**mon·o·'va·len·cy** *n.*

mon·ox·ide (mɒˈnɒksaɪd) *n.* an oxide that contains one oxygen atom per molecule: *carbon monoxide, CO.*

Mon·roe (mənˈrəʊ) *n.* **1. James.** 1758–1831, U.S. statesman; fifth president of U.S. (1817–25). He promulgated the Monroe Doctrine (1823). **2. Mar·i·lyn,** original name *Norma Jean Mortenson.* 1926–62, U.S. film actress.

Mon·roe doc·trine *n.* a principle of U.S. foreign policy that opposes the influence or interference of outside powers in the Americas.

Mon·ro·vi·a (mɒnˈrəʊvɪə) *n.* the capital and chief port of Liberia, on the Atlantic: founded in 1822 as a home for freed American slaves; University of Liberia (1862). Pop.: 100 000 (1972 est.).

Mons (*French* mɔ̃ːs) *n.* a town in SW Belgium, capital of Hainaut province: scene of the first battle (1914) of the British Expeditionary Force during World War I. Pop.: 59 956 (1970).

Mon·sei·gneur *French.* (mɔ̃sɛˈɲœːr) *n., pl.* ***Mes·sei·gneurs.*** a title given to French bishops, prelates, and princes. Abbrev.: **Mgr.** [literally: my lord]

mon·sieur (*French* məˈsjø; *English* məsˈjɜː) *n., pl.* **mes·sieurs** (*French* meːˈsjø; *English* ˈmesəz). a French title of address equivalent to *sir* when used alone or *Mr.* when placed before a name. [literally: my lord]

Mon·sig·nor (mɒnˈsiːnjə; *Italian* ˌmonsiɲˈɲoːr) *n., pl.* **·nors** *or* **·nor·i** (*Italian* -ˈɲoːri). *R.C. Church.* an ecclesiastical title attached to certain offices or distinctions usually bestowed by the Pope. ~Abbrev.: **Mgr., Msgr.** [C17: from Italian, from French MONSEIGNEUR]

mon·soon (mɒnˈsuːn) *n.* **1.** a seasonal wind of S Asia that blows from the southwest in summer, bringing heavy rains, and from the northeast in winter. **2.** the rainy season when the SW monsoon blows, from about April to October. **3.** any wind that changes direction with the seasons. [C16: from obsolete Dutch *monssoen,* from Portuguese *monção,* from Arabic *mawsim* season] —**mon·'soon·al** *adj.*

mons pu·bis (ˈmɒnz ˈpjuːbɪs) *n., pl.* **mon·tes pu·bis** (ˈmɒntiːz). the fatty cushion of flesh in human females situated over the junction of the pubic bones. Also called: **mons veneris.** [C17: New Latin: hill of the pubes]

mon·ster (ˈmɒnstə) *n.* **1.** an imaginary beast, such as a centaur, usually made up of various animal or human parts. **2.** a person, animal, or plant with a marked structural deformity. **3.** a cruel, wicked, or inhuman person. **4. a.** a very large person, animal, or thing. **b.** (*as modifier*): *a monster cake.* [C13: from Old French *monstre,* from Latin *monstrum* portent, from *monēre* to warn]

mon·strance (ˈmɒnstrəns) *n. R.C. Church.* a receptacle, usually of gold or silver, with a transparent container in which the consecrated Host is exposed for adoration. [C16: from Medieval Latin *mōnstrantia,* from Latin *mōnstrāre* to show]

mon·stros·i·ty (mɒnˈstrɒsɪtɪ) *n., pl.* **·ties. 1.** an outrageous or ugly person or thing; monster. **2.** the state or quality of being monstrous.

mon·strous (ˈmɒnstrəs) *adj.* **1.** abnormal, hideous, or unnatural in size, character, etc. **2.** (of plants and animals) abnormal in structure. **3.** outrageous, atrocious, or shocking: *it is monstrous how badly he has been treated.* **4.** huge: *a monstrous audience.* **5.** of, relating to, or resembling a monster. —**'mon·strous·ly** *adv.* —**'mon·strous·ness** *n.*

mons ven·er·is (ˈmɒnz ˈvɛnərɪs) *n., pl.* **mon·tes ven·er·is** (ˈmɒntiːz). another name for **mons pubis.** [C17: New Latin: hill of Venus]

Mont. *abbrev. for* Montana.

mon·tage (mɒnˈtɑːʒ; *French* mɔ̃ˈtaːʒ) *n.* **1.** the art or process of composing pictures by the superimposition or juxtaposition of miscellaneous elements, such as other pictures or photographs. **2.** such a composition. **3.** a method of film editing involving the juxtaposition or partial superimposition of several shots to form a single image. **4.** a rapidly cut film sequence of this kind. [C20: from French, from *monter* to MOUNT¹]

Mon·ta·gnard (ˌmɒntənˈjɑːd, -ˈjɑː) *n., pl.* **·gnards** *or* **·gnard. 1.** a member of a hill people living on the border between Vietnam, Laos, and NE Cambodia. **2.** a member of a North American Indian people living in the N Rocky Mountains. [C19: from French: mountaineer, from *montagne* MOUNTAIN]

Mon·ta·gu (ˈmɒntəˌgjuː) *n.* **1. Charles.** See (Earl of) **Halifax. 2.** Lady **Mar·y Wort·ley.** 1689–1762, English writer, noted for her *Letters from the East* (1763).

Mon·ta·gu's har·ri·er *n.* a brownish European bird of prey, *Circus pygargus,* with long narrow wings and a long tail:

family *Accipitridae* (hawks, harriers, etc.). [C19: named after Col. George *Montagu* (1751–1815), British naturalist]

Mon·taigne (*French* mɔ̃'tɛɲ) *n.* **Mi·chel Ey·quem de** (mi'ʃɛl i'kɛm də). 1533–92, French writer. His life's work, the *Essays* (begun in 1571), established the essay as a literary genre and record the evolution of his moral ideas.

Mon·ta·le (*Italian* mon'ta:le) *n.* **Eu·gen·io** (eu'dʒɛ:njo). 1896–1981, Italian poet: Nobel prize for literature 1975.

Mon·tan·a (mɒn'tænə) *n.* a state of the western U.S.: consists of the Great Plains in the east and the Rocky Mountains in the west. Capital: Helena. Pop.: 694 409 (1970). Area: 377 070 sq. km (145 587 sq. miles). Abbrevs.: **Mont.** or (with zip code) **MT** —**Mon·'tan·an** *adj., n.*

mon·tane ('mɒnteɪn) *adj.* of or inhabiting mountainous regions: *a montane flora.* [C19: from Latin *montānus,* from *mons* MOUNTAIN]

mon·tan wax ('mɒntæn) *n.* a hard wax obtained from lignite and peat, varying in colour from white to dark brown. It is used in polishes and candles. [C20: from Latin *montānus* of a mountain]

Mon·tau·ban (*French* mɔ̃to'bɑ̃) *n.* a city in SW France: a Huguenot stronghold in the 16th and 17th centuries, taken by Richelieu in 1629. Pop.: 50 420 (1975).

Mont·bé·liard (*French* mɔ̃be'lja:r) *n.* an industrial town in E France: former capital of the duchy of Burgundy. Pop.: 31 591 (1975).

Mont Blanc (*French* mɔ̃ 'blɑ̃) *n.* a massif in SW Europe, mainly between France and Italy: the highest mountain in the Alps; beneath it is **Mont Blanc Tunnel,** 12 km (7.5 miles) long. Highest peak (in France): 4807 m (15 772 ft.). Italian name: **Mon·te Bian·co** ('monte 'bjaŋko).

mont·bre·tia (mɒn'bri:ʃə) *n.* any plant of the African iridaceous genus *Montbretia,* with ornamental orange flowers. [C19: New Latin, named after A. F. E. Coquebert de *Montbret* (1780–1801), French botanist]

Mont·calm (mɒnt'kɑ:m; *French* mɔ̃'kalm) *n.* **Louis Jo·seph** (lwi ʒo'zɛf), Marquis de Montcalm de Saint-Véran. 1712–59, French general in Canada (1756); killed in Quebec by British forces under General Wolfe.

Mont Ce·nis (*French* mɔ̃ sə'ni) *n.* See (Mont) **Cenis.**

Mont Cer·vin (mɔ̃ sɛr'vɛ̃) *n.* the French name for the **Matterhorn.**

mont-de-pié·té *French.* (mɔ̃ də pje'te) *n., pl.* ***monts-de-pié·té*** (mɔ̃ də pje'te). (formerly) a public pawnshop. [from Italian *monte di pietà* bank of pity]

mon·te ('mɒntɪ) *n.* **1.** a gambling card game of Spanish origin. **2.** *Austral. informal.* a certainty. [C19: from Spanish: mountain, hence pile of cards]

Mon·te Car·lo ('mɒntɪ 'kɑ:ləʊ; *French* mɔ̃te kar'lo) *n.* a town and resort forming part of the principality of Monaco, on the Riviera: famous casino and the destination of an annual car rally (the **Monte Carlo Rally**). Pop.: 9948 (1968).

Mon·te Car·lo meth·od *n.* a mathematical technique for determining the probability of a given process by constructing a model and using empirical techniques of simulation, and sampling. [C20: named after the casino at Monte Carlo, where systems for winning at roulette, etc., are often tried]

Mon·te Cas·si·no ('mɒntɪ kə'si:nəʊ; *Italian* 'monte kas'si:no) *n.* a hill above Cassino in central Italy: site of Benedictine monastery (530 A.D.) destroyed in 1944 during fighting between the Allies and the Axis powers.

Mon·te Cor·no (*Italian* 'monte 'korno) *n.* See **Corno.**

Mon·te·fio·re (ˌmɒntɪfɪ'ɔ:rɪ) *n.* **Hugh (William).** born 1920, English Anglican prelate; suffragan bishop of Kingston-upon-Thames (1970–77) and bishop of Birmingham since 1977.

Mon·te·go Bay (mɒn'ti:gəʊ) *n.* a port and resort in NW Jamaica: the second largest town on the island. Pop.: 42 800 (1971 est.).

mon·teith (mɒn'ti:θ) *n.* a large ornamental bowl, usually of silver, for cooling wineglasses, which are suspended from the notched rim. [C17: said to be from the name of a Scot who wore a cloak with a scalloped edge]

Mon·te·ne·gro (ˌmɒntɪ'ni:grəʊ) *n.* a constituent republic of Yugoslavia, bordering on the Adriatic: declared a kingdom in 1910 and united with Serbia, Croatia, and other territories in 1918 to form Yugoslavia. Capital: Titograd. Pop.: 529 604 (1971). Area: 13 812 sq. km (5387 sq. miles). —ˌ**Mon·te·'ne·grin** *adj., n.*

Mon·te·rey (ˌmɒntə'reɪ) *n.* a city in W California: capital of Spain's Pacific empire from 1774 to 1825; taken by the U.S. (1846). Pop.: 26 302 (1970).

mon·te·ro (mɒn'tɛərəʊ; *Spanish* mon'tero) *n., pl.* **·ros** (-rəʊz; *Spanish* -ros). a round cap with a flap at the back worn by hunters, esp. in Spain in the 17th and 18th centuries. [C17: from Spanish, literally: mountaineer]

Mon·ter·rey (ˌmɒntə'reɪ; *Spanish* ˌmonte'rrej) *n.* a city in NE Mexico, capital of Nuevo Léon state: the third largest city in Mexico; a major industrial centre, esp. for metals. Pop.: 1 049 957 (1975 est.).

Mon·tes·pan (*French* mɔ̃tɛs'pɑ̃) *n.* **Mar·quise de,** title of *Françoise Athénaïs de Rochechouart.* 1641–1707, French noblewoman; mistress of Louis XIV of France.

Mon·tes·quieu (*French* mɔ̃tɛs'kjø) *n.* **Ba·ron de la Brède et de** (bɑ'rɔ̃ də la 'brɛd e də), title of *Charles Louis de Secondat.* 1689–1755, French political philosopher. His chief works are the satirical *Lettres persanes* (1721) and *L'Esprit des lois* (1748), a comparative analysis of various forms of government, which had a profound influence on political thought in Europe and the U.S.

Mon·tes·so·ri (ˌmɒntɪ'sɔ:rɪ; *Italian* ˌmontes'sɔ:ri) *n.* **Ma·ri·a** (ma'ri:a). 1870–1952, Italian educational reformer, who evolved the Montessori method of teaching children.

Mon·tes·so·ri meth·od *n.* a method of nursery education in which children are provided with generous facilities for practical play and allowed to develop at their own pace.

Mon·teux (*French* mɔ̃'tø) *n.* **Pierre** (pjɛ:r). 1875–1964, U.S. conductor, born in France.

Mon·te·ver·di (ˌmɒntɪ'vɛədɪ) *n.* **Clau·dio** ('klaʊdɪˌəʊ). ?1567–1643, Italian composer, noted esp. for his innovations in opera and for his expressive use of dissonance. His operas include *Orfeo* (1607) and *L'Incoronazione di Poppea* (1642) and he also wrote many motets and madrigals.

Mon·te·vi·de·o (ˌmɒntɪvɪ'deɪəʊ; *Spanish* ˌmonteβi'ðeo) *n.* the capital and chief port of Uruguay, in the south on the Río de la Plata estuary: the largest city in the country: University of the Republic (1849); resort. Pop.: 1 229 748 (1975).

Mon·te·zu·ma II (ˌmɒntɪ'zu:mə) *n.* 1466–1520, Aztec emperor of Mexico (?1502–20). He was overthrown and killed by the Spanish conquistador Cortés.

Mont·fort ('mɒntfət) *n.* **Si·mon de,** Earl of Leicester. ?1208–65, English soldier, born in Normandy. He led the baronial rebellion against Henry III and ruled England from 1264 to 1265; he was killed at Evesham.

mont·gol·fier (mɒnt'gɒlfɪə; *French* mɔ̃gɒl'fje) *n.* a hot-air balloon. [C18: see MONTGOLFIER]

Mont·gol·fier (*French* mɔ̃gɔl'fje) *n.* **Jacques É·tienne** (ʒɑ:k e'tjɛn), 1745–99, and his brother **Jo·seph Mi·chel** (ʒozɛf mi'ʃɛl), 1740–1810, French inventors, who built (1782) and ascended in (1783) the first practical hot-air balloon.

Mont·gom·er·y[1] (mənt'gʌmərɪ) *n.* a city in central Alabama, on the Alabama River: state capital; capital of the Confederacy (1861–65). Pop.: 153 013 (1973 est.).

Mont·gom·er·y[2] (mənt'gʌmərɪ) *n.* **Ber·nard Law,** 1st Viscount Montgomery of Alamein. 1887–1976, British field marshal. As commander of the 8th Army in North Africa, he launched the offensive, beginning with the victory at El Alamein (1942), that drove Rommel's forces back to Tunis. He also commanded the ground forces in the invasion of Normandy (1944).

Mont·gom·er·y·shire (mənt'gʌmərɪˌʃɪə, -ʃə) *n.* (until 1974) a county of central Wales, now part of Powys.

month (mʌnθ) *n.* **1.** one of the twelve divisions (**calendar months**) of the calendar year. **2.** a period of time extending from one date to a corresponding date in the next calendar month. **3.** a period of four weeks or of 30 days. **4.** the period of time (**solar month**) taken by the moon to return to the same longitude after one complete revolution around the earth; 27.321 58 days (approximately 27 days, 7 hours, 43 minutes, 4.5 seconds). **5.** the period of time (**sidereal month**) taken by the moon to make one complete revolution around the earth, measured between two successive conjunctions with a particular star; 27.321 66 days (approximately 27 days, 7 hours, 43 minutes, 11 seconds). **6.** Also called: **lunation.** the period of time (**lunar** or **synodic month**) taken by the moon to make one complete revolution around the earth, measured between two successive new moons; 29.530 59 days (approximately 29 days, 12 hours, 44 minutes, 3 seconds). **7. a month of Sundays.** *Informal.* an extremely long unspecified period of time. [Old English *mōnath;* related to Old High German *mānōd,* Old Norse *mānathr;* compare Gothic *mena* moon]

Mon·ther·lant (*French* mɔ̃tɛr'lɑ̃) *n.* **Hen·ri (Millon) de** (ɑ̃'ri də). 1896–1972, French novelist and dramatist: his novels include *Les Jeunes Filles* (1935–39) and *Le Chaos et la nuit* (1963).

month·ly ('mʌnθlɪ) *adj.* **1.** occurring, done, appearing, payable, etc., once every month. **2.** lasting or valid for a month: *a monthly subscription.* ~*adv.* **3.** once a month. ~*n., pl.* **·lies. 4.** a book, periodical, magazine, etc., published once a month. **5.** *Informal.* a menstrual period.

month's mind *n. R.C. Church.* a Mass celebrated in remembrance of a person one month after his death.

mon·ti·cule ('mɒntɪˌkju:l) *n.* a small hill or mound, such as a secondary volcanic cone. [C18: via French from Late Latin *monticulus,* diminutive of Latin *mons* mountain]

Mont·lu·çon (*French* mɔ̃ly'sɔ̃) *n.* an industrial city in central France, on the Cher River. Pop.: 58 824 (1975).

Mont·mar·tre (*French* mɔ̃'martr) *n.* a district of N Paris, on a hill above the Seine: the highest point in the city; famous for its associations with many artists.

Mont·par·nasse (*French* mɔ̃par'nas) *n.* a district of S Paris, on the left bank of the Seine: noted for its cafés, frequented by artists, writers, and students.

Mont·pel·ier (mɒnt'pi:ljə) *n.* a city in N central Vermont, on the Winooski River: the state capital. Pop.: 8609 (1970).

Mont·pel·lier (*French* mɔ̃pə'lje) *n.* a city in S France, the chief town of Languedoc: its university was founded by Pope Nicholas IV in 1289; wine trade. Pop.: 195 603 (1975).

Mon·tre·al (ˌmɒntrɪ'ɔ:l) *n.* a port in central Canada, in S Quebec on **Montreal Island** at the junction of the Ottawa and St. Lawrence Rivers: the country's largest city and a major port. Pop.: 1 080 546 (1976 est.). French name: **Mont·ré·al** (mɔ̃re'al).

Mon·treuil (*French* mɔ̃'trœj) *n.* an E suburb of Paris: formerly famous for peaches, but now increasingly industrialized. Pop.: 96 684 (1975).

Mon·treux (*French* mɔ̃'trø) *n.* a town and resort in W Switzerland, in Vaud canton on Lake Geneva. Pop.: 20 421 (1970).

Mont·rose (mɒn'trəʊz) *n.* **James Gra·ham,** 1st Marquess and 5th Earl of Montrose. 1612–50, Scottish general, noted for his victories in Scotland for Charles I in the Civil War. He was later captured and hanged.

Mont-Saint-Mi·chel (*French* mɔ̃ sɛ̃ mi'ʃɛl) *n.* a rocky islet off the coast of NW France, accessible at low tide by a causeway, in the **Bay of St. Michel** (an inlet of the Gulf of St. Malo): Benedictine abbey (966), used as a prison from the Revolution until 1863; reoccupied by Benedictine monks since 1966. Area: 1 hectare (3 acres).

Mont+ser+rat *n.* **1.** (ˌmɒntsə'ræt). a volcanic island in the Caribbean, in the Leeward Islands of the West Indies. Capital: Plymouth. Pop.: 13 076 (1970 est.). Area: 103 sq. km (40 sq. miles). **2.** (*Spanish* ˌmonse'rrat). a mountain in NE Spain, northwest of Barcelona: famous Benedictine monastery. Height: 1216 m (4054 ft.). Ancient name: **Mons Serratus.**

mon·u+ment ('mɒnjʊmənt) *n.* **1.** an obelisk, statue, building, etc., erected in commemoration of a person or event or in celebration of something. **2.** a notable building or site, esp. one preserved as public property. **3.** a tomb or tombstone. **4.** a literary or artistic work regarded as commemorative of its creator or a particular period. **5.** *U.S.* a boundary marker. **6.** an exceptional example: *his lecture was a monument of tedium.* **7.** an obsolete word for **statue.** [C13: from Latin *monumentum,* from *monēre* to remind, advise]

mon·u+men+tal (ˌmɒnjʊ'mɛntᵊl) *adj.* **1.** like a monument, esp. in large size, endurance, or importance: *a monumental work of art.* **2.** of, relating to, or being a monument. **3.** *Informal.* (intensifier): *monumental stupidity.* —ˌ**mon·u+men+'tal+i·ty** *n.* —ˌ**mon·u+'men+tal+ly** *adv.*

Mon+za (*Italian* 'montsa) *n.* a city in N Italy, northeast of Milan: the ancient capital of Lombardy; scene of the assassination of King Umberto I in 1900; motor-racing circuit. Pop.: 119 405 (1975 est.).

mon+zo+nite ('mɒnzəˌnaɪt) *n.* a coarse-grained plutonic igneous rock consisting of equal amounts of plagioclase and orthoclase feldspar, with ferromagnesian minerals. [C19: from German, named after *Monzoni,* Tyrolean mountain where it was found] —**mon+zo+nit+ic** (ˌmɒnzə'nɪtɪk) *adj.*

moo (muː) *vb.* **1.** (*intr.*) (of a cow, bull, etc.) to make a characteristic deep long sound; low. ~*interj.* **2.** an instance or imitation of this sound.

mooch (muːtʃ) *vb. Slang.* **1.** (*intr.*) to loiter or walk aimlessly. **2.** (*intr.*) to behave in an apathetic way. **3.** (*intr.*) to sneak or lurk; skulk. **4.** (*tr.*) *Chiefly U.S.* **a.** to cadge. **b.** to steal. [C17: perhaps from Old French *muchier* to skulk] —'**mooch+er** *n.*

mood[1] (muːd) *n.* **1.** a temporary state of mind or temper: *a cheerful mood.* **2.** a sullen or gloomy state of mind, esp. when temporary: *she's in a mood.* **3. in the mood.** in a favourable state of mind (for something or to do something). [Old English *mōd* mind, feeling; compare Old Norse *mōthr* grief, wrath]

mood[2] (muːd) *n.* **1.** *Grammar.* a category of the verb or verbal inflections that expresses semantic and grammatical differences, including such forms as the indicative, subjunctive, and imperative. **2.** *Logic.* one of several forms of a syllogism classified by whether the constituent statements are affirmative, negative, universal, or particular. ~Also called: **mode.** [C16: from MOOD[1], influenced in meaning by MODE]

mood·y ('muːdɪ) *adj.* **mood·i+er, mood·i+est. 1.** sullen, sulky, or gloomy. **2.** temperamental or changeable. —'**mood·i+ly** *adv.* —'**mood·i+ness** *n.*

Moo·dy ('muːdɪ) *n.* **Dwight Ly·man.** 1837–99, U.S. evangelist and hymnodist, noted for his revivalist campaigns in Britain and the U.S. with I. D. Sankey.

Moog syn+the+siz+er (muːg, məʊg) *n. Music, trademark.* an electrophonic instrument operated by means of a keyboard and pedals, in which sounds are produced by a bank of sine-wave and square-wave generators selected and combined by means of patching as in a telephone exchange. Often shortened to **synthesizer** or **Moog.** [C20: named after Robert *Moog* (born 1934), American engineer]

moo+lah ('muːlɑː) *n.* a slang name for **money.**

mool+vie *or* **mool+vi** ('muːlviː) *n.* (esp. in India) a Muslim doctor of the law, teacher, or learned man: also used as a title of respect. [C17: from Urdu, from Arabic *mawlawīy;* compare MULLAH]

moon (muːn) *n.* **1.** the natural satellite of the earth. Diameter: 3476 km; mass: 7.4 x 10^{22} kg; mean distance from earth: 384 400 km; periods of rotation and revolution: 27.32 days. **2.** the face of the moon as it is seen during its revolution around the earth, esp. at one of its phases: *new moon; full moon.* **3.** any natural satellite of a planet. **4.** moonlight; moonshine. **5.** something resembling a moon. **6.** a month, esp. a lunar one. **7. once in a blue moon.** very seldom. **8. reach for the moon.** to desire or attempt something unattainable or difficult to obtain. ~*vb.* **9.** (when *tr.,* often foll. by *away;* when *intr.,* often foll. by *around*) to be idle in a listless way, as if in love, or to idle (time) away. [Old English *mōna;* compare Old Frisian *mōna,* Old High German *māno*] —'**moon+less** *adj.*

moon+beam ('muːnˌbiːm) *n.* a ray of moonlight.

moon blind+ness *n.* **1.** *Ophthalmol.* a nontechnical name for **nyctalopia. 2.** Also called: **mooneye.** *Vet. science.* a disorder affecting horses, inflammation of the eyes and sometimes blindness. —'**moon-**ˌ**blind** *adj.*

moon+calf ('muːnˌkɑːf) *n., pl.* **+calves. 1.** a born fool; dolt. **2.** a person who idles time away. **3.** *Obsolete.* a freak or monster.

Moon Child *n.* a euphemistic name for **Cancer** (sense 2b.).

mooned (muːnd) *adj.* decorated with a moon.

moon+eye ('muːnˌaɪ) *n.* **1.** any of several North American large-eyed freshwater clupeoid fishes of the family *Hiodontidae,* esp. *Hiodon tergisus.* See also **goldeye. 2.** *Vet. science.* another name for **moon blindness.**

moon-eyed *adj.* **1.** having the eyes open wide, as in awe. **2.** *Vet. science.* affected with moon blindness.

moon-faced *adj.* having a round face; full-faced.

moon+fish ('muːnˌfɪʃ) *n., pl.* **+fish·es** *or* **+fish. 1.** any of several deep-bodied silvery carangid fishes, occurring in warm and tropical American coastal waters. **2.** any of various other round silvery fishes, such as the Indo-Pacific *Monodactylus argenteus.* **3.** another name for **opah.**

moon+flow·er ('muːnˌflaʊə) *n.* **1.** any of several night-blooming convolvulaceous plants, esp. the white-flowered *Calonyction* (or *Ipomoea*) *aculeatum.* **2.** Also called: **angels' tears.** a Mexican solanaceous plant, *Datura suaveolens,* planted in the tropics for its white night-blooming flowers.

moon+light ('muːnˌlaɪt) *n.* **1.** Also called: **moonshine.** light from the sun received on earth after reflection by the moon. 2. (*modifier*) illuminated by the moon: *a moonlight walk.* ~*vb.* **+lights, +light+ing. +light+ed. 3.** (*intr.*) *Informal.* to work at a secondary job, esp. at night. —'**moon+**ˌ**light·er** *n.*

moon+light flit *n.* a hurried departure by night to escape from one's creditors.

moon+light+ing ('muːnˌlaɪtɪŋ) *n.* (in 19th-century Ireland) the carrying out of cattle-maiming, murders, etc., during the night in protest against the land-tenure system.

moon+lit ('muːnlɪt) *adj.* illuminated by the moon.

moon+quake ('muːnˌkweɪk) *n.* a light tremor of the moon, detected on the moon's surface.

moon+rak·er ('muːnˌreɪkə) *n. Nautical.* a small square sail set above a skysail.

moon rat *n.* a ratlike SE Asian nocturnal mammal, *Echinosorex gymnurus,* with greyish fur and an elongated snout: family *Erinaceidae* (hedgehogs): the largest living insectivore.

moon+rise ('muːnˌraɪz) *n.* the moment when the moon appears above the horizon.

moon+scape ('muːnˌskeɪp) *n.* the general surface of the moon or a representation of it.

moon+seed ('muːnˌsiːd) *n.* any menispermaceous climbing plant of the genus *Menispermum* and related genera, having red or black fruits with crescent-shaped or ring-shaped seeds.

moon+set ('muːnˌsɛt) *n.* the moment when the moon disappears below the horizon.

moon+shine ('muːnˌʃaɪn) *n.* **1.** another word for **moonlight** (sense 1). **2.** *U.S.* illegally distilled or smuggled whisky or other spirit. **3.** foolish talk or thought.

moon+shin·er ('muːnˌʃaɪnə) *n. U.S.* a person who illegally makes or smuggles distilled spirits.

moon+shot ('muːnˌʃɒt) *n.* the launching of a spacecraft, rocket, etc., to the moon.

moon+stone ('muːnˌstəʊn) *n.* a gem variety of orthoclase or albite that is white and translucent with bluish reflections.

moon+struck ('muːnˌstrʌk) *or* **moon+strick·en** ('muːnˌstrɪkən) *adj.* deranged or mad.

moon+wort ('muːnˌwɜːt) *n.* **1.** Also called in U.S.: **grape fern.** any of various ferns of the genus *Botrychium,* esp. *B. lunaria,* which has crescent-shaped leaflets. **2.** another name for **honesty.**

moon·y ('muːnɪ) *adj.* **moon·i+er, moon·i+est. 1.** *Informal.* dreamy or listless. **2.** of or like the moon. **3.** *Brit. slang.* crazy or foolish. —'**moon·i+ly** *adv.* —'**moon·i+ness** *n.*

moor[1] (mʊə, mɔː) *n.* a tract of unenclosed waste ground, usually having peaty soil covered with heather, coarse grass, bracken, and moss. [Old English *mōr;* related to Old Saxon *mōr,* Old High German *muor* swamp] —'**moor·y** *adj.*

moor[2] (mʊə, mɔː) *vb.* to secure (a vessel, etc.) with cables, ropes, or anchors, or (of a vessel, etc.) to be secured in this way. [C15: of Germanic origin; related to Old English *mǣrelsrāp* rope for mooring]

Moor (mʊə, mɔː) *n.* a member of a Muslim people of North Africa, of mixed Arab and Berber descent. In the 8th century they were converted to Islam and established power in North Africa and Spain, where they established a civilization (756–1492).[C14: via Old French from Latin *Maurus,* from Greek *Mauros,* possibly from Berber]

moor+age ('mʊərɪdʒ, 'mɔːrɪdʒ) *n.* **1.** a place for anchoring a vessel. **2.** a charge for anchoring. **3.** the act of anchoring.

moor+cock ('mʊəˌkɒk, 'mɔː-) *n.* the male of the red grouse.

Moore (mʊə, mɔː) *n.* **1. George.** 1852–1933, Irish novelist. His works include *Esther Waters* (1894) and *The Brook Kerith* (1916). **2. G(eorge) E(dward).** 1873–1958, English philosopher, noted esp.for his *Principia Ethica* (1903). **3. Ger·ald.** born 1899, English pianist, noted as an accompanist esp. to *Lieder* singers. **4. Hen·ry.** born 1898, English sculptor. His works are characterized by monumental organic forms and include the *Madonna and Child* (1943) at St. Matthew's Church, Northampton. **5.** Sir **John.** 1761–1809, British general; commander of the British army (1808–09) in the Peninsular War: killed at Corunna. **6. Mar·i·anne.** 1887–1972, U.S. poet. **7. Thom·as.** 1779–1852, Irish poet, best known for *Irish Melodies* (1807–34).

moor+fowl ('mʊəˌfaʊl, 'mɔː-) *n.* (in Brit. game laws) an archaic name for **red grouse.** Compare **heathfowl.**

moor+hen ('mʊəˌhɛn, 'mɔː-) *n.* **1.** a bird, *Gallinula chloropus,* inhabiting ponds, lakes, etc., having a black plumage, red bill, and a red shield above the bill: family *Rallidae* (rails). **2.** the female of the red grouse.

moor+ing ('mʊərɪŋ, 'mɔː-) *n.* **1.** a place for anchoring a vessel. **2.** a permanent anchor, dropped in the water and equipped with a floating buoy, to which vessels can moor.

moor·ing mast *n.* a mast or tower to which a balloon or airship may be moored. Also called: **mooring tower.**
moor·ings ('mʊərɪŋz, 'mɔː-) *pl. n.* **1.** *Nautical.* the ropes, anchors, etc., used in mooring a vessel. **2.** (*sometimes sing.*) something that provides security or stability.
Moor·ish ('mʊərɪʃ, 'mɔː-) *adj.* **1.** of or relating to the Moors. **2.** denoting the style of architecture used in Spain from the 13th to 16th century, characterized by the horseshoe arch. Also: **Morisco.**
Moor·ish i·dol *n.* a tropical marine spiny-finned fish, *Zanclus canescens,* that is common around coral reefs: family *Zanclidae.* It has a deeply compressed body with yellow and black stripes, a beaklike snout, and an elongated dorsal fin.
moor·land ('mʊələnd, 'mɔː-) *n. Brit.* an area of moor.
moor·wort ('mʊəˌwɜːt, 'mɔː-) *n.* another name for **marsh andromeda.**
moose (muːs) *n., pl.* **moose.** a large North American deer, *Alces alces,* having large flattened palmate antlers: also occurs in Europe and Asia where it is called an elk. [C17: from Algonquian; related to Narragansett *moos,* from *moosu* he strips, alluding to the moose's habit of stripping trees]
Moose Jaw *n.* a city in W Canada, in S Saskatchewan. Pop.: 31 854 (1971).
moot (muːt) *adj.* **1.** subject or open to debate: *a moot point.* ~*vb.* (*tr.*) **2.** to suggest or bring up for debate. **3.** to plead or argue theoretical or hypothetical cases, as an academic exercise or as vocational training for law students. ~*n.* **4.** a discussion or debate of a hypothetical case or point, held as an academic activity. **5.** (in Anglo-Saxon England) an assembly, mainly in a shire or hundred, dealing with local legal and administrative affairs. [Old English *gemōt;* compare Old Saxon *mōt,* Middle High German *muoze* meeting] —**'moot·er** *n.*
moot court *n.* a mock court trying hypothetical legal cases.
mop[1] (mɒp) *n.* **1.** an implement with a wooden handle and a head made of twists of cotton or a piece of synthetic sponge, used for polishing or washing floors, or washing dishes. **2.** something resembling this, such as a tangle of hair. ~*vb.* **mops, mop·ping, mopped.** (*tr.*) **3.** (often foll. by *up*) to clean or soak up with or as if with a mop. ~See also **mop up.** [C15 *mappe,* from earlier *mappel,* from Medieval Latin *mappula* cloth, from Latin *mappa* napkin]
mop[2] (mɒp) *Rare.* ~*vb.* **mops, mop·ping, mopped. 1.** (*intr.*) to make a grimace or sad expression (esp. in the phrase **mop and mow**). —*n.* **2.** such a face or expression. [C16: perhaps from Dutch *moppen* to pour; compare Dutch *mop* pug dog]
mop·board ('mɒpˌbɔːd) *n.* a U.S. word for **skirting board.**
mope (məʊp) *vb.* (*intr.*) **1.** to be gloomy or apathetic. **2.** to move or act in an aimless way. ~*n.* **3.** a gloomy person. [C16: perhaps from obsolete *mope* fool and related to MOP[2]] —**'mop·er** *n.* —**'mop·ing·ly** *adv.*
mo·ped ('məʊpɛd) *n. Brit.* a light motorcycle often fitted with auxiliary pedals. [C20: from MOTOR + PEDAL]
mopes (məʊps) *pl. n.* **the.** low spirits.
mo·poke ('məʊˌpəʊk) *n.* **1.** a small spotted owl, *Ninox novaezeelandiae,* of Australia and New Zealand. **2.** (in Australia) a frogmouth, *Podargus strigoides,* with reddish-brown or grey plumage. ~Also called: **morepork.** [C19: imitative of the bird's cry]
mop·pet ('mɒpɪt) *n.* a less common word for **poppet** (sense 1). [C17: from obsolete *mop* rag doll; of obscure origin]
mop up *vb.* (*tr., adv.*) **1.** to clean with a mop. **2.** *Informal.* to complete (a task, etc.). **3.** *Military.* to clear (remaining enemy forces) after a battle, as by killing, taking prisoner, etc. ~*n.* **mop-up. 4.** the act or an instance of mopping up.
mo·quette (mɒ'kɛt) *n.* a thick velvety fabric used for carpets, upholstery, etc. [C18: from French; of uncertain origin]
mor (mɔː) *n.* a layer of acidic humus formed in cool moist areas where decomposition is slow. [Danish]
mor. *Bookbinding. abbrev. for* morocco.
Mor. *abbrev. for* Morocco.
mo·ra ('mɔːrə) *n., pl.* **·rae** (-riː) *or* **·ras.** *Prosody.* the quantity of a short syllable in verse represented by the breve (˘). [C16: from Latin: pause]
mo·ra·ceous (mɔː'reɪʃəs) *adj.* of, relating to, or belonging to the *Moraceae,* a mostly tropical and subtropical family of trees and shrubs, including fig, mulberry, breadfruit, and hop, many of which have latex in the stems and heads enclosed in a fleshy receptacle. [C20: via New Latin from Latin *morus* mulberry tree]
Mo·ra·da·bad (ˌmɔːrədə'bæd) *n.* a city in N India, in N Uttar Pradesh. Pop.: 258 590 (1971).
mo·raine (mɒ'reɪn) *n.* a mass of debris, carried by glaciers and forming ridges and mounds when deposited. [C18: from French, from Savoy dialect *morena,* of obscure origin] —**mo·'rain·al** *or* **mo·'rain·ic** *adj.*
mor·al ('mɒrəl) *adj.* **1.** concerned with or relating to human behaviour, esp. the distinction between good and bad or right and wrong behaviour: *moral sense.* **2.** adhering to conventionally accepted standards of conduct. **3.** based on a sense of right and wrong according to conscience: *moral courage; moral law.* **4.** having psychological rather than tangible effects: *moral support; a moral defeat.* **5.** *Law.* (of evidence, etc.) based on a knowledge of the tendencies of human nature. ~*n.* **6.** the lesson to be obtained from a fable or event: *point the moral.* **7.** a concise truth; maxim. **8.** (*pl.*) principles of behaviour in accordance with standards of right and wrong. [C14: from Latin *mōrālis* relating to morals or customs, from *mōs* custom] —**'mor·al·ly** *adv.*
mo·rale (mɒ'rɑːl) *n.* the degree of mental or moral confidence of a person or group; spirit of optimism. [C18: morals, from French, n. use of MORAL (adj.)]
mor·al haz·ard *n. Insurance.* a risk incurred by an insurance company with respect to the possible lack of honesty or prudence among policyholders.
mor·al·ism ('mɒrəˌlɪzəm) *n.* **1.** the habit or practice of moralizing. **2.** a moral saying. **3.** the practice of moral principles without reference to religion.
mor·al·ist ('mɒrəlɪst) *n.* **1.** a person who seeks to regulate the morals of others or to imbue others with a sense of morality. **2.** a person who lives in accordance with moral principles. —ˌ**mor·al·'is·tic** *adj.* —ˌ**mor·al·'is·ti·cal·ly** *adv.*
mo·ral·i·ty (mə'rælɪtɪ) *n., pl.* **·ties. 1.** the quality of being moral. **2.** conformity to conventional standards of moral conduct. **3.** a system of moral principles. **4.** an instruction or lesson in morals. **5.** short for **morality play.**
mo·ral·i·ty play *n.* a type of drama written between the 14th and 16th centuries concerned with the conflict between personified virtues and vices.
mor·al·ize *or* **mor·al·ise** ('mɒrəˌlaɪz) *vb.* **1.** (*intr.*) to make moral pronouncements. **2.** (*tr.*) to interpret or explain in a moral sense. **3.** (*tr.*) to improve the morals of. —ˌ**mor·al·i·'za·tion** *or* ˌ**mor·al·i·'sa·tion** *n.* —**'mor·al·ˌiz·er** *or* **'mor·al·ˌis·er** *n.* —**'mor·al·ˌiz·ing·ly** *or* **'mor·al·ˌis·ing·ly** *adv.*
mor·al phil·os·o·phy *n.* the branch of philosophy dealing with ethics.
Mor·al Re·ar·ma·ment *n.* a worldwide movement for moral and spiritual renewal founded by Frank Buchman in 1938. Also called: **Buchmanism.** Former name: **Oxford Group.**
mor·al the·ol·o·gy *n.* the branch of theology dealing with ethics.
Mor·ar ('mɔːrə) *n.* **Loch.** a lake in W Scotland, in the SW Highlands: the deepest in Scotland. Length: 18 km (11 miles). Depth: 296 m (987 ft.).
mo·rass (mə'ræs) *n.* **1.** a tract of swampy low-lying land. **2.** a disordered or muddled situation or circumstance, esp. one that impedes progress. [C17: from Dutch *moeras,* ultimately from Old French *marais* MARSH]
mor·a·to·ri·um (ˌmɒrə'tɔːrɪəm) *n., pl.* **·ri·a** (-rɪə) *or* **·ri·ums. 1.** a legally authorized postponement of the fulfilment of an obligation. **2.** an agreed suspension of activity. [C19: New Latin, from Late Latin *morātōrius* dilatory, from *mora* delay] —**mor·a·to·ry** ('mɒrətərɪ, -trɪ) *adj.*
Mo·ra·va (mə'rɑːvə) *n.* **1.** a river in Czechoslovakia, rising in the Sudeten Mountains and flowing south to the Danube: forms part of the border between Czechoslovakia and Austria. Length: 370 km (230 miles). German name: **March. 2.** a river in E Yugoslavia, formed by the confluence of the Southern Morava and the Western Morava near Stalac: flows north to the Danube. Length: 209 km (130 miles). **3.** ('mɔrava). the Czech name for **Moravia.**
Mo·ra·vi·a[1] (mə'reɪvɪə, mɒ-) *n.* a region of central Czechoslovakia, around the Morava River, bounded by the Bohemian-Moravian Highlands, the Sudeten Mountains, and the W Carpathians: became a separate Austrian crownland in 1848; made part of Czechoslovakia in 1918; valuable mineral resources. Czech name: **Morava.** German name: **Mähren.**
Mo·ra·via[2] (*Italian* mo'raːvja) *n.* **Al·ber·to** (al'bɛrto), pen name of *Alberto Pincherle.* born 1907, Italian novelist and short-story writer: his novels include *The Time of Indifference* (1929) and *The Woman of Rome* (1949).
Mo·ra·vi·an (mə'reɪvɪən, mɒ-) *adj.* **1.** of or relating to Moravia, its people, or their dialect of Czech. **2.** of or relating to the Moravian Church. ~*n.* **3.** the Moravian dialect. **4.** a native or inhabitant of Moravia. **5.** a member of the Moravian Church. —**Mo·'ra·vi·an·ism** *n.*
Mo·ra·vi·an Church *n.* a Protestant Church originating in Moravia in 1722 as a revival of the sect of Bohemian Brethren. It has close links with the Lutheran Church.
Mo·ra·vi·an Gate *n.* a low mountain pass linking S Poland and Moravia (Czechoslovakia), between the SE Sudeten Mountains and the W Carpathian Mountains.
mo·ray (mɒ'reɪ) *n., pl.* **·rays.** any voracious marine coastal eel of the family *Muraenidae,* esp. *Muraena helena,* marked with brilliant patterns and colours. [C17: from Portuguese *moréia,* from Latin *mūrēna,* from Greek *muraina*]
Mor·ay ('mʌrɪ) *n.* (until 1975) a county of NE Scotland, now part of Grampian region. Former name: **Elgin.**
Mor·ay Firth *n.* an inlet of the North Sea on the NE coast of Scotland. Length: about 56 km (35 miles).
mor·bid ('mɔːbɪd) *adj.* **1.** having an unusual interest in death or unpleasant events. **2.** gruesome. **3.** relating to or characterized by disease; pathologic: *a morbid growth.* [C17: from Latin *morbidus* sickly, from *morbus* illness] —**'mor·bid·ly** *adv.* —**'mor·bid·ness** *n.*
mor·bid a·nat·o·my *n.* the branch of medical science concerned with the study of the structure of diseased organs and tissues.
mor·bid·i·ty (mɔː'bɪdɪtɪ) *n.* **1.** the state of being morbid. **2.** Also called: **morbidity rate.** the relative incidence of a particular disease in a specific locality.
mor·bif·ic (mɔː'bɪfɪk) *adj.* causing disease; pathogenic. —**mor·'bif·i·cal·ly** *adv.*
Mor·bi·han (*French* mɔrbi'ã) *n.* a department of NW France, in S Brittany. Capital: Vannes. Pop.: 581 348 (1975). Area: 7092 sq. km (2766 sq. miles).
mor·bil·li (mɔː'bɪlaɪ) *n.* a technical name for **measles.** [C17: from Medieval Latin *morbillus* pustule, diminutive of Latin *morbus* illness]

mor·ceau *French.* (mɔr'so) *n., pl.* **·ceaux** (-'so). **1.** a fragment or morsel. **2.** a short composition, esp. a musical one. [C18: from Old French: MORSEL]
mor·cha ('mɔːtʃɑː) *n.* (in India) a hostile demonstration against the government. [Hindi: entrenchment]
mor·da·cious (mɔː'deɪʃəs) *adj.* sarcastic, caustic, or biting. [C17: from Latin *mordax,* from *mordēre* to bite] —**mor·'da·cious·ly** *adv.* —**mor·dac·i·ty** (mɔː'dæsɪtɪ) *or* **mor·'da·cious·ness** *n.*
mor·dant ('mɔːdᵊnt) *adj.* **1.** sarcastic or caustic. **2.** having the properties of a mordant. **3.** pungent. ~*n.* **4.** a substance used before the application of a dye, possessing the ability to fix colours in textiles, leather, etc. See also **lake**² (sense 1). **5.** an acid or other corrosive fluid used to etch lines on a printing plate. ~*vb.* **6.** (*tr.*) to treat (a fabric, yarn, etc.) with a mordant. [C15: from Old French: biting, from *mordre* to bite, from Latin *mordēre*] —**'mor·dan·cy** *n.* —**'mor·dant·ly** *adv.*
Mor·de·ca·i (ˌmɔːdə'kaɪɪ, 'mɔːdəˌkaɪ) *n. Old Testament.* the cousin of Esther who averted a threatened massacre of the Jews (Esther 2–9).
mor·dent ('mɔːdᵊnt) *n. Music.* a melodic ornament consisting of the rapid alternation of a note with a note one degree lower than it. Also called: **lower mordent.** [C19: from German, from Italian *mordente,* from *mordere* to bite]
Mor·dred ('mɔːdrɛd) *n.* a variant spelling of **Modred.**
Mord·vin ('mɔːdvɪn) *n.* **1.** (*pl.* **·vin** *or* **·vins**) a member of a Finnish people of the middle Volga region, living chiefly in the Mordvinian ASSR. **2.** the language of this people, belonging to the Finno-Ugric family.
Mor·dvin·i·an Au·ton·o·mous So·vi·et So·cial·ist Re·pub·lic (mɔː'dvɪnɪən) *n.* an administrative division of the W central Soviet Union, in the middle Volga basin. Capital: Saransk. Pop.: 1 029 562 (1970). Area: 26 200 sq. km (10 110 sq. miles). Also called: **Mor·do·vi·an Au·ton·o·mous So·vi·et So·cial·ist Re·pub·lic** (mɔː'dəʊvɪən).
more (mɔː) *determiner.* **1. a.** the comparative of **much** or **many:** *more joy than you know; more pork sausages.* **b.** (*as pronoun; functioning as sing. or pl.*): *he has more than she does; even more are dying every day.* **2. a.** additional; further: *no more bananas.* **b.** (*as pronoun; functioning as sing. or pl.*): *I can't take any more; more than expected.* **3. more of.** to a greater extent or degree: *we see more of Sue these days; more of a nuisance than it should be.* ~*adv.* **4.** used to form the comparative of some adjectives and adverbs: *a more believable story; more quickly.* **5.** the comparative of **much:** *people listen to the radio more now.* **6.** additionally; again: *I'll look at it once more.* **7. more or less. a.** as an estimate; approximately. **b.** to an unspecified extent or degree: *the party was ruined, more or less.* **8. more so.** to a greater extent or degree. **9. neither more nor less than.** simply. **10. think more of.** to have a higher opinion of. **11. what is more.** moreover. [Old English *māra;* compare Old Saxon, Old High German *mēro,* Gothic *maiza.* See also MOST]
Usage. See at **most.**
More (mɔː) *n.* **1. Han·nah.** 1745–1833, English writer, noted for her religious tracts, esp. *The Shepherd of Salisbury Plain.* **2.** Sir **Thom·as.** 1478–1535, English statesman, humanist, and Roman Catholic Saint; lord chancellor to Henry VIII (1529–32). His opposition to Henry's divorce from Catharine of Aragon and his refusal to recognize the Act of Supremacy resulted in his execution on a charge of treason. In *Utopia* (1516), he set forth his concept of the ideal state. Feast day: July 9.
Mo·re·a (mɔː'rɪə) *n.* the medieval name for the **Peloponnese.**
Mo·reau (*French* mɔ'ro) *n.* **1. Gus·tave** (gys'tav) 1826–98, French symbolist painter. **2. Jeanne** (ʒan). born 1928, French stage and film actress. Her films include *Jules et Jim* (1961), *Les Liaisons Dangereuses* (1960), *Viva Maria* (1965), *The Bride wore Black* (1967), and *Great Catherine* (1968). **3. Jean Vic·tor** (ʒã vik'tɔːr). 1763–1813, French general in the Revolutionary and Napoleonic Wars.
More·cambe ('mɔːkəm) *n.* a port and resort in NW England, in NW Lancashire on **Morecambe Bay** (an inlet of the Irish Sea). Pop. (with Heysham): 41 863 (1971).
mo·reen (mɒ'riːn) *n.* a heavy, usually watered, fabric of wool or wool and cotton, used esp. in furnishing. [C17: perhaps from MOIRE, influenced by VELVETEEN]
more·ish *or* **mor·ish** (ˌmɔːrɪʃ) *adj. Informal.* (of food) causing a desire for more: *these cakes are very moreish.*
mo·rel (mɒ'rɛl) *n.* any edible saprophytic ascomycetous fungus of the genus *Morchella,* in which the mushroom has a pitted cap: order *Pezizales.* [C17: from French *morille,* probably of Germanic origin; compare Old High German *morhila,* diminutive of *morha* carrot]
Mo·re·lia (*Spanish* mo'relja) *n.* a city in central Mexico, capital of Michoacán state: a cultural centre during colonial times; two universities. Pop.: 209 014 (1975 est.). Former name (until 1828): **Valladolid.**
mo·rel·lo (mə'rɛləʊ) *n., pl.* **·los.** a variety of small very dark sour cherry, *Prunus cerasus austera.* [C17: perhaps from Medieval Latin *amārellum* diminutive of Latin *amārus* bitter, but also influenced by Italian *morello* blackish]
Mo·re·los (*Spanish* mo'relos) *n.* an inland state of S central Mexico, on the S slope of the great plateau. Capital: Cuernavaca. Pop.: 616 119 (1970). Area: 4988 sq. km (1926 sq. miles).
more·o·ver (mɔː'rəʊvə) *sentence connector.* in addition to what has already been said; furthermore.
more·pork ('mɔːˌpɔːk) *n.* another name for **mopoke.**
mo·res ('mɔːreɪz) *pl. n. Sociol.* the customs and conventions embodying the fundamental values of a group or society. [C20: from Latin, plural of *mōs* custom]
Mo·res·co (mə'rɛskəʊ) *n., adj.* a variant spelling of **Morisco.**
Mo·resque (mɔː'rɛsk) *adj.* **1.** (esp. of decoration and architecture) of Moorish style. ~*n.* **2. a.** Moorish design or decoration. **b.** a specimen of this. [C17: from French, from Italian *moresco,* from *Moro* MOOR]
More·ton Bay fig *n.* a large Australian fig tree, *Ficus macrophilla,* having glossy leaves and smooth bark. [named after *Moreton Bay,* Queensland, Australia]
Mor·gan¹ ('mɔːgən) *n.* an American breed of small compact saddle horse. [C19: named after Justin *Morgan,* (1747–98), American owner of the original sire]
Mor·gan² ('mɔːgən) *n.* **1.** Sir **Hen·ry.** 1635–88, Welsh buccaneer, who raided Spanish colonies in the West Indies for the English. **2. John Pier·pont.** 1837–1913, U.S. financier, philanthropist, and art collector. **3. Thom·as Hunt.** 1866–1945, U.S. biologist. He formulated the chromosome theory of heredity. Nobel prize for medicine 1933.
mor·ga·nat·ic (ˌmɔːgə'nætɪk) *adj.* of or designating a marriage between a person of high rank and a person of low rank, by which the latter is not elevated to the higher rank and any issue have no rights to the succession of the higher party's titles, property, etc. [C18: from the Medieval Latin phrase *mātrimōnium ad morganāticum* marriage based on the morning-gift (a token present after consummation representing the husband's only liability); *morganātica,* ultimately from Old High German *morgan* morning; compare Old English *morgengiefu* morning-gift] —ˌ**mor·ga·'nat·i·cal·ly** *adv.*
mor·gan·ite ('mɔːgəˌnaɪt) *n.* a pink variety of beryl, used as a gemstone. [C20: named after J. P. MORGAN]
Mor·gan le Fay ('mɔːgən lə 'feɪ) *or* **Mor·gain le Fay** ('mɔːgaɪn, -gən) *n.* a wicked fairy of Arthurian legend, the half sister of King Arthur.
mor·gen ('mɔːgən) *n.* **1.** a South African unit of area, equal to about two acres or 0.8 hectare. **2.** a unit of area, formerly used in Prussia and Scandinavia, equal to about two thirds of an acre. [C17: from Dutch: morning, a morning's ploughing]
morgue (mɔːg) *n.* **1.** another word for **mortuary** (sense 1). **2.** *Informal.* a room or file containing clippings, etc., used for reference in a newspaper. [C19: from French *le Morgue,* a Paris mortuary]
morgue *French.* (mɔrg) *n.* superiority; haughtiness.
mor·i·bund ('mɒrɪˌbʌnd) *adj.* **1.** near death. **2.** stagnant; without force or vitality. [C18: from Latin, from *morī* to die] —ˌ**mor·i·'bun·di·ty** *n.* —**'mor·i·ˌbund·ly** *adv.*
Mö·ri·ke (*German* 'møːrɪkə) *n.* **E·du·ard** ('eːduart). 1804–1875, German poet, noted for his lyrics, such a *On a Winter's Morning before Sunrise* and *At Midnight.*
mo·ri·on¹ ('mɔːrɪən) *n.* a 16th-century helmet with a brim and wide comb. [C16: via Old French from Spanish *morrión,* perhaps from *morra* crown of the head]
mo·ri·on² ('mɔːrɪən) *n.* a smoky brown, grey, or blackish variety of quartz, used as a gemstone. [C18: via French from Latin *mōrion,* a misreading of *mormorion*]
Mo·ris·co (mə'rɪskəʊ) *or* **Mo·res·co** (mə'rɛskəʊ) *n., pl.* **·cos** *or* **·coes. 1.** a Spanish Moor. **2.** a morris dance. ~*adj.* **3.** another word for **Moorish.** [C16: from Spanish, from *Moro* MOOR]
mor·ish ('mɔːrɪʃ) *adj.* a variant spelling of **moreish.**
Mor·ley¹ ('mɔːlɪ) *n.* an industrial town in N England, in West Yorkshire near Leeds. Pop.: 44 340 (1971).
Mor·ley² ('mɔːlɪ) *n.* **1. Ed·ward Wil·liams.** 1838–1923, U.S. chemist who collaborated with A. A. Michelson in the Michelson-Morley experiment. **2. John,** Viscount Morley of Blackburn. 1838–1923, British Liberal statesman and writer; secretary of state for India (1905–10). **3. Thom·as.** ?1557–?1603, English composer and organist, noted for his madrigals and his textbook on music, *A Plaine and Easie Introduction to Practicall Musicke* (1597).
Mor·mon ('mɔːmən) *n.* **1.** a member of the Church of Jesus Christ of Latter-day Saints, founded in 1830 at La Fayette, New York, by Joseph Smith. **2.** a prophet whose supposed revelations were recorded by Joseph Smith in the Book of Mormon. ~*adj.* **3.** of or relating to the Mormons, their Church, or their beliefs. —**'Mor·mon·ism** *n.*
morn (mɔːn) *n.* **1.** a poetic word for **morning. 2. the morn.** *Scot.* tomorrow. [Old English *morgen;* compare Old High German *morgan,* Old Norse *morginn*]
mor·nay ('mɔːneɪ) *adj.* (*often immediately postpositive*) denoting a cheese sauce used in several dishes: *eggs mornay.* [perhaps named after Philippe de MORNAY]
Mor·nay (*French* mɔr'nɛ) *n.* **Phi·lippe de** (fi'lip də), Seigneur du Plessis-Marly. 1549–1623, French Huguenot leader. Also called: **Duplessis-Mornay.**
morn·ing ('mɔːnɪŋ) *n.* **1.** the first part of the day, ending at or around noon. **2.** sunrise; daybreak; dawn. **3.** the beginning or early period: *the morning of the world.* **4. the morning after.** *Informal.* the aftereffects of excess, esp. a hangover. **5.** (*modifier*) of, used, or occurring in the morning: *morning coffee.* [C13 *morwening,* from MORN, formed on the model of EVENING]
morn·ing coat *n.* a cutaway frock coat, part of morning dress. Also called: **tail coat, swallow-tailed coat.**
morn·ing dress *n.* formal day dress for men, comprising a morning coat, usually with grey trousers and top hat.
morn·ing-glo·ry *n., pl.* **·ries.** any of various mainly tropical convolvulaceous plants of the genus *Ipomoea* and related genera, with trumpet-shaped blue, pink, or white flowers, which close in late afternoon.

morn+ings ('mɔ:nɪŋz) *adv. Informal.* in the morning, esp. regularly, or during every morning.

morn+ing sick+ness *n. Informal.* nausea occurring shortly after rising: an early symptom of pregnancy.

morn+ing star *n.* a planet, usually Venus, seen just before sunrise during the time that the planet is west of the sun. Also called: **daystar.** Compare **evening star.**

morn+ing watch *n. Nautical.* the watch between 4 and 8 a.m.

Mo·ro[1] ('mɔ:rəʊ) *n.* **1.** (*pl.* **·ros** *or* **·ro**) a member of a group of predominantly Muslim peoples of the S Philippines: noted for their manufacture of weapons. **2.** the language of these peoples, belonging to the Malayo-Polynesian family. [C19: via Spanish from Latin *Maurus* MOOR]

Mor·o[2] (*Italian* 'mɔro) *n.* **Al·do** ('aldo). 1916–78, Italian Christian Democrat statesman; prime minister of Italy (1963–68; 1974–76) and minister of foreign affairs (1965–66; 1969–72; 1973–74). He negotiated the entry of the Italian Communist Party into coalition government before being kidnapped by the Red Brigades in 1978 and murdered.

mo+roc+co (mə'rɒkəʊ) *n.* a fine soft leather made from goatskins, used for bookbinding, shoes, etc. [C17: after MOROCCO, where it was originally made]

Mo+roc+co (mə'rɒkəʊ) *n.* a kingdom in NW Africa, on the Mediterranean and the Atlantic: conquered by the Arabs in about 683, who introduced Islam; at its height under Berber dynasties (11th–13th centuries); became a French protectorate in 1912 and gained independence in 1956. It is mostly mountainous, with the Atlas Mountains in the centre and the Rif range along the Mediterranean coast, with the Sahara in the south and southeast; an important exporter of phosphates. Languages: Arabic, Berber, and French. Religion: mostly Sunni Muslim. Currency: dirham. Pop.: 15 329 259 (1971). Area: 500 000 sq. km (166 000 sq. miles). French name: **Maroc.** —**Mo+roc+can** (mə'rɒkən) *adj., n.*

mor+on ('mɔ:rɒn) *n.* **1.** a foolish or stupid person. **2.** a person having an intelligence quotient of between 50 and 70, able to work under supervision. [C20: from Greek *mōros* foolish] —**mo+ron+ic** (mɒ'rɒnɪk) *adj.* —**mo+'ron·i·cal+ly** *adv.* —**'mo+ron+ism** *or* **mo+'ron+i·ty** *n.*

Mo+ro+ni (mə'rəʊnɪ; *French* mɔrɔ'ni) *n.* the capital of the Comoro Islands, on the island of Grande Comore. Pop.: 12 000 (1974 est.).

mo+rose (mə'rəʊs) *adj.* ill-tempered or gloomy. [C16: from Latin *mōrōsus* peevish, capricious, from *mōs* custom, will, caprice] —**mo+'rose+ly** *adv.* —**mo+'rose+ness** *n.*

morph (mɔ:f) *n. Linguistics.* the phonological representation of a morpheme. [C20: shortened form of MORPHEME]

morph. *or* **morphol.** *abbrev. for:* **1.** morphological. **2.** morphology.

-morph *n. combining form.* indicating shape, form, or structure of a specified kind: *ectomorph.* [from Greek *-morphos,* from *morphē* shape] —**-mor·phic** *or* **-mor·phous** *adj. combining form.* —**-mor·phy** *n. combining form.*

mor+phal+lax+is (ˌmɔ:fə'læksɪs) *n., pl.* **+lax·es** (-'læksi:z) *Zoology.* the transformation of one part into another that sometimes occurs during regeneration of organs in certain animals. [C20: New Latin, from MORPHO- + Greek *allaxis* exchange, from *allassein* to exchange, from *allos* other]

mor+pheme ('mɔ:fi:m) *n. Linguistics.* a speech element having a meaning or grammatical function that cannot be subdivided into further such elements. [C20: from French, from Greek *morphē* form, coined on the model of PHONEME; see -EME] —**mor+'phem+ic** *adj.* —**mor+'phem·i+cal+ly** *adv.*

Mor+phe·us ('mɔ:fɪəs, -fju:s) *n. Greek myth.* the god of sleep and dreams. —**'Mor+phe·an** *adj.*

mor+phine ('mɔ:fi:n) *or* **mor+phi·a** ('mɔ:fɪə) *n.* an alkaloid extracted from opium: used in medicine as an anaesthetic and sedative although repeated use causes addiction. Formula: $C_{17}H_{19}NO_3$. [C19: from French, from MORPHEUS]

mor+phin+ism ('mɔ:fɪˌnɪzəm) *n.* morphine addiction.

mor+pho- *or before a vowel* **morph-** *combining form.* **1.** indicating form or structure: *morphology.* **2.** morpheme: *morphophonemics.* [from Greek *morphē* form, shape]

mor+pho+gen+e·sis (ˌmɔ:fəʊ'dʒɛnɪsɪs) *n.* **1.** the development of form and structure in an organism during its growth from embryo to adult. **2.** the evolutionary development of form in an organism or part of an organism. —**mor+pho+ge·net+ic** (ˌmɔ:fəʊdʒɪ'nɛtɪk) *or* ˌ**mor+pho+'gen+ic** *adj.*

mor+phol+o·gy (mɔ:'fɒlədʒɪ) *n.* **1.** the branch of biology concerned with the form and structure of organisms. **2.** the form and structure of words in a language, esp. the consistent patterns of inflection, combination, derivation and change, etc., that may be observed and classified. **3.** the study of linguistic forms and structures. **4.** the form and structure of anything. —**mor+pho+log+ic** (ˌmɔ:fə'lɒdʒɪk) *or* ˌ**mor+pho+'log·i·cal** *adj.* —ˌ**mor+pho+'log·i·cal+ly** *adv.* —**mor+'phol·o·gist** *n.*

mor+pho+pho+neme (ˌmɔ:fəʊ'fəʊni:m) *n. Linguistics.* the set of phonemes or sequences of phonemes that constitute the various allomorphs of a morpheme. [C20: from MORPHEME + PHONEME]

mor+pho+pho+ne·mics (ˌmɔ:fəʊfəʊ'ni:mɪks) *n. Linguistics.* the study of the phonemic realization of the allomorphs of the morphemes of a language. —ˌ**mor+pho+pho+'ne·mic** *adj.*

mor+pho+sis (mɔ:'fəʊsɪs) *n., pl.* **+ses** (-si:z). *Biology.* development in an organism or its parts characterized by structural change. [C17: via New Latin from Greek, from *morphoun* to form, from *morphē* form]

Mor·phy ('mɔ:fɪ) *n.* **Paul.** 1837–84, U.S. chess player, widely considered to have been the world's greatest player.

Mor+ris ('mɒrɪs) *n.* **Wil·liam.** 1834–96, English poet, Pre-Raphaelite painter, craftsman, and socialist writer. He founded the Kelmscott Press (1890).

Mor·ris chair *n.* an armchair with an adjustable back and large cushions. [C19: named after William MORRIS]

mor+ris dance *n.* any of various old English folk dances usually performed by men (**morris men**) to the accompaniment of violin, concertina, etc. The dancers are adorned with bells and often represent characters from folk tales. Often shortened to **morris.** [C15 *moreys daunce* Moorish dance. See MOOR] —**mor+ris danc+ing** *n.*

Mor·ri·son ('mɒrɪsən) *n.* **Her·bert Stan·ley,** Baron Morrison of Lambeth. 1888–1965, British Labour statesman, who served in Churchill's War Cabinet (1942–45).

mor+ro ('mɒrəʊ; *Spanish* 'moro) *n., pl.* **+ros** (-rəʊz; *Spanish* -ros). a rounded hill or promontory. [from Spanish]

mor+row ('mɒrəʊ) *n.* (usually preceded by *the*) *Archaic or poetic.* **1.** the next day. **2.** the period following a specified event. **3.** the morning. [C13 *morwe,* from Old English *morgen* morning; see MORN]

Mors (mɔ:z) *n.* the Roman god of death. Greek counterpart: **Thanatos.**

morse (mɔ:s) *n.* a clasp or fastening on a cope. [C15: from Old French *mors,* from Latin *morsus* clasp, from *mordēre* to bite]

Morse (mɔ:s) *n.* **Sam·u·el Fin·ley Breese** ('fɪnlɪ bri:z). 1791–1872, U.S. inventor and painter. He invented the first electric telegraph and the Morse code.

Morse code *n.* a telegraph code used internationally for transmitting messages. Letters, numbers, etc., are represented by groups of shorter dots and longer dashes, or by groups of the corresponding sounds, *dits* and *dahs,* the groups being separated by spaces. Also called: **international Morse code.**

mor+sel ('mɔ:səl) *n.* **1.** a small slice or mouthful of food. **2.** a small piece; bit. [C13: from Old French, from *mors* a bite, from Latin *morsus,* from *mordēre* to bite]

mort (mɔ:t) *n.* a call blown on a hunting horn to signify the death of the animal hunted. [C16: via Old French from Latin *mors* death]

mor+tal ('mɔ:təl) *adj.* **1.** (of living beings, esp. human beings) subject to death. **2.** of or involving life or the world. **3.** ending in or causing death; fatal: *a mortal blow.* **4.** deadly or unrelenting: *a mortal enemy.* **5.** of or like the fear of death; dire: *mortal terror.* **6.** great or very intense: *mortal pain.* **7.** conceivable or possible: *there was no mortal reason to go.* **8.** *Slang.* long and tedious: *for three mortal hours.* ~*n.* **9.** a mortal being. **10.** *Informal.* a person: *a mean mortal.* [C14: from Latin *mortālis,* from *mors* death] —**'mor+tal+ly** *adv.*

mor+tal+i·ty (mɔ:'tælɪtɪ) *n., pl.* **·ties. 1.** the condition of being mortal. **2.** great loss of life, as in war or disaster. **3.** the number of deaths in a given period. **4.** mankind; humanity. **5.** an obsolete word for **death.**

mor+tal+i·ty rate *n.* another term for **death rate.**

mor+tal+i·ty ta+ble *n. Insurance.* an actuarial table indicating life expectancy and death frequency for a given age, occupation, etc.

mor+tal sin *n. Theol.* a sin regarded as involving total loss of grace. Also called: **deadly sin.** Compare **venial sin.**

mor+tar ('mɔ:tə) *n.* **1.** a mixture of cement or lime or both with sand and water, used as a bond between bricks or stones or as a covering on a wall. **2.** a muzzle-loading cannon having a short barrel and relatively wide bore that fires low-velocity shells in high trajectories over a short range. **3.** a similar device for firing lifelines, etc. **4.** a vessel, usually bowl-shaped, in which substances are pulverized with a pestle. **5.** *Mining.* a cast-iron receptacle in which ore is crushed. ~*vb.* (*tr.*) **6.** to join (bricks or stones) or cover (a wall) with mortar. **7.** to fire on with mortars. [C13: from Latin *mortārium* basin in which mortar is mixed; in some senses, via Old French *mortier* substance mixed inside such a vessel]

mor·tar+board ('mɔ:təˌbɔ:d) *n.* **1.** a black tasselled academic cap with a flat square top covered with cloth. **2.** Also called: **hawk.** a small square board with a handle on the underside for carrying mortar.

mort+gage ('mɔ:gɪdʒ) *n.* **1.** a conditional conveyance of property, esp. real property, as security for the repayment of a loan. **2.** the deed effecting such a transaction. ~*vb.* (*tr.*) **3.** to convey (property) by mortgage. **4.** *Informal.* to pledge. [C14: from Old French, literally: dead pledge, from *mort* dead + *gage* security, GAGE[1]] —**'mort+gage+a·ble** *adj.*

mort+ga+gee (ˌmɔ:gɪ'dʒi:) *n. Law.* **1.** the party to a mortgage who makes the loan. **2.** a person who holds mortgaged property as security for repayment of a loan.

mort+gag+or ('mɔ:gɪdʒə, ˌmɔ:gɪ'dʒɔ:) *or* **mort+gag+er** *n. Property law.* a person who borrows money by mortgaging his property to the lender as security.

mor+ti+cian (mɔ:'tɪʃən) *n. U.S.* another word for **undertaker.** [C19: from MORTUARY + *-ician,* as in *physician*]

mor+ti+fi+ca+tion (ˌmɔ:tɪfɪ'keɪʃən) *n.* **1.** a feeling of loss of prestige or self-respect; humiliation. **2.** something causing this. **3.** *Christianity.* the practice of mortifying the senses, etc. **4.** another word for **gangrene.**

mor+ti+fy ('mɔ:tɪˌfaɪ) *vb.* **+fies, +fy+ing, +fied. 1.** (*tr.*) to humiliate or cause to feel shame. **2.** (*tr.*) *Christianity.* to subdue and bring under control by disciplinary exercises, etc. **3.** to cause or undergo tissue death or gangrene. [C14: via Old French from Church Latin *mortificāre* to put to death, from Latin *mors* death + *facere* to do] —**'mor+ti+ˌfi+er** *n.* —**'mor+ti+ˌfy+ing+ly** *adv.*

Mor·ti·mer ('mɔ:tɪmə) *n.* **Rog·er de,** 8th Baron of Wigmore and

1st Earl of March. 1287–1330, lover of Isabella, the wife of Edward II of England: they invaded England in 1326 and compelled the king to abdicate in favour of his son, Edward III; executed.

mor+tise *or* **mor+tice** ('mɔːtɪs) *n.* **1.** a slot or recess, usually rectangular, cut into a piece of wood, stone, etc., to receive a matching projection (tenon) of another piece, or a mortise lock. **2.** *Printing:* a cavity cut into a letterpress printing plate into which type or another plate is inserted. ~*vb.* (*tr.*) **3.** to cut a slot or recess in (a piece of wood, etc.). **4.** to join (two pieces of wood, etc.) by means of a mortise and tenon. **5.** to cut a cavity in (a letterpress printing plate) for the insertion of type, etc. [C14: from Old French *mortoise,* perhaps from Arabic *murtazza* fastened in position] —'**mor+tis+er** *n.*

mor+tise lock *n.* a lock set into a mortise in a door so that the mechanism of the lock is enclosed by the door.

mort+main ('mɔːtˌmeɪn) *n. Law.* the state or condition of lands, etc., held inalienably, as by an ecclesiastical or other corporation. [C15: from Old French *mortemain,* from Medieval Latin *mortua manus* dead hand, inalienable ownership]

Mor·ton ('mɔːtᵊn) *n.* **Jel·ly Roll,** nickname of *Ferdinand Joseph La Menthe Morton.* 1885–1941, U.S. jazz pianist; one of the creators of New Orleans jazz.

mor+tu+ar·y ('mɔːtʃʊərɪ) *n., pl.* **+ar·ies. 1.** Also called: **morgue.** a building where dead bodies are kept before cremation or burial. ~*adj.* **2.** of or relating to death or burial. [C14 (as n., a funeral gift to a parish priest): via Medieval Latin *mortuārium* (n.) from Latin *mortuārius* of the dead]

mor·u+la ('mɒrjʊlə) *n., pl.* **+las** *or* **+lae** (-ˌliː). *Embryol.* a solid ball of cells resulting from cleavage of a fertilized ovum. [C19: via New Latin, diminutive of Latin *morum* mulberry, from Greek *moron*] —'**mor·u+lar** *adj.*

mor+wong ('mɔːˌwɒŋ) *n.* a food fish of Australasian coastal waters belonging to the genus *Cheilodactylos:* family *Cirrhitidae* (or *Cheilodactylidae*). [from a native Australian language]

mos. *abbrev. for* months.

mo+sa+ic (mə'zeɪɪk) *n.* **1.** a design or decoration made up of small pieces of coloured glass, stone, etc. **2.** the process of making a mosaic. **3. a.** a mottled yellowing that occurs in the leaves of plants affected with any of various virus diseases. **b.** Also called: **mosaic disease.** any of the diseases, such as **tobacco mosaic,** that produce this discoloration. **4.** *Genetics.* another name for **chimera** (sense 4). **5.** an assembly of aerial photographs forming a composite picture of a large area on the ground. **6.** a light-sensitive surface on a television camera tube, consisting of a large number of granules of photoemissive material deposited on an insulating medium. [C16: via French and Italian from Medieval Latin *mōsaicus,* from Late Greek *mouseion* mosaic work, from Greek *mouseios* of the Muses, from *mousa* MUSE] —**mo+sa·i+cist** (mə'zeɪɪsɪst) *n.*

Mo+sa+ic (məʊ'zeɪɪk) *or* **Mo+sa·i+cal** *adj.* of or relating to Moses or the laws and traditions ascribed to him.

mo+sa+ic gold (mə'zeɪɪk) *n.* stannic sulphide, esp. when suspended in lacquer for use in gilding surfaces.

Mo+sa+ic law *n. Old Testament.* the laws of the Hebrews ascribed to Moses and contained in the Pentateuch.

mo+sa+saur ('məʊsəˌsɔː) *or* **mo+sa+sau+rus** (ˌməʊsə'sɔːrəs) *n., pl.* **+saurs** *or* **+sau+ri** (-'sɔːraɪ). any of various extinct Cretaceous giant marine lizards of the genus *Mosasaurus* and related genera, typically having paddle-like limbs. [C18: from Latin *Mosa* the river MEUSE (near which remains were first found) + -SAUR]

mos+cha+tel (ˌmɒskə'tɛl) *n.* a small N temperate plant, *Adoxa moschatellina,* with greenish-white musk-scented flowers: family *Adoxaceae.* Also called: **townhall clock, five-faced bishop.** [C18: via French from Italian *moscatella,* diminutive of *moscato* MUSK]

Mos+cow ('mɒskəʊ) *n.* the capital of the Soviet Union and of the RSFSR, on the Moskva River: dates from the 11th century; capital of the grand duchy of Russia from 1547 to 1712; made capital of the Soviet Union in 1918; centres on the medieval Kremlin; chief political, cultural, and industrial centre of the Soviet Union, with two universities. Pop.: 6 941 961 (1970). Russian name: **Moskva.**

Mose·ley ('məʊzlɪ) *n.* **Hen·ry Gwyn-Jef·freys.** 1887–1915, English physicist. He showed that the wavelengths of x-rays emitted from the elements are related to their atomic numbers.

Mo+selle (məʊ'zɛl) *n.* **1.** a department of NE France, in Lorraine region. Capital: Metz. Pop.: 1 030 957 (1975). Area: 6253 sq. km (2439 sq. miles). **2.** a river in W Europe, rising in NE France and flowing northwest, forming part of the border between Luxembourg and West Germany, then northeast to the Rhine: many vineyards along its lower course. Length: 547 km (340 miles). German name: **Mo+sel** ('moːzᵊl). **3.** (*sometimes not cap.*) a German white wine from the Rhine valley.

Mo·ses ('məʊzɪz) *n.* **1.** *Old Testament.* the Hebrew prophet who led the Israelites out of Egypt to the Promised Land and gave them divinely revealed laws. **2. Grand·ma,** nickname of *Anna Mary Robertson Moses.* 1860–1961, U.S. painter of primitives, who began to paint at the age of 75.

mo+sey ('məʊzɪ) *vb.* (*intr.*) *U.S. slang.* (often foll. by *along* or *on*) to walk in a leisurely manner; amble. [C19: origin unknown]

mo+shav *Hebrew.* (mɔ'ʃav) *n., pl.* **+sha+vim** (-ʃa'vim). a cooperative settlement in Israel, consisting of a number of small farms. [C20: from Hebrew *mōshābh* a dwelling]

Mo·shesh (mɒ'ʃɛʃ) *or* **Mo·shoe·shoe** (mɒ'ʃuʃu) *n.* died 1870, African chief, who founded the Basotho nation, now Lesotho.

Mos+kva (*Russian* mas'kva) *n.* **1.** the Russian name for **Moscow. 2.** a river in the W central Soviet Union, rising in the Smolensk-Moscow upland, and flowing southeast through Moscow to the Oka River: linked with the River Volga by the Moscow Canal. Length: about 500 km (310 miles).

Mos+lem ('mɒzləm) *n., pl.* **+lems** *or* **+lem,** *adj.* a variant spelling of **Muslim.** —**Mos+lem+ic** (mɒz'lɛmɪk) *adj.* —'**Mos+lem+ism** *n.*

Mos·ley ('məʊzlɪ) *n.* Sir **Os·wald Er·nald.** 1896-1980, British politician; founder of the British Union of Fascists (1932).

Mo+so+tho (mʊ'suːtʊ) *n., pl.* **+tho** *or* **+thos.** a member of the Basotho people. Former name: **Basuto.**

mosque (mɒsk) *n.* a Muslim place of worship, usually having one or more minarets and often decorated with elaborate tracery and texts from the Koran. Also called: **masjid, musjid.** [C14: earlier *mosquee,* from Old French via Italian *moschea,* ultimately from Arabic *masjid* temple]

mos+qui+to (mə'skiːtəʊ) *n., pl.* **+toes** *or* **+tos.** any dipterous insect of the family *Culicidae:* the females have a long proboscis adapted for piercing the skin of man and animals to suck their blood. See also **aedes, anopheles, culex.** [C16: from Spanish, diminutive of *mosca* fly, from Latin *musca*]

mos+qui+to boat *n.* another name for **MTB.**

mos+qui+to hawk *n.* another name for **nighthawk** (sense 1).

mos+qui+to net *or* **net+ting** *n.* a fine curtain or net put in windows, around beds, etc., to keep mosquitoes out.

moss (mɒs) *n.* **1.** any bryophyte of the class *Musci,* typically growing in dense mats on trees, rocks, moist ground, etc. See also **peat moss. 2.** a clump or growth of any of these plants. **3.** any of various similar but unrelated plants, such as club moss, Spanish moss, Ceylon moss, rose moss, and reindeer moss. **4.** *Chiefly Scot.* a peat bog or swamp. [Old English *mos* swamp; compare Middle Dutch, Old High German *mos* bog, Old Norse *mosi;* compare also Old Norse *mýrr* MIRE] —'**moss+ˌlike** *adj.* —'**moss·y** *adj.* —'**moss·i+ness** *n.*

Moss (mɒs) *n.* **Stir·ling.** born 1929, English racing driver.

moss ag+ate *n.* a variety of chalcedony with dark greenish mossy markings, used as a gemstone.

moss+back ('mɒsˌbæk) *n. U.S.* **1.** an old turtle, shellfish, etc., that has a growth of algae on its back. **2.** *Informal.* a provincial or conservative person. —'**moss+ˌbacked** *adj.*

Möss·bau·er ef+fect ('mɒsˌbaʊə; *German* 'mœsˌbauər) *n. Physics.* the phenomenon in which an atomic nucleus in a crystal of certain substances emits a gamma ray without any recoil to the atom. The study of the emitted gamma rays (**Mössbauer spectroscopy**) is used to determine the energy levels in a nucleus, the structure of molecules, etc. [C20: named after Rudolf Ludwig *Mössbauer* (born 1929), German physicist]

moss+bunk+er ('mɒsˌbʌŋkə) *n. U.S.* another name for **menhaden.**

moss-grown *adj.* covered with moss.

Mos+si ('mɒsɪ) *n.* **1.** (*pl.* **+sis** *or* **+si**) a member of a Negroid people of S Africa, living chiefly in Upper Volta: noted for their use of cowry shells as currency and for their trading skill. **2.** the language of this people, belonging to the Gur branch of the Niger-Congo family.

mos+sie[1] ('mɒzɪ) *n. Austral.* an informal name for **mosquito.**

mos+sie[2] ('mɒsɪ) *n.* another name for the **Cape sparrow.** [of uncertain origin]

mos+so ('mɒsəʊ) *adv. Music.* to be performed with rapidity. See also **meno mosso.** [Italian, past participle of *muovere* to MOVE]

moss pink *n.* a North American plant, *Phlox subulata,* forming dense mosslike mats: cultivated for its pink, white, or lavender flowers: family *Polemoniaceae.* Also called: **ground pink.**

moss rose *n.* a variety of rose, *Rosa centifolia muscosa,* that has a mossy stem and calyx and fragrant pink flowers.

moss stitch *n.* a knitting stitch made up of alternate plain and purl stitches.

moss+troop·er ('mɒsˌtruːpə) *n.* a raider in the border country of England and Scotland in the mid-17th century. [C17 *moss,* in northern English dialect sense: bog]

most (məʊst) *determiner.* **1. a.** a great majority of; nearly all: *most people like eggs.* **b.** (*as pronoun; functioning as sing. or pl.*): *most of them don't know; most of it is finished.* **2. the most. a.** the superlative of **many** and **much:** *you have the most money; the most apples.* **b.** (*as pronoun*): *the most he can afford is two pounds.* **3. at (the) most.** at the maximum: *that girl is four at the most.* **4. for the most part.** See **part** (sense 12). **5. make the most of.** to use to the best advantage: *she makes the most of her accent.* **6. than most.** short for **than most others:** *the leaves are greener than most.* **7. the most.** *Slang, chiefly U.S.* wonderful: *that chick's the most.* ~*adv.* **8. the most.** used to form the superlative of some adjectives and adverbs: *the most beautiful daughter of all.* **9.** the superlative of **much:** *people welcome a drink most after work.* **10.** (intensifier): *a most absurd story.* **11.** *U.S. informal or dialect.* almost: *most every town in this state.* [Old English *māst* or *mǣst,* whence Middle English *moste, mēst;* compare Old Frisian *maest,* Old High German *meist,* Old Norse *mestr*]

Usage. The meanings of *most* and *mostly* should not be confused. In *she was most affected by the news, most* is equivalent to *very* and is generally acceptable. In *she was mostly affected by the news,* the implication is that there was something else, in addition to the news, which affected her, although less so. *More* and *most* should also be distinguished when used in comparisons. *More* applies to cases involving two persons, objects, etc., *most* to cases involving three or more: *John is the more intelligent of the two; he is the most intelligent of the students.*

-most *suffix.* (*forming the superlative degree of some adjectives and adverbs*): *hindmost; uppermost.* [Old English *-mǣst, -mest,* originally a superlative suffix, later mistakenly taken as derived from *mǣst* (adv.) most]

Most Hon·our·a·ble *n.* a courtesy title applied to marquesses and members of the Privy Council and the Order of Bath.

most·ly ('məʊstlɪ) *adv.* **1.** almost entirely; chiefly. **2.** on many or most occasions; usually.

Most Rev·er·end *n.* a courtesy title applied to Anglican archbishops and Roman Catholic bishops.

Mo·sul ('məʊsᵊl) *n.* a city in N Iraq, on the River Tigris opposite the ruins of Nineveh: an important commercial centre with nearby Ayn Zalah oilfield; university. Pop.: 293 000 (1970 est.).

mot (məʊ) *n.* short for **bon mot.** [C16: via French from Vulgar Latin *mottum* (unattested) utterance, from Latin *muttum* a mutter, from *muttīre* to mutter]

M.O.T. (in Britain) *abbrev. for:* **1.** Ministry of Transport (Industries). **2.** the M.O.T. test or test certificate.

mote[1] (məʊt) *n.* a tiny speck. [Old English *mot;* compare Middle Dutch *mot* grit, Norwegian *mutt* speck]

mote[2] (məʊt) *vb. past* **moste** (məʊst). (takes an infinitive without *to*) *Archaic.* may or might. [Old English *mōt,* first person singular present tense of *mōtan* to be allowed]

mo·tel (məʊ'tɛl) *n.* a roadside hotel for motorists, usually having direct access from each room or chalet to a parking space or garage. [C20: from *motor + hotel*]

mo·tet (məʊ'tɛt) *n.* a polyphonic choral composition used as an anthem in the Roman Catholic service. [C14: from Old French, diminutive of *mot* word; see MOT]

moth (mɒθ) *n.* any of numerous insects of the order *Lepidoptera* that typically have stout bodies with antennae of various shapes (but not clubbed), including large brightly coloured species, such as hawk moths, and small inconspicuous types, such as the clothes moths. Compare **butterfly** (sense 1). [Old English *moththe;* compare Middle Dutch *motte,* Old Norse *motti*]

moth·ball ('mɒθ,bɔ:l) *n.* **1.** Also called: **camphor ball.** a small ball of camphor or naphthalene used to repel clothes moths in stored clothing, etc. **2. put in mothballs.** to postpone work on (a project, activity, etc.). ~*vb.* (*tr.*) **3.** to prepare (a ship) for a long period of storage by sealing all openings with plastic to prevent corrosion. **4.** to postpone work on (a project, activity, etc.).

moth-eat·en *adj.* **1.** decayed, decrepit, or outdated. **2.** eaten away by or as if by moths.

moth·er[1] ('mʌðə) *n.* **1. a.** a female who has given birth to offspring. **b.** (*as modifier*): *a mother bird.* **2.** (*often cap., esp. as a term of address*) a person's own mother. **3.** a female substituting in the function of a mother. **4.** (*often cap.*) *Chiefly archaic.* a term of address for an old woman. **5. a.** motherly qualities, such as maternal affection: *it appealed to the mother in her.* **b.** (*as modifier*): *mother love.* **c.** (*in combination*): *mothercraft.* **6. a.** a female or thing that creates, nurtures, protects, etc., something. **b.** (*as modifier*): *mother church; mother earth.* **7.** a title given to certain members of female religious orders: *mother superior.* **8.** *Christian Science.* God as the eternal Principle. **9.** (*modifier*) native or innate: *mother wit.* **10.** *Offensive taboo slang, chiefly U.S.* short for **motherfucker. 11. be mother.** to pour the tea: *I'll be mother.* ~*vb.* (*tr.*). **12.** to give birth to or produce. **13.** to nurture, protect, etc. as a mother. [Old English *mōdor;* compare Old Saxon *mōdar,* Old High German *muotar,* Latin *māter,* Greek *mētēr*] —**'moth·er·less** *adj.*

moth·er[2] ('mʌðə) *n.* a stringy slime containing various bacteria that forms on the surface of liquids undergoing acetous fermentation. It can be added to wine, etc. to promote vinegar formation. Also called: **mother of vinegar.** [C16: perhaps from MOTHER[1], but compare Spanish *madre* scum, Dutch *modder* dregs, Middle Low German *modder* decaying object, *mudde* sludge] —**'moth·er·y** *adj.*

Moth·er Car·ey's chick·en ('kɛərɪz) *n.* another name for **storm petrel.** [origin unknown]

moth·er coun·try *n.* **1.** the original country of colonists or settlers. **2.** another term for **fatherland.**

moth·er·fuck·er ('mʌðə,fʌkə) *n. Offensive taboo slang, chiefly U.S.* a person or thing, esp. an exasperating or unpleasant one. Often shortened to **mother.**

Moth·er Goose *n.* the imaginary author of the collection of nursery rhymes published in 1781 in London as *Mother Goose's Melody.* [C18: translated from French *Contes de ma mère l'Oye* (1697), title of a collection of tales by Charles PERRAULT]

moth·er·hood ('mʌðə,hʊd) *n.* **1.** the state of being a mother. **2.** the qualities characteristic of a mother.

Moth·er Hub·bard ('hʌbəd) *n.* (*sometimes not cap.*) a woman's full-length unbelted dress. [C19: after *Mother Hubbard,* a character in a nursery rhyme]

Moth·er·ing Sun·day ('mʌðərɪŋ) *n. Brit.* the fourth Sunday in Lent, when mothers traditionally receive presents from their children. Also called: **Mother's Day.**

moth·er-in-law *n., pl.* **moth·ers-in-law.** the mother of one's wife or husband.

moth·er·land ('mʌðə,lænd) *n.* another word for **fatherland.**

moth·er·less ('mʌðələs) *adj.* **1.** not having a mother. ~*adv.* **2.** *Austral.* (intensifier): *motherless broke.*

moth·er lode *n. Mining.* the principal lode in a system.

moth·er·ly ('mʌðəlɪ) *adj.* of or resembling a mother, esp. in warmth, or protectiveness. —**'moth·er·li·ness** *n.*

Moth·er of God *n.* a title given to the Virgin Mary.

Moth·er of Par·lia·ments *n.* **the.** the British Parliament: the model and creator of many other Parliaments.

moth·er-of-pearl *n.* a hard iridescent substance, mostly calcium carbonate, that forms the inner layer of the shells of certain molluscs, such as the oyster. It is used to make buttons, inlay furniture, etc. Also called: **nacre.**

moth·er-of-thou·sands *n.* another name for **mind-your-own-business.**

Moth·er's Day *n.* **1.** *U.S.* the second Sunday in May, observed as a day in honour of mothers. **2.** See **Mothering Sunday.**

moth·er ship *n.* a ship providing facilities and supplies for a number of small vessels, etc.

moth·er su·pe·ri·or *n., pl.* **moth·er su·pe·ri·ors** *or* **moth·ers su·pe·ri·or.** the head of a community of nuns.

moth·er tongue *n.* **1.** the language first learned by a child. **2.** a language from which another has evolved.

Moth·er·well and Wish·aw ('mʌðəwəl; 'wɪʃɔ:) *n.* a town in S central Scotland, in SE Strathclyde region on the River Clyde: formed by the union of the two towns in 1920; a coal-mining and industrial centre. Pop.: 74 184 (1971).

moth·er wit *n.* native practical intelligence; common sense.

moth·er·wort ('mʌðə,wɜ:t) *n.* any of several plants of the Eurasian genus *Leonurus,* esp. *L. cardiaca,* having divided leaves and clusters of small purple or pink flowers: family *Labiatae* (labiates). [C14: so named because it was thought to be beneficial in uterine disorders]

moth·proof ('mɒθ,pru:f) *adj.* **1.** (esp. of clothes) chemically treated so as to repel clothes moths. ~*vb.* **2.** (*tr.*) to make (clothes, etc.) mothproof.

moth·y ('mɒθɪ) *adj.* **moth·i·er, moth·i·est. 1.** ragged; moth-eaten. **2.** containing moths; full of moths.

mo·tif (məʊ'ti:f) *n.* **1.** a distinctive idea, esp. a theme elaborated on in a piece of music, literature, etc. **2.** Also called: **motive.** a recurring form or shape in a design or pattern. [C19: from French. See MOTIVE]

mo·tile ('məʊtaɪl) *adj.* **1.** capable of moving spontaneously and independently. ~*n.* **2.** *Psychol.* a person whose mental imagery strongly reflects movement, esp. his own. [C19: from Latin *mōtus* moved, from *movēre* to move] —**mo·til·i·ty** (məʊ'tɪlɪtɪ) *n.*

mo·tion ('məʊʃən) *n.* **1.** the process of continual change in the physical position of an object; movement: *linear motion.* **2.** a movement or action, esp. of part of the human body; a gesture. **3. a.** the capacity for movement. **b.** a manner of movement, esp. walking; gait. **4.** a mental impulse. **5.** a formal proposal to be discussed and voted on in a debate, meeting, etc. **6.** *Law.* an application made to a judge or court for an order or ruling necessary to the conduct of legal proceedings. **7.** *Brit.* **a.** the evacuation of the bowels. **b.** excrement. **8. a.** part of a moving mechanism. **b.** the action of such a part. **9.** *Music.* the upward or downward course followed by a part or melody. Parts whose progressions are in the same direction exhibit **similar motion,** while two parts whose progressions are in opposite directions exhibit **contrary motion.** See also **parallel** (sense 3). **10. go through the motions. a.** to act or perform the task (of doing something) mechanically or without sincerity. **b.** to mimic the action (of something) by gesture. **11. in motion.** operational or functioning (often in the phrases **set in motion, set the wheels in motion**). ~*vb.* **12.** (*when tr., may take a clause as object or an infinitive*) to signal or direct (a person) by a movement or gesture. [C15: from Latin *mōtiō* a moving, from *movēre* to move] —**'mo·tion·al** *adj.* —**'mo·tion·er** *n.*

mo·tion·less ('məʊʃənlɪs) *adj.* not moving; absolutely still. —**'mo·tion·less·ly** *adv.* —**'mo·tion·less·ness** *n.*

mo·tion pic·ture *n.* a U.S. term for **film** (sense 1).

mo·tion sick·ness *n.* the state or condition of being dizzy or nauseous from riding in a moving vehicle.

mo·tion stud·y *n.* short for **time and motion study.**

mo·ti·vate ('məʊtɪ,veɪt) *vb.* (*tr.*) to give incentive to.

mo·ti·va·tion (,məʊtɪ'veɪʃən) *n.* **1.** the act or an instance of motivating. **2.** desire to do; interest or drive. **3.** incentive or inducement. **4.** *Psychol.* the process that arouses, sustains and regulates human and animal behaviour. —**,mo·ti·'va·tion·al** *adj.* —**'mo·ti·,va·tive** *adj.*

mo·ti·va·tion·al re·search *n.* the application of psychology to the study of consumer behaviour, esp. the planning of advertising and sales campaigns. Also called: **motivation research.**

mo·tive ('məʊtɪv) *n.* **1.** the reason for a certain course of action, whether conscious or unconscious. **2.** a variant spelling of **motif.** ~*adj.* **3.** of or causing motion or action: *a motive force.* **4.** of or acting as a motive; motivating. ~*vb.* (*tr.*) **5.** to motivate. [C14: from Old French *motif,* from Late Latin *mōtīvus* (adj.) moving, from Latin *mōtus,* past participle of *movēre* to move] —**'mo·tive·less** *adj.* —**'mo·tive·less·ly** *adv.* —**'mo·tive·less·ness** *n.*

mo·tive pow·er *n.* **1.** any source of energy used to produce motion. **2.** the means of supplying power to an engine, vehicle, etc. **3.** any driving force.

mo·tiv·i·ty (məʊ'tɪvɪtɪ) *n.* the power of moving or of initiating motion.

mot juste *French.* (mo 'ʒyst) *n., pl.* ***mots justes*** (mo 'ʒyst). the appropriate word or expression.

mot·ley ('mɒtlɪ) *adj.* **1.** made up of elements of varying type, quality, etc. **2.** multicoloured. ~*n.* **3.** a motley collection or mixture. **4.** the particoloured attire of a jester. **5.** *Obsolete.* a jester. [C14: perhaps from *mot* speck, MOTE¹]

mot+mot ('mɒtmɒt) *n.* any tropical American bird of the family *Momotidae,* having a long tail and blue and brownish-green plumage: order *Coraciiformes* (kingfishers, etc.). [C19: from American Spanish, imitative of the bird's call]

mo+to+cross ('məʊtəˌkrɒs) *n.* **1.** a motorcycle race across very rough ground. **2.** another name for **rallycross.** See also **autocross.** [C20: from MOTO(R) + CROSS(-COUNTRY)]

mo+to+neu+ron (ˌməʊtəʊ'njʊərɒn) *n. Anatomy.* an efferent nerve cell; motor neuron.

mo+tor ('məʊtə) *n.* **1. a.** the engine, esp. an internal-combustion engine, of a vehicle. **b.** (*as modifier*): *a motor scooter.* **2.** Also called: **electric motor.** a machine that converts electrical energy into mechanical energy by means of the forces exerted on a current-carrying coil placed in a magnetic field. **3.** any device that converts another form of energy into mechanical energy to produce motion. **4. a.** *Chiefly Brit.* a car or other motor vehicle. **b.** (*as modifier*): *motor spares.* ~*adj.* **5.** producing or causing motion. **6.** *Physiol.* **a.** of or relating to nerves or neurons that carry impulses that cause muscles to contract. **b.** of or relating to movement or to muscles that induce movement. ~*vb.* **7.** (*intr.*) to travel by car. **8.** (*tr.*) *Brit.* to transport by car. [C16: from Latin *mōtor* a mover, from *movēre* to move]

mo+tor+a·ble ('məʊtərəbᵊl) *adj.* (of a road) suitable for use by motor vehicles.

mo·tor+bi·cyc+le ('məʊtəˌbaɪsɪkᵊl) *n.* **1.** a motorcycle. **2.** a moped.

mo·tor+bike ('məʊtəˌbaɪk) *n.* a less formal name for **motorcycle.**

mo·tor+boat ('məʊtəˌbəʊt) *n.* any boat powered by a motor.

mo·tor+bus ('məʊtəˌbʌs) *n.* a bus driven by an internal-combustion engine.

mo·tor+cade ('məʊtəˌkeɪd) *n.* a parade of cars or other motor vehicles. [C20: from MOTOR + CAVALCADE]

mo·tor+car ('məʊtəˌkɑː) *n.* **1.** a more formal word for **car** (sense 1). **2.** a self-propelled electric railway car.

mo·tor car·a+van *n. Brit.* a motor vehicle fitted with equipment for cooking, sleeping, etc., like that of a caravan.

mo·tor+coach ('məʊtəˌkəʊtʃ) *n.* a coach driven by an internal-combustion engine.

mo·tor+cy·cle ('məʊtəˌsaɪkᵊl) *n.* **1.** Also called: **motorbike.** a two-wheeled vehicle, having a stronger frame than a bicycle, that is driven by a petrol engine, usually with a capacity of between 125 cc and 1000 cc. ~*vb.* (*intr.*) **2.** to ride on a motorcycle. —**'mo·tor+ˌcy·clist** *n.*

-mo·tored *adj.* (*in combination*) having a specified type of motor or number of motors.

mo+tor gen+er·a+tor *n.* a generator driven by an electric motor, by means of which the voltage, frequency, or phases of an electrical power supply can be changed.

mo+tor+ist ('məʊtərɪst) *n.* a driver of a car, esp. when considered as a car-owner.

mo+tor+ize *or* **mo+tor+ise** ('məʊtəˌraɪz) *vb.* (*tr.*) **1.** to equip with a motor. **2.** to provide (military units) with motor vehicles. —**ˌmo·tor·i·'za+tion** *or* **ˌmo·tor·i·'sa+tion** *n.*

mo·tor+man ('məʊtəmən) *n., pl.* **+men. 1.** the driver of an electric train. **2.** the operator of a motor.

mo+tor park *n.* a W African name for **car park.**

mo+tor scoot+er *n.* a light motorcycle with small wheels and an enclosed engine. Often shortened to **scooter.**

mo+tor ve+hi+cle *n.* a road vehicle driven by a motor or engine, esp. an internal-combustion engine.

mo+tor ves+sel *or* **ship** *n.* a ship whose main propulsion system is a diesel or other internal-combustion engine.

mo·tor+way ('məʊtəˌweɪ) *n. Brit.* a main road for fast-moving traffic, having limited access, separate carriageways for vehicles travelling in opposite directions, and usually a total of four or six lanes. U.S. name: **superhighway.**

Mo+town ('məʊˌtaʊn) *n.* music combining rhythm and blues and pop, or gospel rhythms and modern ballad harmony. [C20: from *Mo(tor) Town,* a nickname for Detroit, Michigan, where this music originated]

motte (mɒt) *n. History.* a natural or man-made mound on which a castle was erected. [C14: see MOAT]

M.O.T. test *n.* (in Britain) a compulsory annual test of the roadworthiness of motor vehicles over a certain age, carried out on behalf of the Department of the Environment.

mott+le ('mɒtᵊl) *vb.* **1.** (*tr.*) to colour with streaks or blotches of different shades. ~*n.* **2.** a mottled appearance, as of the surface of marble. **3.** one streak or blotch of colour in a mottled surface. [C17: back formation from MOTLEY]

mot+to ('mɒtəʊ) *n., pl.* **+toes** *or* **+tos. 1.** a short saying expressing the guiding maxim or ideal of a family, organization, etc., esp. when part of a coat of arms. **2.** a short explanatory phrase inscribed on or attached to something. **3.** a verse or maxim contained in a paper cracker. **4.** a quotation prefacing a book or chapter of a book. **5.** a recurring musical phrase. [C16: via Italian from Latin *muttum* utterance]

Mo·tu ('məʊtuː) *n.* **1.** (*pl.* **·tu** *or* **·tus**) a member of an aboriginal people of S Papua. **2.** the language of this people, belonging to the Malayo-Polynesian family. **3.** Also called: **Hiri Motu** *or* (esp. formerly) **Police Motu.** a pidgin version of this language, widely used in Papua-New Guinea. Compare **Neo-Melanesian.**

mo·tu pro+pri·o ('məʊtuː 'prəʊprɪˌəʊ) *n.* an administrative papal bull. [Latin: of his own accord]

moue *French.* (mu) *n.* a disdainful or pouting look.

mouf+lon *or* **mouf+flon** ('muːflɒn) *n.* a wild short-fleeced mountain sheep, *Ovis musimon,* of Corsica and Sardinia. [C18: via French from Corsican *mufrone,* from Late Latin *mufrō*]

mouil+lé ('mwiːeɪ) *adj. Phonetics.* palatalized, as in the sounds represented by Spanish *ll* or *ñ,* Italian *gl* or *gn* (pronounced as (ʎ) and (ɲ) respectively), or French *ll* (representing a (j) sound). [C19: from French, past participle of *mouiller* to moisten, from Latin *mollis* soft]

mou+jik ('muːʒɪk) *n.* a variant spelling of **muzhik.**

mould¹ *or U.S.* **mold** (məʊld) *n.* **1.** a shaped cavity used to give a definite form to fluid or plastic material. **2.** a frame on which something may be constructed. **3.** something shaped in or made on a mould. **4.** shape, form, design, or pattern. **5.** specific nature, character, or type: *heroic mould.* ~*vb.* (*tr.*) **6.** to make in a mould. **7.** to shape or form, as by using a mould. **8.** to influence or direct: *to mould opinion.* **9.** to cling to: *the skirt moulds her figure.* **10.** *Metallurgy.* to make (a material such as sand) into a mould that is used in casting. [C13 (n.): changed from Old French *modle,* from Latin *modulus* a small measure, MODULE] —**'mould·a·ble** *or U.S.* **'mold+a·ble** *adj.* —**ˌmould+a·'bil+i·ty** *or U.S.* **ˌmold+a·'bil+i·ty** *n.*

mould² *or U.S.* **mold** (məʊld) *n.* **1.** a coating or discoloration caused by various saprophytic fungi that develop in a damp atmosphere on the surface of stored food, fabrics, wallpaper, etc. **2.** any of the fungi that causes this growth. ~*vb.* **3.** to become or cause to become covered with this growth. ~Also called: **mildew.** [C15: dialect (Northern English) *mowlde* mouldy, from the past participle of *moulen* to become mouldy, probably of Scandinavian origin; compare Old Norse *mugla* mould]

mould³ *or U.S.* **mold** (məʊld) *n.* **1.** loose soil, esp. when rich in organic matter. **2.** *Poetic.* the earth. [Old English *molde;* related to Old High German *molta* soil, Gothic *mulde*]

mould+board *or U.S.* **mold+board** ('məʊldˌbɔːd) *n.* the curved blade of a plough, which turns over the furrow.

mould+er¹ *or U.S.* **mold+er** ('məʊldə) *vb.* (often foll. by *away*) to crumble or cause to crumble, as through decay. [C16: verbal use of MOULD³]

mould+er² *or U.S.* **mold+er** ('məʊldə) *n.* **1.** a person who moulds or makes moulds. **2.** *Printing.* one of the set of electrotypes used for making duplicates.

mould+ing *or U.S.* **mold+ing** ('məʊldɪŋ) *n.* **1.** *Architect.* **a.** a shaped outline, esp. one used on cornices, etc. **b.** a shaped strip made of wood, stone, etc. **2.** something moulded.

mould+ing board *n.* a board on which dough is kneaded.

mould+warp ('məʊldˌwɔːp) *or* **mould·y+warp** ('məʊldɪˌwɔːp) *n.* an archaic or dialect name for a **mole** (the animal). [C14 *moldewarpe;* ultimately from Germanic *moldeworpon* (unattested) earth-thrower, from *moldā* MOULD³ + *wurp, werp* to throw (both unattested)]

mould·y *or U.S.* **mold·y** ('məʊldɪ) *adj.* **mould·i·er, mould·i·est** *or U.S.* **mold·i·er, mold·i·est. 1.** covered with mould. **2.** stale or musty, esp. from age or lack of use. **3.** *Slang.* boring; dull. —**'mould·i·ness** *or U.S.* **'mold·i+ness** *n.*

mould·y fig *n. Slang.* a rigid adherent to older jazz forms.

mou+lin ('muːlɪn) *n.* a vertical shaft in a glacier, maintained by a constant descending stream of water and debris. [C19: from French: a mill]

Mou+lins (*French* mu'lɛ̃) *n.* a market town in central France, on the Allier River. Pop.: 26 906 (1975).

Moul+mein *or* **Maul+main** (maʊl'meɪn) *n.* a port in S Burma, near the mouth of the Salween River: exports teak and rice. Pop.: 172 569 (1970 est.).

moult *or U.S.* **molt** (məʊlt) *vb.* **1.** (of birds, mammals, reptiles, and arthropods) to shed (feathers, hair, skin, or cuticle). ~*n.* **2.** the periodic process of moulting. See also **ecdysis.** [C14 *mouten,* from Old English *mūtian,* as in *bimūtian* to exchange for, from Latin *mūtāre* to change] —**'moult+er** *or U.S.* **'molt+er** *n.*

mound¹ (maʊnd) *n.* **1.** a raised mass of earth, debris, etc. **2.** any heap or pile: *a mound of washing.* **3.** a small natural hill. **4.** *Archaeol.* another word for **barrow**². **5.** an artificial ridge of earth, stone, etc., as used for defence. ~*vb.* **6.** (often foll. by *up*) to gather into a mound; heap. **7.** (*tr.*) to cover or surround with a mound: *to mound a grave.* [C16: earthwork, perhaps from Old English *mund* hand, hence defence: compare Middle Dutch *mond* protection]

mound² (maʊnd) *n. Heraldry.* a rare word for **orb** (sense 1). [C13 (meaning: world, C16: orb): from French *monde,* from Latin *mundus* world]

Mound Build+er *n.* a member of a group of prehistoric inhabitants of the Mississippi region who built altar-mounds, tumuli, etc.

mound-build·er *n.* another name for **megapode.**

mount¹ (maʊnt) *vb.* **1.** to go up (a hill, stairs, etc.); climb. **2.** to get up on (a horse, a platform, etc.). **3.** (*intr.;* often foll. by *up*) to increase; accumulate: *excitement mounted.* **4.** (*tr.*) to fix onto a backing, setting, or support: *to mount a photograph; to mount a slide.* **5.** (*tr.*) to provide with a horse for riding, or to place on a horse. **6.** (of male animals) to climb onto (a female animal) for copulation. **7.** (*tr.*) to prepare (a play, etc.) for production. **8.** (*tr.*) to prepare (a skeleton, etc.) for exhibition as a specimen. **9.** (*tr.*) to place or carry (weapons) in such a position that they can be fired. **10. mount guard.** See **guard** (sense 25). ~*n.* **11.** a backing, setting, or support onto which something is fixed. **12.** the act or manner of mounting. **13.** a horse for riding. **14.** a slide used in microscopy. **15.** *Philately.* **a.** a small transparent pocket in an album for a postage stamp. **b.** another word (esp. U.S.) for **hinge** (sense 4). [C16: from Old French *munter,* from Vulgar Latin *montāre* (unattested) from Latin *mons* MOUNT²] —**'mount+a·ble** *adj.* —**'mount+er** *n.*

mount[2] (maʊnt) *n.* **1.** a mountain or hill: used in literature and (when cap.) in proper names: *Mount Everest.* **2.** (in palmistry) any of the seven cushions of flesh on the palm of the hand. [Old English *munt,* from Latin *mons* mountain, but influenced in Middle English by Old French *mont*]

moun+tain ('maʊntɪn) *n.* **1. a.** a natural upward projection of the earth's surface, higher and steeper than a hill and often having a rocky summit. **b.** (*as modifier*): *mountain people; mountain scenery.* **c.** (*in combination*): *a mountaintop.* **2.** a huge heap or mass: *a mountain of papers.* **3.** anything of great quantity or size. [C13: from Old French *montaigne,* from Vulgar Latin *montānea* (unattested) mountainous, from Latin *montānus,* from *mons* mountain]

Moun+tain ('maʊntɪn) *n.* **the.** an extremist faction during the French Revolution led by Danton and Robespierre. [C18: so called because its members sat in the highest row of seats at the National Convention Hall in 1793]

moun+tain ash *n.* **1.** any of various trees of the rosaceous genus *Sorbus,* such as *S. aucuparia* (**European mountain ash** or **rowan**), having clusters of small white flowers and bright red berries. **2.** any of several Australian eucalyptus trees, such as *Eucalyptus regnans.*

moun+tain av+ens *n.* See **avens** (sense 2).

moun+tain cat *n.* any of various wild feline mammals, such as the bobcat, lynx, or puma.

moun+tain chain *n.* a series of ranges of mountains.

moun+tain dev+il *n.* another name for **moloch.**

moun+tain+eer (ˌmaʊntɪ'nɪə) *n.* **1.** a person who climbs mountains. **2.** a person living in a mountainous area. ~*vb.* **3.** (*intr.*) to climb mountains. —ˌ**moun+tain+'eer+ing** *n.*

moun+tain goat *n.* **1.** short for **Rocky Mountain goat. 2.** any wild goat inhabiting mountainous regions.

moun+tain lau+rel *n.* any of various ericaceous shrubs or trees of the genus *Kalmia,* esp. *K. latifolia* of E North America, which has leathery poisonous leaves and clusters of pink or white flowers. Also called: **calico bush.**

moun+tain li+on *n.* another name for **puma.**

moun+tain+ous ('maʊntɪnəs) *adj.* **1.** of or relating to mountains: *a mountainous region.* **2.** like a mountain, esp. in size or impressiveness. —'**moun+tain+ous+ly** *adv.* —'**moun+tain+ous+ness** *n.*

moun+tain range *n.* a series of adjoining mountains or of lines of mountains of similar origin.

moun+tain sheep *n.* **1.** another name for **bighorn. 2.** any wild sheep inhabiting mountainous regions.

moun+tain sick+ness *n.* nausea and shortness of breath caused by climbing to high altitudes.

Moun+tain Stand+ard Time *n.* one of the standard times used in North America, seven hours behind Greenwich Mean Time. Abbrev.: **M.S.T.**

Mount·bat·ten (maʊnt'bætᵊn) *n.* **Lou·is (Francis Albert Victor Nicholas),** 1st Earl Mountbatten of Burma. 1900-1979, British naval commander; great-grandson of Queen Victoria. During World War II he was supreme allied commander in SE Asia (1943-46). He was the last viceroy of India (1947) and governor general (1947-48). Murdered by the IRA.

Mount Des+ert Is+land *n.* an island off the coast of Maine: lakes and granite peaks. Area: 279 sq. km (108 sq. miles).

moun+te·bank ('maʊntɪˌbæŋk) *n.* **1.** (formerly) a person who sold quack medicines in public places. **2.** a charlatan; fake. ~*vb.* **3.** (*intr.*) to play the mountebank. [C16: from Italian *montambanco* a climber on a bench, from *montare* to MOUNT[1] + *banco* BENCH (see also BANK[1])] —ˌ**moun+te·'bank+er·y** *n.*

mount+ed ('maʊntɪd) *adj.* **1.** equipped with or riding horses: *mounted police.* **2.** provided with a support, backing, etc.

Mount·ie or **Mount·y** ('maʊntɪ) *n., pl.* **Mount·ies.** *Informal.* a member of the Royal Canadian Mounted Police. [nickname evolved from MOUNTED]

mount+ing ('maʊntɪŋ) *n.* another word for **mount** (sense 11).

mount·ing-block *n.* a block of stone formerly used to aid a person when mounting a horse.

Mount I·sa ('aɪzə) *n.* a city in NE Australia in NW Queensland: mining of copper and other minerals. Pop.: 32 850 (1975 est.).

Mount Mc·Kin·ley Na+tion+al Park *n.* a national park in S central Alaska: contains part of the Alaska Range. Area: 7847 sq. km (3030 sq. miles).

Mount Rai+ni+er Na+tion+al Park *n.* a national park in W Washington, in the Cascade Range. Area: 976 sq. km (377 sq. miles).

mourn (mɔːn) *vb.* **1.** to feel or express sadness for the death or loss of (someone or something). **2.** (*intr.*) to observe the customs of mourning, as by wearing black. **3.** (*tr.*) to grieve over (loss or misfortune). [Old English *murnan;* compare Old High German *mornēn* to be troubled, Gothic *maurnan* to grieve, Greek *mermeros* worried]

mourn+er ('mɔːnə) *n.* **1.** a person who mourns, esp. at a funeral. **2.** (at U.S. revivalist meetings) a person who repents publicly.

mourn+ful ('mɔːnfʊl) *adj.* **1.** evoking grief; sorrowful. **2.** gloomy; sad. —'**mourn+ful+ly** *adv.* —'**mourn+ful+ness** *n.*

mourn+ing ('mɔːnɪŋ) *n.* **1.** the act or feelings of one who mourns; grief. **2.** the conventional symbols of grief, such as the wearing of black. **3.** the period of time during which a death is officially mourned. **4. in mourning.** observing the conventions of mourning. ~*adj.* **5.** of or relating to mourning. —'**mourn+ing+ly** *adv.*

mourn+ing band *n.* a piece of black material, esp. an armband, worn to indicate that the wearer is in mourning.

mourn+ing cloak *n.* the U.S. name for **Camberwell beauty.**

mourn+ing dove *n.* a brown North American dove, *Zenaidura macroura,* with a plaintive song.

mouse *n.* (maʊs), *pl.* **mice** (maɪs). **1.** any of numerous small long-tailed rodents of the families *Muridae* and *Cricetidae* that are similar to but smaller than rats. See also **fieldmouse, harvest mouse, house mouse. 2.** any of various related rodents, such as the jumping mouse. **3.** a quiet, timid, or cowardly person. **4.** *Slang.* a black eye. **5.** *Nautical.* another word for **mousing.** ~*vb.* (maʊz). **6.** to stalk and catch (mice, etc.). **7.** (*intr.*) to go about stealthily. **8.** (*tr.*) *Nautical.* to secure (a hook) with mousing. [Old English *mūs;* compare Old Saxon *mūs,* German *maus,* Old Norse *mūs,* Latin *mūs,* Greek *mūs*] —'**mouse+,like** *adj.*

mouse+bird ('maʊsˌbɜːd) *n.* another name for **coly.**

mouse deer *n.* another name for **chevrotain.**

mouse-ear *n.* short for **mouse-ear chickweed** (see **chickweed** (sense 2)).

mous+er ('maʊzə, 'maʊsə) *n.* a cat or other animal that is used to catch mice: usually qualified: *a good mouser.*

mouse+tail ('maʊsˌteɪl) *n.* any of various N temperate ranunculaceous plants of the genus *Myosurus,* esp. *M. minimus,* with tail-like flower spikes.

mouse+trap ('maʊsˌtræp) *n.* **1.** any trap for catching mice, esp. one with a spring-loaded metal bar that is released by the taking of the bait. **2.** *Brit. informal.* cheese of indifferent quality.

mous+ey ('maʊsɪ) *adj.* **mous·i+er, mous·i+est.** a variant spelling of **mousy.** —'**mous·i+ly** *adv.* —'**mous·i+ness** *n.*

mous+ing ('maʊzɪŋ) *n.* *Nautical.* a lashing, shackle, etc., for closing off a hook to prevent a load from slipping off.

mous+sa+ka or **mou+sa+ka** (mʊ'sɑːkə) *n.* a dish originating in the Balkan States, consisting of meat, aubergines, and tomatoes, topped with cheese sauce. [C20: from Modern Greek]

mousse (muːs) *n.* **1.** a light creamy dessert made with eggs, cream, fruit, etc., set with gelatine. **2.** a similar dish made from fish or meat. [C19: from French: froth]

mousse+line (*French* mus'lin) *n.* **1.** a fine fabric made of rayon or silk. **2.** a type of fine glass. [C17: French: MUSLIN]

mousse+line de laine *French.* (muslin də 'lɛn) *n.* a light woollen fabric. [literally: muslin of wool]

mousse+line de soie *French.* (muslin də 'swa) *n.* a thin gauzelike fabric of silk or rayon. [literally: muslin of silk]

mousse+line sauce *n.* a light sweet or savoury sauce, made by adding whipped cream or egg whites to hollandaise sauce. [from French *mousseline,* literally: muslin]

Mous·sorg·sky (mʊ'sɔːgskɪ; *Russian* 'musərkskij) *n.* a variant spelling of (Modest Petrovich) **Mussorgsky.**

mous+tache or *U.S.* **mus+tache** (mə'stɑːʃ) *n.* **1.** the unshaved growth of hair on the upper lip, and sometimes down the sides of the mouth. **2.** a similar growth of hair or bristles (in animals) or feathers (in birds). **3.** a mark like a moustache. [C16: via French from Italian *mostaccio,* ultimately from Doric Greek *mustax* upper lip] —**mous+'tached** or *U.S.* **mus+'tached** *adj.*

mous+tache cup *n.* a cup with a partial cover to protect a drinker's moustache.

Mous·te·ri·an (muː'stɪərɪən) *n.* **1.** a culture characterized by flint flake tools and associated with Neanderthal man, found throughout Europe, North Africa, and the Near East, dating from before 70 000–32 000 B.C. ~*adj.* **2.** of or relating to this culture. [C20: from French *Moustérien* from archaeological finds of the same period in the cave of *Le Moustier,* Dordogne, France]

mous·y or **mous+ey** ('maʊsɪ) *adj.* **mous·i+er, mous·i+est. 1.** resembling a mouse, esp. in colour. **2.** shy or ineffectual: *a mousy little woman.* **3.** infested with mice. —'**mous·i+ly** *adv.* —'**mous·i+ness** *n.*

mouth *n.* (maʊθ), *pl.* **mouths** (maʊðz). **1.** the opening through which many animals take in food and issue vocal sounds. **2.** the system of organs surrounding this opening, including the lips, tongue, teeth, etc. **3.** the visible part of the lips on the face. **4.** a person regarded as a consumer of food: *four mouths to feed.* **5.** verbal expression (esp. in the phrase **give mouth to**). **6.** a particular manner of speaking: *a foul mouth.* **7.** *Informal.* boastful, rude, or excessive talk: *he is all mouth.* **8.** the point where a river issues into a sea or lake. **9.** the opening of a container, such as a jar. **10.** the opening of or place leading into a cave, tunnel, volcano, etc. **11.** that part of the inner lip of a horse on which the bit acts, esp. when specified as to sensitivity: *a hard mouth.* **12.** *Music.* the narrow slit in an organ pipe. **13.** the opening between the jaws of a vice or other gripping device. **14.** a pout; grimace. **15. by word of mouth.** orally rather than by written means. **16. down in** or **at the mouth.** in low spirits. **17. have a big mouth** or **open one's big mouth.** *Informal.* to speak indiscreetly, loudly, or excessively. **18. keep one's mouth shut.** to keep a secret. **19. put words into someone's mouth. a.** to represent, often inaccurately, what someone has said. **b.** to tell someone what to say. **20. put one's money where one's mouth is.** to take appropriate action to support what one has said. ~*vb.* (maʊð). **21.** to speak or say (something) insincerely, esp. in public. **22.** (*tr.*) to form (words) with movements of the lips but without speaking. **23.** (*tr.*) to accustom (a horse) to wearing a bit. **24.** (*tr.*) to take (something) into the mouth or to move (something) around inside the mouth. **25.** (*intr.; usually foll. by at*) to make a grimace. [Old English *mūth;* compare Old Norse *muthr,* Gothic *munths,* Dutch *mond*] —**mouth+er** ('maʊðə) *n.*

mouth+brood·er ('maʊθˌbruːdə) or **mouth+breed·er** ('maʊθˌbriːdə) *n.* any of various African cichlid fishes of the genera *Tilapia* and *Haplochromis* that carry their eggs and young around in the mouth.

mouth·ful ('mauθ,fʊl) *n., pl.* **-fuls.** **1.** as much as is held in the mouth at one time. **2.** a small quantity, as of food. **3.** a long word or phrase that is difficult to say. **4.** *Informal, chiefly U.S.* an impressive remark (esp. in the phrase **say a mouthful**).

mouth or·gan *n.* another name for **harmonica** (sense 1).

mouth·part ('mauθ,pɑ:t) *n.* any of the paired appendages in arthropods that surround the mouth and are specialized for feeding.

mouth·piece ('mauθ,pi:s) *n.* **1.** the part of a wind instrument into which the player blows. **2.** the part of a telephone receiver into which a person speaks. **3.** the part of a container forming its mouth. **4.** a person who acts as a spokesman, as for an organization. **5.** a publication, esp. a periodical, expressing the official views of an organization. **6.** *Boxing.* another name for **gumshield.**

mouth-to-mouth *adj.* designating a method of artificial respiration involving blowing air rhythmically into the mouth of a person who has stopped breathing, to stimulate return of spontaneous breathing.

mouth·wash ('mauθ,wɒʃ) *n.* a medicated aqueous solution, used for gargling and for cleansing the mouth.

mouth·wa·ter·ing ('mauθ,wɔ:tərɪŋ) *adj.* whetting the appetite, as from smell, appearance, or description.

mouth·y ('mauðɪ) *adj.* **mouth·i·er, mouth·i·est.** bombastic; excessively talkative.

mou·ton ('mu:tɒn) *n.* sheepskin processed to resemble the fur of another animal, esp. beaver or seal. [from French: sheep. See MUTTON]

mov·a·ble *or* **move·a·ble** ('mu:vəbᵊl) *adj.* **1.** able to be moved or rearranged; not fixed. **2.** (esp. of religious festivals such as Easter) varying in date from year to year. **3.** (usually spelt **moveable**) *Law.* denoting or relating to personal property as opposed to realty. **4.** *Printing.* (of type) cast singly so that each character is on a separate piece of type suitable for composition by hand, as founder's type. *~n.* **5.** (*often pl.*) a movable article, esp. a piece of furniture. **—,mov·a·'bil·i·ty** *or* **'mov·a·ble·ness** *n.* **—'mov·a·bly** *adv.*

move (mu:v) *vb.* **1.** to go or take from one place to another; change in location or position. **2.** (*usually intr.*) to change (one's dwelling, place of business, etc.). **3.** to be or cause to be in motion; stir. **4.** (*intr.*) (of machines, etc.) to work or operate. **5.** (*tr.*) to cause (to do something); prompt. **6.** (*intr.*) to begin to act: *move soon or we'll lose the order.* **7.** (*intr.*) to associate oneself with a specified social circle: *to move in exalted spheres.* **8.** (*intr.*) to make progress. **9.** (*tr.*) to arouse affection, pity, or compassion in; touch. **10.** (in board games) to change the position of (a piece) or (of a piece) to change position. **11.** (of merchandise) to be disposed of by being bought. **12.** (when *tr., often takes a clause as object;* when *intr.,* often foll. by *for*) to suggest (a proposal) formally, as in debating or parliamentary procedure. **13.** (*intr.;* usually foll. by *on* or *along*) to go away or to another place; leave. **14.** to cause (the bowels) to evacuate or (of the bowels) to be evacuated. **15.** (*intr.*) *Informal.* to be exciting or active: *the party started moving at twelve.* **16. move heaven and earth.** *Informal.* to take every step possible. *~n.* **17.** the act of moving; movement. **18.** one of a sequence of actions, usually part of a plan; manoeuvre. **19.** the act of moving one's residence, place of business, etc. **20.** (in board games) **a.** a player's turn to move his piece or take other permitted action. **b.** a permitted manoeuvre of a piece. **21. get a move on.** *Informal.* **a.** to get started. **b.** to hurry up. **22. make a move.** (*usually used with a negative*) *Informal.* to take even the slightest action: *don't make a move without phoning me.* **23. make one's move.** to commit oneself to a position or course of action. **24. on the move.** *Informal.* **a.** travelling from place to place. **b.** advancing; succeeding. **c.** very active; busy. [C13: from Anglo-French *mover,* from Latin *movēre*]

move in *vb.* (*mainly adv.*) **1.** (*also prep.*) Also (when *prep.*): **move into.** to occupy or take possession of (a new residence, place of business, etc.), or help (someone) to do this. **2.** (*intr.;* often foll. by *on*) *Informal.* to creep close (to), as in preparing to capture. **3.** (*intr.;* often foll. by *on*) *Informal.* to try to gain power or influence (over) or interfere (with).

move·ment ('mu:vmənt) *n.* **1. a.** the act, process, or result of moving. **b.** an instance of moving. **2.** the manner of moving. **3. a.** a group of people with a common ideology, esp. a political or religious one. **b.** the organized action of such a group. **4.** a trend or tendency in a particular sphere. **5.** the driving and regulating mechanism of a watch or clock. **6.** (*often pl.*) a person's location and activities during a specific time. **7. a.** the evacuation of the bowels. **b.** the matter evacuated. **8.** *Music.* a principal self-contained section of a symphony, sonata, etc., usually having its own structure. **9.** tempo or pace, as in music or literature. **10.** *Fine arts.* the appearance of motion in painting, sculpture, etc. **11.** *Prosody.* the rhythmical structure of verse. **12.** a positional change by one or a number of military units. **13.** a change in the market price of a security or commodity.

move out *vb.* (*adv.*) to vacate a residence, place of business, etc., or help (someone) to do this.

mov·er ('mu:və) *n.* **1.** *Informal.* a person, business, idea, etc., that is advancing or progressing. **2.** a person who moves a proposal, as in a debate. **3.** *U.S.* a removal firm or a person who works for one.

mov·ie ('mu:vɪ) *n. U.S.* **a.** an informal word for **film** (sense 1). **b.** (*as modifier*): *movie ticket.*

mov·ie cam·er·a *n.* the U.S. term for **cine camera.**

mov·ie film *n.* the U.S. term for **cine film.**

Mov·ie·tone ('mu:vɪ,təun) *n. U.S. trademark.* the earliest technique of including a soundtrack on film.

mov·ing ('mu:vɪŋ) *adj.* **1.** arousing or touching the emotions. **2.** changing or capable of changing position. **3.** causing motion. **—'mov·ing·ly** *adv.* **—'mov·ing·ness** *n.*

mov·ing av·er·age *n. Statistics.* an average with several successive values obtained by replacing one item in the numerator of the average but keeping the same denominator. It is often used in time series.

mov·ing pic·ture *n.* a U.S. name for **film** (sense 1).

mov·ing stair·case *or* **stair·way** *n.* less common terms for **escalator.**

Mo·vi·o·la (,mu:vɪ'əulə) *n. Trademark.* a viewing machine used in cutting and editing film.

mow[1] (məu) *vb.* **mows, mow·ing, mowed, mowed** *or* **mown. 1.** to cut down (grass, crops, etc.), with a hand implement or machine. **2.** (*tr.*) to cut the growing vegetation of (a field, lawn, etc.). [Old English *māwan;* related to Old High German *māen,* Middle Dutch *maeyen* to mow, Latin *metere* to reap, Welsh *medi*] **—'mow·er** *n.*

mow[2] (mau) *n.* **1.** the part of a barn where hay, straw, etc., is stored. **2.** the hay, straw, etc., stored. [Old English *mūwa;* compare Old Norse *mūgr* heap, Greek *mukōn*]

mow[3] (mau) *n., vb.* an archaic word for **grimace.** [C14: from Old French *moe* a pout, or Middle Dutch *mouwe*]

mow·burnt ('məu,bɜ:nt) *adj.* (of hay, straw, etc.) damaged by overheating in a mow.

mow down *vb.* (*tr., adv.*) to kill in large numbers, esp. by gunfire.

mown (məun) *vb.* the past participle of **mow**[1].

mox·a ('mɒksə) *n.* **1.** a downy material obtained from various plants and used in Oriental medicine as a cauterizing agent or counterirritant for the skin. **2.** any of various plants yielding this material, such as the wormwood *Artemisia chinensis.* [C17: anglicized version of Japanese *mogusa,* contraction of *moe gusa* burning herb]

mox·ie ('mɒksɪ) *n. U.S. slang.* courage, nerve, or vigour. [from the trademark *Moxie,* a soft drink]

Mo·zam·bique *or* **Mo·çam·bique** (,məuzəm'bi:k) *n.* a republic in SE Africa: colonized by the Portuguese from 1505 onwards and a slave-trade centre until 1878; made an overseas province of Portugal in 1951; became an independent republic in 1975. Currency: escudo. Capital: Maputo. Pop.: 8 233 834 (1970). Area: 771 124 sq. km (297 846 sq. miles). Also called (until 1975): **Portuguese East Africa.**

Mo·zam·bique Chan·nel *n.* a strait between Mozambique and Madagascar. Length: about 1600 km (1000 miles). Width: 400 km (250 miles).

Moz·ar·ab (məu'zærəb) *n.* (formerly) a Christian of Moorish Spain. [C18: via Spanish from Arabic *musta'rib* a would-be Arab] **—Moz·'ar·a·bic** *adj.*

Mo·zart ('məutsɑ:t) *n.* **Wolf·gang A·ma·de·us** ('vɔlfgaŋ ,ama'de:ʊs). 1756–91, Austrian composer. A child prodigy and prolific genius, his works include operas, such as *The Marriage of Figaro* (1786), *Don Giovanni* (1787), and *The Magic Flute* (1791), symphonies, concertos for piano, violin, clarinet, and French horn, string quartets and quintets, sonatas, songs, and Masses, such as the unfinished *Requiem* (1791). **—Mo·'zar·te·an** *or* **Mo·'zar·ti·an** *adj.*

moz·za·rel·la (,mɒtsə'rɛlə) *n.* a moist white Italian curd cheese made originally from buffalo milk. [from Italian, diminutive of *mozza* a type of cheese, from *mozzare* to cut off]

moz·zet·ta (məu'zɛtə; *Italian* mot'tsetta) *or* **mo·zet·ta** *n. R.C. Church.* a short hooded cape worn by the pope, cardinals, etc. [C18: from Italian, shortened from *almozzetta,* from Medieval Latin *almutia* AMICE[1]]

mp *or* **m.p.** *Music. abbrev. for* mezzo piano. [Italian: moderately soft]

M.P. *abbrev. for:* **1.** (in Britain) Member of Parliament. **2.** (in Britain) Metropolitan Police. **3.** Military Police. **4.** Mounted Police.

m.p. *abbrev. for* melting point.

m.p.g. *abbrev. for* miles per gallon.

m.p.h. *abbrev. for* miles per hour.

M.Phil. *or* **M.Ph.** *abbrev. for* Master of Philosophy.

M.P.S. *abbrev. for:* **1.** Member of the Pharmaceutical Society. **2.** Member of the Philological Society. **3.** Member of the Physical Society.

M.R. *abbrev. for:* **1.** (in Britain) Master of the Rolls. **2.** motivation(al) research.

Mr. ('mɪstə) *n., pl.* **Messrs.** ('mɛsəz). **1.** a title used before a man's name or names or before some office that he holds: *Mr. Jones; Mr. President.* **2.** (in military contexts) a title used in addressing a warrant officer, officer cadet, or junior naval officer. **3.** a title placed before the surname of a surgeon. [C17: abbreviation of MISTER]

MRA *abbrev. for* Moral Rearmament.

M.R.C. *abbrev. for* (in Britain) Medical Research Council.

mri·dang (mrɪ'dʌŋg) *n.* a drum used in Indian music. [Hindi]

m-RNA *abbrev. for* messenger RNA.

Mrs. ('mɪsɪz) *n., pl.* **Mrs.** *or* **Mesdames.** a title used before the name or names of a married woman. [C17: originally an abbreviation of MISTRESS]

MS *international car registration for* Mauritius.

MS. *or* **ms.** *pl.* **MSS.** *or* **mss.** *abbrev. for* manuscript.

M.S. *abbrev. for:* **1.** Master of Surgery. **2.** (on gravestones, etc.) memoriae sacrum. [Latin: sacred to the memory of] **3.** multiple sclerosis.

Ms. (mɪz, məs) *n.* a title substituted for **Mrs.** or **Miss** before a woman's name to avoid making a distinction between married and unmarried women.

M.Sc. *abbrev. for* Master of Science.

MSG *abbrev. for* monosodium glutamate.

Msgr. *abbrev. for* Monsignor.

MSI *Electronics. abbrev. for* medium scale integration.

m.s.l. *or* **M.S.L.** *abbrev. for* mean sea level.

M.S.T. *abbrev. for* Mountain Standard Time.

Ms-Th *Physics. symbol for* mesothorium.

Mt. *or* **mt.** *abbrev. for:* **1.** mount: *Mt. Everest.* **2.** Also: **mtn.** mountain.

MTB *n. Brit.* a motor torpedo boat.

M.Tech. *abbrev. for* Master of Technology.

Mt. Rev. *abbrev. for* Most Reverend.

mu (mju:) *n.* the 12th letter in the Greek alphabet (M, μ), a consonant, translated as *m.*

Mu·bar·ak (mʊˈbɑːrək) *n.* **Mu·ham·mad Hos·ni** (ˈhʊsnɪ) born 1929, Egyptian politician; president of Egypt from 1981.

muc- *combining form.* variant of **muco-** before a vowel.

much (mʌtʃ) *determiner.* **1. a.** (*usually used with a negative*) a great quantity or degree of: *there isn't much honey left.* **b.** (*as pronoun*): *much has been learned from this.* **2. a bit much.** *Informal.* rather excessive. **3. as much.** exactly that: *I suspected as much when I heard.* **4. make much of. a.** (*used with a negative*) to make sense of: *he couldn't make much of her babble.* **b.** to give importance to: *she made much of this fact.* **c.** to pay flattering attention to: *the reporters made much of the film star.* **5. not much of.** not to any appreciable degree or extent: *he's not much of an actor really.* **6. not up to much.** *Informal.* of a low standard: *this beer is not up to much.* **7. think much of.** (*used with a negative*) to have a high opinion of: *I don't think much of his behaviour.* ~*adv.* **8.** considerably: *they're much better now.* **9.** practically; nearly (esp. in the phrase **much the same**). **10.** (*usually used with a negative*) often; a great deal: *it doesn't happen much in this country.* **11.** (**as**) **much as.** even though; although: *much as I'd like to, I can't come.* ~*adj.* **12.** (*predicative; usually used with a negative*) impressive, or important: *this car isn't much.* ~See also **more, most.** [Old English *mycel;* related to Old English *micel* great, Old Saxon *mikil,* Gothic *mikils;* compare also Latin *magnus,* Greek *megas*]

much+ness (ˈmʌtʃnɪs) *n.* **1.** *Archaic or informal.* magnitude. **2. much of a muchness.** *Brit.* very similar.

mu+cic ac·id (ˈmju:sɪk) *n.* a colourless crystalline solid carboxylic acid found in milk sugar and used in the manufacture of pyrrole. Formula: $C_4H_4(OH)_4(COOH)_2$. [C19: *mucic,* from French *mucique;* see MUCUS, -IC]

mu+cid (ˈmju:sɪd) *adj. Rare.* mouldy, musty, or slimy. [C17: from Latin *mūcidus,* from *mucēre* to be mouldy] —**mu+ˈcid+i·ty** *or* **ˈmu+cid+ness** *n.*

mu+ci+lage (ˈmju:sɪlɪdʒ) *n.* **1.** a sticky preparation, such as gum or glue, used as an adhesive. **2.** a complex glutinous carbohydrate secreted by certain plants. [C14: via Old French from Late Latin *mūcilāgo* mouldy juice; see MUCID] —**mu+ci+lag·i·nous** (ˌmju:sɪˈlædʒɪnəs) *adj.* —**ˌmu+ci+ˈlag·i·nous+ly** *adv.* —**ˌmu+ci+ˈlag·i·nous+ness** *n.*

mu+cin (ˈmju:sɪn) *n. Biochem.* any of a group of nitrogenous mucoproteins occurring in saliva, skin, tendon, etc., that produce a very viscous solution in water. [C19: via French from Latin MUCUS] —**ˈmu+cin+ous** *adj.*

muck (mʌk) *n.* **1.** farmyard dung or decaying vegetable matter. **2.** Also called: **muck soil.** an organic soil rich in humus and used as a fertilizer. **3.** dirt or filth. **4.** earth, rock material, etc., removed during mining excavations. **5.** *Slang, chiefly Brit.* trash. **6. make a muck of.** *Slang, chiefly Brit.* to ruin or spoil. ~*vb.* (*tr.*) **7.** to spread manure upon (fields, etc.). **8.** to soil or pollute. **9.** (usually foll. by *up*) *Brit. slang.* to ruin or spoil. **10.** (often foll. by *out*) to clear muck from. [C13: probably of Scandinavian origin; compare Old Norse *myki* dung, Norwegian *myk*]

muck a·bout *vb. Brit. slang.* **1.** (*intr.*) to waste time; misbehave. **2.** (when *intr.,* foll. by *with*) to interfere with, annoy, or waste the time of.

muck·a·muck (ˈmʌkəˌmʌk) *Canadian W coast.* ~*n.* **1.** food. ~*vb.* **2.** (*intr.*) to consume food; eat. [Chinook Jargon]

muck+er (ˈmʌkə) *n.* **1.** *Mining.* a person who shifts broken rock or waste. **2.** *Brit. slang.* **a.** a friend; mate. **b.** a coarse person.

muck in *vb.* (*intr., adv.*) *Brit. slang.* to share something, such as duties, work, etc., (with other people).

muck+le (ˈmʌkᵊl) *Scot.* ~*adj.* **1.** large; much. ~*adv.* **2.** much; greatly. [dialect variant of MICKLE]

muck+rake (ˈmʌkˌreɪk) *n.* **1.** an agricultural rake for spreading manure. ~*vb.* **2.** (*intr.*) to seek out and expose scandal, esp. concerning public figures. —**ˈmuck+ˌrak+er** *n.* —**ˈmuck+ˌrak+ing** *n.*

muck+sweat (ˈmʌkˌswɛt) *n. Brit. informal.* profuse sweat or a state of profuse sweating.

muck+worm (ˈmʌkˌwɜ:m) *n.* **1.** any larva or worm that lives in mud. **2.** *Informal.* a miser.

muck·y (ˈmʌkɪ) *adj.* **muck·i+er, muck·i+est. 1.** dirty. **2.** of or like muck. —**ˈmuck·i+ly** *adv.* —**ˈmuck·i+ness** *n.*

mu·co- *or before a vowel* **muc-** *combining form.* mucus or mucous: *mucoprotein; mucin.*

mu+coid (ˈmju:kɔɪd) *or* **mu+coi+dal** *adj.* of the nature of or resembling mucin.

mu+co+pol·y+sac+cha+ride (ˌmju:kəʊˌpɒlɪˈsækəraɪd) *n. Biochem.* any of a group of complex polysaccharides composed of hexoses and pentoses with uronic acids, hexosamines, or both.

mu+co+pro+tein (ˌmju:kəʊˈprəʊti:n) *n.* any of a group of conjugated proteins containing small quantities of mucopolysaccharides; glycoprotein.

mu+co+pu+ru+lent (ˌmju:kəʊˈpjʊərələnt) *adj. Pathol.* composed of or containing both mucus and pus.

mu+co+sa (mju:ˈkəʊsə) *n., pl.* **+sae** (-si:). another word for **mucous membrane.** [C19: New Latin, from Latin *mūcōsus* slimy] —**mu+ˈco+sal** *adj.*

mu+cous (ˈmju:kəs) *or* **mu+cose** (ˈmju:kəʊs, -kəʊz) *adj.* of, resembling, or secreting mucus. [C17: from Latin *mūcōsus* slimy, from MUCUS] —**mu+cos+i·ty** (mju:ˈkɒsɪtɪ) *n.*

mu+cous mem+brane *n.* a mucus-secreting membrane that lines body cavities or passages that are open to the external environment. Also called: **mucosa.** —**mu+co+mem+bra+nous** (ˌmju:kəʊˈmɛmbrənəs) *adj.*

mu+cro (ˈmju:krəʊ) *n., pl.* **mu+cro+nes** (mju:ˈkrəʊni:z). *Biology.* a short pointed projection from certain parts or organs, as from the tip of a leaf. [C17: from Latin *mūcrō* point]

mu+cro+nate (ˈmju:krəʊnɪt, -ˌneɪt) *or* **mu+cro+nat+ed** *adj.* terminating in a sharp point. [C18: from Latin *mūcrōnātus* pointed, from MUCRO] —**ˌmu+cro+ˈna+tion** *n.*

mu+cus (ˈmju:kəs) *n.* the slimy protective secretion of the mucous membranes, consisting mainly of mucin. [C17: from Latin: nasal secretions; compare *mungere* to blow the nose; related to Greek *muxa* mucus, *muktēr* nose]

mud (mʌd) *n.* **1.** a fine-grained soft wet deposit that occurs on the ground after rain, at the bottom of ponds, etc. **2.** *Informal.* slander or defamation. **3. clear as mud.** not at all clear. **4. drag (someone's) name in the mud.** to disgrace or defame (someone). **5. here's mud in your eye.** *Informal.* a humorous drinking toast. **6. (someone's) name is mud.** *Informal.* (someone) is disgraced. **7. throw** (*or* **sling**) **mud at.** *Informal.* slander; vilify. ~*vb.* **muds, mud+ding, mud+ded. 8.** (*tr.*) to soil or cover with mud. [C14: probably from Middle Low German *mudde;* compare Middle High German *mot* swamp, mud, Swedish *modd* slush]

mud bath *n.* **1.** a medicinal bath in heated mud. **2.** a dirty or muddy occasion, state, etc.

mud+cat (ˈmʌdˌkæt) *n.* any of several large North American catfish living in muddy rivers, esp. in the Mississippi valley.

mud daub+er *n.* any of various wasps of the family *Sphecidae,* that construct cells of mud or clay in which they lay their eggs and store live insects as food for the developing larvae. See also **digger wasp.**

mud+dle (ˈmʌdᵊl) *vb.* (*tr.*) **1.** (often foll. by *up*) to mix up (objects, items, etc.); jumble. **2.** to confuse. **3.** to make (water) muddy or turbulent. **4.** *U.S.* to mix or stir (alcoholic drinks, etc.). ~*n.* **5.** a state of physical or mental confusion. [C16: perhaps from Middle Dutch *moddelen* to make muddy] —**ˈmud+dled+ness** *or* **ˈmud+dle+ment** *n.* —**ˈmud+dling+ly** *adv.*

mud+dle a·long *or* **on** *vb.* (*intr., adv.*) to proceed in a disorganized way.

mud·dle+head·ed (ˌmʌdᵊlˈhɛdɪd) *adj.* mentally confused or vague. —**ˌmud·dle+ˈhead·ed·ness** *n.*

mud+dler (ˈmʌdlə) *n.* **1.** a person who muddles or muddles through. **2.** an instrument for mixing drinks thoroughly.

mud+dle through *vb.* (*intr., adv.*) *Chiefly Brit.* to succeed in some undertaking in spite of lack of organization.

mud+dy (ˈmʌdɪ) *adj.* **+di+er, +di+est. 1.** covered or filled with mud. **2.** not clear or bright: *muddy colours.* **3.** cloudy: *a muddy liquid.* **4.** (esp. of thoughts) confused or vague. ~*vb.* **+dies, +dy+ing, +died. 5.** to become or cause to become muddy. —**ˈmud+di+ly** *adv.* —**ˈmud+di+ness** *n.*

Mu+dé+jar *Spanish.* (muˈðexar) *n., pl.* **+ja·res** (-xaˌres). **1.** *Medieval history.* a Spanish Moor, esp. one permitted to stay in Spain after the Christian reconquest. ~*adj.* **2.** of or relating to a style of architecture orginated by Mudéjares. [from Arabic *mudajjan* one permitted to remain]

mud+fish (ˈmʌdˌfɪʃ) *n., pl.* **+fish** *or* **+fish·es.** any of various fishes, such as the bowfin and cichlids, that live at or frequent the muddy bottoms of rivers, lakes, etc.

mud flat *n.* a tract of low muddy land, esp. near an estuary, that is covered at high tide and exposed at low tide.

mud+guard (ˈmʌdˌgɑ:d) *n.* a curved part of a motorcycle, bicycle, etc., attached above the wheels to reduce the amount of water or mud thrown up by them. U.S. name: **fender.**

mud hen *n.* any of various birds that frequent marshes or similar places, esp. the coots, rails, etc.

mu+dir (mu:ˈdɪə) *n.* a local governor. [C19: via Turkish, from Arabic, from *adāra* to administrate]

mud+lark (ˈmʌdˌlɑ:k) *n.* **1.** *Slang, now rare.* a street urchin. **2.** *Austral. slang.* a racehorse that runs well on a wet or muddy course.

mud map *n. Austral.* a map drawn on the ground with a stick.

mud+pack (ˈmʌdˌpæk) *n.* a cosmetic astringent paste containing fuller's earth, used to improve the complexion.

mud pie *n.* a mass of mud moulded into a pie-like shape by a child.

mud pup+py *n.* any aquatic North American salamander of the genus *Necturus,* esp. *N. maculosus,* having red feathery external gills and other persistent larval features: family *Proteidae.* See also **neoteny.**

mu+dra (məˈdrɑ:) *n.* any of various ritual hand movements in Hindu religious dancing. [Sanskrit, literally: sign, token]

mud+skip·per (ˈmʌdˌskɪpə) *n.* any of various gobies of the genus *Periophthalmus* and related genera that occur in tropical coastal regions of Africa and Asia and can move on land by means of their strong pectoral fins.

mud+sling·ing ('mʌdˌslɪŋɪŋ) *n.* casting malicious slurs on an opponent, esp. in politics. —'**mud+ˌsling·er** *n.*
mud+stone ('mʌdˌstəʊn) *n.* a dark grey clay rock similar to shale but with the lamination less well developed.
mud tur+tle *n.* any of various small turtles of the genus *Kinosternon* and related genera that inhabit muddy rivers in North and Central America: family *Kinosternidae.*
muen+ster ('mʊnstə) *n.* a whitish-yellow semihard whole milk cheese, often flavoured with caraway or aniseed. [after *Muenster,* Haut-Rhin, France]
mues+li ('mju:zlɪ) *n.* a mixture of rolled oats, nuts, fruit, etc., eaten with milk. [Swiss German, from German (*Ge*)*müse* vegetable + *-li,* diminutive suffix]
mu+ez+zin (mu:'ɛzɪn) *n. Islam.* the official of a mosque who calls the faithful to prayer five times a day from the minaret. [C16: changed from Arabic *mu'adhdhin*]
muff[1] (mʌf) *n.* **1.** an open-ended cylinder of fur or cloth into which the hands are placed for warmth. **2.** the tuft on either side of the head of certain fowls. [C16: probably from Dutch *mof,* ultimately from French *mouffle* MUFFLE[1]]
muff[2] (mʌf) *vb.* **1.** to perform (an action) awkwardly. **2.** (*tr.*) to bungle (a shot, catch, etc.) in a game. ~*n.* **3.** any unskilful play in a game, esp. a dropped catch. **4.** any clumsy or bungled action. **5.** a bungler. [C19: of uncertain origin]
muf+fin ('mʌfɪn) *n.* **1.** *Brit.* a thick round baked yeast roll, usually toasted and served with butter. **2.** *U.S.* a small cup-shaped sweet bread roll, usually eaten hot with butter. [C18: perhaps from Low German *muffen,* cakes]
muf+fin man *n. Brit.* (formerly) an itinerant seller of muffins.
muf+fle[1] ('mʌfᵊl) *vb.* (*tr.*) **1.** (often foll. by *up*) to wrap up (the head) in a scarf, cloak, etc., esp. for warmth. **2.** to deaden (a sound or noise), esp. by wrapping. **3.** to prevent (the expression of something) by (someone). ~*n.* **4.** something that muffles. **5.** a kiln with an inner chamber for firing porcelain, enamel, etc., at a low temperature. [C15: probably from Old French; compare Old French *moufle* mitten, *emmouflé* wrapped up]
muf+fle[2] ('mʌfᵊl) *n.* the fleshy hairless part of the upper lip and nose in ruminants and some rodents. [C17: from French *mufle,* of unknown origin]
muf+fler ('mʌflə) *n.* **1.** a thick scarf, collar, etc. **2.** the U.S. name for **silencer** (sense 1). **3.** something that muffles.
muf+ti ('mʌftɪ) *n., pl.* **+tis.** civilian dress, esp. as worn by a person who normally wears a military uniform. [C19: perhaps from MUFTI]
Muf+ti ('mʌftɪ) *n., pl.* **+tis. 1.** a Muslim legal expert and adviser on the law of the Koran. **2.** (in the former Ottoman empire) the leader of the religious community. [C16: from Arabic *muftī,* from *aftā* to give a (legal) decision]
Mu+fu+li+ra (ˌmu:fu:'lɪərə) *n.* a mining town in the Copper Belt of Zambia. Pop.: 107 802 (1969).
mug[1] (mʌg) *n.* **1.** a drinking vessel with a handle, usually cylindrical and made of earthenware. **2.** Also called: **mugful.** the quantity held by a mug or its contents. [C16: probably from Scandinavian; compare Swedish *mugge* pitcher with handle]
mug[2] (mʌg) *n.* **1.** *Slang.* a person's face or mouth: *get your ugly mug out of here!* **2.** *Slang.* a grimace. **3.** *Slang.* a gullible person; esp. one who is swindled easily. **4. a mug's game.** a worthless activity. ~*vb.* **mugs, mug+ging, mugged. 5.** (*tr.*) *Informal.* to attack or rob (someone) violently. [C18: perhaps from MUG[1], since drinking vessels were sometimes modelled into the likeness of a face]
Mu·ga·be (mʊ'gɑ:bɪ) *n.* **Rob·ert.** born 1925, Zimbabwean politician; leader of one wing of the Patriotic Front and the ZANU (PF) party; prime minister 1980
mug+ger[1] ('mʌgə) *n.* **1.** *Informal.* a person who commits robbery with violence, esp. in the street. **2.** *Chiefly U.S.* a person who overacts.
mug+ger[2], **mug+gar,** *or* **mug+gur** ('mʌgə) *n.* a large freshwater crocodile, *Crocodylus niloticus,* inhabiting marshes and pools of India and Ceylon. Also called: **marsh crocodile.** [C19: from Hindi *magar*]
mug+gins ('mʌgɪnz) *n.* **1.** *Brit. slang.* a simpleton. **2.** a variation on the game of dominoes. **3.** a card game. [C19: probably from the surname *Muggins*]
mug+gy ('mʌgɪ) *adj.* **+gi+er, +gi+est.** (of weather, air, etc.) unpleasantly warm and humid. [C18: dialect *mug* drizzle, probably from Scandinavian; compare Old Norse *mugga* mist] —'**mug+gi+ly** *adv.* —'**mug+gi+ness** *n.*
mug up *vb.* (*adv.*) *Brit. slang.* to study (a subject) hard, esp. for an exam.
mug+wort ('mʌgˌwɜ:t) *n.* **1.** a N temperate perennial herbaceous plant, *Artemisia vulgaris,* with aromatic leaves and clusters of small greenish-white flowers: family *Compositae* (composites). **2.** another name for **crosswort.** [Old English *mucgwyrt,* perhaps from Old English *mycg* MIDGE]
mug+wump ('mʌgˌwʌmp) *n.* a neutral or independent person, esp. in politics. [C19: from Algonquian: great chief, from *mogki* great + *-omp* man] —'**mug+ˌwump+er·y** *or* '**mug+ˌwump+ism** *n.* —'**mug+ˌwump+ish** *adj.*
Mu·ham·mad (mʊ'hæməd) *n.* a variant of **Mohammed.**
Mu·ham·mad A·li ('ɑ:lɪ, ɑ:'li:, 'ælɪ) *n.* former name *Cassius* (*Marcellus*) *Clay.* born 1942, U.S. boxer, who first became world heavyweight champion in 1964.
Mu+ham+mad+an *or* **Mu+ham+med+an** (mʊ'hæmədᵊn) *n., adj.* another word for **Muslim.**
Mu+har+ram (mu:'hærəm) *or* **Mo+har+ram** *n.* the first month of the Islamic year. [From Arabic: sacred]

Mühl+hau+sen ('my:lhaʊzᵊn) *n.* the German name for **Mulhouse.**
Muir (mjʊə) *n.* **Ed·win.** 1887–1959, Scottish novelist, poet, and critic.
Muir Gla+cier *n.* a glacier in SE Alaska, in the St. Elias Mountains, flowing southeast from Mount Fairweather. Area: about 900 sq. km (350 sq. miles).
mu+jik ('mu:ʒɪk) *n.* a variant spelling of **muzhik.**
Muk+den ('mʊkdən) *n.* a former name of **Shenyang.**
muk+luk ('mʌklʌk) *n.* a soft boot, usually of sealskin, worn by Eskimos. [from Eskimo *muklok* large seal]
mu+lat+to (mju:'lætəʊ) *n., pl.* **+tos** *or* **+toes. 1.** a person having one Negro and one White parent. ~*adj.* **2.** of a light brown colour; tawny. [C16: from Spanish *mulato* young mule, variant of *mulo* MULE]
mul+ber·ry ('mʌlbərɪ, -brɪ) *n., pl.* **·ries. 1.** any moraceous tree of the temperate genus *Morus,* having edible blackberry-like fruit, such as *M. alba* (**white mulberry**), the leaves of which are used to feed silkworms. **2.** the fruit of any of these trees. **3.** any of several similar or related trees, such as the paper mulberry and Indian mulberry. **4. a.** a dark purple colour. **b.** (*as adj.*): *a mulberry dress.* [C14: from Latin *mōrum,* from Greek *moron;* related to Old English *mōrberie;* compare Dutch *moerbezie,* Old High German *mūrberi*]
mulch (mʌltʃ) *n.* **1.** half-rotten vegetable matter, peat, etc., used to prevent soil erosion or enrich the soil. ~*vb.* **2.** (*tr.*) to cover (the surface of land) with mulch. [C17: from obsolete *mulch* soft; related to Old English *mylisc* mellow; compare dialect German *molsch* soft, Latin *mollis* soft]
Mul·ci·ber ('mʌlsɪbə) *n.* another name for **Vulcan.**
mulct (mʌlkt) *vb.* (*tr.*) **1.** to cheat or defraud. **2.** to fine (a person). ~*n.* **3.** a fine or penalty. [C15: via French from Latin *multa* a fine]
Mul·doon (ˌmʌl'du:n) *n.* **Rob·ert Da·vid.** born 1921, New Zealand statesman; prime minister of New Zealand since 1975.
mule[1] (mju:l) *n.* **1.** the sterile offspring of a male donkey and a female horse, used as a beast of burden. Compare **hinny**[1]. **2.** any hybrid animal: *a mule canary.* **3.** Also called: **spinning mule.** a machine invented by Samuel Crompton that spins cotton into yarn and winds the yarn on spindles. **4.** *U.S. informal.* an obstinate or stubborn person. [C13: from Old French *mul,* from Latin *mūlus* ass, mule]
mule[2] (mju:l) *n.* a backless shoe or slipper. [C16: from Old French from Latin *mulleus* a magistrate's shoe]
mule deer *n.* a W North American deer, *Odocoileus hemionus,* with long ears and a black-tipped tail.
mule skin+ner *n. U.S.* an informal term for **muleteer.**
mu+le·ta (mju:'lɛtə) *n.* the small cape attached to a stick used by the matador during the final stages of a bullfight. [Spanish: small mule, crutch, from *mula* MULE[1]]
mu+le·teer (ˌmju:lɪ'tɪə) *n.* a person who drives mules.
mul+ey ('mju:lɪ) *or* **mul+ley** ('mʌlɪ) *adj.* **1.** (of cattle) having no horns. ~*n.* **2.** any hornless cow. [C16: variant of dialect *moiley,* from Gaelic *maol,* Welsh *moel* bald]
mul+ga ('mʌlgə) *n. Austral.* **1.** any of various Australian acacia shrubs, esp. *Acacia aneura,* which grows in the central desert regions and has leaflike leafstalks. **2.** scrub comprised of a dense growth of acacia. **3.** the outback; bush. **4.** an Aboriginal shield. [from a native Australian language]
Mul+ha+cén (*Spanish* ˌmula'θen) *n.* a mountain in S Spain, in the Sierra Nevada: the highest peak in Spain. Height: 3478 m (11 410 ft.).
Mül+heim an der Ruhr (*German* 'my:lhaɪm an de:r 'ru:r) *or* **Mül+heim** *n.* an industrial city in W West Germany, in North Rhine-Westphalia on the River Ruhr: river port. Pop.: 190 783 (1974 est.).
Mul+house (*French* my'lu:z) *n.* a city in E France, on the Rhône-Rhine canal: under German rule (1871–1918); textiles. Pop.: 119 326 (1975). German name: **Mühlhausen.**
mu+li+eb+ri+ty (ˌmju:lɪ'ɛbrɪtɪ) *n.* **1.** the condition of being a woman. **2.** femininity. [C16: via Late Latin from Latin *muliēbris* womanly, from *mulier* woman]
mul+ish ('mju:lɪʃ) *adj.* stubborn; obstinate; headstrong. —'**mul+ish+ly** *adv.* —'**mul+ish+ness** *n.*
Mul+ki ('mʊlkɪ) *n.* a native or inhabitant of the former Hyderabad State in India. [Urdu, from *mulk* country]
mull[1] (mʌl) *vb.* (*tr.*) (often foll. by *over*) to study or ponder. [C19: probably from MUDDLE]
mull[2] (mʌl) *vb.* (*tr.*) to heat (wine, ale, etc.) with sugar and spices to make a hot drink. [C17: of unknown origin]
mull[3] (mʌl) *n.* a light muslin fabric of soft texture. [C18: earlier *mulmull,* from Hindi *malmal*]
mull[4] (mʌl) *n.* a layer of non-acidic humus formed in well drained and aerated soils. [C20: from Danish *muld;* see MOULD[3]]
mull[5] (mʌl) *n. Scot.* a promontory. [C14: related to Gaelic *maol,* Icelandic *múli*]
Mull (mʌl) *n.* a mountainous island in W Scotland, the largest island of the Inner Hebrides, separated from the mainland by the **Sound of Mull.** Chief town: Tobermory. Pop.: 1560 (1971). Area: 909 sq. km (351 sq. miles).
mul+lah, mul+la ('mʌlə, 'mʊlə), *or* **mol+lah** ('mɒlə) *n.* a Muslim scholar, teacher, or religious leader: also used as a title of respect. [C17: from Turkish *molla,* Persian and Hindi *mulla,* from Arabic *mawlā* master]
mul+lein *or* **mul+len** ('mʌlɪn) *n.* any of various Mediterranean herbaceous plants of the scrophulariaceous genus *Verbascum,* such as *V. thapsus* (**common mullein** or **Aaron's rod**), typically having tall spikes of yellow flowers and broad hairy leaves.

[C15: from Old French *moleine,* probably from Old French *mol* soft, from Latin *mollis*]

mul+ler ('mʌlə) *n.* a flat heavy implement of stone or iron used to grind material against a slab of stone, etc. [C15: probably from *mullen* to grind to powder; compare Old English *myl* dust]

Mul·ler ('mʌlə) *n.* **Her·mann Jo·seph.** 1890–1967, U.S. geneticist, noted for his work on the transmutation of genes by x-rays: Nobel prize for medicine 1946.

Mül·ler (*German* 'mylər) *n.* **1. Fried·rich Max** ('fri:drɪç 'maks). 1823–1900, British Sanskrit scholar born in Germany. **2. Jo·hann** ('jo:han). See **Regiomontanus. 3. Jo·han·nes Pe·ter** (jo'hanəs 'pe:tər). 1801–58, German physiologist and anatomist. **4. Paul Her·mann** ('paʊl 'hɛrman). 1899–1965, Swiss chemist. He synthesized DDT (1939) and discovered its use as an insecticide: Nobel prize for medicine 1948.

mul+let ('mʌlɪt) *n.* **1.** any of various teleost food fishes belonging to the families *Mugilidae* (see **grey mullet**) or *Mullidae* (see **red mullet**). **2.** the U.S. name for **grey mullet.** [C15: via Old French from Latin *mullus,* from Greek *mullos*]

mul+ley ('mʌlɪ) *adj.* a variant spelling of **muley.**

mul+li·gan ('mʌlɪgən) *n. U.S.* a stew made from odds and ends of food. [C20: perhaps from the surname]

mul+li·ga+taw+ny (ˌmʌlɪgə'tɔ:nɪ) *n.* a curry-flavoured soup of Anglo-Indian origin, made with meat stock. [C18: from Tamil *milakutanni,* from *milaku* pepper + *tanni* water]

Mul·li·ken ('mʌlɪkən) *n.* **Rob·ert San·der·son.** born 1896, U.S. physicist and chemist, who won the Nobel prize for chemistry (1966) for his work on chemical bonding and the electronic structure of molecules.

mul+li·on ('mʌlɪən) *n.* **1.** a vertical member between the casements or panes of a window or the panels of a screen. **2.** one of the ribs on a rock face. ~*vb.* **3.** (*tr.*) to furnish (a window, etc.) with mullions. [C16: variant of Middle English *munial,* from Old French *moinel,* of unknown origin]

mul+lite ('mʌlaɪt) *n.* a colourless mineral consisting of aluminium silicate in orthorhombic crystalline form: used as a refractory. Formula: $Al_6Si_2O_{13}$. [from island of MULL]

mul+lock ('mʌlək) *n.* **1.** *Austral.* waste material from a mine. **2.** *Brit. dialect.* a mess or muddle. **3. poke mullock at.** *Austral. informal.* to ridicule. [C14: related to Old English *myl* dust, Old Norse *mylja* to crush; see MULLER] —**'mul+lock·y** *adj.*

mull·o·way ('mʌləˌweɪ) *n.* a large Australian marine Sciaenid fish, *Sciaena antarctica,* valued for sport and food. [C19: of unknown origin]

Mul+tan (ˌmʊl'tɑ:n) *n.* a city in central Pakistan, near the Chenab River. Pop.: 542 195 (1972).

mul+tan+gu+lar (mʌl'tæŋgjʊlə) *or* **mul·ti·an+gu+lar** *adj.* having many angles.

mul+te·i·ty (mʌl'ti:ɪtɪ) *n.* manifoldness. [C19: from Latin *multus* many, perhaps formed by analogy with HAECCEITY]

mul·ti- *combining form.* **1.** many or much: *multiflorous; multimillion.* **2.** more than one: *multiparous; multistorey.* [from Latin *multus* much, many]

mul·ti+chan+nel an·a+lys+er (ˌmʌltɪ'tʃæn°l) *n.* an electronic instrument, such as a pulse height analyser, that splits an input waveform into a large number of channels in accordance with a particular parameter of the input.

mul·ti+cide ('mʌltɪˌsaɪd) *n.* mass murder.

mul·ti+col+lin+e·ar+i·ty (ˌmʌltɪkəʊˌlɪnɪ'ærɪtɪ) *n. Statistics.* the condition occurring when two or more of the independent variables in a regression equation are correlated.

mul·ti+col+oured ('mʌltɪˌkʌləd) *adj.* having many colours.

mul·ti+dis+ci+pli+nar·y (ˌmʌltɪ'dɪsɪˌplɪnərɪ) *adj.* of or relating to the study of one topic, involving several subject disciplines.

mul·ti+fac+et+ed (ˌmʌltɪ'fæsɪtɪd) *adj.* **1.** (of a gem) having many facets. **2.** having many aspects, abilities, etc.

mul·ti+fac+to+ri·al (ˌmʌltɪfæk'tɔ:rɪəl) *adj. Genetics.* of or designating inheritance that depends on more than one gene.

mul·ti+far·i·ous (ˌmʌltɪ'fɛərɪəs) *adj.* having many parts of great variety. [C16: from Late Latin *multifārius* manifold, from Latin *multifāriam* on many sides] —ˌ**mul·ti+'far·i·ous+ly** *adv.* —ˌ**mul+ti+'far·i·ous+ness** *n.*

mul·ti+fid ('mʌltɪfɪd) *or* **mul+tif·i·dous** (mʌl'tɪfɪdəs) *adj.* having or divided into many lobes or similar segments: *a multifid leaf.* [C18: from Latin *multifidus,* from *multus* many + *findere* to split] —**'mul·ti+ˌfid+ly** *adv.*

mul·ti+flo+ra rose (ˌmʌltɪ'flɔ:rə) *n.* an Asian climbing shrubby rose, *Rosa multiflora,* having clusters of small fragrant flowers: the source of many cultivated roses.

mul·ti+foil ('mʌltɪˌfɔɪl) *n.* an ornamental design having a large number of foils. See also **trefoil, quatrefoil, cinquefoil.**

mul·ti+fold ('mʌltɪˌfəʊld) *adj.* many times doubled; manifold.

mul·ti+fo+li+ate (ˌmʌltɪ'fəʊlɪɪt, -ˌeɪt) *adj. Botany.* having many leaves or leaflets: *a multifoliate compound leaf.*

mul·ti+form ('mʌltɪˌfɔ:m) *adj.* having many forms or kinds. —**mul·ti+for+mi·ty** (ˌmʌltɪ'fɔ:mɪtɪ) *n.*

mul·ti+grav·i·da (ˌmʌltɪ'grævɪdə) *n.* a woman who is pregnant for at least the third time. Compare **multipara.** [C20: New Latin; see MULTI-, GRAVID]

mul·ti+hull ('mʌltɪˌhʌl) *n.* a sailing vessel with two or more hulls. Compare **monohull.**

mul·ti+lat+er+al (ˌmʌltɪ'lætərəl, -'lætrəl) *adj.* **1.** of or involving more than two nations or parties: *a multilateral pact.* **2.** having many sides. —ˌ**mul·ti+'lat+er+al+ly** *adv.*

mul·ti+lin+gual (ˌmʌltɪ'lɪŋgwəl) *adj.* **1.** able to speak more than two languages. **2.** written or expressed in more than two languages. Compare **bilingual, monolingual.**

mul·ti+me·di·a (ˌmʌltɪ'mi:dɪə) *pl. n.* **a.** the combined use of media such as television, slides, etc., esp. in education. **b.** (*as modifier*): *multimedia aids to teaching.*

mul·ti+mil+lion+aire (ˌmʌltɪˌmɪljə'nɛə) *n.* a person with a fortune of several million pounds, dollars, etc.

mul·ti+na+tion+al (ˌmʌltɪ'næʃən°l) *adj.* (of a large business company) operating in several countries.

mul·ti+no+mi·al (ˌmʌltɪ'nəʊmɪəl) *n.* another name for **polynomial** (sense 2b.). [C17: from MULTI- + *-nomial* as in BINOMIAL]

mul·ti+nu+cle·ar (ˌmʌltɪ'nju:klɪə) *or* **mul·ti+nu+cle·ate** (ˌmʌltɪ'nju:klɪɪt, -ˌeɪt) *adj.* (of a cell, microorganism, etc.) having more than two nuclei.

mul·tip·a+ra (mʌl'tɪpərə) *n., pl.* **+rae** (-ˌri:). a woman who has given birth to more than one viable fetus or living child. Compare **multigravida.** [C19: New Latin, feminine of *multiparus* MULTIPAROUS]

mul·tip·a+rous (mʌl'tɪpərəs) *adj.* **1.** (of certain species of mammal) producing many offspring at one birth. **2.** of, relating to, or designating a multipara. [C17: from New Latin *multiparus*] —**mul·ti+par+i·ty** (ˌmʌltɪ'pærɪtɪ) *n.*

mul·ti+par+tite (ˌmʌltɪ'pɑ:taɪt) *adj.* **1.** divided into many parts or sections. **2.** *Government.* a less common word for **multilateral.**

mul·ti+ped ('mʌltɪˌpɛd) *or* **mul·ti+pede** ('mʌltɪˌpi:d) *Rare.* ~*adj.* **1.** having many feet. ~*n.* **2.** an insect or animal having many feet. [C17: from Latin *multipēs*]

mul·ti+phase ('mʌltɪˌfeɪz) *adj.* another word for **polyphase.**

mul·ti+plane ('mʌltɪˌpleɪn) *n.* an aircraft that has more than one pair of wings. Compare **monoplane.**

mul·ti+ple ('mʌltɪp°l) *adj.* **1.** having or involving more than one part, individual, etc. **2.** *Electronics, U.S.* (of a circuit) having a number of conductors in parallel. ~*n.* **3.** the product of a given number or polynomial and any other one: *6 is a multiple of 2.* **4.** *Telephony.* an electrical circuit accessible at a number of points to any one of which a connection can be made. **5.** short for **multiple store.** [C17: via French from Late Latin *multiplus,* from Latin MULTIPLEX] —**'mul·ti+ply** *adv.*

mul·ti+ple al+leles *pl. n.* a group of three or more alleles produced by mutation of the gene. Only two of them are present in a normal diploid cell at the same time. —**mul+ti+ple al+lel+ism** *n.*

mul·ti+ple-choice *adj.* having a number of possible given answers out of which the correct one must be chosen.

mul·ti+ple fac+tors *pl. n. Genetics.* two or more pairs of genes that act as a unit, producing cumulative effects in the phenotype.

mul·ti+ple fruit *n.* a fruit, such as a pineapple, formed from the ovaries of individual flowers in an inflorescence.

mul·ti+ple per+son+al+i·ty *n. Psychiatry.* a mental disorder in which an individual's personality appears to have become separated into two or more distinct personalities, each with its own complex organization. Nontechnical name: **split personality.** See also **schizophrenia.**

mul·ti+ple+poind+ing (ˌmʌltɪp°l'pɔɪndɪŋ) *n. Scot. law.* another name for **interpleader** (sense 1).

mul·ti+ple scle+ro+sis *n.* a chronic progressive disease of the central nervous system characterized by loss of some of the myelin sheath surrounding certain nerve fibres and resulting in speech and visual disorders, tremor, muscular incoordination, partial paralysis, etc. Also called: **disseminated sclerosis.**

mul·ti+ple star *n.* a system of three or more stars associated by gravitation. See also **binary star.**

mul·ti+ple store *n.* one of several retail enterprises under the same ownership and management. Also called: **multiple shop.**

mul·ti+plet ('mʌltɪˌplɛt, -plɪt) *n. Physics.* **1.** a line in a spectrum formed of two or more closely spaced lines, resulting from small differences in energy level of atoms or molecules. **2.** a group of related elementary particles that differ only in electric charge.

mul·ti+ple vot+ing *n.* the practice of voting in more than one constituency in the same election.

mul·ti+plex ('mʌltɪˌplɛks) *n.* **1.** *Telecomm.* **a.** the use of a common communications channel for sending two or more messages or signals. In **frequency-division multiplex** the frequency band transmitted by the common channel is split into narrower bands each of which constitutes a distinct channel. In **time-division multiplex** different channels are established by intermittent connections to the common channel. **b.** (*as modifier*): *a multiplex transmitter.* ~*adj.* **2.** designating a method of map-making using three cameras to produce a stereoscopic effect. **3.** a less common word for **multiple.** [C16: from Latin: having many folds, from MULTI- + *plicāre* to fold] —**'mul·ti+ˌplex+er** *n.*

mul·ti+pli+cand (ˌmʌltɪplɪ'kænd) *n.* a number to be multiplied by another number, the **multiplier.** [C16: from Latin *multiplicandus,* gerund of *multiplicāre* to MULTIPLY]

mul·ti+pli+cate ('mʌltɪplɪˌkeɪt) *adj. Rare.* manifold.

mul·ti+pli+ca+tion (ˌmʌltɪplɪ'keɪʃən) *n.* **1.** a mathematical operation, the inverse of division, in which the product of two or more numbers or quantities is calculated. Usually written $a \times b$, $a.b$, ab. **2.** the act of multiplying or state of being multiplied. **3.** the act or process in animals, plants, or people of reproducing or breeding. —ˌ**mul·ti+pli+'ca+tion+al** *adj.*

ˌ**mul·ti+'ax+i·al** *adj.*
ˌ**mul·ti+'branched** *adj.*
ˌ**mul·ti+'cel+lu+lar** *adj.*
ˌ**mul·ti+'chan+nelled** *adj.*
ˌ**mul·ti+di+'men+sion+al** *adj.*
ˌ**mul·ti+di+'rec+tion+al** *adj.*
ˌ**mul·ti+'po+lar** *adj.*
ˌ**mul·ti+'valve** *adj.*

mul·ti+pli+ca+tion sign *n.* the symbol ×, placed between numbers to be multiplied, as in 3 × 4 × 5 = 60.

mul·ti+pli+ca+tion ta+ble *n.* one of a group of tables giving the results of multiplying two numbers together.

mul·ti+pli+ca+tive ('mʌltɪplɪˌkeɪtɪv, ˌmʌltɪ'plɪkətɪv) *adj.* **1.** tending or able to multiply. **2.** *Maths.* involving multiplication. —**'mul·ti+pli+ˌca+tive+ly** *adv.*

mul·ti+plic+i·ty (ˌmʌltɪ'plɪsɪtɪ) *n., pl.* **·ties. 1.** a large number or great variety. **2.** the state of being multiple. **3.** *Physics.* **a.** the number of levels into which the energy of an atom, molecule, or nucleus splits as a result of coupling between orbital angular momentum and spin angular momentum. **b.** the number of elementary particles in a multiplet.

mul·ti+pli+er ('mʌltɪˌplaɪə) *n.* **1.** a person or thing that multiplies. **2.** the number by which another number, the **multiplicand,** is multiplied. **3.** *Physics.* any device or instrument, such as a photomultiplier, for increasing an effect. **4.** *Economics.* **a.** the ratio of the total expansion in income accruing from an initial autonomous change in expenditure divided by this change in expenditure itself. **b.** (*as modifier*): *multiplier effects.*

mul·ti+ply ('mʌltɪˌplaɪ) *vb.* **+plies, +ply+ing, +plied. 1.** to increase or cause to increase in number, quantity, or degree. **2.** (*tr.*) to increase (one number or quantity) by another number or quantity using multiplication. **3.** (*intr.*) to increase in number by reproduction. [C13: from Old French *multiplier,* from Latin *multiplicāre* to multiply, from *multus* much, many + *plicāre* to fold] —**'mul·ti+ˌpli+a·ble** *or* **'mul·ti+ˌplic+a·ble** *adj.*

mul·ti+pro+gram+ming (ˌmʌltɪ'prəugræmɪŋ) *n.* a time-sharing technique by which several computer programs each run for a short period in rotation.

mul·ti+pur+pose (ˌmʌltɪ'pɜːpəs) *adj.* able to be used for many purposes: *a multipurpose gadget.*

mul·ti+racial (ˌmʌltɪ'reɪʃəl) *adj.* comprising people of many races. —**ˌmul·ti+'ra+cial+ism** *n.*

mul·ti+role ('mʌltɪˌrəul) *adj.* having a number of roles, functions, etc.

mul·ti+screen ('mʌltɪˌskriːn) *adj. Films.* of or relating to a form of presentation in which different images are projected onto three or more screens.

mul·ti+stage ('mʌltɪˌsteɪdʒ) *adj.* **1.** (of a rocket or missile) having several stages, each of which can be jettisoned after it has burnt out. **2.** (of a turbine, compressor, or supercharger) having more than one rotor. **3.** (of any process or device) having more than one stage.

mul·ti+sto+rey (ˌmʌltɪ'stɔːrɪ) *adj.* **1.** (of a building) having many storeys. ~*n.* **2.** a multistorey car park.

mul·ti+tude ('mʌltɪˌtjuːd) *n.* **1.** a large gathering of people. **2. the.** the common people. **3.** a large number. **4.** the state or quality of being numerous. [C14: via Old French from Latin *multitūdō*]

mul·ti+tu+di+nous (ˌmʌltɪ'tjuːdɪnəs) *adj.* **1.** very numerous. **2.** *Rare.* great in extent, variety, etc. **3.** *Poetic.* crowded. —**ˌmul·ti+'tu+di+nous+ly** *adv.* —**ˌmul·ti+'tu+di+nous+ness** *n.*

mul·ti+va+lent (ˌmʌltɪ'veɪlənt) *adj.* another word for **polyvalent.** —**ˌmul·ti+'va+len+cy** *n.*

mul·ti+ver+si·ty (ˌmʌltɪ'vɜːsɪtɪ) *n. Chiefly U.S.* a university with many constituent and affiliated institutions. [C20: MULTI- + UNIVERSITY]

mul·ti+vi+bra+tor (ˌmʌltɪvaɪ'breɪtə) *n.* an electronic oscillator consisting of two transistors or other electronic devices, coupled so that the input of each is derived from the output of the other.

mul·ti+vo+cal (ˌmʌltɪ'vəukᵊl) *adj.* having many meanings.

mul+tum in par+vo ('multum ɪn 'pɑːvəu) much in a small space. [Latin]

mul+ture ('mʌltʃə) *n. Archaic or Scot.* **1.** a fee formerly paid to a miller for grinding grain. **2.** the right to receive such a fee. [C13: from Old French *moulture,* from Medieval Latin *molitūra* a grinding, from Latin *molere*]

mum[1] (mʌm) *n. Chiefly Brit.* an informal word for **mother.** [C19: a child's word]

mum[2] (mʌm) *adj.* **1.** keeping information, etc., to oneself; silent. ~*n.* **2. mum's the word.** (*interj.*) silence or secrecy is to be observed. [C14: suggestive of closed lips]

mum[3] *or* **mumm** (mʌm) *vb.* **mums, mum+ming, mummed.** (*intr.*) to act in a mummer's play. [C16: verbal use of MUM[2]]

mum[4] (mʌm) *n. Brit, obsolete.* a type of beer made from cereals, beans, etc. [C17: from German *Mumme,* perhaps from the name of its original brewer]

mum+ble ('mʌmbᵊl) *vb.* **1.** to utter indistinctly, as with the mouth partly closed; mutter. **2.** *Rare.* to chew (food) ineffectually or with difficulty. ~*n.* **3.** an indistinct or low utterance or sound. [C14 *momelen,* from MUM[2]] —**'mum+bler** *n.* —**'mum+bling+ly** *adv.*

mum+bo jum+bo ('mʌmbəu) *n., pl.* **mum+bo jum+bos. 1.** foolish religious reverence, ritual, or incantation. **2.** meaningless or unnecessarily complicated language. **3.** an object of superstitious awe or reverence. [C18: probably from Mandingo *mama dyumbo,* name of a tribal god]

mum+chance ('mʌmˌtʃɑːns) *adj.* silent; struck dumb. [C16 (masquerade, dumb show): from Middle Low German *mummenschanze* masked serenade; from *mummen* (see MUMMER) + *schanze* CHANCE]

mu me+son (mjuː) *n.* a former name for **muon.**

Mum·ford ('mʌmfəd) *n.* **Lew·is.** born 1895, U.S. sociologist, whose works are chiefly concerned with the relationship between man and his environment. They include *The City in History* (1962) and *Roots of Contemporary Architecture* (1972).

mum+mer ('mʌmə) *n.* **1.** one of a group of masked performers in folk play or mime. **2.** a mime artist. **3.** *Humorous or derogatory.* an actor. [C15: from Old French *momeur,* from *momer* to mime; related to *momon* mask]

mum+mer·y ('mʌmərɪ) *n., pl.* **+mer·ies. 1.** a performance by mummers. **2.** hypocritical or ostentatious ceremony.

mum+mi+fy ('mʌmɪˌfaɪ) *vb.* **+fies, +fy+ing, +fied. 1.** (*tr.*) to preserve the body of a man or animal as a mummy. **2.** (*intr.*) to dry up; shrivel. **3.** (*tr.*) to preserve (an outdated idea, institution, etc.) while making lifeless. —**ˌmum+mi+fi+'ca+tion** *n.*

mum+my[1] ('mʌmɪ) *n., pl.* **+mies. 1.** an embalmed or preserved body, esp. as prepared for burial in ancient Egypt. **2.** *Obsolete.* the substance of such a body used medicinally. **3.** a mass of pulp. **4.** a dark brown pigment. [C14: from Old French *momie,* from Medieval Latin *mumia,* from Arabic *mūmiyah* asphalt, from Persian *mūm* wax]

mum+my[2] ('mʌmɪ) *n., pl.* **+mies.** *Chiefly Brit.* a child's word for **mother.** [C19: variant of MUM[1]]

mump[1] (mʌmp) *vb.* (*intr.*) *Archaic.* to be silent. [C16 (to grimace, sulk, be silent): of imitative origin, alluding to the shape of the mouth when mumbling or chewing]

mump[2] (mʌmp) *Archaic. vb.* (*intr.*) to beg. [C17: perhaps from Dutch *mompen* to cheat]

mumps (mʌmps) *n.* an acute contagious viral disease of the parotid salivary glands, characterized by swelling of the affected parts, fever, and pain beneath the ear: usually affects children. Also called: **epidemic parotitis.** [C16: from MUMP[1] (to grimace)] —**'mum+pish** *adj.*

mun. *abbrev. for* municipal.

munch (mʌntʃ) *vb.* to chew (food, etc.) steadily, esp. with a crunching noise. [C14 *monche,* of imitative origin; compare CRUNCH] —**'munch+er** *n.*

Munch (muŋk) *n.* **Ed·vard** ('ɛdvard). 1863–1944, Norwegian painter and engraver, whose works, often on the theme of death, include *The Cry* (1893); a major influence on the expressionists, esp. on *die Brücke.*

Mün+chen ('mynçᵊn) *n.* the German name for **Munich.**

Mün·chen-Glad·bach ('mynçᵊn 'glatbax) *n.* the former name of **Mönchen-Gladbach.**

Münch·hau·sen (*German* 'mynçˌhauzᵊn) *n.* **1.** an exaggerated story. **2.** a person who tells such a story. ~*adj.* **3.** of or relating to a syndrome in which a patient feigns illness to obtain hospital treatment. [C19: after Baron *Münchhausen,* subject of a series of exaggerated adventure tales written in English by R. E. Raspe (1737–94)]

Mun+da ('mundə) *n.* **1.** a family of languages spoken by scattered peoples throughout central India. **2.** (*pl.* **+das**) a member of any of these peoples.

mun+dane ('mʌndeɪn, mʌn'deɪn) *adj.* **1.** everyday, ordinary, or banal. **2.** relating to the world or worldly matters. [C15: from French *mondain,* via Late Latin, from Latin *mundus* world] —**'mun+dane+ly** *adv.* —**'mun+dane+ness** *n.*

mung·a ('mʌŋgə) *n. Austral. slang.* food. [C20: perhaps from French *manger* to eat]

mung bean (mʌŋ) *n.* **1.** an E Asian bean plant, *Phaseolus aureus,* grown for forage and as the source of bean sprouts used in oriental cookery. **2.** the seed of this plant. [C20 *mung,* changed from *mungo,* from Tamil *mūngu,* ultimately from Sanskrit *mudga*]

mun+go ('mʌŋgəu), **mon+go,** *or* **mon+goe** *n., pl.* **+gos** *or* **+goes.** a cheap felted fabric made from waste wool. [C19: of unknown origin]

Mu+nich ('mjuːnɪk) *n.* a city in SW West Germany, capital of the state of Bavaria, on the Isar River: the third largest city in West Germany; became capital of Bavaria in 1508; headquarters of the Nazi movement in the 1920s; a major financial, commercial, and manufacturing centre. Pop.: 1 336 576 (1974 est.). German name: **München.**

Mu+nich Pact *or* **A·gree+ment** *n.* the pact signed by Germany, Great Britain, France, and Italy on Sept. 29, 1938, to settle the crisis over Czechoslovakia, by which the Sudetenland was ceded to Germany.

mu+nic·i+pal (mjuː'nɪsɪpᵊl) *adj.* of or relating to a town, city, or borough or its local government. [C16: from Latin *mūnicipium* a free town, from *mūniceps* citizen from *mūnia* responsibilities + *capere* to take] —**mu+'nic·i+pal+ism** *n.* —**mu+'nic·i+pal+ist** *n.* —**mu+'nic·i+pal+ly** *adv.*

mu+nic·i+pal+i·ty (mjuːˌnɪsɪ'pælɪtɪ) *n., pl.* **·ties. 1.** a city, town, or district enjoying some degree of local self-government. **2.** the governing body of such a unit.

mu+nic·i+pal+ize *or* **mu+nic·i+pal+ise** (mjuː'nɪsɪpəˌlaɪz) *vb.* (*tr.*) **1.** to bring under municipal ownership or control. **2.** to make a municipality of. —**mu+ˌnic·i+pal·i+'za+tion** *or* **mu+ˌnic·i+pal·i+'sa+tion** *n.*

mu+nif·i·cent (mjuː'nɪfɪsənt) *adj.* **1.** (of a person) very generous; bountiful. **2.** (of a gift, etc.) generous; liberal. [C16: back formation from Latin *mūnificentia* liberality, from *mūnificus,* from *mūnus* gift + *facere* to make] —**mu+'nif·i+cence** *or* **mu+'nif·i·cent+ness** *n.* —**mu+'nif·i·cent+ly** *adv.*

mu+ni+ment ('mjuːnɪmənt) *n. Rare.* a means of defence. [C15: via Old French, from Latin *munīre* to defend]

mu+ni+ments ('mjuːnɪmənts) *pl. n.* **1.** *Law.* the title deeds and other documentary evidence relating to the title to land. **2.** *Archaic.* furnishings or supplies.

mu+ni+tion (mjuː'nɪʃən) *vb.* (*tr.*) to supply with munitions. [C16: via French from Latin *mūnītiō* fortification, from *mūnīre* to fortify. See AMMUNITION] —**mu+'ni+tion+er** *n.*

mu+ni+tions (mjuː'nɪʃənz) *pl. n.* (*sometimes sing.*) military equipment and stores, esp. ammunition.

mun·nion ('mʌnjən) *n.* an archaic word for **mullion.** [C16: from MONIAL]
Mun·ro (mʌn'rəʊ) *n.* **H(ector) H(ugh),** pen name *Saki.* 1870–1916, Scottish author, born in Burma, noted for his collections of satirical short stories, such as *Reginald* (1904) and *Beasts and Superbeasts* (1914).
Mun·sell scale *n.* a standard chromaticity scale used in specifying colour. It gives approximately equal changes in visual hue. [C20: named after *A. H. Munsell* (1858–1918), American inventor]
mün·ster ('mynstə) *n.* a variant spelling of **muenster.**
Mun·ster ('mʌnstə) *n.* a province of SW Ireland: the largest of the four provinces and historically a kingdom; consists of the counties of Clare, Cork, Kerry, Limerick, Tipperary, and Waterford. Capital: Cork. Pop.: 882 002 (1971). Area: 24 125 sq. km (9315 sq. miles).
Mün·ster (*German* 'mynstər) *n.* a city in NW West Germany, capital of North Rhine-Westphalia state on the Dortmund–Ems Canal: scene of the signing of the Treaty of Westphalia (1648); became capital of Prussian Westphalia in 1815. Pop.: 199 748 (1974 est.).
Mün·ster·berg ('mʊnstə,bɜ:g) *n.* **Hu·go.** 1863–1916, German psychologist, in the U.S. from 1897, noted for his pioneering work in applied psychology.
munt (mʊnt) *n. Rhodesian slang, derogatory.* a Black African. [from Zulu *umuntu* person]
mun·tin ('mʌntɪn) *n.* another name (esp. U.S.) for **glazing-bar.** [C17: variant of C15 *mountant,* from Old French *montant,* present participle of *monter* to MOUNT[1]]
munt·jac *or* **munt·jak** ('mʌnt,dʒæk) *n.* any small Asian deer of the genus *Muntiacus,* typically having a chestnut-brown coat, small antlers, and a barklike cry. Also called: **barking deer.** [C18: probably changed from Javanese *mindjangan* deer]
Muntz metal *n.* a type of brass consisting of three parts copper and two parts zinc, used in casting and extrusion. [C19: named after G. F. *Muntz* (1794–1857), English metallurgist]
mu·on ('mju:ɒn) *n.* a positive or negative elementary particle with a mass 207 times that of an electron and spin ½. It was originally called the **mu meson** but is now classified as a lepton. [C20: short for MU MESON]
mu·rage ('mjʊərɪdʒ) *n. Brit., archaic.* a tax levied for the construction or maintenance of town walls. [C13: from Old French, ultimately from Latin *mūrus* wall]
mu·ral ('mjʊərəl) *n.* **1.** a large painting or picture on a wall. ~*adj.* **2.** of or relating to a wall. [C15: from Latin *mūrālis,* from *mūrus* wall] —'**mu·ral·ist** *n.*
Mu·ra·sa·ki Shi·ki·bu (,mjʊərə'sɑ:ki: 'ʃi:ki:,bu:) *n.* **Bar·on·ess.** 11th-century Japanese authoress of *The Tale of Genji,* perhaps the world's first novel.
Mu·rat (*French* my'ra) *n.* **Jo·a·chim** (ʒɔa'ʃɛ̃). 1767?–1815, French marshal, during the Napoleonic Wars; king of Naples (1808–15).
Mur·cia (*Spanish* 'murθja) *n.* **1.** a region and ancient kingdom of SE Spain, on the Mediterranean: taken by the Moors in the 8th century; an independent Muslim kingdom in the 11th and 12th centuries. **2.** a city in SE Spain, capital of Murcia province: trading centre for a rich agricultural region; silk industry; university (1915). Pop.: 243 759 (1970).
mur·da·bad ('mʊdɑ:,bɑ:d) *vb. (tr.) Indian.* down with; death to: used as part of a slogan in India, Pakistan, etc. Compare **zindabad.** [from Urdu, from Persian *murda* dead]
mur·der ('mɜ:də) *n.* **1.** the unlawful premeditated killing of one human being by another. Compare **manslaughter, homicide. 2.** *Informal.* something dangerous, difficult, or unpleasant: *driving around London is murder.* **3. cry blue murder.** *Informal.* to make or cause an outcry. **4. get away with murder.** *Informal.* to escape censure; do as one pleases. ~*vb. (mainly tr.)* **5.** (*also intr.*) to kill (someone) unlawfully with premeditation or during the commission of a crime. **6.** to kill brutally. **7.** *Informal.* to destroy; ruin: *he murdered her chances of happiness.* **8.** *Informal.* to defeat completely; beat decisively: *the home team murdered their opponents.* ~Also (archaic or dialect): **murther.** [Old English *morthor;* related to Old English *morth* Old Norse *morth,* Latin *mors* death; compare French *meurtre*] —'**mur·der·er** *n.* —'**mur·der·ess** *fem. n.*
mur·der·ous ('mɜ:dərəs) *adj.* **1.** intending, capable of, or guilty of murder. **2.** *Informal.* very dangerous, difficult, or unpleasant: *a murderous road.* —'**mur·der·ous·ly** *adv.* —'**mur·der·ous·ness** *n.*
Mur·doch ('mɜ:,dɒk) *n.* **Ir·is.** born 1919, British novelist and philosopher. Her novels include *The Bell* (1958), *A Severed Head* (1961; play 1963), *The Red and the Green* (1965), *A Word Child* (1975), and *Henry and Cato* (1976).
mure (mjʊə) *vb. (tr.)* an archaic or literary word for **immure.** [C14: from Old French *murer,* from Latin *mūrus* wall]
Mu·reş ('mʊərɛʃ) *n.* a river in SE central Europe, rising in central Rumania in the Carpathian Mountains and flowing west to the Tisza River at Szeged, Hungary. Length: 885 km (550 miles). Hungarian name: **Maros.**
mu·rex ('mjʊərɛks) *n., pl.* **mu·ri·ces** ('mjʊərɪ,si:z). any of various spiny-shelled marine gastropods of the genus *Murex* and related genera: formerly used as a source of the dye Tyrian purple. [C16: from Latin *mūrex* purple fish; related to Greek *muax* sea mussel]
mu·ri·ate ('mjʊərɪɪt; -,eɪt) *n.* an obsolete name for a **chloride.** [C18: back formation from *muriatic;* see MURIATIC ACID]
mu·ri·at·ic ac·id (,mjʊərɪ'ætɪk) *n.* a former name for **hydrochloric acid.** [C17: from Latin *muriāticus* pickled, from *muria* brine]
mu·ri·cate ('mjʊərɪ,keɪt) *or* **mu·ri·cat·ed** *adj. Biology.* having a surface roughened by numerous short points: *muricate stems.* [C17: from Latin *mūricātus* pointed like a MUREX]
Mu·ril·lo (mjʊə'rɪləʊ; *Spanish* mu'riʎo) *n.* **Bar·to·lo·mé Es·te·ban** (,bartolo'me es'teβan). 1618–82, Spanish painter, esp. of religious subjects and beggar children.
mu·rine ('mjʊəraɪn, -rɪn) *adj.* **1.** of, relating to, or belonging to the *Muridae,* an Old World family of rodents, typically having long hairless tails: includes rats and mice. **2.** resembling a mouse or rat. ~*n.* **3.** any animal belonging to the *Muridae.* [C17: from Latin *mūrīnus* of mice, from *mūs* MOUSE]
murk *or* **mirk** (mɜ:k) *n.* **1.** gloomy darkness. ~*adj.* **2.** an archaic variant of **murky.** [C13: probably from Old Norse *myrkr* darkness; compare Old English *mirce* dark]
murk·y *or* **mirk·y** ('mɜ:kɪ) *adj.* **murk·i·er, murk·i·est** *or* **mirk·i·er, mirk·i·est. 1.** gloomy or dark. **2.** cloudy or impenetrable as with smoke or fog. —'**murk·i·ly** *or* '**mirk·i·ly** *adv.* —'**murk·i·ness** *or* '**mirk·i·ness** *n.*
Mur·man Coast ('muəmən) *or* **Mur·mansk Coast** *n.* a coastal region of the NW Soviet Union, in the north of the Kola Peninsula: within the Arctic Circle, but ice-free.
Mur·mansk (*Russian* 'murmənsk) *n.* a port in the NW Soviet Union, on the Kola Inlet of the Barents Sea: founded in 1915; the world's largest town north of the Arctic Circle, with a large fishing fleet. Pop.: 358 000 (1975 est.).
mur·mur ('mɜ:mə) *n.* **1.** a continuous low indistinct sound, as of distant voices. **2.** an indistinct utterance: *a murmur of satisfaction.* **3.** a complaint; grumble: *he made no murmur at my suggestion.* **4.** *Med.* any abnormal soft blowing sound heard within the body, usually over the chest. See also **heart murmur.** ~*vb.* **5.** to utter (something) in a murmur. **6.** (*intr.*) to complain in a murmur. [C14: as n., from Latin *murmur;* vb. via Old French *murmurer* from Latin *murmurāre* to rumble] —'**mur·mur·er** *n.* —'**mur·mur·ing·ly** *adv.* —'**mur·mur·ous** *adj.*
mur·phy ('mɜ:fɪ) *n., pl.* **·phies.** a dialect or informal word for **potato.** [C19: from the common Irish surname *Murphy*]
Mur·phy ('mɜ:fɪ) *n.* **Wil·liam Par·ry.** born 1892, U.S. physician: with G. R. Minot, he discovered the liver treatment for anaemia and they shared, with G. H. Whipple, the Nobel prize for medicine in 1934.
Mur·phy bed *n. U.S.* a bed designed to be folded or swung into a cabinet when not in use. [C20: named after William *Murphy,* American inventor]
mur·ra ('mʌrə) *n.* See **murrhine.**
mur·rain ('mʌrɪn) *n.* **1.** any plaguelike disease in cattle. **2.** *Archaic.* a plague. [C14: from Old French *morine,* from *morir* to die, from Latin *morī*]
Mur·ray[1] ('mʌrɪ) *n.* a river in SE Australia, rising in New South Wales and flowing northwest into SE South Australia, then south into the Indian Ocean at Encounter Bay: the main river of Australia, important for irrigation and power. Length: 2590 km (1609 miles).
Mur·ray[2] ('mʌrɪ) *n.* **1.** Sir **(George) Gil·bert (Aimé).** 1866–1957, British classical scholar, born in Australia: noted for his verse translations of Greek dramatists, esp. Euripides. **2.** Sir **James Au·gus·tus Hen·ry.** 1837–1915, Scottish lexicographer; one of the original editors (1879–1915) of what became the *Oxford English Dictionary.* **3. Lio·nel,** known as *Len.* born 1922, English trades union leader; general secretary of the Trades Union Congress since 1973.
murre (mɜ:) *n. U.S.* any guillemot of the genus *Uria.* [C17: origin unknown]
murre·let ('mɜ:lɪt) *n.* any of several small diving birds of the genus *Brachyramphus* and related genera, similar and related to the auks: family *Alcidae,* order *Charadriiformes.*
mur·rey ('mʌrɪ) *adj. Brit., archaic.* mulberry-coloured. [C14: from Old French *moré,* ultimately from Latin *mōrum* mulberry]
mur·rhine *or* **mur·rine** ('mʌraɪn, -ɪn) *adj.* **1.** of or relating to an unknown substance used in ancient Rome to make vases, etc. ~*n.* **2.** Also called: **murra.** the substance so used. [C16: from Latin *murr(h)inus* belonging to *murra*]
mur·rhine glass *n.* a type of Eastern glassware made from fluorspar and decorated with pieces of coloured metal.
Mur·rum·bidg·ee (,mʌrəm'bɪdʒɪ) *n.* a river in SE Australia, rising in S New South Wales and flowing north and west to the Murray River: important for irrigation. Length: 1690 km (1050 miles).
mur·ther ('mɜ:ðə) *n., vb.* an archaic word for **murder.** —'**mur·ther·er** *n.*
mus. *abbrev. for:* **1.** museum. **2.** music. **3.** musical.
mu·sa·ceous (mju:'zeɪʃəs) *adj.* of, relating to, or belonging to the *Musaceae,* a family of tropical flowering plants having large leaves and clusters of elongated berry fruits: includes the banana, plantain, and Manilla hemp. [C19: from New Latin *Mūsāceae,* from *Mūsa* genus name, from Arabic *mawzah* banana]
Mus.B. *or* **Mus.Bac.** *abbrev. for* Bachelor of Music.
Mus·ca ('mʌskə) *n., Latin genitive* **Mus·cae** ('mʌski:). a small constellation in the S hemisphere lying between the Southern Cross and Chamaeleon. [Latin: a fly]
mus·ca·del *or* **mus·ca·delle** (,mʌskə'dɛl) *n.* another name for **muscatel.**
mus·ca·dine ('mʌskədɪn, -,daɪn) *n.* **1.** a woody climbing viceous plant, *Vitis rotundifolia,* of the southeastern U.S. **2.** Also called: **scuppernong, bullace grape.** the thick-skinned

musk-scented purple grape produced by this plant: used to make wine. [C16: from MUSCADEL]

mus+cae vo+li+tan+tes ('mʌsi: vɒlɪ'tænti:z) *n. Pathol.* moving black specks or threads seen before the eyes, caused by opaque fragments floating in the vitreous humour or a defect in the lens. [C18: New Latin: flying flies]

mus+ca+rine ('mʌskərɪn, -ˌri:n) *n.* a poisonous alkaloid occurring in certain mushrooms. Formula: $C_8H_{19}NO_3$. [C19: from Latin *muscārius* of flies, from *musca* fly]

mus+cat ('mʌskət, -kæt) *n.* **1.** any of various grapevines that produce sweet white grapes used for making wine or raisins. **2.** another name for **muscatel.** [C16: via Old French from Provençal *muscat,* from *musc* MUSK]

Mus+cat ('mʌskət, -kæt) *n.* the capital of the Sultanate of Oman, a port on the Gulf of Oman: a Portuguese port from the early 16th century; controlled by Persia (1650–1741). Pop.: 7650 (1971 est.). Arabic name: **Masqat.**

Mus+cat and O·man *n.* the former name (until 1970) of (the Sultanate of) **Oman.**

mus+ca+tel (ˌmʌskə'tɛl), **mus+ca+del,** *or* **mus+ca+delle** *n.* **1.** Also called: **muscat.** a rich sweet wine made from muscat grapes. **2.** the grape or raisin from a muscat vine. [C14: from Old French *muscadel,* from Old Provençal, from *moscadel,* from *muscat* musky. See MUSK]

mus+cid ('mʌsɪd) *n.* **1.** any fly of the dipterous family *Muscidae,* including the housefly and tsetse fly. *~adj.* **2.** of, relating to, or belonging to the *Muscidae.* [C19: via New Latin from Latin *musca* fly]

mus+cle ('mʌsᵊl) *n.* **1.** a tissue composed of bundles of elongated cells capable of contraction and relaxation to produce movement in an organ or part. **2.** an organ composed of muscle tissue. **3.** strength or force. *~vb.* **4.** *(intr.;* often foll. by *in, on,* etc.) *Informal.* to force one's way (in). [C16: from medical Latin *musculus* little mouse, from the imagined resemblance of some muscles to mice, from Latin *mūs* mouse] —**'mus+cly** *adj.*

mus·cle-bound *adj.* **1.** having overdeveloped and inelastic muscles. **2.** lacking flexibility.

mus+cle fi+bre *n.* any of the numerous elongated contractile cells that contain many nuclei and make up striated muscle.

mus+cle+man ('mʌsᵊlˌmæn) *n., pl.* **+men. 1.** a man with highly developed muscles. **2.** a henchman employed by a gangster, etc., to intimidate or use violence upon victims.

mus+cle sense *n.* another name for **kinaesthesia.**

mus+co+va+do *or* **mus+ca+va+do** (ˌmʌskə'vɑ:dəʊ) *n.* raw sugar obtained from the juice of sugar cane by evaporating the molasses. [C17: from Portuguese *açúcar mascavado* separated sugar; *mascavado* from *mascavar* to separate, probably from Latin]

mus+co+vite ('mʌskəˌvaɪt) *n.* a translucent light-coloured mica consisting of a potassium aluminium silicate. Formula: $KAl_3Si_3O_{10}(OH)_2$. See also **mica.** [C19: from the phrase *Muscovy glass,* an early name for mica]

Mus+co+vite ('mʌskəˌvaɪt) *n.* **1.** a native or inhabitant of Moscow. *~adj.* **2.** an archaic word for **Russian.**

Mus+co+vy ('mʌskəvɪ) *n.* **1.** a Russian principality (13th to 16th centuries), of which Moscow was the capital. **2.** an archaic name for **Russia** and **Moscow.**

Mus+co+vy duck *or* **musk duck** *n.* a large crested widely domesticated South American duck, *Cairina moschata,* having a greenish-black plumage with white markings and a large red caruncle on the bill. [C17: originally *musk duck,* a name later mistakenly associated with MUSCOVY]

mus+cu+lar ('mʌskjʊlə) *adj.* **1.** having well-developed muscles; brawny. **2.** of, relating to, or consisting of muscle. [C17: from New Latin *muscularis,* from *musculus* MUSCLE] —**mus+cu+lar+i+ty** (ˌmʌskjʊ'lærɪtɪ) *n.* —**'mus+cu+lar+ly** *adv.*

mus+cu+lar dys+tro+phy *n.* a genetic disease characterized by progressive deterioration and wasting of muscle fibres, causing difficulty in walking.

mus+cu+la+ture ('mʌskjʊlətʃə) *n.* **1.** the arrangement of muscles in an organ or part. **2.** the total muscular system of an organism.

Mus.D. *or* **Mus.Doc.** *abbrev. for* Doctor of Music.

muse[1] (mju:z) *vb.* **1.** (when *intr.,* often foll. by *on* or *about*) to reflect (about) or ponder (on), usually in silence. **2.** *(intr.)* to gaze thoughtfully. *~n.* **3.** a state of abstraction. [C14: from Old French *muser,* perhaps from *mus* snout, from Medieval Latin *mūsus*] —**'mus+er** *n.* —**'muse+ful** *adj.* —**'muse+ful+ly** *adv.*

muse[2] (mju:z) *n.* (often preceded by *the*) a goddess that inspires a creative artist, esp. a poet. [C14: from Old French, from Latin *Mūsa,* from Greek *Mousa* a Muse]

Muse (mju:z) *n. Greek myth.* any of nine sister goddesses, each of whom was regarded as the protectress of a different art or science. Daughters of Zeus and Mnemosyne, the nine are Calliope, Clio, Erato, Euterpe, Melpomene, Polyhymnia, Terpsichore, Thalia, and Urania.

mus+e+ol+o+gy (ˌmju:zɪ'ɒdʒɪ) *n.* the science of museum organisation. —ˌ**mus+e·'ol·o·gist** *n.*

mu+sette (mju:'zɛt; *French* my'zɛt) *n.* **1.** a type of bagpipe with a bellows popular in France during the 17th and 18th centuries. **2.** a dance, with a drone bass originally played by a musette. [C14: from Old French, diminutive of *muse* bagpipe]

mu+sette bag *n. U.S.* an army officer's haversack.

mu+se·um (mju:'zɪəm) *n.* a place or building where objects of historical, artistic, or scientific interest are exhibited, preserved, or studied. [C17: via Latin from Greek *Mouseion* home of the Muses, from *Mousa* MUSE]

mu+se·um piece *n.* **1.** an object of sufficient age or interest to be kept in a museum. **2.** *Informal.* a person or thing regarded as antiquated or decrepit.

mush[1] (mʌʃ) *n.* **1.** a soft pulpy mass or consistency. **2.** *U.S.* a thick porridge made from corn meal. **3.** *Informal.* cloying sentimentality. [C17: from obsolete *moose* porridge; probably related to MASH; compare Old English *mōs* food]

mush[2] (mʌʃ) *interj.* **1.** an order to dogs in a sled team to start up or go faster. *~n.* **2.** a journey with such a sled. [C20: from Canadian French *mouche!* Fly! from French *mouche* a fly, from Latin *musca*] —**'mush+er** *n.*

mush[3] (mʊʃ) *n. Brit.* a slang word for **face.** [C19: from MUSH[1], alluding to the softness of the face]

mush[4] (mʊʃ) *n. Brit. slang.* a familiar or contemptuous term of address. [C19: probably from Gypsy *moosh* a man]

mush+room ('mʌʃru:m, -rʊm) *n.* **1. a.** the fleshy spore-producing body of any of various basidiomycetous fungi, typically consisting of a cap (see **pileus**) at the end of a stem arising from an underground mycelium. Some species, such as the field mushroom, are edible. Compare **toadstool. b.** (*as modifier*)*: mushroom soup.* **2.** the fungus producing any of these structures. **3. a.** something resembling a mushroom in shape or rapid growth. **b.** (*as modifier*)*: mushroom expansion.* *~vb.* *(intr.)* **4.** to grow rapidly: *demand mushroomed overnight.* **5.** to assume a mushroom-like shape. **6.** to gather mushrooms. [C15: from Old French *mousseron,* from Late Latin *mussiriō,* of obscure origin]

mush+room cloud *n.* the large mushroom-shaped cloud of dust, debris, etc. produced by a nuclear explosion.

mush·y ('mʌʃɪ) *adj.* **mush·i·er, mush·i·est. 1.** soft and pulpy. **2.** *Informal.* excessively sentimental or emotional. —**'mush·i·ly** *adv.* —**'mush·i·ness** *n.*

mu+sic ('mju:zɪk) *n.* **1.** an art form consisting of sequences of sounds in time, esp. tones of definite pitch organized melodically, harmonically, rhythmically and according to tone colour. **2.** such an art form characteristic of a particular people, culture, or tradition: *Indian music; rock music; baroque music.* **3.** the sounds so produced, esp. by singing or musical instruments. **4.** written or printed music, such as a score or set of parts. **5.** any sequence of sounds perceived as pleasing or harmonious. **6.** *Rare.* a group of musicians: *the Queen's music.* **7. face the music.** *Informal.* to accept the consequences of one's actions. **8. music to one's ears.** something that is very pleasant to hear: *his news is music to my ears.* [C13: via Old French from Latin *mūsica,* from Greek *mousikē (tekhnē)* (art) belonging to the Muses, from *Mousa* MUSE]

mu+si+cal ('mju:zɪkᵊl) *adj.* **1.** of, relating to, or used in music: *a musical instrument.* **2.** harmonious; melodious: *musical laughter.* **3.** talented in or fond of music. **4.** involving or set to music: *a musical evening.* *~n.* **5.** short for **musical comedy.** —**'mu+si+cal+ly** *adv.* —**'mu+si+cal+ness** *or* ˌ**mu+si+'cal+i+ty** *n.*

mu+si+cal chairs *n.* a party game in which players walk around chairs while music is played, there being one less chair than players. Whenever the music stops, the player who fails to find a chair is eliminated.

mu+si+cal com+e·dy *n.* **1.** a play or film, usually having a light romantic story, that consists of dialogue interspersed with singing and dancing. **2.** such plays and films collectively.

mu+si+cale (ˌmju:zɪ'kɑ:l) *n. U.S.* a party or social evening with a musical programme. [C19: shortened from French *soirée musicale* musical evening]

mu+si+cal glass·es *pl. n.* another term for **glass harmonica.**

mu+sic box *or* **mu+si+cal box** *n.* a mechanical instrument that plays tunes by means of pins on a revolving cylinder striking the tuned teeth of a comblike metal plate.

mu+sic cen+tre *n.* a single hi-fi unit containing a turntable, amplifier, radio and cassette player.

mu+sic dra+ma *n.* **1.** an opera in which the musical and dramatic elements are of equal importance and strongly interfused. **2.** the genre of such operas. [C19: translation of German *Musikdrama,* coined by Wagner to describe his later operas]

mu+sic hall *n. Chiefly Brit.* **1. a.** a variety entertainment consisting of songs, comic turns, etc. U.S. name: **vaudeville. b.** (*as modifier*)*: a music-hall song.* **2.** a theatre at which such entertainments are staged.

mu+si+cian (mju:'zɪʃən) *n.* a person who plays or composes music, esp. as a profession. —**mu+'si+cian+ly** *adj.*

mu+si+cian+ship (mju:'zɪʃən,ʃɪp) *n.* skill or artistry in performing music.

mu+sic of the spheres *n.* inaudible music supposed by Pythagoras to be produced by the movement of the celestial spheres.

mu+si+col+o·gy (ˌmju:zɪ'kɒlədʒɪ) *n.* the scholarly study of music. —**mu+si+co+log·i·cal** (ˌmju:zɪkə'lɒdʒɪkᵊl) *adj.* —ˌ**mu+si+co+'log·i·cal+ly** *adv.* —ˌ**mu+si+'col·o·gist** *n.*

mu+sic pa+per *n.* paper ruled or printed with a stave for writing music.

mu+sic roll *n.* a roll of perforated paper for use in a mechanical instrument such as a player piano.

mu+sic stand *n.* a frame, usually of wood or metal, upon which a musical score or orchestral part is supported.

Mu·sil (*German* 'mu:zɪl) *n.* **Rob·ert** ('ro:bɛrt). 1880–1942, Austrian novelist, whose novel *The Man Without Qualities* (1930–42) is an ironic examination of contemporary ills.

mu+sique con+crète *French.* (myzik kɔ̃'krɛt) *n.* another term for **concrete music.**

mus+jid ('mʌsdʒɪd) *n.* a variant spelling of **masjid.**

musk (mʌsk) *n.* **1.** a strong-smelling glandular secretion of the male musk deer, used in perfumery. **2.** a similar substance produced by certain other animals, such as the civet and otter, or manufactured synthetically. **3.** any of several scrophulariaceous plants of the genus *Mimulus,* esp. the North American *M. moschatus,* which has yellow flowers and was formerly cultivated for its musky scent. See also **monkey flower. 4.** the smell of musk or a similar heady smell. **5.** (*modifier*) containing or resembling musk: *musk oil; a musk flavour.* [C14: from Late Latin *muscus,* from Greek *moskhos,* from Persian *mushk,* probably from Sanskrit *mushká* scrotum (from the appearance of the musk deer's musk bag), diminutive of *mūsh* MOUSE]

musk deer *n.* a small central Asian mountain deer, *Moschus moschiferus.* The male has long tusklike canine teeth and secretes musk.

musk duck *n.* **1.** another name for **Muscovy duck. 2.** a duck, *Biziura lobata,* inhabiting swamps, lakes, and streams in Australia. The male has a leathery pouch beneath the bill and emits a musky odour.

mus+keg ('mʌsˌkɛg) *n. Chiefly Canadian.* an undrained boggy hollow characterized by sphagnum moss vegetation. [C19: from Algonquian: grassy swamp]

mus+kel+lunge ('mʌskəˌlʌndʒ), **mas+ka+longe** ('mæskəˌlɒndʒ), *or* **mas+ka+nonge** ('mæskəˌnɒndʒ) *n., pl.* **+lung·es, +long·es, +nong·es** *or* **+lunge, +longe, +nonge.** a large North American freshwater game fish, *Esox masquinongy:* family *Esocidae* (pikes, etc.). Often shortened (informally) to **musky** *or* **muskie.** [C18 *maskinunga,* of Algonquian origin; compare Ojibwa *mashkinonge* big pike]

mus+ket ('mʌskɪt) *n.* a long-barrelled muzzle-loading shoulder gun used between the 16th and 18th centuries by infantry soldiers. [C16: from French *mousquet,* from Italian *moschetto* arrow, earlier: sparrow hawk, from *moscha* a fly, from Latin *musca*]

mus+ket+eer (ˌmʌskɪ'tɪə) *n.* (formerly) a soldier armed with a musket.

mus+ket+ry ('mʌskɪtrɪ) *n.* **1.** muskets or musketeers collectively. **2.** the technique of using small arms.

Mus+kho+ge·an *or* **Mus+ko+ge·an** (mʌs'kəʊgɪən) *n.* a family of North American Indian languages.

mus+kie ('mʌskɪ) *n. Canadian.* an informal name for the **muskellunge.**

musk mal+low *n.* **1.** a malvaceous plant, *Malva moschata,* of Europe and N Africa, with purple-spotted stems, pink flowers, and a faint scent of musk. **2.** another name for **abelmosk.**

musk+mel·on ('mʌskˌmɛlən) *n.* **1.** any of several varieties of the melon *Cucumis melo,* such as the cantaloupe and honeydew. **2.** the fruit of any of these melons, having ribbed or warty rind and sweet yellow, white, or green flesh with a musky aroma.

musk or+chid *n.* a small Eurasian orchid, *Herminium monorchis,* with dense spikes of musk-scented greenish-yellow flowers.

musk ox *n.* a large bovid mammal, *Ovibos moschatus,* having a dark shaggy coat, short legs, and widely spaced downward-curving horns: now confined to the tundras of Canada and Greenland.

musk+rat ('mʌskˌræt) *n., pl.* **+rats** *or* **+rat. 1.** a North American beaver-like amphibious rodent, *Ondatra zibethica,* closely related to but larger than the voles: family *Cricetidae.* **2.** the brown fur of this animal. **3.** either of two closely related rodents, *Ondatra obscurus* or *Neofiber alleni* (**round-tailed muskrat**). ~Also called: **musquash.**

musk rose *n.* a prickly shrubby Mediterranean rose, *Rosa moschata,* cultivated for its white musk-scented flowers.

musk tur+tle *n.* any of several small turtles of the genus *Sternotherus,* esp. *S. odoratus* (**common musk turtle** or **stinkpot**), that emit a strong unpleasant odour: family *Kinosternidae.*

musk·y[1] ('mʌskɪ) *adj.* **musk·i·er, musk·i·est.** resembling the smell of musk; having a heady or pungent sweet aroma. —**'musk·i·ness** *n.*

mus+ky[2] ('mʌskɪ) *n., pl.* **mus+kies.** an informal name for the **muskellunge.**

Mus+lim ('mʊzlɪm, 'mʌz-) *or* **Mos+lem** *n., pl.* **+lims** *or* **+lim. 1.** a follower of the religion of Islam. ~*adj.* **2.** of or relating to Islam, its doctrines, culture, etc. ~Also: **Mohammedan, Muhammadan.** [C17: from Arabic, literally: one who surrenders] —**'Mus+lim+ism** *or* **'Mos+lem+ism** *n.*

mus+lin ('mʌzlɪn) *n.* a fine plain-weave cotton fabric. [C17: from French *mousseline,* from Italian *mussolina,* from Arabic *mawṣilīy* of Mosul, from *Mawṣil* Mosul, Iraq, where it was first produced]

Mus.M. *abbrev. for* Master of Music.

mus·o ('mju:zəʊ) *n. Austral. slang.* a musician, esp. a professional one.

mus+quash ('mʌskwɒʃ) *n.* another name for **muskrat,** esp. the fur. [C17: from Algonquian: compare Natick *musquash,* Abnaki *muskwessu*]

muss (mʌs) *U.S. informal.* ~*vb.* **1.** (*tr.;* often foll. by *up*) to make untidy; rumple. ~*n.* **2.** a state of disorder; muddle. [C19: probably a blend of MESS + FUSS] —**'muss·y** *adj.* —**'muss·i+ly** *adv.* —**'muss·i·ness** *n.*

mus+sel ('mʌsᵊl) *n.* **1.** any of various marine bivalves of the genus *Mytilus* and related genera, esp. *M. edulis* (**edible mussel**), having a dark slightly elongated shell and living attached to rocks, etc. **2.** any of various freshwater bivalves of the genera *Anodonta, Unio,* etc., attached to rocks, sand, etc., having a flattened oval shell (a source of mother-of-pearl). [Old English *muscle,* from Vulgar Latin *muscula* (unattested), from Latin *musculus,* diminutive of *mūs* mouse]

Mus·set (*French* my'sɛ) *n.* **Al·fred de** (al'frɛd də). 1810–57, French romantic poet and dramatist: his works include the play *Lorenzaccio* (1834) and the lyrics *Les Nuits* (1835–37), tracing his love affair with George Sand.

Mus·so·li·ni (ˌmʊsə'li:nɪ; *Italian* ˌmusso'lini:) *n.* **Be·ni·to** (be'ni:to) known as *il Duce.* 1883–1945, Italian Fascist dictator. After the Fascist march on Rome, he was appointed prime minister by King Victor Emmanuel III (1922) and assumed dictatorial powers. He annexed Abyssinia and allied Italy with Germany (1936), entering World War II in 1940. He was forced to resign following the Allied invasion of Sicily (1943) and was eventually shot by Italian partisans.

Mus·sorg·sky *or* **Mous·sorg·sky** (mʊ'sɔ:gskɪ; *Russian* 'musərkskij) *n.* **Mo·dest Pe·tro·vich** (ma'dɛst pɪ'trɔvitʃ). 1839–81, Russian composer. He translated inflections of speech into melody in such works as the song cycle *Songs and Dances of Death* (1875–77) and the opera *Boris Godunov* (1874). His other works include *Pictures at an Exhibition* (1874) for piano.

Mus+sul+man *or* **Mus+sal+man** ('mʌsᵊlmən) *n., pl.* **+mans.** an archaic word for **Muslim.** [C16: from Persian *Musulmān* (pl.) from Arabic *Muslimūn,* pl. of MUSLIM]

must[1] (mʌst; *unstressed* məst, məs) *vb.* (takes an infinitive without *to* or an implied infinitive) used as an auxiliary: **1.** to express obligation or compulsion: *you must pay your dues.* In this sense, *must* does not form a negative. If used with a negative infinitive it indicates obligatory prohibition. **2.** to indicate necessity: *I must go to the bank tomorrow.* **3.** to indicate the probable correctness of a statement: *he must be there by now.* **4.** to indicate inevitability: *all good things must come to an end.* **5.** to express resolution: **a.** on the part of the speaker when used with *I* or *we: I must finish this.* **b.** on the part of another or others as imputed to them by the speaker, when used with *you, he, she, they,* etc.: *let him get drunk if he must.* **6.** (used emphatically) to express conviction or certainty on the part of the speaker: *he must have reached the town by now, surely; you must be joking.* **7.** (foll. by *away*) used with an implied verb of motion to express compelling haste: *I must away.* ~*n.* **8.** an essential or necessary thing: *a safety belt in a car is a must these days.* [Old English *mōste* past tense of *mōtan* to be allowed, be obliged to; related to Old Saxon *mōtan,* Old High German *muozan,* German *mussen*]

must[2] (mʌst) *n.* the newly pressed juice of grapes or other fruit ready for fermentation. [Old English, from Latin *mustum* new wine, must, from *mustus* (adj.) new-born]

must[3] (mʌst) *n.* mustiness or mould. [C17: back formation from MUSTY]

must[4] (mʌst) *n.* a variant spelling of **musth.**

mus+tache (mə'stɑ:ʃ) *n.* the U.S. spelling of **moustache.** —**mus+'tached** *adj.*

mus+ta+chi·o (mə'stɑ:ʃɪˌəʊ) *n., pl.* **+chi·os.** (*often pl. when considered as two halves*) *Often humorous.* a moustache, esp. when bushy or elaborately shaped. [C16: from Spanish *mostacho* and Italian *mostaccio*] —**mus+'ta+chi+oed** *adj.*

Mus·ta·fa Ke·mal ('mʊstəfə kə'mɑ:l) *n.* See (Kemal) **Atatürk.**

mus+tang ('mʌstæŋ) *n.* a small breed of horse, often wild or half wild, found in the southwestern U.S. [C19: from Mexican Spanish *mestengo,* from *mesta* a group of stray animals]

mus+tard ('mʌstəd) *n.* **1.** any of several Eurasian plants of the cruciferous genus *Brassica,* esp. black mustard and white mustard, having yellow flowers and slender pods: cultivated for their pungent seeds. See also **charlock. 2.** a paste made from the powdered seeds of any of these plants and used as a condiment. **3. a.** a brownish yellow colour. **b.** (*as adj.*): *a mustard carpet.* **4.** *Slang.* zest or enthusiasm. [C13: from Old French *moustarde,* from Latin *mustum* MUST[2], since the original condiment was made by adding must]

mus+tard and cress *n.* seedlings of white mustard and garden cress, used in salads, etc.

mus+tard gas *n.* an oily liquid vesicant compound used in chemical warfare. Its vapour causes blindness and burns. Formula: $(ClCH_2CH_2)_2S$.

mus+tard oil *n.* an oil that is obtained from mustard seeds and used in making soap.

mus+tard plas+ter *n. Med.* a mixture of powdered black mustard seeds and an adhesive agent applied to the skin for its relaxing, stimulating, or counterirritant effects.

mus+tee (mʌ'sti:, 'mʌsti:) *or* **mes+tee** (mɛ'sti:) *n.* **1.** the offspring of a White and a quadroon. **2.** any person of mixed ancestry. [C17: shortened from MESTIZO]

mus+te+line ('mʌstɪˌlaɪn, -lɪn) *adj.* **1.** of, relating to, or belonging to the *Mustelidae,* a family of typically predatory mammals including weasels, ferrets, minks, polecats, badgers, skunks, and otters: order *Carnivora* (carnivores). ~*n.* **2.** any musteline animal. [C17: from Latin *mustēlīnus,* from *mustēla* weasel, from *mūs* mouse + *-tēla,* of unknown origin]

mus+ter ('mʌstə) *vb.* **1.** to call together (numbers of men) for duty, inspection, etc., or (of men) to assemble in this way. **2. muster in** *or* **out.** *U.S.* to enlist into or discharge from military service. **3.** (*tr.;* sometimes foll. by *up*) to summon or gather: *to muster one's arguments; to muster up courage.* ~*n.* **4.** an assembly of military personnel for duty, etc. **5.** a collection, assembly, or gathering. **6.** a flock of peacocks. **7. pass muster.** to be acceptable. [C14: from old French *moustrer,* from Latin *monstrāre* to show, from *monstrum* portent, omen]

mus+ter roll *n.* a list of the officers and men in a regiment, ship's company, etc.

musth *or* **must** (mʌst) *n.* (often preceded by *in*) a state of frenzied sexual excitement in the males of certain large mammals, esp. elephants, associated with discharge from a gland between the ear and eye. [C19: from Urdu *mast,* from Persian: drunk]

mus·ty ('mʌstɪ) *adj.* **·ti·er, ·ti·est. 1.** smelling or tasting old, stale, or mouldy. **2.** old-fashioned, dull, or hackneyed: *musty ideas.* [C16: perhaps a variant of obsolete *moisty,* influenced by MUST[3]] **—'must·i·ly** *adv.* **—'must·i·ness** *n.*

mut (mʌt) *n. Printing.* another word for **em** (sense 1). [C20: shortened from MUTTON]

mu·ta·ble ('mju:təbəl) *adj.* **1.** able to or tending to change. **2.** *Astrology.* of or relating to four of the signs of the zodiac, Gemini, Virgo, Sagittarius, and Pisces, which are associated with the quality of adaptability. Compare **cardinal** (sense 8), **fixed** (sense 10). [C14: from Latin *mūtābilis* fickle, from *mūtāre* to change] **—ˌmu·ta·'bil·i·ty** *or* **'mu·ta·ble·ness** *n.* **—'mu·ta·bly** *adv.*

mu·ta·gen ('mju:tədʒən) *n.* a substance or agent that can induce genetic mutation. [C20: from MUTATION + -GEN] **—mu·ta·gen·ic** (ˌmju:tə'dʒɛnɪk) *adj.*

mu·tant ('mju:tənt) *n.* **1.** Also called: **mutation.** an animal, organism, or gene that has undergone mutation. *—adj.* **2.** of, relating to, undergoing, or resulting from change or mutation. [C20: from Latin *mutāre* to change]

mu·tate (mju:'teɪt) *vb.* to undergo or cause to undergo mutation. [C19: from Latin *mūtātus* changed, from *mūtāre* to change] **—mu·ta·tive** ('mju:tətɪv, mju:'teɪtɪv) *adj.*

mu·ta·tion (mju:'teɪʃən) *n.* **1.** the act or process of mutating; change; alteration. **2.** a change or alteration. **3.** a change in the chromosomes or genes of a cell. When this change occurs in the gametes the structure and development of the resultant offspring may be affected. See also **inversion** (sense 11). **4.** another word for **mutant** (sense 1). **5.** a physical characteristic of an individual resulting from this type of chromosomal change. **6.** *Phonetics.* **a.** (in Germanic languages) another name for **umlaut. b.** (in Celtic languages) a phonetic change in certain initial consonants caused by a preceding word. **—mu·'ta·tion·al** *adj.* **—mu·'ta·tion·al·ly** *adv.*

mu·ta·tion stop *n.* an organ pipe sounding the harmonic of the note normally produced.

mu·ta·tis mu·tan·dis *Latin.* (mu:'tɑ:tɪs mu:'tændɪs) the necessary changes having been made.

Mu·ta·zi·lite (mu:'tɑ:zɪˌlaɪt) *n.* a member of an 8th-century liberal Muslim sect, later merged into the Shiahs. [from Arabic *mu'tazilah* body of seceders + -ITE[1]]

mutch[1] (mʌtʃ) *n.* formerly, a close-fitting linen cap, worn by women and children in Scotland. [C15: from Middle Dutch *mutse* cap, from Medieval Latin *almucia* AMICE]

mutch[2] (mʌtʃ) *vb. Brit. dialect.* **1.** *(tr.)* to cadge; beg. **2.** *(intr.)* another word for **mitch.**

mutch·kin ('mʌtʃkɪn) *n.* a Scottish unit of liquid measure equal to slightly less than one pint. [C15: from Middle Dutch *mudseken,* from Latin *modius* measure for grain]

mute[1] (mju:t) *adj.* **1.** not giving out sound or speech; silent. **2.** unable to speak; dumb. **3.** unspoken or unexpressed: *mute dislike.* **4.** *Law.* (of a person arraigned on indictment) refusing to answer a charge. **5.** another word for **plosive. 6.** (of a letter in a word) silent. *~n.* **7.** a person who is unable to speak. **8.** *Law.* a person who refuses to plead when arraigned on indictment for an offence. **9.** any of various devices used to soften the tone of stringed or brass instruments. **10.** *Phonetics.* a plosive consonant; stop. **11.** a silent letter. **12.** an actor in a dumb-show. **13.** a hired mourner at a funeral. *~vb. (tr.)* **14.** to reduce the volume of (a musical instrument) by means of a mute, soft pedal, etc. **15.** to subdue the strength of (a colour, tone, lighting, etc.). [C14 *muwet* from Old French *mu,* from Latin *mūtus* silent] **—'mute·ly** *adv.* **—'mute·ness** *n.*

mute[2] (mu:t) *Archaic. ~vb.* **1.** (of birds) to discharge (faeces). *~n.* **2.** birds' faeces. [C15: from Old French *meutir,* variant of *esmeltir,* of Germanic origin; probably related to SMELT[1] and MELT]

mute swan *n.* a Eurasian swan, *Cygnus olor,* with a pure white plumage, an orange-red bill with a black base, and a curved neck. Compare **whistling swan.**

mu·ti·cous ('mju:tɪkəs) *adj. Botany.* lacking an awn, spine, or point. [C19: from Latin *muticus* awnless, curtailed]

mu·ti·late ('mju:tɪˌleɪt) *vb. (tr.)* to damage or maim esp. by depriving of a limb, essential part, etc. [C16: from Latin *mutilāre* to cut off; related to *mutilus* maimed] **—ˌmu·ti·'la·tion** *n.* **—'mu·ti·ˌla·tive** *adj.* **—'mu·ti·ˌla·tor** *n.*

mu·ti·neer (ˌmju:tɪ'nɪə) *n.* a person who mutinies.

mu·ti·nous ('mju:tɪnəs) *adj.* **1.** openly rebellious or disobedient: *a mutinous child.* **2.** characteristic or indicative of mutiny. **—'mu·ti·nous·ly** *adv.* **—'mu·ti·nous·ness** *n.*

mu·ti·ny ('mju:tɪnɪ) *n., pl.* **·nies. 1.** open rebellion against constituted authority, esp. by seamen or soldiers against their officers. *~vb.* **·nies, ·ny·ing, ·nied. 2.** *(intr.)* to engage in mutiny. [C16: from obsolete *mutine,* from Old French *mutin* rebellious, from *meute* mutiny, ultimately from Latin *movēre* to move]

mut·ism ('mju:ˌtɪzəm) *n.* **1.** the state of being mute. **2.** *Psychiatry.* **a.** a refusal to speak although the mechanism of speech is not damaged. **b.** the lack of development of speech, due usually to early deafness.

Mut·su·hi·to (ˌmu:tsʊ'hi:təʊ) *n.* See **Meiji.**

mutt (mʌt) *n. Slang.* **1.** an inept, ignorant, or stupid person. **2.** a mongrel dog; cur. [C20: shortened from MUTTONHEAD]

mut·ter ('mʌtə) *vb.* **1.** to utter (something) in a low and indistinct tone. **2.** *(intr.)* to grumble or complain. **3.** *(intr.)* to make a low continuous murmuring sound. *~n.* **4.** a muttered sound or complaint. [C14 *moteren;* related to Norwegian (dialect) *mutra,* Old High German *mutilōn;* compare Old English *mōtian* to speak] **—'mut·ter·er** *n.* **—'mut·ter·ing·ly** *adv.*

mut·ton ('mʌtən) *n.* **1.** the flesh of sheep, esp. of mature sheep, used as food. **2. mutton dressed (up) as lamb.** an older person, thing, or idea dressed up to look young or new. **3.** *Printing.* another word for **em** (sense 1). Compare **nut** (sense 11). [C13 *moton* sheep, from Old French, from Medieval Latin *multō,* of Celtic origin; the term was adopted in printing to distinguish the pronunciation of *em quad* from *en quad*] **—'mut·ton·y** *adj.*

mut·ton bird *n.* any of several shearwaters, having a dark plumage with greyish underparts.

mut·ton chop *n.* a piece of mutton from the loin.

mut·ton·chops ('mʌtənˌtʃɒps) *pl. n.* side whiskers trimmed in the shape of chops, widening out from the temples.

mut·ton·head ('mʌtənˌhɛd) *n. Slang.* a stupid or ignorant person; fool. **—'mut·ton·ˌhead·ed** *adj.*

Mut·tra ('mʌtrə) *n.* the former name of **Mathura.**

mu·tu·al ('mju:tʃʊəl) *adj.* **1.** experienced or expressed by each of two or more people or groups about the other; reciprocal: *mutual distrust.* **2.** common to or shared by both or all of two or more parties: *a mutual friend; mutual interests.* [C15: from Old French *mutuel,* from Latin *mūtuus* reciprocal (originally: borrowed); related to *mūtāre* to change] **—mu·tu·al·i·ty** (ˌmju:tjʊ'ælɪtɪ) *or* **'mu·tu·al·ness** *n.* **—'mu·tu·al·ly** *adv.*

mu·tu·al fund *n.* the U.S. name for **unit trust.**

mu·tu·al in·duct·ance *n.* a measure of the mutual induction between two magnetically linked circuits, given as the ratio of the induced emf to the rate of change of current producing it. It is usually measured in henries. Symbol: *M* or L_{12} Also called: **coefficient of mutual induction.**

mu·tu·al in·duc·tion *n.* the production of an electromotive force in a circuit by a current change in a second circuit magnetically linked to the first. See also **mutual inductance.** Compare **self-induction.**

mu·tu·al in·sur·ance *n.* a system of insurance by which all policyholders become company members under contract to pay premiums into a common fund out of which claims are paid.

mu·tu·al·ism ('mju:tjʊəˌlɪzəm) *n.* another name for **symbiosis.** **—'mu·tu·al·ist** *n., adj.* **—ˌmu·tu·al·'is·tic** *adj.*

mu·tu·al·ize *or* **mu·tu·al·ise** ('mju:tjʊəˌlaɪz) *vb.* **1.** to make or become mutual. **2.** *(tr.) U.S.* to organize or convert (a business enterprise) so that customers or employees own a majority of shares. **—ˌmu·tu·al·i·'za·tion** *or* **ˌmu·tu·al·i·'sa·tion** *n.*

mu·tu·al sav·ings bank *n. Chiefly U.S.* a savings bank having no subscribed capital stock and distributing all available net profit to depositors who, however, remain creditors without voting power.

mu·tu·el ('mju:tjʊəl) *n.* short for **pari-mutuel.**

mu·tule ('mju:tju:l) *n. Architect.* one of a set of flat blocks below the corona of a Doric cornice. Compare **modillion.** [C16: via French from Latin *mūtulus* modillion]

muu-muu ('mu:ˌmu:) *n.* a loose brightly-coloured dress worn by women in Hawaii. [from Hawaiian]

Mu·zak ('mju:zæk) *n. Trademark.* recorded light music played in shops, restaurants, factories, etc., to entertain, increase sales or production, etc.

mu·zhik, mou·jik, *or* **mu·jik** ('mu:ʒɪk) *n.* a Russian peasant, esp. under the tsars. [C16: from Russian: peasant]

Mu·zo·re·wa (ˌmuzə'reɪwə) *n.* **A·bel (Tendekayi)** ('eɪbəl). born 1925, Rhodesian Methodist bishop and politician; president of the African National Council since 1971. He was one of the negotiators of an internal settlement (1978), and was prime minister (1979-81).

muzz (mʌz) *vb. (tr.) Brit. Informal.* to make (something) muzzy.

muz·zle ('mʌzəl) *n.* **1.** the projecting part of the face, usually the jaws and nose, of animals such as the dog and horse. **2.** a guard or strap fitted over an animal's nose and jaws to prevent it biting or eating. **3.** the front end of a gun barrel. *~vb. (tr.)* **4.** to prevent from being heard or noticed: *to muzzle the press.* **5.** to put a muzzle on (an animal). **6.** to take in (a sail). [C15 *mosel,* from Old French *musel,* diminutive of *muse* snout, from Medieval Latin *mūsus,* of unknown origin] **—'muz·zler** *n.*

muz·zle-load·er *n.* a firearm receiving its ammunition through the muzzle. **—'muz·zle-ˌload·ing** *adj.*

muz·zle ve·loc·i·ty *n.* the velocity of a projectile as it leaves a firearm's muzzle.

muz·zy ('mʌzɪ) *adj.* **·zi·er, ·zi·est. 1.** blurred, indistinct, or hazy. **2.** confused, muddled, or befuddled. [C18: origin obscure] **—'muz·zi·ly** *adv.* **—'muz·zi·ness** *n.*

mv *Music. abbrev. for* mezzo voce.

MV *symbol for* megavolt.

M.V. *abbrev. for:* **1.** motor vessel. **2.** muzzle velocity.

M.V.D. *abbrev. for* Ministry of Internal Affairs; the Soviet police organization since 1946. [from Russian *Ministerstvo vnutrennikh del*]

M.V.O. *abbrev. for* (in Britain) Member of the Royal Victorian Order.

M.V.S. *abbrev. for* Master of Veterinary Surgery.

M.V.Sc. *abbrev. for* Master of Veterinary Science.

MW 1. *symbol for* megawatt. **2.** *Radio. abbrev. for* medium wave. **3.** *International car registration for* Malawi.

mwa·li·mu (mwɑ:'li:mu:) *n.* a teacher. [Swahili]

Mwe·ru ('mweəru:) *n.* a lake in central Africa, on the border between Zambia and Zaïre. Area: 4196 sq. km (1620 sq. miles).

Mx *Physics. symbol for* maxwell.
my (maɪ) *determiner.* **1.** of, belonging to, or associated with the speaker or writer (me): *my own ideas; do you mind my smoking?* **2.** used in various forms of address: *my lord; my dear boy.* **3.** used in various exclamations: *my goodness!* ~*interj.* **4.** an exclamation of surprise, awe, etc.: *my, how you've grown!* [C12 *mī*, variant of Old English *mīn* when preceding a word beginning with a consonant]
M.Y. *abbrev. for* motor yacht.
my- *combining form.* variant of **myo-** before a vowel.
my+al·gi·a (maɪ'ældʒɪə) *n.* pain in a muscle or a group of muscles. [C19: from MYO- + -ALGIA] —**my+'al+gic** *adj.*
my·a+lism ('maɪəˌlɪzəm) *n.* a kind of witchcraft, similar to obi, practised esp. in the West Indies. [C19: from *myal*, probably of West African origin] —**'my·a+list** *n.*
my+all ('maɪəl) *n.* **1.** any of several Australian acacias, esp. *Acacia pendula*, having hard scented wood used for fences. **2.** an Australian Aborigine living independently of society. [C19: from a native Australian name]
my+as+the·ni·a (ˌmaɪəs'θiːnɪə) *n.* **1.** any muscular weakness. **2.** short for **myasthenia gravis.** [C19: from MYO- + ASTHENIA] —**my+as+then+ic** (ˌmaɪəs'θɛnɪk) *adj.*
my+as+the·ni·a gra+vis ('grɑːvɪs) *n.* a chronic progressive disease in which the muscles, esp. those of the head and face, become weak and easily fatigued.
myc- *combining form.* variant of **myco-** before a vowel.
my+ce·li·um (maɪ'siːlɪəm) *n., pl.* **·li·a** (-lɪə). the vegetative body of fungi: a mass of branching filaments (hyphae) that spread throughout the nutrient substratum. [C19 (literally: nail of fungus): from MYCO- + Greek *hēlos* nail] —**my+'ce·li·al** *adj.* —**my+ce·loid** ('maɪsɪˌlɔɪd) *adj.*
My+ce·nae (maɪ'siːniː) *n.* an ancient Greek city in the NE Peloponnesus on the plain of Argos.
My+ce·nae·an (ˌmaɪsɪ'niːən) *adj.* **1.** of or relating to ancient Mycenae or its inhabitants. **2.** of or relating to the Aegean civilization of Mycenae (1400 to 1100 B.C.)
-my·cete *n. combining form.* indicating a member of a class of fungi: *myxomycete.* [from New Latin *-mycetes*, from Greek *mukētes*, plural of *mukēs* fungus]
my·ce·to- *or before a vowel* **my·cet-** *combining form.* fungus: *mycetozoan.* [from Greek *mukēs* fungus]
my+ce·to·ma (ˌmaɪsɪ'təʊmə) *n., pl.* **+mas** *or* **+ma+ta** (-mətə). a chronic fungal infection, esp. of the foot, characterized by swelling, usually resulting from a wound.
my+ce·to+zo·an (maɪˌsiːtəʊ'zəʊən) *n.* another name for **myxomycete.**
my·co- *or before a vowel* **myc-** *combining form.* indicating fungus: *mycology.* [from Greek *mukēs* fungus]
my+co+bac+te+ri·um (ˌmaɪkəʊbæk'tɪərɪəm) *n., pl.* **+ri·a** (-rɪə). any rod-shaped Gram-positive bacterium of the genus *Mycobacterium*, esp. the tubercle bacillus: family *Mycobacteriaceae.*
mycol. *abbrev. for:* **1.** mycological. **2.** mycology.
my+col+o·gy (maɪ'kɒlədʒɪ) *n.* **1.** the branch of botany concerned with the study of fungi. **2.** the fungi of a particular region. —**my+co+log·i·cal** (ˌmaɪkə'lɒdʒɪkᵊl) *or* ˌ**my+co+'log+ic** *adj.* —**my+'col·o+gist** *n.*
my+cor+rhi+za *or* **my+co+rhi+za** (ˌmaɪkə'raɪzə) *n., pl.* **+zae** (-ziː) *or* **+zas.** an association of a fungus and a higher plant in which the fungus lives within or on the outside of the roots forming a symbiotic or parasitic relationship. —ˌ**my+cor+'rhi+zal** *or* ˌ**my+co+'rhi+zal** *adj.*
my+co+sis (maɪ'kəʊsɪs) *n.* any infection or disease caused by fungus. —**my+cot+ic** (maɪ'kɒtɪk) *adj.*
My+co+stat+in (ˌmaɪkəʊ'stætɪn) *n. Trademark.* a brand of **nystatin.**
my+dri·a+sis (mɪ'draɪəsɪs, maɪ-) *n.* abnormal dilation of the pupil of the eye, produced by drugs, coma, etc. [C17: via Late Latin from Greek; origin obscure]
myd+ri+at+ic (ˌmɪdrɪ'ætɪk) *adj.* **1.** relating to or causing mydriasis. ~*n.* **2.** a mydriatic drug.
my·el- *or before a consonant* **my·el·o-** *combining form.* the spinal cord or bone marrow: *myeloid.* [from Greek *muelos* marrow, spinal cord, from *mus* muscle]
my+e·len+ceph·a+lon (ˌmaɪɪlɛn'sɛfəˌlɒn) *n., pl.* **+lons** *or* **+la** (-lə). the part of the embryonic hindbrain that develops into the medulla oblongata. Nontechnical name: **afterbrain.** —**my+e·len+ce·phal+ic** (ˌmaɪɪlɛnsə'fælɪk) *adj.*
my+e·lin ('maɪɪlɪn) *or* **my+e·line** ('maɪɪˌliːn) *n.* a white fatlike substance forming a protective sheath around certain nerve fibres. —ˌ**my+e·'lin+ic** *adj.*
my+e·li·tis (ˌmaɪɪ'laɪtɪs) *n.* inflammation of the spinal cord or of the bone marrow.
my+e·loid ('maɪɪˌlɔɪd) *adj.* of or relating to the spinal cord or the bone marrow.
my+e·lo+ma (ˌmaɪə'ləʊmə) *n.* a usually malignant tumour of the bone marrow or composed of cells normally found in bone marrow. —ˌ**my+e·'lo+ma+**ˌ**toid** *adj.*
my·ia+sis ('maɪəsɪs) *n., pl.* **+ses** (-ˌsiːz). **1.** infestation of the body by the larvae of flies. **2.** any disease resulting from such infestation. [C19: New Latin, from Greek *muia* a fly]
My Lai ('maɪ 'laɪ, 'miː) *n.* a village in S Vietnam where in 1968 U.S. troops massacred over 100 civilians.
my+lo+nite ('maɪləˌnaɪt, 'mɪlə-) *n.* a fine-grained metamorphic rock, often showing banding and micaceous fracture, formed by the crushing, grinding, or rolling of the original structure. [C19: from Greek *mulōn* mill]
my·na, my+nah, *or* **mi·na** ('maɪnə) *n.* any of various tropical Asian starlings of the genera *Acridotheres, Gracula*, etc., esp. *G. religiosa* (see **hill myna**), some of which can mimic human speech. [C18: from Hindi *mainā*, from Sanskrit *madana*]
Myn+heer (mə'nɪə) *n.* a Dutch title of address equivalent to *Sir* when used alone or to *Mr.* when placed before a name. [C17: from Dutch *mijnheer*, my lord]
my·o- *or before a vowel* **my-** *combining form.* muscle: *myocardium.* [from Greek *mus* MUSCLE]
my·o+car·di·al in+farc+tion *n.* destruction of an area of heart muscle as the result of occlusion of a coronary artery. Compare **coronary thrombosis.**
my·o+car+di·o+graph (ˌmaɪəʊ'kɑːdɪəˌgræf, -ˌgrɑːf) *n.* an instrument for recording the movements of heart muscle.
my·o+car+di+tis (ˌmaɪəʊkɑː'daɪtɪs) *n.* inflammation of the heart muscle.
my·o+car+di·um (ˌmaɪəʊ'kɑːdɪəm) *n., pl.* **+di·a** (-dɪə). the muscular tissue of the heart. [C19: *myo-* + *cardium*, from Greek *kardia* heart] —ˌ**my·o+'car+di·al** *adj.*
my·o+gen+ic (ˌmaɪə'dʒɛnɪk) *adj.* originating in or forming muscle tissue.
my·o+glo+bin (ˌmaɪəʊ'gləʊbɪn) *n.* a protein that occurs in muscle and is similar to haemoglobin but has a greater affinity for oxygen.
my·o+graph ('maɪəˌgræf, -ˌgrɑːf) *n.* an instrument for recording tracings (**myograms**) of muscular contractions. —ˌ**my·o+'graph+ic** *adj.* —ˌ**my·o+'graph·i+cal+ly** *adv.* —**my+og+ra+phy** (maɪ'ɒgrəfɪ) *n.*
my+ol+o·gy (maɪ'ɒlədʒɪ) *n.* the branch of medical science concerned with the structure and diseases of muscles. —**my·o+log+ic** (ˌmaɪə'lɒdʒɪk) *or* ˌ**my·o+'log·i·cal** *adj.* —**my+'ol·o+gist** *n.*
my·o+ma (maɪ'əʊmə) *n., pl.* **+mas** *or* **+ma·ta** (-mətə). a benign tumour composed of muscle tissue. —**my+om·a+tous** (maɪ'əʊmətəs). *adj.*
my+ope ('maɪəʊp) *n.* any person afflicted with myopia. [C18: via French from Greek *muōps*; see MYOPIA]
my·o+pi·a (maɪ'əʊpɪə) *n.* inability to see distant objects clearly because the images are focused in front of the retina; short-sightedness. [C18: via New Latin from Greek *muōps* short-sighted, from *muein* to close (the eyes), blink + *ōps* eye] —**my+op+ic** (maɪ'ɒpɪk) *adj.* —**my+'op·i+cal+ly** *adv.*
my·o+sin ('maɪəsɪn) *n.* the chief protein of muscle, a globulin that combines with actin to form the complex protein actomyosin. [C19: from MYO- + -OSE[2] + -IN]
my·o+so+tis (ˌmaɪə'səʊtɪs) *or* **my·o+sote** ('maɪəˌsəʊt) *n.* any plant of the boraginaceous genus *Myosotis.* See **forget-me-not.** [C18: New Latin from Greek *muosōtis* mouse-ear (referring to its furry leaves), from *muos*, genitive of *mus* mouse + *-ōt-*, stem of *ous* ear]
my·o+tome ('maɪəˌtəʊm) *n.* **1.** any segment of embryonic mesoderm that develops into skeletal muscle in the adult. **2.** any of the segmentally arranged blocks of muscle in lower vertebrates such as fishes.
my·o+to+ni·a (ˌmaɪə'təʊnɪə) *n.* lack of muscle tone, frequently including muscle spasm or rigidity. Also called: **amyotonia.** —**my·o+ton+ic** (ˌmaɪə'tɒnɪk) *adj.*
myr·i·a- *combining form.* indicating a very great number: *myriapod.* [from Greek *murios* countless]
myr·i·ad ('mɪrɪəd) *adj.* **1.** innumerable. ~*n.* **2.** a large indefinite number. **3.** *Archaic.* ten thousand. [C16: via Late Latin from Greek *murias* ten thousand]
myr·i·a+pod ('mɪrɪəˌpɒd) *n.* **1.** any terrestrial arthropod of the group *Myriapoda*, having a long segmented body and many walking limbs: includes the centipedes and millipedes. ~*adj.* **2.** of, relating to, or belonging to the *Myriapoda.* [C19: from New Latin *Myriapoda.* See MYRIAD, -POD] —**myr·i·ap·o+dan** (ˌmɪrɪ'æpədᵊn) *adj.* —ˌ**myr·i+'ap·o+dous** *adj.*
my+ri+ca (mɪ'raɪkə) *n.* the dried root bark of the wax myrtle, used as a tonic and to treat diarrhoea. [C18: via Latin from Greek *murikē* the tamarisk]
myr·me·co- *combining form.* ant: *myrmecology; myrmecophile.* [from Greek *murmēx*]
myr+me·col·o·gy ('mɜːmɪ'kɒlədʒɪ) *n.* the branch of zoology concerned with the study of ants. —**myr+me·co+log·i·cal** (ˌmɜːmɪkə'lɒdʒɪkᵊl) *adj.* —ˌ**myr+me·'col·o·gist** *n.*
myr+me·coph·a+gous (ˌmɜːmɪ'kɒfəgəs) *adj.* **1.** (of jaws, etc.) specialized for feeding on ants. **2.** feeding on ants.
myr+me·co+phile ('mɜːmɪkəʊˌfaɪl) *n.* an animal that lives in a colony of ants. —**myr+me·coph·i+lous** (ˌmɜːmɪ'kɒfɪləs) *adj.*
Myr+mi+don ('mɜːmɪˌdɒn, -dᵊn) *n., pl.* **Myr+mi+dons** *or* **Myr+mid·o+nes** (mɜː'mɪdᵊˌniːz). **1.** *Greek myth.* one of a race of people whom Zeus made from a nest of ants. They settled in Thessaly and were led against Troy by Achilles. See **Aeacus. 2.** (*often not cap.*) a follower or henchman.
my+rob·a+lan (maɪ'rɒbələn, mɪ-) *n.* **1.** the dried plumlike fruit of various tropical trees of the genus *Terminalia*, used in dyeing, tanning, ink, and medicine. **2.** a dye extracted from this fruit. **3.** another name for **cherry plum.** [C16: via Latin from Greek *murobalanos*, from *muron* ointment + *balanos* acorn]
My+ron ('maɪərən) *n.* 5th-century B.C. Greek sculptor. He worked mainly in bronze and introduced a greater variety of pose into Greek sculpture, as in his *Discobolus.*
myrrh (mɜː) *n.* **1.** any of several burseraceous trees and shrubs of the African and S Asian genus *Commiphora*, esp. *C. myrrha*, that exude an aromatic resin. Compare **balm of gilead** (sense 1). **2.** the resin obtained from such a plant, used in perfume, incense, and medicine. **3.** another name for **sweet cicely** (sense 1). [Old English *myrre*, via Latin from Greek *murrha*, ultimately from Akkadian *murrū*; compare Hebrew *mōr*, Arabic *murr*]

myr·ta·ceous (mɜːˈteɪʃəs) *adj.* of, relating to, or belonging to the *Myrtaceae,* a family of mostly tropical and subtropical trees and shrubs having oil glands in the leaves: includes eucalyptus, clove, myrtle, and guava. [C19: via New Latin from Latin *myrtus* myrtle, from Greek *murtos*]

myr·tle (ˈmɜːtᵊl) *n.* **1.** any evergreen shrub or tree of the myrtaceous genus *Myrtus,* esp. *M. communis,* a S European shrub with pink or white flowers and aromatic blue-black berries. **2.** short for **crape myrtle. 3. creeping** *or* **trailing myrtle.** *U.S.* another name for **periwinkle** (the plant). [C16: from Medieval Latin *myrtilla,* from Latin *myrtus,* from Greek *murtos*]

my·self (maɪˈsɛlf) *pron.* **1. a.** the reflexive form of *I* or *me.* **b.** (intensifier): *I myself know of no answer.* **2.** (*preceded by a copula*) my usual self: *I'm not myself today.* **3.** *Not standard.* used instead of *I* or *me* in compound noun phrases: *John and myself are voting together.*

Usage. The use of *myself* for *I* or *me* is often the result of an attempt to be elegant or correct. However, careful users of English only employ *myself* when it follows *I* or *me* in the same clause: *I cut myself,* but *he gave it to me* (not *myself*). The same is true of the other reflexives. This rule does permit constructions such as *he wrote it himself* (unassisted) and *he himself wrote it* (without an intermediary), but these are only to be used to reinforce a previous reference to the same individual.

My·si·a (ˈmɪsɪə) *n.* an ancient region in the NW corner of Asia Minor. —**ˈMy·si·an** *adj., n.*

My·sore (maɪˈsɔː) *n.* **1. a.** city in S India, in S Karnataka state: former capital of the state of Mysore; manufacturing and trading centre; university (1916). Pop.: 355 685 (1971). **2.** the former name (until 1973) of **Karnataka.**

mys·ta·gogue (ˈmɪstəˌgɒg) *n.* (in Mediterranean mystery religions) a person who instructs those who are preparing for initiation into the mysteries. [C16: via Latin from Greek *mustagōgos,* from *mustēs* candidate for initiation + *agein* to lead. See MYSTIC] —**mys·ta·gog·ic** (ˌmɪstəˈgɒdʒɪk) *or* **ˌmys·ta·ˈgog·i·cal** *adj.* —**ˌmys·taˈgog·i·cal·ly** *adv.* —**mys·ta·go·gy** (ˈmɪstəˌgɒdʒɪ) *n.*

mys·te·ri·ous (mɪˈstɪərɪəs) *adj.* **1.** characterized by or indicative of mystery. **2.** puzzling, curious, or enigmatic. —**mys·ˈte·ri·ous·ly** *adv.* —**mys·ˈte·ri·ous·ness** *n.*

mys·ter·y[1] (ˈmɪstərɪ, -trɪ) *n., pl.* **·ter·ies. 1.** an unexplained or inexplicable event, phenomenon, etc. **2.** a person or thing that arouses curiosity or suspense because of an unknown, obscure, or enigmatic quality. **3.** the state or quality of being obscure, inexplicable, or enigmatic. **4.** a story, film, etc., which arouses suspense and curiosity because of facts concealed. **5.** *Theol.* any truth that is divinely revealed but otherwise unknowable. **6.** *Christianity.* a sacramental rite, such as the Eucharist, or (*when pl.*) the consecrated elements of the Eucharist. **7.** (*often pl.*) any of various rites of certain ancient Mediterranean religions. **8.** *Archaic.* symbolic significance. **9.** short for **mystery play.** [C14: via Latin from Greek *mustērion* secret rites. See MYSTIC]

mys·ter·y[2] (ˈmɪstərɪ) *n., pl.* **·ter·ies.** *Archaic.* **1.** a trade, occupation, or craft. **2.** a guild of craftsmen. [C14: from Medieval Latin *mistērium,* from Latin *ministerium* occupation, from *minister* official]

mys·ter·y play *n.* (in the Middle Ages) a type of drama based on the life of Christ. Compare **miracle play.**

mys·ter·y tour *n.* an excursion to an unspecified destination.

mys·tic (ˈmɪstɪk) *n.* **1.** a person who achieves mystical experience or an apprehension of divine mysteries ~*adj.* **2.** another word for **mystical.** [C14: via Latin from Greek *mustikos,* from *mustēs* mystery initiate]

mys·ti·cal (ˈmɪstɪkᵊl) *adj.* **1.** relating to or characteristic of mysticism. **2.** *Theol.* having a divine or sacred significance that surpasses natural human apprehension. **3.** having occult or metaphysical significance, nature, or force. **4.** a less common word for **mysterious.** —**ˈmys·ti·cal·ly** *adv.* —**ˈmys·ti·cal·ness** *n.*

mys·ti·cism (ˈmɪstɪˌsɪzəm) *n.* **1.** belief in or experience of a reality surpassing normal human understanding or experience, esp. a reality perceived as essential to the nature of life. **2.** a system of contemplative prayer and spirituality aimed at achieving direct intuitive experience of the divine. **3.** obscure or confused belief or thought.

mys·ti·fy (ˈmɪstɪˌfaɪ) *vb.* **·fies, ·fy·ing, ·fied.** (*tr.*) **1.** to confuse, bewilder, or puzzle. **2.** to make mysterious or obscure. [C19: from French *mystifier,* from *mystère* MYSTERY[1] or *mystique* MYSTIC] —**ˌmys·ti·fi·ˈca·tion** *n.* —**ˈmys·ti·ˌfied·ly** *adv.* —**ˈmys·ti·ˌfi·er** *n.* —**ˈmys·ti·ˌfy·ing·ly** *adv.*

mys·tique (mɪˈstiːk) *n.* an aura of mystery, power, and awe that surrounds a person or thing: *the mystique of the theatre; the mystique of computer programming.* [C20: from French (adj.): MYSTIC]

myth (mɪθ) *n.* **1. a.** a story about superhuman beings of an earlier age taken by preliterate society to be a true account, usually of how natural phenomena, social customs, etc., came into existence. **b.** another word for **mythology** (senses 1, 3). **2.** a fictitious or unproven person or thing. **3.** (in modern literature) a theme or character type embodying an idea: *Hemingway's myth of the male hero.* **4.** *Philosophy.* (esp. in the writings of Plato) an allegory or parable. [C19: via Late Latin from Greek *muthos* fable, word]

myth. *abbrev. for:* **1.** mythological. **2.** mythology.

myth·i·cal (ˈmɪθɪkᵊl) *adj.* **1.** of or relating to myth. **2.** imaginary or fictitious. —**ˈmyth·i·cal·ly** *adv.*

myth·i·cize *or* **myth·i·cise** (ˈmɪθɪˌsaɪz) *vb.* (*tr.*) to make into or treat as a myth. —**ˌmyth·i·ci·ˈza·tion** *or* **ˌmyth·i·ci·ˈsa·tion** *n.* —**ˈmyth·i·ˌcist, ˈmyth·i·ˌciz·er,** *or* **ˈmyth·i·ˌcis·er** *n.*

myth·o- *n. combining form.* myth: *mythogenesis; mythography.*

myth·o·log·i·cal (ˌmɪθəˈlɒdʒɪkᵊl) *adj.* **1.** of or relating to mythology. **2.** mythical. —**ˌmyth·o·ˈlog·i·cal·ly** *adv.*

my·thol·o·gist (mɪˈθɒlədʒɪst) *n.* **1.** an expert in or student of mythology. **2.** a writer or editor of myths.

my·thol·o·gize *or* **my·thol·o·gise** (mɪˈθɒləˌdʒaɪz) *vb.* **1.** to tell, study, or explain (myths). **2.** (*intr.*) to create or make up myths. **3.** (*tr.*) to convert into a myth. —**my·ˌthol·o·gi·ˈza·tion** *or* **my·ˌthol·o·gi·ˈsa·tion** *n.* —**my·ˈthol·o·ger, my·ˈthol·o·ˌgiz·er,** *or* **my·ˈthol·o·ˌgis·er** *n.*

my·thol·o·gy (mɪˈθɒlədʒɪ) *n., pl.* **·gies. 1.** a body of myths, esp. one associated with a particular culture, institution, person, etc. **2.** a body of stories about a person, institution, etc.: *the mythology of Hollywood.* **3.** myths collectively. **4.** the study or collecting of myths.

myth·o·ma·ni·a (ˌmɪθəʊˈmeɪnɪə) *n. Psychiatry.* the tendency to lie, exaggerate, or relate incredible imaginary adventures as if they had really happened, occurring in some mental disorders. —**myth·o·ma·ni·ac** (ˌmɪθəʊˈmeɪnɪˌæk) *n., adj.*

myth·o·poe·ia (ˌmɪθəʊˈpiːə) *or* **myth·o·po·e·sis** (ˌmɪθəpəʊˈiːsɪs) *n.* the composition or making of myths. [C19: from Greek, from *muthopoiein,* from *muthos* myth + *poiein* to make]

myth·o·poe·ic (ˌmɪθəʊˈpiːɪk) *adj.* of or relating to the composition of myths; productive of myths. —**ˌmyth·o·ˈpoe·ism** *n.* —**ˌmyth·o·ˈpoe·ist** *n.*

my·thos (ˈmaɪθɒs, ˈmɪθɒs) *n., pl.* **·thoi** (-θɔɪ). **1.** the complex of beliefs, values, attitudes, etc., characteristic of a specific group or society. **2.** another word for **myth** or **mythology.**

Myt·i·le·ne (ˌmɪtɪˈliːnɪ) *n.* **1.** a port on the Greek island of Lesbos: Roman remains; Byzantine fortress. Pop.: 23 447 (1971). Modern Greek name: **Mitilíni. 2.** a former name for **Lesbos.**

myx·o- *or before a vowel* **myx-** *combining form.* mucus or slime: *myxomycete.* [from Greek *muxa* slime, mucus]

myx·oe·de·ma *or U.S.* **myx·e·de·ma** (ˌmɪksɪˈdiːmə) *n.* a disease resulting from underactivity of the thyroid gland characterized by puffy eyes, face, and hands and mental sluggishness. See also **cretinism.** —**myx·oe·dem·ic** (ˌmɪksɪˈdɛmɪk), **myx·oe·dem·a·tous** (ˌmɪksɪˈdɛmətəs, -ˈdiː-) *or U.S.* **ˌmyx·e·ˈdem·ic, ˌmyx·e·ˈdem·a·tous** *adj.*

myx·o·ma (mɪkˈsəʊmə) *n., pl.* **·mas** *or* **·ma·ta** (-mətə). a tumour composed of mucous connective tissue, usually situated in subcutaneous tissue. —**myx·om·a·tous** (mɪkˈsɒmətəs) *adj.*

myx·o·ma·to·sis (ˌmɪksəməˈtəʊsɪs) *n.* an infectious and usually fatal viral disease of rabbits characterized by swelling of the mucous membranes and formation of skin tumours.

myx·o·my·cete (ˌmɪksəʊmaɪˈsiːt) *n.* any of a group of organisms having a naked mass of protoplasm and characteristics of both plants and animals: usually classified as fungi. Also called: **mycetozoan, slime mould.** —**ˌmyx·o·my·ˈce·tous** *adj.*

myx·o·vi·rus (ˈmɪksəʊˌvaɪərəs) *n.* any of a group of viruses that cause influenza, mumps, and certain other diseases.

mzee (ᵊmzeɪ) *E. African.* ~*n.* **1.** an old person. ~*adj.* **2.** advanced in years. [C19: from Swahili]

mzun·gu (ᵊmˈzʊŋguː) *n. E. African.* a White person. [C20: from Swahili]

N

n *or* **N** (ɛn) *n., pl.* **n's, N's,** *or* **Ns. 1.** the 14th letter and 11th consonant of the modern English alphabet. **2.** a speech sound represented by this letter, usually an alveolar nasal, as in *nail.*

n^{1} *symbol for:* **1.** neutron. **2.** *Optics.* index of refraction. **3.** nano-.

n^{2} (ɛn) *determiner.* an indefinite number (of): *there are n objects in a box.*

N *symbol for:* **1.** *Printing.* en. **2.** Also: **kt.** *Chess.* knight. **3.** newton(s). **4.** *Chem.* nitrogen. **5.** North. **6.** Avogadro's number. **7.** noun. ~**8.** *international car registration for* Norway.

n. *abbrev. for:* **1.** natus. [Latin: born] **2.** neuter. **3.** new. **4.** nominative. **5.** noon. **6.** note. **7.** noun. **8.** number.

N. *abbrev. for:* **1.** National(ist). **2.** Navy. **3.** New. **4.** Norse.

Na *the chemical symbol for* sodium. [Latin *natrium*]

NA *international car registration for* Netherlands Antilles.

N.A. *abbrev. for* North America.

N.A.A.C.P. (in the U.S.) *abbrev. for* National Association for the Advancement of Colored People.

NAAFI ('næfɪ) *n.* **1.** *acronym for* Navy, Army, and Air Force Institutes: an organization providing canteens, shops, etc., for British military personnel at home or overseas. **2.** a canteen, shop, etc., run by this organization.

nab (næb) *vb.* **nabs, nab+bing, nabbed.** (*tr.*) *Informal.* **1.** to arrest (a criminal, etc.). **2.** to seize suddenly; snatch. [C17: perhaps of Scandinavian origin; compare Danish *nappe,* Swedish *nappa* to snatch. See KIDNAP]

Nab·a+tae·an *or* **Nab·a+te·an** (ˌnæbə'tiːən) *n.* **1.** a member of an Arab trading people who flourished southeast of Palestine, around Petra, in the Hellenistic and Roman periods. **2.** the extinct form of Aramaic spoken by this people.

Na+bis (*French* na'bi) *pl. n., sing.* **+bi** (-'bi). a group of French artists much influenced by Gauguin, including Bonnard and Vuillard, who reacted against the naturalism of the impressionists. See also **synthetism.** [C19: French, from Hebrew *nābhi* prophet]

Na+blus ('nɑːbləs) *n.* a town west of the River Jordan: near the site of ancient Shechem. Pop.: 444 223 (1967 est.).

na+bob ('neɪbɒb) *n.* **1.** *Informal.* a rich, powerful, or important man. **2.** (formerly) a European who made a fortune in the Orient, esp. in India. **3.** another name for a **nawab.** [C17: from Portuguese *nababo,* from Hindi *nawwāb;* see NAWAB] —**na+bob+er·y** ('neɪbɒbərɪ, neɪ'bɒbərɪ) *or* **'na+bob+ism** *n.* —**'na+bob+ish** *adj.*

Nab·o·kov (nə'bɒkɒf, 'næbəˌkɒf) *n.* **Vla·di·mir Vla·di·mi·ro·vich** (vla'dimir vla'dimirəvitʃ). 1899–1977, U.S. novelist, born in Russia. His works include *Lolita* (1955), *Pnin* (1957), *Pale Fire* (1962), and *Ada* (1969). —**Nab·o·kov+i·an** (ˌnæbə'kəʊvɪən) *adj.*

Na·bo·ni·dus (ˌnæbə'naɪdəs) *n. Old Testament.* the father of Belshazzar; last king of Babylon before it was captured by Cyrus in 539 B.C.

Na·both ('neɪbɒθ) *n. Old Testament.* an inhabitant of Jezreel, murdered by King Ahab at the instigation of his wife Jezebel for refusing to sell his vineyard (I Kings 21).

na+celle (nə'sɛl) *n.* a streamlined enclosure on an aircraft, not part of the fuselage, to accommodate an engine, passengers, crew, etc. [C20: from French: small boat, from Late Latin *nāvicella,* a diminutive of Latin *nāvis* ship]

na+cre ('neɪkə) *n.* the technical name for **mother-of-pearl.** [C16: via French from Old Italian *naccara,* from Arabic *naqqārah* shell, drum] —**'na+cred** *adj.*

na+cre+ous ('neɪkrɪəs) *adj.* **1.** relating to or consisting of mother-of-pearl. **2.** having the lustre of mother-of-pearl: *nacreous minerals.*

NAD *n. Biochem.* nicotinamide adenine dinucleotide; a coenzyme that is a hydrogen carrier in metabolic reactions, esp. in tissue respiration. Former name: **DPN.**

Na-De·ne *or* **Na-Dé·né** (nɑː'deɪnɪ, nə'diːn) *n.* a phylum of North American Indian languages including Athapascan, Tlingit, and Haida. [from Haida *na* to dwell + Athapascan *dene* (unattested) people; coined by Edward Sapir (1884–1939), American anthropologist]

NADH *n. Biochem.* the chemically reduced form of NAD.

na+dir ('neɪdɪə, 'næ-) *n.* **1.** the point on the celestial sphere directly below an observer and diametrically opposite the zenith. **2.** the lowest or deepest point; depths: *the nadir of despair.* [C14: from Old French, from Arabic *nazīr as-samt,* literally: opposite the zenith]

NADP *n. Biochem.* nicotinamide adenine dinucleotide phosphate; a coenzyme with functions similar to those of NAD. Former name: **TPN.**

nae (neɪ) a Scot. word for **no**^{1} or **not.**

nae+vus *or U.S.* **ne+vus** ('niːvəs) *n., pl.* **+vi** (-vaɪ). any congenital growth or pigmented blemish on the skin; birthmark or mole. [C19: from Latin; related to (*g*)*natus* born, produced by nature] —**'nae+void** *adj.*

nag^{1} (næg) *vb.* **nags, nag+ging, nagged. 1.** to scold or annoy constantly . **2.** (when *intr.,* often foll. by *at*) to be a constant source of discomfort or worry (to): *her death nagged him.* ~*n.* **3.** a person, esp. a woman, who nags. [C19: of Scandinavian origin; compare Swedish *nagga* to GNAW, irritate, German *nagen*] —**'nag+ger** *n.* —**'nag+ging+ly** *adv.*

nag^{2} (næg) *n.* **1.** *Often derogatory.* a horse. **2.** a small riding horse. [C14: of Germanic origin; related to NEIGH]

Na·ga ('nɑːgə) *n.* **1.** (*pl.* **·gas** *or* **·ga**) a member of a people of NE India and W Burma: until the early 20th century they practised headhunting. **2.** the language of this people, belonging to the Sino-Tibetan family of languages and having many dialects.

Na+ga+land ('nɑːgəˌlænd) *n.* a state of NE India: formed in 1962 from parts of Assam and the North-East Frontier Agency; inhabited chiefly by Naga tribes; consists of almost inaccessible forested hills and mountains (the **Naga Hills**); shifting cultivation predominates. Capital: Kohima. Pop.: 515 449 (1971). Area: 16 488 sq. km (6366 sq. miles).

na+ga+na (nə'gɑːnə) *n.* a disease of hoofed animals of central and southern Africa, caused by parasitic protozoa of the genus *Trypanosoma* that is transmitted by tsetse flies. [from Zulu *u-nakane*]

Na+ga+no (nə'gɑːnəʊ) *n.* a city in central Japan, on central Honshu: Buddhist shrine; two universities. Pop.: 302 542 (1974 est.).

Na+ga+ri ('nɑːgərɪ) *n.* **1.** a set of scripts, including Devanagari, used as the writing systems for several languages of India. **2.** another word for **Devanagari.**

Na+ga+sa+ki (ˌnɑːgə'sɑːkɪ) *n.* a port in SW Japan, on W Kyushu: almost completely destroyed in 1945 by the second atomic bomb dropped on Japan by the U.S.; shipbuilding industry. Pop.: 445 655 (1974 est.).

na+gor ('neɪgɔː) *n.* another name for **reedbuck.** [C18: from French, arbitrarily named by Buffon, from earlier *nanguer*]

Na·gor·no-Ka·ra·bakh Au·ton·o+mous Re+gion (nə'gɔːnəʊ kərʌ'bɑːk) *n.* an administrative division of the S Soviet Union, in the S Azerbaijan SSR: acquired by Russia in 1813. Capital: Stepanakert. Pop.: 150 313 (1970). Area: 4400 sq. km (1700 sq. miles).

Na·go+ya ('nɑːgəʊjə) *n.* a city in central Japan, on S Honshu on Ise Bay: a major industrial centre. Pop.: 2 080 000 (1975).

Nag+pur (næg'pʊə) *n.* a city in central India, in NE Maharashtra state: became capital of the kingdom of Nagpur (1743); capital of the Central Provinces (later Madhya Pradesh) from 1861 to 1956. Pop.: 866 076 (1971).

Nagy (*Hungarian* nɔdj) *n.* **Im·re** ('imrɛ). 1896–1958, Hungarian statesman; prime minister (1953–55; 1956). He was removed from office and later executed when Soviet forces suppressed the revolution of 1956.

Nagy+sze·ben ('nɔttsɛˌbɛn) *n.* the Hungarian name for **Sibiu.**

Nagy+vá·rad ('nɔdjvaːrɔd) *n.* the Hungarian name for **Oradea.**

Nah. *Bible. abbrev. for* Nahum.

Na·ha ('nɑːhə) *n.* a port in S Japan, on the SW coast of Okinawa Island: chief city of the Ryukyu Islands. Pop.: 276 380 (1970).

Na+hua·tl ('nɑːwɑːtᵊl, nɑː'wɑːtᵊl) *n.* **1.** (*pl.* **·tl** *or* **·tls**) a member of one of a group of Central American and Mexican Indian peoples including the Aztecs. **2.** the language of these peoples, belonging to the Uto-Aztecan family. ~Also called: **Na+hua+tlan.**

Na+hum ('neɪhəm) *n. Old Testament.* **1.** a Hebrew prophet of the 7th century B.C. **2.** the book containing his oracles.

nai+ad ('naɪæd) *n., pl.* **+ads** *or* **+a·des** (-əˌdiːz). **1.** *Greek myth.* a nymph dwelling in a lake, river, spring, or fountain. **2.** the aquatic larva of the dragonfly, mayfly, and related insects. **3.** Also called: **water nymph.** any monocotyledonous submerged aquatic plant of the genus *Naias* (or *Najas*), having narrow leaves and small flowers: family *Naiadaceae* (or *Najadaceae*). **4.** any of certain freshwater mussels of the genus *Unio.* See **mussel** (sense 2). [C17: via Latin from Greek *nāias:* water nymph; related to *náein* to flow]

na+ïf (nɑː'iːf) *adj., n.* a less common word for **naive.**

nail (neɪl) *n.* **1.** a fastening device usually made from round or oval wire, having a point at one end and a head at the other. **2.** anything resembling such a fastening device, esp. in function or shape. **3.** the horny plate covering part of the dorsal surface of the fingers or toes. See **fingernail, toenail. 4.** the claw of a mammal, bird, or reptile. **5.** *Slang.* a hypodermic needle, used for injecting drugs. **6.** a unit of length, formerly used for measuring cloth, equal to two and a quarter inches. **7. a nail in one's coffin.** an experience so shocking as to shorten life. **8. bite one's nails. a.** to chew off the ends of one's fingernails. **b.** to be worried or apprehensive. **9. hard as nails. a.** in tough physical condition. **b.** without sentiment or feelings. **10. hit the nail on the head.** to do or say something correct or telling. **11. on the nail.** *Informal.* (of payments) at once; on the spot (esp. in the phrase **pay on the nail**). ~*vb.* (*tr.*) **12.** to attach with or as if with nails. **13.** *Informal.* to arrest, catch, or seize. **14.** *Informal.* to hit or bring down, as with a shot: *I nailed the sniper.* **15.** *Informal.* to expose or detect (a lie or liar). **16.** to fix or focus (one's eyes, attention, etc.) on an object. **17.** to stud with nails. [Old English *nægl;* related to Old High German *nagal* nail, Latin *unguis* fingernail, claw, Greek *onux*] —**'nail+er** *n.* —**'nail+less** *adj.*

nail-bit·ing *n.* **1.** the act or habit of biting one's fingernails. **2.** **a.** anxiety or tension. **b.** (*as modifier*): *nail-biting suspense.*
nail+brush ('neɪl,brʌʃ) *n.* a small stiff-bristled brush for cleaning the fingernails.
nail down *vb.* (*tr., adv.*) **1.** to fasten down with or as if with nails. **2.** *Informal.* to extort a definite promise or consent from: *I nailed him down on the deadline.* **3.** *Informal.* to settle in a definite way: *they nailed down the agreement.*
nail+file ('neɪl,faɪl) *n.* a small file, chiefly either of metal or of board coated with emery, used to trim the nails.
nail+head ('neɪl,hɛd) *n.* a decorative device, as on tooled leather, resembling the round head of a nail.
nail pol+ish *or* **var+nish** *or esp. U.S.* **e·nam+el** *n.* a quick-drying cosmetic lacquer applied to colour the nails or make them shiny or esp. both.
nail set *n.* a punch for driving the head of a nail below or flush with the surrounding surface.
nail up *vb.* (*tr., adv.*) to shut in or fasten tightly with or as if with nails.
nain+sook ('neɪnsʊk, 'næn-) *n.* a light soft plain-weave cotton fabric, used esp. for babies' wear. [C19: from Hindi *nainsukh,* literally: delight to the eye, from *nain* eye + *sukh* delight, from Sanskrit *sukha*]
na·i+ra (nɑː'ɛrə) *n.* the standard monetary unit of Nigeria.
Nairn (nɛən) *n.* (until 1975) a county of NE Scotland, now part of the Highland region.
Nai+ro+bi (naɪ'rəʊbɪ) *n.* the capital of Kenya, in the southwest at an altitude of 1650 m (5500 ft.): founded in 1899; became capital in 1905; commercial and industrial centre; the **Nairobi National Park** (a game reserve) is nearby. Pop.: 630 000 (1973 est.).
nais+sant ('neɪsᵊnt) *adj. Heraldry.* (of a beast) having only the forepart shown above a horizontal division of a shield. [C16: from Old French, literally: being born. See NASCENT]
na+ive, na+ïve (nɑː'iːv, naɪ'iːv), *or* **na+ïf** *adj.* **1.** **a.** having or expressing innocence and credulity; ingenuous. **b.** (*as n.*): *only the naive believed him.* **2.** artless or unsophisticated. **3.** lacking developed powers of analysis, reasoning, or criticism: *a naive argument.* ~*n.* **4.** *Rare.* a person who is naive, esp. in his artistic style. [C17: from French, feminine of *naïf,* from Old French *naif* native, spontaneous, from Latin *nātīvus* NATIVE, from *nasci* to be born] —**na+'ive+ly, na+'ïve+ly,** *or* **na+'ïf+ly** *adv.* —**na+'ive+ness, na+ïve+ness,** *or* **na+'ïf+ness** *n.*
na+ive+té, na+ïve+té (,nɑːiː'veɪ), *or* **na+ive+ty** (naɪ'iːvtɪ) *n.* **1.** the state or quality of being naive; ingenuousness; simplicity. **2.** a naive act or statement.
na+ked ('neɪkɪd) *adj.* **1.** having the body completely unclothed; undressed. Compare **bare. 2.** having no covering; bare; exposed: *a naked flame.* **3.** with no qualification or concealment; stark; plain: *the naked facts.* **4.** unaided by any optical instrument, such as a telescope or microscope (esp. in the phrase **the naked eye**). **5.** with no defence, protection, or shield. **6.** (usually foll. by *of*) stripped or destitute: *naked of weapons.* **7.** (of the seeds of gymnosperms) not enclosed in a pericarp. **8.** (of flowers) lacking a perianth. **9.** (of stems) lacking leaves and other appendages. **10.** (of animals) lacking hair, feathers, scales, etc. **11.** *Law.* **a.** unsupported by authority or financial or other consideration: *a naked contract.* **b.** lacking some essential condition to render valid; incomplete. [Old English *nacod;* related to Old High German *nackot* (German *nackt*), Old Norse *noktr,* Latin *nudus*] —**'na+ked+ly** *adv.* —**'na+ked+ness** *n.*
na+ked la+dies *n.* (*functioning as sing.*) another name for **autumn crocus.**
na+ked sin+gu+lar+i+ty *n. Astronomy.* a hypothetical location at which there would be a discontinuity in the space-time continuum as a result of the gravitational collapse of a spherical mass. See also **black hole.**
na+ker ('neɪkə, 'næk-) *n.* one of a pair of small kettledrums used in medieval music. [C14: from Old French *nacre,* via Medieval Greek *anakara,* from Arabic *naqāra*]
Na+khi+che+van (*Russian* nəxitʃɪ'vanj) *n.* a city in the SW Soviet Union, capital of the Nakhichevan ASSR: an ancient trading town; ceded to Russia in 1828. Pop.: 33 279 (1970). Ancient name: **Naxuana.**
Na+khi+che+van Au·ton·o+mous So+vi+et So+cial+ist Re+pub+lic (nəkɪtʃɛ'vɑːn) *n.* an administrative division of the S Soviet Union: belongs to the Azerbaijan SSR, from which it is separated by part of the Armenian SSR; annexed by Russia in 1828. Capital: Nakhichevan. Pop.: 202 187 (1970). Area: 5500 sq. km (2120 sq. miles).
Na+ku+ru (nə'kuːruː) *n.* a town in W Kenya, on Lake Nakuru: commercial centre of an agricultural region. Pop.: 47 800 (1969).
Nal+chik (*Russian* 'naljtʃik) *n.* a city in the SW Soviet Union, capital of the Kabardino-Balkar ASSR, in a valley of the Greater Caucasus: health resort. Pop.: 188 000 (1975 est.).
NALGO ('nælgəʊ) *n. acronym for* National and Local Government Officers' Association.
Na·ma ('nɑːmə) *or* **Na+ma+qua** (nə'mɑːkwə) *n.* **1.** (*pl.* **·ma, ·mas** *or* **+qua, +quas**) a member of a Hottentot people living chiefly in Namaqualand. **2.** the dialect of Hottentot spoken by this people, belonging to the Khoisan family. —**'Na+man** *or* **Na+'ma+quan** *n., adj.*
Na+man+gan (*Russian* nəman'gan) *n.* a city in the S central Soviet Union, in the E Uzbek SSR. Pop.: 209 000 (1975 est.).
Na+ma+qua+land (nə'mɑːkwə,lænd) *n.* a semiarid coastal region of South West Africa, extending from near Windhoek into Cape Province, South Africa: divided by the Orange River into **Little Namaqualand** in South Africa, and **Great Namaqualand** in South West Africa; rich mineral resources. Area: 47 961 sq. km (18 518 sq. miles). Also called: **Na+ma+land** ('nɑːmə,lænd).
na+mas kar (nə'mʌs kɑː) *n.* a salutation used in India. [Sanskrit, from *namas* salutation, bow + *kara* doing]
nam·by-pam·by (,næmbɪ'pæmbɪ) *adj.* **1.** sentimental or prim in a weak insipid way: *namby-pamby manners.* **2.** clinging, feeble, or spineless: *a namby-pamby child.* ~*n., pl.* **·bies. 3.** a person who is namby-pamby. [C18: a nickname of Ambrose Phillips (died 1749), whose pastoral verse was ridiculed for being insipid]
name (neɪm) *n.* **1.** a word or term by which a person or thing is commonly and distinctively known. **2.** mere outward appearance or form as opposed to fact (esp. in the phrase **in name**): *he was a ruler in name only.* **3.** a word, title, or phrase descriptive of character, usually abusive or derogatory: *to call a person names.* **4.** reputation, esp., if unspecified, good reputation: *he's made quite a name for himself.* **5.** **a.** a famous person or thing: *a name in the advertising world.* **b.** *Chiefly U.S.* (*as modifier*): *a name product.* **6.** **in** *or* **under the name of.** using as a name. **7.** **in the name of.** **a.** for the sake of. **b.** by the sanction or authority of. **8.** **know by name.** to have heard of without having met. **9.** **name of the game.** *Chiefly U.S.* **a.** anything that is essential, significant, or important. **b.** expected or normal conditions, circumstances, etc.: *in gambling, losing money's the name of the game.* **10.** **to one's name.** belonging to one: *I haven't a penny to my name.* ~*vb.* (*tr.*) **11.** to give a name to; call by a name: *she named the child Edward.* **12.** to refer to by name; cite: *he named three French poets.* **13.** to determine, fix, or specify: *they have named a date for the meeting.* **14.** to appoint to or cite for a particular title, honour, or duty; nominate: *he was named Journalist of the Year.* **15.** **name names.** to cite people, esp. in order to blame or accuse them. **16.** **name the day.** to choose the day for one's wedding. **17.** **you name it.** whatever you need, mention, etc. [Old English *nama,* related to Latin *nomen,* Greek *noma,* Old High German *namo,* German *namen*] —**'nam·a·ble** *or* **'name+a·ble** *adj.*
name-call·ing *n.* verbal abuse, esp. as a crude form of argument.
name day *n.* **1.** *R.C. Church.* the feast day of a saint whose name one bears. **2.** another name for **ticket day.**
name-drop·ping *n. Informal.* the practice of referring frequently to famous or fashionable people, esp. as though they were intimate friends, in order to impress others. —**'name-,drop·per** *n.*
name+less ('neɪmlɪs) *adj.* **1.** without a name; anonymous. **2.** incapable of being named; indescribable: *a nameless horror seized him.* **3.** too unpleasant or disturbing to be mentioned: *nameless atrocities.* **4.** having no legal name; illegitimate: *a nameless child.* —**'name+less+ly** *adv.* —**'name+less+ness** *n.*
name+ly ('neɪmlɪ) *adv.* that is to say: *it was another colour, namely green.*
Na+men ('nɑːmə) *n.* the Flemish name for **Namur.**
name part *n.* another name for **title role.**
name+plate ('neɪm,pleɪt) *n.* a small panel on or next to the door of a room or building, bearing the occupant's name and profession.
name+sake ('neɪm,seɪk) *n.* **1.** a person or thing named after another. **2.** a person or thing with the same name as another. [C17: probably a shortening of the phrase describing people connected *for the name's sake*]
name+tape ('neɪm,teɪp) *n.* a narrow cloth tape attached to clothing, etc., bearing the owner's name.
Nam+hoi ('nɑːm'hɔɪ) *n.* another name for **Fatshan.**
Na+mib·i·a (nɑː'mɪbɪə, nə-) *n.* the name recognized by the United Nations (since 1968) for **South West Africa.** —**Na+'mib+i·an** *adj., n.*
Nam Tso ('nɑːm 'tsɔː) *n.* a salt lake in SW China, in SE Tibet at an altitude of 4629 m (15 186 ft.). Area: about 1800 sq. km (700 sq. miles). Also called: **Tengri Nor.**
Na+mur (næ'mʊə; *French* na'myːr) *n.* **1.** a province of S Belgium. Capital: Namur. Pop.: 390 442 (1975 est.). Area: 3660 sq. km (1413 sq. miles). **2.** a town in S Belgium, capital of Namur province: strategically situated on a promontory between the Sambre and Meuse Rivers, besieged and captured many times. Pop.: 32 269 (1970). Flemish name **Namen.**
nan (næn), **nan·a,** *or* **nan·na** ('nænə) *n.* a child's word for **grandmother.** [see NANNY; compare Greek *nanna* aunt, Medieval Latin *nonna* old woman]
na·na ('nɑːnə) *n. Austral. slang.* **1.** the head. **2.** **do one's nana.** to become very angry. **3.** **off one's nana.** mad; insane. [C19: probably from BANANA]
Na·nak ('nɑːnək) *n.* 1469–1538, Indian religious leader; founder of Sikhism.
Nan+chang *or* **Nan-ch'ang** ('næn'tʃæŋ) *n.* a walled city in SE China, capital of Kiangsi province, on the Kan River: largest city in the Poyang basin. Pop.: 675 000 (1970 est.).
Nan-ching ('næn'tʃɪŋ) *n.* a variant spelling of **Nanking.**
nan+cy *or* **nan+cy boy** ('nænsɪ) *n.* **a.** an effeminate or homosexual boy or man. **b.** (*as modifier*): *his nancy ways.* [C20: from the girl's name *Nancy*]
Nan+cy ('nænsɪ; *French* nɑ̃'si) *n.* a city in NE France: became the capital of the dukes of Lorraine in the 12th century, becoming French in 1766; administrative and financial centre. Pop.: 111 493 (1975).
Nan+da De+vi ('nʌndə 'diːvɪ) *n.* a mountain in N India, in N Uttar Pradesh in the Himalayas. Height: 7817 m (25 645 ft.).

NAND cir·cuit *or* **gate** (nænd) *n. Electronics.* a computer logic circuit having two or more input wires and one output wire that has an output signal if one or more of the input signals are at a low voltage. Compare **OR circuit.** [C20: from *not* + AND; see NOT CIRCUIT, AND CIRCUIT]

Nan·ga Par·bat (ˈnʌŋɡə ˈpɑːbʌt) *n.* a mountain in N India, in NW Kashmir in the W Himalayas. Height: 8126 m (26 660 ft.).

nan·keen (næŋˈkiːn) *or* **nan·kin** (ˈnænkɪn) *n.* **1.** a hard-wearing buff-coloured cotton fabric. **2. a.** a pale greyish-yellow colour. **b.** (*as adj.*): *a nankeen carpet.* [C18: named after NANKING, China, where it originated]

Nan·king (ˈnænˈkɪŋ) *or* **Nan·ching** *n.* a port in E central China, capital of Kiangsu province, on the Yangtze River: capital of the Chinese empire and a literary centre from the 14th to 17th centuries; capital of Nationalist China (1928–37); university (1928). Pop.: 1 750 000 (1970 est.).

Nan·ning *or* **Nan-ning** (ˈnænˈnɪŋ) *n.* a port in S China, capital of Kwangsi-Chuang AR, on the Siang River: rail links with North Vietnam. Pop.: 550 000 (1970 est.).

nan·ny (ˈnænɪ) *n., pl.* **·nies. 1.** a nurse or nursemaid for children. **2.** a child's word for **grandmother.** [C19: child's name for a nurse]

nan·ny goat *n.* a female goat. Compare **billy goat.**

na·no- *combining form.* **1.** denoting 10^{-9}: *nanosecond.* Symbol: n **2.** indicating extreme smallness: *nanoplankton.* [from Latin *nānus* dwarf, from Greek *nanos*]

na·no·me·tre (ˈnænəʊˌmiːtə) *n.* one thousand-millionth of a metre. Symbol: nm

Na·nook (ˈnænuːk) *n.* (*sometimes not cap.*) *North Canadian.* the polar bear.

na·no·plank·ton *or* **nan·no·plank·ton** (ˈnænəʊˌplænktən) *n.* microscopic organisms in plankton.

na·no·sec·ond (ˈnænəʊˌsɛkənd) *n.* one thousand-millionth of a second. Symbol: ns

Nan·sen (ˈnænsən) *n.* **Fridt·jof** (ˈfridjɔf). 1861–1930, Norwegian arctic explorer, statesman, and scientist. He crossed Greenland (1888–89) and attempted to reach the North Pole (1893–96), attaining a record 86° 14′ N (1895). He was the League of Nations' high commissioner for refugees (1920–22): Nobel peace prize 1922.

Nan·sen bot·tle *n.* an instrument used by oceanographers for obtaining samples of seawater from a desired depth. [C19: named after F. NANSEN]

Nan·sen pass·port *n.* a passport issued to stateless persons by the League of Nations after World War I. [C20: named after F. NANSEN]

Nan Shan (ˈnæn ˈʃæn) *pl. n.* a mountain range in N central China, mainly in Tsinghai province, with peaks over 6000 m (20 000 ft.).

Nan·terre (*French* nɑ̃ˈtɛːr) *n.* a town in N France, on the Seine: an industrial suburb of Paris. Pop.: 96 004 (1975).

Nantes (*French* nɑ̃ːt) *n.* **1.** a port in W France, at the head of the Loire estuary: scene of the signing of the Edict of Nantes and of the Noyades (drownings) during the French Revolution; extensive shipyards, and large metallurgical and food processing industries. Pop.: 263 689 (1975). **2.** *History.* See **Edict of Nantes.**

Nan·tuck·et (nænˈtʌkɪt) *n.* an island off SE Massachusetts: formerly a centre of the whaling industry; now a resort. Length: nearly 24 km (15 miles). Width: 5 km (3 miles).

Nan·tung (ˈnænˈtʌŋ) *n.* a city in E China, in Kiangsu province on the Yangtze estuary. Pop.: 260 400 (1953).

Naoi·se (ˈniːsɪ) *n. Irish myth.* the husband of Deirdre, killed by his uncle Conchobar.

Na·o·mi (ˈneɪəmɪ) *n. Old Testament.* the mother-in-law of Ruth (Ruth 1:2). Douay spelling: **No·e·mi.**

na·os (ˈneɪɒs) *n., pl.* **na·oi** (ˈneɪɔɪ). **1.** *Rare.* an ancient classical temple. **2.** *Architect.* another name for **cella.** [C18: from Greek: inner part of temple]

nap[1] (næp) *vb.* **naps, nap·ping, napped.** (*intr.*) **1.** to sleep for a short while; doze. **2.** to be unaware or inattentive; be off guard (esp. in the phrase **catch someone napping**). ~*n.* **3.** a short light sleep; doze. [Old English *hnappian;* related to Middle High German *napfen*]

nap[2] (næp) *n.* **1. a.** the raised fibres of velvet or similar cloth. **b.** the direction in which these fibres lie when smoothed down. **2.** any similar downy coating. ~*vb.* **naps, nap·ping, napped. 3.** (*tr.*) to raise the nap of (velvet, etc.) by brushing or similar treatment. [C15: probably from Middle Dutch *noppe;* related to Old English *hnoppian* to pluck]

nap[3] (næp) *n.* **1.** Also called: **napoleon.** a card game similar to whist, usually played for stakes. **2.** a call in this card game, undertaking to win all five tricks. **3.** *Horse racing.* a tipster's choice for an almost certain winner. **4. go nap. a.** to undertake to win all five tricks at nap. **b.** to risk everything on one chance. **5. nap hand.** a position in which there is a very good chance of success if a risk is taken. ~*vb.* **naps, nap·ping, napped.** (*tr.*) **6.** *Horse racing.* to name (a horse) as likely to win a race. [C19: short for NAPOLEON, the original name of the card game]

na·palm (ˈneɪpɑːm, ˈnæ-) *n.* **1.** a thick and highly incendiary liquid, usually consisting of petrol gelled with aluminium soaps, used in fire bombs, flame throwers, etc. ~*vb.* **2.** (*tr.*) to attack with napalm. [C20: from NA(PHTHENATE) + PALM(ITATE)]

nape (neɪp) *n.* the back of the neck. [C13: of unknown origin]

na·per·y (ˈneɪpərɪ) *n. Rare.* household linen, esp. table linen. [C14: from Old French *naperie,* from *nape* tablecloth, from Latin *mappa.* See NAPKIN]

Naph·ta·li (ˈnæftəˌlaɪ) *n. Old Testament.* **1.** Jacob's sixth son, whose mother was Rachel's handmaid (Genesis 30:7–8). **2.** the tribe descended from him. **3.** the territory of this tribe, between the Sea of Galilee and the mountains of central Galilee. Douay spelling: **Neph·ta·li.**

naph·tha (ˈnæfθə, ˈnæp-) *n.* **1.** a distillation product from coal tar boiling in the approximate range 80–170°C and containing aromatic hydrocarbons. **2.** a distillation product from petroleum boiling in the approximate range 100–200°C and containing aliphatic hydrocarbons: used as a solvent and in petrol. **3.** an obsolete name for **petroleum.** [C16: via Latin from Greek, of Iranian origin; related to Persian *neft* naphtha]

naph·tha·lene, naph·tha·line (ˈnæfθəˌliːn, ˈnæp-), *or* **naph·tha·lin** (ˈnæfθəlɪn, ˈnæp-) *n.* a white crystalline volatile solid with a characteristic penetrating odour: an aromatic hydrocarbon used in moth balls and in the manufacture of dyes, explosives, etc. Formula: $C_{10}H_8$. [C19: from NAPHTHA + ALCOHOL + -ENE] —**naph·thal·ic** (næfˈθælɪk, næp-) *adj.*

naph·thene (ˈnæfθiːn, ˈnæp-) *n.* any of a class of cycloalkanes, mainly derivatives of cyclopentane, found in petroleum. [C20: from NAPHTHA + -ENE]

naph·thol (ˈnæfθɒl, ˈnæp-) *n.* a white crystalline solid having two isomeric forms, **alpha-naphthol,** used in dyes, and **beta-naphthol,** used in dyes and as an antioxidant. Formula: $C_{10}H_7OH$. [C19: from NAPHTHA + -OL[1]]

naph·thyl (ˈnæfθaɪl, -θɪl, ˈnæp-) *n.* (*modifier*) of, consisting of, or containing either of two forms of the monovalent group $C_{10}H_7$-. [C19: from NAPHTHA + -YL]

Na·pier[1] (ˈneɪpɪə) *n.* **1.** Sir **Charles James.** 1782–1853, British general. **2. John.** 1550–1617, Scottish mathematician: invented logarithms and pioneered the decimal notation used today.

Na·pier[2] (ˈneɪpɪə) *n.* a port in New Zealand, on E North Island on Hawke Bay: wool trade centre. Pop.: 40 186 (1971).

Na·pier·i·an log·a·ri·thm (nəˈpɪərɪən, neɪ-) *n.* another name for **natural logarithm.**

Na·pier's bones *n.* a set of graduated rods formerly used for multiplication and division. [C17: based on a method invented by John NAPIER]

na·pi·form (ˈneɪpɪˌfɔːm) *adj. Botany.* shaped like a turnip. [C19: from Latin *nāpus* turnip]

nap·kin (ˈnæpkɪn) *n.* **1.** Also called: **table napkin.** a usually square piece of cloth or paper used while eating to protect the clothes, wipe the mouth, etc.; serviette. **2.** *Rare.* a similar piece of cloth used for example as a handkerchief or headscarf. **3.** a more formal name for **nappy**[1]. **4.** a less common term for **sanitary towel.** [C15: from Old French, from *nape* tablecloth, from Latin *mappa* small cloth, towel; see MAP]

Na·ples (ˈneɪpᵊlz) *n.* **1.** a port in SW Italy, capital of Campania region, on the Bay of Naples: the third largest city in the country; founded by Greeks in the 6th century B.C.; incorporated into the Kingdom of the Two Sicilies in 1140 and its capital (1282–1503); university (1224). Pop.: 1 223 785 (1975 est.). Ancient name: **Neapolis.** Italian name: **Napoli. 2. Bay of.** an inlet of the Tyrrhenian Sea in the SW coast of Italy.

Na·ples yel·low *n.* **1.** a permanent yellow pigment, used by artists; lead antimonate. **2.** a similar pigment consisting of a mixture of zinc oxide with yellow colouring matter. **3.** the colour of either of these pigments.

na·po·le·on (nəˈpəʊlɪən) *n.* **1.** a former French gold coin worth 20 francs bearing a portrait of either Napoleon I or Napoleon III. **2.** *Cards.* the full name for **nap**[3]. [C19: from French *napoléon,* after NAPOLEON I]

Na·po·le·on I (nəˈpəʊlɪən) *n.* full name *Napoleon Bonaparte.* 1769–1821, Emperor of the French (1804–15). He came to power as the result of a coup in 1799 and established an extensive European empire. A brilliant general, he defeated every European coalition against him until, irreparably weakened by the Peninsular War and the Russian campaign (1812), his armies were defeated at Leipzig (1813). He went into exile but escaped and ruled as emperor during the Hundred Days. He was finally defeated at Waterloo (1815). As an administrator, his achievements were of lasting significance and include the *Code Napoléon,* which remains the basis of French law.

Na·po·le·on II *n.* Duke of Reichstadt. 1811–32, son of Napoleon Bonaparte and Marie Louise. He was known as the *King of Rome* during the first French empire and was entitled Napoleon II by Bonapartists after Napoleon I's death (1821).

Na·po·le·on III *n.* known as *Louis-Napoleon;* full name *Charles Louis Napoleon Bonaparte.* 1808–73, Emperor of the French (1852–70); nephew of Napoleon I. He led two abortive Bonapartist risings (1836; 1840) and was elected president of the Second Republic (1848), establishing the Second Empire in 1852. Originally successful in foreign affairs, he was deposed after the disastrous Franco-Prussian War.

Na·po·le·on·ic (nəˌpəʊlɪˈɒnɪk) *adj.* relating to or characteristic of Napoleon I or his era.

Na·po·le·on·ic Code *n.* the English name for the *Code Napoléon.*

Na·po·le·on·ic Wars *pl. n.* the series of wars fought between France, under Napoleon Bonaparte, and (principally) England, Prussia, Russia, and Austria either alone or in alliances (1799–1815).

Na·po·li (ˈnaːpoli) *n.* the Italian name for **Naples.**

nap·pa (ˈnæpə) *n.* a soft leather, used in gloves and clothes, made from sheepskin, lambskin, or kid. [C19: named after *Napa,* California, where it was originally made]

nappe (næp) *n.* **1.** a large sheet or mass of rock, originally a recumbent fold, that has been thrust from its original position by earth movements. **2.** the sheet of water that flows over a dam or weir. **3.** *Geom.* either of the two parts into which a cone (sense 2) is divided by the vertex. [C20: from French: tablecloth]

nap+per[1] ('næpə) *n.* a person or thing that raises the nap on cloth.

nap+per[2] ('næpə) *n. Brit.* a slang or dialect word for **head.** [C20: from NAP[1]]

nap+py[1] ('næpɪ) *n., pl.* **+pies.** *Brit.* a piece of soft material, esp. towelling or a disposable material, wrapped around a baby in order to absorb its excrement. Also called: **napkin.** U.S. name: **diaper.** [C20: changed from NAPKIN]

nap+py[2] ('næpɪ) *adj.* **+pi+er, +pi+est. 1.** having a nap; downy; fuzzy. **2.** (of alcoholic drink, esp. beer) **a.** having a head; frothy. **b.** strong or heady. **3.** *Dialect, chiefly Brit.* slightly intoxicated; tipsy. **4.** (of a horse) jumpy or irritable; nervy. *~n.* **5.** any strong alcoholic drink, esp. heady beer. —**'nap+pi+ness** *n.*

Na+ra ('nɑːrə) *n.* a city in central Japan, on S Honshu: the first capital of Japan (710–784). Pop.: 247 082 (1974 est.).

Na+ra+yan+ganj (nə'rɑːjənˌgʌndʒ) *n.* a city in central Bangladesh, on the Ganges delta just southeast of Dacca. Pop.: 186 769 (1974).

Nar+ba+da (nə'bʌdə) *n.* another name for the **Narmada.**

Nar+bonne (*French* nar'bɔn) *n.* a city in S France: capital of the Roman province of **Gallia Narbonensis**; harbour silted up in the 14th century. Pop.: 40 543 (1975).

nar+ceine *or* **nar+ceen** ('nɑːsiːn) *n.* a narcotic alkaloid that occurs in opium. Formula: $C_{23}H_{27}O_8N$. [C19: via French from Greek *narkē* numbness]

nar+cis+sism ('nɑːsɪˌsɪzəm) *or* **nar+cism** ('nɑːsɪzəm) *n.* **1.** an exceptional interest in or admiration for oneself, esp. one's physical appearance. **2.** sexual satisfaction derived from contemplation of one's own physical or mental endowments. —**'nar+cis+sist** *n.* —**ˌnar+cis+'sis+tic** *adj.*

nar+cis+sus (nɑː'sɪsəs) *n., pl.* **+cis+sus·es** *or* **+cis+si** (-'sɪsaɪ, -'sɪsɪ). any amaryllidaceous plant of the Eurasian genus *Narcissus,* esp. *N. poeticus,* whose yellow, orange, or white flowers have a crown surrounded by spreading segments. [C16: via Latin from Greek *nárkissos,* perhaps from *narkē* numbness, because of narcotic properties attributed to species of the plant]

Nar·cis·sus (nɑː'sɪsəs) *n. Greek myth.* a beautiful youth who fell in love with his reflection in a pool and pined away, becoming the flower that bears his name.

nar·co- *or sometimes before a vowel* **narc-** *combining form.* indicating numbness or torpor: *narcolepsy.* [from Greek *narkē* numbness]

nar+co·a·nal·y·sis (ˌnɑːkəʊə'nælɪsɪs) *n.* psychoanalysis of a patient in a trance induced by a narcotic drug.

nar+co+lep+sy ('nɑːkəˌlɛpsɪ) *n. Pathol.* a rare condition characterized by sudden and uncontrollable episodes of deep sleep. —**ˌnar+co+'lep+tic** *adj.*

nar+co+sis (nɑː'kəʊsɪs) *n.* unconsciousness induced by narcotics or general anaesthetics.

nar+co+syn+the·sis (ˌnɑːkəʊ'sɪnθɪsɪs) *n.* a method of treating severe personality disorders by working with the patient while he is under the influence of a barbiturate drug, such as sodium pentothal.

nar+cot+ic (nɑː'kɒtɪk) *n.* **1.** any of a group of drugs, such as opium and morphine, that produce numbness and stupor. They are used medicinally to relieve pain but are sometimes also taken for their pleasant effects; prolonged use may cause addiction. **2.** anything that relieves pain or induces sleep, mental numbness, etc. *~adj.* **3.** of, relating to, or designating narcotics. **4.** of or relating to narcotics addicts or users. **5.** of or relating to narcosis. [C14: via Medieval Latin from Greek *narkōtikós,* from *narkoūn* to render numb, from *narkē* numbness] —**nar+'cot+i+cal+ly** *adv.*

nar+co+tism ('nɑːkəˌtɪzəm) *n.* stupor or addiction induced by narcotic drugs.

nar+co+tize *or* **nar+co+tise** ('nɑːkəˌtaɪz) *vb. (tr.)* to place under the influence of a narcotic drug. —**ˌnar+co+ti+'za+tion** *or* **ˌnar+co+ti+'sa+tion** *n.*

nard (nɑːd) *n.* **1.** another name for **spikenard** (senses 1, 2). **2.** any of several plants, such as certain valerians, whose aromatic roots were formerly used in medicine. [C14: via Latin from Greek *nárdos,* perhaps ultimately from Sanskrit *nalada* Indian spikenard, perhaps via Semitic (Hebrew *nērd,* Arabic *nārdīn*)]

nar+doo ('nɑːduː) *n.* **1.** any of certain cloverlike ferns of the genus *Marsilea,* which grow in swampy areas. **2.** the spores of such a plant, used as food in Australia. [C19: from a native Australian language]

nar+es ('nɛəriːz) *pl. n., sing.* **nar+is** ('nɛərɪs). *Anatomy.* the nostrils. [C17: from Latin; related to Old English *nasu,* Latin *nāsus* nose]

nar+ghi+le, nar+gi+le, *or* **nar+gi+leh** ('nɑːgɪlɪ, -ˌleɪ) *n.* another name for **hookah.** [C19: from French *narguilé,* from Persian *nārgīleh* a pipe having a bowl made of coconut shell, from *nārgīl* coconut]

nar+i·al ('nɛərɪəl) *or* **nar+ine** ('nɛərɪn, -raɪn) *adj. Anatomy.* of or relating to the nares. [C19: from Latin *nāris* nostril]

nark (nɑːk) *Brit. slang.* *~n.* **1.** an informer or spy, esp. one working for the police (**copper's nark**). *~vb.* **2.** *(tr.)* to annoy, upset, or irritate. **3.** *(intr.)* to inform or spy, esp. for the police. [C19: probably from Romany *nāk* nose]

Nar+ma+da (nə'mʌdə) *or* **Nar+ba+da** *n.* a river in central India, rising in Madhya Pradesh and flowing generally west to the Gulf of Cambay in a wide estuary: the second most sacred river in India. Length: 1290 km (801 miles).

Nar+ra+gan+set *or* **Nar+ra+gan+sett** (ˌnærə'gænsɪt) *n.* **1.** *(pl.* **+set, +sets** *or* **+sett, +setts)** a member of a North American Indian people formerly living in Rhode Island. **2.** the language of this people, belonging to the Algonquian family.

Nar+ra+gan+sett Bay *n.* an inlet of the Atlantic in SE Rhode Island: contains several islands, including Rhode Island, Prudence Island, and Conanicut Island.

nar+rate (nə'reɪt) *vb.* **1.** to tell (a story); relate. **2.** to speak in accompaniment of (a film, television programme, etc.). [C17: from Latin *narrāre* to recount, from *gnārus* knowing] —**nar+'rat+a+ble** *adj.* —**nar+'ra+tor** *or* **nar+'rat+er** *n.*

nar+ra+tion (nə'reɪʃən) *n.* **1.** the act or process of narrating. **2.** a narrated account or story; narrative. **3.** (in traditional rhetoric) the third step in making a speech, the putting forward of the question.

nar+ra+tive ('nærətɪv) *n.* **1.** an account, report, or story, as of events, experiences, etc. **2.** (sometimes preceded by *the*) the part of a literary work, etc., that relates events. **3.** the process or technique of narrating. *~adj.* **4.** telling a story: *a narrative poem.* **5.** of or relating to narration: *narrative art.* —**'nar+ra+tive+ly** *adv.*

nar+row ('nærəʊ) *adj.* **1.** small in breadth, esp. in comparison to length. **2.** limited in range or extent. **3.** limited in outlook; lacking breadth of vision. **4.** limited in means or resources; meagre: *narrow resources.* **5.** barely adequate or successful (esp. in the phrase **a narrow escape**). **6.** painstakingly thorough; minute: *a narrow scrutiny.* **7.** *Brit. dialect.* overcareful with money; parsimonious. **8.** *Phonetics.* **a.** another word for **tense**[1] (sense 4). **b.** relating to or denoting a transcription used to represent phonetic rather than phonemic distinctions. **c.** another word for **close** (sense 33). **9.** (of agricultural feeds) especially rich in protein. *~vb.* **10.** to make or become narrow; limit; restrict. *~n.* **11.** a narrow place, esp. a pass or strait. [Old English *nearu;* related to Old Saxon *naru*] —**'nar+row+ly** *adv.* —**'nar+row+ness** *n.*

nar+row boat *n.* a long narrow bargelike boat with a beam of 2.1 metres (7 feet) or less, used on canals.

nar+row gauge *n.* **1.** a smaller distance between the lines of a railway than the standard gauge of 56½ inches. *~adj.* **nar·row-gauge** *or* **nar·row-gauged. 2.** of, relating to, or denoting a railway with a narrow gauge.

nar·row-mind·ed *adj.* having a biased or illiberal viewpoint; bigoted, intolerant, or prejudiced. —**ˌnar·row-'mind·ed+ly** *adv.* —**ˌnar·row-'mind·ed+ness** *n.*

nar+rows ('nærəʊz) *pl. n.* a narrow part of a strait, river, current, etc.

nar+thex ('nɑːθɛks) *n.* **1.** a portico at the west end of a basilica or church, esp. one that is at right angles to the nave. **2.** a rectangular entrance hall between the porch and nave of a church. [C17: via Latin from Medieval Greek: enclosed porch, enclosure (earlier: box), from Greek *narthēx* giant fennel, the stems of which were used to make boxes]

Nar+va (*Russian* 'narvə) *n.* a port in the W Soviet Union, in the Estonian SSR on the Narva River near the Gulf of Finland: developed around a Danish fortress in the 13th century; textile centre. Pop.: 57 863 (1970).

Nar+vik ('nɑːvɪk; *Norwegian* 'narviːk) *n.* a port in N Norway: scene of two naval battles in 1940; exports iron ore from Kiruna and Gällivare (Sweden). Pop.: 13 182 (1970).

nar+whal, nar+wal ('nɑːwəl), *or* **nar+whale** ('nɑːˌweɪl) *n.* an arctic toothed whale, *Monodon monoceros,* having a black-spotted whitish skin and, in the male, a long spiral tusk: family *Monodontidae.* [C17: of Scandinavian origin; compare Danish, Norwegian *narhval,* from Old Norse *nāhvalr,* from *nār* corpse + *hvalr* whale, from its white colour, supposed to resemble a human corpse]

nar·y ('nɛərɪ) *adv. Dialect.* not; never: *nary a man was left.* [C19: variant of *ne'er a* never a]

N.A.S. *abbrev. for* National Association of Schoolmasters.

NASA ('næsə) *n.* (in the U.S.) *acronym for* National Aeronautics and Space Administration.

na+sal ('neɪzᵊl) *adj.* **1.** of or relating to the nose. **2.** *Phonetics.* pronounced with the soft palate lowered allowing air to escape via the nasal cavity instead of or as well as through the mouth. *~n.* **3.** a nasal speech sound, such as English *m, n,* or *ng.* [C17: from French from Late Latin *nāsālis,* from Latin *nāsus* nose] —**na+sal+i+ty** (neɪ'zælɪtɪ) *n.* —**'na+sal+ly** *adv.*

na+sal in+dex *n.* the ratio of the widest part of the nose to its length multiplied by 100.

na+sal+ize *or* **na+sal+ise** ('neɪzəˌlaɪz) *vb. (tr.)* to pronounce nasally. —**ˌna+sal+i+'za+tion** *or* **ˌna+sal+i+'sa+tion** *n.*

nas+cent ('næsᵊnt, 'neɪ-) *adj.* **1.** starting to grow or develop; being born. **2.** *Chem.* (of an element or simple compound, esp. hydrogen) created within the reaction medium in the atomic form and having a high activity. [C17: from Latin *nascēns* present participle of *nāscī* to be born] —**'nas+cence** *or* **'nas+cen+cy** *n.*

nase+ber·ry ('neɪzˌbɛrɪ) *n., pl.* **+ber·ries.** another name for **sapodilla.** [C17: from Spanish *néspera* medlar + BERRY]

Nase+by ('neɪzbɪ) *n.* a village in Northamptonshire: site of a major Parliamentarian victory (1645) in the Civil War.

Nash (næʃ) *n.* **1. John.** 1752–1835, English town planner and architect. He designed Regent's Park, Regent Street, and the Marble Arch in London. **2. Og·den.** 1902–71, U.S. humorous poet. **3. Paul.** 1889–1946, English painter, noted esp. as a war artist in both World Wars and for his landscapes. **4. Rich·ard,** known as *Beau Nash.* 1674–1762, English dandy. **5.** See

(Thomas) **Nashe. 6.** Sir **Wal·ter.** 1882–1968, New Zealand statesman, born in England: prime minister of New Zealand (1957–60).

Nashe *or* **Nash** (næʃ) *n.* **Thom·as.** 1567–1601, English pamphleteer, satirist, and novelist, author of the first picaresque novel in English, *The Unfortunate Traveller, or the Life of Jack Wilton* (1594).

Nash·o ('næʃəʊ) *n. Obsolete Austral. slang.* **1.** compulsory military training; conscription. **2.** a conscript. [C20: shortening and alteration of *national service*]

Nash+ville ('næʃvɪl) *n.* a city in central Tennessee, the state capital, on the Cumberland River: an industrial and commercial centre, noted for its recording industry. Pop.: 449 109 (1973 est.).

na+si+on ('neɪzɪən) *n.* a craniometric point where the top of the nose meets the ridge of the forehead. [C20: New Latin, from Latin *nāsus* nose] —**'na+si·al** *adj.*

na·so- *combining form.* nose: *nasopharynx.* [from Latin *nāsus* nose]

na+so+fron+tal (ˌneɪzəʊ'frʌntᵊl) *adj. Anatomy.* of or relating to the nasal and frontal bones.

na+so+phar+ynx (ˌneɪzəʊ'færɪŋks) *n., pl.* **+pha+ryn+ges** (-fə'rɪndʒiːz) *or* **+phar+ynx·es.** the part of the pharynx situated above and behind the soft palate. —**na+so+pha+ryn+ge·al** (ˌneɪzəʊfə'rɪndʒɪəl, -ˌfærɪn'dʒɪəl) *adj.*

Nas+sau *n.* **1.** (*German* 'nasaʊ). a region of central West Germany: formerly a duchy (1816–66), from which a branch of the House of Orange arose (represented by the present rulers of the Netherlands and Luxembourg); annexed to the Prussian province of Hesse-Nassau in 1866; corresponds to present-day W Hesse and NE Rhineland-Palatinate states. **2.** ('næsɔː). the capital and chief port of the Bahamas, on the NE coast of New Providence Island: resort. Pop.: 101 503 (1970).

Nas·ser ('nɑːsə, 'næsə) *n.* **Ga·mal Ab·del** (gə'mɑːl 'æbdel). 1918–70, Egyptian soldier and statesman; president of Egypt (1956–70). He was one of the leaders of the coup that deposed King Farouk (1952) and became premier (1954). His nationalization of the Suez Canal (1956) led to an international crisis, and during his presidency Egypt was twice defeated by Israel (1956; 1967).

Nas·ta·se (nə'stɑːzɪ) *n.* **I·lie** ('iːlɪə). born 1946, Rumanian tennis player: U.S. champion 1972.

nas+tic move+ment ('næstɪk) *n.* a response of plant parts that is independent of the direction of the external stimulus, such as the opening of buds caused by an alteration in light intensity. [C19 *nastic*, from Greek *nastos* close-packed, from *nassein* to press down]

na+stur+tium (nə'stɜːʃəm) *n.* **1.** any of various plants of the genus *Tropaeolum*, esp. *T. major*, having round leaves and yellow, red, or orange trumpet-shaped spurred flowers: family *Tropaeolaceae*. **2.** a strong or dark reddish-orange colour. [C17: from Latin: kind of cress, from *nāsus* nose + *tortus* twisted, from *torquēre* to twist, distort; so called because the pungent smell causes one to wrinkle one's nose]

nas+ty ('nɑːstɪ) *adj.* **+ti+er, +ti+est. 1.** unpleasant, offensive, or repugnant. **2.** (of an experience, condition, etc.) unpleasant, dangerous, or painful: *a nasty wound.* **3.** spiteful, abusive, or ill-natured. [C14: origin obscure; probably related to Swedish dialect *nasket* and Dutch *nestig* dirty] —**'nas+ti+ly** *adv.* —**'nas+ti+ness** *n.*

-nas·ty *n. combining form.* indicating a nastic movement to a certain stimulus, etc.: *nyctinasty.* [from Greek *nastos* pressed down, close-pressed] —**-nas·tic** *adj. combining form.*

nat. *abbrev. for:* **1.** national. **2.** native. **3.** natural.

na+tal ('neɪtᵊl) *adj.* **1.** of or relating to birth. **2.** a rare word for **native**: *natal instincts.* [C14: from Latin *nātālis* of one's birth, from *nātus*, from *nascī* to be born]

Na+tal *n.* **1.** (nə'tæl). a province of E South Africa, between the Drakensberg and the Indian Ocean: set up as a republic by the Boers in 1838; became a British colony in 1843; joined South Africa in 1910. Capital: Pietermaritzburg. Pop.: 2 140 166 (1970). Area: 86 967 sq. km (33 578 sq. miles). **2.** (*Portuguese* na'tal) a port in NE Brazil, capital of Rio Grande do Norte state, near the mouth of the Potengi River. Pop.: 250 787 (1970).

na+tal+i+ty (neɪ'tælɪtɪ) *n., pl.* **·ties.** another name (esp. U.S.) for **birth rate.**

na+tant ('neɪtᵊnt) *adj.* **1.** (of aquatic plants) floating on the water. **2.** *Rare.* floating or swimming. [C18: from Latin *natāns*, present participle of *natāre* to swim]

na+ta+tion (nə'teɪʃən) *n.* a formal or literary word for **swimming.** [C16: from Latin *natātiō* a swimming, from *natāre* to swim] —**na+'ta+tion+al** *adj.*

na+ta+to+ri+um (ˌneɪtə'tɔːrɪəm) *n., pl.* **+ri+ums** *or* **+ri+a** (-rɪə). *Rare.* a swimming pool, esp. an indoor pool. [C20: from Late Latin: swimming-place, pool]

na+ta+to+ry (nə'teɪtərɪ) *or* **na+ta+to+ri+al** (ˌnætə'tɔːrɪəl) *adj.* of or relating to swimming. [C18: from Late Latin *natātōrius*, from *natāre* to swim]

natch (nætʃ) *sentence substitute. Informal.* short for **naturally.**

na+tes ('neɪtiːz) *pl. n., sing.* **+tis** (-tɪs). a technical word for the **buttocks.** [C17: from Latin; compare Greek *nōton* back, *nosthi* buttocks]

Na+than ('neɪθən) *n. Old Testament.* a prophet at David's court (II Samuel 7:1–17; 12:1–15).

Na·than·ael (nə'θænjəl) *n. New Testament.* a Galilean who is perhaps to be identified with Bartholomew among the apostles (John 1:45–51; 21:1).

nathe+less ('neɪθlɪs) *or* **nath+less** ('næθlɪs) *Archaic.* **1.** *sentence connector.* another word for **nonetheless.** *~prep.* **2.** notwithstanding; despite. [Old English *nāthylǣs*, from *nā* never + *thȳ* for that + *lǣs* less]

na+tion ('neɪʃən) *n.* **1.** an aggregation of people or peoples of one or more cultures, races, etc., organized into a single state: *the Canadian nation.* **2.** a community of persons not constituting a state but bound by common descent, language, history, etc. **3. a.** a federation of tribes, esp. American Indians. **b.** the territory occupied by such a federation. [C13: via Old French from Latin *nātiō* birth, tribe, from *nascī* to be born] —**'na+tion+ˌhood** *n.* —**'na+tion+less** *adj.*

na+tion+al ('næʃənᵊl) *adj.* **1.** of, involving, or relating to a nation as a whole. **2.** of, relating to, or characteristic of a particular nation: *the national dress of Poland.* **3.** *Rare.* nationalistic or patriotic. *~n.* **4.** a citizen or subject. **5.** a national newspaper. —**'na+tion+al+ly** *adv.*

Na+tion+al ('næʃənᵊl) *n.* **the.** short for the **Grand National.**

na+tion+al ac+count+ing *n.* another name for **social accounting.**

na+tion+al an+them *n.* a patriotic hymn or other song adopted by a nation for use on public or state occasions.

Na+tion+al As+sem+bly *n. French history.* the body constituted by the French third estate in June 1789 after the calling of the Estates General. It was dissolved in Sept. 1791 to be replaced by the new Legislative Assembly.

na+tion+al as+sis+tance *n.* the former name for **supplementary benefit.**

na+tion+al bank *n.* **1.** (in the U.S.) a commercial bank incorporated under a Federal charter and legally required to be a member of the Federal Reserve System. Compare **state bank. 2.** a bank owned and operated by a government.

Na+tion+al Bu+reau of Stand+ards *n. U.S.* an organization, founded in 1901, whose function is to establish and maintain standards for units of measurements. Compare **British Standards Institution, International Standards Organization.**

na+tion+al code *n.* another term for **Australian Rules.**

Na+tion+al Con+ven+tion *n.* **1.** a convention held every four years by each major U.S. political party to choose its presidential candidate. **2.** *French history.* the longest lasting of the revolutionary assemblies, lasting from Sept. 1792 to Oct. 1795, when it was replaced by the Directory.

Na+tion+al Coun+try Par+ty *n.* an Australian political party drawing its main support from rural areas. Often shortened to: **National Party.** Abbrev.: **N.C.P.**

Na+tion+al Cov+e+nant *n.* See **Covenant.**

na+tion+al debt *n.* the total financial obligations incurred by a nation's central government. Also called (esp. U.S.): **public debt.**

Na+tion+al E+co+nom+ic De+vel+op+ment Coun+cil *n.* an advisory body on general economic policy in Britain, composed of representatives of government, management, and trade unions: established in 1962. Abbrevs.: **N.E.D.C.,** (informal) **Neddy.**

Na+tion+al En+ter+prise Board *n.* a public corporation established in 1975 to help the economy of the UK, develop its industrial efficiency and international competitiveness, and support its productive employment: the board's activities include finance for industrial investment and restructuring. Abbrev.: **N.E.B.**

Na+tion+al Front *n.* (in Britain) a small political party of the right with racialist and other extremist policies. Abbrev.: **N.F.**

Na+tion+al Guard *n.* **1.** (*sometimes not cap.*) the armed force, first commanded by Lafayette, that was established in France in 1789 and existed intermittently until 1871. **2.** (in the U.S.) a state military force that can be called into federal service by the president.

Na+tion+al Health Ser+vice *n.* (in Britain) the system of national medical services since 1948, financed mainly by taxation.

na+tion+al in+come *n. Economics.* the total of all incomes accruing over a specified period to residents of a country and consisting of wages, salaries, profits, rent, and interest.

na+tion+al in+sur+ance *n.* (in Britain) state insurance based on weekly contributions from employees and employers and providing payments to the unemployed, the sick, the retired, etc., as well as medical services. See also **social security, supplementary benefit.**

na+tion+al+ism ('næʃənəˌlɪzəm, 'næʃnə-) *n.* **1.** a sentiment based on common cultural characteristics that binds a population and often produces a policy of national independence or separatism. **2.** loyalty or devotion to one's country; patriotism. **3.** exaggerated, passionate, or fanatical devotion to a national community. See also **chauvinism.** —**'na+tion+al+ist** *n., adj.* —**ˌna+tion+al+'is+tic** *adj.*

Na+tion+al+ist Chi+na *n.* an unofficial name for the **Republic of China** (Taiwan).

Na+tion+al+ist Par+ty *n.* (in South Africa) the largest political party in Parliament: composed mainly of right-wing Afrikaners. It has ruled since 1948. See also **United Party, Progressive Party.**

na+tion+al+i+ty (ˌnæʃə'nælɪtɪ) *n., pl.* **·ties. 1.** the state or fact of being a citizen of a particular nation. **2.** a body of people sharing common descent, history, language, etc.; a nation. **3.** a national group: *30 different nationalities are found in this city.* **4.** national character or quality. **5.** the state or fact of being a nation; national status.

na+tion+al+ize *or* **na+tion+al+ise** ('næʃənəˌlaɪz, 'næʃnə-) *vb.* (*tr.*) **1.** to put (an industry, resources, etc.) under state control or ownership. **2.** to make national in scope, character, or status. **3.** a less common word for **naturalize.** —ˌ**na+tion+al·i+'za+tion** *or* ˌ**na+tion+al·i+'sa+tion** *n.*

Na+tion+al Lib+er+a+tion Front *n.* **1.** (*sometimes not cap.*) a revolutionary movement that seeks the national independence of a country, usually by guerrilla warfare. **2.** a political organization formed in South Vietnam in 1960 by the Vietcong. Also called: **National Liberation Front of South Vietnam.**

na+tion+al park *n.* an area of land controlled by the state in order to preserve its natural beauty, wild life, etc.

na+tion+al ser+vice *n. Chiefly Brit.* compulsory military service.

Na+tion+al So+cial+ism *n. German history.* the doctrines and practices of the Nazis, involving the supremacy of Hitler as Führer, anti-Semitism, state control of the economy, and national expansion. Also called: **Nazism, Naziism.** —**Na+tion+al So+cial+ist** *n., adj.*

Na+tion+al Trust *n.* an organization concerned with the preservation of historic buildings and monuments and areas of the countryside of great beauty. It was founded in 1895 and incorporated by act of parliament in 1907.

na·tion-state *n.* an independent state inhabited by all the people of one nation and one nation only.

na·tion+wide ('neɪʃənˌwaɪd) *adj.* covering or available to the whole of a nation; national: *a nationwide survey.*

na+tive ('neɪtɪv) *adj.* **1.** relating or belonging to a person or thing by virtue of conditions existing at the time of birth: *a native language.* **2.** inherent, natural, or innate: *native wit.* **3.** born in a specified place: *a native Indian.* **4.** (when *postpositive*, foll. by *to*) originating in a specific place or area: *kangaroos are native to Australia.* **5.** characteristic of or relating to the indigenous inhabitants of a country or area: *the native art of the New Guinea Highlands.* **6.** (of chemical elements, esp. metals) found naturally in the elemental form; not chemically combined as in an ore. **7.** unadulterated by civilization, artifice, or adornment; natural. **8.** *Archaic.* related by birth or race. ~*n.* **9.** (usually foll. by *of*) a person born in a particular place: *a native of Geneva.* **10.** (usually foll. by *of*) a species of animal or plant originating in a particular place or area: *the kangaroo is a native of Australia.* **11.** a member of an indigenous people of a country or area, esp. a non-White people, as opposed to colonial settlers and immigrants. **12.** *Derogatory, rare.* any non-White. [C14: from Latin *nātīvus* innate, natural, from *nascī* to be born] —**'na+tive+ly** *adv.* —**'na+tive+ness** *n.*

na+tive bear *n.* an Australian name for **koala.**

na·tive-born *adj.* born in the country or area indicated.

na+tive oak *n. Austral.* another name for **Casuarina.**

na+tive speak+er *n.* a person having a specified native language: *a native speaker of Cree.*

Na+tive States *pl. n.* the former 562 semi-independent states of India, ruled by Indians but subject to varying degrees of British authority: merged with provinces by 1948; largest states were Hyderabad, Gwalior, Baroda, Mysore, Cochin, Jammu and Kashmir, Travancore, Sikkim, and Indore. Also called: **Indian States and Agencies.**

na+tiv+ism ('neɪtɪˌvɪzəm) *n.* **1.** *Chiefly U.S.* the policy of favouring the natives of a country over the immigrants. **2.** *Anthropol.* the policy of protecting and reaffirming native tribal cultures in reaction to acculturation. **3.** the philosophical doctrine that some ideas exist innately in the mind. —**'na+tiv+ist** *n., adj.* —ˌ**na+tiv+'is+tic** *adj.*

na+tiv+i·ty (nə'tɪvɪtɪ) *n., pl.* **·ties.** birth or origin, esp. in relation to the circumstances surrounding it.

Na+tiv+i·ty (nə'tɪvɪtɪ) *n.* **1.** the birth of Jesus Christ. **2.** the feast of Christmas as a commemoration of this. **3. a.** an artistic representation of the circumstances of the birth of Christ. **b.** (*as modifier*): *a nativity play.*

natl. *abbrev. for* national.

NATO ('neɪtəʊ) *n. acronym for* North Atlantic Treaty Organization, an international organization composed of the U.S., Canada, Iceland, Britain, and 11 other European countries: established by the **North Atlantic Treaty** (1949) for purposes of collective security.

na+tri·um ('neɪtrɪəm) *n.* an obsolete name for **sodium.** [C19: New Latin; see NATRON]

nat+ro+lite ('nætrəˌlaɪt, 'neɪ-) *n.* a colourless, white, or yellow zeolite mineral consisting of sodium aluminium silicate in the form of needle-like orthorhombic crystals. Formula: $Na_2Al_2Si_3O_{10}.2H_2O$. [C19: from NATRON + -LITE]

na+tron ('neɪtrən) *n.* a whitish or yellow mineral that consists of hydrated sodium carbonate and occurs in saline deposits and salt lakes. Formula: $Na_2CO_3.10H_2O$. [C17: via French and Spanish from Arabic *natrūn*, from Greek *nitron* NITRE]

NATSOPA (ˌnæt'səʊpə) *n. acronym for* National Society of Operative Printers, Graphical and Media Personnel.

nat+ter ('nætə) *Chiefly Brit.* ~*vb.* **1.** (*intr.*) to talk idly and at length; chatter or gossip. ~*n.* **2.** prolonged idle chatter or gossip. [C19: changed from *gnatter* to grumble, of imitative origin; compare Low German *gnatteren*] —**'nat+ter+er** *n.*

nat+ter+jack ('nætəˌdʒæk) *n.* a European toad, *Bufo calamita*, of sandy regions, having a greyish-brown body marked with reddish warty processes: family *Bufonidae.* [C18: of unknown origin]

nat+ty ('nætɪ) *adj.* **+ti+er, +ti+est.** *Informal.* smart in appearance or dress; spruce; dapper: *a natty outfit.* [C18: perhaps from obsolete *netty*, from *net* NEAT; compare Old French *net* trim] —**'nat+ti+ly** *adv.* —**'nat+ti+ness** *n.*

nat·u·ral ('nætʃrəl) *adj.* **1.** of, existing in, or produced by nature: *natural science; natural cliffs.* **2.** in accordance with human nature: *it is only natural to want children.* **3.** as is normal or to be expected; ordinary or logical: *the natural course of events.* **4.** not acquired; innate: *a natural gift for sport.* **5.** being so through innate qualities: *a natural leader.* **6.** not supernatural or strange: *natural phenomena.* **7.** not constrained or affected; genuine or spontaneous. **8.** not artificially dyed or coloured: *a natural blonde.* **9.** following or resembling nature or life; lifelike: *she looked more natural without her make-up.* **10.** not affected by man or civilization; uncultivated; wild: *in the natural state this animal is not ferocious.* **11.** illegitimate; born out of wedlock. **12.** not adopted but rather related by blood: *her natural parents.* **13.** *Music.* **a.** not sharp or flat. **b.** (*postpositive*) denoting a note that is neither sharp nor flat: *B natural.* **c.** (of a key or scale) containing no sharps or flats. **14.** *Music.* of or relating to a trumpet, horn, etc., without valves or keys, on which only notes of the harmonic series of the keynote can be obtained. Compare **flat**[1] (sense 22), **sharp** (sense 12). **15.** determined by inborn conviction: *natural rights.* **16.** *Cards.* **a.** (of a card) not a joker or wild card. **b.** (of a canasta or sequence) containing no wild cards. **c.** (of a bid in bridge) describing genuine values; not conventional. **17.** *Theol.* based on the principles and findings of human reason and what is to be learned of God from nature rather than on revelation: *natural religion.* ~*n.* **18.** *Informal.* a person or thing regarded as certain to qualify for success, selection, etc.: *the horse was a natural for first place.* **19.** *Music.* **a.** an accidental cancelling a previous sharp or flat. Also called (U.S.): **cancel.** Usual symbol: ♮ **b.** a note affected by this accidental. Compare **flat**[1] (sense 33), **sharp** (sense 17). **20.** *Pontoon.* the combination of an ace with a ten or court card when dealt to a player as his first two cards. **21.** *Obsolete.* an imbecile; idiot. —**'nat·u·ral+ly** *adv.* —**'nat·u·ral+ness** *n.*

nat·u·ral-born *adj.* being as specified through one's birth: *a natural-born Irishman.*

nat·u·ral child+birth *n.* a method of childbirth characterized by the absence of anaesthetics, in which the expectant mother is given special breathing and relaxing exercises.

nat·u·ral clas+si+fi+ca+tion *n. Biology.* classification of organisms according to relationships based on descent from a common ancestor.

nat·u·ral gas *n.* a gaseous mixture consisting mainly of methane trapped below ground; used extensively as a fuel.

nat·u·ral gen+der *n.* grammatical gender that reflects, as in English, the sex or animacy of the referent of a noun rather than the form or any other feature of the word.

nat·u·ral his+to+ry *n.* **1.** the study of animals and plants in the wild state. **2.** the study of all natural phenomena. **3.** the sum of these phenomena in a given place or at a given time: *the natural history of Iran.* —**nat·u·ral his+to+ri·an** *n.*

nat·u·ral+ism ('nætʃrəˌlɪzəm) *n.* **1. a.** a movement, esp. in art and literature, advocating detailed realistic and factual description, esp. that in 19th-century France in the writings of Zola, Flaubert, etc. **b.** the characteristics or effects of this movement. **2.** a school of painting or sculpture characterized by the faithful imitation of appearances for their own sake. **3.** *Theol.* the belief that all religious truth is based not on revelation but rather on the study of natural causes and processes. **4.** *Philosophy.* a scientific account of the world in terms of causes and natural forces that rejects all spiritual, supernatural, or teleological explanations. **5.** action or thought caused by natural desires and instincts. **6.** devotion to that which is natural.

nat·u·ral+ist ('nætʃrəlɪst) *n.* **1.** a person who is versed in or interested in botany or zoology. **2.** a person who advocates or practises naturalism, esp. in art or literature.

nat·u·ral+is+tic (ˌnætʃrə'lɪstɪk) *adj.* **1.** of, imitating, or reproducing nature in effect or characteristics. **2.** of or characteristic of naturalism, esp. in art or literature. **3.** of or relating to naturalists. —ˌ**nat·u·ral+'is+ti+cal+ly** *adv.*

nat·u·ral+ize *or* **nat·u·ral+ise** ('nætʃrəˌlaɪz) *vb.* **1.** (*tr.*) to give citizenship to (a person of foreign birth). **2.** to be or cause to be adopted in another place, as a word, custom, etc. **3.** (*tr.*) to introduce (a plant or animal from another region) and cause it to adapt to local conditions. **4.** (*intr.*) (of a plant or animal) to adapt successfully to a foreign environment. **5.** (*tr.*) to explain (something unusual) with reference to nature, excluding the supernatural. **6.** (*tr.*) to make natural or more lifelike. —ˌ**nat·u·ral·i+'za+tion** *or* ˌ**nat·u·ral·i+'sa+tion** *n.*

nat·u·ral lan+guage *n.* **1.** a language that has evolved naturally as a means of communication among people. Compare **artificial language, formal language.** **2.** languages of this kind considered collectively.

nat·u·ral law *n. Philosophy.* a law of conduct or morality supposed to be inherent in human nature and ascertainable by reason, as distinguished from law based on divine revelation or human legislation.

nat·u·ral log·a+rithm *n.* a logarithm to the base e (see **base**[1] (sense 16)). Usually written $\log_e$ or ln. Also called: **Napierian logarithm.** Compare **common logarithm.**

nat·u·ral+ly ('nætʃrəlɪ) *adv.* **1.** in a natural or normal way. **2.** through nature; inherently; instinctively. **3.** of course; surely.

nat·u·ral num+ber *n.* any of the positive integers 1,2,3,4,...

nat·u·ral phi+los·o+phy *n.* (now only used in Scottish universities) physical science, esp. physics. —**nat·u·ral phi+los·o+pher** *n.*

nat·u·ral re+sourc·es *pl. n.* naturally occurring materials such as coal, fertile land, etc., that can be used by man.

nat·u·ral sci+ence *n.* **1.** the sciences collectively that are involved in the study of the physical world and its phenomena, including biology, physics, chemistry, and geology, but excluding social sciences, abstract or theoretical sciences, such as mathematics, and applied sciences. **2.** any one of these sciences. —**nat·u·ral sci·en·tist** *n.*

nat·u·ral se·lec·tion *n.* a process resulting in the survival of those individuals from a population of animals or plants that are best adapted to the prevailing environmental conditions. The survivors tend to produce more offspring than those less well adapted, so that the composition of the population is changed.

nat·u·ral the·ol·o·gy *n.* the branch of theology concerned with the knowledge of God achieved by natural reason. Compare **revealed religion.** —**nat·u·ral the·o·lo·gian** *n.*

nat·u·ral vir·tues *pl. n.* (esp. among the scholastics) those virtues of which man is capable without direct help from God, specifically justice, temperance, prudence, and fortitude. Compare **theological virtues.**

na·ture ('neɪtʃə) *n.* **1.** the fundamental qualities of a person or thing; identity or essential character. **2.** (*often cap., esp. when personified*) the whole system of the existence, arrangement, forces, and events of all physical life that are not controlled by man. **3.** all natural phenomena and plant and animal life, as distinct from man and his creations. **4.** a wild primitive state untouched by man or civilization. **5.** natural unspoilt scenery or countryside. **6.** disposition or temperament. **7.** tendencies, desires, or instincts governing behaviour. **8.** the normal biological needs or urges of the body. **9.** sort; kind; character. **10.** the real appearance of a person or thing: *a painting very true to nature.* **11.** accepted standards of basic morality or behaviour. **12.** *Biology.* the complement of genetic material that partly determines the structure of an organism; genotype. Compare **nurture** (sense 3). **13. against nature.** unnatural or immoral. **14. by nature.** essentially or innately. **15. call of nature.** *Informal, euphemistic or humorous.* the need to urinate or defecate. **16. from nature.** using natural models in drawing, painting, etc. **17. in** (*or* **of**) **the nature of.** essentially the same as; by way of. [C13: via Old French from Latin *nātūra,* from *nātus,* past participle of *nascī* to be born]

na·ture strip *n. Austral. informal.* a grass strip running alongside a road; verge.

na·ture stud·y *n.* the study of the natural world, esp. animals and plants, by direct observation at an elementary level.

na·ture trail *n.* a path through countryside of particular interest to naturalists.

na·tur·ism ('neɪtʃə,rɪzəm) *n.* another name for **nudism.** —'**na·tur·ist** *n., adj.*

na·tur·op·a·thy (,neɪtʃə'rɒpəθɪ) *n.* a method of treating disorders, involving the use of herbs and other naturally grown foods, sunlight, fresh air, etc. Also called: **nature cure.** —**na·tur·o·path** ('neɪtʃərə,pæθ) *n.* —**na·tur·o·path·ic** (,neɪtʃərə'pæθɪk) *adj.*

nauch (nɔ:tʃ) *n.* a variant spelling of **nautch.**

Nau·cra·tis ('nɔ:krətɪs) *n.* an ancient Greek city in N Egypt, in the Nile delta: founded in the 7th century B.C.

naught (nɔ:t) *n.* **1.** *Archaic or literary.* nothing or nothingness; ruin or failure. **2.** a variant spelling (esp. U.S.) of **nought. 3. set at naught.** to have disregard or scorn for; disdain. ~*adv.* **4.** *Archaic or literary.* not at all: *it matters naught.* ~*adj.* **5.** *Obsolete.* worthless, ruined, or wicked. [Old English *nāwiht,* from *nā* NO[1] + *wiht* thing, person; see WIGHT[1], WHIT]

naugh·ty ('nɔ:tɪ) *adj.* **-ti·er, -ti·est. 1.** (esp. of children or their behaviour) mischievous or disobedient; bad. **2.** mildly indecent; titillating. ~*n.* **3.** *Austral. slang.* sexual intercourse. [C14: (originally: needy, of poor quality): from NAUGHT] —'**naugh·ti·ly** *adv.* —'**naugh·ti·ness** *n.*

nau·ma·chi·a (nɔ:'meɪkɪə) *or* **nau·ma·chy** ('nɔ:məkɪ) *n., pl.* **-chi·ae** (-kɪ,i:), **-chi·as,** *or* **-chies.** (in ancient Rome) **1.** a mock sea fight performed as an entertainment. **2.** an artificial lake used in such a spectacle. [C16: via Latin from Greek *naumakhiā,* from *naus* ship + *makhē* battle]

nau·pli·us ('nɔ:plɪəs) *n., pl.* **-pli·i** (-plɪ,aɪ). the larva of many crustaceans, having a rounded unsegmented body with three pairs of limbs. [C19: from Latin: type of shellfish, from Greek *Nauplios,* one of the sons of Poseidon]

Na·u·ru (nɑ:'u:ru:) *n.* an island republic in the SW Pacific, west of the Gilbert Islands: administered jointly by Australia, New Zealand, and Britain as a UN trust territory before becoming an independent member of the Commonwealth in 1968. The economy is based on export of phosphates. Languages: Nauruan (a Malayo-Polynesian language) and English. Religion: Christian. Currency: Australian dollar. Pop.: 8000 (1975 UN est.). Area: 2130 hectares (5263 acres). Former name: **Pleasant Island.** —**Na·'u·ru·an** *adj., n.*

nau·se·a ('nɔ:zɪə, -sɪə) *n.* **1.** the sensation that precedes vomiting. **2.** a feeling of disgust or revulsion. [C16: via Latin from Greek: seasickness, from *naus* ship]

nau·se·ate ('nɔ:zɪ,eɪt, -sɪ-) *vb.* **1.** (*tr.*) to arouse feelings of disgust or revulsion in. **2.** to feel or cause to feel sick. —,**nau·se·'a·tion** *n.*

nau·se·ous ('nɔ:zɪəs, -sɪəs) *adj.* **1.** causing nausea. **2.** distasteful to the mind or senses; repulsive. —'**nau·se·ous·ly** *adv.* —'**nau·se·ous·ness** *n.*

Nau·sic·a·ä (nɔ:'sɪkɪə) *n. Greek myth.* a daughter of Alcinous, king of the Phaeacians, who assisted the shipwrecked Odysseus after discovering him on a beach.

naut. *abbrev. for* nautical.

-naut *n. combining form.* indicating a person engaged in the navigation of a vehicle, esp. one used for scientific investigation: *astronaut.*

nautch *or* **nauch** (nɔ:tʃ) *n.* **a.** an intricate traditional Indian dance performed by professional dancing girls. **b.** (*as modifier*): *a nautch girl.* [C18: from Hindi *nāc,* from Sanskrit *nrtya,* from *nrtyati* he acts or dances]

nau·ti·cal ('nɔ:tɪkᵊl) *adj.* of, relating to, or involving ships, navigation, or seamen. [C16: from Latin *nauticus,* from Greek *nautikos,* from *naus* ship] —'**nau·ti·cal·ly** *adv.*

nau·ti·cal mile *n.* **1.** Also called: **international nautical mile, air mile.** a unit of length, used esp. in navigation, equal to 1852 metres (6076.103 feet). **2.** a British unit of length, equal to 1853.18 metres (6082 feet). Formerly called: **geographical mile.** Compare **sea mile.**

nau·ti·loid ('nɔ:tɪ,lɔɪd) *n.* **1.** any mollusc of the *Nautiloidea,* a group of cephalopods that includes the pearly nautilus and many extinct forms. ~*adj.* **2.** of, relating to, or belonging to the *Nautiloidea.*

nau·ti·lus ('nɔ:tɪləs) *n., pl.* **-lus·es** *or* **-li** (-,laɪ). **1.** any cephalopod mollusc of the genus *Nautilus,* esp. the pearly nautilus. **2.** short for **paper nautilus.** [C17: via Latin from Greek *nautilos* sailor, from *naus* ship]

nav. *abbrev. for:* **1.** naval. **2.** navigable. **3.** navigation. **4.** navigator.

Nav·a·ho *or* **Nav·a·jo** ('nævə,həʊ, 'nɑ:-) *n.* **1.** (*pl.* **-ho, -hos, -hoes** *or* **-jo, -jos, -joes**) a member of a North American Indian people of Arizona, New Mexico, and Utah. **2.** the language of this people, belonging to the Athapascan group of the Na-Dene phylum.

na·val ('neɪvᵊl) *adj.* **1.** of, relating to, characteristic of, or having a navy. **2.** of or relating to ships; nautical. [C16: from Latin *nāvālis,* from *nāvis* ship; related to Greek *naus,* Old Norse *nōr* ship, Sanskrit *nau*]

na·val ar·chi·tec·ture *n.* the designing of ships. —**na·val ar·chi·tect** *n.*

nav·ar ('nævɑ:) *n.* a system of air navigation in which a ground radar station relays signals to each aircraft indicating the relative positions of neighbouring aircraft. [C20: from nav(igational and traffic control rad)ar]

nav·a·rin ('nævərɪn; *French* nava'rɛ̃) *n.* a stew of mutton or lamb with root vegetables. [from French]

Nav·a·ri·no (,nava'ri:no) *n.* the Italian name for **Pylos.**

Na·varre (nə'vɑ:) *n.* a former kingdom of SW Europe: established in the 9th century by the Basques; the parts south of the Pyrenees joined Spain in 1515 and the N parts passed to France in 1589. Capital: Pamplona. Spanish name: **Na·var·ra** (na'βarra).

nave[1] (neɪv) *n.* the central space in a church, extending from the narthex to the chancel and often flanked by aisles. [C17: via Medieval Latin from Latin *nāvis* ship, from the similarity of shape]

nave[2] (neɪv) *n.* the central block or hub of a wheel. [Old English *nafu, nafa;* related to Old High German *naba*]

na·vel ('neɪvᵊl) *n.* **1.** the scar in the centre of the abdomen, usually forming a slight depression, where the umbilical cord was attached. Technical name: **umbilicus. 2.** a central part, location, or point; middle. **3.** short for **navel orange.** [Old English *nafela;* related to Old Frisian *navla,* Old High German *nabulo* (German *Nabel*), Latin *umbilīcus*]

na·vel or·ange *n.* a sweet orange that is usually seedless and has at its apex a navel-like depression enclosing an underdeveloped secondary fruit.

na·vel·wort ('neɪvᵊl,wɜ:t) *n.* another name for **pennywort** (sense 1).

na·vew ('neɪvju:) *n.* another name for **turnip** (senses 1, 2). [C16: from Old French *navel,* from Latin *nāpus*]

nav·i·cert ('nævɪ,sɜ:t) *n.* a certificate specifying the contents of a neutral ship's cargo, issued esp. in time of war by a blockading power. [C20: from Latin *nāvi(s)* ship + English CERT(IFICATE)]

na·vic·u·lar (nə'vɪkjʊlə) *adj. Anatomy.* **1.** shaped like a boat. ~*n. also* **na·vic·u·la·re** (nə,vɪkjʊ'lɑ:rɪ) **2.** a small boat-shaped bone of the wrist or foot. [C16: from Late Latin *nāviculāris,* from Latin *nāvicula,* diminutive of *nāvis* ship]

navig. *abbrev. for* navigation.

nav·i·ga·ble ('nævɪgəbᵊl) *adj.* **1.** wide, deep, or safe enough to be sailed on or through: *a navigable channel.* **2.** capable of being steered or controlled: *a navigable raft.* —,**nav·i·ga·'bil·i·ty** *or* '**nav·i·ga·ble·ness** *n.* —'**nav·i·ga·bly** *adv.*

nav·i·gate ('nævɪ,geɪt) *vb.* **1.** to plan, direct, or plot the path or position of (a ship, an aircraft, etc.). **2.** (*tr.*) to travel over, through, or on (water, air, or land) in a boat, aircraft, etc. **3.** *Informal.* to direct (oneself, one's way, etc.) carefully or safely: *he navigated his way to the bar.* **4.** (*intr.*) *Rare.* to voyage in a ship; sail. [C16: from Latin *nāvigāre* to sail, from *nāvis* ship + *agere* to drive]

nav·i·ga·tion (,nævɪ'geɪʃən) *n.* **1.** the skill or process of plotting a route and directing a ship, aircraft, etc., along it. **2.** the act or practice of navigating: *dredging made navigation of the river possible.* **3.** *U.S., rare.* ship traffic; shipping. **4.** *Midland English dialect.* an inland waterway; canal. —,**nav·i·'ga·tion·al** *adj.*

Nav·i·ga·tion Acts *pl. n.* a series of acts of Parliament, the first of which was passed in 1381, that attempted to restrict to English ships the right to carry goods to and from England and its colonies. The attempt to enforce the acts helped cause the War of American Independence.

nav·i·ga·tor ('nævɪ,geɪtə) *n.* **1.** a person who is skilled in or performs navigation, esp. on a ship or aircraft. **2.** (esp. formerly) a person who explores by ship. **3.** an instrument or device for assisting a pilot to navigate an aircraft.

Náv·pak·tos (*Greek* 'nafpaktos) *n.* a port in W Greece, between the Gulfs of Corinth and Patras: scene of a naval battle (1571) in which the Turkish fleet was defeated by the fleets of the Holy League. Pop.: 8170 (1971). Italian name: **Lepanto.**

Nav·rat·i·lo·va (næˌvrætɪˈləʊvə) *n.* **Mar·ti·na.** born 1956, Czech tennis player, living in the U.S.: Wimbledon champion 1978, 1979, and 1982.

nav+vy (ˈnævɪ) *n., pl.* **+vies.** *Brit. informal.* a labourer on a building site, excavations, etc. [C19: shortened from *navigator,* builder of a navigation (sense 4)]

na·vy (ˈneɪvɪ) *n., pl.* **·vies. 1.** the warships and auxiliary vessels of a nation or ruler. **2.** (*often cap.;* usually preceded by *the*) the branch of a country's armed services comprising such ships, their crews, and all their supporting services and equipment. **3.** short for **navy blue. 4.** *Archaic or literary.* a fleet of ships. **5.** (*as modifier*): *a navy custom.* [C14: via Old French from Vulgar Latin *nāvia* (unattested) ship, from Latin *nāvis* ship]

na·vy blue *n.* **a.** a dark greyish-blue colour. **b.** (*as adj.*): *a navy-blue suit.* Sometimes shortened to **navy.** [C19: from the colour of the British naval uniform]

na·vy cut *n.* tobacco finely cut from a block.

Na·vy List *n. Brit.* an official list of all serving commissioned officers of the Royal Navy and reserve officers liable for recall.

na+wab (nəˈwɑːb) *n.* (formerly) a Muslim ruling prince or powerful landowner in India. [C18: from Hindi *nawwāb,* from Arabic *nuwwāb,* plural of *na'ib* viceroy, governor]

Nax+al+ite (ˈnʌksəˌlaɪt) *n.* a member of an extreme Maoist group in India that originated in 1967 in West Bengal and which employs tactics of agrarian terrorism and direct action. [C20: named after *Naxalbari,* a town in West Bengal where the movement started]

Nax+os (ˈnæksɒs) *n.* a Greek island in the S Aegean, the largest of the Cyclades: ancient centre of the worship of Dionysius. Pop.: 14 201 (1971). Area: 438 sq. km (169 sq. miles).

nay (neɪ) **1.** (*sentence substitute*) a word for **no**[1]: archaic or dialectal except in voting by voice. ~*n.* **2. a.** a person who votes in the negative. **b.** a negative vote. ~*adv.* **3.** (*sentence modifier*) *Archaic.* an emphatic form of **no**[1]. ~Compare **aye.** [C12: from Old Norse *nei,* from *ne* not + *ei* ever, AY[2]]

Na+ya+rit (*Spanish* ˌnajaˈrit) *n.* a state of W Mexico, on the Pacific: includes the offshore Tres Marías Islands. Capital: Tepic. Pop.: 544 031 (1970). Area: 27 621 sq. km (10 772 sq. miles).

Naz·a+rene (ˌnæzəˈriːn) *n.* **1.** an early name for a **Christian** (Acts 24:5) or (when preceded by *the*) for **Jesus Christ. 2.** a member of one of several groups of Jewish-Christians found principally in Syria. ~*adj.* **3.** of or relating to Nazareth or the Nazarenes.

Naz·a+reth (ˈnæzərɪθ) *n.* a town in N Israel, in Lower Galilee: the home of Jesus in his youth. Pop.: 33 300 (1972).

Naz·a+rite (ˈnæzəˌraɪt) *or* **Naz·i+rite** *n. Old Testament.* a religious ascetic of ancient Israel.

Naze (neɪz) *n.* **the. 1.** a flat marshy headland in SE England, in Essex on the North Sea coast. **2.** another name for **Lindesnes.**

Na·zi (ˈnɑːtsɪ) *n., pl.* **·zis. 1.** a member of the National Socialist German Workers' Party, which was founded in 1919 and seized political control in Germany in 1933 under Adolf Hitler. **2.** *Derogatory.* anyone who thinks or acts like a Nazi. ~*adj.* **3.** of, characteristic of, or relating to the Nazis. [C20: from German, phonetic spelling of the first two syllables of *Nationalsozialist* National Socialist] —**Na+zism** (ˈnɑːtsɪzəm) *or* **Na+zi+ism** (ˈnɑːtsɪɪzəm) *n.*

Na+zi+fy (ˈnɑːtsɪˌfaɪ) *vb.* **+fies, +fy+ing, +fied.** (*tr.*) to make Nazi in character. —ˌ**Na+zi+fi+ˈca+tion** *n.*

Nb *the chemical symbol for* niobium.

n.b. *Cricket. abbrev. for* no ball.

NB, N.B., *or* **n.b.** *abbrev. for* nota bene. [Latin: note well]

N.B. *abbrev. for* New Brunswick.

NBC (in the U.S.) *abbrev. for* National Broadcasting Company.

N.B.G. *Informal. abbrev. for* no bloody good. Also: **nbg**

N.C. *abbrev. for* North Carolina.

N.C.B. *abbrev. for* National Coal Board.

N.C.C.L. *abbrev. for* National Council for Civil Liberties.

N.C.O. *abbrev. for* noncommissioned officer.

N.C.P. *Austral. abbrev. for* National Country Party.

n.d. *abbrev. for* no date.

Nd *the chemical symbol for* neodymium.

N. Dak. *abbrev. for* North Dakota.

Ndja+me+na (ᵊndʒɑːˈmeɪnə) *n.* the capital of Chad, in the southwest, at the confluence of the Shari and Logone Rivers: trading centre for livestock. Pop.: 179 000 (1972 est.). Former name (until 1973): **Fort Lamy.**

Ndo+la (ᵊnˈdəʊlə) *n.* a city in N Zambia: copper, cobalt, and sugar refineries. Pop.: 159 786 (1969).

N.D.P. (in Canada) *abbrev. for* New Democratic Party.

Ne *the chemical symbol for* neon.

NE *abbrev. for* northeast(ern).

N.E. *abbrev. for* New England.

ne- *combining form.* variant of **neo-,** esp. before a vowel: *Nearctic.*

Neagh (neɪ) *n.* **Lough.** a lake in Northern Ireland, in SW Co. Antrim: the largest lake in the British Isles. Area: 388 sq. km (150 sq. miles).

Ne+an+der+thal man (nɪˈændəˌtɑːl) *n.* a type of primitive man, *Homo neanderthalensis,* or *H. sapiens neanderthalensis,* occurring throughout much of Europe in late Palaeolithic times. [C19: from the anthropological findings (1857) in the Neandertal, a valley near Düsseldorf, Germany]

neap (niːp) *adj.* **1.** of, relating to, or constituting a neap tide. ~*n.* **2.** short for **neap tide.** [Old English, as in *nēpflōd* neap tide, of uncertain origin]

Ne·a·pol·i·tan (ˌnɪəˈpɒlɪtᵊn) *n.* **1.** a native or inhabitant of Naples. ~*adj.* **2.** of or relating to Naples. [C15: from Latin *Neāpolītānus,* ultimately from Greek *Neapolis* new town]

Ne·a+pol·i+tan ice cream *n.* ice cream, usually in brick form, with several layers of different colours and flavours.

Ne·a+pol·i·tan sixth *n.* (in musical harmony) a chord composed of the subdominant of the key, plus a minor third and a minor sixth. Harmonically it is equivalent to the first inversion of a major chord built upon the flatted supertonic.

neap tide (niːp) *n.* either of the two tides that occur at the first or last quarter of the moon when the attractions of the sun and moon almost balance each other and produce the smallest rise in tidal level. Compare **spring tide** (sense 1).

near (nɪə) *prep.* **1.** at or to a place or time not far away from; close to. ~*adv.* **2.** at or to a place or time not far away; close by. **3. near to.** not far from; near. **4.** short for **nearly** (esp. in phrases such as **damn near**): *I was damn near killed.* ~*adj.* **5.** (*postpositive*) at or in a place not far away. **6.** (*prenominal*) only just successful or only just failing: *a near escape.* ~*vb.* **7.** to come or draw close (to). ~*n.* **8.** Also called: **nearside. a.** the left side of a horse, team of animals, vehicle, etc. **b.** (*as modifier*): *the near foreleg.* [Old English *nēar* (adv.), comparative of *nēah* close, NIGH; related to Old Frisian *niār,* Old Norse *nǣr,* Old High German *nāhōr*] —ˈ**near+ness** *n.*

near- *combining form.* nearly; almost: *a near-perfect landing.*

near+by *adj.* (ˈnɪəˌbaɪ), *adv.* (ˌnɪəˈbaɪ) not far away; close at hand.

Ne+arc+tic (nɪˈɑːktɪk) *adj.* of or denoting a zoogeographical region consisting of North America, north of the tropic of Cancer, and Greenland.

Near East *n.* **1.** another term for the **Middle East. 2.** (formerly) the Balkan States and the area of the Ottoman Empire.

near+ly (ˈnɪəlɪ) *adv.* **1.** not quite; almost; practically. **2. not nearly.** nowhere near; not at all: *not nearly enough money.* **3.** closely: *the person most nearly concerned.*

near miss *n.* **1.** a bomb, shell, etc., that does not exactly hit the target. **2.** any attempt or shot that just fails to be successful. **3.** an incident in which two aircraft, etc., narrowly avoid collision.

near rhyme *n. Prosody.* another term for **half-rhyme.**

near+side (ˈnɪəˌsaɪd) *n.* **1.** (usually preceded by *the*) *Chiefly Brit.* **a.** the side of a vehicle, etc., normally nearer the kerb (in Britain, the left side). **b.** (*as modifier*): *the nearside door.* Compare **offside. 2. a.** the left side of an animal, team of horses, etc. **b.** (*as modifier*): *the nearside flank.*

near-sight·ed (ˌnɪəˈsaɪtɪd) *adj.* relating to or suffering from myopia. —ˌ**near-ˈsight·ed+ly** *adv.* —ˌ**near-ˈsight·ed+ness** *n.*

near thing *n. Informal.* an event or action whose outcome is nearly a failure, success, disaster, etc.

neat[1] (niːt) *adj.* **1.** clean, tidy, and orderly. **2.** liking or insisting on order and cleanliness; fastidious. **3.** smoothly or competently done; efficient: *a neat job.* **4.** pat or slick: *his excuse was suspiciously neat.* **5.** (of alcoholic drinks, etc.) without added water, lemonade, etc.; undiluted. **6.** a less common word for **net**[2]: *neat profits.* **7.** *Slang, chiefly U.S.* good; pleasing; admirable. [C16: from Old French *net,* from Latin *nitidus* clean, shining, from *nitēre* to shine; related to Middle Irish *niam* beauty, brightness, Old Persian *naiba-* beautiful] —ˈ**neat+ly** *adv.* —ˈ**neat+ness** *n.*

neat[2] (niːt) *n., pl.* **neat.** *Archaic or dialect.* a domestic bovine animal. [Old English *neat*]

neat+en (ˈniːtᵊn) *vb.* (*tr.*) to make neat; tidy.

neath *or* **'neath** (niːθ) *prep. Archaic.* short for **beneath.**

neat's-foot oil *n.* a yellow fixed oil obtained by boiling the feet and shinbones of cattle and used esp. to dress leather.

neb (nɛb) *n. Archaic or dialect.* **1.** *Chiefly northern Brit.* the peak of a cap. **2.** the beak of a bird or the nose or snout of an animal. **3.** a person's mouth. **4.** the projecting part or end of anything. [Old English *nebb;* related to Old Norse *nef,* Old High German *snabul* (German *Schnabel*)]

N.E.B. *abbrev. for:* **1.** New English Bible. **2.** National Enterprise Board.

Ne·bo (ˈniːbəʊ) *n.* **Mount.** a mountain in Jordan, northeast of the Dead Sea: the highest point of a ridge known as Pisgah, from which Moses viewed the Promised Land just before his death (Deuteronomy 34:1). Height: 806 m (2646 ft.).

Nebr. *abbrev. for* Nebraska.

Ne+bras+ka (nɪˈbræskə) *n.* a state of the western U.S.: consists of an undulating plain. Capital: Lincoln. Pop.: 1 483 791 (1970). Area: 197 974 sq. km (76 483 sq. miles). Abbrevs.: **Nebr.** or (with zip code) **NB** —**Ne+bras+kan** *adj., n.*

Neb·u+chad+nez+zar[1] (ˌnɛbjʊkədˈnɛzə) *n.* a wine bottle, used esp. for display, holding the equivalent of twenty normal bottles (approximately 520 ounces). [C20: named after NEBUCHADNEZZAR[2], from the custom of naming large wine bottles after Old Testament figures; compare JEROBOAM]

Neb·u·chad·nez·zar[2] (ˌnɛbjʊkədˈnɛzə) *or* **Neb·u·chad·rez·zar** *n. Old Testament.* a king of Babylon, 605–562 B.C., who conquered and destroyed Jerusalem and exiled the Jews to Babylon (II Kings 24–25).

neb·u+la (ˈnɛbjʊlə) *n., pl.* **+lae** (-ˌliː) *or* **+las. 1.** *Astronomy.* a diffuse cloud of particles and gases (mainly hydrogen) that is visible either as a hazy patch of light or an irregular dark region. Compare **extragalactic nebula, planetary nebula. 2.** *Pathol.* **a.** opacity of the cornea. **b.** cloudiness of the urine. **3.** any substance for use in an atomizer spray. [C17: from Latin: mist, cloud; related to Greek *nephétē* cloud, Old High German *nebul* cloud, Old Norse *njól* night] —ˈ**neb·u+lar** *adj.*

neb·u·lar hy·poth·e·sis *n.* the theory that the solar system evolved from nebular matter.

neb·u·lize *or* **neb·u·lise** ('nɛbjʊ,laɪz) *vb.* (*tr.*) to convert (a liquid) into a mist or fine spray; atomize. —,**neb·u·li·'za·tion** *or* ,**neb·u·li·'sa·tion** *n.* —'**neb·u·,liz·er** *or* '**neb·u·,lis·er** *n.*

neb·u·los·i·ty (,nɛbjʊ'lɒsɪtɪ) *n., pl.* **·ties. 1.** the state or quality of being nebulous. **2.** *Astronomy.* a nebula.

neb·u·lous ('nɛbjʊləs) *adj.* **1.** lacking definite form, shape, or content; vague or amorphous: *nebulous reasons.* **2.** of, characteristic of, or resembling a nebula. **3.** *Rare.* misty or hazy. —'**neb·u·lous·ly** *adv.* —'**neb·u·lous·ness** *n.*

ne·ces·sar·ies ('nɛsɪsərɪz) *pl. n.* **1.** (*sometimes sing.*) what is needed, esp. money or provisions for a journey. **2.** *Law.* food, clothing, etc., essential for the maintenance of a dependant in the condition of life to which he or she is accustomed.

nec·es·sar·i·ly ('nɛsɪsərɪlɪ, ,nɛsɪ'sɛrɪlɪ) *adv.* **1.** as an inevitable or natural consequence: *girls do not necessarily like dolls.* **2.** as a certainty: *he won't necessarily come.*

nec·es·sar·y ('nɛsɪsərɪ) *adj.* **1.** needed to achieve a certain desired effect or result; required. **2.** resulting from necessity; inevitable: *the necessary consequences of your action.* **3.** *Logic.* **a.** (of a proposition) inevitably determined as true or false by the meaning of the words or by a natural law, so that a denial would be a contradiction. **b.** (of an inference) always yielding a true conclusion if the premisses are true. **c.** (of a condition) required to be fulfilled to assure the truth of a proposition, event, etc. Compare **sufficient** (sense 2). **4.** *Rare.* compelled, as by necessity or law; not free. [C14: from Latin *necessārius* indispensable, from *necesse* unavoidable]

ne·ces·si·tar·i·an·ism (nɪ,sɛsɪ'tɛərɪə,nɪzəm) *or* **nec·es·sar·i·an·ism** (,nɛsɪ'sɛərɪə,nɪzəm) *n.* *Philosophy.* the belief that human actions and choices are causally determined and cannot be willed. Compare **libertarian.** —**ne·,ces·si·'tar·i·an** *or* ,**nec·es·'sar·i·an** *n., adj.*

ne·ces·si·tate (nɪ'sɛsɪ,teɪt) *vb.* (*tr.*) **1.** to cause as an unavoidable and necessary result. **2.** (*usually passive*) to compel or require (someone to do something). —**ne·,ces·si·'ta·tion** *n.* —**ne·'ces·si·ta·tive** *adj.*

ne·ces·si·tous (nɪ'sɛsɪtəs) *adj.* very needy; destitute; poverty-stricken. —**ne·'ces·si·tous·ly** *adv.*

ne·ces·si·ty (nɪ'sɛsɪtɪ) *n., pl.* **·ties. 1.** (*sometimes pl.*) something needed for a desired result; prerequisite: *necessities of life.* **2.** a condition or set of circumstances, such as physical laws or social rules, that inevitably requires a certain result: *it is a matter of necessity to wear formal clothes when meeting the Queen.* **3.** the state or quality of being obligatory or unavoidable. **4.** urgent requirement, as in an emergency or misfortune: *in time of necessity we must all work together.* **5.** poverty or want. **6.** *Rare.* compulsion through laws of nature; fate. **7.** *Philosophy.* **a.** a condition, principle, or conclusion that cannot be otherwise. **b.** the constraining force of physical determinants on all aspects of life. Compare **freedom** (sense 8). **8. of necessity.** inevitably; necessarily.

neck (nɛk) *n.* **1.** the part of an organism connecting the head with the rest of the body. **2.** the part of a garment around or nearest the neck. **3.** something resembling a neck in shape or position: *the neck of a bottle.* **4.** *Anatomy.* a constricted portion of an organ or part, such as the cervix of the uterus. **5.** a narrow or elongated projecting strip of land; a peninsula or isthmus. **6.** a strait or channel. **7.** the part of a violin, cello, etc., that extends from the body to the tuning pegs and supports the fingerboard. **8.** a solid block of lava from the opening of an extinct volcano, exposed after erosion of the surrounding rock. **9.** *Botany.* the upper, usually tubular, part of the archegonium of mosses, ferns, etc. **10.** the length of a horse's head and neck taken as an approximate distance by which one horse beats another in a race: *to win by a neck.* **11.** *Informal.* a short distance, amount, or margin: *he is always a neck ahead in new techniques.* **12.** *Architect.* the narrow band at the top of the shaft of a column between the necking and the capital, esp. as used in the Tuscan order. **13.** another name for **beard** (on printer's type). **14. break one's neck.** *Informal.* to exert oneself greatly, esp. by hurrying, in order to do something. **15. get it in the neck.** *Informal.* to be reprimanded or punished severely. **16. neck and neck.** absolutely level or even in a race or competition. **17. neck of the woods.** *Informal.* area or locality: *a quiet neck of the woods.* **18. neck or nothing.** whatever the risk; at any cost. **19. risk one's neck.** to take a great risk. **20. save one's** *or* **someone's neck.** *Informal.* to escape from or help someone else to escape from a difficult or dangerous situation. **21. stick one's neck out.** *Informal.* to risk criticism, ridicule, failure, etc., by speaking one's mind. **22. up to one's neck (in).** deeply involved (in). ~*vb.* **23.** (*intr.*) *Informal.* to kiss, embrace, or fondle (someone or one another) passionately. [Old English *hnecca;* related to Old High German *hnack,* Old Irish *cnocc* hill] —'**neck·er** *n.*

Neck·ar ('nɛkɑː) *n.* a river in SW West Germany, rising in the Black Forest and flowing generally north into the Rhine at Mannheim. Length: 394 km (245 miles).

neck·band ('nɛk,bænd) *n.* a band around the neck of a garment as finishing, decoration, or a base for a collar.

neck·cloth ('nɛk,klɒθ) *n.* a large ornamental usually white cravat worn formerly by men.

Neck·er ('nɛkə; *French* nɛ'kɛːr) *n.* **Jacques** (ʒɑːk). 1732–1804, French financier and statesman, born in Switzerland; finance minister of France (1777–81; 1788–90). He attempted to reform the fiscal system and in 1789 he recommended summoning the States General. His subsequent dismissal was one of the causes of the storming of the Bastille (1789).

neck·er·chief ('nɛkətʃɪf, -,tʃiːf) *n.* a piece of ornamental cloth, often square, worn around the neck. [C14: from NECK + KERCHIEF]

neck·ing ('nɛkɪŋ) *n.* **1.** *Informal.* the activity of kissing and embracing lovingly. **2.** Also called: **gorgerin.** *Architect.* one or more mouldings at the top of a column between the shaft and the capital.

neck·lace ('nɛklɪs) *n.* a chain, band, or cord, often bearing beads, pearls, jewels, etc., worn around the neck as an ornament, esp. by women.

neck·line ('nɛk,laɪn) *n.* the shape or position of the upper edge of a dress, blouse, etc.: *a plunging neckline.*

neck·piece ('nɛk,piːs) *n.* a piece of fur, cloth, etc., worn around the neck or neckline.

neck·tie ('nɛk,taɪ) *n.* the U.S. name for **tie** (sense 11).

neck·wear ('nɛk,wɛə) *n.* articles of clothing, such as ties, scarves, etc., worn around the neck.

nec·ro- *or before a vowel* **necr-** *combining form.* indicating death, a dead body, or dead tissue: *necrology; necrophagous; necrosis.* [from Greek *nekros* corpse]

nec·ro·bi·o·sis (,nɛkrəʊbaɪ'əʊsɪs) *n.* *Physiol.* the normal degeneration and death of cells. Compare **necrosis.** —**nec·ro·bi·ot·ic** (,nɛkrəʊbaɪ'ɒtɪk) *adj.*

ne·crol·a·try (nɛ'krɒlətrɪ) *n.* the worship of the dead.

ne·crol·o·gy (nɛ'krɒlədʒɪ) *n., pl.* **·gies. 1.** a list of people recently dead. **2.** a less common word for **obituary.** —**nec·ro·log·i·cal** (,nɛkrə'lɒdʒɪkəl) *adj.* —**ne·'crol·o·gist** *n.*

nec·ro·man·cy ('nɛkrəʊ,mænsɪ) *n.* **1.** the art or practice of supposedly conjuring up the dead, esp. in order to obtain from them knowledge of the future. **2.** black magic; sorcery. [C13: (as in sense 1) ultimately from Greek *nekromanteia,* from *nekros* corpse; (as in sense 2) from Medieval Latin *nigromantia,* from Latin *niger* black, which replaced *necro-* through folk etymology] —'**nec·ro·,man·cer** *n.* —,**nec·ro·'man·tic** *adj.*

nec·ro·ma·ni·a (,nɛkrəʊ'meɪnɪə) *n.* another word for **necrophilia.** —,**nec·ro·'ma·ni·,ac** *n.*

nec·ro·phil·i·a (,nɛkrəʊ'fɪlɪə) *n.* sexual attraction for or sexual intercourse with dead bodies. Also called: **necromania, necrophilism.** —,**nec·ro·'phil·i·,ac** *or* **nec·ro·phile** ('nɛkrəʊ,faɪl) *n.* —,**nec·ro·'phil·ic** *adj.*

ne·croph·i·lism (nɛ'krɒfɪ,lɪzəm) *n.* **1.** another word for **necrophilia. 2.** a strong desire to be dead.

nec·ro·pho·bi·a (,nɛkrəʊ'fəʊbɪə) *n.* an abnormal fear of death or dead bodies. —'**nec·ro·,phobe** *n.* —,**nec·ro·'pho·bic** *adj.*

ne·crop·o·lis (nɛ'krɒpəlɪs) *n., pl.* **·lis·es** *or* **·leis** (-,leɪs). a burial site or cemetery. [C19: from Greek *nekropolis*]

nec·rop·sy ('nɛkrɒpsɪ) *or* **nec·ros·co·py** (nɛ'krɒskəpɪ) *n., pl.* **·sies** *or* **·pies.** another name for **autopsy.** [C19: from Greek *nekros* dead body + *opsis* sight]

ne·crose (nɛ'krəʊs, 'nɛkrəʊs) *vb.* to cause or undergo necrosis. [C19: back formation from NECROSIS]

ne·cro·sis (nɛ'krəʊsɪs) *n.* **1.** the death of one or more cells in the body, usually within a localized area, as from an interruption of the blood supply to that part. **2.** death of plant tissue due to disease, frost, etc. [C17: New Latin from Greek *nekrōsis,* from *nekroun* to kill, from *nekros* corpse] —**ne·crot·ic** (nɛ'krɒtɪk) *adj.*

ne·crot·o·my (nɛ'krɒtəmɪ) *n., pl.* **·mies. 1.** dissection of a dead body. **2.** surgical excision of dead tissue from a living organism.

nec·tar ('nɛktə) *n.* **1.** a sugary fluid produced in the nectaries of flowers and collected by bees and other insects. **2.** *Classical myth.* the drink of the gods. Compare **ambrosia** (sense 1). **3.** any delicious drink, esp. a sweet one. **4.** something very pleasant or welcome: *your words are nectar to me.* **5.** *Chiefly U.S.* **a.** the undiluted juice of a fruit. **b.** a mixture of fruit juices. [C16: via Latin from Greek *néktar,* perhaps *nek-* death (related to *nekros* corpse) + *-tar,* related to Sanskrit *tarati* he overcomes; compare Latin *nex* death and *trans* across] —**nec·tar·e·ous** (nɛk'tɛərɪəs) *or* '**nec·tar·ous** *adj.*

nec·tar·ine ('nɛktərɪn) *n.* **1.** a variety of peach tree, *Prunus persica nectarina.* **2.** the fruit of this tree, which has a smooth skin. [C17: apparently from NECTAR]

nec·ta·ry ('nɛktərɪ) *n., pl.* **·ries. 1.** any of various glandular structures secreting nectar that occur in the flowers, leaves, stipules, etc., of a plant. **2.** any of the abdominal tubes in aphids through which honeydew is secreted. [C18: from New Latin *nectarium,* from NECTAR] —**nec·tar·i·al** (nɛk'tɛərɪəl) *adj.*

N.E.D.C. *abbrev. for* National Economic Development Council. Also: (informal) **Ned·dy** ('nɛdɪ).

ned·dy ('nɛdɪ) *n., pl.* **·dies.** a child's word for a **donkey.** [C18: from *Ned,* pet form of *Edward*]

Ne·der·land ('neːdər,lɑnt) *n.* the Dutch name for the **Netherlands.**

née *or* **nee** (neɪ) *adj.* indicating the maiden name of a married woman: *Mrs. Bloggs née Blandish.* [C19: from French: past participle (fem.) of *naître* to be born, from Latin *nascī*]

need (niːd) *vb.* **1.** to be in want of: *to need money.* **2.** (*tr.*) to require or be required of necessity (to be or do something); be obliged: *to need to do more work.* **3.** (takes an infinitive without *to*) used as an auxiliary in negative and interrogative sentences to express necessity or obligation and does not add *-s* when used with *he, she, it,* and singular nouns: *need he go?* **4.** (*intr.*) *Archaic.* to be essential or necessary to: *there needs no reason for this.* ~*n.* **5.** the fact or an instance of feeling the lack of something: *he has need of a new coat.* **6.** a requirement: *the need for vengeance.* **7.** necessity or obligation resulting from some situation: *no need to be frightened.* **8.** distress or extremity: *a friend in need.* **9.** extreme poverty or destitution;

penury. [Old English *nēad, nied;* related to Old Frisian *nēd,* Old Saxon *nōd,* Old High German *nōt*]

need+ful ('ni:dfʊl) *adj.* **1.** necessary; needed; required. **2.** *Archaic.* needy; poverty-stricken. —**'need+ful+ly** *adv.* —**'need+ful+ness** *n.*

need·i+ness ('ni:dɪnɪs) *n.* the state of being needy; poverty.

nee+dle ('ni:dᵊl) *n.* **1.** a pointed slender piece of metal, usually steel, with a hole or eye in it through which thread is passed for sewing. **2.** a somewhat larger rod with a point at one or each end, used in knitting. **3.** a similar instrument with a hook at one end for crocheting. **4. a.** another name for **stylus** (sense 3). **b.** a small thin pointed device, esp. one made of stainless steel, used to transmit the vibrations from a gramophone record to the pickup. **5.** *Med.* **a.** the long hollow pointed part of a hypodermic syringe, which is inserted into the body. **b.** an informal name for **hypodermic syringe. 6.** *Surgery.* a pointed steel instrument, often curved, for suturing, puncturing, or ligating. **7.** a long narrow stiff leaf in which water loss is greatly reduced: *pine needles.* **8.** any slender sharp spine, such as the spine of a sea urchin. **9.** any slender pointer for indicating the reading on the scale of a measuring instrument. **10.** short for **magnetic needle. 11.** a crystal resembling a needle in shape. **12.** a sharp pointed metal instrument used in engraving and etching. **13.** anything long and pointed, such as an obelisk: *a needle of light.* **14.** a short horizontal beam passed through a wall and supported on vertical posts to take the load of the upper part of the wall. **15.** *Informal.* **a.** anger or intense rivalry, esp. in a sporting encounter. **b.** (*as modifier*): *a needle match.* **16. have** *or* **get the needle (to).** *Brit. slang.* to feel dislike, distaste, nervousness, or annoyance (for): *she got the needle after he had refused her invitation.* ~*vb.* **17.** (*tr.*) *Informal.* to goad or provoke, as by constant criticism. **18.** (*tr.*) to sew, embroider, or prick (fabric) with a needle. **19.** (*tr.*) *U.S.* to increase the alcoholic strength of (beer or other beverages). **20.** (*intr.*) (of a substance) to form needle-shaped crystals. [Old English *nǣdl;* related to Gothic *nēthla,* German *Nadel*]

nee+dle bush *n.* a small Australian tree, *Hakea leucoptera,* having needle-shaped leaves and soft wood used for veneers: family *Proteaceae.*

nee·dle+cord ('ni:dᵊl,kɔ:d) *n.* a corduroy fabric with narrow ribs.

nee·dle+craft ('ni:dᵊl,krɑ:ft) *n.* the art or practice of needlework.

nee·dle+fish ('ni:dᵊl,fɪʃ) *n., pl.* **+fish** *or* **+fish·es. 1.** any ferocious teleost fish of the family *Belonidae* of warm and tropical regions, having an elongated body and long toothed jaws. **2.** another name for **pipefish.**

nee·dle+ful ('ni:dᵊl,fʊl) *n.* a length of thread, etc., cut for use in a needle.

nee·dle+point ('ni:dᵊl,pɔɪnt) *n.* **1.** embroidery done on canvas with the same stitch throughout so as to resemble tapestry. **2.** another name for **point lace.**

need+less ('ni:dlɪs) *adj.* not required or desired; unnecessary. —**'need+less+ly** *adv.* —**'need+less+ness** *n.*

nee+dle time *n. Chiefly Brit.* the limited time allocated by a radio channel to the broadcasting of music from records.

nee+dle valve *n.* a valve with a needle-like part that can be moved to control the flow of a fluid.

nee·dle+wom·an ('ni:dᵊl,wʊmən) *n., pl.* **+wom·en.** a woman who does needlework; seamstress.

nee·dle+work ('ni:dᵊl,wɜ:k) *n.* **1.** work done with a needle, esp. sewing and embroidery. **2.** the result of such work.

needs (ni:dz) *adv.* (preceded or foll. by *must*) of necessity: *we must needs go; we will go, if needs must.*

need·y ('ni:dɪ) *adj.* **need·i·er, need·i·est. a.** in need; poverty-stricken. **b.** (*as n.*): *the needy.*

neep (ni:p) *n. Brit.* a dialect name for a **turnip.** [Old English *nǣp,* from Latin *nāpus* turnip]

ne'er (nɛə) *adv.* a poetic contraction of **never.**

ne'er-do-well *n.* **1.** an improvident, irresponsible, or lazy person. ~*adj.* **2.** useless; worthless: *your ne'er-do-well schemes.*

ne+far·i·ous (nɪ'fɛərɪəs) *adj.* evil; wicked; sinful. [C17: from Latin *nefārius,* from *nefās* unlawful deed, from *nē* not + *fās* divine law] —**ne+'far·i·ous+ly** *adv.* —**ne+'far·i·ous+ness** *n.*

Nef·er·ti·ti (,nɛfə'ti:tɪ) *or* **Nof·re·te·te** *n.* 14th-century B.C. Egyptian queen; wife of Akhenaton.

NEG (in transformational grammar) *abbrev. for* negative.

neg. *abbrev. for* negative(ly).

ne+gate (nɪ'geɪt) *vb.* (*tr.*) **1.** to make ineffective or void; nullify; invalidate. **2.** to deny or contradict. [C17: from Latin *negāre,* from *neg-,* variant of *nec* not + *aio* I say] —**ne+'ga·tor** *or* **ne+'gat+er** *n.*

ne+ga·tion (nɪ'geɪʃən) *n.* **1.** the opposite or absence of something. **2.** a negative thing or condition. **3.** the act or an instance of negating. **4.** *Logic.* a proposition that is the denial of another proposition and is true only if the original proposition is false. Usually written: $\sim p$, $\bar{p}$, or $\neg p$, where p is the original proposition and ~, ¯, and ¬ symbolize *not.* **5.** *Computer technol.* another name for **inversion** (sense 10).

neg·a·tive ('nɛgətɪv) *adj.* **1.** expressing or meaning a refusal or denial: *a negative answer.* **2.** lacking positive or affirmative qualities, such as enthusiasm, interest, or optimism. **3.** showing or tending towards opposition or resistance. **4. a.** measured in a direction opposite to that regarded as positive. **b.** having the same magnitude but opposite sense to an equivalent positive quantity. **5.** *Biology.* indicating movement or growth away from a particular stimulus: *negative geotropism.* **6.** *Med.* (of the results of a diagnostic test) indicating absence of the disease or condition for which the test was made. **7.** another word for **minus** (senses 3b, 5). **8.** *Physics.* **a.** (of an electric charge) having the same polarity as the charge of an electron. **b.** (of a body, system, ion, etc.) having a negative electric charge; having an excess of electrons. **c.** (of a point in an electric circuit) having a lower electrical potential than some other point with an assigned zero potential. **9.** short for **electronegative. 10.** (of a lens) capable of causing divergence of a parallel beam of light. **11.** of or relating to a photographic negative. **12.** *Logic.* (of a proposition) denying the truth of the predicate, as in the proposition *no man is immortal.* **13.** *Astrology.* of, relating to, or governed by the signs of the zodiac of the earth and water classifications, which are thought to be associated with a receptive passive nature. **14.** short for **Rh negative.** ~*n.* **15.** a statement or act of denial, refusal, or negation. **16.** a negative person or thing. **17.** *Photog.* a piece of photographic film or a plate, previously exposed and developed, showing an image that, in black-and-white photography, has a reversal of tones. In colour photography the image is in complementary colours to the subject so that blue sky appears yellow, green grass appears purple, etc. **18.** *Physics.* a negative object, such as a terminal or a plate in a voltaic cell. **19.** a sentence or other linguistic element with a negative meaning, as the English word *not.* **20.** a quantity less than zero or a quantity to be subtracted. **21.** *Logic.* a proposition that denies the truth of the predicate. **22.** *Archaic.* the right of veto. **23. in the negative.** indicating denial or refusal. ~ **24.** (*sentence substitute*) (esp. in military communications) a signal codeword for **no**[1]. ~*vb.* (*tr.*) **25.** to deny or nullify; negate. **26.** to show to be false; disprove. **27.** to refuse consent to or approval of: *the proposal was negatived.* ~Compare **positive, affirmative.** —**'neg·a+tive+ly** *adv.* —**'neg·a+tive+ness** *or* **,neg·a+'tiv+i·ty** *n.*

neg·a+tive feed+back *n.* the return of a proportion of the output of a mechanical, electronic, or other system to the input. See **feedback.**

neg·a+tive hal+lu+ci+na+tion *n. Psychol.* an apparent abnormal inability to perceive an object.

neg·a+tive po+lar+i·ty *n. Grammar.* the grammatical character of a word or phrase, such as *ever* or *any,* that may normally only be used in a semantically or syntactically negative or interrogative context.

neg·a·tive-rais·ing *n. Transformational grammar.* a rule that moves a negative element out of the complement clause of certain verbs, such as *think,* into the main clause, as in the derivation of *He doesn't think that he'll finish.*

neg·a+tive re+sist+ance *n.* a characteristic of certain electronic components in which an increase in the applied voltage increases the resistance, producing a proportional decrease in current.

neg·a+tive sign *n.* the symbol (−) used to indicate a negative quantity or a subtraction; minus sign.

neg·a+tive tax *n.* a payment by the State to a person with a low income, the magnitude of the payment increasing as the income decreases. It is regarded as a form of social welfare. Also called: **negative income tax.**

neg·a·ti+vism ('nɛgətɪv,ɪzəm) *n.* **1.** a tendency to be or a state of being unconstructively critical. **2.** any sceptical or derisive system of thought. **3.** *Psychiatry.* refusal to do what is expected or suggested or the tendency to do the opposite. —**'neg·a·tiv+ist** *n., adj.* —**,neg·a·tiv+'is·tic** *adj.*

ne+ga+tor (nɪ'geɪtə) *n. Electronics.* another name for **NOT circuit.**

neg·a+tron ('nɛgə,trɒn) *n.* an obsolete word for **electron.** [C20: from NEGA(TIVE + ELEC)TRON]

Neg+ev ('nɛgɛv) *or* **Neg+eb** ('nɛgɛb) *n.* the S part of Israel, on the Gulf of Aqaba: a triangular-shaped semidesert region, with large areas under irrigation; scene of fighting between Israeli and Egyptian forces in 1948. Chief town: Beersheba. Area: 12 820 sq. km (4950 sq. miles).

ne+glect (nɪ'glɛkt) *vb.* (*tr.*) **1.** to fail to give due care, attention, or time to: *to neglect a child.* **2.** to fail (to do something) through thoughtlessness or carelessness: *he neglected to tell her.* **3.** to ignore or disregard: *she neglected his frantic signals.* ~*n.* **4.** lack of due care or attention; negligence: *the child starved through neglect.* **5.** the act or an instance of neglecting or the state of being neglected. [C16: from Latin *neglegere* to neglect, from *nec* not + *legere* to select] —**ne+'glect·er** *or* **ne+'glec·tor** *n.*

ne+glect+ful (nɪ'glɛktfʊl) *adj.* (when *postpositive,* foll. by *of*) not giving due care and attention (to); careless; heedless. —**ne+'glect+ful+ly** *adv.* —**ne+'glect+ful+ness** *n.*

neg+li+gee, neg+li+gée, *or* **neg+li+gé** ('nɛglɪ,ʒeɪ) *n.* **1.** a woman's light dressing gown, esp. one that is lace-trimmed. **2.** any informal attire. [C18: from French *négligée,* past participle (fem.) of *négliger* to NEGLECT]

neg+li+gence ('nɛglɪdʒəns) *n.* **1.** the state or quality of being negligent. **2.** a negligent act. **3.** *Law.* a civil wrong whereby the defendant is in breach of a legal duty, resulting in injury to the plaintiff.

neg+li+gent ('nɛglɪdʒənt) *adj.* **1.** habitually neglecting duties, responsibilities, etc.; lacking attention, care, or concern; neglectful. **2.** careless or nonchalant. —**'neg+li+gent+ly** *adv.*

neg+li·gi·ble ('nɛglɪdʒəbᵊl) *adj.* so small, unimportant, etc., as to be not worth considering; insignificant. —**,neg+li·gi·'bil+i·ty** *or* **'neg+li·gi·ble+ness** *n.* —**'neg+li·gi·bly** *adv.*

ne+go+tia·ble (nɪ'gəʊʃəbᵊl) *adj.* **1.** able to be negotiated. **2.** (of a bill of exchange, promissory note, etc.) legally transferable in title from one party to another. —**ne+,go+tia·'bil+i·ty** *n.*

ne+go+ti+ant (nɪˈgəʊʃɪənt) *n.* a person, nation, organization, etc. involved in a negotiation.
ne+go+ti+ate (nɪˈgəʊʃɪˌeɪt) *vb.* **1.** to work or talk (with others) to achieve (a transaction, an agreement, etc.). **2.** (*tr.*) to succeed in passing through, around, or over: *to negotiate a mountain pass.* **3.** (*tr.*) *Finance.* **a.** to transfer (a negotiable commercial paper) by endorsement to another in return for value received. **b.** to sell (financial assets). **c.** to arrange for (a loan). [C16: from Latin *negōtiārī* to do business, from *negōtium* business, from *nec* not + *ōtium* leisure] —**ne+ˈgo+ti+ˌa+tor** *n.*
ne+go+ti·a+tion (nɪˌgəʊʃɪˈeɪʃən) *n.* **1.** a discussion set up or intended to produce a settlement or agreement. **2.** the act or process of negotiating.
Ne+gress (ˈni:grɪs) *n.* a female Negro.
Ne+gril+lo (nɪˈgrɪləʊ) *n., pl.* **+los** *or* **+loes.** a member of a dwarfish Negro race of central and southern Africa. [C19: from Spanish, diminutive of *negro* black]
Neg+ri Sem+bi+lan (ˈnɛgrɪ sɛmˈbi:lən) *n.* a state of S West Malaysia: mostly mountainous, with large areas under paddy and rubber. Capital: Seremban. Pop.: 480 053 (1970). Area: 6643 sq. km (2565 sq. miles).
Ne+grit+ic (nɪˈgrɪtɪk) *adj.* relating to the Negroes or the Negritos.
Ne+gri+to (nɪˈgri:təʊ) *n., pl.* **+tos** *or* **+toes.** a member of any of various dwarfish Negroid peoples of SE Asia and Melanesia. [C19: from Spanish, diminutive of *negro* black]
ne+gri+tude (ˈni:grɪˌtju:d, ˈnɛg-) *n.* **1.** the fact of being a Negro. **2.** awareness and cultivation of the Negro heritage, values, and culture. [C20: from French, from *nègre* NEGRO¹]
Ne+gro[1] (ˈni:grəʊ) *n., pl.* **+groes.** **1.** a member of any of the dark-skinned indigenous peoples of Africa and their descendants elsewhere. ~*adj.* **2.** relating to or characteristic of Negroes. [C16: from Spanish or Portuguese: black, from Latin *niger* black] —**ˈNe+gro+ism** *n.*
Neg+ro[2] (ˈneɪgrəʊ, ˈnɛg-) *n.* **Ri·o. 1.** a river in NW South America, rising in E Colombia (as the Guainía) and flowing east, then south as part of the border between Colombia and Venezuela, entering Brazil and continuing southeast to join the Amazon at Manáus. Length: about 2250 km (1400 miles). **2.** a river in S central Argentina, formed by the confluence of the Neuquén and Limay Rivers and flowing east and southeast to the Atlantic. Length: about 1014 km (630 miles). **3.** a river in central Uruguay, rising in S Brazil and flowing southwest into the Uruguay River. Length: about 467 km (290 miles).
Ne+groid (ˈni:grɔɪd) *adj.* **1.** denoting, relating to, or belonging to one of the major racial groups of mankind, characterized by brown-black skin, crisp or woolly hair, a broad flat nose, and full lips. This group includes the indigenous peoples of Africa south of the Sahara, their descendants elsewhere, and some Melanesian peoples. ~*n.* **2.** a member of this racial group.
Ne+gro+phil (ˈni:grəʊˌfɪl) *or* **Ne+gro+phile** (ˈni:grəʊˌfaɪl) *n.* a person who admires Negroes and their culture. —**Ne+groph+il+ism** (ni:ˈgrɒfɪˌlɪzəm) *n.*
Ne+gro+phobe (ˈni:grəʊˌfəʊb) *n.* a person who dislikes or fears Negroes. —**ˌNe+gro+ˈpho+bi+a** *n.* —**ˌNe+gro+ˈpho+bic** *adj.*
Neg+ro+pont (ˈnɛgrəʊˌpɒnt) *n.* **1.** the former English name for **Euboea. 2.** the medieval English name for **Chalcis.**
Ne+gros (ˈneɪgrəʊs; *Spanish* ˈneɣros) *n.* an island of the central Philippines, one of the Visayan Islands. Capital: Bacolod. Pop.: 2 219 022 (1970). Area: 13 670 sq. km (5278 sq. miles).
Ne+gro spir+i+tu+al *n.* a type of religious song originating among Negro slaves in the American South.
ne+gus (ˈni:gəs) *n., pl.* **+gus·es.** a hot drink of port and lemon juice, usually spiced and sweetened. [C18: named after Col. Francis *Negus* (died 1732), its English inventor]
Ne+gus (ˈni:gəs) *n., pl.* **+gus·es.** a title of the emperor of Ethiopia. [from Amharic: king]
Neh. *Bible. abbrev. for* Nehemiah.
Ne+he+mi+ah (ˌni:ɪˈmaɪə) *n. Old Testament.* **1.** a Jewish official at the court of Artaxerxes, king of Persia, who in 444 B.C. became a leader in the rebuilding of Jerusalem after the Babylonian captivity. **2.** the book recounting the acts of Nehemiah.
Neh·ru (ˈnεəru:) *n.* **1. Ja·wa·har·lal** (dʒəwəhəˈlɑ:l). 1889–1964, Indian statesman and nationalist leader. He spent several periods in prison for his nationalist activities and practised a policy of noncooperation with Britain during World War II. He was the first prime minister of the republic of India (1947–64). **2.** his father, **Mo·ti·lal** (məʊtɪˈlɑ:l). 1861–1931, Indian nationalist, lawyer, and journalist; first president of the reconstructed Indian National Congress.
neigh (neɪ) *n.* **1.** the high-pitched cry of a horse; whinny. ~*vb.* **2.** (*intr.*) to make a neigh or a similar noise. **3.** (*tr.*) to utter with a sound like a neigh. [Old English *hnǣgan;* related to Old Saxon *hnēgian*]
neigh+bour *or U.S.* **neigh+bor** (ˈneɪbə) *n.* **1.** a person who lives near or next to another. **2. a.** a person or thing near or next to another. **b.** (*as modifier*): *neighbour states.* ~*vb.* **3.** (when *intr.*, often foll. by *on*) to be or live close (to a person or thing). [Old English *nēahbūr*, from *nēah* NIGH + *būr*, *gebūr* dweller; see BOOR] —**ˈneigh+bour+less** *or U.S.* **ˈneigh+bor+less** *adj.*
neigh+bour+hood *or U.S.* **neigh+bor+hood** (ˈneɪbəˌhʊd) *n.* **1.** the immediate environment; surroundings; vicinity. **2.** a district where people live. **3.** the people in a particular area; neighbours. **4.** neighbourly feeling. **5. in the neighbourhood of.** approximately (a given number). **6.** *Maths.* the set of all points whose distance from a given point is less than a specified value.
neigh+bour+ly *or U.S.* **neigh+bor+ly** (ˈneɪbəlɪ) *adj.* kind, friendly, or sociable, as befits a neighbour. —**ˈneigh+bour+li+ness** *or U.S.* **ˈneigh+bor+li+ness** *n.*
Neis+se (ˈnaɪsə) *n.* a tributary of the Oder.
nei+ther (ˈnaɪðə) *determiner.* **1. a.** not one nor the other (of two); not either: *neither foot is swollen.* **b.** (*as pronoun*): *neither can win.* ~*conj.* **2.** (*coordinating*) **a.** (used preceding alternatives joined by *nor*) not: *neither John nor Mary nor Joe went.* **b.** another word for **nor** (sense 2). ~*adv.* (*sentence modifier*) **3.** *Not standard.* another word for **either** (sense 4). [C13 (literally: *ne either* not either): changed from Old English *nāwther*, from *nāhwæther*, from *nā* not + *hwæther* which of two; see WHETHER]

Usage. A verb following a compound subject that uses *neither...(nor)* should be in the singular if both subjects are in the singular: *neither Jack nor John has done the work.* Where the subjects are different in number, the verb usually agrees with the subject nearest to it: *neither they nor Jack was able to come.*

Nejd (nɛʒd, neɪd) *n.* a region of central Saudi Arabia: formerly an independent sultanate of Arabia; united with Hejaz to form the kingdom of Saudi Arabia (1932). Capital: Riyadh. Pop.: about 4 000 000 (1970 est.). Area: about 1 087 800 sq. km (420 000 sq. miles).
nek (nɛk) *n.* (*cap. when part of name*) *S. African.* a mountain pass: *Lundeans Nek.*
Ne·kra·sov (*Russian* nɪˈkrasəf) *n.* **Ni·ko·lai A·le·kse·ye·vich** (nikaˈlaj alɪˈksjejɪvitʃ). 1821–77, Russian poet, who wrote chiefly about the sufferings of the peasantry.
nek+ton (ˈnɛktɒn) *n.* the population of free-swimming animals that inhabits the middle depths of a sea or lake. Compare **plankton.** [C19: via German from Greek *nēkton* a swimming thing, from *nēkhein* to swim] —**nek+ˈton+ic** *adj.*
nel+ly (ˈnɛlɪ) *n.* **not on your nelly.** (*sentence substitute*). *Brit. slang.* not under any circumstances; certainly not.
nel+son (ˈnɛlsən) *n.* any wrestling hold in which a wrestler places his arm or arms under his opponent's arm or arms from behind and exerts pressure with his palms on the back of his opponent's neck. See **full nelson, half-nelson.** [C19: from a proper name]
Nel+son[1] (ˈnɛlsən) *n.* **1.** a town in NW England, in E Lancashire: textile industry. Pop.: 31 225 (1971). **2.** a port in New Zealand, on N South Island on Tasman Bay: inter-island shipping. Pop.: 29 282 (1971). **3. River.** a river in central Canada, in N central Manitoba, flowing from Lake Winnipeg northeast to Hudson Bay. Length: about 650 km (400 miles).
Nel·son[2] (ˈnɛlsən) *n.* **Ho·ra·ti·o,** Viscount Nelson. 1758–1805, British naval commander during the Revolutionary and Napoleonic Wars. He became rear admiral in 1797 after the battle of Cape St. Vincent and in 1798 almost destroyed the French fleet at the battle of the Nile. He was killed at Trafalgar (1805) after defeating Villeneuve's fleet.
ne+lum+bo (nɪˈlʌmbəʊ) *n., pl.* **+bos.** either of the two aquatic plants of the genus *Nelumbo:* family *Nelumbonaceae.* See **lotus** (sense 4), **water chinquapin.** [C19: New Latin, from Sinhalese *nelumbu* lotus]
Ne+man *or* **Nye+man** (*Russian* ˈnjɛmən) *n.* a river in the W Soviet Union, rising in the Belorussian SSSR and flowing generally northwest through the Lithuanian SSR to the Baltic. Length: 937 km (582 miles). Polish name: **Niemen.**
nem·a+thel+minth (ˌnɛməˈθɛlmɪnθ) *n.* any unsegmented worm of the group *Nemathelminthes,* including the nematodes, nematomorphs, and acanthocephalans.
ne+mat+ic (nɪˈmætɪk) *adj. Chem.* (of a substance) existing in or having a mesomorphic state in which a linear orientation of the molecules causes anisotropic properties. Compare **smectic.** See also **liquid crystal.** [C20: NEMAT(O)- (referring to the threadlike chains of molecules in liquid) + -IC]
nem·a·to- *or before a vowel* **nem·at-** *combining form.* indicating a threadlike form: *nematocyst.* [from Greek *nēma* thread]
nem·a+to+cyst (ˈnɛmətəˌsɪst, nɪˈmætə-) *n.* a structure in coelenterates, such as jellyfish, consisting of a capsule containing a hollow coiled thread that can be everted to sting or paralyse prey and enemies. —**ˌnem·a+to+ˈcys+tic** *adj.*
nem·a+tode (ˈnɛməˌtəʊd) *n.* any unsegmented worm of the phylum (or class) *Nematoda,* having a tough outer cuticle. The group includes free-living forms and disease-causing parasites, such as the hookworm and filaria. Also called: **nematode worm, roundworm.**
Nem+bu+tal (ˈnɛmbjʊˌtɑ:l) *n.* a trademark for **pentobarbitone sodium.**
nem. con. *abbrev. for* nemine contradicente. [Latin: no one contradicting; unanimously]
Ne+me·a (nɪˈmi:ə) *n.* (in ancient Greece) a valley in N Argolis in the NE Peloponnesus; site of the **Nemean Games,** a Panhellenic festival and athletic competition held every other year. —**Ne+ˈme·an** *adj.*
Ne+me·an li·on *n. Greek myth.* an enormous lion that was strangled by Hercules as his first labour.
ne+mer+te·an (nɪˈmɜ:tɪən) *or* **nem+er+tine** (ˈnɛməˌtaɪn) *n.* **1.** any soft flattened ribbon-like marine worm of the phylum (or class) *Nemertea* (or *Nemertina*), having an eversible threadlike proboscis. Also called: **ribbon worm.** ~*adj.* **2.** of, relating to, or belonging to the *Nemertea.* [C19: via New Latin from Greek *Nēmertēs* a NEREID]
Ne·me·ry (nəˈmɛrɪ) *n.* **Jaa·far Mo·ham·med al** (ˈdʒɑ:ˌfɑ: məˈhæmɪd æl). born 1930, Sudanese statesman and general; president of the Sudan since 1971.
ne+me·sia (nɪˈmi:ʒə) *n.* any plant of the southern African

scrophulariaceous genus *Nemesia:* cultivated for their brightly coloured (often reddish) flowers. [C19: New Latin, from Greek *nemesion,* name of a plant resembling this]

Nem·e·sis ('nɛmɪsɪs) *n., pl.* **·ses** (-ˌsiːz). **1.** *Greek myth.* the goddess of retribution and vengeance. **2.** (*sometimes not cap.*) any agency of retribution and vengeance. [C16: via Latin from Greek: righteous wrath, from *némein* to distribute what is due]

ne·ne ('neɪˌneɪ) *n.* a rare black-and-grey short-winged Hawaiian goose, *Branta sandvicensis,* having partly webbed feet. [from Hawaiian]

ne·o- *or sometimes before a vowel* **ne-** *combining form.* **1.** (*sometimes cap.*) new, recent, or a new or modern form or development: *neoclassicism; neocolonialism.* **2.** (*usually cap.*) the most recent subdivision of a geological period: *Neogene.* [from Greek *neos* new]

ne·o·an·throp·ic (ˌniːəʊæn'θrɒpɪk) *adj. Anthropol.* of, relating to, or resembling modern man.

ne·o·ars·phen·a·mine (ˌniːəʊɑːs'fɛnəˌmiːn, -fɪ'næmɪn) *n.* a derivative of arsenic used in treating syphilis.

Ne·o·cene ('niːəˌsiːn) *adj.* **1.** (formerly) of, denoting, or formed in the Miocene and Pliocene epochs. ~*n.* **2. the.** the Neocene time or rock series. ~Compare **Neogene.**

ne·o·clas·si·cism (ˌniːəʊ'klæsɪˌsɪzəm) *n.* **1.** a late 18th- and early 19th-century style in architecture, decorative art, and fine art, based on the imitation of surviving classical models and types. **2.** *Music.* a movement of the 1920s, involving Hindemith, Stravinsky, etc., that sought to avoid the emotionalism of late romantic music by reviving the use of counterpoint, forms such as the classical suite, and small instrumental ensembles. —**ne·o·clas·si·cal** (ˌniːəʊ'klæsɪkᵊl) *or* ˌ**ne·o·'clas·sic** *adj.* —ˌ**ne·o·'clas·si·cist** *n.*

ne·o·co·lo·ni·al·ism (ˌniːəʊkə'ləʊnɪəˌlɪzəm) *n.* (in the modern world) political control by an outside power of a country that is in theory sovereign and independent, esp. through the domination of its economy. —ˌ**ne·o·co·'lo·ni·al** *adj.* —ˌ**ne·o·co·'lo·ni·al·ist** *n.*

Ne·o-Dar·win·ism (ˌniːəʊ'dɑːwɪˌnɪzəm) *n.* a modern theory of evolution that relates Darwinism to the occurrence of inheritable variation by genetic mutation. —ˌ**Ne·o-Dar·'win·i·an** *adj., n.*

ne·o·dym·i·um (ˌniːəʊ'dɪmɪəm) *n.* a toxic silvery-white metallic element of the lanthanide series, occurring principally in monazite: used in colouring glass. Symbol: Nd; atomic no.: 60; atomic wt.: 144.24; valency: 3; relative density: 6.80 and 7.00 (depending on allotrope); melting pt.: 1024°C; boiling pt.: 3127°C. [C19: New Latin; see NEO- + DIDYMIUM]

Ne·o·gae·a (ˌniːəʊ'dʒiːə) *n.* a zoogeographical area comprising the Neotropical region. Compare **Arctogaea, Notogaea.** [C19: New Latin, from NEO- + GAEA, from Greek *gaia* earth] —ˌ**Ne·o·'gae·an** *adj.*

Ne·o·gene ('niːəˌdʒiːn) *adj.* **1.** of, denoting, or formed during the Miocene, Pliocene, Pleistocene, and Holocene epochs. ~*n.* **2. the.** the Neogene period or system. ~Compare **Neocene.**

ne·o·im·pres·sion·ism (ˌniːəʊɪm'prɛʃəˌnɪzəm) *n.* a movement in French painting initiated mainly by Seurat in the 1880s and combining his vivid colour technique with strictly formal composition. See also **pointillism.** —ˌ**ne·o·im·'pres·sion·ist** *n., adj.*

Ne·o-La·marck·ism (ˌniːəʊlə'mɑːkɪzəm) *n.* a modern theory of evolution based on Lamarckism and emphasizing the influence of environmental factors on genetic changes. —ˌ**Ne·o-La·'marck·i·an** *adj., n.*

Ne·o-Lat·in (ˌniːəʊ'lætɪn) *n.* **1.** another term for **New Latin.** ~*adj.* **2.** denoting or relating to New Latin. **3.** denoting or relating to language that developed from Latin; Romance.

ne·o·lith ('niːəlɪθ) *n.* a Neolithic stone implement.

Ne·o·lith·ic (ˌniːə'lɪθɪk) *n.* **1.** the cultural period that lasted in SW Asia from about 9000 to 6000 B.C. and in Europe from about 4000 to 2400 B.C. and was characterized by primitive crop-growing and stock-rearing and the use of polished stone and flint tools and weapons. ~*adj.* **2.** relating to this period. ~See also **Mesolithic, Palaeolithic.**

ne·ol·o·gism (nɪ'ɒləˌdʒɪzəm) *or* **ne·ol·o·gy** *n., pl.* **·gisms** *or* **·gies.** **1.** a newly coined word, or a phrase or familiar word used in a new sense. **2.** the practice of using or introducing neologisms. **3.** *Rare.* a body of new ideas, esp. in theology. [C18: via French from NEO- + *-logism,* from Greek *logos* word, saying] —**ne·'ol·o·gist** *n.* —**ne·ˌol·o·'gis·tic, ne·ˌol·o·'gis·ti·cal,** *or* **ne·o·log·i·cal** (ˌnɪə'lɒdʒɪkᵊl) *adj.* —**ne·ˌol·o·'gis·ti·cal·ly** *or* ˌ**ne·o·'log·i·cal·ly** *adv.*

ne·ol·o·gize *or* **ne·ol·o·gise** (nɪ'ɒləˌdʒaɪz) *vb.* (*intr.*) to invent or use neologisms.

Ne·o-Mel·a·ne·si·an *n.* an English-based creole language widely spoken in the SW Pacific, with borrowings from other languages, esp. Motu. Also called: **Beach-la-Mar.**

ne·o·my·cin (ˌniːəʊ'maɪsɪn) *n.* an antibiotic obtained from the bacterium *Streptomyces fradiae,* administered locally in the treatment of skin and eye infections or orally for bowel infections. Formula: $C_{12}H_{26}N_4O_6$.

ne·on ('niːɒn) *n.* **1.** a colourless odourless rare gaseous element, an inert gas occurring in trace amounts in the atmosphere: used in illuminated signs and lights. Symbol: Ne; atomic no.: 10; atomic wt.: 20.179; density: 0.8999 kg/m³; melting pt.: –248.67°C; boiling pt.: –246.05°C. **2.** (*modifier*) of or illuminated by neon or neon lamps: *neon sign.* [C19: via New Latin from Greek *neon* new]

ne·o·nate ('niːəʊˌneɪt) *n.* a newborn child. —ˌ**ne·o·'na·tal** *adj.*

ne·on lamp *n.* a glass bulb or tube containing neon at low pressure that gives a pink or red glow when a voltage is applied.

ne·o·or·tho·dox·y (ˌniːəʊ'ɔːθəˌdɒksɪ) *n.* a movement in 20th-century Protestantism, reasserting certain older traditional Christian doctrines. —ˌ**ne·o-'or·tho·dox** *adj.*

ne·o·phyte ('niːəʊˌfaɪt) *n.* **1.** a person newly converted to a religious faith. **2.** *R.C. Church.* a novice in a religious order. **3.** a novice or beginner. [C16: via Church Latin from New Testament Greek *neophutos* recently planted, from *néos* new + *phuton* a plant] —**ne·o·phyt·ic** (ˌniːəʊ'fɪtɪk) *adj.*

ne·o·plasm ('niːəʊˌplæzəm) *n. Pathol.* any abnormal new growth of tissue; tumour. —**ne·o·plas·tic** (ˌniːəʊ'plæstɪk) *adj.*

ne·o·plas·ti·cism (ˌniːəʊ'plæstɪˌsɪzəm) *n.* the style of abstract painting evolved by Mondrian and the Dutch de Stijl movement, characterized by the use of horizontal and vertical lines and planes and by black, white, grey, and primary colours.

ne·o·plas·ty ('niːəʊˌplæstɪ) *n.* the surgical formation of new tissue structures or repair of damaged structures.

Ne·o-Pla·to·nism (ˌniːəʊ'pleɪtəˌnɪzəm) *n.* a philosophical system of the 3rd century A.D. combining elements of the Greek Judeo-Christian and Eastern traditions. —**Ne·o-Pla·ton·ic** (ˌniːəʊplə'tɒnɪk) *adj.* —ˌ**Ne·o-'Pla·to·nist** *n.*

ne·o·prene ('niːəʊˌpriːn) *n.* a synthetic rubber obtained by the polymerization of chloroprene. It is resistant to oil and ageing and is used in waterproof products, such as diving suits, paints, and adhesives. [C20: from NEO- + PR(OPYL) + -ENE]

Ne·op·tol·e·mus (ˌniːɒp'tɒləməs) *n. Greek myth.* a son of Achilles and slayer of King Priam of Troy. Also called: **Pyrrhus.**

Ne·o·scho·las·ti·cism (ˌniːəʊskə'læstɪˌsɪzəm) *n.* a revival of scholasticism that attempts to adapt it to the needs of modern life. —ˌ**Ne·o·scho·'las·tic** *adj.*

ne·ot·e·ny (nɪ'ɒtənɪ) *n.* the persistence of larval features in the adult form of an animal. For example, the adult axolotl, a salamander, retains larval external gills. See also **paedogenesis.** [C19: from New Latin *neotenia,* from Greek NEO- + *teinein* to stretch] —**ne·'ot·e·nous** *adj.*

ne·o·ter·ic (ˌniːəʊ'tɛrɪk) *Rare.* ~*adj.* **1.** belonging to a new fashion or trend; modern: *a neoteric genre.* ~*n.* **2.** a new writer or philosopher. [C16: via Late Latin from Greek *neōterikos* young, fresh, from *neoteros* younger, more recent, from *neos* new, recent] —ˌ**ne·o·'ter·i·cal·ly** *adv.*

Ne·o·trop·i·cal (ˌniːəʊ'trɒpɪkᵊl) *adj.* of or denoting a zoogeographical region consisting of South America and North America south of the tropic of Cancer.

ne·o·type ('niːəʊˌtaɪp) *n. Biology.* a specimen selected to replace a type specimen that has been lost or destroyed.

Ne·o·zo·ic (ˌniːəʊ'zəʊɪk) *adj.* of or formed at any time after the end of the Mesozoic era.

N.E.P. *abbrev. for* New Economic Policy.

Ne·pal (nɪ'pɔːl) *n.* a kingdom in S Asia: the world's only Hindu kingdom; united in 1768 by the Gurkhas; consists of swampy jungle in the south and great massifs, valleys, and gorges of the Himalayas over the rest of the country, with many peaks over 8000 m (26 000 ft.) (notably Everest and Kanchenjunga). Official language: Nepali. Religion: Hindu and Mahayana Buddhist. Currency: rupee. Capital: Katmandu. Pop.: 11 555 983 (1971). Area: 140 797 sq. km (54 362 sq. miles). —**Nep·a·lese** (ˌnɛpə'liːz) *adj., n.*

Ne·pal·i (nɪ'pɔːlɪ) *n.* **1.** the official language of Nepal, also spoken in Sikkim and parts of India. It forms the E group of Pahari and belongs to the Indic branch of Indo-European. **2.** a native or inhabitant of Nepal; a Nepalese. ~*adj.* **3.** of or relating to Nepal, its inhabitants, or their language; Nepalese.

ne·pen·the (nɪ'pɛnθɪ) *n.* **1.** a drug, or the plant providing it, that ancient writers referred to as a means of forgetting grief or trouble. **2.** anything that produces sleep, forgetfulness, or pleasurable dreaminess. [C16: via Latin from Greek *nēpenthes* sedative made from a herb, from *nē-* not + *penthos* grief] —**ne·'pen·the·an** *adj.*

ne·per ('neɪpə, 'niː-) *n.* a unit expressing the ratio of two quantities, esp. amplitudes in telecommunications, equal to the natural logarithm of the ratio of the two quantities. Symbol: Np, N [C20: named after John NAPIER (1550–1617); the name was approved in 1928]

neph·e·line ('nɛfɪlɪn, -ˌliːn) *or* **neph·e·lite** ('nɛfɪˌlaɪt) *n.* a whitish mineral consisting of sodium potassium aluminium silicate in hexagonal crystalline form: used in the manufacture of glass and ceramics. Formula: $(Na,K)(AlSi)_2O_4$. [C19: from French *néphéline,* from Greek *nephelē* cloud, so called because pieces of it become cloudy if dipped in nitric acid]

neph·e·lin·ite ('nɛfɪlɪˌnaɪt) *n.* a fine-grained basic laval rock consisting of pyroxene and nepheline.

neph·e·lom·e·ter (ˌnɛfɪ'lɒmɪtə) *n. Chem.* an instrument for measuring the size or density of particles suspended in a fluid. —**neph·e·lo·me·tric** (ˌnɛfɪləʊ'mɛtrɪk) *adj.* —ˌ**neph·e·'lom·e·try** *n.*

neph·ew ('nɛvjuː, 'nɛf-) *n.* a son of one's sister or brother. [C13: from Old French *neveu,* from Latin *nepōs;* related to Old English *nefa,* Old High German *nevo* relative]

neph·o·gram ('nɛfəˌgræm) *n. Meteorol.* a photograph of a cloud.

neph·o·graph ('nɛfəˌgrɑːf, -ˌgræf) *n.* an instrument for photographing clouds.

ne·phol·o·gy (nɪ'fɒlədʒɪ) *n.* the study of clouds. —**neph·o·log·i·cal** (ˌnɛfə'lɒdʒɪkᵊl) *adj.* —**ne·'phol·o·gist** *n.*

neph·o·scope ('nɛfəˌskəʊp) *n.* an instrument for measuring the altitude, velocity, and direction of movement of clouds.

ne·phral·gi·a (nɪˈfrældʒɪə) *n.* pain in a kidney. —**neˈphral·gic** *adj.*

ne·phrec·to·my (nɪˈfrɛktəmɪ) *n., pl.* **·mies.** surgical removal of a kidney.

ne·phrid·i·um (nɪˈfrɪdɪəm) *n., pl.* **·i·a** (-ɪə). a simple excretory organ of many invertebrates, consisting of a tube through which waste products pass to the exterior. [C19: New Latin: little kidney] —**neˈphrid·i·al** *adj.*

neph·rite (ˈnɛfraɪt) *n.* a tough fibrous amphibole mineral: a variety of jade consisting of calcium magnesium silicate in monoclinic crystalline form. Formula: $Ca_2Mg_5Si_8O_{22}(OH)_2$. [C18: via German *Nephrit* from Greek *nephrós* kidney, so called because it was thought to be beneficial in kidney disorders]

ne·phrit·ic (nɪˈfrɪtɪk) *adj.* **1.** of or relating to the kidneys. **2.** relating to or affected with nephritis.

ne·phri·tis (nɪˈfraɪtɪs) *n.* inflammation of a kidney.

neph·ro- *or before a vowel* **nephr-** *combining form.* kidney or kidneys: *nephrotomy.* [from Greek *nephros*]

neph·ron (ˈnɛfrɒn) *n.* any of the minute urine-secreting tubules that form the functional unit of the kidneys.

ne·phro·sis (nɪˈfrəʊsɪs) *n.* any noninflammatory degenerative kidney disease. —**ne·phrot·ic** (nɪˈfrɒtɪk) *adj.*

ne·phrot·o·my (nɪˈfrɒtəmɪ) *n., pl.* **·mies.** surgical incision into a kidney.

ne·pit (ˈniːpɪt) *n.* another word for **nit**[4].

ne plus ul·tra *Latin.* (ˈneɪ ˈplʊs ˈʊltrɑː) *n.* the extreme or perfect point or state. [literally: not more beyond (that is, go no further), allegedly a warning to sailors inscribed on the Pillars of Hercules at Gibraltar]

Ne·pos (ˈniːpɒs) *n.* **Cor·ne·li·us.** ?100–?25 B.C., Roman historian and biographer; author of *De Viris illustribus.*

nep·o·tism (ˈnɛpəˌtɪzəm) *n.* favouritism shown to relatives or close friends by those with power or influence. [C17: from Italian *nepotismo,* from *nepote* NEPHEW, from the former papal practice of granting special favours to nephews or other relatives] —**ne·pot·ic** (nɪˈpɒtɪk) *or* **ˌnep·o·ˈtis·tic** *adj.* —**ˈnep·o·tist** *n.*

Nep·tune[1] (ˈnɛptjuːn) *n.* the Roman god of the sea. Greek counterpart: **Poseidon.**

Nep·tune[2] (ˈnɛptjuːn) *n.* the eighth planet from the sun, having two satellites, Triton and Nereid. Mean distance from sun: 4497 million km; period of revolution around sun: 164.8 years; period of rotation: 15.8 hours; diameter and mass: 3.5 and 17.46 times that of earth respectively.

Nep·tu·ni·an (nɛpˈtjuːnɪən) *adj.* **1.** of or relating to Neptune or the sea. **2.** of, occurring on, or relating to the planet Neptune. **3.** *Geology.* (of sedimentary rock formations such as dykes) formed under water.

nep·tu·ni·um (nɛpˈtjuːnɪəm) *n.* a silvery metallic transuranic element synthesized in the production of plutonium and occurring in trace amounts in uranium ores. Symbol: Np; atomic no.: 93; half-life of most stable isotope, ^{237}Np: 2.14×10^6 years; valency: 3, 4, 5, or 6; relative density: 20.25; melting pt.: 640°C; boiling pt.: 3902°C (est.).

nep·tu·ni·um se·ries *n.* a radioactive series that starts with plutonium-241 and ends with bismuth-209. Neptunium-237 is the longest-lived member of the series.

ne·ral (ˈnɪəræl) *n. Chem.* the *trans-* isomer of citral.

N.E.R.C. *abbrev. for* Natural Environment Research Council.

Ne·re·id[1] (ˈnɪərɪɪd) *n., pl.* **Ne·re·i·des** (nəˈriːəˌdiːz). *Greek myth.* any of the 50 sea nymphs who were the daughters of the sea god Nereus. [C17: via Latin from Greek *Nērēid,* from NEREUS; compare Latin *nāre* to swim]

Ne·re·id[2] (ˈnɪərɪɪd) *n.* one of the two natural satellites of the planet Neptune. It is the smaller of the two, and the more distant from the planet. Compare **Triton**[2].

ne·re·is (ˈnɪərɪɪs) *n.* any polychaete worm of the genus *Nereis.* See **ragworm.** [C18: from Latin; see NEREID[1]]

Ne·re·us (ˈnɪərɪˌuːs) *n. Greek myth.* a sea god who lived in the depths of the sea with his wife Doris and their daughters the Nereides.

Ne·ri (ˈnɪərɪ) *n.* Saint **Phil·ip.** Italian name *Filippo de' Neri.* 1515–95, Italian priest; founder of the Congregation of the Oratory (1564). Feast day: May 26.

ne·rit·ic (nɛˈrɪtɪk) *adj.* of or formed in the region of shallow seas near a coastline. [C20: perhaps from Latin *nērīta* sea mussel, from Greek *nēritēs,* from NEREUS]

Nernst (*German* nɛrnst) *n.* **Wal·ther Her·mann** (ˈvaltər ˈhɛrman). 1864–1941, German physical chemist who formulated the third law of thermodynamics: Nobel prize for chemistry 1920.

Nernst heat the·o·rem (nɛənst) *n.* the principle that reactions in crystalline solids involve changes in entropy that tend to zero as the temperature approaches absolute zero. See **law of thermodynamics** (sense 1).

Ne·ro (ˈnɪərəʊ) *n.* full name *Nero Claudius Caesar Drusus Germanicus;* original name *Lucius Domitius Ahenobarbus,* 37–68 A.D., Roman emperor (54–68). He became notorious for his despotism and cruelty, and was alleged to have started the fire (64) that destroyed a large part of Rome.

ner·o·li oil *or* **ner·o·li** (ˈnɪərəlɪ) *n.* a brown oil distilled from the flowers of various orange trees, esp. the Seville orange: used in perfumery. [C17: named after Anne Marie de la Tremoïlle of *Neroli,* French-born Italian princess believed to have discovered it]

Ne·ru·da (*Spanish* neˈruða) *n.* **Pa·blo** (ˈpaβlo). pen name of *Neftalí Ricardo Reyes,* 1904–73, Chilean poet. His works include *Veinte poemas de amor y una canción desesperada* (1924) and *Canto general* (1950), an epic history of the Americas: Nobel prize for literature 1971.

Ner·va (ˈnɜːvə) *n.* full name *Marcus Cocceius Nerva.* ?30–98 A.D., Roman emperor (96–98), who introduced some degree of freedom after the repressive reign of Domitian. He adopted Trajan as his son and successor.

Ner·val (*French* nɛrˈval) *n.* **Gé·rard de** (ʒeˈraːr də). pseudonym of *Gérard Labrunie.* 1808–55, French poet, noted esp. for the sonnets of mysticism, myth, and private passion in *Les Chimères* (1854).

ner·vate (ˈnɜːveɪt) *adj.* (of leaves) having veins.

ner·va·tion (nɜːˈveɪʃən) *or* **ner·va·ture** (ˈnɜːvətʃə) *n.* a less common word for **venation.**

nerve (nɜːv) *n.* **1.** any of the cordlike bundles of fibres that conduct sensory or motor impulses between the brain or spinal cord and another part of the body. **2.** courage, bravery, or steadfastness. **3. lose one's nerve.** to become timid, esp. failing to perform some audacious act. **4.** *Informal.* boldness or effrontery; impudence: *he had the nerve to swear at me.* **5.** muscle or sinew (often in the phrase **strain every nerve**). **6.** a large vein in a leaf. **7.** any of the veins of an insect's wing. ~*vb.* (*tr.*) **8.** to give courage to (oneself); steel (oneself). **9.** to provide with nerve or nerves. [C16: from Latin *nervus;* related to Greek *neuron;* compare Sanskrit *snāvan* sinew]

nerve cell *n.* another name for **neuron.**

nerve cen·tre *n.* **1.** a group of nerve cells associated with a specific function. **2.** a principal source of control over any complex activity: *Wall Street is the financial nerve centre of America.*

nerve fi·bre *n.* a threadlike extension of a nerve cell; axon.

nerve gas *n.* (esp. in chemical warfare) any of various poisonous gases that have a paralysing effect on the central nervous system that can be fatal.

nerve im·pulse *n.* the electrical wave transmitted along a nerve fibre, usually following stimulation of the nerve-cell body. See also **action potential.**

nerve·less (ˈnɜːvlɪs) *adj.* **1.** calm and collected. **2.** listless or feeble. —**ˈnerve·less·ly** *adv.* —**ˈnerve·less·ness** *n.*

nerve-rack·ing *or* **nerve-wrack·ing** *adj.* very distressing, exhausting, or harrowing.

nerves (nɜːvz) *pl. n. Informal.* **1.** the imagined source of emotional control: *my nerves won't stand it.* **2.** anxiety, tension, or imbalance: *she's all nerves.* **3. bundle of nerves.** *Informal.* a very nervous person. **4. get on one's nerves.** to irritate, annoy, or upset one.

nerv·ine (ˈnɜːviːn) *adj.* **1.** having a soothing or calming effect upon the nerves. ~*n.* **2.** a nervine drug or agent. [C17: from New Latin *nervīnus,* from Latin *nervus* NERVE]

nerv·ing (ˈnɜːvɪŋ) *n. Vet. science.* surgical removal of part of a nerve trunk, usually because of chronic and disabling inflammation.

nerv·ous (ˈnɜːvəs) *adj.* **1.** very excitable or sensitive; highly strung. **2.** (often foll. by *of*) apprehensive or worried: *I'm nervous of traffic.* **3.** of, relating to, or containing nerves; neural: *nervous tissue.* **4.** affecting the nerves or nervous tissue: *a nervous disease.* **5.** *Archaic.* active, vigorous, or forceful. —**ˈnerv·ous·ly** *adv.* —**ˈnerv·ous·ness** *n.*

nerv·ous break·down *n.* (*not in technical use*) a psychiatric illness characterized by irritability, depression, fatigue, insomnia, and nonspecific or ill-defined physical complaints. Former name: **neurasthenia.**

nerv·ous sys·tem *n.* the sensory and control apparatus of all multicellular animals above the level of sponges, consisting of a network of nerve cells (see **neuron**). See also **central nervous system.**

ner·vure (ˈnɜːvjʊə) *n.* **1.** *Entomol.* any of the stiff chitinous rods that form the supporting framework of an insect's wing; vein. **2.** *Botany.* any of the veins or ribs of a leaf. [C19: from French; see NERVE, -URE]

nerv·y (ˈnɜːvɪ) *adj.* **nerv·i·er, nerv·i·est. 1.** *Brit. informal.* tense or apprehensive. **2.** having or needing bravery or endurance. **3.** *U.S. informal.* brash or cheeky. **4.** *Archaic.* muscular; sinewy. —**ˈnerv·i·ly** *adv.* —**ˈnerv·i·ness** *n.*

nes·ci·ence (ˈnɛsɪəns) *n.* **1.** a formal or literary word for **ignorance. 2.** *Rare.* lack of religious belief; agnosticism. [C17: from Late Latin *nescientia,* from Latin *nescīre* to be ignorant of, from *ne* not + *scīre* to know; compare SCIENCE] —**ˈnes·ci·ent** *adj.*

nesh (nɛʃ) *adj. Brit. dialect.* **1.** sensitive to the cold. **2.** timid or cowardly. [from Old English *hnesce;* related to Gothic *hnasqus* tender, soft; of obscure origin]

ness (nɛs) *n.* **a.** *Archaic.* a promontory or headland. **b.** (*cap. as part of a name*): *Orford Ness.* [Old English *næs* headland; related to Old Norse *nes,* Old English *nasu* NOSE]

Ness (nɛs) *n.* **Loch.** a lake in NW Scotland, in the Great Glen: said to be inhabited by a legendary aquatic monster. Length: 36 km (22.5 miles). Depth: 229 m (754 ft.).

-ness *suffix forming nouns chiefly from adjectives and participles.* indicating state, condition, or quality, or an instance of one of these: *greatness; selfishness; meaninglessness; a kindness.* [Old English *-nes,* of Germanic origin; related to Gothic *-nassus*]

nes·sel·rode (ˈnɛsəlˌrəʊd) *n.* a rich frozen pudding, made of chestnuts, eggs, cream, etc. [C19: named after Count NESSELRODE, whose chef invented the dish]

Nes·sel·rode (ˈnɛsəlˌrəʊd; *Russian* nɪsɪlˈrɔdə) *n.* Count **Karl Rob·ert.** 1780–1862, Russian diplomat: as foreign minister (1822–56), he negotiated the Treaty of Paris after the Crimean War (1856).

Nes·sus ('nɛsəs) *n. Greek myth.* a centaur that killed Hercules. A garment dipped in its blood fatally poisoned Hercules, who had been given it by Deianira who thought it was a love charm.

nest (nɛst) *n.* **1.** a place or structure in which birds, fishes, insects, reptiles, mice, etc., lay eggs or give birth to young. **2.** a number of animals of the same species and their young occupying a common habitat: *an ants' nest.* **3.** a place fostering something undesirable: *a nest of thievery.* **4.** the people in such a place: *a nest of thieves.* **5.** a cosy or secluded place. **6.** a set of things, usually of graduated sizes, designed to fit together: *a nest of tables.* **7.** *Military.* a weapon emplacement: *a machine-gun nest.* ~*vb.* **8.** (*intr.*) to make or inhabit a nest. **9.** (*intr.*) to hunt for birds' nests. **10.** (*tr.*) to place in a nest. [Old English; related to Latin *nīdus* (nest) and to BENEATH, SIT] —'**nest+er** *n.* —'**nest+,like** *adj.*

nest egg *n.* **1.** a fund of money kept in reserve; savings. **2.** a natural or artificial egg left in a nest to induce hens to lay their eggs in it.

nes+tle ('nɛsᵊl) *vb.* **1.** (*intr.;* often foll. by *up* or *down*) to snuggle, settle, or cuddle closely. **2.** (*intr.*) to be in a sheltered or protected position; lie snugly. **3.** (*tr.*) to shelter or place snugly or partly concealed, as in a nest. [Old English *nestlian.* See NEST] —'**nes+tler** *n.*

nest+ling ('nɛstlɪŋ, 'nɛslɪŋ) *n.* **1. a.** a young bird not yet fledged. **b.** (*as modifier*): *a nestling thrush.* **2.** any young person or animal. [C14: from NEST + -LING¹]

Nes·tor ('nɛstɔː) *n.* **1.** *Greek myth.* the oldest and wisest of the Greeks in the Trojan War. **2.** (*sometimes not cap.*) a wise old man; sage.

Nes+to+ri+an+ism (nɛ'stɔːrɪəˌnɪzəm) *n.* the doctrine that Christ was two distinct persons, divine and human, implying a denial that the Virgin Mary was the mother of God. It is attributed to the heresiarch Nestorius and survives in the Iraqi Church. —**Nes+'to+ri+an** *n., adj.*

Nes·to·ri·us (nɛ'stɔːrɪəs) *n.* died ?451 A.D., Syrian churchman; patriarch of Constantinople (428–431). —**Nes+'to+ri+an** *adj.*

net¹ (nɛt) *n.* **1.** an openwork fabric of string, rope, wire, etc.; mesh. **2.** a device made of net, used to protect or enclose things or to trap animals. **3. a.** a thin light mesh fabric of cotton, nylon, or other fibre, used for curtains, dresses, etc. **b.** (*as modifier*): *net curtains.* **4.** a plan, strategy, etc., intended to trap or ensnare: *the murderer slipped through the police net.* **5.** *Tennis, badminton, etc.* **a.** a strip of net that divides the playing area into two equal parts. **b.** a shot that hits the net, whether or not it goes over. **6.** the goal in soccer, hockey, etc. **7.** (*often pl.*) *Cricket.* **a.** a pitch surrounded by netting, used for practice. **b.** a practice session in a net. **8.** another word for **network** (sense 2). ~*vb.* **nets, net+ting, net+ted. 9.** (*tr.*) to catch with or as if with a net; ensnare. **10.** (*tr.*) to shelter or surround with a net. **11.** (*intr.*) *Tennis, badminton, etc.* to hit a shot into the net. **12.** to make a net out of (rope, string, etc.). [Old English *net;* related to Gothic *nati,* Dutch *net*]

net² *or* **nett** (nɛt) *adj.* **1.** remaining after all deductions, as for taxes, expenses, losses, etc.: *net profit.* Compare **gross** (sense 2). **2.** (of weight) after deducting tare. **3.** ultimate; final; conclusive (esp. in the phrase **net result**). ~*n.* **4.** net income, profits, weight, etc. ~*vb.* **nets, net+ting, net+ted. 5.** (*tr.*) to yield or earn as clear profit. [C14: clean, neat, from French *net* NEAT; related to Dutch *net,* German *nett*]

Ne+ta+ji ('neɪtɑːdʒɪ) *n.* the title for Subhash Chandra **Bose.** [Hindi, from *neta* leader + -JI]

net+ball ('nɛtˌbɔl) *n.* a team game similar to basketball played mainly by women. —'**net+,ball+er** *n.*

net do·mes·tic prod+uct *n. Econ.* the gross domestic product minus an allowance for the depreciation of capital goods.

Neth. *abbrev. for* Netherlands.

neth+er ('nɛðə) *adj.* placed or situated below, beneath, or underground: *nether regions; a nether lip.* [Old English *niothera, nithera,* literally: further down, from *nither* down. Related to Old Irish *nitaram,* German *nieder*]

Neth+er+lands ('nɛðələndz) *n.* **the. 1.** Also called: **Holland.** a kingdom in NW Europe, on the North Sea: declared independence from Spain in 1581 as the United Provinces; became a major maritime and commercial power in the 17th century, gaining many overseas possessions; a member of the Common Market. It is mostly flat and low-lying, with about 40 per cent of the land being below sea level, much of it on polders protected by dykes. Language: Dutch. Religion: Christian majority, with both Protestant and Roman Catholic Churches. Currency: guilder. Capital: Amsterdam, with the seat of government at The Hague. Pop.: 13 541 000 (1974 est.). Area: 40 883 sq. km (15 785 sq. miles). Dutch name: **Nederland. 2.** the kingdom of the Netherlands together with the Flemish-speaking part of Belgium, esp. as ruled by Spain and Austria before 1581; the Low Countries. —**Neth+er+land+er** ('nɛðəˌlændə) *n.*

Neth+er+lands An+til+les *pl. n.* **the.** two groups of islands in the Caribbean, in the Lesser Antilles: overseas division of the Netherlands, consisting of the S group of Curaçao, Aruba, and Bonaire, and the N group of St. Eustatius, Saba, and the S part of St. Martin; economy based on refining oil from Venezuela. Capital: Willemstad (on Curaçao). Pop.: 230 824 (1972 est.). Area: 996 sq. km (390 sq. miles). Former names: **Curaçao** (until 1949), **Dutch West Indies, Netherlands West Indies.**

Neth+er+lands East In+dies *n.* **the.** a former name (1798–1945) for **Indonesia.**

Neth+er+lands Gui+an·a *n.* a former name for **Surinam.**

Neth+er+lands West In+dies *n.* **the.** a former name for the **Netherlands Antilles.**

neth·er·most ('nɛðəˌməʊst) *determiner.* **the.** farthest down; lowest.

neth+er world *n.* **1.** the world after death; the underworld. **2.** hell. ~Also called: **nether regions.**

net na+tion+al prod+uct *n.* gross national product minus an allowance for the depreciation of capital goods.

Ne·to ('nɛtəʊ) *n.* **An·to·ni·o (Agostinho).** 1922-79, Angolan statesman; president of the People's Republic of Angola 1975-1979.

net prof+it *n.* gross profit minus all operating costs not included in the calculation of gross profit, esp. wages, overheads, and depreciation.

net+su+ke ('nɛtsʊkɪ) *n.* (in Japan) a carved toggle, esp. of wood or ivory, originally used to tether a medicine box worn dangling from the waist. [C19: from Japanese]

nett (nɛt) *adj., n., vb.* a variant spelling of **net**².

net+ting ('nɛtɪŋ) *n.* any netted fabric or structure.

net+tle ('nɛtᵊl) *n.* **1.** any weedy plant of the temperate urticaceous genus *Urtica,* such as *U. dioica* (**stinging nettle**), having serrated leaves with stinging hairs and greenish flowers. **2.** any of various other urticaceous plants with stinging hairs or spines. **3.** any of various plants that resemble urticaceous nettles, such as the dead-nettle, hemp nettle, and horse nettle. **4. grasp the nettle.** to attempt or approach something with boldness and courage. ~*vb.* (*tr.*) **5.** to bother; irritate. **6.** to sting as a nettle does. [Old English *netele;* related to Old High German *nazza* (German *Nessel*)] —'**net+tle-,like** *adj.* —'**net+tly** *adj.*

net+tle rash *n.* a nontechnical name for **urticaria.**

net+tle+some ('nɛtᵊlsəm) *adj.* causing or susceptible to irritation.

net ton *n.* the full name for **ton**¹ (sense 2).

net+ty ('nɛtɪ) *n., pl.* **+ties.** *Northeast English dialect.* a lavatory, originally an earth closet. [of obscure origin]

net+work ('nɛtˌwɜːk) *n.* **1.** an interconnected group or system: *a network of shops.* **2.** a system of intersecting lines, roads, veins, etc. **3.** another name for **net** (sense 1) or **netting. 4.** *Radio.* a group of broadcasting stations that all transmit the same programme simultaneously. **5.** *Electronics.* a system of interconnected components or circuits.

Neu+bran+den+burg (*German* ˌnɔɪ'brandᵊnˌbʊrk) *n.* a city in N East Germany: 14th-century city walls. Pop.: 52 998 (1972 est.).

Neu+châ+tel (*French* nøʃɑ'tɛl) *n.* **1.** a canton in the Jura Mountains of NW Switzerland. Capital: Neuchâtel. Pop.: 169 173 (1970). Area: 798 sq. km (308 sq. miles). **2.** a town in W Switzerland, capital of Neuchâtel canton, on Lake Neuchâtel: until 1848 the seat of the last hereditary rulers in Switzerland. Pop.: 38 784 (1970). **3. Lake.** a lake in W Switzerland: the largest lake wholly in Switzerland. Area: 216 sq. km (83 sq. miles). ~German name (for senses 1 and 2): **Neu+en+burg** ('nɔɪənˌbʊrk).

Neuf+châ+tel (*French* nøʃɑ'tɛl) *n.* a soft creamy whole milk cheese, similar to cream cheese. [named after *Neufchâtel,* town in N France where it is made]

Neuil·ly-sur-Seine (*French* nœji syr 'sɛn) *n.* a town in N France, on the Seine: a suburb of NW Paris. Pop.: 66 095 (1975).

Neu+mann (*German* 'nɔɪman) *n.* **1. Jo·hann Bal·tha·sar** ('joːhan 'baltazar). 1687–1753, German rococo architect. His masterpiece is the church of Vierzehnheiligen in Bavaria. **2.** See (John) **von Neumann.**

neume *or* **neum** (njuːm) *n. Music.* one of a series of notational symbols used before the 14th century. [C15: from Medieval Latin *neuma* group of notes sung on one breath, from Greek *pneuma* breath] —'**neum+ic** *adj.*

Neu+mün+ster (*German* ˌnɔɪ'mynstər) *n.* a town in N West Germany, in Schleswig-Holstein: manufacturing of textiles and machinery. Pop.: 86 100 (1970).

neu+ral ('njʊərəl) *adj.* of or relating to a nerve or the nervous system. —'**neu+ral+ly** *adv.*

neu+ral+gia (njʊ'rældʒə) *n.* severe spasmodic pain along the course of one or more nerves. —**neu+'ral+gic** *adj.*

neu+ras+the+ni·a (ˌnjʊərəs'θiːnɪə) *n.* an obsolete technical term for **nervous breakdown.** —**neu+ras+then+ic** (ˌnjʊərəs'θɛnɪk) *adj.* —ˌ**neu+ras+'then+i+cal+ly** *adv.*

neu+rec+to+my (njʊ'rɛktəmɪ) *n., pl.* **+mies.** the surgical removal of a nerve segment.

neu+ri+lem+ma (ˌnjʊərɪ'lɛmə) *n.* a variant spelling of **neurolemma.** [C19: from French *névrilème,* from Greek *neuron* nerve + *eilēma* covering, but influenced also by Greek *lemma* husk]

neu+ri+tis (njʊ'raɪtɪs) *n.* inflammation of a nerve or nerves, often accompanied by pain and loss of function in the affected part. —**neu+rit+ic** (njʊ'rɪtɪk) *adj.*

neu+ro- *or before a vowel* **neur-** *combining form.* indicating a nerve or the nervous system: *neuroblast; neurology.* [from Greek *neuron* nerve; related to Latin *nervus*]

neu+ro+blast ('njʊərəʊˌblæst) *n.* an embryonic nerve cell.

neu+ro+coele ('njʊərəˌsiːl) *n. Embryol.* a cavity in the embryonic brain and spinal cord that develops into the ventricles and central canal respectively.

neu+ro+fi+bril (ˌnjʊərəʊ'faɪbrɪl) *n.* any of the delicate threads within the body of a nerve cell that extend into the axon and dendrites. —ˌ**neu+ro+'fi+bri+lar** *adj.*

neu+ro+gen+ic (ˌnjʊərəʊ'dʒɛnɪk) *adj.* originating in or stimulated by the nervous system or nerve impulses.

neu+rog+li·a (njʊ'rɒglɪə) *n.* the delicate web of connective tissue that surrounds and supports nerve cells. [C19: from NEURO- + Late Greek *glia* glue]

neu·ro·gram (ˈnjʊərəʊˌɡræm) *n. Psychol.* another word for **engram.**

neu·ro·hy·poph·y·sis (ˌnjʊərəʊhaɪˈpɒfɪsɪs) *n., pl.* **·ses** (-ˌsiːz). the posterior lobe of the pituitary gland. Compare **adenohypophysis.**

neurol. *abbrev. for* neurology.

neu·ro·lem·ma (ˌnjʊərəʊˈlɛmə) *n.* the thin membrane that forms a sheath around nerve fibres. Also called: **neurilemma.** [C19: New Latin, from NEURO- + Greek *eilēma* covering]

neu·rol·o·gy (njʊˈrɒlədʒɪ) *n.* the study of the anatomy, physiology, and diseases of the nervous system. —**neu·ro·log·i·cal** (ˌnʊərəˈlɒdʒɪkᵊl) *adj.* —**neu·ˈrol·o·gist** *n.*

neu·ro·ma (njʊˈrəʊmə) *n., pl.* **·ma·ta** (-mətə) *or* **·mas.** any tumour composed of nerve tissue. —**neu·rom·a·tous** (njʊˈrɒmətəs) *adj.*

neu·ro·mus·cu·lar (ˌnjʊərəʊˈmʌskjʊlə) *adj.* of, relating to, or affecting nerves and muscles.

neu·ron (ˈnjʊərɒn) *or* **neu·rone** (ˈnjʊərəʊn) *n.* a cell specialized to conduct nerve impulses: consists of a cell body, axon, and dendrites. Also called: **nerve cell.** —**neu·ron·ic** (njʊˈrɒnɪk) *adj.*

neu·ro·path (ˈnjʊərəʊˌpæθ) *n.* a person suffering from or predisposed to a disorder of the nervous system.

neu·ro·pa·thol·o·gy (ˌnjʊərəʊpəˈθɒlədʒɪ) *n.* the study of diseases of the nervous system. —ˌ**neu·ro·pa·ˈthol·o·gist** *n.*

neu·rop·a·thy (njʊˈrɒpəθɪ) *n.* any disease of the nervous system. —**neu·ro·path·ic** (ˌnjʊərəʊˈpæθɪk) *adj.* —ˌ**neu·ro·ˈpath·i·cal·ly** *adv.*

neu·ro·phys·i·ol·o·gy (ˌnjʊərəʊˌfɪzɪˈɒlədʒɪ) *n.* the study of the functions of the nervous system. —**neu·ro·phys·i·o·log·i·cal** (ˌnjʊərəʊˌfɪzɪəˈlɒdʒɪkᵊl) *adj.* —ˌ**neu·ro·ˌphys·i·o·ˈlog·i·cal·ly** *adv.* —ˌ**neu·ro·ˌphys·i·ˈol·o·gist** *n.*

neu·ro·psy·chi·a·try (ˌnjʊərəʊsaɪˈkaɪətrɪ) *n.* the branch of medicine concerned with neurological and mental disorders. —**neu·ro·psy·chi·at·ric** (ˌnjʊərəʊˌsaɪkɪˈætrɪk) *adj.* —ˌ**neu·ro·psy·ˈchi·a·trist** *n.*

neu·rop·ter·an *or* **neu·rop·ter·on** (njʊˈrɒptərən) *n., pl.* **·ter·ans** *or* **·ter·a** (-tərə). any neuropterous insect.

neu·rop·ter·ous (njʊˈrɒptərəs) *or* **neu·rop·ter·an** *adj.* of, relating to, or belonging to the *Neuroptera*, an order of insects having two pairs of large much-veined wings and biting mouthparts: includes the lacewings and antlions. [C18: from New Latin *Neuroptera*; see NEURO-, -PTER]

neu·ro·sis (njʊˈrəʊsɪs) *n., pl.* **·ses** (-siːz). a relatively mild mental disorder, characterized by symptoms such as hysteria, anxiety, or obsessive behaviour. Also called: **psychoneurosis.**

neu·ro·sur·ger·y (ˌnjʊərəʊˈsɜːdʒərɪ) *n.* the branch of surgery concerned with the nervous system. —ˌ**neu·ro·ˈsur·geon** *n.* —ˌ**neu·ro·ˈsur·gi·cal** *adj.* —ˌ**neu·ro·ˈsur·gi·cal·ly** *adv.*

neu·rot·ic (njʊˈrɒtɪk) *adj.* **1.** of, relating to, or afflicted by neurosis. ~*n.* **2.** a person who is afflicted with a neurosis or who tends to be emotionally unstable or unusually anxious. —**neu·ˈrot·i·cal·ly** *adv.*

neu·rot·i·cism (njʊˈrɒtɪsɪzəm) *n.* a personality trait characterized by instability, anxiety, aggression, etc.

neu·rot·o·my (njʊˈrɒtəmɪ) *n., pl.* **·mies.** the surgical cutting of a nerve, esp. to relieve intractable pain. —**neu·ˈrot·o·mist** *n.*

neu·ro·vas·cu·lar (ˌnʊərəʊˈvæskjʊlə) *adj.* of, relating to, or affecting both the nerves and the blood vessels.

Neu·satz (ˈnɔɪzats) *n.* the German name for **Novi Sad.**

Neuss (*German* nɔɪs) *n.* an industrial city in W West Germany, in North Rhine-Westphalia west of Düsseldorf: founded as a Roman fortress in the 1st century A.D. Pop.: 118 607 (1974 est.). Latin name: **Novaesium.**

Neus·tri·a (ˈnjuːstrɪə) *n.* the western part of the kingdom of the Merovingian Franks formed in 561 A.D. in what is now N France. —**ˈNeus·tri·an** *adj.*

neut. *abbrev. for* neuter.

neu·ter (ˈnjuːtə) *adj.* **1.** *Grammar.* **a.** denoting or belonging to a gender of nouns which for the most part have inanimate referents or do not specify the sex of their referents. **b.** (*as n.*): *German "Mädchen" (meaning "girl") is a neuter.* **2.** (of animals and plants) having nonfunctional, underdeveloped, or absent reproductive organs. **3.** sexless or giving no indication of sex: *a neuter sort of name.* ~*n.* **4.** a sexually underdeveloped female insect, such as a worker bee. **5.** a castrated animal, esp. a domestic animal. **6.** a flower in which the stamens and pistil are absent or nonfunctional. ~*vb.* **7.** (*tr.*) to castrate (an animal). [C14: from Latin, from *ne* not + *uter* either (of two)]

neu·tral (ˈnjuːtrəl) *adj.* **1.** not siding with any party to a war or dispute. **2.** of, belonging to, or appropriate to a neutral party, country, etc.: *neutral land.* **3.** of no distinctive quality, characteristics, or type; indifferent. **4.** (of a colour such as white or black) having no hue; achromatic. **5.** (of a colour) dull, but harmonizing with most other colours. **6.** a less common term for **neuter** (sense 2). **7.** *Chem.* neither acidic nor alkaline. **8.** *Physics.* having zero charge or potential. **9.** *Rare.* having no magnetism. **10.** *Phonetics.* (of a vowel) articulated with the tongue relaxed in mid-central position and the lips midway between spread and rounded: *the word "about" begins with a neutral vowel.* ~*n.* **11.** a neutral person, nation, etc. **12.** a citizen of a neutral state. **13.** the position of the controls of a gearbox that leaves the transmission disengaged. [C16: from Latin *neutrālis*; see NEUTER] —**ˈneu·tral·ly** *adv.*

neu·tral·ism (ˈnjuːtrəˌlɪzəm) *n.* (in international affairs) the policy, practice, or attitude of neutrality, noninvolvement, or nonalignment with power blocs. —**ˈneu·tral·ist** *n., adj.*

neu·tral·i·ty (njuːˈtrælɪtɪ) *n.* **1.** the state or character of being neutral, esp. in a dispute, contest, etc. **2.** the condition of being chemically or electrically neutral.

neu·tral·ize *or* **neu·tral·ise** (ˈnjuːtrəˌlaɪz) *vb.* (*mainly tr.*) **1.** (*also intr.*) to render or become ineffective or neutral by counteracting, mixing, etc.; nullify. **2.** to make or become electrically or chemically neutral. **3.** to exclude (a country) from the sphere of warfare or alliances by international agreement: *the great powers neutralized Belgium in the 19th century.* **4.** to render (an army, etc.) incapable of further military action. —ˌ**neu·tral·i·ˈza·tion** *or* ˌ**neu·tral·i·ˈsa·tion** *n.* —**ˈneu·tral·ˌiz·er** *or* **ˈneu·tral·ˌis·er** *n.*

neu·tral spir·its *n. U.S.* ethanol of more than 190° proof.

neu·tret·to (njuːˈtrɛtəʊ) *n., pl.* **·tos.** *Physics.* a hypothetical uncharged particle having the same mass as an electron.

neu·tri·no (njuːˈtriːnəʊ) *n., pl.* **·nos.** *Physics.* a stable leptonic neutral elementary particle with zero rest mass and spin $\frac{1}{2}$ that travels at the speed of light. Two types exist, one being produced with positrons in neutron decay and the other with positive muons in pion decay. [C20: from Italian, diminutive of *neutrone* NEUTRON]

neu·tron (ˈnjuːtrɒn) *n. Physics.* a neutral elementary particle with a rest mass of $1.674\,82 \times 10^{-27}$ kilogram and spin $\frac{1}{2}$; classified as a baryon. In the nucleus of an atom it is stable but when free it decays. [C20: from NEUTRAL, on the model of ELECTRON]

neu·tron bomb *n.* a type of nuclear weapon designed to provide a high yield of neutrons but to cause little blast or long-lived radioactive contamination. The neutrons destroy all life in the target area.

neu·tron num·ber *n.* the number of neutrons in the nucleus of an atom. Symbol: *N*

neu·tron star *n.* a star that has collapsed under its own gravity. It is composed solely of neutrons, has a mass of between 1.4 and about 3 times that of the sun, and a density in excess of 10^7 kilograms per cubic metre.

neu·tro·phil (ˈnjuːtrəfɪl) *or* **neu·tro·phile** (ˈnjuːtrəˌfaɪl) *n.* **1.** Also called: **polymorph.** a leucocyte having a lobed nucleus and a fine granular cytoplasm, which stains with neutral dyes. ~*adj.* **2.** (of cells and tissues) readily stainable by neutral dyes.

Nev. *abbrev. for* Nevada.

Ne·va (ˈniːvə; *Russian* nɪˈva) *n.* a river in the NW Soviet Union, flowing west to the Gulf of Finland by the delta on which Leningrad stands. Length: 74 km (46 miles).

Ne·va·da (nɪˈvɑːdə) *n.* a state of the western U.S.: lies almost wholly within the Great Basin, a vast desert plateau; noted for production of gold and copper. Capital: Carson City. Pop.: 488 738 (1970). Area: 284 612 sq. km (109 889 sq. miles). Abbrevs.: **Nev.** or (with zip code) **NV**

né·vé (ˈnɛveɪ) *n.* **1.** Also called: **firn.** a mass of porous ice, formed from snow, that has not yet become frozen into glacier ice. **2.** a snow field at the head of a glacier that becomes transformed to ice. [C19: from Swiss French *nevé* glacier, from Late Latin *nivātus* snow-cooled, from *nix* snow]

nev·er (ˈnɛvə) *adv., sentence substitute.* **1.** at no time; not ever. **2.** certainly not; by no means; in no case. ~*interj.* **3.** Also: **well I never!** surely not! [Old English *næfre*, from *ne* not + *æfre* EVER]

Usage. In good usage, *never* is not used with simple past tenses to mean *not* (*I was asleep at midnight, so I did not see* (not *never saw*) *her go*).

nev·er·more (ˌnɛvəˈmɔː) *adv. Literary.* never again.

nev·er-nev·er *Informal.* ~*n.* **1.** *Brit.* the hire-purchase system of buying. **2.** *Austral.* remote desert country, as that of W Queensland and central Australia. ~*adj.* **3.** imaginary; idyllic (esp. in the phrase **never-never land**).

Ne·vers (*French* nəˈvɛːr) *n.* a city in central France: capital of the former duchy of Nivernais; engineering industry. Pop.: 47 780 (1975).

nev·er·the·less (ˌnɛvəðəˈlɛs) *sentence connector.* in spite of that; however; yet.

Ne·vis *n.* **1.** (ˈniːvɪs, ˈnɛvɪs). an island in the West Indies, in the Leeward Islands: part of St. Kitts-Nevis-Anguilla; the volcanic cone of **Nevis Peak**, which rises to 1002 m (3287 ft.), lies in the centre of the island. Capital: Charlestown. Pop.: 11 230 (1970). Area: 129 sq. km (50 sq. miles). **2.** (ˈnɛvɪs). See **Ben Nevis.**

Nev·ski (ˈnɛfskɪ; *Russian* ˈnjɛfskij) *n.* See **Alexander Nevski.**

ne·vus (ˈniːvəs) *n., pl.* **·vi** (-vaɪ). the usual U.S. spelling of **naevus.**

new (njuː) *adj.* **1. a.** recently made or brought into being: *a new dress; our new baby.* **b.** (*as n.*): *the new.* **2.** of a kind never before existing; novel: *a new concept in marketing.* **3.** having existed before but only recently discovered: *a new comet.* **4.** markedly different from what was before: *the new liberalism.* **5.** fresh and unused; not second-hand: *a new car.* **6.** (*prenominal*) having just or recently become: *a new bride.* **7.** (often foll. by *to* or *at*) recently introduced (to); inexperienced (in) or unaccustomed (to): *new to this neighbourhood.* **8.** (*cap. in names or titles*) more or most recent of two or more things with the same name: *the New Testament.* **9.** (*prenominal*) fresh; additional: *I'll send some new troops.* **10.** (often foll. by *to*) unknown; novel: *this is new to me.* **11.** (of a cycle) beginning or occurring again: *a new year.* **12.** (*prenominal*) (of crops) harvested early: *new carrots.* **13.** changed, esp. for the better: *she returned a new woman from her holiday.* **14.** up-to-date; fashionable. **15.** (*cap. when part of a name*) (*prenominal*) being the most recent, usually living, form of a language: *New High German.* **16. turn over a new leaf.** to reform; make a fresh start. ~*adv.* (*usually in combination*) **17.** recently, freshly: *new-laid eggs.* **18.** anew; again. [Old English *nīowe*; related to Gothic *niujis*, Old Norse *naujas*, Latin *novus*] —**ˈnew·ness** *n.*

New Am+ster+dam *n.* the Dutch settlement established on Manhattan (1624–26); capital of New Netherlands; captured by the English and renamed New York in 1664.

New+ark ('nju:ək) *n.* **1.** a town in N central England, in Nottinghamshire. Pop.: 24 631 (1971). Official name: **Newark-on-Trent.** **2.** a port in NE New Jersey, just west of New York City, on Newark Bay and the Passaic River: the largest city in the state; founded in 1666 by Puritans from Connecticut; industrial and commercial centre. Pop.: 367 683 (1973 est.).

New Bed+ford *n.* a port and resort in SE Massachusetts, near Buzzards Bay: settled by Plymouth colonists in 1652; a leading whaling port (18th–19th century). Pop.: 101 777 (1970).

new+born ('nju:ˌbɔ:n) *adj.* **1. a.** recently or just born. **b.** (*as n.*): *the newborn.* **2.** (of hope, faith, etc.) reborn.

New Brit+ain *n.* an island in the S Pacific, northeast of New Guinea: the largest island of the Bismarck Archipelago; part of Papua New Guinea; mountainous, with several active volcanoes. Capital: Rabaul. Pop.: 175 264 (1971). Area: 36 519 sq. km (14 100 sq. miles).

new broom *n. Informal.* a person in a new job, etc., eager to make changes.

New Bruns+wick *n.* a province of SE Canada on the Gulf of St. Lawrence and the Bay of Fundy: extensively forested. Capital: Fredericton. Pop.: 677 250 (1976). Area: 72 092 sq. km (27 835 sq. miles).

New+burg ('nju:bɜ:g) *adj.* (*immediately postpositive*) (of shellfish, esp. lobster) cooked in a rich sauce of butter, cream, sherry, and egg yolks. [of unknown origin]

New+bur·y ('nju:bərɪ) *n.* a market town in S England, in Berkshire: scene of a Parliamentarian victory (1643) and a Royalist victory (1644) during the Civil War; racecourse. Pop.: 25 017 (1971).

New Cal+e·do+ni·a *n.* an island in the SW Pacific, east of Australia: forms, with its dependencies, an overseas territory of France; discovered by Captain Cook in 1774; rich mineral resources. Capital: Nouméa. Pop.: 133 000 (1976 est.). Area: 19 103 sq. km (7374 miles). French name: **Nouvelle Calédonie.**

New Cas+tile *n.* a region and former province of central Spain. Chief town: Toledo.

New+cas+tle[1] ('nju:ˌkɑ:səl) *n.* a port in SE Australia, in E New South Wales near the mouth of the Hunter River: important industrial centre, with extensive steel, metalworking, engineering, shipbuilding, and chemical industries. Pop.: 363 010 (1975 est.).

New·cas·tle[2] ('nju:ˌkɑ:səl) *n.* **Duke of,** the title of *Thomas Pelham Holles.* 1693–1768, English Whig prime minister (1754–56; 1757–62).

New+cas+tle dis+ease *n.* an acute viral disease of birds, esp. poultry, characterized by pneumonia and inflammation of the central nervous system. [C20: named after *Newcastle-upon-Tyne,* where it was recorded in 1926]

New+cas·tle-un·der-Lyme *n.* a town in W central England, in Staffordshire. Pop.: 76 970 (1971). Often shortened to **Newcastle.**

New+cas·tle-up·on-Tyne *n.* a port in NE England, administrative centre of Tyne and Wear, near the mouth of the River Tyne opposite Gateshead: Roman remains; engineering and shipbuilding industries; university (1937). Pop.: 222 153 (1971). Often shortened to **Newcastle.**

New Church *n.* another name for the **New Jerusalem Church.**

New·combe ('nju:kəm) *n.* **John.** born 1944, Australian tennis player: Wimbledon champion 1967 and 1970–71; U.S. champion 1967 and 1973; Australian champion 1973 and 1975.

New·com·en ('nju:ˌkʌmən) *n.* **Thom·as.** 1663–1729, English engineer who invented a steam engine, which James Watt later modified and developed.

new+com·er ('nju:ˌkʌmə) *n.* a person who has recently arrived or started to participate in something.

new crit·i+cism *n.* an approach to literary criticism through close analysis of the text. **—new crit·ic** *n.*

New Deal *n.* **1.** the domestic policies of Franklin D. Roosevelt for economic and social reform. **2.** the period of the implementation of these policies. (1933–40). **—New Deal+er** *n.*

New Del+hi *n.* See **Delhi.**

New Dem·o·crat+ic Par+ty *n.* the Canadian social democratic party. Abbrev.: **NDP.**

New E·co+nom+ic Pol·i·cy *n.* an economic programme in the Soviet Union from 1921 to 1928, that permitted private ownership of industries, etc. Abbrev.: **N.E.P.**

new+el ('nju:əl) *n.* **1.** the central pillar of a winding staircase, esp. one that is made of stone. **2.** See **newel post.** [C14: from Old French *nouel* knob, from Medieval Latin *nōdellus,* diminutive of *nōdus* NODE]

new+el post *n.* the post at the top or bottom of a flight of stairs that supports the handrail. Sometimes shortened to **newel.**

New Eng+land *n.* **1.** the NE part of the U.S., consisting of the states of Maine, New Hampshire, Vermont, Massachusetts, Rhode Island, and Connecticut: settled originally chiefly by Puritans in the mid-17th century. **2.** a district in SE Australia, in northern New South Wales. **—New Eng+land+er** *n.*

New Eng+land Range *n.* a mountain range in SE Australia, in NE New South Wales: part of the Great Dividing Range. Highest peak: Ben Lomond, 1520 m (4986 ft.).

New Eng+lish Bi+ble *n.* a new Modern English version of the Bible and Apocrypha, published in full in 1970.

new+fan+gled ('nju:'fæŋgəld) *adj.* **1.** newly come into existence or fashion, esp. excessively modern. **2.** *Rare.* excessively fond of new ideas, fashions, etc. [C14 *newefangel* liking new things, from *new* + *-fangel,* from Old English *fōn* to take] **—'new+'fan+gled+ness** *n.*

new-fash·ioned *adj.* of or following a recent design, trend, etc.

New+fie ('nju:fɪ) *n. Informal.* **1.** a native or inhabitant of Newfoundland. **2.** the province or island of Newfoundland.

New For+est *n.* a region of woodland and heath in S England, in SW Hampshire: a hunting ground of the West Saxon kings; tourist area, noted for its ponies. Area: 336 sq. km (130 sq. miles).

New+found+land ('nju:fəndlənd, -ˌlænd, -fən-; nju:'faʊndlənd) *n.* **1.** an island of E Canada, separated from the mainland by the Strait of Belle Isle: with the Coast of Labrador forms the province of Newfoundland; consists of a rugged plateau with the Long Range Mountains in the west. Area: 110 681 sq. km (42 734 sq. miles). **2.** a province of E Canada, consisting of the island of Newfoundland and the Coast of Labrador. Capital: St. John's. Pop.: 557 725 (1976). Area: 404 519 sq. km (156 185 sq. miles). **3.** a large heavy breed of dog similar to a Saint Bernard with a flat coarse usually black coat. **—New+found+land+er** (nju:'faʊndləndə) *n.*

New France *n.* the former French colonies and possessions in North America, most of which were lost to England and Spain by 1763: often restricted to the French possessions in Canada.

New+gate ('nju:gɪt, -ˌgeɪt) *n.* a famous London prison, in use from the Middle Ages: demolished in 1902.

New Geor+gia *n.* **1.** a group of islands in the SW Pacific, in the Solomon Islands. **2.** the largest island in this group. Area: about 1300 sq. km (500 sq. miles).

New Gra+na+da *n.* **1.** a former Spanish presidency and later viceroyalty in South America. At its greatest extent it consisted of present-day Panama, Colombia, Venezuela, and Ecuador. **2.** the name of Colombia when it formed, with Panama, part of Great Colombia (1819–30).

New Guin·ea *n.* **1.** an island in the W Pacific, north of Australia: divided politically into West Irian (a province of Indonesia) in the west and Papua New Guinea in the east. There is a central chain of mountains and a lowland area of swamps in the south and along the Sepik River in the north. Pop.: 1 795 602 (1971 est.). Area: 775 213 sq. km (299 310 sq. miles). **2. Trust Territory of.** (until 1975) an administrative division of the former Territory of Papua and New Guinea, consisting of the NE part of the island of New Guinea together with the Bismarck Archipelago; now part of Papua New Guinea.

New Guin·ea mac·ro+phy+lum (ˌmækrəʊ'faɪləm) *n.* the older term for **Trans-New Guinea phylum.**

New Guin·ea Pidg+in *n.* the variety of Neo-Melanesian spoken in Papua New Guinea and neighbouring islands.

New+ham ('nju:əm) *n.* a borough of E Greater London, on the River Thames: established in 1965. Pop.: 228 900 (1976 est.).

New Hamp+shire *n.* a state of the northeastern U.S.: generally hilly. Capital: Concord. Pop.: 737 681 (1970). Area: 23 379 sq. km (9027 sq. miles). Abbrevs.: **N.H.** or (with zip code) **NH**

New Har+mo+ny *n.* a village in SW Indiana, on the Wabash River: scene of two experimental cooperative communities, the first founded in 1815 by George Rapp, a German religious leader, and the second by Robert Owen in 1825.

New+ha+ven ('nju:ˌheɪvən) *n.* a ferry port and resort on the S coast of England, in East Sussex. Pop.: 9977 (1971).

New Ha+ven *n.* an industrial city and port in S Connecticut, on Long Island Sound: settled in 1638 by English Puritans, who established it as a colony in 1643; seat of Yale University (1701). Pop.: 131 262 (1973 est.).

New Heb+ri+des *pl. n.* a group of islands in the W Pacific, west of Fiji: Anglo-French joint rule established in 1906; attained partial autonomy in 1978 and full independence in 1980. Economy based chiefly on copra. Capital: Vila (on Efate). Pop.: 97 500 (1976 est.). Area: about 14 760 sq. km (5700 sq. miles). Since 1980 called **Vanuatu.**

Ne Win ('neɪ 'wɪn) *n.* born 1911, Burmese statesman; prime minister (1958–60) and president since 1962.

New Ire+land *n.* an island in the S Pacific, in the Bismarck Archipelago, separated from New Britain by St. George's Channel: part of Papua New Guinea. Chief town and port: Kavieng. Pop.: 59 543 (1971). Area: (including adjacent islands) 9850 sq. km (3800 sq. miles).

new+ish ('nju:ɪʃ) *adj.* fairly new. **—'new+ish+ly** *adv.* **—'new+ish+ness** *n.*

New Jer+sey *n.* a state of the eastern U.S., on the Atlantic and Delaware Bay: mostly low-lying, with a heavy industrial area in the northeast and many coastal resorts. Capital: Trenton. Pop.: 7 168 164 (1970). Area: 19 479 sq. km (7521 sq. miles). Abbrevs.: **N.J.** or (with zip code) **NJ**

New Je+ru+sa+lem *n. Ecclesiast.* heaven regarded as the prototype of the earthly Jerusalem; the heavenly city.

New Je+ru+sa+lem Church *n.* a sect founded in 1787 on the teachings of Swedenborg. Often shortened to **New Church.**

New King+dom *n.* a period of Egyptian history, extending from the 18th to the 20th dynasty (?1570–?1080 B.C.).

New Lat+in *n.* the form of Latin used since the Renaissance, esp. for scientific nomenclature. Also called: **Neo-Latin.**

New Learn+ing *n.* the classical and Biblical studies of Renaissance Europe in the 15th and 16th centuries.

New Left *n.* a loose grouping of leftwing radicals, esp. among students, that arose in many countries after 1960.

New Look *n.* **the.** a fashion in women's clothes introduced in 1947, characterized by long full skirts.

new+ly ('nju:lɪ) *adv.* **1.** recently; lately or just: *a newly built* *shelf.* **2.** again; afresh; anew: *newly raised hopes.* **3.** in a new manner; differently: *a newly arranged hairdo.*

new·ly+wed ('nju:lɪ,wɛd) *n.* (*often pl.*) a recently married person.

New·man ('nju:mən) *n.* **1. John Hen·ry.** 1801–90, English theologian. Originally an Anglican minister, he was a prominent figure in the Oxford Movement. He became a Roman Catholic (1845) and a priest (1847) and was made a cardinal (1879). His writings include the spiritual autobiography, *Apologia pro vita sua* (1864), a treatise on the nature of belief, *The Grammar of Assent* (1870), and many hymns. **2. Paul.** born 1925, U.S. film actor, whose films include *Exodus* (1961), *The Hustler* (1962), *Butch Cassidy and the Sundance Kid* (1969), *The Sting* (1973), and *Slap Shot* (1977).

new+mar+ket ('nju:,mɑ:kɪt) *n.* **1.** a double-breasted waisted coat with a full skirt worn, esp. for riding, in the 19th century. **2.** a simple gambling card game.

New+mar+ket ('nju:,mɑ:kɪt) *n.* a town in SE England, in W Suffolk: a famous horse-racing centre since the reign of James I. Pop.: 12 934 (1971).

new maths *n.* an approach to mathematics in which the basic principles of set theory are introduced at an elementary level.

New Mex·i·co *n.* a state of the southwestern U.S.: consists of high semiarid plateaus and mountains, crossed by the Rio Grande and the Pecos River; large Spanish-American and Indian populations; contains over two-thirds of U.S. uranium reserves. Capital: Santa Fé. Pop.: 1 016 000 (1970). Area: 314 451 sq. km (121 412 sq. miles). Abbrevs.: **N. Mex, N.M.,** or (with zip code) **NM** —**New Mex·i·can** *n.*

New Mod+el Ar·my *n.* the army established (1645) during the Civil War by the English parliamentarians, which exercised considerable political power under Cromwell.

new moon *n.* **1.** the moon when it appears as a narrow waxing crescent. **2.** the time at which this occurs. **3.** *Astronomy.* one of the four principal phases of the moon, occurring when it lies between the earth and the sun.

New Neth+er+land ('nɛðələnd) *n.* a Dutch North American colony of the early 17th century, centred on the Hudson valley. Captured by the English in 1664, it was divided into New York and New Jersey.

New Or+le+ans ('ɔ:lɪənz, -lənz; ɔ:'li:nz) *n.* a port in SE Louisiana, on the Mississippi River about 172 km (107 miles) from the sea: the largest city in the state and the second most important port in the U.S.; founded by the French in 1718; belonged to Spain (1763–1803). It is largely below sea level, built around the Vieux Carré (French quarter); famous for its annual Mardi Gras festival and for its part in the history of jazz; a major commercial, industrial, and transportation centre. Pop.: 513 479 (1973 est.).

New Or+le+ans jazz *n.* the jazz originating in New Orleans from about 1914; traditional jazz.

new plan+ets *pl. n.* the outer planets Uranus, Neptune, and Pluto, only discovered comparatively recently.

New Ply+mouth *n.* a port in New Zealand, on W North Island: founded in 1841. Pop.: 34 314 (1971).

New+port ('nju:,pɔ:t) *n.* **1.** a port in SE Wales on the River Usk, administrative centre of Gwent: steel industry. Pop.: 112 048 (1971). **2.** a port in SE Rhode Island: founded in 1639, it became one of the richest towns of colonial America; centre of a large number of U.S. naval establishments. Pop.: 34 562 (1970). **3.** a town in S England, administrative centre of the Isle of Wight. Pop.: 22 286 (1971).

New+port News *n.* a port in SE Virginia, at the mouth of the James River: an industrial centre, with one of the world's largest shipyards. Pop.: 137 827 (1973 est.).

New Prov·i+dence *n.* an island in the Atlantic, in the Bahamas. Chief town: Nassau. Pop.: 100 553 (1970). Area: 150 sq. km (58 sq. miles).

New Que+bec *n.* a region of E Canada in the N part of the province of Quebec: consists of most of the Labrador-Ungava peninsula and contains extensive iron deposits. Area: about 777 000 sq. km (300 000 sq. miles).

New Rom+ney *n.* a market town in SE England, in Kent on Romney Marsh: of early importance as one of the Cinque Ports, but is now over 1.6 km (1 mile) inland. Pop.: 3414 (1971). Former name (until 1563): **Romney.**

news (nju:z) *n.* (*functioning as sing.*) **1.** current events; important or interesting recent happenings. **2.** information about such events, as in the mass media. **3. a. the.** a presentation, such as a radio broadcast, of information of this type: *the news is at six.* **b.** (*in combination*): *a newscaster.* **4.** interesting or important information not previously known or realized: *it's news to me.* **5.** a person, fashion, etc., widely reported in the mass media: *she is no longer news in the film world.* —**'news+less** *adj.*

news a·gen+cy *n.* an organization that collects news reports for newspapers, etc. Also called: **press agency.**

news+a·gent ('nju:z,eɪdʒənt) *or U.S.* **news+deal·er** *n. Brit.* a shopkeeper who sells newspapers, stationery, etc.

news+boy *or* (*fem.*) **news+girl** *n.* a boy or girl who sells or delivers newspapers.

news+cast ('nju:z,kɑ:st) *n. Chiefly U.S.* a radio or television broadcast of the news. [C20: from NEWS + (BROAD)CAST] —**'news+,cast·er** *n.*

news+hawk ('nju:z,hɔ:k) *n. U.S. informal.* a newspaper reporter. Also called: **newshound** ('nju:z,haund).

New Si+be·ri·an Is+lands *pl. n.* an archipelago in the Arctic Ocean, off the N mainland of the Soviet Union, in the Yakut ASSR. Area: about 37 555 sq. km (14 500 sq. miles).

news+let·ter ('nju:z,lɛtə) *n.* **1.** Also called: **news-sheet.** a printed periodical bulletin circulated to members of a group. **2.** *History.* a written or printed account of the news.

news+mon·ger ('nju:z,mʌŋgə) *n. Old-fashioned.* a gossip.

New South *n. Austral. informal.* See **New South Wales.**

New South Wales *n.* a state of SE Australia: originally contained over half the continent, but was reduced by the formation of other states (1825–1911); consists of a narrow coastal plain, separated from extensive inland plains by the Great Dividing Range; the most populous state; mineral resources. Capital: Sydney. Pop.: 4 776 200 (1976). Area: 801 428 sq. km (309 433 sq. miles).

New Spain *n.* a Spanish viceroyalty of the 16th to 19th centuries, composed of Mexico, Central America north of Panama, the Spanish West Indies, the southwestern U.S., and the Philippines.

news+pa·per ('nju:z,peɪpə) *n.* **1. a.** a weekly or daily publication consisting of folded sheets and containing articles on the news, features, reviews, and advertisements. Often shortened to **paper. b.** (*as modifier*): *a newspaper article.* **2.** a less common name for **newsprint.**

news+pa·per+man ('nju:z,peɪpə,mæn) *or* (*fem.*) **news+pa·per+wom·an** *n., pl.* **+men** *or* **+wom·en. 1.** a person who works for a newspaper as a reporter or editor. **2.** the owner or proprietor of a newspaper.

new+speak ('nju:,spi:k) *n.* the language of bureaucrats and politicians, regarded as deliberately ambiguous and misleading. [C20: from *1984*, a novel by George Orwell]

news+print ('nju:z,prɪnt) *n.* an inexpensive wood-pulp paper used for newspapers.

news+reel ('nju:z,ri:l) *n.* a short film with a commentary presenting current events.

news+stand ('nju:z,stænd) *n.* a portable stand or stall in the street, etc., from which newspapers are sold.

New Stone Age *n.* (not now in technical use) another term for **Neolithic.**

New Style *n.* the present method of reckoning dates using the Gregorian calendar.

news ven+dor *n.* a person who sells newspapers.

news+wor·thy ('nju:z,wɜ:ðɪ) *adj.* sufficiently interesting to be reported in a news bulletin, etc. —**'news+,wor·thi+ness** *n.*

news·y ('nju:zɪ) *adj.* **news·i·er, news·i·est.** full of news, esp. gossipy or personal news: *a newsy letter.* —**'news·i·ness** *n.*

newt (nju:t) *n.* **1.** any of various small semiaquatic urodele amphibians, such as *Triturus vulgaris* (**common newt**) of Europe, having a long slender body and tail and short feeble legs. **2.** *Chiefly Brit.* any other urodele amphibian, including the salamanders. [C15: from *a newt*, a mistaken division of *an ewt; ewt,* from Old English *eveta* EFT[1]]

New Test. *abbrev. for* New Testament.

New Tes+ta+ment *n.* the collection of writings consisting of the Gospels, Acts of the Apostles, Pauline and other Epistles, and the book of Revelation, composed soon after Christ's death and added to the Jewish writings of the Old Testament to make up the Christian Bible.

New Thought *n.* a movement interested in spiritual healing and the power of constructive thinking.

new+ton ('nju:tᵊn) *n.* the derived SI unit of force that imparts an acceleration of 1 metre per second per second to a mass of 1 kilogram; equivalent to 10^5 dynes or 7.233 poundals. Symbol: N [C20: named after Sir Isaac NEWTON]

New+ton[1] ('nju:tᵊn) *n.* **1.** a new town in central Wales, in Powys. Pop.: 5621 (1971). **2.** one of the deepest craters on the moon, over 7300 metres deep and about 112 kilometres in diameter, situated in the SE quadrant.

New·ton[2] ('nju:tᵊn) *n.* Sir **I·saac.** 1643–1727, English mathematician, physicist, astronomer, and philosopher, noted particularly for his law of gravitation, his three laws of motion, his theory that light is composed of corpuscles, and his development of calculus independently of Leibnitz. His works include *Principia Mathematica* (1687) and *Opticks* (1704). —**New+to+ni·an** (nju:'təunɪən) *adj.*

New+to+ni·an me+chan+ics *n.* a system of mechanics based on Newton's laws of motion.

New+to+ni·an tel+e+scope *n.* a type of astronomical reflecting telescope in which light is reflected from a large concave mirror, onto a plane mirror, and through a hole in the side of the body of the telescope to form an image.

New+ton's law of grav·i+ta+tion *n.* the principle that two bodies attract each other with a force directly proportional to the product of their masses and inversely proportional to the square of the distance between them.

New·ton's laws of mo+tion *n.* three laws of mechanics describing the motion of a body. **The first law** states that a body remains at rest or in uniform motion in a straight line unless acted upon by a force. **The second law** states that a body's rate of change of momentum is proportional to the force causing it. **The third law** states that any force on a body produces an equal and opposite reaction.

new town *n. Brit.* a town that has been planned and built by the government, esp. to accommodate overspill population.

New·town+ab·bey (,nju:tᵊn'æbɪ) *n.* a town in Northern Ireland, in Co. Antrim on Belfast Lough; the third largest town in Northern Ireland, formed in 1958 by the amalgamation of seven villages; light industrial centre, esp. for textiles. Pop.: 57 908 (1971).

New+town St. Bos+wells ('nju:taun sənt 'bɒzwəlz) *n.* a village in SE Scotland, administrative centre of Borders region: agricultural centre. Pop.: 1253 (1971).

new wave *n.* a movement in art, film-making, politics, etc., that consciously breaks with traditional ideas.

New Wave[1] *n.* **the.** a movement in the French cinema of the 1960s, led by such directors as Godard, Truffaut, and Resnais, and characterized by a fluid use of the camera and an abandonment of traditional editing techniques. Also called: **Nouvelle Vague.**

New Wave[2] *n.* rock music of the late 1970's, usually characterized by basic rhythms, a strong beat, and simple harmonies, although it is sometimes more complex. It is sometimes also aggressive.

New Wind+sor *n.* the official name of **Windsor**[1] (sense 1).

new wool *n.* wool that is being processed or woven for the first time. Usual U.S. term: **virgin wool.**

New World *n.* **the.** the Americas; the western hemisphere.

New World mon+key *n.* any monkey of the family *Cebidae*, of Central and South America, having widely separated nostrils: many are arboreal and have a prehensile tail. Compare **Old World monkey.**

New Year *n.* the first day or days of the year in various calendars, usually celebrated as a holiday.

New Year's Day *n.* January 1, celebrated as a holiday in many countries. Often shortened to (U.S. informal) **New Year's.**

New Year's Eve *n.* the evening of Dec. 31, often celebrated with parties. See also **Hogmanay.**

New York *n.* **1.** a city in SE New York State, at the mouth of the Hudson River: the largest city and chief port of the U.S.; settled by the Dutch as New Amsterdam in 1624 and captured by the British in 1664, when it was named New York; consists of five boroughs (Manhattan, the Bronx, Queens, Brooklyn, and Richmond) and many islands, with its commercial and financial centre in Manhattan; the country's leading commercial and industrial city. Pop.: 7 646 818 (1973 est.). Also called: **New York City.** Abbrev.: **N.Y.C., NYC 2.** a state of the northeastern U.S.: consists chiefly of a plateau with the Finger Lakes in the centre, the Adirondack Mountains in the northeast, the Catskill Mountains in the southeast, and Niagara Falls in the west. Capital: Albany. Pop.: 18 241 266 (1970). Area: 123 882 sq. km (47 831 sq. miles). Abbrevs.: **N.Y.** or (with zip code) **NY** —**New York+er** *n.*

New York Bay *n.* an inlet of the Atlantic at the mouth of the Hudson River: forms the harbour of the port of New York.

New York State Barge Ca+nal *n.* a system of inland waterways in New York State, connecting the Hudson River with Lakes Erie and Ontario and, via Lake Champlain, with the St. Lawrence. Length: 845 km (525 miles).

New Zea+land ('zi:lənd) *n.* an independent dominion within the Commonwealth, occupying two main islands (North Island and South Island), Stewart Island, the Chatham Islands, and a number of minor islands in the SE Pacific: original Maori inhabitants surrendered sovereignty in 1840 and were finally subdued by 1870; became a dominion in 1907; a major world exporter of dairy products, wool, and meat. Official language: English. Religion: Christian majority. Currency: New Zealand dollar. Capital: Wellington. Pop.: 3 027 000 (1974 est.). Area: 268 867 sq. km (103 736 sq. miles). —**New Zea+land+er** *n.*

Nex·ø (*Danish* 'nɛgsø:) *n.* **Mar·tin An·der·sen** ('martən 'anərsən). 1869–1954, Danish novelist. His chief works are the novels *Pelle the Conqueror* (1906–10), which deals with the labour movement, and *Ditte, Daughter of Man* (1917–21).

next (nɛkst) *adj.* **1.** immediately following: *the next patient to be examined; do it next week.* **2.** immediately adjoining: *the next room.* **3.** closest to in degree: *the tallest boy next to James; the next-best thing.* **4. the next (Sunday) but one.** the (Sunday) after the next. ~*adv.* **5.** at a time or on an occasion immediately to follow: *the patient to be examined next; next, he started to unscrew the telephone receiver.* **6. next to. a.** adjacent to; at or on one side of: *the house next to ours.* **b.** following in degree: *next to your mother, who do you love most?* **c.** almost: *next to impossible.* ~*prep.* **7.** *Archaic.* next to. [Old English *nēhst*, superlative of *nēah* NIGH; compare NEAR, NEIGHBOUR]

next door *adj.* (**next-door** *when prenominal*), *adv.* at, in, or to the adjacent house, flat, building, etc.: *we live next door to the dentist; the next-door house.*

next friend *n. Law.* a person acting on behalf of an infant or other person under legal disability.

next of kin *n.* a person's closest relative or relatives.

nex+us ('nɛksəs) *n., pl.* **nex+us. 1.** a means of connection between members of a group or things in a series; link; bond. **2.** a connected group or series. [C17: from Latin: a binding together, from *nectere* to bind]

Ney (neɪ; *French* nɛ) *n.* **Mi·chel** (mi'ʃɛl), Duc d'Elchingen. 1769–1815, French marshal, who earned the epithet *Bravest of the Brave* at the battle of Borodino (1812) in the Napoleonic Wars. He rallied to Napoleon on his return from Elba and was executed for treason (1815).

Nez Per+cé ('nɛz 'pɜ:s; *French* ne pɛr'se) *n.* **1.** (*pl.* **Nez Per+cés** ('pɜ:sɪz; *French* pɛr'se) *or* **Nez Per+cé**) a member of a North American Indian people of the Pacific coast, a tribe of the Sahaptino. **2.** the Sahaptin language of this people. [French, literally: pierced nose]

NF *or* **N.F.** *abbrev. for:* **1.** Norman French (language). **2.** *Brit.* National Front.

N.F. *or* **N/F** *Banking. abbrev. for* no funds.

NF. *or* **Nfld.** *abbrev. for* Newfoundland.

N.F.S. (in Britain) *abbrev. for* National Fire Service.

N.F.U. (in Britain) *abbrev. for* National Farmers' Union.

N.F.W.I. (in Britain) *abbrev. for* National Federation of Women's Institutes.

N.G. *abbrev. for:* **1.** Also: **NG** (in the U.S.) National Guard. **2.** New Guinea. **3.** Also: **ng** no good.

N.G.A. *abbrev. for* National Graphical Association.

ngai·o ('naɪəʊ) *n.* a small New Zealand tree, *Myoporum laetum*, yielding useful timber: family *Myoporaceae*. [from Maori]

Nga+lie+ma Moun+tain (ᵊŋgɑ:'ljeɪmə) *n.* the Zaïrese name for (Mount) **Stanley.**

NGC *abbrev. for* New General Catalogue of Nebulae and Clusters of Stars; a catalogue in which over 8000 nebulae, galaxies, and clusters are listed numerically.

NGk *or* **NGk.** *abbrev. for* New Greek.

N.G.O. (in India) *abbrev. for* non-gazetted officer.

ngo+ma (ᵊŋ'gəʊmə, ᵊŋ'gɒm-) *n. E. African.* a type of drum. [Swahili]

Ngu+ni (ᵊŋ'gu:nɪ) *n.* a group of Bantu languages of southern Africa, consisting chiefly of Zulu, Xhosa, and Swazi.

ngwee (ᵊŋgweɪ) *n.* a Zambian monetary unit worth one hundredth of a kwacha.

N.H. *abbrev. for* New Hampshire.

Nha Trang ('njɑ: 'træŋ) *n.* a port in SE Vietnam, on the South China Sea: nearby temples of the Cham civilization; fishing industry. Pop.: 194 969 (1971).

N.H.S. (in Britain) *abbrev. for* National Health Service.

Ni *the chemical symbol for* nickel.

N.I. *abbrev. for:* **1.** (in Britain) National Insurance. **2.** Northern Ireland.

ni·a·cin ('naɪəsɪn) *n.* another name for **nicotinic acid.** [C20: from NI(COTINIC) AC(ID) + -IN]

Ni+ag·a+ra (naɪ'ægrə, -'ægərə) *n.* **1.** a river in NE North America, on the border between W New York State and Ontario, Canada, flowing from Lake Erie to Lake Ontario. Length: 45 km (28 miles). **2.** a torrent.

Ni+ag·a+ra Falls *n.* **1.** the falls of the Niagara River, on the border between the U.S. and Canada: divided by Goat Island into the American Falls, 50 m (167 ft.) high, and the Horseshoe or Canadian Falls, 47 m (158 ft.) high. **2.** a city in W New York State, situated at the falls of the Niagara River. Pop.: 86 615 (1970). **3.** a city in S Canada, in SE Ontario on the Niagara River just below the falls: linked to the city of Niagara Falls in the U.S. by three bridges. Pop.: 67 163 (1971).

Nia+mey (njɑ:'meɪ) *n.* the capital of Niger, in the southwest on the River Niger: became capital in 1926; airport and land route centre. Pop.: 130 299 (1975 est.).

nib (nɪb) *n.* **1.** the writing point of a pen, esp. an insertable tapered metal part with a split tip. **2.** a point, tip, or beak. **3.** (*pl.*) crushed cocoa beans. ~*vb.* **nibs, nib+bing, nibbed.** (*tr.*) **4.** to provide with a nib. **5.** to prepare or sharpen the nib of. [C16 (in the sense: beak): origin obscure; compare northern German *nibbe* tip. See NEB, NIBBLE] —'**nib+,like** *adj.*

nib+ble ('nɪbᵊl) *vb.* (when *intr.*, often foll. by *at*) **1.** (esp. of animals, such as mice) to take small repeated bites (of). **2.** to take dainty or tentative bites: *to nibble at a cake.* **3.** to bite (at) gently or caressingly. **4.** (*intr.*) to make petty criticisms. **5.** (*intr.*) to consider tentatively or cautiously: *to nibble at an idea.* ~*n.* **6.** a small mouthful. **7.** an instance or the act of nibbling. [C15: related to Low German *nibbelen*. Compare NIB, NEB] —'**nib+bler** *n.*

Ni+be·lung ('ni:bə,lʊŋ) *n., pl.* **·lungs** *or* **·lung+en** (-,lʊŋən). *German myth.* **1.** any of the race of dwarfs who possessed a treasure hoard stolen by Siegfried. **2.** one of Siegfried's companions or followers. **3.** (in the *Nibelungenlied*) a member of the family of Gunther, king of Burgundy.

Ni+be·lung+en+lied *German.* ('ni:bə,lʊŋən,li:t) *n.* a medieval High German heroic epic of unknown authorship based on German history and legend and written about 1200. [literally: song of the Nibelungs]

nib+lick ('nɪblɪk) *n. Golf.* a club, a No. 9 iron, giving a great deal of lift. [C19: of unknown origin]

nibs (nɪbz) *pl. n.* **his nibs.** *Slang.* a mock title used of someone in authority. [C19: of unknown origin]

Ni+cae·a (naɪ'si:ə) *n.* an ancient city in NW Asia Minor, in Bithynia: site of the **first council of Nicaea** (325 A.D.), which composed the Nicene Creed. Modern Turkish name: **Iznik.** —**Ni+cene** ('naɪsi:n) *or* **Ni+'cae·an** *adj.*

Nic·a+ra+gu·a (,nɪkə'rægjʊə) *n.* **1.** a republic in Central America, on the Caribbean and the Pacific: colonized by the Spanish from the 1520s; gained independence in 1821 and was annexed by Mexico, becoming a republic in 1838. Language: Spanish. Religion: Roman Catholic. Currency: córdoba. Pop.: 1 911 543 (1971). Area: about 148 000 sq. km (57 140 sq. miles). **2. Lake.** a lake in SW Nicaragua, separated from the Pacific by an isthmus 19 km (12 miles) wide: the largest lake in Central America. Area: 8264 sq. km (3191 sq. miles). —,**Nic·a+'ra+gu·an** *adj., n.*

nic+co+lite ('nɪkə,laɪt) *n.* a copper-coloured mineral consisting of nickel arsenide in hexagonal crystalline form, occurring associated with copper and silver ores: a source of nickel. Formula: NiAs. [C19: from New Latin *niccolum* NICKEL + -ITE[1]]

nice (naɪs) *adj.* **1.** pleasant or commendable: *a nice day.* **2.** kind or friendly: *a nice gesture of help.* **3.** subtle, delicate, or discriminating: *a nice point in the argument.* **4.** precise; skilful: *a nice fit.* **5.** *Now rare.* fastidious; respectable: *he was not too nice about his methods.* **6.** *Obsolete.* **a.** foolish or ignorant. **b.** delicate. **c.** shy; modest. **d.** wanton. **7. nice and.** pleasingly: *it's nice and cool.* [C13 (originally: foolish): from Old French *nice* simple, silly, from Latin *nescius* ignorant, from *nescīre* to be ignorant; see NESCIENCE] —'**nice·ly** *adv.* —'**nice·ness** *n.* —'**nic·ish** *adj.*

Nice (*French* nis) *n.* a city in SE France, on the Mediterranean: a leading resort of the French Riviera; founded by Phocaeans from Marseille in about the 3rd century B.C. Pop.: 346 620 (1975).

Ni·cene Coun·cil *n.* **1.** the first council of Nicaea, the first general council of the Church, held in 325 A.D. to settle the Aryan controversy. **2.** the second council of Nicaea, the seventh general council of the Church, held in 787 A.D. to settle the question of images.

Ni·cene Creed *n.* **1.** the formal summary of Christian beliefs promulgated at the first council of Nicaea in 325 A.D. **2.** a longer formulation of Christian beliefs authorized at the council of Constantinople in 381, and now used in most Christian liturgies.

ni·ce·ty ('naɪsɪtɪ) *n., pl.* **·ties. 1.** a subtle point of delicacy or distinction: *a nicety of etiquette.* **2.** (*usually pl.*) a refinement or delicacy: *the niceties of first-class travel.* **3.** subtlety, delicacy, or precision. **4.** excessive refinement; fastidiousness. **5. to a nicety.** with precision.

niche (nɪtʃ, ni:ʃ) *n.* **1.** a recess in a wall, esp. one that contains a statue, etc. **2.** a position particularly suitable for the person occupying it: *he found his niche in politics.* **3.** *Ecology.* the status of a plant or animal within its community, which determines its activities, relationships with other organisms, etc. ~*vb.* **4.** (*tr.*) to place (a statue) in a niche; ensconce (oneself). [C17: from French, from Old French *nichier* to nest, from Vulgar Latin *nīdicāre* (unattested) to build a nest, from Latin *nīdus* NEST]

Nich·o·las ('nɪkələs) *n.* **Saint.** 4th-century A.D. bishop of Myra, in Asia Minor; patron saint of Russia and of children, sailors, merchants, and pawnbrokers. Feast day: Dec. 6. See also **Santa Claus.**

Nich·o·las I *n.* **1. Saint,** called *the Great.* died 867 A.D., Italian ecclesiastic; pope (858–867). He championed papal supremacy. Feast day: Nov. 13. **2.** 1796–1855, tsar of Russia (1825–55). He gained notoriety for his autocracy and his emphasis on military discipline and bureaucracy.

Nich·o·las II *n.* 1868–1918, tsar of Russia (1894–1917). After the disastrous Russo-Japanese War (1904–05), he was forced to summon a representative assembly, but his continued autocracy and incompetence precipitated the Russian Revolution (1917): he abdicated and was shot.

Nich·o·las V *n.* original name *Tommaso Parentucelli.* 1397–1455, Italian ecclesiastic; pope (1447–55). He helped to found the Vatican Library.

Nich·o·las of Cu·sa ('kju:zə) *n.* 1401–64, German cardinal, philosopher, and mathematician: anticipated Copernicus in asserting that the earth revolves around the sun.

Ni·chol·son ('nɪkəlsən) *n.* **Ben.** 1894–1982, English painter, noted for his abstract still lifes.

Ni·chrome ('naɪ,krəum) *n.* *Trademark.* any of various alloys containing nickel, iron, and chromium, with smaller amounts of other components. It is used in electrical heating elements, furnaces, etc.

Ni·ci·as ('nɪsɪəs) *n.* died 414 B.C., Athenian statesman and general. He ended the first part of the Peloponnesian War by making peace with Sparta (421).

nick (nɪk) *n.* **1.** a small notch or indentation on an edge or surface. **2.** a groove on the shank of a printing type, used to orientate type and often to distinguish the fount. **3.** *Brit.* a slang word for **prison** or **police station. 4. in good nick.** in good condition. **5. in the nick of time.** just in time. ~*vb.* **6.** (*tr.*) to chip or cut. **7.** *Slang, chiefly Brit.* **a.** to steal. **b.** to take into legal custody; arrest. **8.** (*intr.;* often foll. by *off*) *Austral. informal.* to move or depart rapidly. **9. nick (someone) for.** *U.S. slang.* to defraud (someone) to the extent of. **10.** to divide and reset (certain of the tail muscles of a horse) to give the tail a high carriage. **11.** (*tr.*) to guess, catch, etc., exactly. **12.** (*intr.*) (of breeding stock) to mate satisfactorily. [C15: perhaps changed from C14 *nocke* NOCK]

nick·el ('nɪkᵊl) *n.* **1.** a malleable ductile silvery-white metallic element that is strong and corrosion-resistant, occurring principally in pentlandite and niccolite: used in alloys, esp. in toughening steel, in electroplating, and as a catalyst in organic synthesis. Symbol: Ni; atomic no.: 28; atomic wt.: 58.71; valency: 1, 2, or 3; relative density: 8.90; melting pt.: 1453°C; boiling pt.: 2732°C. **2.** a U.S. and Canadian coin and monetary unit worth five cents. ~*vb.* **·els, ·el·ling, ·elled** *or U.S.* **·els, ·el·ing, ·eled. 3.** (*tr.*) to plate with nickel. [C18: shortened form of German *Kupfernickel* niccolite, literally: copper demon, so called by miners because it was mistakenly thought to contain copper]

nick·el bloom *n.* another name for **annabergite.**

nick·el·ic (nɪ'kɛlɪk) *adj.* **1.** of or containing metallic nickel. **2.** of or containing nickel in the trivalent state.

nick·el·if·er·ous (,nɪkə'lɪfərəs) *adj.* containing nickel.

nick·el·o·de·on (,nɪkə'ləudɪən) *n. U.S.* **1.** an early form of jukebox. **2.** (formerly) a cinema charging five cents for admission. **3.** (formerly) a Pianola, esp. one operated by inserting a five-cent piece. [C20: from NICKEL + (MEL)ODEON]

nick·el·ous ('nɪkələs) *adj.* of or containing nickel, esp. in the divalent state.

nick·el plate *n.* a thin layer of nickel deposited on a surface, usually by electrolysis.

nick·el sil·ver *n.* any of various white alloys containing copper (46–63 per cent), zinc (18–36 per cent), and nickel (6–30 per cent): used in making tableware, etc. Also called: **German silver.**

nick·er[1] ('nɪkə) *vb.* (*intr.*) **1.** (of a horse) to neigh softly. **2.** to laugh quietly; snigger. [C18: perhaps from NEIGH]

nick·er[2] ('nɪkə) *n., pl.* **·er.** *Brit. slang.* a pound sterling. [C20: of unknown origin]

Nick·laus ('nɪklaus) *n.* **Jack.** born 1940, U.S. professional golfer: won the British Open Championship (1966; 1970) and the U.S. Open Championship (1967; 1972).

nick·nack ('nɪk,næk) *n.* a variant spelling of **knickknack.**

nick·name ('nɪk,neɪm) *n.* **1.** a familiar, pet, or derisory name given to a person, animal, or place: *his nickname was Lefty because he was left-handed.* **2.** a shortened or familiar form of a person's name: *Joe is a nickname for Joseph.* ~*vb.* **3.** (*tr.*) to call by a nickname. [C15: *a nekename,* mistaken division of *an ekename* an additional name, from *eke* addition + NAME]

nick·point ('nɪk,pɔɪnt) *n.* a variant spelling (esp. U.S.) of **knickpoint.**

Nic·o·bar Is·lands ('nɪkə,bɑ:) *pl. n.* a group of 19 islands in the Indian Ocean, south of the Andaman Islands, with which they form a territory of India. Area: 1645 sq. km (635 sq. miles).

Nic·o·de·mus (,nɪkə'di:məs) *n. New Testament.* a Pharisee and a member of the Sanhedrin, who supported Jesus against the other Pharisees (John 8:50–52).

Ni·co·lai (*German* ,niko'laɪ) *n.* **Carl Ot·to Ehr·en·fried** ('karl 'ɔto 'e:rən,fri:t). 1810–49, German composer: noted for his opera *The Merry Wives of Windsor* (1849).

Nic·ol prism ('nɪkᵊl) *n.* a device composed of two prisms of Iceland spar or calcite cut at specified angles and cemented together with Canada balsam. It is used for producing plane-polarized light. [C19: named after William *Nicol* (?1768–1851), Scottish physicist, its inventor]

Nic·ol·son ('nɪkəlsən) *n.* Sir **Har·old (George).** 1886–1968, English diplomat and author.

Nic·o·si·a (,nɪkə'si:ə, -'sɪə) *n.* the capital of Cyprus, in the central part on the Pedieos River: capital since the 10th century. Pop.: 115 700 (1973).

ni·co·ti·a·na (nɪ,kəuʃɪ'ɑ:nə, -'eɪnə) *n.* any solanaceous plant of the American and Australian genus *Nicotiana,* such as tobacco, having white, yellow, or purple fragrant flowers. [C16: see NICOTINE]

nic·o·tin·a·mide (,nɪkə'tɪnə,maɪd, -'ti:n-) *n.* the amide of nicotinic acid: a component of the vitamin B complex and essential in the diet for the prevention of pellagra. Formula: $C_6H_6ON_2$.

nic·o·tine ('nɪkə,ti:n) *n.* a colourless oily acrid toxic liquid that turns yellowish-brown in air and light: the principal alkaloid in tobacco, used as an agricultural insecticide. Formula: $C_{10}H_{14}N_2$. [C19: from French, from New Latin *herba nicotiana* Nicot's plant, named after J. *Nicot* (1530-1600), French diplomat who introduced tobacco into France] —**nic·o·tin·ic** (,nɪkə'tɪnɪk) *adj.*

nic·o·tin·ic ac·id *n.* a vitamin of the B complex that occurs in milk, liver, yeast, etc. Lack of it in the diet leads to the disease pellagra. Formula: $(C_5H_4N)COOH$. Also called: **niacin.**

nic·o·tin·ism ('nɪkəti:,nɪzəm) *n. Pathol.* a toxic condition of the body or a bodily organ or part caused by nicotine.

Nic·the·roy (*Portuguese* ,nite'rɔɪ) *n.* another name for **Niterói.**

nic·ti·tate ('nɪktɪ,teɪt) *or* **nic·tate** ('nɪkteɪt) *vb.* a technical word for **blink.** [C19: from Medieval Latin *nictitāre* to wink repeatedly, from Latin *nictāre* to wink, from *nicere* to beckon] —**,nic·ti·'ta·tion** *or* **nic·'ta·tion** *n.*

nic·ti·tat·ing mem·brane *n.* (in reptiles, birds, and some mammals) a thin fold of skin beneath the eyelid that can be drawn across the eye. Also called: **third eyelid, haw.**

Ni·da·ros (*Norwegian* 'ni:da,ru:s) *n.* the former name (1930–31) of **Trondheim.**

nid·der·ing *or* **nid·er·ing** ('nɪdərɪŋ) *Archaic.* ~*n.* **1.** a coward. ~*adj.* **2.** cowardly. [C16: a mistaken reading of Old English *nithing* coward; related to *nīth* malice]

nid·dle-nod·dle ('nɪdᵊl,nɒdᵊl) *adj.* **1.** nodding. ~*vb.* **2.** to nod rapidly or unsteadily. [C18: reduplication of NOD]

nide (naɪd) *n.* another word for **nye.** [C17: from Latin *nīdus* nest]

ni·dic·o·lous (nɪ'dɪkələs) *adj.* (of young birds) remaining in the nest for some time after hatching. [C19: from Latin *nīdus* nest + *colere* to inhabit]

ni·dif·u·gous (nɪ'dɪfjʊgəs) *adj.* (of young birds) leaving the nest very soon after hatching. [C19: from Latin *nīdus* nest + *fugere* to flee]

nid·i·fy ('nɪdɪ,faɪ) *or* **nid·i·fi·cate** ('nɪdɪfɪ,keɪt) *vb.* **·fies, ·fy·ing, ·fied.** (*intr.*) (of birds) to make or build a nest. [C17: from Latin *nīdificāre,* from *nīdus* a nest + *facere* to make] —**,nid·i·fi·'ca·tion** *n.*

nid-nod ('nɪd,nɒd) *vb.* **-nods, -nod·ding, -nod·ded.** to nod repeatedly. [C18: reduplication of NOD]

ni·dus ('naɪdəs) *n., pl.* **·di** (-daɪ). **1.** the nest in which insects or spiders deposit their eggs. **2.** *Pathol.* a focus of infection. **3.** a cavity in which plant spores develop. [C18: from Latin: NEST] —'**ni·dal** *adj.*

Nie·buhr ('ni:buə) *n.* **1. Bar·thold Ge·org** ('bartɔlt 'ge:ɔrk). 1776–1831, German historian, noted for his critical approach to sources, esp. in *History of Rome* (1811–32). **2. Rein·hold.** 1892–1971, U.S. Protestant theologian. His works include *Moral Man and Immoral Society* (1932) and *The Nature and Destiny of Man* (1941–43).

niece (ni:s) *n.* a daughter of one's sister or brother. [C13: from Old French: niece, granddaughter, ultimately from Latin *neptis* granddaughter]

Nie·der·ö·ster·reich ('ni:dər,ø:stəraɪç) *n.* the German name for **Lower Austria.**

Nie·der·sach·sen ('niːdərˌzaksᵊn) *n.* the German name for **Lower Saxony.**

ni·el·lo (nɪ'ɛləʊ) *n., pl.* **·li** (-lɪ) *or* **·los. 1.** a black compound of sulphur and silver, lead, or copper used to incise a design on a metal surface. **2.** the process of decorating surfaces with niello. **3.** a surface or object decorated with niello. ~*vb.* **·los, ·lo·ing, ·loed. 4.** (*tr.*) to decorate or treat with niello. [C19: from Italian from Latin *nigellus* blackish, from *niger* black] —**ni'el·list** *n.*

Niel·sen ('niːlsən; *Danish* 'nelsən) *n.* **Carl (August)** (karl). 1865–1931, Danish composer. His works include six symphonies and the opera *Masquerade* (1906).

Nie·men ('njɛmɛn) *n.* the Polish name for the **Neman.**

Nie·möl·ler (*German* 'niːmœlər) *n.* **Mar·tin** ('martiːn). born 1892, German Protestant theologian, who was imprisoned (1938–45) for his opposition to Hitler.

Nier·stein·er (*German* 'niːrʃtaɪnər) *n.* a white wine from the region around Nierstein, Germany.

Nie·tzsche ('niːtʃə) *n.* **Frie·drich Wil·helm** ('friːdrɪç 'vɪlhɛlm). 1844–1900, German philosopher, poet, and critic, noted esp. for his concept of the superman and his rejection of traditional Christian values. His chief works are *The Birth of Tragedy* (1872), *Thus Spake Zarathustra* (1883–91), and *Beyond Good and Evil* (1886). —**Nie·tzsche·an** ('niːtʃɪən) *n., adj.* —**'Nie·tzsche·ˌism** *or* **'Nie·tzsche·an·ˌism** *n.*

nieve (niːv) *n. Northern Brit. dialect.* the closed hand; fist. [C14: from Old Norse *hnefi*]

Niè·vre (*French* 'njɛːvr) *n.* a department of central France, in Burgundy region. Capital: Nevers. Pop.: 249 996 (1975). Area: 6888 sq. km (2686 sq. miles).

niff (nɪf) *Brit. slang.* ~*n.* **1.** a bad smell. ~*vb.* **2.** to smell badly; stink. [C20: perhaps from SNIFF] —**'niff·y** *adj.*

Ni·fl·heim ('nɪvᵊlˌheɪm) *n. Norse myth.* the abode of the dead. [Old Norse: literally, mist home]

nif·ty ('nɪftɪ) *adj.* **·ti·er, ·ti·est.** *Informal.* pleasing, apt, or stylish. [C19: of uncertain origin] —**'nif·ti·ly** *adv.* —**'nif·ti·ness** *n.*

NIG *international car registration for* Niger.

Ni·ger ('naɪdʒə) *n.* **1.** a landlocked republic in West Africa: important since earliest times for its trans-Saharan trade routes; made a French colony in 1922 and became fully independent in 1960; exports peanuts and livestock. Official language: French. Religion: mostly Muslim. Currency: franc. Capital: Niamey. Pop.: 4 476 000 (1974 est.). Area: 1 315 640 sq. km (507 969 sq. miles). **2.** a river in West Africa, rising in S Guinea and flowing in a great northward curve through Mali, then southwest through Niger and Nigeria to the Gulf of Guinea: the third longest river in Africa, with the largest delta, covering an area of 36 260 sq. km (14 000 sq. miles). Length: 4184 km (2600 miles). **3.** a state of W central Nigeria, formed in 1976 from part of North-Western State. Capital: Minna. Pop.: 2 900 000 (1976 est.). Area: 17 344 sq. km (6695 sq. miles).

Ni·ger-Con·go *n.* **1.** a family of languages of Africa consisting of the Bantu languages together with most of the languages of the coastal regions of West Africa. The chief branches are Benue-Congo (including Bantu), Kwa, Mande, and West Atlantic. ~*adj.* **2.** relating to or belonging to this family of languages.

Ni·ge·ri·a (naɪ'dʒɪərɪə) *n.* a republic in West Africa, on the Gulf of Guinea: Lagos annexed by the British in 1861; protectorates of Northern and Southern Nigeria formed in 1900 and united as a colony in 1914; gained independence as a member of the Commonwealth in 1960; Eastern Region seceded as the Republic of Biafra for the duration of the severe civil war (1967–70). It consists of a belt of tropical rain forest in the south, with semidesert in the extreme north and highlands in the east; the main export is petroleum. Official language: English; Hausa, Ibo, and Yoruba are the chief regional languages. Religion: animist, Muslim, and Christian. Currency: naira. Capital: Lagos. Pop.: 62 925 000 (1975 UN est.). Area: 923 773 sq. km (356 669 sq. miles). —**Ni'ge·ri·an** *adj., n.*

Ni·ger seed *n.* another name for **ramtil** (sense 2).

nig·gard ('nɪgəd) *n.* **1.** a stingy person. ~*adj. Archaic.* **2.** miserly. [C14: perhaps of Scandinavian origin; related to Swedish dialect *nygg* and Old English *hnēaw* stingy]

nig·gard·ly ('nɪgədlɪ) *adj.* **1.** stingy or ungenerous. **2.** meagre: *a niggardly salary.* ~*adv.* **3.** stingily; grudgingly. —**'nig·gard·li·ness** *n.*

nig·ger ('nɪgə) *Derogatory.* ~*n.* **1. a.** another name for a Negro. **b.** (*as modifier*): *nigger minstrels.* **2.** a member of any dark-skinned race. **3. nigger in the woodpile.** a hidden snag or hindrance. [C18: from C16 dialect *neeger,* from French *nègre,* from Spanish NEGRO¹]

nig·gle ('nɪgᵊl) *vb.* **1.** (*intr.*) to find fault continually. **2.** (*intr.*) to be preoccupied with details; fuss. **3.** (*tr.*) to irritate; worry. [C16: from Scandinavian; related to Norwegian *nigla.* Compare NIGGARD] —**'nig·gler** *n.* —**'nig·gly** *adj.*

nig·gling ('nɪglɪŋ) *adj.* **1.** petty. **2.** fussy. **3.** irritating. **4.** requiring painstaking work. —**'nig·gling·ly** *adv.*

nigh (naɪ) *adj., adv., prep.* an archaic, poetic, or dialect word for **near.** [Old English *nēah, nēh;* related to German *nah,* Old Frisian *nei.* Compare NEAR, NEXT]

night (naɪt) *n.* **1.** the period of darkness each 24 hours between sunset and sunrise, as distinct from day. **2.** (*modifier*) of, occurring, working, etc., at night: *a night nurse.* **3.** the occurrence of this period considered as a unit: *four nights later they left.* **4.** the period between sunset and retiring to bed; evening. **5.** the time between bedtime and morning: *she spent the night alone.* **6.** the weather conditions of the night: *a clear night.* **7.** the activity or experience of a person during a night. **8.** (*sometimes cap.*) any evening designated for a special observance or function. **9.** nightfall or dusk. **10.** a state or period of gloom, ignorance, etc. **11. make a night of it.** to go out and celebrate for most of the night. **12. night and day.** continually: *that baby cries night and day.* ~Related adj.: **nocturnal.** [Old English *niht;* compare Dutch *nacht,* Latin *nox,* Greek *nux*] —**'night·less** *adj.* —**'night·ˌlike** *adj.*

night blind·ness *n. Pathol.* a nontechnical term for **nyctalopia.**

night-bloom·ing ce·re·us *n.* any of several cacti of the genera *Hylocereus, Selenicereus,* etc., having large fragrant flowers that open at night.

night·cap ('naɪtˌkæp) *n.* **1.** a cloth cap formerly worn in bed. **2.** a bedtime drink, esp. an alcoholic or hot one.

night·club ('naɪtˌklʌb) *n.* a place of entertainment open until late at night, usually offering food, drink, a floor show, dancing, etc. —**'night·ˌclub·ber** *n.*

night danc·er *n.* (in Uganda) a person believed to employ the help of the dead in destroying other people.

night·dress ('naɪtˌdrɛs) *n. Brit.* a loose dress worn in bed by women. Also called: **nightgown, nightie.**

night·fall ('naɪtˌfɔːl) *n.* the approach of darkness; dusk.

night·gown ('naɪtˌgaʊn) *n.* **1.** another name for **nightdress. 2.** a man's nightshirt.

night·hawk ('naɪtˌhɔːk) *n.* **1.** Also called: **bullbat, mosquito hawk.** any American nightjar of the genus *Chordeiles* and related genera, having a dark plumage and, in the male, white patches on the wings and tail. **2.** *Informal.* another name for **night owl.**

night her·on *n.* any nocturnal heron of the genus *Nycticorax* and related genera, having short legs and necks, a heavy body, and a short heavy bill.

night·ie *or* **night·y** ('naɪtɪ) *n., pl.* **night·ies.** *Informal.* short for **nightdress** or **nightgown.**

night·in·gale ('naɪtɪŋˌgeɪl) *n.* **1.** a brownish European songbird, *Luscinia megarhynchos,* with a broad reddish-brown tail: well known for its musical song, usually heard at night. **2.** any of various similar or related birds, such as *Luscinia luscinia* (**thrush nightingale**). [Old English *nihtegale,* literally: night-singer, from NIGHT + *galan* to sing]

Night·in·gale ('naɪtɪŋˌgeɪl) *n.* **Flo·rence,** called *the Lady with the Lamp.* 1820–1910, English nurse, famous for her work during the Crimean War. She helped to raise the status and quality of the nursing profession and founded a training school for nurses in London (1860).

night·jar ('naɪtˌdʒɑː) *n.* any nocturnal bird of the family *Caprimulgidae,* esp. *Caprimulgus europaeus* (**European nightjar**): order *Caprimulgiformes.* They have a cryptic plumage and large eyes and feed on insects. [C17: NIGHT + JAR², so called from its discordant cry]

night latch *n.* a door lock that is operated by means of a knob on the inside and a key on the outside.

night let·ter *n. U.S.* a telegram sent for delivery the next day at a cheaper rate than a regular telegram.

night·life ('naɪtˌlaɪf) *n.* social life or entertainment taking place in the late evening or night, as in nightclubs.

night-light *n.* a dim light burning at night, esp. for children.

night·long ('naɪtˌlɒŋ) *adj., adv.* throughout the night.

night·ly ('naɪtlɪ) *adj.* **1.** happening or relating to each night. **2.** happening at night. ~*adv.* **3.** at night or each night.

night·mare ('naɪtˌmɛə) *n.* **1.** a terrifying or deeply distressing dream. **2. a.** an event or condition resembling a terrifying dream: *the nightmare of shipwreck.* **b.** (*as modifier*): *a nightmare drive.* **3.** a thing that is feared. **4.** (formerly) an evil spirit supposed to harass or suffocate sleeping people. [C13 (meaning: incubus; C16: bad dream): from NIGHT + Old English *mare, mære* evil spirit, from Germanic; compare Old Norse *mara* incubus, Polish *zmora,* French *cauchemar* nightmare] —**'night·ˌmar·ish** *adj.* —**'night·ˌmar·ish·ly** *adv.* —**'night·ˌmar·ish·ness** *n.*

night-night *interj.* an informal word for **goodnight.**

night owl *or* **hawk** *n. Informal.* a person who is or prefers to be up and about late at night.

night ra·ven *n. Poetic.* any bird, esp. the night heron, that is most active at night.

night·rid·er ('naɪtˌraɪdə) *n.* a member of a band of mounted and usually masked Whites in the southern U.S. who carried out acts of revenge and intimidation at night after the Civil War. —**'night·ˌrid·ing** *n.*

night robe *n.* a U.S. name for **nightdress.**

nights (naɪts) *adv. Informal.* at night, esp. regularly: *he works nights.*

night school *n.* an educational institution that holds classes in the evening for those who are not free during the day.

night·shade ('naɪtˌʃeɪd) *n.* **1.** any of various solanaceous plants, such as deadly nightshade, woody nightshade, and black nightshade. **2.** See **enchanter's nightshade.** [Old English *nihtscada,* apparently NIGHT + SHADE, referring to the poisonous or soporific qualities of these plants]

night·shirt ('naɪtˌʃɜːt) *n.* a loose knee-length or longer shirtlike garment worn in bed by men.

night soil *n.* human excrement used as a fertilizer.

night·spot ('naɪtˌspɒt) *n.* an informal word for **nightclub.**

night stick *n.* a U.S. name for **truncheon.**

night-time *n.* **a.** the time from sunset to sunrise; night as distinct from day. **b.** (*as modifier*): *a night-time prowler.*

night watch *n.* **1.** a watch or guard kept at night, esp. for security. **2.** the period of time the watch is kept. **3.** a person who keeps such a watch; night watchman.

night watch+man *n.* **1.** Also called: **night watch.** a person who keeps guard at night on a factory, public building, etc. **2.** *Cricket.* a batsman sent in to bat to play out time when a wicket has fallen near the end of a day's play.

night+wear ('naɪt,wɛə) *n.* apparel worn in bed or before retiring to bed; pyjamas, nightdress, dressing gowns, etc.

ni+gres+cent (naɪ'grɛsᵊnt) *adj.* blackish; dark. [C18: from Latin *nigrescere* to grow black, from *niger* black; see NEGRO[1]] —**ni+'gres+cence** *n.*

nig+ri+fy ('nɪgrɪ,faɪ) *vb.* **+fies, +fy+ing, +fied.** a rare word for **blacken.**

nig+ri+tude ('nɪgrɪ,tju:d) *n. Rare.* blackness; darkness. [C17: from Latin *nigritūdō* from *niger* black]

ni+gro+sine ('nɪgrə,si:n, -sɪn) *or* **ni+gro+sin** ('nɪgrəsɪn) *n.* any of a class of black pigments and dyes obtained from aniline: used in inks and shoe polishes and for dyeing textiles, etc. [C19: from Latin *niger* black + -OSE[1] + -INE[1]]

ni+hil *Latin.* ('naɪhɪl, 'ni:hɪl) *n.* nil; nothing. —**ni+'hil+i+ty** *n.*

ni+hil+ism ('naɪɪ,lɪzəm) *n.* **1.** a complete denial of all established authority and institutions. **2.** *Philosophy.* an extreme form of scepticism that systematically rejects all values, belief in existence, the possibility of communication, etc. **3.** a revolutionary doctrine of destruction for its own sake. **4.** the practice or promulgation of terrorism. —**'ni+hil+ist** *n., adj.* —**,ni+hil+'is+tic** *adj.*

Ni+hil+ism ('naɪɪ,lɪzəm) *n.* (in tsarist Russia) any of several revolutionary doctrines that upheld terrorism.

ni+hil ob+stat ('ɒbstæt) the phrase used by a Roman Catholic censor to declare publication inoffensive to faith or morals. [Latin, literally: nothing hinders]

Ni+hon ('ni:'hɒn) *n.* transliteration of a Japanese name for **Japan.**

Ni·i·ga+ta ('ni:ɪ,gɑ:tə) *n.* a port in central Japan, on NW Honshu at the mouth of the Shinano River: the chief port on the Sea of Japan. Pop.: 413 061 (1974 est.).

Ni·jin·sky (nɪ'dʒɪnskɪ) *n.* **Wa·slaw** or **Va·slaw** (vats'laf). 1890–1950, Russian ballet dancer and choreographer, who was associated wth Diaghilev. His creations include settings of Stravinsky's *Petrushka* and *The Rite of Spring.*

Nij+me·gen ('naɪ,meɪgən; *Dutch* 'nɛj,me:xə) *n.* an industrial town in the E Netherlands, in Gelderland province on the Waal River: the oldest town in the country; scene of the signing (1678) of the peace treaty between Louis XIV, the Netherlands, Spain, and the Holy Roman Empire. Pop.: 148 029 (1974 est.). Latin name: **Noviomagus.** German name: **Nimwegen.**

-nik *suffix forming nouns.* denoting a person associated with a specified state or quality: *beatnik.* [C20: from Russian *-nik*, as in SPUTNIK, and influenced by Yiddish *-nik* (agent suffix)]

Ni+kar·i·a (nɪ'kɛərɪə, naɪ-) *n.* another name for **Icaria.**

Ni·ke ('naɪki:) *n. Greek myth.* the winged goddess of victory. Roman counterpart: **Victoria.** [from Greek: victory]

Nik+kǫ ('ni:kəʊ) *n.* a town in central Japan, on NE Honshu: a major pilgrimage centre, with a 4th-century Shinto shrine, a Buddhist temple (767), and the shrines and mausoleums of the Tokugawa shoguns. Pop.: 28 502 (1970).

Ni+ko+lain+kau+pun+ki (*Finnish* ,nikəlaɪn'kaʊpʊŋki) *n.* the former name of **Vaasa.**

Ni+ko+la+yev (*Russian* nika'lajɪf) *n.* a city in the SW Soviet Union, in the S Ukrainian SSR on the Southern Bug about 64 km (40 miles) from the Black Sea: founded as a naval base in 1788; one of the leading Soviet Black Sea ports. Pop.: 424 000 (1975 est.). Former name: **Vernoleninsk.**

nil (nɪl) *n.* another word for **nothing,** used esp. in the scoring of certain games. [C19: from Latin]

nil de+spe+ran+dum ('nɪl ,dɛspə'rændəm) *interj.* never despair. [from Latin, literally: nothing to be despaired of]

Nile (naɪl) *n.* a river in Africa, rising in S central Burundi in its remotest headstream, the **Luvironza:** flows into Lake Victoria and leaves the lake as the **Victoria Nile,** flowing to Lake Albert, which is drained by the **Albert Nile,** becoming the White Nile on the border between Uganda and the Sudan; joined by its chief tributary, the **Blue Nile** (which rises near Lake Tana, Ethiopia) at Khartoum, and flows north to its delta on the Mediterranean; the longest river in the world. Length: (from the source of the Luvironza to the Mediterranean) 6741 km (4187 miles).

Nile blue *n.* **a.** a pale greenish-blue colour. **b.** (*as adj.*): *a Nile-blue carpet.*

Nile green *n.* **a.** a pale bluish-green colour. **b.** (*as adj.*): *a Nile-green dress.*

nil+gai ('nɪlgaɪ) *or* **nil+ghau** *n., pl.* **+gai, +gais** *or* **+ghau, ghaus.** a large Indian antelope, *Boselaphus tragocamelus.* The male is blue-grey with white markings and has small horns; the female is brownish and has no horns. [C19: from Hindi *nīlgāw* blue bull, from Sanskrit *nīla* dark blue + *go* bull]

Nil+gi+ri Hills ('nɪlgɪrɪ) *or* **Nil+gi+ris** *pl. n.* a plateau in S India, in Tamil Nadu. Average height: 2000 m (6500 ft.), reaching 2635 m (8647 ft.) in Doda Betta.

Ni·lo-Sa·har·an ('naɪlɒsə'hɑ:rən) *n.* **1.** a family of languages of Africa, spoken chiefly by Nilotic peoples in a region extending from the Sahara to Kenya and Tanzania, including the Chari-Nile, Saharan, Songhai, and other branches. Classification is complicated by the fact that many languages spoken in this region belong to the unrelated Afro-Asiatic, Kordofanian, and Niger-Congo families. ~*adj.* **2.** relating to or belonging to this family of languages.

Ni+lot+ic (naɪ'lɒtɪk) *adj.* **1.** of or relating to the Nile. **2.** of, relating to, or belonging to a tall Negroid pastoral people inhabiting the S Sudan, parts of Kenya and Uganda, and neighbouring countries. **3.** relating to or belonging to the group of languages spoken by the Nilotic peoples. ~*n.* **4.** a group of languages of E Africa, including Luo, Dinka, and Masai, now generally regarded as belonging to the Chari-Nile branch of the Nilo-Saharan family. [C17: via Latin from Greek *Neilotikós*, from *Neilos* the NILE]

Nils·son (*Swedish* 'nilsɔn) *n.* **Bir·git** ('birgit). born 1918, Swedish operatic soprano.

nim (nɪm) *n.* a game in which two players alternately remove one or more small items, such as matchsticks, from one of several rows or piles, the object being to take (or avoid taking) the last item remaining on the table. [C20: perhaps from archaic *nim* to take, from Old English *niman*]

nim+ble ('nɪmbᵊl) *adj.* **1.** agile, quick, and neat in movement: *nimble fingers.* **2.** alert; acute: *a nimble intellect.* [Old English *næmel* quick to grasp, and *numol* quick at seizing, both from *niman* to take] —**'nim+ble+ness** *n.* —**'nim+bly** *adv.*

nim·ble·wit ('nɪmbəl,wɪt) *n. Chiefly U.S.* an alert, bright, and clever person. —**'nim·ble+,wit+ted** *adj.*

nim+bo+stra+tus (,nɪmbəʊ'streɪtəs, -'strɑ:təs) *n., pl.* **+ti** (-taɪ). a dark-coloured rain-bearing stratus cloud.

nim+bus ('nɪmbəs) *n., pl.* **+bi** (-baɪ) *or* **+bus·es. 1. a.** a dark grey rain-bearing cloud. **b.** (*in combination*): *cumulonimbus clouds.* **2. a.** an emanation of light surrounding a saint or deity. **b.** a representation of this emanation. **3.** a surrounding aura or atmosphere. [C17: from Latin; cloud, radiance] —**'nim+bused** *adj.*

Nîmes (*French* nim) *n.* a city in S France: Roman remains including an amphitheatre and the Pont du Gard aqueduct. Pop.: 133 942 (1975).

ni+mi+e·ty (nɪ'maɪɪtɪ) *n., pl.* **·ties.** a rare word for **excess.** [C16: from Late Latin *nimietās*, from Latin *nimis* too much]

nim·i·ny-pim·i·ny ('nɪmɪnɪ'pɪmɪnɪ) *adj.* excessively refined; prim. [C19: imitative of a prim affected enunciation]

Nim·itz ('nɪmɪts) *n.* **Ches·ter Wil·liam.** 1885–1966, U.S. admiral; commander in chief of the U.S. Pacific fleet in World War II (1941–45).

ni+mon+ic al+loy (nɪ'mɒnɪk) *n.* any of various nickel-based alloys used at high temperatures, as in gas turbine blades. [C20: from NI(CKEL) + MO(LYBDENUM) + -IC]

Nim·rod ('nɪmrɒd) *n.* **1.** *Old Testament.* a hunter, who was famous for his prowess (Genesis 10:8–9). **2.** a person who is dedicated to or skilled in hunting. Douay spelling: **Nem·rod.** ~**Nim+'rod+i·an** *or* **Nim+'rod+ic** *adj.*

Nim+we+gen ('nɪm,ve:gᵊn) *n.* the German name for **Nijmegen.**

Ni·ña ('ni:nə; *Spanish* 'niɲa) *n.* **the.** one of the three ships commanded by Columbus in 1492.

nin+com+poop ('nɪnkəm,pu:p, 'nɪŋ-) *n.* a stupid person; fool; idiot. [C17: of unknown origin]

nine (naɪn) *n.* **1.** the cardinal number that is the sum of one and eight. See also **number** (sense 1). **2.** a numeral, 9, IX, etc., representing this number. **3.** something representing, represented by, or consisting of nine units, such as a playing card with nine symbols on it. **4.** Also: **nine o'clock.** nine hours after noon or midnight: *the play starts at nine.* **5. dressed (up) to the nines.** *Informal.* elaborately dressed. **6. 999** (in Britain) the telephone number of the emergency services. **7. nine to five.** normal office hours: *he works nine to five; a nine-to-five job.* ~*determiner.* **8. a.** amounting to nine: *nine days.* **b.** (*as pronoun*): *nine of the ten are ready.* ~Related prefixes: **nona-, nono-.** [Old English *nigon*; related to Gothic *niun*, Latin *novem*]

Nine (naɪn) *pl. n.* **the. 1.** the nine Muses. **2.** the nine member-states of the Common Market.

nine+fold ('naɪn,fəʊld) *adj.* **1.** equal to or having nine times as many or as much. **2.** composed of nine parts. ~*adv.* **3.** by or up to nine times as many or as much.

nine+pins ('naɪn,pɪnz) *n.* **1.** another name for **skittles. 2.** (*sing.*) one of the pins used in this game.

nine+teen (,naɪn'ti:n) *n.* **1.** the cardinal number that is the sum of ten and nine and is a prime number. See also **number** (sense 1). **2.** a numeral, 19, XIX, etc., representing this number. **3.** something represented by, representing, or consisting of 19 units. **4. talk nineteen to the dozen.** to talk incessantly. ~*determiner.* **5. a.** amounting to nineteen: *nineteen pictures.* **b.** (*as pronoun*): *only nineteen voted.* [Old English *nigontīne*]

nine+teenth (,naɪn'ti:nθ) *adj.* **1.** (*usually prenominal*) **a.** coming after the eighteenth in numbering or counting order, position, time, etc., being the ordinal number of *nineteen.* Often written: 19th. **b.** (*as n.*): *the nineteenth was rainy.* ~*n.* **2. a.** one of 19 approximately equal parts of something. **b.** (*as modifier*): *a nineteenth part.* **3.** the fraction that is equal to one divided by 19 (1/19).

nine+teenth hole *n. Golf, slang.* the bar in a golf clubhouse.

nine+teenth man *n.* **1.** *Australian Rules football.* the first reserve in a team. **2.** any person acting as a reserve or substitute.

nine+ti+eth ('naɪntɪɪθ) *adj.* **1.** (*usually prenominal*) **a.** being the ordinal number of *ninety* in numbering or counting order, position, time, etc. Often written: 90th. **b.** (*as n.*): *ninetieth in succession.* ~*n.* **2. a.** one of 90 approximately equal parts of something. **b.** (*as modifier*): *a ninetieth part.* **3.** the fraction equal to one divided by 90 (1/90).

nine+ty ('naɪntɪ) *n., pl.* **+ties. 1.** the cardinal number that is the product of ten and nine. See also **number** (sense 1). **2.** a numeral, 90, XC, etc., representing this number. **3.** something represented by, representing, or consisting of 90 units.

~*determiner.* **4. a.** amounting to ninety: *ninety times out of a hundred.* **b.** (*as pronoun*): *at least ninety are thought to be missing.* [Old English *nigontig*]

Ni·ne·veh ('nɪnɪvə) *n.* the ancient capital of Assyria, on the River Tigris opposite the present-day city of Mosul (N Iraq): at its height in the 8th and 7th centuries B.C.; destroyed in 612 B.C. by the Medes and Babylonians. —'**Ni+ne·vite** *n.*

Ning+po ('nɪŋ'pəʊ) *n.* a port in E China, in NE Chekiang, on the Yung River, about 20 km (12 miles) from its mouth at Hangchow Bay: one of the first sites of European settlement in China. Pop.: 237 500 (1953).

Ning+sia *or* **Ning+hsia** ('nɪŋ'ʃjɑː) *n.* **1.** a former province of NW China: mostly included in the Inner Mongolian AR in 1956, with the smaller part constituted as the Ningsia Hui AR in 1958. **2.** the former name of **Yinchwan.**

Ning+sia Hu·i Au·ton·o·mous Re+gion ('nɪŋ'ʃjɑː 'huːɪ) *n.* an administrative division of NW China, south of the Inner Mongolian AR. Capital: Yinchwan. Pop.: 3 000 000 (1976 est.). Area: 66 400 sq. km (25 896 sq. miles).

nin+ny ('nɪnɪ) *n., pl.* **+nies.** a dull-witted person. [C16: perhaps from *an innocent* simpleton] —'**nin+ny+ish** *adj.*

ni+non ('niːnɒn, 'naɪnɒn; *French* ninɔ̃) *n.* a fine strong silky fabric. [C20: from French]

ninth (naɪnθ) *adj.* **1.** (*usually prenominal*) **a.** coming after the eighth in counting order, position, time, etc.; being the ordinal number of *nine.* Often written: 9th. **b.** (*as n.*): *he came on the ninth; ninth in line.* ~*n.* **2. a.** one of nine equal or nearly equal parts of an object, quantity, measurement, etc. **b.** (*as modifier*): *a ninth part.* **3.** the fraction equal to one divided by nine (1/9). **4.** *Music.* **a.** an interval of one octave plus a second. **b.** one of tw notes constituting such an interval. **c.** see **ninth chord.** ~*adv.* **5.** Also: **ninthly.** after the eighth person, position, event, etc. ~ **6.** Also: **ninthly.** *sentence connector.* as the ninth point: linking what follows to the previous statement. [Old English *nigotha;* related to Old High German *niunto,* Old Norse *nīundi*]

ninth chord *n.* a chord much used in jazz and pop, consisting of a major or minor triad with the seventh and ninth added above the root. Often shortened to **ninth.**

Ni·nus ('naɪnəs) *n.* a king of Assyria and the legendary founder of Nineveh, husband of Semiramis.

Ni·o·be ('naɪəbɪ) *n. Greek myth.* a daughter of Tantalus, whose children were slain after she boasted of them: although turned into stone, she continued to weep. —**Ni·o+be·an** (naɪ'əʊbɪən) *adj.*

ni·o+bic (naɪ'əʊbɪk, -'ɒbɪk) *adj.* of or containing niobium in the pentavalent state. Also: **columbic.**

ni·o+bite ('naɪəˌbaɪt) *n.* another name for **columbite.** [C19: NIOBIUM + -ITE[1]]

ni·o·bi·um (naɪ'əʊbɪəm) *n.* a ductile white superconductive metallic element that occurs principally in columbite and tantalite: used in steel alloys. Symbol: Nb; atomic no.: 41; atomic wt.: 92.906; valency: 2, 3, or 5; relative density: 8.57; melting pt.: 2468°C; boiling pt.: 4927°C. Former name: **columbium.** [C19: from New Latin, from NIOBE (daughter of Tantalus), so named because it occurred in TANTALITE]

ni·o+bous (naɪ'əʊbəs) *adj.* of or containing niobium in the trivalent state. Also: **columbous.**

Niort (*French* njɔːr) *n.* a market town in W France. Pop.: 63 965 (1975).

nip[1] (nɪp) *vb.* **nips, nip+ping, nipped.** (*mainly tr.*) **1.** to catch or tightly compress, as between a finger and the thumb; pinch. **2.** (often foll. by *off*) to remove by clipping, biting, etc. **3.** (when *intr.,* often foll. by *at*) to give a small sharp bite (to): *the dog nipped at his heels.* **4.** (esp. of the cold) to affect with a stinging sensation. **5.** to harm through cold: *the frost nipped the young plants.* **6.** Also: **nip in the bud.** to check or destroy the growth of. **7.** *Slang.* to steal. **8.** (*intr.;* foll. by *along, up, out,* etc.) *Brit. informal.* to hurry; dart. **9.** *Slang, chiefly U.S.* to snatch. ~*n.* **10.** the act of nipping; a pinch, snip, etc. **11. a.** a frosty or chilly quality. **b.** severe frost or cold: *the first nip of winter.* **12.** a small piece or quantity: *he went out for a nip of fresh air.* **13.** a sharp flavour or tang. **14.** *Archaic.* a taunting remark. **15. nip and tuck.** *U.S.* neck and neck. [C14: of Scandinavian origin; compare Old Norse *hnippa* to prod]

nip[2] (nɪp) *n.* **1.** a small drink of spirits; dram. **2.** *Chiefly Brit.* a measure of spirits usually equal to one sixth of a gill. ~*vb.* **nips, nip+ping, nipped. 3.** to drink spirits, esp. habitually in small amounts. [C18: shortened from *nipperkin* a vessel holding a half pint or less, of uncertain origin; compare Dutch *nippen* to sip]

Nip (nɪp) *n. Slang.* a derogatory word for a Japanese. [C20: short for *Nipponese*]

ni·pa ('niːpə, 'naɪ-) *n.* **1.** a palm tree, *Nipa fruticans,* of S and SE Asia, having feathery leaves, used for thatching, and edible fruit. **2.** the fruit or thatch obtained from this tree. **3.** the sap of this tree, used to make a liquor. [C16: from Malay *nīpah*]

Nip·i+gon ('nɪpəgɒn) *n.* **Lake.** a lake in central Canada, in NW Ontario, draining into Lake Superior via the **Nipigon River.** Area: 4843 sq. km (1870 sq. miles).

Nip+is+sing ('nɪpɪsɪŋ) *n.* **Lake.** a lake in central Canada, in E Ontario between the Ottawa River and Georgian Bay. Area: 855 sq. km (330 sq. miles).

nip+per ('nɪpə) *n.* **1.** a person or thing that nips. **2.** the large pincer-like claw of a lobster, crab, or similar crustacean. **3.** *Informal, chiefly Brit.* a small child.

nip+pers ('nɪpəz) *pl. n.* an instrument or tool, such as a pair of pliers, for snipping, pinching, or squeezing.

nip+ping ('nɪpɪŋ) *adj.* **1.** sharp and biting: *a nipping wind.* **2.** sarcastic; bitter. —'**nip+ping+ly** *adv.*

nip·ple ('nɪpᵊl) *n.* **1.** Also called: **mammilla, papilla, teat.** the small conical projection in the centre of the areola of each breast, which in women contains the outlet of the milk ducts. **2.** something resembling a nipple in shape or function. **3.** Also called: **grease nipple.** a small drilled bush, usually screwed into a bearing, through which grease is introduced. **4.** *U.S.* an informal word for **dummy** (sense 11). [C16: from earlier *neble, nible,* perhaps from NEB, NIB]

nip·ple+wort ('nɪpᵊlˌwɜːt) *n.* an annual Eurasian plant, *Lapsana communis,* with pointed oval leaves and small yellow flower heads: family *Compositae* (composites).

Nip+pon ('nɪpɒn) *n.* transliteration of the Japanese name for **Japan.** —**Nip+pon+ese** (ˌnɪpə'niːz) *adj., n.*

Nip+pur (nɪ'pʊə) *n.* an ancient Sumerian and Babylonian city, the excavated site of which is in SE Iraq: an important religious centre, abandoned in the 12th or 13th century.

nip+py ('nɪpɪ) *adj.* **+pi+er, +pi+est. 1.** biting, sharp, or chilly. **2.** *Brit. informal.* **a.** quick; nimble; active. **b.** (of a motor vehicle) small and relatively powerful. —'**nip+pi+ly** *adv.*

N.I.R.C. *abbrev. for* National Industrial Relations Court.

nir+va+na (nɪə'vɑːnə, nɜː-) *n. Buddhism, Hinduism.* final release from the cycle of reincarnation attained by extinction of all desires and individual existence, culminating (in Buddhism) in absolute blessedness, or (in Hinduism) in absorption into Brahman. [C19: from Sanskrit: extinction, literally: a blowing out, from *nir-* out + *vāti* it blows] —**nir+'va+nic** *adj.*

Niš *or* **Nish** (niːʃ) *n.* an industrial town in E Yugoslavia, in SE Serbia: situated on routes between central Europe and the Aegean. Pop.: 127 654 (1971).

Ni+san *Hebrew.* (niː'san) *n.* the seventh month of the civil year and the first of the ecclesiastical year in the Jewish calendar, falling approximately in March and April.

Ni+sha+pur (ˌniːʃɑː'pʊə) *n.* a town in NE Iran, at an altitude of 1195 m (3920 ft.): birthplace and burial place of Omar Khayyam. Pop.: 33 482 (1966).

Ni+shi+no+mi+ya (ˌniːʃɪ'nɒmɪjə) *n.* an industrial city in central Japan, on S Honshu, northwest of Osaka. Pop.: 383 568 (1974 est.).

ni·si ('naɪsaɪ) *adj.* (*postpositive*) *Law.* (of a court order, etc.) coming into effect on a specified date unless cause is shown within a certain period why it should not: *a decree nisi.* [C19: from Latin: unless, if not]

ni·si pri+us ('praɪəs) *n.* **1.** *English legal history.* **a.** a direction that a case be brought up to Westminster for trial before a single judge and a jury. **b.** the writ giving this direction. **c.** trial before the justices taking the assizes. **2.** (in the U.S.) a court where civil actions are tried by a single judge sitting with a jury as distinguished from an appellate court. [C15: from Latin: unless previously]

Nis·sen hut ('nɪsᵊn) *n.* a military shelter of semicircular cross section, made of corrugated steel sheet. U.S. equivalent: **Quonset hut.** [C20: named after Lt. Col. Peter *Nissen* (1871–1930), British mining engineer, its inventor]

ni+sus ('naɪsəs) *n., pl.* **+sus.** an impulse towards or striving after a goal. [C17: from Latin: effort, from *nītī* to strive]

nit[1] (nɪt) *n.* **1.** the egg of a louse, usually adhering to human hair. **2.** the larva of a louse or similar insect. [Old English *hnitu;* related to Dutch *neet,* Old High German *hniz*]

nit[2] (nɪt) *n.* a unit of luminance equal to 1 candela per square metre. [C20: from Latin *nitor* brightness]

nit[3] (nɪt) *n. Informal, chiefly Brit.* short for **nitwit.**

nit[4] (nɪt) *n.* a unit of information equal to 1.44 bits. Also called: **nepit.** [C20: from *n(apierian dig)it*]

nit[5] (nɪt) *n.* **keep nit.** *Austral. informal.* to keep watch, esp. during illegal activity. [C19: from *nix!* a shout of warning]

ni+ter ('naɪtə) *n.* the usual U.S. spelling of **nitre.**

Ni+te·rói (*Portuguese* ˌnite'rɔɪ) *n.* a port in SE Brazil, on Guanabara Bay opposite Rio de Janeiro: contains Brazil's chief shipyards. Pop.: 291 970 (1970). Also called: **Nictheroy.**

ni+tid ('nɪtɪd) *adj. Poetic.* bright; glistening. [C17: from Latin *nitidus,* from *nitere* to shine]

ni+ton ('naɪtɒn) *n.* a less common name for **radon.** [C20: from Latin *nitēre* to shine]

nit-pick·ing *Informal.* ~*n.* **1.** a concern with insignificant details, esp. with the intention of finding fault. ~*adj.* **2.** showing such a concern; fussy. —'**nit-ˌpick·er** *n.*

ni+tra+mine (ˌnaɪtrəˌmiːn) *n.* another name for **tetryl.**

ni+trate ('naɪtreɪt) *n.* **1.** any salt or ester of nitric acid, such as sodium nitrate, $NaNO_3$. **2.** a fertilizer consisting of or containing nitrate salts. ~*vb.* **3.** (*tr.*) to treat with nitric acid or a nitrate. **4.** to convert or be converted into a nitrate. **5.** to undergo or cause to undergo the chemical process in which a nitro group is introduced into a molecule. —**ni+'tra+tion** *n.*

ni+tre *or U.S.* **ni+ter** ('naɪtə) *n.* another name for **potassium nitrate** *or* **sodium nitrate.** [C14: via Old French from Latin *nitrum* from Greek *nitron* NATRON]

ni+tric ('naɪtrɪk) *adj.* of or containing nitrogen, esp. in the pentavalent state.

ni+tric ac·id *n.* a colourless or yellowish fuming corrosive liquid usually used in aqueous solution. It is an oxidizing agent and a strong monobasic acid: important in the manufacture of fertilizers, explosives, and many other chemicals. Formula: HNO_3. Former name: **aqua fortis.**

ni+tric bac+te+ri·a *n.* bacteria that convert nitrites to nitrates in the soil. See also **nitrobacteria.**

ni+tric ox+ide *n.* a colourless slightly soluble gas forming red fumes of nitrogen dioxide in air. Formula: NO.

ni+tride ('naɪtraɪd) *n.* a compound of nitrogen with a more electropositive element, for example magnesium nitride, Mg_3N_2.

ni+trid+ing ('naɪtraɪdɪŋ) *n.* a type of case-hardening in which steel is heated for long periods in ammonia vapour so that nitrogen produced by dissociation on the surface enters the steel.

ni+tri+fi+ca+tion (ˌnaɪtrɪfɪ'keɪʃən) *n.* **1.** the oxidation of the ammonium compounds in dead organic material into nitrites and nitrates by soil nitrobacteria, making nitrogen available to plants. See also **nitrogen cycle. 2. a.** the addition of a nitro group to an organic compound. **b.** the substitution of a nitro group for another group in an organic compound.

ni+tri+fy ('naɪtrɪˌfaɪ) *vb.* **+fies, +fy+ing, +fied.** (*tr.*) **1.** to treat or cause to react with nitrogen or a nitrogen compound. **2.** to treat (soil) with nitrates. **3.** (of nitrobacteria) to convert (ammonium compounds) into nitrates by oxidation. —**'ni+tri+ˌfi+a·ble** *adj.*

ni+trile ('naɪtrɪl, -traɪl) *n.* any one of a class of organic compounds containing the monovalent group, -CN. Also called (not in technical usage): **cyanide.**

ni+trite ('naɪtraɪt) *n.* any salt or ester of nitrous acid.

ni·tro- *or before a vowel* **nitr-** *combining form.* **1.** indicating that a chemical compound contains a nitro group, $-NO_2$: *nitrobenzene.* **2.** indicating that a chemical compound is a nitrate ester: *nitrocellulose.* [from Greek *nitron* NATRON]

ni+tro+bac+te+ri+a (ˌnaɪtrəubæk'tɪərɪə) *pl. n., sing.* **+te+ri+um** (-'tɪərɪəm). soil bacteria of the order *Pseudomonadales* that are involved in nitrification, including species of *Nitrosomonas* and *Nitrobacter.*

ni+tro+ben+zene (ˌnaɪtrəu'benzi:n) *n.* a yellow oily toxic water-insoluble liquid compound, used as a solvent and in the manufacture of aniline. Formula: $C_6H_5NO_2$.

ni+tro+cel+lu+lose (ˌnaɪtrəu'seljuˌləus) *n.* another name (not in chemical usage) for **cellulose nitrate.**

ni+tro+chlo+ro+form (ˌnaɪtrəu'klɒrəˌfɔ:m) *n.* another name for **chloropicrin.**

ni+tro com+pound *n.* any one of a class of usually organic compounds that contain the monovalent group, $-NO_2$ (**nitro group** or **radical**), linked to a carbon atom. The commonest example is nitrobenzene, $C_6H_5NO_2$.

ni+tro+gen ('naɪtrədʒən) *n.* **a.** a colourless odourless relatively unreactive gaseous element that forms 78 per cent (by volume) of the air, occurs in many compounds, and is an essential constituent of proteins and nucleic acids: used in the manufacture of ammonia and other chemicals and as a refrigerant. Symbol: N; atomic no.: 7; atomic wt.: 14.0067; valency: 3 or 5; density: 1/251 kg/m³; melting pt.: -209.86°C; boiling pt.: -195.8°C. **b.** (*as modifier*): *nitrogen cycle.*

ni+tro+gen cy+cle *n.* the natural circulation of nitrogen by living organisms. Nitrates in the soil, derived from dead organic matter by bacterial action (see **nitrification, nitrogen fixation**), are absorbed and synthesized into complex organic compounds by plants and reduced to nitrates again when the plants and the animals feeding on them die and decay.

ni+tro+gen di+ox+ide *n.* a red-brown poisonous irritating gas that, at ordinary temperatures, exists in equilibrium with dinitrogen tetroxide. It is an intermediate in the manufacture of nitric acid, a nitrating agent, and an oxidizer for rocket fuels. Formula: NO_2.

ni+tro+gen fix+a+tion *n.* **1.** the conversion of atmospheric nitrogen into nitrogen compounds by soil bacteria, such as *Rhizobium,* in the root nodules of legumes, and by certain blue-green algae. **2.** a process, such as the Haber process, in which atmospheric nitrogen is converted into a nitrogen compound, used esp. for the manufacture of fertilizer. —**'ni+tro·gen-ˌfix·ing** *adj.*

ni+trog+en+ize *or* **ni+trog+en+ise** (naɪ'trɒdʒɪˌnaɪz) *vb.* to combine or treat with nitrogen or a nitrogen compound. —**ni+ˌtrog+en+i+'za+tion** *or* **ni+ˌtrog+en+i+'sa+tion** *n.*

ni+tro+gen mus+tard *n.* any of a class of organic compounds resembling mustard gas in their molecular structure. General formula: $RN(CH_2CH_2Cl)_2$, where R is an organic group: important in the treatment of cancer.

ni+trog+e+nous (naɪ'trɒdʒɪnəs) *adj.* containing nitrogen or a nitrogen compound: *a nitrogenous fertilizer.*

ni+tro+gen per+ox+ide *n.* **1.** another name for **nitrogen dioxide. 2.** the equilibrium mixture of nitrogen dioxide and dinitrogen tetroxide.

ni+tro+gen te+trox+ide *n.* **1.** another name for **dinitrogen tetroxide. 2.** a brown liquefied mixture of nitrogen dioxide and dinitrogen tetroxide, used as a nitrating, bleaching, and oxidizing agent.

ni+tro+glyc+er+in (ˌnaɪtrəu'glɪsərɪn) *or* **ni+tro+glyc+er+ine** (ˌnaɪtrəu'glɪsəˌri:n) *n.* a pale yellow viscous explosive liquid substance made from glycerol and nitric and sulphuric acids and used in explosives and in medicine as a vasodilator. Formula: $CH_2NO_3CHNO_3CH_2NO_3$. Also called: **trinitroglycerin.**

ni+tro+hy+dro+chlo+ric ac+id (ˌnaɪtrəuˌhaɪdrəu'klɒrɪk) *n.* another name for **aqua regia.**

ni+trom+e+ter (naɪ'trɒmɪtə) *n.* an instrument for measuring the amount of nitrogen in a substance. —**ni+tro+met+ric** (ˌnaɪtrəu'metrɪk) *adj.*

ni+tro+me+thane (ˌnaɪtrəu'mi:θeɪn) *n.* an oily colourless liquid obtained from methane and used as a solvent and rocket fuel and in the manufacture of synthetic resins. Formula: CH_3NO_2.

ni+tro+par+af+fin (ˌnaɪtrəu'pærəfɪn) *n.* any of a class of colourless toxic compounds with the general formula $C_nH_{2n+1}NO_2$.

ni+tros+a+mine (ˌnaɪtrəusə'mi:n, ˌnaɪtrəus'æmi:n) *n.* any one of a class of neutral, usually yellow oily compounds containing the divalent group =NNO.

ni+tro+so (naɪ'trəusəu) *n.* (*modifier*) of, consisting of, or containing the monovalent group O:N-: *a nitroso compound.* [C19: from Latin *nitrōsus* full of natron; see NITRE]

ni+tro+syl ('naɪtrəsɪl, -ˌsaɪl) *n.* (*modifier*) another word for **nitroso,** esp. when applied to inorganic compounds: *nitrosyl chloride.* [C19: see NITROSO]

ni+trous ('naɪtrəs) *adj.* of, derived from, or containing nitrogen, esp. in a low valency state. [C17: from Latin *nitrōsus* full of natron]

ni+trous ac·id *n.* a weak monobasic acid known only in solution and in the form of nitrite salts. Formula: HNO_2.

ni+trous bac+te+ri+a *pl. n.* bacteria that convert ammonia to nitrites in the soil. See also **nitrobacteria.**

ni+trous ox+ide *n.* a colourless nonflammable slightly soluble gas with a sweet smell: used as an anaesthetic in dentistry and surgery. Formula: N_2O. Also called: **laughing gas.**

nit+ty¹ ('nɪtɪ) *adj.* **+ti+er, +ti+est.** infested with nits.

nit+ty² ('nɪtɪ) *adj.* **+ti+er, +ti+est.** *Informal.* foolish; stupid. [C20: from NITWIT]

nit·ty-grit·ty ('nɪtɪ'grɪtɪ) *n.* **the.** *Slang.* the basic facts of a matter, situation, etc.; the core. [C20: perhaps rhyming compound formed from GRIT]

nit+wit ('nɪtˌwɪt) *n.* a foolish or dull person. [C20: NIT + WIT]

Ni·u·e (nɪ'u:eɪ) *n.* an island in the S Pacific, between Tonga and the Cook Islands: annexed by New Zealand (1901); achieved full internal self-government in 1974. Chief town and port: Alofi. Pop.: 4990 (1971). Area: 260 sq. km (100 sq. miles). Also called: **Savage Island.**

ni+val ('naɪvᵊl) *adj.* of or growing in or under snow. [C17: from Latin *nivālis* from *nix* snow]

ni+va+tion (naɪ'veɪʃən) *n.* the weathering of rock around a patch of snow by alternate freezing and thawing. [C19: from Latin *nix,* stem *niv-* snow]

Niv·en ('nɪvᵊn) *n.* **Da·vid.** born 1909, British film actor and television personality. His films include *Thank You Jeeves* (1936), *Around the World in 80 Days* (1956), *Casino Royale* (1967), and *Paper Tiger* (1975).

niv+e·ous ('nɪvɪəs) *adj.* resembling snow, esp. in colour. [C17: from Latin *niveus* from *nix* snow]

Ni+ver+nais (*French* nivɛr'nɛ) *n.* a former province of central France, around Nevers.

Ni+vôse *French.* (ni'vo:z) *n.* the fourth month of the French revolutionary calendar, extending from Dec. 22 to Jan. 20. [C18: via French from Latin *nivōsus* snowy, from *nix* snow]

nix¹ (nɪks) *U.S. Informal.* **1.** *sentence substitute.* another word for **no**¹. ~*interj.* **2.** be careful! watch out! ~*n.* **3.** a rejection or refusal. **4.** nothing at all. ~*vb.* **5.** (*tr.*) to veto, deny, reject, or forbid (plans, suggestions, etc.). [C18: from German, colloquial form of *nichts* nothing]

nix² (nɪks) *or* (*fem.*) **nix·ie** ('nɪksɪ) *n. Germanic myth.* a water sprite, usually unfriendly to humans. [C19: from German *Nixe* nymph or water spirit, from Old High German *nihhus;* related to Old English *nicor* sea monster]

nix+er ('nɪksə) *n. Dublin dialect.* a spare-time job. [probably from NIX¹, since the income derived from this job alone is too small to support the worker.

Nix·ie tube ('nɪksɪ) *n. Electronics.* another name for **digitron.**

Nix·on ('nɪksən) *n.* **Rich·ard Mil·hous.** born 1913, U.S. politician; 37th president from 1969 until he resigned in 1974.

ni+zam (naɪ'zæm) *n.* (formerly) a Turkish regular soldier. [C18: ultimately from Arabic *nizām* order, arrangement]

Ni+zam (nɪ'zɑ:m) *n.* the title of the ruler of Hyderabad, India, from 1724 to 1948.

Nizh+ni Nov+go+rod (*Russian* 'niʒnij 'nɔvgərət) *n.* the former name (until 1932) of **Gorki**¹.

Nizh+ni Ta+gil (*Russian* 'niʒnij ta'gil) *n.* a city in the central Soviet Union, on the E slopes of the Ural Mountains: a major metallurgical centre. Pop.: 394 000 (1975 est.).

N.J. *abbrev. for* New Jersey.

Njord (njɔ:d) *or* **Njorth** (njɔ:θ) *n. Norse myth.* the god of the sea, fishing, and prosperity.

N.K.G.B. *abbrev. for* People's Commissariat of State Security; the Soviet secret police from 1943 to 1946. [from Russian *Narodny komissariat gosudarstvennoi bezopasnosti*]

Nko·mo (ᵊŋ'kəuməu) *n.* **Josh·u·a.** born 1917, Zimbabwean politician; leader of one wing of the Patriotic Front guerrillas and the Patriotic Front party.

Nkru·mah (ᵊŋ'kru:mə) *n.* **Kwa·me** ('kwɑ:mɪ). 1909–72, Ghanaian statesman, prime minister (1957-60) and president (1960-66). He led demands for self-government in the 1950s, achieving Ghanaian independence in 1957. He was overthrown by a military coup (1966).

NKVD *abbrev.* the Soviet police and secret police from 1934 to 1943: the police from 1943–46. [from Russian *Narodny komissariat vnutrennikh del* People's Commissariat of Internal Affairs]

NL, N.L., *or* **NL.** *abbrev. for* New Latin.

n.l. *abbrev. for:* **1.** *Printing.* new line. **2.** non licet. [Latin: it is not permitted] **3.** non liquet. [Latin: it is not clear]

N.L.C. *abbrev. for* National Liberal Club.

N.L.F. *abbrev. for* National Liberation Front.

N.L.L.S.T. *n. abbrev. for* National Lending Library for Science and Technology.

n.m. *abbrev. for* nautical mile.

N. Mex. *abbrev. for* New Mexico.

NMR *abbrev. for* nuclear magnetic resonance.

NNE *abbrev. for* north-northeast.
NNW *abbrev. for* north-northwest.
no[1] (nəʊ) *sentence substitute.* **1.** used to express denial, disagreement, refusal, disapproval, disbelief, or acknowledgement of negative statements. **2.** used with question intonation to query a previous negative statement, as in disbelief: *Alfred isn't dead yet. No?* ~*adv.* **3.** (*sentence modifier*) used to emphasize a negative statement, esp. when disagreeing: *no you can't.* ~*n., pl.* **noes** *or* **nos. 4.** an answer or vote of *no.* **5.** (*often pl.*) a person who votes in the negative. **6. the noes have it.** there is a majority of votes in the negative. Compare (for senses 4–6) **aye. 7. not take no for an answer.** to continue in a course of action, etc., despite refusals. ~Compare **yes.** [Old English *nā*, from *ne* not, no + *ā* ever; see AY[1]]
no[2] (nəʊ) *determiner.* **1.** not any, not a, or not one: *there's no money left; no card in the file.* **2.** not by a long way; not at all: *she's no youngster.* **3.** (foll. by comparative adjectives and adverbs) not: *no less than forty men; no taller than a child; no more quickly than before.* [Old English *nā*, changed from *nān* NONE[1]]
No[1] *or* **Noh** (nəʊ) *n., pl.* **No** *or* **Noh.** the stylized classic drama of Japan, developed in the 15th century or earlier, using music, dancing, chanting, elaborate costumes, and themes from religious stories or myths. [from Japanese *nō* talent, from Chinese *neng*]
No[2] *the chemical symbol for* nobelium.
No[3] (nəʊ) *n.* **Lake.** a lake in the S central Sudan, where the Bahr el Jebel (White Nile) is joined by the Bahr el Ghazal. Area: about 103 sq. km (40 sq. miles).
No. *abbrev. for:* **1.** north(ern). **2.** (*pl.* **Nos., nos.**) Also: **no.** number. [from French *numéro*]
n.o. *Cricket. abbrev. for* not out.
no-ac·count *U.S. dialect.* ~*adj.* **1.** worthless; good-for-nothing. ~*n.* **2.** a worthless person.
No·a·chi·an (nəʊˈeɪkɪən) *or* **No+ach+ic** (nəʊˈækɪk, -ˈeɪkɪk) *adj. Old Testament.* of or relating to the patriarch Noah.
No·ah (ˈnəʊə) *n. Old Testament.* a Hebrew patriarch, who saved himself, his family, and a pair of each species of animal and bird from the Flood by building a ship (**Noah's Ark**) in which they all survived (Genesis 6–8).
nob[1] (nɒb) *n. Cribbage.* **1.** the jack of the suit turned up. **2. one for his nob.** the call made with this jack, scoring one point. [C19: of uncertain origin]
nob[2] (nɒb) *n. Slang, chiefly Brit.* a person of wealth or social distinction. [C19: of uncertain origin] **—nob+by** *adj.* **—nob+bi+ly** *adv.*
no-ball *n.* **1.** *Cricket.* an illegal ball, as for overstepping the crease, throwing, etc., for which the batting side scores a run unless the batsman hits the ball, in which case he can only be out by being run out. **2.** *Rounders.* an illegal ball, esp. one bowled too high or too low. ~*interj.* **3.** *Cricket, rounders.* a call by the umpire indicating a no-ball.
nob+ble (ˈnɒbᵊl) *vb.* (*tr.*) *Brit. slang.* **1.** to disable (a race horse), esp. with drugs. **2.** to win over or outwit (a person) by underhand means. **3.** to steal; filch. **4.** to get hold of; grab. **5.** to kidnap. [C19: back formation from *nobbler*, from false division of *an hobbler* (one who hobbles horses) as *a nobbler*] **—ˈnob+bler** *n.*
nob+but (ˈnɒbət) *adv. Dialect.* nothing but; only. [C14: from NO[1] + BUT[1]]
No·bel (nəʊˈbɛl) *n.* **Al·fred Bern·hard** (ˈalfreːd ˈbæːrnhard). 1833–96, Swedish chemist, engineer, and philanthropist, noted for his invention of dynamite (1866) and for his bequest for the foundation of the Nobel prizes.
no+be·li·um (nəʊˈbiːlɪəm) *n.* a transuranic element produced artificially from curium. Symbol: No; atomic no.: 102; half-life of most stable isotope, ^{255}No: 180 seconds (approx.). [C20: New Latin, named after *Nobel* Institute, Stockholm, where it was discovered]
No·bel prize *n.* an annual prize awarded since 1901 for outstanding contributions to chemistry, physics, physiology and medicine, literature, economics, and peace. The recipients are chosen by an international committee centred in Sweden.
no+bil·i·a+ry (nəˈbɪlɪərɪ) *adj.* of or relating to the nobility. [C18: from French *nobiliaire*; see NOBLE, -ARY]
no+bil·i·a+ry par+ti+cle *n.* a preposition, such as French *de* or German *von*, occurring as part of a title or surname: *Marquis de Sade; Wernher von Braun.*
no+bil·i·ty (nəʊˈbɪlɪtɪ) *n., pl.* **·ties. 1.** a socially or politically privileged class whose titles are conferred by descent or by royal decree. **2.** the state or quality of being morally or spiritually good; dignity: *the nobility of his mind.* **3.** (in the British Isles) the class of people holding the title of dukes, marquesses, earls, viscounts, or barons and their feminine equivalents collectively; peerage.
no+ble (ˈnəʊbᵊl) *adj.* **1.** of or relating to a hereditary class with special social or political status, often derived from a feudal period. **2.** of or characterized by high moral qualities; magnanimous: *a noble deed.* **3.** having dignity or eminence; illustrious. **4.** grand or imposing; magnificent: *a noble avenue of trees.* **5.** of superior quality or kind; excellent: *a noble strain of horses.* **6.** *Chem.* **a.** (of certain elements) chemically unreactive. **b.** (of certain metals, esp. copper, silver, and gold) resisting oxidation. **7.** *Falconry.* **a.** designating long-winged falcons that capture their quarry by stooping on it from above. Compare **ignoble. b.** designating the type of quarry appropriate to a particular species of falcon. ~*n.* **8.** a person belonging to a privileged social or political class whose status is usually indicated by a title conferred by sovereign authority or descent. **9.** (in the British Isles) a person holding the title of duke, marquess, earl, viscount, or baron, or a feminine equivalent. **10.** a former Brit. gold coin having the value of one third of a pound. [C13: via Old French from Latin *nōbilis*, originally, capable of being known, hence well-known, noble, from *noscere* to know] **—ˈno+ble+ness** *n.* **—ˈno+bly** *adv.*
no+ble art *or* **sci+ence** *n.* **the.** boxing.
no·ble+man (ˈnəʊbᵊlmən) *or* (*fem.*) **no·ble+wom·an** *n., pl.* **+men** *or* **+wom·en.** a person of noble rank, title, or status; peer; aristocrat.
no+ble sav+age *n.* (in romanticism) an idealized view of primitive man.
no+blesse (nəʊˈblɛs) *n. Literary.* **1.** noble birth or condition. **2.** the noble class. [C13: from Old French; see NOBLE]
no+blesse o·blige (nəʊˈblɛs əʊˈbliːʒ; *French* nɔblɛs ɔˈbliːʒ) *n. Often ironic.* the supposed obligation of nobility to be honourable and generous. [French, literally: nobility obliges]
no+bod·y (ˈnəʊbədɪ) *pron.* **1.** no person; no one. ~*n., pl.* **+bod·ies. 2.** an insignificant person.
Usage. See at **everyone.**
no+ci+cep+tive (ˌnəʊsɪˈsɛptɪv) *adj.* causing or reacting to pain. [C20: from Latin *nocēre* to injure + RECEPTIVE]
nock (nɒk) *n.* **1.** a notch on an arrow that fits on the bowstring. **2.** either of the grooves at each end of a bow that hold the bowstring. ~*vb.* (*tr.*) **3.** to fit (an arrow) on a bowstring. **4.** to put a groove or notch in (a bow or arrow). [C14: related to Swedish *nock* tip]
nock+ing point *n.* a marked part of the bowstring where the arrow is placed.
no-claim bo+nus *n.* a reduction on an insurance premium, esp. one covering a motor vehicle, if no claims have been made within a specified period. Also called: **no-claims bonus.**
noc+tam+bu+lism (nɒkˈtæmbjʊˌlɪzəm) *or* **noc+tam+bu+la+tion** *n.* another word for **somnambulism.** [C19: from Latin *nox* night + *ambulāre* to walk] **—noc+ˈtam+bu+list** *n.*
noc·ti- *or before a vowel* **noct-** *combining form.* night: *noctilucent.* [from Latin *nox, noct-*]
noc+ti+lu+ca (ˌnɒktɪˈluːkə) *n., pl.* **+cae** (-siː). any bioluminescent marine dinoflagellate protozoan of the genus *Noctiluca.* [C17: from Latin, from *nox* night + *lūcēre* to shine]
noc+ti+lu+cent (ˌnɒktɪˈluːsᵊnt) *adj.* shining at night, as certain high-altitude clouds, believed to consist of meteor dust that reflects sunlight. **—ˌnoc+ti+ˈlu+cence** *n.*
noc+tu+id (ˈnɒktjʊɪd) *n.* **1.** any nocturnal moth of the family *Noctuidae:* includes the underwings and antler moth. See also **cutworm, army worm.** ~*adj.* **2.** of, relating to, or belonging to the *Noctuidae.* [C19: via New Latin from Latin *noctua* night owl, from *nox* night]
noc+tule (ˈnɒktjuːl) *n.* any of several large Old World insectivorous bats of the genus *Nyctalus,* esp. *N. noctula:* family *Vespertilionidae.* [C18: probably from Late Latin *noctula* small owl, from Latin *noctua* night owl]
noc+turn (ˈnɒktɜːn) *n. R.C. Church.* any of the main sections of the office of matins. [C13: from Medieval Latin *nocturna* (n.), from Latin *nocturnus* nocturnal, from *nox* night]
noc+tur+nal (nɒkˈtɜːnᵊl) *adj.* **1.** of, used during, occurring in, or relating to the night. **2.** (of animals) active at night. **3.** (of plants) having flowers that open at night and close by day. ~Compare **diurnal.** [C15: from Late Latin *nocturnālis*, from Latin *nox* night] **—ˌnoc+tur+ˈnal+i+ty** *n.* **—noc+ˈtur+nal+ly** *adv.*
noc+turne (ˈnɒktɜːn) *n.* **1.** a short, lyrical piece of music, esp. one for the piano. **2.** a painting or tone poem of a night scene.
noc·u·ous (ˈnɒkjʊəs) *adj. Rare.* harmful; noxious. [C17: from Latin *nocuus*, from *nocēre* to hurt] **—ˈnoc·u·ous+ly** *adv.* **—ˈnoc·u·ous+ness** *n.*
nod (nɒd) *vb.* **nods, nod+ding, nod+ded. 1.** to lower and raise (the head) briefly, as to indicate agreement, invitation, etc. **2.** (*tr.*) to express or indicate by nodding: *she nodded approval.* **3.** (*tr.*) to bring or direct by nodding: *she nodded me towards the manager's office.* **4.** (*intr.*) (of flowers, trees, etc.) to sway or bend forwards and back. **5.** (*intr.*) to let the head fall forward through drowsiness; be almost asleep: *the old lady sat nodding by the fire.* **6.** (*intr.*) to be momentarily inattentive or careless: *even Homer sometimes nods.* ~*n.* **7.** a quick down-and-up movement of the head, as in assent, command, etc.: *she greeted him with a nod.* **8.** a short sleep; nap. See also **land of Nod. 9.** a swaying motion, as of flowers, etc., in the wind. **10. the nod.** *Boxing, informal.* the award of a contest to a competitor on the basis of points scored. ~See also **nod off.** [C14 *nodde*, of obscure origin] **—ˈnod+ding+ly** *adv.*
nod+al (ˈnəʊdᵊl) *adj.* of or like a node. **—no+ˈdal+i+ty** *n.*
nod+dle[1] (ˈnɒdᵊl) *n. Informal, chiefly Brit.* the head or brains: *use your noddle!* [C15: origin obscure]
nod+dle[2] (ˈnɒdᵊl) *vb. Informal, chiefly Brit.* to nod (the head), as through drowsiness. [C18: from NOD]
nod+dy (ˈnɒdɪ) *n., pl.* **+dies. 1.** any of several tropical terns of the genus *Anous*, esp. *A. stolidus* (**common noddy**), typically having a dark plumage. **2.** a fool or dunce. [C16: perhaps noun use of obsolete *noddy* foolish, drowsy, perhaps from NOD (vb.); the bird is so called because it allows itself to be caught by hand]
node (nəʊd) *n.* **1.** a knot, swelling, or knob. **2.** the point on a plant stem from which the leaves or lateral branches grow. **3.** *Physics.* a point of zero or minimum displacement in a standing wave. Compare **antinode. 4.** Also called: **crunode.** *Maths.* a point at which two branches of a curve intersect, each branch having a distinct tangent. **5.** *Maths., linguistics.* one of the

objects of which a graph or a tree consists; vertex. **6.** *Astronomy.* either of the two points at which the orbit of a body intersects the plane of the ecliptic. When the body moves from the south to the north side of the ecliptic it passes the **ascending node** and from the north to the south side it passes the **descending node. 7.** *Anatomy.* **a.** any natural bulge or swelling of a structure or part, such as those that occur along the course of a lymphatic vessel (**lymph node**). **b.** a finger joint or knuckle. [C16: from Latin *nōdus* knot]

node house *n.* a prefabricated shelter used by welders during the construction of an oil rig.

node of Ran·vi·er ('rɑːnvɪˌeɪ) *n.* any of the gaps that occur at regular intervals along the length of the sheath of a myelinated nerve fibre, at which the axon is exposed. [C19: named after Louis-Antoine *Ranvier* (1835–1922), French histologist]

nod·i·cal ('nəʊdɪkᵊl, 'nɒdɪ-) *adj.* of or relating to the nodes of a celestial body, esp. of the moon.

nod off *vb.* (*intr., adv.*) *Informal.* to fall asleep.

no·dose ('nəʊdəʊs, nəʊ'dəʊs) *or* **no·dous** ('nəʊdəs) *adj.* having nodes or knotlike swellings: *nodose stems.* [C18: from Latin *nōdōsus* knotty] —**no·dos·i·ty** (nəʊ'dɒsɪtɪ) *n.*

nod·ule ('nɒdjuːl) *n.* **1.** a small knot, lump, or node. **2.** Also called: **root nodule.** any of the knoblike outgrowths on the roots of clover and many other legumes: contain bacteria involved in nitrogen fixation. **3.** *Anatomy.* any small node or knoblike protuberance. **4.** a small rounded lump of rock or mineral substance, esp. in a matrix of different rock material. [C17: from Latin *nōdulus* from *nōdus* knot] —**'nod·u·lar, 'nod·u·lose,** *or* **'nod·u·lous** *adj.*

no·dus ('nəʊdəs) *n., pl.* **-di** (-daɪ). **1.** a problematic idea, situation, etc. **2.** another word for **node.** [C14: from Latin: knot]

No·el *or* **No·ël** (nəʊ'ɛl) *n.* **1.** (in carols, etc.) another word for **Christmas. 2.** (*often not cap.*) *Rare.* a Christmas carol. [C19: from French, from Latin *nātālis* a birthday; see NATAL]

no·e·sis (nəʊ'iːsɪs) *n.* **1.** *Philosophy.* the exercise of reason, esp. in the apprehension of universal forms. Compare **dianoia. 2.** *Psychol.* the mental process used in learning; the functioning of the intellect. See also **cognition.** [C19: from Greek *noēsis* thought, from *noein* to think]

no·et·ic (nəʊ'ɛtɪk) *adj.* of or relating to the mind, esp. to its rational and intellectual faculties. [C17: from Greek *noētikos*, from *noein* to think, from *nous* the mind]

Nof·re·te·te (ˌnɒfrɛ'tiːtɪ) *n.* a variant of **Nefertiti.**

nog[1] *or* **nogg** (nɒg) *n.* **1.** Also called: **flip.** a drink, esp. an alcoholic one, containing beaten egg. **2.** *East Anglian dialect.* strong local beer. [C17 (originally: a strong beer): of obscure origin]

nog[2] (nɒg) *n.* **1.** a wooden peg or block built into a masonry or brick wall to provide a fixing for nails, etc. **2.** short for **nogging** (sense 1). [C17: origin unknown]

nog·gin ('nɒgɪn) *n.* **1.** a small quantity of spirits, usually 1 gill. **2.** a small mug or cup. **3.** an informal word for **head.** [C17: of obscure origin]

nog·ging ('nɒgɪŋ) *n.* **1.** Also called: **nog.** a short horizontal timber member used between the studs of a framed partition. **2.** masonry or brickwork between the timber members of a framed construction. **3.** a number of wooden pieces fitted between the timbers of a half-timbered wall.

no-go ar·e·a *n.* a district in a town that is barricaded off, usually by a paramilitary organization, within which the police, army, etc., can only enter by force.

No·gu·chi (nɔː'guːtʃɪ) *n.* **Hi·de·yo** ('hiːdɛˌjɔː). 1876–1928, Japanese bacteriologist, active in the U.S. He made important discoveries in the treatment of syphilis.

Noh (nəʊ) *n.* a variant spelling of **No**[1].

no-hop·er *n. Austral. slang.* a useless person; failure.

no·how ('nəʊˌhaʊ) *adv. Not standard.* (*in negative constructions*) **a.** under any conditions. **b.** in any manner.

noil (nɔɪl) *n. Textiles.* the short or knotted fibres that are separated from the long fibres, or staple, by combing. [C17: of unknown origin]

noise (nɔɪz) *n.* **1.** a sound, esp. one that is loud or disturbing. **2.** loud shouting; clamour; din. **3.** any undesired electrical disturbance in a circuit, etc., degrading the useful information in a signal. See also **signal-to-noise ratio. 4.** talk or interest: *noise about strikes.* **5. make a noise.** to talk a great deal or complain (about). ~*vb.* **6.** (*tr.;* usually foll. by *abroad* or *about*) to spread (news, gossip, etc.). **7.** (*intr.*) *Rare.* to talk loudly or at length. **8.** (*intr.*) *Rare.* to make a din or outcry; be noisy. [C13: from Old French, from Latin: NAUSEA]

noise·less ('nɔɪzlɪs) *adj.* making little or no sound; silent. —**'noise·less·ly** *adv.* —**'noise·less·ness** *n.*

noise·mak·er ('nɔɪzˌmeɪkə) *n. U.S.* something, such as a clapper or bell, used to make a loud noise at football matches, celebrations, etc. —**'noise·ˌmak·ing** *n., adj.*

noi·sette (nwɑː'zɛt) *adj.* **1.** flavoured or made with hazelnuts. ~*n.* **2.** a small round boneless slice of lamb from the fillet or leg. [from French: hazel nut]

noi·some ('nɔɪsəm) *adj.* **1.** (esp. of smells) offensive. **2.** harmful or noxious. [C14: from obsolete *noy*, variant of ANNOY + -SOME[1]] —**'noi·some·ly** *adv.* —**'noi·some·ness** *n.*

nois·y ('nɔɪzɪ) *adj.* **nois·i·er, nois·i·est. 1.** making a loud or constant noise. **2.** full of or characterized by noise. —**'nois·i·ly** *adv.* —**'nois·i·ness** *n.*

No·lan ('nəʊlən) *n.* **Sid·ney.** born 1917, Australian painter, whose works explore themes in Australian folklore.

Nol·de (*German* 'nɔldə) *n.* **E·mil** ('eːmiːl). 1867–1956, German painter and engraver, noted particularly for his violent use of colour and the primitive masklike quality of his figures.

no·lens vo·lens *Latin.* ('nəʊlɛnz 'vəʊlɛnz) *adv.* whether willing or unwilling.

no·li-me-tan·ge·re ('nəʊlɪˌmeɪ'tæŋgərɪ) *n.* **1.** a warning against interfering or against touching a person or thing. **2.** a work of art depicting Christ appearing to Mary Magdalene after His Resurrection. **3.** another name for **touch-me-not** (the plant). **4.** a cancerous ulcer affecting soft tissue and bone. [from Latin: do not touch me, the words spoken by Christ to Mary Magdalene (Vulgate, John 20:17)]

nol·le pros·e·qui ('nɒlɪ 'prɒsɪˌkwaɪ) *n. Law.* an entry made on the court record when the plaintiff in a civil suit or prosecutor in a criminal prosecution undertakes not to continue the action or prosecution. Compare **non prosequitur.** [Latin: do not pursue (prosecute)]

no·lo con·ten·de·re ('nəʊləʊ kɒn'tɛndərɪ) *n. Law, chiefly U.S.* a plea made by a defendant to a criminal charge having the same effect in those proceedings as a plea of guilty but not precluding him from denying the charge in a subsequent action. [Latin: I do not wish to contend]

nol. pros. *or* **nol·le pros.** *abbrev. for* nolle prosequi.

nom. *abbrev. for:* **1.** nominal. **2.** nominative.

no·ma ('nəʊmə) *n.* a gangrenous inflammation of the mouth, esp. one affecting malnourished children. [C19: New Latin, from Latin *nomē* ulcer, from Greek *nomē* feeding; related to Greek *nemein* to feed]

no·mad ('nəʊmæd) *n.* **1.** a member of a people or tribe who move from place to place to find pasture and food. **2.** a person who continually moves from place to place; wanderer. [C16: via French from Latin *nomas* wandering shepherd, from Greek; related to *nemein* to feed, pasture] —**'no·mad·ism** *n.*

no·mad·ic (nəʊ'mædɪk) *adj.* relating to or characteristic of nomads or their way of life. —**no·'mad·i·cal·ly** *adv.*

no·mad·ize *or* **no·mad·ise** ('nəʊmædˌaɪz) *vb.* **1.** (*intr.*) to live as nomads. **2.** (*tr.*) to make into nomads. **3.** (*tr.*) to people (a place) with nomads.

no-man's-land *n.* **1.** land between boundaries, esp. an unoccupied zone between opposing forces. **2.** an unowned or unclaimed piece of land. **3.** an ambiguous area of activity or thought.

nom·arch ('nɒmɑːk) *n.* **1.** the head of an ancient Egyptian nome. **2.** the senior administrator in a Greek nomarchy. [C17: from Greek *nomarkhēs*]

nom·ar·chy ('nɒmɑːkɪ, -əkɪ) *n., pl.* **-chies.** any of the provinces of modern Greece; nome. [C19: from Greek; see NOME, -ARCHY]

nom·bles ('nʌmbᵊlz) *pl. n.* a variant spelling of **numbles.**

nom·bril ('nɒmbrɪl) *n. Heraldry.* a point on a shield between the fesse point and the lowest point. [C16: from French, literally: navel]

nom de guerre ('nɒm də 'gɛə; *French* nɔ̃ də 'gɛːr) *n., pl.* **noms de guerre.** an assumed name; pseudonym. [literally: war name]

nom de plume ('nɒm də 'pluːm; *French* nɔ̃ də 'plym) *n., pl.* **noms de plume.** another term for **pen name.**

nome (nəʊm) *n.* **1.** any of the provinces of modern Greece; nomarchy. **2.** an administrative division of ancient Egypt. [C18: from Greek *nomos* pasture, region]

no·men ('nəʊmɛn) *n., pl.* **nom·i·na** ('nɒmɪnə). an ancient Roman's second name, designating his gens or clan. See also **agnomen, cognomen, praenomen.** [Latin: a name]

no·men·cla·tor ('nəʊmɛnˌkleɪtə) *n.* a person who invents or assigns names, as in scientific classification. [C16: from Latin, from *nōmen* name + *calāre* to call]

no·men·cla·ture (nəʊ'mɛnklətʃə; *U.S.* 'nəʊmənˌkleɪtʃər) *n.* the terminology used in a particular science, art, activity, etc. [C17: from Latin *nōmenclātūra* list of names; see NOMENCLATOR]

nom·i·nal ('nɒmɪnᵊl) *adj.* **1.** in name only; theoretical: *the nominal leader.* **2.** minimal in comparison with real worth or what is expected; token: *a nominal fee.* **3.** of, relating to, constituting, bearing, or giving a name. **4.** *Grammar.* of or relating to a noun or noun phrase. ~*n.* **5.** *Grammar.* a nominal element; a noun, noun phrase, or syntactically similar structure. **6.** *Bell-ringing.* the harmonic an octave above the strike tone of a bell. [C15: from Latin *nōminālis* of a name, from *nōmen* name] —**'nom·i·nal·ly** *adv.*

nom·i·nal·ism ('nɒmɪnᵊˌlɪzəm) *n.* the philosophical theory that the variety of objects to which a single general word, such as *dog*, applies have nothing in common but the name. Compare **conceptualism, realism.** —**'nom·i·nal·ist** *n.* —**ˌnom·i·nal·'is·tic** *adj.*

nom·i·nal val·ue *n.* another name for **par value.**

nom·i·nal wag·es *pl. n.* another name for **money wages.**

nom·i·nate *vb.* ('nɒmɪˌneɪt). (*mainly tr.*) **1.** to propose as a candidate, esp. for an elective office. **2.** to appoint to an office or position. **3.** (*intr.*) *Austral.* to stand as a candidate in an election. **4.** *Archaic.* to name, entitle, or designate. ~*adj.* ('nɒmɪnɪt). **5.** *Rare.* having a particular name. [C16: from Latin *nōmināre* to call by name, from *nōmen* name] —**'nom·i·ˌna·tor** *n.*

nom·i·na·tion (ˌnɒmɪ'neɪʃən) *n.* the act of nominating or state of being nominated, esp. as an election candidate.

nom·i·na·tive ('nɒmɪnətɪv, 'nɒmnə-) *adj.* **1.** *Grammar.* denoting a case of nouns and pronouns in inflected languages that is used esp. to identify the subject of a finite verb. See also **subjective** (sense 6). **2.** appointed rather than elected to a position, office, etc. **3.** bearing the name of a person. ~*n.* **4.** *Grammar.* **a.** the nominative case. **b.** a word or speech element in the nominative case. [C14: from Latin *nōminātīvus* belonging to naming, from *nōmen* name] —**nom·i·na·ti·val** (ˌnɒmɪnəˈtaɪvᵊl) *adj.* —ˈ**nom·i·na·tive·ly** *adv.*

nom·i·nee (ˌnɒmɪˈniː) *n.* a person who is nominated to an office or as a candidate. [C17: from NOMINATE + -EE]

no·mism (ˈnəʊmɪzəm) *n. Theol.* adherence to a law or laws as a primary exercise of religion. [C20: from Greek *nomos* law, custom] —**no·ˈmis·tic** *adj.*

nom·o- *combining form.* indicating law or custom: *nomology.* [from Greek *nomos* law, custom]

no·moc·ra·cy (nɒˈmɒkrəsɪ, nəʊ-) *n., pl.* **·cries.** government based on the rule of law rather than arbitrary will, terror, etc. [C19: from Greek, from *nomos* law + -CRACY]

nom·o·gram (ˈnɒməˌɡræm, ˈnəʊmə-) *or* **nom·o·graph** *n.* **1.** a graph consisting of three lines graduated for different variables so that a straight line intersecting all three gives the related values of the variables. **2.** any graphic representation of numerical relationships.

no·mog·ra·phy (nɒˈmɒɡrəfɪ) *n., pl.* **·phies.** the science of constructing nomographs. —**no·ˈmog·ra·pher** *n.* —**nom·o·graph·ic** (ˌnɒməˈɡræfɪk) *or* ˌ**nom·o·ˈgraph·i·cal** *adj.* —ˌ**nom·o·ˈgraph·i·cal·ly** *adv.*

no·mol·o·gy (nəʊˈmɒlədʒɪ) *n.* **1.** the science of law and law-making. **2.** the branch of science concerned with the formulation of laws explaining natural phenomena. —**no·mo·log·i·cal** (ˌnəʊməˈlɒdʒɪkᵊl) *adj.* —ˌ**no·mo·ˈlog·i·cal·ly** *adv.* —**no·ˈmol·o·gist** *n.*

nom·o·thet·ic (ˌnɒməˈθɛtɪk) *or* **nom·o·thet·i·cal** *adj.* **1.** giving or enacting laws; legislative. **2.** *Psychol.* of or relating to the search for general laws or traits, esp. in personality theory. Compare **idiographic.** [C17: from Greek *nomothetikos,* from *nomothetēs* law-giver]

-no·my *n. combining form.* indicating a science or the laws governing a certain field of knowledge: *agronomy; economy.* [from Greek *-nomia* law; related to *nemein* to distribute, control] —**-nom·ic** *adj. combining form.*

non- *prefix.* **1.** indicating negation: *nonexistent.* **2.** indicating refusal or failure: *noncooperation.* **3.** indicating exclusion from a specified class of persons or things: *nonfiction.* **4.** indicating lack or absence, esp. of a quality associated with what is specified: *nonobjective; nonevent.* [from Latin *nōn* not]

no·na- *or before a vowel* **non-** *combining form.* nine: *nonagon.* [from Latin *nōnus*]

no·nage (ˈnəʊnɪdʒ) *n.* **1.** *Law.* the state of being under any of various ages at which a person may legally enter into certain transactions, such as the making of binding contracts, marrying, etc. **2.** any period of immaturity.

no·na·ge·nar·i·an (ˌnəʊnədʒɪˈnɛərɪən) *n.* **1.** a person who is from 90 to 99 years old. ~*adj.* **2.** of, relating to, or denoting a nonagenarian. [C19: from Latin *nōnāgēnārius,* from *nōnāginta* ninety]

non·ag·gres·sion (ˌnɒnəˈɡrɛʃən) *n.* **a.** restraint of aggression, esp. between states. **b.** (*as modifier*): *a nonaggression pact.*

non·a·gon (ˈnɒnəˌɡɒn) *n.* a polygon having nine sides. Also called: **enneagon.** —**non·ag·o·nal** (nɒnˈæɡənᵊl) *adj.*

non·a·ligned (ˌnɒnəˈlaɪnd) *adj.* (of states, etc.) not part of a major alliance or power bloc, esp. not allied to the U.S., the Soviet Union, or China. —ˌ**non·a·ˈlign·ment** *n.*

non·a·no·ic ac·id (ˌnɒnəˈnəʊɪk) *n.* a colourless oily fatty acid with a rancid odour: used in making pharmaceuticals, lacquers, and plastics. Formula: $CH_3(CH_2)_7COOH$. Also called: **pelargonic acid.** [C19: from *nonane* a paraffin, ninth in the methane series, from Latin *nōnus* ninth + -ANE]

non·ap·pear·ance (ˌnɒnəˈpɪərəns) *n.* failure to appear or attend, esp. as a defendant or witness in court.

nonce[1] (nɒns) *n.* the present time or occasion (now only in the phrase **for the nonce**). [C12: from the phrase *for the nonce,* a mistaken division of *for then anes,* literally: for the once, from *then* dative singular of *the* + *anes* ONCE]

nonce[2] (nɒns) *n. Prison slang.* a rapist. [C20: of unknown origin]

nonce word *n.* a word coined for a single occasion.

non·cha·lant (ˈnɒnʃələnt) *adj.* casually unconcerned or indifferent; uninvolved. [C18: from French, from *nonchaloir* to lack warmth, from NON- + *chaloir* from Latin *calēre* to be warm] —ˈ**non·cha·lance** *n.* —ˈ**non·cha·lant·ly** *adv.*

non-com (ˈnɒnˌkɒm) *n.* short for **noncommissioned officer.**

non·com·bat·ant (nɒnˈkɒmbətənt) *n.* **1.** a civilian in time of war. **2.** a member of the armed forces whose duties do not include fighting, such as a chaplain or surgeon.

non·com·mis·sioned of·fic·er (ˌnɒnkəˈmɪʃənd) *n.* **1.** a person holding a military rank, such as sergeant or corporal, that involves the exercise of authority but does not carry a commission.

non·com·mit·tal (ˌnɒnkəˈmɪtᵊl) *adj.* **1.** not involving or revealing commitment to any particular opinion or course of action: *a noncommittal reply.* **2.** *Rare.* having no outstanding quality, meaning, etc.

non com·pos men·tis *Latin.* (ˈnɒn ˈkɒmpəs ˈmɛntɪs) *adj.* mentally incapable of managing one's own affairs; of unsound mind. [Latin: not in control of one's mind]

non·con·duc·tor (ˌnɒnkənˈdʌktə) *n.* a substance that is a poor conductor of heat, electricity, or sound.

non·con·form·ist (ˌnɒnkənˈfɔːmɪst) *n.* a person who does not conform to generally accepted patterns of behaviour or thought. —ˌ**non·con·ˈform·ism** *n.*

Non·con·form·ist (ˌnɒnkənˈfɔːmɪst) *n.* **1.** a member of a Protestant denomination that dissents from an Established Church, esp. the Church of England. ~*adj.* **2.** of, relating to, or denoting Nonconformists. —ˌ**Non·con·ˈform·i·ty** *or* ˌ**Non·con·ˈform·ism** *n.*

non·con·form·i·ty (ˌnɒnkənˈfɔːmɪtɪ) *n.* **1.** failure or refusal to conform. **2.** absence of agreement or harmony.

non·con·trib·u·to·ry (ˌnɒnkənˈtrɪbjʊtərɪ, -trɪ) *adj.* **1.** denoting an insurance or pension scheme for employees, the premiums of which are paid entirely by the employer. **2.** not providing contribution; non-contributing.

non·co·op·er·a·tion (ˌnɒnkəʊˌɒpəˈreɪʃən) *n.* **1.** failure or refusal to cooperate. **2.** refusal to pay taxes, obey government decrees, etc., as a protest. —**non·co·op·er·a·tive** (ˌnɒnkəʊˈɒpərətɪv) *adj.* —ˌ**non·co·ˈop·er·ˌa·tor** *n.*

non·de·script (ˈnɒndɪˌskrɪpt) *adj.* **1.** lacking distinct or individual characteristics; having no outstanding features. ~*n.* **2.** a nondescript person or thing. [C17: NON- + Latin *dēscriptus,* past participle of *dēscrībere* to copy, DESCRIBE]

non·de·struc·tive test·ing (ˌnɒndɪˈstrʌktɪv) *n.* any of several methods of detecting flaws in metals, etc., without causing damage. The most common techniques involve the use of x-rays, gamma rays, and ultrasonic vibrations.

non·dis·junc·tion (ˌnɒndɪsˈdʒʌŋkʃən) *n.* the failure of paired homologous chromosomes to move to opposite poles of the cell during meiosis.

none[1] (nʌn) *pron.* (*functioning as sing. or pl.*) **1.** not any of a particular class: *none of my letters has arrived.* **2.** no one; nobody: *there were none to tell the tale.* **3.** no part (of a whole); not any (of): *none of it looks edible.* **4. none other.** no other person: *none other than the Queen herself.* **5. none the.** (*foll. by a comparative adj.*) in no degree: *she was none the worse for her ordeal.* **6. none too.** not very: *he was none too pleased with his car.* [Old English *nān,* literally: not one]

Usage. See at **everyone.**

none[2] (nəʊn) *n.* another word for **nones.**

non·ef·fec·tive (ˌnɒnɪˈfɛktɪv) *Chiefly U.S.* ~*adj.* **1.** not effective. **2.** unfit for or incapable of active military service. ~*n.* **3.** *Military.* a noneffective person.

non·e·go (nɒnˈiːɡəʊ, -ˈɛɡəʊ) *n. Philosophy.* everything that is outside one's conscious self, such as one's environment.

non·en·ti·ty (nɒnˈɛntɪtɪ) *n., pl.* **·ties.** **1.** an insignificant person or thing. **2.** a nonexistent thing. **3.** the state of not existing; nonexistence.

non·e·quiv·a·lence (ˌnɒnɪˈkwɪvələns) *n.* **1.** the relationship of being unequal or incomparable. **2.** *Logic.* the relation between two propositions of which one and only one is true. **3.** *Logic.* a function of two propositions that takes the value *true* only

---

ˌ**non·ac·ˈcept·ance** *n.*
ˌ**non·al·co·ˈhol·ic** *adj.*
ˌ**non·at·ˈtend·ance** *n.*
ˌ**non·at·ˈtrib·u·tive** *adj.*
ˌ**non·au·ˈthor·i·ˌta·tive** *adj.*
non·ˈau·to·ˌmat·ed *adj.*
ˌ**non·au·to·ˈmat·ic** *adj.*
non·ˈba·sic *adj.*
non·ˈbe·ing *n.*
ˌ**non·bel·ˈlig·er·ent** *adj.*
non·ˈbreak·a·ble *adj.*
non·ˈcar·bo·ˌnat·ed *adj.*
ˌ**non·car·ˈniv·o·rous** *adj.*
non-ˈCath·o·lic *adj.*
ˌ**non-Cau·ˈca·sian** *adj.*
non·ˈcaus·al *adj.*
ˌ**non·ce·ˈles·tial** *adj.*
non·ˈcel·lu·lar *adj.*
non·ˈcen·tral *adj.*
non·ˈcer·e·bral *adj.*
non·ˈcharge·a·ble *adj.*
non-ˈChris·tian *adj.*
non·ˈclaim *n.*
non·ˈclas·sic *or* **non·ˈclas·si·cal** *adj.*
non·ˈclas·si·ˌfied *adj.*
non·ˈcler·i·cal *adj.*
non·ˈclin·i·cal *adj.*
ˌ**non·co·ˈag·u·ˌlat·ing** *adj.*
ˌ**non·col·ˈle·gi·ate** *adj.*
ˌ**non·com·ˈbin·ing** *adj.*
ˌ**non·com·ˈmer·cial** *adj.*
ˌ**non·com·ˈmis·sioned** *adj.*
ˌ**non·com·ˈmu·ni·cant** *n.*
ˌ**non·com·ˈmu·ni·ˌca·tive** *adj.*
non·ˈcom·mu·nist *adj., n.*
ˌ**non·com·ˈpet·i·tive** *adj.*
ˌ**non·com·ˈpli·ance** *n.*
ˌ**non·con·ˈcil·i·a·to·ry** *adj.*
ˌ**non·con·ˈclu·sive** *adj.*
ˌ**non·con·ˈcur·rent** *adj.*
ˌ**non·con·ˈduc·tive** *adj.*
ˌ**non·con·fi·ˈden·tial** *adj.*
ˌ**non·con·ˈflict·ing** *adj.*
ˌ**non·con·ˈgen·i·tal** *adj.*
ˌ**non·con·ˈnec·tive** *adj.*
ˌ**non·con·ˈsec·u·tive** *adj.*
ˌ**non·con·ˈsent·ing** *adj.*
ˌ**non·con·sti·ˈtu·tion·al** *adj.*
ˌ**non·con·ˈstrain·ing** *adj.*
ˌ**non·con·ˈstruc·tive** *adj.*
ˌ**non·con·ˈta·gious** *adj.*
ˌ**non·con·ˈtem·po·ˌrar·y** *adj.*
ˌ**non·con·ˈtrib·u·ting** *adj.*
ˌ**non·con·ˈtrol·la·ble** *adj.*
ˌ**non·con·ˈtrol·ling** *adj.*
ˌ**non·con·tro·ˈver·sial** *adj.*
ˌ**non·con·ˈven·tion·al** *adj.*
ˌ**non·con·ˈver·gent** *adj.*
ˌ**non·con·ˈver·sant** *adj.*
ˌ**non·con·ˈvert·i·ble** *adj.*
ˌ**non·cor·ˈrob·o·ˌra·tive** *adj.*
ˌ**non·cor·ˈrod·ing** *adj.*
ˌ**non·cre·ˈa·tive** *adj.*
non·ˈcrim·i·nal *adj.*
non·ˈcrit·i·cal *adj.*
non·ˈcul·ti·ˌvat·ed *adj.*
non·ˈcur·rent *adj.*
ˌ**non·de·ˈcid·u·ous** *adj.*
ˌ**non·de·ˈduct·i·ble** *adj.*
ˌ**non·de·ˈliv·er·y** *n.*
ˌ**non·dem·o·ˈcrat·ic** *adj.*
ˌ**non·de·ˈmon·stra·ble** *adj.*
ˌ**non·de·ˌnom·i·ˈna·tion·al** *adj.*
ˌ**non·de·part·ˈmen·tal** *adj.*
ˌ**non·de·ˈpend·ence** *n.*
ˌ**non·de·ˈtach·a·ble** *adj.*
non·ˈdet·o·ˌnat·ing *adj.*
ˌ**non·dic·ta·ˈto·ri·al** *adj.*
ˌ**non·dif·ˈfus·ing** *adj.*
ˌ**non·dip·lo·ˈmat·ic** *adj.*
ˌ**non·di·ˈrec·tion·al** *adj.*
non·ˈdis·ci·pli·ˌnar·y *adj.*
ˌ**non·dis·ˈcrim·i·ˌnat·ing** *adj.*
ˌ**non·dis·ˈtinc·tive** *adj.*
ˌ**non·di·ˈvis·i·ble** *adj.*
ˌ**non·doc·ˈtri·nal** *adj.*
ˌ**non·dog·ˈmat·ic** *adj.*
ˌ**non·do·ˈmes·ti·ˌcat·ed** *adj.*
ˌ**non·dra·ˈmat·ic** *adj.*
non·ˈdrink·er *n.*
non·ˈdriv·er *n.*
non·ˈearn·ing *adj.*
ˌ**non·e·co·ˈnom·ic** *adj.*
non·ˈed·i·ble *adj.*
ˌ**non·e·ˈlas·tic** *adj.*
ˌ**non·e·ˈlec·tion** *n.*
ˌ**non·e·ˈlec·tive** *adj.*
non·ˈel·i·gi·ble *adj.*
ˌ**non·e·ˈmo·tion·al** *adj.*

when one or other of the propositions, but not both, is true, and the value *false* otherwise.

nones (nəʊnz) *n.* (*functioning as sing. or pl.*) **1.** (in the Roman calendar) the ninth day before the ides of each month: the seventh day of March, May, July, and October, and the fifth of each other month. See also **calends. 2.** *Chiefly R.C. Church.* the fifth of the seven canonical hours of the divine office, originally fixed at the ninth hour of the day, about 3 p.m. [Old English *nōn,* from Latin *nōna hora* ninth hour, from *nōnus* ninth]

non·es·sen·tial (ˌnɒnɪˈsɛnʃəl) *adj.* **1.** not essential; not necessary. **2.** *Biochem.* (of an amino acid in a particular organism) able to be synthesized from other substances. ~*n.* **3.** a nonessential person or thing.

none·such *or* **non·such** (ˈnʌnˌsʌtʃ) *n.* **1.** *Archaic.* a matchless person or thing; nonpareil. **2.** another name for **black medick.**

non·et (nɒˈnɛt) *n.* a piece of music composed for a group of nine instruments. [C19: from Italian *nonetto,* from *nono* ninth, from Latin *nōnus*]

none·the·less (ˌnʌnðəˈlɛs) *sentence connector.* despite that; however; nevertheless.

non-Eu·clid·e·an ge·om·e·try *n.* the branch of modern geometry in which certain axioms of Euclidean geometry are restated. It introduces fundamental changes into the concept of space.

non·e·vent (ˌnɒnɪˈvɛnt) *n.* a disappointing or insignificant occurrence, esp. one predicted to be important.

non·fea·sance (nɒnˈfiːzᵊns) *n. Law.* a failure to act when under an obligation to do so. Compare **malfeasance, misfeasance.**

non·fer·rous (nɒnˈfɛrəs) *adj.* **1.** denoting any metal other than iron. **2.** not containing iron: *a nonferrous alloy.*

non·fic·tion (nɒnˈfɪkʃən) *n.* **1.** writing dealing with facts and events rather than imaginative narration. **2.** (*modifier*) relating to or denoting nonfiction. —**non·ˈfic·tion·al** *adj.* —**non·ˈfic·tion·al·ly** *adv.*

non·flam·ma·ble (nɒnˈflæməbᵊl) *adj.* incapable of burning or not easily set on fire; not flammable.

nong (nɒŋ) *n. Austral. slang.* a stupid or incompetent person. [C19: perhaps alteration of obsolete English dialect *nigmenog* silly fellow, of unknown origin]

non·har·mon·ic (ˌnɒnhɑːˈmɒnɪk) *adj. Music.* not relating to the harmony formed by a chord or chords.

no·nil·lion (nəʊˈnɪljən) *n.* **1.** (in Britain and Germany) the number represented as one followed by 54 zeros (10^{54}). **2.** (in the U.S. and France) the number represented as one followed by 30 zeros (10^{30}). Brit. word: **quintillion.** [C17: from French, from Latin *nōnus* ninth, on the model of MILLION] —**no·ˈnil·lionth** *adj., n.*

non·in·ter·ven·tion (ˌnɒnɪntəˈvɛnʃən) *n.* refusal to intervene, esp. the abstention by a state from intervening in the affairs of other states or in its own internal disputes. —**ˌnon·in·ter·ˈven·tion·al** *adj.* —**ˌnon·in·ter·ˈven·tion·ist** *n., adj.*

non·join·der (nɒnˈdʒɔɪndə) *n. Law.* the failure to join as party to a suit a person who should have been included either as a plaintiff or as a defendant. Compare **misjoinder.**

non·ju·ror (nɒnˈdʒʊərə) *n.* a person who refuses to take an oath, as of allegiance.

Non·ju·ror (nɒnˈdʒʊərə) *n.* any of a group of clergy in England and Scotland who declined to take the oath of allegiance to William and Mary in 1689.

non li·cet (ˈnɒn ˈlaɪsɪt) *adj.* not permitted; unlawful.

non li·quet (ˈnɒn ˈlaɪkwɪt) *adj. Roman law.* (of a cause, evidence, etc.) not clear.

non·met·al (nɒnˈmɛtᵊl) *n.* any of a number of chemical elements that form negative ions, have acidic oxides, and are generally poor conductors of heat and electricity.

non·met·al·lic (ˌnɒnmɪˈtælɪk) *adj.* **1.** not of metal. **2.** of, concerned with, or being a nonmetal.

non·mor·al (nɒnˈmɒrəl) *adj.* not involving or related to morality or ethics; neither moral nor immoral.

No·no (*Italian* ˈnɔːno) *n.* **Lu·i·gi** (luˈiːdʒi). born 1924, Italian composer of 12-tone music.

non·ob·jec·tive (ˌnɒnəbˈdʒɛktɪv) *adj.* of or designating an art movement in which things are depicted in an abstract or purely formalized way, not as they appear in reality.

non·pa·reil (ˈnɒnpərəl, ˌnɒnpəˈreɪl) *n.* **1.** a person or thing that is unsurpassed or unmatched; peerless example. **2.** (formerly) a size of printers' type equal to 6 point. **3.** *U.S.* a small bead of coloured sugar used to decorate cakes, biscuits, etc. **4.** *Chiefly U.S.* a flat round piece of chocolate covered with this sugar. ~*adj.* **5.** having no match or equal; peerless. [C15: from French, from NON- + *pareil* similar]

non·par·ous (nɒnˈpærəs) *adj.* never having given birth.

non·par·tic·i·pat·ing (ˌnɒnpɑːˈtɪsɪˌpeɪtɪŋ) *adj.* **1.** not participating. **2.** (of an assurance policy, share, etc.) not carrying the right to share in a company's profit.

non·par·ti·san *or* **non·par·ti·zan** (ˌnɒnpɑːtɪˈzæn) *adj.* not partisan or aligned, esp. not affiliated to, influenced by, or supporting any one political party. —**ˌnon·par·ti·ˈsan·ˌship** *or* **ˌnon·par·ti·ˈzan·ˌship** *n.*

non·par·ty (nɒnˈpɑːtɪ) *adj.* not connected with any one political party.

non·plus (nɒnˈplʌs) *vb.* **·plus·ses, ·plus·sing, ·plussed** *or U.S.* **·plus·es, ·plus·ing, ·plused. 1.** (*tr.*) to put at a loss; confound: *he was nonplussed by the sudden announcement.* ~*n., pl.* **·plus·es. 2.** a state of utter perplexity prohibiting action or speech. [C16: from Latin *nōn plūs* no further (that is, nothing further can be said or done)]

non·pro·duc·tive (ˌnɒnprəˈdʌktɪv) *adj.* **1.** (of workers, etc.) not directly responsible for producing goods. **2.** having disappointing results; unproductive. —**ˌnon·pro·ˈduc·tive·ness** *n.* —**non·pro·duc·tiv·i·ty** (ˌnɒnprɒdʌkˈtɪvɪtɪ) *n.*

non-prof·it-mak·ing *or U.S.* (*often*) **non·prof·it** *adj.* not yielding a profit, esp. because organized or established for some other reason: *a non-profit-making organization.*

non·pro·lif·er·a·tion (ˌnɒnprəˌlɪfəˈreɪʃən) *n.* **1. a.** limitation of the production or spread of something, esp. nuclear or chemical weapons. **b.** (*as modifier*): *a nonproliferation treaty.* **2.** failure or refusal to proliferate.

non pros. *Law. abbrev. for* non prosequitur.

non-pros (ˌnɒnˈprɒs) *n.* **1.** short for **non prosequitur.** ~*vb.* **-pros·ses, -pros·sing, -prossed. 2.** (*tr.*) to enter a judgment of non prosequitur against (a plaintiff).

non pro·se·qui·tur (ˈnɒn prəʊˈsɛkwɪtə) *n. Law.* (formerly) a judgment in favour of a defendant when the plaintiff failed to take the necessary steps in an action within the time allowed. Compare **nolle prosequi.** [Latin, literally: he does not prosecute]

non·rep·re·sen·ta·tion·al (ˌnɒnrɛprɪzɛnˈteɪʃənᵊl) *adj. Art.* another word for **abstract** (sense 4).

---

non·ˈe·qual *adj.*
ˌnon·e·ˈquiv·a·lent *adj.*
ˌnon·es·ˈtab·lish·ment *n.*
non·ˈeth·i·cal *adj.*
ˌnon·ex·ˈchange·a·ble *adj.*
ˌnon·ex·ˈclu·sive *adj.*
ˌnon·ex·ˈist·ence *n.*
ˌnon·ex·ˈist·ent *adj.*
ˌnon·ex·ˈplo·sive *adj.*
non·ˈfac·tu·al *adj.*
non·ˈfa·tal *adj.*
non·ˈfed·er·al *adj.*
ˌnon·fic·ˈti·tious *adj.*
non·ˈfi·nite *adj.*
non·ˈflex·i·ble *adj.*
non·ˈflu·id *adj.*
ˌnon·for·ˈma·tion *n.*
non·ˈfreez·ing *adj.*
ˌnon·ful·ˈfil·ment *n.*
non·ˈfunc·tion·al *adj.*
non·ˈfu·si·ble *adj.*
non·ˈgas·e·ous *adj.*
ˌnon·gov·ern·ˈmen·tal *adj.*
non·ˈhab·it·a·ble *adj.*
non·ˈhaz·ard·ous *adj.*
non·ˈher·it·a·ble *adj.*
ˌnon·his·ˈtor·i·cal *adj.*
non·ˈhu·man *adj.*
ˌnon·i·ˈden·ti·cal *adj.*
ˌnon·id·i·o·ˈmat·ic *adj.*
ˌnon·in·ˈclu·sion *n.*
ˌnon·in·de·ˈpend·ent *adj.*
ˌnon·in·ˈdict·a·ble *adj.*
ˌnon·in·ˈdus·tri·al *adj.*
ˌnon·in·ˈfec·tious *adj.*
ˌnon·in·ˈflam·ma·ble *adj.*
ˌnon·in·ˈflect·ed *adj.*
ˌnon·in·ˈfor·ma·tive *adj.*
ˌnon·in·ˈher·ent *adj.*
ˌnon·in·ˈher·it·a·ble *adj.*
ˌnon·in·ˈju·ri·ous *adj.*
ˌnon·in·ˈstinc·tive *adj.*
ˌnon·in·sti·ˈtu·tion·al *adj.*
ˌnon·in·tel·ˈlec·tu·al *adj.*
ˌnon·in·ter·ˈchange·a·ble *adj.*
ˌnon·in·ter·ˈsect·ing *adj.*
ˌnon·in·ˈtox·i·ˌcat·ing *adj.*
ˌnon·in·ˈtu·i·tive *adj.*
non·ˈir·ri·tant *adj., n.*
non·ˈju·ry *adj.*
non·ˈko·sher *adj.*
non·ˈlam·i·ˌnat·ed *adj.*
non·ˈle·thal *adj.*
non·ˈlin·e·ar *adj.*
non·ˈlit·er·ˌar·y *adj.*
ˌnon·li·ˈtur·gi·cal *adj.*
non·ˈlo·cal *adj.*
non·ˈlog·i·cal *adj.*
non·ˈlu·mi·nous *adj.*
ˌnon·mag·ˈnet·ic *adj.*
ˌnon·ma·ˈlig·nant *adj.*
non·ˈmar·i·time *adj.*
ˌnon·ma·ˌte·ri·al·ˈis·tic *adj.*
ˌnon·ma·ˈter·nal *adj.*
ˌnon·math·e·ˈmat·i·cal *adj.*
non·ˈmeas·ur·a·ble *adj.*
ˌnon·me·ˈchan·i·cal *adj.*
non·ˈmed·i·cal *adj.*
ˌnon·me·ˈdic·i·nal *adj.*
ˌnon·me·ˈlod·ic *adj.*
non·ˈmem·ber *n.*
non·ˈmem·ber·ˌship *n.*
non·ˈmi·gra·ˌto·ry *adj.*
non·ˈmil·i·tant *adj.*
ˌnon·min·is·ˈte·ri·al *adj.*
non·ˈmoun·tain·ous *adj.*
non·ˈmys·ti·cal *adj.*
non·ˈmyth·i·cal *adj.*
non-ˈna·tion·al *adj.*
non-ˈna·tive *adj.*
non-ˈnat·u·ral *adj.*
non-ˈnav·i·ga·ble *adj.*
ˌnon·ne·ˈgo·ti·a·ble *adj.*
ˌnon·ˈnu·cle·ar *adj.*
ˌnon·ob·ˈlig·a·ˌto·ry *adj.*
ˌnon·ob·ˈserv·ance *n.*
ˌnon·oc·ˈcur·rence *n.*
ˌnon·of·ˈfi·cial *adj.*
ˌnon·ˈop·er·a·ble *adj.*
ˌnon·op·er·ˈa·tion·al *adj.*
ˌnon·ˈop·er·a·tive *adj.*
ˌnon·or·ˈgan·ic *adj.*
non·ˈor·tho·ˌdox *adj.*
ˌnon·os·ˈten·sive *adj.*
non·ˈpar·al·ˌlel *adj.*
ˌnon·par·a·ˈsit·ic *adj.*
ˌnon·pa·ˈren·tal *adj.*
ˌnon·par·lia·ˈmen·ta·ry *adj.*
ˌnon·pa·ˈro·chi·al *adj.*
ˌnon·pa·ˈter·nal *adj.*
non·ˈpay·ing *adj.*
non·ˈpay·ment *n.*
non·ˈper·ma·nent *adj.*
non·ˈper·me·a·ble *adj.*
ˌnon·phil·o·ˈsoph·i·cal *adj.*
ˌnon·pho·ˈne·mic *adj.*
non·ˈphys·i·cal *adj.*
ˌnon·phys·i·o·ˈlog·i·cal *adj.*
non·ˈplay·ing *adj.*
non·ˈpoi·son·ous *adj.*
ˌnon·po·ˈlit·i·cal *adj.*
non·ˈpo·rous *adj.*
ˌnon·pos·ˈses·sion *n.*
non·ˈprac·ti·cal *adj.*
non·ˈpre·cious *adj.*
non·ˈpred·a·ˌto·ry *adj.*
ˌnon·pre·ˈdict·a·ble *adj.*
ˌnon·prej·u·ˈdi·cial *adj.*
ˌnon·pre·ˈscrip·tive *adj.*
ˌnon·pre·ˈserv·a·ble *adj.*
ˌnon·pres·er·ˈva·tion *n.*
ˌnon·pro·ˈfes·sion·al *adj.*
ˌnon·pro·ˈgres·sive *adj.*
ˌnon·pro·ˈpor·tion·al *adj.*
ˌnon·pro·ˈtec·tive *adj.*
non·ˈpun·ish·a·ble *adj.*
non·ˈra·cial *adj.*
non·ˈrad·i·cal *adj.*
ˌnon·ra·di·o·ˈac·tive *adj.*
non·ˈra·tion·al *adj.*
non·ˈread·er *n.*
ˌnon·re·al·ˈis·tic *adj.*
ˌnon·rec·og·ˈni·tion *n.*
ˌnon·re·ˈcov·er·a·ble *adj.*
non·re·ˈflec·tive *adj.*
non·ˈreg·i·ˌment·ed *adj.*
non·ˈreg·is·tered *adj.*
non·re·ˈli·gious *adj.*
non·re·ˈnew·a·ble *adj.*
ˌnon·rep·re·ˈsent·a·tive *adj.*

non+res·i+dent (nɒn'rɛzɪdənt) *n.* **1.** a person who is not residing in the place implied or specified: *the hotel restaurant is open to nonresidents.* ~*adj.* **2.** not residing in the place specified. —**non+'res·i+dence** *or* **non+'res·i+den+cy** *n.*

non+re+sis+tant (ˌnɒnrɪ'zɪstənt) *adj.* **1.** incapable of resisting something, such as a disease; susceptible. **2.** *History.* (esp. in 17th-century England) practising passive obedience to royal authority even when its commands were unjust. —**ˌnon+re+'sis+tance** *n.*

non+re+stric+tive (ˌnɒnrɪ'strɪktɪv) *adj.* **1.** not restrictive or limiting. **2.** *Grammar.* denoting a relative clause that is not restrictive. Compare **restrictive** (sense 2).

non+re+turn+a·ble (ˌnɒnrɪ'tɜːnəbᵊl) *adj.* denoting a container, esp. a bottle, on which no returnable deposit is paid on purchase of the contents.

non+rig+id (nɒn'rɪdʒɪd) *adj.* **1.** not rigid; flexible. **2.** (of the gas envelope of an airship) flexible and held in shape only by the internal gas pressure.

non+sched+uled (nɒn'ʃɛdjuːld) *adj.* **1.** not according to a schedule or plan; unscheduled. **2.** (of an airline) operating without published flight schedules.

non+sense ('nɒnsəns) *n.* **1.** something that has or makes no sense; unintelligible language; drivel. **2.** conduct or action that is absurd. **3.** foolish or evasive behaviour or manners: *she'll stand no nonsense.* **4.** **no-nonsense.** tolerating no nonsense; businesslike. **5.** things of little or no value or importance; trash. ~*interj.* **6.** an exclamation of disagreement. —**non+sen+si+cal** (nɒn'sɛnsɪkᵊl) *adj.* —**non+'sen+si+cal+ly** *adv.* —**non+'sen+si+cal+ness** *or* **non+ˌsen+si+'cal+i+ty** *n.*

non+sense verse *n.* verse in which the sense is nonexistent or absurd, such as that of Edward Lear.

non seq. *abbrev. for* non sequitur.

non se+qui+tur ('nɒn 'sɛkwɪtə) *n.* **1.** a statement having little or no relevance to what preceded it. **2.** *Logic.* a conclusion that does not follow from the premisses. Abbrev.: **non seq.** [Latin, literally: it does not follow]

non+slip (nɒn'slɪp) *adj.* designed to reduce or prevent slipping.

non+smok+er (nɒn'sməʊkə) *n.* **1.** a person who does not smoke. **2.** a train compartment in which smoking is forbidden. —**non+'smok+ing** *adj.*

non+stand+ard (nɒn'stændəd) *adj.* **1.** denoting or characterized by idiom, vocabulary, etc., that is not regarded as correct and acceptable by educated native speakers of a language; not standard. **2.** deviating from a given standard.

non+start+er (nɒn'stɑːtə) *n.* **1.** a horse that fails to run in a race for which it has been entered. **2.** a person or thing that is useless, has little chance of success, etc.

non+sta+tive (nɒn'steɪtɪv) *Grammar.* ~*adj.* **1.** denoting a verb describing an action rather than a state, as for example *throw* or *thank* as opposed to *know* or *hate.* Compare **stative.** ~*n.* **2.** a nonstative verb. ~Also: **active.**

non+stick ('nɒn'stɪk) *adj.* (of saucepans, frying pans, etc.) coated with a substance such as polytetrafluoroethylene (PTFE) that prevents food sticking to them.

non+stop ('nɒn'stɒp) *adj., adv.* without making a stop: *a nonstop flight.*

non+stri+at+ed (nɒn'straɪeɪtɪd) *adj.* (esp. of certain muscle fibres) having no striations.

non-strik·er *n. Cricket.* the batsman who is not facing the bowling.

non+such ('nʌnˌsʌtʃ) *n.* a variant spelling of **nonesuch.**

non+suit (nɒn'sjuːt) *n.* **1.** *Law.* an order of a judge dismissing a suit when the plaintiff fails to show he has a good cause of action or fails to produce any evidence. ~*vb.* **2.** (*tr.*) to order the dismissal of the suit of (a person).

non trop+po ('nɒn 'trɒpəʊ) *adv. Music.* (preceded by a musical direction, esp. a tempo marking) not to be observed too strictly (esp. in the phrases **allegro ma non troppo, adagio ma non troppo**).

non-U (nɒn'juː) *adj. Brit. informal.* (esp. of language) not characteristic of or used by the upper class. Compare **U.**

non+un+ion (nɒn'juːnjən) *adj.* **1.** not belonging or related to a trade union: *nonunion workers.* **2.** not favouring or employing union labour: *a nonunion shop.* **3.** not produced by union labour: *nonunion shirts.* ~*n.* **4.** *Pathol.* failure of broken bones or bone fragments to heal.

non+un+ion+ism (nɒn'juːnjəˌnɪzəm) *n. Chiefly U.S.* opposition to trade unionism. —**non+'un+ion+ist** *n.*

non+ver+bal com+mu+ni+ca+tion (nɒn'vɜːbᵊl) *n. Psychol.* those aspects of communication, such as gestures and facial expressions, that do not involve verbal communication but which may include nonverbal aspects of speech itself (accent, tone of voice, speed of speaking, etc.).

non+vi+o+lence (nɒn'vaɪələns) *n.* abstention from the use of physical force to achieve goals. —**non+'vi+o+lent** *adj.*

non+vot+er (nɒn'vəʊtə) *n.* **1.** a person who does not vote. **2.** a person not eligible to vote.

non+vot+ing (nɒn'vəʊtɪŋ) *adj.* **1.** of or relating to a nonvoter. **2.** *Finance.* (of shares, etc.) not entitling the holder to vote at company meetings.

non-White *n. Chiefly South African.* a person not of the Caucasoid or White race.

noo+dle[1] ('nuːdᵊl) *n.* (*often pl.*) a ribbon-like strip of pasta: noodles are chiefly served in soup or with a sauce. [C18: from German *Nudel,* origin obscure]

noo+dle[2] ('nuːdᵊl) *n.* **1.** *U.S.* a slang word for **head. 2.** a simpleton. [C18: perhaps a blend of NODDLE[1] and NOODLE[1]]

nook (nʊk) *n.* **1.** a corner or narrow recess, as in a room. **2.** a secluded or sheltered place; retreat. [C13: origin obscure; perhaps related to Norwegian dialect *nok* hook]

noon (nuːn) *n.* **1. a.** the middle of the day; 12 o'clock in the daytime or the time or point at which the sun crosses the local meridian. **b.** (*as modifier*): *the noon sun.* **2.** *Poetic.* the highest, brightest, or most important part; culmination. [Old English *nōn,* from Latin *nōna* (*hōra*) ninth hour (originally 3 p.m., the ninth hour from sunrise)]

noon+day ('nuːnˌdeɪ) *n.* **a.** the middle of the day; noon. **b.** (*as modifier*): *the noonday sun.*

no-one *or* **no one** *pron.* no person; nobody.
Usage. See at **everyone.**

noon+ing ('nuːnɪŋ) *n. Dialect, chiefly U.S.* **1.** a midday break for rest or food. **2.** midday; noon.

noon+time ('nuːnˌtaɪm) *or* **noon+tide** *n.* **a.** the middle of the day; noon. **b.** (*as modifier*): *a noontime drink.*

Noord+bra+bant (ˌnoːrd'braːbɑnt) *n.* the Dutch name for **North Brabant.**

Noord+hol+land (ˌnoːrt'hɔlɑnt) *n.* the Dutch name for **North Holland.**

noose (nuːs) *n.* **1.** a loop in the end of a rope or cord, such as a lasso, snare, or hangman's halter, usually tied with a slipknot. **2.** something that restrains, binds, or traps. **3. put one's head in a noose.** to bring about one's own downfall. ~*vb.* (*tr.*) **4.** to secure or catch in or as if in a noose. **5.** to make a noose of or in. [C15: perhaps from Provençal *nous,* from Latin *nōdus* NODE]

no+pal ('nəʊpᵊl) *n.* **1.** any of various cacti of the genus *Nopalea,* esp. the red-flowered *N. cochinellifera,* which is a host plant of the cochineal insect. **2.** a cactus, *Opuntia lindheimeri,* having yellow flowers and purple fruits. See also **prickly pear.** [C18: from Spanish, from Nahuatl *nopálli* cactus]

no-par *adj.* (of securities) without a par value.

nope (nəʊp) *sentence substitute.* an informal word for **no**[1].

nor (nɔː; *unstressed* nə) *conj.* (*coordinating*) **1.** (used to join alternatives, the first of which is preceded by *neither*) and not: *neither measles nor mumps.* **2.** (foll. by an auxiliary verb or *have, do,* or *be* used as main verbs) (and) not...either: *they weren't talented—nor were they particularly funny.* **3.** *Brit. dialect.* than: *better nor me.* **4.** *Poetic.* neither: *nor wind nor rain.* [C13: contraction of Old English *nōther,* from *nahwæther* NEITHER]

Nor. *abbrev. for:* **1.** Norman. **2.** north. **3.** Norway. **4.** Norwegian.

nor- *combining form.* **1.** indicating that a chemical compound is derived from a specified compound by removal of a group or groups: *noradrenaline.* **2.** indicating that a chemical compound is a normal isomer of a specified compound. [by shortening from NORMAL]

nor+a+dren+a+line (ˌnɔːrə'drɛnəlɪn, -liːn) *or* **nor+a+dren+a+lin** *n.* a hormone secreted by the adrenal medulla, increasing blood pressure and heart rate, and by the endings of sympathetic nerves, where it acts as a transmitter of impulses. Formula: $C_8H_{11}NO_3$. U.S. name: **norepinephrine.**

NOR cir+cuit *or* **gate** (nɔː) *n. Computer technol.* a logic circuit having two or more input wires and one output wire that has an output signal only if all input signals are at a low voltage. Compare **AND circuit.** [C20: from NOR, so named because the action performed is similar to the operation of the conjunction *nor* in logic]

Nord (*French* nɔːr) *n.* a department of N France, in Nord-Pas-de-Calais region. Capital: Lille. Pop.: 2 534 906 (1975). Area: 5774 sq. km (2252 sq. miles).

Nor·dau (*German* 'nɔrdaʊ) *n.* **Max Si·mon** (maks 'ziːmɔn), original name *Max Simon Südfeld.* 1849–1923, German author, born in Hungary; a leader of the Zionist movement.

Nor·den·skjöld (*Swedish* 'nuːrdənʃœld) *n.* Baron **Nils A·dolf Er·ik** (nils 'ɑːdɔlf 'eːrik). 1832–1901, Swedish Arctic explorer

---

ˌ**non+res·i+'den+tial** *adj.*
ˌ**non+re+'strict+ed** *adj.*
non+'ru+ral *adj.*
ˌ**non+sci+en+'tif+ic** *adj.*
non+'sea+son+al *adj.*
ˌ**non+sec+'ta+ri+an** *adj.*
non+'sec·u+lar *adj.*
non+'seg+re+ˌgat+ed *adj.*
ˌ**non+se+'lec+tive** *adj.*
non+'sen+si+tive *adj.*
non+'sex+u+al *adj.*
non+'shrink+a+ble *adj.*
ˌ**non+sig+'nif+i+cant** *adj.*
non+'sink+a+ble *adj.*
non+'skilled *adj.*
non+'so+cial *adj.*
non+'sol+u+ble *adj.*
non+'speak+ing *adj.*
non+'spe+cial+ist *n.*
ˌ**non+spe+'cif+ic** *adj.*
non+'spec+u+ˌla+tive *adj.*
non+'spir+it+u+al *adj.*
non+'sport+ing *adj.*
non+'stain+a+ble *adj.*
non+'stain+ing *adj.*
ˌ**non+sta+'tis+ti+cal** *adj.*
ˌ**non+stra+'te+gic** *adj.*
non+'struc+tur+al *adj.*
ˌ**non+sub+'scrib+er** *n.*
ˌ**non+sug+'ges+tive** *adj.*
non+'sul+phur+ous *adj.*
ˌ**non+sup+'pres+sion** *n.*
non+'sur+gi+cal *adj.*
ˌ**non+sus+'tain+ing** *adj.*
non+'swim+mer *n.*
ˌ**non+sym+'bol+ic** *adj.*
ˌ**non+sys+tem+'at+ic** *adj.*
non+'tech+ni+cal *adj.*
non+'tem+po+ral *adj.*
ˌ**non+ter+ri+'to+ri+al** *adj.*
ˌ**non+the+'at+ri+cal** *adj.*
non+'tox+ic *adj.*
ˌ**non+tra+'di+tion+al** *adj.*
ˌ**non+trans+'fer+a+ble** *adj.*
non+'trop+i+cal *adj.*
non+'typ+i+cal *adj.*
non+'u+ni+ˌform *adj.*
non+'us+age *n.*
non+'use *n.*
non+'us+er *n.*
non+'ven+om+ous *adj.*
non+'ver+bal *adj.*
non+'ver+i+ˌfi+a+ble *adj.*
non+'ves+ti+cal *adj.*
non+'vo+cal *adj.*
non+'vol+a+tile *adj.*

and geologist, born in Finland. He was the first to navigate the Northeast Passage (1878–79).

Nor+den+skjöld Sea *n.* the former name of the **Laptev Sea.** [named after N. A. E. NORDENSKJÖLD]

Nor+dic ('nɔːdɪk) *adj.* of, relating to, or belonging to a subdivision of the Caucasoid race typified by the tall blond blue-eyed long-headed inhabitants of N Britain, Scandinavia, N Germany, and the Netherlands. [C19: from French *nordique,* from *nord* NORTH]

Nord+kyn Cape (*Norwegian* 'nuːrçyːn) *n.* a cape in N Norway: the northernmost point of the European mainland.

Nord–Pas-de-Ca·lais (*French* nɔr pɑ də ka'lɛ) *n.* a region of N France, on the Straits of Dover (the **Pas de Calais**): coal-mining, textile and metallurgical industries.

Nord·rhein-West·fa·len ('nɔrtraɪn vɛst'faːlən) *n.* the German name for **North Rhine-Westphalia.**

nor+ep·i+neph+rine (ˌnɔːrɛpɪ'nɛfrɪn, -riːn) *n.* the U.S. name for **noradrenaline.**

Nor+folk ('nɔːfək) *n.* **1.** a county of E England, on the North Sea and the Wash: low-lying, with large areas of fens in the west and the Broads in the east; rich agriculturally. Administrative centre: Norwich. Pop.: 662 500 (1976 est.). Area: 5353 sq. km (2067 sq. miles). **2.** a port in SE Virginia, on the Elizabeth River and Hampton Roads: headquarters of the U.S. Atlantic fleet; shipbuilding. Pop.: 283 064 (1973 est.).

Nor+folk Is+land *n.* an island in the S Pacific, between New Caledonia and N New Zealand: administered by Australia; discovered by Captain Cook in 1774; a penal settlement in early years. Pop.: 1422 (1972). Area: 36 sq. km (14 sq. miles).

Nor+folk jack+et *n.* a man's single-breasted belted jacket with one or two chest pockets and a box pleat down the back. [C19: worn in NORFOLK for duck shooting]

Nor+ge ('nɔrgə) *n.* the Norwegian name for **Norway.**

no+ri·a ('nɔːrɪə) *n.* a waterwheel with buckets attached to its rim for raising water from a stream into irrigation canals, etc.: common in Spain and the Orient. [C18: via Spanish from Arabic *nā'ūra,* from *na'ara* to creak]

Nor·i+cum ('nɒrɪkəm) *n.* an Alpine kingdom of the Celts, south of the Danube: comprises present-day central Austria and parts of Bavaria; a Roman province from about 16 B.C.

nor+ite ('nɔːraɪt) *n.* a variety of gabbro that has hypersthene as the main ferromagnesian mineral. [C19: from Norwegian *norit,* from *Norge* Norway + *-it* -ITE[1]]

nork (nɔːk) *n.* (*usually pl.*) *Austral. slang.* a female breast. [C20: of unknown origin]

nor+land ('nɔːlənd) *n. Archaic.* the north part of a country or the earth.

norm (nɔːm) *n.* **1.** an average level of achievement or performance, as of a group or person. **2.** a standard of achievement or behaviour that is required, desired, or designated as normal. **3.** *Sociol.* an established standard of behaviour shared by members of a social group to which each member is expected to conform. **4.** *Maths.* **a.** the length of a vector expressed as the square root of the sum of the square of its components. **b.** another name for **mode** (sense 6). **5.** *Geology.* the theoretical standard mineral composition of an igneous rock. [C19: from Latin *norma* carpenter's rule, square]

norm. *abbrev. for* normal.

Norm. *abbrev. for* Norman.

Nor+ma ('nɔːmə) *n., Latin genitive* **Nor+mae** ('nɔːmiː). a constellation in the S hemisphere crossed by the Milky Way lying near Scorpius and Ara.

nor+mal ('nɔːmᵊl) *adj.* **1.** usual; regular; common; typical: *the normal way of doing it; the normal level.* **2.** constituting a standard: *if we take this as normal.* **3.** *Psychol.* **a.** being within certain limits of intelligence, educational success or ability, etc. **b.** conforming to the conventions of one's group. **4.** *Biology, med.* (of laboratory animals) maintained in a natural state for purposes of comparison with animals treated with drugs, etc. **5.** *Chem.* (of a solution) containing a number of grams equal to the equivalent weight of the solute in each litre of solvent. Symbol: *N.* **6.** *Geom.* another word for **perpendicular** (sense 1). ~*n.* **7.** the usual, average, or typical state, degree, form, etc. **8.** anything that is normal. **9.** *Geom.* a line or plane perpendicular to another line or plane or to the tangent of a curved line or plane at the point of contact. [C16: from Latin *normālis* conforming to the carpenter's square, from *norma* NORM] —**nor+mal+i·ty** (nɔː'mælɪtɪ) *or esp. U.S.* **'nor+mal+cy** *n.*

nor+mal curve *n. Statistics.* a symmetrical bell-shaped curve representing the normal distribution and showing the probability associated with each variate value.

nor+mal dis+tri+bu+tion *n. Statistics.* a continuous distribution of a random variable with its mean, median, and mode equal. Also called: **Gaussian distribution.**

nor+mal+ize *or* **nor+mal+ise** ('nɔːməˌlaɪz) *vb.* (*tr.*) **1.** to bring or make into the normal state. **2.** to bring into conformity with a standard. **3.** to heat (steel) above a critical temperature and allow it to cool in air to relieve internal stresses; anneal. —ˌ**nor+mal·i·'za+tion** *or* ˌ**nor+mal·i+'sa+tion** *n.*

nor+mal+ly ('nɔːməlɪ) *adv.* **1.** as a rule; usually; ordinarily. **2.** in a normal manner.

nor+mal ma+trix *n.* a square matrix A for which $AA^* = A^*A$, where A^* is the Hermitian conjugate of A.

nor+mal school *n.* a school or institution for training teachers (in France, and formerly the U.S. and Canada).

Nor+man ('nɔːmən) *n.* **1.** (in the Middle Ages) a member of the people of Normandy descended from the 10th-century Scandinavian conquerors of the country and the native French. **2.** a native or inhabitant of Normandy. **3.** another name for **Norman French.** ~*adj.* **4.** of, relating to, or characteristic of the Normans, esp. the Normans in England, or their dialect of French. **5.** of, relating to, or characteristic of Normandy or its inhabitants. **6.** denoting, relating to, or having the style of Romanesque architecture used in Britain from the Norman Conquest until the 12th century. It is characterized by the rounded arch, the groin vault, massive masonry walls, etc.

Nor+man arch *n. Chiefly Brit.* a semicircular arch, esp. one in the Romanesque style of architecture developed by the Normans in England. Also called: **Roman arch.**

Nor+man Con+quest *n.* the invasion and settlement of England by the Normans, following the Battle of Hastings (1066).

Nor+man+dy ('nɔːməndɪ) *n.* a former province of N France, on the English Channel: settled by Vikings under Rollo in the 10th century; scene of the Allied landings in 1944. Chief town: Rouen. French name: **Nor+man+die** (nɔrmã'di).

Nor+man Eng+lish *n.* the dialect of English used by the Norman conquerors of England.

Nor+man French *n.* the medieval Norman and English dialect of Old French. See also **Anglo-French** (sense 3).

Nor+man+ize *or* **Nor+man+ise** ('nɔːməˌnaɪz) *vb.* to make or become Norman in character, style, customs, etc. —ˌ**Nor+man·i+'za+tion** *or* ˌ**Nor+man·i+'sa+tion** *n.*

nor+ma+tive ('nɔːmətɪv) *adj.* **1.** implying, creating or prescribing a norm or standard, as in language: *normative grammar.* **2.** of, relating to, or based on norms. —**'nor+ma+tive+ly** *adv.* —**'nor+ma+tive+ness** *n.*

Norn (nɔːn) *n.* **1.** *Norse myth.* any of the three virgin goddesses of fate, who predestine the lives of the gods and men. **2.** the medieval Norse language of the Orkneys, Shetlands, and parts of N Scotland. It was extinct by 1750.

No·ro·dom Si·han·ouk (ˌnɒrə'dɒm 'siːənʊk) *n.* See **Sihanouk.**

Norr+kö+ping (*Swedish* 'nɔrtçøːpiŋ) *n.* a port in SE Sweden, near the Baltic. Pop.: 119 470 (1974 est.).

Norse (nɔːs) *adj.* **1.** of, relating to, or characteristic of ancient and medieval Scandinavia or its inhabitants. **2.** of, relating to, or characteristic of Norway. ~*n.* **3. a.** the N group of Germanic languages, spoken in Scandinavia; Scandinavian. **b.** any one of these languages, esp. in their ancient or medieval forms. See also **Proto-Norse, Old Norse. 4. the Norse.** (*functioning as pl.*) **a.** the Norwegians. **b.** the Vikings.

Norse+man ('nɔːsmən) *n., pl.* **+men.** another name for a **Viking.**

north (nɔːθ) *n.* **1.** one of the four cardinal points of the compass, at 0° or 360°, that is 90° from east and west and 180° from south. **2.** the direction along a meridian towards the North Pole. **3.** the direction in which a compass needle points; magnetic north. **4. the north.** (*often cap.*) any area lying in or towards the north. ~*adj.* **5.** situated in, moving towards, or facing the north. **6.** (esp. of the wind) from the north. ~*adv.* **7.** in, to, towards, or (esp. of the wind) from the north. ~Abbrev.: **N** [Old English; related to Old Norse *northr,* Dutch *noord,* Old High German *nord*]

North[1] (nɔːθ) *n.* **the. 1.** the northern area of England, generally regarded as reaching approximately the southern boundaries of Yorkshire, Derbyshire, and Cheshire. **2.** (in the U.S.) the area approximately north of Maryland and the Ohio River, esp. those states north of the Mason-Dixon line that were known as the Free States during the Civil War. **3.** the northern part of North America, esp. the area consisting of Alaska and the Yukon; the North Country. **4.** *Poetic.* the north wind. ~*adj.* **5. a.** of or denoting the northern part of a specified country, area, etc. **b.** (*as part of a name*): *North Africa.*

North[2] (nɔːθ) *n.* **1. Fred·er·ick,** 2nd Earl of Guildford, called *Lord North.* 1732–92, English statesman; prime minister (1770–82), dominated by George III. He was held responsible for the loss of the American colonies. **2.** Sir **Thom·as.** ?1535–?1601, English translator of Plutarch's *Lives* (1579), which was the chief source of Shakespeare's Roman plays.

North Af+ri+ca *n.* the part of Africa between the Mediterranean and the Sahara Desert: consists chiefly of Morocco, Algeria, Tunisia, Libya, and N Egypt. —**North Af+ri+can** *adj., n.*

North+al+ler+ton (nɔː'θælətᵊn) *n.* a market town in N England, administrative centre of North Yorkshire. Pop.: 8750 (1971).

North A·mer·i·ca *n.* the third largest continent, linked with South America by the Isthmus of Panama and bordering on the Arctic Ocean, the N Pacific, the N Atlantic, the Gulf of Mexico, and the Caribbean. It consists generally of a great mountain system (the Western Cordillera) extending along the entire W coast, actively volcanic in the extreme north and south, with the Great Plains to the east and the Appalachians still further east, separated from the Canadian Shield by an arc of large lakes (Great Bear, Great Slave, Winnipeg, Superior, Michigan, Huron, Erie, Ontario); reaches its greatest height of 6194 m (20 320 ft.) in Mount McKinley, Alaska, and its lowest point of 85 m (280 ft.) below sea level in Death Valley, California, and ranges from snowfields, tundra, and taiga in the north to deserts in the southwest and tropical forests in the extreme south. Pop.: 315 000 000 (1970 est.). Area: over 24 000 000 sq. km (9 500 000 sq. miles). —**North A·mer·i·can** *adj., n.*

North+amp+ton (nɔː'θæmptən, nɔːθ'hæmp-) *n.* **1.** a town in central England, administrative centre of Northamptonshire, on the River Nene: footwear and engineering industries. Pop.: 126 608 (1971). **2.** short for **Northamptonshire.**

North+amp+ton+shire (nɔː'θæmptənʃɪə, -ʃə, nɔːθ'hæmp-) *n.* a county of central England: agriculture, iron and steel, engineering, and footwear industries. Administrative centre: Northampton. Pop.: 505 900 (1976 est.). Area: 2370 sq. km (915 sq. miles). Abbrev.: **Northants.**

Northants. (nɔːˈθænts) *abbrev. for* Northamptonshire.

North At+lan+tic Drift *or* **Cur+rent** *n.* the warm ocean current flowing northeast, under the influence of prevailing winds, from the Gulf of Mexico towards NW Europe and warming its climate. Also called: **Gulf Stream.**

North At+lan+tic Trea+ty Or+gan·i+za+tion *n.* the full name of **NATO.**

North Bor+ne·o *n.* the former name (until 1963) of **Sabah.**

north+bound (ˈnɔːθ,baʊnd) *adj.* going or leading towards the north.

North Bra+bant *n.* a province of the S Netherlands: formed part of the medieval duchy of Brabant. Capital: 's Hertogenbosch. Pop.: 1 879 800 (1973 est.). Area: 4965 sq. km (1917 sq. miles).

north by east *n.* one point on the compass east of north, 11° 15′ clockwise from north. ~*adj., adv.* in, from, or towards this direction.

north by west *n.* **1.** one point on the compass west of north, 348° 45′ clockwise from north. ~*adj., adv.* **2.** in, from, or towards this direction.

North Cape *n.* **1.** a cape on N Magerøy Island, in the Arctic Ocean off the N coast of Norway. **2.** a cape on N North Island, New Zealand.

North Car·o+li+na *n.* a state of the southeastern U.S., on the Atlantic: consists of a coastal plain rising to the Piedmont Plateau and the Appalachian Mountains in the west. Capital: Raleigh. Pop.: 5 082 059 (1970). Area: 126 387 sq. km (48 798 sq. miles). Abbrevs.: **N.C.** or (with zip code) **NC**

North Chan+nel *n.* a strait between NE Ireland and SW Scotland, linking the North Atlantic with the Irish Sea.

North·cliffe (ˈnɔːθklɪf) *n.* **Vis·count.** title of *Alfred Charles William Harmsworth.* 1865–1922, British newspaper proprietor. With his brother, 1st Viscount Rothermere, he built up a vast chain of newspapers. He founded the *Daily Mail* (1896), the *Daily Mirror* (1903), and acquired *The Times* (1908).

North Coun+try *n.* (usually preceded by *the*) **1.** another name for **North**[1] (sense 1). **2.** the geographic region formed by Alaska and the Yukon.

north·coun·try·man (,nɔːθˈkʌntrɪ,mən) *n., pl.* **+men.** a native or inhabitant of the North of England.

North Da+ko+ta *n.* a state of the western U.S.: mostly undulating prairies and plains, rising from the Red River valley in the east to the Missouri plateau in the west, with the infertile Bad Lands in the extreme west. Capital: Bismarck. Pop.: 617 761 (1970). Area: 183 019 sq. km (70 664 sq. miles). Abbrevs.: **N.Dak., N.D.,** or (with zip code) **ND**

north+east (,nɔːθˈiːst; *Nautical* ,nɔːrˈiːst) *n.* **1.** the point of the compass or direction midway between north and east, 45° clockwise from north. **2.** (*often cap.*; usually preceded by *the*) any area lying in or towards this direction. ~*adj. also* **north+east·ern. 3.** (*sometimes cap.*) of or denoting the northeastern part of a specified country, area, etc.: *northeast Lincolnshire.* **4.** situated in, proceeding towards, or facing the northeast. **5.** (esp. of the wind) from the northeast. ~*adv.* **6.** in, to, towards, or (esp. of the wind) from the northeast. ~Abbrev.: **NE** —,**north+ˈeast·ern·most** *adj.*

North+east (,nɔːθˈiːst) *n.* (usually preceded by *the*) the northeastern part of England, esp. Northumberland and Durham.

north+east by east *n.* **1.** one point on the compass east of northeast, 56° 15′ clockwise from north. ~*adj., adv.* **2.** in, from, or towards this direction.

north+east by north *n.* **1.** one point on the compass north of northeast, 33° 45′ clockwise from north. ~*adj., adv.* **2.** in, from, or towards this direction.

north+east·er (,nɔːθˈiːstə; *Nautical* ,nɔːrˈiːstə) *n.* a strong wind or storm from the northeast.

north+east·er+ly (,nɔːθˈiːstəlɪ; *Nautical* ,nɔːrˈiːstəlɪ) *adj., adv.* **1.** in, towards, or (esp. of a wind) from the northeast. ~*n., pl.* **+lies. 2.** a wind or storm from the northeast.

North East Fron+tier A·gen+cy *n.* the former name (until 1972) of **Arunachal Pradesh.**

North+east Pas+sage *n.* a shipping route along the Arctic coasts of Europe and Asia, between the Atlantic and Pacific: first navigated by Nordenskjöld (1878–79).

north+east·ward (,nɔːθˈiːstwəd; *Nautical* ,nɔːrˈiːstwəd) *adj.* **1.** towards or (esp. of a wind) from the northeast. ~*n.* **2.** a direction towards or area in the northeast. —,**north+ˈeast·ward+ly** *adj., adv.*

north+east·wards (,nɔːθˈiːstwədz; *Nautical* ,nɔːrˈiːstwədz) *or* **north+east·ward** *adv.* to the northeast.

north+er (ˈnɔːðə) *n. Chiefly southern U.S.* a wind or storm from the north.

nor+ther+ly (ˈnɔːðəlɪ) *adj.* **1.** of, relating to, or situated in the north. ~*adv., adj.* **2.** towards or in the direction of the north. **3.** from the north: *a northerly wind.* ~*n., pl.* **+lies. 4.** a wind from the north. —ˈ**nor+ther+li+ness** *n.*

north+ern (ˈnɔːðən) *adj.* **1.** situated in or towards the north: *northern towns.* **2.** directed or proceeding towards the north: *a northern flow of traffic.* **3.** (esp. of winds) proceeding from the north. **4.** (*sometimes cap.*) of, relating to, or characteristic of the north or North. **5.** (*sometimes cap.*) *Astronomy.* north of the celestial equator.

North+ern Cross *n.* a group of the five brightest stars that form a large cross in the constellation Cygnus.

North+ern Dvi+na *n.* See **Dvina.**

North+ern+er (ˈnɔːðənə) *n.* (*sometimes not cap.*) a native or inhabitant of the north of any specified region, esp. England or the U.S.

north+ern hem·i+sphere *n.* (*often caps.*) **1.** that half of the globe lying north of the equator. **2.** *Astronomy.* that half of the celestial sphere north of the celestial equator. ~Abbrev.: **N hemisphere.**

North+ern Ire+land *n.* that part of the United Kingdom occupying the NE part of Ireland: separated from the rest of Ireland, which became independent in 1920, remaining part of the United Kingdom, with a separate Parliament (Stormont) and limited self-government; scene of severe conflict between Catholics and Protestants, including terrorist bombing since 1969. Capital: Belfast. Pop.: 1 527 593 (1971). Area: 14 121 sq. km (5452 sq. miles).

north+ern lights *pl. n.* another name for **aurora borealis.**

north+ern+most (ˈnɔːðən,məʊst) *adj.* situated or occurring farthest north.

North+ern Rho+de·sia *n.* the former name (until 1964) of **Zambia.**

North+ern So+tho *n.* another name for **Pedi** (the language).

North+ern Ter+ri·to·ries *n.* a former British protectorate in W Africa, established in 1897; attached to the Gold Coast in 1901; now constitutes the Northern Region of Ghana (since 1957).

North+ern Ter+ri+to·ry *n.* an administrative division of N central Australia, on the Timor and Arafura Seas: includes Ashmore and Cartier Islands; the Arunta Desert lies in the east, the Macdonnell Ranges in the south, and Arnhem Land in the north (containing Australia's largest Aboriginal reservation). Capital: Darwin. Pop.: 97 100 (1976). Area: 1 347 525 sq. km (520 280 sq. miles).

North Ger+man+ic *n.* a subbranch of the Germanic languages that consists of Danish, Norwegian, Swedish, Icelandic, and their associated dialects. See also **Old Norse.**

North Hol+land *n.* a province of the NW Netherlands, on the peninsula between the North Sea and IJsselmeer: includes the West Frisian Island of Texel. Capital: Haarlem. Pop.: 2 283 400 (1973 est.). Area: 2663 sq. km (1029 sq. miles). Dutch name: **Noordholland.**

north+ing (ˈnɔːθɪŋ, -ðɪŋ) *n.* **1.** *Navigation.* movement or distance covered in a northerly direction, esp. as expressed in the resulting difference in latitude. **2.** *Astronomy.* a north or positive declination. **3.** *Cartography.* **a.** the distance northwards of a point from a given parallel indicated by the second half of a map grid reference. **b.** a latitudinal grid line. Compare **easting** (sense 2).

North Is+land *n.* the northernmost of the two main islands of New Zealand. Pop.: 2 050 208 (1971). Area: 114 729 sq. km (44 297 sq. miles).

North Ko+re·a *n.* a republic in NE Asia, on the Sea of Japan and the Yellow Sea: established in 1948 as a people's republic; mostly rugged and mountainous, with fertile lowlands in the west. Language: Korean. Currency: won. Capital: Pyongyang. Pop.: 15 852 000 (1975 UN est.). Area: 122 313 sq. km (47 225 sq. miles). Official name: **Democratic People's Republic of Korea.** —**North Ko+re·an** *adj., n.*

North+land (ˈnɔːθlənd) *n.* **1.** the peninsula containing Norway and Sweden. **2.** (in Canada) the far north. —ˈ**North+land+er** *n.*

North+man (ˈnɔːθmən) *n., pl.* **+men.** another name for a **Viking.**

north-north·east *n.* **1.** the point on the compass or the direction midway between north and northeast, 22° 30′ clockwise from north. ~*adj., adv.* **2.** in, from, or towards this direction. ~Abbrev.: **NNE**

north-north·west *n.* **1.** the point on the compass or the direction midway between northwest and north, 337° 30′ clockwise from north. ~*adj., adv.* **2.** in, from, or towards this direction. ~Abbrev.: **NNW**

North Os+se·tian Au·ton·o+mous So+vi+et So+cial+ist Re+pub+lic (əˈsiːʃən) *n.* an administrative division of the S Soviet Union, on the N slopes of the central Caucasus Mountains. Capital: Ordzhonikidze. Pop.: 552 581 (1970). Area: about 8000 sq. km (3088 sq. miles).

North Pole *n.* **1.** the northernmost point on the earth's axis, at a latitude of 90°N, characterized by very low temperatures. **2.** Also called: **north celestial pole.** *Astronomy.* the point of intersection of the earth's extended axis and the northern half of the celestial sphere, lying about 1° from Polaris.

North Rhine-West·pha+li·a *n.* a state of W West Germany: formed in 1946 by the amalgamation of the Prussian province of Westphalia with the N part of the Prussian Rhine province and later with the state of Lippe; highly industrialized. Capital: Düsseldorf. Pop.: 16 914 118 (1970). Area: 34 039 sq. km (13 142 sq. miles). German name: **Nordrhein-Westfalen.**

North Rid+ing *n.* (until 1974) an administrative division of Yorkshire, now constituting most of North Yorkshire.

North Sas+katch+e·wan *n.* a river in W Canada, rising in W Alberta and flowing northeast, east, and southeast to join the South Saskatchewan River and form the Saskatchewan River. Length: 1223 km (760 miles).

North Sea *n.* an arm of the Atlantic between Great Britain and the N European mainland. Area: about 569 800 sq. km (220 000 sq. miles). Former name: **German Ocean.**

North-Sea gas *n. Brit.* natural gas obtained from deposits below the North Sea.

North Star *n.* **the.** another name for **Polaris** (sense 1).

Northumb. *or* **Northld.** *abbrev. for* Northumberland.

North+um+ber+land (nɔːˈθʌmbələnd) *n.* the northernmost county of England, on the North Sea: hilly in the north (the Cheviots) and west (the Pennines), with many Roman remains, notably Hadrian's Wall; shipbuilding, coal-mining. Administrative centre: Newcastle. Pop.: 287 300 (1976 est.). Area: 4975 sq. km (1943 sq. miles). Abbrev.: **Northumb.**

North+um+bri+a (nɔːˈθʌmbrɪə) *n.* **1.** (in Anglo-Saxon Britain) a region that stretched from the Humber to the Firth of Forth: formed in the 7th century A.D., it became an important intellectual centre; a separate kingdom until 876 A.D. **2.** another name for **Northumberland.**

North+um+bri+an (nɔːˈθʌmbrɪən) *adj.* **1.** of or relating to the English county of Northumberland, its inhabitants, or their dialect of English. **2.** of or relating to ancient Northumbria, its inhabitants, or their dialect. ~*n.* **3. a.** the dialect of Old and Middle English spoken north of the River Humber. See also **Anglian, Mercian. b.** the dialect of Modern English spoken in Northumberland.

North Vi+et+nam *n.* a region of N Vietnam, on the Gulf of Tonkin: an independent Communist state from 1954 until 1976. Area: 164 061 sq. km (63 344 sq. miles).

north+ward (ˈnɔːθwəd; *Nautical* ˈnɔːðəd) *adj.* **1.** moving, facing, or situated towards the north. ~*n.* **2.** the northward part, direction, etc.; the north. ~*adv.* **3.** a variant of **northwards.** —ˈ**north+ward+ly** *adj., adv.*

north+wards (ˈnɔːθwədz) *or* **north+ward** *adv.* towards the north.

north+west (ˌnɔːθˈwɛst; *Nautical* ˌnɔːˈwɛst) *n.* **1.** the point of the compass or direction midway between north and west, clockwise 315° from north. **2.** (*often cap.;* usually preceded by *the*) any area lying in or towards this direction. ~*adj. also* **north+west+ern. 3.** (*sometimes cap.*) of or denoting the northwestern part of a specified country, area, etc.: *northwest Greenland.* ~*adj., adv.* **4.** in, to, towards, or (esp. of the wind) from the northwest. ~Abbrev.: **NW** —ˌ**north+ˈwest+ern+most** *adj.*

North+west (ˌnɔːθˈwɛst) *n.* (usually preceded by *the*) **1.** the northwestern part of England, esp. Lancashire and the Lake District. **2.** the northwestern part of the U.S., consisting of the states of Washington, Oregon, and sometimes Idaho.

north+west by north *n.* **1.** one point on the compass north of northwest, 326° 15′ clockwise from north. ~*adj., adv.* **2.** in, from, or towards this direction.

north+west by west *n.* **1.** one point on the compass south of northwest, 303° 45′ clockwise from north. ~*adj., adv.* **2.** in, from, or towards this direction.

north+west+er (ˌnɔːθˈwɛstə; *Nautical* ˌnɔːˈwɛstə) *n.* a strong wind or storm from the northwest.

north+west+er+ly (ˌnɔːθˈwɛstəlɪ; *Nautical* ˌnɔːˈwɛstəlɪ) *adj., adv.* **1.** in, towards, or (esp. of a wind) from the northwest. ~*n., pl.* **+lies. 2.** a wind or storm from the northwest.

North-West Fron+tier *n.* a mountainous region of N Pakistan between Afghanistan and Jammu and Kashmir: part of British India from 1901 until 1947; of strategic importance, esp. for the Khyber Pass.

North+west Pas+sage *n.* the passage by sea from the Atlantic to the Pacific along the N coast of America: attempted for over 300 years by Europeans seeking a short route to the Far East, before being successfully navigated by Amundsen (1903–06).

North+west Ter+ri+to+ries *n.* the part of Canada north of the provinces and east of the Yukon Territory, including the islands of the Arctic, Hudson Bay, James Bay, and Ungava Bay; comprises over a third of Canada's total area; rich mineral resources; divided into the three districts of Franklin, Keewatin, and Mackenzie. Pop.: 42 609 (1976). Area: 3 246 404 sq. km (1 253 438 sq. miles).

North+west Ter+ri+to+ry *n.* See **Old Northwest.**

north+west+ward (ˌnɔːθˈwɛstwəd; *Nautical* ˌnɔːˈwɛstwəd) *adj.* **1.** towards or (esp. of a wind) from the northwest. ~*n.* **2.** a direction towards or area in the northwest. —ˌ**north+ˈwest+ward+ly** *adj., adv.*

north+west+wards (ˌnɔːθˈwɛstwədz; *Nautical* ˌnɔːˈwɛstwədz) *or* **north+west+ward** *adv.* towards or (esp. of a wind) from the northwest.

North+wich (ˈnɔːθwɪtʃ) *n.* a town in NW England, in Cheshire: salt and chemical industries. Pop.: 18 109 (1971).

North York+shire *n.* a county in N England, formed in 1974 from most of the North Riding of Yorkshire and parts of the East and West Ridings. Administrative centre: Northallerton. Pop.: 653 000 (1976 est.). Area: 8321 sq. km (3213 sq. miles).

Norw. *abbrev. for:* **1.** Norway. **2.** Norwegian.

Nor+way (ˈnɔːˌweɪ) *n.* a kingdom in NW Europe, occupying the W part of the Scandinavian peninsula: first united in the Viking age (800–1050); under the rule of Denmark (1523–1814) and Sweden (1814–1905); became an independent monarchy in 1905. Its coastline is deeply indented by fjords and fringed with islands, rising inland to plateaus and mountains. Norway has a large fishing fleet and its merchant navy is among the world's largest. Language: Norwegian. Religion: mostly Lutheran. Currency: krone. Capital: Oslo. Pop.: 3 985 000 (1974 est.). Area: 324 218 sq. km (125 181 sq. miles). Norwegian name: **Norge.**

Nor+way lob+ster *n.* a European lobster, *Nephrops norvegicus,* fished for food.

Nor+way ma+ple *n.* a large Eurasian maple tree, *Acer platanoides,* with broad five-lobed pale green leaves.

Nor+way rat *n.* another name for **brown rat.**

Nor+way spruce *n.* a European spruce tree, *Picea abies,* planted for timber and ornament, having drooping branches and dark green needle-like leaves.

Nor+we+gian (nɔːˈwiːdʒən) *adj.* **1.** of, relating to, or characteristic of Norway, its language, or its people. ~*n.* **2.** any of the various North Germanic languages of Norway. See also **Nynorsk, Bokmal.** Compare **Norse. 3.** a native, citizen, or inhabitant of Norway.

Nor+we+gian Sea *n.* part of the Arctic Ocean between Greenland and Norway.

nor'+west+er (ˌnɔːˈwɛstə) *n.* **1.** a less common name for **sou'wester. 2.** a drink of strong liquor.

Nor+wich (ˈnɒrɪdʒ) *n.* a city in E England, administrative centre of Norfolk: cathedral (founded 1096); University of East Anglia (1963); footwear industry. Pop.: 121 688 (1971).

Nos. *or* **nos.** *abbrev. for* numbers.

nose (nəuz) *n.* **1.** the organ of smell and entrance to the respiratory tract, consisting of a prominent structure divided into two hair-lined air passages by a median septum. **2.** the sense of smell itself: in hounds and other animals, the ability to follow trails by scent (esp. in the phrases **a good nose, a bad nose**). **3.** instinctive skill or facility, esp. in discovering things (sometimes in the phrase **follow one's nose**): *he had a nose for good news stories.* **4.** any part regarded as resembling a nose in form or function, such as a nozzle or spout. **5.** the forward part of a vehicle, aircraft, etc., esp. the front end of an aircraft. **6.** narrow margin of victory (in the phrase **(win) by a nose**). **7. cut off one's nose to spite one's face.** to carry out a vengeful action that hurts oneself more than another. **8. keep one's nose clean.** to stay out of trouble; behave properly. **9. keep one's nose to the grindstone.** to work hard and continuously. **10. lead by the nose.** to control; dominate. **11. look down one's nose at.** *Informal.* to be contemptuous or disdainful of. **12. pay through the nose.** *Informal.* to pay an exorbitant price. **13. on the nose.** *Slang.* **a.** (in horse-race betting) to win only: *I bet twenty pounds on the nose on that horse.* **b.** *Chiefly U.S.* precisely; exactly. **c.** *Austral.* bad or bad-smelling. **14. under one's nose. a.** directly in front of one. **b.** unknown to one. **15. with one's nose in the air.** haughtily. **16. poke, stick, etc., one's nose into.** *Informal.* to pry into or interfere in. **17. put someone's nose out of joint.** *Informal.* to thwart or offend someone. **18. rub someone's nose in it.** *Informal.* to remind someone unkindly of a shortcoming. **19. see no further than (the end of) one's nose.** *Informal.* **a.** to be short-sighted; suffer from myopia. **b.** to lack insight or foresight. **20. turn up one's nose (at).** *Informal.* to behave disdainfully (towards). ~*vb.* **21.** (*tr.*) (esp. of horses, dogs, etc.) to rub, touch, or sniff with the nose; nuzzle. **22.** to smell or sniff. **23.** (*intr.;* usually foll. by *after* or *for*) to search (for) by or as if by scent. **24.** to move or cause to move forwards slowly and carefully: *the car nosed along the clifftop; we nosed the car into the garage.* **25.** (*intr.;* foll. by *into, around, about,* etc.) to pry or snoop (into) or meddle (in). [Old English *nosu;* related to Old Frisian *nose,* Norwegian *nosa* to smell and *nus* smell] —ˈ**nose+less** *adj.* —ˈ**nose+ˌlike** *adj.*

nose+bag (ˈnəuzˌbæg) *n.* a bag, fastened around the head of a horse and covering the nose, in which feed is placed.

nose+band (ˈnəuzˌbænd) *n.* the detachable part of a horse's bridle that goes around the nose. Also called: **nosepiece.** —ˈ**nose+ˌband+ed** *adj.*

nose+bleed (ˈnəuzˌbliːd) *n.* bleeding from the nose as the result of injury, etc. Technical name: **epistaxis.**

nose cone *n.* the conical forward section of a missile, spacecraft, etc., designed to withstand high temperatures, esp. during re-entry into the earth's atmosphere.

nose dive *n.* **1.** a sudden plunge with the nose or front pointing downwards, esp. of an aircraft. **2.** *Informal.* a sudden drop or sharp decline: *prices took a nose dive.* ~*vb.* **nose-dive.** (*intr.*) **3.** to perform or cause to perform a nose dive. **4.** *Informal.* to drop suddenly.

nose flute *n.* (esp. in the South Sea Islands) a type of flute blown through the nose.

nose+gay (ˈnəuzˌgeɪ) *n.* a small bunch of flowers; posy. [C15: from NOSE + GAY (in the archaic sense: toy)]

nose out *vb.* (*tr., adv.*) **1.** to discover by smelling. **2.** to discover by cunning or persistence: *the reporter managed to nose out a few facts.* **3.** *Informal.* to beat by a narrow margin: *he was nosed out of first place by the champion.*

nose+piece (ˈnəuzˌpiːs) *n.* **1.** a piece of armour, esp. part of a helmet, that serves to protect the nose. **2.** the connecting part of a pair of spectacles that rests on the nose; bridge. **3.** the part of a microscope to which one or more objective lenses are attached. **4.** a less common word for **noseband.**

nose rag *n. Slang.* a handkerchief.

nose ring *n.* a ring fixed through the nose, as for leading a bull.

nose wheel *n.* a wheel fitted to the forward end of a vehicle, esp. the landing wheel under the nose of an aircraft.

nos+ey (ˈnəuzɪ) *n.* a variant spelling of **nosy.**

nosh (nɒʃ) *Slang.* ~*n.* **1.** food or a meal. ~*vb.* **2.** to eat. [C20: from Yiddish; compare German *naschen* to nibble] —ˈ**nosh+er** *n.*

nosh-up *n. Brit. slang.* a large and satisfying meal.

no-side *n. Rugby.* the end of a match, signalled by the referee's whistle.

nos+ing (ˈnəuzɪŋ) *n.* **1.** the edge of a step or stair tread that projects beyond the riser. **2.** a projecting edge of a moulding, esp. one that is half-round.

no+so- *or before a vowel* **nos-** *combining form.* disease: *nosology.* [from Greek *nosos*]

no+sog+ra+phy (nɒˈsɒgrəfɪ) *n.* a written classification and description of various diseases. —**no+ˈsog+ra+pher** *n.* —**no+so+graph+ic** (ˌnɒsəˈgræfɪk) *adj.*

no+sol+o+gy (nɒˈsɒlədʒɪ) *n.* the branch of medicine concerned with the classification of diseases. —**nos+o+log+i+cal** (ˌnɒsəˈlɒdʒɪkᵊl) *adj.* —ˌ**nos+o+ˈlog+i+cal+ly** *adv.* —**no+ˈsol+o+gist** *n.*

nos+tal+gia (nɒ'stældʒə, -dʒɪə) *n.* **1.** a yearning for the return of past circumstances, events, etc. **2.** the evocation of this emotion, as in a book, film, etc. **3.** longing for home or family; homesickness. [C18: New Latin (translation of German *Heimweh* homesickness), from Greek *nostos* return home + -ALGIA] —**nos+'tal+gic** *adj.* —**nos+'tal+gi+cal+ly** *adv.*

nos+toc ('nɒstɒk) *n.* any blue-green alga of the genus *Nostoc*, occurring in moist places as rounded colonies consisting of coiled filaments in a gelatinous substance. [C17: New Latin, coined by Paracelsus]

nos+tol+o·gy (nɒ'stɒlədʒɪ) *n. Med.* another word for **gerontology.** [C20: from Greek *nostos* a return home (with reference to ageing or second childhood) + -LOGY] —**nos+to+log+ic** (ˌnɒstə'lɒdʒɪk) *adj.*

Nos·tra·da·mus (ˌnɒstrə'dɑːməs) *n.* latinized name of *Michel de Notredame.* 1503–66, French physician and astrologer; author of a book of prophecies in rhymed quatrains, *Centuries* (1555).

nos+tril ('nɒstrɪl) *n.* either of the two external openings of the nose. [Old English *nosthyrl,* from *nosu* NOSE + *thyrel* hole]

nos+trum ('nɒstrəm) *n.* **1.** a patent or quack medicine. **2.** a favourite remedy, as for political or social problems. [C17: from Latin: our own (make), from *noster* our]

nos·y *or* **nos+ey** ('nəʊzɪ) *adj.* **nos·i+er, nos·i+est.** *Informal.* prying or inquisitive. —**'nos·i+ly** *adv.* —**'nos·i+ness** *n.*

nos·y par+ker *n. Informal, chiefly Brit.* a prying person. [C20: apparently arbitrary use of surname *Parker*]

not (nɒt) *adv.* **1. a.** used to negate the sentence, phrase, or word that it modifies: *I will not stand for it.* **b.** (*in combination*): *they cannot go.* **2. not that.** (*conj.*) Also (archaic): **not but what.** which is not to say or suppose that: *I expect to lose the game—not that I mind.* ~ **3.** *sentence substitute.* used to indicate denial, negation, or refusal: *certainly not.* [C14 *not,* variant of *nought* nothing, from Old English *nāwiht,* from *nā* no + *wiht* creature, thing. See NAUGHT, NOUGHT]

not- *combining form.* variant of **noto-** before a vowel.

no·ta be·ne *Latin.* ('nəʊtə 'biːnɪ) *n.* note well; take note. Abbrevs.: **NB, N.B., nb, n.b.**

no+ta·bil+i·ty (ˌnəʊtə'bɪlɪtɪ) *n., pl.* **·ties. 1.** the state or quality of being notable. **2.** a distinguished person; notable.

no+ta·ble ('nəʊtəb^{ə}l) *adj.* **1.** worthy of being noted or remembered; remarkable; distinguished. ~*n.* **2.** a notable person. [C14: via Old French from Latin *notābilis,* from *notāre* to NOTE] —**'no·ta·ble·ness** *n.* —**'no+ta·bly** *adv.*

no+ta+rize *or* **no+ta+rise** ('nəʊtəˌraɪz) *vb.* (*tr.*) to attest to or authenticate (a document, contract, etc.), as a notary.

no+ta+ry ('nəʊtərɪ) *n., pl.* **+ries. 1.** a notary public. **2.** (formerly) a clerk licensed to prepare legal documents. **3.** *Archaic.* a clerk or secretary. [C14: from Latin *notārius* clerk, from *nota* a mark, note] —**no+tar+i·al** (nəʊ'tɛərɪəl) *adj.* —**no+'tar·i·al+ly** *adv.* —**'no+ta+ry+ˌship** *n.*

no+ta+ry pub+lic *n., pl.* **no+ta+ries pub+lic.** a public official, usually a solicitor, who is legally authorized to administer oaths, attest and certify certain documents, etc.

no+tate (nəʊ'teɪt) *vb.* to write (esp. music) in notation. [C20: back formation from NOTATION]

no+ta+tion (nəʊ'teɪʃən) *n.* **1.** any series of signs or symbols used to represent quantities or elements in a specialized system, such as music or mathematics. **2.** the act or process of notating. **3. a.** the act of noting down. **b.** a note or record. [C16: from Latin *notātiō* a marking, from *notāre* to NOTE] —**no+'ta+tion+al** *adj.*

notch (nɒtʃ) *n.* **1.** a V-shaped cut or indentation; nick. **2.** a cut or nick made in a tally stick or similar object. **3.** *U.S.* a narrow pass or gorge. **4.** *Informal.* a step or level (esp. in the phrase **a notch above**). ~*vb.* (*tr.*). **5.** to cut or make a notch. **6.** to record with or as if with a notch. **7.** (usually foll. by *up*) *Informal.* to score or achieve: *the team notched up its fourth win.* [C16: from incorrect division of *an otch* (as *a notch*), from Old French *oche* notch, from Latin *obsecāre* to cut off, from *secāre* to cut] —**'notch·y** *adj.*

NOT cir+cuit *or* **gate** (nɒt) *n. Computer technol.* a logic circuit that has a high-voltage output signal if the input signal is low, and vice versa: used extensively in computers. Also called: **inverter, negator.** [C20: so named because the action performed on electrical signals is similar to the operation of *not* in logical constructions]

note (nəʊt) *n.* **1.** a brief summary or record in writing, esp. a jotting for future reference. **2.** a brief letter, usually of an informal nature. **3.** a formal written communication, esp. from one government to another. **4.** a short written statement giving any kind of information. **5.** a critical comment, explanatory statement, or reference in the text of a book, often preceded by a number. **6.** short for **bank note. 7.** a characteristic element or atmosphere: *a note of sarcasm.* **8.** a distinctive vocal sound, as of a species of bird or animal: *the note of the nightingale.* **9.** any of a series of graphic signs representing a musical sound whose pitch is indicated by position on the stave and whose duration is indicated by the sign's shape, etc. **10.** Also called (esp. U.S.): **tone.** *Chiefly Brit.* a musical sound of definite fundamental frequency or pitch. **11.** *Chiefly Brit.* a key on a piano, organ, etc. **12.** a sound, as from a musical instrument, used as a signal or warning: *the note to retreat was sounded.* **13.** short for **promissory note. 14.** *Archaic or poetic.* a tune or melody. **15. of note. a.** distinguished or famous: *an athlete of note.* **b.** worth noticing or paying attention to; important: *nothing of note.* **16. strike the right** (*or* **a false**) **note.** to behave appropriately (or inappropriately). **17. take note.** (often foll. by *of*) to observe carefully; pay close attention (to). ~*vb.* (*tr.; may take a clause as object*) **18.** to notice; perceive: *he noted that there was a man in the shadows.* **19.** to pay close attention to; observe: *they noted every movement.* **20.** to make a written note or memorandum of: *she noted the date in her diary.* **21.** to make particular mention of; remark upon: *I note that you do not wear shoes.* **22.** to write down (music, a melody, etc.) in notes. **23.** a less common word for **annotate.** [C13: via Old French from Latin *nota* sign, indication] —**'note+less** *adj.*

note+book ('nəʊtˌbʊk) *n.* **1.** a book for recording notes or memoranda. **2.** a book for registering promissory notes.

note+case ('nəʊtˌkeɪs) *n.* a less common word for **wallet.**

not+ed ('nəʊtɪd) *adj.* **1.** distinguished; celebrated; famous. **2.** of special note or significance; noticeable: *a noted increase in the crime rate.* —**'not+ed+ly** *adv.*

note+let ('nəʊtlɪt) *n.* a folded card with a printed design on the front, for writing a short informal letter.

note of hand *n.* another name for **promissory note.**

note+pa·per ('nəʊtˌpeɪpə) *n.* paper for writing letters; writing paper.

note row (rəʊ) *n. Music.* another name for **tone row.**

notes (nəʊts) *pl. n.* **1.** short descriptive or summarized jottings taken down for future reference. **2.** a record of impressions, reflections, etc., esp. as a literary form.

notes in+é·gales *French.* (nɔt ine'gal) *pl. n.* **1.** (in French baroque music, etc.) notes written down evenly but executed as if they were divided into pairs of long and short notes. **2.** the style of playing in this manner. [literally: unequal notes]

note val·ue *n.* another term for **time value.**

note+wor·thy ('nəʊtˌwɜːðɪ) *adj.* worthy of notice; notable. —**'note+ˌwor·thi+ly** *adv.* —**'note+ˌwor·thi+ness** *n.*

noth+ing ('nʌθɪŋ) *pron.* **1.** (*indefinite*) no thing; not anything, as of an implied or specified class of things: *I can give you nothing.* **2.** no part or share: *to have nothing to do with this crime.* **3.** a matter of no importance or significance: *it doesn't matter, it's nothing.* **4.** indicating the absence of anything perceptible; nothingness. **5.** indicating the absence of meaning, value, worth, etc.: *to amount to nothing.* **6.** zero quantity; nought. **7. be nothing to. a.** not to concern or be significant to (someone). **b.** to be not nearly as good, etc., as. **8. have** *or* **be nothing to do with.** to have no connection with. **9. have (got) nothing on. a.** to have no engagements to keep. **b.** to compare unfavourably with. **c.** to be undressed or naked. **10. in nothing flat.** *Informal.* in almost no time; very quickly or soon. **11. nothing but.** no more than; only. **12. nothing doing.** *Informal.* an expression of dismissal, disapproval, lack of compliance with a request, etc. **13. nothing if not.** at the very least; certainly. **14. nothing less than** *or* **nothing short of.** downright; truly. **15. (there's) nothing for it.** *Brit.* an expression of resignation to some course of action. **16. there's nothing like.** a general expression of praise: *there's nothing like a good cup of tea.* **17. there's nothing to it.** it is very simple, easy, etc. **18. think nothing of. a.** to regard as simple or easy. **b.** to have a very low opinion of. **19. to say nothing of.** not to mention. **20. stop at nothing.** to do anything; be ruthless. ~*adv.* **21.** in no way; not at all: *he looked nothing like his brother.* ~*n.* **22.** *Informal.* a person or thing of no importance or significance. **23. sweet nothings.** words of endearment or affection. [Old English *nāthing, nān thing,* from *nān* NONE[1] + THING]

Usage. *Nothing* always takes a singular verb in careful usage, although a plural verb is often heard in informal speech in sentences such as *nothing but books were on the shelf.*

noth+ing+ness ('nʌθɪŋnɪs) *n.* **1.** the state or condition of being nothing; nonexistence. **2.** absence of consciousness or life. **3.** complete insignificance or worthlessness. **4.** something that is worthless or insignificant.

no+tice ('nəʊtɪs) *n.* **1.** the act of perceiving; observation; attention: *to escape notice.* **2. take notice.** to pay attention; attend. **3. take no notice of.** to ignore or disregard. **4.** information about a future event; warning; announcement. **5.** a displayed placard or announcement giving information. **6.** advance notification of intention to end an arrangement, contract, etc., as of renting or employment (esp. in the phrase **give notice**). **7. at short, two hours',** *etc.,* **notice.** with notification only a little, two hours, etc., in advance. **8.** *Chiefly Brit.* dismissal from employment. **9.** favourable, interested, or polite attention: *she was beneath his notice.* **10.** a theatrical or literary review: *the play received very good notices.* ~*vb.* **11.** to become conscious; aware of; perceive; note. **12.** (*tr.*) to point out or remark upon. **13.** (*tr.*) to pay polite or interested attention to. **14.** (*tr.*) to recognize or acknowledge (an acquaintance, etc.). [C15: via Old French from Latin *notitia* fame, from *nōtus* known, celebrated]

no+tice+a·ble ('nəʊtɪsəb^{ə}l) *adj.* easily seen or detected; perceptible: *the stain wasn't noticeable.* —**ˌno+tice+a·'bil+i·ty** *n.* —**'no+tice+a·bly** *adv.*

no+tice board *n. Brit.* a board on which notices, advertisements, bulletins, etc., are displayed. U.S. name: **bulletin board.**

no+ti+fi+a·ble ('nəʊtɪˌfaɪəb^{ə}l) *adj.* denoting certain infectious diseases, such as smallpox and tuberculosis, outbreaks of which must be reported to the public health authorities.

no+ti+fi+ca+tion (ˌnəʊtɪfɪ'keɪʃən) *n.* **1.** the act of notifying. **2.** a formal announcement. **3.** something that notifies; a notice.

no+ti+fy ('nəʊtɪˌfaɪ) *vb.* **+fies, +fy+ing, +fied.** (*tr.*) **1.** to inform of; tell. **2.** *Chiefly Brit.* to draw attention to; to make known; announce. [C14: from Old French *notifier,* from Latin *notificāre* to make known, from *nōtus* known + *facere* to make] —**'no+ti+ˌfi+er** *n.*

no-till·age *n.* a system of farming in which planting is done in a narrow trench, without tillage, and weeds are controlled with herbicide.

no+tion ('nəʊʃən) *n.* **1.** a vague idea; impression. **2.** an idea, concept, or opinion. **3.** an inclination or whim. [C16: from Latin *nōtiō* a becoming acquainted (with), examination (of), from *noscere* to know]

no+tion+al ('nəʊʃən°l) *adj.* **1.** relating to, expressing, or consisting of notions or ideas. **2.** characteristic of a notion or concept, esp. in being speculative or imaginary; abstract. **3.** *Grammar.* **a.** (of a word) having lexical meaning. **b.** another word for **semantic.** —'**no+tion+al+ly** *adv.*

no+tions ('nəʊʃənz) *pl. n. U.S.* pins, cotton, ribbon, and similar wares used for sewing, etc.; haberdashery.

no+tit·i·a (nəʊ'tɪʃɪə) *n.* a register or list, esp. of ecclesiastical districts. [C18: Latin, literally: knowledge, from *notus* known]

no+to- *or before a vowel* **not-** *combining form.* the back: *notochord.* [from Greek *nōton* the back]

no+to+chord ('nəʊtə,kɔ:d) *n.* a fibrous longitudinal rod in all embryo and some adult chordate animals, immediately above the gut, that supports the body. It is replaced in adult vertebrates by the vertebral column. —,**no+to+'chord+al** *adj.*

No+to+gae·a (,nəʊtə'dʒi:ə) *n.* a zoogeographical area comprising the Australasian region. Compare **Arctogaea, Neogaea.** [C19: from Greek *notos* south wind + *gaia* land] —,**No+to+'gae·an** *n., adj.*

no+to+ri+ous (nəʊ'tɔ:rɪəs) *adj.* **1.** well-known for some bad or unfavourable quality, deed, etc.; infamous. **2.** *Rare.* generally known or widely acknowledged. [C16: from Medieval Latin *notōrius* well-known, from *nōtus* known, from *noscere* to know] —**no+to+ri+e·ty** (,nəʊtə'raɪɪtɪ) *or* **no+'to+ri+ous+ness** *n.* —**no+'to+ri+ous+ly** *adv.*

no+tor+nis (nəʊ'tɔ:nɪs) *n.* a rare flightless rail of the genus *Notornis,* of New Zealand. See **takahe.** [C19: New Latin, from Greek *notos* south + *ornis* bird]

no+to+ther+i·um (,nəʊtəʊ'θɪərɪəm) *n.* an extinct Pleistocene rhinoceros-sized marsupial of the genus *Nototherium,* related to the wombats. [C19: New Latin, from Greek *notos* south (referring to their discovery in the S hemisphere) + *thērion* beast]

no+tour ('nəʊtə) *adj.* (in Scots law) short for **notorious.** A **notour bankrupt** is one who has failed to discharge his debts within the days of grace allowed by the court.

not prov+en *adj.* (*postpositive*) a third verdict available to Scottish courts, returned when there is evidence against the defendant but insufficient to convict.

No+tre Dame ('nəʊtrə 'dɑ:m; *French* nɔtrə 'dam) *n.* the early Gothic cathedral of Paris, on the Île de la Cité: built between 1163 and 1257.

no-trump *Bridge.* ~*n. also* **no-trumps. 1.** a bid or contract to play without trumps. ~*adj. also* **no-trump·er. 2.** (of a hand) of balanced distribution suitable for playing without trumps.

Not+ting+ham ('nɒtɪŋəm) *n.* a city in N central England, administrative centre of Nottinghamshire, on the River Trent: scene of the outbreak of the Civil War (1642); famous for its associations with the Robin Hood legend; university (1881). Pop.: 299 758 (1971).

Not+ting+ham+shire ('nɒtɪŋəm,ʃɪə, -ʃə) *n.* an inland county of central England: generally low-lying, with part of the S Pennines and the remnant of Sherwood Forest in the east. Administrative centre: Nottingham. Pop.: 977 500 (1976 est.). Area: 2214 sq. km (859 sq. miles). Abbrev.: **Notts.**

Notts. (nɒts) *abbrev. for* Nottinghamshire.

no+tum ('nəʊtəm) *n., pl.* **+ta** (-tə). a cuticular plate covering the dorsal surface of a thoracic segment of an insect. [C19: New Latin, from Greek *nōton* back] —'**no+tal** *adj.*

No+tus ('nəʊtəs) *n. Classical myth.* a personification of the south or southwest wind.

not+with+stand+ing (,nɒtwɪθ'stændɪŋ, -wɪð-) *prep.* **1.** (*often immediately postpositive*) in spite of; despite. ~*conj.* **2.** (*subordinating*) despite the fact that; although. ~ **3.** *sentence connector.* in spite of that; nevertheless.

Nouak+chott (*French* nwak'ʃɔt) *n.* the capital of Mauritania, near the Atlantic coast: replaced St. Louis as capital in 1957; situated on important caravan routes. Pop.: 104 000 (1975 est.).

nou+gat ('nu:gɑ:) *n.* a hard chewy pink or white sweet containing chopped nuts, cherries, etc. [C19: via French from Provençal *nogat,* from *noga* nut, from Latin *nux* nut]

nought (nɔ:t) *n. also* **naught, ought, aught. 1.** another name for **zero:** used esp. in counting or numbering. ~*n., adj., adv.* **2.** a variant spelling of **naught.** [Old English *nōwiht,* from *ne* not, no + *ōwiht* something; see WHIT]

noughts and cross·es *n.* a game in which two players, one using a nought, "O", the other a cross, "X", alternately mark one square out of nine formed by two pairs of crossed lines, the winner being the first to get three of his symbols in a row. U.S. terms: **tick-tack-toe, crisscross.**

Nou+mé·a (,nu:'meɪə; *French* nume'a) *n.* the capital and chief port of the French Overseas Territory of New Caledonia. Pop.: 60 200 (1975 est.).

nou+me·non ('nu:mɪnən, 'naʊ-) *n., pl.* **·na** (-nə). (in the philosophy of Kant) **1.** a thing as it is in itself, not perceived or interpreted, incapable of being known in practice or in principle, and so existing only as a matter of speculation, but thought by Kant to be of fundamental importance. Compare **phenomenon. 2.** the object of a purely intellectual intuition. [C18: via German from Greek: thing being thought of, from *noein* to think, perceive; related to *nous* mind] —'**nou+me+nal** *adj.* —'**nou+me+nal+ism** *n.* —'**nou+me+nal+ist** *n., adj.* —,**nou+me+'nal+i·ty** *n.* —'**nou+me+nal+ly** *adv.*

noun (naʊn) *n.* **a.** a word or group of words that refers to a person, place, or thing or any syntactically similar word. **b.** (*as modifier*): *a noun phrase.* Abbrev.: **n.** [C14: via Anglo-French from Latin *nōmen* NAME] —'**noun+al** *adj.* —'**noun+al+ly** *adv.* —'**noun+less** *adj.*

noun phrase *n. Grammar.* a constituent of a sentence that consists of a noun and any modifiers it may have, a noun clause, or a word, such as a pronoun, that takes the place of a noun.

nour+ish ('nʌrɪʃ) *vb.* (*tr.*) **1.** to provide with the materials necessary for life and growth. **2.** to support or encourage (an idea, feeling, etc.); foster: *to nourish resentment.* [C14: from Old French *norir,* from Latin *nūtrīre* to feed, care for] —'**nour+ish+er** *n.* —'**nour+ish+ing+ly** *adv.*

nour+ish+ment ('nʌrɪʃmənt) *n.* **1.** the act or state of nourishing. **2.** a substance that nourishes; food; nutriment.

nous (naʊs) *n.* **1.** *Metaphysics.* mind or reason, esp. when regarded as the principle governing all things. **2.** *Brit. slang.* common sense; intelligence. [C17: from Greek]

nou+veau riche *French.* (nuvo 'riʃ) *n., pl.* ***nou+veaux riches*** (nuvo 'riʃ). **1.** (often *pl.* and preceded by *the*) a person who has acquired wealth recently and is regarded as vulgarly ostentatious or lacking in social graces. ~*adj.* **2.** of or characteristic of the *nouveaux riches.* [literally: new rich]

nou+veau ro+man *French.* (nuvo rɔ'mã) *n., pl.* ***nou+veaux ro+mans*** (nuvo rɔ'mã). another term for **anti-roman.** [literally: new novel]

Nou+velle-Ca+lé+do+nie (nuvɛl kaledɔ'ni) *n.* the French name for **New Caledonia.**

Nou+velle Vague *French.* (nuvɛl 'vag) *n. Films.* another term for **New Wave.**

Nov. *abbrev. for* November.

no·va ('nəʊvə) *n., pl.* **·vae** (-vi:) *or* **·vas.** a faint variable star that undergoes an explosion and fast increase of luminosity, decreasing to its original luminosity in months or years. Compare **supernova.** [C19: New Latin *nova* (*stella*) new star, from Latin *novus* new]

no+vac·u+lite (nəʊ'vækjʊ,laɪt) *n.* a fine-grained dense hard rock containing quartz and feldspar: used as a whetstone. [C18: from Latin *novācula* sharp knife, razor, from *novāre* to renew]

No·va·lis (*German* no'va:lɪs) *n.* pen name of *Friedrich von Hardenberg.* 1772–1801, German romantic poet. His works include the mystical *Hymnen an die Nacht* (1797; published 1800) and *Geistliche Lieder* (1799).

No·va Lis+bo·a (*Portuguese* 'nɔvə liʒ'βoə) *n.* the former name (1928–73) of **Huambo.**

No+va+ra (*Italian* no'va:ra) *n.* a city in NW Italy, in NE Piedmont: scene of the Austrian defeat of the Piedmontese in 1849. Pop.: 102 036 (1975 est.).

No·va Sco+tia ('nəʊvə 'skəʊʃə) *n.* **1.** a peninsula in E Canada, between the Gulf of St. Lawrence and the Bay of Fundy. **2.** a province of E Canada, consisting of the Nova Scotia peninsula and Cape Breton Island: first settled by the French as Acadia. Capital: Halifax. Pop.: 828 571 (1976). Area: 52 841 sq. km (20 402 sq. miles).

no+va+tion (nəʊ'veɪʃən) *n.* **1.** *Law.* the substitution of a new obligation for an old one by mutual agreement between the parties, esp. of one debtor or creditor for another. **2.** an obsolete word for **innovation.** [C16: from Late Latin *novātio* a renewing, from Latin *novāre* to renew]

No+va+ya Zem+lya (*Russian* 'nɔvəjə zɪm'lja) *n.* an archipelago in the Arctic Ocean, off the NE coast of the Soviet Union: consists of two large islands and many islets. Area: about 81 279 sq. km (31 382 sq. miles).

nov+el[1] ('nɒv°l) *n.* **1.** an extended work in prose, either fictitious or partly so, dealing with character, action, thought, etc., esp. in the form of a story. **2. the.** the literary genre represented by novels. **3.** (*usually pl.*) *Obsolete.* a short story or novella, as one of those in the *Decameron* of Boccaccio. [C15: from Old French *novelle,* from Latin *novella* (*narrātiō*) new (story); see NOVEL[2]]

nov+el[2] ('nɒv°l) *adj.* of a kind not seen before; fresh; new; original: *a novel suggestion.* [C15: from Latin *novellus* new, diminutive of *novus* new] —'**nov+el+ly** *adv.*

nov+el[3] ('nɒv°l) *n. Roman law.* a new decree or an amendment to an existing statute. See also **Novels.**

nov+el+ese (,nɒvə'li:z) *n. Derogatory.* a style of writing characteristic of poor novels.

nov+el+ette (,nɒvə'lɛt) *n.* **1.** an extended prose narrative story or short novel. **2.** a novel that is regarded as being slight, trivial, or sentimental. **3.** a short piece of lyrical music, esp. one for the piano.

nov+el+et+tish (,nɒvə'lɛtɪʃ) *adj.* characteristic of a novelette; trite or sentimental.

nov+el+ist ('nɒvəlɪst) *n.* a writer of novels.

nov+el+is+tic (,nɒvə'lɪstɪk) *adj.* of or characteristic of novels, esp. in style or method of treatment: *his novelistic account annoyed other historians.*

nov+el+ize *or* **nov+el+ise** ('nɒvə,laɪz) *vb.* to convert (a true story, film, etc.) into a novel. —,**nov+el·i+'za+tion** *or* ,**nov+el·i+'sa+tion** *n.*

no+vel+la (nəʊ'vɛlə) *n., pl.* **+las** *or* **+le** (-leɪ). **1.** (formerly) a short narrative tale, esp. a popular story having a moral or satirical point, such as those in Boccaccio's *Decameron.* **2.** a short novel; novelette. [C20: from Italian; see NOVEL[1]]

No+vel·lo (nə'vɛləʊ) *n.* **I·vor,** original name *Ivor Novello Davies.* 1893–1951, Welsh actor, composer, songwriter, and dramatist.

Nov+els ('nɒv°lz) *pl. n. Roman law.* the new statutes of Justinian and succeeding emperors supplementing the Justinian Code: now forming part of the Corpus Juris Civilis. [Latin *Novellae* (*constitūtiōnēs*) new (laws)]

nov·el·ty ('nɒvəltɪ) *n., pl.* **·ties. 1. a.** the quality of being new and fresh and interesting. **b.** (*as modifier*): *novelty value.* **2.** a new or unusual experience or occurrence. **3.** (*often pl.*) a small usually cheap new toy, ornament, or trinket. [C14: from Old French *novelté;* see NOVEL[2]]

No·vem·ber (nəʊ'vɛmbə) *n.* the eleventh month of the year, consisting of 30 days. [C13: via Old French from Latin: ninth month, from *novem* nine]

no·ve·na (nəʊ'viːnə) *n., pl.* **·nae** (-niː). *R.C. Church.* a devotion consisting of prayers or services on nine consecutive days. [C19: from Medieval Latin, from Latin *novem* nine]

no·ver·cal (nəʊ'vɜːkəl) *adj. Rare.* stepmotherly. [C17: from Latin *novercālis,* from *noverca* stepmother]

Nov·go·rod (*Russian* 'nɔvgərət) *n.* a city in the NW Soviet Union, on the Volkhov River; became a principality in 862 under Rurik, an event regarded as the founding of the Russian state; a major trading centre in the Middle Ages; destroyed by Ivan the Terrible in 1570. Pop.: 165 000 (1975 est.).

nov·ice ('nɒvɪs) *n.* **1.** a person who is new to or inexperienced in a certain task, situation, etc.; beginner; tyro. **2.** a probationer in a religious order. **3.** a sportsman, esp. an oarsman, who has not won a recognized prize, performed to an established level, etc. **4.** a racehorse, esp. a steeplechaser or hurdler, that has not won a specified number of races. [C14: via Old French from Latin *novīcius,* from *novus* new]

No·vi Sad (*Serbo-Croatian* 'nɔviː 'saːd) *n.* a port in NE Yugoslavia, on the River Danube: founded in 1690 as the seat of the Serbian patriarch; university (1960). Pop.: 141 375 (1971). German name: **Neusatz.**

no·vi·ti·ate *or* **no·vi·ci·ate** (nəʊ'vɪʃɪɪt, -ˌeɪt) *n.* **1.** the state of being a novice, esp. in a religious order, or the period for which this lasts. **2.** the part of a religious house where the novices live. **3.** a less common word for **novice.** [C17: from French *noviciat,* from Latin *novīcius* NOVICE]

No·vo·caine ('nəʊvəˌkeɪn) *n.* a trademark for **procaine hydrochloride.** See **procaine.**

No·vo·kuz·netsk (*Russian* nəvəkuz'njɛtsk) *n.* a city in the S central Soviet Union: iron and steel works. Pop.: 524 000 (1975 est.). Former name (1932–61): **Stalinsk.**

No·vo·si·birsk (*Russian* nəvəsi'birsk) *n.* a city in the central Soviet Union, on the River Ob: the largest town in Siberia; developed with the coming of the Trans-Siberian railway in 1893. Pop.: 1 265 000 (1975 est.).

now (naʊ) *adv.* **1.** at or for the present time or moment. **2.** at this exact moment; immediately. **3.** in these times; nowadays. **4.** given the present circumstances: *now we'll have to stay to the end.* **5.** (preceded by *just*) very recently: *he left just now.* **6.** (often preceded by *just*) very soon: *he is leaving just now.* **7. (every) now and again** *or* **then.** occasionally; on and off. **8. for now.** for the time being. **9. now now!** (*interj.*) an exclamation used to rebuke or pacify someone. **10. now then. a.** *sentence connector.* used to preface an important remark, the next step in an argument, etc. **b.** (*interj.*) an expression of mild reproof: *now then, don't tease!* ~*conj.* **11.** (*subordinating;* often foll. by *that*) seeing that; since it has become the case that: *now you're in charge, things will be better.* ~ **12.** *sentence connector.* **a.** used as a transitional particle or hesitation word: *now, I can't really say.* **b.** used for emphasis: *now listen to this.* **c.** used at the end of a command, esp. in dismissal: *run along, now.* ~*n.* **13.** the present moment or time: *now is the time to go.* [Old English *nū;* compare Old Saxon *nū,* German *nun,* Latin *nunc,* Greek *nu*]

now·a·days ('naʊəˌdeɪz) *adv.* in these times.

no·way ('nəʊˌweɪ) *adv. Now chiefly U.S.* in no manner; not at all; nowise. Also (not standard): **noways.**

Now·el *or* **Now·ell** (nəʊ'ɛl) *n.* an archaic spelling of **Noel.**

no·whence ('nəʊwɛns) *adv. Archaic.* from no place; from nowhere.

no·where ('nəʊwɛə) *adv.* **1.** in, at, or to no place; not anywhere. **2. get nowhere (fast).** *Informal.* to fail completely to make any progress. **3. nowhere near.** far from; not nearly. ~*n.* **4.** a nonexistent or insignificant place. **5. middle of nowhere.** a completely isolated, featureless, or insignificant place.

no·whith·er ('nəʊˌwɪðə) *adv. Archaic.* to no place; to nowhere. [Old English *nāhwider.* See NEITHER]

no·wise ('nəʊˌwaɪz) *adv.* another word for **noway.**

nowt[1] (naʊt) *n. Northern Brit.* a dialect word for **nothing.** [from NAUGHT]

nowt[2] (naʊt) *n. Northern Brit.* a dialect word for **cattle.** [C13: from Old Norse *naut;* see NEAT[2]]

Nox (nɒks) *n.* the Roman goddess of the night. Greek counterpart: **Nyx.**

nox·ious ('nɒkʃəs) *adj.* **1.** poisonous or harmful. **2.** harmful to the mind or morals; corrupting. [C17: from Latin *noxius* harmful, from *noxa* injury] —**'nox·ious·ly** *adv.* —**'nox·ious·ness** *n.*

no·yade (nwɑː'jɑːd; *French* nwa'jad) *n. French history.* execution by drowning, esp. as practised during the Reign of Terror at Nantes from 1793 to 1794. [C19: from French, from *noyer* to drown, from Late Latin *necāre* to drown, from Latin: to put to death]

noy·au ('nwaɪəʊ) *n.* a liqueur made from brandy flavoured with nut kernels. [C18: from French: kernel, from Latin *nux* nut]

Noy·on (*French* nwa'jɔ̃) *n.* a town in N France: scene of the coronations of Charlemagne (768) and Hugh Capet (987); birthplace of John Calvin. Pop.: 14 033 (1975).

noz·zle ('nɒzəl) *n.* **1.** a projecting pipe or spout from which fluid is discharged. **2.** Also called: **propelling nozzle.** a pipe or duct, esp. in a jet engine or rocket, that directs the effluent and accelerates or diffuses the flow to generate thrust. **3.** a socket, such as the part of a candlestick that holds the candle. [C17 *nosle, nosel,* diminutive of NOSE]

Np *the chemical symbol for* neptunium.

NP *abbrev. for* **1.** neuropsychiatric. **2.** neuropsychiatry. **3.** new penny *or* pence. Also: **np 4.** noun phrase.

n.p. *abbrev. for:* **1.** *Printing.* new paragraph. **2.** *Law.* nisi prius. **3.** no place of publication.

N.P. *abbrev. for* Notary Public.

N.P.A. *abbrev. for* Newspaper Publishers' Association.

N.P.L. *abbrev. for* National Physical Laboratory.

nr. *or* **nr** *abbrev. for* near.

NS *abbrev. for:* **1.** not sufficient *or* not satisfactory. **2.** nuclear ship.

n.s. *abbrev. for:* **1.** new series. **2.** not specified.

N.S. *abbrev. for:* **1.** New Style (method of reckoning dates). **2.** Nova Scotia.

N.S.B. *abbrev. for* National Savings Bank.

N.S.F. *or* **N/S/F** *Banking. abbrev. for* not sufficient funds.

N.S.P.C.C. *abbrev. for* National Society for the Prevention of Cruelty to Children.

N.S.W. *abbrev. for* New South Wales.

N.T. *abbrev. for:* **1.** Also: **NT** National Trust. **2.** Also: **NT.** New Testament. **3.** Northern Territory. **4.** no trumps.

-n't *contraction of* not: used as an enclitic after *be* and *have* when they function as main verbs and after auxiliary verbs or verbs operating syntactically as auxiliaries: *can't; don't; shouldn't; needn't; daren't; isn't.*

nth (ɛnθ) *adj.* **1.** *Maths.* of or representing an unspecified ordinal number, usually the greatest in a series of values: *the nth power.* **2.** *Informal.* being the last, most recent, or most extreme of a long series: *for the nth time, eat your lunch!* **3. to the nth degree.** *Informal.* to the utmost extreme; as much as possible.

Nth. *abbrev. for* North.

NTP *or* **N.T.P.** *abbrev. for* normal temperature and pressure: standard conditions of 0°C temperature and 101.325 kPa (760 mmHg) pressure. Also: **STP**

nt. wt. *or* **nt wt** *abbrev. for* net weight.

n-type *adj.* **1.** (of a semiconductor) having more conduction electrons than mobile holes. **2.** associated with or resulting from the movement of electrons in a semiconductor: *n-type conductivity.* ~Compare **p-type.**

nu (njuː) *n.* the 13th letter in the Greek alphabet (Ν, ν), a consonant, transliterated as *n.* [from Greek, of Semitic origin; compare NUN[2]]

N.U.A.A.W. *abbrev. for* National Union of Agricultural and Allied Workers.

nu·ance (njuː'ɑːns, 'njuːɑːns) *n.* a subtle difference in colour, meaning, tone, etc.; a shade or graduation. [C18: from French, from *nuer* to show light and shade, ultimately from Latin *nūbēs* a cloud]

nub (nʌb) *n.* **1.** a small lump or protuberance. **2.** a small piece or chunk. **3.** the point or gist: *the nub of a story.* **4.** a small fibrous knot in yarn. [C16: variant of *knub,* from Middle Low German *knubbe* KNOB] —**'nub·bly** *or* **'nub·by** *adj.*

Nu·ba ('njuːbə) *n.* **1.** (*pl.* **·bas** *or* **·ba**) a member of a formerly warlike Nilotic people living chiefly in the hills of S central Sudan. **2.** the language or group of related dialects spoken by this people, belonging to the Chari-Nile branch of the Nilo-Saharan family.

nub·bin ('nʌbɪn) *n. U.S.* something small or undeveloped, esp. a fruit or ear of corn. [C19: diminutive of NUB]

nub·ble ('nʌbəl) *n.* a small lump. [C19: diminutive of NUB]

nu·bec·u·la (njuː'bɛkjʊlə) *n., pl.* **·lae** (-liː). See **Magellanic Cloud.** [C19: from Latin, diminutive of *nubes* cloud]

Nu·bi·a ('njuːbɪə) *n.* an ancient region of NE Africa, on the Nile, extending from Aswan to Khartoum. —**'Nu·bi·an** *n., adj.*

Nu·bi·an Des·ert *n.* a desert in the NE Sudan, between the Nile valley and the Red Sea: mainly a sandstone plateau.

nu·bile ('njuːbaɪl) *adj.* (of a girl or woman) **1.** ready or suitable for marriage by virtue of age or maturity. **2.** sexually attractive. [C17: from Latin *nūbilis,* from *nūbere* to marry] —**nu·bil·i·ty** (njuː'bɪlɪtɪ) *n.*

nu·cel·lus (njuː'sɛləs) *n., pl.* **·li** (-laɪ). the central part of a plant ovule containing the embryo sac. [C19: New Latin, from Latin *nucella* from *nux* nut] —**nu·'cel·lar** *adj.*

nu·cha ('njuːkə) *n., pl.* **·chae** (-kiː). *Zoology, anatomy.* the back or nape of the neck. [C14: from Medieval Latin, from Arabic *nukhā'* spinal marrow] —**'nu·chal** *adj.*

nu·cle·ar ('njuːklɪə) *adj.* **1.** of, concerned with, or involving the nucleus of an atom: *nuclear fission.* **2.** *Biology.* of, relating to, or contained within the nucleus of a cell: *a nuclear membrane.* **3.** of, relating to, forming, or resembling any other kind of nucleus. **4.** of, concerned with, or operated by energy from fission or fusion of atomic nuclei: *a nuclear weapon.* **5.** involving, concerned with, or possessing nuclear weapons: *nuclear war.*

nu·cle·ar bomb *n.* a bomb whose force is due to uncontrolled nuclear fusion or nuclear fission.

nu·cle·ar en·er·gy *n.* energy released during a nuclear reaction as a result of fission or fusion and the conversion of mass into energy. Also called: **atomic energy.**

nu·cle·ar fam·i·ly *n. Sociol., anthropol.* a primary social unit consisting of parents, their offspring, and one or both grandparents or a marital partner of one of the offspring. Compare **extended family.**

nu·cle·ar fis·sion *n.* the splitting of an atomic nucleus into approximately equal parts, either spontaneously or as a result of the impact of a particle usually with an associated release of energy. Sometimes shortened to **fission.** Compare **nuclear fusion.**

nu·cle·ar fu·el *n.* a fuel that provides nuclear energy, used in nuclear power stations, nuclear submarines, etc.

nu·cle·ar fu·sion *n.* a reaction in which two nuclei combine to form a nucleus with the release of energy. Sometimes shortened to **fusion.** Compare **nuclear fission.** See also **thermonuclear reaction.**

nu·cle·ar i·so·mer *n.* the more formal name for **isomer** (sense 2). —**nu·cle·ar i·som·er·ism** *n.*

nu·cle·ar mag·net·ic res·on·ance *n.* a technique for determining the magnetic moments of nuclei by subjecting a substance to high-frequency radiation and a large magnetic field. The technique is used as a method of determining structure. Abbrev.: **NMR.** See also **electron spin resonance.**

nu·cle·ar phys·ics *n.* the branch of physics concerned with the structure and behaviour of the nucleus and the particles of which it consists. —**nu·cle·ar phys·i·cist** *n.*

nu·cle·ar pow·er *n.* power, esp. electrical or motive, produced by a nuclear reactor. Also called: **atomic power.**

nu·cle·ar re·act·ion *n.* a process in which the structure and energy content of an atomic nucleus is changed by interaction with another nucleus or particle.

nu·cle·ar re·ac·tor *n.* a device in which a nuclear reaction is maintained and controlled for the production of nuclear energy. Sometimes shortened to **reactor.** Former name: **atomic pile.** See also **fission reactor, fusion reactor.**

nu·cle·ase (ˈnjuːklɪˌeɪz) *n.* any of a group of enzymes that hydrolyse nucleic acids to simple nucleotides.

nu·cle·ate (ˈnjuːklɪɪt, -ˌeɪt) *adj.* **1.** having a nucleus. ~*vb.* **2.** to form a nucleus. —ˌ**nu·cle·ˈa·tion** *n.* —ˈ**nu·cle·ˌa·tor** *n.*

nu·cle·i (ˈnjuːklɪˌaɪ) *n.* the plural of **nucleus.**

nu·cle·ic ac·id (njuːˈkliːɪk, -ˈkleɪ-) *n. Biochem.* any of a group of complex compounds with a high molecular weight that are vital constituents of all living cells. See also **RNA, DNA.**

nu·cle·in (ˈnjuːklɪɪn) *n.* any of a group of proteins, containing phosphorus, that occur in the nuclei of living cells.

nu·cle·o- *or before a vowel* **nu·cle-** *combining form.* **1.** nucleus or nuclear: *nucleoplasm.* **2.** nucleic acid: *nucleoprotein.*

nu·cle·o·lus (ˌnjuːklɪˈəʊləs) *n., pl.* **·li** (-laɪ). a small rounded body within a resting nucleus that contains RNA and proteins and is involved in protein synthesis. Also called: **nucleole.** [C19: from Latin, diminutive of NUCLEUS] —ˌ**nu·cle·ˈo·lar,** ˈ**nu·cle·o·ˌlate,** *or* ˈ**nu·cle·o·ˌlat·ed** *adj.*

nu·cle·on (ˈnjuːklɪˌɒn) *n.* a proton or neutron, esp. one present in an atomic nucleus.

nu·cle·on·ics (ˌnjuːklɪˈɒnɪks) *n.* (*functioning as sing.*) the branch of physics concerned with the applications of nuclear energy. —ˌ**nu·cle·ˈon·ic** *adj.* —ˌ**nu·cle·ˈon·i·cal·ly** *adv.*

nu·cle·on num·ber *n.* another name for **mass number.**

nu·cle·o·phil·ic (ˌnjuːklɪəʊˈfɪlɪk) *adj. Chem.* having or involving an affinity for positive charge. Nucleophilic reagents (**nucleophiles**) are molecules, atoms, and ions that behave as electron donors. Compare **electrophilic.**

nu·cle·o·plasm (ˈnjuːklɪəˌplæzəm) *n.* the protoplasm constituting the nucleus of a plant or animal cell. Also called: **karyoplasm.** —ˌ**nu·cle·o·ˈplas·mic** *or* ˌ**nu·cle·o·plas·ˈmat·ic** *adj.*

nu·cle·o·pro·tein (ˌnjuːklɪəʊˈprəʊtiːn) *n.* a compound within a cell nucleus that consists of a protein bound to a nucleic acid.

nu·cle·o·side (ˈnjuːklɪəˌsaɪd) *n. Biochem.* a compound containing a purine or pyrimidine base linked to a sugar (usually ribose or deoxyribose).

nu·cle·o·tide (ˈnjuːklɪəˌtaɪd) *n. Biochem.* a compound consisting of a nucleoside linked to phosphoric acid. Nucleic acids are made up of long chains (polynucleotides) of such compounds.

nu·cle·us (ˈnjuːklɪəs) *n., pl.* **·cle·i** (-klɪˌaɪ) *or* **·cle·us·es. 1.** a central or fundamental part or thing around which others are grouped; core. **2.** a centre of growth or development; basis; kernel: *the nucleus of an idea.* **3.** *Biology.* a spherical or ovoid cellular organelle, bounded by a membrane, that consists of DNA, RNA, etc., and is responsible for growth and reproduction of the cell and the transmission of hereditary material. **4.** *Anatomy.* any of various groups of nerve cells in the central nervous system. **5.** *Astronomy.* the central portion in the head of a comet, consisting of small solid particles of ice and frozen gases, which vaporize on approaching the sun to form the coma and tail. **6.** *Physics.* the positively charged dense region at the centre of an atom, composed of protons and neutrons, about which electrons orbit. **7.** *Chem.* a fundamental group of atoms in a molecule serving as the base structure for related compounds and remaining unchanged during most chemical reactions: *the benzene nucleus.* **8.** *Botany.* **a.** the central point of a starch granule. **b.** a rare name for **nucellus. 9.** *Phonetics.* the most sonorous part of a syllable, usually consisting of a vowel or frictionless continuant. [C18: from Latin: kernel, from *nux* nut]

nu·clide (ˈnjuːklaɪd) *n.* a species of atom characterized by its atomic number and its mass number. See also **isotope.** [C20: from NUCLEO- + *-ide,* from Greek *eidos* shape]

nud·dy (ˈnʌdɪ) *n.* **in the nuddy.** *Informal, chiefly Brit. and Austral.* in the nude; naked.

nude (njuːd) *adj.* **1.** completely unclothed; undressed. **2.** having no covering; bare; exposed. **3.** *Law.* **a.** lacking some essential legal requirement, esp. supporting evidence. **b.** (of a contract, agreement, etc.) made without consideration and void unless under seal. ~*n.* **4.** the state of being naked (esp. in the phrase **in the nude**). **5.** a naked figure, esp. in painting, sculpture, etc. [C16: from Latin *nūdus*] —ˈ**nude·ly** *adv.* —ˈ**nude·ness** *n.*

nudge (nʌdʒ) *vb.* (*tr.*) **1.** to push or poke (someone) gently, esp. with the elbow, to get attention; jog. **2.** to push slowly or lightly: *as I drove out, I just nudged the gatepost.* ~*n.* **3.** a gentle poke or push. [C17: perhaps from Scandinavian; compare Icelandic *nugga* to push] —ˈ**nudg·er** *n.*

nu·di- *combining form.* naked or bare: *nudibranch.* [from Latin *nūdus*]

nu·di·branch (ˈnjuːdɪˌbræŋk) *n.* any marine gastropod of the order *Nudibranchia,* characterized by a shell-less, often beautifully coloured, body bearing external gills and other appendages. Also called: **sea slug.** [C19: from NUDI- + *branche,* from Latin *branchia* gills]

nu·di·caul (ˈnjuːdɪˌkɔːl) *or* **nu·di·cau·lous** (ˌnjuːdɪˈkɔːləs) *adj.* (of plants) having stems without leaves. [C20: from NUDI- + *caul,* from Latin *caulis* stem]

nud·ism (ˈnjuːdɪzəm) *n.* the practice of nudity, esp. for reasons of health, religion, etc. —ˈ**nud·ist** *n.*

nu·di·ty (ˈnjuːdɪtɪ) *n., pl.* **·ties. 1.** the state or fact of being nude; nakedness. **2.** *Rare.* a nude figure, esp. in art.

nu·dum pac·tum (ˈnjuːdʊm ˈpæktʊm) *n. Law.* an agreement made without consideration and void unless made under seal. [Latin: nude (sense 3b.) agreement]

Nue·vo La·re·do (*Spanish* ˈnweβo laˈreðo) *n.* a city and port of entry in NE Mexico, in Tamaulipas state on the Rio Grande opposite Laredo, Texas: oil industries. Pop.: 193 145 (1975 est.).

Nue·vo Le·ón (ˈnweɪvəʊ leɪˈəʊn, nuːˈeɪ-; *Spanish* ˈnweβo leˈon) *n.* a state of NE Mexico: the first centre of heavy industry in Latin America. Capital: Monterrey. Pop.: 1 694 689 (1970). Area: 64 555 sq. km (24 925 sq. miles).

Nuf·field (ˈnʌfiːld) *n.* **Wil·liam Rich·ard Mor·ris,** 1st Viscount Nuffield. 1877–1963, English motorcar manufacturer and philanthropist. He endowed Nuffield College at Oxford (1937) and the Nuffield Foundation (1943), a charitable trust for the furtherance of medicine and education.

Nuf·field teach·ing pro·ject *n. Brit.* a complete school programme in mathematics, science, etc., with suggested complementary theory and practical work.

nu·ga·to·ry (ˈnjuːgətərɪ, -trɪ) *adj.* **1.** of little value; trifling. **2.** not valid: *a nugatory law.* [C17: from Latin *nūgātōrius,* from *nūgārī* to jest, from *nūgae* trifles]

nug·gar (ˈnʌgə) *n.* a sailing boat used to carry cargo on the Nile. [from Arabic]

nug·get (ˈnʌgɪt) *n.* **1.** a small piece or lump, esp. of gold in its natural state. **2.** something small but valuable or excellent. ~*vb.* (*tr.*) *Austral.* to pick out (nuggets, etc.) from the surface of rock. [C19: origin unknown]

nug·get·y (ˈnʌgɪtɪ) *adj.* **1.** of or resembling a nugget. **2.** *Austral. informal.* (of a person) thickset; stocky.

N.U.G.M.W. *abbrev. for* National Union of General and Municipal Workers.

nui·sance (ˈnjuːsəns) *n.* **1. a.** a person or thing that causes annoyance or bother. **b.** (*as modifier*): *nuisance value.* **2.** *Law.* something unauthorized that is obnoxious or injurious to the community at large (**public nuisance**) or to an individual, esp. in relation to his ownership or occupation of property (**private nuisance**). [C15: via Old French from *nuire* to injure, from Latin *nocēre*]

Nuits-Saint-Georges (*French* nɥi sɛ̃ ˈʒɔrʒ) *n.* a fine red wine produced near the town of Nuits-Saint-Georges in Burgundy.

N.U.J. *abbrev. for* National Union of Journalists.

nuke (njuːk) *n. Slang, chiefly U.S.* a nuclear bomb.

Nu·ku'·a·lo·fa (ˌnuːkuːəˈlɔːfə) *n.* the capital of Tonga, a port on the N coast of Tongatapu Island. Pop.: 15 545 (1966).

Nu·kus (*Russian* nuˈkus) *n.* a city in the S Soviet Union, capital of the Kara-Kalpak ASSR, on the Amu Darya River. Pop.: 74 103 (1970).

null (nʌl) *adj.* **1.** without legal force; invalid; (esp. in the phrase **null and void**). **2.** without value or consequence; useless. **3.** lacking distinction; characterless: *a null expression.* **4.** nonexistent; amounting to nothing. **5.** *Maths.* **a.** quantitatively zero. **b.** relating to zero. **c.** (of a set) having no members. **d.** (of a sequence) having zero as a limit. **6.** *Physics.* involving measurement in which conditions are adjusted so that an instrument has a zero reading, as with a Wheatstone bridge. [C16: from Latin *nullus* none, from *ne* not + *ullus* any]

nul·lah (ˈnʌlɑː) *n.* (in India) a stream or drain. [C18: from Hindi *nālā*]

nul·la-nul·la (ˌnʌləˈnʌlə) *n. Austral.* a wooden club used by Aborigines. [from a native Australian language]

Null·ar·bor Plain (ˈnʌləˌbɔː) *n.* a vast low plateau of S Australia: extends north from the Great Australian Bight to the Great Victoria Desert; has no surface water or trees. Area: 260 000 sq. km (100 000 sq. miles).

null hy·poth·e·sis *n. Statistics.* a hypothesis that is to be tested against another but is to be nullified in favour of the alternative, subject to a given level of error.

nul·li·fid·i·an (ˌnʌlɪˈfɪdɪən) *n.* **1.** a person who has no faith or belief; sceptic; disbeliever. ~*adj.* **2.** having no faith or belief. [C16: from Latin, from *nullus* no + *fidēs* faith]

nul·li·fy (ˈnʌlɪˌfaɪ) *vb.* **·fies, ·fy·ing, ·fied.** (*tr.*) **1.** to render legally void or of no effect. **2.** to render ineffective or useless; cancel out. [C16: from Late Latin *nullificāre* despise, from Latin *nullus* of no account + *facere* to make] —ˌ**nul·li·fi·ˈca·tion** *n.* —ˈ**nul·li·ˌfi·er** *n.*

nul·lip·a·ra (nʌˈlɪpərə) *n., pl.* **·rae** (-ˌriː). a woman who has never borne a child. [C19: New Latin, from *nullus* no, not any

+ *-para,* from *parere* to bring forth; see -PAROUS] —**nul·'lip·a·rous** *adj.*

nul·li·pore ('nʌlɪˌpɔː) *n.* any of several red seaweeds that secrete and become encrusted with calcium carbonate: family *Rhodophyceae.* [C19: from Latin, from *nullus* no + PORE²]

nul·li·ty ('nʌlɪtɪ) *n., pl.* **·ties.** **1.** the state of being null. **2.** a null or legally invalid act or instrument. **3.** something null, ineffective, characterless, etc. [C16: from Medieval Latin *nullitās,* from Latin *nullus* no, not any]

N.U.M. *abbrev. for* National Union of Mineworkers.

num. *abbrev. for:* **1.** number. **2.** numeral.

Num. *Bible. abbrev. for* Numbers.

Nu·man·ti·a (njuː'mæntɪə) *n.* an ancient city in N Spain: a centre of Celtic resistance to Rome in N Spain: captured by Scipio the Younger in 133 B.C. —**Nu·'man·ti·an** *adj., n.*

Nu·ma Pom·pil·i·us ('njuːmə pɒm'pɪlɪəs) *n.* the legendary second king of Rome (?715–?673 B.C.), said to have instituted religious rites.

numb (nʌm) *adj.* **1.** deprived of feeling through cold, shock, etc. **2.** unable to move; paralysed. **3.** characteristic of or resembling numbness: *a numb sensation.* ~*vb.* **4.** (*tr.*) to make numb; deaden, shock, or paralyse. [C15 *nomen,* literally: taken (with paralysis), from Old English *niman* to take; related to Old Norse *nema,* Old High German *niman*] —**'numb·ly** *adv.* —**'numb·ness** *n.*

num·bat ('nʌmˌbæt) *n.* a small Australian marsupial, *Myrmecobius fasciatus,* having a long snout and tongue and strong claws for hunting and feeding on termites: family *Dasyuridae.* Also called: **banded anteater.** [C20: from a native Australian language]

num·ber ('nʌmbə) *n.* **1.** a concept of quantity that is or can be derived from a single unit, the sum of a collection of units, or zero. Every number occupies a unique position in a sequence, enabling it to be used in counting. It can be assigned to one or more sets that can be arranged in a hierarchical classification: every number is a **complex number;** a complex number is either an **imaginary number** or a **real number,** and the latter can be a **rational number** or an **irrational number;** a rational number is either an **integer** or a **fraction,** while an irrational number can be a **transcendental number** or an **algebraic number.** See also **cardinal number, ordinal number. 2.** the symbol used to represent a number; numeral. **3.** a numeral or string of numerals used to identify a person or thing, esp. in numerical order: *a telephone number.* **4.** the person or thing so identified or designated: *she was number seven in the race.* **5.** the sum or quantity of equal or similar units or things: *a large number of people.* **6.** one of a series, as of a magazine or periodical; issue. **7. a.** a self-contained piece of pop or jazz music. **b.** a self-contained part of an opera or other musical score, esp. one for the stage. **8.** a group or band of people, esp. an exclusive group: *he was not one of our number.* **9.** *Slang.* a person, esp. a sexually attractive girl: *who's that nice little number?* **10.** *Informal.* an admired article, esp. an item of clothing for a woman: *that little number is by Dior.* **11.** a grammatical category for the variation in form of nouns, pronouns, and any words agreeing with them, depending on how many persons or things are referred to, esp. as singular or plural in number and in some languages dual or trial. **12. any number of.** several or many. **13. by numbers.** *Military.* (of a drill procedure, etc.) performed step by step, each move being made on the call of a number. **14. get** *or* **have someone's number.** *U.S. informal.* to discover a person's true character or intentions. **15. in numbers.** in large numbers; numerously. **16. one's number is up.** *Brit. informal.* one is finished; one is dead or ruined. **17. without** *or* **beyond number.** of too great a quantity to be counted; innumerable. ~*vb.* (*mainly tr.*) **18.** to assign a number to. **19.** to add up to; total. **20.** (*also intr.*) to list (items) one by one; enumerate. **21.** (*also intr.*) to put or be put into a group, category, etc.: *they were numbered among the worst hit.* **22.** to limit the number of: *his days were numbered.* [C13: from Old French *nombre,* from Latin *numerus*]

num·ber·less ('nʌmbəlɪs) *adj.* **1.** too many to be counted; countless. **2.** not containing or consisting of numbers. —**'num·ber·less·ly** *adv.* —**'num·ber·less·ness** *n.*

num·ber line *n.* (in number theory) an infinite line on which points are taken to represent the real numbers by their distance from a reference point.

num·ber off *vb.* (*adv.*) to call out or cause to call out one's number or place in a sequence, esp. in a rank of soldiers: *the sergeant numbered his men off from the right.*

num·ber one *n.* **1.** an informal phrase for **oneself, myself,** etc.: *to look after number one.* ~*adj.* **2.** first in importance, urgency, quality, etc.: *number one priority.*

num·ber·plate ('nʌmbəˌpleɪt) *n.* a plate mounted on the front and back of a motor vehicle bearing the registration number. Usual U.S. term: **license plate.**

Num·bers ('nʌmbəz) *n.* the fourth book of the Old Testament, recording the numbers of the Israelites who followed Moses out of Egypt.

Num·ber Ten *n.* 10 Downing Street, the British prime minister's official London residence.

num·ber the·o·ry *n.* the study of integers, their properties, and the relationship between integers.

num·ber work *n.* simple arithmetic and similar mathematical procedures as used and studied at primary level. Also called (esp. formerly): **sums.**

numb·fish ('nʌmˌfɪʃ) *n., pl.* **·fish** *or* **·fish·es.** any of several electric rays, such as *Narcine tasmaniensis* (**Australian numbfish**). [C18: so called because it numbs its victims]

num·bles ('nʌmbᵊlz) *pl. n. Archaic.* the heart, lungs, liver, etc., of a deer or other animal, cooked for food. [C14: from Old French *nombles,* plural of *nomble* thigh muscle of a deer, changed from Latin *lumbulus* a little loin, from *lumbus* loin; see HUMBLE PIE]

numb·skull ('nʌmˌskʌl) *n.* a variant spelling of **numskull.**

num·dah ('nʌmdɑː) *n.* **1.** a coarse felt made in India, etc. **2.** a saddle pad made from this. **3.** an embroidered rug made from this. ~Also called (for senses 1, 2): **numnah.** [C19: from Urdu *namdā*]

nu·men ('njuːmɛn) *n., pl.* **·mi·na** (-mɪnə). **1.** (esp. in ancient Roman religion) a deity or spirit presiding over a thing or place. **2.** a guiding principle, force, or spirit. [C17: from Latin: a nod (indicating a command), divine power; compare *nuere* to nod]

nu·mer·a·ble ('njuːmərəbᵊl) *adj.* able to be numbered or counted. —**'nu·mer·a·bly** *adv.*

nu·mer·al ('njuːmərəl) *n.* **1.** a symbol or group of symbols used to express a number: for example, *6* (*Arabic*), *VI* (*Roman*), *110* (*binary*). ~*adj.* **2.** of, consisting of, or denoting a number. [C16: from Late Latin *numerālis* belonging to number, from Latin *numerus* number]

nu·mer·ar·y ('njuːmərərɪ) *adj.* of or relating to numbers.

nu·mer·ate *adj.* ('njuːmərɪt). **1.** able to use numbers, esp. in arithmetical operations. Compare **literate.** ~*vb.* ('njuːməˌreɪt). **2.** (*tr.*) to read (a numerical expression). **3.** a less common word for **enumerate.** [C18 (vb.): from Latin *numerus* number + -ATE¹, by analogy with *literate*] —**nu·mer·a·cy** ('njuːmərəsɪ) *n.*

nu·mer·a·tion (ˌnjuːmə'reɪʃən) *n.* **1.** the act or process of writing, reading, or naming numbers. **2.** a system of numbering or counting. —**'nu·mer·a·tive** *adj.*

nu·mer·a·tor ('njuːməˌreɪtə) *n.* **1.** *Maths.* the dividend of a fraction: the numerator of 7/8 is 7. Compare **denominator. 2.** a person or thing that numbers; enumerator.

nu·mer·i·cal (njuː'mɛrɪkᵊl) *or* **nu·mer·ic** *adj.* **1.** of, relating to, or denoting a number or numbers. **2.** measured or expressed in numbers: *numerical value.* **3.** *Maths.* **a.** containing or using constants, coefficients, terms, or elements represented by numbers: $3x^2 + 4y = 2$ *is a numerical equation.* Compare **literal** (sense 6). **b.** another word for **absolute** (sense 11a.). —**nu·'mer·i·cal·ly** *adv.*

nu·mer·i·cal a·nal·y·sis *n.* a branch of mathematics concerned with methods, usually iterative, for obtaining solutions to problems by means of a computer.

nu·mer·ol·o·gy (ˌnjuːmə'rɒlədʒɪ) *n.* the study of numbers, such as the figures in a birth date, and of their supposed influence on human affairs. —**nu·mer·o·log·i·cal** (ˌnjuːmərə'lɒdʒɪkᵊl) *adj.* —**ˌnu·mer·'ol·o·gist** *n.*

nu·mer·ous ('njuːmərəs) *adj.* **1.** being many. **2.** consisting of many units or parts: *a numerous collection.* —**'nu·mer·ous·ly** *adv.* —**'nu·mer·ous·ness** *n.*

Nu·mid·i·a (njuː'mɪdɪə) *n.* an ancient country of N Africa, corresponding roughly to present-day Algeria: flourished until its invasion by Vandals in 429; chief towns were Cirta and Hippo Regius. —**Nu·'mid·i·an** *n., adj.*

Nu·mid·i·an crane *n.* another name for **demoiselle crane** (see **demoiselle** (sense 1)).

nu·mi·nous ('njuːmɪnəs) *adj.* **1.** denoting, being, or relating to a numen; divine. **2.** arousing spiritual or religious emotions. **3.** mysterious or awe-inspiring. [C17: from Latin *numin-,* NUMEN + -OUS]

numis. *or* **numism.** *abbrev. for* numismatic(s).

nu·mis·mat·ics (ˌnjuːmɪz'mætɪks) *n.* (*functioning as sing.*) the study or collection of coins, medals, etc. Also called: **nu·mis·ma·tol·o·gy** (ˌnjuːmɪzmə'tɒlədʒɪ). [C18: from French *numismatique,* from Latin *nomisma,* from Greek: piece of currency, from *nomizein* to have in use, from *nōmos* use] —**ˌnu·mis·'mat·ic** *adj.* —**ˌnu·mis·'mat·i·cal·ly** *adv.*

nu·mis·ma·tist (njuː'mɪzmətɪst) *or* **nu·mis·ma·tol·o·gist** (njuːˌmɪzmə'tɒlədʒɪst) *n.* a person who studies or collects coins, medals, etc.

num·ma·ry ('nʌmərɪ) *adj.* of or relating to coins. [C17: from Latin *nummārius*]

num·mu·lar ('nʌmjʊlə) *adj.* shaped like a coin; disc-shaped; circular. [C19: from Latin *nummulus* a small coin]

num·mu·lite ('nʌmjʊˌlaɪt) *n.* any of various large fossil protozoans of the family *Nummulitidae,* common in Tertiary times: order *Foraminifera* (foraminifers). [C19: from New Latin *Nummulites* genus name, from Latin *nummulus,* from *nummus* coin] —**num·mu·lit·ic** (ˌnʌmjʊ'lɪtɪk) *adj.*

num·nah ('nʌmnɑː) *n.* another word for **numdah** (senses 1, 2).

num·skull *or* **numb·skull** ('nʌmˌskʌl) *n.* a stupid person; dolt; blockhead.

nun¹ (nʌn) *n.* **1.** a female member of a religious order. **2.** (*sometimes cap.*) a variety of domestic fancy pigeon having a black-and-white plumage with a ridged peak or cowl of short white feathers. [Old English *nunne,* from Church Latin *nonna,* from Late Latin: form of address used for an elderly woman] —**'nun·like** *adj.*

nun² (nʊn) *n.* the 14th letter in the Hebrew alphabet (נ or, at the end of a word, ן) transliterated as *n.*

nun·a·tak ('nʌnəˌtæk) *n.* an isolated mountain peak projecting through the surface of surrounding glacial ice and supporting a distinct fauna and flora after recession of the ice. [C19: via Danish from Eskimo]

nun buoy (nʌn) *n. Nautical.* a red buoy, conical at the top, marking the right side of a channel leading into a harbour. Compare **can buoy.** [C18: from obsolete *nun* child's spinning top + BUOY]

Nunc Di+mit+tis (ˈnʌŋk dɪˈmɪtɪs, ˈnʊŋk) *n.* **1.** the Latin name for the Canticle of Simeon (Luke 2:29–32). **2.** a musical setting of this. [from the opening words (Vulgate): now let depart]

nun+ci+a+ture (ˈnʌnsɪətʃə) *n.* the office or term of office of a nuncio. [C17: from Italian *nunziatura;* see NUNCIO]

nun+ci+o (ˈnʌnʃɪˌəʊ, -sɪ-) *n., pl.* **+ci+os.** *R.C. Church.* a diplomatic representative of the Holy See, ranking above an internuncio and esp. having ambassadorial status. [C16: via Italian from Latin *nuntius* messenger]

nun+cle (ˈnʌŋk^{ə}l) *n.* an archaic or dialect word for **uncle.** [C16: from division of *mine uncle* as *my nuncle*]

nun+cu+pa+tive (ˈnʌŋkjʊˌpeɪtɪv, nʌŋˈkju:pətɪv) *adj.* (of a will) declared orally by the testator and later written down. [C16: from Late Latin *nuncupātīvus* nominal, from Latin *nuncupāre* to name]

Nun+ea+ton (nʌnˈi:t^{ə}n) *n.* a town in central England, in Warwickshire. Pop.: 66 979 (1971).

nun+hood (ˈnʌnhʊd) *n.* **1.** the condition, practice, or character of a nun. **2.** nuns collectively.

nun+ner+y (ˈnʌnərɪ) *n., pl.* **+ner+ies.** the convent or religious house of a community of nuns.

nun+ny bag (ˈnʌnɪ) *n. Canadian.* a small sealskin haversack, used chiefly in Newfoundland. [C19: *nunny,* probably from Scottish dialect *noony* luncheon, from NOON]

nun's cloth *or* **veil+ing** (nʌnz) *n.* a thin soft plain-weave silk or worsted fabric used for veils, dresses, etc.

Nu+pe (ˈnu:peɪ) *n.* **1.** (*pl.* **·pe** *or* **·pes**) a member of a Negroid people of Nigeria, noted as fishermen, who live near the confluence of the Niger and Benue Rivers. **2.** the language of this people, belonging to the Kwa branch of the Niger-Congo family.

NUPE (ˈnju:pɪ) *n. acronym for* National Union of Public Employees.

nup+tial (ˈnʌpʃəl, -tʃəl) *adj.* **1.** relating to marriage; conjugal: *nuptial vows.* **2.** *Zoology.* of or relating to mating: *the nuptial flight of a queen bee.* [C15: from Latin *nuptiālis,* from *nuptiae* marriage, from *nubere* to marry] —**ˈnup+tial+ly** *adv.*

nup+tials (ˈnʌpʃəlz, -tʃəlz) *pl. n.* (*sometimes sing.*) a marriage ceremony; wedding.

N.U.R. *abbrev. for* National Union of Railwaymen.

Nu+rem+berg (ˈnjʊərəmˌbɜ:g) *n.* a city in SE West Germany, in N Bavaria: scene of annual Nazi rallies (1933–38), the anti-Semitic Nuremberg decrees (1935), and the trials of Nazi leaders for their war crimes (1945–46). Pop.: 514 657 (1974 est.). German name: **Nürnberg.**

Nu+re+yev (ˈnjʊərɪef, njʊˈreɪ-) *n.* **Ru+dolf.** born 1939, ballet dancer, born in the Soviet Union: in England since 1961.

Nu+ri (ˈnʊərɪ) *n.* **1.** (*pl.* **·ris** *or* **·ri**) Also called: **Kafir.** a member of an Indo-European people of Nuristan and neighbouring parts of Pakistan. **2.** Also called: **Kafiri.** the Dardic language of this people.

Nu+ri+stan (ˌnʊərɪˈstɑ:n) *n.* a region of E Afghanistan: consists mainly of high mountains (including part of the Hindu Kush), steep narrow valleys, and forests. Area: about 13 000 sq. km (5000 sq. miles). Former name: **Kafiristan.**

Nur+mi (ˈnɜ:mɪ; *Finnish* ˈnurmi) *n.* **Paa+vo** (ˈpɑ:vɔ), known as *The Flying Finn.* 1897–1973, Finnish runner, winner of the 1500, 5000, and 10 000 metres' races at the 1924 Olympic Games in Paris.

Nürn+berg (ˈnyrnbɛrk) *n.* the German name for **Nuremberg.**

nurse (nɜ:s) *n.* **1.** a person, usually a woman, who tends the sick, injured, or infirm. **2.** short for **nursemaid. 3.** a woman employed to breast-feed another woman's child; wet nurse. **4.** a worker in a colony of social insects that takes care of the larvae. ~*vb.* (*mainly tr.*) **5.** (*also intr.*) to tend (the sick). **6.** (*also intr.*) to feed (a baby) at the breast; suckle. **7.** to try to cure (an ailment). **8.** to clasp carefully or fondly: *she nursed the crying child in her arms.* **9.** (*also intr.*) (of a baby) to suckle at the breast (of). **10.** to look after (a child) as one's employment. **11.** to harbour; preserve: *to nurse a grudge.* **12.** *Billiards.* to keep (the balls) together for a series of cannons. [C16: from earlier *norice,* Old French *nourice,* from Late Latin *nūtrīcia* nurse, from Latin *nūtrīcius* nourishing, from *nūtrīre* to nourish]

nurse+maid (ˈnɜ:sˌmeɪd) *or* **nurse+ry+maid** *n.* a woman or girl employed to look after someone else's children. Often shortened to **nurse.**

nurse+ry (ˈnɜ:srɪ) *n., pl.* **+ries. 1. a.** a room in a house set apart for use by children. **b.** (*as modifier*): *nursery wallpaper.* **2.** a place where plants, young trees, etc., are grown commercially. **3.** an establishment providing residential or day care for babies and very young children; crèche. **4.** short for **nursery school. 5.** anywhere serving to foster or nourish new ideas, etc. **6.** Also called: **nursery cannon.** *Billiards.* **a.** a series of cannons with the three balls adjacent to a cushion, esp. near a corner pocket. **b.** a cannon in such a series.

nurse+ry+man (ˈnɜ:srɪmən) *n., pl.* **+men.** a person who owns or works in a nursery in which plants are grown.

nurse+ry rhyme *n.* a short traditional verse or song for children, such as *Little Jack Horner.*

nurse+ry school *n.* a school for young children, usually from three to five years old.

nurse+ry slopes *pl. n.* gentle slopes used by beginners in skiing.

nurse+ry stakes *n.* a race for two-year-old horses.

nurse shark *n.* any of various sharks of the family *Orectolobidae,* such as *Ginglymostoma cirratum* of the Atlantic Ocean, having an external groove on each side of the head between the mouth and nostril. [C15 *nusse fisshe* (later influenced in spelling by NURSE), perhaps from division of obsolete *an huss* shark, dogfish (of uncertain origin) as *a nuss*]

nurs+ing bot+tle *n.* another term (esp. U.S.) for **feeding bottle.**

nurs+ing fa+ther *n.* another name for a **foster father.**

nurs+ing home *n.* **1.** a private hospital or residence staffed and equipped to care for aged or infirm persons. **2.** *Brit.* a private maternity home.

nurs+ing mo+ther *n.* **1.** another name for a **foster mother. 2.** a mother who is breast-feeding her baby.

nurs+ling *or* **nurse+ling** (ˈnɜ:slɪŋ) *n.* a child or young animal that is being suckled, nursed, or fostered.

nur+ture (ˈnɜ:tʃə) *n.* **1.** the act or process of promoting the development, etc., of a child. **2.** something that nourishes. **3.** *Biology.* the environmental factors that partly determine the structure of an organism. See also **nature** (sense 12). ~*vb.* (*tr.*) **4.** to feed or support. **5.** to educate or train. [C14: from Old French *norriture,* from Latin *nutrīre* to nourish] —**ˈnur+tur+a+ble** *adj.* —**ˈnur+tur+er** *n.*

N.U.S. *abbrev. for:* **1.** National Union of Seamen. **2.** National Union of Students.

Nu+sa Teng+ga+ra (ˈnu:sə tɛŋˈgɑ:rə) *n.* an island chain forming a province of Indonesia, east of Java: the main islands are Bali, Lombok, Sumbawa, Sumba, Flores, Alor, and Timor. Pop.: 7 706 561 (1971). Area: 73 144 sq. km (28 241 sq. miles). Also called: **Lesser Sunda Islands.**

nut (nʌt) *n.* **1.** a dry one-seeded indehiscent fruit that usually possesses a woody wall. **2.** (*not in technical use*) any similar fruit, such as the walnut, having a hard shell and an edible kernel. **3.** the edible kernel of such a fruit. **4.** *Slang.* **a.** an eccentric person. **b.** a person who is mentally disturbed. **5.** a slang word for the **head. 6. do one's nut.** *Brit. slang.* to be extremely angry; go into a rage. **7. off one's nut.** *Slang.* mad, crazy, or foolish. **8.** a person or thing that presents difficulties (esp. in the phrase **a tough** *or* **hard nut to crack**). **9.** a small metallic block, usually hexagonal or square, with an internal screw thread enabling it to be fitted onto a bolt. **10.** Also called (U.S.): **frog.** *Music.* **a.** the ledge or ridge at the upper end of the fingerboard of a violin, cello, etc., over which the strings pass to the tuning pegs. **b.** the end of a violin bow that is held by the player. **11.** *Printing.* another word for **en. 12.** a small usually gingery biscuit. **13.** *Brit.* a small piece of coal. ~See also **nuts.** ~*vb.* **nuts, nut+ting, nut+ted. 14.** (*intr.*) to gather nuts. [Old English *hnutu;* related to Old Norse *hnot,* Old High German *hnuz* (German *Nuss*)] —**ˈnut+ˌlike** *adj.*

N.U.T. *abbrev. for* National Union of Teachers.

nu+tant (ˈnju:t^{ə}nt) *adj. Botany.* having the apex hanging down: *nutant flowers.* [C18: from Latin *nūtāre* to nod]

nu+ta+tion (nju:ˈteɪʃən) *n.* **1.** *Astronomy.* a periodic variation in the precession of the earth's axis causing the earth's poles to oscillate about their mean position. **2.** the spiral growth of a shoot, tendril, or similar plant organ, caused by variation in the growth rate in different parts. **3.** the act or an instance of nodding the head. [C17: from Latin *nūtātiō* from *nūtāre* to nod] —**nu+ˈta+tion+al** *adj.*

nut+brown (ˈnʌtˈbraʊn) *adj.* of a brownish colour, esp. a reddish-brown: *nutbrown hair.*

nut+case (ˈnʌtˌkeɪs) *n. Slang.* an insane or very foolish person.

nut+crack+er (ˈnʌtˌkrækə) *n.* **1.** (*often pl.*) a device for cracking the shells of nuts. **2.** either of two birds, *Nucifraga caryocatactes* of the Old World or *N. columbianus* (**Clark's nutcracker**) of North America, having speckled plumage and feeding on nuts, seeds, etc.: family *Corvidae* (crows).

nut+gall (ˈnʌtˌgɔ:l) *n.* a nut-shaped gall caused by gall wasps on the oak and other trees.

nut+hatch (ˈnʌtˌhætʃ) *n.* any songbird of the family *Sittidae,* esp. *Sitta europaea,* having strong feet and bill, and feeding on insects, seeds, and nuts. [C14 *notehache,* from *note* nut + *hache* hatchet, from the bird's habit of splitting nuts; see NUT, HACK[1]]

nut+house (ˈnʌtˌhaʊs) *n. Slang.* a mental hospital or asylum.

nut+let (ˈnʌtlɪt) *n.* **1.** any of the one-seeded portions of a fruit, such as a labiate fruit, that fragments when mature. **2.** the stone of a drupe, such as a plum. **3.** a small nut.

nut+meg (ˈnʌtmɛg) *n.* **1.** an East Indian evergreen tree, *Myristica fragrans,* cultivated in the tropics for its hard aromatic seed: family *Myristicaceae.* See also **mace**[2]. **2.** the seed of this tree, used as a spice. **3.** any of several similar trees or their fruit. **4.** a greyish-brown colour. [C13: from Old French *nois muguede,* from Old Provençal *noz muscada* musk-scented nut, from Latin *nux* NUT + *muscus* MUSK]

nut oil *n.* oil obtained from walnuts, hazelnuts, etc., used in paints and varnishes.

nut pine *n.* either of two varieties of the pine tree *Pinus cembroides,* of Mexico, Arizona, and California, having edible nuts.

nu+tri+a (ˈnju:trɪə) *n.* **1.** another name for **coypu,** esp. the fur. **2.** a brown colour with a grey tinge. [C19: from Spanish: otter, variant of *lutria,* ultimately from Latin *lūtra* otter]

nu+tri+ent (ˈnju:trɪənt) *n.* **1.** any of the mineral substances that are absorbed by the roots of plants for nourishment. **2.** any substance that nourishes an animal. ~*adj.* **3.** providing or contributing to nourishment: *a nutrient solution.* [C17: from Latin *nūtrīre* to nourish]

nu+tri+ment (ˈnju:trɪmənt) *n.* any material providing nourishment. [C16: from Latin *nūtrīmentum* from *nūtrīre* to nourish] —**nu+tri+ment+al** (ˌnju:trɪˈmɛnt^{ə}l) *adj.*

nu+tri+tion (nju:ˈtrɪʃən) *n.* **1.** a process in animals and plants involving the intake of nutrient materials and their subsequent assimilation into the tissues. **2.** the act or process of nourishing. **3.** the study of nutrition, esp. in humans. [C16: from Late Latin *nūtrītiō*, from *nūtrīre* to nourish] —**nu'tri·tion·al** *or* **nu'tri·tion·ar·y** *adj.* —**nu'tri·tion·al·ly** *adv.*

nu·tri·tion·ist (nju:'trɪʃənɪst) *n.* a person who specializes in nutrition and the nutritive value of various foods.

nu·tri·tious (nju:'trɪʃəs) *adj.* nourishing, sometimes to a high degree. [C17: from Latin *nūtrīcius* nourishing, from *nūtrix* a NURSE] —**nu'tri·tious·ly** *adv.* —**nu'tri·tious·ness** *n.*

nu·tri·tive ('nju:trɪtɪv) *adj.* **1.** providing nourishment. **2.** of, concerning, or promoting nutrition. ~*n.* **3.** a nutritious food. —**'nu·tri·tive·ly** *adv.*

nuts (nʌts) *adj.* **1.** a slang word for **insane. 2.** (foll. by *about* or *on*) *Slang.* extremely fond (of) or enthusiastic (about). ~*interj.* **3.** *Slang.* an expression of disappointment, contempt, refusal, or defiance. ~*pl. n.* **4.** a taboo slang word for **testicles.**

nuts and bolts *pl. n. Informal.* the essential or practical details.

nut·shell ('nʌt,ʃɛl) *n.* **1.** the shell around the kernel of a nut. **2. in a nutshell.** in essence; briefly.

nut·ter ('nʌtə) *n. Brit. slang.* a mad or eccentric person.

nut·ting ('nʌtɪŋ) *n.* the act or pastime of gathering nuts.

nut·ty ('nʌtɪ) *adj.* **·ti·er, ·ti·est. 1.** containing or abounding in nuts. **2.** resembling nuts, esp. in taste. **3.** a slang word for **insane. 4.** (foll. by *over* or *about*) *Informal.* extremely fond (of) or enthusiastic (about). —**'nut·ti·ly** *adv.* —**'nut·ti·ness** *n.*

nut·wood ('nʌt,wud) *n.* **1.** any of various nut-bearing trees, such as walnut. **2.** the wood of any of these trees.

nux vom·i·ca ('nʌks 'vɒmɪkə) *n.* **1.** an Indian spiny loganiaceous tree, *Strychnos nux-vomica*, with orange-red berries containing poisonous seeds. **2.** any of the seeds of this tree, which contain strychnine and other poisonous alkaloids. **3.** a medicine manufactured from the seeds of this tree, formerly used as a heart stimulant. [C16: from Medieval Latin: vomiting nut]

nuz·zle ('nʌz^əl) *vb.* **1.** to push or rub gently against the nose or snout. **2.** (*intr.*) to nestle; lie close. **3.** (*tr.*) to dig out with the snout. [C15 *nosele*, from NOSE (n.)]

NW *abbrev. for* northwest(ern).

N.W.T. *abbrev. for* Northwest Territories (of Canada).

N.Y. *abbrev. for* New York (city or state).

nya·la ('njɑ:lə) *n., pl.* **·la** *or* **·las. 1.** a spiral-horned southern African antelope, *Tragelaphus angasi*, with a fringe of white hairs along the length of the back and neck. **2. mountain nyala.** a similar and related Ethiopian animal, *T. buxtoni*, lacking the white crest. [from Zulu]

Nyan·ja ('njændʒə) *n.* **1.** (*pl.* **·ja** *or* **·jas**) a member of a Negroid people of central Africa, living chiefly in Malawi. **2.** the language of this people, belonging to the Bantu group of the Niger-Congo family. Nyanja forms the basis of a pidgin used as a lingua franca in central Africa.

nyan·za ('njænzə, nɪ'ænzə) *n.* (*cap. when part of a name*) (in E Africa) a lake. [from Bantu]

Ny·as·a *or* **Ny·as·sa** (nɪ'æsə, naɪ'æsə) *n.* **Lake.** the former name of Lake **Malawi.**

Ny·as·a·land (nɪ'æsə,lænd, naɪ'æsə-) *n.* the former name (until 1964) of **Malawi.**

N.Y.C. *abbrev. for* New York City.

nyc·ta·gi·na·ceous (,nɪktədʒɪ'neɪʃəs) *adj.* of, relating to, or belonging to the *Nyctaginaceae*, a family of mostly tropical plants, including bougainvillea, having large coloured bracts surrounding each flower. [from New Latin, from *Nyctago* type genus, from Greek *nukt-, nux* night]

nyc·ta·lo·pi·a (,nɪktə'ləupɪə) *n.* inability to see normally in dim light. Nontechnical name: **night blindness.** Compare **hemeralopia.** [C17: via Late Latin from Greek *nuktálōps*, from *nux* night + *alaos* blind + *ōps* eye]

nyc·ti·nas·ty ('nɪktɪ,næstɪ) *n. Botany.* a nastic movement, such as the closing of petals, that occurs in response to the alternation of day and night. [C20: from Greek *nukt-, nux* night + -NASTY] —,**nyc·ti'nas·tic** *adj.*

nyc·tit·ro·pism (nɪk'tɪtrə,pɪzəm) *n.* a tendency of some plant parts to assume positions at night that are different from their daytime positions. [C19: *nyct-*, from Greek *nukt-, nux* night + -TROPISM] —**nyc·ti·trop·ic** (,nɪktɪ'trɒpɪk) *adj.*

nyc·to·pho·bi·a (,nɪktəu'fəubɪə) *n. Psychiatry.* an abnormal dread of night or darkness. [*nyct-*, from Greek *nukt-, nux* night + -PHOBIA] —,**nyc·to'pho·bic** *adj.*

nye (naɪ) *n.* a flock of pheasants. Also called: **nide, eye.** [C15: from Old French *ni*, from Latin *nīdus* nest]

Nye·man (*Russian* 'njɛmən) *n.* a variant spelling of **Neman.**

Nye·re·re (njə'rɛərɪ, nɪ-) *n.* **Ju·li·us Kam·ba·ra·ge** (kæm'bɑ:rɑ:gə). born 1922, Tanzanian statesman; president since 1964. He became prime minister of Tanganyika (1961) and president (1962), negotiating the union of Tanganyika and Zanzibar to form Tanzania (1964).

Nyí·regy·há·za (*Hungarian* 'nji:rɛtj,ha:zɔ) *n.* a market town in NE Hungary. Pop.: 71 000 (1970).

Ny·kø·bing (*Danish* 'nykø:beŋ) *n.* a port in Denmark, on the W coast of Falster Island. Pop.: 90 332 (1968).

nyl·ghau ('nɪlgɔ:) *n., pl.* **·ghau** *or* **·ghaus.** another name for **nilgai.**

ny·lon ('naɪlɒn) *n.* **1.** a class of synthetic polyamide materials made by copolymerizing dicarboxylic acids with diamines. They can be moulded into a variety of articles, such as combs and machine parts. Nylon monofilaments are used for bristles, etc., and nylon fibres can be spun into yarn. **2. a.** yarn or cloth made of nylon, used for clothing, stockings, etc. **b.** (*as modifier*): *a nylon dress.* [C20: originally a trademark]

ny·lons ('naɪlɒnz) *pl. n.* stockings made of nylon or other manmade material.

nymph (nɪmf) *n.* **1.** *Myth.* a spirit of nature envisaged as a beautiful maiden. **2.** *Chiefly poetic.* a beautiful young woman. **3.** the larva of insects such as the dragonfly and mayfly. It resembles the adult, apart from having underdeveloped wings and reproductive organs, and develops into the adult without a pupal stage. [C14: via Old French from Latin, from Greek *numphē* nymph; related to Latin *nūbere* to marry] —**'nym·phal** *or* **nym·phe·an** ('nɪmfɪən) *adj.* —**'nymph·like** *adj.*

nym·pha ('nɪmfə) *n., pl.* **·phae** (-fi:). *Anatomy.* either one of the labia minora. Also called: **labium minus pudendi.** [C17: from Latin: bride, NYMPH]

nym·phae·a·ceous (,nɪmfɪ'eɪʃəs) *adj.* of, relating to, or belonging to the *Nymphaeaceae*, a family of plants, including the water lilies, that grow in water or marshes and have typically floating leaves and showy flowers. [from New Latin, from Latin *nymphaea* water lily, ultimately from Greek *numphaios* sacred to nymphs]

nym·pha·lid ('nɪmfəlɪd) *n.* **1.** any butterfly of the family *Nymphalidae*, typically having brightly coloured wings: includes the fritillaries, tortoiseshells, red admiral, and peacock. ~*adj.* **2.** of, relating to, or belonging to the *Nymphalidae.* [C19: from New Latin, from *Nymphālis* genus name, from Latin; see NYMPH]

nymph·et ('nɪmfɪt) *n.* a young girl who is sexually precocious and desirable. [C17 (meaning: a young nymph) diminutive of NYMPH]

nym·pho ('nɪmfəu) *n., pl.* **·phos.** *Informal.* short for **nymphomaniac.**

nym·pho·lep·sy ('nɪmfə,lɛpsɪ) *n., pl.* **·sies.** a state of violent emotion, esp. when associated with a desire for something that one cannot have. [C18: from NYMPHOLEPT, on the model of *epilepsy*] —,**nym·pho'lep·tic** *adj.*

nym·pho·lept ('nɪmfə,lɛpt) *n.* a person afflicted by nympholepsy. [C19: from Greek *numpholēptos* caught by nymphs, from *numphē* nymph + *lambanein* to seize]

nym·pho·ma·ni·a (,nɪmfə'meɪnɪə) *n.* an abnormally intense and persistent desire in a woman for sexual intercourse. Compare **satyriasis.** [C18: New Latin, from Greek *númphē* nymph + -MANIA] —,**nym·pho'ma·ni·ac** *n., adj.* —**nym·pho·ma·ni·a·cal** (,nɪmfəumə'naɪək^əl) *adj.*

Ny·norsk (*Norwegian* 'ny:nɔrsk; *English* 'ni:nɔ:sk) *n.* one of the two mutually intelligible official forms of written Norwegian: it also exists in spoken form, and is derived from the dialect of W and N Norway. Also called: **Landsmål.** Compare **Bokmål.** [Norwegian: new Norse]

Nyo·ro ('njɔ:rəu) *n.* **1.** (*pl.* **·ro** *or* **·ros**) a member of a Negroid people of W Uganda. **2.** the language of this people, belonging to the Bantu group of the Niger-Congo family.

nys·tag·mus (nɪ'stægməs) *n. Pathol.* an involuntary movement of the eyeball. [C19: New Latin, from Greek *nustagmos;* related to *nustazein* to nod] —**nys'tag·mic** *adj.*

nys·ta·tin ('nɪstətɪn) *n.* an antibiotic obtained from the bacterium *Streptomyces noursei:* used in the treatment of infections caused by certain fungi, esp. *Candida albicans.* [C20: from *New York State*, where it was originated + -IN]

Nyx (nɪks) *n. Greek myth.* the goddess of the night, daughter of Chaos. Roman counterpart: **Nox.**

NZ *international car registration for* New Zealand.

N.Z. *or* **N. Zeal.** *abbrev. for* New Zealand.

N.Z.B.C. *abbrev. for* New Zealand Broadcasting Commission.

O

o or **O** (əʊ) *n., pl.* **o's, O's,** *or* **Os. 1.** the 15th letter and fourth vowel of the modern English alphabet. **2.** any of several speech sounds represented by this letter, in English as in *code, pot, cow, move,* or *form.* **3.** another name for **nought.**

O[1] *symbol for:* **1.** *Chem.* oxygen. **2.** a human blood type of the ABO group. See **universal donor. 3.** Old.

O[2] (əʊ) *interj.* **1.** a variant of **oh. 2.** an exclamation introducing an invocation, entreaty, wish, etc.: *O God! O for the wings of a dove!*

o. *abbrev. for:* **1.** octavo. **2.** old. **3.** only. **4.** order. **5.** *Pharmacol.* pint. [from Latin *octarius*]

O. *abbrev. for:* **1.** Ocean. **2.** octavo. **3.** old.

o- *prefix.* short for **ortho-** (sense 4).

o' (ə) *prep. Informal or archaic.* shortened form of **of:** *a cup o' tea.*

O'- *prefix.* (in surnames of Irish Gaelic origin) descendant of: *O'Corrigan.* [from Irish Gaelic *ó, ua* descendant]

-o *suffix.* forming informal and slang variants and abbreviations, esp. of nouns: *wino; lie doggo; Jacko.* [probably special use of OH]

-o- *connective vowel.* used to connect elements in a compound word: *chromosome; filmography.* Compare **-i-.** [from Greek, stem vowel of many nouns and adjectives in combination]

oaf (əʊf) *n.* a stupid or loutish person. [C17: variant of Old English *ælf* ELF] —**'oaf+ish** *adj.* —**'oaf+ish+ly** *adv.* —**'oaf+ish+ness** *n.*

O·a·hu (əʊ'ɑːhuː) *n.* an island in central Hawaii: the third largest of the Hawaiian Islands. Chief town: Honolulu. Pop.: 630 528 (1970). Area: 1574 sq. km (608 sq. miles).

oak (əʊk) *n.* **1.** any deciduous or evergreen tree or shrub of the fagaceous genus *Quercus,* having acorns as fruits and lobed leaves. See also **holm oak, cork oak, red oak, Turkey oak, durmast. 2. a.** the wood of any of these trees, used esp. as building timber and for making furniture. **b.** (*as modifier*): *an oak table.* **3.** any of various trees that resemble the oak, such as the poison oak, silky oak, and Jerusalem oak. **4.** anything made of oak, esp. a heavy outer door to a set of rooms in an Oxford or Cambridge college. **5.** the leaves of an oak tree, worn as a garland. **6.** the dark brownish colour of oak wood. [Old English *āc;* related to Old Norse *eik,* Old High German *eih,* Latin *aesculus*]

oak ap+ple *or* **gall** *n.* any of various brownish round galls on oak trees, containing the larva of certain wasps.

oak+en ('əʊkən) *adj.* made of the wood of the oak.

Oak+ham ('əʊkəm) *n.* a market town in E central England, in Leicestershire, formerly county town of Rutland. Pop.: 6411 (1971).

Oak+land ('əʊklənd) *n.* a port and industrial centre in W California, on San Francisco Bay. Pop.: 345 880 (1973 est.).

Oak·ley ('əʊklɪ) *n.* **An·nie.** original name *Phoebe Anne Oakley Mozee.* 1860–1926, U.S. markswoman.

Oaks (əʊks) *n.* **the. 1.** a horse race for fillies held annually at Epsom since 1779: one of the classics of English flat-racing. **2.** any of various similar races.

oa·kum ('əʊkəm) *n.* loose fibre obtained by unravelling old rope, used esp. for caulking seams in wooden ships. [Old English *ācuma,* variant of *ācumba,* literally: off-combings, from *ā-* off + *-cumba,* from *cemban* to COMB]

Oak+ville ('əʊkvɪl) *n.* a city in SE Canada, in SE Ontario on Lake Ontario southwest of Toronto: motor-vehicle industry. Pop.: 61 483 (1971).

O. & M. *n. abbrev. for* organization and method (in studies of working methods).

O.A.P. *abbrev. for* old age pension *or* pensioner.

oar (ɔː) *n.* **1.** a long shaft of wood for propelling a boat by rowing, having a broad blade that is dipped into and pulled against the water. Oars were also used for steering certain kinds of ancient sailing boats. **2.** short for **oarsman. 3. put one's oar in.** to interfere or interrupt. ~*vb.* **4.** to row or propel with or as if with oars: *the two men were oaring their way across the lake.* [*Old English ār,* of Germanic origin; related to Old Norse *ār*] —**'oar+less** *adj.* —**'oar+,like** *adj.*

oared (ɔːd) *adj.* **1.** equipped with oars. **2.** (*in combination*) having oars as specified: *two-oared.*

oar+fish ('ɔː,fɪʃ) *n., pl.* **+fish** *or* **+fish·es.** a very long ribbonfish, *Regalecus glesne,* with long slender ventral fins. Also called: **king of the herrings.** [C19: referring to the flattened oarlike body]

oar+lock ('ɔː,lɒk) *n.* the usual U.S. word for **rowlock.**

oars+man ('ɔːzmən) *n., pl.* **+men.** a man who rows, esp. one who rows in a racing boat. —**'oars+man+,ship** *n.*

OAS *abbrev. for:* **1.** Organization of American States. **2.** *Organisation de l'Armée Secrète;* an organization of European settlers in Algeria who opposed Algerian independence by acts of terrorism (1961–63).

o·a·sis (əʊ'eɪsɪs) *n., pl.* **·ses** (-siːz). **1.** a fertile patch in a desert occurring where the water table approaches or reaches the ground surface. **2.** a refuge; haven. [C17: via Latin from Greek, probably of Egyptian origin]

oast (əʊst) *n. Chiefly Brit.* **1.** a kiln for drying hops. **2.** Also called **oast house.** a building containing such kilns, usually having a conical or pyramidal roof. [Old English *āst;* related to Old Norse *eisa* fire]

oat (əʊt) *n.* **1.** an erect annual grass, *Avena sativa,* grown in temperate regions for its edible seed. **2.** (*usually pl.*) the seeds or fruits of this grass. **3.** any of various other grasses of the genus *Avena,* such as the wild oat. **4.** *Poetic.* a flute made from an oat straw. **5. feel one's oats.** *U.S. informal.* **a.** to feel exuberant. **b.** to feel self-important. **6. get one's oats.** *Slang.* to have sexual intercourse. **7. sow one's (wild) oats.** to indulge in adventure or promiscuity during youth. [Old English *āte,* of obscure origin]

oat+cake ('əʊt,keɪk) *n.* a brittle unleavened cake of oatmeal.

oat+en ('əʊtᵊn) *adj.* made of oats or oat straw.

Oates (əʊts) *n.* **Ti·tus** ('taɪtəs). 1649–1705, English conspirator. He fabricated the Popish Plot (1678), a supposed Catholic conspiracy to kill Charles II, burn London, and massacre Protestants. His perjury caused the execution of many innocent Catholics.

oat grass *n.* any of various oatlike grasses, esp. of the genera *Arrhenatherum* and *Danthonia,* of Eurasia and N. Africa.

oath (əʊθ) *n., pl.* **oaths** (əʊðz). **1.** a solemn pronouncement to affirm the truth of a statement or to pledge a person to some course of action, often involving a sacred being or object as witness. **2.** the form of such a pronouncement. **3.** an irreverent or blasphemous expression, esp. one involving the name of a deity; curse. **4. on, upon,** *or* **under oath. a.** under the obligation of an oath. **b.** *Law.* having sworn to tell the truth, usually with one's hand on the Bible. **5. take an oath.** to declare formally with an oath or pledge, esp. before giving evidence. [Old English *āth;* related to Old Saxon, Old Frisian *ēth,* Old High German *eid*]

oat+meal ('əʊt,miːl) *n.* **1.** meal ground from oats, used for making porridge, oatcakes, etc. **2. a.** a greyish-yellow colour. **b.** (*as adj.*): *an oatmeal coat.*

O.A.U. *abbrev. for* Organization of African Unity; an association of African states, established in 1963 to fight colonialism and promote unity among African nations.

Oa·xa+ca (wə'hɑːkɜː; *Spanish* oa'xaka) *n.* **1.** a state of S Mexico, on the Pacific: includes most of the Isthmus of Tehuantepec; inhabited chiefly by Indians. Capital: Oaxaca de Juárez. Pop.: 2 171 733 (1970). Area: 95 363 sq. km (36 820 sq. miles). **2.** a city in S Mexico, capital of Oaxaca state: founded in 1486 by the Aztecs and conquered by Spain in 1521. Pop.: 118 810 (1975 est.). Official name: **Oa·xa+ca de Juá·rez** (ðe 'xwares).

Ob (*Russian* ɔpj) *n.* a river in the N central Soviet Union, formed at Bisk by the confluence of the Biya and Katun Rivers and flowing generally north to the **Gulf of Ob** (an inlet of the Arctic Ocean): one of the largest rivers in the world, with a drainage basin of about 2 930 000 sq. km (1 131 000 sq. miles). Length: 3682 km (2287 miles).

ob. *abbrev. for:* **1.** (on tombstones, etc.) obiit. [Latin: he (or she) died] **2.** obiter. [Latin: incidentally; in passing] **3.** oboe.

ob- *prefix.* inverse or inversely: *obovate.* [from Old French, from Latin *ob.* In compound words of Latin origin, *ob-* (and *oc-, of-, op-*) indicates: to, towards (*object*); against (*oppose*); away from (*obsolete*); before (*obstetric*); down, over (*obtect*); for the sake of (*obsecrate*); and is used as an intensifier (*oblong*)]

O.B. *Brit. abbrev. for:* **1.** Old Boy. **2.** outside broadcast.

o·ba ('ɔːbɑː, -bə) *n.* (in W Africa) a Yoruba chief or ruler.

Obad. *Bible. abbrev. for* Obadiah.

O·ba·di·ah (,əʊbə'daɪə) *n. Old Testament.* **1.** a Hebrew prophet. **2.** the book containing his oracles, chiefly directed against Edom. Douay spelling: **Ab·di·as** (æb'daɪəs).

O·ban ('əʊbᵊn) *n.* a small port and resort in W Scotland, in NW Strathclyde on the Firth of Lorn. Pop.: 6910 (1971).

O·ba·san·jo (əʊ,basan'dʒəʊ) *n.* **O·lu·se·gun** (əʊ,luːsɛ'gʊn). born 1937, Nigerian general and statesman; head of state since 1976.

obb. *abbrev. for* obbligato.

ob+bli·ga+to *or* **ob+li·ga+to** (,ɒblɪ'gɑːtəʊ) *Music.* ~*adj.* **1.** not to be omitted in performance. ~*n., pl.* **+tos** *or* **+ti** (-tiː). **2.** an essential part in a score: *with oboe obbligato.* ~See **ad lib.** [C18: from Italian, from *obbligare* to OBLIGE]

ob+con+ic (ɒb'kɒnɪk) *adj. Botany.* (of a fruit or similar part) shaped like a cone and attached at the pointed end.

ob+cor+date (ɒb'kɔːdeɪt) *adj. Botany.* heart-shaped and attached at the pointed end: *obcordate leaves.*

obdt. *abbrev. for* obedient.

ob+du+rate ('ɒbdjʊrɪt) *adj.* **1.** not easily moved by feelings or supplication; hard-hearted. **2.** impervious to persuasion, esp. to moral persuasion. [C15: from Latin *obdūrāre* to make hard, from *ob-* (intensive) + *dūrus* hard; compare ENDURE] —**'ob+du+ra+cy** *or* **'ob+du+rate+ness** *n.* —**'ob+du+rate+ly** *adv.*

O.B.E. *abbrev. for* Officer of the Order of the British Empire (a Brit. title).

o·beah ('əʊbɪə) *n.* another word for **obi**[2].

o·be·di+ence (ə'biːdɪəns) *n.* **1.** the condition or quality of being obedient. **2.** the act or an instance of obeying; dutiful or submissive behaviour. **3.** the authority vested in a Church or similar body. **4.** the collective group of persons submitting to this authority. See also: **passive obedience.**

o·be·di+ent (əˈbiːdɪənt) *adj.* obeying or willing to obey. [C13: from Old French, from Latin *oboediens,* present participle of *oboedīre* to OBEY] —**o'be·di+ent+ly** *adv.*

o·be·di+en·tia+ry (əʊˌbiːdɪˈɛnʃərɪ) *n., pl.* **+ries.** *Christianity.* the holder of any monastic office under the superior. [C18: from Medieval Latin *obedientiarius;* see OBEDIENT, -ARY]

o·bei+sance (əʊˈbeɪsəns, əʊˈbiː-) *n.* **1.** an attitude of deference or homage. **2.** a gesture expressing obeisance. [C14: from Old French *obéissant,* present participle of *obéir* to OBEY] —**o'bei+sant** *adj.* —**o'bei+sant+ly** *adv.*

ob+e·lisk (ˈɒbɪlɪsk) *n.* **1.** a stone pillar having a square or rectangular cross section and sides that taper towards a pyramidal top, often used as a monument in ancient Egypt. **2.** *Printing.* another name for **dagger** (sense 2). [C16: via Latin from Greek *obeliskos* a little spit, from *obelos* spit] —ˌ**ob+e'lis+cal** *adj.* —ˌ**ob+e'lis+koid** *adj.*

ob+e·lize *or* **ob+e·lise** (ˈɒbɪˌlaɪz) *vb.* (*tr.*) to mark (a word or passage) with an obelus. [C17: from Greek *obelizein*]

ob+e·lus (ˈɒbɪləs) *n., pl.* **·li** (-ˌlaɪ). **1.** a mark (— or ÷) used in editions of ancient documents to indicate spurious words or passages. **2.** another name for **dagger** (sense 2). [C14: via Late Latin from Greek *obelos* spit]

O·ber+am·mer+gau (*German* ˌoːbərˈamərgaʊ) *n.* a village in S West Germany, in Bavaria in the foothills of the Alps: famous for its Passion Play, performed by the villagers every ten years (except during the World Wars) since 1634, in thanksgiving for the end of the Black Death.

O·ber+hau+sen (*German* ˈoːbərˌhauzᵊn) *n.* an industrial city in W West Germany, in North Rhine-Westphalia on the Rhine-Herne Canal: site of the first ironworks in the Ruhr. Pop.: 240 702 (1974 est.).

O·ber+land (ˈəʊbəˌlænd) *n.* the lower parts of the Bernese Alps in central Switzerland, mostly in S Bern canton.

O·ber·on[1] (ˈəʊbəˌrɒn) *n.* (in medieval folklore) the king of the fairies, husband of Titania.

O·ber+on[2] (ˈəʊbəˌrɒn) *n.* the second largest of the five satellites of Uranus and the furthest from the planet.

O·ber+ö·ster+reich (ˈoːbərˌøːstəraɪç) *n.* the German name for **Upper Austria.**

o·bese (əʊˈbiːs) *adj.* excessively fat or fleshy; corpulent. [C17: from Latin *obēsus,* from *ob-* (intensive) + *edere* to eat] —**o'be·si·ty** *or* **o'bese+ness** *n.*

o·bey (əˈbeɪ) *vb.* **1.** to carry out (instructions or orders); comply with (demands). **2.** to behave or act in accordance with (one's feelings, whims, etc.). [C13: from Old French *obéir,* from Latin *oboedīre,* from *ob-* to, towards + *audīre* to hear] —**o'bey+er** *n.*

ob+fus+cate (ˈɒbfʌsˌkeɪt) *vb.* (*tr.*) **1.** to obscure or darken. **2.** to perplex or bewilder. [C16: from Latin *ob-* (intensive) + *fuscāre* to blacken, from *fuscus* dark] —ˌ**ob+fus'ca+tion** *n.* —**ob+fus'ca·to·ry** *adj.*

o·bi[1] (ˈəʊbɪ) *n., pl.* **o·bis** *or* **o·bi.** a broad sash tied in a large flat bow at the back, worn by Japanese women and children as part of the national costume. [C19: from Japanese]

o·bi[2] (ˈəʊbɪ) *or* **o·be·ah** *n., pl.* **o·bis** *or* **o·be·ahs. 1.** a kind of witchcraft originating in Africa and practised by the Negroes of the West Indies. **2.** a charm or amulet used in this. [of West African origin; compare Edo *obi* poison] —**'o·bi+ism** *n.*

ob·it (ˈɒbɪt, ˈəʊbɪt) *n. Informal.* **1.** short for **obituary. 2.** a memorial service.

ob·i·ter dic+tum (ˈɒbɪtə ˈdɪktəm, ˈəʊ-) *n., pl.* **ob·i+ter dic+ta** (ˈdɪktə). **1.** *Law.* an observation by a judge on some point of law not directly in issue in the case before him and thus neither requiring his decision nor serving as a precedent, but nevertheless of persuasive authority. **2.** any comment, remark, or observation made in passing. [Latin: something said in passing]

o·bi+tu·ar·y (əˈbɪtjʊərɪ) *n., pl.* **+ar·ies.** a published announcement of a death, often accompanied by a short biography of the dead person. [C18: from Medieval Latin *obituārius,* from Latin *obīre* to fall, from *ob-* down + *īre* to go] —**o'bi+tu+ar+ist** *n.*

obj. *abbrev. for:* **1.** *Grammar.* object(ive). **2.** objection.

ob+ject[1] (ˈɒbdʒɪkt) *n.* **1.** a tangible and visible thing. **2.** a person or thing seen as a focus or target for feelings, thought, etc.: *an object of affection.* **3.** an aim, purpose, or objective. **4.** *Informal.* a ridiculous or pitiable person, spectacle, etc. **5.** *Philosophy.* that towards which cognition is directed, esp. the external world as opposed to the ego. **6.** *Grammar.* a noun, pronoun, or noun phrase whose referent is the recipient of the action of a verb. See also **direct object, indirect object. 7.** *Grammar.* a noun, pronoun, or noun phrase that is governed by a preposition. **8. no object.** not a hindrance or obstacle: *money is no object.* [C14: from Late Latin *objectus* something thrown before (the mind), from Latin *obicere;* see OBJECT[2]]

ob+ject[2] (əbˈdʒɛkt) *vb.* **1.** (*tr.; takes a clause as object*) to state as an objection: *he objected that his motives had been good.* **2.** (*intr.;* often foll. by *to*) to raise or state an objection (to); present an argument (against). [C15: from Latin *obicere,* from *ob-* against + *jacere* to throw]

ob+ject ball *n. Billiards, etc.* any ball except the cue ball, esp. one which the striker aims to hit with the cue ball.

ob+ject glass *n. Optics.* another name for **objective** (sense 10).

ob+jec+ti+fy (əbˈdʒɛktɪˌfaɪ) *vb.* **+fies, +fy+ing, +fied.** (*tr.*) to represent concretely; present as an object. —**ob+ˌjec+ti+fi'ca+tion** *n.*

ob+jec+tion (əbˈdʒɛkʃən) *n.* **1.** an expression, statement, or feeling of opposition or dislike. **2.** a cause for such an expression, statement, or feeling. **3.** the act of objecting.

ob+jec+tion+a·ble (əbˈdʒɛkʃənəbᵊl) *adj.* unpleasant, offensive, or repugnant. —**ob+ˌjec+tion+a'bil+i·ty** *or* **ob+'jec+tion+a·ble+ness** *n.* —**ob+'jec+tion+a·bly** *adv.*

ob+jec+tive (əbˈdʒɛktɪv) *adj.* **1.** existing independently of perception; being a material object as opposed to a concept, idea, etc. **2.** undistorted by emotion or personal bias. **3.** of or relating to actual and external phenomena as opposed to thoughts, feelings, etc. **4.** *Med.* (of disease symptoms) perceptible to persons other than the individual affected. **5.** *Grammar.* denoting a case of nouns and pronouns, esp. in languages having only two cases, that is used to identify the direct object of a finite verb or preposition and for various other purposes. In English the objective case of pronouns is also used in many elliptical constructions (as in *Poor me! Who, him?*), as the subject of a gerund (as in *It was me helping him*), informally as a predicate complement (as in *It's me*), and in nonstandard use as part of a compound subject (as in *John, Larry, and me went fishing*). See also **accusative. 6.** of, or relating to a goal or aim. ~*n.* **7.** the object of one's endeavours; goal; aim. **8.** an actual phenomenon; reality. **9.** *Grammar.* **a.** the objective case. **b.** a word or speech element in the objective case. **10.** Also called: **object glass.** *Optics.* **a.** the lens or combination of lenses nearest to the object in an optical instrument. **b.** the lens or combination of lenses forming the image in a camera or projector. ~Abbrev.: **obj.** Compare **subjective.** —**ob+jec+tiv+al** (ˌɒbdʒɛkˈtaɪvəl) *adj.* —**ob+'jec+tive+ly** *adv.* —**ob+'jec+tive+ness** *or* ˌ**ob+jec+'tiv+i·ty** *n.*

ob+jec+tive gen+i·tive *n. Grammar.* a use of the genitive case to express an objective relationship, as in Latin *timor mortis* (fear of death).

ob+jec+tive point *n. Military.* a place or position towards which forces are directed.

ob+jec+tiv+ism (əbˈdʒɛktɪˌvɪzəm) *n.* **1.** the tendency to stress what is objective. **2.** the philosophical doctrine that reality is objective, and that sense data correspond with it. —**ob+'jec+tiv+ist** *n.* —**ob+ˌjec+tiv+'is+tic** *adj.* —**ob+ˌjec+tiv+'is+ti+cal+ly** *adv.*

ob+ject lan+guage *n.* a language described by or being investigated by another language. Compare **metalanguage.**

ob+ject les+son *n.* a practical demonstration of some principle or ideal.

ob+ject pro+gram *n.* a computer program transcribed from the equivalent source program into machine language by the compiler or assembler.

ob+jet d'art *French.* (ɔbʒɛ ˈdaːr) *n., pl.* ***ob+jets d'art*** (ɔbʒɛ ˈdaːr). a small object considered to be of artistic worth. [French: object of art]

ob+jet trou+vé *French.* (ɔbʒɛ truˈve) *n., pl.* ***ob+jets trou+vés*** (ɔbʒɛ truˈve) any ordinary object considered from an aesthetic viewpoint. [C20: French: found object]

ob+jur+gate (ˈɒbdʒəˌgeɪt) *vb.* (*tr.*) to scold or reprimand. [C17: from Latin *objurgāre,* from *ob-* against + *jurgāre* to scold] —ˌ**ob+jur+'ga+tion** *n.* —**'ob+jur+ˌga+tor** *n.* —**ob+jur+ga+to+ry** (ɒbˈdʒɜːgətərɪ, -trɪ) *or* **ob+'jur+ga+tive** *adj.*

obl. *abbrev. for:* **1.** oblique. **2.** oblong.

ob+lan+ce·o·late (ɒbˈlɑːnsɪəlɪt, -ˌleɪt) *adj. Botany.* (esp. of leaves) having a broad rounded apex and a tapering base.

ob+last (ˈɒblɑːst) *n.* an administrative and territorial division in some republics of the Soviet Union. [from Russian, from Old Slavonic, *vlast* government]

ob+late[1] (ˈɒbleɪt) *adj.* having an equatorial diameter of greater length than the polar diameter: *the earth is an oblate sphere.* Compare **prolate.** [C18: from New Latin *oblātus* lengthened, from Latin *ob-* towards + *lātus,* past participle of *ferre* to bring] —**'ob+late+ly** *adv.*

ob+late[2] (ˈɒbleɪt) *n.* a person dedicated to a monastic or religious life. [C19: from French *oblat,* from Medieval Latin *oblātus,* from Latin *offerre* to OFFER]

ob+la+tion (ɒˈbleɪʃən) *n. Christianity.* **1.** the offering of the bread and wine of the Eucharist to God. **2.** any offering made for religious or charitable purposes. [C15: from Church Latin *oblātiō;* see OBLATE[2]] —**ob+la+to+ry** (ˈɒblətərɪ, -trɪ) *or* **ob+'la+tion+al** *adj.*

ob+li+gate (ˈɒblɪˌgeɪt) *vb.* **1.** to compel, constrain, or oblige morally or legally. **2.** (in the U.S.) to bind (property, funds, etc.) as security. ~*adj.* **3.** compelled, bound, or restricted. **4.** *Biology.* able to exist under only one set of environmental conditions: *an obligate parasite cannot live independently of its host.* Compare **facultative** (sense 3). [C16: from Latin *obligāre* to OBLIGE] —**'ob+li+ga·ble** *adj.* —**ob+'lig·a·tive** *adj.* —**'ob+li+ˌga+tor** *n.*

ob+li+ga+tion (ˌɒblɪˈgeɪʃən) *n.* **1.** a moral or legal requirement; duty. **2.** the act of obligating or the state of being obligated. **3.** *Law.* **a.** a legally enforceable agreement to perform some act, esp. to pay money, for the benefit of another party. **4.** *Law.* **a.** a written contract containing a penalty. **b.** an instrument acknowledging indebtedness to secure the repayment of money borrowed. **5.** a person or thing to which one is bound morally or legally. **6.** something owed in return for a service or favour. **7.** a service or favour for which one is indebted. —ˌ**ob+li+'ga+tion+al** *adj.*

ob+li+ga+to (ˌɒblɪˈgɑːtəʊ) *adj. Music.* a variant spelling of **obbligato.**

ob+lig·a·to·ry (ɒˈblɪgətərɪ, -trɪ) *adj.* **1.** required to be done, obtained, possessed, etc. **2.** of the nature of or constituting an obligation. —**ob+'lig·a·to+ri+ly** *adv.*

o·blige (əˈblaɪdʒ) *vb.* **1.** (*tr.; often passive*) to bind or constrain (someone to do something) by legal, moral, or physical means. **2.** (*tr.; usually passive*) to make indebted or grateful to (someone) by doing a favour or service: *we are obliged to you for dinner.* **3.** to do a service or favour to (someone): *she obliged the guest with a song.* [C13: from Old French *obliger*, from Latin *obligāre*, from *ob-* to, towards + *ligāre* to bind] —**o·'blig·er** *n.*

ob·li·gee (ˌɒblɪ'dʒiː) *n.* **1.** a person in whose favour an obligation, contract, or bond is created; creditor. **2.** a person who receives a bond.

o·blig·ing (ə'blaɪdʒɪŋ) *adj.* ready to do favours; agreeable; kindly. —**o·'blig·ing·ly** *adv.* —**o·'blig·ing·ness** *n.*

ob·li·gor (ˌɒblɪ'gɔː) *n.* **1.** a person who binds himself by contract to perform some obligation; debtor. **2.** a person who gives a bond.

o·blique (ə'bliːk) *adj.* **1.** at an angle; slanting; sloping. **2.** *Geom.* **a.** (of lines, planes, etc.) neither perpendicular nor parallel to one another or to another line, plane, etc. **b.** not related to or containing a right angle. **3.** indirect or evasive. **4.** *Grammar.* denoting any case of nouns, pronouns, etc., other than the nominative. **5.** *Biology.* having asymmetrical sides or planes: *an oblique leaf.* **6.** (of a map projection) constituting a type of zenithal projection in which the plane of projection is tangential to the earth's surface at some point between the equator and the poles. ~*n.* **7.** something oblique, esp. a line. **8.** another name for **solidus.** **9.** *Navigation.* the act of changing course by less than 90°. ~*vb.* (*intr.*) **10.** to take or have an oblique direction. **11.** (of a military formation) to move forward at an angle. [C15: from Old French, from Latin *oblīquus*, of obscure origin] —**o·'blique·ly** *adv.* —**o·'blique·ness** *n.*

o·blique an·gle *n.* an angle that is not a right angle or any multiple of a right angle.

o·blique nar·ra·tion *n.* another name for **indirect speech.** Also called: **oblique speech.**

o·blique sail·ing *n.* a ship's movement on a course that is not due north, south, east, or west.

o·bliq·ui·ty (ə'blɪkwɪtɪ) *n., pl.* **·ties.** **1.** the state or condition of being oblique. **2.** a deviation from the perpendicular or horizontal. **3.** a moral or mental deviation. **4.** Also called: **obliquity of the ecliptic.** *Astronomy.* the angle between the plane of the earth's orbit and that of the celestial equator, equal to approximately 23° 27′ at present. —**o·'bliq·ui·tous** *adj.*

o·blit·er·ate (ə'blɪtəˌreɪt) *vb.* (*tr.*) to destroy every trace of; wipe out completely. [C16: from Latin *oblitterāre* to erase, from *ob-* out + *littera* letter] —**o·ˌblit·e·'ra·tion** *n.* —**o·'blit·er·a·tive** *adj.* —**o·'blit·er·ˌa·tor** *n.*

o·bliv·i·on (ə'blɪvɪən) *n.* **1.** the condition of being forgotten or disregarded. **2.** the state of being mentally withdrawn or blank. **3.** *Law.* an intentional overlooking, esp. of political offences; amnesty; pardon. [C14: via Old French from Latin *oblīviō* forgetfulness, from *oblīviscī* to forget]

o·bliv·i·ous (ə'blɪvɪəs) *adj.* (usually foll. by *of*) unaware or forgetful. —**ob·'liv·i·ous·ly** *adv.* —**ob·'liv·i·ous·ness** *n.*

ob·long ('ɒbˌlɒŋ) *adj.* **1.** having an elongated, esp. rectangular, shape. ~*n.* **2.** a figure or object having this shape. [C15: from Latin *oblongus*, from *ob-* (intensive) + *longus* LONG[1]]

ob·lo·quy ('ɒbləkwɪ) *n., pl.* **·quies.** **1.** defamatory or censorious statements, esp. when directed against one person. **2.** disgrace brought about by public abuse. [C15: from Latin *obloquium* contradiction, from *ob-* against + *loquī* to speak]

ob·mu·tes·cence (ˌɒbmjuː'tɛsəns) *n.* *Archaic.* persistent silence. [C17: from Latin *obmūtescere* to become mute] —ˌ**ob·mu·'tes·cent** *adj.*

ob·nox·ious (əb'nɒkʃəs) *adj.* **1.** extremely unpleasant. **2.** *Obsolete.* exposed to harm, injury, etc. [C16: from Latin *obnoxius*, from *ob-* to + *noxa* injury, from *nocēre* to harm] —**ob·'nox·ious·ly** *adv.* —**ob·'nox·ious·ness** *n.*

ob·nu·bil·ate (ɒb'njuːbɪˌleɪt) *vb.* (*tr.*) *Literary.* to darken or obscure. [C16: ultimately from Latin *obnūbilāre* to cover with clouds, from *nubes* cloud]

o·boe ('əʊbəʊ) *n.* **1.** a woodwind instrument of the family that includes the bassoon and cor anglais, consisting of a conical tube fitted with a mouthpiece having a double reed. It has a penetrating nasal tone. Range: about two octaves plus a sixth upwards from B flat below middle C. **2.** a person who plays this instrument in an orchestra: *second oboe.* ~Archaic form: **hautboy.** [C18: via Italian *oboe*, phonetic approximation to French *haut bois*, literally: high wood (referring to its pitch)] —'**o·bo·ist** *n.*

o·boe da cac·cia (də 'kætʃə) *n.* an obsolete member of the oboe family; the predecessor of the cor anglais. [Italian: hunting oboe]

o·boe d'a·mo·re (dɑː'mɔːreɪ) *n.* a type of oboe pitched a minor third lower than the oboe itself. It is used chiefly in the performance of baroque music.

ob·o·lus ('ɒbələs) *or* **ob·ol** ('ɒbɒl) *n., pl.* **·li** (-ˌlaɪ) *or* **·ols.** **1.** a modern Greek unit of weight equal to one tenth of a gram. **2.** a silver coin of ancient Greece worth one sixth of a drachma. [C16: via Latin from Greek *obolos* small coin, nail; related to *obelos* spit, variant of OBELUS]

O·bo·te (ɒ'bəʊteɪ, -tɪ) *n.* **(Apollo) Mil·ton.** born 1924, Ugandan politician; prime minister of Uganda (1962-66) and president (1966-71); deposed by Amin; re-elected prime minister (1980).

ob·o·vate (ɒb'əʊveɪt) *adj.* (of a leaf or similar flat part) shaped like the longitudinal section of an egg with the narrower end at the base; inversely ovate.

ob·o·void (ɒb'əʊvɔɪd) *adj.* (of a fruit or similar solid part) egg-shaped with the narrower end at the base. Compare **ovoid** (sense 2).

ob·rep·tion (ɒ'brɛpʃən) *n.* the obtaining of something, such as a gift, by giving false information. Compare **subreption** (sense 1). [C17: from Latin *obreptio*, from *obrepere* to creep up to]

obs. *abbrev. for:* **1.** obscure. **2.** observation. **3.** Also: **Obs.** observatory. **4.** obsolete.

ob·scene (əb'siːn) *adj.* **1.** offensive or outrageous to accepted standards of decency or modesty. **2.** *Law.* (of publications, etc.) having a tendency to deprave or corrupt. **3.** disgusting; repellent: *an obscene massacre.* [C16: from Latin *obscēnus* inauspicious, perhaps related to *caenum* filth] —**ob·'scene·ly** *adv.*

ob·scen·i·ty (əb'sɛnɪtɪ) *n., pl.* **·ties.** **1.** the state or quality of being obscene. **2.** an obscene act, statement, work, etc.

ob·scur·ant (əb'skjʊərənt) *n.* **1.** an opposer of reform and enlightenment. ~*adj.* **2.** of or relating to an obscurant. **3.** causing obscurity. —ˌ**ob·scu·'rant·ism** *n.* —ˌ**ob·scu·'rant·ist** *n., adj.*

ob·scure (əb'skjʊə) *adj.* **1.** unclear or abstruse. **2.** indistinct, vague, or indefinite. **3.** inconspicuous or unimportant. **4.** hidden, secret, or remote. **5.** (of a vowel) reduced to or transformed into a neutral vowel (ə). **6.** gloomy, dark, clouded, or dim. ~*vb.* (*tr.*) **7.** to make unclear, vague, or hidden. **8.** to cover or cloud over. **9.** *Phonetics.* to pronounce (a vowel) with articulation that causes it to become a neutral sound represented by (ə). ~*n.* **10.** a rare word for **obscurity.** [C14: via Old French from Latin *obscūrus* dark] —**ob·scu·ra·tion** (ˌɒbskjʊ'reɪʃən) *n.* —**ob·'scure·ly** *adv.* —**ob·'scure·ness** *n.*

ob·scu·ri·ty (əb'skjʊərɪtɪ) *n., pl.* **·ties.** **1.** the state or quality of being obscure. **2.** an obscure person or thing.

ob·scur·um per ob·scur·i·us (əb'skjʊərəm pɜː əb'skjʊərɪəs) *n.* another term for **ignotum per ignotius.** [Latin: the obscure by the more obscure]

ob·se·crate ('ɒbsɪˌkreɪt) *vb.* (*tr.*) a rare word for **beseech.** [C16: from Latin *obsecrāre* to entreat (in the name of the gods), from *ob-* for the sake of + *sacrāre* to hold in reverence; see SACRED] —ˌ**ob·se·'cra·tion** *n.*

ob·se·quent ('ɒbsɪkwənt) *adj.* (of a river) flowing into a subsequent stream in the opposite direction to the original slope of the land. [C16 (in the obsolete sense: yielding): from Latin *obsequī*, from *sequī* to follow]

ob·se·quies ('ɒbsɪkwɪz) *pl. n., sing.* **·quy.** funeral rites. [C14: via Anglo-Norman from Medieval Latin *obsequiae* (influenced by Latin *exsequiae*), from *obsequium* compliance]

ob·se·qui·ous (əb'siːkwɪəs) *adj.* **1.** obedient or attentive in an ingratiating or servile manner. **2.** *Now rare.* submissive or compliant. [C15: from Latin *obsequiōsus* compliant, from *obsequium* compliance, from *obsequi* to follow, from *ob-* to + *sequi* to follow] —**ob·'se·qui·ous·ly** *adv.* —**ob·'se·qui·ous·ness** *n.*

ob·ser·vance (əb'zɜːvəns) *n.* **1.** recognition of or compliance with a law, custom, practice, etc. **2.** the act of such recognition. **3.** a ritual, ceremony, or practice, esp. of a religion. **4.** observation or attention. **5.** the degree of strictness of a religious order or community in following its rule. **6.** *Archaic.* respectful or deferential attention.

ob·ser·vant (əb'zɜːvənt) *adj.* **1.** paying close attention to detail; watchful or heedful. **2.** adhering strictly to rituals, ceremonies, laws, etc. —**ob·'ser·vant·ly** *adv.*

ob·ser·va·tion (ˌɒbzə'veɪʃən) *n.* **1.** the act of observing or the state of being observed. **2.** a comment or remark. **3.** detailed examination of phenomena prior to analysis, diagnosis, or interpretation: *the patient was under observation.* **4.** the facts learned from observing. **5.** an obsolete word for **observance.** **6.** *Navigation.* **a.** a sight taken with an instrument to determine the position of an observer relative to that of a given heavenly body. **b.** the data so taken. —ˌ**ob·ser·'va·tion·al** *adj.* —ˌ**ob·ser·'va·tion·al·ly** *adv.*

ob·ser·va·tion car *n.* a railway carriage fitted with large expanses of glass to provide a good view of the scenery.

ob·ser·va·tion post *n.* *Military.* a position from which observations can be made or from which fire can be directed.

ob·ser·va·to·ry (əb'zɜːvətərɪ, -trɪ) *n., pl.* **·ries.** **1.** an institution or building specially designed and equipped for observing meteorological and astronomical phenomena. **2.** any building or structure providing an extensive view of its surroundings.

ob·serve (əb'zɜːv) *vb.* **1.** (*tr.; may take a clause as object*) to see; perceive; notice: *we have observed that you steal.* **2.** (when *tr., may take a clause as object*) to watch (something) carefully; pay attention to (something). **3.** to make observations of (something), esp. scientific ones. **4.** (when *intr.*, usually foll. by *on* or *upon;* when *tr., may take a clause as object*) to make a comment or remark: *the speaker observed that times had changed.* **5.** (*tr.*) to abide by, keep, or follow (a custom, tradition, law, holiday, etc.). [C14: via Old French from Latin *observāre*, from *ob-* to + *servāre* to watch] —**ob·'serv·a·ble** *adj.* —**ob·'serv·a·ble·ness** *or* **ob·ˌserv·a·'bil·i·ty** *n.* —**ob·'serv·a·bly** *adv.*

ob·serv·er (əb'zɜːvə) *n.* **1.** a person or thing that observes. **2.** a person who attends a conference, etc., solely to note the proceedings. **3.** a person trained to identify aircraft, esp. a member of an aircrew.

ob·sess (əb'sɛs) *vb.* (*tr.*) to preoccupy completely; haunt. [C16: from Latin *obsessus* besieged, past participle of *obsidēre*, from *ob-* in front of + *sedēre* to sit] —**ob·'ses·sive** *adj.* —**ob·'ses·sive·ly** *adv.* —**ob·'ses·sive·ness** *n.*

ob·ses·sion (əb'sɛʃən) *n.* **1.** *Psychiatry.* a persistent idea or impulse that continually forces its way into consciousness, esp. one associated with anxiety and mental illness. **2.** a persistent preoccupation, idea, or feeling. **3.** the act of obsessing or the state of being obsessed. —**ob'ses·sion·al** *adj.* —**ob'ses·sion·al·ly** *adv.*

ob·sid·i·an (ɒb'sɪdɪən) *n.* a dark glassy volcanic rock formed by very rapid solidification of lava. [C17: from Latin *obsidiānus*, erroneous transcription of *obsiānus* (*lapis*) (stone of) *Obsius*, the name (in Pliny) of the discoverer of a stone resembling obsidian]

ob·so·lesce (ˌɒbsə'lɛs) *vb.* (*intr.*) to become obsolete.

ob·so·les·cent (ˌɒbsə'lɛsᵊnt) *adj.* becoming obsolete or out of date. [C18: from Latin *obsolescere;* see OBSOLETE] —ˌ**ob·so'les·cence** *n.* —ˌ**ob·so'les·cent·ly** *adv.*

ob·so·lete ('ɒbsəˌliːt, ˌɒbsə'liːt) *adj.* **1.** out of use or practice; not current. **2.** out of date; unfashionable or outmoded. **3.** *Biology.* (of parts, organs, etc.) vestigial; rudimentary. [C16: from Latin *obsolētus* worn out, past participle of *obsolēre* (unattested), from *ob-* opposite to + *solēre* to be used] —'**ob·so·ˌlete·ly** *adv.* —'**ob·so·ˌlete·ness** *n.*

ob·sta·cle ('ɒbstəkᵊl) *n.* **1.** a person or thing that opposes or hinders something. **2.** *Brit.* a fence or hedge used in show jumping. [C14: via Old French from Latin *obstāculum*, from *obstāre*, from *ob-* against + *stāre* to stand]

ob·sta·cle race *n.* a race in which competitors have to negotiate various obstacles.

obstet. *abbrev. for* obstetric(s).

ob·stet·ric (ɒb'stɛtrɪk) *or* **ob·stet·ri·cal** *adj.* of or relating to childbirth or obstetrics. [C18: via New Latin from Latin *obstetrīcius*, from *obstetrix* a midwife, literally: woman who stands opposite, from *obstāre* to stand against; see OBSTACLE] —**ob'stet·ri·cal·ly** *adv.*

ob·ste·tri·cian (ˌɒbstɛ'trɪʃən) *n.* a physician who specializes in obstetrics.

ob·stet·rics (ɒb'stɛtrɪks) *n.* (*functioning as sing.*) the branch of medicine concerned with childbirth and the treatment of women before and after childbirth.

ob·sti·na·cy ('ɒbstɪnəsɪ) *n., pl.* **-cies. 1.** the state or quality of being obstinate. **2.** an obstinate act, attitude, etc.

ob·sti·nate ('ɒbstɪnɪt) *adj.* **1.** adhering fixedly to a particular opinion, attitude, course of action, etc. **2.** self-willed or headstrong. **3.** difficult to subdue or alleviate; persistent: *an obstinate fever.* [C14: from Latin *obstinātus*, past participle of *obstināre* to persist in, from *ob-* (intensive) + *stin-*, variant of *stare* to stand] —'**ob·sti·nate·ly** *adv.*

ob·sti·pa·tion (ˌɒbstɪ'peɪʃən) *n. Pathol.* a severe form of constipation, usually resulting from obstruction of the intestinal tract. [C16: from Latin *obstīpātiō*, from *ob-* (intensive) + *stīpāre* to press together]

ob·strep·er·ous (əb'strɛpərəs) *adj.* noisy or rough, esp. in resisting restraint or control. [C16: from Latin, from *obstrepere*, from *ob-* against + *strepere* to roar] —**ob'strep·er·ous·ly** *adv.* —**ob'strep·er·ous·ness** *n.*

ob·struct (əb'strʌkt) *vb.* (*tr.*) **1.** to block (a road, passageway, etc.) with an obstacle. **2.** to make (progress or activity) difficult. **3.** to impede or block a clear view of. [C17: from Latin: built against, past participle of *obstruere*, from *ob-* against + *struere* to build] —**ob'struct·er** *or* **ob'struc·tor** *n.* —**ob'struc·tive** *adj., n.* —**ob'struc·tive·ly** *adv.* —**ob'struc·tive·ness** *n.*

ob·struc·tion (əb'strʌkʃən) *n.* **1.** a person or thing that obstructs. **2.** the act or an instance of obstructing. **3.** delay of business, esp. in a legislature by means of procedural devices. **4.** *Sport.* the act of unfairly impeding an opposing player. **5.** the state or condition of being obstructed. —**ob'struc·tion·al** *adj.* —**ob'struc·tion·al·ly** *adv.*

ob·struc·tion·ist (əb'strʌkʃənɪst) *n.* a person who deliberately obstructs business, etc., esp. in a legislature. —**ob'struc·tion·ism** *n.*

ob·stru·ent ('ɒbstruənt) *Med.* ~*adj.* **1.** causing obstruction, esp. of the intestinal tract. ~*n.* **2.** anything that causes obstruction. [C17: from Latin *obstruere* to OBSTRUCT]

ob·tain (əb'teɪn) *vb.* **1.** (*tr.*) to gain possession of; acquire; get. **2.** (*intr.*) to be customary, valid, or accepted: *a new law obtains in this case.* **3.** (*tr.*) *Archaic.* to arrive at. **4.** (*intr.*) *Archaic.* to win a victory; succeed. [C15: via Old French from Latin *obtinēre* to take hold of, from *ob-* (intensive) + *tenēre* to hold] —**ob'tain·a·ble** *adj.* —**obˌtain·a'bil·i·ty** *n.* —**ob'tain·er** *n.* —**ob'tain·ment** *n.*

ob·tain·ing by de·cep·tion *n. Law.* the offence of dishonestly obtaining the property of another by some deception or misrepresentation of facts.

ob·tect (ɒb'tɛkt) *adj.* (of a pupa) encased in a hardened secretion so that the wings, legs, etc., are held immovably to the body, as in butterflies. Also: **obtected.** [C19: from Latin *obtectus* covered, past participle of *obtegere*, from *ob-* (intensive) + *tegere* to cover]

ob·test (ɒb'tɛst) *vb. Rare.* **1.** (*tr.; may take a clause as object or an infinitive*) to beg (someone) earnestly. **2.** (when *tr.*, *takes a clause as object;* when *intr.*, may be foll. by *with* or *against*) to object; protest. **3.** (*tr.*) to call (a supernatural power) to witness. [C16: from Latin *obtestārī* to protest, from *ob-* to + *testārī* to bear or call as witness] —ˌ**ob·tes'ta·tion** *n.*

ob·trude (əb'truːd) *vb.* **1.** to push (oneself, one's opinions, etc.) on others in an unwelcome way. **2.** (*tr.*) to push out or forward. [C16: from Latin *obtrūdere*, from *ob-* against + *trūdere* to push forward] —**ob'trud·er** *n.* —**ob·tru·sion** (əb'truːʒən) *n.*

ob·tru·sive (əb'truːsɪv) *adj.* **1.** obtruding or tending to obtrude. **2.** sticking out; protruding; noticeable. —**ob'tru·sive·ly** *adv.* —**ob'tru·sive·ness** *n.*

ob·tund (ɒb'tʌnd) *vb.* (*tr.*) *Rare.* to deaden or dull. [C14: from Latin *obtundere* to beat against, from *ob-* against + *tundere* to belabour] —**ob'tund·ent** *adj., n.*

ob·tu·rate ('ɒbtjʊəˌreɪt) *vb.* (*tr.*) to stop up (an opening, esp. the breech of a gun). [C17: from Latin *obtūrāre* to block up, of obscure origin] —ˌ**ob·tu'ra·tion** *n.* —'**ob·tu·ˌra·tor** *n.*

ob·tuse (əb'tjuːs) *adj.* **1.** mentally slow or emotionally insensitive. **2.** *Maths.* **a.** (of an angle) lying between 90° and 180°. **b.** (of a triangle) having one interior angle greater than 90°. **3.** not sharp or pointed. **4.** indistinctly felt, heard, etc.; dull: *obtuse pain.* **5.** (of a leaf or similar flat part) having a rounded or blunt tip. [C16: from Latin *obtūsus* dulled, past participle of *obtundere* to beat down; see OBTUND] —**ob'tuse·ly** *adv.* —**ob'tuse·ness** *n.*

ob·verse ('ɒbvɜːs) *adj.* **1.** facing or turned towards the observer. **2.** forming or serving as a counterpart. **3.** (of certain plant leaves) narrower at the base than at the top. ~*n.* **4.** a counterpart or complement. **5.** *Logic.* a proposition inferred from another by replacing the original subject and predicate by their contradictions, as with *no sum is incorrect* inferred from *every sum is correct.* **6.** the side of a coin that bears the main design or device. Compare **reverse** (sense 15). [C17: from Latin *obversus* turned towards, past participle of *obvertere*, from *ob-* to + *vertere* to turn] —**ob'verse·ly** *adv.*

ob·vert (ɒb'vɜːt) *vb.* (*tr.*) **1.** *Logic.* to deduce the obverse of (a proposition). **2.** *Rare.* to turn so as to show the main or other side. [C17: from Latin *obvertere* to turn towards; see OBVERSE] —**ob'ver·sion** *n.*

ob·vi·ate ('ɒbvɪˌeɪt) *vb.* (*tr.*) to do away with or counter. [C16: from Late Latin *obviātus* prevented, past participle of *obviāre;* see OBVIOUS] —ˌ**ob·vi'a·tion** *n.*

ob·vi·ous ('ɒbvɪəs) *adj.* **1.** easy to see or understand; evident. **2.** exhibiting motives, feelings, intentions, etc., clearly or without subtlety. **3.** naive or unsubtle: *the play was rather obvious.* **4.** *Obsolete.* being or standing in the way. [C16: from Latin *obvius*, from *obviam* in the way, from *ob-* against + *via* way] —'**ob·vi·ous·ly** *adv.* —'**ob·vi·ous·ness** *n.*

ob·vo·lute ('ɒbvəˌluːt) *adj.* **1.** (of leaves or petals in the bud) folded so that the margins overlap each other. **2.** turned in or rolled. [C18: from Latin *obvolūtus* past participle of *obvolvere*, from *ob-* to, over + *volvere* to roll] —ˌ**ob·vo'lu·tion** *n.* —'**ob·vo·ˌlu·tive** *adj.*

Oc. *abbrev. for* Ocean.

O.C. *abbrev. for* Officer Commanding.

o/c *abbrev. for* overcharge.

o·ca ('əʊkə) *n.* any of various South American herbaceous plants of the genus *Oxalis*, cultivated for their edible tubers: family *Oxalidaceae.* [C20: via Spanish from Quechua *okka*]

OCAM *abbrev. for* Organisation commune africaine et malgache: an association of the 14 principal Francophone states of Africa, established in 1965 to further political cooperation and economic and social development.

oc·a·ri·na (ˌɒkə'riːnə) *n.* an egg-shaped wind instrument with a protruding mouthpiece and six to eight finger holes, producing an almost pure tone. Also called (U.S. informal): **sweet potato.** [C19: from Italian: little goose, from *oca* goose, ultimately from Latin *avis* bird]

O'Ca·sey (əʊ'keɪsɪ) *n.* **Sean** (ʃɔːn). 1880–1964, Irish dramatist. His plays include *Juno and the Paycock* (1924) and *The Plough and the Stars* (1926), which are realistic pictures of Dublin slum life.

Oc·cam ('ɒkəm) *n.* a variant spelling of (William of) **Ockham.**

occas. *abbrev. for* occasional(ly).

oc·ca·sion (ə'keɪʒən) *n.* **1.** (sometimes foll. by *of*) the time of a particular happening or event. **2.** (sometimes foll. by *for*) a reason or cause (to do or be something); grounds: *there was no occasion to complain.* **3.** an opportunity (to do something); chance. **4.** a special event, time, or celebration: *the party was quite an occasion.* **5. on occasion.** every so often. **6. rise to the occasion.** to have the courage, wit, etc., to meet the special demands of a situation. **7. take occasion.** to avail oneself of an opportunity (to do something). ~*vb.* **8.** (*tr.*) to bring about, esp. incidentally or by chance. [C14: from Latin *occāsiō* a falling down, from *occidere*, from *ob-* down + *cadere* to fall]

oc·ca·sion·al (ə'keɪʒənᵊl) *adj.* **1.** taking place from time to time; not frequent or regular. **2.** of, for, or happening on special occasions. **3.** serving as an occasion (for something).

oc·ca·sion·al·ism (ə'keɪʒənəˌlɪzəm) *n.* the post-Cartesian theory that the seeming interconnection of mind and matter is effected by God.

oc·ca·sion·al li·cence *n. Brit.* a licence granted to sell alcohol only at specified times.

oc·ca·sion·al·ly (ə'keɪʒənəlɪ) *adv.* from time to time.

oc·ca·sion·al ta·ble *n.* a small table with no regular use.

oc·ca·sions (ə'keɪʒənz) *pl. n. Archaic.* **1.** (*sometimes sing.*) needs; necessities. **2.** personal or business affairs.

oc·ci·dent ('ɒksɪdənt) *n.* a literary or formal word for **west.** Compare **orient.** [C14: via Old French from Latin *occidere* to fall, go down]

Oc·ci·dent ('ɒksɪdənt) *n.* (usually preceded by *the*) **1.** the countries of Europe and America. **2.** the western hemisphere.

Oc·ci·den·tal (ˌɒksɪ'dɛntᵊl) (*sometimes not cap.*) ~*adj.* **1.** of or relating to the Occident. ~*n.* **2.** an inhabitant, esp. a native, of the Occident. —ˌ**Oc·ci'den·tal·ism** *n.* —ˌ**Oc·ci'den·tal·ist** *n., adj.* —ˌ**Oc·ci'den·tal·ly** *adv.*

Oc·ci·den·tal·ize *or* **Oc·ci·den·tal·ise** (ˌɒksɪ'dɛntəˌlaɪz) *vb.* (*tr.*) to make or become Occidental. —ˌ**Oc·ci·ˌden·tal·i'za·tion** *or* ˌ**Oc·ci·ˌden·tal·i'sa·tion** *n.*

oc·cip·i·tal (ɒk'sɪpɪtᵊl) *adj.* **1.** of or relating to the back of the head or skull. ~*n.* **2.** short for **occipital bone.**

oc+cip·i·tal bone *n.* the saucer-shaped bone that forms the back part of the skull and part of its base.

oc+cip·i·tal lobe *n.* the posterior portion of each cerebral hemisphere, concerned with the interpretation of visual sensory impulses.

oc+ci+put ('ɒksɪˌpʌt, -pət) *n., pl.* **oc+ci+puts** *or* **oc+cip·i·ta** (ɒk'sɪpɪtə). the back part of the head or skull. [C14: from Latin, from *ob-* at the back of + *caput* head]

oc+clude (ə'klu:d) *vb.* **1.** (*tr.*) to block or stop up (a passage or opening); obstruct. **2.** (*tr.*) to prevent the passage of. **3.** (*tr.*) *Chem.* (of a solid) to incorporate (a substance) by absorption or adsorption. **4.** *Meteorol.* to form or cause to form an occluded front. **5.** *Dentistry.* to produce or cause to produce occlusion, as in chewing. [C16: from Latin *occlūdere,* from *ob-* (intensive) + *claudere* to close] —**oc+'clud+ent** *adj.*

oc+clud+ed front *n. Meteorol.* the line or plane occurring where the cold front of a depression has overtaken the warm front, raising the warm sector from ground level. Also called: **occlusion.**

oc+clu+sion (ə'klu:ʒən) *n.* **1.** the act or process of occluding or the state of being occluded. **2.** *Meteorol.* another term for **occluded front. 3.** *Dentistry.* the normal position of the teeth when the jaws are closed. **4.** *Phonetics.* the complete closure of the vocal tract at some point, as in the closure prior to the articulation of a plosive. —**oc+'clu+sal** (ə'klu:səl) *adj.*

oc+clu+sive (ə'klu:sɪv) *adj.* **1.** of or relating to the act of occlusion. ~*n.* **2.** *Phonetics.* an occlusive speech sound. —**oc+'clu+sive+ness** *n.*

oc+cult *adj.* (ɒ'kʌlt, 'ɒkʌlt). **1. a.** of or characteristic of magical, mystical, or supernatural arts, phenomena, or influences. **b.** (*as n.*): *the occult.* **2.** beyond ordinary human understanding. **3.** secret or esoteric. ~*vb.* (ɒ'kʌlt). **4.** *Astronomy.* (of a celestial body) to hide (another celestial body) from view by occultation or (of a celestial body) to become hidden by occultation. **5.** to hide or become hidden or shut off from view. **6.** (*intr.*) (of lights, esp. in lighthouses) to shut off at regular intervals. [C16: from Latin *occultus,* past participle of *occulere,* from *ob-* over, up + *-culere,* related to *celāre* to conceal] —**oc+'cult+ly** *adv.* —**oc+'cult+ness** *n.*

oc+cul+ta+tion (ˌɒkʌl'teɪʃən) *n.* **1.** the temporary disappearance of one celestial body as it moves out of sight behind another body. **2.** the act of occulting or the state of being occulted.

oc+cult+ism ('ɒkʌlˌtɪzəm) *n.* belief in and the study and practice of magic, astrology, etc. —**'oc+cult+ist** *n., adj.*

oc+cu+pan+cy ('ɒkjʊpənsɪ) *n., pl.* **+cies. 1.** the act of occupying; possession of a property. **2.** *Law.* the possession and use of property by or without agreement and without any claim to ownership. **3.** *Law.* the act of taking possession of unowned property, esp. land, with the intent of thus acquiring ownership. **4.** the condition or fact of being an occupant, esp. a tenant. **5.** the period of time during which one is an occupant, esp. of property.

oc+cu+pant ('ɒkjʊpənt) *n.* **1.** a person, thing, etc., holding a position or place. **2.** *Law.* a person who has possession of something, esp. an estate, house, etc.; tenant. **3.** *Law.* a person who acquires by occupancy the title to something previously without an owner.

oc+cu+pa+tion (ˌɒkjʊ'peɪʃən) *n.* **1.** a person's regular work or profession; job or principal activity. **2.** any activity on which time is spent by a person. **3.** the act of occupying or the state of being occupied. **4.** the control of a country by a foreign military power. **5.** the period of time that a nation, place, or position is occupied. **6.** (*modifier*) for the use of the occupier of a particular property: *occupation road; occupation bridge.*

oc+cu+pa+tion+al (ˌɒkjʊ'peɪʃənᵊl) *adj.* of, relating to, or caused by an occupation: *occupational hazards.* —ˌ**oc+cu+'pa+tion+al+ly** *adv.*

oc+cu+pa+tion+al psy+chol+o+gy *n. Psychol.* the study of human behaviour at work, including ergonomics, selection procedures, and the effects of stress.

oc+cu+pa+tion+al ther+a+py *n. Med.* the therapeutic use of crafts, hobbies, etc., esp. in the rehabilitation of emotionally disturbed patients.

oc+cu+pa+tion fran+chise *n. Brit.* the right of a tenant to vote in national and local elections.

oc+cu+pi+er ('ɒkjʊˌpaɪə) *n.* **1.** *Brit.* a person who is in possession or occupation of a house or land. **2.** a person or thing that occupies.

oc+cu+py ('ɒkjʊˌpaɪ) *vb.* **+pies, +py+ing, +pied.** (*tr.*) **1.** to live or be established in (a house, flat, office, etc.). **2.** (*often passive*) to keep (a person) busy or engrossed; engage the attention of. **3.** (*often passive*) to take up (a certain amount of time or space). **4.** to take and hold possession of, esp. as a demonstration: *students occupied the college buildings.* **5.** to fill or hold (a position or rank). [C14: from Old French *occuper,* from Latin *occupāre* to seize hold of, from *ob-* (intensive) + *capere* to take]

oc+cur (ə'kɜ:) *vb.* **+curs, +cur+ring, +curred.** (*intr.*) **1.** to happen; take place; come about. **2.** to be found or be present; exist. **3.** (foll. by *to*) to be realized or thought of (by); suggest itself (to). [C16: from Latin *occurrere* to run up to, from *ob-* to + *currere* to run]

Usage. In careful English, *occur* and *happen* are not used of prearranged events: *the wedding took place* (not *occurred* or *happened*) *in the afternoon.*

oc+cur+rence (ə'kʌrəns) *n.* **1.** something that occurs; a happening; event. **2.** the act or an instance of occurring: *a crime of frequent occurrence.* —**oc+'cur+rent** *adj.*

o+cean ('əʊʃən) *n.* **1.** a very large stretch of sea, esp. one of the five oceans of the world, the Atlantic, Pacific, Indian, Arctic, and Antarctic. **2.** the body of salt water covering approximately 70 per cent of the earth's surface. **3.** a huge quantity or expanse: *an ocean of replies.* **4.** *Literary.* the sea. [C13: via Old French from Latin *ōceanus,* from Greek *ōkeanos* OCEANUS]

o+cean+ar+i+um (ˌəʊʃə'nɛərɪəm) *n., pl.* **+i+ums** *or* **·i·a** (-ɪə). a large salt-water aquarium for marine life.

o+cean-go+ing *adj.* (of a ship, boat, etc.) suited for travel on the open ocean.

o+cean grey+hound *n.* a fast ship, esp. a liner.

O+ce+an+i+a (ˌəʊʃɪ'ɑ:nɪə) *n.* the islands of the central and S Pacific, including Melanesia, Micronesia, and Polynesia: sometimes also including Australasia and the Malay Archipelago. —**O+ce+'an+i+an** *adj., n.*

o+ce+an+ic (ˌəʊʃɪ'ænɪk) *adj.* **1.** of or relating to the ocean. **2.** living in the depths of the ocean: *oceanic fauna.* **3.** huge or overwhelming. **4.** (of geological formations) of volcanic origin, arising from the ocean: *oceanic islands.*

O+ce+an+ic (ˌəʊʃɪ'ænɪk) *n.* **1.** a branch, group, or subfamily of the Malayo-Polynesian family of languages, comprising Polynesian and Melanesian. ~*adj.* **2.** of, relating to, or belonging to this group of languages. **3.** of or relating to Oceania.

O+ce+a+nid (əʊ'sɪənɪd) *n., pl.* **O+ce+a+nids** *or* **O+ce+an+i+des** (ˌəʊsɪ'ænɪˌdi:z). *Greek myth.* any of the ocean nymphs born of Oceanus and Tethys.

O+cean of Storms *n.* the largest of the dark plains (mare) on the surface of the moon, situated in the second and third quadrant. Also called: **Oceanus Procellarum.**

oceanog. *abbrev. for* oceanography.

o+cean+og+ra+phy (ˌəʊʃə'nɒgrəfɪ, ˌəʊʃɪə-) *n.* the branch of science dealing with the physical and biological features of the sea. —ˌ**o+cean+'og+ra+pher** *n.* —**o+cean+o+graph+ic** (ˌəʊʃənə'græfɪk, ˌəʊʃɪə-) *or* ˌ**o+cean+o+'graph+i+cal** *adj.* —ˌ**o+cean+o+'graph+i+cal+ly** *adv.*

o+cean+ol+o+gy (ˌəʊʃə'nɒlədʒɪ, ˌəʊʃɪə-) *n.* the study of the sea, esp. of its economic geography.

O+ce+a+nus (əʊ'sɪənəs) *n. Greek myth.* a Titan, divinity of the stream believed to flow around the earth.

o+cel+lus (ɒ'sɛləs) *n., pl.* **+li** (-laɪ). **1.** the simple eye of insects and some other invertebrates, consisting basically of light-sensitive cells. **2.** any eyelike marking in animals, such as the eyespot on the tail feather of a peacock. **3.** *Botany.* **a.** an enlarged discoloured cell in a leaf. **b.** a swelling on the sporangium of certain fungi. [C19: via New Latin from Latin: small eye, from *oculus* eye] —**o+'cel+lar** *adj.* —**oc+el+late** ('ɒsɪˌleɪt) *or* **oc+el+lated** ('ɒsɪˌleɪtɪd) *adj.* —ˌ**oc+el+'la+tion** *n.*

oc+e+lot ('ɒsɪˌlɒt, 'əʊ-) *n.* a feline mammal, *Felis pardalis,* inhabiting the forests of Central and South America and having a dark-spotted buff-brown coat. [C18: via French from Nahuatl *ocelotl* jaguar]

och (ɒx) *interj. Scot., Irish.* an expression of surprise, contempt, or disagreement.

o+cher ('əʊkə) *n., adj., vb.* the U.S. spelling of **ochre.** —**'o+cher+ous** *or* **'o+cher+y** *adj.* —**o+chroid** ('əʊkrɒɪd) *adj.*

och+loc+ra+cy (ɒk'lɒkrəsɪ) *n., pl.* **+cies.** rule by the mob; mobocracy. [C16: via French, from Greek *okhlokratia,* from *okhlos* mob] —**och+lo+crat** ('ɒkləˌkræt) *n.* —ˌ**och+lo+'crat+ic** *adj.*

och+lo+pho+bi+a (ˌɒklə'fəʊbɪə) *n. Psychol.* the fear of crowds. [C19: from New Latin, from Greek *okhlos* mob]

och+one (ɒ'xəʊn) *interj. Scot., Irish.* an expression of sorrow or regret. [from Gaelic *ochóin*]

o+chre *or U.S.* **o+cher** ('əʊkə) *n.* **1.** any of various natural earths containing ferric oxide, silica, and alumina: used as yellow or red pigments. **2. a.** a moderate yellow-orange to orange colour. **b.** (*as adj.*): *an ochre dress.* ~*vb.* **3.** (*tr.*) to colour with ochre. [C15: from Old French *ocre,* from Latin *ōchra,* from Greek *ōkhra,* from *ōkhros* pale yellow] —**o+chre+ous** ('əʊkrɪəs, 'əʊkərəs), **o+chrous** ('əʊkrəs), **o+chry** ('əʊkərɪ, 'əʊkrɪ) *or U.S.* **'o+cher+ous, 'o+cher+y** *adj.* —**o+chroid** ('əʊkrɔɪd) *adj.*

och+re+a ('ɒkrɪə) *n., pl.* **+re+ae** (-rɪˌi:). a variant spelling of **ocrea.**

-ock *suffix forming nouns.* indicating smallness: *hillock.* [Old English *-oc, -uc*]

Ock+e+ghem *or* **Ok+e+ghem** ('ɒkəˌgɛm; *Dutch* 'ɔkəxəm) *n.* **Jo+han+nes** (jo:'hɑnəs), **Jean d'** (ʒɑ̃ də), or **Jan van** (jɑn vɑn). ?1430–?95, Flemish composer. Also: **Ock+en+heim** ('ɒkənˌhaɪm).

ock+er ('ɒkə) *Austral. slang.* ~*n.* **1.** (*often cap.*) an uncultivated or boorish Australian. ~*adj., adv.* **2.** typical of such a person. [C20: of uncertain origin]

Ock+ham *or* **Oc+cam** ('ɒkəm) *n.* **Wil+liam of.** died ?1349, English nominalist philosopher, who contested the temporal power of the papacy and ended the conflict between nominalism and realism. See **Ockham's razor.**

Ock+ham's ra+zor *or* **Oc+cam's ra+zor** *n.* a maxim, attributed to William of Ockham, stating that in explaining something assumptions must not be needlessly multiplied.

o'clock (ə'klɒk) *adv.* **1.** used after a number from one to twelve to indicate the hour of the day or night. **2.** used after a number to indicate direction or position relative to the observer, twelve o'clock being directly ahead or overhead and other positions being obtained by comparisons with a clock face.

O'Con+nell (əʊ'kɒnᵊl) *n.* **Dan+iel.** 1775–1847, Irish nationalist leader and orator, whose election to the British House of Commons (1828) forced the acceptance of Catholic emancipation (1829).

O'Con+nor (əʊ'kɒnə) *n.* **1. Frank.** pen name of *Michael O'Donovan.* 1903–66, Irish short-story writer and critic. **2.**

Thom·as Pow·er, known as *Tay Pay.* 1848–1929, Irish journalist and nationalist leader.

o·co+til+lo (ˌəʊkə'ti:ljəʊ) *n., pl.* **+los.** a cactus-like tree, *Fouquieria splendens,* of Mexico and the southwestern U.S., with scarlet tubular flowers: used for hedges and candlewood: family *Fouquieriaceae.* [Mexican Spanish: diminutive of *ocote* pine, from Nahuatl *ocotl* torch]

OCR *abbrev. for* optical character reader *or* recognition.

oc+re·a *or* **och+re·a** ('ɒkrɪə) *n., pl.* **+re·ae** (-rɪˌi:). a cup-shaped structure that sheathes the stems of certain plants, formed from united stipules or leaf bases. [C19: from Latin: greave, legging, of obscure origin]

oc+re+ate ('ɒkrɪɪt, -ˌeɪt) *adj.* **1.** *Botany.* possessing an ocrea; sheathed. **2.** *Ornithol.* another word for **booted** (sense 2).

oct. *abbrev. for* octavo.

Oct. *abbrev. for* October.

oct- *combining form.* variant of **octo-** before a vowel.

oc·ta- *combining form.* variant of **octo-.**

oc+ta+chord ('ɒktəˌkɔ:d) *n.* **1.** an eight-stringed musical instrument. **2.** a series of eight notes, esp. a scale.

oc+tad ('ɒktæd) *n.* **1.** a group or series of eight. **2.** *Chem.* an element or group with a valency of eight. [C19: from Greek *oktas,* from *oktō* eight] **—oc+'tad+ic** *adj.*

oc+ta+gon ('ɒktəˌgən) *or* **oc+tan+gle** *n.* a polygon having eight sides. [C17: via Latin from Greek *oktagōnos,* having eight angles]

oc+tag·o·nal (ɒk'tægənᵊl) *adj.* **1.** having eight sides and eight angles. **2.** of or relating to an octagon. **—oc+'tag·o·nal+ly** *adv.*

oc+ta+he+dral (ˌɒktə'hi:drəl) *adj.* **1.** having eight plane surfaces. **2.** shaped like an octahedron.

oc+ta+he+drite (ˌɒktə'hi:draɪt) *n.* another name for **anatase.**

oc+ta+he+dron (ˌɒktə'hi:drən) *n., pl.* **+drons** *or* **+dra** (-drə). a solid figure having eight plane faces.

oc+tal no+ta+tion *or* **oc+tal** ('ɒktəl) *n.* a number system having a base 8: often used in computing, one octal digit being equivalent to a group of three bits.

oc+tam+er+ous (ɒk'tæmərəs) *adj.* consisting of eight parts, esp. (of flowers) having the parts arranged in groups of eight.

oc+tam+e·ter (ɒk'tæmɪtə) *n. Prosody.* a verse line consisting of eight metrical feet.

oc+tane ('ɒkteɪn) *n.* a liquid alkane hydrocarbon found in petroleum and existing in 18 isomeric forms, esp. the isomer *n*-octane. Formula: C_8H_{18}. See also **isooctane.**

oc+tane+di·o+ic ac·id (ˌɒkteɪndaɪ'əʊɪk) *n.* a colourless crystalline dicarboxylic acid found in suberin and castor oil and used in the manufacture of synthetic resins. Formula: HOOC-$(CH_2)_6$COOH. Also called: **suberic acid.** [C20: from OCTANE + DIOL]

oc+tane num+ber *or* **rat+ing** *n.* a measure of the quality of a petrol expressed as the percentage of isooctane in a mixture of isooctane and *n*-heptane that gives a fuel with the same antiknock qualities as the given petrol.

oc+tan+gle ('ɒktæŋgᵊl) *n.* another name for **octagon.**

oc+tan+gu+lar (ɒk'tæŋgjʊlə) *adj.* having eight angles.

Oc+tans ('ɒktænz) *n., Latin genitive* **Oc+tan+tis** (ɒk'tæntɪs). a faint constellation in the S hemisphere in which the S celestial pole is situated.

oc+tant ('ɒktənt) *n.* **1.** *Maths.* **a.** any of the eight parts into which the three planes containing the Cartesian coordinate axes divide space. **b.** an eighth part of a circle. **2.** *Astronomy.* the position of a celestial body when it is at an angular distance of 45° from another body. **3.** an instrument used for measuring angles, similar to a sextant but having a graduated arc of 45°. [C17: from Latin *octans* half quadrant, from *octo* eight]

oc+tar+chy ('ɒktɑ:kɪ) *n., pl.* **+chies. 1.** government by eight rulers. **2.** a confederacy of eight kingdoms, tribes, etc.

oc+ta+roon (ˌɒktə'ru:n) *n.* a variant spelling of **octoroon.**

oc+ta+va+lent (ˌɒktə'veɪlənt) *adj. Chem.* having a valency of eight.

oc+tave ('ɒktɪv) *n.* **1. a.** the interval between two musical notes one of which has twice the pitch of the other and lies eight notes away from it counting inclusively along the diatonic scale. **b.** one of these two notes, esp. the one of higher pitch. **c.** (*as modifier*): *an octave leap.* See also **perfect** (sense 9), **diminished** (sense 2), **interval** (sense 5). **2.** *Prosody.* a rhythmic group of eight lines of verse. **3.** ('ɒkteɪv). **a.** a feast day and the seven days following. **b.** the final day of this period. **4.** the eighth of eight basic positions in fencing. **5.** any set or series of eight. *~adj.* **6.** consisting of eight parts. [C14 (originally: eighth day) via Old French from Medieval Latin *octāva diēs* eighth day (after a festival), from Latin *octo* eight]

oc+tave coup+ler *n.* a mechanism on an organ that enables keys or pedals an octave apart to be played simultaneously.

Oc·ta·vi·a (ɒk'teɪvɪə) *n.* died 11 B.C., wife of Mark Antony; sister of Augustus.

Oc·ta·vi·an (ɒk'teɪvɪən) *n.* the name of **Augustus** before he became emperor (27 B.C.).

oc+ta+vo (ɒk'teɪvəʊ) *n., pl.* **+vos. 1.** Also called: **eightvo.** a book size resulting from folding a sheet of paper of a specified size to form eight leaves: *demi-octavo.* Often written: **8vo, 8°. 2.** a book of this size. [C16: from New Latin phrase *in octavo* in an eighth (of a whole sheet)]

oc+ten+ni·al (ɒk'tɛnɪəl) *adj.* **1.** occurring every eight years. **2.** lasting for eight years. [C17: from Latin *octennium* eight years, from *octo* eight + *annus* year] **—oc+'ten+ni·al·ly** *adv.*

oc+tet (ɒk'tɛt) *n.* **1.** any group of eight, esp. eight singers or musicians. **2.** a piece of music composed for such a group. **3.** *Prosody.* another word for **octave** (sense 2). **4.** *Chem.* a group of eight electrons forming a stable shell in an atom. *~*Also (for senses 1, 2, 3): **octette.** [C19: from Latin *octo* eight, on the model of DUET]

oc+til+lion (ɒk'tɪljən) *n.* **1.** (in Britain and Germany) the number represented as one followed by 48 zeros (10^{48}). **2.** (in the U.S. and France) the number represented as one followed by 27 zeros (10^{27}). [C17: from French, on the model of MILLION] **—oc+'til+lionth** *adj.*

oc·to-, oc·ta-, *or before a vowel* **oct-** *combining form.* eight: *octosyllabic; octagon.* [from Latin *octo,* Greek *oktō*]

Oc+to+ber (ɒk'təʊbə) *n.* the tenth month of the year, consisting of 31 days. [Old English, from Latin, from *octo* eight, since it was the eighth month in Roman reckoning]

Oc+to+ber Rev·o+lu+tion *n.* another name for the **Russian Revolution** (sense 2).

Oc+to+brist (ɒk'təʊbrɪst) *n.* a member of a Russian political party favouring the constitutional reforms granted in a manifesto issued by Nicholas II in Oct. 1905.

oc+to+cen+te+nar·y (ˌɒktəʊsɛn'ti:nərɪ) *n., pl.* **+nar·ies.** an eight-hundredth anniversary.

oc+to+dec·i+mo (ˌɒktəʊ'dɛsɪməʊ) *n., pl.* **+mos.** *Bookbinding.* another word for **eighteenmo.** [C18: from New Latin phrase *in octodecimo* in an eighteenth (of a whole sheet)]

oc+to+ge·nar+i·an (ˌɒktəʊdʒɪ'nɛərɪən) *or* **oc+tog+e·nar·y** (ɒk'tɒdʒɪnərɪ) *n., pl.* **·nar·i·ans** *or* **·nar·ies. 1.** a person who is between 80 and 90 years old. *~adj.* **2.** of or relating to an octogenarian. [C19: from Latin *octōgēnārius* containing eighty, from *octōgēnī* eighty each]

oc+to+nar·y ('ɒktənərɪ) *Rare.* *~adj.* **1.** relating to or based on the number eight. *~n., pl.* **+nar·ies. 2.** *Prosody.* a stanza of eight lines. **3.** a group of eight. [C16: from Latin *octōnārius,* from *octōnī* eight at a time]

oc+to+pod ('ɒktəˌpɒd) *n.* **1.** any cephalopod mollusc of the order *Octopoda,* including octopuses and the paper nautilus, having eight tentacles, and lacking an internal shell. *~adj.* **2.** of, relating to, or belonging to the *Octopoda.*

oc+to+pus ('ɒktəpəs) *n., pl.* **+pus·es. 1.** any cephalopod mollusc of the genera *Octopus, Eledone,* etc., having a soft oval body with eight long suckered tentacles and occurring at the sea bottom: order *Octopoda* (octopods). **2.** a powerful influential organization, etc., with far-reaching effects, esp. harmful ones. **3.** another name for **spider** (sense 8). [C18: via New Latin from Greek *oktōpous* having eight feet]

oc+to+roon (ˌɒktə'ru:n) *n.* a person having one quadroon and one white parent and therefore having one-eighth Negro blood. Compare **quadroon.** [C19: OCTO- + *-roon* as in QUADROON]

oc+to+syl+la+ble ('ɒktəˌsɪləbᵊl) *n.* **1.** a line of verse composed of eight syllables. **2.** a word of eight syllables. **—oc+to+syl+lab+ic** (ˌɒktəʊsɪ'læbɪk) *adj.*

oc+troi ('ɒktrwɑ:) *n.* **1.** a duty on various goods brought into certain towns or cities. **2.** the place where such a duty is collected. **3.** the officers responsible for its collection. [C17: from French *octroyer* to concede, from Medieval Latin *auctorizāre* to AUTHORIZE]

OCTU ('ɒktu:) *n. Brit. acronym for* Officer Cadets Training Unit.

oc+tu+ple ('ɒktjʊpᵊl) *n.* **1.** a quantity or number eight times as great as another. *~adj.* **2.** eight times as much or as many. **3.** consisting of eight parts. *~vb.* **4.** (*tr.*) to multiply by eight. [C17: from Latin *octuplus,* from *octo* eight + *-plus* as in *duplus* double]

oc·u+lar ('ɒkjʊlə) *adj.* **1.** of or relating to the eye. *~n.* **2.** another name for **eyepiece.** [C16: from Latin *oculāris* from *oculus* eye] **—'oc·u·lar+ly** *adv.*

oc·u+lar+ist ('ɒkjʊləˌrɪst) *n.* a person who makes artificial eyes.

oc·u+list ('ɒkjʊlɪst) *n. Med.* a former term for **ophthalmologist.** [C17: via French from Latin *oculus* eye]

oc·u·lo- *or sometimes before a vowel* **oc·ul-** *combining form.* indicating the eye: *oculomotor.* [from Latin *oculus*]

oc·u+lo+mo+tor (ˌɒkjʊləʊ'məʊtə) *adj.* relating to or causing eye movements. [C19: from Latin *oculus* eye + MOTOR]

oc·u+lo+mo+tor nerve *n.* the third cranial nerve, which supplies most of the eye muscles.

od (ɒd, əʊd), **od·yl,** *or* **od+yle** *n. Archaic.* a hypothetical force formerly thought to be responsible for many natural phenomena, such as magnetism, light, and hypnotism. [C19: coined arbitrarily by Baron Karl von Reichenbach (1788–1869), German scientist] **—'od·ic** *adj.*

Od, 'Od, *or* **Odd** (ɒd) *n. Euphemistic.* (used in mild oaths) an archaic word for **God.**

OD *abbrev. for* Old Dutch.

O.D. *abbrev. for:* **1.** Also: **o.d.** *Military.* olive drab. **2.** Officer of the Day. **3.** Also: **O/D** *Banking.* **a.** on demand. **b.** overdraft. **c.** overdrawn. **4.** outside diameter. **5.** ordnance datum.

o·da+lisque *or* **o·da+lisk** ('əʊdəlɪsk) *n.* a female slave or concubine. [C17: via French, changed from Turkish *ōdalik,* from *ōdah* room + *-lik* n. suffix]

odd (ɒd) *adj.* **1.** unusual or peculiar in appearance, character, etc. **2.** occasional, incidental, or random: *odd jobs.* **3.** leftover or additional: *odd bits of wool.* **4. a.** not divisible by two. **b.** represented or indicated by a number that is not divisible by two: *graphs are on odd pages.* Compare **even**[1] (sense 7). **5.** being part of a matched pair or set when the other or others are missing: *an odd sock; odd volumes.* **6.** (*in combination*). used to designate an indefinite quantity more than the quantity specified in round numbers: *fifty-odd pounds.* **7.** out-of-the-way or secluded. **8.** *Maths.* (of a function) changing sign but not absolute value when the sign of the independent variable is changed, as in $y = x^3$. Compare **even**[1] (sense 13). **9. odd man out.** a person or thing excluded from others forming a group, unit, etc. ~*n.* **10.** *Golf.* **a.** one stroke more than the score of one's opponent. **b.** an advantage or handicap of one stroke added to or taken away from a player's score. **11.** a thing or person that is odd in sequence or number. —**'odd·ly** *adv.* —**'odd·ness** *n.*

odd·ball ('ɒd,bɔːl) *U.S. informal.* ~*n.* **1.** a strange or eccentric person or thing. Brit. equivalent: **odd fish.** ~*adj.* **2.** strange or peculiar.

Odd·fel·low ('ɒd,fɛləʊ) *n.* a member of the **Independent Order of Oddfellows,** a secret benevolent and fraternal association founded in England in the 18th century.

odd·i·ty ('ɒdɪtɪ) *n., pl.* **·ties. 1.** an odd person or thing. **2.** an odd quality or characteristic. **3.** the condition of being odd.

odd-job·man *or* **odd-job·ber** *n.* a person who does casual work, esp. domestic repairs.

odd lot *n.* **1.** a batch of merchandise, etc., that contains less than or more than the usual number of units. **2.** *Stock Exchange.* a number of securities less than the standard trading unit of 100.

odd·ment ('ɒdmənt) *n.* **1.** (*often pl.*) an odd piece or thing; leftover. **2.** *Printing.* any individual part of a book, such as the preface, excluding the main text.

odd-pin·nate *adj.* (of a plant leaf) pinnate with a single leaflet at the apex.

odds (ɒdz) *pl. n.* **1.** (foll. by *on* or *against*) the probability, expressed as a ratio, that a certain event will take place: *the odds against the outsider are a hundred to one.* **2.** the amount, expressed as a ratio, by which the wager of one better is greater than that of another: *he was offering odds of five to one.* **3.** the likelihood that a certain state of affairs will be found to be so: *the odds are that he is drunk.* **4.** the chances or likelihood of success in a certain undertaking: *their odds were very poor after it rained.* **5.** an equalizing allowance, esp. one given to a weaker side in a contest. **6.** the advantage that one contender is judged to have over another: *the odds are on my team.* **7.** *Brit.* a significant difference (esp. in the phrase **it makes no odds**). **8. at odds.** on bad terms. **9. give** *or* **lay odds.** to offer a bet with favourable odds. **10. over the odds. a.** *Brit.* more than is expected, necessary, etc.: *he got two pounds over the odds for this job.* **b.** *Austral.* unfair or excessive. **11. take odds.** to accept such a bet. **12. what's the odds?** *Brit. informal.* what difference does it make?

odds and ends *pl. n.* miscellaneous items or articles.

odds and sods *pl. n. Brit.* miscellaneous people or things.

odds-on *adj.* **1.** (of a chance, horse, etc.) rated at even money or less to win. **2.** regarded as more or most likely to win, succeed, happen, etc.

ode (əʊd) *n.* **1.** a lyric poem, typically addressed to a particular subject, with lines of varying lengths and complex rhythms. See also **Horatian ode, Pindaric ode. 2.** (formerly) a poem meant to be sung. [C16: via French from Late Latin *ōda,* from Greek *ōidē,* from *aeidein* to sing]

-ode[1] *n. combining form.* denoting resemblance: *nematode.* [from Greek *-ōdēs,* from *eidos* shape, form]

-ode[2] *n. combining form.* denoting a path or way: *electrode.* [from Greek *-odos,* from *hodos* a way]

O·dels·ting ('əʊdᵊls,tɪŋ) *or* **O·dels·thing** *n.* the lower chamber of the Norwegian parliament. See also **Lagting, Storting.**

O·den·se (*Danish* 'oːðənsə) *n.* a port in S Denmark, on Fyn Island: cathedral founded by King Canute in the 11th century. Pop.: 168 178 (1974 est.).

O·der ('əʊdə) *n.* a river in central Europe, rising in N Czechoslovakia and flowing north and west, forming part of the border between East Germany and Poland to the Baltic. Length: 913 km (567 miles). Czech and Polish name: **Odra.**

O·der-Neis·se Line ('əʊdə 'naɪsə) *n.* the present-day boundary between Germany and Poland along the Rivers Oder and Neisse. Established in 1945, it originally separated the Soviet Zone of Germany from the regions of Germany under Polish administration.

O·des·sa (əʊ'dɛsə; *Russian* a'djɛsə) *n.* a port in the SW Soviet Union, in the S Ukrainian SSR on the Black Sea: the chief Russian grain port in the 19th century; university (1865); industrial centre and one of the largest ports in the Soviet Union. Pop.: 1 002 000 (1975 est.).

o·de·um ('əʊdɪəm) *n., pl.* **o·de·a** ('əʊdɪə). (esp. in ancient Greece and Rome) a building for musical performances. Also called: **odeon.** [C17: from Latin, from Greek *ōideion,* from *ōidē* ODE]

O·din ('əʊdɪn) *or* **O·thin** *n. Norse myth.* the supreme creator god; the divinity of wisdom, culture, war, and the dead. Germanic counterpart: **Wotan, Woden.**

o·di·ous ('əʊdɪəs) *adj.* offensive; repugnant. [C17: from Latin, related to *ōdī* I hate] —**'o·di·ous·ly** *adv.* —**'o·di·ous·ness** *n.*

o·di·um ('əʊdɪəm) *n.* **1.** the dislike accorded to a hated person or thing. **2.** hatred; repugnance. [C17: from Latin; related to *ōdī* I hate, Greek *odussasthai* to be angry]

O.D.M. *abbrev. for* Ministry of Overseas Development.

Od·o·a·cer (,ɒdəʊ'eɪsə) *or* **Od·o·va·car** (,əʊdəʊ'vɑːkə) *n.* ?434–493 A.D., barbarian ruler of Italy (476–493); assassinated by Theodoric.

o·dom·e·ter (ɒ'dɒmɪtə, əʊ-) *n.* the usual U.S. name for **mileometer.** [C18 *hodometer,* from Greek *hodos* way + METER] —**o·'dom·e·try** *n.*

O'Don·o·van (əʊ'dɒnəvᵊn) *n.* **Mi·chael.** the original name of (Frank) **O'Connor.**

-o·dont *adj. and n. combining form.* having teeth of a certain type; -toothed: *acrodont.* [from Greek *odōn* tooth]

od·on·tal·gi·a (,ɒdɒn'tældʒɪə) *n.* a technical name for **toothache.** —**,od·on·'tal·gic** *adj.*

o·don·to- *or before a vowel* **o·dont-** *combining form.* indicating a tooth or teeth: *odontology.* [from Greek *odōn* tooth]

o·don·to·blast (ɒ'dɒntə,blæst) *n.* any of a layer of cells lining the pulp cavity of a tooth and giving rise to the dentine. —**o·,don·to·'blas·tic** *adj.*

o·don·to·glos·sum (ɒ,dɒntə'glɒsəm) *n.* any epiphytic orchid of the tropical American genus *Odontoglossum,* having clusters of brightly coloured flowers.

o·don·to·graph (ɒ'dɒntə,grɑːf, -,græf) *n.* an aid to marking out gear teeth, in which a circular arc is substituted for the true involute curve. —**o·don·to·graph·ic** (ɒ,dɒntə'græfɪk) *adj.* —**od·on·tog·ra·phy** (,ɒdɒn'tɒgrəfɪ) *n.*

o·don·toid (ɒ'dɒntɔɪd) *adj.* **1.** toothlike. **2.** of or relating to the odontoid process.

o·don·toid pro·cess *n. Anatomy.* the toothlike upward projection at the back of the second vertebra of the neck.

od·on·tol·o·gy (,ɒdɒn'tɒlədʒɪ) *n.* the branch of science concerned with the anatomy, development, and diseases of teeth and related structures. —**o·don·to·log·i·cal** (ɒ,dɒntə'lɒdʒɪkᵊl) *adj.* —**,od·on·'tol·o·gist** *n.*

o·don·to·phore (ɒ'dɒntə,fɔː) *n.* an oral muscular protrusible structure in molluscs that supports the radula. —**od·on·toph·o·ral** (,ɒdɒn'tɒfərəl) *or* **,od·on·'toph·or·ous** *adj.*

o·dor ('əʊdə) *n.* the U.S. spelling of **odour.** —**'o·dor·less** *adj.*

o·dor·if·er·ous (,əʊdə'rɪfərəs) *adj.* having or emitting an odour, esp. a fragrant one. —**,o·dor·'if·er·ous·ly** *adv.* —**,o·dor·'if·er·ous·ness** *n.*

o·dor·ous ('əʊdərəs) *adj.* having or emitting a characteristic smell or odour. —**'o·dor·ous·ly** *adv.* —**'o·dor·ous·ness** *n.*

o·dour *or U.S.* **o·dor** ('əʊdə) *n.* **1.** the property of a substance that gives it a characteristic scent or smell. **2.** a pervasive quality about something: *an odour of dishonesty.* **3.** repute or regard (in the phrases **in good odour, in bad odour**). **4.** *Archaic.* a sweet-smelling fragrance. [C13: from Old French *odur,* from Latin *odor;* related to Latin *olēre* to smell, Greek *ōzein*] —**'o·dour·less** *or U.S.* **'o·dor·less** *adj.*

o·dour of sanc·ti·ty *n. Derogatory.* sanctimoniousness. [C18: originally, the sweet smell said to be exhaled by the bodies of dead saints]

Od·o·va·car (,əʊdəʊ'vɑːkə) *n.* a variant spelling of **Odoacer.**

Od·ra ('ɔdra) *n.* the Czech and Polish name for the **Oder.**

od·yl *or* **od·yle** ('ɒdɪl) *n.* another word for **od.**

O·dys·seus (ə'diːsɪəs) *n. Greek myth.* one of the foremost of the Greek heroes at the siege of Troy, noted for his courage and ingenuity. His return to his kingdom of Ithaca was fraught with adventures in which he lost all his companions and he was acknowledged by his wife Penelope only after killing her suitors. Roman name: **Ulysses.**

Od·ys·sey ('ɒdɪsɪ) *n.* **1.** a Greek epic poem, attributed to Homer, describing the ten-year homeward wanderings of Odysseus after the fall of Troy. **2.** (*often not cap.*) any long eventful journey. —**Od·ys·se·an** (,ɒdɪ'siːən) *adj.*

Oe *symbol for* oersted.

OE, O.E., *or* **OE.** *abbrev. for* Old English (language).

o.e. *Commerce. abbrev. for* omissions excepted.

O.E.C.D. *abbrev. for* Organization for Economic Cooperation and Development; an association of 21 nations to promote growth and trade, set up in 1961 to supersede the O.E.E.C.

oe·col·o·gy (iː'kɒlədʒɪ) *n.* a less common spelling of **ecology.** —**oec·o·log·i·cal** (,ɛkə'lɒdʒɪkᵊl, ,iː-) *adj.* —**,oec·o·'log·i·cal·ly** *adv.* —**oe·'col·o·gist** *n.*

oe·cu·men·i·cal (,iːkjʊ'mɛnɪkᵊl) *adj.* a less common spelling of **ecumenical.**

O.E.D. *abbrev. for* Oxford English Dictionary.

oe·de·ma *or* **e·de·ma** (ɪ'diːmə) *n., pl.* **·ma·ta** (-mətə). **1.** *Pathol.* an excessive accumulation of serous fluid in the intercellular spaces of tissue. **2.** *Plant pathol.* an abnormal swelling in a plant caused by a large mass of parenchyma or an accumulation of water in the tissues. [C16: via New Latin from Greek *oidēma,* from *oideîn* to swell] —**oe·dem·a·tous, e·dem·a·tous** (ɪ'dɛmətəs) *or* **oe·'dem·a·,tose, e·'dem·a·,tose** *adj.*

Oe·di·pus ('iːdɪpəs) *n. Greek myth.* the son of Laius and Jocasta, the king and queen of Thebes, who killed his father, being unaware of his identity, and unwittingly married his mother, by whom he had four children. When the truth was revealed, he put out his eyes and Jocasta killed herself.

Oe·di·pus com·plex *n. Psychoanal.* a group of emotions, usually unconscious, involving the desire of a child, esp. a male child, to possess sexually the parent of the opposite sex while excluding the parent of the same sex. Compare **Electra complex.** —**'oe·di·pal** *or* **,oed·i·'pe·an** *adj.*

O.E.E.C. *abbrev. for* Organization for European Economic Cooperation; an organization of European nations set up in 1948 to allocate postwar U.S. aid and to stimulate trade and cooperation. It was superseded by the O.E.C.D. in 1961.

Oeh·len·schlä·ger *or* **Öh·len·schlä·ger** (*Danish* 'øːlən,slɛːgər) *n.* **Ad·am Gott·lob** ('adam 'gɔtlɔp). 1779–1850, Danish romantic poet and dramatist.

oeil-de-boeuf *French.* (œjdə'bœf) *n., pl.* ***oeils-de-boeuf*** (œjdə'bœf). a circular window, esp. in 17th- and 18th-century French architecture. [literally: bull's eye]

oeil·lade (ɜː'jɑːd; *French* œ'jad) *n. Literary.* an amorous or suggestive glance; ogle. [C16: from French, from *oeil* eye, from Latin *oculus* + *-ade* as in FUSILLADE]

oe·nol·o·gy *or* **e·nol·o·gy** (iː'nɒlədʒɪ) *n.* the study of wine. [C19: from Greek *oînos* wine + -LOGY] —**oe·no·log·i·cal** *or* **e·no·log·i·cal** (,iːnə'lɒdʒɪkᵊl) *adj.* —**oe·'nol·o·gist** *or* **e·'nol·o·gist** *n.*

oe·no·mel ('iːnə,mɛl) *n.* **1.** a drink made of wine and honey. **2.**

Literary. a source of strength and sweetness. [C16: via Latin from Greek *oinos* wine + *meli* honey]

Oe·no·ne (iːˈnəʊnɪ) *n. Greek myth.* a nymph of Mount Ida, whose lover Paris left her for Helen.

o'er (ɔː, əʊə) *prep., adv.* a poetic contraction of **over.**

oer+sted (ˈɜːstɛd) *n.* the cgs unit of magnetic field strength; the field strength that would cause a unit magnetic pole to experience a force of 1 dyne in a vacuum. It is equivalent to 79.58 amperes per metre. [C20: named after H. C. *Oersted* (1777–1851), Danish physicist, who discovered electromagnetism]

oe·soph·a+gus *or U.S.* **e·soph·a+gus** (iːˈsɒfəgəs) *n., pl.* **+gi** (-ˌgaɪ). the part of the alimentary canal between the pharynx and the stomach; gullet. [C16: via New Latin from Greek *oisophagos,* from *oisein,* future infinitive of *pherein* to carry + *-phagos,* from *phagein* to eat] —**oe·soph·a·ge·al** *or U.S.* **e·soph·a+ge·al** (iːˌsɒfəˈdʒiːəl) *adj.*

oes+tra+di+ol (ˌiːstrəˈdaɪɒl, ˌɛstrə-) *or U.S.* **es+tra+di+ol** *n.* the most potent oestrogenic hormone secreted by the mammalian ovary: synthesized and used to treat oestrogen deficiency and cancer of the breast. Formula: $C_{18}H_{24}O_2$. [C20: from New Latin, from OESTRIN + DI-[1] + -OL[1]]

oes+trin (ˈiːstrɪn, ˈɛstrɪn) *or U.S.* **es+trin** *n.* an obsolete term for **oestrogen.** [C20: from OESTR(US) + -IN]

oes+tri+ol (ˈiːstrɪˌɒl, ˈɛstrɪ-) *or U.S.* **es+tri+ol** *n.* a weak oestrogenic hormone secreted by the mammalian ovary: a synthetic form is used to treat oestrogen deficiency. Formula: $C_{18}H_{24}O_3$. [C20: from OESTRIN + TRI- + -OL[1]]

oes+tro+gen (ˈiːstrədʒən, ˈɛstrə-) *or U.S.* **es+tro+gen** *n.* any of several steroid hormones, that are secreted chiefly by the ovaries and placenta, that induce oestrus, stimulate changes in the female reproductive organs during the oestrous cycle, and promote development of female secondary sexual characteristics. [C20: from OESTRUS + -GEN] —**oes+tro+gen+ic** (ˌiːstrəˈdʒɛnɪk, ˌɛstrə-) *or U.S.* **es+tro+gen+ic** (ˌɛstrəˈdʒɛnɪk, ˌiːstrə-) *adj.* —**ˌoes+tro+ˈgen·i+cal+ly** *or U.S.* **ˌes+tro+ˈgen·i+cal+ly** *adv.*

oes+trone (ˈiːstrəʊn, ˈɛstrəʊn) *or U.S.* **es+trone** *n.* a weak oestrogenic hormone secreted by the mammalian ovary and having the same medical uses as oestradiol. Formula: $C_{18}H_{22}O_2$. [C20: from OESTR(US) + -ONE]

oes+trous cy+cle *n.* a hormonally controlled cycle of activity of the reproductive organs in many female mammals. The follicular stage (growth of the Graafian follicles, thickening of the lining of the uterus, secretion of oestrogen, and ovulation (see **oestrus**)) is succeeded by the luteal phase (formation of the corpus luteum and secretion of progesterone), followed by regression and a return to the first stage.

oes+trus (ˈiːstrəs, ˈɛstrəs) *or U.S.* **es+trus** *n.* a regularly occurring period of sexual receptivity in most female mammals, except humans, during which ovulation occurs and copulation can take place; heat. [C17: from Latin *oestrus* gadfly, hence frenzy, from Greek *oistros*] —**ˈoes+trous** *or U.S.* **ˈes+trous** *adj.*

oeu·vre *French.* (ˈœːvr) *n.* **1.** a work of art, literature, music, etc. **2.** the total output of a writer, painter, etc. [ultimately from Latin *opera,* plural of *opus* work]

of (ɒv; *unstressed* əv) *prep.* **1.** used with a verbal noun or gerund to link it with a following noun that is either the subject or the object of the verb embedded in the gerund: *the breathing of a fine swimmer* (subject); *the breathing of clean air* (object). **2.** used to indicate possession, origin, or association: *the house of my sister; to die of hunger.* **3.** used after words or phrases expressing quantities: *a pint of milk.* **4.** constituted by, containing, or characterized by: *a family of idiots; a rod of iron; a man of some depth.* **5.** used to indicate separation, as in time or space: *within a mile of the town; within ten minutes of the beginning of the concert.* **6.** used to mark apposition: *the city of Naples; a speech on the subject of archaeology.* **7.** about; concerning: *speak to me of love.* **8.** used in passive constructions to indicate the agent: *he was beloved of all.* **9.** *Informal.* used to indicate a day or part of a period of time when some activity habitually occurs: *I go to the pub of an evening.* **10.** *U.S.* before the hour of: *a quarter of nine.* [Old English (as prep. and adv.); related to Old Norse *af,* Old High German *aba,* Latin *ab,* Greek *apo*]

Usage. See at **off.**

OF, O.F., *or* **OF.** *abbrev. for* Old French (language).

o·fay (ˈəʊfeɪ) *n. U.S. Negro slang.* a derogatory term for a white person. [C20: origin unknown]

off (ɒf) *prep.* **1.** used to indicate actions in which contact is absent or rendered absent, as between an object and a surface: *to lift a cup off the table.* **2.** used to indicate the removal of something that is or has been appended to or in association with something else: *to take the tax off potatoes.* **3.** out of alignment with: *we are off course.* **4.** situated near to or leading away from: *just off the High Street.* **5.** not inclined towards: *I'm off work; I've gone off you.* ~*adv.* **6.** (*particle*) so as to deactivate or disengage: *turn off the radio.* **7.** (*particle*) **a.** so as to get rid of: *sleep off a hangover.* **b.** so as to be removed from, esp. as a reduction: *he took ten per cent off.* **8.** spent away from work or other duties: *take the afternoon off.* **9. a.** on a trip, journey, or race: *I saw her off at the station.* **b.** (*particle*) so as to be completely absent, used up, or exhausted: *this stuff kills off all vermin.* **10.** out from the shore or land: *the ship stood off.* **11. a.** out of contact; at a distance: *the ship was 10 miles off.* **b.** out of the present location: *the girl ran off.* **12.** away in the future: *August is less than a week off.* **13.** (*particle*) so as to be no longer taking place: *the match has been rained off.* **14.** (*particle*) removed from contact with something, as clothing from the body: *the girl took all her clothes off.* **15. off and on** *or* **on and off.** occasionally; intermittently: *he comes here off and on.* **16. off with.** (*interj.*) a command, often peremptory, or an exhortation to remove or cut off (something specified): *off with his head; off with that coat, my dear.* ~*adj.* **17.** not on; no longer operative: *the off position on the dial.* **18.** (*postpositive*) not or no longer taking place; cancelled or postponed: *the meeting is off.* **19.** in a specified condition regarding money, provisions, etc.: *well off; how are you off for bread?* **20.** unsatisfactory or disappointing: *his performance was rather off; an off year for good tennis.* **21.** (*postpositive*) in a condition as specified: *I'd be better off without this job.* **22.** (*postpositive*) no longer on the menu; not being served at the moment: *sorry, love, haddock is off.* **23.** (*postpositive*) (of food or drink) having gone bad, sour, etc.: *this milk is off.* ~*n.* **24.** *Cricket.* **a.** the part of the field on that side of the pitch to which the batsman presents his bat when taking strike: thus for a right-hander, off is on the right-hand side. Compare **leg** (sense 12). **b.** (*in combination*): a fielding position in this part of the field: *mid-off.* **c.** (*as modifier*): *the off stump.* [originally variant of OF; fully distinguished from it in the 17th century]

Usage. In educated usage, *off* is not followed by *from* or *of: he stepped off* (not *off of*) *the platform.* Careful writers also avoid using the word in the place of *from: they bought apples from* (rather than *off*) *the man.*

off. *abbrev. for:* **1.** offer. **2.** office. **3.** officer. **4.** official.

Of·fa (ˈɒfə) *n.* died 796 A.D., king of Mercia (757–796), who constructed an earthwork **(Offa's Dyke)** between Wales and Mercia.

of+fal (ˈɒfˀl) *n.* **1.** the edible internal parts of an animal, such as the heart, liver, and tongue. **2.** dead or decomposing organic matter. **3.** refuse; rubbish. [C14: from OFF + FALL, referring to parts fallen or cut off; compare German *Abfall* rubbish]

Of+fa+ly (ˈɒfəlɪ) *n.* an inland county of E central Ireland, in Leinster province: formerly an ancient kingdom, which also included parts of Tipperary, Leix, and Kildare. County town: Tullamore. Pop.: 51 834 (1971). Area: 2000 sq. km (770 sq. miles).

off+beat (ˈɒfˌbiːt) *n.* **1.** *Music.* any of the normally unaccented beats in a bar, such as the second and fourth beats in a bar of four-four time. They are stressed in some jazz and dance music, such as the bossa nova. ~*adj.* **2. a.** unusual, unconventional, or eccentric. **b.** (*as n.*): *he liked the offbeat in music.*

off-Broad·way *adj.* **1.** designating the kind of experimental, low-budget, or noncommercial productions associated with theatre outside the Broadway area in New York. **2.** (of theatres) not located in Broadway. ~Compare **off-off-Broadway.**

off-cen·tre *adj.* slightly eccentric or unconventional; not completely sound or balanced.

off chance *n.* **1.** a slight possibility. **2. on the off chance.** with the hope: *on the off chance of getting the job.*

off col+our *adj.* (**off-col·our** *when prenominal*). **1.** *Chiefly Brit.* slightly ill; unwell. **2.** indecent or indelicate; risqué.

off cut *n.* a piece of paper, plywood, etc., remaining after the main pieces have been cut; remnant.

Of+fen+bach[1] (*German* ˈɔfˀnˌbax) *n.* a city in S central West Germany, on the River Main in Hesse opposite Frankfurt am Main: leather-goods industry. Pop.: 120 092 (1974 est.).

Of·fen·bach[2] (ˈɒfənˌbɑːk; *French* ɔfɛnˈbaːk) *n.* **Jacques** (ʒɑːk). 1819–80, French composer of operettas, including *Orpheus in the Underworld* (1858) and *The Tales of Hoffmann* (1881).

of+fence *or U.S.* **of+fense** (əˈfɛns) *n.* **1.** a violation or breach of a law, custom, rule, etc. **2. a.** any public wrong or crime. **b.** a nonindictable crime punishable on summary conviction. **3.** annoyance, displeasure, or resentment. **4. give offence (to).** to cause annoyance or displeasure (to). **5. take offence.** to feel injured, humiliated, or offended. **6.** a source of annoyance, displeasure, or anger. **7.** attack; assault. **8.** *Archaic.* injury or harm. —**of+ˈfence+less** *or U.S.* **of+ˈfense+less** *adj.*

of+fend (əˈfɛnd) *vb.* **1.** to hurt the feelings, sense of dignity, etc., of (a person, etc.). **2.** (*tr.*) to be disagreeable to; disgust: *the smell offended him.* **3.** (*intr. except in archaic uses*) to break (a law or laws in general). [C14: via Old French *offendre* to strike against, from Latin *offendere,* from *ob-* against + *fendere* to strike] —**of+ˈfend+er** *n.*

of+fen+sive (əˈfɛnsɪv) *adj.* **1.** unpleasant or disgusting, as to the senses. **2.** causing anger or annoyance; insulting. **3.** for the purpose of attack rather than defence. ~*n.* **4.** (*usually preceded by the*) an attitude or position of aggression. **5.** an assault, attack, or military initiative, esp. a strategic one. —**of+ˈfen+sive+ly** *adv.* —**of+ˈfen+sive+ness** *n.*

of+fer (ˈɒfə) *vb.* **1.** to present or proffer (something, someone, oneself, etc.) for acceptance or rejection. **2.** (*tr.*) to present as part of a requirement: *she offered English as a second subject.* **3.** (*tr.*) to provide or make accessible: *this stream offers the best fishing.* **4.** (*intr.*) to present itself: *if an opportunity should offer.* **5.** (*tr.*) to show or express willingness or the intention (to do something). **6.** (*tr.*) to put forward (a proposal, opinion, etc.) for consideration. **7.** (*tr.*) to present for sale. **8.** (*tr.*) to propose as payment; bid or tender. **9.** (when *tr.,* often foll. by *up*) to present (a prayer, sacrifice, etc.) as or during an act of worship. **10.** (*tr.*) to show readiness for: *to offer battle.* **11.** (*intr.*) to make a proposal of marriage. ~*n.* **12.** something, such as a proposal or bid, that is offered. **13.** the act of offering or the condition of being offered. **14.** *Contract law.* a proposal made by one person that will create a binding contract if accepted unconditionally by the person to whom it is made. See also **acceptance. 15.** a proposal of marriage. **16.** short for **offer price. 17. on offer.** for sale at a reduced price. [Old English, from Latin *offerre* to

present, from *ob-* to + *ferre* to bring] —'**of·fer·er** *or* '**of·fe·ror** *n.*
of·fer·ing ('ɒfərɪŋ) *n.* **1.** something that is offered. **2.** a contribution to the funds of a religious organization. **3.** a sacrifice, as of an animal, to a deity.
of·fer price *n. Stock exchange.* the price at which a stockjobber is prepared to sell a specific security. Often shortened to **offer.** Compare **bid price.**
of·fer·to·ry ('ɒfətərɪ) *n., pl.* **·to·ries.** *Christianity.* **1.** the oblation of the bread and wine at the Eucharist. **2.** the offerings of the worshippers at this service. **3.** the prayers said or sung while the worshippers' offerings are being received. [C14: from Church Latin *offertōrium* place appointed for offerings, from Latin *offerre* to OFFER]
off-glide *n. Phonetics.* a glide caused by the movement of the articulators away from their position in articulating the previous speech sound. Compare **on-glide.**
off·hand (ˌɒf'hænd) *adj. also* **off·hand·ed,** *adv.* **1.** without preparation or warning; impromptu. **2.** without care, thought, attention, or consideration: *an offhand manner.* —ˌ**off·'hand·ed·ly** *adv.* —ˌ**off·'hand·ed·ness** *n.*
of·fice ('ɒfɪs) *n.* **1. a.** a room or set of rooms in which business, professional duties, clerical work, etc., are carried out. **b.** (*as modifier*): *office furniture; an office boy.* **2.** (*often pl.*) the building or buildings in which the work of an organization, such as a business or government department, is carried out. **3.** a commercial or professional business: *the architect's office approved the plans.* **4.** the group of persons working in an office: *it was a happy office until she came.* **5.** (*cap. when part of a name*) (in Britain) a department of the national government: *the Home Office.* **6.** (*cap. when part of a name*) (in the U.S.) **a.** a governmental agency, esp. of the Federal government. **b.** a subdivision of such an agency or of a department: *Office of Science and Technology.* **7. a.** a position of trust, responsibility, or duty, esp. in a government or organization: *the office of president; to seek office.* **b.** (*in combination*): *an office-holder.* **8.** duty or function: *the office of an administrator.* **9.** (*often pl.*) a minor task or service: *domestic offices.* **10.** (*often pl.*) an action performed for another, usually a beneficial action: *through his good offices.* **11.** a place where tickets, information, etc., can be obtained: *a ticket office.* **12.** *Ecclesiast.* **a.** (often *pl.*) a ceremony or service, prescribed by ecclesiastical authorities, esp. one for the dead. **b.** the order or form of these. **c.** *R.C. Church.* the official daily service. **d.** short for **divine office.** **13.** (*pl.*) the parts of a house or estate where work is done, goods are stored, etc. **14.** *Brit.* a euphemistic term for **lavatory.** **15. the office.** a hint or signal. **16. in** (*or* **out**) **of office.** (of a government) in (or out) of power. [C13: via Old French from Latin *officium* service, duty, from *opus* work, service + *facere* to do]
of·fice bear·er *n.* a person who holds an office; official.
of·fice block *n.* a large building designed to provide office accommodation.
of·fice boy *n.* a boy employed in an office for running errands and other minor jobs.
of·fice hours *pl. n.* **1.** the hours during which an office is open for business. **2.** the number of hours worked in an office.
of·fic·er ('ɒfɪsə) *n.* **1.** a person in the armed services who holds a position of responsibility, authority, and duty. **2.** See **police officer.** **3.** a person authorized to serve as master or mate of a vessel. **4.** a person appointed or elected to a position of responsibility or authority in a government, society, etc. **5.** a government official: *a customs officer.* **6.** (in the Order of the British Empire) a member of the grade below commander. ~*vb.* (*tr.*) **7.** to furnish with officers. **8.** to act as an officer over (some section, group, organization, etc.).
of·fic·er of arms *n. Heraldry.* a pursuivant or herald.
of·fic·er of the day *n.* a military officer whose duty is to take charge of the security of the unit or camp for a day.
of·fic·er of the guard *n.* a junior officer whose duty is to command a ceremonial guard.
of·fi·cial (ə'fɪʃəl) *adj.* **1.** of or relating to an office, its administration, or its duration. **2.** sanctioned by, recognized by, or derived from authority: *an official statement.* **3.** appointed by authority, esp. for some special duty. **4.** having a formal ceremonial character: *an official dinner.* ~*n.* **5.** a person who holds a position in an organization, government department, etc., esp. a subordinate position. —**of·'fi·cial·ly** *adv.*
Of·fi·cial (ə'fɪʃəl) *adj.* **1.** of or relating to one of the two factions of the IRA and Sinn Fein, which have existed since a split in 1969. The Official movement emphasizes political rather than guerrilla activity. ~*n.* **2.** a member of the Official IRA and Sinn Fein. ~Compare **Provisional.**
of·fi·cial·dom (ə'fɪʃəldəm) *n.* **1.** the outlook or behaviour of officials, esp. those rigidly adhering to regulations; bureaucracy. **2.** officials or bureaucrats collectively.
of·fi·cial·ese (əˌfɪʃə'li:z) *n.* language characteristic of official documents, esp. when verbose or pedantic.
Of·fi·cial Re·ceiv·er *n.* an officer appointed by the Department of Trade and Industry to receive the income and manage the estate of a bankrupt pending the appointment of a trustee in bankruptcy. See also **receiver.**
Of·fi·cial Ref·er·ee *n. Law.* (in England) a circuit judge attached to the High Court who is empowered to try certain cases, esp. where a detailed examination of accounts or other documents is involved.
Of·fi·cial So·lic·i·tor *n.* an officer of the Supreme Court of Judicature with special responsibilities for protecting the interests of persons under disability.
of·fi·ci·ant (ə'fɪʃɪənt) *n.* a person who presides and officiates at a religious ceremony.
of·fi·ci·ar·y (ə'fɪʃɪərɪ) *n., pl.* **·ar·ies.** **1.** a body of officials. ~*adj.* **2.** of, relating to, or derived from office.
of·fi·ci·ate (ə'fɪʃɪˌeɪt) *vb.* (*intr.*) **1.** to hold the position, responsibility, or function of an official. **2.** to conduct a religious or other ceremony. [C17: from Medieval Latin *officiāre,* from Latin *officium;* see OFFICE] —**ofˌfi·ci·'a·tion** *n.* —**of·'fi·ci·ˌa·tor** *n.*
of·fic·i·nal (ɒ'fɪsɪnəl, ˌɒfɪ'saɪnəl) *Pharmacol., obsolete.* ~*adj.* **1.** (of pharmaceutical products) available without prescription. **2.** (of a plant) having pharmacological properties. ~*n.* **3.** an officinal preparation or plant. [C17: from Medieval Latin *officīnālis,* from Latin *officīna* workshop; see OFFICE] —**of·'fic·i·nal·ly** *adv.*
of·fi·cious (ə'fɪʃəs) *adj.* **1.** unnecessarily or obtrusively ready to offer advice or services. **2.** marked by such readiness. **3.** *Diplomacy.* informal or unofficial. **4.** *Obsolete.* attentive or obliging. [C16: from Latin *officiōsus* kindly, from *officium* service; see OFFICE] —**of·'fi·cious·ly** *adv.* —**of·'fi·cious·ness** *n.*
of·fing ('ɒfɪŋ) *n.* **1.** the part of the sea that can be seen from the shore. **2. in the offing.** likely to occur soon.
of·fish ('ɒfɪʃ) *adj. Informal.* aloof or distant in manner. —'**of·fish·ly** *adv.* —'**of·fish·ness** *n.*
off key *adj.* (**off-key** *when prenominal*) *adv.* **1.** *Music.* **a.** not in the correct key. **b.** out of tune. **2.** out of keeping; discordant.
off-li·cence *n. Brit.* **1.** a shop, counter, etc., where alcoholic drinks are sold for consumption elsewhere. U.S. equivalent: **package store.** **2.** a licence permitting such sales.
off lim·its *adj.* (**off-lim·its** *when prenominal*). **1.** *U.S. Chiefly military.* not to be entered; out of bounds. ~*adv.* **2.** in or into an area forbidden by regulations.
off line *adj.* (**off-line** *when prenominal*). **1.** of, relating to, or concerned with a part of a computer system not connected to the central processing unit but controlled by a computer storage device. Compare **on line.** **2.** disconnected from a computer; switched off.
off-load *vb.* (*tr.*) to get rid of (something unpleasant or burdensome), as by delegation to another.
off-off-Broad·way *adj.* of or relating to highly experimental informal small-scale theatrical productions in New York, usually taking place in cafés, small halls, etc. Compare **off-Broadway.**
off-peak *adj.* of or relating to services as used outside periods of intensive use or electricity supplied at cheaper rates during the night.
off·print ('ɒfˌprɪnt) *n.* **1.** Also called (U.S.): **separate.** a separate reprint of an article that originally appeared in a larger publication. ~*vb.* **2.** (*tr.*) to reprint (an article taken from a larger publication) separately.
off-put·ting *adj. Brit. informal.* disconcerting or disturbing.
off sea·son *adj.* (**off-sea·son** *when prenominal*). **1.** denoting or occurring during a period of little activity in a trade or business. ~*adv.* **2.** in an off-season period.
off·set *n.* ('ɒfˌsɛt). **1.** something that counterbalances or compensates for something else. **2. a.** a printing method in which the impression is made onto an intermediate surface, such as a rubber blanket, which transfers it to the paper. **b.** (*modifier*) relating to, involving, or printed by offset: *offset letterpress; offset lithography.* **3.** another name for **set-off.** **4.** *Botany.* **a.** a short runner in certain plants, such as the houseleek, that produces roots and shoots at the tip. **b.** a plant produced from such a runner. **5.** a ridge projecting from a range of hills or mountains. **6.** a narrow horizontal or sloping surface formed where a wall is reduced in thickness towards the top. **7.** a person or group descended collaterally from a particular group or family; offshoot. **8.** *Surveying.* a measurement of distance to a point at right angles to a survey line. ~*vb.* (ˌɒf'sɛt), **·sets, ·set·ting, ·set.** **9.** (*tr.*) to counterbalance or compensate for. **10.** (*tr.*) to print (pictures, text, etc.) using the offset process. **11.** (*tr.*) to construct an offset in (a wall). **12.** (*intr.*) to project or develop as an offset.
off·shoot ('ɒfˌʃu:t) *n.* **1.** a shoot or branch growing from the main stem of a plant. **2.** something that develops or derives from a principal source or origin.
off·shore (ˌɒf'ʃɔ:) *adj., adv.* from, away from, or at some distance from the shore.
off·side ('ɒf'saɪd) *adj., adv.* **1.** *Sport.* (in football, hockey, etc.) in a position illegally ahead of the ball or puck when it is played, usually when within one's opponents' half or the attacking zone. ~*n.* **2.** (usually preceded by *the*) *Chiefly Brit.* **a.** the side of a vehicle, etc., nearest the centre of the road (in Britain, the right side). **b.** (*as modifier*): *the offside passenger door.* Compare **nearside.**
off-sid·er *n. Austral.* a partner or assistant.
off·spring ('ɒfˌsprɪŋ) *n.* **1.** the immediate descendant or descendants of a person, animal, etc.; progeny. **2.** a product, outcome, or result.
off·stage ('ɒf'steɪdʒ) *adj., adv.* out of the view of the audience; off the stage.
off-street *adj.* located away from a street: *off-street parking.*
off the rec·ord *adj.* (**off-the-rec·ord** *when prenominal*). **1.** not intended to be recorded or stated openly. ~*adv.* **2.** with such an intention; unofficially.
off-white *n.* **1.** a colour, such as cream or bone, consisting of white mixed with a tinge of grey or with a pale hue. ~*adj.* **2.** of such a colour: *an off-white coat.*

off-year e·lec·tion *n.* (in the U.S.) an election held in a year when a presidential election does not take place.
O'Fiaich (əʊ'fi:) *n.* **Tom·as.** born 1923, Irish Roman Catholic prelate; archbishop of Armagh and primate of all Ireland since 1978.
O.F.M. *abbrev. for* Ordo Fratrum Minorum (the Franciscans). [Latin: Order of Minor Friars]
OFris *abbrev. for* Old Frisian.
O.F.S. *abbrev. for* Orange Free State.
oft (ɒft) *adv.* short for **often** (archaic or poetic except in combinations such as **oft-repeated** and **oft-recurring**). [Old English *oft;* related to Old High German *ofto*]
of·ten ('ɒfᵊn) *adv.* **1.** frequently or repeatedly; much of the time. Archaic equivalents: **'of·ten·,times, 'oft·,times. 2. as often as not.** quite frequently. **3. every so often.** at regular intervals. **4. more often than not.** in more than half the instances. ~*adj.* **5.** *Archaic.* repeated; frequent. [C14: variant of OFT before vowels and *h*]
o.g. *abbrev. for* own goal.
O.G. *abbrev. for:* **1.** Officer of the Guard. **2.** Also: **o.g.** *Philately.* original gum.
Og·a·den (,ɒgə'dɛn) *n.* **the.** a region of SE Ethiopia, bordering on Somalia: consists of a desert plateau, inhabited by Somali nomads; a secessionist movement, supported by Somalia, has existed within the region since the early 1960s and led to bitter fighting between Ethiopia and Somalia (1977–78).
O·ga·sa·wa·ra Gun·to (,ɒgəsə'wɑ:rə 'gʌntəʊ) *n.* the Japanese name for the **Bonin Islands.**
Og·bo·mo·sho (,ɒgbə'məʊʃəʊ) *n.* a city in SW Nigeria: the third largest town in Nigeria; trading centre for an agricultural region. Pop.: 432 000 (1975 est.).
Og·den ('ɒgdən) *n.* **C(harles) K(ay).** 1889–1957, English linguist, who, with I. A. Richards, devised Basic English.
og·do·ad ('ɒgdəʊ,æd) *n.* a group of eight. [C17: via Late Latin from Greek *ogdoos* eighth, from *oktō* eight]
o·gee ('əʊdʒi:) *n. Architect.* **1.** Also called: **talon.** a moulding having a cross section in the form of a letter S. **2.** short for **ogee arch.** [C15: probably variant of OGIVE]
o·gee arch *n. Architect.* a pointed arch having an S-shaped curve on both sides. Sometimes shortened to **ogee.** Also called: **keel arch.**
og·ham *or* **og·am** ('ɒgəm) *n.* an ancient alphabetical writing system used by the Celts in Britain, consisting of straight lines drawn or carved perpendicular to or at an angle to another long straight line. [C17: from Old Irish *ogom,* of uncertain origin but associated with the name *Ogma,* legendary inventor of this alphabet]
Og·ham I·rish *n.* another name for **Old Irish:** the language of inscriptions in the ogham alphabet.
o·give ('əʊdʒaɪv, əʊ'dʒaɪv) *n.* **1.** a diagonal rib or groin of a Gothic vault. **2.** another name for **lancet arch. 3.** *Statistics.* a graph the ordinates of which represent cumulative frequencies of the values indicated by the corresponding abscissas. **4.** the conical head of a missile or rocket that protects the payload during its passage through the atmosphere. [C17: from Old French, of uncertain origin] —**o·'giv·al** *adj.*
o·gle ('əʊgᵊl) *vb.* **1.** to look at (someone, esp. an attractive woman) amorously. **2.** (*tr.*) to stare or gape at. ~*n.* **3.** a flirtatious or lewd look. [C17: probably from Low German *oegeln,* from *oegen* to look at] —**'o·gler** *n.*
O·gle·thorpe ('əʊgᵊl,θɔ:p) *n.* **James Ed·ward.** 1696–1785, English general and colonial administrator; founder of the colony of Georgia (1733).
O·go·oué *or* **O·go·we** (ɒ'gəʊweɪ) *n.* a river in W central Africa, rising in the SW Congo Republic and flowing generally northwest and north through Gabon to the Atlantic. Length: about 970 km (683 miles).
Og·pu ('ɒgpu:) *n.* the Soviet police and secret police from 1923 to 1934. [C20: from Russian *O(byedinyonnoye) g(osudarstvennoye) p(oliticheskoye) u(pravleniye)* United State Political Administration]
o·gre ('əʊgə) *n.* **1.** (in folklore) a giant, usually given to eating human flesh. **2.** any monstrous or cruel person. [C18: from French, perhaps from Latin *Orcus* god of the infernal regions] —**'o·gre·ish** *adj.* —**'o·gress** *fem. n.*
O·gun (əʊ'gʊn) *n.* a state of SW Nigeria, formed in 1976 from part of Western State. Capital: Abeokuta. Pop.: 1 448 966 (1976 est.). Area: 13 600 sq. km (5250 sq. miles).
O·gyg·i·an (əʊ'dʒɪdʒɪən) *adj.* of very great age; prehistoric. [C19: from Greek *Ōgugios* relating to *Ogyges,* the most ancient king of Greece, mythical ruler of Boeotia or Attica]
oh (əʊ) *interj.* an exclamation expressive of surprise, pain, pleasure, etc.
O. Hen·ry (əʊ 'hɛnrɪ) *n.* pen name of *William Sidney Porter.* 1862–1910, U.S. short-story writer. His collections of stories, characterized by his use of caricature and surprising endings, include *Cabbages and Kings* (1904) and *The Four Million* (1906).
OHG, O.H.G. *or* **OHG.** *abbrev. for* Old High German.
O'Hig·gins (əʊ'hɪgɪnz; *Spanish* o'iɣins) *n.* **1. Am·bro·sio** (æm'brəʊzɪ,əʊ). ?1720–1801, Irish soldier, who became viceroy of Chile (1789–96) and of Peru (1796–1801). **2.** his son, **Ber·nar·do** (ber'narðo). 1778–1842, Chilean revolutionary. He was one of the leaders in the struggle for independence from Spain and was Chile's first president (1817–23).
O·hi·o (əʊ'haɪəʊ) *n.* **1.** a state of the central U.S., in the Midwest on Lake Erie: consists of prairies in the west and the Allegheny plateau in the east, the Ohio River forming the S and most of the E borders. Capital: Columbus. Pop.: 10 652 017 (1970). Area: 106 125 sq. km (40 975 sq. miles). Abbrev. (with zip code): **OH 2.** a river in the eastern U.S., formed by the confluence of the Allegheny and Monongahela Rivers at Pittsburgh: flows generally west and southwest to join the Mississippi at Cairo, Illinois, as its chief E tributary. Length: 1570 km (975 miles).
ohm (əʊm) *n.* the derived SI unit of electric resistance; the resistance between two points on a conductor when a constant potential difference of 1 volt between them produces a current of 1 ampere. Symbol: Ω [C19: named after Georg Simon OHM]
Ohm (əʊm) *n.* **Ge·org Si·mon** ('ge:ɔrk 'zi:mon). 1787–1854, German physicist, who formulated the law named after him.
ohm·age ('əʊmɪdʒ) *n.* electrical resistance in ohms.
ohm·me·ter ('əʊm,mi:tə) *n.* an instrument for measuring electrical resistance.
O.H.M.S. (in Britain and the dominions of the Commonwealth) *abbrev. for* On Her (*or* His) Majesty's Service.
Ohm's law *n.* the principle that the electric current passing through a conductor is directly proportional to the potential difference across it, the constant of proportionality being the resistance of the conductor.
o·ho (əʊ'həʊ) *interj.* an exclamation expressing surprise, exultation, or derision.
o.h.v. *abbrev. for* overhead valve.
-oid *suffix forming adjectives and associated nouns.* indicating likeness, resemblance, or similarity: *anthropoid.* [from Greek *-oeidēs* resembling, form of, from *eidos* form]
-oi·de·a *suffix forming plural proper nouns.* forming the names of zoological classes or superfamilies: *Crinoidea; Canoidea.* [from New Latin, from Latin *-oīdēs* -OID]
o·id·i·um (əʊ'ɪdɪəm) *n. Botany.* any of various fungal spores produced in the form of a chain by the development of septa in a hypha. [New Latin: from OO- + -IDIUM]
oil (ɔɪl) *n.* **1.** any of a number of viscous liquids with a smooth sticky feel. They are usually flammable, insoluble in water, soluble in organic solvents, and are obtained from plants and animals, from mineral deposits, and by synthesis. They are used as lubricants, fuels, perfumes, foodstuffs, and raw materials for chemicals. See also **essential oil, fixed oil. 2. a.** another name for **petroleum. b.** (*as modifier*)*: an oil engine; an oil rig.* **3. a.** any of a number of substances usually derived from petroleum and used for lubrication. Also called: **lubricating oil. b.** (*in combination*)*: an oilcan; an oilstone.* **c.** (*as modifier*)*: an oil pump.* **4.** a fraction of petroleum used as a fuel in domestic heating, industrial furnaces, marine engines, etc. Also called: **fuel oil. 5.** *Brit.* **a.** paraffin, esp. when used as a domestic fuel. **b.** (*as modifier*)*: an oil lamp; an oil stove.* **6.** any substance of a consistency resembling that of oil: *oil of vitriol.* **7.** the solvent, usually linseed oil, with which pigments are mixed to make artists' paints. **8. a.** (*often pl.*) oil colour or paint. **b.** (*as modifier*)*: an oil painting.* **9.** an oil painting. **10.** *Austral. and N.Z. slang.* facts or news. **11. strike oil. a.** to discover petroleum while drilling for it. **b.** *Informal.* to become very rich or successful. ~*vb.* (*tr.*) **12.** to lubricate, smear, polish, etc., with oil or an oily substance. **13. oil one's tongue.** *Informal.* to speak flatteringly or glibly. **14.** *Informal.* to bribe (esp. in the phrase **oil someone's palm**). **15. oil the wheels.** to make things run smoothly. **16. well oiled.** drunk. [C12: from Old French *oile,* from Latin *oleum* (olive) oil, from *olea* olive tree, from Greek *elaia* OLIVE] —**'oil-,like** *adj.*
oil bee·tle *n.* any of various beetles of the family *Meloidae* that exude an oily evil-smelling substance from their joints, which deters enemies.
oil·bird ('ɔɪl,bɜ:d) *n.* a nocturnal gregarious cave-dwelling bird, *Steatornis caripensis,* of N South America and Trinidad, having a hooked bill and dark plumage: family *Steatornithidae,* order *Caprimulgiformes.* Also called: **guacharo.**
oil cake *n.* stock feed consisting of compressed cubes made from the residue of the crushed seeds of oil-bearing crops such as linseed.
oil·can ('ɔɪl,kæn) *n.* a container with a long nozzle for applying lubricating oil to machinery, etc.
oil·cloth ('ɔɪl,klɒθ) *n.* **1.** waterproof material made by treating one side of a cotton fabric with a drying oil, or a synthetic resin. **2.** another name for **linoleum.**
oil·cup ('ɔɪl,kʌp) *n.* a cup-shaped oil reservoir in a machine providing continuous lubrication for a bearing.
oil drum *n.* a metal drum used to contain or transport oil.
oiled silk *n.* silk treated with oil to make it waterproof.
oil·er ('ɔɪlə) *n.* **1.** a person, device, etc., that lubricates or supplies oil. **2.** an oil tanker. **3.** an oil well.
oil·field ('ɔɪl,fi:ld) *n.* an area containing reserves of petroleum, esp. one that is already being exploited.
oil·fired ('ɔɪl,faɪəd) *adj.* (of central heating, etc.) using oil as fuel.
oil·man ('ɔɪlmən) *n., pl.* **·men. 1.** a person who owns or operates oil wells. **2.** a person who makes or sells oil.
oil of tur·pen·tine *n.* another name for **turpentine** (sense 3).
oil of vit·ri·ol *n.* another name for **sulphuric acid.**
oil paint *or* **col·our** *n.* paint made of pigment ground in oil, usually linseed oil, used for oil painting.
oil paint·ing *n.* **1.** a picture painted with oil paints. **2.** the art or process of painting with oil paints. **3.** *Informal.* a person or thing regarded as good-looking (esp. in the phrase **she's no oil painting**).
oil palm *n.* a tropical African palm tree, *Elaeis guineensis,* the fruits of which yield palm oil.
oil rig *n.* See **rig** (sense 6).

Oil Riv+ers *pl. n.* the delta of the Niger River in S Nigeria.
oil shale *n.* a fine-grained shale containing oil, which can be extracted by heating.
oil+skin ('ɔɪl,skɪn) *n.* **1. a.** a cotton fabric treated with oil and pigment to make it waterproof. **b.** (*as modifier*): *an oilskin hat.* **2.** (*often pl.*) a protective outer garment of this fabric.
oil slick *n.* a mass of floating oil covering an area of water, esp. oil that has leaked or been discharged from a ship.
oil+stone ('ɔɪl,stəʊn) *n.* a stone with a fine grain lubricated with oil and used for sharpening cutting tools. See also **whetstone.**
oil var+nish *n.* another name for **varnish** (sense 1).
oil well *n.* a boring into the earth or sea bed for the extraction of petroleum.
oil·y ('ɔɪlɪ) *adj.* **oil·i·er, oil·i·est. 1.** soaked in or smeared with oil or grease. **2.** consisting of, containing, or resembling oil. **3.** flatteringly servile or obsequious. —**'oil·i·ly** *adv.* —**'oil·i+ness** *n.*
oink (ɔɪŋk) *interj.* an imitation or representation of the grunt of a pig or the cry of a goose.
oint+ment ('ɔɪntmənt) *n.* **1.** a fatty or oily medicated preparation applied to the skin to heal or protect. **2.** a similar substance used as a cosmetic. [C14: from Old French *oignement,* from Latin *unguentum* UNGUENT]
Oi+reach+tas ('ɛrəkθəs; *Gaelic* 'ɛrəxθəs) *n.* the parliament of the Republic of Ireland. See also **Dáil Eireann.** [Irish: assembly, from Old Irish *airech* nobleman]
Oise (*French* wa:z) *n.* **1.** a department of N France, in Picardy region. Capital: Beauvais. Pop.: 620 450 (1975). Area: 5887 sq. km (2296 sq. miles). **2.** a river in N France, rising in Belgium, in the Ardennes, and flowing southwest to join the Seine at Conflans. Length: 302 km (188 miles).
Oi·strakh ('ɔɪstrɑ:k; *Russian* 'ɔjstrəx) *n.* **1. Da·vid** (da'vit). 1908–74, Soviet violinist. **2.** his son, **I·gor** ('igərj). born 1931, Soviet violinist.
Oi·ta ('ɔɪtə) *n.* an industrial city in SW Japan, on NE Kyushu: dominated most of Kyushu in the 16th century. Pop.: 304 922 (1974 est.).
O·jib+wa (əʊ'dʒɪbwə) *n.* **1.** (*pl.* **+was** *or* **+wa**) a member of a North American Indian people living in a region west of Lake Superior. **2.** the language of this people, belonging to the Algonquian family. ~Also called: **Chippewa.**
O.K. (,əʊ'keɪ) *Informal.* **1.** *sentence substitute.* an expression of approvement, agreement, etc. ~*adj.* (*usually postpositive*), *adv.* **2.** in good or satisfactory condition. ~*vb.* **O.K.s, O.K.ing** (,əʊ'keɪɪŋ), **O.K.ed** (,əʊ'keɪd). **3.** (*tr.*) to approve or endorse. ~*n., pl.* **O.K.s. 4.** approval or agreement. ~Also: **okay.** [C19: perhaps after the *O.K. Club* (founded in 1840 by supporters of Martin Van Buren for U.S. president), from *Old Kinderhook,* Van Buren's birthplace in New York]
o·ka ('əʊkə) *or* **oke** (əʊk) *n.* **1.** a unit of weight used in Turkey, equal to about 2.75 pounds or 1.24 kilograms. **2.** a unit of liquid measure used in Turkey, equal to about 1.3 pints or 0.75 litres. [C17: from Turkish *ōqah,* from Arabic *ūqīyya,* probably from Greek *ounkia;* perhaps related to Latin *uncia* one twelfth; see OUNCE]
o·ka+pi (əʊ'kɑ:pɪ) *n., pl.* **+pis** *or* **+pi.** a ruminant mammal, *Okapia johnstoni,* of the forests of central Africa, having a reddish-brown coat with horizontal white stripes on the legs and small horns: family *Giraffidae.* [C20: from a Central African word]
O·ka+van+go *or* **O·ko+van+go** (,əʊkə'vɑ:ŋgəʊ) *n.* a river in SW central Africa, rising in central Angola and flowing southeast, then east as part of the border between Angola and South West Africa, then southeast across the Caprivi Strip to form a great marsh known as the **Okavango Basin.** Length: about 1600 km (1000 miles).
O·ka+ya+ma (,ɒkə'jɑ:mə) *n.* a city in SW Japan, on W Honshu on the Inland Sea. Pop.: 501 220 (1974 est.).
oke[1] (əʊk) *n.* another name for **oka.**
oke[2] (əʊk) *adj. Informal.* another term for **O.K.**
O·kee+cho+bee (,əʊkɪ'tʃəʊbɪ) *n.* **Lake.** a lake in S Florida, in the Everglades: second largest freshwater lake wholly within the U.S. Area: 1813 sq. km (700 sq. miles).
O·ke·fe+no·kee Swamp (,əʊkəfɪ'nəʊkɪ) *n.* a swamp in SE Georgia and N Florida: protected flora and fauna. Area: 1554 sq. km (600 sq. miles).
o·key-doke ('əʊkɪ,dəʊk) *or* **o·key-do·key** ('əʊkɪ'dəʊkɪ) *sentence substitute, adj., adv. Informal.* another term for **O.K.**
O·khotsk ('əʊkɒtsk; *Russian* a'xɔtsk) *n.* **Sea of.** part of the NW Pacific, surrounded by the Kamchatka Peninsula, the Kurile Islands, Sakhalin Island, and the E coast of Siberia. Area: 1 589 840 sq. km (613 838 sq. miles).
O·kie ('əʊkɪ) *n. U.S. slang, sometimes considered offensive.* **1.** an inhabitant of Oklahoma. **2.** an impoverished migrant farm worker, esp. one who left Oklahoma during the Depression of the 1930s to work elsewhere in the U.S.
O·ki+na+wa (,əʊkɪ'nɑ:wə) *n.* a coral island of SW Japan, the largest of the Ryukyu Islands in the N Pacific: scene of heavy fighting in World War II; administered by the U.S. (1945–72); agricultural. Chief town: Naha City. Pop.: 934 176 (1971). Area: 1176 sq. km (454 sq. miles).
Okla. *abbrev. for* Oklahoma.
Ok+la+ho+ma (,əʊklə'həʊmə) *n.* a state in the S central U.S.: consists of plains in the west, rising to mountains in the southwest and east; important for oil. Capital: Oklahoma City. Pop.: 2 559 253 (1970). Area: 178 145 sq. km (68 782 sq. miles). Abbrevs.: **Okla.** or (with zip code) **OK** —**,O·kla+'ho+man** *adj., n.*
O·kla+ho+ma Cit·y *n.* a city in central Oklahoma: the state capital and a major agricultural and industrial centre. Pop.: 373 717 (1973 est.).
o·kra ('əʊkrə) *n.* **1.** an annual malvaceous plant, *Hibiscus esculentus,* of the Old World tropics, with yellow-and-red flowers and edible oblong sticky green pods. **2.** the pod of this plant, eaten in soups, stews, etc. See also **gumbo** (sense 1). [C18: of West African origin]
ok·ta ('ɒktə) *n.* a unit used in meteorology to measure cloud cover, equivalent to a cloud cover of one eighth of the sky. [C20: from Greek *okta-, oktō* eight]
-ol[1] *suffix forming nouns.* denoting an organic chemical compound containing a hydroxyl group, esp. alcohols and phenols: *ethanol; quinol.* [from ALCOHOL]
-ol[2] *n. combining form.* (*not used systematically*) variant of **-ole**[1].
O·laf I ('əʊləf) *or* **O·lav I** ('əʊləv) *n.* called *Olaf Tryggvesson.* ?965–?1000 A.D., king of Norway (995–?1000). He began the conversion of Norway to Christianity.
O·laf II *or* **O·lav II** *n.* **Saint.** 995–1030 A.D., king of Norway (1015–28), who worked to complete the conversion of Norway to Christianity; deposed by Canute; patron saint of Norway. Feast day: July 29.
O·laf V *or* **O·lav V** *n.* born 1903, king of Norway since 1957; son of Haakon VII.
Ö·land (*Swedish* 'ø:,land) *n.* an island in the Baltic Sea, separated from the mainland of SE Sweden by Kalmar Sound: the second largest Swedish island. Chief town: Borgholm. Pop.: 20 361 (1970). Area: 1347 sq. km (520 sq. miles).
Ol·cott ('ɔ:lkɒt) *n.* Colonel **Hen·ry Steel.** ?1832–1907, U.S. theosophist.
old (əʊld) *adj.* **1.** having lived or existed for a relatively long time: *an old man; an old tradition; old wine; an old house; an old country.* **2. a.** of or relating to advanced years or a long life: *old age.* **b. the old.** old people. **c. old and young.** people of all ages. **3.** decrepit or senile. **4.** worn with age or use: *old clothes; an old car.* **5. a.** (*postpositive*) having lived or existed for a specified period: *a child who is six years old.* **b.** (*in combination*): *a six-year-old child.* **c.** (*as n. in combination*): *a six-year-old.* **6.** (*cap. when part of a name or title*) earlier or earliest of two or more things with the same name: *the old edition; the Old Testament; old Norwich.* **7.** (*cap. when part of a name*) designating the form of a language in which the earliest known records are written: *Old English.* **8.** (*prenominal*) familiar through long acquaintance or repetition: *an old friend; an old excuse.* **9.** practised; hardened: *old in cunning.* **10.** (*prenominal*) (often preceded by *good*) cherished; dear: used as a term of affection or familiarity: *good old George.* **11.** *Informal.* (with any of several nouns) used as a familiar form of address to a person: *old thing; old bean; old stick; old fellow.* **12.** skilled through long experience (esp. in the phrase **an old hand**). **13.** out-of-date; unfashionable. **14.** remote or distant in origin or time of origin: *an old culture.* **15.** (*prenominal*) former; previous: *my old house was small.* **16. a.** (*prenominal*) established for a relatively long time: *an old member.* **b.** (*in combination*): *old-established.* **17.** sensible, wise, or mature: *old beyond one's years.* **18.** (of a river, valley, or land surface) in the final stage of the cycle of erosion, characterized by flat extensive flood plains and minimum relief. See also **youthful** (sense 4), **mature** (sense 6). **19.** (intensifier) (esp. in phrases such as **a good old time, any old thing, any old how,** etc.). **20.** (of crops) harvested late. **21. good old days.** an earlier period of time regarded as better than the present. **22. little old.** indicating affection, esp. humorous affection: *my little old wife.* **23. the old one** (*or* **gentleman**). *Informal.* a jocular name for **Satan.** ~*n.* **24.** an earlier or past time (esp. in the phrase **of old**): *in days of old.* [Old English *eald;* related to Old Saxon *ald,* Old High German, German *alt,* Latin *altus* high] —**'old+ish** *adj.* —**'old+ness** *n.*
old age pen+sion *n.* another name for **retirement pension.** —**old age pen+sion+er** *n.*
Old Bai+ley ('beɪlɪ) *n.* the chief court exercising criminal jurisdiction in London; the Central Criminal Court of England.
old bird *n. Jocular.* a wary and astute person.
old boy *n.* **1.** (*sometimes caps.*) *Brit.* a male ex-pupil of a school. **2.** *Informal, chiefly Brit.* **a.** a familiar name used to refer to a man. **b.** an old man.
old boy net+work *n. Brit. informal.* the appointment to power of former pupils of the same small group of public schools or universities.
Old Bul+gar+i·an *n.* another name for **Old Church Slavonic.**
Old Cas+tile *n.* a region of N Spain, on the Bay of Biscay: formerly a province. Spanish name: **Castilla la Vieja.**
Old·cas·tle ('əʊld,kɑ:səl) *n.* Sir **John,** Baron Cobham. ?1378–1417, Lollard leader. In 1411 he led an English army in France but in 1413 he was condemned as a heretic and later hanged and burnt. He is thought to have been a model for Shakespeare's character Falstaff in *Henry IV.*
Old Cath·o·lic *adj.* **1.** of or relating to several small national Churches which have broken away from the Roman Catholic Church on matters of doctrine. ~*n.* **2.** a member of one of these Churches.
Old Church Sla+von+ic *or* **Slav+ic** *n.* the oldest recorded Slavonic language: the form of Old Slavonic into which the Bible was translated in the ninth century, preserved as a liturgical language of various Orthodox Churches: belonging to the South Slavonic subbranch of languages.
old clothes man *n.* a person who deals in second-hand clothes.
old coun+try *n.* the country of origin of an immigrant or an immigrant's ancestors.

Old Dart *n.* **the.** *Austral. slang.* England. [C19: of unknown origin]
Old Del·hi *n.* See **Delhi.**
Old Dutch *n.* the Dutch language up to about 1100, derived from the Low Franconian dialect of Old Low German. See also **Franconian.** Abbrev.: **OD.**
old·en ('əʊldᵊn) *adj.* an archaic or poetic word for **old** (often in phrases such as **in olden days** and **in olden times**).
Ol·den·burg[1] ('əʊldᵊnˈbɜːg; *German* 'ɔldᵊnˌbʊrk) *n.* **1.** a city in NW West Germany, in Lower Saxony: former capital of Oldenburg state. Pop.: 134 168 (1974 est.). **2.** a former state of NW Germany: became part of Lower Saxony in 1946.
Ol·den·burg[2] ('əʊldᵊnˌbɜːg) *n.* **Claes** (klɔːs). born 1929, U.S. pop sculptor and artist, born in Sweden.
Old Eng·lish *n.* **1.** Also called: **Anglo-Saxon.** the English language from the time of the earliest settlements in the fifth century A.D. to about 1100. The main dialects were West Saxon (the chief literary form), Kentish, and Anglian. Compare **Middle English, Modern English.** Abbrev.: **OE. 2.** *Printing.* a Gothic typeface commonly used in England up to the 18th century.
Old Eng·lish sheep·dog *n.* a breed of large sheepdog with a profuse shaggy coat.
old·er ('əʊldə) *adj.* **1.** the comparative of **old. 2.** Also (of people, esp. members of the same family): **elder.** having lived or existed longer; of greater age.
old-es·tab·lished *adj.* established for a long time.
old·e-world·e ('əʊldɪ'wɜːldɪ) *adj. Sometimes facetious.* old-world or quaint.
old face *n. Printing.* a type style that originated in the 18th century, characterized by little contrast between thick and thin strokes. Compare **modern** (sense 5).
old·fan·gled ('əʊldˌfæŋgᵊld) *adj. Derogatory.* out-of-date; old-fashioned. [C20: formed on analogy with NEWFANGLED]
old-fash·ioned *adj.* **1.** belonging to, characteristic of, or favoured by former times; outdated: *old-fashioned ideas.* **2.** favouring or adopting the dress, manners, fashions, etc., of a former time. **3.** *Northern English dialect.* old for one's age: *an old-fashioned child.* ~*n.* **4.** a cocktail containing spirit, bitters, fruit, etc.
Old French *n.* the French language in its earliest forms, from about the ninth century up to about 1400. Abbrev.: **OF.**
Old Fri·sian *n.* the Frisian language up to about 1400. Abbrev.: **OFris.**
old girl *n.* **1.** (*sometimes caps.*) *Brit.* a female ex-pupil of a school. **2.** *Informal, chiefly Brit.* **a.** a familiar name used to refer to a woman. **b.** an old woman.
Old Glo·ry *n.* a nickname for the flag of the United States of America.
old gold *n.* **a.** a dark yellow colour, sometimes with a brownish tinge. **b.** (*as adj.*): *an old-gold carpet.*
old guard *n.* **1.** a group that works for a long-established or old-fashioned cause or principle. **2.** the conservative element in a political party or other group.
Old Guard *n.* the French imperial guard created by Napoleon Bonaparte in 1804.
Old·ham ('əʊldəm) *n.* a town in NW England, in Greater Manchester. Pop.: 105 705 (1971).
old hand *n.* a person who is skilled at something through long experience.
Old Har·ry *n. Informal.* a jocular name for **Satan.**
old hat *adj.* (*postpositive*) old-fashioned or trite.
Old High Ger·man *n.* a group of West Germanic dialects that eventually developed into modern German; High German up to about 1200: spoken in the Middle Ages on the upper Rhine, in Bavaria, Alsace, and elsewhere, including Alemannic, Bavarian, Langobardic, and Upper Franconian. Abbrev.: **OHG.**
Old Ice·land·ic *n.* the dialect of Old Norse spoken and written in Iceland; the Icelandic language up to about 1600.
old·ie ('əʊldɪ) *n. Informal.* an old person or thing.
Old I·rish *n.* **1.** Also called: **Ogham Irish.** the Celtic language of Ireland up to about 900 A.D., of which few records survive. **2.** Irish Gaelic up to about 1100.
Old King·dom *n.* a period of Egyptian history: usually considered to extend from the third to the sixth dynasty (?2700–?2150 B.C.).
old la·dy *n.* an informal term for **mother** or **wife.**
Old Lat·in *n.* the Latin language before the classical period, up to about 100 B.C.
old-line *adj.* **1.** *U.S.* conservative; old-fashioned. **2.** well-established; traditional. —ˌ**old-'lin·er** *n.*
Old Low Ger·man *n.* the Saxon and Low Franconian dialects of German up to about 1200; the old form of modern Low German and Dutch. Abbrev.: **OLG.**
old maid *n.* **1.** a woman regarded as unlikely ever to marry; spinster. **2.** *Informal.* a prim, fastidious, or excessively cautious person. **3.** a card game using a pack from which one card has been removed, in which players try to avoid holding the unpaired card at the end of the game. —ˌ**old-'maid·ish** *adj.*
old man *n.* **1.** an informal term for **father** or **husband. 2.** (*sometimes caps.*) *Informal.* a man in command, such as an employer, foreman, or captain of a ship. **3.** *Sometimes facetious.* an affectionate term used in addressing a man. **4.** another name for **southernwood. 5.** *Austral. informal.* **a.** an adult male kangaroo. **b.** (*as modifier*) very large. **6.** *Christianity.* the unregenerate aspect of human nature.
old man's beard *n.* any of various plants having long trailing parts, esp. traveller's joy and Spanish moss.
old mas·ter *n.* **1.** one of the great European painters of the period 1500 to 1800. **2.** a painting by one of these.
old moon *n.* **1.** a phase of the moon lying between last quarter and new moon, when it appears as a waning crescent. **2.** the moon when it appears as a waning crescent. **3.** the time at which this occurs.
Old Nick *n. Informal.* a jocular name for **Satan.**
Old Norse *n.* the language or group of dialects of medieval Scandinavia and Iceland from about 700 to about 1350, forming the North Germanic branch of the Indo-European family of languages. See also **Proto-Norse, Old Icelandic.** Abbrev.: **ON.**
Old North French *n.* any of the dialects of Old French spoken in N France, such as Norman French.
Old North·west *n.* (in the early U.S.) the land between the Great Lakes, the Mississippi, and the Ohio River. Awarded to the U.S. in 1783, it was organized into the **Northwest Territory** in 1787 and now forms the states of Ohio, Indiana, Illinois, Wisconsin, Michigan, and part of Minnesota.
Old Per·sian *n.* an ancient language belonging to the West Iranian branch of the Indo-European family, recorded in cuneiform inscriptions of the 6th to the 4th centuries B.C. See also **Middle Persian.**
Old Pre·tend·er *n.* See (James Francis Edward) **Stuart.**
Old Prus·sian *n.* the former language of the non-German Prussians, belonging to the Baltic branch of the Indo-European family: extinct by 1700.
old rose *n.* **a.** a greyish-pink colour. **b.** (*as adj.*): *old-rose gloves.*
Old Sax·on *n.* the Saxon dialect of Low German up to about 1200, from which modern Low German is derived. Abbrev.: **OS.**
old school *n.* **1.** *Chiefly Brit.* a school formerly attended by a person. **2.** a group of people favouring traditional ideas or conservative practices.
old school tie *n.* **1.** *Brit.* a distinctive tie that indicates which school the wearer attended. **2.** the attitudes, loyalties, values, etc., associated with British public schools.
Old Sla·von·ic *or* **Slav·ic** *n.* the South Slavonic language up to about 1400: the language of the Macedonian Slavs that developed into Serbo-Croatian and Bulgarian. See also **Old Church Slavonic.**
old sol·dier *n.* **1.** a former soldier or veteran. **2.** an experienced or practised person.
Old South *n.* the American South before the Civil War.
old squaw *n. U.S.* a long-tailed northern sea duck, *Clangula hyemalis,* having dark wings and a white-and-brown head and body. Also called: **oldwife.**
old stag·er *n.* a person with experience; old hand.
old·ster ('əʊldstə) *n.* **1.** *Informal.* an older person. **2.** *Brit. Navy.* a person who has been a midshipman for four years.
Old Stone Age *n.* (*not now in technical usage*) another term for **palaeolithic.**
old style *n. Printing.* a type style reviving the characteristics of old face.
Old Style *n.* the former method of reckoning dates using the Julian calendar. Compare **New Style.**
old talk *Caribbean.* ~*n.* **1.** superficial chatting. ~*vb.* **old-talk. 2.** (*intr.*) to indulge in such chatting.
Old Test. *abbrev. for* Old Testament.
Old Tes·ta·ment *n.* the collection of books comprising the sacred Scriptures of the Hebrews and essentially recording the history of the Hebrew people as the chosen people of God; the first part of the Christian Bible.
old-time *adj.* (*prenominal*) of or relating to a former time; old-fashioned: *old-time dancing.*
old-time dance *n. Brit.* a formal or formation dance, such as the lancers. —**old-time danc·ing** *n.*
old-tim·er *n.* **1.** a person who has been in a certain place, occupation, etc., for a long time. **2.** *U.S.* an old man.
Ol·du·vai Gorge ('ɒldʊˌvaɪ) *n.* a gorge in N Tanzania, north of the Ngorongoro Crater: fossil evidence of early man and other closely related species, together with artifacts.
old·wife ('əʊldˌwaɪf) *n., pl.* **·wives. 1.** another name for **old squaw. 2.** any of various fishes, esp. the menhaden or the alewife.
old wives' tale *n.* a belief passed on by word of mouth as a piece of traditional wisdom.
old wom·an *n.* **1.** an informal term for **mother** or **wife. 2.** a timid, fussy, or cautious person. —**old wom·an·ish** *adj.*
Old World *n.* that part of the world that was known before the discovery of the Americas, comprising Europe, Asia, and Africa; the eastern hemisphere.
old-world *adj.* of or characteristic of former times, esp., in Europe, quaint or traditional. —ˌ**old-'world·ly** *adv.*
Old World mon·key *n.* any monkey of the family *Cercopithecidae,* including macaques, baboons, and mandrills. They are more closely related to anthropoid apes than are the New World monkeys, having nostrils that are close together and nonprehensile tails.
o·lé (əʊ'leɪ) *interj.* **1.** an exclamation of approval or encouragement customary at bullfights, flamenco dancing, and other Spanish or Latin-American events. ~*n.* **2.** a cry of olé. [Spanish, from Arabic *wa-llāh,* from *wa* and + *allāh* God]
-ole[1] *or* **-ol** *n. combining form.* **1.** denoting an organic unsaturated compound containing a 5-membered ring: *thiazole.* **2.** denoting an aromatic organic ether: *anisole.* [from Latin *oleum* oil, from Greek *elaion,* from *elaia* olive]
-ole[2] *suffix of nouns.* indicating something small: *arteriole.* [from Latin *-olus,* diminutive suffix]

o·le·a·ceous (ˌəʊlɪˈeɪʃəs) *adj.* of, relating to, or belonging to the *Oleaceae,* a family of trees and shrubs, including the ash, jasmine, privet, lilac, and olive. [C19: via New Latin from Latin *olea* OLIVE; see also OIL]

o·le·ag·i·nous (ˌəʊlɪˈædʒɪnəs) *adj.* **1.** resembling or having the properties of oil. **2.** containing or producing oil. [C17: from Latin *oleāginus,* from *olea* OLIVE; see also OIL]

o·le·an·der (ˌəʊlɪˈændə) *n.* a poisonous evergreen Mediterranean apocynaceous shrub or tree, *Nerium oleander,* with fragrant white, pink, or purple flowers. Also called: **rosebay.** [C16: from Medieval Latin, variant of *arodandrum,* perhaps from Latin RHODODENDRON]

o·le·as·ter (ˌəʊlɪˈæstə) *n.* any of several shrubs of the genus *Elaeagnus,* esp. *E. angustifolia,* of S Europe, Asia, and North America, having silver-white twigs, yellow flowers, and an olive-like fruit: family *Elaeagnaceae.* Also called: **wild olive.** [Latin: from *olea;* see OLIVE, OIL]

o·le·ate (ˈəʊlɪˌeɪt) *n.* any salt or ester of oleic acid, containing the ion $C_{17}H_{33}COO^-$ or the group $C_{17}H_{33}COO$-: common components of natural fats.

o·lec·ra·non (əʊˈlɛkrəˌnɒn, ˌəʊlɪˈkreɪnən) *n. Anatomy.* the bony projection of the ulna behind the elbow joint. [C18: from Greek, shortened from *ōlenokrānon,* from *ōlenē* elbow + *krānion* head] —**o·lec·ra·nal** (əʊˈlɛkrənᵊl, ˌəʊlɪˈkreɪnᵊl) *adj.*

o·le·fine *or* **o·le·fin** (ˈəʊlɪˌfiːn, -fɪn, ˈɒl-) *n.* another name for **alkene.** [C19: from French *oléfiant,* ultimately from Latin *oleum* oil + *facere* to make] —ˌ**o·le·ˈfin·ic** *adj.*

o·le·ic ac·id (əʊˈliːɪk) *n.* a colourless oily liquid unsaturated acid occurring, as the glyceride, in almost all natural fats; *cis*-9-octadecenoic acid: used in making soaps, ointments, cosmetics, and lubricating oils. Formula: $CH_3(CH_2)_7CH{:}CH(CH_2)_7COOH$. [C19 *oleic,* from Latin *oleum* oil + -IC]

o·le·in (ˈəʊlɪɪn) *n.* another name for **triolein.** [C19: from French *oléine,* from Latin *oleum* oil + -IN]

o·le·o- *combining form.* oil: *oleomargarine.* [from Latin *oleum* OIL]

o·le·o·graph (ˈəʊlɪəˌgrɑːf, -ˌgræf) *n.* **1.** a chromolithograph printed in oil colours to imitate the appearance of an oil painting. **2.** the pattern formed by a drop of oil spreading on water. —**o·le·o·graph·ic** (ˌəʊlɪəˈgræfɪk) *adj.* —**o·le·og·ra·phy** (ˌəʊlɪˈɒgrəfɪ) *n.*

o·le·o·mar·ga·rine (ˌəʊlɪəʊˌmɑːdʒəˈriːn) *or* **o·le·o·mar·ga·rin** (ˌəʊlɪəʊˈmɑːdʒərɪn) *n.* another name (esp. U.S.) for **margarine.**

o·le·o oil *n.* an oil extracted from beef fat, consisting mainly of a mixture of olein and palmitin. It is used in the manufacture of margarine.

o·le·o·res·in (ˌəʊlɪəʊˈrɛzɪn) *n.* **1.** a semisolid mixture of a resin and essential oil, obtained from certain plants. **2.** *Pharmacol.* a liquid preparation of resins and oils, obtained by extraction from plants. —ˌ**o·le·o·ˈres·in·ous** *adj.*

o·le·um (ˈəʊlɪəm) *n., pl.* **o·le·a** (ˈəʊlɪə) *or* **o·le·ums.** another name for **fuming sulphuric acid.** [from Latin: oil, referring to its oily consistency]

O lev·el *n. Brit.* **1. a.** the basic level of the General Certificate of Education. **b.** (*as modifier*): *O level maths.* **2.** a pass in a particular subject at O level: *he has eight O levels.*

ol·fac·tion (ɒlˈfækʃən) *n.* **1.** the sense of smell. **2.** the act or function of smelling.

ol·fac·to·ry (ɒlˈfæktərɪ, -triː) *adj.* **1.** of or relating to the sense of smell. ~*n., pl.* **·ries. 2.** (*usually pl.*) an organ or nerve concerned with the sense of smell. [C17: from Latin *olfactus,* past participle of *olfacere,* from *olere* to smell + *facere* to make]

ol·fac·to·ry bulb *n.* the anterior and slightly enlarged end of the olfactory tract, from which the cranial nerves concerned with the sense of smell originate.

ol·fac·to·ry nerve *n.* either one of the first pair of cranial nerves, supplying the mucous membrane of the nose.

ol·fac·to·ry tract *n.* a long narrow triangular band of white tissue originating in the olfactory bulb and extending back to the point at which its fibres enter the base of the cerebrum.

OLG, O.L.G., *or* **OLG.** *abbrev. for* Old Low German.

o·lib·a·num (ɒˈlɪbənəm) *n.* another name for **frankincense.** [C14: from Medieval Latin, from Greek *libanos*]

ol·id (ˈɒlɪd) *adj.* foul-smelling. [C17: from Latin *olidus,* from *olēre* to smell]

ol·i·garch (ˈɒlɪˌgɑːk) *n.* a member of an oligarchy.

ol·i·gar·chy (ˈɒlɪˌgɑːkɪ) *n., pl.* **·chies. 1.** government by a small group of people. **2.** a state or organization so governed. **3.** a small body of individuals ruling such a state. **4.** *Chiefly U.S.* a small clique of private citizens who exert a strong influence on government. [C16: via Medieval Latin from Greek *oligarkhia,* from *oligos* few + -ARCHY] —ˌ**ol·i·ˈgar·chic** *or* ˌ**ol·i·ˈgar·chi·cal** *adj.* —ˌ**ol·i·ˈgar·chi·cal·ly** *adv.*

ol·i·go- *or before a vowel* **ol·ig-** *combining form.* indicating a few or little: *oligopoly.* [from Greek *oligos* little, few]

Ol·i·go·cene (ˈɒlɪgəʊˌsiːn, ɒˈlɪg-) *adj.* **1.** of, denoting, or formed in the third epoch of the Tertiary period, which lasted for 15 000 000 years. ~*n.* **2.** (preceded by *the*) the Oligocene epoch or rock series. [C19: OLIGO- + -CENE]

ol·i·go·chaete (ˈɒlɪgəʊˌkiːt) *n.* **1.** any freshwater or terrestrial annelid worm of the class *Oligochaeta,* having bristles (chaetae) borne singly along the length of the body: includes the earthworms. ~*adj.* **2.** of, relating to, or belonging to the class *Oligochaeta.* [C19: from New Latin; see OLIGO-, CHAETA]

ol·i·go·clase (ˈɒlɪgəʊˌkleɪs) *n.* a white, bluish, or reddish-yellow feldspar mineral of the plagioclase series, consisting of aluminium silicates of sodium and calcium. Formula: $NaAlSi_3O_8.CaAl_2Si_2O_8$. [C19: from OLIGO- + -CLASE]

ol·i·gop·o·ly (ˌɒlɪˈgɒpəlɪ) *n., pl.* **·lies.** *Economics.* a market situation in which control over the supply of a commodity is held by a small number of producers each of whom is able to influence prices and thus directly affect the position of competitors. —ˌ**ol·i·ˌgop·o·ˈlis·tic** *adj.*

ol·i·gop·so·ny (ˌɒlɪˈgɒpsənɪ) *n., pl.* **·nies.** a market situation in which the demand for a commodity is represented by a small number of purchasers. [C20: from OLIGO- + *-opsony,* from Greek *opsōnia* purchase of food] —ˌ**ol·i·ˌgop·so·ˈnis·tic** *adj.*

ol·i·go·sac·cha·ride (ˌɒlɪgəʊˈsækəˌraɪd, -rɪd) *n.* any one of a class of carbohydrates consisting of a few monosaccharide units linked together. Compare **polysaccharide.**

ol·i·go·troph·ic (ˌɒlɪgəʊˈtrɒfɪk) *adj.* (of lakes and similar habitats) poor in nutrients and plant life and rich in oxygen. Compare **eutrophic.** —**ol·i·got·ro·phy** (ˌɒlɪˈgɒtrəfɪ) *n.*

ol·i·gu·ri·a (ˌɒlɪˈgjʊərɪə) *or* **ol·i·gu·re·sis** (ˌɒlɪgjʊˈriːsɪs) *n.* excretion of an abnormally small volume of urine, often as the result of a kidney disorder. Compare **anuria.** [C19: from OLIGO- + -URIA] —**ol·i·gu·ret·ic** (ˌɒlɪgjʊˈrɛtɪk) *adj.*

Ó·lim·bos (ˈɔlimbɔs) *n.* transliteration of the modern Greek name for **Olympus** (sense 1).

o·li·o (ˈəʊlɪˌəʊ) *n., pl.* **o·li·os. 1.** a dish of many different ingredients. **2.** a miscellany or potpourri. [C17: from Spanish *olla* stew, from Latin: jar]

Ol·i·phant (ˈɒlɪfənt) *n.* Sir **Mar·cus Lau·rence El·win.** born 1901, Australian nuclear physicist.

ol·i·va·ceous (ˌɒlɪˈveɪʃəs) *adj.* of an olive colour.

ol·i·var·y (ˈɒlɪvərɪ) *adj.* **1.** shaped like an olive. **2.** *Anatomy.* of or relating to either of two masses of tissue (**olivary bodies**) on the forward portion of the medulla oblongata. [C16: from Latin *olivārius,* from *oliva* OLIVE]

ol·ive (ˈɒlɪv) *n.* **1.** an evergreen oleaceous tree, *Olea europaea,* of the Mediterranean region but cultivated elsewhere, having white fragrant flowers, and edible shiny black fruits. **2.** the fruit of this plant, eaten as a relish and used as a source of olive oil. **3.** the wood of the olive tree, used for ornamental work. **4.** any of various trees or shrubs resembling the olive. **5. a.** a yellow-green colour. **b.** (*as adj.*): *an olive coat.* ~*adj.* **6.** of, relating to, or made of the olive tree, its wood, or its fruit. [C13: via Old French from Latin *oliva,* related to Greek *elaia* olive tree; compare Greek *elaion* oil]

ol·ive branch *n.* **1.** a branch of an olive tree used to symbolize peace. **2.** any offering of peace or conciliation.

ol·ive brown *n.* **a.** a yellowish-brown to yellowish-green colour. **b.** (*as adj.*): *an olive-brown coat.*

ol·ive crown *n.* (esp. in ancient Greece and Rome) a garland of olive leaves awarded as a token of victory.

ol·ive drab *n.* **1.** *U.S.* **a.** a dull but fairly strong greyish-olive colour. **b.** (*as adj.*): *an olive-drab jacket.* **2.** cloth or clothes in this colour, esp. the uniform of the U.S. Army.

ol·ive green *n.* **a.** a colour that is greener, stronger, and brighter than olive; deep yellowish-green. **b.** (*as adj.*): *an olive-green coat.*

o·liv·en·ite (ɒˈlɪvɪˌnaɪt) *n.* a green to black rare secondary mineral consisting of hydrated basic copper arsenate in orthorhombic crystalline form. Formula: $Cu_2(AsO_4)(OH)$. [C19: from German *Oliven*(*erz*) olive (ore) + -ITE[1]]

ol·ive oil *n.* a pale yellow oil pressed from ripe olive fruits and used in cooking, medicines, soaps, etc.

Ol·i·ver (ˈɒlɪvə) *n.* **1.** one of Charlemagne's 12 paladins. See also **Roland. 2. Joseph,** called *King Oliver.* 1885–1938, U.S. pioneer jazz cornetist.

Ol·ives (ˈɒlɪvz) *n.* **Mount of.** a hill to the east of Jerusalem: in New Testament times the village Bethany (Mark 11:11) was on its eastern slope and Gethsemane on its western one.

O·liv·i·er (əˈlɪvɪˌeɪ) *n.* **Lau·rence (Kerr),** Lord Olivier. born 1907, English actor and director.

ol·i·vine (ˈɒlɪˌviːn, ˌɒlɪˈviːn) *n.* any of a group of hard glassy olive-green or brown minerals consisting of magnesium iron silicate in orthorhombic crystalline form: found in basic igneous rocks such as basalt and gabbro. Formula: $(Mg,Fe)_2SiO_4$. [C18: from German, named after its colour]

ol·la (ˈɒlə; *Spanish* ˈoʎa) *n.* **1.** a cooking pot. **2.** short for **olla podrida.** [Spanish, from Latin *olla,* variant of *aulla* pot]

ol·la po·dri·da (pɒˈdriːdə; *Spanish* poˈðriða) *n.* **1.** a Spanish dish, consisting of a stew with beans, sausages, etc. **2.** an assortment; miscellany. [literally: rotten pot]

olm (əʊlm, ɒlm) *n.* a pale blind eel-like salamander, *Proteus anguinus,* of underground streams in SE Europe, that retains its larval form throughout its life: family *Proteidae.* See also **mud puppy.** [C20: from German]

Ol·mütz (ˈɔlmyts) *n.* the German name for **Olomouc.**

ol·o·gy (ˈɒlədʒɪ) *n., pl.* **·gies.** *Informal.* a science or other branch of knowledge. [C19: abstracted from words with this ending, such as *theology, biology,* etc.; see -LOGY]

O·lo·mouc (*Czech* ˈɔlɔmɔuts) *n.* a city in Czechoslovakia, in North Moravia on the Morava River: capital of Moravia until 1640; university (1576). Pop.: 79 900 (1970). German name: **Olmütz.**

o·lo·ro·so (ˌɒləˈrəʊsəʊ) *n.* a full-bodied golden-coloured sherry. [from Spanish: fragrant]

Ol·szt·yn (*Russian* ˈɔlʃtɪn) *n.* a town in NE Poland: founded in 1334 by the Teutonic Knights; communications centre. Pop.: 107 500 (1974 est.).

O·lym·pi·a (əˈlɪmpɪə) *n.* **1.** a plain in Greece, in the NW Peloponnese: in ancient times a major sanctuary of Zeus and site of the original Olympic Games. **2.** a port in W Washington, the state capital, on Puget Sound. Pop.: 23 111 (1970).

O·lym·pi·ad (əˈlɪmpɪˌæd) *n.* **1.** a staging of the modern Olympic Games. **2.** the four-year period between consecutive celebrations of the Olympic Games; a unit of ancient Greek chronology dating back to 776 B.C. **3.** an international contest in chess, bridge, etc.

O·lym·pi·an (əˈlɪmpɪən) *adj.* **1.** of or relating to Mount Olympus or to the classical Greek gods. **2.** majestic or godlike in manner or bearing. **3.** superior to mundane considerations, esp. when impractical. **4.** of or relating to ancient Olympia or its inhabitants. ~*n.* **5.** a god of Olympus. **6.** an inhabitant or native of ancient Olympia. **7.** *Chiefly U.S.* a competitor in the Olympic Games.

O·lym·pic (əˈlɪmpɪk) *adj.* **1.** of or relating to the Olympic Games. **2.** of or relating to ancient Olympia.

O·lym·pic Games *n.* (*functioning as sing. or pl.*) **1.** the greatest Panhellenic festival, held every fourth year in honour of Zeus at ancient Olympia. From 472 B.C., it consisted of five days of games, sacrifices, and festivities. **2.** Also called: **the Olympics.** the modern revival of these games, consisting of international athletic and sporting contests held every four years in a selected country since their inception in Athens in 1896. See also **Winter Olympic Games.**

O·lym·pic Moun·tains *pl. n.* a mountain range in NW Washington: part of the Coast Range. Highest peak: Mount Olympus, 2427 m (7965 ft.).

O·lym·pic Pen·in·su·la *n.* a large peninsula of W Washington.

O·lym·pus (əʊˈlɪmpəs) *n.* **1. Mount.** a mountain in NE Greece, on the border between Thessaly and Macedonia: the highest mountain in Greece, believed in Greek mythology to be the dwelling place of the greater gods. Height: 2911 m (9550 ft.). Greek name: **Ólimbos. 2. Mount.** a mountain in NW Washington: highest peak of the Olympic Mountains. Height: 2427 m (7965 ft.). **3.** a poetic word for **heaven.**

O·lyn·thus (əʊˈlɪnθəs) *n.* an ancient city in N Greece: the centre of Chalcidice.

Om (əʊm) *n. Hinduism.* a sacred syllable typifying the three gods Brahma, Vishnu, and Siva, who are concerned in the threefold operation of integration, maintenance, and disintegration. [from Sanskrit]

Om. *abbrev. for* Ostmark.

O.M. *abbrev. for* Order of Merit (a Brit. title).

-o·ma *n. combining form.* indicating a tumour: *glaucoma.* [from Greek *-ōma*]

om·a·dhaun (ˈɒməˌdaʊn) *n. Irish.* a fool.

O·magh (əʊˈmɑː, ˈəʊmə) *n.* a market town in Northern Ireland, county town of Co. Tyrone. Pop.: 11 953 (1971).

O·ma·ha (ˈəʊməˌhɑː) *n.* a city in E Nebraska, on the Missouri River opposite Council Bluffs, Iowa: the largest city in the state; the country's largest livestock market and meat-packing centre. Pop.: 377 292 (1973 est.).

O·man (əʊˈmɑːn) *n.* a sultanate in SE Arabia, on the **Gulf of Oman** and the Arabian Sea: the most powerful state in Arabia in the 19th century, ruling Zanzibar, much of the Persian coast, and part of Pakistan. Language: Arabic. Religion: Muslim. Currency: rial. Capital: Muscat. Pop.: 766 000 (1975 UN est.). Area: about 212 400 sq. km (82 000 sq. miles). Former name (until 1970): **Muscat and Oman.** —**O·ˈma·ni** *adj., n.*

O·mar Khay·yam (ˈəʊmɑː kaɪˈɑːm) *n.* ?1050–?1123, Persian poet, mathematician, and astronomer, noted for the *Rubaiyat,* a collection of quatrains, popularized in the West by Edward Fitzgerald's version (1859).

o·ma·sum (əʊˈmeɪsəm) *n., pl.* **-sa** (-sə). another name for **psalterium.** [C18: from Latin: bullock's tripe]

O·may·yad *or* **Om·mi·ad** (əʊˈmaɪæd) *n., pl.* **-yads, -ya·des** (-əˌdiːz) *or* **-ads, -a·des. 1.** a caliph of the dynasty ruling (661–750 A.D.) from its capital at Damascus. **2.** an emir (756–929 A.D.) or caliph (929–1031 A.D.) of the Omayyad dynasty in Spain.

om·bre *or U.S.* **om·ber** (ˈɒmbə) *n.* an 18th-century card game. [C17: from Spanish *hombre* man, referring to the player who attempts to win the stakes]

om·bro- *combining form.* indicating rain: *ombrometer; ombrology.* [from Greek *ombros* shower of rain]

om·buds·man (ˈɒmbʊdzmən) *n., pl.* **-men.** an official who investigates citizens' complaints against the government or its servants. Also called (Brit.): **parliamentary commissioner.** [C20: from Swedish: commissioner]

Om·dur·man (ˌɒmdɜːˈmɑːn) *n.* a city in the central Sudan, on the White Nile, opposite Khartoum: the largest town in the Sudan; scene of the **Battle of Omdurman** (1898), in which the Mahdi's successor was defeated by Lord Kitchener's forces. Pop.: 258 532 (1971 est.).

-ome *suffix forming nouns.* denoting a mass or part of a specified kind: *rhizome.* [variant of -OMA]

o·me·ga (ˈəʊmɪɡə) *n.* **1.** the 24th and last letter of the Greek alphabet (Ω, ω), a long vowel, transliterated as *o* or *ō.* **2.** the ending or last of a series. [C16: from Greek *ō mega* big *o;* see MEGA-, OMICRON]

o·me·ga mi·nus *n.* an unstable negatively charged elementary particle, classified as a baryon, that has a mass 3276 times that of the electron.

ome·lette *or esp. U.S.* **ome·let** (ˈɒmlɪt) *n.* a savoury or sweet dish of beaten eggs cooked in fat. [C17: from French *omelette,* changed from *alumette,* from *alumelle* sword blade, changed by mistaken division from *la lemelle,* from Latin (see LAMELLA); apparently from the flat shape of the omelette]

o·men (ˈəʊmən) *n.* **1.** a phenomenon or occurrence regarded as a sign of future happiness or disaster. **2.** prophetic significance. ~*vb.* **3.** (*tr.*) to portend. [C16: from Latin]

o·men·tum (əʊˈmɛntəm) *n., pl.* **-ta** (-tə). *Anatomy.* a double fold of peritoneum connecting the stomach with other abdominal organs. [C16: from Latin: membrane, esp. a caul, of obscure origin]

o·mer (ˈəʊmə) *n.* an ancient Hebrew unit of dry measure equal to one tenth of an ephah. [C17: from Hebrew *ʿōmer* a measure]

O·mer (ˈəʊmə) *n. Judaism.* a period of seven weeks extending from the second day of Passover to the first day of Shabuoth. Also called: **Counting of the Omer.**

o·mi·cron (əʊˈmaɪkrɒn, ˈɒmɪkrɒn) *n.* the 15th letter in the Greek alphabet (O, ο), a short vowel, transliterated as *o.* [from Greek *ō mikron* small *o;* see MICRO-, OMEGA]

om·i·nous (ˈɒmɪnəs) *adj.* **1.** foreboding evil. **2.** serving as or having significance as an omen. [C16: from Latin *ōminōsus;* see OMEN] —**ˈom·i·nous·ly** *adv.* —**ˈom·i·nous·ness** *n.*

o·mis·sion (əʊˈmɪʃən) *n.* **1.** something that has been omitted or neglected. **2.** the act of omitting or the state of having been omitted. [C14: from Latin *omissiō,* from *omittere* to OMIT] —**o·ˈmis·sive** *adj.* —**o·ˈmis·sive·ness** *n.*

o·mit (əʊˈmɪt) *vb.* **o·mits, o·mit·ting, o·mit·ted.** (*tr.*) **1.** to neglect to do or include. **2.** to fail (to do something). [C15: from Latin *omittere,* from *ob-* away + *mittere* to send] —**o·mis·si·ble** (əʊˈmɪsɪbᵊl) *adj.* —**o·ˈmit·ter** *n.*

om·ma·tid·i·um (ˌɒməˈtɪdɪəm) *n., pl.* **-tid·i·a** (-ˈtɪdɪə). any of the numerous cone-shaped units that make up the compound eyes of some arthropods. [C19: via New Latin from Greek *ommatidion,* from *omma* eye] —**ˌom·ma·ˈtid·i·al** *adj.*

om·mat·o·phore (ɒˈmætəˌfɔː) *n. Zoology.* a movable stalk or tentacle bearing an eye, occurring in lower animals such as crabs and snails. [C19: from Greek *omma* eye + -PHORE] —**om·ma·toph·o·rous** (ˌɒməˈtɒfərəs) *adj.*

Om·mi·ad (əʊˈmaɪæd) *n., pl.* **-ads** *or* **-a·des** (-əˌdiːz). a variant spelling of **Omayyad.**

om·ni- *combining form.* all or everywhere: *omnipresent.* [from Latin *omnis* all]

om·ni·bus (ˈɒmnɪˌbʌs, -bəs) *n., pl.* **-bus·es. 1.** a less common word for **bus. 2.** Also called: **omnibus volume.** a collection of works by one author or several works on a similar topic, reprinted in one volume. ~*adj.* **3.** (*prenominal*) of, dealing with, or providing for many different things or cases. [C19: from Latin, literally: for all, from *omnis* all]

om·ni·com·pe·tent (ˌɒmnɪkɒmpɪtənt) *adj.* able to judge or deal with all matters. —**ˌom·ni·ˈcom·pe·tence** *n.*

om·ni·di·rec·tion·al (ˌɒmnɪdɪˈrɛkʃənᵊl, -ˌdaɪ-) *adj.* (of an antenna) capable of transmitting and receiving radio signals in all directions, radiating properties at any instant being the same on all bearings.

om·ni·far·i·ous (ˌɒmnɪˈfɛərɪəs) *adj.* of many or all varieties or forms. [C17: from Late Latin *omnifārius,* from Latin *omnis* all + *-farius* doing, related to *facere* to do] —**ˌom·ni·ˈfar·i·ous·ly** *adv.* —**ˌom·ni·ˈfar·i·ous·ness** *n.*

om·nif·ic (ɒmˈnɪfɪk) *or* **om·nif·i·cent** (ɒmˈnɪfɪsənt) *adj. Rare.* creating all things. [C17: via Medieval Latin from Latin *omni-* + *-ficus,* from *facere* to do] —**om·ˈnif·i·cence** *n.*

om·nip·o·tent (ɒmˈnɪpətənt) *adj.* **1.** having very great or unlimited power. ~*n.* **2. the Omnipotent.** an epithet for God. [C14: via Old French from Latin *omnipotens* all-powerful, from OMNI- + *potens,* from *posse* to be able] —**om·ˈnip·o·tence** *n.* —**om·ˈnip·o·tent·ly** *adv.*

om·ni·pres·ent (ˌɒmnɪˈprɛzᵊnt) *adj.* (esp. of a deity) present in all places at the same time. —**ˌom·ni·ˈpres·ence** *n.*

om·ni·range (ˈɒmnɪˌreɪndʒ) *n.* a very-high-frequency ground radio navigational system to assist a pilot in plotting his exact position.

om·nis·ci·ent (ɒmˈnɪsɪənt) *adj.* **1.** having infinite knowledge or understanding. **2.** having very great or seemingly unlimited knowledge. [C17: from Medieval Latin *omnisciens,* from Latin OMNI- + *scīre* to know] —**om·ˈnis·ci·ence** *n.* —**om·ˈnis·ci·ent·ly** *adv.*

om·ni·um-gath·er·um (ˈɒmnɪəmˈɡæðərəm) *n. Often facetious.* a miscellaneous collection. [C16: from Latin *omnium* of all, from *omnis* all + Latinized form of English *gather*]

om·ni·vore (ˈɒmnɪˌvɔː) *n.* an omnivorous person or animal.

om·niv·or·ous (ɒmˈnɪvərəs) *adj.* **1.** eating food of both animal and vegetable origin, or any type of food indiscriminately. **2.** taking in or assimilating everything, esp. with the mind. [C17: from Latin *omnivorus* all-devouring, from OMNI- + *vorāre* to eat greedily] —**om·ˈniv·or·ous·ly** *adv.* —**om·ˈniv·or·ous·ness** *n.*

o·mo·pha·gi·a (ˌəʊməˈfeɪdʒɪə) *or* **o·moph·a·gy** (əʊˈmɒfədʒɪ) *n.* the eating of raw food, esp. meat. [C18: via New Latin from Greek *ōmophagia,* from *ōmos* raw + -PHAGIA] —**o·mo·phag·ic** (ˌəʊməˈfædʒɪk) *or* **o·moph·a·gous** (əʊˈmɒfəɡəs) *adj.*

Om·pha·le (ˈɒmfəˌliː) *n. Greek myth.* a queen of Lydia, whom Hercules was required to serve as a slave to atone for the murder of Iphitus.

om·pha·los (ˈɒmfəˌlɒs) *n.* **1.** (in the ancient world) a sacred conical object, esp. a stone. The most famous omphalos at Delphi was assumed to mark the centre of the earth. **2.** the central point. **3.** *Literary.* another word for **navel.** [Greek: navel]

O.M.S. *abbrev. for* Organisation Mondiale de la Santé. [French: World Health Organization]

Omsk (ɒmsk) *n.* a city in the central Soviet Union, at the confluence of the Irtysh and Om Rivers: a major industrial centre, with pipelines from the second Baku oilfield. Pop.: 968 000 (1975 est.).

O·mu·ta (ˈəʊmuːˌtɑː) *n.* a city in SW Japan, on W Kyushu on Ariake Bay: coal-mining centre. Pop.: 169 485 (1974 est.).

on (ɒn) *prep.* **1.** in contact or connection with the surface of; at the upper surface of: *an apple on the ground; a mark on the table cloth.* **2.** attached to: *a puppet on a string.* **3.** carried with: *I've no money on me.* **4.** in the immediate vicinity of; close to or along the side of: *a house on the sea; this verges on the ridiculous!* **5.** within the time limits of a day or date: *he arrived on Thursday.* **6.** being performed upon or relayed through the medium of: *what's on the television?* **7.** at the occasion of: *on his retirement.* **8.** used to indicate support, subsistence, contingency, etc.: *he lives on bread; it depends on what you want.* **9. a.** regularly taking (a drug): *she's on the pill.* **b.** addicted to: *he's on heroin.* **10.** by means of (something considered as a mode of transport) (esp. in such phrases as **on foot, on wheels, on horseback,** etc.). **11.** in the process or course of: *on a journey; on strike.* **12.** concerned with or relating to: *a tax on potatoes; a programme on archaeology.* **13.** used to indicate the basis, grounds, or cause, as of a statement or action: *I have it on good authority.* **14.** against: used to indicate opposition: *they marched on the city at dawn.* **15.** used to indicate a meeting or encounter: *he crept up on her.* **16.** (used with an adj. preceded by *the*) indicating the manner or way in which an action is carried out: *on the sly; on the cheap.* ~*adv.* (*often used as a particle*) **17.** in the position or state required for the commencement or sustained continuation, as of a mechanical operation: *the radio's been on all night.* **18. a.** attached to, surrounding, or placed in contact with something: *the girl had nothing on.* **b.** taking place: *what's on tonight?* **19.** in a manner indicating continuity, persistence, concentration, etc.: *don't keep on about it; the play went on all afternoon.* **20.** in a direction towards something, esp. forwards; so as to make progress: *we drove on towards London; march on!* **21. on and off.** intermittently; from time to time. **22. on and on.** without ceasing, continually. ~*adj.* **23.** functioning; operating: *the on position on a radio control.* **24.** (*postpositive*) *Informal.* **a.** staked or wagered as a bet: *ten pounds on that horse.* **b.** performing, as on stage, etc.: *I'm on in five minutes.* **c.** definitely taking place: *the match is on for Friday; their marriage is still on.* **d.** charged to: *the drinks are on me.* **e.** tolerable or practicable: *your plan just isn't on.* **25. on at.** *Informal.* nagging: *she was always on at her husband.* **26. on it.** *Austral. informal.* drinking alcoholic liquor. **27.** *Cricket.* (of a bowler) bowling. ~*n.* **28.** *Cricket.* **a.** (*modifier*) relating to or denoting the leg side of a cricket field or pitch: *the on side; an on drive.* **b.** (*in combination*) used to designate certain fielding positions on the leg side: *long-on; mid-on.* **29.** (*postpositive*) (of a person) to be willing to do something. [Old English *an, on;* related to Old Saxon *an,* Old High German, Gothic *ana*]

On (ɒn) *n.* the ancient Egyptian and biblical name for **Heliopolis.**

ON *or* **O.N.** *abbrev. for* Old Norse.

-on *suffix forming nouns.* **1.** (in physics) indicating an elementary particle or quantum: *electron; photon.* **2.** (in chemistry) indicating an inert gas: *neon; radon.* [from ION]

on·a·ger ('ɒnədʒə) *n., pl.* **-gri** (-ˌgraɪ) *or* **-gers. 1.** a Persian variety of the wild ass, *Equus hemionus.* Compare **kiang. 2.** an ancient war engine for hurling stones, etc. [C14: from Late Latin: military engine for stone throwing, from Latin: wild ass, from Greek *onagros,* from *onos* ass + *agros* field]

on·a·gra·ceous (ˌɒnə'greɪʃəs) *adj.* of, relating to, or belonging to the *Onagraceae,* a family of flowering plants including fuchsia and willowherb. [C19: via New Latin *Onagrāceae,* from Latin *onager;* see ONAGER]

o·nan·ism ('əunəˌnɪzəm) *n.* another name for **masturbation** or **coitus interruptus.** [C18: after *Onan,* son of Judah; see Genesis 38:9] —**'o·nan·ist** *n.* —**ˌo·nan·'is·tic** *adj.*

O·nas·sis (əu'næsɪs) *n.* **Ar·is·to·tle (Socrates).** 1906–75, Argentinian (formerly Greek) shipowner, born in Turkey. In 1968 he married **Jac·que·line,** born 1929, the widow of U.S. President John F. Kennedy.

O.N.C. (in Britain) *abbrev. for* Ordinary National Certificate; a qualification recognized by many national technical and professional institutions, roughly equivalent to GCE A Level.

once (wʌns) *adv.* **1.** one time; on one occasion or in one case. **2.** at some past time; formerly: *I could speak French once.* **3.** by one step or degree (of relationship): *a cousin once removed.* **4.** (*in conditional clauses, negatives, etc.*) ever; at all: *if you once forget it.* **5.** multiplied by one. **6. once and away. a.** conclusively. **b.** occasionally. **7. once and for all.** conclusively; for the last time. **8. once in a while.** occasionally; now and then. **9. once or twice** *or* **once and again.** a few times. **10. once upon a time.** used to begin fairy tales and children's stories. ~*conj.* **11.** (*subordinating*) as soon as; if ever or whenever: *once you begin, you'll enjoy it.* ~*n.* **12.** one occasion or case: *you may do it, this once.* **13. all at once. a.** suddenly or without warning. **b.** simultaneously. **14. at once. a.** immediately. **b.** simultaneously. **15. for once.** this time, if (or but) at no other time. [C12 *ones, anes,* adverbial genitive of *on, an* ONE]

once-o·ver *n. Informal.* **1.** a quick examination or appraisal. **2.** a quick but comprehensive piece of work. **3.** a violent beating or thrashing. ~(Esp. (for all senses) in the phrase **give (a person** or **thing) the** (or **a**) **once-over**).

onc·er ('wʌnsə) *n.* **1.** *Brit. slang.* a one-pound note. **2.** *Austral. slang.* a person elected to Parliament who can only expect to serve one term. [C20: from ONCE]

on·co- *n. combining form.* denoting a tumour: *oncology.* [from Greek *onkos*]

on·co·gen·ic (ˌɒŋkəu'dʒɛnɪk) *or* **on·cog·e·nous** (ɒŋ'kɒdʒənəs) *adj.* causing the formation of a tumour.

on·col·o·gy (ɒŋ'kɒlədʒɪ) *n.* the branch of medicine concerned with the study, classification, and treatment of tumours. —**on·co·log·i·cal** (ˌɒŋkə'lɒdʒɪkəl) *adj.* —**on·'col·o·gist** *n.*

on·com·ing ('ɒnˌkʌmɪŋ) *adj.* **1.** coming nearer in space or time; approaching. ~*n.* **2.** the approach or onset: *the oncoming of winter.*

on·cost ('ɒnˌkɒst) *n. Brit.* another word for **overhead** (sense 7).

O.N.D. (in Britain) *abbrev. for* Ordinary National Diploma; a nationally recognized qualification in technical subjects, reached after a two-year full-time or sandwich course.

ondes Mar·te·not (*French* ɔ̃d martə'no) *n. Music.* an electronic keyboard instrument in which the frequency of an oscillator is varied to produce separate musical notes. [C20: French, literally: Martenot waves, invented by Maurice *Martenot* (1898–1980)]

on dit *French* (ɔ̃ 'di) *n., pl.* ***on dits*** (ɔ̃ 'di). a rumour; piece of gossip. [literally: it is said, they say]

On·do ('ɒndəu) *n.* a state of SW Nigeria, on the Bight of Benin: formed in 1976 from part of Western State. Capital: Akure. Pop.: 2 727 676 (1976 est.). Area: 14 400 sq. km (5559 sq. miles).

on·do·graph ('ɒndəuˌgrɑːf, -ˌgræf) *n.* an instrument for producing a graphical recording of an alternating current by measuring the charge imparted to a capacitor at different points in the cycle. [C20: from French, from *onde* wave + -GRAPH] —**'on·do·ˌgram** *n.*

on·dom·e·ter (ɒn'dɒmɪtə) *n.* an instrument for measuring the frequency of radio waves. [from French *onde* wave + -METER]

one (wʌn) *determiner.* **1. a.** single; lone; not two or more: *one car.* **b.** (*as pronoun*): *one is enough for now; one at a time.* **c.** (*in combination*): *one-eyed; one-legged.* **2. a.** distinct from all others; only; unique: *one girl in a million.* **b.** (*as pronoun*): *one of a kind.* **3. a.** a specified (person, item, etc.) as distinct from another or others of its kind: *raise one hand and then the other.* **b.** (*as pronoun*): *which one is correct?* **4.** a certain, indefinite, or unspecified (time); some: *one day you'll be sorry.* **5.** *Informal.* an emphatic word for **a** or **an:** *it was one hell of a fight.* **6.** a certain (person): *one Miss Jones was named.* **7. (all) in one.** combined; united. **8. all one. a.** all the same. **b.** of no consequence: *it's all one to me.* **9. at one.** (often foll. by *with*) in a state of agreement or harmony. **10. be made one.** (of a man and a woman) to become married. **11. many a one.** many people. **12. neither one thing nor the other.** indefinite, undecided, or mixed. **13. never a one.** none. **14. one and all.** everyone, without exception. **15. one by one.** one at a time; individually. **16. one or two.** a few. **17. one way and another.** on balance. **18. one with another.** on average. ~*pron.* **19.** an indefinite person regarded as typical of every person: *one can't say any more than that.* **20.** any indefinite person: used as the subject of a sentence to form an alternative grammatical construction to that of the passive voice: *one can catch fine trout in this stream.* **21.** *Archaic.* an unspecified person: *one came to him.* ~*n.* **22.** the smallest whole number and the first cardinal number; unity. See also **number** (sense 1). **23.** a numeral (1, I, i, etc.) representing this number. **24.** *Music.* the numeral 1 used as the lower figure in a time signature to indicate that the beat is measured in semibreves. **25.** something representing, represented by, or consisting of one unit. **26.** Also: **one o'clock.** one hour after noon or midnight. **27.** a blow or setback (esp. in the phrase **one in the eye for**). **28. the one.** (in neo-Platonic philosophy) the ultimate being. **29. the Holy One** *or* **the One above.** God. **30. the Evil one.** Satan; the devil. ~Related prefixes: **mono-, uni-.** [Old English *ān,* related to Old French *ān, ēn,* Old High German *ein,* Old Norse *einn,* Latin *unus,* Greek *oinē* ace]

Usage. Where the pronoun *one* is repeated, as in *one might think one would be unwise to say that, he* is sometimes substituted: *one might think he would be unwise to say that.* Careful writers avoid *one* followed by *he,* however, because of possible ambiguity: *he* in this case could refer either to the same person as *one* or to some other person.

-one *suffix forming nouns.* indicating that a chemical compound is a ketone: *acetone.* [arbitrarily from Greek *-ōnē,* feminine patronymic suffix, but perhaps influenced by *-one* in OZONE]

one an·oth·er *pron.* the reflexive form of plural pronouns when the action, attribution, etc., is reciprocal: *they kissed one another; knowing one another.* Also: **each other.**

one-armed ban·dit *n.* an informal name for **slot machine.**

one-eighty *n., pl.* **-ies.** *Skateboarding.* a manoeuvre in which the rider spins the board half a turn and continues travelling in the original direction. [C20: short for *180 degrees*]

O·ne·ga (*Russian* a'njɛgə) *n.* a lake in the NW Soviet Union, mostly in the Karelian ASSR: the second largest lake in Europe and fourth largest in the Soviet Union. Area: 9891 sq. km (3819 sq. miles).

one-horse *adj.* **1.** drawn by or using one horse. **2.** (*prenominal*) *Informal.* small or obscure: *a one-horse town.*

O·nei·da (əu'naɪdə) *n., pl.* **-das** *or* **-da. 1. Lake.** a lake in central New York State: part of the New York State Barge Canal system. Length: about 35 km (22 miles). Greatest width: 9 km (6 miles). **2.** (preceded by *the; functioning as pl.*) a North American Indian people formerly living east of Lake Ontario; one of the Iroquois peoples. **3.** a member of this people. **4.** the language of this people, belonging to the Iroquoian family. [from Iroquois *onēyóte',* literally: standing stone]

O'Neill (əu'niːl) *n.* **Eu·gene (Gladstone).** 1888–1953, U.S. dramatist. His works, which are notable for their emotional power and psychological analysis, include *Desire under the Elms* (1924), *Strange Interlude* (1928), *Mourning becomes Elektra* (1931), *Long Day's Journey into Night* (1941), and *The Iceman Cometh* (1946): Nobel prize for literature 1936.

o·nei·ric (əu'naɪərɪk) *adj. Rare.* of or relating to dreams.

o·nei·ro- *combining form.* indicating a dream: *oneirocritic.* [from Greek *oneiros* dream]
o·nei·ro·crit·ic (əʊˌnaɪərəʊˈkrɪtɪk) *n.* a person who interprets dreams. [C17: from Greek *oneirokritikos*] **—o·ˌnei·ro·ˈcrit·i·cal** *adj.* **—o·ˌnei·ro·ˈcrit·i·cal·ly** *adv.*
o·nei·ro·man·cy (əʊˈnaɪərəʊˌmænsɪ) *n. Rare.* divination by the interpretation of dreams. [C17: from Greek *oneiros* dream + -MANCY] **—o·ˈnei·ro·ˌman·cer** *n.*
one-man *adj.* consisting of or done by or for one man: *a one-man band; a one-man show.*
one·ness (ˈwʌnnɪs) *n.* **1.** the state or quality of being one; singleness. **2.** the state of being united; agreement. **3.** uniqueness. **4.** sameness.
one-night stand *n.* **1.** a performance given only once at any one place. **2.** *Informal.* **a.** a sexual encounter lasting only one evening or night. **b.** a person regarded as being only suitable for such an encounter.
one-off *n. Brit.* **a.** something that is carried out or made only once. **b.** (*as modifier*): *a one-off job.* Also: **one-shot.**
one-piece *adj.* (of a garment, esp. a bathing costume) made in one piece.
on·er (ˈwʌnə) *n. Brit. informal.* **1.** an outstanding person or thing. **2.** a heavy blow. [C20: from ONE]
on·er·ous (ˈɒnərəs, ˈəʊ-) *adj.* **1.** laborious or oppressive. **2.** *Law.* (of a contract, lease, etc.) having or involving burdens or obligations that counterbalance or outweigh the advantages. [C14: from Latin *onerōsus* burdensome, from *onus* load] **—ˈon·er·ous·ly** *adv.* **—ˈon·er·ous·ness** *n.*
one·self (wʌnˈsɛlf) *pron.* **1. a.** the reflexive form of *one.* **b.** (intensifier): *one doesn't do that oneself.* **2.** (*preceded by a copula*) one's normal or usual self: *one doesn't feel oneself after such an experience.*
one-sid·ed *adj.* **1.** considering or favouring only one side of a matter, problem, etc. **2.** having all the advantage on one side. **3.** larger or more developed on one side. **4.** having, existing on, or occurring on one side only. **5.** another term for **unilateral. 6.** denoting a surface on which any two points can be joined without crossing an edge. See **Möbius strip.** **—ˌone-ˈsid·ed·ly** *adv.* **—ˌone-ˈsid·ed·ness** *n.*
one-step *n.* **1.** an early 20th-century ballroom dance with long quick steps, the precursor of the foxtrot. **2.** a piece of music composed for or in the rhythm of this dance.
One Thou·sand Guin·eas *n.* See **Thousand Guineas.**
one-time *adj.* **1.** (*prenominal*) at some time in the past; former. *~adv.* **2.** *Caribbean informal.* at once.
one-to-one *adj.* **1.** (of two or more things) corresponding exactly. **2.** *Maths.* characterized by or involving the pairing of each member of one set with only one member of another set, without remainder.
one-track *adj.* **1.** *Informal.* obsessed with one idea, subject, etc. **2.** having or consisting of a single track.
one-two *n.* **1.** *Boxing.* a jab with the leading hand followed by a cross with the other hand. **2.** *Soccer.* another term for **wall pass.**
one-up *adj. Informal.* having or having scored an advantage or lead over someone or something.
one-up·man·ship (wʌnˈʌpmənˌʃɪp) *n. Informal.* the art or practice of achieving or maintaining an advantage over others.
one-way *adj.* **1.** moving or allowing travel in one direction only: *one-way traffic; a one-way ticket.* **2.** entailing no reciprocal obligation, action, etc.: *a one-way agreement.*
one-way tick·et *n.* the U.S. word for **single ticket.**
on-glide *n. Phonetics.* a glide immediately preceding a speech sound, for which the articulators are taking position. Compare **off-glide.**
on·go·ing (ˈɒnˌgəʊɪŋ) *adj.* **1.** actually in progress: *ongoing projects.* **2.** continually moving forward; developing.
on·ion (ˈʌnjən) *n.* **1.** an alliaceous plant, *Allium cepa,* having greenish-white flowers: cultivated for its rounded edible bulb. **2.** the bulb of this plant, consisting of concentric layers of white succulent leaf bases with a pungent odour and taste. **3.** any of several related plants similar to *A. cepa,* such as *A. fistulosum* (Welsh onion). **4.** *Austral. slang.* a girl participating in a gangbang. **5. know one's onions.** *Brit. slang.* to be fully acquainted with a subject. [C14: via Anglo-Norman from Old French *oignon,* from Latin *unio* onion, related to UNION] **—ˈon·ion·y** *adj.*
on·ion dome *n.* a bulb-shaped dome characteristic of Byzantine and Russian church architecture.
On·ions (ˈʌnjənz) *n.* **Charles Tal·but.** 1873–1965, English lexicographer; an editor of the *Oxford English Dictionary.*
on·ion·skin (ˈʌnjənˌskɪn) *n.* a glazed translucent paper.
O·nit·sha (əˈnɪtʃə) *n.* a port in S Nigeria, in Anambra State on the Niger River: industrial centre. Pop.: 220 000 (1975 est.).
o·ni·um com·pound *or* **salt** (ˈəʊnɪəm) *n. Chem.* any salt in which the positive ion (**onium ion**) is formed by the attachment of a proton to a neutral compound, as in ammonium, oxonium, and sulphonium compounds.
on key *adj.* (**on-key** *when prenominal*), *adv.* **1.** in the right key. **2.** in tune.
on line *adj.* (**on-line** *when prenominal*). of, relating to, or concerned with a peripheral device that is directly connected to and controlled by the central processing unit of a computer. Compare **off line.**
on·look·er (ˈɒnˌlʊkə) *n.* a person who observes without taking part. **—ˈonˌlook·ing** *adj.*
on·ly (ˈəʊnlɪ) *adj.* (*prenominal*) **1. the.** being single or very few in number: *the only men left in town were too old to bear arms.* **2.** (of a child) having no siblings. **3.** unique by virtue of being superior to anything else; peerless. **4. one and only. a.** (*adj.*) incomparable; unique. **b.** (*as n.*) the object of all one's love: *you are my one and only.* *~adv.* **5.** without anyone or anything else being included; alone: *you have one choice only; only a genius can do that.* **6.** merely or just: *it's only Henry.* **7.** no more or no greater than: *we met only an hour ago.* **8.** used in conditional clauses introduced by *if* to emphasize the impossibility of the condition ever being fulfilled: *if I had only known, this would never have happened.* **9.** not earlier than; not...until: *I only found out yesterday.* **10. if only** *or* **if...only.** an expression used to introduce a wish, esp. one felt to be unrealizable. **11. only if.** never...except when. **12. only too. a.** (intensifier): *he was only too pleased to help.* **b.** most regrettably (esp. in the phrase **only too true**). **13.** *sentence connector.* but; however: used to introduce an exception or condition: *play outside: only don't go into the street.* [Old English *ānlīc,* from *ān* ONE + *-līc* -LY]
Usage. In informal English, *only* is often used as a sentence connector: *it would have been possible, only he was not present at the time.* This use is avoided in careful usage, esp. in formal contexts: *it would have been possible had he been present.*
on·ly-be·got·ten *adj. Archaic.* (of a child) the only offspring of its father.
o.n.o. (in advertisements) *abbrev. for* or near offer: *£50 o.n.o.*
on·o·ma·si·ol·o·gy (ˌɒnəʊˌmeɪsɪˈɒlədʒɪ) *n.* **1.** another name for **onomastics** (sense 1). **2.** the branch of semantics concerned with the meanings of and meaning relations between individual words.
on·o·mas·tic (ˌɒnəˈmæstɪk) *adj.* **1.** of or relating to proper names. **2.** *Law.* denoting a signature in a different handwriting from that to which it is attached. [C17: from Greek *onomastikos,* from *onomazein* to name, from *onoma* NAME]
on·o·mas·tics (ˌɒnəˈmæstɪks) *n.* **1.** (*functioning as sing.*) the study of proper names, esp. of their origins. **2.** (*functioning as sing. or pl.*) a systematization of the facts about how proper names are formed in a given language.
on·o·mat·o·poe·ia (ˌɒnəˌmætəˈpiːə) *n.* **1.** the formation of words whose sound is imitative of the sound of the noise or action designated, such as *hiss, buzz,* and *bang.* **2.** the use of such words for poetic or rhetorical effect. [C16: via Late Latin from Greek *onoma* name + *poiein* to make] **—ˌon·o·ˌmat·o·ˈpoe·ic** *or* **on·o·mat·o·po·et·ic** (ˌɒnəˌmætəpəʊˈɛtɪk) *adj.* **—ˌon·o·ˌmat·o·ˈpoe·i·cal·ly** *or* **ˌon·o·ˌmat·o·po·ˈet·i·cal·ly** *adv.*
On·on·da·ga (ˌɒnənˈdɑːgə) *n.* **1. Lake.** a salt lake in central New York State. Area: about 13 sq. km (5 sq. miles). **2.** (*pl.* **·gas** *or* **·ga**) a member of a North American Indian Iroquois people formerly living between Lake Champlain and the St. Lawrence River. **3.** the language of this people, belonging to the Iroquoian family. [from Iroquois *onōtáge',* literally: on the top of the hill (the name of their principal village)] **—ˌOn·on·ˈda·gan** *adj.*
on·rush (ˈɒnˌrʌʃ) *n.* a forceful forward rush or flow.
on·set (ˈɒnˌsɛt) *n.* **1.** an attack; assault. **2.** a start; beginning.
on·shore (ˈɒnˈʃɔː) *adj., adv.* **1.** towards the land: *an onshore gale.* **2.** on land; not at sea.
on·side (ˌɒnˈsaɪd) *adj., adv. Football, hockey, etc.* (of a player) in a legal position, as when behind the ball or with a required number of opponents between oneself and the opposing team's goal line. Compare **offside.**
on·slaught (ˈɒnˌslɔːt) *n.* a violent attack. [C17: from Middle Dutch *aenslag,* from *aan* ON + *slag* a blow, related to SLAY]
on stream *adj.* (of a manufacturing process, industrial plant, equipment, etc.) in or about to go into operation or production.
Ont. *abbrev. for* Ontario.
On·tar·i·o (ɒnˈtɛərɪəʊ) *n.* **1.** a province of central Canada: lies mostly on the Canadian Shield and contains the fertile plain of the lower Great Lakes and the St. Lawrence River, one of the world's leading industrial areas; the second largest and the most populous province. Capital: Toronto. Pop.: 8 264 465 (1976). Area: 891 198 sq. km (344 092 sq. miles). **2. Lake.** a lake between the U.S. and Canada, bordering on New York State and Ontario province: the smallest of the Great Lakes; linked with Lake Erie by the Niagara River and Welland Canal; drained by the St. Lawrence. Area: 19 684 sq. km (7600 sq. miles).
on·to *or* **on to** (ˈɒntʊ; *unstressed* ˈɒntə) *prep.* **1.** to a position that is on: *step onto the train as it passes.* **2.** having become aware of (something illicit or secret): *the police are onto us.* **3.** into contact with: *get onto the factory.*
Usage. *Onto* is now generally accepted as a word in its own right. *On to* is still used, however, where *on* is considered to be part of the verb: *he moved on to the next platform* as contrasted with *he jumped onto the next platform.*
on·to- *combining form.* existence or being: *ontogeny; ontology.* [from Late Greek, from *ōn* (stem *ont-*) being, present participle of *einai* to be]
on·tog·e·ny (ɒnˈtɒdʒənɪ) *or* **on·to·gen·e·sis** (ˌɒntəˈdʒɛnɪsɪs) *n.* the entire sequence of events involved in the development of an individual organism. Compare **phylogeny.** **—on·to·gen·ic** (ˌɒntəʊˈdʒɛnɪk) *or* **on·to·ge·net·ic** (ˌɒntəʊdʒɪˈnɛtɪk) *adj.* **—ˌon·to·ˈgen·i·cal·ly** *or* **ˌon·to·ge·ˈnet·i·cal·ly** *adv.*
on·to·log·i·cal ar·gu·ment *n. Philosophy.* one of the arguments that attempt to prove that the concept of God is the concept of a being who cannot but exist.
on·tol·o·gy (ɒnˈtɒlədʒɪ) *n.* **1.** *Philosophy.* the branch of metaphysics that deals with the nature of being. **2.** *Logic.* the set of entities presupposed by a theory. **—ˌon·to·ˈlog·i·cal** *adj.* **—ˌon·to·ˈlog·i·cal·ly** *adv.*
o·nus (ˈəʊnəs) *n., pl.* **o·nus·es.** a responsibility, task, or burden. [C17: from Latin: burden]

o·nus pro+ban+di ('əʊnəs prəʊ'bændɪ) *n. Law.* the Latin phrase for **burden of proof.**
on+ward ('ɒnwəd) *adj.* **1.** directed or moving forwards, onwards, etc. ~*adv.* **2.** a variant of **onwards.**
on+wards ('ɒnwədz) *or* **on+ward** *adv.* at or towards a point or position ahead, in advance, etc.
on·y+choph·o+ran (ˌɒnɪ'kɒfərən) *n.* any wormlike invertebrates of the phylum *Onychophora,* having a segmented body, short unjointed limbs, and breathing by means of tracheae: intermediate in structure and evolutionary development between annelids and arthropods. [from New Latin *Onychophora,* from Greek *onukh-* nail, claw + -PHORE]
-o·nym *n. combining form.* indicating a name or word: *acronym; pseudonym.* [from Greek *-onumon,* from *onuma,* Doric variant of *onoma* name]
on·y+mous ('ɒnɪməs) *adj.* (of a book) bearing its author's name. [C18: back formation from ANONYMOUS]
on·yx ('ɒnɪks) *n.* **1.** a variety of chalcedony with alternating black and white parallel bands, used as a gemstone. Formula: SiO_2. **2.** a compact variety of calcite used as an ornamental stone; onyx marble. Formula: $CaCO_3$. [C13: from Latin from Greek: finger nail (so called from its veined appearance)]
o·o- *or* **o·ö-** *combining form.* egg or ovum: *oosperm.* [from Greek *ōion* EGG[1]]
o·o·cyte ('əʊəˌsaɪt) *n.* an immature female germ cell that gives rise to an ovum after two meiotic divisions.
oo·dles ('u:dᵊlz) *pl. n. Informal.* great quantities: *oodles of money.* [C20: of uncertain origin]
oof (u:f) *n. Slang.* money. [C19: from Yiddish *ooftisch,* from German *auf dem Tische* on the table (referring to gambling stakes)] —**'oof·y** *adj.*
o·og+a·my (əʊ'ɒgəmɪ) *n.* sexual reproduction involving a small motile male gamete and a large much less motile female gamete: occurs in all higher animals and some plants. —**o'og·a+mous** *adj.*
o·o·gen+e·sis (ˌəʊə'dʒɛnɪsɪs) *n.* the formation and maturation of ova from undifferentiated cells in the ovary. See also **oocyte.** —**o·o·ge+net+ic** (ˌəʊədʒɪ'nɛtɪk) *adj.*
o·o·go+ni·um (ˌəʊə'gəʊnɪəm) *n., pl.* **·ni·a** (-nɪə) *or* **·ni·ums. 1.** an immature female germ cell forming oocytes by repeated divisions. **2.** a female sex organ of some algae and fungi producing female gametes (oospheres). —**o·o'go+ni·al** *adj.*
ooh (u:) *interj.* an exclamation of surprise, pleasure, pain, etc.
o·o·lite ('əʊəˌlaɪt) *n.* any sedimentary rock, esp. limestone, consisting of tiny spherical concentric grains within a fine matrix. [C18: from French from New Latin *oolitēs,* literally: egg stone; probably a translation of German *Rogenstein* roe stone] —**o·o·lit+ic** (ˌəʊə'lɪtɪk) *adj.*
o·ol+o·gy (əʊ'ɒlədʒɪ) *n.* the branch of ornithology concerned with the study of birds' eggs. —**o·o·log·i·cal** (ˌəʊə'lɒdʒɪkᵊl) *adj.* —**o'ol·o+gist** *n.*
oo·long ('u:ˌlɒŋ) *n.* a kind of dark tea, grown in China, that is partly fermented before being dried. [C19: from Chinese *wu lung,* from *wu* black + *lung* dragon]
oo·mi+ak *or* **oo·mi+ac** ('u:mɪˌæk) *n.* other words for **umiak.**
oom+pah ('u:mˌpɑ:) *n.* a representation of the sound made by a deep brass instrument, esp. in military band music.
oomph (ʊmf) *n. Informal.* **1.** enthusiasm, vigour, or energy. **2.** sex appeal.
oont (ʊnt) *Anglo-Indian dialect.* a camel. [C19: from Hindi *unt*]
o·o·pho+rec+to+my (ˌəʊəfə'rɛktəmɪ) *n., pl.* **·mies.** surgical removal of an ovary or ovarian tumour. Also called: **ovariectomy.** Compare **ovariotomy.**
o·o·pho+ri+tis (ˌəʊəfə'raɪtɪs) *n.* inflammation of an ovary; ovaritis. —**o·o·pho+rit+ic** (ˌəʊəfə'rɪtɪk) *adj.*
o·o·phyte ('əʊəˌfaɪt) *n.* the gametophyte in mosses, liverworts, and ferns. —**o·o·phyt+ic** (ˌəʊə'fɪtɪk) *adj.*
oops (ʊps, u:ps) *interj.* an exclamation of surprise or of apology as when someone drops something or makes a mistake.
oose (u:s) *n. Scot. dialect.* dust; fluff. [of unknown origin]
o·o·sperm ('əʊəˌspɜ:m) *n.* a fertilized ovum; zygote.
o·o·sphere ('əʊəˌsfɪə) *n.* a large female gamete produced in the oogonia of algae and fungi.
o·o·spore ('əʊəˌspɔ:) *n.* a thick-walled sexual spore that develops from a fertilized oosphere in some algae and fungi. —**ˌo·o+'spor+ic** *or* **ˌo·o+'spor+ous** *adj.*
Oost+en+de (o:st'ɛndə) *n.* the Flemish name for **Ostend.**
o·o·the·ca (ˌəʊə'θi:kə) *n., pl.* **·cae** (-si:). a capsule containing eggs that is produced by some insects and molluscs. [C19: New Latin, from OO- + *thēkē* case] —**ˌo·o'the·cal** *adj.*
o·o·tid ('əʊəˌtɪd) *n. Zoology.* an immature female gamete that develops into an ovum. [C20: from OO- + (SPERMA)TID]
ooze[1] (u:z) *vb.* **1.** (*intr.*) to flow or leak out slowly, as through pores or very small holes. **2.** to exude or emit (moisture, gas, etc.). **3.** (*tr.*) to overflow with: *to ooze charm.* **4.** (*intr.;* often foll. by *away*) to disappear or escape gradually. ~*n.* **5.** a slow flowing or leaking. **6.** an infusion of vegetable matter, such as sumac or oak bark, used in tanning. [Old English *wōs* juice]
ooze[2] (u:z) *n.* **1.** a soft thin mud found at the bottom of lakes and rivers. **2.** a fine-grained calcareous or siliceous marine deposit consisting of the hard parts of planktonic organisms. **3.** muddy ground, esp. of bogs. [Old English *wāse* mud; related to Old French *wāse,* Old Norse *veisa*]
ooze leath+er *n.* a very soft leather with a suedelike finish.
ooz·y[1] ('u:zɪ) *adj.* **ooz·i+er, ooz·i+est.** moist or dripping.
ooz·y[2] ('u:zɪ) *adj.* **ooz·i+er, ooz·i+est.** of, resembling, or containing mud; slimy. —**'ooz·i+ly** *adv.* —**'ooz·i+ness** *n.*
OP *Military. abbrev. for* observation post.
op. *abbrev. for:* **1.** opera. **2.** operation. **3.** opposite. **4.** opus. **5.** operator. **6.** optical.
o.p. *or* **O.P.** *abbrev. for* out of print.
O.P. *abbrev. for* Ordo Praedictatorum (the Dominicans). [Latin: Order of Preachers]
o·pac+i·ty (əʊ'pæsɪtɪ) *n., pl.* **·ties. 1.** the state or quality of being opaque. **2.** the degree to which something is opaque. **3.** an opaque object or substance. **4.** obscurity of meaning; unintelligibility. **5.** *Physics, photog.* the ratio of the intensity of light falling on a surface, such as a photographic film, to that transmitted by the surface.
o·pah ('əʊpə) *n.* a large soft-finned deep-sea teleost fish, *Lampris regius* (or *luna*), of the Atlantic and Pacific Oceans and the Mediterranean Sea, having a deep, brilliantly coloured body: family *Lampridae.* Also called: **moonfish, kingfish.** [C18: of West African origin]
o·pal ('əʊpᵊl) *n.* an amorphous form of hydrated silicon dioxide that is colourless or of variable colour and transparent or translucent: found in sedimentary and volcanic rocks and in deposits from hot springs in America and Australia. Some varieties are used as gemstones. Formula: $SiO_2.nH_2O$. [C16: from Latin *opalus,* from Greek *opallios,* from Sanskrit *upala* precious stone] —**'o·pal-ˌlike** *adj.*
o·pa+lesce (ˌəʊpə'lɛs) *vb.* (*intr.*) to exhibit a milky iridescence.
o·pal+es+cent (ˌəʊpə'lɛsᵊnt) *adj.* having or emitting an iridescence like that of an opal. —**ˌo·pal+'es+cence** *n.*
o·pal+ine ('əʊpəˌlaɪn) *adj.* **1.** opalescent. ~*n.* **2.** an opaque or semiopaque whitish glass.
o·paque (əʊ'peɪk) *adj.* **1.** not transmitting light; not transparent or translucent. **2.** not reflecting light; lacking lustre or shine; dull. **3.** not transmitting radiant energy, such as electromagnetic or corpuscular radiation, or sound. **4.** hard to understand; unintelligible. **5.** unintelligent; dense. ~*n.* **6.** *Photog.* an opaque pigment used to block out particular areas on a negative. ~*vb.* **o·paques, o·paqu+ing, o·paqued.** (*tr.*) **7.** to make opaque. **8.** *Photog.* to block out particular areas, such as blemishes, on (a negative), using an opaque. [C15: from Latin *opăcus* shady] —**o'paque+ly** *adv.* —**o'paque+ness** *n.*
o·paque con+text *n. Philosophy.* a context in which replacement of an expression by a coreferential expression may change the truth-value of the whole proposition.
o·paque pro+jec+tor *n.* the U.S. name for **episcope.**
op art (ɒp) *n.* a style of abstract art chiefly concerned with the exploitation of optical effects such as the illusion of movement. [C20: *op,* short for *optical*]
op. cit. (in textual annotations) *abbrev. for* opere citato. [Latin: in the work cited]
ope (əʊp) *vb., adj.* an archaic or poetic word for **open.**
OPEC ('əʊˌpɛk) *n. acronym for* Organization of Petroleum-Exporting Countries: an organization formed in 1961 to administer a common policy for the sale of petroleum. Its members are Iraq, Kuwait, Iran, Qatar, Saudi Arabia, Venezuela, Indonesia, Libya, and Abu Dhabi.
o·pen ('əʊpᵊn) *adj.* **1.** not closed or barred: *the door is open.* **2.** affording free passage, access, view, etc.; not blocked or obstructed: *the road is open for traffic.* **3.** not sealed, fastened, or wrapped: *an open package.* **4.** having the interior part accessible: *an open drawer.* **5.** extended, expanded, or unfolded: *an open newspaper; an open flower.* **6.** ready for business: *the shops are open.* **7.** able to be obtained; available: *the position advertised last week is no longer open.* **8.** unobstructed by buildings, trees, etc.: *open countryside.* **9.** free to all to join, enter, use, visit, etc.: *an open competition.* **10.** unengaged or unoccupied: *the doctor has an hour open for you to call.* **11.** (of a season or period) not restricted for purposes of hunting game or quarry of various kinds. **12.** not decided or finalized: *an open question.* **13.** ready to entertain new ideas; not biased or prejudiced: *an open mind.* **14.** unreserved or candid: *she was very open in her description.* **15.** liberal or generous: *an open hand.* **16.** extended or eager to receive (esp. in the phrase **with open arms**). **17.** exposed to view; blatant: *open disregard of the law.* **18.** liable or susceptible: *you will leave yourself open to attack if you speak.* **19.** (of climate or seasons) free from frost; mild. **20.** free from navigational hazards, such as ice, sunken ships, etc.: *open water.* **21.** *U.S.* without legal restrictions or enforceable regulations, esp. in relation to gambling, vice, etc.: *an open town.* **22.** without barriers to prevent absconding: *an open prison.* **23.** having large or numerous spacing or apertures: *open ranks.* **24.** full of small openings or gaps; porous: *an open texture.* **25.** *Printing.* (of type matter) generously leaded or widely spaced. **26.** *Music.* **a.** (of a violin or guitar string) not stopped with the finger. **b.** (of a pipe, such as an organ pipe) not closed at either end. **c.** (of a note) played on such a string or pipe. **27.** *Commerce.* in operation; active: *an open account.* **28.** (of a cheque) not crossed. **29.** (of a return ticket) not specifying a date for travel. **30.** *Sport.* **a.** (of a goal, court, etc.) unguarded or relatively unprotected: *the forward missed an open goal.* **b.** (of a stance, esp. in golf) characterized by the front of the body being turned forward. **31.** (of a wound) exposed to the air. **32.** (esp. of the large intestine) free from obstruction. **33.** undefended and of no military significance: *an open city.* **34.** *Phonetics.* **a.** denoting a vowel pronounced with the lips relatively wide apart. **b.** denoting a syllable that does not end in a consonant, as in *pa.* **35.** *Maths.* (of a set) containing points whose neighbourhood consists of other points of the same set: *points inside a circle are an open set.* ~*vb.* **36.** to move or cause to move from a closed or fastened position: *to open a window.* **37.** (when *intr.,* foll by *on* or *onto*) to render accessible or unobstructed: *to open a road; to open a parcel; the door*

opens into the hall. **38.** (*intr.*) to come into or appear in view: *the lake opened before us.* **39.** to puncture (a boil, etc.) so as to permit drainage. **40.** to extend or unfold or cause to extend or unfold: *to open a newspaper.* **41.** to disclose or uncover or be disclosed or uncovered: *to open one's heart.* **42.** to cause (the mind) to become receptive or (of the mind) to become receptive. **43.** to operate or cause to operate: *to open a shop.* **44.** (when *intr.*, sometimes foll. by *out*) to make or become less compact or dense in structure: *to open ranks.* **45.** to set or be set in action; start: *to open a discussion; to open the batting.* **46.** (*tr.*) to arrange for (a bank account, savings account, etc.) usually by making an initial deposit. **47.** to turn to a specified point in (a book, magazine, etc.): *open at page one.* **48.** *Law.* to make the opening statement in (a case before a court of law). **49.** (*intr.*) *Cards.* to bet, bid, or lead first on a hand. ~*n.* **50.** (often prec. by *the*) any wide or unobstructed space or expanse, esp. of land or water. **51.** See **open air.** **52.** *Sport.* a competition which all may enter. **53. bring** (or **come**) **into the open.** to make (or become) evident or public. ~See also **open up.** [Old English; related to Old French *open, epen,* Old Saxon *opan,* Old High German *offan*] —**'o·pen+a·ble** *adj.* —**'o·pen+ly** *adv.* —**'o·pen+ness** *n.*

o·pen air *n.* **a.** the place or space where the air is unenclosed; the outdoors. **b.** (*as modifier*): *an open-air concert.*

o·pen-and-shut *adj.* easily decided or solved; obvious: *an open-and-shut case.*

O·pen Breth+ren *n.* one of the two main divisions of the Plymouth Brethren that, in contrast to the Exclusive Brethren, permits contacts with members outside the sect.

o·pen+cast min+ing ('əʊpᵊnˌkɑːst) *n. Brit.* mining by excavating from the surface. Also called (esp. U.S.): **strip mining.**

o·pen chain *n.* a chain of atoms in a molecule that is not joined at its ends into the form of a ring.

o·pen cir+cuit *n.* an incomplete electrical circuit in which no current flows. Compare **closed circuit.**

o·pen court *n.* a court or trial to which members of the public are freely admitted.

o·pen day *n.* an occasion on which an institution, such as a school, is open for inspection by the public. U.S. name: **open house.**

o·pen door *n.* **1.** a policy or practice by which a nation grants opportunities for trade to all other nations equally. **2.** free and unrestricted admission.

o·pen-end·ed *adj.* without definite limits, as of duration or amount: *an open-ended contract.*

o·pen+er ('əʊpənə) *n.* **1.** an instrument used to open sealed containers such as tins or bottles: *a bottle opener.* **2.** a person who opens, esp. the player who makes the first bid or play. **3.** *U.S.* the first song, act, etc., in a variety show.

o·pen-eyed *adj.* **1.** with the eyes wide open, as in amazement. **2.** watchful; alert.

o·pen-faced *adj.* **1.** having an ingenuous expression. **2.** (of a watch) having no lid or cover other than the glass.

o·pen-field *adj.* (*prenominal*) *Medieval history.* of or denoting the system in which an arable area was divided into unenclosed strips, esp. cultivated by different tenants.

o·pen game *n. Chess.* a relatively simple game involving open ranks and files, permitting tactical play, and usually following symmetrical development. Compare **closed game.**

o·pen-hand·ed *adj.* generous; liberal. —**ˌo·pen-'hand·ed+ly** *adv.*

o·pen-heart·ed *adj.* **1.** kindly and warm. **2.** disclosing intentions and thoughts clearly; candid. —**ˌo·pen-'heart·ed+ly** *adv.* —**ˌo·pen-'heart·ed+ness** *n.*

o·pen-hearth fur+nace *n.* a steel-making reverbatory furnace in which pig iron and scrap is contained in a shallow hearth and heated by producer gas.

o·pen-hearth pro+cess *n.* a process for making steel using an open-hearth furnace.

o·pen-heart sur+ger·y *n.* surgical repair of the heart during which the blood circulation is often maintained mechanically.

o·pen house *n.* **1.** a U.S. name for **at-home** or **open day.** **2. keep open house.** to be always ready to receive guests.

o·pen+ing ('əʊpənɪŋ) *n.* **1.** the act of making or becoming open. **2.** a vacant or unobstructed space, esp. one that will serve as a passageway; gap. **3.** *Chiefly U.S.* a tract in a forest in which trees are scattered or absent. **4.** the first part or stage of something. **5. a.** the first performance of something, esp. a theatrical production. **b.** (*as modifier*): *the opening night.* **6.** a specific or formal sequence of moves at the start of any of certain games, esp. chess or draughts. **7.** an opportunity or chance, esp. for employment or promotion in a business concern. **8.** *Law.* the preliminary statement made by counsel to the court or jury before adducing evidence in support of his case.

o·pen+ing time *n. Brit.* the time at which pubs can legally start selling alcoholic drinks.

o·pen let+ter *n.* a letter, esp. one of protest, addressed to a person but also made public, as through the press.

o·pen mar+ket *n.* a market in which prices are determined by supply and demand, there are no barriers to entry, and trading is not restricted to a specific area.

o·pen mar+ket op+er·a+tions *pl. n. Finance.* the purchase and sale on the open market of government securities by the Bank of England for the purpose of regulating the supply of money and credit to the economy.

o·pen-mind·ed *adj.* having a mind receptive to new ideas, arguments, etc.; unprejudiced. —**ˌo·pen-'mind·ed+ly** *adv.* —**ˌo·pen-'mind·ed+ness** *n.*

o·pen-mouthed *adj.* **1.** having an open mouth, esp. in surprise. **2.** greedy or ravenous. **3.** clamorous or vociferous.

o·pen or+der *n. Military.* a formation that allows additional space between the front and near ranks of a guard or inspected unit to allow the inspecting officer to pass.

o·pen-plan *adj.* having no or few dividing walls between areas: *an open-plan office floor.*

o·pen pol+i+cy *n.* an insurance policy in which the amount payable in the event of a claim is settled after the loss or damage has occurred. Compare **valued policy.**

o·pen pri+mar·y *n. U.S. government.* a primary in which any registered voter may participate. Compare **closed primary.**

o·pen-reel *adj.* another term for **reel-to-reel.**

o·pen se+cret *n.* something that is supposed to be secret but is widely known.

o·pen sen+tence *n. Logic.* a formula that contains a free occurrence of a variable. Compare **closed sentence.**

o·pen ses·a+me *n.* a very successful means of achieving a result. [from the magical words used by Ali Baba in the *Arabian Nights* to open the door of the robbers' den]

o·pen shop *n.* **1.** an establishment in which persons are hired and employed irrespective of their membership of a trade union. Compare **closed shop, union shop.** **2.** *U.S.* (formerly) an organization hiring only nonunion labour.

O·pen U·ni+ver+si·ty *n. Brit.* **the.** a university founded in 1969 for mature students studying by television and radio lectures, correspondence courses, local counselling, and summer schools.

o·pen up *vb.* (*adv.*) (*intr.*) *Informal.* **1.** (*intr.*) to start firing a gun or guns. **2.** (*intr.*) to speak freely or without restraint. **3.** (*intr.*) (of a motor vehicle) to accelerate. **4.** (*tr.*) to render accessible: *the motorway opened up the remoter areas.* **5.** to make or become more exciting or lively: *the game opened up after half-time.*

o·pen ver+dict *n.* a finding by a coroner's jury of death without stating the cause.

o·pen+work ('əʊpᵊnˌwɜːk) *n.* ornamental work, as of metal or embroidery, having a pattern of openings or holes.

op+er·a[1] ('ɒpərə, 'ɒprə) *n.* **1.** an extended dramatic work in which music constitutes a dominating feature, either consisting of separate recitatives, arias, and choruses, or having a continuous musical structure. **2.** the branch of music or drama represented by such works. **3.** the score, libretto, etc., of an opera. **4.** a theatre where opera is performed. [C17: via Italian from Latin: work, a work, plural of *opus* work]

op+er·a[2] ('ɒpərə) *n.* a plural of **opus.**

op+er+a·ble ('ɒpərəbᵊl, 'ɒprə-) *adj.* **1.** capable of being treated by a surgical operation. **2.** capable of being operated. **3.** capable of being put into practice. —**ˌop+er+a·'bil+i·ty** *n.* —**'op+er+a·bly** *adv.*

o·pé+ra bouffe ('ɒpərə 'buːf; *French* ɔpera 'buf) *n., pl.* **o·pé+ra bouffes, o·pé+ras bouffe,** *or* **o·pé+ras bouffes** (*French* ɔpera 'buf). a type of light or satirical opera common in France during the 19th century. [from French: comic opera]

o·pe·ra buf+fa ('buːfə; *Italian* 'opera 'buffa) *n., pl.* **o·pe·ra buf+fas, o·pe·ras buf+fa,** *or* **o·pe·re buf·fe** (*Italian* 'opere 'buffe). a kind of comic opera originating in Italy during the 18th century. [from Italian: comic opera]

op+er·a cloak *n.* a large cloak worn over evening clothes. Also called: **opera hood.**

o·pé+ra co+mique ('ɒpərə kɒ'miːk; *French* ɔpera kɔ'mik) *n., pl.* **o·pé+ra co+miques, o·pé+ras co+mique,** *or* **o·pé+ras co+miques** (*French* ɔpera kɔ'mik). any type of opera, current in France during the 19th century and characterized by spoken dialogue.

op+er·a glass·es *pl. n.* small low-powered binoculars used by audiences in theatres, etc.

op+er·a hat *n.* a collapsible top hat operated by a spring.

op+er·a house *n.* a theatre designed for opera.

op+er+and ('ɒpəˌrænd) *n.* a quantity or function upon which a mathematical operation is performed. [C19: from Latin *operandum* (something) to be worked upon, from *operārī* to work]

op+er+ant ('ɒpərənt) *adj.* **1.** producing effects; operating. ~*n.* **2.** a person or thing that operates.

op+er+ant con+di+tion+ing *n. Psychol.* another name for **instrumental conditioning.**

o·pe·ra se+ri·a ('sɪərɪə; *Italian* 'opera 'sɛːrja) *n., pl.* **o·pe·ra se+ri·as, o·pe·ras se+ri·a,** *or* **o·pe·re se+rie** (*Italian* 'opere 'sɛːrje). a type of opera current in 18th century Italy based on a serious plot, esp. a mythological tale. [from Italian: serious opera]

op+er+ate ('ɒpəˌreɪt) *vb.* **1.** to function or cause to function. **2.** (*tr.*) to control the functioning of: *operate a machine.* **3.** to manage, direct, run, or pursue (a business, system, etc.). **4.** to perform a surgical operation upon (a person or animal). **5.** (*intr.*) to produce a desired or intended effect. **6.** (*tr.*; usually foll. by *on*) to treat or process in a particular or specific way. **7.** (*intr.*) to conduct military or naval operations. **8.** (*intr.*) to deal in securities on a stock exchange. [C17: from Latin *operāri* to work]

op+er+at+ic (ˌɒpə'rætɪk) *adj.* **1.** of or relating to opera. **2.** histrionic or exaggerated. —**ˌop+er+'at·i·cal+ly** *adv.*

op+er+at+ing ta+ble *n.* the table on which the patient lies during a surgical operation.

op+er+at+ing the·a+tre *n.* a room in which surgical operations are performed.

op+er+a·tion (ˌɒpə'reɪʃən) *n.* **1.** the act, process, or manner of operating. **2.** the state of being in effect, in action, or operative (esp. in the phrases **in** *or* **into operation**). **3.** a process, method, or series of acts, esp. of a practical or mechanical nature. **4.**

Surgery. any manipulation of the body or one of its organs or parts to repair damage, arrest the progress of a disease, remove foreign matter, etc. **5. a.** a military or naval action, such as a campaign, manoeuvre, etc. **b.** (*cap. and prenominal when part of a name*): *Operation Crossbow.* **6.** *Maths.* any procedure, such as addition, multiplication, involution, or differentiation, in which one or more numbers or quantities are operated upon according to specific rules. **7.** a commercial or financial transaction.

op·er·a·tion·al (ˌɒpəˈreɪʃənᵊl) *adj.* **1.** of or relating to an operation or operations. **2.** in working order and ready for use. **3.** *Military.* capable of, needed in, or actually involved in operations. —ˌ**op·er·ˈa·tion·al·ly** *adv.*

op·er·a·tion·al·ism (ˌɒpəˈreɪʃənəˌlɪzəm) *or* **op·er·a·tion·ism** (ˌɒpəˈreɪʃəˌnɪzəm) *n.* (in the philosophy of science) the belief that a scientific concept should be defined by specifying the operations to be performed in determining its validity. Such operations include the application of test procedures, the taking of measurements, etc. —ˌ**op·er·ˌa·tion·alˈist·ic** *adj.*

op·er·a·tions re·search *n.* the analysis of problems in business and industry involving the construction of models and the application of linear programming, critical path analysis, and other quantitative techniques. Also: **operational research.**

op·er·a·tions room *n.* a room from which operations, esp. military operations, are controlled.

op·er·a·tive (ˈɒpərətɪv) *adj.* **1.** in force, effect, or operation. **2.** exerting force or influence. **3.** producing a desired effect; significant: *the operative word.* **4.** of or relating to a surgical procedure. ~*n.* **5.** a worker, esp. one with a special skill. **6.** *U.S.* a private detective. —ˈ**op·er·a·tive·ly** *adv.* —ˈ**op·er·a·tive·ness** *or* ˌ**op·er·a·ˈtiv·i·ty** *n.*

op·er·a·tize *or* **op·er·a·tise** (ˈɒpərəˌtaɪz) *vb.* (*tr.*) to turn a play, novel, etc., into an opera.

op·er·a·tor (ˈɒpəˌreɪtə) *n.* **1.** a person who operates a machine, instrument, etc. **2.** a person who owns or operates an industrial or commercial establishment. **3.** a speculator, esp. one who operates on currency or stock markets. **4.** *Informal.* a person who manipulates affairs and other people. **5.** *Maths.* any symbol, term, letter, etc., used to indicate or express a specific operation or process, such as ∫ (the integral operator), or Δ (the differential operator).

o·per·cu·lum (əʊˈpɜːkjʊləm) *n., pl.* **·la** (-lə) *or* **·lums. 1.** *Zoology.* **a.** the hard bony flap covering the gill slits in fishes. **b.** the bony plate in certain gastropods covering the opening of the shell when the body is withdrawn. **2.** *Botany.* the covering of the spore-bearing capsule of a moss. **3.** *Biology.* any other covering or lid in various organisms. [C18: via New Latin from Latin: lid, from *operīre* to cover] —**o·ˈper·cu·lar** *or* **o·per·cu·late** (əʊˈpɜːkjʊlɪt, -ˌleɪt) *adj.*

op·er·et·ta (ˌɒpəˈrɛtə) *n.* a type of comic or lighthearted opera. [C18: from Italian: a small OPERA] —ˌ**op·er·ˈet·tist** *n.*

op·er·on (ˈɒpəˌrɒn) *n. Genetics.* a group of adjacent genes functioning as a unit under the control of another gene (the **operator gene**). [C20: from OPERATE]

op·er·ose (ˈɒpəˌrəʊs) *adj. Rare.* **1.** laborious. **2.** industrious; busy. [C17: from Latin *operōsus* painstaking, from *opus* work] —ˈ**op·er·ˌose·ly** *adv.* —ˈ**op·er·ˌose·ness** *n.*

oph·i·cleide (ˈɒfɪˌklaɪd) *n. Music.* an obsolete keyed wind instrument of bass pitch. [C19: from French *ophicléide,* from Greek *ophis* snake + *kleis* key]

o·phid·i·an (əʊˈfɪdɪən) *adj.* **1.** snakelike. **2.** of, relating to, or belonging to the *Ophidia,* a suborder of reptiles that comprises the snakes. ~*n.* **3.** any reptile of the suborder *Ophidia;* a snake. [C19: from New Latin *Ophidia* name of suborder, from Greek *ophidion,* from *ophis* snake]

oph·i·ol·o·gy (ˌɒfɪˈɒlədʒɪ) *n.* the branch of zoology that is concerned with the study of snakes. [C19: from Greek *ophis* snake + -LOGY] —**oph·i·o·log·i·cal** (ˌɒfɪəˈlɒdʒɪkᵊl) *adj.* —ˌ**oph·i·ˈol·o·gist** *n.*

O·phir (ˈəʊfə) *n. Bible.* a region, probably situated on the SW coast of Arabia on the Red Sea, renowned, esp. in King Solomon's reign, for its gold and precious stones (I Kings 9:28; 10:10).

o·phite (ˈəʊfaɪt) *n.* any of several greenish mottled rocks with ophitic texture, such as dolerite and diabase. [C17: from Latin *ophītēs,* from Greek, from *ophis* snake]

o·phit·ic (əʊˈfɪtɪk) *adj.* (of the texture of rocks such as dolerite) having small elongated unorientated feldspar crystals embedded in the ferromagnesian matrix.

Oph·iu·chus (ɒˈfjuːkəs) *n., Latin genitive* **Oph·iu·chi** (ɒˈfjuːkaɪ). a large constellation lying on the celestial equator between Hercules and Scorpius and containing the dark nebula, **Ophiuchus Nebula.** [C17: via Latin from Greek *Ophioukhos,* from *ophis* snake + *ekhein* to hold]

oph·thal·mi·a (ɒfˈθælmɪə) *n.* inflammation of the eye, often including the conjunctiva. [C16: via Late Latin from Greek, from *ophthalmos* eye; see OPTIC]

oph·thal·mic (ɒfˈθælmɪk) *adj.* of or relating to the eye.

oph·thal·mi·tis (ˌɒfθælˈmaɪtɪs) *n.* inflammation of the eye.

oph·thal·mo- *or before a vowel* **oph·thalm-** *combining form.* indicating the eye or the eyeball: *ophthalmoscope.* [from Greek *ophthalmos* EYE]

ophthalmol. *or* **ophthal.** *abbrev. for* ophthalmology.

oph·thal·mol·o·gist (ˌɒfθælˈmɒlədʒɪst) *n.* a medical practitioner specializing in the diagnosis and treatment of eye diseases.

oph·thal·mol·o·gy (ˌɒfθælˈmɒlədʒɪ) *n.* the branch of medicine concerned with the eye and its diseases. —**oph·thal·mo·log·i·cal** (ɒfˌθælməˈlɒdʒɪkᵊl) *adj.*

oph·thal·mo·scope (ɒfˈθælməˌskəʊp) *n.* an instrument for examining the interior of the eye. —**oph·thal·mo·scop·ic** (ɒfˌθælməˈskɒpɪk) *adj.*

oph·thal·mos·co·py (ˌɒfθælˈmɒskəpɪ) *n.* examination of the interior of the eye with an ophthalmoscope.

O·phüls (ˈɔːfəls; *German* ˈɔfyls) *n.* **Max** (maks). 1902–57, German film director, whose films include *Liebelei* (1932), *La Signora di tutti* (1934), *La Ronde* (1950), *Le Plaisir* (1952), and *Lola Montes* (1955).

-o·pi·a *n. combining form.* indicating a visual defect or condition: *myopia.* [from Greek, from *ōps* eye] —**-op·ic** *adj. combining form.*

o·pi·ate *n.* (ˈəʊpɪɪt). **1.** any of various narcotic drugs containing opium or an alkaloid of opium. **2.** any other narcotic or sedative drug. **3.** something that soothes, deadens, or induces sleep. ~*adj.* (ˈəʊpɪɪt). **4.** containing or consisting of opium. **5.** inducing relaxation; soporific. ~*vb.* (ˈəʊpɪˌeɪt). (*tr.*) *Rare.* **6.** to treat with an opiate. **7.** to dull or deaden. [C16: from Medieval Latin *opiātus;* from Latin *opium* poppy juice, OPIUM]

o·pine (əʊˈpaɪn) *vb.* (when *tr., usually takes a clause as object*) to hold or express an opinion: *he opined that it was all a sad mistake.* [C16: from Latin *opīnārī*]

o·pin·ion (əˈpɪnjən) *n.* **1.** judgment or belief not founded on certainty or proof. **2.** the prevailing or popular feeling or view: *public opinion.* **3.** evaluation, impression, or estimation of the value or worth of a person or thing. **4.** an evaluation or judgment given by an expert: *a medical opinion.* **5.** the advice given by counsel on a case submitted to him for his view on the legal points involved. **6. a matter of opinion.** a point open to question. **7. be of the opinion (that).** to believe (that). [C13: via Old French from Latin *opīniō* belief, from *opīnārī* to think; see OPINE]

o·pin·ion·at·ed (əˈpɪnjəˌneɪtɪd) *adj.* holding obstinately and unreasonably to one's own opinions; dogmatic. —**o·ˈpin·ion·ˌat·ed·ly** *adv.* —**o·ˈpin·ion·ˌat·ed·ness** *n.*

o·pin·ion·a·tive (əˈpɪnjəˌneɪtɪv) *adj. Rare.* **1.** of or relating to opinion. **2.** another word for **opinionated.** —**o·ˈpin·ion·ˌa·tive·ly** *adv.* —**o·ˈpin·ion·ˌa·tive·ness** *n.*

o·pin·ion poll *n.* another term for a **poll** (sense 3).

o·pis·tho·branch (əˈpɪsθəˌbræŋk) *n.* any marine gastropod of the class *Opisthobranchia* (or *Opisthobranchiata*), in which the shell is reduced or absent: includes the pteropods, sea hares, and nudibranchs. [via New Latin from Greek *opisthen* behind + -BRANCH]

op·is·thog·na·thous (ˌɒpɪsˈθɒgnəθəs) *adj.* (of a person or animal) having receding jaws. [C19: from Greek *opisthen* behind + -GNATHOUS] —ˌ**op·is·ˈthog·na·thism** *n.*

o·pi·um (ˈəʊpɪəm) *n.* **1.** an addictive narcotic drug extracted from the unripe seed capsules of the opium poppy and containing alkaloids such as morphine and codeine: used in medicine as an analgesic and hypnotic. **2.** something having a tranquillizing or stupefying effect. [C14: from Latin: poppy juice, from Greek *opion,* diminutive of *opos* juice of a plant]

o·pi·um den *n.* a place where opium is sold and used.

o·pi·um·ism (ˈəʊpɪəˌmɪzəm) *n. Pathol.* addiction to opium or a condition resulting from prolonged use of opium.

o·pi·um pop·py *n.* a poppy, *Papaver somniferum,* of SW Asia, with greyish-green leaves and typically white or reddish flowers: widely cultivated as a source of opium.

O·por·to (əˈpɔːtəʊ) *n.* a port in NW Portugal, near the mouth of the Douro River: the second largest city in Portugal, famous for port wine (begun in 1678). Pop.: 311 800 (1974 est.). Portuguese name: **Pôrto.**

o·pos·sum (əˈpɒsəm) *or* **pos·sum** *n., pl.* **·sums** *or* **·sum. 1.** any thick-furred marsupial, esp. *Didelphis marsupialis* (**common opossum**), of the family *Didelphidae* of S North, Central, and South America, having an elongated snout and a hairless prehensile tail. Sometimes (informal) shortened to **possum. 2.** any of various similar animals, esp. a phalanger. [C17: from Algonquian *aposoum;* related to Delaware *apässum,* literally: white beast]

o·pos·sum shrimp *n.* any of various shrimplike crustaceans of the genera *Mysis, Praunus,* etc., of the order *Mysidacea,* in which the females carry the eggs and young around in a ventral brood pouch.

opp. *abbrev. for:* **1.** opposed. **2.** opposite.

Op·pen·hei·mer (ˈɒpənˌhaɪmə) *n.* **J(ulius) Rob·ert.** 1904–67, U.S. nuclear physicist. He was director of the Los Alamos laboratory (1943–45), which produced the first atomic bomb. He opposed the development of the hydrogen bomb (1949) and in 1953 was alleged to be a security risk. He was later exonerated.

op·pi·dan (ˈɒpɪdən) *Rare.* ~*adj.* **1.** of a town; urban. ~*n.* **2.** a person living in a town. [C16: from Latin *oppidānus,* from *oppidum* town]

op·pi·late (ˈɒpɪˌleɪt) *vb.* (*tr.*) *Pathol.* to block (the pores, bowels, etc.). [C16: from Latin *oppīlāre,* from *ob-* against + *pīlāre* to pack closely] —ˌ**op·pi·ˈla·tion** *n.*

op·po·nent (əˈpəʊnənt) *n.* **1.** a person who opposes another in a contest, battle, etc. **2.** *Anatomy.* an opponent muscle. ~*adj.* **3.** opposite, as in position. **4.** *Anatomy.* (of a muscle) bringing two parts into opposition. **5.** opposing; contrary. [C16: from Latin *oppōnere* to oppose, from *ob-* against + *pōnere* to place] —**op·ˈpo·nen·cy** *n.*

op·por·tune (ˈɒpəˌtjuːn) *adj.* **1.** occurring at a time that is suitable or advantageous. **2.** fit or suitable for a particular purpose or occurrence. [C15: via Old French from Latin *opportūnus,* from *ob-* to + *portus* harbour (originally: coming to the harbour, obtaining timely protection)] —'**op+por+,tune+ly** *adv.* —'**op+por+,tune+ness** *n.*

op+por+tun+ist (,ɒpə'tju:nɪst) *n.* **1.** a person who adapts his actions, responses, etc., to take advantage of opportunities, circumstances, etc. ~*adj.* **2.** taking advantage of opportunities and circumstances in this way. —,**op+por+'tun+ism** *n.* —,**op+por+tun+'is+tic** *adj.*

op+por+tu+ni·ty (,ɒpə'tju:nɪtɪ) *n., pl.* **·ties. 1.** a favourable, appropriate, or advantageous combination of circumstances. **2.** a chance or prospect.

op+por+tu+ni·ty cost *n. Economics.* cost in terms of the best alternatives foregone.

op+pos+a·ble (ə'pəuzəb^{ə}l) *adj.* **1.** capable of being opposed. **2.** Also: **apposable.** (of the thumb of primates, esp. man) capable of being moved into a position facing the other digits so as to be able to touch the ends of each. **3.** capable of being placed opposite something else. —**op+'pos+a·bly** *adv.* —**op+,pos+a·'bil+i·ty** *n.*

op+pose (ə'pəuz) *vb.* **1.** (*tr.*) to fight against, counter, or resist strongly. **2.** (*tr.*) to be hostile or antagonistic to; be against. **3.** (*tr.*) to place or set in opposition; contrast or counterbalance. **4.** (*tr.*) to place opposite or facing. **5.** (*intr.*) to be or act in opposition. [C14: via Old French from Latin *oppōnere,* from *ob-* against + *pōnere* to place] —**op+'pos+er** *n.* —**op+'pos+ing+ly** *adv.* —**op+pos+i+tive** (ə'pɒzɪtɪv) *adj.*

op+po+site ('ɒpəzɪt, -sɪt) *adj.* **1.** situated or being on the other side or at each side of something between: *their houses were at opposite ends of the street.* **2.** facing or going in contrary directions: *opposite ways.* **3.** diametrically different in character, tendency, belief, etc.: *opposite views.* **4.** *Botany.* **a.** (of leaves, flowers, etc.) arranged in pairs on either side of the stem. **b.** (of parts of a flower) arranged opposite the middle of another part. **5.** *Maths.* **a.** (of two vertices or sides in an even-sided polygon) separated by the same number of vertices or sides in both a clockwise and anticlockwise direction. **b.** (of a side in a triangle) facing a specified angle. Abbrev.: **opp.** ~*n.* **6.** a person or thing that is opposite; antithesis. **7.** *Maths.* the side facing a specified angle in a right-angled triangle. **8.** a rare word for **opponent.** ~*prep.* **9.** Also: **opposite to.** facing; corresponding to (something on the other side of a division): *the house opposite ours.* **10.** as a co-star with: *she played opposite Olivier in "Hamlet".* ~*adv.* **11.** on opposite sides: *she lives opposite.* —'**op+po+site+ly** *adv.* —'**op+po+site+ness** *n.*

op+po+site num+ber *n.* a person holding an equivalent and corresponding position on another side or situation.

op+po+site prompt *n. Theatre.* another name for **stage right.** See **prompt.**

op+po+site sex *n.* **the.** women in relation to men or men in relation to women.

op+po+si+tion (,ɒpə'zɪʃən) *n.* **1.** the act of opposing or the state of being opposed. **2.** hostility, unfriendliness, or antagonism. **3.** a person or group antagonistic or opposite in aims to another. **4. a.** (usually preceded by *the*) a political party or group opposed to the ruling party or government. **b.** (*cap. as part of a name, esp. in Britain and other Commonwealth countries*): *Her Majesty's Loyal Opposition.* **c. in opposition.** (of a political party) opposing the government. **5.** a position facing or opposite another. **6.** the act of placing something facing or opposite something else. **7.** something that acts as an obstacle to some course or progress. **8.** *Astronomy.* **a.** the position of an outer planet or the moon when it is in line or nearly in line with the earth as seen from the sun and is approximately at its nearest to the earth. **b.** the position of two celestial bodies when they appear to be diametrically opposite each other on the celestial sphere. **9.** *Astrology.* an exact aspect of 180° between two planets, etc., an orb of 8° being allowed. Compare **conjunction** (sense 5), **square** (sense 8), **trine** (sense 1). **10.** *Logic.* the relation between propositions having the same subject and predicate but differing in quality, quantity, or both, as with *all men are wicked; no men are wicked; some men are not wicked.* —,**op+po+'si+tion+al** *adj.* —,**op+po+'si+tion+ist** *n.* —,**op+po+'si+tion+less** *adj.*

op+press (ə'prɛs) *vb.* (*tr.*) **1.** to subjugate by cruelty, force, etc. **2.** to afflict or torment. **3.** to lie heavy on (the mind, imagination, etc.). **4.** an obsolete word for **overwhelm.** [C14: via Old French from Medieval Latin *oppressāre,* from Latin *opprimere,* from *ob-* against + *premere* to press] —**op+'pres+sing+ly** *adv.* —**op+'pres+sion** *n.* —**op+'pres+sor** *n.*

op+pres+sive (ə'prɛsɪv) *adj.* **1.** cruel, harsh, or tyrannical. **2.** heavy, constricting, or depressing. —**op+'pres+sive+ly** *adv.* —**op+'pres+sive+ness** *n.*

op+pro+bri+ous (ə'prəubrɪəs) *adj.* **1.** expressing scorn, disgrace, or contempt. **2.** shameful or infamous. —**op+'pro+bri+ous+ly** *adv.* —**op+'pro+bri+ous+ness** *n.*

op+pro+bri·um (ə'prəubrɪəm) *n.* **1.** the state of being abused or scornfully criticized. **2.** reproach or censure. **3.** a cause of disgrace or ignominy. [C17: from Latin *ob-* against + *probrum* a shameful act]

op+pugn (ə'pju:n) *vb.* (*tr.*) to call into question; dispute. [C15: from Latin *oppugnāre,* from *ob-* against + *pugnāre* to fight, from *pugnus* clenched fist; see PUGNACIOUS] —**op+'pugn+er** *n.*

op+pug+nant (ə'pʌgnənt) *adj. Rare.* combative, antagonistic, or contrary. —**op+'pug+nan+cy** *n.* —**op+'pug+nant+ly** *adv.*

Ops (ɒps) *n.* the Roman goddess of abundance and fertility, wife of Saturn. Greek counterpart: **Rhea.**

op+si+math ('ɒpsɪ,mæθ) *n.* a person who learns late in life. [C19: from Greek *opsimathēs,* from *opse* late + *math-* learn] —**op+sim+a+thy** (ɒp'sɪməθɪ) *n.*

-op·sis *combining form.* indicating a specified appearance or resemblance: *coreopsis.* [from Greek *opsis* sight]

op+son+ic in+dex *n.* the ratio of the number of bacteria destroyed by phagocytes in the blood of a test patient to the number destroyed in the blood of a normal individual.

op+so+nin ('ɒpsənɪn) *n.* a constituent of blood serum that renders invading bacteria more susceptible to ingestion by phagocytes in the serum. [C20: from Greek *opsōnion* victuals] —**op+son+ic** (ɒp'sɒnɪk) *adj.*

op+so+nize, op+so+nise ('ɒpsə,naɪz), *or* **op+son+i+fy** (ɒp'sɒnɪ,faɪ) *vb.* (*tr.*) to subject (bacteria) to the action of opsonins. —,**op+so+ni+'za+tion,** ,**op+so+ni+'sa+tion,** *or* **op+,son+i+fi+'ca+tion** *n.*

opt (ɒpt) *vb.* (when *intr.,* foll. by *for*) to show preference (for) or choose (to do something). ~See also **opt out.** [C19: from French *opter,* from Latin *optāre* to choose]

opt. *abbrev. for:* **1.** *Grammar.* optative. **2.** optical. **3.** optician. **4.** optics. **5.** optimum. **6.** optional.

op+ta+tive ('ɒptətɪv) *adj.* **1.** indicating or expressing choice, preference, or wish. **2.** *Grammar.* denoting a mood of verbs in Greek, Sanskrit, etc., expressing a wish. ~*n.* **3.** *Grammar.* **a.** the optative mood. **b.** a verb in this mood. [C16: via French *optatif,* from Late Latin *optātīvus,* from Latin *optāre* to desire]

op+tic ('ɒptɪk) *adj.* **1.** of or relating to the eye or vision. **2.** a less common word for **optical.** ~*n.* **3.** an informal word for **eye. 4.** *Brit., trademark.* a device attached to an inverted bottle for dispensing measured quantities of liquid, such as whisky, gin, etc. [C16: from Medieval Latin *opticus,* from Greek *optikos,* from *optos* visible, seen; related to *ōps* eye]

op+ti+cal ('ɒptɪk^{ə}l) *adj.* **1.** of, relating to, producing, or involving light. **2.** of or relating to the eye or to the sense of sight; optic. **3.** (esp. of a lens) aiding vision or correcting a visual disorder. —'**op+ti+cal+ly** *adv.*

op+ti+cal ac+tiv+i+ty *n.* the ability of substances that are optical isomers to rotate the plane of polarization of a transmitted beam of plane-polarized light.

op+ti+cal bench *n.* an apparatus for experimentation in optics, typically consisting of an adjustable arrangement of light source, lenses, prisms, etc.

op+ti+cal char+ac+ter read+er *n.* a computer peripheral device enabling letters, numbers, or other characters usually printed on paper to be optically scanned and input to a storage device, such as magnetic tape. The device uses the process of **optical character recognition.** Abbrev. (for both *reader* and *recognition*): **OCR.**

op+ti+cal crown *n.* an optical glass of low dispersion and relatively low refractive index. It is used in the construction of lenses.

op+ti+cal den+si+ty *n. Physics.* the former name for **reflection density** or **transmission density.**

op+ti+cal dou+ble star *n.* two stars that appear close together when viewed through a telescope but are not physically associated and are often separated by a great distance. Compare **binary star.**

op+ti+cal flint *n.* an optical glass of high dispersion and high refractive index containing lead oxide. They are used in the manufacture of lenses, artificial gems, and cut glass. Also called: **flint glass.**

op+ti+cal glass *n.* any of several types of clear homogeneous glass of known refractive index used in the construction of lenses, etc. See **optical flint, optical crown.**

op+ti+cal il+lu+sion *n.* **1.** an object causing a false visual impression. **2.** an instance of deception by such an object.

op+ti+cal i·som+er+ism *n.* isomerism of chemical compounds in which the two isomers differ only in that their molecules are mirror images of each other. See also **dextrorotatory, laevorotatory, racemization.** —**op+ti+cal i·so+mer** *n.*

op+ti+cal ma+ser *n.* another name for **laser.**

op+ti+cal ro+ta+tion *n.* the angle through which plane-polarized light is rotated in its passage through a substance exhibiting optical activity.

op+tic ax+is *n.* the direction in a uniaxial crystal or one of the two directions in a biaxial crystal along which a ray of unpolarized light may pass without undergoing double refraction.

op+tic disc *n.* a small oval-shaped area on the retina marking the site of entrance into the eyeball of the optic nerve. See **blind spot.**

op+ti+cian (ɒp'tɪʃən) *n.* a person who makes or sells spectacles or other optical instruments. Compare **ophthalmologist, optometrist.**

op+tic nerve *n.* the second cranial nerve, which provides a sensory pathway from the retina to the brain.

op+tics ('ɒptɪks) *n.* (*functioning as sing.*) the branch of science concerned with vision and the generation, nature, propagation, and behaviour of electromagnetic light.

op+tic thal+a+mus *n. Anatomy.* an older term for **thalamus.**

op+ti+mal ('ɒptɪməl) *adj.* another word for **optimum.**

op+ti+mism ('ɒptɪ,mɪzəm) *n.* **1.** the tendency to expect the best and see the best in all things. **2.** hopefulness; confidence. **3.** the doctrine of the ultimate triumph of good over evil. **4.** the philosophical doctrine that this is the best of all possible worlds. ~Compare **pessimism.** [C18: from French *optimisme,* from Latin *optimus* best, from *bonus* good] —'**op+ti+mist** *n.* —,**op+ti+'mis+tic** *or* ,**op+ti+'mis+ti+cal** *adj.* —,**op+ti+'mis+ti+cal+ly** *adv.*

op+ti+mize *or* **op+ti+mise** ('ɒptɪ,maɪz) *vb.* **1.** (*tr.*) to take the full advantage of. **2.** (*tr.*) to plan or carry out (an economic activity) with maximum efficiency. **3.** (*intr.*) to be optimistic. **4.** (*tr.*) to write or modify (a computer program) to achieve maximum efficiency in storage capacity, time, cost, etc. —**ˌop·ti·mi·'za·tion** *or* **ˌop·ti·mi·'sa·tion** *n.*

op·ti·mum ('ɒptɪməm) *n., pl.* **·ma** (-mə) *or* **·mums. 1.** a condition, degree, amount or compromise that produces the best possible result. ~*adj.* **2.** most favourable or advantageous; best: *optimum conditions.* [C19: from Latin: the best (thing), from *optimus* best; see OPTIMISM]

op·tion ('ɒpʃən) *n.* **1.** the act or an instance of choosing or deciding. **2.** the power or liberty to choose. **3.** the right, obtained by a fee, to purchase or sell property, esp. shares or commodities, at a specified time in the future at a fixed price. **4.** something chosen; choice. **5. keep** (*or* **leave**) **one's options open.** not to commit oneself. **6. soft option.** an easy alternative. [C17: from Latin *optiō* free choice, from *optāre* to choose]

op·tion·al ('ɒpʃənᵊl) *adj.* possible but not compulsory; left to personal choice. —**'op·tion·al·ly** *adv.*

op·tom·e·ter (ɒp'tɒmɪtə) *n.* any of various instruments for measuring the refractive power of the eye.

op·tom·e·trist (ɒp'tɒmɪtrɪst) *n.* a person, usually without medical qualifications, who tests visual acuity and prescribes corrective lenses. Compare **ophthalmologist, optician.**

op·tom·e·try (ɒp'tɒmɪtrɪ) *n.* the science or practice of testing visual acuity and prescribing corrective lenses. —**op·to·met·ric** (ˌɒptə'mɛtrɪk) *adj.*

opt out *vb.* (*intr., adv.;* often foll. by *of*) to choose not to be involved (in) or part (of).

op·u·lent ('ɒpjʊlənt) *adj.* **1.** having or indicating wealth. **2.** abundant or plentiful. [C17: from Latin *opulens,* from *opēs* (pl.) wealth] —**'op·u·lence** *or* **'op·u·len·cy** *n.* —**'op·u·lent·ly** *adv.*

o·pun·ti·a (ɒ'pʌnʃɪə) *n.* any cactus of the genus *Opuntia,* esp. prickly pear, having fleshy branched stems and green, red, or yellow flowers. [C17: New Latin, from Latin *Opuntia* (*herba*) the Opuntian (plant), from *Opus,* ancient town of Locris, Greece]

o·pus ('əʊpəs) *n., pl.* **o·pus·es** *or* **op·er·a** ('ɒpərə). **1.** an artistic composition, esp. a musical work. **2.** (*often cap.*) (usually followed by a number) a musical composition by a particular composer, generally catalogued in order of publication: *Beethoven's opus 61 is his violin concerto.* Abbrev.: **op.** [C18: from Latin: a work; compare: Sanskrit *apas* work]

o·pus·cule (ɒ'pʌskju:l) *n. Rare.* a small or insignificant artistic work. [C17: via French from Latin *opusculum,* from *opus* work] —**o·'pus·cu·lar** *adj.*

or[1] (ɔ:; *unstressed* ə) *conj.* (*coordinating*) **1.** used to join alternatives: *apples or pears; apples or pears or cheese; apples, pears, or cheese.* **2.** used to join rephrasings of the same thing: *to serve in the army, or rather to fight in the army; twelve, or a dozen.* **3.** used to join two alternatives when the first is preceded by *either* or *whether: whether it rains or not we'll be there; either yes or no.* **4. one or two, four or five,** *etc.* a few. **5. or else.** otherwise; if not: *go home, or else you will get cold.* **6.** a poetic word for **either** or **whether,** as the first element in correlatives, with *or* also preceding the second alternative. ~See also **exclusive or** and **inclusive or.** [C13: contraction of *other,* used to introduce an alternative, changed (through influence of EITHER) from Old English *oththe;* compare Old High German *odar* (German *oder*)]
Usage. See at **either** and **neither.**

or[2] (ɔ:) *Archaic.* ~*conj.* **1.** (*subordinating;* foll. by *ever* or *ere*) before; when. ~*prep.* **2.** before. [Old English *ār* soon; related to Old Norse *ār* early, Old High German *ēr*]

or[3] (ɔ:) *adj.* (*usually postpositive*) *Heraldry.* of the metal gold. [C16: via French from Latin *aurum* gold]

-or[1] *suffix forming nouns from verbs.* a person or thing that does what is expressed by the verb: *actor; conductor; generator; sailor.* [via Old French *-eur, -eor,* from Latin *-or* or *-ātor*]

-or[2] *suffix forming nouns.* **1.** indicating state, condition, or activity: *terror; error.* **2.** the U.S. spelling of **-our.**

o.r. *Commerce. abbrev. for* owner's risk.

O.R. *abbrev. for:* **1.** operational research. **2.** *Military.* other ranks.

o·ra ('ɔ:rə) *n.* a plural of **os**[2].

or·ache *or esp. U.S.* **or·ach** ('ɒrɪtʃ) *n.* any of several herbaceous plants or small shrubs of the chenopodiaceous genus *Atriplex,* esp. *A. hortensis* (**garden orache**), which is cultivated as a vegetable. They have typically greyish-green lobed leaves and inconspicuous flowers. [C15: from Old French *arache,* from Latin *atriplex,* from Greek *atraphaxus,* of obscure origin]

or·a·cle ('ɒrəkᵊl) *n.* **1.** a prophecy, often obscure or allegorical, revealed through the medium of a priest or priestess at the shrine of a god. **2.** a shrine at which an oracular god is consulted. **3.** an agency through which a prophecy is transmitted. **4.** any person or thing believed to indicate future action with infallible authority. **5.** a statement believed to be infallible and authoritative. **6.** *Bible.* **a.** a message from God. **b.** the holy of holies in the Israelite temple. [C14: via Old French from Latin *ōrāculum,* from *ōrāre* to request]

or·a·cles ('ɒrəkᵊlz) *pl. n.* another term for **Scripture** (sense 1).

o·rac·u·lar (ɒ'rækjʊlə) *adj.* **1.** of or relating to an oracle. **2.** wise and prophetic. **3.** mysterious or ambiguous. —**o·'rac·u·lar·ly** *adv.*

or·a·cy ('ɔ:rəsɪ) *n.* the capacity to express oneself in and understand speech. [C20: from Latin *or-, os* mouth, by analogy with *literacy*]

O·ra·dea (*Rumanian* o'radja) *n.* an industrial city in NW Rumania, in Transylvania: ceded by Hungary (1919). Pop.: 153 437 (1974 est.). German name: **Grosswardein.** Hungarian name: **Nagyvárad.**

o·ral ('ɔ:rəl, 'ɒrəl) *adj.* **1.** spoken or verbal: *an oral agreement.* **2.** relating to, affecting, or for use in the mouth: *an oral thermometer.* **3.** of or relating to the surface of an animal, such as a jellyfish, on which the mouth is situated. **4.** denoting a drug to be taken by mouth: *an oral contraceptive.* Compare **parenteral. 5.** of, relating to, or using spoken words. **6.** *Phonetics.* pronounced with the soft palate in a raised position completely closing the nasal cavity and allowing air to pass out only through the mouth. **7.** *Psychoanal.* **a.** relating to a stage of psychosexual development during which the child's interest is concentrated on the mouth. **b.** denoting personality traits, such as dependence, selfishness, and aggression, resulting from fixation at the oral stage. Compare **anal** (sense 2), **genital** (sense 2), **phallic** (sense 2.). ~*n.* **8.** an examination in which the questions and answers are spoken rather than written. [C17: from Late Latin *ōrālis,* from Latin *ōs* face] —**'o·ral·ly** *adv.*

o·ral so·ci·e·ty *n.* a society that has not developed literacy.

O·ran (ɔ'ræn, ɔ'rɑ:n; *French* ɔ'rã) *n.* a port in NW Algeria: the second largest city in the country; scene of the destruction by the British of most of the French fleet in the harbour in 1940 to prevent its capture by the Germans. Pop.: 327 493 (1966).

or·ange ('ɒrɪndʒ) *n.* **1.** any of several citrus trees, esp. *Citrus sinensis* (**sweet orange**) and the Seville orange, cultivated in warm regions for their round edible fruit. See also **tangerine** (sense 1). **2. a.** the fruit of any of these trees, having a yellowish-red bitter rind and segmented juicy flesh. See also **navel orange. b.** (*as modifier*): *orange peel.* **3.** the hard wood of any of these trees. **4.** any of a group of colours, such as that of the skin of an orange, that lie between red and yellow in the visible spectrum in the approximate wavelength range 620–585 nanometres. **5.** a dye or pigment producing these colours. **6.** orange cloth or clothing: *dressed in orange.* **7.** any of several trees or herbaceous plants that resemble the orange, such as mock orange. ~*adj.* **8.** of the colour orange. [C14: via Old French from Old Provençal *auranja,* from Arabic *nāranj,* from Persian *nārang,* from Sanskrit *nāranga,* probably of Dravidian origin]

Or·ange[1] ('ɒrɪndʒ) *n.* **1.** a river in S Africa, rising in NE Lesotho and flowing generally west across the South African plateau to the Atlantic: the longest river in South Africa. Length: 2093 km (1300 miles). **2.** a town in SE France: a small principality in the Middle Ages, the descendants of which formed the House of Orange. Pop.: 26 468 (1975). Ancient name: **Arausio.**

Or·ange[2] ('ɒrɪndʒ) *n.* **1.** a princely family of Europe. Its possessions, originally centred in S France, passed in 1544 to the count of Nassau, who became William I of Orange and helped to found the United Provinces of the Netherlands. Since 1815 it has been the name of the reigning house of the Netherlands. **2.** (*modifier*) of or relating to the Orangemen. **3.** (*modifier*) of or relating to the royal dynasty of Orange.

or·ange·ade (ˌɒrɪndʒ'eɪd) *n.* an effervescent orange-flavoured drink.

or·ange blos·som *n.* the flowers of the orange tree, traditionally worn by brides.

or·ange chro·mide *n.* an Asian cichlid fish, *Etropus maculatus,* with a brownish-orange spotted body.

or·ange flow·er wa·ter *n.* a distilled infusion of orange blossom, used in cakes, confectionery, etc.

Or·ange Free State *n.* a province of central South Africa, between the Orange and Vaal rivers: settled by Boers in 1836 after the Great Trek; annexed by Britain in 1848; became a province of South Africa in 1910; economy based on agriculture and mineral resources (esp. gold and uranium). Capital: Bloemfontein. Pop.: 1 649 306 (1970). Area: 29 152 sq. km (49 866 sq. miles).

Or·ange·ism ('ɒrɪndʒˌɪzəm) *n.* the practices or principles of Orangemen, esp. Protestant supremacy in Ireland, Northern Ireland, or Canada.

Or·ange·man ('ɒrɪndʒmən) *n., pl.* **·men.** a member of a society founded as a secret order in Ireland (1795) to uphold the Protestant religion, the Protestant dynasty, and Protestant supremacy against Irish nationalists and Roman Catholics. **Orange Lodges** have since spread to many parts of the former British Empire. [C18: after William, prince of *Orange* (king of England as William III)]

Or·ange·man's Day *n.* the 12th of July, celebrated by Protestants in Northern Ireland to commemorate the anniversary of the Battle of the Boyne (1690).

or·ange pe·koe *n.* a superior grade of black tea made from the small leaves at the tips of the plant stems and growing in India and Sri Lanka.

or·ang·er·y ('ɒrɪndʒərɪ, -dʒrɪ) *n., pl.* **·er·ies.** a building, such as a greenhouse, in which orange trees are grown.

or·ange stick *n.* a small stick used to clean the fingernails and cuticles, having one pointed and one rounded end.

or·ange-tip *n.* a European butterfly, *Anthocharis cardamines,* having whitish wings with orange tipped forewings: family *Pieridae.*

or·ange·wood ('ɒrɪndʒˌwʊd) *n.* **a.** the hard fine-grained yellowish wood of the orange tree. **b.** (*as modifier*): *an orangewood table.*

o·rang-u·tan (ɔ:ˌræŋu:'tæn, ˌɔ:ræŋ'u:tæn) *or* **o·rang-ou·tang** (ɔ:ˌræŋu:'tæŋ, ˌɔ:ræŋ'u:tæŋ) *n.* a large anthropoid ape, *Pongo pygmaeus,* of the forests of Sumatra and Borneo, with shaggy reddish-brown hair and strong arms. Sometimes shortened to **orang.** [C17: from Malay *orang hutan,* from *ōrang* man + *hūtan* forest]

o·ra pro no·bis *Latin.* (ˈɔːrɑː prəʊ ˈnəʊbɪs) *R.C. Church.* a Latin invocation meaning *pray for us.*

o·rate (ɔːˈreɪt) *vb.* (*intr.*) **1.** to make or give an oration. **2.** to speak pompously and lengthily.

o·ra·tion (ɔːˈreɪʃən) *n.* **1.** a formal public declaration or speech. **2.** any rhetorical, lengthy, or pompous speech. **3.** an academic exercise or contest in public speaking. [C14: from Latin *ōrātiō* speech, harangue, from *ōrāre* to plead, pray]

or·a·tor (ˈɒrətə) *n.* **1.** a public speaker, esp. one versed in rhetoric. **2.** a person given to lengthy or pompous speeches. **3.** *Obsolete.* the plaintiff in a cause of action in chancery.

Or·a·to·ri·an (ˌɒrəˈtɔːrɪən) *n.* a member of the religious congregation of the Oratory.

or·a·to·ri·o (ˌɒrəˈtɔːrɪəʊ) *n., pl.* **·ri·os.** a dramatic but unstaged musical composition for soloists, chorus, and orchestra, based on a religious theme. [C18: from Italian, literally: ORATORY[2], referring to the Church of the Oratory at Rome where musical services were held]

or·a·to·ry[1] (ˈɒrətərɪ, -trɪ) *n.* **1.** the art of public speaking. **2.** rhetorical skill or style. [C16: from Latin (*ars*) *ōrātōria* (the art of) public speaking] —ˌ**or·a·ˈtor·i·cal** *adj.*

or·a·to·ry[2] (ˈɒrətərɪ, -trɪ) *n., pl.* **·ries.** a small room or secluded place, set apart for private prayer. [C14: from Anglo-Norman, from Church Latin *ōrātōrium* place of prayer, from *ōrāre* to plead, pray]

Or·a·to·ry (ˈɒrətərɪ, -trɪ) *n. R.C. Church.* **1.** Also called: **Congregation of the Oratory.** the religious society of secular priests (**Oratorians**) living in a community founded by St. Philip Neri. **2.** any church belonging to this society: *the Brompton Oratory.*

orb (ɔːb) *n.* **1.** (in royal regalia) an ornamental sphere surmounted by a cross, representing the power of a sovereign. **2.** a sphere; globe. **3.** *Poetic.* another word for **eye. 4.** *Obsolete or poetic.* **a.** a celestial body, esp. the earth or sun. **b.** the orbit of a celestial body. **5.** an archaic word for **circle.** ~*vb.* **6.** to make or become circular or spherical. **7.** (*tr.*) an archaic word for **encircle.** [C16: from Latin *orbis* circle, disc]

or·bic·u·lar (ɔːˈbɪkjʊlə), **or·bic·u·late,** *or* **or·bic·u·lat·ed** *adj.* **1.** circular or spherical. **2.** (of a leaf or similar flat part) circular or nearly circular. **3.** *Rare.* rounded or total. —**or·bic·u·lar·i·ty** (ɔːˌbɪkjʊˈlærɪtɪ) *n.* —**or·ˈbic·u·lar·ly** *adv.*

or·bit (ˈɔːbɪt) *n.* **1.** *Astronomy.* the curved path, usually elliptical, followed by a planet, satellite, comet, etc., in its motion around another celestial body under the influence of gravitation. **2.** a range or field of action or influence; sphere: *he is out of my orbit.* **3.** the bony cavity containing the eyeball. Nontechnical name: **eye socket. 4.** *Zoology.* **a.** the skin surrounding the eye of a bird. **b.** the hollow in which lies the eye or eyestalk of an insect or other arthropod. **5.** *Physics.* the path of an electron in its motion around the nucleus of an atom. ~*vb.* **6.** to move around (a body) in a curved path, usually circular or elliptical. **7.** (*tr.*) to send (a satellite, spacecraft, etc.) into orbit. **8.** (*intr.*) to move in or as if in an orbit. [C16: from Latin *orbita* course, from *orbis* circle, ORB] —ˈ**or·bit·al** *adj.* —ˈ**or·bit·al·ly** *adv.*

or·bit·al (ˈɔːbɪtᵊl) *n.* a region surrounding an atomic nucleus in which the distribution of electrons is given by a wave function.

or·bit·al ve·loc·i·ty *n.* the velocity required by a spacecraft, satellite, etc., to enter and maintain a given orbit.

orc (ɔːk) *n.* **1.** any of various whales, such as the killer and grampus. **2.** a mythical monster. [C16: via Latin *orca,* perhaps from Greek *orux* whale]

Or·cad·i·an (ɔːˈkeɪdɪən) *n.* **1.** a native or inhabitant of the Orkneys. ~*adj.* **2.** of or relating to the Orkneys. [from Latin *orcades* the Orkney Islands]

or·ce·in (ˈɔːsɪɪn) *n.* a brown crystalline material formed by the action of ammonia on orcinol and present in orchil: used as a dye, biological stain, and antiseptic. Formula: $C_{28}H_{24}O_7N_2$. [C19: see ORCINOL]

orch. *abbrev. for:* **1.** orchestra(l). **2.** orchestrated by.

or·chard (ˈɔːtʃəd) *n.* **1.** an area of land devoted to the cultivation of fruit trees. **2.** a collection of fruit trees especially cultivated. [Old English *orceard, ortigeard,* from *ort-,* from Latin *hortus* garden + *geard* YARD[2]]

or·chard bush *n. West African.* open savanna country with occasional trees and scrub, as found north of the W African forest belt.

or·chard·man (ˈɔːtʃədmən) *n., pl.* **·men.** a person who grows and sells orchard fruits.

or·ches·tra (ˈɔːkɪstrə) *n.* **1.** a large group of musicians, esp. one whose members play a variety of different instruments. See also **symphony orchestra, string orchestra, chamber orchestra. 2.** a group of musicians, each playing the same type of instrument: *a balalaika orchestra.* **3.** Also called: **orchestra pit.** the space reserved for musicians in a theatre, immediately in front of or under the stage. **4.** *Chiefly U.S.* the stalls in a theatre. **5.** (in the ancient Greek theatre) the semicircular space in front of the stage. [C17: via Latin from Greek: the space in the theatre reserved for the chorus, from *orkheisthai* to dance] —**or·ches·tral** (ɔːˈkɛstrəl) *adj.*

or·ches·trate (ˈɔːkɪˌstreɪt) *vb.* (*tr.*) **1.** to score or arrange a piece of music for orchestra. **2.** *U.S.* to arrange, organize, or build up for special effect. —ˌ**or·ches·ˈtra·tion** *n.* —ˈ**or·ches·ˌtra·tor** *n.*

or·ches·tri·na (ˌɔːkɪsˈtriːnə) or **or·ches·tri·on** (ɔːˈkɛstrɪən) *n.* any of various types of mechanical musical instrument designed to imitate the sound of an orchestra.

or·chid (ˈɔːkɪd) *n.* any terrestrial or epiphytic plant of the family *Orchidaceae,* having flowers of unusual shapes and beautiful colours, specialized for pollination by certain insects. See **purple-fringed orchid, spider orchid, bee orchid.** [C19: from New Latin *Orchideae;* see ORCHIS]

or·chi·da·ceous (ˌɔːkɪˈdeɪʃəs) *adj.* of, relating to, or belonging to the *Orchidaceae,* a family of flowering plants including the orchids.

or·chil (ˈɔːkɪl, -tʃɪl) *or* **ar·chil** *n.* **1.** any of various lichens, esp. any of the genera *Roccella, Dendrographa,* and *Lecanora.* **2.** Also called: **cudbear.** a purplish dye obtained by treating these lichens with aqueous ammonia: contains orcinol, orcein, and litmus. [C15: from Old French *orcheil,* of uncertain origin]

or·chis (ˈɔːkɪs) *n.* **1.** any terrestrial orchid of the N temperate genus *Orchis,* having fleshy tubers and spikes of typically pink flowers. **2.** any of various temperate or tropical orchids of the genus *Habenaria,* such as the fringed orchis. [C16: via Latin from Greek *orkhis* testicle; so called from the shape of its roots]

or·chi·tis (ɔːˈkaɪtɪs) *n.* inflammation of one or both testicles. [C18: from New Latin, from Greek *orkhis* testicle + -ITIS] —**or·chit·ic** (ɔːˈkɪtɪk) *adj.*

or·ci·nol (ˈɔːsɪˌnɒl) *or* **or·cin** (ˈɔːsɪn) *n.* a colourless crystalline water-soluble solid that occurs in many lichens and from which the dyes found in litmus are derived. Formula: $CH_3C_6H_3(OH)_2$. [C20: from New Latin *orcina,* from Italian *orcello* ORCHIL]

OR cir·cuit *or* **gate** (ɔː) *n. Computer technol.* a logic circuit having two or more input wires and one output wire that gives an output signal if one or more input signals are at a high voltage: used extensively as a basic circuit in computers. Compare **AND circuit, NAND circuit.** [C20: so named from its similarity to the function of *or* in logical constructions]

Or·cus (ˈɔːkəs) *n.* another name for **Dis** (sense 1).

Or·czy (ˈɔːtsɪ) *n.* Baroness **Em·mus·ka** (ˈɛmʊʃkə). 1865–1947, British novelist, born in Hungary; author of *The Scarlet Pimpernel* (1905).

ord. *abbrev. for:* **1.** order. **2.** ordinal. **3.** ordinance. **4.** ordnance. **5.** ordinary.

or·dain (ɔːˈdeɪn) *vb.* (*tr.*) **1.** to consecrate (someone) as a priest; confer holy orders upon. **2.** (*may take a clause as object*) to decree, appoint, or predestine irrevocably. **3.** (*may take a clause as object*) to order, establish, or enact with authority. **4.** *Obsolete.* to select for an office. [C13: from Anglo-Norman *ordeiner,* from Late Latin *ordināre* from Latin *ordo* ORDER] —**or·ˈdain·er** *n.* —ˌ**or·ˈdain·ment** *n.*

or·deal (ɔːˈdiːl) *n.* **1.** a severe or trying experience. **2.** *History.* a method of trial in which the guilt or innocence of an accused person was determined by subjecting him to physical danger, esp. by fire or water. The outcome was regarded as an indication of divine judgment. [Old English *ordāl, ordēl;* related to Old Frisian *ordēl,* Old High German *urteili* (German *Urteil*) verdict. See DEAL[1], DOLE[1]]

or·der (ˈɔːdə) *n.* **1.** a state in which all components or elements are arranged logically, comprehensibly, or naturally. **2.** an arrangement or disposition of things in succession; sequence: *alphabetical order.* **3.** an established or customary method or state, esp. of society. **4.** a peaceful or harmonious condition of society: *order reigned in the streets.* **5.** (*often pl.*) a class, rank, or hierarchy: *the lower orders.* **6.** *Biology.* any of the taxonomic groups into which a class is divided and which contains one or more families. *Carnivora, Primates,* and *Rodentia* are three orders of the class *Mammalia.* **7.** an instruction that must be obeyed; command. **8.** a decision or direction of a court or judge entered on the court record but not included in the final judgment. **9. a.** a commission or instruction to produce or supply something in return for payment. **b.** the commodity produced or supplied. **c.** (*as modifier*): *order form.* **10.** a procedure followed by an assembly, meeting, etc. **11.** (*cap. when part of a name*) a body of people united in a particular aim or purpose. **12.** Also called: **religious order.** (*usually cap.*) a group of persons who bind themselves by vows in order to devote themselves to the pursuit of religious aims. **13.** (*often pl.*) another name for **holy orders, major orders,** or **minor orders. 14.** *History.* a society of knights constituted as a fraternity, such as the Knights Templars. **15. a.** a group of people holding a specific honour for service or merit, conferred on them by a sovereign or state. **b.** the insignia of such a group. **16. a.** any of the five major classical styles of architecture classified by the style of columns and entablatures used. See also **Doric, Ionic, Corinthian, Tuscan, Composite. b.** any style of architecture. **17.** *Ecclesiast.* **a.** the sacrament by which bishops, priests, etc., have their offices conferred upon them. **b.** any of the degrees into which the ministry is divided. **c.** the office of an ordained Christian minister. **18.** *Ecclesiast.* a form of Christian Church service prescribed to be used on specific occasions. **19.** *Maths.* **a.** the number of times a function must be differentiated to obtain a given derivative. **b.** the order of the highest derivative in a differential equation. **c.** the number of rows or columns in a determinant or square matrix. **d.** the number of members of a finite group. **20.** *Military.* (often preceded by *the*) the dress, equipment, or formation directed for a particular purpose or undertaking: *drill order; battle order.* **21. a tall order.** something difficult, demanding, or exacting. **22. in order. a.** in sequence. **b.** properly arranged. **c.** appropriate or fitting. **23. in order to.** (*prep., foll. by an infinitive*) so that it is possible to: *to eat in order to live.* **24. in order that.** (*conj.*) with the purpose that; so that. **25. keep order.** to maintain or enforce order. **26. of** *or* **in the order of.** having an approximately specified size or quantity. **27. on order.** having been ordered or commissioned but not having been delivered. **28. out of order. a.** not in sequence. **b.** not working. **c.** not following the rules or customary procedure. **29.**

to order. **a.** according to a buyer's specifications. **b.** on request or demand. ~*vb.* **30.** (*tr.*) to give a command to (a person or animal to do or be something). **31.** to request (something) to be supplied or made, esp. in return for payment: *he ordered a hamburger.* **32.** (*tr.*) to instruct or command to move, go, etc. (to a specified place): *they ordered her into the house.* **33.** (*tr.; may take a clause as object*) to authorize; prescribe: *the doctor ordered a strict diet.* **34.** (*tr.*) to arrange, regulate, or dispose (articles, etc.) in their proper places. **35.** (of fate or the gods) to will; ordain. **36.** (*tr.*) *Rare.* to ordain. ~*interj.* **37.** an exclamation of protest against an infringement of established procedure. **38.** an exclamation demanding that orderly behaviour be restored. [C13: from Old French *ordre,* from Latin *ordō*] —'**or+der+er** *n.* —'**or+der+less** *adj.*

or+der a·bout *or* **a·round** *vb.* (*tr.*) to bully or domineer.

or+der arms *interj., n. Military.* the order in drill to hold the rifle close to the right side with the butt resting on the ground.

or+der in coun+cil *n.* (in Britain and various other Commonwealth countries) a decree of the Cabinet, usually made under the authority of a statute: in theory a decree of the sovereign and Privy Council.

or+der+ly ('ɔːdəlɪ) *adj.* **1.** in order, properly arranged, or tidy. **2.** obeying or appreciating method, system, and arrangement. **3.** harmonious or peaceful. **4.** *Military.* of or relating to orders: *an orderly book.* ~*adv.* **5.** according to custom or rule. ~*n., pl.* **+lies. 6.** *Med.* a male hospital attendant. **7.** *Military.* a junior rank detailed to carry orders for a more senior officer. —'**or+der+li+ness** *n.*

or+der+ly of+fic+er *n.* another name for **officer of the day.**

or+der+ly room *n. Military.* a room in the barracks of a battalion or company used for general administrative purposes.

Or+der of Mer+it *n. Brit.* an order conferred on civilians and servicemen for eminence in any field.

or+der of the day *n.* **1.** the general directive of a commander in chief or the specific instructions of a commanding officer. **2.** *Informal.* the prescribed or only thing offered or available: *prunes were the order of the day.* **3.** (in Parliament and similar legislatures) any item of public business ordered to be considered on a specific day. **4.** an agenda or programme.

Or+der of the Gar+ter *n.* the highest order of British knighthood. It consists of the sovereign, 31 knight companions, and extra members created by statute. Also called: the **Garter.**

or+der pa+per *n.* a list indicating the order in which business is to be conducted, esp. in Parliament.

or+di+nal ('ɔːdɪnᵊl) *adj.* **1.** denoting a certain position in a sequence of numbers. **2.** of, relating to, or characteristic of an order in biological classification. ~*n.* **3.** short for **ordinal number. 4.** a book containing the forms of services for the ordination of ministers. **5.** *R.C. Church.* a service book.

or+di+nal num+ber *n.* **1.** a number denoting order, quality, or degree in a group, such as *first, second, third.* Sometimes shortened to **ordinal. 2.** a symbol denoting the cardinal number of a mathematical set, maintaining the order of the elements in that set.

or+di+nance ('ɔːdɪnəns) *n.* an authoritative regulation, decree, law or practice. [C14: from Old French *ordenance,* from Latin *ordināre* to set in order]

or+di+nand ('ɔːdɪ,nænd) *n. Christianity.* a candidate for ordination.

or+di+nar+i+ly ('ɔːdᵊnrɪlɪ, 'ɔːdᵊ,nɛrɪlɪ) *adv.* in ordinary, normal, or usual practice; usually; normally.

or+di+nar·y ('ɔːdᵊnrɪ) *adj.* **1.** of common or established type or occurrence. **2.** familiar, everyday, or unexceptional. **3.** uninteresting or commonplace. **4.** having regular or *ex officio* jurisdiction: *an ordinary judge.* **5.** *Maths.* (of a differential equation) containing two variables only and derivatives of one of the variables with respect to the other. ~*n., pl.* **+nar·ies. 6.** a common or average situation, amount, or degree (esp. in the phrase **out of the ordinary**). **7.** a normal or commonplace person or thing. **8.** *Civil law.* a judge who exercises jurisdiction in his own right. **9.** (*usually cap.*) an ecclesiastic, esp. a bishop, holding an office to which certain jurisdictional powers are attached. **10.** *R.C. Church.* **a.** the parts of the Mass that do not vary from day to day. Compare **proper** (sense 12). **b.** a prescribed form of divine service, esp. the Mass. **11.** the U.S. name for **penny-farthing. 12.** *Heraldry.* any of several conventional figures, such as the bend, the fesse, and the cross, commonly charged upon shields. **13.** *History.* a clergyman who visited condemned prisoners before their death. **14.** *Brit. obsolete.* **a.** a meal provided regularly at a fixed price. **b.** the inn, etc., providing such meals. **15. in ordinary.** *Brit.* (used esp. in titles) in regular service or attendance: *physician in ordinary to the sovereign.* [C16 (adj.) and C13 (some n. senses): ultimately from Latin *ordinārius* orderly, from *ordō* order]

Or+di+nar·y lev+el *n. Brit.* See **O level.**

or+di+nar·y ray *n.* the plane-polarized ray of light that obeys the laws of refraction in a doubly-refracting crystal. See **double refraction.** Compare **extraordinary ray.**

or+di+nar·y sea+man *n.* a seaman of the lowest rank, being insufficiently experienced to be an able-bodied seaman.

or+di+nar·y shares *pl. n. Brit.* shares representing part of the capital issued by a company and entitling their holders to a share of the profit and to a claim on net assets. U.S. equivalent: **common stock.** Compare **preference shares.**

or+di+nate ('ɔːdɪnɪt) *n.* **1.** the vertical or *y*-coordinate of a point in a two-dimensional system of Cartesian coordinates. Compare **abscissa.** ~*adj.* **2.** *Rare.* regular or ordered. [C16: from New Latin (*linea*) *ordināte* (*applicāta*) (line applied) in an orderly manner, from *ordināre* to arrange in order]

or+di+na+tion (,ɔːdɪ'neɪʃən) *n.* **1. a.** the act of conferring holy orders. **b.** the reception of holy orders. **2.** the condition of being ordained or regulated. **3.** an arrangement or order.

ordn. *abbrev. for* ordnance.

ord+nance ('ɔːdnəns) *n.* **1.** cannon or artillery. **2.** military supplies; munitions. **3. the.** a department of an army or government dealing with military supplies. [C14: variant of ORDINANCE]

ord+nance da+tum *n.* mean sea level calculated from observation taken at Newlyn, Cornwall, and used as the official basis for height calculation on British maps. Abbrev.: **O.D.**

Ord+nance Sur+vey *n.* the official map-making body of the British or Irish government.

or+don+nance ('ɔːdənəns; *French* ɔrdɔ'nɑ̃ːs) *n.* **1.** the proper disposition of the elements of a building or an artistic or literary composition. **2.** an ordinance, law, or decree, esp. in French law. [C17: from Old French *ordenance* arrangement, influenced by *ordonner* to order]

Or+do+vi+ci+an (,ɔːdəʊ'vɪʃɪən) *adj.* **1.** of, denoting, or formed in the second period of the Palaeozoic era, between the Cambrian and Silurian periods, which lasted for 60 000 000 years during which marine invertebrates flourished. ~*n.* **2. the.** the Ordovician period or rock system. [C19: from Latin *Ordovices* ancient Celtic tribe in N Wales]

or+dure ('ɔːdjʊə) *n.* **1.** excrement; dung. **2.** something regarded as being morally offensive. [C14: via Old French, from *ord* dirty, from Latin *horridus* shaggy]

Or+dzho+ni+ki+dze *or* **Or+jo+ni+ki+dze** (*Russian* ardʒəni'kidzɪ) *n.* a city in the S Soviet Union, capital of the North Ossetian ASSR on the N slopes of the Caucasus. Pop.: 270 000 (1975 est.). Former name (until 1944): **Vladikavkaz.**

ore (ɔː) *n.* any naturally occurring mineral or aggregate of minerals from which economically important constituents, esp. metals, can be extracted. [Old English *ār, ōra;* related to Gothic *aiz,* Latin *aes,* Dutch *oer*]

ö·re ('ørə) *n., pl.* **ö·re.** a Scandinavian monetary unit worth one hundredth of a Swedish krona and one hundredth of a Danish and Norwegian krone.

o·re·ad ('ɔːrɪ,æd) *n. Greek myth.* a mountain nymph. [C16: via Latin from Greek *Oreias,* from *oros* mountain]

Ö·re·bro (*Swedish* ,œːrə'bruː) *n.* a town in S Sweden: one of Sweden's oldest towns; scene of the election of Jean Bernadotte as heir to the throne in 1810. Pop.: 117 560 (1974 est.).

o·rec+tic (ɒ'rɛktɪk) *adj.* of or relating to the desires. [C18: from Greek *orektikos* causing desire, from *oregein* to desire]

ore dress+ing *n.* the first stage in the extraction of a metal from an ore in which as much gangue as possible is removed and the ore is prepared for smelting, refining, etc. Also called: **mineral dressing, mineral processing.**

Oreg. *abbrev. for* Oregon.

o·re·ga+no (,ɒrɪ'gɑːnəʊ) *n.* **1.** a Mediterranean variety of wild marjoram (*Origanum vulgare*), with pungent leaves. **2.** the dried powdered leaves of this plant, used to season food. [American Spanish, from Spanish, from Latin *orīganum,* from Greek *origanon* an aromatic herb, perhaps marjoram]

Or+e·gon ('ɒrɪgən) *n.* a state of the northwestern U.S., on the Pacific: consists of the Coast and Cascade Ranges in the west and a plateau in the east; important timber production. Capital: Salem. Pop.: 2 143 010 (1970). Area: 251 180 sq. km (96 981 sq. miles). Abbrevs.: **Oreg.** or (with zip code) **OR**

Or+e·gon fir *or* **pine** *n.* other names for **Douglas fir.**

Or+e·gon grape *n.* **1.** an evergreen berberidaceous shrub, *Mahonia aquifolium,* of NW North America, having yellow fragrant flowers and small blue edible berries. **2.** the berry of this shrub.

Or+e·gon trail *n.* an early pioneering route across the central U.S., from Independence, W Missouri, to the Columbia River country of N Oregon: used chiefly between 1804 and 1860. Length: about 3220 km (2000 miles).

O·rel *or* **O·ryol** (*Russian* a'rjɔl) *n.* a city in the central Soviet Union. Pop.: 273 000 (1975 est.).

O·ren+burg ('ɒrən,bɜːg; *Russian* arɪn'burk) *n.* a city in the E Soviet Union, on the Ural River. Pop.: 419 000 (1975 est.). Former name (1938–57): **Chkalov.**

O·ren+se (*Spanish* o'rense) *n.* a city in NW Spain, in Galicia on the Miño River: warm springs. Pop.: 73 379 (1970).

O·res·tes (ɒ'rɛstiːz) *n. Greek myth.* the son of Agamemnon and Clytemnestra, who killed his mother and her lover Aegisthus in revenge for their murder of his father.

Ø·re·sund (,œːrə'sund) *n.* the Swedish and Danish name for The **Sound.**

orfe (ɔːf) *n.* a small slender European cyprinoid fish, *Idus idus,* occurring in two colour varieties, namely the **silver orfe** and the **golden orfe,** popular aquarium fishes. Compare **goldfish.** [C17: from German; related to Latin *orphus,* Greek *orphos* the sea perch]

Orff (ɔːf) *n.* **Carl** (karl). 1895–1982, German composer. His works include the secular oratorio *Carmina Burana* (1937) and the opera *Antigone* (1949).

or+fray ('ɔːfrɪ) *n.* a less common spelling of **orphrey.**

org. *abbrev. for:* **1.** organic. **2.** organization. **3.** organized.

or+gan ('ɔːgən) *n.* **1. a.** Also called: **pipe organ.** a large complex musical keyboard instrument in which sound is produced by means of a number of pipes arranged in sets or stops, supplied with air from a bellows. The largest instruments possess three or more manuals and one pedal keyboard and have the greatest range of any instrument. **b.** (*as modifier*): *organ pipe; organ stop; organ loft.* **2.** any instrument, such as a harmonium, in which sound is produced in this way. See also **reed organ, harmonica. 3.** short for **electric organ** (sense 1a.), **electronic**

organ. **4.** a fully differentiated structural and functional unit, such as a kidney or a root, in an animal or plant. **5.** an agency or medium of communication, esp. a periodical issued by a specialist group or party. **6.** an instrument with which something is done or accomplished. **7.** a euphemistic word for **penis.** [C13: from Old French *organe*, from Latin *organum* implement, from Greek *organon* tool; compare Greek *ergein* to work]

or+gan+die *or esp. U.S.* **or+gan+dy** ('ɔːgəndɪ) *n., pl.* **+dies.** a fine and slightly stiff cotton fabric used for dresses, etc. [C19: from French *organdi*, of unknown origin]

or+ga+nelle (ˌɔːgə'nɛl) *n.* a structural and functional unit, such as a mitochondrion, in a cell or unicellular organism. [C20: from New Latin *organella*, from Latin *organum*: see ORGAN]

or·gan-grind·er *n.* a street musician playing a hand organ for money.

or+gan+ic (ɔː'gænɪk) *adj.* **1.** of, relating to, derived from, or characteristic of living plants and animals. **2.** of or relating to animal or plant constituents or products having a carbon basis. **3.** of or relating to one or more organs of an animal or plant. **4.** of, relating to, or belonging to the class of chemical compounds that are formed from carbon: *an organic compound.* Compare **inorganic** (sense 2). **5.** constitutional in the structure of something; fundamental; integral. **6.** of or characterized by the coordination of integral parts; organized. **7.** of or relating to the essential constitutional laws regulating the government of a state: *organic law.* **8.** of, relating to, or grown with the use of fertilizers or pesticides deriving from animal or vegetable matter. ~*n.* **9.** any substance, such as a fertilizer or pesticide, that is derived from animal or vegetable matter. —**or+'gan·i+cal+ly** *adv.*

or+gan+ic chem+is+try *n.* the branch of chemistry concerned with the compounds of carbon: originally confined to compounds produced by living organisms but now extended to include man-made substances based on carbon, such as plastics. Compare **inorganic chemistry.**

or+gan+ic dis+ease *n.* any disease in which there is a physical change in the structure of an organ or part. Compare **functional disease.**

or+gan·i+cism (ɔː'gænɪˌsɪzəm) *n.* **1.** the theory that the functioning of living organisms is determined by the working together of all organs as an integrated system. **2.** the theory that all symptoms are caused by organic disease. **3.** the theory that each organ of the body has its own peculiar constitution. —**or+'gan·i+cist** *n., adj.* —**or+ˌgan·i+'cis+tic** *adj.*

or+gan+ism ('ɔːgəˌnɪzəm) *n.* **1.** any living animal or plant, including any bacterium or virus. **2.** anything resembling a living creature in structure, behaviour, etc. —**ˌor+gan+'is+mal** *or* **ˌor+gan+'is+mic** *adj.* —**ˌor+gan+'is+mal+ly** *adv.*

or+gan+ist ('ɔːgənɪst) *n.* a person who plays the organ.

or+gan·i+za+tion *or* **or+gan·i+sa+tion** (ˌɔːgənaɪ'zeɪʃən) *n.* **1.** the act of organizing or the state of being organized. **2.** an organized structure or whole. **3.** a business or administrative concern united and constructed for a particular end. **4.** a body of administrative officials, as of a political party, a government department, etc. **5.** order, tidiness, or system; method. —**ˌor+gan·i+'za+tion+al** *or* **ˌor+gan·i+'sa+tion+al** *adj.* —**ˌor+gan·i+'za+tion+al+ly** *or* **ˌor+gan·i+'sa+tion+al+ly** *adv.*

or+gan·i+za+tion man *n.* **1.** a person who specializes in or is good at organization. **2.** a person who is overconcerned with organization.

Or+gan·i+za+tion of Af+ri+can U·ni·ty *n.* See **OAU.**

Or+gan·i+za+tion of A·mer·i+can States *n.* an association consisting of the U.S. and other republics in the W hemisphere, founded at Bogotá in 1948 to promote military, economic, social, and cultural cooperation among the member states. Abbrev.: **OAS.** See also **Pan American Union.**

or+gan+ize *or* **or+gan+ise** ('ɔːgəˌnaɪz) *vb.* **1.** to form (parts or elements of something) into a structured whole; coordinate. **2.** (*tr.*) to arrange methodically or in order. **3.** (*tr.*) to provide with an organic structure. **4.** (*tr.*) to enlist (the workers) of (a factory or concern) in a trade union. **5.** (*intr.*) to join or form an organization or trade union. **6.** (*tr.*) *Informal.* to put (oneself) in an alert and responsible frame of mind.

or+gan+iz+er *or* **or+gan+is+er** ('ɔːgəˌnaɪzə) *n.* **1.** a person who organizes or is capable of organizing. **2.** *Embryol.* any part of an embryo or any substance produced by it that induces specialization of undifferentiated cells.

or·gan·o- *combining form.* **1.** (in biology or medicine) indicating an organ or organs: *organogenesis.* **2.** (in chemistry) indicating a compound containing an organic group: *organometallic compounds.*

or+gan·o+gen+e·sis (ˌɔːgənəʊ'dʒɛnɪsɪs) *n.* **1.** the formation and development of organs in an animal or plant. **2.** the study of this process. —**or+gan·o+ge·net+ic** (ˌɔːgənəʊdʒɪ'nɛtɪk) *adj.* —**ˌor+gan·o+ge·'net·i+cal+ly** *adv.*

or+gan+og+ra+phy (ˌɔːgə'nɒgrəfɪ) *n.* the description of the organs and major structures of animals and plants. —**or+gan·o+graph+ic** (ˌɔːgənəʊ'græfɪk) *or* **ˌor+gan·o+'graph·i+cal** *adj.* —**ˌor+gan+'og+ra+phist** *n.*

or+gan·o+lep+tic (ˌɔːgənəʊ'lɛptɪk) *adj. Physiol.* **1.** able to stimulate an organ, esp. a special sense organ. **2.** able to perceive a sensory stimulus.

or+gan+ol·o·gy (ˌɔːgə'nɒlədʒɪ) *n.* the study of the structure and function of the organs of animals and plants. —**or+gan·o+log·i+cal** (ˌɔːgənəʊ'lɒdʒɪkᵊl) *adj.* —**ˌor+gan+'ol·o·gist** *n.*

or+gan·o+me·tal+lic (ɔːˌgænəʊmɪ'tælɪk) *adj.* of, concerned with, or being an organic compound with one or more metal atoms in its molecules: *an organometallic compound.*

or+ga+non ('ɔːgəˌnɒn) *or* **or+ga+num** *n., pl.* **+na** (-nə), **+nons** *or* **+na, +nums. 1.** *Epistemology.* an instrument for acquiring knowledge, esp. a system of logical or scientific rules of investigation. **2.** a means of communicating knowledge or thought. [C16: from Greek: implement; see ORGAN]

or+gan·o+ther·a+py (ˌɔːgənəʊ'θɛrəpɪ) *n.* the treatment of disease with extracts of animal endocrine glands. —**or+gan·o+ther·a+peu+tic** (ˌɔːgənəʊˌθɛrə'pjuːtɪk) *adj.*

or+gan screen *n.* a wooden or stone screen that supports the organ in a cathedral or church and divides the choir from the nave.

or+ga+num ('ɔːgənəm) *n., pl.* **+na** (-nə) *or* **+nums. 1.** a form of polyphonic music originating in the ninth century, consisting of a plainsong melody with parts added at the fourth and fifth. **2.** a variant spelling of **organon.** [C17: via Latin from Greek; see ORGAN]

or+gan+za (ɔː'gænzə) *n.* a thin stiff fabric of silk, cotton, nylon, rayon, etc. [C20: perhaps related to ORGANZINE]

or+gan+zine ('ɔːgənˌziːn, ɔː'gænziːn) *n.* **1.** a strong thread made of twisted strands of raw silk. **2.** fabric made of such threads. [C17: from French *organsin*, from Italian *organzino*, probably from *Urgench*, a town in Soviet central Asia where the fabric was originally produced]

or+gasm ('ɔːgæzəm) *n.* **1.** the most intense point during sexual excitement, characterized by extremely pleasurable sensations and in the male accompanied by ejaculation of semen. **2.** *Rare.* intense or violent excitement. [C17: from New Latin *orgasmus*, from Greek *orgasmos*, from *organ* to mature, swell] —**or+'gas+mic** *or* **or+'gas+tic** *adj.*

or+geat ('ɔːʒɑː; *French* ɔr'ʒa) *n.* a drink made from barley or almonds, and orangeflower water. [C18: via French, from *orge* barley, from Latin *hordeum*]

or+gu+lous ('ɔːgjʊləs) *adj. Archaic.* proud. [C13: from Old French, from *orgueil* pride, from Frankish *urgōli* (unattested)]

or·gy ('ɔːdʒɪ) *n., pl.* **·gies. 1.** a wild gathering marked by promiscuous sexual activity, excessive drinking, etc. **2.** an act of immoderate or frenzied indulgence. **3.** (*often pl.*) secret religious rites of Dionysus, Bacchus, etc., marked by drinking, dancing, and songs. [C16: from French *orgies*, from Latin *orgia*, from Greek: nocturnal festival] —**ˌor+gi+'as+tic** *adj.*

o·ri+bi ('ɒrɪbɪ) *n., pl.* **-bi** *or* **+bis.** a small African antelope, *Ourebia ourebi*, of grasslands and bush south of the Sahara, with fawn-coloured coat and, in the male, ridged spikelike horns. [C18: from Afrikaans, probably from Hottentot *arab*]

o·ri+el ('ɔːrɪəl) *n.* a bay window, esp. one that is supported by one or more brackets or corbels. Also called: **oriel window.** [C14: from Old French *oriol* gallery, perhaps from Medieval Latin *auleolum* niche]

o·ri+ent *n.* ('ɔːrɪənt). **1.** *Poetic.* another word for **east.** Compare **occident. 2.** *Archaic.* the eastern sky or the dawn. **3. a.** the iridescent lustre of a pearl. **b.** (*as modifier*): *orient pearls.* **4.** a pearl of high quality. ~*adj.* ('ɔːrɪənt). **5.** *Now chiefly poetic.* oriental. **6.** *Archaic.* (of the sun, stars, etc.) rising. ~*vb.* ('ɔːrɪˌɛnt). **7.** a variant of **orientate.** [C18: via French from Latin *oriēns* rising (sun), from *orīrī* to rise]

O·ri+ent ('ɔːrɪənt) *n.* (usually preceded by *the*) **1.** the countries east of the Mediterranean. **2.** the eastern hemisphere.

o·ri+en+tal (ˌɔːrɪ'ɛntᵊl) *adj.* another word for **eastern.** Compare **occidental.**

O·ri+en+tal (ˌɔːrɪ'ɛntᵊl) *adj.* **1.** (*sometimes not cap.*) of or relating to the Orient. **2.** of or denoting a zoogeographical region consisting of southeastern Asia from India to Borneo, Java, and the Philippines. ~*n.* **3.** (*sometimes not cap.*) an inhabitant, esp. a native, of the Orient.

O·ri+en+tal+ism (ˌɔːrɪ'ɛntəˌlɪzəm) *n.* **1.** knowledge of or devotion to the Orient. **2.** an Oriental quality, style, or trait. —**ˌO·ri+'en+tal+ist** *n.* —**ˌO·ri+ˌen+tal+'ist+ic** *adj.*

O·ri+en+tal+ize *or* **O·ri+en+tal+ise** (ˌɔːrɪ'ɛntəˌlaɪz) *vb.* to make, become, or treat as Oriental. —**ˌO·ri+ˌen+tal·i+'za+tion** *or* **ˌO·ri+ˌen+tal·i+'sa+tion** *n.*

o·ri+en+tate ('ɔːrɪɛnˌteɪt) *vb.* **1.** to adjust or align (oneself or something else) according to surroundings or circumstances. **2.** (*tr.*) to position, align, or set (a map, surveying instrument, etc.) with reference to the points of the compass or other specific directions. **3.** (*tr.*) to set or build (a church) in an easterly direction.

o·ri+en+ta+tion (ˌɔːrɪɛn'teɪʃən) *n.* **1.** the act or process of orientating or the state of being orientated. **2.** position or positioning with relation to the points of the compass or other specific directions. **3.** the adjustment or alignment of oneself or one's ideas to surroundings or circumstances. **4.** Also called: **orientation course.** *Chiefly U.S.* **a.** a course, programme, lecture, etc., introducing a new situation or environment. **b.** (*as modifier*): *an orientation talk.* **5.** *Psychol.* the knowledge of one's own temporal, social, and practical circumstances in life. **6.** *Biology.* the change in position of the whole or part of an organism in response to a stimulus, such as light. **7.** *Chem.* the relative dispositions of atoms, ions, or groups in molecules or crystals. **8.** the siting of a church on an east-west axis, usually with the altar at the E end. —**ˌo·ri+en+'ta+tion+al** *adj.*

O·ri+en+te (ˌɔːrɪ'ɛnteɪ; *Spanish* o'rjente) *n.* a province of E Cuba: the largest province in the country; scene of many revolts, notably of Fidel Castro's overthrow of the Batista regime in 1959. Capital: Santiago de Cuba. Pop.: 2 998 972 (1970). Area: 36 591 sq. km (14 128 sq. miles).

o·ri+en+teer+ing (ˌɔːrɪɛn'tɪərɪŋ) *n.* a sport in which contestants race on foot over a course consisting of checkpoints found with the aid of a map and a compass.

or·i+fice ('ɒrɪfɪs) *n. Chiefly technical.* an opening or mouth into a cavity; vent; aperture. [C16: via French from Late Latin *ōrificium*, from Latin *ōs* mouth + *facere* to make]

or·i·flamme (ˈɒrɪˌflæm) *n.* a scarlet flag, originally of the abbey of St. Denis in N France, adopted as the national banner of France in the Middle Ages. [C15: via Old French, from Latin *aurum* gold + *flamma* flame]

orig. *abbrev. for:* **1.** origin. **2.** original(ly).

o·ri·ga·mi (ˌɒrɪˈgɑːmɪ) *n.* the art or process, originally Japanese, of paper folding. [from Japanese, from *ori* a folding + *kami* paper]

o·ri·gan (ˈɒrɪgən) *n.* another name for **marjoram** (sense 2). [C16: from Latin *orīganum,* from Greek *origanon* an aromatic herb, perhaps marjoram; compare OREGANO]

Or·i·gen (ˈɒrɪˌdʒɛn) *n.* ?185–?254 A.D., Christian theologian, born in Alexandria. His writings include *Hexapla,* a synopsis of the Old Testament, *Contra Celsum,* a defence of Christianity, and *De principiis,* a statement of Christian theology.

or·i·gin (ˈɒrɪdʒɪn) *n.* **1.** a primary source; derivation. **2.** the beginning of something; first stage or part. **3.** (*often pl.*) ancestry or parentage; birth extraction. **4.** *Anatomy.* **a.** the end of a muscle, opposite its point of insertion. **b.** the beginning of a nerve or blood vessel or the site where it first starts to branch out. **5.** *Maths.* **a.** the point of intersection of coordinate axes or planes. **b.** the point whose coordinates are all zero. See also **pole**[2] (sense 7). [C16: from French *origine,* from Latin *origō* beginning, birth, from *orīrī* to rise, spring from]

o·rig·i·nal (əˈrɪdʒɪnᵊl) *adj.* **1.** of or relating to an origin or beginning. **2.** fresh and unusual; novel. **3.** able to think of or carry out new ideas or concepts. **4.** being that from which a copy, translation, etc., is made. ~*n.* **5.** the first and genuine form of something, from which others are derived. **6.** a person or thing used as a model in art or literature. **7.** a person whose way of thinking is unusual or creative. **8.** an unconventional or strange person. **9.** the first form or occurrence of something. **10.** an archaic word for **originator.**

o·rig·i·nal·i·ty (əˌrɪdʒɪˈnælɪtɪ) *n., pl.* **·ties. 1.** the quality or condition of being original. **2.** the ability to create or innovate. **3.** something original.

o·rig·i·nal·ly (əˈrɪdʒɪnəlɪ) *adv.* **1.** in the first place. **2.** in an original way. **3.** with reference to the origin or beginning.

o·rig·i·nal sin *n. Theol.* a state of sin held to be innate in mankind as the descendants of Adam.

o·rig·i·nate (əˈrɪdʒɪˌneɪt) *vb.* **1.** to come or bring into being. **2.** (*intr.*) *U.S.* (of a bus, train, etc.) to begin its journey at a specified point. **—o·ˌrig·i·ˈna·tion** *n.* **—o·ˈrig·iˌna·tor** *n.*

o·ri·na·sal (ˌɔːrɪˈneɪzᵊl) *adj.* **1.** *Phonetics.* pronounced with simultaneous oral and nasal articulation. ~*n.* **2.** *Phonetics.* an orinasal speech sound. [C19: from Latin *ōr-* (from *ōs* mouth) + NASAL] **—ˌo·ri·ˈna·sal·ly** *adv.*

O·ri·no·co (ˌɒrɪˈnəʊkəʊ) *n.* a river in N South America, rising in S Venezuela and flowing west, then north as part of the border between Colombia and Venezuela, then east to the Atlantic by a great delta: the third largest river system in South America, draining an area of 945 000 sq. km (365 000 sq. miles); reaches a width of 22 km (14 miles) during the rainy season. Length: about 2575 km (1600 miles).

o·ri·ole (ˈɔːrɪˌəʊl) *n.* **1.** any songbird of the mainly tropical Old World family *Oriolidae,* such as *Oriolus oriolus* (**golden oriole**), having a long pointed bill and a mostly yellow-and-black plumage. **2.** any American songbird of the family *Icteridae,* esp. those of the genus *Icterus,* such as the Baltimore oriole, with a typical male plumage of black with either orange or yellow. [C18: from Medieval Latin *oryolus,* from Latin *aureolus,* diminutive of *aureus,* from *aurum* gold]

O·ri·on[1] (əˈraɪən) *n. Greek myth.* a Boeotian giant famed as a great hunter, who figures in several tales.

O·ri·on[2] (əˈraɪən) *n., Latin genitive* **O·ri·o·nis** (ˌɔːrɪˈəʊnɪs) constellation near Canis Major containing two first magnitude stars (Betelgeuse and Rigel) and a distant low density emission nebule (the **Orion Nebula**).

or·i·son (ˈɒrɪzᵊn) *n. Literary.* another word for **prayer**[1]. [C12: from Old French *oreison,* from Late Latin *ōrātiō,* from Latin: speech, from *ōrāre* to speak]

O·ris·sa (ɒˈrɪsə) *n.* a state of E India, on the Bay of Bengal: part of the province of Bihar and Orissa (1912–36); enlarged by the addition of 25 native states in 1949. Capital: Bhubaneswar. Pop.: 21 944 615 (1971). Area: 155 825 sq. km (60 164 sq. miles).

O·ri·ya (ɒˈriːə) *n.* **1.** (*pl.* **·ya**) a member of a people of India living chiefly in Orissa and neighbouring states. **2.** the state language of Orissa, belonging to the Indic branch of the Indo-European family.

O·ri·za·ba (ˌɔːrɪˈzɑːbə; *Spanish* ˌoriˈθaβa) *n.* **1.** a city and resort in SE Mexico, in Veracruz state. Pop.: 108 283 (1974 est.). **2. Pico de.** the Spanish name for **Citlaltépetl.**

Or·jo·ni·ki·dze (*Russian* ardʒəniˈkidzɪ) *n.* a variant spelling of **Ordzhonikidze.**

Ork·neys (ˈɔːknɪz) *or* **Ork·ney Is·lands** *pl. n.* a group of over 70 islands off the NE coast of Scotland, separated from the mainland by the Pentland Firth: constitutes an island authority of Scotland; low-lying and treeless; prehistoric remains. Administrative centre: Kirkwall. Pop.: 17 748 (1976 est.). Area: 974 sq. km (376 sq. miles).

orle (ɔːl) *n. Heraldry.* a border around a shield. [C16: from French, from *ourler* to hem]

Or·lé·a·nais (*French* ɔrleaˈnɛ) *n.* a former province of N central France, centred on Orléans.

Or·le·an·ist (ɔːˈlɪənɪst) *n.* an adherent of the Orléans branch of the French Bourbons.

Or·lé·ans[1] (ɔːˈlɪənz; *French* ɔrleˈã) *n.* a city in N central France, on the River Loire: famous for its deliverance by Joan of Arc from the long English siege in 1429; university (1305); an important rail and road junction. Pop.: 105 956 (1975).

Or·lé·ans[2] (*French* ɔrleˈã) *n.* **Lou·is Phi·lippe Joseph** (lwi filip ʒoˈzɛf), Duc d'Orléans, known as *Philippe Egalité* (after 1792). 1747–93, French nobleman, who supported the French Revolution and voted for the death of the king, his cousin, but was executed after his son fled to Austria.

Or·lon (ˈɔːlɒn) *n. Trademark.* a crease-resistant acrylic fibre or fabric used for clothing, furnishings, etc.

or·lop *or* **or·lop deck** (ˈɔːlɒp) *n. Nautical.* (in a vessel with four or more decks) the lowest deck. [C15: from Dutch *overloopen* to run over, spill. See OVER, LEAP]

Or·ly (ˈɔːliː; *French* ɔrˈli) *n.* a suburb of SE Paris, France, with an international airport. Pop.: 26 244 (1975).

Or·man·dy (ˈɔːməndɪ) *n.* **Eu·gene.** born 1899, U.S. conductor born in Hungary.

Or·mazd *or* **Or·muzd** (ˈɔːməzd) *n. Zoroastrianism.* the creative deity, embodiment of good and opponent of Ahriman. Also called: **Ahura Mazda.** [from Persian, from Avestan *Ahura-Mazda,* from *ahura* spirit + *mazdā* wise]

or·mer (ˈɔːmə) *n.* **1.** Also called: **sea-ear.** an edible marine gastropod mollusc, *Haliotis tuberculata,* that has an ear-shaped shell perforated with holes and occurs near the Channel Islands. **2.** any other abalone. [C17: from French (Guernsey dialect), apparently from Latin *auris* ear + *mare* sea]

or·mo·lu (ˈɔːməˌluː) *n.* **1. a.** a gold-coloured alloy of copper, tin, or zinc used to decorate furniture, mouldings, etc. **b.** (*as modifier*): *an ormolu clock.* **2.** gold prepared to be used for gilding. [C18: from French *or moulu* ground gold]

Or·muz (ˈɔːmʌz) *n.* a variant spelling of **Hormuz.**

or·na·ment *n.* (ˈɔːnəmənt). **1.** anything that enhances the appearance of a person or thing. **2.** decorations collectively: *she was totally without ornament.* **3.** a small decorative object. **4.** something regarded as a source of pride or beauty. **5.** *Music.* any of several decorations, such as the trill, mordent, etc., occurring chiefly as improvised embellishments in baroque music. ~*vb.* (ˈɔːnəˌmɛnt). (*tr.*) **6.** to decorate with or as if with ornaments. **7.** to serve as an ornament to. [C14: from Latin *ornāmentum,* from *ornāre* to adorn] **—ˌor·na·men·ˈta·tion** *n.*

or·na·men·tal (ˌɔːnəˈmɛntᵊl) *adj.* **1.** of value as an ornament; decorative. **2.** (of a plant) used to decorate houses, gardens, etc. ~*n.* **3.** a plant cultivated for show or decoration. **—ˌor·na·ˈmen·tal·ly** *adv.*

or·nate (ɔːˈneɪt) *adj.* **1.** heavily or elaborately decorated. **2.** (of style in writing, etc.) over-embellished; flowery. [C15: from Latin *ornāre* to decorate] **—or·ˈnate·ly** *adv.* **—or·ˈnate·ness** *n.*

Orne (*French* ɔrn) *n.* a department of NW France, in Basse-Normandy. Capital: Alençon. Pop.: 300 375 (1975). Area: 6144 sq. km (2396 sq. miles).

or·ner·y (ˈɔːnərɪ) *adj. Dialect or informal.* **1.** *U.S.* stubborn or vile-tempered. **2.** *U.S.* low; treacherous: *an ornery trick.* **3.** ordinary. [C19: alteration of ORDINARY] **—ˈor·ner·i·ness** *n.*

or·nis (ˈɔːnɪs) *n.* a less common word for **avifauna.** [C19: from Greek: bird]

or·nith·ic (ɔːˈnɪθɪk) *adj.* of or relating to birds or a bird fauna. [C19: from Greek *ornithikos,* from *ornis* bird]

or·ni·thine (ˈɔːnɪˌθiːn) *n.* an amino acid produced from arginine by hydrolysis: involved in the formation of urea in the liver; diaminopentanoic acid. Formula: $NH_2(CH_2)_3CHNH_2COOH$. [C19: from *ornithuric* (*acid*) secreted in the urine of birds, from ORNITHO + -URIC]

or·ni·this·chi·an (ˌɔːnɪˈθɪskɪən) *adj.* **1.** of, relating to, or belonging to the *Ornithischia,* an order of dinosaurs that included the ornithopods, stegosaurs, ankylosaurs, and triceratops. ~*n.* **2.** any dinosaur of the order *Ornithischia.* [C20: from ORNITHO- + Greek *ischion* hip joint]

or·nith·o- *or before a vowel* **or·nith-** *combining form.* bird or birds: *ornithology; ornithomancy; ornithopter; ornithoscopy; ornithosis.* [from Greek *ornis, ornith-* bird]

ornithol. *or* **ornith.** *abbrev. for:* **1.** ornithological. **2.** ornithology.

or·ni·thol·o·gy (ˌɔːnɪˈθɒlədʒɪ) *n.* the study of birds, including their physiology, classification, ecology, and behaviour. **—or·ni·tho·log·i·cal** (ˌɔːnɪθəˈlɒdʒɪkᵊl) *adj.* **—ˌor·ni·tho·ˈlog·i·cal·ly** *adv.* **—ˌor·ni·ˈthol·o·gist** *n.*

or·ni·tho·man·cy (ˈɔːnɪθəʊˌmænsɪ) *n.* divination from the flight and cries of birds.

or·ni·tho·pod (ˈɔːnɪθəˌpɒd) *n.* any herbivorous typically bipedal ornithischian dinosaur of the suborder *Ornithopoda,* including the iguanodon.

or·ni·thop·ter (ˈɔːnɪˌθɒptə) *n.* a heavier-than-air craft sustained in and propelled through the air by flapping wings. Also called: **orthopter.**

or·ni·tho·rhyn·chus (ˌɔːnɪθəʊˈrɪŋkəs) *n.* the technical name for **duck-billed platypus.** [C19: New Latin, from ORNITHO- + Greek *rhunkhos* bill]

or·ni·thos·co·py (ˌɔnɪˈθɒskəpɪ) *n.* divination from the observation of birds.

or·ni·tho·sis (ˌɔːnɪˈθəʊsɪs) *n.* a viral disease of birds that is occasionally transmitted to man. See **psittacosis.**

o·ro-[1] *combining form.* mountain: *orogeny; orography.* [from Greek *oros*]

o·ro-[2] *combining form.* oral; mouth: *oromaxillary.* [from Latin, from *ōs*]

or·o·ban·cha·ceous (ˌɔːrəʊbæŋˈkeɪʃəs) *adj.* of, relating to, or belonging to the *Orobanchaceae,* a family of flowering plants all of which are root parasites, including broomrape and toothwort. [via Latin from Greek *orobankhē* broomrape]

o·rog·e·ny (ɒˈrɒdʒɪnɪ) *or* **o·ro·gen·e·sis** (ˌɒrəʊˈdʒɛnɪsɪs) *n.* the formation of mountain ranges by intense upward displacement of the earth's crust. —**o·ro·gen·ic** (ˌɒrəʊˈdʒɛnɪk) *or* **o·ro·ge·net·ic** (ˌɒrəʊdʒɪˈnɛtɪk) *adj.* —ˌ**o·ro·ˈgen·i·cal·ly** *or* ˌ**o·ro·ge·ˈnet·i·cal·ly** *adv.*

o·rog·ra·phy (ɒˈrɒgrəfɪ) *or* **o·rol·o·gy** (ɒˈrɒlədʒɪ) *n.* the study or mapping of relief, esp. of mountains. —**o·ˈrog·ra·pher** *or* **o·ˈrol·o·gist** *n.* —**or·o·graph·ic** (ˌɒrəˈgræfɪk) *or* **or·o·log·i·cal** (ˌɒrəˈlɒdʒɪkᵊl) *adj.* —ˌ**or·o·ˈgraph·i·cal·ly** *or* ˌ**or·o·ˈlog·i·cal·ly** *adv.*

o·ro·ide (ˈɔːrəʊˌaɪd) *n.* an alloy containing copper, tin, and other metals, used as imitation gold. [C19: from French *or* gold + -OID]

o·rom·e·ter (ɒˈrɒmɪtə) *n.* an aneroid barometer with an altitude scale. [C19: from ORO-¹ (mountain, altitude) + -METER]

O·ron·tes (ɒˈrɒntiːz) *n.* a river in SW Asia, rising in Lebanon and flowing north through Syria into Turkey, where it turns west to the Mediterranean. Length: 571 km (355 miles). Arabic name: **Asi.**

or·o·tund (ˈɒrəʊˌtʌnd) *adj.* **1.** (of the voice) resonant; booming. **2.** (of speech or writing) bombastic; pompous. [C18: from Latin phrase *ore rotundo* with rounded mouth]

O·roz·co (*Spanish* oˈrosko) *n.* **Jo·sé Cle·men·te** (xoˈse kleˈmente). 1883–1949, Mexican painter, noted for his monumental humanistic murals.

or·phan (ˈɔːfən) *n.* **1. a.** a child, one or (more commonly) both of whose parents are dead. **b.** (*as modifier*): *an orphan child.* ~*vb.* **2.** (*tr.*) to deprive of one or both parents. [C15: from Late Latin *orphanus,* from Greek *orphanos;* compare Latin *orbus* bereaved]

or·phan·age (ˈɔːfənɪdʒ) *n.* **1.** an institution for orphans and abandoned children. **2.** the state of being an orphan.

or·phar·i·on (ɔːˈfærɪən) *n.* a large lute in use during the 16th and 17th centuries. [C16: from ORPH(EUS) + *Arion,* musicians of Greek mythology]

Or·phe·an (ˈɔːfɪən) *adj.* **1.** of or relating to Orpheus. **2.** melodious or enchanting.

Or·phe·us (ˈɔːfɪəs, -fjuːs) *n. Greek myth.* a poet and lyre-player credited with the authorship of the poems forming the basis of Orphism. He married Eurydice and sought her in Hades after her death. He failed to win her back and was killed by a band of Bacchantes.

Or·phic (ˈɔːfɪk) *adj.* **1.** of or relating to Orpheus or Orphism. **2.** (*sometimes not cap.*) mystical or occult. —**ˈOr·phi·cal·ly** *adv.*

Or·phism (ˈɔːfɪzəm) *n.* a mystery religion of ancient Greece, widespread from the 6th century onwards, combining pre-Hellenic beliefs, the Thracian cult of (Dionysius) Zagreus, etc. —**Or·ˈphis·tic** *adj.*

or·phrey *or* **or·fray** (ˈɔːfrɪ) *n.* a richly embroidered band or border, esp. on an ecclesiastical vestment. [C13 *orfreis,* from Old French, from Late Latin *aurifrisium, auriphrygium,* from Latin *aurum* gold + *Phrygius* Phrygian]

or·pi·ment (ˈɔːpɪmənt) *n.* a yellow mineral consisting of arsenic trisulphide in monoclinic crystalline form occurring in association with realgar: is an ore of arsenic. Formula: As_2S_3. [C14: via Old French from Latin *auripigmentum* gold pigment]

or·pine (ˈɔːpaɪn) *or* **or·pin** (ˈɔːpɪn) *n.* a succulent perennial N temperate crassulaceous plant, *Sedum telephium,* with toothed leaves and heads of small purplish-white flowers. Also called: **livelong** (Brit.), **live-forever** (U.S.). [C14: from Old French, apparently from ORPIMENT (perhaps referring to the yellow flowers of a related species)]

Or·ping·ton¹ (ˈɔːpɪŋtən) *n.* **1.** a heavy breed of domestic fowl of various single colours, laying brown eggs. **2.** a breed of brown duck with an orange bill.

Or·ping·ton² (ˈɔːpɪŋtən) *n.* a district of SE London, part of the Greater London borough of Bromley since 1965.

or·re·ry (ˈɒrərɪ) *n., pl.* **-ries.** a mechanical model of the solar system in which the planets can be moved at the correct relative velocities around the sun. [C18: originally made for Charles Boyle, Earl of *Orrery*]

or·ris *or* **or·rice** (ˈɒrɪs) *n.* **1.** any of various irises, esp. *Iris florentina,* that have fragrant rhizomes. **2.** Also: **orrisroot.** the rhizome of such a plant, prepared and used as perfume. [C16: variant of IRIS]

Or·si·ni (*Italian* orˈsiːni) *n.* an Italian aristocratic family that was prominent in Rome from the 12th to the 18th century.

Orsk (*Russian* ɔrsk) *n.* a city in the S central Soviet Union, on the Ural River: a major railway and industrial centre, with an oil refinery linked by pipeline with the Emba field (on the Caspian). Pop.: 240 000 (1975 est.).

or·ta·nique (ˌɔːtəˈniːk) *n.* a hybrid between an orange and a tangerine. [C20: from OR(ANGE) + TAN(GERINE) + (UN)IQUE]

Or·te·gal (*Spanish* ˌorteˈɣal) *n.* **Cape.** a cape in NW Spain, projecting into the Bay of Biscay.

Or·te·ga y Gas·set (*Spanish* orˈteɣa i gaˈset) *n.* **Jo·sé** (xoˈse). 1883–1955, Spanish essayist and philosopher. His best-known work is *The Revolt of the Masses* (1930).

Orth. *abbrev. for* Orthodox (religion).

or·thi·con (ˈɔːθɪˌkɒn) *n.* short for **image orthicon.** [C20: from ORTHO- + ICON(OSCOPE)]

or·tho- *or before a vowel* **orth-** *combining form.* **1.** straight or upright: *orthotropous.* **2.** perpendicular or at right angles: *orthoclastic.* **3.** correct or right: *orthodontics; orthodox; orthography; orthoptics.* **4.** (*often in italics*) denoting an organic compound containing a benzene ring with substituents attached to adjacent carbon atoms (the 1,2- positions): *orthodinitrobenzene.* Abbrev.: *o-*. Compare **para-**¹ (sense 6), **meta-** (sense 4). **5.** denoting an oxyacid regarded as the highest hydrated form of the anhydride or a salt of such an acid: *orthophosphoric acid.* Compare **meta-** (sense 6). **6.** denoting a diatomic substance in which the spins of the two atoms are parallel: *orthohydrogen.* Compare **para-**¹ (sense 8). [from Greek *orthos* straight, right, upright]

or·tho·bo·ric ac·id (ˌɔːθəʊˈbɔːrɪk) *n.* the more formal name for **boric acid** (sense 1).

or·tho·cen·tre *or U.S.* **or·tho·cen·ter** (ˈɔːθəʊˌsɛntə) *n.* the point of intersection of any two altitudes of a triangle.

or·tho·ce·phal·ic (ˌɔːθəʊsɪˈfælɪk) *or* **or·tho·ceph·a·lous** (ˌɔːθəʊˈsɛfələs) *adj.* having a skull whose breadth is between 70 and 75 per cent of its length. —ˌ**or·tho·ˈceph·a·ly** *n.*

or·tho·chro·mat·ic (ˌɔːθəʊkrəʊˈmætɪk) *adj. Photog.* of or relating to an emulsion giving a rendering of relative light intensities of different colours that corresponds approximately to the colour sensitivity of the eye, esp. one that is insensitive to red light. ~Sometimes shortened to **ortho.** Compare **panchromatic.** —**or·tho·chro·ma·tism** (ˌɔːθəʊˈkrəʊməˌtɪzəm) *n.*

or·tho·clase (ˈɔːθəʊˌkleɪs, -ˌkleɪz) *n.* a white or coloured feldspar mineral consisting of an aluminium silicate of potassium in monoclinic crystalline form used in the manufacture of glass and ceramics and as a gemstone. Formula: $KAlSi_3O_8$.

or·tho·don·tics (ˌɔːθəʊˈdɒntɪks) *or* **or·tho·don·ti·a** (ˌɔːθəʊˈdɒntɪə) *n.* the branch of dentistry concerned with preventing or correcting irregularities of the teeth. Also called: **dental orthopaedics.** —ˌ**or·tho·ˈdon·tic** *adj.* —ˌ**or·tho·ˈdon·tist** *n.*

or·tho·dox (ˈɔːθəˌdɒks) *adj.* **1.** conforming with established or accepted standards, as in religion, behaviour, or attitudes. **2.** conforming to the Christian faith as established by the early Church. [C16: via Church Latin from Greek *orthodoxos,* from *orthos* correct + *doxa* belief] —**ˈor·tho·ˌdox·ly** *adv.*

Or·tho·dox (ˈɔːθəˌdɒks) *adj.* **1.** of or relating to the Orthodox Church of the East. **2.** (*sometimes not cap.*) of or relating to Orthodox Judaism.

Or·tho·dox Church *n.* **1.** Also called: **Byzantine Church, Eastern Orthodox Church, Greek Orthodox Church.** the collective body of those Eastern Churches that were separated from the western Church in the 11th century and are in communion with the Greek patriarch of Constantinople. **2.** any of these Churches.

Or·tho·dox Ju·da·ism *n.* the form of Judaism characterized by strict observance of the Mosaic Law as interpreted in the Talmud and the unfailing practice of personal devotions.

or·tho·dox·y (ˈɔːθəˌdɒksɪ) *n., pl.* **-dox·ies. 1.** orthodox belief or practice. **2.** the quality of being orthodox.

or·tho·ep·y (ˈɔːθəʊˌɛpɪ) *n.* the study of correct or standard pronunciation. [C17: from Greek *orthoepeia,* from ORTHO- straight + *epos* word] —**or·tho·ep·ic** (ˌɔːθəʊˈɛpɪk) *adj.* —ˌ**or·tho·ˈep·i·cal·ly** *adv.*

or·tho·gen·e·sis (ˌɔːθəʊˈdʒɛnɪsɪs) *n.* **1.** *Biology.* **a.** evolution of a group of organisms in a particular direction, which is generally predetermined. **b.** the theory that proposes such a development. **2.** the theory that there is a series of stages through which all cultures pass in the same order. —**or·tho·ge·net·ic** (ˌɔːθəʊdʒɪˈnɛtɪk) *adj.* —ˌ**or·tho·ge·ˈnet·i·cal·ly** *adv.*

or·tho·gen·ic (ˌɔːθəʊˈdʒɛnɪk) *adj.* **1.** *Med.* relating to corrective procedures designed to promote healthy development. **2.** of or relating to orthogenesis. —ˌ**or·tho·ˈgen·i·cal·ly** *adv.*

or·thog·na·thous (ɔːˈθɒgnəθəs) *adj. Anatomy.* having normally aligned jaws. —**or·ˈthog·na·ˌthism** *or* **or·ˈthog·na·thy** *n.*

or·thog·o·nal (ɔːˈθɒgənᵊl) *adj.* **1.** Also: **orthographic.** relating to, consisting of, or involving right angles; perpendicular. **2.** *Maths.* **a.** (of a pair of vectors) having a defined scalar product equal to zero. **b.** (of a pair of functions, etc.) having a defined product equal to zero. —**or·ˈthog·o·nal·ly** *adv.*

or·thog·o·nal ma·trix *n. Maths.* a matrix that is the inverse of its transpose so that any two rows or any two columns are orthogonal vectors. Compare **symmetric matrix.**

or·tho·graph·ic (ˌɔːθəˈgræfɪk) *or* **or·tho·graph·i·cal** *adj.* **1.** of or relating to spelling. **2.** *Maths.* another word for **orthogonal** (sense 1). —ˌ**or·tho·ˈgraph·i·cal·ly** *adv.*

or·thog·ra·phy (ɔːˈθɒgrəfɪ) *n., pl.* **-phies. 1.** a writing system. **2. a.** spelling considered to be correct. **b.** the principles underlying spelling. **3.** the study of spelling. —**or·ˈthog·ra·pher** *or* **or·ˈthog·ra·phist** *n.*

or·tho·hy·dro·gen (ˌɔːθəʊˈhaɪdrədʒən) *n. Chem.* the form of molecular hydrogen, constituting about 75 per cent of the total at normal temperatures, in which the nuclei of the atoms spin in the same direction. Compare **parahydrogen.**

or·tho·mor·phic (ˌɔːθəʊˈmɔːfɪk) *adj. Geography.* another word for **conformal** (sense 2).

or·tho·pae·dics *or U.S.* **or·tho·pe·dics** (ˌɔːθəˈpiːdɪks) *n.* (*functioning as sing.*) **1.** the branch of surgery concerned with disorders of the spine and joints and the repair of deformities of these parts. **2. dental orthopaedics.** another name for **orthodontics.** —ˌ**or·tho·ˈpae·dic** *or U.S.* ˌ**or·tho·ˈpe·dic** *adj.* —ˌ**or·tho·ˈpae·dist** *or U.S.* ˌ**or·tho·ˈpe·dist** *n.*

or·tho·phos·phate (ˌɔːθəʊˈfɒsfeɪt) *n.* any salt or ester of orthophosphoric acid.

or·tho·phos·phor·ic ac·id (ˌɔːθəʊfɒsˈfɒrɪk) *n.* a colourless soluble solid tribasic acid used in the manufacture of fertilizers and soaps. Formula: H_3PO_4. Also called: **phosphoric acid.**

or·tho·phos·pho·rous ac·id (ˌɔːθəʊˈfɒsfərəs) *n.* a white or yellowish hygroscopic crystalline dibasic acid. Formula: H_3PO_3. Also called: **phosphorous acid.**

or·tho·psy·chi·a·try (ˌɔːθəʊsaɪˈkaɪətrɪ) *n.* the study and treatment of mental disorders with emphasis on prevention during childhood. —**or·tho·psy·chi·at·ric** (ˌɔːθəʊˌsaɪkɪˈætrɪk) *adj.* —ˌ**or·tho·psy·ˈchi·a·trist** *n.*

or·thop·ter (ˈɔːθɒptə) *n.* another name for **ornithopter.**

or·thop·ter·an (ɔːˈθɒptərən) *or* **or·thop·ter·on** *n., pl.* **·ter·ans** *or* **·ter·a** (-tərə). any orthopterous insect.

or·thop·ter·ous (ɔːˈθɒptərəs) *or* **or·thop·ter·an** *adj.* of, relating to, or belonging to the *Orthoptera*, a large order of insects, including crickets, locusts, and grasshoppers, having leathery forewings and membranous hind wings, hind legs adapted for leaping, and organs of stridulation.

or·thop·tic (ɔːˈθɒptɪk) *adj.* relating to normal binocular vision.

or·thop·tics (ɔːˈθɒptɪks) *n.* (*functioning as sing.*) the science or practice of correcting defective vision, as by exercises to strengthen weak eye muscles.

or·tho·rhom·bic (ˌɔːθəʊˈrɒmbɪk) *adj. Crystallog.* relating to the crystal system characterized by three mutually perpendicular unequal axes. Also: **rhombic, trimetric.**

or·tho·scope (ˈɔːθəʊˌskəʊp) *n. Med. obsolete.* a 19th-century instrument for viewing the fundus of the eye through a layer of water, which eliminates distortion caused by the cornea.

or·tho·scop·ic (ˌɔːθəʊˈskɒpɪk) *adj.* **1.** of, relating to, or produced by normal vision. **2.** yielding an undistorted image.

or·thos·ti·chy (ɔːˈθɒstɪkɪ) *n., pl.* **·chies. 1.** an imaginary vertical line that connects a row of leaves on a stem. **2.** an arrangement of leaves so connected. ~Compare **parastichy.** [C19: from ORTHO- + Greek *stikhos*] —**or·ˈthos·ti·chous** *adj.*

or·tho·tone (ˈɔːθəʊˌtəʊn) *adj.* **1.** (of a word) having an independent accent. ~*n.* **2.** an independently accented word.

or·tho·trop·ic (ˌɔːθəʊˈtrɒpɪk) *adj.* **1.** *Botany.* relating to or showing growth that is in direct line with the stimulus. **2.** (of a material) having different elastic properties in different planes. —**or·thot·ro·pism** (ɔːˈθɒtrəˌpɪzəm) *n.*

or·thot·ro·pous (ɔːˈθɒtrəpəs) *adj.* (of a plant ovule) growing straight during development so that the micropyle is at the apex. Compare **anatropous.**

Ort·les (*Italian* ˈɔrtles) *pl. n.* a range of the Alps in N Italy. Highest peak: 3899 m (12 792 ft.). Also called: **Ort·ler** (ˈɔːtlə).

or·to·lan (ˈɔːtələn) *n.* **1.** Also called: **ortolan bunting.** a brownish Old World bunting, *Emberiza hortulana,* regarded as a delicacy. **2.** any of various other small birds eaten as delicacies, esp. the bobolink. [C17: via French from Latin *hortulānus,* from *hortulus,* diminutive of *hortus* garden]

orts (ɔːts) *pl. n.* (*sometimes sing.*) *Archaic or dialect.* scraps or leavings. [C15: of Germanic origin; related to Dutch *oorete,* from *oor-* remaining + *ete* food]

O·ru·ro (*Spanish* oˈruro) *n.* a city in W Bolivia: a former silver-mining centre; university (1892); tin, copper, and tungsten. Pop.: 119 700 (1970 est.).

Or·vie·to (*Italian* orˈvjɛːto) *n.* **1.** a market town in central Italy, in Umbria: Etruscan remains. Pop.: 23 220 (1971). Latin name: **Urbs Vetus. 2.** a light white wine from this region.

Or·well (ˈɔːwəl, -wɛl) *n.* **George,** pen name of *Eric Arthur Blair.* 1903–50, English novelist and essayist, born in India. He is notable for his social criticism, as in *The Road to Wigan Pier* (1932); his account of his experiences of the Spanish Civil War *Homage to Catalonia* (1938); and his satirical novels *Animal Farm* (1945), an allegory on the Russian Revolution, and *1984* (1949), in which he depicts an authoritarian state of the future. —**Or·wel·li·an** (ɔːˈwɛlɪən) *adj.*

-o·ry[1] *suffix forming nouns.* **1.** indicating a place for: *observatory.* **2.** something having a specified use: *directory.* [via Old French *-orie,* from Latin *-ōrium, -ōria*]

-o·ry[2] *suffix forming adjectives.* of or relating to; characterized by; having the effect of: *contributory; promissory.* [via Old French *-orie,* from Latin *-ōrius*]

O·ryol (*Russian* aˈrjɔl) *n.* a variant spelling of **Orel.**

or·yx (ˈɒrɪks) *n., pl.* **·yx·es** *or* **·yx.** any large African antelope of the genus *Oryx,* typically having long straight nearly upright horns. [C14: via Latin from Greek *orux* stonemason's axe, used also of the pointed horns of an antelope]

os[1] (ɒs) *n., pl.* **os·sa** (ˈɒsə). *Anatomy.* the technical name for **bone.** [C16: from Latin: bone; compare Greek *osteon*]

os[2] (ɒs) *n., pl.* **o·ra** (ˈɔːrə). *Anatomy, zoology.* a mouth or mouthlike part or opening. [C18: from Latin]

os[3] (əʊs) *n., pl.* **o·sar** (ˈəʊsɑː). another name for **esker.** [C19 *osar* (pl.), from Swedish *ås* (sing.) ridge]

Os *the chemical symbol for* osmium.

o.s. *abbrev. for:* **1.** old series. **2.** only son. **3.** Also: **OS, O/S** out of stock. **4.** Also: **O.S., OS, O/S** *Banking.* outstanding.

O.S. *abbrev. for:* **1.** Old School. **2.** Old Style (method of reckoning dates). **3.** Ordinary Seaman. **4.** (in Britain) Ordnance Survey. **5.** outsize. **6.** Also **OS.** Old Saxon (language).

O.S.A. *abbrev. for* Order of Saint Augustine.

O·sage (əʊˈseɪdʒ, ˈəʊseɪdʒ) *n.* **1.** (*pl.* **O·sag·es** *or* **O·sage**) a member of a North American Indian people formerly living in an area between the Missouri and Arkansas Rivers. **2.** the language of this people, belonging to the Siouan family.

O·sage or·ange *n.* **1.** a North American moraceous tree, *Maclura pomifera,* grown for hedges and ornament. **2.** the warty orange-like fruit of this plant.

O·sa·ka (əʊˈsɑːkə) *n.* a port in S Japan, on S Honshu on **Osaka Bay** (an inlet of the Pacific): the second largest city in Japan (the chief commercial city during feudal times); university (1931); an industrial and commercial centre. Pop.: 2 780 000 (1975).

O.S.B. *abbrev. for* Order of Saint Benedict.

Os·borne (ˈɒzbən, -ˌbɔːn) *n.* **John (James).** born 1929, English dramatist. His plays include *Look Back in Anger* (1956), containing the prototype of the angry young man, Jimmy Porter, *The Entertainer* (1957), and *Inadmissible Evidence* (1965).

Os·can (ˈɒskən) *n.* **1.** an extinct language of ancient S Italy belonging to the Italic branch of the Indo-European family. See also **Osco-Umbrian. 2.** a speaker of this language; a Samnite. ~*adj.* **3.** of or relating to this language.

os·car (ˈɒskə) *n. Austral. slang.* cash; money. [C20: rhyming slang, from *Oscar* Ashe (1871–1936), Australian actor]

Os·car (ˈɒskə) *n.* any of several small gold statuettes awarded annually in the United States by the Academy of Motion Picture Arts and Sciences for outstanding achievements in films. [C20: said to have been named after a remark made by an official on first seeing the statuette, that it reminded him of his uncle Oscar]

Os·car II *n.* 1829–1907, king of Sweden (1872–1907) and of Norway (1872–1905).

os·cil·late (ˈɒsɪˌleɪt) *vb.* **1.** (*intr.*) to move or swing from side to side regularly. **2.** (*intr.*) to waver between opinions, courses of action, etc. **3.** *Physics.* to undergo or produce or cause to undergo or produce oscillation. [C18: from Latin *oscillāre* to swing, from *oscillum* a swing]

os·cil·lat·ing u·ni·verse the·o·ry *n.* the theory that the universe is oscillating between periods of expansion and contraction.

os·cil·la·tion (ˌɒsɪˈleɪʃən) *n.* **1.** *Physics.* **a.** regular fluctuation in value, position, or state about a mean value, such as the variation in an alternating current or the regular swinging of a pendulum. **b.** a single cycle of such a fluctuation. **2.** the act or process of oscillating. —**os·cil·la·to·ry** (ˈɒsɪlətərɪ, -trɪ) *adj.*

os·cil·la·tor (ˈɒsɪˌleɪtə) *n.* **1.** a circuit or instrument for producing an alternating current or voltage of a required frequency. **2.** any instrument for producing oscillations. **3.** a person or thing that oscillates.

os·cil·lo·gram (ɒˈsɪləˌgræm) *n.* the recording obtained from an oscillograph or the trace on an oscilloscope screen.

os·cil·lo·graph (ɒˈsɪləˌgrɑːf, -ˌgræf) *n.* a device for producing a graphical record of the variation of an oscillating quantity, such as an electric current. —**os·cil·lo·graph·ic** (ɒˌsɪləˈgræfɪk) *adj.* —**os·cil·log·ra·phy** (ˌɒsɪˈlɒgrəfɪ) *n.*

os·cil·lo·scope (ɒˈsɪləˌskəʊp) *n.* an instrument for producing a representation of a rapidly changing quantity on the screen of a cathode-ray tube. The rapid changes are converted into electric signals, which are applied to plates in the cathode-ray tube. Changes in the magnitude of the potential across the plates deflect the electron beam and thus produce a trace on the screen.

os·cine (ˈɒsaɪn, ˈɒsɪn) *adj.* of, relating to, or belonging to the *Oscines,* a suborder of passerine birds that includes most of the songbirds. [C17: via New Latin from Latin *oscen* singing bird]

os·ci·tan·cy (ˈɒsɪtənsɪ) *or* **os·ci·tance** *n., pl.* **·tan·cies** *or* **·tanc·es. 1.** the state of being drowsy, lazy, or inattentive. **2.** the act of yawning. ~Also called: **oscitation.** [C17: from Latin *oscitāre* to gape, yawn] —ˈ**os·ci·tant** *adj.*

Os·co-Um·bri·an (ˌɒskəʊˈʌmbrɪən) *n.* **1.** a group of extinct languages of ancient Italy, including Oscan, Umbrian, and Sabellian, which were displaced by Latin. ~*adj.* **2.** relating to or belonging to this group of languages.

os·cu·lant (ˈɒskjʊlənt) *adj.* **1.** *Biology.* (of an organism or group of organisms) possessing some of the characteristics of two different taxonomic groups. **2.** *Zoology.* closely joined or adhering. [C19: from Latin *ōsculārī* to kiss; see OSCULUM]

os·cu·lar (ˈɒskjʊlə) *adj.* **1.** *Zoology.* of or relating to an osculum. **2.** of or relating to the mouth or to kissing.

os·cu·late (ˈɒskjʊˌleɪt) *vb.* **1.** *Usually humorous.* to kiss. **2.** (*intr.*) (of an organism or group of organisms) to be intermediate between two taxonomic groups. **3.** *Geom.* to touch in osculation. [C17: from Latin *ōsculārī* to kiss; see OSCULUM]

os·cu·la·tion (ˌɒskjʊˈleɪʃən) *n.* **1.** *Maths.* a point at which two branches of a curve have a common tangent, each branch extending in both directions of the tangent. Also called: **tacnode. 2.** *Rare.* the act or an instance of kissing. —**os·cu·la·to·ry** (ˈɒskjʊlətərɪ, -trɪ) *adj.*

os·cu·lum (ˈɒskjʊləm) *n., pl.* **·la** (-lə). *Zoology.* a mouthlike aperture, esp. the opening in a sponge out of which water passes. [C17: from Latin a kiss, little mouth, diminutive of *ōs* mouth]

O.S.D. *abbrev. for* Order of Saint Dominic.

-ose[1] *suffix forming adjectives.* possessing; resembling: *verbose; grandiose.* [from Latin *-ōsus;* see -OUS]

-ose[2] *suffix forming nouns.* **1.** indicating a carbohydrate, esp. a sugar: *lactose.* **2.** indicating a decomposition product of protein: *albumose.* [from GLUCOSE]

O.S.F. *abbrev. for* Order of Saint Francis.

Osh·a·wa (ˈɒʃəwə) *n.* a city in central Canada, in SE Ontario on Lake Ontario: motor-vehicle industry. Pop.: 91 587 (1971).

O·shog·bo (əˈʃɒgbəʊ) *n.* a city in SW Nigeria: trade centre. Pop.: 282 000 (1975 est.).

o·si·er (ˈəʊzɪə) *n.* **1.** any of various willow trees, esp. *Salix viminalis,* whose flexible branches or twigs are used for making baskets, etc. **2.** a twig or branch from such a tree. **3.** any of several North American dogwoods, esp. the red osier. [C14: from Old French, probably from Medieval Latin *ausēria,* perhaps of Gaulish origin; compare Breton *aoz*]

O·si·jek (*Serbo-Croatian* ˈɔsijɛk) *n.* a town in N Yugoslavia, in

E Croatia on the Drava River: under Turkish rule from 1526 to 1687. Pop.: 93 912 (1971). Ancient name: **Mursa.**

O·si·ris (əʊˈsaɪrɪs) *n.* an ancient Egyptian god, ruler of the underworld and judge of the dead. —**Oˈsi·ri·an** *adj.*

-o·sis *suffix forming nouns.* **1.** indicating a process or state: *metamorphosis.* **2.** indicating a diseased condition: *tuberculosis.* Compare **-iasis. 3.** indicating the formation or development of something: *fibrosis.* [from Greek, suffix used to form nouns from verbs with infinitives in *-oein* or *-oun*]

Os·lo (ˈɒzləʊ; *Norwegian* ˈuslu) *n.* the capital and chief port of Norway, in the southeast at the head of **Oslo Fjord** (an inlet of the Skagerrak): founded in about 1050; university (1811); a major commercial and industrial centre, producing about a quarter of Norway's total output. Pop.: 465 337 (1974 est.). Former names: **Christiania** (1624–1877), **Kristiania** (1877–1924).

Os·man I (ˈɒzmən, ɒzˈmɑːn) *or* **Oth·man I** *n.* 1259–1326, Turkish sultan; founder of the Ottoman Empire.

Os·man·li (ɒzˈmænlɪ) *adj.* **1.** of or relating to the Ottoman Empire. ~*n.* **2.** (*pl.* **·lis**) (formerly) a subject of the Ottoman Empire. **3.** the Turkish language, esp. as written in Arabic letters under the Ottoman Empire. [C19: from Turkish, from OSMAN I]

os·mic (ˈɒzmɪk) *adj.* of or containing osmium in a high valence state, esp. the tetravalent state.

os·mi·ous (ˈɒzmɪəs) *adj.* another word for **osmous.**

os·mi·rid·i·um (ˌɒzmɪˈrɪdɪəm) *n.* a very hard corrosion-resistant white or grey natural alloy of osmium and iridium in variable proportions, often containing smaller amounts of platinum, ruthenium, and rhodium: used in pen nibs, etc. Also called: **iridosmine.** [C19: from OSM(IUM) + IRIDIUM]

os·mi·um (ˈɒzmɪəm) *n.* a very hard brittle bluish-white metal, the heaviest known element, occurring with platinum and alloyed with iridium in osmiridium: used to produce platinum alloys, mainly for pen tips and instrument pivots, as a catalyst, and in electric-light filaments. Symbol: Os; atomic no.: 76; atomic wt.: 190.2; valency: 1 to 8; relative density: 22.57; melting pt.: 3045°C (approx.); boiling pt.: 5027°C (approx.). [C19: from Greek *osmē* smell, so called from its penetrating odour]

os·mi·um te·trox·ide *n.* a yellowish poisonous water-soluble crystalline substance with a penetrating odour, used as a reagent and catalyst in organic synthesis. Formula: OsO_4.

os·mom·e·ter (ɒzˈmɒmɪtə) *n.* an instrument for measuring osmotic pressure. [C20: from OSMO(SIS) + -METER] —**os·mo·met·ric** (ˌɒzməˈmɛtrɪk) *adj.* —ˌ**os·mo·ˈmet·ri·cal·ly** *adv.* —**os·ˈmom·e·try** *n.*

os·mose (ˈɒzməʊs, -məʊz, ˈɒs-) *vb.* **1.** to undergo or cause to undergo osmosis. ~*n.* **2.** a former name for **osmosis.** [C19 (n.): abstracted from the earlier terms *endosmose* and *exosmose;* related to Greek *ōsmos* push]

os·mo·sis (ɒzˈməʊsɪs, ɒs-) *n.* **1.** the passage of solvent molecules from a less concentrated to a more concentrated solution through a semipermeable membrane until both solutions are of the same concentration. **2.** diffusion through any membrane or porous barrier, as in dialysis. **3.** gradual or unconscious assimilation or adoption, as of ideas. [C19: Latinized form from OSMOSE (n.), from Greek *ōsmos* push, thrust] —**os·mot·ic** (ɒzˈmɒtɪk, ɒs-) *adj.* —**os·ˈmot·i·cal·ly** *adv.*

os·mot·ic pres·sure *n.* the pressure necessary to prevent osmosis into a given solution when the solution is separated from the pure solvent by a semipermeable membrane.

os·mous (ˈɒzməs) *adj.* of or containing osmium in a low valence state, esp. the divalent state. Also: **osmious.**

os·mun·da (ɒzˈmʌndə) *or* **os·mund** (ˈɒzmənd) *n.* any fern of the genus *Osmunda,* such as the royal fern, having large spreading fronds: family *Osmundaceae.* [C13: from Old French *osmonde,* of unknown origin]

Os·na·brück (*German* ˈɔsnaˌbryk) *n.* an industrial city in N West Germany, in Lower Saxony: a member of the Hanseatic League in the Middle Ages. Pop.: 164 060 (1974 est.).

os·na·burg (ˈɒznəˌbɜːg) *n.* a coarse plain-woven cotton used for sacks, furnishings, etc. [C16: corruption of OSNABRÜCK, where it was originally made]

os·prey (ˈɒsprɪ, -preɪ) *n.* **1.** a large broad-winged fish-eating diurnal bird of prey, *Pandion haliaetus,* with a dark back and whitish head and underparts: family *Pandioridae.* Often called in U.S.: **fish hawk. 2.** any of the feathers of various other birds, used esp. as trimming for hats. [C15: from Old French *ospres,* apparently from Latin *ossifraga,* literally: bone-breaker, from *os* bone + *frangere* to break]

Os·sa (ˈɒsə) *n.* a mountain in NE Greece, in E Thessaly: famous in mythology for the attempt of the twin giants, Otus and Ephialtes, to reach heaven by piling Ossa on Olympus and Pelion on Ossa. Height: 1978 m (6489 ft.).

os·se·in (ˈɒsɪɪn) *n.* a protein that forms the organic matrix of bone, constituting about 40 per cent of its matter. [C19: from Latin *osseus* bony, from *os* bone]

os·se·ous (ˈɒsɪəs) *adj.* consisting of or containing bone, bony. [C17: from Latin *osseus,* from *os* bone] —**ˈos·se·ous·ly** *adv.*

Os·set (ˈɒsɪt) *n.* a member of an Iranian people living in the Soviet Union, chiefly in Ossetia in the Caucasus.

Os·se·tia (ɒˈsiːʃə) *n.* a region of the SW Soviet Union, in the Caucasus: consists administratively of the North Ossetian ASSR of the RSFSR and the South Ossetian AR of the Georgian SSR.

Os·set·ic (ɒˈsɛtɪk) *or* **Os·se·tian** (ɒˈsiːtɪən) *adj.* **1.** of or relating to Ossetia, its people, or their language. ~*n.* **2.** the language of the Ossets, belonging to the East Iranian branch of the Indo-European family.

Os·si·an (ˈɒsɪən) *n.* a legendary Irish hero and bard of the 3rd century A.D. See also (James) **Macpherson.** —ˌ**Os·si·ˈan·ic** *adj.*

os·si·cle (ˈɒsɪkᵊl) *n.* a small bone, esp. one of those in the middle ear. [C16: from Latin *ossiculum,* from *os* bone] —**os·sic·u·lar** (ɒˈsɪkjʊlə) *adj.*

Os·sie (ˈɒzɪ) *adj., n.* a variant spelling of **Aussie.**

Os·si·etz·ky (ˌɒsɪˈɛtskɪ) *n.* **Carl von** (karl fɔn). 1889–1938, German pacifist leader. He was imprisoned for revealing Germany's secret rearmament (1931–32) and again under Hitler (1933–36): Nobel peace prize 1935.

os·sif·er·ous (ɒˈsɪfərəs) *adj. Geology.* containing or yielding bones: *ossiferous caves.*

os·si·fi·ca·tion (ˌɒsɪfɪˈkeɪʃən) *n.* **1.** the formation of or conversion into bone. **2.** the process of ossifying or the state of being ossified.

os·si·frage (ˈɒsɪfrɪdʒ, -ˌfreɪdʒ) *n.* an archaic name for the **lammergeier** and **osprey.** [C17: from Latin *ossifraga* sea eagle; see OSPREY]

os·si·fy (ˈɒsɪˌfaɪ) *vb.* **·fies, ·fy·ing, ·fied. 1.** to convert or be converted into bone. **2.** (*intr.*) (of habits, attitudes, etc.) to become inflexible. [C18: from French *ossifier,* from Latin *os* bone + *facere* to make] —**ˈos·si·ˌfi·er** *n.*

os·so buc·co (ˈɒsəʊ ˈbʊkəʊ) *n.* a stew, originally from Italy, made with knuckle of veal, cooked in tomato sauce. [C20: from Italian: marrow bone]

os·su·ar·y (ˈɒsjʊərɪ) *n., pl.* **·ar·ies.** any container for the burial of human bones, such as an urn or vault. [C17: from Late Latin *ossuārium,* from Latin *os* bone]

O.S.T. *U.S. abbrev. for* Office of Science and Technology.

os·te·al (ˈɒstɪəl) *adj.* **1.** of or relating to bone or to the skeleton. **2.** composed of bone; osseous. [C19: from Greek *osteon* bone]

os·te·i·tis (ˌɒstɪˈaɪtɪs) *n.* inflammation of a bone. —**os·te·i·tic** (ˌɒstɪˈɪtɪk) *adj.*

os·te·i·tis de·for·mans (dɪˈfɔːmənz) *n.* another name for **Paget's disease** (sense 1).

Os·tend (ɒsˈtɛnd) *n.* a port and resort in NW Belgium, in West Flanders on the North Sea. Pop.: 71 227 (1970). French name: **Os·tende** (ɔsˈtɑ̃ːd). Flemish name: **Oostende.**

os·ten·si·ble (ɒˈstɛnsɪbᵊl) *adj.* **1.** apparent; seeming. **2.** pretended. [C18: via French from Medieval Latin *ostensibilis,* from Latin *ostendere* to show, from *ob-* before + *tendere* to extend] —**os·ˌten·si·ˈbil·i·ty** *n.* —**os·ˈten·si·bly** *adv.*

os·ten·sive (ɒˈstɛnsɪv) *adj.* **1.** obviously or manifestly demonstrative. **2.** a less common word for **ostensible.** [C17: from Late Latin *ostentīvus,* from Latin *ostendere* to show; see OSTENSIBLE] —**os·ˈten·sive·ly** *adv.*

os·ten·so·ry (ɒsˈtɛnsərɪ) *n. R.C. Church.* another word for **monstrance.** [C18: from Medieval Latin *ostensorium;* see OSTENSIBLE]

os·ten·ta·tion (ˌɒstɛnˈteɪʃən) *n.* **1.** pretentious, showy, or vulgar display. **2.** *Archaic.* false appearance. —ˌ**os·ten·ˈta·tious** *adj.* —ˌ**os·ten·ˈta·tious·ly** *adv.*

os·te·o- *or before a vowel* **os·te-** *combining form.* indicating bone or bones: *osteopathy.* [from Greek *osteon*]

os·te·o·ar·thri·tis (ˌɒstɪəʊɑːˈθraɪtɪs) *n.* chronic inflammation of the joints, esp. those that bear weight, with pain and stiffness. Also called: **degenerative joint disease.** —**os·te·o·ar·thrit·ic** (ˌɒstɪəʊɑːˈθrɪtɪk) *adj., n.*

os·te·o·blast (ˈɒstɪəʊˌblæst) *n.* a bone-forming cell. —ˌ**os·te·o·ˈblas·tic** *adj.*

os·te·oc·la·sis (ˌɒstɪˈɒkləsɪs) *n.* **1.** surgical fracture of a bone to correct deformity. **2.** absorption of bone tissue.

os·te·o·clast (ˈɒstɪəʊˌklæst) *n.* **1.** a surgical instrument for fracturing bone. **2.** a large multinuclear cell formed in bone marrow that is associated with the normal absorption of bone. —ˌ**os·te·o·ˈclas·tic** *adj.*

os·te·o·gen·e·sis (ˌɒstɪəʊˈdʒɛnɪsɪs) *n.* the formation of bone.

os·te·oid (ˈɒstɪˌɔɪd) *adj.* of or resembling bone; bony.

os·te·ol·o·gy (ˌɒstɪˈɒlədʒɪ) *n.* the study of the structure and function of bones. —**os·te·o·log·i·cal** (ˌɒstɪəˈlɒdʒɪkᵊl) *adj.* —ˌ**os·te·o·ˈlog·i·cal·ly** *adv.* —ˌ**os·te·ˈol·o·gist** *n.*

os·te·o·ma (ˌɒstɪˈəʊmə) *n., pl.* **·ma·ta** (-mətə) *or* **·mas.** a benign tumour composed of bone or bonelike tissue.

os·te·o·ma·la·ci·a (ˌɒstɪəʊməˈleɪʃɪə) *n.* a disease in adults characterized by softening of the bones, resulting from a deficiency of vitamin D and of calcium and phosphorus. [C19: from New Latin, from OSTEO- + Greek *malakia* softness] —ˌ**os·te·o·ma·ˈla·ci·al** *or* **os·te·o·ma·lac·ic** (ˌɒstɪəʊməˈlæsɪk) *adj.*

os·te·o·my·e·li·tis (ˌɒstɪəʊˌmaɪɪˈlaɪtɪs) *n.* inflammation of bone marrow, caused by infection.

os·te·o·path (ˈɒstɪəˌpæθ) *or* **os·te·op·a·thist** (ˌɒstɪˈɒpəθɪst) *n.* a person who practises osteopathy.

os·te·op·a·thy (ˌɒstɪˈɒpəθɪ) *n.* a system of healing based on the manipulation of bones or other parts of the body. —**os·te·o·path·ic** (ˌɒstɪəˈpæθɪk) *adj.* —ˌ**os·te·o·ˈpath·i·cal·ly** *adv.*

os·te·o·phyte (ˈɒstɪəˌfaɪt) *n.* a small abnormal bony outgrowth. —**os·te·o·phyt·ic** (ˌɒstɪəˈfɪtɪk) *adj.*

os·te·o·plas·tic (ˌɒstɪəˈplæstɪk) *adj.* **1.** of or relating to osteoplasty. **2.** of or relating to the formation of bone.

os·te·o·plas·ty (ˈɒstɪəˌplæstɪ) *n., pl.* **·ties.** the branch of surgery concerned with bone repair or bone grafting.

os·te·o·por·o·sis (ˌɒstɪəʊpɔːˈrəʊsɪs) *n.* porosity and brittleness of the bones due to loss of protein from the bone matrix. [C19: from OSTEO- + PORE + -OSIS]

os+te·o+tome ('ɒstɪəˌtəʊm) *n.* a surgical instrument for cutting bone, usually a special chisel.
os+te·ot·o+my (ˌɒstɪ'ɒtəmɪ) *n., pl.* **+mies.** the surgical cutting or dividing of bone, usually to correct a deformity.
Ö·ster+reich ('øːstəˌraɪç) *n.* the German name for **Austria.**
Os+ti·a ('ɒstɪə) *n.* an ancient town in W central Italy, originally at the mouth of the Tiber but now about 6 km (4 miles) inland: served as the port of ancient Rome; harbours built by Claudius and Trajan; ruins excavated since 1854.
os+ti+ar·y ('ɒstɪərɪ) *n., pl.* **+ar·ies.** *R.C. Church.* another word for **porter**² (sense 4). [C15: from Latin *ostiārius* door-keeper, from *ostium* door]
os+ti+na+to (ˌɒstɪ'nɑːtəʊ) *n.* **a.** a continuously reiterated musical phrase. **b.** (*as modifier*): *an ostinato passage.* [Italian: from Latin *obstinātus* OBSTINATE]
os+ti+ole ('ɒstɪˌəʊl) *n. Biology.* **1.** the pore in the reproductive bodies of certain algae and fungi through which spores pass. **2.** any small pore. [C19: from Latin *ostiolum,* diminutive of *ostium* door] —**os+ti·o+lar** ('ɒstɪələ) *adj.*
os+ti·um ('ɒstɪəm) *n., pl.* **+ti·a** (-tɪə). *Biology.* **1.** any of the pores in sponges through which water enters the body. **2.** any of the openings in the heart of an arthropod through which blood enters. **3.** any similar opening. [C17: from Latin: door, entrance]
ost+ler ('ɒslə) *or* **host+ler** *n. Archaic.* a stableman, esp. one at an inn. [C15: variant of *hostler,* from HOSTEL]
ost+mark ('ɒstˌmɑːk; *German* 'ɔstˌmark) *n.* the standard monetary unit of East Germany, divided into 100 pfennigs. [literally: east mark]
os+to+sis (ɒs'təʊsɪs) *n.* the formation of bone; ossification.
os+tra+cize *or* **os+tra+cise** ('ɒstrəˌsaɪz) *vb.* (*tr.*) **1.** to exclude or banish (a person) from a particular group, society, etc. **2.** (in ancient Greece) to punish by temporary exile. [C17: from Greek *ostrakizein* to select someone for banishment by voting on potsherds; see OSTRACON] —**'os+tra+cism** *n.* —**'os+tra+ˌciz·a·ble** *or* **'os+tra+ˌcis·a·ble** *adj.* —**'os+tra+ˌciz·er** *or* **'os+tra+ˌcis+er** *n.*
os+tra+cod ('ɒstrəˌkɒd) *n.* any minute crustacean of the mainly freshwater subclass *Ostracoda,* in which the body is enclosed in a transparent two-valved carapace. [C19: via New Latin from Greek *ostrakōdēs* having a shell, from *ostrakon* shell] —**os+tra+co+dan** (ˌɒstrə'kəʊdən) *or* ˌ**os+tra+'co+dous** *adj.*
os+tra+co+derm ('ɒstrəkəˌdɜːm, ɒs'trækə-) *n.* any extinct Palaeozoic fishlike jawless vertebrate of the group *Ostracodermi,* characterized by a heavily armoured body. [C19: via New Latin from Greek *ostrakon* shell + -DERM]
os+tra+con ('ɒstrəˌkɒn) *n.* (in ancient Greece) a potsherd used for ostracizing. [from Greek]
Os+tra+va (*Czech* 'ɔstrava) *n.* an industrial city in N Czechoslovakia, on the River Oder: the chief coal-mining area in Czechoslovakia, in Upper Silesia. Pop.: 292 404 (1974 est.).
os+trich ('ɒstrɪtʃ) *n., pl.* **+trich·es** *or* **+trich. 1.** a fast-running flightless African bird, *Struthio camelus,* that is the largest living bird, with stout two-toed feet and dark feathers, except on the naked head, neck, and legs: order *Struthioniformes* (see **ratite**). **2. American ostrich.** another name for **rhea. 3.** a person who refuses to recognize the truth, reality, etc.: a reference to the ostrich's supposed habit of burying its head in the sand. [C13: from Old French *ostrice,* from Latin *avis* bird + Late Latin *struthio* ostrich, from Greek *strouthion*]
Os+tro+goth ('ɒstrəˌgɒθ) *n.* a member of the eastern group of the Goths, who formed a kingdom in Italy from 493 to 552. [C17: from Late Latin *Ostrogothī,* from *ostro-* east, eastward + GOTH] —ˌ**Os+tro+'goth+ic** *adj.*
Ost·wald (*German* 'ɔstvalt) *n.* **Wil·helm** ('vɪlhɛlm). 1853–1932, German chemist, noted for his pioneering work in catalysis. He also invented a process for making nitric acid from ammonia and developed a new theory of colour: Nobel prize for chemistry 1909.
Os+ty+ak ('ɒstɪˌæk) *n.* **1.** (*pl.* **+aks** *or* **+ak**) a member of an Ugrian people living in NW Siberia E of the Urals. **2.** the language of this people, belonging to the Finno-Ugric family: related to Hungarian.
Oś+wię+cim (*Polish* ɔʃ'fjɛntʃim) *n.* an industrial town in S Poland: site of Nazi concentration camp during World War II. Pop.: 41 000 (1972 est.). German name: **Auschwitz.**
O.T. *abbrev. for:* **1.** occupational therapy. **2.** Old Testament. **3.** overtime. **4.** *Austral.* Overland Telegraph (the line from Adelaide to Darwin).
ot- *combining form.* variant of **oto-** before a vowel: *otalgia.*
o·tal+gi·a (əʊ'tældʒɪə, -dʒə) *n.* the technical name for **earache.**
O.T.C. *abbrev. for:* **1.** (in Britain) Officers' Training Corps. **2.** *Stock Exchange.* over the counter.
oth+er ('ʌðə) *determiner.* **1. a.** (when used before a singular noun, usually preceded by *the*) the remaining (one or ones in a group of which one or some have been specified): *I'll read the other sections of the paper later.* **b. the other** (*as pronoun; functioning as sing.*): *one walks while the other rides.* **2.** (a) different (one or ones from that or those already specified or understood): *he found some other house; no other man but you; other days were happier.* **3.** additional; further: *there are no other possibilities.* **4.** (preceded by *every*) alternate; two: *it buzzes every other minute.* **5. other than. a.** apart from; besides: *a lady other than his wife.* **b.** different from: *he couldn't be other than what he is.* Archaic form: **other from. 6. no other** *Archaic.* nothing else: *I can do no other.* **7. or other.** (preceded by a phrase or word with *some*) used to add vagueness to the preceding pronoun, noun, or noun phrase: *he's somewhere or other; some dog or other bit him.* **8. other things being equal.** conditions being the same or unchanged. **9. the other day, night,** *etc.* a few days, nights, etc., ago. **10. the other thing.** an unexpressed alternative. ~*pron.* **11.** another: *show me one other.* **12.** (*pl.*) additional or further ones: *the police have found two and are looking for others.* **13.** (*pl.*) other people or things. **14. the others.** the remaining ones (of a group): *take these and leave the others.* **15.** different ones (from those specified or understood): *they'd rather have others, not these.* See also **each other, one another.** ~*adv.* **16.** (usually used with a negative and foll. by *than*) otherwise; differently: *they couldn't behave other than they do.* [Old English *ōther;* related to Old Saxon *āthar, ōthar,* Old High German *andar*]
oth·er-di·rect+ed *adj.* guided by values derived from external influences. Compare **inner-directed.**
oth·er+gates ('ʌðəˌgeɪts) *Archaic.* ~*adv.* **1.** differently; otherwise. ~*adj.* **2.** different. [C14: from OTHER + GATE³ + Old English *-s,* adverbial suffix]
oth·er+guess ('ʌðəˌgɛs) *adj. Informal.* another word for **other-gates** (sense 2).
oth+er+ness ('ʌðənɪs) *n.* the quality of being different or distinct in appearance, character, etc.
oth·er+where ('ʌðəˌwɛə) *adv. Archaic, poetic.* elsewhere.
oth·er+wise ('ʌðəˌwaɪz) **1.** *sentence connector.* or else; if not, then: *go home — otherwise your mother will worry.* ~*adv.* **2.** differently: *I wouldn't have thought otherwise.* **3.** in other respects: *an otherwise hopeless situation.* ~*adj.* **4.** (*predicative*) of an unexpected nature; different: *the facts are otherwise.* ~*pron.* **5.** something different in outcome: *success or otherwise.*
oth+er world *n.* the spirit world or afterlife.
oth·er+world·ly (ˌʌðə'wɜːldlɪ) *adj.* **1.** of or relating to the spiritual or imaginative world. **2.** impractical or unworldly. —ˌ**oth·er+'world·li+ness** *n.*
O·thin ('əʊðɪn) *n.* a variant of **Odin.**
Oth+man ('pθmən, pθ'mɑːn) *adj., n.* a variant of **Ottoman.**
Oth·man I *n.* a variant of **Osman I.**
O·tho I ('əʊθəʊ) *n.* a variant of **Otto I.**
o·tic ('əʊtɪk, 'ɒtɪk) *adj.* of or relating to the ear. [C17: from Greek *ōtikos,* from *ous* ear]
-ot·ic *suffix forming adjectives.* **1.** relating to or affected by: *sclerotic.* **2.** causing: *narcotic.* [from Greek *-ōtikos*]
o·ti+ose ('əʊtɪˌəʊs, -ˌəʊz) *adj.* **1.** serving no useful purpose: *otiose language.* **2.** *Rare.* indolent; lazy. [C18: from Latin *ōtiōsus* leisured, from *ōtium* leisure] —**o·ti+os+i·ty** (ˌəʊtɪ'ɒsɪtɪ) *or* **'o·ti+ose+ness** *n.*
o·ti+tis (əʊ'taɪtɪs) *n.* inflammation of the ear, esp. the middle ear (**otitis media**), with pain, impaired hearing, etc.
o·to- *or before a vowel* **ot-** *combining form.* indicating the ear: *otitis; otolith.* [from Greek *ous, ōt-* ear]
o·to+cyst ('əʊtəʊˌsɪst) *n.* **1.** another name for **statocyst. 2.** the embryonic structure in vertebrates that develops into the inner ear in the adult. —ˌ**o·to+'cys+tic** *adj.*
o·to+lar+yn+gol+o·gy (ˌəʊtəʊˌlærɪŋ'gɒlədʒɪ) *n.* the branch of medicine concerned with the ear, nose, and throat and their diseases. Sometimes called: **otorhinolaryngology.** —**o·to+la+ryn+go+log·i+cal** (ˌəʊtəʊləˌrɪŋgə'lɒdʒɪkᵊl) *adj.* —ˌ**o·to+ˌlar+yn+'gol·o+gist** *n.*
o·to+lith ('əʊtəʊˌlɪθ) *n.* **1.** any of the granules of calcium carbonate in the inner ear of vertebrates. Movement of otoliths, caused by a change in position of the animal, stimulates sensory hair cells, which convey the information to the brain. **2.** another name for **statolith** (sense 1). —ˌ**o·to+'lith+ic** *adj.*
o·tol+o·gy (əʊ'tɒlədʒɪ) *n.* the branch of medicine concerned with the ear. —**o·to+log·i+cal** (ˌəʊtə'lɒdʒɪkᵊl) *adj.* —**o·'tol·o+gist** *n.*
o·to+scope ('əʊtəʊˌskəʊp) *n.* a medical instrument for examining the external ear. —**o·to+scop+ic** (ˌəʊtəʊ'skɒpɪk) *adj.*
Ot+ran+to (*Italian* 'ɔːtranto) *n.* a small port in SE Italy, in Apulia on the **Strait of Otranto:** the most easterly town in Italy; dates back to Greek times and was an important Roman port; its ruined castle was the setting of Horace Walpole's *Castle of Otranto.* Pop.: 4151 (1971).
ot+tar ('ɒtə) *n.* a variant spelling of **attar.**
ot+ta+va (əʊ'tɑːvə) *n.* an interval of an octave. See **all' ottava.** [Italian: OCTAVE]
ot+ta+va ri·ma ('riːmə) *n. Prosody.* a stanza form consisting of eight iambic pentameter lines, rhyming a b a b a b c c. [Italian: eighth rhyme]
Ot+ta+wa ('ɒtəwə) *n.* **1.** the capital of Canada, in E Ontario on the Ottawa River: name changed from Bytown to Ottawa in 1854. Pop.: 302 341 (1971). **2.** a river in central Canada, rising in W Quebec and flowing west, then southeast to join the St. Lawrence River as its chief tributary at Montreal; forms the border between Quebec and Ontario for most of its length. Length: 1120 km (696 miles).
ot+ter ('ɒtə) *n., pl.* **+ters** *or* **+ter. 1.** any freshwater carnivorous musteline mammal of the subfamily *Lutrinae,* esp. *Lutra lutra* (**Eurasian otter**), typically having smooth fur, a streamlined body, and webbed feet. **2.** the fur of any of these animals. **3.** a type of fishing tackle consisting of a weighted board to which hooked and baited lines are attached. [Old English *otor;* related to Old Norse *otr,* Old High German *ottar*]
Ot+ter+burn ('ɒtəˌbɜːn) *n.* a village in NE England, in central Northumberland: scene of a battle (1388) in which the English, led by Hotspur, were defeated by the Scots.
ot+ter hound *n.* a dog of a breed used for otter hunting.
ot+ter shrew *n.* any small otter-like amphibious mammal, esp. *Potamogale velox,* of the family *Potamogalidae* of W and central Africa: order *Insectivora* (insectivores).

ot·to ('ɒtəʊ) *n.* another name for **attar.**

Ot·to (*German* 'ɔto) *n.* **Ru·dolf** ('ru:dɔlf). 1869–1937, German theologian: his best-known work is *The Idea of the Holy* (1923).

Ot·to I ('ɒtəʊ) *or* **O·tho I** *n.* called *the Great.* 912–73 A.D., king of Germany (936–73); Holy Roman Emperor (962–73).

Ot·to cy+cle *n.* an engine cycle used on four-stroke petrol engines (**Otto engines**) in which, ideally, combustion and rejection of heat both take place at constant volume. Compare **diesel cycle.** [C19: named after Nikolaus August *Otto* (1832–91), German engineer]

ot+to+man ('ɒtəmən) *n., pl.* **+mans. 1. a.** a low padded seat, usually armless, sometimes in the form of a chest. **b.** a cushioned footstool. **2.** a corded fabric. [C17: from French *ottomane,* feminine of OTTOMAN]

Ot+to+man ('ɒtəmən) *or* **Oth+man** *adj.* **1.** *History.* of or relating to the Ottomans or the Ottoman Empire. **2.** denoting or relating to the Turkish language. ~*n., pl.* **+mans. 3.** a member of a Turkish people who invaded the Near East in the late 13th century. [C17: from French, via Medieval Latin, from Arabic *Othmānī* Turkish, from Turkish *Othman* OSMAN I]

Ot+to+man Em+pire *n.* the former Turkish empire in Europe, Asia, and Africa, which lasted from the late 13th century until the end of World War I. Also called: **Turkish Empire.**

Ot·way ('ɒtweɪ) *n.* **Thom·as.** 1652–85, English dramatist, noted for *The Orphan* (1680) and *Venice Preserv'd* (1682).

O.U. *abbrev. for:* **1.** the Open University. **2.** Oxford University.

oua+ba+in ('wɑ:bɑ:ɪn) *n.* a poisonous white crystalline glucoside extracted from certain trees and used as a heart stimulant and, by some African tribes, on poison darts. Formula: $C_{29}H_{44}O_{12}.8H_2O$. [C19: from French *ouabaïo,* from Somali *waba yo* native name of tree]

Ouach·i+ta *or* **Wash·i+ta** ('wɒʃɪ,tɔ:) *n.* a river in the S central U.S., rising in the **Ouachita Mountains** and flowing east, south, and southeast into the Red River in E Louisiana. Length: 974 km (605 miles).

Oua+ga+dou+gou (,wɑ:gə'du:gu:) *n.* the capital of Upper Volta, on the central plateau: terminus of the railway from Abidjan (Ivory Coast). Pop.: 110 000 (1970 est.).

oua+na+niche (,wɑ:nə'ni:ʃ) *n.* a landlocked variety of the Atlantic salmon, *Salmo salar ouananiche,* found in lakes in SE Canada. [from Canadian French, from Montagnais *wananish,* diminutive of *wanans* salmon]

Ou·ban+gui (u:'bɑ:ŋgi:, ju:'bæŋgɪ) *n.* a variant spelling of **Ubangi.**

ou·bli+ette (,u:blɪ'ɛt) *n.* dungeon the only entrance to which is through the top. [C19: from French, from *oublier* to forget]

ouch[1] (aʊtʃ) *interj.* an exclamation of sharp sudden pain.

ouch[2] (aʊtʃ) *n. Archaic.* **1.** a brooch or clasp set with gems. **2.** the setting of a gem. [C15 *an ouch,* mistaken division of C14 *a nouche,* from Old French *nouche,* of Germanic origin; compare Old High German *nusca* buckle]

Oudh (aʊd) *n.* a region of N India, in central Uttar Pradesh: annexed by Britain in 1856 and a centre of the Indian Mutiny (1857–58); joined with Agra in 1877, becoming the United Provinces of Agra and Oudh in 1902, which were renamed Uttar Pradesh in 1950.

Oues+sant (wɛ'sã) *n.* the French name for **Ushant.**

ought[1] (ɔ:t) *vb.* (foll. by *to; takes an infinitive or implied infinitive*) used as an auxiliary **1.** to indicate duty or obligation: *you ought to pay your dues.* **2.** to express prudent expediency: *you ought to see him.* **3.** (usually with reference to future time) to express probability or expectation: *you ought to finish this work by Friday.* **4.** to express a desire or wish on the part of the speaker: *you ought to come next week.* [Old English *āhte,* past tense of *āgan* to OWE; related to Gothic *aihta*]

Usage. In careful English, *ought* is not used with *did* or *had. I ought not to do it,* not *I didn't ought to do it; I ought not to have done it,* not *I hadn't ought to have done it.*

ought[2] (ɔ:t) *n., adv.* a variant spelling of **aught**[1].

ought[3] (ɔ:t) *n.* a less common word for **nought** (zero). [C19: mistaken division of *a nought* as *an ought;* see NOUGHT]

Oui+ja ('wi:dʒə) *n. Trademark.* a board on which are marked the letters of the alphabet. Answers to questions are spelt out by a pointer or glass held by the fingertips of the participants, and are supposedly formed by spiritual forces. [C20: from French *oui* yes + German *ja* yes]

Ouj+da (u:dʒ'dɑ:) *n.* a city in NE Morocco, near the border with Algeria: frontier post. Pop.: 175 532 (1971).

Ou·lu ('aʊlʊ) *n.* an industrial city and port in W Finland, on the Gulf of Bothnia: university (1959). Pop.: 85 500 (1970). Swedish name: **Uleåborg.**

ounce[1] (aʊns) *n.* **1.** a unit of weight equal to one sixteenth of a pound (avoirdupois); 1 ounce is equal to 437.5 grains or 28.349 grams. Abbrev.: **oz. 2.** a unit of weight equal to one twelfth of a Troy or Apothecaries' pound; 1 ounce is equal to 480 grains or 31.103 grams. **3.** short for **fluid ounce. 4.** a small portion or amount. [C14: from Old French *unce,* from Latin *uncia* a twelfth; from *ūnus* one]

ounce[2] (aʊns) *n.* another name for **snow leopard.** [C18: from Old French *once,* by mistaken division of *lonce* as if *l'once,* from Latin LYNX]

our (aʊə) *determiner.* **1.** of, belonging to, or associated in some way with us: *our best vodka; our parents are good to us.* **2.** belonging to or associated with all people or people in general: *our nearest planet is Venus.* **3.** a formal word for *my* used by editors or other writers, and monarchs. **4.** *Informal.* (often sarcastic) used instead of *your: are our feet hurting?* **5.** *Brit. dialect.* belonging to the family of the speaker: *it's our Sandra's birthday tomorrow.* [Old English *ūre* (genitive plural), from US; related to Old French, Old Saxon *ūser,* Old High German *unsēr,* Gothic *unsara*]

-our *suffix forming nouns.* indicating state, condition, or activity: *behaviour; labour.* [in Old French *-eur,* from Latin *-or,* noun suffix]

Our Fa+ther *n.* another name for the **Lord's Prayer,** taken from its opening words.

Our La·dy *n.* a title given to the Virgin Mary.

ours (aʊəz) *pron.* **1.** something or someone belonging to or associated with us: *ours have blue tags.* **2. of ours.** belonging to or associated with us.

our+self (aʊə'sɛlf) *pron. Archaic.* a variant of **myself,** formerly used by monarchs or editors in formal contexts.

our+selves (aʊə'sɛlvz) *pron.* **1. a.** the reflexive form of *we* or *us.* **b.** (intensifier): *we ourselves will finish it.* **2.** (*preceded by a copula*) our usual selves: *we are ourselves when we're together.* **3.** *Not standard.* used instead of *we* or *us* in compound noun phrases: *other people and ourselves.*

Usage. See at **myself.**

-ous *suffix forming adjectives.* **1.** having or full of: *dangerous; spacious.* **2.** (in chemistry) indicating that an element is chemically combined in the lower of two possible valence states: *ferrous; stannous.* Compare **-ic** (sense 2). [from Old French, from Latin *-ōsus* or *-us,* Greek *-os,* adj. suffixes]

Ouse (u:z) *n.* **1.** Also called: **Great Ouse.** a river in E England, rising in Northamptonshire and flowing northeast to the Wash near King's Lynn; for the last 56 km (35 miles) follows mainly artificial channels. Length: 257 km (160 miles). **2.** a river in NE England, in Yorkshire, formed by the confluence of the Swale and Ure Rivers: flows southeast to the Humber. Length: 92 km (57 miles). **3.** a river in S England, rising in Sussex and flowing south to the English Channel. Length: 48 km (30 miles).

ou·sel ('u:zᵊl) *n.* a variant spelling of **ouzel.**

oust (aʊst) *vb.* (*tr.*) **1.** to eject; expel. **2.** *Property law.* to deprive (a person) of the possession of land, etc. [C16: from Anglo-Norman *ouster,* from Latin *obstāre* to withstand, from *ob-* against + *stāre* to stand]

oust+er ('aʊstə) *n. Property law.* the act of dispossessing of freehold property; eviction; ejection.

out (aʊt) *adv.* **1.** (*often used as a particle*) at or to a point beyond the limits of some location; outside: *get out at once.* **2.** (*particle*) out of consciousness: *she passed out at the sight of blood.* **3.** (*particle*) used to indicate a burst of activity as indicated by the verb: *fever broke out.* **4.** (*particle*) used to indicate obliteration of an object: *the graffiti was painted out.* **5.** (*particle*) used to indicate an approximate drawing or description: *sketch out; chalk out.* **6.** (*often used as a particle*) away from one's custody or ownership, esp. on hire: *to let out a cottage.* **7.** on sale or on view to the public: *the book is being brought out next May.* **8.** (of a young woman) in or into polite society: *Lucinda had a fabulous party when she came out.* **9.** (of a jury) withdrawn to consider a verdict in private. **10.** (*particle*) used to indicate exhaustion or extinction: *the sugar's run out; put the light out.* **11.** (*particle*) used to indicate a goal or object achieved at the end of the action specified by the verb: *he worked it out; let's fight it out, then!* **12.** (*preceded by a superlative*) existing: *the friendliest dog out.* **13.** an expression in signalling, radio, etc., to indicate the end of a transmission. **14. out of. a.** at or to a point outside: *out of his reach.* **b.** away from; not in: *stepping out of line; out of focus.* **c.** because of, motivated by: *doing it out of jealousy.* **d.** from (a material or source): *made out of plastic.* **e.** not or no longer having any of (a substance, material, etc.): *we're out of sugar.* **15. out to it.** *Austral. informal.* asleep or unconscious. ~*adj.* (*postpositive*). **16.** not or not any longer worth considering: *that plan is out because of the weather.* **17.** not allowed: *smoking on duty is out.* **18.** (*also prenominal*) not in vogue; unfashionable: *that sort of dress is out these days.* **19.** (of a fire or light) no longer burning or providing illumination: *the fire is out.* **20.** not working: *the radio's out.* **21.** unconscious: *he was out for two minutes.* **22.** not in; not at home: *call back later, they're out now.* **23.** desirous of or intent on (something or doing something): *I'm out for as much money as I can get.* **24.** Also: **out on strike.** on strike: *the machine shop is out.* **25.** (in several games and sports) denoting the state in which a player is caused to discontinue active participation, esp. in some specified role. **26.** used up; exhausted: *our supplies are completely out.* **27.** worn into holes: *this sweater is out at the elbows.* **28.** inaccurate, deficient, or discrepant: *out by six pence.* **29.** not in office or authority: *his party will be out at the election.* **30.** completed or concluded, as of time: *before the year is out.* **31.** (*also prenominal*) being out: *the out position on the dial.* ~*prep.* **32.** out of; out through: *he ran out the door.* **33.** *Archaic or dialect.* outside; beyond: *he comes from out our domain.* ~*interj.* **34. a.** an exclamation, usually peremptory, of dismissal, reproach, etc. **b.** (in wireless telegraphy) an expression used to signal that the speaker is signing off. **35. out with it.** a command to make something known immediately, without missing any details. ~*n.* **36.** *Chiefly U.S.* a method of escape from a place, difficult situation, punishment, etc. **37.** *Baseball.* an instance of the putting out of a batter; put-out. **38.** *Printing.* **a.** the omission of words, etc., from a printed text; lacuna. **b.** the words, etc., so omitted. **39. ins and outs.** See **in** (sense 28). ~*vb.* **40.** (*tr.*) to put or throw out. **41.** (*intr.*) to be made known or effective despite efforts to the contrary (esp. in the phrase **will out**): *the truth will out.* [Old English *ūt;* related to Old Saxon, Old Norse *ūt,* Old High German *ūz,* German *aus*]

out- *prefix.* **1.** excelling or surpassing in a particular action:

outlast; outlive. **2.** indicating an external location or situation away from the centre: *outpost; outpatient.* **3.** indicating emergence, an issuing forth, etc.: *outcrop; outgrowth.* **4.** indicating the result of an action: *outcome.*

out·age (ˈaʊtɪdʒ) *n.* **1.** a quantity of goods missing or lost after storage or shipment. **2.** a period of power failure, machine stoppage, etc.

out and a·way *adv.* by far.

out-and-out *adj.* (*prenominal*) thoroughgoing; complete.

out-and-out·er *n. Slang.* **1.** a thorough or thoroughgoing person or thing. **2.** a person or thing that is excellent of its kind.

out·a·sight (ˌaʊtəˈsaɪt) *or* **out-of-sight** *adj., interj. Informal.* another term for **far-out.**

out·back (ˈaʊtˌbæk) *n. Austral.* **a.** the remote bush country of Australia. **b.** (*as modifier*): *outback life.*

out·bal·ance (ˌaʊtˈbæləns) *vb.* (*tr.*) another word for **outweigh.**

out·bid (ˌaʊtˈbɪd) *vb.* **·bids, ·bid·ding, ·bid, ·bid·den** *or* **·bid.** (*tr.*) to bid higher than; outdo in bidding.

out·board (ˈaʊtˌbɔːd) *adj.* **1.** (of a boat's engine) portable, with its own propeller, and designed to be attached externally to the stern. Compare **inboard** (sense 1). **2.** in a position away from, or further away from, the centre line of a vessel or aircraft, esp. outside the hull or fuselage. *~adv.* **3.** away from the centre line of a vessel or aircraft, esp. outside the hull or fuselage. *~n.* **4.** an outboard motor. **5.** a boat fitted with an outboard motor.

out·bound (ˈaʊtˌbaʊnd) *adj.* going out; outward bound.

out·brave (ˌaʊtˈbreɪv) *vb.* (*tr.*) **1.** to surpass in bravery. **2.** to confront defiantly.

out·break (ˈaʊtˌbreɪk) *n.* a sudden, violent, or spontaneous occurrence, esp. of disease or strife.

out·breed (ˌaʊtˈbriːd) *vb.* **·breeds, ·breed·ing, ·bred. 1.** (*intr.*) *Anthropol.* to produce offspring through sexual relations outside a particular family or tribe. **2.** to breed (animals that are not closely related) or (of such animals) to be bred. —ˌ**out·ˈbreed·ing** *n.*

out·build·ing (ˈaʊtˌbɪldɪŋ) *n.* a building subordinate to but separate from a main building; outhouse.

out·burst (ˈaʊtˌbɜːst) *n.* **1.** a sudden and violent expression of emotion. **2.** an explosion or eruption.

out·cast (ˈaʊtˌkɑːst) *n.* **1.** a person who is rejected or excluded from a social group. **2.** a vagabond or wanderer. **3.** anything thrown out or rejected. *~adj.* **4.** rejected, abandoned, or discarded; cast out.

out·caste (ˈaʊtˌkɑːst) *n.* **1.** a person who has been expelled from a caste. **2.** a person having no caste. *~vb.* **3.** (*tr.*) to cause (someone) to lose his caste.

out·class (ˌaʊtˈklɑːs) *vb.* (*tr.*) **1.** to surpass in class, quality, etc. **2.** to defeat easily.

out·come (ˈaʊtˌkʌm) *n.* something that follows from an action, dispute, situation, etc.; result; consequence.

out·crop *n.* (ˈaʊtˌkrɒp). **1.** part of a rock formation or mineral vein that appears at the surface of the earth. **2.** an emergence; appearance. *~vb.* (ˌaʊtˈkrɒp), **·crops, ·crop·ping, ·cropped. 3.** (*intr.*) (of rock strata, mineral veins, etc.) to protrude through the surface of the earth. **4.** (*intr.*) another word for **crop out.**

out·cross *vb.* (ˌaʊtˈkrɒs). **1.** to breed (animals or plants of the same breed but different strains). *~n.* (ˈaʊtˌkrɒs). **2.** an animal or plant produced as a result of outcrossing. **3.** an act of outcrossing.

out·cry *n.* (ˈaʊtˌkraɪ), *pl.* **·cries. 1.** a widespread or vehement protest. **2.** clamour; uproar. *~vb.* (ˌaʊtˈkraɪ), **·cries, ·cry·ing, ·cried. 3.** (*tr.*) to cry louder or make more noise than (someone or something).

out·date (ˌaʊtˈdeɪt) *vb.* (*tr.*) (of something new) to cause (something else) to become old-fashioned or obsolete.

out·dat·ed (ˌaʊtˈdeɪtɪd) *adj.* old-fashioned or obsolete.

out·dis·tance (ˌaʊtˈdɪstəns) *vb.* (*tr.*) to leave far behind.

out·do (ˌaʊtˈduː) *vb.* **·does, ·do·ing, ·did, ·done.** (*tr.*) to surpass or exceed in performance or execution.

out·door (ˈaʊtˈdɔː) *adj.* (*prenominal*) Also: **out-of-door.** taking place, existing, or intended for use in the open air: *outdoor games; outdoor clothes.*

out·doors (ˌaʊtˈdɔːz) *adv.* **1.** Also: **out-of-doors.** in the open air; outside. *~n.* **2.** the world outside habitation.

out·er (ˈaʊtə) *adj.* (*prenominal*) **1.** being or located on the outside; external. **2.** further from the middle or central part. *~n.* **3.** *Archery.* **a.** the white outermost ring on a target. **b.** a shot that hits this ring. **4.** *Austral.* the unsheltered part of the spectator area at a sports ground. **5. on the outer.** *Austral.* excluded or neglected.

out·er bar *n.* (in England) a collective name for junior barristers who plead from outside the bar of the court. Compare **Queen's Counsel.**

out·er gar·ments *pl. n.* the garments that are worn over a person's other clothes.

Out·er Mon·go·li·a *n.* the former name (until 1924) of the **Mongolian People's Republic.**

out·er·most (ˈaʊtəˌməʊst) *adj.* furthest from the centre or middle; outmost.

out·er plan·et *n.* any of the planets Jupiter, Saturn, Uranus, Neptune, and Pluto, whose orbit lies outside the asteroid belt.

out·er space *n.* (*not in technical usage*) any region of space beyond the atmosphere of the earth.

out·face (ˌaʊtˈfeɪs) *vb.* (*tr.*) **1.** to face or stare down. **2.** to confront boldly or defiantly.

out·fall (ˈaʊtˌfɔːl) *n.* the end of a river, sewer, drain, etc., from which it discharges.

out·field (ˈaʊtˌfiːld) *n.* **1.** *Cricket.* the area of the field relatively far from the pitch; the deep. Compare **infield. 2.** *Baseball.* **a.** the area of the playing field beyond the lines connecting first, second, and third bases. **b.** the positions of the left fielder, centre fielder, and right fielder taken collectively. Compare **infield. 3.** *Agriculture.* farm land most distant from the farmstead. —ˈ**out·ˌfield·er** *n.*

out·fight·ing *n.* fighting at a distance and not at close range.

out·fit (ˈaʊtˌfɪt) *n.* **1.** a set of articles or equipment for a particular task, occupation, etc. **2.** a set of clothes, esp. a carefully selected one. **3.** *Informal.* any group or association regarded as a cohesive unit, such as a military company, business house, etc. **4.** the act of fitting out. *~vb.* **·fits, ·fit·ting, ·fit·ted. 5.** to furnish or be furnished with an outfit, equipment, etc.

out·fit·ter (ˈaʊtˌfɪtə) *n. Chiefly Brit.* **1.** a shop that sells men's clothes. **2.** a person who provides outfits.

out·flank (ˌaʊtˈflæŋk) *vb.* (*tr.*) **1.** to go around the flank of (an opposing army, etc.). **2.** to get the better of.

out·flow (ˈaʊtˌfləʊ) *n.* **1.** anything that flows out, such as liquid, money, ideas, etc. **2.** the amount that flows out. **3.** the act or process of flowing out.

out·foot (ˌaʊtˈfʊt) *vb.* (*tr.*) **1.** (of a boat) to go faster than (another boat). **2.** to surpass in running, dancing, etc.

out·fox (ˌaʊtˈfɒks) *vb.* (*tr.*) to surpass in guile or cunning.

out·gas (ˌaʊtˈgæs) *vb.* **·gas·ses, ·gas·sing, ·gassed.** to undergo or cause to undergo the removal of adsorbed or absorbed gas from solids, often by heating in a vacuum.

out·gen·er·al (ˌaʊtˈdʒɛnərəl) *vb.* **·als, ·al·ling, ·alled** *or U.S.* **·als, ·al·ing, ·aled.** (*tr.*) to surpass in generalship.

out·go *vb.* (ˌaʊtˈgəʊ), **·goes, ·go·ing, ·went, ·gone. 1.** (*tr.*) to exceed or outstrip. *~n.* (ˈaʊtˌgəʊ). **2.** cost; outgoings; outlay. **3.** something that goes out; outflow.

out·go·ing (ˈaʊtˌgəʊɪŋ) *adj.* **1.** departing; leaving. **2.** leaving or retiring from office: *the outgoing chairman.* **3.** friendly and sociable. *~n.* **4.** the act of going out.

out·go·ings (ˈaʊtˌgəʊɪŋz) *pl. n.* necessary expenditure.

out-group *n. Sociol.* persons excluded from an in-group.

out·grow (ˌaʊtˈgrəʊ) *vb.* **·grows, ·grow·ing, ·grew, ·grown.** (*tr.*) **1.** to grow too large for (clothes, shoes, etc.). **2.** to lose (a habit, idea, reputation, etc.) in the course of development or time. **3.** to grow larger or faster than.

out·growth (ˈaʊtˌgrəʊθ) *n.* **1.** a thing growing out of a main body. **2.** a development, result, or consequence. **3.** the act of growing out.

out·gun (ˌaʊtˈgʌn) *vb.* (*tr.*) **·guns, ·gun·ning, ·gunned. 1.** to surpass in fire power. **2.** to surpass in shooting. **3.** *Informal.* to surpass or excel.

out·haul (ˈaʊtˌhɔːl) *n. Nautical.* a line or cable for tightening the foot of a sail by hauling the clew out along the boom or yard.

out-Her·od *vb.* (*tr.*) to surpass in evil, excesses, or cruelty. [C17: originally *out-Herod Herod,* from Shakespeare's *Hamlet* (act 3, scene 2)]

out·house (ˈaʊtˌhaʊs) *n.* a building near to, but separate from, a main building; outbuilding.

out·ing (ˈaʊtɪŋ) *n.* a short outward and return journey; trip; excursion.

out·jock·ey (ˌaʊtˈdʒɒkɪ) *vb.* (*tr.*) to outwit by deception.

out·land *adj.* (ˈaʊtˌlænd, -lənd). **1.** outlying or distant. **2.** *Archaic.* foreign; alien. *~n.* (ˈaʊtˌlænd). **3.** (*usually pl.*) the outlying areas of a country or region.

out·land·er (ˈaʊtˌlændə) *n.* a foreigner or stranger.

out·land·ish (aʊtˈlændɪʃ) *adj.* **1.** grotesquely unconventional in appearance, habits, etc. **2.** *Archaic.* foreign. —**out·ˈland·ish·ly** *adv.* —**out·ˈland·ish·ness** *n.*

out·law (ˈaʊtˌlɔː) *n.* **1.** (formerly) a person excluded from the law and deprived of its protection. **2.** any fugitive from the law, esp. a habitual transgressor. **3.** a wild or untamed beast. *~vb.* (*tr.*) **4.** to put (a person) outside the law and deprive of its protection. **5.** (in the U.S.) to deprive (a contract, etc.) of legal force. **6.** to ban.

out·law·ry (ˈaʊtˌlɔːrɪ) *n., pl.* **·ries. 1.** the act of outlawing or the state of being outlawed. **2.** disregard for the law.

out·lay *n.* (ˈaʊtˌleɪ). **1.** an expenditure of money, effort, etc. *~vb.* (ˌaʊtˈleɪ), **·lays, ·lay·ing, ·laid. 2.** (*tr.*) to spend (money, etc.).

out·let (ˈaʊtlɛt, -lɪt) *n.* **1.** an opening or vent permitting escape or release. **2.** a means for release or expression of emotion, creative energy, etc. **3. a.** a market for a product or service. **b.** a commercial establishment retailing the goods of a particular producer or wholesaler. **4. a.** a channel that drains a body of water. **b.** the mouth of a river. **5.** a point in a wiring system from which current can be taken to supply electrical devices. **6.** *Anatomy.* the beginning or end of a passage, esp. the lower opening of the pelvis (**pelvic outlet**).

ˌ**out·ˈact** *vb.*
ˌ**out·ˈbar·gain** *vb.*
ˌ**out·ˈbluff** *vb.*
ˌ**out·ˈboast** *vb*
ˌ**out·ˈbox** *vb.*
ˌ**out·ˈdance** *vb.*
ˌ**out·ˈdare** *vb.*
ˌ**out·ˈdodge** *vb.*
ˌ**out·ˈdrink** *vb.,* **·drinks, ·drink·ing, ·drank, ·drunk.**
ˌ**out·ˈeat** *vb.,* **·eats, ·eat·ing, ·ate, ·eat·en.**
ˌ**out·ˈfight** *vb.,* **·fights, ·fight·ing, ·fought.**
ˌ**out·ˈfly** *vb.,* **·flies, ·fly·ing, ·flew, ·flown.**
ˌ**out·ˈguess** *vb.*
ˌ**out·ˈhit** *vb.,* **·hits, ·hit·ting, ·hit.**
ˌ**out·ˈjump** *vb.*

out·li·er ('aʊtˌlaɪə) *n.* **1.** an outcrop of rocks that is entirely surrounded by older rocks. **2.** a person, thing, or part situated away from a main or related body. **3.** a person who lives away from his place of work, duty, etc.

out·line ('aʊtˌlaɪn) *n.* **1.** a preliminary or schematic plan, draft, account, etc. **2.** (*usually pl.*) the important features of an argument, theory, work, etc. **3.** the line by which an object or figure is or appears to be bounded. **4. a.** a drawing or manner of drawing consisting only of external lines. **b.** (*as modifier*): *an outline map.* ~*vb.* (*tr.*) **5.** to draw or display the outline of. **6.** to give the main features or general idea of.

out·live (ˌaʊt'lɪv) *vb.* (*tr.*) **1.** to live longer than (someone). **2.** to live beyond a date or period: *he outlived the century.* **3.** to live through (an experience).

out·look ('aʊtˌlʊk) *n.* **1.** a mental attitude or point of view. **2.** the probable or expected condition or outcome of something: *the weather outlook.* **3.** the view from a place. **4.** view or prospect. **5.** the act or state of looking out.

out·ly·ing ('aʊtˌlaɪɪŋ) *adj.* distant or remote from the main body or centre, as of a town or region.

out·man (ˌaʊt'mæn) *vb.* **·mans, ·man·ning, ·manned.** (*tr.*) **1.** to surpass in manpower. **2.** to surpass in manliness.

out·ma·noeu·vre *or U.S.* **out·ma·neu·ver** (ˌaʊtmə'nu:və) *vb.* (*tr.*) to secure a strategic advantage over by skilful manoeuvre.

out·mod·ed (ˌaʊt'məʊdɪd) *adj.* **1.** no longer fashionable or widely accepted. **2.** no longer practical or usable. —**ˌout·'mod·ed·ly** *adv.* —**ˌout·'mod·ed·ness** *n.*

out·most ('aʊtˌməʊst) *adj.* another word for **outermost.**

out·ness ('aʊtnɪs) *n.* **1.** the state or quality of being external. **2.** outward expression.

out·num·ber (ˌaʊt'nʌmbə) *vb.* (*tr.*) to exceed in number.

out of bounds *adj.* (*postpositive*), *adv.* **1.** (often foll. by *to*) not to be entered (by); barred (to): *out of bounds to civilians.* **2.** outside specified or prescribed limits.

out of date *adj.* (**out-of-date** *when prenominal*), *adv.* no longer valid, current, or fashionable; outmoded.

out-of-door *adj.* (*prenominal*) another word for **outdoor.**

out-of-doors *adv., adj.* (*postpositive*) in the open air; outside. Also: **outdoors.**

out of pock·et *adj.* (**out-of-pock·et** *when prenominal*). **1.** (*postpositive*) having lost money, as in a commercial enterprise. **2.** without money to spend. **3.** (*prenominal*) (of expenses) unbudgeted and paid for in cash.

out-of-the-way *adj.* (*prenominal*) **1.** distant from more populous areas. **2.** uncommon or unusual.

out·pa·tient ('aʊtˌpeɪʃənt) *n.* a non-resident hospital patient. Compare **inpatient.**

out·point (ˌaʊt'pɔɪnt) *vb.* (*tr.*) **1.** to score more points than. **2.** *Nautical.* to sail closer to the wind (point higher) than (another sailing vessel).

out·port ('aʊtˌpɔ:t) *n.* *Chiefly Brit.* a subsidiary port built in deeper water than the original port.

out·por·ter ('aʊtˌpɔ:tə) *n.* *Canadian.* an inhabitant or native of a Newfoundland outport.

out·post ('aʊtˌpəʊst) *n.* **1.** *Military.* **a.** a position stationed at a distance from the area occupied by a major formation. **b.** the troops assigned to such a position. **2.** an outlying settlement or position. **3.** a limit or frontier.

out·pour *n.* ('aʊtˌpɔ:). **1.** the act of flowing or pouring out. **2.** something that pours out. ~*vb.* (ˌaʊt'pɔ:). **3.** to pour or cause to pour out freely or rapidly.

out·pour·ing ('aʊtˌpɔ:rɪŋ) *n.* **1.** a passionate or exaggerated outburst; effusion. **2.** another word for **outpour** (senses 1, 2).

out·put ('aʊtˌpʊt) *n.* **1.** the act of production or manufacture. **2.** the amount produced, as in a given period: *a high weekly output.* **3.** the material produced, manufactured, yielded, etc. **4.** *Electronics.* **a.** the power, voltage, or current delivered by a circuit or component. **b.** the point at which the signal is delivered. **5.** the power, energy, or work produced by an engine or a system. **6.** *Computer technol.* **a.** the information produced by a computer. **b.** the operations and devices involved in producing this information. See also **input/output. 7.** (*modifier*) of or relating to electronic, computer, or other output: *output signal; output device.*

out·rage ('aʊtˌreɪdʒ) *n.* **1.** a wantonly vicious or cruel act. **2.** a gross violation of decency, morality, honour, etc. **3.** profound indignation, anger, or hurt, caused by such an act. ~*vb.* (*tr.*) **4.** to cause profound indignation, anger, or resentment in. **5.** to offend grossly (feelings, decency, human dignity, etc.). **6.** to commit an act of wanton viciousness, cruelty, or indecency on. **7.** a euphemistic word for **rape**[1]. [C13 (meaning: excess): via French from *outré* beyond, from Latin *ultrā*]

out·ra·geous (aʊt'reɪdʒəs) *adj.* **1.** being or having the nature of an outrage. **2.** grossly offensive to decency, authority, etc. **3.** violent or unrestrained in behaviour or temperament. **4.** extravagant or immoderate. —**out·'ra·geous·ly** *adv.* —**out·'ra·geous·ness** *n.*

out·rank (ˌaʊt'ræŋk) *vb.* (*tr.*) **1.** to be of higher rank than. **2.** to take priority over.

ou·tré *French.* (u'tre) *adj.* deviating from what is usual or proper. [past participle of *outrer* to pass beyond]

out·reach *vb.* (ˌaʊt'ri:tʃ). **1.** (*tr.*) to surpass in reach. **2.** (*tr.*) to go beyond. **3.** to reach or cause to reach out. ~*n.* ('aʊtˌri:tʃ). **4.** the act or process of reaching out. **5.** the length or extent of reach.

out·re·lief *n.* *Brit.* (formerly) money given to poor people not living in a workhouse.

out·ride (ˌaʊt'raɪd) *vb.* **·rides, ·rid·ing, ·rode, ·rid·den.** (*tr.*) **1.** to outdo by riding faster, farther, or better than. **2.** (of a vessel) to ride out (a storm). ~*n.* **3.** *Prosody, rare.* an extra unstressed syllable within a metrical foot.

out·rid·er ('aʊtˌraɪdə) *n.* **1.** a person who goes ahead of a car, group of people, etc., to ensure a clear passage. **2.** a person who goes in advance to investigate, discover a way, etc.; scout. **3.** a person who rides in front of or beside a carriage, esp. as an attendant or guard. **4.** *U.S.* a mounted herdsman.

out·rig·ger ('aʊtˌrɪgə) *n.* **1.** a framework for supporting a pontoon outside and parallel to the hull of a boat to provide stability. **2.** a boat equipped with such a framework, esp. one of the canoes of the South Pacific. **3.** any projecting framework attached to a boat, aircraft, building, etc., to act as a support. **4.** *Rowing.* another name for **rigger** (sense 2).

out·right ('aʊtˌraɪt) *adj.* (*prenominal*) **1.** without qualifications or limitations: *outright ownership.* **2.** complete; total: *an outright lie.* **3.** straightforward; direct: *an outright manner.* ~*adv.* **4.** without restrictions: *buy outright.* **5.** without reservation or concealment: *ask outright.* **6.** instantly: *he was killed outright.* **7.** *Obsolete.* straight ahead or out.

out·run (ˌaʊt'rʌn) *vb.* **·runs, ·run·ning, ·ran, ·run.** (*tr.*) **1.** to run faster, farther, or better than. **2.** to escape from by or as if by running. **3.** to go beyond; exceed.

out·run·ner ('aʊtˌrʌnə) *n.* **1.** an attendant who runs in front of a carriage, etc. **2.** the leading dog in a sled team.

out·rush ('aʊtˌrʌʃ) *n.* a flowing or rushing out.

out·sell (ˌaʊt'sɛl) *vb.* **·sells, ·sell·ing, ·sold.** to sell or be sold in greater quantities than.

out·sert ('aʊtˌsɜ:t) *n.* another word for **wrapround** (sense 4). [C20: based on INSERT]

out·set ('aʊtˌsɛt) *n.* a start; beginning (esp. in the phrase **from** (*or* **at**) **the outset**).

out·shine (ˌaʊt'ʃaɪn) *vb.* **·shines, ·shin·ing, ·shone. 1.** (*tr.*) to shine more brightly than. **2.** (*tr.*) to surpass in excellence, beauty, wit, etc. **3.** (*intr.*) *Rare.* to emit light.

out·shoot *vb.* (ˌaʊt'ʃu:t), **·shoots, ·shoot·ing, ·shot. 1.** (*tr.*) to surpass or excel in shooting. **2.** to go or extend beyond (something). ~*n.* ('aʊtˌʃu:t). **3.** a thing that projects or shoots out. **4.** the act or state of shooting out or protruding.

out·side *prep.* (ˌaʊt'saɪd) **1.** (sometimes foll. by *of*) on or to the exterior of: *outside the house.* **2.** beyond the limits of: *outside human comprehension.* **3.** apart from; other than: *no-one knows outside you and me.* ~*adj.* ('aʊtˌsaɪd). **4.** (*prenominal*) situated on the exterior: *an outside lavatory.* **5.** remote; unlikely: *an outside chance.* **6.** not a member of. **7.** the greatest possible or probable (prices, odds, etc.). ~*adv.* (ˌaʊt'saɪd). **8.** outside a specified thing or place; out of doors. **9.** *Slang.* not in prison. ~*n.* ('aʊt'saɪd). **10.** the external side or surface: *the outside of the garage.* **11.** the external appearance or aspect. **12.** the exterior or outer part of something. **13.** (of a path, pavement, etc.) the side nearest the road or away from a wall or building. **14.** *Sport.* an outside player, as in football. **15.** (*pl.*) the outer sheets of a ream of paper. **16.** *Canadian.* (in the north) the settled parts of Canada. **17. at the outside.** *Informal.* at the most or at the greatest extent: *two days at the outside.* **18. outside in.** See **inside out.**

Usage. In careful usage, *outside* and *inside* are preferred to *outside of* and *inside of*: *she waits outside* (not *outside of*) *the school.*

out·side broad·cast *n.* *Radio, television.* a broadcast not made from a studio.

out·sid·er (ˌaʊt'saɪdə) *n.* **1.** a person or thing excluded from or not a member of a set, group, etc. **2.** a contestant, esp. a horse, thought unlikely to win in a race. **3.** *Canadian.* a person who does not live in the arctic regions.

out·side work *n.* work done off the premises of a business.

out sis·ter *n.* a member of a community of nuns who performs tasks in the outside world on behalf of the community.

out·size ('aʊtˌsaɪz) *adj.* **1.** Also: **out·sized.** very large or larger than normal: *outsize tomatoes.* ~*n.* **2.** something outsize, such as a garment or person. **3.** (*modifier*) relating to or dealing in outsize clothes: *an outsize shop.*

out·skirts ('aʊtˌskɜ:ts) *pl. n.* (*sometimes sing.*) outlying or bordering areas, districts, etc., as of a city.

out·smart (ˌaʊt'smɑ:t) *vb.* (*tr.*) *Informal.* to get the better of; outwit.

out·sole ('aʊtˌsəʊl) *n.* the outermost sole of a shoe.

out·span *South African.* ~*n.* ('aʊtˌspæn). **1.** an area on a farm kept available for travellers to rest and refresh animals, etc. **2.** the act of unharnessing or unyoking. ~*vb.* ('aʊt'spæn), **·spans, ·span·ning, ·spanned. 3.** to unharness or unyoke (animals). [C19: partial translation of Afrikaans *uitspan*, from *uit* out + *spannen* to stretch]

out·spo·ken (ˌaʊt'spəʊkən) *adj.* **1.** candid or bold in speech. **2.** said or expressed with candour or boldness.

out·spread *vb.* (ˌaʊt'sprɛd), **·spreads, ·spread·ing, ·spread. 1.** to spread out or cause to spread out. ~*adj.* ('aʊt'sprɛd). **2.** spread or stretched out. **3.** scattered or diffused widely. ~*n.* ('aʊtˌsprɛd). **4.** a spreading out.

ˌout·'last *vb.*
ˌout·'laugh *vb.*
ˌout·'live *vb.*
ˌout·'match *vb.*
ˌout·'pace *vb.*
ˌout·per·'form *vb.*
ˌout·'play *vb.*
ˌout·pro·'duce *vb.*
ˌout·'race *vb.*
ˌout·'range *vb.*
ˌout·'ri·val *vb.*, **·vals, ·val·ling, ·valled** *or U.S.* **·vals, ·valing, ·valed.**
ˌout·'root *vb.*
ˌout·'sing *vb.*, **·sings, ·sing·ing, ·sang, ·sung.**

out+stand (ˌaʊtˈstænd) *vb.* **+stands, +stand+ing, +stood. 1.** (*intr.*) to be outstanding or excel. **2.** (*intr.*) *Nautical.* to stand out to sea. **3.** (*tr.*) *Archaic.* to last beyond.

out+stand+ing (ˌaʊtˈstændɪŋ) *adj.* **1.** superior; excellent; distinguished. **2.** prominent, remarkable, or striking. **3.** still in existence; unsettled, unpaid, or unresolved. **4.** (of shares, bonds, etc.) issued and sold. **5.** projecting or jutting upwards or outwards.

out+sta+tion (ˈaʊtˌsteɪʃən) *n.* **1.** a station or post in a remote or unsettled region. *~adv.* **2.** (in Malaysia) away from (the speaker's) town or area.

out+stay (ˌaʊtˈsteɪ) *vb.* (*tr.*) **1.** to stay longer than. **2.** to stay too long. **3. outstay one's welcome.** See **overstay** (sense 3).

out+stretch (ˌaʊtˈstrɛtʃ) *vb.* (*tr.*) **1.** to extend or expand; stretch out. **2.** to stretch or extend beyond.

out+strip (ˌaʊtˈstrɪp) *vb.* **+strips, +strip+ping, +stripped.** (*tr.*) **1.** to surpass in a sphere of activity, competition, etc. **2.** to be or grow greater than. **3.** to go faster than and leave behind.

out+swing (ˈaʊtˌswɪŋ) *n. Cricket.* the movement of a bowled ball from leg to off through the air. Compare **inswing.** —ˈ**out+ˌswing+er** *n.*

out+think (ˌaʊtˈθɪŋk) *vb.* **+thinks, +think+ing, +thought.** (*tr.*) **1.** to outdo in thinking. **2.** to outwit.

out tray *n.* (in an office, etc.) a tray for outgoing correspondence, documents, etc.

out+turn (ˈaʊtˌtɜːn) *n.* a rare word for **output** (sense 2).

out+vote (ˌaʊtˈvəʊt) *vb.* (*tr.*) to defeat by a majority of votes.

out+ward (ˈaʊtwəd) *adj.* **1.** of or relating to what is apparent or superficial. **2.** of or relating to the outside of the body. **3.** belonging or relating to the external, as opposed to the mental, spiritual, or inherent. **4.** of, relating to, or directed towards the outside or exterior. **5.** (of a ship, part of a voyage, etc.) leaving for a particular destination. **6. the outward man. a.** *Theol.* the body as opposed to the soul. **b.** *Facetious.* clothing. *~adv.* **7.** (of a ship) away from port. **8.** a variant of **outwards.** *~n.* **9.** the outward part; exterior. —ˈ**out+ward+ness** *n.*

Out+ward Bound move+ment *n. Brit.* a scheme to provide adventure training for young people.

out+ward+ly (ˈaʊtwədlɪ) *adv.* **1.** in outward appearance: *outwardly she looked calm.* **2.** with reference to the outside or outer surface; externally.

out+wards (ˈaʊtwədz) *or* **out+ward** *adv.* towards the outside; out.

out+wash (ˈaʊtˌwɒʃ) *n.* a mass of gravel, sand, etc., carried and deposited by the water derived from melting glaciers.

out+wear (ˌaʊtˈwɛə) *vb.* **+wears, +wear+ing, +wore, +worn.** (*tr.*) **1.** to use up or destroy by wearing. **2.** to last or wear longer than. **3.** to outlive, outgrow, or develop beyond. **4.** to deplete or exhaust in strength, determination, etc.

out+weigh (ˌaʊtˈweɪ) *vb.* (*tr.*) **1.** to prevail over; overcome: *his desire outweighed his discretion.* **2.** to be more important or significant than. **3.** to be heavier than.

out+wit (ˌaʊtˈwɪt) *vb.* **+wits, +wit+ting, +wit+ted.** (*tr.*) **1.** to get the better of by cunning or ingenuity. **2.** *Archaic.* to be of greater intelligence than.

out+with (ˈaʊtˌwɪθ) *prep. Scot.* outside.

out+work *n.* (ˈaʊtˌwɜːk). **1.** (*often pl.*) defences which lie outside main defensive works. **2.** work performed away from the factory, office, etc., by which it has been commissioned. *~vb.* (ˌaʊtˈwɜːk), **+works, +work+ing, +worked** *or* **+wrought.** (*tr.*) **3.** to work better, harder, etc., than. **4.** to work out to completion. —ˈ**out+ˌwork+er** *n.*

ou·zel *or* **ou·sel** (ˈuːzᵊl) *n.* **1.** short for **ring ouzel** or **water ouzel. 2.** an archaic name for the (European) **blackbird.** [Old English *ōsle,* related to Old High German *amsala* (German *Amsel*), Latin *merula* MERLE]

ou·zo (ˈuːzəʊ) *n.* a strong aniseed-flavoured spirit from Greece. [Modern Greek *ouzon,* of obscure origin]

o·va (ˈəʊvə) *n.* the plural of **ovum.**

o·val (ˈəʊvᵊl) *adj.* **1.** having the shape of an ellipse or ellipsoid. *~n.* **2.** anything that is oval in shape, such as a sports ground. [C16: from Medieval Latin *ōvālis,* from Latin *ōvum* egg] —ˈ**o·val+ly** *adv.* —ˈ**o·val+ness** *or* **o·val+i·ty** (əʊˈvælɪtɪ) *n.*

O·val (ˈəʊvᵊl) *n.* **the.** a cricket ground in central London, in the borough of Lambeth.

o·vals of Cas·si·ni (kəˈsiːnɪ) *pl. n. Maths.* the locus of a point *x,* whose distance from two fixed points, *a* and *b,* is such that $|x-a||x-b|$ is a constant. [C18: named after J. D. *Cassini* (1625–1712), Italian-French astronomer and mathematician]

O·vam+bo (əʊˈvæmbəʊ, ɔːˈvambɔː) *n.* **1.** (*pl.* **+bo** *or* **+bos**) a member of a mixed Hottentot and Negroid people of southern Africa, living chiefly in N South West Africa: noted for their skill in metal work. **2.** the language of this people, belonging to the Bantu group of the Niger-Congo family.

o·var·i·ec·to·my (əʊˌvɛərɪˈɛktəmɪ) *n., pl.* **+mies.** *Surgery.* another name for **oophorectomy.**

o·var·i·ot·o·my (əʊˌvɛərɪˈɒtəmɪ) *n., pl.* **+mies.** surgical incision into an ovary. Compare **oophorectomy.**

o·va+ri+tis (ˌəʊvəˈraɪtɪs) *n.* inflammation of an ovary; oophoritis.

o·va+ry (ˈəʊvərɪ) *n., pl.* **+ries. 1.** either of the two female reproductive organs, which produce ova and secrete oestrogen hormones. **2.** the corresponding organ in vertebrate and invertebrate animals. **3.** *Botany.* the hollow basal region of a carpel containing one or more ovules. In some plants the carpels are united to form a single compound ovary. [C17: from New Latin *ōvārium,* from Latin *ōvum* egg] —**o·var+i·an** (əʊˈvɛərɪən) *adj.*

o·vate (ˈəʊveɪt) *adj.* **1.** shaped like an egg. **2.** (esp. of a leaf) shaped like the longitudinal section of an egg, with the broader end at the base. Compare **obovate.** [C18: from Latin *ōvātus* egg-shaped; see OVUM] —ˈ**o·vate+ly** *adv.*

o·va+tion (əʊˈveɪʃən) *n.* **1.** an enthusiastic reception, esp. one of prolonged applause: *a standing ovation.* **2.** a victory procession less glorious than a triumph awarded to a Roman general. [C16: from Latin *ovātiō* rejoicing, from *ovāre* to exult] —**o·ˈva+tion+al** *adj.*

ov·en (ˈʌvᵊn) *n.* **1.** an enclosed heated compartment or receptacle for baking or roasting food. **2.** a similar device, usually lined with a refractory material, used for drying substances, firing ceramics, heat-treating, etc. [Old English *ofen;* related to Old High German *ofan,* Old Norse *ofn*] —ˈ**ov·en-ˌlike** *adj.*

ov·en+bird (ˈʌvᵊnˌbɜːd) *n.* **1.** any of numerous small brownish South American passerine birds of the family *Furnariidae* that build oven-shaped clay nests. **2.** a common North American warbler, *Seiurus aurocapillus,* that has an olive-brown striped plumage with an orange crown and builds a cup-shaped nest on the ground.

ov·en-read·y *adj.* (of various foods) bought already prepared so that they are ready to be cooked in the oven.

ov·en+ware (ˈʌvᵊnˌwɛə) *n.* heat-resistant dishes in which food can be both cooked and served.

o·ver (ˈəʊvə) *prep.* **1.** directly above; on the top of; via the top or upper surface of: *over one's head.* **2.** on or to the other side of: *over the river.* **3.** during; through, or throughout (a period of time). **4.** in or throughout all parts of: *to travel over England.* **5.** throughout the whole extent of: *over the racecourse.* **6.** above; in preference to: *I like that over everything else.* **7.** by the agency of (an instrument of telecommunication): *we heard it over the radio.* **8.** more than: *over a century ago.* **9.** on the subject of; about: *an argument over nothing.* **10.** while occupied in: *discussing business over golf.* **11.** having recovered from the effects of: *she's not over that last love affair yet.* **12. over and above.** added to; in addition to: *he earns a large amount over and above his salary.* *~adv.* **13.** in a state, condition, situation, or position that is or has been placed or put over something: *to climb over.* **14.** (*particle*) so as to cause to fall: *knocking over a policeman.* **15.** at or to a point across intervening space, water, etc.: *come over and see us; over in America.* **16.** throughout a whole area: *the world over.* **17.** (*particle*) from beginning to end, usually cursorily: *to read a document over.* **18.** throughout a period of time: *stay over for this week.* **19.** (esp. in signalling and radio) it is now your turn to speak, act, etc. **20.** more than is expected or usual: *not over well.* **21. over again.** once more. **22. over against. a.** opposite to. **b.** contrasting with. **23. over and over.** (often followed by **again**) repeatedly. **24. over the odds.** in addition, esp. when not expected. *~adj.* **25.** (*postpositive*) finished; no longer in progress: *is the concert over yet?* *~adv., adj.* **26.** remaining; surplus (often in the phrase **left over**). *~n.* **27.** *Cricket.* a set of six balls (eight in Australia) bowled by a bowler from the same end of the pitch. [Old English *ofer;* related to Old High German *ubir, obar,* Old Norse *yfir,* Latin *super,* Greek *huper*]

o·ver- *prefix.* **1.** excessive or excessively; beyond an agreed or desirable limit: *overcharge; overdue; oversimplify.* **2.** indicating superior rank: *overseer.* **3.** indicating location or movement above: *overhang.* **4.** indicating movement downwards: *overthrow.*

o·ver+a·chieve (ˌəʊvərəˈtʃiːv) *vb.* (*intr.*) to perform better than expected or predicted, as in an examination. —ˌ**o·ver+a·ˈchiev+er** *n.*

o·ver+act (ˌəʊvərˈækt) *vb.* to act or behave in an exaggerated manner, as in a theatrical production. Also: **overplay.**

o·ver+age (ˌəʊvərˈeɪdʒ) *adj.* beyond a specified age.

o·ver+all *adj.* (ˈəʊvərˌɔːl). **1.** (*prenominal*) from one end to the other. **2.** (*prenominal*) including or covering everything: *the overall cost.* *~adv.* (ˌəʊvərˈɔːl). **3.** in general; on the whole. *~n.* (ˈəʊvərˌɔːl). **4.** *Brit.* a protective work garment usually worn over ordinary clothes. **5.** (*pl.*) hard-wearing work trousers with a bib and shoulder-straps or jacket attached.

o·ver+arch (ˌəʊvərˈɑːtʃ) *vb.* (*tr.*) to form an arch over.

o·ver+arm (ˈəʊvərˌɑːm) *adj.* **1.** *Sport, esp. cricket.* bowled, thrown, or performed with the arm raised above the shoulder. *~adv.* **2.** with the arm raised above the shoulder.

o·ver+awe (ˌəʊvərˈɔː) *vb.* (*tr.*) to subdue, restrain, or overcome by affecting with a feeling of awe.

o·ver+bal+ance *vb.* (ˌəʊvəˈbæləns). **1.** to lose or cause to lose

ˌ**out+ˈsit** *vb.,* **+sits, +sit+ting, +sat.**
ˌ**out+ˈspeak** *vb.,* **+speaks, +speak+ing, +spoke, +spo+ken.**
ˌ**out+ˈstare** *vb.*
ˌ**out+ˈstep** *vb.*
ˌ**out+ˈtalk** *vb.*
ˌ**out+ˈva+lue** *vb.*
ˌ**out+ˈwalk** *vb.*
ˌ**o·ver+a·ˈbound** *vb.*
ˌ**o·ver+a·ˈbun+dance** *n.*
ˌ**o·ver+ac+ˈcen+tu+ˌate** *vb.*
ˌ**o·ver+ac+ˌcu+mu+ˈla+tion** *n.*
ˌ**o·ver+ˈac+tive** *adj.*
ˌ**o·ver+a·ˈdorned** *adj.*
ˌ**o·ver+ad+ˈvance** *vb.*
ˌ**o·ver+af+ˈfect** *vb.*
ˌ**o·ver+ag+ˈgres+sive** *adj.*
ˌ**o·ver+am+ˈbi+tious** *adj.*
ˌ**o·ver+am+ˈbi+tious+ly** *adv.*
ˌ**o·ver+ˈan+a+ˌlyse** *vb.*
ˌ**o·ver+ˈan+gry** *adj.*
ˌ**o·ver+ˈan+i+ˌmat+ed** *adj.*
ˌ**o·ver+ˈan+i+ˌmat+ed+ly** *adv.*
ˌ**o·ver+ˌan+i+ˈma+tion** *n.*
ˌ**o·ver+ˈanx+ious** *adj.*
ˌ**o·ver+ap+ˌpre+ci+ˈa+tion** *n.*
ˌ**o·ver+ap+ˈpre+ci+a+tive** *adj.*
ˌ**o·ver+ˌap+pre+ˈhen+sive** *adj.*
ˌ**o·ver+ˌap+pre+ˈhen+sive+ly** *adv.*
ˌ**o·ver+ˌap+pre+ˈhen+sive+ness** *n.*
ˌ**o·ver+ˌar+gu+ˈmen+ta+tive** *adj.*
ˌ**o·ver+as+ˈsert** *vb.*
ˌ**o·ver+as+ˈser+tion** *n.*
ˌ**o·ver+as+ˈser+tive** *adj.*
ˌ**o·ver+as+ˈser+tive+ly** *adv.*
ˌ**o·ver+as+ˈser+tive+ness** *n.*
ˌ**o·ver+as+ˈsess+ment** *n.*
ˌ**o·ver+as+ˈsured** *adj.*
ˌ**o·ver+at+ˈtached** *adj.*
ˌ**o·ver+at+ˈten+tive** *adj.*

balance. **2.** (*tr.*) another word for **outweigh.** ~*n.* (ˈəʊvəˌbæləns). **3.** excess of weight, value, etc.

o·ver+bear (ˌəʊvəˈbɛə) *vb.* **+bears, +bear+ing, +bore, +borne. 1.** (*tr.*) to dominate or overcome: *to overbear objections.* **2.** (*tr.*) to press or bear down with weight or physical force. **3.** to produce or bear (fruit, progeny, etc.) excessively.

o·ver+bear+ing (ˌəʊvəˈbɛərɪŋ) *adj.* **1.** domineering or dictatorial in manner or action. **2.** of particular or overriding importance or significance. —**ˌo·ver+ˈbear+ing+ly** *adv.*

o·ver+bid *vb.* (ˌəʊvəˈbɪd), **+bids, +bid+ding, +bid, +bid+den** *or* **+bid. 1.** (*intr.*) *Bridge.* to bid for more tricks than one can expect to win. **2.** to bid more than the value of (something). ~*n.* (ˈəʊvəˌbɪd). **3.** a bid higher than someone else's bid.

o·ver+bite (ˈəʊvəˌbaɪt) *n. Dentistry.* an extension of the upper front teeth over the lower front teeth when the mouth is closed. Also called: **vertical overlap.**

o·ver+blouse (ˈəʊvəˌblaʊz) *n.* a blouse designed to fit loosely over the waist or hips.

o·ver+blow (ˌəʊvəˈbləʊ) *vb.* **+blows, +blow+ing, +blew, +blown. 1.** *Music.* to blow into (a wind instrument) with greater force than normal in order to obtain the octave above the fundamental in the harmonic series. **2.** to blow (a wind instrument) or (of a wind instrument) to be blown too hard. **3.** to blow over, away, or across.

o·ver+blown (ˌəʊvəˈbləʊn) *adj.* **1.** overdone or excessive. **2.** bombastic; turgid: *overblown prose.* **3.** (of flowers, such as the rose) past the stage of full bloom.

o·ver+board (ˈəʊvəˌbɔːd) *adv.* **1.** from on board a vessel into the water. **2. go overboard.** *Informal.* **a.** to be extremely enthusiastic. **b.** to go to extremes. **3. throw overboard.** to reject or abandon.

o·ver+boot (ˈəʊvəˌbuːt) *n.* a protective boot worn over an ordinary boot or shoe.

o·ver+build (ˌəʊvəˈbɪld) *vb.* **+builds, +build+ing, +built.** (*tr.*) **1.** to build over or on top of. **2.** to erect too many buildings in (an area). **3.** to build too large or elaborately.

o·ver+bur+den *vb.* (ˌəʊvəˈbɜːdᵊn). **1.** (*tr.*) to load with excessive weight, work, etc. ~*n.* (ˈəʊvəˌbɜːdᵊn). **2.** an excessive burden or load. **3.** *Geology.* the sedimentary rock material that covers coal seams, mineral veins, etc. —**ˌo·ver+ˈbur+den+some** *adj.*

o·ver+call *Bridge.* ~*n.* (ˈəʊvəˌkɔːl). **1.** a bid higher than the preceding one. ~*vb.* (ˌəʊvəˈkɔːl). **2.** to bid higher than (an opponent).

o·ver+cap·i·tal+ize *or* **o·ver+cap·i·tal+ise** (ˌəʊvəˈkæpɪtəˌlaɪz) *vb.* (*tr.*) **1.** to provide or issue capital for (an enterprise) in excess of profitable investment opportunities. **2.** to estimate the capital value of (a company) at an unreasonably or unlawfully high level. **3.** to overestimate the market value of (property, etc.). —**ˌo·ver+ˌcap·i·tal·i+ˈza+tion** *or* **ˌo·ver+ˌcap·i·tal·i+ˈsa+tion** *n.*

o·ver+cast *adj.* (ˈəʊvəˌkɑːst). **1.** covered over or obscured, esp. by clouds. **2.** *Meteorol.* (of the sky) more than 95 per cent cloud-covered. **3.** gloomy or melancholy. **4.** sewn over by overcasting. ~*vb.* (ˌəʊvəˈkɑːst). **5.** to make or become overclouded or gloomy. **6.** to sew (an edge, as of a hem) with long stitches passing successively over the edge. ~*n.* (ˈəʊvəˌkɑːst). **7.** a covering, as of clouds or mist. **8.** *Meteorol.* the state of the sky when more than 95 per cent of it is cloud-covered. **9.** *Mining.* a crossing of two passages without an intersection.

o·ver+charge *vb.* (ˌəʊvəˈtʃɑːdʒ). **1.** to charge too much. **2.** (*tr.*) to fill or load beyond capacity. **3.** *Literary.* another word for **exaggerate.** ~*n.* (ˈəʊvəˌtʃɑːdʒ). **4.** an excessive price or charge. **5.** an excessive load.

o·ver+check (ˈəʊvəˌtʃɛk) *n.* **1.** a thin leather strap attached to a horse's bit to keep its head up. **2.** (in textiles) **a.** a checked pattern laid over another checked pattern. **b.** a fabric patterned in such a way.

o·ver+cloud (ˌəʊvəˈklaʊd) *vb.* **1.** to make or become covered with clouds. **2.** to make or become dark or dim.

o·ver+coat (ˈəʊvəˌkəʊt) *n.* a warm heavy coat worn over the outer clothes in cold weather.

o·ver+come (ˌəʊvəˈkʌm) *vb.* **+comes, +com+ing, +came, +come. 1.** (*tr.*) to get the better of in a conflict. **2.** (*often passive*) to render incapable or powerless by laughter, sorrow, exhaustion, etc.: *he was overcome by fumes.* **3.** (*tr.*) to surmount obstacles, objections, etc. **4.** (*intr.*) to be victorious.

o·ver+com+pen+sate (ˌəʊvəˈkɒmpənˌseɪt) *vb.* **1.** to compensate (a person or thing) excessively. **2.** (*intr.*) *Psychol.* to engage in overcompensation. —**ˌo·ver+ˌcom+pen+ˈsa+to·ry** *adj.*

o·ver+com+pen+sa+tion (ˌəʊvəˌkɒmpɛnˈseɪʃən) *n. Psychol.* an attempt to make up for a character trait by overexaggerating its opposite.

o·ver+crop (ˌəʊvəˈkrɒp) *vb.* **+crops, +crop+ping, +cropped.** (*tr.*) to exhaust (land) by excessive cultivation.

o·ver+de·vel+op (ˌəʊvədɪˈvɛləp) *vb.* (*tr.*) **1.** to develop too much or too far. **2.** *Photog.* to process (a film, plate, or print) in developer for more than the required time, at too great a concentration, etc. —**ˌo·ver+de·ˈvel+op+ment** *n.*

o·ver+do (ˌəʊvəˈduː) *vb.* **+does, +do+ing, +did, +done.** (*tr.*) **1.** to take or carry too far; do to excess. **2.** to exaggerate, overelaborate, or overplay. **3.** to cook or bake too long. **4. overdo it, things,** *etc.* to overtax one's strength, capacity, etc.

o·ver+dose *n.* (ˈəʊvəˌdəʊs). **1.** (esp. of drugs) an excessive dose. ~*vb.* (ˌəʊvəˈdəʊs). **2.** (*tr.*) to give an excessive dose to. —**ˌo·ver+ˈdos+age** *n.*

o·ver+draft (ˈəʊvəˌdrɑːft) *n.* **1.** a draft or withdrawal of money in excess of the credit balance on a bank account. **2.** the amount of money drawn or withdrawn thus.

o·ver+draught (ˈəʊvəˌdrɑːft) *n.* a current of air passed above a fire, as in a furnace.

o·ver+draw (ˌəʊvəˈdrɔː) *vb.* **+draws, +draw+ing, +drew, +drawn. 1.** to draw on (a bank account) in excess of the credit balance. **2.** (*tr.*) to strain or pull (a bow, etc.) too far. **3.** (*tr.*) to exaggerate in describing or telling.

o·ver+dress *vb.* (ˌəʊvəˈdrɛs). **1.** to dress (oneself or another) too elaborately or finely. ~*n.* (ˈəʊvəˌdrɛs). **2.** a dress that may be worn over a jumper, blouse, etc.

o·ver+drive *n.* (ˈəʊvəˌdraɪv). **1.** a very high gear in a motor vehicle used at high speeds to reduce wear and save fuel. ~*vb.* (ˌəʊvəˈdraɪv), **+drives, +driv+ing, +drove, +driv+en. 2.** (*tr.*) to drive too hard or too far; overwork or overuse.

o·ver+due (ˌəʊvəˈdjuː) *adj.* past the time specified, required, or preferred for arrival, occurrence, payment, etc.

o·ver+dye (ˌəʊvəˈdaɪ) *vb.* (*tr.*) **1.** to dye (a fabric, yarn, etc.) excessively. **2.** to dye for a second or third time with a different colour.

o·ver+es+ti+mate *vb.* (ˌəʊvəˈɛstɪˌmeɪt). **1.** (*tr.*) to value or estimate too highly. ~*n.* (ˌəʊvəˈɛstɪmɪt). **2.** an estimate that is too high. —**ˌo·ver+ˌes+ti+ˈma+tion** *n.*

o·ver+ex+pose (ˌəʊvərɪksˈpəʊz) *vb.* (*tr.*) **1.** to expose too much or for too long. **2.** *Photog.* to expose (a film, plate, or paper) for too long a period or with too bright a light.

o·ver+fall (ˈəʊvəˌfɔːl) *n.* **1.** a turbulent stretch of water caused by marine currents over an underwater ridge. **2.** a mechanism that allows excess water to escape from a dam or lock.

o·ver+flight (ˈəʊvəˌflaɪt) *n.* the flight of an aircraft over a specific area or territory.

o·ver+flow *vb.* (ˌəʊvəˈfləʊ), **+flows, +flow+ing, +flowed, +flown. 1.** to flow or run over (a limit, brim, bank, etc.). **2.** to fill or be filled beyond capacity so as to spill or run over. **3.** (*intr.; usually foll. by* with) to be filled with happiness, tears, etc. **4.** (*tr.*) to spread or cover over; flood or inundate. ~*n.* (ˈəʊvəˌfləʊ). **5.** overflowing matter, esp. liquid. **6.** any outlet that enables surplus liquid to be discharged or drained off, esp. one just below the top of a tank or cistern. **7.** the amount by which a limit, capacity, etc., is exceeded.

o·ver+fly (ˌəʊvəˈflaɪ) *vb.* **+flies, +fly+ing, +flew, +flown.** (*tr.*) to fly an aircraft over (a territory) or past (a point).

o·ver+fold (ˈəʊvəˌfəʊld) *n. Geology.* a fold in the form of an anticline in which one limb is more steeply inclined than the other.

ˌo·ver+at+ˈten+tive+ly *adv.*
ˌo·ver+at+ˈten+tive+ness *n.*
ˌo·ver+ˈbold *adj.*
ˌo·ver+ˈbrave *adj.*
ˌo·ver+ˈbulk·y *adj.*
ˌo·ver+ˈbur+den+some *adj.*
ˌo·ver+ˈbus·y *adj.*
ˌo·ver+ˈbuy *vb.*, **+buys, +buy+ing, +bought.**
ˌo·ver+ca+ˈpac+i·ty *n.*
ˌo·ver+ˈcare+ful *adj.*
ˌo·ver+ˈcas+u·al *adj.*
ˌo·ver+ˈcau+tious *adj.*
ˌo·ver+ˌcen+tral+i+ˈza+tion *or* **ˌo·ver+ˌcen+tral·i+ˈsa+tion** *n.*
ˌo·ver+ˈce+re+bral *adj.*
ˌo·ver+ˈciv+il *adj.*
ˌo·ver+ˈciv·i+ˌlize *or* **ˌo·ver+ˈciv·i+ˌlise** *vb.*
ˌo·ver+ˈcom+mon *adj.*
ˌo·ver+com+ˈpet·i+tive *adj.*
ˌo·ver+com+ˈpla+cen+cy *n.*
ˌo·ver+com+ˈpla+cent *adj.*
ˌo·ver+ˈcom+plex *adj.*
ˌo·ver+ˈcom+pli+ˌcate *vb.*
ˌo·ver+con+ˈcern *n.*
ˌo·ver+ˈcon+fi+dent *adj.*
ˌo·ver+ˌcon+sci+ˈen+tious *adj.*
ˌo·ver+con+ˈserv+a+tive *adj.*
ˌo·ver+con+ˈsid+er+ate *adj.*
ˌo·ver+con+ˈsume *vb.*
ˌo·ver+con+ˈsump+tion *n.*
ˌo·ver+ˈcook *vb.*
ˌo·ver+ˈcool *vb., adj.*
ˌo·ver+cor+ˈrect *adj., vb.*
ˌo·ver+cor+ˈrec+tion *n.*
ˌo·ver+ˈcost+ly *adj.*
ˌo·ver+ˈcrit·i+cal *adj.*
ˌo·ver+ˈcrit·i+ˌcize *or* **ˌo·ver+ˈcrit·i+ˌcise** *vb.*
ˌo·ver+ˈcrowd *vb.*
ˌo·ver+ˈcul+ti+ˌvate *vb.*
ˌo·ver+ˈcu+ri+ous *adj.*
ˌo·ver+ˈdec·o+ˌrate *vb.*
ˌo·ver+de+ˈfen+sive *adj.*
ˌo·ver+ˌdef+er+ˈen+tial *adj.*
ˌo·ver+de+ˈlib+er+ˌate *vb., adj.*
ˌo·ver+ˈdel·i+cate *adj.*
ˌo·ver+de+ˈpend+ent *adj.*
ˌo·ver+de+ˈsir+ous *adj.*
ˌo·ver+ˈde+tailed *adj.*
ˌo·ver+ˈdil·i+gent *adj.*
ˌo·ver+ˈdil·i+gent+ly *adv.*
ˌo·ver+di+ˈlute *vb.*
ˌo·ver+ˈdis+tant *adj.*
ˌo·ver+di+ˌver+si+fi+ˈca+tion *n.*
ˌo·ver+di+ˈver+si+ˌfy *vb.*, **+fies, +fy+ing, +fied.**
ˌo·ver+di+ˈver+si+ty *n.*
ˌo·ver+ˈdram·a+tize *or* **ˌo·ver+ˈdram·a+tise** *vb.*
ˌo·ver+ˈdrink *vb.*, **+drinks, +drink+ing, +drank, +drunk.**
ˌo·ver+ˈeag+er *adj.*
ˌo·ver+ˈear+nest *adj.*
ˌo·ver+ˈeat *vb.*, **+eats, +eat+ing, +ate, +eat+en.**
ˌo·ver+ˈed+u+ˌcate *vb.*
ˌo·ver+ef+ˈfu+sive *adj.*
ˌo·ver+e·ˈlab+o+rate *adj., vb.*
ˌo·ver+e·ˈlate *vb.*
ˌo·ver+em+ˈbel+lish *vb.*
ˌo·ver+em+ˈbroi+der *vb.*
ˌo·ver+e·ˈmo+tion+al *adj.*
ˌo·ver+ˈem+pha+sis *n.*
ˌo·ver+ˈem+pha+ˌsize *or* **ˌo·ver+ˈem+pha+ˌsise** *vb.*
ˌo·ver+em+ˈphat+ic *adj.*
ˌo·ver+ˌem+u+ˈla+tion *n.*
ˌo·ver+en+ˈthu+si+asm *n.*
ˌo·ver+en+ˌthu+si+ˈas+tic *adj.*
ˌo·ver+ex+ˈact+ing *adj.*
ˌo·ver+ex+ˈcit+a+ble *adj.*
ˌo·ver+ex+ˈcit+a+bly *adv.*
ˌo·ver+ex+ˈcite *vb.*
ˌo·ver+ˈex+er+ˌcise *vb.*
ˌo·ver+ex+ˈert *vb.*
ˌo·ver+ex+ˈpand *vb.*
ˌo·ver+ex+ˈpan+sion *n.*
ˌo·ver+ex+ˈpect+ant *adj.*
ˌo·ver+ex+ˈpen+di+ture *n.*
ˌo·ver+ex+ˈplic+it *adj.*
ˌo·ver+ex+ˈpres+sive *adj.*
ˌo·ver+ex+ˈtend *vb.*
ˌo·ver+ˈfac+ile *adj.*
ˌo·ver+fa+ˈmil+iar *adj.*
ˌo·ver+fa+ˌmil·i+ˈar+i·ty *n.*
ˌo·ver+ˈfan+ci+ful *adj.*
ˌo·ver+ˈfar *adj., adv.*
ˌo·ver+fas+ˈtid+i+ous *adj.*
ˌo·ver+ˈfear+ful *adj.*
ˌo·ver+ˈfeed *vb.*, **+feeds, +feed+ing, +fed.**
ˌo·ver+ˈfill *vb.*

o·ver+gar+ment ('əʊvəˌgɑːmənt) *n.* any garment worn over other clothes, esp. to protect them from wear or dirt.

o·ver+glaze ('əʊvəˌgleɪz) *adj.* (of decoration or colours) applied to porcelain or pottery above the glaze.

o·ver+ground ('əʊvəˌgraʊnd) *adj.* on or above the surface of the ground: *an overground railway.*

o·ver+grow (ˌəʊvə'grəʊ) *vb.* **+grows, +grow+ing, +grew, +grown. 1.** (*tr.*) to grow over or across (an area, path, etc.). **2.** (*tr.*) to choke or supplant by a stronger growth. **3.** (*tr.*) to grow too large for. **4.** (*intr.*) to grow beyond normal size. —**'o·ver+ˌgrowth** *n.*

o·ver+hand ('əʊvəˌhænd) *adj.* **1.** *Chiefly U.S.* thrown or performed with the hand raised above the shoulder. **2.** sewn with thread passing over two edges in one direction. ~*adv.* **3.** *Chiefly U.S.* with the hand above the shoulder; overarm. **4.** with shallow stitches passing over two edges. ~*vb.* **5.** to sew (two edges) overhand.

o·ver+hand knot *n.* a knot formed by making a loop in a piece of cord and drawing one end through it.

o·ver+hang *vb.* (ˌəʊvə'hæŋ), **+hangs, +hang+ing, +hung. 1.** to project or extend beyond (a surface, building, etc.). **2.** (*tr.*) to hang or be suspended over. **3.** (*tr.*) to menace, threaten, or dominate. ~*n.* ('əʊvəˌhæŋ). **4.** a formation, object, part of a structure, etc., that extends beyond or hangs over something, such as an outcrop of rock overhanging a mountain face. **5.** the amount or extent of projection. **6.** *Aeronautics.* **a.** half the difference in span of the main supporting surfaces of a biplane or other multiplane. **b.** the distance from the outer supporting strut of a wing to the wing tip.

o·ver+haul *vb.* (ˌəʊvə'hɔːl). (*tr.*) **1.** to examine carefully for faults, necessary repairs, etc. **2.** to make repairs or adjustments to (a car, machine, etc.). **3.** to overtake. ~*n.* ('əʊvəˌhɔːl). **4.** a thorough examination and repair.

o·ver+head *adj.* ('əʊvəˌhɛd). **1.** situated or operating above head height or some other reference level. **2.** (*prenominal*) inclusive: *the overhead price included meals.* ~*adv.* (ˌəʊvə'hɛd). **3.** over or above head height, esp. in the sky. ~*n.* ('əʊvəˌhɛd). **4. a.** a stroke in racket games played from above head height. **b.** (*as modifier*): *an overhead smash.* **5.** *Nautical.* the interior lining above one's head below decks in a vessel. **6.** short for **overhead door. 7.** (*modifier*) of, concerned with, or resulting from overheads: *overhead costs.*

o·ver+head cam+shaft *n.* a type of camshaft situated above the cylinder head in an internal-combustion engine. It is usually driven by a shaft from the crankshaft and the cams bear directly onto the valve stems or rocker arms.

o·ver+head door *n.* a door that rotates on a horizontal axis and is supported horizontally when open. Sometimes shortened to **overhead.**

o·ver+heads ('əʊvəˌhɛdz) *pl. n.* business expenses, such as rent, that are not directly attributable to any department or product and can therefore be assigned only arbitrarily. Also called: **burden, oncost.** Compare **prime cost.**

o·ver·head-valve en+gine *n.* a type of internal-combustion engine in which the inlet and exhaust valves are in the cylinder head above the pistons. U.S. name: **valve-in-head engine.** Compare **side-valve engine.**

o·ver+hear (ˌəʊvə'hɪə) *vb.* **+hears, +hear+ing, +heard.** (*tr.*) to hear (a person, remark, etc.) without the knowledge of the speaker.

o·ver+heat (ˌəʊvə'hiːt) *vb.* **1.** to make or become excessively hot. **2.** (*tr.; often passive*) to make very agitated, irritated, etc. ~*n.* **3.** the condition of being overheated.

O·ver+ijs+sel (*Dutch* ˌoːvər'ɛjsəl) *n.* a province of the E Netherlands: generally low-lying. Capital: Zwolle. Pop.: 956 300 (1973 est.). Area: 3929 sq. km (1517 sq. miles).

o·ver+is+sue ('əʊvərˌɪsjuː, -ˌɪʃuː) *vb.* **+sues, +su+ing, +sued.** (*tr.*) **1.** to issue (shares, banknotes, etc.) in excess of demand or ability to pay. ~*n.* **2.** shares, etc., thus issued.

o·ver+joy (ˌəʊvə'dʒɔɪ) *vb.* (*tr.*) to give great delight to.

o·ver+kill ('əʊvəˌkɪl) *n.* **1.** the capability to deploy more weapons, esp. nuclear weapons, than is necessary to ensure military advantage. **2.** any capacity or treatment that is greater than that required.

o·ver+land ('əʊvəˌlænd) *adj.* (*prenominal*), *adv.* **1.** over or across land. ~*vb.* **2.** *Austral.* to drive (animals) overland. —**'o·ver+ˌland+er** *n.*

o·ver+lap *vb.* (ˌəʊvə'læp), **+laps, +lap+ping, +lapped. 1.** (of two things) to extend or lie partly over (each other). **2.** to cover and extend beyond (something). **3.** (*intr.*) to coincide partly in time, subject, etc. ~*n.* ('əʊvəˌlæp). **4.** a part that overlaps or is overlapped. **5.** the amount, length, etc., overlapping. **6.** the act or fact of overlapping. **7.** a place of overlapping. **8.** *Geology.* the horizontal extension of the lower beds in a series of rock strata beyond the upper beds, usually caused by submergence of the land.

o·ver+lay *vb.* (ˌəʊvə'leɪ), **+lays, +lay+ing, +laid.** (*tr.*) **1.** to lay or place over or upon something else. **2.** (often foll. by *with*) to cover, overspread, or conceal with. **3.** (foll. by *with*) to cover a surface with an applied decoration: *ebony overlaid with silver.* **4.** to achieve the correct printing pressure all over (a forme or plate) by adding to the appropriate areas of the packing. ~*n.* ('əʊvəˌleɪ). **5.** something that is laid over something else; covering. **6.** an applied decoration or layer, as of gold leaf. **7.** a transparent sheet giving extra details to a map or diagram over which it is designed to be placed. **8.** *Printing.* material, such as paper, used to overlay a forme or plate.

o·ver+leaf ('əʊvəˌliːf) *adv.* on the other side of the page.

o·ver+lie (ˌəʊvə'laɪ) *vb.* **+lies, +ly+ing, +lay, +lain.** (*tr.*) **1.** to lie or rest upon. Compare **overlay. 2.** to kill (a baby or newborn animal) by lying upon it.

o·ver+live (ˌəʊvə'lɪv) *vb.* **1.** to live longer than (another person). **2.** to survive or outlive (an event).

o·ver+load *vb.* (ˌəʊvə'ləʊd). **1.** (*tr.*) to put too large a load on or in. ~*n.* ('əʊvəˌləʊd). **2.** an excessive load.

o·ver+long (ˌəʊvə'lɒŋ) *adj., adv.* too or excessively long.

o·ver+look *vb.* (ˌəʊvə'lʊk). (*tr.*) **1.** to fail to notice or take into account. **2.** to disregard deliberately or indulgently. **3.** to look at or over from above: *the garden is overlooked by the prison.* **4.** to afford a view of from above: *the house overlooks the bay.* **5.** to rise above. **6.** to look after. **7.** to look at carefully. **8.** to bewitch or cast the evil eye upon (someone). ~*n.* ('əʊvəˌlʊk). *U.S.* **9.** a high place affording a view. **10.** an act of overlooking.

o·ver+lord ('əʊvəˌlɔːd) *n.* a supreme lord or master. —**'o·ver+ˌlord·ship** *n.*

o·ver+ly ('əʊvəlɪ) *adv.* too; excessively.

o·ver+man *vb.* (ˌəʊvə'mæn), **+mans, +man+ning, +manned. 1.** (*tr.*) to supply with an excessive number of men. ~*n.* ('əʊvəˌmæn), *pl.* **+men. 2.** a man who oversees others. **3.** the Nietzschean superman.

o·ver+man+tel ('əʊvəˌmæntəl) *n.* a shelf over a mantelpiece.

o·ver+mas·ter (ˌəʊvə'mɑːstə) *vb.* (*tr.*) to overpower.

o·ver+match *Chiefly U.S.* ~*vb.* (ˌəʊvə'mætʃ). (*tr.*) **1.** to be more than a match for. **2.** to match with a superior opponent. ~*n.* ('əʊvəˌmætʃ). **3.** a person superior in ability. **4.** a match in which one contestant is superior.

o·ver+mat·ter ('əʊvəˌmætə) *n. Printing.* type that has been set but cannot be used for printing owing to lack of space. Also called: **overset.**

o·ver+much (ˌəʊvə'mʌtʃ) *adv., adj.* **1.** too much; very much. ~*n.* **2.** an excessive amount.

o·ver+nice (ˌəʊvə'naɪs) *adj.* too fastidious, precise, etc.

o·ver+night *adv.* (ˌəʊvə'naɪt). **1.** for the duration of the night: *we stopped overnight.* **2.** in or as if in the course of one night; suddenly: *the situation changed overnight.* ~*adj.* ('əʊvəˌnaɪt). (*usually prenominal*) **3.** done in, occurring in, or lasting the night: *an overnight stop.* **4.** staying for one night: *overnight guests.* **5.** lasting one night: *an overnight trip.* **6.** for use during a single night: *overnight clothes.* **7.** occurring in or as if in the course of one night; sudden: *an overnight victory.*

o·ver+night tel·e+gram *n. Brit.* a cheap internal telegram, usually delivered on the following day.

o·ver+pass *n.* ('əʊvəˌpɑːs). **1.** another name for **flyover** (sense 1). ~*vb.* (ˌəʊvə'pɑːs), **+pass·es, +pas+sing, +passed, +past.** (*tr.*) *Now rare.* **2.** to pass over, through, or across. **3.** to exceed. **4.** to get over. **5.** to ignore.

o·ver+pay (ˌəʊvə'peɪ) *vb.* **+pays, +pay+ing, +paid. 1.** to pay (someone) at too high a rate. **2.** to pay (someone) more than is due, as by an error.

o·ver+per+suade (ˌəʊvəpɜː'sweɪd) *vb.* (*tr.*) to persuade (someone) against his inclination or judgment.

o·ver+pitch (ˌəʊvə'pɪtʃ) *vb. Cricket.* to bowl a ball so that it pitches too close to the stumps.

o·ver+play (ˌəʊvə'pleɪ) *vb.* **1.** (*tr.*) to exaggerate the importance of. **2.** another word for **overact. 3. overplay one's hand.** to overestimate the worth or strength of one's position.

o·ver+plus ('əʊvəˌplʌs) *n.* surplus or excess quantity.

o·ver+pow+er (ˌəʊvə'paʊə) *vb.* (*tr.*) **1.** to conquer or subdue by superior force. **2.** to have such a strong effect on as to make helpless or ineffective. **3.** to supply with more power than necessary.

o·ver+pow+er+ing (ˌəʊvə'paʊərɪŋ) *adj.* **1.** so strong or intense as to be unbearable. **2.** so powerful as to crush or conquer. —**ˌo·ver+'pow+er+ing+ly** *adv.*

ˌo·ver+'fish *vb.*
ˌo·ver+'fond *adj.*
ˌo·ver+'frag+ile *adj.*
ˌo·ver+'full *adj.*
ˌo·ver+'fur+nish *vb.*
ˌo·ver+ˌgen+er+al·i+'za+tion *or* ˌo·ver+ˌgen+er+al·i+'sa+tion *n.*
ˌo·ver+'gen+er+al+ˌize *or* ˌo·ver+'gen+er+al+ˌise *vb.*
ˌo·ver+'gen+er+ous *adj.*
ˌo·ver+'hast·i+ly *adv.*
ˌo·ver+'hast·i+ness *n.*
ˌo·ver+'hast·y *adj.*
ˌo·ver+'hur+ried *adj.*
ˌo·ver+ˌi·de·al+'is+tic *adj.*
ˌo·ver+i·'de·al+ˌize *or* ˌo·ver+i·'de·al+ˌise *vb.*
ˌo·ver+im+'ag·i+na+tive *adj.*
ˌo·ver+im+'press *vb.*
ˌo·ver+im+'pres+sion+a·ble *adj.*
ˌo·ver+in+'cline *vb.*
ˌo·ver+in+'dulge *vb.*
ˌo·ver+in+'dus+tri+al+ˌize *or* ˌo·ver+in'dus+tri+al+ˌise *vb.*
ˌo·ver+in+'flate *vb.*
ˌo·ver+'in+flu+ence *vb.*
ˌo·ver+ˌin+flu+'en+tial *adj.*
ˌo·ver+in+'sist+ence *n.*
ˌo·ver+in+'sist+ent *adj.*
ˌo·ver+in+'sist+ent+ly *adv.*
ˌo·ver+in+'sure *vb.*
ˌo·ver+ˌin+tel+'lec+tu·al *adj.*
ˌo·ver+ˌin+tel+'lec+tu+al+ly *adv.*
ˌo·ver+in+'tense *adj.*
ˌo·ver+in+'tense+ly *adv.*
ˌo·ver+'in+ter+est *n.*
ˌo·ver+in+'vest *vb.*
ˌo·ver+'la+den *adj.*
ˌo·ver+'large *adj.*
ˌo·ver+'lav+ish *adj.*
ˌo·ver+'leap *vb.*, +leaps, +leap+ing; +leaped *or* +leapt.
ˌo·ver+'long *adj., adv.*
ˌo·ver+'mag+ni+ˌfy *vb.*, +fies, +fy+ing, +fied.
ˌo·ver+'man·y *adj.*
ˌo·ver+'meas+ure *n.*
ˌo·ver+'mod+est *adj.*
ˌo·ver+'mod+est+ly *adv.*
ˌo·ver+'mod·i+ˌfy *vb.*, +fies, +fy+ing, +fied.
ˌo·ver+par+'tic·u+lar *adj.*
ˌo·ver+'peo+pled *adj.*
ˌo·ver+ˌpes+si+'mis+tic *adj.*
ˌo·ver+'pop·u+late *vb.*
ˌo·ver+pop·u+'la+tion *n.*
ˌo·ver+'pow+er+ful *adj.*
ˌo·ver+'praise *vb.*
ˌo·ver+pre+'cise *adj.*
ˌo·ver+'price *vb.*

o·ver+print *vb.* (ˌəʊvəˈprɪnt). **1.** (*tr.*) to print (additional matter or another colour) on a sheet of paper. ~*n.* (ˈəʊvəˌprɪnt). **2.** additional matter or another colour printed onto a previously printed sheet. **3.** additional matter, other than a change in face value, applied to a finished postage stamp by printing, stamping, etc. See also **surcharge** (sense 5), **provisional** (sense 2).

o·ver+pro+tect (ˌəʊvəprəˈtɛkt) *vb.* (*tr.*) to protect more than necessary, esp. to shield a child excessively so as to inhibit its development. —ˌ**o·ver+pro+ˈtec+tion** *n.*

o·ver+rate (ˌəʊvəˈreɪt) *vb.* (*tr.*) to assess too highly.

o·ver+reach (ˌəʊvəˈriːtʃ) *vb.* **1.** (*tr.*) to defeat or thwart (oneself) by attempting to do or gain too much. **2.** (*tr.*) to aim for but miss by going too far or attempting too much. **3.** to get the better of (a person) by trickery. **4.** (*tr.*) to reach or extend beyond or over. **5.** (*intr.*) to reach or go too far. **6.** (*intr.*) (of a horse) to strike the back of a forefoot with the edge of the opposite hind foot.

o·ver+re·act (ˌəʊvərɪˈækt) *vb.* (*intr.*) to react excessively to something. —ˌ**o·ver+re·ˈac+tion** *n.*

o·ver+re+fine (ˌəʊvərɪˈfaɪn) *vb.* **1.** to refine (something) to excess. **2.** to make excessively fine distinctions.

o·ver+ride (ˌəʊvəˈraɪd) *vb.* +**rides,** +**rid+ing,** +**rode,** +**rid+den.** (*tr.*) **1.** to set aside or disregard with superior authority or power. **2.** to supersede or annul. **3.** to dominate or vanquish by or as if by trampling down. **4.** to extend or pass over, esp. to overlap. **5.** to ride (a horse, etc.) too hard. **6.** to ride over or across.

o·ver+rid+er (ˈəʊvəˌraɪdə) *n.* either of two metal or rubber attachments fitted to the bumper of a motor vehicle to prevent the bumpers interlocking with those of another vehicle.

o·ver-rid+ing *adj.* taking precedence.

o·ver+rule (ˌəʊvəˈruːl) *vb.* (*tr.*) **1.** to disallow the arguments of (a person) by the use of authority. **2.** to rule or decide against (an argument, decision, etc.). **3.** to prevail over, dominate, or influence. **4.** to exercise rule over.

o·ver+run *vb.* (ˌəʊvəˈrʌn), +**runs,** +**run+ning,** +**ran,** +**run. 1.** (*tr.*) to attack or invade and defeat conclusively. **2.** (*tr.*) to swarm or spread over rapidly. **3.** to run over (something); overflow. **4.** to extend or run beyond a limit). **5.** (*intr.*) (of an engine) to run with a closed throttle at a speed dictated by that of the vehicle it drives, as on a decline. **6.** (*tr.*) **a.** to print (a book, journal, etc.) in a greater quantity than ordered. **b.** to print additional copies of (a publication). **7.** (*tr.*) *Printing.* to transfer (set type and other matter) from one column, line, or page, to another. **8.** (*tr.*) *Archaic.* to run faster than. ~*n.* (ˈəʊvəˌrʌn). **9.** the act or an instance of overrunning. **10.** the amount or extent of overrunning. **11.** the number of copies of a publication in excess of the quantity ordered. **12.** the cleared level area at the end of an airport runway.

o·ver+score (ˌəʊvəˈskɔː) *vb.* (*tr.*) to cancel or cross out by drawing a line or lines over or through.

o·ver+seas *adv.* (ˌəʊvəˈsiːz). **1.** beyond the sea; abroad. ~*adj.* (ˈəʊvəˈsiːz). **2.** of, to, in, from, or situated in countries beyond the sea. **3.** Also: **o·ver+sea** (ˌəʊvəˈsiː). of or relating to passage over the sea. ~*n.* (ˌəʊvəˈsiːz). **4.** (*functioning as sing.*) *Informal.* a foreign country or foreign countries collectively.

o·ver+seas tel·e+gram *n. Brit.* another name for **cable** (sense 5).

o·ver+see (ˌəʊvəˈsiː) *vb.* +**sees,** +**see+ing,** +**saw,** +**seen.** (*tr.*) **1.** to watch over and direct; supervise. **2.** to watch secretly or accidentally. **3.** *Archaic.* to scrutinize; inspect.

o·ver+se·er (ˈəʊvəˌsiːə) *n.* **1.** a person who oversees others, esp. workmen. **2.** *British history.* short for **overseer of the poor;** a minor official of a parish attached to the workhouse or poorhouse.

o·ver+sell (ˌəʊvəˈsɛl) *vb.* +**sells,** +**sell+ing,** +**sold. 1.** (*tr.*) to sell more of (a commodity, etc.) than can be supplied. **2.** to use excessively aggressive methods in selling (commodities). **3.** (*tr.*) exaggerate the merits of.

o·ver+set (ˌəʊvəˈsɛt) *vb.* +**sets,** +**set+ting,** +**set. 1.** (*tr.*) to disturb or upset. **2.** (*tr.*) *Printing.* to set (type or copy) in excess of the space available.

o·ver+sew (ˈəʊvəˌsəʊ, ˌəʊvəˈsəʊ) *vb.* +**sews,** +**sew+ing,** +**sewed,** +**sewn.** to sew (two edges) with close stitches that pass over them both.

o·ver+sexed (ˌəʊvəˈsɛkst) *adj.* having an excessive preoccupation with or need for sexual activity.

o·ver+shad+ow (ˌəʊvəˈʃædəʊ) *vb.* (*tr.*) **1.** to render insignificant or less important in comparison. **2.** to cast a shadow or gloom over.

o·ver+shoe (ˈəʊvəˌʃuː) a protective shoe worn over an ordinary shoe.

o·ver+shoot (ˌəʊvəˈʃuːt) *vb.* +**shoots,** +**shoot+ing,** +**shot. 1.** to shoot or go beyond (a mark or target). **2.** to cause (an aircraft) to fly or taxi too far along (a runway) during landing or taking off, or (of an aircraft) to fly or taxi too far along a runway. **3.** (*tr.*) to pass swiftly over or down over, as water over a wheel.

o·ver+shot (ˈəʊvəˌʃɒt) *adj.* **1.** having or designating an upper jaw that projects beyond the lower jaw, esp. when considered as an abnormality. **2.** (of a water wheel) driven by a flow of water that passes over the wheel rather than under it. Compare **undershot.**

o·ver+side (ˈəʊvəˌsaɪd) *adv.* over the side (of a ship).

o·ver+sight (ˈəʊvəˌsaɪt) *n.* **1.** an omission or mistake, esp. one made through failure to notice something. **2.** supervision.

o·ver+sim+pli+fy (ˌəʊvəˈsɪmplɪˌfaɪ) *vb.* +**fies,** +**fy+ing,** +**fied.** to simplify (something) to the point of distortion or error. —ˌ**o·ver+ˌsim+pli+fi+ˈca+tion** *n.*

o·ver+size (ˌəʊvəˈsaɪz) *adj.* **1.** Also: **oversized.** larger than the usual size. ~*n.* **2.** a size larger than the usual or proper size. **3.** something that is oversize.

o·ver+skirt (ˈəʊvəˌskɜːt) *n.* an outer skirt, esp. one that reveals a decorative underskirt.

o·ver+slaugh (ˈəʊvəˌslɔː) *n. Military.* **1.** the passing over of one duty for another that takes precedence. ~*vb.* **2.** (*tr.*) *U.S.* to pass over; ignore. [C18: from Dutch *overslaan* to pass over]

o·ver+sleep (ˌəʊvəˈsliːp) *vb.* +**sleeps,** +**sleep+ing,** +**slept.** (*intr.*) to sleep beyond the intended time for getting up.

o·ver+sleeve (ˈəʊvəˌsliːv) *n.* a protective sleeve covering an ordinary sleeve.

o·ver+soul (ˈəʊvəˌsəʊl) *n.* the spiritual essence of all things, transcending and uniting individual souls.

o·ver+spend (ˌəʊvəˈspɛnd) *vb.* +**spends,** +**spend+ing,** +**spent. 1.** to spend in excess of (one's desires or what one can afford). **2.** (*tr.; usually passive*) to wear out; exhaust.

o·ver+spill *n.* (ˈəʊvəˌspɪl). **1. a.** something that spills over or is in excess. **b.** (*as modifier*): *overspill population.* ~*vb.* (ˌəʊvəˈspɪl), +**spills,** +**spill+ing,** +**spilt** *or* +**spilled. 2.** (*intr.*) to overflow.

o·ver+staff (ˌəʊvəˈstɑːf) *vb.* (*tr.*) to provide an excessive number of staff (for a factory, hotel, etc.).

o·ver+state (ˌəʊvəˈsteɪt) *vb.* (*tr.*) to state too strongly; exaggerate or overemphasize. —ˌ**o·ver+ˈstate+ment** *n.*

o·ver+stay (ˌəʊvəˈsteɪ) *vb.* (*tr.*) **1.** to stay beyond the time, limit, or duration of. **2.** *Finance.* to delay a transaction in (a market) until after the point at which the maximum profit would have been made. **3. overstay** *or* **outstay one's welcome.** to stay (at a party, etc.) longer than pleases the host.

o·ver+steer (ˌəʊvəˈstɪə) *vb.* (*intr.*) (of a vehicle) to turn more sharply, for a particular turn of the steering wheel, than is desirable or anticipated.

o·ver+step (ˌəʊvəˈstɛp) *vb.* +**steps,** +**step+ping,** +**stepped.** (*tr.*) to go beyond (a certain or proper limit).

o·ver+strung (ˌəʊvəˈstrʌŋ) *adj.* **1.** too highly strung; tense. **2.** (of a piano) having two sets of strings crossing each other at an oblique angle.

o·ver+stuff (ˌəʊvəˈstʌf) *vb.* (*tr.*) **1.** to force too much into. **2.** to cover (furniture, etc.) entirely with upholstery.

o·ver+sub+scribe (ˌəʊvəsəbˈskraɪb) *vb.* (*tr.; often passive*) to subscribe or apply for in excess of available supply.

o·vert (ˈəʊvɜːt) *adj.* **1.** open to view; observable. **2.** *Law.* open; deliberate. Criminal intent may be inferred from an overt act. [C14: via Old French, from *ovrir* to open, from Latin *aperire*]

o·ver+take (ˌəʊvəˈteɪk) *vb.* +**takes,** +**tak+ing,** +**took,** +**tak+en. 1.** *Chiefly Brit.* to move past (another vehicle or person) travelling in the same direction. **2.** (*tr.*) to pass or do better than, after catching up with. **3.** (*tr.*) to come upon suddenly or unexpectedly: *night overtook him.* **4.** (*tr.*) to catch up with; draw level with.

o·ver+task (ˌəʊvəˈtɑːsk) *vb.* (*tr.*) to impose too heavy a task upon.

o·ver+tax (ˌəʊvəˈtæks) *vb.* (*tr.*) **1.** to tax too heavily. **2.** to impose too great a strain on.

o·ver-the-coun·ter *adj.* **1. a.** (of securities) not listed or quoted on a stock exchange. **b.** (of a security market) dealing in such securities. **c.** (of security transactions) conducted through a broker's office directly between purchaser and seller and not on a stock exchange. Abbrev.: **OTC, O.T.C. 2.** (of medicinal drugs) able to be sold without a prescription.

o·ver+throw *vb.* (ˌəʊvəˈθrəʊ), +**throws,** +**throw+ing,** +**threw,** +**thrown. 1.** (*tr.*) to effect the downfall or destruction of (a ruler, institution, etc.), esp. by force. **2.** (*tr.*) to throw or turn over. **3.** to throw (something, esp. a ball) too far. **4.** (*tr.*) *Archaic.* to make mad. ~*n.* (ˈəʊvəˌθrəʊ). **5.** an act of overthrowing. **6.** downfall; destruction. **7.** *Cricket.* **a.** a ball thrown back too far by a fielder. **b.** a run scored because of this.

o·ver+thrust (ˈəʊvəˌθrʌst) *n. Geology.* a reverse fault in which the rocks on the upper surface of a fault plane have moved over the rocks on the lower surface. Compare **underthrust.**

o·ver+time *n.* (ˈəʊvəˌtaɪm). **1. a.** work at a regular job done in addition to regular working hours. **b.** (*as modifier*): *overtime pay.* **2.** the rate of pay established for such work. **3.** time in excess of a set period. **4.** *Sport, U.S.* extra time. ~*adv.* (ˈəʊvə-

---

ˌ**o·ver+pro+ˈduce** *vb.*
ˌ**o·ver+pro+ˈduc+tion** *n.*
ˌ**o·ver+ˈprom·i+nent** *adj.*
ˌ**o·ver+ˈprompt** *adj.*
ˌ**o·ver+ˈprompt+ly** *adv.*
ˌ**o·ver+pro+ˈpor+tion** *vb.*
ˌ**o·ver+ˈproud** *adj.*
ˌ**o·ver+ˈpub+li+ˌcize** *or* ˌ**o·ver+ˈpub+li+ˌcise** *vb.*
ˌ**o·ver+ˈright+eous** *adj.*
ˌ**o·ver+ˈright+eous+ly** *adv.*
ˌ**o·ver+ˈright+eous+ness** *n.*
ˌ**o·ver+ˈripe** *adj.*
ˌ**o·ver+ˈroast** *vb.*
ˌ**o·ver+ro+ˈman+ti+ˌcize** *or* ˌ**o·ver+ro+ˈman+ti+ˌcise** *vb.*
ˌ**o·ver+ˈscep+ti+cal** *adj.*
ˌ**o·ver+ˈscru+pu+lous** *adj.*
ˌ**o·ver+ˈsen+si+tive** *adj.*
ˌ**o·ver+se+ˈvere** *adj.*
ˌ**o·ver+ˈsharp** *adj.*
ˌ**o·ver+ˈskep+ti+cal** *adj.*
ˌ**o·ver+so+ˈlic+i+tous** *adj.*
ˌ**o·ver+so+ˈphis+ti+ˌcat+ed** *adj.*
ˌ**o·ver+ˈspar+ing** *adj.*
ˌ**o·ver+ˌspe+cial+i+ˈza+tion** *or* ˌ**o·ver+ˌspe+cial·i+ˈsa+tion** *n.*
ˌ**o·ver+ˈspe+cial+ˌize** *or* ˌ**o·ver+ˈspe+cial+ˌise** *vb.*
ˌ**o·ver+ˈspread** *vb.,* +**spreads,** +**spread+ing,** +**spread.**
ˌ**o·ver+ˈstim+u+ˌlate** *vb.*
ˌ**o·ver+ˈstock** *vb.*
ˌ**o·ver+ˈstretch** *vb.*
ˌ**o·ver+ˈstrict** *adj.*
ˌ**o·ver+ˈstride** *vb.,* +**strides,** +**strid+ing,** +**strode,** +**strid+den.**
ˌ**o·ver+ˈsub+tle** *adj.*
ˌ**o·ver+ˈsub+tle+ty** *n.*
ˌ**o·ver+sup+ˈply** *vb.,* +**plies,** +**ply+ing,** +**plied.**
ˌ**o·ver+sus+ˈcep+ti+ble** *adj.*
ˌ**o·ver+sus+ˈpi+cious** *adj.*
ˌ**o·ver+ˌsys+tem+ˈat+ic** *adj.*

ˌtaɪm). **5.** beyond the regular or stipulated time. ~*vb.* (ˌəʊvəˈtaɪm). **6.** (*tr.*) to exceed the required time for (a photographic exposure, etc.).

o·ver+tone (ˈəʊvəˌtəʊn) *n.* **1.** (*often pl.*) additional meaning or nuance: *overtones of despair.*. **2.** *Music, acoustics.* any of the tones, with the exception of the fundamental, that constitute a musical sound and contribute to its quality, each having a frequency that is a multiple of the fundamental frequency. See also **harmonic** (sense 6), **partial** (sense 6).

o·ver+top (ˌəʊvəˈtɒp) *vb.* **+tops, +top+ping, +topped.** (*tr.*) **1.** to exceed in height. **2.** to surpass; excel.

o·ver+trade (ˌəʊvəˈtreɪd) *vb.* (*intr.*) (of an enterprise) to trade in excess of capacity or working capital.

o·ver+trick (ˈəʊvəˌtrɪk) *n. Bridge.* a trick by which a player exceeds his contract.

o·ver+trump (ˌəʊvəˈtrʌmp) *vb. Cards.* to play a trump higher than (one previously played to the trick).

o·ver+ture (ˈəʊvəˌtjʊə) *n.* **1.** *Music.* **a.** a piece of orchestral music containing contrasting sections that is played at the beginning of an opera or oratorio, often containing the main musical themes of the work. **b.** a similar piece preceding the performance of a play. **c.** Also called: **concert overture.** a one-movement orchestral piece, usually having a descriptive or evocative title. **d.** a short piece in three movements (**French overture** or **Italian overture**) common in the 17th and 18th centuries. **2.** (*often pl.*) a proposal, act, or gesture initiating a relationship, negotiation, etc. **3.** something that introduces what follows. ~*vb.* (*tr.*) **4.** to make or present an overture to. **5.** to introduce with an overture. [C14: via Old French, from Late Latin *apertūra* opening, from Latin *aperīre* to open; see OVERT]

o·ver+turn *vb.* (ˌəʊvəˈtɜːn). **1.** to turn or cause to turn from an upright or normal position. **2.** (*tr.*) to overthrow or destroy. ~*n.* (ˈəʊvəˌtɜːn). **3.** the act of overturning or the state of being overturned.

o·ver-un·der *U.S.* ~*adj.* **1.** (of a two-barrelled firearm) having one barrel on top of the other. ~*n.* **2.** an over-under firearm.

o·ver+view (ˈəʊvəˌvjuː) *n. Chiefly U.S.* a general survey.

o·ver+watch (ˌəʊvəˈwɒtʃ) *vb.* (*tr.*) **1.** to watch over. **2.** *Archaic.* to fatigue with long watching or lack of sleep.

o·ver+ween+ing (ˌəʊvəˈwiːnɪŋ) *adj.* **1.** (of a person) excessively arrogant or presumptuous. **2.** (of opinions, appetites, etc.) excessive; immoderate. —**ˌo·ver+ˈween+ing+ly** *adv.* —**ˌo·ver+ˈween+ing+ness** *n.*

o·ver+weigh (ˌəʊvəˈweɪ) *vb.* (*tr.*) **1.** to exceed in weight; overbalance. **2.** to weigh down; oppress.

o·ver+weight *adj.* (ˌəʊvəˈweɪt). **1.** weighing more than is usual, allowed, or healthy. ~*n.* (ˈəʊvəˌweɪt). **2.** extra or excess weight. **3.** *Archaic.* greater importance or effect. ~*vb.* (ˌəʊvəˈweɪt). (*tr.*) **4.** to give too much emphasis or consideration to. **5.** to add too much weight to. **6.** to weigh down.

o·ver+whelm (ˌəʊvəˈwelm) *vb.* (*tr.*) **1.** to overpower the thoughts, emotions, or senses of. **2.** to overcome with irresistible force. **3.** to overcome, as with a profusion or concentration of something. **4.** to cover over or bury completely. **5.** to weigh or rest upon overpoweringly. **6.** *Archaic.* to overturn.

o·ver+whelm+ing (ˌəʊvəˈwelmɪŋ) *adj.* overpowering in effect or force.

o·ver+wind (ˌəʊvəˈwaɪnd) *vb.* **+winds, +wind+ing, +wound.** (*tr.*) to wind (a watch, etc.) beyond the proper limit.

o·ver+win+ter (ˌəʊvəˈwɪntə) *vb.* (*intr.*) to spend winter (in or at a particular place).

o·ver+word (ˈəʊvəˌwɜːd) *n.* a repeated word or phrase.

o·ver+work *vb.* (ˌəʊvəˈwɜːk). (*mainly tr.*) **1.** (*also intr.*) to work or cause to work too hard or too long. **2.** to use too much: *to overwork an excuse.* **3.** to decorate the surface of. **4.** to work up. ~*n.* (ˈəʊvəˌwɜːk). **5.** excessive or excessively tiring work.

o·ver+write (ˌəʊvəˈraɪt) *vb.* **+writes, +writ+ing, +wrote, +writ+ten.** **1.** to write (something) in an excessively ornate or prolix style. **2.** to write too much about (someone or something). **3.** to write on top of (other writing).

o·ver+wrought (ˌəʊvəˈrɔːt) *adj.* **1.** full of nervous tension; agitated. **2.** too elaborate; fussy: *an overwrought style.* **3.** (*often postpositive* and foll. by *with*) with the surface decorated or adorned.

o·vi- *or* **o·vo-** *combining form.* egg or ovum: *oviform; ovotestis.* [from Latin *ōvum*]

Ov·id (ˈɒvɪd) *n.* Latin name *Publius Ovidius Naso.* 43 B.C.–?17 A.D., Roman poet. His verse includes poems on love, *Ars Amatoria,* on myths, *Metamorphoses,* and on his sufferings in exile, *Tristia.* —**O·vid+i·an** (ɒˈvɪdɪən) *adj.*

ov·i+duct (ˈɒvɪˌdʌkt, ˈəʊ-) *n.* the tube through which ova are conveyed from an ovary. Also called (in mammals): **Fallopian tube.** —**ov·i+du·cal** (ˌɒvɪˈdjuːkᵊl, ˌəʊ-) *or* **ˌov·i·ˈduc·tal** *adj.*

O·vie+do (*Spanish* oˈβjeðo) *n.* a city in NW Spain: capital of Asturias from 810 until 1002; centre of a coal and iron mining area. Pop.: 154 177 (1970).

o·vif+er·ous (əʊˈvɪfərəs) *adj. Zoology.* carrying or producing eggs or ova: *the oviferous legs of certain spiders.*

o·vi+form (ˈəʊvɪˌfɔːm) *adj. Biology.* shaped like an egg.

o·vine (ˈəʊvaɪn) *adj.* of, relating to, or resembling a sheep. [C19: from Late Latin *ovīnus,* from Latin *ovis* sheep]

o·vip·a+rous (əʊˈvɪpərəs) *adj.* (of fishes, reptiles, birds, etc.) producing eggs that hatch outside the body of the mother. Compare **ovoviviparous, viviparous** (sense 1). —**o·vi+par+i·ty** (ˌəʊvɪˈpærɪtɪ) *n.* —**o·ˈvip·a·rous+ly** *adv.*

o·vi+pos+it (ˌəʊvɪˈpɒzɪt) *vb.* (*intr.*) (of insects and fishes) to deposit eggs through an ovipositor. —**o·vi+po+si·tion** (ˌəʊvɪpəˈzɪʃən) *n.*

o·vi+pos·i+tor (ˌəʊvɪˈpɒzɪtə) *n.* **1.** the egg-laying organ of most female insects, consisting of a pair of specialized appendages at the end of the abdomen. **2.** a similar organ in certain female fishes, formed by an extension of the edges of the genital opening.

o·vi+sac (ˈəʊvɪˌsæk) *n.* a capsule or sac, such as an ootheca, in which egg cells are produced.

o·vo- *combining form.* variant of **ovi-**.

o·void (ˈəʊvɔɪd) *adj.* **1.** egg-shaped. **2.** *Botany.* (of a fruit or similar part) egg-shaped with the broader end at the base. Compare **obovoid.** ~*n.* **3.** something that is ovoid.

o·vo+lo (ˈəʊvəˌləʊ) *n., pl.* **+li** (-ˌlaɪ). *Architect.* a convex moulding having a cross section in the form of a quarter of a circle or ellipse. Also called: **quarter round, thumb.** Compare **congé** (sense 3), **echinus** (sense 1). [C17: from Italian: a little egg, from *ovo* egg, from Latin *ōvum*]

o·vo+tes+tis (ˌəʊvəʊˈtɛstɪs) *n., pl.* **+tes** (-tiːz). the reproductive organ of snails, which produces both ova and spermatozoa.

o·vo+vi·vip·a+rous (ˌəʊvəʊvaɪˈvɪpərəs) *adj.* (of certain reptiles, fishes, etc.) producing eggs that hatch within the body of the mother. Compare **oviparous, viviparous** (sense 1). —**o·vo+vi+vi+par+i·ty** (ˌəʊvəʊˌvaɪvɪˈpærɪtɪ) *n.*

ov·u+late (ˈɒvjʊˌleɪt) *vb.* (*intr.*) to produce or discharge eggs from an ovary. [C19: from OVULE] —**ˌov·u+ˈla+tion** *n.*

ov·ule (ˈɒvjuːl) *n.* **1.** a small body in seed-bearing plants that contains the egg cell and develops into the seed after fertilization. **2.** *Zoology.* an immature ovum. [C19: via French from Medieval Latin *ōvulum* a little egg, from Latin *ōvum* egg] —**ˈov·u+lar** *adj.*

o·vum (ˈəʊvəm) *n., pl.* **o·va** (ˈəʊvə). an unfertilized female gamete; egg cell. [from Latin: egg]

ow (aʊ) *interj.* an exclamation of pain.

owe (əʊ) *vb.* (*mainly tr.*) **1.** to be under an obligation to pay (someone) to the amount of. **2.** (*intr.*) to be in debt: *he still owes for his house.* **3.** (often foll. by *to*) to have as a result (of): *he owes his success to chance.* **4.** to feel the need or obligation to do, give, etc.: *to owe somebody thanks; to owe it to oneself to rest.* **5.** to hold or maintain in the mind or heart (esp. in the phrase **owe a grudge**). [Old English *āgan* to have (C12: to have to); related to Old Saxon *ēgan,* Old High German *eigan*]

ow+el+ty (ˈəʊəltɪ) *n., pl.* **+ties.** *Law.* equality, esp. in financial transactions. [C16: from Anglo-French *owelté,* ultimately from Latin *aequalitas,* from *aequalis* EQUAL]

Ow·en (ˈəʊɪn) *n.* **1. Da·vid (Anthony Llewellyn).** born 1938, English Labour politician; foreign secretary (1977–79); cofounder of Social Democratic Party (1981). **2.** Sir **Rich·ard.** 1804–1892, English comparative anatomist and palaeontologist. **3. Rob·ert.** 1771–1858, Welsh industrialist and social reformer. He formed a model industrial community at New Lanark, Scotland, and pioneered co-operative societies. His books include *New View of Society* (1813). **4. Wil·fred.** 1893–1918, English poet of World War I; killed in action.

Ow·ens (ˈəʊɪnz) *n.* **Jes·se.** original name *John Cleveland.* 1913-80, U.S. athlete.

Ow·en Stan·ley Range *n.* a mountain range in SE New Guinea. Highest peak: Mount Victoria, 4073 m (13 363 ft.).

O·wer+ri (əˈwɛrɪ) *n.* a market town in S Nigeria, capital of Imo state. Pop.: 26 000 (1973 est.).

ow+ing (ˈəʊɪŋ) *adj.* **1.** (*postpositive*) owed; due. **2. owing to.** (*prep.*) because of or on account of.

Usage. See at **due.**

owl (aʊl) *n.* **1.** any nocturnal bird of prey of the order *Strigiformes,* having large front-facing eyes, a small hooked bill, soft feathers, and a short neck. **2.** any of various breeds of owl-like fancy domestic pigeon (esp. the **African owl, Chinese owl,** and **English owl**). **3.** a person who looks or behaves like an owl, esp. in having a solemn manner. [Old English *ūle;* related to Dutch *uil,* Old High German *ūwila,* Old Norse *ugla*]

owl+et (ˈaʊlɪt) *n.* a young or nestling owl.

owl+ish (ˈaʊlɪʃ) *adj.* **1.** like an owl. **2.** solemn and wise in appearance. —**ˈowl+ish+ly** *adv.* —**ˈowl+ish+ness** *n.*

own (əʊn) *determiner.* (*preceded by a possessive*) **1. a.** (intensifier): *John's own idea; your own mother.* **b.** (*as pronoun*): *I'll use my own.* **2.** on behalf of oneself or in relation to oneself: *he is his own worst enemy.* **3. come into one's own. a.** to fulfil one's potential. **b.** to receive what is due to one. **4. get one's own back.** *Informal.* to have revenge. **5. hold one's own.** to maintain one's situation or position, esp. in spite of opposition or difficulty. **6. on one's own. a.** without help. **b.** by oneself; alone. ~*vb.* **7.** (*tr.*) to have as one's possession. **8.** (when *intr.,* often foll. by *up, to,* or *up to*) to confess or admit; acknowledge. **9.** (*tr.; takes a clause as object*) *Now rare.* to concede: *I own that you are right.* [Old English *āgen,* originally past participle of *āgan* to have; related to Old Saxon *ēgan,* Old Norse *eiginn.* See OWE]

own+er (ˈəʊnə) *n.* a person who owns; legal possessor.

ˌ**o·ver+ˈtask** *vb.*
ˌ**o·ver+ˈtech+ni+cal** *adj.*
ˌ**o·ver+ˈtire** *vb.*
ˌ**o·ver+ˈtrain** *vb.*
ˌ**o·ver+ˈuse** *vb.*
ˌ**o·ver+ˈuse** *n.*
ˌ**o·ver+ˈval·ue** *vb.,* **·ues, ·u+ing, ·ued.**
ˌ**o·ver+ˈvi·o+lent** *adj.*
ˌ**o·ver+ˈwill+ing** *adj.*
ˌ**o·ver+ˈwise** *adj.*
ˌ**o·ver+ˈzeal+ous** *adj.*

own+er+ship ('əʊnəˌʃɪp) *n.* **1.** the state or fact of being an owner. **2.** legal right of possession; proprietorship.

owt (aʊt) *pron. Northern Brit.* a dialect word for **anything.** [a variant of AUGHT]

ox (ɒks) *n., pl.* **ox·en. 1.** an adult castrated male of any domesticated species of cattle, esp. *Bos taurus,* used for draught work and meat. **2.** any bovine mammal, esp. any of the domestic cattle. [Old English *oxa;* related to Old Saxon, Old High German *ohso,* Old Norse *oxi*]

ox·a- *or before a vowel* **ox-** *combining form.* indicating that a chemical compound contains oxygen, used esp. to denote that a heterocyclic compound is derived from a specified compound by replacement of a carbon atom with an oxygen atom: *oxalic acid; oxazine.*

ox·a+late ('ɒksəˌleɪt) *n.* a salt or ester of oxalic acid.

ox+al+ic ac·id (ɒk'sælɪk) *n.* a colourless poisonous crystalline dicarboxylic acid found in many plants: used as a bleach and a cleansing agent for metals. Formula: $(COOH)_2$. Also called: **ethanedioic acid.** [C18: from French *oxalique,* from Latin *oxalis* garden sorrel; see OXALIS]

ox·a+lis ('ɒksəlɪs, ɒk'sælɪs) *n.* any plant of the genus *Oxalis,* having clover-like leaves which contain oxalic acid and white, pink, red, or yellow flowers: family *Oxalidaceae.* See also **wood sorrel.** [C18: via Latin from Greek: sorrel, sour wine, from *oxus* acid, sharp]

ox·a+zine ('ɒksəˌzi:n) *n.* any of 13 heterocyclic compounds with the formula C_4H_5NO. [from OXY- + AZINE]

ox+blood ('ɒksˌblʌd) *or* **ox+blood red** *adj.* of a dark reddish-brown colour.

ox+bow ('ɒksˌbəʊ) *n.* **1.** a U-shaped piece of wood fitted under and around the neck of a harnessed ox and attached to the yoke. **2.** Also called: **oxbow lake, cutoff.** a small curved lake lying on the flood plain of a river and constituting the remnant of a former meander.

Ox+bridge ('ɒksˌbrɪdʒ) *n.* **a.** the British universities of Oxford and Cambridge, esp. considered as ancient and prestigious academic institutions, bastions of privilege and superiority, etc. **b.** (*as modifier*)*: Oxbridge arrogance.*

ox·en ('ɒksən) *n.* the plural of **ox.**

Ox·en·stier·na *or* **Ox·en·stjer·na** (*Swedish* 'uksənˌʃæ:rna) *n.* **Count Ax·el** ('aksəl). 1583–1654, Swedish statesman. He was chancellor (1612–54) and successfully directed Swedish foreign policy for most of the Thirty Years' War.

ox+eye ('ɒksˌaɪ) *n.* **1.** any Eurasian plant of the genus *Buphthalmum,* having daisy-like flower heads with yellow rays and dark centres: family *Compositae* (composites). **2.** any of various North American plants of the related genus *Heliopsis,* having daisy-like flowers. **3. oxeye daisy.** another name for **daisy** (sense 2).

ox-eyed *adj.* having large round eyes, like those of an ox.

Ox+ford[1] ('ɒksfəd) *n.* **1.** a city in S England, administrative centre of Oxfordshire, at the confluence of the Rivers Thames and Cherwell: Royalist headquarters during the Civil War; university, consisting of 30 separate colleges, the oldest being University College (1249); motor-vehicle industry. Pop.: 108 564 (1971). **2.** Also called: **Oxford Down.** a breed of sheep with short wool and a dark brown face and legs. **3.** a type of stout laced shoe with a low heel. **4.** a lightweight fabric of plain or twill weave used for men's shirts, etc.

Ox·ford[2] ('ɒksfəd) *n.* **1st Earl of.** title of (Robert) **Harley.**

Ox+ford ac+cent *n.* the accent associated with Oxford English.

Ox+ford bags *pl. n.* trousers with very wide baggy legs, originally popular in the 1920s. Often shortened to **bags.**

Ox+ford blue *n.* **1. a.** a dark blue colour. **b.** (*as adj.*)*: an Oxford-blue scarf.* **2.** a person who has been awarded a blue from Oxford University.

Ox+ford Eng+lish *n.* that form of the received pronunciation of English supposed to be typical of Oxford University and regarded by many as affected or pretentious.

Ox+ford frame *n.* a type of picture frame in which the sides of the frame cross each other and project outwards.

Ox+ford grey *n.* **a.** a dark grey colour. **b.** (*as adj.*)*: an Oxford-grey suit.*

Ox+ford Group *n.* an early name for **Moral Rearmament.**

Ox+ford Move+ment *n.* the movement within the Church of England initiated by the Tractarians at Oxford in 1833, insisting upon the continuity of the Church with patristic Christianity and opposing liberalizing and rationalizing tendencies.

Ox+ford+shire ('ɒksfədˌʃɪə, -ʃə) *n.* an inland county of S central England: situated mostly in the basin of the Upper Thames, with the Cotswolds in the west and the Chilterns in the southeast. Administrative centre: Oxford. Pop.: 541 800 (1976 est.). Area: 2680 sq. km (1035 sq. miles). Abbrev.: **Oxon.**

ox+heart ('ɒksˌhɑ:t) *n.* a variety of sweet cherry having large heart-shaped fruit.

ox+hide ('ɒksˌhaɪd) *n.* leather made from the hide of an ox.

ox·i+dant ('ɒksɪdənt) *n.* a substance that acts or is used as an oxidizing agent. Also called (esp. in rocketry): **oxidizer.**

ox·i+dase ('ɒksɪˌdeɪs, -ˌdeɪz) *n.* any of a group of enzymes that bring about biological oxidation.

ox·i+date ('ɒksɪˌdeɪt) *vb.* another word for **oxidize.**

ox·i+da·tion (ˌɒksɪ'deɪʃən) *n.* **a.** the act or process of oxidizing. **b.** (*as modifier*)*: an oxidation state; an oxidation potential.* —**ˌox·i·'da+tion+al** *adj.* —**'ox·i+ˌda+tive** *adj.*

ox·i+da·tion-re·duc·tion *n.* **a.** a reversible chemical process usually involving the transfer of electrons, in which one reaction is an oxidation and the reverse reaction is a reduction. **b.** Also **redox.** (*as modifier*)*: an oxidation-reduction reaction.*

ox+ide ('ɒksaɪd) *n.* **1.** any compound of oxygen with another element. **2.** any organic compound in which an oxygen atom is bound to two alkyl or aryl groups; an ether. [C18: from French, from *ox*(*ygène*) + (*ac*)*ide;* see OXYGEN, ACID]

ox·i+dim+e·try (ˌɒksɪ'dɪmɪtrɪ) *n. Chem.* a branch of volumetric analysis in which oxidizing agents are used in titrations. [C20: from OXID(ATION) + -METRY] —**ox·i+di+met+ric** (ˌɒksɪdɪ'metrɪk) *adj.*

ox·i+dize *or* **ox·i+dise** ('ɒksɪˌdaɪz) *vb.* **1.** to undergo or cause to undergo a chemical reaction with oxygen, as in formation of an oxide. **2.** to form or cause to form a layer of metal oxide, as in rusting. **3.** to lose or cause to lose hydrogen atoms. **4.** to undergo or cause to undergo a decrease in the number of electrons. Compare **reduce** (sense 11). —**ˌox·i+di+'za+tion** *or* **ˌox·i+di+'sa+tion** *n.*

ox·i+diz+er *or* **ox·i+dis+er** ('ɒksɪˌdaɪzə) *n.* an oxidant, esp. a substance that combines with the fuel in a rocket engine.

ox·i+diz+ing a·gent *n. Chem.* a substance that oxidizes another substance, being itself reduced in the process. Common oxidizing agents are oxygen, hydrogen peroxide, and ferric salts. Compare **reducing agent.**

ox+ime ('ɒksi:m) *n.* any of a class of compounds with the general formula RR′NOH, where R is an organic group and R′ is either an organic group (**ketoxime**) or hydrogen atom (**aldoxime**): used in the chemical analysis of carbonyl compounds. [C19: from OX(YGEN) + IM(ID)E]

ox+lip ('ɒksˌlɪp) *n.* **1.** Also called: **paigle.** a primulaceous Eurasian woodland plant, *Primula elatior,* with small drooping pale yellow flowers. **2.** a similar and related plant that is a natural hybrid between the cowslip and primrose. [Old English *oxanslyppe,* literally: ox's slippery dropping; see SLIP[3], compare COWSLIP]

ox·o- *or before a vowel* **ox-** *combining form.* indicating that a chemical compound contains oxygen linked to another atom by a double bond, used esp. to denote that a compound is derived from a specified compound by replacement of a methylene group with a carbonyl group: *oxobutanoic acid.*

Oxon. ('ɒksən) *abbrev. for:* **1.** (in degree titles, etc.) of Oxford. [from Latin *Oxoniensis*] **2.** Oxfordshire. [from Latin *Oxonia*]

Ox·o·ni·an (ɒk'səʊnɪən) *adj.* **1.** of or relating to Oxford or Oxford University. ~*n.* **2.** a member of Oxford University. **3.** an inhabitant or native of Oxford.

ox·o+ni·um com+pound *or* **salt** (ɒk'səʊnɪəm) *n. Chem.* any of a class of salts derived from certain organic ethers or alcohols by adding a proton to the oxygen atom and thus producing a positive ion (**oxonium ion**).

ox+peck·er ('ɒksˌpɛkə) *n.* either of two African starlings, *Buphagus africanus* or *B. erythrorhynchus,* having flattened bills with which they obtain food from the hides of cattle, etc. Also called: **tick bird.**

ox+tail ('ɒksˌteɪl) *n.* the skinned tail of an ox, used esp. in soups and stews.

ox+ter ('ɒkstə) *n. Scot. and northern Brit. dialect.* the armpit. [C16: from Old English *oxta;* related to Old High German *Ahsala,* Latin *axilla*]

ox+tongue ('ɒksˌtʌŋ) *n.* **1.** any of various Eurasian plants of the genus *Picris,* having oblong bristly leaves and clusters of dandelion-like flowers: family *Compositae* (composites). **2.** any of various other plants having bristly tongue-shaped leaves, such as alkanet. **3.** the tongue of an ox, braised or boiled as food.

Ox·us ('ɒksəs) *n.* the ancient name for the **Amu Darya.**

ox·y-[1] *combining form.* denoting something sharp; acute: *oxytone.* [from Greek, from *oxus*]

ox·y-[2] *combining form.* **1.** containing or using oxygen: *oxyacetylene.* **2.** a former equivalent of **hydroxy-.**

ox·y+a·cet·y+lene (ˌɒksɪə'sɛtɪˌli:n) *n.* **a.** a mixture of oxygen and acetylene; used in a blowpipe for cutting or welding metals at high temperatures. **b.** (*as modifier*)*: an oxyacetylene burner.*

ox·y+ac·id (ˌɒksɪ'æsɪd) *n.* any acid that contains oxygen. Also called: **oxygen acid.**

ox·y+ceph·a+ly (ˌɒksɪ'sɛfəlɪ) *n. Pathol.* the condition of having a conical skull. —**ox·y+ce·phal+ic** (ˌɒksɪsɪ'fælɪk) *or* **ˌox·y+'ceph·a+lous** *adj.*

ox·y+gen ('ɒksɪdʒən) *n.* **a.** a colourless odourless highly reactive gaseous element: the most abundant element in the earth's crust (49.2 per cent). It is essential for aerobic respiration and almost all combustion and is widely used in industry. Symbol: O; atomic no.: 8; atomic wt.: 15.9994; valency: 2; density: 1.429 kg/m^3; melting pt.: –218.4°C; boiling pt.: –182.96°C. **b.** (*as modifier*)*: an oxygen mask.* —**ox·y+gen+ic** (ˌɒksɪ'dʒɛnɪk) *or* **ox+yg+e·nous** (ɒk'sɪdʒɪnəs) *adj.*

ox·y+gen ac·id *n.* another name for **oxyacid.**

ox·y+gen+ate ('ɒksɪdʒɪˌneɪt), **ox·y+gen+ize,** *or* **ox·y+gen+ise** *vb.* to enrich or be enriched with oxygen: *to oxygenate blood.* —**ˌox·y+gen+'a+tion** *n.* —**ˌox·y+gen+'iz+a·ble** *or* **ˌox·y+gen+'is+a·ble** *adj.* —**'ox·y+ge+ˌniz+er** *or* **'ox·y+ge+ˌnis+er** *n.*

ox·y+gen ef+fect *n. Biology.* the increased sensitivity to radiation of living organisms, tissues, etc., when they are exposed in the presence of oxygen.

ox·y+gen mask *n.* a device, worn over the nose and mouth, to which oxygen is supplied from a cylinder or other source: used to aid breathing.

ox·y+gen tent *n. Med.* a transparent enclosure covering a bedridden patient, into which oxygen is released to help maintain respiration.

ox·y+hae+mo+glo+bin (ˌɒksɪˌhi:məʊ'gləʊbɪn) *n. Biochem.* the bright red product formed when oxygen from the lungs combines with haemoglobin in the blood.

ox·y+hy+dro+gen (ˌɒksɪ'haɪdrədʒən) *n.* **a.** a mixture of hydrogen and oxygen used to provide an intense flame for welding. **b.** (*as modifier*): *an oxyhydrogen blowpipe.*

ox·y+mo+ron (ˌɒksɪˈmɔːrɒn) *n., pl.* **+mo+ra** (-ˈmɔːrə). *Rhetoric.* an epigrammatic effect, by which contradictory terms are used in conjunction: *beautiful tyrant; fiend angelical.* [C17: via New Latin from Greek *oxumōron,* from *oxus* sharp + *mōros* stupid]

ox·y+salt (ˌɒksɪˈsɔːlt) *n.* any salt of an oxyacid.

ox·y+sul+phide (ˌɒksɪˈsʌlfaɪd) *n. Chem.* a compound containing an element combined with oxygen and sulphur.

ox·y+tet+ra+cy+cline (ˌɒksɪˌtɛtrəˈsaɪklɪn) *n.* a broad-spectrum antibiotic, obtained from the bacterium *Streptomyces rimosus,* used in treating various infections. Formula: $C_{22}H_{24}N_2O_9$.

ox·y+to+cic (ˌɒksɪˈtəʊsɪk) *adj.* **1.** accelerating childbirth by stimulating uterine contractions. ~*n.* **2.** an oxytocic drug or agent. [C19: from Greek, from OXY-[1] + *tokos* childbirth]

ox·y+to+cin (ˌɒksɪˈtəʊsɪn) *n.* a polypeptide hormone, secreted by the pituitary gland, that stimulates contractions of the uterus or oviduct and ejection of milk in mammals; alpha-hypophame: used therapeutically for aiding childbirth. Formula: $C_{43}H_{66}N_{12}O_{12}S_2$. Compare **vasopressin.**

ox·y+tone (ˈɒksɪˌtəʊn) (in the classical Greek language) ~*adj.* **1.** (of a word) having an accent on the final syllable. ~*n.* **2.** an oxytone word. ~Compare **paroxytone, proparoxytone.**

oy·er (ˈɔɪə) *n.* **1.** *English legal history.* (in the 13th century) an assize. **2.** (formerly) the reading out loud of a document in court. **3.** See **oyer and terminer.**

oy·er and ter+mi+ner (ˈtɜːmɪnə) *n.* **1.** *English law.* (formerly) a commission issued to judges to try cases on assize. It became obsolete with the abolition of assizes and the setting up of crown courts in 1972. **2.** the court in which such hearing was held. **3.** (in the U.S.) a court exercising higher criminal jurisdiction. [C15: from Anglo-Norman, from *oyer* to hear + *terminer* to judge]

o·yez *or* **o·yes** (ˈəʊjɛs, -jɛz) *interj.* **1.** a cry, usually uttered three times, by a public crier or court official for silence and attention before making a proclamation. ~*n.* **2.** such a cry. [C15: via Anglo-Norman from Old French *oiez!* hear!]

O·yo (ˈəʊjəʊ) *n.* a state of SW Nigeria, formed in 1976 from part of Western State. Capital: Ibadan. Pop.: 5 208 904 (1976 est.). Area: 17 600 sq. km (6794 sq. miles).

oys+ter (ˈɔɪstə) *n.* **1. a.** any edible marine bivalve mollusc of the genus *Ostrea,* having a rough irregularly shaped shell and occurring on the sea bed, mostly in coastal waters. **b.** (*as modifier*): *oyster farm; oyster knife.* **2.** any of various similar and related molluscs, such as the pearl oyster and the **saddle oyster** (*Anomia ephippium*). **3.** the oyster-shaped piece of dark meat in the hollow of the pelvic bone of a fowl. **4.** something from which advantage, delight, profit, etc., may be derived: *the world is his oyster.* **5.** *Informal.* a very uncommunicative person. ~*vb.* **6.** (*intr.*) to dredge for, gather, or raise oysters. [C14 *oistre,* from Old French *uistre,* from Latin *ostrea,* from Greek *ostreon;* related to Greek *osteon* bone, *ostrakon* shell]

oys+ter bed *n.* a place, esp. on the sea bed, where oysters breed and grow naturally or are cultivated for food or pearls. Also called: **oyster bank, oyster park.**

oys·ter+catch·er (ˈɔɪstəˌkætʃə) *n.* any shore bird of the genus *Haematopus* and family *Haematopodidae,* having a black or black-and-white plumage and a long stout laterally compressed red bill.

oys+ter crab *n.* any of several small soft-bodied crabs of the genus *Pinnotheres,* esp. *P. ostreum,* that live as commensals in the mantles of oysters.

oys·ter+man (ˈɔɪstəmən) *n., pl.* **+men.** *Chiefly U.S.* **1.** a person who gathers, cultivates, or sells oysters. **2.** a boat used in gathering oysters.

oys+ter pink *n.* **a.** a delicate pinkish-white colour, sometimes with a greyish tinge. **b.** (*as adj.*): *oyster-pink shoes.*

oys+ter plant *n.* another name for **salsify** (sense 1).

oys+ter white *n.* **a.** a greyish-white colour. **b.** (*as adj.*): *oyster-white walls.*

oz *or* **oz.** *abbrev. for* ounce. [from Italian *onza*]

Oz (ɒz) *n. Austral. slang.* Australia.

Oz·a+lid (ˈɒzəlɪd) *n.* **1.** *Trademark.* a method of duplicating type matter, illustrations, etc., when printed on translucent paper. It is used for proofing. **2.** a reproduction produced by this method.

O·zark Moun+tains, O·zark Plat+eau (ˈəʊzɑːk), *or* **O·zarks** *pl. n.* an eroded plateau in S Missouri, N Arkansas, and NE Oklahoma. Area: about 130 000 sq. km (50 000 sq. miles).

o·zo+ce·rite *or* **o·zo+ke·rite** (əʊˈzəʊkəˌraɪt) *n.* a brown or greyish wax that occurs associated with petroleum and is used for making candles and waxed paper. Also called: **earth wax, mineral wax.** [C19: from German *ozokerit,* from Greek *ozein* odour + *kēros* beeswax]

o·zone (ˈəʊzəʊn, əʊˈzəʊn) *n.* **1.** a colourless gas with a chlorine-like odour, formed by an electric discharge in oxygen: a strong oxidizing agent, used in bleaching, sterilizing water, purifying air, etc. Formula: O_3; density: 2.14 kg/m³; melting pt.: –192°C; boiling pt.: –110.51. **2.** *Informal.* clean bracing air, as found at the seaside. [C19: from German *ozon,* from Greek: smell] —**o·zon+ic** (əʊˈzɒnɪk) *or* **ˈo·zo+nous** *adj.*

o·zo+nide (əʊˈzəʊnaɪd) *n.* any of a class of unstable explosive compounds produced by the addition of ozone to a double bond in an organic compound.

o·zo+nif+er+ous (ˌəʊzəʊˈnɪfərəs) *adj.* containing ozone.

o·zo+nize *or* **o·zo+nise** (ˈəʊzəʊˌnaɪz) *vb.* (*tr.*) **1.** to convert (oxygen) into ozone. **2.** to treat (a substance) with ozone. —ˌ**o·zo+ni+ˈza+tion** *or* ˌ**o·zo+ni+ˈsa+tion** *n.* —**ˈo·zo+ˌniz+er** *or* **ˈo·zo+ˌnis+er** *n.*

o·zo+nol·y+sis (ˌəʊzəʊˈnɒlɪsɪs) *n. Chem.* the process of treating an organic compound with ozone to form an ozonide: used to locate double bonds in molecules.

o·zo+no+sphere (əʊˈzəʊnəˌsfɪə, -ˈzɒnə-) *or* **o·zone lay+er** *n.* a region of ozone concentration in the stratosphere that absorbs high-energy solar ultraviolet rays.

ozs *or* **ozs.** *abbrev. for* ounces.

P

p *or* **P** (piː) *n., pl.* **p's, P's,** or **Ps. 1.** the 16th letter and 12th consonant of the modern English alphabet. **2.** a speech sound represented by this letter, usually a voiceless bilabial stop, as in *pig.* **3. mind one's p's and q's.** to be careful to use polite or suitable language.

p *symbol for:* **1.** (in Britain) penny *or* pence. **2.** *Music.* piano: an instruction to play quietly. **3.** *Physics.* pico-. **4.** *Physics.* **a.** momentum. **b.** proton. **c.** pressure.

P *symbol for:* **1.** *Chem.* phosphorus. **2.** *Physics.* **a.** pressure. **b.** power. **c.** parity. **d.** poise. **3.** (on road signs) parking. **4.** *Chess.* pawn. ~**5.** *international car registration for* Portugal.

p. *abbrev. for:* **1.** (*pl.* **pp.**) page. **2.** part. **3.** participle. **4.** past. **5.** per. **6.** *Currency.* **a.** peseta. **b.** peso. **7.** pint. **8.** pipe. **9.** population. **10.** post [Latin: after] **11.** pro [Latin: in favour of; for]

P. *abbrev. for:* **1.** Pastor. **2.** President. **3.** Priest. **4.** Prince.

pa (pɑː) *n.* an informal word for **father.**

Pa *the chemical symbol for* protactinium.

PA *international car registration for* Panama.

P.A. *abbrev. for:* **1.** personal assistant. **2.** *Military.* Post Adjutant. **3.** power of attorney. **4.** press agent. **5.** Press Association. **6.** *Banking.* private account. **7.** public-address system. **8.** publicity agent. **9.** Publishers Association. **10.** purchasing agent. **11.** personal appearance.

Pa. *abbrev. for* Pennsylvania.

p.a. *abbrev. for* per annum. [Latin: yearly]

paal (pɑːl) *n. Caribbean.* a stake driven into the ground. [from Dutch: a pile, stake]

PABA (ˈpɑːbə) *n. acronym for* para-aminobenzoic acid.

Pabst (*German* paːpst) *n.* **G(eorge) W(ilhelm).** 1885–1967, German film director, whose films include *Joyless Street* (1925), *Pandora's Box* (1929), and *The Last Act* (1954).

pab·u·lum (ˈpæbjʊləm) *n. Rare.* **1.** food. **2.** food for thought; mental nourishment. [C17: from Latin: from *pascere* to feed]

PABX *Brit. abbrev. for* private automatic branch exchange. See also **PBX.**

Pac. *abbrev. for* Pacific.

pa·ca (ˈpɑːkə, ˈpækə) *n.* a large burrowing hystricomorph rodent, *Cuniculus paca,* of Central and South America, having white-spotted brown fur and a large head: family *Dasyproctidae.* [C17: from Spanish, from Tupi]

pace[1] (peɪs) *n.* **1. a.** a single step in walking. **b.** the distance covered by a step. **2.** a measure of length equal to the average length of a stride, approximately 3 feet. See also **Roman pace, geometric pace, military pace. 3.** speed of movement, esp. of walking or running. **4.** rate or style of proceeding at some activity: *to live at a fast pace.* **5.** manner or action of stepping, walking, etc.; gait. **6.** any of the manners in which a horse or other quadruped walks or runs, the three principal paces being the walk, trot, and canter (or gallop). **7.** a manner of moving, natural to the camel and sometimes developed in the horse, in which the two legs on the same side of the body are moved and put down at the same time. **8.** *Chiefly Brit.* a step or small raised platform. **9. put (someone) through his paces.** to test the ability of (a person). **10. keep pace with.** to proceed at the same speed as. **11. set the pace.** to determine the rate at which a group runs or walks or proceeds at some other activity. **12. stand** *or* **stay the pace.** to keep up with the speed or rate of others. ~*vb.* **13.** (*tr.*) to set or determine the pace for, as in a race. **14.** (often foll. by *about, up and down,* etc.) to walk with regular slow or fast paces, as in boredom, agitation, etc.: *to pace the room.* **15.** (*tr.*; often foll. by *out*) to measure by paces: *to pace out the distance.* **16.** (*intr.*) to walk with slow regular strides: *to pace along the street.* **17.** (*intr.*) (of a horse) to move at the pace (the specially developed gait). [C13: via Old French from Latin *passūs* step, from *pandere* to spread, unfold, extend (the legs as in walking)]

pa·ce[2] (ˈpeɪsɪ; *Latin* ˈpɑːkɛ) *prep.* with due deference to: used to acknowledge politely someone who disagrees with the speaker or writer. [C19: from Latin, from *pāx* peace]

pace+mak·er (ˈpeɪsˌmeɪkə) *n.* **1.** a person, horse, vehicle, etc., used in a race or speed trial to set the pace. **2.** a person, organization, etc., regarded as being the leader in a particular field of activity. **3.** Also called: **cardiac pacemaker.** a small area of specialized tissue within the wall of the right atrium of the heart whose spontaneous electrical activity initiates and controls the beat of the heart. **4.** Also called: **artificial pacemaker.** an electronic device for use in certain cases of heart disease to assume the functions of the natural cardiac pacemaker.

pac+er (ˈpeɪsə) *n.* **1.** a horse trained to move at a special gait, esp. for racing. **2.** another word for **pacemaker.**

pace+set·ter (ˈpeɪsˌsɛtə) *n.* another word for **pacemaker** (senses 1, 2).

pace+way (ˈpeɪsweɪ) *n. Austral.* a racecourse for trotting and pacing.

pa+cha (ˈpɑːʃə) *n.* a variant spelling of **pasha.**

pa+cha+lic (ˈpɑːʃəlɪk) *n.* a variant spelling of **pashalik.**

pa+chi+si (pəˈtʃiːzɪ, pɑː-) *n.* an Indian game somewhat resembling backgammon, played on a cruciform board using six cowries as dice. [C18: from Hindi *pacīsī,* from *pacīs* twenty-five (the highest score possible in one throw)]

pach·ou+li (ˈpætʃʊlɪ, pəˈtʃuːlɪ) *n.* a variant spelling of **patchouli.**

Pa+chu+ca (*Spanish* paˈtʃuka) *n.* a city in central Mexico, capital of Hidalgo state, in the Sierra Madre Oriental: silver mines; university (1961). Pop.: 84 543 (1970).

Pa+chu+co (pəˈtʃuːkəʊ) *n., pl.* **+cos.** *U.S.* a young Mexican living in the U.S., esp. one of low social status who belongs to a street gang. [C20: from Mexican Spanish]

pach·y+derm (ˈpækɪˌdɜːm) *n.* any very large thick-skinned mammal, such as an elephant, rhinoceros, or hippopotamus. [C19: from French *pachyderme,* from Greek *pakhudermos* thick-skinned, from *pakhus* thick + *derma* skin] —**ˌpach·y+ˈder+ma+tous** *adj.*

pach·y+tene (ˈpækɪˌtiːn) *n.* the third stage of the prophase of meiosis during which the chromosomes become shorter and thicker and divide into chromatids. [from Greek *pakhus* thick + *tainia* band]

pa+cif+ic (pəˈsɪfɪk) *adj.* **1.** tending or conducive to peace; conciliatory. **2.** not aggressive; opposed to the use of force. **3.** free from conflict; peaceful. [C16: from Old French *pacifique,* from Latin *pācificus,* from *pāx* peace + *facere* to make] —**pa+ˈcif·i·cal+ly** *adv.*

Pa+cif+ic (pəˈsɪfɪk) *n.* **1. the.** short for **Pacific Ocean.** ~*adj.* **2.** of or relating to the Pacific Ocean or its islands.

pac·i+fi+ca+tion (ˌpæsɪfɪˈkeɪʃən) *n.* the act, process, or policy of pacifying. —**ˌpac·i·fi·ˈca·to·ry** *adj.*

Pa+cif+ic Is+lands *n.* **Trust Ter+ri+to·ry of the.** an island group in the W Pacific Ocean, mandated to Japan after World War I and assigned to the U.S. by the United Nations in 1947: consists of 2141 islands (96 inhabited) of the Caroline, Marshall, and Mariana groups. Administrative centre: Saipan (Mariana Islands). Pop.: 107 054 (1971). Land area: about 1800 sq. km (700 sq. miles), scattered over about 7 500 000 sq. km (3 000 000 sq. miles) of ocean. Compare **Micronesia.**

Pa+cif+ic North+west *n.* the region of North America lying north of the Columbia River and west of the Rockies.

Pa+cif+ic O·cean *n.* the world's largest and deepest ocean, lying between Asia and Australia and North and South America: almost landlocked in the north, linked with the Arctic Ocean only by the Bering Strait, and extending to Antarctica in the south; has exceptionally deep trenches, and a large number of volcanic and coral islands. Area: about 165 760 000 sq. km (64 000 000 sq. miles). Average depth: 4215 m (14 050 ft.). Greatest depth: Challenger Deep (in the Marianas Trench), 11 033 m (37 073 ft.). Greatest width: (between Panama and Mindanao, Philippines) 17 066 km (10 600 miles).

Pa+cif+ic Stand+ard Time *n.* one of the standard times used in North America, based on the local time of the 120° meridian, eight hours behind Greenwich Mean Time. Abbrev.: **PST.**

pac·i+fi+er (ˈpæsɪˌfaɪə) *n.* **1.** a person or thing that pacifies. **2.** *U.S.* a baby's dummy or teething ring.

pac·i+fism (ˈpæsɪˌfɪzəm) *n.* **1.** the belief that violence of any kind is unjustifiable and that one should not participate in war, etc. **2.** the belief that international disputes can be settled by arbitration rather than war.

pac·i+fist (ˈpæsɪfɪst) *n.* **1.** a person who supports pacifism. **2.** a person who refuses military service.

pac·i+fy (ˈpæsɪˌfaɪ) *vb.* **+fies, +fy+ing, +fied.** (*tr.*) **1.** to calm the anger or agitation of; mollify. **2.** to restore to peace or order, esp. by the threat or use of force. [C15: from Old French *pacifier;* see PACIFIC] —**ˈpac·i·fi+a·ble** *adj.*

pack[1] (pæk) *n.* **1. a.** a bundle or load, esp. one carried on the back. **b.** (*as modifier*): *a pack animal.* **2.** a collected amount of anything. **3.** a complete set of similar things, esp. a set of 52 playing cards. **4.** a group of animals of the same kind, esp. hunting animals: *a pack of hounds.* **5.** any group or band that associates together, esp. for criminal purposes. **6.** *Rugby.* the forwards of a team or both teams collectively, as in a scrum or in rucking. **7.** the basic organizational unit of Cub Scouts and Brownies. **8. a.** a small package, carton, or container, used to retail commodities, esp. foodstuffs, cigarettes, etc. **b.** (*in combination*): *pack-sealed.* **9.** short for **pack ice. 10.** the quantity of something, such as food, packaged for preservation. **11.** *Med.* **a.** a sheet or blanket, either damp or dry, for wrapping about the body, esp. for its soothing effect. **b.** a material such as cotton or gauze for temporarily filling a bodily cavity, esp. to control bleeding. **12.** *Austral.* another name for **rucksack. 13.** *Mining.* a roof support, esp. one made of rubble. **14.** short for **face pack. 15.** a parachute folded and ready for use. **16. go to the pack.** *Austral. informal.* to fall into a lower state or condition. **17.** *Computer technol.* another name for **deck** (sense 5). ~*vb.* **18.** to place or arrange (articles) in (a container), such as clothes in a suitcase. **19.** (*tr.*) to roll up into a bundle. **20.** (when passive, often foll. by *out*) to press tightly together; cram: *the audience packed into the foyer; the hall was packed out.* **21.** to form (snow, ice, etc.) into a hard compact mass or (of snow, etc.) to become compacted. **22.** (*tr.*) to press in or cover tightly: *to pack a hole with cement.* **23.** (*tr.*) to load (a horse, donkey, etc.) with a burden. **24.** (often foll. by *off* or *away*) to send away or go away, esp. hastily. **25.** (*tr.*) to seal (a joint) by inserting a layer of compressible material between the faces. **26.** (*tr.*) to fill (a bearing or gland) with grease to lubricate it. **27.** (*tr.*) to separate (two adjoining components) so that they have a predetermined gap between them, by introducing shims, washers, plates, etc. **28.** (*tr.*) *Med.* to treat with a pack. **29.** (*tr.*) *Slang.* to be capable of inflicting (a blow, etc.): *he packs a mean punch.* **30.** (*tr.*) *U.S. informal.* to carry or wear habitually: *he packs a gun.* **31.** (*intr.*; often foll. by *down*) *Rugby.* to form a scrum. **32.** (*tr.*; often foll. by *into, to,* etc.) *U.S.* to carry (goods, etc.), esp. on the back: *will you pack your camping equipment into the mountains?* **33. pack one's bags.** *Informal.* to get ready to leave. **34. send packing.** *Informal.* to dismiss peremptorily. ~See also **pack in, pack up.** [C13: related to Middle Low German *pak,* of obscure origin] —**'pack·a·ble** *adj.*

pack[2] (pæk) *vb.* (*tr.*) to fill (a legislative body, committee, etc.) with one's own supporters: *to pack a jury.* [C16: perhaps changed from PACT]

pack·age ('pækɪdʒ) *n.* **1.** any wrapped or boxed object or group of objects. **2. a.** a proposition, offer, or thing for sale in which separate items are offered together as a single or inclusive unit. **b.** (*as modifier*): *a package holiday; a package deal.* **3.** a complete unit consisting of a number of component parts sold separately. **4.** the act or process of packing or packaging. **5.** *Computer technol.* a set of programs designed for a specific type of problem in statistics, production control, etc., making it unnecessary for a separate program to be written for each problem. **6.** the usual U.S. word for **packet** (sense 1). ~*vb.* (*tr.*) **7.** to wrap in or put into a package. **8.** to design and produce a package for (retail goods). **9.** to group (separate items) together as a single unit. —**'pack·ag·er** *n.*

pack·age store *n. U.S.* a store where alcoholic drinks are sold for consumption elsewhere. Also called: **liquor store.** Brit. equivalent: **off-licence.**

pack·ag·ing ('pækɪdʒɪŋ) *n.* **1.** the design and manufacture of packages for retail commodities. **2.** material suitable for making packages.

pack drill *n.* a military punishment by which the offender is made to march about carrying a full pack of equipment.

pack·er ('pækə) *n.* **1.** a person or company whose business is to pack goods, esp. food: *a meat packer.* **2.** a person or machine that packs.

pack·et ('pækɪt) *n.* **1.** a small or medium-sized container of cardboard, paper, etc., often together with its contents: *a packet of biscuits.* Usual U.S. word: **package. 2.** a small package; parcel. **3.** Also called: **packet boat.** a boat that transports mail, passengers, goods, etc., on a fixed short route. **4.** *Slang.* a large sum of money: *to cost a packet.* **5. catch, cop,** *or* **get a packet.** *Brit. slang.* to suffer an unpleasant experience, injury, etc. ~*vb.* **6.** (*tr.*) to wrap up in a packet or as a packet. [C16: from Old French *pacquet,* from *pacquer* to pack, from Old Dutch *pak* a pack]

pack·horse ('pæk,hɔːs) *n.* a horse used to transport goods, equipment, etc.

pack ice *n.* a large area of floating ice, usually occurring in polar seas, consisting of separate pieces that have become massed together. Also called: **ice pack.**

pack in *vb.* (*tr., adv.*) *Brit. informal.* to stop doing (something) (often in the phrase **pack it in**).

pack·ing ('pækɪŋ) *n.* **1. a.** material used to cushion packed goods. **b.** (*as modifier*): *a packing needle.* **2.** the packaging of foodstuffs. **3.** *Med.* **a.** the application of a medical pack. **b.** gauze or other absorbent material for packing a wound, etc. **4.** *Printing.* sheets of material, esp. paper, used to cover the platen or impression cylinder of a letterpress machine. **5.** any substance or material used to make watertight or gastight joints, esp. in a stuffing box.

pack·ing box *n.* another name for **stuffing box.**

pack·ing frac·tion *n.* a measure of the stability of a nucleus, equal to the difference between its mass in amu and its mass number, divided by the mass number.

pack of lies *n.* a completely false story, account, etc.

pack rat *n.* any rat of the genus *Neotoma,* of W North America, having a long tail that is furry in some species: family *Cricetidae.* Also called: **wood rat.**

pack·sack ('pæk,sæk) *n. U.S.* another word for **knapsack.**

pack·sad·dle ('pæk,sædᵊl) *n.* a saddle hung with packs, equipment, etc., used on a pack animal.

pack·thread ('pæk,θrɛd) *n.* a strong twine for sewing or tying up packages.

pack up *vb.* (*adv.*) **1.** to put (things) away in a proper or suitable place. **2.** *Informal.* to give up (an attempt) or stop doing (something): *if you don't do your work better, you might as well pack up.* **3.** (*intr.*) (of an engine, etc.) to fail to operate; break down.

pact (pækt) *n.* an agreement or compact between two or more parties, nations, etc., for mutual advantage. [C15: from Old French *pacte,* from Latin *pactum,* from *pacīscī* to agree]

pad[1] (pæd) *n.* **1.** a thick piece of soft material used to make something comfortable, give it shape, or protect it. **2.** a guard made of flexible resilient material worn in various sports to protect parts of the body. **3.** Also called: **stamp pad, ink pad.** a block of firm absorbent material soaked with ink for transferring to a rubber stamp. **4.** Also called: **notepad, writing pad.** a number of sheets of paper fastened together along one edge. **5.** a flat piece of stiff material used to back a piece of blotting paper. **6. a.** the fleshy cushion-like underpart of the foot of a cat, dog, etc. **b.** any of the parts constituting such a structure. **7.** any of various level surfaces or flat-topped structures, such as a launch pad. **8.** *Entomol.* a nontechnical name for **pulvillus. 9.** the large flat floating leaf of the waterlily. **10.** *Slang.* a person's residence. **11.** *U.S. slang.* a bed or bedroom. **12.** *Austral.* a path or track: *a cattle pad.* ~*vb.* **pads, pad·ding, pad·ded.** (*tr.*) **13.** to line, stuff, or fill out with soft material, esp. in order to protect or give shape to. **14.** (often foll. by *out*) to inflate with irrelevant or false information: *to pad out a story.* [C16: origin uncertain; compare Low German *pad* sole of the foot]

pad[2] (pæd) *vb.* **pads, pad·ding, pad·ded. 1.** (*intr.*; often foll. by *along, up,* etc.) to walk with a soft or muffled tread. **2.** (when *intr.,* often foll. by *around*) to travel (a route, etc.) on foot, esp. at a slow pace; tramp: *to pad around the country.* ~*n.* **3.** a dull soft sound, esp. of footsteps. **4.** *Archaic.* short for **footpad. 5.** *Archaic or dialect.* a slow-paced horse; nag. **6.** *Brit. dialect.* a path, etc. [C16: perhaps from Middle Dutch *paden,* from *pad* PATH]

pa·dang ('pædæŋ) *n.* (in Malaysia) a playing field. [from Malay: plain]

Pa·dang ('pɑːdɑːŋ) *n.* a port in W Indonesia, in W Sumatra at the foot of the **Padang Highlands** on the Indian Ocean. Pop.: 196 339 (1971).

pa·dauk *or* **pa·douk** (pə'daʊk, -'dɔːk) *n.* **1.** any of various tropical African or Asian papilionaceous trees of the genus *Pterocarpus* that have reddish wood. **2.** the wood of any of these trees, used in decorative cabinetwork. ~See also **amboyna.** [from a native Burmese word]

pad·ded cell *n.* a room, esp. one in a mental hospital, with padded surfaces in which violent inmates are placed.

pad·ding ('pædɪŋ) *n.* **1.** any soft material used to pad clothes, etc. **2.** superfluous material put into a speech or written work to pad it out; waffle. **3.** inflated or false entries in a financial account, esp. an expense account.

pad·dle[1] ('pædᵊl) *n.* **1.** a short light oar with a flat blade at one or both ends, used without a rowlock to propel a canoe or small boat. **2.** Also called: **float.** a blade of a water wheel or paddle wheel. **3.** a period of paddling: *to go for a paddle upstream.* **4. a.** a paddle wheel used to propel a boat. **b.** (*as modifier*): *a paddle steamer.* **5.** the sliding panel in a lock or sluice gate that regulates the level or flow of water. **6.** any of various instruments shaped like a paddle and used for beating, mixing, etc. **7.** a table-tennis bat. **8.** the flattened limb of a seal, turtle, or similar aquatic animal, specialized for swimming. ~*vb.* **9.** to propel (a canoe, etc.) with a paddle. **10. paddle one's own canoe. a.** to be self-sufficient. **b.** to mind one's own business. **11.** (*tr.*) to convey by paddling: *we paddled him to the shore.* **12.** (*tr.*) to stir or mix with or as if with a paddle. **13.** to row (a boat) steadily, esp. (of a racing crew) to row firmly but not at full pressure. **14.** (*intr.*) (of steamships) to be propelled by paddle wheels. **15.** (*intr.*) to swim with short rapid strokes, like a dog. **16.** *U.S. informal.* to spank. [C15: of unknown origin] —**'pad·dler** *n.*

pad·dle[2] ('pædᵊl) *vb.* (*mainly intr.*) **1.** to walk or play barefoot in shallow water, mud, etc. **2.** to dabble the fingers, hands, or feet in water. **3.** to walk unsteadily, like a baby. **4.** (*tr.*) *Archaic.* to fondle with the fingers. ~*n.* **5.** the act of paddling in water. [C16: of uncertain origin] —**'pad·dler** *n.*

pad·dle·fish ('pædᵊl,fɪʃ) *n., pl.* **·fish** *or* **·fish·es. 1.** a primitive bony fish, *Polyodon spathula,* of the Mississippi River, having a long paddle-like projection to the snout: family *Polyodontidae.* **2.** a similar and related Chinese fish, *Psephurus gladius,* of the Yangtze River.

pad·dle wheel *n.* a large wheel fitted with paddles, turned by an engine to propel a vessel on the water.

pad·dock[1] ('pædək) *n.* **1.** a small enclosed field, usually near a house or stable. **2.** (in horse racing) the enclosure in which horses are paraded and mounted before a race, together with the accompanying rooms, etc. **3.** (in motor racing) an area near the pits where cars are worked on before races. **4.** *Austral.* any area of fenced land. ~*vb.* **5.** (*tr.*) to confine (horses, etc.) in a paddock. [C17: variant of dialect *parrock,* from Old English *pearruc* enclosure, of Germanic origin. See PARK]

pad·dock[2] ('pædək) *n. Archaic or Brit. dialect.* a frog or toad. [C12: from *pad* toad, probably from Old Norse *padda;* see -OCK]

pad·dy[1] ('pædɪ) *n., pl.* **·dies. 1.** Also called: **paddy field.** a field planted with rice. **2.** rice as a growing crop or when harvested but not yet milled. [from Malay *pādī*]

pad·dy[2] ('pædɪ) *n., pl.* **·dies.** *Brit. informal.* a fit of temper. [C19: from PADDY]

Pad·dy ('pædɪ) *n., pl.* **·dies.** (*sometimes not cap.*) an informal name for an Irishman. [from *Patrick*]

pad·dy wag·on *n. U.S.* a slang word for **patrol wagon.**

pad·dy·whack *or* **pad·dy·wack** ('pædɪ,wæk) *n. Informal.* **1.** *Brit.* another word for **paddy**[2]. **2.** a spanking or smack.

pad·e·mel·on *or* **pad·dy·mel·on** ('pædɪ,mɛlən) *n.* a small wallaby of the genus *Thylogale,* of coastal scrubby regions of Australia. [C19: from a native Australian name]

Pa·der·born (*German* ,paːdər'bɔrn) *n.* a market town in NW West Germany, in North Rhine-Westphalia: scene of the meeting between Charlemagne and Pope Leo III (799 A.D.) that led to the foundation of the Holy Roman Empire. Pop.: 68 200 (1970).

Pa·de·rew·ski (*Polish* ,padɛ'rɛfski) *n.* **Ignace Jan** (i'ɲas jan). 1860–1941, Polish pianist, composer, and statesman; prime minister (1919).

Pa·di·shah ('pɑːdɪ,ʃɑː) *n.* a title of the Shah of Iran. [from Persian *pādi* lord + SHAH]

pad·lock ('pæd,lɒk) *n.* **1.** a detachable lock having a hinged or sliding shackle, which can be used to secure a door, lid, etc., by passing the shackle through rings or staples. ~*vb.* **2.** (*tr.*) to fasten with or as if with a padlock. [C15 *pad*, of obscure origin]

Pad+ma Shri ('pʌdmə 'ʃri:) *n.* (in India) an award for distinguished service in any field. [Hindi: lotus decoration]

pa+douk (pə'daʊk, -'dɔ:k) *n.* a variant spelling of **padauk.**

Pa+do+va ('pa:dova) *n.* the Italian name for **Padua.**

pa+dre ('pɑ:drɪ) *n. Informal.* (*sometimes cap.*) **1.** father: used to address or refer to a clergyman, esp. a priest. **2.** a chaplain to the armed forces. [via Spanish or Italian]

pa+dro+ne (pə'drəʊnɪ) *n.* **1.** the owner or proprietor of an inn, esp. in Italy. **2.** *U.S.* an employer who completely controls his workers, esp. a man who exploits Italian immigrants in the U.S. [C17: from Italian see PATRON]

pad+saw ('pæd,sɔ:) *n.* a small narrow saw used for cutting curves. [C19: from PAD[1] (in the sense: a handle that can be fitted to various tools) + SAW[1]]

Pad+u·a ('pædʒʊə, 'pædjʊə) *n.* a city in NE Italy, in Veneto: important in Roman and Renaissance times; university (1222); botanical garden (1545). Pop.: 240 013 (1975 est.). Latin name: **Patavium.** Italian name: **Padova.**

pad·u·a+soy ('pædjʊə,sɔɪ) *n.* **1.** a rich strong silk fabric used for hangings, vestments, etc. **2.** a garment made of this. [C17: changed (through influence of PADUA) from earlier *poudesoy*, from French *pou-de-soie*, of obscure origin]

Pa+dus ('peɪdəs) *n.* the Latin name for the **Po.**

pae·an *or U.S.* (*sometimes*) **pe·an** ('pi:ən) *n.* **1.** a hymn sung in ancient Greece in invocation of or thanksgiving to a deity. **2.** any song of praise. **3.** enthusiastic praise: *the film received a paean from the critics.* [C16: via Latin from Greek *paiān* hymn to Apollo, from his title *Paiān*, denoting the physician of the gods]

paed+er+ast ('pɛdə,ræst) *n.* a less common spelling of **pederast.** —,**paed+er+'as+tic** *adj.* —'**paed+er+,as+ty** *n.*

pae+di·a+tri+cian *or U.S.* **pe+di·a+tri+cian** (,pi:dɪə'trɪʃən) *n.* a medical practitioner who specializes in paediatrics.

pae+di+at+rics *or U.S.* **pe+di+at+rics** (,pi:dɪ'ætrɪks) *n.* the branch of medical science concerned with children and their diseases. —,**pae+di+'at+ric** *or U.S.* ,**pe+di+'at+ric** *adj.*

pae·do-, pe·do- *or before a vowel* **paed-, ped-** *combining form.* indicating a child or children: *paedology.* [from Greek *pais, paid-* child]

pae+do+gen+e·sis (,pi:dəʊ'dʒɛnɪsɪs) *n.* sexual reproduction in an animal that retains its larval features. See also **neoteny.** —**pae+do+ge·net+ic** (,pi:dəʊdʒə'nɛtɪk) *or* ,**pae+do+'gen+ic** *adj.*

pae+dol+o·gy *or U.S.* **pe+dol+o·gy** (pi:'dɒlədʒɪ) *n.* the study of the character, growth, and development of children. —**pae+do+log·i·cal** *or U.S.* **pe+do+log·i·cal** (,pi:dᵊ'lɒdʒɪkᵊl) *adj.* —**pae+'dol·o+gist** *or U.S.* **pe+'dol·o+gist** *n.*

pae+do+mor+pho+sis (,pi:də'mɔ:fəsɪs) *n.* the resemblance of adult animals to the young of their ancestors: seen in the evolution of modern man, who shows resemblances to the young stages of australopithecines.

pae+do+phil·i·a (,pi:dəʊ'fɪlɪə) *n.* the condition of being sexually attracted to children. —**pae+do+phile** ('pi:dəʊ,faɪl) *or* ,**pae+do+'phil·i·ac** *n., adj.*

pa+el+la (paɪ'ɛlə; *Spanish* pa'eʎa) *n., pl.* **+las** (-ləz; *Spanish* -ʎas). **1.** a Spanish dish made from rice, shellfish, chicken, and vegetables. **2.** the large flat frying pan in which a paella is cooked. [from Catalan, from Old French *paelle*, from Latin *patella* small pan]

pae+on ('pi:ən) *n. Prosody.* a metrical foot of four syllables, with one long one and three short ones in any order. [C17: via Latin *paeon* from Greek *paiōn*; variant of PAEAN] —**pae+'on+ic** *adj.*

pae·o+ny ('pi:ənɪ) *n., pl.* **+nies.** a variant spelling of **peony.**

Paes+tum ('pɛstəm) *n.* an ancient Greek colony on the coast of Lucania in S Italy.

pa+gan ('peɪgən) *n.* **1.** a member of a group professing a polytheistic religion or any religion other than Christianity, Judaism, or Islam. **2.** a person without any religion; heathen. ~*adj.* **3.** of or relating to pagans or their faith or worship. **4.** heathen; irreligious. [C14: from Church Latin *pāgānus* civilian (hence, not a soldier of Christ), from Latin: countryman, villager, from *pāgus* village] —'**pa+gan+dom** *n.* —'**pa+gan+ish** *adj.* —'**pa+gan+ism** *n.* —'**pa+gan+ist** *adj., n.* —,**pa+gan+'ist+ic** *adj.* —,**pa+gan+'ist·i·cal+ly** *adv.*

Pa·ga·ni·ni (*Italian* ,paga'ni:ni) *n.* **Nic·co·lò** (,niko'lɔ). 1782–1840, Italian violinist and composer.

pa+gan+ize *or* **pa+gan+ise** ('peɪgə,naɪz) *vb.* to become pagan, render pagan, or convert to paganism. —,**pa+gan·i+'za+tion** *or* ,**pa+gan·i+'sa+tion** *n.* —'**pa+gan+,iz+er** *or* '**pa+gan+,is+er** *n.*

page[1] (peɪdʒ) *n.* **1.** one side of one of the leaves of a book, newspaper, letter, etc. or the written or printed matter it bears. Abbrev.: **p.** (*pl.* **pp.**) **2.** such a leaf considered as a unit: *insert a new page.* **3.** an episode, phase, or period: *a glorious page in the revolution.* **4.** *Printing.* the type as set up for printing a page. ~*vb.* **5.** (*tr.*) another word for **paginate.** [C15: via Old French from Latin *pāgina*]

page[2] (peɪdʒ) *n.* **1.** a boy employed to run errands, carry messages, etc., for the guests in a hotel, club, etc., usually wearing a uniform. **2.** a youth in attendance at official functions or ceremonies, esp. weddings. **3.** *Medieval history.* **a.** a boy in training for knighthood in personal attendance on a knight. **b.** a youth in the personal service of a person of rank, esp. in a royal household: *page of the chamber.* **4.** *U.S.* an attendant at Congress or other legislative body. ~*vb.* (*tr.*) **5.** to call out the name of a person, esp. by a loudspeaker system, so as to give him a message. **6.** to act as a page to or attend as a page. [C13: via Old French from Italian *paggio*, probably from Greek *paidion* boy, from *pais* child]

Page (peɪdʒ) *n.* **1.** Sir **Fred·er·ick Hand·ley.** 1885–1962, English pioneer in the design and manufacture of aircraft. **2.** Sir **Earle (Christmas Grafton).** 1880–1961, Australian statesman; co-leader, with S. M. Bruce, of the federal government of Australia (1923–29).

pag+eant ('pædʒənt) *n.* **1.** an elaborate colourful parade or display portraying scenes from history, etc., esp. one involving rich costume. **2.** any magnificent or showy display, procession, etc. [C14: from Medieval Latin *pāgina* scene of a play, from Latin: PAGE[1]]

pag+eant+ry ('pædʒəntrɪ) *n., pl.* **+ries. 1.** spectacular display or ceremony. **2.** *Archaic.* pageants collectively.

page+boy ('peɪdʒ,bɔɪ) *n.* **1.** a smooth medium-length hair style with the ends of the hair curled under. **2.** a less common word for **page**[2] (sense 1).

Pa·get's dis+ease ('pædʒɪts) *n.* **1.** Also called: **osteitis deformans.** a chronic disease of the bones characterized by inflammation and deformation. **2.** Also called: **Paget's cancer.** cancer of the nipple and surrounding tissue. [C19: named after Sir James *Paget* (1814–99), English surgeon and pathologist, who described these diseases]

pag·i+nal ('pædʒɪnᵊl) *adj.* **1.** page-for-page: *paginal facsimile.* **2.** of, like, or consisting of pages.

pag·i+nate ('pædʒɪ,neɪt) *vb.* (*tr.*) to number the pages of (a book, manuscript, etc.) in sequence. Compare **foliate.** —,**pag·i+'na+tion** *n.*

pa+go+da (pə'gəʊdə) *n.* an Indian or Far Eastern temple, esp. a tower, usually pyramidal and having many storeys. [C17: from Portuguese *pagode*, ultimately from Sanskrit *bhagavatī* divine]

pa+go+da tree *n.* a Chinese leguminous tree, *Sophora japonica*, with ornamental white flowers and dark green foliage.

Pa·go Pa·go ('pɑ:ŋgəʊ 'pɑ:ŋgəʊ) *n.* a port in American Samoa, on SE Tutuila Island. Pop.: 2451 (1970). Former name: **Pango Pango.**

pa+gu+ri+an (pə'gjʊərɪən) *or* **pa+gu+rid** (pə'gjʊərɪd, 'pægjʊrɪd) *n.* **1.** any decapod crustacean of the family *Paguridae*, which includes the hermit crabs. ~*adj.* **2.** of, relating to, or belonging to the *Paguridae.* [C19: from Latin *pagurus*, from Greek *pagouros* kind of crab]

pah (pɑ:) *interj.* an exclamation of disgust, disbelief, etc.

Pa+hang (pə'hʌŋ) *n.* a state of West Malaysia, on the South China Sea: the largest Malayan state; mountainous and heavily forested. Capital: Kuala Lipis. Pop.: 503 131 (1970). Area: 35 964 sq. km (13 886 sq. miles).

Pa+ha+ri (pə'hɑ:rɪ) *n.* a group of Indo-European languages spoken in the Himalayas, divided into **Eastern Pahari** (Nepali) and **Western Pahari** (consisting of many dialects).

Pah·la·vi[1] ('pɑ:ləvɪ) *n.* **1. Mo·ham·med Re·za** ('ri:zə). 1919-80, shah of Iran 1941; deposed and exiled in 1978. **2.** his father, **Re·za.** 1877-1944, shah of Iran (1925-41). Originally an army officer, he gained power by a coup d'état (1921) and was chosen shah by the National Assembly. He reorganized the army and did much to modernize Iran.

Pah+la+vi[2] ('pɑ:ləvɪ) *n.* the Middle Persian language, esp. as used in classical Zoroastrian and Manichean literature. [C18: from Persian *pahlavī*, from Old Persian *Parthava* PARTHIA]

Pa+hsien ('pɑ:'ʃjɛn) *n.* another name for **Chungking.**

paid (peɪd) *vb.* **1.** the past tense or past participle of **pay**[1]. **2. put paid to.** *Chiefly Brit.* to end or destroy: *breaking his leg put paid to his hopes of running in the Olympics.*

pai+gle ('peɪgᵊl) *n.* another name for the **cowslip** and **oxlip.**

Paign+ton ('peɪntən) *n.* a town and resort in SW England, in Devon: administratively part of Torbay since 1968.

pail (peɪl) *n.* **1.** a bucket, esp. one made of wood or metal. **2.** Also called: **pailful.** the quantity that fills a pail. [Old English *pægel*; compare Catalan *paella* frying pan, PAELLA]

pail+lasse ('pælɪ,æs, ,pælɪ'æs) *n.* a variant spelling (esp. U.S.) of **palliasse.**

pail+lette (pæl'jɛt; *French* pa'jɛt) *n.* **1.** a sequin or spangle sewn onto a costume, etc. **2.** a small piece of metal or foil, used in enamelling for decoration. [C19: from French, diminutive of *paille* straw, from Latin *palea*]

pain (peɪn) *n.* **1.** the sensation of acute physical hurt or discomfort caused by injury, illness, etc. **2.** emotional suffering or mental distress. **3. on pain of.** subject to the penalty of. **4.** Also called: **pain in the neck.** *Informal.* a person or thing that is a nuisance. ~*vb.* (*tr.*) **5.** to cause (a person) hurt, grief, anxiety, etc. **6.** *Informal.* to annoy; irritate. [C13: from Old French *peine*, from Latin *poena* punishment, grief, from Greek *poinē* penalty]

Paine (peɪn) *n.* **Thom·as.** 1737–1809, American political pamphleteer, born in England. His works include the pamphlets *Common Sense* (1776) and *Crisis* (1776–83), supporting the American colonists' fight for independence; *The Rights of Man* (1791–92), a justification of the French Revolution; and *The Age of Reason* (1794–96), a defence of deism.

pained (peɪnd) *adj.* having or expressing pain or distress, esp. mental or emotional distress: *a pained expression.*

pain+ful ('peɪnfʊl) *adj.* **1.** causing pain; distressing: *a painful duty.* **2.** affected with pain: *a painful leg.* **3.** tedious or difficult. **4.** *Informal.* extremely bad: *a painful performance.* —'**pain+ful+ly** *adv.* —'**pain+ful+ness** *n.*

pain+kill·er ('peɪn,kɪlə) *n.* **1.** an analgesic drug or agent. **2.** anything that relieves pain.

pain+less ('peɪnlɪs) *adj.* **1.** not causing pain or distress. **2.** not affected by pain. —'**pain+less+ly** *adv.* —'**pain+less+ness** *n.*

pains (peɪnz) *pl. n.* **1.** care, trouble, or effort (esp. in the phrases **take pains, be at pains to**). **2.** labour pains.

pains+tak·ing ('peɪnz,teɪkɪŋ) *adj.* extremely careful, esp. as to fine detail: *painstaking research.* —**'pains+,tak·ing+ly** *adv.* —**'pains+,tak·ing+ness** *n.*

paint (peɪnt) *n.* **1.** a substance used for decorating or protecting a surface, esp. a mixture consisting of a solid pigment suspended in a liquid, that when applied to a surface dries to form a hard coating. **2.** a dry film of paint on a surface. **3.** the solid pigment of a paint before it is suspended in liquid. **4.** *Informal.* face make-up, such as rouge. **5.** short for **greasepaint.** ~*vb.* **6.** to make (a picture) of (a figure, landscape, etc.) with paint applied to a surface such as canvas. **7.** to coat (a surface, etc.) with paint, as in decorating. **8.** (*tr.*) to apply (liquid, etc.) onto (a surface): *her mother painted the cut with antiseptic.* **9.** (*tr.*) to apply make-up onto (the face, lips, etc.). **10.** (*tr.*) to describe vividly in words. **11. paint the town red.** *Informal.* to celebrate uninhibitedly; go on a spree. [C13: from Old French *peint* painted, from *peindre* to paint, from Latin *pingere* to paint, adorn] —**'paint·y** *adj.*

paint+box ('peɪnt,bɒks) *n.* a box containing a tray of dry watercolour paints.

paint+brush ('peɪnt,brʌʃ) *n.* a brush used to apply paint.

Paint+ed Des+ert *n.* a section of the high plateau country of N central Arizona, along the N side of the Little Colorado River Valley: brilliant coloured rocks; occupied largely by Navaho and Hopi Indians. Area: about 20 000 sq. km (7500 sq. miles).

paint+ed la·dy *n.* a migratory nymphalid butterfly, *Vanessa cardui,* with pale brownish-red mottled wings.

paint+ed wom+an *n.* a woman of low moral character.

paint+er[1] ('peɪntə) *n.* **1.** a person who paints surfaces as a trade. **2.** an artist who paints pictures.

paint+er[2] ('peɪntə) *n.* a line attached to the bow of a boat for tying it up. [C15: probably from Old French *penteur* strong rope]

paint+er+ly ('peɪntəlɪ) *adj.* **1.** having qualities peculiar to painting, esp. the depiction of shapes by means of solid masses of colour, rather than by lines, etc. Compare **linear** (sense 5). **2.** of or characteristic of a painter; artistic.

paint+er's col+ic *n. Pathol.* another name for **lead colic.**

paint+ing ('peɪntɪŋ) *n.* **1.** the art or process of applying paints to canvas, etc., to make a picture or other artistic composition. **2.** a composition or picture made in this way. **3.** the act of applying paint to a surface with a brush.

pair (pɛə) *n., pl.* **pairs** *or informal* **pair. 1.** two identical or similar things matched for use together: *a pair of socks.* **2.** two persons, animals, things, etc., used or grouped together: *a pair of horses; a pair of scoundrels.* **3.** an object considered to be two identical or similar things joined together: *a pair of trousers.* **4.** two people joined in love or marriage. **5.** a male and a female animal of the same species, esp. such animals kept for breeding purposes. **6.** *Parliamentary procedure.* **a.** two opposed members who both agree not to vote on a specified motion or for a specific period of time. **b.** the agreement so made. **7.** two playing cards of the same rank or denomination: *a pair of threes.* **8.** one member of a matching pair: *I can't find the pair to this glove.* **9.** *Rowing.* see **pair-oar. 10.** *Brit. and U.S. dialect.* a group or set of more than two. ~*vb.* **11.** (often foll. by *off*) to arrange or fall into groups of twos. **12.** to group or be grouped in matching pairs: *to pair socks.* **13.** to join or be joined in marriage; mate or couple. **14.** (when *tr., usually passive*) *Parliamentary procedure.* to form or cause to form a pair: *18 members were paired for the last vote.* [C13: from Old French *paire,* from Latin *paria* equal (things), from *pār* equal]

Usage. Like other collective nouns, *pair* takes a singular or a plural verb according to whether it is seen as a unit or as a collection of two things: *the pair of cuff links was gratefully received; that pair* (the two of them) *are on very good terms with each other.*

pair-oar *n. Rowing.* a racing shell in which two oarsmen sit one behind the other and pull one oar each. Also called: **pair.** Compare **double scull.**

pair pro+duc+tion *n.* the production of an electron and a positron from a gamma-ray photon that passes close to an atomic nucleus.

pair roy+al *n.* (in some card games) a set of three cards of the same denomination.

pairs (pɛəz) *pl. n.* another name for **Pelmanism.**

pai+sa ('paɪsɑː) *n., pl.* **+se** (-seɪ). a monetary unit of India and Pakistan worth one hundredth of a rupee. [from Hindi]

pai+sa+no (paɪ'sɑːnəʊ; *Spanish* paj'sano) *n., pl.* **+nos** (-nəʊz; *Spanish* -nos). *Southwestern U.S.* (often a term of address) **1.** *Informal.* a friend; pal. **2.** a fellow countryman. [C20: via Spanish from French *paysan* PEASANT]

pais+ley ('peɪzlɪ) *n.* **1.** a pattern of small curving shapes with intricate detailing, usually printed in bright colours. **2.** a soft fine wool fabric traditionally printed with this pattern. **3.** a garment made of this fabric, esp. a shawl popular in the late 19th century. **4.** (*modifier*) of or decorated with this pattern: *a paisley scarf.* [C19: named after PAISLEY, Scotland]

Pais+ley[1] ('peɪzlɪ) *n.* an industrial town in SW Scotland, in central Strathclyde region: one of the world's chief centres for the manufacture of thread, linen, and gauze in the 19th century. Pop.: 96 134 (1971).

Pais·ley[2] ('peɪzlɪ) *n.* Rev. **I·an (Richard Kyle).** born 1926, Northern Ireland politician; Protestant and Loyalist.

Pai+ute *or* **Pi+ute** ('paɪ,uːt, paɪ'juːt) *n.* **1.** (*pl.* **+utes** *or* **+ute**) a member of either of two North American Indian peoples (**Northern Paiute** and **Southern Paiute**) of the Southwestern U.S., related to the Aztecs. **2.** the language of either of these peoples, belonging to the Shoshonean subfamily of the Uto-Aztecan family.

pa+jam+as (pə'dʒɑːməz) *pl. n.* the U.S. spelling of **pyjamas.**

PAK *international car registration for* Pakistan.

pak-choi cab+bage ('pɑːk'tʃɔɪ) *n.* another name for **Chinese cabbage** (sense 2). [from Chinese (Cantonese dialect), literally: white vegetable]

pa+ke·ha ('pɑːkɪ,hɑː) *n. N.Z.* a person who is not of Maori ancestry, esp. a White person. [from Maori]

Pak·i ('pækɪ) *n. Brit. slang, derogatory.* a Pakistani immigrant residing in Britain.

Pak·i-bash·ing *n. Brit. slang.* the activity of making vicious and unprovoked physical assaults upon Pakistani immigrants residing in Britain. —**'Pak·i-,bash·er** *n.*

Pa+ki+stan (,pɑːkɪ'stɑːn) *n.* **1.** a republic in S Asia, on the Arabian Sea: formerly West Pakistan until East Pakistan gained independence as Bangladesh in 1971; contains the fertile plains of the Indus valley rising to mountains in the north and west. Official language: Urdu. Religion: mostly Muslim. Currency: rupee. Capital: Islamabad. Pop.: 64 892 000 (1972). Area: 801 508 sq. km (309 463 sq. miles). **2.** a former republic in S Asia consisting of the provinces of West Pakistan and East Pakistan (now Bangladesh), 1500 km (900 miles) apart: formed in 1947 from the predominantly Muslim parts of India. —**,Pa+ki+'stan·i** *n., adj.*

pal (pæl) *Informal.* ~*n.* **1.** a close friend; comrade. **2.** an accomplice. ~*vb.* **pals, pal+ling, palled. 3.** (*intr.;* usually foll. by *with* or *around*) to associate as friends. ~See also **pal up.** [C17: from English Gypsy: brother, ultimately from Sanskrit *bhrātar* BROTHER]

Pal. *abbrev. for* Palestine.

PAL (pæl) *n. acronym for* phase alternation line: a colour-television broadcasting system used generally in Europe.

pal+ace ('pælɪs) *n.* (*cap. when part of a name*) **1.** the official residence of a reigning monarch or member of a royal family: *Buckingham Palace.* **2.** the official residence of various high-ranking church dignitaries or members of the nobility, as of an archbishop. **3.** a large and richly furnished building resembling a royal palace. [C13: from Old French *palais,* from Latin *Palātium* PALATINE[2], the site of the palace of the emperors]

pal+ace rev·o+lu+tion *n.* a coup d'état made by those already in positions of power, usually with little violence.

Pa·la·cio Val·dés (*Spanish* pa'laθjo bal'des) *n.* **Ar·man·do** (ar'mando). 1853–1938, Spanish novelist and critic.

pal·a+din ('pælədɪn) *n.* **1.** one of the legendary twelve peers of Charlemagne's court. **2.** a knightly champion. [C16: via French from Italian *paladino,* from Latin *palātīnus* imperial official, from *Palātium* PALATINE[2]]

pal·ae+an+throp+ic (,pælɪæn'θrɒpɪk) *adj.* relating to or denoting the earliest variety of man.

Pal·ae+arc+tic (,pælɪ'ɑːktɪk) *adj.* of or denoting a zoogeographical region consisting of Europe, Africa north of the Sahara, and most of Asia north of the Himalayas.

pal·ae+eth+nol+o·gy (,pælɪɛθ'nɒlədʒɪ) *n.* the study of prehistoric man. —**pal·ae+eth+no+log·i+cal** (,pælɪ,ɛθnə'lɒdʒɪkᵊl) *adj.* —**,pal·ae+eth+'nol·o+gist** *n.*

pal·ae·o-, *before a vowel* **pal·ae-** *or esp. U.S.* **pal·e·o-, pal·e-** *combining form.* old, ancient, or prehistoric: *palaeography.* [from Greek *palaios* old]

pal·ae·o+an+thro+pol+o·gy (,pælɪəʊ,ænθrə'pɒlədʒɪ) *n.* the branch of anthropology concerned with primitive man.

pal·ae·o+bot·a+ny (,pælɪəʊ'bɒtənɪ) *n.* the study of fossil plants. —**pal·ae·o+bo+tan·i+cal** (,pælɪəʊbə'tænɪkᵊl) *or* **,pal·ae·o+bo+'tan+ic** *adj.* —**,pal·ae·o+'bot·a+nist** *n.*

Pal·ae·o+cene ('pælɪəʊ,siːn) *adj.* **1.** of, denoting, or formed in the first epoch of the Tertiary period, which lasted for 10 million years. ~*n.* **2. the.** the Palaeocene epoch or rock series.

pal·ae·o+cli+ma+tol+o·gy (,pælɪəʊ,klaɪmə'tɒlədʒɪ) *n.* the study of climates of the geological past.

pal·ae·o+eth+no+bot·a+ny (,pælɪəʊ,ɛθnəʊ'bɒtənɪ) *n.* the study of fossil seeds and grains to further archaeological knowledge, esp. of the domestication of cereals.

Pal·ae·o+gene ('pælɪə,dʒiːn) *adj.* **1.** of or formed in the Palaeocene, Eocene, and Oligocene epochs. ~*n.* **2. the.** the Palaeogene period or system.

pal·ae+og+ra+phy (,pælɪ'ɒgrəfɪ) *n.* **1.** the study of the handwritings of the past, and often the manuscripts, etc., as well, so that they may be dated, read, etc., and may serve as historical and literary sources. **2.** a handwriting of the past. —**pal·ae+'og+ra+pher** *n.* —**pal·ae·o+graph+ic** (,pælɪəʊ'græfɪk) *or* **,pal·ae·o+'graph·i+cal** *adj.*

pal·ae·o+lith ('pælɪəʊ,lɪθ) *n.* a stone tool dating to the Palaeolithic.

Pal·ae·o+lith+ic (,pælɪəʊ'lɪθɪk) *n.* **1.** the period of the emergence of primitive man and the manufacture of unpolished chipped stone tools, about 2.5 million to 3 million years ago until about 12 000 B.C. See also **Lower Palaeolithic, Middle Palaeolithic, Upper Palaeolithic.** ~*adj.* **2.** (*sometimes not cap.*) of or relating to this period.

Pal·ae·o+lith+ic man *n.* any of various primitive types of man, such as Neanderthal man and Java man, who lived in the Palaeolithic Age.

pal·ae·o+mag+net+ism (,pælɪəʊ'mægnɪtɪzəm) *n.* the study of magnetism in rocks, used to investigate the past configuration of the earth's magnetic field.

pal·ae+on+tog+ra+phy (,pælɪɒn'tɒgrəfɪ) *n.* the branch of palaeontology concerned with the description of fossils. —**pal·ae+**

on+to·graph+ic (ˌpælɪˌɒntəˈgræfɪk) *or* **ˌpal·ae+ˌon+to+ˈgraph·i+cal** *adj.*

palaeontol. *abbrev. for* palaeontology.

pal·ae+on+tol+o·gy (ˌpælɪɒnˈtɒlədʒɪ) *n.* **1.** the study of fossils to determine the structure and evolution of extinct animals and plants and the age and conditions of deposition of the rock strata in which they are found. See also **palaeobotany, palaeozoology. 2.** another name for **palaeozoology.** —**pal·ae+on+to+log·i+cal** (ˌpælɪˌɒntəˈlɒdʒɪkᵊl) *adj.* —**ˌpal·ae+ˌon+to+ˈlog·i+cal+ly** *adv.* —**ˌpal·ae+on+ˈtol·o+gist** *n.*

Pal·ae·o+zo+ic (ˌpælɪəʊˈzəʊɪk) *adj.* **1.** of, denoting, or relating to an era of geological time that began 600 million years ago with the Cambrian period and lasted about 375 million years until the end of the Permian period. *~n.* **2. the.** the Palaeozoic era.

pal·ae·o+zo+ol+o·gy *or* **pal·ae·o+zo+öl+o·gy** (ˌpælɪəʊzuːˈɒlədʒɪ) *n.* the study of fossil animals. Also called: **palaeontology.** —**pal·ae·o+zo·o+log·i+cal** *or* **pal·ae·o+zo·ö+log·i+cal** (ˌpælɪəʊˌzuəˈlɒdʒɪkᵊl) *adj.* —**ˌpal·ae·o+zo+ˈol·o+gist** *or* **ˌpal·ae·o+zo+ˈöl·o+gist** *n.*

pa+laes+tra *or esp. U.S.* **pa+les+tra** (pəˈlɛstrə, -ˈliː-) *n., pl.* **+tras** *or* **+trae** (-triː). (in ancient Greece or Rome) a public place devoted to the training of athletes. [C16: via Latin from Greek *palaistra,* from *palaiein* to wrestle]

pal+ais glide (ˈpæleɪ) *n.* a dance with high kicks and gliding steps in which performers link arms in a row. [C20: from French *palais de danse* public dance hall]

pal+an+quin *or* **pal+an+keen** (ˌpælənˈkiːn) *n.* a covered litter, formerly used in the Orient, carried on the shoulders of four men. [C16: from Portuguese *palanquim,* from Prakrit *pallanka,* from Sanskrit *paryanka* couch]

pal+at+a·ble (ˈpælətəbᵊl) *adj.* pleasant or acceptable or satisfactory: *a palatable suggestion.* —**ˌpal+at+a·ˈbil+i·ty** *or* **ˈpal+at+a·ble+ness** *n.* —**ˈpal+at+a·bly** *adv.*

pal·a+tal (ˈpælətᵊl) *adj.* **1.** Also: **palatine.** of or relating to the palate. **2.** *Phonetics.* of, relating to, or denoting a speech sound articulated with the blade of the tongue touching the hard palate. *~n.* **3.** Also called: **palatine.** the bony plate that forms the palate. **4.** *Phonetics.* a palatal speech sound, such as the semivowel (j). —**ˈpal·a+tal+ly** *adv.*

pal·a+tal+ize *or* **pal·a+tal+ise** (ˈpælətəˌlaɪz) *vb.* (*tr.*) to pronounce (a speech sound) with the blade of the tongue touching the palate. —**ˌpal·a+tal·i+ˈza+tion** *or* **ˌpal·a·tal·i·ˈsa+tion** *n.*

pal+ate (ˈpælɪt) *n.* **1.** the roof of the mouth, separating the oral and nasal cavities. See **hard palate, soft palate. 2.** the sense of taste: *she had no palate for the wine.* **3.** relish or enjoyment. **4.** *Botany.* (in some two-lipped corollas) the projecting part of the lower lip that closes the opening of the corolla. [C14: from Latin *palātum,* perhaps of Etruscan origin]

pa+la+tial (pəˈleɪʃəl) *adj.* of, resembling, or suitable for a palace; sumptuous. —**pa+ˈla+tial+ly** *adv.* —**pa+ˈla+tial+ness** *n.*

pa+lat·i+nate (pəˈlætɪnɪt) *n.* a territory ruled by a palatine prince or noble or count palatine.

Pa+lat·i+nate (pəˈlætɪnɪt) *n.* **1. the.** a territory in SW Germany once ruled by the counts palatine. Through the centuries it has changed in size and location. German name: **Pfalz.** See also **Upper Palatinate, Lower Palatinate. 2.** a native or inhabitant of the Palatinate.

pal·a+tine[1] (ˈpæləˌtaɪn) *adj.* **1.** (of an individual) possessing royal prerogatives in a territory. **2.** of, belonging to, characteristic of, or relating to a count palatine, county palatine, palatinate, or palatine. **3.** of or relating to a palace. *~n.* **4.** *Feudal history.* the lord of a palatinate. **5.** any of various important officials at the late Roman, Merovingian, or Carolingian courts. **6.** (in Colonial America) any of the proprietors of a palatine colony, such as Carolina. [C15: via French from Latin *palātīnus* belonging to the palace, from *palātium;* see PALACE]

pal·a+tine[2] (ˈpæləˌtaɪn) *adj.* **1.** of or relating to the palate. *~n.* **2.** either of two bones forming the hard palate. [C17: from French *palatin,* from Latin *palātum* palate]

Pal·a+tine[1] (ˈpæləˌtaɪn) *adj.* **1.** of or relating to the Palatinate. *~n.* **2.** a Palatinate.

Pal·a+tine[2] (ˈpæləˌtaɪn) *n.* **1.** one of the Seven Hills of Rome: traditionally the site of the first settlement of Rome. *~adj.* **2.** of, relating to, or designating this hill.

Pa+lau Is+lands (pɑːˈlaʊ) *pl. n.* a group of islands in the W Pacific, in the W Caroline Islands: administratively part of the U.S. Trust Territory of the Pacific Islands. Chief island: Babelthuap. Pop.: 13 025 (1972 est.). Area: 476 sq. km (184 sq. miles). Former name: **Pelew Islands.**

pa+la+ver (pəˈlɑːvə) *n.* **1.** tedious or time-consuming business, esp. when of a formal nature: *all the palaver of filling in forms.* **2.** loud and confused talk and activity; hubbub. **3.** (often used humorously) a conference. **4.** *Now rare.* talk intended to flatter or persuade. **5.** *W. African.* **a.** an argument. **b.** trouble arising from an argument. *~vb.* **6.** (*intr.*) (often used humorously) to have a conference. **7.** (*intr.*) to talk loudly and confusedly. **8.** (*tr.*) to flatter or cajole. [C18: from Portuguese *palavra* talk, from Latin *parabola* PARABLE]

Pa+la+wan (*Spanish* paˈlavan) *n.* an island of the SW Philippines between the South China Sea and the Sulu Sea: the westernmost island in the country; mountainous and forested. Capital: Puerto Princesa. Pop.: 236 635 (1970). Area: 11 785 sq. km (4550 sq. miles).

pale[1] (peɪl) *adj.* **1.** lacking brightness of colour; whitish: *pale morning light.* **2.** (of a colour) whitish; produced by a relatively small quantity of colouring agent. **3.** dim or wan: *the pale stars.* **4.** feeble: *a pale effort.* *~vb.* **5.** to make or become pale or paler; blanch. **6.** (*intr.;* often foll. by *before*) to lose superiority or importance (in comparison to): *her dress paled before that of her hostess.* [C13: from Old French *palle,* from Latin *pallidus* pale, from *pallēre* to look wan] —**ˈpale+ly** *adv.* —**ˈpale+ness** *n.*

pale[2] (peɪl) *n.* **1.** a wooden post or strip used as an upright member in a fence. **2.** an enclosing barrier, esp. a fence made of pales. **3.** an area enclosed by a pale. **4.** a sphere of activity within which certain restrictions, etc., are applied. **5.** *Heraldry.* an ordinary consisting of a vertical stripe, usually in the centre of a shield. **6. beyond the pale.** outside the limits of social convention. *~vb.* **7.** (*tr.*) to enclose with pales. [C14: from Old French *pal,* from Latin *pālus* stake; compare POLE[1]]

pa+le·a (ˈpeɪlɪə) *or* **pale** *n., pl.* **pa+le·ae** (ˈpeɪlɪˌiː) *or* **pales.** *Botany.* **1.** the scalelike membranous bract that partly encloses a grass flower. **2.** any small membranous bract or scale. [C18: from Latin: straw, chaff; see PALLET] —**pa+le·a+ceous** (ˌpeɪlɪˈeɪʃəs) *adj.*

pale+face (ˈpeɪlˌfeɪs) *n.* a derogatory term for a White person, said to have been used by North American Indians.

Pa+lem+bang (pɑːˈlɛmbɑːŋ) *n.* a port in W Indonesia, in S Sumatra; oil refineries; university (1955). Pop.: 582 961 (1971).

Pa+len+cia (*Spanish* paˈlenθja) *n.* a city in N central Spain: earliest university in Spain (1208); seat of Castilian kings (12th–13th centuries); communications centre. Pop.: 58 370 (1970).

Pa+len+que (*Spanish* paˈleŋke) *n.* the site of an ancient Mayan city in S Mexico famous for its architectural ruins.

pal·e·o- *or before a vowel* **pal·e-** *combining form.* variants (esp. U.S.) of **palaeo-.**

Pa+ler+mo (pəˈlɛəməʊ, -ˈlɜː-; *Italian* paˈlɛrmo) *n.* the capital of Sicily, on the NW coast: founded by the Phoenicians in the 8th century. Pop.: 662 567 (1975 est.).

Pal+es+tine (ˈpælɪˌstaɪn) *n.* **1.** Also called: (the) **Holy Land.** an ancient country in the Middle East, between the Jordan and the Mediterranean, and Lebanon and the Sinai peninsula. **2.** a former British mandate in this region, divided in 1948 between Israel and Jordan. —**Pal+es+tin+i+an** (ˌpælɪˈstɪnɪən) *adj., n.*

Pal+es+tine Lib+er+a+tion Or+gan+i+za+tion *n.* an organization founded in 1964 with the aim of creating a state for Palestinian Arabs and removing the state of Israel.

pa+les+tra (pəˈlɛstrə, -ˈliː-) *n., pl.* **+tras** *or* **+trae** (-triː). the usual U.S. spelling of **palaestra.**

Pa·le·stri·na (ˌpæleˈstriːnə) *n.* **Gio·van·ni Pier·lu·i·gi da** (dʒoˈvanni ˌpjerluˈiːdʒi da). ?1525–94, Italian composer and master of counterpoint. His works, nearly all for unaccompanied choir and religious in nature, include the *Missa Papae Marcelli* (1555).

pale·tot (ˈpæltəʊ) *n.* **1.** a loose outer garment. **2.** a woman's fitted coat often worn over a crinoline or bustle. [C19: from French]

pal+ette *or* **pal+let** (ˈpælɪt) *n.* **1.** a flat piece of wood, plastic, etc., used by artists as a surface on which to mix their paints. **2.** the range of colours characteristic of a particular artist, painting, or school of painting: *a restricted palette.* **3.** either of the plates of metal attached by a strap to the cuirass in a suit of armour to protect the armpits. [C17: from French, diminutive of *pale* shovel, from Latin *pala* spade]

pal+ette knife *n.* a round-ended spatula with a thin flexible blade used esp. by artists for mixing, applying, and scraping off paint, esp. oil paint.

Pa·ley (ˈpeɪlɪ) *n.* **Wil·liam.** 1743–1805, English theologian and utilitarian philosopher. His chief works are *The Principles of Moral and Political Philosophy* (1785), *Horae Paulinae* (1790), *A View of the Evidences of Christianity* (1794), and *Natural Theology* (1802).

pal+frey (ˈpɔːlfrɪ) *n. Archaic.* a light saddle horse, esp. ridden by women. [C12: from Old French *palefrei,* from Medieval Latin *palafredus,* from Late Latin *paraverēdus,* from Greek *para* beside + Latin *verēdus* light fleet horse, of Celtic origin]

Pa·li (ˈpɑːlɪ) *n.* an ancient language of India derived from Sanskrit; the language of the Buddhist scriptures. [C19: from Sanskrit *pāli-bhāsa,* from *pāli* canon + *bhāsa* language, of Dravidian origin]

pal·i+kar (ˈpælɪˌkɑː) *n.* a Greek soldier in the war of independence against Turkey (1821–28). [C19: from Modern Greek *palikari* youth]

pal+imp+sest (ˈpælɪmpˌsɛst) *n.* **1.** a manuscript on which two or more successive texts have been written, each one being erased to make room for the next. *~adj.* **2.** (of a text) written on a palimpsest. **3.** (of a document, etc.) used as a palimpsest. [C17: from Latin *palimpsestus* parchment cleaned for reuse, from Greek *palimpsēstos,* from *palin* again + *psēstos* rubbed smooth, from *psēn* to scrape]

pal+in+drome (ˈpælɪnˌdrəʊm) *n.* a word or phrase the letters of which, when taken in reverse order, give the same word or phrase, such as *able was I ere I saw Elba.* [C17: from Greek *palindromos* running back again, from *palin* again + -DROME] —**pal+in+drom+ic** (ˌpælɪnˈdrɒmɪk) *adj.*

pal+ing (ˈpeɪlɪŋ) *n.* **1.** a fence made of pales. **2.** pales collectively. **3.** a single pale. **4.** the act of erecting pales.

pal+in+gen+e·sis (ˌpælɪnˈdʒɛnɪsɪs) *n., pl.* **·ses** (-ˌsiːz). **1.** *Theol.* spiritual rebirth through metempsychosis of Christian baptism. **2.** *Biology.* another name for **recapitulation** (sense 2). [C19: from Greek *palin* again + *genesis* birth, GENESIS] —**pal+in·ge·net+ic** (ˌpælɪndʒəˈnɛtɪk) *adj.* —**ˌpal+in+ge·ˈnet·i+cal+ly** *adv.*

pal·i+node (ˈpælɪˌnəʊd) *n.* **1.** a poem in which the poet recants something he has said in a former poem. **2.** *Rare.* a recantation. [C16: from Latin *palinōdia* repetition of a song, from Greek, from *palin* again + *ōidē* song, ODE]

pal·i+sade (ˌpælɪˈseɪd) *n.* **1.** a strong fence made of stakes driven into the ground, esp. for defence. **2.** one of the stakes used in such a fence. **3.** *Botany.* a layer of elongated mesophyll cells containing many chloroplasts, situated below the outer epidermis of a leaf blade. ~*vb.* **4.** (*tr.*) to enclose with a palisade. [C17: via French, from Old Provençal *palissada,* ultimately from Latin *pālus* stake; see PALE², POLE¹]

pal·i·sades (ˌpælɪˈseɪdz, ˈpælɪˌseɪdz) *pl. n. U.S.* high cliffs in a line, often along a river, resembling a palisade.

pal·ish (ˈpeɪlɪʃ) *adj.* rather pale.

Palk Strait (pɔːk, pɔːlk) *n.* a channel between SE India and N Ceylon. Width: about 64 km (40 miles).

pall¹ (pɔːl) *n.* **1.** a cloth covering, usually black, spread over a coffin or tomb. **2.** a coffin, esp. during the funeral ceremony. **3.** a dark heavy covering; shroud: *the clouds formed a pall over the sky.* **4.** a depressing or oppressive atmosphere: *her bereavement cast a pall on the party.* **5.** *Heraldry.* an ordinary consisting of a Y-shaped bearing. **6.** *Christianity.* **a.** a small square linen cloth with which the chalice is covered at the Eucharist. **b.** an archaic word for **pallium** (sense 2). **7.** an obsolete word for **cloak.** ~*vb.* **8.** (*tr.*) to cover or depress with a pall. [Old English *pæll,* from Latin: PALLIUM]

pall² (pɔːl) *vb.* **1.** (*intr.;* often foll. by *on*) to become or appear boring, insipid, or tiresome (to): *history classes palled on me.* **2.** to cloy or satiate, or become cloyed or satiated. [C14: variant of APPAL]

Pal·la·di·an¹ (pəˈleɪdɪən) *adj.* denoting, relating to, or having the style of architecture created by Andrea Palladio. [C18: after Andrea PALLADIO] —**Pal·ˈla·di·an·ism** *n.*

Pal·la·di·an² (pəˈleɪdɪən) *adj.* **1.** of or relating to the goddess Pallas Athena. **2.** *Literary.* wise or learned. [C16: from Latin *Palladius,* from Greek: belonging to Pallas Athena]

pal·lad·ic (pəˈlædɪk, -ˈleɪ-) *adj.* of or containing palladium in the trivalent or tetravalent state.

Pal·la·dio (*Italian* palˈlaːdjo) *n.* **An·dre·a** (anˈdrɛːa). 1508–80, Italian architect who revived and developed classical architecture, esp. the ancient Roman ideals of symmetrical planning and harmonic proportions. His treatise *Four Books on Architecture* (1570) and his designs for villas and palaces profoundly influenced 18th-century domestic architecture in England and the U.S.

pal·la·di·um¹ (pəˈleɪdɪəm) *n.* a ductile malleable silvery-white element of the platinum metal group occurring principally in nickel-bearing ores: used as a hydrogenation catalyst and, alloyed with gold, in jewellery, etc. Symbol: Pd; atomic no.: 46; atomic wt.: 106.4; valency: 2, 3, or 4; relative density: 12.02; melting pt.: 1552°C; boiling pt.: 3140°C. [C19: named after the asteroid *Pallas,* at the time (1803) a recent discovery]

pal·la·di·um² (pəˈleɪdɪəm) *n.* something believed to ensure protection; safeguard. [C17: after the PALLADIUM]

Pal·la·di·um (pəˈleɪdɪəm) *n.* a statue of Pallas Athena, esp. the one upon which the safety of Troy depended.

pal·la·dous (pəˈleɪdəs, ˈpælədəs) *adj.* of or containing palladium in the divalent state.

Pal·las (ˈpæləs) *n. Astronomy.* the second largest asteroid (approximate diameter 450 kilometres), revolving around the sun in a period of 4.62 years.

Pal·las A·the·na *or* **Pal·las** (ˈpæləs) *n.* another name for **Athena.**

pall·bear·er (ˈpɔːlˌbɛərə) *n.* a person who carries or escorts the coffin at a funeral.

pal·let¹ (ˈpælɪt) *n.* **1.** a straw-filled mattress or bed. **2.** any hard or makeshift bed. [C14: from Anglo-Norman *paillet,* from Old French *paille* straw, from Latin *palea* straw]

pal·let² (ˈpælɪt) *n.* **1.** an instrument with a handle and a flat, sometimes flexible, blade used by potters for shaping. **2.** a portable platform for storing and moving goods. **3.** *Horology.* the locking lever that engages and disengages alternate end pawls with the escape wheel to give impulses to the balance. **4.** a variant spelling of **palette** (sense 1). **5.** *Music.* a flap valve of wood faced with leather that opens to admit air to the wind chest of an organ. [C16: from Old French *palette* a little shovel, from *pale* spade, from Latin *pala* spade]

pal·let knife *n.* a variant spelling of **palette knife.**

pal·li·asse *or* **pail·lasse** (ˈpælɪˌæs, ˌpælɪˈæs) *n.* a straw-filled mattress; pallet. [C18: from French *paillasse,* from Italian *pagliaccio,* ultimately from Latin *palea* PALLET¹]

pal·li·ate (ˈpælɪˌeɪt) *vb.* (*tr.*) **1.** to lessen the severity of (pain, disease, etc.) without curing or removing; alleviate; mitigate. **2.** to cause (an offence, etc.) to seem less serious by concealing evidence, etc.; extenuate. [C16: from Late Latin *palliāre* to cover up, from Latin *pallium* a cloak, PALLIUM] —**ˌpal·li·ˈa·tion** *n.* —**ˈpal·li·ˌa·tor** *n.*

pal·li·a·tive (ˈpælɪətɪv) *adj.* **1.** serving to palliate; relieving without curing. ~*n.* **2.** something that palliates, such as a sedative drug or agent. —**ˈpal·li·a·tive·ly** *adv.*

pal·lid (ˈpælɪd) *adj.* lacking colour, brightness, or vigour; wan or vapid: *a pallid complexion; a pallid performance.* [C17: from Latin *pallidus,* from *pallēre* to be PALE¹] —**ˈpal·lid·ly** *adv.* —**ˈpal·lid·ness** *or* **pal·ˈlid·i·ty** *n.*

pal·li·um (ˈpælɪəm) *n., pl.* **·li·a** (-lɪə) *or* **·li·ums. 1.** a garment worn by men in ancient Greece or Rome, made by draping a large rectangular cloth about the body. **2.** *Chiefly R.C. Church.* a woollen vestment consisting of a band encircling the shoulders with two lappets hanging from it front and back: worn by the pope, all archbishops, and (as a mark of special honour) some bishops. **3.** Also called: **mantle.** *Anatomy.* the cerebral cortex and contiguous white matter. **4.** *Zoology.* another name for **mantle** (sense 4). [C16: from Latin: cloak; related to Latin *palla* mantle]

pall-mall (ˈpælˈmæl) *n. Obsolete.* **1.** a game in which a ball is driven by a mallet along an alley and through an iron ring. **2.** the alley itself. [C17: from obsolete French, from Italian *pallamaglio,* from *palla* ball + *maglio* mallet]

Pall Mall (ˈpæl ˈmæl) *n.* a street in London, noted for its many clubs.

pal·lor (ˈpælə) *n.* a pale condition, esp. when unnatural: *fear gave his face a deathly pallor.* [C17: from Latin: whiteness (of the skin), from *pallēre* to be PALE¹]

pal·ly (ˈpælɪ) *adj.* **·li·er, ·li·est.** *Informal.* on friendly or familiar terms.

palm¹ (pɑːm) *n.* **1.** the inner part of the hand from the wrist to the base of the fingers. **2.** a corresponding part in animals, esp. apes and monkeys. **3.** a linear measure based on the breadth or length of a hand, equal to three to four inches (7.5 to 10 centimetres) or seven to ten inches (17.5 to 25 centimetres) respectively. **4.** the part of a glove that covers the palm. **5.** a hard leather shield worn by sailmakers to protect the palm of the hand. **6. a.** the side of the blade of an oar that faces away from the direction of a boat's movement during a stroke. **b.** the face of the fluke of an anchor. **7.** a flattened or expanded part of the antlers of certain deer. **8. in the palm of one's hand.** at one's mercy or command. ~*vb.* (*tr.*) **9.** to conceal in or about the hand, as in sleight-of-hand tricks, etc. **10.** to touch or soothe with the palm of the hand. ~See also **palm off.** [C14 *paume,* via Old French from Latin *palma;* compare Old English *folm* palm of the hand, Greek *palamē*]

palm² (pɑːm) *n.* **1.** any treelike plant of the tropical and subtropical monocotyledonous family *Palmaceae* (or *Palmae*), having a straight unbranched trunk crowned with large pinnate or palmate leaves. **2.** a leaf or branch of any of these trees, a symbol of victory, success, etc. **3.** merit or victory. **4.** an emblem or insignia representing a leaf or branch worn on certain military decorations. [Old English, from Latin *palma,* from the likeness of its spreading fronds to a hand; see PALM¹]

Pal·ma (*Spanish* ˈpalma) *n.* the capital of the Balearic Islands, on the SW coast of Majorca: a tourist centre. Pop.: 234 098 (1970). Official name: **Palma de Mallorca.**

pal·ma·ceous (pælˈmeɪʃəs) *adj.* of, relating to, or belonging to the palm family, *Palmaceae* (or *Palmae*).

pal·mar (ˈpælmə) *adj.* of or relating to the palm of the hand.

pal·ma·ry (ˈpælmərɪ) *adj. Rare.* worthy of praise. [C17: from Latin *palmārius* relating to the palm of victory; see PALM²]

pal·mate (ˈpælmeɪt, -mɪt) *or* **pal·mat·ed** *adj.* **1.** shaped like an open hand: *palmate antlers.* **2.** *Botany.* having five lobes or segments that spread out from a common point: *palmate leaves.* **3.** (of the feet of most water birds) having three toes connected by a web.

pal·ma·tion (pælˈmeɪʃən) *n.* **1.** the state of being palmate. **2.** a projection or division of a palmate structure.

Palm Beach *n.* a town in SE Florida, on an island between Lake Worth (a lagoon) and the Atlantic: major resort and tourist centre. Pop.: 9086 (1970).

palm civ·et *n.* any of various small civet-like arboreal viverrine mammals of the genera *Paradoxurus, Hemigalus,* etc., of Africa and S and SE Asia.

palm·er (ˈpɑːmə) *n.* (in medieval Europe) **1.** a pilgrim bearing a palm branch as a sign of his visit to the Holy Land. **2.** an itinerant monk. **3.** any pilgrim. [C13: from Old French *palmier,* from Medieval Latin *palmārius,* from Latin *palma* palm]

Palm·er (ˈpɑːmə) *n.* **1. Ar·nold.** born 1929, U.S. professional golfer: won the U.S. Open Championship (1960) and the British Open Championship (1961; 1962). **2. Sam·u·el.** 1805–81, English painter of visionary landscapes, influenced by William Blake.

Palm·er Ar·chi·pel·a·go *pl. n.* a group of islands between South America and Antarctica: part of the British colony of Falkland Islands and Dependencies. Former name: **Antarctic Archipelago.**

Palm·er Land *n.* the S part of the Antarctic Peninsula.

Palm·er Pen·in·su·la *n.* the former name (until 1964) for the **Antarctic Peninsula.**

Palm·er·ston¹ (ˈpɑːməstən) *n.* the former name (1869–1911) of **Darwin¹.**

Palm·er·ston² (ˈpɑːməstən) *n.* **Hen·ry John Tem·ple,** 3rd Viscount Palmerston. 1784–1865, British statesman; foreign secretary (1830–34; 1835–41; 1846–51); prime minister (1855–58; 1859–65). His talent was for foreign affairs, in which he earned a reputation as a British nationalist and for high-handedness and gunboat diplomacy.

Palm·er·ston North *n.* a city in New Zealand, in S North Island on the Manawatu River. Pop.: 51 893 (1971).

pal·mette (pælˈmɛt) *n. Archaeol.* an ornament or design resembling the palm leaf. [C19: from French: a little PALM²]

pal·met·to (pælˈmɛtəʊ) *n., pl.* **·tos** *or* **·toes. 1.** any of several small chiefly tropical fan palms, esp. any of the genus *Sabal,* of the southeastern U.S. See also **cabbage palmetto, saw palmetto. 2.** any of various other fan palms such as palms of the genera *Serenoa, Thrinax,* and *Chamaerops.* [C16: from Spanish *palmito* a little PALM²]

Pal·mi·ra (*Spanish* palˈmira) *n.* a city in W Colombia: agricultural trading centre. Pop.: 140 481 (1973).

palm·is·try (ˈpɑːmɪstrɪ) *n.* the process or art of interpreting character, telling fortunes, etc., by the configuration of lines, marks, and bumps on a person's hand. Also called: **chiromancy.** [C15 *pawmestry,* from *paume* PALM¹; the second element is unexplained] —**ˈpalm·ist** *n.*

pal·mi·tate (ˈpælmɪˌteɪt) *n.* any salt or ester of palmitic acid.

pal·mit·ic ac·id (pælˈmɪtɪk) *n.* a white crystalline solid that is a saturated fatty acid: used in the manufacture of soap and candles. Formula: $CH_3(CH_2)_4COOH$. [C19: from French *palmitique;* see PALM², -ITE², -IC]

pal·mi·tin ('pælmɪtɪn) *n.* the colourless glyceride of palmitic acid, occurring in many natural oils and fats. Formula: $(C_{15}H_{13}COO)_3C_3H_5$. Also called: **tripalmitin.** [C19: from French *palmitine,* probably from *palmite* pith of the palm tree; see PALM²]

palm off *vb.* (*tr., adv.,* often foll. by *on*) **1.** to offer, sell or spend fraudulently: *to palm off a counterfeit coin.* **2.** to divert in order to be rid of: *I palmed the unwelcome visitor off on John.*

palm oil *n.* a yellow butter-like oil obtained from the fruit of the oil palm, used as an edible fat and in soap, etc.

palm-oil chop *n.* a W African dish made with meat and palm oil.

palm sug·ar *n.* sugar obtained from the sap of certain species of palm trees.

Palm Sun·day *n.* the Sunday before Easter commemorating Christ's triumphal entry into Jerusalem.

palm vault·ing *n.* a less common name for **fan vaulting.**

palm wine *n.* (esp. in W Africa) the sap drawn from the palm tree, esp. when allowed to ferment.

palm·y ('pɑːmɪ) *adj.* **palm·i·er, palm·i·est. 1.** prosperous, flourishing, or luxurious: *a palmy life.* **2.** covered with, relating to, or resembling palms: *a palmy beach.*

pal·my·ra (pæl'maɪrə) *n.* a tall tropical Asian palm, *Borassus flabellifer* with large fan-shaped leaves used for thatching and weaving and edible seedlings. [C17: from Portuguese *palmeira* palm tree (see PALM²); perhaps influenced by PALMYRA, city in Syria]

Pal·my·ra (pæl'maɪrə) *n.* **1.** an ancient city in central Syria: said to have been built by Solomon. Biblical name: **Tadmor. 2.** an island in the central Pacific, in the Line Islands: under U.S. administration.

Pal·o Al·to *n.* **1.** ('pæləʊ 'æltəʊ). a city in W California, southeast of San Francisco: founded in 1891 as the seat of Stanford University. Pop.: 55 996 (1970). **2.** (*Spanish* 'palo 'alto). a battlefield in E Mexico, northwest of Monterrey, where the first battle (1846) of the Mexican War took place, in which the Mexicans under General Mariano Arista were defeated by the Americans under General Zachary Taylor.

pa·lo·lo worm (pə'ləʊləʊ) *n.* any of several polychaete worms of the family *Eunicidae,* esp. *Eunice viridis,* of the S Pacific Ocean: reproductive segments are shed from the posterior end of the body when breeding. [C20 *palolo,* from Samoan or Tongan]

Pal·o·mar ('pælə,mɑː) *n.* **Mount.** a mountain in S California, northeast of San Diego: site of **Mount Palomar Observatory,** which has a large (200-inch) reflecting telescope. Height: 1870 m (6140 ft.).

pal·o·mi·no (,pælə'miːnəʊ) *n., pl.* **·nos.** a golden horse with a cream or white mane and tail. [American Spanish, from Spanish: dovelike, from Latin *palumbīnus,* from *palumbēs* ring dove]

pa·loo·ka (pə'luːkə) *n. U.S. slang.* a stupid or clumsy boxer or other person. [C20: origin uncertain]

Pa·los (*Spanish* 'palos) *n.* a village and former port in SW Spain: starting point of Columbus' voyage of discovery to America (1492).

palp (pælp) *or* **pal·pus** *n., pl.* **palps** *or* **pal·pi** ('pælpaɪ). **1.** either of a pair of sensory appendages that arise from the mouthparts of crustaceans and insects. **2.** either of a pair of tactile organs arising from the head or anterior end of certain annelids and molluscs. [C19: from French, from Latin *palpus* a touching]

pal·pa·ble ('pælpəbᵊl) *adj.* **1.** (*usually prenominal*) easily perceived by the senses or the mind; obvious: *the excuse was a palpable lie.* **2.** capable of being touched; tangible. **3.** *Med.* capable of being discerned by the sense of touch: *a palpable tumour.* [C14: from Late Latin *palpābilis* that may be touched, from Latin *palpāre* to stroke, touch] —**,pal·pa·'bil·i·ty** *or* **'pal·pa·ble·ness** *n.* —**'pal·pa·bly** *adv.*

pal·pate¹ ('pælpeɪt) *vb.* (*tr.*) *Med.* to examine (an area of the body) by the sense of touch and pressure. [C19: from Latin *palpāre* to stroke] —**pal·'pa·tion** *n.*

pal·pate² ('pælpeɪt) *adj. Zoology.* of, relating to, or possessing a palp or palps.

pal·pe·bral ('pælpɪbrəl) *adj.* of or relating to the eyelid. [C19: from Late Latin *palpebrālis,* from Latin *palpebra* eyelid; probably related to *palpāre* to stroke]

pal·pe·brate ('pælpɪ,brɪt, -,breɪt) *adj.* **1.** having eyelids. ~*vb.* **2.** (*intr.*) to wink or blink, esp. repeatedly.

pal·pi·tate ('pælpɪ,teɪt) *vb.* (*intr.*) **1.** (of the heart) to beat with abnormal rapidity. **2.** to flutter or tremble. [C17: from Latin *palpitāre* to throb, from *palpāre* to stroke] —**'pal·pi·tant** *adj.* —**,pal·pi·'ta·tion** *n.*

pals·grave ('pɔːlzgreɪv) *n. Archaic.* a German count palatine. [C16: from Dutch, from Middle Dutch *paltsgrave,* from *palts* estate of a palatine + *grave* count] —**pals·gra·vine** ('pɔːlzgrə,viːn) *fem. n.*

pal·stave ('pɔːl,steɪv) *n. Archaeol.* a kind of celt, usually of bronze, made to fit into a split wooden handle rather than having a socket for the handle. [C19: from Danish *paalstav,* from Old Norse, from *páll* spade + *stafr* STAFF]

pal·sy ('pɔːlzɪ) *n., pl.* **·sies. 1.** *Pathol.* paralysis, esp. of a specified type: *cerebral palsy. vb.* **·sies, ·sy·ing, ·sied.** (*tr.*) **2.** to paralyse. [C13 *palesi,* from Old French *paralisie,* from Latin PARALYSIS] —**'pal·sied** *adj.*

pal·ter ('pɔːltə) *vb.* (*intr.*) **1.** to act or talk insincerely. **2.** to haggle. [C16: of unknown origin] —**'pal·ter·er** *n.*

pal·try ('pɔːltrɪ) *adj.* **·tri·er, ·tri·est. 1.** insignificant; meagre. **2.** worthless or petty. [C16: from Low Germanic *palter, paltrig* ragged] —**'pal·tri·ly** *adv.* —**'pal·tri·ness** *n.*

pa·lu·dal (pə'ljuːdᵊl, 'pæljʊdᵊl) *adj. Rare.* **1.** of, relating to, or produced by marshes. **2.** malarial. [C19: from Latin *palus* marsh; related to Sanskrit *palvala* pond]

pal·u·dism ('pælju,dɪzəm) *n. Pathol.* a rare word for **malaria.** [C19: from Latin *palus* marsh]

pal up *vb.* (intr., adv.; often foll. by *with*) *Informal.* to become friends (with): *he palled up with the other boys.*

pal·y ('peɪlɪ) *adj.* (*usually postpositive*) *Heraldry.* vertically striped. [C15: from Old French *palé,* from Latin *pālus* stake; see PALE²]

pal·y·nol·o·gy (,pælɪ'nɒlədʒɪ) *n.* the study of living and fossil pollen grains and plant spores. [C20: from Greek *palunein* to scatter + -LOGY] —**pal·y·no·log·i·cal** (,pælɪnə'lɒdʒɪkᵊl) *adj.* —**,pal·y·'nol·o·gist** *n.*

pam. *or* **pamph.** *abbrev. for* pamphlet.

Pa·ma-Nyun·gan ('pɑːmə'njʊŋgən) *adj.* **1.** of or relating to the largest family within the phylum of languages spoken by the Australian Aborigines. ~*n.* **2.** this phylum.

Pa·mirs (pə'mɪəz) *pl. n.* **the.** a mountainous area of central Asia, mainly in the Tadzhik SSR of the Soviet Union and partly in the Kirghiz SSR, extending into China and Afghanistan: consists of a complex of high ranges, from which the Tien Shan projects to the north, the Kunlun and Karakoram to the east, and the Hindu Kush to the west. Highest peak: Kungur, 7719 m (25 326 ft.). Also called: **Pamir.**

Pam·li·co Sound ('pæmlɪkəʊ) *n.* an inlet of the Atlantic between the E coast of North Carolina and its chain of offshore islands. Length: 130 km (80 miles).

pam·pas ('pæmpəz) *n.* (*often functioning as pl.*) **a.** the extensive grassy plains of temperate South America, esp. in Argentina. **b.** (*as modifier*): *pampas dwellers.* [C18: from American Spanish *pampa* (sing.), from Quechua *bamba* plain] —**pam·pe·an** ('pæmpɪən, pæm'piːən) *adj.*

pam·pas grass ('pæmpəs, -pəz) *n.* any of various large grasses of the South American genus *Cortaderia* and related genera, widely cultivated for their large feathery silver-coloured flower branches.

pam·per ('pæmpə) *vb.* (*tr.*) **1.** to treat with affectionate and usually excessive indulgence; coddle; spoil. **2.** *Archaic.* to feed to excess. [C14: of Germanic origin; compare German dialect *pampfen* to gorge oneself] —**'pam·per·er** *n.*

pam·pe·ro (pæm'pɛərəʊ; *Spanish* pam'pero) *n., pl.* **·ros** (-rəʊz; *Spanish* -ros). a dry cold wind in South America blowing across the pampas from the south or southwest. [C19: from American Spanish: (wind) of the PAMPAS]

pam·phlet ('pæmflɪt) *n.* **1.** a brief publication generally having a paper cover; booklet. **2.** a brief treatise, often on a subject of current interest, published in pamphlet form. [C14 *pamflet,* from Anglo-Latin *panfletus,* from Medieval Latin *Pamphilus* title of a popular 12th-century amatory poem from Greek *Pamphilos* masculine proper name]

pam·phlet·eer (,pæmflɪ'tɪə) *n.* **1.** a person who writes or issues pamphlets, esp. of a controversial nature. ~*vb.* **2.** (*intr.*) to write or issue pamphlets.

pam·phrey ('pæmfrɪ) *n. Ulster dialect.* a cabbage. [of unknown origin]

Pam·phyl·i·a (pæm'fɪlɪə) *n.* an area on the S coast of ancient Asia Minor.

Pam·plo·na (pæm'pləʊnə; *Spanish* pam'plona) *n.* a city in N Spain in the foothills of the Pyrenees: capital of the kingdom of Navarre from the 11th century until 1841. Pop.: 147 168 (1970). Former name: **Pampeluna.**

pan¹ (pæn) *n.* **1. a.** a wide metal vessel used in cooking. **b.** (*in combination*): *saucepan.* **2.** Also called: **pan·ful.** the amount such a vessel will hold. **3.** any of various similar vessels used in industry, etc., as for boiling liquids. **4.** a dish used by prospectors, esp. gold prospectors, for separating a valuable mineral from the gravel or earth containing it by washing and agitating. **5.** either of the two dishlike receptacles on a balance. **6.** Also called: **lavatory pan.** *Brit.* the bowl of a lavatory. **7. a.** a natural or artificial depression in the ground where salt can be obtained by the evaporation of brine. **b.** a natural depression containing water or mud. **8.** *Caribbean.* the indented top from an oil drum used as an instrument in a steel band. **9.** see **hardpan** or **brainpan. 10.** a small ice floe. **11.** a slang word for **face. 12.** a small cavity containing priming powder in the locks of old guns. **13.** a hard substratum of soil. ~*vb.* **pans, pan·ning, panned. 14.** (when *tr.,* often foll. by *off* or *out*) to wash (gravel) in a pan to separate particles of (valuable minerals) from it. **15.** (*intr.;* often foll. by *out*) (of gravel, etc.) to yield valuable minerals by this process. **16.** (*tr.*) *Informal.* to criticize harshly: *the critics panned his new play.* ~See also **pan out.** [Old English *panne;* related to Old Saxon, Old Norse *panna,* Old High German *pfanna*]

pan² (pæn) *n.* **1.** the leaf of the betel tree. **2.** a preparation of this leaf which is chewed, together with betel nuts and lime, in India and the East Indies. [C17: from Hindi, from Sanskrit *parna* feather, wing, leaf]

pan³ (pæn) *vb.* **pans, pan·ning, panned. 1.** to move (a film camera) or (of a film camera) to be moved so as to follow a moving object or obtain a panoramic effect. ~*n.* **2. a.** the act of panning. **b.** (*as modifier*): *a pan shot.* [C20: shortened from PANORAMIC]

Pan (pæn) *n. Greek myth.* the god of fields, woods, shepherds, and flocks, represented as a man with a goat's legs, horns, and ears.

Pan. *abbrev. for* Panama.

pan- *combining form.* **1.** all or every: *panchromatic.* **2.** including or relating to all parts or members: *Pan-African; pantheistic.* [from Greek *pan,* neuter of *pas* all]

pan·a·ce·a (ˌpænəˈsɪə) *n.* a remedy for all diseases or ills. [C16: via Latin from Greek *panakeia* healing everything, from *pan* all + *akēs* remedy] —**ˌpan·a·ˈce·an** *adj.*

pa+nache (pəˈnæʃ, -ˈnɑːʃ) *n.* **1.** a dashing manner; style; swagger: *he rides with panache.* **2.** a feathered plume on a helmet. [C16: via French from Old Italian *pennacchio,* from Late Latin *pinnāculum* feather, from Latin *pinna* feather; compare Latin *pinnāculum* PINNACLE]

pa+na+da (pəˈnɑːdə) *n.* a mixture of flour, water, etc., or of breadcrumbs soaked in milk, used as a thickening. [C16: from Spanish, from *pan* bread, from Latin *pānis*]

Pan-Af·ri·can *adj.* **1.** of or relating to all African countries or the advocacy of political unity among African countries. ~*n.* **2.** a supporter of the Pan-African movement. —**ˈPan-ˈAf·ri·can+ism** *n.* —**ˈPan-ˈAf·ri·can+ist** *n.*

Pan·a+ma (ˌpænəˈmɑː, ˈpænəˌmɑː) *n.* **1.** a republic in Central America, occupying the Isthmus of Panama: gained independence from Spain in 1821 and joined Greater Colombia; became independent in 1903, with the immediate area around the canal forming the Canal Zone under U.S. jurisdiction. Languages: Spanish and English. Religion: chiefly Roman Catholic. Currency: balboa. Capital: Panama City. Pop.: 1 428 082 (1970). Area: 75 650 sq. km (29 201 sq. miles). **2. Isthmus of.** an isthmus linking North and South America, between the Pacific and the Caribbean. Length: 676 km (420 miles). Width (at its narrowest point): 50 km (31 miles). Former name: (Isthmus of) **Darien. 3. Gulf of.** a wide inlet of the Pacific in Panama. —**Pan·a+ma+ni·an** (ˌpænəˈmeɪnɪən) *adj., n.*

Pan·a+ma Ca+nal *n.* a canal across the Isthmus of Panama, linking the Atlantic and Pacific Oceans: extends from Colón on the Caribbean Sea southeast to Balboa on the Gulf of Panama; built by the U.S. (1904–14), after an unsuccessful previous attempt (1881–89) by the French under de Lesseps. Length: 64 km (40 miles).

Pan·a+ma Ca+nal Zone *n.* See **Canal Zone.**

Pan·a+ma Cit·y *n.* the capital of Panama, near the Pacific entrance of the Panama Canal: developed rapidly with the building of the Panama Canal; seat of the University of Panama (1935). Pop.: 576 645 (1970).

Pan·a+ma hat *n.* (*sometimes not cap.*) a hat made of the plaited leaves of the jipijapa plant of Central and South America. Often shortened to **panama** or **Panama.**

Pan-A·mer·i+can *adj.* of, relating to, or concerning North, South, and Central America collectively or the advocacy of political or economic unity among American countries. —**ˈPan-Aˈmer·i+can+ism** *n.*

Pan A·mer·i+can Un+ion *n.* the secretariat and major official agency of the Organization of American States.

Pan-Ar·ab·ism *n.* the principle of, support for, or the movement towards Arab political union or cooperation. —**ˈPan-ˈAr·ab** *or* **ˈPan-ˈAr·ab·ic** *adj., n.*

pan·a+tel+la (ˌpænəˈtɛlə) *n.* a long slender cigar. [American Spanish *panetela* long slim biscuit, from Italian *panatella* small loaf, from *pane* bread, from Latin *pānis*]

Pan+ath+e·nae·a (pæˌnæθɪˈniːə) *n.* (in ancient Athens) a summer festival on the traditional birthday of Athena.

Pa+nay (pɑːˈnaɪ) *n.* an island in the central Philippines, the westernmost of the Visayan Islands. Pop.: 2 144 544 (1970). Area: 12 300 sq. km (4750 sq. miles).

pan+cake (ˈpænˌkeɪk) *n.* **1. a.** a thin flat cake, often rolled and filled, made from batter and fried on both sides. **b.** (*as modifier*): *pancake mix.* **2.** a stick or flat cake of compressed make-up. **3.** Also called: **pancake landing.** an aircraft landing made by levelling out a few feet from the ground and then dropping onto it. ~*vb.* **4.** to cause (an aircraft) to make a pancake landing or (of an aircraft) to make a pancake landing.

Pan+cake Day *n.* another name for **Shrove Tuesday.**

pan+cake ice *n.* thin slabs of newly formed ice in polar seas.

pan+chax (ˈpænˌtʃæks) *n.* any of several brightly coloured tropical Asian cyprinodont fishes of the genus *Aplocheilus,* such as *A. panchax* (**blue panchax**). [C19: from New Latin (former generic name), of obscure origin]

Pan+cha+yat (pənˈtʃɑːjət) *n.* a village council in India. [Hindi, from Sanskrit *panch* five, because such councils originally consisted of five members]

Pan+chen La·ma (ˈpɑːntʃən) *n.* one of the two Grand Lamas of Tibet, ranking below the Dalai Lama. Also called: **Tashi Lama.** [from Tibetan *panchen,* literally: great jewel, from the title of the lama (in full: great jewel among scholars)]

pan+chro+mat+ic (ˌpænkrəʊˈmætɪk) *adj. Photog.* (of an emulsion or film) made sensitive to all colours by the addition of suitable dyes to the emulsion. Compare **orthochromatic.** —**pan+chro+ma+tism** (pænˈkrəʊməˌtɪzəm) *n.*

pan+cos+mism (pænˈkɒzmɪzəm) *n.* the philosophical doctrine that the material universe is all that exists. [C19: see PAN-, COSMOS, -ISM]

pan+cra+ti·um (pænˈkreɪʃɪəm) *n., pl.* **+ti·a** (-ʃɪə). (in ancient Greece) a wrestling and boxing contest. [C17: via Latin from Greek *pankration,* from PAN- + *kratos* strength] —**pan+crat+ic** (pænˈkrætɪk) *adj.*

pan+cre+as (ˈpæŋkrɪəs) *n.* a large elongated glandular organ, situated behind the stomach, that secretes insulin and pancreatic juice. [C16: via New Latin from Greek *pankreas,* from *pan-* + *kreas* flesh] —**pan+cre+at+ic** (ˌpæŋkrɪˈætɪk) *adj.*

pan+cre+at+ic juice *n.* the clear alkaline secretion of the pancreas that is released into the duodenum and contains several digestive enzymes.

pan+cre·a+tin (ˈpæŋkrɪətɪn) *n.* the powdered extract of the pancreas of certain animals, such as the pig, used in medicine as an aid to the digestion.

pan+da (ˈpændə) *n.* **1.** Also called: **giant panda.** a large black-and-white herbivorous bearlike mammal, *Ailuropoda melanoleuca,* related to the raccoons and inhabiting the bamboo forests of China: family *Procyonidae.* **2. lesser** or **red panda.** a closely related smaller animal resembling a raccoon, *Ailurus fulgens,* of the mountain forests of S Asia, having a reddish-brown coat and ringed tail. [C19: via French from a native Nepalese word]

pan+da car *n.Brit.* a police patrol car, esp. a blue and white one.

pan+da+na+ceous (ˌpændəˈneɪʃəs) *adj.* of, relating to, or belonging to the *Pandanaceae,* an Old World tropical family of monocotyledonous plants including the screw pines.

pan+da+nus (pænˈdeɪnəs) *n., pl.* **+nus·es.** any of various Old World tropical palmlike plants of the genus *Pandanus,* having leaves and roots yielding a fibre used for making mats, etc., and prop roots: family *Pandanaceae.* See also **screw pine.** [C19: via New Latin from Malay *pandan*]

Pan·da·rus (ˈpændərəs) *n.* **1.** *Greek myth.* the leader of the Lycians, allies of the Trojans in their war with the Greeks. He broke the truce by shooting Menelaus with an arrow and was killed in the ensuing battle by Diomedes. **2.** (in medieval legend) the procurer of Cressida on behalf of Troilus.

Pan+de·an (pænˈdiːən) *adj.* of or relating to the god Pan.

pan+dect (ˈpændɛkt) *n.* **1.** a treatise covering all aspects of a particular subject. **2.** (*often pl.*) the complete body of laws of a country; legal code. [C16: via Late Latin from Greek *pandektēs* containing everything, from PAN- + *dektēs* receiver, from *dekhesthai* to receive]

pan+dem+ic (pænˈdɛmɪk) *adj.* **1.** (of a disease) affecting persons over a wide geographical area; extensively epidemic. **2.** *Rare.* widespread; general. ~*n.* **3.** a pandemic disease. [C17: from Late Latin *pandēmus,* from Greek *pandēmos* general, from PAN- + *dēmos* the people]

pan+de+mo+ni·um (ˌpændɪˈməʊnɪəm) *n.* **1.** wild confusion; uproar. **2.** a place of uproar and chaos. [C17: coined by Milton to designate the capital of hell in *Paradise Lost,* from PAN- + Greek *daimōn* DEMON] —**pan+de+mo+ni+ac** (ˌpændɪˈməʊnɪˌæk) *or* **pan+de+mon+ic** (ˌpændɪˈmɒnɪk) *adj.*

pan+der (ˈpændə) *vb.* **1.** (*intr.; foll. by to*) to give gratification (to weaknesses or desires). **2.** (*archaic when tr.*) to act as a go-between in a sexual intrigue (for). ~*n. also* **pan+der+er. 3.** a person who caters for vulgar desires, esp. in order to make money. **4.** a person who procures a sexual partner for another; pimp. [C16 (n.): from *Pandare* PANDARUS]

pan+dit (ˈpʌndɪt; *spelling pron.* ˈpændɪt) *n. Hinduism.* a variant spelling of **pundit.**

P. & L. *abbrev. for* profit and loss.

P. & O. *abbrev. for* Peninsular and Oriental (Steamship Company).

Pan·do·ra (pænˈdɔːrə) *or* **Pan·dore** (pænˈdɔː, ˈpændɔː) *n. Greek myth.* the first woman, made out of earth as the gods' revenge on man for obtaining fire from Prometheus. Given a box (**Pandora's box**) that she was forbidden to open, she disobeyed out of curiosity and released from it all the ills that beset man, leaving only hope within. [from Greek, literally: all-gifted]

pan+dore (ˈpændɔː) *n. Music.* another word for **bandore.**

pan+dour (ˈpænduə) *n.* one of an 18th-century force of Croatian soldiers in the Austrian service notorious for their brutality. [C18: via French from Hungarian *pandur,* from Croat: guard, probably from Medieval Latin *banderius* summoner, from *bannum* BAN]

pan+dow+dy (pænˈdaʊdɪ) *n., pl.* **+dies.** *U.S.* a deep-dish pie made from fruit, esp. apples, with a cake topping: *apple pandowdy.* [C19: of unknown origin]

p. & p. *Brit. abbrev. for* postage and packing.

pan+du+rate (ˈpændjʊˌreɪt) *or* **pan+du+ri+form** (pænˈdjʊərɪˌfɔːm) *adj.* (of plant leaves) shaped like the body of a fiddle. [C19: from Late Latin *pandūra* BANDORE]

pan+dy (ˈpændɪ) *Chiefly Scot. or Irish.* ~*n., pl.* **+dies. 1.** (in schools) a stroke on the hand with a strap, etc., as a punishment. ~*vb.* **+dies, +dy+ing, +died. 2.** (*tr.*) to punish with such strokes. [C19: from Latin *pande* (*manum*) stretch out (the hand), from *pandere* to spread or extend]

pan+dy+bat (ˈpændɪˌbæt) *n. Obsolete, chiefly Scot. and Irish.* (in boys' schools) a leather strap used in pandying.

pane[1] (peɪn) *n.* **1.** a sheet of glass in a window or door. **2.** a panel of a window, door, wall, etc. **3.** a flat section or face, as of a cut diamond. **4.** *Philately.* **a.** any rectangular marked divisions of a sheet of stamps made for convenience in selling. **b.** a single page in a stamp booklet. See also **tête-bêche, se tenant.** [C13: from Old French *pan* portion, from Latin *pannus* rag]

pane[2] (peɪn) *n.* a variant of **peen.**

pa·né *French.* (paˈne) *adj.* (of fish, meat, etc.) dipped or rolled in breadcrumbs before cooking.

pan+e·gyr+ic (ˌpænɪˈdʒɪrɪk) *n.* a public formal commendation; eulogy. [C17: via French and Latin from Greek, from *panēguris* public gathering, from PAN- + *aguris* assembly] —**ˌpan+e·ˈgyr·i·cal** *adj.* —**ˌpan+e·ˈgyr·i·cal+ly** *adv.* —**ˌpan+e·ˈgyr+ist** *n.*

pan+e·gy+rize *or* **pan+e·gy+rise** (ˈpænɪdʒɪˌraɪz) *vb.* to make a eulogy or eulogies (about).

pan+el ('pænᵊl) *n.* **1.** a flat section of a wall, door, etc. **2.** any distinct section or component of something, esp. of a car body, the spine of a book, etc. **3.** a piece of material inserted in a skirt, etc. **4. a.** a group of persons selected to act as a team in a quiz, to judge a contest, to discuss a topic before an audience, etc. **b.** (*as modifier*): *a panel game.* **5.** a public discussion by such a group: *a panel on public health.* **6.** *Law.* **a.** a list of persons summoned for jury service. **b.** the persons on a specific jury. **7.** *Scots law.* a person indicted or accused of a crime after appearing in court. **8. a.** a thin board used as a surface or backing for an oil painting. **b.** a painting done on such a surface. **9.** any picture with a length much greater than its breadth. **10.** See **instrument panel. 11.** *Brit.* (formerly) **a.** a list of patients insured under the National Health Insurance Scheme. **b.** a list of medical practitioners within a given area available for consultation by these patients. **12. on the panel.** *Brit. informal.* receiving sickness benefit, esp. from the government. ~*vb.* **+els, +el+ling, +elled** *or U.S.* **+els, +el+ing, +eled.** (*tr.*) **13.** to furnish or decorate with panels. **14.** to divide into panels. **15.** *Law.* **a.** to empanel (a jury). **b.** (in Scotland) to bring (a person) to trial; indict. [C13: from Old French: portion, from *pan* piece of cloth, from Latin *pannus;* see PANE]

pan+el beat+er *n.* a person who beats out the bodywork of motor vehicles, etc.

pan+el heat+ing *n.* a system of space heating with panels that contain heating pipes or electrical conductors.

pan+el+ling *or U.S.* **pan+el+ing** ('pænᵊlɪŋ) *n.* **1.** panels collectively, as on a wall or ceiling. **2.** material used for making panels.

pan+el+list *or U.S.* **pan+el+ist** ('pænᵊlɪst) *n.* a member of a panel, esp. on a radio or television programme.

pan+el pin *n.* a light slender nail with a narrow head.

pan+el saw *n.* a saw with a long narrow blade for cutting thin wood.

pan+el truck *n.* the U.S. name for **delivery van.**

pan+el van *n. Austral.* a small van, esp. one having windows and seats in the rear.

pan+et+to+ne (ˌpænəˈtəʊnɪ; *Italian* ˌpanetˈtoːne) *n., pl.* **+nes** *or* **+ni** (-nɪ). a kind of Italian spiced brioche containing sultanas: traditionally eaten at Christmas in Italy. [Italian, from *panetto* small loaf, from *pane* bread, from Latin *pānis*]

pang (pæŋ) *n.* a sudden brief sharp feeling, as of loneliness, physical pain, or hunger. [C16: variant of earlier *prange,* of Germanic origin]

pan+ga ('pæŋgə) *n.* a broad heavy knife of E Africa, used as a tool or weapon. [from a native E African word]

Pan+gae·a (pænˈdʒiːə) *n.* an ancient landmass that is thought to have split up at the end of the Palaeozoic era into the continents of Gondwanaland and Laurasia. [C20: from Greek, literally: all-earth]

pan+gen+e·sis (pænˈdʒɛnɪsɪs) *n.* a former theory of heredity, that each body cell produces hereditary particles that circulate in the blood before collecting in the reproductive cells. See also **blastogenesis** (sense 1). —**pan+ge·net+ic** (ˌpændʒəˈnɛtɪk) *adj.* —ˌ**pan+geˈnet+i·cal+ly** *adv.*

Pan-Ger·man+ism *n.* (esp. in the 19th century) the movement for the unification of Germany.

Pang-fou ('pæŋˈfuː) *n.* a variant spelling of **Pengpu.**

pan+go+lin (pæŋˈgəʊlɪn) *n.* any mammal of the order *Pholidota* found in tropical Africa, S Asia, and Indonesia, having a body covered with overlapping horny scales and a long snout specialized for feeding on ants and termites. Also called: **scaly anteater.** [C18: from Malay *peng-gōling,* from *gōling* to roll over; from its ability to roll into a ball]

Pan+go Pan+go ('pɑːŋgəʊ 'pɑːŋgəʊ) *n.* the former name of **Pago Pago.**

pan+han+dle[1] ('pænˌhændᵊl) *n.* **1.** (*sometimes cap.*) *U.S.* a narrow strip of land that projects from one state into another. **2.** (in a South African city) a plot of land without street frontage.

pan+han+dle[2] ('pænˌhændᵊl) *vb. U.S. informal.* to accost and beg from (passers-by), esp. on the street. [C19: probably a back formation from *panhandler* a person who begs with a pan] —**ˈpan+ˌhan+dler** *n.*

Pan+hel+len+ic (ˌpænhɛˈlɛnɪk) *adj.* of or relating to all the Greeks, all Greece, or Panhellenism.

Pan+hel+len+ism (ˌpænˈhɛlɪˌnɪzəm) *n.* the principle of or support for the union of all Greeks or all Greece. —ˌ**Pan+ˈhel+len+ist** *n.* —ˌ**Pan+ˌhel+len+ˈis+tic** *adj.*

pan+ic ('pænɪk) *n.* **1.** a sudden overwhelming feeling of terror or anxiety, esp. one affecting a whole group of people. **2.** (*modifier*) of or resulting from such terror: *panic measures.* ~*vb.* **+ics, +ick+ing, +icked. 3.** to feel or cause to feel panic. [C17: from French *panique,* from New Latin *pānicus,* from Greek *panikos* emanating from PAN, considered as the source of irrational fear] —**ˈpan+ick·y** *adj.*

Pan+ic ('pænɪk) *adj.* of or relating to the god Pan.

pan+ic grass *n.* any of various grasses of the genus *Panicum,* such as millet, grown in warm and tropical regions for fodder and grain. [C15 *panic,* from Latin *pānicum,* probably a back formation from *pānicula,* PANICLE]

pan·i·cle ('pænɪkᵊl) *n.* a compound raceme, as in the oat. [C16: from Latin *pānicula* tuft, diminutive of *panus* thread, ultimately from Greek *penos* web; related to *penion* bobbin] —**ˈpan·i+cled** *adj.*

pan·ic+mon·ger ('pænɪkˌmʌŋgə) *n.* a person who spreads panic.

pan·ic-strick·en *or* **pan·ic-struck** *adj.* affected by panic.

pa+nic·u+late (pəˈnɪkjʊˌleɪt, -lɪt) *or* **pa+nic·u+lat+ed** *adj. Botany.* growing or arranged in panicles: *a paniculate inflorescence.* —**pa+ˈnic·u+ˌlate+ly** *adv.*

Pan+ja+bi (pʌnˈdʒɑːbɪ) *adj., n.* a variant spelling of **Punjabi.**

pan+jan+drum (pænˈdʒændrəm) *n.* a pompous self-important man. [C18: after a character, the *Grand Panjandrum,* in a nonsense work (1755) by Samuel Foote, English playwright and actor]

Pan+jim ('pɑːnˌʒɪm) *n.* the capital of the Indian union territory of Goa, Daman, and Diu: a port on the Arabian Sea on the coast of Goa. Pop.: 34 953 (1971).

Pank·hurst ('pæŋkhɜːst) *n.* **1.** Dame **Chris·ta·bel.** 1880–1958, English suffragette. **2.** her mother, **Em·me·line.** 1858–1928, English suffragette leader, who founded the militant Women's Social and Political Union (1903). **3. Syl·vi·a,** daughter of Emmeline Pankhurst. 1882–1960, English suffragette and pacifist.

pan-loaf *or* **pen-loaf** *n. Irish and central Scot. dialect.* a loaf of bread with a light crust all the way round. Often shortened to **pan.**

pan+mix·i·a (pænˈmɪksɪə) *or* **pan+mix+is** (pænˈmɪksɪs) *n.* (in population genetics) random mating within an interbreeding population. [C20: from New Latin, from Greek PAN- + *mixis* act of mating]

Pan+mun+jom ('pɑːnˈmʊnˈdʒɒm) *n.* a village in the demilitarized zone of Korea: site of truce talks leading to the end of the Korean War (1950–53).

pan+nage ('pænɪdʒ) *n. Archaic.* **1.** pasturage for pigs, esp. in a forest. **2.** the right to pasture pigs in a forest. **3.** payment for this. **4.** acorns, beech mast, etc., on which pigs feed. [C13: from Old French *pasnage,* ultimately from Latin *pastiō-, pastiō* feeding, from *pascere* to feed]

panne (pæn) *n.* a lightweight velvet fabric. [C19: via Old French, from Latin *pinna* wing, feather]

pan+ni+er ('pænɪə) *n.* **1.** a large basket, esp. one of a pair slung over a beast of burden. **2.** one of a pair of bags slung either side of the back wheel of a motor cycle, etc. **3.** (esp. in the 18th century) **a.** a hooped framework to distend a woman's skirt. **b.** one of two puffed out loops of material worn drawn back onto the hips to reveal the underskirt. [C13: from Old French *panier,* from Latin *pānārium* basket for bread, from *pānis* bread]

pan+ni+kin ('pænɪkɪn) *n. Chiefly Brit.* a small metal cup or pan. [C19: from PAN[1] + -KIN]

pan+ni+kin boss *n. Austral. informal.* a person in charge of a few fellow-workers.

Pan+no+ni·a (pəˈnəʊnɪə) *n.* a region of the ancient world south and west of the Danube: made a Roman province in 6 A.D.

pa+no+cha (pəˈnəʊtʃə) *n.* **1.** a coarse grade of sugar made in Mexico. **2.** *U.S.* a sweet made from brown sugar and milk, often with chopped nuts. [Mexican Spanish, diminutive of Spanish *pan* bread, from Latin *pānis*]

pan·o·ply ('pænəplɪ) *n., pl.* **+plies. 1.** a complete or magnificent array. **2.** the entire equipment of a warrior. [C17: via French from Greek *panoplia* complete armour, from PAN- + *hopla* armour, pl. of *hoplon* tool] —**ˈpan·o·plied** *adj.*

pan+op+tic (pænˈɒptɪk) *or* **pan+op+ti+cal** *adj.* taking in all parts, aspects, etc., in a single view; all-embracing: *a panoptic survey.* [C19: from Greek *panoptēs* seeing everything, from PAN- + *optos* visible] —**pan+ˈop+ti+cal+ly** *adv.*

pan·o+ra+ma (ˌpænəˈrɑːmə) *n.* **1.** an extensive unbroken view, as of a landscape, in all directions. **2.** a wide or comprehensive survey: *a panorama of the week's events.* **3.** a large extended picture or series of pictures of a scene, unrolled before spectators a part at a time so as to appear continuous. **4.** another name for **cyclorama.** [C18: from PAN- + Greek *horāma* view] —**pan·o·ram+ic** (ˌpænəˈræmɪk) *adj.* —ˌ**pan·o·ˈram·i+cal+ly** *adv.*

pan·o·ram+ic sight *n.* a type of artillery sight with a large field of view.

pan out *vb.* (*intr., adv.*) *Informal.* to work out; turn out; result.

pan+pipes ('pænˌpaɪps) *pl. n.* (*often sing.; often cap.*) a number of reeds or whistles of graduated lengths bound together to form a musical wind instrument. Also called: **pipes of Pan, syrinx.**

Pan-Slav·ism *n.* (esp. in the 19th century) the movement for the union of the Slavic peoples, esp. under the hegemony of tsarist Russia. —**ˈPan-ˈSlav·ic** *adj.*

pan+so·phy ('pænsəfɪ) *n.* universal knowledge. [C17: from New Latin *pansophia;* see PAN-, -SOPHY] —**pan+soph+ic** (pænˈsɒfɪk) *or* **pan+ˈsoph·i·cal** *adj.* —**pan+ˈsoph·i·cal+ly** *adv.*

pan+sy ('pænzɪ) *n., pl.* **+sies. 1.** any violaceous garden plant that is a variety of *Viola tricolor,* having flowers with rounded velvety petals, white, yellow, or purple in colour. See also **wild pansy. 2.** *Slang.* an effeminate or homosexual man or boy. **3. a.** a strong violet colour. **b.** (*as adj.*): *a pansy carpet.* [C15: from Old French *pensée* thought, from *penser* to think, from Latin *pensāre*]

pant (pænt) *vb.* **1.** to breathe with noisy deep gasps, as when out of breath from exertion or excitement. **2.** to say (something) while breathing thus. **3.** (*intr.;* often foll. by *for*) to have a frantic desire (for); yearn. **4.** (*intr.*) to pulsate; throb rapidly. ~*n.* **5.** the act or an instance of panting. **6.** a short deep gasping noise; puff. [C15: from Old French *pantaisier,* from Greek *phantasioun* to have visions, from *phantasia* FANTASY]

Pan·ta·gru·el (ˌpæntəgruːˈɛl) *n.* a gigantic prince, noted for his ironical buffoonery, in Rabelais' satire *Gargantua and Pantagruel* (1534). —ˌ**Pan+ta+gru+ˈel+i·an** *adj.* —ˌ**Pan+ta+ˈgru+el+ism** *n.* —ˌ**Pan+ta+ˈgru+el+ist** *n.*

pan+ta+lets *or* **pan+ta+lettes** (ˌpæntəˈlɛts) *pl. n.* **1.** long drawers, usually trimmed with ruffles, extending below the skirts: worn during the early and mid-19th century. **2.** a pair of ruffles for the ends of such drawers. [C19: diminutive of PANTALOONS]

pan+ta+loon (ˌpæntəˈluːn) *n. Theatre.* **1.** (in pantomime) an absurd old man, the butt of the clown's tricks. **2.** (*usually cap.*) (in commedia dell'arte) a lecherous old merchant dressed in pantaloons. [C16: from French *Pantalon,* from Italian *Pantalone,* local nickname for a Venetian, probably from *San Pantaleone,* a fourth-century Venetian saint]

pan+ta+loons (ˌpæntəˈluːnz) *pl. n.* **1.** men's tight-fitting trousers: worn in the 19th century. **2.** *Informal or facetious.* any trousers, esp. baggy ones.

pan+tech+ni+con (pænˈtɛknɪkən) *n. Brit.* **1.** a large van, esp. one used for furniture removals. **2.** a warehouse where furniture is stored. [C19: from PAN- + Greek *tekhnikon* relating to the arts, from *tekhnē* art; originally the name of a London bazaar, the building later being used as a furniture warehouse]

Pan+tel+le+ri·a (*Italian* ˌpantelleˈriːa) *n.* an Italian island in the Mediterranean, between Sicily and Tunisia: of volcanic origin; used by the Romans as a place of banishment. Pop.: 8327 (1971). Area: 83 sq. km (32 sq. miles). Ancient name: **Cossyra.**

Pan-Teu·ton+ism *n.* another name for **Pan-Germanism.**

pan+the·ism (ˈpænθɪˌɪzəm) *n.* **1.** the doctrine that God is the transcendent reality of which man, nature, and the material universe are manifestations. **2.** any doctrine that regards God as identical with the material universe or the forces of nature. **3.** readiness to worship all or a large number of gods. —**ˈpan+the·ist** *n.* —**ˌpan+the·ˈis+tic** *or* **ˌpan+the·ˈis+ti+cal** *adj.* —**ˌpan+the·ˈis+ti+cal+ly** *adv.*

pan+the+on (pænˈθiːən, ˈpænθɪən) *n.* **1.** (esp. in ancient Greece or Rome) a temple to all the gods. **2.** all the gods collectively of a religion. **3.** a monument or building commemorating a nation's dead heroes. [C14: via Latin from Greek *Pantheion,* from PAN- + *-theios* divine, from *theos* god]

Pan+the+on (pænˈθiːən, ˈpænθɪən) *n.* a circular temple in Rome dedicated to all the gods, built by Agrippa in 27 B.C., rebuilt by Hadrian 120–24 A.D., and used since 609 A.D. as a Christian church.

pan+ther (ˈpænθə) *n., pl.* **+thers** *or* **+ther. 1.** another name for **leopard** (sense 1), esp. the black variety (**black panther**). **2.** *U.S.* any of various related animals, esp. the puma. [C14: from Old French *pantère,* from Latin *panthēra,* from Greek *panthēr;* perhaps related to Sanskrit *pundarīka* tiger]

pant·ies (ˈpæntɪz) *pl. n.* a pair of women's or children's underpants.

pan+ti+hose (ˈpæntɪˌhəʊz) *n.* a less common word for **tights.**

pan+tile (ˈpænˌtaɪl) *n.* **1.** a roofing tile, with an S-shaped cross section, laid so that the downward curve of one tile overlaps the upward curve of the adjoining tile. **2.** a tapering roofing tile with a semicircular cross section, laid alternately so that the convex side of one tile overlaps the concave side of adjoining tiles.

pan+ti+soc+ra+cy (ˌpæntɪˈsɒkrəsɪ) *n.* a community, social group, etc., in which all have rule and everyone is equal. [C18: from Greek, from PANTO- + *isos* equal + -CRACY]

pan+to (ˈpæntəʊ) *n., pl.* **+tos.** *Brit. informal.* short for **pantomime.**

pan·to- *or before a vowel* **pant-** *combining form.* all: *pantisocracy; pantofle; pantograph; pantomime.* [from Greek *pant-, pas*]

pan+tof+le, pan+tof+fle (pænˈtɒfᵊl), *or* **pan+tou+fle** (pænˈtuːfᵊl) *n. Archaic.* a kind of slipper. [C15: from French *pantoufle,* from Old Italian *pantofola,* perhaps from Medieval Greek *pantophellos* shoe made of cork, from PANTO- + *phellos* cork]

pan+to+graph (ˈpæntəˌgrɑːf) *n.* **1.** an instrument consisting of pivoted levers for copying drawings, maps, etc., to any desired scale. **2.** a sliding type of current collector, esp. a diamond-shaped frame mounted on a train roof in contact with an overhead wire. —**pan+tog+ra+pher** (pænˈtɒgrəfə) *n.* —**pan+to+graph+ic** (ˌpæntəˈgræfɪk) *adj.* —**ˌpan+to+ˈgraph·i+cal+ly** *adv.* —**pan+ˈtog+ra+phy** *n.*

pan+to+mime (ˈpæntəˌmaɪm) *n.* **1.** (in Britain) **a.** a kind of play performed at Christmas time characterized by farce, music, lavish sets, stock roles, and topical jokes. **b.** (*as modifier*): *a pantomime horse.* **2.** a theatrical entertainment in which words are replaced by gestures and bodily actions. **3.** action without words as a means of expression. **4.** (in ancient Rome) an actor in a dumbshow. **5.** *Informal, chiefly Brit.* a confused or farcical situation. ~*vb.* **6.** another word for **mime.** [C17: via Latin from Greek *pantomīmos;* see PANTO-, MIME] —**pan+to+mim+ic** (ˌpæntəˈmɪmɪk) *adj.* —**pan+to+mim+ist** (ˈpæntəˌmaɪmɪst) *n.*

pan+to+then+ic ac·id (ˌpæntəˈθɛnɪk) *n.* an oily acid that is a vitamin of the B complex: occurs widely in animal and vegetable foods and is essential for cell growth. Formula: $C_{19}H_{17}NO_5$. [C20: from Greek *pantothen* from every side]

pan+toum (pænˈtuːm) *n. Prosody.* a verse form consisting of a series of quatrains in which the second and fourth lines of each verse are repeated as the first and third lines of the next. [C19: via French from Malay *pantun*]

pan+try (ˈpæntrɪ) *n., pl.* **+tries.** a small room or cupboard in which provisions, cooking utensils, etc., are kept; larder. [C13: via Anglo-Norman, from Old French *paneterie* store for bread, ultimately from Latin *pānis* bread]

pants (pænts) *pl. n.* **1.** *Brit.* an undergarment reaching from the waist to the thighs or knees. **2.** the usual U.S. name for **trousers. 3. bore, scare, etc., the pants off.** *Informal.* to bore, scare, etc., extremely. [C19: shortened from *pantaloons;* see PANTALOON]

pant+suit (ˈpæntˌsjuːt, -ˌsuːt) *n.* the U.S. term for **trouser suit.**

pant·y gir+dle *n.* a foundation garment with a crotch, often of lighter material than a girdle.

pant·y+waist (ˈpæntɪˌweɪst) *n. U.S. informal.* a man or boy considered as childish, lacking in courage, etc. [C20: originally a child's garment of trousers buttoned to a jacket at the waist]

pan+zer (ˈpænzə; *German* ˈpantsər) *n.* **1.** (*modifier*) of, relating to, or characteristic of the fast mechanized armoured units employed by the German army in World War II: *a panzer attack.* **2.** a vehicle belonging to a panzer unit, esp. a tank. **3.** (*pl.*) armoured troops. [C20: from German, from Middle High German, from Old French *panciere* coat of mail, from Latin *pantex* PAUNCH]

Pão de A·çú+car (ˈpɐ̃ʊn di aˈsukar) *n.* the Brazilian name for the **Sugar Loaf Mountain.**

Pao+ting *or* **Pao-ting** (ˈpaʊˈtɪŋ) *n.* a city in NE China, in N Hopeh province. Former name: **Tsingyuan.**

Pao+tow (ˈpaʊˈtaʊ) *n.* an industrial city in N China, in the central Inner Mongolian AR on the Yellow River. Pop.: 920 000 (1970 est.).

pap[1] (pæp) *n.* **1.** any soft or semiliquid food, such as bread softened with milk, esp. for babies or invalids; mash. **2.** worthless or oversimplified ideas, etc.; drivel: *intellectual pap.* [C15: from Middle Low German *pappe,* via Medieval Latin from Latin *pappāre* to eat; compare Dutch *pap,* Italian *pappa*]

pap[2] (pæp) *n.* **1.** *Archaic or northern Brit. dialect.* a nipple or teat. **2. a.** something resembling a breast or nipple, such as (formerly) one of a pair of rounded hilltops. **b.** (*cap. as part of a name*): *the Pap of Glencoe.* [C12: of Scandinavian origin, imitative of a sucking sound; compare Latin *papilla* nipple, Sanskrit *pippalaka*]

pa·pa[1] (pəˈpɑː) *n. Archaic.* an informal word for **father.** [C17: from French, a children's word for father; compare Late Latin *pāpa,* Greek *pappa*]

pa·pa[2] (ˈpɑːpɑː) *n. R.C. Church.* another name for the **pope.** [C16: from Italian]

pa+pa+cy (ˈpeɪpəsɪ) *n., pl.* **+cies. 1.** the office or term of office of a pope. **2.** the system of government in the Roman Catholic Church in which the pope is head. [C14: from Medieval Latin *pāpātia,* from *pāpa* POPE]

Pa·pa·do·pou·los (ˌpæpəˈdɒpələs; *Greek* papaˈðɔpulɔs) *n.* **George.** born 1919, Greek army officer and statesman; prime minister (1967–73) and president (1973) in Greece's military government.

pa+pa+in (pəˈpeɪɪn, -ˈpaɪɪn) *n.* a proteolytic enzyme occurring in the unripe fruit of the papaya tree, *Carica papaya:* used as a meat tenderizer and in medicine as an aid to protein digestion. [C19: from PAPAYA]

pa+pal (ˈpeɪpᵊl) *adj.* of or relating to the pope or the papacy. —**ˈpa+pal+ly** *adv.*

pa+pal cross *n.* a cross with three crosspieces.

Pa+pal States *n.* the temporal domain of the popes in central Italy from 756 A.D. until the unification of Italy in 1870. Also called: **States of the Church.**

Pa·pan·dre·ou (ˌpæpənˈdreɪuː; *Greek* papanˈðrɛu) *n.* **An·dre·as (George)** (anˈdrɛas). born 1919, Greek economist and socialist politician; prime minister from 1981.

pa+pa+ver·a+ceous (pəˌpeɪvəˈreɪʃəs) *adj.* of, relating to, or belonging to the *Papaveraceae,* a family of plants having large showy flowers and a cylindrical seed capsule with pores beneath the lid: includes the poppies and greater celandine. [C19: from New Latin, from Latin *papāver* POPPY]

pa+pa+ver+ine (pəˈpeɪvəˌriːn, -rɪn) *n.* a white crystalline almost insoluble alkaloid found in opium and used as an antispasmodic to treat coronary spasms and certain types of colic. Formula: $C_{20}H_{21}NO_4$. [C19: from Latin *papāver* POPPY]

pa+paw *or* **paw+paw** (ˈpɔːˌpɔː) *n.* **1.** Also called: **custard apple. a.** a bush or small tree, *Asimina triloba,* of central North America, having small fleshy edible fruit: family *Annonaceae.* **b.** the fruit of this tree. **2.** another name for **papaya.** [C16: from Spanish PAPAYA]

pa+pa+ya (pəˈpaɪə) *n.* **1.** a West Indian evergreen tree, *Carica papaya,* with a crown of large dissected leaves and large green hanging fruit: family *Caricaceae.* **2.** the fruit of this tree, having a yellow sweet edible pulp and small black seeds. ~Also called: **pawpaw.** [C15 *papaye,* from Spanish *papaya,* from an American Indian language; compare Carib *ababai*] —**pa+ˈpa+yan** *adj.*

Pa+pe+e+te (ˌpɑːpɪˈiːtɪ) *n.* the capital of French Polynesia, on the NW coast of Tahiti: one of the largest towns in the S Pacific. Pop.: 25 342 (1971).

Pa+pen (*German* ˈpaːpᵊn) *n.* **Franz von** (frants fɔn). 1879–1969, German statesman; chancellor (1932) and vice chancellor (1933–34) under Hitler, whom he was instrumental in bringing to power.

pa+per (ˈpeɪpə) *n.* **1.** a substance made from cellulose fibres derived from rags, wood, etc., often with other additives, and formed into flat thin sheets suitable for writing on, decorating walls, etc. **2.** a single piece of such material, esp. if written or printed on. **3.** (*usually pl.*) documents for establishing the identity of the bearer; credentials. **4.** (*pl.*) Also called: **ship's papers.** official documents relating to the ownership, cargo, etc., of a ship. **5.** (*pl.*) collected diaries, letters, etc. **6.** See **newspaper** or **wallpaper. 7.** *Government.* See **white paper, green paper, command paper. 8.** a lecture or short published treatise on a specific subject. **9.** a short essay, as by a student. **10. a.** a set of written examination questions. **b.** the student's answers. 11. *Commerce.* See **commercial paper.** 12. *Theatre slang.* a free ticket. 13. **on paper.** in theory, as opposed to fact: *it was a good idea on paper, but failed in practice.* ~*adj.* 14. made of paper: *paper cups do not last long.* 15. thin like paper: *paper walls.* 16. (*prenominal*) existing only in theory: *paper expenditure.* 17. taking place in writing: *paper battles.* ~*vb.* 18. to cover (walls) with wallpaper. 19. (*tr.*) to cover or furnish with paper. 20. (*tr.*) *Theatre slang.* to fill (a performance, etc.) by giving away free tickets (esp. in the phrase **paper the house**). [C14: from Latin PAPYRUS] —**'pa+per+er** *n.* —**'pa+per·y** *adj.* —**'pa+per·i+ness** *n.*

pa·per+back ('peɪpəˌbæk) *n.* 1. a book or edition with covers made of flexible card, sold relatively cheaply. Compare **hardback.** ~*adj. also* **pa·per+bound, soft-cover.** 2. of or denoting a paperback or publication of paperbacks.

pa·per+bark ('peɪpəˌbɑːk) *n.* any of several Australian myrtaceous trees of the genus *Melaleuca*, esp. *M. quinquenervia*, of swampy regions, having spear-shaped leaves and papery bark that can be peeled off in thin layers.

pa·per+board ('peɪpəˌbɔːd) *n.* **a.** a thick cardboard made of compressed layers of paper pulp; pasteboard. **b.** (*as modifier*): *a paperboard box.*

pa·per+boy ('peɪpəˌbɔɪ) *n.* a boy employed to deliver newspapers, etc. —**'pa·per+ˌgirl** *fem. n.*

pa+per chase *n.* a cross-country run in which a runner lays a trail of paper for others to follow.

pa·per+clip ('peɪpəˌklɪp) *n.* a clip for holding sheets of paper together; esp. one made of bent wire.

pa·per-cut·ter *n.* a machine for cutting paper, usually a blade mounted over a table on which paper can be aligned.

pa·per+hang·er ('peɪpəˌhæŋə) *n.* 1. a person who hangs wallpaper as an occupation. 2. *U.S. slang.* a counterfeiter. —**'pa·per+ˌhang·ing** *n.*

pa·per+knife ('peɪpəˌnaɪf) *n., pl.* **+knives.** a knife with a comparatively blunt blade, esp. one of wood, bone, etc., for opening sealed envelopes, etc.

pa+per mon+ey *n.* paper currency issued by the government or the central bank as legal tender and which circulates as a substitute for specie.

pa+per mul+ber·ry *n.* a small moraceous E Asian tree, *Broussonetia papyrifera*, the inner bark of which was formerly used for making paper in Japan. See also **tapa.**

pa+per nau+ti+lus *n.* any cephalopod mollusc of the genus *Argonauta*, esp. *A. argo*, of warm and tropical seas, having a papery external spiral shell: order *Octopoda* (octopods). Also called **argonaut.** Compare **pearly nautilus.**

pa+per o·ver *vb.* (*tr., adv.*) to conceal (something controversial or unpleasant).

pa+per tape *n.* a strip of paper used in computers, telex machines etc., for recording information in the form of rows of either six or eight holes, some or all of which are punched to produce a combination used as a discrete code symbol.

pa+per ti+ger *n.* a nation, institution, etc., that appears powerful but is in fact weak or insignificant. [C20: translation of a Chinese phrase first applied to the U.S.]

pa·per+weight ('peɪpəˌweɪt) *n.* a small heavy object, placed on loose papers to prevent them from scattering.

pa·per+work ('peɪpəˌwɜːk) *n.* clerical work, such as the completion of forms or the writing of reports or letters.

pap+e·terie ('pæpətrɪ; *French* pap'tri) *n.* a box or case for papers and other writing materials. [C19: from French, from *papetier* maker of paper, from *papier* PAPER]

Pa+phi+an ('peɪfɪən) *adj.* 1. of or relating to Paphos. 2. of or relating to Aphrodite. 3. *Literary.* of sexual love.

Paph+la+go+ni·a (ˌpæflə'gəʊnɪə) *n.* an ancient country and Roman province in N Asia Minor, on the Black Sea.

Pa+phos[1] ('peɪfɒs) *n.* a village in SW Cyprus, near the sites of two ancient cities: famous as the centre of Aphrodite worship and traditionally the place at which she landed after her birth among the waves.

Pa·phos[2] ('peɪfɒs) *or* **Pa·phus** ('peɪfəs) *n. Greek myth.* the son of Pygmalion and Galatea, who succeeded his father on the throne of Cyprus.

Pa+pia+men+to (*Spanish* ˌpapja'mento) *n.* a creolized Spanish spoken in the Netherlands Antilles. [Spanish, from *papia* talk]

pa+pier col+lé (*French* papje kɔ'le) *n.* a type of collage, usually of an abstract design. [French, literally: glued paper]

pa·pier-mâ·ché (ˌpæpjeɪ'mæʃeɪ; *French* papjemɑ'ʃe) *n.* 1. a hard strong substance suitable for painting on, made of paper pulp or layers of paper mixed with paste, size, etc., and moulded when moist. ~*adj.* 2. made of papier-mâché. [C18: from French, literally: chewed paper]

pa+pil·i·o+na+ceous (pəˌpɪlɪə'neɪʃəs) *adj.* of, relating to, or belonging to the *Papilionaceae*, a family of leguminous plants having irregular flowers: includes peas, beans, clover, alfalfa, gorse, and broom. [C17: from New Latin, from Latin *pāpiliō* butterfly]

pa+pil+la (pə'pɪlə) *n., pl.* **+lae** (-liː). 1. the small projection of tissue at the base of a hair, tooth, or feather. 2. any other similar protuberance. 3. any minute blunt hair or process occurring in plants. [C18: from Latin: nipple; related to Latin *papula* pimple] —**pa+'pil+lar·y, 'pap+il+late,** *or* **'pap+il+lose** *adj.*

pap+il+lo+ma (ˌpæpɪ'ləʊmə) *n., pl.* **+ma+ta** (-mətə) *or* **+mas.** *Pathol.* a benign tumour derived from epithelial tissue and forming a rounded or lobulated mass. [C19: from PAPILLA + -OMA] —**ˌpap+il+'lo+ma+tous** *adj.* —**ˌpap+il+ˌlo+ma+'to+sis** *n.*

pap+il+lon ('pæpɪˌlɒn) *n.* a breed of toy spaniel with large ears. [French: butterfly, from Latin *pāpiliō*]

pap+il+lote ('pæpɪˌləʊt) *n.* 1. a paper frill around cutlets, etc. 2. **en papillote.** (of food) cooked in oiled greaseproof paper or foil. [C18: from French PAPILLON]

pa+pist ('peɪpɪst) *n., adj.* (*often cap.*) *Usually disparaging.* another term for **Roman Catholic.** [C16: from French *papiste*, from Church Latin *pāpa* POPE] —**pa+'pis+ti+cal** *or* **pa+'pis+tic** *adj.* —**'pa+pist+ry** *n.*

pa+poose *or* **pap+poose** (pə'puːs) *n.* an American Indian baby or child. [C17: from Algonquian *papoos*]

pap+pus ('pæpəs) *n., pl.* **pap+pi** ('pæpaɪ). a ring of fine feathery hairs surrounding the fruit in composite plants, such as thistle; aids dispersal of the fruits by the wind. [C18: via New Latin, from Greek *pappos* grandfather, old man, old man's beard, hence: pappus, down] —**'pap+pose** *or* **'pap+pous** *adj.*

pap+py[1] ('pæpɪ) *adj.* **+pi+er, +pi+est.** resembling pap; mushy.

pap+py[2] ('pæpɪ) *n., pl.* **+pies.** *U.S.* an informal word for **father.**

pap+ri+ka ('pæprɪkə, pæ'priː-) *n.* 1. a mild powdered seasoning made from a sweet variety of red pepper. 2. the fruit or plant from which this seasoning is obtained. [C19: via Hungarian from Serbian, from *papar* PEPPER]

Pap test *or* **smear** *n. Med.* an examination of stained cells in a smear taken of bodily secretions, esp. those from the vagina or uterus, for detection of cancer. [C20: named after George *Papanicolaou* (1883–1962), U.S. anatomist, who devised it]

Pa+pu·a ('pæpjʊə) *n.* 1. **Territory of.** a former territory of Australia, consisting of SE New Guinea and adjacent islands: now part of Papua New Guinea. Former name (1888–1906): **British New Guinea.** 2. **Gulf of.** an inlet of the Coral Sea in the SE coast of New Guinea.

Pa+pu·an ('pæpjʊən) *adj.* 1. of or relating to Papua or any of the languages spoken there. ~*n.* 2. a native or inhabitant of Papua New Guinea. 3. any of several languages of Papua New Guinea that apparently do not belong to the Malayo-Polynesian family.

Pa+pu·a New Guin·ea *n.* a country in the SW Pacific; consists of the E half of New Guinea, the Bismarck Archipelago, the W Solomon Islands, Trobriand Islands, D'Entrecasteaux Islands, Woodlark Island, and the Louisiade Archipelago; administered by Australia from 1949 until 1975, when it became an independent member of the Commonwealth. Currency: kina. Capital: Port Moresby. Pop.: 2 184 986 (1966). Area: 461 693 sq. km (178 260 sq. miles).

pap+ule ('pæpjuːl) *or* **pap·u·la** ('pæpjʊlə) *n., pl.* **+ules** *or* **·u·lae** (-jʊˌliː). *Pathol.* a small solid usually round elevation of the skin. [C19: from Latin *papula* pustule, pimple] —**'pap·u·lar** *adj.* —**ˌpap·u+'lif+er+ous** *adj.*

pap·y+ra+ceous (ˌpæpɪ'reɪʃəs) *adj.* of, relating to, made of, or resembling paper.

pap·y+rol+o·gy (ˌpæpɪ'rɒlədʒɪ) *n.* the study of ancient papyri. —**pap·y+ro+log·i·cal** (ˌpæpɪrə'lɒdʒɪkəl) *adj.* —**ˌpap·y+'rol·o·gist** *n.*

pa+py+rus (pə'paɪrəs) *n., pl.* **+ri** (-raɪ) *or* **+rus·es.** 1. a tall aquatic cyperaceous plant, *Cyperus papyrus*, of S Europe and N and central Africa with small green-stalked flowers arranged like umbrella spokes around the stem top. 2. a kind of paper made from the stem pith of this plant, used by the ancient Egyptians, Greeks, and Romans. 3. an ancient document written on this paper. [C14: via Latin from Greek *papūros* reed used in making paper]

par (pɑː) *n.* 1. an accepted level or standard, such as an average (esp. in the phrase **up to par**). 2. a state of equality (esp. in the phrase **on a par with**). 3. *Finance.* the established value of the unit of one national currency in terms of the unit of another where both are based on the same metal standard. 4. *Commerce.* **a.** See **par value. b.** the condition of equality between the current market value of a share, bond, etc., and its face value (the **nominal par**). This equality is indicated by **at par,** while **above** (*or* **below**) **par** indicates that the market value is above (or below) face value. 5. *Golf.* an estimated standard score for a hole or course that a good player should make: *par for the course was 72.* ~*adj.* 6. average or normal. 7. (*usually prenominal*) *Commerce.* of or relating to par: *par value.* [C17: from Latin *pār* equal, on a level; see PEER[1]]

par. *abbrev. for:* 1. paragraph. 2. parallel. 3. parenthesis. 4. parish.

Par. *abbrev. for* Paraguay.

par- *prefix.* variant of **para-**[1] before a vowel.

pa·ra ('pɑːrə) *n., pl.* **·ras** *or* **·ra.** a Yugoslavian monetary unit worth one hundredth of a dinar. [C17: Serbo-Croatian, via Turkish from Persian *pārah* piece, portion]

pa·ra ('pærə) *n. Informal.* 1. a parachutist, esp. a soldier. 2. paragraph.

Pa·rá (*Portuguese* pa'ra) *n.* 1. a state of N Brazil, on the Atlantic: mostly dense tropical rain forest. Capital: Belém. Pop.: 2 167 018 (1970). Area: 1 248 042 sq. km (474 896 sq. miles). 2. another name for **Belém.** 3. an estuary in N Brazil into which flow the Tocantins River and a branch of the Amazon. Length: about 320 km (200 miles).

par·a-[1] *or before a vowel* **par-** *prefix.* 1. beside; near: *parameter; parathyroid.* 2. beyond: *parapsychology.* 3. resembling: *paramnesia.* 4. defective; abnormal: *paraesthesia.* 5. subsidiary to: *paraphysis.* 6. (*usually in italics*) denoting that an organic compound contains a benzene ring with substituents attached to atoms that are directly opposite across the ring (the 1,4- positions): *paradinitrobenzene; para*-cresol. Abbrev.: *p*-. Compare **ortho-** (sense 4), **meta-** (sense 4). 7. denoting an isomer, polymer, or compound related to a specified compound: *paraldehyde; paracasein.* 8. denoting the form of a diatomic substance in which the spins of the two constituent atoms are antiparallel: *parahydrogen.* Compare **ortho-** (sense 6). [from Greek *para* (prep.) alongside, beyond]

par·a-[2] *combining form.* indicating an object that acts as a protection against something: *parachute; parasol.* [via French from Italian *para-*, from *parare* to defend, shield against, ultimately from Latin *parāre* to prepare]

par·a·a·mi·no·ben·zo·ic ac·id *n. Biochem.* an acid present in yeast and liver: used in the manufacture of dyes and pharmaceuticals. Formula: $C_6H_4(NH_2)COOH$.

pa·rab·a·sis (pə'ræbəsɪs) *n., pl.* **·ses** (-ˌsiːz). (in classical Greek comedy) an address from the chorus to the audience. [C19: from Greek, from *parabanein* to step forward]

par·a·bi·o·sis (ˌpærəbaɪ'əʊsɪs) *n.* **1.** the natural union of two individuals, such as Siamese twins, so that they share a common circulation of the blood. **2.** a similar union induced for experimental or therapeutic purposes. [C20: from PARA-[1] + Greek *biōsis* manner of life, from *bios* life] **—par·a·bi·ot·ic** (ˌpærəbaɪ'ɒtɪk) *adj.*

par·a·blast ('pærəˌblæst) *n.* the yolk of an egg, such as a hen's egg, that undergoes meroblastic cleavage. [C19: from PARA-[1] + -BLAST] **—ˌpar·a·'blas·tic** *adj.*

par·a·ble ('pærəbᵊl) *n.* **1.** a short story that uses familiar events to illustrate a religious or ethical situation. **2.** any of the stories of this kind told by Jesus Christ. [C14: from Old French *parabole,* from Latin *parabola* comparison, from Greek *parabolē* analogy, from *paraballein* to throw alongside, from PARA-[1] + *ballein* to throw] **—pa·rab·o·list** (pə'ræbəlɪst) *n.*

pa·rab·o·la (pə'ræbələ) *n.* a conic section formed by the intersection of a cone by a plane parallel to the generator. Standard equation: $y^2 = 4ax$, where $2a$ is the distance between focus and directrix. [C16: via New Latin from Greek *parabolē* a setting alongside; see PARABLE]

par·a·bol·ic[1] (ˌpærə'bɒlɪk) *adj.* **1.** of, relating to, or shaped like a parabola. **2.** shaped like a paraboloid: *a parabolic mirror.*

par·a·bol·ic[2] (ˌpærə'bɒlɪk) *or* **par·a·bol·i·cal** *adj.* of or resembling a parable. **—ˌpar·a·'bol·i·cal·ly** *adv.*

par·a·bol·ic aer·i·al *n.* a microwave aerial, used esp. in radar and radio telescopes, consisting of a parabolic reflector. Informal name: **dish.**

pa·rab·o·lize[1] *or* **pa·rab·o·lise** (pə'ræbəˌlaɪz) *vb. (tr.)* to explain by a parable.

pa·rab·o·lize[2] *or* **pa·rab·o·lise** (pə'ræbəˌlaɪz) *vb. (tr.)* to shape like a parabola or parabaloid. **—pa·ˌrab·o·li·'za·tion** *or* **pa·ˌrab·o·li·'sa·tion** *n.*

pa·rab·o·loid (pə'ræbəˌlɔɪd) *n.* a geometric surface whose sections parallel to two coordinate planes are parabolic and whose sections parallel to the third plane are either elliptical or hyperbolic. Equations: $x^2/a^2 \pm y^2/b^2 = 2cz$ **—pa·ˌrab·o·'loi·dal** *adj.*

par·a·brake ('pærəˌbreɪk) *n.* another name for **brake parachute.**

par·a·ca·se·in (ˌpærə'keɪsɪɪn, -siːn) *n. U.S.* another name for **casein.**

Par·a·cel·sus (ˌpærə'sɛlsəs) *n.* **Phi·lip·pus Au·re·o·lus** ('fɪlɪpəs ɔː'riː'əʊləs). original name *Theophrastus Bombastus von Hohenheim.* 1493–1541, Swiss physician and alchemist, who pioneered the use of specific treatment, based on observation and experience, to remedy particular diseases.

pa·ra·ce·ta·mol (ˌpærə'siːtəˌmɒl, -'sɛtə-) *n.* a mild analgesic drug used as an alternative to aspirin. [C20: from *para-acetamidophenol*]

pa·rach·ro·nism (pə'rækrəˌnɪzəm) *n.* an error in dating, esp. by giving too late a date. Compare **prochronism.** [C17: from PARA-[1] + *-chronism,* as in ANACHRONISM]

par·a·chute ('pærəˌʃuːt) *n.* **1. a.** a device used to retard the fall of a man or package from an aircraft, consisting of a large fabric canopy connected to a harness. **b.** (*as modifier*): *parachute troops.* Sometimes shortened to **chute.** See also **brake parachute.** *~vb.* **2.** (of troops, supplies, etc.) to land or cause to land by parachute from an aircraft. [C18: from French, from PARA-[2] + *chute* fall] **—'par·a·ˌchut·ist** *n.*

par·a·clete ('pærəˌkliːt) *n. Rare.* a mediator or advocate.

Par·a·clete ('pærəˌkliːt) *n. Theol.* the Holy Ghost as comforter or advocate. [C15: via Old French from Church Latin *Paraclētus,* from Late Greek *Paraklētos* advocate, from Greek *parakalein* to summon as a helper, from PARA-[1] + *kalein* to call]

pa·rade (pə'reɪd) *n.* **1.** an ordered, esp. ceremonial, march, assembly, or procession, as of troops being reviewed: *on parade.* **2.** Also called: **parade ground.** a place where military formations regularly assemble. **3.** a visible show or display: *to make a parade of one's grief.* **4.** a public promenade or street of shops. **5.** a successive display of things or people. **6.** the interior area of a fortification. **7.** a parry in fencing. **8. on parade.** exhibiting oneself. *~vb.* **9.** (when *intr.*, often foll. by *through* or *along*) to walk or march, esp. in a procession (through): *to parade the streets.* **10.** (*tr.*) to exhibit or flaunt: *he was parading his medals.* **11.** (*tr.*) to cause to assemble in formation, as for a military parade. **12.** (*intr.*) to walk about in a public place. [C17: from French: a making ready, a setting out, a boasting display; compare Italian *parata,* Spanish *parada,* all ultimately from Latin *parāre* to prepare] **—pa·'rad·er** *n.*

par·a·digm ('pærəˌdaɪm) *n.* **1.** the set of all the inflected forms of a word or a systematic arrangement displaying these forms. **2.** a pattern or model. [C15: via French and Latin from Greek *paradeigma* pattern, from *paradeiknunai* to compare, from PARA-[1] + *deiknunai* to show] **—par·a·dig·mat·ic** (ˌpærədɪg'mætɪk) *adj.*

par·a·dise ('pærəˌdaɪs) *n.* **1.** heaven as the ultimate abode or state of the righteous. **2.** *Islam.* the sensual garden of delights that the Koran promises the faithful after death. **3.** Also called: **limbo.** (according to some theologians) the intermediate abode or state of the just prior to the Resurrection of Jesus, as in Luke 23:43. **4.** the place or state of happiness enjoyed by Adam before the first sin; the Garden of Eden. **5.** any place or condition that fulfils all one's desires or aspirations. **6.** a park in which foreign animals are kept. [Old English, from Church Latin *paradīsus,* from Greek *paradeisos* garden, of Persian origin; compare Avestan *pairidaēza* enclosed area, from *pairi-* around + *daēza* wall]

par·a·dise fish *n.* any of several beautifully coloured labyrinth fishes of the genus *Macropodus,* esp. *M. opercularis,* of S and SE Asia.

par·a·di·si·a·cal (ˌpærədɪ'saɪəkᵊl), **par·a·dis·i·ac** (ˌpærə'dɪsɪˌæk), *or* **par·a·di·sa·i·cal** (ˌpærədɪ'seɪɪkᵊl) *adj.* of, relating to, or resembling paradise. **—ˌpar·a·di·'si·a·cal·ly** *or* **ˌpar·a·di·'sa·i·cal·ly** *adv.*

par·a·dos ('pærəˌdɒs) *n.* a bank behind a trench or other fortification, giving protection from being fired on from the rear. [C19: from French, from PARA-[2] + *dos* back, from Latin *dorsum;* compare PARASOL, PARAPET]

par·a·dox ('pærəˌdɒks) *n.* **1.** a seemingly absurd or self-contradictory statement that is or may be true: *religious truths are often expressed in paradox.* **2.** a self-contradictory proposition, such as *I am always a liar.* **3.** a person or thing exhibiting apparently contradictory characteristics. **4.** an opinion that conflicts with common belief. [C16: from Late Latin *paradoxum,* from Greek *paradoxos* opposed to existing notions, from PARA-[1] + *doxa* opinion] **—ˌpar·a·'dox·i·cal** *adj.* **—ˌpar·a·'dox·i·cal·ly** *adv.*

par·a·dox·i·cal sleep *n. Physiol.* sleep that appears to be deep but that is characterized by rapid eye movements, heavier breathing, and increased electrical activity of the brain.

par·a·drop ('pærəˌdrɒp) *n.* the delivery of personnel or equipment from an aircraft by parachute.

par·aes·the·si·a *or U.S.* **par·es·the·si·a** (ˌpærɛs'θiːzɪə) *n. Pathol.* an abnormal sensation in an organ, part, or area of the skin, as of burning, prickling, tingling, etc. **—par·aes·thet·ic** *or U.S.* **par·es·thet·ic** (ˌpærɛs'θɛtɪk) *adj.*

par·af·fin ('pærəfɪn) *or* **par·af·fine** ('pærəˌfiːn) *n.* **1.** Also called: **paraffin oil,** (esp. U.S.) **kerosene.** a liquid mixture consisting mainly of alkane hydrocarbons with boiling points in the range 150°–300°C, used as an aircraft fuel, in domestic heaters, and as a solvent. **2.** another name for **alkane. 3.** See **paraffin wax. 4.** See **liquid paraffin.** *~vb. (tr.)* **5.** to treat with paraffin. [C19: from German, from Latin *parum* too little + *affinis* adjacent; so called from its chemical inertia]

par·af·fin wax *n.* a white insoluble odourless waxlike solid consisting mainly of alkane hydrocarbons with melting points in the range 50°–60°C, used in candles, waterproof paper, and as a sealing agent. Also called: **paraffin.**

par·a·form·al·de·hyde (ˌpærəfɔː'mældɪˌhaɪd) *or* **par·a·form** *n.* a white amorphous solid polymeric form of formaldehyde: used as a convenient source of formaldehyde. Formula: $(CH_2O)_n$, where n lies between 6 and 50.

par·a·gen·e·sis (ˌpærə'dʒɛnɪsɪs) *or* **par·a·ge·ne·si·a** (ˌpærədʒɪ'niːzɪə) *n.* the order in which the constituent minerals of a rock mass have been formed. **—par·a·ge·net·ic** (ˌpærədʒɪ'nɛtɪk) *adj.* **—ˌpar·a·ge·'net·i·cal·ly** *adv.*

par·a·go·ge (ˌpærə'gəʊdʒɪ) *or* **par·a·gogue** ('pærəˌgɒg) *n.* the addition of a sound or a syllable to the end of a word. [C17: via Late Latin from Greek *paragōgē* an alteration, ultimately from *paragein* to lead past, change] **—par·a·gog·ic** (ˌpærə'gɒdʒɪk) *or* **ˌpar·a·'gog·i·cal** *adj.* **—ˌpar·a·'gog·i·cal·ly** *adv.*

par·a·gon ('pærəgən) *n.* **1.** a model of excellence; pattern: *a paragon of virtue.* **2.** a size of printer's type, approximately equal to 20 point. *~vb. (tr.)* **3.** *Archaic.* **a.** to equal or surpass. **b.** to compare. **c.** to regard as a paragon. [C16: via French from Old Italian *paragone* comparison, from Medieval Greek *parakonē* whetstone, from Greek *parakonan* to sharpen against, from PARA-[1] + *akonan* to sharpen, from *akonē* whetstone]

par·a·graph ('pærəˌgrɑːf, -ˌgræf) *n.* **1.** one of a number of blocks into which a text is subdivided in order to separate ideas, etc., usually marked by the beginning of a new line, indention, increased interlinear space, etc. **2.** *Printing.* the character ¶, used as a reference mark or to indicate the beginning of a new paragraph. **3.** a short article, etc., in a newspaper. *~vb. (tr.)* **4.** to form into paragraphs. **5.** to express or report in a paragraph. [C16: from Medieval Latin *paragraphus,* from Greek *paragraphos* line drawing attention to part of a text, from *paragraphein* to write beside, from PARA-[1] + *graphein* to write] **—par·a·graph·ic** (ˌpærə'græfɪk) *or* **ˌpar·a·'graph·i·cal** *adj.* **—ˌpar·a·'graph·i·cal·ly** *adv.*

par·a·graph·i·a (ˌpærə'grɑːfɪə) *n. Psychiatry.* the accidental insertion or omission of words in what one writes, often the result of a mental disorder. [C20: from New Latin; see PARA-[1], -GRAPH]

Par·a·guay ('pærəˌgwaɪ) *n.* **1.** an inland republic in South America: colonized by the Spanish from 1537 gaining independence in 1811; lost 142 500 sq. km (55 000 sq. miles) of territory and over half its population after its defeat in the war against Argentina, Brazil, and Uruguay (1865–70). It is divided by the Paraguay River into a sparsely inhabited semiarid region (Chaco) in the west, and a central region of wooded hills, tropical forests, and rich grasslands, rising to the Paraná plateau in the east. Official languages: Spanish and Guarani. Religion: Roman Catholic. Currency: guarani. Capital: Asunción. Pop.: 2 357 955 (1972). Area: 406 750 sq. km (157 047 sq. miles). **2.** a river in South America flowing south through

Brazil and Paraguay to the Paraná River. Length: about 2400 km (1500 miles). —ˌ**Par·a·'guay·an** *adj., n.*

Par·a·guay tea *n.* another name for **maté.**

par·a·hy·dro·gen (ˌpærə'haɪdrədʒən) *n. Chem.* the form of molecular hydrogen (constituting about 25 per cent of the total at normal temperatures) in which the nuclei of the two atoms in each molecule spin in opposite directions. Compare **orthohydrogen.**

Pa·ra·í·ba (*Portuguese* ˌpara'iba) *n.* **1.** a state of NE Brazil, on the Atlantic: consists of a coastal strip, with hills and plains inland; irrigated agriculture. Capital: João Pessoa. Pop.: 2 382 617 (1970). Area: 56 371 sq. km (21 765 sq. miles). **2.** Also called: **Pa·ra·í·ba do Sul** (dɔ 'sul). a river in SE Brazil, flowing southwest and then northeast to the Atlantic near Campos. Length: 1060 km (660 miles). **3.** Also called: **Pa·ra·í·ba do Nor·te** (dɔ 'nɔrtɛ). a river in NE Brazil, in Paraíba state, flowing northeast and east to the Atlantic. Length: 386 km (240 miles). **4.** the former name (until 1930) of **João Pessoa.**

par·a·keet *or* **par·ra·keet** ('pærəˌkiːt) *n.* any of numerous small long-tailed parrots, such as *Psittacula krameri* (**ring-necked parakeet**), of Africa. [C16: from Spanish *periquito* and Old French *paroquet* parrot, of uncertain origin]

par·a·lan·guage ('pærəˌlæŋgwɪdʒ) *n. Linguistics.* suprasegmental elements in speech, such as intonation, that may affect the meaning of an utterance.

par·al·de·hyde (pə'rældɪˌhaɪd) *n.* a colourless liquid substance that is a cyclic trimer of acetaldehyde: used in making dyestuffs and as a sedative. Formula: $(C_2H_4O)_3$.

par·a·leip·sis (ˌpærə'laɪpsɪs) *or* **par·a·lip·sis** *n., pl.* **·ses** (-siːz). a rhetorical device in which an idea is emphasized by the pretence that it is too obvious to discuss, as in *there are many drawbacks to your plan, not to mention the cost.* [C16: via Late Latin from Greek: neglect, from *paraleipein* to leave aside, from PARA-[1] + *leipein* to leave]

pa·ra·li·pom·e·na (ˌpærəlaɪ'pɒmənə) *pl. n.* **1.** things added in a supplement to a work. **2.** *Old Testament.* an obsolete name for the Books of **Chronicles.** [C14: via late Latin from Greek *paraleipomena,* from PARA- (on one side) + *leipein* to leave]

par·al·lax ('pærəˌlæks) *n.* **1.** an apparent change in the position of an object resulting from a change in position of the observer. **2.** *Astronomy.* the angle subtended at a celestial body, esp. a star, by the radius of the earth's orbit. **Annual** or **heliocentric parallax** is the apparent displacement of a nearby star resulting from its observation from the earth. **Diurnal** or **geocentric parallax** results from the observation of a planet, the sun, or the moon from the surface of the earth. [C17: via French from New Latin *parallaxis,* from Greek: change, from *parallassein* to change, from PARA-[1] + *allassein* to alter] —**par·al·lac·tic** (ˌpærə'læktɪk) *adj.* —ˌ**par·al·'lac·ti·cal·ly** *adv.*

par·al·lel ('pærəˌlɛl) *adj.* (when *postpositive,* usually foll. by *to*) **1.** separated by an equal distance at every point; never touching or intersecting: *parallel walls, parallel lines.* **2.** corresponding; similar: *parallel situations.* **3.** *Music.* **a.** Also: **consecutive.** (of two or more parts or melodies) moving in similar motion but keeping the same interval apart throughout: *parallel fifths.* **b.** denoting successive chords in which the individual notes move in parallel motion. **4.** *Grammar.* denoting syntactic constructions in which the constituents of one construction correspond to those of the other. **5.** *Computer technol.* operating on several items of information, instructions, etc., simultaneously. Compare **serial.** ~*n.* **6.** *Maths.* one of a set of parallel lines, planes, etc. **7.** an exact likeness. **8.** a comparison. **9.** Also called: **parallel of latitude.** any of the imaginary lines around the earth parallel to the equator, designated by degrees of latitude ranging from 0° at the equator to 90° at the poles. **10. a.** a configuration of two or more electrical components connected between two points in a circuit so that the same voltage is applied to each (esp. in the phrase **in parallel**). Compare **series** (sense 6). **b.** (*as modifier*): *a parallel circuit.* **11.** *Printing.* the character (‖) used as a reference mark. **12.** a trench or line lying in advance of and parallel to other defensive positions. ~*vb.* **·lels, ·lel·ing, ·leled.** (*tr.*) **13.** to make parallel. **14.** to supply a parallel to. **15.** to be a parallel to or correspond with: *your experience parallels mine.* [C16: via French and Latin from Greek *parallēlos* alongside one another, from PARA-[1] + *allēlos* one another]

par·al·lel bars *n. Gymnastics.* **a.** a pair of wooden bars on uprights, sometimes at different heights, for various exercises. **b.** this event in competitions.

par·al·lel·e·pi·ped, par·al·lel·o·pi·ped (ˌpærəˌlɛlə'paɪpɛd), *or* **par·al·lel·e·pi·pe·don** (ˌpærəˌlɛlɪ'paɪpɪdən) *n.* a geometric solid whose six faces are parallelograms. [C16: from Greek *parallēlepipedon;* from *parallēlos* PARALLEL + *epipedon* plane surface, from EPI- + *pedon* ground]

par·al·lel·ism ('pærəˌlɛlɪzəm) *n.* **1.** the state of being parallel. **2.** *Grammar.* the use of parallel constructions. **3.** *Philosophy.* the doctrine that mental and physical processes are concomitant but not causally connected. **4.** *Music.* the characteristic use of parallel chords common in music since Debussy, Ravel, etc. —'**par·al·ˌlel·ist** *n., adj.*

par·al·lel·o·gram (ˌpærə'lɛləˌgræm) *n.* a quadrilateral whose opposite sides are parallel and equal in length. See also **rhombus, rectangle, trapezium, trapezoid.** [C16: via French from Late Latin, from Greek *parallēlogrammon,* from *parallēlos* PARALLEL + *grammē* line, related to *graphein* to write]

par·al·lel·o·gram rule *n. Maths, physics.* a rule for finding the resultant of two vectors by constructing a parallelogram with two adjacent sides representing the magnitudes and directions of the vectors, the diagonal through the point of intersection of the vectors representing their resultant.

par·al·lel turn *n. Skiing.* a turn, executed by shifting one's weight, in which the skis stay parallel.

pa·ral·o·gism (pə'rælәˌdʒɪzəm) *n.* **1.** *Logic.* an argument that is unintentionally invalid. Compare **sophism. 2.** any invalid argument or conclusion. [C16: via Late Latin from Greek *paralogismos,* from *paralogizesthai* to argue fallaciously, from PARA-[1] + *-logizesthai,* ultimately from *logos* word] —**pa·'ral·o·gist** *n.* —**pa·ˌral·o·'gis·tic** *adj.*

par·a·lyse *or U.S.* **par·a·lyze** ('pærəˌlaɪz) *vb.* (*tr.*) **1.** *Pathol.* to affect with paralysis. **2.** *Med.* to render (a part of the body) insensitive to pain, touch, etc., esp. by injection of an anaesthetic. **3.** to make immobile; transfix. [C19: from French *paralyser,* from *paralysie* PARALYSIS] —ˌ**par·a·ly·'sa·tion** *or U.S.* ˌ**par·a·ly·'za·tion** *n.* —'**par·a·ˌlys·er** *or U.S.* '**par·a·ˌlyz·er** *n.*

pa·ral·y·sis (pə'rælɪsɪs) *n., pl.* **·ses** (-ˌsiːz) **1.** *Pathol.* **a.** impairment or loss of voluntary muscle function or of sensation (**sensory paralysis**) in a part or area of the body, usually caused by a lesion or disorder of the muscles or the nerves supplying them. **b.** a disease characterized by such impairment or loss; palsy. **2.** cessation or impairment of activity: *paralysis of industry by strikes.* [C16: via Latin from Greek *paralusis;* see PARA[1], -LYSIS]

pa·ral·y·sis ag·i·tans ('ædʒɪˌtænz) *n.* another name for **Parkinson's disease.**

par·a·lyt·ic (ˌpærə'lɪtɪk) *adj.* **1.** of, relating to, or of the nature of paralysis. **2.** afflicted with or subject to paralysis. **3.** *Brit. informal.* drunk. ~*n.* **4.** a person afflicted with paralysis. —ˌ**par·a·'lyt·i·cal·ly** *adv.*

par·a·mag·net·ism (ˌpærə'mægnɪˌtɪzəm) *n. Physics.* the phenomenon exhibited by substances that have a relative permeability slightly greater than unity and a positive susceptibility. The effect is due to the alignment of unpaired spins of electrons in atoms of the material. —**par·a·mag·net·ic** (ˌpærəmæg'netɪk) *adj.* Compare **diamagnetism, ferromagnetism.**

Par·a·mar·i·bo (ˌpærə'mærɪˌbəʊ; *Dutch* ˌpaːraː'maːriːboː) *n.* the capital and chief port of Surinam, 27 km (17 miles) from the Atlantic on the Suriname River: the only large town in the country. Pop.: 151 500 (1971 est.).

par·a·mat·ta *or* **par·ra·mat·ta** (ˌpærə'mætə) *n.* a lightweight twill-weave fabric of wool with silk or cotton, used for dresses, etc. [C19: named after *Parramatta,* New South Wales, Australia, where it was originally produced]

par·a·me·ci·um (ˌpærə'miːsɪəm) *n., pl.* **·ci·a** (-sɪə). any freshwater protozoan of the genus *Paramecium,* having an oval body covered with cilia and a ventral ciliated groove for feeding: class *Ciliata* (ciliates). [C18: New Latin, from Greek *paramēkēs* elongated, from PARA-[1] + *mēkos* length]

par·a·med·i·cal (ˌpærə'mɛdɪk[ə]l) *adj.* of or designating a person, such as a laboratory technician, who supplements the work of the medical profession.

par·a·ment ('pærəmənt) *n., pl.* **par·a·ments** *or* **par·a·men·ta** (ˌpærə'mɛntə). (*often pl.*) an ecclesiastical vestment or decorative hanging. [C14: from Old French *parament,* from Medieval Latin *paramentum,* from Latin *parāre* to prepare]

pa·ram·e·ter (pə'ræmɪtə) *n.* **1.** an arbitrary constant that determines the specific form of a mathematical expression, such as *a* and *b* in $y = ax^2 + b$. **2.** *Informal.* any constant or limiting factor: *a designer must work within the parameters of budget and practicality.* [C17: from New Latin; see PARA-[1], -METER] —**par·a·met·ric** (ˌpærə'mɛtrɪk) *or* ˌ**par·a·'met·ri·cal** *adj.*

par·a·met·ric am·pli·fi·er *n.* a type of high-frequency amplifier in which energy from a pumping oscillator is transferred to the input signal through a circuit with a varying parameter, usually a varying reactance.

par·a·mil·i·tar·y (ˌpærə'mɪlɪtərɪ, -trɪ) *adj.* denoting or relating to a group of personnel with military structure functioning either as a civil force or in support of military forces.

par·am·ne·si·a (ˌpæræm'niːzɪə) *n. Psychiatry.* a disorder of the memory or the faculty of recognition in which dreams may be confused with reality.

par·a·mo ('pærəˌməʊ) *n., pl.* **·mos.** a high plateau in the Andes between the tree line and the permanent snow line. [C18: American Spanish, from Spanish: treeless plain]

par·a·morph ('pærəˌmɔːf) *n.* **1.** a mineral that has undergone paramorphism. **2.** a plant or animal that is classified on the basis of inadequate data and differs taxonomically from other members of the species in which it has been placed. —ˌ**par·a·'mor·phic** *or* ˌ**par·a·'mor·phous** *adj.*

par·a·mor·phine (ˌpærə'mɔːfiːn) *n.* another name for **thebaine.**

par·a·mor·phism (ˌpærə'mɔːfɪzəm) *n.* a process by which the crystalline structure of a mineral alters without any change in its chemical composition.

par·a·mount ('pærəˌmaʊnt) *adj.* **1.** of the greatest importance or significance; pre-eminent. ~*n.* **2.** *Rare.* a supreme ruler. [C16: via Anglo-Norman from Old French *paramont,* from *par* by + *-amont* above, from Latin *ad montem* to the mountain] —'**par·a·ˌmount·cy** *n.* —'**par·a·ˌmount·ly** *adv.*

par·a·mour ('pærəˌmʊə) *n.* **1.** *Now usually derogatory.* a lover, esp. an adulterous woman. **2.** an archaic word for **beloved.** [C13: from Old French, literally: through love]

Pa·ra·ná (*Portuguese, Spanish* ˌpara'na) *n.* **1.** a state of S Brazil, on the Atlantic: consists of a coastal plain and a large rolling plateau with extensive forests. Capital: Curitiba. Pop.: 6 929 868 (1970). Area: 199 555 sq. km (77 048 sq. miles). **2.** a city in E Argentina, on the Paraná River opposite Santa Fé:

capital of Argentina (1853–1862). Pop.: 127 836 (1970). **3.** a river in central South America, formed in S Brazil by the confluence of the Rio Grande and the Paranaíba River and flowing generally south to the Atlantic through the Rio de la Plata estuary. Length: 2900 km (1800 miles).

pa+rang ('pɑ:ræŋ) *n.* a short stout straight-edged knife used by the Dyaks of Borneo. [C19: from Malay]

par·a+noi·a (ˌpærə'nɔɪə) *n.* **1.** a form of schizophrenia characterized by a slowly progressive deterioration of the personality, involving delusions and often hallucinations. **2.** a mental disorder characterized by any of several types of delusions, in which the personality otherwise remains relatively intact. **3.** *Informal.* intense fear or suspicion, esp. when unfounded. [C19: via New Latin from Greek: frenzy, from *paranoos* distraught, from PARA-[1] + *noos* mind] —**par·a·noi+ac** (ˌpærə'nɔɪɪk) *adj., n.*

par·a+noid ('pærəˌnɔɪd) *adj.* **1.** of, characterized by, or resembling paranoia. **2.** exhibiting undue suspicion, fear of persecution, etc. ~*n.* **3.** a person who shows the behaviour patterns associated with paranoia.

par·a+nor+mal (ˌpærə'nɔ:məl) *adj.* beyond normal explanation.

par·a+nymph ('pærəˌnɪmf) *n. Archaic.* a bridesmaid or best man. [C16: via Late Latin from Greek *paranumphos,* from PARA-[1] + *numphē* bride (literally: person beside the bride)]

par·a+pet ('pærəpɪt, -ˌpɛt) *n.* **1.** a low wall or railing along the edge of a balcony, roof, etc. **2.** another word for **breastwork.** [C16: from Italian *parapetto,* literally: chest-high wall, from PARA-[2] + *petto,* from Latin *pectus* breast]

par+aph ('pærəf) *n.* a flourish after a signature, originally to prevent forgery. [C14: via French from Medieval Latin *paraphus,* variant of *paragraphus* PARAGRAPH]

par·a+pher+na+li·a (ˌpærəfə'neɪlɪə) *pl. n.* (*sometimes functioning as sing.*) **1.** elaborate procedure; rigmarole: *the paraphernalia of getting a visa.* **2.** miscellaneous articles or equipment. **3.** *Law.* (formerly) articles of personal property given to a married woman by her husband before or during marriage and regarded in law as her possessions over which she had some measure of control. [C17: via Medieval Latin from Latin *parapherna* personal property of a married woman, apart from her dowry, from Greek, from PARA-[1] + *phernē* dowry, from *pherein* to carry]

par·a+phrase ('pærəˌfreɪz) *n.* **1.** an expression of a statement or text in other words, esp. in order to clarify. **2.** the practice of making paraphrases. ~*vb.* **3.** to put into other words; restate. [C16: via French from Latin *paraphrasis,* from Greek, from *paraphrazein* to recount] —**par·a·phras+tic** (ˌpærə'fræstɪk) *adj.*

pa+raph·y+sis (pə'ræfɪsɪs) *n., pl.* **+ses** (-ˌsi:z). any of numerous sterile cells occurring between the sex organs of mosses and algae and between the spore-producing bodies of basidiomycetous and ascomycetous fungi. [C19: New Latin from Greek: subsidiary growth, from PARA-[1] + *phusis* growth] —**pa+'raph·y+sate** *adj.*

par·a+ple·gia (ˌpærə'pli:dʒə) *n. Pathol.* paralysis of the lower half of the body, usually as the result of disease or injury of the spine. Compare **hemiplegia, quadriplegia.** [C17: via New Latin from Greek: a blow on one side, from PARA-[1] + *plēssein* to strike] —ˌ**par·a+'ple·gic** *adj., n.*

par·a+po+di·um (ˌpærə'pəʊdɪəm) *n., pl.* **+di·a** (-dɪə). **1.** any of the paired unjointed lateral appendages of polychaete worms, used in locomotion, respiration, etc. **2.** any of various similar appendages of other invertebrates, esp. certain molluscs. [New Latin: from PARA-[1] + -PODIUM]

par·a+prax+is (ˌpærə'præksɪs) *n. Psychoanal.* minor errors in action, such as slips of the tongue, supposedly the result of repressed impulses. See also **Freudian slip.** [C20: from PARA-[1] + Greek *praxis* a doing, deed]

par·a+psy+chol+o·gy (ˌpærəsaɪ'kɒlədʒɪ) *n.* the study of mental phenomena, such as telepathy, which are beyond the scope of normal physical explanation.

Par·a+quat ('pærəˌkwɒt) *n. Trademark.* a yellow extremely poisonous soluble solid used in solution as a weedkiller.

Pa·rá rub+ber (pə'rɑ:, 'pɑ:rə) *n.* a South American rubber obtained from any of various euphorbiaceous trees of the genus *Hevea,* esp. *H. brasiliensis.* See also **rubber tree.**

par·a+sang ('pærəˌsæŋ) *n.* a Persian unit of distance equal to about 3.4 miles or 5.5 kilometres. [C16: via Latin and Greek from a Persian word related to modern Persian *farsang*]

par·a+se·le+ne (ˌpærəsɪ'li:nɪ) *n., pl.* **+nae** (-ni:). *Meteorol.* a bright image of the moon on a lunar halo. Also called: **mock moon.** Compare **parhelion.** [C17: New Latin, from PARA-[1] + Greek *selēnē* moon] —ˌ**par·a·se·'le+nic** *adj.*

Pa+ra+shah ('pærəˌʃɑ:; *Hebrew* para'ʃa) *n., pl.* **+shoth** (-ˌʃəʊt; *Hebrew* -'ʃɔt). *Judaism.* **1.** any of the sections of the Torah read in the synagogue. **2.** any of the subsections of the weekly lessons read on Sabbaths in the synagogue. [from Hebrew *pārāshāh,* literally: explanation]

par·a+site ('pærəˌsaɪt) *n.* **1.** an animal or plant that lives in or on another (the host) from which it obtains nourishment. The host does not benefit from the association and is often harmed by it. **2.** a person who habitually lives at the expense of others; sponger. **3.** (formerly) a sycophant. [C16: via Latin from Greek *parasitos* one who lives at another's expense, from PARA-[1] + *sitos* grain] —**par·a+sit+ic** (ˌpærə'sɪtɪk) *or* ˌ**par·a+'sit·i·cal** *adj.* —ˌ**par·a+'sit·i·cal+ly** *adv.*

par·a+site drag *n.* the part of the drag on an aircraft that is contributed by nonlifting surfaces, such as fuselage, nacelles, etc. Also called: **parasite resistance.**

par·a+sit·i+cide (ˌpærə'sɪtɪˌsaɪd) *n.* **1.** any substance capable of destroying parasites. ~*adj.* **2.** destructive to parasites. —ˌ**par·a+ˌsit·i+'cid+al** *adj.*

par·a+sit+ism ('pærəsaɪˌtɪzəm) *n.* **1.** the relationship between a parasite and its host. **2.** the state of being infested with parasites. **3.** the state of being a parasite.

par·a+si+tize *or Brit.* (*often*) **par·a+si+tise** ('pærəsɪˌtaɪz, -saɪ-) *vb.* (*tr.*) **1.** to infest or infect with parasites. **2.** to live on (another organism) as a parasite.

par·a+sit+ol+o·gy (ˌpærəsaɪ'tɒlədʒɪ) *n.* the branch of biology that is concerned with the study of parasites. —**par·a+si+to+log·i+cal** (ˌpærəˌsaɪtə'lɒdʒɪkəl) *adj.* —ˌ**par·a+sit+'ol·o+gist** *n.*

par·a+sol ('pærəˌsɒl) *n.* an umbrella used for protection against the sun; sunshade. [C17: via French from Italian *parasole,* from PARA-[2] + *sole* sun, from Latin *sōl*]

pa+ras+ti+chy (pə'ræstɪkɪ) *n., pl.* **+chies. 1.** a hypothetical spiral line connecting the bases of a series of leaves on a stem. **2.** an arrangement of leaves so connected. ~Compare **orthostichy.** —**pa+'ras+ti+chous** *adj.*

par·a+sym+pa+thet+ic (ˌpærəˌsɪmpə'θɛtɪk) *adj. Anatomy. Physiol.* of or relating to the division of the autonomic nervous system that acts in opposition to the sympathetic system by slowing the heartbeat, constricting the bronchi of the lungs, stimulating the smooth muscles of the digestive tract, etc. Compare **sympathetic** (sense 4).

par·a+syn+ap+sis (ˌpærəsɪ'næpsɪs) *n.* another name for **synapsis** (sense 1). —ˌ**par·a+syn+'ap+tic** *adj.*

par·a+syn+the+sis (ˌpærə'sɪnθɪsɪs) *n.* formation of words by means of compounding a phrase and adding an affix, as for example *light-headed,* which is *light* + *head* with the affix *-ed.* —**par·a+syn+thet+ic** (ˌpærəsɪn'θɛtɪk) *adj.*

par·a+syn+the+ton (ˌpærə'sɪnθətɒn) *n., pl.* **+ta** (-tə). a word formed by parasynthesis; for example, *kind-hearted.* [from Greek]

par·a+tax+is (ˌpærə'tæksɪs) *n.* the juxtaposition of clauses in a sentence without the use of a conjunction, as for example *None of my friends stayed—they all left early.* [C19: New Latin from Greek, from *paratassein,* literally: to arrange side by side, PARA-[1] + *tassein* to arrange] —**par·a+tac+tic** (ˌpærə'tæktɪk) *adj.* —ˌ**par·a+'tac+ti+cal+ly** *adv.*

par·a+thi+on (ˌpærə'θaɪɒn) *n.* a slightly water-soluble toxic oil, odourless and colourless when pure, used as an insecticide. Formula: $C_{10}H_{14}NO_5PS$.

par·a+thy+roid (ˌpærə'θaɪrɔɪd) *adj.* **1.** situated near the thyroid gland. **2.** of or relating to the parathyroid glands. ~*n.* **3.** See **parathyroid gland.**

par·a+thy+roid gland *n.* any one of the small egg-shaped endocrine glands situated near or embedded within the thyroid gland: they secrete parathyroid hormone.

par·a+thy+roid hor+mone *n.* the hormone secreted by the parathyroid glands that controls the level of calcium in the blood: a deficiency of the hormone often results in tentany. Also called: **parathormone.**

par·a+troops ('pærəˌtru:ps) *pl. n.* troops trained and equipped to be dropped by parachute into a battle area. Also called: **paratroopers, parachute troops.**

par·a+ty+phoid (ˌpærə'taɪfɔɪd) *Pathol.* ~*adj.* **1.** resembling typhoid fever or its causative agent. **2.** of or relating to paratyphoid fever. ~*n.* **3.** See **paratyphoid fever.**

par·a+ty+phoid fe+ver *n.* a disease resembling but less severe than typhoid fever, characterized by chills, headache, nausea, vomiting, and diarrhoea, caused by bacteria of the genus *Salmonella.*

par·a+vane ('pærəˌveɪn) *n.* a torpedo-shaped device towed from the bow of a vessel so that the cables will cut the anchors of any moored mines.

par a·vion *French.* (par a'vjɔ̃) by aeroplane: used in labelling mail sent by air.

par·a+zo+an (ˌpærə'zəʊən). *n., pl.* **+zo·a** (-'zəʊə). any multicellular invertebrate of the group *Parazoa,* which includes only the sponges (phylum *Porifera*). Compare **metazoan.** [C19: from *parazoa,* formed on the model of *protozoa* and *metazoa,* from PARA-[1] + Greek *zōon* animal]

par+boil ('pɑ:ˌbɔɪl) *vb.* (*tr.*) **1.** to boil until partially cooked, often before further cooking. **2.** to subject to uncomfortable heat. [C15: from Old French *parboillir,* from Late Latin *perbullīre* to boil thoroughly (see PER-, BOIL[1]); modern meaning due to confusion of *par-* with *part*]

par+buck+le ('pɑ:ˌbʌkəl) *n.* **1.** a rope sling for lifting or lowering a heavy cylindrical object, such as a cask or tree trunk. ~*vb.* **2.** (*tr.*) to raise or lower (an object) with such a sling. [C17: of uncertain origin]

Par+cae ('pɑ:si:) *pl. n., sing.* **Par·ca** ('pɑ:kə). **The.** the Roman goddesses of fate. Greek counterparts: The **Moirai.**

par+cel ('pɑ:səl) *n.* **1.** something wrapped up: package. **2.** a group of people or things having some common characteristic. **3.** a quantity of some commodity offered for sale; lot. **4.** a distinct portion of land. **5.** an essential part of something (esp. in the phrase **part and parcel**). ~*vb.* **+cels, +cel+ling, +celled** *or U.S.* **+cels, +cel+ing, +celed.** (*tr.*) **6.** (often foll. by *up*) to make a parcel of; wrap up. **7.** (often foll. by *out*) to divide (up) into portions. **8.** *Nautical.* to bind strips of canvas around (a rope). ~*adv.* **9.** an archaic word for **partly.** [C14: from Old French *parcelle,* from Latin *particula* PARTICLE]

par+ce·nar·y ('pɑ:sɪnərɪ) *n.* joint heirship. Also called: **coparcenary.** [C16: from Old French *parçonerie,* from *parçon* distribution; see PARCENER]

par+ce·ner ('pɑ:sɪnə) *n.* a person who takes an equal share with another or others; coheir. Also called: **coparcener.** [C13: from

Old French *parçonier,* from *parçon* distribution, from Latin *partītiō* a sharing, from *partīre* to divide]

parch (pɑːtʃ) *vb.* **1.** to deprive or be deprived of water; dry up: *the sun parches the fields.* **2.** (*tr.; usually passive*) to make very thirsty: *I was parched after the run.* **3.** (*tr.*) to roast (corn, etc.) lightly. [C14: of obscure origin]

Par·chee·si (pɑːˈtʃiːzɪ) *n. Trademark.* a modern board game derived from the ancient game of pachisi.

parch·ment (ˈpɑːtʃmənt) *n.* **1.** the skin of certain animals, such as sheep, treated to form a durable material, as for bookbinding, or (esp. formerly) manuscripts. **2.** a manuscript, etc., made of or resembling this material. **3.** a type of stiff yellowish paper resembling parchment. [C13: from Old French *parchemin,* via Latin from Greek *pergamēnē,* from *Pergamēnos* of Pergamum (where parchment was made); the form of Old French *parchemin* was influenced by *parche* leather, from Latin *Parthica* (*pellis*) Parthian (leather)] —**ˈparch·ment·y** *adj.*

par·close (ˈpɑːˌkləʊz) *n.* a screen or railing in a church separating off an altar, chapel, etc. [C14: from Old French, noun use of past participle of *parclore* to close off; see PER-, CLOSE]

pard[1] (pɑːd) *n. U.S.* short for **pardner.**

pard[2] (pɑːd) *n. Archaic.* a leopard or panther. [C13: via Old French from Latin *pardus,* from Greek *pardos*]

par·da·lote (ˈpɑːdəˌləʊt) *n.* another name for **diamond bird.** [C19: from New Latin, from Greek *pardalōtos* spotted like a leopard; see PARD[2]]

pard·ner (ˈpɑːdnə) *n. U.S. dialect.* friend or partner: used as a term of address.

par·don (ˈpɑːdᵊn) *vb.* (*tr.*) **1.** to excuse or forgive (a person) for (an offence, mistake, etc.): *to pardon someone; to pardon a fault.* ~*n.* **2.** forgiveness; allowance. **3. a.** release from punishment for an offence. **b.** the warrant granting such release. **4.** a Roman Catholic indulgence. ~*interj.* **5.** Also: **pardon me; I beg your pardon. a.** sorry; excuse me. **b.** what did you say? [C13: from Old French, from Medieval Latin *perdōnum,* from *perdōnāre* to forgive freely, from Latin *per* (intensive) + *dōnāre* to grant] —**ˈpar·don·a·ble** *adj.* —**ˈpar·don·a·bly** *adv.* —**ˈpar·don·less** *adj.*

par·don·er (ˈpɑːdᵊnə) *n.* (before the Reformation) a person licensed to sell ecclesiastical indulgences.

Par·du·bi·ce (*Czech* ˈpardubitʃɛ) *n.* a city in NW Czechoslovakia, on the Elbe River: 13th-century cathedral; oil refinery. Pop.: 70 777 (1968).

pare (pɛə) *vb.* (*tr.*) **1.** to peel or cut (the outer layer) from (something). **2.** to cut the edges from (the nails); trim. **3.** to decrease bit by bit. [C13: from Old French *parer* to adorn, from Latin *parāre* to make ready] —**ˈpar·er** *n.*

Pa·ré (*French* paˈre) *n.* **Am·broise** (ãˈbrwaːz). ?1517–90, French surgeon. He reintroduced ligature of arteries following amputation instead of cauterization.

par·e·gor·ic (ˌpærəˈgɒrɪk) *n.* a medicine consisting of opium, benzoic acid, camphor, and anise oil, formerly widely used to relieve diarrhoea and coughing in children. [C17 (meaning: relieving pain): via Late Latin from Greek *parēgorikos* soothing, from *parēgoros* relating to soothing speech, from PARA-[1] (beside, alongside of) + *-ēgor-,* from *agoreuein* to speak in assembly, from *agora* assembly]

pa·rei·ra (pəˈrɛərə) *n.* the root of a South American menispermaceous climbing plant, *Chondrodendron tomentosum,* used as a diuretic, tonic, and as a source of curare. [C18: from Portuguese *pareira brava,* literally: wild vine]

paren. *abbrev. for* parenthesis.

pa·ren·chy·ma (pəˈrɛŋkɪmə) *n.* **1.** a soft plant tissue consisting of simple thin-walled cells with intervening air spaces: constitutes the greater part of fruits, stems, roots, etc. **2.** animal tissue that constitutes the essential or specialized part of an organ as distinct from the blood vessels, connective tissue, etc., associated with it. **3.** loosely-packed tissue filling the spaces between the organs in lower animals such as flatworms. [C17: via New Latin from Greek *parenkhuma* something poured in beside, from PARA-[1] + *enkhuma* infusion] —**par·en·chym·a·tous** (ˌpærɛŋˈkɪmətəs) *adj.*

par·ent (ˈpɛərənt) *n.* **1.** a father or mother. **2.** a person acting as a father or mother; guardian. **3.** *Rare.* an ancestor. **4.** a source or cause. **5. a.** an organism or organization that has produced one or more organisms similar to itself. **b.** (*as modifier*): *a parent organism.* **6.** *Physics, chem.* **a.** a precursor, such as a nucleus or compound, of a derived entity. **b.** (*as modifier*): *a parent nucleus; a parent ion.* [C15: via Old French from Latin *parens* parent, from *parere* to bring forth] —**ˈpar·ent·hood** *n.*

par·ent·age (ˈpɛərəntɪdʒ) *n.* **1.** ancestry. **2.** derivation from a particular origin. **3.** a less common word for **parenthood.**

pa·ren·tal (pəˈrɛntᵊl) *adj.* **1.** of or relating to a parent or parenthood. **2.** *Genetics.* designating the first generation in a line, which gives rise to all succeeding (filial) generations. —**paˈren·tal·ly** *adv.*

par·en·ter·al (pæˈrɛntərəl) *adj. Med.* **1.** (esp. of the route by which a drug is administered) by means other than through the digestive tract, esp. by injection. **2.** designating a drug to be injected. [C20: from PARA-[1] + ENTERO- + -AL[1]] —**parˈen·ter·al·ly** *adv.*

pa·ren·the·sis (pəˈrɛnθɪsɪs) *n., pl.* **·ses** (-ˌsiːz). **1.** a phrase, often explanatory or qualifying, inserted into a passage with which it is not grammatically connected, and marked off by brackets, dashes, etc. **2.** Also called: **bracket.** either of a pair of characters, (), used to enclose such a phrase or as a sign of aggregation in mathematical or logical expressions. **3.** an intervening occurrence; interlude; interval. **4. in parenthesis.** inserted as a parenthesis. [C16: via Late Latin from Greek: something placed in besides, from *parentithenai,* from PARA-[1] + EN-[2] + *tithenai* to put] —**par·en·thet·ic** (ˌpærənˈθɛtɪk) *or* **ˌpar·en·ˈthet·i·cal** *adj.* —**ˌpar·en·ˈthet·i·cal·ly** *adv.*

pa·ren·the·size *or* **pa·ren·the·sise** (pəˈrɛnθɪˌsaɪz) *vb.* (*tr.*) **1.** to place in parentheses. **2.** to insert as a parenthesis. **3.** to intersperse (a speech, writing, etc.) with parentheses.

par·er·gon (pəˈrɛəgɒn) *n., pl.* **·ga** (-gə). work that is not one's main employment. [C17: from Latin, from Greek, from PARA-[1] + *ergon* work]

pa·re·sis (pəˈriːsɪs, ˈpærɪsɪs) *n. Pathol.* **1.** incomplete or slight paralysis of motor functions. **2.** short for **general paresis.** See **general paralysis of the insane.** [C17: via New Latin from Greek: a relaxation, from *parienai* to let go, from PARA-[1] + *hienai* to release] —**pa·ret·ic** (pəˈrɛtɪk) *adj.*

par·es·the·si·a (ˌpærɛsˈθiːzɪə) *n. Pathol.* the usual U.S. spelling of **paraesthesia.** —**par·es·thet·ic** (ˌpærɛsˈθɛtɪk) *adj.*

Pa·re·to (*Italian* paˈreːto) *n.* **Vil·fre·do** (vilˈfreːdo). 1848–1923, Italian sociologist and economist. He anticipated Fascist principles of government in his *Mind and Society* (1916).

pa·re·u (ˈpɑːreɪˌuː) *n.* a rectangle of fabric worn by Polynesians as a skirt or loincloth. [from Tahitian]

pa·re·ve (ˈpɑːvə, ˈpɑːrəvə) *adj. Judaism.* a variant of **parve.**

par ex·cel·lence *French.* (par ɛksɛˈlɑ̃ːs; *English* pɑːr ˈɛksələns) to a degree of excellence; beyond comparison: *she is the charitable lady par excellence.* [French, literally: by (way of) excellence]

par·fait (pɑːˈfeɪ) *n.* a rich frozen dessert made from eggs and cream with ice cream, fruit, etc. [from French: PERFECT]

par·fleche (ˈpɑːflɛʃ) *n. U.S.* **1.** rawhide that has been dried after soaking in lye and water to remove the hair. **2.** an object, such as a case, made of this. [C19: from Canadian French, from French *parer* to ward off, protect + *flèche* arrow]

par·get (ˈpɑːdʒɪt) *n.* **1.** Also called: **pargeting. a.** plaster, mortar, etc., used to line chimney flues or cover walls. **b.** plasterwork that has incised ornamental patterns. **2.** another name for **gypsum** (esp. when used in building). ~*vb. tr.* **3.** to cover or decorate with parget. [C14: from Old French *pargeter* to throw over, from *par* PER- + *geter,* from Medieval Latin *jactāre* to throw]

par·he·lic cir·cle (pɑːˈhiːlɪk, -ˈhɛlɪk) *n. Meteorol.* a luminous band at the same altitude as the sun, parallel to the horizon, caused by reflection of the sun's rays by ice crystals in the atmosphere.

par·he·li·on (pɑːˈhiːlɪən) *n., pl.* **·li·a** (-lɪə). one of several bright spots on the parhelic circle or solar halo, caused by the diffraction of light by ice crystals in the atmosphere, esp. around sunset. Also called: **mock sun, sundog.** Compare **anthelion.** [C17: via Latin from Greek *parēlion,* from PARA-[1] (beside) + *hēlios* sun] —**par·he·lic** (pɑːˈhiːlɪk, -ˈhɛlɪk) *or* **par·he·li·a·cle** (ˌpɑːhɪˈlaɪəkᵊl) *adj.*

par·i- *combining form.* equal or equally; even (in number): *parisyllabic; paripinnate.* [from Latin *par*]

pa·ri·ah (pəˈraɪə; ˈpærɪə) *n.* **1.** a social outcast. **2.** (formerly) a member of a low caste in South India. [C17: from Tamil *paraiyan* drummer, from *parai* drum; so called because members of the caste were the drummers at festivals]

pa·ri·ah dog *n.* another term for **pye-dog.**

Par·i·an (ˈpɛərɪən) *adj.* **1.** denoting or relating to a fine white marble mined in classical times in Paros. **2.** denoting or relating to a fine biscuit porcelain used mainly for statuary. **3.** of or relating to Paros. ~*n.* **4.** a native or inhabitant of Paros. **5.** Parian marble. **6.** Parian porcelain.

Pa·ri·cu·tín (*Spanish* ˌparikuˈtin) *n.* a volcano in W central Mexico, in Michoacán state, formed in 1943 after a week of earth tremors; grew to a height of 2500 m (8200 ft.) in a year and buried the village of Paricutín.

par·i·es (ˈpɛərɪˌiːz) *n., pl.* **pa·ri·e·tes** (pəˈraɪɪˌtiːz). the wall of an organ or bodily cavity. [C18: from Latin: wall]

pa·ri·e·tal (pəˈraɪɪtᵊl) *adj.* **1.** *Anatomy, biology.* of, relating to, or forming the walls or part of the walls of a bodily cavity or similar structure: *the parietal bones of the skull.* **2.** of or relating to the side of the skull. **3.** (of plant ovaries) having ovules attached to the walls. **4.** *U.S.* living or having authority within a college. ~*n.* **5.** a parietal bone. [C16: from Late Latin *parietālis,* from Latin *pariēs* wall]

pa·ri·e·tal bone *n.* either of the two bones forming part of the roof and sides of the skull.

pa·ri·e·tal cell *n.* any one of the cells in the lining of the stomach that produce hydrochloric acid.

pa·ri·e·tal lobe *n.* the portion of each cerebral hemisphere concerned with the perception and interpretation of sensations of touch, temperature, and taste and with muscular movements.

par·i·mu·tu·el (ˌpærɪˈmjuːtjʊəl) *n., pl.* **par·i·mu·tu·els** *or* **par·is·mu·tu·els** (ˌpærɪˈmjuːtjʊəlz). **a.** a system of betting in which those who have bet on the winners of a race share in the total amount wagered less a percentage for the management. **b.** (*as modifier*): *the pari-mutuel machine.* [C19: from French, literally: mutual wager]

par·ing (ˈpɛərɪŋ) *n.* (*often pl.*) something pared or cut off.

pa·ri pas·su *Latin.* (ˌpærɪ ˈpæsuː, ˈpɑːrɪ) *adv. Usually legal.* with equal speed or progress; equably: often used to refer to the right of creditors to receive assets from the same source without one taking precedence.

par·i·pin·nate (ˌpærɪˈpɪneɪt) *adj.* (of pinnate leaves) having an even number of leaflets and no terminal leaflet. Compare **imparipinnate.**

Par·is[1] (ˈpærɪs; *French* paˈri) *n.* **1.** the capital of France, in the north on the River Seine: constitutes a department; dates from the 3rd century B.C., becoming capital of France in 987; centre of the French Revolution; centres around its original site on an island in the Seine, the **Île de la Cité,** containing Notre Dame; university (1150). Pop.: 2 317 227 (1975). Ancient name: **Lutetia. 2. Treaty of Paris. a.** a treaty of 1783 between the U.S., Britain, France, and Spain, ending the War of American Independence. **b.** a treaty of 1763 signed by Britain, France, and Spain that ended their involvement in the Seven Years' War. **c.** a treaty of 1898 between Spain and the U.S. bringing to an end the Spanish-American War. [via French and Old French, from Late Latin (*Lūtētia*) *Parisiōrum* (marshes) of the *Parisii*, a tribe of Celtic Gaul] —**Pa+ris+i+an** (pə'rɪzɪən) *n., adj.*

Par·is[2] ('pærɪs) *n.* **1.** *Greek myth.* a prince of Troy, whose abduction of Helen from her husband Menelaus started the Trojan War. **2. Mat·thew.** ?1200–59, English chronicler, whose principal work is the *Chronica Majora*.

Par+is Com+mune *n. French history.* the council established in Paris in the spring of 1871 in opposition to the National Assembly and esp. to the peace negotiated with Prussia following the Franco-Prussian War. Troops of the Assembly crushed the Commune with great bloodshed.

Par+is green *n.* an emerald-green poisonous insoluble substance used as a pigment and insecticide. It is a double salt of copper arsenite and copper acetate. Formula: $3Cu(AsO_2)_2.Cu(C_2H_3O_2)_2$.

par+ish ('pærɪʃ) *n.* **1.** a subdivision of a diocese, having its own church and a clergyman. **2.** the churchgoers of such a subdivision. **3.** (in England and, formerly, Wales) the smallest unit of local government in rural areas. **4.** (in Louisiana) a unit of local government corresponding to a county in other states of the U.S. **5.** the people living in a parish. **6. on the parish.** *History.* receiving parochial relief. [C13: from Old French *paroisse*, from Church Latin *parochia*, from Late Greek *paroikia*, from *paroikos* Christian, sojourner, from Greek: neighbour, from PARA-[1] (beside) + *oikos* house]

Pa+ri+shad ('pʌrɪʃəd) *n.* (in India) an assembly. [Hindi]

par+ish clerk *n.* a person designated to assist in various church duties.

par+ish coun+cil *n. Brit.* the administrative body of a parish. See **parish** (sense 3).

pa+rish+ion+er (pə'rɪʃənə) *n.* a member of a particular parish.

par+ish reg+is+ter *n.* a book in which the births, baptisms, marriages, and deaths in a parish are recorded.

par·i+son ('pærɪsᵊn) *n.* an unshaped mass of glass before it is moulded into its final form. [C19: from French *paraison*, from *parer* to prepare]

par·i+syl+lab+ic (ˌpærɪsɪ'læbɪk) *adj.* (of a noun or verb, in inflected languages) containing the same number of syllables in all or almost all inflected forms. Compare **imparisyllabic.**

par·i·ty[1] ('pærɪtɪ) *n., pl.* **·ties. 1.** equality of rank, pay, etc. **2.** close or exact analogy or equivalence. **3.** *Finance.* **a.** the amount of a foreign currency equivalent at the established exchange rate to a specific sum of domestic currency. **b.** a similar equivalence between different forms of the same national currency, esp. the gold equivalent of a unit of gold-standard currency. **4.** equality between prices of commodities or securities in two separate markets. **5.** *Physics.* **a.** a property of a physical system characterized by the behaviour of the sign of its wave function when reflected in space. The wave function either remains unchanged (**even parity**) or changes in sign (**odd parity**). **b.** a quantum number describing this property, equal to +1 for even parity systems and −1 for odd parity systems. Symbol: *P.* See also **conservation of parity. 6.** *Maths.* a relationship between two integers. If both are odd or both even they have the same parity; if one is odd and one even they have different parity. **7.** *U.S.* a system of government support for farm products. [C16: from Late Latin *pāritās*; see PAR]

par·i·ty[2] ('pærɪtɪ) *n.* **1.** the condition or fact of having given birth. **2.** the number of children to which a woman has given birth. [C19: from Latin *parere* to bear]

par·i·ty check *n.* a check made of computer data to ensure that the total number of bits of value 1 (or 0) in each unit of information remains odd or even after transfer between a peripheral device and the memory or vice versa.

park (pɑːk) *n.* **1.** a large area of land preserved in a natural state for recreational use by the public. See also **national park. 2.** a piece of open land in a town with public amenities. **3.** a large area of land forming a private estate. **4.** *English law.* an enclosed tract of land where wild beasts are protected, acquired by a subject by royal grant or prescription. Compare **forest** (sense 4). **5.** *U.S.* See **amusement park. 6.** *U.S.* See **car park. 7.** *U.S.* a playing field or sports stadium. **8. the park.** *Brit. informal.* a soccer pitch. **9.** a gear selector position on the automatic transmission of a motor vehicle that acts as a parking brake. **10.** the area in which the equipment and supplies of a military formation are assembled. **11.** a high valley surrounded by mountains in the western U.S. ~*vb.* **12.** to stop and leave (a vehicle) temporarily. **13.** to manoeuvre (a motor vehicle) into a space for it to be left: *try to park without hitting the kerb.* **14.** (*tr.*) *Informal.* to leave or put somewhere: *park yourself in front of the fire.* **15.** *Military.* to arrange equipment in a park. **16.** (*tr.*) to enclose in or as a park. [C13: from Old French *parc*, from Medieval Latin *parricus* enclosure, from Germanic; compare Old High German *pfarrih* pen, Old English *pearruc* PADDOCK[1]] —**'park+ˌlike** *adj.*

Park (pɑːk) *n.* **1. Mun·go** ('mʌŋgəʊ). 1771–1806, Scottish explorer. He led two expeditions (1795–97; 1805–06) to trace the course of the Niger in Africa. He was drowned during the second expedition. **2. Chung Hee** ('tʃʊŋ 'hiː). 1917-79, South Korean politician; president of the Republic of Korea 1963-79; assassinated.

par+ka ('pɑːkə) *n.* a warm knee-length weatherproof coat, often with a hood, originally worn by Eskimos. [C19: from Aleutian: skin]

Par·ker ('pɑːkə) *n.* **1. Char·lie.** nickname *Bird* or *Yardbird.* 1920–55, U.S. jazz alto saxophonist and composer; the leading exponent of early bop. **2. Dor·o·thy (Rothschild).** 1893–1967, U.S. writer, noted esp. for the ironical humour of her short stories. **3. Mat·thew.** 1504–75, English prelate. As archbishop of Canterbury (1559–75), he supervised Elizabeth I's religious settlement.

par+kin ('pɑːkɪn) *n. Brit.* moist spicy ginger cake usually containing oatmeal. [C19: of unknown origin]

park+ing disc *n.* See **disc** (sense 7).

park+ing lot *n.* the U.S. term for **car park.**

park+ing me+ter *n.* a timing device, usually coin-operated, that indicates how long a vehicle may be left parked.

park+ing or+bit *n.* an orbit around the earth or moon in which a spacecraft can be placed temporarily in order to prepare for the next step in its programme.

park+ing tick+et *n.* a summons served for a parking offence.

Par·kin·son's dis+ease ('pɑːkɪnsənz) *n.* a progressive chronic disorder of the central nervous system characterized by impaired muscular coordination and tremor. Also called: **parkinsonism, Parkinson's syndrome, paralysis agitans, shaking palsy.** [C19: named after James *Parkinson* (1755–1824), English surgeon, who first described it]

Par·kin·son's law *n.* the notion, expressed facetiously as a law of economics, that work expands to fill the time allotted to it. [C20: named after C. N. *Parkinson* (born 1909), English economist, who formulated it]

park+land ('pɑːkˌlænd) *n.* grassland with scattered trees.

park sa+van+na *n.* savanna grassland scattered with trees.

park+way ('pɑːkˌweɪ) *n. U.S.* a wide road planted with trees, etc.

park·y ('pɑːkɪ) *adj.* **park·i+er, park·i+est.** (*usually postpositive*) *Brit. informal.* (of the weather) chilly; cold. [C19: perhaps from PERKY]

Parl. *abbrev. for:* **1.** Parliament. **2.** Also: **parl.** parliamentary.

par+lance ('pɑːləns) *n.* **1.** a particular manner of speaking, esp. when specialized; idiom: *political parlance.* **2.** *Archaic.* any discussion, such as a debate. [C16: from Old French, from *parler* to talk, via Medieval Latin from Late Latin *parabola* speech, PARABLE; compare PARLEY]

par+lan+do (pɑː'lændəʊ) *adj., adv. Music.* to be performed as though speaking. [Italian: speaking, from *parlare* to speak]

par+lay ('pɑːlɪ) *U.S.* ~*vb.* (*tr.*) **1.** to stake (winnings from one bet) on a subsequent wager. Brit. term: **double up. 2.** to exploit (one's talent, etc.) to achieve worldly success. ~*n.* **3.** a bet in which winnings from one wager are staked on another, or a series of such bets. [C19: variant of *paroli*, via French from Neapolitan Italian *parolo*, from *paro* a pair, from Latin *pār* equal, PAR]

par+ley ('pɑːlɪ) *n.* **1.** a discussion, esp. between enemies under a truce to decide terms of surrender, etc. ~*vb.* **2.** (*intr.*) to discuss, esp. with an enemy under a truce. **3.** (*tr.*) to speak (a foreign language). [C16: from French, from *parler* to talk, from Medieval Latin *parabolāre*, from Late Latin *parabola* speech, PARABLE] —**'par+ley+er** *n.*

parl+ey+voo (ˌpɑːlɪ'vuː) *vb.* (*intr.*) *Informal.* **1.** to speak French. ~*n.* **2.** the French language. **3.** a Frenchman. [C20: jocular respelling of *parlez-vous (français)?* do you speak (French)?]

par+lia+ment ('pɑːləmənt) *n.* **1.** an assembly of the representatives of a political nation or people, often the supreme legislative authority. **2.** any legislative or deliberative assembly, conference, etc. **3.** Also: **'par+le+ment.** (in France before the Revolution) any of several high courts of justice in which royal decrees, etc., were registered. [C13: from Anglo-Latin *parliamentum*, from Old French *parlement*, from *parler* to speak; see PARLEY]

Par+lia+ment ('pɑːləmənt) *n.* **1.** the highest legislative authority in Britain, consisting of the House of Commons, which exercises effective power, the House of Lords, and the sovereign. **2.** a similar legislature in another country. **3.** the two chambers of a Parliament. **4.** the lower chamber of a Parliament. **5.** any of the assemblies of such a body created by a general election and royal summons and dissolved before the next election.

par+lia+men+tar+i+an (ˌpɑːləmɛn'tɛərɪən) *n.* **1.** an expert in parliamentary procedures, etc. **2.** (*sometimes cap.*) *Brit.* a Member of Parliament. ~*adj.* **3.** of or relating to a parliament or parliaments.

Par+lia+men+tar+i+an (ˌpɑːləmɛn'tɛərɪən) *n.* **1.** a supporter of Parliament during the Civil War. ~*adj.* **2.** of or relating to Parliament or its supporters during the Civil War.

par+lia+men+tar+i+an+ism (ˌpɑːləmɛn'tɛərɪəˌnɪzəm) *or* **par+lia+men+tar+ism** *n.* the system of parliamentary government.

par+lia+men+ta+ry (ˌpɑːlə'mɛntərɪ, -trɪ) *adj.* (*sometimes cap.*) **1.** of or characteristic of a parliament or Parliament. **2.** proceeding from a parliament or Parliament: *a parliamentary decree.* **3.** conforming to or derived from the procedures of a parliament or Parliament: *parliamentary conduct.* **4.** having a parliament or Parliament. **5.** of or relating to Parliament or its supporters during the Civil War.

par+lia+men+ta+ry a·gent *n.* (in Britain) a person who is employed to manage the parliamentary business of a private group.

Par+lia+men+ta+ry Com+mis+sion+er *n.* (in Britain) the official name for **ombudsman.**

par+lia+men+ta+ry pri+vate sec+re+tar·y *n.* (in Britain) a backbencher in Parliament who assists a minister, esp. in liaison with backbenchers. Abbrev.: **PPS** or **P.P.S.**

par+lia+men+ta+ry sec+re+tar·y *n.* a member of Parliament appointed, usually as a junior minister, to assist a minister of the Crown with his departmental responsibilities.

par+lour *or U.S.* **par+lor** ('pɑːlə) *n.* **1.** *Old-fashioned.* a living room, esp. one kept tidy for the reception of visitors. **2.** a reception room in a priest's house, convent, etc. **3.** a small room for guests away from the public rooms in an inn, club, etc. **4.** *Chiefly U.S.* a room or shop equipped as a place of business: *a billiard parlor.* **5.** *Caribbean.* a small shop, esp. one selling cakes and nonalcoholic drinks. **6.** a building equipped for milking cows in. [C13: from Anglo-Norman *parlur,* from Old French *parleur* room in convent for receiving guests, from *parler* to speak; see PARLEY]

par+lour car *n. U.S.* a comfortable railway coach with individual reserved seats.

par+lour game *n.* an informal indoor game.

par+lous ('pɑːləs) *Archaic.* ~*adj.* **1.** dangerous or difficult. **2.** cunning. ~*adv.* extremely. [C14 *perlous,* variant of PERILOUS] —**'par+lous+ly** *adv.* —**'par+lous+ness** *n.*

parl. proc. *abbrev. for* parliamentary procedure.

Par+ma ('pɑːmə) *n.* **1.** (*Italian* 'parma) a city in N Italy, in Emilia-Romagna: capital of the duchy of Parma and Piacenza from 1545 until it became part of Italy in 1860; important food industry (esp. Parmesan cheese). Pop.: 177 210 (1975 est.). **2.** a city in NE Ohio, south of Cleveland. Pop.: 101 482 (1973 est.). —**Par+me+san** (ˌpɑːmɪ'zæn, 'pɑːmɪˌzæn).

Par+men·i·des (pɑː'mɛnɪˌdiːz) *n.* 5th-century B.C. Greek Eleatic philosopher, born in Italy. He held that the universe is single and unchanging and denied the existence of change and motion. His doctrines are expounded in his poem *On Nature,* of which only fragments are extant.

Par+men+tier ('pɑːmənˌtjeɪ; *French* parmɑ̃'tje) *adj.* (of soups, etc.) containing or garnished with potatoes. [C19: named after A. *Parmentier* (1780–1813), French horticulturist]

Par+me+san cheese (ˌpɑːmɪ'zæn, 'pɑːmɪˌzæn) *n.* a hard dry cheese made from skimmed milk, used grated, esp. on pasta dishes and soups.

Par·mi·gia·ni·no (*Italian* ˌparmidʒa'niːno) *n.* original name *Girolamo Francesco Maria Mazzola.* 1503–40, Italian painter, one of the originators of mannerism. Also called: **Par·mi·gia·no** (ˌparmi'dʒaːno).

Par+na·i·ba *or* **Par+na+hi+ba** (*Portuguese* parna'iba) *n.* a river in NE Brazil, rising in the Serra das Mangabeiras and flowing generally northeast, to the Atlantic. Length: about 1450 km (900 miles).

Par+nas+si·an[1] (pɑː'næsɪən) *adj.* of or relating to Mount Parnassus or poetry.

Par+nas+si·an[2] (pɑː'næsɪən) *n.* **1.** one of a school of French poets of the late 19th century who wrote verse that emphasized metrical form and restricted emotion. ~*adj.* **2.** of or relating to the Parnassians or their poetry. [C19: from French *parnassien,* from *Parnasse* PARNASSUS; from *Le Parnasse contemporain,* title of an anthology produced by these poets] —**Par+'nas+si+an+ism** *or* **Par+'nas+sism** *n.*

Par+nas+sus (pɑː'næsəs) *n.* **1. Mount.** a mountain in central Greece, in NW Boeotia: in ancient times sacred to Dionysus, Apollo, and the Muses, with the Castalian Spring and Delphi on its slopes. Height: 2457 m (8061 ft.). Modern Greek names: **Par+nas+sós** (ˌparna'sɔs), **Liákoura. 2. a.** the world of poetry. **b.** a centre of poetic or other creative activity. **3.** a collection of verse or belles-lettres.

Par+nell ('pɑːnᵊl, pɑː'nɛl) *n.* **Charles Stew·art.** 1846–91, Irish nationalist, who led the Irish Home Rule movement in Parliament (1880–90) with a calculated policy of obstruction. Although Gladstone was converted to Home Rule (1886), Parnell's career was ruined by the scandal over his adultery with Mrs. O'Shea. —**'Par+nel+lism** *n.* —**'Par+nel+lite** *n., adj.*

pa+ro+chi·al (pə'rəʊkɪəl) *adj.* **1.** narrow in outlook or scope; provincial. **2.** of or relating to a parish or parishes. [C14: via Old French from Church Latin *parochiālis;* see PARISH] —**pa+'ro+chi+al+ism** *n.* —**pa+ˌro+chi+'al+i+ty** *n.* —**pa+'ro+chi+al+ly** *adv.*

pa+ro+chi·al church coun+cil *n. Church of England.* an elected body of lay representatives of the members of a parish that administers the affairs of the parish.

par·o+dy ('pærədɪ) *n., pl.* **+dies. 1.** a musical, literary, or other composition that mimics the style of another composer, author, etc., in a humorous or satirical way. **2.** mimicry of someone's individual manner in a humorous or satirical way. **3.** something so badly done as to seem an intentional mockery; travesty. ~*vb.* **+dies, +dy+ing, +died. 4.** (*tr.*) to make a parody of. [C16: via Latin from Greek *paroidiā* satirical poem, from PARA-[1] + *ōidē* song] —**pa+rod+ic** (pə'rɒdɪk) *or* **pa+'rod·i·cal** *adj.* —**'par·o+dist** *n.*

pa+roi+cous (pə'rɔɪkəs) *or* **pa+roe+cious** (pə'riːʃəs) *adj.* (of mosses and related plants) having the male and female reproductive organs at different levels on the same stem. [C19: from Greek *paroikos* living near by, from PARA-[1] (beside) + *oikos* house; compare PARISH]

pa+rol (pə'rəʊl) *Law.* ~*n.* **1.** (formerly) the pleadings in an action when presented by word of mouth. **2.** an oral statement; word of mouth (now only in the phrase **by parol**). ~*adj.* **3. a.** (of a contract, lease, etc.) made orally or in writing but not under seal. **b.** expressed or given by word of mouth: *parol evidence.* [C15: from Old French *parole* speech; see PAROLE]

pa+role (pə'rəʊl) *n.* **1. a.** the freeing of a prisoner before his sentence has expired, on the condition that he is of good behaviour. **b.** the duration of such conditional release. **2.** a promise given by a prisoner, as to be of good behaviour if granted liberty or partial liberty. **3.** a variant spelling of **parol. 4.** *U.S. military.* a password. **5.** *Linguistics.* language as manifested in the individual speech acts of particular speakers. Compare **langue. 6. on parole. a.** conditionally released from detention. **b.** *Informal.* (of a person) under scrutiny, esp. for a recurrence of an earlier shortcoming. ~*vb.* (*tr.*) **7.** to place (a person) on parole. [C17: from Old French, from the phrase *parole d'honneur* word of honour; *parole* from Late Latin *parabola* speech] —**pa+'rol+a·ble** *adj.* —**pa+rol·ee** (pərəʊ'liː) *n.*

par·o+no+ma+si·a (ˌpærənəʊ'meɪzɪə) *n. Rhetoric.* a play on words, esp. a pun. [C16: via Latin from Greek: a play on words, from *paronomazein* to make a change in naming, from PARA-[1] (besides) + *onomazein* to name, from *onoma* a name] —**par·o+no+mas+tic** (ˌpærənəʊ'mæstɪk) *adj.* —**ˌpar·o+no+'mas+ti+cal+ly** *adv.*

par·o+nym ('pærənɪm) *n. Linguistics.* a cognate word. [C19: via Late Latin from Greek *paronumon, from* PARA-[1] (beside) + *onoma* a name] —**ˌpar·o+'nym+ic** *or* **pa+ron·y+mous** (pə'rɒnɪməs) *adj.* —**pa+'ron·y+mous+ly** *adv.*

Pár+os ('pɛərɒs) *n.* a Greek island in the S Aegean Sea, in the Cyclades: site of the discovery (1627) of the Parian Chronicle, a marble tablet outlining Greek history from before 1000 B.C. to about 354 B.C. (now at Oxford University). Pop.: 7314 (1971). Area: 166 sq. km (64 sq. miles).

pa+rot+ic (pə'rɒtɪk) *adj.* situated near the ear. [C19: from New Latin *paroticus,* from Greek PARA-[1] (near) + *-oticus,* from *ous* ear]

pa+rot+id (pə'rɒtɪd) *adj.* **1.** relating to or situated near the parotid gland. ~*n.* **2.** See **parotid gland.** [C17: via French via Latin from Greek *parōtis,* from PARA-[1] (near) + *-ōtis* from *ous* ear]

pa+rot+id gland *n.* a large salivary gland, in man situated in front of and below each ear.

par·o+ti+tis (ˌpærə'taɪtɪs) *or* **pa+rot·i+di+tis** (pəˌrɒtɪ'daɪtɪs) *n.* inflammation of the parotid gland. See also **mumps.** —**par·o+tit+ic** (ˌpærə'tɪtɪk) *or* **pa+rot·i+dit+ic** (pəˌrɒtɪ'dɪtɪk) *adj.*

pa+ro+toid (pə'rɒtɔɪd) *n.* **1.** Also called: **paratoid gland.** any of various warty poison glands on the head and back of certain toads and salamanders. —*adj.* **2.** resembling a parotid gland. [C19: from Greek *parot(is)* (see PAROTID) + -OID]

-par·ous *adj. combining form.* giving birth to: *oviparous.* [from Latin *-parus,* from *parere* to bring forth]

par·ou+si·a (pə'ruːsɪə) *n. Theol.* another term for the **Second Coming.** [C19: from Greek: presence]

par+ox+ysm ('pærəkˌsɪzəm) *n.* **1.** an uncontrollable outburst: *a paroxysm of giggling.* **2.** *Pathol.* **a.** a sudden attack or recurrence of a disease. **b.** any fit or convulsion. [C17: via French from Medieval Latin *paroxysmus* annoyance, from Greek *paroxusmos,* from *paroxunein* to goad, from PARA-[1] (intensifier) + *oxunein* to sharpen, from *oxus* sharp] —**ˌpar+ox+'ys+mal** *or* **ˌpar+ox+'ys+mic** *adj.* —**ˌpar+ox+'ys+mal+ly** *adv.*

par+ox·y+tone (pə'rɒksɪˌtəʊn) *adj.* **1.** (in the classical Greek language) of, relating to, or denoting words having an acute accent on the next to last syllable. ~*n.* **2.** a paroxytone word. ~Compare **oxytone.** [C18: via New Latin from Greek *paroxutonos,* from PARA-[1] (beside) + *-oxutonos* OXYTONE] —**par+ox·y+ton+ic** (ˌpærɒksɪ'tɒnɪk) *adj.*

par+pend ('pɑːpənd) *or U.S.* **par+pen** ('pɑːpən) *n.* another name for **perpend**[1].

par+quet ('pɑːkeɪ, -kɪ) *n.* **1.** a floor covering of pieces of hardwood fitted in a decorative pattern; parquetry. **2.** Also called: **parquet floor.** a floor so covered. **3.** *U.S.* the stalls of a theatre. **4.** the main part of the Paris Bourse, where officially listed securities are traded. Compare **coulisse** (sense 3). **5.** (in France) the department of government responsible for the prosecution of crimes. ~*vb.* (*tr.*) **6.** to cover a floor with parquet. [C19: from Old French: small enclosure, from *parc* enclosure; see PARK]

par+quet cir+cle *n. U.S.* the seating area of the main floor of a theatre that lies to the rear of the auditorium and underneath the balcony. Also called: **parterre.**

par+quet+ry ('pɑːkɪtrɪ) *n.* a geometric pattern of inlaid pieces of wood, often of different kinds, esp. as used to cover a floor or to ornament furniture. Compare **marquetry.**

parr (pɑː) *n., pl.* **parrs** *or* **parr.** a salmon up to two years of age, with dark spots and transverse bands. [C18: of unknown origin]

Parr (pɑː) *n.* **Ca·the·rine.** 1512–48, sixth wife of Henry VIII of England.

par+ra+keet ('pærəˌkiːt) *n.* a variant spelling of **parakeet.**

par+ra+mat+ta (ˌpærə'mætə) *n.* a variant spelling of **paramatta.**

par+rel *or* **par+ral** ('pærəl) *n. Nautical.* a ring that holds the jaws of a boom to the mast but lets it slide up and down. [C15: probably from *aparail* equipment, APPAREL]

par+ri+cide ('pærɪˌsaɪd) *n.* **1.** the act of killing either of one's parents. **2.** a person who kills his or her parent. [C16: from Latin *parricīdium* murder of a parent or relative, and from *parricīda* one who murders a relative, from *parri-* (element related to Greek *pēos* kinsman) + *-cīdium, -cīda* -CIDE] —**ˌpar+ri+'cid+al** *adj.*

par+rot ('pærət) *n.* **1.** any bird of the tropical and subtropical order *Psittaciformes,* having a short hooked bill, compact body, bright plumage, and an ability to mimic sounds. **2.** a person who repeats or imitates the words or actions of another unintelligently. ~*vb.* **3.** (*tr.*) to repeat or imitate mechanically without understanding. [C16: probably from French *paroquet;* see PARAKEET] —**'par+rot+ry** *n.*

par·rot-fash·ion *adv. Informal.* without regard for meaning; by rote: *she learned it parrot-fashion.*

par+rot fe+ver *or* **dis+ease** *n.* another name for **psittacosis.**

par·rot+fish ('pærətˌfɪʃ) *n., pl.* **+fish** *or* **+fish·es. 1.** any brightly coloured tropical marine percoid fish of the family *Scaridae,* having parrot-like jaws. **2.** any of various similar fishes.

par+ry ('pærɪ) *vb.* **+ries, +ry+ing, +ried. 1.** to ward off (an attack, etc.) by blocking or deflecting, as in fencing. **2.** (*tr.*) to evade (questions, etc.), esp. adroitly. ~*n., pl.* **+ries. 3.** an act of parrying, esp. (in fencing) using a stroke or circular motion of the blade. **4.** a skilful evasion, as of a question. [C17: from French *parer* to ward off, from Latin *parāre* to prepare]

Par·ry ('pærɪ) *n.* **1.** Sir **(Charles) Hu·bert (Hastings).** 1848–1918, English composer, noted esp. for his choral works. **2.** Sir **Wil·liam Ed·ward.** 1790–1855, English arctic explorer, who searched for the Northwest Passage (1819–25) and attempted to reach the North Pole (1827).

parse (pɑːz) *vb. Grammar.* **1.** to assign constituent structure to (a sentence or the words in a sentence). **2.** (*intr.*) (of a word or linguistic element) to play a specified role in the structure of a sentence. [C16: from Latin *pars* (*ōrātionis*) part (of speech)] —**'pars+a·ble** *adj.* —**'pars+er** *n.*

par+sec ('pɑːˌsɛk) *n.* a unit of astronomical distance equal to the distance from earth at which stellar parallax would be 1 second of arc; equivalent to 3.0857×10^{16} metres or 3.262 light-years. [C20: from PARALLAX + SECOND[2]]

Par+see ('pɑːsiː) *n.* **1.** an adherent of a monotheistic religion of Zoroastrian origin, the practitioners of which were driven out of Persia by the Muslims in the eighth century A.D. It is now found chiefly in western India. ~*adj.* **2.** of or relating to the Parsees or their religion. [C17: from Persian *Pārsī* a Persian, from Old Persian *Pārsa* PERSIA] —**'Par+see+ism** *n.*

Par+si+fal ('pɑːsɪfᵊl, -ˌfɑːl) *n.* a variant of **Parzival.**

par+si+mo+ny ('pɑːsɪmənɪ) *n.* extreme care or reluctance in spending; frugality; niggardliness. [C15: from Latin *parcimōnia,* from *parcere* to spare] —**par+si+mo+ni+ous** (ˌpɑːsɪ'məʊnɪəs) *adj.* —**ˌpar+si+'mo+ni+ous+ly** *adv.*

pars+ley ('pɑːslɪ) *n.* **1.** a S European umbelliferous plant, *Petroselinum crispum,* widely cultivated for its curled aromatic leaves, which are used in cooking. **2.** any of various similar and related plants, such as fool's-parsley, stone parsley, and cow parsley. [C14 *persely,* from Old English *petersilie* + Old French *persil, peresil,* both ultimately from Latin *petroselīnum* rock parsley, from Greek *petroselinon,* from *petra* rock + *selinon* parsley]

pars+ley piert (pɪət) *n.* a small N temperate rosaceous plant, *Aphanes arvensis,* having fan-shaped leaves and small greenish flowers.

pars+nip ('pɑːsnɪp) *n.* **1.** a strong-scented umbelliferous plant, *Pastinaca sativa,* cultivated for its long whitish root. **2.** the root of this plant, eaten as a vegetable. **3.** any of several similar plants, esp. the cow parsnip. [C14: from Old French *pasnaie,* from Latin *pastināca,* from *pastināre* to dig, from *pastinum* two-pronged tool for digging; also influenced by Middle English *nepe* TURNIP]

par+son ('pɑːsᵊn) *n.* **1.** a parish priest in the Church of England, formerly applied only to those who held ecclesiastical benefices. **2.** any clergyman. [C13: from Medieval Latin *persōna* parish priest, representative of the parish, from Latin: personage; see PERSON] —**par+son+ic** (pɑː'sɒnɪk) *or* **par+'son·i·cal** *adj.*

par+son+age ('pɑːsᵊnɪdʒ) *n.* the residence of a parson who is not a rector or vicar, as provided by the parish.

par+son bird *n.* another name for **tui.**

Par·sons ('pɑːsənz) *n.* Sir **Charles Al·ger·non.** 1854–1931, English engineer, who developed the steam turbine.

par+son's nose *n.* the fatty extreme end portion of the tail of a fowl when cooked. Also called: **pope's nose.**

part (pɑːt) *n.* **1.** a piece or portion of a whole. **2.** an integral constituent of something: *dancing is part of what we teach.* **3. a.** an amount less than the whole; bit: *they only recovered part of the money.* **b.** (*as modifier*)*: an old car in part exchange for a new one.* **4.** one of several equal or nearly equal divisions: *mix two parts flour to one part water.* **5. a.** an actor's role in a play. **b.** the speech and actions which make up such a role. **c.** a written copy of these. **6.** a person's proper role or duty: *everyone must do his part.* **7.** (*often pl.*) region; area: *you're well-known in these parts.* **8.** *Anatomy.* any portion of a larger structure. **9.** a component that can be replaced in a machine, etc.: *spare parts.* **10.** the U.S. word for **parting** (sense 1). **11.** *Music.* **a.** one of a number of separate melodic lines making up the texture of music. **b.** one of such melodic lines, which is assigned to one or more instrumentalists or singers: *the viola part; the soprano solo part.* **c.** such a line performed from a separately written or printed copy. See **part song. 12. for the most part.** generally. **13. for one's part.** as far as one is concerned. **14. in part.** to some degree; partly. **15. of many parts.** having many different abilities. **16. on the part of.** on behalf of. **17. part and parcel.** an essential ingredient. **18. play a part. a.** to pretend to be what one is not. **b.** to have something to do with; be instrumental: *to play a part in the king's downfall.* **19. take in good part.** to respond to (teasing, etc.) with good humour. **20. take part in.** to participate in. **21. take someone's part.** to support one person in an argument, etc. ~*vb.* **22.** to divide or separate from one another; take or come apart: *to part the curtains; the seams parted when I washed the dress.* **23.** to go away or cause to go away from one another; stop or cause to stop seeing each other: *the couple parted amicably.* **24.** (*intr.;* foll. by *from*) to leave; say goodbye to. **25.** (*intr.;* foll. by *with*) to relinquish, esp. reluctantly: *I couldn't part with my teddy bear.* **26.** (*tr.;* foll. by *from*) to cause to relinquish, esp. reluctantly: *he's not easily parted from his cash.* **27.** (*intr.*) to split; separate: *the path parts here.* **28.** (*tr.*) to arrange (the hair) in such a way that a line of scalp is left showing. **29.** (*intr.*) a euphemism for **die. 30.** (*intr.*) *Archaic.* to depart. **31. part company. a.** to separate from one another: *they were in partnership, but parted company last year.* **b.** (foll. by *with*) to leave; go away from. ~*adv.* **32.** to some extent; partly. [C13: via Old French from Latin *partīre* to divide, from *pars* a part]

part. *abbrev. for:* **1.** participle. **2.** particular.

par+take (pɑː'teɪk) *vb.* **+takes, +tak+ing, +took, +tak+en.** (*mainly intr.*) **1.** (foll. by *in*) to have a share; participate: *to partake in the excitement.* **2.** (foll. by *of*) to take or receive a portion, esp. of food or drink: *each partook of the food offered to them.* **3.** (foll. by *of*) to suggest or have some of the quality (of): *music partaking of sadness.* **4.** (*tr.*) *Archaic.* to share in. [C16: back formation from *partaker,* earlier *part taker,* based on Latin *particeps* participant; see PART, TAKE] —**par+'tak+er** *n.*

par+tan ('pɑːtᵊn) *n.* a Scot. word for **crab**[1]. [C15: of Celtic origin]

part+ed ('pɑːtɪd) *adj.* **1.** *Botany.* divided almost to the base: *parted leaves.* **2.** *Heraldry.* showing two coats of arms divided by a vertical central line.

par+terre (pɑː'tɛə) *n.* **1.** a formally patterned flower garden. **2.** *Chiefly U.S.* another name for **parquet circle.** [C17: from French, from *par* along + *terre* ground]

part ex+change *n.* a transaction in which used goods are taken as partial payment for more expensive ones of the same type.

par+the·no+car+py (pɑː'θiːnəʊˌkɑːpɪ) *n.* the development of fruit without fertilization or formation of seeds. [C20: from Greek *parthenos* virgin + *karpos* fruit] —**par+ˌthe·no+'car+pic** *or* **par+ˌthe·no+'car+pous** *adj.*

par+the·no+gen+e·sis (ˌpɑːθɪnəʊ'dʒɛnɪsɪs) *n.* **1.** a type of reproduction, occurring in some insects and flowers, in which the unfertilized ovum develops directly into a new individual. **2.** human conception without fertilization by a male; virgin birth. [C19: from Greek *parthenos* virgin + *genesis* birth] —**par+the·no+ge·net+ic** (ˌpɑːθɪˌnəʊdʒɪ'nɛtɪk) *adj.* —**ˌpar+the·ˌno+ge·'net+i·cal+ly** *adv.*

Par+the+non ('pɑːθəˌnɒn, -nən) *n.* the temple on the Acropolis in Athens built in the 5th century B.C. and regarded as the finest example of the Greek Doric order.

Par·the·no·pae·us (ˌpɑːθənəʊ'piːəs) *n. Greek myth.* one of the Seven against Thebes, son of Atalanta.

Par·then·o·pe (pɑː'θɛnəpɪ) *n. Greek myth.* a siren, who drowned herself when Odysseus evaded the lure of the sirens' singing. Her body was said to have been cast ashore at what became Naples.

Par+the·nos ('pɑːθɪˌnɒs) *n.* an epithet meaning "Virgin", applied by the Greeks to several goddesses, esp. Athena.

Par+thi·a ('pɑːθɪə) *n.* a country in ancient Asia, southeast of the Caspian Sea, that expanded into a great empire dominating SW Asia in the 2nd century B.C. It was destroyed by the Seleucids in the 3rd century A.D. —**'Par+thi·an** *n., adj.*

Par+thi·an shot *n.* a hostile remark or gesture delivered while departing. [alluding to the custom of Parthian archers who shot their arrows backwards while retreating]

par+tial ('pɑːʃəl) *adj.* **1.** relating to only a part; not general or complete: *a partial eclipse.* **2.** biased: *a partial judge.* **3.** (*postpositive;* foll. by *to*) having a particular liking (for). **4.** *Botany.* **a.** constituting part of a larger structure: *a partial umbel.* **b.** used for only part of the life cycle of a plant: *a partial habitat.* **c.** (of a parasite) not exclusively parasitic. **5.** *Maths.* designating or relating to an operation in which only one of a set of independent variables is considered at a time. ~*n.* **6.** Also called: **partial tone.** *Music and acoustics.* any of the component tones of a single musical sound, including both those that belong to the harmonic series of the sound and those that do not. **7.** *Maths.* a partial derivative. [C15: from Old French *parcial,* from Late Latin *partiālis* incomplete, from Latin *pars* PART] —**'par+tial+ly** *adv.* —**'par+tial+ness** *n.*

par+tial de+riv·a+tive *n.* the derivative of a function of two or more variables with respect to one of the variables, the other or others being considered constant. Written $\partial f/\partial x$.

par+tial e·clipse *n.* an eclipse, esp. of the sun, in which the body is only partially hidden. Compare **total eclipse, annular eclipse.**

par+tial frac+tion *n. Maths.* one of a set of fractions into which a more complicated fraction can be resolved.

par+ti·al+i+ty (ˌpɑːʃɪ'ælɪtɪ) *n., pl.* **·ties. 1.** favourable prejudice or bias. **2.** (usually foll. by *for*) liking or fondness. **3.** the state or condition of being partial.

par+tial pres+sure *n.* the pressure that a gas, in a mixture of gases, would exert if it alone occupied the whole volume occupied by the mixture.

par+tial prod+uct *n.* the result obtained when a number is multiplied by one digit of a multiplier.

part+i·ble ('pɑːtəbᵊl) *adj.* (esp. of property or an inheritance) divisible; separable. [C16: from Late Latin *partibilis,* from *part-, pars* part]

par+tic·i+pate (pɑː'tɪsɪˌpeɪt) *vb.* (*intr.;* often foll. by *in*) to take part, be or become actively involved, or share (in). [C16: from Latin *participāre,* from *pars* part + *capere* to take] —**par+'tic·i+pant** *adj., n.* —**par+ˌtic·i+'pa·tion** *or* **par+'tic·i·pance** *n.* —**par+'tic·i+ˌpa·tor** *n.* —**par+ˌtic·i+'pa·tor·y** *adj.*

par·tic·i·pat·ing in·sur·ance *n.* a system of insurance by which policyholders receive dividends from the company's profit or surplus.

par·ti·ci·ple ('pɑːtɪsɪpᵊl, pɑː'tɪsɪpᵊl) *n.* a nonfinite form of verbs, in English and other languages, used adjectivally and in the formation of certain compound tenses. See also **present participle, past participle.** [C14: via Old French from Latin *participium* participle, from *particeps* partaker, from *pars* PART + *capere* to take] —**par·ti·cip·i·al** (ˌpɑːtɪ'sɪpɪəl) *adj., n.* —ˌ**par·ti·'cip·i·al·ly** *adv.*

par·ti·cle ('pɑːtɪkᵊl) *n.* **1.** an extremely small piece of matter; speck. **2.** a very tiny amount; iota: *it doesn't make a particle of difference.* **3.** a function word, esp. (in certain languages) a word belonging to an uninflected class having suprasegmental or grammatical function: *the Greek particles "mēn" and "de" are used to express contrast; questions in Japanese are indicated by the particle "ka"; English* up *is sometimes regarded as an adverbial particle.* **4.** a common affix, such as *re-*, *un-*, or *-ness.* **5.** *Physics.* a body with finite mass that can be treated as having negligible size, and internal structure. **6.** See **elementary particle.** **7.** *R.C. Church.* a small piece broken off from the Host at Mass. **8.** *Archaic.* a section or clause of a document. [C14: from Latin *particula* a small part, from *pars* PART]

par·ti·cle ac·cel·er·a·tor *n.* a machine for accelerating charged elementary particles to very high energies, used for research in nuclear physics. See also **linear accelerator, cyclotron, betatron, synchrotron, synchrocyclotron.**

par·ti·cle sep·ar·a·tion *n. Transformational grammar.* a rule that moves the particle of a phrasal verb, thus deriving a sentence like *He looked the answer up* from a structure that also underlies *He looked up the answer.*

par·ti-col·oured *or* **par·ty-col·oured** ('pɑːtɪˌkʌləd) *adj.* having different colours in different parts; variegated. [C16: *parti,* from (obsolete) *party* of more than one colour, from Old French: striped, from Latin *partīrī* to divide]

par·tic·u·lar (pə'tɪkjʊlə) *adj.* **1.** (*prenominal*) of or belonging to a single or specific person, thing, category, etc.; specific; special: *the particular demands of the job; no particular reason.* **2.** (*prenominal*) exceptional or marked: *a matter of particular importance.* **3.** (*prenominal*) relating to or providing specific details or circumstances: *a particular account.* **4.** exacting or difficult to please, esp. in details; fussy. **5.** (of the solution of a differential equation) obtained by giving specific values to the arbitrary constants in a general equation. **6.** *Logic.* (of a proposition) affirming or denying something about only some members of a class of objects, as in *some men are not wicked.* Compare **universal** (sense 9). **7.** *Property law.* denoting an estate that precedes the passing of the property into ultimate ownership. See also **remainder, reversion.** ~*n.* **8.** a separate distinct item that helps to form a generalization: opposed to *general.* **9.** (*often pl.*) an item of information; detail: *complete in every particular.* **10.** *Logic.* a particular proposition. **11. in particular.** especially, particularly, or exactly. [C14: from Old French *particuler,* from Late Latin *particulāris* concerning a part, from Latin *particula* PARTICLE] —**par·'tic·u·lar·ly** *adv.*

par·tic·u·lar av·er·age *n. Insurance.* partial damage to or loss of a ship or its cargo affecting only the shipowner or one cargo owner.

par·tic·u·lar·ism (pə'tɪkjʊləˌrɪzəm) *n.* **1.** exclusive attachment to the interests of one group, class, sect, etc., esp. at the expense of the community as a whole. **2.** the principle of permitting each state or minority in a federation the right to further its own interests or retain its own laws, traditions, etc. **3.** *Theol.* the doctrine that divine grace is restricted to the elect. —**par·'tic·u·lar·ist** *n., adj.* —**par·ˌtic·u·lar·'is·tic** *adj.*

par·tic·u·lar·i·ty (pəˌtɪkjʊ'lærɪtɪ) *n., pl.* **·ties.** **1.** (*often pl.*) a specific circumstance: *the particularities of the affair.* **2.** great attentiveness to detail; fastidiousness. **3.** the quality of being precise: *a description of great particularity.* **4.** the state or quality of being particular as opposed to general; individuality: *the particularity of human situations.*

par·tic·u·lar·ize *or* **par·tic·u·lar·ise** (pə'tɪkjʊləˌraɪz) *vb.* **1.** to treat in detail; give details (about). **2.** (*tr.*) to apply to a particular case. —**par·ˌtic·u·lar·i·'za·tion** *or* **par·ˌtic·u·lar·i·'sa·tion** *n.* —**par·'tic·u·lar·ˌiz·er** *or* **par·'tic·u·lar·ˌis·er** *n.*

Par·tic·u·lars of Claim *pl. n. Law.* (in England) the first reading made by the plaintiff in a county court action, showing the facts upon which he relies in support of his claim and the relief asked for.

par·tic·u·late (pɑː'tɪkjʊlɪt, -ˌleɪt) *adj.* **1.** of or made up of separate particles. **2.** *Genetics.* of, relating to, or designating inheritance of characteristics, esp. with emphasis on the role of genes.

part·ing ('pɑːtɪŋ) *n.* **1.** *Brit.* the line of scalp showing when sections of hair are combed in opposite directions. U.S. equivalent: **part.** **2.** the act of separating or the state of being separated. **3. a.** a departure or leave-taking, esp. one causing a final separation. **b.** (*as modifier*): *a parting embrace.* **4.** a place or line of separation or division. **5.** *Chem.* a division of a crystal along a plane that is not a cleavage plane. **6.** a euphemism for **death.** ~*adj.* (*prenominal*) **7.** *Literary.* departing: *the parting day.* **8.** serving to divide or separate.

part·ing strip *n.* a thin strip of wood, metal, etc., used to separate two adjoining materials.

par·ti pris *French.* (parti 'pri) *n.* a preconceived opinion.

par·ti·san[1] *or* **par·ti·zan** (ˌpɑːtɪ'zæn, 'pɑːtɪˌzæn) *n.* **1.** an adherent or devotee of a cause, party, etc. **2. a.** a member of an armed resistance group within occupied territory. **b.** (*as modifier*): *partisan forces.* ~*adj.* **3.** of, relating to, or characteristic of a partisan. **4.** relating to or excessively devoted to one party, faction, etc.; one-sided: *partisan control.* [C16: via French, from Old Italian *partigiano,* from *parte* faction, from Latin *pars* PART] —ˌ**par·ti·'san·ship** *or* ˌ**par·ti·'zan·ship** *n.*

par·ti·san[2] *or* **par·ti·zan** ('pɑːtɪzᵊn) *n.* a spear or pike with a long tapering double-edged blade. [C16: from French *partizane,* from Old Italian *partigiana,* from *partigiano* PARTISAN[1]]

par·ti·ta (pɑː'tiːtə) *n. Music.* a type of suite. [Italian: divided (piece), from Latin *partīrī* to divide]

par·tite ('pɑːtaɪt) *adj.* **1.** (*in combination*) composed of or divided into a specified number of parts: *bipartite.* **2.** (esp. of plant leaves) divided almost to the base to form two or more parts. [C16: from Latin *partīre* to divide]

par·ti·tion (pɑː'tɪʃən) *n.* **1.** a division into parts; separation. **2.** something that separates, such as a large screen dividing a room in two. **3.** a part or share. **4.** *Property law.* a division of property, esp. realty, among joint owners. **5.** *Maths.* any of the ways by which an integer can be expressed as a sum of integers. **6.** *Logic.* the analysis of a class into its elements or parts. **7.** *Biology.* a structure that divides or separates. **8.** *Rhetoric.* the second part of a speech where the chief lines of thought are announced. ~*vb.* (*tr.*) **9.** (often foll. by *off*) to separate or apportion into sections: *to partition a room off with a large screen.* **10.** *Property law.* to divide (property, esp. realty) among joint owners, by dividing either the property itself or the proceeds of sale. [C15: via Old French from Latin *partītiō,* from *partīre* to divide] —**par·'ti·tion·er** *or* **par·'ti·tion·ist** *n.*

par·ti·tive ('pɑːtɪtɪv) *adj.* **1.** *Grammar.* indicating that a noun involved in a construction refers only to a part or fraction of what it otherwise refers to. The phrase *some of the butter* is a partitive construction; in some inflected languages it would be translated by the genitive case of the noun. **2.** serving to separate or divide into parts. ~*n.* **3.** *Grammar.* a partitive linguistic element or feature. [C16: from Medieval Latin *partītīvus* serving to divide, from Latin *partīre* to divide] —**'par·ti·tive·ly** *adv.*

part·let ('pɑːtlɪt) *n.* a woman's garment covering the neck and shoulders, worn esp. during the 16th century. [C14 *Pertelote,* name of the hen in Chaucer's "Nun's Priest's Tale", from Old French, of unknown origin]

part·ly ('pɑːtlɪ) *adv.* to some extent; not completely.

part·ner ('pɑːtnə) *n.* **1.** an ally or companion: *a partner in crime.* **2.** a member of a partnership. **3.** one of a pair of dancers or players on the same side in a game: *my bridge partner.* **4.** either member of a married couple. ~*vb.* **5.** to be or cause to be a partner (of). [C14: variant (influenced by PART) of PARCENER] —**'part·ner·less** *adj.*

part·ners ('pɑːtnəz) *pl. n. Nautical.* a wooden construction around an opening in a deck, as to support a mast.

part·ner·ship ('pɑːtnəˌʃɪp) *n.* **1. a.** a contractual relationship between two or more persons carrying on a joint business venture with a view to profit, each incurring liability for losses and the right to share in the profits. **b.** the deed creating such a relationship. **c.** the persons associated in such a relationship. **2.** the state or condition of being a partner.

part-off *n. Caribbean.* a screen used to divide off part of a room, such as the eating place of a parlour.

part of speech *n.* a class of words sharing important syntactic or semantic features; a group of words in a language that may occur in similar positions or fulfil similar functions in a sentence. The chief parts of speech in English are noun, pronoun, adjective, determiner, adverb, verb, preposition, conjunction, and interjection.

par·ton ('pɑːˌtɒn) *n. Physics.* a hypothetical elementary particle postulated as a constituent of neutrons and protons. [from PART + -ON]

par·took (pɑː'tʊk) *vb.* the past tense of **partake.**

par·tridge ('pɑːtrɪdʒ) *n., pl.* **·tridg·es** *or* **·tridge.** **1.** any of various small Old World gallinaceous game birds of the genera *Perdix, Alectoris,* etc., esp. *P. perdix* (**common** or **European partridge**): family *Phasianidae* (pheasants). **2.** *U.S.* any of various other gallinaceous birds, esp. the bobwhite and ruffed grouse. [C13: from Old French *perdriz,* from Latin *perdix,* from Greek]

par·tridge·ber·ry ('pɑːtrɪdʒˌbɛrɪ) *n., pl.* **·ries.** **1.** Also called: **boxberry, twinberry.** a creeping woody rubiaceous plant, *Mitchella repens,* of E North America with small white fragrant flowers and scarlet berries. **2.** the berry of the wintergreen. **3.** another name for **wintergreen** (sense 1).

par·tridge-wood *n.* the dark striped wood of the tropical American papilionaceous tree, *Andira inermis,* used for cabinetwork.

parts (pɑːts) *pl. n.* **1.** personal abilities or talents: *a man of many parts.* **2. private parts.** *Euphemistic.* external genital regions.

Parts of Hol·land *n.* See (Parts of) **Holland.**

Parts of Kes·te·ven *n.* See (Parts of) **Kesteven.**

Parts of Lind·sey *n.* See (Parts of) **Lindsey.**

part song *n.* **1.** a song composed in harmonized parts and usually contrapuntal in style. **2.** (*in more technical usage*) a piece of homophonic choral music in which the topmost part carries the melody.

part-time *adj.* **1.** for less than the entire time appropriate to an activity: *a part-time job; a part-time waitress.* ~*adv.* **2.** on a part-time basis: *he works part time.* ~Compare **full-time.** —**part-'tim·er** *n.*

par·tu·ri·ent (pɑː'tjʊərɪənt) *adj.* **1.** of or relating to childbirth. **2.** giving birth. **3.** producing or about to produce a new idea, etc. [C16: via Latin *parturīre*, from *parere* to bring forth] —**par·'tu·ri·en·cy** *n.*

par·tu·ri·fa·cient (pɑːˌtjʊərɪ'feɪʃənt) *adj., n. Med.* another word for **oxytocic.** [C19: from Latin *parturīre* to be in travail + *facere* to make]

par·tu·ri·tion (ˌpɑːtjʊ'rɪʃən) *n.* the act or process of giving birth. [C17: from Late Latin *parturītiō*, from *parturīre* to be in labour]

part work *n. Brit.* a series of magazines issued as at weekly or monthly intervals, which are designed to be bound together to form a complete course or book.

part-writ·ing *n. Music.* the aspect of composition concerned with the writing of parts, esp. counterpoint.

par·ty ('pɑːtɪ) *n., pl.* **·ties. 1. a.** a social gathering for pleasure, often held as a celebration. **b.** (*as modifier*): *party spirit.* **c.** (*in combination*): *partygoer.* **2.** a group of people associated in some activity: *a rescue party.* **3. a.** (*often cap.*) a group of people organized together to further a common political aim, etc., such as the election of its candidates to public office. **b.** (*as modifier*): *party politics.* **4.** the practice of taking sides on public issues. **5.** a person, esp. one who participates in some activity such as entering into a contract. **6.** the person or persons taking part in legal proceedings, such as plaintiff or prosecutor: *a party to the action.* ~*adj.* **7.** *Heraldry.* (of a shield) divided vertically into two colours, metals, or furs. [C13: from Old French *partie* part, faction, from Latin *partīrī* to divide; see PART]

par·ty line *n.* **1.** a telephone line serving two or more subscribers. **2.** the policies or dogma of a political party, etc., to which all members are expected to subscribe. **3.** *Chiefly U.S.* the boundary between adjoining property.

par·ty man *n.* a loyal member of a political party, esp. one who is slavishly loyal or extremely devoted.

par·ty pol·i·tics *n.* politics conducted through, by, or for parties, as opposed to other interests or the public good.

par·ty wall *n. Property law.* a wall separating two properties or pieces of land and over which each of the adjoining owners has certain rights.

pa·ru·lis (pə'ruːlɪs) *n., pl.* **·li·des** (-lɪˌdiːz). *Pathol.* another name for **gumboil.**

pa·rure (pə'rʊə) *n.* a set of jewels or other ornaments. [C15: from Old French *pareure* adornment, from *parer* to embellish, from Latin *parāre* to arrange]

par val·ue *n.* the value imprinted on the face of a share certificate or bond and used to assess dividend, capital ownership, or interest. Also called: **face value.** Compare **market value, book value** (sense 2).

par·ve ('pɑːvə) *or* **pa·re·ve** *adj. Judaism.* containing no milk, meat, nor their derivatives, and so admissible for use with them: *parvebread.* [from Yiddish *parev,* of obscure origin]

par·ve·nu *or* (*fem.*) **par·ve·nue** ('pɑːvəˌnjuː) *n.* **1.** a person who, having risen socially or economically, is considered to be an upstart or to lack the appropriate refinement for his new position. ~*adj.* **2.** of or characteristic of a parvenu. [C19: from French, from *parvenir* to attain, from Latin *pervenīre*, from *per* through + *venīre* to come]

par·vis *or* **par·vise** ('pɑːvɪs) *n.* a court or portico in front of a building, esp. a church. [C14: via Old French from Late Latin *paradīsus* PARADISE]

Par·zi·val (*German* 'partsiˌfal) *or* **Par·si·fal** *n. German myth.* the hero of a medieval cycle of legends about the Holy Grail. English equivalent: **Percival.**

pas (pɑː; *French* pɑ) *n., pl.* **pas. 1.** a dance step or movement, esp. in ballet. **2.** *Rare.* the right to precede; precedence. [C18: from French, literally: step]

Pas·a·de·na (ˌpæsə'diːnə) *n.* a city in SW California, east of Los Angeles. Pop.: 109 241 (1973 est.).

Pa·sar·ga·dae (pæ'sɑːgəˌdiː) *n.* an ancient city in Persia, northeast of Persepolis in present-day Iran: built by Cyrus the Great.

Pa·say ('pɑːsaɪ) *n.* a city in the Philippines, on central Luzon just south of Manila, on Manila Bay. Pop.: 240 913 (1975 est.). Also called: **Rizal.**

pas·cal ('pæskᵊl) *n.* the derived SI unit of pressure; the pressure exerted on an area of 1 square metre by a force of 1 newton; equivalent to 10 dynes per square centimetre or 1.45×10^{-4} pound per square inch. Symbol: Pa [C20: named after B. PASCAL]

Pas·cal (*French* pas'kal) *n.* **Blaise** (blɛːz). 1623–62, French philosopher, mathematician, and physicist. As a scientist, he made important contributions to hydraulics and differential calculus and, with Fermat, developed the theory of probability. His chief philosophical works are *Lettres provinciales* (1656–57), written in defence of Jansenism and against the Jesuits, and *Pensées* (1670), fragments of a Christian apologia.

Pas·cal's tri·an·gle *n.* a triangular figure consisting of rows of numbers, each number being obtained by adding together the two numbers on either side of it in the row above. [C17: named after B. PASCAL]

Pasch (pɑːsk, pæsk) *n.* an archaic name for **Passover** or **Easter.** [C12: from Old French *pasche,* via Church Latin and Greek from Hebrew *pesakh,* PESACH] —**'Pas·chal** *adj.*

pas·chal flow·er *n.* another name for **pasqueflower.**

pas·chal lamb *n.* **1.** (*sometimes caps.*) *Old Testament.* the lamb killed and eaten on the first day of the Passover. **2.** (*caps.*) Christ regarded as this sacrifice.

Pas-de-Ca·lais (*French* pɑd ka'lɛ) *n.* a department of N France, in Nord–Pas-de-Calais region, on the Straits of Dover (the **Pas de Calais**): the part of France closest to the British Isles. Capital: Arras. Pop.: 1 420 960 (1975). Area: 6752 sq. km (2633 sq. miles).

pas de chat (*French* pɑ də 'ʃa) *n., pl.* **pas de chat** *Ballet.* a cat-like leap. [French: cat's step]

pas de deux (*French* pɑ də 'dø) *n., pl.* **pas de deux.** *Ballet.* a sequence for two dancers. [French: step for two]

pa·se ('pɑːseɪ) *n. Bullfighting.* a movement of the cape or muleta by a matador to attract the bull's attention and guide its attack. [from Spanish, literally: pass]

pash[1] (pæʃ) *n. Slang.* infatuation. [C20: from PASSION]

pash[2] (pæʃ) *Obsolete or dialect.* ~*vb.* **1.** to throw or be thrown and break or be broken to bits; smash. ~*n.* **2.** a crushing blow. [C17 (n.): from earlier *passhen* to throw with violence, probably of imitative origin]

pa·sha *or* **pa·cha** ('pɑːʃə, 'pæʃə) *n.* (formerly) a provincial governor or other high official of the Ottoman Empire or the modern Egyptian kingdom: placed after a name when used as a title. [C17: from Turkish *paşa*]

pa·sha·lik *or* **pa·sha·lic** ('pɑːʃəlɪk) *n.* the province or jurisdiction of a pasha. [C18: from Turkish]

pash·ka ('pæʃkə) *n.* a rich Russian dessert made of cottage cheese, cream, almonds, currants, etc., set in a special wooden mould and traditionally eaten at Easter.

pashm ('pæʃəm) *n.* the under-fur of various Tibetan animals, esp. goats, used for Cashmere shawls. [from Persian, literally: wool]

Pash·to ('pʌʃtəʊ) *n., pl.* **·to** *or* **·tos. 1.** a language of Afghanistan and NW Pakistan, belonging to the East Iranian branch of the Indo-European family: since 1936 the official language of Afghanistan. **2.** a speaker of the Pashto language; a Pathan. ~*adj.* **3.** denoting or relating to this language or a speaker of it.

Pa·sio·na·ria (*Spanish* ˌpasjo'narja) *n.* **La** (la). pseudonym of *Dolores Ibarruri.* born 1895, Spanish Communist leader, who lived in exile in the Soviet Union (1939–75).

Pa·siph·a·ë (pə'sɪfɪiː) *n. Greek myth.* the wife of Minos and mother (by a bull) of the Minotaur.

pa·so do·ble ('pæsəʊ 'dəʊbleɪ; *Spanish* 'paso 'doble) *n., pl.* **pa·so do·bles** *or* **pa·sos do·bles** (*Spanish* 'pasos 'dobles). **1.** a modern ballroom dance in fast duple time. **2.** a piece of music composed for or in the rhythm of this dance. [Spanish: double step]

Pa·so·li·ni (*Italian* ˌpazo'liːni) *n.* **Pier Pa·o·lo** (pjɛːr 'paːolo). 1922–77, Italian film director. His films include *Oedipus Rex* (1967), *The Gospel according to St. Matthew* (1964), *Theorem* (1968), *Pigsty* (1969), and *Decameron* (1970).

pasque·flow·er ('pɑːskˌflaʊə, 'pæsk-) *n.* **1.** a small purple-flowered ranunculaceous plant, *Anemone pulsatilla* (or *Pulsatilla vulgaris*), of N and Central Europe and W Asia. **2.** any of several related North American plants, such as *A. patens.* ~ Also called: **paschal flower.** [C16: from French *passefleur,* from *passer* to excel + *fleur* flower; changed to *pasqueflower* Easter flower, because it blooms at Easter]

pas·quin·ade (ˌpæskwɪ'neɪd) *or* **pas·quil** ('pæskwɪl) *n.* **1.** an abusive lampoon or satire, esp. one posted in a public place. ~*vb.* **·ades, ·ad·ing, ·ad·ed** *or* **·quils, ·quil·ling, ·quilled. 2.** (*tr.*) to ridicule with pasquinade. [C17: from Italian *Pasquino* name given to an ancient Roman statue disinterred in 1501, which was annually posted with satirical verses] —ˌ**pas·quin·'ad·er** *n.*

pass (pɑːs) *vb.* **1.** to go onwards or move by or past (a person, thing, etc.). **2.** to run, extend, or lead through, over, or across (a place): *the route passes through the city.* **3.** to go through or cause to go through (an obstacle or barrier): *to pass a needle through cloth.* **4.** to move or cause to move onwards or over: *he passed his hand over her face.* **5.** (*tr.*) to go beyond or exceed: *this victory passes all expectation.* **6.** to gain or cause to gain an adequate or required mark, grade, or rating in (an examination, course, etc.): *the examiner passed them all.* **7.** (often foll. by *away* or *by*) to elapse or allow to elapse: *we passed the time talking.* **8. pass the time of day (with).** to spend time amicably, esp. in chatting, with no particular purpose. **9.** (*intr.*) to take place or happen: *what passed at the meeting?* **10.** to speak or exchange or be spoken or exchanged: *angry words passed between them.* **11.** to spread or cause to spread: *we passed the news round the class.* **12.** to transfer or exchange or be transferred or exchanged: *the bomb passed from hand to hand.* **13.** (*intr.*) to undergo change or transition: *to pass from joy to despair.* **14.** (when *tr.*, often foll. by *down*) to transfer or be transferred by inheritance: *the house passed to the younger son.* **15.** to agree to or sanction or to be agreed to or receive the sanction of a legislative body, person of authority, etc.: *the assembly passed 10 resolutions.* **16.** (*tr.*) (of a legislative measure) to undergo (a procedural stage) and be agreed: *the bill passed the committee stage.* **17.** (when *tr.*, often foll. by *on* or *upon*) to pronounce or deliver (judgment, findings, etc.): *the court passed sentence.* **18.** to go or allow to go without comment or censure: *the intended insult passed unnoticed.* **19.** (*intr.*) to opt not to exercise a right, as by not answering a question or not making a bid or a play in card games. **20.** *Physiol.* to discharge (urine, etc.) from the body. **21.** (*intr.*) to come to an end or disappear: *his anger soon passed.* **22.** (*intr.;* usually foll. by *for* or *as*) to be likely to be mistaken for or accepted as (someone or something else): *you could easily pass for your sister.* **23.** (*intr.;* foll. by *away, on,* or *over*) a euphemism for **die. 24.** (*tr.*) *Chiefly U.S.* to fail to declare (a dividend). **25.** (*intr.;* usually foll. by *on* or *upon*) *Chiefly U.S.* (of a court, jury, etc.) to sit in judgment; adjudicate. **26.** *Sport.* to hit, kick, or throw (the ball, etc.) to another player. **27. bring to pass.** *Archaic.* to cause to happen. **28. come to pass.** *Archaic.* to happen. ~*n.* **29.** the act of passing. **30. a.** a route through a range of mountains where the summit is lower or where there is a gap between peaks. **b.** (*cap. as part of a name*): *the Simplon Pass.* **31.** a way through any difficult region. **32.** a permit, licence, or authorization to do something without restriction: *she has a pass to visit the museum on Sundays.* **33. a.** a document allowing entry to and exit from a military installation. **b.** a document authorizing leave of absence. **34.** *Brit.* **a.** the passing of a college or university examination to a satisfactory standard but not as high as honours. Compare **honours** (sense 2). **b.** (*as modifier*): *a pass degree.* **35.** a dive, sweep, or bombing or landing run by an aircraft. **36.** a motion of the hand or of a wand as a prelude to or part of a conjuring trick. **37.** *Informal.* an attempt, in words or action, to invite sexual intimacy. **38.** a state of affairs or condition, esp. a bad or difficult one (esp. in the phrase **a pretty pass**). **39.** *Sport.* the transfer of a ball, etc., from one player to another. **40.** *Fencing.* a thrust or lunge with a sword. **41.** *Bridge, etc.* the act of passing (making no bid). **42.** *Bullfighting.* another word for **pase. 43.** *Archaic.* a witty sally or remark. ~*interj.* **44.** *Bridge, etc.* a call indicating that a player has no bid to make. ~See also **pass by, pass off, pass out, pass over, pass up.** [C13: from Old French *passer* to pass, surpass, from Latin *passūs* step, PACE[1]]

pass. *abbrev. for:* **1.** passive. **2.** passenger. **3.** passage.

pass·a·ble ('pɑːsəb°l) *adj.* **1.** adequate, fair, or acceptable: *a passable but not outstanding speech.* **2.** (of an obstacle) capable of being passed or crossed. **3.** (of currency) valid for general circulation. **4.** (of a proposed law) able to be ratified or enacted. —'**pass·a·ble·ness** *n.*

pass·a·bly ('pɑːsəblɪ) *adv.* **1.** fairly; somewhat. **2.** acceptably; well enough: *she sings passably.*

pas·sa·ca·glia (ˌpæsə'kɑːljə) *n.* **1.** an old Spanish dance in slow triple time. **2.** a slow instrumental piece characterized by a series of variations on a particular theme played over a repeated bass part. See also **chaconne** (sense 1). [C17: earlier *passacalle*, from Spanish *pasacalle* street dance, from *paso* step + *calle* street; the ending *-alle* was changed to *-aglia* to suggest an Italian origin]

pas·sade (pæ'seɪd) *n. Dressage.* the act of moving back and forth in the same place. [C17: via French from Italian *passata*, from *passare* to PASS]

pas·sage[1] ('pæsɪdʒ) *n.* **1.** a channel, opening, etc., through or by which a person may pass. **2.** *Music.* a section or division of a piece, movement, etc. **3.** a way, as in a hall or lobby. **4.** a section of a written work, speech, etc., esp. one of moderate length. **5.** a journey, esp. by ship: *the outward passage took a week.* **6.** the act or process of passing from one place, condition, etc., to another: *passage of a gas through a liquid.* **7.** the permission, right, or freedom to pass: *to be denied passage through a country.* **8.** the enactment of a law or resolution by a legislative or deliberative body. **9.** an evacuation of the bowels. **10.** *Rare.* an exchange or interchange, as of blows, words, etc. (esp. in the phrase **passage at arms**). [C13: from Old French from *passer* to PASS]

pas·sage[2] ('pæsɪdʒ, 'pæsɑːʒ) *Dressage.* ~*n.* **1.** a sideways walk in which diagonal pairs of feet are lifted alternatively. **2.** a cadenced lofty trot, the moment of suspension being clearly defined. ~*vb.* **3.** to move or cause to move at a passage. [C18: from French *passager*, variant of *passéger*, from Italian *passeggiare* to take steps, ultimately from Latin *passūs* step, PACE[1]]

pas·sage hawk *or* **pas·sag·er hawk** *n.* a young hawk or falcon caught while on migration. Compare **eyas, haggard.**

pas·sage·way ('pæsɪdʒˌweɪ) *n.* a way, esp. one in or between buildings; passage.

pas·sage work *n. Music.* scales, runs, etc., in a piece of music which have no structural significance but provide an opportunity for virtuoso display.

Pas·sa·ma·quod·dy Bay (ˌpæsəmə'kwɒdɪ) *n.* an inlet of the Bay of Fundy between New Brunswick (Canada) and Maine (U.S.) at the mouth of the St. Croix River.

pas·sant ('pæs°nt) *adj.* (*usually postpositive*) *Heraldry.* (of a beast) walking, with the right foreleg raised. [C14: from Old French, present participle of *passer* to PASS]

pass band *n.* the band of frequencies that is transmitted with maximum efficiency through a circuit, filter, etc.

pass·book ('pɑːsˌbʊk) *n.* **1.** a book for keeping a record of withdrawals from and payments into a building society. **2.** another name for **bankbook. 3.** a customer's book in which is recorded by a trader a list of credit sales to that customer. **4.** *S. African.* an official document serving to identify the bearer, his race, his residence, and his employment.

pass by *vb.* **1.** (*intr.*) to go or move past. **2.** (*tr., adv.*) to overlook or disregard: *to pass by difficult problems.*

pas·sé ('pɑːseɪ, 'pæseɪ; *French* pa'se) *adj.* **1.** out-of-date: *passé ideas.* **2.** past the prime; faded: *a passé society beauty.* [C18: from French, past participle of *passer* to PASS]

pas·sel ('pæs°l) *n. Informal or dialect, chiefly U.S.* a group or quantity of no fixed number. [variant of PARCEL]

passe·men·terie (pæs'mɛntrɪ; *French* pasmɑ̃'tri) *n.* a decorative trimming of gimp, cord, beads, braid, etc. [C16: from Old French *passement*, from *passer* to trim, PASS]

pas·sen·ger ('pæsɪndʒə) *n.* **1. a.** a person travelling in a car, train, boat, etc., not driven by him. **b.** (*as modifier*): *a passenger seat.* **2.** *Chiefly Brit.* a member of a group or team who is a burden on the others through not participating fully in the work. **3.** *Archaic.* a wayfarer. [C14: from Old French *passager* passing, from PASSAGE]

pas·sen·ger pi·geon *n.* a gregarious North American pigeon, *Ectopistes migratorius:* became extinct at the beginning of the 20th century.

passe-par·tout (ˌpæspɑː'tuː; *French* paspar'tu) *n.* **1.** a mounting for a picture in which strips of strong gummed paper are used to bind together the glass, picture and backing. **2.** the gummed paper used for this. **3.** a mat, often decorated, on which a photograph, etc., is mounted. **4.** something that secures entry everywhere, esp. a master key. [C17: from French, literally: pass everywhere]

passe·pied (pɑːs'pjeɪ) *n., pl.* **·pieds** (-'pjeɪ). **1.** a lively minuet of Breton origin, in triple time, popular in the 17th century. **2.** a piece of music composed for or in the rhythm of this dance. [C17: from French: pass the foot]

pass·er-by *n., pl.* **pass·ers-by.** a person that is passing or going by, esp. on foot.

pas·ser·ine ('pæsəˌraɪn, -ˌriːn) *adj.* **1.** of, relating to, or belonging to the *Passeriformes*, an order of birds characterized by the perching habit: includes the larks, finches, crows, thrushes, starlings, etc. ~*n.* **2.** any bird belonging to the order *Passeriformes.* [C18: from Latin *passer* sparrow]

pas seul (*French* pɑ 'sœl) *n.* a dance sequence for one person. [French, literally: step on one's own]

pas·si·ble ('pæsɪb°l) *adj.* susceptible to emotion or suffering; able to feel. [C14: from Medieval Latin *passibilis*, from Latin *patī* to suffer; see PASSION] —ˌ**pas·si·'bil·i·ty** *n.*

pas·si·flo·ra·ceous (ˌpæsɪflɔː'reɪʃəs) *adj.* of, relating to, or belonging to the *Passifloraceae*, a tropical and subtropical family of climbing plants including the passion flowers: the flowers have five petals and threadlike parts forming a dense mass (corona) around the central disc. [C19: from New Latin *Passiflora*, the type genus (passion flower)]

pas·sim *Latin.* ('pæsɪm) *adv.* here and there; throughout: used to indicate that what is referred to occurs frequently in the work cited.

pass·ing ('pɑːsɪŋ) *adj.* **1.** transitory or momentary: *a passing fancy.* **2.** cursory or casual in action or manner: *a passing reference.* ~*adv., adj. Archaic.* **3.** to an extreme degree: *the events were passing strange.* ~*n.* **4.** a place where or means by which one may pass, cross, ford, etc. **5.** a euphemistic word for **death. 6. in passing.** by the way; incidentally: *he mentioned your visit in passing.*

pass·ing bell *n.* a bell rung to announce a death or a funeral. Also called: **death bell, death knell.**

pass·ing note *or U.S.* **pass·ing tone** *n. Music.* a nonharmonic note through which a melody passes from one harmonic note to the next. Compare **auxiliary note.**

pass·ing shot *n. Tennis.* a winning shot hit outside an opponent's reach.

pas·sion ('pæʃən) *n.* **1.** ardent love or affection. **2.** intense sexual love. **3.** a strong affection or enthusiasm for an object, concept, etc.: *a passion for poetry.* **4.** any strongly felt emotion, such as love, hate, envy, etc. **5.** the object of an intense desire, ardent affection, or enthusiasm. **6.** an outburst expressing intense emotion: *he burst into a passion of sobs.* **7.** *Philosophy.* the state of being acted upon by external forces, esp. by those that are false to one's nature as a rational being: usually contrasted with *action.* **8.** the sufferings and death of a Christian martyr. [C12: via French from Church Latin *passiō* suffering, from Latin *patī* to suffer]

Pas·sion ('pæʃən) *n.* **1.** the sufferings of Christ from the Last Supper to his death on the cross. **2.** any of the four Gospel accounts of this. **3.** a musical setting of this: *the St. Matthew Passion.*

pas·sion·al ('pæʃən°l) *adj.* **1.** of, relating to, or due to passion or the passions. ~*n.* **2.** a book recounting the sufferings of Christian martyrs or saints.

pas·sion·ate ('pæʃənɪt) *adj.* **1.** manifesting or exhibiting intense sexual feeling or desire: *a passionate lover.* **2.** capable of, revealing, or characterized by intense emotion: *a passionate plea.* **3.** easily roused to anger; quick-tempered. —'**pas·sion·ate·ly** *adv.* —'**pas·sion·ate·ness** *n.*

pas·sion·flow·er ('pæʃənˌflaʊə) *n.* any passifloraceous plant of the tropical American genus *Passiflora*, cultivated for their red, yellow, greenish, or purple showy flowers: some species have edible fruit. See also **granadilla.**

pas·sion fruit *n.* the edible fruit of any of various passion-flowers, esp. granadilla.

pas·sion·less ('pæʃənlɪs) *adj.* **1.** empty of emotion or feeling: *a passionless marriage.* **2.** calm and detached; dispassionate. —'**pas·sion·less·ly** *adv.* —'**pas·sion·less·ness** *n.*

Pas·sion play *n.* a play depicting the Passion of Christ.

Pas·sion Sun·day *n.* the fifth Sunday in Lent (the second Sunday before Easter), when Passiontide begins.

Pas·sion·tide ('pæʃənˌtaɪd) *n.* the last two weeks of Lent, extending from Passion Sunday to Holy Saturday.

Pas·sion Week *n.* **1.** the week between Passion Sunday and Palm Sunday. **2.** (formerly) Holy Week; the week before Easter.

pas·sive ('pæsɪv) *adj.* **1.** not active or not participating perceptibly in an activity, organization, etc. **2.** unresisting and receptive to external forces; submissive. **3.** not working or operating. **4.** affected or acted upon by an external object or force. **5.** *Grammar.* denoting a voice of verbs in sentences in which the grammatical subject is not the logical subject but rather the recipient of the action described by the verb, as *was broken* in the sentence *The glass was broken by a boy.* Compare **active** (sense 5a). **6.** *Chem.* (of a substance, esp. a metal) apparently chemically unreactive, usually as a result of the formation of a thin protective layer that prevents further reaction. **7.** *Electronics, telecomm.* **a.** containing no source of power and therefore capable only of attenuating a signal: *a* *passive network.* **b.** not capable of amplifying a signal or controlling a function: *a passive communications satellite.* **8.** *Finance.* (of a bond, share, debt, etc.) yielding no interest. ~*n.* **9.** *Grammar.* **a.** the passive voice. **b.** a passive verb. [C14: from Latin *passīvus* susceptible of suffering, from *patī* to undergo] —**'pas+sive+ly** *adv.* —**'pas+sive+ness** *or* **pas+'siv+i·ty** *n.*

pas+sive o·be·di+ence **1.** unquestioning obedience to authority. **2.** the surrender of a person's will to another person.

pas+sive re+sist+ance *n.* resistance to a government, law, etc., made without violence, as by fasting, demonstrating peacefully, or refusing to cooperate.

pas+siv+ism ('pæsɪˌvɪzəm) *n.* **1.** the theory, belief, or practice of passive resistance. **2.** the quality, characteristics, or fact of being passive. —**'pas+siv+ist** *n.*

pass+key ('pɑːsˌkiː) *n.* **1.** any of various keys, esp. a latchkey. **2.** another term for **master key** or **skeleton key.**

pass law *n.* (in South Africa) a law restricting the movement of Black Africans, esp. from rural to urban areas.

pass off *vb.* (*adv.*) **1.** to be or cause to be accepted or circulated in a false character or identity: *he passed the fake diamonds off as real.* **2.** (*intr.*) to come to a gradual end; disappear: *eventually the pain passed off.* **3.** to emit (a substance) as a gas or vapour, or (of a substance) to be emitted in this way. **4.** (*intr.*) to take place: *the meeting passed off without disturbance.* **5.** (*tr.*) to set aside or disregard: *I managed to pass off his insult.*

pass out *vb.* (*adv.*) **1.** (*intr.*) *Informal.* to become unconscious; faint. **2.** (*intr.*) *Brit.* (esp. of an officer cadet) to qualify for a military commission, etc.; complete a course of training satisfactorily: *General Smith passed out from Sandhurst in 1933.* **3.** (*tr.*) to distribute.

pass o·ver *vb.* **1.** (*tr., adv.*) to take no notice of; disregard: *they passed me over in the last round of promotions.* **2.** (*intr., prep.*) to disregard (something bad or embarrassing): *we shall pass over your former faults.*

Pass+o·ver ('pɑːsˌəʊvə) *n.* Also called: **Pesach, Pesah, Feast of the Unleavened Bread. 1.** an eight-day Jewish festival beginning on Nisan 15 and celebrated in commemoration of the passing over or sparing of the Israelites in Egypt, when God smote the firstborn of the Egyptians (Exodus 12). **2.** another term for the **Paschal Lamb.** [C16: from *pass over,* translation of Hebrew *pesah,* from *pāsah* to pass over]

pass+port ('pɑːspɔːt) *n.* **1.** an official document issued by a government, identifying an individual, granting him permission to travel abroad, and requesting the protection of other governments for him. **2.** a licence granted by a state to a foreigner, allowing the passage of his person or goods through the country. **3.** another word for **sea letter** (sense 1). **4.** a quality, asset, etc., that gains a person admission or acceptance. [C15: from French *passeport,* from *passer* to PASS + PORT[1]]

pass up *vb.* (*tr., adv.*) **1.** *Informal.* to refuse or reject: *I won't pass up this opportunity.* **2.** to take no notice of (someone).

pas+sus ('pæsəs) *n., pl.* **+sus** *or* **+sus·es.** (esp. in medieval literature) a division or section of a poem, story, etc. [C16: from Latin: step, PACE[1]]

pass+word ('pɑːsˌwɜːd) *n.* **1.** a secret word, phrase, etc., that ensures admission or acceptance by proving identity, membership, etc. **2.** an action, quality, etc., that gains admission or acceptance.

past (pɑːst) *adj.* **1.** completed, finished, and no longer in existence: *past happiness.* **2.** denoting or belonging to all or a segment of the time that has elapsed at the present moment: *the past history of the world.* **3.** denoting a specific unit of time that immediately precedes the present one: *the past month.* **4.** (*prenominal*) denoting a person who has held and relinquished an office or position; former: *a past president.* **5.** *Grammar.* denoting any of various tenses of verbs that are used in describing actions, events, or states that have been begun or completed at the time of utterance. Compare **aorist, imperfect, perfect.** ~*n.* **6. the past.** the period of time or a segment of it that has elapsed: *forget the past.* **7.** the history, experience, or background of a nation, person, etc.: *a soldier with a distinguished past.* **8.** an earlier period of someone's life, esp. one that contains events kept secret or regarded as disreputable. **9.** *Grammar.* **a.** a past tense. **b.** a verb in a past tense. ~*adv.* **10.** at a specified or unspecified time before the present; ago: *three years past.* **11.** on or onwards: *I greeted him but he just walked past.* ~*prep.* **12.** beyond in time: *it's past midnight.* **13.** beyond in place or position: *the library is past the church.* **14.** moving beyond; in a direction that passes: *he walked past me.* **15.** beyond or above the reach, limit, or scope of: *his foolishness is past comprehension.* **16.** beyond or above in number or amount: *to count past ten.* **17. past it.** *Informal.* unable to perform the tasks one could do when one was younger. **18. not put it past someone.** to consider a person capable of (something). [C14: from *passed,* past participle of PASS]

pas+ta ('pæstə) *n.* any of several variously shaped edible preparations made from a flour and water dough, such as spaghetti. [Italian, from Late Latin: PASTE]

paste[1] (peɪst) *n.* **1.** a mixture or material of a soft or malleable consistency, such as toothpaste. **2.** an adhesive made from water and flour or starch, used for joining pieces of paper, etc. **3.** a preparation of food, such as meat, that has been powdered to a creamy mass, for spreading on bread, etc. **4.** any of various sweet doughy confections: *almond paste.* **5.** dough, esp. when prepared with shortening, as for making pastry. **6. a.** Also called: **strass.** a hard shiny glass used for making imitation gems. **b.** an imitation gem made of this glass. **7.** the combined ingredients of porcelain. See also **hard paste, soft paste.** ~*vb.* (*tr.*) **8.** (often foll. by *on* or *onto*) to attach by or as if by using paste: *he pasted posters onto the wall.* **9.** (usually foll. by *with*) to cover (a surface) with paper, etc., usually attached with an adhesive: *he pasted the wall with posters.* [C14: via Old French from Late Latin *pasta* dough, from Greek *pastē* barley porridge, from *pastos,* from *passein* to sprinkle]

paste[2] (peɪst) *vb.* (*tr.*) *Slang.* to hit, esp. with the fists; punch or beat soundly. [C19: variant of BASTE to beat]

paste+board ('peɪstˌbɔːd) *n.* **1. a.** a stiff board formed from layers of paper or pulp pasted together, esp. as used in bookbinding. **b.** (*as modifier*): *a pasteboard bookcover.* **2.** *Chiefly U.S.* a board on which pastry dough is rolled out. **3.** *Slang.* a card or ticket. ~*adj.* **4.** flimsy or fake.

pas+tel ('pæstᵊl, pæ'stɛl) *n.* **1. a.** a substance made of ground pigment bound with gum, used for making sticks for drawing. **b.** a crayon of this. **c.** a drawing done in such crayons. **2.** the medium or technique of pastel drawing. **3.** a pale delicate colour. **4.** a light prose work, esp. a poetic one. **5.** another name for **woad** (the dye and plant). ~*adj.* **6.** (of a colour) pale; delicate: *pastel blue.* [C17: via French from Italian *pastello,* from Late Latin *pastellus* woad compounded into a paste, diminutive of *pasta* PASTE[1]] —**'pas+tel+ist** *or* **'pas+tel+list** *n.*

pas+tern ('pæstən) *n.* **1.** the part of a horse's foot between the fetlock and the hoof. **2.** Also called: **fetter bone.** either of the two bones that constitute this part. [C14: from Old French *pasturon,* from *pasture* a hobble, from Latin *pāstōrius* of a shepherd, from PĀSTOR]

Pas·ter·nak ('pæstəˌnæk; *Russian* pəstɪr'nak) *n.* **Bo·ris Le·o·ni·do·vich** (ba'ris lɪa'nidəvitʃ). 1890–1960, Soviet lyric poet, novelist, and translator, noted particularly for his novel of the Russian Revolution, *Dr. Zhivago* (1957). He was awarded the Nobel prize for literature in 1958, but was forced to decline it.

paste-up *n.* **1.** Also called (in the U.S.): **mechanical.** *Printing.* a sheet of paper or board on which are pasted artwork, proofs, etc., for photographing prior to making a plate. **2.** another name for **collage.**

Pas·teur (*French* pas'tœːr) *n.* **Louis** (lwi). 1822–95, French chemist and bacteriologist. His discovery that the fermentation of milk and alcohol was caused by microorganisms resulted in the process of pasteurization. He also devised methods of immunization against anthrax and rabies and pioneered stereochemistry.

pas+teur+ism ('pæstəˌrɪzəm, -stjə-, 'pɑː-) *n. Med.* **1.** a method of securing immunity from rabies in a person who has been bitten by a rabid animal, by daily injections of progressively virulent suspensions of the infected spinal cord of a rabbit that died of rabies. **2.** a similar method of treating patients with other viral infections by the serial injection of progressively virulent suspensions of the causative virus. ~Also called: **Pasteur treatment.**

pas+teur·i+za+tion *or* **pas+teur·i+sa+tion** (ˌpæstəraɪ'zeɪʃən, -stjə-, ˌpɑː-) *n.* the process of heating beverages, such as milk, beer, wine, or cider, or solid foods, such as cheese or crab meat, to destroy harmful or undesirable microorganisms or to limit the rate of fermentation by the application of controlled heat.

pas+teur+ize *or* **pas+teur+ise** ('pæstəˌraɪz, -stjə-, 'pɑː-) *vb.* (*tr.*) **1.** to subject (milk, beer, etc.) to pasteurization. **2.** *Rare.* to subject (a patient) to pasteurism.

pas+teur+iz+er *or* **pas+teur+is+er** ('pæstəˌraɪzə, -stjə-, 'pɑː-) *n.* **1.** an apparatus for pasteurizing substances (esp. milk). **2.** a person who carries out pasteurization.

pas+tiche (pæ'stiːʃ) *or* **pas+tic+cio** (pæ'stɪtʃəʊ) *n.* **1.** a work of art that mixes styles, materials, etc. **2.** a work of art in the style of another artist. [C19 French *pastiche,* Italian *pasticcio,* literally: pie crust (hence, something blended) from Late Latin *pasta* PASTE[1]]

pas+tille *or* **pas+til** ('pæstɪl) *n.* **1.** a small flavoured or medicated lozenge for chewing. **2.** an aromatic substance burnt to fumigate the air. **3.** *Med.* a small coated paper disc formerly used to estimate the dose or intensity of radiation (esp. of x-rays): it changes colour when exposed. **4.** a variant of **pastel** (sense 1). [C17: via French from Latin *pastillus* small loaf, from *pānis* bread]

pas+time ('pɑːsˌtaɪm) *n.* an activity or entertainment which makes time pass pleasantly: *golf is my favourite pastime.*

pas+tis (pæ'stɪs, -'stiːs) *n.* an anise-flavoured alcoholic drink. [from French, of uncertain origin]

past mas+ter *n.* **1.** a person with talent for, or experience in, a particular activity: *a past master of tact.* **2.** a person who has held the office of master in a guild, etc.

Pas+to (*Spanish* 'pasto) *n.* a city in SE Colombia, at an altitude of 2590 m (8500 ft.). Pop.: 119 339 (1973).

pas+tor ('pɑːstə) *n.* **1.** a clergyman or priest in charge of a congregation. **2.** a person who exercises spiritual guidance over a number of people. **3.** an archaic word for **shepherd. 4.** Also called: **rosy pastor.** an S Asian starling, *Sturnus roseus,* having glossy black head and wings and a pale pink body. [C14: from Latin: shepherd, from *pascere* to feed] —**'pas+tor+ˌship** *n.*

pas+to+ral ('pɑːstərəl) *adj.* **1.** of, characterized by, or depicting rural life, scenery, etc. **2.** (of a literary work) dealing with an idealized form of rural existence in a conventional way. **3.** (of land) used for pasture. **4.** denoting or relating to the branch of theology dealing with the duties of a clergyman or priest to his congregation. **5.** of or relating to a clergyman or priest in charge of a congregation or his duties as such. **6.** of or relating to shepherds, their work, etc. ~*n.* **7.** a literary work or picture portraying rural life, esp. the lives of shepherds in an idealizing way. See also **eclogue. 8.** *Music.* a variant spelling of **pastorale. 9.** *Ecclesiast.* **a.** a letter from a clergyman to the people under his charge. **b.** the letter of a bishop to the clergy or people of his diocese. **c.** Also called: **pastoral staff.** the crosier or staff carried by a bishop as a symbol of his pastoral responsibilities. [C15: from Latin, from PASTOR] **—'pas+to+ral+ism** *n.* **—'pas+to+ral+ly** *adv.*

pas+to+rale (ˌpæstəˈrɑːl) *n., pl.* **+rales** *or* **+ra+li** (*Italian* -ˈraːli). *Music.* **1.** a composition evocative of rural life, characterized by moderate compound duple or quadruple time and sometimes a droning accompaniment. **2.** a musical play based on a rustic story, popular during the 16th century. [C18: Italian, from Latin: PASTORAL]

pas+tor+al+ist (ˈpɑːstərəlɪst) *n. Austral.* a grazier or land-holder raising sheep, cattle, etc., on a large scale.

pas+tor+ate (ˈpɑːstərɪt) *n.* **1.** the office or term of office of a pastor. **2.** a body of pastors; pastors collectively.

past par+ti+ci+ple *n.* a participial form of verbs used to modify a noun that is logically the object of a verb, also used in certain compound tenses and passive forms of the verb in English and other languages.

past per+fect *Grammar.* ~*adj.* **1.** denoting a tense of verbs used in relating past events where the action had already occurred at the time of the action of a main verb that is itself in a past tense. In English this is a compound tense formed with *had* plus the past participle. ~*n.* **2. a.** the past perfect tense. **b.** a verb in this tense.

pas+tra+mi (pəˈstrɑːmɪ) *n.* highly seasoned smoked beef, esp. prepared from a shoulder cut. [from Yiddish, from Rumanian *pastramă,* from *păstra* to preserve]

pas+try (ˈpeɪstrɪ) *n., pl.* **+tries. 1.** a dough of flour, water, shortening and sometimes other ingredients. **2.** baked foods, such as tarts, made with this dough. **3.** an individual cake or pastry pie. [C16: from PASTE[1]]

pas+try cream *n.* a creamy custard, often flavoured, used as a filling for eclairs, flans, etc. Also called: **pastry custard.**

pas+tur+age (ˈpɑːstʃərɪdʒ) *n.* **1.** the right to graze or the business of grazing cattle. **2.** another word for **pasture.**

pas+ture (ˈpɑːstʃə) *n.* **1.** land covered with grass or herbage and grazed by or suitable for grazing by livestock. **2.** a specific tract of such land. **3.** the grass or herbage growing on it. ~*vb.* **4.** (*tr.*) to cause (livestock) to graze or (of livestock) to graze (a pasture). [C13: via Old French from Late Latin *pāstūra,* from *pascere* to feed]

past·y[1] (ˈpeɪstɪ) *adj.* **past·i+er, past·i+est. 1.** of or like the colour, texture, etc., of paste. **2.** (esp. of the complexion) pale or unhealthy-looking. ~*n., pl.* **past·ies. 3.** either one of a pair of small round coverings for the nipples used by striptease dancers. **—'past·i+ly** *adv.* **—'past·i+ness** *n.*

past·y[2] (ˈpæstɪ) *n., pl.* **past·ies.** a round of pastry folded over a filling of meat, vegetables, etc.: *Cornish pasty.* [C13: from Old French *pastée,* from Late Latin *pasta* dough]

PA sys+tem *n.* See **public-address system.**

pat[1] (pæt) *vb.* **pats, pat+ting, pat+ted. 1.** to hit (something) lightly with the palm of the hand or some other flat surface: *to pat a ball.* **2.** to slap (a person or animal) gently, esp. on the back, as an expression of affection, congratulation, etc. **3.** (*tr.*) to shape, smooth, etc., with a flat instrument or the palm. **4.** (*intr.*) to walk or run with light footsteps. **5. pat (someone) on the back.** *Informal.* to congratulate or encourage. ~*n.* **6.** a light blow with something flat. **7.** a gentle slap. **8.** a small mass of something: *a pat of butter.* **9.** the sound made by a light stroke or light footsteps. **10. pat on the back.** *Informal.* a gesture or word indicating approval or encouragement. [C14: perhaps imitative]

pat[2] (pæt) *adv.* **1.** Also: **off pat.** exactly or fluently memorized or mastered: *he recited it pat.* **2.** opportunely or aptly. **3. stand pat. a.** *Chiefly U.S.* to refuse to abandon a belief, decision, etc. **b.** (in poker, etc.) to play without adding new cards to the hand dealt. ~*adj.* **4.** exactly right for the occasion; apt: *a pat reply.* **5.** too exactly fitting; glib: *a pat answer to a difficult problem.* **6.** exactly right: *a pat hand in poker.* [C17: perhaps adverbial use ("with a light stroke") of PAT[1]]

pat[3] (pæt) *n.* **on one's pat.** *Austral. informal.* alone; on one's own. [C20: rhyming slang, from *Pat* Malone]

Pat (pæt) *n.* an informal name for an Irishman.

pat. *abbrev. for* patent(ed).

pa+ta+gi·um (pəˈteɪdʒɪəm) *n., pl.* **+gi·a** (-dʒɪə). **1.** a web of skin between the neck, limbs, and tail in bats and gliding mammals that functions as a wing. **2.** a membranous fold of skin connecting margins of a bird's wing to the shoulder. [C19: New Latin from Latin, from Greek *patageion* gold border on a tunic]

Pat·a+go+ni·a (ˌpætəˈgəʊnɪə) *n.* **1.** the southernmost region of South America, in Argentina and Chile extending from the Andes to the Atlantic. **2.** an arid tableland in the southernmost part of Argentina, rising towards the Andes in the west.

patch (pætʃ) *n.* **1. a.** a piece of material used to mend a garment, etc., or to make a patchwork, sewn-on pocket, etc. **b.** (*as modifier*): *a patch pocket.* **2.** a small piece, area, expanse, etc. **3. a.** a small plot of land. **b.** its produce: *a patch of cabbages.* **4.** *Pathol.* any discoloured area on the skin, mucous membranes, etc., usually being one sign of a specific disorder. **5.** *Med.* **a.** a protective covering for an injured eye. **b.** any protective dressing. **6.** an imitation beauty spot made of black or coloured silk, etc., worn by both sexes, esp. in the 18th century. **7.** an identifying piece of fabric worn on the shoulder of a uniform, on a vehicle, etc. **8.** a small contrasting section or stretch: *a patch of cloud in the blue sky.* **9.** a scrap; remnant. **10.** a small set of instructions to correct or improve a computer program. **11. not a patch on.** not nearly as good as. **12. strike** or **hit a bad patch.** to have a difficult time. ~*vb.* (*tr.*) **13.** to mend or supply (a garment, etc.) with a patch or patches. **14.** to put together or produce with patches. **15.** (of material) to serve as a patch to. **16.** (often foll. by *up*) to mend hurriedly or in a makeshift way. **17.** (often foll. by *up*) to make (up) or settle (a quarrel, etc.). **18.** to connect (electric circuits) together temporarily by means of a patch board. [C16 *pacche,* perhaps from French *pieche* PIECE] **—'patch+a·ble** *adj.* **—'patch+er** *n.*

patch board *or* **pan+el** *n.* a device with a large number of sockets into which electrical plugs can be inserted to form many different temporary circuits: used in telephone exchanges, computer systems, etc. Also called: **plugboard.**

patch·ou+li, pach·ou+li, *or* **patch·ou+ly** (ˈpætʃʊlɪ, pəˈtʃuːlɪ) *n.* **1.** any of several Asiatic trees of the genus *Pogostemon,* the leaves of which yield a heavy fragrant oil: family *Labiatae* (labiates). **2.** the perfume made from this oil. [C19: from Tamil *paccilai,* from *paccu* green + *ilai* leaf]

patch pock+et *n.* a pocket on the outside of a garment.

patch test *n. Med.* a test to detect an allergic reaction by applying small amounts of a suspected substance to the skin and then examining the area for signs of irritation.

patch+work (ˈpætʃˌwɜːk) *n.* **1.** needlework done by sewing pieces of different materials together. **2.** something, such as a theory, made up of various parts: *a patchwork of cribbed ideas.*

patch·y (ˈpætʃɪ) *adj.* **patch·i+er, patch·i+est. 1.** irregular in quality, occurrence, intensity, etc.: *a patchy essay.* **2.** having or forming patches. **—'patch·i+ly** *adv.* **—'patch·i+ness** *n.*

patd. *abbrev. for* patented.

pate (peɪt) *n.* the head, esp. with reference to baldness or (in facetious use) intelligence. [C14: of unknown origin]

pâ+té (ˈpæteɪ; *French* pɑˈte) *n.* **1.** a spread of very finely minced liver, poultry, etc., served usually as an hors d'oeuvre. **2.** a savoury pie of meat or fish. [from French: PASTE[1]]

pâ+té de foie gras (*French* pɑte də fwa ˈgrɑ) *n., pl.* **pâ+tés de foie gras** (*French* pɑte də fwa ˈgrɑ). a smooth rich paste made from the liver of a specially fattened goose, considered a great delicacy. [French: pâté of fat liver]

pa+tel+la (pəˈtɛlə) *n., pl.* **+lae** (-liː). **1.** *Anatomy.* a small flat triangular bone in front of and protecting the knee joint. Nontechnical name: **kneecap. 2.** *Biology.* a cuplike structure, such as the spore-producing body of certain ascomycetous fungi. **3.** *Archaeol.* a small pan. [C17: from Latin, from *patina* shallow pan] **—pa+'tel+lar** *adj.*

pa+tel+late (pəˈtɛlɪt, -leɪt) *adj.* Also: **pa+tel+li+form** (pəˈtɛlɪˌfɔːm). having the shape of a patella.

pat+en (ˈpætᵊn), **pat+in,** *or* **pat+ine** (ˈpætɪn) *n.* a plate, usually made of silver or gold, esp. the plate on which the bread is placed in the Eucharist. [C13: from Old French *patene,* from Medieval Latin, from Latin *patina* pan]

pa+ten+cy (ˈpeɪtᵊnsɪ) *n.* **1.** the condition of being obvious. **2.** the state of a bodily passage, duct, etc., of being open or unobstructed. **3.** *Phonetics.* the degree to which the vocal tract remains unobstructed in the articulation of a speech sound. See also **closure** (sense 6).

pa+tent (ˈpeɪtᵊnt, ˈpætᵊnt) *n.* **1. a.** a government grant to an inventor assuring him the sole right to make, use, and sell his invention for a limited period. **b.** a document conveying such a grant. **2.** an invention, privilege, etc., protected by a patent. **3. a.** an official document granting a right. **b.** any right granted by such a document. **4.** (in the U.S.) **a.** a grant by the government of title to public lands. **b.** the instrument by which such title is granted. **c.** the land so granted. **5.** a sign that one possesses a certain quality. ~*adj.* **6.** open or available for inspection (esp. in the phrases **letters patent, patent writ**). **7.** (ˈpeitᵊnt). obvious: *their scorn was patent to everyone.* **8.** concerning protection, appointment, etc., of or by a patent or patents. **9.** proprietary. **10.** (esp. of a bodily passage or duct) being open or unobstructed. **11.** *Biology.* spreading out widely: *patent branches.* **12.** (of plate glass) ground and polished on both sides. ~*vb.* (*tr.*) **13.** to obtain a patent for. **14.** to grant (public land, etc.) by a patent. **15.** *Metallurgy.* to heat (a metal) above a transformation temperature and cool it at a rate that allows cold working. [C14: via Old French from Latin *patēre* to lie open; n. use, short for *letters patent,* from Medieval Latin *litterae patentes* letters lying open (to public inspection)] **—'pa+tent+a·ble** *adj.* **—ˌpa+tent+a·'bil+i·ty** *n.*

pa+tent·ee (ˌpeɪtᵊnˈtiː, ˌpæ-) *n.* a person, group, company, etc., that has been granted a patent.

pa+tent leath+er (ˈpeɪtᵊnt) *n.* leather or imitation leather processed with lacquer to give a hard glossy surface.

pa+tent log *n. Nautical.* any of several mechanical devices for measuring the speed of a vessel and the distance travelled, consisting typically of a trailing rotor that registers its rotations on a meter. Compare **chip log.**

pa+tent+ly (ˈpeɪtᵊntlɪ) *adv.* obviously: *he was patently bored.*

pa+tent med+i+cine (ˈpeɪtᵊnt) *n.* a medicine, usually of low potency; protected by a patent and available without a doctor's prescription.

Pa+tent Of+fice *n.* a government department that issues patents.

pa+ten+tor (ˌpeɪtᵊnˈtɔː, ˌpæ-) *n.* a person who or official body that grants a patent or patents.

pa+tent right *n.* the exclusive right granted by a patent.

Pa+tent Rolls *pl. n.* (in Britain) the register of patents issued.

pa+tent still *n.* a type of still in which the distillation is continuous.

pa·ter ('peɪtə) *n. Brit. public school slang.* another word for **father:** now chiefly used facetiously. [from Latin]

Pa·ter ('peɪtə) *n.* **Wal·ter (Horatio).** 1839–94, English essayist and critic, noted for his prose style and his advocation of the "love of art for its own sake". His works include the philosophical romance *Marius the Epicurean* (1885), *Studies in the History of the Renaissance* (1873), and *Imaginary Portraits* (1887).

pa·ter·fa·mil·i·as (ˌpeɪtəfə'mɪlɪˌæs) *n., pl.* **pa·tres·fa·mil·i·as** (ˌpɑːtreɪzfə'mɪlɪˌæs). **1.** the male head of a household. **2.** *Roman law.* **a.** the head of a household having authority over its members. **b.** the parental or other authority of another person. [Latin: father of the family]

pa·ter·nal (pə'tɜːnəl) *adj.* **1.** relating to or characteristic of a father, esp. in showing affection, encouragement, etc.; fatherly. **2.** (*prenominal*) related through the father: *his paternal grandfather.* **3.** inherited or derived from the male parent. [C17: from Late Latin *paternālis,* from Latin *pater* father] —**pa·'ter·nal·ly** *adv.*

pa·ter·nal·ism (pə'tɜːnəˌlɪzəm) *n.* the attitude or policy of a government or other authority that manages the affairs of a country, company, community, etc., in the manner of a father, esp. in usurping individual responsibility and the liberty of choice. —**pa·'ter·nal·ist** *n., adj.* —**pa·ˌter·nal·'is·tic** *adj.* —**pa·ˌter·nal·'is·ti·cal·ly** *adv.*

pa·ter·ni·ty (pə'tɜːnɪtɪ) *n.* **1. a.** the fact or state of being a father. **b.** (*as modifier*): *a paternity suit was filed against the man.* **2.** descent or derivation from a father. **3.** authorship or origin: *the paternity of the theory is disputed.* [C15: from Late Latin *paternitās,* from Latin *pater* father]

pa·ter·ni·ty suit *n. Law.* the U.S. or nontechnical term for **affiliation proceedings.**

pat·er·nos·ter (ˌpætə'nɒstə) *n.* **1.** *R.C. Church.* the beads at the ends of each decade of the rosary marking the points at which the Paternoster is recited. **2.** any fixed form of words used as a prayer or charm. **3.** Also called: **paternoster line.** a type of fishing tackle in which short lines and hooks are attached at intervals to the main line. **4.** a type of lift in which platforms are attached to continuous chains. The lift does not stop at each floor but passengers enter while it is moving. [Latin, literally: our father (from the opening of the Lord's Prayer)]

Pat·er·nos·ter (ˌpætə'nɒstə) *n.* (*sometimes not cap.*) *R.C. Church.* **1.** The Lord's Prayer, esp. in Latin. **2.** the recital of this as an act of devotion. [see PATERNOSTER]

Pat·er·son ('pætəsən) *n.* a city in NE New Jersey: settled by the Dutch in the late 17th century. Pop.: 143 372 (1973 est.).

Pat·er·son's curse *n.* the Austral. name for **viper's bugloss.**

path (pɑːθ) *n., pl.* **paths** (pɑːðz). **1.** a road or way, esp. a narrow trodden track. **2.** a surfaced walk, as through a garden. **3.** the course or direction in which something moves: *the path of a whirlwind.* **4.** a course of conduct: *the path of virtue.* [Old English *pæth;* related to Old High German, German *Pfad*] —**'path·less** *adj.*

path. (pæθ) *abbrev. for:* **1.** pathological. **2.** pathology.

-path *suffix forming nouns.* **1.** denoting a person suffering from a specified disease or disorder: *neuropath.* **2.** denoting a practitioner of a particular method of treatment: *osteopath.* [back formation from -PATHY]

Pa·than (pə'tɑːn) *n.* a member of the Pashto-speaking people of Afghanistan, NW Pakistan, and elsewhere, most of whom are Muslim in religion. [C17: from Hindi]

pa·thet·ic (pə'θɛtɪk) *adj.* **1.** evoking or expressing pity, sympathy, etc. **2.** distressingly inadequate: *a pathetic fire flickered in the hearth.* **3.** *Brit. slang.* uninteresting; worthless: *the people at the party were pathetic!* **4.** *Obsolete.* of or affecting the feelings. ~*pl. n.* **5.** pathetic sentiments. [C16: from French *pathétique,* via Late Latin from Greek *pathetikos* sensitive, from *pathos* suffering; see PATHOS] —**pa·'thet·i·cal·ly** *adv.*

pa·thet·ic fal·la·cy *n.* (in literature) the presentation of nature, etc., as possessing human feelings.

path·find·er ('pɑːθˌfaɪndə) *n.* **1.** a person who makes or finds a way, esp. through unexplored areas or fields of knowledge. **2.** an aircraft or parachutist who indicates a target area by dropping flares, etc. **3.** a radar device used for navigation or homing onto a target. —**'path·ˌfind·ing** *n.*

path·ic ('pæθɪk) *n. Obsolete.* **1.** a catamite. **2.** a person who suffers; victim. ~*adj.* **3.** of or relating to a catamite. **4.** of or relating to suffering. [C17: via Latin from Greek *pathikos* passive, see PATHOS]

path·o- *or before a vowel* **path-** *combining form.* disease: *pathology.* [from Greek *pathos* suffering; see PATHOS]

path·o·gen ('pæθəˌdʒɛn) *or* **path·o·gene** ('pæθəˌdʒiːn) *n.* any agent that can cause disease.

path·o·gen·e·sis (ˌpæθə'dʒɛnɪsɪs) *or* **pa·thog·e·ny** (pə'θɒdʒɪnɪ) *n.* the origin, development, and resultant effects of a disease. —**path·o·ge·net·ic** (ˌpæθəʊdʒɪ'nɛtɪk) *adj.*

path·o·gen·ic (ˌpæθə'dʒɛnɪk) *adj.* able to cause or produce disease: *pathogenic bacteria.*

path·og·no·mon·ic (ˌpæθəgnə'mɒnɪk) *adj. Pathol.* characteristic or indicative of a particular disease. [C17: from Greek *pathognōmonikos* expert in judging illness, from PATHO- + *gnōmōn* judge] —ˌ**path·og·no·'mon·i·cal·ly** *adv.*

path·og·no·my (pə'θɒgnəmɪ) *n.* study or knowledge of the passions or emotions or their manifestations. [C18: from PATHO- + *-gnomy,* as in PHYSIOGNOMY]

pathol. *abbrev. for:* **1.** pathological. **2.** pathology.

path·o·log·i·cal (ˌpæθə'lɒdʒɪkəl) *or* **path·o·log·ic** *adj.* **1.** of or relating to pathology. **2.** relating to, involving, or caused by disease. **3.** *Informal.* compulsively motivated: *a pathological liar.* —ˌ**path·o·'log·i·cal·ly** *adv.*

pa·thol·o·gy (pə'θɒlədʒɪ) *n., pl.* **·gies. 1.** the branch of medicine concerned with the cause, origin, and nature of disease, including the changes occurring as a result of disease. **2.** the manifestations of disease, esp. changes occurring in tissues or organs. **3.** any variant or deviant condition from normal. —**pa·'thol·o·gist** *n.*

pa·thos ('peɪθɒs) *n.* **1.** the quality or power, esp. in literature or speech, of arousing feelings of pity, sorrow, etc. **2.** a feeling of sympathy or pity: *a stab of pathos.* **3.** *Rare or poetic.* a condition of misery. [C17: from Greek: suffering; related to *penthos* sorrow]

path·way ('pɑːθˌweɪ) *n.* **1.** another word for **path. 2.** *Biochem.* a chain of reactions associated with a particular metabolic process.

-pa·thy *n. combining form.* **1.** indicating feeling, sensitivity, or perception: *telepathy.* **2.** indicating disease or a morbid condition: *psychopathy.* **3.** indicating a method of treating disease: *osteopathy.* [from Greek *patheia* suffering; see PATHOS] —**-path·ic** *adj. combining form.*

Pa·ti·a·la (ˌpʌtɪ'ɑːlə) *n.* a city in N India, in E Punjab: seat of the Punjabi University (1962). Pop.: 148 686 (1971).

pa·tience ('peɪʃəns) *n.* **1.** tolerant and even-tempered perseverance. **2.** the capacity for calmly enduring pain, trying situations, etc. **3.** *Brit.* any of various card games for one player only, in which the cards may be laid out in various combinations as the player tries to use up the whole pack. U.S. word: **solitaire. 4.** *Obsolete.* permission; sufferance. [C13: via Old French from Latin *patientia* endurance, from *patī* to suffer]

pa·tient ('peɪʃənt) *adj.* **1.** enduring trying circumstances with even temper. **2.** tolerant; understanding. **3.** capable of accepting delay with equanimity. **4.** persevering or diligent: *a patient worker.* **5.** *Archaic.* admitting of a certain interpretation. ~*n.* **6.** a person who is receiving medical care. **7.** *Rare.* a person or thing that is the recipient of some action. [C14: see PATIENCE] —**'pa·tient·ly** *adv.*

pat·in ('pætɪn) *n.* a variant spelling of **paten.**

pat·i·na[1] ('pætɪnə) *n.* **1.** a film of oxide formed on the surface of a metal, esp. the green oxidation of bronze or copper. See also **verdigris. 2.** any fine layer on a surface: *a patina of frost.* **3.** the sheen on a surface that is caused by long handling. [C18: from Italian: coating, from Latin: PATINA[2]]

pat·i·na[2] ('pætɪnə) *n., pl.* **·nae** (-ˌniː). a broad shallow dish used in ancient Rome. [from Latin, from Greek *patanē* platter]

pa·ti·o ('pætɪˌəʊ) *n., pl.* **·os. 1.** an open inner courtyard, esp. one in a Spanish or Spanish-American house. **2.** an area adjoining a house, esp. one that is paved and used for outdoor activities. [C19: from Spanish: courtyard]

pa·tis·se·rie (pə'tiːsərɪ) *n.* **1.** a shop where fancy pastries are sold. **2.** such pastries. [C18: French, from *pâtissier* pastry cook, ultimately from Late Latin *pasta* PASTE[1]]

Pat·more ('pætmɔː) *n.* **Cov·en·try (Kersey Dighton).** 1823–96, English poet. His works, celebrating both conjugal and divine love, include *The Angel in the House* (1854–62) and *The Unknown Eros* (1877).

Pat·mos ('pætmɒs) *n.* a Greek island in the Aegean, in the NW Dodecanese: St. John's place of exile (about 95 A.D.), where he wrote the Apocalypse. Pop.: 2486 (1971). Area: 34 sq. km (13 sq. miles).

Pat·na ('pætnə) *n.* a city in NE India, capital of Bihar state, on the River Ganges: founded in the 5th century B.C.; university (1917); centre of a rice growing region. Pop.: 473 001 (1971).

Pat·na rice *n.* a variety of long-grain rice, used for savoury dishes.

Pat. Off. *abbrev. for* Patent Office.

pat·ois ('pætwɑː; *French* pa'twa) *n., pl.* **pat·ois** ('pætwɑːz; *French* pa'twa). an unwritten regional dialect of a language, esp. of French, usually considered substandard. [C17: from Old French: rustic speech, perhaps from *patoier* to handle awkwardly, from *patte* paw]

Pa·ton ('peɪtən) *n.* **Al·an (Stewart).** born 1903, South African writer, noted esp. for his novel dealing with the racial problem in South Africa, *Cry, the Beloved Country* (1965).

pat. pend. *abbrev. for* patent pending.

Pa·tras (pə'træs, 'pætrəs) *n.* a port in W Greece, in the NW Peloponnese on the **Gulf of Patras** (an inlet of the Ionian Sea): one of the richest cities in Greece until the 3rd century B.C.; under Turkish rule from 1458 to 1687 and from 1715 until the War of Greek Independence, which began here in 1821. Pop.: 112 228 (1971). Modern Greek name: **Pá·trai** ('patrɛ).

pat·ri- *combining form.* father: *patricide; patrilocal.* [from Latin *pater,* Greek *patēr* FATHER]

pa·tri·al ('peɪtrɪəl) *n. Brit.* a person who has rights of nationality by virtue of the birth of a parent or grandparents. [C20: from Latin *patria* native land]

pa·tri·arch ('peɪtrɪˌɑːk) *n.* **1.** the male head of a tribe or family. Compare **matriarch. 2.** a very old or venerable man. **3.** *Old Testament.* any of a number of persons regarded as the fathers of the human race, divided into the antediluvian patriarchs, from Adam to Noah, and the postdiluvian, from Noah to Abraham. **4.** *Old Testament.* any of the three ancestors of the Hebrew people: Abraham, Isaac, or Jacob. **5.** *Old Testament.* any of Jacob's twelve sons, regarded as the ancestors of the twelve tribes of Israel. **6.** *Early Christian Church.* the bishop of one of several principal sees, esp. those of Rome, Antioch, and Alexandria. **7.** *Eastern Orthodox.* the bishops of the four ancient principal sees of Constantinople, Antioch, Alexandria, and Jerusalem, and also of Russia,

Rumania, and Serbia, the bishop of Constantinople (the **ecumenical Patriarch**) being highest in dignity among these. **8.** *R.C. Church.* **a.** a title given to the Pope. **b.** a title given to a number of bishops, esp. of the Uniat Churches, indicating their rank as immediately below that of the Pope. **9.** *Mormon Church.* another word for **Evangelist** (sense 2). **10.** *Eastern Christianity.* the head of the Coptic, Armenian, Syrian Jacobite, or Nestorian Churches, and of certain other non-Orthodox Churches in the East. **11.** the oldest or most venerable member of a group, community, etc.: *the patriarch of steam engines.* **12.** a person regarded as the founder of a community, tradition, etc. [C12: via Old French from Church Latin *patriarcha*] —ˌ**pa+tri+'ar+chal** *adj.* —ˌ**pa+tri+'ar+chal+ly** *adv.*

pa+tri+ar+chal cross *n.* a cross with two high horizontal bars, the upper one shorter than the lower.

pa+tri+ar+chate ('peɪtrɪˌɑːkɪt) *n.* **1.** the office, jurisdiction, province, or residence of a patriarch. **2.** a family or people under male domination or government.

pa+tri+ar+chy ('peɪtrɪˌɑːkɪ) *n., pl.* **+chies. 1.** a form of social organization in which a male is the head of the family and descent, kinship, and title are traced through the male line. **2.** any society governed by such a system.

pa+tri+cian (pə'trɪʃən) *n.* **1.** a member of the hereditary aristocracy of ancient Rome. In the early republic the patricians held almost all the higher offices. Compare **plebs** (sense 2). **2.** a high nonhereditary title awarded by Constantine and his eastern Roman successors for services to the empire. **3.** (in medieval Europe) **a.** a title borne by numerous princes including several emperors from the 8th to the 12th century. **b.** a member of the upper class in numerous Italian republics and German free cities. **4.** an aristocrat. **5.** a person of refined conduct, tastes, etc. ~*adj.* **6.** (esp. in ancient Rome) of, relating to, or composed of patricians. **7.** aristocratic. **8.** oligarchic and often antidemocratic or nonpopular: *patrician political views.* [C15: from Old French *patricien,* from Latin *patricius* noble, from *pater* father]

pa+tri+ci+ate (pə'trɪʃɪɪt, -ˌeɪt) *n.* **1.** the dignity, position, or rank of a patrician. **2.** the class or order of patricians.

pat+ri+cide ('pætrɪˌsaɪd) *n.* **1.** the act of killing one's father. **2.** a person who kills his father. —ˌ**pat+ri+'cid+al** *adj.*

Pat·rick ('pætrɪk) *n.* **Saint.** 5th-century A.D. English missionary in Ireland; patron saint of Ireland. He left an account of his life and work in his *Confession.* Feast day: March 17.

pat+ri+cli+nous (ˌpætrɪ'klaɪnəs), **pat+ro+cli+nous,** *or* **pat+ro+cli+nal** *adj.* (of animals and plants) showing the characters of the male parent. Compare **matriclinous.** [C20: from Latin *pater* father + *clināre* to incline]

pat+ri+lin+e·al (ˌpætrɪ'lɪnɪəl) *or* **pat+ri+lin+e+ar** *adj.* tracing descent, kinship, or title through the male line. —ˌ**pat+ri+'lin+e·al+ly** *or* ˌ**pat+ri+'lin+e·ar+ly** *adv.*

pat+ri+lo+cal (ˌpætrɪ'ləʊkᵊl) *adj.* having or relating to a marriage pattern in which the couple live with the husband's family. —ˌ**pat+ri+'lo+cal+ly** *adv.*

pat+ri+mo+ny ('pætrɪmənɪ) *n., pl.* **+nies. 1.** an inheritance from one's father or other ancestor. **2.** the endowment of a church. [C14 *patrimoyne,* from Old French from Latin *patrimonium* paternal inheritance] —**pat+ri+mo+ni·al** (ˌpætrɪ'məʊnɪəl) *adj.* —ˌ**pat+ri+'mo+ni+al+ly** *adv.*

pa+tri+ot ('peɪtrɪət, 'pæt-) *n.* a person who vigorously supports his country and its way of life. [C16: via French from Late Latin *patriōta,* from Greek *patriotēs,* from *patris* native land; related to Greek *patēr* father; compare Latin *pater* father, *patria* fatherland] —**pat+ri+ot+ic** (ˌpætrɪ'ɒtɪk) *adj.* —ˌ**pat+ri+'ot·i·cal+ly** *adv.*

pat+ri+ot+ism ('pætrɪəˌtɪzəm) *n.* devotion to one's own country and concern for its defence. Compare **nationalism.**

pa+tris+tic (pə'trɪstɪk) *or* **pa+tris+ti+cal** *adj.* of or relating to the Fathers of the Church, their writings, or the study of these. —**pa+'tris+ti+cal+ly** *adv.* —**pa+'tris+tics** *n.*

Pa·troc·lus (pə'trɒkləs) *n. Greek myth.* a friend of Achilles, killed in the Trojan War by Hector. His death made Achilles return to the fight after his quarrel with Agamemnon.

pa+trol (pə'trəʊl) *n.* **1.** the action of going through or around a town, etc., at regular intervals for purposes of security or observation. **2.** a person or group that carries out such an action. **3.** a military detachment with the mission of security, gathering information, or the destruction of enemy forces. **4.** a division of a troop of Scouts or Guides. ~*vb.* **+trols, +trol+ling, +trolled. 5.** to engage in a patrol of (a place). [C17: from French *patrouiller,* from *patouiller* to flounder in mud, from *patte* paw] —**pa+'trol+ler** *n.*

pa+trol car *n.* a police car with a radio telephone used for patrolling streets and motorways. See also **panda car.**

pa·trol+man (pə'trəʊlmən) *n., pl.* **+men. 1.** *Chiefly U.S.* a man, esp. a policeman, who patrols a certain area. **2.** *Brit.* a man employed to patrol an area to help motorists in difficulty.

pa+trol+o·gy (pə'trɒlədʒɪ) *n.* **1.** the study of the writings of the Fathers of the Church. **2.** a collection of such writings. [C17: from Greek *patr-, patēr* father + -LOGY] —**pat+ro+log·i·cal** (ˌpætrə'lɒdʒɪkᵊl) *adj.* —**pa+'trol·o·gist** *n.*

pa+trol wag+on *or* **po+lice wag+on** *n.* the usual U.S. term for **Black Maria.**

pa+tron ('peɪtrən) *n.* **1.** a person who sponsors or aids artists, charities, etc.; protector or benefactor. **2.** a customer of a shop, hotel, etc., esp. a regular one. **3.** See **patron saint. 4.** (in ancient Rome) the protector of a dependant or client, often the former master of a freedman still retaining certain rights over him. **5.** *Church of England, etc.* a person or body having the right to present a clergyman to a benefice. [C14: via Old French from Latin *patrōnus* protector, from *pater* father] —'**pa+tron+al** *adj.* —'**pa+tron+ess** *fem. n.* —'**pa+tron+ly** *adj.*

pat+ron+age ('pætrənɪdʒ) *n.* **1. a.** the support given or custom brought by a patron. **b.** the position of a patron. **2.** (in politics) **a.** the practice of making appointments to office, granting contracts, etc. **b.** the favours, etc., so distributed. **3. a.** a condescending manner. **b.** any kindness done in a condescending way. **4.** *Church of England, etc.* the right to present a clergyman to a benefice.

pat+ron+ize *or* **pat+ron+ise** ('pætrəˌnaɪz) *vb.* **1.** to behave or treat in a condescending way. **2.** to act as a patron by sponsoring or bringing trade to. —'**pat+ron+ˌiz+er** *or* '**pat+ron+ˌis+er** *n.* —'**pat+ron+ˌiz+ing+ly** *or* '**pat+ron+ˌis+ing+ly** *adv.*

pa+tron saint *n.* a saint regarded as the particular guardian of a country, church, trade, person, etc.

pat+ro+nym+ic (ˌpætrə'nɪmɪk) *adj.* **1.** (of a name) derived from the name of its bearer's father. In Western cultures, many surnames are patronymic in origin, as for example Irish names beginning with *O'* and English names ending with *-son;* in other cultures, such as Russian, a special patronymic name is used in addition to the surname. ~*n.* **2.** a patronymic name. [C17: via Late Latin from Greek *patronumikos,* from *pater* father + *onoma* NAME]

pa+troon (pə'truːn) *n. U.S.* a Dutch landholder in New Netherland and New York with manorial rights in the colonial era. [C18: from Dutch: PATRON] —**pa+'troon+ˌship** *n.*

pat+sy ('pætsɪ) *n., pl.* **+sies.** *U.S. slang.* a person who is easily cheated, victimized, etc. [C20: of unknown origin]

pat+tée ('pæteɪ, 'pætɪ) *adj.* (*often postpositive*) (of a cross) having triangular arms widening outwards. [from French *patte* paw]

pat+ten ('pætᵊn) *n.* a wooden clog or sandal on a raised wooden platform or metal ring. [C14: from Old French *patin,* probably from *patte* paw]

pat+ter¹ ('pætə) *vb.* **1.** (*intr.*) to walk or move with quick soft steps. **2.** (*intr.*) to strike with or make a quick succession of light tapping sounds. **3.** (*tr.*) *Rare.* to cause to patter. ~*n.* **4.** a quick succession of light tapping sounds, as of feet: *the patter of mice.* [*C17: from* PAT¹]

pat+ter² ('pætə) *n.* **1.** the glib rapid speech of comedians, etc. **2.** quick idle talk; chatter. **3.** the jargon of a particular group, etc.; lingo. ~*vb.* **4.** to speak glibly and rapidly. **5.** to repeat (prayers, etc.) in a mechanical or perfunctory manner. [C14: from Latin *pater* in *Pater Noster* Our Father]

pat+tern ('pætᵊn) *n.* **1.** an arrangement of repeated or corresponding parts, decorative motifs, etc.: *although the notes seemed random, a careful listener could detect a pattern.* **2.** a decorative design: *a paisley pattern.* **3.** a style: *various patterns of cutlery.* **4.** a plan or diagram used as a guide in making something: *a paper pattern for a dress.* **5.** a standard way of moving, acting, etc.: *traffic patterns.* **6.** a model worthy of imitation: *a pattern of kindness.* **7.** a representative sample. **8.** a wooden or metal shape or model used in a foundry to make a mould. **9. a.** the arrangement of marks made in a target by bullets. **b.** a diagram displaying such an arrangement. ~*vb. tr.* **10.** (often foll. by *after* or *on*) to model. **11.** to arrange as or decorate with a pattern. [C14 *patron,* from Medieval Latin *patrōnus* example, from Latin: PATRON]

pat+ter song *n. Music.* a humorous song or aria, the text of which consists of rapid strings of words.

Pat·ti ('pætɪ) *n.* **A·de·li·na** (ˌade'liːna). 1843–1919, Italian operatic coloratura soprano, born in Spain.

Pat·ton ('pætᵊn) *n.* **George Smith.** 1885–1945, U.S. general, who held command during World War II.

pat+ty ('pætɪ) *n., pl.* **+ties. 1.** a small flattened cake of minced food. **2.** a small pie. [C18: from French PÂTÉ]

pat+u+lous ('pætjʊləs) *adj.* **1.** *Botany.* spreading widely or expanded: *patulous branches.* **2.** *Rare.* gaping. [C17: from Latin *patulus* open, from *patēre* to lie open] —'**pat+u+lous+ly** *adv.* —'**pat+u+lous+ness** *n.*

Pau (*French* po) *n.* a city in SW France: residence of the French kings of Navarre; tourist centre for the Pyrenees. Pop.: 85 860 (1975).

PAU *or* **P.A.U.** *abbrev. for* Pan American Union.

pau·a ('paʊə) *n.* an edible abalone, *Haliotis iris,* of New Zealand, having an iridescent shell used for jewellery, etc. [from Maori]

pau+cal ('pɔːkᵊl) *Grammar.* ~*n.* **1.** a grammatical number occurring in some languages for words in contexts where a few of their referents are described or referred to. ~*adj.* **2.** relating to or inflected for this number. [from Latin *paucus* few]

pau+ci·ty ('pɔːsɪtɪ) *n.* **1.** smallness of quantity; insufficiency; dearth. **2.** smallness of number; fewness. [C15: from Latin *paucitās* scarcity, from *paucus* few]

Paul (pɔːl) *n.* **1. Saint.** Also called: **Paul the Apostle, Saul of Tarsus.** original name *Saul.* died ?67 A.D. one of the first Christian missionaries to the Gentiles, who died a martyr in Rome. Until his revelatory conversion he had assisted in persecuting the Christians. He wrote many of the Epistles in the New Testament. Feast day: June 29. **2. Jean.** See **Jean Paul.**

Paul III *n.* original name *Alessandro Farnese.* 1468–1549, Italian ecclesiastic; pope (1534–49). He excommunicated Henry VIII of England (1538) and inaugurated the Counter-Reformation by approving the establishment of the Jesuits (1540), instituting the Inquisition in Italy, and convening the Council of Trent (1545).

Paul VI *n.* original name *Giovanni Battista Montini.* 1897–1978, Italian ecclesiastic; pope (1963–1978).

paul+dron ('pɔːldrən) *n.* either of two metal plates worn with armour to protect the shoulders. [C15: from French *espauleron*, from *espaule* shoulder; see EPAULET]

Pau·li ('pɔːlɪ, 'paʊlɪ) *n.* **Wolf·gang.** 1900–58, U.S. physicist, born in Austria. He formulated the exclusion principle (1924) and postulated the existence of the neutrino (1931), later confirmed by Fermi: Nobel prize for physics 1945.

Pau·li ex+clu+sion prin+ci+ple *n. Physics.* the principle that two similar particles cannot occupy the same quantum state; sometimes shortened to **exclusion principle.**

Paul+ine ('pɔːlaɪn) *adj.* relating to Saint Paul or his doctrines.

Pau·ling ('pɔːlɪŋ) *n.* **Li·nus Carl.** born 1901, U.S. chemist, noted particularly for his work on the nature of the chemical bond and his opposition to nuclear tests: Nobel prize for chemistry 1954; Nobel peace prize 1962.

Pau·li·nus (pɔː'laɪnəs) *n.* **Saint.** died 644 A.D., Roman missionary to England; first bishop of York and archbishop of Rochester. Feast day: Oct. 10.

Paul Jones *n.* an old-time dance in which partners are exchanged. [C19: named after John Paul JONES]

pau+low+ni·a (pɔː'ləʊnɪə) *n.* any scrophulariaceous tree of the Japanese genus *Paulownia*, esp. *P. tomentosa*, having large heart-shaped leaves and clusters of purplish or white flowers. [C19: New Latin, named after Anna *Paulovna*, daughter of Paul I of Russia]

Paul Pry *n.* a nosy person. [C19: from a character in the play *Paul Pry* by John Poole (1825)]

Pau+mo+tu Ar+chi+pel·a+go (paʊ'məʊtuː) *n.* another name for the **Tuamotu Archipelago.**

paunch (pɔːntʃ) *n.* **1.** the belly or abdomen, esp. when protruding. **2.** another name for **rumen. 3.** *Nautical.* a thick mat that prevents chafing. ~*vb. tr.* **4.** to stab in the stomach; disembowel. [C14: from Anglo-Norman *paunche*, from Old French *pance*, from Latin *panticēs* (pl.) bowels] —**'paunch·y** *adj.* —**'paunch·i+ness** *n.*

pau+per ('pɔːpə) *n.* **1.** a person who is extremely poor. **2.** (formerly) a destitute person supported by public charity. [C16: from Latin: poor] —**'pau+per+ism** *n.*

pau+per+ize or **pau+per+ise** ('pɔːpəˌraɪz) *vb.* (*tr.*) to make a pauper of; impoverish.

Pau·sa·ni·as (pɔː'seɪnɪəs) *n.* 2nd-century A.D. Greek geographer and historian. His *Description of Greece* gives a valuable account of the topography of ancient Greece.

pause (pɔːz) *vb.* (*intr.*) **1.** to cease an action temporarily; stop. **2.** to hesitate; delay: *she replied without pausing.* ~*n.* **3.** a temporary stop or rest, esp. in speech or action; short break. **4.** *Prosody.* another word **caesura. 5.** Also called: **fermata.** *Music.* a continuation of a note or rest beyond its normal length. Usual symbol: 𝄐 **6. give pause (to).** to cause to hesitate. [C15: from Latin *pausa* pause, from Greek *pausis*, from *pauein* to halt] —**'paus+al** *adj.* —**'paus+er** *n.* —**'paus+ing+ly** *adv.*

pav (pæv) *n. Austral. informal.* short for **pavlova.**

pav+age ('peɪvɪdʒ) *n.* **1.** a tax towards paving streets. **2.** the right to levy such a tax. **3.** the act of paving.

pa+vane or **pa+van** (pə'vɑːn, -'væn, 'pævᵊn) *n.* **1.** a slow and stately dance of the 16th and 17th centuries. **2.** a piece of music composed for or in the rhythm of this dance, usually characterized by a slow stately triple time. [C16 *pavan*, via French from Spanish *pavana*, from Old Italian *padovana* Paduan (dance), from *Padova* Padua]

pave (peɪv) *vb.* (*tr.*) **1.** to cover (a road, etc.) with a firm surface suitable for travel, as with paving stones or concrete. **2.** to serve as the material for a pavement or other hard layer: *bricks paved the causeway.* **3.** (often foll. by *with*) to cover with a hard layer (of): *shelves paved with marble.* **4.** to prepare or make easier (esp. in the phrase **pave the way**): *to pave the way for future development.* [C14: from Old French *paver*, from Latin *pavīre* to ram down] —**'pav+er** *n.*

pa·vé ('pæveɪ) *n.* **1.** a paved surface, esp. an uneven one. **2.** a style of setting gems so closely that no metal shows.

pave+ment ('peɪvmənt) *n.* **1.** a hard-surfaced path for pedestrians alongside and a little higher than a road. U.S. word: **sidewalk. 2.** a paved surface, esp. one that is a thoroughfare. **3.** the material used in paving. [C13: from Latin *pavīmentum* a hard floor, from *pavīre* to beat hard]

Pa·ve·se (*Italian* pa'veːse) *n.* **Ce·sa·re** ('tʃeːzare). 1908–50, Italian writer and translator. His works include collections of poems, such as *Verrà la morte e avrà i tuoi occhi* (1953), short stories, such as the collection *Notte di festa* (1953), and the novel *La Luna e i falò* (1950).

pav+id ('pævɪd) *adj. Rare.* fearful; timid. [C17: from Latin *pavidus* fearful, from *pavēre* to tremble with fear]

pa+vil+ion (pə'vɪljən) *n.* **1.** *Brit.* a building at a sports ground, esp. a cricket pitch, in which players change, etc. **2.** a summerhouse or other decorative shelter. **3.** a building or temporary structure, esp. one that is open and ornamental, for housing exhibitions, etc. **4.** a large ornate tent, esp. one with a peaked top, as used by medieval armies. **5.** one of a set of buildings that together form a hospital or other large institution. **6.** one of four main facets on a brilliant-cut stone between the girdle and the culet. ~*vb.* (*tr.*) *Literary.* **7.** to place or set in or as if in a pavilion: *pavilioned in splendour.* **8.** to provide with a pavilion or pavilions. [C13: from Old French *pavillon* canopied structure, from Latin *pāpiliō* butterfly, tent]

pav+ing ('peɪvɪŋ) *n.* **1.** a paved surface; pavement. **2.** material used for a pavement.

pav+ing stone *n.* a concrete or stone slab for paving.

pav+iour or *U.S.* **pav+ior** ('peɪvjə) *n.* **1.** a person who lays paving. **2.** a machine for ramming down paving. **3.** material used for paving. [C15: from *paver*, from PAVE]

pav+is or **pav+ise** ('pævɪs) *n.* a large square shield, developed in the 15th century, at first portable but later heavy and set up in a permanent position. [C14: from Old French *pavais*, from Italian *pavese* of *Pavia*, Italian city where these shields were originally made]

Pav+lo+dar (*Russian* pəvla'dar) *n.* a port in the S Soviet Union, in the NE Kazakh SSR on the Irtysh River: major industrial centre with an oil refinery. Pop.: 283 000 (1975 est.).

Pav·lov ('pævlɒv; *Russian* 'pavləf) *n.* **I·van Pe·tro·vich** (i'van pɪ'trɔvitʃ). 1849–1936, Soviet physiologist. His study of conditioned reflexes in dogs influenced behaviourism. He also made important contributions to the study of digestion: Nobel prize for medicine 1904.

Pav+lo+va (pæv'ləʊvə) *n.* a meringue cake topped with whipped cream and fruit, popular in Australia. Often shortened (Austral. informal) to **pav.** [C20: named after Anna PAVLOVA]

Pav·lo·va (pæv'ləʊvə; *Russian* 'pavləvə) *n.* **An·na** ('annə). 1885–1931, Russian ballerina.

Pa·vo ('pɑːvəʊ) *n., Latin genitive* **Pa+vo+nis** (pə'vəʊnɪs). a small constellation near the South Pole lying between Tucana and Ara. [Latin: peacock]

pav·o+nine ('pævəˌnaɪn) *adj.* of or resembling a peacock or the colours, design, or iridescence of a peacock's tail. [C17: from Latin *pāvōnīnus*, from *pāvō* peacock]

paw (pɔː) *n.* **1.** any of the feet of a four-legged mammal, bearing claws or nails. **2.** *Informal.* a hand, esp. one that is large, clumsy, etc. ~*vb.* **3.** to scrape or contaminate with the paws or feet. **4.** (*tr.*) *Informal.* to touch or caress in a clumsy, rough, or overfamiliar manner; maul. [C13: via Old French from Germanic; related to Middle Dutch *pōte*, German *Pfote*]

pawk·y ('pɔːkɪ) *adj.* **pawk·i+er, pawk·i+est.** *Dialect or Scot.* having a dry wit. [C17: from Scottish *pawk* trick, of unknown origin] —**'pawk·i+ly** *adv.* —**'pawk·i·ness** *n.*

pawl (pɔːl) *n.* a pivoted lever shaped to engage with a ratchet wheel to prevent motion in a particular direction. [C17: perhaps from Dutch *pal* pawl]

pawn[1] (pɔːn) *vb.* (*tr.*) **1.** to deposit (an article) as security for the repayment of a loan, esp. from a pawnbroker. **2.** to stake: *to pawn one's honour.* ~*n.* **3.** an article deposited as security. **4.** the condition of being so deposited (esp. in the phrase **in pawn**). **5.** a person or thing that is held as a security, esp. a hostage. **6.** the act of pawning. [C15: from Old French *pan* security, from Latin *pannus* cloth, apparently because clothing was often left as a surety; compare Middle Flemish *paen* pawn, German *Pfand* pledge] —**'pawn+age** *n.*

pawn[2] (pɔːn) *n.* **1.** a chess piece of the lowest theoretical value, limited to forward moves of one square at a time with the option of two squares on its initial move: it captures with a diagonal move only. Abbrev.: **P** Compare **piece** (sense 12). **2.** a person, group, etc., manipulated by another. [C14: from Anglo-Norman *poun*, from Old French *pehon*, from Medieval Latin *pedō* infantryman, from Latin *pēs* foot]

pawn+bro·ker ('pɔːnˌbrəʊkə) *n.* a dealer licensed to lend money at a specified rate of interest on the security of movable personal property, which can be sold if the loan is not repaid within a specified period. —**'pawn+ˌbro·king** *n.*

Paw+nee (pɔː'niː) *n.* **1.** (*pl.* **+nees** or **+nee**) a member of a confederacy of related North American Indian peoples, formerly living in Nebraska and Kansas, now chiefly in Oklahoma. **2.** the language of these peoples, belonging to the Caddoan family.

pawn+shop ('pɔːnˌʃɒp) *n.* the premises of a pawnbroker.

pawn tick+et *n.* a receipt for goods pawned.

paw+paw ('pɔːˌpɔː) *n.* another name for **papaw** or **papaya.**

pax (pæks) *n.* **1.** *Chiefly R.C. Church.* **a.** a greeting signifying Christian love transmitted from one to another of those assisting at the Eucharist; kiss of peace. **b.** a small metal or ivory plate, often with a representation of the Crucifixion, formerly used to convey the kiss of peace from the celebrant at Mass to those attending it, who kissed the plate in turn. ~*interj.* **2.** *Brit. school slang.* a call signalling an end to hostilities or claiming immunity from the rules of a game: usually accompanied by a crossing of the fingers. [Latin: peace]

Pax (pæks) *n.* **1.** the Roman goddess of peace. Greek counterpart: **Irene. 2.** a period of general peace, esp. one in which there is one dominant nation. [Latin: peace]

P.A.X. *abbrev. for* private automatic exchange.

Pax Ro+ma+na ('pæks rəʊ'mɑːnə) *n.* the Roman peace; the long period of stability under the Roman Empire.

Pax·ton ('pækstən) *n.* Sir **Jo·seph.** 1801–65, English architect, who designed Crystal Palace (1851), the first large structure of prefabricated glass and iron parts.

pax+wax ('pæksˌwæks) *n. Brit. dialect.* a strong ligament in the neck of many mammals, which supports the head. [C15: changed from C14 *fax wax*, probably from Old English *feax* hair of the head, *wax* growth]

pay[1] (peɪ) *vb.* **pays, pay+ing, paid. 1.** to discharge (a debt, obligation, etc.) by giving or doing something: *he paid his creditors.* **2.** (when intr., often foll. by *for*) to give (money, etc.) to (a person) in return for goods or services: *they pay their workers well; they pay by the hour.* **3.** to give or afford (a person, etc.) a profit or benefit: *it pays one to be honest.* **4.** (*tr.*) to give or bestow (a compliment, regards, attention, etc.). **5.** (*tr.*) to make (a visit or call). **6.** (*intr.*; often foll. by *for*) to give compensation or make amends. **7.** (*tr.*) to yield a return of: *the shares pay 15 per cent.* **8.** to give or do (something equivalent) in return; pay back: *he paid for the insult with a blow.* **9.** (*tr.; past tense and past participle* **paid** *or* **payed**) *Nautical.* to allow (a vessel) to make leeway. **10.** *Austral. informal.* to acknowledge or accept (something) as true, just, etc. **11. pay one's way. a.** to contribute one's share of expenses. **b.** to remain solvent without outside help. ~*n.* **12. a.** money given in return for work or services; a salary or wage. **b.** (*as modifier*): *a pay slip; pay claim.* **13.** paid employment (esp. in the phrase **in the pay of**). **14.** *Rare.* a person considered in regard to his ability to pay or promptitude in paying debts, bills, etc. **15.** (*modifier*) *Chiefly U.S.* requiring the insertion of money or discs before or during use: *a pay phone; a pay toilet.* **16.** (*modifier*) rich enough in minerals to be profitably mined or worked: *pay gravel.* ~See also **pay back, pay down, pay for, pay in, pay off, pay out, pay up.** [C12: from Old French *payer,* from Latin *pācāre* to appease (a creditor), from *pāx* PEACE]

pay[2] (peɪ) *vb.* **pays, pay·ing, payed.** (*tr.*) *Nautical.* to caulk (the seams of a wooden vessel) with pitch or tar. [C17: from Old French *peier,* from Latin *picāre,* from *pix* pitch]

pay·a·ble (ˈpeɪəbᵊl) *adj.* **1.** (often foll. by *on*) to be paid: *payable on the third of each month.* **2.** that is capable of being paid. **3.** capable of being profitable. **4.** (of a debt, etc.) imposing an obligation on the debtor to pay, esp. at once.

pay back *vb.* (*tr., adv.*) **1.** to retaliate against: *to pay someone back for an insult.* **2.** to give or do (something equivalent) in return for a favour, insult, etc. **3.** to repay (a loan, etc.). ~*n.* **pay·back. 4. a.** the return on an investment. **b.** Also called: **payback period.** the time taken for a project to cover its outlay.

pay bed *n.* a bed in a hospital for which the user has paid as a private patient.

pay·day (ˈpeɪˌdeɪ) *n.* the day on which wages or salaries are paid.

pay down *vb.* (*adv.*) to pay (a sum of money) at the time of purchase as the first of a series of instalments.

P.A.Y.E. (in Britain) *abbrev. for* pay as you earn; a system by which income tax levied on wage and salary earners is paid by employers directly to the government.

pay·ee (peɪˈiː) *n.* **1.** the person to whom a cheque, money order, etc., is made out. **2.** a person to whom money is paid or due.

pay·er (ˈpeɪə) *n.* **1.** a person who pays. **2.** the person named in a commercial paper as responsible for its payment on redemption.

pay for *vb.* (*prep.*) **1.** to make (payment) (for). **2.** (*intr.*) to suffer or be punished, as for a mistake, wrong decision, etc.: *in his old age he paid for the laxity of his youth.*

pay in *vb.* (*tr., adv.*) to hand (money, etc.) to a cashier for depositing in a bank account.

pay·ing guest *n.* a euphemism for **lodger.** Abbrev.: **PG**

pay·load (ˈpeɪˌləʊd) *n.* **1.** that part of a cargo earning revenue. **2. a.** the passengers, cargo, or bombs carried by an aircraft. **b.** the equipment carried by a rocket, satellite, or spacecraft. **3.** the explosive power of a warhead, bomb, etc., carried by a missile, or aircraft: *a missile carrying a 50-megaton payload.*

pay·mas·ter (ˈpeɪˌmɑːstə) *n.* an official of a government, business, etc., responsible for the payment of wages and salaries.

pay·ment (ˈpeɪmənt) *n.* **1.** the act of paying. **2.** a sum of money paid. **3.** something given in return; punishment or reward.

pay·nim (ˈpeɪnɪm) *n. Archaic.* **1.** a heathen or pagan. **2.** a Muslim. [C13: from Old French *paienime,* from Late Latin *pāgānismus* paganism, from *pāgānus* PAGAN]

pay off *vb.* **1.** (*tr., adv.*) to pay all that is due in wages, etc., and discharge from employment. **2.** (*tr., adv.*) to pay the complete amount of (a debt, bill, etc.). **3.** (*intr., adv.*) to turn out to be profitable, effective, etc.: *the gamble paid off.* **4.** (*tr., adv.* or *intr., prep.*) to take revenge on (a person) or for (a wrong done): *to pay someone off for an insult.* **5.** (*tr., adv.*) *Informal.* to give a bribe to. **6.** (*intr., adv.*) *Nautical.* (of a vessel) to make leeway. ~*n.* **pay·off. 7.** the final settlement, esp. in retribution: *the payoff came when the gang besieged the squealer's house.* **8.** *Informal.* the climax, consequence, or outcome of events, a story, etc., esp. when unexpected or improbable. **9.** the final payment of a debt, salary, etc. **10.** the time of such a payment. **11.** *Informal.* a bribe.

pay·o·la (peɪˈəʊlə) *n. U.S. informal.* **1.** a bribe given to secure special treatment, esp. to a disc jockey to promote a commercial product. **2.** the practice of paying or receiving such bribes. [C20: from PAY[1] + *-ola,* as in *Victrola*]

pay out *vb.* (*adv.*) **1.** to distribute (money, etc.); disburse. **2.** (*tr.*) to release (a rope) gradually, hand over hand. **3.** (*tr.*) to retaliate against.

pay·roll (ˈpeɪˌrəʊl) *n.* **1.** a list of employees, specifying the salary or wage of each. **2.** the total of these amounts or the actual money equivalent: *the total payroll.*

Pay·san·dú (*Spanish* ˌpajsanˈdu) *n.* a port in W Uruguay, on the Uruguay River: the third largest city in the country. Pop.: 80 000 (1975 est.).

Pays de la Loire (*French* pei də la ˈlwaːr) *n.* a region of W France, on the Bay of Biscay: generally low-lying, drained by the River Loire and its tributaries; agricultural.

payt. *abbrev. for* payment.

pay up *vb.* (*adv.*) to pay (money) promptly, in full, or on demand.

Pb *the chemical symbol for* lead. [from New Latin *plumbum*]

P.B. *abbrev. for:* **1.** British Pharmacopoeia. **2.** Prayer Book.

P.B.X. *Brit. abbrev. for* private branch exchange; a telephone system that handles the internal and external calls of a building, firm, etc.

P.C. *abbrev. for:* **1.** Parish Council(lor). **2.** Past Commander. **3.** (in Britain) Police Constable. **4.** Post Commander. **5.** Prince Consort. **6.** (in Britain) Privy Council(lor). **7.** (in Canada) Progressive Conservative.

pc. *abbrev. for:* **1.** piece. (*pl.* **pcs.**) **2.** price.

p.c. *abbrev. for:* **1.** per cent. **2.** post card. **3.** (in prescriptions) post cibum. [Latin *after meals*]

P/C, p/c, *or* **p.c.** *abbrev. for:* **1.** petty cash. **2.** price current.

pct. *U.S. abbrev. for* per cent.

P.D. *U.S. abbrev. for* Police Department.

Pd *the chemical symbol for* palladium.

pd. *abbrev. for* paid.

p.d. *abbrev. for:* **1.** Also: **P.D.** per diem. **2.** potential difference.

P.D.S.A. (in Britain) *abbrev. for* People's Dispensary for Sick Animals.

pe (peɪ; *Hebrew* pe) *n.* the 17th letter in the Hebrew alphabet (פ or, at the end of a word, ף) transliterated as *p* or, when final, *ph.* [from Hebrew *peh* mouth]

PE *international car registration for* Peru.

P.E. *abbrev. for:* **1.** physical education. **2.** potential energy. **3.** Presiding Elder. **4.** Also: **p.e.** printer's error. **5.** *Statistics.* probable error. **6.** Protestant Episcopal.

pea (piː) *n.* **1.** an annual climbing papilionaceous plant, *Pisum sativum,* with small white flowers and long green pods containing edible green seeds: cultivated in temperate regions. **2. a.** the seed of this plant, eaten as a vegetable. **b.** (*as modifier*): *pea soup.* **3.** any of several other leguminous plants, such as the sweet pea, chickpea, and cowpea. **4. the pea.** *Austral. informal.* the favourite to succeed. [C17: from PEASE (incorrectly assumed to be a plural)] —ˈ**pea·ˌlike** *adj.*

Pea·bod·y (ˈpiːˌbɒdɪ) *n.* **George.** 1795–1869, U.S. merchant, banker, and philanthropist in the U.S. and England.

peace (piːs) *n.* **1. a.** the state existing during the absence of war. **b.** (*as modifier*): *peace negotiations.* **2.** (*often cap.*) a treaty marking the end of a war. **3.** a state of harmony between people or groups; freedom from strife. **4.** law and order within a state; absence of violence or other disturbance: *a breach of the peace.* **5.** absence of mental anxiety (often in the phrase **peace of mind**). **6.** a state of stillness, silence, or serenity. **7. at peace. a.** in a state of harmony or friendship. **b.** in a state of serenity. **c.** dead: *the old lady is at peace now.* **8. hold** *or* **keep one's peace.** to keep silent, esp. about something secret. **9. keep the peace.** to maintain or refrain from disturbing law and order. **10. make one's peace with.** to become reconciled with. **11. make peace.** to bring hostilities to an end. ~*vb.* **12.** (*intr.*) *Obsolete except as an imperative.* to be or become silent or still. [C12: from Old French *pais,* from Latin *pāx*]

peace·a·ble (ˈpiːsəbᵊl) *adj.* **1.** inclined towards peace. **2.** tranquil; calm. —ˈ**peace·a·ble·ness** *n.* —ˈ**peace·a·bly** *adv.*

Peace Corps *n.* an agency of the U.S. government that sends American volunteers to developing countries, where they work on educational projects, etc.: established in 1961.

peace·ful (ˈpiːsfʊl) *adj.* **1.** not in a state of war or disagreement. **2.** calm; tranquil. **3.** of, relating to, or in accord with a time of peace: *peaceful uses of atomic energy.* **4.** inclined towards peace. —ˈ**peace·ful·ly** *adv.* —ˈ**peace·ful·ness** *n.*

peace·mak·er (ˈpiːsˌmeɪkə) *n.* a person who establishes peace, esp. between others. —ˈ**peace·ˌmak·ing** *n.*

peace of·fer·ing *n.* **1.** something given to an adversary in the hope of procuring or maintaining peace. **2.** *Judaism.* a sacrificial meal shared between the offerer and Jehovah to intensify the union between them.

peace pipe *n.* a long decorated pipe smoked by North American Indians on ceremonial occasions, esp. as a token of peace. Also called: **calumet, pipe of peace.**

Peace Riv·er *n.* a river in W Canada, rising in British Columbia as the Finlay River and flowing northeast into the Slave River. Length: 1715 km (1065 miles).

peace·time (ˈpiːsˌtaɪm) *n.* **a.** a period without war; time of peace. **b.** (*as modifier*): *a peacetime agreement.*

peach[1] (piːtʃ) *n.* **1.** a small rosaceous tree, *Prunus persica,* with pink flowers and rounded edible fruit: cultivated in temperate regions. See also **nectarine** (sense 1). **2.** the soft juicy fruit of this tree, which has a downy reddish-yellow skin, yellowish-orange sweet flesh, and a single stone. See also **nectarine** (sense 2). **3. a.** a pinkish-yellow to orange colour. **b.** (*as adj.*): *a peach dress.* **4.** *Informal.* a person or thing that is especially pleasing. [C14 *peche,* from Old French, from Medieval Latin *persica,* from Latin *Persicum mālum* Persian apple]

peach[2] (piːtʃ) *vb.* (*intr. except in obsolete uses*) *Slang.* to inform against (an accomplice). [C15: variant of earlier *apeche,* from French, from Late Latin *impedicāre* to entangle; see IMPEACH] —ˈ**peach·er** *n.*

peach-blow *n., adj.* **1. a.** a delicate purplish-pink colour. **b.** (*as adj.*): *a peach-blow vase.* **2.** a glaze of this colour on Oriental porcelain.

peach mel·ba *n.* a dessert made of halved peaches, vanilla ice cream, and melba sauce.

peach·y (ˈpiːtʃɪ) *adj.* **peach·i·er, peach·i·est. 1.** of or like a peach, esp. in colour or texture. **2.** *Informal.* excellent; fine. —ˈ**peach·i·ly** *adv.* —ˈ**peach·i·ness** *n.*

pea·cock (ˈpiːˌkɒk) *n., pl.* **·cocks** *or* **·cock. 1.** a male peafowl, having a crested head and a very large fan-like tail marked with blue and green eyelike spots. **2.** another name for **peafowl. 3.** a vain strutting person. ~*vb.* **4.** to display (oneself) proudly. **5.** *Obsolete slang, Austral.* to acquire (the best pieces of land) in such a way that the surrounding land is useless to others. [C14 *pecok, pe-* from Old English *pāwa* (from Latin *pāvō* peacock) + COCK[1]] —ˈ**pea·ˌcock·ish** *adj.* —ˈ**pea·ˌhen** *fem. n.*

Pea·cock ('piː,kɒk) *n.* **Thom·as Love.** 1785–1866, English novelist and poet, noted for his satirical romances, including *Headlong Hall* (1816) and *Nightmare Abbey* (1818).

pea+cock blue *n., adj.* (**peacock-blue** *when prenominal*). **a.** a greenish-blue colour. **b.** (*as adj.*): *a peacock-blue car.*

pea+cock but+ter+fly *n.* a European nymphalid butterfly, *Inachis io*, having reddish-brown wings each marked with a purple eyespot.

pea+cock ore *n.* another name for **bornite.**

pea crab *n.* any of various globular soft-bodied crabs of the genus *Pinnotheres* and related genera that live commensally in the mantles of certain bivalves.

pea+fowl ('piː,faʊl) *n., pl.* **+fowls** *or* **+fowl.** **1.** either of two large pheasants, *Pavo cristatus* (**blue peafowl**) of India and Ceylon and *P. muticus* (**green peafowl**) of SE Asia. The males (see **peacock** (sense 1)) have a characteristic bright plumage. **2.** a rare closely related African species, *Afropavo congensis* (**Congo peafowl**), both sexes of which are brightly coloured.

peag *or* **peage** (piːg) *n.* a less common word for **wampum.** [shortened from Narraganset *wampompeag* WAMPUM]

pea green *n., adj.* (**pea-green** *when prenominal*). **a.** a yellowish-green colour. **b.** (*as adj.*): *a pea-green teapot.*

pea jack+et *or* **pea+coat** ('piː,kəʊt) *n.* a sailor's short heavy double-breasted overcoat of navy wool. [C18: from Dutch *pijjekker*, from *pij* coat of coarse cloth + *jekker* jacket]

peak[1] (piːk) *n.* **1.** a pointed end, edge, or projection: *the peak of a roof.* **2.** the pointed summit of a mountain. **3.** a mountain with a pointed summit. **4.** the point of greatest development, strength, etc.: *the peak of his career.* **5. a.** a sharp increase in a physical quantity followed by a sharp decrease: *a voltage peak.* **b.** the maximum value of this quantity. **c.** (*as modifier*): *peak voltage.* **6.** Also called: **visor.** a projecting piece on the front of some caps. **7. a.** see **widow's peak. b.** the pointed end of a beard. **8.** *Nautical.* **a.** the extreme forward (**forepeak**) or aft (**afterpeak**) parts of the hull. **b.** (of a fore-and-aft quadrilateral sail) the after uppermost corner. **c.** the after end of a gaff. ~*vb.* **9.** (*tr.*) *Nautical.* to set (a gaff) or tilt (oars) vertically. **10.** to form or reach or cause to form or reach a peak. [C16: perhaps from PIKE, influenced by BEAK; compare Spanish *pico*, French *pic*, Middle Low German *pēk*] —**'peak·y** *adj.*

peak[2] (piːk) *vb.* (*intr.*) to become wan, emaciated, or sickly. [C16: of uncertain origin] —**'peak·y** *or* **'peak+ish** *adj.*

Peak Dis+trict *n.* a region of N central England, in N Derbyshire at the S end of the Pennines: consists of moors in the north and a central limestone plateau; many caves. Highest point: 727 m (2088 ft.).

Peake (piːk) *n.* **Mer·vyn.** 1911–68, English novelist, poet, and illustrator. In his trilogy *Gormenghast* (1946–59), he creates, with vivid imagination, a grotesque Gothic world.

peaked (piːkt) *adj.* having a peak; pointed.

peak load *n.* the maximum load on an electrical power-supply system. Compare **base load.**

peal (piːl) *n.* **1.** a loud prolonged usually reverberating sound, as of bells, thunder or laughter. **2.** *Bell-ringing.* a series of changes rung in accordance with specific rules, consisting of not less than 5000 permutations in a ring of eight bells. **3.** (*not in technical usage*) the set of bells in a belfry. ~*vb.* **4.** (*intr.*) to sound with a peal or peals. **5.** (*tr.*) to give forth loudly and sonorously. **6.** (*tr.*) to ring (bells) in peals. [C14: *pele*, variant of *apele* APPEAL]

pe·an[1] ('piːən) *n.* a less common U.S. spelling of **paean.**

pean[2] (piːn) *n. Heraldry.* a fur of sable spotted with or. [C16: of uncertain origin]

pea+nut ('piː,nʌt) *n.* **1.** Also called: **goober** and, in Britain, **groundnut, monkey nut. a.** a leguminous plant, *Arachis hypogaea*, of tropical America: widely cultivated for its edible seeds. The seed pods are forced underground where they ripen. See also **hog peanut. b.** the edible nutlike seed of this plant, used for food and as a source of oil. **2.** *U.S. slang.* a small or insignificant person.

pea+nut but+ter *n.* a brownish oily paste made from peanuts.

pea+nut oil *n.* oil that is made from peanut seeds and used for cooking, in soaps, and in pharmaceutical products.

pea+nuts ('piː,nʌts) *n. Slang.* a trifling amount of money.

pear (pɛə) *n.* **1.** a widely cultivated rosaceous tree, *Pyrus communis*, having white flowers and edible fruits. **2.** the sweet gritty-textured juicy fruit of this tree, which has a globular base and tapers towards the apex. **3.** the wood of this tree, used for making furniture. [Old English *pere*, ultimately from Latin *pirum*]

pearl[1] (pɜːl) *n.* **1.** a hard smooth lustrous typically rounded structure occurring on the inner surface of the shell of a clam or oyster: consists of calcium carbonate secreted in layers around an invading particle such as a sand grain; much valued as a gem. **2.** any artificial gem resembling this. **3.** See **mother-of-pearl. 4.** a person or thing that is like a pearl, esp. in beauty or value. **5.** a pale greyish-white colour, often with a bluish tinge. **6.** a size of printer's type, approximately equal to 5 point. ~*adj.* **7.** of, made of, or set with pearl or mother-of-pearl. **8.** having the shape or colour of a pearl. ~*vb.* **9.** (*tr.*) to set with or as if with pearls. **10.** to shape into or assume a pearl-like form or colour. **11.** (*intr.*) to dive or search for pearls. [C14: from Old French, from Vulgar Latin *pernula* (unattested), from Latin *perna* sea mussel]

pearl[2] (pɜːl) *n., vb.* a variant spelling of **purl**[1] (senses 2,3,5).

pearl ash *n.* the granular crystalline form of potassium carbonate.

pearl bar+ley *n.* barley ground into small round grains, used in cooking, esp. in soups and stews.

pearl+er ('pɜːlə) *n.* **1.** a person who dives for or trades in pearls. **2.** a boat used while searching for pearls. **3.** Also: **purler.** *Austral. informal.* something outstandingly good.

pearl grey *n., adj.* (**pearl-grey** *when prenominal*). **a.** a light bluish-grey colour. **b.** (*as adj.*): *pearl-grey shoes.*

Pearl Har+bor *n.* an almost landlocked inlet of the Pacific on the S coast of the island of Oahu, Hawaii: site of a U.S. naval base attacked by the Japanese in 1941, resulting in the U.S. entry into World War II.

pearl+ite ('pɜːlaɪt) *n.* **1.** the lamellar structure in carbon steels and some cast irons that consists of alternate plates of pure iron and iron carbide. **2.** a variant spelling of **perlite.** —**pearl+it+ic** (pɜː'lɪtɪk) *adj.*

pearl+ized *or* **pearl+ised** ('pɜːlaɪzd) *adj.* having or given a pearly lustre: *a pearlized lipstick.*

pearl mil+let *n.* a tall grass, *Pennisetum glaucum*, cultivated in Africa, E Asia, and the southern U.S. as animal fodder and for its pearly white seeds, which are used as grain.

pearl oys+ter *n.* any of various tropical marine bivalves of the genus *Pinctada* and related genera: a major source of pearls.

Pearl Riv+er *n.* **1.** a river in central Mississippi, flowing southwest and south to the Gulf of Mexico. Length: 789 km (490 miles). **2.** the English name for the **Chu Chiang.**

pearl+wort ('pɜːl,wɜːt) *n.* any caryophyllaceous plant of the genus *Sagina*, having small white flowers that are spherical in bud.

pearl·y ('pɜːlɪ) *adj.* **pearl·i+er, pearl·i+est. 1.** resembling a pearl, esp. in lustre. **2.** of the colour pearl; pale bluish-grey. **3.** decorated with pearls or mother-of-pearl. ~*n., pl.* **pearl·ies.** *Brit.* **4.** a London costermonger or the wife of one who wears on ceremonial occasions a traditional dress of dark clothes covered with pearl buttons. **5.** (*pl.*) the clothes or the buttons themselves. —**'pearl·i+ness** *n.*

Pearl·y Gates *pl. n.* **1.** *Informal.* the entrance to heaven. **2.** (*not caps.*) *Brit. slang.* teeth.

pearl·y king *or* (*fem.*) **pearl·y queen** *n.* the London costermonger whose ceremonial clothes display the most lavish collection of pearl buttons. See also **pearly.**

pearl·y nau+ti+lus *n.* any of several cephalopod molluscs of the genus *Nautilus*, esp. *N. pompilius*, of warm and tropical seas, having a partitioned pale pearly external shell with brown stripes. Also called: **chambered nautilus.** Compare **paper nautilus.**

pear+main ('pɛə,meɪn) *n.* any of several varieties of apple having a red skin. [C15: from Old French *permain* a type of pear, perhaps from Latin *Parmēnsis* of *Parma*]

Pears (pɪəz) *n.* **Pe·ter.** born 1910, English operatic tenor.

peart (pɪət) *adj. Dialect.* lively; spirited; brisk. [C15: variant of PERT] —**'peart+ly** *adv.* —**'peart+ness** *n.*

Pea·ry ('pɪərɪ) *n.* **Rob·ert Ed·win.** 1856–1920, U.S. arctic explorer, generally regarded as the first man to reach the North Pole (1909).

peas+ant ('pɛzᵊnt) *n.* **1. a.** a member of a class of low social status that depends on either cottage industry or agricultural labour as a means of subsistence. **b.** (*as modifier*): *peasant dress.* **2.** *Informal.* a person who lives in the country; rustic. **3.** *Informal.* an uncouth or uncultured person. [C15: from Anglo-French, from Old French *païsant*, from *païs* country, from Latin *pāgus* rural area; see PAGAN]

peas+ant+ry ('pɛzᵊntrɪ) *n.* **1.** peasants as a class. **2.** conduct characteristic of peasants. **3.** the status of a peasant.

pease (piːz) *n., pl.* **pease.** *Archaic or dialect.* another word for **pea.** [Old English *peose*, via Late Latin from Latin *pisa* peas, pl. of *pisum*, from Greek *pison*]

pease+cod *or* **peas+cod** ('piːz,kɒd) *n. Archaic.* the pod of a pea plant. [C14: from PEASE + COD[2]]

pease pud+ding *n. Chiefly Brit.* a dish of split peas that have been soaked and boiled, served with ham or pork.

pea+shoot·er ('piː,ʃuːtə) *n.* a tube through which pellets such as dried peas are blown, used as a toy weapon.

pea+soup+er ('piː,suːpə) *n.* **1.** *Informal, chiefly Brit.* dense dirty yellowish fog. **2.** *Canadian.* a disparaging name for a **French Canadian.**

peat[1] (piːt) *n.* **a.** a compact brownish deposit of partially decomposed vegetable matter saturated with water: found in uplands and bogs in temperate and cold regions and is used as a fuel (when dried) and as a fertilizer. **b.** (*as modifier*): *peat bog.* [C14: from Anglo-Latin *peta*, perhaps from Celtic; compare Welsh *peth* thing] —**'peat·y** *adj.*

peat[2] (piːt) *n.* **1.** *Archaic, derogatory.* a person, esp. a woman. **2.** *Obsolete.* a term of endearment for a girl or woman. [C16: of uncertain origin]

peat moss *n.* any of various mosses, esp. sphagnum, that grow in wet places in dense masses and decay to form peat. Also called: **bog moss.** See also **sphagnum.**

peat reek *n.* **1.** the smoke of a peat fire. **2.** whisky distilled over a peat fire.

peau de soie ('pəʊ də 'swɑː; *French* po də 'swa) *n.* a rich reversible silk or rayon fabric. [literally: skin of silk]

pea+vey *or* **pea+vy** ('piːvɪ) *n., pl.* **+veys** *or* **+vies.** *U.S.* a wooden lever with a metal pointed end and a hinged hook used for handling logs. Compare **cant hook.** [C19: named after Joseph *Peavey*, American who invented it]

peb+ble ('pɛbᵊl) *n.* **1.** a small smooth rounded stone, esp. one worn by the action of water. **2. a.** a transparent colourless variety of rock crystal, used for making certain lenses. **b.** such a lens. **3.** (*modifier*) *Informal.* (of a lens or of spectacles) thick, with a high degree of magnification or distortion. **4. a.** a grainy irregular surface, esp. on leather. **b.** leather having such a surface. **5.** *Informal, chiefly Austral.* a troublesome or obstinate person or animal. ~*vb.* **6.** to pave, cover, or pelt with pebbles. **7.** (*tr.*) to impart a grainy surface to (leather). [Old English *papolstān*, from *papol-* (perhaps of imitative origin) + *stān* stone] —ˈ**peb·bly** *adj.*

peb·ble dash *n. Brit.* a finish for external walls consisting of small stones embedded in plaster.

peb·bling (ˈpɛblɪŋ) *n. Curling.* the act of spraying the rink with drops of hot water to slow down the stone.

pe·can (pɪˈkæn, ˈpiːkən) *n.* **1.** a hickory tree, *Carya pecan* (or *C. illinoensis*), of the southern U.S., having deeply furrowed bark and edible nuts. **2.** the smooth oval nut of this tree, which has a sweet oily kernel. [C18: from Algonquian *paccan;* related to Ojibwa *pagân* nut with a hard shell, Cree *pakan*]

pec·ca·ble (ˈpɛkəbᵊl) *adj.* liable to sin; susceptible to temptation. [C17: via French from Medieval Latin *peccābilis,* from Latin *peccāre* to sin] —ˌ**pec·ca·ˈbil·i·ty** *n.*

pec·ca·dil·lo (ˌpɛkəˈdɪləʊ) *n., pl.* **·los** *or* **·loes.** a petty sin or trifling fault. [C16: from Spanish *pecadillo,* from *pecado* sin, from Latin *peccātum,* from *peccāre* to transgress]

pec·cant (ˈpɛkənt) *adj. Rare.* **1.** guilty of an offence; corrupt. **2.** violating or disregarding a rule; faulty. **3.** producing disease; morbid. [C17: from Latin *peccans,* from *peccāre* to sin] —ˈ**pec·can·cy** *n.* —ˈ**pec·cant·ly** *adv.*

pec·ca·ry (ˈpɛkərɪ) *n., pl.* **·ries** *or* **·ry.** either of two pig-like artiodactyl mammals, *Tayassu tajacu* (**collared peccary**) or *T. albirostris* (**white-lipped peccary**) of forests of southern North America, Central and South America: family *Tayassuidae.* [C17: from Carib]

pec·ca·vi (pɛˈkɑːviː) *n., pl.* **·vis.** a confession of guilt. [C16: from Latin, literally: I have sinned, from *peccāre*]

Pe·cho·ra (*Russian* pɪˈtʃɔrə) *n.* a river in the NW Soviet Union, rising in the Ural Mountains and flowing north in a great arc to the **Pechora Sea** (the SE part of the Barents Sea). Length: 1814 km (1127 miles).

peck[1] (pɛk) *n.* **1.** a unit of dry measure equal to 8 quarts or one quarter of a bushel. **2.** a container used for measuring this quantity. **3.** a large quantity or number. [C13: from Anglo-Norman, of uncertain origin]

peck[2] (pɛk) *vb.* **1.** (when *intr.,* sometimes foll. by *at*) to strike with the beak or with a pointed instrument. **2.** (*tr.;* sometimes foll. by *out*) to dig (a hole, etc.) by pecking. **3.** (*tr.*) (of birds) to pick up (corn, worms, etc.) by pecking. **4.** (*intr.;* often foll. by *at*) to nibble or pick (at one's food). **5.** *Informal.* to kiss (a person) quickly and lightly. **6.** (*intr.;* foll. by *at*) to nag. ~*n.* **7.** a quick light blow, esp. from a bird's beak. **8.** a mark made by such a blow. **9.** *Informal.* a quick light kiss. [C14: of uncertain origin; compare PICK[1], Middle Low German *pekken* to jab with the beak]

peck·er (ˈpɛkə) *n.* **1.** *Brit. slang.* good spirits (esp. in the phrase **keep one's pecker up**). **2.** *Informal.* short for **woodpecker. 3.** *U.S. slang.* a taboo word for **penis.**

peck·ing or·der *n.* **1.** Also called: **peck order.** a natural hierarchy in a group of gregarious birds, such as domestic fowl. **2.** any hierarchical order, as among people in a particular group.

Peck·in·pah (ˈpɛkɪnˌpɑː) *n.* **Sam.** born 1926, U.S. film director, esp. of westerns, such as *The Wild Bunch* (1969). Among his other films are *Straw Dogs* (1971), *Bring me the Head of Alfredo Garcia* (1974), and *Cross of Iron* (1977).

peck·ish (ˈpɛkɪʃ) *adj. Informal, chiefly Brit.* feeling slightly hungry; having an appetite. [C18: from PECK[2]]

Peck·sniff·i·an (pɛkˈsnɪfɪən) *adj.* affecting benevolence or high moral principles. [C19: after Seth *Pecksniff,* character in *Martin Chuzzlewit* (1843), a novel by Dickens]

Pe·cos (ˈpeɪkəs; *Spanish* peˈkos) *n.* a river in the southwestern U.S., rising in N central New Mexico and flowing southeast to the Rio Grande. Length: about 1180 km (735 miles).

Pécs (*Hungarian* peːtʃ) *n.* an industrial city in SW Hungary: university (1367). Pop.: 160 488 (1974 est.).

pec·tase (ˈpɛkteɪs) *n.* an enzyme occurring in certain ripening fruits: involved in transforming pectin into a soluble form. [C19: from PECTIN + -ASE]

pec·tate (ˈpɛkteɪt) *n.* a salt or ester of pectic acid. [C19: from PECTIC + -ATE[1]]

pec·ten (ˈpɛktɪn) *n., pl.* **·tens** *or* **·ti·nes** (-tɪˌniːz). **1.** a comblike structure in the eye of birds and reptiles, consisting of a network of blood vessels projecting inwards from the retina, which it is thought to supply with oxygen. **2.** any other comblike part or organ. **3.** any scallop of the genus *Pecten,* which swim by expelling water from their shell valves in a series of snapping motions. [C18: from Latin: a comb, from *pectere,* related to Greek *pekein* to comb]

pec·tic ac·id *n.* a complex acid containing arabinose and galactose that occurs in ripe fruit, beets, and other vegetables. Formula: $C_{35}H_{50}O_{33}$.

pec·tin (ˈpɛktɪn) *n. Biochem.* any of the acidic hemicelluloses that occur in ripe fruit and vegetables: used in the manufacture of jams because of their ability to solidify to a gel when heated in a sugar solution. [C19: from Greek *pēktos* congealed, from *pegnuein* to set] —ˈ**pec·tic** *or* ˈ**pec·tin·ous** *adj.*

pec·ti·nate (ˈpɛktɪˌneɪt) *or* **pec·ti·nat·ed** *adj.* shaped like a comb: *pectinate antennae.* [C18: from Latin *pectinātus* combed; see PECTEN] —ˌ**pec·ti·ˈna·tion** *n.*

pec·tize *or* **pec·tise** (ˈpɛktaɪz) *vb.* to change into a jelly; gel. [C19: from Greek *pēktos* solidified; see PECTIN] —ˈ**pec·tiz·a·ble** *or* ˈ**pec·tis·a·ble** *adj.* —ˌ**pec·ti·ˈza·tion** *or* ˌ**pec·ti·ˈsa·tion** *n.*

pec·to·ral (ˈpɛktərəl) *adj.* **1.** of or relating to the chest, breast, or thorax: *pectoral fins.* **2.** worn on the breast or chest: *a pectoral medallion.* **3.** *Rare.* heartfelt or sincere. ~*n.* **4.** a pectoral organ or part, esp. a muscle or fin. **5.** a medicine or remedy for disorders of the chest or lungs. **6.** anything worn on the chest or breast for decoration or protection. [C15: from Latin *pectorālis,* from *pectus* breast] —ˈ**pec·to·ral·ly** *adv.*

pec·to·ral fin *n.* either of a pair of fins, situated just behind the head in fishes, that help to control the direction of movement during locomotion.

pec·to·ral gir·dle *or* **arch** *n.* a skeletal support to which the front or upper limbs of a vertebrate are attached.

pec·to·ral mus·cle *n.* either of two large chest muscles (**pectoralis major** and **pectoralis minor**), that assist in movements of the shoulder and upper arm.

pec·u·late (ˈpɛkjʊˌleɪt) *vb.* to appropriate or embezzle (public money, etc.). [C18: from Latin *pecūlārī,* from *pecūlium* private property (originally, cattle); see PECULIAR] —ˌ**pec·u·ˈla·tion** *n.* —ˈ**pec·u·ˌla·tor** *n.*

pe·cu·li·ar (pɪˈkjuːlɪə) *adj.* **1.** strange or unusual; odd: *a peculiar individual; a peculiar idea.* **2.** distinct from others; special. **3.** (*postpositive;* foll. by *to*) belonging characteristically or exclusively (to): *peculiar to North America.* ~*n.* **4.** Also called: **arbitrary.** *Printing.* a special sort, esp. an accented letter. **5.** *Church of England.* a church or parish that is exempt from the jurisdiction of the ordinary in whose diocese it lies. [C15: from Latin *pecūliāris* concerning private property, from *pecūlium* literally: property in cattle, from *pecus* cattle] —**pe·ˈcu·li·ar·ly** *adv.*

pe·cu·li·ar·i·ty (pɪˌkjuːlɪˈærɪtɪ) *n., pl.* **·ties. 1.** a strange or unusual habit or characteristic. **2.** a distinguishing trait, etc., that is characteristic of a particular person; idiosyncrasy. **3.** the state or quality of being peculiar.

pe·cu·li·ar peo·ple *pl. n.* **1.** (*sometimes caps.*) a small sect of faith healers founded in London in 1838, having no ministers or external organization. **2.** the Jews considered as God's elect.

pe·cu·li·um (pɪˈkjuːlɪəm) *n. Roman law.* property that a father or master allowed his child or slave to hold as his own. [C17: from Latin; see PECULIAR]

pe·cu·ni·ar·y (pɪˈkjuːnɪərɪ) *adj.* **1.** consisting of or relating to money. **2.** *Law.* (of an offence) involving a monetary penalty. [C16: from Latin *pecūniāris,* from *pecūnia* money] —**pe·ˈcu·ni·ar·i·ly** *adv.*

pe·cu·ni·ar·y ad·van·tage *n. Law.* financial advantage that is dishonestly obtained by deception and that constitutes a criminal offence.

ped. *abbrev. for:* **1.** pedal. **2.** pedestal.

ped- *combining form.* variant of **paed-.**

-ped *or* **-pede** *n. combining form.* foot or feet: *quadruped; centipede.* [from Latin *pēs, ped-* foot]

ped·a·gog·ics (ˌpɛdəˈgɒdʒɪks, -ˈgəʊ-) *n.* (*functioning as sing.*) another word for **pedagogy.**

ped·a·gogue *or U.S.* (*sometimes*) **ped·a·gog** (ˈpɛdəˌgɒg) *n.* **1.** a teacher or educator. **2.** a pedantic or dogmatic teacher. [C14: from Latin *paedagōgus,* from Greek *paidagōgos* slave who looked after his master's son, from *pais* boy + *agōgos* leader] —ˌ**ped·a·ˈgog·ic** *or* ˌ**ped·a·ˈgog·i·cal** *adj.* —ˌ**ped·a·ˈgog·i·cal·ly** *adv.* —ˈ**ped·a·ˌgog·ism** *or* ˈ**ped·a·ˌgogu·ism** *n.*

ped·a·go·gy (ˈpɛdəˌgɒgɪ, -ˌgɒdʒɪ, -ˌgəʊdʒɪ) *n.* the principles, practice, or profession of teaching.

ped·al[1] (ˈpɛdᵊl) *n.* **1. a.** any foot-operated lever or other device, esp. one of the two levers that drive the chainwheel of a bicycle, the foot-brake, clutch control, or accelerator of a car, one of the levers on an organ controlling deep bass notes, or one of the levers on a piano used to create a muted effect or sustain tone. **b.** (*as modifier*)*: a pedal cycle; a pianist's pedal technique.* ~*vb.* **·als, ·al·ling, ·alled** *or U.S.* **·als, ·al·ing, ·aled. 2.** to propel (a bicycle, etc.) by operating the pedals. **3.** (*intr.*) to operate the pedals of an organ, piano, etc., esp. in a certain way. **4.** to work (pedals of any kind). [C17: from Latin *pedālis;* see PEDAL[2]]

pe·dal[2] (ˈpiːdᵊl) *adj.* of or relating to the foot or feet. [C17: from Latin *pedālis,* from *pēs* foot]

pe·dal·fer (pɪˈdælfə) *n.* a type of zonal soil deficient in lime but containing deposits of aluminium and iron, found in wet areas, esp. those with high temperatures. Compare **pedocal.** [C20: PEDO-[2] + ALUM + *-fer,* from Latin *ferrum* iron]

ped·a·lo (ˈpɛdᵊləʊ) *n., pl.* **·los** *or* **·loes.** a pleasure craft driven by pedal-operated paddle wheels. [C20: from PEDAL]

ped·al point (ˈpɛdᵊl) *n. Music.* a sustained bass note, over which the other parts move bringing about changing harmonies. Often shortened to **pedal.**

ped·ant (ˈpɛdᵊnt) *n.* **1.** a person who relies too much on academic learning or who is concerned chiefly with insignificant detail. **2.** *Archaic.* a schoolmaster or teacher. [C16: via Old French from Italian *pedante* teacher; perhaps related to Latin *paedagōgus* PEDAGOGUE] —**pe·dan·tic** (pɪˈdæntɪk) *adj.* —**pe·ˈdan·ti·cal·ly** *adv.*

ped·ant·ry (ˈpɛdᵊntrɪ) *n., pl.* **·ries.** the habit or an instance of being a pedant, esp. in the display of useless knowledge or minute observance of petty rules or details.

ped·ate (ˈpɛdeɪt) *adj.* **1.** (of a plant leaf) deeply divided into several lobes with the lateral lobes divided into smaller lobes. **2.** *Zoology.* having or resembling a foot: *a pedate appendage.* [C18: from Latin *pedātus* equipped with feet, from *pēs* foot] —ˈ**ped·ate·ly** *adv.*

pe·dat·i·fid (pɪˈdætɪfɪd, -ˈdeɪ-) *adj.* (of a plant leaf) pedately divided, with the divisions less deep than in a pedate leaf.

ped·dle (ˈpɛdᵊl) *vb.* **1.** to go from place to place selling (goods, esp. small articles). **2.** (*tr.*) to sell (illegal drugs, esp. narcotics). **3.** (*tr.*) to advocate (ideas, etc.) persistently or importunately: *to peddle a new philosophy.* **4.** (*intr.*) *Archaic.* to trifle. [C16: back formation from PEDLAR]

ped+dler ('pɛdlə) *n.* **1.** a person who sells illegal drugs, esp. narcotics. **2.** the usual U.S. spelling of **pedlar.**

-pede *n. combining form.* variant of **-ped.**

ped+er+ast *or* **paed+er+ast** ('pɛdəˌræst) *n.* a man who practises pederasty.

ped+er+as+ty *or* **paed+er+as+ty** ('pɛdəˌræstɪ) *n.* homosexual relations between men and boys. [C17: from New Latin *paederastia,* from Greek, from *pais* boy + *erastēs* lover, from *eran* to love] —ˌ**ped+er+'as+tic** *or* ˌ**paed+er+'as+tic** *adj.*

ped+es+tal ('pɛdɪstᵊl) *n.* **1.** a base that supports a column, statue, etc., as used in classical architecture. **2.** a position of eminence or supposed superiority (esp. in the phrases **place, put,** *or* **set on a pedestal**). **3. a.** either of a pair of sets of drawers used as supports for a writing surface. **b.** (*as modifier*): *a pedestal desk.* [C16: from French *piédestal,* from Old Italian *piedestallo,* from *pie* foot + *di* of + *stallo* a stall]

pe+des+tri+an (pɪ'dɛstrɪən) *n.* **1. a.** a person travelling on foot; walker. **b.** (*as modifier*): *a pedestrian precinct.* ~*adj.* **2.** dull; commonplace: *a pedestrian style of writing.* [C18: from Latin *pedester,* from *pēs* foot]

pe+des+tri+an cross+ing *n. Brit.* a path across a road marked as a crossing for pedestrians. See also **zebra crossing, pelican crossing.** U.S. name: **crosswalk.**

pe+des+tri+an+ize *or* **pe+des+tri+an+ise** (pɪ'dɛstrɪəˌnaɪz) *vb.* (*tr.*) to convert (a street, etc.) into an area for the use of pedestrians only, by excluding all motor vehicles. —**pe+ˌdes+tri+a+ni+'za+tion** *or* **pe+ˌdes+tri+a+ni+'sa+tion** *n.*

ped+i- *combining form.* indicating the foot: *pedicure.* [from Latin *pēs, ped-* foot]

Ped+i ('pɛdɪ) *n.* **1.** Also called: **Northern Sotho.** a member of a subgroup of the Sotho people resident in the Transvaal. **2.** the dialect of Sotho spoken by this people.

ped+i+cab ('pɛdɪˌkæb) *n.* a pedal-operated tricycle, available for hire in some Asian countries, with an attached seat for one or two passengers.

ped+i+cel ('pɛdɪˌsɛl) *n.* **1.** the stalk bearing a single flower of an inflorescence. **2.** Also called: **peduncle.** *Biology.* any short stalk bearing an organ or organism. **3.** the second segment of an insect's antenna. [C17: from New Latin *pedicellus,* from Latin *pedīculus,* from *pēs* foot]

ped+i+cle ('pɛdɪkᵊl) *n. Biology.* any small stalk; pedicel; peduncle. [C17: from Latin *pedīculus* small foot; see PEDICEL]

pe+dic+u+lar (pɪ'dɪkjʊlə) *adj.* **1.** relating to, infested with, or caused by lice. **2.** *Biology.* of or relating to a stem, stalk, or pedicle. [C17: from Latin *pedīculāris,* from *pedīculus,* diminutive of *pedis* louse]

pe+dic+u+late (pɪ'dɪkjʊlɪt, -ˌleɪt) *adj.* **1.** of, relating to, or belonging to the *Pediculati,* a large order of teleost fishes containing the anglers. ~*n.* **2.** any fish belonging to the order *Pediculati.* [C19: from Latin *pedīculus* little foot; see PEDICEL]

pe+dic+u+lo+sis (pɪˌdɪkjʊ'ləʊsɪs) *n. Pathol.* the state of being infested with lice. [C19: via New Latin from Latin *pedīculus* louse; see PEDICULAR] —**pe+dic+u+lous** (pɪ'dɪkjʊləs) *adj.*

ped+i+cure ('pɛdɪˌkjʊə) *n.* professional treatment of the feet, either by a medical expert or a cosmetician. [C19: via French from Latin *pēs* foot + *curāre* to care for]

ped+i+form ('pɛdɪˌfɔ:m) *adj.* shaped like a foot.

ped+i+gree ('pɛdɪˌgri:) *n.* **1. a.** the line of descent of a pure-bred animal. **b.** (*as modifier*): *a pedigree bull.* **2.** a document recording this. **3.** a genealogical table, esp. one indicating pure ancestry. **4.** derivation or background: *the pedigree of an idea.* [C15: from Old French *pie de grue* crane's foot, alluding to the spreading lines used in a genealogical chart] —'**ped+i+ˌgreed** *adj.*

ped+i+ment ('pɛdɪmənt) *n.* **1.** a low-pitched gable, esp. one that is triangular as used in classical architecture. **2.** a gently sloping rock surface, formed through denudation under arid conditions. [C16: from obsolete *periment,* perhaps workman's corruption of PYRAMID] —ˌ**ped+i+'ment+al** *adj.*

ped+i+palp ('pɛdɪˌpælp) *n.* either member of the second pair of head appendages of arachnids: specialized for feeding, locomotion, etc. [C19: from New Latin *pedipalpi,* from Latin *pēs* foot + *palpus* palp]

ped+lar *or esp. U.S.* **ped+dler, ped+ler** ('pɛdlə) *n.* a person who peddles; hawker. [C14: changed from *peder,* from *ped, pedde* basket, of obscure origin]

pe+do-[1] *or before a vowel* **ped-** *combining form.* a U.S. spelling of **paedo-.**

ped+o-[2] *combining form.* indicating soil: *pedocal.* [from Greek *pedon*]

ped+o+cal ('pɛdəˌkæl) *n.* a type of zonal soil that is rich in lime and characteristic of relatively dry areas. Compare **pedalfer.** [from PEDO-[2] + CAL(CIUM)]

pe+dol+o+gy[1] (pɪ'dɒlədʒɪ) *n.* a U.S. spelling of **paedology.**

pe+dol+o+gy[2] (pɪ'dɒlədʒɪ) *n.* the study of the formation, characteristics, and distribution of soils. —**pe+do+log+i+cal** (ˌpi:də'lɒdʒɪkᵊl) *adj.* —**pe+'dol+o+gist** *n.*

pe+dom+e+ter (pɪ'dɒmɪtə) *n.* a device containing a pivoted weight that records the number of steps taken in walking and hence the distance travelled.

pe+dun+cle (pɪ'dʌŋkᵊl) *n.* **1.** the stalk of a plant bearing an inflorescence or solitary flower. **2.** *Anatomy.* a stalklike structure, esp. a large bundle of nerve fibres within the brain. **3.** *Pathol.* a slender process of tissue by which a polyp or tumour is attached to the body. **4.** *Biology.* another name for **pedicel** (sense 2). [C18: from New Latin *pedunculus,* from Latin *pedīculus* little foot; see PEDICLE] —**pe+'dun+cled** *or* **pe+dun+cu+lar** (pɪ'dʌŋkjʊlə) *adj.*

pe+dun+cu+late (pɪ'dʌŋkjʊlɪt, -ˌleɪt) *or* **pe+dun+cu+lat+ed** *adj.* having, supported on, or growing from a peduncle. —**pe+ˌdun+cu+'la+tion** *n.*

pe+dun+cu+late oak *n.* a large deciduous oak tree, *Quercus robur,* of Eurasia, having lobed leaves and stalked acorns. Also called: **common oak.**

pee (pi:) *Slang.* ~*vb.* **pees, pee+ing, peed. 1.** (*intr.*) to urinate. ~*n.* **2.** urine. **3.** the act of urinating. [C18: euphemistic for PISS, based on the initial letter]

Pee+bles ('pi:bᵊlz) *n.* (until 1975) a county of SE Scotland, now part of the Borders region.

peek (pi:k) *vb.* **1.** (*intr.*) to glance quickly or furtively; peep. ~*n.* **2.** a quick or furtive glance. [C14 *pike,* related to Middle Dutch *kiken* to peek]

peek·a+boo ('pi:kəˌbu:) *n.* **1.** a game for young children, in which one person hides his face and suddenly reveals it and cries "peekaboo." ~*adj.* **2.** (of a garment) made of fabric that is almost transparent or patterned with small holes. [C16: from PEEK]

peel[1] (pi:l) *vb.* **1.** (*tr.*) to remove (the skin, rind, outer covering, etc.) of (a fruit, egg, etc.). **2.** (*intr.*) (of paint, etc.) to be removed from a surface, esp. through weathering. **3.** (*intr.*) (of a surface) to lose its outer covering of paint, etc., esp. through weathering. **4.** (*intr.*) (of a person or part of the body) to shed skin in flakes or (of skin) to be shed in flakes, esp. as a result of sunburn. **5.** (*intr.;* often foll. by *off*) *Slang.* to undress. **6.** *Croquet.* to put (another player's ball) through a hoop or hoops. **7. keep one's eyes peeled** (*or* **skinned**). to keep a sharp lookout. ~*n.* **8.** the skin or rind of a fruit, etc. ~See also **peel off.** [Old English *pilian* to strip off outer layer, from Latin *pilāre* to make bald, from *pilus* a hair]

peel[2] (pi:l) *n.* a long-handled shovel used by bakers for moving bread, etc., in an oven. [C14 *pele,* from Old French, from Latin *pāla* spade, from *pangere* to drive in; see PALETTE]

peel[3] (pi:l) *n. Brit.* a fortified tower of the 16th century on the borders between England and Scotland, built to withstand raids. [C14 (fence made of stakes): from Old French *piel* stake, from Latin *pālum;* see PALE[2], PALING]

Peel (pi:l) *n.* Sir **Rob·ert.** 1788–1850, British statesman; Conservative prime minister (1834–35; 1841–46). As Home Secretary (1828–30) he founded the Metropolitan Police and in his second ministry carried through a series of free-trade budgets culminating in the repeal of the Corn Laws (1846), which split the Tory party. —'**Peel+ite** *n.*

Peele (pi:l) *n.* **George.** ?1556–?96, English dramatist and poet. His works include the pastoral drama *The Arraignment of Paris* (1584) and the comedy *The Old Wives' Tale* (1595).

peel+er[1] ('pi:lə) *n.* **1.** a special knife or mechanical device for peeling vegetables, fruit, etc.: *a potato peeler.* **2.** *U.S. slang.* a striptease dancer.

peel+er[2] ('pi:lə) *n. Brit. slang.* an obsolete word for **policeman.** [C19: from the founder of the police force, Sir Robert PEEL]

pee·lie-wal·ly ('pi:lɪ'wælɪ) *adj. Central Scot. urban dialect.* off colour; pale: *he's a wee bit peelie-wally this morning.* [apparently a reduplicated form of WALLY in the sense: faded]

peel+ing ('pi:lɪŋ) *n.* a strip of skin, rind, bark, etc., that has been peeled off: *a potato peeling.*

peel off *vb.* (*adv.*) **1.** to remove or be removed by peeling. **2.** (*intr.*) (of an aircraft) to turn away as by banking, and leave a formation. **3.** *Slang.* to go away or cause to go away.

peen (pi:n) *n.* **1.** the end of a hammer head opposite the striking face, often rounded or wedge-shaped. ~*vb.* **2.** (*tr.*) to strike with the peen of a hammer or with a stream of metal shot in order to bend or shape (a sheet of metal). [C17: variant of *pane,* perhaps from French *panne,* ultimately from Latin *pinna* point]

peep[1] (pi:p) *vb.* (*intr.*) **1.** to look furtively or secretly, as through a small aperture or from a hidden place. **2.** to appear partially or briefly: *the sun peeped through the clouds.* ~*n.* **3.** a quick or furtive look. **4.** the first appearance: *the peep of dawn.* [C15: variant of PEEK] —'**peep+er** *n.*

peep[2] (pi:p) *vb.* (*intr.*) **1.** (esp. of young birds) to utter shrill small noises. **2.** to speak in a thin shrill voice. ~*n.* **3.** a peeping sound. **4.** *U.S.* any of various small sandpipers of the genus *Calidris* (or *Erolia*) and related genera, such as the pectoral sandpiper. [C15: of imitative origin] —'**peep+er** *n.*

peep+er ('pi:pə) *n.* **1.** a person who peeps. **2.** (*often pl.*) a slang word for **eye.**

peep+hole ('pi:pˌhəʊl) *n.* a small aperture, such as one in the door of a flat for observing callers before opening.

Peep+ing Tom *n.* a man who furtively observes women undressing; voyeur. [C19: after the tailor who, according to legend, peeped at Lady Godiva when she rode naked through Coventry]

peep+show ('pi:pˌʃəʊ) *n.* a small box with a peephole through which a series of pictures, esp. of erotic poses, can be seen. Also called: **raree show.**

peep sight *n.* a rear gunsight having an adjustable eyepiece fitted with a narrow aperture through which the target and the front sight are aligned when aiming.

pee+pul ('pi:pᵊl) *or* **pi+pal** *n.* an Indian moraceous tree, *Ficus religiosa,* resembling the banyan: regarded as sacred by Buddhists. Also called: **bo tree.** [C18: from Hindi *pīpal,* from Sanskrit *pippala*]

peer[1] (pɪə) *n.* **1.** a member of a nobility; nobleman. **2.** a person who holds any of the five grades of the British nobility: duke, marquess, earl, viscount, and baron. See also **life peer.** **3.** a person who is an equal in social standing, rank, age, etc.: *to be tried by one's peers.* **4.** *Archaic.* a companion; mate. [C14 (in sense 3): from Old French *per,* from Latin *pār* equal]

peer[2] (pɪə) *vb.* (*intr.*) **1.** to look intently with or as if with difficulty: *to peer into the distance.* **2.** to appear partially or dimly: *the sun peered through the fog.* [C16: from Flemish *pieren* to look with narrowed eyes]

peer·age ('pɪərɪdʒ) *n.* **1.** the whole body of peers; aristocracy. **2.** the position, rank, or title of a peer. **3.** (esp. in the British Isles) a book listing the peers and giving genealogical and other information about them.

peer·ess ('pɪərɪs) *n.* **1.** the wife or widow of a peer. **2.** a woman holding the rank of a peer in her own right.

peer group *n.* a social group composed of individuals of approximately the same age.

peer·less ('pɪəlɪs) *adj.* having no equals; matchless.

peer of the realm *n., pl.* **peers of the realm.** (in Great Britain and Northern Ireland) any member of the nobility entitled to sit in the House of Lords.

peet·weet ('piːtˌwiːt) *n. U.S.* another name for the **spotted sandpiper.** [C19: imitative of its cry]

peeve (piːv) *Informal.* ~*vb.* **1.** (*tr.*) to irritate; vex; annoy. ~*n.* **2.** something that irritates; vexation: *it was a pet peeve of his.* [C20: back formation from PEEVISH]

peev·ers ('piːvəz) *n. Scot. dialect.* hopscotch. [from *peever* (the stone used in the game), of obscure origin]

peev·ish ('piːvɪʃ) *adj.* **1.** fretful or irritable: *a peevish child.* **2.** *Obsolete.* perverse. [C14: of unknown origin] —**'peev·ish·ly** *adv.* —**'peev·ish·ness** *n.*

pee·wit *or* **pe·wit** ('piːwɪt) *n.* another name for **lapwing.** [C16: imitative of its call]

peg (pɛg) *n.* **1.** a small cylindrical pin or dowel, sometimes slightly tapered, used to join two parts together. **2.** a pin pushed or driven into a surface: used to mark scores, define limits, support coats, etc. **3.** any of several pins passing through the head (**peg box**) of a violin, etc., which can be turned so as to tune strings wound around them. See also **pin** (sense 11). **4.** Also called: **clothes peg.** *Brit.* a split or hinged pin for fastening wet clothes to a line to dry. U.S. equivalent: **clothespin.** **5.** *Brit.* a small drink of wine or spirits, esp. of brandy or whisky and soda. **6.** an opportunity or pretext for doing something: *a peg on which to hang a theory.* **7.** a mountaineering piton. **8.** *Croquet.* a post that a player's ball must strike to win the game. **9.** *Informal.* a level of self-esteem, importance, etc. (esp. in the phrases **come** *or* **take down a peg**). **10.** *Informal.* See **peg leg.** **11. off the peg.** *Chiefly Brit.* (of clothes) ready-to-wear, as opposed to tailor-made. ~*vb.* **pegs, peg·ging, pegged.** **12.** (*tr.*) to knock or insert a peg into or pierce with a peg. **13.** (*tr.*; sometimes foll. by *down*) to secure with pegs: *to peg a tent.* **14.** (*tr.*) to mark (a score) with pegs, as in some card games. **15.** (*tr.*) *Informal.* to aim and throw (stones, etc.) at a target. **16.** (*intr.*; foll. by *away, along,* etc.) *Chiefly Brit.* to work steadily: *he pegged away at his job for years.* **17.** (*tr.*) to stabilize (the price of a commodity, an exchange rate, etc.) by legislation or market operations. [C15: from Low Germanic *pegge*]

Peg·a·sus[1] ('pɛgəsəs) *n. Greek myth.* an immortal winged horse, which sprang from the blood of the slain Medusa and enabled Bellerophon to achieve many great deeds as his rider.

Peg·a·sus[2] ('pɛgəsəs) *n., Latin genitive* **Peg·a·si** ('pɛgəˌsaɪ). a constellation in the N hemisphere lying close to Andromeda and Pisces.

peg·board ('pɛgˌbɔːd) *n.* **1.** a board having a pattern of holes into which small pegs can be fitted, used for playing certain games or keeping a score. **2.** another name for **solitaire** (sense 1). **3.** hardboard perforated by a pattern of holes in which articles may be pegged or hung, as for display.

peg down *vb.* (*tr., adv.*) to make (a person) committed to a course of action or bound to follow rules: *you won't peg him down on any decision.*

peg leg *n. Informal.* **1.** an artificial leg, esp. one made of wood. **2.** a person with an artificial leg.

peg·ma·tite ('pɛgməˌtaɪt) *n.* any of a class of coarse-grained intrusive igneous rocks consisting chiefly of quartz and feldspar: usually occur as dykes among igneous rocks of finer grain. [C19: from Greek *pegma* something joined together] —**peg·ma·tit·ic** (ˌpɛgmə'tɪtɪk) *adj.*

peg out *vb.* (*adv.*) **1.** (*intr.*) *Informal.* to collapse or die. **2.** *Croquet.* **a.** (*intr.*) to win a game by hitting the peg. **b.** (*tr.*) to cause (an opponent's ball) to hit the peg, rendering it out of the game. **3.** *Cribbage.* (*intr.*) to score the point that wins the game. **4.** (*tr.*) to mark or secure with pegs: *to peg out one's claims to a piece of land.*

peg top *n.* a child's spinning top, usually made of wood with a metal centre pin.

peg-top *adj.* (of skirts, trousers, etc.) wide at the hips then tapering off towards the ankle.

Pe·gu (pɛ'guː) *n.* a city in S Burma: capital of a united Burma (16th century). Pop.: 122 000 (1969 est.).

Peh·le·vi ('peɪləvɪ) *n.* a variant spelling of **Pahlavi**[2].

P.E.I. *abbrev. for* Prince Edward Island.

peign·oir ('peɪnwɑː) *n.* a woman's dressing gown or negligee. [C19: from French, from *peigner* to comb, since the garment was worn while the hair was combed]

Pei·pus ('paɪpəs) *n.* a lake in the W Soviet Union, on the boundary between the RSFSR and Estonia: drains into the Gulf of Finland. Area: 3512 sq. km (1356 sq. miles). Russian name: **Chudskoye Ozero.**

Pei·rae·us (paɪ'riːəs) *n.* a variant spelling of **Piraeus.**

Peirce (pɪəs) *n.* **Charles San·ders.** 1839–1914, U.S. logician, philosopher, and mathematician; pioneer of pragmatism.

pej·o·ra·tion (ˌpiːdʒə'reɪʃən) *n.* **1.** semantic change whereby a word acquires unfavourable connotations: *the English word "silly" changed its meaning from "holy" or "happy" by pejoration.* Compare **amelioration.** **2.** the process of worsening; deterioration.

pe·jo·ra·tive (pɪ'dʒɒrətɪv, 'piːdʒər-) *adj.* **1.** (of words, expressions, etc.) having an unpleasant or disparaging connotation. ~*n.* **2.** a pejorative word, etc. [C19: from French *péjoratif,* from Late Latin *pējōrātus,* past participle of *pējōrāre* to make worse, from Latin *pēior* worse] —**pe·'jo·ra·tive·ly** *adv.*

pek·an ('pɛkən) *n.* another name for **fisher** (the animal). [C18: from Canadian French *pékan,* of Algonquian origin; compare Abnaki *pékané*]

peke (piːk) *n. Informal.* a Pekingese dog.

Pe·kin (piː'kɪn) *n.* a breed of white or cream duck with a bright orange bill. [C18: via French from PEKING]

Pe·king (piː'kɪŋ) *n.* the capital of the People's Republic of China, in the northeast in central Hopeh province: dates back to the 12th century B.C.; consists of two central walled cities, the Outer City (containing the commercial quarter) and the Inner City, which contains the Imperial City, within which is the Purple or Forbidden City; three universities. Pop.: 8 000 000 (1976 est.).

Pe·king·ese (ˌpiːkɪŋ'iːz) *or* **Pe·kin·ese** (ˌpiːkə'niːz) *n.* **1.** (*pl.* **·ese**) a small breed of pet dog with a profuse straight coat, curled plumed tail, and short wrinkled muzzle. **2.** the dialect of Mandarin Chinese spoken in Peking, the pronunciation of which serves as a standard for the language. **3.** (*pl.* **·ese**) a native or inhabitant of Peking. ~*adj.* **4.** of or relating to Peking or its inhabitants.

Pe·king man *n.* an early type of man, *Homo erectus,* remains of which, of the Lower Palaeolithic age, were found in a cave near Peking, China, in 1927.

pe·koe ('piːkəʊ) *n.* a high-quality tea made from the downy tips of the young buds of the tea plant. [C18: from Chinese (Amoy) *peh ho,* from *peh* white + *ho* down]

pel·age ('pɛlɪdʒ) *n.* the coat of a mammal, consisting of hair, wool, fur, etc. [C19: via French from Old French *pel* animal's coat, from Latin *pilus* hair]

Pe·la·gi·an Is·lands (pɛ'leɪdʒɪən) *pl. n.* a group of Italian islands (Lampedusa, Linosa, and Lampione) in the Mediterranean, between Tunisia and Malta. Pop.: 4620 (1968 est.). Area: about 27 sq. km (11 sq. miles). Italian name: **I·so·le Pe·la·gie** ('iːzole pe'ladʒe).

Pe·la·gi·an·ism (pɛ'leɪdʒɪəˌnɪzəm) *n. Christianity.* a heretical doctrine, first formulated by Pelagius, that rejected the concept of original sin and maintained that the individual takes the initial steps towards salvation by his own efforts and not by the help of divine grace.

pe·lag·ic (pɛ'lædʒɪk) *adj.* **1.** of or relating to the open sea: *pelagic whaling.* **2.** (of marine life) living or occurring in the upper waters of open sea. **3.** (of geological formations) derived from material that has fallen to the bottom from the upper waters of the sea. [C17: from Latin *pelagicus,* from *pelagus,* from Greek *pelagos* sea]

Pe·la·gi·us (pɛ'leɪdʒɪəs) *n.* ?360–?420 A.D., British monk, who originated the body of doctrines known as Pelagianism and was condemned for heresy (1417). —**Pe·'la·gi·an** *n., adj.*

pel·ar·gon·ic ac·id (ˌpɛlə'gɒnɪk) *n.* another name for **nonanoic acid.**

pel·ar·go·ni·um (ˌpɛlə'gəʊnɪəm) *n.* any plant of the chiefly southern African geraniaceous genus *Pelargonium,* having circular or lobed leaves and red, pink, or white aromatic flowers: includes many cultivated geraniums. [C19: via New Latin from Greek *pelargos* stork, on the model of GERANIUM; from the likeness of the seed vessels to a stork's bill]

Pe·las·gi·an (pɛ'læzdʒɪən) *n.* **1.** a member of any of the pre-Hellenic peoples (the **Pelasgi**) who inhabited Greece and the islands and coasts of the Aegean Sea before the arrival of the Bronze Age Greeks. ~*adj. also* **Pe·las·gic.** **2.** of or relating to these peoples.

Pe·lé ('pɛleɪ) *n.* original name *Edson Arantes do Nascimento.* born 1940, Brazilian footballer.

pe·lec·y·pod (pɪ'lɛsɪˌpɒd) *n., adj.* another word for **bivalve** (senses 1, 2). [C19: from Greek *pelekus* hatchet + -POD]

Pe·lée (pə'leɪ) *n.* **Mount.** a volcano in the West Indies, in N Martinique: erupted in 1902, killing every person but one in the town of St. Pierre. Height: 1463 m (4800 ft.).

pel·er·ine ('pɛləˌriːn) *n.* a woman's narrow cape with long pointed ends in front. [C18: from French *pèlerine,* feminine of *pèlerin* PILGRIM, that is, a pilgrim's cape]

Pe·le's hair ('peɪleɪz, 'piːliːz) *n.* fine threads of volcanic rock material formed from molten lava by the action of wind, explosion, etc. [C20: translation of Hawaiian *lauoho-o Pele,* from Pele, name of the goddess of volcanoes]

Pel·e·us ('pɛlɪəs, 'piːlɪəs) *n. Greek myth.* a king of the Myrmidons; father of Achilles.

Pe·lew Is·lands (piː'luː) *pl. n.* the former name of the **Palau Islands.**

pelf (pɛlf) *n. Contemptuous.* money or wealth, esp. if dishonestly acquired; lucre. [C14: from Old French *pelfre* booty; related to Latin *pilāre* to despoil]

pel·ham ('pɛləm) *n.* a horse's bit for a double bridle, less severe than a curb but more severe than a snaffle. [probably from the proper name *Pelham*]

Pe·li·as ('piːlɪˌæs) *n. Greek myth.* a son of Poseidon and Tyro.

He feared his nephew Jason and sent him to recover the Golden Fleece, hoping he would not return.

pel·i·can ('pɛlɪkən) *n.* any aquatic bird of the tropical and warm water family *Pelecanidae,* such as *P. onocrotalus* (**white pelican**): order *Pelecaniformes.* They have a long straight flattened bill, with a distensible pouch for engulfing fish. [Old English *pellican,* from Late Latin *pelicānus,* from Greek *pelekān;* perhaps related to Greek *pelekus* axe, perhaps from the shape of the bird's bill; compare Greek *pelekas* woodpecker]

pel·i·can cross·ing *n.* a type of road crossing marked by black and white stripes or by two rows of metal studs and consisting of a pedestrian-operated traffic-light system. [C20: from *pe(destrian) li(ght) con(trolled) crossing,* with *-con* adapted to *-can* of *pelican*]

Pe·li·on ('pi:lɪən) *n.* a mountain in NE Greece, in E Thessaly. In Greek mythology it was the home of the centaurs. Height: 1548 m (5079 ft.). Modern Greek name: **Pílion.**

pe·lisse (pɛ'li:s) *n.* **1.** a fur-trimmed cloak. **2.** a high-waisted loose coat, usually fur-trimmed, worn esp. by women in the early 19th century. [C18: via Old French from Medieval Latin *pellicia* cloak, from Latin *pellis* skin]

pe·lite ('pi:laɪt) *n.* any argillaceous rock such as shale. [C19: from Greek *pēlos* mud] —**pe·lit·ic** (pɪ'lɪtɪk) *adj.*

Pel·la ('pɛlə) *n.* an ancient city in N Greece: the capital of Macedonia under Philip II.

pel·la·gra (pə'leɪgrə, -'læ-) *n. Pathol.* a disease caused by a dietary deficiency of niacin, characterized by burning or itching often followed by scaling of the skin, inflammation of the mouth, diarrhoea, mental impairment, etc. [C19: via Italian from *pelle* skin + *-agra,* from Greek *agra* paroxysm] —**pel·'la·grous** *adj.*

Pel·les ('pɛli:z) *n.* (in Arthurian legend) the father of Elaine and one of the searchers for the Holy Grail.

pel·let ('pɛlɪt) *n.* **1.** a small round ball, esp. of compressed matter: *a wax pellet.* **2. a.** an imitation bullet used in toy guns. **b.** a piece of small shot. **3.** a stone ball formerly used as a catapult or cannon missile. **4.** Also called: **cast, casting.** *Ornithol.* a mass of undigested food, including bones, fur, feathers, etc., that is regurgitated by certain birds, esp. birds of prey. **5.** a small pill. **6.** a raised area on coins and carved or moulded ornaments. ~*vb.* (*tr.*) **7.** to strike with pellets. **8.** to make or form into pellets. [C14: from Old French *pelote,* from Vulgar Latin *pilota* (unattested), from Latin *pila* ball]

Pelle·tier (*French* pɛl'tje) *n.* **Pierre Jo·seph** (pjɛ:r ʒo'zɛf). 1788–1842, French chemist, who isolated quinine, chlorophyll, and other chemical substances.

pel·li·cle ('pɛlɪk^{ə}l) *n.* **1.** a thin skin or film. **2.** the hard protective outer layer of certain protozoans, such as those of the genus *Paramecium.* **3.** *Botany.* **a.** the thin outer layer of a mushroom cap. **b.** a growth on the surface of a liquid culture. **4.** *Photog.* the thin layer of emulsion covering a plate, film, or paper. [C16: via French from Latin *pellicula,* from *pellis* skin] —**pel·lic·u·lar** (pɛ'lɪkjʊlə) *adj.*

pel·li·to·ry ('pɛlɪtərɪ, -trɪ) *n., pl.* **·ries. 1.** any of various urticaceous plants of the S and W European genus *Parietaria,* esp. *P. diffusa* (**pellitory-of-the-wall** or **wall pellitory**), that grow in crevices and have long narrow leaves and small pink flowers. **2. pellitory of Spain.** a small Mediterranean plant, *Anacyclus pyrethrum,* the root of which contains an oil formerly used to relieve toothache: family *Compositae* (composites). [C16 *peletre,* from Old French *piretre,* from Latin *pyrethrum* from Greek *purethron,* from *pur* fire, from the hot pungent taste of the root]

pell-mell ('pɛl'mɛl) *adv.* **1.** in a confused headlong rush: *the hounds ran pell-mell into the yard.* **2.** in a disorderly manner: *the things were piled pell-mell in the room.* ~*adj.* **3.** disordered; tumultuous: *a pell-mell rush for the exit.* ~*n.* **4.** disorder; confusion. [C16: from Old French *pesle-mesle,* jingle based on *mesler* to MEDDLE]

pel·lu·cid (pɛ'lu:sɪd) *adj.* **1.** transparent or translucent. **2.** extremely clear in style and meaning; limpid. [C17: from Latin *pellūcidus,* variant of *perlūcidus,* from *perlūcēre* to shine through, from *per* through + *lūcēre* to shine] —**pel·'lu·cid·ly** *adv.* —**ˌpel·lu·'cid·i·ty** *or* **pel·'lu·cid·ness** *n.*

Pel·man·ism ('pɛlməˌnɪzəm) *n.* **1.** a system of training to improve the memory. **2.** (*often not cap.*) a memory card game in which a pack of cards is spread out face down and players try to turn up pairs with the same number. Also called: **pairs,** (esp. U.S.) **concentration.** [named after the *Pelman* Institute, founded in London in 1898]

pel·met ('pɛlmɪt) *n.* an ornamental drapery or board fixed above a window to conceal the curtain rail. [C19: probably from French *palmette* palm-leaf decoration on cornice moulding; see PALMETTE]

Pel·o·pon·nese (ˌpɛləpə'ni:s) *n.* the S peninsula of Greece, joined to central Greece by the Isthmus of Corinth: chief cities in ancient times were Sparta and Corinth, now Patras. Pop.: 986 912 (1971). Area: 21 439 sq. km (8361 sq. miles). Medieval name: **Morea.** Greek name: **Peloponnesos.** Also called: **Peloponnesus.** —**Pel·o·pon·ne·sian** (ˌpɛləpə'ni:ʃən) *adj.*

Pel·o·pon·ne·sian War *n.* a war fought for supremacy in Greece from 431 to 404 B.C., in which Athens and her allies were defeated by the league centred on Sparta.

Pe·lops ('pi:lɒps) *n. Greek myth.* the son of Tantalus, who as a child was killed by his father and served up as a meal for the gods.

pe·lo·ri·a (pɛ'lɔ:rɪə) *n.* the abnormal production of regular flowers in a plant of a species that usually produces irregular flowers. [C19: via New Latin from Greek *pelōros,* from *pelōr* monster] —**pe·lor·ic** (pɛ'lɔ:rɪk, -'lɒ-) *adj.*

pe·lo·rus (pɪ'lɔ:rəs) *n., pl.* **·rus·es.** a gyrocompass over which two sight vanes are mounted for measuring the relative bearings of observed points. [of uncertain origin, perhaps from Latin *Pelōrus* a dangerous Sicilian promontory, now called Cape Faro]

pe·lo·ta (pə'lɒtə)) *n.* any of various games played in Spain, Spanish America, SW France, etc., by two players who use a basket strapped to their wrists to propel a ball against a specially marked wall. [C19: from Spanish: ball, from Old French *pelote;* see PELLET]

Pe·lo·tas (*Portuguese* pe'lɔtas) *n.* a port in S Brazil, in Rio Grande do Sul on the Canal de São Gonçalo. Pop.: 150 278 (1970).

pelt[1] (pɛlt) *vb.* **1.** (*tr.*) to throw (missiles, etc.) at (a person, etc.). **2.** (*tr.*) to hurl (insults, etc.) at (a person, etc.). **3.** (*intr.;* foll. by *along,* etc.) to move rapidly; hurry. **4.** (*intr.;* often foll. by *down*) to rain heavily. ~*n.* **5.** a blow. **6.** speed (esp. in the phrase **at full pelt**). [C15: of uncertain origin, perhaps from PELLET] —**'pelt·er** *n.*

pelt[2] (pɛlt) *n.* **1.** the skin of a fur-bearing animal, such as a mink, esp. when it has been removed from the carcass. **2.** the hide of an animal, stripped of hair and ready for tanning. [C15: perhaps back formation from PELTRY]

pel·tast ('pɛltæst) *n.* (in ancient Greece) a lightly armed foot soldier. [C17: from Latin *peltasta,* from Greek *peltastēs* soldier equipped with a *pelta* small leather shield]

pel·tate ('pɛlteɪt) *adj.* (of leaves) having the stalk attached to the centre of the lower surface. [C18: from Latin *peltātus* equipped with a *pelta* small shield; see PELTAST] —**'pel·tate·ly** *adv.* —**pel·'ta·tion** *n.*

Pel·ti·er ef·fect ('pɛltɪˌeɪ) *n. Physics.* the production of heat at either junction of a thermocouple when a current is passed around the thermocouple circuit. The heat produced is additional to the heat arising from the resistance of the wires. Compare **Seebeck effect.** [C19: named after Jean *Peltier* (1785–1845), French physicist, who discovered it]

Pel·ti·er el·e·ment *n.* an electronic device consisting of metal strips between which alternate strips of n-type and p-type semiconductors are connected. Passage of a current causes heat to be absorbed from one set of metallic strips and emitted from the other by the Peltier effect.

pelt·ry ('pɛltrɪ) *n., pl.* **·ries.** the pelts of animals collectively. [C15: from Old French *peleterie* collection of pelts, from Latin *pilus* hair]

pel·vic ('pɛlvɪk) *adj.* of, near, or relating to the pelvis.

pel·vic fin *n.* either of a pair of fins attached to the pelvic girdle of fishes that help to control the direction of movement during locomotion.

pel·vic gir·dle *or* **arch** *n.* the skeletal structure supporting the lower limbs in man and the hind limbs or corresponding parts in other vertebrates.

pel·vis ('pɛlvɪs) *n., pl.* **·vis·es** *or* **·ves** (-vi:z). **1.** the large funnel-shaped structure at the lower end of the trunk of most vertebrates: in man it is formed by the hipbones and sacrum. **2.** the bones that form this structure. **3.** any anatomical cavity or structure shaped like a funnel or cup. **4.** short for **renal pelvis.** [C17: from Latin: basin, laver]

Pem·ba ('pɛmbə) *n.* an island in the Indian Ocean, off the E coast of Africa north of Zanzibar: part of Tanzania; produces most of the world's cloves. Chief town: Chake Chake. Pop.: 164 243 (1967). Area: 984 sq. km (380 sq. miles).

Pem·broke ('pɛmbrʊk) *n.* **1.** a town in SW Wales, on Milford Haven: 11th-century castle where Henry VII was born. Pop.: 14 092 (1971). **2.** the smaller variety of corgi, usually having a docked or short tail.

Pem·broke·shire ('pɛmbrʊkˌʃɪə, -ʃə) *n.* (until 1974) a county of SW Wales, now part of Dyfed.

Pem·broke ta·ble *n.* a small table with drop leaves and often one or more drawers. [perhaps named after Mary Herbert, Countess of *Pembroke* (1561–1621), who originally ordered its design]

pem·mi·can *or* **pem·i·can** ('pɛmɪkən) *n.* a small pressed cake of shredded dried meat, pounded into paste with fat and berries or dried fruits, used originally by American Indians and now chiefly for emergency rations. [C19: from Cree *pimikân,* from *pimii* fat, grease]

pem·phi·gus ('pɛmfɪgəs, pɛm'faɪ-) *n. Pathol.* any of a group of blistering skin diseases, esp. a potentially fatal form (**pemphigus vulgaris**) characterized by large blisters on the skin, mucous membranes of the mouth, genitals, intestines, etc., which eventually rupture and form painful denuded areas from which critical amounts of bodily protein, fluid, and blood may be lost. [C18: via New Latin from Greek *pemphix* bubble]

pen[1] (pɛn) *n.* **1.** an implement for writing or drawing using ink, formerly consisting of a sharpened and split quill, and now of a metal nib attached to a holder. See also **ballpoint, fountain pen. 2.** the writing end of such an implement; nib. **3.** style of writing. **4. the pen. a.** writing as an occupation. **b.** the written word: *the pen is mightier than the sword.* **5.** the long horny internal shell of a squid. ~*vb.* **pens, pen·ning, penned. 6.** (*tr.*) to write or compose. [Old English *pinne,* from Late Latin *penna* (quill) pen, from Latin: feather]

pen[2] (pɛn) *n.* **1.** an enclosure in which domestic animals are kept: *sheep pen.* **2.** any place of confinement. **3.** a dock for servicing submarines, esp. one having a bombproof roof. ~*vb.* **pens, pen·ning, penned** *or* **pent. 4.** (*tr.*) to enclose or keep in a pen. [Old English *penn,* perhaps related to PIN]

pen[3] (pɛn) *n. U.S. informal.* short for **penitentiary.**

pen[4] (pɛn) *n.* a female swan. [C16: of unknown origin]

Pen. *abbrev. for* Peninsula.
P.E.N. (pɛn) *abbrev. for* International Association of Poets, Playwrights, Editors, Essayists, and Novelists.
pe+nal ('pi:nᵊl) *adj.* **1.** of, relating to, constituting, or prescribing punishment. **2.** payable as a penalty: *a penal sum.* **3.** used or designated as a place of punishment: *a penal institution.* [C15: from Late Latin *poenālis* concerning punishment, from *poena* penalty] —**'pe+nal+ly** *adv.*
pe+nal code *n.* the codified body of the laws in any legal system that relate to crime and its punishment.
pe+nal+ize *or* **pe+nal+ise** ('pi:nə,laɪz) *vb.* (*tr.*) **1.** to impose a penalty on (someone), as for breaking a law or rule. **2.** to inflict a handicap or disadvantage on. **3.** *Sport.* to award a free stroke, point, or penalty against (a player or team). **4.** to declare (an act) legally punishable; make subject to a penalty. —**,pe+nal·i+'za+tion** *or* **,pe+nal·i+'sa+tion** *n.*
pe+nal ser+vi+tude *n. English criminal law.* (formerly) the imprisonment of an offender and his subjection to hard labour. It was substituted for transportation in 1853 and abolished in 1948. Compare **hard labour.**
pen+al+ty ('pɛnᵊltɪ) *n., pl.* **+ties. 1.** a legal or official punishment, such as a term of imprisonment. **2.** some other form of punishment, such as a fine or forfeit for not fulfilling a contract. **3.** loss, suffering, or other unfortunate result of one's own action, error, etc. **4.** *Sport, games, etc.* a handicap awarded against a player or team for illegal play, such as a free shot at goal by the opposing team, loss of points, etc. [C16: from Medieval Latin *poenālitās* penalty; see PENAL]
pen+al+ty ar·e·a *n. Soccer.* a rectangular area in front of the goal, within which the goalkeeper may handle the ball and within which a penalty is awarded for a foul by the attacking team.
pen+al+ty box *n.* **1.** *Soccer.* another name for **penalty area. 2.** *Ice hockey.* a bench for players serving time penalties.
pen+al+ty kill+er *n. Ice hockey.* a good player who, when his team is shorthanded because of a penalty, is sent onto the ice to prevent the other side from scoring.
pen+al+ty rates *pl. n. Austral.* rates of pay, such as double time, paid to employees working outside normal working hours.
pen+ance ('pɛnəns) *n.* **1.** voluntary self-punishment to atone for a sin, crime, etc. **2.** a feeling of regret for one's wrongdoings. **3.** *Christianity.* **a.** a punishment usually consisting of prayer, fasting, etc., undertaken voluntarily as an expression of penitence for sin. **b.** a punishment of this kind imposed by church authority as a condition of absolution. **4.** *R.C. Church.* a sacrament in which repentant sinners are absolved on condition of confession of their sins to a priest and of performing a penance. ~*vb.* **5.** (*tr.*) (of ecclesiastical authorities) to impose a penance upon (a sinner). [C13: via Old French from Latin *paenitentia* repentance; related to Latin *poena* penalty]
Pe+nang (pɪ'næŋ) *n.* **1.** a state of West Malaysia: consists of the island of Penang and the province Wellesley on the mainland, which first united administratively in 1798 as a British colony. Capital: George Town. Pop.: 773 327 (1970). Area: 1031 sq. km (398 sq. miles). **2.** a forested island off the NW coast of Malaya, in the Strait of Malacca. Area: 293 sq. km (113 sq. miles). Former name (until about 1867): **Prince of Wales Island. 3.** another name for **George Town.**
pe+na+tes (pə'nɑ:ti:z) *pl. n.* See **lares and penates.**
pence (pɛns) *n.* the plural of **penny.**
Usage. Since the decimalization of British currency and the introduction of the abbreviation **p,** as in *10p, 85p,* etc., the abbreviation has tended to replace *pence* in speech, as in *4p* (,fɔ:'pi:), *12p* (,twɛlv'pi:), etc.
pen+cel, pen+sel, *or* **pen+sil** ('pɛnsᵊl) *n.* a small pennon, originally one carried by a knight's squire. [C13: via Anglo-French from Old French *penoncel* a little PENNON]
pen+chant ('pɛntʃənt; *French* pɑ̃'ʃɑ̃) *n.* strong inclination or liking; bent or taste. [C17: from French, from *pencher* to incline, from Latin *pendēre* to be suspended]
Pen+chi *or* **Pen+ki** ('pɛn'tʃi:) *n.* an industrial city in NE China, in S Liaoning province. Pop.: 600 000 (1970 est.).
pen+cil ('pɛnsᵊl) *n.* **1. a.** a thin cylindrical instrument used for writing, drawing, etc., consisting of a central rod of graphite either encased in wood and sharpened or held in a mechanical metal device. **b.** (*as modifier*): *a pencil drawing.* **2.** something similar in shape or function: *a styptic pencil.* **3.** a narrow set of lines or rays, such as light rays, diverging from or converging to a point. **4.** *Rare.* an artist's individual style or technique in drawing. ~*vb.* **+cils, +cil+ling, +cilled** *or U.S.* **+cils, +cil+ing, +ciled.** (*tr.*) **5.** to draw, colour, or write with a pencil. **6.** to mark with a pencil. [C14: from Old French *pincel,* from Latin *pēnicillus* painter's brush, from *pēniculus* a little tail, from *pēnis* tail] —**'pen+cil+ler** *or U.S.* **'pen+cil+er** *n.*
pend (pɛnd) *vb.* (*intr.*) **1.** to await judgment or settlement. **2.** *Dialect.* to hang; depend. [C15: from Latin *pendēre* to hang; related to Latin *pendere* to suspend]
pen+dant ('pɛndənt) *n.* **1. a.** an ornament that hangs from a piece of jewellery. **b.** a necklace with such an ornament. **2.** a hanging light, esp. a chandelier. **3.** a carved ornament that is suspended from a ceiling or roof. **4.** something that matches or complements something else. **5.** Also called: **pennant.** *Nautical.* a length of wire or rope secured at one end to a mast or spar and having a block or other fitting at the lower end. ~*adj.* **6.** a variant spelling of **pendent.** [C14: from Old French, from *pendre* to hang, from Latin *pendēre* to hang down; related to Latin *pendere* to hang, *pondus* weight, Greek *span* to pull]
pen+dent ('pɛndənt) *adj.* **1.** dangling. **2.** jutting. **3.** (of a grammatical construction) incomplete: *a pendent nominative is a construction having no verb.* **4.** a less common word for **pending.** ~*n.* **5.** a variant spelling of **pendant.** [C15: from Old French *pendant,* from *pendre* to hang; see PENDANT] —**'pen+den+cy** *n.* —**'pen+dent+ly** *adv.*
pen+den+te li·te (pɛn'dɛntɪ 'laɪtɪ) *adj. Law.* while a suit is pending. [Latin, literally: with litigation pending]
pen+den+tive (pɛn'dɛntɪv) *n.* any of four triangular sections of vaulting with concave sides, positioned at a corner of a rectangular space to support a circular or polygonal dome. [C18: from French *pendentif,* from Latin *pendens* hanging, from *pendere* to hang]
Pen·de·rec·ki (*Polish* ,pɛndɛ'rɛtski) *n.* **Krzy·stof** ('kʃɪʃtɔf). born 1933, Polish composer, noted for his highly individual orchestration. His works include *Threnody for the Victims of Hiroshima* for strings (1960), *Stabat Mater* (1962), and the *Passion According to St. Luke* (1963–66).
pend+ing ('pɛndɪŋ) *prep.* **1.** while waiting for or anticipating. ~*adj.* (*postpositive*) **2.** not yet decided, confirmed, or finished: *what are the matters pending?* **3.** imminent: *these developments have been pending for some time.*
pen+drag·on (pɛn'drægən) *n.* a supreme war chief or leader of the ancient Britons. [Welsh, literally: head dragon] —**pen+'drag·on+,ship** *n.*
pen+du+lous ('pɛndjʊləs) *adj.* **1.** hanging downwards, esp. so as to swing from side to side. **2.** *Rare.* in a state of indecision; vacillating. [C17: from Latin *pendulus,* from *pendēre* to hang down] —**'pen+du+lous+ly** *adv.*
pen+du+lum ('pɛndjʊləm) *n.* **1.** a body mounted so that it can swing freely under the influence of gravity. It is either a bob hung on a light thread **(simple pendulum)** or a more complex structure **(compound pendulum). 2.** such a device used to regulate a clockwork mechanism. **3.** something that changes its position, attitude, etc. fairly regularly: *the pendulum of public opinion.* [C17: from Latin *pendulus* PENDULOUS]
pene- *or before a vowel* **pen-** *prefix.* almost: *peneplain.* [from Latin *paene*]
Pe·nel·o·pe (pə'nɛləpɪ) *n. Greek myth.* the wife of Odysseus, who remained true to him during his long absence despite the importunities of many suitors.
pe+ne·plain *or* **pe+ne·plane** ('pi:nɪ,pleɪn, ,pi:nɪ'pleɪn) *n.* a relatively flat land surface produced by a long period of erosion. [C19: from PENE- + PLAIN[1]] —**,pe+ne·pla+'na+tion** *n.*
pen+e·tra·li·a (,pɛnɪ'treɪlɪə) *pl. n.* **1.** the innermost parts. **2.** secret matters. [C17: from Latin, from *penetrālis* inner, from *penetrāre* to PENETRATE] —**,pen+e·'tra+li·an** *adj.*
pen+e·trance ('pɛnɪtrəns) *n. Genetics.* the percentage frequency with which a gene exhibits its effect.
pen+e·trant ('pɛnɪtrənt) *adj.* **1.** sharp; penetrating. ~*n.* **2.** *Chem.* a substance that lowers the surface tension of a liquid and thus causes it to penetrate or be absorbed more easily. **3.** a person or thing that penetrates.
pen+e·trate ('pɛnɪ,treɪt) *vb.* **1.** to find or force a way into or through (something); pierce; enter. **2.** to diffuse through (a substance, etc.); permeate. **3.** (*tr.*) to see through: *their eyes could not penetrate the fog.* **4.** (*tr.*) (of a man) to insert the penis into the vagina of (a woman). **5.** (*tr.*) to grasp the meaning of (a principle, etc.). **6.** (*intr.*) to be understood: *his face lit up as the new idea penetrated.* [C16: from Latin *penetrāre;* related to *penitus* inner, and *penus* the interior of a house] —**'pen+e·tra·ble** *adj.* —**,pen+e·tra·'bil+i·ty** *n.* —**'pen+e·tra·bly** *adv.* —**'pen+e·,tra+tor** *n.*
pen+e·trat+ing ('pɛnɪ,treɪtɪŋ) *adj.* tending to or able to penetrate: *a penetrating mind; a penetrating voice.* —**'pen+e·,trat+ing+ly** *adv.*
pen+e·tra+tion (,pɛnɪ'treɪʃən) *n.* **1.** the act or an instance of penetrating. **2.** the ability to penetrate. **3.** insight or perception. **4.** *Military.* an offensive manoeuvre that breaks through an enemy's defensive position. **5.** another name for **depth of field.**
Pe+ne+us (pɪ'ni:əs) *n.* the ancient name for the **Salambria.**
pen friend *n.* another name for **pen pal.**
P'eng+hu ('pɛŋ'hu:) *n.* transliteration of the Chinese name for the **Pescadores.**
pen+gö ('pɛŋgɜ:) *n., pl.* **+gös.** (formerly) the standard monetary unit of Hungary, replaced by the forint in 1946. [from Hungarian, from *pengeni* to sound]
Peng+pu ('pɛŋ'pu:) *or* **Pang-fou** *n.* a city in E China, in Anhwei province. Pop.: 253 000 (1953).
pen+guin ('pɛŋgwɪn) *n.* **1.** any flightless marine bird, such as *Aptenodytes patagonica* (king penguin) and *Pygoscelis adeliae* (**Adélie penguin**), of the order *Sphenisciformes* of cool southern, esp. Antarctic, regions: they have wings modified as flippers, webbed feet, and feathers lacking barbs. See also **emperor penguin. 2.** an obsolete name for **great auk.** [C16: perhaps from Welsh *pen gwyn,* from *pen* head + *gwyn* white]
pen·i·cil+late (,pɛnɪ'sɪlɪt, -eɪt) *adj. Biology.* having or resembling one or more tufts of fine hairs: *a penicillate caterpillar.* [C19: from Latin *pēnicillus* brush, PENCIL] —**,pen·i·'cil+late+ly** *adv.* —**,pen·i·cil+'la+tion** *n.*
pen·i·cil+lin (,pɛnɪ'sɪlɪn) *n.* an antibiotic with powerful bacteriostatic action, used to treat pneumonia, gonorrhoea, and infections caused by streptococci and staphylococci: obtained from the fungus *Penicillium,* esp. *P. notatum.* Formula: R-$C_9H_{11}N_2O_4S$ where R is one of several side chains. [C20: from PENICILLIUM]
pen·i·cil+li·um (,pɛnɪ'sɪlɪəm) *n., pl.* **+cil+li·ums** *or* **+cil+li·a** (-'sɪlɪə). any ascomycetous saprophytic fungus of the genus *Penicillium,* which commonly grow as a green or blue mould on stale food: some species are used in cheesemaking and others

as a source of penicillin. [C19: New Latin, from Latin *pēnicillus* tuft of hairs; named from the tufted appearance of the sporangia of this fungus]

pe·nile ('pi:naɪl) *adj.* of or relating to the penis.

pe·nil·li·on *or* **pen·nil·li·on** (pɪ'nɪlɪən) *pl. n., sing.* **pe·nill** (pɪ'nɪl). the Welsh art or practice of singing poetry in counterpoint to a traditional melody played on the harp. [from Welsh: verses, plural of *penill* verse, stanza]

pen·in·su·la (pɪ'nɪnsjʊlə) *n.* a narrow strip of land projecting into a sea or lake from the mainland. [C16: from Latin, literally: almost an island, from *paene* PENE- + *insula* island] —**pen·'in·su·lar** *adj.*

Pen·in·su·la *n.* **the.** short for the **Iberian Peninsula.**

Pen·in·su·lar War *n.* the war (1808–14) fought in the Iberian Peninsula by British, Portuguese, and Spanish forces against the French: part of the Napoleonic Wars.

pen·in·su·late (pɪ'nɪnsjʊˌleɪt) *vb.* (*tr.*) to cause (land) to become peninsular.

pe·nis ('pi:nɪs) *n., pl.* **·nis·es** *or* **·nes** (-ni:z). the male organ of copulation in higher vertebrates, also used for urine excretion in many mammals. [C17: from Latin: penis]

pe·nis en·vy *n. Psychoanal.* a Freudian concept in which envy of the penis is postulated as the cause for some of the characteristics of femininity.

pen·i·tent ('pɛnɪtənt) *adj.* **1.** feeling regret for one's sins; repentant. ~*n.* **2.** a person who is penitent. **3.** *Christianity.* **a.** a person who repents his sins and seeks forgiveness for them. **b.** *R.C. Church.* a person who confesses his sins to a priest and submits to a penance imposed by him. [C14: from Church Latin *paenitēns* regretting, from *paenitēre* to repent, of obscure origin] —**'pen·i·tence** *n.* —**'pen·i·tent·ly** *adv.*

pen·i·ten·tial (ˌpɛnɪ'tɛnʃəl) *adj.* **1.** of, showing, or constituting penance. ~*n.* **2.** *Chiefly R.C. Church.* a book or compilation of instructions for confessors. **3.** a less common word for **penitent** (senses 2, 3). —ˌ**pen·i·'ten·tial·ly** *adv.*

pen·i·ten·tia·ry (ˌpɛnɪ'tɛnʃərɪ) *n., pl.* **·ries.** **1.** (in the U.S.) a state prison. **2.** *R.C. Church.* **a.** a cleric appointed to supervise the administration of the sacrament of penance in a particular area. **b.** a priest who has special faculties to absolve particularly grave sins. **c.** a cardinal who presides over a tribunal that decides all matters affecting the sacrament of penance. **d.** this tribunal itself. ~*adj.* **3.** another word for **penitential.** **4.** (of an offence) punishable by imprisonment in a penitentiary. [C15 (meaning also: an officer dealing with penances): from Medieval Latin *poenitentiārius,* from Latin *paenitēns* PENITENT]

Pen·ki ('pɛn'tʃi:) *n.* a variant spelling of **Penchi.**

pen·knife ('pɛnˌnaɪf) *n., pl.* **·knives.** a small knife with one or more blades that fold into the handle; pocketknife.

pen·man ('pɛnmən) *n., pl.* **·men.** **1.** a person skilled in handwriting. **2.** a person who writes by hand in a specified way: *a bad penman.* **3.** an author. **4.** *Rare.* a scribe.

pen·man·ship ('pɛnmənˌʃɪp) *n.* style or technique of writing by hand. Also called: **calligraphy.**

Penn (pɛn) *n.* **1.** **Wil·liam.** 1644–1718, English Quaker and founder of Pennsylvania. **2.** **Ar·thur.** born 1922, U.S. film director: films include *Bonnie and Clyde* (1967), *Alice's Restaurant* (1969), *Little Big Man* (1970), *The Missouri Breaks* (1976); and *Night Moves* (1978).

Penn. *abbrev. for* Pennsylvania.

pen·na ('pɛnə) *n., pl.* **·nae** (-ni:). *Ornithol.* any large feather that has a vane and forms part of the main plumage of a bird. [Latin: feather] —**pen·na·ceous** (pɛ'neɪʃəs) *adj.*

pen name *n.* an author's pseudonym. Also called: **nom de plume.**

pen·nant ('pɛnənt) *n.* **1.** a type of pennon, esp. one flown from vessels as identification or for signalling. **2.** *Chiefly U.S. and Austral.* **a.** a flag serving as an emblem of championship in certain sports. **b.** (*as modifier*): *pennant cricket.* **3.** *Nautical.* another word for **pendant** (sense 5). [C17: probably a blend of PENDANT and PENNON]

pen·nate ('pɛneɪt) *or* **pen·nat·ed** *adj. Biology.* **1.** having feathers, wings, or winglike structures. **2.** another word for **pinnate.** [C19: from Latin *pennātus,* from *penna* wing]

pen·ni ('pɛnɪ) *n., pl.* **·ni·a** (-nɪə) *or* **·nis.** a Finnish monetary unit worth one hundredth of a markka. [Finnish, from Low German *pennig* PENNY]

pen·ni·less ('pɛnɪlɪs) *adj.* very poor; almost totally without money. —**'pen·ni·less·ly** *adv.* —**'pen·ni·less·ness** *n.*

Pen·nine Alps ('pɛnaɪn) *pl. n.* a range of the Alps between Switzerland and Italy. Highest peak: Monte Rosa, 4634 m (15 204 ft.).

Pen·nines ('pɛnaɪnz) *pl. n.* a system of hills in England, extending from the Cheviot Hills in the north to the River Trent in the south: forms the watershed for the main rivers of N England. Highest peak: Cross Fell, 893 m (2930 ft.). Also called: (the) **Pennine Chain.**

Pen·nine Way *n.* a footpath extending from Edale, Derbyshire, for 402 km (250 miles) to Kirk Yetholm, Roxburghshire.

pen·ni·nite ('pɛnɪˌnaɪt) *n.* a bluish-green variety of chlorite occurring in the form of thick crystals. [C20: from German *Pennin* Pennine (Alps) + ITE[1]]

pen·non ('pɛnən) *n.* **1.** a long flag, often tapering and rounded, divided, or pointed at the end, originally a knight's personal flag. **2.** a small tapering or triangular flag borne on a ship or boat. **3.** a poetic word for **wing.** [C14: via Old French ultimately from Latin *penna* feather]

pen·non·cel *or* **pen·on·cel** ('pɛnənˌsɛl) *n.* another word for **pencel.** [C14: from Old French *penoncel* a little PENNON]

Penn·syl·va·ni·a (ˌpɛnsɪl'veɪnɪə) *n.* a state of the northeastern U.S.: almost wholly in the Appalachians, with the Allegheny Plateau to the west and a plain in the southeast; the second most important U.S. state for manufacturing. Capital: Harrisburg. Pop.: 11 793 909 (1970). Area: 116 462 sq. km (44 966 sq. miles). Abbrevs.: **Pa., Penn., Penna.,** or (with zip code) **PA**

Penn·syl·va·ni·a Dutch *n.* **1.** Also called: **Pennsylvania German.** a dialect of German spoken in E Pennsylvania. **2.** (preceded by *the; functioning as pl.*) a group of German-speaking people in E Pennsylvania, descended from 18th-century settlers from SW Germany and Switzerland.

Penn·syl·va·ni·an (ˌpɛnsɪl'veɪnɪən) *adj.* **1.** of the state of Pennsylvania. **2.** (in North America) of, denoting, or formed in the upper of two divisions of the Carboniferous period (see also **Mississippian** (sense 2)), which lasted 30 million years, during which coal measures were formed. ~*n.* **3.** an inhabitant or native of the state of Pennsylvania. **4.** (preceded by *the*) the Pennsylvanian period or rock system, equivalent to the Upper Carboniferous of Europe.

pen·ny ('pɛnɪ) *n., pl.* **pen·nies** *or* **pence** (pɛns). **1.** Also called: **new penny.** *Brit.* a bronze coin having a value equal to one hundredth of a pound. Abbrev.: **p.** **2.** *Brit.* (before 1971) a bronze or copper coin having a value equal to one twelfth of a shilling or one two-hundred-and-fortieth of a pound. Symbol: **d.** **3.** (*pl.* **pen·nies**) *U.S.* a cent. **4.** a coin of similar value, as used in several other countries. **5.** (*used with negative*)*Informal, chiefly Brit.* the least amount of money: *I don't have a penny.* **6.** **a bad penny.** *Informal, chiefly Brit.* an objectionable person or thing. **7.** **a pretty penny.** *Informal.* a considerable sum of money. **8.** **spend a penny.** *Brit. informal.* to urinate. **9.** **the penny dropped.** *Informal, chiefly Brit.* the explanation of something was finally realized. [Old English *penig, pening;* related to Old Saxon *penni(n)g,* Old High German *pfeni(n)c,* German *Pfennig*]

pen·ny-a-lin·er *n. Now rare.* a hack writer or journalist.

pen·ny ar·cade *n.* a public place with various coin-operated machines for entertainment.

Pen·ny Black *n.* the first adhesive postage stamp, issued in Britain in 1840; an imperforate stamp bearing the profile of Queen Victoria on a dark background.

pen·ny·cress ('pɛnɪˌkrɛs) *n.* any of several cruciferous plants of the genus *Thlaspi* of temperate Eurasia and North America, typically having small white or mauve flowers and rounded or heart-shaped leaves.

pen·ny-dread·ful *n., pl.* **·fuls.** *Brit. informal.* a cheap, often lurid or sensational book or magazine.

pen·ny-far·thing *n. Brit.* an early type of bicycle with a large front wheel and a small rear wheel, the pedals being attached to the front wheel. U.S. name: **ordinary.**

pen·ny-pinch·er *n. Informal.* a person who is excessively careful with money. —**'pen·ny-ˌpinch·ing** *n., adj.*

pen·ny·roy·al (ˌpɛnɪ'rɔɪəl) *n.* **1.** a Eurasian plant, *Mentha pulegium,* with hairy leaves, small mauve flowers, and yielding an aromatic oil used in medicine: family *Labiatae* (labiates). **2.** Also called: **mock pennyroyal.** a similar and related plant, *Hedeoma pulegioides,* of E North America. [C16: variant of Anglo-Norman *puliol real,* from Old French *pouliol* (from Latin *pūleium* pennyroyal) + *real* ROYAL]

pen·ny·weight ('pɛnɪˌweɪt) *n.* a unit of weight equal to 24 grains or one twentieth of an ounce (Troy).

pen·ny whis·tle *n.* a type of flageolet with six finger holes, esp. a cheap one made of metal. Also called: **tin whistle.**

pen·ny-wise *adj.* **1.** greatly concerned with saving small sums of money. **2.** **penny-wise and pound-foolish.** careful about trifles but wasteful in large ventures.

pen·ny·wort ('pɛnɪˌwɜ:t) *n.* **1.** Also called: **navelwort.** a crassulaceous Eurasian rock plant, *Umbilicus rupestris* (or *Cotyledon umbilicus*), with whitish-green tubular flowers and rounded leaves. **2.** a marsh plant, *Hydrocotyle vulgaris,* of Europe and North Africa, having circular leaves and greenish-pink flowers: family *Hydrocotylaceae.* **3.** a gentianaceous plant, *Obolaria virginica,* of E North America, with fleshy scalelike leaves and small white or purplish flowers. **4.** any of various other plants with rounded penny-like leaves.

pen·ny·worth ('pɛnɪˌwɜ:θ) *n.* **1.** the amount that can be bought for a penny. **2.** a small amount: *he hasn't got a pennyworth of sense.*

pe·nol·o·gy *or* **poe·nol·o·gy** (pi:'nɒlədʒɪ) *n.* **1.** the branch of the social sciences concerned with the punishment of crime. **2.** the science of prison management. [C19: from Greek *poinē* punishment] —**pe·no·log·i·cal** *or* **poe·no·log·i·cal** (ˌpi:nɪ'lɒdʒɪkᵊl) *adj.* —ˌ**pe·no·'log·i·cal·ly** *or* ˌ**poe·no·'log·i·cal·ly** *adv.* —**pe·'nol·o·gist** *or* **poe·'nol·o·gist** *n.*

pen pal *n.* a person with whom one regularly exchanges letters, often a person in another country whom one has not met. Also called: **pen friend.**

pen·push·er *n.* a person who writes a lot, esp. a clerk involved with boring paperwork. —**'pen·ˌpush·ing** *adj., n.*

Pen·rith (pɛn'rɪθ) *n.* a market town in NW England, in Cumbria. Pop.: 11 299 (1971).

pen·sile ('pɛnsaɪl) *adj. Ornithol.* designating or building a hanging nest: *pensile birds.* [C17: from Latin *pensilis* hanging down, from *pendēre* to hang] —**pen·sil·i·ty** (pɛn'sɪlɪtɪ) *or* **'pen·sile·ness** *n.*

pen·sion[1] ('pɛnʃən) *n.* **1.** a regular payment made by the state to people over a certain age to enable them to subsist without having to work. **2.** a regular payment made by an employer to former employees after they retire. **3.** any regular payment made on charitable grounds, by way of patronage, or in recognition of merit, service, etc.: *a pension paid to a disabled soldier.* ~*vb.* **4.** (*tr.*) to grant a pension to. [C14: via Old

French from Latin *pēnsiō* a payment, from *pendere* to pay] —**'pen+sion+a·ble** *adj.* —**'pen+sion+less** *adj.*

pen+sion² *French.* (pɑ̃'sjɔ̃) *n.* (in France and some other countries) **1.** a relatively cheap boarding house. **2.** another name for **full board.** [C17: from French; extended meaning of French *pension* grant; see PENSION¹]

pen+sion+ar·y ('pɛnʃənərɪ) *adj.* **1.** constituting a pension. **2.** maintained by or receiving a pension. **3.** *Archaic.* bought with money. ~*n., pl.* **+ar·ies. 4.** a rare word for **pensioner. 5.** a person whose service can be bought.

pen+sion+er ('pɛnʃənə) *n.* **1.** a person who is receiving a pension, esp. an old-age pension from the state. **2.** a person dependent on the pay or bounty of another. **3.** *Obsolete, Brit.* another name for **gentleman-at-arms.**

pen+sion off *vb. (tr., adv.)* **1.** to cause to retire from a job, etc., and pay a pension to. **2.** to discard, because old and worn: *to pension off submarines.*

pen+sive ('pɛnsɪv) *adj.* **1.** deeply or seriously thoughtful, often with a tinge of sadness. **2.** expressing or suggesting pensiveness. [C14: from Old French *pensif,* from *penser* to think, from Latin *pensāre* to consider; compare PENSION¹] —**'pen+sive+ly** *adv.* —**'pen+sive+ness** *n.*

pen+ste+mon (pɛn'stiːmən) *n.* a variant spelling (esp. U.S.) of **pentstemon.**

pen+stock ('pɛn,stɒk) *n.* **1.** a conduit that supplies water to a hydroelectric power plant. **2.** a channel bringing water from the head gates to a water wheel. **3.** a sluice for controlling water flow. [C17: from PEN² + STOCK]

pent (pɛnt) *vb.* a past tense of **pen².**

pen+ta- *combining form.* five: *pentagon; pentameter; pentaprism.* [from Greek *pente*]

pen+ta+chlo+ro+phe+nol (,pɛntə,klɔːrə'fiːnɒl) *n.* a white crystalline water-insoluble compound used as a fungicide, herbicide, and preservative for wood. Formula: C_6Cl_5OH.

pen+ta+cle ('pɛntəkᵊl) *n.* **1.** Also called: **pentagram, pentangle.** a star-shaped figure formed by extending the sides of a regular pentagon to meet at five points. **2.** such a figure used as a magical or symbolic figure by the Pythagoreans, black magicians, etc. [C16: from Italian *pentacolo* something having five corners; see PENTA-]

pen+tad ('pɛntæd) *n.* **1.** a group or series of five. **2.** the number or sum of five. **3.** a period of five years. **4.** *Chem.* a pentavalent element, atom, or radical. [C17: from Greek *pentas* group of five]

pen+ta+dac+tyl (,pɛntə'dæktɪl) *adj.* (of the limbs of amphibians, reptiles, birds, and mammals) consisting of an upper arm or thigh, a forearm or shank, and a hand or foot bearing five digits.

pen+ta+gon ('pɛntə,gɒn) *n.* a polygon having five sides. —**pen+tag·o·nal** (pɛn'tægənᵊl) *adj.*

Pen+ta+gon ('pɛntə,gɒn) *n.* **1.** the five-sided building in Arlington, Virginia, that houses the headquarters of the U.S. armed forces. **2.** the military leadership of the U.S.

pen+ta+he+dron (,pɛntə'hiːdrən) *n., pl.* **+drons** *or* **+dra** (-drə). a solid figure having five plane faces. See also **polyhedron.** —**,pen+ta+'he+dral** *adj.*

pen+tam+er+ous (pɛn'tæmərəs) *adj.* consisting of five parts, esp. (of flowers) having the petals, sepals, and other parts arranged in groups of five. —**pen+'tam+er+ism** *n.*

pen+tam+e·ter (pɛn'tæmɪtə) *n.* **1.** a verse line consisting of five metrical feet. **2.** (in classical prosody) a verse line consisting of two dactyls, one stressed syllable, two dactyls, and a final stressed syllable. ~*adj.* **3.** designating a verse line consisting of five metrical feet.

pen+tane ('pɛnteɪn) *n.* an alkane hydrocarbon having three isomers, esp. the isomer with a straight chain of carbon atoms (*n*-pentane) which is a colourless flammable liquid used as a solvent. Formula: C_5H_{12} (*n*-).

pen+tan+gu+lar (pɛn'tæŋgjʊlə) *adj.* having five angles.

pen+ta+no+ic ac+id (,pɛntə'nəʊɪk) *n.* a colourless liquid carboxylic acid with an unpleasant odour, used in making perfumes, flavourings, and pharmaceuticals. Formula: $CH_3(CH_2)_3COOH$. Also called: **valeric acid.** [from PENTANE + -OIC]

pen+ta+prism ('pɛntə,prɪzəm) *n.* a five-sided prism that deviates light from any direction through an angle of 90°.

pen+ta+quine ('pɛntə,kwiːn, -kwɪn) *n.* a synthetic drug used to treat malaria. Formula: $C_{18}H_{27}N_3O$. [C20: from PENTA- + QUINOLINE]

pen+tar+chy ('pɛntɑːkɪ) *n., pl.* **+chies. 1.** government by five rulers. **2.** a ruling body of five. **3.** a union or association of five kingdoms, provinces, etc., each under its own ruler. **4.** a country ruled by a body of five. —**pen+'tar+chi+cal** *adj.*

pen+ta+stich ('pɛntə,stɪk) *n.* a poem, stanza, or strophe that consists of five lines.

Pen+ta+teuch ('pɛntə,tjuːk) *n.* the first five books of the Old Testament regarded as a unity. [C16: from Church Latin *pentateuchus,* from Greek PENTA- + *teukhos* tool (in Late Greek: scroll)] —**'Pen+ta+,teuch+al** *adj.*

pen+tath+lon (pɛn'tæθlən) *n.* an athletic contest consisting of five different events, based on a competition in the ancient Greek Olympics. Compare **decathlon.** [C18: from Greek *pentathlon,* from PENTA- + *athlon* contest]

pen+ta+tom+ic (,pɛntə'tɒmɪk) *adj. Chem.* having five atoms in the molecule.

pen+ta+ton+ic scale (,pɛntə'tɒnɪk) *n. Music.* any of several scales consisting of five notes, the most commonly encountered one being composed of the first, second, third, fifth, and sixth degrees of the major diatonic scale.

pen+ta+va+lent (,pɛntə'veɪlənt) *adj. Chem.* having a valency of five. Also: **quinquevalent.**

Pen+te·cost ('pɛntɪ,kɒst) *n.* **1.** a Christian festival occurring on Whit Sunday commemorating the descent of the Holy Ghost on the apostles. **2.** another name for **Feast of Weeks. 3.** *Judaism.* **a.** the Jewish harvest festival of Weeks occurring on the fiftieth day after the second day of Passover. **b.** another name for **Shabuoth.** [Old English, from Church Latin *pentēcostē,* from Greek *pentēkostē* fiftieth (day after the Resurrection)]

Pen+te·cos+tal (,pɛntɪ'kɒstᵊl) *adj.* **1.** (*usually prenominal*) of or relating to any of various Christian groups that emphasize the charismatic aspects of Christianity and adopt a fundamental attitude to the Bible. **2.** of or relating to Pentecost or the influence of the Holy Ghost. ~*n.* **3.** a member of a Pentecostal Church. —**,Pen+te·'cos+tal+ism** *n.* —**,Pen+te·'cos+tal+ist** *n., adj.*

Pen+tel+i+kon (pɛn'tɛlɪkɒn) *n.* a mountain in SE Greece, near Athens: famous for its white marble, worked regularly from the 6th century B.C., from which the chief buildings and sculptures in Athens are made. Height: 1109 m (3638 ft.). Latin name: **Pentelicus.**

pen+tene ('pɛntiːn) *n.* a colourless flammable liquid alkene having several straight-chained isomeric forms, used in the manufacture of organic compounds. Formula: C_5H_{10}. Also called: **amylene.**

Pen·the·si·le·ia *or* **Pen·the·si·le·a** (,pɛnθəsɪ'leɪə) *n. Greek myth.* the daughter of Ares and queen of the Amazons, who she led to the aid of Troy. She was slain by Achilles.

Pen·the·us ('pɛnθɪəs) *n. Greek myth.* the grandson of Cadmus and his successor as king of Thebes, who resisted the introduction of the cult of Dionysus. In revenge the god drove him mad and he was torn to pieces by a group of Bacchantes, one of whom was his mother.

pent+house ('pɛnt,haʊs) *n.* **1.** a flat or maisonette built onto the top floor or roof of a block of flats. **2.** a construction on the roof of a building, esp. one used to house machinery, etc. **3.** a shed built against a building, esp. one that has a sloping roof. **4.** *Real tennis.* the roofed corridor that runs along three sides of the court. [C14 *pentis* (later *penthouse,* by folk etymology), from Old French *apentis,* from Late Latin *appendicium* appendage, from Latin *appendere* to hang from; see APPENDIX]

pen+ti+men+to (,pɛntɪ'mɛntəʊ) *n., pl.* **+ti** (-tiː). **1.** the revealing of a painting or part of a painting that has been covered over by a later painting. **2.** the part of a painting thus revealed. [C20: Italian, literally: correction]

Pent+land Firth ('pɛntlənd) *n.* a channel between the mainland of N Scotland and the Orkney Islands: notorious for rough seas. Length: 32 km (20 miles). Width: up to 13 km (8 miles).

pent+land+ite ('pɛntlən,daɪt) *n.* a brownish-yellow mineral consisting of an iron and nickel sulphide in cubic crystalline form: the principal ore of nickel. Formula: (Fe,Ni)S. [C19: from French; after J. B. *Pentland* (died 1873)]

pen+to+bar+bi+tone so+di·um (,pɛntə'bɑːbɪ,təʊn) *n.* a barbiturate drug used in medicine as a sedative and hypnotic. U.S. name **sodium pentabarbital.** Formula: $C_{11}H_{17}N_2O_3Na$.

pen+tode ('pɛntəʊd) *n.* **1.** an electronic valve having five electrodes: a cathode, anode, and three grids. **2.** (*modifier*) (of a transistor) having three terminals at the base or gate. [C20: from PENTA- + Greek *odos* way]

pen+tom+ic (pɛn'tɒmɪk) *adj.* denoting or relating to the subdivision of an army division into five battle groups, esp. for nuclear warfare. [C20: from PENTA- + ATOMIC]

pen+to+san ('pɛntə,sæn) *n. Biochem.* any of a group of polysaccharides, having the general formula $(C_5H_8O_4)_n$: occur in plants, humus, etc. [C20: from PENTOSE + -AN]

pen+tose ('pɛntəʊs) *n.* any monosaccharide containing five atoms of carbon per molecule: occur mainly in plants and the nucleic acids. [C20: from PENTA- + -OSE²]

Pen+to+thal so+di·um ('pɛntə,θæl) *n.* a trademark for **thiopentone sodium.**

pent+ox+ide (pɛnt'ɒksaɪd) *n.* an oxide of an element with five atoms of oxygen per molecule.

pent+ste+mon (pɛnt'stiːmən) *or* **pen+ste+mon** *n.* any scrophulariaceous plant of the North American genus *Pentstemon* (or *Penstemon*), having white, pink, red, blue, or purple flowers with five stamens, one of which is bearded and sterile. [C18: New Latin, from PENTA- + Greek *stēmōn* thread (here: stamen)]

pent-up *adj.* not released; repressed: *pent-up emotions.*

pen+tyl ('pɛntaɪl, -tɪl) *n.* (*modifier*) of, consisting of, or containing the monovalent group $CH_3CH_2CH_2CH_2CH_2$-: *a pentyl group or radical.*

pen+tyl ac+e+tate *n.* a colourless combustible liquid used as a solvent for paints, in the extraction of penicillin, in photographic film, and as a flavouring. Formula: $CH_3COOC_5H_{11}$. Also called: **amyl acetate.** Nontechnical name: **banana oil.**

pen·tyl·ene·tet·ra·zol (,pɛntɪliːn'tɛtrə,zɒl) *n.* a white crystalline water-soluble substance with a bitter taste, used in medicine to stimulate the central nervous system. Formula: $C_6H_{10}N_4$. [C20: from *penta-methylene-tetrazole*]

pe+nu+che (pə'nuːtʃɪ) *n.* a variant spelling of **panocha.**

pe+nuch+le *or* **pe+nuck+le** ('piːnʌkᵊl) *n.* less common spellings of **pinochle.**

pen+ult ('pɛnʌlt, pɪ'nʌlt) *or* **pe+nul+ti+ma** (pɪ'nʌltɪmə) *n.* the last syllable but one in a word. [C16: Latin *paenultima syllaba,* from *paene ultima* almost the last]

pe+nul+ti+mate (pɪ'nʌltɪmɪt) *adj.* **1.** next to the last. ~*n.* **2.** anything that is next to the last, esp. a penult.

pe+num+bra (pɪ'nʌmbrə) *n., pl.* **+brae** (-briː) *or* **+bras. 1.** a fringe region of half shadow resulting from the partial obstruction of light by an opaque object. **2.** *Astronomy.* the lighter and outer region of a sunspot. **3.** *Painting.* the point or area in which light and shade blend. ~Compare **umbra.** [C17: via New Latin from Latin *paene* almost + *umbra* shadow] —**pe+'num+bral** *or* **pe+'num+brous** *adj.*

pe+nu+ri+ous (pɪ'njʊərɪəs) *adj.* **1.** niggardly with money. **2.** lacking money or means. **3.** yielding little; scanty. —**pe+'nu+ri+ous+ly** *adv.* —**pe+'nu+ri+ous+ness** *n.*

pen·u+ry ('pɛnjʊrɪ) *n.* **1.** extreme poverty. **2.** extreme scarcity. [C15: from Latin *pēnūria* dearth, of obscure origin]

Pe+nu+ti·an (pɪ'njuːtɪən, -ʃən) *n.* a family or stock of North American Indian languages of the Pacific coast, related to Chinookan.

Pen+za (*Russian* 'pjɛnzə) *n.* a city in the W Soviet Union: manufacturing centre. Pop.: 426 000 (1975 est.).

Pen+zance (pɛn'zæns) *n.* a town in SW England, in SW Cornwall: the westernmost town in England; resort and fishing port. Pop.: 19 352 (1971).

pe·on[1] ('piːən, 'piːɒn) *n.* **1.** a Spanish-American farm labourer or unskilled worker. **2.** (formerly in Spanish America) a debtor compelled to work off his debts. **3.** any very poor person. [C19: from Spanish *peón* peasant, from Medieval Latin *pedō* man who goes on foot, from Latin *pēs* foot; compare Old French *paon* PAWN[2]]

peon[2] (pjuːn, 'piːən, 'piːɒn) *n.* (in India, Ceylon, etc., esp. formerly) **1.** a messenger or attendant, esp. in an office. **2.** a native policeman. **3.** a foot soldier. [C17: from Portuguese *peão* orderly; see PEON[1]]

pe+on+age ('piːənɪdʒ) *or* **pe+on+ism** ('piːəˌnɪzəm) *n.* **1.** the state of being a peon. **2.** a system in which a debtor must work for his creditor until the debt is paid off.

pe·o+ny ('piːənɪ) *n., pl.* **+nies. 1.** any of various ranunculaceous shrubs and plants of the genus *Paeonia,* of Eurasia and North America, having large pink, red, white, or yellow flowers. **2.** the flower of any of these plants. [Old English *peonie,* from Latin *paeōnia,* from Greek *paiōnia;* related to *paiōnios* healing, from *paiōn* physician]

peo+ple ('piːpᵊl) *n.* (*usually functioning as pl.*) **1.** persons collectively or in general. **2.** a group of persons considered together: *blind people.* **3.** (*pl.* **peo+ples**) the persons living in a country and sharing the same nationality: *the French people.* **4.** one's family: *he took her home to meet his people.* **5.** persons loyal to someone powerful: *the king's people accompanied him in exile.* **6. the people. a.** the mass of persons without special distinction, privileges, etc. **b.** the body of persons in a country, etc., esp. those entitled to vote. ~*vb.* **7.** (*tr.*) to provide with or as if with people or inhabitants. [C13: from Old French *pople,* from Latin *populus;* see POPULACE]
Usage. See at **person.**

peo+ple's de+moc+ra+cy *n.* (in Communist ideology) a country or form of government in transition from bourgeois democracy to socialism. In this stage there is more than one class, the largest being the proletariat, led by the Communist Party, which is therefore the dominant power.

peo+ple's front *n.* a less common term for **popular front.**

Peo+ple's Par+ty *n. U.S. history.* the political party of the Populists.

Pe·o+ri·a (piː'ɔːrɪə) *n.* a port in N central Illinois, on the Illinois River. Pop.: 127 898 (1973 est.).

pep (pɛp) *n.* **1.** high spirits, energy, or vitality. ~*vb.* **peps, pep+ping, pepped. 2.** (*tr.;* usually foll. by *up*) to liven by imbuing with new vigour. [C20: short for PEPPER]

P.E.P. *abbrev. for* political and economic planning.

Pep·in the Short ('pɛpɪn) *n.* died 768 A.D., king of the Franks (751–768); son of Charles Martel and father of Charlemagne. He deposed the Merovingian king (751) and founded the Carolingian dynasty.

pep+los *or* **pep+lus** ('pɛpləs) *n., pl.* **+los·es** *or* **+lus·es.** (in ancient Greece) the top part of a woman's attire, caught at the shoulders and hanging in folds to the waist. Also called: **peplum.** [C18: from Greek, of obscure origin]

pep+lum ('pɛpləm) *n., pl.* **+lums** *or* **+la** (-lə). **1.** a flared ruffle attached to the waist of a jacket, bodice, etc. **2.** a variant of **peplos.** [C17: from Latin: full upper garment, from Greek *peplos* shawl]

pe·po ('piːpəʊ) *n., pl.* **+pos.** the fruit of any of various cucurbitaceous plants, such as the melon, squash, cucumber, and pumpkin, having a firm rind, fleshy watery pulp, and numerous seeds. [C19: from Latin: pumpkin, from Greek *pepōn* edible gourd, from *peptein* to ripen]

pep+per ('pɛpə) *n.* **1.** a woody climbing plant, *Piper nigrum,* of the East Indies, having small black berry-like fruits: family *Piperaceae.* **2.** the dried fruit of this plant, which is ground to produce a sharp hot condiment. See also **black pepper, white pepper. 3.** any of various other plants of the genus *Piper.* See **cubeb, betel, kava. 4.** Also called: **capsicum.** any of various tropical plants of the solanaceous genus *Capsicum,* esp. *C. frutescens,* the fruits of which are used as a vegetable and a condiment. See also **bird pepper, sweet pepper, red pepper, cayenne pepper. 5.** the fruit of any of these capsicums, which has a mild or pungent taste. **6.** the condiment made from the fruits of any of these plants. **7.** any of various similar but unrelated plants, such as water pepper. ~*vb.* (*tr.*) **8.** to season with pepper. **9.** to sprinkle liberally; dot: *his prose was peppered with alliteration.* **10.** to pelt with small missiles. [Old English, *piper,* from Latin, from Greek *peperi;* compare French *poivre,* Old Norse *piparr*]

pep·per-and-salt *adj.* **1.** (of cloth, etc.) marked with a fine mixture of black and white. **2.** (of hair) streaked with grey.

pep·per+corn ('pɛpəˌkɔːn) *n.* **1.** the small dried berry of the pepper plant (*Piper nigrum*). **2.** something trifling.

pep·per+corn rent *n.* a rent that is very low or nominal.

pep+pered moth *n.* a European geometrid moth, *Biston betularia,* occurring in a pale grey speckled form in rural areas and a black form in industrial regions. See also **melanism** (sense 1).

pep·per+grass ('pɛpəˌgrɑːs) *n.* the usual U.S. name for **pepperwort** (sense 2).

pep+per mill *n.* a small hand mill used to grind peppercorns.

pep·per+mint ('pɛpəˌmɪnt) *n.* **1.** a temperate mint plant, *Mentha piperita,* with purple or white flowers: cultivated for its downy leaves, which yield a pungent oil. **2.** the oil from this plant, which is used as a flavouring. **3.** a sweet flavoured with peppermint.

pep+per pot *n.* **1.** a small container with perforations in the top for sprinkling pepper. **2.** a West Indian stew of meat, rice, vegetables, etc., highly seasoned with cassareep.

pep+per tree *n.* any of several evergreen anacardiaceous trees of the chiefly South American genus *Schinus,* esp. *S. molle* (also called: **mastic tree**), having yellowish-white flowers and bright red ornamental fruits.

pep·per+wort ('pɛpəˌwɜːt) *n.* **1.** any of various temperate and tropical aquatic or marsh ferns of the genus *Marsilea,* having floating leaves consisting of four leaflets: family *Marsileaceae.* **2.** any of several cruciferous plants of the genus *Lepidium,* esp. *L. campestre,* of dry regions of Eurasia, having small white flowers and pungent seeds. Usual U.S. name: **peppergrass.**

pep+per·y ('pɛpərɪ) *adj.* **1.** flavoured with or tasting of pepper. **2.** quick-tempered; irritable. **3.** full of bite and sharpness: *a peppery speech.* —**'pep+per·i+ness** *n.*

pep pill *n. Informal.* a tablet containing a stimulant drug.

pep+py ('pɛpɪ) *adj.* **+pi+er, +pi+est.** *Informal.* full of vitality; bouncy or energetic. —**'pep+pi+ly** *adv.* —**'pep+pi+ness** *n.*

pep+sin *or* **pep+sine** ('pɛpsɪn) *n.* a proteolytic enzyme produced in the stomach in the inactive form pepsinogen, which, when activated by acid, splits proteins into peptones. [C19: via German from Greek *pepsis,* from *peptein* to digest]

pep+si+nate ('pɛpsɪˌneɪt) *vb.* (*tr.*) **1.** to treat (a patient) with pepsin. **2.** to mix or infuse (something) with pepsin.

pep+sin·o+gen (pɛp'sɪnədʒən) *n.* the inactive precursor of pepsin produced by the stomach.

pep talk *n. Informal.* an enthusiastic talk designed to increase confidence, production, cooperation, etc.

pep+tic ('pɛptɪk) *adj.* **1.** of, relating to, or promoting digestion. **2.** of, relating to, or caused by pepsin or the action of the digestive juices. [C17: from Greek *peptikos* capable of digesting, from *pepsis* digestion, from *peptein* to digest]

pep+tic ul+cer *n. Pathol.* an ulcer of the mucous membrane lining those parts of the alimentary tract exposed to digestive juices, including the oesophagus, the stomach, the duodenum, and parts of the small intestine.

pep+ti+dase ('pɛptɪˌdeɪs, -ˌdeɪz) *n.* any of a group of proteolytic enzymes that hydrolyse peptides to amino acids.

pep+tide ('pɛptaɪd) *n.* any of a group of compounds consisting of two or more amino acids linked by chemical bonding between their respective carboxyl and amino groups. See also **peptide bond, polypeptide.**

pep+tide bond *n. Biochem.* a chemical amide linkage, =CHCONHCH=, formed by the condensation of the amino group of one amino acid with the carboxyl group of another.

pep+tize *or* **pep+tise** ('pɛptaɪz) *vb.* (*tr.*) *Chem.* to disperse (a substance) into a colloidal state, usually to form a sol. —**'pep+tiz+a·ble** *or* **'pep+tis+a·ble** *adj.* —**ˌpep+ti+'za+tion** *or* **ˌpep+ti+'sa+tion** *n.* —**'pep+tiz+er** *or* **'pep+tis+er** *n.*

pep+tone ('pɛptəʊn) *n. Biochem.* any of a group of compounds that form an intermediary group in the digestion of proteins to amino acids. See also **metaprotein, proteose.** [C19: from German *Pepton,* from Greek *pepton* something digested, from *peptein* to digest] —**pep+ton+ic** (pɛp'tɒnɪk) *adj.*

pep+to+nize *or* **pep+to+nise** ('pɛptəˌnaɪz) *vb.* (*tr.*) to hydrolyse (a protein) to peptones by enzymic action, esp. by pepsin or pancreatic extract. —**ˌpep+to+ni+'za+tion** *or* **ˌpep+to+ni+'sa+tion** *n.* —**'pep+to+ˌniz+er** *or* **'pep+to+ˌnis+er** *n.*

Pepys (piːps) *n.* **Sam·u·el.** 1633–1703, English diarist and naval administrator. His diary, which covers the period 1660–69, is a vivid account of London life through such disasters as the Great Plague, the Fire of London, and the intrusion of the Dutch fleet up the Thames.

Pe+quot ('piːkwɒt) *n.* **1.** (*pl.* **+quot** *or* **+quots**) a member of a North American Indian people formerly living in S New England. **2.** the language of this people, belonging to the Algonquian family. [probably based on Narraganset *paquatanog* destroyers]

per (pɜː; *unstressed* pə) *determiner.* **1.** for every: *three pence per pound.* ~*prep.* **2.** (esp. in some Latin phrases) by; through. **3. as per.** according to: *as per specifications.* **4. as per usual.** *Informal.* as usual. [C15: from Latin: by, for each]

per. *abbrev. for:* **1.** period. **2.** person.

per- *prefix.* **1.** indicating that a chemical compound contains a high proportion of a specified element: *peroxide; perchloride.* **2.** indicating that a chemical element is in a higher than usual state of oxidation: *permanganate; perchlorate.* **3.** (*not in technical usage*) variant of **peroxy-:** *persulphuric acid.* [from Latin *per* through. In compound words borrowed from Latin, *per-* indicates: through (*pervade*); throughout (*permanent*); away (*perfidy*); and is used as an intensifier (*permutation*)]

Pe·ra ('pɪərə) *n.* the former name of **Beyoğlu.**

per·ac·id (pɜːˈræsɪd) *n.* **1.** an acid, such as perchloric acid, in which the element forming the acid radical exhibits its highest valency. **2.** (*not in technical usage*) an acid, such as persulphuric acid, that contains the -OOH group. Recommended names: **peroxo acid, peroxy acid.** —**per·a·cid·i·ty** (ˌpɛrəˈsɪdɪtɪ) *n.*

per·ad·ven·ture (pərədˈvɛntʃə, ˌpɜːr-) *Archaic.* ~*adv.* **1.** by chance; perhaps. ~*n.* **2.** chance, uncertainty, or doubt. [C13: from Old French *par aventure* by chance]

Pe·rae·a *or* **Pe·re·a** (pəˈriːə) *n.* a region of ancient Palestine, east of the River Jordan and the Dead Sea.

Pe·rak (ˈpɛərə, ˈpɪərə, pɪˈræk) *n.* a state of NW West Malaysia, on the Strait of Malacca: tin-mining. Capital: Ipoh. Pop.: 1 561 184 (1970). Area: 20 680 sq. km (8030 sq. miles).

per·am·bu·late (pəˈræmbjʊˌleɪt) *vb.* **1.** to walk about (a place). **2.** (*tr.*) to walk round in order to inspect. [C16: from Latin *perambulāre* to traverse, from *per* through + *ambulāre* to walk] —**per·ˌam·bu·ˈla·tion** *n.* —**per·am·bu·la·to·ry** (pəˈræmbjʊlətərɪ, -trɪ) *adj.*

per·am·bu·la·tor (pəˈræmbjʊˌleɪtə) *n.* **1.** a formal word for **pram**[1]. **2.** a wheel-like instrument used by surveyors to measure distances.

per an·num (pər ˈænəm) *adv.* every year or by the year.

p/e ratio *n.* short for price/earnings ratio.

per·bo·rate (pəˈbɔːreɪt) *n.* any of certain salts derived, or apparently derived, from perboric acid. See **sodium perborate.**

per·cale (pəˈkeɪl, -ˈkɑːl) *n.* a close-textured woven cotton fabric, plain or printed, used esp. for sheets. [C17: via French from Persian *pargālah* piece of cloth]

per·ca·line (ˈpɜːkəˌliːn, -lɪn) *n.* a fine light cotton fabric, used esp. for linings. [C19: from French; see PERCALE]

per cap·i·ta (pə ˈkæpɪtə) *adj., adv.* of or for each person. [Latin, literally: according to heads]

per·ceive (pəˈsiːv) *vb.* **1.** to become aware of (something) through the senses, esp. the sight; recognize or observe. **2.** (*tr.; may take a clause as object*) to come to comprehend; grasp. [C13: from Old French *perçoivre*, from Latin *percipere* seize entirely, from PER- (thoroughly) + *capere* to grasp] —**per·ˈceiv·a·ble** *adj.* —**per·ˌceiv·a·ˈbil·i·ty** *n.* —**per·ˈceiv·a·bly** *adv.* —**per·ˈceiv·er** *n.*

per·ceived noise dec·i·bel *n.* a unit for measuring perceived levels of noise by comparison with the sound pressure level of a reference sound judged equally noisy by a normal listener. Abbrev.: **PNdB**

per cent (pə ˈsɛnt) *adv.* **1.** Also: **per centum.** in or for every hundred. ~*n. also* **percent. 2.** a percentage or proportion. **3.** (*often pl.*) securities yielding a rate of interest as specified: *he bought three percents.* [C16: from Medieval Latin *per centum* out of every hundred]

per·cent·age (pəˈsɛntɪdʒ) *n.* **1.** proportion or rate per hundred parts. **2.** *Commerce.* the interest, tax, commission, or allowance on a hundred items. **3.** any proportion in relation to the whole. **4.** *Informal.* profit or advantage.

per·cen·tile (pəˈsɛntaɪl) *n.* one of 99 actual or notional values of a variable dividing its distribution into 100 groups with equal frequencies. Also called (in the U.S.): **centile.**

per·cept (ˈpɜːsɛpt) *n.* **1.** a concept that depends on recognition by the senses, such as sight, of some external object or phenomenon. **2.** an object or phenomenon that is perceived. [C19: from Latin *perceptum*, from *percipere* to PERCEIVE]

per·cep·ti·ble (pəˈsɛptəbᵊl) *adj.* able to be perceived; noticeable or recognizable. —**per·ˌcep·ti·ˈbil·i·ty** *or* **per·ˈcep·ti·ble·ness** *n.* —**per·ˈcep·ti·bly** *adv.*

per·cep·tion (pəˈsɛpʃən) *n.* **1.** the act or the effect of perceiving. **2.** insight or intuition gained by perceiving. **3.** the ability or capacity to perceive. **4.** the process by which an organism detects and interprets information from the external world by means of the sensory receptors. **5.** *Law.* the collection, receipt, or taking into possession of rents, crops, etc. [C15: from Latin *perceptiō* comprehension; see PERCEIVE] —**per·ˈcep·tion·al** *adj.*

per·cep·tive (pəˈsɛptɪv) *adj.* **1.** quick at perceiving; observant. **2.** perceptual. **3.** able to perceive. —**per·ˈcep·tive·ly** *adv.* —**ˌper·cep·ˈtiv·i·ty** *or* **per·ˈcep·tive·ness** *n.*

per·cep·tu·al (pəˈsɛptjʊəl) *adj.* of or relating to perception. —**per·ˈcep·tu·al·ly** *adv.*

per·cep·tu·al de·fence *n. Psychol.* the process by which certain stimuli are either not perceived or are distorted due to their offensive, unpleasant, or threatening nature.

Per·ce·val (ˈpɜːsɪvᵊl) *n.* **Spen·cer.** 1762–1812, British statesman; prime minister (1809–12); assassinated.

perch[1] (pɜːtʃ) *n.* **1.** a pole, branch, or other resting place above ground on which a bird roosts or alights. **2.** a similar resting place for a person or thing. **3.** another name for **rod** (sense 7). **4.** a solid measure for stone, usually taken as 198 inches by 18 inches by 12 inches. **5.** a pole joining the front and rear axles of a carriage. **6.** a frame on which cloth is placed for inspection. **7.** *Obsolete or dialect.* a pole. ~*vb.* **8.** (usually foll. by *on*) to alight, rest, or cause to rest on or as if on a perch: *the bird perched on the branch; the cap was perched on his head.* **9.** (*tr.*) to inspect (cloth) on a perch. [C13 *perche* stake, from Old French, from Latin *pertica* long staff] —**ˈperch·er** *n.*

perch[2] (pɜːtʃ) *n., pl.* **perch** *or* **perch·es. 1.** any freshwater spiny-finned teleost fish of the family *Percidae*, esp. those of the genus *Perca*, such as *P. fluviatilis* of Europe and *P. flavescens* (**yellow perch**) of North America: valued as food and game fishes. **2.** any of various similar or related fishes. [C13: from Old French *perche*, from Latin *perca*, from Greek *perkē*; compare Greek *perkos* spotted]

per·chance (pəˈtʃɑːns) *adv. Archaic or poetic.* **1.** perhaps; possibly. **2.** by chance; accidentally. [C14: from Anglo-French *par chance*; see PER, CHANCE]

Per·che·ron (ˈpɜːʃəˌrɒn) *n.* a compact heavy breed of carthorse, grey or black in colour. [C19: from French, from *le Perche*, region of NW France where the breed originated]

per·chlo·rate (pəˈklɔːreɪt) *n.* any salt or ester of perchloric acid. Perchlorate salts contain the ion ClO_4^-.

per·chlo·ric ac·id (pəˈklɔːrɪk) *n.* a colourless syrupy oxyacid of chlorine containing a greater proportion of oxygen than chloric acid. It is a powerful oxidizing agent and is used as a laboratory reagent. Formula: $HClO_4$.

per·chlo·ride (pəˈklɔːraɪd) *n.* a chloride that contains more chlorine than other chlorides of the same element.

per·cip·i·ent (pəˈsɪpɪənt) *adj.* **1.** able to perceive. **2.** perceptive. ~*n.* **3.** a person or thing that perceives. [C17: from Latin *percipiens* observing, from *percipere* to grasp; see PERCEIVE] —**per·ˈcip·i·ence** *n.* —**per·ˈcip·i·ent·ly** *adv.*

Per·ci·val *or* **Per·ce·val** (ˈpɜːsɪvᵊl) *n.* (in Arthurian legend) a knight in King Arthur's court. German equivalent: **Parzival.**

per·coid (ˈpɜːkɔɪd) *or* **per·coi·de·an** (pəˈkɔɪdɪən) *adj.* **1.** of, relating to, or belonging to the *Percoidea*, a suborder of spiny-finned teleost fishes including the perches, sea bass, red mullet, cichlids, etc. **2.** of, relating to, or resembling a perch. ~*n.* **3.** any fish belonging to the suborder *Percoidea.* [C19: from Latin *perca* PERCH[2] + -OID]

per·co·late *vb.* (ˈpɜːkəˌleɪt). **1.** to cause (a liquid) to pass through a fine mesh, porous substance, etc. or (of a liquid) to pass through a fine mesh, etc.; trickle: *rain percolated through the roof.* **2.** to permeate; penetrate gradually: *water percolated the road.* **3.** (*intr.*) *U.S. informal.* to become active or lively: *she percolated with happiness.* **4.** to make (coffee) or (of coffee) to be made in a percolator. ~*n.* (ˈpɜːkəlɪt, -ˌleɪt). **5.** a product of percolation. [C17: from Latin *percolāre*, from PER + *cōlāre* to strain, from *cōlum* a strainer; see COLANDER] —**per·co·la·ble** (ˈpɜːkələbᵊl) *adj.* —**ˌper·co·ˈla·tion** *n.* —**ˈper·co·la·tive** *adj.*

per·co·la·tor (ˈpɜːkəˌleɪtə) *n.* a kind of coffeepot in which boiling water is forced up through a tube and filters down through the coffee grounds into a container.

per con·tra (ˈpɜː ˈkɒntrə) *adv.* on the contrary. [from Latin]

per·cuss (pəˈkʌs) *vb.* (*tr.*) **1.** to strike sharply, rapidly, or suddenly. **2.** *Med.* to tap on (a body surface) with the fingertips or a special hammer to aid diagnosis or for therapeutic purposes. [C16: from Latin *percutere*, from *per-* through + *quatere* to shake] —**per·ˈcus·sor** *n.*

per·cus·sion (pəˈkʌʃən) *n.* **1.** the act, an instance, or an effect of percussing. **2.** *Music.* the family of instruments in which sound arises from the striking of materials with sticks or hammers. **3.** *Music.* **a.** instruments of this family constituting a section of an orchestra, etc. **b.** (as modifier): *a percussion ensemble.* **4.** *Med.* the act of percussing a body surface. **5.** the act of exploding a percussion cap. [C16: from Latin *percussiō*, from *percutere* to hit; see PERCUSS]

per·cus·sion cap *n.* a detonator consisting of a paper or thin metal cap containing material that explodes when struck and formerly used in certain firearms.

per·cus·sion in·stru·ment *n.* any of various musical instruments that produce a sound when their resonating surfaces are struck directly, as with a stick or mallet, or by leverage action. They may be of definite pitch (as a kettledrum or xylophone), indefinite pitch (as a gong or rattle), or a mixture of both (as various drums).

per·cus·sion·ist (pəˈkʌʃənɪst) *n. Music.* a person who plays any of several percussion instruments, esp. in an orchestra.

per·cus·sion lock *n.* a gunlock in which the hammer strikes a percussion cap.

per·cus·sive (pəˈkʌsɪv) *adj.* of, caused by, or relating to percussion. —**per·ˈcus·sive·ly** *adv.* —**per·ˈcus·sive·ness** *n.*

per·cu·ta·ne·ous (ˌpɜːkjuˈteɪnɪəs) *adj. Med.* effected through the skin, as in the absorption of an ointment.

Per·cy (ˈpɜːsɪ) *n.* **1.** Sir **Hen·ry,** called *Harry Hotspur.* 1364–1403, English rebel, who was killed leading an army against Henry IV. **2. Thom·as.** 1729–1811, English bishop and antiquary. His *Reliques of Ancient English Poetry* (1765) stimulated the interest of Romantic writers in old English and Scottish ballads.

Per·di·do (*Spanish* perˈðiðo) *n.* **Monte.** a mountain in NE Spain, in the central Pyrenees. Height: 3352 m (10 997 ft.). French name: (Mont) **Perdu.**

per di·em (ˈpɜː ˈdaɪɛm, ˈdiːɛm) *adv.* **1.** every day or by the day. ~*n.* **2.** an allowance for daily expenses, usually those incurred while working. [from Latin]

per·di·tion (pəˈdɪʃən) *n.* **1.** *Christianity.* **a.** final and irrevocable spiritual ruin. **b.** this state as one that the wicked are said to be destined to endure forever. **2.** another word for **hell. 3.** *Archaic.* utter disaster, ruin, or destruction. [C14: from Late Latin *perditiō* ruin, from Latin *perdere* to lose, from PER- (away) + *dāre* to give]

per·du *or* **per·due** (ˈpɜːdjuː) *n.* **1.** *Obsolete.* a soldier placed at hazard or in a situation from which there is little chance of recovery. ~*adj.* **2.** hidden. [C16: via French: lost, from *perdre* to lose, from Latin *perdere* to destroy]

Per·du (pɛrˈdy) *n.* **Mont.** the French name for (Monte) **Perdido.**

per·dur·a·ble (pəˈdjʊərəbᵊl) *adj. Rare.* extremely durable. [C13: from Late Latin *perdūrābilis*, from Latin *per-* (intensive) + *dūrābilis* long-lasting, from *dūrus* hard] —**ˌper·dur·a·ˈbil·i·ty** *n.* —**ˈper·dur·a·bly** *adv.*

père *French.* (pɛːr; *English* pɛə) *n.* an addition to a French surname to specify the father rather than the son of the same name: *Dumas père.* Compare **fils.**

Père Da·vid's deer *n.* a large grey deer, *Elaphurus davidianus,* surviving only in captivity as descendants of a herd preserved in the Imperial hunting park near Peking. [C20: named after Father A. *David* (d. 1900), French missionary]

per+e·gri+nate (ˈpɛrɪgrɪˌneɪt) *vb.* **1.** (*intr.*) to travel or wander about from place to place; voyage. **2.** (*tr.*) to travel through (a place). ~*adj.* **3.** an obsolete word for **foreign.** [C16: from Latin, from *peregrīnārī* to travel; see PEREGRINE] —**ˈper+e·gri+ˌna+tor** *n.*

per+e·gri+na+tion (ˌpɛrɪgrɪˈneɪʃən) *n.* **1.** a voyage, esp. an extensive one. **2.** the act or process of travelling.

per+e·grine (ˈpɛrɪgrɪn) *adj. Archaic.* **1.** coming from abroad. **2.** travelling or migratory; wandering. [C14: from Latin *peregrīnus* foreign, from *pereger* being abroad, from *per* through + *ager* land (that is, beyond one's own land)]

per+e·grine fal+con *n.* a falcon, *Falco peregrinus,* occurring in most parts of the world, having a dark plumage on the back and wings and lighter underparts. See also **duck hawk.**

Pe+rei+ra (*Spanish* peˈrejra) *n.* a town in W central Colombia: cattle trading and coffee processing. Pop.: 174 128 (1973).

pe+rei+ra bark (pəˈrɛərə) *n.* the bark of a South American apocynaceous tree, *Geissospermum vellosii:* source of a substance formerly used for treating malaria.

per+emp+to·ry (pəˈrɛmptərɪ) *adj.* **1.** urgent or commanding: *a peremptory ring on the bell.* **2.** not able to be remitted or debated; decisive. **3.** positive or assured in speech, manner, etc.; dogmatic. **4.** *Law.* **a.** admitting of no denial or contradiction; precluding debate. **b.** obligatory rather than permissive. [C16: from Anglo-Norman *peremptorie,* from Latin *peremptōrius* decisive, from *perimere* to take away completely, from PER- (intensive) + *emere* to take] —**per+ˈemp+to+ri+ly** *adv.* —**per+ˈemp+to+ri+ness** *n.*

pe+ren+nate (ˈpɛrɪˌneɪt, pəˈrɛneɪt) *vb.* (*intr.*) (of plants) to live from one growing season to another, usually with a period of reduced activity between seasons. [C17: from Latin *perennātus,* from *perennāre,* from PER- (through) + *annus* year]

per+en+ni·al (pəˈrɛnɪəl) *adj.* **1.** lasting throughout the year or through many years. **2.** everlasting; perpetual. ~*n.* **3.** a woody or herbaceous plant that continues its growth for at least three years. Compare **annual** (sense 3), **biennial** (sense 3). [C17: from Latin *perennis* continual, from *per* through + *annus* year] —**per+ˈen+ni+al+ly** *adv.*

perf. *abbrev. for:* **1.** perfect. **2.** perforated. **3.** perforation.

per+fect *adj.* (ˈpɜːfɪkt). **1.** having all essential elements. **2.** unblemished; faultless: *a perfect gemstone.* **3.** correct or precise: *perfect timing.* **4.** utter or absolute: *a perfect stranger.* **5.** excellent in all respects: *a perfect day.* **6.** *Maths.* exactly divisible into equal integral or polynomial roots: *36 is a perfect square.* **7.** *Botany.* **a.** (of flowers) having functional stamens and pistils. **b.** (of plants) having all parts present. **8.** *Grammar.* denoting a tense of verbs used in describing an action that has been completed by the subject. In English this is a compound tense, formed with *have* or *has* plus the past participle. **9.** *Music.* **a.** of or relating to the intervals of the unison, fourth, fifth, and octave. **b.** (of a cadence) ending on the tonic chord, giving a feeling of conclusion. Also: **full, final.** Compare **imperfect** (sense 6). **10.** *Archaic.* positive, certain, or assured. ~*n.* (ˈpɜːfɪkt). **11.** *Grammar.* **a.** the perfect tense. **b.** a verb in this tense. ~*vb.* (pəˈfɛkt). (*tr.*) **12.** to make perfect; improve to one's satisfaction: *he is in Paris to perfect his French.* **13.** to make fully accomplished. **14.** *Printing.* to print the reverse side of (a printed sheet of paper). [C13: from Latin *perfectus,* from *perficere* to perform, from *per* through + *facere* to do] —**per+ˈfect+er** *n.* —**ˈper+fect+ness** *n.*

Usage. See at **unique.**

per+fect com+pe+ti+tion *n. Economics.* a market situation in which there exits a homogeneous product, freedom of entry, and a large number of buyers and sellers none of whom individually can affect price.

per+fect gas *n.* another name for **ideal gas.**

per+fect+i·ble (pəˈfɛktəbᵊl) *adj.* capable of becoming or being made perfect. —**per+ˌfect+i·ˈbil+i·ty** *n.*

per+fec+tion (pəˈfɛkʃən) *n.* **1.** the act of perfecting or the state or quality of being perfect. **2.** the highest degree of a quality, etc.: *the perfection of faithfulness.* **3.** an embodiment of perfection. [C13: from Latin *perfectiō* a completing, from *perficere* to finish]

per+fec+tion+ism (pəˈfɛkʃəˌnɪzəm) *n.* **1.** *Philosophy.* the doctrine that man can attain perfection in this life. **2.** the demand for the highest standard of excellence.

per+fec+tion+ist (pəˈfɛkʃənɪst) *n.* **1.** a person who strives for or demands the highest standards of excellence in work, etc. **2.** a person who believes the doctrine of perfectionism. ~*adj.* **3.** of or relating to perfectionism.

per+fec+tive (pəˈfɛktɪv) *adj.* **1.** tending to perfect. **2.** *Grammar.* denoting an aspect of verbs in some languages, including English, used to express that the action or event described by the verb is or was completed: *I lived in London for ten years* is perfective; *I have lived in London for ten years* is imperfective, since the implication is that I still live in London.

per+fect+ly (ˈpɜːfɪktlɪ) *adv.* **1.** completely, utterly, or absolutely. **2.** in a perfect way; extremely well.

per+fect num+ber *n.* an integer, such as 28, that is equal to the sum of all its possible factors, excluding itself.

per+fec+to (pəˈfɛktəʊ) *n., pl.* **+tos.** a large cigar that is tapered from both ends. [Spanish, literally: perfect]

per+fect par+ti+ci+ple *n.* another name for **past participle.**

per+fect pitch *n.* another name (not in technical usage) for **absolute pitch.**

per+fect rhyme *n.* **1.** Also called: **full rhyme.** rhyme between words in which the stressed vowels and any succeeding consonants are identical although the consonants preceding the stressed vowels may be different, as between *part/hart* or *believe/conceive.* **2.** a rhyme between two words that are pronounced the same although differing in meaning: *bough/bow.*

per+fer+vid (pɜːˈfɜːvɪd) *adj. Literary.* extremely ardent, enthusiastic, or zealous. [C19: from New Latin *perfervidus,* from Latin *per-* (intensive) + *fervidus* FERVID] —**per+ˈfer+vid+ly** *adv.* —**per+ˈfer+vid+ness** *n.*

per+fid+i+ous (pəˈfɪdɪəs) *adj.* guilty, treacherous, or faithless; deceitful. —**per+ˈfid·i+ous+ly** *adv.* —**per+ˈfid·i+ous+ness** *n.*

per+fi+dy (ˈpɜːfɪdɪ) *n., pl.* **+dies.** a perfidious act. [C16: from Latin *perfidia,* from *perfidus* faithless, from *per* beyond + *fidēs* faith]

per+fin (ˈpɜːfɪn) *n. Philately.* the former name for **spif.** [from *perf(orated with) in(itials)*]

per+fo+li+ate (pəˈfəʊlɪɪt, -ˌeɪt) *adj.* (of a leaf) having a base that completely encloses the stem, so that the stem appears to pass through it. [C17: from New Latin *perfoliātus,* from Latin *per-* through + *folium* leaf] —**per+ˌfo+li·ˈa+tion** *n.*

per+fo+rate *vb.* (ˈpɜːfəˌreɪt). **1.** to make a hole or holes in (something); penetrate. **2.** (*tr.*) to punch rows of holes between (stamps, etc.) for ease of separation. ~*adj.* (ˈpɜːfərɪt). **3.** *Biology.* **a.** pierced by small holes: *perforate shells.* **b.** marked with small transparent spots. **4.** *Philately.* another word for **perforated.** [C16: from Latin *perforāre,* from *per-* through + *forāre* to pierce] —**per+fo+ra·ble** (ˈpɜːfərəbᵊl) *adj.* —**ˈper+fo+ra+tive** *or* **ˈper+fo+ra+to·ry** *adj.* —**ˈper+fo+ˌra+tor** *n.*

per+fo+rat+ed (ˈpɜːfəˌreɪtɪd) *adj.* **1.** pierced with one or more holes. **2.** (esp. of stamps) having perforations. Abbrev.: **perf.**

per+fo+rat+ed tape *n.* a U.S. name for **paper tape.**

per+fo+ra+tion (ˌpɜːfəˈreɪʃən) *n.* **1.** the act of perforating or the state of being perforated. **2.** a hole or holes made in something. **3. a.** a method of making individual stamps, etc. easily separable by punching holes along their margins. **b.** the holes punched in this way. Abbrev.: **perf.**

per+fo+ra+tion gauge *n.* a graduated scale for measuring perforations and roulettes of postage stamps.

per+force (pəˈfɔːs) *adv.* by necessity; unavoidably. [C14: from Old French *par force;* see PER, FORCE]

per+form (pəˈfɔːm) *vb.* **1.** to carry out or do (an action). **2.** (*tr.*) to fulfil or comply with: *to perform someone's request.* **3.** to present or enact (a play, concert, etc.) before or otherwise entertain an audience: *the group performed Hamlet.* **4.** (*intr.*) *Informal.* to accomplish sexual intercourse: *he performed well.* [C14: from Anglo-Norman *perfourmer* (influenced by *forme* FORM), from Old French *parfournir,* from *par-* PER- + *fournir* to provide; see FURNISH] —**per+ˈform+a·ble** *adj.* —**per+ˈform+er** *n.*

per+for+mance (pəˈfɔːməns) *n.* **1.** the act, process, or art of performing. **2.** an artistic or dramatic production: *last night's performance was terrible.* **3.** manner or quality of functioning: *a machine's performance.* **4.** *Informal.* mode of conduct or behaviour, esp. when distasteful or irregular: *what did you mean by that performance at the restaurant?* **5.** any accomplishment.

per+for+mance test *n. Psychol.* a test designed to assess a person's manual ability.

per+for+ma+tive (pəˈfɔːmətɪv) *adj. Linguistics, philosophy.* **1. a.** denoting an utterance that itself constitutes the act described by the verb. For example, the sentence *I confess that I was there* is itself a confession. **b.** (*as n.*): *that sentence is a performative.* **2. a.** denoting a verb that may be used as the main verb in such an utterance. **b.** (*as n.*): *"promise" is a performative.* —**per+ˈform·a+tive+ly** *adv.*

per+form+ing (pəˈfɔːmɪŋ) *adj.* (of an animal) trained to perform tricks before an audience, as in a circus.

per+form+ing arts *pl. n.* the arts that are primarily performed before an audience, such as dance and drama.

per+fume *n.* (ˈpɜːfjuːm). **1.** a mixture of alcohol and fragrant essential oils extracted from flowers, etc., or made synthetically, used esp. to impart a pleasant long-lasting scent to the body, etc. See also **cologne, toilet water. 2.** a scent or odour, esp. a fragrant one. ~*vb.* (pəˈfjuːm). **3.** (*tr.*) to impart a perfume to. [C16: from French *parfum,* probably from Old Provençal *perfum,* from *perfumar* to make scented, from *per* through (from Latin) + *fumar* to smoke, from Latin *fumāre* to smoke]

per+fum+er (pəˈfjuːmə) *n.* a person who makes or sells perfume.

per+fum+er·y (pəˈfjuːmərɪ) *n., pl.* **+er·ies. 1.** a place where perfumes are sold. **2.** a factory where perfumes are made. **3.** the process of making perfumes. **4.** perfumes in general.

per+func+to·ry (pəˈfʌŋktərɪ) *adj.* **1.** done superficially, only as a matter of routine; careless or cursory. **2.** dull or indifferent. [C16: from Late Latin *perfunctōrius* negligent, from *perfunctus* dispatched, from *perfungī* to fulfil; see FUNCTION] —**per+ˈfunc+to+ri+ly** *adv.* —**per+ˈfunc+to+ri+ness** *n.*

per+fuse (pəˈfjuːz) *vb.* (*tr.*) to suffuse or permeate (a liquid, colour, etc.) through or over (something). [C16: from Latin *perfūsus* wetted, from *perfundere* to pour over, from PER- + *fundere* to pour] —**per+ˈfu+sion** *n.* —**per+ˈfu+sive** *adj.*

Per+ga+mum (ˈpɜːgəməm) *n.* **1.** an ancient city in NW Asia Minor, in Mysia: capital of a major Hellenistic monarchy of the same name that later became a Roman province. **2.** the ancient name for **Bergama.**

per·go·la (ˈpɜːgələ) *n.* a horizontal trellis or framework, supported on posts, that carries climbing plants and may form a covered walk. [C17: via Italian from Latin *pergula* projection from a roof, from *pergere* to go forward]

Per·go·le·si (*Italian* ˌpergoˈleːsi) *n.* **Gio·van·ni Bat·tis·ta** (dʒoˈvanni batˈtista). 1710–36, Italian composer: his works include the operetta *La Serva padrona* (1733) and the *Stabat Mater* (1736) for women's voices.

per·haps (pəˈhæps; *informal* præps) *adv.* **1. a.** possibly; maybe. **b.** (*as sentence modifier*): *he'll arrive tomorrow, perhaps; perhaps you'll see him tomorrow.* ~ **2.** *sentence substitute.* it may happen, be so, etc.; maybe. [C16 *perhappes,* from *per* by + *happes* chance, HAP]

pe·ri (ˈpɪərɪ) *n., pl.* **·ris. 1.** (in Persian folklore) one of a race of beautiful supernatural beings. **2.** any beautiful fairy-like creature. [C18: from Persian: fairy, from Avestan *pairikā* witch]

per·i- *prefix.* **1.** enclosing, encircling, or around: *pericardium; pericarp; perigon.* **2.** near or adjacent: *perihelion.* [from Greek *peri* around, near, about]

per·i·anth (ˈpɛrɪˌænθ) *n.* the outer part of a flower, consisting of the calyx and corolla. [C18: from French *périanthe,* from New Latin, from PERI- + Greek *anthos* flower]

per·i·apt (ˈpɛrɪˌæpt) *n. Rare.* a charm or amulet. [C16: via French from Greek *periapton,* from PERI- + *haptos* clasped, from *haptein* to fasten]

per·i·blem (ˈpɛrɪˌblɛm) *n. Botany.* a layer of meristematic tissue in stems and roots that gives rise to the cortex. [C19: via German from Greek *periblēma* protection, from *periballein* to throw around, from PERI- + *ballein* to throw]

per·i·car·di·tis (ˌpɛrɪkɑːˈdaɪtɪs) *n.* inflammation of the pericardium. —**per·i·car·dit·ic** (ˌpɛrɪkɑːˈdɪtɪk) *adj.*

per·i·car·di·um (ˌpɛrɪˈkɑːdɪəm) *n., pl.* **·di·a** (-dɪə). the membranous sac enclosing the heart. [C16: via New Latin from Greek *perikardion,* from PERI- + *kardia* heart] —ˌ**per·i·ˈcar·di·al** *or* ˌ**per·i·ˈcar·di·ac** *adj.*

per·i·carp (ˈpɛrɪˌkɑːp) *n.* **1.** the part of a fruit enclosing the seeds that develops from the wall of the ovary. **2.** a layer of tissue around the reproductive bodies of some algae and fungi. [C18: via French from New Latin *pericarpium*] —ˌ**per·i·ˈcar·pi·al** *or* ˌ**per·i·ˈcar·pic** *adj.* —ˌ**per·i·car·ˈpoi·dal** *adj.*

per·i·chon·dri·um (ˌpɛrɪˈkɒndrɪəm) *n., pl.* **·dri·a** (-drɪə). the white fibrous membrane that covers the surface of cartilage. [C18: New Latin, from PERI- + Greek *chondros* cartilage] —ˌ**per·i·ˈchon·dri·al** *adj.*

per·i·clase (ˈpɛrɪˌkleɪs) *n.* a mineral consisting of magnesium oxide in the form of isometric crystals or grains: occurs in limestone masses. [C19: from New Latin *periclasia,* from Greek *peri* very + *klasis* a breaking, referring to its perfect cleavage] —**per·i·clas·tic** (ˌpɛrɪˈklæstɪk) *adj.*

Per·i·cle·an (ˌpɛrɪˈkliːən) *adj.* of or relating to Pericles or to the period when Athens was the intellectual and artistic leader of the Greek city-states.

Per·i·cles (ˈpɛrɪˌkliːz) *n.* died 429 B.C., Athenian statesman and leader of the popular party, who contributed greatly to Athens' political and cultural supremacy in Greece. In power from about 460, he was responsible for the construction of the Parthenon. He conducted the Peloponnesian War (431–404) successfully until his death.

per·i·cli·nal (ˌpɛrɪˈklaɪnᵊl) *adj.* **1.** of or relating to a pericline. **2.** *Botany.* **a.** denoting or relating to cell walls that are parallel to the surface of a plant part, such as a meristem. **b.** (of chimeras) having one component completely enclosed by the other component.

per·i·cline (ˈpɛrɪˌklaɪn) *n.* **1.** a white translucent variety of albite in the form of elongated crystals. **2.** Also called: **dome.** a dome-shaped formation of stratified rock with its slopes following the direction of folding. [C19: from Greek *periklinēs* sloping on all sides, from PERI- + *klinein* to lean]

pe·ric·o·pe (pəˈrɪkəpɪ) *n.* a selection from a book, esp. a passage from the Bible read at religious services. [C17: via Late Latin from Greek *perikopē* piece cut out, from PERI- + *kopē* a cutting] —**per·i·cop·ic** (ˌpɛrɪˈkɒpɪk) *adj.*

per·i·cra·ni·um (ˌpɛrɪˈkreɪnɪəm) *n., pl.* **·ni·a** (-nɪə). the fibrous membrane covering the external surface of the skull. [C16: New Latin, from Greek *perikranion*] —ˌ**per·i·ˈcra·ni·al** *adj.*

per·i·cy·cle (ˈpɛrɪˌsaɪkᵊl) *n.* a layer of plant tissue beneath the endodermis: surrounds the conducting tissue in roots and certain stems. [C19: from Greek *perikuklos*] —**per·i·cy·clic** (ˌpɛrɪˈsaɪklɪk, -ˈsɪk-) *adj.*

per·i·cyn·thi·on (ˌpɛrɪˈsɪnθɪən) *n.* the point at which a spacecraft launched from earth into a lunar orbit is nearest the moon. Compare **perilune, apocynthion.** [C20: from PERI- + *-cynthion,* from CYNTHIA]

per·i·derm (ˈpɛrɪˌdɜːm) *n.* the outer corky protective layer of woody stems and roots, consisting of cork cambium, phelloderm and cork. [C19: from New Latin *peridermis*] —ˌ**per·i·ˈder·mal** *or* ˌ**per·i·ˈder·mic** *adj.*

pe·rid·i·um (pəˈrɪdɪəm) *n., pl.* **·rid·i·a** (-ˈrɪdɪə). the distinct outer layer of the spore-bearing organ in many fungi. [C19: from Greek *pēridion* a little wallet, from *pēra* leather bag, of obscure origin]

per·i·dot (ˈpɛrɪˌdɒt) *n.* a pale green transparent variety of the olivine chrysolite, used as a gemstone. [C14: from Old French *peritot,* of unknown origin]

per·i·do·tite (ˌpɛrɪˈdəʊtaɪt) *n.* a dark coarse-grained ultrabasic plutonic igneous rock consisting principally of olivine. [C19: from French, from PERIDOT] —**per·i·do·tit·ic** (ˌpɛrɪdəʊˈtɪtɪk) *adj.*

per·i·gee (ˈpɛrɪˌdʒiː) *n.* the point in its orbit around the earth when the moon or an artificial satellite is nearest the earth. Compare **apogee.** [C16: via French from Greek *perigeion,* from PERI- + *gea* earth] —ˌ**per·i·ˈge·an** *or* ˌ**per·i·ˈge·al** *adj.*

per·i·gla·cial (ˌpɛrɪˈgleɪʃəl) *adj.* relating to a region bordering a glacier: *periglacial climate.*

per·i·gon (ˈpɛrɪgən) *n.* an angle of 360°. Also called: **round angle.**

Per·i·gor·di·an (ˌpɛrɪˈgɔːdɪən) *adj.* **1.** of, relating to, or characteristic of an Upper Palaeolithic culture in Europe, esp. in France. ~*n.* **2.** (preceded by *the*) the Perigordian culture. [C20: after *Périgord,* district in France]

pe·rig·y·nous (pəˈrɪdʒɪnəs) *adj.* **1.** (of a flower) having a concave or flat receptacle with a distinct gynoecium surrounded by the other floral parts, as in the rose hip. **2.** of or relating to the parts of a flower arranged in this way. [C19: from New Latin *perigynus;* see PERI-, -GYNOUS] —**pe·ˈrig·y·ny** *n.*

per·i·he·li·on (ˌpɛrɪˈhiːlɪən) *n., pl.* **·li·a** (-lɪə). the point in its orbit when a planet or comet is nearest the sun. Compare **aphelion.** [C17: from New Latin *perihēlium,* from PERI- + Greek *hēlios* sun]

per·il (ˈpɛrɪl) *n.* exposure to risk or harm; danger or jeopardy. [C13: via Old French from Latin *perīculum*]

per·i·lous (ˈpɛrɪləs) *adj.* very hazardous or dangerous: *a perilous journey.* —ˈ**per·i·lous·ly** *adv.* —ˈ**per·i·lous·ness** *n.*

per·i·lune (ˈpɛrɪˌluːn) *n.* the point in a lunar orbit when a spacecraft launched from the moon is nearest the moon. Compare **apolune, pericynthion.** [C20: from PERI- + *-lune* from Latin *lūna* moon]

per·i·lymph (ˈpɛrɪˌlɪmf) *n.* the fluid filling the space between the membranous and bony labyrinths of the internal ear.

pe·rim·e·ter (pəˈrɪmɪtə) *n.* **1.** *Maths.* **a.** the curve or line enclosing a plane area. **b.** the length of this curve or line. **2. a.** any boundary around something, such as a field, etc. **b.** (*as modifier*): *a perimeter fence; a perimeter patrol.* **3.** a medical instrument for measuring the limits of the field of vision. [C16: from French *périmètre,* from Latin *perimetros;* see PERI-, -METER] —**per·i·met·ric** (ˌpɛrɪˈmɛtrɪk), ˌ**per·i·ˈmet·ri·cal,** *or* **pe·ˈrim·e·tral** *adj.* —ˌ**per·i·ˈmet·ri·cal·ly** *adv.* —**pe·ˈrim·e·try** *n.*

per·i·morph (ˈpɛrɪˌmɔːf) *n.* a mineral that encloses another mineral of a different type. —ˌ**per·i·ˈmor·phic** *or* ˌ**per·i·ˈmor·phous** *adj.* —ˌ**per·i·ˈmor·phism** *n.*

per·i·mys·i·um (ˌpɛrɪˈmɪzɪəm) *n. Anatomy.* the sheath of fibrous connective tissue surrounding the primary bundles of muscle fibres. [C19: from PERI- + *-mysium,* from Greek *mus* muscle]

per·i·na·tal (ˌpɛrɪˈneɪtᵊl) *adj.* of, relating to, or occurring in the period immediately before or after birth.

per·i·neph·ri·um (ˌpɛrɪˈnɛfrɪəm) *n., pl.* **·ri·a** (-rɪə). *Anatomy.* the fatty and connective tissue surrounding the kidney. [C19: from PERI- + *-nephrium,* from Greek *nephros* kidney] —ˌ**per·i·ˈneph·ric** *adj.*

per·i·ne·um (ˌpɛrɪˈniːəm) *n., pl.* **·ne·a** (-ˈniːə). **1.** the region of the body between the anus and the genital organs, including some of the underlying structures. **2.** the nearly diamond-shaped surface of the human trunk between the thighs. [C17: from New Latin, from Greek *perinaion,* from PERI- + *inein* to empty out] —ˌ**per·i·ˈne·al** *adj.*

per·i·neu·ri·tis (ˌpɛrɪnjʊˈraɪtɪs) *n.* inflammation of the perineurium. —**per·i·neu·rit·ic** (ˌpɛrɪnjʊˈrɪtɪk) *adj.*

per·i·neu·ri·um (ˌpɛrɪˈnjʊərɪəm) *n.* the connective tissue forming a sheath around a single bundle of nerve fibres. [C19: from New Latin, from PERI- + Greek *neuron* nerve] —ˌ**per·i·ˈneu·ri·al** *adj.*

pe·ri·od (ˈpɪərɪəd) *n.* **1.** a portion of time of indefinable length: *he spent a period away from home.* **2. a.** a portion of time specified in some way: *the Arthurian period; Picasso's blue period.* **b.** (*as modifier*): *period costume.* **3.** a nontechnical name for **menstruation. 4.** *Geology.* a unit of geological time during which a system of rocks is formed: *the Jurassic period.* **5.** a division of time, esp. of the academic day. **6.** *Physics, maths.* **a.** the time taken to complete one cycle of a regularly recurring phenomenon; the reciprocal of frequency. Symbol: *T.* **b.** an interval in which the values of a periodic function follow a certain pattern that is duplicated over successive intervals: $\sin x = \sin (x + 2\pi)$, *where* 2π *is the period.* **7.** *Astronomy.* **a.** the time required by a body to make one complete rotation on its axis. **b.** the time interval between two successive maxima or minima of light variation of a variable star. **8.** *Chem.* one of the horizontal rows of elements in the periodic table. Each period starts with an alkali metal and ends with a rare gas. Compare **group** (sense 11). **9.** another term (esp. U.S.) for **full stop. 10.** a complete sentence, esp. a complex one with several clauses. **11.** *Music.* a passage or division of a piece of music, usually consisting of two or more contrasting or complementary musical phrases and ending on a cadence. Also called: **sentence. 12.** (in classical prosody) a unit consisting of two or more cola. **13.** *Rare.* a completion or end. [C14 *peryod,* from Latin *periodus,* from Greek *periodos* circuit, from PERI- + *hodos* way]

pe·ri·o·date (pɜːˈraɪəˌdeɪt) *n.* any salt or ester of a periodic acid.

pe·ri·od·ic (ˌpɪərɪˈɒdɪk) *adj.* **1.** happening or recurring at intervals; intermittent. **2.** of, relating to, or resembling a period. **3.** having or occurring in repeated periods or cycles. —ˌ**pe·ri·ˈod·i·cal·ly** *adv.* —**pe·ri·o·dic·i·ty** (ˌpɪərɪəˈdɪsɪtɪ) *n.*

per·i·od·ic ac·id (ˌpɜːraɪˈɒdɪk) *n.* any of various oxyacids of iodine containing a greater proportion of oxygen than iodic acid and differing from each other in water content, esp. either of the crystalline compounds HIO_4 (**metaperiodic acid**) and H_5IO_6 (**paraperiodic acid**). [C19: from PER- + IODIC]

pe+ri+od·i+cal (ˌpɪərɪˈɒdɪkəl) *n.* **1.** a publication issued at regular intervals, usually monthly or weekly. *~adj.* **2.** of or relating to such publications. **3.** published at regular intervals. **4.** periodic or occasional.

pe+ri+od+ic func+tion (ˌpɪərɪˈɒdɪk) *n. Maths.* a function, such as sin *x*, whose value is repeated at constant intervals.

pe+ri+od+ic law (ˌpɪərɪˈɒdɪk) *n.* the principle that the chemical properties of the elements are periodic functions of their atomic weights (also called **Mendeleev's law**) or, more accurately, of their atomic numbers.

pe+ri+od+ic sen+tence (ˌpɪərɪˈɒdɪk) *n. Rhetoric.* a sentence in which the completion of the main clause is left to the end, thus creating an effect of suspense.

pe+ri+od+ic sys+tem (ˌpɪərɪˈɒdɪk) *n.* the classification of the elements based on the periodic law.

pe+ri+od+ic ta+ble (ˌpɪərɪˈɒdɪk) *n.* a table of the elements, arranged in order of increasing atomic number, based on the periodic law. Elements having similar chemical properties and electronic structures appear in vertical columns (groups).

pe+ri+od·i+za+tion *or* **pe+ri+od·i+sa+tion** (ˌpɪərɪədaɪˈzeɪʃən) *n.* the act or process of dividing history into periods.

per·i·o+don+tal (ˌpɛrɪəˈdɒntəl) *adj. Dentistry.* situated around a tooth.

per·i·o+don+tics (ˌpɛrɪəˈdɒntɪks) *or* **per·i·o+don+ti·a** (ˌpɛrɪəˈdɒnʃɪə) *n.* the branch of dentistry concerned with diseases affecting the tissues and structures that surround teeth. [C19: from PERI- + *-odontics,* from Greek *odōn* tooth] —ˌ**per·i·o+ˈdon+tic** *adj.* —ˌ**per·i·o+ˈdon+ti+cal+ly** *adv.*

pe+ri+od piece *n.* an object, piece of music, etc., valued for its quality of evoking a particular historical period.

per·i·o+nych·i·um (ˌpɛrɪəʊˈnɪkɪəm) *n., pl.* **·i·a** (-ɪə). the skin that surrounds a fingernail or toenail. [C19: New Latin, from PERI- + Greek *onux* a nail]

per·i·os+te·um (ˌpɛrɪˈɒstɪəm) *n., pl.* **+te·a** (-tɪə). a thick fibrous two-layered membrane covering the surface of bones. [C16: New Latin, from Greek *periosteon,* from PERI- + *osteon* bone] —ˌ**per·i+ˈos·te·al** *adj.*

per·i·os+ti+tis (ˌpɛrɪɒˈstaɪtɪs) *n.* inflammation of the periosteum. —**per·i+os+tit+ic** (ˌpɛrɪɒˈstɪtɪk) *adj.*

per·i·o+tic (ˌpɛrɪˈəʊtɪk, -ˈɒtɪk) *adj.* **1.** of or relating to the structures situated around the internal ear. **2.** situated around the ear. [C19: from PERI- + *-otic,* from Greek *ous* ear]

per·i·pa+tet+ic (ˌpɛrɪpəˈtɛtɪk) *adj.* **1.** itinerant. **2.** *Brit.* employed in two or more educational establishments and travelling from one to another: *a peripatetic football coach.* *~n.* **3.** a peripatetic person. [C16: from Latin *peripatēticus,* from Greek *peripatētikos,* from *peripatein* to pace to and fro] —ˌ**per·i·pa+ˈtet·i·cal+ly** *adv.*

Per·i·pa+tet+ic (ˌpɛrɪpəˈtɛtɪk) *adj.* **1.** of or relating to the teachings of Aristotle, who used to teach philosophy while walking about the Lyceum in ancient Athens. *~n.* **2.** a student of Aristotelianism.

per·i·pe·tei·a, per·i·pe·ti·a (ˌpɛrɪpɪˈtaɪə, -ˈtɪə), *or* **pe+rip+e·ty** (pəˈrɪpətɪ) *n.* (esp. in drama) an abrupt turn of events or reversal of circumstances. [C16: from Greek, from PERI- + *piptein* to fall (to change suddenly, literally: to fall around)] —ˌ**per·i·pe·ˈtei·an** *or* ˌ**per·i·pe·ˈti·an** *adj.*

pe+riph+er+al (pəˈrɪfərəl) *adj.* **1.** not relating to the most important part of something; incidental, minor, or superficial. **2.** of, relating to, or of the nature of a periphery. **3.** *Anatomy.* of, relating to, or situated near the surface of the body: *a peripheral nerve.* —**pe+ˈriph+er+al+ly** *adv.*

pe+riph+er+al de+vice *or* **u·nit** *n. Computer technol.* any device, such as a card punch, line printer, or magnetic tape unit, concerned with input/output, storage, etc. Often shortened to **peripheral.**

pe+riph+er·y (pəˈrɪfərɪ) *n., pl.* **+er·ies.** **1.** the outermost boundary of an area. **2.** the outside surface of something. **3.** *Anatomy.* the surface or outermost part of the body or one of its organs or parts. [C16: from Late Latin *peripherīa,* from Greek, from PERI- + *pherein* to bear]

pe+riph+ra+sis (pəˈrɪfrəsɪs) *n., pl.* **+ra+ses** (-rəˌsiːz) **1.** a roundabout way of expressing something; circumlocution. **2.** an expression of this kind. [C16: via Latin from Greek, from PERI- + *phrazein* to declare]

per·i·phras+tic (ˌpɛrɪˈfræstɪk) *adj.* **1.** employing or involving periphrasis. **2.** expressed in two or more words rather than by an inflected form of one: used esp. of a tense of a verb where the second element is an auxiliary verb. For example, *He does go* and *He will go* involve periphrastic tenses. —ˌ**per·i+ˈphras+ti+cal+ly** *adv.*

pe+riph·y·ton (pəˈrɪfɪˌtɒn) *n.* aquatic organisms, such as certain algae, that live attached to rocks or other surfaces. [C20: from Greek, from PERI- + *phutos,* from *phuein* to grow]

pe+rip+te·ral (pəˈrɪptərəl) *adj.* having a row of columns on all sides. [C19: from PERI- + *-pteral,* from Greek *pteron* wing]

pe+rique (pəˈriːk) *n.* a strong highly-flavoured tobacco cured in its own juices and grown in Louisiana. [C19: apparently from *Périque,* nickname of Pierre Chenet, American tobacco planter who first grew it in Louisiana]

per·i+sarc (ˈpɛrɪˌsɑːk) *n.* the outer chitinous layer secreted by colonial hydrozoan coelenterates, such as species of *Obelia.* [C19: from PERI- + *-sarc,* from Greek *sarx* flesh] —ˌ**per·i+ˈsar+cal** *or* ˌ**per·i+ˈsar+cous** *adj.*

per·i·scope (ˈpɛrɪˌskəʊp) *n.* any of a number of optical instruments that enable the user to view objects that are not in the direct line of vision, such as one in a submarine for looking above the surface of the water. They have a system of mirrors or prisms to reflect the light and often contain focusing lenses. [C19: from Greek *periskopein* to look around; see PERI-, -SCOPE]

per·i+scop+ic (ˌpɛrɪˈskɒpɪk) *adj.* (of a lens) having a wide field of view. —ˌ**per·i+ˈscop·i+cal+ly** *adv.*

per+ish (ˈpɛrɪʃ) *vb.* (*intr.*) **1.** to be destroyed or die, esp. in an untimely way. **2.** to rot: *leather perishes if exposed to bad weather.* **3. do a perish.** *Austral. informal.* to die or come near to dying of thirst or starvation. [C13: from Old French *périr,* from Latin *perīre* to pass away entirely, from PER- (away) + *īre* to go]

per+ish+a·ble (ˈpɛrɪʃəbəl) *adj.* **1.** liable to rot or wither. *~n.* **2.** (*often pl.*) a perishable article, esp. food. —ˌ**per+ish+a·ˈbil+i·ty** *or* ˈ**per+ish+a·ble+ness** *n.* —ˈ**per+ish+a·bly** *adv.*

per+ished (ˈpɛrɪʃt) *adj. Informal.* (of a person, part of the body, etc.) extremely cold.

per+ish+ing (ˈpɛrɪʃɪŋ) *adj.* **1.** *Informal.* (of weather, etc.) extremely cold. **2.** *Slang.* (intensifier qualifying something undesirable): *you perishing blighter!* —ˈ**per+ish+ing+ly** *adv.*

per·i+sperm (ˈpɛrɪˌspɜːm) *n.* the nutritive tissue surrounding the embryo in certain seeds, and developing from the nucellus of the ovule. —ˌ**per·i+ˈsper+mal** *adj.*

per·i+spo+me·non (ˌpɛrɪˈspəʊməˌnɒn) *adj.* **1.** (of a Greek word) bearing a circumflex accent on the last syllable. *~n.* **2.** a word having such an accent. [from Greek, from PERI- (around) + *spaein* to pull, draw]

pe+ris+so+dac+tyl (pəˌrɪsəʊˈdæktɪl) *or* **pe+ris+so+dac+tyle** (pəˌrɪsəʊˈdæktaɪl) *n.* **1.** any placental mammal of the order *Perissodactyla,* having hooves with an odd number of toes: includes horses, tapirs, and rhinoceroses. *~adj.* **2.** of, relating to, or belonging to the *Perissodactyla.* [C19: from New Latin *perissodactylus,* from Greek *perissos* uneven + *daktulos* digit] —**pe+ˌris+so+ˈdac+ty+lous** *adj.*

per·i+stal+sis (ˌpɛrɪˈstælsɪs) *n., pl.* **+ses** (-siːz). *Physiol.* the succession of waves of involuntary muscular contraction of various bodily tubes, esp. of the alimentary tract, where it effects transport of food and waste products. [C19: from New Latin, from PERI- + Greek *stalsis* compression, from *stellein* to press together] —ˌ**per·i+ˈstal+tic** *adj.* —ˌ**per·i+ˈstal+ti+cal+ly** *adv.*

per·i+stome (ˈpɛrɪˌstəʊm) *n.* **1.** a fringe of pointed teeth surrounding the opening of a moss capsule. **2.** any of various parts surrounding the mouth of invertebrates such as echinoderms, earthworms, and protozoans. [C18: from New Latin *peristoma,* from PERI- + Greek *stoma* mouth] —ˌ**per·i+ˈsto+mal** *or* ˌ**per·i+ˈsto+mi·al** *adj.*

per·i+style (ˈpɛrɪˌstaɪl) *n.* **1.** a colonnade that surrounds a court or building. **2.** an area that is surrounded by a colonnade. [C17: via French from Latin *peristȳlum,* from Greek *peristulon,* from PERI- + *stulos* column] —ˌ**per·i+ˈsty+lar** *adj.*

per·i+the·ci·um (ˌpɛrɪˈθiːsɪəm) *n., pl.* **·ci·a** (-sɪə). *Botany.* a flask-shaped structure containing asci that are discharged from an apical pore; a type of ascocarp. [C19: from New Latin, from PERI- + Greek *thēkē* case]

per·i+to+ne·um (ˌpɛrɪtəˈniːəm) *n., pl.* **+ne·a** (-ˈniːə) *or* **+ne·ums.** a thin translucent serous sac that lines the walls of the abdominal cavity and covers most of the viscera. [C16: via Late Latin from Greek *peritonaion,* from *peritonos* stretched around, from PERI- + *teinein* to stretch] —ˌ**per·i+to+ˈne·al** *adj.*

per·i+to+ni+tis (ˌpɛrɪtəˈnaɪtɪs) *n.* inflammation of the peritoneum. —**per·i+to+nit+ic** (ˌpɛrɪtəˈnɪtɪk) *adj.*

per·i+track (ˈpɛrɪˌtræk) *n.* another name for **taxiway.**

pe+rit+ri+cha (pəˈrɪtrɪkə) *pl. n., sing.* **per·i+trich** (ˈpɛrɪˌtrɪk). **1.** ciliate protozoans, of the order *Peritrichida,* in which the cilia are restricted to a spiral around the mouth. **2.** bacteria having the entire cell surface covered with cilia. [C19: from New Latin, from PERI- + Greek *thrix* hair] —**pe+ˈrit+ri+chous** *adj.*

per·i+wig (ˈpɛrɪˌwɪg) *n.* a wig, such as a peruke. [C16 *perwyke,* changed from French *perruque* wig, PERUKE]

per·i+win+kle[1] (ˈpɛrɪˌwɪŋkəl) *n.* any of various edible marine gastropods of the genus *Littorina,* esp. *L. littorea,* having a spirally coiled shell. Often shortened to **winkle.** [C16: of unknown origin]

per·i+win+kle[2] (ˈpɛrɪˌwɪŋkəl) *n.* **1.** Also called (U.S.): **creeping myrtle, trailing myrtle.** any of several Eurasian apocynaceous evergreen plants of the genus *Vinca,* such as *V. minor* (**lesser periwinkle**) and *V. major* (**greater periwinkle**), having trailing stems and blue flowers. **2. a.** a light purplish-blue colour. **b.** (*as adj.*): *a periwinkle coat.* [C14 *pervenke,* from Old English *perwince,* from Late Latin *pervinca*]

per+jure (ˈpɜːdʒə) *vb.* (*tr.*) *Criminal law.* to render (oneself) guilty of perjury. [C15: from Old French *parjurer,* from Latin *perjūrāre,* from PER- + *jūrāre* to make an oath, from *jūs* law] —ˈ**per+jur+er** *n.*

per+jured (ˈpɜːdʒəd) *adj. Criminal law.* **1. a.** having sworn falsely. **b.** having committed perjury. **2.** involving or characterized by perjury: *perjured evidence.*

per+jur·y (ˈpɜːdʒərɪ) *n., pl.* **+jur·ies.** *Criminal law.* the offence committed by a witness in judicial proceedings who, having been lawfully sworn or having affirmed, wilfully gives false evidence. [C14: from Anglo-French *parjurie,* from Latin *perjūrium* a false oath; see PERJURE] —**per+jur·i·ous** (pɜːˈdʒʊərɪəs) *adj.* —**per+ˈjur·i·ous+ly** *adv.*

perk[1] (pɜːk) *adj.* **1.** pert; brisk; lively. *~vb.* **2.** See **perk up.** [C16: see PERK UP]

perk[2] (pɜːk) *vb.* (*intr.*) *Informal.* (of coffee) to percolate.

perk[3] (pɜːk) *n. Brit. informal.* short for **perquisite.**

Per·kin's mauve (ˈpɜːkɪnz) *n.* another name for **mauve** (the dye). [C19: named after Sir William Henry *Perkin* (1838–1907), who first synthesized it]

perk up *vb.* (*adv.*) **1.** to make or become more cheerful, hopeful, or lively. **2.** to rise or cause to rise up briskly: *the dog's ears perked up.* **3.** (*tr.*) to make smarter in appearance: *she perked up her outfit with a bright scarf.* **4.** (*intr.*) *Austral. slang.* to vomit. [C14 *perk:* perhaps from Norman French *perquer;* see PERCH[1]]

perk·y ('pɜːkɪ) *adj.* **perk·i·er, perk·i·est. 1.** jaunty; lively. **2.** confident; spirited. —'**perk·i·ly** *adv.* —'**perk·i·ness** *n.*

Per·lis ('pɛəlɪs, 'pɜː-) *n.* a state of NW West Malaysia, on the Andaman Sea: a dependency of Thailand until 1909. Capital: Kangar. Pop.: 120 996 (1970). Area: 803 sq. km (310 sq. miles).

per·lite *or* **pearl·ite** ('pɜːlaɪt) *n.* a variety of obsidian consisting of masses of small pearly globules: used as a filler, insulator, and soil-conditioner. [C19: from French, from *perle* PEARL] —**per·lit·ic** *or* **pearl·it·ic** (pɜː'lɪtɪk) *adj.*

per·lo·cu·tion (ˌpɜːlɒ'kjuːʃən) *n. Philosophy.* the effect that someone has by uttering certain words, such as frightening a person. Compare **illocution.** [C16 (in the obsolete sense: the action of speaking): from Medieval or New Latin *perlocūtiō;* see PER-, LOCUTION] —ˌ**per·lo·'cu·tion·ar·y** *adj.*

perm[1] (pɜːm) *Informal.* ~*n.* **1.** short for **permanent wave.** ~*vb.* (*tr.*) **2.** to give (hair) a permanent wave.

perm[2] (pɜːm) *n. Informal.* short for **permutation** (sense 4).

Perm (*Russian* pjermj) *n.* a port in the central Soviet Union, on the Kama River: oil refinery; university (1916). Pop.: 939 000 (1975 est.). Former name (1940–62): **Molotov.**

per·ma·frost ('pɜːməˌfrɒst) *n.* ground that is permanently frozen, often to great depths, the surface sometimes thawing in the summer. [C20: from PERMA(NENT) + FROST]

perm·al·loy (pɜːm'ælɔɪ) *n.* any of various alloys containing iron and nickel (45–80 per cent) and sometimes smaller amounts of chromium and molybdenum.

per·ma·nence ('pɜːmənəns) *n.* the state or quality of being permanent.

per·ma·nen·cy ('pɜːmənənsɪ) *n., pl.* **·cies. 1.** a person or thing that is permanent. **2.** another word for **permanence.**

per·ma·nent ('pɜːmənənt) *adj.* **1.** existing or intended to exist for an indefinite period: *a permanent structure.* **2.** not expected to change for an indefinite time; not temporary: *a permanent condition.* [C15: from Latin *permanens* continuing, from *permanēre* to stay to the end, from *per-* through + *manēre* to remain] —'**per·ma·nent·ly** *adv.*

Per·ma·nent Court of Ar·bi·tra·tion *n.* the official name of the **Hague Tribunal.**

per·ma·nent mag·net *n.* a magnet, often of steel, that retains its magnetization after the magnetic field producing it has been removed. —**per·ma·nent mag·net·ism** *n.*

per·ma·nent press *n.* **a.** a chemical treatment for clothing that makes the fabric crease-resistant and sometimes provides a garment with a permanent crease or pleats. **b.** (*as modifier*): *permanent-press skirts.*

per·ma·nent wave *n.* a series of waves or curls made in the hair by application of heat or chemicals, lasting several months. Often shortened to **perm.**

per·ma·nent way *n. Chiefly Brit.* the track of a railway, including the ballast, sleepers, rails, etc.

per·man·ga·nate (pə'mæŋgəˌneɪt, -nɪt) *n.* a salt of permanganic acid.

per·man·gan·ic ac·id (ˌpɜːmæn'gænɪk) *n.* a monobasic acid known only in solution and in the form of permanganate salts. Formula: $HMnO_4$.

per·me·a·bil·i·ty (ˌpɜːmɪə'bɪlɪtɪ) *n.* **1.** the state or quality of being permeable. **2.** a measure of the ability of a medium to modify a magnetic field, expressed as the ratio of the magnetic flux density in the medium to the field strength; measured in henries per metre. Symbol: μ See also **relative permeability, magnetic constant. 3.** the rate at which gas diffuses through the surface of a balloon or airship, usually expressed in litres per square metre per day.

per·me·a·ble ('pɜːmɪəbᵊl) *adj.* capable of being permeated, esp. by liquids. [C15: from Late Latin *permeābilis,* from Latin *permeāre* to pervade; see PERMEATE] —'**per·me·a·ble·ness** *n.* —'**per·me·a·bly** *adv.*

per·me·ance ('pɜːmɪəns) *n.* **1.** the act of permeating. **2.** the reciprocal of the reluctance of a magnetic circuit. Symbol: Λ —'**per·me·ant** *adj., n.*

per·me·ate ('pɜːmɪˌeɪt) *vb.* **1.** to penetrate or pervade (a substance, area, etc.): *a lovely smell permeated the room.* **2.** to pass through or cause to pass through by osmosis or diffusion: *to permeate a membrane.* [C17: from Latin *permeāre,* from *per-* through + *meāre* to pass] —ˌ**per·me·'a·tion** *n.* —'**per·me·a·tive** *adj.* —'**per·me·ˌa·tor** *n.*

per men·sem *Latin.* ('pɜː 'mɛnsəm) *adv.* every month or by the month.

Per·mi·an ('pɜːmɪən) *adj.* **1.** of, denoting, or formed in the last period of the Palaeozoic era, between the Carboniferous and Triassic periods, which lasted for 45 000 000 years. ~*n.* **2. the.** the Permian period or rock system. [C19: after PERM, Russia]

per mill *or* **mil** (pə 'mɪl) *adv.* by the thousand or in each thousand.

per·mis·si·ble (pə'mɪsəbᵊl) *adj.* permitted; allowable. —**per·ˌmis·si·'bil·i·ty** *n.* —**per·'mis·si·bly** *adv.*

per·mis·sion (pə'mɪʃən) *n.* authorization to do something.

per·mis·sive (pə'mɪsɪv) *adj.* **1.** tolerant; lenient: *permissive parents.* **2.** indulgent in matters of sex: *a permissive society.* **3.** granting permission. **4.** *Archaic.* not obligatory. —**per·'mis·sive·ly** *adv.* —**per·'mis·sive·ness** *n.*

per·mit *vb.* (pə'mɪt), **·mits, ·mit·ting, ·mit·ted. 1.** (*tr.*) to grant permission to do something: *you are permitted to smoke.* **2.** (*tr.*) to consent to or tolerate: *she will not permit him to come.* **3.** (when *intr.,* often foll. by *of;* when *tr.,* often foll. by an infinitive) to allow the possibility (of): *the passage permits of two interpretations; his work permits him to relax nowadays.* ~*n.* ('pɜːmɪt). **4.** an official certificate or document granting authorization; licence. **5.** permission, esp. written permission. [C15: from Latin *permittere,* from *per-* through + *mittere* to send] —**per·'mit·ter** *n.*

per·mit·tiv·i·ty (ˌpɜːmɪ'tɪvɪtɪ) *n., pl.* **·ties.** a measure of the ability of a substance to transmit an electric field, expressed as the ratio of its electric displacement to the applied field strength; measured in farads per metre. Symbol: ϵ See also **relative permittivity, electric constant.**

per·mu·ta·tion (ˌpɜːmjʊ'teɪʃən) *n.* **1.** *Maths.* **a.** an ordered arrangement of the numbers, terms, etc., of a set into specified groups: *the permutations of a, b, and c, taken two at a time, are ab, ba, ac, ca, bc, cb.* **b.** a group formed in this way. The number of permutations of *n* objects taken *r* at a time is $n!/(n-r)!$. Symbol: $_nP_r$. Compare **combination** (sense 6). **2.** a combination of items, etc., made by reordering. **3.** an alteration; transformation. **4.** a fixed combination for selections of results on football pools. Usually shortened to **perm.** [C14: from Latin *permūtātiō,* from *permūtāre* to change thoroughly; see MUTATION] —ˌ**per·mu·'ta·tion·al** *adj.*

per·mute (pə'mjuːt) *vb.* (*tr.*) **1.** to change the sequence of. **2.** *Maths.* to subject to permutation. [C14: from Latin *permūtāre,* from PER- + *mūtāre* to change, alter] —**per·'mut·a·ble** *adj.* —**per·ˌmut·a·'bil·i·ty** *or* **per·'mut·a·ble·ness** *n.* —**per·'mut·a·bly** *adv.*

Per·nam·bu·co (ˌpɜːnəm'bjuːkəʊ; *Portuguese* ˌpernəm'buku) *n.* **1.** a state of NE Brazil, on the Atlantic: consists of a humid coastal plain rising to a high inland plateau. Capital: Recife. Pop.: 5 160 640 (1970). Area: 98 280 sq. km (37 946 sq. miles). **2.** the former name of **Recife.**

per·ni·cious (pə'nɪʃəs) *adj.* **1.** wicked or malicious: *pernicious lies.* **2.** causing grave harm; deadly. [C16: from Latin *perniciōsus,* from *perniciēs* ruin, from PER- (intensive) + *nex* death] —**per·'ni·cious·ly** *adv.* —**per·'ni·cious·ness** *n.*

per·ni·cious a·nae·mi·a *n.* a form of anaemia characterized by lesions of the spinal cord, weakness, sore tongue, numbness in the arms and legs, diarrhoea, etc.: associated with inadequate absorption of vitamin B_{12}.

per·nick·et·y (pə'nɪkɪtɪ) *or U.S.* **per·snick·et·y** *adj. Informal.* **1.** excessively precise and attentive to detail; fussy. **2.** (of a task) requiring close attention; exacting. [C19: originally Scottish, of unknown origin] —**per·'nick·et·i·ness** *or U.S.* **per·'snick·et·i·ness** *n.*

Per·nik (*Bulgarian* 'pɛrnik) *n.* an industrial town in W Bulgaria, on the Struma River. Pop.: 79 335 (1970). Former name (1949–62): **Dimitrovo.**

Per·nod ('pɛənəʊ; *French* pɛr'no) *n. Trademark.* an aniseed-flavoured apéritif from France.

Pe·rón (*Spanish* pe'ron) *n.* **1. Juan Do·ming·o** (xwan do'miŋgo). 1895–1974, Argentine soldier and statesman; president (1946–55; 1973–74). He was deposed in 1955, remaining in exile until 1973. **2.** his third wife **Ma·rí·a Es·tell·a** (ma'ria es'tela), known as *Isabel.* born 1930, president of Argentina (1974–76); deposed. **3. (María) E·va (Duarte) de Pe·rón** ('eva), known as *Evita.* Second wife of Juan Domingo Perón. 1919–52, Argentine film actress: active in politics and social welfare (1946–52).

pe·ro·ne·al (ˌpɛrə'niːəl) *adj. Anatomy.* of or relating to the fibula or the outer side of the leg. [C19: from New Latin *peronē* fibula, from Greek: fibula]

per·o·rate ('pɛrəˌreɪt) *vb.* (*intr.*) **1.** to speak at length, esp. in a formal manner. **2.** to conclude a speech or sum up, esp. with a formal recapitulation.

per·o·ra·tion (ˌpɛrə'reɪʃən) *n. Rhetoric.* the conclusion of a speech or discourse, in which points made previously are summed up or recapitulated, esp. with greater emphasis. [C15: from Latin *perōrātiō,* from *perōrāre,* from PER- (thoroughly) + *ōrāre* to speak]

pe·rox·i·dase (pə'rɒksɪˌdeɪs, -ˌdeɪz) *n.* any of a group of enzymes that catalyse the oxidation of a compound by the decomposition of hydrogen peroxide or an organic peroxide. They generally consist of a protein combined with haem.

per·ox·ide (pə'rɒksaɪd) *n.* **1.** short for **hydrogen peroxide,** esp. when used for bleaching hair. **2.** any of a class of metallic oxides, such as sodium peroxide, Na_2O_2, that contain the divalent ion $^-O\text{-}O^-$. **3.** (*not in technical usage*) any of certain dioxides, such as manganese peroxide, MnO_2, that resemble peroxides in their formula but do not contain the $^-O\text{-}O^-$ ion. **4.** any of a class of organic compounds whose molecules contain two oxygen atoms bound together. They tend to be explosive. **5.** (*modifier*) of, relating to, bleached with, or resembling peroxide: *a peroxide blonde.* ~*vb.* **6.** (*tr.*) to bleach (the hair) with peroxide.

per·ox·y- *or esp. for inorganic compounds* **per·ox·o-** *combining form.* indicating the presence of the peroxide group, -O-O-: *peroxysulphuric acid.* Also (not in technical usage): **per-.**

per·ox·y·sul·phu·ric ac·id (pəˌrɒksɪsʌl'fjʊərɪk) *n.* a white hygroscopic crystalline unstable oxidizing acid. Formula: H_2SO_5. Also called (not in technical usage): **persulphuric acid, Caro's acid.**

per·pend[1] ('pɜːpənd) *or* **per·pent** *n.* a large stone that passes through a wall from one side to the other. Also called: **parpend,**

perpend stone. [C15: from Old French *parpain,* of uncertain origin]

per+pend[2] (pəˈpɛnd) *vb.* an archaic word for **ponder.** [C16: from Latin *perpendere* to examine, from PER- (thoroughly) + *pendere* to weigh]

per+pen+dic·u+lar (ˌpɜːpənˈdɪkjʊlə) *adj.* **1.** Also: **normal.** at right angles. **2.** denoting, relating to, or having the style of Gothic architecture used in England during the 14th and 15th centuries, characterized by tracery having vertical lines, a four-centred arch, and fan vaulting. **3.** upright; vertical. ~*n.* **4.** *Geom.* a line or plane perpendicular to another. **5.** any instrument used for indicating the vertical line through a given point. **6.** *Mountaineering.* a nearly vertical face. [C14: from Latin *perpendiculāris,* from *perpendiculum* a plumbline, from *per-* through + *pendēre* to hang] —**per+pen+dic·u+lar+i·ty** (ˌpɜːpənˌdɪkjʊˈlærɪtɪ) *n.* —ˌ**per+pen+ˈdic·u+lar+ly** *adv.*

per+pe+trate (ˈpɜːpɪˌtreɪt) *vb.* (*tr.*) to perform or be responsible for (a deception, crime, etc.). [C16: from Latin *perpetrāre,* from *per-* (thoroughly) + *patrāre* to perform, perhaps from *pater* father, leader in the performance of sacred rites] —ˌ**per+pe+ˈtra+tion** *n.* —ˈ**per+pe+ˌtra+tor** *n.*

per+pet+u·al (pəˈpɛtjʊəl) *adj.* **1.** (*usually prenominal*) eternal; permanent. **2.** (*usually prenominal*) seemingly ceaseless because often repeated: *your perpetual complaints.* **3.** *Horticulture.* blooming throughout the growing season or year. ~*n.* **4.** a plant that blooms throughout the growing season. [C14: via Old French from Latin *perpetuālis* universal, from *perpes* continuous, from *per-* (thoroughly) + *petere* to go towards] —**per+ˈpet+u·al+ly** *adv.*

per+pet+u·al mo+tion *n.* **1.** Also called: **perpetual motion of the first kind.** motion of a hypothetical mechanism that continues indefinitely without any external source of energy. It is impossible in practice because of friction. **2.** Also called: **perpetual motion of the second kind.** motion of a hypothetical mechanism that derives its energy from a source at a lower temperature. It is impossible in practice because of the second law of thermodynamics.

per+pet·u+ate (pəˈpɛtjʊˌeɪt) *vb.* (*tr.*) to cause to continue or prevail: *to perpetuate misconceptions.* [C16: from Latin *perpetuāre* to continue without interruption, from *perpetuus* PERPETUAL] —**per+ˌpet·u·ˈa+tion** *n.*

per+pe+tu+i+ty (ˌpɜːpɪˈtjuːɪtɪ) *n., pl.* **·ties. 1.** eternity. **2.** the state or quality of being perpetual. **3.** *Property law.* a limitation preventing the absolute disposal of an estate for longer than the period allowed by law. **4.** an annuity with no maturity date and payable indefinitely. **5. in perpetuity.** for ever. [C15: from Old French *perpetuite,* from Latin *perpetuitās* continuity]

Per+pi+gnan (*French* pɛrpiˈɲɑ̃) *n.* a town in S France: historic capital of Roussillon. Pop.: 107 971 (1975).

per+plex (pəˈplɛks) *vb.* (*tr.*) **1.** to puzzle; bewilder; confuse. **2.** to complicate: *to perplex an issue.* [C15: from obsolete *perplex* (adj.) intricate, from Latin *perplexus* entangled, from *per-* (thoroughly) + *plectere* to entwine]

per+plex+i·ty (pəˈplɛksɪtɪ) *n., pl.* **·ties. 1.** the state of being perplexed. **2.** the state of being intricate or complicated. **3.** something that perplexes.

per pro. *abbrev. for* per procurationem. [Latin: through the agency of; by delegation to]

per+qui+site (ˈpɜːkwɪzɪt) *n.* **1.** an incidental benefit gained from a certain type of employment, such as the use of a company car. **2.** a customary benefit received in addition to a regular income. **3.** a customary tip. **4.** something expected or regarded as an exclusive right. ~Often shortened (informal) to **perk.** [C15: from Medieval Latin *perquīsītum* an acquired possession, from Latin *perquīrere* to seek earnestly for something, from *per-* (thoroughly) + *quaerere* to ask for, seek]

Per+rault (*French* pɛˈro) *n.* **Charles** (ʃarl). 1628–1703, French author, noted for his *Contes de ma mère l'oye* (1697), which contains the fairytales *Little Red Riding Hood, Cinderella,* and *The Sleeping Beauty.*

Per+rin (*French* pɛˈrɛ̃) *n.* **Jean Bap·tiste** (ʒɑ̃ baˈtist). 1870–1942, French physicist, noted for his work on cathode rays: Nobel prize for physics 1926.

per+ron (ˈpɛrən) *n.* an external flight of steps, esp. one at the front entrance of a building. [C14: from Old French, from *pierre* stone, from Latin *petra*]

per+ry (ˈpɛrɪ) *n., pl.* **+ries.** wine made of pears, similar in taste to cider. [C14 *pereye,* from Old French *pere,* ultimately from Latin *pirum* pear]

Per·ry (ˈpɛrɪ) *n.* **1. Mat·thew Cal·braith.** 1794–1858, U.S. naval officer, who led a naval expedition to Japan that obtained a treaty (1854) opening up Japan to western trade. **2.** his brother, **Ol·i·ver Haz·ard.** 1785–1819, U.S. naval officer: defeated a British squadron on Lake Erie (1813).

pers. *abbrev. for:* **1.** person. **2.** personal.

Pers. *abbrev. for* Persia(n).

per+salt (ˈpɜːˌsɔːlt) *n.* any salt of a peracid.

per se (ˈpɜː ˈseɪ) *adv.* by or in itself; intrinsically. [Latin]

perse (pɜːs) *adj.* of a dark greyish-blue colour. [C14: from Old French, from Medieval Latin *persus,* perhaps changed from Latin *Persicus* Persian]

per+se+cute (ˈpɜːsɪˌkjuːt) *vb.* (*tr.*) **1.** to oppress, harass, or maltreat, esp. because of race, religion, etc. **2.** to bother persistently. [C15: from Old French *persecuter,* back formation from *persecuteur,* from Late Latin *persecūtor* pursuer, from *persequī* to take vengeance upon] —ˈ**per+se·ˌcu+tive** *or* ˈ**per+se·ˌcu+to·ry** *adj.* —ˈ**per+se·ˌcu+tor** *n.*

per+se·cu+tion (ˌpɜːsɪˈkjuːʃən) *n.* the act of persecuting or the state of being persecuted.

per+se·cu+tion com+plex *n. Psychol.* an acute irrational fear that other people are plotting one's downfall and that they are responsible for one's failures.

Per+se·id (ˈpɜːsɪɪd) *n.* any member of a meteor shower occurring annually during early August and appearing to radiate from a point in the constellation Perseus. [C19: from Greek *Persēides* daughters of PERSEUS[1]]

Per·seph·o·ne (pəˈsɛfənɪ) *n. Greek myth.* a daughter of Zeus and Demeter, abducted by Hades and made his wife and queen of the underworld, but allowed part of each year to leave it. Roman counterpart: **Proserpina.**

Per+sep·o+lis (pəˈsɛpəlɪs) *n.* the capital of ancient Persia in the Persian Empire and under the Seleucids: founded by Darius; sacked by Alexander the Great in 330 B.C.

Per·seus[1] (ˈpɜːsjuːs) *n. Greek myth.* a son of Zeus and Danaë, who with Athena's help slew the Gorgon Medusa and rescued Andromeda from a sea monster.

Per+seus[2] (ˈpɜːsjuːs) *n., Latin genitive* **Per+se·i** (ˈpɜːsɪˌaɪ). a conspicuous constellation in the N hemisphere lying between Auriga and Cassiopeia and crossed by the Milky Way. It contains the eclipsing binary, Algol.

per+se·ver+ance (ˌpɜːsɪˈvɪərəns) *n.* **1.** continued steady belief or efforts, withstanding discouragement or difficulty; persistence. **2.** *Theol.* persistence in remaining in a state of grace until death. —ˌ**per+se+ˈver+ant** *adj.*

per+sev+e·ra+tion (pɜːˌsɛvəˈreɪʃən) *n. Psychol.* **1.** the tendency for an impression, idea, or feeling to dissipate only slowly and to recur during subsequent experiences. **2.** an inability to change one's method of working when transferred from one task to another.

per+se+vere (ˌpɜːsɪˈvɪə) *vb.* (*intr.;* often foll. by *in*) to show perseverance. [C14: from Old French *perseverer,* from Latin *persevērāre,* from *perseverus* very strict; see SEVERE]

Per·shing (ˈpɜːʃɪŋ) *n.* **John Jo·seph,** nickname *Black Jack.* 1860–1948, U.S. general. He was commander in chief of the American Expeditionary Force in Europe (1917–19).

Per+sia (ˈpɜːʃə) *n.* **1.** the former name (until 1935) of **Iran. 2.** another name for **Persian Empire.**

Per+sian (ˈpɜːʃən) *adj.* **1.** of or relating to ancient Persia or modern Iran, their inhabitants, or their languages. ~*n.* **2.** a native, citizen, or inhabitant of modern Iran; an Iranian. **3.** a member of an Indo-European people of West Iranian speech who established a great empire in SW Asia in the 6th century B.C. **4.** the language of Iran or Persia in any of its ancient or modern forms, belonging to the West Iranian branch of the Indo-European family. See also **Avestan, Old Persian, Pahlavi**[2]**.**

Per+sian blinds *n.* another term for **persiennes.**

Per+sian car+pet *or* **rug** *n.* a carpet or rug made in Persia or other countries of the Near East by knotting silk or wool yarn by hand onto a woven backing, characterized by rich colours and flowing or geometric designs.

Per+sian cat *n.* a long-haired variety of domestic cat with a stocky body, round face, and short thick legs.

Per+sian Em+pire *n.* the S Asian empire established by Cyrus the Great in the 6th century B.C. and overthrown by Alexander the Great in the 4th century B.C. At its height it extended from India to Europe.

Per+sian Gulf *n.* a shallow arm of the Arabian Sea between SW Iran and Arabia: linked with the Arabian Sea by the Strait of Hormus and the Gulf of Oman; important for the oilfields on its shores. Area: 233 000 sq. km (90 000 sq. miles).

Per+sian lamb *n.* **1.** a black loosely curled fur obtained from the skin of the karakul lamb. **2.** a karakul lamb.

Per+sian mel+on *n.* another name for **winter melon.**

per+si+car·i·a (ˌpɜːsɪˈkɛərɪə) *n.* another name for **red shank** (the plant).

per+si+ennes (ˌpɜːsɪˈɛnz) *pl. n.* outside window shutters having louvres to keep out the sun while maintaining ventilation. Also called: **Persian blinds.** [C19: from French, from *persien* Persian]

per+si+flage (ˈpɜːsɪˌflɑːʒ) *n.* light frivolous conversation, style, or treatment; friendly teasing. [C18: via French, from *persifler* to tease, from *per-* (intensive) + *siffler* to whistle, from Latin *sībilāre* to whistle]

per+sim+mon (pɜːˈsɪmən) *n.* **1.** any of several tropical trees of the genus *Diospyros,* typically having hard wood and large orange-red fruit: family *Ebenaceae.* **2.** the sweet fruit of any of these trees, which is edible when completely ripe. ~See also **ebony** (sense 1). [C17: of Algonquian origin; related to Delaware *pasimēnan* dried fruit]

Per+sis (ˈpɜːsɪs) *n.* an ancient region of SW Iran: homeland of the Achamenid dynasty.

per+sist (pəˈsɪst) *vb.* (*intr.*) **1.** (often foll. by *in*) to continue steadfastly or obstinately despite opposition or difficulty. **2.** to continue to exist or occur without interruption: *the rain persisted throughout the night.* [C16: from Latin *persistere,* from *per-* (intensive) + *sistere,* to stand steadfast, from *stāre* to stand] —**per+ˈsist+er** *n.*

per+sis+tence (pəˈsɪstəns) *or* **per+sis+ten+cy** *n.* **1.** the quality of persisting; tenacity. **2.** the act of persisting; continued effort or existence. **3.** the continuance of an effect after the cause of it has stopped: *persistence of vision.*

per+sis+tent (pəˈsɪstənt) *adj.* **1.** showing persistence. **2.** incessantly repeated; unrelenting: *your persistent questioning.* **3.** (of plant parts) remaining attached to the plant after the normal time of withering: *a fruit surrounded by a persistent perianth.* **4.** *Zoology.* **a.** (of parts normally present only in young stages) present in the adult: *persistent gills in axolotls.*

b. continuing to grow or develop after the normal period of growth: *persistent teeth.* **—per+'sis+tent+ly** *adv.*

per+sis+tent cru+el+ty *n. Brit. law.* conduct causing fear of danger to the life or health of a spouse (used in matrimonial proceedings before magistrates).

per+snick+et·y (pəˈsnɪkɪtɪ) *adj.* the U.S. word for **pernickety.**

per+son (ˈpɜːsᵊn) *n., pl.* **per+sons. 1.** an individual human being. **2.** the body of a human being, sometimes including his or her clothing: *guns hidden on his person.* **3.** a grammatical category into which pronouns and forms of verbs are subdivided depending on whether they refer to the speaker, the person addressed, or some other individual, thing, etc. **4.** a human being or a corporation recognized in law as having certain rights and obligations. **5.** *Philosophy.* a being characterized by a personality, consciousness, rationality, a moral sense, and self-awareness. **6.** *Archaic.* a character or role; guise. **7. in person. a.** actually present: *the author will be there in person.* **b.** without the help or intervention of others. [C13: from Old French *persone,* from Latin *persōna* mask, perhaps from Etruscan *phersu* mask]

Usage. *People* is the word usually used to refer to more than one individual: *there were a hundred people at the reception. Persons* is rarely used, except in official English: *several persons were interviewed.*

-per·son *suffix of nouns.* sometimes used instead of *-man* and *-woman* or *-lady: chairperson; salesperson.*

Per·son (ˈpɜːsᵊn) *n. Theol.* any of the three hypostases existing as distinct in the one God and constituting the Trinity. They are the **First Person,** the Father, the **Second Person,** the Son, and the **Third Person,** the Holy Ghost.

per+so+na (pɜːˈsəʊnə) *n., pl.* **+nae** (-niː). **1.** (*often pl.*) a character in a play, novel, etc. **2.** an assumed identity or character. **3.** (in Jungian psychology) the mechanism that conceals a person's true thoughts and feelings, esp. in his adaptation to the outside world. [Latin: mask]

per+son+a·ble (ˈpɜːsənəbᵊl) *adj.* pleasant in appearance and personality. **—'per+son+a·ble+ness** *n.* **—'per+son+a·bly** *adv.*

per+son+age (ˈpɜːsənɪdʒ) *n.* **1.** an important or distinguished person. **2.** another word for **person:** *a strange personage.* **3.** *Rare.* a figure in literature, history, etc.

per+so+na gra+ta *Latin.* (pɜːˈsəʊnə ˈgrɑːtə) *n., pl.* ***per+so+nae gra+tae*** (pɜːˈsəʊniː ˈgrɑːtiː) an acceptable person, esp. a diplomat acceptable to the government of the country to which he is sent.

per+son+al (ˈpɜːsənᵊl) *adj.* **1.** of or relating to the private aspects of a person's life: *personal letters; a personal question.* **2.** (*prenominal*) of or relating to a person's body, its care, or its appearance: *personal hygiene; great personal beauty.* **3.** (*prenominal*) belonging to or intended for a particular person and no one else: *as a personal favour; for your personal use.* **4.** (*prenominal*) undertaken by an individual himself: *a personal appearance by a celebrity.* **5.** referring to, concerning, or involving a person's individual personality, intimate affairs, etc., esp. in an offensive way: *personal remarks; don't be so personal.* **6.** having the attributes of an individual conscious being: *a personal God.* **7.** of or arising from the personality: *personal magnetism.* **8.** of, relating to, or denoting grammatical person. **9.** *Law.* of or relating to moveable property, as money, etc. Compare **real**[1] (sense 7). *~n.* **10.** *Law.* an item of moveable property.

per+son+al col+umn *n.* a newspaper column containing personal messages, advertisements by charities, requests for friendship, holiday companions, etc.

per+son+al e·qua+tion *n.* **1.** the variation or error in observation or judgment caused by individual characteristics. **2.** the allowance made for such variation.

per+son+al+ism (ˈpɜːsənəˌlɪzəm) *n.* **1.** a philosophical movement that stresses the value of persons. **2.** an idiosyncratic mode of behaviour or expression. **—ˌper+son+al+'is+tic** *adj.* **—'per+son+al+ist** *n., adj.*

per+son+al+i·ty (ˌpɜːsəˈnælɪtɪ) *n., pl.* **·ties. 1.** *Psychol.* the sum total of all the behavioural and mental characteristics by means of which an individual is recognized as being unique. **2.** the distinctive character of a person that makes him socially attractive: *a salesman needs a lot of personality.* **3.** a well-known person in a certain field, such as sport or entertainment. **4.** a remarkable person: *the old fellow is a real personality.* **5.** the quality of being a unique person. **6.** the distinctive atmosphere of a place or situation. **7.** (*often pl.*) a personal remark.

per+son+al+i·ty dis+or+der *n. Psychiatry.* any of a group of mental disorders characterized by a permanent disposition to behave in ways causing suffering to oneself or others.

per+son+al+i·ty in+ven+to·ry *n. Psychol.* a form of personality test in which the subject answers questions about himself. The results are used to determine dimensions of personality, such as extroversion.

per+son+al+i·ty test *n. Psychol.* any test designed to assess a subject's personality.

per+son+al+i·ty type *n. Psychol.* a cluster of personality traits commonly occurring together.

per+son+al+ize *or* **per+son+al+ise** (ˈpɜːsənəˌlaɪz) *vb.* (*tr.*) **1.** to endow with personal or individual qualities or characteristics. **2.** to mark (stationery, clothing, etc.) with a person's initials, name, etc. **3.** to take (a remark, etc.) personally. **4.** another word for **personify. —ˌper+son+al+i+'za+tion** *or* **ˌper+son+al·i+'sa+tion** *n.*

per+son+al+ly (ˈpɜːsənəlɪ) *adv.* **1.** without the help or intervention of others: *I'll attend to it personally.* **2.** (*sentence modifier*) in one's own opinion or as regards oneself: *personally, I hate onions.* **3.** as if referring to oneself: *to take the insults personally.* **4.** as a person: *we like him personally, but professionally he's incompetent.*

per+son+al pro+noun *n.* a pronoun having a definite person or thing as an antecedent and functioning grammatically in the same way as the noun that it replaces. In English, the personal pronouns include *I, you, he, she, it, we,* and *they,* and are inflected for case.

per+son+al prop+er+ty *n. Law.* moveable property, as furniture, money, etc. Compare **real property.**

per+son+al+ty (ˈpɜːsənəltɪ) *n., pl.* **+ties.** *Law.* another word for **personal property.** [C16: from Anglo-French, from Late Latin *persōnālitās* personality]

per+so+na non gra+ta *Latin.* (pɜːˈsəʊnə nɒn ˈgrɑːtə) *n., pl.* ***per+so+nae non gra+tae*** (pɜːˈsəʊniː nɒn ˈgrɑːtiː). **1.** an unacceptable or unwelcome person. **2.** a diplomatic or consular officer who is not acceptable to the government or sovereign to whom he is accredited.

per+son+ate[1] (ˈpɜːsəˌneɪt) *vb.* (*tr.*) **1.** to act the part of (a character in a play); portray. **2.** a less common word for **personify. 3.** *Criminal law.* to assume the identity of (another person) with intent to deceive. **—ˌper+son·'a+tion** *n.* **—'per+son·a+tive** *adj.* **—'per+son·ˌa+tor** *n.*

per+son+ate[2] (ˈpɜːsənɪt, -ˌneɪt) *adj.* (of the corollas of certain flowers) having two lips in the form of a face. [C18: from New Latin *persōnātus* masked, from Latin *persōna;* see PERSON]

per+son+i+fi+ca+tion (pɜːˌsɒnɪfɪˈkeɪʃən) *n.* **1.** the attribution of human characteristics to things, abstract ideas, etc., as for literary or artistic effect. **2.** the representation of an abstract quality or idea in the form of a person, creature, etc., as in art and literature. **3.** a person or thing that personifies. **4.** a person or thing regarded as an embodiment of a quality: *he is the personification of optimism.*

per+son+i+fy (pɜːˈsɒnɪˌfaɪ) *vb.* **+fies, +fy+ing, +fied.** (*tr.*) **1.** to attribute human characteristics to (a thing or abstraction). **2.** to represent (an abstract quality) in human or animal form. **3.** (of a person or thing) to represent (an abstract quality), as in art or literature. **4.** to be the embodiment of. **—per+'son+i+ˌfi+a·ble** *adj.* **—per+'son+i+ˌfi+er** *n.*

per+son+nel (ˌpɜːsəˈnɛl) *n.* **1.** the people employed in an organization or for a service or undertaking. Compare **materiel. 2. a.** the office or department that interviews, appoints, or keeps records of employees. **b.** (*as modifier*): *a personnel officer.* [C19: from French, ultimately from Late Latin *persōnālis* personal (adj.); see PERSON]

per+spec+tive (pəˈspɛktɪv) *n.* **1.** a way of regarding situations, facts, etc., and judging their relative importance. **2.** the proper or accurate point of view or the ability to see it; objectivity: *try to get some perspective on your troubles.* **3.** *Philosophy.* **a.** the relationship of the aspects of anything to one another and to the whole. **b.** any one of the aspects of something. **4.** the theory or art of suggesting three dimensions on a two-dimensional surface, in order to recreate the dimensions and spatial relationships that objects or a scene in recession present to the eye. **5.** the appearance of objects, buildings, etc., relative to each other, as determined by their distance from the viewer, or the effects of this distance on their appearance. **6.** a picture in perspective. [C14: from Medieval Latin *perspectīva ars* the science of optics, from Latin *perspicere* to inspect carefully, from *per-* (intensive) + *specere* to behold] **—per+'spec+tive+ly** *adv.*

Per+spec+tiv+ism (pəˈspɛktɪˌvɪzəm) *n. Philosophy.* **1.** the doctrine that reality can only be known from several given points of view. **2.** the doctrine that only aspects of reality, never the whole, can be known.

Per+spex (ˈpɜːspɛks) *n. Trademark.* any of various clear acrylic resins, used chiefly as a substitute for glass.

per+spi+ca+cious (ˌpɜːspɪˈkeɪʃəs) *adj.* **1.** acutely perceptive or discerning. **2.** *Archaic.* having keen eyesight. [C17: from Latin *perspicax,* from *perspicere* to look at closely; see PERSPECTIVE] **—ˌper+spi+'ca+cious+ly** *adv.* **—ˌper+spi+'ca+cious+ness** *or* **per+spi+cac+i+ty** (ˌpɜːspɪˈkæsɪtɪ) *n.*

per+spi+cu+i+ty (ˌpɜːspɪˈkjuːɪtɪ) *n.* **1.** the quality of being perspicuous. **2.** another word for **perspicacity.**

per+spic·u·ous (pəˈspɪkjʊəs) *adj.* (of speech or writing) easily understood; lucid. [C15: from Latin *perspicuus* transparent, from *perspicere* to explore thoroughly; see PERSPECTIVE] **—per+'spic·u·ous+ly** *adv.* **—per+'spic·u·ous+ness** *n.*

per+spi+ra+tion (ˌpɜːspəˈreɪʃən) *n.* **1.** the salty fluid secreted by the sweat glands of the skin. **2.** the act or process of secreting this fluid.

per+spir+a·to·ry (pəˈspaɪərətərɪ, -trɪ) *adj.* of, relating to, or stimulating perspiration.

per+spire (pəˈspaɪə) *vb.* to secrete or exude (perspiration) through the pores of the skin. [C17: from Latin *perspīrāre* to blow, from *per-* (through) + *spīrare* to breathe; compare INSPIRE] **—per+'spir+ing+ly** *adv.*

per+suade (pəˈsweɪd) *vb.* (*tr.; may take a clause as object or an infinitive*) **1.** to induce, urge, or prevail upon successfully: *he finally persuaded them to buy it.* **2.** to cause to believe; convince: *even with the evidence, the police were not persuaded.* [C16: from Latin *persuādēre,* from *per-* (intensive) + *suādēre* to urge, advise] **—per+'suad+a·ble** *or* **per+'sua+si·ble** *adj.* **—per+ˌsuad+a·'bil+i·ty** *or* **per+ˌsua+si+'bil+i·ty** *n.* **—per+'suad+er** *n.*

per+sua+sion (pəˈsweɪʒən) *n.* **1.** the act of persuading or of trying to persuade. **2.** the power to persuade. **3.** the state of being persuaded; strong belief. **4.** an established creed or belief, esp. a religious one. **5.** a sect, party, or faction. [C14: from Latin *persuāsiō;* see PERSUADE]

per+sua+sive (pəˈsweɪsɪv) *adj.* having the power or ability to persuade; tending to persuade: *a persuasive salesman.* —**per+ˈsua+sive+ly** *adv.* —**per+ˈsua+sive+ness** *n.*

per+sul+phu+ric ac·id *or U.S.* **per+sul+fu+ric ac·id** (ˌpɜːsʌlˈfjʊərɪk) *n.* another name (not in technical usage) for **peroxysulphuric acid.**

pert (pɜːt) *adj.* **1.** saucy, impudent, or forward. **2.** jaunty: *a pert little bow.* **3.** *Obsolete.* clever or brisk. [C13: variant of earlier *apert,* from Latin *apertus* open, from *aperīre* to open; influenced by Old French *aspert,* from Latin *expertus* EXPERT] —**ˈpert+ly** *adv.* —**ˈpert+ness** *n.*

pert. *abbrev. for* pertaining.

per+tain (pəˈteɪn) *vb.* (*intr.;* often foll. by *to*) **1.** to have reference, relation, or relevance. **2.** to be appropriate. **3.** to belong (to) or be a part (of); be an adjunct, attribute, or accessory (of). [C14: from Latin *pertinēre,* from *per-* (intensive) + *tenēre* to hold]

Perth (pɜːθ) *n.* **1.** a city in central Scotland, on the River Tay: capital of Scotland from the 12th century until the assassination of James I here in 1437. Pop.: 43 051 (1971). **2.** (until 1975) a county of central Scotland, now part of Central and Tayside regions. **3.** a city in SW Australia, capital of Western Australia, on the Swan River: major industrial centre; University of Western Australia (1911). Pop.: 787 300 (1975 est.).

per+ti+na+cious (ˌpɜːtɪˈneɪʃəs) *adj.* **1.** doggedly resolute in purpose or belief; unyielding. **2.** stubbornly persistent. [C17: from Latin *pertināx,* from *per-* (intensive) + *tenāx* clinging, from *tenēre* to hold] —**ˌper+ti+ˈna+cious+ly** *adv.* —**per+ti+nac+i+ty** (ˌpɜːtɪˈnæsɪtɪ) *or* **ˌper+ti+ˈna+cious+ness** *n.*

per+ti+nent (ˈpɜːtɪnənt) *adj.* relating to the matter at hand; relevant. [C14: from Latin *pertinēns,* from *pertinēre* to PERTAIN] —**ˈper+ti+nence** *n.* —**ˈper+ti+nent+ly** *adv.*

per+turb (pəˈtɜːb) *vb.* (*tr.; often passive*) **1.** to disturb the composure of; trouble. **2.** to throw into disorder. **3.** *Physics, astronomy.* to cause (a planet, electron, etc.) to undergo a perturbation. [C14: from Old French *pertourber,* from Latin *perturbāre* to confuse, from *per-* (intensive) + *turbāre* to agitate, from *turba* confusion] —**per+ˈturb+a·ble** *adj.* —**per+ˈturb+a·bly** *adv.* —**per+ˈturb+ing+ly** *adv.*

per+tur+ba+tion (ˌpɜːtəˈbeɪʃən) *n.* **1.** the act of perturbing or the state of being perturbed. **2.** a cause of disturbance or upset. **3.** *Physics.* a secondary influence on a system that modifies simple behaviour, such as the effect of the other electrons on one electron in an atom. **4.** *Astronomy.* a small continuous deviation in the inclination and eccentricity of the orbit of a planet or comet, due to the attraction of neighbouring planets.

per+tus+sis (pəˈtʌsɪs) *n.* the technical name for **whooping cough.** [C18: New Latin, from Latin *per-* (intensive) + *tussis* cough] —**per+ˈtus+sal** *adj.*

Pe·ru (pəˈruː) *n.* a republic in W South America, on the Pacific: the centre of the great Inca Empire when conquered by the Spanish in 1532; gained independence in 1824 by defeating Spanish forces with armies led by San Martín and Bolívar; consists of a coastal desert, rising to the Andes; an important exporter of minerals and a major fishing nation. Official languages: Spanish and Quechua. Religion: Roman Catholic. Currency: sol. Capital: Lima. Pop.: 13 538 208 (1972). Area: 1 285 215 sq. km (496 222 sq. miles). —**Pe+ru+vi·an** (pəˈruːvɪən) *adj., n.*

Pe·ru Cur+rent *n.* a cold ocean current flowing northwards off the Pacific coast of South America. Also called: **Humboldt Current.**

Pe+ru+gia (pəˈruːdʒə; *Italian* peˈruːdʒa) *n.* **1.** a city in central Italy, in Umbria: centre of the Umbrian school of painting (15th century); university (1308); Etruscan and Roman remains. Pop.: 135 011 (1975 est.). Ancient name: **Perusia. 2. Lake.** another name for (Lake) **Trasimene.**

Pe·ru·gi·no (*Italian* ˌperuˈdʒiːno) *n.* **Il** (il). original name *Pietro Vannucci.* 1446–1523, Italian painter; master of Raphael. His works include the fresco *Christ giving the Keys to Peter* in the Sistine Chapel, Rome.

pe+ruke (pəˈruːk) *n.* a type of wig for men, fashionable in the 17th and 18th centuries. Also called: **periwig.** [C16: from French *perruque,* from Italian *perrucca* wig, of obscure origin]

pe+ruse (pəˈruːz) *vb.* (*tr.*) **1.** to read or examine with care; study. **2.** to browse or read through in a leisurely way. [C15 (meaning: to use up): from PER- (intensive) + USE] —**pe+ˈrus+al** *n.* —**pe+ˈrus+er** *n.*

Pe+rutz (pəˈrʊts) *n.* **Max Fer·di·nand.** born 1914, British biochemist, born in Austria. With J. C. Kendrew, he worked on the structure of haemoglobin and shared the Nobel prize for chemistry (1962).

Pe+ru+vi·an bark *n.* another name for **cinchona** (sense 2).

Pe+ruz·zi (*Italian* peˈruttsi) *n.* **Bal·das·sa·re Tom·ma·so** (ˌbaldasˈsaːre tomˈmaːzo). 1481–1536, Italian architect and painter of the High Renaissance. The design of the Palazzo Massimo, Rome, is attributed to him.

perv (pɜːv) *Austral. slang.* ~*n.* **1.** a pervert. **2.** an erotic glance or look. ~*vb.* (*intr.*) *also* **perve. 3.** to give a person an erotic look.

per+vade (pɜːˈveɪd) *vb.* (*tr.*) to spread through or throughout, esp. subtly or gradually; permeate. [C17: from Latin *pervādere,* from *per-* through + *vādere* to go] —**per+ˈvad+er** *n.* —**per+va+sion** (pɜːˈveɪʒən) *n.*

per+va+sive (pɜːˈveɪsɪv) *adj.* pervading or tending to pervade. [C18: from Latin *pervāsus,* past participle of *pervādere* to PERVADE] —**per+ˈva+sive+ly** *adv.* —**per+ˈva+sive+ness** *n.*

per+verse (pəˈvɜːs) *adj.* **1.** deliberately deviating from what is regarded as normal, good, or proper. **2.** persistently holding to what is wrong. **3.** wayward or contrary; obstinate; cantankerous. **4.** *Archaic.* perverted. [C14: from Old French *pervers,* from Latin *perversus* turned the wrong way] —**per+ˈverse+ly** *adv.* —**per+ˈverse+ness** *n.*

per+ver+sion (pəˈvɜːʃən) *n.* **1.** any abnormal means of obtaining sexual satisfaction. **2.** the act of perverting or the state of being perverted. **3.** a perverted form or usage.

per+ver+si·ty (pəˈvɜːsɪtɪ) *n., pl.* **·ties. 1.** the quality or state of being perverse. **2.** a perverse action, comment, etc.

per+ver+sive (pəˈvɜːsɪv) *adj.* perverting or tending to pervert.

per+vert *vb.* (pəˈvɜːt). (*tr.*) **1.** to use wrongly or badly. **2.** to interpret wrongly or badly; distort. **3.** to lead into deviant or perverted beliefs or behaviour; corrupt. **4.** to debase. ~*n.* (ˈpɜːvɜːt). **5.** a person who practises sexual perversion. [C14: from Old French *pervertir,* from Latin *pervertere* to turn the wrong way, from *per-* (indicating deviation) + *vertere* to turn] —**per+ˈvert+er** *n.* —**per+ˈver+ti·ble** *adj.*

per+vert+ed (pəˈvɜːtɪd) *adj.* **1.** deviating greatly from what is regarded as normal or right; distorted. **2.** of or practising sexual perversion. **3.** incorrectly interpreted. —**per+ˈvert+ed+ly** *adv.* —**per+ˈvert+ed+ness** *n.*

per+vi+ous (ˈpɜːvɪəs) *adj.* **1.** able to be penetrated; permeable. **2.** receptive to new ideas, etc.; open-minded. [C17: from Latin *pervius,* from *per-* (through) + *via* a way] —**ˈper+vi+ous+ly** *adv.* —**ˈper+vi+ous+ness** *n.*

pes (peɪz, piːz) *n., pl.* **ped·es** (ˈpɛdiːz). **1.** the technical name for the human **foot. 2.** the corresponding part in higher vertebrates. **3.** any footlike part. [C19: New Latin: foot]

Pe+sach *or* **Pe+sah** (ˈpeɪsɑːk; *Hebrew* ˈpɛsax) *n.* another word for **Passover.** [from Hebrew *pesah;* see PASSOVER]

pe+sade (pɛˈsɑːd) *n. Dressage.* a position in which the horse stands on the hind legs with the forelegs in the air. [C18: from French, from *posade,* from Italian *posata* a halt, from *posare* to stop, from Latin *pausa* end]

Pe+sa+ro (*Italian* ˈpeːzaro) *n.* a port and resort in E central Italy, in the Marches on the Adriatic. Pop.: 84 373 (1971). Ancient name: **Pisaurum.**

Pes+ca+do+res (ˌpɛskəˈdɔːrɪz) *pl. n.* a group of 64 islands in Formosa Strait, separated from Taiwan (to which it belongs) by the **Pescadores Channel.** Pop.: 118 355 (1972 est.). Area: 127 sq. km (49 sq. miles). Chinese name: **P'eng-hu.**

Pe+sca+ra (*Italian* pesˈkaːra) *n.* a city and resort in E central Italy, on the Adriatic. Pop.: 132 458 (1975 est.).

pe+se·ta (pəˈseɪtə; *Spanish* peˈseta) *n.* the standard monetary unit of Spain and its dependencies, divided into 100 centimos. [C19: from Spanish, diminutive of PESO]

pe+se·wa (pɪˈseɪwɑː) *n.* a Ghanaian monetary unit worth one hundredth of a cedi.

Pesh·a·war (pəˈʃɔːə) *n.* a city in N Pakistan, at the E end of the Khyber Pass: one of the oldest cities in Pakistan and capital of the ancient kingdom of Gandhara; university (1950). Pop.: 268 366 (1972).

Pe+shit+ta (pəˈʃiːtə) *or* **Pe+shi+to** (pəˈʃiːtəʊ) *n.* the principal Syriac version of the Bible. [C18 *Peshito,* from Syriac]

pesk·y (ˈpɛskɪ) *adj.* **pesk·i·er, pesk·i·est.** *U.S. informal.* troublesome: *pesky flies.* [C19: probably changed from *pesty;* see PEST] —**ˈpesk·i·ly** *adv.* —**ˈpesk·i·ness** *n.*

pe·so (ˈpeɪsəʊ; *Spanish* ˈpeso) *n., pl.* **·sos** (-səʊz; *Spanish* -sos). **1.** the standard monetary unit, comprising 100 centavos, of Argentina, Bolivia, Colombia, Cuba, the Dominican Republic, Mexico, and the Philippines. **2.** the standard monetary unit of Uruguay, divided into 100 centesimos. **3.** a coin or currency note worth a peso. **4.** another name for **piece of eight.** [C16: from Spanish: weight, from Latin *pēnsum* something weighed out, from *pendere* to weigh]

pes+sa+ry (ˈpɛsərɪ) *n., pl.* **+ries.** *Med.* **1.** a device for inserting into the vagina, either as a support for the uterus or (**diaphragm pessary**) as a contraceptive. **2.** a medicated vaginal suppository. [C14: from Late Latin *pessārium,* from Latin *pessum,* from Greek *pessos* plug]

pes+si+mism (ˈpɛsɪˌmɪzəm) *n.* **1.** the tendency to expect the worst and see the worst in all things. **2.** the doctrine of the ultimate triumph of evil over good. **3.** the doctrine that this is the worst of all possible worlds. [C18: from Latin *pessimus* worst, from *malus* bad] —**ˈpes+si+mist** *n.* —**ˌpes+si+ˈmis+tic** *or* **ˌpes+si+ˈmis+ti+cal** *adj.* —**ˌpes+si+ˈmis+ti+cal+ly** *adv.*

pest (pɛst) *n.* **1.** a person or thing that annoys, esp. by imposing itself when it is not wanted; nuisance. **2. a.** any organism that damages crops, injures or irritates livestock or man, or reduces the fertility of land. **b.** (*as modifier*): *pest control.* **3.** *Rare.* an epidemic disease or pestilence. [C16: from Latin *pestis* plague, of obscure origin]

Pes·ta·loz·zi (ˌpɛstəˈlɒtsɪ) *n.* **Jo·hann Hein·rich** (ˈjoːhan ˈhaɪnrɪç). 1746–1827, Swiss educational reformer. His emphasis on learning by observation exerted a wide influence on elementary education.

pes+ter (ˈpɛstə) *vb.* (*tr.*) to annoy or nag continually. [C16: from Old French *empestrer* to hobble (a horse), from Vulgar Latin *impāstōriāre* (unattested) to use a hobble, from *pāstōria* (unattested) a hobble, from Latin *pāstōrius* relating to a herdsman, from *pastor* herdsman] —**ˈpes+ter+er** *n.* —**ˈpes+ter+ing+ly** *adv.*

pest+hole (ˈpɛstˌhəʊl) *n.* any filthy or squalid place that is seemingly or actually overrun with an epidemic disease.

pest+house ('pɛstˌhaʊs) *n. Obsolete.* a hospital for treating persons with infectious diseases. Also called: **lazaretto.**

pes·ti+cide ('pɛstɪˌsaɪd) *n.* a chemical used for killing pests, esp. insects and rodents. —ˌ**pes+ti+'cid+al** *adj.*

pes+tif+er+ous (pɛ'stɪfərəs) *adj.* **1.** *Informal.* troublesome; irritating. **2.** breeding, carrying, or spreading infectious disease. **3.** corrupting; pernicious. [C16: from Latin *pestifer,* from *pestis* contagious disease, PEST + *ferre* to bring] —**pes+'tif+er+ous+ly** *adv.* —**pes+'tif+er+ous+ness** *n.*

pes+ti+lence ('pɛstɪləns) *n.* **1. a.** any epidemic outbreak of a deadly and highly infectious disease, such as the plague. **b.** such a disease. **2.** an evil influence or idea.

pes+ti+lent ('pɛstɪlənt) *adj.* **1.** annoying; irritating. **2.** highly destructive morally or physically; pernicious. **3.** infected with or likely to cause epidemic or infectious disease. [C15: from Latin *pestilens* unwholesome, from *pestis* plague] —**'pes+ti+lent+ly** *adv.*

pes+ti+len+tial (ˌpɛstɪ'lɛnʃəl) *adj.* **1.** dangerous or troublesome; harmful or annoying. **2.** of, causing, or resembling pestilence. —ˌ**pes+ti+'len+tial+ly** *adv.*

pes+tle ('pɛsᵊl) *n.* **1.** a club-shaped instrument for mixing or grinding substances in a mortar. **2.** a tool for pounding or stamping. ~*vb.* **3.** to pound (a substance or object) with or as if with a pestle. [C14: from Old French *pestel,* from Latin *pistillum;* related to *pinsāre* to crush]

pet[1] (pɛt) *n.* **1.** a tame animal kept in a household for companionship, amusement, etc. **2.** a person who is fondly indulged; favourite: *teacher's pet.* ~(*modifier*) **3.** kept as a pet: *a pet dog.* **4.** of or for pet animals: *pet food.* **5.** particularly cherished; favourite: *a pet theory; a pet hatred.* ~*vb.* **pets, pet+ting, pet+ted. 6.** (*tr.*) to treat (a person, animal, etc.) as a pet; pamper. **7.** (*tr.*) to pat or fondle (an animal, child, etc.). **8.** (*intr.*) *Informal.* (of two people) to caress each other in an erotic manner, as during lovemaking (often in the phrase **heavy petting**). [C16: origin unknown] —**'pet+ter** *n.*

pet[2] (pɛt) *n.* **1.** a fit of sulkiness, esp. at what is felt to be a slight; pique. ~*vb.* **pets, pet+ting, pet+ted. 2.** (*intr.*) to take offence; sulk. [C16: of uncertain origin]

Pet. *Bible. abbrev. for* Peter.

pet·a- *prefix.* denoting 10^{15}: *petametres.* Symbol: P.

Pé·tain (*French* pe'tɛ̃) *n.* **Hen·ri Phi·lippe O·mer** (ãri filip ɔ'mɛ:r). 1856–1951, French marshal, noted for his victory at Verdun (1916) in World War I and his leadership of the pro-Nazi government of unoccupied France at Vichy (1940–44); imprisoned for treason (1945).

pet+al ('pɛtᵊl) *n.* any of the separate parts of the corolla of a flower: often brightly coloured. [C18: from New Latin *petalum,* from Greek *petalon* leaf; related to *petannunai* to lie open] —**'pet+al+ine** *adj.* —**'pet·al-ˌlike** *adj.* —**'pet+alled** *adj.*

-pe·tal *adj. combining form.* seeking: *centripetal.* [from New Latin *-petus,* from Latin *petere* to seek]

pet+al+if+er+ous (ˌpɛtə'lɪfərəs) *or* **pet+al+ous** *adj.* bearing or having petals.

pet+al·o·dy ('pɛtəˌləʊdɪ) *n.* a condition in certain plants in which stamens or other parts of the flower assume the form and function of petals. [C19: from Greek *petalōdēs* like a leaf, from *petalon* leaf] —**pet·a+lod+ic** (ˌpɛtə'lɒdɪk) *adj.*

pet+al+oid ('pɛtəˌlɔɪd) *adj. Biology.* resembling a petal, esp. in shape: *the petaloid pattern on a sea urchin.*

pe+tard (pɪ'tɑ:d) *n.* **1.** (formerly) a device containing explosives used to breach a wall, doors, etc. **2. hoist with one's own petard.** being the victim of one's own schemes, etc. **3.** a type of explosive firework. [C16: from French: firework, from *péter* to break wind, from Latin *pēdere*]

pet·a+sus ('pɛtəsəs) *or* **pet·a+sos** ('pɛtəsəs, -ˌsɒs) *n.* a broad-brimmed hat worn by the ancient Greeks, such as one with wings on either side as traditionally worn by Mercury. [C16: via Latin from Greek *petasos*]

pet+cock ('pɛtˌkɒk) *n.* a small valve for checking the water content of a steam boiler or draining waste from the cylinder of a steam engine. [C19: from PET[1] or perhaps French *pet,* from *peter* to break wind + COCK[1]]

pe·te·chi·a (pɪ'ti:kɪə) *n.* a minute discoloured spot on the surface of the skin or mucous membrane, caused by an underlying ruptured blood vessel. [C18: via New Latin from Italian *petecchia* freckle, of obscure origin] —**pe+'te·chi·al** *adj.*

pe+ter[1] ('pi:tə) *vb.* (*intr.;* foll. by *out* or *away*) to fall (off) in volume, intensity, etc., and finally cease: *the cash petered out in three months.* [C19: of unknown origin]

pe+ter[2] ('pi:tə) *Bridge, whist.* ~*n.* **1.** a signal to a partner by playing a high card followed by a low one. ~*vb.* **2.** (*intr.*) to play a high card followed by a low one. [C20: perhaps a special use of PETER[1] (to fall off in power)]

pe+ter[3] ('pi:tə) *n. Slang.* **1.** a safe, till, or cashbox. **2.** a prison cell. **3.** the witness box in a courtroom. [C20: from the name *Peter*]

Pe·ter ('pi:tə) *n. New Testament.* **1.** Also called: **Simon Peter. Saint.** died ?67 A.D., a fisherman of Bethsaida, who became leader of the apostles and is regarded by Roman Catholics as the first pope; probably martyred at Rome. **2.** either of two epistles traditionally ascribed to Peter (in full **The First Epistle** and **The Second Epistle of Peter**).

Pe·ter I *n.* known as *Peter the Great.* 1672–1725, tsar of Russia (1682–1725), who assumed sole power in 1689. He introduced many reforms in government, technology, and the western European ideas. He also acquired new territories for Russia in the Baltic and founded the new capital of St. Petersburg (1703).

Pe·ter III *n.* 1728–62, grandson of Peter I and tsar of Russia (1762): deposed in a coup d'état led by his wife (later Catherine II); assassinated.

Pe+ter+bor+ough ('pi:təbərə, -brə) *n.* **1.** a city in central England, in N Cambridgeshire on the River Nene: industrial centre; under development as a new town since 1968. Pop.: 87 493 (1971). **2. Soke of.** a former administrative county of Northamptonshire: part of Northamptonshire since 1965. **3.** a city in SE Canada, in SE Ontario: manufacturing centre. Pop.: 58 111 (1971).

Pe+ter+lee ('pi:təˌli:) *n.* a new town in Co. Durham, founded in 1968. Pop.: 21 836 (1971).

Pe+ter+loo Mas+sa+cre (ˌpi:tə'lu:) *n.* an incident at St. Peter's Fields, Manchester, in 1819 in which a radical meeting was broken up by a cavalry charge, resulting in about 500 injuries and 11 deaths. [C19: from *St. Peter's Fields* + WATERLOO]

pe·ter+man ('pi:təmən) *n., pl.* **+men.** *Slang.* a burglar skilled in safe-breaking. [C19: from PETER[3]]

Pe+ter+mann Peak ('pi:təmən) *n.* a mountain in E Greenland. Height: 2932 m (9645 ft.).

Pe·ter Pan *n.* a youthful, boyish, or immature man. [C20: after the main character in *Peter Pan* (1904), a play by J. M. BARRIE]

Pe·ter Pan col+lar *n.* a collar on a round neck, having two rounded ends at the front.

Pe·ter Prin+ci·ple *n.* **the.** the theory, usually taken facetiously, that all members in a hierarchy rise to their own level of incompetence. [C20: from the book *The Peter Principle* (1969) by Dr. Lawrence J. Peter and Raymond Hull, in which the theory was originally propounded]

Pe+ters+burg ('pi:təzˌbɜ:g) *n.* a city in SE Virginia, on the Appomattox River: scene of prolonged fighting (1864–65) during the final months of the American Civil War. Pop.: 36 103 (1970).

pe·ter+sham ('pi:təʃəm) *n.* **1.** a thick corded ribbon used to stiffen belts, etc. **2.** a heavy woollen fabric used for coats, etc. **3.** a kind of overcoat made of such fabric. [C19: named after Viscount *Petersham* (d.1851), English army officer]

Pe·ter·son ('pi:təsᵊn) *n.* **Os·car (Emmanuel).** born 1925, Canadian jazz pianist and singer, who led his own trio from the early 1950s.

Pe·ter's pence *or* **Pe·ter pence** *n.* **1.** an annual tax, originally of one penny, formerly levied for the maintenance of the Papal See: abolished by Henry VIII in 1534. **2.** a voluntary contribution made by Roman Catholics in many countries for the same purpose. [C13: referring to St. PETER, considered as the first pope]

Pe·ter the Her·mit *n.* ?1050–1115, French monk and preacher of the First Crusade.

peth·i·dine ('pɛθɪˌdi:n) *n.* another name for **meperidine hydrochloride.** [C20: perhaps a blend of PIPERIDINE + ETHYL]

pet·i·o+late ('pɛtɪəˌleɪt) *or* **pet·i·o·lat+ed** *adj.* (of a plant or leaf) having a leafstalk. Compare **sessile** (sense 1).

pet·i+ole ('pɛtɪˌəʊl) *n.* **1.** the stalk by which a leaf is attached to the rest of the plant. **2.** *Zoology.* a slender stalk or stem, such as the connection between the thorax and abdomen of ants. [C18: via French from Latin *petiolus* little foot, from *pēs* foot]

pe·ti·o+lule ('pi:tɪəʊlˌju:l) *n.* the stalk of any of the leaflets making up a compound leaf. [C19: from New Latin *petiolūlus,* diminutive of Latin PETIOLUS]

pet+it ('pɛtɪ) *adj.* (*prenominal*) *Chiefly law.* of little or lesser importance; small: *petit jury.* [C14: from Old French: little, of obscure origin]

pet+it bour+geois ('pɛtɪ 'bʊəʒwɑ:; *French* pəti bur'ʒwa) *n., pl.* **pet+its bour+geois** ('pɛtɪ 'bʊəʒwɑ:z; *French* pəti bur'ʒwa). **1.** Also called: **petite bourgeoisie, petty bourgeoisie.** the section of the middle class with the lowest social status, generally composed of shopkeepers, lower clerical staff, etc. **2.** a member of this stratum. ~*adj.* **3.** of, relating to, or characteristic of the petit bourgeois, esp. indicating a sense of self-righteousness and a high degree of conformity to established standards of behaviour.

pe+tite (pə'ti:t) *adj.* (of women) small, delicate, and dainty. [C18: from French, feminine of *petit* small]

pet+it four ('pɛtɪ 'fɔ:; *French* pəti 'fu:r) *n., pl.* **pet+its fours** ('pɛtɪ 'fɔ:z; *French* pəti 'fu:r). any of various very small rich sweet cakes and biscuits, usually decorated with fancy icing, marzipan, etc. [French, literally: little oven]

pe+ti+tion (pɪ'tɪʃən) *n.* **1.** a written document signed by a large number of people demanding some form of action from a government or other authority. **2.** any formal request to a higher authority or deity; entreaty. **3.** *Law.* a formal application in writing made to a court asking for some specific judicial action: *a petition for divorce.* **4.** the action of petitioning. ~*vb.* **5.** (*tr.*) to address or present a petition to (a person in authority, government, etc.): *to petition Parliament.* **6.** (*intr.;* foll by *for*) to seek by petition: *to petition for a change in the law.* [C14: from Latin *petītiō,* from *petere* to seek] —**pe+'ti+tion+ar·y** *adj.*

pe+ti+tion+er (pɪ'tɪʃənə) *n.* **1.** a person who presents a petition. **2.** *Chiefly Brit.* the plaintiff in a divorce suit.

pe+ti+ti·o prin+ci+pi·i (pɪ'tɪʃɪˌəʊ prɪn'kɪpɪˌaɪ) *n. Logic.* a form of fallacious reasoning in which the conclusion has been assumed in the premisses; begging the question. Sometimes shortened to **petitio.** [C16: Latin, translation of Greek *to en arkhei aiteisthai* an assumption at the beginning]

pet+it ju·ry *n.* a jury of 12 persons empanelled to determine the facts of a case and decide the issue pursuant to the direction of the court on points of law. Also called: **petty jury.** Compare **grand jury.** —**pet+it ju+ror** *n.*

pet+it lar+ce·ny *n.* **1.** (formerly in England) the stealing of property valued at 12 pence or under. Abolished 1827. **2.** (in some states of the U.S.) the theft of property having a value below a certain figure. Also called: **petty larceny.** Compare **grand larceny.** —**pet+it lar+ce·nist** *n.*

pet+it mal ('pɛtɪ 'mæl; *French* pəti 'mal) *n.* a mild form of epilepsy characterized by periods of impairment or loss of consciousness for up to 30 seconds. Compare **grand mal.** [C19: French: little illness]

pet+it point ('pɛtɪ 'pɔɪnt; *French* pəti 'pwɛ̃) *n.* **1.** Also called: **tent stitch.** a small diagonal needlepoint stitch used for fine detail. **2.** work done with such stitches, esp. fine tapestry. Compare **gros point.** [French: small point]

pe+tits pois (*French* pəti 'pwa) *pl. n.* small green peas. [French: small peas]

Pe·tö·fi (*Hungarian* 'pɛtø:fi) *n.* **Sán·dor** ('ʃa:ndor). 1823–49, Hungarian lyric poet and patriot.

Pet+ra ('pɛtrə, 'pi:trə) *n.* an ancient city in the south of present-day Jordan; capital of the Nabataean kingdom.

Pet·rarch ('pɛtrɑ:k) *n.* Italian name *Francesco Petrarca.* 1304–74, Italian lyric poet and scholar, who greatly influenced the values of the Renaissance. His collection of poems *Canzoniere,* inspired by his ideal love for Laura, was written in the Tuscan dialect. He also wrote much in Latin, esp. the epic poem *Africa* (1341) and the *Secretum* (1342), a spiritual self-analysis. —'**Pet+rar+chan** *adj.*

Pet+rar+chan son+net *n.* a sonnet form associated with the poet Petrarch, having an octave rhyming a b b a a b b a and a sestet rhyming either c d e c d e or c d c d c d. Also called: **Italian sonnet.**

pet+rel ('pɛtrəl) *n.* any oceanic bird of the order *Procellariiformes,* having a hooked bill and tubular nostrils: includes albatrosses, storm petrels, and shearwaters. See also **storm petrel.** [C17: variant of earlier *pitteral,* associated by folk etymology with St. *Peter,* because the bird appears to walk on water]

Pe+tri dish ('pi:trɪ) *n.* a shallow circular flat-bottomed dish, often with a fitting cover, used in laboratories, esp. for producing cultures of microorganisms. [C19: named after J. R. *Petri* (1852–1921), German bacteriologist]

Pe·trie ('pɛtrɪ) *n.* Sir (**William Matthew**) **Flin·ders.** 1853–1942, English Egyptologist and archaeologist.

pet+ri+fac+tion (ˌpɛtrɪ'fækʃən) *or* **pet+ri+fi+ca+tion** (ˌpɛtrɪfɪ'keɪʃən) *n.* **1.** the act or process of forming petrified organic material. **2.** the state of being petrified.

Pet+ri+fied For+est *n.* a national park in E Arizona, containing petrified coniferous trees about 170 000 000 years old.

pet+ri+fy ('pɛtrɪˌfaɪ) *vb.* **+fies, +fy+ing, +fied. 1.** (*tr.; often passive*) to convert (organic material, esp. plant material) into a fossilized form by impregnation with dissolved minerals so that the original appearance is preserved. **2.** to make or become dull, unresponsive, insensitive, etc.; deaden. **3.** (*tr.; often passive*) to stun or daze with horror, fear, etc. [C16: from French *pétrifier,* ultimately from Greek *petra* stone, rock] —'**pe+tri+ˌfi+er** *n.*

Pe+trine ('pi:traɪn) *adj.* **1.** *New Testament.* of or relating to St. Peter, his position of leadership, or the epistles, etc., attributed to him. **2.** *R.C. Church.* of or relating to the supremacy in the Church that the pope is regarded as having inherited from St. Peter: *the Petrine claims.*

pet+ro- *or before a vowel* **petr-** *combining form.* **1.** indicating stone or rock: *petrology.* **2.** indicating petroleum, its products, etc.: *petrochemical.* [from Greek *petra* rock or *petros* stone]

pet+ro+chem·i+cal (ˌpɛtrəʊ'kɛmɪkᵊl) *n.* **1.** any substance, such as acetone or ethanol, obtained from petroleum or natural gas. ~*adj.* **2.** of, concerned with, or obtained from petrochemicals or related to petrochemistry. —ˌ**pet+ro+'chem·i+cal+ly** *adv.*

pet+ro+chem+is+try (ˌpɛtrəʊ'kɛmɪstrɪ) *n.* **1.** the chemistry of petroleum and its derivatives. **2.** the branch of chemistry concerned with the chemical composition of rocks.

pet+ro+dol+lar ('pɛtrəʊˌdɒlə) *n.* money, paid in dollars, earned by a country for the exporting of petroleum.

petrog. *abbrev. for* petrography.

pet+ro+glyph ('pɛtrəˌglɪf) *n.* a drawing or carving on rock, esp. a prehistoric one. [C19: via French from Greek *petra* stone + *gluphē* carving]

Pet+ro+grad ('pɛtrəʊˌgræd; *Russian* pɪtra'grat) *n.* a former name (1914–24) of **Leningrad.**

pe+trog+ra+phy (pɛ'trɒgrəfɪ) *n.* the branch of petrology concerned with the description and classification of rocks. Abbrev.: **petrog.** —**pe+'trog+ra+pher** *n.* —**pet+ro+graph+ic** (ˌpɛtrə'græfɪk) *or* ˌ**pet+ro+'graph·i+cal** *adj.* —ˌ**pet+ro+'graph·i+cal+ly** *adv.*

pet+rol ('pɛtrəl) *n.* any one of various volatile flammable liquid mixtures of hydrocarbons, mainly hexane, heptane, and octane, obtained from petroleum and used as a solvent and a fuel for internal-combustion engines. Usually petrol also contains additives such as antiknock compounds and corrosion inhibitors. U.S. name: **gasoline.** [C16: via French from Medieval Latin PETROLEUM]

petrol. *abbrev. for* petrology.

pet+ro+la+tum (ˌpɛtrə'leɪtəm) *n.* a translucent gelatinous substance obtained from petroleum; used as a lubricant and in medicine as an ointment base and protective dressing. Also called: **mineral jelly, petroleum jelly.**

pe+tro+le·um (pə'trəʊlɪəm) *n.* a dark-coloured thick flammable crude oil occurring in sedimentary rocks around the Persian Gulf and parts of North and South America, consisting mainly of hydrocarbons: Fractional distillation separates the crude oil into petrol, paraffin, diesel oil, lubricating oil, etc. Fuel oil, paraffin wax, asphalt, and carbon black are extracted from the residue. [C16: from Medieval Latin, from Latin *petra* stone + *oleum* oil]

pe+tro+le·um e·ther *n.* a volatile mixture of the higher alkane hydrocarbons, obtained as a fraction of petroleum and used as a solvent.

pe+tro+le·um jel+ly *n.* another name for **petrolatum.**

pe+trol+ic (pɛ'trɒlɪk) *adj.* of, relating to, containing, or obtained from petroleum.

pe+trol·o·gy (pɛ'trɒlədʒɪ) *n., pl.* **·gies.** the study of the composition, origin, structure, and formation of rocks. Abbrev.: **petrol.** —**pet+ro·log·i·cal** (ˌpɛtrə'lɒdʒɪkᵊl) *adj.* —ˌ**pet+ro+'log·i·cal+ly** *adv.* —**pe+'trol·o+gist** *n.*

pet+rol sta+tion *n. Brit.* another term for **filling station.**

pet+ro+nel ('pɛtrəˌnɛl) *n.* a firearm of large calibre used in the 16th and early 17th centuries, esp. by cavalry soldiers. [C16: from French, literally: of the breast, from *poitrine* breast, from Latin *pectus*]

Pe·tro·ni·us (pɪ'trəʊnɪəs) *n.* **Gai·us** ('gaɪəs), known as *Petronius Arbiter.* died 66 A.D., Roman satirist, supposed author of the *Satyricon,* a picaresque account of the licentiousness of contemporary society.

Pet+ro+pav+lovsk (*Russian* pɪtra'pavləfsk) *n.* a city in the S Soviet Union, in the N Kazakh SSR on the Ishim River. Pop.: 193 000 (1975 est.).

Pe+tró+po+lis (*Portuguese* pe'trɔpulis) *n.* a city in SE Brazil, north of Rio de Janeiro: resort. Pop.: 116 080 (1970).

pe+tro+sal (pɛ'trəʊsᵊl) *adj. Anatomy.* of, relating to, or situated near the dense part of the temporal bone that surrounds the inner ear. [C18: from Latin *petrōsus* full of rocks, from *petra* a rock, from Greek]

Pe·tro·sian (pɪ'trəʊʒən) *n.* **Tig·ran** (tig'ran). born 1929, Soviet chess player; world champion (1963–69).

pet+rous ('pɛtrəs, 'pi:-) *adj.* **1.** *Anatomy.* denoting the dense part of the temporal bone that surrounds the inner ear. **2.** *Rare.* like rock or stone. [C16: from Latin *petrōsus* full of rocks]

Pe+trovsk (*Russian* pɪ'trɔfsk) *n.* the former name (until 1921) of **Makhachkala.**

Pet+ro+za+vodsk (*Russian* pɪtrəza'vɔtsk) *n.* a city in the NW Soviet Union, capital of the Karelian ASSR, on Lake Onega: developed around ironworks established by Peter the Great in 1703; university (1940). Pop.: 210 000 (1975 est.).

pe-tsai cab+bage ('peɪ'tsaɪ) *n.* another name for **Chinese cabbage** (sense 1). [from Chinese (Peking) *pe ts'ai,* literally: white vegetable]

Pet+sa+mo (*Finnish* 'pɛtsɑmɔ) *n.* a former territory of N Finland ceded by the Soviet Union to Finland in 1920 and taken back in 1940; now part of the northwest RSFSR.

pet+ti+coat ('pɛtɪˌkəʊt) *n.* **1.** a woman's light undergarment in the form of an underskirt or including a bodice supported by shoulder straps. **2.** *Informal.* **a.** a humorous or mildly disparaging name for a woman. **b.** (*as modifier*): *petticoat politics.* [C15: see PETTY, COAT]

pet+ti+fog ('pɛtɪˌfɒg) *vb.* **+fogs, +fog+ging, +fogged.** (*intr.*) to be a pettifogger.

pet+ti+fog+ger ('pɛtɪˌfɒgə) *n.* **1.** a lawyer of inferior status who conducts unimportant cases, esp. one who is unscrupulous or resorts to trickery. **2.** any person who quibbles or fusses over details. [C16: from PETTY + *fogger,* of uncertain origin, perhaps from *Fugger,* name of a family (C15–16) of German financiers] —'**pet+ti+ˌfog+ger·y** *n.*

pet+ti+fog+ging ('pɛtɪˌfɒgɪŋ) *adj.* **1.** petty: *pettifogging details.* **2.** mean; quibbling: *pettifogging lawyers.*

pet+tish ('pɛtɪʃ) *adj.* peevish; petulant: *a pettish child.* [C16: from PET[2]] —'**pet+tish+ly** *adv.* —'**pet+tish+ness** *n.*

pet+ti+toes ('pɛtɪˌtəʊz) *pl. n.* pig's trotters, esp. when used as food. [C16: from Old French *petite oie,* literally: little goose (giblets of a goose)]

pet+ty ('pɛtɪ) *adj.* **+ti+er, +ti+est. 1.** trivial; trifling; inessential: *petty details.* **2.** of a narrow-minded, mean, or small-natured disposition or character: *petty spite.* **3.** minor or subordinate in rank: *petty officialdom.* [C14: from Old French PETIT] —'**pet+ti+ly** *adv.* —'**pet+ti+ness** *n.*

pet+ty cash *n.* a small cash fund kept on a firm's premises for the payment of minor incidental expenses.

pet+ty ju+ry *n.* a variant of **petit jury.** —**pet+ty ju+ror** *n.*

pet+ty lar+ce·ny *n. Criminal law.* a variant of **petit larceny.**

pet+ty of+fic+er *n.* a noncommissioned officer in a naval service comparable in rank to a sergeant in an army or marine corps.

pet+ty ses+sions *n.* another term for **magistrates' court.**

pet·u+lant ('pɛtjʊlənt) *adj.* irritable, impatient, or sullen in a peevish or capricious way. [C16: via Old French from Latin *petulāns* bold, from *petulāre* (unattested) to attack playfully, from *petere* to assail] —'**pet·u+lance** *or* '**pet·u+lan+cy** *n.* —'**pet·u+lant+ly** *adv.*

pe+tu+ni·a (pɪ'tju:nɪə) *n.* any solanaceous plant of the tropical American genus *Petunia:* cultivated for their white or purple funnel-shaped flowers. [C19: via New Latin from obsolete French *petun* variety of tobacco, from Tupi *petyn*]

pe+tun+tse *or* **pe+tun+tze** (pɪ'tʌntsɪ, -'tʊn-) *n.* a fusible feldspathic mineral used in hard-paste porcelain; china stone. [C18: from Chinese (Peking) *pe tun tzu,* from *pe* white + *tun* heap + *tzu* offspring]

Pevs·ner ('pɛvznə) *n.* **1. An·toine** (ɑ̃'twan). 1886–1962, French constructivist sculptor and painter, born in Russia; brother of Naum Gabo. **2.** Sir **Nik·o·laus** ('nɪkəlaus). born 1903, British architectural historian, born in Germany: his monumental series *Buildings of England* (1951–74) describes every structure of account in the country.

pew (pju:) *n.* **1.** (in a church) **a.** one of several long benchlike seats with backs, used by the congregation. **b.** an enclosed compartment reserved for the use of a family or other small group. **2.** *Brit. informal.* a seat (esp. in the phrase **take a pew**). [C14 *pywe,* from Old French *puye,* from Latin *podium* a balcony, from Greek *podion* supporting structure, from *pous* foot]

pe+wee *or* **pee+wee** ('pi:wi:) *n.* any of several small North American flycatchers of the genus *Contopus,* having a greenish-brown plumage. [C19: imitative of its cry]

pe+wit *or* **pee+wit** ('pi:wɪt) *n.* other names for **lapwing.** [C13: imitative of the bird's cry]

pew+ter ('pju:tə) *n.* **1. a.** any of various alloys containing tin (80–90 per cent), lead (10–20 per cent), and sometimes small amounts of other metals, such as copper and antimony. **b.** (*as modifier*): *pewter ware; a pewter tankard.* **2.** a bluish-grey colour. **3.** plate or kitchen utensils made from pewter. ~*adj.* **4.** of a bluish-grey colour. [C14: from Old French *peaultre,* of obscure origin; related to Old Provençal *peltre* pewter] —'**pew+ter+er** *n.*

pe+yo+te (peɪ'əʊtɪ, pɪ-) *n.* another name for **mescal** (the plant). [Mexican Spanish, from Nahuatl *peyotl*]

pf. *abbrev for:* **1.** perfect. **2.** Also: **pfg.** pfennig. **3.** preferred.

Pfalz (pfalts) *n.* the German name for the **Palatinate.**

pfen+nig ('fɛnɪg; *German* 'pfɛnɪç) *n., pl.* **+nigs** *or* **+ni+ge** (*German* -nɪgə). a German monetary unit worth either one hundredth of a West German deutsche mark or of an East German ostmark. [German: PENNY]

Pforz+heim (*German* 'pfɔrtshaɪm) *n.* a city in West Germany, in W Baden-Württemberg: centre of the German watch and jewellery industry. Pop.: 91 100 (1970).

P.G. *abbrev. for:* **1.** paying guest. **2.** postgraduate.

pg. *abbrev. for* page.

Pg. *abbrev. for:* **1.** Portugal. **2.** Portuguese.

PGA *abbrev. for* Professional Golfers' Association.

pH *n.* potential of hydrogen; a measure of the acidity or alkalinity of a solution equal to the common logarithm of the reciprocal of the concentration of hydrogen ions in moles per cubic decimetre of solution. Pure water has a pH of 7, acid solutions have a pH less than 7, and alkaline solutions a pH greater than 7.

Ph *chemical symbol for* phenyl group or radical.

ph. *abbrev. for* phase.

Phae·a·cian (fi:'eɪʃən) *n. Greek myth.* one of a race of people inhabiting the island of Scheria visited by Odysseus on his way home from the Trojan War.

Phae·dra ('fi:drə) *n. Greek myth.* the wife of Theseus, who falsely accused her stepson Hippolytus of raping her because he spurned her amorous advances.

Phae·drus ('fi:drəs) *n.* ?15 B.C.–?50 A.D., Roman author of five books of Latin verse fables, based chiefly on Aesop.

Pha·ë·thon ('feɪəθən) *n. Greek myth.* the son of Helios (the sun god) who borrowed his father's chariot and nearly set the earth on fire by approaching too close to it. Zeus averted the catastrophe by striking him down with a thunderbolt.

phae+ton ('feɪtᵊn) *n.* a light four-wheeled horse-drawn carriage with or without a top, usually having two seats.

phage (feɪdʒ) *n.* short for **bacteriophage.**

-phage *n. combining form.* indicating something that eats or consumes something specified: *bacteriophage.* [from Greek *-phagos;* see PHAGO-] —**-pha·gous** *adj. combining form.*

phag+e·dae+na *or* **phag+e·de·na** (ˌfædʒɪ'di:nə) *n. Pathol.* a rapidly spreading ulcer that destroys tissues as it increases in size. [C17: via Latin from Greek, from *phagein* to eat]

phag·o- *or before a vowel* **phag-** *combining form.* eating, consuming, or destroying: *phagocyte.* [from Greek *phagein* to consume]

phag·o+cyte ('fægəˌsaɪt) *n.* an amoeboid cell or protozoan that engulfs particles, such as food substances or invading microorganisms. —**phag·o+cyt+ic** (ˌfægə'sɪtɪk) *adj.*

phag·o+cy+to+sis (ˌfægəsaɪ'təʊsɪs) *n.* the process by which a cell, such as a white blood cell, ingests microorganisms, other cells, and foreign particles.

phag·o+ma+ni·a (ˌfægəʊ'meɪnɪə) *n.* a compulsive desire to eat. —ˌ**phag·o+'ma+ni+ac** *n.*

phag·o+pho+bi·a (ˌfægəʊ'fəʊbɪə) *n.* an abnormal fear of eating. —ˌ**phag·o+'pho+bic** *adj.*

-pha·gy *or* **-pha·gi·a** *n. combining form.* indicating an eating or devouring: *anthropophagy.* [from Greek *-phagia;* see PHAGO-]

phal+ange ('fælændʒ) *n., pl.* **pha+lan+ges** (fæ'lændʒi:z). *Anatomy.* another name for **phalanx** (sense 5). [C16: via French, ultimately from Greek PHALANX]

pha+lan+ge·al (fə'lændʒɪəl) *adj. Anatomy.* of or relating to a phalanx or phalanges.

pha+lan+ger (fə'lændʒə) *n.* any of various Australasian arboreal marsupials, such as *Trichosurus vulpecula* (**brush-tailed phalanger**), having dense fur and a long tail: family *Phalangeridae.* Also called (in Australia): **possum.** See also **flying phalanger.** [C18: via New Latin from Greek *phalaggion* spider's web, referring to its webbed hind toes]

phal+an+ster·y ('fælənstərɪ, -strɪ) *n., pl.* **+ster·ies.** **1.** (in Fourierism) **a.** buildings occupied by a phalanx. **b.** a community represented by a phalanx. **2.** any similar association or the buildings occupied by such an association. [C19: from French *phalanstère,* from *phalange* PHALANX, on the model of *monastère* MONASTERY]

phal+anx ('fælæŋks) *n., pl.* **phal+anx·es** *or* **pha+lan+ges** (fæ'lændʒi:z). **1.** an ancient Greek and Macedonian battle formation of hoplites presenting long spears from behind a wall of overlapping shields. **2.** any closely ranked unit or mass of people: *the police formed a phalanx to protect the embassy.* **3.** a number of people united for a common purpose. **4.** (in Fourierism) a group of approximately 1800 persons forming a commune in which all property is collectively owned. **5.** any of the bones of the fingers or toes. **6.** *Botany.* a bundle of stamens, joined together by their stalks (filaments). [C16: via Latin from Greek: infantry formation in close ranks, bone of finger or toe]

phal·a+rope ('fæləˌrəʊp) *n.* any aquatic shore bird of the family *Phalaropidae,* such as *phalaropus fulicarius* (**grey phalarope**), of northern oceans and lakes, having a long slender bill and lobed toes: order *Charadriiformes.* [C18: via French from New Latin *Phalaropus,* from Greek *phalaris* coot + *pous* foot]

phal+lic ('fælɪk) *adj.* **1.** of, relating to, or resembling a phallus: *a phallic symbol.* **2.** *Psychoanal.* **a.** relating to a stage of psychosexual development during which the child's interest is concentrated on the genital organs. **b.** designating personality traits, such as conceit and self-assurance, due to fixation at the phallic stage of development. Compare **anal** (sense 2), **oral** (sense 7), **genital** (sense 2). **3.** of or relating to phallicism.

phal+li+cism ('fælɪˌsɪzəm) *or* **phal+lism** *n.* the worship or veneration of the phallus. —'**phal+li+cist** *or* '**phal+list** *n.*

phal+lic stage *n. Psychol.* a stage in the development of a male child in which he becomes preoccupied with his own penis as an object of gratification.

phal+lus ('fæləs) *n., pl.* **+li** (-laɪ) *or* **+lus·es.** **1.** another word for **penis.** **2.** an image of the male sexual organ, esp. one venerated as a religious symbol of reproductive power. [C17: via Late Latin from Greek *phallos*]

-phane *n. combining form.* indicating something resembling a specified substance: *cellophane.* [from Greek *phainein* to shine, (in passive) appear]

phan+er·o+crys+tal+line (ˌfænərəʊ'krɪstəlɪn, -ˌlaɪn) *adj.* (of igneous and metamorphic rocks) having a crystalline structure in which the crystals are large enough to be seen with the naked eye.

phan+er·o+gam ('fænərəʊˌgæm) *n.* any plant of the former major division *Phanerogamae,* which included all seed-bearing plants; a former name for **spermatophyte.** Compare **cryptogam.** [C19: from New Latin *phanerogamus,* from Greek *phaneros* visible + *gamos* marriage] —ˌ**phan+er·o+'gam+ic** *or* **phan+er+og·a+mous** (ˌfænə'rɒgəməs) *adj.*

phan+er·o+phyte ('fænərəˌfaɪt, fə'nɛrə-) *n.* a tree or shrub that bears its perennating buds more than 25 centimetres above the level of the soil. [C20: from Greek *phanero-* visible + -PHYTE]

Phan+er·o+zo+ic (ˌfænərə'zəʊɪk) *adj.* of or relating to rock strata, fauna, etc., of the Palaeozoic, Mesozoic, or Cenozoic eras. Compare **Cryptozoic.**

phan+tasm ('fæntæzəm) *n.* **1.** a phantom. **2.** an illusory perception of an object, person, etc. **3.** (in the philosophy of Plato) objective reality as distorted by perception. [C13: from Old French *fantasme,* from Latin *phantasma,* from Greek; related to Greek *phantazein* to cause to be seen, from *phainein* to show] —**phan+'tas+mal** *or* **phan+'tas+mic** *adj.* —**phan+'tas+mal+ly** *or* **phan+'tas+mi+cal+ly** *adv.*

phan+tas+ma+go+ri·a (ˌfæntæzmə'gɔ:rɪə) *or* **phan+tas+ma+go·ry** (fæn'tæzməgərɪ) *n.* **1.** *Psychol.* a shifting medley of real or imagined figures, as in a dream. **2.** *Films.* a sequence of pictures made to vary in size rapidly while remaining in focus. **3.** *Rare.* a shifting scene composed of different elements. [C19: probably from French *fantasmagorie* production of phantasms, from PHANTASM + *-agorie,* perhaps from Greek *ageirein* to gather together] —**phan+tas+ma+go+ric** (ˌfæntæzmə'gɒrɪk) *or* ˌ**phan+tas+ma+'go+ri+cal** *adj.* —ˌ**phan+tas+ma+'go+ri+cal+ly** *adv.*

phan+ta+sy ('fæntəsɪ) *n., pl.* **+sies.** an archaic spelling of **fantasy.**

phan+tom ('fæntəm) *n.* **1. a.** an apparition or spectre. **b.** (*as modifier*): *a phantom army marching through the sky.* **2.** the visible representation of something abstract, esp. as appearing in a dream or hallucination: *phantoms of evil haunted his sleep.* **3.** something apparently unpleasant or horrific that has no material form. **4.** *Med.* another name for **manikin** (sense 2b.). [C13: from Old French *fantosme,* from Latin *phantasma,* PHANTASM]

phan+tom limb *n.* the illusion that a limb still exists following its amputation, sometimes with the sensation of pain (**phantom limb pain**).

-pha·ny *n. combining form.* indicating a manifestation: *theophany.* [from Greek *-phania,* from *phainein* to show; see -PHANE] —**-pha·nous** *adj. combining form.*

phar., Phar., pharm., *or* **Pharm.** *abbrev. for:* **1.** pharmaceutical. **2.** pharmacist. **3.** pharmacopoeia. **4.** pharmacy.

Phar+aoh ('fɛərəʊ) *n.* the title of the ancient Egyptian kings. [Old English *Pharaon,* via Latin, Greek, and Hebrew ultimately from Egyptian *pr-'o* great house] —**Phar+aon+ic** (fɛə'rɒnɪk) *adj.*

Phar+aoh ant *n.* a small yellowish-red ant, *Monomorium pharaonis,* of warm regions: accidentally introduced into many countries, infesting heated buildings.

Phar·i+sa+ic (ˌfærɪ'seɪɪk) *or* **Phar·i+sa·i·cal** *adj.* **1.** *Judaism.* of, relating to, or characteristic of the Pharisees or Pharisaism. **2.** (*often not cap.*) righteously hypocritical. —ˌ**Phar·i+'sa·i·cal+ly** *adv.* —ˌ**Phar·i+'sa·i·cal+ness** *n.*

Phar·i·sa·ism ('færɪseɪˌɪzəm) *or* **Phar·i·see·ism** ('færɪsiːˌɪzəm) *n.* **1.** *Judaism.* the tenets and customs of the Pharisees. **2.** (*often not cap.*) observance of the external forms of religion without genuine belief; hypocrisy.

Phar·i·see ('færɪˌsiː) *n.* **1.** *Judaism.* a member of an ancient Jewish sect that was opposed to the Sadducees, teaching strict observance of Jewish traditions and believing in life after death and in the coming of the Messiah. **2.** (*often not cap.*) a self-righteous or hypocritical person. [Old English *Farisēus,* ultimately from Aramaic *perīshāiyā*, pl. of *perīsh* separated]

phar·ma·ceu·ti·cal (ˌfɑːmə'sjuːtɪkᵊl), **phar·ma·ceu·tic,** *or* **phar·ma·cal** ('fɑːməkᵊl) *adj.* of or relating to drugs or pharmacy. [C17: from Late Latin *pharmaceuticus,* from Greek *pharmakeus* purveyor of drugs; see PHARMACY] —ˌ**phar·ma·'ceu·ti·cal·ly** *adv.*

phar·ma·ceu·tics (ˌfɑːmə'sjuːtɪks) *n.* **1.** (*functioning as sing.*) another term for **pharmacy** (sense 1). **2.** pharmaceutical remedies.

phar·ma·cist ('fɑːməsɪst) *or* **phar·ma·ceu·tist** (ˌfɑːmə'sjuːtɪst) *n.* a person qualified to prepare and dispense drugs.

phar·ma·co- *combining form.* indicating drugs: *pharmacology; pharmacopoeia.* [from Greek *pharmakon* drug, potion]

phar·ma·co·dy·nam·ics (ˌfɑːməkəʊdaɪ'næmɪks) *n.* (*functioning as sing.*) the branch of pharmacology concerned with the action of drugs on the physiology of the body. —ˌ**phar·ma·co·dy·'nam·ic** *adj.*

phar·ma·cog·no·sy (ˌfɑːmə'kɒgnəsɪ) *n.* the branch of pharmacology concerned with the study of crude drugs of plant and animal origin. [C19: from PHARMACO- + *gnosy,* from Greek *gnosis* knowledge] —ˌ**phar·ma·'cog·no·sist** *n.* —**phar·ma·cog·nos·tic** (ˌfɑːməkɒg'nɒstɪk) *adj.*

pharmacol. *abbrev. for* pharmacology.

phar·ma·col·o·gy (ˌfɑːmə'kɒlədʒɪ) *n.* the science or study of drugs, including their characteristics, action, and uses. —**phar·ma·co·log·i·cal** (ˌfɑːməkə'lɒdʒɪkᵊl) *adj.* —ˌ**phar·ma·co·'log·i·cal·ly** *adv.* —ˌ**phar·ma·'col·o·gist** *n.*

phar·ma·co·poe·ia *or U.S.* (*sometimes*) **phar·ma·co·pe·ia** (ˌfɑːməkə'piːə) *n.* an authoritative book containing a list of medicinal drugs with their uses, preparation, dosages, formulas, etc. [C17: via New Latin from Greek *pharmakopoiia* art of preparing drugs, from PHARMACO- + *-poiia,* from *poiein* to make] —ˌ**phar·ma·co·'poe·ial** *or* ˌ**phar·ma·co·'poe·ic** *adj.* —ˌ**phar·ma·co·'poe·ist** *n.*

phar·ma·cy ('fɑːməsɪ) *n., pl.* **-cies. 1.** Also: **pharmaceutics.** the practice or art of preparing and dispensing drugs. **2.** a dispensary. [C14: from Medieval Latin *pharmacia,* from Greek *pharmakeia* making of drugs, from *pharmakon* drug]

Pha·ros ('fɛərɒs) *n.* a large Hellenistic lighthouse built on an island off Alexandria in Egypt in about 280 B.C. and destroyed by an earthquake in the 14th century: usually included among the Seven Wonders of the World.

Phar·sa·lus (fɑː'seɪləs) *n.* an ancient town in Thessaly in N Greece. Several major battles were fought nearby, including Caesar's victory over Pompey (48 B.C.).

phar·yn·ge·al (ˌfærɪn'dʒiːəl) *or* **pha·ryn·gal** (fə'rɪŋgᵊl) *adj.* **1.** of, relating to, or situated in or near the pharynx. **2.** *Phonetics.* pronounced or supplemented in pronunciation with an articulation in or constriction of the pharynx. ~*n.* **3.** *Phonetics.* a pharyngeal speech sound. [C19: from New Latin *pharyngeus;* see PHARYNX]

phar·yn·ge·al ton·sil *n.* the technical name for **adenoids.**

phar·yn·gi·tis (ˌfærɪn'dʒaɪtɪs) *n.* inflammation of the pharynx.

pha·ryn·go- *or before a vowel* **pha·ryng-** *combining form.* pharynx: *pharyngoscope.*

phar·yn·gol·o·gy (ˌfærɪŋ'gɒlədʒɪ) *n.* the branch of medical science concerned with the pharynx and its diseases. —**phar·yn·go·log·i·cal** (ˌfærɪŋgə'lɒdʒɪkᵊl) *adj.* —ˌ**phar·yn·'gol·o·gist** *n.*

pha·ryn·go·scope (fə'rɪŋgəˌskəʊp) *n.* a medical instrument for examining the pharynx. —**pha·ryn·go·scop·ic** (fəˌrɪŋgə'skɒpɪk) *adj.* —**phar·yn·gos·co·py** (ˌfærɪŋ'gɒskəpɪ) *n.*

phar·yn·got·o·my (ˌfærɪŋ'gɒtəmɪ) *n., pl.* **-mies.** surgical incision into the pharynx.

phar·ynx ('færɪŋks) *n., pl.* **pha·ryn·ges** (fæ'rɪndʒiːz) *or* **phar·ynx·es.** the part of the alimentary canal between the mouth and the oesophagus. Compare **nasopharynx.** [C17: via New Latin from Greek *pharunx* throat; related to Greek *pharanx* chasm]

phase (feɪz) *n.* **1.** any distinct or characteristic period or stage in a sequence of events or chain of development: *there were two phases to the resolution; his immaturity was a passing phase.* **2.** *Astronomy.* one of the recurring shapes of the portion of the moon or an inferior planet illuminated by the sun: *the new moon, first quarter, full moon, and last quarter are the four principal phases of the moon.* **3.** *Physics.* **a.** the fraction of a cycle of a periodic quantity that has been completed at a specific reference time, expressed as an angle. **b.** (*as modifier*): *a phase shift.* **4.** *Physics.* a particular stage in a periodic process or phenomenon. **5. in phase.** (of two waveforms) reaching corresponding phases at the same time. **6. out of phase.** (of two waveforms) not in phase. **7.** *Chem.* a distinct state of matter characterized by homogeneous composition and properties and the possession of a clearly defined boundary. **8.** *Zoology.* a variation in the normal form of an animal, esp. a colour variation, brought about by seasonal or geographical change. **9.** *Biology.* (*usually in combination*) a stage in mitosis or meiosis: *prophase; metaphase.* **10.** *Electrical engineering.* one of the circuits in a system in which there are two or more alternating voltages displaced by equal amounts in phase (sense 5). See also **polyphase.** ~*vb.* (*tr.*) **11.** (*often passive*) to execute, arrange, or introduce gradually or in stages: *a phased withdrawal.* **12.** (sometimes foll. by *with*) to cause (a part, process, etc.) to function or coincide with (another part, etc.): *he tried to phase the intake and output of the machine; he phased the intake with the output.* **13.** *Chiefly U.S.* to arrange (processes, goods, etc.) to be supplied or executed when required. [C19: from New Latin *phases,* pl. of *phasis,* from Greek: aspect; related to Greek *phainein* to show] —'**phase·less** *adj.* —'**pha·sic** *or* '**phase·al** *adj.*

phase in *vb.* (*tr., adv.*) to introduce in a gradual or cautious manner: *the legislation was phased in over two years.*

phase mod·u·la·tion *n.* **1.** a type of modulation, used in communication systems, in which the phase of a radio carrier wave is varied by an amount proportional to the instantaneous amplitude of the modulating signal. **2.** a wave that has undergone this process.

phase out *vb.* **1.** (*tr., adv.*) to discontinue or withdraw gradually. ~*n.* **phase-out. 2.** *Chiefly U.S.* the action or an instance of phasing out: *a phase-out of conventional forces.*

phase rule *n.* the principle that in any system in equilibrium the number of degrees of freedom is equal to the number of components less the number of phases plus two. See also **degree of freedom, component** (sense 4).

-pha·si·a *n. combining form.* indicating speech disorder of a specified kind: *aphasia.* [from Greek, from *phanai* to speak] —**-pha·sic** *adj. and n. combining form.*

phas·mid ('fæzmɪd) *n.* **1.** any plant-eating insect of the mainly tropical order *Phasmida:* includes the leaf insects and stick insects. ~*adj.* **2.** of, relating to, or belonging to the order *Phasmida.* [C19: from New Latin *Phasmida,* from Greek *phasma* spectre]

phat·ic ('fætɪk) *adj.* (of speech, esp. of conversational phrases) used to establish social contact and to express sociability rather than specific meaning. [C20: from Greek *phat(os)* spoken + -IC]

PH.C. *abbrev. for* Pharmaceutical Chemist.

Ph.D. *abbrev. for* Doctor of Philosophy. Also: **D.Phil.**

pheas·ant ('fɛzᵊnt) *n.* **1.** any of various long-tailed gallinaceous birds of the family *Phasianidae,* esp. *Phasianus colchicus* (**ring-necked pheasant**), having a brightly-coloured plumage in the male: native to Asia but introduced elsewhere. **2.** any of various other gallinaceous birds of the family *Phasianidae,* including the quails and partridges. **3.** *U.S.* any of several other gallinaceous birds, esp. the ruffed grouse. [C13: from Old French *fesan,* from Latin *phāsiānus,* from Greek *phasianos ornis* Phasian bird, named after the River *Phasis,* in Colchis]

pheas·ant's eye *n.* an annual ranunculaceous plant, *Adonis annua* (or *autumnalis*), with scarlet flowers and finely divided leaves: native to S Europe but naturalized elsewhere.

Phe·be ('fiːbɪ) *n.* a variant spelling of **Phoebe**[1].

Phei·dip·pi·des *or* **Phi·dip·pi·des** (faɪ'dɪpɪˌdiːz) *n.* Athenian athlete, who ran to Sparta to seek help against the Persians before the Battle of Marathon (490 B.C.).

phel·lem ('fɛləm) *n. Botany.* the technical name for **cork** (sense 4). [C20: from Greek *phellos* cork + PHLOEM]

phel·lo·derm ('fɛləʊˌdɜːm) *n.* a layer of thin-walled cells produced by the inner surface of the cork cambium. [C19: from Greek *phellos* cork + -DERM] —ˌ**phel·lo·'der·mal** *adj.*

phel·lo·gen ('fɛlədʒən) *n. Botany.* the technical name for **cork cambium.** [C19: from Greek *phellos* cork + -GEN] —**phel·lo·ge·net·ic** (ˌfɛləʊdʒɪ'nɛtɪk) *or* **phel·lo·gen·ic** (ˌfɛləʊ'dʒɛnɪk) *adj.*

phe·na·caine ('fiːnəˌkeɪn, 'fɛn-) *n.* a crystalline basic compound that is the hydrochloride of holocaine: used as a local anaesthetic in ophthalmic medicine. Formula: $C_{18}H_{22}N_2O_2HCl$. [C20: from PHENO- + ACETO- + COCAINE]

phe·nac·e·tin (fɪ'næsɪtɪn) *n.* a white crystalline solid used in medicine to relieve pain and fever. Formula: $CH_3CONHC_6H_4OC_2H_5$. Also called: **acetophenetidin.** [C19: from PHENETIDINE + ACETYL + -IN]

phen·a·cite ('fɛnəˌsaɪt) *or* **phen·a·kite** ('fɛnəˌkaɪt) *n.* a colourless or white glassy mineral consisting of beryllium silicate in hexagonal crystalline form: occurs in veins in granite. Formula: Be_2SiO_4. [C19: from Greek *phenax* a cheat, because of its deceptive resemblance to quartz]

phe·nan·threne (fɪ'nænθriːn) *n.* a colourless crystalline aromatic compound isomeric with anthracene: used in the manufacture of dyes, drugs, and explosives. Formula: $C_{14}H_{10}$. [C19: from PHENO- + ANTHRACENE]

phen·a·zine ('fɛnəˌziːn) *n.* a yellow crystalline compound that is the parent compound of many azine dyes and some antibiotics. Formula: $C_6H_4N_2C_6H_4$. [C19: from PHENO- + AZINE]

phe·net·ic (fɪ'nɛtɪk) *adj. Biology.* of, relating to, or designating a system of classification based on similarities between organisms without regard to their evolutionary relationships. [C20: from PHEN(OTYPE) + (GEN)ETIC]

phe·net·i·dine (fɪ'nɛtɪˌdiːn, -dɪn) *n.* a liquid amine that is a derivative of phenetole, existing in three isomeric forms: used in the manufacture of dyestuffs. Formula: $C_6H_4(NH_2)(OC_2H_5)$. [C19: from PHENETOLE + -ID[3] + -INE[2]]

phen·e·tole ('fɛnɪˌtəʊl, -ˌtɒl) *n.* a colourless oily compound; phenyl ethyl ether. Formula: $C_6H_5OC_2H_5$. [C19: from PHENO- + ETHYL + -OLE[1]]

phen·for·min (fɛn'fɔːmɪn) *n.* a biguanide administered orally in the treatment of diabetes to lower blood levels of glucose. Formula: $C_{10}H_{15}N_5$. [C20: from PHEN(YL) + FORM(AMIDE) + -IN]

phe·nix ('fiːnɪks) *n. U.S.* a variant spelling of **phoenix.**

phe·no- *or before a vowel* **phen-** *combining form.* **1.** showing or manifesting: *phenotype.* **2.** indicating that a molecule contains benzene rings: *phenobarbitone.* [from Greek *phaino-* shining, from *phainein* to show; its use in a chemical sense is exemplified in *phenol,* so called because originally prepared from illuminating gas]

phe+no+bar+bi+tone (ˌfiːnəʊˈbɑːbɪˌtəʊn) *or* **phe+no+bar+bi+tal** (ˌfiːnəʊˈbɑːbɪtᵊl) *n.* a white crystalline derivative of barbituric acid used as a sedative for treating insomnia and epilepsy. Formula: $C_{12}H_{12}N_2O_3$.

phe+no+cop·y (ˈfiːnəʊˌkɒpɪ) *n., pl.* **+cop·ies.** a noninheritable change in an organism that is caused by environmental influence during development but resembles the effects of a genetic mutation.

phe+no+cryst (ˈfiːnəˌkrɪst, ˈfɛn-) *n.* any of several large crystals that are embedded in a mass of smaller crystals in igneous rocks such as porphyry. [C19: from PHENO- (shining) + CRYSTAL]

phe+nol (ˈfiːnɒl) *n.* **1.** Also called: **carbolic acid.** a white crystalline soluble poisonous acidic derivative of benzene, used as an antiseptic and disinfectant and in the manufacture of resins, nylon, dyes, explosives, and pharmaceuticals; hydroxybenzene. Formula: C_6H_5OH. **2.** *Chem.* any of a class of weakly acidic organic compounds whose molecules contain one or more hydroxyl groups bound directly to a carbon atom in an aromatic ring.

phe+no+late (ˈfiːnəˌleɪt) *vb.* **1.** (*tr.*) Also: **carbolize.** to treat or disinfect with phenol. ~*n.* **2.** another name (not in technical usage) for **phenoxide.**

phe+nol+ic (fɪˈnɒlɪk) *adj.* of, containing, or derived from phenol.

phe+nol+ic res+in *n.* any one of a class of resins derived from phenol, used in paints, adhesives, and as thermosetting plastics. See also **Bakelite.**

phe+nol+o·gy (fɪˈnɒlədʒɪ) *n.* the study of recurring phenomena, such as animal migration, esp. as influenced by climatic conditions. [C19: from PHENO(MENON) + -LOGY] —**phe+no+log·i·cal** (ˌfiːnəˈlɒdʒɪkᵊl) *adj.* —**phe+ˈnol·o+gist** *n.*

phe+nol+phtha+lein (ˌfiːnɒlˈθeɪliːn, -lɪɪn, -ˈθæl-) *n.* a colourless crystalline compound used in medicine as a laxative and in chemistry as an indicator. Formula: $C_{20}H_{14}O_4$.

phe+nom+e·na (fɪˈnɒmɪnə) *n.* the plural of **phenomenon.**

phe+nom+e·nal (fɪˈnɒmɪnᵊl) *adj.* **1.** of or relating to a phenomenon. **2.** extraordinary; outstanding; remarkable: *a phenomenal achievement.* **3.** *Philosophy.* known or perceived by the senses rather than the mind. —**phe+ˈnom+e·nal+ly** *adv.*

phe+nom+e·nal+ism (fɪˈnɒmɪnəˌlɪzəm) *n.* **1.** the theory that only phenomena are real and can be known. Compare **idealism, realism. 2.** the tendency to think about things as phenomena only. Compare **positivism.** —**phe+ˈnom+e·nal+ist** *n., adj.* —**phe+ˌnom+e·nal+ˈis+ti+cal+ly** *adv.*

phe+nom+e·nol+o·gy (fɪˌnɒmɪˈnɒlədʒɪ) *n. Philosophy.* **1.** the movement founded by Husserl that concentrates on the detailed description of conscious experience, without recourse to explanation, metaphysical assumptions, and traditional philosophical questions. **2.** the science of phenomena as opposed to the science of being. —**phe+nom+e·no+log·i·cal** (fɪˌnɒmɪnəˈlɒdʒɪkᵊl) *adj.* —**phe+ˌnom+e·no+ˈlog·i·cal+ly** *adv.*

phe+nom+e·non (fɪˈnɒmɪnən) *n., pl.* **+e·na** (-ɪnə) *or* **+e·nons. 1.** anything that can be perceived as an occurrence or fact by the senses. **2.** any remarkable occurrence or person. **3.** *Philosophy.* **a.** the object of perception, experience, etc. **b.** (in the writings of Kant) a thing as it appears and is interpreted in perception and reflection, as distinguished from its real nature as a thing-in-itself. Compare **noumenon.** [C16: via Late Latin from Greek *phainomenon,* from *phainesthai* to appear, from *phainein* to show]

Usage. Although *phenomena* is often treated as if it were singular, correct usage is to employ *phenomenon* with a singular construction and *phenomena* with a plural: *that is an interesting phenomenon* (not *phenomena*); *several new phenomena were recorded in his notes.*

phe+no+thi·a+zine (ˌfiːnəʊˈθaɪəziːn) *n.* a colourless to light yellow insoluble crystalline compound that darkens to olive green when exposed to light: used as an anthelmintic for livestock and in insecticides. Formula: $C_{12}H_9NS$.

phe+no+type (ˈfiːnəʊˌtaɪp) *n.* the physical constitution of an organism as determined by the interaction of its genetic constitution and the environment. Compare **genotype.** —**phe+no+typ+ic** (ˌfiːnəʊˈtɪpɪk) *or* ˌ**phe+no+ˈtyp·i·cal** *adj.* —ˌ**phe+no+ˈtyp·i+cal+ly** *adv.*

phe+nox+ide (fɪˈnɒksaɪd) *n.* any of a class of salts of phenol. They contain the ion $C_6H_5O^-$. Also called: **phenolate.**

phe+nyl (ˈfiːnaɪl, ˈfɛnɪl) *n.* (*modifier*) of, containing, or consisting of the monovalent group C_6H_5, derived from benzene: *a phenyl group or radical.*

phe·nyl+al·a·nine (ˌfiːnaɪlˈæləˌniːn, ˌfɛnɪl-) *n.* a colourless soluble crystalline optically active amino acid that must be introduced into the body by diet. Formula: $C_9H_{11}NO_2$.

phe·nyl+a·mine (ˌfiːnaɪləˈmiːn, ˌfɛnɪl-) *n.* another name for **aniline.**

phe·nyl+ke·ton+u·ri·a (ˌfiːnaɪlˌkiːtəˈnjʊərɪə) *n.* a congenital metabolic disorder characterized by the abnormal accumulation of phenylalanine in the body fluids, resulting in various degrees of mental deficiency. [C20: New Latin; see PHENYL, KETONE, -URIA]

pher·o+mone (ˈfɛrəˌməʊn) *n.* a chemical substance, secreted externally by certain animals, such as insects, affecting the behaviour or physiology of other animals of the same species. [C20: *phero-,* from Greek *pherein* to bear + (HOR)MONE]

phew (fjuː) *interj.* an exclamation of relief, surprise, disbelief, weariness, etc.

phi (faɪ) *n., pl.* **phis.** the 21st letter in the Greek alphabet, Φ, φ, a consonant, transliterated as *ph* or *f.*

phi·al (ˈfaɪəl) *n.* a small bottle for liquids, etc.; vial. [C14: from Old French *fiole,* from Latin *phiola* saucer, from Greek *phialē* wide shallow vessel]

Phi Be·ta Kap+pa (ˈfaɪ ˈbeɪtə ˈkæpə, ˈbiːtə) *n. U.S.* **1.** a national honorary society, founded in 1776, membership of which is based on high academic ability. **2.** a member of this society. [from the initials of the Greek motto *philosophia biou kubernētēs* philosophy the guide of life]

Phid·i·as (ˈfɪdɪˌæs) *n.* 5th-century B.C. Greek sculptor, regarded as one of the greatest of sculptors. He executed the sculptures of the Parthenon and the colossal statue of Zeus at Olympia, one of the Seven Wonders of the World: neither survives in the original. —**ˈPhid+i·an** *adj.*

Phi·dip·pi·des (faɪˈdɪpɪˌdiːz) *n.* a variant spelling of **Pheidippides.**

phil. *abbrev. for:* **1.** philosophy. **2.** philharmonic.

Phil. *abbrev. for:* **1.** Philippians. **2.** Philippines. **3.** Philadelphia.

Phil·a+del+ph·i·a (ˌfɪləˈdɛlfɪə) *n.* a city and port in SE Pennsylvania, at the confluence of the Delaware and Schuylkill Rivers: the fourth largest city in the U.S.; founded by Quakers in 1682; cultural and financial centre of the American colonies and the federal capital (1790–1800); scene of the Continental Congresses (1774–83) and the signing of the Declaration of Independence (1776). Pop.: 1 861 719 (1973 est.).

phil·a+del+phus (ˌfɪləˈdɛlfəs) *n.* any shrub of the N temperate genus *Philadelphus,* cultivated for their strongly scented showy flowers: family *Philadelphaceae.* See also **mock orange.** [C19: New Latin, from Greek *philadelphon* mock orange, literally: loving one's brother]

Phi+lae (ˈfaɪliː) *n.* an island in Upper Egypt, in the Nile north of the Aswan Dam: of religious importance in ancient times; almost submerged since the raising of the level of the dam.

phi+lan+der (fɪˈlændə) *vb.* (*intr.,* often foll. by *with*) (of a man) to flirt with women. [C17: from Greek *philandros* fond of men, from *philos* loving + *anēr* man; used as a name for a lover in literary works] —**phi+ˈlan+der+er** *n.*

phil+an+throp+ic (ˌfɪlənˈθrɒpɪk) *or* **phil+an+throp·i·cal** *adj.* showing concern for humanity, esp. by performing charitable actions, donating money, etc. —ˌ**phil+an+ˈthrop·i·cal+ly** *adv.*

phi+lan+thro+py (fɪˈlænθrəpɪ) *n., pl.* **+pies. 1.** the practice of performing charitable or benevolent actions. **2.** love of mankind in general. [C17: from Late Latin *philanthrōpia,* from Greek: love of mankind, from *philos* loving + *anthrōpos* man] —**phi+ˈlan+thro+pist** *or* **phil+an+thrope** (ˈfɪlənˌθrəʊp) *n.*

phi+lat+e·ly (fɪˈlætəlɪ) *n.* the collection and study of postage stamps and all related material concerned with postal history. [C19: from French *philatélie,* from PHILO- + Greek *ateleia* exemption from charges (here referring to stamps), from A-[1] + *telos* tax, payment] —**phil·a+tel+ic** (ˌfɪləˈtɛlɪk) *adj.* —ˌ**phil·a+ˈtel·i+cal+ly** *adv.* —**phi+ˈlat+e·list** *n.*

Phil·by (ˈfɪlbɪ) *n.* **Har·old,** called *Kim.* born 1912, English double agent; defected to Russia (1963).

-phile *or* **-phil** *n. combining form.* indicating a person or thing having a fondness or preference for something specified: *bibliophile; Francophile.* [from Greek *philos* loving]

Philem. *Bible. abbrev. for* Philemon.

Phi·le·mon[1] (faɪˈliːmɒn) *n. New Testament.* **1.** a Christian of Colossae whose escaped slave came to meet Paul. **2.** the book (in full **The Epistle of Paul the Apostle to Philemon**), asking Philemon to forgive the slave for escaping.

Phi·le·mon[2] (faɪˈliːmɒn) *n. Greek myth.* a poor Phrygian, who with his wife Baucis offered hospitality to the disguised Zeus and Hermes.

phil+har+mon+ic (ˌfɪlhɑːˈmɒnɪk, ˌfɪlə-) *adj.* **1.** fond of music. **2.** (*cap. when part of a name*) denoting an orchestra, choir, society, etc., devoted to the performance, appreciation, and study of music. ~*n.* **3.** (*cap. when part of a name*) a specific philharmonic choir, orchestra, or society. [C18: from French *philharmonique,* from Italian *filarmonico* music-loving; see PHILO-, HARMONY]

phil+hel+lene (fɪlˈhɛliːn) *or* **phil+hel+len+ist** (fɪlˈhɛlɪnɪst) *n.* **1.** a lover of Greece and Greek culture. **2.** *European history.* a supporter of the cause of Greek national independence. —**phil+hel+le·nic** (ˌfɪlhɛˈliːnɪk) *adj.* —**phil+hel+len+ism** (fɪlˈhɛlɪˌnɪzəm) *n.*

-phil·i·a *n. combining form.* **1.** indicating a tendency towards: *haemophilia.* **2.** indicating an abnormal liking for: *necrophilia.* [from Greek *philos* loving] —**-phil·i·ac** *n. combining form.* —**-phi·lous** *or* **-phil·ic** *adj. combining form.*

phil·i·beg (ˈfɪlɪˌbɛg) *n.* a variant spelling of **filibeg.**

Phil·ip (ˈfɪlɪp) *n.* **1.** *New Testament.* **a.** an apostle from Bethsaida (John 1:43–51; 6:5–7; 12:21; 14:8). **b.** Also called: **Philip the Evangelist.** one of the seven deacons appointed by the early Church. **c.** Also called: **Philip the Tetrarch.** one of the sons of Herod the Great, who was ruler of part of former Judaea (4 B.C.–34 A.D.) (Luke 3:1). **2. King,** American Indian name *Metacomet.* died 1676, American Indian chief, the son of Massasoit. He waged King Philip's War against the colonists of New England (1675–76) and was killed in battle. **3. Prince.** another name for the (Duke of) **Edinburgh.**

Phil·ip II *n.* **1.** 382–36 B.C., king of Macedonia (359–36); the father of Alexander the Great. **2.** called *Philip Augustus.* 1165–1223, Capetian king of France (1180–1223); set out on the Third Crusade with Richard I of England (1190). **3.** 1527–98, king of Spain (1556–98) and king of Portugal (1580–98) as *Philip I;* the husband of Mary I of England (1554–58). He championed the Counter-Reformation, sending the Armada against England (1588).

Phil·ip IV *n.* called *the Fair.* 1268–1314, king of France (1285–1314): he challenged the power of the papacy, obtaining the elevation of Clement V as pope residing at Avignon (the beginning of the Babylonian captivity of the papacy).

Phil·ip V *n.* 1683–1746, king of Spain (1700–46) and founder of the Bourbon dynasty in Spain. His accession began the War of Spanish Succession (1701–13).

Phil·ip VI *n.* 1293–1350, first Valois king of France (1328–50). Edward III of England claimed his throne, which with other disputes led to the beginning of the Hundred Years' War (1337).

Phil+ippe+ville (ˈfɪlɪpˌvɪl) *n.* the former name of **Skikda.**

Phi+lip+pi (fɪˈlɪpaɪ, ˈfɪl-) *n.* an ancient city in NE Macedonia: scene of the victory of Antony and Octavian over Brutus and Cassius (42 B.C.). **—Phi+ˈlip+pi·an** *adj.*

Phi+lip+pi·ans (fɪˈlɪpɪənz) *n.* (*functioning as sing.*) a book of the New Testament (in full **The Epistle of Paul the Apostle to the Philippians**).

phi+lip+pic (fɪˈlɪpɪk) *n.* a bitter or impassioned speech of denunciation; invective.

Phi+lip+pics (fɪˈlɪpɪks) *pl. n.* **1.** Demosthenes' orations against Philip of Macedon. **2.** Cicero's orations against Antony.

Phil+ip+pine ma+hog·a+ny (ˈfɪlɪˌpiːn) *n.* any of various Philippine hardwood trees of the genus *Shorea* and related genera: family *Dipterocarpaceae.*

Phil+ip+pines (ˈfɪlɪˌpiːnz, ˌfɪlɪˈpiːnz) *n.* **Republic of the.** a republic in SE Asia, occupying an archipelago of about 7100 islands (including Luzon, Mindanao, Samar, and Negros): became a Spanish colony in 1571 but ceded to the U.S. in 1898 after the Spanish-American War; gained independence in 1946. The islands are generally mountainous and volcanic. Languages: chiefly Tagalog and English. Religion: chiefly Roman Catholic. Currency: peso. Capital: Quezon City. Pop.: 36 684 486 (1970). Area: 299 765 sq. km (115 740 sq. miles).

Phil+ip+pine Sea *n.* part of the NW Pacific Ocean, east and north of the Philippines.

Phil+ip+pop·o+lis (ˌfɪlɪˈpɒpəlɪs) *n.* transliteration of the Greek name for **Plovdiv.**

Phil·ips (ˈfɪlɪps) *n.* **Am·brose.** 1674–1749, English pastoral poet and dramatist.

Phil·ip the Good *n.* 1396–1467, duke of Burgundy (1419–67), under whose rule Burgundy was one of the most powerful states in Europe.

Phi+lis+ti·a (fɪˈlɪstɪə) *n.* an ancient country on the coast of SW Palestine. **—Phi+ˈlis+ti·an** *adj.*

Phil+is+tine (ˈfɪlɪˌstaɪn) *n.* **1.** a person who is unreceptive to or hostile towards culture, the arts, etc.; a smug boorish person. **2.** a member of the non-Semitic people who inhabited ancient Philistia. ~*adj.* **3.** (*sometimes not cap.*) boorishly uncultured. **4.** of or relating to the ancient Philistines. **—Phil+is+tin+ism** (ˈfɪlɪstɪˌnɪzəm) *n.*

Phil·lip (ˈfɪlɪp) *n.* **Ar·thur.** 1738–1814, English naval commander; captain general of the First Fleet, which carried convicts from Portsmouth to Sydney Cove, Australia, where he founded New South Wales.

Phil·lips (ˈfɪlɪps) *n.* Captain **Mark.** born 1948, English three-day-event horseman; husband of Princess Anne.

phil+lu+men+ist (fɪˈljuːmənɪst, -ˈluː-) *n.* a person who collects matchbox labels. [C20: from PHILO- + Latin *lumen* light + -IST]

phil·o- *or before a vowel* **phil-** *combining form.* indicating a love of: *philology; philanthropic.* [from Greek *philos* loving]

Phil·oc·te·tes (ˌfɪlɒkˈtiːtiːz, fɪˈlɒktɪˌtiːz) *n. Greek myth.* a hero of the Trojan War, in which he killed Paris with the bow and poisoned arrows given to him by Hercules.

phil·o+den+dron (ˌfɪləˈdɛndrən) *n., pl.* **+drons** *or* **+dra** (-drə). any aroid evergreen climbing plant of the tropical American genus *Philodendron:* cultivated as house plants. [C19: New Latin from Greek: lover of trees]

phi+log·y+ny (fɪˈlɒdʒɪnɪ) *n. Rare.* fondness for women. Compare **misogyny.** [C17: from Greek *philogunia,* from PHILO- + *gunē* woman] **—phi+ˈlog·y+nist** *n.* **—phi+ˈlog·y+nous** *adj.*

Phi·lo Ju·dae·us (ˈfaɪləʊ dʒuːˈdiːəs) *n.* ?20 B.C.–?54 A.D., Jewish philosopher, born in Alexandria. He sought to reconcile Judaism with Greek philosophy.

philol. *abbrev. for:* **1.** philological. **2.** philology.

phi+lol+o·gy (fɪˈlɒlədʒɪ) *n.* (no longer in scholarly use) **1.** comparative and historical linguistics. **2.** the scientific analysis of written records and literary texts. **3.** the study of literature in general. [C17: from Latin *philologia,* from Greek: love of language] **—phil·o+log·i·cal** (ˌfɪləˈlɒdʒɪkᵊl) *adj.* **—ˌphil·o+ˈlog·i·cal+ly** *adv.* **—phi+ˈlol·o·gist** *or* **phi+ˈlol·o·ger** *n.*

phil·o+mel (ˈfɪləˌmɛl) *or* **phil·o·me·la** (ˌfɪləʊˈmiːlə) *n.* poetic names for a **nightingale.** [C14 *philomene,* via Medieval Latin from Latin *philomēla,* from Greek]

Phil·o·me·la (ˌfɪləʊˈmiːlə) *n. Greek myth.* an Athenian princess, who was raped and had her tongue cut out by her brother-in-law Tereus, and subsequently was transformed into a nightingale. See **Procne.**

phil·o+pro+gen·i+tive (ˌfɪləʊprəʊˈdʒɛnɪtɪv) *adj. Rare.* **1.** fond of children. **2.** producing many offspring.

philos. *abbrev. for:* **1.** philosopher. **2.** philosophical.

phi+los·o+pher (fɪˈlɒsəfə) *n.* **1.** a student or adherent of a particular philosophy or system of values. **2.** a person of philosophical temperament, esp. one who is patient, wise, and stoical. **3.** (formerly) an alchemist or devotee of occult science. **4.** a person who establishes the ideology of a cult or movement: *the philosopher of the revolution.*

phi+los·o+pher's stone *n.* a stone or substance thought by alchemists to be capable of transmuting base metals into gold.

phil·o+soph·i+cal (ˌfɪləˈsɒfɪkᵊl) *or* **phil·o+soph+ic** *adj.* **1.** of or relating to philosophy or philosophers. **2.** reasonable, wise, or learned. **3.** having a calm and stoical disposition. **4.** (formerly) of or relating to science or natural philosophy. **—ˌphil·o+ˈsoph·i+cal+ly** *adv.* **—ˌphil·o+ˈsoph·i·cal+ness** *n.*

phi+los·o+phize *or* **phi+los·o+phise** (fɪˈlɒsəˌfaɪz) *vb.* **1.** (*intr.*) to make philosophical pronouncements and speculations. **2.** (*tr.*) to explain philosophically. **—phi+ˌlos·o·phi+ˈza·tion** *or* **phi+ˌlos·o·phi+ˈsa·tion** *n.* **—phi+ˈlos·o+ˌphiz+er** *or* **phi+ˈlos·o+ˌphis+er** *n.*

phi+los·o+phy (fɪˈlɒsəfɪ) *n., pl.* **+phies. 1.** the rational investigation of being, knowledge, and right conduct. **2.** a system or school of thought: *the philosophy of Descartes.* **3.** the critical study of the basic principles and concepts of a discipline: *the philosophy of law.* **4.** *Archaic or literary.* the investigation of natural phenomena, esp. alchemy, astrology, and astronomy. **5.** any system of belief, values, or tenets. **6.** a personal outlook or viewpoint. **7.** serenity of temper. [C13: from Old French *filosofie,* from Latin *philosophia,* from Greek, from *philosophos* lover of wisdom]

-phi·lous *or* **-phil·ic** *adj. combining form.* indicating love of or fondness of: *heliophilous.* [from Latin *-philus,* from Greek *-philos;* see -PHILE]

phil+tre *or U.S.* **phil+ter** (ˈfɪltə) *n.* a drink supposed to arouse love, desire, etc. [C16: from Latin *philtrum,* from Greek *philtron* love-potion, from *philos* loving]

phi+mo+sis (faɪˈməʊsɪs) *n.* abnormal tightness of the foreskin, preventing its being retracted over the tip of the penis. [C17: via New Latin from Greek: a muzzling, from *phimos* a muzzle]

phi-phe·nom+e·non (ˈfaɪfɪˌnɒmɪnən) *n., pl.* **·na** (-nə). *Psychol.* an illusion in which two lights turned on and off alternately are seen as one light moving to and fro. [C20: arbitrary use of Greek *phi*]

phiz (fɪz) *n. Slang, chiefly Brit.* the face or a facial expression: *an ugly phiz.* Also called: **phiz+og** (ˈfɪzɒg). [C17: colloquial shortening of PHYSIOGNOMY]

Phiz (fɪz) *n.* pseudonym of *Hablot Knight Browne.* 1815–82, English painter, noted for his illustrations for Dickens' novels.

phle+bi+tis (flɪˈbaɪtɪs) *n.* inflammation of a vein. [C19: via New Latin from Greek; see PHLEBO-, -ITIS] **—phle+bit+ic** (flɪˈbɪtɪk) *adj.*

phle·bo- *or before a vowel* **phleb-** *combining form.* indicating a vein: *phlebotomy.* [from Greek *phleps, phleb-,* vein]

phleb·o+scle+ro+sis (ˌflɛbəʊsklɪˈrəʊsɪs) *n. Pathol.* hardening and loss of elasticity of the veins.

phle+bot·o+mize *or* **phle+bot·o+mise** (flɪˈbɒtəˌmaɪz) *vb.* (*tr.*) *Surgery.* to perform phlebotomy on (a patient).

phle+bot·o+my (flɪˈbɒtəmɪ) *n., pl.* **+mies.** surgical incision into a vein. Also called: **venesection.** [C14: from Old French *flebothomie,* from Late Latin *phlebotomia,* from Greek] **—phleb·o+tom+ic** (ˌflɛbəˈtɒmɪk) *or* **ˌphleb·o+ˈtom·i+cal** *adj.* **—phle+ˈbot·o+mist** *n.*

Phleg+e·thon (ˈflɛgɪˌθɒn) *n. Greek myth.* a river of fire in Hades. [C14: from Greek, literally: blazing, from *phlegethein* to flame, blaze]

phlegm (flɛm) *n.* **1.** the viscid mucus secreted by the walls of the respiratory tract. **2.** *Archaic.* one of the four bodily humours. **3.** apathy; stolidity; indifference. **4.** self-possession; imperturbability; coolness. [C14: from Old French *fleume,* from Late Latin *phlegma,* from Greek: inflammation, from *phlegein* to burn] **—ˈphlegm·y** *adj.*

phleg+mat+ic (flɛgˈmætɪk) *or* **phleg+mat·i·cal** *adj.* **1.** having a stolid or unemotional disposition. **2.** not easily excited. **—phleg+ˈmat·i·cal+ly** *adv.* **—phleg+ˈmat·i·cal+ness** *or* **phleg+ˈmat·ic+ness** *n.*

phlo+em (ˈfləʊɛm) *n.* tissue in higher plants that conducts synthesized food substances to all parts of the plant. [C19: via German from Greek *phloos* bark]

phlo+gis+tic (flɒˈdʒɪstɪk) *adj.* **1.** *Pathol.* of inflammation; inflammatory. **2.** *Chem.* of, concerned with, or containing phlogiston.

phlo+gis+ton (flɒˈdʒɪstɒn, -tən) *n. Chem.* a hypothetical substance formerly thought to be present in all combustible materials and to be released during burning. [C18: via New Latin from Greek, from *phlogizein* to set alight; related to *phlegein* to burn]

phlog·o+pite (ˈflɒgəˌpaɪt) *n.* a brownish mica consisting of a hydrous silicate of potassium, magnesium, and aluminium, occurring principally in marble and dolomite. Formula: $KMg_3AlSi_3O_{10}(OH)_2$. See also **mica.** [C19: from Greek *phlogōpos* of fiery appearance, from *phlox* flame + *ōps* eye]

phlox (flɒks) *n., pl.* **phlox** *or* **phlox·es.** any polemoniaceous plant of the chiefly North American genus *Phlox:* cultivated for their clusters of white, red, or purple flowers. [C18: via Latin from Greek: a plant of glowing colour, literally: flame]

phlyc+te·na *or* **phlyc+tae+na** (flɪkˈtiːnə) *n., pl.* **+nae** (-niː). *Pathol.* a small blister, vesicle, or pustule. [C17: via New Latin from Greek *phluktaina,* from *phluzein* to swell]

Phnom Penh *or* **Pnom Penh** (ˈnɒm ˈpɛn) *n.* the capital of Cambodia, a port in the south at the confluence of the Mekong and Tonle Sap Rivers: capital of the country since 1865; university (1960). Pop.: 468 900 (1970).

-phobe *n. combining form.* indicating a person or thing that fears or hates: *Germanophobe; xenophobe.* [from Greek *-phobos* fearing] **—-pho·bic** *adj. combining form.*

pho·bi·a ('fəʊbɪə) *n.* a compelling fear or dread, esp. of a particular object or situation. [C19: from Greek *phobos* fear] **—'pho·bic** *adj.*

-pho·bi·a *n. combining form.* indicating an extreme abnormal fear of or aversion to: *acrophobia; claustrophobia.* [via Latin from Greek, from *phobos* fear] **—-pho·bic** *adj. combining form.*

Pho·bos ('fəʊbɒs) *n.* the larger of the two satellites of Mars and the closer to the planet. Approximate diameter: 23 km. Compare **Deimos.**

Pho·cae·a (fəʊ'siːə) *n.* an ancient port in Asia Minor, the northernmost of Ionian cities on the W coast of Asia Minor: an important maritime state (about 1000–600 B.C.).

pho·cine ('fəʊsaɪn) *adj.* **1.** of, relating to, or resembling a seal. **2.** of, relating to, or belonging to the *Phocinae,* a subfamily that includes the harbour seal and grey seal. [C19: ultimately from Greek *phōkē* a seal]

Pho·cis ('fəʊsɪs) *n.* an ancient district of central Greece, on the Gulf of Corinth: site of the Delphic oracle.

pho·co·me·li·a (ˌfəʊkəʊ'miːlɪə) *or* **pho·com·e·ly** (fəʊ'kɒməlɪ) *n.* a congenital deformity resulting from prenatal interference with the development of the fetal limbs, characterized esp. by short stubby hands or feet attached close to the body. [C19: via New Latin from Greek *phōkē* a seal + *melos* a limb] **—ˌpho·co·'me·lic** *adj.*

phoe·be ('fiːbɪ) *n.* any of several greyish-brown North American flycatchers of the genus *Sayornis,* such as *S. phoebe* (**eastern phoebe**). [C19: imitative of the bird's call]

Phoe·be[1] *or* **Phe·be** ('fiːbɪ) *n.* **1.** *Classical myth.* a Titaness, who later became identified with Artemis (Diana) as goddess of the moon. **2.** *Poetic.* a personification of the moon.

Phoe·be[2] ('fiːbɪ) *n.* the smallest of the nine satellites of Saturn and the furthest from the planet. It has retrograde motion.

Phoe·bus ('fiːbəs) *n.* **1.** Also called: **Phoebus Apollo.** *Greek myth.* Apollo as the sun god. **2.** *Poetic.* a personification of the sun. [C14: via Latin from Greek *Phoibos* bright; related to *phaos* light]

Phoe·ni·ci·a (fə'nɪʃɪə, -'niː-) *n.* an ancient maritime country extending from the Mediterranean Sea to the Lebanon Mountains, now occupied by the coastal regions of Lebanon and parts of Syria and Israel: consisted of a group of city-states, at their height between about 1200 and 1000 B.C., that were leading traders of the ancient world.

Phoe·ni·ci·an (fə'nɪʃɪən, -'niːʃən) *n.* **1.** a member of an ancient Semitic people of NW Syria who dominated the trade of the ancient world in the first millennium B.C. and founded colonies throughout the Mediterranean. **2.** the extinct language of this people, belonging to the Canaanitic branch of the Semitic subfamily of the Afro-Asiatic family. *~adj.* **3.** of or relating to Phoenicia, the Phoenicians, or their language.

phoe·nix *or U.S.* **phe·nix** ('fiːnɪks) *n.* **1.** a legendary Arabian bird said to set fire to itself and rise anew from the ashes every 500 years. **2.** a person or thing of surpassing beauty or quality. [Old English *fenix,* via Latin from Greek *phoinix;* identical in form with Greek *Phoinix* Phoenician, purple]

Phoe·nix[1] ('fiːnɪks) *n., Latin genitive* **Phoe·ni·ces** ('fiːnɪˌsiːz). a constellation in the S hemisphere lying between Grus and Eridanus.

Phoe·nix[2] ('fiːnɪks) *n.* a city in central Arizona, capital city of the state, on the Salt River. Pop.: 637 121 (1973 est.).

Phoe·nix Is·lands *pl. n.* a group of eight coral islands in the central Pacific: administratively part of the Gilbert Islands. Pop.: 2192 (1968). Area: 28 sq. km (11 sq. miles).

Phom·vi·hane ('pɒmvɪhɑːn) *n.* **Kay·sone** ('kaɪsɒn). born 1920, Laotian Communist statesman; prime minister of Laos since 1975.

phon (fɒn) *n.* a unit of loudness that measures the intensity of a sound by the number of decibels it is above a reference tone having a frequency of 1000 hertz and a root-mean-square sound pressure of 20×10^{-6} pascal.

phon. *abbrev. for:* **1.** Also: **phonet.** phonetics. **2.** phonology.

pho·nate (fəʊ'neɪt) *vb.* (*intr.*) to articulate speech sounds, esp. to cause the vocal cords to vibrate in the execution of a voiced speech sound. [C19: from Greek *phōnē* voice] **—pho·'na·tion** *n.* **—pho·na·to·ry** ('fəʊnətərɪ, -trɪ) *adj.*

phone[1] (fəʊn) *n., vb. Informal.* short for **telephone.**

phone[2] (fəʊn) *n. Phonetics.* a single uncomplicated speech sound. [C19: from Greek *phōnē* sound, voice]

-phone *combining form.* **1.** (*forming nouns*) indicating voice, sound, or a device giving off sound: *microphone; telephone.* **2.** (*forming adjectives*) speaking a particular language: *Francophone.* [from Greek *phōnē* voice, sound] **—-phon·ic** *adj. combining form.*

phone-in *n.* **a.** a radio or television programme in which listeners' or viewers' questions, comments, etc., are telephoned to the studio and broadcast live as part of a discussion. **b.** (*as modifier*): *a phone-in programme.*

pho·neme ('fəʊniːm) *n. Linguistics.* one of the set of speech sounds in any given language that serve to distinguish one word from another. A phoneme may consist of several phonetically distinct articulations, which are regarded as identical by native speakers, since one articulation may be substituted for another without any change of meaning. Thus /p/ and /b/ are separate phonemes in English because they distinguish such words as *pet* and *bet,* whereas the light and dark /l/ sounds in *little* are not separate phonemes since they may be transposed without changing meaning. [C20: via French from Greek *phōnēma* sound, speech]

pho·ne·mic (fə'niːmɪk) *adj. Linguistics.* **1.** of or relating to the phoneme. **2.** relating to or denoting speech sounds that belong to different phonemes rather than being allophonic variants of the same phoneme. Compare **phonetic** (sense 2). **3.** of or relating to phonemics. **—pho·'ne·mi·cal·ly** *adv.*

pho·ne·mics (fə'niːmɪks) *n.* (*functioning as sing.*) that aspect of linguistics concerned with the classification, analysis, interrelation, and environmental changes of the phonemes of a language. **—pho·'ne·mi·cist** *n.*

pho·nen·do·scope (fə'nɛndəˌskəʊp) *n.* an instrument that amplifies small sounds, esp. within the human body. [C20: from PHONO- + ENDO- + -SCOPE]

pho·net·ic (fə'nɛtɪk) *adj.* **1.** of or relating to phonetics. **2.** denoting any perceptible distinction between one speech sound and another, irrespective of whether the sounds are phonemes or allophones. Compare **phonemic** (sense 2). **3.** conforming to pronunciation: *phonetic spelling.* [C19: from New Latin *phōnēticus,* from Greek *phōnētikos,* from *phōnein* to make sounds, speak] **—pho·'net·i·cal·ly** *adv.*

pho·net·ic al·pha·bet *n.* a list of the words used in communications to represent the letters of the alphabet, as in E for Echo, T for Tango.

pho·ne·ti·cian (ˌfəʊnɪ'tɪʃən) *n.* a person skilled in phonetics or one who employs phonetics in his work.

pho·net·ics (fə'nɛtɪks) *n.* (*functioning as sing.*) the science concerned with the study of speech processes, including the production, perception, and analysis of speech sounds from both an acoustic and a physiological point of view. This science, though capable of being applied to language studies, technically excludes linguistic considerations. Compare **phonology.**

pho·net·ist ('fəʊnɪtɪst) *n.* **1.** another name for **phonetician. 2.** a person who advocates or uses a system of phonetic spelling.

pho·ney *or* **pho·ny** ('fəʊnɪ) *Slang.* *~adj.* **·ni·er, ·ni·est. 1.** not genuine; fake. **2.** (of a person) insincere or pretentious. *~n., pl.* **·neys** *or* **·nies. 3.** an insincere or pretentious person. **4.** something that is not genuine; a fake. [C20: origin uncertain] **—'pho·ney·ness** *or* **'pho·ni·ness** *n.*

phon·ics ('fɒnɪks) *n.* (*functioning as sing.*) **1.** an obsolete name for **acoustics. 2.** a method of teaching people to read by training them to associate letters with their phonetic values. **—'phon·ic** *adj.* **—'phon·i·cal·ly** *adv.*

pho·no- *or before a vowel* **phon-** *combining form.* indicating a sound or voice: *phonograph; phonology.* [from Greek *phōnē* sound, voice]

pho·no·gram ('fəʊnəˌgræm) *n.* **1.** any written symbol standing for a sound, syllable, morpheme, or word. **2.** a sequence of written symbols having the same sound in a variety of different words; for example, *ough* in *bought, ought,* and *brought.* **—ˌpho·no·'gram·ic** *or* **ˌpho·no·'gram·mic** *adj.*

pho·no·graph ('fəʊnəˌgrɑːf, -ˌgræf) *n.* **1.** an early form of gramophone capable of recording and reproducing sound on wax cylinders. **2.** the usual U.S. word for **gramophone.**

pho·nog·ra·phy (fəʊ'nɒgrəfɪ) *n.* **1.** a writing system that represents sounds by individual symbols. Compare **logography. 2.** the employment of such a writing system. **—pho·'nog·ra·pher** *or* **pho·'nog·ra·phist** *n.* **—pho·no·graph·ic** (ˌfəʊnə'græfɪk) *adj.*

phonol. *abbrev. for* phonology.

pho·no·lite ('fəʊnəˌlaɪt) *n.* a fine-grained volcanic igneous rock consisting of alkaline feldspars and nepheline. [C19: via French from German *Phonolith;* see PHONO-, -LITE] **—pho·no·lit·ic** (ˌfəʊnə'lɪtɪk) *adj.*

pho·nol·o·gy (fə'nɒlədʒɪ) *n., pl.* **·gies. 1.** the study of the sound system of a language or of languages in general. Compare **syntax** (senses 1, 2), **semantics. 2.** such a sound system. **—pho·no·log·i·cal** (ˌfəʊnə'lɒdʒɪkᵊl, 'fɒn-) *adj.* **—ˌpho·no·'log·i·cal·ly** *adv.* **—pho·'nol·o·gist** *n.*

pho·nom·e·ter (fə'nɒmɪtə) *n.* an apparatus that measures the intensity of sound, esp. one calibrated in phons. **—pho·no·met·ric** (ˌfəʊnə'mɛtrɪk) *or* **ˌpho·no·'met·ri·cal** *adj.*

pho·non ('fəʊnɒn) *n. Physics.* a quantum of vibrational energy in the acoustic vibrations of a crystal lattice.

pho·no·scope ('fəʊnəˌskəʊp) *n.* a device that renders visible the mechanical vibrations of a sounding instrument.

pho·no·tac·tics ('fəʊnəʊˌtæktɪks) *n. Linguistics.* the study of the possible arrangement of the sounds of a language in the words of that language. [C20: from PHONO- + *-tactics,* on the model of *syntactic;* see SYNTAX]

pho·no·type ('fəʊnəˌtaɪp) *n. Printing.* **1.** a type bearing a phonetic symbol. **2.** text printed in phonetic symbols. **—pho·no·typ·ic** (ˌfəʊnə'tɪpɪk) *or* **ˌpho·no·'typ·i·cal** *adj.*

pho·no·typ·y ('fəʊnəˌtaɪpɪ) *n.* the transcription of speech into phonetic symbols. **—'pho·no·ˌtyp·ist** *or* **'pho·no·ˌtyp·er** *n.*

pho·ny ('fəʊnɪ) *adj.* **·ni·er, ·ni·est,** *n., pl.* **·nies.** a variant spelling (esp. U.S.) of **phoney. —'pho·ni·ness** *n.*

-pho·ny *n. combining form.* indicating a specified type of sound: *cacophony; euphony.* [from Greek *-phōnia,* from *phōnē* sound] **—-phon·ic** *adj. combining form.*

phoo·ey ('fuːɪ) *interj. Informal.* an exclamation of scorn, contempt, disbelief, etc. [C20: probably variant of PHEW]

-phore *n. combining form.* indicating a person or thing that bears or produces: *gonophore; semaphore.* [from New Latin *-phorus,* from Greek *-phoros* bearing, from *pherein* to bear] **—-pho·rous** *adj. combining form.*

-pho·re·sis *n. combining form.* indicating a transmission: *electrophoresis.* [from Greek *phorēsis* being carried, from *pherein* to bear]

phos·gene ('fɒzdʒiːn) *n.* a colourless easily liquefied poisonous gas with an odour resembling that of new-mown hay: used in chemical warfare and in the manufacture of pesticides, dyes, and polyurethane resins. [C19: from Greek *phos* light + *-gene*, variant of -GEN]

phos·ge·nite ('fɒzdʒɪˌnaɪt) *n.* a rare fluorescent secondary mineral consisting of lead chloro-carbonate in the form of greyish tetragonal crystals. Formula: $Pb_2(Cl_2CO_3)$.

phos·pha·tase ('fɒsfəˌteɪs, -ˌteɪz) *n.* any of a group of enzymes that catalyse the hydrolysis of organic phosphates.

phos·phate ('fɒsfeɪt) *n.* **1.** any salt or ester of any phosphoric acid, esp. a salt of orthophosphoric acid. **2.** (*often pl.*) any of several chemical fertilizers containing phosphorous compounds. [C18: from French *phosphat;* see PHOSPHORUS, -ATE[1]] —**phos·phat·ic** (fɒs'fætɪk) *adj.*

phos·pha·tide ('fɒsfəˌtaɪd) *n.* another name for **phospholipid.**

phos·pha·tize *or* **phos·pha·tise** ('fɒsfəˌtaɪz) *vb.* **1.** (*tr.*) to treat with a phosphate or phosphates, as by applying a fertilizer. **2.** to change or be changed into a phosphate. —ˌ**phos·pha·ti·'za·tion** *or* ˌ**phos·pha·ti·'sa·tion** *n.*

phos·pha·tu·ri·a (ˌfɒsfə'tjʊərɪə) *n. Pathol.* an abnormally large amount of phosphates in the urine. [C19: New Latin, from PHOSPHATE + -URIA] —ˌ**phos·pha·'tu·ric** *adj.*

phos·phene ('fɒsfiːn) *n.* the sensation of light caused by pressure on the eyelid of a closed eye. [C19: from Greek *phos* light + *phainein* to show]

phos·phide ('fɒsfaɪd) *n.* any compound of phosphorus with another element, esp. a more electropositive element.

phos·phine ('fɒsfiːn) *n.* a colourless inflammable gas that is slightly soluble in water and has a strong fishy odour: used as a pesticide. Formula: PH_3.

phos·phite ('fɒsfaɪt) *n.* any salt or ester of phosphorous acid.

phos·pho- *or before a vowel* **phosph-** *combining form.* containing phosphorus: *phosphocreatine.* [from French, from *phosphore* PHOSPHORUS]

phos·pho·cre·a·tine (ˌfɒsfə'kriːəˌtiːn) *or* **phos·pho·cre·a·tin** *n.* a compound of phosphoric acid and creatine found in vertebrate muscle.

phos·pho·lip·id (ˌfɒsfə'lɪpɪd) *n.* any of a group of compounds composed of fatty acids, phosphoric acid, and a nitrogenous base: important constituents of all membranes. Also called: **phosphatide.**

phos·pho·pro·tein (ˌfɒsfə'prəʊtiːn) *n.* any of a group of conjugated proteins, esp. casein, in which the protein molecule is bound to phosphoric acid.

phos·phor ('fɒsfə) *n.* a substance, such as the coating on a cathode-ray tube, capable of emitting light when irradiated with particles or electromagnetic radiation. [C17: from French, ultimately from Greek *phōsphoros* PHOSPHORUS]

phos·pho·rate ('fɒsfəˌreɪt) *vb.* **1.** to treat or combine with phosphorus. **2.** (*tr.*) *Rare.* to cause (a substance) to exhibit phosphorescence.

phos·phor bronze *n.* any of various hard corrosion-resistant alloys containing copper, tin (2–8 per cent), and phosphorus (0.1–0.4 per cent): used in gears, bearings, cylinder casings, etc.

phos·pho·resce (ˌfɒsfə'rɛs) *vb.* (*intr.*) to exhibit phosphorescence.

phos·pho·res·cence (ˌfɒsfə'rɛsəns) *n.* **1.** *Physics.* **a.** a fluorescence that persists after the bombarding radiation producing it has stopped. **b.** a fluorescence for which the average lifetime of the excited atoms is greater than 10^{-8} seconds. **2.** the light emitted in phosphorescence. **3.** the emission of light during a chemical reaction, such as bioluminescence, in which insufficient heat is evolved to cause fluorescence. Compare **fluorescence.**

phos·pho·res·cent (ˌfɒsfə'rɛsᵊnt) *adj.* exhibiting or having the property of phosphorescence. —ˌ**phos·pho·'res·cent·ly** *adv.*

phos·phor·ic (fɒs'fɒrɪk) *adj.* of or containing phosphorus in the pentavalent state.

phos·phor·ic ac·id *n.* **1.** another name for **orthophosphoric acid. 2.** any oxyacid of phosphorus produced by reaction between phosphorus pentoxide and water. See also **metaphosphoric acid, pyrophosphoric acid, hypophosphoric acid.**

phos·pho·rism ('fɒsfəˌrɪzəm) *n.* poisoning caused by prolonged exposure to phosphorus.

phos·pho·rite ('fɒsfəˌraɪt) *n.* **1.** a fibrous variety of the mineral apatite. **2.** any of various mineral deposits that consist mainly of calcium phosphate. —**phos·pho·rit·ic** (ˌfɒsfə'rɪtɪk) *adj.*

phos·phor·o·scope (fɒs'fɒrəˌskəʊp) *n.* an instrument for measuring the duration of phosphorescence after the source of radiation causing it has been removed.

phos·pho·rous ('fɒsfərəs) *adj.* of or containing phosphorus in the trivalent state.

phos·pho·rous ac·id *n.* **1.** another name for **orthophosphorous acid. 2.** any oxyacid of phosphorus containing less oxygen than the corresponding phosphoric acid. See also **hypophosphorous acid.**

phos·pho·rus ('fɒsfərəs) *n.* **1.** an allotropic nonmetallic element occurring in phosphates and living matter. Ordinary phosphorus is a toxic flammable phosphorescent white solid; the red form is less reactive and nontoxic: used in matches, pesticides, and alloys. The radioisotope **phosphorus-32 (radiophosphorus),** with a half-life of 14.3 days, is used in radiotherapy and as a tracer. Symbol: P; atomic no.: 15; atomic wt.: 30.974; valency: 3 or 5; relative density: 1.82 (white), 2.20 (red); melting pt.: 44.1°C (white); boiling pt.: 280°C (white). **2.** *Rare.* another name for a **phosphor.** [C17: via Latin from Greek *phōsphoros* light-bringing, from *phōs* light + *pherein* to bring]

Phos·pho·rus ('fɒsfərəs) *n.* a morning star, esp. Venus.

phos·pho·rus pent·ox·ide *n.* a white odourless solid produced when phosphorus burns: has a strong affinity for water with which it forms phosphoric acids. Formula: P_2O_5 (commonly existing as the dimer P_4O_{10}). Also called: **phosphoric anhydride.**

phos·phor·y·lase (fɒs'fɒrɪˌleɪs, -ˌleɪz) *n.* any of a group of enzymes that catalyse the hydrolysis of glycogen to glucose-1-phosphate. [C20: from PHOSPHORUS + -YL + -ASE]

phos·sy jaw ('fɒsɪ) *n.* a gangrenous condition of the lower jawbone caused by prolonged exposure to phosphorus fumes. [C19: *phossy,* colloquial shortening of PHOSPHORUS]

phot (fɒt, fəʊt) *n.* a unit of illumination equal to one lumen per square centimetre. 1 phot is equal to 10 000 lux. [C20: from Greek *phōs* light]

phot. *abbrev. for:* **1.** photograph. **2.** photographic. **3.** photography.

pho·tic ('fəʊtɪk) *adj.* **1.** of or concerned with light. **2.** *Biology.* of or relating to the production of light by organisms. **3.** Also: **photobathic.** designating the zone of the sea where photosynthesis takes place.

pho·to ('fəʊtəʊ) *n., pl.* **·tos.** *Informal.* short for **photograph.**

pho·to- *combining form.* **1.** of, relating to, or produced by light: *photosynthesis.* **2.** indicating a photographic process: *photolithography.* [from Greek *phōs, phōt-*, light]

pho·to·ac·tin·ic (ˌfəʊtəʊæk'tɪnɪk) *adj.* emitting actinic radiation.

pho·to·ac·tive (ˌfəʊtəʊ'æktɪv) *adj.* (of a substance) capable of responding to light or other electromagnetic radiation.

pho·to·au·to·troph·ic (ˌfəʊtəʊˌɔːtəʊ'trɒfɪk) *adj.* (of plants) capable of using light as the energy source in the synthesis of food from inorganic matter. See also **photosynthesis.**

pho·to·bath·ic (ˌfəʊtəʊ'bæθɪk) *adj.* another word for **photic** (sense 3).

pho·to·cath·ode (ˌfəʊtəʊ'kæθəʊd) *n.* a cathode that undergoes or is used for photoemission.

pho·to·cell ('fəʊtəʊˌsɛl) *n.* a device in which the photoelectric or photovoltaic effect or photoconductivity is used to produce a current or voltage when exposed to light or other electromagnetic radiation. They are used in exposure meters, burglar alarms, etc. Also called: **photoelectric cell, electric eye.**

pho·to·chem·is·try (ˌfəʊtəʊ'kɛmɪstrɪ) *n.* the branch of chemistry concerned with the chemical effects of light and other electromagnetic radiations. Also called: **actinochemistry.** —**pho·to·chem·i·cal** (ˌfəʊtəʊ'kɛmɪkᵊl) *adj.* —ˌ**pho·to·'chem·i·cal·ly** *adv.* —ˌ**pho·to·'chem·ist** *n.*

pho·to·chron·o·graph (ˌfəʊtəʊ'krɒnəˌgrɑːf, -ˌgræf) *n. Physics.* an instrument for measuring very small time intervals by the trace made by a beam of light on a moving photographic film. —**pho·to·chron·og·ra·phy** (ˌfəʊtəʊkrə'nɒgrəfɪ) *n.*

pho·to·com·pose (ˌfəʊtəʊkəm'pəʊz) *vb.* (*tr.*) the U.S. word for **filmset.** —ˌ**pho·to·com·'pos·er** *n.*

pho·to·com·po·si·tion (ˌfəʊtəʊˌkɒmpə'zɪʃən) *n.* the usual U.S. name for **filmsetting.**

pho·to·con·duc·tion (ˌfəʊtəʊkən'dʌkʃən) *n.* conduction of electricity resulting from the absorption of light. See **photoconductivity.**

pho·to·con·duc·tiv·i·ty (ˌfəʊtəʊˌkɒndʌk'tɪvɪtɪ) *n.* the change in the electrical conductivity of certain substances, such as selenium, as a result of the absorption of electromagnetic radiation. —**pho·to·con·duc·tive** (ˌfəʊtəʊkən'dʌktɪv) *adj.* —ˌ**pho·to·con·'duc·tor** *n.*

pho·to·cop·i·er ('fəʊtəʊˌkɒpɪə) *n.* an instrument using light-sensitive photographic materials to reproduce written, printed, or graphic work.

pho·to·cop·y ('fəʊtəʊˌkɒpɪ) *n., pl.* **·cop·ies. 1.** a photographic reproduction of written, printed, or graphic work. See also **microcopy.** ~*vb.* **·cop·ies, ·cop·y·ing, ·cop·ied. 2.** to reproduce (written, printed, or graphic work) on photographic material.

pho·to·cur·rent ('fəʊtəʊˌkʌrənt) *n.* an electric current produced by electromagnetic radiation in the photoelectric effect, photovoltaic effect, or photoconductivity.

pho·to·dis·in·te·gra·tion (ˌfəʊtəʊdɪˌsɪntɪ'greɪʃən) *n.* disintegration of an atomic nucleus as a result of its absorption of a photon, usually a gamma ray.

pho·to·dy·nam·ics (ˌfəʊtəʊdaɪ'næmɪks) *n.* (*functioning as sing.*) the branch of biology concerned with the effects of light on the actions of plants and animals. —ˌ**pho·to·dy·'nam·ic** *adj.*

pho·to·e·las·tic·i·ty (ˌfəʊtəʊɪlæ'stɪsɪtɪ) *n.* the effects of stress, such as double refraction, on the optical properties of transparent materials.

pho·to·e·lec·tric (ˌfəʊtəʊɪ'lɛktrɪk) *or* **pho·to·e·lec·tri·cal** *adj.* of or concerned with electric or electronic effects caused by light or other electromagnetic radiation. —ˌ**pho·to·e·'lec·tri·cal·ly** *adv.* —**pho·to·e·lec·tric·i·ty** (ˌfəʊtəʊɪlɛk'trɪsɪtɪ) *n.*

pho·to·e·lec·tric cell *n.* another name for **photocell.**

pho·to·e·lec·tric ef·fect *n.* **1.** the ejection of electrons from a solid by an incident beam of sufficiently energetic electromagnetic radiation. **2.** any phenomenon involving electricity and electromagnetic radiation, such as photoemission.

pho·to·e·lec·tron (ˌfəʊtəʊɪ'lɛktrɒn) *n.* an electron ejected from an atom, molecule, or solid by an incident photon.

pho·to·e·lec·tro·type (ˌfəʊtəʊɪ'lɛktrəʊˌtaɪp) *n.* an electrotype mode using photography.

pho·to·e·mis·sion (ˌfəʊtəʊɪ'mɪʃən) *n.* the emission of electrons due to the impact of electromagnetic radiation, esp. as a result of the photoelectric effect. —ˌ**pho·to·e·'mis·sive** *adj.*

pho·to·en·grave (ˌfəʊtəʊɪn'greɪv) *vb. (tr.)* to reproduce (an illustration, etc.) by photoengraving. —ˌ**pho·to·en·'grav·er** *n.*

pho·to·en·grav·ing (ˌfəʊtəʊɪn'greɪvɪŋ) *n.* **1.** a photomechanical process for producing letterpress printing plates. **2.** a plate made by this process. **3.** a print made from such a plate.

pho·to fin·ish *n.* **1.** a finish of a race in which contestants are so close that a photograph is needed to decide the result. **2.** *Informal.* any race or competition in which the winners or placed contestants are separated by a very small margin.

Pho·to·fit ('fəʊtəʊˌfɪt) *n. Trademark.* **a.** a method of combining photographs of facial features, hair, etc., into a composite picture of a face: used by the police to trace suspects, criminals, etc., from witnesses' descriptions. **b.** (*as modifier*): *a Photofit picture.*

pho·to·flash ('fəʊtəʊˌflæʃ) *n.* another name for **flashbulb.**

pho·to·flood ('fəʊtəʊˌflʌd) *n.* a highly incandescent tungsten lamp used as an artificial light source for indoor photography, television, etc. The brightness is obtained by overloading the voltage.

pho·to·fluo·rog·ra·phy (ˌfəʊtəʊflʊə'rɒgrəfɪ) *n. Med.* the process of taking a photograph (**photofluorogram**) of a fluoroscopic image: used in diagnostic screening.

photog. *abbrev. for:* **1.** photograph. **2.** photographer. **3.** photographic. **4.** photography.

pho·to·gel·a·tin pro·cess (ˌfəʊtəʊ'dʒɛlətɪn) *n.* another name for **collotype** (sense 1).

pho·to·gene ('fəʊtəʊˌdʒiːn) *n.* another name for **afterimage.**

pho·to·gen·ic (ˌfəʊtə'dʒɛnɪk) *adj.* **1.** (esp. of a person) having features, colouring, and a general facial appearance that look attractive in photographs. **2.** *Biology.* producing or emitting light: *photogenic bacteria.* —ˌ**pho·to·'gen·i·cal·ly** *adv.*

pho·to·ge·ol·o·gy (ˌfəʊtəʊdʒɪ'ɒlədʒɪ) *n.* the study and identification of geological phenomena using aerial photographs.

pho·to·gram ('fəʊtəˌgræm) *n.* **1.** a picture, usually abstract, produced on a photographic material without the use of a camera, as by placing an object on the material and exposing to light. **2.** *Obsolete.* a photograph, often of the more artistic kind rather than a mechanical record.

pho·to·gram·me·try (ˌfəʊtəʊ'græmɪtrɪ) *n.* the process of making measurements from photographs, used esp. in the construction of maps from aerial photographs and also in medical and industrial research, etc. —**pho·to·gram·met·ric** (ˌfəʊtəʊgrə'mɛtrɪk) *adj.* —ˌ**pho·to·'gram·me·trist** *n.*

pho·to·graph ('fəʊtəˌgrɑːf, -ˌgræf) *n.* **1.** Also called: **exposure.** an image of an object, person, scene, etc., in the form of a print or slide recorded by a camera on photosensitive material. Often (informal) shortened to **photo.** ~*vb.* **2.** to take photographs of (an object, person, scene, etc.).

pho·tog·ra·pher (fə'tɒgrəfə) *n.* a person who takes photographs, either as a hobby or a profession.

pho·to·graph·ic (ˌfəʊtə'græfɪk) *adj.* **1.** of or relating to photography: *a photographic society; photographic materials.* **2.** like a photograph in accuracy or detail. **3.** (of a person's memory) able to retain facts, appearances, etc., in precise detail, often after only a very short view of or exposure to them. —ˌ**pho·to·'graph·i·cal·ly** *adv.*

pho·to·graph·ic mag·ni·tude *n. Astronomy.* the magnitude of a star as determined from photographic plates. It depends on the colour of the starlight and differs from the **visual magnitude** since an emulsion has a different colour sensitivity from that of the eye.

pho·tog·ra·phy (fə'tɒgrəfɪ) *n.* **1.** the process of recording images on sensitized material by the action of light, x-rays, etc., and the chemical processing of this material to produce a print, slide, or cine film. **2.** the art, practice, or occupation of taking and printing photographs, making cine films, etc.

pho·to·gra·vure (ˌfəʊtəʊgrə'vjʊə) *n.* **1.** any of various methods in which an intaglio plate for printing is produced by the use of photography. Former name: **heliogravure. 2.** matter printed from such a plate. [C19: from PHOTO- + French *gravure* engraving]

pho·to·jour·nal·ism (ˌfəʊtəʊ'dʒɜːnᵊˌlɪzəm) *n.* journalism in which photographs are the predominant feature. —ˌ**pho·to·'jour·nal·ist** *n.* —ˌ**pho·to·ˌjour·nal·'is·tic** *adj.*

pho·to·ki·ne·sis (ˌfəʊtəʊkɪ'niːsɪs, -kaɪ-) *n. Biology.* the movement of an organism in response to the stimulus of light. —**pho·to·ki·net·ic** (ˌfəʊtəʊkɪ'nɛtɪk, -kaɪ-) *adj.* —ˌ**pho·to·ki·'net·i·cal·ly** *adv.*

pho·to·lith·o·graph (ˌfəʊtəʊ'lɪθəˌgrɑːf, -ˌgræf) *n.* **1.** a picture printed by photolithography. ~*vb.* **2.** (*tr.*) to reproduce (pictures, text, etc.) by photolithography.

pho·to·li·thog·ra·phy (ˌfəʊtəʊlɪ'θɒgrəfɪ) *n.* **1.** a lithographic printing process using photographically made plates. Often shortened to **photolitho. 2.** *Electronics.* a process used in the manufacture of semiconductor devices, thin-film circuits, and printed circuits in which a particular pattern is transferred from a photograph onto a substrate, producing a pattern that acts as a mask during an etching or diffusion process. See also **planar process.** —ˌ**pho·to·li·'thog·ra·pher** *n.*

pho·to·lu·mi·nes·cence (ˌfəʊtəʊˌluːmɪ'nɛsəns) *n.* luminescence resulting from the absorption of light or infrared or ultraviolet radiation. —ˌ**pho·to·ˌlu·mi·'nes·cent** *adj.*

pho·tol·y·sis (fəʊ'tɒlɪsɪs) *n.* chemical decomposition caused by light or other electromagnetic radiation. Compare **radiolysis.** —**pho·to·lyt·ic** (ˌfəʊtəʊ'lɪtɪk) *adj.*

photom. *abbrev. for* photometry.

pho·to·map ('fəʊtəʊˌmæp) *n.* **1.** a map constructed by adding grid lines, place names, etc., to one or more aerial photographs. ~*vb.* **-maps, -map·ping, -mapped. 2.** (*tr.*) to map (an area) using aerial photography.

pho·to·me·chan·i·cal (ˌfəʊtəʊmɪ'kænɪkᵊl) *adj.* **1.** of or relating to any of various methods by which printing plates are made using photography. ~*n.* **2.** a final paste-up of artwork or typeset matter or both for photographing and processing into a printing plate. Often shortened to **mechanical.** —ˌ**pho·to·me·'chan·i·cal·ly** *adv.*

pho·tom·e·ter (fəʊ'tɒmɪtə) *n.* an instrument used in photometry, usually one that compares the illumination produced by a particular light source with that produced by a standard source. See also **spectrophotometer.**

pho·tom·e·try (fəʊ'tɒmɪtrɪ) *n.* **1.** the measurement of the intensity of light. **2.** the branch of physics concerned with such measurements. —**pho·to·met·ric** (ˌfəʊtə'mɛtrɪk) *adj.* —ˌ**pho·to·'met·ri·cal·ly** *adv.* —**pho·'tom·e·trist** *n.*

pho·to·mi·cro·graph (ˌfəʊtəʊ'maɪkrəˌgrɑːf, -ˌgræf) *n.* **1.** a photograph of a microscope image. Sometimes called: **microphotograph. 2.** a less common name for **microphotograph** (sense 1). —**pho·to·mi·crog·ra·pher** (ˌfəʊtəʊmaɪ'krɒgrəfə) *n.* —**pho·to·mi·cro·graph·ic** (ˌfəʊtəʊˌmaɪkrə'græfɪk) *adj.* —ˌ**pho·to·ˌmi·cro·'graph·i·cal·ly** *adv.* —ˌ**pho·to·mi·'crog·ra·phy** *n.*

pho·to·mon·tage (ˌfəʊtəʊmɒn'tɑːʒ) *n.* **1.** the technique of producing a composite picture by combining several photographs: used esp. in advertising. **2.** the composite picture so produced.

pho·to·mul·ti·pli·er (ˌfəʊtəʊ'mʌltɪˌplaɪə) *n.* a sensitive device for measuring electromagnetic radiation, consisting of a photocathode, from which electrons are released by incident photons, and an electron multiplier, which amplifies and produces a detectable pulse of current.

pho·to·mu·ral (ˌfəʊtəʊ'mjʊərəl) *n.* a decoration covering all or part of a wall consisting of a single enlarged photograph or a montage.

pho·ton ('fəʊtɒn) *n.* a quantum of electromagnetic radiation, regarded as a particle with zero rest mass and charge, unit spin, and energy equal to the product of the frequency of the radiation and the Planck constant.

pho·to·nas·ty ('fəʊtəʊˌnæstɪ) *n. Botany.* a nastic movement in response to a change in light intensity. —ˌ**pho·to·'nas·tic** *adj.*

pho·to·neu·tron (ˌfəʊtəʊ'njuːtrɒn) *n.* a neutron emitted from a nucleus as a result of photodisintegration.

pho·to·nu·cle·ar (ˌfəʊtəʊ'njuːklɪə) *adj. Physics.* of or concerned with a nuclear reaction caused by a photon.

pho·to-off·set *n. Printing.* an offset process in which the plates are produced photomechanically.

pho·to·per·i·od (ˌfəʊtəʊ'pɪərɪəd) *n.* the period of daylight in every 24 hours, esp. in relation to its effects on plants and animals. See also **photoperiodism.** —ˌ**pho·to·ˌper·i·'od·ic** *adj.* —ˌ**pho·to·ˌper·i·'od·i·cal·ly** *adv.*

pho·to·per·i·od·ism (ˌfəʊtəʊ'pɪərɪəˌdɪzəm) *n.* the response of plants and animals by behaviour, growth, etc., to photoperiods.

pho·toph·i·lous (fəʊ'tɒfələs) *adj.* (esp. of plants) growing best in strong light. —**pho·'toph·i·ly** *n.*

pho·to·pho·bi·a (ˌfəʊtəʊ'fəʊbɪə) *n.* **1.** *Pathol.* abnormal sensitivity of the eyes to light, as the result of inflammation, etc. **2.** *Psychiatry.* abnormal fear of or aversion to sunlight or well-lit places. —ˌ**pho·to·'pho·bic** *adj.*

pho·to·phore ('fəʊtəˌfɔː) *n. Zoology.* any light-producing organ in animals, esp. in certain fishes.

pho·to·pi·a (fəʊ'təʊpɪə) *n.* the normal adaptation of the eye to light; day vision. [C20: New Latin, from PHOTO- + -OPIA] —**pho·top·ic** (fəʊ'tɒpɪk, -'təʊ-) *adj.*

pho·to·pol·y·mer (ˌfəʊtəʊ'pɒlɪmə) *n.* a polymeric material that is sensitive to light: used in printing plates, microfilms, etc.

pho·to·re·cep·tor (ˌfəʊtəʊrɪ'sɛptə) *n. Zoology, physiol.* a light-sensitive cell or organ that conveys impulses through the sensory neuron connected to it.

pho·to·re·con·nais·sance (ˌfəʊtəʊrɪ'kɒnɪsəns) *n. Chiefly military.* reconnaissance from the air by camera.

pho·to re·lief *n.* a method of showing the configuration of the relief of an area by photographing a model of it that is illuminated by a lamp in the northwest corner.

pho·to·sen·si·tive (ˌfəʊtəʊ'sɛnsɪtɪv) *adj.* sensitive to electromagnetic radiation, esp. light: *a photosensitive photographic film.* —ˌ**pho·to·ˌsen·si·'tiv·i·ty** *n.*

pho·to·sen·si·tize *or* **pho·to·sen·si·tise** (ˌfəʊtəʊ'sɛnsɪˌtaɪz) *vb. (tr.)* to make (an organism or substance) photosensitive. —ˌ**pho·to·ˌsen·si·ti·'za·tion** *or* ˌ**pho·to·ˌsen·si·ti·'sa·tion** *n.*

pho·to·set ('fəʊtəʊˌsɛt) *vb.* **-sets, -set·ting, -set.** (*tr.*) another word for **filmset.** —'**pho·to·ˌset·ter** *n.*

pho·to·sphere ('fəʊtəʊˌsfɪə) *n.* the visible surface of the sun. —**pho·to·spher·ic** (ˌfəʊtəʊ'sfɛrɪk) *adj.*

Pho·to·stat ('fəʊtəʊˌstæt) *n.* **1.** *Trademark.* a machine or process used to make quick positive or negative photographic copies of written, printed, or graphic matter. **2.** any copy made by such a machine. ~*vb.* **3.** to make a Photostat copy. —ˌ**pho·to·'stat·ic** *adj.*

pho·to·syn·the·sis (ˌfəʊtəʊ'sɪnθɪsɪs) *n.* **1.** (in plants) the synthesis of organic compounds from carbon dioxide and water (with the release of oxygen) using light energy absorbed by chlorophyll. **2.** the corresponding process in certain bacteria. —**pho·to·syn·thet·ic** (ˌfəʊtəʊsɪn'θɛtɪk) *adj.* —ˌ**pho·to·syn·'thet·i·cal·ly** *adv.*

pho·to·syn·the·size *or* **pho·to·syn·the·sise** (ˌfəʊtəʊ'sɪnθɪˌsaɪz) *vb.* (of plants and some bacteria) to carry out photosynthesis.

pho·to+tax+is (ˌfəʊtəʊˈtæksɪs) *or* **pho·to+tax·y** *n.* the movement of an entire organism in response to light. —**pho·to+tac+tic** (ˌfəʊtəʊˈtæktɪk) *adj.*

pho·to+te·leg+ra+phy (ˌfəʊtəʊtɪˈlɛgrəfɪ) *n.* a system of facsimile telegraphy in which a transmitted image (a **phototelegram**) is reproduced, esp. using a halftone process. —**pho·to+tel·e+graph+ic** (ˌfəʊtəʊˌtɛlɪˈgræfɪk) *adj.* —**ˌpho·to+ˌtel·e·ˈgraph·i+cal+ly** *adv.*

pho·to+ther·a+py (ˌfəʊtəʊˈθɛrəpɪ) *or* **pho·to+ther·a+peu+tics** (ˌfəʊtəʊˌθɛrəˈpjuːtɪks) *n.* the use of light in the treatment of disease. —**ˌpho·to+ˌther·a+ˈpeu+tic** *adj.* —**ˌpho·to+ˌther·a+ˈpeu+ti+cal+ly** *adv.*

pho·to+ther+mic (ˌfəʊtəʊˈθɜːmɪk) *or* **pho·to+ther+mal** *adj.* of or concerned with light and heat, esp. the production of heat by light. —**ˌpho·to+ˈther+mi+cal+ly** *or* **ˌpho·to+ˈther+mal+ly** *adv.*

pho+tot·o+nus (fəʊˈtɒtənəs) *n.* the condition of plants that enables them to respond to the stimulus of light. —**pho·to+ton+ic** (ˌfəʊtəʊˈtɒnɪk) *adj.*

pho·to+to+pog+ra+phy (ˌfəʊtəʊtəˈpɒgrəfɪ) *n.* the preparation of topographic maps from photographs.

pho·to+tran+sis+tor (ˌfəʊtəʊtrænˈsɪstə) *n.* a junction transistor, whose base signal is generated by illumination of the base. The emitter current, and hence collector current, increases with the intensity of the light.

pho·to+trop+ism (ˌfəʊtəʊˈtrəʊpɪzəm) *n.* the growth response of plant parts to the stimulus of light. —**ˌpho·to+ˈtrop+ic** *adj.*

pho·to+tube (ˈfəʊtəʊˌtjuːb) *n.* a type of photocell in which radiation falling on a photocathode causes electrons to flow to an anode and thus produce an electric current.

pho·to+type (ˈfəʊtəʊˌtaɪp) *Printing.* ~*n.* **1. a.** a printing plate produced by photography. **b.** a print produced from such a plate. ~*vb.* **2.** (*tr.*) to reproduce (an illustration, etc.) using a phototype. —**pho·to+typ+ic** (ˌfəʊtəʊˈtɪpɪk) *adj.* —**ˌpho·to+ˈtyp·i+cal+ly** *adv.*

pho·to+type+set+ting (ˌfəʊtəʊˈtaɪpˌsɛtɪŋ) *n.* a U.S. name for **filmsetting.**

pho·to+ty+pog+ra+phy (ˌfəʊtəʊtaɪˈpɒgrəfɪ) *n.* any printing process involving the use of photography. —**pho·to+ty·po+graph·i·cal** (ˌfəʊtəʊˌtaɪpəˈgræfɪkᵊl) *adj.* —**ˌpho·to+ˌty·po+ˈgraph·i+cal+ly** *adv.*

pho·to+vol+ta+ic (ˌfəʊtəʊvɒlˈteɪɪk) *adj.* of, concerned with, or producing electric current or voltage caused by electromagnetic radiation.

pho·to+vol+ta+ic ef+fect *n.* the effect observed when electromagnetic radiation falls on a thin film of one solid deposited on the surface of a dissimilar solid producing a difference in potential between the two materials.

pho·to+zin+cog+ra+phy (ˌfəʊtəʊzɪŋˈkɒgrəfɪ) *n.* a photoengraving process using a printing plate made of zinc. —**pho·to+zin+co+graph** (ˌfəʊtəʊˈzɪŋkəˌgrɑːf, -ˌgræf) *n.*

phr. *abbrev. for* phrase.

phras+al (ˈfreɪzᵊl) *adj.* of, relating to, or composed of phrases. —**ˈphras+al+ly** *adv.*

phras+al verb *n.* (in English grammar) a phrase that consists of a verb plus an adverbial or prepositional particle, esp. one the meaning of which cannot be deduced by analysis of the meaning of the constituents: *"take in" meaning "deceive" is a phrasal verb.*

phrase (freɪz) *n.* **1.** a group of words forming together a syntactic constituent of a sentence but (in English) not containing a finite verb. Compare **clause** (sense 1), **noun phrase, verb phrase. 2.** an idiomatic or original expression. **3.** manner or style of speech or expression. **4.** *Music.* a small group of notes forming a coherent unit of melody. **5.** (in choreography) a short sequence of dance movements. ~*vb.* (*tr.*) **6.** *Music.* to divide (a melodic line, part, etc.) into musical phrases, esp. in performance. **7.** to express orally or in a phrase. [C16: from Latin *phrasis,* from Greek: speech, from *phrazein* to declare, tell]

phrase mark+er *n. Linguistics.* a representation, esp. one in the form of a tree diagram, of the constituent structure of a sentence.

phra+se·o+gram (ˈfreɪzɪəˌgræm) *n.* a symbol representing a phrase, as in shorthand.

phra+se·o+graph (ˈfreɪzɪəˌgrɑːf) *n.* a phrase for which there exists a phraseogram. —**phra+se·o+graph+ic** (ˌfreɪzɪəˈgræfɪk) *adj.* —**phra+se·og+ra+phy** (ˌfreɪzɪˈɒgrəfɪ) *n.*

phra+se·ol·o+gist (ˌfreɪzɪˈɒlədʒɪst) *n.* a person who is interested in or collects phrases or who affects a particular phraseology.

phra+se·ol·o·gy (ˌfreɪzɪˈɒlədʒɪ) *n., pl.* **·gies. 1.** the manner in which words or phrases are used. **2.** a set of phrases used by a particular group of people. —**phra+se·o+log·i·cal** (ˌfreɪzɪəˈlɒdʒɪkᵊl) *adj.* —**ˌphra+se·o+ˈlog·i+cal+ly** *adv.*

phrase-struc·ture rule *n. Generative grammar.* a rule of the form A → X where A is a syntactic category label, such as *noun phrase* or *sentence,* and X is a sequence of such labels and/or morphemes. Also called: **rewrite rule.** Compare **transformational rule.**

phras+ing (ˈfreɪzɪŋ) *n.* **1.** the way in which something is expressed, esp. in writing; wording. **2.** *Music.* the division of a melodic line, part, etc., into musical phrases.

phra+try (ˈfreɪtrɪ) *n., pl.* **+tries.** *Anthropol.* a group of people within a tribe who have a common ancestor. [C19: from Greek *phratria* clan, from *phratēr* fellow clansman; compare Latin *frāter* brother] —**ˈphra+tric** *adj.*

phre+at+ic (frɪˈætɪk) *adj. Geography.* of or relating to ground water occurring below the water table. Compare **vadose.** [C19: from Greek *phrear* a well]

phren. *or* **phrenol.** *abbrev. for* phrenology.

phre+net+ic (frɪˈnɛtɪk) *adj.* an obsolete spelling of **frenetic.** —**phre+ˈnet·i+cal+ly** *adv.* —**phre+ˈnet+ic+ness** *n.*

phren+ic (ˈfrɛnɪk) *adj.* **1. a.** of or relating to the diaphragm. **b.** (*as n.*): *the phrenic.* **2.** *Obsolete.* of or relating to the mind. [C18: from New Latin *phrenicus,* from Greek *phrēn* mind, diaphragm]

phre+ni+tis (frɪˈnaɪtɪs) *n. Rare.* **1.** another name for **encephalitis. 2.** a state of frenzy; delirium. [C17: via Late Latin from Greek: delirium, from *phrēn* mind, diaphragm + -ITIS] —**phre+nit+ic** (frɪˈnɪtɪk) *adj.*

phren·o- *or before a vowel* **phren-** *combining form.* **1.** mind or brain: *phrenology.* **2.** of or relating to the diaphragm: *phrenic.* [from Greek *phrēn* mind, diaphragm]

phre+nol+o·gy (frɪˈnɒlədʒɪ) *n.* (formerly) the branch of science concerned with localization of function in the human brain, esp. determination of the strength of the faculties by the shape and size of the skull overlying the parts of the brain thought to be responsible for them. —**phren·o+log·i·cal** (ˌfrɛnəˈlɒdʒɪkᵊl) *adj.* —**phre+ˈnol·o+gist** *n.*

phren+sy (ˈfrɛnzɪ) *n., pl.* **+sies.** an obsolete spelling of **frenzy.**

Phrix·us (ˈfrɪksəs) *n. Greek myth.* the son of Athamas and Nephele who escaped the wrath of his father's mistress, Ino, by flying to Colchis on a winged ram with a golden fleece. See also **Helle, Golden Fleece.**

Phryg·i·a (ˈfrɪdʒɪə) *n.* an ancient country of W central Asia Minor.

Phryg+i·an (ˈfrɪdʒɪən) *adj.* **1.** of or relating to ancient Phrygia, its inhabitants, or their extinct language. **2.** *Music.* of or relating to an authentic mode represented by the natural diatonic scale from E to E. See **Hypo-. 3.** *Music.* (of a cadence) denoting a progression that leads a piece of music out of the major key and ends on the dominant chord of the relative minor key. ~*n.* **4.** a native or inhabitant of ancient Phrygia. **5.** an ancient language of Phrygia, belonging to the Thraco-Phrygian branch of the Indo-European family: recorded in a few inscriptions.

Phryg+i·an cap *n.* a conical cap of soft material worn during ancient times that became a symbol of liberty during the French Revolution.

P.H.S. (in the U.S.) *abbrev. for* Public Health Service.

phtha+lein (ˈθeɪliːn, -lɪɪn, ˈθæl-, ˈfθæl-) *n.* any of a class of organic compounds obtained by the reaction of phthalic anhydride with a phenol and used in dyes. [C19: from *phthal-,* shortened form of NAPHTHALENE + -IN]

phthal+ic ac·id (ˈθælɪk, ˈfθæl-) *n.* a soluble colourless crystalline acid used in the synthesis of dyes and perfumes; 1,2-benzenedicarboxylic acid. Formula: $C_6H_4(COOH)_2$. [C19 *phthalic,* from *phthal-* (see PHTHALEIN) + -IC]

phthal+ic an+hy+dride *n.* a white crystalline substance used mainly in producing dyestuffs. Formula: $C_6H_4(CO)_2O$.

phthal·o+cy·a+nine (ˌθæləʊˈsaɪəˌniːn, ˌθeɪ-, ˌfθæl-) *n.* **1.** a cyclic blue-green organic pigment. Formula: $(C_6H_4C_2N)_4N_4$. **2.** any of a class of compounds derived by coordination of this compound with a metal atom. They are blue or green pigments used in printing inks, plastics, and enamels. [C20: from *phthal-* (see PHTHALEIN) + CYANINE]

phthi+ri·a+sis (θɪˈraɪəsɪs) *n. Pathol.* the state or condition of being infested with lice; pediculosis. [C16: via Latin from Greek, from *phtheir* louse]

phthi+sic (ˈθaɪsɪk, ˈfθaɪsɪk, ˈtaɪsɪk) *Obsolete.* ~*adj.* **1.** relating to or affected with phthisis. ~*n.* **2.** another name for **asthma.** [C14: from Old French *tisike,* from Latin *phthisicus,* from Greek *phthisikos;* see PHTHISIS] —**ˈphthis·i+cal** *adj.*

phthi+sis (ˈθaɪsɪs, ˈfθaɪ-, ˈtaɪ-) *n. Rare.* any disease that causes wasting of the body, esp. pulmonary tuberculosis. [C16: via Latin from Greek: a wasting away, from *phthinein* to waste away]

phut (fʌt) *Informal.* ~*n.* **1.** a representation of a dull heavy sound. ~*adv.* **2. to go phut.** to break down or collapse. [C19: of imitative origin]

phy·co- *combining form.* seaweed: *phycology.* [from Greek *phukos*]

phy+col·o·gy (faɪˈkɒlədʒɪ) *n.* the study of algae. —**phy+co+log·i+cal** (ˌfaɪkəˈlɒdʒɪkᵊl) *adj.* —**phy+ˈcol·o+gist** *n.*

phy+co+my+cete (ˌfaɪkəʊˈmaɪsiːt) *n.* any filamentous fungus of the class *Phycomycetes,* in which the spores are produced sexually or asexually: includes certain mildews and moulds. —**ˌphy+co+my+ˈce·tous** *adj.*

Phyfe (faɪf) *n.* **Dun·can.** ?1768–1854, U.S. cabinet maker, born in Scotland.

phy+la (ˈfaɪlə) *n.* the plural of **phylum.**

phy+lac+ter·y (fɪˈlæktərɪ) *n., pl.* **+ter·ies. 1.** *Judaism.* either of two small leather cases containing strips of parchment inscribed with religious texts, worn by Jewish men during morning prayer. **2.** a reminder or aid to remembering. **3.** *Archaic.* an amulet or charm. [C14: from Late Latin *phylactērium,* from Greek *phulaktērion* outpost, from *phulax* a guard]

phy+le (ˈfaɪlɪ) *n., pl.* **+lae** (-liː). a tribe or clan of an ancient Greek people such as the Ionians. [C19: from Greek *phulē* tribe, clan] —**ˈphy+lic** *adj.*

phy+let+ic (faɪˈlɛtɪk) *or* **phy+lo+ge·net+ic** (ˌfaɪləʊdʒɪˈnɛtɪk) *adj.* of or relating to the evolutionary development of organisms. [C19: from Greek *phuletikos* tribal] —**phy+ˈlet·i·cal+ly** *or* **ˌphy+lo+ge·ˈnet·i·cal+ly** *adv.*

-phyll *or* **-phyl** *n. combining form.* leaf: *chlorophyll.* [from Greek *phullon*]

phyl+lite (ˈfɪlaɪt) *n.* a compact lustrous metamorphic rock, rich in mica, derived from a clay rock. —**phyl+lit+ic** (fɪˈlɪtɪk) *adj.*

phyl·lo- *or before a vowel* **phyll-** *combining form.* leaf: *phyllopod.* [from Greek *phullon* leaf]

phyl·lo·clade ('fɪləʊˌkleɪd) *or* **phyl·lo·clad** ('fɪləʊˌklæd) *n.* another name for **cladode.** [C19: from New Latin *phyllocladium,* from PHYLLO- + Greek *klados* branch]

phyl·lode ('fɪləʊd) *n.* a flattened leafstalk that resembles and functions as a leaf. [C19: from New Latin *phyllodium,* from Greek *phullōdēs* leaflike] —**phyl·'lo·di·al** *adj.*

phyl·loid ('fɪlɔɪd) *adj.* resembling a leaf.

phyl·lome ('fɪləʊm) *n.* a leaf or a leaflike organ. —**phyl·lom·ic** (fɪ'lɒmɪk, -'ləʊ-) *adj.*

phyl·lo·qui·none (ˌfɪləʊkwɪ'nəʊn) *n.* a viscous fat-soluble liquid occurring in plants: essential for the production of prothrombin, required in blood clotting. Formula: $C_{31}H_{46}O_2$. Also called: **vitamin K$_1$**.

phyl·lo·tax·is (ˌfɪlə'tæksɪs) *or* **phyl·lo·tax·y** *n., pl.* **·tax·es** (-'tæksi:z) *or* **·tax·ies. 1.** the arrangement of the leaves on a stem. **2.** the study of this arrangement in different plants. —ˌ**phyl·lo·'tac·tic** *adj.*

-phyl·lous *adj. combining form.* having leaves of a specified number or type: *monophyllous.* [from Greek *-phullos* of a leaf]

phyl·lox·e·ra (ˌfɪlɒk'sɪərə, fɪ'lɒksərə) *n., pl.* **·rae** (-ri:) *or* **·ras.** any homopterous insect of the genus *Phylloxera,* such as *P. vitifolia* (or *Viteus vitifolii*) (**vine phylloxera**), typically feeding on plant juices: family *Phylloxeridae.* [C19: New Latin, from PHYLLO- + *xēros* dry]

phy·log·e·ny (faɪ'lɒdʒɪnɪ) *or* **phy·lo·gen·e·sis** (ˌfaɪləʊ'dʒɛnɪsɪs) *n., pl.* **·nies** *or* **·gen·e·ses** (-'dʒɛnɪˌsi:z). *Biology.* the sequence of events involved in the evolution of a species, genus, etc. Compare **ontogeny.** [C19: from PHYLO- + -GENY] —**phy·lo·gen·ic** (ˌfaɪləʊ'dʒɛnɪk) *or* **phy·lo·ge·net·ic** (ˌfaɪləʊdʒɪ'nɛtɪk) *adj.*

phy·lum ('faɪləm) *n., pl.* **·la** (-lə). **1.** a major taxonomic division of the animals and plants that contain one or more classes. An example is the phylum *Arthropoda* (insects, crustaceans, arachnids, etc. and myriapods). **2.** any analogous group, such as a group of related language families or linguistic stocks. [C19: New Latin, from Greek *phulon* race]

phys. *abbrev. for:* **1.** physical. **2.** physician. **3.** physics. **4.** physiological. **5.** physiology.

phys·i·at·rics (ˌfɪzɪ'ætrɪks) *n.* (*functioning as sing.*) *Med., U.S.* another name for **physiotherapy.** [C19: from PHYSIO- + -IATRICS] —ˌ**phys·i·'at·ric** *or* ˌ**phys·i·'at·ri·cal** *adj.*

phys·ic ('fɪzɪk) *n.* **1.** *Rare.* a medicine or drug, esp. a cathartic or purge. **2.** *Archaic.* the art or skill of healing. **3.** an archaic term for **physics.** ~*vb.* **·ics, ·ick·ing, ·icked.** (*tr.*) *Archaic.* **4.** to treat (a patient) with medicine. [C13: from Old French *fisique,* via Latin, from Greek *phusikē,* from *phusis* nature] —**'phys·ick·y** *adj.*

phys·i·cal ('fɪzɪkᵊl) *adj.* **1.** of or relating to the body, as distinguished from the mind or spirit. **2.** of, relating to, or resembling material things or nature: *the physical universe.* **3.** of or concerned with matter and energy. **4.** of or relating to physics. **5.** perceptible to the senses; apparent: *a physical manifestation.* ~*n.* **6.** short for **physical examination.** —**'phys·i·cal·ly** *adv.* —**'phys·i·cal·ness** *n.*

phys·i·cal an·thro·pol·o·gy *n.* the branch of anthropology dealing with the genetic aspect of human development and its physical variations.

phys·i·cal chem·is·try *n.* the branch of chemistry concerned with the way in which the physical properties of substances depend on and influence their chemical structure, properties, and reactions.

phys·i·cal ed·u·ca·tion *n.* training and practice in sports, gymnastics, etc., as in schools and colleges. Abbrev.: **PE**

phys·i·cal ex·am·i·na·tion *n. Med.* the process of examining the body by means of sight, touch, percussion, or auscultation to diagnose disease or verify fitness.

phys·i·cal ge·og·ra·phy *n.* the branch of geography that deals with the natural features of the earth's surface.

phys·i·cal·ism ('fɪzɪkᵊˌlɪzəm) *n. Philosophy.* the doctrine that all phenomena can be described in terms of space and time and that all meaningful statements are either analytic, as in logic and mathematics, or can be reduced to empirically verifiable assertions. —**'phys·i·cal·ist** *n., adj.* —ˌ**phys·i·cal·'is·tic** *adj.*

phys·i·cal jerks *pl. n. Slang.* See **jerk**[1] (sense 6).

phys·i·cal med·i·cine *n.* the branch of medicine devoted to the management of physical disabilities, as resulting from rheumatic disease, asthma, poliomyelitis, etc. See also **rehabilitation** (sense 2).

phys·i·cal sci·ence *n.* any of the sciences concerned with nonliving matter, energy, and the physical properties of the universe, such as physics, chemistry, astronomy, and geology. Compare **life science.**

phys·i·cal ther·a·py *n.* another term for **physiotherapy.**

phy·si·cian (fɪ'zɪʃən) *n.* **1.** a person legally qualified to practise medicine, esp. one specializing in areas of treatment other than surgery; doctor of medicine. **2.** *Archaic.* any person who treats diseases; healer. [C13: from Old French *fisicien,* from *fisique* PHYSIC]

phys·i·cist ('fɪzɪsɪst) *n.* a person versed in or studying physics.

phys·i·co·chem·i·cal (ˌfɪzɪkəʊ'kɛmɪkᵊl) *adj.* of, concerned with, or relating to physical chemistry or both physics and chemistry. —ˌ**phys·i·co·'chem·i·cal·ly** *adv.*

phys·ics ('fɪzɪks) *n.* (*functioning as sing.*) **1.** the branch of science concerned with the properties of matter and energy and the relationships between them. It is based on mathematics and traditionally includes mechanics, optics, electricity and magnetism, acoustics, and heat. Modern physics, based on quantum theory, includes atomic, nuclear, particle, and solid-state studies. It can also embrace applied fields such as geophysics and meteorology. **2.** physical properties of behaviour: *the physics of the electron.* **3.** *Archaic.* natural science or natural philosophy. [C16: from Latin *physica,* translation of Greek *ta phusika* natural things, from *phusis* nature]

phys·i·o- *or before a vowel* **phys-** *combining form.* **1.** of or relating to nature or natural functions: *physiology.* **2.** physical: *physiotherapy.* [from Greek *phusio,* from *phusis* nature, from *phuein* to make grow]

phys·i·o·crat ('fɪzɪəʊˌkræt) *n.* a follower of Quesnay's doctrines of government: believing that the inherent natural order governing society was based on land and its natural products as the only true form of wealth. [C18: from French *physiocrate;* see PHYSIO-, -CRAT] —**phys·i·oc·ra·cy** (ˌfɪzɪ'ɒkrəsɪ) *n.* —ˌ**phys·i·o·'crat·ic** *adj.*

phys·i·og·no·my (ˌfɪzɪ'ɒnəmɪ) *n.* **1.** a person's features or characteristic expression considered as an indication of personality. **2.** the art or practice of judging character from facial features. **3.** the outward appearance of something, esp. the physical characteristics of a geographical region. [C14: from Old French *phisonomie,* via Medieval Latin, from Late Greek *phusiognōmia,* erroneous for Greek *phusiognōmonia,* from *phusis* nature + *gnōmōn* judge] —**phys·i·og·nom·ic** (ˌfɪzɪə'nɒmɪk) *or* ˌ**phys·i·og·'nom·i·cal** *adj.* —ˌ**phys·i·og·'nom·i·cal·ly** *adv.* —ˌ**phys·i·'og·no·mist** *n.*

phys·i·og·ra·phy (ˌfɪzɪ'ɒgrəfɪ) *n.* another name for **geomorphology** or **physical geography.** —ˌ**phys·i·'og·ra·pher** *n.* —**phys·i·o·graph·ic** (ˌfɪzɪə'græfɪk) *or* ˌ**phys·i·o·'graph·i·cal** *adj.* —ˌ**phys·i·o·'graph·i·cal·ly** *adv.*

physiol. *abbrev. for:* **1.** physiological. **2.** physiology.

phys·i·o·log·i·cal (ˌfɪzɪə'lɒdʒɪkᵊl) *adj.* **1.** of or relating to physiology. **2.** of or relating to normal healthful functioning; not pathological. —ˌ**phys·i·o·'log·i·cal·ly** *adv.*

phys·i·o·log·i·cal psy·chol·o·gy *n.* the branch of psychology concerned with the study and correlation of physiological and psychological events.

phys·i·ol·o·gy (ˌfɪzɪ'ɒlədʒɪ) *n.* **1.** the branch of science concerned with the functioning of organisms. **2.** the processes and functions of all or part of an organism. [C16: from Latin *physiologia,* from Greek] —ˌ**phys·i·'ol·o·gist** *n.*

phys·i·o·ther·a·py (ˌfɪzɪəʊ'θɛrəpɪ) *n.* the therapeutic use of physical agents or means, such as massage, exercises, etc. Also called: **physical therapy, physiatrics** (U.S.). —ˌ**phys·i·o·'ther·a·pist** *n.*

phy·sique (fɪ'zi:k) *n.* the general appearance of the body with regard to size, shape, muscular development, etc. [C19: via French, from *physique* (adj.) natural, from Latin *physicus* physical]

phy·so·clis·tous (ˌfaɪsəʊ'klɪstəs) *adj.* (of fishes) having an air bladder that is not connected to the alimentary canal. Compare **physostomous.** [C19: PHYSO- + *-clistous,* from Greek *kleistos* closed]

phy·so·stig·mine (ˌfaɪsəʊ'stɪgmi:n) *or* **phy·so·stig·min** (ˌfaɪsəʊ'stɪgmɪn) *n.* an alkaloid found in the Calabar bean used esp. in eye drops to reduce pressure inside the eyeball. Formula: $C_{15}H_{21}N_3O_2$. Also called: **eserine.** [C19: from New Latin *Physostigma* genus name, from PHYSO- + Greek *stigma* mark]

phy·sos·to·mous (faɪ'sɒstəməs) *adj.* (of fishes) having a duct connecting the air bladder to part of the alimentary canal. Compare **physoclistous.** [C19: from PHYSO- + *-stomous,* from Greek *stoma* mouth]

-phyte *n. combining form.* indicating a plant of a specified type or habitat: *lithophyte; thallophyte.* [from Greek *phuton* plant] —**-phyt·ic** *adj. combining form.*

phy·to- *or before a vowel* **phyt-** *combining form.* indicating a plant or vegetation: *phytogenesis.* [from Greek *phuton* plant, from *phuein* to make grow]

phy·to·gen·e·sis (ˌfaɪtəʊ'dʒɛnɪsɪs) *or* **phy·tog·e·ny** (faɪ'tɒdʒənɪ) *n.* the branch of botany concerned with the origin and evolution of plants. —**phy·to·ge·net·ic** (ˌfaɪtəʊdʒɪ'nɛtɪk) *adj.* —ˌ**phy·to·ge·'net·i·cal·ly** *adv.*

phy·to·gen·ic (ˌfaɪtəʊ'dʒɛnɪk) *adj.* derived from plants: *coal is a phytogenic substance.*

phy·to·ge·og·ra·phy (ˌfaɪtəʊdʒɪ'ɒgrəfɪ) *n.* the branch of botany that is concerned with the geographical distribution of plants. —ˌ**phy·to·ge·'og·ra·pher** *n.*

phy·tog·ra·phy (faɪ'tɒgrəfɪ) *n.* the branch of botany that is concerned with the detailed description of plants.

phy·to·hor·mone (ˌfaɪtəʊ'hɔ:məʊn) *n.* a hormone-like substance produced by a plant.

phy·tol·o·gy (faɪ'tɒlədʒɪ) *n.* a rare name for **botany.** —**phy·to·log·i·cal** (ˌfaɪtə'lɒdʒɪkᵊl) *adj.* —ˌ**phy·to·'log·i·cal·ly** *adv.* —**phy·'tol·o·gist** *n.*

phy·ton ('faɪtɒn) *n.* a unit of plant structure, usually considered as the smallest part of the plant that is capable of growth when detached from the parent plant. [C20: from Greek. See -PHYTE]

phy·to·pa·thol·o·gy (ˌfaɪtəʊpə'θɒlədʒɪ) *n.* the branch of botany concerned with diseases of plants. —**phy·to·path·o·log·i·cal** (ˌfaɪtəʊˌpæθə'lɒdʒɪkᵊl) *adj.* —ˌ**phy·to·pa·'thol·o·gist** *n.*

phy·toph·a·gous (faɪ'tɒfəgəs) *adj.* (esp. of insects) feeding on plants. —**phy·toph·a·gy** (faɪ'tɒfədʒɪ) *n.*

phy·to·plank·ton (ˌfaɪtə'plæŋktən) *n.* the plant constituent of plankton, mainly unicellular algae. Compare **zooplankton.** —**phy·to·plank·ton·ic** (ˌfaɪtəplæŋk'tɒnɪk) *adj.*

phy·to·so·ci·ol·o·gy (ˌfaɪtəʊˌsəʊsɪ'ɒlədʒɪ, -ˌsəʊʃɪ-) *n.* the branch of ecology that is concerned with the origin, development, etc., of plant communities. —**phy·to·so·ci·o·log·i·cal** (ˌfaɪtəʊˌsəʊsɪəˈlɒdʒɪkəl, -ˌsəʊʃɪə-) —ˌ**phy·to·so·ci·o·ˈlog·i·cal·ly** *adv.* —ˌ**phy·to·ˌso·ci·ˈol·o·gist** *n.*

phy·to·tox·in (ˌfaɪtəˈtɒksɪn) *n.* a toxin, such as strychnine, that is produced by a plant. Compare **zootoxin.**

phy·to·tron (ˈfaɪtəʊˌtrɒn) *n.* a building in which plants can be grown on a large scale, under controlled conditions.

pi[1] (paɪ) *n., pl.* **pis. 1.** the 16th letter in the Greek alphabet (Π, π), a consonant, transliterated as *p.* **2.** *Maths.* a transcendental number, fundamental to mathematics, that is the ratio of the circumference of a circle to its diameter. Approximate value: 3.141 592... ; symbol: π [C18 (mathematical use): representing the first letter of Greek *periphereia* PERIPHERY]

pi[2] *or* **pie** (paɪ) *n., pl.* **pies. 1.** a jumbled pile of printer's type. **2.** a jumbled mixture. ~*vb.* **pies, pi·ing, pied** *or* **pies, pie·ing, pied.** (*tr.*) **3.** to spill and mix (set type) indiscriminately. **4.** to mix up. [C17: of uncertain origin]

pi[3] (paɪ) *Brit. slang.* See **pious** (senses 2, 3).

PI *international car registration for* Philippine Islands.

P.I. *abbrev. for* Philippine Islands.

Pia·cen·za (*Italian* pjaˈtʃɛntsa) *n.* a town in N Italy, in Emilia-Romagna on the River Po. Pop.: 108 775 (1975 est.). Latin name: **Placentia.**

pi·ac·u·lar (paɪˈækjʊlə) *adj. Ecclesiast.* **1.** making expiation for a sacrilege. **2.** requiring expiation. [C17: from Latin *piāculum* propitiatory sacrifice, from *piāre* to appease]

Piaf (*French* pjaf) *n.* **E·dith** (eˈdit), known as *the Little Sparrow.* original name *Edith Giovanna Gassion.* 1915–63, French singer.

pi·affe (pɪˈæf) *n. Dressage.* a passage done on the spot. [C18: from French, from *piaffer* to strut]

Pia·get (*French* pjaˈʒɛ) *n.* **Jean** (ʒɑ̃). 1896-1980, Swiss psychologist, noted for his work on the development of the cognitive functions in children.

pi·a ma·ter (ˈpaɪə ˈmeɪtə) *n.* the innermost of the three membranes (see **meninges**) that cover the brain and spinal cord. [C16: from Medieval Latin, literally: pious mother, intended to translate Arabic *umm raqīqah* tender mother]

pi·a·nism (ˈpiːəˌnɪzəm) *n.* technique, skill, or artistry in playing the piano. —ˌ**pi·a·ˈnis·tic** *adj.*

pi·a·nis·si·mo (pɪəˈnɪsɪˌməʊ) *adj., adv. Music.* to be performed very quietly. Symbol: *pp* [C18: from Italian, superlative of *piano* soft]

pi·a·nist (ˈpɪənɪst) *n.* a person who plays the piano.

pi·an·o[1] (pɪˈænəʊ) *n., pl.* **·an·os.** a musical stringed instrument resembling a harp set in a vertical or horizontal frame, played by depressing keys that cause hammers to strike the strings and produce audible vibrations. See also: **grand piano, upright piano.** [C19: short for PIANOFORTE]

pia·no[2] (ˈpjɑːnəʊ) *adj., adv. Music.* to be performed softly. Symbol: *p* [C17: from Italian, from Latin *plānus* flat; see PLAIN]

pi·an·o ac·cor·di·on *n.* an accordion in which the right hand plays a piano-like keyboard. See **accordion.** —**pi·an·o ac·cor·di·on·ist** *n.*

pi·an·o·for·te (pɪˈænəʊˈfɔːtɪ) *n.* the full name for **piano**[1]. [C18: from Italian, originally (*gravecembalo col*) *piano e forte* (harpsichord with) soft and loud; see PIANO[2], FORTE[2]]

Pi·a·no·la (pɪəˈnəʊlə) *n. Trademark.* a type of mechanical piano in which the keys are depressed by air pressure from bellows, this air flow being regulated by perforations in a paper roll. Also called: **player piano.**

pi·an·o play·er *n.* **1.** another word for **pianist. 2.** any of various devices for playing a piano automatically.

pi·an·o roll *n.* a perforated roll of paper actuating the playing mechanism of a Pianola. Also called: **music roll.**

pi·an·o stool *n.* a stool on which a pianist sits when playing a piano, esp. one whose height is adjustable.

pi·an·o tri·o *n.* **1.** an instrumental ensemble consisting of a piano, a violin, and a cello. **2.** a piece of music written for such an ensemble, usually having the form and commonest features of a sonata.

pi·as·sa·va (ˌpiːəˈsɑːvə) *or* **pi·as·sa·ba** (ˌpiːəˈsɑːbə) *n.* **1.** either of two South American palm trees, *Attalea funifera* or *Leopoldinia piassaba.* **2.** the coarse fibre obtained from either of these trees, used to make brushes and rope. [C19: via Portuguese from Tupi *piaçaba*]

pi·as·tre *or* **pi·as·ter** (pɪˈæstə) *n.* **1.** the standard monetary unit of South Vietnam, divided into 100 cents. **2. a.** a fractional monetary unit of Egypt, Lebanon, Sudan, and Syria worth one hundredth of a pound. **b.** Also called: **kurus.** a Turkish monetary unit worth one hundredth of a lira. **c.** a Libyan monetary unit worth one hundredth of a dinar. **3.** a rare word for **piece of eight.** [C17: from French *piastre,* from Italian *piastra d'argento* silver plate; related to Italian *piastro* PLASTER]

Piau·í (*Portuguese* pjauˈi) *n.* a state of NE Brazil, on the Atlantic: rises to a semiarid plateau, with the more humid Paranaíba valley in the west. Capital: Teresina. Pop.: 1 680 573 (1970). Area: 250 934 sq. km (96 886 sq. miles).

Pia·ve (*Italian* ˈpjaːve) *n.* a river in NE Italy, rising near the border with Austria and flowing south and southeast to the Adriatic: the main line of Italian defence during World War I. Length: 220 km (137 miles).

pi·az·za (pɪˈætsə, -ˈædzə; *Italian* ˈpjattsa) *n.* **1.** a large open square in an Italian town. **2.** *Chiefly Brit.* a covered passageway or gallery. [C16: from Italian: marketplace, from Latin *platēa* courtyard, from Greek *plateia;* see PLACE]

pi·broch (ˈpiːbrɒk; *Gaelic* ˈpiːbrɒx) *n.* a piece of music for Scottish bagpipes, consisting of a theme and variations. [C18: from Gaelic *piobaireachd,* from *piobair* piper]

pi·ca[1] (ˈpaɪkə) *n.* **1.** Also called: **em, pica em.** a printer's unit of measurement, equal to 12 points or 0.166 ins. **2.** (formerly) a size of printer's type equal to 12 point. [C15: from Anglo-Latin *pīca* list of ecclesiastical regulations, apparently from Latin *pīca* magpie, with reference to its habit of making collections of miscellaneous items; the connection between the original sense (ecclesiastical list) and the typography meanings is obscure]

pi·ca[2] (ˈpaɪkə) *n. Pathol.* an abnormal craving to ingest substances such as clay, dirt, or hair, sometimes occurring during pregnancy, in persons with chlorosis, etc. [C16: from medical Latin, from Latin: magpie, being an allusion to its omnivorous feeding habits]

pic·a·dor (ˈpɪkəˌdɔː) *n. Bullfighting.* a horseman who pricks the bull with a lance in the early stages of a fight to goad and weaken it. [C18: from Spanish, literally: pricker, from *picar* to prick; see PIQUE]

Pi·card (*French* piˈkaːr) *n.* **Jean** (ʒɑ̃). 1620–82, French astronomer. He was the first to make a precise measurement of a longitude line, enabling him to estimate the earth's radius.

Pic·ar·dy (ˈpɪkədɪ) *n.* a region of N France: mostly low-lying; scene of heavy fighting in World War I. French name: **Pi·car·die** (pikarˈdi).

Pic·ar·dy third *n. Music.* a major chord used in the final chord of a piece of music in the minor mode. Also called: **tierce de Picardie.** [translation of French *tierce de Picardie,* from its use in the church music of Picardy]

pic·a·resque (ˌpɪkəˈrɛsk) *adj.* **1.** of or relating to a type of fiction in which the hero, a rogue, goes through a series of episodic adventures. It originated in Spain in the 16th century. **2.** of or involving rogues or picaroons. [C19: via French from Spanish *picaresco,* from *pícaro* a rogue]

pic·a·roon *or* **pick·a·roon** (ˌpɪkəˈruːn) *n. Archaic.* an adventurer or rogue. [C17: from Spanish *picarón,* from *pícaro*]

Pi·cas·so (pɪˈkæsəʊ) *n.* **Pa·blo** (ˈpæbləʊ). 1881–1973, Spanish painter and sculptor, resident in France: a highly influential figure in 20th-century art and a founder, with Braque, of cubism. A prolific artist, his works include *The Dwarf Dancer* (1901), belonging to his blue period; the first cubist painting *Les Demoiselles d'Avignon* (1907); *Three Dancers* (1925), which appeared in the first surrealist exhibition; and *Guernica* (1937), inspired by an event in the Spanish Civil War.

pic·a·yune (ˌpɪkəˈjuːn) *adj. also* **pic·a·yun·ish.** *U.S.* **1.** *Informal.* of small value or importance. **2.** *Informal.* mean; petty. ~*n.* **3.** the half real, an old Spanish-American coin. **4.** *U.S.* any coin of little value, esp. a five-cent piece. [C19: from French *picaillon* coin from Piedmont, from Provençal *picaioun,* of unknown origin] —ˌ**pic·a·ˈyun·ish·ly** *adv.* —ˌ**pic·a·ˈyun·ish·ness** *n.*

Pic·ca·dil·ly (ˌpɪkəˈdɪlɪ) *n.* one of the main streets of London, running from Piccadilly Circus to Hyde Park Corner.

pic·ca·lil·li (ˈpɪkəˌlɪlɪ) *n.* a pickle of mixed vegetables, esp. onions, cauliflower, and cucumber, in a mustard sauce. [C18: *piccalillo,* perhaps a coinage based on PICKLE]

pic·ca·nin (ˈpɪkəˌnɪn, ˌpɪkəˈnɪn) *n. S. African informal.* a Black African child. [variant of PICCANINNY]

pic·ca·nin·ny *or* **pick·a·nin·ny** (ˌpɪkəˈnɪnɪ) *n., pl.* **a.** a small Negro or Aboriginal child. **b.** (*as modifier*): tiny: *a piccaninny fire won't last long.* [C17: perhaps from Portuguese *pequenino* tiny one, from *pequeno* small]

Pic·card (*French* piˈkaːr) *n.* **1. Au·guste** (oˈgyst). 1884–1962, Swiss physicist, whose study of cosmic rays led to his pioneer balloon ascents in the stratosphere (1931–32). **2.** his twin brother, **Jean Fé·lix** (ʒɑ̃ feˈliks). 1884–1963, U.S. chemist and aeronautical engineer, born in Switzerland, noted for his balloon ascent into the stratosphere (1934).

pic·co·lo (ˈpɪkəˌləʊ) *n., pl.* **·los.** a woodwind instrument, the smallest member of the flute family, lying an octave above that of the flute. See **flute** (sense 1). [C19: from Italian: small; compare English PETTY, French *petit*]

pice (paɪs) *n., pl.* **pice. 1.** a former Indian coin worth one sixty-fourth of a rupee. **2.** a fractional monetary unit of Nepal worth one hundredth of a rupee. [C17: from Mahratti *paisā*]

pic·e·ous (ˈpɪsɪəs, ˈpaɪsɪəs) *adj.* of, relating to, or resembling pitch. [C17: from Latin *piceus,* from *pix* PITCH[2]]

pich·i·ci·e·go (ˌpɪtʃɪsɪˈeɪgəʊ) *n., pl.* **·gos. 1.** a very small Argentinian armadillo, *Chlamyphorous truncatus,* with white silky hair and pale pink plates on the head and back. **2. greater pichiciego.** a similar but larger armadillo, *Burmeisteria retusa.* [C19: from Spanish, probably from Guarani *pichey* small armadillo + Spanish *ciego* blind]

pick[1] (pɪk) *vb.* **1.** to choose (something) deliberately or carefully, from or as if from a group or number; select. **2.** to pluck or gather (fruit, berries, or crops) from (a tree, bush, field, etc.): *to pick hops; to pick a whole bush.* **3.** (*tr.*) to clean or prepare (fruit, poultry, etc.) by removing the indigestible parts. **4.** (*tr.*) to remove loose particles from (the teeth, the nose, etc.). **5.** (esp. of birds) to nibble or gather (corn, etc.). **6.** (*tr.*) to pierce, dig, or break up (a hard surface) with a pick. **7.** (*tr.*) to form (a hole, etc.) in this way. **8.** (when *intr.,* foll. by *at*) to nibble (at) fussily or without appetite. **9.** to separate (strands, fibres, etc.), as in weaving. **10.** (*tr.*) to deliberately provoke (an argument, fight, etc.). **11.** (*tr.*) to steal (money or valuables) from (a person's pocket). **12.** (*tr.*) to open (a lock) with an instrument other than a key. **13.** to pluck the strings of (a guitar, banjo, etc.). **14.** (*tr.*) to make (one's way) carefully on foot: *they picked their way through the rubble.* **15. pick and choose.** to select fastidiously, fussily, etc. **16. pick someone's brains.** *Informal.* to obtain information or ideas from someone. ~*n.* **17.** freedom or right of selection (esp. in the phrase **take**

one's pick). **18.** a person, thing, etc., that is chosen first or preferred: *the pick of the bunch.* **19.** the act of picking. **20.** the amount of a crop picked at one period or from one area. **21.** *Printing.* a speck of dirt or metal or a blob of ink on the surface of set type or a printing plate. See also **pick at, pick off, pick on, pick out, pick-up.** [C15: from earlier *piken* to pick, influenced by French *piquer* to pierce; compare Middle Low German *picken,* Dutch *pikken*] —**'pick·a·ble** *adj.*

pick[2] (pɪk) *n.* **1.** a tool with a handle carrying a long steel head curved and tapering to a point at one or both ends, used for loosening soil, breaking rocks, etc. **2.** any of various tools used for picking, such as an ice pick or toothpick. [C14: perhaps a variant of PIKE[2]]

pick[3] (pɪk) (in weaving) ~*vb.* **1.** (*tr.*) to cast (a shuttle). ~*n.* **2.** one casting of a shuttle. **3.** a weft or filling thread. [C14: variant of PITCH[1]]

pick·a·back ('pɪkəˌbæk) *n., adv.* another word for **piggyback.**

pick·a·nin·ny ('pɪkəˌnɪnɪ) *n., pl.* **·nies.** a variant spelling (esp. U.S.) of **piccaninny.**

pick·a·roon (ˌpɪkə'ru:n) *n.* a variant spelling of **picaroon.**

pick at *vb.* (*intr., prep.*) to make criticisms of in a niggling or petty manner.

pick·axe *or U.S.* **pick·ax** ('pɪkˌæks) *n.* **1.** a large pick or mattock. ~*vb.* **2.** to use a pickaxe on (earth, rocks, etc.). [C15: from earlier *pikois* (but influenced also by AXE) from Old French *picois,* from *pic* PICK[2]; compare also PIQUE]

pick·er ('pɪkə) *n.* **1.** a person or thing that picks, esp. that gathers fruit, crops, etc. **2.** (in weaving) a person or the part of the loom that casts the shuttle.

pick·er·el ('pɪkərəl, 'pɪkrəl) *n., pl.* **·el** *or* **·els.** any of several North American freshwater game fishes, such as *Esox americanus* and *E. niger:* family *Esocidae* (pikes, etc.). [C14: a small pike; see PIKE[1], -REL]

pick·er·el·weed ('pɪkərəlˌwi:d, 'pɪkrəl-) *n.* any of several North American freshwater plants of the genus *Pontederia,* esp. *P. cordata,* having arrow-shaped leaves and purple flowers: family *Pontederiaceae.*

Pick·er·ing ('pɪkərɪŋ) *n.* **1. Ed·ward Charles.** 1846–1919, U.S. astronomer, who invented the meridian photometer. **2.** his brother, **Wil·liam Hen·ry.** 1858–1938, U.S. astronomer, who discovered Phoebe, the ninth satellite of Saturn, and predicted (1919) the existence and position of Pluto.

pick·et ('pɪkɪt) *n.* **1.** a pointed stake, post, or peg that is driven into the ground to support a fence, provide a marker for surveying, etc. **2.** an individual or group, who stand outside an establishment to make a protest, to dissuade or prevent employees or clients from entering, etc. **3.** a small detachment of troops or warships positioned towards the enemy to give early warning of attack. ~*vb.* **4.** to post or serve as pickets at (a factory, embassy, etc.): *let's go and picket the shop.* **5.** to guard (a main body or place) by using or acting as a picket. **6.** (*tr.*) to fasten (a horse or other animal) to a picket. **7.** (*tr.*) to fence (an area, boundary, etc.) with pickets. [C18: from French *piquet,* from Old French *piquer* to prick; see PIKE[2]] —**'pick·et·er** *n.*

pick·et fence *n.* a fence consisting of pickets supported at close regular intervals by being driven into the ground, by interlacing with strong wire, or by nailing to horizontal timbers fixed to posts in the ground.

pick·et line *n.* a line of people acting as pickets.

Pick·ford ('pɪkfəd) *n.* **Mar·y.** original name *Gladys Smith.* 1893–1979, U.S. actress in silent films, born in Canada.

pick·in ('pɪkɪn) *n. W. African.* a small child. [from Portuguese *pequeno;* see PICCANINNY]

pick·ings ('pɪkɪŋz) *pl. n.* (*sometimes sing.*) money, profits, etc., acquired easily or by more or less dishonest means; spoils.

pick·le ('pɪk[ə]l) *n.* **1.** (*often pl.*) vegetables, such as cauliflowers, onions, etc., preserved in vinegar, brine, etc.. **2.** any food preserved in this way. **3.** a liquid or marinade, such as spiced vinegar, for preserving vegetables, meat, fish, etc. **4.** *U.S.* a cucumber that has been preserved and flavoured in a pickling solution, as brine or vinegar. **5.** *Informal.* an awkward or difficult situation: *to be in a pickle.* **6.** *Brit. informal.* a mischievous child. ~*vb.* (*tr.*) **7.** to preserve in a pickling liquid. **8.** to immerse (a metallic object) in a liquid, such as an acid, to remove surface scale. [C14: perhaps from Middle Dutch *pekel;* related to German *Pökel* brine] —**'pick·ler** *n.*

pick·led ('pɪk[ə]ld) *adj.* **1.** preserved in a pickling liquid. **2.** *Informal.* intoxicated; drunk.

pick·lock ('pɪkˌlɒk) *n.* **1.** a person who picks locks, esp. one who gains unlawful access to premises by this means. **2.** an instrument for picking locks.

pick-me-up *n. Informal.* a tonic or restorative, esp. a special drink taken as a stimulant.

pick off *vb.* (*tr., adv.*) to aim at and shoot one by one.

pick on *vb.* (*intr., prep.*) to select for something unpleasant, esp. in order to bully, blame, or cause to perform a distasteful task.

pick out *vb.* (*tr., adv.*) **1.** to select for use or special consideration, illustration, etc., as from a group. **2.** to distinguish (an object from its surroundings), as in painting: *she picked out the woodwork in white.* **3.** to perceive or recognize (a person or thing previously obscured): *we picked out his face among the crowd.* **4.** to distinguish (sense or meaning) from or as if from a mass of detail or complication. **5.** to play (a tune) tentatively, by or as if by ear.

pick·pock·et ('pɪkˌpɒkɪt) *n.* a person who steals from the pockets or handbags of others in public places.

pick-up *n.* **1.** Also called: **pick-up arm, tone arm.** the light balanced arm of a gramophone that carries the wires from the cartridge to the preamplifier. **2.** an electromagnetic transducer that converts the vibrations of the steel strings of an electric guitar or other amplified instrument into electric signals. **3.** another name for **cartridge** (sense 3). **4.** a small truck with an open body and low sides used for light deliveries. **5.** *Informal.* an ability to accelerate rapidly: *this car has good pick-up.* **6.** *Informal.* a casual acquaintance, usually one made for the purpose of a sexual liaison. **7.** *Informal.* **a.** a stop to collect passengers, goods, etc. **b.** the people or things collected. **8.** *Slang.* a free ride in a motor vehicle. **9.** *Informal.* an improvement. **10.** *Slang.* a pick-me-up. ~*vb.* **pick up.** (*adv.*) **11.** (*tr.*) to gather up in the hand or hands. **12.** (*tr.*) to obtain or purchase casually, incidentally, etc. **13.** (*intr.*) to improve in health, condition, activity, etc.: *the market began to pick up.* **14.** (*tr.*) to learn gradually or as one goes along. **15.** (*tr.*) to collect or give a lift to (passengers, hitchhikers, goods, etc.). **16.** (*tr.*) *Informal.* to become acquainted with, esp. with a view to having sexual relations. **17.** (*tr.*) *Slang.* to arrest. **18.** to increase (speed): *the cars picked up down the straight.* **19.** (*tr.*) to receive (electrical signals, a radio signal, sounds, etc.), as for transmission or amplification.

Pick·wick·i·an (pɪk'wɪkɪən) *adj.* **1.** of, relating to, or resembling Mr. Pickwick in Charles Dickens' *The Pickwick Papers,* esp. in being naive or benevolent. **2.** (of the use or meaning of a word, etc.) odd or unusual.

pick·y ('pɪkɪ) *adj.* **pick·i·er, pick·i·est.** *Informal.* fussy; finicky; choosy. —**'pick·i·ly** *adv.* —**'pick·i·ness** *n.*

pic·nic ('pɪknɪk) *n.* **1.** a trip or excursion to the country, seaside, etc., on which people bring food to be eaten in the open air. **2. a.** any informal meal eaten outside. **b.** (*as modifier*)*: a picnic lunch.* **3.** *Informal.* an easy or agreeable task. **4.** *Informal, chiefly Austral.* a troublesome experience. ~*vb.* **·nics, ·nick·ing, ·nicked. 5.** (*intr.*) to eat a picnic. [C18: from French *piquenique,* of unknown origin] —**'pic·nick·er** *n.*

pic·nic rac·es *pl. n. Austral.* horse races for amateur riders held in rural areas.

pi·co- *prefix.* denoting 10^{-12}: *picofarad.* Symbol: p [from Spanish *pico* small quantity, odd number, peak]

Pi·co de A·ne·to (*Spanish* 'piko ðe a'neto) *n.* See **Aneto.**

Pi·co del·la Mi·ran·do·la (*Italian* 'pi:ko ˌdɛlla miran'dola) *n.* Count **Gio·van·ni** (dʒo'vanni). 1463–94, Italian Platonist philosopher. His attempt to reconcile the ideas of classical, Christian, and Arabic writers in a collection of 900 theses, prefaced by his *Oration on the Dignity of Man* (1486), was condemned by the pope.

Pi·co de Tei·de (*Spanish* 'piko ðe 'tejðe) *n.* See **Teide.**

pic·o·line ('pɪkəˌli:n, -lɪn) *n.* a liquid derivative of pyridine found in bone oil and coal tar; methylpyridene. Formula: $C_5H_4N(CH_3)$. [C19: from Latin *pic-, pix* PITCH[2] + -OL[2] + -INE[2]] —**pic·o·lin·ic** (ˌpɪkə'lɪnɪk) *adj.*

pic·ong ('pɪkɒŋ) *n. Caribbean.* any teasing or satirical banter, originally a verbal duel in song. [from Spanish *picón* mocking, from *picar* to pierce; compare PICADOR]

pi·cot ('pi:kəʊ) *n.* any of a pattern of small loops, as on lace. [C19: from French: small point, from *pic* point]

pic·o·tee (ˌpɪkə'ti:) *n.* a type of carnation having pale petals edged with a darker colour, usually red. [C18: from French *picoté* marked with points, from *picot* PICOT]

pic·rate ('pɪkreɪt) *n.* **1.** any salt or ester of picric acid, such as sodium picrate. **2.** a charge-transfer complex formed by picric acid.

pic·ric ac·id ('pɪkrɪk) *n.* a toxic sparingly soluble crystalline yellow acid; 2,4,6-trinitrophenol: used as a dye, antiseptic, and explosive. Formula: $C_6H_2OH(NO_2)_3$. See also **lyddite.**

pic·rite ('pɪkraɪt) *n.* a coarse-grained ultrabasic igneous rock consisting of olivine and augite with small amounts of plagioclase feldspar.

pic·ro- *or before a vowel* **picr-** *combining form.* bitter: *picrotoxin.* [from Greek *pikros*]

pic·ro·tox·in (ˌpɪkrə'tɒksɪn) *n.* a bitter poisonous crystalline compound used as an antidote for barbiturate poisoning. Formula: $C_{30}H_{34}O_{13}$.

Pict (pɪkt) *n.* a member of a pre-Celtic people of N Britain. Throughout Roman times the Picts carried out border raids, esp. from Scotland. [Old English *Peohtas;* later forms from Late Latin *Pictī* painted men, from *pingere* to paint]

Pict·ish ('pɪktɪʃ) *n.* the language of the Picts, of which few records survive. It was almost certainly not an Indo-European language and was extinct by about 900 A.D.

pic·to·gram ('pɪktəˌgræm) *n.* another word for **pictograph.**

pic·to·graph ('pɪktəˌgrɑ:f) *n.* **1.** a picture or symbol standing for a word or group of words, as in written Chinese. **2.** a chart on which symbols are used to represent values, such as population levels or consumption. [C19: from Latin *pictus,* from *pingere* to paint] —**pic·to·graph·ic** (ˌpɪktə'græfɪk) *adj.* —**pic·tog·ra·phy** (pɪk'tɒgrəfɪ) *n.*

Pic·tor ('pɪktə) *n., Latin genitive* **Pic·to·ris** (pɪk'tɔ:rɪs). a faint constellation in the S hemisphere lying between Dorado and Carina. [Latin: painter]

pic·to·ri·al (pɪk'tɔ:rɪəl) *adj.* **1.** relating to, consisting of, or expressed by pictures. **2.** (of books, etc.) containing pictures. **3.** of or relating to painting or drawing. **4.** (of language, style, etc.) suggesting a picture; vivid; graphic. ~*n.* **5. a.** a magazine, newspaper, etc., containing many pictures. **b.** (*cap. as part of a name*)*: the Sunday Pictorial.* [C17: from Late Latin *pictōrius,* from Latin *pictor* painter, from *pingere* to paint] —**pic·'to·ri·al·ly** *adv.*

pic·ture ('pɪktʃə) *n.* **1. a.** a visual representation of something, such as a person or scene, produced on a surface, as in a photograph, painting, etc. **b.** (*as modifier*): *picture gallery; picture postcard.* **2.** a mental image or impression: *a clear picture of events.* **3.** a verbal description, esp. one that is vivid. **4.** a situation considered as an observable scene: *the political picture.* **5.** a person or thing that bears a close resemblance to another: *he was the picture of his father.* **6.** a person, scene, etc., considered as typifying a particular state or quality: *the picture of despair.* **7.** a beautiful person or scene: *you'll look a picture.* **8. a.** a motion picture; film. **b.** (*as modifier*): *picture theatre.* **9. the pictures.** *Chiefly Brit.* a cinema or film show. **10.** another name for **tableau vivant. 11. in the picture.** informed about a given situation. ~*vb.* (*tr.*) **12.** to visualize or imagine. **13.** to describe or depict, esp. vividly. **14.** (*often passive*) to put in a picture or make a picture of: *they were pictured sitting on the rocks.* [C15: from Latin *pictūra* painting, from *pingere* to paint]

pic·ture card *n.* another name for **court card.**

pic·ture·go·er ('pɪktʃə,gəʊə) *n. Brit., old-fashioned.* a person who goes to the cinema, esp. frequently.

pic·ture hat *n.* any hat with a very wide brim, esp. one worn by women during the 18th century.

pic·ture pal·ace *n. Brit., old-fashioned.* another name for **cinema.**

pic·tur·esque (,pɪktʃə'rɛsk) *adj.* **1.** visually pleasing, esp. in being striking or vivid: *a picturesque view.* **2.** having a striking or colourful character, nature, etc. **3.** (of language) graphic; vivid. C18: from French *pittoresque* (but also influenced by PICTURE), from Italian *pittoresco,* from *pittore* painter, from Latin *pictor*] —,**pic·tur·'esque·ly** *adv.* —,**pic·tur·'esque·ness** *n.*

pic·ture tube *n.* another name for **television tube.**

pic·ture win·dow *n.* a large window having a single pane of glass, usually placed so that it overlooks a view.

pic·ture writ·ing *n.* **1.** any writing system that uses pictographs. **2.** a system of artistic expression and communication using pictures or symbolic figures.

pic·ul ('pɪkᵊl) *n.* a unit of weight, used in China, Japan, and in SE Asia, equal to approximately 133 pounds or 60 kilograms. [C16: from Malay *pīkul* a grown man's load]

pid·dle ('pɪdᵊl) *vb.* **1.** (*intr.*) an informal word for **urinate. 2.** (when *tr.,* often foll. by *away*) to spend (one's time) aimlessly; fritter. [C16: origin unknown] —'**pid·dler** *n.*

pid·dling ('pɪdlɪŋ) *adj. Informal.* petty; trifling; trivial. —'**pid·dling·ly** *adv.*

pid·dock ('pɪdək) *n.* any marine bivalve of the family *Pholadidae,* boring into rock, clay, or wood by means of sawlike shell valves. See also **shipworm.** [C19: origin uncertain]

pidg·in ('pɪdʒɪn) *n.* a language made up of elements of two or more other languages and used for contacts, esp. trading contacts, between the speakers of other languages. Unlike creoles, pidgins do not constitute the mother tongue of any speech community. [C19: perhaps from Chinese pronunciation of English *business*]

pidg·in Eng·lish *n.* a pidgin in which one of the languages involved is English.

pie[1] (paɪ) *n.* **1.** a baked food consisting of a sweet or savoury filling in a pastry-lined dish, often covered with a pastry crust. **2. have a finger in the pie.** to have a share or stake in something. **3. pie in the sky.** *Informal.* illusory hope of some future good; false optimism. [C14: of obscure origin]

pie[2] (paɪ) *n.* an archaic or dialect name for **magpie.** [C13: via Old French from Latin *pīca* magpie; related to Latin *pīcus* woodpecker]

pie[3] (paɪ) *n. Printing.* a variant spelling of **pi**[2]**.**

pie[4] (paɪ) *n.* a very small former Indian coin worth one third of a pice. [C19: from Hindi *pā'ī,* from Sanskrit *pādikā* a fourth]

pie[5] *or* **pye** (paɪ) *n. History.* a book for finding the Church service for any particular day. [C15: from Medieval Latin *pica* almanac; see PICA]

pie·bald ('paɪ,bɔ:ld) *adj.* **1.** marked or spotted in two different colours, esp. black and white: *a piebald horse.* ~*n.* **2.** a black-and-white pied horse. [C16: PIE[2] + BALD; see also PIED]

piece (pi:s) *n.* **1.** an amount or portion forming a separate mass or structure; bit: *a piece of wood.* **2.** a small part, item, or amount forming part of a whole, esp. when broken off or separated: *a piece of bread.* **3.** a length by which a commodity is sold, esp. cloth, wallpaper, etc. **4.** an instance or occurrence: *a piece of luck.* **5.** *Slang.* a girl or woman regarded as an object of sexual attraction: *a nice piece.* **6.** an example or specimen of a style or type, such as an article of furniture: *a beautiful piece of Dresden.* **7.** *Informal.* an opinion or point of view: *to state one's piece.* **8.** a literary, musical, or artistic composition. **9.** a coin having a value as specified: *fifty-pence piece.* **10.** a small object, often individually shaped and designed, used in playing certain games, esp. board games: *chess pieces.* **11. a.** a firearm or cannon. **b.** (*in combination*): *fowling-piece.* **12.** any chessman other than a pawn. **13.** *U.S.* a short time or distance: *down the road a piece.* **14.** *Northern Brit. dialect.* a packed lunch taken to work. **15. give someone a piece of one's mind.** *Informal.* to criticize or censure a person frankly or vehemently. **16. go to pieces. a.** (of a person) to lose control of oneself; have a breakdown. **b.** (of a building, organization, etc.) to disintegrate. **17. nasty piece of work.** *Brit. informal.* a cruel or mean person. **18. of a piece.** of the same kind; alike. **19. piece of cake.** *Brit. informal.* something easily obtained or achieved. ~*vb.* (*tr.*) **20.** (often foll. by *together*) to fit or assemble piece by piece. **21.** (often foll. by *up*) to patch or make up (a garment, etc.) by adding pieces. **22.** *Textiles.* to join (broken threads, etc.) during spinning. [C13 *pece,* from Old French, of Gaulish origin; compare Breton *pez* piece, Welsh *peth* portion]

pièce de ré·sis·tance *French.* (pjɛs də rezis'tɑ̃:s) *n.* **1.** the principal or most outstanding item in a series or creative artist's work. **2.** the main dish of a meal.

piece-dyed *adj.* (of fabric) dyed after weaving. Compare **yarn-dyed.**

piece goods *pl. n.* goods, esp. fabrics, made in standard widths and lengths. Also called: **yard goods.**

piece·meal ('pi:s,mi:l) *adv.* **1.** by degrees; bit by bit; gradually. **2.** in or into pieces or piece from piece: *to tear something piecemeal.* ~*adj.* **3.** fragmentary or unsystematic: *a piecemeal approach.* [C13 *pecemele,* from PIECE + *-mele,* from Old English *mælum* quantity taken at one time]

piece of eight *n., pl.* **piec·es of eight.** a former Spanish coin worth eight reals; peso.

piece out *vb.* (*tr., adv.*) **1.** to extend by adding pieces. **2.** to cause to last longer by using only a small amount at a time: *to piece out rations.*

piec·er ('pi:sə) *n. Textiles.* a person who mends, repairs, or joins something, esp. broken threads on a loom.

piece rate *n.* a fixed rate paid according to the quantity produced.

piece·work ('pi:s,wɜ:k) *n.* work paid for according to the quantity produced. Compare **timework.**

pie chart *n.* a circular graph divided into sectors proportional to the magnitudes of the quantities represented.

pie·crust ta·ble ('paɪ,krʌst) *n.* a round table, ornamented with carved moulding suggestive of a piecrust.

pied (paɪd) *adj.* having markings of two or more colours.

pied-à-terre *French.* (pjeta'tɛ:r) *n., pl.* ***pieds-à-terre*** (pjeta'tɛ:r). a flat, house, or other lodging for secondary or occasional use. [literally: foot on (the) ground]

pied·mont ('pi:dmɒnt) *adj.* (*prenominal*) (of glaciers, plains, etc.) formed or situated at the foot of a mountain or mountain range. [via French from Italian *piémonte,* from *pié,* variant of *piede* foot + *mont* mountain]

Pied·mont ('pi:dmɒnt) *n.* **1.** a region of NW Italy: consists of the upper Po Valley; mainly agricultural. Chief town: Turin. Pop.: 4 434 802 (1971). Area: 25 399 sq. km (9807 sq. miles). Italian name: **Piemonte. 2.** a low plateau of the eastern U.S., between the coastal plain and the Appalachian Mountains.

pied·mont·ite ('pi:dmɒn,taɪt, -mən-) *n.* a dark red mineral occurring in metamorphic rocks: consists of a hydrated silicate of calcium, aluminium, iron, and manganese. Formula: $Ca_2(Al,Fe,Mn)_3(SiO_4)_3OH$. [C19: from *Piedmont* (Italian *Piemonte*) in Italy]

Pied Pip·er *n.* **1.** Also called: **The Pied Piper of Hamelin.** (in German legend) a piper who rid the town of Hamelin of rats by luring them away with his music and then, when he was not paid for his services, lured away its children. **2.** (*sometimes not cap.*) a person who entices others to follow him.

pied-pip·ing *n. Transformational grammar.* the principle that a noun phrase may take with it the rest of a prepositional phrase or a larger noun phrase in which it is contained, when moved in a transformation. For example, when the interrogative pronoun is moved to initial position, other words are moved too, as in *to whom did you speak?*

pied wag·tail *n.* a British songbird, *Motacilla alba yarrellii,* with a black throat and back, long black tail, and white underparts and face: family *Motacillidae* (wagtails and pipits).

pie-eat·er *n. Austral. informal, offensive.* a person of little account or importance.

pie-eyed *adj.* a slang expression for **drunk.**

pie·man ('paɪmən) *n., pl.* **·men.** *Brit., obsolete.* a seller of pies.

Pie·mon·te (*Italian* pje'monte) *n.* the Italian name for **Piedmont** (sense 1).

pier (pɪə) *n.* **1.** a structure with a deck that is built out over water, and used as a landing place, promenade, etc. **2.** a pillar that bears heavy loads, esp. one of rectangular cross section. **3.** the part of a wall between two adjacent openings. **4.** another name for **buttress.** [C12 *per,* from Anglo-Latin *pera* pier supporting a bridge]

pierce (pɪəs) *vb.* (*mainly tr.*) **1.** to form or cut (a hole) in (something) with or as if with a sharp instrument. **2.** to thrust into or penetrate sharply or violently: *the thorn pierced his heel.* **3.** to force (a way, route, etc.) through (something) **4.** (of light, etc.) to shine through or penetrate (darkness). **5.** (*also intr.*) to discover or realize (something) suddenly or (of an idea, etc.) to become suddenly apparent. **6.** (of sounds or cries) to sound sharply through (the silence, etc.). **7.** to move or affect (a person's emotions, bodily feelings, etc.) deeply or sharply: *the cold pierced their bones.* **8.** (*intr.*) to penetrate or be capable of penetrating: *piercing cold.* [C13 *percen,* from Old French *percer,* ultimately from Latin *pertundere,* from *per* through + *tundere* to strike] —'**pierc·a·ble** *adj.* —'**pierc·er** *n.* —'**pierc·ing** *adj.* —'**pierc·ing·ly** *adv.*

Pierce (pɪəs) *n.* **Frank·lin.** 1804–69, U.S. statesman; 14th president of the U.S. (1853–57).

pier glass *n.* a tall narrow mirror, usually one of a pair or set, designed to hang on the wall between windows, usually above a pier table.

Pi·e·ri·a (paɪ'ɪərɪə) *n.* a region of ancient Macedonia, west of the Gulf of Salonika: site of the Pierian Spring.

Pi·e·ri·an (paɪ'ɪərɪən) *adj.* **1.** of or relating to the Muses or artistic or poetic inspiration. **2.** of or relating to Pieria.

Pi·e·ri·an Spring *n.* a sacred fountain in Pieria, in Greece, fabled to inspire those who drank from it.

Pi·e·ri·des (paɪ'ɪərɪ,di:z) *pl. n. Greek myth.* **1.** another name for the Muses (see **Muse**). **2.** nine maidens of Thessaly, who were defeated in a singing contest by the Muses and turned into magpies for their effrontery.

pi+e·ri+dine (paɪ'ɛrɪˌdaɪn) *adj.* of, relating to, or belonging to the *Pieridae*, a family of butterflies including the whites and brimstones.

Pie·ro Del·la Fran·ces·ca (*Italian* 'pjɛ:ro 'dɛlla fran'tʃeska) *n.* ?1420–92, Italian painter, noted particularly for his frescoes of the *Legend of the True Cross* in San Francesco, Arezzo.

Pie·ro di Co·si·mo (*Italian* 'pjɛ:ro di 'kɔ:zimo) *n.* 1462–1521, Italian painter, noted for his mythological works.

Pierre (pɪə) *n.* a city in central South Dakota, capital of the state, on the Missouri River: the smallest state capital of the U.S. Pop.: 9699 (1970).

Pi+er+rot ('pɪərəʊ; *French* pjɛ'ro) *n.* **1.** a male character from French pantomime with a whitened face, white costume, and pointed hat. **2.** (*usually not cap.*) a clown or masquerader so made up.

pier ta+ble *n.* a side table designed to stand against a wall between windows.

pi+e·tà (pɪɛ'tɑ:) *n.* a sculpture, painting, or drawing of the dead Christ, supported by the Virgin Mary. [Italian: pity, from Latin *pietās* PIETY]

Pie+ter+mar+itz+burg (ˌpi:tə'mærɪtsˌbɜ:g) *n.* a city in E South Africa, capital of Natal province: founded in 1839 by the Boers: gateway to Natal's mountain resorts. Pop.: 112 666 (1970).

pi+e·tism ('paɪɪˌtɪzəm) *n.* **1.** a less common word for **piety**. **2.** excessive, exaggerated, or affected piety or saintliness. —'**pi+e·tist** *n.* —ˌ**pi+e·'tis+tic** *or* ˌ**pi+e·'tis+ti+cal** *adj.*

Pi+e·tism ('paɪɪˌtɪzəm) *n. History.* a reform movement in the German Lutheran Churches during the 17th and 18th centuries that strived to renew the devotional ideal. —'**Pi+e·tist** *n.*

pi+e·ty ('paɪɪtɪ) *n., pl.* **·ties. 1.** dutiful devotion to God and observance of religious principles. **2.** the quality or characteristic of being pious. **3.** a pious action, saying, etc. **4.** *Now rare.* devotion and obedience to parents or superiors. [C13 *piete*, from Old French, from Latin *pietās* piety, dutifulness, from *pius* PIOUS]

pi·e·zo- *combining form.* pressure: *piezometer.* [from Greek *piezein* to press]

pi+e·zo+chem+is+try (paɪˌi:zəʊ'kɛmɪstrɪ) *n.* the study of chemical reactions at high pressures.

pi+e·zo+e·lec+tric crys+tal (paɪˌi:zəʊɪ'lɛktrɪk) *n.* a crystal, such as quartz, that produces a potential difference across its opposite faces when under mechanical stress. See also **piezoelectric effect.**

pi+e·zo+e·lec+tric ef+fect *or* **pi+e·zo+e·lec+tric+i·ty** (paɪˌi:zəʊɪlɛk'trɪsɪtɪ) *n. Physics.* **a.** the production of electricity or electric polarity by applying a mechanical stress to certain crystals. **b.** the converse effect in which stress is produced in a crystal as a result of an applied potential difference. —**pi+ˌe·zo+e·'lec+tri+cal+ly** *adv.*

pi+e·zom+e·ter (ˌpaɪɪ'zɒmɪtə) *n.* any instrument for the measurement of pressure (**pi+e·zom+e·try**), esp. very high pressure, or for measuring the compressibility of materials under pressure. —**pi+e·zo+met+ric** (paɪˌi:zəʊ'mɛtrɪk) *adj.* —**piˌ+e·zo+'met+ri+cal+ly** *adv.*

pif+fle ('pɪfᵊl) *n. Informal.* **1.** nonsense: *to talk piffle.* ~*vb.* **2.** (*intr.*) to talk or behave feebly. [C19: origin uncertain]

pig (pɪg) *n.* **1.** any artiodactyl mammal of the African and Eurasian family *Suidae*, esp. *Sus scrofa* (**domestic pig**), typically having a long head with a movable snout, a thick bristle-covered skin, and, in wild species, long curved tusks. **2.** a domesticated pig weighing more than 120 pounds. **3.** *Informal.* a dirty, greedy, or bad-mannered person. **4.** the meat of swine; pork. **5.** *Derogatory.* a slang word for **policeman. 6. a.** a mass of metal, such as iron, copper, or lead, cast into a simple shape for ease of storing or transportation. **b.** a mould in which such a mass of metal is formed. **7.** *Brit. informal.* something that is difficult or unpleasant. **8. a pig in a poke.** something bought or received without prior sight or knowledge. **9. make a pig of oneself.** *Informal.* to overindulge oneself. ~*vb.* **pigs, pig+ging, pigged. 10.** (*intr.*) (of a sow) to give birth. **11.** (*intr.*) Also: **pig it.** *Informal.* to live in squalor. **12.** (*tr.*) *Informal.* to devour (food) greedily. [C13 *pigge*, of obscure origin]

pig bed *n.* a bed of sand in which pig iron is cast.

pi+geon ('pɪdʒɪn) *n.* **1.** any of numerous birds of the family *Columbidae*, having a heavy body, small head, short legs and long pointed wings: order *Columbiformes.* See **rock dove. 2.** *Slang.* a victim or dupe. **3.** *Brit. informal.* concern or responsibility (often in the phrase **it's his, her,** etc., **pigeon**). [C14: from Old French *pijon* young dove, from Late Latin *pīpiō* young bird, from *pīpīre* to chirp]

pi+geon breast *n.* a deformity of the chest characterized by an abnormal protrusion of the breastbone, caused by rickets or by obstructed breathing during infancy. Also called: **chicken breast.**

pi+geon hawk *n.* the North American variety of the merlin.

pi·geon-heart·ed *or* **pi·geon-liv·ered** *adj.* of a timid or fearful disposition.

pi·geon+hole ('pɪdʒɪnˌhəʊl) *n.* **1.** a small compartment for papers, letters, etc., as in a bureau. **2.** a hole or recess in a dovecote for pigeons to nest in. **3.** *Informal.* a category or classification. ~*vb.* (*tr.*) **4.** to put aside or defer. **5.** to classify or categorize, esp. in a rigid manner.

pi+geon pea *n.* another name for **dhal.**

pi·geon-toed *adj.* having the toes turned inwards.

pi·geon+wing ('pɪdʒɪnˌwɪŋ) *n. Chiefly U.S.* a fancy step in dancing in which the feet are clapped together.

pig+face ('pɪgˌfeɪs) *n. Austral.* a creeping succulent plant of the genus *Carpobrotus*, having bright-coloured flowers and red fruits and often grown for ornament: family *Aizoaceae.*

pig+fish ('pɪgˌfɪʃ) *n., pl.* **+fish** *or* **+fish·es. 1.** Also called: **hogfish.** any of several grunts, esp. *Orthopristis chrysopterus*, of the North American Atlantic coast. **2.** any of several wrasses, such as *Achoerodus gouldii* (**giant pigfish**), that occur around the Great Barrier Reef.

pig+ger·y ('pɪgərɪ) *n., pl.* **+ger·ies. 1.** a place where pigs are kept and reared. **2.** great greediness; piggishness.

pig+gin ('pɪgɪn) *n.* a small wooden bucket or tub. Also called: **pipkin.** [C16: origin unknown]

pig+gish ('pɪgɪʃ) *adj.* **1.** like a pig, esp. in appetite or manners. **2.** *Informal, chiefly Brit.* obstinate or mean. —'**pig+gish+ly** *adv.* —'**pig+gish+ness** *n.*

Pig·gott ('pɪgət) *n.* **Les·ter (Keith).** born 1935. English flat-racing jockey: by 1977 he had won the Derby eight times.

pig+gy ('pɪgɪ) *n., pl.* **+gies. 1.** a child's word for a pig, esp. a piglet. **2.** a child's word for toe or, sometimes, finger. ~*adj.* **+gi+er, +gi+est. 3.** another word for **piggish.**

pig·gy+back ('pɪgɪˌbæk) *or* **pick·a+back** ('pɪkəˌbæk) *n.* **1. a.** a ride on the back and shoulders of another person. **b.** (*as modifier*): *a piggyback ride.* ~*adv.* **2.** on the back and shoulders of another person.

pig+gy bank *n.* a child's coin bank shaped like a pig with a slot for coins.

pig-head·ed *adj.* stupidly stubborn. —'**pig-ˌhead·ed+ly** *adv.* —'**pig-ˌhead·ed+ness** *n.*

pig i·ron *n.* crude iron produced in a blast furnace and poured into moulds in preparation for making wrought iron, steels, alloys, etc.

Pig Lat+in *n.* a secret language used by children in which any consonants at the beginning of a word are placed at the end, followed by *-ay;* for example *cathedral* becomes *athedralcay.*

pig+let ('pɪglɪt) *n.* a young pig.

pig+meat ('pɪgˌmi:t) *n.* a less common name for **pork, ham,** or **bacon.**

pig+ment ('pɪgmənt) *n.* **1.** a substance occurring in plant or animal tissue and producing a characteristic colour, such as chlorophyll in green plants and haemoglobin in red blood. **2.** any substance used to impart colour. **3.** a powder that is mixed with a liquid to give a paint, ink, etc. [C14: from Latin *pigmentum*, from *pingere* to paint] —'**pig+men+tar·y** *adj.*

pig+men+ta+tion (ˌpɪgmən'teɪʃən) *n.* **1.** coloration in plants, animals, or man caused by the presence of pigments. **2.** the deposition of pigment in animals, plants, or man.

Pig+my ('pɪgmɪ) *n., pl.* **+mies.** a variant spelling of **Pygmy.**

pig+nut ('pɪgˌnʌt) *n.* **1.** Also called: **hognut. a.** the bitter nut of any of several North American hickory trees, esp. *Carya glabra* (**brown hickory**). **b.** any of the trees bearing such a nut. **2.** another name for **earthnut.**

pig+pen ('pɪgˌpɛn) *n.* another word for **pigsty.**

Pigs (pɪgz) *n.* **Bay of.** See **Bay of Pigs.**

pig's ear *n.* **1.** *Cockney rhyming slang.* beer. **2.** something that has been badly or clumsily done; a botched job (esp. in the phrase **make a pig's ear of (something)**).

pig's fry *n.* the heart, liver, lights, and sweetbreads of a pig cooked, esp. fried, together.

pig+skin ('pɪgˌskɪn) *n.* **1.** the skin of the domestic pig. **2.** leather made of this skin. **3.** *U.S. informal.* a football. ~*adj.* **4.** made of pigskin.

pig+stick ('pɪgˌstɪk) *vb.* (*intr.*) (esp. in India) to hunt and spear wild boar, esp. from horseback. —'**pig+ˌstick+er** *n.*

pig+stick+ing ('pɪgˌstɪkɪŋ) *n.* the sport of hunting wild boar.

pig+sty ('pɪgˌstaɪ) *or U.S.* **pig+pen** *n., pl.* **+sties. 1.** a pen for pigs; sty. **2.** *Brit.* a dirty or untidy place.

pig+swill ('pɪgˌswɪl) *n.* waste food or other edible matter fed to pigs. Also called: **pig's wash.**

pig+tail ('pɪgˌteɪl) *n.* **1.** a bunch of hair or one of two bunches on either side of the face, worn loose or plaited. **2.** a twisted roll of tobacco. —'**pig+ˌtailed** *adj.*

pig+weed ('pɪgˌwi:d) *n.* **1.** Also called: **redroot.** any of several coarse North American amaranthaceous weeds of the genus *Amaranthus*, esp. *A. retroflexus*, having hair leaves and green flowers. **2.** a U.S. name for **fat hen.**

pi·ka ('paɪkə) *n.* any burrowing lagomorph mammal of the family *Ochotonidae* of mountainous regions of North America and Asia, having short rounded ears, a rounded body, and rudimentary tail. Also called: **cony.** [C19: from Tungusic *piika*]

pike[1] (paɪk) *n., pl.* **pike** *or* **pikes. 1.** any of several large predatory freshwater teleost fishes of the genus *Esox*, esp. *E. lucius* (**northern pike**), having a broad flat snout, strong teeth, and an elongated body covered with small scales: family *Esocidae.* **2.** any of various similar fishes. [C14: short for *pikefish*, from Old English *pīc* point, with reference to the shape of its jaw]

pike[2] (paɪk) *n.* **1.** a medieval weapon consisting of a metal spearhead joined to a long pole, the pikestaff. **2.** a point or spike. ~*vb.* **3.** (*tr.*) to stab or pierce using a pike. [Old English *pīc* point, of obscure origin]

pike[3] (paɪk) *n.* short for **turnpike** (senses 1, 2).

pike[4] (paɪk) *n. Northern English dialect.* a pointed or conical hill. [Old English *pīc*, of obscure origin]

pike+let ('paɪklɪt) *n. Brit. dialect.* a type of crumpet. [C18: from Welsh *bara pyglyd* pitchy bread]

pike+man ('paɪkmən) *n., pl.* **+men.** (formerly) a soldier armed with a pike.

pike+perch ('paɪkˌpɜ:tʃ) *n., pl.* **+perch** *or* **+perch·es.** any of various pikelike freshwater teleost fishes of the genera *Stizostedion* (or *Lucioperca*), such as *S. lucioperca* of Europe: family *Percidae* (perches).

pik·er ('paɪkə) *n. Austral. slang.* **1.** a wild bullock. **2.** a lazy person; shirker. [C19: perhaps related to PIKE[3]]

Pikes Peak *n.* a mountain in central Colorado, in the Rockies. Height: 4300 m (14 109 ft.).

pike·staff ('paɪkˌstɑːf) *n.* the wooden handle of a pike.

pi·las·ter (pɪ'læstə) *n.* a shallow rectangular column attached to the face of a wall. [C16: from French *pilastre,* from Latin *pīla* pillar] —**pi·'las·tered** *adj.*

Pi·late ('paɪlət) *n.* **Pon·tius** ('pɒnʃəs, 'pɒntɪəs). Roman procurator of Judaea (?26–?36 A.D.), who ordered the crucifixion of Jesus.

Pi·la·tus (*German* pi'la:tʊs) *n.* a mountain in central Switzerland, in Unterwalden canton: derives its name from the legend that the body of Pontius Pilate lay in a former lake on the mountain. Height: 2122 m (6962 ft.).

pi·lau (pɪ'laʊ), **pil·af, pil·aff** ('pɪlæf), **pi·lao** (pɪ'laʊ), *or* **pi·law** (pɪ'lɔː) *n.* a dish originating from the East, consisting of rice flavoured with spices and cooked in stock, to which meat, poultry, or fish may be added. [C17: from Turkish *pilāw,* from Persian]

pilch (pɪltʃ) *n. Brit., archaic.* an infant's outer garment. [C17: from Old English *pylce* a garment made of skin and fur, from Late Latin *pellicia,* from Latin *pellis* fur]

pil·chard ('pɪltʃəd) *n.* a European food fish, *Sardina* (or *Clupea*) *pilchardus,* with a rounded body covered with large scales: family *Clupeidae* (herrings). [C16 *pylcher,* of obscure origin]

Pil·co·ma·yo (*Spanish* ˌpilko'majo) *n.* a river in S central South America, rising in W central Bolivia and flowing southeast, forming the border between Argentina and Paraguay, to the Paraguay River at Asunción. Length: about 1600 km (1000 miles).

pile[1] (paɪl) *n.* **1.** a collection of objects laid on top of one another or of other material stacked vertically; heap; mound. **2.** *Informal.* a large amount of money (esp. in the phrase **make a pile**). **3.** (*often pl.*) *Informal.* a large amount: *a pile of work.* **4.** a less common word for **pyre. 5.** a large building or group of buildings. **6.** *Physics.* a structure of uranium and a moderator used for producing atomic energy; nuclear reactor. **7.** *Metallurgy.* an arrangement of wrought-iron bars that are to be heated and worked into a single bar. **8.** the point of an arrow. ~*vb.* **9.** (often foll. by *up*) to collect or be collected into or as if into a pile: *snow piled up in the drive.* **10.** (*intr.;* foll. by *in, into, off, out,* etc.) to move in a group, esp. in a hurried or disorganized manner: *to pile off the bus.* **11. pile arms.** to prop a number of rifles together, muzzles together and upwards, butts forming the base. **12. pile it on.** *Informal.* to exaggerate. ~See also **pile up.** [C15: via Old French from Latin *pīla* stone pier]

pile[2] (paɪl) *n.* **1.** a long column of timber, concrete, or steel that is driven into the ground to provide a foundation for a structure. **2.** *Heraldry.* an ordinary shaped like a wedge, usually displayed point downwards. ~*vb.* (*tr.*) **3.** to drive (piles) into the ground. **4.** to provide or support (a structure) with piles. [Old English *pīl,* from Latin *pīlum*]

pile[3] (paɪl) *n.* **1.** *Textiles.* **a.** the yarns in a fabric that stand up or out from the weave, as in carpeting, velvet, etc. **b.** one of these yarns. **2.** soft fine hair, fur, wool, etc. [C15: from Anglo-Norman *pyle,* from Latin *pilus* hair]

pi·le·ate ('paɪlɪɪt, -ˌeɪt, 'pɪl-) *or* **pi·le·at·ed** ('paɪlɪˌeɪtɪd, 'pɪl-) *adj.* **1.** (of birds) having a crest. **2.** *Botany,* having a pileus. [C18: from Latin *pīleātus* wearing a felt cap, from PILEUS]

pile-driv·er *n.* **1.** a machine that drives piles into the ground either by repeatedly allowing a heavy weight to fall on the head of the pile or by using a steam hammer. **2.** *Informal.* a forceful punch or kick.

pi·le·ous ('paɪlɪəs, 'pɪl-) *adj. Biology.* **1.** hairy. **2.** of or relating to hair. [C19: ultimately from Latin *pilus* a hair]

piles (paɪlz) *pl. n.* a nontechnical name for **haemorrhoids.** [C15: from Latin *pilae* balls (referring to the appearance of external piles)]

pile shoe *n.* an iron casting shaped to a point and fitted to a lower end of a wooden or concrete pile. Also called: **shoe.**

pi·le·um ('paɪlɪəm, 'pɪl-) *n., pl.* **·le·a** (-lɪə). the top of a bird's head from the base of the bill to the occiput. [C19: New Latin, from Latin PILEUS]

pile up *vb.* (*adv.*) **1.** to gather or be gathered in a pile; accumulate. **2.** *Informal.* to crash or cause to crash. ~*n.* **pile-up. 3.** *Informal.* a multiple collision of vehicles.

pi·le·us ('paɪlɪəs, 'pɪl-) *n., pl.* **·le·i** (-lɪˌaɪ). the upper cap-shaped part of a mushroom or similar spore-producing body. [C18: (botanical use) New Latin, from Latin: felt cap]

pile·wort ('paɪlˌwɜːt) *n.* any of several plants, such as lesser celandine, thought to be effective in treating piles.

pil·fer ('pɪlfə) *vb.* to steal (minor items), esp. in small quantities. [C14 *pylfre* (n.) from Old French *pelfre* booty; see PELF] —**'pil·fer·er** *n.*

pil·fer·age ('pɪlfərɪdʒ) *n.* **1.** the act or practice of stealing small quantities or articles. **2.** the amount so stolen.

pil·gar·lic (pɪl'gɑːlɪk) *n.* **1.** *Obsolete.* a bald head or a man with a bald head. **2.** *Dialect.* a pitiable person. [C16: literally, peeled garlic]

pil·grim ('pɪlgrɪm) *n.* **1.** a person who undertakes a journey to a sacred place as an act of religious devotion. **2.** any wayfarer. [C12: from Provençal *pelegrin,* from Latin *peregrīnus* foreign, from *per* through + *ager* field, land; see PEREGRINE]

pil·grim·age ('pɪlgrɪmɪdʒ) *n.* **1.** a journey to a shrine or other sacred place. **2.** a journey or long search made for exalted or sentimental reasons. ~*vb.* **3.** (*intr.*) to make a pilgrimage.

Pil·grim·age of Grace *n.* a rebellion in 1536 in N England against the Reformation and Henry VIII's government.

Pil·grim Fa·thers *or* **Pil·grims** *pl. n.* **the.** the English Puritans who sailed on the Mayflower to New England, where they founded Plymouth Colony in SE Massachusetts (1620).

pi·li (pɪ'liː) *n., pl.* **·lis. 1.** a burseraceous Philippine tree, *Canarium ovatum,* with edible seeds resembling almonds. **2.** Also called: **pili nut.** the seed of this tree. [from Tagalog]

pi·lif·er·ous (paɪ'lɪfərəs) *adj.* **1.** (esp. of plants or their parts) bearing or ending in a hair or hairs. **2.** designating the outer layer of root epidermis, which bears the root hairs.

pil·i·form ('pɪlɪˌfɔːm) *adj. Botany.* resembling a long hair.

pil·ing ('paɪlɪŋ) *n.* **1.** the act of driving piles. **2.** a number of piles. **3.** a structure formed of piles.

Pi·lion ('piljɔn) *n.* transliteration of the Modern Greek name for **Pelion.**

pill[1] (pɪl) *n.* **1.** a small spherical or ovoid mass of a medicinal substance, intended to be swallowed whole. **2. the.** (*sometimes cap.*) *Informal.* an oral contraceptive. **3.** something unpleasant that must be endured (esp. in the phrase **bitter pill to swallow**). **4.** *Slang.* a ball or disc. **5.** *Slang.* an unpleasant or boring person. ~*vb.* **6.** (*tr.*) to give pills to. **7.** (*tr.*) to make pills of. **8.** (*intr.*) to form into small balls. **9.** (*tr.*) *Slang.* to blackball. [C15: from Middle Flemish *pille,* from Latin *pilula* a little ball, from *pila* ball]

pill[2] (pɪl) *vb.* **1.** *Archaic or dialect.* to peel or skin (something). **2.** *Archaic.* to pillage or plunder (a place, etc.). **3.** *Obsolete.* to make or become bald. [Old English *pilian,* from Latin *pilāre* to strip]

pil·lage ('pɪlɪdʒ) *vb.* **1.** to rob (a town, village, etc.) of (booty or spoils), esp. during a war. ~*n.* **2.** the act of pillaging. **3.** something obtained by pillaging; booty. [C14: via Old French from *piller* to despoil, probably from *peille* rag, from Latin *pīleus* felt cap] —**'pil·lag·er** *n.*

pil·lar ('pɪlə) *n.* **1.** an upright structure of stone, brick, metal, etc. that supports a superstructure or is used for ornamentation. **2.** something resembling this in shape or function: *a pillar of stones; a pillar of smoke.* **3.** a prominent supporter: *a pillar of the Church.* **4. from pillar to post.** from one place to another. ~*vb.* **5.** (*tr.*) to support with or as if with pillars. [C13: from Old French *pilier,* from Latin *pīla;* see PILE[1]]

pil·lar box *n.* **1.** *Brit.* a red pillar-shaped public letter box situated on a pavement. ~*adj.* **pil·lar-box. 2.** characteristic of a pillar box (in the phrase **pillar-box red).**

Pil·lars of Her·cu·les *n.* the two promontories at the E end of the Strait of Gibraltar: the Rock of Gibraltar on the European side and the Jebel Musa on the African side; according to legend, formed by Hercules.

pill·box ('pɪlˌbɒks) *n.* **1.** a box for pills. **2.** a small enclosed fortified emplacement, usually made of reinforced concrete. **3.** a small round hat, now worn esp. by women.

pill bug *n.* any of various woodlice of the genera *Armadillidium* and *Oniscus,* capable of rolling up into a ball when disturbed.

pil·lion ('pɪljən) *n.* **1.** a seat or place behind the rider of a motorcycle, scooter, horse, etc. ~*adv.* **2.** on a pillion: *to ride pillion.* [C16: from Gaelic; compare Scottish *pillean,* Irish *pillīn* couch; related to Latin *pellis* skin]

pil·li·winks ('pɪlɪˌwɪŋks) *n.* a medieval instrument of torture for the fingers and thumbs. [C14: of uncertain origin]

pil·lo·ry ('pɪlərɪ) *n., pl.* **·ries. 1.** a wooden framework into which offenders were formerly locked by the neck and wrists and exposed to public abuse and ridicule. **2.** exposure to public scorn or abuse. ~*vb.* **·ries, ·ry·ing, ·ried.** (*tr.*) **3.** to expose to public scorn or ridicule. **4.** to punish by putting in a pillory. [C13: from Anglo-Latin *pillorium,* from Old French *pilori,* of uncertain origin; related to Provençal *espillori*]

pil·low ('pɪləʊ) *n.* **1.** a cloth case stuffed with feathers, foam rubber, etc., used to support the head, esp. during sleep. **2.** Also called: **cushion.** a padded cushion or board on which pillow lace is made. **3.** anything like a pillow in shape or function. ~*vb.* **4.** (*tr.*) to rest (one's head) on or as if on a pillow. **5.** (*tr.*) to serve as a pillow for. [Old English *pylwe,* from Latin *pulvīnus* cushion; compare German *Pfühl*]

pil·low block *n.* a block, such as a simple journal, that supports a shaft.

pil·low·case ('pɪləʊˌkeɪs) *or* **pil·low·slip** ('pɪləʊˌslɪp) *n.* a removable washable cover of cotton, linen, nylon, etc., for a pillow.

pil·low lace *n.* lace made by winding thread around bobbins on a padded cushion or board. Compare **point lace.**

pil·low sham *n. Chiefly U.S.* a decorative cover for a bed pillow.

pills (pɪlz) *pl. n. Taboo slang.* another word for **testicles.**

pill·wort ('pɪlˌwɜːt) *n.* a small Eurasian water fern, *Pilularia globulifera,* with globular spore-producing bodies. [C19: from PILL[1] + WORT]

pi·lo·car·pine (ˌpaɪləʊ'kɑːpaɪn, -pɪn) *or* **pi·lo·car·pin** (ˌpaɪləʊ'kɑːpɪn) *n.* an alkaloid extracted from the leaves of the jaborandi tree, formerly used to induce sweating. Formula: $C_{11}H_{16}N_2O_2$. [C19: from New Latin *Pilocarpus* genus name, from Greek *pilos* hair + *karpos* fruit]

Pi·los ('pilɔs) *n.* transliteration of the Modern Greek name for **Pylos.**

pi·lose ('paɪləʊz) *adj. Biology.* covered with fine soft hairs: *pilose leaves.* [C18: from Latin *pilōsus,* from *pilus* hair] —**pi·los·i·ty** (paɪ'lɒsɪtɪ) *n.*

pi·lot ('paɪlət) *n.* **1. a.** a person who is qualified to operate an aircraft or spacecraft in flight. **b.** (*as modifier*): *pilot error.* **2. a.** a person who is qualified to steer or guide a ship into or out of a port, river mouth, etc. **b.** (*as modifier*): *a pilot ship.* **3.** a person who steers a ship. **4.** a person who acts as a leader or guide. **5.** *Machinery.* a guide, often consisting of a tongue or dowel, used to assist in joining two mating parts together. **6.** *Machinery.* a plug gauge for measuring an internal diameter. **7.** *Films.* a colour test strip accompanying black-and-white rushes from colour originals. **8.** an experimental programme on radio or television. **9.** See **pilot film. 10.** (*modifier*) used in or serving as a test or trial: *a pilot project.* **11.** (*modifier*) serving as a guide: *a pilot beacon.* ~*vb.* (*tr.*) **12.** to act as pilot of. **13.** to control the course of. **14.** to guide or lead (a project, people, etc.). [C16: from French *pilote,* from Medieval Latin *pilotus,* ultimately from Greek *pēdon* oar; related to Greek *pous* foot]

pi·lot·age ('paɪlətɪdʒ) *n.* **1.** the act of piloting an aircraft or ship. **2.** a pilot's fee. **3.** the navigation of an aircraft by the observation of ground features and use of charts.

pi·lot bal·loon *n.* a meteorological balloon used to observe air currents.

pi·lot bis·cuit *n.* another term for **hardtack.**

pi·lot cloth *n.* a type of thick blue cloth used to make sailor's coats, etc.

pi·lot en·gine *n.* a locomotive that clears or tests the way ahead for a train engine.

pi·lot film *n.* a film of short duration serving as a guide to a projected series.

pi·lot fish *n.* **1.** a small carangid fish, *Naucrates ductor,* of tropical and subtropical seas, marked with dark vertical bands: often accompanies sharks and other large fishes. **2.** any of various similar or related fishes.

pi·lot house *n. Nautical.* an enclosed structure on the bridge of a vessel from which it can be navigated; wheelhouse.

pi·lot·ing ('paɪlətɪŋ) *n.* **1.** the navigational handling of a ship near land using buoys, soundings, landmarks, etc., or the finding of a ship's position by such means. **2.** the occupation of a pilot.

pi·lot lamp *n.* a small light in an electric circuit or device that lights up when the circuit is closed or when certain conditions prevail.

pi·lot light *n.* **1.** a small auxiliary flame that ignites the main burner of a gas appliance when the control valve opens. **2.** a small electric light used as an indicator.

pi·lot of·fic·er *n.* the most junior commissioned rank in the British Royal Air Force and in certain other air forces.

pi·lot whale *n.* any of several black toothed whales of the genus *Globicephala,* such as *G. melaena,* that occur in all seas except polar seas: family *Delphinidae.* Also called: **black whale, blackfish.**

Pil·sen ('pɪlzᵊn) *n.* the German name for **Plzeň.**

Pils·ner ('pɪlznə) *or* **Pil·sen·er** *n.* a type of pale beer with a strong flavour of hops. [named after PILSEN, where it was originally brewed]

Pił·sud·ski (*Polish* piwˈsutski) *n.* **Jó·zef** ('juzɛf). 1867–1935, Polish nationalist leader and statesman; president (1918–21) and premier (1926–28; 1930).

Pilt·down man ('pɪlt,daʊn) *n.* an advanced hominid postulated from fossil bones found in Sussex in 1912, but shown by modern dating methods in 1953 to be a hoax.

pil·ule ('pɪlju:l) *n.* a small pill. [C16: via French from Latin *pilula* little ball, from *pila* ball] —**'pil·u·lar** *adj.*

pi·men·to (pɪ'mɛntəʊ) *n., pl.* **·tos.** another name for **allspice** or **pimiento.** [C17: from Spanish *pimiento* pepper plant, from Medieval Latin *pigmenta* spiced drink, from Latin *pigmentum* PIGMENT]

pi me·son *n.* another name for **pion.**

pi·mien·to (pɪ'mjɛntəʊ, -'mɛn-) *n., pl.* **·tos.** a Spanish pepper, *Capsicum annuum,* with a red fruit used raw in salads, cooked as a vegetable, and as a stuffing for green olives. Also called: **pimento.** [variant of PIMENTO]

pimp[1] (pɪmp) *n.* **1.** a man who solicits for a prostitute or brothel and lives off the earnings. **2.** a man who procures sexual gratification for another; procurer; pander. ~*vb.* **3.** (*intr.*) to act as a pimp. [C17: of unknown origin]

pimp[2] (pɪmp) *Slang, chiefly Austral.* ~*n.* **1.** a spy or informer. ~*vb.* **2.** (*intr.;* often foll. by *on*) to inform (on). [of unknown origin]

pim·per·nel ('pɪmpə,nɛl, -nᵊl) *n.* **1.** any of several plants of the primulaceous genus *Anagallis,* such as the scarlet pimpernel, typically having small star-shaped flowers. **2.** any of several similar and related plants, such as *Lysimachia nemorum* (**yellow pimpernel**). [C15: from Old French *pimpernelle,* ultimately from Latin *piper* PEPPER; compare Old English *pipeneale*]

pim·ple ('pɪmpᵊl) *n.* a small round usually inflamed swelling of the skin. [C14: related to Old English *pipilian* to break out in spots; compare Latin *papula* pimple] —**'pim·pled** *adj.* —**'pim·ply** *adj.* —**'pim·pli·ness** *n.*

pin (pɪn) *n.* **1. a.** a short stiff straight piece of wire pointed at one end and either rounded or having a flattened head at the other: used mainly for fastening pieces of cloth, paper, etc., esp. temporarily. **b.** (*in combination*): *pinhole.* **2.** short for **cotter pin, hairpin, panel pin, rolling pin,** or **safety pin. 3.** an ornamental brooch, esp. a narrow one. **4.** a badge worn fastened to the clothing by a pin. **5.** something of little or no importance (esp. in the phrase **not care** or **give a pin (for)**). **6.** a peg or dowel. **7.** anything resembling a pin in shape, function, etc. **8.** (in various bowling games) a usually club-shaped wooden object set up in groups as a target. **9.** Also called: **safety pin.** a clip on a hand grenade that prevents its detonation until removed or released. **10.** *Nautical.* **a.** See **belaying pin. b.** the axle of a sheave. **c.** the sliding closure for a shackle. **11.** *Music.* a metal tuning peg on a piano, the end of which inserted into a detachable key by means of which it is turned. **12.** *Surgery.* a metal rod, esp. of stainless steel, for holding together adjacent ends of broken or fractured bones during healing. **13.** *Chess.* a position in which a piece is pinned against a more valuable piece or the king. **14.** *Golf.* the flagpole marking the hole on a green. **15.** the cylindrical part of a key that enters a lock. **16.** *Wrestling.* a position in which a person is held tight or immobile, esp. with both shoulders touching the ground. **17.** a dovetail tenon used to make a dovetail joint. **18.** *Brit.* a miniature beer cask containing 4½ gallons. **19.** (*usually pl.*) *Informal.* legs. ~*vb.* **pins, pin·ning, pinned.** (*tr.*) **20.** to attach, hold, or fasten with or as if with a pin or pins. **21.** to transfix with a pin, spear, etc. **22.** (foll. by *on*) *Informal.* to place (the blame for something): *he pinned the charge on his accomplice.* **23.** *Chess.* to cause (an enemy piece) to be effectively immobilized by attacking it with a queen, rook, or bishop so that moving it would reveal a check or expose a more valuable piece to capture. **24.** Also: **underpin.** to support (masonry, etc.), as by driving in wedges over a beam. ~See also **pin down.** [Old English *pinn;* related to Old High German *pfinn,* Old Norse *pinni* nail]

pi·na·ceous (paɪ'neɪʃəs) *adj.* of, relating to, or belonging to the *Pinaceae,* a family of conifers with needle-like leaves: includes pine, spruce, fir, larch, and cedar. [C19: via New Latin from Latin *pīnus* a pine]

pi·ña cloth ('pi:njə) *n.* a fine fabric made from the fibres of the pineapple leaf. [C19: from Spanish *piña* pineapple]

pin·a·fore ('pɪnə,fɔ:) *n.* **1.** *Chiefly Brit.* an apron, esp. one with a bib. **2.** *Chiefly U.S.* an overdress buttoning at the back. [C18: from PIN + AFORE]

pin·a·fore dress *n.* a sleeveless dress worn over a blouse or sweater. U.S. name: **jumper.**

Pi·nar del Rí·o (*Spanish* pi'nar ðel 'rio) *n.* a city in W Cuba: tobacco industry. Pop.: 73 200 (1970).

pi·nas·ter (paɪ'næstə, pɪ-) *n.* a Mediterranean pine tree, *Pinus pinaster,* with paired needles and prickly cones. Also called: **maritime** (or **cluster**) **pinaster.** [C16: from Latin: wild pine, from *pīnus* pine]

pin·ball ('pɪn,bɔ:l) *n.* **a.** a game in which the player shoots a small ball through several hazards on a table, electrically operated machine, etc. **b.** (*as modifier*): *a pinball machine.*

pince-nez ('pæns,neɪ, 'pɪns-; *French* pɛ̃s'ne) *n., pl.* **pince-nez.** eyeglasses that are held in place only by means of a clip over the bridge of the nose. [C19: French, literally: pinch-nose]

pin·cer move·ment ('pɪnsə) *n.* a military manoeuvre in which the two flanks of an army attempt to break through the opposing army with the aim of complete encirclement.

pin·cers ('pɪnsəz) *pl. n.* **1.** Also called: **pair of pincers.** a gripping tool consisting of two hinged arms with handles at one end and, at the other, curved bevelled jaws that close on the workpiece: used esp. for extracting nails. **2.** the pair or pairs of jointed grasping appendages in lobsters and certain other arthropods. [C14: from Old French *pinceour,* from Old French *pincier* to PINCH]

pinch (pɪntʃ) *vb.* **1.** to press (something, esp. flesh) tightly between two surfaces, esp. between a finger and thumb. **2.** to confine, squeeze, or painfully press (toes, fingers, etc.) because of lack of space: *these shoes pinch.* **3.** (*tr.*) to cause stinging pain to: *the cold pinched his face.* **4.** (*tr.*) to make thin or drawn-looking, as from grief, lack of food, etc. **5.** (usually foll. by *on*) to provide (oneself or another person) with meagre allowances, amounts, etc. **6. pinch pennies.** to live frugally because of meanness or to economize. **7.** (*tr.*) *Nautical.* to sail (a sailing vessel) so close to the wind that her sails begin to luff and she loses way. **8.** (*intr.;* sometimes foll. by *out*) (of a vein of ore) to narrow or peter out. **9.** (usually foll. by *off, out,* or *back*) to remove the tips of (buds, shoots, etc.) to correct or encourage growth. **10.** (*tr.*) *Informal.* to steal or take without asking. **11.** (*tr.*) *Informal.* to arrest. ~*n.* **12.** a squeeze or sustained nip. **13.** the quantity of a substance, such as salt, that can be taken between a thumb and finger. **14.** a very small quantity. **15.** (usually preceded by *the*) sharp, painful, or extreme stress, need, etc.: *the pinch of poverty.* **16.** See **pinch bar. 17.** *Slang.* a robbery. **18.** *Slang.* a police raid or arrest. **19. at a pinch.** if absolutely necessary. **20. with a pinch** *or* **grain of salt.** without wholly believing. [C16: probably from Old Norman French *pinchier* (unattested); related to Old French *pincier* to pinch; compare Late Latin *punctiāre* to prick]

pinch bar *n.* a crowbar with a lug formed on it to provide a fulcrum.

pinch·beck ('pɪntʃ,bɛk) *n.* **1.** an alloy of copper and zinc, used as imitation gold. **2.** a spurious or cheap imitation; sham. ~*adj.* **3.** made of pinchbeck. **4.** sham, spurious, or cheap. [C18 (the alloy), C19 (something spurious): after Christopher *Pinchbeck* (?1670–1732), English watchmaker who invented it]

pinch·cock ('pɪntʃ,kɒk) *n.* a clamp used to compress a flexible tube to control the flow of fluid through it.

pinch ef·fect *n.* the constriction of a beam of charged particles, caused by a force on each particle due to its motion in the magnetic field generated by the movement of the other particles.

pinch-hit *vb.* **-hits, -hit·ting, -hit.** (*intr.*) **1.** *Baseball.* to bat as a substitute for the scheduled batter. **2.** *U.S. informal.* to act as a substitute. —**pinch hit·ter** *n.*

pinch·pen·ny ('pɪntʃ,pɛnɪ) *adj.* **1.** niggardly; miserly. ~*n., pl.* **·nies. 2.** a miserly person; niggard.

Pinck·ney ('pɪŋknɪ) *n.* **1. Charles Cotes·worth.** 1746–1825, U.S. statesman, who was a member of the convention that framed the U.S. Constitution (1787). **2.** his brother, **Thom·as.** 1750–1828, U.S. soldier and politician. He was U.S. minister to Britain (1792–96) and special envoy to Spain (1795–96).

pin curl *n.* a small section of hair wound in a circle and secured with a hairpin to set it in a curl.

pin+cush·ion ('pɪnˌkʊʃən) *n.* a small well-padded cushion in which pins are stuck ready for use.

Pin·dar ('pɪndə) *n.* ?518–?438 B.C., Greek lyric poet, noted for his *Epinikia,* odes commemorating victories in the Greek games.

Pin+dar+ic (pɪn'dærɪk) *adj.* **1.** of, relating to, or resembling the style of Pindar. **2.** *Prosody.* having a complex metrical structure, either regular or irregular. ~*n.* **3.** See **Pindaric ode.**

Pin+dar+ic ode *n.* a form of ode associated with Pindar consisting of a triple unit or groups of triple units, with a strophe and an antistrophe of identical structure followed by an epode of a different structure. Often shortened to **Pindaric.**

pind+ling ('pɪndlɪŋ) *adj.* *Dialect.* **1.** *Western Brit.* peevish or fractious. **2.** *U.S.* sickly or puny. [C19: perhaps changed from *spindling*]

pin down *vb.* (*tr., adv.*) **1.** to force (someone) to make a decision or carry out a promise. **2.** to define clearly: *he had a vague suspicion that he couldn't quite pin down.* **3.** to confine to a place: *the fallen tree pinned him down.*

Pin+dus ('pɪndəs) *pl. n.* a mountain range in central Greece between Epirus and Thessaly. Highest peak: Mount Smólikas, 2633 m (8639 ft.). Modern Greek name: **Pín+dhos** ('pinðɔs).

pine[1] (paɪn) *n.* **1.** any evergreen resinous coniferous tree of the genus *Pinus,* of the N hemisphere, with long needle-shaped leaves and brown cones: family *Pinaceae.* See also **longleaf pine, nut pine, pitch pine, Scots pine. 2.** any other tree or shrub of the family *Pinaceae.* **3.** the wood of any of these trees. **4.** any of various similar but unrelated plants, such as ground pine and screw pine. [Old English *pīn,* from Latin *pīnus* pine]

pine[2] (paɪn) *vb.* **1.** (*intr.;* often foll. by *for* or an infinitive) to feel great longing or desire; yearn. **2.** (*intr.;* often foll. by *away*) to become ill, feeble, or thin through worry, longing, etc. **3.** (*tr.*) *Archaic.* to mourn or grieve for. ~*n.* **4.** *Archaic.* a deep longing. [Old English *pīnian* to torture, from *pīn* pain, from Medieval Latin *pēna,* from Latin *poena* PAIN]

pin+e·al ('pɪnɪəl, paɪ'ni:əl) *adj.* **1.** resembling a pine cone. **2.** of or relating to the pineal gland. [C17: via French from Latin *pīnea* pine cone]

pin+e·al eye *n.* an outgrowth of the pineal gland that forms an eyelike structure on the top of the head in certain cold-blooded vertebrates.

pin+e·al gland *or* **bod·y** *n.* a pea-sized organ in the brain, situated beneath the posterior part of the corpus callosum, that secretes melatonin into the blood stream. Technical names: **epiphysis, epiphysis cerebri.**

pine+ap·ple ('paɪnˌæpᵊl) *n.* **1.** a tropical American bromeliaceous plant, *Ananas comosus,* cultivated in the tropics for its large fleshy edible fruit. **2.** the fruit of this plant, consisting of an inflorescence clustered around a fleshy axis and surmounted by a tuft of leaves. **3.** *Military slang.* a hand grenade. [C14 *pinappel* pine cone; C17: applied to the fruit because of its appearance]

pine+ap·ple weed *n.* an Asian plant, *Matricaria matricarioides,* naturalized in Europe and North America, having greenish-yellow flower heads, and smelling of pineapple when crushed: family *Compositae* (composites).

pine cone *n.* the seed-producing structure of a pine tree. See **cone** (sense 3a).

pine end *n.* *Brit. dialect.* the gable or gable end of a building.

pine mar+ten *n.* a marten, *Martes martes,* of N European and Asian coniferous woods, having dark brown fur with a creamy-yellow patch on the throat.

pi+nene ('paɪni:n) *n.* either of two isomeric terpenes, found in many essential oils and constituting the main part of oil of turpentine. The commonest structural isomer (**α-pinene**) is used in the manufacture of camphor, solvents, plastics, and insecticides. Formula: $C_{10}H_{16}$. [C20: from PINE[1] + -ENE]

pine nee+dle *n.* any of the fine pointed leaves of a pine.

Pi·ne·ro (pɪ'nɪərəʊ) *n.* Sir **Ar·thur Wing.** 1855–1934, English dramatist. His works include the farce *Dandy Dick* (1887) and the problem play *The Second Mrs. Tanqueray* (1893).

pi+ner·y ('paɪnərɪ) *n., pl.* **+ner·ies. 1.** a place, esp. a hothouse, where pineapples are grown. **2.** a forest of pine trees, esp. one cultivated for timber.

Pines *n.* **Isle of.** an island in the NW Caribbean, south of Cuba: administratively part of Cuba since 1925. Chief town: Nueva Gerona. Pop.: 30 103 (1970). Area: 3061 sq. km (1182 sq. miles). Spanish name: **Isla de Pinos.**

pine tar *n.* a brown or black semisolid or viscous substance, produced by the destructive distillation of pine wood, used in roofing compositions, paints, medicines, etc.

pi+ne·tum (paɪ'ni:təm) *n., pl.* **·ta** (-tə). an area of land where pine trees and other conifers are grown. [C19: from Latin, from *pīnus* PINE[1]]

pin+fall ('pɪnˌfɔ:l) *n.* *Wrestling.* another name for **fall** (sense 48).

pin+feath·er ('pɪnˌfɛðə) *n.* *Ornithol.* a feather emerging from the skin and still enclosed in its horny sheath.

pin+fish ('pɪnˌfɪʃ) *n., pl.* **+fish** *or* **+fish·es.** a small porgy, *Lagodon rhomboides,* occurring off the SE North American coast of the Atlantic. Also called: **sailor's choice.**

pin+fold ('pɪnˌfəʊld) *n.* **1. a.** a pound for stray cattle. **b.** a fold or pen for sheep or cattle. ~*vb.* **2.** (*tr.*) to gather or confine in or as if in a pinfold. [Old English *pundfald,* from POUND[3] + FOLD[2]]

ping (pɪŋ) *n.* **1.** a short high-pitched resonant sound, as of a bullet striking metal or a sonar echo. ~*vb.* **2.** (*intr.*) to make such a noise. [C19: of imitative origin] —**'ping+er** *n.*

pin+go ('pɪŋgəʊ) *n., pl.* **+gos.** a mound of earth or gravel formed through pressure from a layer of water trapped between newly frozen ice and underlying permafrost in Arctic regions. [C20: from Eskimo]

Ping-Pong ('pɪŋˌpɒŋ) *n.* *Trademark.* another name for **table tennis.** Also called: **ping pong.**

pin+guid ('pɪŋgwɪd) *adj.* fatty, oily, or greasy; soapy. [C17: from Latin *pinguis* fat, rich] —**pin+'guid+i·ty** *n.*

pin+head ('pɪnˌhɛd) *n.* **1.** the head of a pin. **2.** something very small. **3.** *Slang.* a stupid or contemptible person.

pin+head+ed ('pɪnˌhɛdɪd) *adj.* stupid or silly. —**'pin+ˌhead+ed+ness** *n.*

pin+hole ('pɪnˌhəʊl) *n.* **1.** a small hole made with or as if with a pin. **2.** *Archery.* the exact centre of an archery target, in the middle of the Gold zone.

pin+hole cam+er+a *n.* a camera with a pinhole as an aperture instead of a lens.

pin+ion[1] ('pɪnjən) *n.* **1.** *Chiefly poetic.* a bird's wing. **2.** the part of a bird's wing including the flight feathers. ~*vb.* (*tr.*) **3.** to hold or bind (the arms) of (a person) so as to restrain or immobilize him. **4.** to confine or shackle. **5.** to make (a bird) incapable of flight by removing that part of (the wing) from which the flight feathers grow. [C15: from Old French *pignon* wing, from Latin *pinna* wing]

pin+ion[2] ('pɪnjən) *n.* a cogwheel that engages with a larger wheel or rack, which it drives or by which it is driven. [C17: from French *pignon* cogwheel, from Old French *peigne* comb, from Latin *pecten* comb; see PECTEN]

Pi+niós (pi'njɔs) *n.* transliteration of the Modern Greek name for the **Salambria.**

pin+ite ('pɪnaɪt, 'paɪ-) *n.* a greyish-green or brown mineral containing amorphous aluminium and potassium sulphates. [C19: from German *Pinit,* named after the *Pini* mine, Schneeberg, Saxony]

pink[1] (pɪŋk) *n.* **1.** any of a group of colours with a reddish hue that are of low to moderate saturation and can usually reflect or transmit a large amount of light; a pale reddish tint. **2.** pink cloth or clothing: *dressed in pink.* **3.** any of various Old World plants of the caryophyllaceous genus *Dianthus,* such as *D. plumarius* (**garden pink**), cultivated for their fragrant flowers. See also **carnation** (sense 1). **4.** any of various plants of other genera, such as the moss pink. **5.** the flower of any of these plants. **6.** the highest or best degree, condition, etc. (esp. in the phrases **in the pink of health, in the pink**). **7. a.** a huntsman's scarlet coat. **b.** a huntsman who wears a scarlet coat. ~*adj.* **8.** of the colour pink. **9.** *Brit. informal.* left wing. **10.** *U.S. derogatory.* **a.** sympathetic to or influenced by Communism. **b.** leftist or radical, esp. half-heartedly. **11.** (of a huntsman's coat) scarlet or red. ~*vb.* **12.** (*intr.*) another word for **knock** (sense 7). [C16 (the flower), C18 (the colour): perhaps a shortening of PINKEYE] —**'pink+ish** *adj.* —**'pink+ness** *n.* —**'pink·y** *adj.*

pink[2] (pɪŋk) *vb.* (*tr.*) **1.** to prick lightly with a sword, etc. **2.** to decorate (leather, cloth, etc.) with a perforated or punched pattern. **3.** to cut with pinking shears. [C14: perhaps of Low German origin; compare Low German *pinken* to peck]

pink[3] (pɪŋk) *n.* a sailing vessel with a narrow overhanging transom. [C15: from Middle Dutch *pinke,* of obscure origin]

pink el·e+phant *n.* (*often pl.*) a facetious name applied to hallucinations caused by drunkenness.

Pink·er·ton ('pɪŋkətən) *n.* **Al·lan.** 1819–84, U.S. private detective, born in Scotland. He founded the first detective agency in the U.S. (1850).

pink+eye ('pɪŋkˌaɪ) *n.* **1.** Also called: **acute conjunctivitis.** an acute contagious inflammation of the conjunctiva of the eye, characterized by redness, discharge, etc.: usually caused by bacterial infection. **2.** Also called: **infectious keratitis.** a similar condition affecting the cornea of horses and cattle. [C16: partial translation of obsolete Dutch *pinck oogen* small eyes]

pink-eye ('pɪŋkˌaɪ) or **pink-hi** *n.* *Austral.* a holiday or celebration, esp. among Aboriginals. [C20: from a native Australian language]

Pink Floyd (flɔɪd) *n.* English rock group (formed 1966): comprising Dave Gilmour (born 1944; lead guitar and vocals; replaced Syd Barrett, born 1946, in 1968), Rick Wright (born 1945; keyboards), Roger Waters (born 1944; bass guitar), and Nick Mason (born 1945; drums). Their albums include *A Saucerful of Secrets* (1968), *Atom Heart Mother* (1970), *Dark Side of the Moon* (1973), and *Animals* (1977).

pink gin *n.* a mixture of gin and bitters.

pink·ie *or* **pink·y** ('pɪŋkɪ) *n., pl.* **·ies.** *U.S., Scot.* the little finger. [C19: from Dutch *pinkje,* diminutive of *pink;* compare PINKEYE]

pink+ing shears *pl. n.* scissors with a serrated edge on one or both blades, producing a wavy edge to material cut, thus preventing fraying.

pink·o ('pɪŋkəʊ) *n., pl.* **·os** *or* **·oes.** *U.S. derogatory.* a person regarded as mildly left wing.

pink+root ('pɪŋkˌru:t) *n.* **1.** any of several loganiaceous plants of the genus *Spigelia,* esp. *S. marilandica,* of the southeastern U.S., having red-and-yellow flowers and pink roots. **2.** the powdered root of this plant, used as a vermifuge. **3.** a fungal disease of onions and related plants resulting in stunted growth and shrivelled pink roots.

pink sal·mon *n.* **1.** any salmon having pale pink flesh, esp. *Oncorhynchus gorbuscha,* of the Pacific Ocean. **2.** the flesh of such a fish.
pink slip *n. U.S. informal.* a notice of redundancy issued to an employee.
Pink·ster *or* **Pinx·ter** ('pɪŋkstə) *n. U.S.* a dialect word for **Whit Sunday** or **Whitsuntide.** [C19: from Dutch, from an unattested West Germanic word ultimately derived from Greek *pentēkostē* PENTECOST]
pin mon·ey *n.* **1.** an allowance by a husband to his wife for personal expenditure. **2.** money saved or earned to be used for incidental expenses.
pin·na ('pɪnə) *n., pl.* **·nae** (-ni:) *or* **·nas. 1.** any leaflet of a pinnate compound leaf. **2.** *Zoology.* a feather, wing, fin, or similarly shaped part. **3.** another name for **auricle** (sense 2). [C18: via New Latin from Latin: wing, feather, fin]
pin·nace ('pɪnɪs) *n.* any of various kinds of ship's tender. [C16: from French *pinace,* apparently from Old Spanish *pinaza,* literally: something made of pine, ultimately from Latin *pīnus* pine]
pin·na·cle ('pɪnək^əl) *n.* **1.** the highest point or level, esp. of fame, success, etc. **2.** a towering peak, as of a mountain. **3.** a slender upright structure in the form of a cone, pyramid, or spire on the top of a buttress, gable, or tower. ~*vb.* (*tr.*) **4.** to set on or as if on a pinnacle. **5.** to furnish with a pinnacle or pinnacles. **6.** to crown with a pinnacle. [C14: via Old French from Late Latin *pinnāculum* a peak, from Latin *pinna* wing]
pin·nate ('pɪneɪt, 'pɪnɪt) *or* **pin·nat·ed** *adj.* **1.** like a feather in appearance. **2.** (of compound leaves) having the leaflets growing opposite each other in pairs on either side of the stem. [C18: from Latin *pinnātus,* from *pinna* feather] —'**pin·nate·ly** *adv.* —**pin'na·tion** *n.*
pin·nat·i- *combining form.* pinnate or pinnately: *pinnatifid.*
pin·nat·i·fid (pɪ'nætɪfɪd) *adj.* (of leaves) pinnately divided into lobes reaching more than half way to the midrib. —**pin'nat·i·fid·ly** *adv.*
pin·nat·i·par·tite (pɪˌnætɪ'pɑ:taɪt) *adj.* (of leaves) pinnately divided into lobes reaching just over half way to the midrib.
pin·nat·i·ped (pɪ'nætɪˌpɛd) *adj.* (of birds) having lobate feet.
pin·nat·i·sect (pɪ'nætɪˌsɛkt) *adj.* (of leaves) pinnately divided almost to the midrib but not into separate leaflets.
pin·ner ('pɪnə) *n.* **1.** a person or thing that pins. **2.** a small dainty apron. **3.** a cap with two long flaps pinned on.
pin·ni·ped ('pɪnɪˌpɛd) *or* **pin·ni·pe·di·an** (ˌpɪnɪ'pi:dɪən) *adj.* **1.** of, relating to, or belonging to the *Pinnipedia,* an order of aquatic placental mammals having a streamlined body and limbs specialized as flippers: includes seals, sea lions, and the walrus. ~*n.* **2.** any pinniped animal. ~Compare **fissiped.** [C19: from New Latin *pinnipēs,* from Latin *pinna* feather, fin + *pēs* foot]
pin·nule ('pɪnju:l) *or* **pin·nu·la** ('pɪnjʊlə) *n., pl.* **pin·nules** *or* **pin·nu·lae** ('pɪnjʊˌli:). **1.** any of the lobes of a leaflet of a pinnate compound leaf, which is itself pinnately divided. **2.** *Zoology.* any feather-like part, such as any of the arms of a sea lily. [C16: from Latin *pinnula* diminutive of *pinna* feather] —'**pin·nu·lar** *adj.*
pin·ny ('pɪnɪ) *n., pl.* **·nies.** a child's or informal name for **pinafore.**
Pi·no·chet (U·gar·te) ('pi:nəˌʃeɪ) *n.* **Au·gus·to** (aʊ'gusto). born 1915, Chilean general and statesman; president of Chile since 1974, following his overthrow of Allende (1973).
pi·noch·le, pe·nuch·le, *or* **pi·noc·le** ('pi:nʌk^əl) *n.* **1.** a card game for two to four players similar to bezique. **2.** the combination of queen of spades and jack of diamonds in this game. [C19: of unknown origin]
pi·no·le (pɪ'nəʊlɪ) *n.* (in the southwestern United States) flour made of parched ground corn, mesquite beans, sugar, etc. [from American Spanish, from Nahuatl]
pin·point ('pɪnˌpɔɪnt) *vb.* (*tr.*) **1.** to locate or identify exactly: *to pinpoint a problem; to pinpoint a place on a map.* ~*n.* **2.** an insignificant or trifling thing. **3.** the point of a pin. **4.** (*modifier*) exact: *a pinpoint aim.*
pin·prick ('pɪnˌprɪk) *n.* **1.** a slight puncture made by or as if by a pin. **2.** a small irritation. ~*vb.* **3.** (*tr.*) to puncture with or as if with a pin.
pin rail *n. Nautical.* a strong wooden rail or bar containing holes for belaying pins to which lines are fastened on sailing vessels. Compare **fife rail.**
pins and nee·dles *n. Informal.* **1.** a tingling sensation in the fingers, toes, legs, etc., caused by the return of normal blood circulation after its temporary impairment. **2. on pins and needles.** in a state of anxious suspense or nervous anticipation.
Pinsk (*Russian* pinsk) *n.* a city in the W Soviet Union, in the SW Byelorussian SSR: capital of a principality (13th–14th centuries). Pop.: 61 752 (1970).
pin·stripe ('pɪnˌstraɪp) *n.* (in textiles) a very narrow stripe in fabric or the fabric itself, used esp. for men's suits.
pint (paɪnt) *n.* **1.** a unit of liquid measure of capacity equal to one eighth of a gallon. 1 Brit. pint is equal to 0.568 litre, 1 U.S. pint to 0.473 litre. **2.** a unit of dry measure of capacity equal to one half of a quart. 1 U.S. dry pint is equal to one sixtyfourth of a U.S. bushel or 0.5506 litre. **3.** a measure having such a capacity. **4.** *Brit. informal.* **a.** a pint of beer. **b.** a drink of beer: *he's gone out for a pint.* [C14: from Old French *pinte,* of uncertain origin; perhaps from Medieval Latin *pincta* marks used in measuring liquids, ultimately from Latin *pingere* to paint; compare Middle Low German, Middle Dutch *pinte*]
pin·ta[1] ('pɪntə) *n.* a tropical infectious skin disease caused by the bacterium *Treponema carateum* and characterized by the formation of papules and loss of pigmentation in circumscribed areas. Also called: **mal de pinto.** [C19: from American Spanish, from Spanish: spot, ultimately from Latin *pictus* painted, from *pingere* to paint]
pint·a[2] ('paɪntə) *n.* an informal word for **pint,** esp. of milk or beer. [C20: phonetic rendering of *pint of*]
Pin·ta ('pɪntə) *n.* **the.** one of the three ships commanded by Columbus on his first voyage to America (1492).
pin·ta·de·ra (ˌpɪntə'dɛərə) *n.* a decorative stamp, usually made of clay, found in the Neolithic of the E Mediterranean and in many American cultures. [from Spanish, literally: an instrument for making decorations on bread, from *pintado* mottled, from *pintar* to PAINT]
pin·tail ('pɪnˌteɪl) *n., pl.* **·tails** *or* **·tail.** a greyish-brown duck, *Anas acuta,* with slender pointed wings and a pointed tail.
Pin·ter ('pɪntə) *n.* **Har·old.** born 1930, English dramatist. His plays, such as *The Caretaker* (1960), *The Homecoming* (1965), and *Landscape* (1968), are noted for their equivocal and halting dialogue.
pin·tle ('pɪnt^əl) *n.* **1.** a pin or bolt forming the pivot of a hinge. **2.** the link bolt, hook, or pin on a vehicle's towing bracket. **3.** the needle or plunger of the injection valve of an oil engine. [Old English *pintel* penis]
pin·to ('pɪntəʊ) *U.S.* ~*adj.* **1.** marked with patches of white; piebald. ~*n., pl.* **·tos. 2.** a pinto horse. [C19: from American Spanish (originally: painted, spotted), ultimately from Latin *pingere* to paint]
pin·to bean *n.* a variety of kidney bean that has mottled seeds and is grown for fodder in the southwestern U.S.
pint-size *or* **pint-sized** *adj. Informal.* very small; tiny.
Pin·tu·ric·chio (*Italian* ˌpintu'rikkjo) *or* **Pin·to·ric·chio** (*Italian* ˌpinto'rikkjo) *n.* real name *Bernardino di Betto.* ?1454–1513, Italian painter of the Umbrian school.
pin-up *n.* **1.** *Informal.* **a.** a picture of a sexually attractive girl, esp. when partially or totally undressed. **b.** (*as modifier*): *a pin-up magazine.* **2.** *Slang.* a girl who has appeared in such a picture. **3.** a photograph of a famous personality. **4.** (*modifier*) *U.S.* designed to be hung from a wall: *a pin-up lamp.*
pin·wheel ('pɪnˌwi:l) *n.* **1.** another name for **Catherine wheel** (sense 1). **2.** a cogwheel whose teeth are formed by small pins projecting either axially or radially from the rim of the wheel. **3.** the U.S. name for **windmill** (the toy).
pin·work ('pɪnˌwɜ:k) *n.* (in needlepoint lace) the fine raised stitches.
pin·worm ('pɪnˌwɜ:m) *n.* a parasitic nematode worm, *Enterobius vermicularis,* infecting the colon, rectum, and anus of humans: family *Oxyuridae.* Also called: **threadworm.**
pin wrench *n.* a wrench fitted with a cylindrical pin that registers in a hole in the part to be rotated, used to improve the application of the turning moment.
pinx·it *Latin.* ('pɪŋksɪt) *n.* he (or she) painted it: an inscription sometimes found on paintings following the artist's name.
pin·y *or* **pine·y** ('paɪnɪ) *adj.* **pin·i·er, pin·i·est.** of, resembling, or covered with pine trees.
Pin·zón (*Spanish* pin'θon) *n.* **1. Mar·tín A·lon·zo** (mar'tin a'lonθo). ?1440–93, Spanish navigator, who commanded the *Pinta* on Columbus' first expedition (1492–93), which he abandoned in a vain attempt to be the first to arrive back in Spain. **2.** his brother, **Vi·cen·te Yá·ñez** (bi'θente 'jaɲeθ). ?1460–?1524, Spanish navigator, who commanded the *Niña* on Columbus' first expedition (1492–93).
pio·let (pjəʊ'leɪ) *n.* a type of iceaxe.
pi·on ('paɪɒn) *or* **pi me·son** *n. Physics.* a meson having a positive or negative charge and a rest mass 273 times that of the electron, or no charge and a rest mass 264 times that of the electron.
pi·o·neer (ˌpaɪə'nɪə) *n.* **1. a.** a colonist, explorer, or settler of a new land, region, etc. **b.** (*as modifier*): *a pioneer wagon.* **2.** an innovator or developer of something new. **3.** *Military.* a member of an infantry group that digs entrenchments, makes roads, etc. **4.** *Ecology.* the first species of plant or animal to colonize an area of bare ground. ~*vb.* **5.** to be a pioneer (in or of something). **6.** (*tr.*) to initiate, prepare, or open up: *to pioneer a medical programme.* [C16: from Old French *paonier* infantryman, from *paon* PAWN[2]; see also PEON[1]]
pi·ous ('paɪəs) *adj.* **1.** having or expressing reverence for a god or gods; religious; devout. **2.** marked by reverence. **3.** marked by false reverence; sanctimonious. **4.** sacred; not secular. **5.** *Archaic.* having or expressing devotion for one's parents or others. [C17: from Latin *pius,* related to *piāre* to expiate] —'**pi·ous·ly** *adv.* —'**pi·ous·ness** *n.*
pip[1] (pɪp) *n.* **1.** the seed of a fleshy fruit, such as an apple or pear. **2.** any of the segments marking the surface of a pineapple. **3.** a rootstock or flower of the lily of the valley or certain other plants. [C18: short for PIPPIN]
pip[2] (pɪp) *n.* **1.** a short high-pitched sound, a sequence of which can act as a time signal, esp. on radio. **2.** a radar blip. **3. a.** a spot or single device, such as a spade, diamond, heart, or club on a playing card. **b.** any of the spots on dice or dominoes. **4.** *Informal.* the emblem worn on the shoulder by junior officers in the British Army, indicating their rank. ~*vb.* **pips, pip·ping, pipped. 5.** (of a young bird) **a.** (*intr.*) to chirp; peep. **b.** to pierce (the shell of its egg) while hatching. **6.** (*intr.*) to make a short high-pitched sound. [C16 (in the sense: spot or speck); C17 (vb.); C20 (in the sense: short high-pitched sound): of obscure, probably imitative origin; senses 1 and 5 are probably related to PEEP[2]]
pip[3] (pɪp) *n.* **1.** a contagious disease of poultry characterized by the secretion of thick mucus in the mouth and throat. **2.**

Facetious slang. a minor human ailment. **3.** *Brit. slang.* a bad temper or depression (esp. in the expression **give (someone) the pip**). ~*vb.* **pips, pip+ping, pipped. 4.** *Brit. slang.* to be or cause to be annoyed or depressed. [C15: from Middle Dutch *pippe*, ultimately from Latin *pituita* phlegm; see PITUITARY]

pip[4] (pɪp) *vb.* **pips, pip+ping, pipped.** (*tr.*) *Brit. slang.* **1.** to wound or kill, esp. with a gun. **2.** to defeat (a person), esp. when his success seems certain (often in the phrase **pip at the post**). **3.** to blackball or ostracize. [C19 (originally in the sense: to blackball): probably from PIP[2]]

pi·pa (ˈpiːpə) *n.* a tongueless South American toad, *Pipa pipa*, that carries its young in pits in the skin of its back. [C18: from Surinam dialect, probably of African origin]

pip+age (ˈpaɪpɪdʒ) *n.* **1.** pipes collectively. **2.** conveyance by pipes. **3.** the money charged for such conveyance.

pi+pal (ˈpaɪpᵊl) *n.* a variant spelling of **peepul.**

pipe[1] (paɪp) *n.* **1.** a long tube of metal, plastic, etc. used to convey water, oil, gas, etc. **2.** a long tube or case. **3. a.** an object made in various shapes and sizes, consisting of a small bowl with an attached tubular stem, in which tobacco or other substances are smoked. **b.** (*as modifier*): *a pipe bowl.* **4.** Also called: **pipe+ful.** the amount of tobacco that fills the bowl of a pipe. **5.** *Zoology, botany.* any of various hollow organs, such as the respiratory passage of certain animals. **6. a.** any musical instrument whose sound production results from the vibration of an air column in a simple tube. **b.** any of the tubular devices on an organ, in which air is made to vibrate either directly, as in a flue pipe, or by means of a reed. **7.** an obsolete three-holed wind instrument, held in the left hand while played and accompanied by the tabor. See **tabor. 8. the pipes.** See **bagpipes. 9.** a shrill voice or sound, as of a bird. **10. a.** a boatswain's pipe. **b.** the sound it makes. **11.** (*pl.*) *Informal.* the respiratory tract or vocal cords. **12.** *Metallurgy.* a conical hole in the head of an ingot, made by escaping gas as the metal cools. **13.** a cylindrical vein of rich ore, such as one of the vertical diamond-bearing veins at Kimberley, South Africa. **14.** Also called: **volcanic pipe.** a vertical cylindrical passage in a volcano through which molten lava is forced during eruption. **15.** *U.S. slang.* something easy to do, esp. a simple course in college. **16. put that in your pipe and smoke it.** *Informal.* accept that fact if you can. ~*vb.* **17.** to play (music) on a pipe. **18.** (*tr.*) to summon or lead by a pipe: *to pipe the dancers.* **19.** to utter (something) shrilly. **20. a.** to signal orders to (the crew) by a boatswain's pipe. **b.** (*tr.*) to signal the arrival or departure of: *to pipe the admiral aboard.* **21.** (*tr.*) to convey (water, gas, etc.) by a pipe or pipes. **22.** (*tr.*) to provide with pipes. **23.** (*tr.*) to trim (an article, esp. of clothing) with piping. ~See also **pipe down, pipe up.** [Old English *pīpe* (n.), *pīpian* (vb.), ultimately from Latin *pīpāre* to chirp] —**ˈpipe+less** *adj.* —**ˈpip·y** *adj.*

pipe[2] (paɪp) *n.* **1.** a large cask for wine, oil, etc. **2.** a measure of capacity for wine equal to four barrels. 1 pipe is equal to 126 U.S. gallons or 105 Brit. gallons. **3.** a cask holding this quantity with its contents. [C14: via Old French (in the sense: tube), ultimately from Latin *pīpāre* to chirp; compare PIPE[1]]

pipe+clay (ˈpaɪpˌkleɪ) *n.* **1.** a fine white pure clay, used in the manufacture of tobacco pipes and pottery and for whitening leather and similar materials. ~*vb.* **2.** (*tr.*) to whiten with pipeclay.

pipe clean+er *n.* a short length of thin wires twisted so as to hold tiny tufts of yarn: used to clean the stem of a tobacco pipe.

pipe down *vb.* (*intr., adv.*) *Slang.* to stop talking, making noise, etc.

pipe dream *n.* a fanciful or impossible plan or hope. [alluding to dreams produced by smoking an opium pipe]

pipe+fish (ˈpaɪpˌfɪʃ) *n., pl.* **+fish** *or* **+fish·es.** any of various teleost fishes of the genera *Nerophis, Syngnathus,* etc., having a long tubelike snout and an elongated body covered with bony plates: family *Syngnathidae.* Also called: **needlefish.**

pipe+fit·ting (ˈpaɪpˌfɪtɪŋ) *n.* **1. a.** the act or process of bending, cutting to length, and joining pipes. **b.** the branch of plumbing involving this. **2.** the threaded gland nuts, unions, adapters, etc., used for joining pipes. —**ˈpipe+ˌfit·ter** *n.*

pipe+line (ˈpaɪpˌlaɪn) *n.* **1.** a long pipe, esp. underground, used to transport oil, natural gas, etc., over long distances. **2.** a medium of communication, esp. a private one. **3. in the pipeline.** in the process of being completed, delivered, or produced. ~*vb.* (*tr.*) **4.** to convey by pipeline. **5.** to supply with a pipeline.

pipe maj+or *n.* the chief player in a band of bagpipe players.

pipe or+gan *n.* another name for **organ** (the musical instrument). Compare **reed organ.**

pip+er (ˈpaɪpə) *n.* **1.** a person who plays a pipe or bagpipes. **2. pay the piper and call the tune.** to bear the cost of an undertaking and control it.

pip+e·ra+ceous (ˌpɪpəˈreɪʃəs) *adj.* of, relating to, or belonging to the *Piperaceae,* a family of pungent tropical shrubs and climbing flowering plants: includes pepper, betel, and cubeb. [C17: via New Latin from Latin *piper* PEPPER]

pi+per·a+zine (pɪˈpɛrəˌziːn, -zɪn) *n.* a white crystalline deliquescent heterocyclic nitrogen compound used as an insecticide, corrosion inhibitor, and veterinary anthelmintic. Formula: $C_4H_{10}N_2$.

pi+per·i+dine (pɪˈpɛrɪˌdiːn, -dɪn) *n.* a colourless liquid heterocyclic compound with a peppery ammoniacal odour: used in making rubbers and curing epoxy resins. Formula: $C_5H_{11}N$.

pip+er+ine (ˈpɪpəˌraɪn, -rɪn) *n.* a crystalline insoluble alkaloid that is the active ingredient of pepper, used as a flavouring and as an insecticide. Formula: $C_{17}H_{19}NO_3$. [C19: from Latin *piper* PEPPER]

pip+er·o+nal (ˈpɪpərəʊˌnæl) *n.* a white fragrant aldehyde used in flavourings, perfumery, and suntan lotions. Formula: $C_6H_3O_2$-CH_2CHO. Also called: **heliotropin.**

pipes of Pan *pl. n.* another term for **panpipes.**

pipe+stone (ˈpaɪpˌstəʊn) *n.* a variety of consolidated red clay used by American Indians to make tobacco pipes.

pi+pette (pɪˈpɛt) *n.* **1.** a slender glass tube drawn to a fine bore at one end and usually graduated, for transferring or measuring out known volumes of liquid. ~*vb.* **2.** (*tr.*) to transfer or measure out (a liquid) using a pipette. [C19: via French: little pipe, from *pipe* PIPE[1]]

pipe up *vb.* (*intr., adv.*) **1.** to commence singing or playing a musical instrument: *the band piped up.* **2.** to speak up, esp. in a shrill voice.

pipe+wort (ˈpaɪpˌwɜːt) *n.* a perennial plant, *Eriocaulon septangulare,* of wet places in W Ireland, the Scottish Hebrides, and the eastern U.S., having a twisted flower stalk and a greenish-grey scaly flower head: family *Eriocaulaceae.*

pip+ing (ˈpaɪpɪŋ) *n.* **1.** pipes collectively, esp. pipes formed into a connected system, as in the plumbing of a house. **2.** a cord of icing, whipped cream, etc., often used to decorate desserts and cakes. **3.** a thin strip of covered cord or material, used to edge hems, etc. **4.** the sound of a pipe or a set of bagpipes. **5.** the art or technique of playing a pipe or bagpipes. **6.** a shrill voice or sound, esp. a whistling sound. ~*adj.* **7.** making a shrill sound. **8.** *Archaic.* relating to the pipe (associated with peace), as opposed to martial instruments, such as the fife or trumpet. **9. piping hot.** extremely hot.

pip·i+strelle (ˌpɪpɪˈstrɛl) *n.* any of numerous small brownish insectivorous bats of the genus *Pipistrellus,* occurring in most parts of the world: family *Vespertilionidae.* [C18: via French from Italian *pipistrello,* from Latin *vespertīliō* a bat, from *vesper* evening, because of its nocturnal habits]

pip+it (ˈpɪpɪt) *n.* any of various songbirds of the genus *Anthus* and related genera, having brownish speckled plumage and a long tail: family *Motacillidae.* Also called: **titlark.** [C18: probably of imitative origin]

pip+kin (ˈpɪpkɪn) *n.* **1.** a small metal or earthenware vessel. **2.** another name for **piggin.** [C16: perhaps a diminutive of PIPE[2]; see -KIN]

pip+pin (ˈpɪpɪn) *n.* **1.** any of several varieties of eating apple with a rounded oblate shape. **2.** the seed of any of these fruits. [C13: from Old French *pepin,* of uncertain origin]

pip+sis+se·wa (pɪpˈsɪsəwə) *n.* any of several ericaceous plants of the Asian and American genus *Chimaphila,* having jagged evergreen leaves and white or pinkish flowers. Also called: **wintergreen.** [C19: from Cree *pipisisikweu,* literally: it breaks it into pieces, so called because it was believed to be efficacious in treating bladder stones]

pip+squeak (ˈpɪpˌskwiːk) *n. Informal.* a person or thing that is insignificant or contemptible.

pi+quant (ˈpiːkənt, -kɑːnt) *adj.* **1.** having an agreeably pungent or tart taste. **2.** lively or stimulating to the mind, **3.** *Archaic.* cutting or severe. [C16: from French (literally: prickling), from *piquer* to prick, goad; see PIQUE[1]] —**ˈpi+quan+cy** *or* **ˈpi+quant+ness** *n.* —**ˈpi+quant+ly** *adv.*

pique[1] (piːk) *n.* **1.** a feeling of resentment or irritation, as from having one's pride wounded. ~*vb.* **piques, piqu+ing, piqued.** (*tr.*) **2.** to cause to feel resentment or irritation. **3.** to excite or arouse. **4.** (foll. by *on* or *upon*) to pride or congratulate (oneself). [C16: from French, from *piquer* to prick, sting; see PICK[1]]

pique[2] (piːk) *Piquet.* ~*n.* **1.** a score of 30 points made by a player while his opponent's score is nil. ~*vb.* **2.** to score a pique (against someone). [C17: from French *pic,* of uncertain origin]

pi+qué (ˈpiːkeɪ) *n.* a close-textured fabric of cotton, silk, or spun rayon woven with lengthwise ribs. [C19: from French *piqué* pricked, from *piquer* to prick]

pi+quet (pɪˈkɛt, -ˈkeɪ) *n.* a card game for two people playing with a reduced pack and scoring points for card combinations and tricks won. [C17: from French, of unknown origin; compare PIQUE[2]]

pi+ra+cy (ˈpaɪrəsɪ) *n., pl.* **+cies. 1.** *Brit.* robbery on the seas within admiralty jurisdiction. **2.** a felony, such as robbery or hijacking, committed aboard a ship or aircraft. **3.** the unauthorized use or appropriation of patented or copyrighted material, ideas, etc. [C16: from Anglo-Latin *pirātia,* from Late Greek *peirāteia;* see PIRATE]

Pi+rae+us *or* **Pei+rae+us** (paɪˈriːəs, pɪˈreɪ-) *n.* a port in SE Greece, adjoining Athens: the country's chief port; founded in the 5th century B.C. as the port of Athens. Pop.: 187 458 (1971). Modern Greek name: **Pi+rai+évs** (ˌpirɛˈɛfs).

pi+ra+gua (pɪˈrɑːgwə, -ˈræg-) *n.* another word for **pirogue.** [C17: via Spanish from Carib: dugout canoe]

Pi·ran·del·lo (*Italian* ˌpiranˈdɛllo) *n.* **Lu·i·gi** (luˈiːdʒi). 1867–1936, Italian short-story writer, novelist, and dramatist. His plays include *Right you are* (*If you think so*) (1917), *Six Characters in Search of an Author* (1921), and *Henry IV* (1922): Nobel prize for literature 1934.

Pi·ra·ne·si (*Italian* ˌpiraˈneːsi) *n.* **Giam·bat·tis·ta** (ˌdʒambatˈtista). 1720–78, Italian etcher and architect: etchings include *Imaginary Prisons* and *Views of Rome.*

pi+ra+nha *or* **pi+ra+ña** (pɪˈrɑːnjə) *n.* any of various small freshwater voracious fishes of the genus *Serrasalmus* and related genera, of tropical America, having strong jaws and sharp teeth: family *Characidae* (characins). [C19: via Portuguese from Tupi: fish with teeth, from *pirá* fish + *sainha* tooth]

pi+rate (ˈpaɪrɪt) *n.* **1.** a person who commits piracy. **2. a.** a vessel used by pirates. **b.** (*as modifier*): *a pirate ship.* **3.** a person who uses or appropriates literary, artistic, or other work of someone else illicitly. **4. a.** a person or group of people who broadcast illegally. **b.** (*as modifier*): *a pirate radio station.* ~*vb.* **5.** (*tr.*) to use, appropriate, or reproduce (artistic work, ideas, etc.) illicitly. [C15: from Latin *pīrāta,* from Greek *peirātēs* one who attacks, from *peira* an attempt, attack] —**pi+rat+ic** (paɪˈrætɪk) *or* **pi+ˈrat·i·cal** *adj.* —**pi+ˈrat·i+cal+ly** *adv.*

Pi·rith·o·üs (paɪˈrɪθəʊəs) *n. Greek myth.* a prince of the Lapiths, who accomplished many great deeds with his friend Theseus.

pirn (pɜːn) *n. Scot.* **1.** a fishing rod or reel. **2.** (in weaving) the spool of a shuttle. [C15: of uncertain origin]

pi+rog (pɪˈrəʊg) *n., pl.* **+ro+gi** (-ˈrəʊgɪ). a large pie filled with meat, vegetables etc. [from Russian: pie]

pi+rogue (pɪˈrəʊg) *or* **pi+ra+gua** *n.* any of various kinds of dugout canoes. [C17: via French from Spanish PIRAGUA]

pir·ou+ette (ˌpɪrʊˈɛt) *n.* **1.** a body spin, esp. in dancing, on the toes or the ball of the foot. ~*vb.* **2.** (*intr.*) to perform a pirouette. [C18: from French, from Old French *pirouet* spinning top; related to Italian *pirolo* little peg]

pi+rozh+ki *or* **pi+rosh+ki** (pɪˈrɒʃkɪ) *pl. n., sing.* **pir·o·zhok** (ˈpɪrəˌʒɒk). small triangular pastries filled with meat, vegetables, etc. [C20: from Russian, diminutive of PIROG]

Pi·sa (ˈpiːzə; *Italian* ˈpiːsa) *n.* a city in NW Italy, in Tuscany near the mouth of the River Arno: flourishing maritime republic (11th–12th centuries), contains a university (1343), a cathedral (1063), and the Leaning Tower (begun in 1174 and about 5 m (17ft.) from perpendicular); tourism. Pop.: 103 412 (1965 est.).

pis al+ler *French.* (pi zaˈle) *n.* a last resort; final expedient. [literally: (at) the worst going]

Pi·sa·nel·lo (*Italian* ˌpisaˈnɛllo) *n.* **An·to·nio** (anˈtɔːnjo). ?1395–?1455, Italian painter and medallist; a major exponent of the International Gothic style. He is best known for his portrait medals and drawings of animals.

Pi·sa·no (*Italian* piˈsaːno) *n.* **1. Gio·van·ni** (dʒoˈvanni). ?1250–?1320, Italian sculptor, who successfully integrated classical and Gothic elements in his sculptures, esp. in his pulpit in St. Andrea, Pistoia. **2.** his father, **Ni·co·la** (niˈkɔːla). ?1220–?84, Italian sculptor, who pioneered the classical style and is often regarded as a precursor of the Italian Renaissance: noted esp. for his pulpit in the baptistery of Pisa Cathedral.

pis+ca+ry (ˈpɪskərɪ) *n., pl.* **+ries. 1.** a place where fishing takes place. **2.** the right to fish in certain waters. [C15: from Latin *piscārius* fishing, from *piscis* a fish]

pis+ca+to+ri·al (ˌpɪskəˈtɔːrɪəl) *or* **pis+ca·to·ry** (ˈpɪskətərɪ, -trɪ) *adj.* **1.** of or relating to fish, fishing, or fishermen. **2.** devoted to fishing. [C19: from Latin *piscātōrius,* from *piscātor* fisherman] —**ˌpis+ca+ˈto+ri+al+ly** *adv.*

Pi+sces (ˈpaɪsiːz, ˈpɪ-) *n.,* Latin genitive **Pi+sci·um** (ˈpaɪsɪəm). **1.** *Astronomy.* a faint extensive zodiacal constellation lying between Aquarius and Aries on the ecliptic. **2.** *Astrology.* **a.** Also called: the **Fishes.** the twelfth sign of the zodiac, symbol ♓, having a mutable water classification and ruled by the planets Jupiter and Neptune. The sun is in this sign between about Feb. 19 and March 20. **b.** a person born when the sun is in this sign. **3. a.** a taxonomic group that comprises all fishes. See **fish** (sense 1). **b.** a taxonomic group that comprises the bony fishes only. See **teleost.** ~*adj.* **4.** *Astrology.* born under or characteristic of Pisces. ~Also (for senses 2b., 4): **Pis+ce·an** (ˈpaɪsɪən). [C14: Latin: the fish (plural)]

pis·ci- *combining form.* fish: *pisciculture.* [from Latin *piscis*]

pis+ci+cul+ture (ˈpɪsɪˌkʌltʃə) *n.* the rearing and breeding of fish under controlled conditions. —**ˌpis+ci+ˈcul+tur+al** *adj.* —**ˌpis+ci+ˈcul+tur+al+ly** *adv.* —**ˌpis+ci+ˈcul+tur+ist** *n., adj.*

pis+ci+na (pɪˈsiːnə) *n., pl.* **+nae** (-niː) *or* **+nas.** *R.C. Church.* a stone basin, with a drain, in a church or sacristy where water used at Mass is poured away. [C16: from Latin: fishpond, from *piscis* a fish] —**pis+ci+nal** (ˈpɪsɪnᵊl) *adj.*

pis+cine (ˈpɪsaɪn) *adj.* of, relating to, or resembling a fish.

Pis+cis Aus+tri+nus (ˈpɪsɪs ɒˈstraɪnəs, ˈpaɪ-) *n., Latin genitive* **Pis+cis Aus+tri+ni** (ɒˈstraɪnaɪ). a small constellation in the S hemisphere lying between Aquarius and Grus and containing the first-magnitude star Fomalhaut. [Latin: the Southern Fish]

pis+civ·o+rous (pɪˈsɪvərəs) *adj.* feeding on fish: *piscivorous birds.*

Pis+gah (ˈpɪzgə) *n.* **Mount.** *Old Testament.* the mountain slopes to the northeast of the Dead Sea, from one of which, Mount Nebo, Moses viewed Canaan.

pish (pʃ, pɪʃ) *interj.* **1.** an exclamation of impatience or contempt. ~*vb.* **2.** to make this exclamation at (someone or something).

pi+shogue (pɪˈʃəʊg) *n. Irish.* sorcery; witchcraft. [from Irish *piseog, pisreog*]

Pish+pek (pɪʃˈpɛk) *n.* the former name (until 1926) of **Frunze.**

pis·i+form (ˈpɪsɪˌfɔːm) *adj.* **1.** *Zoology, botany.* resembling a pea. ~*n.* **2.** a small pea-like bone on the ulnar side of the carpus. [C18: via New Latin from Latin *pīsum* pea + *forma* shape]

Pi·sis·tra·tus (paɪˈsɪstrətəs) *n.* ?600–527 B.C., tyrant of Athens: he established himself in firm control of the city following his defeat of his aristocratic rivals at Pallene (546).

pis+mire (ˈpɪsˌmaɪə) *n.* an archaic or dialect word for an **ant.** [C14 (literally: urinating ant, from the odour of formic acid characteristic of an anthill): from PISS + obsolete *mire* ant, of Scandinavian origin; compare Old Norse *maurr,* Middle Low German *mīre* ant]

pi+so+lite (ˈpaɪsəʊˌlaɪt) *n.* any sedimentary rock consisting of pea-sized concentric formations within a fine matrix. [C18: from New Latin *pisolithus* pea stone, from Greek *pisos* pea + *lithos* -LITE] —**pi+so+lit+ic** (ˌpaɪsəʊˈlɪtɪk) *adj.*

piss (pɪs) *Taboo slang.* ~*vb.* **1.** (*intr.*) to urinate. **2.** (*tr.*) to discharge as or in one's urine: *to piss blood.* ~*n.* **3.** an act of urinating. **4.** urine. **5.** *Austral.* beer. [C13: from Old French *pisser,* probably of imitative origin] —**ˈpiss+er** *n.*

piss a·bout *or* **a·round** *vb.* (*intr., adv.*) *Taboo slang.* to behave in a casual or silly way.

Pis·sar·ro (pɪˈsɑːrəʊ; *French* pisaˈro) *n.* **Ca·mille** (kaˈmij). 1830–1903, French impressionist painter, esp. of landscapes.

piss art+ist *n. Brit. slang.* a person who drinks heavily and gets drunk frequently.

pissed (pɪst) *adj. Brit. taboo slang.* intoxicated; drunk.

piss off *vb.* (*adv.*) *Taboo slang.* **1.** (*tr.; often passive*) to annoy, irritate, or disappoint. **2.** (*intr.*) *Chiefly Brit.* to go away; depart, often used to dismiss a person.

pis+ta+chi·o (pɪˈstɑːʃɪˌəʊ) *n., pl.* **·os. 1.** an anacardiaceous tree, *Pistacia vera,* of the Mediterranean region and W Asia, with small hard-shelled nuts. **2.** Also called: **pistachio nut.** the nut of this tree, having an edible green kernel. **3.** the sweet flavour of the pistachio nut, used in ice creams, etc. ~*adj.* **4.** of a yellowish-green colour. [C16: via Italian and Latin from Greek *pistakion* pistachio nut, from *pistakē* pistachio tree, from Persian *pistah*]

pis+ta+reen (ˌpɪstəˈriːn) *n.* a Spanish coin, used in the U.S. and the West Indies until the 18th century. [C18: perhaps changed from PESETA]

piste (piːst) *n.* **1.** a trail, slope, or course for skiing. **2.** a rectangular area for fencing bouts. [C18: via Old French from Old Italian *pista,* from *pistare* to tread down]

pis+til (ˈpɪstɪl) *n.* the female reproductive part of a flower, consisting of one or more separate or fused carpels; gynoecium. [C18: from Latin *pistillum* PESTLE]

pis+til+late (ˈpɪstɪlɪt, -ˌleɪt) *adj.* (of plants) **1.** having pistils but no anthers. **2.** having or producing pistils.

Pis+to·ia (*Italian* pisˈtoːja) *n.* a city in N Italy, in N Tuscany: scene of the defeat and death of Catiline in 62 B.C. Pop.: 93 263 (1971).

pis+tol (ˈpɪstᵊl) *n.* **1.** a short-barrelled handgun. **2. hold a pistol to a person's head.** to threaten a person in order to force him to do what one wants. ~*vb.* **+tols, +tol+ling, +tolled** *or U.S.* **+tols, +tol+ing, +toled. 3.** (*tr.*) to shoot with a pistol. [C16: from French *pistole,* from German, from Czech *pišťala* pistol, pipe; related to Russian *pischal* shepherd's pipes]

pis+tole (pɪsˈtəʊl) *n.* any of various gold coins of varying value, formerly used in Europe. [C16: from Old French, shortened from *pistolet,* literally: little PISTOL]

pis+to+leer (ˌpɪstəˈlɪə) *n.* a person, esp. a soldier, who is armed with or fires a pistol.

pis+tol grip *n.* **a.** a handle shaped like the butt of a pistol. **b.** (*as modifier*): *a pistol-grip camera.*

pis·tol-whip *vb:* **-whips, -whip·ping, -whipped.** (*tr.*) *U.S.* to beat or strike with a pistol barrel.

pis+ton (ˈpɪstən) *n.* a disc or cylindrical part that slides to and fro in a hollow cylinder. In an internal-combustion engine it is forced to move by the expanding gases in the cylinder head and is attached by a pivoted connecting rod to a crankshaft or flywheel, thus converting reciprocating motion into rotation. [C18: via French from Old Italian *pistone,* from *pistare* to pound, grind, from Latin *pinsere* to crush, beat]

pis+ton ring *n.* a split ring, usually made of cast iron, that fits into a groove on the rim of a piston to provide a spring-loaded seal against the cylinder wall.

pis+ton rod *n.* **1.** the rod that connects the piston of a reciprocating steam engine to the crosshead. **2.** a less common name for a **connecting rod.**

pit[1] (pɪt) *n.* **1.** a large, usually deep opening in the ground. **2. a.** a mine or excavation, esp. for coal. **b.** the shaft in a mine. **c.** (*as modifier*): *pit pony; pit prop.* **3.** a concealed danger or difficulty. **4. the pit.** hell. **5.** Also called: **orchestra pit.** the area that is occupied by the orchestra in a theatre, located in front of the stage. **6.** an enclosure for fighting animals or birds, esp. gamecocks. **7.** *Anatomy.* **a.** a small natural depression on the surface of a body, organ, structure, or part; fossa. **b.** the floor of any natural bodily cavity: *the pit of the stomach.* **8.** *Pathol.* a small indented scar at the site of a former pustule; pockmark. **9.** any of various small areas in a plant cell wall that remain unthickened when the rest of the cell becomes lignified. **10.** a working area at the side of a motor-racing track for servicing or refuelling vehicles. **11.** *U.S.* a section on the floor of a commodity exchange devoted to a special line of trading. **12.** an area of sand or other soft material at the end of a long jump approach, behind the bar of a pole vault, etc., on which an athlete may land safely. **13.** the ground floor of the auditorium of a theatre. **14.** *Brit.* a slang word for **bed** or **bedroom. 15.** another word for **pitfall** (sense 2). **16. dig a pit for.** try to ensnare or trick. ~*vb.* **pits, pit+ting, pit+ted. 17.** (*tr.;* often foll. by *against*) to match in opposition, esp. as antagonists. **18.** to mark or become marked with pits. **19.** (*tr.*) to place or bury in a pit. [Old English *pytt,* from Latin *puteus;* compare Old French *pet,* Old High German *pfuzzi*]

pit[2] (pɪt) *Chiefly U.S.* ~*n.* **1.** the stone of a cherry, plum, etc. ~*vb.* **pits, pit+ting, pit+ted. 2.** (*tr.*) to extract the stone from (a fruit). [C19: from Dutch: kernel; compare PITH]

pit[3] (pɪt) *n.* a rowdy card game in which players bid for commodities.

pi·ta (ˈpiːtə) *n.* **1.** any of several agave plants yielding a strong fibre. See also **istle. 2.** a species of pineapple, *Ananas magdalenae,* the leaves of which yield a white fibre. **3.** Also called: **pita fibre.** the fibre obtained from any of these plants, used in making cordage and paper. [C17: via Spanish from Quechua]

pit·a·pat ('pɪtəˌpæt) *adv.* **1.** with quick light taps or beats. ~*vb.* **+pats, +pat+ting, +pat+ted.** **2.** (*intr.*) to make quick light taps or beats. ~*n.* **3.** such taps or beats.

Pit+cairn Is+land (pɪt'kɛən, 'pɪtkɛən) *n.* an island in the S Pacific: forms with other islands a British colony; uninhabited until the landing in 1790 of the mutineers of H.M.S. *Bounty* and their Tahitian companions. Pop.: 169 (1971 UN est.). Area: 4.6 sq. km (1.75 sq. miles).

pitch[1] (pɪtʃ) *vb.* **1.** to hurl or throw (something); cast; fling. **2.** (*usually tr.*) to set up (a camp, tent, etc.). **3.** (*tr.*) to place or thrust (a stake, etc.) into the ground. **4.** (*intr.*) to move vigorously or irregularly to and fro or up and down. **5.** (*tr.*) to set the level, character, or slope of. **6.** (*intr.*) to slope downwards. **7.** (*intr.*) to fall forwards or downwards. **8.** (*intr.*) (of a vessel) to alternatively dip and raise its bow and stern. **9.** (*tr.*; foll. by *up*) *Cricket.* to bowl (a ball) so that it bounces near the batsman. **10.** (*intr.*) (of a missile, aircraft, etc.) to deviate from a stable flight attitude by movement of the longitudinal axis about the lateral axis. Compare **yaw, roll** (sense 14). **11.** (*tr.*) (in golf, etc.) to hit (a ball) steeply into the air, esp. with backspin to minimize roll. **12.** (*tr.*) *Music.* **a.** to sing or play accurately (a note, interval, etc.). **b.** (*usually passive*) (of a wind instrument) to specify or indicate its basic key or harmonic series by its size, manufacture, etc. **13.** (*tr.*) *Cards.* to lead (a suit) and so determine trumps for that trick. **14.** *Southwest English dialect.* (used with *it* as subject) to snow without the settled snow melting. **15. in there pitching.** *U.S. informal.* taking part with enthusiasm. **16. pitch a tale** (*or* **yarn**). to tell a story, usually of a fantastic nature. ~*n.* **17.** the degree of elevation or depression. **18. a.** the angle of descent of a downward slope. **b.** such a slope. **19.** the extreme height or depth. **20.** a section of a route up a slope between two belay points. **21.** the degree of slope of a roof, esp. when expressed as a ratio of height to span. **22.** the distance between corresponding points on adjacent members of a body of regular form, esp. the distance between teeth on a gearwheel or between threads on a screw thread. **23.** the distance between regularly spaced objects such as rivets, bolts, etc. **24.** the pitching motion of a ship, missile, etc. **25. a.** the distance a propeller advances in one revolution, assuming no slip. **b.** the blade angle of a propeller or rotor. **26.** *Music.* **a.** the auditory property of a note that is conditioned by its frequency relative to other notes: *high pitch; low pitch.* **b.** an absolute frequency assigned to a specific note, fixing the relative frequencies of all other notes. The fundamental frequencies of the notes A–G, in accordance with the frequency A = 440 hertz, were internationally standardized and accepted in 1939. See also **concert pitch** (sense 1), **international pitch.** **27.** *Cricket.* the rectangular area between the stumps, 22 yards long and 10 feet wide; the wicket. **28.** *Geology.* the inclination of the axis of an anticline or syncline or of a stratum or vein from the horizontal. **29.** another name for **seven-up.** **30.** the act or manner of pitching a ball, as in cricket, etc. See also **full pitch.** **31.** *Chiefly Brit.* a vendor's station, esp. on a pavement. **32.** *Slang.* a persuasive sales talk, esp. one routinely repeated. **33.** *Chiefly Brit.* (in many sports) the field of play. **34.** Also called: **pitch shot.** *Golf.* an approach shot in which the ball is struck in a high arc. **35. make a pitch for.** *U.S. slang.* **a.** to give verbal support to. **b.** to attempt to attract someone sexually or romantically. **36. queer someone's pitch.** *Brit. informal.* to upset the plans of another. ~See also **pitch in, pitch into, pitch on.** [C13 *picchen;* possibly related to PICK[1]]

pitch[2] (pɪtʃ) *n.* **1.** any of various heavy dark viscid substances obtained as a residue from the distillation of tars. See also **coal-tar pitch.** **2.** any of various similar substances, such as asphalt, occurring as natural deposits. **3.** any of various similar substances obtained by distilling certain organic substances so that they are incompletely carbonized. **4.** crude turpentine obtained as sap from pine trees. ~*vb.* **5.** (*tr.*) to apply pitch to (something). [Old English *pic,* from Latin *pix*]

pitch ac+cent *n.* (in languages such as Ancient Greek or modern Swedish) an accent in which emphatic syllables are pronounced on a higher musical pitch relative to other syllables. Also called: **tonic accent.**

pitch-and-toss *n.* a game of skill and chance in which the player who pitches a coin nearest to a mark has the first chance to toss all the coins, winning those that land heads up.

pitch-black *adj.* **1.** extremely dark; unlit: *the room was pitch-black.* **2.** of a deep black colour.

pitch+blende ('pɪtʃˌblɛnd) *n.* a blackish mineral that is a type of uraninite and occurs in veins, frequently associated with silver: the principal source of uranium and radium. Formula: UO_2. [C18: partial translation of German *Pechblende,* from *Pech* PITCH[2] (from its black colour) + BLENDE]

pitch cir+cle *n.* an imaginary circle passing through the teeth of a gearwheel, concentric with the gearwheel, and having a radius that would enable it to be in contact with a similar circle around a mating gearwheel.

pitch-dark *adj.* extremely or completely dark.

pitched bat+tle *n.* **1.** a battle ensuing from the deliberate choice of time and place, engaging all the planned resources. **2.** any fierce encounter, esp. one with large numbers.

pitch+er[1] ('pɪtʃə) *n.* **1.** a large jug, usually rounded with a narrow neck and often of earthenware, used mainly for holding water. **2.** *Botany.* any of the urn-shaped leaves of the pitcher plant. [C13: from Old French *pichier,* from Medieval Latin *picārium,* variant of *bicārium* BEAKER]

pitch+er[2] ('pɪtʃə) *n.* **1.** *Baseball.* the player on the fielding team who pitches the ball to the batter. **2.** Also called: **pitching niblick.** *Golf.* an iron with a steep-angled head, similar to a niblick. **3.** a granite stone used in paving.

pitch+er plant *n.* any of various insectivorous plants of the genera *Sarracenia, Nepenthes,* and *Darlingtonia,* having leaves modified to form pitcher-like organs that attract and trap insects, which are then digested. See also **huntsman's-cup.**

pitch+fork ('pɪtʃˌfɔːk) *n.* **1.** a long-handled fork with two long curved tines for lifting, turning, or tossing hay. ~*vb.* (*tr.*) **2.** to use a pitchfork on (something). **3.** to thrust (someone) unwillingly into a position.

pitch in *vb.* (*intr., adv.*) **1.** to cooperate or contribute. **2.** to begin energetically.

pitch+ing tool *n.* a masonry chisel for rough work.

pitch in·to *vb.* (*intr., prep.*) **1.** to assail physically or verbally. **2.** to get on with doing (something).

Pitch Lake *n.* a deposit of natural asphalt in the West Indies, in SW Trinidad. Area: 46 hectares (114 acres).

pitch+man ('pɪtʃmən) *n., pl.* **+men.** *U.S.* **1.** an itinerant pedlar of small merchandise who operates from a stand at a fair, etc. **2.** any high-pressure salesman or advertiser.

pitch+om+e+ter (pɪtʃ'ɒmɪtə) *n.* an instrument embodying a clinometer, for measuring the pitch of a ship's propeller.

pitch on *or* **up·on** *vb.* (*intr., prep.*) to determine or decide.

pitch pine *n.* **1.** any of various coniferous trees of the genus *Pinus,* esp. *P. rigida,* of North America, having red-brown bark and long lustrous light brown cones: valued as a source of turpentine and pitch. **2.** the wood of any of these trees.

pitch pipe *n.* a small pipe, esp. one having a reed like a harmonica, that sounds a note or notes of standard frequency. It is used for establishing the correct starting note for unaccompanied singing.

pitch+stone ('pɪtʃˌstəʊn) *n.* a dark glassy acid volcanic rock similar in composition to granite, usually intruded as dykes, sills, etc. [C18: translation of German *Pechstein*]

pitch·y ('pɪtʃɪ) *adj.* **pitch·i·er, pitch·i·est.** **1.** full of or covered with pitch. **2.** resembling pitch. —**'pitch·i·ness** *n.*

pit·e·ous ('pɪtɪəs) *adj.* **1.** exciting or deserving pity. **2.** *Archaic.* having or expressing pity. —**'pit·e·ous·ly** *adv.* —**'pit·e·ous·ness** *n.*

pit+fall ('pɪtˌfɔːl) *n.* **1.** an unsuspected difficulty or danger. **2.** a trap in the form of a concealed pit, designed to catch men or wild animals. [Old English *pytt* PIT[1] + *fealle* trap]

pith (pɪθ) *n.* **1.** the soft fibrous tissue lining the inside of the rind in fruits such as the orange and grapefruit. **2.** the essential or important part, point, etc. **3.** weight; substance. **4.** Also called: **medulla.** *Botany.* the central core of unspecialized cells surrounded by conducting tissue in stems. **5.** the soft central part of a bone, feather, etc. ~*vb.* (*tr.*) **6.** to destroy the brain and spinal cord of (a laboratory animal) by piercing or severing. **7.** to kill (animals) by severing the spinal cord. **8.** to remove the pith from (a plant). [Old English *pitha;* compare Middle Low German *pedik,* Middle Dutch *pitt(e)*]

pit+head ('pɪtˌhɛd) *n.* the top of a mine shaft and the buildings, hoisting gear, etc., situated around it.

pith+e·can+thro+pus (ˌpɪθɪkæn'θrəʊpəs, -'kænθrə-) *n., pl.* **+pi** (-ˌpaɪ). any primitive apelike man of the former genus *Pithecanthropus,* now included in the genus *Homo.* See **Java man, Peking man.** [C19: New Latin, from Greek *pithēkos* ape + *anthrōpos* man] —**ˌpith+e·'can+thro+ˌpine** *or* **ˌpith+e·'can+thro+ˌpoid** *adj.*

pith hel+met *n.* a lightweight hat made of pith that protects the wearer from the sun. Also called: **topee, topi.**

pi+thos ('pɪθɒs, 'paɪ-) *n., pl.* **+thoi** (-θɔɪ). a large ceramic container for oil or grain. [from Greek]

pith·y ('pɪθɪ) *adj.* **pith·i·er, pith·i·est.** **1.** terse and full of meaning or substance. **2.** of, resembling, or full of pith. —**'pith·i·ly** *adv.* —**'pith·i·ness** *n.*

pit·i+a·ble ('pɪtɪəbᵊl) *adj.* exciting or deserving pity or contempt. —**'pit·i·a·ble·ness** *n.* —**'pit·i·a·bly** *adv.*

pit·i+ful ('pɪtɪfʊl) *adj.* **1.** arousing or deserving pity. **2.** arousing or deserving contempt. **3.** *Archaic.* full of pity or compassion. —**'pit·i·ful·ly** *adv.* —**'pit·i·ful·ness** *n.*

pit·i+less ('pɪtɪlɪs) *adj.* having or showing little or no pity or mercy. —**'pit·i·less·ly** *adv.* —**'pit·i·less·ness** *n.*

pit+man ('pɪtmən) *n., pl.* **+men.** *Chiefly Northern Brit.* a person who works down a mine, esp. a coal-miner.

Pit·man ('pɪtmən) *n.* Sir **I·saac.** 1813–97, English inventor of a system of phonetic shorthand (1837).

pi+ton ('piːtɒn; *French* pi'tɔ̃) *n. Mountaineering.* a metal spike that may be driven into a crevice and used to secure a rope, etc. [C20: from French: ringbolt]

Pi·tot-stat·ic tube ('piːtəʊ'stætɪk) *n.* combined Pitot and static pressure tubes placed in a fluid flow to measure the total and static pressures. The difference in pressures, as recorded on a manometer or airspeed indicator, indicates the fluid velocity. Also called: **Pitot tube.**

Pi·tot tube ('piːtəʊ) *n.* **1.** a small tube placed in a fluid with its open end upstream and the other end connected to a manometer. It measures the total pressure of the fluid and indirectly its velocity. **2.** short for **Pitot-static tube,** esp. one fitted to an aircraft. [C18: named after its inventor, Henri *Pitot* (1695–1771), French physicist]

pit+saw ('pɪtˌsɔː) *n.* a large saw formerly used for cutting logs into planks, operated by two men, one standing on top of the log and the other in a pit underneath it.

Pitt (pɪt) *n.* **1. Wil·liam,** called *Pitt the Elder,* 1st Earl of Chatham. 1708–78, English statesman. He was first minister

(1756–57; 1757–61; 1766–68) and achieved British victory in the Seven Years' War (1756–63). **2.** his son **Wil·liam,** called *Pitt the Younger.* 1759–1806, English statesman. As prime minister (1783–1801; 1804–06), he carried through important fiscal and tariff reforms. From 1793, his attention was focused on the wars with revolutionary and Napoleonic France.

pit+ta ('pɪtə) *n.* a flat rounded slightly leavened bread, originally from the Middle East, with a hollow inside like a pocket, which can be filled with food. Also called: **Arab bread, Greek bread.** [from Modern Greek: a cake]

pit+tance ('pɪtᵊns) *n.* a small amount or portion, esp. a meagre allowance of money. [C16: from Old French *pietance* ration, ultimately from Latin *pietās* duty]

pit·ter-pat·ter ('pɪtə,pætə) *n.* **1.** the sound of light rapid taps or pats, as of raindrops. ~*vb.* **2.** (*intr.*) to make such a sound. ~*adv.* **3.** with such a sound: *the rain fell pitter-patter on the window.*

Pitts+burgh ('pɪtsbɜ:g) *n.* a port in SW Pennsylvania, at the confluence of the Allegheny and Monongahela Rivers, which form the Ohio River: settled around Fort Pitt in 1758; developed rapidly with the discovery of iron deposits and one of the world's richest coalfields; the largest river port in the U.S. and an important industrial centre, with large steel mills. Pop.: 479 276 (1973 est.).

Pitt Street Farm+er *n. Austral. slang.* another name for **Collins Street Farmer.** [C20: after a principal business street in Sydney]

pi+tu·i·tar·y (pɪ'tju:ɪtərɪ, -trɪ) *n., pl.* **+tar·ies. 1.** See **pituitary gland, pituitary extract.** ~*adj.* **2.** of or relating to the pituitary gland. **3.** *Archaic.* of or relating to phlegm or mucus. [C17: from Late Latin *pītuītārius* slimy, from *pītuīta* phlegm]

pi+tu·i·tar·y ex+tract *n.* a preparation of the pituitary gland, used in medicine for the therapeutic effects of its hormones.

pi+tu·i·tar·y gland *or* **bod·y** *n.* the master endocrine gland, attached by a stalk to the base of the brain. Its two lobes (see **adenohypophysis** and **neurohypophysis**) secrete hormones affecting skeletal growth, development of the sex glands, and the functioning of the other endocrine glands. Also called: **hypophysis, hypophysis cerebri.**

pit·u+ri ('pɪtərɪ) *n.* an Australian solanaceous shrub, *Duboisia hopwoodi,* the leaves of which are the source of a narcotic used by the Aborigines. [C19: from a native Australian name]

pit vi·per *n.* any venomous snake of the New World family *Crotalidae,* having a heat-sensitive organ in a pit on each side of the head: includes the rattlesnakes.

pit·y ('pɪtɪ) *n., pl.* **pit·ies. 1.** sympathy or sorrow felt for the sufferings of another. **2. have** (*or* **take**) **pity on.** to have sympathy or show mercy for. **3.** something that causes regret or pity. **4.** an unfortunate chance: *what a pity you can't come.* ~*vb.* **pit·ies, pit·y+ing, pit+ied. 5.** to feel pity (for). [C13: from Old French *pité,* from Latin *pietās* duty] —**'pit·y+ing·ly** *adv.*

pit·y+ri·a+sis (,pɪtə'raɪəsɪs) *n.* **1.** any of a group of skin diseases characterized by the shedding of dry flakes of skin. **2.** a similar skin disease of certain domestic animals. [C17: via New Latin from Greek *pituriasis* scurfiness, from *pituron* bran]

più (pju:) *adv. Music.* (*in combination*) more (quickly, softly, etc.): *più allegro, più mosso, più lento.* [Italian, from Latin *plus* more]

Piu+ra (*Spanish* 'pjura) *n.* a city in NW Peru: the oldest colonial city in Peru, founded by Pizarro in 1532; commercial centre of an agricultural district. Pop.: 126 010 (1972).

Pi·us II ('paɪəs) *n.* pen name *Aeneas Silvius,* original name *Enea Silvio de' Piccolomini.* 1405–64, Italian ecclesiastic, humanist, poet, and historian; pope (1458–64).

Pi·us IV *n.* original name *Giovanni Angelo de' Medici.* 1499–1565, pope (1559–65). He reconvened the Council of Trent (1562), confirming its final decrees.

Pi·us V *n.* **Saint.** original name *Michele Ghislieri.* 1504–72, pope (1566–72). He attempted to enforce the reforms decreed by the Council of Trent, excommunicated Elizabeth I of England (1570), and organized the alliance that defeated the Turks at Lepanto (1571). Feast day: May 5.

Pi·us VII *n.* original name *Luigi Barnaba Chiaramonti.* 1740–1823, Italian ecclesiastic; pope (1800–23). He concluded a concordat with Napoleon (1801) and consecrated him as emperor of France (1804), but resisted his annexation of the Papal States (1809).

Pi·us IX *n.* original name *Giovanni Maria Mastai-Ferretti.* 1792–1878, Italian ecclesiastic; pope (1846–78). He refused to recognize the incorporation of Rome and the Papal States in the kingdom of Italy, confining himself to the Vatican after 1870. He decreed the dogma of the Immaculate Conception (1854) and convened the Vatican Council, which laid down the doctrine of papal infallibility (1870).

Pi·us X *n.* **Saint.** original name *Giuseppe Sarto.* 1835–1914, Italian ecclesiastic; pope (1903–14). He condemned Modernism (1907) and initiated a new codification of canon law. Feast day: Sept. 3.

Pi·us XI *n.* original name *Achille Ratti.* 1857–1939, Italian ecclesiastic; pope (1922–39). He signed the Lateran Treaty (1929), by which the Vatican City was recognized as an independent state. His encyclicals condemned Nazism and Communism.

Pi·us XII *n.* original name *Eugenio Pacelli.* 1876–1958, Italian ecclesiastic; pope (1939–58): his attitude towards Nazi German anti-Semitism has been a matter of controversy.

piv+ot ('pɪvət) *n.* **1.** a short shaft or pin supporting something that turns; fulcrum. **2.** the end of a shaft or arbor that terminates in a bearing. **3.** a person or thing upon which progress, success, etc., depends. **4.** the person or position from which a military formation takes its reference when altering position, etc. ~*vb.* **5.** (*tr.*) to mount on or provide with a pivot or pivots. **6.** (*intr.*) to turn on or as if on a pivot. [C17: from Old French; perhaps related to Old Provençal *pua* tooth of a comb]

piv+ot+al ('pɪvətᵊl) *adj.* **1.** of, involving, or acting as a pivot. **2.** of crucial importance. —**'piv+ot+al+ly** *adv.*

piv+ot bridge *n.* another name for **swing bridge.**

pix¹ (pɪks) *pl. n. Informal.* photographs; prints.

pix² (pɪks) *n.* a less common spelling of **pyx.**

pix·ie *or* **pix·y** ('pɪksɪ) *n., pl.* **pix·ies.** (in folklore) a fairy or elf. [C17: of obscure origin]

pix·i+lat+ed ('pɪksɪ,leɪtɪd) *adj. Chiefly U.S.* **1.** eccentric or whimsical. **2.** *Slang.* drunk. [C20: from PIXIE + *-lated,* as in *stimulated, titillated,* etc.] —**,pix·i·'la+tion** *n.*

Pi·zar·ro (pɪ'zɑ:rəʊ; *Spanish* pi'θarro) *n.* **Fran·cis·co** (fran'θisko). ?1475–1541, Spanish conqueror of Peru. He landed in Peru (1532), murdered the Inca King Atahualpa (1533), and founded Lima as the new capital of Peru (1535). He was murdered by his own followers.

pize (paɪz) *vb.* (*tr.*) *Yorkshire dialect.* to strike (someone a blow). [of obscure origin]

pizz. *Music. abbrev. for* pizzicato.

piz+za ('pi:tsə) *n.* a dish of Italian origin consisting of a baked disc of dough covered with cheese and tomatoes, usually with the addition of mushrooms, anchovies, sausage, or ham. [C20: from Italian, perhaps from Vulgar Latin *picea* (unattested), translation of Medieval Greek *pitta* cake, from Latin *piceus* relating to PITCH²]

piz+ze+ri·a (,pi:tsə'ri:ə) *n.* a place where pizzas are made, sold, or eaten.

piz+zi+ca+to (,pɪtsɪ'kɑ:təʊ) *Music.* ~*adj., adv.* **1.** (in music for the violin family) to be plucked with the finger. ~*n.* **2.** the style or technique of playing a normally bowed stringed instrument in this manner. [C19: from Italian: pinched, from *pizzicare* to twist, twang]

piz+zle ('pɪzᵊl) *n. Archaic or dialect.* the penis of an animal, esp. a bull. [C16: of Germanic origin; compare Low German *pēsel,* Flemish *pēzel,* Middle Dutch *pēze* sinew]

PK *abbrev. for* psychokinesis.

pk. *pl.* **pks.** *abbrev. for:* **1.** pack. **2.** park. **3.** peak.

pkg. *pl.* **pkgs.** *abbrev. for* package.

pkt. *abbrev. for* packet.

PL **1.** *international car registration for* Poland. ~**2.** (in transformational grammar) *abbrev. for* plural.

pl. *abbrev. for:* **1.** place. **2.** plate. **3.** plural.

Pl. (in street names) *abbrev. for* Place.

PL/1 *n.* programming language 1: a high-level computer programming language designed for mathematical and scientific purposes.

P.L.A. *abbrev. for* Port of London Authority.

plac+a·ble ('plækəbᵊl) *adj.* easily placated or appeased. [C15: via Old French from Latin *plācābilis,* from *plācāre* to appease; related to *placēre* to please] —**,plac·a·'bil+i·ty** *or* **'plac·a·ble+ness** *n.*

plac+ard ('plækɑ:d) *n.* **1.** a printed or written notice for public display; poster. **2.** a small plaque or card. ~*vb.* (*tr.*) **3.** to post placards on or in. **4.** to publicize or advertise by placards. **5.** to display as a placard. [C15: from Old French *plaquart,* from *plaquier* to plate, lay flat; see PLAQUE]

pla+cate (plə'keɪt) *vb.* (*tr.*) to pacify or appease. [C17: from Latin *plācāre;* see PLACABLE] —**pla+'ca·tion** *n.*

plac·a·to·ry ('plækətərɪ, -trɪ; plə'keɪtərɪ) *or* **plac·a+tive** ('plækətɪv, plə'keɪtɪv) *adj.* placating or intended to placate.

place (pleɪs) *n.* **1.** a particular point or part of space or of a surface, esp. that occupied by a person or thing. **2.** a geographical point, such as a town, city, etc. **3.** a position or rank in a sequence or order. **4. a.** an open square lined with houses of a similar type in a city or town. **b.** (*cap. when part of a street name*): *Grosvenor Place.* **5.** space or room. **6.** a house or living quarters. **7.** any building or area set aside for a specific purpose. **8.** a passage in a book, play, film, etc.: *to lose one's place.* **9.** proper or appropriate position or time: *a woman's place is no longer in the home.* **10.** right or original position: *put it back in its place.* **11.** suitable, appropriate, or customary surroundings (esp. in the phrases **out of place, in place**). **12.** right, prerogative, or duty: *it is your place to give a speech.* **13.** appointment, position, or job: *a place at college.* **14.** position, condition, or state: *if I were in your place.* **15. a.** a space or seat, as at a dining table. **b.** (*as modifier*): *place mat.* **16.** *Maths.* the relative position of a digit in a number. See also **decimal place. 17.** any of the best times in a race. **18.** *Horse racing.* **a.** *Brit.* the first, second, or third position at the finish. **b.** *U.S.* the first or usually the second position at the finish. **c.** (*as modifier*): *a place bet.* **19.** *Theatre.* one of the three unities. See **unity** (sense 8). **20.** *Archaic.* an important position, rank, or role. **21. all over the place.** in disorder or disarray. **22. another place.** *Brit., Parliamentary procedure.* **a.** (in the House of Commons) the House of Lords. **b.** (in the House of Lords) the House of Commons. **23. give place (to).** to make room (for) or be superceded (by). **24. go places.** *Informal.* **a.** to travel. **b.** to become successful. **25. in place of. a.** instead of; in lieu of: *go in place of my sister.* **b.** in exchange for: *he gave her it in place of her ring.* **26. know one's place.** to be aware of one's inferior position. **27. pride of place.** the highest or foremost position. **28. put someone in his** (*or* **her**) **place.** to humble someone who is arrogant, conceited, forward, etc. **29. take one's place.** to take up one's usual or specified position. **30. take the place**

of. to be a substitute for. **31. take place.** to happen or occur. **32. the other place.** *Facetious.* **a.** (at Oxford university) Cambridge university. **b.** (at Cambridge university) Oxford university. ~*vb.* (*mainly tr.*) **33.** to put or set in a particular or appropriate place. **34.** to find or indicate the place of. **35.** to identify or classify by linking with an appropriate context: *to place a face.* **36.** to regard or view as being: *to place prosperity above sincerity.* **37.** to make (an order, bet, etc.). **38.** to find a home or job for (someone). **39.** to appoint to an office or position. **40.** (often foll. by *with*) to put under the care (of). **41.** to direct or aim carefully. **42.** (*passive*) *Brit.* to cause (a racehorse, greyhound, athlete, etc.) to arrive in first, second, third, or sometimes fourth place. **43.** (*intr.*) *U.S.* (of a racehorse, greyhound, etc.) to finish among the first three in a contest, esp. in second position. **44.** to invest (funds). **45.** to sing (a note) with accuracy of pitch. **46.** to insert (an advertisement) in a newspaper, journal, etc. [C13: via Old French from Latin *platēa* courtyard, from Greek *plateia,* from *platus* broad; compare French *plat* flat]

pla+ce·bo (plə'siːbəʊ) *n., pl.* **·bos** *or* **·boes. 1.** *Med.* an inactive substance administered to a patient who insists on receiving medication or who would benefit by the psychological deception or who is used in the investigation of the efficacy of an active drug. See also **control group, placebo effect. 2.** something said or done to please or humour another. **3.** *R.C. Church.* a traditional name for the vespers of the office for the dead. [C13 (in the ecclesiastical sense): from Latin *Placebo Domino* I shall please the Lord (from the opening of the office for the dead); C19 (in the medical sense)]

pla+ce·bo ef+fect *n. Med.* a positive therapeutic effect claimed by a patient after receiving a placebo believed by him to be an active drug. See **control group.**

place card *n.* a card placed on a dinner table before a seat, as at a formal dinner, indicating the name of the person who is to sit there.

place kick *Football.* ~*n.* **1.** a kick in which the ball is placed in position before it is kicked. ~*vb.* **place-kick. 2.** to kick (a ball) using a place kick. ~Compare **drop kick, punt**[2].

place+man ('pleɪsmən) *n., pl.* **+men.** *Brit., rare and derogatory.* a person who holds a public office, esp. for private profit and as a reward for political support.

place+ment ('pleɪsmənt) *n.* **1.** the act of placing or the state of being placed. **2.** arrangement or position. **3.** the process or business of finding employment.

place name *n.* the name of a geographical location, such as a town or area.

pla+cen+ta (plə'sɛntə) *n., pl.* **+tas** *or* **+tae** (-tiː). **1.** the vascular organ formed in the uterus of most mammals during pregnancy, consisting of both maternal and embryonic tissues and providing oxygen and nutrients for the fetus and transfer of waste products from the fetal to the maternal blood circulation. See also **afterbirth. 2.** the corresponding organ or part in certain other mammals. **3.** *Botany.* **a.** the part of the ovary of flowering plants to which the ovules are attached. **b.** the mass of tissue in nonflowering plants that bears the sporangia or spores. [C17: via Latin from Greek *plakoeis* flat cake, from *plax* flat]

pla+cen+tal (plə'sɛntᵊl) *or* **pla+cen+tate** *adj.* (esp. of animals) having a placenta: *placental mammals.* See also **eutherian.**

plac+en+ta+tion (ˌplæsɛn'teɪʃən) *n.* **1.** *Botany.* the way in which ovules are attached in the ovary. **2.** *Zoology.* **a.** the way in which the placenta is attached in the uterus. **b.** the process of formation of the placenta.

plac+er ('plæsə) *n.* **a.** surface sediment containing particles of gold or some other valuable mineral. **b.** (*in combination*): *placer-mining.* [C19: from American Spanish: deposit, from Spanish *plaza* PLACE]

place set+ting *n.* the set of items of cutlery, crockery, and glassware laid for one person at a dining table.

pla+cet ('pleɪsɛt) *n.* a vote or expression of assent by saying the word *placet.* [C16: from Latin, literally: it pleases]

plac+id ('plæsɪd) *adj.* having a calm appearance or nature. [C17: from Latin *placidus* peaceful; related to *placēre* to please] —**pla+cid+i+ty** (plə'sɪdɪtɪ) *or* '**plac+id+ness** *n.* —'**plac+id+ly** *adv.*

plack+et ('plækɪt) *n. Dressmaking.* **1.** a piece of cloth sewn in under a closure with buttons, hooks and eyes, zips, etc. **2.** the closure itself. [C16: perhaps from Middle Dutch *plackaet* breastplate, from Medieval Latin *placca* metal plate]

plac·o+derm ('plækəˌdɜːm) *n.* any extinct bony-plated fishlike vertebrate of the class *Placodermi,* of Silurian to Permian times: thought to have been the earliest vertebrates with jaws. [C19: from Greek *plac-, plax* a flat plate + -DERM]

plac+oid ('plækɔɪd) *adj.* **1.** platelike or flattened. **2.** (of the scales of sharks and other elasmobranchs) toothlike; composed of dentine with an enamel tip and basal pulp cavity. [C19: from Greek *plac-, plax* flat]

pla+fond[1] (plə'fɒn; *French* pla'fɔ̃) *n.* a ceiling, esp. one having ornamentation. [C17: from French, from *plat* flat + *fond* bottom, from Latin *fundus* bottom]

pla+fond[2] (plə'fɒn; *French* pla'fɔ̃) *n.* a card game, a precursor of contract bridge. [French, literally: ceiling, maximum]

pla+gal ('pleɪgᵊl) *adj.* **1.** (of a cadence) progressing from the subdominant to the tonic chord, as in the *Amen* of a hymn. **2.** (of a mode) commencing upon the dominant of an authentic mode, but sharing the same final as the authentic mode. Plagal modes are designated by the prefix *Hypo-* before the name of their authentic counterparts: *the Hypodorian mode.* ~Compare **authentic** (sense 4). [C16: from Medieval Latin *plagālis,* from *plaga,* perhaps from Greek *plagos* side]

plage (plɑːʒ) *n.* another name for **flocculus** (sense 1). [French, literally: beach, strand]

pla+gia+rism ('pleɪdʒəˌrɪzəm) *n.* **1.** the act of plagiarizing. **2.** something plagiarized. —'**pla+gia+rist** *n.* —ˌ**pla+gia+'ris+tic** *adj.*

pla+gia+rize *or* **pla+gia+rise** ('pleɪdʒəˌraɪz) *vb.* to appropriate (ideas, passages, etc.) from (another work or author). —'**pla+gia+ˌriz+er** *or* '**pla+gia+ˌris+er** *n.*

pla+gia+ry ('pleɪdʒərɪ) *n., pl.* **+ries.** *Archaic.* a person who plagiarizes or a piece of plagiarism. [C16: from Latin *plagiārus* plunderer, from *plagium* kidnapping; related to *plaga* snare]

pla·gi·o- *combining form.* slanting, inclining, or oblique: *plagiotropism.* [from Greek *plagios,* from *plagos* side]

pla+gi·o+clase ('pleɪdʒɪəʊˌkleɪz) *n.* a series of feldspar minerals consisting of a mixture of sodium and calcium aluminium silicates in triclinic crystalline form: includes albite, oligoclase, and labradorite. —**pla+gi·o·clas+tic** (ˌpleɪdʒɪəʊ'klæstɪk) *adj.*

pla+gi·o+cli+max (ˌpleɪdʒɪəʊ'klaɪmæks) *n. Ecology.* the climax stage of a community, influenced by man or some other outside factor.

pla+gi·o+trop+ism (ˌpleɪdʒɪəʊ'trəʊpɪzəm) *n.* the growth of a plant at an angle to the vertical in response to a stimulus. —ˌ**pla+gi·o+'trop+ic** *adj.*

plague (pleɪg) *n.* **1.** any widespread and usually highly contagious disease with a high fatality rate. **2.** an infectious disease of rodents, esp. rats, transmitted to man by the bite of the rat flea (*Xenopsylla cheopis*). **3.** See **bubonic plague. 4.** something that afflicts or harasses. **5.** *Informal.* an annoyance or nuisance. **6.** a pestilence, affliction, or calamity on a large scale. esp. when regarded as sent by God. **7.** *Archaic.* used to express annoyance, disgust, etc.: *a plague on you.* ~*vb.* **plagues, plagu+ing, plagued.** (*tr.*) **8.** to afflict or harass. **9.** to bring down a plague upon. **10.** *Informal.* to annoy. [C14: from Late Latin *plāga* pestilence, from Latin: a blow; related to Greek *plēgē* a stroke, Latin *plangere* to strike] —'**plagu+er** *n.*

pla+guy *or* **pla+guey** ('pleɪgɪ) *Informal.* ~*adj.* **1.** disagreeable or vexing. ~*adv.* **2.** disagreeably or annoyingly. —'**pla+gui+ly** *adv.*

plaice (pleɪs) *n., pl.* **plaice** *or* **plaic·es. 1.** a European flatfish, *Pleuronectes platessa,* having an oval brown body marked with red or orange spots and valued as a food fish: family *Pleuronectidae.* **2.** *U.S.* any of various other fishes of the family *Pleuronectidae,* esp. *Hippoglossoides platessoides.* [C13: from Old French *plaïz,* from Late Latin *platessa* flatfish, from Greek *platus* flat]

plaid (plæd) *n.* **1.** a long piece of cloth of a tartan pattern, worn over the shoulder as part of Highland costume. **2. a.** a crisscross weave or cloth. **b.** (*as modifier*): *a plaid scarf.* [C16: from Scottish Gaelic *plaide,* of obscure origin]

plain[1] (pleɪn) *adj.* **1.** flat or smooth; level. **2.** not complicated; clear: *the plain truth.* **3.** not difficult; simple or easy: *a plain task.* **4.** honest or straightforward. **5.** lowly, esp. in social rank or education. **6.** without adornment or show: *a plain coat.* **7.** (of fabric) without pattern or of simple untwilled weave. **8.** not attractive. **9.** not mixed; simple: *plain vodka.* **10.** *Knitting.* of or done in plain. ~*n.* **11.** a level or almost level tract of country, esp. an extensive treeless region. **12.** a simple stitch in knitting. **13.** (in billiards) **a.** the unmarked white ball, as distinguished from the spot balls. **b.** the player using this ball. ~*adv.* **14.** (intensifier): *just plain tired.* [C13: from Old French: simple, from Latin *plānus* level, distinct, clear] —'**plain+ly** *adv.* —'**plain+ness** *n.*

plain[2] (pleɪn) *vb.* a dialect or poetic word for **complain.** [C14 *pleignen,* from Old French *plaindre* to lament, from Latin *plangere* to beat]

plain+chant ('pleɪnˌtʃɑːnt) *n.* another name for **plainsong.** See also **Gregorian chant.** [C18: from French, rendering Medieval Latin *cantus plānus;* see PLAIN[1]]

plain choc·o+late *n.* chocolate with a slightly bitter flavour and dark colour. Compare **milk chocolate.**

plain clothes *pl. n.* **a.** ordinary clothes, as distinguished from uniform, as worn by a police detective on duty. **b.** (*as modifier*): *a plain-clothes policeman.*

plain-laid *adj.* (of a cable or rope) made of three strands twisted together in the usual right-handed direction.

plains (pleɪnz) *pl. n. Chiefly U.S.* extensive tracts of level or almost level treeless countryside; prairies.

plain sail+ing *n.* **1.** *Informal.* smooth or easy progress. **2.** *Nautical.* sailing in a body of water that is unobstructed; clear sailing. Compare **plane sailing.**

Plains In+di·an *n.* a member of any of the North American Indian peoples formerly living in the Great Plains of the U.S. and Canada.

plains+man ('pleɪnzmən) *n., pl.* **+men.** a person who lives in a plains region, esp. in the Great Plains of North America.

Plains of A·bra+ham *n.* a field in E Canada between Quebec City and the St. Lawrence River: site of an important British victory (1759) in the Seven Years' War, which cost the French their possession of Canada.

plain+song ('pleɪnˌsɒŋ) *n.* the style of unison unaccompanied vocal music used in the medieval Church, esp. in Gregorian chant. Also called: **plainchant.** [C16: translation of Medieval Latin *cantus plānus*]

plain-spo·ken *adj.* candid; frank; blunt.

plaint (pleɪnt) *n.* **1.** *Archaic.* a complaint or lamentation. **2.** *Law.* a statement in writing of grounds of complaint made to a court of law and asking for redress of the grievance. [C13: from Old French *plainte,* from Latin *planctus* lamentation, from *plangere* to beat]

plain text *n. Telecomm.* a message set in a directly readable form rather than in coded groups.
plain+tiff ('pleɪntɪf) *n.* a person who brings a civil action in a court of law. Compare **defendant** (sense 1). [C14: from legal French *plaintif,* from Old French *plaintif* (adj.) complaining, from *plainte* PLAINT]
plain+tive ('pleɪntɪv) *adj.* expressing melancholy; mournful. [C14: from Old French *plaintif* grieving, from *plainte* PLAINT] —**'plain+tive+ly** *adv.* —**'plain+tive+ness** *n.*
plais+ter ('pleɪstə) *n. Obsolete.* plaster.
plait (plæt) *n.* **1.** a length of hair, etc., that has been plaited. **2.** *Brit.* a loaf of bread of several twisting or intertwining parts. **3.** a rare spelling of **pleat.** ~*vb.* **4.** (*tr.*) to intertwine (strands or strips) in a pattern. [C15: *pleyt,* from Old French *pleit,* from Latin *plicāre* to fold; see PLY[2]]
plan (plæn) *n.* **1.** a detailed scheme, method, etc., for attaining an objective. **2.** (*sometimes pl.*) a proposed, usually tentative idea for doing something. **3.** a drawing to scale of a horizontal section through a building taken at a given level. Compare **ground plan** (sense 1), **elevation** (sense 5). **4.** an outline, sketch, etc. **5.** (in perspective drawing) any of several imaginary planes perpendicular to the line of vision and between the eye and object depicted. ~*vb.* **plans, plan+ning, planned. 6.** to form a plan (for) or make plans (for). **7.** (*tr.*) to make a plan of (a building). **8.** (*tr.; takes a clause as object or an infinitive*) to have in mind as a purpose; intend. [C18: via French from Latin *plānus* flat; compare PLANE[1], PLAIN[1]]
pla+nar ('pleɪnə) *adj.* **1.** of or relating to a plane. **2.** lying in one plane; flat. [C19: from Late Latin *plānāris* on level ground, from Latin *plānus* flat] —**pla+nar+i+ty** (pleɪ'nærɪtɪ) *n.*
pla+nar+i+an (plə'nɛərɪən) *n.* any free-living turbellarian flatworm of the mostly aquatic suborder *Tricladida,* having a three-branched intestine. [C19: from New Latin *Plānāria* type genus, from Late Latin *plānārius* level, flat; see PLANE[1]]
pla+nar pro+cess *n.* a method of producing diffused junctions in semiconductor devices. A pattern of holes is etched into an oxide layer formed on a silicon substrate, into which impurities are diffused through the holes.
pla+na+tion (pleɪ'neɪʃən) *n.* the erosion of a land surface until it is basically flat.
planch+et ('plɑːntʃɪt) *n.* a piece of metal ready to be stamped as a coin, medal, etc.; flan. [C17: from French: little board, from *planche* PLANK]
plan+chette (plɑː'n'ʃɛt) *n.* a heart-shaped board on wheels with a pencil attached that writes messages under supposed spirit guidance. [C19: from French: little board, from *planche* PLANK]
Planck (plæŋk; *German* plaŋk) *n.* **Max** (**Karl Ernst Ludwig**) (maks). 1858–1947, German physicist who first formulated the quantum theory (1900): Nobel prize for physics 1918.
Planck con+stant *or* **Planck's con+stant** *n.* a fundamental constant equal to the energy of any quantum of radiation divided by its frequency. It has a value of 6.6262×10^{-34} joule seconds. Symbol: *h* See also **Dirac constant.**
plane[1] (pleɪn) *n.* **1.** *Maths.* a flat surface in which a straight line joining any two of its points lies entirely on that surface. **2.** a flat or level surface. **3.** a level of existence, performance, attainment, etc. **4. a.** short for **aeroplane. b.** an aerofoil or supporting surface of an aircraft or hydroplane. ~*adj.* **5.** level or flat. **6.** *Maths.* (of a curve, figure, etc.) lying entirely in one plane. ~*vb.* (*intr.*) **7.** to fly without moving wings or using engines; glide. **8.** (of a boat) to rise partly and skim over the water when moving at a certain speed. **9.** to travel by aeroplane. [C17: from Latin *plānum* level surface] —**'plane+ness** *n.*
plane[2] (pleɪn) *n.* **1.** a tool with an adjustable sharpened steel blade set obliquely in a wooden or iron body, for levelling or smoothing timber surfaces, cutting mouldings or grooves, etc. **2.** a flat tool, usually metal, for smoothing the surface of clay or plaster in a mould. ~*vb.* **3.** (*tr.*) to level, smooth, or cut (timber, wooden articles, etc.) using a plane or similar tool. **4.** (*tr.; often foll. by off*) to remove using a plane. [C14: via Old French from Late Latin *plāna* plane, from *plānāre* to level]
plane[3] (pleɪn) *n.* See **plane tree.**
plane an+gle *n.* an angle between two intersecting lines.
plane chart *n.* a chart used in plane sailing, in which the lines of latitude and longitude are straight and parallel.
plane ge+om+e+try *n.* the study of the properties of and relationships between plane curves, figures, etc.
plane po+lar+i+za+tion *n.* a type of polarization in which waves of light or other electromagnetic radiation are restricted to vibration in a single plane.
plan+er ('pleɪnə) *n.* **1.** a machine with a cutting tool that makes repeated horizontal strokes across the surface of a workpiece: used to cut flat surfaces into metal. **2.** a machine for planing wood, esp. one in which the cutting blades are mounted on a rotating drum. **3.** *Printing.* a flat piece of wood used to level type in a chase. **4.** any person or thing that planes.
plane sail+ing *n. Nautical.* navigation without reference to the earth's curvature. Compare **plain sailing.**
plane sur+vey+ing *n.* the surveying of areas of limited size, making no corrections for the earth's curvature.
plan+et ('plænɪt) *n.* **1.** Also called: **major planet.** any of the nine celestial bodies, Mercury, Venus, earth, Mars, Jupiter, Saturn, Uranus, Neptune, or Pluto, that revolve around the sun in elliptical orbits and are illuminated by light from the sun. **2.** any celestial body revolving around a star, illuminated by light from that star. **3.** *Astrology.* any of the planets of the solar system, excluding the earth but including the sun and moon, each thought to rule one or sometimes two signs of the zodiac. See also **house** (sense 9). [C12: via Old French from Late Latin *planēta,* from Greek *planētēs* wanderer, from *planan* to wander]
plane ta+ble *n.* **1.** a surveying instrument consisting of a drawing board mounted on adjustable legs, and used in the field for plotting measurements directly. ~*vb.* **plane-ta·ble. 2.** to survey (a plot of land) using a plane table.
plan+e+tar+i+um (ˌplænɪ'tɛərɪəm) *n., pl.* **+i+ums** *or* **·i·a** (-ɪə). **1.** an instrument for simulating the apparent motions of the sun, moon, and planets against a background of constellations by projecting images of these bodies onto the inside of a domed ceiling. **2.** a building in which such an instrument is housed. **3.** a model of the solar system, sometimes mechanized to show the relative motions of the planets.
plan+e+tar·y ('plænɪtərɪ, -trɪ) *adj.* **1.** of or relating to a planet. **2.** mundane; terrestrial. **3.** wandering or erratic. **4.** *Astrology.* under the influence of one of the planets. **5.** (of a gear, esp. an epicyclic gear) having an axis that rotates around that of another gear. **6.** (of an electron) having an orbit around the nucleus of an atom. ~*n., pl.* **·tar·ies. 7.** a train of planetary gears.
plan+e+tar·y neb·u·la *n.* a very faint hot star surrounded by an expanding envelope of tenuous ionized gases, mainly hydrogen, that emit a fluorescent glow because of intense short-wave radiation from the star.
plan+e+tes·i+mal hy+poth+e+sis (ˌplænɪ'tɛsɪməl) *n.* the discredited theory that the close passage of a star to the sun caused many small bodies (**planetesimals**) to be drawn from the sun, eventually coalescing to form the planets. [C20: *planetesimal,* from PLANET + INFINITESIMAL]
plan+et+oid ('plænɪˌtɔɪd) *n.* another name for **asteroid** (sense 1). —ˌ**plan+e+'toi+dal** *adj.*
plane tree *or* **plane** *n.* any tree of the genus *Platanus,* having ball-shaped heads of fruits and leaves with pointed lobes: family *Platanaceae.* The hybrid *P.* × *hispanica* (**London plane**) is frequently planted in towns. Also called: **platan.** [C14 *plane,* from Old French, from Latin *platanus,* from Greek *platanos,* from *platos* wide, referring to the leaves]
plan·et-struck *or* **plan·et-strick·en** *adj. Astrology.* affected by the influence of a planet, esp. malignly.
plan+et wheel *or* **gear** *n.* any one of the wheels of an epicyclic gear train that orbits the central axis of the train.
plan+form ('plænˌfɔːm) *n.* the outline or silhouette of an object, esp. an aircraft, as seen from above.
plan+gent ('plændʒənt) *adj.* **1.** having a loud deep sound. **2.** resonant and mournful in sound. [C19: from Latin *plangere* to beat (esp. the breast, in grief); see PLAIN[2]] —**'plan+gen+cy** *n.* —**'plan+gent+ly** *adv.*
pla+nim+e+ter (plæ'nɪmɪtə) *n.* a mechanical integrating instrument for measuring the area of an irregular plane figure, such as the area under a curve, by moving a point attached to an arm around the perimeter of the figure.
pla+nim+e+try (plæ'nɪmɪtrɪ) *n.* the measurement of plane areas. —**pla+ni+met+ric** (ˌplænɪ'mɛtrɪk) *or* ˌ**pla+ni+'met+ri+cal** *adj.*
plan+ish ('plænɪʃ) *vb.* (*tr.*) to give a final finish to (metal, etc.) by hammering or rolling to produce a smooth surface. [C16: from Old French *planir* to smooth out, from Latin *plānus* flat, PLAIN[1]] —**'plan+ish+er** *n.*
plan·i+sphere ('plænɪˌsfɪə) *n.* a projection or representation of all or part of a sphere on a plane surface, such as a polar projection of the celestial sphere onto a chart. [C14: from Medieval Latin *plānisphaerium,* from Latin *plānus* flat + Greek *sphaira* globe] —**plan·i+spher+ic** (ˌplænɪ'sfɛrɪk) *adj.*
plank (plæŋk) *n.* **1.** a stout length of sawn timber. **2.** something that supports or sustains. **3.** *Chiefly U.S.* one of the policies in a political party's programme. **4. walk the plank.** to be forced by pirates, etc., to walk to one's death off the end of a plank jutting out over the water from the side of a ship. ~*vb.* **5.** (*tr.*) to cover or provide (an area) with planks. **6.** (*tr.*) to beat (meat, etc.) to make it tender. **7.** (*tr.*) *Chiefly U.S.* to cook or serve (meat or fish) on a special wooden board. [C13: from Old Norman French *planke,* from Late Latin *planca* board, from *plancus* flat-footed; probably related to Greek *plax* flat surface]
plank+ing ('plæŋkɪŋ) *n.* a number of planks.
plank-sheer *n. Nautical.* a plank or timber covering the upper ends of the frames of a wooden vessel. [C14 *plancher,* from Old French *planchier,* from *planche* plank, from Latin *planca;* spelling influenced by PLANK, SHEER[1]]
plank+ton ('plæŋktən) *n.* the organisms inhabiting the surface layer of a sea or lake, consisting of small drifting plants and animals, such as diatoms. Compare **nekton.** [C19: via German from Greek *planktos* wandering, from *plazesthai* to roam] —**plank+ton+ic** (plæŋk'tɒnɪk) *adj.*
plan+ning blight *n.* the harmful effects on property values caused by uncertainty about development.
pla·no- *or sometimes before a vowel* **plan-** *combining form.* indicating flatness or planeness: *plano-concave.* [from Latin *plānus* flat, level]
pla·no-con·cave (ˌpleɪnəʊ'kɒnkeɪv) *adj.* (of a lens) having one side concave and the other side plane.
pla·no-con·vex (ˌpleɪnəʊ'kɒnvɛks) *adj.* (of a lens) having one side convex and the other side plane.
plan·o+gam+ete ('plænəgəˌmiːt) *n.* a motile gamete, such as a spermatozoon.
pla+nog+ra+phy (plə'nɒgrəfɪ) *n. Printing.* any process, such as

lithography, for printing from a flat surface. —**pla·no·graph·ic** (ˌpleɪnəˈɡræfɪk) *adj.* —ˌ**pla·no·ˈgraph·i·cal·ly** *adv.*
pla·nom·e·ter (plæˈnɒmɪtə) *n.* a flat metal plate used for directly testing the flatness of metal surfaces in accurate metalwork. —**pla·no·met·ric** (ˌpleɪnəˈmɛtrɪk) *adj.* —ˌ**pla·no·ˈmet·ri·cal·ly** *adv.* —**pla·ˈnom·e·try** *n.*
pla·no·sol (ˈpleɪnəˌsɒl) *n.* a type of intrazonal soil of humid or subhumid uplands having a strongly leached upper layer overlying a clay hardpan. [C20: from Latin PLANO- + *solum* soil]
plant (plɑːnt) *n.* **1.** any living organism that typically synthesizes its food from inorganic substances, possesses cellulose cell walls, responds slowly and often permanently to a stimulus, lacks specialized sense organs and nervous system, and has no powers of locomotion. **2.** such an organism that is green, terrestrial, and smaller than a shrub or tree; a herb. **3.** a cutting, seedling, or similar structure, esp. when ready for transplantation. **4. a.** a factory or works. **b.** specialized mechanical apparatus: *generating plant.* **c.** *Austral.* portable equipment, as used by a bushworker, cattle drover, etc. **5.** *Informal.* a thing positioned secretly for discovery by another, esp. in order to incriminate an innocent person. **6.** *Snooker, etc.* a position in which the cue ball can be made to strike an intermediate which then pockets another ball. ~*vb.* (*tr.*) **7.** (often foll. by *out*) to set (seeds, crops, etc.) into (ground) to grow. **8.** to place firmly in position. **9.** to establish; found. **10.** to implant in the mind. **11.** *Slang.* to deliver (a blow). **12.** *Slang.* to position or hide, esp. in order to deceive or observe. **13.** to place (young fish, oysters, spawn, etc.) in (a lake, river, etc.) in order to stock the water. [Old English, from Latin *planta* a shoot, cutting] —**ˈplant·a·ble** *adj.* —**ˈplant·like** *adj.*
Plan·tag·e·net (plænˈtædʒɪnɪt) *n.* a line of English kings, ruling from the ascent of Henry II (1154) to the death of Richard III (1485). [C12: from Old French, literally: sprig of broom, with reference to the crest of the Angevin kings, from Latin *planta* sprig + *genista* broom]
plan·tain[1] (ˈplæntɪn) *n.* any of various N temperate plants of the genus *Plantago,* esp. *P. major* (**great plantain**), which has a rosette of broad leaves and a slender spike of small greenish flowers: family *Plantaginaceae.* See also **ribwort.** [C16: from Spanish *platano* plantain, PLANE TREE]
plan·tain[2] (ˈplæntɪn) *n.* **1.** a large tropical musaceous plant, *Musa paradisiaca.* **2.** the green-skinned banana-like fruit of this plant, eaten as a staple food in many tropical regions. [C14 *plauntein,* from Old French *plantein,* from Latin *plantāgō,* from *planta* sole of the foot]
plan·tain-eat·er *n.* another name for **touraco.**
plan·tain lil·y *n.* any of several Asian plants of the liliaceous genus *Hosta,* having broad ribbed leaves and clusters of white, blue, or lilac flowers. Also called: **day lily.**
plan·tar (ˈplæntə) *adj.* of, relating to, or occurring on the sole of the foot or a corresponding part: *plantar warts.* [C18: from Latin *plantāris,* from *planta* sole of the foot]
plan·ta·tion (plænˈteɪʃən) *n.* **1.** an estate, esp. in tropical countries, where cash crops such as rubber, oil palm, etc., are grown on a large scale. **2.** a group of cultivated trees or plants. **3.** (formerly) a colony or group of settlers. **4.** *Rare.* the planting of seeds, shoots, etc.
plant·er (ˈplɑːntə) *n.* **1.** the owner or manager of a plantation. **2.** a machine designed for rapid, uniform, and efficient planting of seeds in the ground. **3.** a colonizer or settler. **4.** a decorative pot or stand for house plants.
plan·ti·grade (ˈplæntɪˌɡreɪd) *adj.* **1.** walking with the entire sole of the foot touching the ground, as, for example, man and bears. ~*n.* **2.** a plantigrade animal. [C19: via French from New Latin *plantigradus,* from Latin *planta* sole of the foot + *gradus* a step]
plant king·dom *n.* a category of living organisms comprising all plants. Compare **animal kingdom, mineral kingdom.**
plant louse *n.* **1.** another name for an **aphid. 2. jumping plant louse.** any small active cicada-like insect of the homopterous family *Psyllidae* (or *Chermidae*), having hind legs adapted for leaping, and feeding on plant juices.
plan·toc·ra·cy (plɑːnˈtɒkrəsɪ) *n.* a ruling social class composed of planters.
plan·u·la (ˈplænjʊlə) *n., pl.* **-lae** (-ˌliː). the ciliated free-swimming larva of hydrozoan coelenterates such as the hydra. [C19: from New Latin: a little plane, from Latin *plānum* level ground] —**ˈplan·u·lar** *adj.*
plaque (plæk, plɑːk) *n.* **1.** an ornamental or commemorative inscribed tablet or plate of porcelain, wood, etc. **2.** a small flat brooch or badge, as of a club, etc. **3.** *Pathol.* any small abnormal patch on or within the body, such as the typical lesion of psoriasis. **4.** short for **dental plaque. 5.** *Bacteriol.* a clear area within a bacterial or tissue culture caused by localized destruction of the cells by a bacteriophage or other virus. [C19: from French, from *plaquier* to plate, from Middle Dutch *placken* to beat (metal) into a thin plate]
plash[1] (plæʃ) *n., vb.* a less common word for **splash.** [Old English *plæsc,* probably imitative; compare Dutch *plas*]
plash[2] (plæʃ) *vb.* another word for **pleach.** [C15: from Old French *plassier,* from *plais* hedge, woven fence, from Latin *plectere* to plait; compare PLEACH]
plash·y (ˈplæʃɪ) *adj.* **plash·i·er, plash·i·est. 1.** wet or marshy. **2.** splashing or splashy.
-pla·si·a *or* **-pla·sy** *n. combining form.* indicating growth, development, or change: *hypoplasia.* [from New Latin, from Greek *plasis* a moulding, from *plassein* to mould] —**-plas·tic** *adj. combining form.*
plasm (ˈplæzəm) *n.* **1.** protoplasm of a specified type: *germ plasm.* **2.** a variant of **plasma.**
-plasm *n. combining form.* (in biology) indicating the material forming cells: *protoplasm.* [from Greek *plasma* something moulded; see PLASMA] —**-plas·mic** *adj. combining form.*
plas·ma (ˈplæzmə) *or* **plasm** (ˈplæzəm) *n.* **1.** the clear yellowish fluid portion of blood or lymph in which the corpuscles and cells are suspended. **2.** short for **blood plasma. 3.** a former name for **protoplasm** or **cytoplasm. 4.** *Physics.* **a.** a hot ionized material consisting of nuclei and electrons. It is sometimes regarded as a fourth state of matter and is the material present in the sun, most stars, and fusion reactors. **b.** the ionized gas in an electric discharge or spark, containing positive ions and electrons and a small number of negative ions together with unionized material. **5.** a green slightly translucent variety of chalcedony, used as a gemstone. **6.** a less common term for **whey.** [C18: from Late Latin: something moulded, from Greek, from *plassein* to mould] —**plas·mat·ic** (plæzˈmætɪk) *or* **ˈplas·mic** *adj.*
plas·ma en·gine *n.* an engine that generates thrust by reaction to the emission of a jet of plasma.
plas·ma·gel (ˈplæzməˌdʒɛl) *n.* another name for **ectoplasm** (sense 1).
plas·ma·gene (ˈplæzməˌdʒiːn) *n. Biology.* a self-replicating particle occurring in the cytoplasm of a cell and functioning in a way similar to but independent of chromosomal genes. —**plas·ma·gen·ic** (ˌplæzməˈdʒɛnɪk) *adj.*
plas·ma mem·brane *n.* another name for **cell membrane.**
plas·ma·sol (ˈplæzməˌsɒl) *n.* another name for **endoplasm.**
plas·ma torch *n.* an electrical device for converting a gas into a plasma, used for melting metal, etc.
plas·min (ˈplæzmɪn) *n.* another name for **fibrinolysin.**
plas·mo- *or before a vowel* **plasm-** *combining form.* of, relating to, or resembling plasma: *plasmolysis.* [from Greek *plasma;* see PLASMA]
plas·mo·des·ma (ˌplæzməˈdɛzmə) *or* **plas·mo·desm** (ˈplæzməˌdɛzəm) *n., pl.* **-des·ma·ta** (-ˈdɛzmətə) *or* **-desms.** *Botany.* any of various very fine cytoplasmic threads connecting the cytoplasm of adjacent cells via minute holes in the cell walls. [C20: from PLASMO- + Greek *desma* bond]
plas·mo·di·um (plæzˈməʊdɪəm) *n., pl.* **-di·a** (-dɪə). **1.** an amoeboid mass of protoplasm, containing many nuclei: a stage in the life cycle of certain organisms, esp. the nonreproductive stage of the slime moulds. **2.** any parasitic sporozoan protozoan of the genus *Plasmodium,* esp. *P. vivax,* which causes malaria. [C19: New Latin; see PLASMA, -ODE[1]] —**plas·ˈmo·di·al** *adj.*
plas·mo·lyse *or U.S.* **plas·mo·lyze** (ˈplæzməˌlaɪz) *vb.* to subject (a cell) to plasmolysis or (of a cell) to undergo plasmolysis.
plas·mol·y·sis (plæzˈmɒlɪsɪs) *n.* the shrinkage of protoplasm away from the cell walls that occurs as a result of excessive water loss, esp. in plant cells (see **exosmosis).** —**plas·mo·lyt·ic** (ˌplæzməˈlɪtɪk) *adj.* —ˌ**plas·mo·ˈlyt·i·cal·ly** *adv.*
plas·mon (ˈplæzmɒn) *n. Genetics.* the sum total of plasmagenes in a cell.
plas·mo·some (ˈplæzməˌsəʊm) *n.* another name for **nucleolus.**
Plas·sey (ˈplæsɪ) *n.* a village in NE India, in W Bengal: scene of Clive's victory (1757) over Siraj-ud-daula, which established British supremacy over India.
-plast *n. combining form.* indicating an organized living cell or particle of living matter: *protoplast.* [from Greek *plastos* formed, from *plassein* to form]
plas·ter (ˈplɑːstə) *n.* **1.** a mixture of lime, sand, and water, sometimes stiffened with hair or other fibres, that is applied to the surface of a wall or ceiling as a soft paste that hardens when dry. **2.** *Brit.* an adhesive strip of material, usually medicated, for dressing a cut, wound, etc. **3.** short for **mustard plaster** or **plaster of Paris.** ~*vb.* **4.** to coat (a wall, ceiling, etc.) with plaster. **5.** (*tr.*) to apply like plaster: *she plastered make-up on her face.* **6.** (*tr.*) to cause to lie flat or to adhere. **7.** (*tr.*) to apply a plaster cast to. **8.** (*tr.*) *Slang.* to strike or defeat with great force. [Old English, from Medieval Latin *plastrum* medicinal salve, building plaster, via Latin from Greek *emplastron* curative dressing, from EM- + *plassein* to form] —**ˈplas·ter·er** *n.* —**ˈplas·ter·y** *adj.*
plas·ter·board (ˈplɑːstəˌbɔːd) *n.* a thin rigid board, in the form of a layer of plaster compressed between two layers of fibreboard, used to form or cover walls, etc.
plas·ter cast *n.* **1.** *Surgery.* a cast made of plaster of Paris. See **cast** (sense 38). **2.** a copy or mould of a sculpture or other object cast in plaster of Paris.
plas·tered (ˈplɑːstəd) *adj. Slang.* intoxicated; drunk.
plas·ter·ing (ˈplɑːstərɪŋ) *n.* a coating or layer of plaster.
plas·ter of Par·is *n.* **1.** a white powder that sets to a hard solid when mixed with water, used for making sculptures and casts, as an additive for lime plasters, and for making casts for setting broken limbs. It is usually the hemihydrate of calcium sulphate, $2CaSO_4.H_2O$. **2.** the hard plaster produced when this powder is mixed with water: a fully hydrated form of calcium sulphate. ~Sometimes shortened to **plaster.** [C15: from Medieval Latin *plastrum parisiense,* originally made from the gypsum of *Paris*]
plas·tic (ˈplæstɪk) *n.* **1.** any one of a large number of synthetic usually organic materials that have a polymeric structure and can be moulded when soft and then set, esp. such a material in a finished state containing plasticizer, stabilizer, filler, pigments, etc. Plastics are classified as thermosetting (such as Bakelite) or thermoplastic (such as PVC) and are used in the

manufacture of many articles and in coatings, artificial fibres, etc. Compare **resin** (sense 2). ~*adj.* **2.** made of plastic. **3.** easily influenced; impressionable: *the plastic minds of children.* **4.** capable of being moulded or formed. **5.** *Fine arts.* **a.** of or relating to moulding or modelling: *the plastic arts.* **b.** produced or apparently produced by moulding: *the plastic draperies of Giotto's figures.* **6.** having the power to form or influence: *the plastic forces of the imagination.* **7.** *Biology.* of or relating to any formative process; able to change, develop, or grow: *plastic tissues.* **8.** of or relating to plastic surgery. **9.** *Slang.* superficially attractive yet unoriginal or artificial: *plastic food.* [C17: from Latin *plasticus* relating to moulding, from Greek *plastikos,* from *plassein* to form] —**'plas·ti·cal·ly** *adv.*

-plas·tic *adj. combining form.* growing or forming: *neoplastic.* [from Greek *plastikos;* see PLASTIC]

plas·tic bomb *n.* a bomb consisting of an adhesive jelly-like explosive fitted around a detonator.

Plas·ti·cine ('plæstɪˌsiːn) *n. Trademark.* a soft coloured material used, esp. by children, for modelling.

plas·tic·i·ty (plæ'stɪsɪtɪ) *n.* **1.** the quality of being plastic or able to be moulded. **2.** (in pictorial art) the quality of depicting space and form so that they appear three-dimensional.

plas·ti·cize *or* **plas·ti·cise** ('plæstɪˌsaɪz) *vb.* to make or become plastic, as by the addition of a plasticizer. —**ˌplas·ti·ci·'za·tion** *or* **ˌplas·ti·ci·'sa·tion** *n.*

plas·ti·ciz·er *or* **plas·ti·cis·er** ('plæstɪˌsaɪzə) *n.* any of a number of substances added to materials in order to modify their physical properties. Their uses include softening and improving the flexibility of plastics and preventing dried paint coatings from becoming too brittle.

plas·tic sur·ger·y *n.* the branch of surgery concerned with therapeutic or cosmetic repair or reformation of missing, injured, or malformed tissues or parts. Also called: **anaplasty.** —**plas·tic sur·geon** *n.*

plas·tid ('plæstɪd) *n.* any of various small particles in the cytoplasm of the cells of plants and some animals: contain pigments (see **chromoplast**), starch, oil, protein, etc. [C19: via German from Greek *plastēs* sculptor, from *plassein* to form]

plas·tom·e·ter (plæ'stɒmɪtə) *n.* an instrument for measuring plasticity. —**plas·to·met·ric** (ˌplæstəʊ'mɛtrɪk) *adj.* —**plas·'tom·e·try** *n.*

plas·tron ('plæstrən) *n.* the bony plate forming the ventral part of the shell of a tortoise or turtle. [C16: via French from Italian *piastrone,* from *piastra* breastplate, from Latin *emplastrum* PLASTER] —**'plas·tral** *adj.*

-plas·ty *n. combining form.* indicating plastic surgery involving a bodily part, tissue, or a specified process: *rhinoplasty; neoplasty.* [from Greek *-plastia;* see -PLAST]

plat[1] (plæt) *n. U.S.* a small area of ground; plot. [C16: (also occurring in Middle English in place names): originally a variant of PLOT[2]]

plat[2] (plæt) *vb.* **plats, plat·ting, plat·ted,** *n.* a dialect variant of **plait.** [C16: variant of PLAIT]

plat. *abbrev. for:* **1.** plateau. **2.** platoon.

Pla·ta (*Spanish* 'plata) *n.* **Rí·o de la** ('rio ðe la). an estuary on the SE coast of South America, between Argentina and Uruguay, formed by the Uruguay and Paraná Rivers. Length: 275 km (171 miles). Width: (at its mouth) 225 km (140 miles). Also called: **La Plata.** English name: (River) **Plate.**

Pla·tae·a (plə'tiːə) *n.* an ancient city in S Boeotia, traditionally an ally of Athens: scene of the defeat of a great Persian army by the Greeks in 479 B.C.

plat·an ('plætᵊn) *n.* another name for **plane tree.** [C14: from Latin *platanus,* from Greek *platanos;* see PLANE TREE]

plat du jour ('plɑː də 'ʒʊə; *French* pla dy 'ʒuːr) *n., pl.* **plats du jour** ('plɑːz də 'ʒʊə; *French* pla dy 'ʒuːr). the specially prepared or recommended dish of the day on a restaurant's menu. [French, literally: dish of the day]

plate (pleɪt) *n.* **1. a.** a shallow usually circular dish made of porcelain, earthenware, glass, etc., on which food is served or from which food is eaten. **b.** (*as modifier*): *a plate rack.* **2. a.** Also called: **plateful.** the contents of a plate or the amount a plate will hold. **b.** *Austral.* a plate of cakes, sandwiches, etc., brought by a guest to a party: *everyone was asked to bring a plate.* **3.** an entire course of a meal: *a cold plate.* **4.** any shallow or flat receptacle, esp. for receiving a collection in church. **5.** flat metal of uniform thickness obtained by rolling, usually having a thickness greater than about three millimetres. **6.** a thin coating of metal on another metal, as produced by electrodeposition, chemical action, etc. **7.** metal or metalware that has been coated in this way, esp. with gold or silver: *Sheffield plate.* **8.** dishes, cutlery, etc., made of gold or silver. **9.** a sheet of metal, plastic, rubber, etc., having a printing surface produced by a process such as stereotyping, moulding, or photographic deposition. **10.** a print taken from such a sheet or from a woodcut, esp. when appearing in a book. **11.** a thin flat sheet of a substance, such as metal or glass. **12.** armour made of overlapping or articulated pieces of thin metal. **13.** *Photog.* **a.** a sheet of glass, or sometimes metal, coated with photographic emulsion on which an image can be formed by exposure to light. **b.** (*as modifier*): *a plate camera.* **14.** an orthodontic device, esp. one used for straightening children's teeth. **15.** an informal word for **denture. 16.** *Anatomy.* any flat platelike structure or part. **17. a.** a cup or trophy awarded to the winner of a sporting contest, esp. a horse race. **b.** a race or contest for such a prize. **18.** any of the rigid layers of the earth's lithosphere of which there are believed to be at least 15. See also **plate tectonics. 19.** *Electronics.* **a.** *Chiefly U.S.* the anode in an electronic valve. **b.** an electrode in an accumulator or capacitor. **20.** a horizontal timber joist that supports rafters or studs. **21.** a light horseshoe for flat racing. **22.** a thin cut of beef from the brisket. **23.** *Railways.* See **plate rail. 24.** Also called: **Communion plate.** *R.C. Church.* a flat plate held under the chin of a communicant in order to catch any fragments of the consecrated Host. **25.** *Archaic.* a coin, esp. one made of silver. **26. on a plate.** in such a way as to be acquired without further trouble: *he was handed the job on a plate.* **27. on one's plate.** waiting to be done or dealt with: *he has a lot on his plate at the moment.* ~*vb.* (*tr.*) **28.** to coat (a metal) with a thin layer of other metal by electrolysis, chemical reaction, etc. **29.** to cover with metal plates, as for protection. **30.** *Printing.* to make a stereotype or electrotype from (type or another plate). **31.** to form (metal) into plate, esp. by rolling. **32.** to give a glossy finish to (paper) by calendering. **33.** to grow (microorganisms) in a culture medium. [C13: from Old French: thin metal sheet, something flat, from Vulgar Latin *plattus* (unattested); related to Greek *platus* flat]

Plate (pleɪt) *n.* **Riv·er.** the English name for the (Río de la) **Plata.**

plate ar·mour *n.* armour made of thin metal plates, which superseded mail during the 14th century.

plat·eau ('plætəʊ) *n., pl.* **·eaus** *or* **·eaux** (-əʊz). **1.** a wide mainly level area of elevated land. **2.** a relatively long period of stability; levelling off: *the rising prices reached a plateau.* [C18: from French, from Old French *platel* something flat, from *plat* flat; see PLATE]

Plat·eau ('plætəʊ) *n.* a state of central Nigeria, formed in 1976 from part of Benue-Plateau State: tin mining. Capital: Jos. Pop.: 1 421 481 (1976 est.). Area: 31 350 sq. km (12 102 sq. miles).

plat·ed ('pleɪtɪd) *adj.* **1. a.** coated with a layer of metal. **b.** (*in combination*): *goldplated.* **2.** (of a fabric) knitted in two different yarns so that one appears on the face and the other on the back.

plate glass *n.* glass formed into a thin sheet by rolling, used for windows, etc.

plate·lay·er ('pleɪtˌleɪə) *n. Brit.* a workman who lays and maintains railway track. U.S. equivalent: **trackman.**

plate·let ('pleɪtlɪt) *n.* a minute particle occurring in the blood of vertebrates and involved in clotting of the blood. Formerly called: **thrombocyte.** [C19: a small PLATE]

plate·mark ('pleɪtˌmɑːk) *n., vb.* another name for **hallmark** (senses 1, 4).

plat·en ('plætᵊn) *n.* **1.** a flat plate in a printing press that presses the paper against the type. **2.** the roller on a typewriter, against which the keys strike. **3.** the work table of a machine tool, esp. one that is slotted to enable clamping belts to be used. [C15: from Old French *platine,* from *plat* flat; see PLATE]

plat·er ('pleɪtə) *n.* **1.** a person or thing that plates. **2.** *Horse racing.* **a.** a mediocre horse entered chiefly for minor races. **b.** a blacksmith who shoes racehorses with the special type of light shoe used for racing.

plate rail *n. Railways.* an early flat rail with an extended flange on its outer edge to retain wheels on the track. Sometimes shortened to **plate.**

plate tec·ton·ics *n. Geology.* the study of the structure of the earth's crust with reference to the theory of its formation through the gradual movements of rigid layers of the lithosphere (plates).

plat·form ('plætfɔːm) *n.* **1.** a raised floor or other horizontal surface, such as a stage for speakers. **2.** a raised area at a railway station, from which passengers have access to the trains. **3.** the declared principles, aims, etc., of a political party. **4.** a plan of action; design; scheme. **5.** a level raised area of ground. **6. a.** the thick raised sole of some high-heeled shoes. **b.** (*as modifier*): *platform shoes.* **7.** a vehicle or level place on which weapons are mounted and fired. [C16: from French *plateforme,* from *plat* flat + *forme* form, layout]

plat·form rock·er *n. U.S.* a rocking-chair supported on a stationary base.

plat·form tick·et *n.* a ticket for admission to railway platforms but not for travel.

Plath (plæθ) *n.* **Syl·vi·a.** 1932–63, U.S. poet living in England. She wrote two volumes of verse, *The Colossus* (1960) and *Ariel* (1965), and a novel, *The Bell Jar* (1963).

plat·i·na ('plætɪnə, plə'tiːnə) *n.* an alloy of platinum and several other metals, including palladium, osmium, and iridium. [C18: from Spanish: silvery element, from *plata* silver, from Provençal: silver plate]

plat·ing ('pleɪtɪŋ) *n.* **1.** a coating or layer of material, esp. metal. **2.** a layer or covering of metal plates.

pla·tin·ic (plə'tɪnɪk) *adj.* of or containing platinum, esp. in the tetravalent state.

plat·i·nif·er·ous (ˌplætɪ'nɪfərəs) *adj.* platinum-bearing.

plat·in·i·rid·i·um (ˌplætɪnɪ'rɪdɪəm) *n.* any alloy of platinum and iridium: used in jewellery, electrical contacts, and hypodermic needles.

plat·i·nize *or* **plat·i·nise** ('plætɪˌnaɪz) *vb.* (*tr.*) to coat with platinum. —**ˌplat·i·ni·'za·tion** *or* **ˌplat·i·ni·'sa·tion** *n.*

plat·i·no-, plat·i·ni-, *or before a vowel* **plat·in-** *combining form.* of, relating to, containing, or resembling platinum: *platinotype.*

plat·i·no·cy·an·ic ac·id (ˌplætɪnəʊsaɪ'ænɪk) *n.* a hypothetical tetrabasic acid known only in the form of platinocyanide salts. Formula: $H_2Pt(CN)_4$.

plat·i·no·cy·a·nide (ˌplætɪnəʊ'saɪəˌnaɪd, -nɪd) *n.* any salt containing the divalent complex cation $[Pt(CN)_4]^{2-}$

plat·i·noid ('plætɪˌnɔɪd) *adj.* containing or resembling platinum: *a platinoid metal.*

plat·i+no+type ('plætɪnəʊˌtaɪp) *n.* an obsolete process for producing photographic prints using paper coated with an emulsion containing platinum salts, the resulting image in platinum black being more permanent and of a richer tone than the usual silver image.

plat·i+nous ('plætɪnəs) *adj.* of or containing platinum, esp. in the divalent state.

plat·i+num ('plætɪnəm) *n.* **1.** a ductile malleable silvery-white metallic element, very resistant to heat and chemicals. It occurs free and in association with other platinum metals, esp. in osmiridium: used in jewellery, laboratory apparatus, electrical contacts, dentistry, electroplating, and as a catalyst. Symbol: Pt; atomic no.: 78; atomic wt.: 195.09; valency: 1–4; relative density: 21.45; melting pt.: 1772°C; boiling pt.: 3827°C (approx.). **2. a.** a medium to light grey colour. **b.** (*as adj.*)*: a platinum carpet.* [C19: New Latin, from PLATINA, on the model of other metals with the suffix *-um*]

plat·i+num black *n. Chem.* a black powder consisting of very finely divided platinum metal. It is used as a catalyst, esp. in hydrogenation reactions.

plat·i·num-blond *or* (*fem.*) **plat·i·num-blonde** *adj.* **1.** (of hair) of a pale silver-blond colour. **2. a.** having hair of this colour. **b.** (*as n.*)*: she was a platinum blonde.*

plat·i+num met+al *n.* any of the group of precious metallic elements consisting of ruthenium, rhodium, palladium, osmium, iridium, and platinum.

plat·i+tude ('plætɪˌtju:d) *n.* **1.** a trite, dull, or obvious remark or statement; a commonplace. **2.** staleness or insipidity of thought or language; triteness. [C19: from French, literally: flatness, from *plat* flat] —ˌ**plat·i+'tu+di+nous** *adj.*

plat·i+tu+di+nize *or* **plat·i+tu+di+nise** (ˌplætɪ'tju:dɪˌnaɪz) *vb.* (*intr.*) to speak or write in platitudes. —ˌ**plat·i·'tu+di+ˌniz+er** *or* ˌ**plat·i+'tu+di+ˌnis+er** *n.*

Pla·to[1] ('pleɪtəʊ) *n.* ?427–?347 B.C., Greek philosopher: with his teacher Socrates and his pupil Aristotle, he is regarded as the initiator of western philosophy. His influential theory of ideas, which makes a distinction between objects of sense perception and the universal ideas or forms of which they are an expression, is formulated in such dialogues as *Phaedo, Symposium,* and *The Republic.* Other works include *The Apology* and *Laws.*

Pla+to[2] ('pleɪtəʊ) *n.* a crater in the NE quadrant of the moon, about 100 kilometres in diameter, that has a conspicuous dark floor.

Pla+ton+ic (plə'tɒnɪk) *adj.* **1.** of or relating to Plato or his teachings. **2.** (*often not cap.*) free from physical desire: *Platonic love.* —**Pla+'ton·i·cal+ly** *adv.*

Pla+ton+ic sol+id *n.* any of the five possible regular polyhedra: cube, tetrahedron, octahedron, icosahedron, and dodecahedron.

Pla+to+nism ('pleɪtəˌnɪzəm) *n.* **1.** the teachings of Plato and his followers. **2.** the philosophical theory that the meanings of general words are real existing abstract entities (forms) and describe particular objects, etc., by virtue of some relationship of these to the form. Compare **nominalism, conceptualism, intuitionism.** —**'Pla+ton+ist** *n.*

Pla+to+nize *or* **Pla+to+nise** ('pleɪtəˌnaɪz) *vb.* to think or explain by Platonic principles.

pla+toon (plə'tu:n) *n.* **1.** *Military.* a subdivision of a company comprising one or more sections of an army formation. **2.** a group or unit of people, esp. one sharing a common activity, characteristic, etc. [C17: from French *peloton* little ball, group of men, from *pelote* ball; see PELLET]

Platt+deutsch (*German* 'platˌdɔɪtʃ) *n.* another name for **Low German.** [literally: flat (that is, low) German]

Platte (plæt) *n.* a river system of the central U.S., formed by the confluence of the **North Platte** and **South Platte** at North Platte, Nebraska: flows generally east to the Missouri River. Length: 499 km (310 miles).

plat+te+land ('platəˌlant) *n.* **the.** (in South Africa) the area outside the cities and chief towns.

plat+ter ('plætə) *n.* **1.** a large shallow usually oval dish or plate, used for serving food. **2.** *U.S. slang.* a gramophone record. [C14: from Anglo-Norman *plater,* from *plat* dish, from Old French *plat* flat; see PLATE]

plat·y[1] ('pleɪtɪ) *adj.* **plat·i·er, plat·i+est.** of, relating to, or designating rocks, etc., the constituents of which occur in flaky layers: *platy fracture.* [C19: from PLATE + -Y[1]]

plat·y[2] ('plætɪ) *n., pl.* **plat·y, plat·ys,** *or* **plat·ies.** any of various small brightly coloured freshwater cyprinodont fishes of the Central American genus *Xiphophorus,* esp. *X. maculatus.* [C20: shortened from New Latin *Platypoecilus* former genus name, from PLATY- + *-poecilus* from Greek *poikilos* spotted]

plat·y- *combining form.* indicating something flat: *platyhelminth.* [from Greek *platus* flat]

plat·y+hel+minth (ˌplætɪ'hɛlmɪnθ) *n.* any invertebrate of the phylum *Platyhelminthes* (the flatworms). [C19: from New Latin *Platyhelmintha* flatworm, from PLATY- + Greek *helmins* worm] —ˌ**plat·y+hel+'min+thic** *adj.*

plat·y+pus ('plætɪpəs) *n., pl.* **+pus·es.** See **duck-billed platypus.** [C18: New Latin, from PLATY- + *-pus,* from Greek *pous* foot]

plat+yr+rhine ('plætɪˌraɪn) *or* **plat+yr+rhin+i·an** (ˌplætɪ'rɪnɪən) *adj.* **1.** (esp. of New World monkeys) having widely separated nostrils opening to the side of the face. **2.** (of humans) having an unusually short wide nose. ~*n.* **3.** an animal or person with this characteristic. ~Compare **catarrhine.** [C19: from New Latin *platyrrhinus,* from PLATY- + *-rrhinus,* from Greek *rhis* nose]

plau+dit ('plɔ:dɪt) *n.* (*usually pl.*) **1.** an expression of enthusiastic approval or approbation. **2.** a round of applause. [C17: shortened from earlier *plaudite,* from Latin: applaud!, from *plaudere* to APPLAUD]

Plau+en (*German* 'plauən) *n.* a city in S central East Germany: textile centre. Pop.: 81 279 (1972 est.).

plau+si·ble ('plɔ:zəb°l) *adj.* **1.** apparently reasonable, valid, truthful, etc.: *a plausible excuse.* **2.** apparently trustworthy or believable: *a plausible speaker.* [C16: from Latin *plausibilis* worthy of applause, from *plaudere* to APPLAUD] —ˌ**plau+si·'bil+i·ty** *or* **'plau+si·ble+ness** *n.* —**'plau+si·bly** *adv.*

plau+sive ('plɔ:sɪv) *adj.* **1.** expressing praise or approval; applauding. **2.** *Obsolete.* plausible.

Plau·tus ('plɔ:təs) *n.* **Ti·tus Mac·ci·us** ('taɪtəs 'mæksɪəs). ?254–?184 B.C., Roman comic dramatist. His 21 extant works, adapted from Greek plays, esp. those by Menander, include *Menaechmi* (the basis of Shakespeare's *Comedy of Errors*), *Miles Gloriosus, Rudens,* and *Captivi.*

play (pleɪ) *vb.* **1.** to occupy oneself in (a sport or diversion); amuse oneself in (a game, etc.). **2.** (*tr.*) to contend against (an opponent) in a sport or game: *Ed played Tony at chess and lost.* **3.** to fulfil or cause to fulfil (a particular role) in a team game: *he plays defence; he plays in the defence.* **4.** (*tr.*) to address oneself to (a ball, etc.) in a game: *play the ball not the man.* **5.** (*intr.;* often foll. by *about* or *around*) to behave carelessly, esp. in a way that is unconsciously cruel or hurtful; trifle or dally (with): *to play about with a young girl's affections.* **6.** (when *intr.;* often foll. by *at*) to perform or act the part (of) in or as in a dramatic production; assume or simulate the role (of): *to play the villain; just what are you playing at?* **7.** to act out or perform (a dramatic production). **8.** to give a performance in (a place) or (of a performance) to be given in a place. **9. a.** to have the ability to perform on (a musical instrument): *David plays the harp.* **10.** to perform (on a musical instrument) as specified: *he plays out of tune.* **11.** (*tr.*) **a.** to reproduce (a tune, melody, piece of music, note, etc.) on an instrument. **b.** to perform works by (a specific composer): *to play Brahms.* **12.** to discharge or cause to discharge: *he played the water from the hose onto the garden.* **13.** to operate, esp. to cause (a record player, radio, etc.) to emit sound or (of a record player, radio, etc.) to emit (sound): *he played a record; the radio was playing loudly.* **14.** to move or cause to move freely, quickly, or irregularly: *lights played on the scenery.* **15.** (*tr.*) *Stock exchange.* to speculate or operate aggressively for gain in (a market). **16.** (*tr.*) *Angling.* to attempt to tire (a hooked fish) by alternately letting out and reeling in line and by using the rod's flexibility. **17.** to put (a card, counter, piece, etc.) into play. **18.** to gamble (money) on a game, etc. **19. play fair** (*or* **false**). (often foll. by *with*) to prove oneself fair (or unfair) in one's dealings. **20. play by ear.** See **ear**[1] (sense 20). **21. play for time.** to delay the outcome of some activity so as to gain time to one's own advantage. **22. play into the hands of.** to act directly to the advantage of (an opponent). **23. play the fool.** to act as if one is a fool or idiot. **24. play the game.** to act in accordance with acknowledged rules or principles. ~*n.* **25.** a dramatic composition written for performance by actors on a stage, etc.; drama. **26. a.** the performance of a dramatic composition. **b.** (*in combination*)*: playreader.* **27. a.** games, exercise, or other activity undertaken for pleasure, diversion, etc., esp. by children. **b.** (*in combination*)*: playroom.* **c.** (*as modifier*)*: a play group.* **28.** manner of action, conduct, or playing: *fair play.* **29.** the playing or conduct of a game or the period during which a game is in progress: *rain stopped play.* **30.** *U.S.* a move or manoeuvre in a game: *a brilliant play.* **31.** the situation of a ball, etc., that is within the defined area and being played according to the rules (in the phrases **in play, out of play**). **32.** a turn to play: *it's my play.* **33.** the act of playing for stakes; gambling. **34.** action, activity, or operation: *the play of the imagination.* **35.** freedom of or scope or space for movement: *too much play in the rope.* **36.** light, free, or rapidly shifting motion: *the play of light on the water.* **37.** fun, jest, or joking: *I only did it in play.* **38. make a play for.** *Informal.* **a.** to make an obvious attempt to gain. **b.** to attempt to attract or seduce. ~See also **play along, playback, play down, play off, play on, play out, play up, play with.** [Old English *plega* (n.), *plegan* (vb.); related to Middle Dutch *pleyen*] —**'play+a·ble** *adj.*

pla+ya ('plɑ:jə; *Spanish* 'plaja) *n. U.S.* a temporary lake, or its dry often salty bed, in a desert basin. [Spanish: shore, from Late Latin *plagia,* from Greek *plagios* slanting, from *plagos* side; compare French *plage* beach]

play-act *vb.* **1.** (*intr.*) to pretend or make believe. **2.** (*intr.*) to behave in an overdramatic or affected manner. **3.** to act in or as in (a play). —**'play-ˌact·ing** *n.* —**'play-ˌact·or** *n.*

play a·long *vb.* (*adv.*) **1.** (*intr.;* usually foll. by *with*) to cooperate (with), esp. as a temporary measure. **2.** (*tr.*) to manipulate as if in a game, esp. for one's own advantage: *he played the widow along until she gave him her money.*

play+back ('pleɪˌbæk) *n.* **1.** the act or process of reproducing a recording, esp. a sound recording on magnetic tape. **2.** the part of a tape recorder serving to or used for reproducing recorded material. **3.** (*modifier*) of or relating to the reproduction of signals from a recording: *the playback head of a tape recorder.* ~*vb.* **play back.** (*adv.*) **4.** to reproduce (recorded material) on (a magnetic tape) by means of a tape recorder.

play+bill ('pleɪˌbɪl) *n.* **1.** a poster or bill advertising a play. **2.** the programme of a play.

play+boy ('pleɪˌbɔɪ) *n.* a man, esp. one of private means, who devotes himself to the pleasures of nightclubs, expensive holiday resorts, female company, etc.

play down *vb.* (*tr., adv.*) to make little or light of; minimize the importance of.

play·er ('pleɪə) *n.* **1.** a person who participates in or is skilled at some game or sport. **2.** a person who plays a game or sport professionally. **3.** a person who plays a musical instrument. **4.** an actor. **5.** a trifler. **6.** See **record-player. 7.** the playing mechanism in a Pianola.

Play·er ('pleɪə) *n.* **Ga·ry** ('gærɪ). born 1935, South African professional golfer: won the British Open Championship (1959; 1968) and the U.S. Open Championship (1965).

play·er pi·an·o *n.* a mechanical piano; Pianola.

play·ful ('pleɪfʊl) *adj.* **1.** full of high spirits and fun: *a playful kitten.* **2.** good-natured and humorous: *a playful remark.* —'**play·ful·ly** *adv.* —'**play·ful·ness** *n.*

play·go·er ('pleɪˌgəʊə) *n.* a person who goes to theatre performances, esp. frequently.

play·ground ('pleɪˌgraʊnd) *n.* **1.** an outdoor area for children's play, esp. one having swings, slides, etc., or adjoining a school. **2.** a place or region particularly popular as a sports or holiday resort. **3.** a sphere of activity: *reading was his private playground.*

play·house ('pleɪˌhaʊs) *n.* **1.** a theatre where live dramatic performances are given. **2.** a toy house, small room, etc., for children to play in.

play·ing card *n.* one of a pack of 52 rectangular pieces of stiff card, used for playing a wide variety of games, each card having one or more symbols of the same kind (diamonds, hearts, clubs, or spades) on the face, but an identical design on the reverse. See also **suit** (sense 4).

play·ing field *n. Chiefly Brit.* a field or open space used for sport.

play·let ('pleɪlɪt) *n.* a short play.

play·mate ('pleɪˌmeɪt) *or* **play·fel·low** *n.* a friend or partner in play or recreation: *childhood playmates.*

play off *vb.* (*adv.*) **1.** (*tr.*; usually foll. by *against*) to deal with or manipulate as if in playing a game: *to play one person off against another.* **2.** (*intr.*) to take part in a play-off. ~*n.* **play-off. 3.** *Sport.* an extra contest to decide the winner when two or more competitors are tied. **4.** *Chiefly U.S.* a contest or series of games to determine a championship, as between the winners of two competitions.

play on *vb.* (*intr.*) **1.** (*adv.*) to continue to play. **2.** (*prep.*) Also: **play upon.** to exploit or impose upon (the feelings or weakness of another) to one's own advantage.

play on words *n.* another term for **pun.**

play out *vb.* (*tr., adv.*) **1.** to finish: *let's play the game out if we aren't too late.* **2.** (*often passive*) *Informal.* to use up or exhaust. **3.** to release gradually: *he played the rope out.*

play·pen ('pleɪˌpɛn) *n.* a small enclosure, usually portable, in which a young child can be left to play in safety.

play·room ('pleɪˌru:m, -ˌrʊm) *n.* a recreation room, esp. for children.

play·school ('pleɪˌsku:l) *n.* an informal nursery group taking preschool children in half-day sessions. Also called: **play group.**

play·suit ('pleɪˌsju:t) *n.* a woman's or child's outfit, usually comprising shorts and a top.

play·thing ('pleɪˌθɪŋ) *n.* **1.** a toy. **2.** a person regarded or treated as a toy: *he thinks she is just his plaything.*

play·time ('pleɪˌtaɪm) *n.* a time for play or recreation, esp. the school break.

play up *vb.* (*adv.*) **1.** (*tr.*) to emphasize or highlight: *to play up one's best features.* **2.** *Brit. informal.* to behave irritatingly (towards). **3.** (*intr.*) *Brit. informal.* (of a machine, etc.) to function erratically: *the car is playing up again.* **4. play up to. a.** to support (another actor) in a performance. **b.** *Informal.* to try to gain favour with, by flattery.

play with *vb.* (*intr., prep.*) **1.** to consider without giving deep thought to or coming to a conclusion concerning: *we're playing with the idea of emigrating.* **2.** to behave carelessly with: *to play with a girl's affections.*

play·wright ('pleɪˌraɪt) *n.* a person who writes plays.

pla·za ('plɑ:zə; *Spanish* 'plaθa) *n.* **1.** an open space or square, esp. in Spain or a Spanish-speaking country. **2.** *Chiefly U.S.* **a.** a modern complex of shops, buildings, and parking areas. **b.** (*cap. as part of a name*): *Rockefeller Plaza.* [C17: from Spanish, from Latin *platēa* courtyard, from Greek *plateia*; see PLACE]

plea (pli:) *n.* **1.** an earnest entreaty or request: *a plea for help.* **2. a.** *Law.* something alleged or pleaded by or on behalf of a party to legal proceedings in support of his claim or defence. **b.** *Criminal law.* the answer made by an accused to the charge: *a plea of guilty.* **c.** (formerly in England) a suit or action at law. **3.** an excuse, justification, or pretext: *he gave the plea of a previous engagement.* [C13: from Anglo-Norman *plai*, from Old French *plaid* lawsuit, from Medieval Latin *placitum* court order (literally: what is pleasing), from Latin *placēre* to please]

pleach (pli:tʃ) *vb. Chiefly Brit.* to construct or repair (a hedge) by interlacing the shoots. Also: **plash.** [C14 *plechen*, from Old North French *plechier*, from Latin *plectere* to weave, plait; compare PLASH[2]]

plead (pli:d) *vb.* **pleads, plead·ing; plead·ed, plead** (plɛd), *or* **pled. 1.** (when *intr.*, often foll. by *with*) to appeal earnestly or humbly (to). **2.** (*tr.; may take a clause as object*) to give as an excuse; offer in justification or extenuation: *to plead ignorance; he pleaded that he was insane.* **3.** (*intr.*; often foll. by *for*) to provide an argument or appeal (for): *her beauty pleads for her.* **4.** *Law.* to declare oneself to be (guilty or not guilty) in answer to the charge. **5.** *Law.* to advocate (a case) in a court of law. **6.** (*intr.*) *Law.* **a.** to file a pleading. **b.** to address a court as an advocate. [C13: from Old French *plaidier*, from Medieval Latin *placitāre* to have a lawsuit, from Latin *placēre* to please; see PLEA] —'**plead·a·ble** *adj.* —'**plead·er** *n.*

plead·ing ('pli:dɪŋ) *n. Law.* **1.** the act of presenting a case in court, as by a lawyer on behalf of his client. **2.** the art or science of preparing the formal written statements of the parties to a legal action. See also **pleadings.**

plead·ings ('pli:dɪŋz) *pl. n. Law.* the formal written statements presented alternately by the plaintiff and defendant in a lawsuit setting out the respective matters relied upon.

pleas·ance ('plɛzəns) *n.* **1.** a secluded part of a garden laid out with trees, walks, etc. **2.** *Archaic.* enjoyment or pleasure. [C14 *plesaunce*, from Old French *plaisance*, from *plaisant* pleasant, from *plaisir* to PLEASE]

pleas·ant ('plɛzᵊnt) *adj.* **1.** giving or affording pleasure; enjoyable. **2.** having pleasing or agreeable manners, appearance, habits, etc. **3.** *Obsolete.* merry and lively. [C14: from Old French *plaisant*, from *plaisir* to PLEASE] —'**pleas·ant·ly** *adv.* —'**pleas·ant·ness** *n.*

Pleas·ant Is·land *n.* the former name of **Nauru.**

pleas·ant·ry ('plɛzᵊntrɪ) *n., pl.* **-ries. 1.** (*often pl.*) an agreeable or amusing remark, etc., often one made in order to be polite: *they exchanged pleasantries.* **2.** an agreeably humorous manner or style. **3.** *Rare.* enjoyment; pleasantness: *a pleasantry of life.* [C17: from French *plaisanterie*, from *plaisant* PLEASANT]

please (pli:z) *vb.* **1.** to give satisfaction, pleasure, or contentment to (a person); make or cause to be glad. **2.** to be the will of or have the will (to): *if it pleases you; the court pleases.* **3. if you please.** if you will or wish, sometimes used in ironic exclamation. **4. pleased with.** happy because of. **5. please oneself.** to do as one likes. ~*adv.* **6.** (*sentence modifier*) used in making polite requests and in pleading, asking for a favour, etc.: *please don't tell the police where I am.* **7. yes please.** a polite formula for accepting an offer, invitation, etc. [C14 *plese*, from Old French *plaisir*, from Latin *placēre* to please, satisfy] —'**pleas·a·ble** *adj.* —**pleas·ed·ly** ('pli:zɪdlɪ) *adv.* —'**pleas·er** *n.*

pleas·ing ('pli:zɪŋ) *adj.* giving pleasure; likeable or gratifying. —'**pleas·ing·ly** *adv.* —'**pleas·ing·ness** *n.*

pleas·ur·a·ble ('plɛʒərəbᵊl) *adj.* enjoyable, agreeable, or gratifying. —'**pleas·ur·a·ble·ness** *n.* —'**pleas·ur·a·bly** *adv.*

pleas·ure ('plɛʒə) *n.* **1.** an agreeable or enjoyable sensation or emotion: *the pleasure of hearing good music.* **2.** something that gives or affords enjoyment or delight: *his garden was his only pleasure.* **3. a.** amusement, recreation, or enjoyment. **b.** (*as modifier*): *a pleasure boat; pleasure ground.* **4.** *Euphemistic.* sexual gratification or enjoyment: *he took his pleasure of her.* **5.** a person's preference or choice. ~*vb.* **6.** (when *intr.*, often foll. by *in*) *Archaic.* to give pleasure to or take pleasure (in). [C14 *plesir*, from Old French; related to Old French *plaisir* to PLEASE] —'**pleas·ure·ful** *adj.* —'**pleas·ure·less** *adj.*

pleas·ure prin·ci·ple *n. Psychoanal.* the idea that psychological processes and actions are governed by the gratification of needs. It is seen as the governing process of the id, whereas the reality principle is the governing process of the ego. See also **hedonism.**

pleat (pli:t) *n.* **1.** any of various types of fold formed by doubling back fabric, etc., and pressing, stitching, or steaming into place. See also **box pleat, inverted pleat, kick pleat, knife pleat, sunburst pleats.** ~*vb.* **2.** (*tr.*) to arrange (material, part of a garment, etc.) in pleats. [C16: variant of PLAIT]

pleat·er ('pli:tə) *n.* an attachment on a sewing machine that makes pleats.

pleb (plɛb) *n.* **1.** short for **plebeian. 2.** *Brit. slang.* a common vulgar person.

pleb·by ('plɛbɪ) *adj.* **-bi·er, -bi·est.** *Brit. slang.* common or vulgar: *a plebby party.* [C20: shortened from PLEBEIAN]

plebe (pli:b) *n. Informal.* a member of the lowest class at the U.S. Naval Academy or Military Academy; freshman. [C19: shortened from PLEBEIAN]

ple·be·ian (plə'bi:ən) *adj.* **1.** of, relating to, or characteristic of the common people, esp. those of Rome. **2.** lacking refinement; philistine or vulgar: *plebeian tastes.* ~*n.* **3.** one of the common people, esp. one of the Roman plebs. **4.** a person who is coarse, vulgar, or lacking in refinement or discernment. [C16: from Latin *plēbēius* belonging to the people, from *plēbs* the common people of ancient Rome] —**ple'be·ian·ism** *n.*

pleb·i·scite ('plɛbɪˌsaɪt, -sɪt) *n.* **1.** a direct vote by the electorate of a state, region, etc., on some question of usually national importance, such as union with another state or acceptance of a government programme. **2.** any expression or determination of public opinion on some matter. ~See also **referendum.** [C16: from Old French *plébiscite*, from Latin *plēbiscītum* decree of the people, from *plēbs* the populace + *scītum* from *scīscere* to decree, approve, from *scīre* to know] —**ple·bis·ci·ta·ry** (plə'bɪsɪtərɪ) *adj.*

plebs (plɛbz) *n.* **1.** (*functioning as pl.*) the common people; the masses. **2.** (*functioning as sing. or pl.*) common people of ancient Rome. Compare **patrician.** [C17: from Latin: the common people of ancient Rome]

plec·tog·nath ('plɛktɒgˌnæθ) *n.* **1.** any spiny-finned marine fish of the mainly tropical order *Plectognathi* (or *Tetraodontiformes*), having a small mouth, strong teeth, and small gill openings: includes puffers, triggerfish, trunkfish, sunfish, etc. ~*adj.* **2.** of, relating to, or belonging to the order *Plectognathi.* [C19: via New Latin from Greek *plektos* twisted + *gnathos* jaw]

plec·trum ('plɛktrəm) *or* **plec·tron** ('plɛktrən) *n., pl.* **-tra** (-trə), **-trums** *or* **-tra, -trons.** any implement for plucking a string, such as a small piece of plastic, wood, etc., used to strum a guitar or the quill that plucks the string of a harpsichord. [C17: from Latin *plēctrum* quill, plectrum, from Greek *plektron,* from *plessein* to strike]

pled (plɛd) *vb. U.S. or (esp. in legal usage) Scot.* a past tense or past participle of **plead.**

pledge (plɛdʒ) *n.* **1.** a formal or solemn promise or agreement, esp. to do or refrain from doing something. **2. a.** collateral for the payment of a debt or the performance of an obligation. **b.** the condition of being collateral (esp. in the phrase **in pledge**). **3.** a sign, token, or indication: *the gift is a pledge of their sincerity.* **4.** an assurance of support or goodwill, conveyed by drinking to a person, cause, etc.; toast: *we drank a pledge to their success.* **5.** a person who binds himself, as by becoming bail or surety for another. **6. take** *or* **sign the pledge.** to make a vow to abstain from alcoholic drink. ~*vb.* **7.** to promise formally or solemnly: *he pledged allegiance.* **8.** (*tr.*) to bind or secure by or as if by a pledge: *they were pledged to secrecy.* **9.** to give, deposit, or offer (one's word, freedom, property, etc.) as a guarantee, as for the repayment of a loan. **10.** to drink a toast to (a person, cause, etc.). [C14: from Old French *plege,* from Late Latin *plebium* gage, security, from *plebīre* to pledge, of Germanic origin; compare Old High German *pflegan* to look after, care for] —**'pledg+a·ble** *adj.* —**'pledg+er** *n.*

pledg·ee (plɛdʒ'iː) *n.* **1.** a person to whom a pledge is given. **2.** a person to whom property is delivered as a pledge.

pledg+et ('plɛdʒɪt) *n.* a small flattened pad of wool, cotton, etc., esp. for use as a pressure bandage to be applied to wounds or sores. [C16: of unknown origin]

pledg+or *or* **pledge+or** (plɛdʒ'ɔː) *n.* a person who gives or makes a pledge.

-ple·gi·a *n. combining form.* indicating a specified type of paralysis: *paraplegia.* [from Greek, from *plēgē* stroke, from *plēssein* to strike] —**-ple·gic** *adj. and n. combining form.*

plei+ad ('plaɪəd) *n.* a brilliant or talented group, esp. one with seven members. [C16: originally French *Pléiade,* name given by Ronsard to himself and six other poets after a group of Alexandrian Greek poets who were called this after PLEIADES[1]]

Plei+ad ('plaɪəd) *n.* one of the Pleiades (stars or daughters of Atlas).

Plei·a·des[1] ('plaɪəˌdiːz) *n. Greek myth.* the seven daughters of Atlas, placed as stars in the sky either to save them from the pursuit of Orion or, in another account, after they had killed themselves for grief over the death of their half sisters the Hyades.

Plei·a·des[2] ('plaɪəˌdiːz) *n.* a conspicuous open star cluster in the constellation Taurus, containing several hundred stars only six or seven of which are visible to the naked eye. Compare **Hyades**[1].

plein-air (ˌpleɪn'ɛə; *French* plɛ'nɛːr) *adj.* of or in the manner of various French 19th-century schools of painting, esp. impressionism, concerned with the observation of light and atmosphere effects outdoors. [C19: from French phrase *en plein air* in the open (literally, full) air] —**plein-air·ist** (pleɪn'ɛərɪst) *n.*

plei·o- *combining form.* variant of **plio-.**

Plei·o+cene ('plaɪəʊˌsiːn) *adj., n.* a variant spelling of **Pliocene.**

plei+ot+ro+pism (plaɪ'ɒtrəˌpɪzəm) *n. Genetics.* the condition of a gene of affecting more than one characteristic of the phenotype.

Pleis+to+cene ('plaɪstəˌsiːn) *adj.* **1.** of, denoting, or formed in the first epoch of the Quaternary period, which lasted for about 990 000 years. It was characterized by extensive glaciations of the N hemisphere and the evolutionary development of man. ~*n.* **2. the Pleistocene.** the Pleistocene epoch or rock series. [C19: from Greek *pleistos* most + *kainos* recent]

ple+na+ry ('pliːnərɪ, 'plɛn-) *adj.* **1.** full, unqualified, or complete: *plenary powers; plenary indulgence.* **2.** (of assemblies, councils, etc.) attended by all the members. ~*n.* **3.** a book of the gospels or epistles and homilies read at the Eucharist. [C15: from Late Latin *plēnārius,* from Latin *plēnus* full; related to Middle English *plener;* see PLENUM] —**'ple+na+ri+ly** *adv.*

ple+nip·o·tent (plə'nɪpətənt) *adj.* a less common word for **plenipotentiary.**

plen·i+po+ten+ti+ar·y (ˌplɛnɪpə'tɛnʃərɪ) *adj.* **1.** (esp. of a diplomatic envoy) invested with or possessing full power or authority. **2.** conferring full power or authority. **3.** (of power or authority) full; absolute. ~*n., pl.* **+ar·ies. 4.** a person invested with full authority to transact business, esp. a diplomat authorized to represent a country. See also **envoy**[1] (sense 1). [C17: from Medieval Latin *plēnipotentiārius,* from Latin *plēnus* full + *potentia* POWER]

plen+ish ('plɛnɪʃ) *vb.* (*tr.*) *Archaic or Scot.* to fill, stock, or resupply. [C15: from Old French *pleniss-,* from *plenir,* from Latin *plēnus* full] —**'plen+ish+er** *n.* —**'plen+ish+ment** *n.*

plen·i+tude ('plɛnɪˌtjuːd) *n.* **1.** abundance; copiousness. **2.** the condition of being full or complete. [C15: via Old French from Latin *plēnitūdō,* from *plēnus* full]

plen+te·ous ('plɛntɪəs) *adj.* **1.** ample; abundant: *a plenteous supply of food.* **2.** producing or yielding abundantly: *a plenteous grape harvest.* [C13 *plenteus,* from Old French *plentivous,* from *plentif* abundant, from *plenté* PLENTY] —**'plen+te·ous+ly** *adv.* —**'plen+te·ous+ness** *n.*

plen+ti+ful ('plɛntɪfʊl) *adj.* **1.** ample; abundant. **2.** having or yielding an abundance: *a plentiful year.* —**'plen+ti+ful+ly** *adv.* —**'plen+ti+ful+ness** *n.*

plen+ty ('plɛntɪ) *n., pl.* **+ties. 1.** (often foll. by *of*) a great number, amount, or quantity; lots: *plenty of time; there are plenty of cars on display here.* **2.** generous or ample supplies of wealth, produce, or resources: *the age of plenty.* **3. in plenty.** existing in abundance: *food in plenty.* ~*determiner.* **4. a.** very many; ample: *plenty of people believe in ghosts.* **b.** (*as pronoun*): *there's plenty more; that's plenty, thanks.* ~*adv.* **5.** *Not standard, chiefly U.S.* (intensifier): *he was plenty mad.* [C13: from Old French *plenté,* from Late Latin *plēnitās* fullness, from Latin *plēnus* full]

Plen+ty ('plɛntɪ) *n.* **Bay of.** a large bay of the Pacific on the NE coast of North Island, New Zealand.

ple+num ('pliːnəm) *n., pl.* **+nums** *or* **+na** (-nə). **1.** an enclosure containing gas at a higher pressure than the surrounding environment. **2.** a fully attended meeting or assembly, esp. of a legislative body. **3.** (esp. in the philosophy of the Stoics) space regarded as filled with matter. Compare **vacuum** (sense 1). **4.** the condition or quality of being full. [C17: from Latin: space filled by matter, from *plēnus* full]

ple+num sys+tem *n.* a type of air-conditioning system in which air is passed into a room at a pressure greater than atmospheric pressure.

ple·o- *combining form.* variant of **plio-**: *pleochroism; pleomorphism.*

ple+och+ro+ism (plɪ'ɒkrəʊˌɪzəm) *n.* a property of certain crystals of absorbing light to an extent that depends on the orientation of the electric vector of the light with respect to the optic axes of the crystal. The effect occurs in uniaxial crystals (**dichroism**) and esp. in biaxial crystals (**trichroism**). [C19: PLEO- + *-chroism* from Greek *khrōs* skin colour] —**ple·o+chro+ic** (ˌpliːə'krəʊɪk) *adj.*

ple·o+mor+phism (ˌpliːə'mɔːfɪzəm) *or* **ple·o+mor+phy** ('pliːəˌmɔːfɪ) *n.* the occurrence of more than one different form in the life cycle of a plant or animal. —**ˌple·o+'mor+phic** *adj.*

ple·o+nasm ('pliːəˌnæzəm) *n. Rhetoric.* **1.** the use of more words than necessary or an instance of this, such as *a tiny little child.* **2.** a word or phrase that is superfluous. [C16: from Latin *pleonasmus,* from Greek *pleonasmos* excess, from *pleonazein* to be redundant] —**ˌple·o+'nas+tic** *adj.* —**ˌple·o+'nas+ti+cal+ly** *adv.*

ple·o+pod ('pliːəˌpɒd) *n.* another name for **swimmeret.** [C19: from Greek *plein* to swim + *pous* foot]

ple+si·o+saur ('pliːsɪəˌsɔː) *n.* any of various extinct marine reptiles of the order *Sauropterygia,* esp. any of the suborder *Plesiosauria,* of Jurassic and Cretaceous times, having a long neck, short tail, and paddle-like limbs. See also **ichthyosaur.** Compare **dinosaur, pterosaur.** [C19: from New Latin *plēsiosaurus,* from Greek *plēsios* near + *sauros* a lizard]

ples+sor ('plɛsə) *n. Med.* another name for **plexor.**

pleth·o+ra ('plɛθərə) *n.* **1.** superfluity or excess; overabundance. **2.** *Pathol, obsolete.* a condition caused by dilation of superficial blood vessels, characterized esp. by a reddish face. [C16: via Medieval Latin from Greek *plēthōrē* fullness, from *plēthein* to grow full] —**ple+tho+ric** (plɛ'θɒrɪk) *adj.* —**ple+tho+ri+cal+ly** *adv.*

ple+thys+mo+graph (plə'θɪzməˌgrɑːf, -ˌgræf, -'θɪs-) *n.* a device for measuring the fluctuations in volume of a bodily organ or part, such as those caused by variations in the amount of blood it contains. [C19: from Greek *plēthusmos* enlargement + *graphein* to write]

pleu+ra ('plʊərə) *n., pl.* **pleu+rae** ('plʊəriː). **1.** the thin transparent serous membrane enveloping the lungs and lining the walls of the thoracic cavity. **2.** the plural of **pleuron.** [C17: via Medieval Latin from Greek: side, rib] —**'pleu+ral** *adj.*

pleu+ri+sy ('plʊərɪsɪ) *n.* inflammation of the pleura, characterized by pain that is aggravated by deep breathing or coughing. [C14: from Old French *pleurisie,* from Late Latin *pleurisis,* from Greek *pleuritis,* from *pleura* side] —**pleu+rit+ic** (plʊ'rɪtɪk) *adj., n.*

pleu+ri+sy root *n.* **1.** the root of the butterfly weed, formerly used as a cure for pleurisy. **2.** another name for **butterfly weed.**

pleu·ro- *or before a vowel* **pleur-** *combining form.* **1.** of or relating to the side: *pleurodont; pleurodynia.* **2.** indicating the pleura: *pleurotomy.* [from Greek *pleura* side]

pleu+ro+dont ('plʊərəʊˌdɒnt) *adj.* **1.** (of the teeth of some reptiles) having no roots and being fused by their lateral sides only to the inner surface of the jawbone. See also **acrodont** (sense 1). **2.** having pleurodont teeth: *pleurodont lizards.* ~*n.* **3.** an animal having pleurodont teeth.

pleu+ro+dy+ni·a (ˌplʊərəʊ'daɪnɪə) *n.* pain in the muscles between the ribs.

pleu+ron ('plʊərɒn) *n., pl.* **pleu+ra** ('plʊərə). the part of the cuticle of arthropods that covers the lateral surface of a body segment. [C18: from Greek: side]

pleu+ro+pneu+mo+ni·a (ˌplʊərəʊnjuː'məʊnɪə) *n.* the combined disorder of pleurisy and pneumonia.

pleu+rot·o+my (plʊ'rɒtəmɪ) *n., pl.* **+mies.** surgical incision into the pleura, esp. to drain fluid, as in pleurisy.

pleus+ton ('pluːstən, -stɒn) *n.* a mass of small organisms, esp. algae, floating at the surface of shallow pools. [C20: from Greek *pleusis* sailing, from *plein* to sail; for form, compare PLANKTON]

Plev+en (*Bulgarian* 'plɛvɛn) *or* **Plev+na** (*Bulgarian* 'plɛvna) *n.* a town in N Bulgaria: taken by Russia from the Turks in 1877 after a siege of 143 days. Pop.: 89 814 (1970).

plew, plu, *or* **plue** (pluː) *n. Canadian history.* a beaver skin used as a standard unit of value in the fur trade. [from Canadian French *pelu* (adj.) hairy, from French *poilu,* from *poil* hair, from Latin *pilus*]

plex·i+form ('plɛksɪˌfɔːm) *adj.* like or having the form of a network or plexus; intricate or complex.

Plex·i+glass ('plɛksɪˌglɑːs) *n. U.S. Trademark.* a transparent plastic, polymethyl methacrylate, used for combs, plastic sheeting, etc.

plex+or ('plɛksə) *or* **ples+sor** *n. Med.* a small hammer with a rubber head for use in percussion of the chest and testing reflexes. [C19: from Greek *plēxis* a stroke, from *plēssein* to strike]

plex+us ('plɛksəs) *n., pl.* **+us·es** *or* **+us. 1.** any complex network of nerves, blood vessels, or lymphatic vessels. **2.** an intricate network or arrangement. [C17: New Latin, from Latin *plectere* to braid, PLAIT]

pli+a·ble ('plaɪəbᵊl) *adj.* easily moulded, bent, influenced, or altered. **—,pli+a·'bil+i·ty** *or* **'pli+a·ble+ness** *n.* **—'pli+a·bly** *adv.*

pli+ant ('plaɪənt) *adj.* **1.** easily bent; supple: *a pliant young tree.* **2.** easily modified; adaptable; flexible: *a pliant system.* **3.** yielding readily to influence; compliant. [C14: from Old French, from *plier* to fold, bend; see PLY²] **—'pli+an+cy** *or* **'pli+ant+ness** *n.* **—'pli+ant+ly** *adv.*

pli+ca ('plaɪkə) *n., pl.* **pli+cae** ('plaɪsiː). **1.** Also called: **fold.** *Anatomy.* a folding over of parts, such as a fold of skin, muscle, peritoneum, etc. **2.** *Pathol.* a condition of the hair characterized by matting, filth, and the presence of parasites. [C17: from Medieval Latin: a fold, from Latin *plicāre* to fold; see PLY²] **—'pli+cal** *adj.*

pli+cate ('plaɪkeɪt) *or* **pli+cat+ed** *adj.* having or arranged in parallel folds or ridges; pleated: *a plicate leaf; plicate rock strata.* [C18: from Latin *plicātus* folded, from *plicāre* to fold] **—'pli+cate+ly** *adv.* **—'pli+cate+ness** *n.*

pli+ca+tion (plaɪ'keɪʃən) *or* **plic·a+ture** ('plɪkətʃə) *n.* **1.** the act of folding or the condition of being folded or plicate. **2.** a folded part or structure, esp. a fold in a series of rock strata. **3.** *Surgery.* the act or process of suturing together the walls of a hollow organ or part to reduce its size.

pli·é ('pliːeɪ) *n.* a classic ballet practice posture with back erect and knees bent. [French: bent, from *plier* to bend]

pli+er *or* **ply+er** ('plaɪə) *n.* a person who plies a trade.

pli+ers ('plaɪəz) *pl. n.* a gripping tool consisting of two hinged arms with usually serrated jaws that close on the workpiece.

plight¹ (plaɪt) *n.* a condition of extreme hardship, danger, etc. [C14 *plit*, from Old French *pleit* fold, PLAIT; probably influenced by Old English *pliht* peril, PLIGHT²]

plight² (plaɪt) *vb.* (*tr.*) **1.** to give or pledge (one's word, etc.): *he plighted his word to attempt it.* **2.** to promise formally or pledge (allegiance, support, etc.): *to plight aid.* **3. plight one's troth. a.** to make a promise of marriage. **b.** to give one's solemn promise. *~n.* **4.** *Archaic or Brit. dialect.* a solemn promise, esp. of engagement; pledge. [Old English *pliht* peril; related to Old High German, German *Pflicht duty*] **—'plight+er** *n.*

plim+soll *or* **plim+sole** ('plɪmsəl) *n. Brit.* a light rubber-soled canvas shoe worn for various sports. Also called: **gym shoe.** [C20: so called because of the resemblance of the rubber sole to a Plimsoll line]

Plim+soll line ('plɪmsəl) *n.* another name for **load line.** [C19: named after Samuel *Plimsoll* (1824–98), English M.P., who advocated its adoption]

plinth (plɪnθ) *n.* **1.** Also called: **socle.** the rectangular slab or block that forms the lowest part of the base of a column, pedestal, or pier. **2.** Also called: **plinth course.** the lowest part of the wall of a building that appears above ground level, esp. one that is formed of a course of stone or brick. **3.** a flat block on either side of a door frame, where the architrave meets the skirting. [C17: from Latin *plinthus*, from Greek *plinthos* brick, shaped stone]

Plin·y ('plɪnɪ) *n.* **1.** called *Pliny the Elder.* Latin name *Gaius Plinius Secundus.* 23–79 A.D., Roman writer, the author of the encyclopedic *Natural History* (77). **2.** his nephew, called *Pliny the Younger.* Latin name *Gaius Plinius Caecilius Secundus.* ?62–?113 A.D., Roman writer and administrator, noted for his letters.

pli·o-, pleo-, *or* **plei·o-** *combining form.* greater in size, extent, degree, etc.; more: *Pliocene.* [from Greek *pleiōn* more, from *polus* much, many]

Pli·o+cene *or* **Plei·o+cene** ('plaɪəʊˌsiːn) *adj.* **1.** of, denoting, or formed in the last epoch of the Tertiary period, which lasted for ten million years, during which many modern mammals appeared. *~n.* **2. the Pliocene.** the Pliocene epoch or rock series. [C19: PLIO- + *-cene* from Greek *kainos* recent]

plis+sé ('pliːseɪ, 'plɪs-) *n.* **1.** fabric with a wrinkled finish, achieved by treatment involving caustic soda: *cotton plissé.* **2.** such a finish on a fabric. [French: *plissé* pleated, from *plisser* to pleat; see PLY²]

P.L.O. *abbrev. for* Palestine Liberation Organization.

ploat (pləʊt) *vb.* (*tr.*) *Northeastern English dialect.* **1.** to thrash; beat soundly. **2.** to pluck (a fowl). [from Dutch or Flemish *ploten* to pluck the feathers or fur from]

plod (plɒd) *vb.* **plods, plod+ding, plod+ded. 1.** to make (one's way) or walk along (a path, etc.) with heavy usually slow steps. **2.** (*intr.*) to work slowly and perseveringly. *~n.* **3.** the act of plodding. **4.** the sound of slow heavy steps. [C16: of imitative origin] **—'plod+der** *n.* **—'plod+ding+ly** *adv.* **—'plod+ding+ness** *n.*

plodge (plɒdʒ) *Northeastern English dialect.* *~vb.* **1.** (*intr.*) to wade in water, esp. the sea. *~n.* **2.** the act of wading. [of imitative origin; related to PLOD]

Plo+eş+ti (*Rumanian* plo'jeʃtj) *n.* a city in SE central Rumania: centre of the Rumanian petroleum industry. Pop.: 175 527 (1974 est.).

-ploid *adj. and n. combining form.* indicating a specific multiple of a single set of chromosomes: *diploid.* [from Greek *-pl(oos)* -fold + -OID] **—-ploi·dy** *n. combining form.*

plonk¹ (plɒŋk) *vb.* **1.** (often foll. by *down*) to drop or be dropped, esp. heavily or suddenly: *he plonked the money on the table.* *~n.* **2.** the act or sound of plonking. *~interj.* **3.** an exclamation imitative of this sound.

plonk² (plɒŋk) *n. Brit. and Austral. informal.* alcoholic drink, usually wine, esp. of inferior quality. [C20: perhaps from French *blanc* white, as in *vin blanc* white wine]

plonk·o ('plɒŋkəʊ) *n., pl.* **plonk·os.** *Austral. slang.* an alcoholic, esp. one who drinks wine. [C20: from PLONK²]

plop (plɒp) *n.* **1.** the characteristic sound made by an object dropping into water without a splash. *~vb.* **plops, plop+ping, plopped. 2.** to fall or cause to fall with the sound of a plop: *the stone plopped into the water.* *~interj.* **3.** an exclamation imitative of this sound: *to go plop.* [C19: imitative of the sound]

plo+sion ('pləʊʒən) *n. Phonetics.* the sound of an abrupt break of closure, esp. the audible release of a stop. Also called: **explosion.**

plo+sive ('pləʊsɪv) *Phonetics.* *~adj.* **1.** articulated with or accompanied by plosion. *~n.* **2.** a plosive consonant; stop. [C20: from French, from *explosif* EXPLOSIVE]

plot¹ (plɒt) *n.* **1.** a secret plan to achieve some purpose, esp. one that is illegal or underhand: *a plot to overthrow the government.* **2.** the story or plan of a play, novel, etc. **3.** *Military.* a graphic representation of an individual or tactical setting that pinpoints an artillery target. **4.** *Chiefly U.S.* a diagram or plan, esp. a surveyor's map. *~vb.* **plots, plot+ting, plot+ted. 5.** to plan secretly (something illegal, revolutionary, etc.); conspire. **6.** (*tr.*) to mark (a course, as of a ship or aircraft) on a map. **7.** (*tr.*) to make a plan or map of. **8. a.** to locate and mark (one or more points) on a graph by means of coordinates. **b.** to draw (a curve) through these points. **9.** (*tr.*) to construct the plot of (a literary work, etc.). [C16: from PLOT², influenced in use by COMPLOT]

plot² (plɒt) *n.* **1.** a small piece of land: *a vegetable plot.* *~vb.* **plots, plot+ting, plot+ted. 2.** (*tr.*) to arrange or divide (land) into plots. [Old English: piece of land, plan of an area]

plot³ (plɒt) *n. Northern Brit. dialect.* a bonfire made on Guy Fawkes Day (Nov. 5). [special use of PLOT¹, by association with the Gunpowder Plot]

Plo·ti·nus (plɒ'taɪnəs) *n.* ?205–?270 A.D., Roman neo-Platonist philosopher, born in Egypt.

plot+ter ('plɒtə) *n.* an instrument for plotting lines or angles on a chart.

plough *or esp. U.S.* **plow** (plaʊ) *n.* **1.** an agricultural implement with sharp blades, attached to a horse, tractor, etc., for cutting or turning over the earth. **2.** any of various similar implements, such as a device for clearing snow. **3.** a plane with a narrow blade for cutting grooves in wood. **4.** (in agriculture) ploughed land. **5. put one's hand to the plough.** to perform a task. *~vb.* **6.** to till (the soil, etc.) with a plough. **7.** to make (furrows or grooves) in (something) with or as if with a plough. **8.** (when *intr.*, usually foll. by *through*) to move (through something) in the manner of a plough: *the ship ploughed the water.* **9.** (*intr.*; foll. by *through*) to work at slowly or perseveringly. **10.** (*intr.*) *Brit. slang.* to fail an examination. [Old English *plōg* plough land; related to Old Norse *plogr*, Old High German *pfluoc*] **—'plough+er** *or esp. U.S.* **'plow+er** *n.*

Plough *or esp. U.S.* **Plow** (plaʊ) *n.* **the.** the group of the seven brightest stars in the constellation Ursa Major. Also called: **Charles's Wain.** Usual U.S. name: the **Big Dipper.**

plough back *vb.* (*tr., adv.*) to reinvest (the profits of a business) in the same business.

plough+boy *or esp. U.S.* **plow+boy** ('plaʊˌbɔɪ) *n.* **1.** a boy who guides the animals drawing a plough. **2.** any country boy.

plough+man *or esp. U.S.* **plow+man** ('plaʊmən) *n., pl.* **+men. 1.** a man who ploughs, esp. using horses, etc. **2.** any farm labourer. **—'plough+man+ship** *or esp. U.S.* **'plow+man+ship** *n.*

plough+man's spike+nard *n.* a European plant, *Inula conyza*, with tubular yellowish flower heads surrounded by purple bracts: family *Compositae* (composites). Also called: **fleawort.**

plough+share *or esp. U.S.* **plow+share** ('plaʊˌʃɛə) *n.* the horizontal pointed cutting blade of a mouldboard plough.

plough+staff *or esp. U.S.* **plow+staff** ('plaʊˌstɑːf) *n.* **1.** Also called: **ploughtail.** one of the handles of a plough. **2.** a spade-shaped tool used to clean the ploughshare and mouldboard.

Plov+div (*Bulgarian* 'plɔvdif) *n.* a city in S Bulgaria on the Maritsa River: the second largest town in Bulgaria; conquered by Philip II of Macedonia in 341 B.C.; capital of Roman Thracia; commercial centre of a rich agricultural region. Pop.: 305 091 (1974 est.). Greek name: **Philippopolis.**

plov+er ('plʌvə) *n.* **1.** any shore birds of the family *Charadriidae*, typically having a round head, straight bill, and large pointed wings: order *Charadriiformes.* **2.** any of similar and related birds, such as the Egyptian plover (see **crocodile bird**) and the upland plover. **3. green plover.** another name for **lapwing.** [C14: from Old French *plovier* rain bird, from Latin *pluvia* rain]

plow (plaʊ) *n., vb.* the usual U.S. spelling of **plough.** **—'plow+er** *n.*

ploy (plɔɪ) *n.* **1.** a manoeuvre or tactic in a game, conversation, etc.; stratagem; gambit. **2.** any business, job, hobby, etc., with which one is occupied: *angling is his latest ploy.* **3.** *Chiefly Brit.* a frolic, escapade, or practical joke. [variant of EMPLOY]

P.L.P. (in Britain) *abbrev. for* Parliamentary Labour Party.

P.L.R. *abbrev. for* Public Lending Right.

plu *or* **plue** (pluː) *n.* variant spellings of **plew.**

pluck (plʌk) *vb.* **1.** (*tr.*) to pull off (feathers, fruit, etc.) from (a fowl, tree, etc.). **2.** (when *intr.*, foll. by *at*) to pull or tug. **3.** (*tr.*; foll. by *off, away,* etc.) *Archaic.* to pull (something) forcibly or violently (from something or someone). **4.** (*tr.*) to sound (the strings) of (a musical instrument) with the fingers, a plectrum, etc. **5.** (*tr.*) *Slang.* to fleece or swindle. ~*n.* **6.** courage, usually in the face of difficulties or hardship. **7.** a sudden pull or tug. **8.** the heart, liver, and lungs, esp. of an animal used for food. [Old English *pluccian, plyccan;* related to German *pflücken*] —**'pluck·er** *n.*

pluck up *vb.* (*tr., adv.*) **1.** to pull out; uproot. **2.** to muster (courage, one's spirits, etc.).

pluck·y ('plʌkɪ) *adj.* **pluck·i·er, pluck·i·est.** having or showing courage in the face of difficulties, danger, etc. —**'pluck·i·ly** *adv.* —**'pluck·i·ness** *n.*

plug (plʌg) *n.* **1.** a piece of wood, cork, or other material, often cylindrical in shape, used to stop up holes and gaps or as a wedge for taking a screw or nail. **2.** a device usually having three pins to which the terminals of a flex or cable are attached: used to make an electrical connection when inserted into a socket. **3.** Also called: **volcanic plug.** a mass of solidified magma filling the neck of an extinct volcano. **4.** See **sparking plug. 5. a.** a cake of pressed or twisted tobacco, esp. for chewing. **b.** a small piece of such a cake. **6.** *Angling.* a weighted artificial lure with one or more sets of hooks attached, used in spinning. **7.** *Informal.* a recommendation or other favourable mention of a product, show, etc., as on television, radio, or in newspapers. **8.** *Slang.* a shot, blow, or punch (esp. in the phrase **take a plug at**). **9.** *Chiefly U.S.* an old horse. ~*vb.* **plugs, plug·ging, plugged. 10.** (*tr.*) to stop up or secure (a hole, gap, etc.) with or as if with a plug. **11.** (*tr.*) to insert or use (something) as a plug: *to plug a finger into one's ear.* **12.** (*tr.*) *Informal.* to make favourable and often-repeated mentions of (a song, product, show, etc.), esp. on television, radio, or in newspapers. **13.** (*tr.*) *Slang.* to shoot with a gun: *he plugged six rabbits.* **14.** (*tr.*) *Slang.* to punch or strike. **15.** (*intr.;* foll. by *along, away,* etc.) *Informal.* to work steadily or persistently. [C17: from Middle Dutch *plugge;* related to Middle Low German *plugge,* German *Pflock*] —**'plug·ger** *n.*

plug·board ('plʌgˌbɔ:d) *n.* another name for **patch board.**

plug in *vb.* (*tr., adv.*) to connect (an electrical appliance, etc.) with a power source by means of an electrical plug.

plug-ug·ly *adj.* **1.** *Informal.* extremely ugly. ~*n., pl.* **·lies. 2.** *U.S. slang.* a city tough; ruffian. [C19: origin obscure; originally applied to ruffians in New York who attempted to exert political pressure]

plum[1] (plʌm) *n.* **1.** a small rosaceous tree, *Prunus domestica,* with white flowers and an edible oval fruit that is purple, yellow, or green and contains an oval stone. See also **greengage, damson. 2.** the fruit of this tree. **3.** a raisin, as used in a cake or pudding. **4. a.** a dark reddish-purple colour. **b.** (*as adj.*): *a plum carpet.* **5.** *Informal.* **a.** something of a superior or desirable kind, such as a financial bonus. **b.** (*as modifier*): *a plum job.* [Old English *plūme;* related to Latin *prunum,* German *Pflaume*] —**'plum·ˌlike** *adj.*

plum[2] (plʌm) *adj., adv.* a variant spelling of **plumb** (senses 3–6).

plum·age ('plu:mɪdʒ) *n.* the layer of feathers covering the body of a bird. [C15: from Old French, from *plume* feather, from Latin *plūma* down]

plu·mate ('plu:meɪt, -mɪt) *or* **plu·mose** *adj. Zoology, botany.* **1.** of, relating to, or possessing one or more feathers or plumes. **2.** resembling a plume; covered with small hairs: *a plumate seed.* [C19: from Latin *plumātus* covered with feathers; see PLUME]

plumb (plʌm) *n.* **1.** a weight, usually of lead, suspended at the end of a line and used to determine water depth or verticality. **2.** the perpendicular position of a freely suspended plumb line (esp. in the phrases **out of plumb, off plumb**). ~*adj. also* **plum. 3.** (*prenominal*) *Informal, chiefly U.S.* (intensifier): *a plumb nuisance.* ~*adv. also* **plum. 4.** in a vertical or perpendicular line. **5.** *Informal, chiefly U.S.* (intensifier): *plumb idiotic.* **6.** *Informal.* exactly; precisely (also in the phrase **plumb on**). ~*vb.* **7.** (*tr.;* often foll. by *up*) to test the alignment of or adjust to the vertical with a plumb line. **8.** (*tr.*) to undergo or experience (the worst extremes of misery, sadness, etc.): *to plumb the depths of despair.* **9.** (*tr.*) to understand or master (something obscure): *to plumb a mystery.* **10.** to connect or join (a device, such as a tap, etc.) to a waterpipe or drainage system. [C13: from Old French *plomb* (unattested) lead line, from Old French *plon* lead, from Latin *plumbum* lead] —**'plumb·a·ble** *adj.*

plum·bag·i·na·ceous (plʌmˌbædʒɪ'neɪʃəs) *adj.* of, relating to, or belonging to the *Plumbaginaceae,* a family of typically coastal plants having flowers with a brightly coloured calyx and five styles: includes leadwort, thrift, and sea lavender.

plum·ba·go (plʌm'beɪgəʊ) *n., pl.* **·gos. 1.** any plumbaginaceous plant of the genus *Plumbago,* of warm regions, having clusters of blue, white, or red flowers. See also **leadwort. 2.** another name for **graphite.** [C17: from Latin: lead ore, leadwort, translation of Greek *polubdaina* lead ore, from *polubdos* lead]

plumb bob *n.* the weight, usually of lead, at the end of a plumb line; plummet.

plum·be·ous ('plʌmbɪəs) *adj.* made of or relating to lead or resembling lead in colour. [C16: from Latin *plumbeus* leaden, from *plumbum* lead]

plumb·er ('plʌmə) *n.* a person who installs and repairs pipes, fixtures, etc., for water, drainage, and gas. [C14: from Old French *plommier* worker in lead, from Late Latin *plumbārius,* from Latin *plumbum* lead]

plumb·er·y ('plʌmərɪ) *n., pl.* **·er·ies. 1.** the workshop of a plumber. **2.** another word for **plumbing** (sense 1).

plum·bic ('plʌmbɪk) *adj.* of or containing lead in the tetravalent state.

plum·bi·con ('plʌmbɪˌkɒn) *n.* a development of the vidicon television camera tube in which the photoconductive material is replaced by semiconductor material.

plum·bif·er·ous (plʌm'bɪfərəs) *adj.* (of ores, rocks, etc.) containing or yielding lead.

plumb·ing ('plʌmɪŋ) *n.* **1.** Also called: **plumbery.** the trade or work of a plumber. **2.** the pipes, fixtures, etc., used in a water, drainage, or gas installation. **3.** the act or procedure of using a plumb to gauge depth, a vertical, etc.

plum·bism ('plʌmbɪzəm) *n.* chronic lead poisoning. [C19: from Latin *plumbum* lead]

plumb line *n.* **1.** a string with a metal weight at one end that, when suspended, points directly towards the earth's centre of gravity and so is used to determine verticality, the depth of water, etc. **2.** another name for **plumb rule.**

plum·bous ('plʌmbəs) *adj.* of or containing lead in the divalent state. [C17: from Late Latin *plumbōsus* full of lead, from Latin *plumbum* lead]

plumb rule *n.* a plumb line attached to a narrow board, used by builders, surveyors, etc.

plum·bum ('plʌmbəm) *n.* an obsolete name for **lead**[2] (the metal). [from Latin]

plume (plu:m) *n.* **1.** a feather, esp. one that is large or ornamental. **2.** a feather or cluster of feathers worn esp. formerly as a badge or ornament in a headband, hat, etc. **3.** *Biology.* any feathery part, such as the structure on certain fruits and seeds that aids dispersal by wind. **4.** something that resembles a plume: *a plume of smoke.* **5.** a token or decoration of honour; prize. ~*vb.* (*tr.*) **6.** to adorn or decorate with feathers or plumes. **7.** (of a bird) to clean or preen (itself or its feathers). **8.** (foll. by *on* or *upon*) to pride or congratulate (oneself). [C14: from Old French, from Latin *plūma* downy feather] —**'plume·less** *adj.* —**'plume·ˌlike** *adj.*

plum·met ('plʌmɪt) *vb.* **1.** (*intr.*) to drop down; plunge. ~*n.* **2.** another word for **plumb bob. 3.** a lead plumb used by anglers to determine the depth of water. [C14: from Old French *plommet* ball of lead, from *plomb* lead, from Latin *plumbum*]

plum·my ('plʌmɪ) *adj.* **·mi·er, ·mi·est. 1.** of, full of, or resembling plums. **2.** *Brit. informal.* (of speech) having a deep tone and a refined and somewhat drawling articulation. **3.** *Brit. informal.* choice; desirable.

plu·mose ('plu:məʊs, -məʊz) *adj.* another word for **plumate.** [C17: from Latin *plūmōsus* feathery] —**'plu·mose·ly** *adv.* —**plu·mos·i·ty** (plu:'mɒsɪtɪ) *n.*

plump[1] (plʌmp) *adj.* **1.** well filled out or rounded; fleshy or chubby: *a plump turkey.* **2.** bulging, as with contents; full: *a plump wallet.* **3.** (of amounts of money, etc.) generous; ample: *a plump cheque.* ~*vb.* **4.** (often foll. by *up* or *out*) to make or become plump: *to plump up a pillow.* [C15 (meaning: dull, rude), C16 (in current senses): perhaps from Middle Dutch *plomp* dull, blunt] —**'plump·ly** *adv.* —**'plump·ness** *n.*

plump[2] (plʌmp) *vb.* **1.** (often foll. by *down, into,* etc.) to drop or fall suddenly and heavily: *to plump down on the sofa.* **2.** (*intr.;* foll. by *for*) to give support (to) or make a choice (of) one out of a group or number. **3.** (*intr.;* foll. by *in* or *out*) to enter or exit abruptly. ~*n.* **4.** a heavy abrupt fall or the sound of this. ~*adv.* **5.** suddenly or heavily: *he ran plump into the old lady.* **6.** straight down; directly: *the helicopter landed plump in the middle of the field.* ~*adj., adv.* **7.** in a blunt, direct, or decisive manner. [C14: probably of imitative origin; compare Middle Low German *plumpen,* Middle Dutch *plompen*]

plump[3] (plʌmp) *n. Archaic or dialect.* a group of people, animals, or things; troop; cluster. [C15: of uncertain origin]

plump·er ('plʌmpə) *n.* a pad carried in the mouth by actors to round out the cheeks.

plum pud·ding *n. Brit.* a dark brown rich boiled or steamed pudding made with flour, suet, sugar, and dried fruit.

plu·mule ('plu:mju:l) *n.* **1.** the embryonic shoot of seed-bearing plants. **2.** a down feather of young birds that persists in some adults. [C18: from Late Latin *plūmula* a little feather]

plum·y ('plu:mɪ) *adj.* **plum·i·er, plum·i·est. 1.** plumelike; feathery. **2.** consisting of, covered, or adorned with feathers.

plun·der ('plʌndə) *vb.* **1.** to steal (valuables, goods, sacred items, etc.) from (a town, church, etc.) by force, esp. in time of war; loot. **2.** (*tr.*) to rob or steal (choice or desirable things) from (a place): *to plunder an orchard.* ~*n.* **3.** anything taken by plundering or theft; booty. **4.** the act of plundering; pillage. [C17: probably from Dutch *plunderen* (originally: to plunder household goods); compare Middle High German *plunder* bedding, household goods] —**'plun·der·a·ble** *adj.* —**'plun·der·er** *n.* —**'plun·der·ous** *adj.*

plun·der·age ('plʌndərɪdʒ) *n.* **1.** *Maritime law.* **a.** the embezzlement of goods on board a ship. **b.** the goods embezzled. **2.** the act of plundering.

plunge (plʌndʒ) *vb.* **1.** (usually foll. by *into*) to thrust or throw (something, oneself, etc.): *they plunged into the sea.* **2.** to throw or be thrown into a certain state or condition: *the room was plunged into darkness.* **3.** (usually foll. by *into*) to involve or become involved deeply (in): *he plunged himself into a course of Sanskrit.* **4.** (*intr.*) to move or dash violently or with great speed or impetuosity. **5.** (*intr.*) to descend very suddenly or steeply: *the ship plunged in heavy seas; a plunging neckline.* **6.** (*intr.*) *Informal.* to speculate or gamble recklessly, for high stakes, etc. ~*n.* **7.** a leap or dive into water, etc. **8.** *Informal.* a swim; dip. **9.** a place where one can swim or dive, such as a swimming pool. **10.** a headlong rush: *a plunge for the exit.* **11.** a pitching or tossing motion. **12. take the plunge.** *Informal.* **a.** to resolve to do something dangerous or irrevocable. **b.** to get married. [C14: from Old French *plongier,* from Vulgar Latin *plumbicāre* (unattested) to sound with a plummet, from Latin *plumbum* lead]

plunge bath *n.* a bath large enough to immerse the whole body or to dive into.

plung·er ('plʌndʒə) *n.* **1.** a rubber suction cup fixed to the end of a rod, used to clear a blocked drain, etc. **2.** a device or part of a machine that has a plunging or thrusting motion; piston. **3.** *Informal.* a reckless gambler.

plunk (plʌŋk) *vb.* **1.** to pluck (the strings) of (a banjo, etc.) or (of such an instrument) to give forth a sound when plucked. **2.** (often foll. by *down*) to drop or be dropped, esp. heavily or suddenly. ~*n.* **3.** the act or sound of plunking. **4.** *Informal.* a hard blow. ~*interj.* **5.** an exclamation imitative of the sound of something plunking. ~*adv.* **6.** *Informal.* exactly; squarely: *plunk into his lap.* [C20: imitative]

plu·per·fect (plu:'pɜ:fɪkt) *adj., n. Grammar.* another term for **past perfect.** [C16: from the Latin phrase *plūs quam perfectum* more than perfect]

plur. *abbrev. for:* **1.** plural. **2.** plurality.

plu·ral ('plʊərəl) *adj.* **1.** containing, involving, or composed of more than one person, thing, item, etc.: *a plural society.* **2.** denoting a word indicating that more than one referent is being referred to or described. ~*n.* **3.** *Grammar.* **a.** the plural number. **b.** a plural form. [C14: from Old French *plurel,* from Late Latin *plūrālis* concerning many, from Latin *plūs* more] —'**plu·ral·ly** *adv.*

plu·ral·ism ('plʊərə,lɪzəm) *n.* **1.** the holding by a single person of more than one ecclesiastical benefice or office; plurality. **2.** *Sociol.* a theory of society as several autonomous but interdependent groups having equal power. **3.** the existence in a society of groups having distinctive ethnic origin, cultural forms, religions, etc. **4.** *Philosophy.* the doctrine that reality consists of several basic substances or elements. Compare **dualism, monism.** —'**plu·ral·ist** *n., adj.* —,**plu·ral·'ist·ic** *adj.*

plu·ral·i·ty (plʊə'rælɪtɪ) *n., pl.* **·ties. 1.** the state of being plural or numerous. **2.** *Maths.* a number greater than one. **3.** the U.S. term for **relative majority. 4.** a large number. **5.** the greater number; majority. **6.** another word for **pluralism** (sense 1).

plu·ral·ize *or* **plu·ral·ise** ('plʊərə,laɪz) *vb.* **1.** (*intr.*) to hold more than one ecclesiastical benefice or office at the same time. **2.** to make or become plural. —,**plu·ral·i·'za·tion** *or* ,**plu·ral·i·'sa·tion** *n.* —'**plu·ral·,iz·er** *or* '**plu·ral·,is·er** *n.*

plu·ral·vot·ing *n.* **1.** a system that enables an elector to vote more than once in an election. **2.** (in Britain before 1948) a system enabling certain electors to vote in more than one constituency.

plu·ri- *combining form.* denoting several: *pluriliteral; pluripresence.* [from Latin *plur-, plus* more, *plures* several]

plu·ri·lit·e·ral (,plʊrɪ'lɪtərəl) *adj.* (in Hebrew grammar) containing more than three letters in the root.

plu·ri·pres·ence (,plʊrɪ'prɛzəns) *n. Theol.* presence in more than one place at the same time.

plus (plʌs) *prep.* **1.** increased by the addition of: *four plus two* (written 4 + 2). **2.** with or with the addition of: *a good job, plus a new car.* ~*adj.* **3.** (*prenominal*) Also: **positive.** indicating or involving addition: *a plus sign.* **4.** another word for **positive** (senses 8, 9). **5.** on the positive part of a scale or coordinate axis: *a value of* +*x.* **6.** involving positive advantage or good: *a plus factor.* **7.** (*postpositive*) *Informal.* having a value above that which is stated or expected: *she had charm plus.* **8.** (*postpositive*) slightly above a specified standard on a particular grade or percentage: *he received a B+ rating on his essay.* **9.** *Botany.* designating the strain of fungus that can only undergo sexual reproduction with a minus strain. ~*n.* **10.** short for **plus sign. 11.** a positive quantity. **12.** *Informal.* something positive or to the good. **13.** a gain, surplus, or advantage. ~Mathematical symbol: + [C17: from Latin: more; compare Greek *pleiōn,* Old Norse *fleiri* more, German *viel* much]

Usage. *Plus, together with,* and *along with* do not create compound subjects in the way that *and* does: the number of the verb depends on that of the subject to which *plus, together with,* or *along with* are added: *this task, plus all the others, was* (not *were*) *undertaken by the government; the doctor, together with the nurses, was* (not *were*) *waiting for the patient.*

plus fours *pl. n.* men's baggy knickerbockers reaching below the knee, now only worn for hunting, golf, etc. [C20: so called because the trousers are made with four inches of material to hang over at the knee]

plush (plʌʃ) *n.* **1. a.** a fabric with a cut pile that is longer and softer than velvet. **b.** (*as modifier*): *a plush chair.* ~*adj.* **2.** Also: **plushy.** *Informal.* lavishly appointed; rich; costly. [C16: from French *pluche,* from Old French *peluchier* to pluck, ultimately from Latin *pilus* a hair, PILE[3]] —'**plush·ly** *adv.* —'**plush·ness** *n.*

plus sign *n.* the symbol +, indicating addition or positive quantity.

Plu·tarch ('plu:tɑ:k) *n.* ?46–?120 A.D., Greek biographer and philosopher, noted for his *Parallel Lives* of distinguished Greeks and Romans.

Plu·to[1] ('plu:təʊ) *n. Greek myth.* the god of the underworld; Hades.

Plu·to[2] ('plu:təʊ) *n.* the second smallest planet and the farthest known from the sun. Its existence was predicted before it was discovered in 1930. Mean distance from sun: 5907 million km; period of revolution around sun: 248.4 years; period of axial rotation: 6.4 days; diameter and mass: 47 and 10 per cent that of earth respectively. [Latin, from Greek *Ploutōn,* literally: the rich one]

plu·toc·ra·cy (plu:'tɒkrəsɪ) *n., pl.* **·cies. 1.** the rule or control of society by the wealthy. **2.** a state or government characterized by the rule of the wealthy. **3.** a class that exercises power by virtue of its wealth. [C17: from Greek *ploutokratia* government by the rich, from *ploutos* wealth + *-kratia* rule, power] —**plu·to·crat·ic** (,plu:tə'krætɪk) *or* ,**plu·to·'crat·i·cal** *adj.* —,**plu·to·'crat·i·cal·ly** *adv.*

plu·to·crat ('plu:tə,kræt) *n.* a member of a plutocracy.

plu·ton ('plu:tɒn) *n.* any mass of igneous rock that has solidified below the surface of the earth. [C20: back formation from PLUTONIC]

Plu·to·ni·an (plu:'təʊnɪən) *adj.* of or relating to Pluto (the god) or the underworld; infernal.

plu·ton·ic (plu:'tɒnɪk) *adj.* (of igneous rocks) derived from magma that has cooled and solidified below the surface of the earth. [C20: named after PLUTO[1]]

plu·to·ni·um (plu:'təʊnɪəm) *n.* a highly toxic metallic transuranic element. It occurs in trace amounts in uranium ores and is produced in a nuclear reactor by neutron bombardment of uranium-238. The most stable and important isotope, **plutonium-239,** readily undergoes fission and is used as a reactor fuel in nuclear power stations and in nuclear weapons. Symbol: Pu; atomic no.: 94; half-life of ^{239}Pu: 24 360 years; valency: 3, 4, 5, or 6; melting pt.: 641°C; boiling pt.: 3327°C. [C20: named after the planet *Pluto* because Pluto lies beyond Neptune and plutonium was discovered soon after NEPTUNIUM]

Plu·tus ('plu:tʊs) *n.* the Greek god of wealth. [from Greek *ploutos* wealth]

plu·vi·al ('plu:vɪəl) *adj.* **1.** of, characterized by, or due to the action of rain; rainy. ~*n.* **2.** *Geology.* a period of persistent heavy rainfall, esp. one occurring in unglaciated regions during the Pleistocene epoch. [C17: from Latin *pluviālis* rainy, from *pluvia* rain]

plu·vi·om·e·ter (,plu:vɪ'ɒmɪtə) *n.* another word for **rain gauge.** —**plu·vi·o·met·ric** (,plu:vɪə'mɛtrɪk) *adj.* —,**plu·vi·o·'met·ri·cal·ly** *adv.* —,**plu·vi·'om·e·try** *n.*

Plu·viôse *French.* (ply'vjo:z) *n.* the rainy month: the fifth month of the French revolutionary calendar, extending from Jan. 21 to Feb. 19. [C19 *pluviose,* C15 *pluvious;* see PLUVIOUS]

plu·vi·ous ('plu:vɪəs) *or* **plu·vi·ose** *adj.* of or relating to rain; rainy. [C15: from Late Latin *pluviōsus* full of rain, from *pluvia* rain, from *pluere* to rain]

ply[1] (plaɪ) *vb.* **plies, ply·ing, plied.** (*mainly tr.*) **1.** to carry on, pursue, or work at (a job, trade, etc.). **2.** to manipulate or wield (a tool, etc.). **3.** to sell (goods, wares, etc.) esp. at a regular place. **4.** (usually foll. by *with*) to provide (with) or subject (to) repeatedly or persistently: *he plied us with drink the whole evening; to ply a horse with a whip; he plied the speaker with questions.* **5.** (*intr.*) to perform or work at steadily or diligently: *to ply with a spade.* **6.** (*also intr.*) (esp. of a ship, etc.) to travel regularly along (a route) or in (an area): *to ply between Dover and Calais; to ply the trade routes.* [C14 *plye,* short for *aplye* to APPLY]

ply[2] (plaɪ) *n., pl.* **plies. 1. a.** a layer, fold, or thickness, as of cloth, wood, yarn, etc. **b.** (*in combination*): *four-ply.* **2.** a thin sheet of wood glued to other similar sheets to form plywood. **3.** one of the strands twisted together to make rope, yarn, etc. [C15: from Old French *pli* fold, from *plier* to fold, from Latin *plicāre*]

Plym·outh ('plɪməθ) *n.* **1.** a port in SW England, in SW Devon on **Plymouth Sound** (an inlet of the English Channel): Britain's chief port in Elizabethan times; the last port visited by the Pilgrim Fathers in the *Mayflower* before sailing to America; naval base. Pop.: 239 314 (1971). **2.** a city in SE Massachusetts, on **Plymouth Bay**: the first permanent European settlement in New England; founded by the Pilgrim Fathers. Pop.: 18 606 (1970).

Plym·outh Breth·ren *n.* a religious sect founded about 1827, strongly Puritanical in outlook and prohibiting many secular occupations for its members. It combines elements of Calvinism, Pietism, and often of millenarianism, having no organized ministry and emphasizing the autonomy of each local church.

Plym·outh Col·o·ny *n.* the Puritan colony founded by the Pilgrim Fathers in SE Massachusetts (1620). See also **Mayflower.**

Plym·outh Rock *n.* **1.** a heavy American breed of domestic fowl. **2.** a boulder on the coast of Massachusetts: traditionally thought to be the landing place of the Pilgrim Fathers (1620). See also **Mayflower.**

ply·wood ('plaɪ,wʊd) *n.* a structural board consisting of an odd number of thin layers of wood glued together under pressure, with the grain of one layer at right angles to the grain of the adjoining layer.

Pl·zeň (*Czech* 'pᵊlzɛnj) *n.* an industrial city in W Czechoslovakia. Pop.: 154 126 (1974 est.). German name: **Pilsen.**

Pm *the chemical symbol for* promethium.

p.m. *or* **P.M.** *abbrev. for:* **1.** (indicating the time period from midday to midnight) post meridiem. [Latin: after noon] Compare **a.m. 2.** post-mortem (examination).

P.M. *abbrev. for:* **1.** Prime Minister. **2.** Past Master (of a fraternity). **3.** Paymaster. **4.** Postmaster. **5.** *Military.* Provost Marshal.

pm. *abbrev. for* premium.

P.M.G. *abbrev. for:* **1.** Paymaster General. **2.** Postmaster General. **3.** *Military.* Provost Marshal General.

P.N., P/N, *or* **p.n.** *abbrev. for* promissory note.

PNdB *abbrev. for* perceived noise decibel.

pneu·ma ('nju:mə) *n. Philosophy.* a person's vital spirit or soul. [C19: from Greek: breath, spirit, wind; related to *pnein* to blow, breathe]

pneu·mat·ic (nju'mætɪk) *adj.* **1.** of or concerned with air, gases, or wind. Compare **hydraulic. 2.** (of a machine or device) operated by compressed air or by a vacuum: *a pneumatic drill; pneumatic brakes.* **3.** containing compressed air: *a pneumatic tyre.* **4.** of or concerned with pneumatics. **5.** *Theol.* **a.** of or relating to the soul or spirit. **b.** of or relating to the Holy Ghost or other spiritual beings. **6.** (of the bones of birds) containing air spaces which reduce their weight as an adaptation to flying. ~*n.* **7.** short for **pneumatic tyre.** [C17: from Late Latin *pneumaticus* of air or wind, from Greek *pneumatikos* of air or breath, from PNEUMA] **—pneu+ˈmat+i+cal+ly** *adv.*

pneu+mat+ics (njʊˈmætɪks) *n.* (*functioning as sing.*) the branch of physics concerned with the mechanical properties of gases, esp. air. Also called: **aerometry, pneumodynamics.**

pneu+mat+ic trough *n. Chem.* a shallow dishlike vessel filled with a liquid, usually water, and used in collecting gases by displacement of liquid from a filled jar held with its open end under the surface of the liquid.

pneu+mat+ic tyre *n.* a rubber tyre filled with air under pressure, used esp. on motor vehicles.

pneu·ma·to- *combining form.* air; breath or breathing; spirit: *pneumatophore; pneumatology.* [from Greek *pneuma, pneumat-*, breath; see PNEUMA]

pneu+ma+tol+o·gy (ˌnjuːməˈtɒlədʒɪ) *n.* **1.** the branch of theology concerned with the Holy Ghost and other spiritual beings. **2.** an obsolete name for **psychology** (the science). **3.** an obsolete term for **pneumatics.** **—pneu+ma+to+log+i+cal** (ˌnjuːmətəˈlɒdʒɪkᵊl) *adj.* **—ˌpneu+ma+ˈtol·o+gist** *n.*

pneu+ma+tol·y+sis (ˌnjuːməˈtɒlɪsɪs) *n.* a type of metamorphism in which hot gases from solidifying magma react with surrounding rock.

pneu+ma+tom+e·ter (ˌnjuːməˈtɒmɪtə) *n.* an instrument for measuring the pressure exerted by air being inhaled or exhaled during a single breath. Compare **spirometer.** **—ˌpneu+ma+ˈtom+e·try** *n.*

pneu+mat·o+phore (njuːˈmætəʊˌfɔː) *n.* **1.** a specialized root of certain swamp plants, such as the mangrove, that branches upwards and undergoes gaseous exchange with the atmosphere. **2.** a polyp in coelenterates of the order *Siphonophora,* such as the Portuguese man-of-war, that is specialized as a float.

pneu+mec+to+my (njuːˈmɛktəmɪ) *n., pl.* **+mies.** *Surgery.* another word for **pneumonectomy.**

pneu·mo-, pneu·mon·o- *or before a vowel* **pneum-, pneu·mon-** *combining form.* of or related to a lung or the lungs; respiratory: *pneumoconiosis; pneumonitis.* [from Greek *pneumōn* lung or *pneuma* breath]

pneu+mo+ba+cil+lus (ˌnjuːməʊbəˈsɪləs) *n., pl.* **+li** (-laɪ). a rod-shaped bacterium that occurs in the respiratory tract, esp. the Gram-negative *Klebsiella pneumoniae,* which causes pneumonia.

pneu+mo+coc+cus (ˌnjuːməʊˈkɒkəs) *n., pl.* **+coc+ci** (-ˈkɒksaɪ). a spherical bacterium that occurs in the respiratory tract, esp. the Gram-positive *Diplococcus pneumoniae,* which causes pneumonia. **—ˌpneu+mo+ˈcoc+cal** *adj.*

pneu+mo+co+ni+o+sis (ˌnjuːməʊˌkəʊnɪˈəʊsɪs) *or* **pneu+mo+no+co+ni+o+sis** (ˌnjuːmənəʊˌkəʊnɪˈəʊsɪs) *n.* any disease of the lungs or bronchi caused by the inhalation of metallic or mineral particles: characterized by inflammation, cough, and fibrosis. [C19: shortened from *pneumonoconiosis,* from PNEUMO- + *-coniosis,* from Greek *konis* dust]

pneu+mo+dy+nam+ics (ˌnjuːməʊdaɪˈnæmɪks) *n.* (*functioning as sing.*) another name for **pneumatics.**

pneu+mo+en+ceph·a+lo+gram (ˌnjuːməʊɛnˈsɛfələˌɡræm) *n.* See **encephalogram.** **—pneu+mo+en+ceph+al+og+ra+phy** (ˌnjuːməʊɛnˌsɛfəˈlɒɡrəfɪ) *n.*

pneu+mo+gas+tric (ˌnjuːməʊˈɡæstrɪk) *adj. Anatomy.* **1.** of or relating to the lungs and stomach. **2.** a former term for **vagus.**

pneu+mo+graph (ˈnjuːməˌɡrɑːf, -ˌɡræf) *n. Med.* an instrument for making a record (**pneumogram**) of respiratory movements.

pneu+mo+nec+to+my (ˌnjuːməʊˈnɛktəmɪ) *or* **pneu+mec+to+my** *n., pl.* **+mies.** surgical removal of a lung or part of a lung. [C20: from Greek *pneumōn* lung + -ECTOMY]

pneu+mo+ni+a (njuːˈməʊnɪə) *n.* inflammation of one or both lungs, in which the air sacs (alveoli) become filled with liquid, which renders them useless for breathing. It is usually caused by bacterial (esp. pneumococcal) or viral infection. [C17: New Latin from Greek from *pneumōn* lung]

pneu+mon+ic (njuːˈmɒnɪk) *adj.* **1.** of, relating to, or affecting the lungs; pulmonary. **2.** of or relating to pneumonia. [C17: from New Latin *pneumonicus,* from Greek, from *pneumon* lung]

pneu+mon+it+is (ˌnjuːmɒnˈaɪtɪs) *n.* inflammation of the lungs.

pneu+mo+tho+rax (ˌnjuːməʊˈθɔːræks) *n.* **1.** the abnormal presence of air between the lung and the wall of the chest (pleural cavity), resulting in collapse of the lung. **2.** *Med.* the introduction of air into the pleural cavity to collapse the lung: a former treatment for tuberculosis.

p-n junc+tion *n. Electronics.* a boundary between a p-type and n-type semiconductor that functions as a rectifier and is used in diodes and junction transistors.

Pnom Penh (ˈnɒm ˈpɛn) *n.* a variant spelling of **Phnom Penh.**

po (pəʊ) *n., pl.* **pos.** *Brit.* an informal word for **chamber pot.** [C19: from POT[1]]

Po[1] *the chemical symbol for* polonium.

Po[2] (pəʊ) *n.* a river in N Italy, rising in the Cottian Alps and flowing northeast to Turin, then east to the Adriatic: the longest river in Italy. Length: 652 km (405 miles). Latin name: **Padus.**

P.O. *abbrev. for:* **1.** Post Office. **2.** Personnel Officer. **3.** petty officer. **4.** Pilot Officer. **5.** Also: **p.o.** postal order.

po·a+ceous (pəʊˈeɪʃəs) *adj.* (in former botanic classification) of, relating to, or belonging to the plant family *Poaceae* (grasses). [C18: via New Latin from Greek *poa* grass]

poach[1] (pəʊtʃ) *vb.* **1.** to catch (game, fish, etc.) illegally by trespassing on private property. **2.** to encroach on or usurp (another person's rights, duties, etc.) or steal (an idea, employee, etc.). **3.** *Tennis, badminton, etc.* to take or play (shots that should belong to one's partner). **4.** to break up (land) into wet muddy patches, as by riding over it, or (of land) to become broken up in this way. **5.** (*intr.*) (of the feet, shoes, etc.) to sink into heavy wet ground. [C17: from Old French *pocher,* of Germanic origin; compare Middle Dutch *poken* to prod; see POKE[1]]

poach[2] (pəʊtʃ) *vb.* to simmer (eggs, fish, etc.) very gently in water, milk, stock, etc. [C15: from Old French *pochier* to enclose in a bag (as the yolks are enclosed by the whites); compare POKE[2]]

poach+er[1] (ˈpəʊtʃə) *n.* a person who illegally hunts game, fish, etc., on someone else's property.

poach+er[2] (ˈpəʊtʃə) *n.* a metal pan with individual cups for poaching eggs.

P.O.B. *abbrev. for* Post Office Box.

Po·ca·hon·tas (ˌpɒkəˈhɒntəs) *n.* original name *Matoaka;* married name *Rebecca Rolfe.* ?1595–1617, American Indian, who allegedly saved the colonist Captain John Smith from being killed.

po+chard (ˈpəʊtʃəd) *n., pl.* **+chards** *or* **+chard.** any of various diving ducks of the genera *Aythya* and *Netta,* esp. *A. ferina* of Europe, the male of which has a grey-and-black body and a reddish head. [C16: of unknown origin]

pock (pɒk) *n.* **1.** any pustule resulting from an eruptive disease, esp. from smallpox. **2.** another word for **pockmark.** [Old English *pocc;* related to Middle Dutch *pocke,* perhaps to Latin *bucca* cheek] **—ˈpock·y** *adj.*

pock+et (ˈpɒkɪt) *n.* **1.** a small bag or pouch in a garment for carrying small articles, money, etc. **2.** any bag or pouch or anything resembling this. **3. a.** a cavity or hollow in the earth, etc., such as one containing gold or other ore. **b.** the ore in such a place. **4.** a small enclosed or isolated area: *a pocket of resistance.* **5.** any of the six holes with pouches or nets let into the corners and sides of a billiard table. **6.** a position in a race in which a competitor is hemmed in. **7.** *Australian Rules football.* a player in one of two side positions at the ends of the ground: *back pocket; forward pocket.* **8. in one's pocket.** under one's control. **9. in** *or* **out of pocket.** having made a profit or loss, as after a transaction. **10. line one's pockets.** to make money, esp. by dishonesty when in a position of trust. **11.** (*modifier*) suitable for fitting in a pocket; small: *a pocket edition.* ~*vb.* (*tr.*) **12.** to put into one's pocket. **13.** to take surreptitiously or unlawfully; steal. **14.** (*usually passive*) to enclose or confine in or as if in a pocket. **15.** *Billiards, etc.* to drive (a ball) into a pocket. **16.** *U.S.* (esp. of the President) to retain (a bill) without acting on it in order to prevent it from becoming law. See also **pocket veto.** **17.** to hem in (an opponent), as in racing. [C15: from Anglo-Norman *poket* a little bag, from *poque* bag, from Middle Dutch *poke* POKE[2], bag; related to French *poche* pocket] **—ˈpock+et+a·ble** *adj.* **—ˈpock+et+ˌless** *adj.*

pock+et bat·tle+ship *n.* a small warship specially built to conform with treaty limitations on tonnage and armament.

pock+et bil+liards *n. Billiards.* **1.** another name for **pool**[2] (sense 5). **2.** any game played on a table in which the object is to pocket the balls, esp. snooker and pool.

pock·et+book (ˈpɒkɪtˌbʊk) *n. U.S.* a small bag or case for money, papers, etc., carried by a handle or in the pocket.

pock+et bor+ough *n.* (before the Reform Act of 1832) an English borough constituency controlled by one person or family who owned the land. Such a borough normally had few if any inhabitants. Compare **rotten borough.**

pock+et+ful (ˈpɒkɪtˌfʊl) *n., pl.* **+fuls.** **1.** as much as a pocket will hold. **2.** *Informal.* a large amount: *it cost him a pocketful of money.*

pock+et go+pher *n.* the full name for **gopher** (sense 1).

pock·et+knife (ˈpɒkɪtˌnaɪf) *n., pl.* **+knives.** a small knife with one or more blades that fold into the handle; penknife.

pock+et mon+ey *n.* **1.** *Brit.* a small weekly sum of money given to children by parents as an allowance. **2.** money for day-to-day spending, incidental expenses, etc.

pock+et mouse *n.* any small mouselike rodent with cheek pouches, of the genus *Perognathus,* of desert regions of W North America: family *Heteromyidae.*

pock+et ve·to *n. U.S.* **1.** the action of the President in retaining unsigned a bill passed by Congress within the last ten days of a session and thus causing it to die. **2.** any similar action by a state governor or other chief executive.

pock+mark (ˈpɒkˌmɑːk) *n.* **1.** Also called: **pock.** a pitted scar left on the skin after the healing of a smallpox or similar pustule. **2.** any pitting of a surface that resembles or suggests such scars. ~*vb.* **3.** (*tr.*) to scar or pit (a surface) with pockmarks.

po·co (ˈpəʊkəʊ; *Italian* ˈpɔːko) *or* **un po·co** *adj., adv. Music.* (*in combination*) a little; to a small degree: *poco rit.; un poco meno mosso.* [from Italian: little, from Latin *paucus* few, scanty]

po·co a po·co *Music. adv.* (*in combination*) little by little: *poco a poco rall.* [Italian]

po+co+cu+ran+te (ˌpəʊkəʊkjʊˈræntɪ) *n.* **1.** a person who is careless or indifferent. ~*adj.* **2.** indifferent or apathetic. [C18: from Italian, from *poco* little + *curante* caring] **—ˌpo+co+cu+ˈran+te+ism** *or* **ˌpo+co+cu+ˈran+tism** *n.*

pod[1] (pɒd) *n.* **1. a.** the fruit of any leguminous plant, consisting of a long two-valved case that contains several seeds and splits along both sides when ripe. **b.** the seed case as distinct from the seeds. **2.** any similar fruit. **3.** a streamlined structure attached by a pylon to an aircraft and used to house a jet engine (**podded engine**), fuel tank, armament, etc. ~*vb.* **pods, pod+ding, pod+ded. 4.** (*tr.*) to remove the pod or shell from (peas, beans, etc.). **5.** (*intr.*) (of a plant) to produce pods. [C17: perhaps back formation from earlier *podware* bagged vegetables, probably from *pod*, variant of COD[2] + WARE[1]]

pod[2] (pɒd) *n.* a small group of animals, esp. seals, whales, or birds.

pod[3] (pɒd) *n.* **1.** a straight groove along the length of certain augers and bits. **2.** the socket that holds the bit in a boring tool. [C16: of unknown origin]

P.O.D. *abbrev. for* pay on delivery.

-pod *or* **-pode** *n. combining form.* indicating a certain type or number of feet: *arthropod; tripod.* [from Greek *-podos* footed, from *pous* foot]

po+dag+ra (pəˈdægrə) *n.* gout of the foot or big toe. [C15: via Latin from Greek, from *pous* foot + *agra* a trap] —**po+ˈdag+ral, po+ˈdag+ric, po+ˈdag+ri+cal,** *or* **po+ˈdag+rous** *adj.*

pod+dy (ˈpɒdɪ) *n., pl.* **+dies.** *Austral.* a hand-fed calf or lamb. [perhaps from *poddy* (adj.) fat]

po+des+ta (pɒˈdɛstə; *Italian* ˌpodeˈsta) *n.* **1.** (in modern Italy) a subordinate magistrate in some towns. **2.** (in Fascist Italy) the chief magistrate of a commune. **3.** (in medieval Italy) **a.** any of the governors of the Lombard cities appointed by Frederick Barbarossa. **b.** a chief magistrate in any of various republics, such as Florence. [C16: from Italian: power, from Latin *potestās* ability, power, from *posse* to be able]

Pod+go+ri+ca *or* **Pod+go+rit+sa** (*Russian* ˈpɔdgɔˌriːtsa) *n.* the former name (until 1946) of **Titograd.**

podg·y (ˈpɒdʒɪ) *adj.* **podg·i·er, podg·i·est.** short and fat; chubby. —**ˈpodg·i·ly** *adv.* —**ˈpodg·i·ness** *n.*

po+di·a·try (pɒˈdiːətrɪ, -ˈdaɪ-) *n. U.S.* another word for **chiropody.** [C20: from Greek *pous* foot] —**po+ˈdi·a·trist** *n.*

po+di·um (ˈpəʊdɪəm) *n., pl.* **+di·ums** *or* **+di·a** (-dɪə). **1.** a small raised platform used by lecturers, orchestra conductors, etc.; dais. **2.** a plinth that supports a colonnade or wall. **3.** a low wall surrounding the arena of an ancient amphitheatre. **4.** *Zoology.* **a.** the terminal part of a vertebrate limb. **b.** any footlike organ, such as the tube foot of a starfish. [C18: from Latin: platform, balcony, from Greek *podion* little foot, from *pous* foot]

-po·di·um *n. combining form.* a part resembling a foot: *pseudopodium.* [from New Latin: footlike; see PODIUM]

Po+dolsk (*Russian* paˈdɔljsk) *n.* an industrial city in the W central Soviet Union, near Moscow. Pop.: 187 000 (1975 est.).

pod·o·phyl+lin *or* **pod·o·phy+lin res+in** (ˌpɒdəʊˈfɪlɪn) *n.* a bitter yellow resin obtained from the dried underground stems of the May apple and mandrake: used as a cathartic and to treat warts. [C19: from New Latin *Podophyllum* genus of herbs including the May apple, from *podo-*, from Greek *pous* foot + *phullon* leaf]

-pod·ous *adj. combining form.* having feet of a certain kind or number: *cephalopodous.*

pod+zol (ˈpɒdzɒl) *or* **pod+sol** (ˈpɒdsɒl) *n.* a type of soil characteristic of coniferous forest regions having a greyish-white colour in its upper leached layers. [C20: from Russian: ash ground, from *pod* ground + *zola* ashes] —**pod+ˈzol+ic** *or* **pod+ˈsol+ic** *adj.*

pod+zol·i·za+tion (ˌpɒdzɒlaɪˈzeɪʃən), **pod+sol·i·za+tion** (ˌpɒdsɒlaɪˈzeɪʃən) *or* **pod+zol·i·sa+tion, pod+sol·i·sa+tion** *n.* the process by which the upper layer of a soil becomes acidic through the leaching of bases which are deposited in the lower horizons.

pod+zo+lize (ˈpɒdzɒˌlaɪz), **pod+so+lize** (ˈpɒdsɒˌlaɪz) *or* **pod+zo+lise, pod+so+lise** *vb.* (*usually passive*) to make into or form a podzol: *podzolized soil.*

Poe (pəʊ) *n.* **Ed·gar Al·lan.** 1809–49, U.S. short-story writer, poet, and critic. Most of his short stories, such as *The Fall of the House of Usher* (1839) and the *Tales of the Grotesque and Arabesque* (1840), are about death, decay, and madness. *The Murders in the Rue Morgue* (1841) is regarded as the first modern detective story.

P.O.E. *abbrev. for:* **1.** *Military.* port of embarkation. **2.** port of entry.

po·em (ˈpəʊɪm) *n.* **1.** a composition in verse, usually characterized by concentrated and heightened language in which words are chosen for their sound and suggestive power as well as for their sense, and using such techniques as metre, rhyme, and alliteration. **2.** a literary composition that is not in verse but exhibits the intensity or imagination and language common to it: *a prose poem.* **3.** anything resembling a poem in beauty, effect, etc. [C16: from Latin *poēma*, from Greek, variant of *poiēma* something composed, created, from *poiein* to make]

poe+nol·o·gy (piːˈnɒlədʒɪ) *n.* a variant spelling of **penology.**

po+e·sy (ˈpəʊɪzɪ) *n., pl.* **·sies. 1.** an archaic word for **poetry. 2.** *Poetic.* the art of writing poetry. **3.** *Archaic or poetic.* a poem or verse, esp. one used as a motto. [C14: via Old French from Latin *poēsis*, from Greek, from *poiēsis* poetic art, creativity, from *poiein* to make]

po·et (ˈpəʊɪt) *or* (*sometimes when fem.*) **po+et+ess** *n.* **1.** a person who writes poetry. **2.** a person with great imagination and creativity. [C13: from Latin *poēta*, from Greek *poiētēs* maker, poet, from *poiein* to make]

poet. *abbrev. for:* **1.** poetic(al). **2.** poetry.

po+et+as+ter (ˌpəʊɪˈtæstə, -ˈteɪ-) *n.* a writer of inferior verse. [C16: from Medieval Latin; see POET, -ASTER]

po+et+ic (pəʊˈɛtɪk) *or* **po+et·i·cal** *adj.* **1.** of or relating to poetry. **2.** characteristic of or befitting poetry, as in being elevated, sublime, etc. **3.** characteristic of a poet. **4.** recounted in verse. —**po+ˈet·i·cal+ly** *adv.*

po+et·i·cize (pəʊˈɛtɪˌsaɪz), **po+et+ize** (ˈpəʊɪˌtaɪz) *or* **po+et·i+cise, po+et+ise** *vb.* **1.** (*tr.*) to put into poetry or make poetic. **2.** (*intr.*) to speak or write poetically.

po+et+ic jus+tice *n.* fitting retribution; just deserts.

po+et+ic li+cence *n.* justifiable departure from conventional rules of form, fact, logic, etc., as in poetry.

po+et+ics (pəʊˈɛtɪks) *n.* (*usually functioning as sing.*) **1.** the principles and forms of poetry or the study of these, esp. as a form of literary criticism. **2.** a treatise on poetry.

po·et lau+re·ate *n., pl.* **po·ets lau+re·ate.** *Brit.* the poet appointed as court poet of Britain who is given a lifetime post as an officer of the Royal Household. The first was Ben Jonson in 1616.

po+et+ry (ˈpəʊɪtrɪ) *n.* **1.** literature in metrical form; verse. **2.** the art or craft of writing verse. **3.** poetic qualities, spirit, or feeling in anything. **4.** anything resembling poetry in rhythm, beauty, etc. [C14: from Medieval Latin *poētria*, from Latin *poēta* POET]

po-faced *adj.* (of a person) wearing a disapproving, stern expression. [C20: changed from *poor-faced*]

po+gey *or* **po·gy** (ˈpəʊgɪ) *n., pl.* **+geys** *or* **·gies.** *Canadian slang.* **1.** financial or other relief given to the unemployed by the government; dole. **2.** unemployment insurance. **3. a.** the office distributing relief to the unemployed. **b.** (*as modifier*): *pogey clothes.* [C20: from earlier *pogie* workhouse, of unknown origin]

pogge (pɒg) *n.* **1.** Also called: **armed bullhead.** a European marine scorpaenoid fish, *Agonus cataphractus*, of northern European waters, with a large head, long thin tail, and body completely covered with bony plates: family *Agonidae.* **2.** any other fish of the family *Agonidae.*

po+go·ni·a (pəˈgəʊnɪə) *n.* any orchid of the chiefly American genus *Pogonia*, esp. the snakesmouth, having pink or white fragrant flowers. [C19: New Latin, from Greek *pōgōnias* bearded, from *pōgōn* a beard]

po·go stick (ˈpəʊgəʊ) *n.* a stout pole with a handle at the top, steps for the feet and a spring at the bottom, so that the user can spring up, down, and along on it. [C20: of uncertain origin]

pog+rom (ˈpɒgrəm) *n.* an organized persecution or extermination of an ethnic group, esp. of Jews. [C20: via Yiddish from Russian: destruction, from *po-* like + *grom* thunder]

po·gy (ˈpəʊgɪ, ˈpɒgɪ) *n.* **1.** (*pl.* **po·gies** *or* **po·gy**) another name for the **porgy. 2.** (*pl.* **po·gies**) a variant spelling of **pogey.** [C19: perhaps from Algonquian *pohegan* menhaden]

Po+hai (ˌpəʊˈhaɪ) *n.* a large inlet of the Yellow Sea on the coast of NE China. Also called: (Gulf of) **Chihli.**

po+hu+tu+ka+wa (pəˌhuːtəˈkaːwə) *n.* a myrtaceous New Zealand tree, *Metrosideros tomentosa*, with red flowers and hard red wood. [from Maori]

poi (pɔɪ, ˈpəʊɪ) *n.* a Hawaiian dish made of the root of the taro baked, pounded to a paste, and fermented. [C19: from Hawaiian]

-poi·e·sis *n. combining form.* indicating the act of making or producing something specified: *haematopoiesis.* [from Greek, from *poiēsis* a making; see POESY] —**-poi·et·ic** *adj. combining form.*

poign+ant (ˈpɔɪnjənt, -nənt) *adj.* **1.** sharply distressing or painful to the feelings. **2.** to the point; cutting or piercing: *poignant wit.* **3.** keen or pertinent in mental appeal: *a poignant subject.* **4.** pungent in smell. [C14: from Old French, from Latin *pungens* pricking, from *pungere* to sting, pierce, grieve] —**ˈpoign+an+cy** *or* **ˈpoign+ance** *n.* —**ˈpoign+ant+ly** *adv.*

poi+ki+lo+ther+mic (ˌpɔɪkɪləʊˈθɜːmɪk) *or* **poi+ki+lo+ther+mal** (ˌpɔɪkɪləʊˈθɜːməl) *adj.* (of all animals except birds and mammals) having a body temperature that varies with the temperature of the surroundings. Compare **homoiothermic.** [C19: from Greek *poikilos* various + THERMAL] —**ˌpoi+ki+lo+ˈther+mism** *or* **ˌpoi+ki+lo+ˈther+my** *n.*

poi+lu (ˈpwɑːluː; *French* pwaˈly) *n.* an infantryman in the French Army, esp. one in the front lines in World War I. [C20: from French, literally: hairy (that is, virile), from *poil* hair, from Latin *pilus* a hair]

Poin·ca·ré (*French* pwɛ̃kaˈre) *n.* **1. Jules Hen·ri** (ʒyl ãˈri). 1854–1912, French mathematician, physicist, and philosopher. He made important contributions to the theory of functions and to astronomy and electromagnetic theory. **2.** his cousin, **Ray·mond** (rɛˈmɔ̃). 1860–1934, French statesman; premier of France (1912–13; 1922–24; 1926–29); president (1913–20).

poin+ci·a+na (ˌpɔɪnsɪˈɑːnə) *n.* **1.** any tree of the tropical caesalpiniaceous genus *Poinciana*, having large orange or red flowers. **2.** See **royal poinciana.** [C17: New Latin, named after M. de *Poinci*, 17th-century governor of the French Antilles]

poind (pɔɪnd) *vb.* (*tr.*) *Scot. law.* **1.** to take (property of a debtor, etc.) in execution or by way of distress; distrain. **2.** to impound (stray cattle, etc.). [C15: from Scots, variant of Old English *pyndan* to impound]

poin+set+ti·a (pɔɪnˈsɛtɪə) *n.* a euphorbiaceous shrub, *Euphorbia* (or *Poinsettia*) *pulcherrima*, of Mexico and Central America widely cultivated for its showy scarlet bracts, which resemble petals. [C19: New Latin, from the name of J. P. *Poinsett* (1799–1851), U.S. Minister to Mexico, who introduced it to the U.S.]

point (pɔɪnt) *n.* **1.** a dot or tiny mark. **2.** a location, spot, or position. **3.** any dot or mark used in writing or printing, such as a decimal point or a full stop. **4.** the sharp tapered end of a pin, knife, etc. **5.** a pin, needle, or other object having such a point. **6.** *Maths.* **a.** a geometric element having no dimensions and whose position in space is located by means of its coordinates. **b.** a location: *point of inflection.* **7.** a promontory, usually smaller than a cape. **8.** a specific condition or degree. **9.** a moment: *at that point he left the room.* **10.** an important or fundamental reason, aim, etc.: *the point of this exercise is to train new teachers.* **11.** an essential element or thesis in an argument: *you've made your point; I take your point.* **12.** a suggestion or tip. **13.** a detail or item. **14.** an important or outstanding characteristic, physical attribute, etc.: *he has his good points.* **15.** a distinctive characteristic or quality of an animal, esp. one used as a standard in judging livestock. **16.** (*often pl.*) any of the extremities, such as the tail, ears, or feet, of a domestic animal. **17.** a single unit for measuring or counting, as in scoring of a game. **18.** *Australian Rules football.* an informal name for **behind** (sense 9). **19.** *Printing.* a unit of measurement equal to one twelfth of a pica, or approximately 0.01384 inch. There are approximately 72 points to the inch. **20.** *Finance.* **a.** a unit of value used to quote security and commodity prices and their fluctuations. **b.** a percentage unit sometimes payable by a borrower as a premium on a loan. **21.** *Navigation.* **a.** one of the 32 marks on the circumference of a compass card indicating direction. **b.** the angle of 11°15′ between two adjacent marks. **c.** a point on the horizon indicated by such a mark. **22.** *Cricket.* **a.** a fielding position at right angles to the batsman on the off side and relatively near the pitch. **b.** a fielder in this position. **23.** any of the numbers cast in the first throw in craps with which one neither wins nor loses by throwing them: 4, 5, 6, 8, 9, or 10. **24.** either of the two electrical contacts that make or break the current flow in the distributor of an internal-combustion engine. **25.** *Brit.* (*often pl.*) a junction of railway tracks in which a pair of rails can be moved so that a train can be directed onto either of two lines. U.S. equivalent: **switch. 26.** (*often pl.*) a piece of ribbon, cord, etc., with metal tags at the end: used during the 16th and 17th centuries to fasten clothing. **27.** *Backgammon.* a place or position on the board. **28.** *Brit.* an informal name for **socket** (sense 2). **29.** an aggressive position adopted in bayonet or sword drill. **30.** the position of the body of a pointer or setter when it discovers game. **31.** *Boxing.* a mark awarded for a scoring blow, knockdown, etc. **32.** any diacritic used in a writing system, esp. in a phonetic transcription, to indicate modifications of vowels or consonants. See also **vowel point. 33.** *Jewellery.* a unit of weight equal to 0.01 carat. **34.** the act of pointing. **35.** *Ice hockey.* the position just inside the opponents' blue line. **36. at** (*or* **on**) **the point of.** at the moment immediately before a specified condition, action, etc., is expected to begin: *on the point of leaving the room.* **37. beside the point.** not pertinent; irrelevant. **38. case in point.** a specific, appropriate, or relevant instance or example. **39. in point of.** in the matter of; regarding. **40. make a point of. a.** to make (something) one's regular habit. **b.** to do (something) because one thinks it important. **41. not to put too fine a point on it.** to speak plainly and bluntly. **42. score points off.** to gain an advantage at someone else's expense. **43. stretch a point.** to make a concession or exception. **44. to the point.** pertinent. **45. up to a point.** not completely. ~*vb.* **46.** (usually foll. by *at* or *to*) to indicate the location or direction of by or as by extending (a finger or other pointed object) towards it. **47.** (*intr.*; usually foll. by *at* or *to*) to indicate or identify a specific person or thing among several: *all evidence pointed to Donald as the murderer.* **48.** (*tr.*) to direct or cause to go or face in a specific direction or towards a place or goal. **49.** (*tr.*) to sharpen or taper. **50.** (*intr.*) (of gun dogs) to indicate the place where game is lying by standing rigidly with the muzzle turned in its direction. **51.** (*tr.*) to finish or repair the joints of (brickwork, masonry, etc.) with mortar or cement. **52.** (*tr.*) *Music.* to mark (a psalm text) with vertical lines to indicate the points at which the music changes during chanting. **53.** to steer (a sailing vessel) close to the wind or (of a sailing vessel) to sail close to the wind. **54.** (*tr.*) *Phonetics.* to provide (a letter or letters) with diacritics. **55.** (*tr.*) to provide (a Hebrew or similar text) with vowel points. ~See also **point off, point out, point up.** [C13: from Old French: spot, from Latin *punctum* a point, from *pungere* to pierce; also influenced by Old French *pointe* pointed end, from Latin *pungere*]

point-blank *adj.* **1. a.** aimed or fired horizontally at a target without making allowance for the drop in the course of the projectile. **b.** permitting such aim or fire without loss of accuracy: *at point-blank range.* **2.** aimed or fired at nearly zero range. **3.** plain or blunt: *a point-blank question.* ~*adv.* **4.** directly or straight. **5.** plainly or bluntly.

Point Cook *n.* the Royal Australian Air Force College in SE Australia, in S Victoria on Port Phillip Bay.

point d'ap+pui *French.* (pwɛ̃ da'pwi) *n., pl.* ***points d'ap+pui*** (pwɛ̃ da'pwi). **1.** a support or prop. **2.** (formerly) the base or area upon which a battle line was centred.

point de+fect *n.* an imperfection in a crystal, characterized by one unoccupied lattice position or one interstitial atom, molecule, or ion.

point-de·vice *Obsolete.* ~*adj.* **1.** very correct or perfect; precise. ~*adv.* **2.** to perfection; perfectly; precisely.

point du·ty *n.* the stationing of a policeman or traffic warden at a road junction to control and direct traffic.

pointe (pɔɪnt) *n. Ballet.* the tip of the toe (esp. in the phrase **on pointes**). [from French: point]

Pointe-à-Pi·tre (*French* pwɛ̃t a 'pitr) *n.* the chief port of Guadeloupe, on SW Grande Terre Island in the Caribbean. Pop.: 29 522 (1967).

point+ed ('pɔɪntɪd) *adj.* **1.** having a point. **2.** cutting or incisive: *a pointed wit.* **3.** obviously directed at or intended for a particular person: *pointed criticism.* **4.** emphasized or made conspicuous: *pointed ignorance.* **5.** (of an arch or style of architecture employing such an arch) Gothic. —**'point+ed+ly** *adv.* —**'point+ed+ness** *n.*

point+ed arch *n.* another name for **lancet arch.**

Pointe-Noire (*French* pwɛ̃t 'nwa:r) *n.* a port in the S Congo Republic, on the Atlantic: the country's chief port and former capital (1950–58). Pop.: 150 000 (1970 est.).

point+er ('pɔɪntə) *n.* **1.** a person or thing that points. **2.** an indicator on a measuring instrument. **3.** a long rod or cane used by a lecturer to point to parts of a map, blackboard, etc. **4.** one of a breed of large swift hunting dogs, usually white with black, liver, or lemon markings. **5.** a helpful piece of information or advice.

Point+ers ('pɔɪntəz) *pl. n.* **the.** the two brightest stars in the Plough, which lie in the direction pointing towards the Pole Star and are therefore used to locate it.

point group *n. Crystallog.* another term for **crystal class.**

poin+til+lism ('pwæntɪˌlɪzəm, -ti:ˌɪzəm, 'pɔɪn-) *n.* the technique of painting elaborated from impressionism, in which dots of unmixed colour are juxtaposed on a white ground so that from a distance they fuse in the viewer's eye into appropriate intermediate tones. Also called: **divisionism.** [C19: from French, from *pointiller* to mark with tiny dots, from *pointille* little point, from Italian *puntiglio,* from *punto* POINT] —**'poin+til+list** *n., adj.*

point+ing ('pɔɪntɪŋ) *n.* the act or process of repairing or finishing joints in brickwork, masonry, etc., with mortar.

point lace *n.* lace made by a needle with buttonhole stitch on a paper pattern. Also called: **needlepoint.** Compare **pillow lace.**

point+less ('pɔɪntlɪs) *adj.* **1.** without a point. **2.** without meaning, relevance, or force. **3.** *Sport.* without a point scored. —**'point+less+ly** *adv.* —**'point+less+ness** *n.*

point off *vb.* (*tr., adv.*) to mark off from the right-hand side (a number of decimal places) in a whole number to create a mixed decimal: *point off three decimal places in 12345 and you get 12.345.*

point of hon+our *n., pl.* **points of hon+our.** a circumstance, event, etc., that involves the defence of one's principles, social honour, etc.

point of in+flec+tion *n., pl.* **points of in+flec+tion.** *Maths.* a stationary point on a curve at which the tangent is horizontal or vertical and where tangents on either side have the same sign.

point of no re+turn *n.* a point at which an irreversible commitment must be made to an action, progression, etc.

point of or+der *n., pl.* **points of or+der.** a question raised in a meeting or deliberative assembly by a member as to whether the rules governing procedures are being breached.

point of view *n., pl.* **points of view. 1.** a position from which someone or something is observed. **2.** a mental viewpoint or attitude. **3.** the mental position from which a story is observed or narrated: *the omniscient point of view.*

point out *vb.* (*tr., adv.*) to indicate or specify.

points+man ('pɔɪntsˌmæn, -mən) *n., pl.* **+men.** a person who operates railway points. U.S. equivalent: **switchman.**

point source *n. Optics.* a source of light or other radiation that can be considered to have negligible dimensions.

point sys+tem *n.* **1.** *Printing.* a system of measurement using the **point** (see sense 19) as its unit. **2.** a system for evaluation of achievement, as in education or industry, based on awarding points. **3.** any system of writing or printing, such as Braille, that uses protruding dots.

point-to-point *n. Brit.* **a.** a steeplechase organized by a recognized hunt or other body, usually restricted to amateurs riding horses that have been regularly used in hunting. **b.** (*as modifier*): *a point-to-point race.*

point up *vb.* (*tr., adv.*) to emphasize, esp. by identifying: *he pointed up the difficulties we would encounter.*

poise[1] (pɔɪz) *n.* **1.** composure or dignity of manner. **2.** physical balance or assurance in movement or bearing. **3.** the state of being balanced or stable; equilibrium; stability. **4.** the position of hovering. **5.** suspense or indecision. ~*vb.* **6.** to be or cause to be balanced or suspended. **7.** (*tr.*) to hold, as in readiness: *to poise a lance.* **8.** (*tr.*) a rare word for **weigh.** [C16: from Old French *pois* weight, from Latin *pēnsum,* from *pendere* to weigh]

poise[2] (pwa:z) *n.* the cgs unit of viscosity; the viscosity of a fluid in which a tangential force of 1 dyne per square centimetre maintains a difference in velocity of 1 centimetre per second between two parallel planes 1 centimetre apart. It is equivalent to 0.1 newton second per square metre. Symbol: P [C20: named after Jean Louis Marie *Poiseuille* (1799–1869), French physician]

poised (pɔɪzd) *adj.* **1.** self-possessed; dignified; exhibiting composure. **2.** balanced and prepared for action: *a skier poised at the top of the slope.*

poi+son ('pɔɪzᵊn) *n.* **1.** any substance that can impair function, cause structural damage, or otherwise injure the body. **2.** something that destroys, corrupts, etc.: *the poison of fascism.* **3.** a substance that retards a chemical reaction or destroys or inhibits the activity of a catalyst. **4.** a substance that absorbs neutrons in a nuclear reactor and thus slows down the reaction. It may be added deliberately or formed during fission. **5. what's your poison?** *Informal.* what would you like to drink? *~vb. (tr.)* **6.** to give poison to (a person or animal) esp. with intent to kill. **7.** to add poison to. **8.** to taint or infect with or as if with poison. **9.** (foll. by *against*) to turn (a person's mind) against: *he poisoned her mind against me.* **10.** to retard or stop (a chemical or nuclear reaction) by the action of a poison. **11.** to inhibit or destroy (the activity of a catalyst) by the action of a poison. [C13: from Old French *puison* potion, from Latin *pōtiō* a drink, esp. a poisonous one, from *pōtāre* to drink] —**'poi·son·er** *n.*

poi·son dog·wood *or* **el·der** *n.* another name for **poison sumach.**

poi·son gas *n.* a gaseous substance, such as chlorine, phosgene, or lewisite, used in warfare to kill or harm.

poi·son hem·lock *n.* the U.S. name for **hemlock** (sense 1).

poi·son i·vy *n.* any of several North American anacardiaceous shrubs or vines of the genus *Rhus* (or *Toxicodendron*), esp. *R. radicans,* which has small green flowers and whitish berries that cause an itching rash on contact. See also **sumach** (sense 1).

poi·son oak *n.* **1.** either of two North American anacardiaceous shrubs, *Rhus toxicodendron* or *R. diversiloba,* that are related to the poison ivy and cause a similar rash. See also **sumach** (sense 1). **2.** (*not in technical use*) another name for **poison ivy.**

poi·son·ous ('pɔɪzənəs) *adj.* **1.** having the effects or qualities of a poison. **2.** capable of killing or inflicting injury; venomous. **3.** corruptive or malicious. —**'poi·son·ous·ly** *adv.* —**'poi·son·ous·ness** *n.*

poi·son-pen let·ter *n.* a letter written in malice, usually anonymously, and intended to abuse, frighten, or insult the recipient.

poi·son su·mach *n.* an anacardiaceous swamp shrub, *Rhus* (or *Toxicodendron*) *vernix* of the southeastern U.S., that has greenish-white berries and causes an itching rash on contact with the skin. Also called: **poison dogwood, poison elder.** See also **sumach.**

Pois·son dis·tri·bu·tion ('pwɑːsᵊn) *n. Statistics.* a distribution that approximates in the limit to the binomial distribution when the probability of success in a single trial is small and the number of trials is large. [C19: named after S. D. *Poisson* (1781–1840), French mathematician]

Pois·son's ra·ti·o *n.* a measure of the elastic properties of a material expressed as the ratio of the fractional contraction in breadth to the fractional increase in length when the material is stretched. Symbol: μ or ν

Poi·tiers (*French* pwa'tje) *n.* a city in S central France: capital of the former province of Poitou until 1790; scene of the battle (1356) in which the English under the Black Prince defeated the French; university (1432). Pop.: 85 466 (1975).

Poi·tou (*French* pwa'tu) *n.* a former province of W central France, on the Atlantic. Chief town: Poitiers.

Poi·tou-Cha·rentes (*French* pwatu ʃa'rɑ̃ːt) *n.* a region of W central France, on the Bay of Biscay: mainly low-lying.

poke[1] (pəʊk) *vb.* **1.** (*tr.*) to jab or prod, as with the elbow, the finger, a stick, etc. **2.** (*tr.*) to make (a hole, opening, etc.) by or as by poking. **3.** (when *intr.*, often foll. by *at*) to thrust (at). **4.** (*tr.*) *Informal.* to hit with the fist; punch. **5.** (usually foll. by *in, out, out of, through,* etc.) to protrude or cause to protrude: *don't poke your arm out of the window.* **6.** (*tr.*) to stir (a fire, pot, etc.) by poking. **7.** (*intr.*) to meddle or intrude. **8.** (*intr.;* often foll. by *about* or *around*) to search or pry. **9.** (*intr.;* often foll. by *along*) to loiter, potter, dawdle, etc. **10. poke fun at.** to mock or ridicule. **11. poke one's nose into.** to interfere with or meddle in. *~n.* **12.** a jab or prod. **13.** short for **slowpoke. 14.** *Informal.* a blow with one's fist; punch. [C14: from Low German and Middle Dutch *poken* to thrust, prod, strike]

poke[2] (pəʊk) *n.* **1.** *Dialect.* a pocket or bag. **2. a pig in a poke.** See **pig** (sense 8). [C13: from Old Northern French *poque,* of Germanic origin; related to Old English *pocca* bag, Old Norse *poki* POUCH, Middle Dutch *poke* bag; compare POACH[2]]

poke[3] (pəʊk) *n.* **1.** Also called: **poke bonnet.** a woman's bonnet with a brim that projects at the front, popular in the 18th and 19th centuries. **2.** the brim itself. [C18: from POKE[1] (in the sense: to thrust out, project)]

poke[4] (pəʊk) *n.* short for **pokeweed.**

poke·ber·ry ('pəʊkbərɪ) *n., pl.* **·ries. 1.** Also called: **inkberry.** the berry of the pokeweed. **2.** another name for the **pokeweed.**

poke·lo·gan ('pəʊk,ləʊgən) *n. Canadian.* another name for **bogan.**

pok·er[1] ('pəʊkə) *n.* **1.** a metal rod, usually with a handle, for stirring a fire. **2.** a person or thing that pokes.

pok·er[2] ('pəʊkə) *n.* a card game of bluff and skill in which bets are made on the hands dealt, the highest-ranking hand (containing the most valuable combinations of sequences and sets of cards) winning the pool. [C19: probably from French *poque* similar card game]

pok·er face *n. Informal.* a face without expression, as that of a poker player attempting to conceal the value of his cards. —**'pok·er-,faced** *adj.*

pok·er ma·chine *n. Austral.* a fruit machine. Often shortened to **pokie.**

poke·weed ('pəʊk,wiːd), **poke·ber·ry,** *or* **poke·root** *n.* a tall North American plant, *Phytolacca americana,* that has small white flowers, juicy purple berries, and a poisonous purple root used medicinally: family *Phytolaccaceae.* Sometimes shortened to **poke.** Also called: **inkberry.** [C18 *poke,* shortened from Algonquian *puccoon* plant used in dyeing, from *pak* blood]

pok·ie ('pəʊkɪ) *n. Austral. informal.* short for **poker machine.**

pok·y *or* **pok·ey** ('pəʊkɪ) *adj.* **pok·i·er, pok·i·est. 1.** *Informal.* without speed or energy; slow. **2.** (esp. of rooms) small and cramped. *~n., pl.* **pok·ies** *or* **pok·eys. 3.** a U.S. slang word for **jail.** [C19: from POKE[1] (in slang sense: to confine)] —**'pok·i·ly** *adv.* —**'pok·i·ness** *n.*

POL *Military. abbrev. for* petroleum, oil, and lubricants.

pol. *abbrev. for:* **1.** political. **2.** politics.

Pol. *abbrev. for:* **1.** Poland. **2.** Polish.

Po·la ('pɔːla) *n.* the Italian name for **Pula.**

Po·lack ('pəʊlæk) *n. Derogatory slang.* a Pole or a person of Polish descent. [C16: from Polish *Polak* Pole]

po·la·cre (pəʊ'lɑːkə) *or* **po·lac·ca** (pəʊ'lækə) *n.* a three-masted sailing vessel used in the Mediterranean. [C17: from either French *polacre* or Italian *polacca* Pole or Polish; origin unknown]

Po·land ('pəʊlənd) *n.* a republic in central Europe, on the Baltic: first united in the 10th century; dissolved after the third partition effected by Austria, Russia, and Prussia in 1795; re-established independence in 1918; invaded by Germany in 1939; ruled by a Communist government since 1947. It consists chiefly of a low undulating plain in the north, rising to a low plateau in the south, with the Sudeten and Carpathian Mountains along the S border. Language: Polish. Currency: zloty. Capital: Warsaw. Pop.: 33 691 000 (1974 est.). Area: 311 730 sq. km (120 359 sq. miles). Polish name: **Polska.**

Po·lan·ski (pə'lænskɪ) *n.* **Ro·man.** born 1933, Polish film director with a taste for the macabre, as in *Repulsion* (1965) and *Rosemary's Baby* (1968).

po·lar ('pəʊlə) *adj.* **1.** situated at or near, coming from, or relating to either of the earth's poles or the area inside the Arctic or Antarctic Circles: *polar regions.* **2.** having or relating to a pole or poles. **3.** pivotal or guiding in the manner of the Pole Star. **4.** directly opposite, as in tendency or character. **5.** *Chem.* **a.** (of a molecule or compound) being or having a molecule in which there is an uneven distribution of electrons and thus a permanent dipole moment: *water has polar molecules.* **b.** (of a crystal or substance) being or having a crystal that is bound by ionic bonds: *sodium chloride forms polar crystals.*

po·lar ax·is *n.* the fixed line in a system of polar coordinates from which the polar angle, θ, is measured anticlockwise.

po·lar bear *n.* a white carnivorous bear, *Thalarctos maritimus,* of coastal regions of the North Pole.

po·lar bod·y *n. Physiology.* a tiny cell containing little cytoplasm that is produced with the ovum during oogenesis when the oocyte undergoes meiosis.

po·lar cir·cle *n.* a term for either the **Arctic Circle** or **Antarctic Circle.**

po·lar co·or·di·nates *pl. n.* a pair of coordinates for locating a point in a plane by means of the length of a radius vector, *r,* which pivots about the origin to establish the angle, θ, that the position of the point makes with a fixed line. Usually written (r, θ). See also **Cartesian coordinates, spherical coordinates.**

po·lar dis·tance *n.* the angular distance of a star, planet, etc., from the celestial pole; the complement of the declination. Also called: **codeclination.**

po·lar e·qua·tion *n.* an equation in polar coordinates.

po·lar front *n. Meteorol.* a front dividing cold polar air from warmer temperate or tropical air.

po·lar·im·e·ter (,pəʊlə'rɪmɪtə) *n.* **1.** an instrument for measuring the amount of polarization of light. **2.** an instrument for measuring the rotation of the plane of polarization of light as a result of its passage through a liquid or solution. See **optical activity.** —**po·lar·i·met·ric** (,pəʊlərɪ'metrɪk) *adj.* —**,po·lar·'im·e·try** *n.*

Po·la·ris (pə'lɑːrɪs) *n.* **1.** Also called: the **Pole Star,** the **North Star.** the brightest star in the constellation Ursa Minor, situated slightly less than 1° from the north celestial pole. It is a Cepheid variable, with a period of four days. Visual magnitude: 2.08–2.17; spectral type: F8. **2. a.** a type of U.S. two-stage intermediate-range ballistic missile, usually fired by a submerged submarine. **b.** (*as modifier*): *a Polaris submarine.* [shortened from Medieval Latin *stella polāris* polar star]

po·lar·i·scope (pəʊ'lærɪ,skəʊp) *n.* an instrument for detecting polarized light or for observing objects under polarized light, esp. for detecting strain in transparent materials. See **photoelasticity.**

po·lar·i·ty (pəʊ'lærɪtɪ) *n., pl.* **·ties. 1.** the condition of having poles. **2.** the condition of a body or system in which it has opposing physical properties at different points, esp. magnetic poles or electric charge. **3.** the particular state of a part of a body or system that has polarity: *an electrode with positive polarity.* **4.** the state of having or expressing two directly opposite tendencies, opinions, etc.

po·lar·i·za·tion *or* **po·lar·i·sa·tion** (,pəʊləraɪ'zeɪʃən) *n.* **1.** the condition of having or giving polarity. **2.** *Physics.* the process or phenomenon in which the waves of light or other electromagnetic radiation are restricted to certain directions of vibration.

po·lar·ize *or* **po·lar·ise** ('pəʊlə,raɪz) *vb.* **1.** to acquire or cause to acquire polarity. **2.** to acquire or cause to acquire polarization: *to polarize light.* —**'po·lar·,iz·a·ble** *or* **'po·lar·,is·a·ble** *adj.* —**'po·lar·,iz·er** *or* **'po·lar·,is·er** *n.*

po·lar lights *n.* the aurora borealis in the N hemisphere or the aurora australis in the S hemisphere.

po·lar·og·ra·phy (,pəʊlə'rɒgrəfɪ) *n.* a technique for analysing and studying ions in solution by using an electrolytic cell with a very small cathode and obtaining a graph (**polarogram**) of the current against the potential to determine the concentration and nature of the ions. Because the cathode is small, polarization occurs and each type of anion is discharged at a different potential. The apparatus (**polarograph**) usually employs a dropping-mercury cathode.

Po·lar·oid (ˈpəʊləˌrɔɪd) *Trademark.* ~*n.* **1.** a type of plastic sheet that can polarize a transmitted beam of normal light because it is composed of long parallel molecules. It only transmits plane-polarized light if these molecules are parallel to the plane of polarization and, since reflected light is partly polarized, it is often used in sunglasses to eliminate glare. **2. Polaroid Land Camera.** any of several types of camera yielding a finished print by means of a special developing and processing technique that occurs inside the camera and takes only a few seconds to complete. ~*adj.* **3.** of, relating to, using, or used in this type of camera: *Polaroid film.*

po·lar se·quence *n. Astronomy.* a series of stars in the vicinity of the N celestial pole whose accurately determined magnitudes serve as the standard for visual and photographic magnitudes of stars.

pol·der (ˈpəʊldə, ˈpɒl-) *n.* a stretch of land reclaimed from the sea or a lake, esp. in the Netherlands. [C17: from Middle Dutch *polre*]

pole[1] (pəʊl) *n.* **1.** a long slender usually round piece of wood, metal, or other material. **2.** the piece of timber on each side of which a pair of carriage horses are hitched. **3.** another name for **rod** (sense 7). **4.** *Horse racing, chiefly U.S.* **a.** the inside lane of a racecourse. **b.** (*as modifier*): *the pole position.* **c.** one of a number of markers placed at intervals of one sixteenth of a mile along the side of a racecourse. **5.** *Nautical.* **a.** any light spar. **b.** the part of a mast between the head and the attachment of the uppermost shrouds. **6. under bare poles.** *Nautical.* (of a sailing vessel) with no sails set. **7. up the pole.** *Brit. and Austral. informal.* **a.** slightly mad. **b.** mistaken; on the wrong track. ~*vb.* **8.** (*tr.*) to strike or push with a pole. **9.** (*tr.*) **a.** to set out (an area of land or garden) with poles. **b.** to support (a crop, such as hops or beans) on poles. **10.** (*tr.*) to deoxidize (a molten metal, esp. copper) by stirring it with green wood. **11.** to punt (a boat). **12.** (usually foll. by *on*) *Austral. informal.* to scrounge (from) or impose (on). [Old English *pāl,* from Latin *pālus* a stake, prop; see PALE[2]]

pole[2] (pəʊl) *n.* **1.** either of the two antipodal points where the earth's axis of rotation meets the earth's surface. See also **North Pole, South Pole. 2.** *Astronomy.* short for **celestial pole. 3.** *Physics.* **a.** either of the two regions at the extremities of a magnet to which the lines of force converge or from which they diverge. **b.** either of two points or regions in a piece of material, system, etc., at which there are opposite electric charges, as at the two terminals of a battery. **4.** *Biology.* **a.** either end of the axis of a cell, spore, ovum, or similar body. **b.** either end of the spindle formed during the metaphase of mitosis and meiosis. **5.** *Physiol.* the point on a neuron from which the axon or dendrites project from the cell body. **6.** either of two mutually exclusive or opposite actions, opinions, etc. **7.** *Geom.* the origin in a system of polar or spherical coordinates. **8.** any fixed point of reference. **9. poles apart** (*or* **asunder**). having widely divergent opinions, tastes, etc. **10. from pole to pole.** throughout the entire world. [C14: from Latin *polus* end of an axis, from Greek *polos* pivot, axis, pole; related to Greek *kuklos* circle]

Pole[1] (pəʊl) *n.* a native, inhabitant, or citizen of Poland or a speaker of Polish.

Pole[2] (pəʊl) *n.* **Reg·i·nald.** 1500–58, English cardinal; last Roman Catholic archbishop of Canterbury (1556–58).

pole·axe *or U.S.* **pole·ax** (ˈpəʊlˌæks) *n.* **1.** another term for battle-axe. ~*vb.* **2.** (*tr.*) to hit or fell with or as if with a poleaxe. [C14 *pollax* battle-axe, from POLL + AXE]

pole·cat (ˈpəʊlˌkæt) *n., pl.* **·cats** *or* **·cat. 1.** a dark brown musteline mammal, *Mustela putorius,* of woodlands of Europe, Asia, and N Africa, that is closely related to but larger than the weasel and gives off an unpleasant smell. **2.** any of various related animals, such as the **marbled polecat,** *Vormela peregusna.* **3.** *U.S.* a nontechnical name for **skunk.** [C14 *polcat,* perhaps from Old French *pol* cock, from Latin *pullus,* + CAT; from its habit of preying on poultry]

pole horse *n.* a horse harnessed alongside the shaft (pole) of a vehicle. Also called: **poler.**

pol·e·march (ˈpɒlɪˌmɑːk) *n.* (in ancient Greece) a civilian official, originally a supreme general. [C16: from Greek *polemarchos,* from *polemos* war + *archos* ruler]

po·lem·ic (pəˈlɛmɪk) *adj. also* **polemical. 1.** of or involving dispute or controversy. ~*n.* **2.** an argument or controversy, esp. over a doctrine, belief, etc. **3.** a person engaged in such an argument or controversy. [C17: from Medieval Latin *polemicus,* from Greek *polemikos* relating to war, from *polemos* war] —**po·ˈlem·i·cal·ly** *adv.* —**po·lem·i·cist** (pəˈlɛmɪsɪst) *or* **pol·e·mist** (ˈpɒlɪmɪst) *n.*

po·lem·ics (pəˈlɛmɪks) *n.* (*functioning as sing.*) the art or practice of dispute or argument, as in attacking or defending a doctrine or belief.

pol·e·mo·ni·a·ceous (ˌpɒlɪˌməʊnɪˈeɪʃəs) *adj.* of, relating to, or belonging to the *Polemoniaceae,* a chiefly North American family of plants that includes phlox and Jacob's ladder. [C19: from New Latin *Polemōnium* type genus, from Greek *polemōnion* a plant, perhaps valerian]

po·len·ta (pəʊˈlɛntə) *n.* a thick porridge made in Italy, usually from maize. [C16: via Italian from Latin: pearl barley, perhaps from Greek *palē* pollen]

pol·er (ˈpəʊlə) *n.* **1.** another name for **pole horse. 2.** a person or thing that poles, esp. a punter. **3.** *Austral. slang.* an idler or sponger.

pole star *n.* a guiding principle, rule, standard, etc.

Pole Star *n.* **the.** the star closest to the N celestial pole at any particular time. At present this is Polaris, but it will eventually be replaced by some other star owing to precession of the earth's axis.

pole vault *n.* **1. the.** a field event in which competitors attempt to clear a high bar with the aid of an extremely flexible long pole. **2.** a single attempt in the pole vault. ~*vb.* **pole-vault. 3.** (*intr.*) to perform a pole vault or compete in the pole vault. —**ˈpole-ˌvault·er** *n.*

po·leyn (ˈpəʊleɪn) *n.* a piece of armour for protecting the knee. Also called: **kneecap.** [from Old French *polain*]

po·lice (pəˈliːs) *n.* **1. a.** (often preceded by *the*) the organized civil force of a state, concerned with maintenance of law and order, the detection and prevention of crime, etc. **b.** (*as modifier*): *a police inquiry.* **2.** (*functioning as pl.*) the members of such a force collectively. **3.** *Archaic.* **a.** the regulation and control of a community, esp. in regard to the enforcement of law, the prevention of crime, etc. **b.** the department of government concerned with this. ~*vb.* (*tr.*) **4.** to regulate, control, or keep in order by means of a police or similar force. **5.** *U.S.* to make or keep (a military camp, etc.) clean and orderly. [C16: via French from Latin *polītīa* administration, government; see POLITY]

po·lice court *n.* **1.** another name for **magistrates' court. 2.** (in Scotland) an inferior court with limited jurisdiction, presided over by lay magistrates.

po·lice dog *n.* a dog, esp. an Alsatian, trained to help the police, as in tracking.

po·lice·man (pəˈliːsmən) *or* (*fem.*) **po·lice·wom·an** *n., pl.* **·men** *or* **·wom·en.** a member of a police force, esp. one holding the rank of constable.

po·lice·man's hel·met *n.* a Himalayan balsaminaceous plant, *Impatiens glandulifera,* with large purplish-pink flowers, introduced into Britain.

Po·lice Mo·tu *n.* a pidginized version of the Motu language, used as a lingua franca in Papua, originally chiefly by the police. Also called: **Hiri Motu.**

po·lice of·fic·er *n.* a member of a police force, esp. a constable; policeman. Often shortened to (esp. as form of address): **officer.**

po·lice state *n.* a state or country in which a repressive government maintains control through the police.

po·lice sta·tion *n.* the office or headquarters of the police force of a district.

pol·i·cy[1] (ˈpɒlɪsɪ) *n., pl.* **·cies. 1.** a plan of action adopted or pursued by an individual, government, party, business, etc. **2.** wisdom, prudence, shrewdness, or sagacity. **3.** *Scot.* the improved grounds surrounding a country house. [C14: from Old French *policie,* from Latin *polītīa* administration, POLITY]

pol·i·cy[2] (ˈpɒlɪsɪ) *n., pl.* **·cies.** a document containing a contract of insurance. [C16: from Old French *police* certificate, from Old Italian *polizza,* from Latin *apodixis* proof, from Greek *apodeixis* demonstration, proof]

pol·i·cy·hold·er (ˈpɒlɪsɪˌhəʊldə) *n.* a person or organization in whose name an insurance policy is registered.

pol·i·cy sci·ence *n.* a branch of the social sciences concerned with the formulation and implementation of policy in bureaucracies, etc.

po·li·o (ˈpəʊlɪəʊ) *n.* short for **poliomyelitis.**

po·li·o·my·e·li·tis (ˌpəʊlɪəʊˌmaɪəˈlaɪtɪs) *n.* an acute infectious viral disease, esp. affecting children. In its paralytic form (**acute anterior poliomyelitis**) the brain and spinal cord are involved, causing weakness, paralysis, and wasting of muscle. Often shortened to **polio.** Also called: **infantile paralysis.** [C19: New Latin, from Greek *polios* grey + *muelos* marrow]

pol·is (ˈpɒlɪs) *n., pl.* **pol·eis** (ˈpɒlaɪs). an ancient Greek city-state. [from Greek: city]

pol·ish (ˈpɒlɪʃ) *vb.* **1.** to make or become smooth and shiny by rubbing, esp. with wax or an abrasive. **2.** (*tr.*) to make perfect or complete. **3.** to make or become elegant or refined. ~*n.* **4.** a finish or gloss. **5.** the act of polishing or the condition of having been polished. **6.** a substance used to produce a smooth and shiny, often protective surface. **7.** elegance or refinement, esp. in style, manner, etc. [C13 *polis,* from Old French *polir,* from Latin *polīre* to polish] —**ˈpol·ish·a·ble** *adj.* —**ˈpol·ish·er** *n.*

Po·lish (ˈpəʊlɪʃ) *adj.* **1.** of, relating to, or characteristic of Poland, its people, or their language. ~*n.* **2.** the official language of Poland, belonging to the West Slavonic branch of the Indo-European family. **3. the Polish.** (*functioning as pl.*) the people of Poland or Polish speakers collectively.

Po·lish Cor·ri·dor *n.* the strip of land through E Pomerania providing Poland with access to the sea (1919–39), given to her in 1919 in the Treaty of Versailles, and separating East Prussia from the rest of Germany. It is now part of Poland.

pol·ished (ˈpɒlɪʃt) *adj.* **1.** accomplished: *a polished actor.* **2.** impeccably or professionally done: *a polished performance.* **3.** (of rice) having had the outer husk removed by milling.

pol·ish off *vb.* (*tr., adv.*) *Informal.* **1.** to finish or process completely. **2.** to dispose of or kill; eliminate.

pol·ish up *vb.* (*adv.*) **1.** to make or become smooth and shiny by polishing. **2.** (when *intr.,* foll. by *on*) to study or practise until adept at; improve: *polish up your spelling; he's polishing up on his German.*

polit. *abbrev. for:* **1.** political. **2.** politics.

Pol·it·bu·ro (ˈpɒlɪtˌbjʊərəʊ) *n.* **1.** the executive and policy-making committee of a Communist Party. **2.** the supreme policy-making authority in the Soviet Union and most other Communist countries. [C20: from Russian: contraction of *Politicheskoe Buro* political bureau]

po·lite (pəˈlaɪt) *adj.* **1.** showing a great regard for others, as in manners, speech, behaviour, etc.; courteous. **2.** cultivated or refined: *polite society.* **3.** elegant or polished: *polite letters.* [C15: from Latin *polītus* polished; see POLISH] —**po·ˈlite·ly** *adv.* —**po·ˈlite·ness** *n.*

pol·i·tesse (ˌpɒlɪˈtɛs) *n.* formal or genteel politeness. [C18: via French from Italian *politezza,* ultimately from Latin *polīre* to POLISH]

Po·li·tian (pəʊˈlɪʃən, pɒ-) *n.* Italian name *Angelo Polliziano;* original name *Angelo Ambrogini.* 1454–94, Florentine humanist and poet.

pol·i·tic (ˈpɒlɪtɪk) *adj.* **1.** artful or shrewd; ingenious: *a politic manager.* **2.** crafty or unscrupulous; cunning: *a politic old scoundrel.* **3.** sagacious, wise, or prudent, esp. in statesmanship: *a politic choice.* **4.** an archaic word for **political.** See **body politic.** [C15: from Old French *politique,* from Latin *polīticus* concerning civil administration, from Greek *politikos,* from *politēs* citizen, from *polis* city] —**ˈpol·i·tic·ly** *adv.*

po·lit·i·cal (pəˈlɪtɪkᵊl) *adj.* **1.** of or relating to the state, government, the body politic, public administration, policy-making, etc. **2. a.** of, involved in, or relating to government policy-making as distinguished from administration or law. **b.** of or relating to the civil aspects of government as distinguished from the military. **3.** of, dealing with, or relating to politics: *a political person.* **4.** of, characteristic of, or relating to the parties and the partisan aspects of politics. **5.** organized or ordered with respect to government: *a political unit.* —**po·ˈlit·i·cal·ly** *adv.*

po·lit·i·cal e·con·o·my *n.* the former name for **economics** (sense 1).

po·lit·i·cal sci·ence *n.* (esp. as an academic subject) the study of the state, government, and politics: one of the social sciences. —**po·lit·i·cal sci·en·tist** *n.*

pol·i·ti·cian (ˌpɒlɪˈtɪʃən) *n.* **1.** a person actively engaged in politics, esp. a full-time professional member of a deliberative assembly. **2.** a person who is experienced or skilled in the art or science of politics, government, or administration; statesman. **3.** *Disparaging, chiefly U.S.* a person who engages in politics out of a wish for personal gain, as realized by holding a public office.

po·lit·i·cize *or* **po·lit·i·cise** (pəˈlɪtɪˌsaɪz) *vb.* **1.** (*tr.*) to render political in tone, interest, or awareness. **2.** (*intr.*) to participate in political discussion or activity. —**po·ˌlit·i·ci·ˈza·tion** *or* **po·ˌlit·i·ci·ˈsa·tion** *n.*

pol·i·tick·ing (ˈpɒlɪˌtɪkɪŋ) *n.* political activity, esp. seeking votes.

po·lit·i·co (pəˈlɪtɪˌkəʊ) *n., pl.* **·cos.** *Chiefly U.S.* an informal word for a **politician** (senses 1, 3). [C17: from Italian or Spanish]

po·lit·i·co- *combining form.* denoting political or politics: *politicoeconomic.*

pol·i·tics (ˈpɒlɪtɪks) *n.* **1.** (*functioning as sing.*) the practice or study of the art and science of forming, directing, and administrating states and other political units; the art and science of government; political science. **2.** (*functioning as sing.*) the complex or aggregate of relationships of men in society, esp. those relationships involving authority or power. **3.** (*functioning as pl.*) political activities or affairs: *party politics.* **4.** (*functioning as sing.*) the business or profession of politics. **5.** (*functioning as sing. or pl.*) any activity concerned with the acquisition of power, gaining one's own ends, etc.: *company politics are frequently vicious.* **6.** (*functioning as pl.*) opinions, principles, sympathies, etc., with respect to politics: *his conservative politics.* **7.** (*functioning as pl.*) **a.** the policy-formulating aspects of government as distinguished from the administrative, or legal. **b.** the civil functions of government as distinguished from the military.

pol·i·ty (ˈpɒlɪtɪ) *n., pl.* **·ties.** **1.** a form of government or organization of a state, church, society, etc.; constitution. **2.** a politically organized society, state, city, etc. **3.** the management of public or civil affairs. **4.** political organization. [C16: from Latin *polītīa,* from Greek *politeia* citizenship, civil administration, from *politēs* citizen, from *polis* city]

pol·je (ˈpəʊljɛ) *n. Geography.* a large elliptical depression in karst regions, sometimes containing a marsh or small lake. [Serbo-Croatian, literally: field; related to FLOOR]

Polk (pəʊk) *n.* **James Knox.** 1795–1849, U.S. statesman; 11th president of the U.S. (1845–49). During his administration, Texas and territory now included in New Mexico, Colorado, Utah, Nevada, Arizona, Oregon, and California were added to the Union.

pol·ka (ˈpɒlkə) *n., pl.* **·kas.** **1.** a 19th-century Bohemian dance with three steps and a hop, in fast duple time. **2.** a piece of music composed for or in the rhythm of this dance. ~*vb.* **·kas, ·ka·ing, ·kaed. 3.** (*intr.*) to dance a polka. [C19: via French from Czech *pulka* half-step, from *pul* half]

pol·ka dot *n.* **1.** one of a pattern of small circular regularly spaced spots on a fabric. **2. a.** a fabric or pattern with such spots. **b.** (*as modifier*): *a polka-dot dress.* [C19: of uncertain origin]

poll (pəʊl) *n.* **1.** the casting, recording, or counting of votes in an election; a voting. **2.** the result or quantity of such a voting: *a heavy poll.* **3.** Also called: **opinion poll. a.** a canvassing of a representative sample of a large group of people on some question in order to determine the general opinion of the group. **b.** the results or record of such a canvassing. **4.** any counting or enumeration: *a poll of the number of men with long hair.* **5.** short for **poll tax. 6.** a list or enumeration of people, esp. for taxation or voting purposes. **7.** the striking face of a hammer. **8.** the occipital or back part of the head of an animal. ~*vb.* (*mainly tr.*) **9.** to receive (a vote or quantity of votes): *he polled 10 000 votes.* **10.** to receive, take, or record the votes of: *he polled the whole town.* **11.** to canvass (a person, group, area, etc.) as part of a survey of opinion. **12.** *Chiefly U.S.* to take the vote, verdict, opinion, etc., individually of each member (of a jury, conference, etc.). **13.** (*sometimes intr.*) to cast (a vote) in an election. **14.** to clip or shear. **15.** to remove or cut short the horns of (cattle). [C13 (in the sense: a human head) and C17 (in the modern sense: a counting of heads, votes): from Middle Low German *polle* hair of the head, head, top of a tree; compare Swedish *pull* crown of the head]

pol·lack *or* **pol·lock** (ˈpɒlək) *n., pl.* **·lacks, ·lack** *or* **·locks, ·lock.** a gadoid food fish, *Pollachius pollachius,* that has a dark green back and a projecting lower jaw and occurs in northern seas, esp. the North Atlantic Ocean. [C17: from earlier Scottish *podlok,* of obscure origin]

Pol·lai·uo·lo (*Italian* ˌpollajˈwɔːlo) *n.* **1. An·to·nio** (anˈtɔːnjo), ?1432–98, Florentine painter, sculptor, goldsmith, and engraver: his paintings include the *Martyrdom of St. Sebastian.* **2.** his brother **Pie·ro** (ˈpjɛːro). ?1443–96, Florentine painter and sculptor.

pol·lan (ˈpɒlən) *n.* any of several varieties of the whitefish *Coregonus pollan* that occur in lakes in Scotland and Northern Ireland. [C18: probably from Irish *poll* lake]

pol·lard (ˈpɒləd) *n.* **1.** an animal, such as a sheep or deer, that has either shed its horns or antlers or has had them removed. **2.** a tree that has had its branches cut back to encourage a more bushy growth. ~*vb.* **3.** (*tr.*) to convert into a pollard; poll. [C16: hornless animal; see POLL]

polled (pəʊld) *adj.* **1.** (of animals, esp. cattle) having the horns cut off or being naturally hornless. **2.** *Archaic.* shorn of hair; bald.

pol·len (ˈpɒlən) *n.* a fine powdery substance produced by the anthers of seed-bearing plants, consisting of numerous fine grains containing the male gametes. [C16: from Latin: powder; compare Greek *palē* pollen] —**pol·lin·ic** (pəˈlɪnɪk) *adj.*

Pol·len (ˈpɒlən) *n.* **Dan·iel.** 1813–96, New Zealand statesman, born in Ireland: prime minister of New Zealand (1876).

pol·len a·nal·y·sis *n.* another name for **palynology.**

pol·len bas·ket *n.* the part of the hind leg of a bee that is specialized for carrying pollen, typically consisting of a trough bordered by long hairs. Technical name: **corbicula.**

pol·len count *n.* a measure of the pollen present in the air over a 24-hour period, often published to enable sufferers from hay fever to predict the severity of their attacks.

pol·len tube *n.* a hollow tubular outgrowth that develops from a pollen grain after pollination, grows down the style to the ovule, and conveys male gametes to the egg cell.

pol·lex (ˈpɒlɛks) *n., pl.* **·li·ces** (-lɪˌsiːz). the first digit of the forelimb of amphibians, reptiles, birds, and mammals, such as the thumb of man and other primates. [C19: from Latin: thumb, big toe] —**pol·li·cal** (ˈpɒlɪkᵊl) *adj.*

pol·li·nate *or* **pol·le·nate** (ˈpɒlɪˌneɪt) *vb.* (*tr.*) to transfer pollen from the anthers to the stigma of (a flower). —**ˌpol·li·ˈna·tion** *or* **ˌpol·le·ˈna·tion** *n.* —**ˈpol·li·ˌna·tor** *or* **ˈpol·le·ˌna·tor** *n.*

pol·li·nif·er·ous *or* **pol·le·nif·er·ous** (ˌpɒlɪˈnɪfərəs) *adj.* **1.** producing pollen: *polliniferous plants.* **2.** specialized for carrying pollen: *the polliniferous legs of bees.*

pol·lin·i·um (pəˈlɪnɪəm) *n., pl.* **·i·a** (-ɪə). a mass of cohering pollen grains, produced by plants such as orchids and transported as a whole during pollination. [C19: New Latin; see POLLEN]

pol·lin·o·sis *or* **pol·len·o·sis** (ˌpɒlɪˈnəʊsɪs) *n. Pathol.* a technical name for **hay fever.**

pol·li·wog *or* **pol·ly·wog** (ˈpɒlɪˌwɒg) *n.* **1.** *Informal.* a sailor who has not crossed the equator. Compare **shellback. 2.** *U.S. dialect.* another name for **tadpole.** [C15 *polwygle;* see POLL, WIGGLE]

Pol·lock (ˈpɒlək) *n.* **1.** Sir **Fred·er·ick.** 1845–1937, English legal scholar: with Maitland, he wrote *History of English Law before the Time of Edward I* (1895). **2. Jack·son.** 1912–56, U.S. abstract expressionist painter; chief exponent of action painting in the U.S.

poll·ster (ˈpəʊlstə) *n.* a person who conducts opinion polls.

poll tax *n.* a tax levied as a prerequisite for voting.

pol·lu·cite (ˈpɒljʊˌsaɪt, pəˈluːˌsaɪt) *n.* a colourless rare mineral consisting of a hydrated caesium aluminium silicate, often containing some rubidium. It occurs in coarse granite, esp. in Manitoba, and is an important source of caesium. Formula: $CsAlSi_2O_6 \cdot \frac{1}{2}H_2O$. [C19: from Latin *polluc-,* stem of *Pollux* + -ITE[1]; originally called *pollux,* alluding to Castor and Pollux, since it was associated with another mineral called *castor* or *castorite*]

pol·lu·tant (pəˈluːtᵊnt) *n.* a substance that pollutes, esp. a chemical or similar substance that is produced as a waste product of an industrial process.

pol·lute (pəˈluːt) *vb.* (*tr.*) **1.** to contaminate, as with poisonous or harmful substances. **2.** to make morally corrupt or impure; sully. **3.** to desecrate or defile. [C14 *polute,* from Latin *polluere* to defile] —**pol·ˈlut·er** *n.* —**pol·ˈlu·tion** *n.*

pol·lut·ed (pəˈluːtɪd) *adj.* **1.** made unclean or impure; contaminated. **2.** *U.S. slang.* intoxicated; drunk.

Pol·lux (ˈpɒləks) *n.* **1.** the brightest star in the constellation Gemini, lying close to the star **Castor.** Visual magnitude: 1.2;

spectral type: K0; distance: 35 light years. **2.** *Classical myth.* See **Castor and Pollux.**

Pol·ly·an·na (ˌpɒlɪˈænə) *n.* a person who is constantly or excessively optimistic. [C20: after the chief character in *Pollyanna* (1913), a novel by Eleanor Porter (1868–1920), U.S. writer]

po·lo (ˈpəʊləʊ) *n.* **1.** a game similar to hockey played on horseback using long-handled mallets (**polo sticks**) and a wooden ball. **2.** any of several similar games, such as one played on bicycles. **3.** short for **water polo. 4.** Also called: **polo neck. a.** a collar on a garment, worn rolled over to fit closely round the neck. **b.** a garment, esp. a sweater, with such a collar. [C19: from Balti (dialect of Kashmir): ball, from Tibetan *pulu*]

Po·lo (ˈpəʊləʊ) *n.* **Mar·co** (ˈmɑːkəʊ). 1254–1324, Venetian merchant, famous for his account of his travels in Asia. After travelling overland to China (1271–75), he spent 17 years serving Kublai Khan before returning to Venice by sea (1292–95).

pol·o·naise (ˌpɒləˈneɪz) *n.* **1.** a ceremonial marchlike dance in three-four time from Poland. **2.** a piece of music composed for or in the rhythm of this dance. **3.** a woman's costume with a tight bodice and an overskirt drawn back to show a decorative underskirt. [C18: from French *danse polonaise* Polish dance]

po+lo+ni·um (pəˈləʊnɪəm) *n.* a very rare radioactive element that occurs in trace amounts in uranium ores. The isotope **polonium-210** is produced artificially and is used as a lightweight power source in satellites and to eliminate static electricity in certain industries. Symbol: Po; atomic no.: 84; half-life of most stable isotope, ^{209}Po: 103 years; valency: 2,4, or 6; melting pt.: 254°C; boiling pt.: 962°C. [C19: New Latin, from Medieval Latin *Polōnia* Poland; named in honour of the Polish nationality of its discoverer, Marie Curie]

po+lo+ny (pəˈləʊnɪ) *n., pl.* **+nies.** *Brit.* another name for **Bologna sausage.**

Pol Pot (ˈpɒl ˈpɒt) *n.* born 1925, Cambodian Communist statesman; prime minister of Cambodia (1976; 1977-1979).

Pol+ska (ˈpɔlska) *n.* the Polish name for **Poland.**

Pol+ta+va (*Russian* palˈtavə) *n.* a city in the SW Soviet Union, in the E Ukrainian SSR: scene of the victory (1709) of the Russians under Peter the Great over the Swedes under Charles XII. Pop.: 263 000 (1975 est.).

pol+ter+geist (ˈpɒltəˌgaɪst) *n.* a spirit believed to manifest its presence by rappings and other noises and also by acts of mischief, such as throwing furniture about. [C19: from German, from *poltern* to be noisy + *Geist* GHOST]

pol+troon (pɒlˈtruːn) *n.* **1.** an abject or contemptible coward. *~adj.* **2.** a rare word for **cowardly.** [C16: from Old French *poultron,* from Old Italian *poltrone* lazy good-for-nothing, apparently from *poltrire* to lie indolently in bed, from *poltro* bed]

pol·y (ˈpɒlɪ) *n., pl.* **pol·ys.** *Informal.* short for **polytechnic.**

pol·y- *combining form.* **1.** more than one; many or much: *polyhedron.* **2.** having an excessive or abnormal number or amount: *polycythaemia.* [from Greek *polus* much, many; related to Old English *fela* many]

pol·y·a+del+phous (ˌpɒlɪəˈdɛlfəs) *adj.* **1.** (of stamens) having united filaments so that they are arranged in three or more groups. **2.** (of flowers) having polyadelphous stamens. [C19: from New Latin, from POLY- + *-adelphous* from Greek *adelphos* brother]

pol·y+am+ide (ˌpɒlɪˈæmaɪd, -mɪd) *n.* any one of a class of synthetic polymeric materials containing recurring -CONH- groups. See also **nylon.**

pol·y+an+dry (ˈpɒlɪˌændrɪ) *n.* **1.** the practice or condition of being married to more than one husband at the same time. Compare **polygamy. 2.** the practice in animals of a female mating with more than one male during one breeding season. **3.** the condition in flowers of having a large indefinite number of stamens. ~Compare (for senses 2 and 3) **polygyny.** [C18: from Greek *poluandria,* from POLY- + *-andria* from *anēr* man] —ˌ**pol·y+ˈan+drous** *adj.*

pol·y+an+thus (ˌpɒlɪˈænθəs) *n., pl.* **+thus·es. 1.** any of several hybrid garden primroses, esp. *Primula polyantha,* which has brightly coloured flowers. **2. polyanthus narcissus.** a Eurasian amaryllidaceous plant, *Narcissus tazetta,* having clusters of small yellow or white fragrant flowers. [C18: New Latin, Greek: having many flowers]

pol·y+a·tom+ic (ˌpɒlɪəˈtɒmɪk) *adj.* (of a molecule) containing more than two atoms.

pol·y+ba+sic (ˌpɒlɪˈbeɪsɪk) *adj.* (of an acid) having two or more replaceable hydrogen atoms per molecule.

pol·y+ba+site (ˌpɒlɪˈbeɪsaɪt, pəˈlɪbəˌsaɪt) *n.* a grey to black metallic mineral consisting of a sulphide of silver, antimony, and copper in the form of platelike monoclinic crystals. It occurs in veins of silver ore. Formula: $(Ag,Cu)_{16}Sb_2S_{11}$.

Po·lyb·i·us (pəʊˈlɪbɪəs) *n.* ?205–?123 B.C., Greek historian. Under the patronage of Scipio the Younger, he wrote in 40 books a history of Rome from 264 B.C. to 146 B.C.

Pol·y·carp (ˈpɒlɪˌkɑːp) *n.* **Saint.** ?69–?155 A.D., Christian martyr and bishop of Smyrna, noted for his letter to the church at Philippi. Feast day: Jan. 26.

pol·y+car+pel+lar·y (ˌpɒlɪkɑːˈpɛlərɪ) *adj.* (of a plant gynoecium) having or consisting of many carpels.

pol·y+car+pic (ˌpɒlɪˈkɑːpɪk) *or* **pol·y+car+pous** *adj.* (of a plant) able to produce flowers and fruit several times in succession. —ˈ**pol·y+ˌcar+py** *n.*

pol·y+car+pous (ˌpɒlɪˈkɑːpəs) *or* **pol·y+car+pic** *adj.* (of plants) having a gynoecium consisting of many distinct carpels.

pol·y+cen+trism (ˌpɒlɪˈsɛntrɪzəm) *n.* the fact, principle, or advocacy of the existence of more than one guiding or predominant ideological or political centre in a political system, alliance, etc., in the Communist world today.

pol·y+chaete (ˈpɒlɪˌkiːt) *n.* **1.** any marine annelid worm of the class *Polychaeta,* having a distinct head and paired fleshy appendages (parapodia) that bear bristles (chaetae or setae) and are used in swimming: includes the lugworms, ragworms, and sea mice. *~adj. also* **pol·y+chae+tous. 2.** of, relating to, or belonging to the class *Polychaeta.* [C19: from New Latin, from Greek *polukhaitēs:* having much hair; see CHAETA]

pol·y+cha+si·um (ˌpɒlɪˈkeɪzɪəm) *n., pl.* **+si·a** (-zɪə). *Botany.* a cymose inflorescence in which three or more branches arise from each node. [C20: from New Latin, from POLY- + *-chasium* as in DICHASIUM]

pol·y+chro+mat+ic (ˌpɒlɪkrəʊˈmætɪk), **pol·y+chro+mic** (ˌpɒlɪˈkrəʊmɪk), *or* **pol·y+chro+mous** *adj.* **1.** having various or changing colours. **2.** (of light or other electromagnetic radiation) containing radiation with more than one wavelength. —**pol·y+chro+ma+tism** (ˌpɒlɪˈkrəʊməˌtɪzəm) *n.*

pol·y+chrome (ˈpɒlɪˌkrəʊm) *adj.* **1.** having various or changing colours; polychromatic. **2.** made with or decorated in various colours. *~n.* **3.** a work of art or artefact in many colours.

pol·y+chro+my (ˈpɒlɪˌkrəʊmɪ) *n.* decoration in many colours, esp. in architecture or sculpture.

pol·y+clin+ic (ˌpɒlɪˈklɪnɪk) *n.* a hospital or clinic able to treat a wide variety of diseases: general hospital.

Pol·y·cli·tus, Pol·y·clei·tus (ˌpɒlɪˈklaɪtəs), *or* **Pol·y·cle·tus** (ˌpɒlɪˈkliːtəs) *n.* 5th century B.C. Greek sculptor, noted particularly for his idealized bronze sculptures of the male nude, such as the *Doryphoros.*

pol·y+con+ic pro+jec+tion (ˌpɒlɪˈkɒnɪk) *n.* a type of conic projection in which the parallels are not concentric and all meridians except the central one are curved lines. It is neither equal-area nor conformal, but is suitable for maps of areas or countries of great longitudinal extent.

pol·y+cot·y+le·don (ˌpɒlɪˌkɒtɪˈliːdᵊn) *n.* any of various plants, esp. gymnosperms, that have or appear to have more than two cotyledons. —ˌ**pol·y+ˌcot·y+ˈle·don+ous** *adj.*

Po·lyc·ra·tes (pəˈlɪkrəˌtiːz) *n.* died ?522 B.C., Greek tyrant of Samos, who was crucified by a Persian satrap.

pol·y+crys+tal (ˈpɒlɪˌkrɪstᵊl) *n.* an object composed of randomly orient crystals, formed by rapid solidification.

pol·y+cy+clic (ˌpɒlɪˈsaɪklɪk) *adj.* **1.** (of a molecule or compound) containing or having molecules that contain two or more closed rings of atoms. **2.** *Biology.* having two or more rings or whorls: *polycyclic shells; a polycyclic stele.* *~n.* **3.** a polycyclic compound: *anthracene is a polycyclic.*

pol·y+cy+the·mi·a (ˌpɒlɪsaɪˈθiːmɪə) *n.* an abnormal condition of the blood characterized by an increase in the number of red blood cells. [C19: from POLY- + CYTO- + -HAEMIA]

pol·y+dac+tyl (ˌpɒlɪˈdæktɪl) *adj. also* **pol·y+dac+ty+lous. 1.** (of man and other vertebrates) having more than the normal number of digits. *~n.* **2.** a human or other vertebrate having more than the normal number of digits.

pol·y+dem+ic (ˌpɒlɪˈdɛmɪk) *adj. Ecology, rare.* growing in or inhabiting more than two regions. [C20: from POLY- + ENDEMIC]

Pol·y·deu·ces (ˌpɒlɪˈdjuːsiːz) *n.* the Greek name of **Pollux.** See **Castor and Pollux.**

pol·y+dip+si·a (ˌpɒlɪˈdɪpsɪə) *n. Pathol.* excessive thirst. [C18: New Latin, from POLY- + *-dipsia,* from Greek *dipsa* thirst] —ˌ**pol·y+ˈdip+sic** *adj.*

pol·y+em+bry+o·ny (ˌpɒlɪˈɛmbrɪənɪ) *n.* the production of more than one embryo from a single fertilized egg cell: occurs in certain plants and parasitic hymenopterous insects. —**pol·y+em+bry+on+ic** (ˌpɒlɪˌɛmbrɪˈɒnɪk) *adj.*

pol·y+es+ter (ˈpɒlɪˌɛstə) *n.* any of a large class of synthetic materials that are polymers containing recurring -COO- groups: used as plastics, textile fibres, and adhesives.

pol·y+eth+yl+ene (ˌpɒlɪˈɛθɪˌliːn) *n.* another name (esp. U.S.) for **polythene.**

po+lyg·a+la (pəˈlɪgələ) *n.* any herbaceous plant or small shrub of the polygalaceous genus *Polygala.* See also **milkwort.** [C18: New Latin, from Greek *polugalon,* from POLY- + *gala* milk]

pol·y+ga+la+ceous (ˌpɒlɪgəˈleɪʃəs, pəˌlɪg-) *adj.* of, relating to, or belonging to the *Polygalaceae,* a family of plants having flowers with two large outer petal-like sepals, three small sepals, and three to five petals: includes milkwort.

po+lyg·a+my (pəˈlɪgəmɪ) *n.* **1.** the practice of being married to more than one woman at the same time. Compare **polyandry. 2. a.** the condition of having male, female, and hermaphrodite flowers on the same plant. **b.** the condition of having these different types of flower on separate plants of the same species. **3.** the practice in male animals of having more than one mate during one breeding season. [C16: via French from Greek *polugamia* from POLY- + -GAMY] —**po+ˈlyg·a+mist** *n.* —**po+ˈlyg·a+mous** *adj.* —**po+ˈlyg·a+mous+ly** *adv.*

pol·y+gene (ˈpɒlɪˌdʒiːn) *n.* any of a group of genes that each produce a small quantitative effect on a particular characteristic of the phenotype, such as height.

pol·y+gen·e·sis (ˌpɒlɪˈdʒɛnɪsɪs) *n.* **1.** *Biology.* evolution of a polyphyletic organism or group. **2.** the hypothetical descent of the different races of man from different ultimate ancestors. ~Compare **monogenesis.** —**pol·y+ge·net+ic** (ˌpɒlɪdʒəˈnɛtɪk) *adj.* —ˌ**pol·y+ge·net·i+cal+ly** *adv.*

pol·y+glot (ˈpɒlɪˌglɒt) *adj.* **1.** having a command of many languages. **2.** written in, composed of, or containing many languages. ~*n.* **3.** a person with a command of many languages. **4.** a book, esp. a Bible, containing several versions of the same text written in various languages. **5.** a mixture or confusion of languages. [C17: from Greek *poluglōttos* literally: many-tongued, from POLY- + *glōtta* tongue] —**'pol·y·ˌglot·ism** *or* **'pol·y·ˌglot·tism** *n.*

Pol·yg·no·tus (ˌpɒlɪg'nəʊtəs) *n.* 5th-century B.C. Greek painter: associated with Cimon in rebuilding Athens.

pol·y·gon ('pɒlɪˌgɒn) *n.* a closed plane figure consisting of three or more straight sides that connect three or more points (the vertices), none of the sides intersecting. The sum of the interior angles is $(n - 2) \times 180°$ for n sides; the sum of the exterior angles is 360°. A **regular polygon** has all its sides and angles equal. Specific polygons are named according to the number of sides, such as triangle, pentagon, etc. [C16: via Latin from Greek *polugōnon* figure with many angles] —**po·lyg·o·nal** (pə'lɪgənᵊl) *adj.* —**po·'lyg·o·nal·ly** *adv.*

pol·y·go·na·ceous (ˌpɒlɪgə'neɪʃəs, pəˌlɪgə-) *adj.* of, relating to, or belonging to the *Polygonaceae*, a chiefly N temperate family of plants having a sheathing stipule (ocrea) clasping the stem and small inconspicuous flowers: includes dock, sorrel, buckwheat, knotgrass, and rhubarb.

po·lyg·o·num (pə'lɪgənəm) *n.* any polygonaceous plant of the genus *Polygonum*, having stems with knotlike joints and spikes of small white, green, or pink flowers. See also **knotgrass, bistort, prince's-feather** (sense 2). [C18: New Latin, from Greek *polugonon* knotgrass, from *polu-* POLY- + *-gonon*, from *gonu* knee]

pol·y·graph ('pɒlɪˌgrɑːf, -ˌgræf) *n.* **1.** an instrument for the simultaneous electrical or mechanical recording of several involuntary physiological activities, including blood pressure, pulse rate, respiration, and perspiration, used esp. as a lie detector. **2.** a device for producing copies of written, printed, or drawn matter. [C18: from Greek *polugraphos* writing copiously] —**pol·y·graph·ic** (ˌpɒlɪ'græfɪk) *adj.* —**ˌpol·y·'graph·i·cal·ly** *adv.*

po·lyg·y·ny (pə'lɪdʒənɪ) *n.* **1.** the practice in animals of a male mating with more than one female during one breeding season. **2.** the condition in flowers of having many styles. ~Compare **polyandry.** [C18: from POLY- + *-gyny*, from Greek *gunē* a woman] —**po·'lyg·y·nist** *n.* —**po·'lyg·y·nous** *adj.*

pol·y·he·dral an·gle (ˌpɒlɪ'hiːdrəl) *n.* a geometric configuration formed by the intersection of three or more planes, such as the faces of a polyhedron, that have a common vertex. See also **solid angle.**

pol·y·he·dron (ˌpɒlɪ'hiːdrən) *n., pl.* **·drons** *or* **·dra** (-drə). a solid figure consisting of four or more plane faces (all polygons), pairs of which meet along an edge, three or more edges meeting at a vertex. In a **regular polyhedron** all the faces are identical regular polygons making equal angles with each other. Specific polyhedrons are named according to the number of faces, such as tetrahedron, icosahedron, etc. [C16: from Greek *poluedron*, from POLY- + *hedron* side, base] —**ˌpol·y·'he·dral** *adj.*

pol·y·hy·dric (ˌpɒlɪ'haɪdrɪk) *adj.* another word for **polyhydroxy**, esp. when applied to alcohols.

pol·y·hy·drox·y (ˌpɒlɪhaɪ'drɒksɪ) *adj.* (of a chemical compound) containing two or more hydroxyl groups per molecule. Also: **polyhydric.**

Pol·y·hym·ni·a (ˌpɒlɪ'hɪmnɪə) *n. Greek myth.* the Muse of singing, mime, and sacred dance. [Latin, from Greek *Polumnia* full of songs; see POLY-, HYMN]

pol·y·i·so·prene (ˌpɒlɪ'aɪsəˌpriːn) *n.* any of various polymeric forms of isoprene, occurring in rubbers.

pol·y·math ('pɒlɪˌmæθ) *n.* a person of great and varied learning. [C17: from Greek *polumathēs* having much knowledge] —**ˌpol·y·'math·ic** *adj.* —**po·lym·a·thy** (pə'lɪməθɪ) *n.*

pol·y·mer ('pɒlɪmə) *n.* a naturally occurring or synthetic compound, such as starch or Perspex, that has large molecules made up of many relatively simple repeated units. Compare **copolymer.** —**po·lym·er·ism** (pə'lɪməˌrɪzəm, 'pɒlɪmə-) *n.*

pol·y·mer·ic (ˌpɒlɪ'mɛrɪk) *adj.* of, concerned with, or being a polymer: *a polymeric compound.* [C19: from Greek *polumerēs* having many parts]

po·lym·er·i·za·tion (pəˌlɪməraɪ'zeɪʃən, ˌpɒlɪməraɪ-) *n.* the act or process of forming a polymer or copolymer, esp. a chemical reaction in which a polymer is formed.

pol·y·mer·ize *or* **pol·y·mer·ise** ('pɒlɪməˌraɪz, pə'lɪmə-) *vb.* to react or cause to react to form a polymer.

po·lym·er·ous (pə'lɪmərəs) *adj.* **1.** (of flowers) having the petals, sepals, and other parts arranged in whorls of many parts. **2.** *Biology.* having or being composed of many parts.

pol·y·morph ('pɒlɪˌmɔːf) *n.* **1.** a species of animal or plant that exhibits polymorphism. **2.** any of the crystalline forms of a chemical compound that exhibits polymorphism. **3.** Also called: **polymorphonuclear leucocyte.** a common type of white blood cell that has a lobed nucleus and granular cytoplasm and functions as a phagocyte. [C19: from Greek *polumorphos* having many forms]

pol·y·mor·phism (ˌpɒlɪ'mɔːfɪzəm) *n.* **1.** *Biology.* **a.** the occurrence of more than one form of individual in a single species within an interbreeding population. **b.** the occurrence of more than one form in the individual polyps of a coelenterate colony. **2.** the existence or formation of different types of crystal of the same chemical compound.

pol·y·mor·pho·nu·cle·ar (ˌpɒlɪˌmɔːfəʊ'njuːklɪə) *adj.* (of a leucocyte) having a lobed or segmented nucleus. See also **polymorph** (sense 3).

pol·y·mor·phous (ˌpɒlɪ'mɔːfəs) *or* **pol·y·mor·phic** *adj.* **1.** having, taking, or passing through many different forms or stages. **2.** (of a substance) exhibiting polymorphism. **3.** (of an animal or plant) displaying or undergoing polymorphism.

pol·y·myx·in (ˌpɒlɪ'mɪksɪn) *n.* any of several toxic polypeptide antibiotics active against Gram-negative bacteria, obtained from the soil bacterium *Bacillus polymyxa.* [C20: from New Latin *Bacillus polymyxa;* see POLY-, MYXO-, -IN]

Pol·y·ne·sia (ˌpɒlɪ'niːʒə, -ʒɪə) *n.* one of the three divisions of islands in the Pacific, the others being Melanesia and Micronesia: includes Samoa, Society, Marquesas, Mangareva, Tuamotu, Cook, and Tubuai Islands, and Tonga.

Pol·y·ne·sian (ˌpɒlɪ'niːʒən, -ʒɪən) *adj.* **1.** of or relating to Polynesia, its people, or any of their languages. ~*n.* **2.** a member of the people that inhabit Polynesia, generally of Caucasoid features with light skin and wavy hair. **3.** a branch of the Malayo-Polynesian family of languages, including Maori and Hawaiian and a number of other closely related languages of the S and central Pacific.

pol·y·neu·ri·tis (ˌpɒlɪnjʊ'raɪtɪs) *n.* inflammation of many nerves at the same time.

Pol·y·ni·ces (ˌpɒlɪ'naɪsiːz) *n. Greek myth.* a son of Oedipus and Jocasta, for whom the Seven Against Thebes sought to regain Thebes. He and his brother Eteocles killed each other in single combat before its walls.

pol·y·no·mi·al (ˌpɒlɪ'nəʊmɪəl) *adj.* **1.** of, consisting of, or referring to two or more names or terms. ~*n.* **2. a.** a mathematical expression consisting of a sum of terms each of which is the product of a constant and one or more variables raised to a positive or zero integral power. For one variable, x, the general form is given by: $a_0x^n + a_1x^{n-1} + \ldots + a_{n-1}x + a_n$, where a_0, a_1, etc., are real numbers. **b.** Also called: **multinomial.** any mathematical expression consisting of the sum of a number of terms. **3.** *Biology.* a taxonomic name consisting of more than two terms, such as *Parus major minor* in which *minor* designates the subspecies.

pol·y·nu·cle·ar (ˌpɒlɪ'njuːklɪə) *or* **pol·y·nu·cle·ate** *adj.* having many nuclei; multinuclear.

pol·y·nu·cle·o·tide (ˌpɒlɪ'njuːklɪəˌtaɪd) *n. Biochem.* a molecular chain of nucleotides chemically bonded by a series of ester linkages between the phosphoryl group of one nucleotide and the hydroxyl group of the sugar in the adjacent nucleotide. Nucleic acids consist of long chains of polynucleotides.

po·lyn·ya ('pɒlənˌjɑː) *n.* a stretch of open water surrounded by ice, esp. near the mouths of large rivers, in arctic seas. [C19: from Russian, from *poly* open, hollowed-out]

pol·y·on·y·mous (ˌpɒlɪ'ɒnɪməs) *adj.* having or known by several different names.

pol·yp ('pɒlɪp) *n.* **1.** *Zoology.* one of the two forms of individual that occur in coelenterates. It usually has a hollow cylindrical body with a ring of tentacles around the mouth. Compare **medusa** (sense 2). **2.** Also called: **polypus.** *Pathol.* a small vascularized growth arising from the surface of a mucous membrane, having a rounded base or a stalklike projection. [C16 *polip*, from French *polype* nasal polyp, from Latin *pōlypus* sea animal, nasal polyp, from Greek *polupous* having many feet] —**'pol·yp·ous** *or* **'pol·yp·oid** *adj.*

pol·y·par·y ('pɒlɪpərɪ) *or* **pol·y·par·i·um** (ˌpɒlɪ'pɛərɪəm) *n., pl.* **·par·ies** *or* **·par·i·a** (-'pɛərɪə). the common base and connecting tissue of a colony of coelenterate polyps, esp. coral. [C18: from New Latin *polypārium;* see POLYP]

pol·y·pep·tide (ˌpɒlɪ'pɛptaɪd) *n.* any of a group of relatively short-chained proteins consisting of several amino acids linked by peptide bonds. See also **peptide.**

pol·y·pet·al·ous (ˌpɒlɪ'pɛtələs) *adj.* (of flowers) having many distinct or separate petals. Compare **gamopetalous.**

pol·y·pha·gia (ˌpɒlɪ'feɪdʒə) *n.* **1. a.** an abnormal desire to consume excessive amounts of food, esp. as the result of a neurological disorder. **b.** an insatiable appetite. **2.** the habit of certain animals, esp. certain insects, of feeding on many different types of food. [C17: New Latin, from Greek, from *poluphagos* eating much; see POLY-, -PHAGOUS] —**po·lyph·a·gous** (pə'lɪfəgəs) *adj.*

pol·y·phase ('pɒlɪˌfeɪz) *adj.* **1.** Also: **multiphase.** (of an electrical system, circuit, or device) having, generating, or using two or more alternating voltages of the same frequency, the phases of which are cyclically displaced by fractions of a period. See also **single-phase, two-phase, three-phase. 2.** having more than one phase.

Pol·y·phe·mus (ˌpɒlɪ'fiːməs) *n. Greek myth.* a cyclops who imprisoned Odysseus and his companions in his cave. To effect his escape, Odysseus blinded him.

pol·y·phone ('pɒlɪˌfəʊn) *n.* a letter or character having more than one phonetic value, such as English *c*, pronounced (k) before *a, o,* or *u* or (s) before *e* or *i.*

pol·y·phon·ic (ˌpɒlɪ'fɒnɪk) *adj.* **1.** *Music.* composed of relatively independent melodic lines or parts; contrapuntal. **2.** many-voiced. **3.** *Phonetics.* of, relating to, or denoting a polyphone. —**ˌpol·y·'phon·i·cal·ly** *adv.*

pol·y·phon·ic prose *n.* a rhythmically free prose employing poetic devices, such as assonance and alliteration.

po·lyph·o·ny (pə'lɪfənɪ) *n., pl.* **·nies. 1.** polyphonic style of composition or a piece of music utilizing it. **2.** the use of polyphones in a writing system. [C19: from Greek *poluphōnia* diversity of tones, from POLY- + *phōnē* speech, sound] —**po·'lyph·o·nous** *adj.* —**po·'lyph·o·nous·ly** *adv.*

pol·y·phos·phor·ic ac·id (ˌpɒlɪfɒs'fɒrɪk) *n.* **1.** any one of a series of oxyacids of phosphorus with the general formula $H_{n+2}P_nO_{3n+1}$. The first member is pyrophosphoric acid ($n = 2$) and the series includes the highly polymeric metaphosphoric acid. The higher acids exist in an equilibrium mixture. **2.** a glassy or liquid mixture of orthophosphoric and polyphosphoric

acids: used industrially as a dehydrating agent, catalyst, and oxidizing agent.
pol·y·phy·let·ic (ˌpɒlɪfaɪˈlɛtɪk) *adj. Biology.* relating to or characterized by descent from more than one ancestral group of animals or plants. [C19: from POLY- + PHYLETIC] —ˌ**pol·y·phy·ˈlet·i·cal·ly** *adv.*
pol·y·phy·o·dont (ˌpɒlɪˈfaɪəʊˌdɒnt) *adj.* having many successive sets of teeth, as fishes and other lower vertebrates. Compare **diphyodont.**
pol·y·ploid (ˈpɒlɪˌplɔɪd) *adj.* **1.** (of cells, organisms, etc.) having more than twice the basic (haploid) number of chromosomes. ~*n.* **2.** an individual or cell of this type. —ˌ**pol·y·ˈploi·dal** *or* ˌ**pol·y·ˈploi·dic** *adj.* —ˈ**pol·y·ˌploi·dy** *n.*
pol·y·pod (ˈpɒlɪˌpɒd) *adj. also* **po·lyp·o·dous** (pəˈlɪpədəs). **1.** (esp. of insect larvae) having many legs or similar appendages. ~*n.* **2.** an animal of this type.
pol·y·po·dy (ˈpɒlɪˌpəʊdɪ) *n., pl.* **·dies.** any of various ferns of the genus *Polypodium,* esp. *P. vulgare,* having deeply divided leaves and round naked sori: family *Polypodiaceae.* [C15: from Latin *polypodium,* from Greek, from POLY- + *pous* foot]
pol·y·poid (ˈpɒlɪˌpɔɪd) *adj.* **1.** of, relating to, or resembling a polyp. **2.** (of a coelenterate) having the body in the form of a polyp.
pol·y·pro·pyl·ene (ˌpɒlɪˈprəʊpɪˌliːn) *n.* any of various tough flexible synthetic thermoplastic materials made by polymerizing propylene and used for making moulded articles, laminates, bottles, pipes, and fibres for ropes, bristles, upholstery, and carpets.
pol·y·pro·to·dont (ˌpɒlɪˈprəʊtəʊˌdɒnt) *n.* any marsupial of the group *Polyprotodontia,* characterized by four or more upper incisor teeth on each side of the jaw: includes the opossums and bandicoots. Compare **diprotodont.**
pol·yp·tych (ˈpɒlɪptɪk) *n.* an altarpiece consisting of more than three panels, set with paintings or carvings, and usually hinged for folding. Compare **diptych, triptych.** [C19: via Late Latin from Greek *poluptuchon* something folded many times, from POLY- + *ptuchē* a fold]
pol·y·pus (ˈpɒlɪpəs) *n., pl.* **·pi** (paɪ). *Pathol.* another word for **polyp** (sense 2). [C16: via Latin from Greek: POLYP]
pol·y·rhythm (ˈpɒlɪˌrɪðəm) *n. Music.* a style of composition in which each part exhibits different rhythms. —ˌ**pol·y·ˈrhyth·mic** *adj.*
pol·y·sac·cha·ride (ˌpɒlɪˈsækəˌraɪd, -rɪd) *or* **pol·y·sac·cha·rose** (ˌpɒlɪˈsækəˌrəʊz, -ˌrəʊs) *n.* any one of a class of carbohydrates whose molecules contain linked monosaccharide units: includes starch, inulin, and cellulose. General formula: $(C_6H_{10}O_5)_n$. See also **oligosaccharide.**
pol·y·se·my (ˌpɒlɪˈsiːmɪ, pəˈlɪsəmɪ) *n.* ambiguity of individual words. Compare **monosemy.** [C20: from New Latin *polysēmia,* from Greek *polusēmos* having many meanings, from POLY- + *sēma* a sign] —ˌ**pol·y·ˈse·mous** *adj.*
pol·y·sep·al·ous (ˌpɒlɪˈsɛpələs) *adj.* (of flowers) having distinct separate sepals. Compare **gamosepalous.**
pol·y·so·mic (ˌpɒlɪˈsəʊmɪk) *adj.* of, relating to, or designating a basically diploid chromosome complement, in which some but not all the chromosomes are represented more than twice.
pol·y·sty·rene (ˌpɒlɪˈstaɪriːn) *n.* a synthetic thermoplastic material obtained by polymerizing styrene; used as a white rigid foam (**expanded polystyrene**) for insulating and packing and as a glasslike material in light fittings and water tanks.
pol·y·sul·phide (ˌpɒlɪˈsʌlfaɪd) *n.* any sulphide of a metal containing divalent anions in which there are chains of sulphur atoms, as in the polysulphides of sodium, Na_2S_2, Na_2S_3, Na_2S_4, etc.
pol·y·syl·la·ble (ˈpɒlɪˌsɪləbᵊl) *n.* a word consisting of more than two syllables. —**pol·y·syl·lab·ic** (ˌpɒlɪsɪˈlæbɪk) *or* ˌ**pol·y·syl·ˈlab·i·cal** *adj.* —ˌ**pol·y·syl·ˈlab·i·cal·ly** *adv.*
pol·y·syl·lo·gism (ˌpɒlɪˈsɪləˌdʒɪzəm) *n.* a chain of syllogisms in which the conclusion of one syllogism serves as a premiss for the next.
pol·y·syn·de·ton (ˌpɒlɪˈsɪndɪtən) *n.* **1.** *Rhetoric.* the use of several conjunctions in close succession, esp. where some might be omitted, as in *he ran and jumped and laughed for joy.* **2.** Also called: **syndesis.** *Grammar.* a sentence containing more than two coordinate clauses. [C16: POLY- + *-syndeton,* from Greek *sundetos* bound together]
pol·y·syn·thet·ic (ˌpɒlɪsɪnˈθɛtɪk) *adj.* denoting languages, such as Eskimo, in which the meanings of whole phrases or clauses are expressed in a single word. Compare **synthetic** (sense 3), **analytic** (sense 3), **agglutinative** (sense 2). —**pol·y·syn·the·sis** (ˌpɒlɪˈsɪnθɪsɪs) *n.* —ˌ**pol·y·ˈsyn·the·sism** *n.* —ˌ**pol·y·syn·ˈthet·i·cal·ly** *adv.*
pol·y·tech·nic (ˌpɒlɪˈtɛknɪk) *n.* **1.** *Brit.* a college offering advanced full- and part-time courses in many fields at and below degree standard. ~*adj.* **2.** of or relating to technical instruction and training.
pol·y·tet·ra·flu·o·ro·eth·y·lene (ˌpɒlɪˌtɛtrəˌfluərəʊˈɛθɪˌliːn) *n.* a white thermoplastic material with a waxy texture, made by polymerizing tetrafluoroethylene. It is nonflammable, resists chemical action and radiation, and has a high electrical resistance and an extremely low coefficient of friction. It is used for making gaskets, hoses, insulators, bearings, and for coating metal surfaces in chemical plants and in nonstick cooking vessels. Abbrev.: **PTFE.** Also called (trademark): **Teflon.**
pol·y·the·ism (ˈpɒlɪθiːˌɪzəm, ˌpɒlɪˈθiːɪzəm) *n.* the worship of or belief in more than one god. —ˈ**pol·y·ˌthe·ist** *n.* —ˌ**pol·y·the·ˈis·tic** *adj.* —ˌ**pol·y·the·ˈis·ti·cal·ly** *adv.*
pol·y·thene (ˈpɒlɪˌθiːn) *n.* any one of various light thermoplastic materials made from ethylene with properties depending on the molecular weight of the polymer. The common forms are a waxy flexible plastic (**low-density polythene**) and a tougher rigid more crystalline from (**high-density polythene**). Polythene is used for packaging, moulded articles, pipes and tubing, insulation, textiles, and coatings on metal. Also called (esp. U.S.): **polyethylene.**
pol·y·to·nal·i·ty (ˌpɒlɪtəʊˈnælɪtɪ) *or* **pol·y·to·nal·ism** *n. Music.* the simultaneous use of more than two different keys or tonalities. —ˌ**pol·y·ˈto·nal** *adj.* —ˌ**pol·y·ˈto·nal·ly** *adv.* —ˌ**pol·y·ˈto·nal·ist** *n.*
pol·y·troph·ic (ˌpɒlɪˈtrɒfɪk) *adj.* (esp. of bacteria) obtaining food from several different organic sources.
pol·y·typ·ic (ˌpɒlɪˈtɪpɪk) *or* **pol·y·typ·i·cal** *adj.* **1.** existing in, consisting of, or incorporating several different types or forms. **2.** *Biology.* (of a taxonomic group) having many subdivisions, esp. (of a species) having many subspecies and geographical races.
pol·y·un·sat·u·rat·ed (ˌpɒlɪʌnˈsætʃʊˌreɪtɪd) *adj.* of or relating to a class of animal and vegetable fats, the molecules of which consist of long carbon chains with many double bonds. Polyunsaturated compounds are widely used in some margarines and in paints and varnishes.
pol·y·u·re·thane (ˌpɒlɪˈjʊərəˌθeɪn) *or* **pol·y·u·re·than** (ˌpɒlɪˈjʊərəˌθæn) *n.* a class of synthetic materials made by copolymerizing an isocyanate and a polyhydric alcohol and commonly used as a foam (**polyurethane foam**) for insulation and packing, as fibres and hard inert coatings, and in a flexible form (**polyurethane rubber**) for diaphragms and seals.
pol·y·u·ri·a (ˌpɒlɪˈjʊərɪə) *n. Pathol, physiol.* the state or condition of discharging abnormally large quantities of urine, often accompanied by a need to urinate frequently. —ˌ**pol·y·ˈur·ic** *adj.*
pol·y·va·lent (ˌpɒlɪˈveɪlənt, pəˈlɪvələnt) *adj.* **1.** *Chem.* having more than one valency. **2.** (of a vaccine) **a.** effective against several strains of the same disease-producing microorganism, antigen, or toxin. **b.** produced from cultures containing several strains of the same microorganism. —ˌ**pol·y·ˈva·len·cy** *n.*
pol·y·vi·nyl (ˌpɒlɪˈvaɪnɪl, -ˈvaɪnᵊl) *n.* (*modifier*) designating a plastic or resin formed by polymerization of a vinyl derivative.
pol·y·vi·nyl ac·e·tate *n.* a colourless odourless tasteless resin used in emulsion paints and adhesives and for sealing porous surfaces. Abbrev.: **PVA.**
pol·y·vi·nyl chlo·ride *n.* the full name of **PVC.**
pol·y·vi·nyl·i·dene chlo·ride (ˌpɒlɪvaɪˈnɪlɪˌdiːn) *n.* any one of a class of thermoplastic materials formed by the polymerization of vinylidene chloride: used in packaging and for making pipes and fittings for chemical equipment. Also called: **saran.**
pol·y·vi·nyl res·in *n.* any of a class of thermoplastic resins that are made by polymerizing or copolymerizing a vinyl compound. The commonest type is PVC.
Po·lyx·e·na (pɒˈlɪksɪnə) *n. Greek myth.* a daughter of King Priam of Troy, who was sacrificed on the command of Achilles' ghost.
pol·y·zo·an (ˌpɒlɪˈzəʊən) *n., adj.* another word for **bryozoan.** [C19: from New Latin, *Polyzoa* class name, from POLY- + *-zoan,* from Greek *zōion* an animal]
pol·y·zo·ar·i·um (ˌpɒlɪzəʊˈɛərɪəm) *n., pl.* **·i·a** (-ɪə). a colony of bryozoan animals or its supporting skeletal framework. —ˌ**pol·y·zo·ˈar·i·al** *adj.*
pol·y·zo·ic (ˌpɒlɪˈzəʊɪk) *adj. Zoology.* **1.** (of certain colonial animals) having many zooids or similar polyps. **2.** producing or containing many sporozoites.
pom (pɒm) *Slang, chiefly Austral. n.* short for **pommy.**
pom·ace (ˈpʌmɪs) *n.* **1.** the pulpy residue of apples or similar fruit after crushing and pressing, as in cider-making. **2.** any pulpy substance left after crushing, mashing, etc. [C16: from Medieval Latin *pōmācium* cider, from Latin *pōmum* apple]
po·ma·ceous (pɒˈmeɪʃəs) *adj.* of, relating to, or bearing pomes, such as the apple, pear, and quince trees. [C18: from New Latin *pōmāceus,* from Latin *pōmum* apple]
po·made (pəˈmɑːd, -ˈmeɪd) *n.* **1.** a perfumed oil or ointment put on the hair, as to make it smooth and shiny. ~*vb.* **2.** (*tr.*) to put pomade on. ~Also: **pomatum.** [C16: from French *pommade,* from Italian *pomato* (originally made partly from apples), from Latin *pōmum* apple]
po·man·der (pəʊˈmændə) *n.* **1.** a mixture of aromatic substances in a sachet or an orange, formerly carried as scent or as a protection against disease. **2.** a container for such a mixture. [C15: from Old French *pome d'ambre,* from Medieval Latin *pōmum ambrae* apple of amber]
Pom·bal (*Portuguese* pomˈbal) *n.* **Mar·quês de** (ˈmarkɛʃ de). title of *Sebastião José de Carvalho e Mello.* 1699–1782, Portuguese statesman, who dominated Portuguese government from 1750 to 1777 and instituted many administrative and economic reforms.
pom·be (ˈpɒmbɛ) *n. E. African.* any alcoholic drink. [Swahili]
pome (pəʊm) *n.* the fleshy fruit of the apple and related plants, consisting of an enlarged receptacle enclosing the ovary and seeds. [C15: from Old French, from Late Latin *pōma* apple, pl. (assumed to be sing.) of Latin *pōmum* apple]
pom·e·gran·ate (ˈpɒmɪˌgrænɪt, ˈpɒmˌgrænɪt) *n.* **1.** an Asian shrub or small tree, *Punica granatum,* cultivated in semitropical regions for its edible fruit: family *Punicaceae.* **2.** the many-chambered globular fruit of this tree, which has tough reddish rind, juicy red pulp, and many seeds. [C14: from Old French *pome grenate,* from Latin *pōmum* apple + *grenate,* from Latin *grānātum,* from *grānātus* full of seeds]
pom·e·lo (ˈpɒmɪˌləʊ) *n., pl.* **·los.** *Chiefly U.S.* another name for

the **grapefruit** and **shaddock.** [C19: from Dutch *pompelmoes* shaddock, perhaps from *pompoen* big + Portuguese *limão* a lemon]

Pom·er·a·ni·a (ˌpɒməˈreɪnɪə) *n.* a region of N central Europe, extending along the S coast of the Baltic Sea from Stralsund to the Vistula River: now chiefly in Poland, with a small area in NE East Germany. German name: **Pommern.** Polish name: **Pomorze.**

Pom·er·a·ni·an (ˌpɒməˈreɪnɪən) *adj.* **1.** of or relating to Pomerania or its inhabitants. ~*n.* **2.** a native or inhabitant of Pomerania, esp. a German. **3.** a breed of toy dog with a long thick straight coat, related to the Spitz.

pom·fret *or* **pom·fret-cake** (ˈpʌmfrɪt, pɒm-) *n.* a small black rounded confection of liquorice. Also called: **Pontefract cake.** [C19: from *Pomfret,* earlier form of PONTEFRACT, where the cake was originally made]

pom·i·cul·ture (ˈpɒmɪˌkʌltʃə) *n.* the cultivation of fruit. [C19: from Latin *pōmum* apple, fruit + CULTURE]

pom·if·er·ous (pɒˈmɪfərəs) *adj.* (of the apple, pear, etc.) producing pomes or pomelike fruits. [C17: from Latin *pomifer* fruit-bearing]

pom·mel (ˈpʌməl, ˈpɒm-) *n.* **1.** the raised part on the front of a saddle. **2.** a knob at the top of a sword or similar weapon. ~*vb.* ·**mels,** ·**mel·ling,** ·**melled** *or U.S.* ·**mels,** ·**mel·ing,** ·**meled. 3.** a less common word for **pummel.** [C14: from Old French *pomel* knob, from Vulgar Latin *pōmellum* (unattested) little apple, from Latin *pōmum* apple]

Pom·mern (ˈpɔmərn) *n.* the German name for **Pomerania.**

pom·my (ˈpɒmɪ) *n., pl.* ·**mies.** (*sometimes cap.*) *Slang.* a mildly offensive word used by Australians and New Zealanders for an English person. Sometimes shortened to **pom.** [C20: of uncertain origin. Among a number of explanations are: (1) based on a blend of IMMIGRANT and POMEGRANATE (alluding to the red cheeks of English immigrants); (2) from the abbreviation *P.O.M.E.,* Prisoner of Mother England (referring to convicts)]

pom·ol·o·gy (pɒˈmɒlədʒɪ) *n.* the branch of horticulture that is concerned with the study and cultivation of fruit. [C19: from New Latin *pōmologia,* from Latin *pōmum* apple, fruit] —**pom·o·log·i·cal** (ˌpɒməˈlɒdʒɪkəl) *adj.* —ˌ**pom·o·ˈlog·i·cal·ly** *adv.* —**pom·ˈol·o·gist** *n.*

Po·mo·na[1] (pəˈməʊnə) *n.* another name for **Mainland** (in the Orkneys).

Po·mo·na[2] (pəˈməʊnə) *n.* the Roman goddess of fruit trees.

Po·mo·rze (pɔˈmɔʒɛ) *n.* the Polish name for **Pomerania.**

pomp (pɒmp) *n.* **1.** stately or magnificent display; ceremonial splendour. **2.** vain display, esp. of dignity or importance. **3.** *Obsolete.* a procession or pageant. [C14: from Old French *pompe,* from Latin *pompa* procession, from Greek *pompē;* related to Greek *pompein* to send]

pom·pa·dour (ˈpɒmpəˌdʊə) *n.* an early 18th-century hair style for women, having the front hair arranged over a pad to give it greater height and bulk. [C18: named after the Marquise de POMPADOUR, who originated it]

Pom·pa·dour (*French* pɔ̃paˈduːr) *n.* **Mar·quise de,** title of *Jeanne Antoinette Poisson.* 1721–64, mistress of Louis XV of France (1745–64), whom she greatly influenced.

pom·pa·no (ˈpɒmpəˌnəʊ) *n., pl.* ·**no** *or* ·**nos. 1.** any of several deep-bodied carangid food fishes of the genus *Trachinotus,* esp. *T. carolinus,* of American coastal regions of the Atlantic. **2.** a spiny-finned food fish, *Palometa simillima,* of North American coastal regions of the Pacific: family *Stromateidae* (butterfish, etc.). [C19: from Spanish *pámpano* type of fish, of uncertain origin]

Pom·pei·i (pɒmˈpeɪiː) *n.* an ancient city in Italy, southeast of Naples: buried by an eruption of Vesuvius (79 A.D.); excavation of the site, which is extremely well preserved, began in 1748. —**Pom·pei·ian** (pɒmˈpeɪən, -ˈpiː-) *adj., n.*

Pom·pey[1] (ˈpɒmpɪ) *n.* an informal name for **Portsmouth.**

Pom·pey[2] (ˈpɒmpɪ) *n.* called **Pompey the Great;** Latin name *Gnaeus Pompeius Magnus.* 106–48 B.C., Roman general and statesman; a member with Caesar and Crassus of the first triumvirate (60). He later quarrelled with Caesar, who defeated him at Pharsalus (48). He fled to Egypt and was murdered.

Pom·pi·dou (*French* pɔ̃piˈdu) *n.* **Georges** (ʒɔrʒ). 1911–74, French statesman; president of France 1969–74.

pom-pom (ˈpɒmpɒm) *n.* an automatic rapid-firing cannon, esp. a type of antiaircraft cannon used in World War II. Also called: **pompom.**

pom·pon (ˈpɒmpɒn) *or* **pom·pom** *n.* **1.** a ball of tufted silk, wool, feathers, etc., worn on a hat for decoration. **2. a.** the small globelike flower head of certain cultivated varieties of dahlia and chrysanthemum. **b.** (*as modifier*): *pompon dahlia.* [C18: from French, from Old French *pompe* knot of ribbons, of uncertain origin]

pom·pos·i·ty (pɒmˈpɒsɪtɪ) *n., pl.* ·**ties. 1.** vain or ostentatious display of dignity or importance. **2.** the quality of being pompous. **3.** ostentatiously lofty style, language, etc. **4.** a pompous action, remark, etc.

pomp·ous (ˈpɒmpəs) *adj.* **1.** exaggeratedly or ostentatiously dignified or self-important. **2.** ostentatiously lofty in style: *a pompous speech.* **3.** *Rare.* characterized by ceremonial pomp or splendour. —ˈ**pomp·ous·ly** *adv.* —ˈ**pomp·ous·ness** *n.*

'pon (pɒn) *prep. Poetic or archaic. contraction of* upon.

ponce (pɒns) *Slang, chiefly Brit.* ~*n.* **1.** a man given to ostentatious or effeminate display in manners, speech, dress, etc. **2.** another word for **pimp**[1]. ~*vb.* **3.** (*intr.;* often foll. by *around* or *about*) to act like a ponce.

Pon·ce (*Spanish* ˈponse) *n.* a port in S Puerto Rico, on the Caribbean: the second largest town on the island; settled in the 16th century. Pop.: 128 233 (1970).

Ponce de Le·ón (ˈpɒns də ˈliːən; *Spanish* ponθe ðe leˈon) *n.* **Juan** (xwan). ?1460–1521, Spanish explorer. He settled (1509) and governed (1510–12) Puerto Rico and discovered (1513) Florida.

pon·cho (ˈpɒntʃəʊ) *n., pl.* ·**chos.** a cloak of a kind originally worn in South America, made of a rectangular or circular piece of cloth, esp. wool, with a hole in the middle to put the head through. [C18: from American Spanish, from Araucanian *pantho* woollen material]

pond (pɒnd) *n.* **a.** a pool of still water, often artificially created. **b.** (*in combination*): *a fishpond.* [C13 *ponde* enclosure; related to POUND[3]]

pon·der (ˈpɒndə) *vb.* (when *intr.,* sometimes foll. by *on* or *over*) to give thorough or deep consideration (to); meditate (upon). [C14: from Old French *ponderer,* from Latin *ponderāre* to weigh, consider, from *pondus* weight; related to *pendere* to weigh] —ˈ**pon·der·ing·ly** *adv.*

pon·der·a·ble (ˈpɒndərəbəl) *adj.* **1.** able to be evaluated or estimated; appreciable. **2.** capable of being weighed or measured. ~*n.* **3.** (*often pl.*) something that can be evaluated or appreciated; a substantial thing. —ˌ**pon·der·a·ˈbil·i·ty** *n.* —ˈ**pon·der·a·bly** *adv.*

pon·der·ous (ˈpɒndərəs) *adj.* **1.** of great weight; heavy; huge. **2.** (esp. of movement) lacking ease or lightness; awkward, lumbering, or graceless. **3.** dull or laborious: *a ponderous oration.* [C14: from Latin *ponderōsus* of great weight, from *pondus* weight] —ˈ**pon·der·ous·ly** *adv.* —ˈ**pon·der·ous·ness** *or* **pon·der·os·i·ty** (ˌpɒndəˈrɒsɪtɪ) *n.*

Pon·di·cher·ry (ˌpɒndɪˈtʃɛrɪ) *n.* **1.** a Union Territory of SE India: transferred from French to Indian administration in 1954 and made a Union Territory in 1962. Capital: Pondicherry. Pop.: 471 707 (1971). Area: 479 sq. km (185 sq. miles). **2.** a port in SE India, capital of the Union Territory of Pondicherry, on the Coromandel Coast. Pop.: 90 639 (1971).

pond lil·y *n.* another name for **water lily.**

Pon·do (ˈpɒndəʊ) *n.* **1.** (*pl.* ·**do** *or* ·**dos**) a member of a Negro people of southern Africa, living chiefly in Pondoland. **2.** the language of this people, belonging to the Bantu group of the Niger-Congo family.

pon·dok·kie (pɒnˈdɒkɪ) *or* **pon·dok** (ˈpɒndɒk) *n. Derogatory.* (in southern Africa) a crudely made house built of tin sheet, reeds, etc. [C20: from Malay *pondók* leaf house]

Pon·do·land (ˈpɒndəʊˌlænd) *n.* part of the Transkei, South Africa: inhabited chiefly by the Pondo people.

pond scum *n.* a greenish layer floating on the surface of stagnant waters, consisting of various freshwater algae.

pond-skat·er *n.* any of various heteropterous insects of the family *Gerridae,* esp. *Gerris lacustris* (**common pond-skater**), having a slender hairy body and long hairy legs with which they skim about on the surface of ponds. Also called: **water strider, water skater.**

pond·weed (ˈpɒndˌwiːd) *n.* **1.** any of various water plants of the genus *Potamogeton,* which grow in ponds and slow streams: family *Potamogetonaceae.* **2.** Also called: **waterweed.** *Brit.* any of various unrelated water plants, such as Canadian pondweed, mare's-tail, and water milfoil, that have thin or much divided leaves.

pone[1] (pəʊn) *n. Southern U.S.* **1.** Also called: **pone bread, corn pone.** bread made of maize. **2.** a loaf or cake of this. [C17: from Algonquian; compare Delaware *apán* baked]

pone[2] (pəʊn, ˈpəʊnɪ) *n. Cards.* the player to the right of the dealer, or the nondealer in two-handed games. [C19: from Latin: put!, that is, play, from *ponere* to put]

pong (pɒŋ) *Brit. informal.* ~*n.* **1.** a disagreeable or offensive smell; stink. ~*vb.* **2.** (*intr.*) to give off an unpleasant smell; stink. [C20: perhaps from Romany *pan* to stink]

pon·gee (pɒnˈdʒiː, ˈpɒndʒiː) *n.* **1.** a thin plain-weave silk fabric from China or India, left in its natural colour. **2.** a cotton or rayon fabric similar to or in imitation of this. [C18: from Mandarin Chinese (Peking) *pen-chī* woven at home, on one's own loom, from *pen* own + *chi* loom]

pon·gid (ˈpɒŋgɪd, ˈpɒndʒɪd) *n.* **1.** any primate of the family *Pongidae,* which includes the gibbons and the great apes. ~*adj.* **2.** of, relating to, or belonging to the family *Pongidae.* [from New Latin *Pongo* type genus, from Kongo *mpongi* ape]

pon·iard (ˈpɒnjəd) *n.* **1.** a small dagger with a slender blade. ~*vb.* **2.** (*tr.*) to stab with a poniard. [C16: from Old French *poignard* dagger, from *poing* fist, from Latin *pugnus;* related to Latin *pugnāre* to fight]

pons (pɒnz) *n., pl.* **pon·tes** (ˈpɒntiːz). **1.** a bridge of connecting tissue. **2.** short for **pons Varolii.** [Latin: bridge]

pons as·i·no·rum (ˌæsɪˈnɔːrəm) *n.* the geometric proposition that the angles opposite the two equal sides of an isosceles triangle are equal. [Latin: bridge of asses, referring originally to the fifth proposition of the first book of Euclid, which was considered difficult for students to learn]

pons Va·ro·li·i (vəˈrəʊlɪˌaɪ) *n., pl.* **pon·tes Va·ro·li·i** (ˈpɒntiːz). a broad white band of connecting nerve fibres that bridges the hemispheres of the cerebellum in mammals. Sometimes shortened to **pons.** [C16: New Latin, literally: bridge of Varoli, after Costanzo *Varoli* (?1543–75), Italian anatomist]

pont (pɒnt) *n.* (in South Africa) a river ferry, esp. one that is guided by a cable from one bank to the other. [C17: from Dutch: ferryboat, PUNT[1]; reintroduced through Afrikaans in 19th or 20th century]

Pon·ta Del·ga·da (*Portuguese* ˈpontə ðɛlˈgaðə) *n.* a port in the E Azores, on S São Miguel Island: chief commercial centre of the archipelago. Pop.: 69 930 (1970).

Pont+char+train ('pɒntʃə,treɪn) *n.* **Lake.** a shallow lagoon in SE Louisiana, linked with the Gulf of Mexico by a narrow channel, the **Rigolets:** resort and fishing centre. Area: 1620 sq. km (625 sq. miles).

Pon+te+fract ('pɒntɪ,frækt) *n.* an industrial town in N England, in West Yorkshire: castle (1069), in which Richard II was imprisoned and murdered (1400). Pop.: 31 335 (1971).

Pon+te+fract cake *n.* another name for **pomfret.**

Pon+te+ve+dra (*Spanish* ,ponte'βeðra) *n.* a port in NW Spain: takes its name from a 12-arched Roman bridge, the Pons Vetus. Pop.: 52 452 (1970).

Pon·ti·ac ('pɒntɪ,æk) *n.* died 1769, chief of the Ottawa Indians, who led a rebellion against the British (1763–66).

pon+ti·a+nak (,pɒntɪ'ɑ:næk) *n.* (in Malay folklore) a female vampire; the ghost of a woman who has died in childbirth. [from Malay]

Pon+ti·a+nak (,pɒntɪ'ɑ:næk) *n.* a port in Indonesia, on W coast of Borneo almost exactly on the equator. Pop.: 217 555 (1971).

Pon+tic ('pɒntɪk) *adj.* denoting or relating to the Black Sea. [C15: from Latin *Ponticus,* from Greek, from *Pontos* PONTUS]

pon+ti+fex ('pɒntɪ,fɛks) *n., pl.* **pon+tif·i·ces** (pɒn'tɪfɪ,si:z). (in ancient Rome) any of the senior members of the Pontifical College, presided over by the **Pontifex Maximus.** [C16: from Latin, perhaps from Etruscan but influenced by folk etymology as if meaning literally: bridge-maker, from *pons* bridge + *-fex* from *facere* to make]

pon+tiff ('pɒntɪf) *n.* a former title of the pagan high priest at Rome, later used of popes and occasionally of other bishops, and now confined exclusively to the pope. [C17: from French *pontife,* from Latin PONTIFEX]

pon+tif·i·cal (pɒn'tɪfɪkəl) *adj.* **1.** of, relating to, or characteristic of a pontiff, the pope, or a bishop. **2.** having an excessively authoritative manner; pompous. ~*n. R.C. Church, Church of England.* **3.** a book containing the prayers and ritual instructions for ceremonies restricted to a bishop. —**pon+'tif·i+cal+ly** *adv.*

Pon+tif·i·cal Col+lege *n. R.C. Church.* **1.** a major theological college under the direct control of the Roman Curia. **2.** the council of priests, being the chief hieratic body of the Church.

Pon+tif·i·cal Mass *n. R.C. Church, Church of England.* a solemn celebration of Mass by a bishop.

pon+tif·i+cals (pɒn'tɪfɪkəlz) *pl. n. Chiefly R.C. Church.* the insignia and special vestments worn by a bishop, esp. when celebrating High Mass.

pon+tif·i·cate *vb.* (pɒn'tɪfɪ,keɪt). (*intr.*) **1.** Also: **pontify.** to speak or behave in a pompous or dogmatic manner. **2.** to serve or officiate as a pontiff, esp. in celebrating a Pontifical Mass. ~*n.* (pɒn'tɪfɪkɪt). **3.** the office or term of office of a pontiff, now usually the pope.

pon+til ('pɒntɪl) *n.* a less common word for **punty.** [C19: from French, apparently from Italian *puntello;* see PUNTY]

pon+tine ('pɒntaɪn) *adj.* **1.** of or relating to bridges. **2.** of or relating to the pons Varolii. [C19: from Latin *pons* bridge]

Pon+tine Marsh·es ('pɒntaɪn) *pl. n.* an area of W Italy, southeast of Rome: formerly malarial swamps, drained in 1932–34 after numerous attempts since 160 B.C. had failed. Italian name: **A·gro Pon+ti+no** ('a:gro pon'ti:no).

Pon·tius Pi·late ('pɒnʃəs, 'pɒntɪəs 'paɪlət) *n.* See **Pilate.**

pon+to+nier (,pɒntə'nɪə) *n. Military.* a person in charge of or involved in building a pontoon bridge. [C19: from French *pontonnier,* from Latin *pontō* ferry boat, PONTOON[1]]

pon+toon[1] (pɒn'tu:n) *n.* **1. a.** a watertight float or vessel used where buoyancy is required in water, as in supporting a bridge, in salvage work, or where a temporary or mobile structure is required in military operations. **b.** (*as modifier*): *a pontoon bridge.* **2.** *Nautical.* a float, often inflatable, for raising a vessel in the water. [C17: from French *ponton,* from Latin *pontō* punt, floating bridge, from *pōns* bridge]

pon+toon[2] (pɒn'tu:n) *n.* **1.** Also called: **twenty-one** (esp. U.S.), **vingt-et-un.** a gambling game in which players try to obtain card combinations better than the banker's but never worth more than 21 points. **2.** (in this game) the combination of an ace with a ten or court card when dealt to a player as his first two cards. [C20: probably an alteration of French *vingt-et-un,* literally: twenty-one]

Pon·tor·mo (*Italian* pon'tormo) *n.* **Ja·co·po da** ('ja:kopo da). original name *Jacopo Carrucci.* 1494–1556, Italian mannerist painter.

Pon+tus ('pɒntəs) *n.* an ancient region of NE Asia Minor, on the Black Sea: became a kingdom in the 4th century B.C.; at its height under Mithridates VI (about 115–63 B.C.), when it controlled all Asia Minor; defeated by the Romans in the mid-1st century B.C.

Pon+tus Eux·i+nus (ju:k'saɪnəs) *n.* the Latin name of the **Black Sea.**

Pon+ty+pool (,pɒntɪ'pu:l) *n.* an industrial town in E Wales, in Gwent: famous for lacquered ironware in the 18th century. Pop.: 37 014 (1971).

Pon+ty+pridd (,pɒntɪ'pri:ð) *n.* an industrial town in S Wales, in SE Mid Glamorgan. Pop.: 34 465 (1971).

po·ny ('pəʊnɪ) *n., pl.* **·nies. 1.** any of various breeds of small horse, usually under 14.2 hands. **2. a.** a small drinking glass, esp. for liqueurs. **b.** the amount held by such a glass. **3.** anything small of its kind. **4.** *Brit. slang.* a sum of £25, esp. in bookmaking. **5.** Also called: **trot.** *U.S. slang.* a literal translation used by students, often illicitly, in preparation for foreign language lessons or examinations; crib. [C17: from Scottish *powney,* perhaps from obsolete French *poulenet* a little colt, from *poulain* colt, from Latin *pullus* young animal, foal]

po·ny ex+press *n.* (in the American West) a system of mail transport that employed relays of riders and mounts, esp. that operating from Missouri to California in 1860–61.

po·ny+tail ('pəʊnɪ,teɪl) *n.* a hair style for women and girls in which the hair is pulled tightly into a band or ribbon at the back of the head into a loose hanging fall.

po·ny trek+king *n.* the act of riding ponies cross-country, esp. as a pastime.

pooch (pu:tʃ) *n. Chiefly U.S.* a slang word for **dog.** [of unknown origin]

pood (pu:d) *n.* a unit of weight, used in Russia, equal to 36.1 pounds or 16.39 kilograms. [C16: from Russian *pud,* probably from Old Norse *pund* POUND[2]]

poo+dle ('pu:dəl) *n.* an intelligent breed of dog, with curly hair, which is generally clipped from ribs to tail: originally bred as a hunting dog. [C19: from German *Pudel,* short for *Pudelhund,* from *pudeln* to splash + *Hund* dog; the dogs were formerly trained as water dogs; see PUDDLE, HOUND]

poof (pʊf, pu:f) *or* **poove** *n. Brit. slang.* a male homosexual. [C20: from French *pouffe* puff]

poof+tah *or* **poof+ter** ('pʊftə, 'pu:f-) *n. Chiefly Austral. slang.* a man who is considered effeminate or homosexual. [C20: expanded form of POOF]

pooh (pu:) *interj.* an exclamation of disdain, contempt, or disgust.

Pooh-Bah ('pu:'bɑ:) *n.* a pompous self-important official holding several offices at once and fulfilling none of them. [C19: after the character, the Lord-High-Everything-Else, in *The Mikado* (1885), a light opera by Gilbert and Sullivan]

pooh-pooh ('pu:'pu:) *vb.* (*tr.*) to express disdain or scorn for; dismiss or belittle.

pool[1] (pu:l) *n.* **1.** a small body of still water, usually fresh; small pond. **2.** a small isolated collection of liquid spilt or poured on a surface; puddle: *a pool of blood.* **3.** a deep part of a stream or river where the water runs very slowly. **4.** an underground accumulation of oil or gas, usually forming a reservoir in porous sedimentary rock. **5.** See **swimming pool.** [Old English *pōl;* related to Old Frisian *pōl,* German *Pfuhl*]

pool[2] (pu:l) *n.* **1.** any communal combination of resources, funds, etc.: *a typing pool.* **2.** the combined stakes of the betters in many gambling sport or games; kitty. **3.** *Commerce.* a group of producers who conspire to establish and maintain output levels and high prices, each member of the group being allocated a maximum quota; price ring. **4.** *Finance, chiefly U.S.* **a.** a joint fund organized by security-holders for speculative or manipulative purposes on financial markets. **b.** the persons or parties involved in such a combination. **5.** any of various billiard games in which the object is to pot all the balls with the cue ball, esp. that played with 15 coloured and numbered balls, popular in the U.S.; pocket billiards. ~*vb.* (*tr.*) **6.** to combine (investments, money, interests, etc.) into a common fund, as for a joint enterprise. **7.** *Commerce.* to organize a pool of (enterprises). **8.** *Austral. informal.* to inform on or incriminate (someone). [C17: from French *poule,* literally: hen used to signify stakes in a card game, from Medieval Latin *pulla* hen, from Latin *pullus* young animal]

Poole (pu:l) *n.* a port and resort in S England, in Dorset on **Poole Harbour.** Pop.: 106 697 (1971).

Pool Ma+le·bo ('pu:l mə'li:bəʊ) *n.* the Zaïrese name for **Stanley Pool.**

pool+room ('pu:l,ru:m, -,rʊm) *n. U.S.* a hall or establishment where pool, billiards, etc., are played.

pools (pu:lz) *pl. n. Brit.* an organized nationwide principally postal gambling pool betting on the result of football matches. Also called: **football pools.**

pool ta+ble *n.* a billiard table on which pool is played.

poon[1] (pu:n) *n.* **1.** any of several trees of the SE Asian genus *Calophyllum* having lightweight hard wood and shiny leathery leaves: family *Guttiferae.* **2.** the wood of any of these trees, used to make masts and spars. [C17: from Singhalese *pūna*]

poon[2] (pu:n) *n. Austral. slang.* a stupid or ineffectual person. [C20: from English dialect]

Poo+na *or* **Pu+ne** ('pu:nə) *n.* a city in W India, in W Maharashtra: under British rule served as the seasonal capital of the Bombay Presidency. Pop.: 856 105 (1971).

poonce (pu:ns) *n. Austral. slang.* **1.** a male homosexual. **2.** a stupid person. [C20: perhaps a blend of POOF and NANCE]

poon up *vb.* (*intr., adv.*) *Austral. slang.* to dress flashily: *to get pooned up for the evening.* [C20: from POON[2]]

poop[1] (pu:p) *Nautical.* ~*n.* **1.** a raised structure at the stern of a vessel, esp. a sailing ship. **2.** See **poop deck.** ~*vb.* **3.** (*tr.*) (of a wave or sea) to break over the stern of (a vessel). **4.** (*intr.*) (of a vessel) to ship a wave or sea over the stern, esp. repeatedly. [C15: from Old French *pupe,* from Latin *puppis* poop, ship's stern]

poop[2] (pu:p) *vb. U.S. slang.* **1.** (*tr.; usually passive*) to cause to become exhausted; tire: *he was pooped after the race.* **2.** (*intr.;* usually foll. by *out*) to give up or fail, esp. through tiredness: *he pooped out of the race.* [C14 *poupen* to blow, make a sudden sound, perhaps of imitative origin]

poop[3] (pu:p) *n. U.S. slang.* **a.** information; the facts. **b.** (*as modifier*): *a poop sheet.* [of unknown origin]

poop deck *n. Nautical.* the deck on top of the poop.

Po·o·pó (*Spanish* ,poo'po) *n.* **Lake.** a lake in SW Bolivia, at an altitude of 3688 m (12 100 ft.): fed by the Desaguadero River. Area: 2540 sq. km (980 sq. miles).

poor (pʊə, pɔ:) *adj.* **1. a.** lacking financial or other means of subsistence; needy. **b.** (*as n.*): *the poor.* **2.** characterized by or indicating poverty: *the country had a poor economy.* **3.** deficient in amount; scanty or inadequate: *a poor salary.* **4.** (when *postpositive,* usually foll. by *in*) badly supplied (with resources, materials, etc.): *a region poor in wild flowers.* **5.** lacking in quality; inferior. **6.** giving no pleasure; disappointing or disagreeable: *a poor play.* **7.** (*prenominal*) deserving of pity; unlucky: *poor John is ill again.* [C13: from Old French *povre,* from Latin *pauper;* see PAUPER, POVERTY] —**'poor·ness** *n.*

poor box *n.* a box, esp. one in a church, used for the collection of alms or money for the poor.

poor·house ('pʊəˌhaʊs, 'pɔː-) *n.* (formerly) a publicly maintained institution offering accommodation to the poor.

poor law *n. English history.* a law providing for the relief or support of the poor from public, esp. parish, funds.

poor·ly ('pʊəlɪ, 'pɔː-) *adv.* **1.** in a poor way or manner; badly. ~*adj.* **2.** (*usually postpositive*) *Informal.* in poor health; rather ill: *she's poorly today.*

poor re·la·tion *n.* a person or thing considered inferior to another or others: *plastic is a poor relation of real leather.*

poort (pʊət) *n.* (in South Africa) a steep narrow mountain pass, usually following a river or stream. [C19: from Afrikaans, from Dutch: gateway; see PORT[4]]

poor White *n. Often offensive.* **a.** a poverty-stricken and underprivileged White person, esp. in the southern U.S. and South Africa. **b.** (*as modifier*): *poor White trash.*

poove (puːv) *n. Brit. slang.* a variant of **poof.**

pop[1] (pɒp) *vb.* **pops, pop·ping, popped. 1.** to make or cause to make a light sharp explosive sound. **2.** to burst open or cause to burst open with such a sound. **3.** (*intr.; often foll. by in, out,* etc.) *Informal.* to come (to) or go (from) rapidly or suddenly; to pay a brief or unexpected visit (to). **4.** (*intr.*) (esp. of the eyes) to protrude: *her eyes popped with amazement.* **5.** to shoot or fire at (a target) with a firearm. **6.** (*tr.*) to place or put with a sudden movement: *she popped some tablets into her mouth.* **7.** (*tr.*) *Informal.* to pawn: *he popped his watch yesterday.* **8. pop the question.** *Informal.* to propose marriage. ~*n.* **9.** a light sharp explosive sound; crack. **10.** *Informal.* a flavoured nonalcoholic carbonated beverage. ~*adv.* **11.** with a popping sound. ~*interj.* **12.** an exclamation denoting a sharp explosive sound. ~See also **pop off.** [C14: of imitative origin]

pop[2] (pɒp) *n.* **1. a.** music of general appeal, esp. among young people, that originated as a distinctive genre in the 1950s. It is generally characterized by a heavy rhythmic element and the use of electrical amplification. **b.** (*as modifier*): *pop music; a pop record; a pop group.* **2.** *Informal.* a piece of popular or light classical music. ~*adj.* **3.** *Informal.* short for **popular.**

pop[3] (pɒp) *n.* **1.** an informal word for **father. 2.** *Informal.* a name used in addressing an old or middle-aged man.

pop. *abbrev. for:* **1.** popular. **2.** popularly. **3.** population.

P.O.P. *abbrev. for* Post Office Preferred (size of envelopes, etc.).

pop art *n.* a movement in modern art that imitates the methods, styles, and themes of popular culture and mass media, such as comic strips, advertising, and science fiction.

pop·corn ('pɒpˌkɔːn) *n.* **1.** a variety of maize having hard pointed kernels that puff up when heated. **2.** the puffed edible kernels of this plant.

pope[1] (pəʊp) *n.* **1.** (*often cap.*) the bishop of Rome as head of the Roman Catholic Church. **2.** *Eastern Orthodox Churches.* **a.** a title sometimes given to a parish priest. **b.** a title sometimes given to the Greek Orthodox patriarch of Alexandria. **3.** a person assuming or having a status or authority resembling that of a pope. [Old English *papa,* from Church Latin: bishop, esp. of Rome, from Late Greek *papas* father-in-God, from Greek *pappas* father]

pope[2] (pəʊp) *n.* another name for **ruffe** (the fish).

Pope (pəʊp) *n.* **Al·ex·an·der.** 1688–1744, English poet, regarded as the most brilliant satirist of the Augustan period, esp. with his *Imitations of Horace* (1733–38). His technical virtuosity, particularly his fluent use of the heroic couplet, is most evident in *The Rape of the Lock* (*1712–14*). *The Dunciad* (1728; 1742) is an elaborate satire on contemporary hack writers. In the *Moral Essays* (1731–35) and *An Essay on Man* (1733–34) he elaborated the moral values behind his satire.

pope·dom ('pəʊpdəm) *n.* **1.** the office or dignity of a pope. **2.** the tenure of office of a pope. **3.** the dominion of a pope; papal government.

pop·er·y ('pəʊpərɪ) *n.* a derogatory name for **Roman Catholicism.**

pope's nose *n. Chiefly U.S.* another name for **parson's nose.**

pop·eyed ('pɒpˌaɪd) *adj.* **1.** having bulging prominent eyes. **2.** staring in astonishment; amazed.

pop·gun ('pɒpˌgʌn) *n.* a toy gun that fires a pellet or cork by means of compressed air and makes a popping sound.

pop·in·jay ('pɒpɪnˌdʒeɪ) *n.* **1.** a conceited, foppish, or excessively talkative person. **2.** an archaic word for **parrot. 3.** the figure of a parrot used as a target. [C13 *papeniai,* from Old French *papegay* a parrot, from Spanish *papagayo,* from Arabic *babaghā*]

pop·ish ('pəʊpɪʃ) *adj. Derogatory.* belonging to or characteristic of Roman Catholicism. —**'pop·ish·ly** *adv.*

Pop·ish Plot *n.* See (Titus) **Oates.**

pop·lar ('pɒplə) *n.* **1.** any tree of the salicaceous genus *Populus,* of N temperate regions, having triangular leaves, flowers borne in catkins, and light soft wood. See also **aspen, balsam poplar, Lombardy poplar, white poplar. 2.** any of various trees resembling the true poplars, such as the tulip tree. **3.** the wood of any of these trees. [C14: from Old French *poplier,* from *pouple,* from Latin *pōpulus*]

pop·lin ('pɒplɪn) *n.* **a.** a strong fabric, usually of cotton, in plain weave with fine ribbing, used for dresses, children's wear, etc. **b.** (*as modifier*): *a poplin shirt.* [C18: from French *papeline,* perhaps from *Poperinge,* a centre of textile manufacture in Flanders]

pop·lit·e·al (pɒp'lɪtɪəl, ˌpɒplɪ'tiːəl) *adj.* of, relating to, or near the part of the leg behind the knee. [C18: from New Latin *popliteus* the muscle behind the knee joint, from Latin *poples* the ham of the knee]

Po·po·ca·té·petl (ˌpɒpə'kætəpɛtəl, -ˌkætə'pɛtəl; *Spanish* ˌpopoka'tepetl) *n.* a volcano in SE central Mexico, southeast of Mexico City. Height: 5452 m (17 887 ft.).

pop off *vb.* (*intr., adv.*) *Informal.* **1.** to depart suddenly or unexpectedly. **2.** to die, esp. suddenly or unexpectedly: *he popped off at the age of sixty.* **3.** to speak out angrily or indiscreetly: *he popped off at his boss and got fired.*

Po·pov (*Russian* pa'pɔf) *n.* **A·le·xan·der Ste·pa·no·vich** (alɪ'ksandər stɪ'panəvitʃ). 1859–1906, Russian physicist, the first to use an aerial in experiments with radio waves.

pop·o·ver ('pɒpˌəʊvə) *n.* **1.** *Brit.* an individual Yorkshire pudding, often served with roast beef. **2.** *U.S.* a light puffy hollow muffin made from a batter mixture.

pop·pa·dom *or* **pop·pa·dum** ('pɒpədəm) *n.* a thin round crisp Indian bread, fried or roasted and served with curry, etc. [from Hindi]

pop·per ('pɒpə) *n.* **1.** a person or thing that pops. **2.** *Brit.* an informal name for **press stud. 3.** *Chiefly U.S.* a container for cooking popcorn in.

Pop·per ('pɒpə) *n.* Sir **Karl.** born 1902, British philosopher, born in Vienna. In *The Logic of Scientific Discovery* (1934), he proposes that knowledge cannot be absolute and that scientific theories must inevitably be superseded as new problems arising from existing theories are identified. *The Open Society and its Enemies* (1945) is a critique of dogmatic political philosophies, such as Marxism. Other works are *The Poverty of Historicism* (1957), *Conjectures and Refutations* (1963), and *Objective Knowledge* (1972). —**Pop·per·i·an** (pɒ'pɪərɪən) *n., adj.*

pop·pet ('pɒpɪt) *n.* **1.** a term of affection for a small child or sweetheart. **2.** Also called: **poppet valve.** a mushroom-shaped valve that is lifted from its seating by applying an axial force to its stem: commonly used as exhaust or inlet valve in an internal-combustion engine. **3.** *Nautical.* a temporary supporting brace for a vessel hauled on land or in a dry dock. [C14: early variant of PUPPET]

pop·pet head *n.* the framework above a mining shaft that supports the winding mechanism.

pop·pied ('pɒpɪd) *adj.* **1.** covered with poppies. **2.** of or relating to the effects of poppies, esp. in inducing drowsiness or sleep.

pop·ping crease *n. Cricket.* a line four feet in front of and parallel with the bowling crease, at or behind which the batsman stands.

pop·ple ('pɒpəl) *vb.* (*intr.*) **1.** (of boiling water or a choppy sea) to heave or toss; bubble. **2.** (often foll. by *along*) (of a stream or river) to move with an irregular tumbling motion: *the small rivulet poppled along over rocks and stones for half a mile.* [C14: of imitative origin; compare Middle Dutch *popelen* to bubble, throb]

pop·py ('pɒpɪ) *n., pl.* **·pies. 1.** any of numerous papaveraceous plants of the temperate genus *Papaver,* having red, orange, or white flowers and a milky sap: see **corn poppy, Iceland poppy, opium poppy. 2.** any of several similar or related plants, such as the California poppy, prickly poppy, horned poppy, and Welsh poppy. **3.** any of the drugs, such as opium, that are obtained from these plants. **4. a.** a strong red to reddish-orange colour. **b.** (*as adj.*): *a poppy dress.* **5.** a less common name for **poppyhead** (sense 2). **6.** an artificial red poppy flower worn to mark Remembrance Day. [Old English *popæg,* ultimately from Latin *papāver*]

pop·py·cock ('pɒpɪˌkɒk) *n. Informal.* senseless chatter; nonsense. [C19: from Dutch dialect *pappekak,* literally: soft excrement, from *pap* soft + *kak* dung; see PAP[1]]

Pop·py Day *n.* an informal name for **Remembrance Sunday.**

pop·py·head ('pɒpɪˌhɛd) *n.* **1.** the hard dry seed-containing capsule of a poppy. See also **capsule** (sense 3a.). **2.** a carved ornament, esp. one used on the top of the end of a pew or bench in Gothic church architecture.

pop·py seed *n.* the small grey seeds of one type of poppy flower, used esp. on loaves and as a cake filling.

Pop·si·cle ('pɒpsɪkəl) *n. U.S. Trademark.* an ice lolly.

pop·sy ('pɒpsɪ) *n., pl.* **·sies.** *Old-fashioned Brit. slang.* an attractive young woman. [C19: diminutive formed from *pop,* shortened from POPPET; originally a nursery term]

pop·u·lace ('pɒpjʊləs) *n.* (*sometimes functioning as pl.*) **1.** the inhabitants of an area. **2.** the common people; masses. [C16: via French from Italian *popolaccio* the common herd, from *popolo* people, from Latin *populus*]

pop·u·lar ('pɒpjʊlə) *adj.* **1.** appealing to the general public; widely favoured or admired. **2.** favoured by an individual or limited group: *I'm not very popular with her.* **3.** connected with, representing, or prevailing among the general public; common: *popular discontent.* **4.** appealing to or comprehensible to the layman: *a popular lecture on physics.* [C15: from Latin *populāris* belonging to the people, democratic, from *populus* people] —**pop·u·lar·i·ty** (ˌpɒpjʊ'lærɪtɪ) *n.*

pop·u·lar et·y·mol·o·gy *n. Linguistics.* another name for **folk etymology.**

pop·u·lar front *n.* (*often cap.*) any of the left-wing groups or parties that were organized from 1935 onwards to oppose the spread of fascism.

pop·u·lar·ize *or* **pop·u·lar·ise** ('pɒpjʊləˌraɪz) *vb.* (*tr.*) **1.** to make popular; make attractive to the general public. **2.** to make or cause to become easily understandable or acceptable. —ˌ**pop·u·lar·i·'za·tion** *or* ˌ**pop·u·lar·i·'sa·tion** *n.* —'**pop·u·lar·ˌiz·er** *or* '**pop·u·lar·ˌis·er** *n.*

pop·u·lar·ly ('pɒpjʊləlɪ) *adv.* **1.** by the public as a whole; generally or widely. **2.** usually; commonly: *his full name is Robert, but he is popularly known as Bob.* **3.** in a popular manner.

pop·u·lar mu·sic *n.* music having wide appeal, esp. characterized by lightly romantic or sentimental melodies. See also **pop**².

pop·u·lar sov·er·eign·ty *n.* (in the pre-Civil War U.S.) the doctrine that the inhabitants of a territory should be free from federal interference in determining their own domestic policy, esp. in deciding whether or not to allow slavery.

pop·u·late ('pɒpjʊˌleɪt) *vb.* (*tr.*) **1.** (*often passive*) to live in; inhabit. **2.** to provide a population for; colonize or people. [C16: from Medieval Latin *populāre* to provide with inhabitants, from Latin *populus* people]

pop·u·la·tion (ˌpɒpjʊ'leɪʃən) *n.* **1.** (*sometimes functioning as pl.*) all the persons inhabiting a country, city, or other specified place. **2.** the number of such inhabitants. **3.** (*sometimes functioning as pl.*) all the people of a particular race or class in a specific area: *the Chinese population of San Francisco.* **4.** the act or process of providing a place with inhabitants; colonization. **5.** *Ecology.* a group of individuals of the same species inhabiting a given area. **6.** *Astronomy.* either of two main groups of stars classified according to age and location. **Population I** consists of hot white stars, many occurring in galactic clusters and forming the arms of spiral galaxies. Stars of **population II** are older, the brightest being red giants, and are found in the centre of spiral and elliptical galaxies in globular clusters. **7.** Also called: **universe.** *Statistics.* the entire finite or infinite aggregate of individuals or items from which samples are drawn.

pop·u·la·tion ex·plo·sion *n.* a rapid increase in the size of a population caused by such factors as a sudden decline in infant mortality, an increase in life expectancy, etc.

Pop·u·list ('pɒpjʊlɪst) *n.* **1.** *U.S. history.* a member of the People's Party, formed largely by agrarian interests to contest the 1892 presidential election. The movement gradually dissolved after the 1904 election. **2.** (*often not cap.*) a politician or other person who claims to support the interests of the ordinary people. ~*adj. also* **Pop·u·lis·tic. 3.** of, characteristic of, or relating to the People's Party, the Populists, or any individual or movement with similar aims. —'**Pop·u·lism** *n.*

pop·u·lous ('pɒpjʊləs) *adj.* containing many inhabitants; abundantly populated. [C15: from Late Latin *populōsus*] —'**pop·u·lous·ly** *adv.* —'**pop·u·lous·ness** *n.*

pop-up *adj.* **1.** (of an appliance) characterized by or having a mechanism that pops up: *a pop-up toaster.* **2.** (of a book) having pages that rise when opened to simulate a three-dimensional form.

por·bea·gle ('pɔːˌbiːgəl) *n.* any of several voracious sharks of the genus *Lamna,* esp. *L. nasus,* of northern seas: family *Isuridae.* Also called: **mackerel shark.** [C18: from Cornish *porgh-bugel,* of obscure origin]

porce·lain ('pɔːslɪn, -leɪn, 'pɔːsə-) *n.* **1.** a more or less translucent ceramic material, the principal ingredients being kaolin and petuntse (hard paste) or other clays, ground glassy substances, soapstone, bone ash, etc. **2.** an object made of this or such objects collectively. **3.** (*modifier*) of, relating to, or made from this material: *a porcelain cup.* [C16: from French *porcelaine,* from Italian *porcellana* cowrie shell, porcelain (from its shell-like finish), literally: relating to a sow (from the resemblance between a cowrie shell and a sow's vulva), from *porcella* little sow, from *porca* sow, from Latin; see PORK] —**por·cel·la·ne·ous** (ˌpɔːsə'leɪnɪəs) *adj.*

porce·lain clay *n.* another name for **kaolin.**

porch (pɔːtʃ) *n.* **1.** a low structure projecting from the doorway of a house and forming a covered entrance. **2.** *U.S.* an exterior roofed gallery, often partly enclosed; veranda. [C13: from French *porche,* from Latin *porticus* portico]

por·cine ('pɔːsaɪn) *adj.* of, connected with, or characteristic of pigs. [C17: from Latin *porcīnus,* from *porcus* a pig]

por·cu·pine ('pɔːkjʊˌpaɪn) *n.* any of various large hystricomorph rodents of the families *Hystricidae,* of Africa, Indonesia, S Europe, and S Asia, and *Erethizontidae,* of the New World. All species have a body covering of protective spines or quills. [C14 *porc despyne* pig with spines, from Old French *porc espin;* see PORK, SPINE] —'**por·cu·ˌpin·ish** *adj.* —'**por·cu·ˌpin·y** *adj.*

por·cu·pine fish *n.* any of various plectognath fishes of the genus *Diodon* and related genera, of temperate and tropical seas, having a body that is covered with sharp spines and can be inflated into a globe: family *Diodontidae.* Also called: **globefish.**

por·cu·pine grass *n. Austral.* another name for **spinifex.**

pore¹ (pɔː) *vb.* (*intr.*) **1.** (foll. by *over*) to make a close intent examination or study (of a book, map, etc.): *he pored over the documents for several hours.* **2.** (foll. by *over, on,* or *upon*) to think deeply (about): *he pored on the question of their future.* **3.** (foll. by *over, on,* or *upon*) *Rare.* to look earnestly or intently (at); gaze fixedly (upon). [C13 *pouren;* perhaps related to PEER²]

pore² (pɔː) *n.* **1.** *Anatomy, zoology.* any small opening in the skin or outer surface of an animal. **2.** *Botany.* any small aperture, esp. that of a stoma through which water vapour and gases pass. **3.** any other small hole, such as a space in a rock, soil, etc. [C14: from Late Latin *porus,* from Greek *poros* passage, pore]

por·gy ('pɔːgɪ) *n., pl.* **·gy** *or* **·gies. 1.** Also called: **pogy.** any of various sparid fishes, many of which occur in American Atlantic waters. See also **scup, sheepshead. 2.** any of various similar or related fishes. [C18: from Spanish *pargo,* from Latin *phager* type of fish, from Greek *phagros* sea-bream]

Po·ri (*Finnish* 'pɔri) *n.* a port in SW Finland, on the Gulf of Bothnia. Pop.: 73 626 (1970). Swedish name: **Björneborg.**

po·rif·er·an (pɔː'rɪfərən) *n.* **1.** any invertebra of the phylum *Porifera,* which comprises the sponges. ~*adj. also* **po·rif·er·ous. 2.** of, relating to, or belonging to the phylum *Porifera.* [C19: from New Latin *porifer* bearing pores]

po·rif·er·ous (pɔː'rɪfərəs) *adj.* **1.** *Biology.* having many pores. **2.** another word for **poriferan** (sense 2).

Po·ri·ru·a (ˌpɔːrɪ'ruːə) *n.* a city in New Zealand, on North Island just north of Wellington. Pop.: 30 372 (1971).

po·rism ('pɔːrɪzəm) *n.* a type of mathematical proposition considered by Euclid, the meaning of which is now obscure. It is thought to be a proposition affirming the possibility of finding such conditions as will render a certain problem indeterminate or capable of innumerable solutions. [C14: from Late Latin *porisma,* from Greek: deduction, from *porizein* to deduce, carry; related to Greek *poros* passage]

pork (pɔːk) *n.* the flesh of pigs used as food. [C13: from Old French *porc,* from Latin *porcus* pig]

pork bar·rel *n. U.S. slang.* a bill or project requiring considerable government spending in a locality to the benefit of the legislator's constituents who live there. [C20: term originally applied to the Federal treasury considered as a source of lucrative grants]

pork·er ('pɔːkə) *n.* a pig, esp. a young one weighing between 40 and 67 kg, fattened to provide meat such as pork chops.

pork pie *n.* a pie filled with minced seasoned pork.

pork·pie hat ('pɔːkˌpaɪ) *n.* a hat with a round flat crown and a brim that can be turned up or down.

pork pig *n.* a pig, typically of a lean type, bred and used principally for pork.

pork·y ('pɔːkɪ) *adj.* **pork·i·er, pork·i·est. 1.** belonging to or characteristic of pork: *a porky smell.* **2.** *Informal.* fat; obese. —'**pork·i·ness** *n.*

por·noc·ra·cy (pɔː'nɒkrəsɪ) *n.* government or domination of government by whores. [C19: from Greek, from *pornē* a prostitute, harlot + -CRACY]

por·nog·ra·phy (pɔː'nɒgrəfɪ) *n.* **1.** writings, pictures, films, etc., designed to stimulate sexual excitement. **2.** the production of such material. ~Sometimes (informal) shortened to **porn** (pɔːn) or **por·no** ('pɔːnəʊ). [C19: from Greek *pornographos* writing of harlots, from *pornē* a harlot + *graphein* to write] —**por·'nog·ra·pher** *n.* —**por·no·graph·ic** (ˌpɔːnə'græfɪk) *adj.* —ˌ**por·no·'graph·i·cal·ly** *adv.*

por·o·mer·ic (ˌpɔːrə'mɛrɪk) *adj.* **1.** (of a plastic) permeable to water vapour. ~*n.* **2.** a substance having this characteristic, esp. one based on polyurethane and used in place of leather in making shoe uppers. [C20: from PORO(SITY) + (POLY)MER + -IC]

po·ros·i·ty (pɔː'rɒsɪtɪ) *n., pl.* **·ties. 1.** the state or condition of being porous. **2.** *Geology.* the ratio of the volume of space to the total volume of a rock. [C14: from Medieval Latin *porōsitās,* from Late Latin *porus* PORE²]

po·rous ('pɔːrəs) *adj.* **1.** able to absorb water, air, or other fluids. **2.** *Biology, geology.* having pores; poriferous. [C14: from Medieval Latin *porōsus,* from Late Latin *porus* PORE²] —'**po·rous·ly** *adv.* —'**po·rous·ness** *n.*

por·phy·ri·a (pɔː'fɪrɪə) *n.* a hereditary disease of body metabolism, producing abdominal pain, mental confusion, etc. [C19: from New Latin, from *porphyrin* a purple substance excreted by patients suffering from this condition, from Greek *porphura* purple]

por·phy·rin ('pɔːfɪrɪn) *n.* any of a group of pigments occurring widely in animal and plant tissues and having a heterocyclic structure formed from four pyrrole rings linked by four methylene groups. [C20: from Greek *porphura* purple, referring to its colour]

por·phy·rit·ic (ˌpɔːfɪ'rɪtɪk) *adj.* **1.** (of rocks) having large crystals in a fine groundmass of minerals. **2.** consisting of porphyry.

por·phy·rog·e·nite (ˌpɔːfə'rɒdʒɪˌnaɪt) *n.* (*sometimes cap.*) a prince born after his father has succeeded to the throne. [C17: via Medieval Latin from Late Greek *porphurogenētos* born in the purple, from Greek *porphuros* purple]

por·phy·roid ('pɔːfɪˌrɔɪd) *adj.* **1.** (of metamorphic rocks) having a texture characterized by large crystals set in a finer groundmass. ~*n.* **2.** a metamorphic rock having this texture.

por·phy·rop·sin (ˌpɔːfɪ'rɒpsɪn) *n.* a purple pigment occurring in the retina of the eye of certain freshwater fishes.

por·phy·ry ('pɔːfɪrɪ) *n., pl.* **·ries. 1.** a reddish-purple rock consisting of large crystals of feldspar in a finer groundmass of feldspar, hornblende, etc. **2.** any igneous rock with large crystals embedded in a finer groundmass of minerals. [C14 *porfurie,* from Late Latin *porphyrītēs,* from Greek *porphuritēs* (*lithos*) purple (stone), from *porphuros* purple]

por·poise ('pɔːpəs) *n., pl.* **·poise** *or* **·pois·es. 1.** any of various small cetacean mammals of the genus *Phocaena* and related genera, having a blunt snout and many teeth: family *Delphinidae* (or *Phocaenidae*). **2.** (*not in technical use*) any of various related cetaceans, esp. the dolphin. [C14: from French *pourpois,* from Medieval Latin *porcopiscus* (from Latin *porcus* pig + *piscis* fish), replacing Latin *porcus marīnus* sea pig]

por·ridge ('pɒrɪdʒ) *n.* **1.** a dish made from oatmeal or another cereal, cooked in water or milk to a thick consistency. **2.** (in Malaysia) rice broth. [C16: variant (influenced by Middle English *porray* pottage) of POTTAGE]

por·rin·ger ('pɒrɪndʒə) *n.* a small dish, often with a handle, for soup, porridge, etc. [C16: changed from Middle English *potinger, poteger,* from Old French *potager,* from *potage* soup, contents of a pot; see POTTAGE]

Por·se·na ('pɔːsɪnə) *or* **Por·sen·na** (pɔː'sɛnə) *n.* **Lars** (lɑːz). 6th century B.C., a legendary Etruscan king, alleged to have besieged Rome in a vain attempt to reinstate Tarquinius Superbus on the throne.

Por·son ('pɔːsᵊn) *n.* **Rich·ard.** 1759–1808, English classical scholar, noted for his editions of Aeschylus and Euripides.

port[1] (pɔːt) *n.* **1.** a town or place alongside navigable water with facilities for the loading and unloading of ships. **2.** See **port of entry.** [Old English, from Latin *portus* harbour, port]

port[2] (pɔːt) *n.* **1.** Also called (formerly): **larboard. a.** the left side of an aircraft or vessel when facing the nose or bow. **b.** (*as modifier*): *the port bow.* Compare **starboard.** ~*vb.* **2.** to turn or be turned towards the port. [C17: origin uncertain]

port[3] (pɔːt) *n.* a sweet fortified dessert wine. [C17: after *Oporto,* Portugal, from where it came originally]

port[4] (pɔːt) *n.* **1.** *Nautical.* **a.** an opening in the side of a ship, fitted with a watertight door, for access to the holds. **b.** See **porthole** (sense 1). **2.** a small opening in a wall, armoured vehicle, etc., for firing through. **3.** an aperture, esp. one controlled by a valve, by which fluid enters or leaves the cylinder head of an engine, compressor, etc. **4.** *Electronics.* a logical circuit for the input and ouput of data. **5.** *Chiefly Scot.* a gate or portal in a town or fortress. [Old English, from Latin *porta* gate]

port[5] (pɔːt) *Military.* ~*vb.* **1.** (*tr.*) to carry (a rifle, etc.) in a position diagonally across the body with the muzzle near the left shoulder. ~*n.* **2.** this position. [C14: from Old French, from *porter* to carry, from Latin *portāre*]

port[6] (pɔːt) *n. Austral. informal.* **1.** a travelling bag, such as a suitcase. **2.** any other kind of bag, such as a shopping bag. [C20: shortened from PORTMANTEAU]

Port. *abbrev. for:* **1.** Portugal. **2.** Portuguese.

port·a·ble ('pɔːtəbᵊl) *adj.* **1.** able to be carried or moved easily, esp. by hand. **2.** *Archaic.* able to be endured; bearable. ~*n.* **3.** an article that can be readily carried by hand, such as a tape recorder, typewriter, etc. [C14: from Late Latin *portābilis,* from Latin *portāre* to carry] —ˌ**port·a·'bil·i·ty** *or* **'port·a·ble·ness** *n.* —**'port·a·bly** *adv.*

Port Ad·e·laide *n.* the chief port of South Australia, near Adelaide on St. Vincent Gulf. Pop.: 39 000 (1971).

Por·ta·down (ˌpɔːtə'daʊn) *n.* a town in S Northern Ireland, in Co. Armagh. Pop.: 21 906 (1971).

por·tage ('pɔːtɪdʒ) *n.* **1.** the act of carrying; transport. **2.** the cost of carrying or transporting. **3.** the act or process of transporting boats supplies, etc., overland between navigable waterways. **4.** the route overland used for such transport. ~*vb.* **5.** to transport (boats, supplies, etc.) overland between navigable waterways. [C15: from French, from Old French *porter* to carry]

por·tal ('pɔːtᵊl) *n.* **1.** an entrance, gateway, or doorway, esp. one that is large and impressive. **2.** any entrance or access to a place. [C14: via Old French from Medieval Latin *portāle,* from Latin *porta* gate, entrance]

por·tal-to-por·tal *adj.* of or relating to the period between the actual times workers enter and leave their mine, factory, etc.: *portal-to-portal pay.*

por·tal vein *n.* any vein connecting two capillary networks, esp. in the liver (**hepatic portal vein**).

por·ta·men·to (ˌpɔːtə'mɛntəʊ) *n., pl.* **·ti** (-tɪ). *Music.* a smooth slide from one note to another in which intervening notes are not separately discernible. Compare **glissando.** [C18: from Italian: a carrying, from Latin *portāre* to carry]

Port Ar·thur *n.* **1.** a former penal settlement (1833–70) in Australia, on the S coast of the Tasman Peninsula, Tasmania. **2.** the former name of **Lüshun.**

por·ta·tive ('pɔːtətɪv) *adj.* **1.** a less common word for **portable. 2.** concerned with the act of carrying. [C14: from French, from Latin *portāre* to carry]

por·ta·tive or·gan *n. Music.* a small portable organ with arm-operated bellows popular in medieval times.

Port-au-Prince ('pɔːt əʊ 'prɪns; *French* pɔr to 'prɛ̃ːs) *n.* the capital and chief port of Haiti, in the south on the Gulf of Gonaïves: founded in 1749 by the French; university (1944). Pop.: 458 675 (1971 est.).

Port Blair (blɛə) *n.* the capital of the Indian Union Territory of the Andaman and Nicobar Islands, a port on the SE coast of South Andaman Island: a former penal colony. Pop.: 26 218 (1971).

port·cul·lis (pɔːt'kʌlɪs) *n.* an iron or wooden grating suspended vertically in grooves in the gateway of a castle or fortified town and able to be lowered so as to bar the entrance. [C14 *port colice,* from Old French *porte coleïce* sliding gate, from *porte* door, entrance + *coleïce,* from *couler* to slide, flow, from Late Latin *cōlāre* to filter]

Porte (pɔːt) *n.* short for **Sublime Porte;** the court or government of the Ottoman Empire. [C17: shortened from French *Sublime Porte* High Gate, rendering the Turkish title *Babi Ali,* the imperial gate, which was regarded as the seat of government]

porte-co·chere (ˌpɔːtkɒ'ʃɛə) *n.* **1.** a large covered entrance for vehicles leading into a courtyard. **2.** a large roof projecting over a drive to shelter travellers entering or leaving vehicles. [C17: from French: carriage entrance, from *porte* gateway + *coche* coach]

Port E·liz·a·beth *n.* a port in South Africa, in SE Cape Province on Algoa Bay: motor-vehicle manufacture; resort. Pop.: 386 577 (1970).

por·tend (pɔː'tɛnd) *vb.* (*tr.*) **1.** to give warning of; predict or foreshadow. **2.** *Obsolete.* to indicate or signify; mean. [C15: from Latin *portendere* to indicate, foretell; related to *prōtendere* to stretch out]

por·tent ('pɔːtɛnt) *n.* **1.** a sign or indication of a future event, esp. a momentous or calamitous one; omen. **2.** momentous or ominous significance: *a cry of dire portent.* **3.** a miraculous occurrence; marvel. [C16: from Latin *portentum* sign, omen, from *portendere* to PORTEND]

por·ten·tous (pɔː'tɛntəs) *adj.* **1.** of momentous or ominous significance. **2.** miraculous, amazing, or awe-inspiring; prodigious. **3.** self-important or pompous. —**por·'ten·tous·ly** *adv.* —**por·'ten·tous·ness** *n.*

por·ter[1] ('pɔːtə) *n.* **1.** a man employed to carry luggage, parcels, supplies, etc., esp. at a railway station or hotel. **2.** *U.S.* a railway employee who waits on passengers, esp. in a sleeper. **3.** *East African.* a manual labourer. [C14: from Old French *portour,* from Late Latin *portātōr,* from Latin *portāre* to carry]

por·ter[2] ('pɔːtə) *n.* **1.** *Chiefly Brit.* a person in charge of a gate or door; doorman or gatekeeper. **2.** a person employed by a university or college as a caretaker and doorkeeper who also answers enquiries. **3.** a person in charge of the maintenance of a building, esp. a block of flats. **4.** Also called: **ostiary.** *R.C. Church.* a person ordained to what was formerly the lowest in rank of the minor orders. [C13: from Old French *portier,* from Late Latin *portārius* doorkeeper, from Latin *porta* door]

por·ter[3] ('pɔːtə) *n. Brit.* a dark sweet ale brewed from black malt. [C18: shortened from *porter's ale,* apparently because it was a favourite beverage of porters]

Por·ter ('pɔːtə) *n.* **1. Cole.** 1893–1964, U.S. composer and lyricist of musical comedies. His most popular songs include *Night and Day* and *Let's do It.* **2.** Sir **George.** born 1920, British chemist, who shared a Nobel prize for chemistry in 1967 for his work on flash photolysis. **3. Kath·er·ine Anne.** born 1894, U.S. short-story writer and novelist. Her best-known collections of stories are *Flowering Judas* (1930) and *Pale Horse, Pale Rider* (1939). **4. Pe·ter.** born 1929, Australian poet, living in Britain. **5. Wil·liam Sid·ney.** original name of **O. Henry.**

por·ter·age ('pɔːtərɪdʒ) *n.* **1.** the work of carrying supplies, goods, etc., done by porters. **2.** the charge made for this.

por·ter·house ('pɔːtəˌhaʊs) *n.* **1.** Also called: **porterhouse steak.** a thick choice steak of beef cut from the middle ribs or sirloin. **2.** *Archaic.* a house at which porter is served. [C19 (sense 1): said to be named after a porterhouse or chop-house in New York]

port·fire ('pɔːtˌfaɪə) *n.* a device used for firing rockets and fireworks and, in mining, for igniting explosives.

port·fo·li·o (pɔːt'fəʊlɪəʊ) *n., pl.* **·os. 1.** a flat case, esp. of leather, used for carrying maps, drawings, etc. **2.** such a case used for carrying ministerial or state papers. **3.** the responsibilities or role of the head of a government department: *the portfolio for foreign affairs.* **4. Minister without portfolio.** a cabinet minister who is not responsible for any government department. **5.** a list of financial assets, such as shares, bonds, bills of exchange, etc. [C18: from Italian *portafoglio,* from *portāre* to carry + *foglio* leaf, paper, from Latin *folium* leaf]

Port-Gen·til (*French* pɔr ʒɑ̃'ti) *n.* the chief port of Gabon, in the west near the mouth of the Ogooué River: oil refinery. Pop.: 88 146 (1972).

Port Har·court ('hɑːkət, -kɔːt) *n.* a port in S Nigeria, capital of Rivers state on the Niger delta: the nation's second largest port; industrial centre. Pop.: 242 000 (1975 est.).

port·hole ('pɔːtˌhəʊl) *n.* **1.** a small aperture in the side of a vessel to admit light and air, usually fitted with a watertight glass or metal cover, or both. Sometimes shortened to **port. 2.** an opening in a wall or parapet through which a gun can be fired; embrasure.

por·ti·co ('pɔːtɪkəʊ) *n., pl.* **·coes** *or* **·cos. 1.** a covered entrance to a building; porch. **2.** a covered walkway in the form of a roof supported by columns or pillars, esp. one built on to the exterior of a building. [C17: via Italian from Latin *porticus* PORCH]

por·ti·ère (ˌpɔːtɪ'ɛə; *French* pɔr'tjɛːr) *n.* a curtain hung in a doorway. [C19: via French from Medieval Latin *portāria,* from Latin *porta* door] —**por·ti·èred** *adj.*

Por·ţi·le de Fier (pɔr'tsiːlɛ dɛ 'fjɛr) *n.* the Rumanian name for the **Iron Gate.**

por·tion ('pɔːʃən) *n.* **1.** a part of a whole; fraction. **2.** a part allotted or belonging to a person or group. **3.** an amount of food served to one person; helping. **4.** *Law.* **a.** a share of property, esp. one coming to a child from the estate of his parents. **b.** the property given by a woman to her husband at marriage; dowry. **5.** a person's lot or destiny. ~*vb.* (*tr.*) **6.** to divide up; share out. **7.** to give a share to (a person); assign or allocate. **8.** *Law.* to give a dowry or portion to (a person); endow. [C13: via Old French from Latin *portiō* portion, allocation; related to *pars* PART] —**'por·tion·less** *adj.*

Port Jack·son *n.* an inlet of the Pacific on the coast of SE Australia, forming a fine natural harbour: site of the city of Sydney, spanned by Sydney Harbour Bridge.

Port·land ('pɔːtlənd) *n.* **1. Isle of.** a rugged limestone peninsula in SW England, in Dorset, connected to the mainland by a narrow isthmus and by Chesil Bank: the lighthouse of **Portland Bill** lies at the S tip; famous for the quarrying of **Portland stone,** a fine building material. Pop.: 12 306 (1971). **2.** an inland port in NW Oregon, on the Willamette River: the largest city in the state; shipbuilding and chemical industries. Pop.: 378 134 (1973 est.). **3.** a port in SW Maine, on Casco Bay: the largest city in the state; settled by Englishmen in 1632, destroyed successively by French, Indian, and British attacks, and rebuilt; capital of Maine (1820–32). Pop.: 65 116 (1970).

Port+land ce+ment *n.* a cement that hardens under water and is made by mixing, burning, and grinding certain limestones and clays. [C19: named after the ISLE OF PORTLAND, because its colour resembles that of the stone quarried there]

Port+laoi·se (ˌpɔːtˈliːʃə) *n.* a town in central Ireland, county town of Co. Laoighis: site of a top-security prison. Pop.: 6470 (1971).

Port Lou+is (ˈluːɪs, ˈluːɪ) *n.* the capital and chief port of Mauritius, on the NW coast on the Indian Ocean. Pop.: 142 300 (1971 est.).

port+ly (ˈpɔːtlɪ) *adj.* **+li+er, +li+est. 1.** stout or corpulent. **2.** *Archaic.* stately; impressive. [C16: from PORT[5] (in the sense: deportment, bearing)] **—ˈport+li+ness** *n.*

Port Lyau+tey (ljəʊˈteɪ) *n.* the former name (1932–56) of **Mina Hassan Tani.**

port+man+teau (pɔːtˈmæntəʊ) *n., pl.* **+teaus** *or* **+teaux** (-təʊz). **1.** a large travelling case made of stiff leather, esp. one hinged at the back so as to open out into two compartments. **2.** (*modifier*) embodying several uses or qualities: *the heroine is a portmanteau figure of all the virtues.* [C16: from French: cloak carrier, from *porter* to carry + *manteau* cloak MANTLE]

port+man+teau word *n.* another name for **blend** (sense 7). [C19: from the idea that two meanings are packed into one word]

Port Mores+by (ˈmɔːzbɪ) *n.* the capital and chief port of Papua New Guinea, on the SE coast on the Gulf of Papua: important Allied base in World War II. Pop.: 76 507 (1971).

Pôr+to (ˈportu) *n.* the Portuguese name for **Oporto.**

Pôr+to A·le·gre (*Portuguese* ˈportu aˈlɛgri) *n.* a port in S Brazil, capital of the Rio Grande do Sul state: the country's chief inland port; the chief commercial centre of S Brazil, with two universities (1936 and 1948). Pop.: 869 795 (1970).

Por+to+bel+lo (ˌpɔːtəʊˈbɛləʊ) *n.* a small port in Panama, on the Caribbean northeast of Colón: the most important port in South America in colonial times; declined with the opening of the Panama Canal. Pop.: 1980 (1970).

port of call *n.* **1.** any port where a ship stops, excluding its home port. **2.** any place visited on a traveller's itinerary.

port of en+try *n. Law.* an airport, harbour, etc., where customs officials are stationed to supervise the entry into and exit from a country of persons and merchandise.

Port of Spain *n.* the capital and chief port of Trinidad and Tobago, on the W coast of Trinidad. Pop.: 11 032 (1970).

Por+to No·vo (ˈpɔːtəʊ ˈnəʊvəʊ) *n.* the capital of Benin, in the southwest on a coastal lagoon: formerly a centre of Portuguese settlement and the slave trade. Pop.: 104 000 (1975 est.).

Por+to Ri·co (ˈpɔːtə ˈriːkəʊ) *n.* the former name (until 1932) of **Puerto Rico. —Por+to Ri+can** *adj., n.*

Pôr+to Ve+lho (*Portuguese* ˈportu ˈvelju) *n.* a city in W Brazil, capital of the federal territory of Rondônia on the Madeira River. Pop.: 88 856 (1970).

Port Phil+lip Bay *or* **Port Phil+lip** *n.* a bay in SE Australia, which forms the harbour of Melbourne.

por+trait (ˈpɔːtrɪt, -treɪt) *n.* **1. a.** a painting, drawing, sculpture, photograph, or other likeness of an individual, esp. of the face. **b.** (*as modifier*): *a portrait gallery.* **2.** a verbal description or picture, esp. of a person's character. [C16: from French, from *portraire* to PORTRAY]

por+trait+ist (ˈpɔːtrɪtɪst, -treɪ-) *n.* an artist, photographer, etc., who specializes in portraits.

por+trai+ture (ˈpɔːtrɪtʃə) *n.* **1.** the practice or art of making portraits. **2. a.** another term for **portrait** (sense 1). **b.** portraits collectively. **3.** a verbal description.

por+tray (pɔːˈtreɪ) *vb.* (*tr.*) **1.** to represent in a painting, drawing, sculpture, etc.; make a portrait of. **2.** to make a verbal picture of; depict in words. **3.** to play the part of (a character) in a play or film. [C14: from Old French *portraire* to depict, from Latin *prōtrahere* to drag forth, bring to light, from PRO-[1] + *trahere* to drag] **—por+ˈtray+a·ble** *adj.* **—por+ˈtray+al** *n.* **—por+ˈtray+er** *n.*

port+ress (ˈpɔːtrɪs) *n.* a female porter, esp. a doorkeeper.

Port Roy+al *n.* **1.** a fortified town in SE Jamaica, at the entrance to Kingston harbour: capital of Jamaica in colonial times. **2.** the former name (until 1710) of **Annapolis Royal. 3.** (*French* pɔr rwaˈjal) an educational institution about 27 km (17 miles) west of Paris that flourished from 1638 to 1704, when it was suppressed by papal bull as it had become a centre of Jansenism. Its teachers were noted esp. for their work on linguistics: their *Grammaire générale et raisonnée* exercised much influence.

Port Sa·id (ˈsɑːiːd, saɪd) *n.* a port in NE Egypt, at the N end of the Suez Canal: founded in 1859 when the Suez Canal was begun; became the largest coaling station in the world and later an oil-bunkering port; damaged in the Arab–Israeli wars of 1967 and 1973. Pop.: 342 000 (1974 est.).

Port-Sa·lut (ˈpɔː səˈluː; *French* pɔr saˈly) *or* **Port du Sa+lut** *n.* a mild semihard whole-milk cheese of a round flat shape.

Ports+mouth (ˈpɔːtsməθ) *n.* **1.** a port in S England, in Hampshire on the English Channel: Britain's chief naval base. Pop.: 196 973 (1971). Informal name: **Pompey. 2.** a port in SE Virginia, on the Elizabeth River: naval base; shipyards. Pop.: 109 295 (1973 est.).

Port Su+dan *n.* the chief port of the Sudan, in the NE on the Red Sea. Pop.: 110 091 (1971 est.).

Port Tal+bot (ˈtɔːlbət, ˈtæl-) *n.* a port in SE Wales, in West Glamorgan on Swansea Bay: established as a coal port in the mid-19th century; large steelworks; ore terminal. Pop.: 50 658 (1971).

Por+tu+gal (ˈpɔːtjʊgᵊl) *n.* a republic in SW Europe, on the Atlantic: became an independent monarchy in 1139 and expelled the Moors in 1249 after more than four centuries of Muslim rule; became a republic in 1910; under the dictatorship of Salazar from 1932 until 1968, when he was succeeded by Dr. Caetano, who was overthrown by a junta in 1974. Language: Portuguese. Religion: Roman Catholic. Currency: escudo. Capital: Lisbon. Pop.: 8 762 000 (1975 UN est.). Area: 91 530 sq. km (35 340 sq. miles).

Por+tu+guese (ˌpɔːtjʊˈgiːz) *n.* **1.** the official language of Portugal, its overseas territories, and Brazil: the native language of approximately 110 million people. It belongs to the Romance group of the Indo-European family and is derived from the Galician dialect of Vulgar Latin. **2.** (*pl.* **+guese**) a native, citizen, or inhabitant of Portugal. *~adj.* **3.** relating to, denoting, or characteristic of Portugal, its inhabitants, or their language.

Por+tu+guese East Af+ri+ca *n.* a former name (until 1975) of **Mozambique.**

Por+tu+guese Guin·ea *n.* the former name (until 1974) of **Guinea-Bissau. —Por+tu+guese Guin+e·an** *adj., n.*

Por+tu+guese In+di·a *n.* a former Portuguese overseas province on the W coast of India, consisting of Goa, Daman, and Diu: established between 1505 and 1510; annexed by India in 1961.

Por+tu+guese man-of-war *n.* any of several large complex colonial hydrozoans of the genus *Physalia,* esp. *P. physalis,* having an aerial float and long stinging tentacles: order *Siphonophora.* Sometimes shortened to **man-of-war.**

Por+tu+guese Ti+mor *n.* a former Portuguese overseas province in the Malay Archipelago, consisting of the island of Timor, an enclave on the NW coast, and the islands of Ataúro and Jaco.

Por+tu+guese West Af+ri+ca *n.* a former name (until 1975) for **Angola.**

por+tu+lac·a (ˌpɔːtjʊˈlækə, -ˈleɪkə) *n.* any portulacaceous plant of the genus *Portulaca,* such as rose moss and purslane, of tropical and subtropical America, having yellow, pink, or purple showy flowers. [C16: from Latin: PURSLANE]

por+tu+la+ca+ceous (ˌpɔːtjʊləˈkeɪʃəs) *adj.* of, relating to, or belonging to the *Portulacaceae,* a family of fleshy-leaved flowering plants that are common in the U.S.

pos. *abbrev. for:* **1.** position. **2.** positive.

po+sa+da *Spanish.* (poˈsaða) *n., pl.* **+das** (-ðas). an inn in a Spanish-speaking country. [literally: place for stopping]

pose[1] (pəʊz) *vb.* **1.** to assume or cause to assume a physical attitude, as for a photograph or painting. **2.** (*intr.;* often foll. by *as*) to pretend to be or present oneself (as something one is not). **3.** (*intr.*) to affect an attitude or play a part in order to impress others. **4.** (*tr.*) to put forward, ask, or assert: *to pose a question.* *~n.* **5.** a physical attitude, esp. one deliberately adopted for or represented by an artist or photographer. **6.** a mode of behaviour that is adopted for effect. [C14: from Old French *poser* to set in place, from Late Latin *pausāre* to cease, put down (influenced by Latin *pōnere* to place)]

pose[2] (pəʊz) *vb.* (*tr.*) **1.** *Rare.* to puzzle or baffle. **2.** *Archaic.* to question closely. [C16: from obsolete *appose,* from Latin *appōnere* to put to, set against; see OPPOSE]

Po·sei·don (pɒˈsaɪdᵊn) *n. Greek myth.* the god of the sea and of earthquakes; brother of Zeus, Hades, and Hera. He is generally depicted in art wielding a trident. Roman counterpart: **Neptune.**

Po+sen (ˈpoːzᵊn) *n.* the German name for **Poznań.**

pos+er[1] (ˈpəʊzə) *n.* a person who poses.

pos+er[2] (ˈpəʊzə) *n.* a baffling or insoluble question.

po+seur (pəʊˈzɜː) *n.* a person who strikes an attitude or assumes a pose in order to impress others. [C19: from French, from *poser* to POSE[1]]

posh (pɒʃ) *adj. Informal, chiefly Brit.* **1.** smart, elegant, or fashionable; exclusive: *posh clothes.* **2.** upper-class or genteel. *~adv.* **3.** in a manner associated with the upper class: *to talk posh.* [C19: supposedly an acronym of the phrase *port out, starboard home,* the most desirable location for a cabin in British ships sailing to and from the East, being the north-facing or shaded side]

po+sho (ˈpɔʃɔ) *n. E. African.* corn meal. Also called: **ugali.** [from Swahili]

pos+it (ˈpɒzɪt) *vb.* (*tr.*) **1.** to assume or put forward as fact or the factual basis for an argument; postulate. **2.** to put in position. *~n.* **3.** a fact, idea, etc., that is posited; assumption. [C17: from Latin *pōnere* to place, position]

pos+i+tif (ˈpɒsɪtɪf) *n.* (on older organs) a manual controlling soft stops. [from French: positive]

po+si+tion (pəˈzɪʃən) *n.* **1.** the place, situation, or location of a person or thing: *he took up a position to the rear.* **2.** the appropriate or customary location: *the telescope is in position for use.* **3.** the arrangement or disposition of the body or a part of the body: *the corpse was found in a sitting position.* **4.** the manner in which a person or thing is placed; arrangement. **5.** *Military.* an area or point occupied for tactical reasons. **6.** mental attitude; point of view; stand: *what's your position on this issue?* **7.** social status or standing, esp. high social standing. **8.** a post of employment; job. **9.** the act of positing a fact or viewpoint. **10.** something posited, such as an idea, proposition, etc. **11.** *Sport.* the part of a field or playing area where a player is placed or where he generally operates. **12.** *Music.* **a.** the vertical spacing or layout of the written notes in a chord. Chords arranged with the three upper voices close together are in **close position.** Chords whose notes are evenly or widely distributed are in **open position.** See also **root position. b.** one of the points on the fingerboard of a stringed instrument, determining where a string is to be stopped. **13.** (in classical prosody) **a.** the situation in which a short vowel may be regarded as long, that is, when it occurs before two or more consonants. **b. make position.** (of a consonant, either on its own or in combination with other consonants, such as x in Latin) to cause a short vowel to become metrically long when placed after it. **14.** *Finance.* the market commitment of an investor in securities or a trader in commodities: *a long position; a short position.* **15. in a postion.** (foll. by an infinitive) able (to): *I'm not in a position to reveal these figures.* ~*vb.* (*tr.*) **16.** to put in the proper or appropriate place; locate. **17.** *Sport.* to place (oneself or another player) in a particular part of the field or playing area. **18.** *Rare.* to locate or ascertain the position of. [C15: from Late Latin *positiō* a positioning, affirmation, from *pōnere* to place, lay down] —**po'si·tion·al** *adj.*

po·si·tion·al no·ta·tion *n.* the method of denoting numbers by the use of a finite number of digits, each digit having its value multiplied by its place value, as in 936 = (9 × 100) + (3 × 10) + 6.

po·si·tion ef·fect *n.* the effect on the phenotype of interacting genes when their relative positions on the chromosome are altered, as by inversion.

pos·i·tive ('pɒzɪtɪv) *adj.* **1.** characterized by or expressing certainty or affirmation: *a positive answer.* **2.** composed of or possessing actual or specific qualities; real: *a positive benefit.* **3.** tending to emphasize what is good or laudable; constructive: *he takes a very positive attitude when correcting pupils' mistakes.* **4.** tending towards progress or improvement; moving in a beneficial direction. **5.** *Philosophy.* **a.** of or relating to positivism. **b.** constructive rather than sceptical. **6.** independent of circumstances; absolute or unqualified. **7.** (*prenominal*) *Informal.* (intensifier): *a positive delight.* **8.** *Maths.* **a.** having a value greater than zero: *a positive number.* **b.** designating, consisting of, or graduated in one or more quantities greater than zero: *positive direction.* **9.** *Maths.* **a.** measured in a direction opposite to that regarded as negative. **b.** having the same magnitude as but opposite sense to an equivalent negative quantity. **10.** *Grammar.* denoting the usual form of an adjective as opposed to its comparative or superlative form. **11.** *Biology.* indicating movement or growth towards a particular stimulus. **12.** *Physics.* **a.** (of an electric charge) having an opposite polarity to the charge of an electron and the same polarity as the charge of a proton. **b.** (of a body, system, ion, etc.) having a positive electric charge; having a deficiency of electrons: *a positive ion.* **c.** (of a point in an electric circuit) having a higher electric potential than some other point with an assigned zero potential. **13.** short for **electropositive. 14.** (of a lens) capable of causing convergence of a parallel beam of light. **15.** *Med.* (of the results of an examination or test) indicating the existence or presence of a suspected disorder or pathogenic organism. **16.** *Med.* (of the effect of a drug or therapeutic regimen) beneficial or satisfactory. **17.** short for **Rh positive. 18.** (of a machine part) having precise motion with no hysteresis or backlash. **19.** *Chiefly U.S.* (of a government) directly involved in activities beyond the minimum maintenance of law and order, such as social welfare or the organization of scientific research. **20.** *Astrology.* of, relating to, or governed by the group of signs of the zodiac that belong to the air and fire classifications, which are associated with a self-expressive spontaneous nature. ~*n.* **21.** something that is positive. **22.** *Maths.* a quantity greater than zero. **23.** *Photog.* a print or slide showing a photographic image whose colours or tones correspond to those of the original subject. **24.** *Grammar.* the positive degree of an adjective or adverb. **25.** a positive object, such as a terminal or plate in a voltaic cell. **26.** *Music.* **a.** Also called: **positive organ.** a medieval nonportable organ with one manual and no pedals. Compare **portative organ. b.** a variant spelling of **positif.** ~Compare **negative.** [C13: from Late Latin *positīvus* positive, agreed on an arbitrary basis, from *pōnere* to place] —**'pos·i·tive·ness** *n.*

pos·i·tive feed·back *n.* See **feedback** (sense 1).

pos·i·tive·ly ('pɒzɪtɪvlɪ) *adv.* **1.** in a positive manner. **2.** (intensifier): *he disliked her; in fact, he positively hated her.* ~ **3.** *sentence substitute.* unquestionably; absolutely.

pos·i·tive po·lar·i·ty *n. Grammar.* the grammatical characteristic of a word or phrase, such as *delicious* or *rather,* that may normally only be used in a semantically or syntactically positive or affirmative context.

pos·i·tiv·ism ('pɒzɪtɪˌvɪzəm) *n.* **1. a.** a philosophical system that bases knowledge on perception. **b.** the application of this doctrine. See also **logical positivism. 2.** the philosophical system of Auguste Comte, in which the importance of positive science is stressed, esp. that of sociology over religion and metaphysics. **3.** the quality of being definite, certain, etc. —**'pos·i·tiv·ist** *n., adj.* —**ˌpos·i·tiv·'is·tic** *adj.* —**ˌpos·i·tiv·'is·ti·cal·ly** *adv.*

pos·i·tron ('pɒzɪˌtrɒn) *n. Physics.* the antiparticle of the electron, having the same mass and an equal and opposite charge. It is produced in certain decay processes and in pair production, annihilation occurring when it collides with an electron. [C20: from *posi*(*tive* + *elec*)*tron*]

pos·i·tro·ni·um (ˌpɒzɪ'trəʊnɪəm) *n. Physics.* a short-lived entity consisting of a positron and an electron bound together. It decays by annihilation to produce two or three photons.

po·sol·o·gy (pə'sɒlədʒɪ) *n.* the branch of medicine concerned with the determination of appropriate doses of drugs or agents. [C19: from French *posologie,* from Greek *posos* how much]

poss (pɒs) *vb.* (*tr.*) to wash (clothes) by agitating them with a long rod, pole, etc. [of uncertain origin]

poss. *abbrev. for:* **1.** possession. **2.** possessive. **3.** possible. **4.** possibly.

pos·se ('pɒsɪ) *n.* **1.** *U.S.* short for **posse comitatus,** the able-bodied men of a district assembled together and forming a group upon whom the sheriff may call for assistance in maintaining law and order. **2.** *Law.* possibility (esp. in the phrase **in posse**). [C16: from Medieval Latin (*n.*): power, strength, from Latin (vb.): to be able, have power]

pos·se co·mi·ta·tus (ˌkɒmɪ'tɑːtəs) *n.* the formal legal term for **posse** (sense 1). [Medieval Latin: strength (manpower) of the county]

pos·sess (pə'zɛs) *vb.* (*tr.*) **1.** to have as one's property; own. **2.** to have as a quality, faculty, characteristic, etc.: *to possess good eyesight.* **3.** to have knowledge or mastery of: *to possess a little French.* **4.** to gain control over or dominate: *whatever possessed you to act so foolishly?* **5.** (foll. by *of*) to cause to be the owner or possessor: *I am possessed of the necessary information.* **6.** (often foll. by *with*) to cause to be influenced or dominated (by): *the news possessed him with anger.* **7.** to have sexual intercourse with. **8.** *Now rare.* to keep control over or maintain (oneself or one's feelings) in a certain state or condition: *possess yourself in patience until I tell you the news.* **9.** *Archaic.* to gain or seize. [C15: from Old French *possesser,* from Latin *possidēre* to own, occupy; related to Latin *sedēre* to sit] —**pos'ses·sor** *n.*

pos·sessed (pə'zɛst) *adj.* **1.** (foll. by *of*) owning or having. **2.** (*usually postpositive*) under the influence of a powerful force, such as a spirit or strong emotion. **3.** a less common word for **self-possessed.**

pos·ses·sion (pə'zɛʃən) *n.* **1.** the act of possessing or state of being possessed: *in possession of the crown.* **2.** anything that is owned or possessed. **3.** (*pl.*) wealth or property. **4.** the state of being controlled or dominated by or as if by evil spirits. **5.** the physical control or occupancy of land, property, etc., whether or not accompanied by ownership: *to take possession of a house.* **6.** a territory subject to a foreign state or to a sovereign prince: *colonial possessions.* **7.** *Sport.* control of the ball, puck, etc., as exercised by a player or team: *he got possession in his own half.*

pos·ses·sive (pə'zɛsɪv) *adj.* **1.** of or relating to possession or ownership. **2.** having or showing an excessive desire to possess, control, or dominate: *a possessive mother.* **3.** *Grammar.* **a.** another word for **genitive** (sense 1). **b.** denoting an inflected form of a noun or pronoun used to convey the idea of possession, association, etc., as *my* or *Harry's.* ~*n.* **4.** *Grammar.* **a.** the possessive case. **b.** a word or speech element in the possessive case. —**pos'ses·sive·ly** *adv.* —**pos'ses·sive·ness** *n.*

pos·ses·so·ry (pə'zɛsərɪ) *adj.* **1.** of, relating to, or having possession. **2.** *Law.* arising out of, depending upon, or concerned with possession: *a possessory title.*

pos·set ('pɒsɪt) *n.* a drink of hot milk curdled with ale, beer, etc., flavoured with spices, formerly used as a remedy for colds. [C15 *poshoote,* of unknown origin]

pos·si·bil·i·ty (ˌpɒsɪ'bɪlɪtɪ) *n., pl.* **·ties. 1.** the state or condition of being possible. **2.** anything that is possible. **3.** a competitor, candidate, etc., who has a moderately good chance of winning, being chosen, etc. **4.** (*often pl.*) a future prospect or potential: *my new house has great possibilities.*

pos·si·ble ('pɒsɪbᵊl) *adj.* **1.** capable of existing, taking place, or proving true without contravention of any natural law. **2.** capable of being achieved: *it is not possible to finish in three weeks.* **3.** having potential or capabilities for favourable use or development: *the idea is a possible money-spinner.* **4.** that may or may not happen or have happened; feasible but less than probable: *it is possible that man will live on Mars.* ~*n.* **5.** another word for **possibility** (sense 3). [C14: from Latin *possibilis* that may be, from *posse* to be able, have power]

pos·si·bly ('pɒsɪblɪ) *sentence substitute, adv.* **1. a.** perhaps or maybe. **b.** (*as sentence modifier*): *possibly he'll come.* ~*adv.* **2.** by any chance; at all: *he can't possibly come.*

pos·sie *or* **poz·zy** ('pɒzɪ) *n. Austral. informal.* a place; position: *if we're early for the film we'll get a good possie at the back.*

pos·sum ('pɒsəm) *n.* **1.** an informal name for **opossum. 2.** an Austral. and N. Z. name for **phalanger. 3. play possum.** to pretend to be dead, ignorant, asleep, etc., in order to deceive an opponent.

post[1] (pəʊst) *n.* **1.** a length of wood, metal, etc., fixed upright in the ground to serve as a support, marker, point of attachment, etc. **2.** *Horse racing.* **a.** either of two upright poles marking the beginning (**starting post**) and end (**winning post**) of a racecourse. **b.** the finish of a horse race. **3.** any of the main upright supports of a piece of furniture, such as a four-poster bed. ~*vb.* (*tr.*) **4.** (sometimes foll. by *up*) to fasten or put up (a notice) in a public place. **5.** to announce by means of or as if by means of a poster: *to post banns.* **6.** to publish (a name) on a list. **7.** to denounce publicly; brand. [Old English, from Latin *postis;* related to Old High German *first* ridgepole, Greek *pastas* colonnade]

post[2] (pəʊst) *n.* **1.** a position to which a person is appointed or elected; appointment; job. **2.** a position or station to which a person, such as a sentry, is assigned for duty. **3.** a permanent military establishment. **4.** *Brit.* either of two military bugle calls (**first post** and **last post**) ordering or giving notice of the time to retire for the night. **5.** See **trading post** (senses 1, 2). *~vb.* **6.** (*tr.*) to assign to or station at a particular place or position. **7.** *Chiefly Brit.* to transfer to a different unit or ship on taking up a new appointment, etc. [C16: from French *poste,* from Italian *posto,* ultimately from Latin *pōnere* to place]

post[3] (pəʊst) *n.* **1.** *Chiefly Brit.* letters, packages, etc., that are transported and delivered by the Post Office; mail. **2.** *Chiefly Brit.* a single collection or delivery of mail. **3.** *Brit.* an official system of mail delivery. **4.** (formerly) any of a series of stations furnishing relays of men and horses to deliver mail over a fixed route. **5.** a rider who carried mail between such stations. **6.** *Brit.* another word for **pillar box. 7.** *Brit.* short for **post office. 8.** a size of writing or printing paper, 15¼ by 19 inches or 16½ by 21 inches (**large post**). **9.** any of various book sizes, esp. 5¼ by 8¼ inches (**post octavo**) and 8¼ by 10¼ inches (**post quarto**). **10. by return of post.** by the next mail in the opposite direction. *~vb.* **11.** (*tr.*) *Chiefly Brit.* to send by post. U.S. word: **mail. 12.** (*tr.*) *Book-keeping.* **a.** to enter (an item) in a ledger. **b.** (often foll. by *up*) to compile or enter all paper items in (a ledger). **13.** (*tr.*) to inform of the latest news. **14.** (*intr.*) (of a rider) to rise from and reseat oneself in a saddle in time with the motions of a trotting horse; perform a rising trot. **15.** (*intr.*) (formerly) to travel with relays of post horses. **16.** *Archaic.* to travel or dispatch with speed; hasten. *~adv.* **17.** with speed; rapidly. **18.** by means of post horses. [C16: via French from Italian *poste,* from Latin *posita* something placed, from *pōnere* to put, place]

post- *prefix.* **1.** after in time or sequence; following; subsequent: *postgraduate.* **2.** behind; posterior to: *postorbital.* [from Latin, from *post* after, behind]

post+age ('pəʊstɪdʒ) *n.* **a.** the charge for delivering a piece of mail. **b.** (*as modifier*): *postage charges.*

post+age due stamp *n.* a stamp affixed by a Post Office to a letter, parcel, etc., indicating that insufficient or no postage has been prepaid and showing the amount to be paid by the addressee on delivery.

post+age me+ter *n. Chiefly U.S.* a postal franking machine. Also called: **postal meter.**

post+age stamp *n.* **1.** a printed paper label with a gummed back for attaching to mail as an official indication that the required postage has been paid. **2.** a mark directly printed or embossed on an envelope, postcard, etc., serving the same function.

post+al ('pəʊstᵊl) *adj.* of or relating to a Post Office or to the mail-delivery service. **—'post+al+ly** *adv.*

post+al card *n. U.S.* another term for **postcard.**

post+al note *n. Austral.* the usual name for **postal order.**

post+al or+der *n.* a written order for the payment of a sum of money, to a named payee, obtainable and payable at a post office.

post+ax+i+al (pəʊst'æksɪəl) *adj. Anatomy.* **1.** situated or occurring behind the axis of the body. **2.** of or relating to the posterior part of a vertebrate limb.

post+bag ('pəʊstˌbæg) *n.* **1.** *Chiefly Brit.* another name for **mailbag. 2.** the mail received by a magazine, radio programme, public figure, etc.

post-bel·lum ('pəʊst'bɛləm) *adj.* (*prenominal*) of or during the period after a war, esp. the American Civil War. [C19: Latin *post* after + *bellum* war]

post+box ('pəʊstˌbɒks) *n. Chiefly Brit.* a box into which mail is put for collection by the postal service.

post+boy ('pəʊstˌbɔɪ) *n.* **1.** another name for **postilion. 2.** *Obsolete.* a man or boy who rode with the post.

post+card ('pəʊstˌkɑːd) *n.* a card, often bearing a photograph, picture, etc., on one side, (**picture postcard**), for sending a message by post without an envelope. Also called (U.S.): **postal card.**

post+ca+va (pəʊst'kɑːvə, -'keɪvə) *n. Anatomy.* the inferior vena cava. [C19: New Latin; see POST-, VENA CAVA] **—post+'ca+val** *adj.*

post chaise *n.* a closed four-wheeled horse-drawn coach used as a rapid means for transporting mail and passengers in the 18th and 19th centuries. [C18: from POST³ + CHAISE]

post+code ('pəʊstˌkəʊd) *n. Brit.* a code of letters and digits used as part of a postal address to aid the sorting of mail. Also called: **postal code.** U.S. equivalent: **zip code.**

post-cy·clic *adj. Transformational grammar.* denoting rules that apply only after the transformations of a whole cycle. Compare **cyclic** (sense 6), **last-cyclic.**

post+date (pəʊst'deɪt) *vb.* (*tr.*) **1.** to write a future date on (a document, etc.), as on a cheque to prevent it being paid until then. **2.** to assign a date to (an event, period, etc.) that is later than its previously assigned date of occurrence. **3.** to be or occur at a later date than.

post+di+lu+vi·an (ˌpəʊstdɪ'luːvɪən, -daɪ-) *adj. also* **post+di+lu+vi·al. 1.** existing or occurring after the biblical Flood. *~n.* **2.** a person or thing existing after the biblical Flood. [C17: from POST- + *diluvian,* from Latin *diluvium* deluge, flood]

post+doc+tor+al (pəʊst'dɒktərəl) *adj.* of, relating to, or designating studies, research, or professional work above the level of a doctorate.

post+er ('pəʊstə) *n.* **1.** a placard or bill posted in a public place as an advertisement. **2.** a person who posts bills.

poste res+tante ('pəʊst rɪ'stænt; *French* pɔst rɛs'tɑ̃ːt) *n.* **1.** (not in the U.S. and Canada) an address on mail indicating that it should be kept at a specified post office until collected by the addressee. **2.** the mail-delivery service or post-office department that handles mail having this address. ~U.S. and Canadian equivalent: **general delivery.** [French, literally: mail remaining]

pos+te·ri+or (pɒ'stɪərɪə) *adj.* **1.** situated at the back of or behind something. **2.** coming after or following another in a series. **3.** coming after in time. **4.** *Zoology.* (of lower animals) of or near the hind end. **5.** *Botany.* (of a flower) situated nearest to the main stem. **6.** *Anatomy.* dorsal or towards the spine. ~Compare **anterior.** *~n.* **7.** the buttocks; rump. [C16: from Latin: latter, from *posterus* coming next, from *post* after] **—pos+'te·ri+or+ly** *adv.*

pos+ter+i·ty (pɒ'stɛrɪtɪ) *n.* **1.** future or succeeding generations. **2.** all of one's descendants. [C14: from French *postérité,* from Latin *posteritās* future generations, from *posterus* coming after, from *post* after]

pos+tern ('pɒstən) *n.* **1.** a back door or gate, esp. one that is for private use. *~adj.* **2.** situated at the rear or the side. [C13: from Old French *posterne,* from Late Latin *posterula* (*jānua*) a back (entrance), from *posterus* coming behind; see POSTERIOR, POSTERITY]

post+er paint *or* **col+our** *n.* a gum-based opaque watercolour paint used for writing posters, etc.

post ex+change *n. U.S.* a government-subsidized shop operated mainly for military personnel. Abbrev.: **PX**

post+ex+il+i·an (ˌpəʊstɪg'zɪlɪən) *or* **post+ex+il+ic** *adj. Old Testament.* existing or occurring after the Babylonian exile of the Jews (587–539 B.C.).

post+fix *vb.* (pəʊst'fɪks). **1.** (*tr.*) to add or append at the end of something; suffix. *~n.* ('pəʊstˌfɪks). **2.** a less common word for **suffix.**

post-free *adv., adj.* **1.** *Brit.* with the postage prepaid; post-paid. **2.** free of postal charge.

post+gla+ci·al (pəʊst'gleɪsɪəl) *adj.* formed or occurring after a glacial period, esp. after the Pleistocene epoch.

post+grad·u·ate (pəʊst'grædjʊɪt) *n.* **1.** a student who has obtained a degree from a university, etc., and is pursuing studies for a more advanced qualification. **2.** (*modifier*) of or relating to such a student or to his studies. ~Also (U.S.): **graduate.**

post+haste ('pəʊst'heɪst) *adv.* **1.** with great haste; as fast as possible. *~n.* **2.** *Archaic.* great haste.

post hoc ('pəʊst 'hɒk) *n. Logic.* the fallacy of assuming that temporal succession is evidence of causal relation. [from Latin, short for *Post hoc ergo propter hoc* after this, therefore on account of this]

post horn *n.* a simple valveless natural horn consisting of a long tube of brass or copper, either straight or coiled.

post horse *n.* (formerly) a horse kept at an inn or post house for use by postriders or for hire to travellers.

post house *n.* (formerly) a house or inn where horses were kept for postriders or for hire to travellers.

post+hu+mous ('pɒstjʊməs) *adj.* **1.** happening or continuing after one's death. **2.** (of a book, etc.) published after the author's death. **3.** (of a child) born after the father's death. [C17: from Latin *postumus* the last, but modified as though from Latin *post* after + *humus* earth, that is, after the burial] **—'post+hu+mous+ly** *adv.*

post+hyp+not+ic sug+ges+tion (ˌpəʊsthɪp'nɒtɪk) *n.* a suggestion made to the subject while in a hypnotic trance, to be acted upon at some time after emerging from the trance.

pos+tiche (pɒ'stiːʃ) *adj.* **1.** (of architectural ornament) inappropriately applied; sham. **2.** false or artificial; spurious. *~n.* **3.** another term for **hairpiece. 4.** an imitation, counterfeit, or substitute. **5.** anything that is false; sham or pretence. [C19: from French, from Italian *apposticcio* (n.), from Late Latin *appositīcius* (adj.); see APPOSITE]

pos+ti+cous (pɒ'stiːkəs, -'staɪ-) *adj.* (of the position of plant parts) behind another part; posterior. [C19: from Latin *postīcus* that is behind, from *post* after]

post·ie ('pəʊstɪ) *n. Austral. informal.* a postman.

pos+til ('pɒstɪl) *n.* **1.** a commentary or marginal note, as in a Bible. **2.** a homily or collection of homilies. *~vb.* **+tils, +til+ing, +tiled** *or* **+tils, +til+ling, +tilled. 3.** *Obsolete.* to annotate (a biblical passage). [C15 (*postille*): from Old French *postille* from Medieval Latin *postilla,* perhaps from *post illa* (*verba textus*), after these words in the text, often the opening phrase of such an annotation]

pos+til+ion *or* **pos+til+lion** (pɒ'stɪljən) *n.* a person who rides the near horse of the leaders in order to guide a team of horses drawing a coach. [C16: from French *postillon,* from Italian *postiglione,* from *posta* POST³]

post+im+pres+sion+ism (ˌpəʊstɪm'prɛʃəˌnɪzəm) *n.* a movement in painting in France at the end of the 19th century, begun by Cézanne and exemplified by Gauguin, Van Gogh, and Matisse, which rejected the naturalism and momentary effects of impressionism but adapted its use of pure colour to paint

---

post+'a·nal *adj.*
ˌpost-Ar·is·to+'te·li·an *adj.*
ˌpost-Au·'gus·tan *adj.*
post-'Cam·bri·an *adj.*
ˌpost-Car·bon+'if·er+ous *adj.*
ˌpost-Car·o·'lin+gi·an *adj.*
ˌpost-Car·'te·sian *adj.*
post+'clas+si·cal *adj.*
post+'coit+al *adj.*
ˌpost+con+so+'nan+tal *adj.*
ˌpost+con+va+'les+cent *adj.*
ˌpost-Co·'per·ni·can *adj.*
ˌpost-Dar·'win·i·an *adj.*
ˌpost+de+ˌvel+op+'men+tal *adj.*
ˌpost-De·'vo·ni·an *adj.*
ˌpost+di+ag+'nos+tic *adj.*
ˌpost+di+'ges+tive *adj.*
ˌpost+e·'lec+tion *adj.*
post-'E·o·cene *adj.*
ˌpost+hyp+'not+ic *adj.*

subjects with greater subjective emotion. —ˌ**post·im·'pres·sion·ist** *n., adj.* —ˌ**post·im·ˌpres·sion·'ist·ic** *adj.*

post·ing[1] ('pəʊstɪŋ) *n.* a wrestling attack in which the opponent is hurled at the post in one of the corners of the ring.

post·ing[2] ('pəʊstɪŋ) *n.* an appointment to a position or post.

post·lim·i·ny (pəʊst'lɪmɪnɪ) *or* **post·li·min·i·um** (ˌpəʊstlɪ'mɪnɪəm) *n., pl.* **·i·nies** *or* **·i·a** (-ɪə). *International law.* the right by which persons and property seized in war are restored to their former status on recovery.

post·lude ('pəʊstlu:d) *n.* **1.** *Music.* a final or concluding piece or movement. **2.** a voluntary played at the end of a Church service. [C19: from POST- + *-lude,* from Latin *lūdus* game; compare PRELUDE]

post·man ('pəʊstmən) *or (fem.)* **post·wom·an** *n., pl.* **·men** *or* **·wom·en.** a person who carries and delivers mail as a profession.

post·mark ('pəʊstˌmɑ:k) *n.* any mark stamped on mail by postal officials, such as a simple obliteration, date mark, or indication of route. See also **cancellation.**

post·mas·ter ('pəʊstˌmɑ:stə) *or (fem.)* **post·mis·tress** *n.* an official in charge of a local post office.

post·mas·ter gen·er·al *n., pl.* **post·mas·ters gen·er·al.** the executive head of the postal service in certain countries.

post·me·rid·i·an (ˌpəʊstmə'rɪdɪən) *adj.* after noon; in the afternoon or evening. [C17: from Latin *postmerīdiānus* in the afternoon; see POST-, MERIDIAN]

post me·rid·i·em ('pəʊst mə'rɪdɪəm) the full form of **p.m.** [C17: Latin: after noon]

post·mil·len·ni·al (ˌpəʊstmɪ'lɛnɪəl) *adj.* existing or taking place after the millenium.

post·mil·len·ni·al·ism (ˌpəʊstmɪ'lɛnɪəˌlɪzəm) *n. Theol.* the doctrine or belief that the Second Coming of Christ will be preceded by the millenium. —ˌ**post·mil·'len·ni·al·ist** *n.*

post·mor·tem (pəʊst'mɔ:təm) *adj.* **1.** *(prenominal)* occurring after death. *~n.* **2.** analysis or study of a recently completed event: *a postmortem on a game of chess.* **3.** See **postmortem examination.** [C18: from Latin, literally: after death]

post·mor·tem ex·am·i·na·tion *n.* dissection and examination of a dead body to determine the cause of death. Also called: **autopsy, necropsy.**

post·na·sal drip (pəʊst'neɪzᵊl) *n. Med.* a mucus secretion from the rear part of the nasal cavity into the nasopharynx, usually as the result of a cold or an allergy.

post-o·bit (pəʊst'əʊbɪt, -'ɒbɪt) *Chiefly law.* *~n.* **1.** Also called: **post-obit bond.** a bond given by a borrower, payable after the death of a specified person, esp. one given to a moneylender by an expectant heir promising to repay when his interest falls into possession. *~adj.* **2.** taking effect after death. [C18: from Latin *post obitum* after death]

post of·fice *n.* a building or room where postage stamps are sold and other postal business is conducted.

Post Of·fice *n.* a government department or authority in many countries responsible for postal services and often telecommunications.

post of·fice box *n.* a private numbered place in a post office, in which letters received are kept until called for.

post·op·er·a·tive (pəʊst'ɒpərətɪv, -'ɒprətɪv) *adj.* of, relating to, or occurring in the period following a surgical operation. —**post·'op·er·a·tive·ly** *adv.*

post·or·bit·al (pəʊst'ɔ:bɪtᵊl) *adj. Anatomy.* situated behind the eye or the eye socket.

post paid ('pəʊst'peɪd) *adv., adj.* with the postage prepaid.

post·par·tum (pəʊst'pɑ:təm) *adj. Med.* following childbirth. [Latin: after the act of giving birth]

post·pone (pəʊst'pəʊn, pə'spəʊn) *vb. (tr.)* **1.** to put off or delay until a future time. **2.** to put behind in order of importance; defer. [C16: from Latin *postpōnere* to put after, neglect, from POST- + *ponere* to place] —**post·'pon·a·ble** *adj.* —**post·'pone·ment** *n.* —**post·'pon·er** *n.*

post·po·si·tion (ˌpəʊstpə'zɪʃən) *n.* **1.** placement of a modifier or other speech element after the word that it modifies or to which it is syntactically related. **2.** a word or speech element so placed. —ˌ**post·po·'si·tion·al** *adj.* —ˌ**post·po·'si·tion·al·ly** *adv.*

post·pos·i·tive (pəʊst'pɒzɪtɪv) *adj.* **1.** (of an adjective or other modifier) placed after the word modified, either immediately after, as in *two men abreast,* or as part of a complement, as in *those men are bad.* *~n.* **2.** a postpositive modifier. —**post·'pos·i·tive·ly** *adv.*

post·rid·er ('pəʊstˌraɪdə) *n.* (formerly) a person who delivered post on horseback.

post road *n.* a road or route over which post is carried and along which post houses were formerly sited.

post·script ('pəʊsˌskrɪpt) *n.* **1.** a message added at the end of a letter, after the signature. **2.** any supplement, as to a document or book. [C16: from Late Latin *postscribere* to write after, from POST- + *scribere* to write]

post town *n.* a town having a main Post Office branch.

pos·tu·lant ('pɒstjʊlənt) *n.* **1.** a person who makes a request or application. **2.** a candidate for admission to a religious order. [C18: from Latin *postulāns* asking, from *postulāre* to ask, demand] —'**pos·tu·lan·cy** *or* '**pos·tu·lant·ˌship** *n.*

pos·tu·late *vb.* ('pɒstjʊˌleɪt). *(tr.; may take a clause as object)* **1.** to assume to be true or existent; take for granted. **2.** to ask, demand, or claim. **3.** to nominate (a person) to a post or office subject to approval by a higher authority. *~n.* ('pɒstjʊlɪt). **4.** something taken as self-evident or assumed as the basis of an argument. **5.** a necessary condition or prerequisite. **6.** a fundamental principle. **7.** *Logic, maths.* an unproved and indemonstrable statement that should be taken for granted: used as an initial premiss or underlying hypothesis in a process of reasoning. [C16: from Latin *postulāre* to ask for, require; related to *pōscere* to request] —ˌ**pos·tu·'la·tion** *n.*

pos·tu·la·tor ('pɒstjʊˌleɪtə) *n. R.C. Church.* a person, usually a priest, deputed to prepare and present a plea for the beatification or canonization of some deceased person.

pos·ture ('pɒstʃə) *n.* **1.** a position or attitude of the limbs or body. **2.** a characteristic manner of bearing the body; carriage: *to have good posture.* **3.** the disposition of the parts of a visible object. **4.** a mental attitude or frame of mind. **5.** a state, situation, or condition. **6.** a false or affected attitude; pose. *~vb.* **7.** to assume or cause to assume a bodily position or attitude. **8.** *(intr.)* to assume an affected or unnatural bodily or mental posture; pose. [C17: via French from Italian *postura,* from Latin *positūra,* from *pōnere* to place] —'**pos·tur·al** *adj.* —'**pos·tur·er** *n.*

pos·tur·ize *or* **pos·tur·ise** ('pɒstʃəˌraɪz) *vb.* a less common word for **posture** (senses 7, 8).

po·sy ('pəʊzɪ) *n., pl.* **·sies.** **1.** a small bunch of flowers or a single flower; nosegay. **2.** *Archaic.* a brief motto or inscription, esp. one on a trinket or a ring. [C16: variant of POESY]

pot[1] (pɒt) *n.* **1.** a container made of earthenware, glass, or similar material; usually round and deep, often having a handle and lid, used for cooking and other domestic purposes. **2.** the amount that a pot will hold; potful. **3.** a large mug or tankard, as for beer. **4.** *Austral.* any of various measures used for serving beer. **5.** the money or stakes in the pool in gambling games, esp. poker. **6.** a wicker trap for catching fish, esp. crustaceans: *a lobster pot.* **7.** *Billiards, etc.* a shot by which a ball is pocketed. **8.** *Chiefly Brit.* short for **chimneypot. 9.** *U.S. informal.* a joint fund created by a group of individuals or enterprises and drawn upon by them for specified purposes. **10.** *Hunting.* See **pot shot. 11.** See **chamber pot. 12.** See **potbelly. 13. go to pot.** to go to ruin; deteriorate. *~vb.* **pots, pot·ting, pot·ted.** *(mainly tr.)* **14.** to put or preserve (goods, meat, etc.) in a pot. **15.** to cook (food) in a pot. **16.** to shoot (game) for food rather than for sport. **17.** to shoot (game birds or animals) while they are on the ground or immobile rather than flying or running. **18.** *(also intr.)* to shoot casually or without careful aim at (an animal, etc.). **19.** *Billiards, etc.* to pocket (a ball). **20.** *Informal.* to capture or win; secure. [Late Old English *pott,* from Medieval Latin *pottus* (unattested), perhaps from Latin *pōtus* a drink; compare Middle Low German *pot,* Old Norse *pottr*]

pot[2] (pɒt) *n.* **a.** *Northern Brit. dialect.* a deep hole or pothole. **b.** *(cap. when part of a name): Pen-y-Ghent Pot.* [C14: perhaps identical with POT[1] but possibly of Scandinavian origin; compare Swedish dialect *putt* water hole, pit]

pot[3] (pɒt) *n. Slang.* cannabis used as a drug in any form, such as leaves (marijuana or hemp) or resin (hashish). [C20: perhaps shortened from Mexican Indian *potiguaya*]

pot[4] (pɒt) *n. Informal.* short for **potentiometer.**

pot. *abbrev. for* potential.

po·ta·ble ('pəʊtəbᵊl) *adj.* **1.** a less common word for **drinkable.** *~n.* **2.** something fit to drink; a beverage. [C16: from Late Latin *pōtābilis* drinkable, from Latin *pōtāre* to drink] —ˌ**po·ta·'bil·i·ty** *or* '**po·ta·ble·ness** *n.*

po·tage *French.* (pɔ'ta:ʒ; *English* pəʊ'tɑ:ʒ) *n.* any thick soup. [C16: from Old French; see POTTAGE]

po·tam·ic (pə'tæmɪk) *adj.* of or relating to rivers. [C19: from Greek *potamos* river]

po·ta·mol·o·gy (ˌpɒtə'mɒlədʒɪ) *n.* the scientific study of rivers. [C19: from Greek *potamos* river + -LOGY]

pot·ash ('pɒtˌæʃ) *n.* **1.** another name for **potassium carbonate,** esp. the form obtained by leaching wood ash. **2.** another name for **potassium hydroxide. 3.** potassium chemically combined in certain compounds: *chloride of potash.* [C17 *pot ashes,* translation of obsolete Dutch *potaschen;* so called because originally obtained by evaporating the lye of wood ashes in pots]

pot·ash al·um *n.* the full name for **alum** (sense 1).

po·tas·si·um (pə'tæsɪəm) *n.* a light silvery element of the alkali metal group that is highly reactive and rapidly oxidizes in air; occurs principally in carnallite and sylvite. It is used when alloyed with sodium as a cooling medium in nuclear reactors and its compounds are widely used, esp. in fertilizers. Symbol: K; atomic no.: 19; atomic wt.: 39.102; valency: 1; relative

---

ˌ**post-Ju·'ras·sic** *adj.*
post-'Kan·ti·an *adj.*
post-'Marx·i·an *adj.*
ˌ**post·men·o·'pau·sal** *adj.*
post·'men·stru·al *adj.*
ˌ**post-Mes·o·'zo·ic** *adj.*
post-'Mi·o·ˌcene *adj.*
ˌ**post-Mo·'sa·ic** *adj.*
ˌ**post-My·'ce·nae·an** *adj.*
ˌ**post-Na·ˌpo·le·'on·ic** *adj.*
post·'na·sal *adj.*
post·'na·tal *adj.*
ˌ**post-New·'to·ni·an** *adj.*
post·'nup·tial *adj.*
post-'Ol·i·go·ˌcene *adj.*
post·'o·ral *adj.*
ˌ**post-Or·do·'vi·cian** *adj.*
ˌ**post-Pa·le·o·'zo·ic** *adj.*
post-'Paul·ine *adj.*
post-'Per·mi·an *adj.*
ˌ**post·pi·'tu·i·ˌtar·y** *adj.*
post-'Pleis·to·ˌcene *adj.*
post-'Pli·o·ˌcene *adj.*
post·'pran·di·al *adj.*
ˌ**post-Ref·or·'ma·tion** *adj.*
ˌ**post-Rev·o·'lu·tion·ˌar·y** *adj.*
post·'sea·son *adj.*
post·'sea·son·al *adj.*
ˌ**post-Si·'lu·ri·an** *adj.*
ˌ**post-So·'crat·ic** *adj.*
ˌ**post-Tal·'mud·ic** *adj.*
post-'Ter·ti·ˌar·y *adj.*
ˌ**post-Tri·'as·sic** *adj.*
post-'Ved·ic *adj.*
ˌ**post-Vic·'to·ri·an** *adj.*
'**post·war** *adj.*

density: 0.86; melting pt.: 63.65°C; boiling pt.: 774°C. [C19: New Latin *potassa* potash] —**po·'tas·sic** *adj.*

po·tas·si·um-ar·gon dat·ing *n.* a technique for determining the age of minerals based on the occurrence in natural potassium of a small fixed amount of radioisotope ^{40}K that decays to the stable argon isotope ^{40}Ar with a half-life of 1.28×10^9 years. Measurement of the ratio of these isotopes thus gives the age of the mineral. Compare **radiocarbon dating, rubidium-strontium dating.**

po·tas·si·um bi·tar·trate *n.* another name (not in technical usage) for **potassium hydrogen tartrate.**

po·tas·si·um bro·mide *n.* a white crystalline soluble substance with a bitter saline taste used in making photographic papers and plates and in medicine as a sedative. Formula: KBr.

po·tas·si·um car·bon·ate *n.* a white odourless substance used in making glass and soft soap and as an alkaline cleansing agent. Formula: K_2CO_3.

po·tas·si·um chlo·rate *n.* a white crystalline soluble substance used in fireworks, matches, and explosives, and as a disinfectant and bleaching agent. Formula: $KClO_3$.

po·tas·si·um cy·a·nide *n.* a white poisonous granular soluble solid substance used in photography and in extracting gold from its ores. Formula: KCN.

po·tas·si·um di·chro·mate *n.* an orange-red crystalline soluble solid substance that is a good oxidizing agent and is used in making chrome pigments and as a bleaching agent. Formula: $K_2Cr_2O_7$.

po·tas·si·um fer·ri·cy·a·nide *n.* a bright red soluble crystalline substance used in making dyes, pigments, and light-sensitive paper. Formula: $K_3Fe(CN)_6$. Also called: **red prussiate of potash.**

po·tas·si·um fer·ro·cy·a·nide *n.* a yellow soluble crystalline compound used in case-hardening steel and making dyes and pigments. Formula: $K_4Fe(CN)_6$. Also called: **yellow prussiate of potash.**

po·tas·si·um hy·dro·gen tar·trate *n.* a colourless or white soluble crystalline salt used in baking powders, soldering fluxes, and laxatives. Formula: $KHC_4H_4O_6$. Also called (not in technical usage): **potassium bitartrate, cream of tartar.**

po·tas·si·um hy·drox·ide *n.* a white deliquescent alkaline solid used in the manufacture of soap, liquid shampoos, and detergents. Formula: KOH. Also called: **caustic potash.** See also **lye.**

po·tas·si·um ni·trate *n.* a colourless or white crystalline compound used in gunpowders, pyrotechnics, fertilizers, and as a preservative. Formula: KNO_3. Also called: **saltpetre, nitre.**

po·tas·si·um per·man·ga·nate *n.* a dark purple poisonous odourless soluble crystalline solid, used as a bleach, disinfectant, and antiseptic. Formula: $KMnO_4$.

po·tas·si·um sul·phate *n.* a soluble substance usually obtained as colourless crystals of the decahydrate: used in making glass and as a fertilizer. Formula: K_2SO_4.

po·ta·tion (pəʊ'teɪʃən) *n.* **1.** the act of drinking. **2.** a drink or draught, esp. of alcoholic drink. [C15: from Latin *pōtātiō* a drinking, from *pōtāre* to drink]

po·ta·to (pə'teɪtəʊ) *n., pl.* **·toes. 1.** Also called: **Irish potato, white potato. a.** a solanaceous plant, *Solanum tuberosum*, of South America: widely cultivated for its edible tubers. **b.** the starchy oval tuber of this plant, which has a brown or red skin and is cooked and eaten as a vegetable. **2.** any of various similar plants, esp. the sweet potato. **3. hot potato.** *Slang.* a delicate or awkward matter. [C16: from Spanish *patata* white potato, from Taino *batata* sweet potato]

po·ta·to bee·tle *n.* another name for the **Colorado beetle.**

po·ta·to chip *n.* **1.** (*usually pl.*) another name for **chip** (sense 4). **2.** (*usually pl.*) the U.S. term for **crisp** (sense 10).

po·ta·to crisp *n.* (*usually pl.*) another name for crisp (sense 10).

po·ta·to·ry ('pəʊtətərɪ, -trɪ) *adj. Rare.* of, relating to, or given to drinking. [C19: from Late Latin *pōtātōrius* concerning drinking, from Latin *pōtāre* to drink]

pot-au-feu (*French* poto'fø) *n.* **1.** a traditional French stew of beef and vegetables. **2.** the large earthenware casserole in which this is cooked. [literally: pot on the fire]

pot·bel·ly ('pɒt,bɛlɪ) *n., pl.* **·lies. 1.** a protruding or distended belly. **2.** a person having such a belly. **3.** *U.S.* a small bulbous stove in which wood or coal is burned. —**'pot·,bel·lied** *adj.*

pot·boil·er ('pɒt,bɔɪlə) *n. Informal.* a literary or artistic work of little merit produced quickly in order to make money.

pot-bound *adj.* (of a pot plant) having grown to fill all the available root space, resulting in retarded growth of the aerial parts.

pot·boy ('pɒt,bɔɪ) *or* **pot·man** ('pɒtmən) *n., pl.* **·boys** *or* **·men.** *Chiefly Brit.* (esp. formerly) a youth or man employed at a public house to serve beer, etc.

potch (pɒtʃ) *n. Chiefly Austral., slang.* inferior quality opal used in jewellery for mounting precious opals. [C20: of uncertain origin]

pot cheese *n. U.S.* a type of coarse dry cottage cheese.

po·teen (pɒ'ti:n) *n.* (in Ireland) illicit spirit, often distilled from potatoes. [C19: from Irish *poitīn* little pot, from *pota* pot]

Po·tem·kin *or* **Po·tyom·kin** (pɒ'tɛmkɪn; *Russian* pa'tjɔmkin) *n.* **Gri·go·ri A·le·ksan·dro·vich** (gri'gɔrij alɪ'ksandrəvitʃ). 1739–91, Russian soldier and statesman; lover of Catherine II, whose favourite he remained until his death.

po·ten·cy ('pəʊtᵊnsɪ) *or* **po·tence** *n., pl.* **·ten·cies** *or* **·tenc·es. 1.** the state or quality of being potent. **2.** latent or inherent capacity for growth or development. [C16: from Latin *potentia* power, from *posse* to be able]

po·tent[1] ('pəʊtᵊnt) *adj.* **1.** possessing great strength; powerful. **2.** (of arguments, etc.) persuasive or forceful. **3.** influential or authoritative. **4.** tending to produce violent physical or chemical effects: *a potent poison.* **5.** (of a male) capable of having sexual intercourse. [C15: from Latin *potēns* able, from *posse* to be able] —**'po·tent·ly** *adv.* —**'po·tent·ness** *n.*

po·tent[2] ('pəʊtᵊnt) *adj. Heraldry.* (of a cross) having flat bars across the ends of the arms. [C17: from obsolete *potent* a crutch, from Latin *potentia* power]

po·ten·tate ('pəʊtᵊn,teɪt) *n.* a man who possesses great power or authority, esp. a ruler or monarch. [C14: from Late Latin *potentātus* ruler, from Latin: rule, command, from *potens* powerful, from *posse* to be able]

po·ten·tial (pə'tɛnʃəl) *adj.* **1. a.** possible but not yet actual. **b.** (*prenominal*) capable of being or becoming but not yet in existence; latent. **2.** *Grammar.* (of a verb or form of a verb) expressing possibility, as English *may* and *might.* **3.** an archaic word for **potent.** ~*n.* **4.** latent but unrealized ability or capacity: *Jones has great potential as a sales manager.* **5.** *Grammar.* a potential verb or verb form. **6.** short for **electric potential.** [C14: from Old French *potencial*, from Late Latin *potentiālis*, from Latin *potentia* power] —**po·'ten·tial·ly** *adv.*

po·ten·tial dif·fer·ence *n.* the difference in electric potential between two points in an electric field; the work that has to be done in transferring unit positive charge from one point to the other, measured in volts. Abbrev.: **p.d.** Symbol: U, ΔV, or $\Delta\phi$ Compare **electromotive force.**

po·ten·tial di·vid·er *n.* a tapped or variable resistor or a chain of fixed resistors in series, connected across a source of voltage and used to obtain a desired fraction of the total voltage. Also called: **voltage divider.**

po·ten·tial en·er·gy *n.* the energy of a body or system as a result of its position in an electric, magnetic, or gravitational field. It is measured in joules (SI units), electronvolts, ergs, etc. Symbol: E_p, V, U, or ϕ Abbrev.: **P.E.**

po·ten·ti·al·i·ty (pə,tɛnʃɪ'ælɪtɪ) *n., pl.* **·ties. 1.** latent or inherent capacity or ability for growth, fulfilment, etc. **2.** a person or thing that possesses such a capacity.

po·ten·ti·ate (pə'tɛnʃɪ,eɪt) *vb.* (*tr.*) **1.** to cause to be potent. **2.** *Med.* to increase (the individual action or effectiveness) of two drugs by administering them in combination with each other.

po·ten·til·la (,pəʊtᵊn'tɪlə) *n.* any rosaceous plant or shrub of the N temperate genus *Potentilla*, having five-petalled flowers. See also **cinquefoil** (sense 1), **silverweed** (sense 1), **tormentil.** [C16: New Latin, from Medieval Latin: garden valerian, from Latin *potēns* powerful, POTENT[1]]

po·ten·ti·om·e·ter (pə,tɛnʃɪ'ɒmɪtə) *n.* **1.** an instrument for determining a potential difference or electromotive force by measuring the fraction of it that balances a standard electromotive force. **2.** a type of rheostat, usually with three terminals, two of which are connected to a resistance wire and the third to a brush moving along the wire, so that a variable potential can be tapped off: used in electronic circuits, esp. as volume controls. Sometimes shortened to **pot.** —**po·,ten·ti·'om·e·try** *n.*

pot·ful ('pɒt,fʊl) *n.* the amount held by a pot.

pot·head ('pɒt,hɛd) *n. Slang.* a habitual user of cannabis.

poth·e·car·y ('pɒθɪkərɪ) *n., pl.* **·car·ies.** an archaic or Brit. dialect variant of **apothecary.**

po·theen (pɒ'θi:n) *n.* a rare variant of **poteen.**

poth·er ('pɒðə) *n.* **1.** a commotion, fuss, or disturbance. **2.** a choking cloud of smoke, dust, etc. ~*vb.* **3.** to make or be troubled or upset. [C16: of unknown origin]

pot·herb ('pɒt,hɜ:b) *n.* any plant having leaves, flowers, stems, etc., that are used in cooking for seasoning and flavouring or are eaten as a vegetable.

pot·hole ('pɒt,həʊl) *n.* **1.** *Geography.* **a.** a deep hole in limestone areas resulting from action by running water. See also **sinkhole** (sense 1). **b.** a circular hole in the bed of a river produced by abrasion. **2.** a deep hole, esp. one produced in a road surface by wear or weathering.

pot·hol·ing ('pɒt,həʊlɪŋ) *n. Brit.* a sport in which participants explore underground caves. —**'pot·,hol·er** *n.*

pot·hook ('pɒt,hʊk) *n.* **1.** a curved or S-shaped hook used for suspending a pot over a fire. **2.** a long hook used for lifting hot pots, lids, etc. **3.** an S-shaped mark, often made by children when learning to write.

pot·house ('pɒt,haʊs) *n. Brit.* (formerly) a small tavern or pub.

pot·hunt·er ('pɒt,hʌntə) *n.* **1.** a person who hunts for food or for profit without regard to the rules of sport. **2.** *Informal.* a person who enters competitions for the sole purpose of winning prizes. —**'pot·,hunt·ing** *n., adj.*

po·tiche (pɒ'ti:ʃ) *n., pl.* **·tich·es** (-'ti:ʃɪz, -'ti:ʃ). a tall vase or jar, as of porcelain, with a round or polygonal body that narrows towards the neck and a detached lid or cover. [French, from *pot* pot; compare POTTAGE]

po·tion ('pəʊʃən) *n.* **1.** a drink, esp. of medicine, poison, or some supposedly magic beverage. **2.** a rare word for **beverage.** [C13: via Old French from Latin *pōtiō* a drink, especially a poisonous one, from *pōtāre* to drink]

Pot·i·phar ('pɒtɪfə) *n. Old Testament.* one of Pharaoh's officers, who bought Joseph as a slave (Genesis 37:36).

pot·latch ('pɒt,lætʃ) *n.* **1.** *Anthropol.* a competitive ceremonial activity among certain North American Indians, esp. the Kwakiutl, involving a lavish distribution of gifts and the destruction of property to emphasize the wealth and status of the chief or clan. **2.** *U.S. informal.* a wild party or revel. [C19: from Chinook, from Nootka *patshatl* a giving, present]

pot liq·uor *n. Chiefly U.S.* the broth in which meat, esp. pork or bacon, and vegetables have been cooked.

pot·luck ('pɒt'lʌk) *n. Informal.* **1.** whatever food happens to be available without special preparation. **2.** a choice dictated by lack of alternative (esp. in the phrase **take potluck**).

pot·man ('pɒtmən) *n., pl.* ·**men.** *Chiefly Brit.* another word for **potboy.**

pot mar·i·gold *n.* a Central European and Mediterranean plant, *Calendula officinalis,* grown for its rayed orange-and-yellow showy flowers: family *Compositae* (composites). See also **calendula.**

Po·to·mac (pə'təʊmək) *n.* a river in the E central U.S., rising in the Appalachian Mountains of West Virginia: flows northeast, then generally southeast to Chesapeake Bay. Length (from the confluence of headstreams): 462 km (287 miles).

pot·o·roo (ˌpɒtə'ru:) *n.* another name for **kangaroo rat.** [from a native Australian language]

Po·to·sí (*Spanish* ˌpoto'si) *n.* a city in S Bolivia, at an altitude of 4066 m (13 340 ft.): one of the highest cities in the world; developed with the discovery of local silver in 1545; tin mining; university (1571). Pop.: 96 800 (1970 est.).

pot·pie ('pɒtˌpaɪ) *n.* a meat and vegetable stew with a pie crust on top.

pot plant *n.* a plant grown in a flowerpot, esp. indoors.

pot·pour·ri (ˌpəʊ'pʊərɪ) *n., pl.* ·**ris.** **1.** a collection of mixed flower petals dried and preserved in a pot to scent the air. **2.** a collection of unrelated or disparate items; miscellany. **3.** a medley of popular tunes. **4.** a stew of meat and vegetables. [C18: from French, literally: rotten pot, translation of Spanish *olla podrida* miscellany]

pot roast *n.* meat, esp. beef, that is browned and cooked slowly in a covered pot with very little water, often with vegetables added.

Pots·dam ('pɒtsdæm; *German* 'pɔtsdam) *n.* a city in central East Germany, on the Havel River: residence of Prussian kings and German emperors and scene of the **Potsdam Conference** of 1945. Pop.: 118 134 (1975 est.).

pot·sherd ('pɒtˌʃɜ:d) *or* **pot·shard** ('pɒtˌʃɑ:d) *n.* a broken fragment of pottery. [C14: from POT[1] + *schoord* piece of broken crockery; see SHARD]

pot shot *n.* **1.** a chance shot taken casually, hastily, or without careful aim. **2.** a shot fired to kill game in disregard of the rules of sport. **3.** a shot fired at quarry within easy range, often from an ambush.

pot·stone ('pɒtˌstəʊn) *n.* an impure massive variety of soapstone, formerly used for making cooking vessels.

pot·tage ('pɒtɪdʒ) *n.* a thick meat or vegetable soup. [C13: from Old French *potage* contents of a pot, from *pot* POT[1]]

pot·ted ('pɒtɪd) *adj.* **1.** placed or grown in a pot. **2.** cooked or preserved in a pot: *potted shrimps.* **3.** *Informal.* summarized or abridged: *a potted version of a novel.*

pot·ter[1] ('pɒtə) *n.* a person who makes pottery.

pot·ter[2] ('pɒtə) *or esp. U.S.* **put·ter** *Chiefly Brit.* ~*vb.* **1.** (*intr.;* often foll. by *about* or *around*) to busy oneself in a desultory though agreeable manner. **2.** (*intr.;* often foll. by *along* or *about*) to move with little energy or direction: *to potter about town.* **3.** (*tr.;* usually foll. by *away*) to waste (time): *to potter the day away.* ~*n.* **4.** the act of pottering. [C16 (in the sense: to poke repeatedly): from Old English *potian* to thrust; see PUT] —'**pot·ter·er** *or esp. U.S.* '**put·ter·er** *n.*

Pot·ter ('pɒtə) *n.* **1. Be·a·trix.** 1866–1943, English author and illustrator of children's animal stories, such as *The Tale of Peter Rabbit* (1902). **2. Paul·us.** 1625–54, Dutch painter, esp. of animals.

Pot·ter·ies ('pɒtərɪz) *pl. n.* **the.** a region of W central England, in Staffordshire, in which the china and earthenware industries are concentrated.

pot·ter's field *n.* **1.** *U.S.* a cemetery where the poor or unidentified are buried at the public expense. **2.** *New Testament.* the land bought by the Sanhedrin with the money paid for the betrayal of Jesus (which Judas had returned to them) to be used as a burial place for strangers and the friendless poor (Acts 1:19; Matthew 27:7).

pot·ter's wheel *n.* a device with a horizontal rotating disc, on which clay is moulded into pots, bowls, etc., by hand.

pot·ter wasp *n.* any of various solitary wasps of the genus *Eumenes,* which construct vaselike cells of mud or clay, in which they lay their eggs: family *Vespidae.*

pot·ter·y ('pɒtərɪ) *n., pl.* ·**ter·ies.** **1.** articles, vessels, etc., made from earthenware and dried and baked in a kiln. **2.** a place where such articles are made. **3.** the craft or business of making such articles. [C15: from Old French *poterie,* from *potier* potter, from *pot* POT[1]]

pot·ting shed ('pɒtɪŋ) *n.* a building in which plants are grown in flowerpots before being planted outside.

pot·tle ('pɒtᵊl) *n. Archaic.* a liquid measure equal to half a gallon. [C14: *potel,* from Old French: a small POT]

pot·to ('pɒtəʊ) *n., pl.* ·**tos.** **1.** Also called: **kinkajou.** a short-tailed prosimian primate, *Perodicticus potto,* having vertebral spines protruding through the skin in the neck region: family *Lorisidae.* **2. golden potto.** another name for **angwantibo. 3.** another name for **kinkajou** (sense 1). [C18: of West African origin; compare Wolof *pata* type of tailless monkey]

Pott's dis·ease (pɒts) *n.* a disease of the spine, usually caused by tubercular infection and characterized by weakening and gradual disintegration of the vertebrae and the intervertebral discs. [C18: named after Percivall *Pott* (1714–88), English surgeon]

pot·ty[1] ('pɒtɪ) *adj.* ·**ti·er,** ·**ti·est.** *Brit. informal.* **1.** foolish or slightly crazy. **2.** trivial or insignificant. [C19: perhaps from POT[1]] —'**pot·ti·ness** *n.*

pot·ty[2] ('pɒtɪ) *n., pl.* ·**ties.** a child's word for **chamber pot.**

pot·wal·lop·er *or* **pot·wal·ler** ('pɒtˌwɒlə) *n.* (in some English boroughs) a man entitled to the franchise before 1832 by virtue of possession of his own fireplace. [C18: from POT[1] + *wallop* to boil furiously, from Old English *weallan* to boil]

Po·tyom·kin (*Russian* pa'tjɔmkin) *n.* a variant spelling of **Potemkin.**

pouch (paʊtʃ) *n.* **1.** a small flexible baglike container: *a tobacco pouch.* **2.** a saclike structure in any of various animals, such as the abdominal receptacle marsupium in marsupials or the cheek fold in rodents. **3.** *Anatomy.* any sac, pocket, or pouchlike cavity or space in an organ or part. **4.** another word for **mailbag. 5.** a Scot. word for **pocket.** ~*vb.* **6.** (*tr.*) to place in or as if in a pouch. **7.** to arrange or become arranged in a pouchlike form. **8.** (*tr.*) (of certain birds and fishes) to swallow. [C14: from Old Norman French *pouche,* from Old French *poche* bag; see POKE] —'**pouch·y** *adj.*

pouched (paʊtʃt) *adj.* having a pouch or pouches.

pouf *or* **pouffe** (pu:f) *n.* **1.** a large solid cushion, usually cylindrical or cubic in shape, used as a seat. **2. a.** a woman's hair style, fashionable esp. in the 18th century, in which the hair is piled up in rolled puffs. **b.** a pad set in the hair to make such puffs. **3.** a stuffed pad worn under panniers. **4.** (pʊf, pu:f). *Brit. slang.* less common spellings of **poof.** [C19: from French; see PUFF]

pou·lard *or* **pou·larde** ('pu:lɑ:d) *n.* a hen that has been spayed for fattening. Compare **capon.** [C18: from Old French *pollarde,* from *polle* hen; see PULLET]

Pou·lenc (*French* pu'lɛ̃:k) *n.* **Fran·cis** (frɑ̃'sis). 1899–1963, French composer; a member of Les Six. His works include the operas *Les Mamelles de Tirésias* (1947) and *Dialogues des Carmélites* (1957), and the ballet *Les Biches* (1924).

poult (pəʊlt) *n.* the young of a gallinaceous bird, esp. of domestic fowl. [C15: syncopated variant of *poulet* PULLET]

poul·ter·er ('pəʊltərə) *n. Brit.* another word for a **poultryman.** [C17: from obsolete *poulter,* from Old French *pouletier,* from *poulet* PULLET]

poul·tice ('pəʊltɪs) *n.* **1.** Also called: **cataplasm.** *Med.* a local moist and often heated application for the skin consisting of substances such as kaolin, linseed, or mustard, used to improve the circulation, treat inflamed areas, etc. **2.** *Austral. slang.* a large sum of money, esp. a debt. [C16: from earlier *pultes,* from Latin *puls* a thick porridge]

poul·try ('pəʊltrɪ) *n.* domestic fowls collectively. [C14: from Old French *pouletrie,* from *pouletier* poultry-dealer]

poul·try·man ('pəʊltrɪmən) *or* **poul·ter·er** *n., pl.* ·**try·men** *or* ·**ter·ers. 1.** Also called: **chicken farmer.** a person who rears domestic fowls, esp. chickens, for their eggs or meat. **2.** a dealer in poultry, esp. one who sells the dressed carcasses.

pounce[1] (paʊns) *vb.* **1.** (*intr.;* often foll. by *on* or *upon*) to spring or swoop, as in capturing prey. ~*n.* **2.** the act of pouncing; a spring or swoop. **3.** the claw of a bird of prey. [C17: apparently from Middle English *punson* pointed tool; see PUNCHEON[2]] —'**pounc·er** *n.*

pounce[2] (paʊns) *vb.* (*tr.*) to emboss (metal) by hammering from the reverse side. [C15 *pounsen,* from Old French *poinçonner* to stamp; perhaps the same as POUNCE[1]]

pounce[3] (paʊns) *n.* **1.** a very fine resinous powder, esp. of cuttlefish bone, formerly used to dry ink or sprinkled over parchment or unsized writing paper to stop the ink from running. **2.** a fine powder, esp. of charcoal, that is tapped through perforations in paper corresponding to the main lines of a design in order to transfer the design to another surface. **3.** (*as modifier*): *a pounce box.* ~*vb.* (*tr.*) **4.** to dust (paper) with pounce. **5.** to transfer (a design) by means of pounce. [C18: from Old French *ponce,* from Latin *pūmex* PUMICE] —'**pounc·er** *n.*

poun·cet box ('paʊnsɪt) *n.* a box with a perforated top used for containing perfume. [C16 *pouncet,* perhaps alteration of *pounced* punched, perforated; see POUNCE[1]]

pound[1] (paʊnd) *vb.* **1.** (when *intr.,* often foll. by *on* or *at*) to strike heavily and often. **2.** (*tr.*) to beat to a pulp; pulverize. **3.** (*tr.*) to instill by constant drilling: *to pound Latin into him.* **4.** (*tr.;* foll. by *out*) to produce, as by typing heavily. **5.** to walk (the pavement, street, etc.) repeatedly: *he pounded the pavement looking for a job.* **6.** (*intr.*) to throb heavily. ~*n.* **7.** a heavy blow; thump. **8.** the act of pounding. [Old English *pūnian;* related to Dutch *puin* rubble] —'**pound·er** *n.*

pound[2] (paʊnd) *n.* **1.** an avoirdupois unit of weight that is divided into 16 ounces and is equal to 0.453 592 kilograms. Abbrev.: **lb. 2.** a troy unit of weight divided into 12 ounces equal to 0.373 242 kilograms. Abbrev.: **lb tr** *or* **lb t. 3.** an apothecaries' unit of weight, used in the U.S., that is divided into 5760 grains and is equal to one pound troy. **4.** (*not in technical usage*) a unit of force equal to the mass of 1 pound avoirdupois where the acceleration of free fall is 32.174 feet per second per second. Abbrev.: **lbf. 5. a.** the standard monetary unit of the United Kingdom and its dependencies, divided into 100 pence. Official name: **pound sterling. b.** (*as modifier*): *a pound note.* **6.** the standard monetary unit of the following countries: **a.** Cyprus: divided into 1000 mils. **b.** Egypt: divided into 100 piastres. **c.** Ireland: divided into 100 pence. **d.** Israel: divided into 100 agorot. **e.** Lebanon: divided into 100 piastres. **f.** Malta: divided into 100 pence. **g.** Sudan: divided into 100 piastres. **h.** Syria: divided into 100 piastres. **7.** another name for **lira** (sense 2). **8.** Also called: **pound Scots.** a former Scottish monetary unit originally worth an English pound but later declining in value to 1 shilling 8 pence. [Old English *pund*, from Latin *pondō* pound; related to German *Pfund* pound, Latin *pondus* weight]

pound[3] (paʊnd) *n.* **1.** an enclosure, esp. one maintained by a public authority, for keeping officially removed vehicles or distrained goods or animals, esp. stray dogs. **2.** a place where people are confined. **3. a.** a trap for animals. **b.** a trap or keepnet for fish. See **pound net.** ~*vb.* **4.** (*tr.*) to confine in or as if in a pound; impound, imprison, or restrain. [C14: from Late Old English *pund-* as in *pundfeald* PINFOLD]

Pound (paʊnd) *n.* **Ez·ra (Loomis).** 1885–1972, U.S. poet, translator, and critic, living in Europe. Indicted for treason by the U.S. government (1945) for pro-Fascist broadcasts during World War II, he was committed to a mental hospital until 1958. He was a founder of imagism and championed the early work of such writers as T. S. Eliot, Joyce, and Hemingway. His life work, the *Cantos* (1925–70), is an unfinished sequence of poems, which incorporates mythological and historical materials in several languages as well as political, economic, and autobiographical elements.

pound·age[1] (ˈpaʊndɪdʒ) *n.* **1.** a tax, charge, or other payment of so much per pound of weight. **2.** a tax, charge, or other payment of so much per pound sterling. **3.** a weight expressed in pounds.

pound·age[2] (ˈpaʊndɪdʒ) *n. Agriculture.* **a.** confinement of livestock within a pound. **b.** the fee required for freeing a head of livestock from a pound.

pound·al (ˈpaʊndᵊl) *n.* the fps unit of force; the force that imparts an acceleration of 1 foot per second per second to a mass of 1 pound. 1 poundal is equivalent to 0.1382 newton or 1.382×10^4 dynes. Abbrev.: **pdl** [C19: from POUND[2] + QUINTAL]

pound cake *n.* a rich fruit cake originally made with a pound each of butter, sugar, and flour.

-pound·er (ˈpaʊndə) *n.* (*in combination*) **1.** something weighing a specified number of pounds: *a 200-pounder.* **2.** something worth a specified number of pounds: *a ten-pounder.* **3.** a gun that discharges a shell weighing a specified number of pounds: *a two-pounder.*

pound net *n.* a fishing trap having an arrangement of standing nets directing the fish into an enclosed net.

pound of flesh *n.* something that is one's legal right but is an unreasonable demand (esp. in the phrase **to have one's pound of flesh**). [from Shakespeare's *The Merchant of Venice* (1600), Act IV, scene i]

pour (pɔː) *vb.* **1.** to flow or cause to flow in a stream. **2.** (*tr.*) to issue, emit, etc., in a profuse way. **3.** (*intr.*; *often foll. by down*) Also: **pour with rain.** to rain heavily: *it's pouring down outside.* **4.** (*intr.*) to move together in large numbers; swarm. **5.** (*intr.*) to serve tea, coffee, etc.: *shall I pour?* **6. it never rains but it pours.** events, esp. unfortunate ones, come together or occur in rapid succession. **7. pour cold water on.** *Informal.* to discourage or disparage. **8. pour oil on troubled waters.** to try to calm a quarrel, etc. ~*n.* **9.** a pouring, downpour, etc. [C13: of unknown origin] —ˈ**pour·er** *n.*

pour·boire *French.* (purˈbwaːr) *n.* a tip; gratuity. [literally: for drinking]

pour·par·ler *French.* (purparˈle; *English* pʊəˈpɑːleɪ) *n.* an informal or preliminary conference. [literally: for speaking]

pour·point (ˈpʊəˌpɔɪnt) *n.* a man's stuffed quilted doublet of a kind worn between the Middle Ages and the 17th century. [C15: from Old French, from *pourpoindre* to stick, from *pour-* variant of *par-*, from Latin *per* through + *poindre* to pierce, from Latin *pungere* to puncture]

pousse-ca·fé *French.* (puskaˈfe) *n.* **1.** a drink of liqueurs of different colours in unmixed layers. **2.** any liqueur taken with coffee at the end of a meal. [literally: coffee-pusher]

pous·sette (puːˈsɛt) *n.* **1.** a figure in country dancing in which couples hold hands and swing round. ~*vb.* **2.** (*intr.*) to perform such a figure. [C19: from French, from *pousser* to push]

pous·sin (*French* puˈsɛ̃) *n.* a young chicken reared for eating. [from French]

Pous·sin (*French* puˈsɛ̃) *n.* **Ni·co·las** (nikɔˈlɑ). 1594–1665, French painter, regarded as a leader of French classical painting. He is best known for the austere historical and biblical paintings and landscapes of his later years.

pou sto (ˈpuː ˈstəʊ) *n., pl.* **pou stos.** *Literary.* **1.** a place upon which to stand. **2.** a basis of operation. [Greek: where I may stand, from Archimedes' saying that he could move the earth if given a place to stand]

pout[1] (paʊt) *vb.* **1.** to thrust out (the lips), as when sullen, or (of the lips) to be thrust out. **2.** (*intr.*) to swell out; protrude. **3.** (*tr.*) to utter with a pout. ~*n.* **4.** (*sometimes* **the pouts.**) a fit of sullenness. **5.** the act or state of pouting. [C14: of uncertain origin; compare Swedish dialect *puta* inflated, Danish *pude* PILLOW] —ˈ**pout·ing·ly** *adv.*

pout[2] (paʊt) *n., pl.* **pout** *or* **pouts. 1.** short for **horned pout** or **eelpout. 2.** any of various gadoid food fishes, esp. the bib (also called **whiting pout**). **3.** any of certain other stout-bodied fishes. [Old English *-pūte* as in *ǣlepūte* eelpout; related to Dutch *puit* frog]

pout·er (ˈpaʊtə) *n.* **1.** a person or thing that pouts. **2.** a breed of domestic pigeon with a large crop capable of being greatly puffed out.

pov·er·ty (ˈpɒvətɪ) *n.* **1.** the condition of being without adequate food, money, etc. **2.** scarcity or dearth: *a poverty of wit.* **3.** a lack of elements conducive to fertility in land or soil. [C12: from Old French *poverté*, from Latin *paupertās* restricted means, from *pauper* POOR]

pov·er·ty-strick·en *adj.* suffering from extreme poverty.

pow (paʊ) *interj.* an exclamation imitative of a collision, explosion, etc.

P.O.W. *abbrev. for* prisoner of war.

pow·an (ˈpaʊən) *n.* **1.** a freshwater whitefish, *Coregonus clupeoides*, occurring in some Scottish lakes. **2.** any of certain similar related fishes, such as the vendace. ~Also called: **lake herring.** [C17: Scottish variant of POLLAN]

pow·der (ˈpaʊdə) *n.* **1.** a solid substance in the form of tiny loose particles. **2.** preparations in this form, such as gunpowder, face powder, or soap powder. **3.** fresh loose snow, esp. when considered as skiing terrain. **4. take a powder.** *U.S. slang.* to run away or disappear. ~*vb.* **5.** to turn into powder; pulverize. **6.** (*tr.*) to cover or sprinkle with or as if with powder. [C13: from Old French *poldre*, from Latin *pulvis* dust] —ˈ**pow·der·er** *n.* —ˈ**pow·der·y** *adj.*

pow·der blue *n.* **a.** a dusty pale blue colour. **b.** (*as adj.*) *a powder-blue coat.*

pow·der burn *n.* a superficial burn of the skin caused by a momentary intense explosion, esp. of gunpowder.

pow·der com·pact *n.* See **compact** (sense 10).

pow·der flask *n.* a small flask or case formerly used to carry gunpowder.

pow·der horn *n.* a powder flask consisting of the hollow horn of an animal.

pow·der keg *n.* **1.** a small barrel used to hold gunpowder. **2.** *Informal, chiefly U.S.* a potential source or scene of violence, disaster, etc.

pow·der me·tal·lur·gy *n.* the science and technology of producing solid metal components from metal powder by compaction and sintering.

pow·der mon·key *n.* (formerly) a boy who carried powder from the magazine to the guns on warships.

pow·der puff *n.* a soft pad or ball of fluffy material used for applying cosmetic powder to the skin.

pow·der room *n. Euphemistic.* a public lavatory for women.

pow·der·y mil·dew *n.* **1.** a plant disease characterized by a superficial white powdery growth on stems and leaves, caused by parasitic ascomycetous fungi of the family *Erysiphaceae*: affects the rose, aster, apple, vine, oak, etc. **2.** any of the fungi causing this disease. ~Compare **downy mildew.**

Pow·ell (ˈpaʊəl) *n.* **1. An·tho·ny Dym·oke** (ˈdɪməʊk). born 1905, English novelist, best known for his sequence of novels under the general title *A Dance to the Music of Time* (1951–75). **2. Cec·il Frank.** 1903–69, English physicist who was awarded the Nobel prize for physics in 1950 for his discovery of the pi meson. **3. Earl,** called *Bud.* 1924–66, U.S. modern-jazz pianist. **4. (John) E·noch.** born 1912, British politician. An outspoken opponent of Commonwealth immigration into Britain and of British membership of the Common Market, in 1974 he resigned from the Conservative Party, returning to Parliament as a United Ulster Unionist Council member.

pow·er (ˈpaʊə) *n.* **1.** ability or capacity to do something. **2.** (*often pl.*) a specific ability, capacity, or faculty. **3.** political, financial, social, etc., force or influence. **4.** control or dominion or a position of control, dominion, or authority. **5.** a state or other political entity with political, industrial, or military strength. **6.** a person who exercises control, influence, or authority: *he's a power in the state.* **7.** a prerogative, privilege, or liberty. **8. a.** legal authority to act, esp. in a specified capacity, for another. **b.** the document conferring such authority. **9. a.** a military force. **b.** military potential. **10.** *Maths.* **a.** the value of a number or quantity raised to some exponent. **b.** another name for **exponent** (sense 4). **11.** *Physics, engineering.* a measure of the rate of doing work expressed as the work done per unit time. It is measured in watts, horsepower, etc. Symbol: *P* **12. a.** the rate at which electrical energy is fed into or taken from a device or system. It is expressed, in a direct-current circuit, as the product of current and voltage and, in an alternating-current circuit, as the product of the effective values of the current and voltage and the cosine of the phase angle between them. It is measured in watts. **b.** (*as modifier*): *a power amplifier.* **13.** the ability to perform work. **14. a.** mechanical energy as opposed to manual labour. **b.** (*as modifier*): *a power tool.* **15.** a particular form of energy: *nuclear power.* **16. a.** a measure of the ability of a lens or optical system to magnify an object, equal to the reciprocal of the focal length. It is measured in dioptres. **b.** another word for **magnification. 17.** a large amount or quantity: *a power of good.* **18. in one's power.** (*often foll. by an infinitive*) able or allowed (to). **19. in (someone's) power.** under the control or sway of (someone). **20. the powers that be.** the established authority or administration. ~*vb.* (*tr.*) **21.** to give or provide power to. **22.** to fit (a machine) with a motor or engine. **23.** (*intr.*) *Slang.* to travel with great speed or force. [C13: from Anglo-Norman *poer*, from Vulgar Latin *potēre* (unattested), from Latin *posse* to be able]

pow·er·boat (ˈpaʊəˌbəʊt) *n.* a boat propelled by an inboard or outboard motor.

pow·er cut *n.* a temporary interruption or reduction in the supply of electrical power to a particular area. Sometimes shortened to **cut.**

pow·er dive *n.* **1.** a steep dive by an aircraft with its engines at high power. ~*vb.* **pow·er-dive. 2.** to cause (an aircraft) to perform a power dive or (of an aircraft) to perform a power dive.

pow·er drill *n.* a hand tool with a rotating chuck driven by an electric motor and designed to take an assortment of tools for drilling, grinding, polishing, etc.

pow·er·ful (ˈpaʊəfʊl) *adj.* **1.** having great power, force,

potency, or effect. **2.** extremely effective or efficient in action: *a powerful drug; a powerful lens.* **3.** *Dialect.* large or great: *a powerful amount of trouble.* ~*adv.* **4.** *Dialect.* extremely; very: *he ran powerful fast.* —**'pow+er+ful+ly** *adv.* —**'pow+er+ful+ness** *n.*
pow·er+house ('paʊə,haus) *n.* **1.** an electrical generating station or plant. **2.** *Slang.* a forceful or powerful person or thing.
pow+er+less ('paʊəlɪs) *adj.* without power or authority. —**'pow+er+less+ly** *adv.* —**'pow+er+less+ness** *n.*
pow+er line *n.* a set of conductors used to transmit and distribute electrical energy. Sometimes shortened to **line.**
pow+er of ap+point+ment *n. Property law.* authority to appoint persons either from a particular class (**special power**) or selected by the donee of the power (**general power**) to take an estate or interest in property.
pow+er of at+tor+ney *n.* **1.** legal authority to act for another person in certain specified matters. **2.** the document conferring such authority.
pow+er pack *n.* a device for converting the current from a supply into direct or alternating current at the voltage required by a particular electrical or electronic device.
pow+er plant *n.* **1.** the complex, including machinery, associated equipment, and the structure housing it, that is used in the generation of power, esp. electrical power. **2.** the equipment supplying power to a particular machine or for a particular operation or process.
pow+er point *n.* **1.** an electrical socket mounted on or recessed into a wall. **2.** such a socket, esp. one installed before the introduction of 13 ampere ring mains, that is designed to provide a current of up to 15 amperes for supplying heaters, etc., rather than lights.
pow+er pol·i·tics *n.* (in international affairs) the threat or use of force as an instrument of national policy.
pow+er se+ries *n.* a mathematical series whose terms contain ascending positive integral powers of a variable, such as $a_0 + a_1x + a_2x^2 + \ldots$
pow+er sta+tion *n.* an electrical generating station.
pow+er steer+ing *n.* a form of steering used on vehicles, where the torque applied to the steering wheel is augmented by engine power. Also called: **power-assisted steering.**
pow+er struc+ture *n. Chiefly U.S.* **1.** the structure or distribution of power and authority in a community. **2.** the people and groups who are part of such a structure.
Pow·ha·tan (,pauhə'tæn, paʊ'hætᵊn) *n.* American Indian name *Wahunsonacock,* died 1618, American Indian chief of a confederacy of tribes; father of Pocahontas.
pow+wow ('paʊ,waʊ) *n.* **1.** a talk, conference, or meeting. **2.** a magical ceremony of certain North American Indians, usually accompanied by feasting and dancing. **3.** (among certain North American Indians) a medicine man. **4.** a meeting of or negotiation with North American Indians. ~*vb.* **5.** (*intr.*) to hold a powwow. [C17: from Algonquian; related to Natick *pauwau* one who practises magic, Narragansett *powwaw*]
Pow+ys[1] ('paʊɪs) *n.* a county in E Wales, formed in 1974 from most of Breconshire, Montgomeryshire, and Radnorshire. Administrative centre: Llandrindod Wells. Pop.: 101 500 (1976 est.). Area: 5144 sq. km (1986 sq. miles).
Pow·ys[2] ('pəʊɪs) *n.* **John Cow·per** ('ku:pə). 1872–1963, English novelist, essayist, and poet, who spent much of his life in the U.S. His novels include *Wolf Solent* (1929), *A Glastonbury Romance* (1932), and *Owen Glendower* (1940).
pox (pɒks) *n.* **1.** any disease characterized by the formation of pustules on the skin that often leave pockmarks when healed. **2.** (usually preceded by *the*) an informal name for **syphilis. 3. a pox on (someone** *or* **something).** (*interj.*) *Archaic.* an expression of intense disgust or aversion for (someone or something). [C15: changed from *pocks,* plural of POCK]
Po+yang *or* **P'o-yang** ('pɔ:'jæŋ) *n.* a lake in E China, in N Kiangsi province, connected by canal with the Yangtze River: the second largest lake in China. Area: (at its greatest) 2780 sq. km (1073 sq. miles).
Poz+nań (*Polish* 'pɔznajn) *n.* a city in W Poland, on the Warta River: the centre of Polish resistance to German rule (1815–1918, 1939–45). Pop.: 502 800 (1974 est.). German name: **Posen.**
Po+zsony ('poʒonj) *n.* the Hungarian name for **Bratislava.**
poz+zuo+la+na (,pɒtswə'lɑ:nə) *or* **poz+zo+la+na** (,pɒtsə'lɑ:nə) *n.* **1.** a type of porous volcanic ash used in making hydraulic cements. **2.** any of various artificial substitutes for this ash used in cements. [C18: from Italian: of POZZUOLI]
Poz+zuo+li (*Italian* pot'tswɔ:li) *n.* a port in SW Italy, in Campania on the **Gulf of Pozzuoli** (an inlet of the Bay of Naples): in a region of great volcanic activity; founded in the 6th century B.C. by the Greeks. Pop.: 59 813 (1971).
poz+zy ('pɒzɪ) *n.* a variant spelling of **possie.**
pp *abbrev. for:* **1.** pages. **2.** *Music* [Italian *pianissimo*] very quietly.
pp. *abbrev. for:* pages.
p.p. *abbrev. for:* **1.** parcel post. **2.** past participle. **3.** prepaid. **4.** post paid. **5.** privately printed. **6.** [Latin *per procurationem*] through the agency of; by delegation to. **7.** [Latin *post prandium*] (on prescriptions) after a meal.
P.P. *abbrev. for:* **1.** Parish priest. **2.** Past President.
ppd. *abbrev. for:* **1.** post paid. **2.** prepaid.
P.P.E. *abbrev. for* philosophy, politics, and economics: a university course.
ppm, p.p.m., *or* **ppm.** *Chem. abbrev. for* parts per million.
ppr. *or* **p.pr.** *abbrev. for* present participle.
P.P.S. *abbrev. for:* **1.** parliamentary private secretary. **2.** Also: **p.p.s.** post postscriptum. [Latin: after postscript; additional postscript]
p.q. *abbrev. for* previous question.
P.Q. *abbrev. for* Province of Quebec.
Pr *the chemical symbol for* praseodymium.
pr. *abbrev. for:* **1.** (*pl.* **prs.**) pair. **2.** paper. **3.** Also: **Pr.** preferred stock. **4.** price. **5.** pronoun. **6.** power.
Pr. *abbrev. for:* **1.** Priest. **2.** Prince.
p.r. (in prescriptions, etc.) *abbrev. for* per rectum. [Latin: through rectum; to be inserted into the anus]
P.R. *abbrev. for:* **1.** proportional representation. **2.** public relations. **3.** Puerto Rico.
pra+cha+rak (prə'tʃɑ:rək) *n.* (in India) a person appointed to propagate a cause through personal contact, meetings, public lectures, etc. [Hindi]
prac+ti+ca·ble ('præktɪkəbᵊl) *adj.* **1.** capable of being done; feasible. **2.** usable. [C17: from French *praticable,* from *pratiquer* to practise; see PRACTICAL] —**,prac+ti+ca·'bil·i·ty** *or* **'prac+ti+ca·ble+ness** *n.* —**'prac+ti+ca·bly** *adv.*
Usage. See at **practical.**
prac+ti·cal ('præktɪkᵊl) *adj.* **1.** of, involving, or concerned with experience or actual use; not theoretical. **2.** of or concerned with ordinary affairs, work, etc. **3.** adapted or adaptable for use. **4.** of, involving, or trained by practice. **5.** being such for all useful or general purposes; virtual. [C17: from earlier *practic,* from French *pratique,* via Late Latin from Greek *praktikos,* from *prassein* to experience, negotiate, perform] —**,prac+ti+'cal+i·ty** *or* **'prac+ti+cal+ness** *n.* —**'prac+ti+cal+ly** *adv.*
Usage. In careful usage, a distinction is made between *practical* and *practicable. Practical* refers to a person, idea, project, etc., as being more concerned with or relevant to practice than theory: *he is a very practical person; the idea had no practical application. Practicable* refers to a project or idea as being capable of being done or put into effect: *the plan was expensive, yet practicable.*
prac+ti+cal joke *n.* a prank or trick usually intended to make the victim appear foolish. —**prac+ti+cal jok+er** *n.*
prac+tice ('præktɪs) *n.* **1.** a usual or customary action or proceeding: *it was his practice to rise at six; he made a practice of stealing stamps.* **2.** repetition or exercise of an activity in order to achieve mastery and fluency. **3.** the condition of having mastery of a skill or activity through repetition (esp. in the phrases **in practice, out of practice**). **4.** the exercise of a profession: *he set up practice as a lawyer.* **5.** the act of doing something: *he put his plans into practice.* **6.** the established method of conducting proceedings in a court of law. ~*vb.* **7.** the U.S. spelling of **practise.** [C16: from Medieval Latin *practicāre* to practise, from Greek *praktikē* practical science, practical work, from *prattein* to do, act]
prac+tise *or U.S.* **prac+tice** ('præktɪs) *vb.* **1.** to do or cause to do repeatedly in order to gain skill. **2.** (*tr.*) to do (something) habitually or frequently: *they practise ritual murder.* **3.** to observe or pursue (something, such as a religion): *to practise Christianity.* **4.** to work at (a profession, job, etc.): *he practises medicine.* **5.** (foll. by *on* or *upon*) to take advantage of (someone, someone's credulity, etc.). [C15: see PRACTICE]
prac+tised *or U.S.* **prac+ticed** ('præktɪst) *adj.* **1.** expert; skilled; proficient. **2.** acquired or perfected by practice.
prac+ti+tion+er (præk'tɪʃənə) *n.* **1.** a person who practises a profession or art. **2.** *Christian Science.* a person authorized to practise spiritual healing. [C16: from *practician,* from Old French *praticien,* from *pratiquer* to PRACTISE]
Pra+desh (prə'deɪʃ) *n. Indian.* a state, esp. a state in the Union of India. [Hindi]
prae- *prefix.* an archaic variant of **pre-.**
prae+di·al *or* **pre+di·al** ('pri:dɪəl) *adj.* **1.** of or relating to land, farming, etc. **2.** attached to or occupying land. [C16: from Medieval Latin *praediālis,* from Latin *praedium* farm, estate] —**,prae+di+'al+i·ty** *or* **,pre+di+'al+i·ty** *n.*
prae+fect ('pri:fɛkt) *n.* a variant spelling of **prefect** (senses 4–7). —**prae+fec+to+ri+al** (,pri:fɛk'tɔ:rɪəl) *adj.*
prae+mu+ni+re (,pri:mjʊ'naɪərɪ) *n. English history.* **1.** a writ charging with the offence of resorting to a foreign jurisdiction, esp. to that of the Pope, in a matter determinable in a royal court. **2.** the statute of Richard II defining this offence. [C14: from the Medieval Latin phrase (in the text of the writ) *praemūnīre faciās,* literally: that you cause (someone) to be warned in advance, from Latin *praemūnīre* to fortify or protect in front, from *prae* in front + *mūnīre* to fortify; in Medieval Latin the verb was confused with Latin *praemonēre* to forewarn]
prae+no+men (pri:'nəʊmɛn) *n., pl.* **+nom+i+na** (-'nɒmɪnə) *or* **+no+mens.** an ancient Roman's first or given name. See also **agnomen, cognomen, nomen.** [C18: from Latin, from *prae-* before + *nōmen* NAME] —**prae+nom+i+nal** (pri:'nɒmɪnᵊl) *adj.* —**prae+'nom+i+nal+ly** *adv.*
Prae+se+pe (praɪ'si:pɪ) *n.* an open cluster of several hundred stars in the constellation Cancer, visible to the naked eye as a hazy patch of light.
prae+tor *or* **pre+tor** ('pri:tə, -tɔ:) *n.* (in ancient Rome) any of several senior magistrates ranking just below the consuls. [C15: from Latin: one who leads the way, probably from *praeīre,* from *prae-* before + *īre* to go] —**prae+'to+ri+al** *or* **pre+'to+ri+al** *adj.* —**'prae+tor+ship** *or* **'pre+tor+ship** *n.*
prae+to+ri+an *or* **pre+to+ri+an** (pri:'tɔ:rɪən) *adj.* **1.** of or relating to a praetor. ~*n.* **2.** a person holding praetorian rank; a praetor or ex-praetor.

Prae+to+ri+an *or* **Pre+to+ri+an** (priː'tɔːrɪən) *adj.* **1.** of or relating to the Praetorian Guard. **2.** (*sometimes not cap.*) resembling the Praetorian Guard, esp. with regard to corruption. ~*n.* **3.** a member of the Praetorian Guard.

Prae+to+ri+an Guard *n.* **1.** the bodyguard of the Roman emperors, noted for its political corruption, which existed from 27 B.C. to 312 A.D. **2.** a member of this bodyguard.

Prae·to·ri·us (*German* prɛ'toːrius) *n.* **Mi·cha·el** ('mɪça,eːl). 1571–1621, German composer and musicologist, noted esp. for his description of contemporary musical practices and instruments, *Syntagma musicum* (1615–19).

prag+mat+ic (præg'mætɪk) *adj.* **1.** advocating behaviour that is dictated more by practical consequences than by theory or dogma. **2.** *Philosophy.* of or relating to pragmatism. **3.** involving everyday or practical business. **4.** of or concerned with the affairs of a state or community. **5.** *Rare.* interfering or meddlesome; officious. Also (for senses 3, 5): **pragmatical.** [C17: from Late Latin *prāgmaticus*, from Greek *prāgmatikos* from *pragma* act, from *prattein* to do] —**prag+,mat·i+'cal+i·ty** *n.* —**prag+'mat·i·cal+ly** *adv.*

prag+mat+ics (præg'mætɪks) *n.* (*functioning as sing.*) **1.** the study of those aspects of language that cannot be considered in isolation from its use. **2.** the study of the relation between symbols and those who use them.

prag+mat+ic sanc+tion *n.* an edict, decree, or ordinance issued with the force of fundamental law by a sovereign.

prag+ma+tism ('prægmə,tɪzəm) *n.* **1.** a philosophical movement holding that practical consequences are the criterion of knowledge, meaning, and value. **2.** the condition of being pragmatic. —**'prag+ma+tist** *n., adj.* —**,prag+ma+'tis+tic** *adj.*

Prague (prɑːg) *n.* the capital and largest city of Czechoslovakia, on the Vltava River: a rich commercial centre during the Middle Ages; site of Charles University (1348) and a technical university (1707); scene of defenestrations (1419 and 1618) that contributed to the outbreak of the Hussite Wars and the Thirty Years' War respectively. Pop.: 1 095 615 (1974 est.). Czech name: **Praha.**

Pra+ha ('praha) *n.* the Czech name for **Prague.**

Prai+ri·al *French.* (prɛri'al) *n.* the month of meadows: the ninth month of the French Revolutionary calendar, extending from May 21 to June 19. [C18: from French *prairie* meadow]

prai+rie ('prɛərɪ) *n.* (*often pl.*) a treeless grassy plain of the central U.S. and S Canada. Compare **pampas, steppe, savanna.** [C18: from French, from Old French *praierie*, from Latin *prātum* meadow]

prai+rie chick+en, fowl, grouse, *or* **hen** *n.* either of two mottled brown-and-white grouse, *Tympanuchus cupido* or *T. pallidicinctus*, of North America.

prai+rie dog *n.* any of several gregarious sciurine rodents of the genus *Cynomys*, such as *C. ludovicianus*, that live in large complex burrows in the prairies of North America. Also called: **prairie marmot.**

prai+rie oys+ter *n.* **1.** a drink consisting of raw unbeaten egg, vinegar or Worcester sauce (**Worcester oyster**), salt, and pepper: a supposed cure for a hangover. **2.** the testicles of a bull calf cooked and eaten.

Prai+rie Prov+inc·es *pl. n.* the Canadian provinces of Manitoba, Saskatchewan, and Alberta, which lie in the N Great Plains region of North America: the chief wheat and petroleum producing area of Canada.

prai+rie schoon+er *n. U.S.* a horse-drawn covered wagon similar to but smaller than a Conestoga wagon, used in the 19th century to cross the prairies of North America.

prai+rie soil *n.* a soil type occurring in temperate areas formerly under prairie grasses and characterized by a black A horizon, rich in plant foods.

prai+rie tur+nip *n.* another name for **breadroot.**

prai+rie wolf *n.* another name for **coyote** (sense 1).

praise (preɪz) *n.* **1.** the act of expressing commendation, admiration, etc. **2.** the extolling of a deity or the rendering of homage and gratitude to a deity. **3.** the condition of being commended, admired, etc. **4.** *Archaic.* the reason for praise. **5.** **sing someone's praises.** to commend someone highly. ~*vb.* (*tr.*) **6.** to express commendation, admiration, etc., for. **7.** to proclaim or describe the glorious attributes of (a deity) with homage and thanksgiving. [C13: from Old French *preisier*, from Late Latin *pretiāre* to esteem highly, from Latin *pretium* prize; compare PRIZE, PRECIOUS] —**'prais+er** *n.*

praise+wor·thy ('preɪz,wɜːðɪ) *adj.* deserving of praise; commendable. —**'praise+,wor·thi+ly** *adv.* —**'praise+,wor·thi+ness** *n.*

praj+na ('prʊdʒnə, -njɑː) *n.* wisdom or understanding considered as the goal of Buddhist contemplation. [from Sanskrit *prajñā*, from *prajānāti* he knows]

Pra+krit ('prɑːkrɪt) *n.* any of the vernacular Indic languages as distinguished from Sanskrit: spoken from about 300 B.C. to the Middle Ages. See also **Pali.** [C18: from Sanskrit *prākrta* original, from *pra-* before + *kr* to do, make + *-ta* indicating a participle] —**Pra+'krit+ic** *adj.*

pra+line ('prɑːliːn) *n.* **1.** a confection of nuts with caramelized sugar, used in desserts and as a filling for chocolates. **2.** Also called: **sugared almond.** a sweet consisting of an almond encased in sugar. [C18: from French, named after César de Choiseul, comte de Plessis-*Praslin* (1598–1675), French field marshal whose chef first concocted it]

prall+tril·ler ('prɑːl,trɪlə) *n.* **1.** an ornament used in 18th-century music consisting of an inverted mordent with an added initial upper note. **2.** another word for **inverted mordent.** [German: bouncing trill]

pram[1] (præm) *n. Brit.* a cotlike four-wheeled carriage for a baby. U.S. term: **baby carriage.** [C19: shortened and altered from PERAMBULATOR]

pram[2] (prɑːm) *n. Nautical.* a light tender with a flat bottom and a bow formed from the ends of the side and bottom planks meeting in a small raised transom. [C16: from Middle Dutch *prame*; related to Old Frisian *prām*]

prance (prɑːns) *vb.* **1.** (*intr.*) to swagger or strut. **2.** (*intr.*) to caper, gambol, or dance about. **3.** (*intr.*) **a.** (of a horse) to move with high lively springing steps. **b.** to ride a horse that moves in this way. **4.** (*tr.*) to cause to prance. ~*n.* **5.** the act or an instance of prancing. [C14 *prauncen*; perhaps related to German *prangen* to be in full splendour; compare Danish (dialect) *pransk* lively, spirited, used of a horse] —**'pranc+er** *n.* —**'pranc+ing+ly** *adv.*

pran+di·al ('prændɪəl) *adj.* of or relating to a meal. [C19: from Latin *prandium* meal, luncheon] —**'pran+di+al+ly** *adv.*

prang (præŋ) *Chiefly Brit. informal.* ~*n.* **1.** an accident or crash in an aircraft, car, etc. **2.** an aircraft bombing raid. **3.** an achievement. ~*vb.* **4.** to crash or damage (an aircraft, car, etc.). **5.** to damage (a town, etc.) by bombing. [C20: imitative of an explosion]

prank[1] (præŋk) *n.* a mischievous trick or joke, esp. one in which something is done rather than said. [C16: of unknown origin] —**'prank+ish** *adj.*

prank[2] (præŋk) *vb.* **1.** (*tr.*) to dress or decorate showily or gaudily. **2.** (*intr.*) to make an ostentatious display. [C16: from Middle Dutch *pronken*; related to German *Prunk* splendour, *prangen* to be in full splendour]

prank+ster ('præŋkstə) *n.* a practical joker.

prase (preɪz) *n.* a light green translucent variety of chalcedony. [C14: from French, from Latin *prasius* a leek-green stone, from Greek *prasios*, from *prason* a leek]

pra+se·o+dym+i·um (,preɪzɪəʊ'dɪmɪəm) *n.* a malleable ductile silvery-white element of the lanthanide series of metals. It occurs principally in monazite and bastnaesite and is used with other rare earths in carbon-arc lights and as a pigment in glass. Symbol: Pr; atomic no.: 59; atomic wt.: 140.91; valency: 3 or 4; relative density: 6.77; melting pt.: 931°C; boiling pt.: 3212°C. [C20: New Latin, from Greek *prasios* of a leek-green colour + DIDYMIUM]

prat (præt) *n.* an incompetent or ineffectual person: often used as a term of abuse. [C20: probably special used of C16 *prat* buttocks, of unknown origin]

prate (preɪt) *vb.* **1.** (*intr.*) to talk idly and at length; chatter. **2.** (*tr.*) to utter in an idle or empty way. ~*n.* **3.** idle or trivial talk; prattle; chatter. [C15: of Germanic origin; compare Middle Dutch *prāten*, Icelandic and Norwegian *prata*, Danish *prate*] —**'prat+er** *n.* —**'prat+ing+ly** *adv.*

prat+fall ('præt,fɔːl) *n. U.S. slang.* a fall upon one's buttocks. [C20: from C16 *prat* buttocks (of unknown origin) + FALL]

prat+in+cole ('prætɪŋ,kəʊl, 'preɪ-) *n.* any of various swallow-like shore birds of the southern Old World genus *Glareola* and related genera, esp. *G. pratincola*, having long pointed wings, short legs, and a short bill: family *Glareolidae*, order *Charadriiformes.* [C18: from New Latin *pratincola* field-dwelling, from Latin *prātum* meadow + *incola* inhabitant]

pra+tique ('prætiːk, præ'tiːk) *n.* formal permission given to a vessel to use a foreign port upon satisfying the requirements of local health authorities. [C17: from French, from Medieval Latin *practica* PRACTICE]

Pra+to (*Italian* 'praːto) *n.* a walled city in central Italy, in Tuscany: woollen industry. Pop.: 151 365 (1975 est.). Official name: **Pra+to in To+sca+na** (in tos'kaːna).

prat+tle ('prætᵊl) *vb.* **1.** (*intr.*) to talk in a foolish or childish way; babble. **2.** (*tr.*) to utter in a foolish or childish way. ~*n.* **3.** foolish or childish talk. [C16: from Middle Low German *pratelen* to chatter; see PRATE] —**'prat+tler** *n.* —**'prat+tling+ly** *adv.*

prau (praʊ) *n.* another word for **proa.**

prawn (prɔːn) *n.* **1.** any of various small, edible marine decapod crustaceans of the genera *Palaemon, Penaeus,* etc., having a slender flattened body with a long tail and two pairs of pincers. **2.** **come the raw prawn.** *Austral. informal.* to attempt deception. [C15: of obscure origin] —**'prawn+er** *n.*

prax+is ('præksɪs) *n., pl.* **prax+is·es** *or* **prax·es** ('præksiːz). **1.** the practice and practical side of a profession or field of study, as opposed to the theory. **2.** a practical exercise. **3.** accepted practice or custom. [C16: via Medieval Latin from Greek: deed, action, from *prassein* to do]

Prax·it·e·les (præk'sɪtɪ,liːz) *n.* 4th-century B.C. Greek sculptor: his works include statues of Hermes at Olympia, which survives, and of Aphrodite at Cnidus.

pray (preɪ) *vb.* **1.** (when *intr.*, often foll. by *for*; when *tr.*, *usually takes a clause as object*) to utter prayers (to God or other object of worship): *we prayed to God for the sick child.* **2.** (when *tr.*, *usually takes a clause as object or an infinitive*) to make an earnest entreaty (to or for); beg or implore: *she prayed to be allowed to go; leave, I pray you.* **3.** (*tr.*) *Rare.* to accomplish or bring by praying: *to pray a soul into the kingdom.* ~*interj.* **4.** *Archaic.* I beg you; please: *pray, leave us alone.* [C13: from Old French *preier*, from Latin *precārī* to implore, from *prex* an entreaty; related to Old English *fricgan*, Old High German *frāgēn* to ask, Old Norse *fregna* to enquire]

prayer[1] (preə) *n.* **1. a.** a personal communication or petition addressed to a deity, esp. in the form of supplication, adoration, praise, contrition, or thanksgiving. **b.** any other form of spiritual communion with a deity. **2.** a similar personal communication that does not involve adoration, addressed to beings venerated as being closely associated with a deity, such as angels or saints. **3.** the practice of praying: *prayer is our solution to human problems.* **4.** (*often pl.*) a form of devotion, either public or private, spent mainly or wholly praying: *morning prayers.* **5.** (*cap. when part of a recognized name*) a form of words used in praying: *the Lord's Prayer.* **6.** an object or benefit prayed for. **7.** an earnest request, petition, or entreaty. **8.** *Law.* a request contained in a petition to a court for the relief sought by the petitioner. **9.** *U.S. slang.* a chance or hope: *she doesn't have a prayer of getting married.* [C13 *preiere,* from Old French, from Medieval Latin *precāria,* from Latin *precārius* obtained by begging, from *prex* prayer] —**'prayer·less** *adj.*

pray·er[2] ('preɪə) *n.* a person who prays.

prayer beads (prɛə) *pl. n. R.C. Church.* the beads of the rosary.

prayer book (prɛə) *n.* **1.** *Ecclesiast.* a book containing the prayers used at church services or recommended for private devotions. **2.** *Church of England.* (*often caps.*) another name for **Book of Common Prayer.**

prayer·ful ('prɛəfʊl) *adj.* inclined to or characterized by prayer. —**'prayer·ful·ly** *adv.* —**'prayer·ful·ness** *n.*

prayer meet·ing (prɛə) *n. Chiefly Protestantism.* a service at which the participants sing hymns, testify, and offer up individual and often extempore prayers to God.

prayer rug (prɛə) *n.* the small carpet on which a Muslim kneels and prostrates himself while saying his prayers. Also called: **prayer mat.**

prayer shawl (prɛə) *n. Judaism.* another word for **tallith.**

prayer wheel (prɛə) *n. Buddhism.* (esp. in Tibet) a wheel or cylinder inscribed with or containing prayers, each revolution of which is counted as an uttered prayer, so that such prayers can be repeated by turning it.

pray·ing man·tis *or* **man·tid** *n.* another name for **mantis.**

P.R.B. *abbrev. for* (after the signatures of Pre-Raphaelite painters) Pre-Raphaelite Brotherhood.

pre- *prefix.* before in time, rank, order, position, etc.: *predate; pre-eminent; premeditation; prefrontal; preschool.* [from Latin *prae-,* from *prae* before, beforehand, in front]

preach (priːtʃ) *vb.* **1.** to make known (religious truth) or give religious or moral instruction or exhortation in (sermons). **2.** to advocate (a virtue, action, etc.), esp. in a moralizing way. [C13: from Old French *prechier,* from Church Latin *praedicāre,* from Latin: to proclaim in public; see PREDICATE] —**'preach·a·ble** *adj.*

preach·er ('priːtʃə) *n.* **1.** a person who has the calling and function of preaching the Christian Gospel, esp. a Protestant clergyman. **2.** a person who preaches.

Preach·er ('priːtʃə) *n.* **the.** *Bible.* the author of Ecclesiastes or the book of Ecclesiastes.

preach·i·fy ('priːtʃɪˌfaɪ) *vb.* **·fies, ·fy·ing, ·fied.** (*intr.*) *Informal, chiefly U.S.* to preach or moralize in a tedious manner. —**ˌpreach·i·fi·'ca·tion** *n.*

preach·ment ('priːtʃmənt) *n.* **1.** the act of preaching. **2.** a tedious or pompous sermon or discourse.

preach·y ('priːtʃɪ) *adj.* **preach·i·er, preach·i·est.** *U.S. informal.* inclined to or marked by preaching.

pre·ad·am·ite (priːˈædəˌmaɪt) *n.* **1.** a person who believes that there were people on earth before Adam. **2.** a person assumed to have lived before Adam. ~*adj. also* **pre·a·dam·ic** (ˌpriːəˈdæmɪk). **3.** of or relating to a preadamite.

pre·ad·ap·ta·tion (ˌpriːædæpˈteɪʃən) *n. Biology.* the possession by a species or other group of characteristics that may favour survival in a changed environment, such as the limblike fins of crossopterygian fishes, which are preadaptation to terrestrial life.

pre·am·ble (priːˈæmbᵊl) *n.* **1.** a preliminary or introductory statement, esp. attached to a statute or constitution setting forth its purpose. **2.** a preliminary or introductory conference, event, fact, etc. [C14: from Old French *préambule,* from Late Latin *praeambulum* walking before, from Latin *prae-* before + *ambulāre* to walk] —**pre·am·bu·lar** (priːˈæmbjʊlə), **pre·am·bu·la·to·ry** (priːˈæmbjʊlətərɪ, -trɪ), *or* **pre·'am·bu·lar·y** *adj.*

pre·am·pli·fi·er (priːˈæmplɪˌfaɪə) *n.* an electronic amplifier used to improve the signal-to-noise ratio of an electronic device. It boosts a low-level signal to an intermediate level before it is transmitted to the main amplifier. Sometimes shortened to **preamp.**

pre·ax·i·al (priːˈæksɪəl) *adj. Anatomy.* **1.** situated or occurring in front of the axis of the body. **2.** of or relating to the anterior part of a vertebrate limb. —**pre·'ax·i·al·ly** *adv.*

preb·end ('prɛbənd) *n.* **1.** the stipend assigned by a cathedral or collegiate church to a canon or member of the chapter. **2.** the land, tithe, or other source of such a stipend. **3.** a less common word for **prebendary. 4.** *Church of England.* the office, formerly with an endowment, of a prebendary. [C15: from Old French *prébende,* from Medieval Latin *praebenda* pension, stipend, from Latin *praebēre* to offer, supply, from *prae* forth + *habēre* to have, offer] —**pre·ben·dal** (prɪˈbɛndᵊl) *adj.*

preb·en·dar·y ('prɛbəndərɪ, -drɪ) *n., pl.* **·dar·ies. 1.** a canon or member of the chapter of a cathedral or collegiate church who holds a prebend. **2.** *Church of England.* an honorary canon with the title of prebendary.

prec. *abbrev. for* preceding.

Pre·cam·bri·an *or* **Pre-Cam·bri·an** (priːˈkæmbrɪən) *adj.* **1.** of, denoting, or formed in the earliest geological era, which lasted for about 4 000 000 000 years before the Cambrian period. ~*n.* **2. the Precambrian.** the Precambrian era. See **Archaeozoic, Proterozoic.**

pre·can·cel (priːˈkænsᵊl) *vb.* **·cels, ·cel·ling, ·celled** *or U.S.* **·cels, ·cel·ing, ·celed. 1.** (*tr.*) to cancel (postage stamps) before placing them on mail. ~*n.* **2.** a precancelled stamp. —**pre·ˌcan·cel·'la·tion** *n.*

pre·car·i·ous (prɪˈkɛərɪəs) *adj.* **1.** liable to failure or catastrophe; insecure; perilous. **2.** *Archaic.* dependent on another's will. [C17: from Latin *precārius* obtained by begging (hence, dependent on another's will), from *prex* PRAYER] —**pre·'car·i·ous·ly** *adv.* —**pre·'car·i·ous·ness** *n.*

pre·cast *adj.* ('priːˌkɑːst). **1.** (esp. of concrete when employed as a structural element in building) cast in a particular form before being used. ~*vb.* (priːˈkɑːst), **·casts, ·cast·ing, ·cast. 2.** (*tr.*) to cast (concrete) in a particular form before use.

prec·a·to·ry ('prɛkətərɪ, -trɪ) *adj. Rare.* of, involving, or expressing entreaty; supplicatory. Also: **prec·a·tive** ('prɛkətɪv). [C17: from Late Latin *precātōrius* relating to petitions, from Latin *precārī* to beg, PRAY]

pre·cau·tion (prɪˈkɔːʃən) *n.* **1.** an action taken to avoid a dangerous or undesirable event. **2.** caution practised beforehand; circumspection. [C17: from French, from Late Latin *praecautiō,* from Latin *praecavēre* to guard against, from *prae* before + *cavēre* to beware] —**pre·'cau·tion·ar·y** *or* **pre·'cau·tion·al** *adj.* —**pre·'cau·tious** *adj.*

pre·cede (prɪˈsiːd) *vb.* **1.** to go or be before (someone or something) in time, place, rank, etc. **2.** (*tr.*) to preface or introduce. [C14: via Old French from Latin *praecēdere* to go before, from *prae* before + *cēdere* to move]

prec·e·dence ('prɛsɪdəns) *or* **prec·e·den·cy** *n.* **1.** the act of preceding or the condition of being precedent. **2.** the ceremonial order or priority to be observed by persons of different stations on formal occasions: *the officers are seated according to precedence.* **3.** a right to preferential treatment: *I take precedence over you.*

prec·e·dent *n.* ('prɛsɪdənt). **1.** *Law.* a judicial decision that serves as an authority for deciding a later case. **2.** an example or instance used to justify later similar occurrences. ~*adj.* (prɪˈsiːdᵊnt, ˈprɛsɪdənt). **3.** preceding.

prec·e·dent·ed ('prɛsɪˌdɛntɪd) *adj.* (of a decision, etc.) supported by having a precedent.

prec·e·den·tial (ˌprɛsɪˈdɛnʃəl) *adj.* **1.** of, involving, or serving as a precedent. **2.** having precedence. —**ˌprec·e·'den·tial·ly** *adv.*

pre·ced·ing (prɪˈsiːdɪŋ) *adj.* (*prenominal*) going or coming before; former.

pre·cen·tor (prɪˈsɛntə) *n.* **1.** a cleric who directs the choral services in a cathedral. **2.** a person who leads a congregation or choir in the sung parts of church services. [C17: from Late Latin *praecentor* leader of the music, from *prae* before + *canere* to sing] —**pre·cen·to·ri·al** (ˌpriːsɛnˈtɔːrɪəl) *adj.* —**pre·'cen·tor·ˌship** *n.*

pre·cept ('priːsɛpt) *n.* **1.** a rule or principle for action. **2.** a guide or rule for morals; maxim. **3.** a direction, esp. for a technical operation. **4.** *Law.* **a.** a writ or warrant. **b.** a written order to a sheriff to arrange an election, the empanelling of a jury, etc. **c.** (in England) an order to collect money under a rate. [C14: from Latin *praeceptum* maxim, injunction, from *praecipere* to admonish, from *prae* before + *capere* to take]

pre·cep·tive (prɪˈsɛptɪv) *adj.* **1.** of, resembling, or expressing a precept or precepts. **2.** didactic. —**pre·'cep·tive·ly** *adv.*

pre·cep·tor (prɪˈsɛptə) *n.* **1.** a practising physician giving practical training to a medical student. **2.** the head of a preceptory. **3.** *Rare.* a tutor or instructor. —**pre·'cep·tor·ate** *n.* —**pre·cep·to·ri·al** (ˌpriːsɛpˈtɔːrɪəl) *or* **pre·'cep·to·ral** *adj.* —**pre·'cep·tor·ˌship** *n.* —**pre·'cep·tress** *fem. n.*

pre·cep·to·ry (prɪˈsɛptərɪ) *n., pl.* **·ries.** (formerly) a subordinate house or community of the Knights Templars.

pre·cess (prɪˈsɛs) *vb.* to undergo or cause to undergo precession.

pre·ces·sion (prɪˈsɛʃən) *n.* **1.** the act of preceding. **2.** See **precession of the equinoxes. 3.** the motion of a spinning body, such as a top, gyroscope, or planet, in which it wobbles so that the axis of rotation sweeps out a cone. [C16: from Late Latin *praecessiō* a going in advance, from Latin *praecēdere* to PRECEDE] —**pre·'ces·sion·al** *adj.* —**pre·'ces·sion·al·ly** *adv.*

pre·ces·sion of the e·qui·nox·es *n.* the slightly earlier occurrence of the equinoxes each year due to the slow continuous westward shift of the equinoctial points along the ecliptic by 50 seconds of arc per year. It is caused by the precession of the earth's axis.

ˌpre·ab·'sorb *vb.*
ˌpre·ac·'cept *vb.*
ˌpre·ac·'cus·tom *vb.*
ˌpre·ac·'quaint *vb.*
ˌpre·a·'dapt *vb.*
ˌpre·ad·'dress *vb.*
ˌpre·ad·'just *vb.*
ˌpre·ad·o·'les·cence *n.*
ˌpre·ad·o·'les·cent *n., adj.*
ˌpre·a·'dult *adj.*
pre·'ad·ver·ˌtise *vb.*
ˌpre·al·'lot *vb.,* **·lots, ·lot·ting, ·lot·ted.**
ˌpre·an·'nounce *vb.*
ˌpre·an·'tiq·ui·ty *n.*
ˌpre·ap·'pear·ance *n.*
ˌpre·ap·pli·'ca·tion *n.*
ˌpre·ap·'point *vb.*
pre·'arm *vb.*
ˌpre·ar·'range *vb.*
ˌpre·ar·'range·ment *n.*
ˌpre·ar·'rang·er *n.*
ˌpre·as·cer·'tain *vb.*
ˌpre·as·'sem·ble *vb.*
ˌpre·as·'sign *vb.*
ˌpre·as·'sump·tion *n.*
ˌpre·as·'sur·ance *n.*
ˌpre·at·'tune *vb.*
ˌpre-Au·'gus·tan *adj.*
ˌpre-Bab·y·'lo·ni·an *adj.*
pre·'boil *vb.*
pre-'Brit·ish *adj.*
pre-'Bud·dhist *adj.*
pre-Byz·'an·tine *adj.*
pre·'can·cer·ous *adj.*
ˌpre·cap·i·tal·'is·tic *adj.*
ˌpre-Car·bon·'if·er·ous *adj.*
pre-'Celt·ic *adj.*
pre·'cen·sor *vb.*
ˌpre-Chau·'ce·ri·an *adj.*

pre·cinct ('pri:sɪŋkt) *n.* **1. a.** an enclosed area or building marked by a fixed boundary such as a wall. **b.** such a boundary. **2.** a limited area, esp. of thought. **3.** *U.S.* **a.** a district of a city for administrative or police purposes. **b.** the police responsible for such a district. **4.** *U.S.* a polling or electoral district. [C15: from Medieval Latin *praecinctum* (something) surrounded, from Latin *praecingere* to gird around, from *prae* before, around + *cingere* to gird]

pre·cincts ('pri:sɪŋkts) *pl. n.* the surrounding region or area.

pre·ci·os·i·ty (ˌprɛʃɪ'ɒsɪtɪ) *n., pl.* **·ties.** fastidiousness or affectation, esp. in speech or manners.

pre·cious ('prɛʃəs) *adj.* **1.** beloved; dear; cherished. **2.** very costly or valuable. **3.** held in high esteem, esp. in moral or spiritual matters. **4.** very fastidious or affected, as in speech, manners, etc. [C13: from Old French *precios*, from Latin *pretiōsus* valuable, from *pretium* price, value] —**'pre·cious·ly** *adv.* —**'pre·cious·ness** *n.*

pre·cious cor·al *n.* another name for **red coral.**

pre·cious met·al *n.* any of the metals gold, silver, or platinum.

pre·cious stone *n.* any of certain rare minerals, such as diamond, ruby, sapphire, emerald, or opal, that are highly valued as gemstones.

prec·i·pice ('prɛsɪpɪs) *n.* **1. a.** the steep sheer face of a cliff or crag. **b.** the cliff or crag itself. **2.** a precarious situation. [C16: from Latin *praecipitium* steep place, from *praeceps* headlong] —**'prec·i·piced** *adj.*

pre·cip·i·tant (prɪ'sɪpɪtənt) *adj.* **1.** hasty or impulsive; rash. **2.** rushing or falling rapidly or without heed. **3.** abrupt or sudden. ~*n.* **4.** *Chem.* a substance or agent that causes a precipitate to form. —**pre'cip·i·tance** *or* **pre'cip·i·tan·cy** *n.* —**pre'cip·i·tant·ly** *adv.*

pre·cip·i·tate *vb.* (prɪ'sɪpɪˌteɪt). **1.** (*tr.*) to cause to happen too soon or sooner than expected; bring on. **2.** to throw or fall from or as from a height. **3.** to cause (moisture) to condense and fall as snow, rain, etc., or (of moisture, rain, etc.) to condense and fall thus. **4.** *Chem.* to undergo or cause to undergo a process in which a dissolved substance separates from solution as a fine suspension of solid particles. ~*adj.* (prɪ'sɪpɪtɪt). **5.** rushing ahead. **6.** done rashly or with undue haste. **7.** sudden and brief. ~*n.* (prɪ'sɪpɪtɪt). **8.** *Chem.* a precipitated solid in its suspended form or after settling or filtering. [C16: from Latin *praecipitāre* to throw down headlong, from *praeceps* headlong, steep, from *prae* before, in front + *caput* head] —**pre'cip·i·ta·ble** *adj.* —**preˌcip·i·ta'bil·i·ty** *n.* —**pre'cip·i·tate·ly** *adv.* —**pre'cip·i·tate·ness** *n.* —**pre'cip·i·ta·tive** *adj.* —**pre'cip·iˌta·tor** *n.*

pre·cip·i·ta·tion (prɪˌsɪpɪ'teɪʃən) *n.* **1.** *Meteorol.* **a.** rain, snow, sleet, dew, etc., formed by condensation of water vapour in the atmosphere. **b.** the deposition of these on the earth's surface. **c.** the amount precipitated. **2.** the production or formation of a chemical precipitate. **3.** the act of precipitating or the state of being precipitated. **4.** rash or undue haste. **5.** *Spiritualism.* the appearance of a spirit in bodily form; materialization.

pre·cip·i·ta·tion hard·en·ing *n.* *Metallurgy.* a process in which alloys are strengthened by the formation, in their lattice, of a fine dispersion of one component when the metal is quenched from a high temperature and aged at an intermediate temperature.

pre·cip·i·tin (prɪ'sɪpɪtɪn) *n.* *Immunol.* an antibody that causes precipitation when mixed with its specific antigen.

pre·cip·i·tous (prɪ'sɪpɪtəs) *adj.* **1.** resembling a precipice or characterized by precipices. **2.** very steep. **3.** hasty or precipitate. —**pre'cip·i·tous·ly** *adv.* —**pre'cip·i·tous·ness** *n.*

pre·cis *or* **pré·cis** ('preɪsi:) *n., pl.* **pre·cis** *or* **pré·cis** ('preɪsi:z). **1.** a summary of the essentials of a text; abstract. ~*vb.* **2.** (*tr.*) to make a précis of. [C18: from French: PRECISE]

pre·cise (prɪ'saɪs) *adj.* **1.** strictly correct in amount or value: *a precise sum.* **2.** designating a certain thing and no other; particular: *this precise location.* **3.** using or operating with total accuracy: *precise instruments.* **4.** strict in observance of rules, standards, etc.: *a precise mind.* [C16: from French *précis*, from Latin *praecīdere* to curtail, from *prae* before + *caedere* to cut] —**pre'cise·ly** *adv.* —**pre'cise·ness** *n.*

pre·ci·sian (prɪ'sɪʒən) *n.* a punctilious observer of rules or forms, esp. in the field of religion. —**pre'ci·sian·ism** *n.*

pre·ci·sion (prɪ'sɪʒən) *n.* **1.** the quality of being precise; accuracy. **2.** (*modifier*) characterized by or having a high degree of exactness: *precision grinding; a precision instrument.* [C17: from Latin *praecīsiō* a cutting off; see PRECISE] —**pre'ci·sion·ism** *n.* —**pre'ci·sion·ist** *n.*

Pre·ci·sion Club *n.* *Bridge.* a popular modern bidding system of which an important feature is an artificial one-club opening bid showing 16 points or more, with an artificial response of one diamond to show weakness.

pre·clin·i·cal (pri:'klɪnɪkᵊl) *adj.* *Med.* of, relating to, or occurring during the early phases of a disease before accurate diagnosis is possible. —**pre'clin·i·cal·ly** *adv.*

pre·clude (prɪ'klu:d) *vb.* (*tr.*) **1.** to exclude or debar. **2.** to make impossible, esp. beforehand. [C17: from Latin *praeclūdere* to shut up, from *prae* in front, before + *claudere* to close] —**pre'clud·a·ble** *adj.* —**pre·clu·sion** (prɪ'klu:ʒən) *n.* —**pre·clu·sive** (prɪ'klu:sɪv) *adj.* —**pre'clu·sive·ly** *adv.*

pre·co·cial (prɪ'kəʊʃəl) *adj.* **1.** (of young birds) covered with down, having open eyes, and capable of leaving the nest within a few days of hatching. ~*n.* **2.** a precocial bird. ~Compare **altricial.**

pre·co·cious (prɪ'kəʊʃəs) *adj.* **1.** ahead in development, such as the mental development of a child. **2.** *Botany.* (of plants, fruit, etc.) flowering or ripening early. [C17: from Latin *praecox* early maturing, from *prae* early + *coquere* to ripen] —**pre'co·cious·ly** *adv.* —**pre'co·cious·ness** *or* **pre·coc·i·ty** (prɪ'kɒsɪtɪ) *n.*

pre·cog·ni·tion (ˌpri:kɒg'nɪʃən) *n.* *Psychol.* the alleged ability to foresee future events. See also **clairvoyance, clairaudience.** [C17: from Late Latin *praecognitiō* foreknowledge, from *praecognoscere* to foresee, from *prae* before + *cognoscere* to know, ascertain] —**pre·cog·ni·tive** (pri:'kɒgnɪtɪv) *adj.*

pre-Co·lum·bi·an *adj.* of or relating to the Americas before they were discovered by Columbus.

pre·con·ceive (ˌpri:kən'si:v) *vb.* (*tr.*) to form an idea beforehand; conceive of ahead in time.

pre·con·cep·tion (ˌpri:kən'sɛpʃən) *n.* **1.** an idea or opinion formed beforehand. **2.** a bias; prejudice.

pre·con·di·tion (ˌpri:kən'dɪʃən) *n.* **1.** a necessary or required condition; prerequisite. ~*vb.* **2.** (*tr.*) *Psychology.* to present two stimuli to (an organism) consecutively and repeatedly so that they become associated.

pre·co·nize *or* **pre·co·nise** ('pri:kəˌnaɪz) *vb.* (*tr.*) **1.** to announce or commend publicly. **2.** to summon publicly. **3.** (of the pope) to approve the appointment of (a nominee) to one of the higher dignities in the Roman Catholic Church. [C15: from Medieval Latin *praecōnīzāre* to make an announcement, from Latin *praecō* herald] —**ˌpre·co·ni'za·tion** *or* **ˌpre·co·ni'sa·tion** *n.*

pre·con·scious (pri:'kɒnʃəs) *adj.* **1.** *Psychol.* prior to the development of consciousness. ~*n.* **2.** *Psychoanal.* mental contents or activity not immediately in consciousness but readily brought there. Compare **subconscious, unconscious.** —**pre'con·scious·ly** *adv.* —**pre'con·scious·ness** *n.*

pre·con·tract *n.* (pri:'kɒntrækt). **1.** a contract or arrangement made beforehand, esp. a betrothal. ~*vb.* (ˌpri:kən'trækt). **2.** to betroth or enter into a betrothal by previous agreement. **3.** to make (an agreement, etc.) by prior arrangement.

pre·crit·i·cal (pri:'krɪtɪkᵊl) *adj.* of, relating to, or occurring during the period preceding a crisis or a critical state or condition: *a precritical phase of a disease.*

pre·cur·sor (prɪ'kɜ:sə) *n.* **1.** a person or thing that precedes and shows or announces someone or something to come; harbinger. **2.** a predecessor or forerunner. [C16: from Latin *praecursor* one who runs in front, from *praecurrere,* from prae in front + *currere* to run]

pre·cur·so·ry (prɪ'kɜ:sərɪ) *or* **pre·cur·sive** *adj.* **1.** serving as a precursor. **2.** preliminary or introductory.

pred. *abbrev. for* predicate.

pre·da·cious *or* **pre·da·ceous** (prɪ'deɪʃəs) *adj.* **1.** (of animals) habitually hunting and killing other animals for food. **2.** preying on others. [C18: from Latin *praeda* plunder; compare PREDATORY] —**pre'da·cious·ness, pre'da·ceous·ness,** *or* **pre·dac·i·ty** (prɪ'dæsɪtɪ) *n.*

pre·date (pri:'deɪt) *vb.* (*tr.*) **1.** to affix a date to (a document, paper, etc.) that is earlier than the actual date. **2.** to assign a date to (an event, period, etc.) that is earlier than the actual or previously assigned date of occurrence. **3.** to be or occur at an earlier date than; precede in time.

pre·da·tion (prɪ'deɪʃən) *n.* a relationship between two species of animal in a community, in which one (the predator) hunts, kills, and eats the other (the prey).

pred·a·tor ('prɛdətə) *n.* **1.** any carnivorous animal. **2.** a predatory person or thing.

pred·a·to·ry ('prɛdətərɪ, -trɪ) *adj.* **1.** *Zoology.* another word for **predacious** (sense 1). **2.** of, involving, or characterized by plundering, robbing, etc. [C16: from Latin *praedātōrius* rapacious, from *praedārī* to pillage, from *praeda* booty] —**'pred·a·to·ri·ly** *adv.* —**'pred·a·to·ri·ness** *n.*

pre·de·cease (ˌpri:dɪ'si:s) *vb.* **1.** to die before (some other person). ~*n.* **2.** *Rare.* earlier death.

pre·de·ces·sor ('pri:dɪˌsɛsə) *n.* **1.** a person who precedes another, as in an office. **2.** something that precedes something else. [C14: via Old French from Late Latin *praedēcessor,* from *prae* before + *dēcēdere* to go away, from *dē* away + *cēdere* to go]

pre·del·la (prɪ'dɛlə; *Italian* pre'dɛlla) *n., pl.* **·le** (-li:; *Italian* -le). **1.** a small painting or group of paintings as appended to a larger painting, etc. **2.** a platform in a church upon which the altar stands. [C19: from Italian: stool, step, probably from Old High German *bret* board]

pre·des·ti·nar·i·an (ˌpri:dɛstɪ'nɛərɪən) *Theol.* ~*n.* **1.** a person who believes in divine predestination. ~*adj.* **2.** of or relating to predestination or characterizing those who believe in it. —**ˌpre·des·ti'nar·i·an·ism** *n.*

---

pre'check *vb.*
pre'chill *vb.*
ˌpre-Chi'nese *adj.*
pre-'Chris·tian *adj.*
pre-'Christ·mas *adj.*
ˌpre·civ·i·li'za·tion *n.*
pre'clas·si·cal *adj.*
pre'clean *vb.*
pre'cog·iˌtate *vb.*
pre'col·lege *adj.*
ˌpre·col'le·giate *adj.*
ˌpre·con'cert *vb.*
ˌpre·con'ces·sion *n.*
ˌpre·con'demn *vb.*
ˌpre·con·dem'na·tion *n.*
ˌpre·con'jec·ture *vb.*
ˌpre·con'nec·tion *n.*
ˌpre·conˌsid·er'a·tion *n.*
ˌpre·con'struct *vb.*
ˌpre·con·sul'ta·tion *n.*
ˌpre·con'trive *vb.*
ˌpre·con'vic·tion *n.*
pre'cook *vb.*
pre-'Dan·te·an *adj.*
ˌpre-Dar'win·i·an *adj.*
ˌpre·de'sign *vb.*
pre'des·igˌnate *vb.*
ˌpre·de'ter·mi·na·ble *adj.*

pre·des·ti·nate *vb.* (priːˈdɛstɪˌneɪt). **1.** (*tr.*) another word for **predestine.** ~*adj.* (priːˈdɛstɪnɪt, -ˌneɪt). **2.** predestined or foreordained. **3.** *Theol.* subject to predestination; decided by God from all eternity.

pre·des·ti·na·tion (priːˌdɛstɪˈneɪʃən) *n.* **1.** *Theol.* **a.** the act of God foreordaining every event from eternity. **b.** the doctrine or belief, esp. associated with Calvin, that the final salvation of some of mankind is foreordained from eternity by God. **2.** the act of predestining or the state of being predestined.

pre·des·tine (priːˈdɛstɪn) *or* **pre·des·ti·nate** *vb.* (*tr.*) **1.** to foreordain; determine beforehand. **2.** *Theol.* (of God) to decree from eternity (any event, esp. the final salvation of individuals). [C14: from Latin *praedestināre* to resolve beforehand, from *destināre* to determine, DESTINE] —**preˈdes·ti·na·ble** *adj.*

pre·de·ter·mi·nate (ˌpriːdɪˈtɜːmɪnɪt, -ˌneɪt) *adj.* determined beforehand; predetermined. —ˌ**pre·deˈter·mi·nate·ly** *adv.*

pre·de·ter·mine (ˌpriːdɪˈtɜːmɪn) *vb.* (*tr.*) **1.** to determine beforehand. **2.** to influence or incline towards an opinion beforehand; bias. —ˌ**pre·deˌter·miˈna·tion** *n.* —ˌ**pre·deˈter·mi·na·tive** *adj.* —ˌ**pre·deˈter·min·er** *n.*

pre·di·al (ˈpriːdɪəl) *adj.* a variant spelling of **praedial.**

pred·i·ca·ble (ˈprɛdɪkəbᵊl) *adj.* **1.** capable of being predicated or asserted. ~*n.* **2.** a quality, attribute, etc., that can be predicated. **3.** *Logic.* any of the five general forms of attribution, namely genus, species, differentia, property, and accident. [C16: from Latin *praedicābilis,* from *praedicāre* to assert publicly; see PREDICATE, PREACH] —ˌ**pred·i·caˈbil·i·ty** *or* ˈ**pred·i·ca·ble·ness** *n.*

pre·dic·a·ment (prɪˈdɪkəmənt) *n.* **1.** a perplexing, embarrassing, or difficult situation. **2.** (ˈprɛdikəmənt). *Logic.* a logical class or category. **3.** *Archaic.* a specific condition, circumstance, state, position, etc. [C14: from Late Latin *praedicāmentum* what is predicated, from *praedicāre* to announce, assert; see PREDICATE]

pred·i·cant (ˈprɛdɪkənt) *adj.* **1.** of or relating to preaching. ~*n.* **2.** a member of a religious order founded for preaching, esp. a Dominican. **3.** (ˌprɛdɪˈkænt). a variant spelling of **predikant.** [C17: from Latin *praedicāns* preaching, from *praedicāre* to say publicly; see PREDICATE]

pred·i·cate *vb.* (ˈprɛdɪˌkeɪt). (*mainly tr.*) **1.** (*also intr.; when tr., may take a clause as object*) to proclaim, declare, or affirm. **2.** to imply or connote. **3.** (foll. by *on* or *upon*) to base or found (a proposition, argument, etc.). **4.** *Logic.* **a.** to assert or affirm (a property, characteristic, or condition) of the subject of a proposition. **b.** to make (a term, expression, etc.) the predicate of a proposition. ~*n.* (ˈprɛdɪkɪt). **5.** *Grammar.* **a.** the part of a sentence in which something is asserted or denied of the subject of a sentence. **b.** (*as modifier*): *a predicate adjective.* **6.** *Logic.* a term, property, characteristic, or condition that is affirmed or denied concerning the subject of a proposition. ~*adj.* (ˈprɛdɪkɪt). **7.** of or relating to something that has been predicated. [C16: from Latin *praedicāre* to assert publicly, from *prae* in front, in public + *dīcere* to say] —ˌ**pred·iˈca·tion** *n.*

pred·i·cate cal·cu·lus *n.* the system of symbolic logic concerned not only with relations between propositions as wholes but also with the representation by symbols of individuals and predicates in propositions and with quantification over individuals. Also called: **functional calculus.** See also **propositional calculus.**

pre·dic·a·tive (prɪˈdɪkətɪv) *adj. Grammar.* relating to or occurring within the predicate of a sentence: *a predicative adjective.* Compare **attributive.** —**preˈdic·a·tive·ly** *adv.*

pred·i·ca·to·ry (ˈprɛdɪˌkeɪtərɪ, ˌprɛdɪˈkeɪtərɪ) *adj.* of, relating to, or characteristic of preaching or a preacher. [C17: from Late Latin *praedicātōrius,* from *praedicāre* to proclaim]

pre·dict (prɪˈdɪkt) *vb.* (*tr.; may take a clause as object*) to state or make a declaration about in advance, esp. on a reasoned basis; foretell. [C17: from Latin *praedīcere* to mention beforehand, from *prae* before + *dīcere* to say] —**preˈdict·a·ble** *adj.* —**preˌdict·aˈbil·i·ty** *or* **preˈdict·a·ble·ness** *n.* —**preˈdict·a·bly** *adv.*

pre·dic·tion (prɪˈdɪkʃən) *n.* **1.** the act of predicting. **2.** something predicted; a forecast, prophecy, etc. —**preˈdic·tive** *adj.* —**preˈdic·tive·ly** *adv.*

pre·dic·tor (prɪˈdɪktə) *n.* **1.** a person or thing that predicts. **2.** an instrument, used in conjunction with an anti-aircraft gun, that determines the speed, distance, height, and direction of hostile aircraft.

pre·di·gest (ˌpriːdaɪˈdʒɛst, -dɪ-) *vb.* (*tr.*) to treat (food) artificially to aid subsequent digestion in the body. —ˌ**pre·diˈges·tion** *n.*

pred·i·kant *or* **pred·i·cant** (ˌprɛdɪˈkænt) *n.* a minister in the Dutch Reformed Church, esp. in South Africa. [from Dutch, from Old French *predicant,* from Late Latin *praedicans* preaching, from *praedicāre* to PREACH]

pre·di·lec·tion (ˌpriːdɪˈlɛkʃən) *n.* a predisposition, preference, or bias. [C18: from French *prédilection,* from Medieval Latin *praedīligere* to prefer, from Latin *prae* before + *dīligere* to love]

pre·dis·pose (ˌpriːdɪˈspəʊz) *vb.* (*tr.*) **1.** (often foll. by *to* or *towards*) to incline or make (someone) susceptible to something beforehand. **2.** *Chiefly law.* to dispose of (property, etc.) beforehand; bequeath. —ˌ**pre·disˈpos·al** *n.*

pre·dis·po·si·tion (ˌpriːdɪspəˈzɪʃən) *n.* **1.** the condition of being predisposed. **2.** *Med.* susceptibility to a specific disease. Compare **diathesis.**

pred·ni·sone (ˈprɛdnɪˌsəʊn) *n.* a steroid drug derived from cortisone and having the same uses. [C20: perhaps from PRE(GNANT) + D(IE)N(E) + (CORT)ISONE]

pre·dom·i·nant (prɪˈdɒmɪnənt) *adj.* **1.** having superiority in power, influence, etc., over others. **2.** prevailing; prominent. —**preˈdom·i·nance** *or* **preˈdom·i·nan·cy** *n.* —**preˈdom·i·nant·ly** *adv.*

pre·dom·i·nate (prɪˈdɒmɪˌneɪt) *vb.* **1.** (*intr.;* often foll. by *over*) to have power, influence, or control. **2.** (*intr.*) to prevail or preponderate. **3.** (*tr.*) *Rare.* to dominate or have control over. ~*adj.* (prɪˈdɒmɪnɪt). **4.** another word for **predominant.** [C16: from Medieval Latin *praedominārī,* from Latin *prae* before + *dominārī* to bear rule, domineer] —**preˈdom·i·nate·ly** *adv.* —**preˈdom·iˌna·tor** *n.* —**preˌdom·iˈna·tion** *n.*

pre-ec·lamp·si·a (ˌpriːɪˈklæmpsɪə) *n. Pathol.* a toxic condition of pregnancy characterized by high blood pressure, protein in the urine, abnormal weight gain, and oedema. Compare **eclampsia.**

pree·mie *or* **pre·mie** (ˈpriːmɪ) *n. Slang, chiefly U.S.,* a premature infant. [C20: altered from PREMATURE]

pre-em·i·nent (prɪˈɛmɪnənt) *adj.* extremely eminent or distinguished; outstanding. —**pre-ˈem·i·nence** *n.* —**pre-ˈem·i·nent·ly** *adv.*

pre-empt (prɪˈɛmpt) *vb.* **1.** (*tr.*) to acquire in advance of or to the exclusion of others; appropriate. **2.** (*tr.*) *Chiefly U.S.* to occupy (public land) in order to acquire a prior right to purchase. **3.** (*intr.*) *Bridge.* to make a high opening bid, often on a weak hand, to shut out opposition bidding. —**pre-ˈemp·tor** *n.* —**pre-ˈemp·to·ry** *adj.*

pre-emp·tion (prɪˈɛmpʃən) *n.* **1.** *Law.* the purchase of or right to purchase property in advance of or in preference to others. **2.** *International law.* the right of a government to intercept and seize for its own purposes goods or property of the subjects of another state while in transit, esp. in time of war. [C16: from Medieval Latin *praeemptiō,* from *praeemere* to buy beforehand, from *emere* to buy]

pre-emp·tive (prɪˈɛmptɪv) *adj.* **1.** of, involving, or capable of pre-emption. **2.** *Bridge.* (of a high bid) made to shut out opposition bidding. **3.** *Military.* designed to reduce an enemy's attacking strength before it can use it: *a pre-emptive strike.* —**pre-ˈemp·tive·ly** *adv.*

preen[1] (priːn) *vb.* **1.** (of birds) to maintain (feathers) in a healthy condition by arrangement, cleaning, and other contact with the bill. **2.** to dress or array (oneself) carefully; primp. **3.** (usually foll. by *on*) to pride or congratulate (oneself). [C14 *preinen,* probably from *prunen* to PRUNE[3], influenced by *prenen* to prick, pin (see PREEN[2]); suggestive of the pricking movement of the bird's beak] —ˈ**preen·er** *n.*

preen[2] (priːn) *n. Scot.* a pin, esp. a decorative one. [Old English *prēon* a pin; related to Middle High German *pfrieme* awl, Dutch *priem* bodkin]

pre-ex·il·i·an (ˌpriːɪgˈzɪlɪən) *or* **pre-ex·il·ic** *adj. Old Testament.* prior to the Babylonian exile of the Jews (587–539 B.C.).

pref. *abbrev. for:* **1.** preface. **2.** prefatory. **3.** preference. **4.** preferred. **5.** prefix.

pre·fab (ˈpriːˌfæb) *n.* **a.** a building that is prefabricated, esp. a small house. **b.** (*as modifier*): *a prefab house.*

pre·fab·ri·cate (priːˈfæbrɪˌkeɪt) *vb.* (*tr.*) to manufacture sections of (a building), esp. in a factory, so that they can be easily transported to and rapidly assembled on a building site. —**preˌfab·riˈca·tion** *n.* —**preˈfab·riˌca·tor** *n.*

pref·ace (ˈprɛfɪs) *n.* **1.** a statement written as an introduction to a literary or other work, typically explaining its scope, intention, method, etc.; foreword. **2.** anything introductory. **3.** *R.C. Church.* a prayer of thanksgiving and exhortation serving as an introduction to the canon of the Mass. ~*vb.* (*tr.*) **4.** to furnish with a preface. **5.** to serve as a preface to. [C14: from Medieval Latin *praefātia,* from Latin *praefātiō* a saying beforehand, from *praefārī* to utter in advance, from *prae* before + *fārī* to say] —ˈ**pref·ac·er** *n.*

pref·a·to·ry (ˈprɛfətərɪ, -trɪ) *or* **pref·a·to·ri·al** (ˌprɛfəˈtɔːrɪəl) *adj.* of, involving, or serving as a preface; introductory. [C17: from Latin *praefārī* to say in advance; see PREFACE] —ˈ**pref·a·to·ri·ly** *or* ˌ**pref·aˈto·ri·al·ly** *adv.*

pre·fect (ˈpriːfɛkt) *n.* **1.** (in France, Italy, etc.) the chief administrative officer in a department. **2.** (in France, etc.) the head of a police force. **3.** *Brit.* a schoolchild appointed to a position of limited power over his fellows. **4.** (in ancient Rome) any of several magistrates or military commanders. **5.** Also called: **prefect apostolic.** *R.C. Church.* an official having jurisdiction over a missionary district that has no ordinary. **6.** *R.C. Church.* one of two senior masters in a Jesuit school or college (the **prefect of studies** and the **prefect of discipline** or **first prefect**). **7.** *R.C. Church.* a cardinal in charge of a congregation of the Curia. ~Also (for senses 4–7): **praefect.** [C14: from Latin *praefectus* one put in charge, from *praeficere* to place in authority over, from *prae* before + *facere* to do, make] —**pre·fec·to·ri·al** (ˌpriːfɛkˈtɔːrɪəl) *adj.*

pre·fec·ture (ˈpriːfɛkˌtjʊə) *n.* **1.** the office, position, or area of authority of a prefect. **2.** the official residence of a prefect in France, Italy, etc. —**preˈfec·tur·al** *adj.*

ˌ**pre·disˈsolve** *vb.*
ˌ**pre·disˈtin·guish** *vb.*
ˌ**pre·diˈvide** *vb.*
preˈdoom *vb.*
pre·dyˈnas·tic *adj.*
pre·eˈlect *vb.*
pre·eˈlec·tion *n.*
pre-ˈEm·pire *adj.*
ˌ**pre·enˈgage** *vb.*
ˌ**pre·enˈgage·ment** *n.*
ˌ**pre·enˈlist·ment** *n.*
ˌ**pre·esˈtab·lish** *vb.*
preˈes·ti·ˌmate *vb.*
ˌ**pre·exˈam·ine** *vb.*
ˌ**pre·exˈist** *vb.*
ˌ**pre·exˈist·ence** *n.*

pre·fer (prɪˈfɜː) *vb.* ·**fers,** ·**fer·ring,** ·**ferred. 1.** (when *tr., may take a clause as object or an infinitive*) to like better or value more highly: *I prefer to stand.* **2.** *Law.* to give preference, esp. to one creditor over others. **3.** (esp. of the police) to put (charges) before a court, judge, magistrate, etc., for consideration and judgment. **4.** (*tr.; often passive*) to advance in rank over another or others; promote. [C14: from Latin *praeferre* to carry in front, prefer, from *prae* in front + *ferre* to bear] —**pre·ˈfer·rer** *n.*

pref·er·a·ble (ˈprɛfərəbᵊl) *adj.* preferred or more desirable. —ˌ**pref·er·a·ˈbil·i·ty** *or* ˈ**pref·er·a·ble·ness** *n.* —ˈ**pref·er·a·bly** *adv.*

pref·er·ence (ˈprɛfərəns, ˈprɛfrəns) *n.* **1.** the act of preferring. **2.** something or someone preferred. **3.** *Law.* **a.** the settling of the claims of one or more creditors before or to the exclusion of those of the others. **b.** a prior right to payment, as of a dividend or share in the assets of a company in the event of liquidation. **4.** *International trade.* the granting of favour or precedence to particular foreign countries, as by levying differential tariffs.

pref·er·ence shares *pl. n. Brit.* shares representing part of the capital issued by a company and entitling their holders to priority with respect to both net profit and net assets. Preference shares usually carry a definite rate of dividend that is generally lower than that declared on ordinary shares. U.S. name: **preferred stock.** Compare **ordinary shares.**

pref·er·en·tial (ˌprɛfəˈrɛnʃəl) *adj.* **1.** showing or resulting from preference. **2.** giving, receiving, or originating from preference in international trade. —**pref·er·en·ti·al·i·ty** (ˌprɛfəˌrɛnʃɪˈælɪtɪ) *n.* —ˌ**pref·er·ˈen·tial·ly** *adv.*

pref·er·en·tial vot·ing *n.* a system of voting in which the electors signify their choices, as of candidates, in order of preference.

pre·fer·ment (prɪˈfɜːmənt) *n.* **1.** the act of promoting or advancing to a higher position, office, etc. **2.** the state of being preferred for promotion or social advancement. **3.** the act of preferring.

pre·ferred stock *n.* the U.S. name for **preference shares.**

pre·fig·u·ra·tion (ˌpriːfɪgəˈreɪʃən) *n.* **1.** the act of prefiguring. **2.** something that prefigures, such as a prototype. —**pre·ˈfig·u·ra·tive** *adj.* —**pre·ˈfig·u·ra·tive·ly** *adv.* —**pre·ˈfig·u·ra·tive·ness** *n.*

pre·fig·ure (priːˈfɪgə) *vb.* (*tr.*) **1.** to represent or suggest in advance. **2.** to imagine or consider beforehand. —**pre·ˈfig·ure·ment** *n.*

pre·fix *n.* (ˈpriːfɪks). **1.** *Grammar.* an affix that precedes the stem to which it is attached, as for example *un-* in *unhappy.* Compare **suffix** (sense 1). **2.** something coming or placed before. ~*vb.* (priːˈfɪks, ˈpriːfɪks). (*tr.*) **3.** to put or place before. **4.** *Grammar.* to add (a morpheme) as a prefix to the beginning of a word. —**pre·fix·al** (ˈpriːfɪksəl, priːˈfɪk-) *adj.* —ˈ**pre·fix·al·ly** *adv.* —**pre·fix·ion** (priːˈfɪkʃən) *n.*

pre·for·ma·tion (ˌpriːfɔːˈmeɪʃən) *n.* **1.** the act of forming in advance; previous formation. **2.** *Biology.* the theory, now discredited, that an individual develops by simple enlargement of a fully differentiated egg cell. Compare **epigenesis** (sense 1).

pre·fron·tal (priːˈfrʌntᵊl) *adj.* situated in, involving, or relating to the foremost part of the frontal lobe of the brain.

preg·gers (ˈprɛgəz) *adj. Chiefly Brit.* an informal word for **pregnant** (sense 1).

pre·gla·ci·al (priːˈgleɪsɪəl) *adj.* formed or occurring before a glacial period, esp. before the Pleistocene epoch.

preg·na·ble (ˈprɛgnəbᵊl) *adj.* capable of being assailed or captured. [C15 *prenable,* from Old French *prendre* to take, from Latin *prehendere* to lay hold of, catch] —ˌ**preg·na·ˈbil·i·ty** *n.*

preg·nan·cy (ˈprɛgnənsɪ) *n., pl.* ·**cies. 1.** the state or condition of being pregnant. **2.** the period from conception to childbirth.

preg·nant (ˈprɛgnənt) *adj.* **1.** carrying a fetus or fetuses within the womb. **2.** full of meaning or significance. **3.** inventive or imaginative. **4.** prolific or fruitful. [C16: from Latin *praegnāns* with child, from *prae* before + (*g*)*nascī* to be born] —ˈ**preg·nant·ly** *adv.*

pre·hen·sile (prɪˈhɛnsaɪl) *adj.* adapted for grasping, esp. by wrapping around a support: *a prehensile tail.* [C18: from French *préhensile,* from Latin *prehendere* to grasp] —**pre·hen·sil·i·ty** (ˌpriːhɛnˈsɪlɪtɪ) *n.*

pre·hen·sion (prɪˈhɛnʃən) *n.* **1.** the act of grasping. **2.** apprehension by the senses or the mind.

pre·his·tor·ic (ˌpriːhɪˈstɒrɪk) *or* **pre·his·tor·i·cal** *adj.* of or relating to man's development before the appearance of the written word. —ˌ**pre·his·ˈtor·i·cal·ly** *adv.*

pre·his·to·ry (priːˈhɪstərɪ) *n., pl.* ·**ries. 1.** the prehistoric period. **2.** the study of this period, relying entirely on archaeological evidence. —**pre·his·to·ri·an** (ˌpriːhɪˈstɔːrɪən) *n.*

pre·hom·i·nid (priːˈhɒmɪnɪd) *n.* any of various extinct manlike primates. See **australopithecine.**

pre-ig·ni·tion (ˌpriːɪgˈnɪʃən) *n.* ignition of all or part of the explosive charge in an internal-combustion engine before the exact instant necessary for correct operation.

pre·judge (priːˈdʒʌdʒ) *vb.* (*tr.*) to judge beforehand, esp. without sufficient evidence. —**pre·ˈjudg·ment** *or* **pre·ˈjudge·ment** *n.* —**pre·ˈjudg·er** *n.*

prej·u·dice (ˈprɛdʒʊdɪs) *n.* **1.** an opinion formed beforehand, esp. an unfavourable one based on inadequate facts. **2.** the act or condition of holding such opinions. **3.** intolerance of or dislike for people of a specific race, religion, etc. **4.** disadvantage or injury resulting from prejudice. **5. in** (*or* **to**) **the prejudice of.** to the detriment of. **6. without prejudice.** *Law.* without dismissing or detracting from an existing right or claim. ~*vb.* (*tr.*) **7.** to cause to be prejudiced. **8.** to disadvantage or injure by prejudice. [C13: from Old French *préjudice,* from Latin *praejūdicium* a preceding judgment, disadvantage, from *prae* before + *jūdicium* trial, sentence, from *jūdex* a judge]

prej·u·di·cial (ˌprɛdʒʊˈdɪʃəl) *adj.* causing prejudice; detrimental or damaging. —ˌ**prej·u·ˈdi·cial·ly** *adv.*

prel·a·cy (ˈprɛləsɪ) *n., pl.* ·**cies. 1.** Also called: **prel·a·ture** (ˈprɛlɪtʃə). **a.** the office or status of a prelate. **b.** prelates collectively. **2.** Also called: **prel·a·tism** (ˈprɛləˌtɪzəm). *Often derogatory.* government of the Church by prelates.

prel·ate (ˈprɛlɪt) *n.* a Church dignitary of high rank, such as a cardinal, bishop, or abbot. [C13: from Old French *prélat,* from Church Latin *praelātus,* from Latin *praeferre* to hold in special esteem, PREFER] —**pre·lat·ic** (prɪˈlætɪk) *or* **pre·ˈlat·i·cal** *adj.*

prel·a·tism (ˈprɛləˌtɪzəm) *n.* government of the Church by prelates; episcopacy. —ˈ**prel·a·tist** *n.*

pre·lect (prɪˈlɛkt) *vb.* (*intr.*) *Rare.* to lecture or discourse in public. [C17: from Late Latin *praelegere* to instruct by reading, lecture, from *prae* in front of, in public + *legere* to read, choose] —**pre·ˈlec·tion** *n.* —**pre·ˈlec·tor** *n.*

pre·lex·i·cal (priːˈlɛksɪkᵊl) *adj. Transformational grammar.* denoting or applicable at a stage in the formation of a sentence at which words and phrases have not yet replaced all of the underlying grammatical and semantic material of that sentence in the speaker's mind.

pre·li·ba·tion (ˌpriːlaɪˈbeɪʃən) *n. Rare.* an advance taste or sample; foretaste. [C16: from Late Latin *praelībātiō* a tasting beforehand, offering of the first fruits, from Latin *prae* before + *lībāre* to taste]

prelim. *abbrev. for* preliminary.

pre·lim·i·nar·ies (prɪˈlɪmɪnərɪz) *pl. n.* the full word for **prelims.**

pre·lim·i·nar·y (prɪˈlɪmɪnərɪ) *adj.* **1.** (*usually prenominal*) occurring before or in preparation; introductory. ~*n., pl.* ·**nar·ies. 2.** a preliminary event or occurrence. **3.** an eliminating contest held before the main competition. [C17: from New Latin *praelīmināris,* from Latin *prae* before + *līmen* threshold] —**pre·ˈlim·i·nar·i·ly** *adv.*

pre·lims (ˈpriːlɪmz, prəˈlɪmz) *pl. n.* **1.** Also called: **front matter.** the pages of a book, such as the title page and contents, before the main text. **2.** the first public examinations taken for the bachelor's degree in some universities.

pre·lit·er·ate (priːˈlɪtərɪt) *adj.* relating to a society that has not developed a written language. —**pre·lit·er·a·cy** (priːˈlɪtərəsɪ) *n.*

prel·ude (ˈprɛljuːd) *n.* **1. a.** a piece of music that precedes a fugue, or forms the first movement of a suite, or an introduction to an act in an opera, etc. **b.** (esp. for piano) a self-contained piece of music. **2.** something serving as an introduction or preceding event, occurrence, etc. ~*vb.* **3.** to serve as a prelude to (something). **4.** (*tr.*) to introduce by a prelude. [C16: (n.) from Medieval Latin *praelūdium,* from *prae* before + *-lūdium* entertainment, from Latin *lūdus* play; (vb.) from Late Latin *praelūdere* to play beforehand, rehearse, from *lūdere* to play] —**pre·lud·er** (prɪˈljuːdə, ˈprɛljədə) *n.* —**pre·ˈlu·di·al** *adj.* —**pre·lu·sion** (prɪˈljuːʒən) *n.* —**pre·lu·sive** (prɪˈljuːsɪv) *or* **pre·lu·so·ry** (prɪˈljuːsərɪ) *adj.* —**pre·ˈlu·sive·ly** *or* **pre·ˈlu·so·ri·ly** *adv.*

prem. *abbrev. for* premium.

pre·mar·i·tal (priːˈmærɪtᵊl) *adj.* (esp. of sexual relations) occurring before marriage. Compare **extramarital.**

prem·a·ture (ˌprɛməˈtjʊə, ˈprɛməˌtjʊə) *adj.* **1.** occurring or existing before the normal or expected time. **2.** impulsive or hasty: *a premature judgment.* **3.** (of an infant) born before the end of the full period of gestation. [C16: from Latin *praemātūrus,* very early from *prae* in advance + *mātūrus* ripe] —ˌ**prem·a·ˈture·ly** *adv.* —ˌ**prem·a·ˈture·ness** *or* ˌ**prem·a·ˈtur·i·ty** *n.*

pre·max·il·la (ˌpriːmækˈsɪlə) *n., pl.* ·**lae** (-liː). either of two bones situated in the upper jaw between the maxillary bones. —ˌ**pre·max·ˈil·lar·y** *adj.*

pre·med (priːˈmɛd) *Informal.* ~*adj.* **1.** short for **premedical.** ~*n. also* **pre·med·ic. 2.** short for **premedication. 3.** a premedical student.

pre·med·i·cal (priːˈmɛdɪkᵊl) *adj.* **1.** of or relating to a course of study prerequisite for entering medical school. **2.** of or relating to a person engaged in such a course of study: *a premedical student.* —**pre·ˈmed·i·cal·ly** *adv.*

pre·med·i·ca·tion (ˌpriːmɛdɪˈkeɪʃən) *n. Surgery.* any drugs administered to sedate and otherwise prepare a patient for general anaesthesia.

pre·med·i·tate (prɪˈmɛdɪˌteɪt) *vb.* to plan or consider (something, such as a violent crime) beforehand. —**pre·ˈmed·i·ˌtat·ed·ly** *adv.* —**pre·ˈmed·i·ˌta·tive** *adj.* —**pre·ˈmed·i·ˌta·tor** *n.*

pre·med·i·ta·tion (prɪˌmɛdɪˈteɪʃən) *n.* **1.** *Law.* prior resolve to do some act or to commit a crime. **2.** the act of premeditating.

ˌ**pre·ex·ˈpose** *vb.*
ˈ**pre·ˈflight** *adj.*
pre·ˈform *vb.*
ˌ**pre·for·ˈma·tion** *n.*
pre·ˈfranked *adj.*
pre·ˈfreeze *vb.,* ·**freez·es,** ·**freez·ing,** ·**froze,** ·**fro·zen.**
ˌ**pre-Ger·ˈman·ic** *adj.*
pre-ˈGoth·ic *adj.*
pre-ˈGreek *adj.*
pre·ˈhard·en *vb.*
pre·ˈheat *vb.*
pre-Ho·ˈmer·ic *adj.*
pre·ˈhu·man *adj.*
pre·ˈin·di·ˌcate *vb.*
ˌ**pre·in·ˈform** *vb.*
ˌ**pre·in·ˈstruct** *vb.*
pre·ˈkin·der·ˌgar·ten *adj.*
pre·lo·ˈcate *vb.*
pre-ˈMarx·i·an *adj.*

pre+mie ('pri:mɪ) *n.* a variant spelling of **preemie.**

prem+ier ('prɛmjə) *n.* **1.** another name for **prime minister. 2.** any of the heads of governments of the Canadian provinces and the Australian states. **3.** (*pl.*) *Austral.* the winners of a premiership. ~*adj.* (*prenominal*) **4.** first in importance, rank, etc. **5.** first in occurrence; earliest. [C15: from Old French: first, from Latin *prīmārius* principal, from *prīmus* first]

prem·i·ere ('prɛmɪˌɛə, 'prɛmɪə) *n.* **1.** the first public performance of a film, play, opera, etc. **2.** the leading lady in a theatre company. [C19: from French, feminine of *premier* first]

prem+ier+ship ('prɛmjəˌʃɪp) *n.* **1.** the office of premier. **2.** *Austral.* a championship competition held among a number of sporting clubs.

pre+mil+le·nar+i·an (ˌpri:mɪlɪ'nɛərɪən) *or* **pre+mil+le·nar·i+an+ist** *n.* a believer in or upholder of the doctrines of premillennialism. —ˌ**pre+mil+le·'nar·i+an+ism** *n.*

pre+mil+len·ni·al (ˌpri:mɪ'lɛnɪəl) *adj.* of or relating to the period preceding the millennium.

pre+mil+len+ni·al+ism (ˌpri:mɪ'lɛnɪəˌlɪzəm) *n.* the doctrine or belief that the millennium will be preceded by the Second Coming of Christ. —ˌ**pre+mil+'len+ni·al+ist** *n.*

prem+ise (prɪ'maɪz, 'prɛmɪs) *vb.* (when *tr., may take a clause as object*) to state or assume (a proposition) as a premiss in an argument, theory, etc. [C14: from Old French *prémisse,* from Medieval Latin *praemissa* sent on before, from Latin *praemittere* to despatch in advance, from *prae* before + *mittere* to send]

prem+is·es ('prɛmɪsɪz) *pl. n.* **1.** a piece of land together with its buildings, esp. considered as a place of business. **2.** *Law.* **a.** (in a deed, etc.) the matters referred to previously; the aforesaid; the foregoing. **b.** the introductory part of a grant, conveyance, etc. **3.** *Law.* (in the U.S.) the part of a bill in equity that states the names of the parties, details of the plaintiff's claims, etc.

prem+iss *or* **prem+ise** ('prɛmɪs) *n.* **1.** a statement that is assumed or believed to be true and from which a conclusion can logically be drawn. **2.** *Logic.* either of the two propositions of a syllogism. [see PREMISE]

pre+mi·um ('pri:mɪəm) *n.* **1.** an amount paid in addition to a standard rate, price, wage, etc.; bonus. **2.** the amount paid or payable, usually in regular instalments, for an insurance policy. **3.** the amount above nominal or par value at which something sells. **4. a.** an offer of something free or at a specially reduced price as an inducement to buy a commodity or service. **b.** (*as modifier*): *a premium offer.* **5.** a prize given to the winner of a competition; award. **6.** *U.S.* an amount sometimes charged for a loan of money in addition to the interest. **7.** great value or regard: *to put a premium on someone's services.* **8.** a fee, now rarely required, for instruction or apprenticeship in a profession or trade. **9. at a premium. a.** in great demand or of high value, usually because of scarcity. **b.** above par. [C17: from Latin *praemium* prize, booty, reward]

Pre+mi·um Sav+ings Bonds *pl. n.* (in Britain) bonds issued by the Treasury since 1956 for purchase by the public. No interest is paid but there is a monthly draw for cash prizes of various sums. Also called: **premium bonds.**

pre+mo+lar (pri:'məʊlə) *adj.* **1.** situated before a molar tooth. ~*n.* **2.** any one of eight bicuspid teeth in the human adult, two situated on each side of both jaws between the first molar and the canine.

pre+mon+ish (prɪ'mɒnɪʃ) *vb.* (*tr.*) *Rare.* to admonish beforehand; forewarn.

prem·o+ni+tion (ˌprɛmə'nɪʃən) *n.* **1.** an intuition of a future, usually unwelcome, occurrence; foreboding. **2.** an early warning of a future event; forewarning. [C16: from Late Latin *praemonitiō,* from Latin *praemonēre* to admonish beforehand, from *prae* before + *monēre* to warn, advise] —**pre+mon+i·to·ry** (prɪ'mɒnɪtərɪ, -trɪ) *adj.*

pre+morse (prɪ'mɔ:s) *adj. Biology.* appearing as though the end had been bitten off: *a premorse leaf.* [C18: from Latin *praemorsus* bitten off in front, from *praemordēre,* from *prae* in front + *mordēre* to bite]

pre+mu+ni+tion (ˌpri:mjʊ'nɪʃən) *n. Med.* a state of immunity acquired as the result of a persistent latent infection. [C15 (in the sense: to protect beforehand): from Latin *praemūnitiō,* from *praemūnīre,* from *prae* before + *mūnīre* to fortify]

pre+na+tal (pri:'neɪtᵊl) *adj.* **1.** occurring or present before birth; during pregnancy. ~*n.* **2.** *Informal.* a prenatal examination. ~Also: **antenatal.** —**pre+'na+tal+ly** *adv.*

pre+no+men (pri:'nəʊmɛn) *n., pl.* **+nom+i+na** (-'nɒmɪnə) *or* **+no+mens.** *U.S.* a less common spelling of **praenomen.**

pre+nom·i·nal (pri:'nɒmɪnᵊl) *adj.* **1.** placed before a noun, esp. (of an adjective or sense of an adjective) used only before a noun. **2.** of or relating to a praenomen.

pre+no+tion (pri:'nəʊʃən) *n.* a rare word for **preconception.**

pren+tice ('prɛntɪs) *n.* an archaic word for **apprentice.**

pre+oc+cu+pa+tion (pri:ˌɒkjʊ'peɪʃən) *or* **pre+oc+cu+pan+cy** (pri:'ɒkjʊpənsɪ) *n.* **1.** the state of being preoccupied, esp. mentally. **2.** something that holds the attention or preoccupies the mind.

pre+oc+cu+pied (pri:'ɒkjʊˌpaɪd) *adj.* **1.** engrossed or absorbed in something, esp. one's own thoughts. **2.** already or previously occupied. **3.** *Biology.* (of a taxonomic name) already used to designate a genus, species, etc.

pre+oc+cu+py (pri:'ɒkjʊˌpaɪ) *vb.* **+pies, +py+ing, +pied.** (*tr.*) **1.** to engross the thoughts or mind of. **2.** to occupy before or in advance of another. [C16: from Latin *praeoccupāre* to capture in advance, from *prae* before + *occupāre* to seize, take possession of]

pre+or+dain (ˌpri:ɔ:'deɪn) *vb.* (*tr.*) to ordain, decree, or appoint beforehand. —**pre+or+di+na+tion** (ˌpri:ɔ:dɪ'neɪʃən) *n.*

prep (prɛp) *n. Informal.* short for **preparation** (sense 5) or (chiefly U.S.) **preparatory school.**

prep. *abbrev. for:* **1.** preparation. **2.** preparatory. **3.** preposition.

prep·a+ra+tion (ˌprɛpə'reɪʃən) *n.* **1.** the act or process of preparing. **2.** the state of being prepared; readiness. **3.** (*often pl.*) a measure done in order to prepare for something; provision: *to make preparations for something.* **4.** something that is prepared, esp. a medicine. **5.** (esp. in a boarding school) **a.** homework. **b.** the period reserved for this. Usually shortened to **prep 6.** *Music.* **a.** the anticipation of a dissonance so that the note producing it in one chord is first heard in the preceding chord as a consonance. **b.** a note so employed. **7.** (*often cap.*) the preliminary prayers at Mass or divine service. **8.** the Friday before the Jewish Sabbath or any of the major Jewish festivals.

pre+par·a+tive (prɪ'pærətɪv) *adj.* **1.** serving to prepare; preparatory. ~*n.* **2.** something that prepares. —**pre+'par·a+tive+ly** *adv.*

pre+par·a+to·ry (prɪ'pærətərɪ, -trɪ) *adj.* **1.** serving to prepare. **2.** introductory or preliminary. **3.** occupied in preparation. **4. preparatory to.** as a preparation to; before: *a drink preparatory to eating.* —**pre+'par·a+to+ri+ly** *adv.*

pre+par·a+to·ry school *n.* **1.** (in Britain) a private school, usually single-sex and for children between the ages of 6 and 13, generally preparing pupils for public school. **2.** (in the U.S.) a private secondary school preparing pupils for college. ~Often shortened to **prep school.**

pre+pare (prɪ'pɛə) *vb.* **1.** to make ready or suitable in advance for a particular purpose or for some use, event, etc.: *to prepare a meal; to prepare to go.* **2.** to put together using parts or ingredients; compose or construct. **3.** (*tr.*) to equip or outfit, as for an expedition. **4.** (*tr.*) *Music.* to soften the impact of (a dissonant note) by the use of preparation. **5. be prepared.** (*foll. by an infinitive*) willing and able (to do something): *I'm not prepared to reveal these figures.* [C15: from Latin *praeparāre, from prae* before + *parāre* to make ready] —**pre+'par+er** *n.*

pre+par+ed+ness (prɪ'pɛərɪdnɪs) *n.* the state of being prepared or ready, esp. militarily ready for war. —**pre+'par+ed+ly** *adv.*

pre+pay (pri:'peɪ) *vb.* **+pays, +pay+ing, +paid.** (*tr.*) to pay for in advance. —**pre+'pay+a·ble** *adj.* —**pre+'pay+ment** *n.*

pre+pense (prɪ'pɛns) *adj.* (*postpositive*) (usually in legal contexts) arranged in advance; premeditated (esp. in the phrase **malice prepense**). [C18: from Anglo-Norman *purpensé,* from Old French *purpenser* to consider in advance, from *penser* to think, from Latin *pēnsāre* to weigh, consider]

pre+pon+der+ant (prɪ'pɒndərənt) *adj.* greater in weight, force, influence, etc. —**pre+'pon+der+ance** *or* **pre+'pon+der+an+cy** *n.* —**pre+'pon+der+ant+ly** *adv.*

pre+pon+der+ate (prɪ'pɒndəˌreɪt) *vb.* (*intr.*) **1.** (often foll. by *over*) to be more powerful, important, numerous, etc., (than). **2.** to be of greater weight than something else. **3.** *Archaic.* to be weighed down. [C17: from Late Latin *praeponderāre* to be of greater weight, from *pondus* weight] —**pre+'pon+der+ˌat+ing+ly** *adv.* —**pre+'pon+der+ate+ly** *adv.* —**pre+ˌpon+der·'a+tion** *n.*

prep·o+si+tion (ˌprɛpə'zɪʃən) *n.* a word or group of words used before a noun or pronoun to relate it grammatically or semantically to some other constituent of a sentence. Abbrev.: **prep.** [C14: from Latin *praepositiō* a putting before, from *pōnere* to place] —ˌ**prep·o+'si+tion+al** *adj.* —ˌ**prep·o+'si+tion+al+ly** *adv.*

Usage. The practice of ending a sentence with a preposition (*they are the people I hate talking to*) has been much condemned, but careful users avoid it only where it would be stylistically clumsy.

pre+pos·i+tive (pri:'pɒzɪtɪv) *adj.* **1.** (of a word or speech element) placed before the word governed or modified. ~*n.* **2.** a prepositive element. —**pre+'pos·i+tive+ly** *adv.*

pre+pos·i+tor (pri:'pɒzɪtə) *or* **pre+pos+tor** (pri:'pɒstə) *n. Brit., rare.* a prefect in any of certain public schools. [C16: from Latin *praepositus* placed before]

pre+pos+sess (ˌpri:pə'zɛs) *vb.* (*tr.*) **1.** to preoccupy or engross mentally. **2.** to influence in advance for or against a person or thing; prejudice; bias. **3.** to make a favourable impression on beforehand.

pre+pos+sess+ing (ˌpri:pə'zɛsɪŋ) *adj.* creating a favourable impression; attractive. —ˌ**pre+pos+'sess+ing+ly** *adv.* —ˌ**pre+pos+'sess+ing+ness** *n.*

pre+pos+ses+sion (ˌpri:pə'zɛʃən) *n.* **1.** the state or condition of being prepossessed. **2.** a prejudice or bias, esp. a favourable one.

pre+pos+ter+ous (prɪ'pɒstərəs) *adj.* contrary to nature, reason, or sense; absurd; ridiculous. [C16: from Latin *praeposterus* reversed, from *prae* in front, before + *posterus* following] —**pre+'pos+ter+ous+ly** *adv.* —**pre+'pos+ter+ous+ness** *n.*

pre+po+ten+cy (prɪ'pəʊtᵊnsɪ) *n.* **1.** the state or condition of being prepotent. **2.** *Genetics.* the ability of one parent to transmit more characteristics to its offspring than the other parent. **3.** *Botany.* the ability of pollen from one source to bring about fertilization more readily than that from other sources.

pre+po+tent (prɪ'pəʊtᵊnt) *adj.* **1.** greater in power, force, or

ˌ**pre-Men+'de·li·an** *adj.*
pre+'men+stru+al *adj.*
pre+'mix *vb.*
pre+'nup+tial *adj.*
pre+'pack *vb.*
pre+'pack+age *vb.*
pre+'pal·a+tal *adj.*
pre+'plan *vb.,* **+plans, +plan+ning, +planned.**
pre+'pran+di·al *adj.*
ˌ**pre+pub+li+'ca+tion** *adj.*
ˌ**pre+re+'cord** *vb.*

influence. **2.** *Biology.* showing prepotency. [C15: from Latin *praepotens* very powerful, from *posse* to be able] —**pre·'po·tent·ly** *adv.*

prep school *n. Informal.* See **preparatory school.**

pre·puce ('pri:pju:s) *n.* **1.** the retractable fold of skin covering the tip of the penis. Nontechnical name: **foreskin. 2.** a similar fold of skin covering the tip of the clitoris. [C14: from Latin *praepūtium*] —**pre·pu·tial** (pri:'pju:ʃəl) *adj.*

Pre-Raph·ael·ite (ˌpri:'ræfəˌlaɪt) *n.* **1.** a member of the **Pre-Raphaelite Brotherhood,** an association of painters and writers including Rossetti, Holman Hunt, and Millais, founded in 1848 to combat the shallow conventionalism of academic painting and revive the fidelity to nature and the vivid realistic colour that they considered typical of Italian painting before Raphael. ~*adj.* **2.** of, in the manner of, or relating to Pre-Raphaelite painting and painters. —**ˌPre-'Raph·ael·ˌit·ism** *n.*

pre·req·ui·site (pri:'rɛkwɪzɪt) *adj.* **1.** required as a prior condition. ~*n.* **2.** something required as a prior condition.

pre·rog·a·tive (prɪ'rɒgətɪv) *n.* **1.** an exclusive privilege or right exercised by a person or group of people holding a particular office or hereditary rank. **2.** any privilege or right. **3.** a power, privilege, or immunity restricted to a sovereign or sovereign government. **4.** *Archaic.* precedence or pre-eminence. ~*adj.* **5.** having or able to exercise a prerogative. [C14: from Latin *praerogātīva* privilege, earlier: group with the right to vote first, from *prae* before + *rogāre* to ask, beg for]

pres. *abbrev. for:* **1.** present (time). **2.** presidential.

Pres. *abbrev. for* President.

pre·sa ('prɛsɑ:) *n., pl.* **·se** (-seɪ). *Music.* a sign or symbol used in a canon, round, etc., to indicate the entry of each part. Usual signs: :S: or ※ [Italian, literally: a taking up, from *prendere* to take, from Latin *prehendere* to grasp]

pres·age *n.* ('prɛsɪdʒ). **1.** an intimation or warning of something about to happen; portent; omen. **2.** a sense of what is about to happen; foreboding. **3.** *Archaic.* a forecast or prediction. ~*vb.* ('prɛsɪdʒ, prɪ'seɪdʒ). **4.** (*tr.*) to have a presentiment of. **5.** (*tr.*) to give a forewarning of; portend. **6.** (*intr.*) to make a prediction. [C14: from Latin *praesāgium* presentiment, from *praesāgīre* to perceive beforehand, from *sāgīre* to perceive acutely] —**pre·'sage·ful** *adj.* —**pre·'sage·ful·ly** *adv.* —**pre·'sag·er** *n.*

Presb. *abbrev. for* Presbyterian.

pres·by·o·pi·a (ˌprɛzbɪ'əʊpɪə) *n.* a progressively diminishing ability of the eye to focus, noticeable from middle to old age, caused by loss of elasticity of the crystalline lens. [C18: New Latin, from Greek *presbus* old man + *ōps* eye] —**pres·by·op·ic** (ˌprɛzbɪ'ɒpɪk) *adj.*

pres·by·ter ('prɛzbɪtə) *n.* **1. a.** an elder of a congregation in the early Christian Church. **b.** (in some Churches having episcopal politics) an official who is subordinate to a bishop and has administrative, teaching, and sacerdotal functions. **2.** (in some hierarchical Churches) another name for **priest. 3.** (in the Presbyterian Church) **a.** a teaching elder. **b.** a ruling elder. [C16: from Late Latin, from Greek *presbuteros* an older man, from *presbus* old man]

pres·byt·er·ate (prɛz'bɪtərɪt, -ˌreɪt) *n.* **1.** the status or office of a presbyter. **2.** a group of presbyters.

pres·by·ter·i·al (ˌprɛzbɪ'tɪərɪəl) *adj.* of or relating to a presbyter or presbytery. Also: **pres·byt·er·al** (prɛz'bɪtərəl). —**ˌpres·by·'ter·i·al·ly** *adv.*

pres·by·ter·i·an (ˌprɛzbɪ'tɪərɪən) *adj.* **1.** of, relating to, or designating Church government by presbyters or lay elders. ~*n.* **2.** an upholder of this type of Church government. —**ˌpres·by·'ter·i·an·ism** *n.* —**ˌpres·by·ˌter·i·an·'is·tic** *adj.*

Pres·by·ter·i·an (ˌprɛzbɪ'tɪərɪən) *adj.* **1.** of or relating to any of various Protestant Churches governed by presbyters or lay elders and adhering to various modified forms of Calvinism. In 1972 the Presbyterian Church of England became part of the United Reformed Church. ~*n.* **2.** a member of a Presbyterian Church. —**ˌPres·by·'ter·i·an·ism** *n.*

pres·by·ter·y ('prɛzbɪtərɪ, -trɪ) *n., pl.* **·ter·ies. 1.** *Presbyterian Church.* **a.** a local Church court composed of ministers and elders. **b.** the congregations or churches within the jurisdiction of any such court. **2.** the part of a cathedral or church east of the choir, in which the main altar is situated; sanctuary. **3.** presbyters or elders collectively. **4.** government of a church by presbyters or elders. **5.** *R.C. Church.* the residence of a parish priest. [C15: from Old French *presbiterie,* from Church Latin *presbyterium,* from Greek *presbyterion;* see PRESBYTER]

pres·ci·ence ('prɛsɪəns) *n.* knowledge of events before they take place; foreknowledge. [C14: from Latin *praescīre* to foreknow, from *prae* before + *scīre* to know] —**'pres·ci·ent** *adj.* —**'pres·ci·ent·ly** *adv.*

pre·scind (prɪ'sɪnd) *vb. Rare.* **1.** (*intr.;* usually foll. by *from*) to withdraw attention (from something). **2.** (*tr.*) to isolate, remove, or separate, as for special consideration. [C17: from Late Latin *praescindere* to cut off in front, from Latin *prae* before + *scindere* to split]

Pres·cott ('prɛskət) *n.* **Wil·liam Hick·ling** ('hɪklɪŋ). 1796–1858, U.S. historian, noted for his work on the history of Spain and her colonies.

pre·scribe (prɪ'skraɪb) *vb.* **1.** to lay down as a rule or directive. **2.** *Law.* to claim or acquire (a right, title, etc.) by prescription. **3.** *Law.* to make or become invalid or unenforceable by lapse of time. **4.** *Med.* to recommend or order the use of (a drug or other remedy). [C16: from Latin *praescrībere* to write previously, from *prae* before + *scrībere* to write] —**pre·'scrib·er** *n.*

pre·script *n.* ('pri:skrɪpt). **1.** something laid down or prescribed. ~*adj.* (prɪ'skrɪpt, 'pri:skrɪpt). **2.** prescribed as a rule. [C16: from Latin *praescriptum* something written down beforehand, from *praescrībere* to PRESCRIBE]

pre·scrip·ti·ble (prɪ'skrɪptəbᵊl) *adj.* **1.** subject to prescription. **2.** depending on or derived from prescription. —**pre·ˌscrip·ti·'bil·i·ty** *n.*

pre·scrip·tion (prɪ'skrɪpʃən) *n.* **1. a.** written instructions from a physician, dentist, etc., to a pharmacist stating the form, dosage strength, etc., of a drug to be issued to a specific patient. **b.** the drug or remedy prescribed. **2.** (*modifier*) (of drugs) available legally only with a doctor's prescription. **3. a.** written instructions for an optician on the proper grinding of lenses for spectacles. **b.** (*as modifier*): *prescription glasses.* **4.** the act of prescribing. **5.** something that is prescribed. **6.** a long established custom or a claim based on one. **7.** *Law.* **a.** the uninterrupted possession of property over a stated period of time, after which a right or title is acquired (**positive prescription**). **b.** the barring of adverse claims to property, etc., after a specified period of time has elapsed, allowing the possessor to acquire title (**negative prescription**). **c.** the right or title acquired in either of these ways. [C14: from legal Latin *praescriptiō* an order, prescription; see PRESCRIBE]

pre·scrip·tive (prɪ'skrɪptɪv) *adj.* **1.** making or giving directions, rules, or injunctions. **2.** sanctioned by long-standing usage or custom. **3.** derived from or based upon legal prescription: *a prescriptive title.* —**pre·'scrip·tive·ly** *adv.* —**pre·'scrip·tive·ness** *n.*

pre·scrip·tiv·ism (prɪ'skrɪptɪˌvɪzəm) *n. Ethics.* the theory that moral utterances have no truth value but prescribe attitudes to others and express the conviction of the speaker. Compare **descriptivism, emotivism.**

pres·ence ('prɛzəns) *n.* **1.** the state or fact of being present. **2.** the immediate proximity of a person or thing. **3.** personal appearance or bearing, esp. of a dignified nature. **4.** an imposing or dignified personality. **5.** an invisible spirit felt to be nearby. **6.** *Obsolete.* assembly or company. **7.** *Obsolete.* short for **presence chamber.** [C14: via Old French from Latin *praesentia* a being before, from *praeesse* to be before, from *prae* before + *esse* to be]

pres·ence cham·ber *n.* the room in which a great person, such as a monarch, receives guests, assemblies, etc.

pres·ence of mind *n.* the ability to remain calm and act constructively during times of crisis.

pres·ent[1] ('prɛzᵊnt) *adj.* **1.** (*prenominal*) in existence at the moment in time at which an utterance is spoken or written. **2.** (*postpositive*) being in a specified place, thing, etc.: *the murderer is present in this room.* **3.** (*prenominal*) now in consideration or under discussion: *the present topic; the present author.* **4.** *Grammar.* denoting a tense of verbs used when the action or event described is occurring at the time of utterance or when the speaker does not wish to make any explicit temporal reference. **5.** *Archaic.* readily available; instant: *present help is at hand.* **6.** *Archaic.* mentally alert; attentive. ~*n.* **7. the present.** the time being; now. **8.** *Grammar.* **a.** the present tense. **b.** a verb in this tense. **9. at present.** at the moment; now. **10. for the present.** for the time being; temporarily. [C13: from Latin *praesens,* from *praeesse* to be in front of, from *prae-* before, in front + *esse* to be]

pre·sent[2] *vb.* (prɪ'zɛnt). (*tr.*) **1.** to introduce (a person) to another, esp. to someone of higher rank. **2.** to introduce to the public; show; exhibit: *to present a play.* **3.** to bring or suggest to the mind: *to present a problem.* **4.** to give or award: *to present a prize.* **5.** to endow with or as if with a gift or award: *to present a university with a foundation scholarship.* **6.** to offer formally: *to present one's compliments.* **7.** to offer or hand over for action or settlement: *to present a bill.* **8.** to represent or depict in a particular manner: *the actor presented Hamlet as a very young man.* **9.** to salute someone with (one's weapon) (usually in the phrase **present arms**). **10.** to aim or point (a weapon). **11.** to nominate (a clergyman) to a bishop for institution to a benefice in his diocese. **12.** to lay (a charge, etc.) before a court, magistrate, etc., for consideration or trial. **13.** to bring a formal charge or accusation against (a person); indict. **14.** *Chiefly U.S.* (of a grand jury) to take notice of (an offence) from personal knowledge or observation, before any bill of indictment has been drawn up. **15. present oneself.** to appear, esp. at a specific time and place. ~*n.* ('prɛzᵊnt). **16.** anything that is presented; a gift. **17. make someone a present of.** to give someone something: *I'll make you a present of a new car.* [C13: from Old French *presenter,* from Latin *praesentāre* to exhibit, offer, from *praesens* PRESENT[1]] —**pre·'sent·er** *n.*

pre·sent·a·ble (prɪ'zɛntəbᵊl) *adj.* **1.** fit to be presented or introduced to other people. **2.** fit to be displayed or offered. —**pre·'sent·a·ble·ness** *or* **pre·ˌsent·a·'bil·i·ty** *n.* —**pre·'sent·a·bly** *adv.*

pres·en·ta·tion (ˌprɛzən'teɪʃən) *n.* **1.** the act of presenting or state of being presented. **2.** the manner of presenting; delivery. **3. a.** an offering or bestowal, as of a gift. **b.** (*as modifier*): *a presentation copy of a book.* **4.** a performance or representation, as of a play. **5.** the formal introduction of a person, as into society or at court; debut. **6.** the act or right of nominating

ˌpre-Ref·or·'ma·tion *n.*
pre·'reg·is·ter *vb.*
ˌpre·reg·is·'tra·tion *n.*
ˌpre-Ren·'ais·sance *n.*
pre-'Ro·man *adj.*
ˌpre·ro·'man·tic *adj.*
'pre·'school *adj.*
ˌpre·sci·en·'ti·fic *adj.*
pre·'sea·son·al *adj.*
ˌpre·se·'lect *vb.*
pre·'set *vb.*
pre·'shape *vb.*

a clergyman to a benefice. **7.** *Med.* the position of a baby relative to the birth canal at the time of birth. **8.** *Commerce.* another word for **presentment** (sense 4). **9.** an archaic word for **gift. 10.** *Philosophy.* a sense datum. **11.** (*often cap.*) another name for (feast of) **Candlemas.** —ˌ**pres+en+'ta+tion+al** *adj.*

pres+en+ta+tion+ism (ˌprɛzənˈteɪʃəˌnɪzəm) *n. Philosophy.* the theory that objects are identical with our perceptions of them. Compare **representationalism.** —ˌ**pres+en+'ta+tion+ist** *n., adj.*

pre+sent·a+tive (prɪˈzɛntətɪv) *adj.* **1.** *Philosophy.* **a.** able to be known or perceived immediately. **b.** capable of knowing or perceiving in this way. **2.** subject to or conferring the right of ecclesiastical presentation. —**pre+'sent·a+tive+ness** *n.*

pres·ent-day *n.* (*modifier*) of the modern day; current: *I don't like present-day fashions.*

pres+en+tee (ˌprɛzənˈtiː) *n.* **1.** a person who is presented, as at court. **2.** a person to whom something is presented.

pre+sen+tient (prɪˈsɛnʃənt, -ˈzɛn-, priː-) *adj.* characterized by or experiencing a presentiment. [C19: from Latin *praesentiens* present participle of *praesentire,* from *prae-* PRE- + *sentire* to feel]

pre+sen+ti+ment (prɪˈzɛntɪmənt) *n.* a sense of something about to happen; premonition. [C18: from obsolete French, from *pressentir* to sense beforehand; see PRE-, SENTIMENT]

pres+ent+ly (ˈprɛzəntlɪ) *adv.* **1.** in a short while; soon. **2.** *Chiefly U.S.* at the moment. **3.** an archaic word for **immediately.**

pre+sent+ment (prɪˈzɛntmənt) *n.* **1.** the act of presenting or state of being presented; presentation. **2.** something presented, such as a picture, play, etc. **3.** *Law, chiefly U.S.* a statement on oath by a grand jury of something within their own knowledge or observation, esp. the commission of an offence when the indictment has been laid before them. **4.** *Commerce.* the presenting of a bill of exchange, promissory note, etc.

pres+ent par+ti+ci+ple *n.* a participial form of verbs used adjectivally when the action it describes is contemporaneous with that of the main verb of a sentence and also used in the formation of certain compound tenses. In English this form ends in *-ing.* Compare **gerund.**

pres+ent per+fect *adj., n. Grammar.* another term for **perfect** (senses 8, 11).

pres+ents (ˈprɛzənts) *pl. n. Law.* used in a deed or document to refer to itself: *know all men by these presents.*

pres+ent val·ue *n.* the current capital value of a future income or outlay or of a series of such incomes or outlays. It is computed by the process of discounting at a predetermined rate of interest.

pre+serv·a+tive (prɪˈzɜːvətɪv) *n.* **1.** something that preserves or tends to preserve, esp. a chemical added to foods to inhibit decomposition. ~*adj.* **2.** tending or intended to preserve.

pre+serve (prɪˈzɜːv) *vb.* (*mainly tr.*) **1.** to keep safe from danger or harm; protect. **2.** to protect from decay or dissolution; maintain: *to preserve old buildings.* **3.** to maintain possession of; keep up: *to preserve a facade of indifference.* **4.** to prevent from decomposition or chemical change. **5.** to prepare (food), as by freezing, drying, or salting, so that it will resist decomposition. **6.** to make preserves of (fruit, etc.). **7.** to rear and protect (game) in restricted places for hunting or fishing. **8.** (*intr.*) to maintain protection and favourable conditions for game in preserves. ~*n.* **9.** something that preserves or is preserved. **10.** a special area or domain: *archaeology is the preserve of specialists.* **11.** (*usually pl.*) fruit, etc., prepared by cooking with sugar. **12.** areas where game is reared for private hunting or fishing. [C14: via Old French, from Late Latin *praeservāre* literally: to keep safe in advance, from Latin *prae* before + *servāre* to keep safe] —**pre+'serv+a·ble** *adj.* —**pre+ˌserv+a·'bil+i·ty** *n.* —**pre+'serv+a·bly** *adv.* —**pres+er+va+tion** (ˌprɛzəˈveɪʃən) *n.* —**pre+'serv+er** *n.*

pre+shrunk (priːˈʃrʌŋk) *adj.* (of fabrics, garments, etc.) having undergone a shrinking process during manufacture so that further shrinkage will not occur.

pre+side (prɪˈzaɪd) *vb.* (*intr.*) **1.** to sit in or hold a position of authority, as over a meeting. **2.** to exercise authority; control. **3.** to occupy a position as an instrumentalist: *he presided at the organ.* [C17: via French from Latin *praesidēre* to superintend, from *prae* before + *sedēre* to sit] —**pre+'sid+er** *n.*

pres·i+den+cy (ˈprɛzɪdənsɪ) *n., pl.* **+cies. 1. a.** the office, dignity, or term of a president. **b.** (*often cap.*) the office of president of a republic, esp. the office of the President of the U.S. **2.** *Mormon Church.* **a.** a local administrative council consisting of a president and two executive members. **b.** (*often cap.*) the supreme administrative body composed of the Prophet and two councillors.

pres·i+dent (ˈprɛzɪdənt) *n.* **1.** (*often cap.*) the chief executive or head of state of a republic, esp. of the U.S. **2.** (in the U.S.) the chief executive officer of a company, corporation, etc. **3.** a person who presides over an assembly, meeting, etc. **4.** the chief executive officer of certain establishments of higher education. [C14: via Old French from Late Latin *praesidens* ruler; see PRESIDE] —**pres·i+den+tial** (ˌprɛzɪˈdɛnʃəl) *adj.* —ˌ**pres·i+'den+tial+ly** *adv.* —**'pres·i+dent+ˌship** *n.*

pres·i·dent-e·lect *n.* a person who has been elected president but has not yet entered office.

pre+sid·i·o (prɪˈsɪdɪˌəʊ; *Spanish* preˈsiðjo) *n., pl.* **+sid·i·os** (-ˈsɪdɪˌəʊz; *Spanish* -ˈsiðjos). a military post or establishment, esp. in countries under Spanish control. [C19: from Spanish: garrison, from Latin *praesidium* a guard, protection; see PRESIDE]

pre+sid+i·um (prɪˈsɪdɪəm) *n.* **1.** (*often cap.*) (in Communist countries) a permanent committee of a larger body, such as a legislature, that acts for it when it is recessed. **2.** a collective presidency, esp. of a nongovernmental organization. [C20: from Russian *prezidium,* from Latin *praesidium,* from *praesidēre* to superintend; see PRESIDE]

pre+sig+ni+fy (priːˈsɪgnɪˌfaɪ) *vb.* **+fies, +fy+ing, +fied.** (*tr.*) to signify beforehand; foreshadow; foretell.

Pres·ley (ˈprɛzlɪ) *n.* **El·vis.** 1935–77, U.S. rock-and-roll singer, who turned to singing ballads after 1960. His early recordings include the singles *Heartbreak Hotel, Hound Dog, All shook up,* and *Don't be cruel* (all 1956–58) and numbers from the soundtracks of films in which he appeared, including *Jailhouse Rock* and *King Creole* (both 1958).

press[1] (prɛs) *vb.* **1.** to apply or exert weight, force, or steady pressure on: *he pressed the button on the camera.* **2.** (*tr.*) to squeeze or compress so as to alter in shape or form. **3.** to apply heat or pressure to (clothing) so as to smooth out or mark with creases; iron. **4.** to make (objects) from soft material by pressing with a mould, form, etc., esp. to make gramophone records from plastic. **5.** (*tr.*) to hold tightly or clasp, as in an embrace. **6.** (*tr.*) to extract or force out (juice) by pressure (from). **7.** (*tr.*) *Weightlifting.* to successfully lift (a weight) with a press: *he managed to press 280 pounds.* **8.** (*tr.*) to force, constrain, or compel. **9.** to importune or entreat (a person) insistently; urge: *they pressed for an answer.* **10.** to harass or cause harassment. **11.** (*tr.*) to plead or put forward strongly or importunately: *to press a claim.* **12.** (*intr.*) to be urgent. **13.** (*tr.*; usually passive) to have little of: *we're hard pressed for time.* **14.** (when *intr.,* often foll. by *on* or *forward*) to hasten or advance or cause to hasten or advance in a forceful manner. **15.** (*tr.*) (formerly) to put to death or subject to torture by placing heavy weights upon. **16.** (*tr.*) *Archaic.* to trouble or oppress. ~*n.* **17.** any machine that exerts pressure to form, shape, or cut materials or to extract liquids, compress solids, or hold components together while an adhesive joint is formed. **18.** See **printing press. 19.** the art or process of printing. **20. at** *or* **in (the) press.** being printed. **21. to (the) press.** to be printed: *when is this book going to press?* **22. a. the press.** news media and agencies collectively, esp. newspapers. **b.** (*as modifier*): *a press matter; press relations.* **23. the press.** those who work in the news media, esp. newspaper reporters and photographers. **24.** the opinions and reviews in the newspapers, etc.: *the play received a poor press.* **25.** the act of pressing or state of being pressed. **26.** the act of crowding, thronging, or pushing together. **27.** a closely packed throng of people; crowd; multitude. **28.** urgency or hurry in business affairs. **29.** a cupboard, esp. a large one used for storing clothes or linen. **30.** a wood or metal clamp or vice to prevent tennis rackets, etc., from warping when not in use. **31.** *Weightlifting.* a lift in which the weight is raised to shoulder level and then above the head. [C14 *pressen,* from Old French *presser,* from Latin *pressāre,* from *premere* to press]

press[2] (prɛs) *vb.* (*tr.*) **1.** to recruit (men) by forcible measures for military service. **2.** to use for a purpose other than intended, (esp. in the phrase **press into service**). ~*n.* **3.** recruitment into military service by forcible measures, as by a press gang. [C16: back formation from *prest* to recruit soldiers; see PREST[2]; also influenced by PRESS[1]]

press a·gen+cy *n.* another name for **news agency.**

press a·gent *n.* a person employed to obtain favourable publicity, such as notices in newspapers, for an organization, actor, etc. Abbrev.: **PA**

press box *n.* an area reserved for reporters, as in a sports stadium.

Press+burg (ˈprɛsˌbʊrk) *n.* the German name for **Bratislava.**

press con+fer+ence *n.* an interview for press and television reporters given by a politician, film star, etc.

press gal+ler+y *n.* an area set apart for newspaper reporters, esp. in a legislative assembly.

press gang *n.* **1.** (formerly) a detachment of men used to press civilians for service in the navy or army. ~*vb.* **press-gang.** (*tr.*) **2.** to force (a person) to join the navy or army by a press gang. **3.** to induce (a person) to perform a duty by forceful persuasion: *his friends press-ganged him into joining the committee.*

pres+sie *or* **prez+zie** (ˈprɛzɪ) *n.* an informal word for **present**[2] (sense 16).

press+ing (ˈprɛsɪŋ) *adj.* **1.** demanding immediate attention. **2.** persistent or importunate. ~*n.* **3.** a large specified number of gramophone records produced at one time from a master record. —**'press+ing+ly** *adv.* —**'press+ing+ness** *n.*

press+man (ˈprɛsmən, -ˌmæn) *n., pl.* **+men. 1.** a person who works for the press. **2.** a person who operates a printing press.

press+mark (ˈprɛsˌmɑːk) *n. Library science.* a location mark on a book indicating a specific bookcase.

press of sail *n. Nautical.* the most sail a vessel can carry under given conditions. Also called: **press of canvas.**

pres+sor (ˈprɛsə, -sɔː) *adj. Physiol.* relating to or producing an increase in blood pressure. [C19: from Latin *premere* to press]

press re+lease *n.* an official announcement or account of a news item circulated to the press.

press+room (ˈprɛsˌruːm, -ˌrʊm) *n.* the room in a printing establishment that houses the printing presses.

press stud *n.* a fastening device consisting of one part with a projecting knob that snaps into a hole on another like part, used esp. in closures in clothing. Also called: **popper, snap fastener.**

press-up *n.* an exercise in which the body is alternately raised from and lowered to the floor by the arms only, the trunk being kept straight with the toes and hands resting on the floor. Also called (U.S.): **push-up.**

pres+sure (ˈprɛʃə) *n.* **1.** the state of pressing or being pressed. **2.**

the exertion of force by one body on the surface of another. **3.** a moral force that compels: *to bring pressure to bear.* **4.** an urgent claim or demand or series of urgent claims or demands: *to work under pressure.* **5.** a burdensome condition that is hard to bear: *the pressure of grief.* **6.** the force applied to a unit area of a surface, usually measured in pascals (newtons per square metre), millibars, torr, or atmospheres. Symbol: *p* or *P* **7.** short for **atmospheric pressure** or **blood pressure.** ~*vb.* **8.** (*tr.*) *Chiefly U.S.* to constrain or compel, as by the application of moral force. **9.** another word for **pressurize.** [C14: from Late Latin *pressūra* a pressing, from Latin *premere* to press] —**'pres·sure·less** *adj.*

pres·sure cab·in *n.* the pressurized cabin of an aircraft or spacecraft.

pres·sure-cook *vb.* to cook (food) in a pressure cooker.

pres·sure cook·er *n.* a strong hermetically sealed pot in which food may be cooked quickly under pressure at a temperature above the normal boiling point of water.

pres·sure drag *n.* the part of the total drag of a body moving through a gas or liquid caused by the components of the pressures at right angles to the surface of the body.

pres·sure gauge *n.* any instrument for measuring fluid pressure. See also **Bourdon gauge, manometer.**

pres·sure gra·di·ent *n. Meteorol.* the decrease in atmospheric pressure per unit of horizontal distance, shown on a synoptic chart by the spacing of the isobars.

pres·sure group *n.* a group of people who seek to exert pressure on legislators, public opinion, etc., in order to promote their own ideas or welfare.

pres·sure head *n. Physics.* a more formal name for **head** (sense 24a.).

pres·sure point *n.* any of several points on the body above an artery that, when firmly pressed, will control bleeding from the artery at a point farther away from the heart.

pres·sure suit *n.* an inflatable suit worn by a person flying at high altitudes or in space, to provide protection from low pressure.

pres·sur·ize *or* **pres·sur·ise** ('prɛʃə,raɪz) *vb.* (*tr.*) **1.** to increase the pressure in (an enclosure, such as an aircraft cabin) in order to maintain approximately atmospheric pressure when the external pressure is low. **2.** to increase pressure on (a fluid). —**,pres·sur·i·'za·tion** *or* **,pres·sur·i·'sa·tion** *n.* —**'pres·sur·,iz·er** *or* **'pres·sur·,is·er** *n.*

press·work ('prɛs,wɜ:k) *n.* **1.** the operation of a printing press. **2.** the matter printed by a printing press.

prest[1] (prɛst) *adj. Obsolete.* prepared for action or use; ready. [C13: via Old French from Late Latin *praestus* ready to hand; see PRESTO]

prest[2] (prɛst) *n. Obsolete.* a loan of money. [C16: originally, loan money offered as an inducement to recruits, from Old French: advance pay in the army, from *prester* to lend, from Latin *praestāre* to provide, from *prae* before + *stāre* to stand]

Pres·ter John ('prɛstə) *n.* a legendary Christian priest and king, believed in the Middle Ages to have ruled in the Far East, but identified in the 14th century with the king of Ethiopia. [C14 *Prestre Johan,* from Medieval Latin *presbyter Iohannes* Priest John]

pres·ti·dig·i·ta·tion (,prɛstɪ,dɪdʒɪ'teɪʃən) *n.* another name for **sleight of hand.** [C19: from French: quick-fingeredness, from Latin *praestigiae* feats of juggling, tricks, probably influenced by French *preste* nimble, and Latin *digitus* finger; see PRESTIGE] —**,pres·ti·'dig·i·,ta·tor** *n.*

pres·tige (prɛ'sti:ʒ) *n.* **1.** high status or reputation achieved through success, influence, wealth, etc.; renown. **2. a.** the power to influence or impress; glamour. **b.** (*modifier*): *a prestige car.* [C17: via French from Latin *praestigiae* feats of juggling, tricks; apparently related to Latin *praestringere* to bind tightly, blindfold, from *prae* before + *stringere* to draw tight, bind]

pres·tig·ious (prɛ'stɪdʒəs) *adj.* **1.** having status or glamour; impressive or influential. **2.** *Rare.* characterized by or using deceit, cunning, or illusion; fraudulent. —**pres·'tig·ious·ly** *adv.* —**pres·'tig·ious·ness** *n.*

pres·tis·si·mo (prɛ'stɪsɪ,məʊ) *Music. adj., adv.* **1.** to be played as fast as possible. ~*n., pl.* **·mos. 2.** a piece or passage directed to be played in this way. [C18: from Italian: very quickly, from *presto* fast]

pres·to ('prɛstəʊ) *adj., adv.* **1.** *Music.* to be played very fast. ~*adv.* **2.** immediately, suddenly, or at once (esp. in the phrase **hey presto**). ~*n., pl.* **·tos. 3.** *Music.* a movement or passage directed to be played very quickly. [C16: from Italian: fast, from Late Latin *praestus* (adj.) ready to hand, Latin *praestō* (adv.) present]

Pres·ton ('prɛstən) *n.* a town in NW England, administrative centre of Lancashire, on the River Ribble: developed as a weaving centre (17th–18th centuries). Pop.: 97 365 (1971).

Pres·ton·pans (,prɛstən'pænz) *n.* a small town and resort in SE Scotland, in Lothian region on the Firth of Forth: scene of the battle (1745) in which Prince Charles Edward and the Highlanders defeated the English. Pop.: 3138 (1971).

pre·stress (pri:'strɛs) *vb.* (*tr.*) to apply tensile stress to (the steel cables, wires, etc., of a precast concrete part) before the load is applied.

pre·stressed con·crete *n.* concrete that contains steel wires, cables, etc., that are prestressed within their elastic limit to counteract the stresses that will occur under load.

Prest·wich ('prɛstwɪtʃ) *n.* a town in NW England, in Greater Manchester. Pop.: 32 838 (1971).

pre·sum·a·ble (prɪ'zju:məbᵊl) *adj.* able to be presumed or taken for granted.

pre·sum·a·bly (prɪ'zju:məblɪ) *adv.* (*sentence modifier*) one presumes or supposes that: *presumably he won't see you, if you're leaving tomorrow.*

pre·sume (prɪ'zju:m) *vb.* **1.** (when *tr., often takes a clause as object*) to take (something) for granted; assume. **2.** (when *tr., often foll. by an infinitive*) to take upon oneself (to do something) without warrant or permission; dare: *do you presume to copy my work?* **3.** (*intr.;* foll. by *on* or *upon*) to rely or depend: *don't presume on his agreement.* **4.** *Law.* to take as proved until contrary evidence is produced. **5.** (*tr.*) *Rare.* to constitute proof of or evidence for. [C14: via Old French from Latin *praesūmere* to take in advance, from *prae* before + *sūmere* to ASSUME] —**pre·sum·ed·ly** (prɪ'zju:mɪdlɪ) *adv.* —**pre·'sum·er** *n.* —**pre·'sum·ing·ly** *adv.*

pre·sump·tion (prɪ'zʌmpʃən) *n.* **1.** the act of presuming. **2.** bold or insolent behaviour or manners. **3.** a belief or assumption based on reasonable evidence. **4.** a ground or basis on which to presume. **5.** *Law.* an inference of the truth of a fact from other facts proved, admitted, or judicially noticed. [C13: via Old French from Latin *praesumptiō* a using in advance, anticipation, from *praesūmere* to take beforehand; see PRESUME]

pre·sump·tive (prɪ'zʌmptɪv) *adj.* **1.** based on presumption or probability. **2.** affording reasonable ground for belief. **3.** of or relating to embryonic tissues that become differentiated into a particular tissue or organ: *presumptive epidermis.* —**pre·'sump·tive·ly** *adv.* —**pre·'sump·tive·ness** *n.*

pre·sump·tu·ous (prɪ'zʌmptjʊəs) *adj.* **1.** characterized by presumption or tending to presume; bold; forward. **2.** an obsolete word for **presumptive.** —**pre·'sump·tu·ous·ly** *adv.* —**pre·'sump·tu·ous·ness** *n.*

pre·sup·pose (,pri:sə'pəʊz) *vb.* (*tr.*) **1.** to take for granted; assume. **2.** to require or imply as a necessary prior condition. —**pre·sup·po·si·tion** (,pri:sʌpə'zɪʃən) *n.*

pret. *abbrev. for* preterite.

pre·tence *or U.S.* **pre·tense** (prɪ'tɛns) *n.* **1.** the act of pretending. **2.** a false display; affectation. **3.** a claim, esp. a false one, to a right, title, or distinction. **4.** make-believe or feigning. **5.** a false claim or allegation; pretext. **6.** a less common word for **pretension** (sense 3).

pre·tend (prɪ'tɛnd) *vb.* **1.** (when *tr., usually takes a clause as object or an infinitive*) to claim or allege (something untrue). **2.** (*tr.; may take a clause as object or an infinitive*) to make believe, as in a play: *you pretend to be Ophelia.* **3.** (*intr.;* foll. by *to*) to present a claim, esp. a dubious one: *to pretend to the throne.* **4.** (*intr.;* foll. by *to*) *Obsolete.* to aspire as a candidate or suitor (for). [C14: from Latin *praetendere* to stretch forth, feign, from *prae* in front + *tendere* to stretch]

pre·tend·er (prɪ'tɛndə) *n.* **1.** a person who pretends or makes false allegations. **2.** a person who mounts a claim, as to a throne or title.

pre·ten·sion (prɪ'tɛnʃən) *n.* **1.** (*often pl.*) a false or unsupportable claim, esp. to merit, worth, or importance. **2.** a specious or unfounded allegation; pretext. **3.** the state or quality of being pretentious.

pre·ten·sive (prɪ'tɛnsɪv) *adj. Caribbean.* pretentious.

pre·ten·tious (prɪ'tɛnʃəs) *adj.* **1.** making claim to distinction or importance, esp. undeservedly. **2.** having or creating a deceptive outer appearance of great worth; ostentatious. —**pre·'ten·tious·ly** *adv.* —**pre·'ten·tious·ness** *n.*

pre·ter- *prefix.* beyond, more than, or exceeding: *preternatural.* [from Latin *praeter-*, from *praeter*]

pre·ter·hu·man (,pri:tə'hju:mən) *adj. Rare.* beyond what is human.

pret·er·ite *or* **pret·er·it** ('prɛtərɪt) *Grammar.* ~*n.* **1.** a tense of verbs used to relate past action, formed in English by inflection of the verb, as *jumped, swam.* **2.** a verb in this tense. ~*adj.* **3.** denoting this tense. [C14: from Late Latin *praeteritum* (*tempus*) past (time, tense), from Latin *praeterīre* to go by, from PRETER- + *īre* to go]

pret·er·i·tion (,prɛtə'rɪʃən) *n.* **1.** the act of passing over or omitting. **2.** *Roman law.* the failure of a testator to name one of his children in his will, thus invalidating it. **3.** (in Calvinist theology) the doctrine that God passed over or left unpredestined those not elected to final salvation. [C17: from Late Latin *praeteritiō* a passing over]

pre·ter·i·tive (prɪ'tɛrɪtɪv) *adj.* (of a verb) having only past tense forms.

pre·ter·mit (,pri:tə'mɪt) *vb.* **·mits, ·mit·ting, ·mit·ted.** (*tr.*) *Rare.* **1.** to overlook intentionally; disregard. **2.** to fail to do; neglect; omit. [C16: from Latin *praetermittere* to let pass, from PRETER- + *mittere* to send, release] —**pre·ter·mis·sion** (,pri:tə'mɪʃən) *n.* —**,pre·ter·'mit·ter** *n.*

pre·ter·nat·u·ral (,pri:tə'nætʃrəl) *adj.* **1.** beyond what is ordinarily found in nature; abnormal. **2.** another word for **supernatural.** [C16: from Medieval Latin *praeternātūrālis,* from Latin *praeter natūram* beyond the scope of nature] —**,pre·ter·'nat·u·ral·ly** *adv.* —**,pre·ter·'nat·u·ral·ism** *n.* —**,pre·ter·'nat·u·ral·ness** *or* **,pre·ter·,nat·u·'ral·i·ty** *n.*

pre·text ('pri:tɛkst) *n.* **1.** a fictitious reason given in order to conceal the real one. **2.** a specious excuse; pretence. [C16: from Latin *praetextum* disguise, from *praetexere* to weave in front, disguise; see TEXTURE]

pre·'shrink *vb.*
pre·'sift *vb.*
,pre-So·'crat·ic *adj.*
pre·'sur·gi·cal *adj.*
'pre·test *n.*
pre·'test *vb.*
'pre·'war *adj.*
pre·'warm *vb.*

pre+ton+ic (priːˈtɒnɪk) *adj.* denoting or relating to the syllable before the one bearing the primary stress in a word.
pre+tor (ˈpriːtə) *n.* a variant spelling of **praetor.**
Pre+to+ri+a (prɪˈtɔːrɪə) *n.* the administrative capital of South Africa and capital of Transvaal province: two universities (1873, 1930); large steelworks. Pop.: 543 950 (1970).
Pre·to·ri·us (prɪˈtɔːrɪəs) *n.* **1. An·dries Wil·hel·mus Ja·co·bus** (ˈɑndriːs wɪlˈhɛlmys jaːˈkoːbys). 1799–1853, a Boer leader in the Great Trek (1838) to escape British sovereignty; he also led an expedition to the Transvaal (1848). The town Pretoria was named after him. **2.** his son, **Mar·thi·nus Wes·sels** (maːrˈtiːnys ˈwɛsəls). 1819–1901, first president of the South African Republic (1857–71) and of the Orange Free State (1859–63).
pret+ti+fy (ˈprɪtɪˌfaɪ) *vb.* **+fies, +fy+ing, +fied.** (*tr.*) *Often ironical.* to make pretty; embellish. —ˌ**pret+ti+fi+ˈca+tion** *n.* —ˈ**pret+ti+ˌfi+er** *n.*
pret+ty (ˈprɪtɪ) *adj.* **+ti+er, +ti+est. 1.** pleasing or appealing in a delicate or graceful way. **2.** dainty, neat, or charming. **3.** *Informal, often ironical.* excellent, grand, or fine: *here's a pretty mess!* **4.** *Informal.* lacking in masculinity; effeminate; foppish. **5.** *Archaic or Scot.* vigorous or brave. **6.** an archaic word for **elegant. 7. a pretty penny.** *Informal.* a large sum of money. **8. sitting pretty.** *Informal.* in a favourable or satisfactory state or condition. ~*n., pl.* **+ties. 9.** a pretty person or thing. ~*adv.* **10.** *Informal.* fairly or moderately; somewhat. **11.** *Informal.* quite or very. ~*vb.* **+ties, +ty+ing, +tied. 12.** (*tr.;* often foll. by *up*) to make pretty; adorn. [Old English *prættig* clever; related to Middle Low German *prattich* obstinate, Dutch *prettig* glad, Old Norse *prettugr* cunning] —ˈ**pret+ti+ly** *adv.* —ˈ**pret+ti+ness** *n.*
pret·ty-pret·ty *adj. Informal.* excessively or ostentatiously pretty.
pret+zel (ˈprɛtsəl) *n.* a brittle savoury biscuit, in the form of a knot or stick, glazed and salted on the outside, eaten esp. in Germany. [C19: from German, from Old High German *brezitella;* perhaps related to Medieval Latin *bracellus* bracelet, from Latin *bracchium* arm]
Preus+sen (ˈprɔɪsᵊn) *n.* the German name for **Prussia.**
pre+vail (prɪˈveɪl) *vb.* (*intr.*) **1.** (often foll. by *over* or *against*) to prove superior; gain mastery: *skill will prevail.* **2.** to be or appear as the most important feature; be prevalent. **3.** to exist widely; be in force. **4.** (often foll. by *on* or *upon*) to succeed in persuading or inducing. [C14: from Latin *praevalēre* to be superior in strength, from *prae* beyond + *valēre* to be strong] —**pre+ˈvail+er** *n.*
pre+vail+ing (prɪˈveɪlɪŋ) *adj.* **1.** generally accepted; widespread: *the prevailing opinion.* **2.** most frequent or conspicuous; predominant: *the prevailing wind is from the north.* —**pre+ˈvail+ing+ly** *adv.*
prev·a·lent (ˈprɛvələnt) *adj.* **1.** widespread or current. **2.** superior in force or power; predominant. —ˈ**prev·a+lence** *or* ˈ**prev·a+lent+ness** *n.* —ˈ**prev·a+lent+ly** *adv.*
pre+var·i·cate (prɪˈværɪˌkeɪt) *vb.* (*intr.*) to speak or act falsely or evasively with intent to deceive. [C16: from Latin *praevāricārī* to walk crookedly, from *prae* beyond + *vāricare* to straddle the legs; compare Latin *vārus* bent] —**pre+ˌvar+i+ˈca+tion** *n.* —**pre+ˈvar+i+ˌca+tor** *n.*
pre+ve+ni+ent (prɪˈviːnɪənt) *adj.* coming before; anticipating or preceding. [C17: from Latin *praevenīre* to precede, PREVENT] —**pre+ˈve+ni+ent+ly** *adv.*
pre+vent (prɪˈvɛnt) *vb.* **1.** (*tr.*) to keep from happening, esp. by taking precautionary action. **2.** (*tr.;* often foll. by *from*) to keep (someone from doing something); hinder; impede. **3.** (*intr.*) to interpose or act as a hindrance. **4.** (*tr.*) *Archaic.* to anticipate or precede. [C15: from Latin *praevenīre,* from *prae* before + *venīre* to come] —**pre+ˈvent+a+ble** *or* **pre+ˈvent+i+ble** *adj.* —**pre+ˈvent+a+bly** *or* **pre+ˈvent+i+bly** *adv.*
pre+vent+er (prɪˈvɛntə) *n.* **1.** a person or thing that prevents. **2.** *Nautical.* a rope or other piece of gear rigged to prevent a sail from gybing.
pre+ven+tion (prɪˈvɛnʃən) *n.* **1.** the act of preventing. **2.** a hindrance, obstacle, or impediment.
pre+ven+tive (prɪˈvɛntɪv) *or* **pre+ven+ta+tive** (prɪˈvɛntətɪv) *adj.* **1.** tending or intended to prevent or hinder. **2.** *Med.* **a.** tending to prevent disease; prophylactic. **b.** of or relating to the branch of medicine concerned with prolonging life and preventing disease. **3.** (in Britain) of, relating to, or belonging to the customs and excise service or the coastguard. ~*n.* **4.** something that serves to prevent or hinder. **5.** *Med.* any drug or agent that tends to prevent or protect against disease. **6.** another name for **contraceptive.** —**pre+ˈven+tive+ly** *or* **pre+ˈven+ta+tive+ly** *adv.* —**pre+ˈven+tive+ness** *or* **pre+ˈven+ta+tive+ness** *n.*
Pré·vert (*French* preˈvɛːr) *n.* **Jacques** (ʒɑːk). born 1900, Parisian poet, satirist, and writer of film scripts, noted esp. for his song poems. He was a member of the surrealist group from 1925 to 1929.
pre+view *or* **pre+vue** (ˈpriːvjuː) *n.* **1.** an advance or preliminary view or sight. **2.** an advance showing before public presentation of a film, art exhibition, etc., usually before an invited audience of celebrities and journalists. ~*vb.* **3.** (*tr.*) to view in advance.
Pre·vin (ˈprɛvɪn) *n.* **An·dré** (ˈɒndreɪ). born 1929, U.S. orchestral conductor, born in Germany; living in Britain.
pre+vi+ous (ˈpriːvɪəs) *adj.* **1.** (*prenominal*) existing or coming before something else in time or position; prior. **2.** (*postpositive*) *Informal.* taking place or done too soon; premature. **3. previous to.** before; prior to. [C17: from Latin *praevius* leading the way, from *prae* before + *via* way] —ˈ**pre+vi+ous+ly** *adv.* —ˈ**pre+vi+ous+ness** *n.*
pre+vi+ous ques+tion *n.* **1.** (in the House of Commons) a motion to drop the present topic under debate, put in order to prevent a vote. **2.** (in the House of Lords and U.S. legislative bodies) a motion to vote on a bill or other question without delay. ~See also **closure** (sense 4).
pre+vise (prɪˈvaɪz) *vb.* (*tr.*) *Rare.* **1.** to predict or foresee. **2.** to notify in advance. [C16: from Latin *praevidēre* to foresee, from *prae* before + *vidēre* to see]
pre+vi+sion (prɪˈvɪʒən) *n. Rare.* **1.** the act or power of foreseeing; prescience. **2.** a prophetic vision or prophecy.
pre+vo+cal+ic (ˌpriːvəʊˈkælɪk) *adj.* (of a consonant) coming immediately before a vowel. —ˌ**pre+vo+ˈcal+i+cal+ly** *adv.*
Pré·vost d'Ex·iles (*French* prevo dɛgˈzil) *n.* **An·toine Fran·çois** (ãtwan frãˈswa), known as *Abbé Prévost.* 1697–1763, French novelist, noted for his romance *Manon Lescaut* (1731), which served as the basis for operas by Puccini and Massenet.
prey (preɪ) *n.* **1.** an animal hunted or captured by another for food. **2.** a person or thing that becomes the victim of a hostile person, influence, etc. **3. bird** *or* **beast of prey.** a bird or animal that preys on others for food. **4.** an archaic word for **booty.** ~*vb.* (*intr.;* often foll. by *on* or *upon*) **5.** to hunt or seize food by killing other animals. **6.** to make a victim (of others), as by profiting at their expense. **7.** to exert a depressing or obsessive effect (on the mind, spirits, etc.); weigh heavily (upon). [C13: from Old French *preie,* from Latin *praeda* booty; see PREDATORY] —ˈ**prey+er** *n.*
Pri·am (ˈpraɪəm) *n. Greek myth.* the last king of Troy, killed at its fall. He was father by Hecuba of Hector, Paris, and Cassandra.
pri+ap+ic (praɪˈæpɪk, -ˈeɪ-) *or* **pri·a·pe·an** (ˌpraɪəˈpiːən) *adj.* **1.** (*sometimes cap.*) of or relating to Priapus. **2.** a less common word for **phallic.**
pri+a+pism (ˈpraɪəˌpɪzəm) *n. Pathol.* prolonged painful erection of the penis, caused by neurological disorders, obstruction of the penile blood vessels, etc. [C17: from Late Latin *priāpismus,* ultimately from Greek PRIAPUS]
Pri·a·pus (praɪˈeɪpəs) *n.* **1.** (in classical antiquity) the god of the male procreative power and of gardens and vineyards. **2.** (*often not cap.*) a representation of the penis.
Prib·i·lof Is+lands (ˈprɪbɪləf) *pl. n.* a group of islands in the Bering Sea, off SW Alaska, belonging to the U.S.: the breeding ground of the northern fur seal. Area: about 168 sq. km (65 sq. miles). Also called: **Fur Seal Islands.**
price (praɪs) *n.* **1.** the sum in money or goods for which anything is or may be bought or sold. **2.** the cost at which anything is obtained. **3.** the cost of bribing a person. **4.** a sum of money offered or given as a reward for a capture or killing. **5.** value or worth, esp. high worth. **6.** *Gambling.* another word for **odds. 7. at any price.** whatever the price or cost. **8. at a price.** at a high price. **9. beyond** (*or* **without**) **price.** invaluable or priceless. **10. what price** (**something**)? what are the chances of (something) happening now? ~*vb.* (*tr.*) **11.** to fix or establish the price of. **12.** to ascertain or discover the price of. **13. price out of the market.** to charge so highly for as to prevent the sale, hire, etc., of. [C13 *pris,* from Old French, from Latin *pretium* price, value, wage] —ˈ**pric+er** *n.*
Price Com+mis+sion *n.* (in Britain) a commission established by the government in 1973 with authority to control prices as a measure against inflation.
price con+trol *n.* the establishment and maintenance of maximum price levels for basic goods and services by a government, esp. during periods of war or inflation.
price dis+crim+i+na+tion *n. Economics.* the setting of different prices to be charged to different consumers or in different markets for the same goods or services.
price-fix+ing *n. Chiefly U.S.* **1.** the setting of prices by agreement among producers and distributors. **2.** another name for **price control** or **resale price maintenance.**
price+less (ˈpraɪslɪs) *adj.* **1.** of inestimable worth; beyond valuation; invaluable. **2.** *Informal.* extremely amusing or ridiculous. —ˈ**price+less+ly** *adv.* —ˈ**price+less+ness** *n.*
price ring *n.* a group of traders formed to maintain the prices of their goods.
price sup+port *n. U.S.* government maintenance of specified price levels at a minimum above market equilibrium by subsidy or by purchase of the market surplus at the guaranteed levels.
price war *n.* a period of intense competition among enterprises, esp. retail enterprises, in the same market, characterized by repeated price reductions rather than advertising, brand promotion, etc.
price·y *or* **pric·y** (ˈpraɪsɪ) *adj.* **pric·i·er, pric·i·est.** an informal word for **expensive.**
prick (prɪk) *vb.* (*mainly tr.*) **1. a.** to make (a small hole) in (something) by piercing lightly with a sharp point. **b.** to wound in this manner. **2.** (*intr.*) to cause or have a piercing or stinging sensation. **3.** to cause to feel a sharp emotional pain: *knowledge of such poverty pricked his conscience.* **4.** to puncture or pierce something. **5.** to mark, delineate, or outline by dots or punctures. **6.** (*also intr.;* usually foll. by *up*) to rise or raise erect; point: *the dog pricked his ears up at his master's call.* **7.** (usually foll. by *out* or *off*) to transplant (seedlings) into a larger container. **8.** (often foll. by *off*) *Navigation.* to measure or trace (a course, distance, etc.) on a chart with dividers. **9.** *Archaic.* to rouse or impel; urge on. **10.** (*intr.*) *Archaic.* to ride fast on horseback; spur a horse on. **11. prick up one's ears.** to listen closely and attentively. ~*n.* **12.** the act of pricking or the condition or sensation of being pricked. **13.** a mark made by a sharp point; puncture. **14.** a sharp emotional pain resembling the physical pain caused by being pricked: *a prick of conscience.* **15.** a taboo slang word for **penis. 16.** *Slang,*

derogatory. an obnoxious or despicable person. **17.** an instrument or weapon with a sharp point, such as a thorn, goad, bee sting, etc. **18.** the footprint or track of an animal, esp. a hare. **19.** *Obsolete.* a small mark caused by pricking a surface; dot; point. **20. kick against the pricks.** to hurt oneself by struggling against something in vain. [Old English *prica* point, puncture; related to Dutch *prik,* Icelandic *prik* short stick, Swedish *prick* point, stick]

prick·er ('prɪkə) *n.* **1.** a person or thing that pricks. **2.** *U.S.* a thorn; prickle.

prick·et ('prɪkɪt) *n.* **1.** a male deer in the second year of life having unbranched antlers. **2.** a sharp metal spike on which to stick a candle. **3.** a candlestick having such a spike. [C14 *priket,* from *prik* PRICK]

prick·le ('prɪkᵊl) *n.* **1.** *Botany.* a pointed process arising from the outer layer of a stem, leaf, etc., and containing no woody or conducting tissue. Compare **thorn** (sense 1). **2.** a pricking or stinging sensation. ~*vb.* **3.** to feel or cause to feel a stinging sensation. **4.** (*tr.*) to prick, as with a thorn. [Old English *pricel;* related to Middle Low German *prekel,* German *Prickel*]

prick·ly ('prɪklɪ) *adj.* **·li·er, ·li·est. 1.** having or covered with prickles. **2.** stinging or tingling. **3.** bad-tempered or irritable. **4.** full of difficulties; knotty: *a prickly problem.* —**'prick·li·ness** *n.*

prick·ly ash *n.* a North American rutaceous shrub or small tree, *Zanthoxylum americanum,* having prickly branches, feathery aromatic leaves, and bark used as a remedy for toothache. Also called: **toothache tree.**

prick·ly heat *n.* a nontechnical name for **miliaria.**

prick·ly pear *n.* **1.** any of various tropical cacti of the genus *Opuntia,* having flattened or cylindrical spiny joints and oval fruit that is edible in some species. See also **cholla, nopal** (sense 2). **2.** the fruit of any of these plants.

prick·ly pop·py *n.* an annual papaveraceous plant, *Argemone mexicana,* of tropical America, having prickly stems and leaves and large yellow or white flowers.

prick song *n. Obsolete.* **a.** a piece of written vocal music. **b.** vocal music sung from a copy.

pride (praɪd) *n.* **1.** a feeling of honour and self-respect; a sense of personal worth. **2.** excessive self-esteem; conceit. **3.** a source of pride. **4.** satisfaction or pleasure taken in one's own or another's success, achievements, etc. (esp. in the phrase **take (a) pride in**). **5.** the better or most superior part of something; flower. **6.** the most flourishing time. **7.** a group (of lions). **8.** the mettle of a horse; courage; spirit. **9.** *Archaic.* sexual desire, esp. in a female animal. **10.** *Archaic.* display, pomp, or splendour. **11. pride of place.** the most important position. ~*vb.* **12.** (*tr.;* foll. by *on* or *upon*) to take pride in (oneself) for. **13.** (*intr.*) to glory or revel (in). [Old English *prȳda;* related to Latin *prodesse* to be useful, Old Norse *prūthr* stately; see PROUD] —**'pride·ful** *adj.* —**'pride·ful·ly** *adv.*

Pride (praɪd) *n.* **Thom·as.** died 1658, English soldier on the Parliamentary side during the Civil War. He expelled members of the Long Parliament hostile to the army (**Pride's Purge,** 1648) and signed Charles I's death warrant.

prie-dieu (priː'djɜː) *n.* a piece of furniture consisting of a low surface for kneeling upon and a narrow front surmounted by a rest for the elbows or for books, for use when praying. [C18: from French, from *prier* to pray + *Dieu* God]

pri·er *or* **pry·er** ('praɪə) *n.* a person who pries.

priest (priːst) *or* (*fem.*) **priest·ess** *n.* **1.** a person ordained to act as a mediator between God and man in administering the sacraments, preaching, blessing, guiding, etc. **2.** (in episcopal Churches) a minister in the second grade of the hierarchy of holy orders, ranking below a bishop but above a deacon. **3.** a minister of any religion. **4.** an official who offers sacrifice on behalf of the people and performs other religious ceremonies. **5.** (*sometimes cap.*) a variety of fancy pigeon having a bald pate with a crest or peak at the back of the head. ~*vb.* (*tr.*) **6.** to make a priest; ordain. [Old English *prēost,* apparently from PRESBYTER; related to Old High German *prēster,* Old French *prestre*] —**'priest,like** *adj.*

priest·craft ('priːst,krɑːft) *n.* **1.** the art and skills involved in the work of a priest. **2.** *Derogatory.* the influence of priests upon politics or the use by them of secular power.

priest-hole *or* **priest's hole** *n.* a secret chamber in certain houses in England, built as a hiding place for Roman Catholic priests when they were proscribed in the 16th and 17th centuries.

priest·hood ('priːst,hʊd) *n.* **1.** the state, order, or office of a priest. **2.** priests collectively.

Priest·ley ('priːstlɪ) *n.* **1. J(ohn) B(oynton).** born 1894, English author. His works include the novels *The Good Companions* (1929) and *Angel Pavement* (1930) and the comedy *Laburnum Grove* (1933). **2. Jo·seph.** 1733–1804, English chemist, political theorist, and clergyman, in the U.S. from 1794. He discovered oxygen (1774) independently of Scheele and isolated and described many other gases.

priest·ly ('priːstlɪ) *adj.* **·li·er, ·li·est.** of, relating to, characteristic of, or befitting a priest. —**'priest·li·ness** *n.*

priest-rid·den *adj.* dominated or governed by or excessively under the influence of priests.

prig[1] (prɪg) *n.* a person who is smugly self-righteous and narrow-minded. [C18: of unknown origin] —**'prig·ger·y** *or* **'prig·gish·ness** *n.* —**'prig·gish** *adj.* —**'prig·gish·ly** *adv.* —**'prig·gism** *n.*

prig[2] (prɪg) *Brit. slang.* ~*vb.* **prigs, prig·ging, prigged. 1.** another word for **steal.** ~*n.* **2.** another word for **thief.** [C16: of unknown origin]

prill (prɪl) *vb.* **1.** (*tr.*) to convert (a material) into a granular free-flowing form. ~*n.* **2.** prilled material. [C18: originally a Cornish copper-mining term, of obscure origin]

prim *adj.* **prim·mer, prim·mest. 1.** affectedly proper, precise, or formal. ~*vb.* **prims, prim·ming, primmed. 2.** (*tr.*) to make prim. **3.** to purse (the mouth) primly or (of the mouth) to be so pursed. [C18: of unknown origin] —**'prim·ly** *adv.* —**'prim·ness** *n.*

prim. *abbrev. for:* **1.** primary. **2.** primitive.

pri·ma bal·le·ri·na ('priːmə) *n.* a leading female ballet dancer. [from Italian, literally: first ballerina]

pri·ma·cy ('praɪməsɪ) *n., pl.* **·cies. 1.** the state of being first in rank, grade, etc. **2.** *Ecclesiast.* the office, rank, or jurisdiction of a primate or senior bishop or (in the Roman Catholic Church) the pope.

pri·ma don·na ('priːmə 'dɒnə) *n., pl.* **pri·ma don·nas. 1.** a female operatic star; diva. **2.** *Informal.* a temperamental person. [C19: from Italian: first lady]

pri·ma fa·cie ('praɪmə 'feɪʃɪ) at first sight; as it seems at first. [C15: from Latin, from *prīmus* first + *faciēs* FACE]

pri·ma-fa·cie ev·i·dence *n. Law.* evidence that is sufficient to establish a fact or to raise a presumption of the truth of a fact unless controverted.

pri·mal ('praɪməl) *adj.* **1.** first or original. **2.** chief or most important. [C17: from Medieval Latin *prīmālis,* from Latin *prīmus* first]

pri·ma·quine ('praɪmə,kwiːn) *n.* a synthetic drug used in the treatment of malaria. Formula: $C_{15}H_{21}N_3O$. [C20: from *prima-,* from Latin *prīmus* first + QUIN(OLIN)E]

pri·mar·i·ly ('praɪmərəlɪ) *adv.* **1.** principally; chiefly; mainly. **2.** at first; originally.

pri·ma·ry ('praɪmərɪ) *adj.* **1.** first in importance, degree, rank, etc. **2.** first in position or time, as in a series. **3.** fundamental; basic. **4.** being the first stage; elementary. **5.** (*prenominal*) of or relating to the education of children up to the age of 11. **6.** (of the flight feathers of a bird's wing) growing from the manus. **7. a.** being the part of an electric circuit, such as a transformer or induction coil, in which a changing current induces a current in a neighbouring circuit: *a primary coil.* **b.** (of a current) flowing in such a circuit. Compare **secondary. 8. a.** (of a product) consisting of a natural raw material; unmanufactured. **b.** (of production or industry) involving the extraction or winning of such products. Agriculture, fishing, forestry, hunting, and mining are primary industries. Compare **secondary** (sense 7), **tertiary** (sense 2). **9.** *Chem.* **a.** (of an organic compound) having a functional group attached to a carbon atom that is attached to at least two hydrogen atoms. **b.** (of an amine) having only one organic group attached to the nitrogen atom; containing the group NH_2. **c.** (of a salt) derived from a tribasic acid by replacement of one acidic hydrogen atom with a metal atom or electropositive group. **10.** *Linguistics.* **a.** derived from a word that is not a derivation but the ultimate form itself. *Lovable* is a primary derivative of *love.* **b.** (of Latin, Greek, or Sanskrit tenses) referring to present or future time. Compare **historic** (sense 3). **11.** *Geology, obsolete.* relating to the Palaeozoic or earlier eras. ~*n., pl.* **·ries. 12.** a person or thing that is first in rank, occurrence, etc. **13.** (in the U.S.) **a.** a preliminary election in which the voters of a state or region choose a party's convention delegates, nominees for office, etc. See also **closed primary, direct primary, open primary. b.** a local meeting of voters registered with one party to nominate candidates, select convention delegates, etc. Full name: **primary election. 14.** See **primary colour. 15.** any of the flight feathers growing from the manus of a bird's wing. **16.** a primary coil, winding, inductance, or current in an electric circuit. **17.** *Astronomy.* a celestial body around which one or more specified secondary bodies orbit: *the sun is the primary of the earth.* [C15: from Latin *prīmārius* of the first rank, principal, from *prīmus* first]

pri·ma·ry ac·cent *or* **stress** *n. Linguistics.* the strongest accent in a word or breath group, as that on the first syllable of *agriculture.* Compare **secondary accent.**

pri·ma·ry cell *n.* an electric cell that generates an electromotive force by the direct and usually irreversible conversion of chemical energy into electrical energy. It cannot be recharged efficiently by an electric current. Also called: **voltaic cell.** Compare **secondary cell.**

pri·ma·ry col·our *n.* **1.** Also called: **additive primary.** any of the colours red, green, or blue. An equal mixture of the three gives white light. **2.** Also called: **subtractive primary.** any one of the colours magenta, yellow, or cyan. An equal mixture of the three produces a black pigment. **3.** Also called: **psychological primary.** any one of the colours red, yellow, green, blue, black, or white. Any colour can be regarded as formed from a mixture of two or more of these. ~See also **secondary colour, complementary colour.**

pri·ma·ry e·lec·tion *n.* See **primary** (sense 13).

pri·ma·ry pro·cess·es *n. Psychoanal.* unconscious, irrational thought processes, such as condensation or displacement, governed by the pleasure principle. Compare **secondary processes.**

pri·ma·ry school *n.* **1.** (in Britain) a school for children below the age of 11. It is usually divided into an infant and a junior section. **2.** (in the U.S.) a school equivalent to the first three or four grades of elementary school, sometimes including a kindergarten.

pri·ma·ry stress *n. Linguistics.* another term for **primary accent.**

pri·mate[1] ('praɪmeɪt) *n.* **1.** any placental mammal of the order *Primates,* typically having flexible hands and feet with opposable first digits, good eyesight, and, in the higher apes, a highly developed brain: includes lemurs, lorises, monkeys, apes, and man. ~*adj.* **2.** of, relating to, or belonging to the order *Primates.* [C18: from New Latin *primates,* plural of *prīmās* principal, from *prīmus* first] —**pri+ma+tial** (praɪˈmeɪʃəl) *adj.*

pri+mate[2] (ˈpraɪmeɪt) *n.* **1.** another name for **archbishop. 2. Primate of all England.** the Archbishop of Canterbury. **3. Primate of England.** Archbishop of York. [C13: from Old French, from Latin *prīmās* principal, from *prīmus* first]

pri+ma+tol+o+gy (ˌpraɪməˈtɒlədʒɪ) *n.* the branch of zoology that is concerned with the study of primates.

prime (praɪm) *adj.* **1.** (*prenominal*) first in quality or value; first-rate. **2.** (*prenominal*) fundamental; original. **3.** (*prenominal*) first in importance, authority, etc.; chief. **4.** *Maths.* **a.** having no factors except itself or one: *$x^2 + x + 3$ is a prime polynomial.* **b.** (foll. by *to*) having no common factors (with): *20 is prime to 21.* **5.** *Finance.* having the best credit rating: *prime investments.* ~*n.* **6.** the time when a thing is at its best. **7.** a period of power, vigour, etc., usually following youth (esp. in the phrase **the prime of life**). **8.** the beginning of something, such as the spring. **9.** *Maths.* short for **prime number. 10.** *Linguistics.* a semantically indivisible element; minimal component of the sense of a word. **11.** *Music.* **a.** unison. **b.** the tonic of a scale. **12.** *Chiefly R.C. Church.* the second of the seven canonical hours of the divine office, originally fixed for the first hour of the day, at sunrise. **13.** the first of eight basic positions from which a parry or attack can be made in fencing. ~*vb.* **14.** to prepare (something); make ready. **15.** (*tr.*) to apply a primer, such as paint or size, to (a surface). **16.** (*tr.*) to fill (a pump) with its working fluid before starting, in order to improve the sealing of the pump elements and to expel air from it before starting. **17.** (*tr.*) to increase the quantity of fuel in the float chamber of (a carburettor) in order to facilitate the starting of an engine. **18.** (*tr.*) to insert a primer into (a gun, mine, charge, etc.) preparatory to detonation or firing. **19.** (*intr.*) (of a steam engine or boiler) to operate with or produce steam mixed with large amounts of water. **20.** (*tr.*) to provide with facts, information, etc., beforehand; brief. [(adj.) C14: from Latin *prīmus* first; (n.) C13: from Latin *prīma* (*hora*) the first (hour); (vb.) C16: of uncertain origin, probably connected with n.] —**ˈprime+ly** *adv.* —**ˈprime+ness** *n.*

prime cost *n.* the portion of the cost of a commodity that varies directly with the amount of it produced, principally comprising materials and labour. Also called: **variable cost.** Compare **overheads.**

prime me+rid+i+an *n.* the 0° meridian from which the other meridians or lines of longitude are calculated, usually taken to pass through Greenwich.

prime min+is+ter *n.* **1.** the head of a parliamentary government. **2.** the chief minister of a sovereign or a state. —**prime min+is+ter+ship** *or* **prime min+is+try** *n.*

prime mov+er *n.* **1.** the original or primary force behind an idea, enterprise, etc. **2. a.** the source of power, such as fuel, wind, electricity, etc., for a machine. **b.** the means of extracting power from such a source, such as a steam engine, electric motor, etc. **3.** (in the philosophy of Aristotle) that which is the cause of all movement.

Prime Mov+er *n.* (usually preceded by *the*) *Philosophy.* God, esp. when considered as a first cause.

prime num+ber *n.* an integer that cannot be factorized into other integers but is only divisible by itself or 1, such as 2, 3, 7, and 11. Sometimes shortened to **prime.** Compare **composite number.**

pri+mer[1] (ˈpraɪmə) *n.* **1.** an introductory text, such as a school textbook. **2.** *Printing.* See **long primer, great primer.** [C14: via Anglo-Norman from Medieval Latin *primārius* (*liber*) a first (book), from Latin *prīmārius* PRIMARY]

prim+er[2] (ˈpraɪmə) *n.* **1.** a person or thing that primes. **2.** a device, such as a tube containing explosive, for detonating the main charge in a gun, mine, etc. **3.** a substance, such as paint, applied to a surface as a base, sealer, etc. Also called (for senses 2, 3): **priming.** [C15: see PRIME (vb.)]

prime rate *n.* the lowest commercial interest rate charged by a bank at a particular time.

pri+mer+o (prɪˈmɛərəʊ) *n. Chiefly Brit.* a 16th- and 17th-century card game. [C16: from Spanish *primera* card game, from *primero* first, from Latin *prīmārius* chief]

prime time *n.* the peak viewing time on television, for which advertising rates are the highest.

pri+me+val *or* **pri+mae+val** (praɪˈmiːvəl) *adj.* of or belonging to the first age or ages, esp. of the world. [C17: from Latin *prīmaevus* youthful, from *prīmus* first + *aevum* age] —**priˈme+val+ly** *or* **pri+ˈmae+val+ly** *adv.*

prime ver+ti+cal *n. Astronomy.* the great circle passing through the observer's zenith and meeting the horizon due east and west.

prim+i+grav+i+da (ˌpraɪmɪˈgrævɪdə) *n., pl.* **+das** *or* **+dae** (-ˌdiː). *Obstetrics.* a woman who is pregnant for the first time. [C19: New Latin, from Latin *prima* first + *gravida* GRAVID (woman)]

pri+mine (ˈpraɪmɪn) *n. Botany.* the integument surrounding an ovule or the outer of two such integuments. Compare **secundine.** [C19: via French from Latin *prīmus* first]

prim+ing (ˈpraɪmɪŋ) *n.* **1.** something used to prime. **2.** a substance, used to ignite an explosive charge.

pri+mip+a+ra (praɪˈmɪpərə) *n., pl.* **+ras** *or* **+rae** (-ˌriː). *Obstetrics.* a woman who has borne only one child. Also written: **Para I.** [C19: from Latin, from *prīmus* first + *parere* to bring forth] —**prim+i+par+i+ty** (ˌprɪmɪˈpærɪtɪ) *n.* —**pri+ˈmip+a+rous** *adj.*

prim+i+tive (ˈprɪmɪtɪv) *adj.* **1.** of or belonging to the first or beginning; original. **2.** characteristic of an early state, esp. in being crude or uncivilized: *a primitive dwelling.* **3.** *Anthropol.* denoting or relating to a preliterate and nonindustrial social system. **4.** *Biology.* **a.** of, relating to, or resembling an early stage in the evolutionary development of a particular group of organisms: *primitive amphibians.* **b.** another word for **primordial** (sense 3). **5.** showing the characteristics of primitive painters; untrained, childlike, or naive. **6.** *Geology.* of, relating to, or denoting rocks formed in or before the Palaeozoic era. **7.** denoting a word from which another word is derived, as for example *hope,* from which *hopeless* is derived. **8.** *Protestant theol.* of, relating to, or associated with a minority group that breaks away from a sect, denomination, or Church in order to return to what is regarded as the original simplicity of the Gospels. ~*n.* **9.** a primitive person or thing. **10. a.** an artist whose work does not conform to traditional, academic, or avant-garde standards of Western painting, such as a painter from an African or Oceanic civilization. **b.** a painter of the pre-Renaissance era in European painting. **c.** a painter of any era, whose work appears childlike or untrained. Also called (for a., c.): **naive. 11.** a work by such an artist. **12.** a word from which another word is derived. **13.** *Maths.* a curve, function, or other form from which another is derived. [C14: from Latin *prīmitīvus* earliest of its kind, primitive, from *prīmus* first] —**ˈprim+i+tive+ly** *adv.* —**ˈprim+i+tive+ness** *n.*

prim+i+tiv+ism (ˈprɪmɪtɪˌvɪzəm) *n.* **1.** the condition of being primitive. **2.** the notion that the value of primitive cultures is superior to that of the modern world. **3.** the principles, characteristics, etc., of primitive art and artists. —**ˈprim+i+tiv+ist** *n., adj.* —**ˌprim+i+tiv+ˈis+tic** *adj.*

pri+mo (ˈpriːməʊ) *n., pl.* **+mos** *or* **+mi** (-mɪ). *Music.* the upper or right-hand part in a piano duet. Compare **secondo.** [Italian: first, from Latin *prīmus*]

Pri+mo de Ri+ve+ra (*Spanish* ˈprimo ðe riˈβera) *n.* **1. José An+to+nio** (xoˈse anˈtonjo). 1903–36, Spanish politician; founded Falangism. **2.** his father, **Mi+guel** (miˈɣel). 1870–1930, Spanish general; dictator of Spain (1923–30).

pri+mo+gen+i+tor (ˌpraɪməʊˈdʒɛnɪtə) *n.* **1.** a forefather; ancestor. **2.** an earliest parent or ancestor, as of a race. [C17: alteration of PROGENITOR after PRIMOGENITURE]

pri+mo+gen+i+ture (ˌpraɪməʊˈdʒɛnɪtʃə) *n.* **1.** the state of being a first-born. **2.** *Law.* the right of an eldest son to succeed to the estate of his ancestor to the exclusion of all others. Compare **ultimogeniture.** [C17: from Medieval Latin *prīmōgenitūra* birth of a first child, from Latin *prīmō* at first + Late Latin *genitūra* a birth] —**pri+mo+gen+i+tar+y** (ˌpraɪməʊˈdʒɛnɪtərɪ, -trɪ) *adj.*

pri+mor+di+al (praɪˈmɔːdɪəl) *adj.* **1.** existing at or from the beginning; earliest; primeval. **2.** constituting an origin; fundamental. **3.** *Biology.* of or relating to an early stage of development: *primordial germ cells.* ~*n.* **4.** an elementary or basic principle. [C14: from Late Latin *prīmōrdiālis* original, from Latin *prīmus* first + *ōrdīrī* to begin] —**pri+ˌmor+di+ˈal+i+ty** *n.* —**pri+ˈmor+di+al+ly** *adv.*

pri+mor+di+um (praɪˈmɔːdɪəm) *n., pl.* **+di+a** (-dɪə). *Biology.* an organ or part in the earliest stage of development.

primp (prɪmp) *vb.* to dress (oneself), esp. in fine clothes; prink. [C19: probably from PRIM]

prim+rose (ˈprɪmˌrəʊz) *n.* **1.** any of various temperate primulaceous plants of the genus *Primula,* esp. *P. vulgaris* of Europe, which has pale yellow flowers. **2.** short for **evening primrose. 3.** Also called: **primrose yellow.** a light to moderate yellow, sometimes with a greenish tinge. ~*adj.* **4.** of, relating to, or abounding in primroses. **5.** of the colour primrose. **6.** pleasant or gay. [C15: from Old French *primerose,* from Medieval Latin *prīma rosa* first rose]

prim+rose path *n.* (often preceded by *the*) a pleasurable way of life.

prim+u+la (ˈprɪmjʊlə) *n.* any primulaceous plant of the N temperate genus *Primula,* having white, yellow, pink, or purple funnel-shaped flowers with five spreading petals: includes the primrose, oxlip, cowslip, and polyanthus. [C18: New Latin, from Medieval Latin *prīmula* (*vēris*) little first one (of the spring)]

prim+u+la+ceous (ˌprɪmjʊˈleɪʃəs) *adj.* of, relating to, or belonging to the *Primulaceae,* a family of plants having funnel-shaped or bell-shaped flowers: includes primrose, moneywort, pimpernel, and loosestrife.

pri+mum mo+bi+le *Latin.* (ˈpraɪmʊm ˈməʊbɪlɪ) *n.* **1.** a prime mover. **2.** *Astronomy.* the outermost empty sphere, in the Ptolemaic system that was thought to revolve around the earth from east to west in 24 hours carrying with it the inner spheres of the planets, sun, moon, and fixed stars. [C15: from Medieval Latin: first moving (thing)]

pri+mus (ˈpraɪməs) *n. Scottish Episcopal Church.* the presiding bishop in the Synod. [from Latin: first]

Pri+mus (ˈpraɪməs) *n. Trademark.* a portable paraffin cooking stove, used esp. by campers. Also called: **Primus stove.**

pri+mus in+ter pa+res *Latin.* (ˈpraɪməs ɪntə ˈpɑːrɪz) first among equals.

prin. *abbrev. for:* **1.** principal. **2.** principle.

prince (prɪns) *n.* **1.** (in Britain) a son of the sovereign or of one of the sovereign's sons. **2.** a nonreigning male member of a sovereign family. **3.** the monarch of a small territory, such as Monaco, usually called a principality, that was at some time subordinate to an emperor or king. **4.** any sovereign; monarch. **5.** a nobleman in various countries, such as Italy and Germany. **6.** *Chiefly U.S.* an outstanding member of a specified group: *a merchant prince.* **7.** *U.S. informal.* a generous and charming man. [C13: via Old French from Latin *princeps* first man, ruler, chief] —**ˈprince+ˌlike** *adj.*

Prince Al·bert *n.* a man's double-breasted frock coat worn esp. in the early 20th century.

prince con·sort *n.* the husband of a female sovereign, who is himself a prince.

prince·dom ('prɪnsdəm) *n.* **1.** the dignity, rank, or position of a prince. **2.** a land ruled by a prince; principality.

Prince Ed·ward Is·land *n.* an island in the Gulf of St. Lawrence that constitutes the smallest Canadian province. Capital: Charlottetown. Pop.: 118 229 (1976). Area: 5656 sq. km (2184 sq. miles).

prince·ling ('prɪnslɪŋ) *n.* **1.** Also called: **princekin.** a young prince. **2.** Also called: **princelet.** the ruler of an insignificant territory; petty or minor prince.

prince·ly ('prɪnslɪ) *adj.* **·li·er, ·li·est. 1.** generous or lavish. **2.** of, belonging to, or characteristic of a prince. ~*adv.* **3.** in a princely manner. —**'prince·li·ness** *n.*

Prince of Dark·ness *n.* another name for **Satan.**

Prince of Peace *n. Bible.* the future Messiah (Isaiah 9:6): held by most Christians to be Christ.

Prince of Wales[1] *n.* the eldest son and heir apparent of the British sovereign.

Prince of Wales[2] *n.* **Cape.** a cape in W Alaska, on the Bering Strait opposite the coast of the extreme NE Soviet Union: the westernmost point of North America.

Prince of Wales Is·land *n.* **1.** an island in N Canada, in the Northwest Territories. Area: about 36 000 sq. km (14 000 sq. miles). **2.** an island in SE Alaska, the largest island in the Alexander Archipelago. Area: about 4000 sq. km (1500 sq. miles). **3.** an island in NE Australia, in N Queensland in the Torres Strait. **4.** the former name (until about 1867) of the island of **Penang.**

prince re·gent *n.* a prince who acts as regent during the minority, disability, or absence of the legal sovereign.

Prince Re·gent *n.* George IV as regent of Great Britain and Ireland during the insanity of his father (1811–20).

prince roy·al *n.* the eldest son of a monarch.

Prince Ru·pert *n.* a port in W Canada, on the coast of British Columbia: one of the W termini of the Canadian National transcontinental railway. Pop.: 15 747 (1971).

prince's-feath·er *n.* **1.** an amaranthaceous garden plant, *Amaranthus hybridus hypochondriacus,* with spikes of bristly brownish-red flowers. **2.** a tall tropical polygonaceous plant, *Polygonum orientale,* with hanging spikes of pink flowers.

prin·cess (prɪn'sɛs) *n.* **1.** (in Britain) a daughter of the sovereign or of one of the sovereign's sons. **2.** a nonreigning female member of a sovereign family. **3.** the wife and consort of a prince. **4.** any very attractive or outstanding woman. **5.** *Archaic.* a female sovereign.

prin·cess roy·al *n.* the eldest daughter of a British or (formerly) a Prussian sovereign: a title not always conferred.

Prince·ton ('prɪnstən) *n.* a town in central New Jersey: settled by Quakers in 1696; an important educational centre, seat of Princeton University (founded at Elizabeth in 1747 and moved here in 1756); scene of the battle (1777) during the War of American Independence in which Washington's troops defeated the British on the university campus. Pop.: 12 311 (1970).

prin·ci·pal ('prɪnsɪpᵊl) *adj.* (*prenominal*) **1.** first in importance, rank, value, etc.; chief. **2.** denoting or relating to capital or property as opposed to interest, etc. ~*n.* **3.** a person who is first in importance or directs some event, action, organization, etc. **4.** *Law.* **a.** a person who engages another to act as his agent. **b.** an active participant in a crime. **c.** the person primarily liable to fulfil an obligation. **5.** the head of a school or other educational institution. **6.** *U.S.* a supervisory administrator of a group of schools. **7.** *Finance.* **a.** capital or property, as contrasted with the income derived from it. **b.** the original amount of a debt on which interest is calculated. **8.** a main roof truss or rafter. **9.** *Music.* **a.** the chief instrumentalist in a section of the orchestra. **b.** one of the singers in an opera company. **c.** either of two types of open diapason organ stops, one of four-foot length and pitch and the other of eight-foot length and pitch. [C13: via Old French from Latin *principālis* chief, from *princeps* chief man, PRINCE] —**'prin·ci·pal·ly** *adv.* —**'prin·ci·pal·ˌship** *n.*

prin·ci·pal ax·is *n.* **1.** the line passing through the centres of curvature of the faces of a lens or a curved mirror. **2.** any of three mutually perpendicular axes about which the moment of inertia of a body is maximum.

prin·ci·pal boy *n.* the leading male role in a pantomime, played by a woman.

prin·ci·pal fo·cus *n.* another name for **focal point.**

prin·ci·pal·i·ties (ˌprɪnsɪ'pælɪtɪz) *pl. n.* (*often cap.*) the seventh of the nine orders into which the angels are divided in medieval angelology.

prin·ci·pal·i·ty (ˌprɪnsɪ'pælɪtɪ) *n., pl.* **·ties. 1. a.** a territory ruled by a prince. **b.** a territory from which a prince draws his title. **2.** the dignity or authority of a prince.

prin·ci·pal parts *pl. n.* **1.** *Grammar.* the main inflected forms of a verb, from which other inflections may be deduced. In English they are generally considered to consist of the third person present singular, present participle, past tense, and past participle. **2.** the sides and interior angles of a triangle.

Prin·ci·pe ('prɪnsɪpiː; *Portuguese* 'prĩsipə) *n.* an island in the Gulf of Guinea, off the W coast of Africa: part of São Tomé and Príncipe. Area: 150 sq. km (58 sq. miles).

prin·cip·i·um (prɪn'sɪpɪəm) *n., pl.* **·i·a** (-ɪə). (*usually pl.*) a principle, esp. a fundamental one. [C17: Latin: an origin, beginning]

prin·ci·ple ('prɪnsɪpᵊl) *n.* **1.** a standard or rule of personal conduct. **2.** a set of such moral rules: *a man of principle.* **3.** a fundamental or general truth or law. **4.** the essence of something. **5.** a source or fundamental cause; origin. **6.** a rule or law concerning a natural phenomenon or the behaviour of a system: *the principle of the conservation of mass.* **7.** *Chem.* a constituent of a substance that gives the substance its characteristics and behaviour. **8. in principle.** in theory or essence. **9. on principle.** because of or in demonstration of a principle. [C14: from Latin *principium* beginning, basic tenet]

Prin·ci·ple ('prɪnsɪpᵊl) *n. Christian Science.* another word for **God.**

prin·ci·pled ('prɪnsɪpᵊld) *adj.* **a.** having high moral principles. **b.** (*in combination*): *high-principled.*

prin·ci·ple of least ac·tion *n.* the principle that motion between any two points in a conservative dynamical system is such that the action has a minimum value with respect to all paths between the points that correspond to the same energy. Also called: **Maupertuis principle.**

prink (prɪŋk) *vb.* **1.** to dress (oneself, etc.) finely; deck out. **2.** (*intr.*) to preen oneself. [C16: probably changed from PRANK[2] (to adorn, decorate)] —**'prink·er** *n.*

print (prɪnt) *vb.* **1.** to reproduce (text, pictures, etc.), esp. in large numbers, by applying ink to paper or other material by one of various processes. **2.** to produce or reproduce (a manuscript, a book, data, etc.) in print, as for publication. **3.** to write (letters, etc.) in the style of printed matter. **4.** to mark or indent (a surface) by pressing (something) onto it. **5.** to produce a photographic print from (a negative). **6.** (*tr.*) to implant or fix in the mind or memory. **7.** (*tr.*) to make (a mark or indentation) by applying pressure. ~*n.* **8.** printed matter such as newsprint. **9.** a printed publication such as a newspaper or book. **10. in print. a.** in printed or published form. **b.** (of a book, etc.) offered for sale by the publisher. **11. out of print.** no longer available from a publisher. **12.** a design or picture printed from an engraved plate, wood block, or other medium. **13.** printed text, esp. with regard to the typeface used: *small print.* **14.** a positive photographic image in colour or black and white produced, usually on paper, from a negative image on film. Compare **slide** (sense 13). **15. a.** a fabric with a printed design. **b.** (*as modifier*): *a print dress.* **16. a.** a mark or indentation made by pressing something onto a surface. **b.** a stamp, die, etc., that makes such an impression. **c.** the surface subjected to such an impression. **17.** See **fingerprint.** ~See also **print out.** [C13 *priente,* from Old French: something printed, from *preindre* to make an impression, from Latin *premere* to press]

print·a·ble ('prɪntəbᵊl) *adj.* **1.** capable of being printed or of producing a print. **2.** suitable for publication. —**ˌprint·a·'bil·i·ty** *or* **'print·a·ble·ness** *n.*

print·ed cir·cuit *n.* an electronic circuit in which certain components and the connections between them are formed by etching a metallic coating or by electrodeposition on one or both sides of a thin insulating board.

print·er ('prɪntə) *n.* **1.** a person or business engaged in printing. **2.** a machine or device that prints. **3.** *Computer technol.* an output device for printing results on paper.

print·er's dev·il *n.* an apprentice or errand boy in a printing establishment.

print·er·y ('prɪntərɪ) *n., pl.* **·er·ies. 1.** *Chiefly U.S.* an establishment in which typographic printing is carried out. **2.** an establishment in which fabrics are printed.

print·ing ('prɪntɪŋ) *n.* **1. a.** the process, business, or art of producing printed matter. **b.** (*as modifier*): *printing ink.* **2.** printed text. **3.** Also called: **impression.** all the copies of a book or other publication printed at one time. **4.** a form of writing in which letters resemble printed letters.

print·ing press *n.* any of various machines used for printing.

print·mak·er ('prɪntˌmeɪkə) *n.* a person who makes print, esp. a craftsman or artist in this field.

print out *vb.* (*tr., adv.*) **1.** (of a computer output device, such as a line printer) to produce (printed information). ~*n.* **print-out. 2.** such printed information.

print shop *n.* a place in which printing is carried out.

pri·or[1] ('praɪə) *adj.* **1.** (*prenominal*) previous; preceding place. **2. prior to.** before; until. [C18: from Latin: previous]

pri·or[2] ('praɪə) *n.* **1.** the superior of a house and community in certain religious orders. **2.** the deputy head of a monastery or abbey, ranking immediately below the abbot. **3.** (formerly) a chief magistrate in medieval Florence and other Italian republics. [C11: from Late Latin: head, from Latin (adj.): previous, from Old Latin *pri* before]

Pri·or ('praɪə) *n.* **Mat·thew.** 1664–1721, English poet and diplomat, noted for his epigrammatic occasional verse.

pri·or·ate ('praɪərɪt) *n.* the office, status, or term of office of a prior.

pri·or·ess ('praɪərɪs) *n.* a nun holding an office in her convent corresponding to that of a prior in a male religious order.

pri·or·i·ty (praɪ'ɒrɪtɪ) *n., pl.* **·ties. 1.** the condition of being prior; antecedence; precedence. **2.** the right of precedence over others. **3.** something given specified attention: *my first priority.*

pri·or·y ('praɪərɪ) *n., pl.* **·or·ies.** a religious house governed by a prior, sometimes being subordinate to an abbey. [C13: from Medieval Latin *priōria*; see PRIOR[2]]

Pri·pet (*Russian* 'pripɪtj) *n.* a river in the W Soviet Union, rising in the NW Ukrainian SSR and flowing northeast into the Belorussian SSR across the **Pripet Marshes** (the largest swamp in Europe), then east into the Dnieper River. Length: about 800 km (500 miles).

pris·age ('praɪzɪdʒ) *n.* a customs duty levied until 1809 upon wine imported into England. [C16: from Anglo-French, from Old French *prise* a taking or requisitioning, duty, from *prendre* to take; see PRISE]

Pris·ci·an ('prɪʃɪən) *n.* Latin name *Priscianus Caesariensis.* 6th century A.D. Latin grammarian.

prise *or* **prize** (praɪz) *vb.* (*tr.*) **1.** to force open by levering. **2.** to extract or obtain with difficulty: *they had to prise the news out of him.* ~*n.* **3.** *Rare or dialect.* a tool involving leverage in its use or the leverage so employed. ~U.S. equivalent: **pry.** [C17: from Old French *prise* a taking, from *prendre* to take, from Latin *prehendere;* see PRIZE[1]]

prism ('prɪzəm) *n.* **1.** a transparent polygonal solid, often having triangular ends and rectangular sides, for dispersing light into a spectrum or for reflecting and deviating light. They are used in spectroscopes, binoculars, periscopes, etc. **2.** a form of crystal with faces parallel to the vertical axis. **3.** *Maths.* a polyhedron having parallel, polygonal, and congruent bases and sides that are parallelograms. [C16: from Medieval Latin *prisma,* from Greek: something shaped by sawing, from *prizein* to saw]

pris·mat·ic (prɪz'mætɪk) *adj.* **1.** concerned with, containing, or produced by a prism. **2.** exhibiting bright spectral colours: *prismatic light.* **3.** *Crystallog.* another word for **orthorhombic.** —**pris'mat·i·cal·ly** *adv.*

pris·ma·toid ('prɪzmə,tɔɪd) *n.* a polyhedron whose vertices lie in either one of two parallel planes. Compare **prism** (sense 3), **prismoid.** [C19: from Greek *prismatoeidēs* shaped like a prism; see PRISM, -OID] —,**pris·ma'toi·dal** *adj.*

pris·moid ('prɪzmɔɪd) *n.* a prismatoid having an equal number of vertices in each of the two parallel planes and whose sides are trapeziums or parallelograms. [C18: from French *prismoïde;* see PRISM, -OID] —**pris'moi·dal** *adj.*

pris·on ('prɪzᵊn) *n.* **1.** a public building used to house convicted criminals and accused persons remanded in custody and awaiting trial. See also **jail, penitentiary, reformatory. 2.** any place of confinement or seeming confinement. [C12: from Old French *prisun,* from Latin *prēnsiō* a capturing, from *prehendere* to lay hold of]

pris·on·er ('prɪzənə) *n.* **1.** a person deprived of liberty and kept in prison or some other form of custody as a punishment for a crime, while awaiting trial, or for some other reason. **2.** a person confined by any of various restraints: *we are all prisoners of time.* **3. take (someone) prisoner.** to capture and hold as a prisoner, esp. as a prisoner of war.

pris·on·er of war *n.* a person, esp. a serviceman, captured by an enemy in time of war. Abbrev.: **P.O.W.**

pris·on·er's base *n.* a children's game involving two teams, members of which chase and capture each other to increase the number of children in their own base.

pris·sy ('prɪsɪ) *adj.* **·si·er, ·si·est.** *Informal.* fussy and prim, esp. in a prudish way. [C20: probably from PRIM + SISSY] —'**pris·si·ly** *adv.* —'**pris·si·ness** *n.*

Priš·ti·na (*Serbo-Croatian* 'pri:ʃtina) *n.* a city in S Yugoslavia, capital of the Kosovo-Metohija autonomous region: under Turkish control until 1912; nearby is the 14th-century Gračanica monastery. Pop.: 69 524 (1971).

pris·tine ('prɪstaɪn, -ti:n) *adj.* **1.** of or involving the earliest period, state, etc.; original. **2.** pure; uncorrupted. [C15: from Latin *pristinus* primitive; related to *prīmus* first, PRIME]

prith·ee ('prɪðɪ) *interj. Archaic.* pray thee; please. [C16: shortened from *I pray thee*]

prit·tle-prat·tle ('prɪtᵊl,prætᵊl) *n.* foolish or idle talk; babble. [C16: reduplication of PRATTLE]

priv. *abbrev. for:* **1.** private. **2.** privative.

pri·va·cy ('praɪvəsɪ, 'prɪvəsɪ) *n., pl.* **·cies. 1.** the condition of being private or withdrawn; seclusion. **2.** the condition of being secret; secrecy.

Pri·vat·do·cent (*German* pri'va:tdo'tse:nt) *n.* (esp. in German-speaking countries) a university lecturer who formerly received fees from his students rather than a university salary. [German, from *privat* PRIVATE + *docent* (for *Dozent* lecturer) from Latin *docēre* to teach]

pri·vate ('praɪvɪt) *adj.* **1.** not widely known; confidential; secret: *a private conversation.* **2.** not for general or public use: *a private bathroom.* **3.** (*prenominal*) individual; special: *my own private recipe.* **4.** (*prenominal*) having no public office, rank, etc.: *a private man.* **5.** (*prenominal*) denoting a soldier of the lowest military rank: *a private soldier.* **6. in private.** in secret; confidentially. ~*n.* **7.** a soldier of the lowest rank, sometimes separated into qualification grades, in many armies and marine corps: *private first class.* [C14: from Latin *prīvātus* belonging to one individual, withdrawn from public life, from *prīvāre* to deprive, bereave] —'**pri·vate·ly** *adv.*

pri·vate bill *n.* a bill presented to Parliament or Congress on behalf of a private individual, corporation, etc.

pri·vate com·pa·ny *n.* a limited company that does not issue shares for public subscription and whose owners do not enjoy an unrestricted right to transfer their shareholdings. Compare **public company.**

pri·vate en·ter·prise *n.* **1.** economic activity undertaken by private individuals or organizations under private ownership. Compare **public enterprise. 2.** another name for **capitalism.**

pri·va·teer (,praɪvə'tɪə) *n.* **1.** an armed, privately owned vessel commissioned for war service by a government. **2.** Also called: **privateersman.** an officer or member of the crew of a privateer. ~*vb.* **3.** (*intr.*) to serve as a privateer.

pri·vate eye *n. Chiefly U.S.* a private detective.

pri·vate ho·tel *n.* **1.** a hotel in which the proprietor has the right to refuse to accept a person as a guest, esp. a person arriving by chance. **2.** *Austral.* a hotel not having a licence to sell alcoholic liquor.

pri·vate in·come *n.* an income from sources other than employment, such as investment. Also called: **private means.**

pri·vate mem·ber *n.* a member of a legislative assembly, such as the House of Commons, not having an appointment in the government.

pri·vate parts *or* **pri·vates** ('praɪvɪts) *pl. n.* euphemistic terms for **genitals.**

pri·vate pa·tient *n. Brit.* a patient receiving medical treatment not paid for by the National Health Service.

pri·vate prac·tice *n. Brit.* medical practice that is not part of the National Health Service.

pri·vate press *n.* a printing establishment primarily run as a pastime.

pri·vate school *n.* a school under the financial and managerial control of a private body or charitable trust, accepting mostly fee-paying pupils.

pri·vate sec·re·tar·y *n.* a secretary entrusted with the personal and confidential matters of a business executive.

pri·vate trea·ty *n.* a sale of property for a price agreed directly between seller and buyer.

pri·va·tion (praɪ'veɪʃən) *n.* **1.** loss or lack of the necessities of life, such as food and shelter. **2.** hardship resulting from this. **3.** the state of being deprived. **4.** *Logic.* the absence from an object of what ordinarily or naturally belongs to such objects. [C14: from Latin *prīvātiō* deprivation]

priv·a·tive ('prɪvətɪv) *adj.* **1.** causing privation. **2.** expressing lack or negation, as for example the English suffix *-less* and prefix *un-*. **3.** *Logic.* (of a proposition) that predicates a logical privation. [C16: from Latin *prīvātīvus* indicating loss, negative] —'**priv·a·tive·ly** *adv.*

priv·et ('prɪvɪt) *n.* **a.** any oleaceous shrub of the genus *Ligustrum,* esp. *L. vulgare,* having oval dark green leaves, white flowers, and purplish-black berries. **b.** (*as modifier*): *a privet hedge.* [C16: of unknown origin]

priv·et hawk *n.* a hawk moth, *Sphinx ligustri,* with a mauve-and-brown striped body: frequents privets.

priv·i·lege ('prɪvɪlɪdʒ) *n.* **1.** a benefit, immunity, etc., granted under certain conditions. **2.** the advantages and immunities enjoyed by a small usually powerful group or class, esp. to the disadvantage of others: *one of the obstacles to social harmony is privilege.* **3.** any of the fundamental rights guaranteed to the citizens of a country by its constitution. **4. a.** the right of a lawyer to refuse to divulge information obtained in confidence from a client. **b.** the right claimed by any of certain other functionaries to refuse to divulge information: *executive privilege.* **5.** the rights and immunities enjoyed by members of most legislative bodies, such as freedom of speech, freedom from arrest in civil cases during a session, etc. **6.** *U.S. stock exchange.* a speculative contract permitting its purchaser to make optional purchases or sales of securities at a specified time over a limited period of time. See also **call** (sense 58), **put** (sense 20), **spread** (sense 24c.), **straddle** (sense 9). ~*vb.* (*tr.*) **7.** to bestow a privilege or privileges upon. **8.** (foll. by *from*) to free or exempt. [C12: from Old French *privilēge,* from Latin *prīvilēgium* law relevant to rights of an individual, from *prīvus* an individual + *lēx* law]

priv·i·leged ('prɪvɪlɪdʒd) *adj.* **1.** enjoying or granted as a privilege or privileges. **2.** *Law.* **a.** not actionable as a libel or slander. **b.** (of a communication, document, etc.) that a witness cannot be compelled to divulge. **3.** *Nautical.* (of a vessel) having the right of way.

priv·i·ly ('prɪvɪlɪ) *adv. Archaic or literary.* in a secret way.

priv·i·ty ('prɪvɪtɪ) *n., pl* **·ties. 1.** a legally recognized relationship existing between two parties, such as that between lessor and lessee and between the parties to a contract: *privity of estate; privity of contract.* **2.** secret knowledge that is shared. [C13: from Old French *priveté*]

priv·y ('prɪvɪ) *adj.* **priv·i·er, priv·i·est. 1.** (*postpositive;* foll. by *to*) participating in the knowledge of something secret. **2.** *Archaic.* secret, hidden, etc. **3.** *Archaic.* of or relating to one person only. ~*n., pl.* **priv·ies. 4.** a small lavatory, esp. an outhouse. **5.** *Law.* a person in privity with another. See **privity** (sense 1). [C13: from Old French *privé* something private, from Latin *prīvātus* PRIVATE]

priv·y cham·ber *n.* **1.** a private apartment inside a royal residence. **2.** *Archaic.* a private room reserved for the use of a specific person or group.

priv·y coun·cil *n.* **1.** the council of state of a monarch or noble, esp. formerly. **2.** *Archaic.* a private or secret council.

Priv·y Coun·cil *n.* the private council of the British sovereign, consisting of all current and former ministers of the Crown and other distinguished subjects, all of whom are appointed for life. See also **Judicial Committee of the Privy Council.** —**Priv·y Coun·cil·lor** *n.*

priv·y purse *n.* (*often cap.*) **1. a.** (in Britain) an allowance voted by Parliament for the private expenses of the monarch: part of the civil list. **b.** (in other countries) a similar sum of money for the monarch. **2.** an official of the royal household responsible for dealing with the monarch's private expenses. Full name: **Keeper of the Privy Purse.**

priv·y seal *n.* (*often cap.*) (in Britain) a seal affixed to certain documents issued by royal authority: of less rank and importance than the great seal.

prix fixe (*French* pri 'fiks) *n., pl.* **prix fixes** ('fiks). a fixed price charged for one of a set number of meals offered on a menu. Compare **à la carte, table d'hôte.**

prize[1] (praɪz) *n.* **1. a.** a reward or honour for victory or for having won a contest, competition, etc. **b.** (*as modifier*): *prize jockey; prize essay.* **2.** something given to the winner of any game of chance, lottery, etc. **3.** something striven for. **4.** any valuable property captured in time of war, esp. a vessel. [C14: from Old French *prise* a capture, from Latin *prehendere* to seize; influenced also by Middle English *prise* reward; see PRICE]

prize[2] (praɪz) *vb.* (*tr.*) to esteem greatly; value highly. [C15 *prise,* from Old French *preisier* to PRAISE]

prize[3] (praɪz) *vb., n.* a variant spelling of **prise.**

prize court *n. Law.* a court having jurisdiction to determine how property captured at sea in wartime is to be distributed.

prize+fight ('praɪzˌfaɪt) *n.* a boxing match for a prize or purse, esp. one of the fights popular in the 18th and 19th centuries. —**'prize+ˌfight·er** *n.* —**'prize+ˌfight·ing** *n.*

prize mon+ey *n.* **1.** any money offered, paid, or received as a prize. **2.** (formerly) a part of the money realized from the sale of a captured vessel.

prize ring *n.* **1.** the enclosed area or ring used by prize-fighters. **2. the prize ring.** the sport of prizefighting.

p.r.n. (in prescriptions, etc.) *abbrev. for* pro re nata. [Latin: as the situation demands; as needed]

pro[1] (prəʊ) *adv.* **1.** in favour of a motion, issue, course of action, etc. Compare **anti.** ~*prep.* **2.** in favour of. ~*n., pl.* **pros. 3.** (*usually pl.*) an argument or vote in favour of a proposal or motion. See also **pros and cons. 4.** (*usually pl.*) a person who votes in favour of a proposal, motion, etc. ~Compare **con**[2]. [from Latin *prō* (prep.) in favour of]

pro[2] (prəʊ) *n, pl.* **pros.,** *adj. Informal.* short for **professional.** [C19: by shortening]

P.R.O. *abbrev. for:* **1.** Public Records Office. **2.** public relations officer.

pro-[1] *prefix.* **1.** in favour of; supporting: *pro-Chinese.* **2.** acting as a substitute for: *proconsul; pronoun.* [from Latin *prō* (adv. and prep.). In compound words borrowed from Latin, *prō-* indicates: forward, out (*project*); forward and down (*prostrate*); away from a place (*prodigal*); onward in time or space (*proceed*); extension outwards (*propagate*); before in time or place (*provide, protect*); on behalf of (*procure*); acting as a substitute for (*pronominal*); and sometimes intensive force (*promiscuous*)]

pro-[2] *prefix.* before in time or position; anterior; forward: *prophase; procephalic; prognathous.* [from Greek *pro* (prep.) before (in time, position, rank, etc.)]

pro·a ('prəʊə) *or* **prau** *n.* any of several kinds of canoe-like boats used in the South Pacific, esp. one equipped with an outrigger and sails. [C16: from Malay *parāhū* a boat]

pro+ac+tive in+hi+bi+tion (prəʊ'æktɪv) *n. Psychol.* the tendency for earlier memories to interfere with the retrieval of material learned later. Compare **retroactive inhibition.**

pro-am ('prəʊ'æm) *adj. Chiefly U.S.* (of a golf tournament, etc.) involving both professional and amateur players.

prob. *abbrev. for:* **1.** probable. **2.** probably. **3.** problem.

prob·a+bil+ism ('prɒbəbɪˌlɪzəm) *n.* **1.** *Philosophy.* the doctrine that although certainty is impossible, probability is a sufficient basis for belief and action. **2.** a system of moral theology based on the principle that when the lawfulness or unlawfulness of an action is in doubt it is permissible to follow the more dubious course so long as solid arguments support it. —**'prob+a·bil+ist** *n., adj.* —**ˌprob+a·bil+'is·tic** *adj.*

prob+a·bil+i·ty (ˌprɒbə'bɪlɪtɪ) *n., pl.* **·ties. 1.** the condition of being probable. **2.** an event or other thing that is probable. **3.** *Statistics.* a measure of the relative frequency or likelihood of occurrence of an event. Values lie between zero (impossibility) and one (certainty) and are derived from a theoretical distribution or from observations.

prob+a·ble ('prɒbəbᵊl) *adj.* **1.** likely to be or to happen but not necessarily so. **2.** most likely: *the probable cause of the accident.* ~*n.* **3.** a person who is probably to be chosen for a team, event, etc. [C14: via Old French from Latin *probābilis* that may be proved, from *probāre* to prove]

prob+a·ble cause *n. Law.* reasonable grounds for holding a belief, esp. such as will justify bringing legal proceedings against a person or will constitute a defence to a charge of malicious prosecution.

prob+a·bly ('prɒbəblɪ) *adv.* **1.** (*sentence modifier; not used with a negative or in a question*) in all likelihood or probability: *I'll probably see you tomorrow.* ~ **2.** *sentence substitute.* I believe such a thing or situation may be the case.

pro+band ('prəʊbænd) *n.* a person considered as the starting point of a genealogical study, esp. in a familial study of a hereditary disease. [C20: from Latin *probandus,* gerundive of *probāre* to test]

pro+bang ('prəʊbæŋ) *n. Surgery.* a long flexible rod, often with a small sponge at one end, for inserting into the oesophagus, as to apply medication. [C17: variant, apparently by association with PROBE, of *provang,* name coined by W. Rumsey (1584–1660), Welsh judge, its inventor; of unknown origin]

pro+bate ('prəʊbɪt, -beɪt) *n.* **1.** the act or process of officially proving the authenticity and validity of a will. **2. a.** the official certificate stating a will to be genuine and conferring on the executors power to administer the estate. **b.** the probate copy of a will. **3.** (in the U.S.) all matters within the jurisdiction of a probate court. **4.** (*modifier*) of, relating to, or concerned with probate: *a probate court.* ~*vb.* **5.** (*tr.*) *Chiefly U.S.* to establish officially the authenticity and validity of (a will). [C15: from Latin *probāre* to inspect]

pro+ba+tion (prə'beɪʃən) *n.* **1.** a system of dealing with offenders by placing them under the supervision of a probation officer. **2. on probation. a.** under the supervision of a probation officer. **b.** undergoing a test period. **3.** a trial period, as for a teacher, religious novitiate, etc. **4.** the act of proving or testing. —**pro+'ba+tion+al** *or* **pro+'ba+tion+ar·y** *adj.* —**pro+'ba+tion+al+ly** *adv.*

pro+ba+tion+er (prə'beɪʃənə) *n.* a person on probation.

pro+ba+tion of+fic+er *n.* an officer of a court who supervises offenders placed on probation and assists and befriends them.

pro+ba+tive ('prəʊbətɪv) *or* **pro+ba+to·ry** ('prəʊbətərɪ, -trɪ) *adj.* **1.** serving to test or designed for testing. **2.** providing proof or evidence. [C15: from Late Latin *probātīvus* concerning proof] —**'pro+ba+tive+ly** *adv.*

probe (prəʊb) *vb.* **1.** (*tr.*) to search into or question closely. **2.** to examine (something) with or as if with a probe. ~*n.* **3.** something that probes, examines, or tests. **4.** *Surgery.* a slender and usually flexible instrument for exploring a wound, sinus, etc. **5.** a thorough inquiry, such as one by a newspaper into corrupt practices. **6.** *Electronics.* a lead connecting to or containing a measuring· or monitoring circuit used for testing. **7.** *Electronics.* a conductor inserted into a waveguide or cavity resonator to provide coupling to an external circuit. **8.** See **space probe.** [C16: from Medieval Latin *proba* investigation, from Latin *probāre* to test] —**'probe+a·ble** *adj.* —**'prob+er** *n.*

pro+bi·ty ('prəʊbɪtɪ) *n.* confirmed integrity; uprightness. [C16: from Latin *probitās* honesty, from *probus* virtuous]

prob+lem ('prɒbləm) *n.* **1. a.** any thing, matter, person, etc., that is difficult to deal with, solve, or overcome. **b.** (*as modifier*): *a problem child.* **2.** a puzzle, question, etc., set for solution. **3.** *Maths.* a statement requiring a solution usually by means of one or more operations or geometric constructions. **4.** (*modifier*) designating a literary work that deals with difficult moral questions: *a problem play.* [C14: from Late Latin *problēma,* from Greek: something put forward; related to *proballein* to throw forwards, from PRO-[2] + *ballein* to throw]

prob+lem+at+ic (ˌprɒblə'mætɪk) *or* **prob+lem+at·i·cal** *adj.* **1.** having the nature or appearance of a problem; questionable. **2.** *Logic.* (of a proposition or judgment) that may or may not be true. —**ˌprob+lem+'at·i·cal+ly** *adv.*

pro bo·no pub+li+co *Latin.* ('prəʊ 'bəʊnəʊ 'publɪkəʊ) for the public good.

pro+bos+cid+e·an *or* **pro+bos+cid+i·an** (ˌprəʊbɒ'sɪdɪən) *adj.* **1.** of, relating to, or belonging to the *Proboscidea,* an order of massive herbivorous placental mammals having tusks and a long trunk: contains the elephants. ~*n.* **2.** any proboscidean animal.

pro+bos+cis (prəʊ'bɒsɪs) *n., pl.* **+cis·es** *or* **+ci·des** (-sɪˌdi:z). **1.** a long flexible prehensile trunk or snout, as of an elephant. **2.** the elongated mouthparts of certain insects, adapted for piercing or sucking food. **3.** any similar part or organ. **4.** *Informal, facetious.* a person's nose, esp. if large. [C17: via Latin from Greek *proboskis* trunk of an elephant, from *boskein* to feed]

pro+bos+cis mon+key *n.* an Old World Monkey, *Nasalis larvatus,* of Borneo, with an elongated bulbous nose.

proc. *abbrev. for:* **1.** procedure. **2.** proceedings. **3.** process.

pro+caine ('prəʊkeɪn, prəʊ'keɪn) *n.* a colourless or white crystalline water-soluble substance used, as the hydrochloride, as a local anaesthetic; 2-diethylaminoethyl-4-amino benzoate. Formula: $NH_2C_6H_4COOC_2H_4N(C_2H_5)_2$. See also **Novocaine.** [C20: from PRO-[1] + (CO)CAINE]

pro+cam+bi·um (prəʊ'kæmbɪəm) *n.* undifferentiated plant tissue, just behind the growing tip in stems and roots, that develops into conducting tissues. —**pro+'cam+bi·al** *adj.*

pro+carp ('prəʊkɑ:p) *n.* a female reproductive organ in red algae. [C19: from New Latin *procarpium,* from PRO-[2] + *-carpium,* from Greek *karpos* fruit]

pro+ca+the·dral (ˌprəʊkə'θi:drəl) *n.* a church serving as a cathedral.

pro+ce·dure (prə'si:dʒə) *n.* **1.** a way of acting or progressing in a course of action, esp. an established method. **2.** the established mode or form of conducting the business of a legislature, the enforcement of a legal right, etc. **3.** *Computer technol.* another name for **subroutine.** —**pro+'ce·dur+al** *adj.* —**pro+'ce·dur+al+ly** *adv.*

pro+ceed (prə'si:d) *vb.* (*intr.*) **1.** (often foll. by *to*) to advance or carry on, esp. after stopping. **2.** (often foll. by *with*) to undertake and continue (something or to do something): *he proceeded with his reading.* **3.** (often foll. by *against*) to institute or carry on a legal action. **4.** to emerge or originate; arise: *evil proceeds from the heart.* [C14: from Latin *prōcēdere* to advance, from PRO-[1] + *cēdere* to go] —**pro+'ceed+er** *n.*

pro+ceed+ing (prə'si:dɪŋ) *n.* **1.** an act or course of action. **2. a.** the institution of a legal action. **b.** any step taken in a legal action. **3.** (*pl.*) the minutes of the meetings of a club, society, etc. **4.** (*pl.*) legal action; litigation. **5.** (*pl.*) the events of an occasion, meeting, etc.

pro+ceeds ('prəʊsi:dz) *pl. n.* **1.** the profit or return derived from a commercial transaction, investment, etc. **2.** the result, esp. the revenue or total sum, accruing from some undertaking or course of action, as in commerce.

ˌpro+a·bo·'li·tion *adj.*
ˌpro+a·'mend+ment *adj.*
ˌpro-A·'mer·i·can *adj., n.*
ˌpro+an+nex·'a·tion *adj.*
ˌpro+ap+'prov·al *adj.*
ˌpro+ar+bi+'tra·tion *adj.*
ˌpro+au·to·'ma·tion *adj.*
pro+'bib+li+cal *adj.*
pro-'Bol·she+vik *adj., n.*
pro-'Bud·dhist *n., adj.*
pro+'busi+ness *adj.*
pro+'cap·i+tal+ist *adj.*

proc·e·leus·mat·ic (ˌprɒsɪluːs'mætɪk) *Prosody.* ~*adj.* **1.** denoting or consisting of a metrical foot of four short syllables. ~*n.* **2.** a proceleusmatic metrical foot. [C18: from Late Latin *proceleusmaticus,* from Greek *prokeleusmatikos,* from *prokeleuein* to drive on, from PRO-² + *keleuein* to give orders]

pro·ce·phal·ic (ˌprəʊsɪ'fælɪk) *adj. Anatomy.* of or relating to the anterior part of the head.

pro·cess¹ ('prəʊsɛs) *n.* **1.** a series of actions directed to achieving a result or condition. **2.** a method of doing or producing something. **3.** a forward movement. **4.** the course of time. **5. a.** a summons, writ, etc., commanding a person to appear in court. **b.** the whole proceedings in an action at law. **6.** a natural outgrowth or projection of a part, organ, or organism. **7.** (*modifier*) relating to the general preparation of a printing forme or plate by the use, at some stage, of photography. **8.** (*modifier*) denoting a film, film scene, shot, etc., made by techniques that produce unusual optical effects. ~*vb.* (*tr.*) **9.** to subject to a routine procedure; handle. **10.** to treat or prepare by a special method: *to process cheese.* **11. a.** to institute legal proceedings against. **b.** to serve a process on. **12.** *Photog.* **a.** to develop, rinse, fix, wash, and dry (exposed film, etc.). **b.** to produce final prints or slides from (undeveloped film). **13.** *Computer technol.* to perform mathematical and logical operations on (data) according to programmed instructions in order to obtain the required information. [C14: from Old French *procès,* from Latin *prōcessus* an advancing, from *prōcēdere* to PROCEED]

pro·cess² (prə'sɛs) *vb.* (*intr.*) to proceed in or as if in a procession. [C19: back formation from PROCESSION]

pro·ces·sion (prə'sɛʃən) *n.* **1.** the act of proceeding in a regular formation. **2.** a group of people or things moving forwards in an orderly, regular, or ceremonial manner. **3.** a hymn, litany, etc., sung in a procession. **4.** the emanation of the Holy Spirit. ~*vb.* **5.** (*intr.*) *Rare.* to go in procession. [C12: via Old French from Latin *prōcessiō* a marching forwards]

pro·ces·sion·al (prə'sɛʃənəl) *adj.* **1.** of, relating to, or suitable for a procession. ~*n.* **2.** *Christianity.* **a.** a book containing the prayers, hymns, litanies, and liturgy prescribed for processions. **b.** a hymn, litany, etc., used in a procession. —**pro'ces·sion·al·ly** *adv.*

pro·ces·sor ('prəʊsɛsə) *n.* **1.** *Computer technol.* another name for **central processing unit. 2.** a person or thing that carries out a process.

pro·cess print·ing *n.* a method of making reproductions of a coloured picture, usually by using four halftone plates for different coloured inks.

pro·cess-serv·er *n.* a sheriff's officer who serves legal documents such as writs for appearance in court.

pro·cès-ver·bal *French.* (prɔsɛvɛr'bal) *n., pl.* ***·baux*** (-'bo). a written record of an official proceeding; minutes. [C17: from French: see PROCESS, VERBAL]

pro·chro·nism ('prəʊkrəˌnɪzəm) *n.* an error in dating that places an event earlier than it actually occurred. Compare **parachronism.** [C17: from PRO- + Greek *khronos* time + -ISM, by analogy with ANACHRONISM]

pro·claim (prə'kleɪm) *vb.* (*tr.*) **1.** (*may take a clause as object*) to announce publicly; declare. **2.** (*may take a clause as object*) to show or indicate plainly. **3.** to praise or extol. [C14: from Latin *prōclāmāre* to shout aloud] —**proc·la·ma·tion** (ˌprɒklə'meɪʃən) *n.* —**pro·clam·a·to·ry** (prə'klæmətərɪ, -trɪ) *adj.* —**pro'claim·er** *n.*

pro·clit·ic (prəʊ'klɪtɪk) ~*adj.* **1. a.** relating to or denoting a monosyllabic word or form having no stress or accent and pronounced as a prefix of the following word, as in English *'t* for *it* in *'twas.* **b.** (in classical Greek) relating to or denoting a word that throws its accent onto the following word. ~*n.* **2.** a proclitic word or form. ~Compare **enclitic.** [C19: from New Latin *proclīticus,* from Greek *proklinein* to lean forwards; formed on the model of ENCLITIC]

pro·cliv·i·ty (prə'klɪvɪtɪ) *n., pl.* **·ties.** a tendency or inclination. [C16: from Latin *prōclīvitās,* from *prōclīvis* steep, from PRO-¹ + *clīvus* a slope]

Pro·clus ('prəʊkləs, 'prɒk-) *n.* ?410–485 A.D., Greek neo-Platonist philosopher.

Proc·ne ('prɒknɪ) *n. Greek myth.* a princess of Athens, who punished her husband for raping her sister Philomela by feeding him the flesh of their son. She was changed at her death into a swallow. See **Philomela.**

pro·con·sul (prəʊ'kɒnsəl) *n.* **1.** an administrator or governor of a colony, occupied territory, or other dependency. **2.** (in ancient Rome) the governor of a senatorial province. —**pro·con·su·lar** (prəʊ'kɒnsjʊlə) *adj.* —**pro'con·su·late** *or* **pro'con·sul·ship** *n.*

Pro·co·pi·us (prəʊ'kəʊpɪəs) *n.* ?490–?562 A.D., Byzantine historian, noted for his account of the wars of Justinian I against the Persians, Vandals, and Ostrogoths.

pro·cras·ti·nate (prəʊ'kræstɪˌneɪt, prə-) *vb.* (*usually intr.*) to put off or defer (an action) until a later time; delay. [C16: from Latin *prōcrāstināre* to postpone until tomorrow, from PRO-¹ + *crās* tomorrow] —**pro·ˌcras·ti·'na·tion** *n.* —**pro'cras·ti·ˌna·tor** *n.*

pro·cre·ate ('prəʊkrɪˌeɪt) *vb.* **1.** to beget or engender (offspring). **2.** (*tr.*) to bring into being. [C16: from Latin *prōcreāre,* from PRO-¹ + *creāre* to create] —**ˌpro·cre·'a·tion** *n.* —'**pro·cre·ant** *or* '**pro·cre·ˌa·tive** *adj.* —'**pro·cre·ˌa·tor** *n.*

Pro·crus·te·an (prəʊ'krʌstɪən) *adj.* tending or designed to produce conformity by violent or ruthless methods.

Pro·crus·tes (prəʊ'krʌstiːz) *n. Greek myth.* a robber, who put travellers in his bed, stretching or lopping off their limbs so that they fitted it. [C16: from Greek *Prokroustēs* the stretcher, from *prokrouein* to extend by hammering out]

pro·cryp·tic (prəʊ'krɪptɪk) *adj.* (of animals) having protective coloration. [C19: from PRO-² + Greek *kruptein* to conceal] —**pro'cryp·ti·cal·ly** *adv.*

proc·to- *or before a vowel* **proct-** *combining form.* indicating the anus or rectum: *proctology.* [from Greek *prōktos*]

proc·tol·o·gy (prɒk'tɒlədʒɪ) *n.* the branch of medical science concerned with the rectum. —**proc·to·log·i·cal** (ˌprɒktə'lɒdʒɪkəl) *adj.* —**proc'tol·o·gist** *n.*

proc·tor ('prɒktə) *n.* **1.** a member of the teaching staff of certain universities having the duties of invigilating at examinations, enforcing discipline, etc. **2.** (formerly) an agent, esp. one engaged to conduct another's case in a court. **3.** (formerly) an agent employed to collect tithes. **4.** *Church of England.* one of the elected representatives of the clergy in Convocation and the General Synod. [C14: syncopated variant of PROCURATOR] —**proc·to·ri·al** (prɒk'tɔːrɪəl) *adj.* —**proc'to·ri·al·ly** *adv.*

proc·to·scope ('prɒktəˌskəʊp) *n.* a medical instrument for examining the rectum. —**proc·to·scop·ic** (ˌprɒktə'skɒpɪk) *adj.* —**proc·tos·co·py** (prɒk'tɒskəpɪ) *n.*

pro·cum·bent (prəʊ'kʌmbənt) *adj.* **1.** Also: **prostrate.** (of stems) growing along the ground. **2.** leaning forwards or lying on the face. [C17: from Latin *prōcumbere* to fall forwards; compare INCUMBENT]

proc·u·ra·tion (ˌprɒkjʊ'reɪʃən) *n.* **1.** the act of procuring. **2.** *Law.* **a.** the appointment of an agent, procurator, or attorney. **b.** the office, function, or authority of such an official. **c.** the formal written authority given to such an official. See also **power of attorney. 3.** *Criminal law.* the offence of procuring women for immoral purposes. **4.** *Archaic.* the management of another person's affairs.

proc·u·ra·tor ('prɒkjʊˌreɪtə) *n.* **1.** (in ancient Rome) a civil official of the emperor's administration, often employed as the governor of a minor province or as a financial agent. **2.** *Rare.* a person engaged and authorized by another to manage his affairs. [C13: from Latin: a manager, from *prōcūrāre* to attend to] —**proc·u·ra·cy** ('prɒkjʊrəsɪ) *or* '**proc·u·ˌra·tor·ship** *n.* —**proc·u·ra·to·ri·al** (ˌprɒkjʊrə'tɔːrɪəl) *or* **proc·u·ra·to·ry** ('prɒkjʊrətərɪ, -trɪ) *adj.*

proc·u·ra·tor fis·cal *n.* (in Scotland) a legal officer who performs the functions of public prosecutor and coroner.

proc·u·ra·tor·y ('prɒkjʊrətərɪ) *n. Law.* authorization to act on behalf of someone else.

pro·cure (prə'kjʊə) *vb.* **1.** (*tr.*) to obtain or acquire; secure. **2.** to obtain (women or girls) to act as prostitutes. [C13: from Latin *prōcūrāre* to look after, from PRO-¹ + *cūrāre* to care for] —**pro'cur·a·ble** *adj.* —**pro'cure·ment, pro'cur·ance,** *or* **pro'cur·al** *n.*

pro·cur·er (prə'kjʊərə) *n.* a person who procures, esp. a man who procures women or girls as prostitutes.

Pro·cy·on ('prəʊsɪən) *n.* the brightest star in the constellation Canis Minor, a binary with a very faint companion. Visual magnitude: 0.4; spectral type: F3; distance: 11 light years. [C17: via Latin from Greek *Prokuōn* literally: before the Dog, from PRO-² + *kuōn* dog; so named because it rises just before Sirius, the Dog Star]

prod (prɒd) *vb.* **prods, prod·ding, prod·ded. 1.** to poke or jab with or as if with a pointed object. **2.** (*tr.*) to rouse or urge to action. ~*n.* **3.** the act or an instance of prodding. **4.** a sharp or pointed object. **5.** a stimulus or reminder. [C16: of uncertain origin] —'**prod·der** *n.*

prod. *abbrev. for:* **1.** produce. **2.** produced. **3.** product.

prod·i·gal ('prɒdɪgəl) *adj.* **1.** recklessly wasteful or extravagant, as in disposing of goods or money. **2.** lavish in giving or yielding: *prodigal of compliments.* ~*n.* **3.** a person who spends lavishly or squanders money. [C16: from Medieval Latin *prōdigālis* wasteful, from Latin *prōdigus* lavish, from *prōdigere* to squander, from PRO-¹ + *agere* to drive] —**ˌprod·i'gal·i·ty** *n.* —'**prod·i·gal·ly** *adv.*

pro·di·gious (prə'dɪdʒəs) *adj.* **1.** vast in size, extent, power, etc. **2.** wonderful or amazing. **3.** *Obsolete.* threatening. [C16: from Latin *prōdigiōsus* marvellous, from *prōdigium* see PRODIGY] —**pro'di·gious·ly** *adv.* —**pro'di·gious·ness** *n.*

prod·i·gy ('prɒdɪdʒɪ) *n., pl* **·gies. 1.** a person, esp. a child, of unusual or marvellous talents. **2.** anything that is a cause of wonder and amazement. **3.** something monstrous or abnormal. **4.** an archaic word for **omen.** [C16: from Latin *prōdigium* an unnatural happening, from PRO-¹ + *-igium,* probably from *āio* I say]

pro·drome ('prəʊdrəʊm) *n. Med.* any symptom that signals the impending onset of a disease. [C19: via French from New Latin *prodromus,* from Greek *prodromos* forerunner, from PRO-² + *dramein* to run] —**pro'dro·mal** *or* **pro·drom·ic** (prəʊ'drɒmɪk) *adj.*

pro·duce *vb.* (prə'djuːs). **1.** to bring (something) into existence; yield. **2.** to bring forth (a product) by mental or physical effort; make: *she produced a delicious dinner for us.* **3.** (*tr.*) to give birth to. **4.** (*tr.*) to present to view: *to produce evidence.* **5.** to bring before the public: *he produced two plays and a film last year.* **6.** (*tr.*) *Geom.* to extend (a

---

pro-'Cath·o·lic *n., adj.*
ˌpro-Ca·'thol·i·cism *n.*
ˌpro·cen·tral·i·'za·tion *or* ˌpro·cen·tral·i·'sa·tion *adj.*
pro·'church *adj.*
pro·'cler·i·cal *adj.*
pro-'Com·mu·nism *n.*
pro-'Com·mu·nist *adj., n.*
ˌpro-Con·'fed·er·ate *adj.*
ˌpro·con·'scrip·tion *adj.*
ˌpro·con·ser·'va·tion *adj.*
ˌpro-Dar·'win·i·an *adj.*
ˌpro·dem·o·'crat·ic *adj.*
ˌpro·dis·'ar·ma·ment *adj.*
ˌpro·dis·so·'lu·tion *adj.*
ˌpro·en·'force·ment *adj.*

line). ~*n.* ('prɒdju:s). **7.** anything that is produced; product. **8.** agricultural products regarded collectively: *farm produce.* [C15: from Latin *prōdūcere* to bring forward, from PRO-¹ + *dūcere* to lead] —**pro·'duc·i·ble** *adj.* —**pro·,duc·i·'bil·i·ty** *n.*

pro·duc·er (prə'dju:sə) *n.* **1.** a person or thing that produces. **2.** *Brit.* a person responsible for the artistic direction of a play, including interpretation of the script, preparation of the actors, and overall design. **3.** *U.S.* a person who organizes the stage production of a play, including the finance, management, etc. **4.** *Economics.* a person or business enterprise that generates goods or services for sale. Compare **consumer** (sense 1). **5.** *Chem.* an apparatus or plant for making producer gas. **6.** (*often pl.*) *Ecology.* an organism, esp. a green plant, that builds up its own tissues from simple inorganic compounds. See also **consumer** (sense 3), **decomposer.**

pro·duc·er gas *n.* a mixture of carbon monoxide and nitrogen produced by passing air over hot coke, used mainly as a fuel. Also called: **air gas.** See also **water gas.**

pro·duc·er goods *or* **pro·duc·er's goods** *pl. n.* other terms for **capital goods.**

prod·uct ('prɒdʌkt) *n.* **1.** something produced by effort, or some mechanical or industrial process. **2.** the result of some natural process. **3.** a result or consequence. **4.** a substance formed in a chemical reaction. **5.** *Maths.* **a.** the result of the multiplication of two or more numbers, quantities, etc. **b.** another name for **intersection** (sense 3). [C15: from Latin *prōductum* (something) produced, from *prōdūcere* to bring forth]

pro·duc·tion (prə'dʌkʃən) *n.* **1.** the act of producing. **2.** anything that is produced; product. **3.** the amount produced or the rate at which it is produced. **4.** *Economics.* the creation or manufacture for sale of goods and services with exchange value. **5.** any work created as a result of literary or artistic effort. **6.** the organization and presentation of a play, opera, etc. **7.** *Brit.* the artistic direction of a play. **8.** (*modifier*) manufactured by a mass-production process: *a production model of a car.* **9. make a production (out) of.** *Informal.* to make an unnecessary fuss about. —**pro·'duc·tion·al** *adj.*

pro·duc·tion line *n.* a factory system in which parts or components of the end product are transported by a conveyor through a number of different sites at each of which a manual or machine operation is performed on them without interrupting the flow of production.

pro·duc·tive (prə'dʌktɪv) *adj.* **1.** producing or having the power to produce; fertile. **2.** yielding favourable or effective results. **3.** *Economics.* **a.** producing or capable of producing goods and services that have monetary or exchange value: *productive assets.* **b.** of or relating to such production: *the productive processes of an industry.* **4.** (*postpositive;* foll. by *of*) resulting in: *productive of good results.* **5.** denoting an affix or combining form used to produce new words. —**pro·'duc·tive·ly** *adv.* —**prod·uc·tiv·i·ty** (,prɒdʌk'tɪvɪtɪ) *or* **pro·'duc·tive·ness** *n.*

pro·em ('prəʊɛm) *n.* an introduction or preface, such as to a work of literature. [C14: from Latin *prooemium* introduction, from Greek *prooimion,* from PRO-² + *hoimē* song] —**pro·e·mi·al** (prəʊ'i:mɪəl) *adj.*

pro·es·trus (prəʊ'ɛstrəs, -'i:strəs) *n.* the usual U.S. spelling of **pro-oestrus.**

prof (prɒf) *n. Informal.* short for **professor.**

Prof. *abbrev. for* Professor.

pro·fane (prə'feɪn) *adj.* **1.** having or indicating contempt, irreverence, or disrespect for a divinity or something sacred. **2.** not designed or used for religious purposes; secular. **3.** not initiated into the inner mysteries or sacred rites. **4.** vulgar, coarse, or blasphemous: *profane language.* ~*vb.* (*tr.*) **5.** to treat or use (something sacred) with irreverence. **6.** to put to an unworthy or improper use. [C15: from Latin *profānus* outside the temple, from PRO-¹ + *fānum* temple] —**prof·a·na·tion** (,prɒfə'neɪʃən) *n.* —**pro·fan·a·to·ry** (prə'fænətərɪ, -trɪ) *adj.* —**pro·'fan·er** *n.* —**pro·'fane·ly** *adv.* —**pro·'fane·ness** *n.*

pro·fan·i·ty (prə'fænɪtɪ) *n., pl.* **·ties. 1.** the state or quality of being profane. **2.** vulgar or irreverent action, speech, etc.

pro·fess (prə'fɛs) *vb.* **1.** to affirm or announce (something, such as faith); acknowledge: *to profess ignorance; to profess a belief in God.* **2.** (*tr.*) to claim (something, such as a feeling or skill, or to be or do something), often insincerely or falsely: *to profess to be a skilled driver.* **3.** to receive or be received into a religious order, as by taking vows. [C14: from Latin *prōfitērī* to confess openly, from PRO-¹ + *fatērī* to confess]

pro·fessed (prə'fɛst) *adj.* (*prenominal*) **1.** avowed or acknowledged. **2.** alleged or pretended. **3.** professing to be qualified as: *a professed philosopher.* **4.** having taken vows of a religious order. —**pro·fess·ed·ly** (prə'fɛsɪdlɪ) *adv.*

pro·fes·sion (prə'fɛʃən) *n.* **1.** an occupation requiring special training in the liberal arts or sciences, esp. one of the three learned professions, law, theology, or medicine. **2.** the body of people in such an occupation. **3.** the act of professing; avowal; declaration. **4. a.** Also called: **profession of faith.** a declaration of faith in a religion, esp. as made on entering the Church of that religion or an order belonging to it. **b.** the faith or the religion that is the subject of such a declaration. [C13: from Medieval Latin *professiō* the taking of vows upon entering a religious order, from Latin: public acknowledgment; see PROFESS]

pro·fes·sion·al (prə'fɛʃənᵊl) *adj.* **1.** of, relating to, suitable for, or engaged in as a profession. **2.** engaging in an activity for gain or as a means of livelihood. **3.** extremely competent in a job, etc. **4.** undertaken or performed for gain or by people who are paid. ~*n.* **5.** a person who belongs to or engages in one of the professions. **6.** a person who engages for his livelihood in some activity also pursued by amateurs. **7.** a person who engages in an activity with great competence. **8.** an expert player of a game who gives instruction, esp. to members of a club by whom he is hired. —**pro·'fes·sion·al·ly** *adv.*

pro·fes·sion·al·ism (prə'fɛʃənə,lɪzəm) *n.* **1.** the methods, character, status, etc., of a professional. **2.** the pursuit of an activity for gain or livelihood. —**pro·'fes·sion·al·ist** *n., adj.*

pro·fes·sor (prə'fɛsə) *n.* **1.** Also called (esp. in the U.S.): **full professor.** the principal lecturer or teacher in a field of learning at a university or college; a holder of a university chair. **2.** *Chiefly U.S.* any teacher in a university or college. See also **associate professor, assistant professor. 3.** a person who claims skill and instructs others in some sport, occupation, etc. **4.** a person who professes his opinions, beliefs, etc. [C14: from Medieval Latin: one who has made his profession in a religious order, from Latin: a public teacher; see PROFESS] —**prof·es·so·ri·al** (,prɒfɪ'sɔ:rɪəl) *adj.* —**,prof·es·'so·ri·al·ly** *adv.*

prof·es·sor·i·ate (,prɒfɪ'sɔ:rɪɪt) *or* **pro·fes·so·rate** (prə'fɛsərɪt) *n.* **1.** a group of professors. **2.** Also called (esp. Brit.): **pro·fes·sor·ship** (prə'fɛsəʃɪp). the rank or position of university professor.

prof·fer ('prɒfə) *vb.* **1.** (*tr.*) to offer for acceptance; tender. ~*n.* **2.** the act of proffering. [C13: from Old French *proffrir,* from PRO-¹ + *offrir* to offer] —**'prof·fer·er** *n.*

pro·fi·cient (prə'fɪʃənt) *adj.* **1.** having great facility (in an art, occupation, etc.); skilled. ~*n.* **2.** an archaic word for an **expert.** [C16: from Latin *prōficere* to make progress, from PRO-¹ + *facere* to make] —**pro·'fi·cien·cy** *n.* —**pro·'fi·cient·ly** *adv.*

pro·file ('prəʊfaɪl) *n.* **1.** a side view, outline, or representation of an object, esp. of a human face or head. **2.** a view or representation of an object, esp. a building, in contour or outline. **3.** a short biographical sketch of a subject. **4.** a graph or table representing the extent to which a person, field, or object exhibits various tested characteristics or tendencies: *a population profile.* **5.** a vertical section of soil from the ground surface to the parent rock showing the different horizons. **6. a.** a vertical section of part of the earth's crust showing the layers of rock. **b.** a representation of such a section. **7.** the outline of the shape of a river valley either from source to mouth (**long profile**) or at right angles to the flow of the river (**cross profile**). ~*vb.* **8.** (*tr.*) to draw, write, or make a profile of. [C17: from Italian *profilo,* from *profilare* to sketch lightly, from PRO-¹ + Latin *fīlum* thread] —**pro·fil·ist** ('prəʊfɪlɪst) *n.*

pro·file drag *n.* the sum of the surface friction drag and the form drag for a body moving subsonically through a fluid.

prof·it ('prɒfɪt) *n.* **1.** (*often pl.*) excess of revenues over outlays and expenses in a business enterprise over a given period of time, usually a year. **2.** the monetary gain derived from a transaction. **3. a.** income derived from property or an investment, as contrasted with capital gains. **b.** the ratio of this income to the investment or principal. **4.** *Economics.* the income or reward accruing to a successful entrepreneur and held to be the motivating factor of all economic activity in a capitalist economy. **5.** a gain, benefit, or advantage. ~*vb.* **6.** to gain or cause to gain profit. [C14: from Latin *prōfectus* advance, from *prōficere* to make progress; see PROFICIENT] —**'prof·it·er** *n.* —**'prof·it·less** *adj.*

prof·it·a·ble ('prɒfɪtəbᵊl) *adj.* affording gain, benefit, or profit. —**'prof·it·a·bly** *adv.* —**'prof·it·a·ble·ness** *or* **,prof·it·a·'bil·i·ty** *n.*

prof·it and loss *n. Book-keeping.* an account compiled at the end of a financial year showing that year's revenue and expense items and indicating gross and net profit or loss.

prof·i·teer (,prɒfɪ'tɪə) *n.* **1.** a person who makes excessive profits, esp. by charging exorbitant prices for goods in short supply. ~*vb.* **2.** (*intr.*) to make excessive profits.

pro·fit·er·ole (,prɒfɪtə'rəʊl, 'prɒfɪtə,rəʊl, prə'fɪtə,rəʊl) *n.* a small case of choux pastry with a sweet or savoury filling. [C16: from French, literally: a small profit, (related to the gifts, etc., given to a servant), from *profiter* to PROFIT]

prof·it-shar·ing *n.* a system in which a portion of the net profit of a business is distributed to its employees, usually in proportion to their wages or their length of service.

prof·li·gate ('prɒflɪgɪt) *adj.* **1.** shamelessly immoral or debauched. **2.** wildly extravagant or wasteful. ~*n.* **3.** a profligate person. [C16: from Latin *prōflīgātus* corrupt, from *prōflīgāre* to overthrow, from PRO-¹ + *flīgere* to beat] —**prof·li·ga·cy** ('prɒflɪgəsɪ) *n.* —**'prof·li·gate·ly** *adv.*

prof·lu·ent ('prɒfluənt) *adj.* flowing smoothly or abundantly. [C15: from Latin *prōfluere* to flow along]

pro-form *n.* a word having grammatical function but assuming the meaning of an antecedent word or phrase for which it substitutes: *the word "does" is a pro-form for "understands Greek" in "I can't understand Greek but he does."*

pro for·ma *Latin.* ('prəʊ 'fɔ:mə) *adj.* **1.** prescribing a set form or procedure. ~*adv.* **2.** performed in a set manner.

pro·found (prə'faʊnd) *adj.* **1.** penetrating deeply into subjects or ideas: *a profound mind.* **2.** situated at or extending to a great depth. **3.** reaching to or stemming from the depths of one's nature: *profound regret.* **4.** intense or absolute: *profound silence.* **5.** thoroughgoing; extensive: *profound changes.* ~*n.* **6.** *Archaic or literary.* a great depth; abyss. [C14: from Old French *profund,* from Latin *profundus* deep, from PRO-¹ + *fundus* bottom] —**pro·'found·ly** *adv.* —**pro·'found·ness** *or* **pro·fun·di·ty** (prə'fʌndɪtɪ) *n.*

pro+fuse (prə'fju:s) *adj.* **1.** plentiful, copious, or abundant: *profuse compliments.* **2.** (often foll. by *in*) free or generous in the giving (of): *profuse in thanks.* [C15: from Latin *profundere* to pour lavishly] —**pro+'fuse+ly** *adv.* —**pro+'fuse+ness** *or* **pro+'fu+sion** *n.*

prog (prɒg) *vb.* **progs, prog+ging, progged. 1.** (*intr.*) *Brit. slang or dialect.* to prowl about for or as if for food or plunder. ~*n.* **2.** *Brit. slang or dialect.* food obtained by begging. **3.** *Canadian dialect.* a Newfoundland word for **food.** [C17: of unknown origin]

prog. *abbrev. for:* **1.** programme. **2.** progress. **3.** progressive.

Prog. *abbrev. for* Progressive (Party, etc.).

pro+gen·i·tive (prəʊ'dʒɛnɪtɪv) *adj.* capable of bearing offspring. —**pro+'gen·i·tive+ness** *n.*

pro+gen·i·tor (prəʊ'dʒɛnɪtə) *n.* **1.** a direct ancestor. **2.** an originator or founder of a future development; precursor. [C14: from Latin: ancestor, from PRO-[1] + *genitor* parent, from *gignere* to beget]

prog+e·ny ('prɒdʒɪnɪ) *n., pl.* **·nies. 1.** the immediate descendant or descendants of a person, animal, etc. **2.** a result or outcome. [C13: from Latin *prōgeniēs* lineage; see PROGENITOR]

pro+ges+ta+tion+al (ˌprəʊdʒɛ'steɪʃənᵊl) *adj. Physiol.* **1.** of or relating to the phase of the menstrual cycle, lasting approximately 14 days, during which the uterus is prepared for pregnancy by the secretion of progesterone from the corpus luteum. **2.** preceding gestation; before pregnancy.

pro+ges+ter+one (prəʊ'dʒɛstəˌrəʊn) *n.* a steroid hormone, secreted mainly by the corpus luteum in the ovary, that prepares and maintains the uterus for pregnancy. Formula: $C_{21}H_{30}O_2$. Also called: **corpus luteum hormone.** [C20: from PRO-[1] + GE(STATION) + STER(OL) + -ONE]

pro+ges+tin (prəʊ'dʒɛstɪn) *or* **pro+ges+to+gen** *n.* any of a group of steroid hormones that have progesterone-like activity. [C20: from PROGEST(ERONE) + -IN]

pro+glot+tis (prəʊ'glɒtɪs) *or* **pro+glot+tid** *n., pl.* **+glot+ti+des** (-'glɒtɪˌdi:z). any of the segments that make up the body of a tapeworm. Each contains reproductive organs and separates from the worm when filled with fertilized eggs. —**pro+'glot+tic** *or* **ˌpro+glot+'tid+e·an** *adj.*

prog+na+thous (prɒg'neɪθəs) *or* **prog+nath+ic** (prɒg'næθɪk) *adj.* having a projecting lower jaw. [C19: from PRO-[2] + Greek *gnathos* jaw] —**prog+na+thism** ('prɒgnəˌθɪzəm) *n.*

prog+no+sis (prɒg'nəʊsɪs) *n., pl.* **+no+ses** (-'nəʊsi:z). **1.** *Med.* **a.** a prediction of the course or outcome of a disease or disorder. **b.** the chances of recovery from a disease. **2.** any forecast or prediction. [C17: via Latin from Greek: knowledge beforehand]

prog+nos+tic (prɒg'nɒstɪk) *adj.* **1.** of, relating to, or serving as a prognosis. **2.** foretelling or predicting. ~*n.* **3.** *Med.* any symptom or sign used in making a prognosis. **4.** a sign or forecast of some future occurrence. [C15: from Old French *pronostique,* from Latin *prognōsticum,* from Greek *prognōstikon,* from *progignōskein* to know in advance]

prog+nos+ti+cate (prɒg'nɒstɪˌkeɪt) *vb.* **1.** to foretell (future events) according to present signs or indications; prophesy. **2.** (*tr.*) to foreshadow or portend. [C16: from Medieval Latin *prognōsticāre* to predict] —**prog+ˌnos+ti+'ca+tion** *n.* —**prog+'nos+ti+ca+tive** *adj.* —**prog+'nos+ti+ˌca+tor** *n.*

pro+gram *or* (*sometimes*) **pro+gramme** ('prəʊgræm) *n.* **1.** a sequence of coded instructions fed into a computer, enabling it to perform specified logical and arithmetical operations on data. ~*vb.* **+grams, +gram+ming, +grammed** *or* **+grammes, +gram+ming, +grammed. 2.** (*tr.*) to feed a program into (a computer). **3.** (*tr.*) to arrange (data) into a suitable form so that it can be processed by a computer. **4.** (*intr.*) to write a program.

pro+gram+ma+ble *or* **pro+gram+able** (prəʊ'græməbəl) *adj.* capable of being programmed.

pro+gram+mat+ic (ˌprəʊgrə'mætɪk) *adj.* **1.** of or relating to programme music. **2.** of or relating to a programme.

pro+gramme *or U.S.* **pro+gram** ('prəʊgræm) *n.* **1.** a written or printed list of the events, performers, etc., in a public performance. **2.** a performance or series of performances, often presented at a scheduled time, esp. on radio or television. **3.** a specially arranged selection of things to be done. *what's the programme for this afternoon?* **4.** a plan, schedule, or procedure. **5.** a syllabus or curriculum. ~*vb.* **+grammes, +gram+ming, +grammed** *or U.S.* **+grams, +gram+ing, +gramed. 6.** to design or schedule (something) as a programme. ~*n., vb.* **7.** *Computer technol.* a variant spelling of **program.** [C17: from Late Latin *programma,* from Greek: written public notice, from PRO-[2] + *graphein* to write]

pro+grammed learn+ing *n.* a teaching method in which the material to be learnt is broken down into easily understandable parts on which the pupil is able to test himself.

pro+gramme mu+sic *n.* music that is intended to depict or evoke a scene or idea. Compare **absolute music.**

pro+gram+mer ('prəʊgræmə) *n.* a person who analyses a particular problem and writes a program so that the relevant data may be processed by a computer.

pro+gram+ming lan+guage *n.* a language system by which instructions to a computer are put into a coded form, using a well-defined set of characters that is mutually comprehensible to user and computer. See also **FORTRAN, ALGOL, COBOL, PL/1, machine language.**

pro+gress *n.* ('prəʊgrɛs). **1.** movement forwards, esp. towards a place or objective. **2.** satisfactory development, growth, or advance. **3.** advance towards completion, maturity, or perfection. **4.** (*modifier*) of or relating to progress: *a progress report.* **5.** *Biology.* increasing complexity, adaptation, etc., during the development of an individual or evolution of a group. **6.** *Brit.* a stately royal journey. **7. in progress.** taking place; under way. ~*vb.* (prə'grɛs). **8.** (*intr.*) to move forwards or onwards, as towards a place or objective. **9.** to move towards or bring nearer to completion, maturity, or perfection. [C15: from Latin *prōgressus* a going forwards, from *prōgredī* to advance, from PRO-[1] + *gradī* to step]

pro+gres+sion (prə'grɛʃən) *n.* **1.** the act of progressing; advancement. **2.** the act or an instance of moving from one thing or unit in a sequence to the next. **3.** *Maths.* a sequence of numbers in which each term differs from the succeeding term by a constant relation. See also **arithmetic progression, geometric progression, harmonic progression. 4.** *Music.* movement, esp. of a logical kind, from one note to the next (**melodic progression**) or from one chord to the next (**harmonic progression**). **5.** *Astrology.* one of several calculations, based on the movement of the planets, from which it is supposed that one can find the expected developments in a person's birth chart and the probable trends of circumstances for a year in his life. —**pro+'gres+sion+al** *adj.* —**pro+'gres+sion+al+ly** *adv.*

pro+gres+sion+ist (prə'grɛʃənɪst) *or* **pro+gres+sist** (prə'grɛsɪst) *n. Rare.* an advocate of social, political, or economic progress; a member of a progressive political party. —**pro+'gres+sion+ism** *n.*

pro+gres+sive (prə'grɛsɪv) *adj.* **1.** of or relating to progress. **2.** proceeding or progressing by steps or degrees. **3.** (*often cap.*) favouring or promoting political or social reform through government action, or even revolution, to improve the lot of the majority: *a progressive policy.* **4.** denoting or relating to an educational system that allows flexibility in learning procedures, based on activities determined by the needs and capacities of the individual child, the aim of which is to integrate academic with social development. **5.** (of a tax or tax system) graduated so that the rate increases relative to the amount taxed. Compare **regressive** (sense 2). **6.** (esp. of a disease) advancing in severity, complexity, or extent. **7.** (of a dance, card game, etc.) involving a regular change of partners after one figure, one game, etc. **8.** denoting an aspect of verbs in some languages, including English, used to express prolonged or continuous activity as opposed to momentary or habitual activity: *a progressive aspect of the verb "to walk" is "is walking."* ~*n.* **9.** a person who advocates progress, as in education, politics, etc. **10. a.** the progressive aspect of a verb. **b.** a verb in this aspect. —**pro+'gres+sive+ly** *adv.* —**pro+'gres+sive+ness** *n.* —**pro+'gres+siv+ism** *n.* —**pro+'gress+siv+ist** *n.*

Pro+gres+sive (prə'grɛsɪv) *n.* **1.** *U.S. history.* a member or supporter of a Progressive Party. **2.** *Canadian history.* a member or supporter of a chiefly agrarian reform movement advocating the nationalization of railways, low tariffs, an end to party politics, and similar measures: important in the early 1920s. ~*adj.* **3.** of, relating to, or characteristic of a Progressive Party, Progressive movement, or Progressives.

Pro+gres+sive Con+serv·a+tive Par+ty *n.* (in Canada) a major political party with conservative policies.

Pro+gres+sive Par+ty *n.* **1.** a U.S. political party, made up chiefly of dissident Republicans, that nominated Theodore Roosevelt as its presidential candidate in 1912 and supported primaries, progressive labour legislation, and other reforms. **2.** a U.S. political party, composed mostly of farmers, socialists, and unionists, that nominated Robert La Follette for president in 1924 and supported public ownership of railways and of public utilities and other reforms. **3.** a U.S. political party, composed chiefly of dissident Democrats, that nominated Henry Wallace for president in 1948 and supported the nationalization of key industries, advocated social reforms, and opposed the Cold War. **4.** (in South Africa) the most liberal of the legally allowed political parties: formed by secession from the United Party in 1959. The Progressive Party supports a qualified franchise for all South Africans irrespective of colour. See also **Nationalist Party, United Party.**

pro+hib+it (prə'hɪbɪt) *vb.* (*tr.*) **1.** to forbid by law or other authority. **2.** to hinder or prevent. [C15: from Latin *prohibēre* to prevent, from PRO-[1] + *habēre* to hold] —**pro+'hib·it+er** *or* **pro+'hib·i+tor** *n.*

pro+hi+bi+tion (ˌprəʊɪ'bɪʃən) *n.* **1.** the act of prohibiting or state of being prohibited. **2.** an order or decree that prohibits. **3.** (*sometimes cap.*) (esp. in the U.S.) a policy of legally forbidding the manufacture, transportation, sale, or consumption of alcoholic beverages except for medicinal or scientific purposes. **4.** *Law.* a writ from a superior court (in Britain the High Court) forbidding an inferior court to determine a matter outside its jurisdiction. —**ˌpro+hi+'bi+tion+ar·y** *adj.*

Pro+hi+bi+tion (ˌprəʊɪ'bɪʃən) *n.* the period (1920–33) when the manufacture, sale, and transportation of intoxicating liquors was banned by constitutional amendment in the U.S. —**ˌPro+hi+'bi+tion+ist** *n.*

pro+hi+bi+tion+ist (ˌprəʊɪ'bɪʃənɪst) *n.* (*sometimes cap.*) a person who favours prohibition, esp. of alcoholic beverages. —**ˌpro+hi+'bi+tion+ism** *n.*

pro+hib·i+tive (prə'hɪbɪtɪv) *or* **pro+hib·i+to·ry** (prə'hɪbɪtərɪ,

pro+'fas+cist *adj., n.*
ˌpro+fed+er+'a+tion *adj.*
pro+'fem+i+nist *adj., n.*
pro+'for+eign *adj.*
pro-'Freud·i·an *adj., n.*
pro-'Gen·tile *adj., n.*
pro-'Hit·ler *adj.*
ˌpro+im+mi+'gra+tion *adj.*
ˌpro+in+ˌdus+tri+al+i+'za+tion *or* ˌpro+in+ˌdus+tri+al+i+'sa+tion *adj.*
pro+'in+dus+try *adj.*

-trɪ) *adj.* **1.** prohibiting or tending to prohibit. **2.** (esp. of prices) tending or designed to discourage sale or purchase. —**pro**+**'hib·i**+**tive**+**ly** *adv.* —**pro**+**'hib·i**+**tive**+**ness** *n.*

proj+**ect** *n.* ('prɒdʒɛkt). **1.** a proposal, scheme, or design. **2. a.** a task requiring considerable or concerted effort, such as one by students. **b.** the subject of such a task. ~*vb.* (prə'dʒɛkt). **3.** (*tr.*) to propose or plan. **4.** (*tr.*) to throw or cast forwards. **5.** to jut or cause to jut out. **6.** (*tr.*) to send forth or transport in the imagination: *to project oneself into the future.* **7.** (*tr.*) to cause (an image) to appear on a surface. **8.** to cause (one's voice) to be heard clearly at a distance. **9.** *Psychol.* **a.** (*intr.*) (esp. of a child) to believe that others share one's subjective mental life. **b.** to impute to others (one's hidden desires and impulses), esp. as a means of defending oneself. Compare **introject. 10.** (*tr.*) *Geom.* to draw a projection of. **11.** (*intr.*) to communicate effectively, esp. to a large gathering. [C14: from Latin *prōicere* to throw down, from PRO-[1] + *iacere* to throw]

pro+**jec**+**tile** (prə'dʒɛktaɪl) *n.* **1.** an object or body thrown forwards. **2.** any self-propelling missile, esp. one powered by a rocket or the rocket itself. **3.** any object that can be fired from a gun, such as a bullet or shell. ~*adj.* **4.** capable of being or designed to be hurled forwards. **5.** projecting or thrusting forwards. **6.** *Zoology.* another word for **protrusile.** [C17: from New Latin *prōjectilis* jutting forwards]

pro+**jec**+**tion** (prə'dʒɛkʃən) *n.* **1.** the act of projecting or the state of being projected. **2.** an object or part that juts out. **3.** see **map projection. 4.** the representation of a line, figure, or solid on a given plane as it would be seen from a particular direction or in accordance with an accepted set of rules. **5.** a scheme or plan. **6.** a prediction based on known evidence and observations. **7. a.** the process of showing film on a screen. **b.** the image or images shown. **8.** *Psychol.* **a.** the belief, esp. in children, that others share one's subjective mental life. **b.** the process of projecting one's own hidden desires and impulses. See also **defence mechanism. 9.** the mixing by alchemists of powdered philosopher's stone with molten base metals in order to transmute them into gold. —**pro**+**'jec**+**tion**+**al** *adj.*

pro+**jec**+**tion**+**ist** (prə'dʒɛkʃənɪst) *n.* a person responsible for the operation of film projection machines.

pro+**jec**+**tive** (prə'dʒɛktɪv) *adj.* relating to or concerned with projection: *projective geometry.* —**pro**+**'jec**+**tive**+**ly** *adv.*

pro+**jec**+**tive ge**+**om**+**e·try** *n.* the branch of geometry concerned with the properties of solids that are invariant under projection and section.

pro+**jec**+**tive test** *n.* any psychological test, such as the Rorschach test, in which the subject is presented with vague stimuli. The interpretation, by means of projection, is believed to contain important information about personality.

pro+**jec**+**tor** (prə'dʒɛktə) *n.* **1.** an optical instrument that projects an enlarged image of individual slides onto a screen or wall. Full name: **slide projector. 2.** an optical instrument in which a strip of film is wound past a lens at a fixed speed so that the frames can be viewed as a continuously moving sequence on a screen or wall. Full name: **film** *or* **cine projector. 3.** a device for projecting a light beam. **4.** a person who devises projects.

pro+**jet** ('prɒʒeɪ) *n. Diplomacy.* a draft of a proposed treaty; plan or proposition. [C19: via French from Latin *prōjectum* something projecting]

Pro+**ko·fi·ev** (prə'kɒfɪˌɛf; *Russian* pra'kɔfjɪf) *n.* **Ser·gei Ser·ge·ye·vich** (sɪr'gjej sɪr'gjejɪvitʃ). 1891–1953, Soviet composer. His compositions include the orchestral fairy tale *Peter and the Wolf* (1936), the opera *The Love for Three Oranges* (1921), and seven symphonies.

Pro+**kop**+**yevsk** (*Russian* pra'kɔpjɪfsk) *n.* a city in the S Soviet Union, in Kemerovo Region: the chief coal-mining centre of the Kuznetsk Basin. Pop.: 268 000 (1975 est.).

pro+**lac**+**tin** (prəʊ'læktɪn) *n.* a gonadotropic hormone secreted by the anterior lobe of the pituitary gland. In mammals it stimulates the secretion of progesterone by the corpus luteum and initiates and maintains lactation. See also **follicle-stimulating hormone, luteinizing hormone.**

pro+**la**+**mine** ('prəʊləˌmiːn, -mɪn; prəʊ'læmiːn) *n.* any of a group of simple plant proteins, including gliadin, hordein, and zein. [C20: from PROL(INE) + AM(MONIA) + -INE[2]]

pro+**lapse** ('prəʊlæps, prəʊ'læps) *Pathol. n.* **1.** Also: **pro**+**lap**+**sus** (prəʊ'læpsəs). the sinking or falling down of an organ or part. Compare **proptosis.** ~*vb.* (*intr.*) **2.** (of an organ, etc.) to sink from its normal position. [C17: from *prōlābi* to slide along, from PRO-[1] + *lābī* to slip]

pro+**late** ('prəʊleɪt) *adj.* having a polar diameter of greater length than the equatorial diameter. Compare **oblate**[1]. [C17: from Latin *prōferre* to enlarge] —**'pro**+**late**+**ly** *adv.* —**'pro**+**late**+**ness** *n.*

prole (prəʊl) *n. Derogatory slang, chiefly Brit.* See **proletarian.**

pro+**leg** ('prəʊˌlɛg) *n.* any of the short paired unjointed appendages on each abdominal segment of a caterpillar or certain other insect larvae. [C19: from PRO-[1] + LEG]

pro+**le**·**gom**+**e**·**non** (ˌprəʊlɛ'gɒmɪnən) *n., pl.* ·**na** (-nə). (*often pl.*) a preliminary discussion, esp. a formal critical introduction to a lengthy text. [C17: from Greek, from *prolegein,* from PRO-[2] + *legein* to say] —ˌ**pro**+**le**·**'gom**+**e**·**nal** *adj.*

pro+**lep**+**sis** (prəʊ'lɛpsɪs) *n., pl.* +**ses** (-siːz). **1.** a rhetorical device by which objections are anticipated and answered in advance. **2.** use of a word after a verb in anticipation of its becoming applicable through the action of the verb, as *flat* in *hammer it flat.* [C16: via Late Latin from Greek: anticipation, from *prolambanein* to anticipate, from PRO-[2] + *lambanein* to take] —**pro**+**'lep**+**tic** *adj.*

pro+**le**·**tar**+**i**·**an** (ˌprəʊlɪ'tɛərɪən) *or* **pro**+**le**·**tar**·**y** ('prəʊlɪtərɪ, -trɪ) *adj.* **1.** of, relating, or belonging to the proletariat. ~*n., pl.* ·**tar**+**i**·**ans** *or* ·**tar**·**ies. 2.** a member of the proletariat. [C17: from Latin *prōlētārius* one whose only contribution to the state was his offspring, from *prōlēs* offspring] —ˌ**pro**+**le**·**'tar**+**i**·**an**+**ism** *n.* —ˌ**pro**+**le**·**'tar**+**i**·**an**+**ness** *n.*

pro+**le**·**tar**·**i**·**at** (ˌprəʊlɪ'tɛərɪət) *n.* **1.** all wage-earners collectively. **2.** the lower or working class. **3.** (in Marxist theory) the class of wage-earners, esp. industrial workers, in a capitalist society, whose only possession of significant material value is their labour. **4.** (in ancient Rome) the lowest class of citizens who had no property. [C19: via French from Latin *prōlētārius* PROLETARIAN]

pro+**lif**+**er**+**ate** (prə'lɪfəˌreɪt) *vb.* **1.** to grow or reproduce (new parts, cells, etc.) rapidly. **2.** to grow or increase or cause to grow or increase rapidly. [C19: from Medieval Latin *prōlifer* having offspring, from Latin *prōlēs* offspring + *ferre* to bear] —**pro**+ˌ**lif**+**er**·**'a**+**tion** *n.* —**pro**+**'lif**+**er**·**a**+**tive** *adj.*

pro+**lif**+**er**+**ous** (prə'lɪfərəs) *adj.* **1.** (of plants) producing many side branches or offshoots. **2.** (of plants and certain animals) reproducing by means of buds, offshoots, etc. [C17: from Medieval Latin *prōlifer* having offspring]

pro+**lif**+**ic** (prə'lɪfɪk) *adj.* **1.** producing fruit, offspring, etc., in abundance. **2.** producing constant or successful results. **3.** (often foll. by *in* or *of*) rich or fruitful. [C17: from Medieval Latin *prōlificus,* from Latin *prōlēs* offspring] —**pro**+**'lif**·**i**·**cal**+**ly** *adv.* —**pro**+**'lif**+**ic**+**ness** *or* **pro**+**'lif**·**i**·**ca**+**cy** *n.*

pro+**line** ('prəʊliːn, -lɪn) *n.* a water-soluble crystalline amino acid that occurs in protein. 2-pyrrolidinecarboxylic acid. Formula: C_4H_8NCOOH. [C20: from PYRROLIDINE]

pro+**lix** ('prəʊlɪks, prəʊ'lɪks) *adj.* **1.** (of a speech, book, etc.) so long as to be boring; verbose. **2.** indulging in prolix speech or writing; long-winded. [C15: from Latin *prōlixus* stretched out widely, from PRO-[1] + *līquī* to flow] —**pro**+**'lix**+**i**·**ty** *or* **pro**+**'lix**+**ness** *n.* —**pro**+**'lix**+**ly** *adv.*

pro+**loc**·**u**·**tor** (prəʊ'lɒkjʊtə) *n.* a chairman, esp. of the lower house of clergy in a convocation of the Anglican Church. [C15: from Latin: advocate, from PRO-[1] + *loquī* to speak] —**pro**+**'loc**·**u**·**tor**+ˌ**ship** *n.*

pro+**logue** *or U.S.* (*often*) **pro**+**log** ('prəʊlɒg) *n.* **1. a.** the prefatory lines introducing a play or speech. **b.** the actor speaking these lines. **2.** a preliminary act or event. ~*vb.* +**logues,** +**logu**+**ing,** +**logued** *or U.S.* +**logs,** +**log**+**ing,** +**loged. 3.** (*tr.*) to introduce or preface with or as if with a prologue. [C13: from Latin *prologus,* from Greek *prologos,* from PRO-[2] + *logos* discourse]

pro+**long** (prə'lɒŋ) *vb.* (*tr.*) to lengthen in duration or space; extend. [C15: from Late Latin *prōlongāre* to extend, from Latin PRO-[1] + *longus* long] —**pro**+**lon**+**ga**+**tion** (ˌprəʊlɒŋ'geɪʃən) *n.* —**pro**+**'long**+**er** *n.* —**pro**+**'long**+**ment** *n.*

pro+**longe** (prə'lɒndʒ) *n.* a specially fitted rope used as part of the towing equipment of a gun carriage. [C19: from French, from *prolonger* to PROLONG]

pro+**lu**+**sion** (prə'luːʒən) *n.* **1.** a preliminary written exercise. **2.** an introductory essay, sometimes of a slight or tentative nature. [C17: from Latin *prōlūsiō* preliminary exercise, from *prōlūdere* to practise beforehand, from PRO-[1] + *lūdere* to play] —**pro**+**lu**+**so**·**ry** (prə'luːzərɪ) *adj.*

prom (prɒm) *n.* **1.** *Brit.* short for **promenade** or **promenade concert. 2.** *U.S. informal.* a formal dance held at a high school or college.

PROM (prɒm) *n. Computer technol. acronym for* Programmable Read Only Memory.

prom. *abbrev. for* promontory.

prom+**e**·**nade** (ˌprɒmə'nɑːd) *n.* **1.** *Chiefly Brit.* a public walk, esp. at a seaside resort. **2.** a leisurely walk, esp. one in a public place for pleasure or display. **3.** a ball or formal dance. **4.** a marchlike step in dancing. **5.** a marching sequence in a square or country dance. ~*vb.* **6.** to take a promenade in or through (a place). **7.** (*intr.*) *Dancing.* to perform a promenade. **8.** (*tr.*) to display or exhibit (someone or oneself) on or as if on a promenade. [C16: from French, from *promener* to lead out for a walk, from Late Latin *prōmināre* to drive (cattle) along, from PRO-[1] + *mināre* to drive, probably from *minārī* to threaten] —ˌ**prom**+**e**·**'nad**+**er** *n.*

prom+**e**·**nade con**+**cert** *n.* a concert at which some of the audience stand rather than sit. Often shortened to **prom.**

prom+**e**·**nade deck** *n.* an upper covered deck of a passenger ship for the use of the passengers.

pro+**meth**+**a**·**zine** (prəʊ'mɛθəˌziːn) *n.* an antihistamine drug used to treat allergies and to prevent vomiting, esp. in motion sickness. [C20: from PRO(PYL) + (DI)METH(YLAMINE) + (PHENOTHI)AZINE]

Pro+**me**·**the**·**an** (prə'miːθɪən) *adj.* **1.** of or relating to Prometheus. **2.** creative, original, or life-enhancing. ~*n.* **3.** a person who resembles Prometheus.

Pro·**me**·**the**·**us** (prə'miːθɪəs) *n. Greek myth.* a Titan, who stole fire from Olympus to give to mankind and in punishment was chained to a rock, where an eagle tore at his liver until Hercules freed him.

pro+**me**·**thi**·**um** (prə'miːθɪəm) *n.* a radioactive element of the

ˌ**pro**+**in**+**te**+**'gra**+**tion** *adj.*
ˌ**pro**+**in**+**ter**+**'ven**+**tion** *adj.*
ˌ**pro**+**in**+**'vest**+**ment** *adj.*
ˌ**pro**+**ir**+**ri**+**'ga**+**tion** *adj.*
pro-**'Jew**·**ish** *adj.*
pro+**'la**+**bour** *adj.*
pro+**'mil**·**i**+ˌ**tar**·**y** *adj.*
ˌ**pro**+**mi**+**'nor**+**i**·**ty** *adj.*

lanthanide series artificially produced by the fission of uranium. Symbol: Pm; atomic no.: 61; half-life of most stable isotope, ^{145}Pm: 17.7 years; valency: 3; melting pt.: 1080°C (approx.); boiling pt.: 2460°C (approx.). [C20: New Latin from PROMETHEUS]

prom·i·nence ('prɒmɪnəns) *n.* **1.** the state or quality of being prominent. **2.** something that is prominent, such as a protuberance. **3.** relative importance or consequence. **4.** *Astronomy.* an eruption of incandescent gas from the sun's surface that can reach an altitude of several hundred thousand kilometres. It is visible during a total eclipse.

prom·i·nent ('prɒmɪnənt) *adj.* **1.** jutting or projecting outwards. **2.** standing out from its surroundings; noticeable. **3.** widely known; eminent. [C16: from Latin *prōminēre* to jut out, from PRO-[1] + *ēminēre* to project] —**'prom·i·nent·ly** *adv.* —**'prom·i·nent·ness** *n.*

prom·is·cu·i·ty (ˌprɒmɪ'skjuːɪtɪ) *n., pl.* **·ties.** **1.** promiscuous sexual behaviour. **2.** indiscriminate mingling, mixture, or confusion, as of parts or elements.

pro·mis·cu·ous (prə'mɪskjʊəs) *adj.* **1.** indulging in casual and indiscriminate sexual relationships. **2.** consisting of a number of dissimilar parts or elements mingled in a confused or indiscriminate manner. **3.** indiscriminate in selection. **4.** casual or heedless. [C17: from Latin *prōmiscuus* indiscriminate, from PRO[1] + *miscēre* to mix] —**pro·'mis·cu·ous·ly** *adv.* —**pro·'mis·cu·ous·ness** *n.*

prom·ise ('prɒmɪs) *vb.* **1.** (often foll. by *to;* when *tr., may take a clause as object or an infinitive*) to give an assurance of (something to someone); undertake (to do something) in the future: *I promise that I will come.* **2.** (*tr.*) to undertake to give (something to someone): *he promised me a car for my birthday.* **3.** (when *tr., takes an infinitive*) to cause one to expect that in the future one is likely (to be or do something): *she promises to be a fine soprano.* **4.** (*usually passive*) to engage to be married; betroth: *I'm promised to Bill.* **5.** (*tr.*) to assure (someone) of the authenticity or inevitability of something (often in the parenthetic phrase **I promise you,** used to emphasize a statement): *there'll be trouble, I promise you.* ~*n.* **6.** an undertaking or assurance given by one person to another agreeing or guaranteeing to do or give something, or not to do or give something, in the future. **7.** indication of forthcoming excellence or goodness: *a writer showing considerable promise.* **8.** the thing of which an assurance is given. [C14: from Latin *prōmissum* a promise, from *prōmittere* to send forth] —**'prom·is·er** *n.*

Prom·ised Land *n.* **1.** *Old Testament.* the land of Canaan, promised by God to Abraham and his descendants as their heritage (Genesis 12:7). **2.** heaven, esp. when considered as the goal towards which Christians journey in their earthly lives. **3.** any longed-for place where one expects to find greater happiness or fulfilment.

prom·i·see (ˌprɒmɪ'siː) *n. Contract law.* a person to whom a promise is made. Compare **promisor.**

prom·is·ing ('prɒmɪsɪŋ) *adj.* showing promise of favourable development or future success. —**'prom·is·ing·ly** *adv.* —**'prom·is·ing·ness** *n.*

prom·i·sor (ˌprɒmɪ'sɔː, 'prɒmɪˌsɔː) *n. Contract law.* a person who makes a promise. Compare **promisee.**

prom·is·so·ry ('prɒmɪsərɪ) *adj.* **1.** containing, relating to, or having the nature of a promise. **2.** *Insurance.* stipulating how the provisions of an insurance contract will be fulfilled after it has been signed.

prom·is·so·ry note *n. Commerce.* a document, usually negotiable, containing a signed promise to pay a stated sum of money to a specified person at a designated date or on demand. Also called: **note, note of hand.**

prom·on·to·ry ('prɒməntərɪ, -trɪ) *n., pl.* **·ries.** **1.** a high point of land, esp. of rocky coast, that juts out into the sea. **2.** *Anatomy.* any of various projecting structures. [C16: from Latin *prōmunturium* headland; related to *prōminēre;* see PROMINENT]

pro·mote (prə'məʊt) *vb.* (*tr.*) **1.** to further or encourage the progress or existence of. **2.** to raise to a higher rank, status, degree, etc. **3.** to advance (a pupil or student) to a higher course, class, etc. **4.** to urge the adoption of; work for: *to promote reform.* **5.** to encourage the sale of (a product) by advertising or securing financial support. [C14: from Latin *prōmovēre* to push onwards, from PRO-[1] + *movēre* to move] —**pro·'mot·a·ble** *adj.* —**pro·'mo·tion** *n.* —**pro·'mo·tion·al** *adj.*

pro·mot·er (prə'məʊtə) *n.* **1.** a person or thing that promotes. **2.** a person who helps to organize, develop, or finance an undertaking. **3.** a person who organizes and finances a sporting event, esp. a boxing match. **4.** *Chem.* a substance added in small amounts to a catalyst to increase its activity.

pro·mo·tive (prə'məʊtɪv) *adj.* tending to promote. —**pro·'mo·tive·ness** *n.*

prompt (prɒmpt) *adj.* **1.** performed or executed without delay. **2.** quick or ready to act or respond. ~*adv.* **3.** *Informal.* punctually. ~*vb.* **4.** (*tr.*) to urge (someone to do something). **5.** to remind (an actor, singer, etc.) of lines forgotten during a performance. **6.** (*tr.*) to refresh the memory of. **7.** (*tr.*) to give rise to by suggestion: *his affairs will prompt discussion.* ~*n.* **8.** *Commerce.* **a.** the time limit allowed for payment of the debt incurred by purchasing goods or services on credit. **b.** the contract specifying this time limit. **c.** Also called: **prompt note.** a memorandum sent to a purchaser to remind him of the time limit and the sum due. **9.** the act of prompting. **10.** anything that serves to remind. [C15: from Latin *promptus* evident, from *prōmere* to produce, from PRO-[1] + *emere* to buy] —**'prompt·ly** *adv.* —**'prompt·ness** *n.*

prompt·book ('prɒmptˌbʊk) *n.* the production script of a play containing notes, cues, etc.

prompt·er ('prɒmptə) *n.* **1.** a person offstage who reminds the actors of forgotten lines or cues. **2.** a person, thing, etc., that prompts.

promp·ti·tude ('prɒmptɪˌtjuːd) *n.* the quality of being prompt; punctuality.

prompt side *n. Theatre.* the side of the stage where the prompter is, usually to the actor's left in Britain and to his right in the United States.

prom·ul·gate ('prɒməlˌgeɪt) *vb.* (*tr.*) **1.** to put into effect (a law, decree, etc.), esp. by formal proclamation. **2.** to announce or declare officially. **3.** to make widespread. ~Also (archaic): **pro·mulge** (prəʊ'mʌldʒ). [C16: from Latin *prōmulgāre* to bring to public knowledge; probably related to *provulgāre* to publicize, from PRO-[1] + *vulgāre* to make common, from *vulgus* the common people] —ˌ**prom·ul·'ga·tion** *n.* —**'prom·ul·ˌga·tor** *n.*

pro·my·ce·li·um (ˌprəʊmaɪ'siːlɪəm) *n., pl.* **·li·a** (-lɪə). *Botany.* a short tubular outgrowth from certain germinating fungal spores that produces spores itself and then dies. [C19: New Latin from PRO-[1] + MYCELIUM] —ˌ**pro·my·'ce·li·al** *adj.*

pron. *abbrev. for:* **1.** pronominal. **2.** pronoun. **3.** pronounced. **4.** pronunciation.

pro·nate (prəʊ'neɪt) *vb.* (*tr.*) to turn (the forearm or hand) so that the palmar surface is directed downwards. [C19: from Late Latin *prōnāre* to bend forwards, bow] —**pro·'na·tion** *n.*

pro·na·tor (prəʊ'neɪtə) *n.* any muscle that effects pronation.

prone (prəʊn) *adj.* **1.** lying flat or face downwards; prostrate. **2.** sloping or tending downwards. **3.** having an inclination to do something. [C14: from Latin *prōnus* bent forward, from PRO-[1]] —**'prone·ly** *adv.* —**'prone·ness** *n.*

-prone *adj. combining form.* liable or disposed to suffer: *accident-prone.*

pro·neph·ros (prəʊ'nɛfrɒs) *n., pl.* **·roi** (-rɔɪ) *or* **·ra** (-rə). the first-formed anterior part of the embryonic kidney in vertebrates, which remains functional in the larvae of the lower vertebrates. See also **mesonephros, metanephros.** [C19: New Latin, from PRO-[2] + Greek *nephros* kidney] —**pro·'neph·ric** *adj.*

prong (prɒŋ) *n.* **1.** a sharply pointed end of an instrument, such as on a fork. **2.** any pointed projecting part. ~*vb.* **3.** (*tr.*) to prick or spear with or as if with a prong. [C15: related to Middle Low German *prange* a stake, Gothic *anaprangan* to afflict] —**pronged** *adj.*

prong·horn ('prɒŋˌhɔːn) *n.* a ruminant mammal, *Antilocapra americana,* inhabiting rocky deserts of North America and having small branched horns: family *Antilocapridae.* Also called: **American antelope.**

pro·nom·i·nal (prəʊ'nɒmɪnᵊl) *adj.* relating to or playing the part of a pronoun. [C17: from Late Latin *prōnōminālis,* from *prōnōmen* a PRONOUN] —**pro·'nom·i·nal·ly** *adv.*

pro·nom·i·nal·ize *or* **pro·nom·i·nal·ise** (prəʊ'nɒmɪnəˌlaɪz) *vb.* (*tr.*) to make (a word) into or treat as a pronoun. —**pro·ˌnom·i·nal·i·'za·tion** *or* **pro·ˌnom·i·nal·i·'sa·tion** *n.*

pro·noun ('prəʊˌnaʊn) *n.* one of a class of words that serves to replace a noun phrase that has already or is about to be mentioned in the sentence or context. Abbrev.: **pron.** [C16: from Latin *prōnōmen,* from PRO-[1] + *nōmen* noun]

pro·nounce (prə'naʊns) *vb.* **1.** to utter or articulate (a sound or sequence of sounds). **2.** (*tr.*) to utter or articulate (sounds or words) in the correct way. **3.** (*tr.; may take a clause as object*) to proclaim officially and solemnly: *I now pronounce you man and wife.* **4.** (when *tr., may take a clause as object*) to declare as one's judgment: *to pronounce the death sentence upon someone.* **5.** (*tr.*) to make a phonetic transcription of (sounds or words). [C14: from Latin *prōnuntiāre* to announce, from PRO-[1] + *nuntiāre* to announce] —**pro·'nounce·a·ble** *adj.* —**pro·'nounc·er** *n.*

pro·nounced (prə'naʊnst) *adj.* **1.** strongly marked or indicated. **2.** (of a sound) articulated with vibration of the vocal cords; voiced. —**pro·nounc·ed·ly** (prə'naʊnsɪdlɪ) *adv.*

pro·nounce·ment (prə'naʊnsmənt) *n.* **1.** an official or authoritative statement or announcement. **2.** the act of pronouncing, declaring, or uttering formally.

pron·to ('prɒntəʊ) *adv. U.S. informal.* at once; promptly. [C20: from Spanish: quick, from Latin *promptus* PROMPT]

pro·nu·cle·us (ˌprəʊ'njuːklɪəs) *n., pl.* **·cle·i** (-klɪˌaɪ). the nucleus of a mature ovum or spermatozoan before fertilization. —ˌ**pro·'nu·cle·ar** *adj.*

pro·nun·ci·a·men·to (prəˌnʌnsɪə'mɛntəʊ) *n., pl.* **·tos.** **1.** an edict, proclamation, or manifesto, esp. one issued by rebels in a Spanish-speaking country. **2.** an authoritarian announcement. [C19: from Spanish: pronouncement]

pro·nun·ci·a·tion (prəˌnʌnsɪ'eɪʃən) *n.* **1.** the act, instance, or manner of pronouncing sounds. **2.** the supposedly correct manner of pronouncing sounds in a given language. **3.** a phonetic transcription of a word.

pro-oes·trus (prəʊ'iːstrəs, -'ɛstrəs) *or U.S.* **pro·es·trus** *n.* the period in the oestrous cycle that immediately precedes oestrus.

proof (pruːf) *n.* **1.** any evidence that establishes or helps to establish the truth, validity, quality, etc., of something. **2.** *Law.*

---

pro·'mod·ern *adj.*
pro·'mon·ar·chist *adj., n.*
pro-'Mus·lim *adj., n.*
pro·'na·tion·al·ist *adj., n.*
ˌpro·na·tion·al·'is·tic *adj.*
pro-'Ne·gro *adj.*
pro-'Prot·es·tant *adj., n.*
ˌpro·re·'form *adj.*

the whole body of evidence upon which the verdict of a court is based. **3.** *Maths, logic.* a sequence of steps or statements that establishes the truth of a proposition. See also **direct** (sense 17b.), **indirect** (sense 5), **induction** (senses 3, 6). **4.** the act of testing the truth of something (esp. in the phrase **put to the proof**). **5.** *Scot. law.* trial before a judge without a jury. **6.** *Printing.* a trial impression made from composed type for the correction of errors. **7.** (in engraving, etc.) a print made by an artist or under his supervision for his own satisfaction before he hands the plate over to a professional printer. **8.** *Photog.* a trial print from a negative. **9. a.** the alcoholic strength of proof spirit. **b.** the strength of a beverage or other alcoholic liquor as measured on a scale in which the strength of proof spirit is 100 degrees. ~*adj.* **10.** (*usually postpositive;* foll. by *against*) able to resist; impervious (to): *the roof is proof against rain.* **11.** having the alcoholic strength of proof spirit. **12.** of proved strength or impenetrability: *proof armour.* ~*vb.* **13.** (*tr.*) to take a proof from (type matter, a plate, etc.). **14.** to proofread (text) or inspect (a print, etc.), as for approval. **15.** to render (something) proof, esp. to waterproof. [C13: from Old French *preuve* a test, from Late Latin *proba,* from Latin *probāre* to test]

-proof *adj. combining form.* impervious to; resisting the effects of: *waterproof; mothproof.* [from PROOF (adj.)]

proof·read ('pru:f,ri:d) *vb.* **·reads, ·read·ing, ·read** (-,rɛd). to read (copy or printer's proofs) to detect and mark errors to be corrected. —**'proof·,read·er** *n.*

proof spir·it *n.* **1.** (in Britain) a mixture of alcohol and water or an alcoholic beverage that contains 49.28 per cent of alcohol by weight, 57.1 per cent by volume at 60°F (15.6°C): used as a standard of alcoholic liquids. **2.** (in the U.S.) a similar standard mixture containing 50 per cent of alcohol by volume at 60°F.

prop¹ (prɒp) *vb.* **props, prop·ping, propped.** (when *tr.,* often foll. by *up*) **1.** (*tr.*) to support with a rigid object, such as a stick. **2.** (*tr.;* usually also foll. by *against*) to place or lean. **3.** (*tr.*) to sustain or support. **4.** (*intr.*) *Austral.* to stop suddenly or unexpectedly. ~*n.* **5.** something that gives rigid support, such as a stick. **6.** a person or thing giving support, as of a moral or spiritual nature. **7.** *Rugby.* either of the forwards at either end of the front row of a scrum. [C15: related to Middle Dutch *proppe* vine prop; compare Old High German *pfropfo* shoot, German *Pfropfen* stopper]

prop² (prɒp) *n.* short for **property** (sense 8).

prop³ (prɒp) *n.* an informal word for **propeller.**

prop. *abbrev. for:* **1.** proper(ly). **2.** property. **3.** proposition. **4.** proprietor.

pro·pae·deu·tic (,prəupɪ'dju:tɪk) *n.* **1.** (*often pl.*) preparatory instruction basic to further study of an art or science. ~*adj. also* **pro·pae·deu·ti·cal. 2.** of, relating to, or providing such instruction. [C19: from Greek *propaideuein* to teach in advance, from PRO-² + *paideuein* to rear]

prop·a·ga·ble ('prɒpəgəbᵊl) *adj.* capable of being propagated. —**,prop·a·ga·'bil·i·ty** *or* **'prop·a·ga·ble·ness** *n.*

prop·a·gan·da (,prɒpə'gændə) *n.* **1.** the organized dissemination of information, allegations, etc., to assist or damage the cause of a government, movement, etc. **2.** such information, allegations, etc. [C18: from Italian, use of *propāgandā* in the New Latin title *Sacra Congregatio de Propaganda Fide* Sacred Congregation for Propagating the Faith] —**,prop·a·'gan·dism** *n.* —**,prop·a·'gan·dist** *n., adj.*

Prop·a·gan·da (,prɒpə'gændə) *n. R.C. Church.* a congregation responsible for directing the work of the foreign missions and the training of priests for these.

prop·a·gan·dize *or* **prop·a·gan·dise** (,prɒpə'gændaɪz) *vb.* **1.** (*tr.*) to spread by propaganda. **2.** (*tr.*) to subject to propaganda. **3.** (*intr.*) to spread or organize propaganda.

prop·a·gate ('prɒpə,geɪt) *vb.* **1.** *Biology.* to reproduce or cause to reproduce; breed. **2.** *Horticulture.* (*tr.*) to produce (plants) by layering, grafting, cuttings, etc. **3.** (*tr.*) to promulgate; disseminate. **4.** *Physics.* to move through, cause to move through, or transmit, esp. in the form of a wave: *to propagate sound.* **5.** (*tr.*) to transmit (characteristics) from one generation to the next. [C16: from Latin *propāgāre* to increase (plants) by cuttings, from *propāgēs* a cutting, from *pangere* to fasten] —**,prop·a·'ga·tion** *n.* —**,prop·a·'ga·tion·al** *adj.* —**'prop·a·ga·tive** *adj.* —**'prop·a·,ga·tor** *n.*

prop·a·gule ('prɒpə,gju:l) *or* **pro·pag·u·lum** (prəu'pægjuləm) *n.* a plant part, such as a bud, that becomes detached from the rest of the plant and grows into a new plant. [C20: from PROPAG(ATE) + -ULE]

pro·pane ('prəupeɪn) *n.* a colourless flammable gaseous alkane found in petroleum and used as a fuel. Formula: $CH_3CH_2CH_3$. [C19: from PROPIONIC + -ANE]

pro·pa·no·ic ac·id (,prəupə'nəuɪk) *n.* another name for **propionic acid.**

pro·pa·rox·y·tone (,prəupə'rɒksɪ,təun) *adj.* **1.** (in Ancient Greek) of, relating to, or denoting words having an acute accent on the third syllable from the end. ~*n.* **2.** a proparoxytone word. ~Compare **paroxytone.** [C18: from Greek *proparoxutonos;* see PRO-², PAROXYTONE]

pro pa·tri·a *Latin.* ('prəu 'pætrɪ,ɑ:) for one's country.

pro·pel (prə'pɛl) *vb.* **·pels, ·pel·ling, ·pelled.** (*tr.*) to impel, drive, or cause to move forwards. [C15: from Latin *prōpellere* to drive onwards, from PRO-¹ + *pellere* to drive]

pro·pel·lant *or* **pro·pel·lent** (prə'pɛlənt) *n.* **1.** something that provides or causes propulsion, such as the explosive charge in a gun or the fuel in a rocket. **2.** the gas used to carry the liquid droplets in an aerosol spray.

pro·pel·lent (prə'pɛlənt) *adj.* able or tending to propel.

pro·pel·ler (prə'pɛlə) *n.* **1.** a device having blades radiating from a central hub that is rotated to produce thrust to propel a ship, aircraft, etc. **2.** a person or thing that propels.

pro·pel·ler shaft *n.* the shaft in a motor vehicle that transmits power from the gearbox to the differential gear.

pro·pel·ling pen·cil *n.* a pencil consisting of a metal or plastic case containing a replaceable lead. As the point is worn away the lead can be extended, usually by turning part of the case.

pro·pend (prəu'pɛnd) *vb.* (*intr.*) *Obsolete.* to be inclined or disposed. [C16: from Latin *prōpendēre* to hang forwards]

pro·pene ('prəupi:n) *n.* a colourless gaseous alkene obtained by cracking petroleum: used in synthesizing many organic compounds. Formula: $CH_3CH{:}CH_2$. Also called: **propylene.**

pro·pen·si·ty (prə'pɛnsɪtɪ) *n., pl.* **·ties. 1.** a natural tendency or disposition. **2.** *Obsolete.* partiality. [C16: from Latin *prōpensus* inclined to, from *prōpendēre* to PROPEND]

prop·er ('prɒpə) *adj.* **1.** (*usually prenominal*) appropriate or suited for some purpose: *in its proper place.* **2.** correct in behaviour or conduct. **3.** excessively correct in conduct; vigorously moral. **4.** up to a required or regular standard. **5.** (*immediately postpositive*) (of an object, quality, etc.) referred to or named specifically so as to exclude anything not directly connected with it: *his claim is connected with the deed proper.* **6.** (*postpositive;* foll. by *to*) belonging to or characteristic of a person or thing. **7.** (*prenominal*) *Brit. informal.* (intensifier): *I felt a proper fool.* **8.** (*usually postpositive*) (of heraldic colours) considered correct for the natural colour of the object or emblem depicted: *three martlets proper.* **9.** *Archaic.* pleasant or good. ~*adv.* **10.** *Brit. dialect.* (intensifier): *he's proper stupid.* **11. good and proper.** *Informal.* thoroughly: *to get drunk good and proper.* ~*n.* **12.** the parts of the Mass that vary according to the particular day or feast on which the Mass is celebrated. Compare **ordinary** (sense 10). [C13: via Old French from Latin *prōprius* special] —**'prop·er·ly** *adv.* —**'prop·er·ness** *n.*

prop·er frac·tion *n.* a fraction in which the numerator has a lower absolute value than the denominator, as $\frac{1}{2}$ or $x/(3 + x^2)$.

prop·er mo·tion *n.* the very small continuous change in the direction of motion of a star relative to the sun. It is determined from its radial and tangential motion.

prop·er noun *or* **name** *n.* the name of a person, place, or object, as for example *Iceland, Patrick,* or *Uranus.* Compare **common noun.**

prop·er·tied ('prɒpətɪd) *adj.* owning land or property.

Pro·per·ti·us (prə'pɜ:ʃɪəs, -ʃəs) *n.* **Sex·tus** ('sɛkstəs). ?50–?15 B.C., Roman elegiac poet.

prop·er·ty ('prɒpətɪ) *n., pl.* **·ties. 1.** something of value, either tangible, such as land, or intangible, such as patents, copyrights. **2.** *Law.* the right to possess, use, and dispose of anything. **3.** possessions collectively or the fact of owning possessions of value. **4. a.** a piece of land or real estate, esp. used for agricultural purposes. **b.** (*as modifier*): *property rights.* **5.** *Chiefly Austral.* a ranch or station. **6.** a quality, attribute, or distinctive feature of anything, esp. a characteristic attribute such as the density or strength of a material. **7.** *Logic.* an attribute that is not essential to a species but is common and peculiar to it. **8.** any movable object used on the set of a stage play or film. Usually shortened to **prop.** [C13: from Old French *propriété,* from Latin *proprietās* something personal, from *proprius* one's own]

prop·er·ty man *n.* a member of the stage crew in charge of the stage properties. Usually shortened to **propman.**

pro·phage ('prəufeɪdʒ) *n.* a virus that exists in a bacterial cell and undergoes division with its host without destroying it. Compare **bacteriophage.**

pro·phase ('prəu,feɪz) *n.* **1.** the first stage of mitosis, during which the nuclear membrane disappears and the nuclear material resolves itself into chromosomes. See also **metaphase, anaphase, telophase. 2.** the first stage of meiosis, divided into leptotene, zygotene, pachytene, diplotene, and diakinesis phases.

proph·e·cy ('prɒfɪsɪ) *n., pl.* **·cies. 1. a.** a message of divine truth revealing God's will. **b.** the act of uttering such a message. **2.** a prediction or guess. **3.** the function, activity, or charismatic endowment of a prophet or prophets. [C13: ultimately from Greek *prophētēs* PROPHET]

proph·e·sy ('prɒfɪ,saɪ) *vb.* **·sies, ·sy·ing, ·sied. 1.** to reveal or foretell (something, esp. a future event) by or as if by divine inspiration. **2.** (*intr.*) *Archaic.* to give instructions in religious subjects. [C14 *prophecien, from* PROPHECY] —**'proph·e·,si·a·ble** *adj.* —**'proph·e·,si·er** *n.*

proph·et ('prɒfɪt) *n.* **1.** a person who speaks by divine inspiration, esp. one through whom a divinity expresses his will. **2.** a person who predicts the future: *a prophet of doom.* **3.** a spokesman for a movement, doctrine, etc. **4.** *Christian Science.* **a.** a seer in spiritual matters. **b.** the vanishing of material sense to give way to the conscious facts of spiritual truth. [C13: from Old French *prophète,* from Latin *prophēta,* from Greek *prophētēs* one who declares the divine will, from PRO-² + *phanai* to speak] —**'proph·et·ess** *fem. n.* —**'pro·ph·et-,like** *adj.*

Proph·et ('prɒfɪt) *n.* **the. 1.** the principal designation of Mohammed as the founder of Islam. **2.** a name for Joseph Smith as founder of the Mormon Church.

pro·phet·ic (prə'fɛtɪk) *adj.* **1.** of or relating to a prophet or prophecy. **2.** containing or of the nature of a prophecy; predictive. —**pro·'phet·i·cal·ly** *adv.*

Proph·ets ('prɒfɪts) *n.* the books constituting the second main part of the Hebrew Bible, which in Jewish tradition is subdivided into the **Former Prophets,** Joshua, Judges, I-II

Samuel, and I-II Kings, and the **Latter Prophets,** comprising those books which in Christian tradition are alone called the **Prophets** and which are divided into **Major Prophets** and **Minor Prophets.** Compare **Law of Moses, Hagiographa.**

proph·y+lac+tic (ˌprɒfɪˈlæktɪk) *adj.* **1.** protecting from or preventing disease. **2.** protective or preventive. ~*n.* **3.** a prophylactic drug or device. **4.** *Chiefly U.S.* another name for **condom.** [C16: via French from Greek *prophulaktikos,* from *prophulassein* to guard by taking advance measures, from PRO-[2] + *phulax* a guard]

proph·y+lax+is (ˌprɒfɪˈlæksɪs) *n.* the prevention of disease or control of its possible spread.

pro+pin+qui·ty (prəˈpɪŋkwɪtɪ) *n.* **1.** nearness in place or time. **2.** nearness in relationship. [C14: from Latin *propinquitās* closeness, from *propinquus* near, from *prope* near by]

pro+pi·o+nate (ˈprəʊpɪəˌneɪt) *n.* any ester or salt of propionic acid.

pro+pi+on+ic ac·id (ˌprəʊpɪˈɒnɪk) *n.* a colourless liquid carboxylic acid used, as propionates, in inhibiting the growth of moulds in bread. Formula: CH_3CH_2COOH. Also called: **propanoic acid.** [C19: from Greek *pro-* first + *pionic* from *piōn* fat, because it is first in order of the fatty acids]

pro+pi+ti+ate (prəˈpɪʃɪˌeɪt) *vb.* (*tr.*) to appease or make well disposed; conciliate. [C17: from Latin *propitiāre* to appease, from *propitius* gracious] **—pro+ˈpi+ti+a·ble** *adj.* **—pro+ˌpi+ti·ˈa+tion** *n.* **—pro+ˌpi+ti·ˈa+tious** *adj.* **—pro+ˈpi+ti·a+tive** *adj.* **—pro+ˈpi+ti·ˌa+tor** *n.*

pro+pi+tious (prəˈpɪʃəs) *adj.* **1.** favourable or auspicious. **2.** gracious or favourably inclined. [C15: from Latin *propitius* well disposed, from *prope* close to] **—pro+ˈpi+tious+ly** *adv.* **—pro+ˈpi+tious+ness** *n.*

prop+jet (ˈprɒpˌdʒɛt) *n.* another name for **turboprop.**

prop+man (ˈprɒpˌmæn) *n., pl.* **+men.** short for **property man.**

prop·o+lis (ˈprɒpəlɪs) *n.* a greenish-brown resinous aromatic substance collected by bees from the buds of trees for use in the construction of hives. Also called: **bee glue, hive dross.** [C17: via Latin from Greek: suburb, bee glue, from *pro-* before + *polis* city]

pro+po+nent (prəˈpəʊnənt) *n.* **1.** a person who argues in favour of something. **2.** *Law.* a person who seeks probate of a will. [C16: from Latin *prōpōnere* to PROPOSE]

Pro+pon+tis (prəˈpɒntɪs) *n.* the ancient name for (the Sea of) **Marmara.**

pro+por+tion (prəˈpɔːʃən) *n.* **1.** the relationship between different things or parts with respect to comparative size, number, or degree; relative magnitude or extent; ratio. **2.** the correct or desirable relationship between parts of a whole; balance or symmetry. **3.** a part considered with respect to the whole. **4.** (*pl.*) dimensions or size: *a building of vast proportions.* **5.** a share, part, or quota. **6.** *Maths.* a relationship that maintains a constant ratio between two variable quantities: *x increases in direct proportion to y.* **7.** *Maths.* a relationship between four numbers or quantities in which the ratio of the first pair equals the ratio of the second pair. ~*vb.* (*tr.*) **8.** to adjust in relative amount, size, etc. **9.** to cause to be harmonious in relationship of parts. [C14: from Latin *prōportiō* (a translation of Greek *analogia*), from phrase *prō portione,* literally: for (its, his, one's) PORTION] **—pro+ˈpor+tion+a·ble** *adj.* **—pro+ˌpor+tion+a·ˈbil+i·ty** *n.* **—pro+ˈpor+tion+a·bly** *adv.* **—pro+ˈpor+tion+ment** *n.*

pro+por+tion+al (prəˈpɔːʃənᵊl) *adj.* **1.** of, involving, or being in proportion. **2.** *Maths.* having or related by a constant ratio. ~*n.* **3.** *Maths.* an unknown term in a proportion: *in* $a/b = c/x$, *x is the fourth proportional.* **—pro+ˌpor+tion+ˈal+i·ty** *n.* **—pro+ˈpor+tion+al+ly** *adv.*

pro+por+tion+al rep+re+sen+ta+tion *n.* representation of parties in an elective body in proportion to the votes they win. Abbrev.: **P.R.**

pro+por+tion+ate *adj.* (prəˈpɔːʃənɪt). **1.** being in proper proportion. ~*vb.* (prəˈpɔːʃəˌneɪt). **2.** (*tr.*) to make proportionate. **—pro+ˈpor+tion+ate+ly** *adv.* **—pro+ˈpor+tion+ate+ness** *n.*

pro+po+sal (prəˈpəʊzᵊl) *n.* **1.** the act of proposing. **2.** something proposed, as a plan. **3.** an offer, esp. of marriage.

pro+pose (prəˈpəʊz) *vb.* **1.** (when *tr., may take a clause as object*) to put forward (a plan, etc.) for consideration or action. **2.** (*tr.*) to nominate, as for a position. **3.** (*tr.*) to plan or intend (to do something): *I propose to leave town now.* **4.** (*tr.*) to announce the drinking of (a toast) to (the health of someone, etc.). **5.** (*intr.; often foll. by to*) to make an offer of marriage (to someone). [C14: from Old French *proposer,* from Latin *prōpōnere* to display, from PRO-[1] + *pōnere* to place] **—pro+ˈpos+a·ble** *adj.* **—pro+ˈpos+er** *n.*

prop·o+si+tion (ˌprɒpəˈzɪʃən) *n.* **1.** a proposal or topic presented for consideration. **2.** *Logic.* a statement that affirms or denies something and that is or can be shown to be either true or false. **3.** *Maths.* a statement or theorem, usually containing its proof. **4.** *Informal.* **a.** a person or matter to be dealt with: *he's a difficult proposition.* **b.** an invitation to engage in sexual intercourse. ~*vb.* **5.** (*tr.*) to propose a plan, deal, etc., to, esp. to engage in sexual intercourse. [C14 *proposicioun,* from Latin *prōpositiō* a setting forth; see PROPOSE] **—ˌprop·o·ˈsi+tion+al** *adj.* **—ˌprop·o·ˈsi+tion+al+ly** *adv.*

prop·o+si+tion+al cal+cu+lus *n.* the system of symbolic logic concerned only with the relations between propositions as wholes, taking no account of their internal structure. Compare **predicate calculus.**

pro+pos·i+tus (prəˈpɒzɪtəs) *n., pl.* **+ti** (-ˌtaɪ). *Law.* the person from whom a line of descent is traced. [from New Latin, from Latin *prōpōnere* to set forth; see PROPOUND]

pro+pound (prəˈpaʊnd) *vb.* (*tr.*) **1.** to suggest or put forward for consideration. **2.** *English law.* **a.** to produce (a will or similar instrument) to the proper court or authority in order for its validity to be established. **b.** (of an executor) to bring (an action to obtain probate) in solemn form. [C16 *propone,* from Latin *prōpōnere* to set forth from PRO-[1] + *pōnere* to place] **—pro+ˈpound+er** *n.*

propr. *abbrev. for* proprietor.

pro+prae+tor *or* **pro+pre+tor** (prəʊˈpriːtə) *n.* (in ancient Rome) a citizen, esp. an ex-praetor, granted a praetor's imperium to be exercised outside Rome, esp. in the provinces. [Latin, from *prō praetōre* one who acts for a praetor]

pro+pran·o+lol (prəʊˈprænəˌlɒl) *n.* a drug used in the treatment of angina pectoris, arrhythmia, hypertension, and other forms of heart disease. Formula: $C_{16}H_{21}NO_2$.

pro+pri+e·tar·y (prəˈpraɪɪtərɪ, -trɪ) *adj.* **1.** of, relating to, or belonging to property or proprietors. **2.** privately owned and controlled. **3.** *Med.* of or denoting a drug or agent manufactured and distributed under a trade name. Compare **ethical** (sense 3). ~*n., pl.* **·tar·ies. 4.** *Med.* a proprietary drug or agent. **5.** a proprietor or proprietors collectively. **6. a.** right to property. **b.** property owned. **7.** Also called: **lord proprietary.** (in Colonial America) an owner, governor, or grantee of a proprietary colony. [C15: from Late Latin *proprietārius* an owner, from *proprius* one's own] **—pro+ˈpri+e·tar·i+ly** *adv.*

pro+pri+e·tar·y col·o+ny *n. U.S. history.* any of various colonies, granted by the Crown in the 17th century to a person or group of people with full governing rights.

pro+pri+e·tor (prəˈpraɪətə) *n.* **1.** an owner of an unincorporated business enterprise. **2.** a person enjoying exclusive right of ownership to some property. **3.** *U.S. history.* a governor or body of governors of a proprietary colony.

pro+pri+e·ty (prəˈpraɪətɪ) *n., pl.* **·ties. 1.** the quality or state of being appropriate or fitting. **2.** conformity to the prevailing standard of behaviour, speech, etc. **3.** (*pl.*) **the proprieties.** the standards of behaviour considered correct by polite society. [C15: from Old French *propriété,* from Latin *proprietās* a peculiarity, from *proprius* one's own]

pro+pri·o+cep+tor (ˌprəʊprɪəˈsɛptə) *n. Physiol.* any of the special nerve endings (esp. in the inner ear) that are sensitive to changes in bodily position and movement. [C20: from *proprio-,* from Latin *proprius* one's own + RECEPTOR] **—ˌpro+pri·o·ˈcep+tive** *adj.*

prop root *n.* a root that grows from and supports the stem above the ground in plants such as mangroves.

prop+to+sis (prɒpˈtəʊsɪs) *n., pl.* **+ses** (-siːz). *Pathol.* the forward displacement of an organ or part, such as the eyeball. See also **exophthalmos.** Compare **prolapse.** [C17: via Late Latin from Greek, from *propiptein* to fall forwards]

pro+pul+sion (prəˈpʌlʃən) *n.* **1.** the act of propelling or the state of being propelled. **2.** a propelling force. [C15: from Latin *prōpellere* to PROPEL] **—pro+pul+sive** (prəˈpʌlsɪv) *or* **pro+ˈpul+so·ry** *adj.*

pro+pyl (ˈprəʊpɪl) *n.* (*modifier*) of, consisting of, or containing the monovalent group of atoms C_3H_7-: *a propyl group or radical.*

prop·y+lae·um (ˌprɒpɪˈliːəm) *or* **prop·y+lon** (ˈprɒpɪˌlɒn) *n., pl.* **+lae·a** (-ˈliːə) *or* **+lons, +la.** a portico, esp. one that forms the entrance to a temple. [C18: via Latin from Greek *propulaion* before the gate, from PRO-[2] + *pulē* gate]

pro+pyl+ene (ˈprəʊpɪˌliːn) *n.* another name for **propene.** [C19: from PROPYL + -ENE]

pro+pyl+ene gly+col *n.* a colourless viscous hydroscopic sweet-tasting compound used as an antifreeze and brake fluid. Formula: $CH_3CHOHCH_2OH$.

prop·y+lite (ˈprɒpɪˌlaɪt) *n. Geology.* an altered andesite or similar rock containing calcite, chlorite, etc., produced by the action of hot water.

pro ra·ta (ˈprəʊ ˈrɑːtə) in proportion. [Medieval Latin]

pro+rate (prəʊˈreɪt, ˈprəʊreɪt) *vb. Chiefly U.S.* to divide, assess, or distribute (something) proportionately. [C19: from PRO RATA] **—pro+ˈrat+a·ble** *adj.* **—pro+ˈra+tion** *n.*

pro+rogue (prəˈrəʊg) *vb.* to discontinue the meetings of (a legislative body) without dissolving it. [C15: from Latin *prorogāre* literally: to ask publicly, from *prō-* in public + *rogāre* to ask] **—pro+ro+ga+tion** (ˌprəʊrəˈgeɪʃən) *n.*

pros. *abbrev. for* prosody.

pro+sa+ic (prəʊˈzeɪɪk) *adj.* **1.** lacking imagination. **2.** having the characteristics of prose. [C16: from Late Latin *prōsaicus,* from Latin *prōsa* PROSE] **—pro+ˈsa+i+cal+ly** *adv.* **—pro+ˈsa+ic+ness** *n.*

pro+sa+ism (prəʊˈzeɪɪzəm) *or* **pro+sa+i+cism** (prəʊˈzeɪɪˌsɪzəm) *n.* **1.** prosaic quality or style. **2.** a prosaic expression, thought, etc.

pros and cons *pl. n.* the various arguments in favour of and against a motion, course of action, etc. [C16: from Latin *prō* for + *con,* from *contrā* against]

pro+sce+ni+um (prəˈsiːnɪəm) *n., pl.* **·ni·a** (-nɪə) *or* **·ni+ums. 1.** the arch or opening separating the stage from the auditorium together with the area immediately in front of the arch. **2.** (in ancient theatres) the stage itself. [C17: via Latin from Greek *proskēnion,* from *pro-* before + *skēnē* scene]

pro+sciut+to (prəʊˈʃuːtəʊ; *Italian* proˈʃutto) *n.* cured ham from Italy: usually served as an hors d'oeuvre. [Italian, literally: dried beforehand, from *pro-* PRE- + *asciutto* dried]

pro+scribe (prəʊˈskraɪb) *vb.* (*tr.*) **1.** to condemn or prohibit. **2.** to outlaw; banish; exile. **3.** (in ancient Rome) to outlaw (a citizen) by posting his name in public. [C16: from Latin *prōscrībere* to put up a written public notice, from *prō-* in public + *scrībere* to write] **—pro+ˈscrib+er** *n.*

pro+scrip+tion (prəʊ'skrɪpʃən) *n.* **1.** the act of proscribing or the state of being proscribed. **2.** denunciation, prohibition, or exclusion. **3.** outlawry or ostracism. [C14: from Latin *prōscrip-tiō;* see PROSCRIBE] —**pro+'scrip+tive** *adj.* —**pro+'scrip+tive+ly** *adv.* —**pro+'scrip+tive+ness** *n.*

prose (prəʊz) *n.* **1.** spoken or written language as in ordinary usage, distinguished from poetry by its lack of a marked metrical structure. **2.** commonplace or dull discourse, expression, etc. **3.** *R.C. Church.* a hymn recited or sung after the gradual at Mass. **4.** (*modifier*) written in prose. **5.** (*modifier*) matter-of-fact. ~*vb.* **6.** to write or say (something) in prose. [C14: via Old French from Latin phrase *prōsa ōrātiō* straightforward speech, from *prorsus* prosaic, from *prōvertere* to turn forwards, from PRO-[1] + *vertere* to turn] —**'prose+,like** *adj.*

pro+sec+tor (prəʊ'sɛktə) *n.* a person who prepares or dissects anatomical subjects for demonstration.

pros+e+cute ('prɒsɪ,kju:t) *vb.* **1.** (*tr.*) to bring a criminal action against (a person) for some offence. **2.** (*intr.*) **a.** to seek redress by legal proceedings. **b.** to institute or conduct a prosecution. **3.** (*tr.*) to engage in or practise (a profession or trade). **4.** (*tr.*) to continue to do (a task, etc.). [C15: from Latin *prōsequī* to follow, from *prō-* forward + *sequī* to follow] —**'pros+e+,cut+a+ble** *adj.*

pros+e+cut+ing at+tor+ney *n. U.S. Law.* (in some states) an officer in a judicial district appointed to conduct criminal prosecutions on behalf of the state and people.

pros+e+cu+tion (,prɒsɪ'kju:ʃən) *n.* **1.** the act of prosecuting or the state of being prosecuted. **2. a.** the institution and conduct of legal proceedings against a person. **b.** the proceedings brought in the name of the Crown to put an accused on trial. **3.** the lawyers acting for the Crown to put the case against a person. Compare **defence** (sense 6). **4.** the following up or carrying on of something begun, esp. with a view to its accomplishment or completion.

pros+e+cu+tor ('prɒsɪ,kju:tə) *n.* a person who institutes or conducts legal proceedings, esp. in a criminal court.

pros+e+lyte ('prɒsɪ,laɪt) *n.* **1.** a person newly converted to a religious faith or sect; a convert, esp. a gentile converted to Judaism. ~*vb.* **2.** a less common word for **proselytize.** [C14: from Church Latin *prosēlytus,* from Greek *prosēlutos* recent arrival, convert, from *proserchesthai* to draw near] —**pros+e+lyt+ism** ('prɒsɪlɪ,tɪzəm) *n.* —**pros+e+lyt+ic** (,prɒsɪ'lɪtɪk) *adj.*

pros+e+lyt+ize or **pros+e+lyt+ise** ('prɒsɪlɪ,taɪz) *vb.* to convert (someone) from one religious faith to another. —**,pros+e+lyt+i+'za+tion** or **,pros+e+lyt+i+'sa+tion** *n.* —**'pros+e+lyt+,iz+er** or **'pros+e+lyt+,is+er** *n.*

pros+en+ceph+a+lon (,prɒsɛn'sɛfəlɒn) *n., pl.* **+la** (-lə). the part of the brain that develops from the anterior portion of the neural tube. Compare **mesencephalon, rhombencephalon.** Nontechnical name: **forebrain.** [C19: from New Latin, from Greek *prosō* forward + *enkephalos* brain] —**pros+en+ce+phal+ic** (,prɒsɛnsɪ'fælɪk) *adj.*

pros+en+chy+ma (prɒs'ɛŋkɪmə) *n.* a plant tissue consisting of long narrow cells with pointed ends: occurs in conducting tissue. [C19: from New Latin, from Greek *pros-* towards + *enkhuma* infusion; compare PARENCHYMA] —**pros+en+chy+ma+tous** (,prɒsɛn'kaɪmətəs) *adj.*

prose po+em *n.* a prose composition characterized by a poetic style.

Pro+ser+pi+na (prəʊ'sɜ:pɪnə) *n.* the Roman goddess of the underworld. Greek counterpart: **Persephone.**

pro+sim+i+an (prəʊ'sɪmɪən) *n.* **1.** any primate of the primitive suborder *Prosimii,* including lemurs, tree shrews, lorises, and tarsiers. ~*adj.* **2.** of, relating to, or belonging to the *Prosimii.* ~Compare **anthropoid** (sense 4). [C19: via New Latin from PRO-[1] + Latin *sīmia* ape]

pro+sit *German.* ('pro:zɪt) *interj.* good health! cheers! [German, from Latin, literally: may it prove beneficial]

pros+o+dy ('prɒsədɪ) *n.* **1.** the study of poetic metre and of the art of versification, including rhyme, stanzaic forms, and the quantity and stress of syllables. **2.** a system of versification. **3.** the patterns of stress and intonation in a language. [C15: from Latin *prosōdia* accent of a syllable, from Greek *prosōidia* song set to music, from *pros* towards + *ōidē,* from *aoidē* song; see ODE] —**pro+sod+ic** (prə'sɒdɪk) *adj.* —**'pros+o+dist** *n.*

pros+o+po+poe+ia or **pros+o+po+pe+ia** (,prɒsəpə'pi:ə) *n.* **1.** *Rhetoric.* another word for **personification. 2.** a figure of speech that represents an imaginary, absent, or dead person speaking or acting. [C16: via Latin from Greek *prosōpopoiia* dramatization, from *prosōpon* face + *poiein* to make] —**,pros+o+po+'poe+ial** or **,pros+o+po+'pe+ial** *adj.*

pros+pect ('prɒspɛkt) *n.* **1.** (*sometimes pl.*) a probability or chance for future success, esp. as based on present work or aptitude. **2.** a view or scene, esp. one offering an extended outlook. **3.** a prospective buyer, project, etc. **4.** a survey or observation. **5.** *Mining.* **a.** a known or likely deposit of ore. **b.** the location of a deposit of ore. **c.** a sample of ore for testing. **d.** the yield of mineral obtained from a sample of ore. ~*vb.* **6.** (prə'spɛkt) (when *intr.,* often foll. by *for*) to explore (a region) for gold or other valuable minerals. **7.** (*tr.*) to work (a mine) to discover its profitability. **8.** (*intr.;* often foll. by *for*) to search (for). [C15: from Latin *prōspectus* distant view, from *prōspicere* to look into the distance, from *prō-* forward + *specere* to look] —**'pros+pect+less** *adj.*

pro+spec+tive (prə'spɛktɪv) *adj.* **1.** looking towards the future. **2.** (*prenominal*) anticipated or likely. —**pro+'spec+tive+ly** *adv.*

pro+spec+tor (prə'spɛktə) *n.* a person who searches for the natural occurrence of gold, petroleum, etc.

pro+spec+tus (prə'spɛktəs) *n., pl.* **+tus+es. 1.** a formal statement giving details of a forthcoming event, such as the publication of a book or issue of shares. **2.** a pamphlet or brochure giving details of courses, as at a college or school.

pros+per ('prɒspə) *vb.* (*usually intr.*) to thrive, succeed, etc., or cause to thrive, etc. in a healthy way. [C15: from Latin *prosperāre* to succeed, from *prosperus* fortunate, from PRO-[1] + *spēs* hope]

pros+per+i+ty (prɒ'spɛrɪtɪ) *n., pl.* **+i+ties.** the condition of prospering; success or wealth.

pros+per+ous ('prɒspərəs) *adj.* **1.** flourishing; prospering. **2.** rich; affluent; wealthy. **3.** favourable or promising. —**'pros+per+ous+ly** *adv.* —**'pros+per+ous+ness** *n.*

pros+ta+glan+din (,prɒstə'glændɪn) *n.* any of a group of potent hormone-like compounds composed of essential fatty acids and found in all mammalian tissues, esp. human semen. Prostaglandins stimulate the muscles of the uterus and affect the nervous system, blood vessels, and metabolism. [C20: from *prosta(te) gland* + -IN; it was originally believed to be secreted by the prostate gland]

pros+tate ('prɒsteɪt) *n.* **1.** Also called: **prostate gland.** a gland in male mammals that surrounds the neck of the bladder and urethra and secretes a liquid constituent of the semen. ~*adj.* **2.** Also: **pros+tat+ic** (prɒ'stætɪk). of or relating to the prostate gland. [C17: via Medieval Latin from Greek *prostatēs* something standing in front (of the bladder), from *pro-* in front + *histanai* to cause to stand]

pros+ta+tec+to+my (,prɒstə'tɛktəmɪ) *n., pl.* **+mies.** surgical removal of all or a part of the prostate gland.

pros+ta+ti+tis (,prɒstə'taɪtɪs) *n.* inflammation of the prostate gland.

pros+the+sis ('prɒsθɪsɪs, prɒs'θi:sɪs) *n., pl.* **+ses** (-,si:z). **1.** *Surgery.* **a.** the replacement of a missing bodily part with an artificial substitute. **b.** an artifical part such as a limb, eye, or tooth. **2.** *Linguistics.* another word for **prothesis.** [C16: via Late Latin from Greek: an addition, from *prostithenai* to add, from *pros-* towards + *tithenai* to place] —**pros+thet+ic** (prɒs'θɛtɪk) *adj.* —**pros+'thet+i+cal+ly** *adv.*

pros+thet+ic group *n.* the nonprotein component of a conjugated protein, such as the lipid group in a lipoprotein.

pros+thet+ics (prɒs'θɛtɪks) *n.* (*functioning as sing.*) the branch of surgery concerned with prosthesis.

pros+tho+don+tics (,prɒsθə'dɒntɪks) *n.* (*functioning as sing.*) the branch of dentistry concerned with the artificial replacement of missing teeth. [C20: from PROSTH(ESIS) + -ODONT + -ICS] —**,pros+tho+'don+tist** *n.*

pros+ti+tute ('prɒstɪ,tju:t) *n.* **1.** a woman who engages in sexual intercourse for money. **2.** a man who engages in such activity, esp. in homosexual practices. **3.** a person who offers his talent or work for unworthy purposes. ~*vb.* (*tr.*) **4.** to offer (oneself or another) in sexual intercourse for money. **5.** to offer (a person, esp. oneself, or a person's talent) for unworthy purposes. [C16: from Latin *prōstituere* to expose to prostitution, from *prō-* in public + *statuere* to cause to stand] —**,pros+ti+'tu+tion** *n.* —**'pros+ti+,tu+tor** *n.*

pro+sto+mi+um (prəʊ'stəʊmɪəm) *n., pl.* **+mi+a** (-mɪə). the lobe at the head end of earthworms and other annelids: bears tentacles, palps, etc., or forms part of a sucker or proboscis. [via New Latin from Greek *prostomion* mouth] —**pro+'sto+mi+al** *adj.*

pros+trate *adj.* ('prɒstreɪt). **1.** lying with the face downwards, as in submission. **2.** exhausted physically or emotionally. **3.** helpless or defenceless. **4.** *Botany.* another word for **procumbent** (sense 1). ~*vb.* (prɒ'streɪt). (*tr.*) **5.** to bow or cast (oneself) down, as in submission. **6.** to lay or throw down flat, as on the ground. **7.** to make helpless or defenceless. **8.** to make exhausted. [C14: from Latin *prōsternere* to throw to the ground, from *prō-* before + *sternere* to lay low] —**pros+'tra+tion** *n.*

pro+style ('prəʊstaɪl) *adj.* **1.** (of a building) having a row of columns in front, esp. as in the portico of a Greek temple. ~*n.* **2.** a prostyle building, portico, etc. [C17: from Latin *prostȳlos,* from Greek: with pillars in front, from PRO-[2] + *stulos* pillar]

pros+y ('prəʊzɪ) *adj.* **pros+i+er, pros+i+est. 1.** of the nature of or similar to prose. **2.** dull, tedious, or long-winded. —**'pros+i+ly** *adv.* —**'pros+i+ness** *n.*

Prot. *abbrev. for:* **1.** Protestant. **2.** Protectorate.

prot- *combining form.* variant of **proto-** before a vowel.

pro+tac+tin+i+um (,prəʊtæk'tɪnɪəm) *n.* a toxic radioactive metallic element that occurs in uranium ores and is produced by neutron irradiation of thorium. Symbol: Pa; atomic no.: 91; half-life of the most stable isotope, ^{231}Pa: 32 500 years; valency: 4 or 5; relative density: 15.4 (calc.); melting pt.: below 1600°C. Former name: **protoactinium.**

pro+tag+o+nist (prəʊ'tægənɪst) *n.* **1.** the principal character in a play, story, etc. **2.** a supporter, esp. when important or respected, of a cause, political party, etc. [C17: from Greek *prōtagōnistēs,* from *prōtos* first + *agōnistēs* actor] —**pro+'tag+o+nism** *n.*

Pro+tag+o+ras (prəʊ'tægə,ræs) *n.* ?485–?411 B.C., Greek philoso-

,pro+res+to+'ra+tion *adj.*
,pro+re+'vi+sion *adj.*
,pro+rev+o+'lu+tion+,ar+y *adj.*
,pro+'slav+er+y *adj.*
pro-'So+vi+et *adj.*
,pro+su+per+'vi+sion *adj.*
,pro+sur+'ren+der *adj.*
pro+'syn+di+cal+ism *n.*
pro+'un+ion *adj.*
,pro-U+'nit+ed 'States *adj.*
,pro+u+ni+'ver+si+ty *adj.*
pro+'war *adj.*

pher and sophist, famous for his dictum "Man is the measure of all things."

pro+ta+mine ('prəʊtə,mi:n) *n.* any of a group of basic simple proteins that occur, in association with nucleic acids, in the sperm of some fish.

pro+tan+drous (prəʊ'tændrəs) *adj.* (of plants and hermaphrodite animals) producing male gametes before female gametes. Compare **protogynous.** —**pro+'tan+dry** *n.*

pro+ta+no+pi·a (,prəʊtə'nəʊpɪə) *n.* inability to see the colour red; red blindness. [C20: New Latin, from PROTO- + AN- + -OPIA] —**pro+ta+nop+ic** (,prəʊtə'nɒpɪk) *adj.*

prot·a·sis ('prɒtəsɪs) *n., pl.* +**ses** (-si:z). **1.** the clause that states the condition in a conditional sentence. In English the protasis is generally introduced by *if* or *unless.* Compare **apodosis. 2.** (in classical drama) the introductory part of a play. [C17: via Latin from Greek: a proposal, from *pro-* before + *teinein* to extend]

pro·te·a ('prəʊtɪə) *n.* any shrub or small tree of the genus *Protea,* of tropical and southern Africa, having flowers with coloured bracts arranged in showy heads: family *Proteaceae.* [C20: from New Latin, from PROTEUS, referring to the large number of different forms of the plant]

pro·te·an (prəʊ'ti:ən, 'prəʊtɪən) *adj.* readily taking on various shapes or forms; variable. [C16: from PROTEUS]

pro·te·ase ('prəʊtɪ,eɪs) *n.* any enzyme involved in proteolysis. [C20: from PROTEIN + -ASE]

pro+tect (prə'tɛkt) *vb.* (*tr.*) **1.** to defend from trouble, harm, attack, etc. **2.** *Economics.* to assist (domestic industries) by the imposition of protective tariffs on imports. **3.** *Commerce.* to provide funds in advance to guarantee payment of (a note, draft, etc.). [C16: from Latin *prōtegere* to cover before, from PRO-[1] + *tegere* to cover]

pro+tec+tion (prə'tɛkʃən) *n.* **1.** the act of protecting or the condition of being protected. **2.** something that protects. **3. a.** the imposition of duties or quotas on imports, designed for the protection of domestic industries against overseas competition, expansion of domestic employment, etc. **b.** Also called: **protectionism.** the system, policy, or theory of such restrictions. Compare **free trade. 4.** a document that grants protection or immunity from arrest or harassment to a person, esp. a traveller. **5.** *Informal.* **a.** Also called: **protection money.** money demanded by gangsters for freedom from molestation. **b.** freedom from molestation purchased in this way. —**pro+'tec+tion+,ism** *n.* —**pro+'tec+tion+ist** *n.*

pro+tec+tive (prə'tɛktɪv) *adj.* **1.** giving or capable of giving protection. **2.** *Economics.* of, relating to, or intended for protection of domestic industries. ~*n.* **3.** something that protects. —**pro+'tec+tive+ly** *adv.* —**pro+'tec+tive+ness** *n.*

pro+tec+tive col+or·a·tion *n.* the coloration of an animal that enables it to blend with its surroundings and therefore escape the attention of predators.

pro+tec+tive tar+iff *n.* a tariff levied on imports to protect the domestic economy rather than to raise revenue.

pro+tec+tor (prə'tɛktə) *n.* **1.** a person or thing that protects. **2.** *History.* a person who exercised royal authority during the minority, absence, or incapacity of the monarch. —**pro+'tec+to+ral** *adj.* —**pro+'tec+tress** *fem. n.*

Pro+tec+tor (prə'tɛktə) *n.* short for **Lord Protector,** the title borne by Oliver Cromwell (1653–58) and by Richard Cromwell (1658–59) as heads of state during the period known as the **Protectorate.**

pro+tec+tor+ate (prə'tɛktərɪt) *n.* **1. a.** a territory largely controlled by but not annexed to a stronger state. **b.** the relation of a protecting state to its protected territory. **2.** the office or period of office of a protector.

pro+tec+to·ry (prə'tɛktərɪ) *n., pl.* **·ries.** an institution for the care of homeless, delinquent, or destitute children.

pro+té+gé *or* (*fem.*) **pro+té+gée** ('prəʊtɪ,ʒeɪ) *n.* a person who is protected and aided by the patronage of another person. [C18: from French *protéger* to PROTECT]

pro+tein ('prəʊti:n) *n.* any of a large group of nitrogenous compounds of high molecular weight that are essential constituents of all living organisms. They consist of one or more chains of amino acids linked by peptide bonds and are folded into a specific three-dimensional shape maintained by further chemical bonding. [C19: via German from Greek *prōteios* primary, from *protos* first + -IN] —**,pro+tein·'a+ceous, pro+'tein+ic,** *or* **pro+'tei+nous** *adj.*

pro+tein+ase ('prəʊtɪ,neɪs, -,neɪz) *n.* another name for **endopeptidase.**

pro+tein+u·ri·a (,prəʊtɪ'njʊərɪə) *n. Med.* another name for **albuminuria.**

pro tem+po+re *Latin.* ('prəʊ 'tɛmpərɪ) for the time being; temporarily. Often shortened to **pro tem** ('prəʊ'tɛm).

pro+te·ol·y+sis (,prəʊtɪ'ɒlɪsɪs) *n.* the hydrolysis of proteins into simpler compounds by the action of enzymes: occurs esp. during digestion. [C19: from New Latin, from *proteo-* (from PROTEIN) + -LYSIS] —**pro+te·o+lyt+ic** (,prəʊtɪə'lɪtɪk) *adj.*

pro+te·ose ('prəʊtɪ,əʊs, -,əʊz) *n. Now rare.* any of a group of compounds formed during proteolysis that are less complex than metaproteins but more so than peptones. Also called (esp. U.S.): **albumose.** [C20: from PROTEIN + -OSE[2]]

pro·ter·o- *combining form.* anterior or former in time, place, order, etc.: *proterozoic.* [from Greek *proteros* fore]

Pro+te·ro+zo+ic (,prəʊtərəʊ'zəʊɪk) *n.* **1.** the later of two divisions of the Precambrian era, during which the earliest plants and animals are assumed to have lived. Compare **Archaeozoic.** ~*adj.* **2.** of or formed in the late Precambrian era.

pro+test *n.* ('prəʊtɛst). **1. a.** public, often organized, dissent or manifestation of such dissent. **b.** (*as modifier*): *a protest march.* **2.** a declaration or objection that is formal or solemn. **3. a.** a formal notarial statement drawn up on behalf of a creditor and declaring that the debtor has dishonoured a bill of exchange or promissory note. **b.** the action of drawing up such a statement. **c.** a formal declaration by a taxpayer disputing the legality or accuracy of his assessment. **4.** a statement made by the master of a vessel attesting to the circumstances in which his vessel was damaged or imperilled. **5.** the act of protesting. ~*vb.* (prə'tɛst). **6.** (when *intr.,* foll. by *against, at, about,* etc.; when *tr., may take a clause as object*) to make a strong objection (to something, esp. a supposed injustice or offence). **7.** (when *tr., may take a clause as object*) to assert or affirm in a formal or solemn manner. **8.** (*tr.*) to declare that (a bill of exchange or promissory note) has been dishonoured. [C14: from Latin *prōtestārī* to make a formal declaration, from *prō-* before + *testārī* to assert] —**pro+'test+ant** *adj., n.* —**pro+'test+er** *n.* —**pro+'test+ing+ly** *adv.*

Prot+es+tant ('prɒtɪstənt) *n.* **a.** an adherent of Protestantism. **b.** (*as modifier*): *the Protestant Church.*

Prot+es+tant E·pis+co+pal Church *n.* the full title of the **Episcopal Church.**

Prot+es+tant+ism ('prɒtɪstən,tɪzəm) *n.* **1.** the religion or religious system of any of the Churches of Western Christendom that are separated from the Roman Catholic Church and adhere substantially to principles established by Luther, Calvin, etc., in the Reformation. **2.** the Protestant Churches collectively. **3.** adherence to the principles of the Reformation.

pro+tes+ta+tion (,prəʊtɛs'teɪʃən) *n.* **1.** the act of protesting. **2.** something protested about. **3.** a strong declaration.

Pro·teus ('prəʊtɪəs) *n. Greek myth.* a prophetic sea god capable of changing his shape at will.

pro+tha+la+mi+on (,prəʊθə'leɪmɪən) *or* **pro+tha+la+mi+um** *n., pl.* +**mi·a** (-mɪə). a song or poem in celebration of a marriage. [C16: from Greek *pro-* before + *thalamos* marriage; coined by Edmund Spenser, on the model of EPITHALAMION]

pro+thal+lus (prəʊ'θæləs) *or* **pro+thal+li·um** (prəʊ'θælɪəm) *n., pl.* +**li** (-laɪ) *or* +**li·a** (-lɪə). *Botany.* the small flat free-living green disc of tissue that bears the reproductive organs of pteridophytes. [C19: from New Latin, from *pro-* before + Greek *thallus* a young shoot] —**pro+'thal+lic** *or* **pro+'thal+li·al** *adj.*

proth+e·sis ('prɒθɪsɪs) *n.* **1.** a process in the development of a language by which a phoneme or syllable is prefixed to a word to facilitate pronunciation: *Latin "scala" gives Spanish "escala" by prothesis.* **2.** *Eastern Orthodox Church.* the solemn preparation of the Eucharistic elements before consecration. [C16: via Late Latin from Greek: a setting out in public, from *pro-* forth + *thesis* a placing] —**pro+thet +ic** (prə'θɛtɪk) *adj.* —**pro+'thet·i+cal+ly** *adv.*

pro+tho+no+tar·y (,prəʊθə'nəʊtərɪ, -trɪ, prəʊ'θɒnə-) *or* **pro·to+no+tar·y** *n., pl.* +**tar·ies.** (formerly) a chief clerk in certain law courts. [C15: from Medieval Latin *prōthonotārius,* from *prōtho-* PROTO- + Late Latin *notārius* NOTARY] —**pro+thon·o+tar·i·al** (prəʊ,θɒnə'tɛərɪəl) *or* **pro+,ton·o+'tar+i·al** *adj.*

pro+tho+rax (prəʊ'θɔ:ræks) *n., pl.* +**tho+rax·es** *or* +**tho+ra+ces** (-'θɔ:rə,si:z). the first segment of the thorax of an insect, which bears the first pair of walking legs. See also **mesothorax, metathorax.**

pro+throm+bin (prəʊ'θrɒmbɪn) *n. Biochem.* a constituent of blood plasma that is the inactive precursor of thrombin. See also **phylloquinone.**

pro+tist ('prəʊtɪst) *n.* any organism belonging to the kingdom *Protista,* including bacteria, protozoans, unicellular algae and fungi, regarded as distinct from plants and animals. [C19: from New Latin *Protista* most primitive organisms, from Greek *prōtistos* the very first, from *protos* first]

pro+ti·um ('prəʊtɪəm) *n.* the most common isotope of hydrogen, having a mass number of 1. [C20: New Latin, from PROTO- + -IUM]

pro·to- *or sometimes before a vowel* **prot-** *combining form.* **1.** indicating the first in time, order, or rank: *protomartyr.* **2.** primitive, ancestral, or original: *prototype.* **3.** indicating the reconstructed earliest stage of a language: *Proto-Germanic.* **4.** indicating the first in a series of chemical compounds: *protoxide.* **5.** indicating the parent of a chemical compound or an element: *protoactinium.* [from Greek *prōtos* first, from *pro* before; see PRO-[2]]

pro·to+ac+tin+i·um (,prəʊtəʊæk'tɪnɪəm) *n.* the former name of **protactinium.**

pro·to+chor+date (,prəʊtəʊ'kɔ:deɪt) *n.* **1.** any chordate animal of the subphyla *Hemichordata* (acorn worms), *Urochordata* (tunicates), and *Cephalochordata* (lancelets) ~*adj.* **2.** of or relating to protochordates.

pro·to+col ('prəʊtə,kɒl) *n.* **1.** the formal etiquette and code of behaviour, precedence, and procedure for state and diplomatic ceremonies. **2.** a memorandum or record of an agreement, esp. one reached in international negotiations, a meeting, etc. **3. a.** an amendment to a treaty or convention. **b.** an annex appended to a treaty to deal with subsidiary matters or to render the treaty more lucid. **c.** a formal international agreement or understanding on some matter. **4.** *Philosophy.* a statement that records an event objectively. [C16: from Medieval Latin *prōtocollum,* from Late Greek *prōtokollon* sheet glued to the front of a manuscript, from PROTO- + *kolla* glue]

Pro·to-Ger·man+ic *n.* the prehistoric unrecorded language that was the ancestor of all Germanic languages.

pro+tog·y+nous (prəʊ'tɒdʒɪnəs) *adj.* (of plants and hermaphrodite animals) producing female gametes before male ones. Compare **protandrous.** —**pro+'tog·y+ny** *n.*

pro·to+his+to+ry (,prəʊtəʊ'hɪstərɪ) *n.* the period or stage of human development or of a particular culture immediately prior to the emergence of writing. —**pro·to·his·tor·ic** (ˌprəʊtəʊhɪˈstɒrɪk) *adj.*

pro·to·hu·man (ˌprəʊtəʊˈhjuːmən) *n.* **1.** any of various prehistoric primates that resembled modern man. ~*adj.* **2.** of or relating to any of these primates.

Pro·to-In·do-Eu·ro·pe·an *n.* the prehistoric unrecorded language that was the ancestor of all Indo-European languages.

pro·to·lan·guage (ˌprəʊtəʊˈlæŋgwɪdʒ) *n.* an extinct and unrecorded language reconstructed by comparison of its recorded or living descendants. Also called: **Ursprache.**

pro·to·lith·ic (ˌprəʊtəʊˈlɪθɪk) *adj.* of or referring to the earliest Stone Age.

pro·to·mar·tyr (ˌprəʊtəʊˈmɑːtə) *n.* **1.** St. Stephen as the first Christian martyr. **2.** the first martyr to lay down his life in any cause.

pro·to·mor·phic (ˌprəʊtəʊˈmɔːfɪk) *adj. Biology.* primitive in structure; primordial.

pro·ton (ˈprəʊtɒn) *n.* a stable, positively charged elementary particle, found in atomic nuclei in numbers equal to its atomic number. It is a baryon with a charge of 1.6022×10^{-19} coulomb, a rest mass of $1.672\,52 \times 10^{-27}$ kilogram, and spin ½. [C20: from Greek *protos* first]

pro·to·ne·ma (ˌprəʊtəˈniːmə) *n., pl.* **·ne·ma·ta** (-ˈniːmətə). a branched threadlike structure that grows from a moss spore and eventually develops into the moss plant. [C19: from New Latin, from PROTO- + Greek *nema* thread] —ˌ**pro·to·ˈne·mal** *or* **pro·to·ne·ma·tal** (ˌprəʊtəˈniːmətᵊl, -ˈnɛmətᵊl) *adj.*

pro·ton num·ber *n.* another name for **atomic number.** Symbol: *Z.*

Pro·to-Norse *n.* the North Germanic language of Scandinavia up to about 700 A.D. See also **Old Norse.**

pro·to·path·ic (ˌprəʊtəˈpæθɪk) *adj. Physiol.* **1.** of or relating to a sensory nerve that perceives only coarse stimuli, such as pain. **2.** of or relating to such perception. —**pro·top·a·thy** (prəʊˈtɒpəθɪ) *n.*

pro·to·plasm (ˈprəʊtəˌplæzəm) *n. Biology.* the living contents of a cell: a complex translucent colourless colloidal substance differentiated into cytoplasm and nucleoplasm. [C19: from New Latin, from PROTO- + Greek *plasma* form] —ˌ**pro·to·ˈplas·mic,** ˌ**pro·to·ˈplas·mal,** *or* ˌ**pro·to·plas·ˈmat·ic** *adj.*

pro·to·plast (ˈprəʊtəˌplæst) *n.* another name for **energid.** [C16: from Late Latin *prōtoplastus* the first-formed, from Greek *prōtoplastos,* from PROTO- + *plassein* to shape] —ˌ**pro·to·ˈplas·tic** *adj.*

Pro·to·se·mit·ic (ˌprəʊtəʊsɪˈmɪtɪk) *n.* the hypothetical parent language of the Semitic group of languages.

pro·to·star (ˈprəʊtəʊˌstɑː) *n.* a condensation, interstellar gas, or dust, from which a star is thought to develop.

pro·to·stele (ˈprəʊtəˌstiːl, -ˌstiːlɪ) *n.* a simple type of stele with a central core of xylem surrounded by a cylinder of phloem: occurs in most roots and the stems of ferns, etc. —ˌ**pro·to·ˈste·lic** *adj.*

pro·to·the·ri·an (ˌprəʊtəʊˈθɪərɪən) *adj.* **1.** of, relating to, or belonging to the *Prototheria,* a subclass of mammals that includes the monotremes. ~*n.* **2.** any prototherian mammal; a monotreme. ~Compare **eutherian, metatherian.**

pro·to·troph·ic (ˌprəʊtəˈtrɒfɪk) *adj.* **1.** (esp. of bacteria) feeding solely on inorganic matter. **2.** (of cultured bacteria, fungi, etc.) having no specific food requirements.

pro·to·type (ˈprəʊtəˌtaɪp) *n.* **1.** an original model upon which copies are based, from which improved types can be made or that has analogies at a later period. **2.** a person or thing that serves as an example of a type. **3.** *Biology.* the ancestral or primitive form of a species or other group; an archetype. —ˌ**pro·to·ˈty·pal, pro·to·typ·ic** (ˌprəʊtəˈtɪpɪk), *or* ˌ**pro·to·ˈtyp·i·cal** *adj.*

pro·tox·ide (prəʊˈtɒksaɪd) *n.* the oxide of an element that contains the smallest amount of oxygen of any of its oxides.

pro·to·xy·lem (ˌprəʊtəˈzaɪləm) *n.* the first-formed xylem tissue, consisting of extensible thin-walled cells thickened with rings or spirals of lignin. Compare **metaxylem.**

pro·to·zo·an (ˌprəʊtəˈzəʊən) *or* **pro·to·zo·on** (ˌprəʊtəˈzəʊɒn) *n., pl.* **·zo·a** (-ˈzəʊə), **·zo·ans,** *or* **·zo·a.** **1.** any minute invertebrate of the phylum *Protozoa,* including flagellates, ciliates, sporozoans, amoebas, and foraminifers. ~*adj. also* **pro·to·zo·ic. 2.** of, relating to, or belonging to the *Protozoa.* [C19: via New Latin from Greek PROTO- + *zoion* animal]

pro·to·zo·ol·o·gy (ˌprəʊtəʊzəʊˈɒlədʒɪ) *n.* the branch of zoology concerned with the study of protozoans. —**pro·to·zo·o·log·i·cal** (ˌprəʊtəʊˌzəʊəˈlɒdʒɪkᵊl) *adj.* —ˌ**pro·to·zo·ˈol·o·gist** *n.*

pro·tract (prəˈtrækt) *vb.* (*tr.*) **1.** to lengthen or extend (a speech, etc.); prolong in time. **2.** (of a muscle) to draw, thrust, or extend (a part, etc.) forwards. **3.** to plot or draw using a protractor and scale. [C16: from Latin *prōtrahere* to prolong, from PRO-[1] + *trahere* to drag] —**pro·ˈtract·ed·ly** *adv.* —**pro·ˈtract·ed·ness** *n.* —**pro·ˈtrac·tive** *adj.*

pro·trac·tile (prəˈtræktaɪl) *or* **pro·tract·i·ble** *adj.* able to be extended or protruded: *protractile muscle.*

pro·trac·tion (prəˈtrækʃən) *n.* **1.** the act or process of protracting. **2.** the state or condition of being protracted. **3.** a prolongation or protrusion. **4.** an extension of something in time or space. **5.** something that is extended in time or space. **6.** the irregular lengthening of a syllable that is usually short.

pro·trac·tor (prəˈtræktə) *n.* **1.** an instrument for measuring or drawing angles on paper, usually a flat semicircular transparent plastic sheet graduated in degrees. **2.** a person or thing that protracts. **3.** a surgical instrument for removing a bullet from the body. **4.** *Anatomy.* a former term for **extensor.**

pro·trude (prəˈtruːd) *vb.* **1.** to thrust or cause to thrust forwards or outwards. **2.** to project or cause to project from or as if from a surface. [C17: from Latin, from PRO- + *trudere* to thrust] —**pro·ˈtrud·a·ble** *adj.* —**pro·ˈtru·dent** *adj.*

pro·tru·sile (prəˈtruːsaɪl) *adj. Zoology.* capable of being thrust forwards: *protrusile jaws.* Also: **projectile.**

pro·tru·sion (prəˈtruːʒən) *n.* **1.** something that protrudes. **2.** the state or condition of being protruded. **3.** the act or process of protruding.

pro·tru·sive (prəˈtruːsɪv) *adj.* **1.** tending to project or jut outwards. **2.** a less common word for **obtrusive. 3.** *Archaic.* causing propulsion. —**pro·ˈtru·sive·ly** *adv.* —**pro·ˈtru·sive·ness** *n.*

pro·tu·ber·ant (prəˈtjuːbərənt) *adj.* swelling out from the surrounding surface; bulging. [C17: from Late Latin *prōtūberāre* to swell, from PRO-[1] + *tūber* swelling] —**pro·ˈtu·ber·ance** *or* **pro·ˈtu·ber·an·cy** *n.* —**pro·ˈtu·ber·ant·ly** *adv.*

pro·tu·ber·ate (prəˈtjuːbəˌreɪt) *vb.* (*intr.*) *Rare.* to swell out or project from the surrounding surface; bulge out.

pro·tyle (ˈprəʊtaɪl) *or* **pro·tyl** (ˈprəʊtɪl) *n.* a hypothetical primitive substance from which the chemical elements were supposed to have been formed. [C19: from Greek *prōt-* PROTO- + *hylē* substance]

proud (praʊd) *adj.* **1.** (foll. by *of,* an infinitive, or a clause) pleased or satisfied, as with oneself, one's possessions, achievements, etc. **2.** feeling honoured or gratified by or as if by some distinction. **3.** having an inordinately high opinion of oneself; arrogant or haughty. **4.** characterized by or proceeding from a sense of pride: *a proud moment.* **5.** stately or distinguished. **6.** bold or fearless. **7.** *Northern Brit. dialect.* (of a surface, edge, etc.) projecting or protruding from the surrounding area. **8.** (of animals) restive or excited, often sexually; in heat. ~*adv.* **9. do (someone) proud. a.** to entertain (a person) on a grand scale: *they did us proud at the hotel.* **b.** to honour or distinguish (a person): *his honesty did him proud.* [Late Old English *prūd,* from Old French *prud, prod* brave, from Late Latin *prōde* useful, from Latin *prōdesse* to be of value, from *prōd-,* variant of *prō-* for + *esse* to be] —ˈ**proud·ly** *adv.* —ˈ**proud·ness** *n.*

proud flesh *n.* a nontechnical name for **granulation tissue.**

Prou·dhon (*French* pruˈdɔ̃) *n.* **Pierre Jo·seph** (pjɛːr ʒoˈzɛf). 1809–65, French socialist, whose pamphlet *What is Property?* (1840) declared that property is theft.

Proust (*French* prust) *n.* **1. Jo·seph Louis** (ʒozɛf ˈlwi). 1754–1826, French chemist, who formulated the law of constant proportions. **2. Mar·cel** (marˈsɛl). 1871–1922, French novelist whose long novel *À la recherche du temps perdu* (1913–27) deals with the relationship of the narrator to themes such as art, time, memory, and society.

proust·ite (ˈpruːstaɪt) *n.* a red mineral consisting of silver arsenic sulphide in hexagonal crystalline form. Formula: Ag_3AsS_3. [C19: from French, named after J. L. PROUST]

Prout (praʊt) *n.* **1. Eb·e·ne·zer.** 1835–1909, English musicologist and composer, noted for his editions of works by Handel and J. S. Bach. **2. Wil·liam.** 1785–1850, English chemist, noted for his modification of the atomic theory.

prov. *abbrev. for:* **1.** province. **2.** provincial. **3.** provisional.

Prov. *abbrev. for:* **1.** Provençal. **2.** *Bible.* Proverbs. **3.** Province. **4.** Provost.

prove (pruːv) *vb.* **proves, prov·ing, proved; proved** *or* **prov·en.** (*mainly tr.*) **1.** (*may take a clause as object or an infinitive*) to establish or demonstrate the truth or validity of; verify, esp. by using an established sequence of procedures or statements. **2.** to establish the quality of, esp. by experiment or scientific analysis. **3.** *Law.* to establish the validity and genuineness of (a will). **4.** to show (oneself) able or courageous. **5.** (*copula*) to be found or shown (to be): *this has proved useless; he proved to be invaluable.* **6.** *Printing.* to take a trial impression of (type, etc.). **7.** (*intr.*) (of dough) to rise in a warm place before baking. **8.** *Archaic.* to undergo. [C12: from Old French *prover,* from Latin *probāre* to test, from *probus* honest] —ˈ**prov·a·ble** *adj.* —ˌ**prov·a·ˈbil·i·ty** *n.* —ˈ**prov·a·bly** *adv.*

prov·en (ˈpruːvᵊn) *vb.* **1.** a past participle of **prove. 2. not proven.** *Scot. law.* (of a verdict, etc.) pronounced when a jury finds the case against the accused neither disproved nor proved. ~*adj.* **3.** tried; tested: *a proven method.* —ˈ**prov·en·ly** *adv.*

prov·e·nance (ˈprɒvɪnəns) *or* **pro·ve·ni·ence** (prɒˈviːnɪəns) *n.* a place of origin, esp. that of a work of art or archaeological specimen. [C19: from French, from *provenir,* from Latin *prōvenīre* to originate, from *venīre* to come]

Pro·ven·çal (ˌprɒvɒnˈsɑːl; *French* prɔvɑ̃ˈsal) *adj.* **1.** relating to, denoting, or characteristic of Provence, its inhabitants, their dialect of French, or their Romance language. ~*n.* **2.** a language of Provence, closely related to Catalan, French, and Italian, belonging to the Romance group of the Indo-European family. It was important in the Middle Ages as a literary language, and attempts have been made since the 19th century to revive its literary status. See also **langue d'oc. 3.** a native or inhabitant of Provence.

Pro·ven·çale (ˌprɒvɒnˈsɑːl; *French* prɔvɑ̃ˈsal) *adj.* (of dishes) prepared with garlic, oil, and often tomatoes.

Pro·vence (*French* prɔˈvɑ̃ːs) *n.* a former province of SE France, on the Mediterranean, and the River Rhone: forms an administrative region with **Côte d'Azur.**

prov·en·der (ˈprɒvɪndə) *n.* **1.** any dry feed or fodder for domestic livestock. **2.** food in general. [C14: from Old French *provendre,* from Late Latin *praebenda* grant, from Latin *praebēre* to proffer; influenced also by Latin *prōvidēre* to look after]

pro+ven+tric·u+lus (ˌprəuvɛnˈtrɪkjʊləs) *n., pl.* **+tric·u+li** (-ˈtrɪkjʊˌlaɪ). **1.** the first part of the stomach of birds, the gizzard. **2.** the thick muscular stomach of crustaceans and insects; gizzard. [C19: from New Latin, from Latin PRO-[1] + *ventriculus* little belly, from *venter* belly] —ˌ**pro+ven+ˈtric·u+lar** *adj.*

prov+erb (ˈprɒvɜːb) *n.* **1.** a short, memorable, and often highly condensed saying embodying, esp. with bold imagery, some commonplace fact of experience. **2.** a person or thing exemplary in respect of a characteristic: *Antarctica is a proverb for extreme cold.* **3.** *Ecclesiast.* a wise saying or admonition providing guidance. ~*vb.* (*tr.*) **4.** to utter or describe (something) in the form of a proverb. **5.** to make (something) a proverb. [C14: via Old French from Latin *prōverbium,* from *verbum* word]

pro+ver+bi·al (prəˈvɜːbɪəl) *adj.* **1.** (*prenominal*) commonly or traditionally referred to, esp. as being an example of some peculiarity, characteristic, etc. **2.** of, connected with, embodied in, or resembling a proverb. —**pro+ˈver+bi+al+ly** *adv.*

Prov+erbs (ˈprɒvɜːbz) *n.* a book of the Old Testament consisting of the proverbs of various Israelite sages including Solomon.

pro+vide (prəˈvaɪd) *vb.* (*mainly tr.*) **1.** to put at the disposal of; furnish or supply. **2.** to afford; yield: *this meeting provides an opportunity to talk.* **3.** (*intr.;* often foll. by *for* or *against*) to take careful precautions (over): *he provided against financial ruin by wise investment.* **4.** (*intr.;* foll. by *for*) to supply means of support (to), esp. financially: *he provides for his family.* **5.** (in statutes, documents, etc.) to determine (what is to happen in certain contingencies), esp. by including a proviso condition. **6.** to confer and induct into ecclesiastical offices. **7.** *Now rare.* to have or get in store: *in summer many animals provide their winter food.* [C15: from Latin *prōvidēre* to provide for, from *prō-* beforehand + *vidēre* to see] —**pro+ˈvid+er** *n.*

prov·i+dence (ˈprɒvɪdəns) *n.* **1. a.** God's foreseeing protection and care of his creatures. **b.** such protection and care as manifest by some other force. **2.** a manifestation of such care and guidance. **3.** the foresight or care exercised by a person in the management of his affairs or resources.

Prov·i+dence[1] (ˈprɒvɪdəns) *n.* God, esp. as showing foreseeing care and protection of his creatures.

Prov·i+dence[2] (ˈprɒvɪdəns) *n.* a port in NE Rhode Island, capital of the state, at the head of Narragansett Bay: founded by Roger Williams in 1636. Pop.: 169 931 (1973 est.).

prov·i+dent (ˈprɒvɪdənt) *adj.* **1.** providing for future needs. **2.** exercising foresight in the management of one's affairs or resources. **3.** characterized by or proceeding from foresight. [C15: from Latin *prōvidens* foreseeing, from *prōvidēre* to PROVIDE] —ˈ**prov·i+dent+ly** *adv.*

prov·i+dent club *n. Brit.* a hire-purchase system offered by some large retail organizations.

prov·i+den+tial (ˌprɒvɪˈdɛnʃəl) *adj.* relating to, characteristic of, or presumed to proceed from or as if from divine providence. —ˌ**prov·i+ˈden+tial+ly** *adv.*

prov·i+dent so+ci+e·ty *n.* another name for **friendly society.**

pro+vid+ing (prəˈvaɪdɪŋ) *or* **pro+vid+ed** *conj.* (*subordinating;* sometimes foll. by *that*) on the condition or understanding (that): *I'll play, providing you pay me.*

prov+ince (ˈprɒvɪns) *n.* **1.** a territory governed as a unit of a country or empire. **2.** a district, territory, or region. **3.** (*pl;* usually preceded by *the*) those parts of a country lying outside the capital and other large cities and regarded as outside the mainstream of sophisticated culture. **4.** *Ecology.* a subdivision of a region, characterized by a particular fauna and flora. **5.** an area or branch of learning, activity, etc. **6.** the field or extent of a person's activities or office. **7.** *R.C. Church, Church of England.* an ecclesiastical territory, usually consisting of several dioceses, and having an archbishop or metropolitan at its head. **8.** a major administrative and territorial subdivision of a religious order. **9.** *History.* a region of the Roman Empire outside Italy ruled by a governor from Rome. [C14: from Old French, from Latin *prōvincia* conquered territory]

Prov·ince+town (ˈprɒvɪnsˌtaun) *n.* a village in SE Massachusetts, at the tip of Cape Cod: scene of the first landing place of the Pilgrims (1620) and of the signing of the Mayflower Compact (1620). Pop.: 2911 (1971).

pro+vin+cial (prəˈvɪnʃəl) *adj.* **1.** of or connected with a province. **2.** characteristic of or connected with the provinces; local. **3.** having attitudes and opinions supposedly common to people living in the provinces; rustic or unsophisticated; limited. ~*n.* **4.** a person lacking the sophistications of city life; rustic or narrow-minded individual. **5.** a person coming from or resident in a province or the provinces. **6.** the head of an ecclesiastical province. **7.** the head of a major territorial subdivision of a religious order. —**pro+vin+ci+al+i·ty** (prəˌvɪnʃɪˈælɪtɪ) *n.* —**pro+ˈvin+cial+ly** *adv.*

pro+vin+cial+ism (prəˈvɪnʃəˌlɪzəm) *n.* **1.** narrowness of mind or outlook; lack of sophistication. **2.** a word or attitude characteristic of a provincial. **3.** attention to the affairs of one's province rather than the whole nation. **4.** the state or quality of being provincial. ~Also called: **localism.**

prov+ing ground *n.* a place or situation in which something new, such as equipment or a theory, can be tested.

pro+vi+sion (prəˈvɪʒən) *n.* **1.** the act of supplying or providing food, etc. **2.** something that is supplied or provided. **3.** preparations made beforehand (esp. in the phrase **make provision for**). **4.** (*pl.*) food and other necessities, esp. for an expedition. **5.** (*pl.*) food obtained for a household. **6.** a demand, condition, or stipulation formally incorporated in a document; proviso. **7.** the conferring of and induction into ecclesiastical offices. ~*vb.* **8.** (*tr.*) to supply with provisions. [C14: from Latin *prōvīsiō* a providing; see PROVIDE] —**pro+ˈvi+sion+er** *n.*

pro+vi+sion+al (prəˈvɪʒənᵊl) *or* **pro+vi+sion+ar·y** (prəˈvɪʒənərɪ) *adj.* **1.** subject to later alteration; temporary or conditional: *a provisional decision.* ~*n.* **2.** a postage stamp surcharged during an emergency to alter the stamp's denomination or significance until a new or regular issue is printed. —**pro+ˈvi+sion+al+ly** *adv.*

Pro+vi+sion+al (prəˈvɪʒənᵊl) *adj.* **1.** of, designating, or relating to one of the two factions of the IRA and Sinn Fein that have existed since a split in late 1969. The Provisional movement follows the traditional policy of terrorism to achieve Irish unity. ~*n.* **2.** Also called: **Provo.** a member of the Provisional IRA or Sinn Fein. ~Compare **Official.**

pro+vi+so (prəˈvaɪzəu) *n., pl.* **+sos** *or* **+soes. 1.** a clause in a document or contract that embodies a condition or stipulation. **2.** a condition or stipulation. [C15: from Medieval Latin phrase *prōvīsō quod* it being provided that, from Latin *prōvīsus* provided]

pro+vi+so·ry (prəˈvaɪzərɪ) *adj.* **1.** containing a proviso; conditional. **2.** another word for **provisional.** —**pro+ˈvi+so+ri+ly** *adv.*

pro+vit·a+min (prəuˈvɪtəmɪn) *n.* a substance, such as carotene, that is converted into a vitamin in animal tissues.

Pro+vo (ˈprəuvəu) *n., pl.* **+vos.** another name for a **Provisional.**

prov·o+ca+tion (ˌprɒvəˈkeɪʃən) *n.* **1.** the act of provoking or inciting. **2.** something that causes indignation, anger, etc. **3.** *English criminal law.* words or conduct that incite a person to attack another with fatal results.

pro+voc·a+tive (prəˈvɒkətɪv) *adj.* acting as a stimulus or incitement, esp. to anger or sexual desire; provoking: *a provocative woman; a provocative remark.* —**pro+ˈvoc·a+tive+ly** *adv.* —**pro+ˈvoc·a+tive+ness** *n.*

pro+voke (prəˈvəuk) *vb.* (*tr.*) **1.** to anger or infuriate. **2.** to cause to act or behave in a certain manner; incite or stimulate. **3.** to promote (certain feelings, esp. anger, indignation, etc.) in a person. **4.** *Obsolete.* to summon. [C15: from Latin *prōvocāre* to call forth, from *vocāre* to call] —**pro+ˈvok+ing+ly** *adv.*

pro+vo+lo+ne (ˌprəuvəˈləunɪ) *n.* a mellow, pale yellow, soft, and sometimes smoked cheese, made of cow's milk: usually moulded in the shape of a pear. [Italian, from *provola,* apparently from Medieval Latin *probula* cheese made from buffalo milk]

prov+ost (ˈprɒvəst) *n.* **1.** an appointed person who superintends or presides. **2.** the head of certain university colleges or schools. **3.** the principal magistrate of a Scottish burgh. **4.** *Church of England.* the senior dignitary of one of the more recent cathedral foundations. **5.** *R.C. Church.* **a.** the head of a cathedral chapter in England and some other countries. **b.** (formerly) the member of a monastic community second in authority under the abbot. **6.** (in medieval times) an overseer, steward, or bailiff in a manor. **7.** *Obsolete.* a prison warder. [Old English *profost,* from Medieval Latin *prōpositus* placed at the head (of), from Latin *praepōnere* to place first, from *prae-* before + *pōnere* to put]

pro+vost court (prəˈvəu) *n.* a military court for trying people charged with minor offences in an occupied area.

pro+vost guard (prəˈvəu) *n.* (esp. in the U.S.) a detachment under command of the provost marshal.

pro+vost mar+shal (prəˈvəu) *n.* the officer in charge of military police and thus responsible for military discipline in a large camp, area, or city.

prow (prau) *n.* the bow of a vessel. [C16: from Old French *proue,* from Latin *prora,* from Greek *prōra;* related to Latin *pro* in front]

prow+ess (ˈprauɪs) *n.* **1.** outstanding or superior skill or ability. **2.** bravery or fearlessness, esp. in battle. [C13: from Old French *proesce,* from *prou* good; see PROUD]

prowl (praul) *vb.* **1.** (when *intr.,* often foll. by *around* or *about*) to move stealthily around (a place) as if in search of prey or plunder. ~*n.* **2.** the act of prowling. **3. on the prowl. a.** moving around stealthily. **b.** zealously pursuing members of the opposite sex. [C14 *prollen,* of unknown origin] —ˈ**prowl+er** *n.*

prox. *abbrev. for* proximo (next month).

Prox·i+ma (ˈprɒksɪmə) *n.* a flare star in the constellation Centaurus that is the nearest star to the sun. It is a red dwarf of very low magnitude. Distance: 4.3 light years. Also called: **Proxima Centauri.** See also **Rigil Kent.**

prox·i+mal (ˈprɒksɪməl) *adj.* **1.** *Anatomy.* situated close to the centre, median line, or point of attachment or origin. Compare **distal. 2.** another word for **proximate.** —ˈ**prox·i+mal+ly** *adv.*

prox·i+mate (ˈprɒksɪmɪt) *or* **prox·i+mal** *adj.* **1.** next or nearest in space or time. **2.** very near; close. **3.** immediately preceding or following in a series. **4.** a less common word for **approximate.** [C16: from Late Latin *proximāre* to draw near, from Latin *proximus* next, from *prope* near] —ˈ**prox·i+mate+ly** *adv.* —ˈ**prox·i+mate+ness** *n.* —ˌ**prox·i+ˈma+tion** *n.*

prox+im+i·ty (prɒkˈsɪmɪtɪ) *n.* **1.** nearness in space or time. **2.** nearness or closeness in a series. [C15: from Latin *proximitās* closeness; see PROXIMATE]

prox+im+i·ty fuse *n.* an electronically triggered device designed to detonate an explosive charge in a missile, etc., at a predetermined distance from the target.

prox·i+mo (ˈprɒksɪməu) *adv. Now rare except when abbreviated in formal correspondence.* in or during the next or coming month: *a letter of the seventh proximo.* Abbrev.: **prox.** Compare **instant, ultimo.** [C19: from Latin: in or on the next, from *proximus* next]

prox·y (ˈprɒksɪ) *n., pl.* **prox·ies. 1.** a person authorized to act on behalf of someone else; agent: *to vote by proxy.* **2.** the authority, esp. in the form of a document, given to a person to act on behalf of someone else. [C15 *prokesye,* contraction of *procuracy,* from Latin *prōcūrātiō* procuration; see PROCURE]

prs. *abbrev. for* pairs.

prude (pru:d) *n.* a person who affects or shows an excessively modest, prim, or proper attitude, esp. regarding sex. [C18: from French, from *prudefemme,* from Old French *prode femme* respectable woman; see PROUD] —**'prud·ish** *adj.* —**'prud·ish·ly** *adv.* —**'prud·ish·ness** *or* **'prud·er·y** *n.*

pru·dence ('pru:dəns) *n.* **1.** caution in practical affairs; discretion or circumspection. **2.** care taken in the management of one's resources. **3.** consideration for one's own interests. **4.** the condition or quality of being prudent.

pru·dent ('pru:dᵊnt) *adj.* **1.** discreet or cautious in managing one's activities; circumspect. **2.** practical and careful in providing for the future. **3.** exercising good judgment or common sense. [C14: from Latin *prūdēns* farsighted, contraction of *prōvidens* acting with foresight; see PROVIDENT] —**'pru·dent·ly** *adv.* —**'pru·dent·ness** *n.*

pru·den·tial (pru:'dɛnʃəl) *adj.* **1.** characterized by or resulting from prudence. **2.** exercising prudence or sound judgment. —**pru·'den·tial·ly** *adv.*

Pru·den·tius (pru:'dɛnʃəs) *n.* **Au·re·li·us Clem·ens** (ɔ:'ri:lɪəs 'klɛmɛnz). 348–410 A.D., Latin Christian poet, born in Spain. His works include the allegory *Psychomachia.*

Pru·d'hon (*French* pry'dɔ̃) *n.* **Pierre Paul** (pjɛ:r 'pɔl). 1758–1823, French painter, noted for the romantic and mysterious aura of his portraits.

pru·i·nose ('pru:ɪ,nəʊs, -,nəʊz) *adj. Botany.* coated with a powdery or waxy bloom. [C19: from Latin *pruīnōsus* frost-covered, from *pruīna* hoarfrost]

prune[1] (pru:n) *n.* **1.** a purplish-black partially dried fruit of any of several varieties of plum tree. **2.** *Slang, chiefly Brit.* a dull, uninteresting, or foolish person. [C14: from Old French *prune,* from Latin *prūnum* plum, from Greek *prounon*]

prune[2] (pru:n) *vb.* **1.** to remove (dead or superfluous twigs, branches, etc.) from (a tree, shrub, etc.), esp. by cutting off. **2.** to remove (anything undesirable or superfluous) from (a book, etc.). [C15: from Old French *proignier* to clip; probably from *provigner* to prune vines, from *provain* layer (of a plant,) from Latin *propāgo* a cutting] —**'prun·a·ble** *adj.* —**'prun·er** *n.*

prune[3] (pru:n) *vb.* an archaic word for **preen.**

pru·nel·la (pru:'nɛlə), **pru·nelle** (pru:'nɛl), *or* **pru·nel·lo** (pru:'nɛləʊ) *n.* a strong fabric, esp. a twill-weave worsted, used for gowns and the uppers of some shoes. [C17: perhaps from PRUNELLE, with reference to the colour of the cloth]

pru·nelle (pru:'nɛl) *n.* a green French liqueur made from sloes. [C18: from French: a little plum, from *prune* PRUNE[1]]

prun·ing hook *n.* a tool with a curved steel blade terminating in a hook, used for pruning.

pru·ri·ent ('prʊərɪənt) *adj.* **1.** unusually or morbidly interested in sexual thoughts or practices. **2.** exciting or encouraging lustfulness; erotic. [C17: from Latin *prūrīre* to lust after] —**'pru·ri·ence** *n.* —**'pru·ri·ent·ly** *adv.*

pru·ri·go (prʊə'raɪgəʊ) *n.* a chronic inflammatory disease of the skin characterized by the formation of papules and intense itching. [C19: from Latin: an itch] —**pru·ri·gi·nous** (prʊə'rɪdʒɪnəs) *adj.*

pru·ri·tus (prʊə'raɪtəs) *n. Pathol.* **1.** any intense sensation of itching. **2.** any of various conditions characterized by intense itching. [C17: from Latin: an itching; see PRURIENT] —**pru·rit·ic** (prʊə'rɪtɪk) *adj.*

Prus. *abbrev. for* Prussia(n).

Prus·sia ('prʌʃə) *n.* a former German state in N and central Germany, extending from France and the Low Countries to the Baltic Sea and Poland: developed as the chief military power of the Continent, leading the North German Confederation from 1867–71, when the German Empire was established; dissolved in 1947 and divided between East and West Germany, Poland, and the Soviet Union. Area: (in 1939) 294 081 sq. km (113 545 sq. miles). German name: **Preussen.**

Prus·sian ('prʌʃən) *adj.* **1.** of, relating to, or characteristic of Prussia or its people, esp. of the Junkers and their formal military tradition. ~*n.* **2.** a German native or inhabitant of Prussia. **3.** a member of a Baltic people formerly inhabiting the coastal area of the SE Baltic. **4.** See **Old Prussian.**

Prus·sian blue *n.* **1.** a dark blue insoluble crystalline compound of iron, ferric ferrocyanide, used as a pigment in paints and fabric printing. Formula: $Fe_4[Fe(CN)_6]_3$. **2. a.** the blue or deep greenish-blue colour of this pigment. **b.** (*as adj.*): *a Prussian-blue carpet.*

Prus·sian·ism ('prʌʃə,nɪzəm) *n.* the ethos of the Prussian state and aristocracy, esp. militarism and stern discipline.

Prus·sian·ize *or* **Prus·sian·ise** ('prʌʃə,naɪz) *vb.* (*tr.*) to make Prussian in character, esp. with respect to military matters. —**,Prus·sian·i·'za·tion** *or* **,Prus·sian·i·'sa·tion** *n.*

prus·si·ate ('prʌʃɪɪt) *n.* any cyanide, ferrocyanide, or ferricyanide.

prus·sic ac·id ('prʌsɪk) *n.* the weakly acidic extremely poisonous aqueous solution of hydrogen cyanide. [C18: from French *acide prussique* Prussian acid, so called because obtained from Prussian blue]

Prut (*Russian* prut) *n.* a river in E Europe, rising in the SW Ukrainian SSR and flowing generally southeast, forming part of the border between Rumania and the Soviet Union, to join the River Danube. Length: 853 km (530 miles).

pry[1] (praɪ) *vb.* **pries, pry·ing, pried.** **1.** (*intr.;* often foll. by *into*) to make an impertinent or uninvited inquiry (about a private matter, topic, etc.). ~*n., pl.* **pries.** **2.** the act of prying. **3.** a person who pries. [C14: of unknown origin]

pry[2] (praɪ) *vb.* **pries, pry·ing, pried.** the U.S. word for **prise.** [C14: of unknown origin]

pry·er ('praɪə) *n.* a variant spelling of **prier.**

Prynne (prɪn) *n.* **Wil·liam.** 1600–69, English Puritan leader and pamphleteer, whose ears were cut off in punishment for his attacks on Laud.

pryt·a·ne·um (,prɪtə'ni:əm) *n., pl.* **·ne·a** (-'ni:ə). the public hall of a city in ancient Greece. [Latin, from Greek *prutaneion,* from *prutanis, prutaneus*]

Prze·myśl (*Polish* 'pʃɛmɪʃl) *n.* a city in SE Poland, near the border with the Soviet Union on the San River: a fortress in the early Middle Ages; belonged to Austria (1722–1918). Pop.: 54 800 (1972 est.).

Prze·wal·ski's horse (,pɜ:ʒə'vælskɪz) *n.* a rare wild horse, *Equus przewalskii,* of W Mongolia, having an erect mane and no forelock. [C19: named after the Russian explorer Nikolai Mikhailovich *Przewalski* (1839–1888), who discovered it]

P.S. *abbrev. for:* **1.** Passenger Steamer. **2.** phrase structure. **3.** Police Sergeant. **4.** Also: **p.s.** postscript. **5.** private secretary. **6.** prompt side.

ps. *abbrev. for* pieces.

Ps. *or* **Psa.** *Bible. abbrev. for* Psalm.

psalm (sɑ:m) *n.* **1.** (*often cap.*) any of the 150 sacred songs, lyric poems, and prayers that together constitute a book (Psalms) of the Old Testament. **2.** a musical setting of one of these poems. **3.** any sacred song or hymn. [Old English, from Late Latin *psalmus,* from Greek *psalmos* song accompanied on the harp, from *psallein* to play (the harp)] —**'psalm·ic** *adj.*

psalm·ist ('sɑ:mɪst) *n.* the composer of a psalm or psalms, esp. (when *cap.* and preceded by *the*) David, traditionally regarded as the author of the Book of Psalms.

psalm·o·dy ('sɑ:mədɪ, 'sæl-) *n., pl.* **·dies.** **1.** the act of singing psalms or hymns. **2.** the art or practice of the setting to music or singing of psalms. —**'psalm·o·dist** *n.* —**psalm·od·ic** (sɑ:'mɒdɪk, sæl-) *adj.*

Psalms (sɑ:mz) *n.* the collection of 150 psalms in the Old Testament, the full title of which is **The Book of Psalms.**

Psal·ter ('sɔ:ltə) *n.* **1.** another name for **Psalms,** esp. in the version in the Book of Common Prayer. **2.** a translation, musical, or metrical version of the Psalms. **3.** a devotional or liturgical book containing a version of Psalms, often with a musical setting. [Old English *psaltere,* from Late Latin *psaltērium,* from Greek *psaltērion* stringed instrument, from *psallein* to play a stringed instrument]

psal·ter·i·um (sɔ:l'tɪərɪəm) *n., pl.* **·ter·i·a** (-'tɪərɪə). the third compartment of the stomach of ruminants, between the reticulum and abomasum. Also called: **omasum.** [C19: from Latin *psaltērium* PSALTER; from the similarity of its folds to the pages of a book]

psal·ter·y ('sɔ:ltərɪ) *n., pl.* **·ter·ies.** *Music.* an ancient stringed instrument similar to the lyre, but having a trapezoidal sounding board over which the strings are stretched.

psam·mite ('sæmaɪt) *n.* a rare name for **sandstone.** [C19: from Greek *psammos* sand] —**psam·mit·ic** (sæ'mɪtɪk) *adj.*

p's and q's *pl. n.* behaviour within social conventions; manners (esp. in the phrase **to mind one's p's and q's**). [perhaps alluding to a child's difficulty in distinguishing these letters when learning to write]

pse·phite ('si:faɪt) *n.* any rock, such as a breccia, that consists of large fragments embedded in a finer matrix. [C19: via French from Greek *psēphos* a pebble] —**pse·phit·ic** (si:'fɪtɪk) *adj.*

pse·phol·o·gy (sɛ'fɒlədʒɪ) *n.* the statistical and sociological study of elections. [C20: from Greek *psephos* pebble, vote + -LOGY, from the ancient Greeks' custom of voting with pebbles] —**pseph·o·log·i·cal** (,sɛfə'lɒdʒɪkᵊl) *adj.* —**,pseph·o·'log·i·cal·ly** *adv.* —**pse·'phol·o·gist** *n.*

pseud (sju:d) *n.* **1.** *Slang.* a false, artificial, or pretentious person. ~*adj.* **2.** another word for **pseudo.**

pseud. *abbrev. for* pseudonym.

pseud·ax·is (sju:'dæksɪs) *n. Botany.* another name for **sympodium.**

Pseud·e·pig·ra·pha (,sju:dɪ'pɪgrəfə) *pl. n.* various Jewish writings from the first century B.C. to the first century A.D. that claim to have been divinely revealed but which have been excluded from the Greek canon of the Old Testament. Also called (R.C. Church): **Apocrypha.** [C17: from Greek *pseudepigraphos* falsely entitled, from PSEUDO- + *epigraphein* to inscribe] —**Pseud·ep·i·graph·ic** (,sju:dɛpɪ'græfɪk), **,Pseud·ep·i·'graph·i·cal,** *or* **,Pseud·e·'pig·ra·phous** *adj.*

pseu·do ('sju:dəʊ) *adj. Informal.* not genuine; pretended.

pseu·do- *or sometimes before a vowel* **pseud-** *combining form.* **1.** false, pretending, or inauthentic: *pseudo-intellectual.* **2.** having a close resemblance to: *pseudopodium.* [from Greek *pseudēs* false, from *pseudein* to lie]

pseu·do·carp ('sju:dəʊ,kɑ:p) *n.* a fruit, such as the strawberry and apple, that includes parts other than the ripened ovary. Also called: **false fruit, accessory fruit.** —**,pseu·do·'car·pous** *adj.*

,pseu·do·an·'tique *adj.*
,pseu·do·ar·'cha·ic *adj.*
,pseu·do·,a·ris·to·'crat·ic *adj.*
,pseu·do·ar·'tis·tic *adj.*
,pseu·do·,bi·o·'graph·ic *or*
,pseu·do·,bi·o·'graph·i·cal *adj.*
,pseu·do-Bo·'he·mi·an *adj.*
,pseu·do·'clas·sic *or*
,pseu·do·'clas·si·cal *adj.*
,pseu·do·'clas·si·cism *n.*
,pseu·do·'cul·ti·,vat·ed *adj.*
,pseu·do·,dem·o·'crat·ic *adj.*

pseu·do+her+maph+ro+dit+ism (ˌsjuːdəʊhɜːˈmæfrədaɪˌtɪzəm) *n.* the congenital condition of having the organs of reproduction of one sex and the external genitalia, usually malformed, of the opposite sex. Compare **hermaphroditism.**

pseu·do-in·tran+si+tive *adj.* denoting an occurrence of a normally transitive verb in which a direct object is not explicitly stated or forms the subject of the sentence, as in *Margaret is cooking* or *these apples cook well.*

pseu·do+morph (ˈsjuːdəʊˌmɔːf) *n.* a mineral that has an uncharacteristic crystalline form as a result of assuming the shape of another mineral that it has replaced. —ˌ**pseu·do+ˈmor+phic** *or* ˌ**pseu·do+ˈmor+phous** *adj.* —ˌ**pseu·do+ˈmor+phism** *n.*

pseu·do+mu+tu+al+i·ty (ˌsjuːdəʊˌmjuːtjʊˈælɪtɪ) *n., pl.* **·ties.** *Psychol.* a relationship between two persons in which conflict of views or opinions is solved by simply ignoring it.

pseu·do+nym (ˈsjuːdəˌnɪm) *n.* a fictitious name adopted, esp. by an author. [C19: via French from Greek *pseudōnumon*] —ˌ**pseu·do+ˈnym+i·ty** *n.*

pseu+don·y+mous (sjuːˈdɒnɪməs) *adj.* **1.** having or using a false or assumed name. **2.** writing or having been written under a pseudonym. —**pseu+ˈdon·y+mous+ly** *adv.*

pseu·do+po+di·um (ˌsjuːdəʊˈpəʊdɪəm) *n., pl.* **+di·a** (-dɪə). a temporary projection from the cell of a protozoan, leucocyte, etc., used for feeding and locomotion.

psf *or* **p.s.f.** *abbrev. for* pounds per square foot.

pshaw (pʃɔː) *interj. Becoming rare.* an exclamation of disgust, impatience, disbelief, etc.

psi *or* **p.s.i.** *abbrev. for* pounds per square inch.

psi (psaɪ) *n.* the 23rd letter of the Greek alphabet (Ψ, ψ), a composite consonant, transliterated as *ps.*

psia *abbrev. for* pounds per square inch, absolute.

psid *abbrev. for* pounds per square inch, differential.

psig *abbrev. for* pounds per square inch, gauge.

psil·o+cy+bin (ˌsɪləˈsaɪbɪn, ˌsaɪlə-) *n.* a crystalline phosphate ester that is the active principle of the hallucinogenic fungus *Psilocybe mexicana.* Formula: $C_{12}H_{17}N_2O_4P$. [C20: from New Latin *Psilocybe* (from Greek *psilos* bare + *kubē head*) + -IN]

psi+lom+e·lane (sɪˈlɒmɪˌleɪn) *n.* a common black to grey secondary mineral consisting of hydrated basic oxide of manganese and barium: a source of manganese. Formula: $BaMn_9O_{16}(OH)_4$. [C19: from Greek *psilos* bare + *melas* black]

psi par+ti+cle *n.* a type of elementary particle thought to be formed from charmed quarks. See **charm** (sense 7).

psit+ta+cine (ˈsɪtəˌsaɪn, -sɪn) *adj.* of, relating to, or resembling a parrot. [C19: from Late Latin *psittacīnus,* from Latin *psittacus* a parrot]

psit+ta+co+sis (ˌsɪtəˈkəʊsɪs) *n.* a viral disease of parrots and other birds that can be transmitted to man, in whom it produces inflammation of the lungs and pneumonia. Also called: **parrot fever.** [C19: from New Latin, from Latin *psittacus* a parrot, from Greek *psittakos;* see -OSIS]

Pskov (*Russian* pskɔf) *n.* **1.** a city in the W Soviet Union, on the Velikaya River: one of the oldest Russian cities, at its height in the 13th and 14th centuries. Pop.: 151 000 (1975 est.). **2. Lake.** the S part of Lake Peipus in the W Soviet Union, linked to the main part by a channel 24 km (15 miles) long. Area: about 1000 sq. km (400 sq. miles).

pso+as (ˈsəʊəs) *n.* either of two muscles of the loins that aid in flexing and rotating the thigh. [C17: from New Latin, from Greek *psoai* (pl.)]

pso+ra+le·a (səˈreɪlɪə) *n.* any plant of the tropical and subtropical leguminous genus *Psoralea,* having curly leaves, white or purple flowers, and short one-seeded pods. See **breadroot.** [C19: via New Latin from Greek *psōraleos* mangy, from *psōra* mange, an allusion to the glandular dots of the plant]

pso+ri·a+sis (səˈraɪəsɪs) *n.* a skin disease characterized by the formation of reddish spots and patches covered with silvery scales: tends to run in families. [C17: via New Latin from Greek: itching disease, from *psōra* itch] —**pso+ri+at+ic** (ˌsɔːrɪˈætɪk) *adj.*

PSS, P.SS., *or* **p.ss.** *abbrev. for* postscripts.

psst (pst) *interj.* an exclamation of beckoning, esp. one made surreptitiously.

P.S.T. *abbrev. for* (in the U.S.) Pacific Standard Time.

P.S.V. *abbrev. for* public service vehicle.

psych. *abbrev. for:* **1.** psychological. **2.** psychology.

psych *or* **psyche** (saɪk) *vb. (tr.) Informal.* **1.** to psychoanalyse. **2.** (often foll. by *out*) **a.** to guess correctly the intentions of (another); outguess. **b.** to analyse or solve (a problem, etc. psychologically. **3.** to intimidate or frighten. **4.** (usually foll. by *up*) to prepare (oneself) for an action, performance, etc. [C20: shortened from PSYCHOANALYSE]

psy+chas+the·ni·a (ˌsaɪkæsˈθiːnɪə, -θɪˈniːə) *n. Psychiatry, obsolete.* any neurosis characterized by phobias, anxiety, or obsessions. [C20: from New Latin, from PSYCHO- + ASTHENIA] —**psy+chas+then+ic** (ˌsaɪkæsˈθɛnɪk) *adj.*

psy+che (ˈsaɪkɪ) *n.* the human mind or soul. [C17: from Latin, from Greek *psukhē* breath, soul; related to Greek *psukhein* to breathe]

Psy·che (ˈsaɪkɪ) *n. Greek myth.* a beautiful girl loved by Eros (Cupid), who became the personification of the soul.

psy·che·del·i·a (ˌsaɪkəˈdɛlɪə) *n.* (*functioning as sing. or pl.*) psychedelic objects, dress, music, etc.

psy·che·del+ic *or* **psy·cho+del+ic** (ˌsaɪkɪˈdɛlɪk) *adj.* **1.** relating to or denoting new or altered perceptions or sensory experiences, as through the use of hallucinogenic drugs. **2.** denoting any of the drugs, esp. LSD, that produce these effects. **3.** *Informal.* (of painting, fabric design, etc.) having the vivid colours and complex patterns popularly associated with the visual effects of psychedelic states. [C20: from PSYCHE + Greek *delos* visible] —ˌ**psy·che·ˈdel·i·cal+ly** *or* ˌ**psy·cho+ˈdel·i+cal+ly** *adv.*

psy+chi·a+try (saɪˈkaɪətrɪ) *n.* the branch of medicine concerned with the diagnosis and treatment of mental disorders. —**psy+chi+at+ric** (ˌsaɪkɪˈætrɪk) *or* ˌ**psy+chi+ˈat+ri+cal** *adj.* —ˌ**psy+chi+ˈat+ri+cal+ly** *adv.* —**psy+ˈchi·a+trist** *n.*

psy+chic (ˈsaɪkɪk) *adj.* **1. a.** outside the possibilities defined by natural laws, as mental telepathy. **b.** (of a person) sensitive to forces not recognized by natural laws. **2.** mental as opposed to physical; psychogenic. **3.** *Bridge.* (of a bid) based on less strength than would normally be required to make the bid. ~*n.* **4.** a person who is sensitive to parapsychological forces or influences. —**ˈpsy+chi+cal** *adj.* —**ˈpsy+chi+cal+ly** *adv.*

psy+chic de+ter+min+ism *n. Psychol.* the assumption, made esp. by Freud, that mental processes do not occur by chance but that a cause can always be found for them.

psy+chic en+er+giz+er *n. Chiefly U.S.* another name for **antidepressant.**

psy+cho (ˈsaɪkəʊ) *n., pl.* **+chos,** *adj.* a slang word for **psychopath** or **psychopathic.**

psy·cho- *or sometimes before a vowel* **psych-** *combining form.* indicating the mind or psychological or mental processes: *psychology; psychogenesis; psychosomatic.* [from Greek *psukhē* spirit, breath]

psy·cho+a·cous+tics (ˌsaɪkəʊəˈkuːstɪks) *n.* (*functioning as sing.*) *Psychol.* the study of the relationship between sounds and their physiological and psychological effects.

psy·cho+ac+tive (ˌsaɪkəʊˈæktɪv) *adj.* (of drugs such as LSD, opium, and the barbiturates) capable of affecting mental activity. Also: **psychotropic.**

psychoanal. *abbrev. for* psychoanalysis.

psy·cho+an·a+lyse *or* **psy·cho+an·a+lyze** (ˌsaɪkəʊˈænəˌlaɪz) *vb.* (*tr.*) to examine or treat (a person) by psychoanalysis. —ˌ**psy·cho+ˈan·a+lys+er** *or* ˌ**psy·cho+ˈan·a+ˌlyz+er** *n.*

psy·cho+a·nal·y·sis (ˌsaɪkəʊəˈnælɪsɪs) *n.* a method of studying the mind and treating mental and emotional disorders based on revealing and investigating the role of the unconscious mind. —**psy·cho+an·a+lyst** (ˌsaɪkəʊˈænəlɪst) *n.* —**psy·cho+an·a+lyt+ic** (ˌsaɪkəʊˌænəˈlɪtɪk) *or* ˌ**psy·cho+ˌan·a+ˈlyt·i·cal** *adj.* —ˌ**psy·cho+ˌan·a+ˈlyt·i·cal+ly** *adv.*

psy·cho+bi+ol+o·gy (ˌsaɪkəʊbaɪˈɒlədʒɪ) *n. Psychol.* the study of mental illness and processes in relation to the genetics, physiology, and environment of the patient. —**psy·cho+bi·o+log·i·cal** (ˌsaɪkəʊˌbaɪəˈlɒdʒɪkᵊl) *adj.* —ˌ**psy·cho+bi·o+ˈlog·i·cal+ly** *adv.* —ˌ**psy·cho+bi+ˈol·o+gist** *n.*

psy·cho+chem·i·cal (ˌsaɪkəʊˈkɛmɪkᵊl) *n.* **1.** any of various chemical compounds whose primary effect is the alteration of the normal state of consciousness. ~*adj.* **2.** of or relating to such chemical compounds.

psy·cho+dra+ma (ˈsaɪkəʊˌdrɑːmə) *n. Psychiatry.* a form of group therapy in which individuals act out, before an audience, situations from their past. —**psy·cho+dra+mat+ic** (ˌsaɪkəʊdrəˈmætɪk) *adj.*

psy·cho+dy+nam+ics (ˌsaɪkəʊdaɪˈnæmɪks) *n.* (*functioning as sing.*) *Psychol.* the study of mental processes and forces. —ˌ**psy·cho+dy+ˈnam+ic** *adj.* —ˌ**psy·cho+dy+ˈnam·i·cal+ly** *adv.*

psy·cho+gen+e·sis (ˌsaɪkəʊˈdʒɛnɪsɪs) *n. Psychol.* the study of the origin and development of personality, human behaviour, and mental processes. —**psy·cho+ge·net+ic** (ˌsaɪkəʊdʒɪˈnɛtɪk) *adj.* —ˌ**psy·cho+ge·ˈnet·i·cal+ly** *adv.*

psy·cho+gen+ic (ˌsaɪkəʊˈdʒɛnɪk) *adj. Psychol.* (esp. of disorders or symptoms) of mental, rather than organic, origin. —ˌ**psy·cho+ˈgen·i·cal+ly** *adv.*

psy+chog+no+sis (saɪˈkɒgnəsɪs) *Psychol.* ~*n.* **1.** the use of hypnosis to study mental phenomena. **2.** the study of personality by observation of outward bodily signs. —**psy+chog+nos+tic** (ˌsaɪkɒgˈnɒstɪk) *adj.*

psy·cho+his+to+ry (ˌsaɪkəʊˈhɪstərɪ, -ˈhɪstrɪ) *n., pl.* **+ries. 1.** biography based on psychological theories of personality development.

psy·cho+ki+ne·sis (ˌsaɪkəʊkɪˈniːsɪs, -kaɪ-) *n.* **1.** (in parapsychology) alteration of the state of an object by mental influence alone, without any physical intervention. **2.** *Psychiatry.* a state of violent uncontrolled motor activity. —**psy·cho+ki+net+ic** (ˌsaɪkəʊkɪˈnɛtɪk) *adj.*

psychol. *abbrev. for:* **1.** psychological. **2.** psychology.

psy·cho+lin+guis+tics (ˌsaɪkəʊlɪŋˈgwɪstɪks) *n.* (*functioning as sing.*) the psychology of language, including language acquisition by children, the mental processes underlying adult comprehension and production of speech, language disorders, etc. —ˌ**psy·cho+ˈlin+guist** *n.* —ˌ**psy·cho+lin+ˈguis+tic** *adj.*

psy·cho+log·i·cal (ˌsaɪkəˈlɒdʒɪkᵊl) *adj.* **1.** of or relating to psychology. **2.** of or relating to the mind or mental activity. **3.** having no real or objective basis; arising in the mind: *his*

ˌ**pseu·do-E·ˌliz·a·ˈbe+than** *adj.*
ˌ**pseu·do-ˈGeor·gi·an** *adj.*
ˌ**pseu·do-ˈGoth·ic** *adj.*
ˌ**pseu·do-ˈGre·cian** *adj.*
ˌ**pseu·do+his+ˈtor+ic** *or*
ˌ**pseu·do+his+ˈtor·i·cal** *adj.*
ˌ**pseu·do+ˈlit+er+ˌar·y** *adj.*
ˌ**pseu·do+ˌme·di+ˈe·val** *adj.*
ˌ**pseu·do+ˈmod+ern** *adj.*
ˌ**pseu·do+ˈmyth·i·cal** *adj.*
ˌ**pseu·do+ˌo·ri+ˈen·tal** *adj.*
ˌ**pseu·do+ˌpa·tri+ˈot·ic** *adj.*
ˌ**pseu·do+ˌphil·o+ˈsoph·i·cal** *adj.*
ˌ**pseu·do+pro+ˈfes+sion·al** *adj.*
ˌ**pseu·do+ˌpsy·cho+ˈlog·i·cal** *adj.*
ˌ**pseu·do+ˈschol·ar+ly** *adj.*
ˈ**pseu·do+ˌsci+ence** *n.*
ˌ**pseu·do+ˌsci+en+ˈtif+ic** *adj.*
ˌ**pseu·do+ˌso·cial+ˈis+tic** *adj.*
ˌ**pseu·do-Vic·ˈto·ri·an** *adj.*

backaches are all psychological. **4.** affecting the mind. —ˌ**psy·cho+'log·i+cal+ly** *adv.*
psy·cho+log·i+cal block *n.* See **block** (sense 19).
psy·cho+log·i+cal mo+ment *n.* the most appropriate time for producing a desired effect: *he proposed to her at the psychological moment.*
psy·cho+log·i+cal war+fare *n.* the military application of psychology, esp. to the manipulation of morale in time of war.
psy+chol·o+gism (saɪˈkɒləˌdʒɪzəm) *n.* **1.** the belief in the importance and relevance of psychology for other sciences. **2.** the belief that psychology is the basis for all other natural and social sciences. —**psy+ˌchol·o+'gist+ic** *adj.*
psy+chol·o+gize *or* **psy+chol·o+gise** (saɪˈkɒləˌdʒaɪz) *vb.* (*intr.*) **1.** to make interpretations of behaviour and mental processes. **2.** to carry out investigation in the field of psychology.
psy+chol·o·gy (saɪˈkɒlədʒɪ) *n., pl.* **·gies. 1.** the scientific study of all forms of human and animal behaviour, sometimes concerned with the methods through which behaviour can be modified. See also **analytic psychology, comparative psychology. 2.** *Informal.* the mental make-up or structure of an individual that causes him to think or act in the way he does. —**psy+'chol·o·gist** *n.*
psy·cho+met+rics (ˌsaɪkəʊˈmɛtrɪks) *n.* (*functioning as sing.*) **1.** the branch of psychology concerned with the design and use of psychological tests. **2.** the application of statistical and mathematical techniques to psychological testing.
psy+chom+e·try (saɪˈkɒmɪtrɪ) *Psychol.* ~*n.* **1.** measurement and testing of mental states and processes. See also **psychometrics. 2.** (in parapsychology) the supposed ability to deduce facts about events by touching objects related to them. —**psy·cho+met+ric** (ˌsaɪkəʊˈmɛtrɪk) *or* ˌ**psy·cho+'met+ri+cal** *adj.* —ˌ**psy·cho+'met+ri+cal+ly** *adv.* —**psy·cho+me·tri+cian** (ˌsaɪkəʊməˈtrɪʃən) *or* **psy+'chom+e·trist** *n.*
psy·cho+mo+tor (ˌsaɪkəʊˈməʊtə) *adj.* of, relating to, or characterizing movements of the body associated with mental activity.
psy·cho+neu+ro+sis (ˌsaɪkəʊnjʊˈrəʊsɪs) *n., pl.* **+ro+ses** (-ˈrəʊsiːz). another word for **neurosis.** —**psy·cho+neu+rot+ic** (ˌsaɪkəʊnjʊˈrɒtɪk) *adj.*
psy·cho+path (ˈsaɪkəʊˌpæθ) *n.* a person afflicted with a personality disorder characterized by a tendency to commit antisocial and sometimes violent acts and a failure to feel guilt for such acts. —ˌ**psy·cho+'path+ic** *adj.* —ˌ**psy·cho+'path+i·cal+ly** *adv.*
psy·cho+path+ic per+son+al+i+ty *n. Psychiatry.* an antisocial personality characterized by the failure to develop any sense of moral responsibility and the capability of performing violent or antisocial acts.
psy·cho+pa+thol+o·gy (ˌsaɪkəʊpəˈθɒlədʒɪ) *n.* the scientific study of mental disorders. —**psy·cho+path·o+log·i·cal** (ˌsaɪkəʊˌpæθəˈlɒdʒɪkᵊl) *adj.* —ˌ**psy·cho+pa+'thol·o+gist** *n.*
psy+chop·a·thy (saɪˈkɒpəθɪ) *n. Psychiatry.* **1.** another name for **psychopathic personality. 2.** any mental disorder or disease.
psy·cho+phar+ma+col+o·gy (ˌsaɪkəʊˌfɑːməˈkɒlədʒɪ) *n.* the study of drugs that affect the mind. —**psy·cho+phar+ma+co+log·i·cal** (ˌsaɪkəʊˌfɑːməkəˈlɒdʒɪkᵊl) *adj.* —ˌ**psy·cho+ˌphar+ma+'col·o+gist** *n.*
psy·cho+phys+ics (ˌsaɪkəʊˈfɪzɪks) *n.* (*functioning as sing.*) the branch of psychology concerned with the relationship between physical stimuli and the effects they produce in the organism. —ˌ**psy·cho+'phys+i·cal** *adj.*
psy·cho+phys·i+ol+o·gy (ˌsaɪkəʊˌfɪzɪˈɒlədʒɪ) *n.* the branch of psychology concerned with the physiological basis of mental processes. —**psy·cho+phys·i·o+log·i·cal** (ˌsaɪkəʊˌfɪzɪəˈlɒdʒɪkᵊl) *adj.* —ˌ**psy·cho+ˌphys·i+'ol·o+gist** *n.*
psy·cho+sex+u·al (ˌsaɪkəʊˈsɛksjʊəl) *adj.* of or relating to the mental aspects of sex, such as sexual fantasies. —ˌ**psy·cho+ˌsex·u+'al+i+ty** *n.* —ˌ**psy·cho+'sex·u+al+ly** *adv.*
psy+cho+sis (saɪˈkəʊsɪs) *n., pl.* **+cho+ses** (-ˈkəʊsiːz). any form of severe mental disorder in which the individual's contact with reality becomes highly distorted. Compare **neurosis.** [C19: New Latin, from PSYCHO- + -OSIS]
psy·cho+so+cial (ˌsaɪkəʊˈsəʊʃəl) *adj.* of or relating to processes or factors that are both social and psychological in origin.
psy·cho+so+mat+ic (ˌsaɪkəʊsəˈmætɪk) *adj.* of or relating to disorders, such as stomach ulcers, thought to be caused or aggravated by psychological stress.
psy·cho+sur+ger·y (ˌsaɪkəʊˈsɜːdʒərɪ) *n.* any surgical procedure on the brain, such as a frontal lobotomy, to relieve serious mental disorders. —**psy·cho+sur+gi+cal** (ˌsaɪkəʊˈsɜːdʒɪkᵊl) *adj.*
psy·cho+tech+nics (ˌsaɪkəʊˈtɛknɪks) *n.* (*functioning as sing.*) *Psychol, U.S.* the use of psychological knowledge and methods in the modification and control of human behaviour. —ˌ**psy·cho+'tech+ni+cal** *adj.* —**psy·cho+tech+ni+cian** (ˌsaɪkəʊtɛkˈnɪʃən) *n.*
psy·cho+ther·a+py (ˌsaɪkəʊˈθɛrəpɪ) *or* **psy·cho+ther·a+peu+tics** (ˌsaɪkəʊˌθɛrəˈpjuːtɪks) *n.* the use of psychological (as opposed to physical) methods to treat mental disorders. —ˌ**psy·cho+ˌther·a+'peu+tic** *adj.* —ˌ**psy·cho+ˌther·a+'peu+ti+cal+ly** *adv.* —ˌ**psy·cho+'ther·a+pist** *n.*
psy+chot+ic (saɪˈkɒtɪk) *Psychiatry.* ~*adj.* **1.** of, relating to, or characterized by psychosis. ~*n.* **2.** a person suffering from psychosis. —**psy+'chot·i+cal+ly** *adv.*
psy+chot·o+mi+met+ic (saɪˌkɒtəʊmɪˈmɛtɪk) *adj.* (of drugs such as LSD and mescaline) capable of inducing psychotic symptoms.
psy·cho+trop+ic (ˌsaɪkəʊˈtrɒpɪk) *adj.* another word for **psychoactive.**
psy·chro- *combining form.* cold: *psychrometer.* [from Greek *psukhros*]
psy+chrom+e·ter (saɪˈkrɒmɪtə) *n.* a type of hygrometer consisting of two thermometers, one of which has a dry bulb and the other a bulb that is kept moist and ventilated. The difference between the readings of the thermometers gives an indication of atmospheric humidity. Also called: **wet-and-dry-bulb thermometer.**
psy+chro+phil+ic (ˌsaɪkrəʊˈfɪlɪk) *adj.* (esp. of bacteria) showing optimum growth at low temperatures.
psyl+lid (ˈsɪlɪd) *or* **psyl+la** (ˈsɪlə) *n.* any homopterous insect of the family *Psyllidae,* which comprises the jumping plant lice. See **plant louse** (sense 2). [C19: from Greek *psulla* flea]
Pt *the chemical symbol for* platinum.
pt. *abbrev. for:* **1.** part. **2.** patient. **3.** payment. **4.** pint. **5.** point. **6.** port. **7.** preterite.
Pt. (in place names) *abbrev. for:* **1.** Point. **2.** Port.
p.t. *abbrev. for:* **1.** past tense. **2.** pro tempore.
P.T. *abbrev. for:* **1.** physical therapy. **2.** physical training. **3.** postal telegraph. **4.** pupil teacher. **5.** (in Britain, formerly) purchase tax.
P.T.A. *abbrev. for:* **1.** Parent-Teacher Association. **2.** (in Britain) Passenger Transport Authority.
pta. *abbrev. for* peseta.
Ptah (ptɑː, tɑː) *n.* (in ancient Egypt) a major god worshipped as the creative power, esp. at Memphis.
ptar+mi+gan (ˈtɑːmɪgən) *n., pl.* **+gans** *or* **+gan. 1.** any of several arctic and subarctic grouse of the genus *Lagopus,* esp. *L. mutus,* which has a white winter plumage. **2.** (*sometimes cap.*) a created domestic fancy pigeon with ruffled or curled feathers on the wings and back. [C16: changed (perhaps influenced by Greek *pteron* wing) from Scottish Gaelic *tarmachan,* diminutive of *tarmach,* of obscure origin]
PT boat *n.* the U.S. term for an **MTB.**
Pte. *Military. abbrev. for* private.
P.T.E. *abbrev. for* (in Britain) Passenger Transport Executive.
pter·i+dol+o·gy (ˌtɛrɪˈdɒlədʒɪ) *n.* the branch of botany concerned with the study of ferns and related plants. [C19: from *pterido-,* from Greek *pteris* fern + -LOGY] —**pter·i+do+log·i+cal** (ˌtɛrɪdəʊˈlɒdʒɪkᵊl) *adj.* —ˌ**pter·i·'dol·o+gist** *n.*
pter·i+do+phyte (ˈtɛrɪdəʊˌfaɪt) *n.* any plant of the division *Pteridophyta,* reproducing by spores and having vascular tissue, roots, stems, and leaves: includes the ferns, horsetails, and club mosses. [C19: from *pterido-,* from Greek *pteris* fern + -PHYTE] —**pter·i+do+phyt+ic** (ˌtɛrɪdəʊˈfɪtɪk) *or* **pter·i+doph·y+tous** (ˌtɛrɪˈdɒfɪtəs) *adj.*
pter·i+do+sperm (ˈtɛrɪdəˌspɜːm) *n.* any extinct seed-producing fernlike plant of the group *Pteridospermae.* Also called: **seed fern.** [C19: from Greek *pteris* a fern + -SPERM]
pter·o- *combining form.* wing, feather, or a part resembling a wing: *pterodactyl.* [from Greek *pteron* wing, feather]
pter·o+dac+tyl (ˌtɛrəˈdæktɪl) *n.* any extinct flying reptile of the genus *Pterodactylus* and related genera, having membranous wings supported on an elongated fourth digit. See also **pterosaur.**
pter·o+pod (ˈtɛrəˌpɒd) *n.* any small marine gastropod mollusc of the group or order *Pteropoda,* in which the foot is expanded into two winglike lobes for swimming and the shell is absent or thin-walled. Also called: **sea butterfly.**
pter·o+saur (ˈtɛrəˌsɔː) *n.* any extinct flying reptile of the order *Pterosauria,* of Jurassic and Cretaceous times: included the pterodactyls. Compare **dinosaur, plesiosaur.**
-pter·ous *or* **-pter·an** *adj. combining form.* indicating a specified number or type of wings: *dipterous.* [from Greek *-pteros,* from *pteron* wing]
pter·y+goid pro+cess (ˈtɛrɪˌgɔɪd) *n. Anatomy.* either of two long bony plates extending downwards from each side of the sphenoid bone within the skull. [C18 *pterygoid,* from Greek *pterugoeidēs,* from *pterux* wing; see -OID]
pter·y+la (ˈtɛrɪlə) *n., pl.* **+lae** (-ˌliː). *Ornithol.* any of the tracts of skin that bear contour feathers, arranged in lines along the body of a bird. [C19: from New Latin, from Greek *pteron* feather + *hulē* wood, forest]
PTFE *abbrev. for* polytetrafluoroethylene.
ptg. *abbrev. for* printing.
pti+san (tɪˈzæn) *n.* **1.** grape juice drained off without pressure. **2.** a variant spelling of **tisane.** [C14: from Old French *tisane,* from Latin *ptisana,* from Greek *ptisanē* barley groats]
P.T.O. *or* **p.t.o.** *abbrev. for* please turn over.
pto+choc+ra+cy (təʊˈkɒkrəsɪ) *n., pl.* **+cies.** government by the poor. [C18: from Greek, from *ptochos* poor + -CRACY]
Ptol+e+mae+us (ˌtɒlɪˈmiːəs) *n.* a crater in the SE quadrant of the moon, about 140 kilometres (90 miles) in diameter.
Ptol+e+ma+ic (ˌtɒlɪˈmeɪɪk) *adj.* **1.** of or relating to the ancient astronomer Ptolemy or to his conception of the universe. **2.** of or relating to the Macedonian dynasty that ruled Egypt from the death of Alexander the Great (323 B.C.) to the death of Cleopatra (30 B.C.).
Ptol+e+ma+ic sys+tem *n.* the theory of planetary motion developed by Ptolemy from the hypotheses of earlier philosophers, stating that the earth lay at the centre of the universe with the sun, the moon, and the known planets revolving around it in complicated orbits. Beyond the largest of these orbits lay a sphere of fixed stars. See also **epicycle** (sense 1). Compare **Copernican system.**
Ptol+e+ma+ist (ˌtɒlɪˈmeɪɪst) *n.* a believer in or adherent of the Ptolemaic system of the universe.
Ptol·e·my (ˈtɒlɪmɪ) *n.* Latin name *Claudius Ptolemaeus.* 2nd-century A.D. Greek astronomer, mathematician, and geog-

rapher. His *Geography* was the standard geographical textbook until the discoveries of the 15th century. His system of astronomy (see **Ptolemaic system**), as expounded in the *Almagest*, remained undisputed until the Copernican system was evolved.

Ptol·e·my I *n.* called *Ptolemy Soter.* ?367–283 B.C., king of Egypt (323–285 B.C.), a general of Alexander the Great, who obtained Egypt on Alexander's death and founded the Ptolemaic dynasty: his capital Alexandria became the centre of Greek culture.

Ptol·e·my II *n.* called *Philadelphus.* 309–246 B.C., the son of Ptolemy I; king of Egypt (285–246). Under his rule the power, prosperity, and culture of Egypt was at its height.

pto+maine *or* **pto+main** ('təʊmeɪn) *n.* any of a group of amines, such as cadaverine or putrescine, formed by decaying organic matter. [C19: from Italian *ptomaina*, from Greek *ptoma* corpse, from *piptein* to fall]

pto+maine poi+son+ing *n.* a popular term for **food poisoning.** Ptomaines were once erroneously thought to be a cause of food poisoning.

pto+sis ('təʊsɪs) *n., pl.* **pto+ses** ('təʊsiːz). prolapse or drooping of a part, esp. the eyelid. [C18: from Greek: a falling] —**ptot+ic** ('tɒtɪk) *adj.*

pts. *abbrev. for:* **1.** parts. **2.** payments. **3.** pints. **4.** points. **5.** ports.

pty. *Chiefly Austral. abbrev. for* proprietary.

pty·a+lin ('taɪəlɪn) *n. Biochem.* an amylase secreted in the saliva of man and other animals. [C19: from Greek *ptualon* saliva, from *ptuein* to spit]

pty·a+lism ('taɪəˌlɪzəm) *n.* excessive secretion of saliva. [C17: from Greek *ptualismos*, from *ptualizein* to produce saliva, from *ptualon* saliva]

p-type *adj.* **1.** (of a semiconductor) having a density of mobile holes in excess of that of conduction electrons. **2.** associated with or resulting from the movement of holes in a semiconductor: *p-type conductivity.* Compare **n-type.**

Pu *the chemical symbol for* plutonium.

pub (pʌb) *Informal.* ~*n.* **1.** *Chiefly Brit.* a building with a bar and one or more public rooms licensed for the sale and consumption of alcoholic drink, often also providing light meals. Formal name: **public house. 2.** *Austral.* a hotel. ~*vb.* **pubs, pub+bing, pubbed. 3.** (*intr.*) to visit a pub or pubs (esp. in the phrase **go pubbing**).

pub. *abbrev. for:* **1.** public. **2.** publication. **3.** published. **4.** publisher. **5.** publishing.

pub-crawl *Slang, chiefly Brit.* ~*n.* **1.** a drinking tour of a number of pubs or bars. ~*vb.* **2.** (*intr.*) to make such a tour.

pu+ber+ty ('pjuːbətɪ) *n.* the period at the beginning of adolescence when the sex glands become functional and the secondary sexual characteristics emerge. Also called: **pubescence.** [C14: from Latin *pūbertās* maturity, from *pūber* adult] —'**pu+ber+tal** *adj.*

pu+ber+u+lent (pjʊ'bɛrjʊlənt) *adj. Biology.* covered with very fine down; finely pubescent. [C19: from Latin *pūber*]

pu+bes ('pjuːbiːz) *n., pl.* **pu+bes** ('pjuːbiːz). **1.** the region above the external genital organs, covered with hair from the time of puberty. **2.** pubic hair. **3.** the pubic bones. **4.** the plural of **pubis.** [from Latin]

pu+bes+cent (pjuː'bɛsᵊnt) *adj.* **1.** arriving or having arrived at puberty. **2.** (of certain plants and animals or their parts) covered with a layer of fine short hairs or down. [C17: from Latin *pūbēscere* to reach manhood, from *pūber* adult] —**pu+'bes+cence** *n.*

pu+bic ('pjuːbɪk) *adj.* of or relating to the pubes or pubis: *pubic hair.*

pu+bis ('pjuːbɪs) *n., pl.* **+bes** (-biːz). one of the three sections of the hipbone that forms part of the pelvis. [C16: shortened from New Latin *os pūbis* bone of the PUBES]

publ. *abbrev. for:* **1.** publication. **2.** published. **3.** publisher.

pub+lic ('pʌblɪk) *adj.* **1.** of, relating to, or concerning the people as a whole. **2.** open or accessible to all: *public gardens.* **3.** performed or made openly or in the view of all: *public proclamation.* **4.** (*prenominal*) well-known or familiar to people in general: *a public figure.* **5.** (*usually prenominal*) maintained at the expense of, serving, or for the use of a community: *a public library.* **6.** open, acknowledged, or notorious: *a public scandal.* **7. go public.** (of a private company) to issue shares for subscription by the public. ~*n.* **8.** the community or people in general. **9.** a part or section of the community grouped because of a common interest, activity, etc.: *the racing public.* [C15: from Latin *pūblicus*, changed from *pōplicus* of the people, from *populus* people]

pub·lic-ad·dress sys+tem *n.* a system of one or more microphones, amplifiers, and loudspeakers for increasing the sound level of speech or music, used in auditoriums, public gatherings, etc. Sometimes shortened to **PA system.**

pub+li+can ('pʌblɪkən) *n.* **1.** (in Britain) a person who keeps a public house. **2.** (in ancient Rome) a public contractor, esp. one who farmed the taxes of a province. [C12: from Old French *publicain*, from Latin *pūblicānus* tax gatherer, from *pūblicum* state revenues]

pub+lic as+sis+tance *n. U.S.* payment given to individuals by government agencies on the basis of need.

pub+li+ca+tion (ˌpʌblɪ'keɪʃən) *n.* **1.** the act or process of publishing a printed work. **2.** any printed work offered for sale or distribution. **3.** the act or an instance of making information public. **4.** the act of disseminating defamatory matter, esp. by communicating it to a third person. See **libel, slander.** Archaic word: **pub+lish+ment.** [C14: via Old French from Latin *pūblicātiō* confiscation of an individual's property, from *pūblicāre* to seize and assign to public use]

pub+lic com+pa+ny *n.* a limited company whose shares may be purchased by the public and traded freely on the open market. Compare **private company.**

pub+lic con+ve+ni+ence *n.* a public lavatory, esp. one in a public place.

pub+lic debt *n. Chiefly U.S.* **1.** the total financial obligations incurred by all governmental bodies of a nation. **2.** another name for **national debt.**

pub+lic de+fend+er *n.* (in the U.S.) a lawyer engaged at public expense to represent indigent defendants.

pub+lic do+main *n. U.S.* **1.** lands owned by a state or by the federal government. **2.** the status of a published work or invention upon which the copyright or patent has expired or which has not been patented or subject to copyright. It may thus be freely used by the public.

pub+lic en+e·my *n.* a notorious person, such as a criminal, who is regarded as a menace to the public.

pub+lic en+ter+prise *n.* economic activity by governmental organizations. Compare **private enterprise** (sense 1).

pub+lic gal+ler·y *n.* the gallery in a chamber of Parliament reserved for members of the public who wish to listen to the proceedings. Also called: **strangers' gallery.**

pub+lic house *n.* **1.** *Brit.* the formal name for **pub. 2.** *U.S.* an inn, tavern, or small hotel.

pub+li+cist ('pʌblɪsɪst) *n.* **1.** a person who publicizes something, esp. a press or publicity agent. **2.** a journalist. **3.** *Rare.* a person learned in public or international law.

pub+lic+i+ty (pʌ'blɪsɪtɪ) *n.* **1. a.** the technique or process of attracting public attention to people, products, etc., as by the use of the mass media. **b.** (as modifier): *a publicity agent.* **2.** public interest resulting from information supplied by such a technique or process. **3.** information used to draw public attention to people, products, etc. **4.** the state of being public. [C18: via French from Medieval Latin *pūblicitās*; see PUBLIC]

pub+li+cize *or* **pub+li+cise** ('pʌblɪˌsaɪz) *vb.* (*tr.*) to bring to public notice; advertise.

pub+lic law *n.* **1.** a law that applies to the public of a state or nation.

pub+lic lend+ing right *n.* the right of authors to receive payment when their books are borrowed from public libraries.

pub+lic+ly ('pʌblɪklɪ) *adv.* **1.** in a public manner; without concealment; openly. **2.** in the name or with the consent of the public.

pub+lic nui+sance *n.* **1.** *Law.* an illegal act causing harm to members of a particular community rather than to any individual. **2.** *Informal.* a person who is generally considered objectionable.

pub+lic o·pin+ion *n.* the attitude of the public, esp. as a factor in determining the actions of government.

pub+lic pros+e·cu+tor *n. Law.* an official in charge of prosecuting important cases.

Pub+lic Rec+ord Of+fice *n.* an institution in which official records are stored and kept available for inspection by the public.

pub+lic re+la·tions *n.* **1. a.** the practice of creating, promoting, or maintaining good will and a favourable image among the public towards an institution, public body, etc. **b.** the methods and techniques employed. **c.** (*as modifier*): *the public relations industry.* **2.** the condition of the relationship between an organization and the public. **3.** the professional staff employed to create, promote, or maintain a favourable relationship between an organization and the public. Abbrev.: **P.R.**

pub+lic school *n.* **1.** *Chiefly Brit.* a private independent fee-paying secondary school. **2.** any school that is part of a free local educational system.

pub+lic serv+ant *n.* an elected or appointed holder of a public office.

pub+lic serv+ice *n.* **1. a.** government employment. **b.** the management and administration of the affairs of a political unit, esp. the civil service. **2. a.** a service provided for the community: *buses provide a public service.* **b.** (*as modifier*): *a public-service announcement.*

pub·lic-serv·ice cor+po+ra+tion *n. U.S.* a private corporation that provides services to the community, such as telephone service, public transport.

pub·lic-spir·it+ed *adj.* having or showing active interest in public welfare or the good of the community.

pub+lic u·til+i·ty *n.* an enterprise concerned with the provision to the public of essentials, such as electricity or water. Also called (in the U.S.): **public-service corporation.**

pub+lic works *pl. n.* engineering projects and other constructions, financed and undertaken by a government for the community.

pub+lish ('pʌblɪʃ) *vb.* **1.** to produce and issue (printed matter) for distribution and sale. **2.** (*intr.*) to have one's written work issued for publication. **3.** (*tr.*) to announce formally or in public. **4.** (*tr.*) to communicate (defamatory matter) to someone other than the person defamed: *to publish a libel.* [C14: from Old French *puplier*, from Latin *pūblicāre* to make PUBLIC] —'**pub+lish+a·ble** *adj.*

pub+lish+er ('pʌblɪʃə) *n.* **1.** a company or person engaged in publishing periodicals, books, music, etc. **2.** *U.S.* the proprietor of a newspaper or his representative.

Puc·ci·ni (pʊ'tʃiːnɪ) *n.* **Gia·co·mo** ('dʒaːkomo). 1858–1924, Italian operatic composer, noted for the dramatic realism of his operas, which include *Manon Lescaut* (1893), *La Bohème* (1896), *Tosca* (1900), and *Madame Butterfly* (1904).

puc+coon (pə'ku:n) *n.* **1.** Also called: **alkanet.** any of several North American boraginaceous plants of the genus *Lithospermum,* esp. *L. canescens,* that yield a red dye. See also **gromwell. 2.** any of several other plants that yield a reddish dye, esp. the bloodroot (**red puccoon**). **3.** the dye from any of these plants. [C17: of Algonquian origin; see POKEWEED]

puce (pju:s) *n.* **a.** a colour varying from deep red to dark purplish-brown. **b.** (*as adj.*): *a puce carpet.* [C18: shortened from French *couleur puce* flea colour, from Latin *pūlex* flea]

puck[1] (pʌk) *n.* a small disc of hard rubber used in ice hockey. [C19: of unknown origin]

puck[2] (pʌk) *n.* a mischievous or evil spirit. [Old English *pūca,* of obscure origin] —**'puck+ish** *adj.*

puck·a ('pʌkə) *adj.* a less common spelling of **pukka.**

puck+er ('pʌkə) *vb.* **1.** to gather or contract (a soft surface such as the skin of the face) into wrinkles or folds, or (of such a surface) to be so gathered or contracted. ~*n.* **2.** a wrinkle, crease, or irregular fold. [C16: perhaps related to POKE², from the creasing into baglike wrinkles]

pud+ding ('pʊdɪŋ) *n.* **1.** a sweetened usually cooked dessert made in many forms and of various ingredients, such as flour, milk, and eggs, with fruit, etc. **2.** a savoury dish, usually soft and consisting partially of pastry or batter: *steak-and-kidney pudding.* **3.** the dessert course in a meal. **4.** a sausage-like mass of seasoned minced meat, oatmeal, etc., stuffed into a prepared skin or bag and boiled. [C13 *poding;* compare Old English *puduc* a wart, Low German *puddek* sausage] —**'pud+ding·y** *adj.*

pud+ding club *n. Slang.* the state of being pregnant (esp. in the phrase **in the pudding club**).

pud+ding stone *n.* a conglomerate rock in which there is a difference in colour and composition between the pebbles and the matrix.

pud+dle ('pʌdᵊl) *n.* **1.** a small pool of water, esp. of rain. **2.** a small pool of any liquid. **3.** a worked mixture of wet clay and sand that is impervious to water and is used to line a pond or canal. **4.** *Rowing.* the patch of eddying water left by the blade of an oar after completion of a stroke. ~*vb.* (*tr.*) **5.** to make (clay, etc.) into puddle. **6.** to subject (iron) to puddling. [C14 *podel,* diminutive of Old English *pudd* ditch, of obscure origin] —**'pud+dler** *n.* —**'pud+dly** *adj.*

pud+dling ('pʌdlɪŋ) *n.* **1.** a process for converting pig iron into wrought iron by heating it with ferric oxide in a furnace to oxidize the carbon. **2.** *Building.* the process of making a puddle.

pu+den+cy ('pju:dᵊnsɪ) *n.* modesty, shame, or prudishness. [C17: from Late Latin *pudentia,* from Latin *pudēre* to feel shame]

pu+den+dum (pju:'dɛndəm) *n., pl.* **+da** (-də). **1.** (*often pl.*) the human external genital organs collectively, esp. of a female. [C17: from Late Latin, from Latin *pudenda* the shameful (parts), from *pudēre* to be ashamed] —**pu+'den+dal** *or* **pu+dic** ('pju:dɪk) *adj.*

pudg·y ('pʌdʒɪ) *adj.* **pudg·i+er, pudg·i+est.** a variant spelling (esp. U.S.) of **podgy.** [C19: of uncertain origin; compare earlier *pudsy* plump, perhaps from Scottish *pud* stomach, plump child] —**'pudg·i+ly** *adv.* —**'pudg·i+ness** *n.*

Pud+sey ('pʊdzɪ) *n.* a town in N England, in West Yorkshire between Leeds and Bradford. Pop.: 38 127 (1971).

Pue+bla (*Spanish* 'pweβla) *n.* **1.** an inland state of S central Mexico, situated on the Anáhuac Plateau. Capital: Puebla. Pop.: 2 508 226 (1970). Area: 33 919 sq. km (13 096 sq. miles). **2.** a city in S Mexico, capital of Puebla state: founded in 1532; university (1537). Pop.: 482 155 (1975 est.). Full name: **Pue+bla de Za+ra+go+za** (ðe ˌsara'ɣosa).

pueb+lo ('pwɛbləʊ; *Spanish* 'pweβlo) *n., pl.* **+los** (-ləuz; *Spanish* -los). **1.** a communal village, built by certain Indians of the southwestern U.S. and parts of Latin America, consisting of one or more flat-roofed stone or adobe houses. **2.** (in Spanish America) a village or town. **3.** (in the Philippines) a town or township. [C19: from Spanish: people, from Latin *populus*]

Pueb+lo ('pwɛbləʊ) *n., pl.* **+lo** *or* **+los.** a member of any of the North American Indian peoples who live in pueblos, including the Tanoans, Zuñi, and Hopi.

pu+er+ile ('pjʊəraɪl) *adj.* **1.** exhibiting or characteristic of silliness; immature; trivial. **2.** of or characteristic of a child. [C17: from Latin *puerīlis* childish, from *puer* a boy] —**'pu+er+ile+ly** *adv.* —**pu+er+il+i·ty** (pjʊə'rɪlɪtɪ) *n.*

pu+er+il+ism ('pjʊərɪˌlɪzəm) *n. Psychiatry.* immature or childish behaviour by an adult.

pu+er+per+al (pju:'ɜ:pərəl) *adj.* of, relating to, or occurring during the puerperium. [C18: from New Latin *puerperālis* relating to childbirth; see PUERPERIUM]

pu+er+per+al fe+ver *n.* a serious, formerly widespread, form of blood poisoning caused by infection contracted during childbirth.

pu+er+per+al psy+cho+sis *n.* a mental disorder sometimes occurring in women after childbirth, characterized by deep depression, delusions of the child's death, and homicidal feelings towards the child.

pu+er+per+i·um (pjʊə'pɪərɪəm) *n.* the period following childbirth, lasting approximately six weeks, during which the uterus returns to its normal size and shape. [C17: from Latin: childbirth, from *puerperus* relating to a woman in labour, from *puer* boy + *parere* to bear]

Puer+to Ri·co ('pwɜ:təʊ 'ri:kəʊ, 'pwɛə-) *n.* an autonomous commonwealth (in association with the U.S.) occupying the smallest and easternmost of the Greater Antilles in the Caribbean: one of the most densely populated areas in the world; ceded by Spain to the U.S. in 1899. Capital: San Juan. Pop.: 3 087 000 (1975 est.). Area: 8674 sq. km (3349 sq. miles). Former name (until 1932): **Porto Rico.** Abbrev.: **P.R.** —**Puer+to Ri+can** *adj., n.*

puff (pʌf) *n.* **1.** a short quick draught, gust, or emission, as of wind, smoke, air, etc., esp. a forceful one. **2.** the amount of wind, smoke, etc., released in a puff. **3.** the sound made by or associated with a puff. **4.** an instance of inhaling and expelling the breath as in smoking. **5.** a swelling. **6.** a light aerated pastry usually filled with cream, jam, etc. **7.** a powder puff. **8.** exaggerated praise, as of a book, product, etc., esp. through an advertisement. **9.** a piece of clothing fabric gathered up so as to bulge in the centre while being held together at the edges. **10.** a loose piece of hair wound into a cylindrical roll, usually over a pad, and pinned in place in a coiffure. **11.** a less common word for **quilt** (sense 1). **12.** one's breath (esp. in the phrase **out of puff**). **13.** *Slang.* a male homosexual. **14.** a dialect word for **puffball.** ~*vb.* **15.** to blow or breathe or cause to blow or breathe in short quick draughts or blasts. **16.** (*tr.;* often foll. by *out;* usually passive) to cause to be out of breath. **17.** to take puffs or draws at (a cigarette, cigar, or pipe). **18.** to move with or by the emission of puffs: *the steam train puffed up the incline.* **19.** (often foll. by *up, out,* etc.) to swell, as with air, pride, etc. **20.** (*tr.*) to praise with exaggerated empty words, often in advertising. **21.** (*tr.*) to apply (cosmetic powder) from a powder puff to (the face). **22.** *Auctioneering.* to increase the price of (a lot) artificially by having an accomplice make false bids. [Old English *pyffan;* related to Dutch German *puffen,* Swiss *pfuffen,* Norwegian *puffa,* all of imitative origin]

puff ad+der *n.* **1.** a large African viper, *Bitis arietans,* that is yellowish-grey with brown markings and inflates its body when alarmed. **2.** another name for **hognose snake.**

puff+ball ('pʌfˌbɔ:l) *n.* any of various basidiomycetous saprophytic fungi of the genera *Calvatia* and *Lycoperdon,* having a round fruiting body that discharges a cloud of brown spores when mature.

puff+bird ('pʌfˌbɜ:d) *n.* any of various brownish tropical American birds of the family *Bucconidae,* having a large head: order *Piciformes* (woodpeckers, etc.).

puff+er ('pʌfə) *n.* **1.** a person or thing that puffs. **2.** Also called: **globefish.** any marine plectognath fish of the family *Tetraodontidae,* having an elongated spiny body that can be inflated to form a globe.

puff+er·y ('pʌfərɪ) *n., pl.* **+er·ies.** *Informal.* exaggerated praise, esp. in publicity or advertising.

puf+fin ('pʌfɪn) *n.* any of various northern diving birds of the family Alcidae (auks, etc.), esp. genera *Fratercula arctica* (**common** or **Atlantic puffin**), having a black-and-white plumage and a brightly coloured vertically flattened bill: order *Charadriiformes.* [C14: perhaps of Cornish origin]

puff pas+try *or U.S.* **puff paste** *n.* a dough used for making a rich flaky pastry for pies, rich pastries, etc.

puff-puff *n. Brit.* a children's name for a steam locomotive or railway train.

puff·y ('pʌfɪ) *adj.* **puff·i+er, puff·i+est. 1.** short of breath. **2.** swollen or bloated: *a puffy face.* **3.** pompous or conceited. **4.** blowing in gusts. —**'puff·i+ly** *adv.* —**'puff·i+ness** *n.*

pug[1] (pʌg) *n.* a small compact breed of dog with a smooth coat, lightly curled tail, and a short wrinkled nose. [C16: of uncertain origin] —**'pug+gish** *adj.*

pug[2] (pʌg) *vb.* **pugs, pug+ging, pugged.** (*tr.*) **1.** to mix or knead (clay) with water to form a malleable mass or paste, often in a **pug mill. 2.** to fill or stop with clay or a similar substance. [C19: of uncertain origin]

pug[3] (pʌg) *n.* a slang name for **boxer.** [C20: shortened from PUGILIST]

Pu+get Sound ('pju:dʒɪt) *n.* an inlet of the Pacific in NW Washington. Length: about 130 km (80 miles).

pug+ging ('pʌgɪŋ) *n.* material such as clay, mortar, sawdust, sand, etc., inserted between wooden flooring and ceiling to reduce the transmission of sound. Also called: **pug.**

pug+gree, pug+ree ('pʌgrɪ) *or* **pug+ga+ree, pug·a+ree** ('pʌgərɪ) *n.* **1.** the usual Indian word for **turban. 2.** a scarf, usually pleated, around the crown of some hats, esp. sun helmets. [C17: from Hindi *pagrī,* from Sanskrit *parikara*]

pu+gi+lism ('pju:dʒɪˌlɪzəm) *n.* the art, practice, or profession of fighting with the fists; boxing. [C18: from Latin *pugil* a boxer; related to *pugnus* fist, *pugna* a fight] —**ˌpu+gi+list** *n.* —**ˌpu+gi+'lis+tic** *adj.* —**ˌpu+gi+'lis+ti+cal+ly** *adv.*

Pu+glia ('puʎʎa) *n.* the Italian name for **Apulia.**

pug+na+cious (pʌg'neɪʃəs) *adj.* readily disposed to fight; belligerent. [C17: from Latin *pugnāx*] —**pug+'na+cious+ly** *adv.* —**pug+nac+i·ty** (pʌg'næsɪtɪ) *or* **pug+'na+cious+ness** *n.*

pug nose *n.* a short stubby upturned nose. [C18: from PUG¹] —**'pug-ˌnosed** *adj.*

Pug+wash con+fer+enc·es ('pʌgˌwɒʃ) *pl. n.* international peace conferences of scientists held regularly to discuss world problems. [C20: from *Pugwash,* Nova Scotia, where the first conference was held]

puis+ne ('pju:nɪ) *adj.* (esp. of a subordinate judge) of lower rank. [C16: from Anglo-French, from Old French *puisné* born later, from *puis* at a later date, from Latin *posteā* afterwards + *né* born, from *naistre* to be born, from Latin *nascī*]

pu+is+sance ('pju:ɪsᵊns, 'pwi:sɑ:ns) *n.* **1.** a competition in show jumping that tests a horse's ability to jump a limited number of large obstacles. **2.** *Archaic or poetic.* power. [C15: from Old French; see PUISSANT]

pu+is+sant ('pju:ɪsᵊnt) *adj. Archaic or poetic.* powerful. [C15: from Old French, ultimately from Latin *potēns* mighty, from *posse* to have power] —**'pu+is+sant+ly** *adv.*

puke (pju:k) *Slang.* ~*vb.* **1.** to vomit (matter). ~*n.* **2.** the act of vomiting. **3.** the matter vomited. [C16: probably of imitative origin; compare German *spucken* to spit]

puk·ka *or* **puck·a** ('pʌkə) *adj.* (esp. in India) properly or perfectly done, constructed, etc.: *a pukka road.* [C17: from Hindi *pakkā* firm, from Sanskrit *pakva*]

pul (pu:l) *n., pl.* **puls** *or* **pu·li** ('pu:lɪ). an Afghan monetary unit worth one hundredth of an afghani. [via Persian from Turkish: small coin, from Late Greek *phollis* bag for money, from Latin *follis* bag]

Pu·la (*Serbo-Croatian* 'pu:la) *n.* a port in NW Yugoslavia, in NW Croatia at the S tip of the Istrian Peninsula: made a Roman military base in 178 B.C.; became the main Austro-Hungarian naval station and passed to Italy in 1919, then to Yugoslavia in 1947. Pop.: 47 414 (1971). Latin name: **Pietas Julia.** Italian name: **Pola.**

pul·chri·tude ('pʌlkrɪˌtju:d) *n. Formal or literary.* physical beauty. [C15: from Latin *pulchritūdō,* from *pulcher* beautiful] —ˌ**pul·chri·'tud·i·nous** *adj.*

pule (pju:l) *vb.* (*intr.*) to cry plaintively; whimper. [C16: perhaps of imitative origin] —'**pul·er** *n.*

Pu·litz·er ('pulɪtsə) *n.* **Jo·seph.** 1847–1911, U.S. newspaper publisher, born in Hungary. He established the Pulitzer prizes.

Pu·litz·er prize *n.* one of a group of prizes established by Joseph Pulitzer and awarded yearly since 1917 for excellence in American journalism, literature, and music.

pull (pul) *vb.* (*mainly tr.*) **1.** (*also intr.*) to exert force on (an object) so as to draw it towards the source of the force. **2.** to exert force on so as to remove; extract: *to pull a tooth.* **3.** to strip of feathers, hair, etc.; pluck. **4.** to draw the entrails from (a fowl). **5.** to rend or tear. **6.** to strain (a muscle, ligament, or tendon) injuriously. **7.** (usually foll. by *off*) *Informal.* to perform or bring about: *to pull off a million-pound deal.* **8.** *Informal.* (often foll. by *on*) to draw out (a weapon) for use: *he pulled a knife on his attacker.* **9.** *Informal.* to attract: *the pop group pulled a crowd.* **10.** (*intr.;* usually foll. by *on* or *at*) to drink or inhale deeply: *to pull at one's pipe; pull on a bottle of beer.* **11.** to put on or make (a grimace): *to pull a face.* **12.** (also *intr.;* foll by *away, out, over,* etc.) to move (a vehicle) or (of a vehicle) be moved in a specified manner: *he pulled his car away from the roadside.* **13.** *Printing.* to take (a proof) from type. **14.** *Golf, baseball, etc.* to hit (a ball) so that it veers away from the direction in which the player intended to hit it (to the left for a right-handed player). **15.** *Cricket.* to hit (a ball pitched straight or on the off side) to the leg side. **16.** (*also intr.*) to row (a boat) or take a stroke of (an oar) in rowing. **17.** to be rowed by: *a racing shell pulls one, two, four, or eight oars.* **18.** (of a rider) to restrain (a horse), esp. to prevent it from winning a race. **19.** (*intr.*) (of a horse) to resist strongly the attempts of a rider to rein in or check it. **20. pull a fast one.** *Slang.* to play a sly trick. **21. pull apart** *or* **to pieces.** to criticize harshly. **22. pull your head in.** *Austral. informal.* be quiet! **23. pull (one's) punches. a.** *Boxing.* to restrain the force of one's blows, esp. when deliberately losing after being bribed, etc. **b.** *Informal.* to restrain the force of one's criticisms or actions. **24. pull one's weight.** *Informal.* to do a fair or proper share of a task. **25. pull strings.** *Brit. informal.* to exercise personal influence. **26. pull (someone's) leg.** *Informal.* to make fun of or tease. ~*n.* **27.** an act or an instance of pulling or being pulled. **28.** the force or effort used in pulling: *the pull of the moon affects the tides on earth.* **29.** the act or an instance of taking in drink or smoke. **30.** *Printing.* a proof taken from type: *the first pull was smudged.* **31.** something used for pulling, such as a knob or handle. **32.** *Informal.* special advantage or influence: *his uncle is chairman of the company, so he has quite a lot of pull.* **33.** *Informal.* the power to attract attention or support. **34.** a period of rowing. **35.** a single stroke of an oar in rowing. **36.** the act of pulling the ball in golf, cricket, etc. **37.** the act of checking or reining in a horse. **38.** the amount of resistance in a bowstring, trigger, etc. ~See also **pull about, pull back, pull down, pull in, pull off, pull on, pull out, pull through, pull together, pull up.** [Old English *pullian;* related to Icelandic *pūla* to beat] —'**pull·er** *n.*

pull a·bout *vb.* (*tr., adv.*) to handle roughly: *the thugs pulled the old lady about.*

pull back *vb.* (*adv.*) **1.** to return or be returned to a rearward position by pulling: *the army pulled back.* ~*n.* **pull·back. 2.** the act of pulling back. **3.** a device for restraining the motion of a mechanism, etc., or for returning it to its original position.

pull down *vb.* (*tr., adv.*) to destroy or demolish: *the old houses were pulled down.*

pul·let ('pulɪt) *n.* a young hen of the domestic fowl, less than one year old. [C14: from Old French *poulet* chicken, from Latin *pullus* a young animal or bird]

pul·ley ('pulɪ) *n.* **1.** a wheel with a grooved rim in which a rope, chain, or belt can run in order to change the direction or point of application of a force applied to the rope, etc. **2.** a number of such wheels pivoted in parallel in a block, used to raise heavy loads. **3.** a wheel with a flat, convex, or grooved rim mounted on a shaft and driven by or driving a belt passing around it. [C14 *poley,* from Old French *polie,* from Vulgar Latin *polidium* (unattested), apparently from Late Greek *polidion* (unattested) a little pole, from Greek *polos* axis]

pull in *vb.* (*adv.*) **1.** (*intr.;* often foll. by *to*) to reach a destination: *the train pulled in at the station.* **2.** (*intr.*) Also: **pull over.** (of a motor vehicle, driver, etc.) **a.** to draw in to the side of the road in order to stop or to allow another vehicle to pass. **b.** to stop (at a café, lay-by, etc.). **3.** (*tr.*) to draw or attract: *his appearance will pull in the crowds.* **4.** (*tr.*) *Brit. slang.* to arrest. **5.** (*tr.*) to earn or gain (money). ~*n.* **pull-in. 6.** *Brit.* a roadside café, esp. for lorry drivers.

Pull·man ('pulmən) *n., pl.* **·mans.** a luxurious railway coach. Also called: **Pullman car.** [C19: named after George M. *Pullman* (1831–97), its U.S. inventor]

pull off *vb.* (*tr.*) **1.** to remove (clothing) forcefully. **2.** (*adv.*) to succeed in performing (a difficult feat).

pull on *vb.* (*tr., adv.*) to don (clothing).

pul·lo·rum dis·ease (pu'lɔ:rəm) *n.* an acute serious bacterial disease of very young birds, esp. chickens, characterized by a whitish diarrhoea: caused by *Salmonella pullorum,* transmitted during egg production. Also called: **bacillary white diarrhoea.** [Latin *pullōrum* of chickens, from *pullus* chicken]

pull out *vb.* (*adv.*) **1.** (*tr.*) to extract. **2.** (*intr.*) to depart: *the train pulled out of the station.* **3.** *Military.* to withdraw or escape or be withdrawn or rescued, as from a difficult situation: *the troops were pulled out of the ruined city.* **4.** (*intr.*) (of a motor vehicle, driver, etc.) **a.** to draw away from the side of the road. **b.** to draw out from behind another vehicle to overtake. **5.** (*intr.*) to abandon a position or situation, esp. a dangerous or embarrassing one. **6.** (foll. by *of*) to level out or cause to level out (from a dive). ~*n.* **pull-out. 7.** an extra leaf of a book that folds out. **8.** a removable section of a magazine, etc. **9.** a flight manoeuvre during which an aircraft levels out after a dive.

pull·o·ver ('pulˌəuvə) *n.* a garment, esp. a sweater, that is pulled on over the head.

pull through *vb.* to survive or recover or cause to survive or recover, esp. after a serious illness or crisis. Also: **pull round.**

pull to·geth·er *vb.* **1.** (*intr., adv.*) to cooperate or work harmoniously. **2. pull oneself together.** *Informal.* to regain one's self-control or composure.

pul·lu·late ('pʌljuˌleɪt) *vb.* (*intr.*) **1.** (of animals, etc.) to breed rapidly or abundantly; teem; swarm. **2.** (of plants or plant parts) to sprout, bud, or germinate. [C17: from Latin *pullulāre* to sprout, from *pullulus* a baby animal, from *pullus* young animal] —ˌ**pul·lu·'la·tion** *n.*

pull up *vb.* (*adv.*) **1.** (*tr.*) to remove by the roots. **2.** (often foll. by *with* or *on*) to move level (with) or ahead (of) or cause to move level (with) or ahead (of), esp. in a race. **3.** to stop: *the car pulled up suddenly.* **4.** (*tr.*) to rebuke.

pul·mo·nar·y ('pʌlmənərɪ, -mənrɪ, 'pul-) *adj.* **1.** of, or relating to or affecting the lungs. **2.** having lungs or lunglike organs. [C18: from Latin *pulmōnārius,* from *pulmō* a lung; related to Greek *pleumōn* a lung]

pul·mo·nar·y ar·ter·y *n.* either of the two arteries that convey oxygen-depleted blood from the heart to the lungs.

pul·mo·nar·y vein *n.* any one of the four veins that convey oxygen-rich blood from the lungs to the heart.

pul·mo·nate ('pʌlmənɪt, 'pul-) *adj.* **1.** having lungs or lunglike organs. **2.** of, relating to, or belonging to the *Pulmonata,* a mostly terrestrial subclass or order of gastropod molluscs, including snails and slugs, in which the mantle is adapted as a lung. ~*n.* **3.** any pulmonate mollusc. [C19: from New Latin *pulmōnātus*]

pul·mon·ic (pʌl'mɒnɪk, pul-) *adj.* **1.** of or relating to the lungs; pulmonary. ~*n.* **2.** *Rare.* **a.** a person with lung disease. **b.** a drug or remedy for lung disease. [C17: from French *pulmonique,* from Latin *pulmō* a lung; see PULMONARY]

Pul·mo·tor ('pʌlˌməutə, 'pul-) *n. Trademark.* an apparatus for pumping oxygen into the lungs during artificial respiration.

pulp (pʌlp) *n.* **1.** soft or fleshy plant tissue, such as the succulent part of a fleshy fruit. **2.** a moist mixture of cellulose fibres, as obtained from wood, from which paper is made. **3.** *U.S.* a magazine or book containing trite or sensational material, and usually printed on cheap rough paper. **4.** *Dentistry.* the soft innermost part of a tooth, containing nerves and blood vessels. **5.** any soft soggy mass or substance. **6.** *Mining.* pulverized ore, esp. when mixed with water. ~*vb.* **7.** to reduce (a material or solid substance) to pulp or (of a material, etc.) to be reduced to pulp. **8.** (*tr.*) to remove the pulp from (fruit, etc.). [C16: from Latin *pulpa*]

pul·pit ('pulpɪt) *n.* **1.** a raised platform, usually surrounded by a barrier, set up in churches as the appointed place for preaching, leading in prayer, etc. **2.** any similar raised structure, such as a lectern. **3.** a medium for expressing an opinion, such as a column in a newspaper. **4.** (usually preceded by *the*) **a.** the preaching of the Christian message. **b.** the clergy or their message and influence. [C14: from Latin *pulpitum* a platform]

pulp·wood ('pʌlpˌwud) *n.* pine, spruce, or any other soft wood used to make paper.

pulp·y ('pʌlpɪ) *adj.* **pulp·i·er, pulp·i·est.** having a soft or soggy consistency. —'**pulp·i·ness** *n.*

pul·que ('pulkɪ; *Spanish* 'pulke) *n.* a light alcoholic drink from Mexico made from the juice of various agave plants, esp. the maguey. [C17: from Mexican Spanish, apparently from Nahuatl, from *puliuhqui* decomposed, since it will only keep for a day]

pul·sar ('pʌlˌsɑ:) *n.* any of a number of very small extremely dense stars first discovered in 1967, which rotate very fast emitting regular pulses of polarized radiation, esp. radio waves. They are thought to be neutron stars formed during supernova explosions.

pul·sate (pʌl'seɪt) *vb.* (*intr.*) **1.** to expand and contract with a rhythmical beat; throb. **2.** *Physics.* to vary in intensity, magnitude, size, etc.: *the current was pulsating.* **3.** to quiver or vibrate. [C18: from Latin *pulsāre* to push] —**pul·sa·tive** ('pʌlsətɪv) *adj.* —'**pul·sa·tive·ly** *adv.*

pul+sa+tile ('pʌlsəˌtaɪl) *adj.* beating rhythmically; pulsating or throbbing. —**pul+sa+til+i+ty** (ˌpʌlsə'tɪlɪtɪ) *n.*

pul+sat+ing star *n.* a type of variable star, the variation in brightness resulting from expansion and subsequent contraction of the star.

pul+sa+tion (pʌl'seɪʃən) *n.* **1.** the act of pulsating. **2.** *Physiol.* a rhythmic beating or pulsing esp. of the heart or an artery.

pul+sa+tor (pʌl'seɪtə) *n.* **1.** a device that stimulates rhythmic motion of a body; a vibrator. **2.** any pulsating machine, device, or part.

pul+sa+to·ry ('pʌlsətərɪ, -trɪ) *adj.* **1.** of or relating to pulsation. **2.** throbbing or pulsating.

pulse[1] (pʌls) *n.* **1.** *Physiol.* **a.** the rhythmical contraction and expansion of an artery at each beat of the heart, often discernible to the touch at points such as the wrists. **b.** a single pulsation of the heart or arteries. **2.** *Physics, electronics.* **a.** a transient sharp change in voltage, current, or some other quantity normally constant in a system. **b.** one of a series of such transient disturbances, usually recurring at regular intervals and having a characteristic geometric shape. **c.** (*as modifier*): *a pulse generator.* Less common name: **impulse. 3. a.** a recurrent rhythmical series of beats, waves, vibrations, etc. **b.** any single beat, wave, etc., in such a series. **4.** bustle, vitality, or excitement: *the pulse of a city.* **5.** the feelings or thoughts of a group or society as they can be measured: *the pulse of the voters.* **6. keep one's finger on the pulse.** to be well-informed about current events. ~*vb.* **7.** (*intr.*) to beat, throb, or vibrate. [C14 *pous,* from Latin *pulsus* a beating, from *pellere* to beat] —'**pulse+less** *adj.*

pulse[2] (pʌls) *n.* **1.** the edible seeds of any of several papilionaceous plants, such as peas, beans, and lentils. **2.** the plant producing any of these seeds. [C13 *pols,* from Old French, from Latin *puls* pottage of pulse]

pulse height an·a+lys+er *n.* a multichannel analyser that sorts pulses into selected amplitude ranges.

pulse+jet ('pʌlsˌdʒɛt) *n.* a type of ramjet engine in which air is admitted through movable vanes that are closed by the pressure resulting from each intermittent explosion of the fuel in the combustion chamber, thus causing a pulsating thrust. Also called: **pulsejet engine, pulsojet.**

pulse mod·u·la+tion *n.* **1.** a type of modulation in which a train of pulses is used as the carrier wave, one or more of its parameters, such as amplitude, being modulated or modified in order to carry information. **2.** the modulation of a continuous carrier wave by means of pulses.

pul+sim+e·ter (pʌl'sɪmɪtə) *or* **pul+som+e·ter** (pʌl'sɒmɪtə) *n.* *Med.* an instrument for measuring the strength and rate of the pulse.

pul+ver+a·ble ('pʌlvərəbᵊl) *adj.* able to be pulverized.

pul+ver+ize *or* **pul+ver+ise** ('pʌlvəˌraɪz) *vb.* **1.** to reduce (a substance) to fine particles, as by crushing or grinding, or (of a substance) to be so reduced. **2.** (*tr.*) to destroy completely; defeat or injure seriously. —'**pul+ver+ˌiz+a·ble** *or* '**pul+ver+ˌis+a·ble** *adj.* —ˌ**pul+ver·i+'za+tion** *or* ˌ**pul+ver·i+'sa+tion** *n.* —'**pul+ver+ˌiz+er** *or* '**pul+ver+ˌis+er** *n.*

pul+ver·u+lent (pʌl'vɛrʊlənt) *adj.* consisting of, covered with, or crumbling to dust or fine particles. [C17: from Latin *pulverulentus,* from *pulvis* dust] —**pul+'ver·u+lence** *n.*

pul+vil+lus (pʌl'vɪləs) *n., pl.* **+li** (-laɪ). a small pad between the claws at the end of an insect's leg. [C18: from Latin, from *pulvīnulus,* diminutive of *pulvīnus* cushion]

pul+vi+nate ('pʌlvɪˌneɪt) *or* **pul+vi+nat+ed** *adj.* **1.** *Architect.* (of a frieze) curved convexly; having a swelling. **2.** *Botany.* **a.** shaped like a cushion. **b.** (of a leafstalk) having a pulvinus. [C19: from Latin *pulvīnātus* cushion-shaped]

pul+vi+nus (pʌl'vaɪnəs) *n., pl.* **+ni** (-naɪ). a swelling at the base of a leafstalk: changes in its turgor pressure cause changes in the position of the leaf. [C19: from Latin: cushion]

pu·ma ('pju:mə) *n.* a large American feline mammal, *Felis concolor,* that resembles a lion, having a plain greyish-brown coat and long tail. Also called: **cougar, mountain lion.** [C18: via Spanish from Quechuan]

pum+ice ('pʌmɪs) *n.* **1.** Also called: **pumice stone.** a light porous acid volcanic rock having the composition of rhyolite, used for scouring and, in powdered form, as an abrasive and for polishing. ~*vb.* **2.** (*tr.*) to rub or polish with pumice. [C15 *pomys,* from Old French *pomis,* from Latin *pūmex*] —**pu+mi+ceous** (pju:'mɪʃəs) *adj.*

pum+mel ('pʌməl) *vb.* **+mels, +mel+ling, +melled** *or U.S.* **+mels, +mel+ing, +meled.** (*tr.*) to strike repeatedly with or as if with the fists. Also (less common): **pommel.** [C16: see POMMEL]

pump[1] (pʌmp) *n.* **1.** any device for compressing, driving, raising, or reducing the pressure of a fluid, esp. by means of a piston or set of rotating impellers. ~*vb.* **2.** (when *tr.,* usually foll. by *from, out, into, away,* etc.) to raise or drive (air, liquid, etc., esp. into or from something) with a pump or similar device. **3.** (*tr.;* usually foll. by *in* or *into*) to supply in large amounts: *to pump capital into a project.* **4.** (*tr.*) to deliver (shots, bullets, etc.) repeatedly with great force. **5.** to operate (something, esp. a handle or lever) in the manner of a pump or (of something) to work in this way: *to pump the pedals of a bicycle.* **6.** (*tr.*) to obtain (information) from (a person) by persistent questioning. **7.** (*intr.;* usually foll. by *from* or *out of*) (of liquids) to flow freely in large spurts: *oil pumped from the fissure.* [C15: from Middle Dutch *pumpe* pipe, probably from Spanish *bomba,* of imitative origin]

pump[2] (pʌmp) *n.* **1.** a low-cut low-heeled shoe without fastenings, worn esp. for dancing. **2.** a type of shoe with a rubber sole, used in games such as tennis; plimsoll. [C16: of unknown origin]

pum+per+nick+el ('pʌmpəˌnɪkᵊl) *n.* a slightly sour black bread, originating in Germany, made of coarse rye flour. [C18: from German, of uncertain origin]

pump gun *n.* a repeating gun operated by a slide-action mechanism.

pump+kin ('pʌmpkɪn) *n.* **1.** any of several creeping cucurbitaceous plants of the genus *Cucurbita,* esp. *C. pepo* of North America and *C. maxima* of Europe. **2. a.** the large round fruit of any of these plants, which has a thick orange rind, pulpy flesh, and numerous seeds. **b.** (*as modifier*): *pumpkin pie.* [C17: from earlier *pumpion,* from Old French *pompon,* from Latin *pepo,* from Greek *pepōn,* from *pepōn* ripe, from *peptein* to ripen]

pump·kin+seed ('pʌmpkɪnˌsi:d) *n.* **1.** the seed of the pumpkin. **2.** a common North American freshwater sunfish, *Lepomis gibbosus,* with brightly coloured markings: family *Centrarchidae.*

pump prim+ing *n.* **1.** the act or process of introducing fluid into a pump to improve the sealing of the pump parts on starting and to expel air from it. **2.** *U.S.* government expenditure designed to stimulate economic activity in stagnant or depressed areas.

pun[1] (pʌn) *n.* **1.** the use of words or phrases to exploit ambiguities and innuendoes in their meaning, usually for humorous effect; a play on words. An example is: *"Ben Battle was a soldier bold, And used to war's alarms: But a cannonball took off his legs, So he laid down his arms."* (Thomas Hood). ~*vb.* **puns, pun+ning, punned. 2.** (*intr.*) to make puns. [C17: possibly from Italian *puntiglio* point of detail, wordplay; see PUNCTILIO]

pun[2] (pʌn) *vb.* **puns, pun+ning, punned.** (*tr.*) *Brit.* to pack (earth, rubble, etc.) by pounding. [C16: dialectal variant of POUND[1]] —'**pun+ner** *n.*

pu·na *Spanish.* ('puna) *n.* **1.** a high cold dry plateau, esp. in the Andes. **2.** another name for **mountain sickness.** [C17: from American Spanish, from Quechuan]

Pu+na+kha *or* **Pu+na+ka** ('pu:nəkə) *n.* a town in W central Bhutan: a former capital of the country.

punce (pʌns) *Northern Brit. dialect.* ~*vb.* **1.** (*tr.*) to kick, beat, or hit. ~*n.* **2.** a kick or punch. [perhaps a blend of PUNCH[1] and POUNCE]

punch[1] (pʌntʃ) *vb.* **1.** to strike blows at, esp. with a clenched fist. **2.** (*tr.*) *Western U.S.* to herd or drive (cattle), esp. for a living. **3.** (*tr.*) to poke or prod with a stick or similar object. ~*n.* **4.** a blow with the fist. **5.** *Informal.* telling force, point, or vigour: *his arguments lacked punch.* **6. pull (one's) punches.** *Informal.* **a.** to lessen the weight of one's blows purposely, as in theatrical fighting. **b.** to soften one's criticism. [C15: perhaps a variant of POUNCE[2]] —'**punch+er** *n.*

punch[2] (pʌntʃ) *n.* **1.** a tool or machine for piercing holes in a material. **2.** any of various tools used for knocking a bolt, rivet, etc., out of a hole. **3.** a tool or machine used for stamping a design on something or shaping it by impact. **4.** the solid die of a punching machine for cutting, stamping, or shaping material. **5.** *Computer technol.* a device, such as a card punch or tape punch, used for making holes in a card or paper tape. **6.** see **centre punch.** ~*vb.* **7.** (*tr.*) to pierce, cut, stamp, shape, or drive with a punch. [C14: shortened from *puncheon,* from Old French *ponçon;* see PUNCHEON[2]]

punch[3] (pʌntʃ) *n.* any mixed drink containing fruit juice and, usually, alcoholic liquor, generally hot and spiced. [C17: perhaps from Hindi *pānch,* from Sanskrit *pañca* five; the beverage originally included five ingredients]

Punch (pʌntʃ) *n.* the main character in the traditional children's puppet show **Punch and Judy.**

punch+ball ('pʌntʃˌbɔ:l) *n.* **1.** Also called (*U.S.*): **punching bag.** a stuffed or inflated ball or bag, either suspended or supported by a flexible rod, that is punched for exercise, esp. boxing training. **2.** *U.S.* a game resembling baseball in which a light ball is struck with the fist.

punch+board ('pʌntʃˌbɔ:d) *n.* a board full of holes into which numbers on pieces of paper have been pushed, which a player attempts to push out.

punch+bowl ('pʌntʃˌbəʊl) *n.* **1.** a large bowl for serving punch, lemonade, etc., usually with a ladle and often having small drinking glasses hooked around the rim. **2.** *Brit.* a bowl-shaped depression in the land.

punch-drunk *adj.* **1.** demonstrating or characteristic of the behaviour of a person who has suffered repeated blows to the head, esp. a professional boxer. **2.** dazed; stupefied.

punched card *or esp. U.S.* **punch card** *n.* a card on which data can be coded in the form of punched holes. In computing, there are usually 80 columns and 12 rows, each column containing a pattern of holes representing one character. Sometimes shortened to **card.**

punched tape *or U.S.* (*sometimes*) **per+fo+rat+ed tape** *n.* other terms for **paper tape.**

pun+cheon[1] ('pʌntʃən) *n.* **1.** a large cask of variable capacity, usually between 70 and 120 gallons. **2.** the volume of such a cask used as a liquid measure. [C15 *poncion,* from Old French *ponchon,* of uncertain origin]

pun+cheon[2] ('pʌntʃən) *n.* **1.** a short wooden post that is used as a vertical strut. **2.** a less common name for **punch**[2] (sense 1). [C14 *ponson,* from Old French *ponçon,* from Latin *punctiō* a puncture, from *pungere* to prick]

Pun+chi+nel+lo (ˌpʌntʃɪ'nɛləʊ) *n., pl.* **+los** *or* **+loes. 1.** a type of clown from Italian burlesque or puppet shows, the prototype of Punch. **2.** (*sometimes not cap.*) any grotesque or absurd character. [C17: from earlier *Polichinello,* from Italian

(Neapolitan dialect) *Polecenella,* from Italian *pulcino* chicken, ultimately from Latin *pullus* young animal]

punch line *n.* the culminating part of a joke, funny story, etc., that gives it its humorous or dramatic point.

punch-up *n. Brit. slang.* a fight, brawl, or violent argument.

punch·y ('pʌntʃɪ) *adj.* **punch·i·er, punch·i·est. 1.** an informal word for **punch-drunk. 2.** *Informal.* incisive or forceful: *a punchy article.* —'**punch·i·ly** *adv.* —'**punch·i·ness** *n.*

punc·tate ('pʌŋkteɪt) *or* **punc·tat·ed** *adj.* having or marked with minute spots, holes, or depressions. [C18: from New Latin *punctātus,* from Latin *punctum* a point] —**punc'ta·tion** *n.*

punc·til·i·o (pʌŋk'tɪlɪˌəʊ) *n., pl.* **·os. 1.** strict attention to minute points of etiquette. **2.** a petty formality or fine point of etiquette. [C16: from Italian *puntiglio* small point, from *punto* point, from Latin *punctum* point]

punc·til·i·ous (pʌŋk'tɪlɪəs) *adj.* **1.** paying scrupulous attention to correctness in etiquette. **2.** attentive to detail. —**punc'til·i·ous·ly** *adv.* —**punc'til·i·ous·ness** *n.*

punc·tu·al ('pʌŋktjʊəl) *adj.* **1.** arriving or taking place at an arranged time; prompt. **2.** (of a person) having the characteristic of always keeping to arranged times, as for appointments, meetings, etc. **3.** *Obsolete.* precise; exact; apposite. **4.** *Maths.* consisting of or confined to a point in space. [C14: from Medieval Latin *punctuālis* concerning detail, from Latin *punctum* point] —ˌ**punc·tu'al·i·ty** *n.* —'**punc·tu·al·ly** *adv.*

punc·tu·ate ('pʌŋktjʊˌeɪt) *vb. (mainly tr.)* **1.** *(also intr.)* to insert punctuation marks into (a written text). **2.** to interrupt or insert at frequent intervals: *a meeting punctuated by heckling.* **3.** to give emphasis to. [C17: from Medieval Latin *punctuāre* to prick, from Latin *punctum* a prick, from *pungere* to puncture] —'**punc·tuˌa·tor** *n.*

punc·tu·a·tion (ˌpʌŋktjʊ'eɪʃən) *n.* **1.** the use of symbols not belonging to the alphabet of a writing system to indicate aspects of the intonation and meaning not otherwise conveyed in the written language. **2.** the symbols used for this purpose. **3.** the act or an instance of punctuating.

punc·tu·a·tion mark *n.* any of the signs used in punctuation, such as a comma or question mark.

punc·ture ('pʌŋktʃə) *n.* **1.** a small hole made by a sharp object. **2.** a perforation and loss of pressure in a pneumatic tyre, made by sharp stones, glass, etc. **3.** the act of puncturing or perforating. ~*vb.* **4.** *(tr.)* to pierce (a hole) in (something) with a sharp object. **5.** to cause (something pressurized, esp. a tyre) to lose pressure by piercing, or (of a tyre, etc.) to be pierced and collapse in this way. **6.** *(tr.)* to depreciate (a person's self-esteem, pomposity, etc.). [C14: from Latin *punctūra,* from *pungere* to prick] —'**punc·tur·a·ble** *adj.* —'**punc·tur·er** *n.*

pun·dit *or* **pan·dit** ('pʌndɪt) *n.* **1.** a self-appointed expert. **2.** (formerly) a learned person. **3.** a Brahman learned in Sanskrit and, esp. in Hindu religion, philosophy or law. [C17: from Hindi *pandit,* from Sanskrit *pandita* learned man, from *pandita* learned]

Pu·ne ('pu:nə) *n.* another name for **Poona.**

pung (pʌŋ) *n. U.S.* a horse-drawn sleigh with a boxlike body on runners. [C19: shortened from Algonquian *tom-pung;* compare TOBOGGAN]

pun·gent ('pʌndʒənt) *adj.* **1.** having an acrid smell or sharp bitter flavour. **2.** (of wit, satire, etc.) biting; caustic. **3.** *Biology.* ending in a sharp point: *a pungent leaf.* [C16: from Latin *pungens* piercing, from *pungere* to prick] —'**pun·gen·cy** *n.* —'**pun·gent·ly** *adv.*

Pu·nic ('pju:nɪk) *adj.* **1.** of or relating to ancient Carthage or the Carthaginians. **2.** characteristic of the treachery of the Carthaginians. ~*n.* **3.** the language of the ancient Carthaginians; a late form of Phoenician. [C15: from Latin *Pūnicus,* variant of *Poenicus* Carthaginian, from Greek *Phoinix*]

Pu·nic Wars *pl. n.* three wars (264–241 B.C., 218–201 B.C., and 149–146 B.C.), in which Rome crushed Carthaginian power, destroying Carthage itself.

pun·ish ('pʌnɪʃ) *vb.* **1.** to force (someone) to undergo a penalty or sanction, such as imprisonment, fines, death, etc., for some crime or misdemeanour. **2.** *(tr.)* to inflict punishment for (some crime, etc.). **3.** *(tr.)* to use or treat harshly or roughly, esp. as by overexertion: *to punish a horse.* **4.** *(tr.) Informal.* to consume (some commodity) in large quantities: *to punish the bottle.* [C14 *punisse,* from Old French *punir,* from Latin *pūnīre* to punish, from *poena* penalty] —'**pun·ish·er** *n.* —'**pun·ish·ing·ly** *adv.*

pun·ish·a·ble ('pʌnɪʃəbᵊl) *adj.* liable to be punished or deserving of punishment. —ˌ**pun·ish·a'bil·i·ty** *n.*

pun·ish·ment ('pʌnɪʃmənt) *n.* **1.** a penalty or sanction given for any crime or offence. **2.** the act of punishing or state of being punished. **3.** *Informal.* rough treatment.

pu·ni·tive ('pju:nɪtɪv) *or* **pu·ni·to·ry** ('pju:nɪtərɪ, -trɪ) *adj.* relating to, involving, or with the intention of inflicting punishment: *a punitive expedition.* [C17: from Medieval Latin *pūnītīvus* concerning punishment, from Latin *pūnīre* to punish] —'**pu·ni·tive·ly** *adv.* —'**pu·ni·tive·ness** *n.*

Pun·jab (pʌn'dʒɑ:b, 'pʌndʒɑ:b) *n.* **1.** (formerly) a province in NW British India: divided between India and Pakistan in 1947. **2.** a state of NW India: reorganized in 1966 as a Punjabi-speaking state, a large part forming the new state of Haryana; mainly agricultural. Capital: Chandigarh. Pop.: 13 551 060 (1971). Area: 50 255 sq. km (19 403 sq. miles).

Pun·ja·bi *or* **Pan·ja·bi** (pʌn'dʒɑ:bɪ) *n.* **1.** a member of the chief people of the Punjab. **2.** the state language of the Punjab, belonging to the Indic branch of the Indo-European family. ~*adj.* **3.** of or relating to the Punjab, its people, or their language.

Pun·jab States *pl. n.* (formerly) a group of states in NW India, amalgamated in 1956 with Punjab state.

punk[1] (pʌŋk) *n.* **1.** an inferior, rotten, or worthless person or thing. **2.** a follower or practitioner of punk rock, esp. one wearing worthless articles such as safety pins and razor blades for decoration. **3.** worthless articles collectively. **4.** short for **punk rock. 5.** a petty criminal or hoodlum. **6.** *Obsolete.* a young male homosexual; catamite. **7.** *Obsolete.* a prostitute. ~*adj.* **8.** inferior, rotten, or worthless. **9.** denoting or relating to punk rock. [C16: of unknown origin]

punk[2] (pʌŋk) *n.* **1.** dried decayed wood that smoulders when ignited: used as tinder. **2.** any of various other substances that smoulder when ignited, esp. one used to light fireworks. [C18: of uncertain origin]

pun·ka *or* **pun·kah** ('pʌŋkə) *n.* a fan made of a palm leaf or leaves. [C17: from Hindi *pankhā,* from Sanskrit *paksaka* fan, from *paksa* wing]

punk rock *n.* rock music in a style of the late 1970s, characterized by obscene and offensive lyrics, an energetic beat, simple harmonies, and aggressive performance. —**punk 'rock·er** *n.*

pun·net ('pʌnɪt) *n. Chiefly Brit.* a small basket for fruit, such as strawberries. [C19: perhaps diminutive of dialect *pun* POUND[2]]

pun·ster ('pʌnstə) *n.* a person who is fond of making puns, esp. one who makes a tedious habit of this.

punt[1] (pʌnt) *n.* **1.** an open flat-bottomed boat with square ends, propelled by a pole. See **quant.** ~*vb.* **2.** to propel (a boat, esp. a punt) by pushing with a pole on the bottom of a river, etc. [Old English *punt* shallow boat, from Latin *pontō* punt, PONTOON] —'**punt·er** *n.*

punt[2] (pʌnt) *n.* **1.** a kick in certain sports, such as rugby, in which the ball is released and kicked before it hits the ground. ~*vb.* **2.** to kick (a ball, etc.) using a punt. [C19: perhaps a variant of English dialect *bunt* to push, perhaps a nasalized variant of BUTT] —'**punt·er** *n.*

punt[3] (pʌnt) *Chiefly Brit.* ~*vb.* **1.** *(intr.)* to gamble; bet. ~*n.* **2.** a gamble or bet, esp. against the bank, as in roulette, or on horses. **3.** Also called: **punter.** a person who bets. **4. take a punt at.** *Austral. informal.* to have an attempt or try at (something). [C18: from French *ponter* to punt, from *ponte* bet laid against the banker, from Spanish *punto* point, from Latin *punctum*] —'**punt·er** *n.*

Pun·ta A·re·nas (*Spanish* 'punta a'renas) *n.* a port in S Chile, on the Strait of Magellan: the southernmost city in the world. Pop.: 64 450 (1970 est.). Former name: **Magallanes.**

pun·ty ('pʌntɪ) *n., pl.* **·ties.** a long iron rod used in the finishing process of glass-blowing. [C17: see PONTIL]

pu·ny ('pju:nɪ) *adj.* **·ni·er, ·ni·est. 1.** having a small physique or weakly constitution. **2.** paltry; insignificant. [C16: from Old French *puisne* PUISNE] —'**pu·ni·ness** *n.*

pup (pʌp) *n.* **1. a.** a young dog, esp. when under one year of age; puppy. **b.** the young of various other animals, such as the seal. **2. in pup.** (of a bitch) pregnant. **3.** *Informal, chiefly Brit., contemptuous.* a conceited young man (esp. in the phrase **young pup**). **4.** *Informal.* a worthless purchase (esp. in the phrase **be sold a pup**). ~*vb.* **pups, pup·ping, pupped. 5.** (of dogs, seals, etc.) to give birth to (young). [C18: back formation from PUPPY]

pu·pa ('pju:pə) *n., pl.* **·pae** (-pi:) *or* **·pas.** an insect at the immobile nonfeeding stage of development between larva and adult, when many internal changes occur. See **coarctate, exarate, obtect.** [C19: via New Latin, from Latin: a doll, puppet] —'**pu·pal** *adj.*

pu·par·i·um (pju:'pɛərɪəm) *n., pl.* **·i·a** (-ɪə). a hard barrel-shaped case enclosing the pupae of the housefly and other dipterous insects. —**pu'par·i·al** *adj.*

pu·pate (pju:'peɪt) *vb. (intr.)* (of an insect larva) to develop into a pupa. —**pu'pa·tion** *n.*

pu·pil[1] ('pju:pᵊl) *n.* **1.** a student who is taught by a teacher, esp. a young student. **2.** *Civil and Scot. law.* a boy under 14 or a girl under 12 who is in the care of a guardian. [C14: from Latin *pupillus* an orphan, from *pūpus* a child]

pu·pil[2] ('pju:pᵊl) *n.* the dark circular aperture at the centre of the iris of the eye, through which light enters. [C16: from Latin *pūpilla,* diminutive of *pūpa* girl, puppet; from the tiny reflections in the eye]

pu·pil·lage *or U.S.* **pu·pil·age** ('pju:pɪlɪdʒ) *n.* **1.** the condition of being a pupil or duration for which one is a pupil. **2.** (in England) the period spent by a newly called barrister in the chambers of a member of the bar.

pu·pil·lar·y[1] *or* **pu·pi·lar·y** ('pju:pɪlərɪ) *adj.* of or relating to a pupil or legal ward. [C17: from PUPIL[1] + -ARY] —ˌ**pu·pil'lar·i·ty** *or* ˌ**pu·pi'lar·i·ty** *n.*

pu·pil·lar·y[2] *or* **pu·pi·lar·y** ('pju:pɪlərɪ) *adj.* of or relating to the pupil of the eye. [C18: from Latin *pūpilla* PUPIL[2]]

pu·pip·a·rous (pju:'pɪpərəs) *adj.* (of certain dipterous flies) producing young that have already reached the pupa stage at the time of hatching. [C19: from New Latin *pupiparus,* from PUPA + *parere* to bring forth]

pup·pet ('pʌpɪt) *n.* **1. a.** a small doll or figure of a person or animal moved by strings attached to its limbs or by the hand inserted in its cloth body. **b.** *(as modifier): a puppet theatre.* **2. a.** a person, group, state, etc., that appears independent but is in fact controlled by another. **b.** *(as modifier): a puppet government.* [C16 *popet,* perhaps from Old French *poupette* little doll, ultimately from Latin *pūpa* girl, doll]

pup·pet·eer (ˌpʌpɪ'tɪə) *n.* a person who manipulates puppets.

pup+pet+ry ('pʌpɪtrɪ) *n.* **1.** the art of making and manipulating puppets and presenting puppet shows. **2.** unconvincing or specious presentation.

Pup+pis ('pʌpɪs) *n., Latin genitive* **Pup+pis.** a constellation in the S hemisphere lying between Vela and Canis Major, a section of which is crossed by the Milky Way. [Latin: the ship, the POOP of a ship]

pup+py ('pʌpɪ) *n., pl.* **+pies. 1.** a young dog; pup. **2.** *Informal, contemptuous.* a brash or conceited young man; pup. [C15 *popi,* from Old French *popée* doll; compare PUPPET] —**'pup+py+ˌhood** *n.* —**'pup+py+ish** *adj.*

pup+py fat *n.* fatty tissue in a child or adolescent, usually disappearing with age.

pup+py love *n.* another term for **calf love.**

pup tent *n.* another name for **shelter tent.**

Pu+ra+na (pʊ'rɑːnə) *n.* any of a class of Sanskrit writings not included in the Vedas, characteristically recounting the birth and deeds of Hindu gods and the creation, destruction, or recreation of the universe. [C17: from Sanskrit: ancient, from *purā* formerly] —**Pu+'ra+nic** *adj.*

Pur+beck mar+ble *or* **stone** ('pɜːbɛk) *n.* a fossil-rich limestone that takes a high polish: used for building, etc. [C15: named after *Purbeck,* Dorset, where it is quarried]

pur+blind ('pɜːˌblaɪnd) *adj.* **1.** partly or nearly blind. **2.** lacking in insight or understanding; obtuse. [C13: see PURE, BLIND; compare PARBOIL]

Pur·cell ('pɜːsᵊl) *n.* **1. Ed·ward Mills.** born 1912, U.S. physicist, noted for his work on the magnetic moments of atomic nuclei: shared the Nobel prize for physics (1952). **2. Hen·ry.** ?1659–95, English composer, noted chiefly for his rhythmic and harmonic subtlety in setting words. His works include the opera *Dido and Aeneas* (1689), music for the theatrical pieces *King Arthur* (1691) and *The Fairy Queen* (1692), several choral odes, fantasias, sonatas, and church music.

pur+chas+a·ble ('pɜːtʃɪsəbᵊl) *adj.* **1.** able to be bribed or corrupted. **2.** able to be bought. —**ˌpur+chas·a·'bil·i·ty** *n.*

pur+chase ('pɜːtʃɪs) *vb.* (*tr.*) **1.** to obtain (goods, etc.) by payment. **2.** to obtain by effort, sacrifice, etc.: *to purchase one's freedom.* **3.** to draw, haul, or lift (a load) with the aid of mechanical apparatus. **4.** to acquire (an estate) other than by inheritance. ~*n.* **5.** something that is purchased, esp. an article bought with money. **6.** the act of buying. **7.** acquisition of an estate by any lawful means other than inheritance. **8.** a tackle or lever used to provide mechanical advantage in moving a heavy load. **9.** a firm foothold, grasp, etc., as for climbing or levering something. **10.** a means of achieving some influence, advantage, etc. [C13: from Old French *porchacier* to strive to obtain, from *por-* for + *chacier* to CHASE] —**'pur+chas+er** *n.*

pur+chase tax *n. Brit.* a tax levied on nonessential consumer goods and added to selling prices by retailers.

pur+dah, pur+da, *or* **par+dah** ('pɜːdə) *n.* **1.** the custom in some Muslim and Hindu communities of keeping women in seclusion, with clothing that conceals them completely when they go out. **2.** a screen in a Hindu house used to keep the women out of view. **3.** a veil worn by Hindu women of high caste. [C19: from Hindi *parda* veil, from Persian *pardah*]

pure (pjʊə) *adj.* **1.** not mixed with any extraneous or dissimilar materials, elements, etc.: *pure nitrogen.* **2.** free from tainting or polluting matter; clean; wholesome: *pure water.* **3.** free from moral taint or defilement: *pure love.* **4.** (*prenominal*) (intensifier): *pure stupidity; a pure coincidence.* **5.** (of a subject, etc.) studied in its theoretical aspects rather than for its practical applications: *pure mathematics; pure science.* Compare **applied. 6.** (of a vowel) pronounced with more or less unvarying quality without any glide; monophthongal. **7.** (of a consonant) not accompanied by another consonant. **8.** of supposedly unmixed racial descent: *a pure Negro.* **9.** *Genetics, biology.* breeding true for one or more characteristics; homozygous. **10.** *Philosophy.* independent of empirical concepts: *pure reason.* **11.** *Music.* **a.** (of a sound) composed of a single frequency without overtones. **b.** (of intervals in the system of just intonation) mathematically accurate in respect to the ratio of one frequency to another. [C13: from Old French *pur,* from Latin *pūrus* unstained] —**'pure+ness** *n.*

pure+bred *adj.* ('pjʊə'brɛd). **1.** denoting a pure strain obtained through many generations of controlled breeding. ~*n.* ('pjʊəˌbrɛd). **2.** a purebred animal. Compare **grade** (sense 9), **crossbred** (sense 2).

pure cul+ture *n. Bacteriol.* a culture containing a single species of microorganism.

pu+ree *or* **pu·ri** ('puːrɪ) *n.* an unleavened flaky Indian bread, that is deep-fried in ghee and served hot. [Hindi]

pu+rée ('pjʊəreɪ) *n.* **1.** a smooth thick pulp of cooked and sieved fruit, vegetables, meat, or fish. ~*vb.* **+rées, +rée+ing, +réed. 2.** (*tr.*) to make (cooked foods) into a purée. [C19: from French *purer* to PURIFY]

Pure Land sects *pl. n.* Mahayana Buddhist sects venerating the Buddha as the compassionate saviour.

pure line *n.* a breed or strain of animals or plants in which certain characters appear in successive generations as a result of inbreeding or self-fertilization.

pure+ly ('pjʊəlɪ) *adv.* **1.** in a pure manner. **2.** entirely: *purely by chance.* **3.** in a chaste or innocent manner.

pur+fle ('pɜːfᵊl) *n. also* **pur+fling. 1.** a ruffled or curved ornamental band, as on clothing, furniture, etc. ~*vb.* **2.** (*tr.*) to decorate with such a band or bands. [C14: from Old French *purfiler* to decorate with a border, from *filer* to spin, from *fil* thread, from Latin *fīlum*]

pur+ga+tion (pɜː'geɪʃən) *n.* the act of purging or state of being purged; purification.

pur+ga+tive ('pɜːgətɪv) *Med.* ~*n.* **1.** a drug or agent for purging the bowels. ~*adj.* **2.** causing evacuation of the bowels; cathartic. —**'pur+ga+tive+ly** *adv.*

pur+ga+to+ri+al (ˌpɜːgə'tɔːrɪəl) *adj.* **1.** serving to purify from sin. **2.** of, relating to, or like purgatory. —**ˌpur+ga+'to+ri+al+ly** *adv.*

pur+ga+to·ry ('pɜːgətərɪ, -trɪ) *n.* **1.** *Chiefly R.C. Church.* a state or place in which the souls of those who have died in a state of grace are believed to undergo a limited amount of suffering to expiate their venial sins and become purified of the remaining effects of mortal sin. **2.** a place or condition of suffering or torment, esp. one that is temporary. [C13: from Old French *purgatoire,* from Medieval Latin *pūrgātōrium,* literally: place of cleansing, from Latin *pūrgāre* to PURGE]

purge (pɜːdʒ) *vb.* **1.** (*tr.*) to rid (something) of (impure or undesirable elements). **2.** (*tr.*) to rid (a state, political party, etc.) of (dissident or troublesome people). **3.** (*tr.*) **a.** to empty (the bowels) by evacuation of faeces. **b.** to cause (a person) to evacuate his bowels. **4. a.** to clear (a person) of a charge. **b.** to free (oneself) of guilt, as by atonement: *to purge contempt.* **5.** (*intr.*) to be cleansed or purified. ~*n.* **6.** the act or process of purging. **7.** the elimination of opponents or dissidents from a state, political party, etc. **8.** a purgative drug or agent; cathartic. [C14: from Old French *purger,* from Latin *pūrgāre* to purify] —**'purg+er** *n.*

Pu+ri ('pʊəriː, pʊə'riː) *n.* a port in E India, in Orissa on the Bay of Bengal: 12th-century temple of Jagannath. Pop.: 72 712 (1971).

Pu+ri+fi+ca+tion of the Vir+gin Mar·y *n.* **the.** *Christianity.* **1.** the presentation of Jesus in the Temple after the completion of Mary's purification (Luke 2:22). **2.** Also called: **Candlemas.** the feast commemorating this (Feb. 2).

pu+ri+fi+ca+tor ('pjʊərɪfɪˌkeɪtə) *n. Ecclesiast.* a small white linen cloth used to wipe the chalice and paten and also the lips and fingers of the celebrant at the Eucharist.

pu+ri+fy ('pjʊərɪˌfaɪ) *vb.* **+fies, +fy+ing, +fied. 1.** to free (something) of extraneous, contaminating, or debasing matter. **2.** (*tr.*) to free (a person, etc.) from sin or guilt. **3.** (*tr.*) to make clean, as in a ritual, esp. the churching of women after childbirth. [C14: from Old French *purifier,* from Late Latin *pūrificāre* to cleanse, from *pūrus* pure + *facere* to make] —**ˌpu+ri+fi+'ca+tion** *n.* —**pu+rif·i+ca+to+ry** ('pjʊərɪfɪˌkeɪtərɪ) *adj.* —**'pu+ri+ˌfi+er** *n.*

Pu+rim ('pʊərɪm; *Hebrew* puː'riːm) *n.* a Jewish holiday celebrated on Adar 14, in February or March, to commemorate the deliverance of the Jews from the massacre planned for them by Haman (Esther 9). [Hebrew *pūrīm,* plural of *pūr* lot; from the casting of lots by Haman]

pu+rine ('pjʊəriːn) *or* **pu+rin** ('pjʊərɪn) *n.* **1.** a colourless crystalline solid that can be prepared from uric acid. Formula: $C_5H_5N_4$. **2.** any of a number of nitrogenous bases, such as guanine and adenine, that are derivatives of purine and constituents of nucleic acids and certain coenzymes. [C19: from German *Purin;* see PURE, URIC, -INE[2]]

pur+ism ('pjʊəˌrɪzəm) *n.* insistence on traditional canons of correctness of form or purity of style or content, esp. in language, art, or music. —**'pur+ist** *adj., n.* —**pu+'rist+ic** *adj.* —**pu+'ris+ti+cal+ly** *adv.*

pu+ri+tan ('pjʊərɪtᵊn) *n.* **1.** a person who adheres to strict moral or religious principles, esp. one opposed to luxury and sensual enjoyment. ~*adj.* **2.** characteristic of a puritan. [C16: from Late Latin *pūritās* PURITY] —**'pu+ri+tan+ˌism** *n.*

Pu+ri+tan ('pjʊərɪtᵊn) (in the late 16th and 17th centuries) ~*n.* **1.** any of the more extreme English Protestants, most of whom were Calvinists, who wished to purify the Church of England of most of its ceremony and other aspects that they deemed to be Catholic. ~*adj.* **2.** of, characteristic of, or relating to the Puritans. —**'Pu+ri+tan+ˌism** *n.*

pu+ri+tan+i+cal (ˌpjʊərɪ'tænɪkᵊl) *or* **pu+ri+tan+ic** *adj.* **1.** *Usually disparaging.* strict in moral or religious outlook, esp. in shunning sensual pleasures. **2.** (*sometimes cap.*) of or relating to a puritan or the Puritans. —**ˌpu+ri+'tan·i+cal+ly** *adv.* —**ˌpu+ri+'tan·i+cal+ness** *n.*

pu+ri·ty ('pjʊərɪtɪ) *n.* **1.** the state or quality of being pure. **2.** *Physics.* a measure of the amount of a single-frequency colour in a mixture of spectral and achromatic colours.

purl[1] (pɜːl) *n.* **1.** Also called: **purl stitch.** a knitting stitch made by doing a plain stitch backwards. **2.** a decorative border, as of lace. **3.** gold or silver wire thread. ~*vb.* **4.** to knit (a row or garment) in purl stitch. **5.** to edge (something) with a purl. ~Also (for senses 2, 3, 5): **pearl.** [C16: from dialect *pirl* to twist into a cord]

purl[2] (pɜːl) *vb.* **1.** (*intr.*) (of a stream, etc.) to flow with a gentle curling or rippling movement and a murmuring sound. ~*n.* **2.** a curling movement of water; eddy. **3.** a murmuring sound, as of a shallow stream. [C16: related to Norwegian *purla* to bubble]

pur+ler ('pɜːlə) *n. Informal.* **1.** a headlong or spectacular fall (esp. in the phrase **come a purler**). **2.** *Austral.* See **pearler.**

pur+lieu ('pɜːljuː) *n.* **1.** *English history.* land on the edge of a forest that was once included within the bounds of the royal forest but was later separated although still subject to some of the forest laws, esp. regarding hunting. **2.** (*usually pl.*) a neighbouring area; outskirts. **3.** (*often pl.*) a place one frequents; haunt. **4.** *Rare.* a district or suburb, esp. one that is poor or squalid. [C15 *purlewe,* from Anglo-French *puralé* a going through (influenced also by Old French *lieu* place), from Old French *puraler* to traverse, from *pur* through + *aler* to go]

pur+lin *or* **pur+line** ('pɜːlɪn) *n.* a horizontal beam that provides intermediate support for the common rafters of a roof construction. [C15: of uncertain origin]

pur·loin (pɜːˈlɔɪn) *vb.* to take (something) dishonestly; steal. [C15: from Old French *porloigner* to put at a distance, from *por-* for + *loin* distant, from Latin *longus* long] —**purˈloin·er** *n.*

pur·ple (ˈpɜːpᵊl) *n.* **1.** any of various colours with a hue lying between red and blue and often highly saturated; a nonspectral colour. **2.** a dye or pigment producing such a colour. **3.** cloth of this colour, often used to symbolize royalty or nobility. **4.** (usually preceded by *the*) high rank; nobility. **5. a.** the official robe of a cardinal. **b.** the rank, office, or authority of a cardinal as signified by this. **6. the purple.** bishops collectively. ~*adj.* **7.** of the colour purple. **8.** (of writing) excessively elaborate or full of imagery: *purple prose.* **9.** noble or royal. [Old English, from Latin *purpura* purple dye, from Greek *porphura* a purple fish] —ˈ**pur·ple·ness** *n.* —ˈ**pur·plish** *adj.* —ˈ**pur·ply** *adj.*

pur·ple-fringed or·chid *or* **or·chis** *n.* either of two North American orchids, *Habenaria psychodes* or *H. fimbriata,* having purple fringed flowers.

pur·ple gal·li·nule *n.* a long-toed purple aquatic bird, *Porphyrio porphyrio* (or *Porphyrula martinica*), of the southern U.S. and Europe, with red legs and red bill: family *Rallidae* (rails, etc.).

pur·ple heart *n.* **1.** any of several tropical American leguminous trees of the genus *Peltogyne.* **2.** the decorative purple heartwood of any of these trees. **3.** *Informal, chiefly Brit.* a heart-shaped purple tablet consisting mainly of amphetamine.

Pur·ple Heart *n.* a decoration awarded to members of the U.S. Armed Forces for a wound incurred in action.

pur·ple med·ic *n.* another name for **alfalfa.**

pur·ple patch *n.* **1.** Also called: **purple passage.** a section in a piece of writing characterized by rich, fanciful, or ornate language. **2.** *Austral. slang.* a period of success, good fortune, etc.

pur·port *vb.* (pɜːˈpɔːt). (*tr.*) **1.** to claim to be (true, official, etc.) by manner or appearance, esp. falsely. **2.** to signify or imply. ~*n.* (ˈpɜːpɔːt). **3.** meaning; significance; import. **4.** purpose; object; intention. [C15: from Anglo-French: contents, from Old French *porporter* to convey, from *por-* forth + *porter* to carry, from Latin *portāre*]

pur·pose (ˈpɜːpəs) *n.* **1.** the reason for which anything is done, created, or exists. **2.** a fixed design, outcome, or idea that is the object of an action or other effort. **3.** fixed intention in doing something; determination: *a man of purpose.* **4.** practical advantage or use: *to work to good purpose.* **5.** that which is relevant or under consideration (esp. in the phrase **to** or **from the purpose**). **6.** *Archaic.* purport. **7. on purpose.** intentionally. ~*vb.* **8.** (*tr.*) to intend or determine to do (something). [C13: from Old French *porpos,* from *porposer* to plan, from Latin *prōpōnere* PROPOSE]

pur·pose-built *adj.* made to serve a specific purpose.

pur·pose·ful (ˈpɜːpəsful) *adj.* **1.** having a definite purpose in view. **2.** fixed in one's purpose; determined. —ˈ**pur·pose·ful·ly** *adv.* —ˈ**pur·pose·ful·ness** *n.*

pur·pose·less (ˈpɜːpəslɪs) *adj.* having no fixed plan or intention. —ˈ**pur·pose·less·ly** *adv.* —ˈ**pur·pose·less·ness** *n.*

pur·pose·ly (ˈpɜːpəslɪ) *adv.* for a definite reason; on purpose.

pur·pos·ive (ˈpɜːpəsɪv) *adj.* **1.** relating to, having, or indicating conscious intention. **2.** serving a purpose; useful. —ˈ**pur·pos·ive·ly** *adv.* —ˈ**pur·pos·ive·ness** *n.*

pur·pu·ra (ˈpɜːpjʊrə) *n. Pathol.* any of several blood diseases causing purplish spots or patches due to subcutaneous bleeding. [C18: via Latin from Greek *porphura* a shellfish yielding purple dye] —ˈ**pur·pu·ric** *adj.*

pur·pure (ˈpɜːpjʊə) *n., adj.* (*usually postpositive*) *Heraldry.* purple. [Old English from Latin *purpura* PURPLE]

pur·pu·rin (ˈpɜːpjʊrɪn) *n.* a red crystalline compound used as a stain for biological specimens; 1,2,4-trihydroxyanthraquinone. Formula: $C_{14}H_5O_2(OH)_3$. [C19: from Latin *purpura* PURPLE + -IN]

purr (pɜː) *vb.* **1.** (*intr.*) (esp. of cats) to make a low vibrant sound, usually considered as expressing pleasure, etc. **2.** (*tr.*) to express (pleasure, etc.) by this sound. ~*n.* **3.** a purring sound. [C17: of imitative origin; compare French *ronronner* to purr, German *schnurren,* Dutch *snorren*]

purse (pɜːs) *n.* **1.** a small bag or pouch, often made of soft leather, for carrying money, esp. coins. **2.** *U.S.* a woman's handbag. **3.** anything resembling a small bag or pouch in form or function. **4.** wealth; funds; resources. **5.** a sum of money that is offered, esp. as a prize. ~*vb.* **6.** (*tr.*) to contract (the mouth, lips, etc.) into a small rounded shape. [Old English *purs,* probably from Late Latin *bursa* bag, ultimately from Greek: leather]

purs·er (ˈpɜːsə) *n.* an officer aboard a passenger ship, merchant ship, or aircraft who keeps the accounts and attends to the welfare of the passengers.

purse seine *n.* a large net towed, usually by two boats, that encloses a school of fish and is then closed at the bottom by means of a line resembling a purse string.

purse strings *pl. n.* control of finance or expenditure (esp. in such phrases as **hold** or **control the purse strings**).

purs·lane (ˈpɜːslɪn, -leɪn) *n.* **1.** a weedy portulacaceous plant, *Portulaca oleracea,* with small yellow flowers and fleshy leaves, which are used in salads and as a potherb. **2.** any of various similar or related plants, such as sea purslane and water purslane. [C14 *purcelane,* from Old French *porcelaine,* from Late Latin *porcillāgō,* from Latin *porcillāca,* variant of *portulāca*]

pur·su·ance (pəˈsjuːəns) *n.* the carrying out or pursuing of an action, plan, etc.

pur·su·ant (pəˈsjuːənt) *adj.* **1.** (*usually postpositive;* often foll. by *to*) *Chiefly law.* in agreement or conformity. **2.** *Archaic.* pursuing. [C17: related to Middle English *poursuivant* following after, from Old French; see PURSUE] —**purˈsu·ant·ly** *adv.*

pur·sue (pəˈsjuː) *vb.* **·sues, ·su·ing, ·sued.** (*mainly tr.*) **1.** (*also intr.*) to follow (a fugitive, etc.) in order to capture or overtake. **2.** (esp. of something bad or unlucky) to follow closely or accompany: *ill health pursued her.* **3.** to seek or strive to attain (some object, desire, etc.). **4.** to follow the precepts of (a plan, policy, etc.). **5.** to apply oneself to (one's studies, hobbies, interests, etc.). **6.** to follow persistently or seek to become acquainted with. **7.** to continue to discuss or argue (a point, subject, etc.). [C13: from Anglo-Norman *pursiwer,* from Old French *poursivre,* from Latin *prōsequī* to follow after] —**purˈsu·er** *n.*

pur·suit (pəˈsjuːt) *n.* **1. a.** the act of pursuing, chasing, or striving after. **b.** (*as modifier*): *a pursuit plane.* **2.** an occupation, hobby, or pastime. **3.** (in cycling) a race in which the riders set off at intervals along the track and attempt to overtake each other. [C14: from Old French *poursieute,* from *poursivre* to prosecute, PURSUE]

pur·sui·vant (ˈpɜːsɪvənt) *n.* **1.** the lowest rank of heraldic officer. **2.** *History.* a state or royal messenger. **3.** *History.* a follower or attendant. [C14: from Old French, from *poursivre* to PURSUE]

purs·y (ˈpɜːsɪ) *adj.* **1.** short-winded. **2.** *Archaic.* fat; overweight. [C15: alteration of earlier *pursive,* from Anglo-French *porsif,* ultimately from Latin *pulsāre* to PULSATE]

pur·te·nance (ˈpɜːtɪnəns) *n. Archaic.* the inner organs, viscera. [C14: from Old French *pertinance* something that belongs; see APPURTENANCE]

pu·ru·lent (ˈpjʊərulənt) *adj.* of, relating to, or containing pus. [C16: from Latin *pūrulentus,* from PUS] —ˈ**pu·ru·lence** *or* ˈ**pu·ru·len·cy** *n.* —ˈ**pu·ru·lent·ly** *adv.*

Pu·rús (*Spanish, Portuguese* puˈrus) *n.* a river in NW central South America, rising in SE Peru and flowing northeast to the Amazon. Length: about 3200 km (2000 miles).

pur·vey (pəˈveɪ) *vb.* (*tr.*) **1.** to sell or provide (commodities, esp. foodstuffs) on a large scale. **2.** to publish or make available (lies, scandal, etc.). [C13: from Old French *porveeir,* from Latin *prōvidēre* to PROVIDE]

pur·vey·ance (pəˈveɪəns) *n.* **1.** *Rare.* the act of purveying. **2.** *Rare.* that which is purveyed. **3.** *History.* the collection or requisition of provisions for a sovereign.

pur·vey·or (pəˈveɪə) *n.* **1.** (*often pl.*) *Rare.* a person, organization, etc., that supplies food and provisions. **2.** a person who spreads, repeats, or sells (information, lies, etc.). **3.** *History.* an officer providing or exacting provisions, lodging, etc., for a sovereign.

pur·view (ˈpɜːvjuː) *n.* **1.** the scope of operation or concern of something. **2.** the breadth or range of outlook or understanding. **3.** *Law.* the body of a statute, containing the enacting clauses. [C15: from Anglo-Norman *purveu,* from *porveeir* to furnish; see PURVEY]

pus (pʌs) *n.* the yellow or greenish fluid product of inflammation, composed largely of dead leucocytes, exuded plasma, and liquefied tissue cells. [C16: from Latin *pūs;* related to Greek *puon* pus]

Pu·san (ˈpuːˈsæn) *n.* a port in SE South Korea, on the Korean Strait: the second largest city and chief port of the country; industrial centre; two universities. Pop.: 2 450 977 (1975).

Pu·sey (ˈpjuːzɪ) *n.* **Ed·ward Bou·ve·rie** (ˈbuːvərɪ). 1800–82, English ecclesiastic; a leader with Keble and Newman of the Oxford Movement.

Pu·sey·ism (ˈpjuːzɪˌɪzəm) *n.* a derogatory term for the **Oxford Movement,** used by its contemporary opponents. [C19: after E. B. PUSEY] —ˈ**Pu·sey·ite** *n., adj.*

push (pʊʃ) *vb.* **1.** (when *tr.,* often foll. by *off, away,* etc.) to apply steady force to in order to move it. **2.** to thrust (one's way) through something, such as a crowd, by force. **3.** (when *intr.,* often foll. by *for*) to apply oneself vigorously (to achieving a task, plan, etc.). **4.** (*tr.*) to encourage or urge (a person) to some action, decision, etc.: *she was a woman who liked to push her husband.* **5.** (when *intr.,* often foll. by *for*) to be an advocate or promoter (of): *to push for acceptance of one's theories.* **6.** (*tr.*) to use one's influence to help (a person): *to push one's own candidate.* **7.** to bear upon (oneself or another person) in order to achieve more effort, better results, etc. **8.** (*tr.*) to rely too much on (something): *to push one's luck.* **9.** *Tennis, cricket, etc.* to hit (a ball) with a stiff pushing stroke. **10.** (*tr.*) *Informal.* to sell (narcotic drugs) illegally. **11.** (*intr.;* foll. by *out, into,* etc.) (esp. of geographical features) to reach or extend: *the cliffs pushed out to the sea.* **12. push up (the) daisies.** *Slang.* to be dead and buried. ~*n.* **13.** the act of pushing; thrust. **14.** a part or device that is pressed to operate some mechanism. **15.** *Informal.* ambitious or enterprising drive, energy, etc. **16.** *Informal.* a special effort or attempt to advance, as of an army in a war: *to make a push.* **17.** *Informal.* a number of people gathered in one place, such as at a party. **18.** *Austral. slang.* a group or gang, esp. one considered to be a clique. **19.** *Tennis, cricket, etc.* a stiff pushing stroke. **20. at a push.** *Informal.* with difficulty; only just. **21. the push.** *Slang, chiefly Brit.* dismissal from employment. ~See also **push about, push along, push off, push through.** [C13: from Old French *pousser,* from Latin *pulsāre,* from *pellere* to drive]

push a·bout *or* **a·round** *vb.* (*tr., adv.*) *Slang.* to bully; keep telling (a person) what to do in a bossy manner.

push a·long *vb.* (*intr., adv.*) *Informal.* to go away; leave.

push+ball ('pʊʃˌbɔːl) *n. Chiefly U.S.* a game in which two teams try to push a heavy ball towards opposite goals.

push-bike *n. Brit.* an informal name for **bicycle.**

push but·ton *n.* **1.** an electrical switch operated by pressing a button, which closes or opens a circuit. **2.** (*modifier*) **push-but·ton. a.** operated by a push button: *a push-button radio.* **b.** initiated as simply as by pressing a button: *push-button warfare.*

push+cart ('pʊʃˌkɑːt) *n.* another name (esp. U.S.) for **barrow**[1] (sense 3).

push+chair ('pʊʃˌtʃɛə) *n. Brit.* a usually collapsible chair-shaped carriage in which a small child may be wheeled. U.S. word: **stroller.** Austral. words: **pusher, stroller.**

pushed (pʊʃt) *adj.* (often foll. by *for*) *Informal.* short (of) or in need (of time, money, etc.).

push+er ('pʊʃə) *n.* **1.** *Informal.* a person who sells illegal drugs, esp. narcotics such as heroin and morphine. **2.** *Informal.* an actively or aggressively ambitious person. **3. a.** a type of aircraft propeller placed behind the engine. **b.** a type of aircraft using such a propeller. **4.** a person or thing that pushes. **5.** *Brit.* a rakelike implement used by small children to push food onto a spoon. **6.** *Austral.* the usual name for **pushchair.**

push+ing ('pʊʃɪŋ) *adj.* **1.** enterprising, resourceful, or aggressively ambitious. **2.** impertinently self-assertive. ~*adv.* **3.** almost or nearly (a certain age, speed, etc.): *pushing fifty.* —'**push+ing+ly** *adv.* —'**push+ing+ness** *n.*

Push·kin ('pʊʃkɪn) *n.* **A·le·ksan·der Ser·ge·ye·vich** (alɪ'ksandᵊr sɪr'gjejɪvitʃ). 1799–1837, Russian poet, novelist, and dramatist. His works include the romantic verse tale *The Prisoner of the Caucasus* (1822), the verse novel *Eugene Onegin* (1833), the tragedy *Boris Godunov* (1825), and the novel *The Captain's Daughter* (1836).

push off *vb.* (*adv.*) **1.** Also: **push out.** to move into open water, as by being cast off from a mooring. **2.** (*intr.*) *Informal.* to go away; leave.

push+o·ver ('pʊʃˌəʊvə) *n. Slang.* **1.** something that is easily achieved or accomplished. **2.** a person, team, etc., that is easily taken advantage of or defeated.

push+pin ('pʊʃˌpɪn) *n. U.S.* a large-headed drawing pin.

push-pull *n.* (*modifier*) using two similar electronic devices, such as matched valves, made to operate 180° out of phase with each other. The outputs are combined to produce a signal that replicates the input waveform: *a push-pull amplifier.*

push+rod ('pʊʃˌrɒd) *n.* a metal rod transmitting the reciprocating motion that operates the valves of an internal-combustion engine having the camshaft in the crankcase.

push-start *vb.* (*tr.*) **1.** to start (a motor vehicle) by pushing it while it is in gear, thus turning the engine. ~*n.* **2.** the act or process of starting a vehicle in this way.

push through *vb.* (*tr.*) to compel to accept: *the bill was pushed through Parliament.*

Push+to ('pʌʃtəʊ) *or* **Push+tu** ('pʌʃtuː) *n., adj.* variant spellings of **Pashto.**

push-up *n.* the U.S. term for **press-up.**

push·y ('pʊʃɪ) *adj.* **push·i+er, push·i+est.** *Informal.* **1.** offensively assertive or forceful. **2.** aggressively or ruthlessly ambitious. —'**push·i+ly** *adv.* —'**push·i·ness** *n.*

pu·sil·lan·i·mous (ˌpjuːsɪ'lænɪməs) *adj.* characterized by a lack of courage or determination. [C16: from Late Latin *pusillanimis,* from Latin *pusillus* weak + *animus* courage] —**pu+sil+la+nim+i·ty** (ˌpjuːsɪlə'nɪmɪtɪ) *n.* —ˌ**pu+sil+'lan·i·mous+ly** *adv.*

puss[1] (pʊs) *n.* **1.** an informal name for a **cat.** See also **pussy**[1] (sense 1). **2.** *Slang.* a girl or woman. **3.** an informal name for a **hare.** [C16: related to Middle Low German *pūs,* Dutch *poes,* Lithuanian *puz*]

puss[2] (pʊs) *n. Slang.* the face. [C17: from Irish *pus*]

puss moth *n.* a large pale European moth, *Cerura* (or *Dicranura*) *vinula,* having a thick furry body and a tuft of scales on each forewing: family *Notodontidae.*

puss·y[1] ('pʊsɪ) *n., pl.* **puss·ies. 1.** Also called: **puss, pus·sy+cat** ('pʊsɪˌkæt). an informal name for a **cat. 2.** a furry catkin, esp. that of the pussy willow. **3.** a rare word for **tipcat.** [C18: from PUSS[1]]

puss·y[2] ('pʊsɪ) *n., pl.* **puss·ies.** *Taboo slang.* **1.** the female genitals. **2.** a woman considered as a sexual object.

pus+sy[3] ('pʌsɪ) *adj.* **+si+er, +si+est.** containing or full of pus.

puss·y+foot ('pʊsɪˌfʊt) *Informal.* ~*vb.* (*intr.*) **1.** to move about stealthily or warily like a cat. **2.** to avoid committing oneself. ~*n., pl.* **+foots. 3.** a person who pussyfoots.

puss·y wil+low ('pʊsɪ) *n.* **1.** an American willow tree, *Salix discolor,* with silvery silky catkins: widely planted for ornament. **2.** any of various similar willows.

pus+tu+lant ('pʌstjʊlənt) *adj.* **1.** causing the formation of pustules. ~*n.* **2.** an agent causing such formation.

pus+tu+late *vb.* ('pʌstjʊˌleɪt). **1.** to form or cause to form into pustules. ~*adj.* ('pʌstjʊlɪt, -ˌleɪt). **2.** covered with pustules. —ˌ**pus+tu+'la+tion** *n.*

pus+tule ('pʌstjuːl) *n.* **1.** a small inflamed elevated area of skin containing pus. **2.** any small distinct spot resembling a pimple or blister. [C14: from Latin *pustula* a blister, variant of *pūsula;* compare Greek *phusallis* bladder, *phusa* bellows] —**pus+tu+lar** ('pʌstjʊlə) *adj.*

put (pʊt) *vb.* **puts, put+ting, put.** (*mainly tr.*) **1.** to cause to be (in a position or place): *to put a book on the table.* **2.** to cause to be (in a state, relation, etc.): *to put one's things in order.* **3.** (foll. by *to*) to cause (a person) to experience the endurance or suffering (of): *to put to death; to put to the sword.* **4.** to set or commit (to an action, task, or duty), esp. by force: *he put him to work.* **5.** to render, transform, or translate: *to put into English.* **6.** to set (words) in a musical form (esp. in the phrase **put to music**). **7.** (foll. by *at*) to estimate: *he put the distance at fifty miles.* **8.** (foll. by *to*) to utilize (for the purpose of): *he put his knowledge to good use.* **9.** (foll. by *to*) to couple a female animal (with a male) for the purpose of breeding: *the farmer put his heifer to the bull.* **10.** to state; express: *to put it bluntly.* **11.** to set or make (an end or limit): *he put an end to the proceedings.* **12.** to present for consideration in anticipation of an answer or vote; propose: *he put the question to the committee; I put it to you that one day you will all die.* **13.** to invest (money) in; give (support) to: *he put five thousand pounds into the project.* **14.** to impart: *to put zest into a party.* **15.** to throw or cast. **16. not know where to put oneself.** to feel awkward or embarrassed. **17. put paid to.** to destroy irrevocably and utterly: *the manager's disfavour put paid to their hopes for promotion.* **18. stay put.** to remain in one place without leaving it; remain stationary. ~*n.* **19.** a throw or cast, esp. in putting the shot. **20.** Also called: **put option.** *Stock Exchange.* an option to sell a stated amount of securities at a specified price during a specified limited period. Compare **call** (sense 58). ~See also **put about, put across, put aside, put away, put back, put down, put forth, put forward, put in, put off, put on, put on to, put out, put over, put through, put up, put upon.** [C12 *puten* to push; related to Old English *potian* to push, Norwegian, Icelandic *pota* to poke]

put a·bout *vb.* (*adv.*) **1.** *Nautical.* to change course or cause to change course: *we put about and headed for home.* **2.** (*tr.*) to make widely known: *he put about the news of the air disaster.* **3.** (*tr.; usually passive*) to disconcert or disturb: *she was quite put about by his appearance.*

put a·cross *vb.* (*tr.*) **1.** (*adv.*) to communicate in a comprehensible way: *he couldn't put things across very well.* **2. put one across.** *Informal.* to get (someone) to accept or believe a claim, excuse, etc., by deception: *they put one across their teacher.*

pu+ta+men (pjuː'teɪmɛn) *n., pl.* **+tam·i+na** (-'tæmɪnə). the hard endocarp or stone of fruits such as the peach, plum, and cherry. [C19: from Latin: clippings, from *putāre* to prune]

put a·side *or* **by** *vb.* (*tr., adv.*) **1.** to move (an object, etc.) to one side, esp. in rejection. **2.** to store up; save: *to put money aside for a rainy day.* **3.** to ignore or disregard: *let us put aside our differences.*

pu+ta+tive ('pjuːtətɪv) *adj.* **1.** (*prenominal*) commonly regarded as being: *the putative father.* **2.** (*prenominal*) considered to exist or have existed; inferred. **3.** *Grammar.* denoting a mood of the verb in some languages used when the speaker does not have direct evidence of what he is asserting, but has inferred it on the basis of something else. [C15: from Late Latin *putātīvus* supposed, from Latin *putāre* to consider] —'**pu+ta+tive+ly** *adv.*

put a·way *vb.* (*tr., adv.*) **1.** to return (something) to the correct or proper place: *he put away his books.* **2.** to save: *to put away money for the future.* **3.** to lock up in a prison, mental institution, etc.: *they put him away for twenty years.* **4.** to eat or drink, esp. in large amounts. **5.** to put to death, because of old age or illness: *the dog had to be put away.*

put back *vb.* (*tr., adv.*) **1.** to return to its former place. **2.** to move to a later time or date: *the wedding was put back a fortnight.* **3.** to delay or impede the progress of: *the strike put back production severely.*

put down *vb.* (*tr., adv.*) **1.** to make a written record of. **2.** to repress: *to put down a rebellion.* **3.** to consider; account: *they put him down for an ignoramus.* **4.** to attribute: *I put the mistake down to his inexperience.* **5.** to put to death, because of old age or illness: *the vet put the cat down.* **6.** to table on the agenda: *the MPs put down a motion on the increase in crime.* **7.** *Slang.* to dismiss, reject, or humiliate. ~*n.* **put-down. 8.** a cruelly critical remark.

put forth *vb.* (*tr., adv.*) *Formal.* **1.** to present; propose. **2.** (of a plant) to produce or bear (leaves, branches, shoots, etc.).

put for+ward *vb.* (*tr., adv.*) **1.** to propose; suggest. **2.** to offer the name of; nominate.

put in *vb.* (*adv.*) **1.** (*intr.*) *Nautical.* to bring a vessel into port, esp. for a brief stay: *we put in for fresh provisions.* **2.** (often foll. by *for*) to apply or cause to apply (for a job, in a competition, etc.). **3.** (*tr.*) to submit: *he put in his claims form.* **4.** to intervene with (a remark) during a conversation. **5.** (*tr.*) to devote (time, effort, etc.) to a task: *he put in three hours overtime last night.* **6.** (*tr.*) *Cricket.* to cause (a team, esp. the opposing one) to bat: *England won the toss and put the visitors in to bat.* ~*n.* **put-in. 7.** *Rugby.* the act of throwing the ball into a scrum.

put+log ('pʌtˌlɒg) *or* **put+lock** *n.* a short horizontal beam that with others supports the floor planks of a scaffold. [C17: changed (through influence of LOG[1]) from earlier *putlock,* probably from PUT (past participle) + LOCK]

Put·nam ('pʌtnəm) *n.* **1. Is·ra·el.** 1718–90, American general in the War of Independence. **2.** his cousin **Ru·fus.** 1738–1824, American soldier in the War of Independence; surveyor general of the U.S. (1796–1803).

put off *vb.* **1.** (*tr., adv.*) to postpone or delay: *they have put off the dance until tomorrow.* **2.** (*tr., adv.*) to evade (a person) by postponement or delay: *they tried to put him off, but he came anyway.* **3.** (*tr., adv.*) to confuse; disconcert: *he was put off by her appearance.* **4.** (*tr., prep.*) to cause to lose interest in or enjoyment of: *the accident put him off driving.* **5.** (*intr., adv.*) *Nautical.* to be launched off from shore or from a ship: *we put* *off in the lifeboat towards the ship.* **6.** (*tr., adv.*) *Archaic.* to remove (clothes). *~n.* **put+off. 7.** *Chiefly U.S.* a pretext or delay.

put on *vb.* (*tr., mainly adv.*) **1.** to clothe oneself in: *to put on a coat.* **2.** (*usually passive*) to adopt (an attitude or feeling) insincerely: *his misery was just put on.* **3.** to present or stage (a play, show, etc.). **4.** to increase or add: *she put on weight; the batsman put on fifty runs before lunch.* **5.** to cause (an electrical device) to function. **6.** (*also prep.*) to wager (money) on a horse race, game, etc.: *he put ten pounds on the favourite.* **7.** (*also prep.*) to impose as a burden or levy: *to put a tax on cars.* **8.** *Cricket.* to cause (a bowler) to bowl. **9. put (someone) on. a.** to connect (a person) by telephone. **b.** *Slang, chiefly U.S.* to mock or tease. *~n.* **put-on. 10.** *U.S. slang.* a hoax or piece of mockery. **11.** *U.S. slang.* an affected manner or mode of behaviour.

put on to *vb.* (*tr., prep.*) **1.** to connect by telephone. **2.** to inform (someone) of (a person's location or activities): *I'll put the police on to you if you don't stop.* **3.** to tell (a person) about (someone or something beneficial): *can you put me on to a cheap supermarket?*

put out *vb.* (*tr., adv.*) **1.** (*often passive*) **a.** to annoy; anger. **b.** to confound or disturb; confuse. **2.** to extinguish or douse (a fire, light, etc.): *he put out the fire.* **3.** to poke forward: *to put out one's tongue.* **4.** to be or present a source of inconvenience or annoyance to (a person): *I hope I'm not putting you out.* **5.** to issue or publish; broadcast: *the authorities put out a leaflet.* **6.** to render unconscious. **7.** to dislocate: *he put out his shoulder in the accident.* **8.** to show or exert: *the workers put out all their energy in the campaign.* **9.** to pass, give out (work to be done) at different premises. **10.** to lend (money) at interest. **11.** *Cricket.* to dismiss (a player or team). **12.** *Baseball.* to cause (a batter or runner) to be out by a fielding play. *~n.* **put+out. 13.** *Baseball.* a play in which the batter or runner is put out.

put o·ver *vb.* (*tr., adv.*) **1.** *Informal.* to communicate (facts, information, etc.) comprehensibly: *he puts his thoughts over badly.* **2.** *Chiefly U.S.* to postpone; defer: *the match was put over a week.* Brit. equivalent: **put off. 3. put (a fast) one over on.** *Informal.* to get (someone) to accept or believe a claim, excuse, etc., by deception: *he put one over on his boss.*

put-put ('pʌtˌpʌt) *Informal.* *~n.* **1.** a light chugging or popping sound, as made by a petrol engine. **2.** a vehicle powered by an engine making such a sound. *~vb.* **-puts, -put·ting, -put·ted. 3.** (*intr.*) to make or travel along with such a sound.

pu+tre+fy ('pjuːtrɪˌfaɪ) *vb.* **+fies, +fy+ing, +fied.** (of organic matter) to decompose or rot with an offensive smell. [C15: from Old French *putrefier* + Latin *putrefacere*, from *puter* rotten + *facere* to make] **—pu+tre+fac+tion** (ˌpjuːtrɪ'fækʃən) *n.* **—ˌpu+tre+'fac·tive** *or* **pu+tre+fa+cient** (ˌpjuːtrɪ'feɪʃənt) *adj.* **—'pu+tre+ˌfi·a·ble** *adj.* **—'pu+tre+ˌfi·er** *n.*

pu+tres+cent (pjuː'trɛsᵊnt) *adj.* **1.** becoming putrid; rotting. **2.** characterized by or undergoing putrefaction. [C18: from Latin *putrescere* to become rotten] **—pu+'tres+cence** *n.*

pu+tres+ci·ble (pjuː'trɛsɪbᵊl) *~adj.* **1.** liable to become putrid. *~n.* **2.** a putrescible substance. [C18: from Latin *putrescere* to decay] **—pu+ˌtres+ci·'bil+i·ty** *n.*

pu+tres+cine (pjuː'trɛsiːn, -ɪn) *n.* a colourless crystalline amine produced by decaying animal matter; 1,4-diaminobutane. Formula: $H_2N(CH_2)_4NH_2$. [C20: from Latin *putrescere* + -INE[2]]

pu+trid ('pjuːtrɪd) *adj.* **1.** (of organic matter) in a state of decomposition, usually giving off a foul smell: *putrid meat.* **2.** morally corrupt or worthless. **3.** sickening; foul: *a putrid smell.* **4.** *Informal.* deficient in quality or value: *a putrid film.* [C16: from Latin *putridus* rotten, from *putrēre* to be rotten] **—pu+'trid+i·ty** *or* **'pu+trid+ness** *n.* **—'pu+trid+ly** *adv.*

Putsch *German.* (pʊtʃ) *n.* a violent and sudden uprising; political revolt. [German: from Swiss German: a push, of imitative origin]

putt (pʌt) *Golf.* *~n.* **1.** a stroke on the green with a putter to roll the ball into or near the hole. *~vb.* **2.** to strike (the ball) in this way. [C16: of Scottish origin; related to PUT]

put+tee *or* **put+ty** ('pʌtɪ) *n., pl.* **+tees** *or* **+ties.** (*often pl.*) a strip of cloth worn wound around the legs from the ankle to the knee, esp. as part of a uniform in World War I. [C19: from Hindi *paṭṭī*, from Sanskrit *paṭṭikā*, from *paṭṭa* cloth]

putt+er[1] ('pʌtə) *n. Golf.* **1.** a club with a short shaft for putting, usually having a solid metal head. **2.** a golfer who putts: *he is a good putter.*

putt+er[2] ('pʌtə) *vb.* the usual U.S. spelling of **potter**[2]. **—'put+ter+er** *n.*

put+ter[3] ('pʊtə) *n.* **1.** a person who puts: *the putter of a question.* **2.** a person who puts the shot.

put through *vb.* (*tr., mainly adv.*) **1.** to carry out to a conclusion: *he put through his plan.* **2.** (*also prep.*) to organize the processing of: *she put through his application to join the organization.* **3.** to connect by telephone. **4.** to make (a telephone call).

putt+ing green ('pʌtɪŋ) *n.* **1.** (on a golf course) the area of closely mown grass at the end of a fairway where the hole is. **2.** an area of smooth grass with several holes for putting games.

put+to ('pʊtəʊ) *n., pl.* **+ti** (-tɪ). a representation of a small boy, a cherub or cupid, esp. in baroque painting or sculpture. See also **amoretto.** [from Italian, from Latin *putus* boy]

put+ty ('pʌtɪ) *n., pl.* **+ties. 1.** a stiff paste made of whiting and linseed oil that is used to fix glass panes into frames and to fill cracks or holes in woodwork, etc. **2.** any substance with a similar consistency, function, or appearance. **3.** a mixture of lime and water with sand or plaster of Paris used on plaster as a finishing coat. **4.** (*as modifier*): *a putty knife.* **5.** See **putty powder. 6.** a person who is easily influenced or persuaded: *he's putty in her hands.* **7. a.** a colour varying from a greyish-yellow to a greyish-brown or brownish-grey. **b.** (*as adj.*): *putty-coloured.* **8. up to putty.** *Austral. informal.* worthless or useless. *~vb.* **+ties, +ty+ing, +tied. 9.** (*tr.*) to fix, fill, or coat with putty. [C17: from French *potée* a potful]

put+ty pow+der *n.* a powder, either tin oxide or tin and lead oxide, used for polishing glassware, metal, etc.

put·ty+root ('pʌtɪˌruːt) *n.* a North American orchid, *Aplectrum hyemale*, bearing a single leaf and yellowish-brown or purple flowers. Also called: **adam-and-eve.**

Pu+tu+ma+yo (*Spanish* ˌputu'majo) *n.* a river in NW South America, rising in S Colombia and flowing southeast as most of the border between Colombia and Peru, entering the Amazon in Brazil: scene of the Putumayo rubber scandal (1910–11) during the rubber boom, in which many Indians were enslaved and killed by rubber exploiters. Length: 1578 km (980 miles). Brazilian name: **Içá.**

put up *vb.* (*adv., mainly tr.*) **1.** to build; erect: *to put up a statue.* **2.** to accommodate or be accommodated at: *can you put me up for tonight?* **3.** to increase (prices). **4.** to submit or present (a plan, case, etc.). **5.** to offer: *to put a house up for sale.* **6.** to provide or supply; give: *to put up a good fight.* **7.** to provide (money) for; invest in: *they put up five thousand for the new project.* **8.** to preserve or can (jam, etc.). **9.** to pile up (long hair) on the head in any of several styles. **10.** (*also intr.*) to nominate or be nominated as a candidate, esp. for a political or society post: *he put his wife up as secretary; he put up for president.* **11.** *Archaic.* to return (a weapon) to its holder, as a sword to its sheath: *put up your pistol!* **12. put up to. a.** to inform or instruct (a person) about (tasks, duties, etc.). **b.** to urge or goad (a person) on to; incite to. **13. put up with.** (*intr.*) *Informal.* to endure; tolerate. *~adj.* **put-up. 14.** dishonestly or craftily prearranged or conceived (esp. in the phrase **put-up job**).

put up·on *vb.* (*intr., prep., usually passive*) **1.** to presume on (a person's generosity, good nature, etc.); take advantage of: *he's always being put upon.* **2.** to impose hardship on; maltreat: *he was sorely put upon.*

Pu·vis de Cha·vannes (*French* pyvis də ʃa'van) *n.* **Pierre Cé·cile** (pjɛːr se'sil). 1824–98, French mural painter.

Puy de Dôme (pwi də 'doːm) *n.* **1.** a department of central France in Auvergne region. Capital: Clermont-Ferrand. Pop.: 596 699 (1975). Area: 8016 sq. km (3126 sq. miles). **2.** a mountain in central France, in the Auvergne Mountains: a volcanic plug. Height: 1463 m (4800 ft.).

Puy de San+cy (*French* pwi də sã'si) *n.* a mountain in S central France: highest peak of the Monts Dore. Height: 1886 m (6188 ft.).

Pu-yi ('puː'jiː) *n.* **Hen·ry.** 1906–67, last emperor of China as Hsüan T'ung (1908–12); emperor of the Japanese puppet state of Manchukuo as K'ang Te (1934–45).

puz+zle ('pʌzᵊl) *vb.* **1.** to perplex or be perplexed. **2.** (*intr.;* foll. by *over*) to attempt the solution (of); ponder (about): *he puzzled over her absence.* **3.** (*tr.;* usually foll. by *out*) to solve by mental effort: *he puzzled out the meaning of the inscription.* *~n.* **4.** a person or thing that puzzles. **5.** a problem that cannot be easily or readily solved. **6.** the state or condition of being puzzled. **7.** a toy, game, or question presenting a problem that requires skill or ingenuity for its solution. See **jigsaw puzzle, Chinese puzzle.** [C16: of unknown origin] **—'puz+zling+ly** *adv.*

puz+zle+ment ('pʌzᵊlmənt) *n.* the state or condition of being puzzled; perplexity.

puz+zler ('pʌzlə) *n.* a person or thing that puzzles.

PVA *abbrev. for* polyvinyl acetate.

PVC *abbrev. for* polyvinyl chloride; a synthetic thermoplastic material made by polymerizing vinyl chloride. The properties depend on the added plasticizer. The flexible forms are used in hosepipes, insulation, shoes, garments, etc. Rigid PVC is used for moulded articles.

Pvt. *Military. abbrev. for* private.

P.W. *abbrev. for* policewoman.

P.W.D. *abbrev. for* Public Works Department.

pwt *or* **pwt.** *abbrev. for* pennyweight.

PX *Military. abbrev. for* Post Exchange.

PY *international car registration for* Paraguay.

py- *combining form.* variant of **pyo-** before a vowel.

pya (pjɑː, pɪ'ɑː) *n.* a Burmese monetary unit worth one hundredth of a kyat. [from Burmese]

py+ae·mi·a *or* **py+e·mi·a** (paɪ'iːmɪə) *n.* blood poisoning characterized by pus-forming microorganisms in the blood. [C19: from New Latin, from Greek *puon* pus + *haima* blood] **—py+'ae·mic** *or* **py+'e·mic** *adj.*

pyc+nid+i·um (pɪk'nɪdɪəm) *n., pl.* **·i·a** (-ɪə). a small flask-shaped structure containing spores that occurs in ascomycetes and certain other fungi. [C19: from New Latin, from Greek *puknos* thick]

pyc·no- *or before a vowel* **pycn-** *combining form.* indicating thickness or density: *pycnometer.* [via New Latin from Greek *puknos* thick]

pyc+nom+e·ter (pɪk'nɒmɪtə) *n.* a small glass bottle of known volume for determining the relative density of liquids and solids by weighing. **—pyc+no+met+ric** (ˌpɪknə'mɛtrɪk) *adj.*

Pyd+na ('pɪdnə) *n.* a town in ancient Macedonia: site of a major Roman victory over the Macedonians, resulting in the downfall of their kingdom (168 B.C.).

pye (paɪ) *n. Ecclesiast.* a variant spelling of **pie**[5].

pye-dog *or* **pie-dog** *n.* an ownerless half-wild Asian dog.

py+e·li+tis (ˌpaɪəˈlaɪtɪs) *n.* inflammation of the pelvis of the kidney. Compare **pyelonephritis.** —**py+e·lit+ic** (ˌpaɪəˈlɪtɪk) *adj.*

py+e·log+ra+phy (ˌpaɪəˈlɒgrəfɪ) *n. Med.* the branch of radiology concerned with examination of the kidney and associated structures by means of an x-ray picture called a **py+e·lo+gram** (ˈpaɪələʊˌgræm). —**py+e·lo+graph+ic** (ˌpaɪələʊˈgræfɪk) *adj.*

py+e·lo+ne·phri+tis (ˌpaɪələʊnɪˈfraɪtɪs) *n.* inflammation of the kidney and renal pelvis. Compare **pyelitis.**

py+gid+i·um (paɪˈdʒɪdɪəm, -ˈgɪd-) *n., pl.* **·i·a** (-ɪə). the terminal segment, division, or other structure in certain annelids, arthropods, and other invertebrates. [C19: from New Latin, from Greek *pugē* rump] —**py+ˈgid+i·al** *adj.*

Pyg·ma·li·on (pɪgˈmeɪlɪən) *n. Greek myth.* a king of Cyprus, who fell in love with the statue of a woman he had sculpted and which his prayers brought to life as Galatea.

pyg+my *or* **pig+my** (ˈpɪgmɪ) *n., pl.* **+mies.** **1.** an abnormally undersized person. **2.** something that is a very small example of its type. **3.** a person of little importance or significance. **4.** (*modifier*) of very small stature or size. [C14 *pigmeis* the Pygmies, from Latin *Pygmaeus* a Pygmy, from Greek *pugmaios* undersized, from *pugmē* fist] —**pyg+mae·an** *or* **pyg+me·an** (pɪgˈmiːən) *adj.*

Pyg+my *or* **Pig+my** (ˈpɪgmɪ) *n., pl.* **+mies.** a member of one of the dwarf peoples of Equatorial Africa, noted for their hunting and forest culture.

py+ja+ma *or U.S.* **pa+ja+ma** (pəˈdʒɑːmə) *n.* (*modifier*) **1.** of or forming part of pyjamas: *pyjama top.* **2.** requiring pyjamas to be worn: *a pyjama party.*

py+ja+mas *or U.S.* **pa+ja+mas** (pəˈdʒɑːməz) *pl. n.* **1.** loose-fitting nightclothes comprising a jacket or top and trousers. **2.** full loose-fitting ankle-length trousers worn by either sex in various Eastern countries. **3.** women's flared trousers or trouser suit used esp. for leisure wear.

pyk+nic (ˈpɪknɪk) *adj.* (of a physical type) characterized by a broad squat fleshy physique with a large chest and abdomen. [C20: from Greek *puknos* thick]

py+lon (ˈpaɪlən) *n.* **1.** a large vertical steel tower-like structure supporting high-tension electrical cables. **2.** a post or tower for guiding pilots or marking a turning point in a race. **3.** a streamlined aircraft structure for attaching an engine pod, external fuel tank, etc., to the main body of the aircraft. **4.** a monumental gateway, such as one at the entrance to an ancient Egyptian temple. **5.** a temporary artificial leg. [C19: from Greek *pulōn* a gateway]

py+lo+rec+to+my (ˌpaɪlɔːˈrɛktəmɪ) *n., pl.* **+mies.** surgical removal of all or part of the pylorus, often including the adjacent portion of the stomach (**partial gastrectomy**).

py+lo+rus (paɪˈlɔːrəs) *n., pl.* **+ri** (-raɪ). the small circular opening at the base of the stomach through which partially digested food (chyme) passes to the duodenum. [C17: via Late Latin from Greek *pulōrus* gatekeeper, from *pulē* gate + *ouros* guardian] —**py+ˈlo+ric** *adj.*

Py+los (ˈpaɪlɒs) *n.* a port in SW Greece, in the SW Peloponnese; scene of a defeat of the Spartans by the Athenians (425 B.C.) during the Peloponnesian War and of the Battle of Navarino (1827) during the War of Greek Independence. Italian name: **Navarino.** Modern Greek name: **Pílos.**

Pym (pɪm) *n.* **John.** ?1584–1643, leading English parliamentarian during the events leading to the Civil War. He took a prominent part in the impeachment of Buckingham (1626) and of Strafford and Laud (1640).

py·o- *or before a vowel* **py-** *combining form.* denoting pus: *pyosis.* [from Greek *puon*]

py·o+der+ma (ˌpaɪəʊˈdɜːmə) *n. Pathol.* any skin eruption characterized by pustules or the formation of pus.

py·o+gen+e·sis (ˌpaɪəʊˈdʒɛnɪsɪs) *n. Pathol.* the formation of pus. —ˌ**py·o+ˈgen+ic** *adj.*

py+oid (ˈpaɪɔɪd) *adj.* resembling pus.

Pyong+yang *or* **P'yŏng-yang** (ˈpjɒŋˈjæŋ) *n.* the capital of North Korea, in the southwest on the Taedong River: industrial centre; university (1946). Pop.: 1 500 000 (1971 est.).

py+or+rhoe·a *or esp. U.S.* **py+or+rhe·a** (ˌpaɪəˈrɪə) *n. Pathol.* **1.** any condition characterized by a discharge of pus. **2.** See **pyorrhoea alveolaris.** —ˌ**py+or+ˈrhoe·al,** ˌ**py+or+ˈrhoe+ic** *or esp. U.S.* ˌ**py+or+ˈrhe·al,** ˌ**py+or+ˈrhe+ic** *adj.*

py+or+rhoe·a al+ve·o+lar+is (ˌælvɪəˈlɑːrɪs) *n. Dentistry.* inflammation of the gums characterized by the discharge of pus and loosening of the teeth.

py·o+sis (paɪˈəʊsɪs) *n. Pathol.* the formation of pus.

pyr- *combining form.* variant of **pyro-** before a vowel.

py+ra+can+tha (ˌpaɪrəˈkænθə) *n.* any rosaceous shrub of the genus *Pyracantha,* esp. the firethorn, widely cultivated for ornament. [C17: from Greek *purakantha* name of a shrub, from PYRO- + *akantha* thorn]

pyr·a+lid (ˈpɪrəlɪd) *n.* **1.** any moth of the mostly tropical family *Pyralidae,* typically having narrow forewings and broad fringed hind wings: includes the bee moths and the corn borer. ~*adj.* **2.** of, relating to, or belonging to the family *Pyralidae.* [C19: via New Latin from Greek *puralis:* a mythical winged insect believed to live in fire, from *pur* fire]

pyr·a+mid (ˈpɪrəmɪd) *n.* **1.** a huge masonry construction that has a square base and, as in the case of the ancient Egyptian royal tombs, four sloping triangular sides. **2.** an object, formation, or structure resembling such a construction. **3.** *Maths.* a solid having a polygonal base and triangular sides that meet in a common vertex. **4.** *Crystallog.* a crystal form in which three planes intersect all three axes of the crystal. **5.** *Anatomy.* any pointed or cone-shaped bodily structure or part. **6.** *Finance.* a group of enterprises containing a series of holding companies structured so that the top holding company controls the entire group with a relatively small proportion of the total capital invested. **7.** *Chiefly U.S.* the series of transactions involved in pyramiding securities. **8.** (*pl.*) a game similar to billiards with fifteen coloured balls. ~*vb.* **9.** to build up or be arranged in the form of a pyramid. **10.** *Chiefly U.S.* to speculate in (securities or property) by increasing purchases on additional margin or collateral derived from paper profits associated with high prices of securities and property in a boom. **11.** *Finance.* to form (companies) into a pyramid. **12.** (*tr.*) *Logic.* to build up (an argument, thesis, etc.) systematically from a basic general premiss. [C16 (earlier *pyramis*): from Latin *pyramis,* from Greek *puramis,* probably from Egyptian] —**py+ram·i·dal** (pɪˈræmɪdᵊl), ˌ**pyr·a+ˈmid·i·cal,** *or* ˌ**pyr·a+ˈmid+ic** *adj.* —**py+ˈram·i·dal+ly** *or* ˌ**pyr·a+ˈmid·i·cal+ly** *adv.*

py+ram·i+dal peak *n. Geology.* a sharp peak formed where the ridges separating three or more cirques intersect; horn.

pyr·a+mid sell+ing *n.* a practice adopted by some manufacturers of advertising for distributors and selling them batches of goods. The first distributors then advertise for more distributors who are sold subdivisions of the original batches at an increased price. This process continues until the final distributors are left with a stock that is unsaleable except at a loss.

Pyr·a·mus and This·be (ˈpɪrəməs; ˈθɪzbɪ) *n.* (in Greek legend) two lovers of Babylon: Pyramus, wrongly supposing Thisbe to be dead, killed himself and she, encountering him in his death throes, did the same.

py+ran (ˈpaɪræn, paɪˈræn) *n.* an unsaturated heterocyclic compound having a ring containing five carbon atoms and one oxygen atom and two double bonds. It has two isomers depending on the position of the saturated carbon atom relative to the oxygen. [C20: from PYRO- + -AN]

py+ra+nom+e·ter (ˌpaɪrəˈnɒmɪtə) *n. Physics.* another name for **solarimeter.**

py+rar+gy+rite (paɪˈrɑːdʒɪˌraɪt) *n.* a dark red to black mineral consisting of silver antimony sulphide in hexagonal crystalline form: occurs in silver veins and is an important ore of silver. Formula: Ag_3SbS_3. [C19: from German *Pyrargyrit,* from PYRO- + Greek *arguros* silver]

py+ra+zole (ˈpaɪrəˌzɒl) *n.* a crystalline soluble basic heterocyclic compound; 1,2-diazole. Formula: $C_3H_4N_2$.

pyre (paɪə) *n.* a heap or pile of wood or other combustible material, esp. one used for cremating a corpse. [C17: from Latin *pyra,* from Greek *pura* hearth, from *pur* fire]

py+rene[1] (ˈpaɪriːn) *n.* a solid polynuclear aromatic hydrocarbon extracted from coal tar. Formula: $C_{16}H_{10}$. [C19: from PYRO- + -ENE]

py+rene[2] (ˈpaɪriːn) *n. Botany.* any of several small hard stones that occur in a single fruit and contain a single seed each. [C19: from New Latin *pyrena,* from Greek *purēn*]

Pyr+e·nees (ˌpɪrəˈniːz) *pl. n.* a mountain range between France and Spain, extending from the Bay of Biscay to the Mediterranean. Highest peak: Pico de Aneto, 3404 m (11 168 ft.). —ˌ**Pyr+e·ˈne·an** *adj.*

Py+ré+nées *or* **Py+ré+nées At+lan+tiques** (*French* pirenez atlãˈtik) *n.* a department of SW France in Aquitaine region. Capital: Pau. Pop.: 552 615 (1975). Area: 7712 sq. km (3008 sq. miles). Former name: **Basses-Pyrénées.**

Py+ré·nées-O·ri·en·tales (*French* pirenezɔriãˈtal) *n.* a department of S France, in Languedoc-Roussillon region. Capital: Perpignan. Pop.: 305 730 (1975). Area: 4144 sq. km (1616 sq. miles).

pyr+e·noid (ˈpaɪrəˌnɔɪd) *n.* any of various small protein granules that occur in certain algae, mosses, and protozoans and are involved in the synthesis of starch.

py+re·thrin (paɪˈriːθrɪn) *n.* **1.** Also called: **pyrethrin I.** an oily water-insoluble compound used as an insecticide. Formula: $C_{21}H_{28}O_3$. **2.** Also called: **pyrethrin II.** a compound of similar chemical structure and action, also found in pyrethrum. Formula: $C_{22}H_{28}O_5$. [C19: from PYRETHRUM + -IN]

py+re·thrum (paɪˈriːθrəm) *n.* **1.** any of several cultivated Eurasian chrysanthemums, such as *Chrysanthemum coccineum* and *C. roseum,* with white, pink, red, or purple flowers. **2.** any insecticide prepared from the dried flowers of any of these plants, esp. *C. roseum.* [C16: via Latin from Greek *purethron* feverfew, probably from *puretos* fever; see PYRETIC]

py+ret+ic (paɪˈrɛtɪk) *adj. Pathol.* of, relating to, or characterized by fever. Compare **antipyretic.** [C18: from New Latin *pyreticus,* from Greek *puretos* fever, from *pur* fire]

Py+rex (ˈpaɪrɛks) *n. Trademark.* **a.** any of a variety of borosilicate glasses that have low coefficients of expansion, making them suitable for heat-resistant glassware used in cookery and chemical apparatus. **b.** (*as modifier*): *a Pyrex dish.*

py+rex·i·a (paɪˈrɛksɪə) *n.* a technical name for **fever.** [C18: from New Latin, from Greek *purexis,* from *puressein* to be feverish, from *pur* fire] —**py+ˈrex·i·al** *or* **py+ˈrex+ic** *adj.*

pyr+he·li+om+e·ter (pəˌhiːlɪˈɒmɪtə) *n.* an instrument for measuring the intensity of the sun's radiant energy. —**pyr+he·li·o·met+ric** (pəˌhiːlɪəʊˈmɛtrɪk) *adj.*

pyr·i·dine (ˈpɪrɪˌdiːn) *n.* a colourless hygroscopic liquid with a characteristic odour. It is a basic heterocyclic compound containing one nitrogen atom and five carbon atoms in its molecules and is used as a solvent and in preparing other organic chemicals. Formula: C_5H_5N. [C19: from PYRO- + -ID[3] + -INE[2]]

pyr·i·dox·al (ˌpɪrɪˈdɒksəl) *n. Biochem.* a naturally occurring derivative of pyridoxine that is a precursor of a coenzyme (**pyridoxal phosphate**) involved in several enzymic reactions. Formula: $(CH_2OH)(CHO)C_5HN(OH)(CH_3)$.

pyr·i·dox·a·mine (ˌpɪrɪˈdɒksəmiːn) *n. Biochem.* a metabolic form of pyridoxine.

pyr·i·dox·ine (ˌpɪrɪˈdɒksiːn) *n. Biochem.* a derivative of pyridine that is a precursor of the compounds pyridoxal and pyridoxamine. Also called: **vitamin B_6**. [C20: from PYRID(INE) + OX(YGEN) + -INE[2]]

pyr·i·form (ˈpɪrɪˌfɔːm) *adj.* (esp. of organs of the body) pear-shaped. [C18: from New Latin *pyriformis*, from *pyri-*, erroneously from Latin *pirum* pear + *-formis* -FORM]

py·rim·i·dine (paɪˈrɪmɪˌdiːn) *n.* **1.** a liquid or crystalline organic compound with a penetrating odour; 1,3-diazine. It is a weakly basic soluble heterocyclic compound and can be prepared from barbituric acid. Formula: $C_4H_4N_2$. **2.** any of a number of similar compounds having a basic structure that is derived from pyrimidine, including cytosine, thymine, and uracil, which are constituents of nucleic acids. [C20: variant of PYRIDINE]

py·rim·i·dine base *n. Biochem.* a pyrimidine, esp. the compounds cytosine, thymine, and uracil, which occur in nucleic acids.

py·rite (ˈpaɪraɪt) *n.* a hard brittle yellow mineral consisting of iron sulphide in cubic crystalline form. It occurs in all types of rocks and veins, associated with various metals, and is used mainly in the manufacture of sulphuric acid and paper. Formula: FeS_2. Also called: **iron pyrites, pyrites.** [C16: from Latin *pyrites* flint, from Greek *puritēs* (*lithos*) fire (stone), that is, capable of withstanding or striking fire, from *pur* fire] —**py·rit·ic** (paɪˈrɪtɪk) *or* **py·ˈri·tous** *adj.*

py·ri·tes (paɪˈraɪtiːz) *n., pl.* **·tes. 1.** another name for **pyrite. 2.** any of a number of other disulphides of metals, esp. of copper and tin.

py·ro- *or before a vowel* **pyr-** *combining form.* **1.** denoting fire, heat, or high temperature: *pyromania; pyrometer.* **2.** caused or obtained by fire or heat: *pyroelectricity.* **3.** *Chem.* **a.** denoting a new substance obtained by heating another: *pyroboric acid is obtained by heating boric acid.* **b.** denoting an acid or salt with a water content intermediate between that of the ortho- and meta- compounds: *pyro-phosphoric acid.* **4.** *Mineralogy.* **a.** having a property that changes upon the application of heat: *pyromorphite.* **b.** having a flame-coloured appearance: *pyroxylin.*

py·ro·cat·e·chol (ˌpaɪrəʊˈkætɪˌtʃɒl, -kɒl) *or* **py·ro·cat·e·chin** (ˌpaɪrəʊˈkætɪkɪn) *n.* another name for **catechol.**

py·ro·chem·i·cal (ˌpaɪrəʊˈkɛmɪkəl) *adj.* of, concerned with, being, producing, or resulting from chemical changes at high temperatures. —ˌ**py·ro·ˈchem·i·cal·ly** *adv.*

py·ro·clas·tic (ˌpaɪrəʊˈklæstɪk) *adj.* (of rocks) formed from the solid fragments ejected during a volcanic eruption.

py·ro·con·duc·tiv·i·ty (ˌpaɪrəʊˌkɒndʌkˈtɪvɪtɪ) *n.* conductivity that can be induced in certain solids by heating them.

py·ro·e·lec·tric (ˌpaɪrəʊɪˈlɛktrɪk) *adj.* **1.** of, concerned with, or exhibiting pyroelectricity. ~*n.* **2.** a pyroelectric substance.

py·ro·e·lec·tric·i·ty (ˌpaɪrəʊɪlɛkˈtrɪsɪtɪ, -ˌiːlɛk-) *n.* the development of opposite charges at the ends of the axis of certain hemihedral crystals, such as tourmaline, as a result of a change in temperature.

py·ro·gal·late (ˌpaɪrəʊˈgæleɪt) *n.* any salt or ester of pyrogallol.

py·ro·gal·lol (ˌpaɪrəʊˈgælɒl) *n.* a white lustrous crystalline soluble phenol with weakly acidic properties; 1,2,3-trihydroxybenzene: used as a photographic developer and for absorbing oxygen in gas analysis. Formula: $C_6H_3(OH)_3$. [C20: from PYRO- + GALL(IC)[2] + -OL[1]] —ˌ**py·ro·ˈgal·lic** *adj.*

py·ro·gen (ˈpaɪrəʊˌdʒɛn) *n.* any of a group of substances that cause a rise in temperature in an animal body.

py·ro·gen·ic (ˌpaɪrəʊˈdʒɛnɪk) *or* **py·rog·e·nous** (paɪˈrɒdʒɪnəs) *adj.* **1.** produced by or producing heat. **2.** *Pathol.* causing or resulting from fever. **3.** *Geology.* less common words for **igneous.**

py·rog·nos·tics (ˌpaɪrɒgˈnɒstɪks) *pl. n.* the characteristics of a mineral, such as fusibility and flame coloration, that are revealed by the application of heat. [C19: from PYRO- + *-gnostics*, from Greek *gnōsis* knowledge]

py·rog·ra·phy (paɪˈrɒgrəfɪ) *n., pl.* **·phies. 1.** the art or process of burning designs on wood or leather with heated tools or a fire flame. **2.** a design made by this process. —**py·ˈrog·ra·pher** *n.* —**py·ro·graph·ic** (ˌpaɪrəʊˈgræfɪk) *adj.*

py·ro·lig·ne·ous (ˌpaɪrəʊˈlɪgnɪəs) *or* **py·ro·lig·nic** *adj.* (of a substance) produced by the action of heat on wood, esp. by destructive distillation.

py·ro·lig·ne·ous ac·id *n.* the crude reddish-brown acidic liquid obtained by the distillation of wood and containing acetic acid, methanol, and acetone. Also called: **wood vinegar.**

py·ro·lu·site (ˌpaɪrəʊˈluːsaɪt) *n.* a blackish fibrous or soft powdery mineral consisting of manganese dioxide in tetragonal crystalline form. It occurs in association with other manganese ores and is an important source of manganese. Formula: MnO_2. [C19: from PYRO- + Greek *lousis* a washing + ITE[1], from its use in purifying glass]

py·rol·y·sis (paɪˈrɒlɪsɪs) *n.* **1.** the application of heat to chemical compounds in order to cause decomposition. **2.** chemical decomposition of compounds caused by high temperatures. —**py·ro·lyt·ic** (ˌpaɪrəʊˈlɪtɪk) *adj.*

py·ro·mag·net·ic (ˌpaɪrəʊmægˈnɛtɪk) *adj.* a former term for **thermomagnetic.**

py·ro·man·cy (ˈpaɪrəʊˌmænsɪ) *n.* divination by fire or flames. —ˈ**py·ro·ˌman·cer** *n.* —ˌ**py·ro·ˈman·tic** *adj.*

py·ro·ma·ni·a (ˌpaɪrəʊˈmeɪnɪə) *n. Psychiatry.* the uncontrollable impulse and practice of setting things on fire. —ˌ**py·ro·ˈma·ni·ˌac** *n.* —**py·ro·ma·ni·a·cal** (ˌpaɪrəʊməˈnaɪəkəl) *adj.*

py·ro·met·al·lur·gy (ˌpaɪrəʊmɛˈtælədʒɪ, -ˈmɛtəˌlɜːdʒɪ) *n.* the branch of metallurgy involving processes performed at high temperatures, including sintering, roasting, smelting, casting, refining, alloying, and heat treatment.

py·rom·e·ter (paɪˈrɒmɪtə) *n.* an instrument for measuring high temperatures, esp. by measuring the brightness (**optical pyrometer**) or total quantity (**radiation pyrometer**) of the radiation produced by the source. Other types include the resistance thermometer and the thermocouple. —**py·ro·met·ric** (ˌpaɪrəʊˈmɛtrɪk) *or* ˌ**py·ro·ˈmet·ri·cal** *adj.* —ˌ**py·ro·ˈmet·ri·cal·ly** *adv.* —**py·ˈrom·e·try** *n.*

py·ro·mor·phite (ˌpaɪrəʊˈmɔːfaɪt) *n.* a green, yellow, brown, or grey secondary mineral that consists of lead chloro-phosphate in the form of hexagonal crystals. Formula: $Pb_5Cl(PO_4)_3$. [C19: from German *Pyromorphit*, from PYRO- + Greek *morphē* form + ITE[1], an allusion to the fact that it assumes a crystalline form when heated]

py·rone (ˈpaɪrəʊn, paɪˈrəʊn) *n.* **1.** either of two heterocyclic compounds that have a ring containing five carbon atoms and one oxygen atom with two double bonds and a second oxygen atom attached to a carbon atom in either the *ortho*-position (**alpha pyrone**) or the *para*-position (**gamma pyrone**). **2.** any one of a class of compounds that are substituted derivatives of a pyrone.

py·rope (ˈpaɪrəʊp) *n.* a deep yellowish-red garnet that consists of magnesium aluminium silicate and is used as a gemstone. Formula: $Mg_3Al_2(SiO_4)_3$. [C14 (used loosely of a red gem; modern sense C19): from Old French *pirope*, from Latin *pyrōpus* bronze, from Greek *purōpus* fiery-eyed, from *pur* fire + *ōps* eye]

py·ro·phor·ic (ˌpaɪrəʊˈfɒrɪk) *adj.* **1.** (of a chemical) igniting spontaneously on contact with air. **2.** (of an alloy) producing sparks when struck or scraped: *lighter flints are made of pyrophoric alloy.* [C19: from New Latin *pyrophorus*, from Greek *purophoros* fire-bearing, from *pur* fire + *pherein* to bear]

py·ro·phos·phate (ˌpaɪrəʊˈfɒsfeɪt) *n.* any salt or ester of pyrophosphoric acid.

py·ro·phos·phor·ic ac·id (ˌpaɪrəʊfɒsˈfɒrɪk) *n.* a crystalline soluble solid acid formed by the reaction between one molecule of phosphorus pentoxide and two water molecules. Formula: $H_4P_2O_7$. See also **polyphosphoric acid.**

py·ro·pho·tom·e·ter (ˌpaɪrəʊfəʊˈtɒmɪtə) *n.* a type of pyrometer in which the temperature of an incandescent body is determined by photometric measurement of the light it emits. —ˌ**py·ro·pho·ˈtom·e·try** *n.*

py·ro·phyl·lite (ˌpaɪrəʊˈfɪlaɪt) *n.* a white, silvery, or green micaceous mineral that consists of hydrated aluminium silicate in monoclinic crystalline form and occurs in metamorphic rocks. Formula: $Al_2Si_4O_{10}(OH)_2$.

py·ro·sis (paɪˈrəʊsɪs) *n. Pathol.* a technical name for **heartburn.** [C18: from New Latin, from Greek: a burning, from *puroun* to burn, from *pur* fire]

py·ro·stat (ˈpaɪrəʊˌstæt) *n.* **1.** a device that activates an alarm or extinguisher in the event of a fire. **2.** a thermostat for use at high temperatures. —ˌ**py·ro·ˈstat·ic** *adj.*

py·ro·sul·phate (ˌpaɪrəʊˈsʌlfeɪt) *n.* any salt of pyrosulphuric acid. Also called: **disulphate.**

py·ro·sul·phur·ic ac·id (ˌpaɪrəʊsʌlˈfjʊərɪk) *n.* a fuming liquid acid made by adding sulphur trioxide to concentrated sulphuric acid. Formula: $H_2S_2O_7$. Also called: **disulphuric acid.** See also **fuming sulphuric acid.**

py·ro·tech·nics (ˌpaɪrəʊˈtɛknɪks) *n.* **1.** (*functioning as sing.*) the art or craft of making fireworks. **2.** (*functioning as sing. or pl.*) a firework display. **3.** (*functioning as sing. or pl.*) brilliance of display, as in the performance of music. ~Also called: **py·ro·tech·ny.** —ˌ**py·ro·ˈtech·nic** *or* ˌ**py·ro·ˈtech·ni·cal** *adj.*

py·rox·ene (paɪˈrɒksiːn) *n.* any of a large group of dark coloured minerals consisting of the silicates of magnesium, iron, and calcium. They occur in basic igneous rocks and in some metamorphic rocks. [C19: PYRO- + *-xene* from Greek *xenos* foreign, because it was mistakenly thought to have originated elsewhere when found in igneous rocks] —**py·rox·en·ic** (ˌpaɪrɒkˈsɛnɪk) *adj.*

py·rox·e·nite (paɪˈrɒksɪˌnaɪt) *n.* a very dark coarse-grained ultrabasic rock consisting entirely of pyroxene minerals.

py·rox·y·lin (paɪˈrɒksɪlɪn) *n.* a yellow substance obtained by nitrating cellulose with a mixture of nitric and sulphuric acids; guncotton: used to make collodion, plastics, lacquers, and adhesives. [C19: from PYRO- + XYL- + -IN]

Pyr·rha (ˈpɪrə) *n. Greek myth.* the wife of Deucalion, saved with him from the flood loosed upon mankind by Zeus.

pyr·rhic[1] (ˈpɪrɪk) *Prosody.* ~*n.* **1.** a metrical foot of two short or unstressed syllables. ~*adj.* **2.** of or relating to such a metrical foot. **3.** (of poetry) composed in pyrrhics. [C16: via Latin, from Greek *purrhikhē*, traditionally said to be named after its inventor *Purrhikhos*]

pyr·rhic[2] (ˈpɪrɪk) *n.* **1.** a war dance of ancient Greece. ~*adj.* **2.** of or relating to this dance. [C17: Latin from Greek *purrhikhios* belonging to the *purrhikhē* war dance performed in armour; see PYRRHIC[1]]

Pyr·rhic vic·to·ry *n.* a victory in which the victor's losses are as great as those of the defeated. Also called: **Cadmean victory.** [named after PYRRHUS, who defeated the Romans at Asculum in 279 B.C. but suffered heavy losses]

Pyr·rho ('pɪrəʊ) *n.* ?365–?275 B.C., Greek philosopher; founder of scepticism. He maintained that true wisdom and happiness lie in suspension of judgment, since certain knowledge is impossible to attain. —**'Pyr·rho·nism** *n.* —**'Pyr·rho·nist** *n., adj.*

pyr·rho·tite ('pɪrəˌtaɪt) *or* **pyr·rho·tine** ('pɪrəˌtiːn, -ˌtaɪn, -ˌtɪn) *n.* a common bronze-coloured magnetic mineral consisting of ferrous sulphide in hexagonal crystalline form. Formula: FeS. [C19: from Greek *purrhotēs* redness, from *purrhos* fiery, from *pur* fire]

pyr·rhu·lox·i·a (ˌpɪrə'lɒksɪə) *n.* a grey-and-pink crested bunting, *Pyrrhuloxia sinuata*, of Central and SW North America, with a short parrot-like bill. [from New Latin *Pyrrhula* genus of the finches (from Greek *purrhoulas* a flame-coloured bird, from *purrhos* red, from *pur* fire) + *Loxia* genus of the crossbills, from Greek *loxos* oblique]

Pyr·rhus ('pɪrəs) *n.* **1.** 319–272 B.C., king of Epirus (306–272). He invaded Italy but was ultimately defeated by the Romans (275 B.C.). **2.** another name for **Neoptolemus.** —**'Pyr·rhic** *adj.*

pyr·role ('pɪrəʊl, pɪ'rəʊl) *n.* a colourless insoluble toxic liquid having a five-membered ring containing one nitrogen atom, found in many naturally occurring compounds, such as chlorophyll. Formula: C_4H_5N. Also called: **azole.** [C19: from Greek *purrhos* red, from *pur* fire + -OLE] —**pyr·rol·ic** (pɪ'rɒlɪk) *adj.*

pyr·rol·i·dine (pɪ'rɒlɪˌdiːn) *n.* an almost colourless liquid occurring in tobacco leaves and made commercially by hydrogenating pyrrole. It is a strongly alkaline heterocyclic base with molecules that contain a ring of four carbon atoms and one nitrogen atom. Formula: C_4H_9N.

pyr·ru·vic ac·id (paɪ'ruːvɪk) *n.* a colourless pleasant-smelling liquid formed as an intermediate in the metabolism of proteins and carbohydrates; 2-oxopropanoic acid. Formula: CH_3COCH_2OH. [C19: *pyruvic* from PYRO- + Latin *ūva* grape]

Py·thag·o·ras[1] (paɪ'θægərəs) *n.* ?580–?500 B.C., Greek philosopher and mathematician. He founded a religious brotherhood, which followed a life of strict asceticism and greatly influenced the development of mathematics and its application to music and astronomy.

Py·thag·o·ras[2] (paɪ'θægərəs) *n.* a deep crater in the NE quadrant of the moon, 136 kilometres in diameter.

Py·thag·o·ras' the·o·rem *n.* the theorem that in a right-angled triangle the square of the length of the hypotenuse equals the sum of the squares of the other two sides.

Py·thag·o·re·an (paɪˌθægə'riːən) *adj.* **1.** of or relating to Pythagoras. **2.** *Music.* denoting the diatonic scale of eight notes arrived at by Pythagoras and based on a succession of fifths. ~*n.* **3.** a follower of Pythagoras.

Py·thag·o·re·an·ism (paɪˌθægə'riːəˌnɪzəm) *n.* the teachings of Pythagoras and his followers, esp. that the universe is essentially a manifestation of mathematical relationships.

Pyth·i·a ('pɪθɪə) *n. Greek myth.* the priestess of Apollo at Delphi, who transmitted the oracles.

Pyth·i·an ('pɪθɪən) *adj. also* **Pyth·ic. 1.** of or relating to Delphi or its oracle. ~*n.* **2.** the priestess of Apollo at the oracle of Delphi. **3.** an inhabitant of ancient Delphi. [C16: via Latin *Pȳthius* from Greek *Puthios* of Delphi]

Pyth·i·an Games *n.* (in ancient Greece) the second most important Panhellenic festival, celebrated in the third year of each Olympiad near Delphi. The four-year period between celebrations was known as a **Pyth·i·ad** ('pɪθɪˌæd).

Pyth·i·as ('pɪθɪˌæs) *n.* See **Damon and Pythias.**

py·thon ('paɪθən) *n.* any large nonvenomous snake of the family *Pythonidae* of Africa, S Asia, and Australia, such as *Python reticulatus* (**reticulated python**). They reach a length of more than 20 feet and kill their prey by constriction. [C16: New Latin, after PYTHON] —**py·thon·ic** (paɪ'θɒnɪk) *adj.*

Py·thon ('paɪθən) *n. Greek myth.* a dragon, killed by Apollo at Delphi.

py·thon·ess ('paɪθəˌnɛs) *n.* **1.** a woman, such as Apollo's priestess at Delphi, believed to be possessed by an oracular spirit. **2.** a female soothsayer. [C14 *phitonesse*, ultimately from Greek *Puthōn* PYTHON]

py·u·ri·a (paɪ'jʊərɪə) *n. Pathol.* any condition characterized by the presence of pus in the urine. [C19: from New Latin, from Greek *puon* pus + *ouron* urine]

pyx *or* **pix** (pɪks) *n.* **1.** Also called: **pyx chest.** the chest in which coins from the British mint are placed to be tested for weight, etc. **2.** *Christianity.* any receptacle in which the Eucharistic Host is kept. [C14: from Latin *pyxis* small box, from Greek, from *puxos* box-tree; see BOX]

pyx·id·i·um (pɪk'sɪdɪəm) *or* **pyx·is** ('pɪksɪs) *n., pl.* **·i·a** (-ɪə) *or* **pyx·i·des** ('pɪksɪˌdiːz). the dry fruit of such plants as the plantain: a capsule whose upper part falls off when mature so that the seeds are released. [C19: via New Latin from Greek *puxidion* a little box, from *puxis* box, PYX]

pyx·ie ('pɪksɪ) *n.* a creeping evergreen shrub, *Pyxidanthera barbulata*, of the eastern U.S. with small white or pink star-shaped flowers: family *Diapensiaceae*. [C19: shortened from New Latin *Pyxidanthera*, from PYXIS + ANTHER]

pyx·is ('pɪksɪs) *n., pl.* **pyx·i·des** ('pɪksɪˌdiːz). **1.** a small box used by the ancient Greeks and Romans to hold medicines, etc. **2.** a rare word for **pyx. 3.** another name for **pyxidium.** [C14: via Latin from Greek: box]

Pyx·is ('pɪksɪs) *n., Latin genitive* **Pyx·i·dis** ('pɪksɪdɪs). an inconspicuous constellation close to Puppis.

Q

q *or* **Q** (kjuː) *n., pl.* **q's, Q's,** *or* **Qs. 1.** the 17th letter and 13th consonant of the modern English alphabet. **2.** a speech sound represented by this letter, in English usually a voiceless velar stop, as in *unique* and *quick*.
q *symbol for* quintal.
Q *symbol for:* **1.** *Chess.* queen. **2.** question. **3.** *Physics.* heat.
q. *abbrev. for:* **1.** quart. **2.** quarter. **3.** quarterly. **4.** query. **5.** question. **6.** quire.
Q. *abbrev. for:* **1.** quartermaster. **2.** (*pl.* **Qq., qq.**) Also: **q.** quarto. **3.** Quebec. **4.** Queen. **5.** question. **6.** *Electronics.* Q factor.
Qa·boos bin Said (kəˈbuːs bɪn ˈsaɪd) *n.* born 1940, sultan of Oman since 1970.
Qad·da·fi (gəˈdɑːfɪ) *n.* **Mo·a·mar** (ˈməʊəˌmɑː). See (Moamar) **Gaddafi.**
Qad+dish (ˈkædɪʃ) *n., pl.* **Qad+dish+im.** a variant spelling of **Kaddish.**
qa·di (ˈkɑːdɪ, ˈkeɪdɪ) *n., pl.* **·dis.** a variant spelling of **cadi.**
Qair+wan (kaɪəˈwæn) *n.* a variant spelling of **Kairouan.**
Q.A.R.A.N.C. *abbrev. for* Queen Alexandra's Royal Army Nursing Corps.
Qa+tar *or* **Ka+tar** (kæˈtɑː) *n.* a state in E Arabia, occupying a peninsula in the Persian Gulf: under Persian rule until the 19th century; became a British protectorate in 1916; declared independence in 1970; exports petroleum and natural gas. Language: Arabic. Religion: Sunni Muslim. Currency: riyal. Capital: Doha. Pop.: 89 000 (1974 UN est.). Area: about 11 000 sq. km (4250 sq. miles). **—Qa+ˈta+ri** *or* **Ka+ˈta+ri** *adj., n.*
Qat+tar·a De+pres+sion (kəˈtɑːrə) *n.* an arid basin in the Sahara Desert, in NW Egypt, impassable to vehicles. Area: about 18 000 sq. km. (7000 sq. miles). Lowest point: 133 m (435 ft.) below sea level.
QB *Chess. symbol for* queen's bishop.
Q.B. *abbrev. for* Queen's Bench.
QBP *Chess. symbol for* queen's bishop's pawn.
Q.C. *abbrev. for* Queen's Counsel.
q.e. *abbrev. for* quod est. [Latin: which is]
Q.E.D. *abbrev. for* quod erat demonstrandum. [Latin: which was to be shown or proved]
Q.E.F. *abbrev. for* quod erat faciendum. [Latin: which was to be done]
Qeshm (ˈkɛʃəm) *or* **Qishm** (ˈkɪʃəm) *n.* **1.** an island in the Persian Gulf: part of Iran; the largest island in the Persian Gulf. Area: 1336 sq. km (516 sq. miles). **2.** the chief town of this island.
Q.F. *abbrev. for* quick-firing (rifle).
Q fac+tor *n.* **1.** a measure of the relationship between stored energy and rate of energy dissipation in certain electrical components, devices, etc., thus indicating their efficiency. Symbol: Q **2.** Also called: **Q value.** the heat released in a nuclear reaction, usually expressed in millions of electronvolts for each individual reaction. Symbol: Q [C20: short for *quality factor*]
Q fe+ver *n.* an acute disease characterized by fever and pneumonia, transmitted to man by the rickettsia *Coxiella burnetii.* [C20: from *q(uery) fever* (the cause being unknown when it was named)]
qib+la (ˈkɪblə) *n.* a variant spelling of **kiblah.**
qin+tar (kɪnˈtɑː, ˈkɪntɑː) *or* **qin+dar** (kɪnˈdɑː) *n.* an Albanian monetary unit worth one hundredth of a lek.
Qishm (ˈkɪʃəm) *n.* a variant spelling of **Qeshm.**
QKt *Chess. symbol for* queen's knight.
QKtP *Chess. symbol for* queen's knight's pawn.
ql. *abbrev. for* quintal.
q.l. (in prescriptions) *abbrev. for* quantum libet. [Latin: as much as you please]
Qld. *abbrev. for* Queensland.
q.m. (in prescriptions) *abbrev. for* quaque mane. [Latin: every morning]
Q.M. *abbrev. for* Quartermaster.
Q.M.C. *abbrev. for* Quartermaster Corps.
Q.M.G. *abbrev. for* Quartermaster General.
Q.M.S. *abbrev. for* Quartermaster Sergeant.
QN *Chess. symbol for* queen's knight.
q.n. (in prescriptions) *abbrev. for* quaque nocte. [Latin: every night]
QNP *Chess. symbol for* queen's knight's pawn.
qoph (kʊf, kɒf; *Hebrew* kɔf) *n.* a variant spelling of **koph.**
QP *Chess. symbol for* queen's pawn.
Qq. *or* **qq.** *abbrev. for:* **1.** quartos. **2.** questions.
qq.v. *abbrev. for* quae vide (denoting a cross reference to more than one item). Compare **q.v.** [New Latin: which (words, items, etc.) see]
QR *Chess. symbol for* queen's rook.
qr. *pl.* **qrs.** *abbrev. for:* **1.** quarter. **2.** quarterly. **3.** quire.
QRP *Chess. symbol for* queen's rook's pawn.
q.s. *abbrev. for:* **1.** (in prescriptions) quantum sufficit. [Latin: as much as will suffice] **2.** quarter section (of land).
Q.S. *abbrev. for* quarter sessions.
Q-ship *n.* a merchant ship with concealed guns, used to decoy enemy ships into the range of its weapons.
QSL *Telecommunications. symbol for:* **1.** acknowledgment of receipt of a communication. **2.** a card sent by post to confirm a communication.
QSO *symbol for:* **1.** *Telecommunications.* conversation or communication. **2.** *Astronomy.* quasi-stellar object.
QST *n. Telecommunications.* a general signal to all licensed amateur radio operators.
QSY *Telecommunications. symbol for* change transmission to another frequency: *I am going to QSY from 40 to 20 metres.*
qt. *pl.* **qt.** *or* **qts.** *abbrev. for* quart.
q.t. *Informal.* **1.** *abbrev. for* quiet. **2. on the q.t.** secretly.
qto. *abbrev. for* quarto.
qty. *abbrev. for* quantity.
qu. *abbrev. for:* **1.** queen. **2.** query. **3.** question.
qua (kweɪ, kwɑː) *prep.* in the capacity of; by virtue of being. [C17: from Latin, ablative singular (feminine) of *qui* who]
quack[1] (kwæk) *vb.* (*intr.*) **1.** (of a duck) to utter a harsh guttural sound. **2.** to make a noise like a duck. ~*n.* **3.** the harsh guttural sound made by a duck. [C17: of imitative origin; related to Dutch *kwakken,* German *quacken*]
quack[2] (kwæk) *n.* **1. a.** an unqualified person who claims medical knowledge or other skills. **b.** (*as modifier*): *a quack doctor.* **2.** *Informal, chiefly Austral.* a doctor; physician or surgeon. ~*vb.* **3.** (*intr.*) to act in the manner of a quack. [C17: short for QUACKSALVER] **—ˈquack+ish** *adj.*
quack+er·y (ˈkwækərɪ) *n., pl.* **+er·ies.** the activities or methods of a quack.
quack grass *n.* another name for **couch grass.**
quack+sal+ver (ˈkwækˌsælvə) *n.* an archaic word for **quack**[2]. [C16: from Dutch, from *quack,* apparently: to hawk + *salf* SALVE]
quad[1] (kwɒd) *n. Informal.* short for **quadrangle.**
quad[2] (kwɒd) *n. Printing.* a block of type metal used for spacing. [C19: shortened from QUADRAT]
quad[3] (kwɒd) *n.* a variant spelling of **quod** (prison).
quad[4] (kwɒd) *n. Informal.* short for **quadruplet.**
quad. *abbrev. for:* **1.** quadrangle. **2.** quadrant. **3.** quadrilateral.
quad+dy (ˈkwɒdɪ) *n.* (in Australia) a form of betting in which the punter must select the winner of four specified races. Full name: **quadrella.**
quad+ra+ge+nar+i·an (ˌkwɒdrədʒɪˈnɛərɪən) *n.* **1.** a person who is between 40 and 49 years old. ~*adj.* **2.** being from 40 to 49 years old. [C19: from Latin *quadrāgēnārius* consisting of forty, from *quādrāgintā* forty]
Quad+ra+ges+i+ma (ˌkwɒdrəˈdʒɛsɪmə) *n.* **1.** Also called: **Quadragesima Sunday.** the first Sunday in Lent. **2.** *Obsolete.* the forty days of Lent. [C16: from Medieval Latin *quadrāgēsima dies* the fortieth day]
Quad+ra+ges+i+mal (ˌkwɒdrəˈdʒɛsɪməl) *adj.* of, relating to, or characteristic of Lent or the season of Lent.
quad+ran+gle (ˈkwɒdˌræŋgəl) *n.* **1.** *Geom.* a plane figure consisting of four points connected by four lines that may or may not intersect. In a **complete quadrangle,** six lines connect all pairs of points. **2.** a rectangular courtyard, esp. one having buildings on all four sides. Often shortened to **quad. 3.** the building surrounding such a courtyard. [C15: from Late Latin *quadrangulum* figure having four corners] **—quad+ran+gu+lar** (kwɒˈdræŋgjʊlə) *adj.*
quad+rant (ˈkwɒdrənt) *n.* **1.** *Geom.* **a.** a quarter of the circumference of a circle. **b.** the area enclosed by two perpendicular radii of a circle. **c.** any of the four sections into which a plane is divided by two coordinate axes. **2.** a piece of a mechanism in the form of a quarter circle, esp. one used as a cam or a gear sector. **3.** an instrument formerly used in astronomy and navigation for measuring the altitudes of stars, consisting of a graduated arc of 90° and a sighting mechanism attached to a movable arm. [C14: from Latin *quadrāns* a quarter] **—quad+ran+tal** (kwɒˈdræntəl) *adj.*
quad+ra+phon+ics *or* **quad+ro+phon+ics** (ˌkwɒdrəˈfɒnɪks) *n.* (*functioning as sing.*) a system of sound recording and reproduction that uses four independent loudspeakers to give directional sources of sound. The speakers are fed by four separate amplified signals. **—ˌquad+ra+ˈphon+ic** *or* **ˌquad+ro+ˈphon+ic** *adj.* **—quad+raph·o+ny** *or* **quad+roph·o+ny** (kwɒdˈrɒfənɪ) *n.*
quad+rat (ˈkwɒdrət) *n.* **1.** *Ecology.* an area of vegetation, usually one square metre, randomly selected for study of the plants in the surrounding area. **2.** *Printing.* an archaic name for **quad**[2]. [C14 (meaning "a square"): variant of QUADRATE]
quad+rate *n.* (ˈkwɒdrɪt, -reɪt). **1.** a cube, square, or a square or cubelike object. **2.** one of a pair of bones of the upper jaw of fishes, amphibians, reptiles, and birds that articulates with the lower jaw. In mammals it forms the incus. ~*adj.* (ˈkwɒdrɪt, -reɪt). **3.** of or relating to this bone. **4.** square or rectangular. ~*vb.* (kwɒˈdreɪt). **5.** (*tr.*) to make square or rectangular. **6.**

(often foll. by *with*) to conform or cause to conform. [C14: from Latin *quadrāre* to make square]

quad+rat+ic (kwɒ'drætɪk) *Maths.* ~*n.* **1.** Also called: **quadratic equation.** an equation containing one or more terms in which the variable is raised to the power of two, but no terms in which it is raised to a higher power. ~*adj.* **2.** of or relating to the second power.

quad+rat+ics (kwɒ'drætɪks) *n.* (*functioning as sing.*) the branch of algebra concerned with quadratic equations.

quad+ra+ture ('kwɒdrətʃə) *n.* **1.** *Maths.* the process of determining a square having an area equal to that of a given figure or surface. **2.** the process of making square or dividing into squares. **3.** *Astronomy.* a configuration in which two celestial bodies, usually the sun and the moon or a planet, form an angle of 90° with a third body, usually the earth. **4.** *Electronics.* the relationship between two waves that are 90° out of phase.

quad+rel+la (kwɒ'drɛlə) *n.* the full name for a **quaddy.**

quad+ren+ni+al (kwɒ'drɛnɪəl) *adj.* **1.** occurring every four years. **2.** relating to or lasting four years. ~*n.* **3.** a period of four years. —**quad+'ren+ni+al+ly** *adv.*

quad+ren+ni+um (kwɒ'drɛnɪəm) *n., pl.* **+ni·ums** *or* **+ni·a** (-nɪə). a period of four years. [C17: from Latin *quadriennium,* from QUADRI- + *annus* year]

quad·ri- *or before a vowel* **quadr-** *combining form.* four: *quadrilateral; quadrilingual; quadrisyllabic.* [from Latin; compare *quattuor* four]

quad+ric ('kwɒdrɪk) *Maths.* ~*adj.* **1.** having or characterized by an equation of the second degree, usually in two or three variables. **2.** of the second degree. ~*n.* **3.** a quadric curve, surface, or function.

quad+ri+cen+ten+ni+al (ˌkwɒdrɪsɛn'tɛnɪəl) *n.* **1.** a 400th anniversary. ~*adj.* **2.** of, relating to, or celebrating a 400th anniversary.

quad+ri+ceps ('kwɒdrɪˌsɛps) *n., pl.* **+ceps·es** (-ˌsɛpsɪz) *or* **+ceps.** *Anatomy.* a large four-part muscle of the front of the thigh, which extends the leg. [C19: New Latin, from QUADRI- + *-ceps* as in BICEPS] —**quad+ri+cip+i+tal** (ˌkwɒdrɪ'sɪpɪtᵊl) *adj.*

quad+ri+fid ('kwɒdrɪfɪd) *adj. Botany.* divided into four lobes or other parts: *quadrifid leaves.*

quad+ri+ga (kwɒ'dri:gə) *n., pl.* **+gas** *or* **+gae** (-dʒi:). (in the classical world) a two-wheeled chariot drawn by four horses abreast. [C18: from Latin, from earlier *quadrijugae* a team of four, from QUADRI- + *jugum* yoke]

quad+ri+lat+er+al (ˌkwɒdrɪ'lætərəl) *adj.* **1.** having or formed by four sides. ~*n.* **2.** Also called: **tetragon.** a polygon having four sides. A **complete quadrilateral** consists of four lines and their six points of intersection.

quad+rille[1] (kwɒ'drɪl, kwə-) *n.* **1.** a square dance of five or more figures for four or more couples. **2.** a piece of music for such a dance, alternating between simple duple and compound duple time. [C18: via French from Spanish *cuadrilla,* diminutive of *cuadro* square, from Latin *quadra*]

quad+rille[2] (kwɒ'drɪl, kwə-) *n.* an old card game for four players. [C18: from French, from Spanish *cuartillo,* from *cuarto* fourth, from Latin *quartus,* influenced by QUADRILLE[1]]

quad+ril+lion (kwɒ'drɪljən) *n.* **1.** (in Britain and Germany) the number represented as one followed by 24 zeros (10^{24}). U.S. word: **septillion. 2.** (in the U.S. and France) the number represented as one followed by 15 zeros (10^{15}). ~*determiner.* **3.** (preceded by *a* or a numeral) **a.** amounting to this number: *a quadrillion atoms.* **b.** (*as pronoun*): *a quadrillion.* [C17: from French *quadrillon,* from QUADRI- + *-illion,* on the model of *million*] —**quad+'ril+lionth** *adj.*

quad+ri+no+mi+al (ˌkwɒdrɪ'nəʊmɪəl) *n.* an algebraic expression containing four terms.

quad+ri+par+tite (ˌkwɒdrɪ'pɑ:taɪt) *adj.* **1.** divided into or composed of four parts. **2.** maintained by or involving four participants or groups of participants.

quad+ri+ple·gia (ˌkwɒdrɪ'pli:dʒɪə, -dʒə) *n. Pathol.* paralysis of all four limbs, usually as the result of injury to the spine. Also called: **tetraplegia.** Compare **hemiplegia, paraplegia.** —**quad+ri+ple·gic** (ˌkwɒdrɪ'pli:dʒɪk) *adj.*

quad+ri+sect ('kwɒdrɪˌsɛkt) *vb.* to divide into four parts, esp. into four equal parts. —ˌ**quad+ri+'sec+tion** *n.*

quad+ri+va+lent (ˌkwɒdrɪ'veɪlənt) *adj. Chem.* another word for **tetravalent.** —ˌ**quad+ri+'va+len+cy** *or* ˌ**quad+ri+'va+lence** *n.*

quad+riv+i+al (kwɒ'drɪvɪəl) *adj.* **1.** having or consisting of four roads meeting at a point. **2.** (of roads or ways) going in four directions. **3.** of or relating to the quadrivium.

quad+riv+i+um (kwɒ'drɪvɪəm) *n.* (in medieval learning) the higher division of the seven liberal arts, consisting of arithmetic, geometry, astronomy, and music. Compare **trivium.** [from Medieval Latin, from Latin: crossroads, meeting of four ways, from QUADRI- + *via* way]

quad+roon (kwɒ'dru:n) *n.* the offspring of a Mulatto and a White; a person who is one-quarter Negro. [C18: from Spanish *cuarterón,* from *cuarto* quarter, from Latin *quartus*]

quad+ro+phon+ics (ˌkwɒdrə'fɒnɪks) *adj.* a variant spelling of **quadraphonics.**

quad+ru+ma+nous (kwɒ'dru:mənəs) *adj.* (of monkeys and apes) having all four feet specialized for use as hands. [C18: from New Latin *quadrumanus,* from QUADRI- + Latin *manus* hand]

quad+ru+ped ('kwɒdrʊˌpɛd) *n.* **1.** an animal, esp. a mammal, that has all four limbs specialized for walking. ~*adj.* **2.** having four feet. [C17: from Latin *quadrupēs,* from *quadru-* (see QUADRI-) + *pēs* foot] —**quad+ru+ped+al** (kwɒ'dru:pɪdᵊl, ˌkwɒdrʊ'pɛdᵊl) *adj.*

quad+ru+ple ('kwɒdrʊpᵊl, kwɒ'dru:pᵊl) *vb.* **1.** to multiply by four or increase fourfold. ~*adj.* **2.** four times as much or as many; fourfold. **3.** consisting of four parts. ~*n.* **4.** a quantity or number four times as great as another. [C16: via Old French from Latin *quadruplus,* from *quadru-* (see QUADRI-) + *-plus* -fold] —**'quad+ru+ply** *adv.*

quad+ru+plet ('kwɒdrʊplɪt, kwɒ'dru:plɪt) *n.* **1.** one of four offspring born at one birth. Often shortened to **quad. 2.** a group or set of four similar things. **3.** *Music.* a group of four notes to be played in a time value of three.

quad+ru+ple time *n.* musical time in which there are four beats in each bar.

quad+ru+plex ('kwɒdrʊˌplɛks, kwɒ'dru:plɛks) *adj.* consisting of four parts; fourfold. [C19: from Latin, from *quadru-* (see QUADRI-) + *-plex* -fold] —**quad+ru+plic+i+ty** (ˌkwɒdrʊ'plɪsɪtɪ) *n.*

quad+ru+pli+cate *adj.* (kwɒ'dru:plɪkɪt, -ˌkeɪt). **1.** fourfold or quadruple. ~*vb.* (kwɒ'dru:plɪˌkeɪt). **2.** to multiply or be multiplied by four. ~*n.* (kwɒ'dru:plɪkɪt, -ˌkeɪt). **3.** a group or set of four things. [C17: from Latin *quadruplicāre* to increase fourfold] —**quad+ˌru+pli+'ca+tion** *n.*

quae+re ('kwɪərɪ) *Rare.* ~*n.* **1.** a query or question. ~*interj.* **2.** ask or inquire: used esp. to introduce a question. [C16: Latin, from *quaerere* to enquire]

quaes+tor ('kwi:stə, -tɔ:) *or U.S.* (*sometimes*) **ques+tor** ('kwɛstə) *n.* any of several magistrates of ancient Rome, usually a financial administrator. [C14: from Latin, from *quaerere* to enquire] —**quaes+to+ri+al** (kwɛ'stɔ:rɪəl) *adj.* —**'quaes+tor+ˌship** *n.*

quaff (kwɒf, kwɑ:f) *vb.* to drink heartily or in one draught. [C16: perhaps of imitative origin; compare Middle Low German *quassen* to eat or drink excessively] —**'quaff+er** *n.*

quag (kwæg, kwɒg) *n.* another word for **quagmire.** [C16: perhaps related to QUAKE; compare Middle Low German *quabbe*]

quag+ga ('kwægə) *n., pl.* **+gas** *or* **+ga.** a recently extinct member of the horse family (*Equidae*), *Equus quagga,* of southern Africa: it had a sandy brown colouring with zebra-like stripes on the head and shoulders. [C18: from obsolete Afrikaans, from Hottentot *qŭagga;* compare Xhosa *i-qwara* something striped]

quag+gy ('kwægɪ, 'kwɒgɪ) *adj.* **+gi+er, +gi+est. 1.** resembling a marsh or quagmire; boggy. **2.** yielding, soft, or flabby. —**'quag+gi+ness** *n.*

quag+mire ('kwægˌmaɪə, 'kwɒg-) *n.* **1.** a soft wet area of land that gives way under the feet; bog. **2.** an awkward, complex, or embarrassing situation. [C16: from QUAG + MIRE]

qua+hog ('kwɑ:ˌhɒg) *n.* an edible clam, *Venus* (or *Mercenaria*) *mercenaria,* native to the Atlantic coast of North America, having a large heavy rounded shell. Also called: **hard-shell clam, hard-shell, round clam.** Compare **soft-shell clam.** [C18: from Narragansett, short for *poquauhock,* from *pohkeni* dark + *hogki* shell]

Quai d'Or·say (*French* kɛ dɔr'sɛ) *n.* the quay along the S bank of the Seine, Paris, where the French foreign office is situated.

quail[1] (kweɪl) *n., pl.* **quails** *or* **quail. 1.** any small Old World gallinaceous game bird of the genus *Coturnix* and related genera, having a rounded body and small tail: family *Phasianidae* (pheasants). **2.** any of various similar and related American birds, such as the bobwhite. [C14: from Old French *quaille,* from Medieval Latin *quaccula,* probably of imitative origin]

quail[2] (kweɪl) *vb.* (*intr.*) to shrink back with fear; cower. [C15: perhaps from Old French *quailler,* from Latin *coāgulāre* to curdle]

quaint (kweɪnt) *adj.* **1.** attractively unusual, esp. in an old-fashioned style: *a quaint village.* **2.** odd, peculiar, or inappropriate: *a quaint sense of duty.* [C13 (in the sense: clever): from Old French *cointe,* from Latin *cognitus* known, from *cognoscere* to ascertain] —**'quaint+ly** *adv.* —**'quaint+ness** *n.*

quake (kweɪk) *vb.* (*intr.*) **1.** to shake or tremble with or as with fear. **2.** to convulse or quiver, as from instability. ~*n.* **3.** the act or an instance of quaking. **4.** *Informal.* short for **earthquake.** [Old English *cwacian;* related to Old English *cweccan* to shake, Old Irish *bocaim,* German *wackeln*]

Quak+er ('kweɪkə) *n.* **1.** a member of the Society of Friends, a Christian sect founded by George Fox about 1650, whose central belief is the doctrine of the Inner Light. Quakers reject sacraments, ritual, and formal ministry, hold meetings at which any member may speak, and have promoted many causes for social reform. ~*adj.* **2.** of, relating to, or designating the Society of Friends or its religious beliefs or practices. —**'Quak+er+ess** *fem. n.* —**'Quak+er+ish** *adj.* —**'Quak+er+ism** *n.*

Quak+er gun *n.* a dummy gun, as of wood. [alluding to the Quakers' traditional pacifism]

Qua+ker meet+ing *n.* a gathering of the Quakers for worship, characterized by periods of silence and by members' speaking as moved by the Spirit.

quak+ing grass *n.* any grass of the genus *Briza,* of N temperate regions and South America, having delicate flower branches that shake in the wind.

quak·y ('kweɪkɪ) *adj.* **quak·i+er, quak·i+est.** inclined to quake; shaky; tremulous. —**'quak·i+ly** *adv.* —**'quak·i+ness** *n.*

qua+le ('kwɑ:lɪ, 'kweɪ-) *n., pl.* **+li·a** (-lɪə). *Philosophy.* an essential property or quality. [C17: Latin, neuter singular of *qualis* of what kind]

qual+i+fi+ca+tion (ˌkwɒlɪfɪ'keɪʃən) *n.* **1.** an ability, quality, or attribute, esp. one that fits a person to perform a particular job or task: *he has no qualifications to be a teacher.* **2.** a condition that modifies or limits; restriction. **3.** the act of qualifying or state of being qualified.

qual·i·fied ('kwɒlɪˌfaɪd) *adj.* **1.** having the abilities, qualities, attributes, etc., necessary to perform a particular job or task. **2.** limited, modified, or restricted; not absolute.

qual·i·fi·er ('kwɒlɪˌfaɪə) *n.* **1.** a person or thing that qualifies, esp. a contestant in a competition who wins a preliminary heat or contest and so earns the right to take part in the next round. **2.** a preliminary heat or contest. **3.** *Grammar.* another word for **modifier** (sense 1).

qual·i·fy ('kwɒlɪˌfaɪ) *vb.* **·fies, ·fy·ing, ·fied. 1.** to provide or be provided with the abilities or attributes necessary for a task, office, duty, etc.: *his degree qualifies him for the job; he qualifies for the job, but would he do it well?* **2.** (*tr.*) to make less strong, harsh, or violent; moderate or restrict. **3.** (*tr.*) to modify or change the strength or flavour of. **4.** (*tr.*) *Grammar.* another word for **modify** (sense 3). **5.** (*tr.*) to attribute a quality to; characterize. **6.** (*intr.*) to progress to the final stages of a competition, as by winning preliminary contests. [C16: from Old French *qualifier,* from Medieval Latin *quālificāre* to characterize, from Latin *quālis* of what kind + *facere* to make] —**'qual·i·ˌfi·a·ble** *adj.* —**qual·i·fi·ca·to·ry** ('kwɒlɪfɪkətərɪ, -ˌkeɪ-) *adj.*

qual·i·ta·tive ('kwɒlɪtətɪv, -ˌteɪ-) *adj.* involving or relating to distinctions based on quality or qualities. Compare **quantitative.** —**'qual·i·ta·tive·ly** *adv.*

qual·i·ta·tive a·nal·y·sis *n.* See **analysis** (sense 4).

qual·i·ty ('kwɒlɪtɪ) *n., pl.* **·ties. 1.** a distinguishing characteristic, property, or attribute. **2.** the basic character or nature of something. **3.** a trait or feature of personality. **4.** degree or standard of excellence, esp. a high standard. **5.** (formerly) high social status or the distinction associated with it. **6.** musical tone colour; timbre. **7.** *Logic.* the characteristic of a proposition that is dependent on whether it is affirmative or negative. **8.** *Phonetics.* the distinctive character of a vowel, determined by the configuration of the mouth, tongue, etc., when it is articulated and distinguished from the pitch and stress with which it is uttered. **9.** (*modifier*) having or showing excellence or superiority: *a quality product.* [C13: from Old French *qualité,* from Latin *quālitās* state, nature, from *quālis* of what sort]

qual·i·ty con·trol *n.* control of the relative quality of a manufactured product, usually by statistical sampling techniques.

qualm (kwɑːm) *n.* **1.** a sudden feeling of sickness or nausea. **2.** a pang or sudden feeling of doubt, esp. concerning moral conduct; scruple. **3.** a sudden sensation of misgiving or unease. [Old English *cwealm* death or plague; related to Old High German *qualm* despair, Dutch *kwalm* smoke, stench] —**'qualm·ish** *adj.* —**'qualm·ish·ly** *adv.* —**'qualm·ish·ness** *n.*

quam·ash ('kwɒmæʃ, kwə'mæʃ) *n.* another name for **camass** (sense 1).

quan·da·ry ('kwɒndrɪ, -dərɪ) *n., pl.* **·ries.** a situation or circumstance that presents problems difficult to solve; predicament; dilemma. [C16: of uncertain origin; perhaps related to Latin *quandō* when]

quan·dong, quan·dang ('kwɒnˌdɒŋ), *or* **quan·tong** ('kwɒnˌtɒŋ) *n.* **1.** Also called: **native peach. a.** a small Australian santalaceous tree, *Eucarya acuminata* (or *Fusanus acuminatus*). **b.** the edible fruit or nut of this tree, used in preserves. **2.** **silver quandong. a.** an Australian tree, *Elaeocarpus grandis:* family *Elaeocarpaceae.* **b.** the pale easily worked timber of this tree. [from a native Australian language]

quan·go ('kwæŋgəʊ) *n., pl.* **·gos.** *acronym for* quasi-autonomous national government organization or quasi-autonomous non-governmental organization.

quant (kwɒnt) *n.* **1.** a long pole for propelling a boat, esp. a punt, by pushing on the bottom of a river or lake. ~*vb.* **2.** to propel (a boat) with a quant. [C15: probably from Latin *contus* a pole, from Greek *kontos*]

Quant (kwɒnt) *n.* **Mar·y.** born 1934, English fashion designer, whose Chelsea Look of mini-skirts and geometrically patterned fabrics dominated London fashion in the 1960s.

quan·ta ('kwɒntə) *n.* the plural of **quantum.**

quan·tal ('kwɒntəl) *adj.* **1.** of or relating to a quantum or an entity that is quantized. **2.** denoting something that is capable of existing in only one of two states.

quan·tic ('kwɒntɪk) *n.* a homogeneous function of two or more variables in a rational and integral form, as in $x^2 + 3xy + y^2$. [C19: from Latin *quantus* how great]

quan·ti·fi·er ('kwɒntɪˌfaɪə) *n.* **1.** *Logic.* a symbol indicating the quantity of a term: *the existential quantifier,* ($\exists x$), *corresponds to the words "there is something, x, such that..."* **2.** *Grammar.* a word or phrase in a natural language having this role, such as *some, all,* or *many* in English.

quan·ti·fy ('kwɒntɪˌfaɪ) *vb.* **·fies, ·fy·ing, ·fied.** (*tr.*) **1.** to discover or express the quantity of. **2.** *Logic.* to specify the quantity of (a term) by using a quantifier, such as *all, some,* or *no.* [C19: from Medieval Latin *quantificāre,* from Latin *quantus* how much + *facere* to make] —**'quan·ti·fi·a·ble** *adj.* —**ˌquan·ti·fi·'ca·tion** *n.*

quan·ti·ta·tive ('kwɒntɪtətɪv, -ˌteɪ-) *or* **quan·ti·tive** *adj.* **1.** involving or relating to considerations of amount or size. Compare **qualitative. 2.** capable of being measured. **3.** *Prosody.* denoting or relating to a metrical system, such as that in Latin and Greek verse, that is based on the relative length rather than stress of syllables. —**'quan·ti·ta·tive·ly** *or* **'quan·ti·tive·ly** *adv.*

quan·ti·ta·tive a·nal·y·sis *n.* See **analysis** (sense 4).

quan·ti·ty ('kwɒntɪtɪ) *n., pl.* **·ties. 1. a.** a specified or definite amount, weight, number, etc. **b.** (*as modifier*): *a quantity estimate.* **2.** the aspect or property of anything that can be measured, weighed, counted, etc. **3.** a large or considerable amount. **4.** *Maths.* an entity having a magnitude that is denoted by a constant, a variable, or a combination of both. **5.** *Physics.* a specified magnitude or amount; the product of a number and a unit. **6.** *Logic.* the characteristic of a proposition dependent on whether it is a universal or particular statement, considering all or only part of a class. **7.** *Prosody.* the relative duration of a syllable or the vowel in it. [C14: from Old French *quantité,* from Latin *quantitās* extent, amount, from *quantus* how much]

quan·ti·ty sur·vey·or *n.* a person who estimates the cost of the materials and labour necessary for a construction job.

quan·ti·ty the·o·ry *n. Economics.* a theory stating that the general price level varies directly with the quantity of money in circulation and the velocity with which it is circulated, and inversely with the volume of production expressed by the total number of money transactions.

quan·tize *or* **quan·tise** ('kwɒntaɪz) *vb.* (*tr.*) **1.** *Physics.* to restrict (a physical quantity) to one of a set of values characterized by quantum numbers. **2.** *Maths.* to limit (a variable) to values that are integral multiples of a basic unit. —**ˌquan·ti·'za·tion** *or* **ˌquan·ti·'sa·tion** *n.*

quan·tum ('kwɒntəm) *n., pl.* **·ta** (-tə). **1.** *Physics.* **a.** the smallest quantity of some physical property, such as energy, that a system can possess according to the quantum theory. **b.** a particle with such a unit of energy. **2.** amount or quantity, esp. a specific amount. **3.** (*often used with a negative*) the least possible amount that can suffice: *there is not a quantum of evidence for your accusation.* **4.** something that can be quantified or measured. [C17: from Latin *quantus* (adj.) how much]

quan·tum me·chan·ics *n.* the branch of mechanics, based on the quantum theory used for interpreting the behaviour of elementary particles and atoms, which do not obey Newtonian mechanics.

quan·tum num·ber *n. Physics.* one of a set of integers or half-integers characterizing the energy levels of a particle or system of particles. The number multiplied by a fixed quantity gives the amount of some specified physical quantity possessed by the system.

quan·tum sta·tis·tics *n. Physics.* statistics concerned with the distribution of a large collection of elementary particles or atoms among possible quantized energy levels.

quan·tum the·o·ry *n.* a theory concerning the behaviour of physical systems based on Planck's idea that they can only possess certain properties, such as energy and angular momentum, in discrete amounts (quanta). The theory later developed in several equivalent mathematical forms based on De Broglie's theory (see **wave mechanics**) and on the Heisenberg uncertainty principle.

qua·qua·ver·sal (ˌkwɑːkwə'vɜːsəl) *adj. Geology.* directed outwards in all directions from a common centre: *the quaquaversal dip of a pericline.* [C18: from Latin *quāquā* in every direction + *versus* towards]

quar. *abbrev. for:* **1.** quarter. **2.** quarterly.

quar·an·tine ('kwɒrənˌtiːn) *n.* **1.** a period of isolation or detention, esp. of persons or animals arriving from abroad, to prevent the spread of disease, usually consisting of the maximum known incubation period of the suspected disease. **2.** the place or area where such detention is enforced. **3.** any period or state of enforced isolation. ~*vb.* **4.** (*tr.*) to isolate in or as if in quarantine. [C17: from Italian *quarantina* period of forty days, from *quaranta* forty, from Latin *quadrāgintā*]

quar·an·tine flag *n. Nautical.* the yellow signal flag for the letter Q, flown alone from a vessel to indicate that there is no disease aboard and to request pratique or, with a second signal flag, to indicate that there is disease aboard. Also called: **yellow jack.**

quare (kwɛə) *adj. Irish dialect.* **1.** remarkable or strange: *a quare fellow.* **2.** great or good: *you're in a quare mess.* [probably variant of QUEER]

quark (kwɑːk) *n. Physics.* any of three hypothetical elementary particles postulated together with their antiparticles to be fundamental units of all baryons and mesons. The magnitude of their charge is either two thirds or one third of that of the electron. [C20: coined by James Joyce in the novel *Finnegans Wake,* and given special application in physics]

quar·rel[1] ('kwɒrəl) *n.* **1.** an angry disagreement; argument. **2.** a cause of disagreement or dispute; grievance. ~*vb.* **·rels, ·rel·ling, ·relled** *or U.S.* **·rels, ·rel·ing, ·reled.** (*intr.;* often foll. by *with*) **3.** to engage in a disagreement or dispute; argue. **4.** to find fault; complain. [C14: from Old French *querele,* from Latin *querēlla* complaint, from *querī* to complain]

quar·rel[2] ('kwɒrəl) *n.* **1.** an arrow having a four-edged head, fired from a crossbow. **2.** a small square or diamond-shaped pane of glass, usually one of many in a fixed or casement window and framed with lead. [C13: from Old French *quarrel* pane, from Medieval Latin *quadrellus,* diminutive of Latin *quadrus* square]

quar·rel·some ('kwɒrəlsəm) *adj.* inclined to quarrel or disagree; belligerent. —**'quar·rel·some·ly** *adv.* —**'quar·rel·some·ness** *n.*

quar·rian *or* **quar·rion** ('kwɒrɪən) *n.* a cockatiel, *Leptolophus hollandicus,* of scrub and woodland regions of inland Australia, that feeds on seeds and grasses.

quar·ri·er ('kwɒrɪə) *n.* another word for **quarryman.**

quar·ry[1] ('kwɒrɪ) *n., pl.* **·ries. 1.** an open surface excavation for the extraction of building stone, slate, marble, etc., by drilling, blasting, or cutting. **2.** a copious source of something, esp. information. ~*vb.* **·ries, ·ry·ing, ·ried. 3.** to extract (stone, etc.) from or as if from a quarry. **4.** (*tr.*) to excavate a quarry in. **5.** to obtain (something, esp. information) diligently and laboriously: *he was quarrying away in the reference library.* [C15: from Old French *quarriere,* from *quarre* (unattested) square-shaped stone, from Latin *quadrāre* to make square]

quar·ry[2] ('kwɒrɪ) *n., pl.* **·ries. 1.** an animal, bird, or fish that is hunted, esp. by other animals; prey. **2.** anything pursued or hunted. [C14 *quirre* entrails offered to the hounds, from Old French *cuirée* what is placed on the hide, from *cuir* hide, from Latin *corium* leather; probably also influenced by Old French *coree* entrails, from Latin *cor* heart]

quar·ry[3] ('kwɒrɪ) *n., pl.* **·ries. 1.** a square or diamond shape. **2.** something having this shape. **3.** another word for **quarrel**[2]. [C16: from Old French *quarré;* see QUARREL[2]]

quar·ry·man ('kwɒrɪmən) *n., pl.* **·men.** a man who works in or manages a quarry.

quar·ry tile *n.* a square or diamond-shaped unglazed floor tile.

quart[1] (kwɔːt) *n.* **1.** a unit of liquid measure equal to a quarter of a gallon or two pints. 1 U.S. quart (0.946 litre) is equal to 0.8326 U.K. quart. 1 U.K. quart (1.136 litres) is equal to 1.2009 U.S. quarts. **2.** a unit of dry measure equal to 2 pints or one eighth of a peck. [C14: from Old French *quarte,* from Latin *quartus* fourth]

quart[2] (kɑːt) *n.* **1.** *Piquet, etc.* a sequence of four cards in the same suit. **2.** *Fencing.* a variant spelling of **quarte.** [C17: from French *quarte* fourth]

quart. *abbrev. for:* **1.** quarter. **2.** quarterly.

quar·tan ('kwɔːtᵊn) *adj.* (esp. of a malarial fever) occurring every third day. [C13: from Latin *febris quartāna* fever occurring every fourth day, reckoned inclusively]

quarte *French.* (kart) *n.* the fourth of eight basic positions from which a parry or attack can be made in fencing.

quar·ter ('kwɔːtə) *n.* **1.** one of four equal or nearly equal parts of an object, quantity, amount, etc. **2.** Also called: **fourth.** the fraction equal to one divided by four (1/4). **3.** *U.S., Canada, etc.* a quarter of a dollar; 25-cent piece. **4.** a unit of weight equal to a quarter of a hundredweight. 1 U.S. quarter is equal to 25 pounds; 1 Brit. quarter is equal to 28 pounds. **5.** short for **quarter-hour. 6.** a fourth part of a year; three months. **7.** *Astronomy.* **a.** one fourth of the moon's period of revolution around the earth. **b.** either of two phases of the moon, **first quarter** or **last quarter,** when half of the lighted surface is visible from the earth. **8.** *Informal.* a unit of weight equal to a quarter of a pound or 4 ounces. **9.** *Brit.* a unit of capacity for grain, etc., usually equal to 8 U.K. bushels. **10.** *Sport.* one of the four periods into which certain games are divided. **11.** *Nautical.* the part of a vessel's side towards the stern, usually aft of the aftermost mast: *the port quarter.* **12.** *Nautical.* the general direction along the water in the quadrant between the beam of a vessel and its stern: *the wind was from the port quarter.* **13.** a region or district of a town or city: *the Spanish quarter.* **14.** a region, direction, or point of the compass. **15.** (*sometimes pl.*) an unspecified person or group of people: *to get word from the highest quarter.* **16.** mercy or pity, as shown to a defeated opponent (esp. in the phrases **ask for** or **give quarter**). **17.** any of the four limbs, including the adjacent parts, of the carcass of a quadruped or bird: *a hind quarter of beef.* **18.** *Vet. science.* the side part of the wall of a horse's hoof. **19.** the part of a shoe or boot covering the heel and joining the vamp. **20.** *Heraldry.* one of four more or less equal quadrants into which a shield may be divided. **21.** *Military slang.* short for **quartermaster.** ~*vb.* **22.** (*tr.*) to divide into four equal or nearly equal parts. **23.** (*tr.*) to divide into any number of parts. **24.** (*tr.*) (esp. formerly) to dismember (a human body): *to be drawn and quartered.* **25.** to billet or be billeted in lodgings, esp. (of military personnel) in civilian lodgings. **26.** (*intr.*) (of gun dogs or hounds) to range over an area of ground in search of game or the scent of quarry. **27.** (*intr.*) *Nautical.* (of the wind) to blow onto a vessel's quarter: *the wind began to quarter.* **28.** (*tr.*) *Heraldry.* **a.** to divide (a shield) into four separate bearings with a cross. **b.** to place (one set of arms) in diagonally opposite quarters to another. ~*adj.* **29.** being or consisting of one of four equal parts: *a quarter pound of butter.* ~See also **quarters.** [C13: from Old French *quartier,* from Latin *quartārius* a fourth part, from *quartus* fourth]

quar·ter·age ('kwɔːtərɪdʒ) *n.* **1.** an allowance or payment made quarterly. **2.** *Rare.* shelter or lodging.

quar·ter·back ('kwɔːtə,bæk) *n. U.S.* **1.** a player in American football, positioned usually behind the centre, who directs attacking play. **2. Monday-morning quarterbacking.** wisdom after the event, esp. by spectators.

quar·ter-bound *adj.* (of a book) having a binding consisting of two types of material, the better type being used on the spine.

quar·ter crack *n. Vet. science.* a sand crack on the inside of the forefoot of a horse.

quar·ter day *n.* any of four days in the year when certain payments become due. In England, Wales, and Ireland these are Lady Day, Midsummers Day, Michaelmas, and Christmas. In Scotland they are Candlemas, Whit Sunday, Lammas, and Martinmas.

quar·ter·deck ('kwɔːtə,dɛk) *n. Nautical.* the after part of the weather deck of a ship, traditionally the deck on a naval vessel for official or ceremonial use.

quar·tered ('kwɔːtəd) *adj.* **1.** *Heraldry.* (of a shield) divided into four sections, each having contrasting arms or having two sets of arms, each repeated in diagonally opposite corners. **2.** (of a log) sawn into four equal parts along two diameters at right angles to each other; quartersawn.

quar·ter·fi·nal ('kwɔːtə,faɪnᵊl) *n.* the round before the semifinal in a competition.

quar·ter grain *n.* the grain of quartersawn timber.

quar·ter horse *n.* a small powerful breed of horse, originally bred for sprinting in quarter-mile races in Virginia in the late 18th century.

quar·ter-hour *n.* **1.** a period of 15 minutes. **2.** any of the points on the face of a timepiece that mark 15 minutes before or after the hour, and sometimes 30 minutes after. —,**quar·ter-'hour·ly** *adv., adj.*

quar·ter·ing ('kwɔːtərɪŋ) *n.* **1.** *Military.* the allocation of accommodation to service personnel. **2.** *Heraldry.* **a.** the marshalling of several coats of arms on one shield, usually representing intermarriages. **b.** any coat of arms marshalled in this way.

quar·ter·light ('kwɔːtə,laɪt) *n. Brit.* a small pivoted window in the door of a car for ventilation.

quar·ter·ly ('kwɔːtəlɪ) *adj.* **1.** occurring, done, paid, etc., at intervals of three months. **2.** of, relating to, or consisting of a quarter. ~*n., pl.* **·lies. 3.** a periodical issued every three months. ~*adv.* **4.** once every three months. **5.** *Heraldry.* into or in quarters: *a shield divided quarterly.*

quar·ter·mas·ter ('kwɔːtə,mɑːstə) *n.* **1.** an officer responsible for accommodation, food, and equipment in a military unit. **2.** a rating in the navy, usually a petty officer, with particular responsibility for steering a ship and other navigational duties.

quar·ter-mil·er *n.* an athlete who specializes in running the quarter mile.

quar·tern ('kwɔːtən) *n.* **1.** a fourth part of certain weights or measures, such as a peck or a pound. **2.** Also called: **quartern loaf.** *Brit.* **a.** a type of loaf 4 inches square, used esp. for making sandwiches. **b.** any loaf weighing 1600 g when baked. [C13: from Old French *quarteron, from quart* a quarter]

quar·ter note *n.* the usual U.S. name for **crotchet** (sense 1).

quar·ter-phase *adj.* another term for **two-phase.**

quar·ter plate *n.* a photographic plate measuring 8.3 × 10.8 cm.

quar·ter round *n. Architect.* another name for **ovolo.**

quar·ters ('kwɔːtəz) *pl. n.* **1.** housing or accommodation, esp. as provided for military personnel and their families. **2.** the stations assigned to military personnel, esp. to each crew member of a warship: *general quarters.* **3.** (in India) housing provided by an employer or by the government.

quar·ter·saw ('kwɔːtə,sɔː) *vb.* **·saws, ·saw·ing, ·sawed** *or* **·sawn.** (*tr.*) to saw (timber) into quarters along two diameters of a log at right angles to each other.

quar·ter sec·tion *n. U.S.* a land measure, used in surveying, with sides half a mile long; 160 acres.

quar·ter ses·sions *n.* (formerly) a criminal court held four times a year before justices of the peace or a recorder, empowered to try all but the most serious offences and to hear appeals from petty sessions. Replaced in 1972 by **crown courts.** Compare **assizes.**

quar·ter·staff ('kwɔːtə,stɑːf) *n., pl.* **·staves** (-,steɪvz, -,stɑːvz). **1.** a stout iron-tipped wooden staff about 6ft. long, formerly used in England as a weapon. **2.** the use of such a staff in fighting, sport, or exercise.

quar·ter tone *n. Music.* a quarter of a whole tone; a pitch interval corresponding to 50 cents measured on the well-tempered scale.

quar·tet *or* **quar·tette** (kwɔː'tɛt) *n.* **1.** a group of four singers or instrumentalists or a piece of music composed for such a group. See **string quartet. 2.** any group of four. [C18: from Italian *quartetto,* diminutive of *quarto* fourth]

quar·tic ('kwɔːtɪk) *adj., n.* another word for **biquadratic.** [C19: from Latin *quartus* fourth]

quar·tile ('kwɔːtaɪl) *n.* **1.** *Statistics.* one of three actual or notional values of a variable dividing its distribution into four groups with equal frequencies. ~*adj.* **2.** *Statistics.* denoting or relating to a quartile. **3.** *Astrology.* denoting an aspect of two heavenly bodies when their longitudes differ by 90°. [C16: from Medieval Latin *quartīlis,* from Latin *quartus* fourth]

quar·to ('kwɔːtəʊ) *n., pl.* **·tos.** a book size resulting from folding a sheet of paper, usually crown or demy, into four leaves or eight pages, each one quarter the size of the sheet. Often written: **4to, 4°.** [C16: from New Latin phrase *in quartō* in quarter]

quartz (kwɔːts) *n.* **1.** a hard glossy mineral consisting of silicon dioxide in hexagonal crystalline form: present in most rocks, esp. sandstone and granite. It occurs as colourless rock crystal and as several impure coloured varieties including agate, chalcedony, flint, and amethyst. Formula: SiO_2. **2.** short for **quartz glass.** [C18: from German *Quarz,* of Slavic origin]

quartz crys·tal *n.* a thin plate or rod cut in certain directions from a piece of piezoelectric quartz and accurately ground so that it vibrates at a particular frequency.

quartz glass *n.* a colourless glass composed of almost pure silica, resistant to very high temperatures and transparent to near-ultraviolet radiation. Sometimes shortened to **quartz.**

quartz·if·er·ous (kwɔː'tsɪfərəs) *adj.* containing or composed of quartz.

quartz-i·o·dine lamp *or* **quartz lamp** *n.* an electric light bulb consisting of a quartz envelope enclosing an inert gas containing iodine vapour and a tungsten filament. It is used in some car headlights, etc.

quartz·ite ('kwɔːtsaɪt) *n.* **1.** a white or grey sandstone composed of quartz. **2.** a very hard metamorphic rock consisting of a mosaic of intergrown quartz crystals.

qua·sar ('kweɪzɑː, -sɑː) *n.* any of a class of quasi-stellar objects, first detected in 1963, that are powerful sources of radio waves and other forms of energy. Many have large red shifts (greater than 1.5), which imply enormous velocities of recession, distances of several thousand million light-years, and luminosities 200 times greater than that of an ordinary galaxy. [C20: *quas*(*i-stell*)*ar* (*radio source*)]

quash (kwɒʃ) *vb.* (*tr.*) **1.** to subdue forcefully and completely; put down; suppress. **2.** to annul or make void (a law, decision, etc.). **3.** to reject (an indictment, writ, etc.) as invalid. [C14: from Old French *quasser*, from Latin *quassāre* to shake]

Qua+shi *or* **Qua+shie** (ˈkwɑːʃɪ) *n. Caribbean.* an unsophisticated or gullible male Negro peasant: *I'm not a Quashi that anyone can fool.* [from Twi]

qua·si- *combining form.* **1.** almost but not really; seemingly: *a quasi-religious cult.* **2.** resembling but not actually being; so-called: *a quasi-scholar.* [from Latin, literally: as if]

qua·si-con·tract (ˈkwɑːzɪ, ˈkweɪsaɪ, -zaɪ) *n.* an implied contract which arises without the express agreement of the parties.

qua·si-ju·di·cial *adj.* denoting or relating to powers and functions similar to those of a judge, such as those exercised by an arbitrator, administrative tribunal, etc.

Qua·si·mo·do *n.* **1.** (ˌkwɑːzɪˈməʊdəʊ). a character in Victor Hugo's novel *Notre-Dame de Paris* (1831), a grotesque hunchbacked bellringer of the cathedral of Notre Dame. **2.** (*Italian* kwaˈziːmoˌdo) **Sal·va·to·re** (ˌsalvaˈtɔre). 1901–68, Italian poet, whose early work expresses symbolist ideas and techniques. His later work is more concerned with political and social issues: Nobel prize for literature 1959.

qua·si-stel·lar ob·ject *n.* a member of any of several classes of astronomical bodies, including **quasars** (strong radio sources) and **quasi-stellar galaxies** (no traceable radio emission), both of which have exceptionally large red shifts. Abbrev.: **QSO**

quass (kvɑːs, kwɑːs) *n.* a variant spelling of **kvass.**

quas+sia (ˈkwɒʃə) *n.* **1.** any tree of the tropical American simaroubaceous genus *Quassia,* having bitter bark and wood. **2.** the bark and wood of *Quassia amara* and of a related tree, *Picrasma excelsa,* used in furniture making. **3.** a bitter compound extracted from this bark and wood, formerly used as a tonic and anthelmintic, now used in insecticides. [C18: from New Latin, named after Graman *Quassi,* a slave who discovered (1730) the medicinal value of the root]

qua+ter+cen+te+nar·y (ˌkwætəsenˈtiːnərɪ) *n., pl.* **+nar·ies.** a 400th anniversary or the year or celebration marking it. —**ˌqua+ter+cen+ˈten+ni+al** *adj., n.*

qua+ter+nar·y (kwəˈtɜːnərɪ) *adj.* **1.** consisting of fours or by fours. **2.** fourth in a series. **3.** *Chem.* containing or being an atom bound to four other atoms or groups: *a quaternary ammonium compound.* **4.** *Maths.* having four variables. ~*n., pl.* **+nar·ies. 5.** the number four or a set of four. [C15: from Latin *quaternārius* each containing four, from *quaternī* by fours, distributive of *quattuor* four]

Qua+ter+nar·y (kwəˈtɜːnərɪ) *adj.* **1.** of, denoting, or formed in the most recent period of geological time, which succeeded the Tertiary period one million years ago. ~*n.* **2. the.** the Quaternary period or rock system, divided into Pleistocene and Holocene (Recent) epochs or series.

qua+ter+nar·y am+mo+ni·um com+pound *n.* a type of ionic compound that can be regarded as derived from ammonium compounds by replacing the hydrogen atoms with organic groups.

qua+ter+ni+on (kwəˈtɜːnɪən) *n.* **1.** *Maths.* a generalized complex number consisting of four components, $x = x_0 + x_1\mathrm{i} + x_2\mathrm{j} + x_3\mathrm{k}$, where x, $x_0 ... x_3$ are real numbers and $\mathrm{i}^2 = \mathrm{j}^2 = \mathrm{k}^2 = -1$, $\mathrm{ij} = -\mathrm{ji} = \mathrm{k}$, etc. **2.** another word for **quaternary** (sense 5). [C14: from Late Latin *quaterniōn,* from Latin *quaternī* four at a time]

qua+ter+ni+ty (kwəˈtɜːnɪtɪ) *n.* a group of four, esp. a concept of God as consisting of four persons. [C16: from Late Latin *quaternitās,* from Latin *quaternī* by fours; see QUATERNARY]

Quath+lam+ba (kwɑːtˈlɑːmbɑː) *n.* the Sesuto name for the **Drakensberg.**

quat+rain (ˈkwɒtreɪn) *n.* a stanza or poem of four lines, esp. one having alternate rhymes. [C16: from French, from *quatre* four, from Latin *quattuor*]

qua+tre (ˈkætrə; *French* ˈkatr) *n.* a playing card with four pips. [French: four]

Qua+tre Bras (*French* katr ˈbra) *n.* a village in Belgium near Brussels; site of a battle in June 1815 where Wellington defeated the French under Marshal Ney, immediately preceding the battle of Waterloo.

quat·re·foil (ˈkætrəˌfɔɪl) *n.* **1.** a leaf, such as that of certain clovers, composed of four leaflets. **2.** *Architect.* a carved ornament having four foils arranged about a common centre, esp. one used in tracery. [C15: from Old French, from *quatre* four + *-foil* leaflet; compare TREFOIL]

quat+tro+cen+to (ˌkwætrəʊˈtʃɛntəʊ; *Italian* ˌkwatroˈtʃento) *n.* the 15th century, esp. in reference to Renaissance Italian art and literature. [Italian, literally: four hundred (short for fourteen hundred)]

qua+ver (ˈkweɪvə) *vb.* **1.** to say or sing (something) with a trembling voice. **2.** (*intr.*) (esp. of the voice) to quiver, tremble, or shake. **3.** (*intr.*) *Rare.* to sing or play quavers or ornamental trills. ~*n.* **4.** *Music.* a note having the time value of an eighth of a semibreve. Usual U.S. name: **eighth note. 5.** a tremulous sound or note. [C15 (in the sense: to vibrate, QUIVER): from *quaven* to tremble, of Germanic origin; compare Low German *quabbeln* to tremble] —**ˈqua+ver+er** *n.* —**ˈqua+ver+ing+ly** *adv.* —**ˈqua+ver·y** *or* **ˈqua+ver+ous** *adj.*

quay (kiː) *n.* a wharf, typically one built parallel to the shoreline. Compare **pier** (sense 1). [C14 *keye,* from Old French *kai,* of Celtic origin; compare Cornish *kē* hedge, fence, Old Breton *cai* fence]

quay+age (ˈkiːɪdʒ) *n.* **1.** a system of quays. **2.** a charge for the use of a quay.

quay+side (ˈkiːˌsaɪd) *n.* the edge of a quay along the water.

Que. *abbrev. for* Quebec.

quean (kwiːn) *n.* **1.** *Archaic.* **a.** a boisterous, impudent, or disreputable woman. **b.** a prostitute; whore. **2.** *Scot.* a young unmarried woman or girl. [Old English *cwene;* related to Old Saxon, Old High German *quena,* Gothic *qino,* Old Norse *kona,* Greek *gunē* woman. Compare QUEEN]

quea+sy (ˈkwiːzɪ) *adj.* **+si+er, +si+est. 1.** having the feeling that one is about to vomit; nauseous. **2.** feeling or causing uneasiness: *a queasy conscience.* [C15: of uncertain origin] —**ˈquea+si+ly** *adv.* —**ˈquea+si+ness** *n.*

Que+bec (kwɪˈbɛk, kə-, kɛ-) *n.* **1.** a province of E Canada: the largest Canadian province; a French colony from 1608 to 1763, when it passed to Britain; lying mostly on the Canadian Shield, it has vast areas of forest and extensive tundra and is populated mostly in the plain around the St. Lawrence River. Capital: Quebec. Pop.: 6 234 445 (1976). Area: 1 540 680 sq. km (594 860 sq. miles). **2.** a port in E Canada, capital of the province of Quebec, situated on the St. Lawrence River: founded in 1608 by Champlain; scene of the battle of the Plains of Abraham (1759), by which the British won Canada from the French. Pop.: 186 088 (1971).

Qué+be+cois (*French* kebɛˈkwa) *n., pl.* **+cois** (-ˈkwa). a native or inhabitant of the province of Quebec, esp. a French-speaking one.

que+bra+cho (keɪˈbrɑːtʃəʊ; *Spanish* kɛˈβratʃɔ) *n., pl.* **+chos** (-tʃəuz; *Spanish* -tʃɛʃ). **1.** either of two anacardiaceous South American trees, *Schinopsis lorentzii* or *S. balansae,* having a tannin-rich hard wood used in tanning and dyeing. **2.** an apocynaceous South American tree, *Aspidosperma quebracho-blanco,* whose bark yields alkaloids used in medicine and tanning. **3.** the wood or bark of any of these trees. **4.** any of various other South American trees having hard wood. [C19: from American Spanish, from *quiebracha,* from *quebrar* to break (from Latin *crepāre* to rattle) + *hacha* axe (from French *hache*)]

Quech·ua, Kech·ua (ˈkɛtʃwə), *or* **Quich·ua** *n.* **1.** (*pl.* **·uas** *or* **·ua**) a member of any of a group of South American Indian peoples of the Andes, including the Incas. **2.** the language or family of languages spoken by these peoples. —**ˈQuech+uan, ˈKech+uan,** *or* **ˈQuich+uan** *adj., n.*

queen (kwiːn) *n.* **1.** the wife or widow of a king. **2.** a female sovereign who is the official ruler or head of state. **3.** a woman or a thing personified as a woman considered the best or most important of her kind: *a beauty queen; the queen of ocean liners.* **4.** *Informal.* a male homosexual. **5. a.** the only fertile female in a colony of social insects, such as bees, ants, and termites, from the eggs of which the entire colony develops. **b.** (*as modifier*): *a queen bee.* **6.** one of four playing cards in a pack, one for each suit, bearing the picture of a queen. **7.** a chess piece, theoretically the most powerful piece, able to move in a straight line in any direction or diagonally, over any number of squares. ~*vb.* **8.** *Chess.* to promote (a pawn) to a queen when it reaches the eighth rank. **9.** (*tr.*) to crown as queen. **10.** (*intr.*) to reign as queen. **11. queen it.** (often foll. by *over*) *Informal.* to behave in an overbearing manner. [Old English *cwēn;* related to Old Saxon *quān* wife, Old Norse *kvæn,* Gothic *qēns* wife]

Queen-Anne *n.* **1.** a style of furniture popular in England about 1700–20 and in America about 1720–70, characterized by the use of unencumbered curves, walnut veneer, and the cabriole leg. ~*adj.* **2.** in or of this style. **3.** denoting or relating to a style of architecture popular in England during the early 18th century, characterized by red-brick construction with classical ornamentation.

Queen Anne's Boun+ty *Church of England.* ~*n.* **1.** a fund formed by Queen Anne in 1704 for the augmentation of the livings of the poorer Anglican clergy. In 1948 the administrators of the fund were replaced by the Church Commissioners for England. **2.** the office or board administering this fund.

Queen Anne's lace *n.* another name for the **wild carrot.**

Queen Anne's War *n.* those conflicts (1702–13) of the War of the Spanish Succession that were fought in North America.

Queen+bor+ough in Shep+pey (ˈkwiːnbərə) *n.* a town in SE England, in Kent: formed in 1968 by the amalgamation of Queenborough, Sheerness, and Sheppey. Pop.: 31 541 (1971).

queen+cake (ˈkwiːnˌkeɪk) *n.* a small heart-shaped cake containing currants.

Queen Char+lotte Is+lands *pl. n.* a group of about 150 islands off the W coast of Canada: part of British Columbia. Pop.: 3000 (1972 est.). Area: 9596 sq. km (3705 sq. miles).

queen con+sort *n.* the wife of a reigning king.

queen dow·a+ger *n.* the widow of a king.

Queen E·liz·a+beth Is+lands *pl. n.* a group of islands off the N coast of Canada: the northernmost islands of the Canadian Arctic archipelago, lying N of latitude 74°N; part of the Northwest Territories. Area: about 390 000 sq. km (150 000 sq. miles).

queen+ly (ˈkwiːnlɪ) *adj.* **+li+er, +li+est. 1.** resembling or appropriate to a queen. **2.** having the rank of queen. ~*adv.* **3.** in a manner appropriate to a queen. —**ˈqueen+li+ness** *n.*

Queen Mab (mæb) *n.* (in British folklore) a bewitching fairy who rules over men's dreams.

Queen Maud Land (mɔːd) *n.* the large section of Antarctica between Coats Land and Enderby Land: claimed by Norway in 1939.
Queen Maud Range *n.* a mountain range in Antarctica, in S Ross Dependency, extending for about 800 km (500 miles).
queen moth·er *n.* the widow of a former king who is also the mother of the reigning sovereign.
queen of pud·dings *n.* a pudding of meringue and breadcrumbs, with various flavourings.
queen ol·ive *n.* a variety of olive having large fleshy fruit suitable for pickling, esp. one from around Seville in Spain.
queen post *n.* one of a pair of vertical posts that connect the tie beam of a truss to the principal rafters.
queen re·gent *n.* a queen who acts as regent.
queen reg·nant *n.* a queen who reigns on her own behalf.
Queens (kwiːnz) *n.* a borough of E New York City, on Long Island. Pop.: 1 986 473 (1970).
Queen's Bench Division *n.* (in England when the sovereign is female) one of the divisions of the High Court of Justice. Also called (when the sovereign is male): **King's Bench.**
Queens·ber·ry rules ('kwiːnzbərɪ, -brɪ) *pl. n.* **1.** the code of rules followed in modern boxing, requiring the use of padded gloves, rounds of three minutes, and restrictions on the types of blows allowed. **2.** *Informal.* gentlemanly or polite conduct, esp. in a dispute. [C19: named after the ninth Marquess of *Queensberry,* who originated the rules in 1869]
Queen's Coun·sel *n.* (in England when the sovereign is female) a barrister appointed Counsel to the Crown on the recommendation of the Lord Chancellor, entitled to sit within the bar of the court and to wear a silk gown. Also called (when the sovereign is male): **King's Counsel.**
Queen's Coun·ty *n.* the former name of **Laoighis.**
queen's Eng·lish *n.* (when the British sovereign is female) standard Southern British English.
queen's ev·i·dence *n. English law.* (when the sovereign is female) evidence given for the Crown against his former associates in crime by an accomplice (esp. in the phrase **turn queen's evidence).** Also called (when the sovereign is male): **king's evidence.** U.S. equivalent: **state's evidence.**
Queen's Guide *n.* (in Britain and the Commonwealth when the sovereign is female) a Guide who has passed the highest tests of proficiency.
queen's high·way *n.* (in Britain when the sovereign is female) any public road or right of way.
Queens·land ('kwiːnzˌlænd, -lənd) *n.* a state of NE Australia: fringed on the Pacific side by the Great Barrier Reef; the Great Dividing Range lies in the east, separating the coastal lowlands from the dry Great Artesian Basin in the south. Capital: Brisbane. Pop.: 2 037 000 (1976). Area: 1 727 500 sq. km (667 000 sq. miles). —**'Queens·land·er** *n.*
Queens·land lung·fish *n.* a lungfish, *Neoceratodus forsteri,* reaching a length of six feet: occurs in Queensland rivers but introduced elsewhere.
Queens·land nut *n.* another name for **macadamia.**
Queen's proc·tor *n.* (in England when the sovereign is female) an official empowered to intervene in divorce and certain other cases when it is alleged that material facts are being suppressed.
Queen's Reg·u·la·tions *pl. n.* (in Britain and certain other Commonwealth countries when the sovereign is female) the code of conduct for members of the armed forces.
Queen's Scout *n.* (in Britain and the Commonwealth when the sovereign is female) a Scout who has passed the highest tests of endurance, proficiency, and skill. U.S. equivalent: **Eagle Scout.**
queen's shil·ling *n.* See **king's shilling.**
Queen's speech *n.* (in Britain and certain other Commonwealth countries when the sovereign is female) another name for the **speech from the throne.**
Queens·town ('kwiːnzˌtaʊn) *n.* the former name (1849–1922) of **Cóbh.**
queen sub·stance *n.* a pheromone secreted by queen honeybees and consumed by the workers, in whom it causes suppression of egg-laying.
queer (kwɪə) *adj.* **1.** differing from the normal or usual in a way regarded as odd or strange. **2.** suspicious, dubious, or shady. **3.** faint, giddy, or queasy. **4.** *Informal.* homosexual. **5.** *Informal.* odd or unbalanced mentally; eccentric or slightly mad. **6.** *Slang.* worthless or counterfeit. ~*n.* **7.** *Informal.* a homosexual, usually a male. ~*vb.* (*tr.*) *Informal.* **8.** to spoil or thwart (esp. in the phrase **queer someone's pitch).** **9.** to put in a difficult or dangerous position. [C16: perhaps from German *quer* oblique, ultimately from Old High German *twërh*] —**'queer·ish** *adj.* —**'queer·ly** *adv.* —**'queer·ness** *n.*
queer-bash·ing *n. Brit. slang.* the activity of making vicious and unprovoked physical assaults upon homosexuals or supposed homosexuals. —**'queer-bash·er** *n.*
queer street *n.* (*sometimes cap.*) *Informal.* a difficult situation, such as debt or bankruptcy (in the phrase **in queer street).**
quell (kwɛl) *vb.* (*tr.*) **1.** to suppress or beat down (rebellion, disorder, etc.); subdue. **2.** to overcome or allay: *to quell pain; to quell grief.* [Old English *cwellan* to kill; related to Old Saxon *quellian,* Old High German *quellen,* Old Norse *kvelja* to torment] —**'quell·er** *n.*
Quel·part ('kwɛlˌpɑːt) *n.* another name for **Cheju.**
quel·que·chose ('kɛlkə'ʃəʊz) *n.* an insignificant thing; mere trifle. [French, literally: something]
Que·moy (kɛ'mɔɪ) *n.* an island in Formosa Strait, off the SE coast of China: administratively part of Taiwan. Pop. (with associated islets): 61 305 (1971). Area: 130 sq. km (50 sq. miles).
quench (kwɛntʃ) *vb.* (*tr.*) **1.** to satisfy (one's thirst, desires, etc.); slake. **2.** to put out (a fire, flame, etc.); extinguish. **3.** to put down or quell; suppress: *to quench a rebellion.* **4.** to cool (hot metal) by plunging it into cold water. **5.** *Physics.* to reduce the degree of (luminescence or phosphorescence) in (excited molecules or a material) by adding a suitable substance. **6.** *Electronics.* **a.** to suppress (sparking) when the current is cut off in an inductive circuit. **b.** to suppress (an oscillation or discharge) in a component or device. [Old English *ācwencan* to extinguish; related to Old Frisian *quinka* to vanish] —**'quench·a·ble** *adj.* —**'quench·er** *n.* —**'quench·less** *adj.*
Que·neau (*French* kə'no) *n.* **Ray·mond** (rɛ'mɔ̃). 1903–76, French writer, influenced in the 1920s by surrealism. His novels include *Zazie dans le métro* (1959).
que·nelle (kə'nɛl) *n.* a finely sieved mixture of cooked meat or fish, shaped into various forms and cooked in stock or fried as croquettes. [C19: from French, from German *Knödel* dumpling, from Old High German *knodo* knot]
quer·ce·tin *or* **quer·ci·tin** ('kwɜːsɪtɪn) *n.* a yellow crystalline pigment found naturally as its glycosides in the rind and bark of many plants. It is used in medicine to treat fragile capillaries. Formula: $C_{15}H_{10}O_7$; melting pt: 316–7°C. Also called: **flavin.** [C19: from Latin *quercētum* an oak forest (from *quercus* an oak) + -IN] —**quer·cet·ic** (kwɜː'sɛtɪk, -'siː-) *adj.*
quer·cine ('kwɜːsaɪn) *adj. Rare.* of or relating to the oak. [C17: from Latin *quercus* an oak]
Que·ré·ta·ro (*Spanish* ke'retaro) *n.* **1.** an inland state of central Mexico: economy based on agriculture and mining. Capital: Querétaro. Pop.: 485 523 (1970). Area: 11 769 sq. km (4544 sq. miles). **2.** a city in central Mexico, capital of Querétaro state: scene of the signing (1848) of the treaty ending the U.S.-Mexican War and of the execution of Emperor Maximilian (1867). Pop.: 150 226 (1975 est.).
que·rist ('kwɪərɪst) *n.* a person who makes inquiries or queries; questioner.
quern (kwɜːn) *n.* a stone hand mill for grinding corn. [Old English *cweorn;* related to Old Frisian *quern,* Old High German *kurn,* Old Norse *kverna,* Gothic *quairnus* millstone]
quer·u·lous ('kwɛruləs, 'kwɛrjʊ-) *adj.* **1.** inclined to make whining or peevish complaints. **2.** characterized by or proceeding from a complaining fretful attitude or disposition: *a querulous tone.* [C15: from Latin *querulus* from *querī* to complain] —**'quer·u·lous·ly** *adv.* —**'quer·u·lous·ness** *n.*
que·ry ('kwɪərɪ) *n., pl.* **·ries.** **1.** a question, esp. one expressing doubt, uncertainty, or an objection. **2.** a less common name for **question mark.** ~*vb.* **·ries, ·ry·ing, ·ried.** (*tr.*) **3.** to express uncertainty, doubt, or an objection concerning (something). **4.** to put a question to (a person); ask. [C17: from earlier *quere,* from Latin *quaere* ask!, from *quaerere* to seek, enquire]
ques. *abbrev. for* question.
Ques·nay (*French* kɛ'nɛ) *n.* **Fran·çois** (frɑ̃'swa). 1694–1774, French political economist, encyclopedist, and physician. He propounded the theory championed by the physiocrats in his *Tableau économique* (1758).
quest (kwɛst) *n.* **1.** the act or an instance of looking for or seeking; search: *a quest for diamonds.* **2.** (in medieval romance) an expedition by a knight or company of knights to accomplish some prescribed task, such as finding the Holy Grail. **3.** the object of a search; goal or target: *my quest is the treasure of the king.* **4.** *Rare.* a collection of alms. ~*vb.* (*mainly intr.*) **5.** (foll. by *for* or *after*) to go in search (of). **6.** to go on a quest. **7.** (of gun dogs or hounds) **a.** to search for game. **b.** to bay when in pursuit of game. **8.** *Rare.* to collect alms. **9.** (*also tr.*) *Archaic.* to go in search of (a thing); seek or pursue. [C14: from Old French *queste,* from Latin *quaesita* sought, from *quaerere* to seek] —**'quest·er** *n.* —**'quest·ing·ly** *adv.*
ques·tion ('kwɛstʃən) *n.* **1.** a form of words addressed to a person in order to elicit information or evoke a response; interrogative sentence. **2.** a point at issue: *it's only a question of time until she dies; the question is how long they can keep up the pressure.* **3.** a difficulty or uncertainty; doubtful point: *a question of money; there's no question about it.* **4. a.** an act of asking. **b.** an investigation into some problem or difficulty. **5.** a motion presented for debate by a deliberative body. **6. put the question.** to require members of a deliberative assembly to vote on a motion presented. **7.** *Law.* a matter submitted to a court or other tribunal for judicial or quasi-judicial decision. **8. question of fact.** (in English law) that part of the issue before a court that is decided by the jury. **9. question of law.** (in English law) that part of the issue before a court that is decided by the judge. **10. beg the question. a.** to avoid giving a direct answer by posing another question. **b.** to assume the truth of that which is intended to be proved. See **petitio principii.** **11. beyond (all) question.** beyond (any) dispute or doubt. **12. call in** *or* **into question. a.** to make (something) the subject of disagreement. **b.** to cast doubt upon the validity, truth, etc., of (something). **13. in question.** under discussion: *this is the man in question.* **14. out of the question.** beyond consideration; unthinkable or impossible: *the marriage is out of the question.* **15. pop the question.** *Informal.* to ask a girl to marry one. **16. put to the question.** (formerly) to interrogate (a person accused of heresy) by torture. ~*vb.* (*mainly tr.*) **17.** to put a question or questions to (a person); interrogate. **18.** to make (something) the subject of dispute or disagreement. **19.** to express uncertainty about the validity, truth, etc., of (something); doubt. [C13: via Old French from Latin *quaestiō,* from *quaerere* to seek] —**'ques·tion·er** *n.*

ques·tion·a·ble ('kwɛstʃənəbᵊl) *adj.* **1.** (esp. of a person's morality or honesty) admitting of some doubt; dubious. **2.** of disputable value or authority: *a questionable text.* —**'ques·tion·a·ble·ness** *or* **ˌques·tion·a·'bil·i·ty** *n.* —**'ques·tion·a·bly** *adv.*

ques·tion·ing ('kwɛstʃənɪŋ) *adj.* **1.** proceeding from or characterized by a feeling of doubt or uncertainty. **2.** enthusiastic or eager for philosophical or other investigations; intellectually stimulated: *an alert and questioning mind.* —**'ques·tion·ing·ly** *adv.*

ques·tion·less ('kwɛstʃənlɪs) *adj.* **1.** blindly adhering, as to a principle or course of action; unquestioning. **2.** a less common word for **unquestionable.** —**'ques·tion·less·ly** *adv.*

ques·tion mark *n.* **1.** the punctuation mark ?, used at the end of questions and in other contexts where doubt or ignorance is implied. **2.** this mark used for any other purpose, as to draw attention to a possible mistake, as in a chess commentary.

ques·tion mas·ter *n. Brit.* the chairman of a radio or television quiz or panel game.

ques·tion·naire (ˌkwɛstʃə'nɛə, ˌkɛs-) *n.* a set of questions on a form, submitted to a number of people in order to collect statistical information.

ques·tion time *n.* (in parliamentary bodies of the British type) a period of time set aside each day for members to question government ministers.

ques·tor ('kwɛstə) *n. U.S.* a variant spelling of **quaestor.** —**ques·to·ri·al** (kwɛ'stɔːrɪəl) *adj.* —**'ques·tor·ˌship** *n.*

Quet·ta ('kwɛtə) *n.* a city in W central Pakistan, at an altitude of 1650 m (5500 ft.): a summer resort, military station, and trading centre. Pop.: 156 000 (1972).

quet·zal ('kɛtsəl) *or* **que·zal** (kɛ'sɑːl) *n., pl.* **·zals** *or* **·zal·es** (-'sɑːlɛs). **1.** Also called: **resplendent trogon.** a crested bird, *Pharomachrus mocinno,* of Central and N South America, which has a brilliant green, red, and white plumage and, in the male, long tail feathers: family *Trogonidae,* order *Trogoniformes* (trogons). **2.** the standard monetary unit of Guatemala, divided into 100 centavos. [via American Spanish from Nahuatl *quetzalli* brightly coloured tail feather]

Quet·zal·co·a·tl (ˌkɛtsəlkəʊ'ætᵊl) *n.* a god of the Aztecs and Toltecs, represented as a feathered serpent.

queue (kjuː) *Chiefly Brit.* ~*n.* **1.** a line of people, vehicles, etc., waiting for something: *a queue at the theatre.* ~*vb.* **queues, queu·ing, queued. 2.** (*intr.,* often foll. by *up*) to form or remain in a line while waiting. ~U.S. word: **line.** [C16 (in the sense: tail); C18 (in the sense: pigtail): via French from Latin *cauda* tail]

Que·zon Cit·y ('keɪzɒn) *n.* the capital of the Philippines, on central Luzon: replaced Manila (which it adjoins) as capital in 1948; seat of the University of the Philippines (1908). Pop.: 994 679 (1975 est.).

Que·zon y Mo·li·na ('keɪzɒn iː mɒ'liːnə; *Spanish* 'keθon i mo'lina) *n.* **Ma·nuel Lu·is** (ma'nwɛl lwiz). 1878–1944, Philippine statesman: first president of the Philippines (from 1935) and head of the government in exile after the Japanese conquest of the islands in World War II.

quib·ble ('kwɪbᵊl) *vb.* (*intr.*) **1.** to make trivial objections; prevaricate. **2.** *Archaic.* to play on words; pun. ~*n.* **3.** a trivial objection or equivocation, esp. one used to avoid an issue. **4.** *Archaic.* a pun. [C17: probably from obsolete *quib,* perhaps from Latin *quibus* (from *quī* who, which), as used in legal documents, with reference to their obscure phraseology] —**'quib·bler** *n.* —**'quib·bling·ly** *adv.*

Qui·be·ron (*French* ki'brɔ̃) *n.* a peninsula of NW France, on the S coast of Brittany: a naval battle was fought off its coast in 1759 during the Seven Years' War, in which the English defeated the French.

quiche (kiːʃ) *n.* an open savoury tart with a rich custard filling to which bacon, onion, cheese, etc., are added: *quiche Lorraine.* [French, from German *Kuchen* cake]

Quich·ua ('kɪtʃwə) *n., pl.* **·uas** *or* **·ua.** a variant of **Quechua.**

quick (kwɪk) *adj.* **1.** (of an action, movement, etc.) performed or occurring during a comparatively short time: *a quick move.* **2.** lasting a comparatively short time; brief: *a quick flight.* **3.** accomplishing something in a time that is shorter than normal: *a quick worker.* **4.** characterized by rapidity of movement; swift or fast: *a quick walker.* **5.** immediate or prompt: *a quick reply.* **6.** (*postpositive*) eager or ready to perform (an action): *quick to criticize.* **7.** responsive to stimulation; perceptive or alert; lively: *a quick eye.* **8.** eager or enthusiastic for learning: *a quick intelligence.* **9.** easily excited or aroused: *a quick temper.* **10.** skilfully swift or nimble in one's movements or actions; deft: *quick fingers.* **11.** *Archaic.* **a.** alive; living. **b.** (*as n.*) living people (esp. in the phrase **the quick and the dead**). **12.** *Archaic or northern Brit. dialect.* lively or eager: *a quick dog.* **13.** (of a fire) burning briskly. **14.** composed of living plants: *a quick hedge.* **15.** *Brit. dialect.* (of sand) lacking firmness through being wet. **16. quick with child.** *Archaic.* pregnant, esp. being in an advanced state of pregnancy, when the movements of the fetus can be felt. ~*n.* **17.** any area of living flesh that is highly sensitive to pain or touch, esp. that under a toenail or fingernail or around a healing wound. **18.** the vital or most important part (of a thing). **19.** short for **quickset** (sense 1). **20. cut (someone) to the quick.** to hurt (a person's) feelings deeply; offend gravely. ~*adv. Informal.* **21.** in a rapid or speedy manner; swiftly. **22.** soon: *I hope he comes quick.* ~*interj.* **23.** a command requiring the hearer to perform an action immediately or in as short a time as possible. [Old English *cwicu* living; related to Old Saxon *quik,* Old High German *queck,* Old Norse *kvikr* alive, Latin *vīvus* alive, Greek *bios* life] —**'quick·ly** *adv.* —**'quick·ness** *n.*

quick as·sets *pl. n. Accounting.* assets readily convertible into cash; liquid current assets.

quick-change art·ist *n.* an actor or entertainer who undertakes several rapid changes of costume during his performance.

quick·en ('kwɪkən) *vb.* **1.** to make or become faster; accelerate: *he quickened his walk; her heartbeat quickened with excitement.* **2.** to impart to or receive vigour, enthusiasm, etc.; stimulate or be stimulated: *science quickens man's imagination.* **3.** to make or become alive; revive. **4. a.** (of an unborn fetus) to begin to show signs of life. **b.** (of a pregnant woman) to reach the stage of pregnancy at which movements of the fetus can be felt.

quick fire *n.* **1.** rapid continuous gunfire, esp. at a moving target. ~*adj.* **quick-fire. 2.** Also: **quick-firing.** capable of or designed for quick fire. **3.** *Informal.* rapid or following one another in rapid succession: *quick-fire questions.*

quick-freeze *vb.* **-freez·es, -freez·ing, -froze, -fro·zen.** (*tr.*) to preserve (food) by subjecting it to rapid refrigeration at temperatures of 0°C or lower.

quick grass *n.* another name for **couch grass.**

quick·ie ('kwɪkɪ) *Informal.* ~*n.* **1.** Also called (esp. Brit.): **quick one.** a speedily consumed alcoholic drink. **2.** anything made, done, produced, or consumed rapidly or in haste.

quick·lime ('kwɪkˌlaɪm) *n.* another name for **calcium oxide.**

quick march *n.* **1.** a march at quick time or the order to proceed at such a pace. ~*interj.* **2.** a command to commence such a march.

quick·sand ('kwɪkˌsænd) *n.* a deep mass of loose wet sand that sucks anything on top of it inextricably into it.

quick·set ('kwɪkˌsɛt) *Chiefly Brit.* ~*n.* **1. a.** a plant or cutting, esp. of hawthorn, set so as to form a hedge. **b.** such plants or cuttings collectively. **2.** a hedge composed of such plants. ~*adj.* **3.** composed of such plants.

quick·sil·ver ('kwɪkˌsɪlvə) *n.* **1.** another name for **mercury** (sense 1). ~*adj.* **2.** rapid or unpredictable in movement or change: *a quicksilver temper.*

quick·step ('kwɪkˌstɛp) *n.* **1.** a modern ballroom dance in rapid quadruple time. **2.** a piece of music composed for or in the rhythm of this dance. ~*vb.* **·steps, ·step·ping, ·stepped. 3.** (*intr.*) to perform this dance.

quick-tem·pered *adj.* readily roused to anger; irascible.

quick time *n. Military.* the normal marching rate of 120 paces to the minute. Compare **double time.**

quick trick *n. Bridge.* a high card almost certain to win a trick, usually an ace or a king: the unit in one of the systems of hand valuation.

quick-wit·ted *adj.* having a keenly alert mind, esp. as used to avert danger, make effective reply, etc. —**ˌquick-'wit·ted·ly** *adv.* —**ˌquick-'wit·ted·ness** *n.*

quid[1] (kwɪd) *n.* a piece of tobacco, suitable for chewing. [Old English *cwidu* chewing resin; related to Old High German *quiti* glue, Old Norse *kvātha* resin; see CUD]

quid[2] (kwɪd) *n., pl.* **quid. 1.** *Brit.* a slang word for **pound** (sterling). **2. not the full quid.** *Austral. slang.* mentally subnormal. [C17: of obscure origin]

quid·di·ty ('kwɪdɪtɪ) *n., pl.* **·ties. 1.** *Philosophy.* the essential nature of something. Compare **haecceity. 2.** a petty or trifling distinction; quibble. [C16: from Medieval Latin *quidditās,* from Latin *quid* what]

quid·nunc ('kwɪdˌnʌŋk) *n.* a person eager to learn news and scandal; gossipmonger. [C18: from Latin, literally: what now]

quid pro quo ('kwɪd prəʊ 'kwəʊ) *n., pl.* **quid pro quos. 1.** a reciprocal exchange. **2.** something given in compensation, esp. an advantage or object given in exchange for another. [C16: from Latin: something for something]

qui·es·cent (kwɪ'ɛsᵊnt) *adj.* quiet, inactive, or dormant. [C17: from Latin *quiescere* to rest] —**qui·'es·cence** *or* **qui·'es·cen·cy** *n.* —**qui·'es·cent·ly** *adv.*

qui·et ('kwaɪət) *adj.* **1.** characterized by an absence or near absence of noise: *a quiet street.* **2.** characterized by an absence of turbulent motion or disturbance; peaceful, calm, or tranquil: *a quiet glade; the sea is quiet tonight.* **3.** free from activities, distractions, worries, etc.; untroubled: *a quiet life; a quiet day at work.* **4.** private; not public; secret: *a quiet word with someone.* **5.** free from anger, impatience, or other extreme emotion: *a quiet disposition.* **6.** free from pretentiousness or vain display; modest or reserved: *quiet humour.* **7.** *Astronomy.* (of the sun) exhibiting a very low number of sunspots, solar flares, and other surface phenomena; inactive. Compare **active** (sense 8). ~*n.* **8.** the state of being silent, peaceful, or untroubled. **9. on the quiet.** without other people knowing; secretly. ~*vb.* **10.** a less common word for **quieten.** [C14: from Latin *quiētus,* past participle of *quiēscere* to rest, from *quiēs* repose, rest] —**'qui·et·ness** *n.*

qui·et·en ('kwaɪətᵊn) *vb. Chiefly Brit.* **1.** (often foll. by *down*) to make or become calm, silent, etc.; pacify or become peaceful. **2.** (*tr.*) to allay (fear, doubts, etc.).

qui·et·ism ('kwaɪəˌtɪzəm) *n.* a form of religious mysticism originating in Spain in the late 17th century, requiring withdrawal of the spirit from all human effort and complete passivity to God's will. —**qui·et·ist** *n., adj.*

qui·et·ly ('kwaɪətlɪ) *adv.* **1.** in a quiet manner. **2. just quietly.** *Austral.* between you and me; confidentially.

qui·e·tude ('kwaɪəˌtjuːd) *n.* the state or condition of being quiet, peaceful, calm, or tranquil.

qui·e·tus (kwaɪ'iːtəs, -'eɪtəs) *n., pl.* **·tus·es. 1.** anything that serves to quash, eliminate, or kill; *to give the quietus to a rumour.* **2.** a release from life; death. **3.** the discharge or settlement of debts, duties, etc. [C16: from Latin *quiētus est,* literally: he is at rest, QUIET]

quiff (kwɪf) *n. Brit.* a prominent tuft of hair, esp. one brushed up above the forehead. [C19: of unknown origin]

quill (kwɪl) *n.* **1. a.** any of the large stiff feathers of the wing or tail of a bird. **b.** the long hollow central part of a bird's feather; calamus. **2.** a bird's feather made into a pen for writing. **3.** any of the stiff hollow spines of a porcupine or hedgehog. **4.** a device, formerly usually a crow's feather, for plucking a harpsichord string. **5.** a small roll of bark, esp. one of dried cinnamon. **6.** (in weaving) a bobbin or spindle. **7.** a fluted fold, as in a ruff. **8.** a hollow shaft that rotates upon an inner spindle or concentrically about an internal shaft. ~*vb.* (*tr.*) **9.** to wind (thread, etc.) onto a spool or bobbin. **10.** to make or press fluted folds in (a ruff, etc.). [C15 (in the sense: hollow reed or pipe): of uncertain origin; compare Middle Low German *quiele* quill]

quil+lai (kɪ'laɪ) *n.* another name for **soapbark** (sense 1). [C19: via American Spanish from Araucanian]

quil+let ('kwɪlɪt) *n. Archaic.* a quibble or subtlety. [C16: from earlier *quillity,* perhaps an alteration of QUIDDITY]

quil+lon (*French* ki'jɔ̃) *n.* (*often pl.*) either half of the extended crosspiece of a sword or dagger. [C19: from French, diminutive of *quille* bowling pin, ultimately from Old High German *kegil* club, stake]

quill pen *n.* another name for **quill** (sense 2).

quill+wort ('kwɪl,wɜːt) *n.* any aquatic pteridophyte plant of the genus *Isoetes,* with quill-like leaves at the bases of which are spore-producing structures: family *Isoetaceae.*

Quil+mes (*Spanish* 'kilmes) *n.* a city in E Argentina: a resort and suburb of Buenos Aires. Pop.: 355 300 (1971 est.).

quilt (kwɪlt) *n.* **1.** a thick warm cover for a bed, consisting of a soft filling sewn between two layers of material, usually with criss-cross seams. **2.** a bedspread or counterpane. **3.** anything quilted or resembling a quilt. ~*vb.* (*tr.*) **4.** to stitch together (two pieces of fabric) with (a thick padding or lining) between them: *to quilt cotton and wool.* **5.** to create (a garment, covering, etc.) in this way. **6.** to pad with material. **7.** *Austral. informal.* to strike; clout. [C13: from Old French *coilte* mattress, from Latin *culcita* stuffed item of bedding] —**'quilt+er** *n.*

quilt+ing ('kwɪltɪŋ) *n.* **1.** material used for making a quilt. **2.** the act or process of making a quilt. **3.** quilted work.

quim (kwɪm) *n. Brit. taboo.* the female genitals. [C19: of uncertain origin]

Quim+per (*French* kɛ̃'pɛr) *n.* a city in NW France: capital of Finistère department. Pop.: 60 510 (1975).

quin (kwɪn) *n. Brit. informal.* short for **quintuplet** (sense 2). U.S. word: **quint.**

quin·a+crine ('kwɪnə,kriːn) *n.* the U.S. name for **mepacrine.** [C20: from QUIN(INE) + ACR(ID) + -INE²]

qui+na+ry ('kwaɪnərɪ) *adj.* **1.** consisting of fives or by fives. **2.** fifth in a series. **3.** (of a number system) having a base of five. ~*n., pl.* **+ries. 4.** a set of five. [C17: from Latin *quīnārius* containing five, from *quīnī* five each]

qui+nate ('kwaɪneɪt) *adj. Botany.* arranged in or composed of five parts: *quinate leaflets.* [C19: from Latin *quīnī* five each]

quince (kwɪns) *n.* **1.** a small widely cultivated Asian rosaceous tree, *Cydonia oblonga,* with pinkish-white flowers and edible pear-shaped fruits. **2.** the acid-tasting fruit of this tree, much used in preserves. [C14 *qwince* plural of *quyn* quince, from Old French *coin,* from Latin *cotōneum,* from Greek *kudōnion* quince, Cydonian (apple)]

quin+cen+te+nar·y (,kwɪnsɛn'tiːnərɪ) *n., pl.* **+nar·ies.** a 500th anniversary or the year or celebration marking it. [C19: irregularly from Latin *quinque* five + CENTENARY] —**quin+cen+ten+ni·al** (,kwɪnsɛn'tɛnɪəl) *adj., n.*

quin+cun+cial (kwɪn'kʌnʃəl) *adj.* **1.** consisting of or having the appearance of a quincunx. **2.** (of the petals or sepals of a five-membered corolla or calyx in the bud) arranged so that two members overlap another two completely and the fifth overlaps on one margin and is itself overlapped on the other. —**quin+'cun+cial+ly** *adv.*

quin+cunx ('kwɪnkʌŋks) *n.* **1.** a group of five objects arranged in the shape of a rectangle with one at each of the four corners and the fifth in the centre. **2.** *Botany.* a quincuncial arrangement of sepals or petals in the bud. **3.** *Astrology.* an aspect of 150° between two planets, etc. [C17: from Latin: five twelfths, from *quinque* five + *uncia* twelfth; in ancient Rome, this was a coin worth five twelfths of an AS² and marked with five spots]

quin+dec·a+gon (kwɪn'dɛkəgən) *n.* a geometric figure having 15 sides and 15 angles. [C16: from Latin *quindecim* fifteen + *-agon,* as in *decagon*]

quin+dec·a+plet (kwɪn'dɛkə,plɛt) *n.* **1.** a group of 15. **2.** one of a group of 15. [C20: irregularly formed on the models of *quadruplet, quintuplet,* etc.]

quin+de+cen+ni·al (,kwɪndɪ'sɛnɪəl) *adj.* **1.** occurring once every 15 years or over a period of 15 years. ~*n.* **2.** a 15th anniversary. [C20: from Latin *quindecim* fifteen + *annus* year, on the model of *biennial*]

Qui Nhong ('kwiː 'njɒŋ) *n.* a port in SE Vietnam, on the South China Sea. Pop.: 188 717 (1971).

quin+ic ac·id ('kwɪnɪk) *n.* a white crystalline soluble optically active carboxylic acid, found in cinchona bark, bilberries, coffee beans, and the leaves of certain other plants; 1,3,4,5-tetrahydroxycyclohexanecarboxylic acid. Formula: $C_6H_7(OH)_4COOH$.

quin·i+dine ('kwɪnɪ,diːn) *n.* a crystalline alkaloid drug that is an optically active isomer of quinine: used to treat heart arrhythmias. Formula: $C_{20}H_{24}N_2O_2$.

qui+nine (kwɪ'niːn; *U.S.* 'kwaɪnaɪn) *n.* a bitter crystalline alkaloid extracted from cinchona bark, the salts of which are used as a tonic, antipyretic, analgesic, etc., and (usually in combination with chloroquine and similar drugs) in malaria therapy. Formula: $C_{20}H_{24}N_2O_2$. [C19: from Spanish *quina* cinchona bark, from Quechua *kina* bark]

Quinn (kwɪn) *n.* **An·tho·ny.** born 1915, U.S. film actor, born in Mexico: noted esp. for his performances in *La Strada* (1954) and *Zorba the Greek* (1964).

quin+nat salm+on ('kwɪnæt) *n.* another name for **Chinook salmon.** [C19: from Salish *t'kwinnat*]

quin·o- *or before a vowel* **quin-** *combining form.* indicating cinchona, cinchona bark, or quinic acid: *quinidine; quinol; quinoline.* [see QUININE]

quin+ol ('kwɪnɒl) *n.* another name for **hydroquinone.**

quin·o+line ('kwɪnə,liːn, -lɪn) *n.* **1.** an oily colourless insoluble basic heterocyclic compound synthesized by heating aniline, nitrobenzene, glycerol, and sulphuric acid: used as a food preservative and in the manufacture of dyes and antiseptics. Formula: C_9H_7N. **2.** any substituted derivative of quinoline.

qui+none (kwɪ'nəʊn, 'kwɪnəʊn) *n.* another name for **benzoquinone.**

quin·o+noid ('kwɪnə,nɔɪd, kwɪ'nəʊnɔɪd) *or* **quin+oid** *adj.* of, resembling, or derived from quinone.

quin+qua+ge+nar+i·an (,kwɪŋkwədʒɪ'nɛərɪən) *n.* **1.** a person between 50 and 59 years old. ~*adj.* **2.** being between 50 and 59 years old. **3.** of or relating to a quinquagenarian. [C16: from Latin *quinquāgēnārius* containing fifty, from *quinquāgēnī* fifty each]

Quin+qua+ges·i+ma (,kwɪŋkwə'dʒɛsɪmə) *n.* the Sunday preceding Ash Wednesday, the beginning of Lent. Also called: **Quinquagesima Sunday.** [C14: via Medieval Latin from Latin *quinquāgēsima diēs* fiftieth day]

quin·que- *combining form.* five: *quinquevalent.* [from Latin *quinque*]

quin+que+cen+te+nar·y (,kwɪŋkwɪsɛn'tiːnərɪ) *n., pl.* **+nar·ies.** another name for **quincentenary.**

quin+que+fo+li+ate (,kwɪŋkwɪ'fəʊlɪɪt, -,eɪt) *adj.* (of leaves) having or consisting of five leaflets.

quin+quen+ni·al (kwɪn'kwɛnɪəl) *adj.* **1.** occurring once every five years or over a period of five years. ~*n.* **2.** another word for **quinquennium. 3.** a fifth anniversary. —**quin+'quen+ni+al+ly** *adv.*

quin+quen+ni·um (kwɪn'kwɛnɪəm) *n., pl.* **+ni·a** (-nɪə). a period or cycle of five years. [C17: from Latin *quinque* five + *annus* year]

quin+que+par+tite (,kwɪŋkwɪ'pɑːtaɪt) *adj.* **1.** divided into or composed of five parts. **2.** maintained by or involving five participants or groups of participants.

quin+que+reme (,kwɪŋkwɪ'riːm) *n.* an ancient Roman galley with five banks of oars on each side. [C16: from Latin *quinquerēmis,* from QUINQUE- + *rēmus* oar]

quin+que+va+lent (,kwɪŋkwɪ'veɪlənt, kwɪn'kwɛvələnt) *adj. Chem.* another word for **pentavalent.** —**,quin+que+'va+len+cy** *or* **quin+que+va+lence** (,kwɪŋkwɪ'veɪləns, kwɪn'kwɛvələns) *n.*

quin+sy ('kwɪnzɪ) *n.* inflammation of the tonsils and surrounding tissues with the formation of abscesses. [C14: via Old French and Medieval Latin from Greek *kunankhē,* from *kuōn* dog + *ankhein* to strangle]

quint *n.* **1.** (kwɪnt). an organ stop sounding a note a fifth higher than that normally produced by the key depressed. **2.** (kɪnt). *Piquet.* a sequence of five cards in the same suit. [C17: from French *quinte,* from Latin *quintus* fifth]

quin+tain ('kwɪntɪn) *n.* (esp. in medieval Europe) **1.** a post or target set up for tilting exercises for mounted knights or foot soldiers. **2.** the exercise of tilting at such a target. [C14: from Old French *quintaine,* from Latin: street in a Roman camp between the fifth and sixth maniples, from *quintus (manipulus)* fifth (maniple)]

quin+tal ('kwɪntᵊl) *n.* **1.** a unit of weight equal to 100 pounds. **2.** a unit of weight equal to 100 kilograms. [C15: via Old French from Arabic *qintār,* possibly from Latin *centēnārius* consisting of a hundred]

quin+tan ('kwɪntən) *adj.* (of a fever) occurring every fourth day. [C17: from Latin *febris quintāna* fever occurring every fifth day, reckoned inclusively]

Quin+ta+na Ro·o (*Spanish* kin'tana 'roo) *n.* a state of SE Mexico, on the E Yucatán Peninsula: hot, humid, forested, and inhabited chiefly by Maya Indians. Capital: Chetumal. Pop.: 88 150 (1970). Area: 42 031 sq. km (16 228 sq. miles).

quinte *French.* (kɛ̃t) *n.* the fifth of eight basic positions from which a parry or attack can be made in fencing.

quin+tes+sence (kwɪn'tɛsəns) *n.* **1.** the most typical representation of a quality, state, etc. **2.** an extract of a substance containing its principle in its most concentrated form. **3.** (in ancient and medieval philosophy) ether, the fifth and highest essence or element after earth, water, air, and fire, which was thought to be the constituent matter of the heavenly bodies and latent in all things. [C15: via French from Medieval Latin *quinta essentia* the fifth essence, translation of Greek *pemptē ousia*] —**quin+tes+sen+tial** (,kwɪntɪ'sɛnʃəl) *adj.* —**,quin+tes+'sen+tial+ly** *adv.*

quin+tet *or* **quin+tette** (kwɪn'tɛt) *n.* **1.** a group of five singers or instrumentalists or a piece of music composed for such a group. **2.** any group of five. [C19: from Italian *quintetto,* from *quinto* fifth]

quin·tic ('kwɪntɪk) *adj. Maths.* of or relating to the fifth degree: *a quintic equation.*
quin·tile ('kwɪntaɪl) *n. Astrology.* an aspect of 72° between two heavenly bodies. [C17: from Latin *quintus* fifth]
Quin·til·ian (kwɪn'tɪljən) *n.* Latin name *Marcus Fabius Quintilianus.* ?35–?96 A.D., Roman rhetorician and teacher.
quin·til·lion (kwɪn'tɪljən) *n., pl.* **·lions** *or* **·lion. 1.** (in Britain and Germany) the number represented as one followed by 30 zeros (10^{30}). U.S. word: **nonillion. 2.** (in the U.S. and France) the number represented as one followed by 18 zeros (10^{18}). Brit. word: **trillion.** [C17: from Latin *quintus* fifth + *-illion,* as in MILLION] —**quin·'til·lionth** *adj.*
quin·tu·ple ('kwɪntjʊpᵊl, kwɪn'tju:pᵊl) *vb.* **1.** to multiply by five. ~*adj.* **2.** five times as much or as many; fivefold. **3.** consisting of five parts. ~*n.* **4.** a quantity or number five times as great as another. [C16: from French, from Latin *quintus,* on the model of QUADRUPLE]
quin·tu·plet ('kwɪntjʊplɪt, kwɪn'tju:plɪt) *n.* **1.** a group or set of five similar things. **2.** one of five offspring born at one birth. Often shortened to **quin. 3.** *Music.* a group of five notes to be played in a time value of three, four, or some other value.
quin·tu·pli·cate *adj.* (kwɪn'tju:plɪkɪt). **1.** fivefold or quintuple. ~*vb.* (kwɪn'tju:plɪˌkeɪt). **2.** to multiply or be multiplied by five. ~*n.* (kwɪn'tju:plɪkɪt). **3.** a group or set of five things. —**quin·ˌtu·pli·'ca·tion** *n.*
quinze (*French* kɛ̃z) *n.* a card game with rules similar to those of vingt-et-un, except that the score aimed at is 15 rather than 21. [French: fifteen]
quip (kwɪp) *n.* **1.** a sarcastic or cutting remark; gibe. **2.** a witty or clever saying: *a merry quip.* **3.** *Archaic.* another word for **quibble.** ~*vb.* **quips, quip·ping, quipped. 4.** (*intr.*) to make a quip. [C16: from earlier *quippy,* probably from Latin *quippe* indeed, to be sure]
quip·ster ('kwɪpstə) *n.* a person inclined to make sarcastic or witty remarks.
qui·pu *or* **quip·pu** ('ki:pu:, 'kwɪpu:) *n.* a device of the Incas of Peru used to record information, consisting of an arrangement of variously coloured and knotted cords attached to a base cord. [C17: from Spanish *quipo,* from Quechua *quipu,* literally: knot]
quire[1] (kwaɪə) *n.* **1.** a set of 24 or 25 sheets of paper; a twentieth of a ream. **2. a.** four sheets of paper folded once to form a section of 16 pages. **b.** a section or gathering. **3.** a set of all the sheets in a book. [C15 *quayer,* from Old French *quaier,* from Latin *quaternī* four at a time, from *quater* four times]
quire[2] (kwaɪə) *n.* an obsolete spelling of **choir.**
Quir·i·nal ('kwɪrɪnᵊl) *n.* one of the seven hills on which ancient Rome was built.
Qui·ri·nus (kwɪ'raɪnəs) *n. Roman myth.* a god of war, who came to be identified with the deified Romulus.
Qui·ri·tes (kwɪ'raɪti:z) *pl. n.* the citizens of ancient Rome. [from Latin: inhabitants of *Cures,* later applied generally to Roman citizens]
quirk (kwɜ:k) *n.* **1.** an individual peculiarity of character; mannerism or foible. **2.** an unexpected twist or turn: *a quirk of fate.* **3.** a continuous groove in an architectural moulding. **4.** a flourish, as in handwriting. [C16: of unknown origin] —**'quirk·y** *adj.* —**'quirk·i·ly** *adv.* —**'quirk·i·ness** *n.*
quirt (kwɜ:t) *U.S. n.* **1.** a whip with a leather thong at one end. ~*vb.* (*tr.*). **2.** to strike with a quirt. [C19: from Spanish *cuerda* CORD]
quis·ling ('kwɪzlɪŋ) *n.* a traitor who aids an occupying enemy force; collaborator. [C20: after Major Vidkun *Quisling* (1887–1945), Norwegian collaborator with the Nazis]
quist (kwɪst) *n., pl.* **quists** *or* **quist.** *West Midland and southwestern English dialect.* a wood pigeon. [of obscure origin]
quit (kwɪt) *vb.* **quits, quit·ting, quit** *or* **quit·ted. 1.** to desist or cease from (something or doing something); break off: *quit laughing.* **2.** (*tr.*) to depart from; leave: *he quit the place hastily.* **3.** to resign; give up (a job): *he quit his job today.* **4.** to release one's grasp upon (something held): *the child would not quit her mother's hand because of fear.* **5.** (*tr.*) to pay off (a debt); discharge or settle. **6.** (*tr.*) *Archaic.* to conduct or acquit (oneself); comport (oneself): *he quit himself with great dignity.* ~*adj.* **7.** (*usually predicative;* foll. by *of*) free (from); released (from): *he was quit of all responsibility for their safety.* [C13: from Old French *quitter,* from Latin *quiētus* QUIET; see QUIETUS] —**'quit·ter** *n.*
quitch grass (kwɪtʃ) *n.* another name for **couch grass.** Sometimes shortened to **quitch.** [Old English *cwice;* perhaps related to *cwicu* living, QUICK (with the implication that the grass cannot be killed); compare Dutch *kweek,* Norwegian *kvike,* German *Queckengras*]
quit·claim ('kwɪtˌkleɪm) *Law.* ~*n.* **1.** a formal renunciation of any claim against a person or of a right to land. ~*vb.* **2.** (*tr.*) **a.** to renounce (a claim, etc.) formally. **b.** to declare (a person) free from liability. [C14: from Anglo-French *quiteclame,* from *quite* QUIT + *clamer* to declare (from Latin *clamāre* to shout)]
quite (kwaɪt) *adv.* **1.** to the greatest extent; completely or absolutely: *you're quite right; quite the opposite.* **2.** (*not used with a negative*) to a noticeable or partial extent; somewhat: *she's quite pretty.* **3.** in actuality; truly: *he thought the bag was heavy, but it was quite light; it's quite the thing to do.* **4. quite a** *or* **an.** (*not used with a negative*) of an exceptional, considerable, or noticeable kind: *quite a girl; quite a long walk.* **5. quite something.** a remarkable or noteworthy thing or person. ~*sentence substitute.* **6.** Also: **quite so.** an expression used to indicate agreement or assent. [C14: adverbial use of *quite* (adj.) QUIT]
Usage. See at **very.**
Qui·to ('ki:təʊ; *Spanish* 'kito) *n.* the capital of Ecuador, in the north at an altitude of 2850 m (9350 ft.), just south of the equator: the oldest capital in South America, existing many centuries before the Incan conquest in 1487; a cultural centre since the beginning of Spanish rule (1534); two universities. Pop.: 564 900 (1972 est.).
quit·rent ('kwɪtˌrent) *n.* (formerly) a rent payable by a freeholder or copyholder to his lord that released him from liability to perform services.
quits (kwɪts) *Informal.* ~*adj.* (*postpositive*) **1.** on an equal footing; even: *now we are quits.* **2. call it quits.** to agree to end a dispute, contest, etc., agreeing that honours are even. ~*interj.* **3.** an exclamation indicating willingness to give up.
quit·tance ('kwɪtᵊns) *n.* **1.** release from debt or other obligation. **2.** a receipt or other document certifying this. [C13: from Old French, from *quitter* to release from obligation; see QUIT]
quit·tor ('kwɪtə) *n. Vet. science.* infection of the cartilages on the side of a horse's foot, characterized by inflammation and the formation of pus. [C13: perhaps from Old French *cuiture* a boiling, from Latin *coctūra* a cooking, from *coquere* to cook]
quiv·er[1] ('kwɪvə) *vb.* **1.** (*intr.*) to shake with a rapid tremulous movement; tremble. ~*n.* **2.** the state, process, or noise of shaking or trembling. [C15: from obsolete *cwiver* quick, nimble; compare QUAVER] —**'quiv·er·er** *n.* —**'quiv·er·ing·ly** *adv.* —**'quiv·er·y** *adj.*
quiv·er[2] ('kwɪvə) *n.* a case for arrows. [C13: from Old French *cuivre;* related to Old English *cocer,* Old Saxon *kokari,* Old High German *kohhari,* Medieval Latin *cucurum*]
quiv·er·ful ('kwɪvəˌful) *n.* **1.** the amount that a quiver can hold. **2.** *Literary.* a fair number or full complement: *a quiverful of children.*
qui vive (ˌki: 'vi:v) *n.* **on the qui vive.** on the alert; attentive. [C18: from French, literally: long live who?, sentry's challenge (equivalent to "To whose party do you belong?" or "Whose side do you support?")]
Quix·ote ('kwɪksət; *Spanish* ki'xote) *n.* See **Don Quixote.**
quix·ot·ic (kwɪk'sɒtɪk) *adj.* preoccupied with an unrealistically optimistic or chivalrous approach to life; impractically idealistic. [C18: after DON QUIXOTE] —**quix·'ot·i·cal·ly** *adv.* —**quix·o·tism** ('kwɪksəˌtɪzəm) *n.*
quiz (kwɪz) *n., pl.* **quiz·zes. 1. a.** an entertainment in which the general or specific knowledge of the players is tested by a series of questions, esp. as a radio or television programme. **b.** (*as modifier*): *a quiz programme.* **2.** any set of quick questions designed to test knowledge. **3.** an investigation by close questioning; interrogation. **4.** *Obsolete.* a practical joke; hoax. **5.** *Obsolete.* a puzzling or eccentric individual. **6.** *Obsolete.* a person who habitually looks quizzically at others, esp. through a small monocle. ~*vb.* **quiz·zes, quiz·zing, quizzed.** (*tr.*) **7.** to investigate by close questioning; interrogate. **8.** *U.S. informal.* to test or examine the knowledge of (a student or class). **9.** (*tr.*) *Obsolete.* to look quizzically at, esp. through a small monocle. [C18: of unknown origin] —**'quiz·zer** *n.*
quiz·mas·ter ('kwɪzˌmɑ:stə) *n.* a person who puts questions to contestants on a quiz programme.
quiz·zi·cal ('kwɪzɪkᵊl) *adj.* questioning and mocking or supercilious: *a quizzical look.* —**ˌquiz·zi·'cal·i·ty** *n.* —**'quiz·zi·cal·ly** *adv.*
Qum *or* **Kum** (kʊm) *n.* a city in NW central Iran: a place of pilgrimage for Shiite Muslims. Pop.: 140 000 (1972 est.).
Qum·ran ('kʊmrɑ:n) *n.* See **Khirbet Qumran.**
quod (kwɒd) *n. Chiefly Brit.* a slang word for **jail.** [C18: of unknown origin]
quod e·rat de·mon·stran·dum *Latin.* ('kwɒd 'ɛræt ˌdɛmən'strændʊm) (at the conclusion of a proof, esp. of a theorem in Euclidean geometry) which was to be proved. Abbrev.: **Q.E.D.**
quod·li·bet ('kwɒdlɪˌbɛt) *n.* **1.** a light piece of music based on two or more popular tunes. **2.** a subtle argument, esp. one prepared as an exercise on a theological topic. [C14: from Latin, from *quod* what + *libet* pleases, that is, whatever you like] —**ˌquod·li·'bet·i·cal** *adj.* —**ˌquod·li·'bet·i·cal·ly** *adv.*
quoin, coign, *or* **coigne** (kɔɪn, kwɔɪn) *n.* **1.** an external corner of a wall. **2.** Also called: **cornerstone.** a stone forming the external corner of a wall. **3.** another name for **keystone** (sense 1). **4.** *Printing.* a metal or wooden wedge or an expanding mechanical device used to lock type up in a chase. **5.** a wedge used for any of various other purposes. [C16: variant of COIN (corner)]
quoit (kɔɪt) *n.* **1.** a ring of iron, plastic, rope, etc., used in the game of quoits. **2.** *Austral. slang.* a variant spelling of **coit.** [C15: of unknown origin]
quoits (kɔɪts) *pl. n.* (*usually functioning as sing.*) a game in which quoits are tossed at a stake in the ground in attempts to encircle it.
quok·ka ('kwɒkə) *n.* a small wallaby, *Setonix brachyurus,* formerly abundant in swampy coastal regions of Western Australia but now rare, occurring mostly on offshore islands. [from a native Australian language]
quon·dam ('kwɒndæm) *adj.* (*prenominal*) of an earlier time; former: *her quondam lover.* [C16: from Latin]
Quon·set hut ('kwɒnsɪt) *n. Trademark, U.S.* a military shelter made of corrugated steel sheet, having a semicircular cross section. Brit. equivalent: **Nissen hut.**
quor·um ('kwɔ:rəm) *n.* a minimum number of members in an

assembly, society, board of directors, etc., required to be present before any valid business can be transacted: *the quorum is forty.* [C15: from Latin, literally: of whom, occurring in Latin commissions in the formula *quorum vos...duos* (etc.) *volumus* of whom we wish that you be...two]

quot. *abbrev. for* quotation.

quo·ta ('kwəʊtə) *n.* **1.** the proportional share or part of a whole that is due from, due to, or allocated to a person or group. **2.** a prescribed number or quantity, as of items to be manufactured, imported, or exported, immigrants admitted to a country, or students admitted to a college. [C17: from Latin *quota pars* how big a share?, from *quotus* of what number]

quot·a·ble ('kwəʊtəbᵊl) *adj.* apt or suitable for quotation: *his remarks are not quotable in mixed company.* —,**quot·a·'bil·i·ty** *n.*

quo·ta·tion (kwəʊ'teɪʃən) *n.* **1.** a phrase or passage from a book, poem, play, etc., remembered and spoken, esp. to illustrate succinctly or support a point or an argument. **2.** the act or habit of quoting from books, plays, poems, etc. **3.** *Commerce.* a statement of the current market price of a security or commodity. **4.** an estimate of costs submitted by a contractor to a prospective client; tender. **5.** *Stock Exchange.* registration granted to a company or governmental body, enabling the shares and other securities of the company or body to be officially listed and traded. **6.** *Printing.* a large quadrat that is less than type-high and is used to fill up spaces.

quo·ta·tion mark *n.* either of the punctuation marks used to begin or end a quotation, respectively " and " or ' and ' in English printing and writing. When double marks are used, single marks indicate a quotation within a quotation, and vice versa. Also called: **inverted comma.**

quote (kwəʊt) *vb.* **1.** to recite a quotation (from a book, play, poem, etc.), esp. as a means of illustrating or supporting a statement. **2.** (*tr.*) to put quotation marks round (a word, phrase, etc.). **3.** *Stock Exchange.* to state (a current market price) of (a security or commodity). ~*n.* **4.** an informal word for **quotation** (senses 1–4). **5.** (*often pl.*) an informal word for **quotation mark:** *put it in quotes.* ~*interj.* **6.** an expression used parenthetically to indicate that the words that follow it form a quotation: *the president said, quote, I shall not run for office in November, unquote.* [C14: from Medieval Latin *quotāre* to assign reference numbers to passages, from Latin *quot* how many]

quoth (kwəʊθ) *vb. Archaic.* (used with all pronouns except *thou* and *you,* and with nouns) another word for **said**[1] (sense 2). [Old English *cwæth,* third person singular of *cwethan* to say; related to Old Frisian *quetha* to say, Old Saxon, Old High German *quethan;* see BEQUEATH]

quoth·a ('kwəʊθə) *interj. Archaic.* an expression of mild sarcasm, used in picking up a word or phrase used by someone else: *Art thou mad? Mad, quotha! I am more sane than thou.* [C16: from *quoth a* quoth he]

quo·tid·i·an (kwəʊ'tɪdɪən) *adj.* **1.** (esp. of attacks of malarial fever) recurring daily. **2.** every day; commonplace. ~*n.* **3.** a malarial fever characterized by attacks that recur daily. [C14: from Latin *quotīdiānus,* variant of *cottīdiānus* daily]

quo·tient ('kwəʊʃənt) *n.* **1. a.** the result of the division of one number or quantity by another. **b.** the integral part of the result of division. **2.** a ratio of two numbers or quantities to be divided. [C15: from Latin *quotiens* how often]

quo war·ran·to ('kwəʊ wɒ'ræntəʊ) *n. Law.* a proceeding initiated to determine or (formerly) a writ demanding by what authority a person claims an office, franchise, or privilege. [from Medieval Latin: by what warrant]

Qur'·an (kʊ'rɑːn, -'ræn) *n.* a variant spelling of **Koran.**

q.v. (denoting a cross reference) *abbrev. for* quod vide. [New Latin: which (word, item, etc.) see]

qy. *abbrev. for* query.

R

r *or* **R** (ɑː) *n., pl.* **r's, R's,** *or* **Rs. 1.** the 18th letter and 14th consonant of the modern English alphabet. **2.** a speech sound represented by this letter, in English usually an alveolar semivowel, as in *red.* **3.** See **three Rs, the.**

R *symbol for:* **1.** *Chem.* radical. **2.** *Currency.* **a.** rand. **b.** rupee. **3.** Réaumur (scale). **4.** *Physics, electronics.* resistance. **5.** röntgen. **6.** *Chess.* rook. **7.** Royal. **8.** *Chem.* gas constant. ~**9.** *international car registration for* Rumania.

r. *abbrev. for:* **1.** rare. **2.** recipe. **3.** recto. **4.** Also: **r** rod (unit of length). **5.** ruled. **6.** *Cricket, baseball, etc.* run(s).

R. *abbrev. for:* **1.** rabbi. **2.** rector. **3.** Regiment. **4.** Regina. [Latin: Queen] **5.** Republican. **6.** *Ecclesiast.* response. **7.** Rex. [Latin: King] **8.** River. **9.** Royal.

R. *or* **r.** *abbrev. for:* **1.** radius. **2.** railway. **3.** registered (trademark). **4.** right. **5.** river. **6.** road. **7.** rouble.

Ra *the chemical symbol for* radium.

Ra (rɑː) *or* **Re** *n.* the ancient Egyptian sun god, depicted as a man with a hawk's head surmounted by a solar disc and serpent.

RA *international car registration for* Argentina (officially Argentine Republic).

R.A. *abbrev. for:* **1.** rear admiral. **2.** *Astronomy.* right ascension. **3.** (in Britain) Royal Academician *or* Academy. **4.** (in Britain) Royal Artillery.

R.A.A.F. *abbrev. for* Royal Australian Air Force.

Ra+bat (rəˈbɑːt) *n.* the capital of Morocco, in the northwest on the Atlantic coast: became a fortified military centre in the 12th century and a Corsair republic in the 17th century. Pop.: (with Salé) 530 366 (1971).

ra+ba+to *or* **re+ba+to** (rəˈbɑːtəʊ) *n., pl.* **+tos.** a wired or starched collar, often of intricate lace, that stood up at the back and sides: worn in the 17th century. [C16: from French *rabat* collar, with the ending *-o* added as if the word were from Italian]

Ra+baul (rɑːˈbaʊl) *n.* a port on NE New Britain Island, in the Bismarck Archipelago: capital of the Territory of New Guinea until 1941; almost surrounded by volcanoes. Pop.: 24 778 (1970).

Rab+bath Am+mon (ˈræbəθ ˈæmən) *n. Old Testament.* the ancient royal city of the Ammonites, on the site of modern Amman.

rab+bet (ˈræbɪt) *n., vb.* another word for **rebate**[2].

rab+bi (ˈræbaɪ) *n., pl.* **+bis. 1.** the chief religious minister of a synagogue; the spiritual leader of a Jewish congregation. **2.** Also: **rab+bin** (ˈræbɪn). **a.** a scholar learned in Jewish Law, esp. one authorized to teach it. **b.** one of the early Jewish scholars whose teachings are included in the Talmud. [Hebrew, from *rabh* master + *-ī* my]

rab+bin+ate (ˈræbɪnɪt) *n.* **1.** the position, function, or tenure of office of a rabbi. **2.** rabbis collectively.

Rab+bin+ic (rəˈbɪnɪk) *n.* the form of the Hebrew language used by the rabbis of the Middle Ages.

rab+bin·i+cal (rəˈbɪnɪkəl) *or* **rab+bin+ic** *adj.* of or relating to the rabbis, their teachings, writings, views, language, etc. —**rab+ˈbin·i+cal+ly** *adv.*

rab+bin+ism (ˈræbɪˌnɪzəm) *n.* the teachings and traditions of the rabbis of the Talmudic period. —**ˈrab+bi+nist** *n., adj.* —**ˌrab+bi+ˈnis+tic** *adj.*

rab+bit (ˈræbɪt) *n., pl.* **+bits** *or* **+bit. 1.** any of various common gregarious burrowing leporid mammals, esp. *Oryctolagus cuniculus* of Europe and North Africa and the cottontail of America. They are closely related and similar to hares but are smaller and have shorter ears. **2.** the fur of such an animal. **3.** *Brit. informal.* a novice or poor performer at a game or sport. ~*vb. (intr.)* **4.** to hunt or shoot rabbits. **5.** (often foll. by *on* or *away*) *Brit. slang.* to talk inconsequentially; chatter. [C14: perhaps from Walloon *robett,* diminutive of Flemish *robbe* rabbit, of obscure origin]

rab+bit+er (ˈræbɪtə) *n. Chiefly Austral.* a person who traps and sells rabbits.

rab+bit fe+ver *n. Pathol.* another name for **tularaemia.**

rab·bit+fish (ˈræbɪtˌfɪʃ) *n., pl.* **+fish** *or* **+fish·es. 1.** a large chimaera, *Chimaera monstrosa,* common in European seas, with separate caudal and anal fins and a long whiplike tail. **2.** any of the spiny-finned tropical marine fishes of the family *Siganidae* of Indo-Pacific waters. They have a rabbit-like snout and spines on the pelvic or ventral fins.

rab·bit·oh *or* **rab+bit·o** *n. Austral. informal.* an itinerant seller of rabbits for eating. [C20: from such a seller's cry]

rab·bit-proof fence *n.* **a.** a fence through which rabbits are unable to pass. **b.** *Austral. informal.* a boundary between certain Australian states, marked by such a fence.

rab+bit punch *n.* a short sharp blow to the back of the neck that can cause loss of consciousness or even death. Austral. name: **rabbit killer.**

rab+bit+ry (ˈræbɪtrɪ) *n., pl.* **+ries. 1.** a place where tame rabbits are kept and bred. **2.** the rabbits kept in such a place.

rab+ble[1] (ˈræbəl) *n.* **1.** a disorderly crowd; mob. **2. the.** *Contemptuous.* the common people. [C14 (in the sense: a pack of animals): of uncertain origin; perhaps related to Middle Dutch *rabbelen* to chatter, rattle]

rab+ble[2] (ˈræbəl) *n.* **1.** Also called: **rab+bler.** an iron tool or mechanical device for stirring, mixing, or skimming a molten charge in a roasting furnace. ~*vb.* **2.** *(tr.)* to stir, mix, or skim (the molten charge) in a roasting furnace. [C17: from French *râble,* from Latin *rutābulum* rake for a furnace, from *ruere* to rake, dig up]

rab·ble-rous·er *n.* a person who manipulates the passions of the mob; demagogue. —**ˈrab·ble-ˌrous·ing** *adj., n.*

Rab·e·lais (ˈræbəˌleɪ; *French* raˈblɛ) *n.* **Fran·çois** (frɑ̃ˈswa). ?1494–1553, French writer. His written works, esp. *Gargantua and Pantagruel* (1534), contain a lively mixture of earthy wit, common sense, and satire.

Rab+e·lai·si·an (ˌræbəˈleɪzɪən, -ʒən) *adj.* **1.** of, relating to, or resembling the work of Rabelais, esp. by broad, often bawdy humour and sharp satire. ~*n.* **2.** a student or admirer of Rabelais. —**ˌRab+e·ˈlai+si+an+ism** *n.*

ra·bi (ˈrʌbɪ) *n.* (in Pakistan, India, etc.) a crop that is harvested at the end of winter. Compare **kharif.** [Urdu: spring crop, from Arabic *rabī'* spring]

Ra+bi·a (rəˈbɪə) *n.* either the third or the fourth month of the Muslim year, known as **Rabia I** and **Rabia II** respectively; the Muslim spring.

rab+id (ˈræbɪd, ˈreɪ-) *adj.* **1.** relating to or having rabies. **2.** zealous; fanatical; violent; raging. [C17: from Latin *rabidus* frenzied, mad, from *rabere* to be mad] —**ra+bid+i·ty** (rəˈbɪdɪtɪ) *or* **ˈrab+id+ness** *n.* —**ˈrab+id+ly** *adv.*

ra+bies (ˈreɪbiːz) *n. Pathol.* an acute infectious viral disease of the nervous system transmitted by the saliva of infected animals, esp. dogs. It is characterized by excessive salivation, aversion to water, convulsions, and paralysis. Also called: **hydrophobia, lyssa.** [C17: from Latin: madness, from *rabere* to rave] —**rab+ic** (ˈræbɪk) *or* **ra+bi+et+ic** (ˌreɪbɪˈɛtɪk) *adj.*

R.A.C. *abbrev. for:* **1.** Royal Automobile Club. **2.** Royal Armoured Corps.

rac+coon *or* **ra+coon** (rəˈkuːn) *n., pl.* **+coons** *or* **+coon. 1.** any omnivorous mammal of the genus *Procyon,* esp. *P. lotor* (**North American raccoon**), inhabiting forests of North and Central America and the West Indies: family *Procyonidae,* order *Carnivora* (carnivores). Raccoons have a pointed muzzle, long tail, and greyish-black fur with black bands around the tail and across the face. **2.** the fur of the North American raccoon. [C17: from Algonquian *ärähkun,* from *ärähkuněm* he scratches with his hands]

rac+coon dog *n.* a canine mammal, *Nyctereutes procyonoides,* inhabiting woods and forests near rivers in E Asia. It has long yellowish-brown black-tipped hair and facial markings resembling those of a raccoon.

race[1] (reɪs) *n.* **1.** a contest of speed, as in running, swimming, driving, riding, etc. **2.** any competition or rivalry: *the race for the White House.* **3.** rapid or constant onward movement: *the race of time.* **4.** a rapid current of water, esp. one through a narrow channel that has a tidal range greater at one end than the other. **5.** a channel of a stream, esp. one for conducting water to or from a water wheel or other device for utilizing its energy: *a mill race.* **6. a.** a channel or groove that contains ball bearings or roller bearings or that restrains a sliding component. **b.** the inner or outer cylindrical ring in a ball bearing or roller bearing. **7.** *Austral., N.Z.* a narrow passage or enclosure in a sheep yard through which sheep pass individually, as to a sheep dip. **8.** *Austral.* a wire tunnel through which footballers pass from the changing room onto a football field. **9.** another name for **slipstream** (sense 1). **10.** *Archaic.* the span or course of life. **11. not in the race.** *Austral. informal.* given or having no chance. ~*vb.* **12.** to engage in a contest of speed with (another). **13.** to engage (oneself or one's representative) in a race, esp. as a profession or pastime: *to race pigeons.* **14.** to move or go as fast as possible. **15.** to run (an engine, shaft, propeller, etc.) or (of an engine, shaft, propeller, etc.) to run at high speed, esp. after reduction of the load or resistance. ~See also **race off.** [C13: from Old Norse *rās* running; related to Old English *rǣs* attack]

race[2] (reɪs) *n.* **1.** a group of people of common ancestry, distinguished from others by physical characteristics, such as hair type, colour of eyes and skin, stature, etc. Principal races are Caucasoid, Mongoloid, and Negroid. **2. the human race.** human beings collectively. **3.** a group of animals or plants having common characteristics that distinguish them from other members of the same species, usually forming a geographically isolated group; subspecies. **4.** a group of people sharing the same interests, characteristics, etc.: *the race of authors.* [C16: from French, from Italian *razza,* of uncertain origin]

race[3] (reɪs) *n.* a ginger root. [C15: from Old French *rais,* from Latin *rādīx* a root]

Race (reɪs) *n.* **Cape.** a cape at the SE extremity of Newfoundland, Canada.

race+card (ˈreɪsˌkɑːd) *n.* a card or booklet at a race meeting with the times of the races, names of the runners, etc., printed on it.

race·course (ˈreɪsˌkɔːs) *n.* a long broad track, usually of grass, enclosed between rails, and with starting and finishing points marked upon it, over which horses are raced. Also called (esp. U.S.): **racetrack.**

race·go·er (ˈreɪsˌgəʊə) *n.* one who attends a race meeting, esp. a habitual frequenter of race meetings.

race·horse (ˈreɪsˌhɔːs) *n.* a horse specially bred for racing.

ra·ceme (rəˈsiːm) *n.* an inflorescence in which the flowers are borne along the main stem, with the oldest flowers at the base. It can be simple, as in the foxglove, or compound (see **panicle**). [C18: from Latin *racēmus* bunch of grapes]

race meet·ing *n.* a prearranged fixture for racing horses (or sometimes greyhounds) over a set course at set times.

ra·ce·mic (rəˈsiːmɪk, -ˈsɛm-) *adj. Chem.* of, concerned with, or being a mixture of dextrorotatory and laevorotatory isomers in such proportions that the mixture has no optical activity. [C19: from RACEME (as in *racemic acid*) + -IC] —**rac·e·mism** (ˈræsɪˌmɪzəm, rəˈsiːmɪzəm) *n.*

ra·ce·mic ac·id *n.* the optically inactive form of tartaric acid that is sometimes found in grape juice.

rac·e·mize *or* **rac·e·mise** (ˈræsɪˌmaɪz) *vb.* to change or cause to change into a racemic mixture. —ˌ**rac·e·mi·ˈza·tion** *or* ˌ**rac·e·mi·ˈsa·tion** *n.*

rac·e·mose (ˈræsɪˌməʊs, -ˌməʊz) *or* **rac·e·mous** *adj.* being or resembling a raceme. [C17: from Latin *racēmōsus* clustering] —ˈ**rac·e·ˌmose·ly** *or* ˈ**rac·e·mous·ly** *adv.*

race off *vb.* (*tr., adv.*) *Austral. informal.* to entice (a person) away with a view to seduction.

rac·er (ˈreɪsə) *n.* **1.** a person, animal, or machine that races. **2.** a turntable used to traverse a heavy gun. **3.** any of several long slender nonvenomous North American snakes of the colubrid genus *Coluber* and related genera, such as *C. lateralis* (**striped racer**).

race re·la·tions *n.* **1.** (*functioning as pl.*) the relations between members of two or more human races, esp. within a single community. **2.** (*functioning as sing.*) the branch of sociology concerned with such relations.

race ri·ot *n.* a riot among members of different races in the same community.

rac·es (ˈreɪsɪz) *pl. n.* **the.** a series of contests of speed between horses (or sometimes greyhounds) over a set course at prearranged times; a race meeting.

race·track (ˈreɪsˌtræk) *n.* **1.** a circuit or course, esp. an oval one, used for motor racing, speedway, etc. **2.** the usual U.S. word for a **racecourse.**

race·way (ˈreɪsˌweɪ) *n.* **1.** another word for **race**[1] (sense 6). **2.** a racetrack, esp. one for banger racing.

Ra·chel (ˈreɪtʃəl) *n. Old Testament.* the second and best-loved wife of Jacob; mother of Joseph and Benjamin (Genesis 29–35).

ra·chis *or* **rha·chis** (ˈreɪkɪs) *n., pl.* **ra·chis·es, rha·chis·es** *or* **ra·chi·des, rha·chi·des** (ˈrækɪˌdiːz, ˈreɪ-). **1.** *Botany.* the main axis or stem of an inflorescence or compound leaf. **2.** *Ornithol.* the shaft of a feather, esp. the part that carries the barbs. **3.** another name for **vertebral column.** [C17: via New Latin from Greek *rhakhis* ridge] —**ra·chi·al, rha·chi·al** (ˈreɪkɪəl) *or* **ra·chid·i·al, rha·chid·i·al** (rəˈkɪdɪəl) *adj.*

ra·chi·tis (rəˈkaɪtɪs) *n. Pathol.* another name for **rickets.** —**ra·chit·ic** (rəˈkɪtɪk) *adj.*

Rach·ma·ni·noff *or* **Rach·ma·ni·nov** (rækˈmænɪˌnɒf; *Russian* raxˈmaninəf) *n.* **Ser·gei Vas·si·lie·vich** (sɪrˈgjej vaˈsiljɪvɪtʃ). 1873–1943, Russian piano virtuoso and composer.

Rach·man·ism (ˈrækməˌnɪzəm) *n.* extortion or exploitation by a landlord of tenants of dilapidated or slum property, esp. when involving intimidation or use of racial fears to drive out sitting tenants whose rent is fixed at a low rate. [C20: after Perec *Rachman* (1920–62), British property-owner born in Poland]

ra·cial (ˈreɪʃəl) *adj.* **1.** denoting or relating to the division of the human species into races on grounds of physical characteristics. **2.** characteristic of any such group. **3.** relating to or arising from differences between the races: *racial harmony.* **4.** of or relating to a subspecies. —ˈ**ra·cial·ly** *adv.*

ra·cial·ism (ˈreɪʃəˌlɪzəm) *or* **rac·ism** *n.* **1.** the belief that races have distinctive cultural characteristics determined by hereditary factors and that this endows some races with an intrinsic superiority over others. **2.** abusive or aggressive behaviour towards members of another race on the basis of such a belief. —ˈ**ra·cial·ist** *or* ˈ**rac·ist** *n., adj.*

ra·cial un·con·scious *n. Psychol.* another term for **collective unconscious.**

Ra·cine (*French* raˈsin) *n.* **Jean Bap·tiste** (ʒã baˈtist). 1639–99, French tragic poet and dramatist. His plays include *Andromaque* (1667), *Bérénice* (1670), and *Phèdre* (1677).

rac·ing (ˈreɪsɪŋ) *adj.* **1.** denoting or associated with horse races: *the racing fraternity; a racing man.* ~*n.* **2.** the practice of engaging horses or sometimes greyhounds in contests of speed.

rack[1] (ræk) *n.* **1.** a framework for holding, carrying, or displaying a specific load or object: *a plate rack; a hat rack; a hay rack; a luggage rack.* **2.** a toothed bar designed to engage a pinion to form a mechanism that will interconvert rotary and rectilinear motions. **3.** a framework fixed to an aircraft for carrying bombs, rockets, etc. **4.** (usually preceded by *the*) an instrument of torture that stretched the body of the victim. **5.** a cause or state of mental or bodily stress, suffering, etc.; anguish; torment (esp. in the phrase **on the rack**). **6.** *U.S.* (in pool, snooker, etc.) **a.** the triangular frame used to arrange the balls for the opening shot. **b.** the balls so grouped. Brit. equivalent: **frame.** ~*vb.* (*tr.*) **7.** to torture on the rack. **8.** to cause great stress or suffering to: *guilt racked his conscience.* **9.** to strain or shake (something) violently, as by great physical force: *the storm racked the town.* **10.** to place or arrange in or on a rack: *to rack bottles of wine.* **11.** to move (parts of machinery or a mechanism) using a toothed rack. **12.** to raise (rents) exorbitantly; rack-rent. **13. rack one's brains.** to strain in mental effort, esp. to remember something or to find the solution to a problem. ~See also **rack up.** [C14 *rekke,* probably from Middle Dutch *rec* framework; related to Old High German *recchen* to stretch, Old Norse *rekja* to spread out] —ˈ**rack·er** *n.*

rack[2] (ræk) *n.* destruction; wreck (obsolete except in the phrase **go to rack and ruin**). [C16: variant of WRACK[1]]

rack[3] (ræk) *n.* another word for **single-foot,** a gait of the horse. [C16: perhaps based on ROCK[2]]

rack[4] *or* **wrack** (ræk) *n.* **1.** a group of broken clouds moving in the wind. ~*vb.* **2.** (*intr.*) (of clouds) to be blown along by the wind. [Old English *wrǣc* what is driven; related to Gothic *wraks* persecutor, Swedish *vrak* wreckage]

rack[5] (ræk) *vb.* (*tr.*) **1.** to clear (wine, beer, etc.) as by siphoning it off from the dregs. **2.** to fill a container with (beer, wine, etc.). [C15: from Old Provençal *arraca,* from *raca* dregs of grapes after pressing]

rack[6] (ræk) *n.* the neck or rib section of mutton, pork, or veal. [Old English *hrace;* related to Old High German *rahho,* Danish *harke,* Swedish *harkla* to clear one's throat]

rack-and-pin·ion *n.* **1.** a device for converting rotary into linear motion and vice versa, in which a gearwheel (the pinion) engages with a flat toothed bar (the rack). ~*adj.* **2.** (of a type of steering gear in motor vehicles) having a track rod with a rack along part of its length that engages with a pinion attached to the steering column.

rack·et[1] (ˈrækɪt) *n.* **1.** a noisy disturbance or loud commotion; clamour; din. **2.** gay or excited revelry, dissipation, etc. **3.** an illegal enterprise carried on for profit, such as extortion, fraud, prostitution, drug peddling, etc. **4.** *Slang.* a business or occupation: *what's your racket?* **5.** *Music.* **a.** a medieval woodwind instrument of deep bass pitch. **b.** a reed stop on an organ of deep bass pitch. ~*vb.* **6.** (*intr.;* often foll. by *about*) *Now rare.* to go about gaily or noisily, in search of pleasure, excitement, etc. [C16: probably of imitative origin; compare RATTLE[1]]

rack·et[2] *or* **rac·quet** (ˈrækɪt) *n.* **1.** a bat consisting of an open network of nylon or other strings stretched in an oval frame with a handle, used to strike the ball in tennis, etc. **2.** a snowshoe shaped like a tennis racket. ~*vb.* **3.** (*tr.*) to strike (a ball, etc.) with a racket. [C16: from French *raquette,* from Arabic *rāhat* palm of the hand]

rack·et·eer (ˌrækɪˈtɪə) *n.* **1.** a person engaged in illegal enterprises for profit. ~*vb.* **2.** (*intr.*) to operate a racket. —ˌ**rack·et·ˈeer·ing** *n.*

rack·et press *n.* a device consisting of a frame closed by a spring mechanism, for keeping taut the strings of a tennis racket, squash racket, etc.

rack·ets (ˈrækɪts) *n.* (*functioning as sing.*) **a.** a game similar to squash played in a large four-walled court by two or four players using rackets and a small hard ball. **b.** (*as modifier*): *a rackets court; a rackets championship.*

rack·et-tail *n.* any of several birds with a racket-shaped tail, such as certain hummingbirds and kingfishers.

rack·et·y (ˈrækɪtɪ) *adj.* noisy, rowdy, or boisterous.

Rack·ham (ˈrækəm) *n.* **Ar·thur.** 1867–1939, English artist, noted for his book illustrations, esp. of fairy tales.

rack rail·way *n.* a steep mountain railway having a middle rail fitted with a rack that engages a pinion on the locomotive to provide traction. Also called: **cog railway.**

rack-rent *n.* **1.** a high rent that annually equals or nearly equals the value of the property upon which it is charged. **2.** any extortionate rent. ~*vb.* **3.** to charge an extortionate rent for (property, land, etc.). —ˈ**rack-ˌrent·er** *n.*

rack up *vb.* (*tr., adv.*) **1.** to accumulate (points). **2.** to arrange or straighten (frames) in a film projector.

ra·con (ˈreɪkɒn) *n.* another name for **radar beacon.**

rac·on·teur (ˌrækɒnˈtɜː) *n.* a person skilled in telling stories. [C19: French, from *raconter* to tell]

ra·coon (rəˈkuːn) *n., pl.* **·coons** *or* **·coon.** a variant spelling of **raccoon.**

rac·quet (ˈrækɪt) *n.* a variant spelling of **racket**[2].

rac·y (ˈreɪsɪ) *adj.* **rac·i·er, rac·i·est. 1.** (of a person's manner, literary style, etc.) having a distinctively lively and spirited quality; fresh. **2.** having a characteristic or distinctive flavour: *a racy wine.* **3.** suggestive; slightly indecent; risqué: *a racy comedy.* —ˈ**rac·i·ly** *adv.* —ˈ**rac·i·ness** *n.*

rad (ræd) *n.* a unit of absorbed ionizing radiation dose equivalent to an energy absorption per unit mass of 0.01 joule per kilogram of irradiated material. [C20: shortened from RADIATION]

rad. *abbrev. for:* **1.** radian. **2.** radical. **3.** radius. **4.** radix.

RADA (ˈrɑːdə) *n.* (in Britain) *acronym for* Royal Academy of Dramatic Art.

ra·dar (ˈreɪdɑː) *n.* **1.** a method for detecting the position and velocity of a distant object, such as an aircraft. A narrow beam of extremely high-frequency radio pulses is transmitted and reflected by the object back to the transmitter, the signal being displayed on a radarscope. The direction of the reflected beam and the time between transmission and reception of a pulse determine the position of the object. Former name: **radiolocation. 2.** the equipment used in such detection. [C20: *ra(dio) d(etecting) a(nd) r(anging)*]

ra·dar bea·con *n.* a device for transmitting a coded radar signal in response to a signal from an aircraft or ship. The coded signal is then used by the navigator to determine his position. Also called: **racon.**

ra·dar·scope ('reɪdɑːˌskəʊp) *n.* a cathode-ray oscilloscope on which radar signals can be viewed. In a **plan position indicator,** the target is represented by a blip on a radial line that rotates around a point, representing the antenna.

ra·dar trap *n.* See **speed trap.**

Rad·cliffe ('rædklɪf) *n.* **Ann.** 1764–1823, English novelist, noted for her Gothic romance *The Mysteries of Udolpho* (1794).

rad·dle[1] ('rædᵊl) *vb.* (*tr.*) another name for **interweave.**

rad·dle[2] ('rædᵊl) *vb.* **1.** (*tr.*) *Chiefly Brit.* to paint (the face) with rouge. ~*n., vb.* **2.** another word for **ruddle.**

rad·dled ('rædᵊld) *adj.* (esp. of a person) unkempt or run-down in appearance.

Ra·detz·ky (*German* ra'dɛtski) *n.* Count **Jo·seph** ('joːzɛf). 1766–1858, Austrian field marshal in the campaigns against Napoleon; governor of Lombardy-Venetia in N Italy (1850-57).

ra·di·al ('reɪdɪəl) *adj.* **1.** (of lines, bars, beams of light, etc.) emanating from a common central point; arranged like the radii of a circle. **2.** of, like, or relating to a radius or ray. **3.** spreading out or developing uniformly on all sides. **4.** of or relating to the arms of a starfish or similar radiating structures. **5.** *Anatomy.* of or relating to the radius or forearm. **6.** *Astronomy.* (of velocity) in a direction along the line of sight of a celestial object and measured by means of the red shift (or blue shift) of the spectral lines of the object. Compare **tangential** (sense 2). ~*n.* **7.** a radial part or section. **8.** *Zoology.* **a.** any of the basal fin rays of most bony fishes. **b.** a radial or radiating structure, such as any of the ossicles supporting the oral disc of a sea star. **9.** short for **radial tyre.** [C16: from Medieval Latin *radiālis,* from RADIUS] —'**ra·di·al·ly** *adv.*

ra·di·al en·gine *n.* an internal-combustion engine having a number of cylinders arranged about a central crankcase.

ra·di·al-ply *adj.* (of a motor tyre) having the fabric cords in the outer casing running radially to enable the sidewalls to be flexible. Compare **cross-ply.**

ra·di·al sym·me·try *n.* a type of structure of an organism or part of an organism in which a vertical cut through the axis in any of two or more planes produces two halves that are mirror images of each other. Compare **bilateral symmetry.**

ra·di·al tyre *n.* a motor-vehicle tyre having a radial-ply casing. Often shortened to **radial.**

ra·di·al ve·loc·i·ty *n.* the component of the velocity of an object, esp. a celestial body, directed along a line from the observer to the object.

ra·di·an ('reɪdɪən) *n.* an SI unit of plane angle; the angle between two radii of a circle that cut off on the circumference an arc equal in length to the radius. 1 radian is equivalent to 57.296 degrees. Abbrev. **rad.** [C19: from RADIUS]

ra·di·ance ('reɪdɪəns) *or* **ra·di·an·cy** *n., pl.* **·anc·es** *or* **·an·cies. 1.** the quality or state of being radiant. **2.** a measure of the amount of electromagnetic radiation leaving or arriving at a point on a surface. It is the radiant intensity in a given direction of a small element of surface area divided by the orthogonal projection of this area onto a plane at right angles to the direction. Symbol: L_e

ra·di·ant ('reɪdɪənt) *adj.* **1.** sending out rays of light; bright; shining. **2.** characterized by health, intense joy, happiness, etc.: *a radiant countenance.* **3.** emitted or propagated by or as radiation; radiated: *radiant heat.* **4.** *Physics.* (of a physical quantity in photometry) evaluated by absolute energy measurements: *radiant flux; radiant efficiency.* Compare **luminous.** ~*n.* **5.** a point or object that emits radiation, esp. the part of a heater that gives out heat. **6.** *Astronomy.* the point in space from which a meteor shower appears to emanate. [C15: from Latin *radiāre* to shine, from *radius* ray of light, RADIUS] —'**ra·di·ant·ly** *adv.*

ra·di·ant ef·fi·cien·cy *n.* the ratio of the power emitted by a source of radiation to the power consumed by it. Symbol: η_e

ra·di·ant en·er·gy *n.* energy that is emitted or propagated in the form of particles or electromagnetic radiation. It is measured in joules. Symbol: Q_e

ra·di·ant ex·it·ance *n.* the ability of a surface to emit radiation expressed as the radiant flux emitted per unit area at a specified point on the surface. Symbol: M_e

ra·di·ant flux *n.* the rate of flow of energy as radiation. It is measured in watts. Symbol: Φ_e

ra·di·ant heat *n.* heat transferred in the form of electromagnetic radiation rather than by conduction or convection; infrared radiation.

ra·di·ant heat·ing *n.* a system of heating a building by radiant heat emitted from panels containing electrical conductors, hot water, etc.

ra·di·ant in·ten·si·ty *n.* a measure of the amount of radiation emitted from a point expressed as the radiant flux per unit solid angle leaving this source. Symbol: I_e

ra·di·ate *vb.* ('reɪdɪˌeɪt). **1.** Also: **eradiate.** to emit (heat, light, or some other form of radiation) or (of heat, light, etc.) to be emitted as radiation. **2.** (*intr.*) (of lines, beams, etc.) to spread out from a centre or be arranged in a radial pattern. **3.** (*tr.*) (of a person) to show (happiness, health, etc.) to a great degree. ~*adj.* ('reɪdɪɪt, -eɪt). **4.** having rays; radiating. **5.** (of a capitulum) consisting of ray flowers. **6.** (of animals or their parts) showing radial symmetry. **7.** adorned or decorated with rays: *a radiate head on a coin.* [C17: from Latin *radiāre* to emit rays]

ra·di·a·tion (ˌreɪdɪ'eɪʃən) *n.* **1.** *Physics.* **a.** the emission or transfer of radiant energy as particles, electromagnetic waves, sound, etc. **b.** the particles, etc., emitted, esp. the particles and gamma rays emitted in nuclear decay. **2.** Also called: **radiation therapy.** *Med.* treatment using a radioactive substance. **3.** *Anatomy.* a group of nerve fibres that diverge from their common source. **4.** See **adaptive radiation. 5.** the act, state, or process of radiating or being radiated. **6.** *Surveying.* the fixing of points around a central plane table by using an alidade and measuring tape. —ˌ**ra·di'a·tion·al** *adj.*

ra·di·a·tion pat·tern *n.* the graphic representation of the strength and direction of electromagnetic radiation in the vicinity of a transmitting aerial.

ra·di·a·tion sick·ness *n. Pathol.* illness caused by overexposure of the body or a part of the body to ionizing radiations from radioactive material or x-rays. It is characterized by vomiting, diarrhoea, and in severe cases by sterility and cancer.

ra·di·a·tive ('reɪdɪətɪv) *or* **ra·di·a·to·ry** ('reɪdɪətərɪ, -trɪ) *adj. Physics.* emitting or causing the emission of radiation: *a radiative collision.*

ra·di·a·tor ('reɪdɪˌeɪtə) *n.* **1.** a device for heating a room, building, etc., consisting of a series of pipes through which hot water or steam passes. **2.** a device for cooling an internal-combustion engine, consisting of a metal honeycomb through which water passes. Heat is transferred from the water through the thin walls of the honeycomb to the airstream, which is created either by the motion of the vehicle or by a fan. **3.** *Austral.* an electric fire. **4.** *Electronics.* the part of an aerial or transmission line that radiates electromagnetic waves. **5.** an electric space heater.

rad·i·cal ('rædɪkᵊl) *adj.* **1.** of, relating to, or characteristic of the basic or inherent constitution of a person or thing; fundamental: *a radical fault.* **2.** concerned with or tending to concentrate on fundamental aspects of a matter; searching or thoroughgoing: *radical thought; a radical re-examination.* **3.** favouring or tending to produce extreme or fundamental changes in political, economic, or social conditions, institutions, habits of mind, etc.: *a radical party.* **4.** of, relating to, or arising from the root or the base of the stem of a plant: *radical leaves.* **5.** *Maths.* of, relating to, or containing roots of numbers or quantities. **6.** *Linguistics.* of or relating to the root of a word. **7.** *Slang.* terrific: used as a general term of approbation, esp. among skateboarders. ~*n.* **8.** a person who favours extreme or fundamental change in existing institutions or in political, social, or economic conditions. **9.** *Maths.* a root of a number or quantity, such as $\sqrt[3]{5}$, $\sqrt{x}$. **10.** *Chem.* **a.** short for **free radical. b.** another name for **group** (sense 10). **11.** *Linguistics.* another word for **root**[1] (sense 9). **12.** (in logographic writing systems such as that used for Chinese) a character conveying lexical meaning. [C14: from Late Latin *rādīcālis* having roots, from Latin *rādix* a root] —'**rad·i·cal·ness** *n.*

rad·i·cal ax·is *n.* a line from any point of which tangents to two given circles are of equal length. It is the line joining the points of intersection of two circles.

rad·i·cal·ism ('rædɪkəˌlɪzəm) *n.* **1.** the principles, desires, or practices of political radicals. **2.** a radical movement, esp. in politics. **3.** the state or nature of being radical, esp. in politics. —ˌ**rad·i·cal'is·tic** *adj.* —ˌ**rad·i·cal'is·ti·cal·ly** *adv.*

rad·i·cal·ly ('rædɪklɪ) *adv.* thoroughly; completely; fundamentally: *to alter radically.*

rad·i·cal sign *n.* the symbol $\sqrt{}$ placed before a number or quantity to indicate the extraction of a root, esp. a square root. The value of a higher root is indicated by a raised digit, as in $\sqrt[3]{}$.

rad·i·cand ('rædɪˌkænd, ˌrædɪ'kænd) *n.* a number or quantity from which a root is to be extracted, usually preceded by a radical sign: 3 *is the radicand of* $\sqrt{3}$. [C20: from Latin *rādīcandum,* literally: that which is to be rooted, from *rādīcāre* to take root, from *rādīx* root]

rad·i·cel ('rædɪˌsɛl) *n.* a very small root; radicle. [C19: from New Latin *radicella* a little root, from Latin *rādix* root]

rad·i·ces ('reɪdɪˌsiːz) *n.* the plural of **radix.**

rad·i·cle ('rædɪkᵊl) *n.* **1.** *Botany.* **a.** part of the embryo of seed-bearing plants that develops into the main root. **b.** a very small root or rootlike part. **2.** *Anatomy.* any bodily structure resembling a rootlet, esp. one of the smallest branches of a vein or nerve. **3.** *Chem.* a variant spelling of **radical** (sense 10). [C18: from Latin *rādīcula* a little root, from *rādīx* root]

Ra·di·guet (*French* radi'gɛ) *n.* **Ray·mond** (rɛ'mɔ̃). 1903–23, French novelist; the author of *The Devil in the Flesh* (1923) and *Count d'Orgel* (1924).

ra·di·i ('reɪdɪˌaɪ) *n.* a plural of **radius.**

ra·di·o ('reɪdɪəʊ) *n., pl.* **·os. 1.** the use of electromagnetic waves, lying in the radio-frequency range, for broadcasting, two-way communications, etc. **2.** an electronic device designed to receive, demodulate, and amplify radio signals from broadcasting stations, etc. **3.** a similar device permitting both transmission and reception of radio signals for two-way communications. **4.** the broadcasting, content, etc., of radio programmes: *he thinks radio is poor these days.* **5.** the occupation or profession concerned with any aspect of the broadcasting of radio programmes: *he's in radio.* **6.** short for **radiotelegraph, radiotelegraphy,** or **radiotelephone. 7.** (*modifier*) **a.** of, relating to, employed in, or sent by radio signals: *a radio station.* **b.** of, concerned with, using, or operated by radio frequencies: *radio spectrum.* ~*vb.* **·os, ·o·ing, ·oed. 8.** to transmit (a message, etc.) to (a person, radio station, etc.) by means of radio waves. ~Also called (esp. Brit.): **wireless.** [C20: short for *radiotelegraphy*]

ra·di·o- *combining form.* **1.** denoting radio, broadcasting, or radio frequency: *radiogram.* **2.** indicating radioactivity or radiation: *radiochemistry; radiolucent.* [from French, from Latin *radius* ray; see RADIUS]

ra·di·o+ac+ti+vate (ˌreɪdɪəʊ'æktɪˌveɪt) *vb.* (*tr.*) to make radioactive. —**ˌra·di·o+ˌac+ti+'va+tion** *n.*

ra·di·o+ac+tive (ˌreɪdɪəʊ'æktɪv) *adj.* exhibiting, using, or concerned with radioactivity. —**ˌra·di·o+'ac+tive+ly** *adv.*

ra·di·o+ac+tive de+cay *n.* disintegration of a nucleus that occurs spontaneously or as a result of electron capture. One or more different nuclei are formed and usually particles and gamma rays are emitted. Sometimes shortened to **decay.** Also called: **disintegration.**

ra·di·o+ac+tive se+ries *n. Physics.* a series of nuclides each of which undergoes radioactive decay into the next member of the series, ending with a stable element, usually lead. See **uranium series, neptunium series, thorium series, actinium series.**

ra·di·o+ac+tiv+i·ty (ˌreɪdɪəʊæk'tɪvɪtɪ) *n.* the spontaneous emission of radiation from atomic nuclei. The radiation consists of alpha, beta, and gamma radiation.

ra+di·o as+tron·o+my *n.* a branch of astronomy in which the radio telescope is used to detect and analyse radio signals received on earth from radio sources in space.

ra·di·o+au·to+graph (ˌreɪdɪəʊ'ɔːtəˌgrɑːf, -ˌgræf) *n.* another name for **autoradiograph.**

ra+di·o bea+con *n.* a fixed radio transmitting station that broadcasts a characteristic signal by means of which a vessel or aircraft can determine its bearing or position. Sometimes shortened to **beacon.**

ra+di·o beam *n.* a narrow beam of radio signals transmitted by a radio or radar beacon, radio telescope, or some other directional aerial, used for communications, navigation, etc. Sometimes shortened to **beam.**

ra·di·o+bi+ol+o·gy (ˌreɪdɪəʊbaɪ'ɒlədʒɪ) *n.* the branch of biology concerned with the effects of radiation on living organisms and the study of biological processes using radioactive substances as tracers. —**ra·di·o+bi·o+log·i+cal** (ˌreɪdɪəʊˌbaɪə'lɒdʒɪkᵊl) *adj.* —**ˌra·di·o+ˌbi·o+'log·i+cal+ly** *adv.* —**ˌra·di·o+bi+'ol·o+gist** *n.*

ra·di·o+car+bon (ˌreɪdɪəʊ'kɑːbᵊn) *n.* a radioactive isotope of carbon, esp. carbon-14. See **carbon.**

ra·di·o+car+bon dat+ing *n.* a technique for determining the age of organic materials, such as wood, based on their content of the radioisotope ^{14}C acquired from the atmosphere when they formed part of a living plant. The ^{14}C decays to the nitrogen isotope ^{14}N with a half-life of 5730 years. Measurement of the amount of radioactive carbon remaining in the material thus gives an estimate of its age. Also called: **carbon-14 dating.**

ra·di·o+chem+is+try (ˌreɪdɪəʊ'kɛmɪstrɪ) *n.* the chemistry of radioactive elements and their compounds. —**ˌra·di·o+'chem·i+cal** *adj.* —**ˌra·di·o+'chem+ist** *n.*

ra·di·o+com+mu+ni+ca+tion (ˌreɪdɪəʊkəˌmjuːnɪ'keɪʃən) *n.* communication by means of radio waves.

ra+di·o com+pass *n.* any navigational device that gives a bearing by determining the direction of incoming radio waves transmitted from a particular radio station or beacon. See also **goniometer** (sense 2).

ra+di·o con+trol *n.* remote control by means of radio signals from a transmitter. —**'ra·di·o-con·'trolled** *adj.*

ra·di·o+el+e·ment (ˌreɪdɪəʊ'ɛlɪmənt) *n.* an element that is naturally radioactive.

ra+di·o fre+quen+cy *n.* **1. a.** a frequency or band of frequencies that lie in the range 10 kilohertz to 300 000 megahertz and can be used for radio communications and broadcasting. Abbrev.: **rf, RF.** See also **frequency band. b.** (*as modifier*): *a radio-frequency amplifier.* **2.** the frequency transmitted by a particular radio station.

ra·di·o+gen+ic (ˌreɪdɪəʊ'dʒɛnɪk) *adj.* produced or caused by radioactive decay: *a radiogenic element; radiogenic heat.*

ra·di·o+gram ('reɪdɪəʊˌgræm) *n.* **1.** *Brit.* a unit comprising a radio and gramophone. **2.** a message transmitted by radiotelegraphy. **3.** another name for **radiograph.**

ra·di·o+graph ('reɪdɪəʊˌgrɑːf, -ˌgræf) *n.* an image produced on a specially sensitized photographic film or plate by radiation, usually by x-rays or gamma-rays. Also called: **radiogram, shadowgraph.**

ra+di+og+ra+phy (ˌreɪdɪ'ɒgrəfɪ) *n.* the production of radiographs of opaque objects for use in medicine, surgery, industry, etc. —**ˌra+di+'og+ra+pher** *n.* —**ra·di·o+graph+ic** (ˌreɪdɪəʊ'græfɪk) *adj.* —**ˌra·di·o+'graph·i+cal+ly** *adv.*

ra+di·o in+ter+fer+om+e·ter *n.* a type of radio telescope in which two or more aerials connected to the same receiver produce interference patterns that can be analysed to provide information about the source of the radio waves.

ra·di·o+i·so+tope (ˌreɪdɪəʊ'aɪsətəʊp) *n.* an isotope that is radioactive. —**ra·di·o+i·so+top+ic** (ˌreɪdɪəʊˌaɪsə'tɒpɪk) *adj.*

ra·di·o+lar+i·an (ˌreɪdɪəʊ'lɛərɪən) *n.* any of various marine protozoans constituting the order *Radiolaria,* typically having a siliceous shell and stiff radiating pseudopodia: class *Sarcodina* (amoeba, etc.). [C19: from New Latin *Radiolaria,* from Late Latin *radiolus* little sunbeam, from Latin *radius* ray, RADIUS]

ra·di·o+lo+ca+tion (ˌreɪdɪəʊləʊ'keɪʃən) *n.* a former name for **radar.** —**ˌra·di·o+lo+'ca+tion+al** *adj.*

ra·di·o+log·i+cal (ˌreɪdɪə'lɒdʒɪkᵊl) *adj.* **1.** of, relating to, or concerning radiology or the equipment used in radiology. **2.** of, relating to, or involving radioactive materials: *radiological warfare.* —**ˌra·di·o+'log·i+cal+ly** *adv.*

ra+di+ol+o·gy (ˌreɪdɪ'ɒlədʒɪ) *n.* the use of x-rays and radioactive substances in the diagnosis and treatment of disease. —**ˌra+di+'ol·o+gist** *n.*

ra·di·o+lu+cent (ˌreɪdɪəʊ'luːsᵊnt) *adj.* almost transparent to electromagnetic radiation, esp. x-rays.

ra·di·o+lu+mi+nes+cence (ˌreɪdɪəʊˌluːmɪ'nɛsəns) *n. Physics.* luminescence that is induced by radiation from a radioactive material. —**ˌra·di·o+ˌlu+mi+'nes+cent** *adj.*

ra+di+ol·y+sis (ˌreɪdɪ'ɒlɪsɪs) *n.* chemical decomposition caused by radiation, such as a beam of electrons or x-rays.

ra·di·o+me·te·or·o+graph (ˌreɪdɪəʊ'miːtɪərəˌgrɑːf, -ˌgræf) *n.* another name for **radiosonde.**

ra+di+om+e·ter (ˌreɪdɪ'ɒmɪtə) *n.* any instrument for the detection or measurement of radiant energy. —**ra·di·o+met+ric** (ˌreɪdɪəʊ'mɛtrɪk) *adj.* —**ˌra+di+'om+e·try** *n.*

ra+di·o+mi+crom+e·ter (ˌreɪdɪəʊmaɪ'krɒmɪtə) *n.* an instrument for detecting and measuring small amounts of radiation, usually by a sensitive thermocouple.

ra·di·o+nu+clide (ˌreɪdɪəʊ'njuːklaɪd) *n.* a nuclide that is radioactive.

ra·di·o+paque (ˌreɪdɪəʊ'peɪk) *or* **ra·di·o-o·paque** *adj.* not permitting x-rays or other radiation to pass through. —**ra·di·o+pac+i·ty** (ˌreɪdɪəʊ'pæsɪtɪ) *or* **ˌra·di·o-o·'pac·i·ty** *n.*

ra·di·o+phone ('reɪdɪəʊˌfəʊn) *n.* another name for **radiotelephone.**

ra·di·o+phon+ic (ˌreɪdɪə'fɒnɪk) *adj.* denoting or relating to music produced by electronic means. —**ˌra·di·o+'phon·i·cal+ly** *adv.* —**ra+di+oph·o+ny** (ˌreɪdɪ'ɒfənɪ) *n.*

ra·di·o+scope ('reɪdɪəʊˌskəʊp) *n.* an instrument, such as a fluoroscope, capable of detecting radiant energy.

ra+di+os+co+py (ˌreɪdɪ'ɒskəpɪ) *n.* another word for **fluoroscopy.** —**ra·di·o+scop+ic** (ˌreɪdɪəʊ'skɒpɪk) *adj.* —**ˌra·di·o+'scop·i+cal+ly** *adv.*

ra·di·o+sen+si+tive (ˌreɪdɪəʊ'sɛnsɪtɪv) *adj.* affected by or sensitive to radiation. —**ˌra·di·o+'sen+si+tive+ly** *adv.* —**ˌra·di·o+ˌsen+si+'tiv+i·ty** *n.*

ra·di·o+sonde ('reɪdɪəʊˌsɒnd) *n.* an airborne instrument to send meteorological information back to earth by radio. Also called: **radiometeorograph.** [C20: RADIO- + French *sonde* sounding line]

ra+di·o source *n.* a celestial object, such as a supernova remnant or quasar, that is a source of radio waves.

ra+di·o spec+trum *n.* the range of electromagnetic frequencies used in radio transmission, lying between 10 kilohertz and 300 000 megahertz.

ra+di·o star *n.* a former name for **radio source.**

ra+di·o sta+tion *n.* **1.** an installation consisting of one or more transmitters or receivers, etc., used for radiocommunications. **2.** a broadcasting organization.

ra·di·o+tel·e+gram (ˌreɪdɪəʊ'tɛlɪˌgræm) *n.* a message transmitted by radiotelegraphy. Also called: **radiogram.**

ra·di·o+tel·e+graph (ˌreɪdɪəʊ'tɛlɪˌgrɑːf) *vb.* **1.** to send (a message) by radiotelegraphy. ~*n.* **2.** a message sent by radiotelegraphy.

ra·di·o+te·leg+ra+phy (ˌreɪdɪəʊtɪ'lɛgrəfɪ) *n.* a type of telegraphy in which messages (usually in Morse code) are transmitted by radio waves. Also called: **wireless telegraphy.** —**ra·di·o+tel·e+graph+ic** (ˌreɪdɪəʊˌtɛlɪ'græfɪk) *adj.* —**ˌra·di·o+ˌtel·e+'graph·i+cal+ly** *adv.*

ra·di·o+te·lem+e·try (ˌreɪdɪəʊtɪ'lɛmɪtrɪ) *n.* the use of radio waves for transmitting information from a distant instrument to a device that indicates or records the measurements. Sometimes shortened to **telemetry.**

ra·di·o+tel·e+phone (ˌreɪdɪəʊ'tɛlɪˌfəʊn) *n.* **1.** Also called: **radiophone, wireless telephone.** a device for communications by means of radio waves rather than by transmitting along wires or cables. ~*vb.* **2.** to telephone (a person) by radiotelephone. ~Sometimes shortened to **radio.** —**ra·di·o+tel·e+phon+ic** (ˌreɪdɪəʊˌtɛlɪ'fɒnɪk) *adj.* —**ra·di·o+te·leph·o+ny** (ˌreɪdɪəʊtɪ'lɛfənɪ) *n.*

ra+di·o tel·e+scope *n.* an instrument used in radio astronomy to pick up and analyse radio waves from space and also to transmit radio waves.

ra·di·o+tel·e+type (ˌreɪdɪəʊ'tɛlɪˌtaɪp) *n.* **1.** a teleprinter that transmits or receives information by means of radio waves rather than by cable or wire. **2.** a network of such devices widely used for communicating news, messages, information, etc. Abbrevs.: **RTT, RTTY**

ra·di·o+ther·a+py (ˌreɪdɪəʊ'θɛrəpɪ) *n.* the treatment of disease, esp. cancer, by means of alpha or beta particles emitted from an implanted or ingested radioisotope, or by means of a beam of high-energy radiation. —**ra·di·o+ther·a+peu+tic** (ˌreɪdɪəʊˌθɛrə'pjuːtɪk) *adj.* —**ˌra·di·o+ˌther·a+'peu+ti+cal+ly** *adv.* —**ˌra·di·o+'ther·a+pist** *n.*

ra·di·o+therm·y ('reɪdɪəʊˌθɜːmɪ) *n. Med.* the treatment of disease by means of heat generated by electromagnetic radiation.

ra·di·o+tox+ic (ˌreɪdɪəʊ'tɒksɪk) *adj.* of or denoting the toxic effects of radiation or radioactive substances.

ra+di·o valve *n.* another name for **valve** (sense 3).

ra+di·o wave *n.* an electromagnetic wave of radio frequency.

ra+di·o win+dow *n.* a gap in ionospheric reflection that allows radio waves, with frequencies in the range 10 000 to 40 000 megahertz, to pass from or into space.

rad+ish ('rædɪʃ) *n.* **1.** any of various cruciferous plants of the genus *Raphanus,* esp. *R. sativus* of Europe and Asia, cultivated for its edible root. **2.** the root of this plant, which has a pungent taste and is eaten raw in salads. **3. wild radish.** another name for **white charlock.** See **charlock** (sense 2). [Old English *rædic,* from Latin *rādīx* root]

ra+di+um ('reɪdɪəm) *n.* **a.** a highly radioactive luminescent white element of the alkaline earth group of metals. It occurs in pitchblende, carnotite, and other uranium ores, and is used in radiotherapy and in luminous paints. Symbol: Ra; atomic no.: 88; half-life of most stable isotope, ^{226}Ra: 1620 years; valency: 2; relative density: 5 (approx.); melting pt.: 700°C; boiling pt.: 1140°C. **b.** (*as modifier*): *radium needle.* [C20: from Latin *radius* ray]

ra·di·um ther·a·py *n.* treatment of disease, esp. cancer, by exposing affected tissues to radiation from radium.

ra·di·us ('reɪdɪəs) *n., pl.* **-di·i** (-dɪˌaɪ) *or* **-di·us·es.** **1.** a straight line joining the centre of a circle or sphere to any point on the circumference or surface. **2.** the length of this line, usually denoted by the symbol *r*. **3.** the distance from the centre of a regular polygon to a vertex (**long radius**) or the perpendicular distance to a side (**short radius**). **4.** *Anatomy.* the outer and slightly shorter of the two bones of the human forearm, extending from the elbow to the wrist. **5.** a corresponding bone in other vertebrates. **6.** any of the veins of an insect's wing. **7.** a group of ray flowers, occurring in such plants as the daisy. **8. a.** any radial or radiating part, such as a spoke. **b.** (*as modifier*): *a radius arm.* **9.** the lateral displacement of a cam or eccentric wheel. **10.** a circular area of a size indicated by the length of its radius: *the police stopped every lorry within a radius of four miles.* **11.** the operational limit of a ship, aircraft, etc. [C16: from Latin: rod, ray, spoke]

ra·di·us of cur·va·ture *n.* the absolute value of the reciprocal of the curvature of a curve at a given point. See also **centre of curvature.**

ra·di·us vec·tor *n.* **1.** *Maths.* a line joining a point in space to the origin of polar or spherical coordinates. **2.** *Astronomy.* an imaginary line joining a satellite to the planet or star around which it is orbiting.

ra·dix ('reɪdɪks) *n., pl.* **-di·ces** (-dɪˌsiːz) *or* **-dix·es.** **1.** *Maths.* any number that is the base of a number system or of a system of logarithms: *10 is the radix of the decimal system.* **2.** *Biology.* the root or point of origin of a part or organ. **3.** *Linguistics.* a less common word for **root**[1] (sense 9). [C16: from Latin *rādīx* root; compare Greek *rhadix* small branch, *rhiza* root]

ra·dix point *n.* a point, such as the decimal point in the decimal system, separating the integral part of a number from the fractional part.

Rad·nor·shire ('rædnəˌʃɪə, -ʃə) *or* **Rad·nor** *n.* (until 1974) a county of E Wales, now part of Powys.

Ra·dom (*Polish* 'radɔm) *n.* a city in E Poland: under Austria from 1795 to 1815 and Russia from 1815 to 1918. Pop.: 168 700 (1974 est.).

ra·dome ('reɪdəum) *n.* a protective housing for a radar antenna made from a material that is transparent to radio waves. [C20: RA(DAR) + DOME]

ra·don ('reɪdɒn) *n.* a colourless radioactive element of the rare gas group, the most stable isotope of which, radon-222, is a decay product of radium. It is used as an alpha particle source in radiotherapy. Symbol: Rn; atomic no.: 86; half-life of ^{222}Rn: 3.82 days; density: 9.73 kg/m^3; melting pt.: -71°C; boiling pt.: -61.8°C. [C20: from RADIUM + -ON]

rad·u·la ('rædjʊlə) *n., pl.* **-lae** (-ˌliː). a horny tooth-bearing strip on the tongue of molluscs that is used for rasping food. [C19: from Late Latin: a scraping iron, from Latin *rādere* to scrape] —**'rad·u·lar** *adj.*

Rae·burn ('reɪˌbɜːn) *n.* Sir **Hen·ry.** 1756–1823, Scottish portrait painter.

R.A.E.C. *abbrev. for* Royal Army Educational Corps.

RAF (*Not standard* ræf) *or* **R.A.F.** *abbrev. for* Royal Air Force.

raff (ræf) *n. Archaic or dialect.* **1.** rubbish; refuse. **2.** rabble or riffraff. [C14: perhaps from Old French *rafle* a snatching up; compare RAFFLE, RIFFRAFF]

Raf·fer·ty ('ræfətɪ) *or* **Raf·fer·ty's rules** *pl. n. Austral. slang.* no rules at all. [C20: of uncertain origin]

raf·fi·a *or* **raph·i·a** ('ræfɪə) *n.* **1.** Also called: **raffia palm.** a palm tree, *Raphia ruffia*, native to Madagascar, that has large plumelike leaves, the stalks of which yield a useful fibre. **2.** the fibre obtained from this plant, used for tying, weaving, etc. **3.** any of several related palms or the fibre obtained from them. [C19: from Malagasy]

raf·fi·nate ('ræfɪˌneɪt) *n.* the liquid left after a solute has been extracted by solvent extraction.

raf·fi·nose ('ræfɪˌnəuz, -ˌnəus) *n. Biochem.* a trisaccharide of fructose, glucose, and galactose that occurs in sugar beet, cotton seed, certain cereals, etc. Formula: $C_{18}H_{32}O_{16}$. [C19: from French *raffiner* to refine + -OSE[2]]

raff·ish ('ræfɪʃ) *adj.* **1.** careless or unconventional in dress, manners, etc.; rakish. **2.** tawdry; flashy; vulgar. [C19: see RAFF] —**'raff·ish·ly** *adv.* —**'raff·ish·ness** *n.*

raf·fle ('ræfᵊl) *n.* **1. a.** a lottery in which the prizes are goods rather than money. **b.** (*as modifier*): *a raffle ticket.* ~*vb.* **2.** (*tr.;* often foll. by *off*) to dispose of (goods) in a raffle. [C14 (a dice game): from Old French, of obscure origin] —**'raf·fler** *n.*

Raf·fles ('ræfᵊlz) *n.* Sir **Thom·as Stam·ford.** 1781–1826, English colonial administrator: founded Singapore (1819).

raf·fle·si·a (ræ'fliːzɪə) *n.* any of various tropical Asian parasitic leafless plants constituting the genus *Rafflesia*, esp. *R. arnoldi*, the flowers of which grow up to 45 cm (18 inches) across, smell of putrid meat, and are pollinated by carrion flies: family *Rafflesiaceae.* [C19: New Latin, named after Sir Stamford RAFFLES, who discovered it]

raft (rɑːft) *n.* **1.** a buoyant platform of logs, planks, etc., used as a vessel or moored platform. **2.** a thick slab of reinforced concrete laid over soft ground to provide a foundation for a building. **3.** *Slang.* cigarette papers stuck together for rolling a joint (cannabis cigarette). ~*vb.* **4.** to convey or travel by raft, or make a raft from. [C15: from Old Norse *raptr* RAFTER]

raft·er ('rɑːftə) *n.* any one of a set of parallel sloping beams that form the framework of a roof. [Old English *ræfter;* related to Old Saxon *rehter*, Old Norse *raptr*, Old High German *rāvo;* see RAFT]

R.A.F.V.R. *abbrev. for* Royal Air Force Volunteer Reserve.

rag[1] (ræg) *n.* **1. a.** a small piece of cloth, such as one torn from a discarded garment, or such pieces of cloth collectively. **b.** (*as modifier*): *a rag doll; a rag book; rag paper.* **2.** a fragmentary piece of any material; scrap; shred. **3.** *Informal.* a newspaper or other journal, esp. one considered as worthless, sensational, etc. **4.** *Informal.* an item of clothing. **5.** *Informal.* a handkerchief. **6.** *Brit. slang, esp. naval.* a flag or ensign. **7. chew the rag.** *Slang.* to argue or grumble. [C14: probably back formation from RAGGED from Old English *raggig;* related to Old Norse *rögg* tuft]

rag[2] (ræg) *vb.* **rags, rag·ging, ragged.** (*tr.*) **1.** to draw attention facetiously and persistently to the shortcomings or alleged shortcomings of (a person). **2.** *Brit.* to play rough practical jokes on. ~*n.* **3.** *Brit.* a boisterous practical joke, esp. one on a fellow student. **4.** (in British universities, etc.) **a.** a period, usually a week, in which various events are organized to raise money for charity, including a procession of decorated floats and tableaux. **b.** (*as modifier*): *rag day.* [C18: of uncertain origin]

rag[3] (ræg) *Jazz.* ~*n.* **1.** a piece of ragtime music. ~*vb.* **rags, rag·ging, ragged.** **2.** (*tr.*) to compose or perform in ragtime. [C20: shortened from RAGTIME]

rag[4] (ræg) *n.* a roofing slate that is rough on one side. [C13: of obscure origin]

ra·ga ('rɑːgə) *n.* (in Indian music) **1.** any of several conventional patterns of melody and rhythm that form the basis for freely interpreted compositions. Each pattern is associated with different aspects of religious devotion. **2.** a composition based on one of these patterns. [from Sanskrit *rāga* tone, colour]

rag·a·muf·fin ('rægəˌmʌfɪn) *n.* a ragged unkempt person, esp. a child. [C14 *Ragamoffyn*, name of a demon in the poem *Piers Plowman* (1393); probably based on RAG[1]]

rag-and-bone man *n. Brit.* a man who buys and sells discarded clothing, furniture, etc. Also called: **rag·man, rag·pick·er.** U.S. equivalent: **junkman.**

rag·bag ('rægˌbæg) *n.* **1.** a bag for storing odd rags. **2.** a confused assortment; jumble: *a ragbag of ideas.*

rag·bolt ('rægˌbəult) *n.* a bolt that has angled projections on it to prevent it working loose once it has been driven home.

rage (reɪdʒ) *n.* **1.** intense anger; fury. **2.** violent movement or action, esp. of the sea, wind, etc. **3.** great intensity of hunger, sexual desire, or other feelings. **4.** a fashion or craze (esp. in the phrase **all the rage**). ~*vb.* (*intr.*) **5.** to feel or exhibit intense anger. **6.** (esp. of storms, fires, etc.) to move or surge with great violence. **7.** (esp. of a disease or epidemic) to spread rapidly and uncontrollably. [C13: via Old French from Latin *rabiēs* madness]

rag·ged ('rægɪd) *adj.* **1.** (of clothes) worn to rags; tattered. **2.** (of a person) dressed in shabby tattered clothes. **3.** having a neglected or unkempt appearance: *ragged weeds.* **4.** having a loose, rough, or uneven surface or edge; jagged. **5.** uneven or irregular: *a ragged beat; a ragged shout.* [C13: probably from *ragge* RAG[1]] —**'rag·ged·ly** *adv.* —**'rag·ged·ness** *n.*

rag·ged rob·in *n.* a caryophyllaceous plant, *Lychnis flos-cuculi*, native to Europe and Asia, that has pink or white flowers with ragged petals. Also called: **cuckooflower.** See also **catchfly.**

rag·ged school *Brit.* (formerly) a free elementary school for poor children.

rag·ged·y ('rægɪdɪ) *adj. Informal, chiefly U.S.* somewhat ragged; tattered: *a raggedy doll.*

rag·gle-tag·gle ('rægᵊl'tægᵊl) *adj.* motley or unkempt: *a raggle-taggle Gypsy.* [augmented form of RAG-TAG]

rag·i, rag·gee, *or* **rag·gy** ('rægɪ) *n.* a cereal grass, *Eleusine coracana*, cultivated in Africa and Asia for its edible grain. [C18: from Hindi]

rag·lan ('ræglən) *n.* **1.** a coat with sleeves that continue to the collar instead of having armhole seams. ~*adj.* **2.** cut in this design: *a raglan sleeve.* [C19: named after Lord RAGLAN]

Rag·lan ('ræglən) *n.* **Fitz·roy James Hen·ry Som·er·set,** 1st Baron Raglan. 1788–1855, English field marshal, who commanded British troops (1854–55) in the Crimean War.

Rag·na·rök *or* **Rag·na·rok** ('rɑːgnəˌrɒk) *n. Norse myth.* the ultimate destruction of the gods in a cataclysmic battle with evil, out of which a new order will arise. German equivalent: **Götterdämmerung.** [Old Norse *ragnarökkr*, from *regin* the gods + *rökkr* twilight]

ra·gout (ræ'guː) *n.* **1.** a richly seasoned stew of meat or poultry and vegetables. ~*vb.* **-gouts** (-'guːz), **-gout·ing** (-'guːɪŋ), **-gouted** (-'guːd). **2.** (*tr.*) to make into a ragout. [C17: from French, from *ragoûter* to stimulate the appetite again, from *ra-* RE- + *goûter* from Latin *gustāre* to taste]

rags (rægz) *pl. n.* **1.** torn, old, or shabby clothing. **2.** cotton or linen cloth waste used in the manufacture of rag paper. **3. glad rags.** *Informal.* best clothes; finery.

rag·tag ('rægˌtæg) *n. Disparaging.* the common people; rabble (esp. in the phrase **ragtag and bobtail**). [C19]

rag·time ('rægˌtaɪm) *n.* a style of jazz piano music, developed by Scott Joplin around 1900, having a two-four rhythm base and a syncopated melody. [C20: probably from RAGGED + TIME]

rag trade *n. Informal.* the clothing business, esp. the aspects concerned with the manufacture and sale of dresses.

Ra·gu·sa (*Italian* ra'gu:za) *n.* **1.** an industrial town in SE Sicily. Pop.: 59 509 (1971). Ancient name: **Hybla Heraea. 2.** the Italian name (until 1918) for **Dubrovnik.**

rag·weed ('ræg,wi:d) *n.* Also called: **ambrosia.** any North American plant of the genus *Ambrosia,* such as *A. artemisiifolia* **(common ragweed)**: family *Compositae* (composites). Their green tassel-like flowers produce large amounts of pollen, which causes hay fever.

rag·worm ('ræg,wɜ:m) *n.* any polychaete worm of the genus *Nereis,* living chiefly in burrows in sand or mud and having a flattened body with a row of fleshy parapodia along each side. U.S. name: **clamworm.**

rag·wort ('ræg,wɜ:t) *n.* any of several plants of the genus *Senecio,* esp. *S. jacobaea* of Europe, that have yellow daisy-like flowers: family *Compositae* (composites). See also **groundsel.**

rah (rɑ:) *interj. Informal, chiefly U.S.* short for **hurrah.**

Rah·man (Put·ra Al-Haj) ('rɑ:mən 'pu:trə æl'hædʒ) *n.* **Tun·ku Ab·dul** ('tuŋku: 'æbdʊl). born 1903, Malaysian statesman; prime minister of Malaya (1957–59 and 1959–63); prime minister of Malaysia since 1964.

ra·ia ('rɑ:jə, 'raɪə) *n.* a less common word for **rayah.**

raid (reɪd) *n.* **1.** a sudden surprise attack, as for catching someone or seizing something. **2.** an attempt by speculators to force down security or commodity prices by rapid selling. ~*vb.* **3.** to make a raid against (a person, thing, etc.). [C15: Scottish dialect, from Old English *rād* military expedition; see ROAD] —**'raid·er** *n.*

rail[1] (reɪl) *n.* **1.** a horizontal bar of wood, metal, etc., supported by vertical posts, functioning as a fence, barrier, handrail, etc. **2.** a horizontal bar fixed to a wall on which to hang things: *a picture rail.* **3.** a horizontal framing member in a door or piece of panelling. **4.** short for **railing. 5.** one of a pair of parallel bars laid on a prepared track, roadway, etc., that serve as a guide and running surface for the wheels of a railway train, tramcar, etc. **6. a.** short for **railway. b.** (*as modifier*): *rail transport.* **7.** *Nautical.* a trim for finishing the top of a bulwark. **8. off the rails. a.** into or in a state of dysfunction or disorder. **b.** eccentric or mad. ~*vb.* (*tr.*) **9.** to provide with a rail or railings. **10.** (usually foll. by *in* or *off*) to fence (an area) with rails. [C13: from Old French *raille* rod, from Latin *rēgula* ruler, straight piece of wood] —**'rail·less** *adj.*

rail[2] (reɪl) *vb.* (*intr.;* foll. by *at* or *against*) to complain bitterly or vehemently: *to rail against fate.* [C15: from Old French *railler* to mock, from Old Provençal *ralhar* to chatter, joke, from Late Latin *ragere* to yell, neigh] —**'rail·er** *n.*

rail[3] (reɪl) *n.* any of various small wading marsh birds of the genus *Rallus* and related genera: family *Rallidae,* order *Gruiformes* (cranes, etc.). They have short wings and neck, long legs, and dark plumage. [C15: from Old French *raale,* perhaps from Latin *rādere* to scrape]

rail·car ('reɪl,kɑ:) *n.* a passenger-carrying railway vehicle consisting of a single coach with its own power unit.

rail·head ('reɪl,hɛd) *n.* **1.** a terminal of a railway. **2.** the farthest point reached by completed track on an unfinished railway.

rail·ing ('reɪlɪŋ) *n.* **1.** a fence, balustrade, or barrier that consists of rails supported by posts. **2.** rails collectively or material for making rails.

rail·ler·y ('reɪlərɪ) *n., pl.* **·ler·ies. 1.** light-hearted satire or ridicule; banter. **2.** an example of this, esp. a bantering remark. [C17: from French, from *railler* to tease, banter; see RAIL[2]]

rail·road ('reɪl,rəʊd) *n.* **1.** the usual U.S. word for **railway.** ~*vb.* **2.** (*tr.*) *Informal.* to force (a person) into (an action) with haste or by unfair means.

rail·way ('reɪl,weɪ) *or U.S.* **rail·road** *n.* **1.** a permanent track composed of a line of parallel metal rails fixed to sleepers, for transport of passengers and goods in trains. **2.** any track for the wheels of a vehicle to run on: *a cable railway.* **3.** the entire equipment, rolling stock, buildings, property, and system of tracks used in such a transport system. **4.** the organization responsible for operating a railway network. **5.** (*modifier*) of, relating to, or used on a railway or railways: *a railway engine; a railway strike.*

rail·way·man ('reɪl,weɪmən) *n., pl.* **·men.** *Brit.* a worker on a railway, esp. one other than a driver.

rai·ment ('reɪmənt) *n. Archaic or poetic.* attire; clothing; garments. [C15: shortened from *arrayment,* from Old French *areement;* see ARRAY]

rain (reɪn) *n.* **1. a.** precipitation from clouds in the form of drops of water, formed by the condensation of water vapour in the atmosphere. **b.** a fall of rain; shower. **c.** (*in combination*): *a raindrop.* **2.** a large quantity of anything falling rapidly or in quick succession: *a rain of abuse.* **3. (come) rain or shine. a.** regardless of the weather. **b.** regardless of circumstances. **4. right as rain.** *Brit. informal.* perfectly all right; perfectly fit. ~*vb.* **5.** (*intr.;* with *it* as subject) to be the case that rain is falling. **6.** (often with *it* as subject) to fall or cause to fall like rain: *the lid flew off and popcorn rained on everyone.* **7.** (*tr.*) to bestow in large measure: *to rain abuse on someone.* **8. rain cats and dogs.** *Informal.* to rain heavily; pour. **9. rained off.** cancelled or postponed on account of rain. U.S. term: **rained out.** [Old English *regn;* related to Old Frisian *rein,* Old High German *regan,* Gothic *rign*] —**'rain·less** *adj.*

rain·band ('reɪn,bænd) *n.* a dark band in the solar spectrum caused by water in the atmosphere.

rain·bird ('reɪn,bɜ:d) *n.* any of various birds, such as (in Britain) the green woodpecker, whose cry is supposed to portend rain.

rain·bow ('reɪn,bəʊ) *n.* **1.** a bow-shaped display in the sky of the colours of the spectrum, caused by the refraction and reflection of the sun's rays through rain or mist. **2. a.** any similar display of bright colours. **b.** (*as modifier*): *a rainbow pattern.* **3.** an illusory hope: *to chase rainbows.*

rain·bow bird *n.* an Australian bee-eater, *Merops ornatus,* with a brightly-coloured plumage. It feeds in flight and nests in sandy burrows.

Rain·bow Bridge *n.* a natural stone bridge over a creek in SE Utah. Height: 94 m (309 ft.). Span: 85 m (278 ft.).

rain·bow trout *n.* a freshwater trout of North American origin, *Salmo gairdneri,* having a body marked with many black spots and two longitudinal red stripes.

rain·check ('reɪn,tʃɛk) *n. U.S.* **1.** a ticket stub for a baseball or other game that allows readmission on a future date if the event is cancelled because of rain. **2. take a raincheck.** *Informal.* to accept the postponement of an offer.

rain·coat ('reɪn,kəʊt) *n.* a coat worn for protection against rain.

rain·fall ('reɪn,fɔ:l) *n.* **1.** precipitation in the form of raindrops. **2.** *Meteorol.* the amount of precipitation in a specified place and time.

rain·for·est ('reɪn,fɒrɪst) *n.* dense forest found in tropical areas of heavy rainfall. The trees are broad-leaved and evergreen, and the vegetation tends to grow in three layers (undergrowth, intermediate trees and shrubs, and very tall trees, which form a canopy). Also called: **selva.**

rain gauge *n.* an instrument for measuring rainfall or snowfall, consisting of a cylinder covered by a funnel-like lid. Also called: **pluviometer.**

Rai·ni·er III ('reɪnɪ,eɪ; *French* rɛ'nje) *n.* full name *Rainier Louis Henri Maxence Bertrand de Grimaldi.* born 1923, ruling prince of Monaco since 1949. He married (1956) the U.S. actress Grace Kelly (1928–82).

Rai·ni·er ('reɪnɪə; reɪ'nɪə, rə-) *n.* **Mount.** a mountain in W Washington State: the highest mountain in the state and in the Cascade Range. Height: 4392 m (14 410 ft.).

rain·mak·er ('reɪn,meɪkə) *n.* (among American Indians, etc.) a professional practitioner of ritual incantations or other actions intended to cause rain to fall. —**'rain·,mak·ing** *n.*

rain·out ('reɪn,aʊt) *n.* radioactive fall-out or atmospheric pollution carried to the earth by rain.

rain·proof ('reɪn,pru:f) *adj.* **1.** Also: **rain·tight.** (of garments, materials, buildings, etc.) impermeable to rainwater. ~*vb.* **2.** (*tr.*) to make rainproof.

rains (reɪnz) *pl. n.* **the.** the season of heavy rainfall, esp. in the tropics.

rain shad·ow *n.* the relatively dry area on the leeward side of high ground in the path of rain-bearing winds.

rain·storm ('reɪn,stɔ:m) *n.* a storm with heavy rain.

rain tree *n.* a leguminous tree, *Samanea saman,* native to Central America and widely planted in the tropics for ornament. It has red-and-yellow feathery flowers and pinnate leaves whose leaflets close at the approach of rain.

rain·wa·ter ('reɪn,wɔ:tə) *n.* pure water from rain (as distinguished from spring water, tap water, etc., which may contain minerals and impurities).

rain·wa·ter pipe *n. Brit.* another name for **downpipe.**

rain·y ('reɪnɪ) *adj.* **rain·i·er, rain·i·est. 1.** characterized by a large rainfall: *a rainy climate.* **2.** wet or showery; bearing rain. —**'rain·i·ly** *adv.* —**'rain·i·ness** *n.*

rain·y day *n.* a future time of need, esp. financial.

raise (reɪz) *vb.* (*mainly tr.*) **1.** to move, cause to move, or elevate to a higher position or level; lift. **2.** to set or place in an upright position. **3.** to construct, build, or erect: *to raise a barn.* **4.** to increase in amount, size, value, etc.: *to raise prices.* **5.** to increase in degree, strength, intensity, etc.: *to raise one's voice.* **6.** to advance in rank or status; promote. **7.** to arouse or awaken from or as if from sleep or death. **8.** to stir up or incite; activate: *to raise a mutiny.* **9. raise Cain** (*or* **the devil, hell, the roof,** etc.). to create a disturbance, esp. by making a great noise. **10.** to give rise to; cause or provoke: *to raise a smile.* **11.** to put forward for consideration: *to raise a question.* **12.** to cause to assemble or gather together; collect: *to raise an army.* **13.** to grow or cause to grow: *to raise a crop.* **14.** to bring up; rear: *to raise a family.* **15.** to cause to be heard or known; utter or express: *to raise a shout; to raise a protest.* **16.** to bring to an end; remove: *to raise a siege; raise a ban.* **17.** to cause (dough, bread, etc.) to rise, as by the addition of yeast. **18.** *Poker.* to bet more than (the previous player). **19.** *Bridge.* to bid (one's partner's suit) at a higher level. **20.** *Nautical.* to cause (something) to seem to rise above the horizon by approaching: *we raised land after 20 days.* **21.** to establish radio communications with: *we managed to raise Moscow last night.* **22.** to obtain (money, funds, capital, etc.). **23.** to bring (a surface, a design, etc.) into relief; cause to project. **24.** to cause (a blister, welt, etc.) to form on the skin. **25.** to expel (phlegm) by coughing. **26.** *Phonetics.* to modify the articulation of (a vowel) by bringing the tongue closer to the roof of the mouth. **27.** *Maths.* to multiply (a number) by itself a specified number of times: *8 is 2 raised to the power 3.* **28. a.** to institute (a suit or action at law). **b.** to draw up (a summons, etc.). **29.** *Chiefly U.S.* to increase the amount payable on (a cheque, money order, etc.) fraudulently. **30.** *Curling.* to push (a stone) towards the tee with another stone. **31. raise an eyebrow** *or* **one's eyebrows.** to look quizzical or surprised. **32. raise one's glass (to).** to drink the health of (someone); drink a toast (to). **33. raise one's hat.** *Old-fashioned.* to take one's hat briefly off one's head as a greeting or mark of respect. ~*n.* **34.** the act or an instance of raising. **35.** *Chiefly U.S.* an increase, esp. in salary, wages, etc.;

rise. [C12: from Old Norse *reisa;* related to Old English *rǣran* to REAR] —'**rais·a·ble** *or* '**raise·a·ble** *adj.* —'**rais·er** *n.*
raised beach *n.* a wave-cut platform raised above the shoreline by a relative fall in the water level.
rai·sin ('reɪzᵊn) *n.* a dried grape. [C13: from Old French: grape, ultimately from Latin *racēmus* cluster of grapes; compare Greek *rhax* berry, grape] —'**rai·sin·y** *adj.*
rais·ing ('reɪzɪŋ) *n. Transformational grammar.* a rule that moves a constituent from an embedded clause into the main clause. See also **subject-raising, negative-raising.**
rai·son d'ê·tre *French.* (rɛzɔ̃ 'dɛtr) *n., pl.* ***rai·sons d'ê·tre*** (rɛzɔ̃ 'dɛtr). reason or justification for existence.
raj (rɑːdʒ) *n.* (in India) government; rule. [C19: from Hindi, from Sanskrit *rājya,* from *rājati* he rules]
Raj (rɑːdʒ) *n.* **the.** the British government in India before 1947.
Ra·jab (rəˈdʒæb) *n.* the seventh month of the Muslim year.
ra·jah *or* **ra·ja** ('rɑːdʒə) *n.* **1.** (in India, formerly) a ruler or landlord: sometimes used as a form of address or as a title preceding a name. **2.** a Malayan or Javanese prince or chieftain. [C16: from Hindi *rājā,* from Sanskrit *rājan* king; see RAJ; compare Latin *rex* king]
Ra·ja·sthan (ˌrɑːdʒəˈstɑːn) *n.* a state of NW India, bordering on Pakistan: formed in 1958; contains the Thar Desert in the west. Capital: Jaipur. Pop.: 25 765 806 (1971). Area: 342 274 sq. km (132 152 sq. miles).
Raj·kot ('rɑːdʒkəʊt) *n.* a city in W India, in S Gujerat. Pop.: 300 612 (1971).
Raj·put *or* **Raj·poot** ('rɑːdʒpʊt) *n. Hinduism.* one of a Hindu military caste claiming descent from the Kshatriya, the original warrior caste. [C16: from Hindi, from Sanskrit *rājan* king; see RAJ]
Raj·pu·ta·na (ˌrɑːdʒpʊˈtɑːnə) *n.* a former group of princely states in NW India: now mostly part of Rajasthan.
Ra·jya Sa·bha ('rɑːdʒjə 'sʌbə) *n.* the upper chamber of India's Parliament. Compare **Lok Sabha.** [Hindi, *rajya* state + *sabha* assembly]
Ra·ka·ta (rəˈkɑːtə) *n.* another name for **Krakatoa.**
rake[1] (reɪk) *n.* **1.** a hand implement consisting of a row of teeth set in a headpiece attached to a long shaft and used for gathering hay, straw, leaves, etc., or for smoothing loose earth. **2.** any of several mechanical farm implements equipped with rows of teeth or rotating wheels mounted with tines and used to gather hay, straw, etc. **3.** any of various implements similar in shape or function, such as a tool for drawing out ashes from a furnace. **4.** the act of raking. ~*vb.* **5.** to scrape, gather, or remove (leaves, refuse, etc.) with or as if with a rake. **6.** to level or prepare (a surface, such as a flower bed) with a rake or similar implement. **7.** (*tr.;* sometimes foll. by *out*) to clear (ashes, etc.) from (a fire or furnace). **8.** (*tr.;* foll. by *up* or *together*) to gather (items or people) with difficulty, as from a scattered area or limited supply. **9.** (*tr.;* often foll. by *through, over,* etc.) to search or examine carefully. **10.** (when *intr.,* foll. by *against, along,* etc.) to scrape or graze: *the ship raked the side of the quay.* **11.** (*tr.*) to direct (gunfire) along the length of (a target): *machine-guns raked the column.* **12.** (*tr.*) to sweep (one's eyes) along the length of (something); scan. ~See also **rake in, rake-off, rake up.** [Old English *raca;* related to Old Norse *raka,* Old High German *rehho* a rake, Gothic *rikan* to heap up, Latin *rogus* funeral pile] —'**rak·er** *n.*
rake[2] (reɪk) *n.* a dissolute man, esp. one in fashionable society; roué. [C17: short for RAKEHELL]
rake[3] (reɪk) *vb.* (*mainly intr.*) **1.** to incline from the vertical by a perceptible degree, esp. (of a ship's mast or funnel) towards the stern. **2.** (*tr.*) to construct with a backward slope. ~*n.* **3.** the degree to which an object, such as a ship's mast, inclines from the perpendicular, esp. towards the stern. **4.** *Theatre.* the slope of a stage from the back towards the footlights. **5.** *Aeronautics.* **a.** the angle between the wings of an aircraft and the line of symmetry of the aircraft. **b.** the angle between the line joining the centroids of the section of a propeller blade and a line perpendicular to the axis. **6.** the angle between the working face of a cutting tool and a plane perpendicular to the surface of the workpiece. [C17: of uncertain origin; perhaps related to German *ragen* to project, Swedish *raka*]
rake[4] (reɪk) *vb.* (*intr.*) **1.** (of gun dogs or hounds) to hunt with the nose to the ground. **2.** (of hawks) **a.** to pursue quarry in full flight. **b.** (often foll. by *away*) to fly wide of the quarry, esp. beyond the control of the falconer. [Old English *racian* to go forward, of uncertain origin]
rake·hell ('reɪkˌhɛl) *Archaic.* ~*n.* **1.** a dissolute man; rake. ~*adj. also* **rake·hell·y. 2.** profligate; dissolute. [C16: from RAKE[1] + HELL; but compare Middle English *rakel* rash]
rake in *vb.* (*tr., adv.*) *Informal.* to acquire (money) in large amounts.
rake-off *Slang.* ~*n.* **1.** a share of profits, esp. one that is illegal or given as a bribe. ~*vb.* **rake off. 2.** (*tr., adv.*) to take or receive (such a share of profits).
rake up *vb.* (*tr., adv.*) to revive, discover, or bring to light (something forgotten): *to rake up an old quarrel.*
ra·ki *or* **ra·kee** (rɑːˈkiː, 'rækɪ) *n.* a strong spirit distilled in Turkey, Yugoslavia, etc., from grain, usually flavoured with aniseed or other aromatics. [C17: from Turkish *rāqī*]
rak·ish[1] ('reɪkɪʃ) *adj.* dissolute; profligate. —'**rak·ish·ly** *adv.* —'**rak·ish·ness** *n.*
rak·ish[2] ('reɪkɪʃ) *adj.* **1.** dashing; jaunty: *a hat set at a rakish angle.* **2.** *Nautical.* (of a ship or boat) having lines suggestive of speed.
rale *or* **râle** (rɑːl) *n. Med.* an abnormal crackling sound heard on auscultation of the chest, usually caused by the accumulation of fluid in the lungs. [C19: from French *râle,* from *râler* to breathe with a rattling sound; compare RAIL[3]]
Ra·leigh[1] ('rɔːlɪ, 'rɑː-) *n.* a city in E central North Carolina, capital of the state. Pop.: 133 050 (1973 est.).
Ra·leigh[2] *or* **Ra·legh** ('rɔːlɪ, 'rɑː-) *n.* Sir **Wal·ter.** ?1552–1618, English courtier, explorer, and writer; favourite of Elizabeth I. After unsuccessful attempts to colonize Virginia (1584–89), he led two expeditions to the Orinoco to search for gold (1595; 1616). He introduced tobacco and potatoes into England, and was imprisoned (1603–16) for conspiracy under James I. He was beheaded in 1618.
rall. *Music. abbrev. for* rallentando.
ral·len·tan·do (ˌrælɛnˈtændəʊ) *adj., adv. Music.* becoming slower. Abbrev.: **rall.** Also: **ritardando, ritenuto.** [C19: Italian, from *rallentare* to slow down]
ral·line ('rælaɪn, -ɪn) *adj.* of, relating to, or belonging to the *Rallidae,* a family of birds that includes the rails, crakes, and coots. [C19: from New Latin *Rallus* RAIL[3]]
ral·ly[1] ('rælɪ) *vb.* **·lies, ·ly·ing, ·lied. 1.** to bring (a group, unit, etc.) into order, as after dispersal, or (of such a group) to reform and come to order: *the troops rallied for a final assault.* **2.** (when *intr.,* foll. by *to*) to organize (supporters, etc.) for a common cause or (of such people) to come together for a purpose. **3.** to summon up (one's strength, spirits, etc.) or (of a person's health, strength, or spirits) to revive or recover. **4.** (*intr.*) *Stock Exchange.* to increase sharply after a decline: *steels rallied after a bad day.* **5.** (*intr.*) *Tennis, squash, etc.* to engage in a rally. ~*n., pl.* **·lies. 6.** a large gathering of people for a common purpose, esp. for some political cause: *the Nuremberg Rallies.* **7.** a marked recovery of strength or spirits, as during illness. **8.** a return to order after dispersal or rout, as of troops, etc. **9.** *Stock Exchange.* a sharp increase in price or trading activity after a decline. **10.** *Tennis, squash, etc.* an exchange of several shots before one player wins the point. **11.** a type of motoring competition over public and closed roads. [C16: from Old French *rallier,* from RE- + *alier* to write; see ALLY] —'**ral·li·er** *n.*
ral·ly[2] ('rælɪ) *vb.* **·lies, ·ly·ing, ·lied.** to mock or ridicule (someone) in a good-natured way; chaff; tease. [C17: from Old French *railler* to tease; see RAIL[2]]
ral·ly·cross ('rælɪˌkrɒs) *n.* a form of motor sport in which cars race over a one-mile circuit of rough grass with some hard-surfaced sections. See also **autocross, motocross.**
ral·ly round *vb.* (*intr.*) to come to the aid of (someone); offer moral or practical support.
ram (ræm) *n.* **1.** an uncastrated adult male sheep. **2.** a piston or moving plate, esp. one driven hydraulically or pneumatically. **3.** the falling weight of a pile driver or similar device. **4.** short for **battering ram. 5.** Also called: **rostrum, beak.** a pointed projection in the stem of an ancient warship for puncturing the hull of enemy ships. **6.** a warship equipped with a ram. **7.** *Slang.* a sexually active man. ~*vb.* **rams, ram·ming, rammed. 8.** (*tr.;* usually foll. by *into*) to force or drive, as by heavy blows: *to ram a post into the ground.* **9.** (of a moving object) to crash with force (against another object) or (of two moving objects) to collide in this way: *the Athenian ships rammed the enemy.* **10.** (*tr.;* often foll. by *in* or *down*) to stuff or cram (something into a hole, etc.). **11.** (*tr.;* foll. by *onto, against,* etc.) to thrust violently: *he rammed the books onto the desk.* **12.** (*tr.*) *Slang.* to instil (knowledge, etc.) into a person, esp. by repetition (esp. in the phrase **ram (something) down someone's throat**). **13.** (*tr.*) to drive (a charge) into a firearm. [Old English *ramm;* related to Old High German *ram* ram, Old Norse *ramr* fierce, *rimma* to fight] —'**ram·mer** *n.*
Ram (ræm) *n.* **the.** the constellation Aries, the first sign of the zodiac.
RAM (ræm) *n. Computer technol. acronym for* random access memory.
R.A.M. *abbrev. for* Royal Academy of Music.
Ra·ma ('rɑːmə) *n.* (in Hindu mythology) any of Vishnu's three incarnations (the heroes Balarama, Parashurama, or Ramachandra). [from Sanskrit *Rāma* black, dark]
Ra·ma·chan·dra (ˌrɑːməˈtʃʌndrə) *n.* (in Hindu mythology) an incarnation of Vishnu; the hero of the *Ramayana* and a character in the *Mahabharata.* See also **Rama.**
Ram·a·dan, Rham·a·dhan (ˌræməˈdɑːn), *or* **Ram·a·zan** (ˌræməˈzɑːn) *n.* **1.** a period of 30 days in the ninth month of the Muslim year, during which strict fasting is observed from sunrise to sunset. **2.** the fast itself. [C16: from Arabic, literally: the hot month, from *ramad* dryness]
ram-air tur·bine *n.* a small air-driven turbine fitted to an aircraft to provide power in the event of a failure of the normal systems.
Ra·ma·krish·na (ˌrɑːməˈkrɪʃnə) *n.* **Sri** (sriː). 1834–86, Hindu yogi and religious reformer. He preached the equal value of all religions as different paths to God.
Ra·man ef·fect ('rɑːmən) *n.* the change in wavelength of light that is scattered by electrons within a material. The effect is used in **Raman spectroscopy** for studying the properties of molecules. [C20: named after Sir Chandasekhara *Raman* (born 1888), Indian physicist]
Ra·mat Gan (rɑːˈmɑːt ˈgɑːn) *n.* a city in Israel, E of Tel Aviv. Pop.: 120 200 (1974 est.).
Ra·ma·ya·na (rɑːˈmaɪənə) *n.* a Sanskrit epic poem, composed about 300 B.C., recounting the feats of Ramachandra.
Ram·bert ('rɒmbɛə) *n.* Dame **Ma·rie.** 1888–1982, British ballet dancer and teacher, born in Poland: founded the **Ballet Rambert** (1926).
ram·ble ('ræmbᵊl) *vb.* (*intr.*) **1.** to stroll about freely, as for

relaxation, with no particular direction. **2.** (of paths, streams, etc.) to follow a winding course; meander. **3.** (of plants) to grow in a random fashion. **4.** (of speech, writing, etc.) to lack organization. ~*n.* **5.** a leisurely stroll, esp. in the countryside. [C17: probably related to Middle Dutch *rammelen* to ROAM (of animals); see RAM]

ram+bler ('ræmblə) *n.* **1.** a weak-stemmed plant, esp. any of various cultivated hybrid roses that straggle over other vegetation. **2.** a person who rambles, esp. one who takes country walks. **3.** a person who lacks organization in his speech or writing.

Ram+bouil+let ('rɒmbʊˌjeɪ, 'ræmbʊˌleɪ; *French* rãbu'jɛ) *n.* a fine-woolled merino-like breed of sheep. [C19: from *Rambouillet* town in northern France]

ram+bunc+tious (ræm'bʌŋkʃəs) *adj. Informal.* boisterous; unruly. [C19: RAM- + *-bunctious,* from BUMPTIOUS] **—ram+'bunc+tious+ly** *adv.* **—ram+'bunc+tious+ness** *n.*

ram+bu+tan (ræm'buːtᵊn) *n.* **1.** a sapindaceous tree, *Nephelium lappaceum,* native to SE Asia, that has bright red edible fruit covered with hairs. **2.** the fruit of this tree. [C18: from Malay, from *rambut* hair]

R.A.M.C. *abbrev. for* Royal Army Medical Corps.

Ra·meau (*French* ra'mo) *n.* **Jean Phi·lippe** (ʒã fi'lip). 1683–1764, French composer. His works include the opera *Castor et Pollux* (1737), chamber music, harpsichord pieces, church music, and cantatas. His *Traité de l'harmonie* (1722) was of fundamental importance in the development of modern harmony.

ram+e·kin *or* **ram+e·quin** ('ræmɪkɪn) *n.* **1.** a savoury dish made from a cheese mixture baked in a fireproof dish. **2.** the dish itself. [C18: French *ramequin,* of Germanic origin]

ra+men+tum (rə'mɛntəm) *n., pl.* **+ta** (-tə). any of the thin brown scales that cover the stems and leaves of young ferns. [C17: from Latin *rādere* to scrape] **—ram+en+ta+ceous** (ˌræmɛn'teɪʃəs) *adj.*

Ram·e·ses ('ræmɪˌsiːz) *n.* a variant spelling of **Ramses.**

ra·mi ('reɪmaɪ) *n.* the plural of **ramus.**

ram·ie *or* **ram·ee** ('ræmɪ) *n.* **1.** a woody urticaceous shrub of Asia, *Boehmeria nivea,* having broad leaves and a stem that yields a flaxlike fibre. **2.** the fibre from this plant, used in making fabrics, etc. [C19: from Malay *rami*]

ram·i+fi+ca+tion (ˌræmɪfɪ'keɪʃən) *n.* **1.** the act or process of ramifying or branching out. **2.** an offshoot or subdivision. **3.** a subsidiary consequence, esp. one that complicates. **4.** a structure of branching parts.

ram·i+form ('ræmɪˌfɔːm) *adj.* having a branchlike shape. [C19: from Latin *rāmus* branch + -FORM]

ram·i+fy ('ræmɪˌfaɪ) *vb.* **+fies, +fy+ing, +fied. 1.** to divide into branches or branchlike parts. **2.** (*intr.*) to develop complicating consequences; become complex. [C16: from French *ramifier,* from Latin *rāmus* branch + *facere* to make]

Ra+mil+lies ('ræmɪliːz; *French* rami'ji) *n.* a village in central Belgium where the Duke of Marlborough defeated the French in 1706.

ram+jet *or* **ram+jet en+gine** ('ræmˌdʒɛt) *n.* **a.** a type of jet engine in which fuel is burned in a duct using air compressed by the forward speed of the aircraft. **b.** an aircraft powered by such an engine. Also called: **athodyd.**

ram+mish ('ræmɪʃ) *adj.* like a ram, esp. in being lustful or foul-smelling. **—'ram+mish+ly** *adv.* **—'ram+mish+ness** *n.*

ra+mose ('reɪməʊs, ræ'məʊs) *or* **ra+mous** ('reɪməs) *adj.* having branches. [C17: from Latin *rāmōsus,* from *rāmus* branch] **—'ra+mose+ly** *or* **'ra+mous+ly** *adv.* **—ra+mos+i·ty** (ræ'mɒsɪtɪ) *n.*

ramp (ræmp) *n.* **1.** a sloping floor, path, etc., that joins two surfaces at different levels. **2.** a movable stairway by which passengers enter and leave an aircraft. **3.** the act of ramping. **4.** *Brit. slang.* a swindle, esp. one involving exorbitant prices. ~*vb.* (*intr.*) **5.** (often foll. by *about* or *around*) (esp. of animals) to rush around in a wild excited manner. **6.** to act in a violent or threatening manner, as when angry (esp. in the phrase **ramp and rage).** [C18 (n.): from C13 *rampe,* from Old French *ramper* to crawl or rear, probably of Germanic origin; compare Middle Low German *ramp* cramp]

ram+page *vb.* (ræm'peɪdʒ). **1.** (*intr.*) to rush about in an angry, violent, or agitated fashion. ~*n.* ('ræmpeɪdʒ, ræm'peɪdʒ). **2.** angry or destructive behaviour. **3. on the rampage.** behaving violently or destructively. [C18: from Scottish, of uncertain origin; perhaps based on RAMP] **—ram+'pa+geous** *adj.* **—ram+'pa+geous+ly** *adv.* **—ram+'pa+geous+ness** *n.* **—'ram+pag+er** *n.*

ram+pant ('ræmpənt) *adj.* **1.** unrestrained or violent in behaviour, desire, opinions, etc. **2.** growing or developing unchecked. **3.** (*postpositive*) *Heraldry.* (of a beast) standing on the hind legs, the right foreleg raised above the left. **4.** (of an arch) having one abutment higher than the other. [C14: from Old French *ramper* to crawl, rear; see RAMP] **—'ram+pan+cy** *n.* **—'ram+pant+ly** *adv.*

ram+part ('ræmpɑːt) *n.* **1.** the surrounding embankment of a fort, often including any walls, etc., that are built on the bank. **2.** anything resembling a rampart in form or function, esp. in being a defence or bulwark. ~*vb.* **3.** (*tr.*) to provide with a rampart; fortify. [C16: from Old French, from *remparer* to fortify, from RE- + *emparer* to take possession of, from Old Provençal *antparar,* from Latin *ante* before + *parāre* to prepare]

ram+pi+on ('ræmpɪən) *n.* **1.** a campanulaceous plant, *Campanula rapunculus,* native to Europe and Asia, that has clusters of bluish flowers and an edible white tuberous root used in salads. **2.** any of several plants of the related genus *Phyteuma* that are native to Europe and Asia and have heads of blue flowers. [C16: probably from Old French *raiponce,* from Old Italian *raponzo,* from *rapa* turnip, from Latin *rāpum* turnip; see RAPE[2]]

Ram+pur ('rɑːmpʊə) *n.* a city in N India, in N Uttar Pradesh. Pop.: 161 417 (1971).

ram+rod ('ræmˌrɒd) *n.* **1.** a rod for cleaning the barrel of a rifle, etc. **2.** a rod for ramming in the charge of a muzzle-loading firearm.

Ram·say ('ræmzɪ) *n.* **1. Al·lan.** 1686–1758, Scottish poet, noted particularly for his pastoral comedy *The Gentle Shepherd* (1725). **2. James An·drew Broun.** See (10th Earl of) **Dalhousie. 3.** Sir **Wil·liam.** 1852–1916, Scottish chemist. He discovered argon (1894) with Rayleigh, isolated helium (1895), and identified neon, krypton, and xenon: Nobel prize for chemistry (1904).

Ram+ses ('ræmsiːz) *or* **Ram·e·ses** *n.* any of 12 kings of ancient Egypt, who ruled from ?1315 to ?1090 B.C.

Ram·ses II *or* **Ram·e·ses II** *n.* died ?1225 B.C., king of ancient Egypt (?1292–?25). His reign was marked by war with the Hittites and the construction of many colossal monuments, esp. the rock temple at Abu Simbel.

Ram·ses III *or* **Ram·e·ses III** *n.* died ?1167 B.C., king of ancient Egypt (?1198–?67). His reign was marked by wars in Libya and Syria.

Ram·sey ('ræmzɪ) *n.* **Ar·thur Mi·chael.** born 1904, Archbishop of Canterbury (1961–74).

Rams+gate ('ræmzˌgeɪt) *n.* a port and resort in SE England, in E Kent on the North Sea coast. Pop.: 39 482 (1971).

ram+shack+le ('ræmˌʃækᵊl) *adj.* (esp. of buildings) badly constructed or maintained; rickety, shaky, or derelict. [C17 *ramshackled,* from obsolete *ransackle* to RANSACK]

ram+sons ('ræmzənz, -sənz) *pl. n.* (*usually functioning as sing.*) **1.** a broad-leaved garlic, *Allium ursinum,* native to Europe and Asia. **2.** the bulbous root of this plant, eaten as a relish. [Old English *hramesa;* related to Middle Low German *ramese,* Norwegian *rams*]

ram+til ('ræmtɪl) *n.* **1.** an African plant, *Guizotia abyssinica,* grown in India: family *Compositae* (composites). **2.** Also called: **Niger seed.** the seed of this plant, used as a source of oil and a bird food. [from Hindi, from Sanskrit *rāma* black + *tila* sesame]

ram·u·lose ('ræmjʊˌləʊs) *or* **ram·u·lous** ('ræmjʊləs) *adj.* (of the parts or organs of animals and plants) having many small branches. [C18: from Latin *rāmulōsus* full of branching veins, from *rāmulus* twig, from *rāmus* branch]

ra+mus ('reɪməs) *n., pl.* **·mi** (-maɪ). **1.** the barb of a bird's feather. **2.** either of the two parts of the lower jaw of a vertebrate. **3.** any part or organ that branches from another part. [C19: from Latin: branch]

ran (ræn) *vb.* the past tense of **run.**

R.A.N. *abbrev. for* Royal Australian Navy.

Ran+ca+gua (*Spanish* raŋ'kagwa) *n.* a city in central Chile. Pop.: 108 010 (1975 est.).

rance (rɑːns) *n.* a type of red marble, often with white or blue graining, that comes from Belgium. [C19: apparently from French *ranche* rod, pole]

ranch (rɑːntʃ) *n.* **1.** a large tract of land, esp. one in North America, together with the necessary personnel, buildings, and equipment, for rearing livestock, esp. cattle. **2. a.** any large farm for the rearing of a particular kind of livestock or crop: *a mink ranch.* **b.** the buildings, land, etc., connected with it. ~*vb.* **3.** (*intr.*) to manage or run a ranch. [C19: from Mexican Spanish *rancho* small farm; see RANCHO]

ranch+er ('rɑːntʃə) *n.* a person who owns, manages, or works on a ranch.

ranch+er·ie ('rɑːntʃərɪ) *n.* a W Canadian word for Indian **reservation.** [from Spanish *rancheria*]

ran+che+ro (rɑːn'tʃɛərəʊ) *n., pl.* **+ros.** *Southwestern U.S.* another word for **rancher.** [C19: from American Spanish]

Ran+chi ('ræntʃɪ) *n.* an industrial city in E India, in S Bihar between the coal and iron belts of the Chota Nagpur Plateau. Pop.: 175 934 (1971).

ran+cho ('rɑːntʃəʊ) *n., pl.* **+chos.** *Southwestern U.S.* **1.** a hut or group of huts for housing ranch workers. **2.** another word for **ranch.** [C17: from Mexican Spanish: camp, from Old Spanish *ranchar* to be billeted, from Old French *ranger* to place]

ran+cid ('rænsɪd) *adj.* **1.** (of butter, bacon, etc.) having an unpleasant stale taste or smell as the result of decomposition. **2.** (of a taste or smell) rank or sour; stale. [C17: from Latin *rancidus* rank, from *rancēre* to stink] **—'ran+cid+ness** *or* **ran+cid·i·ty** (ræn'sɪdɪtɪ) *n.*

ran+cour *or* *U.S.* **ran+cor** ('ræŋkə) *n.* malicious resentfulness or hostility; spite. [C14: from Old French, from late Latin *rancor* rankness] **—'ran+cor+ous** *adj.* **—'ran+cor+ous+ly** *adv.* **—'ran+cor+ous+ness** *n.*

rand[1] (rænd, rɒnt) *n.* the standard monetary unit of the Republic of South Africa, divided into 100 cents. [C20: from Afrikaans, shortened from WITWATERSRAND, referring to the gold-mining there; related to RAND[2]]

rand[2] (rænd) *n.* **1.** *Shoemaking.* a leather strip put in the heel of a shoe before the lifts are put on. **2.** *Brit. dialect.* **a.** a strip or margin; border. **b.** a strip of cloth; selvage. [Old English; related to Old High German *rant* border, rim of a shield, Old Norse *rönd* shield, rim]

Rand (rænd) *n.* **the.** short for **Witwatersrand.**

ran+dan ('rændæn) *n.* a boat rowed by three people, in which the person in the middle uses two oars and the people fore and aft use one oar each. [C19: of uncertain origin]

R & B *abbrev. for* rhythm and blues.
R & D *abbrev. for* research and development.
Rand+ers (*Danish* 'ranərs) *n.* a port and industrial centre in Denmark, in E Jutland on **Randers Fjord** (an inlet of the Kattegat). Pop.: 57 318 (1970).
Ran·dolph ('rændɒlf, -dəlf) *n.* **1. Ed·mund Jen·nings,** 1753–1813, U.S. politician. He was a member of the convention that framed the U.S. constitution (1787), attorney general (1789–94), and secretary of state (1794–95). **2. John,** called *Randolph of Roanoke.* 1773–1833, U.S. politician, noted for his eloquence: in 1820 he opposed the Missouri Compromise that outlawed slavery. **3.** Sir **Thom·as;** 1st Earl of Moray. Died 1332, Scottish soldier: regent after the death of Robert the Bruce (1329).
ran+dom ('rændəm) *adj.* **1.** lacking any definite plan or prearranged order; haphazard: *a random selection.* **2.** *Statistics.* **a.** (of a variable) having several possible experimental values any one of which is uncertain and depends on chance. **b.** (of a sampling process) carried out so that each member of the population has an equal probability of being selected. ~*n.* **3.** *Chiefly Brit.* another word for **bank**[3] (sense 3). **4. at random.** in a purposeless fashion; not following any prearranged order. [C14: from Old French *randon,* from *randir* to gallop, of Germanic origin; compare Old High German *rinnan* to run] —'**ran+dom+ly** *adv.* —'**ran+dom+ness** *n.*
ran+dom ac+cess *n.* another name for **direct access.**
ran+dom+ize *or* **ran+dom+ise** ('rændə,maɪz) *vb.* (*tr.*) to set up (a selection process, sample, etc.) in a deliberately random way in order to enhance the statistical validity of any results obtained. —,**ran+dom·i+'za·tion** *or* ,**ran+dom·i+'sa·tion** *n.* —'**ran+dom+,iz+er** *or* '**ran+dom+,is+er** *n.*
R and R *U.S. military. abbrev. for* rest and recreation.
rand·y ('rændɪ) *adj.* **rand·i+er, rand·i+est. 1.** *Slang, chiefly Brit.* **a.** sexually excited or aroused. **b.** sexually eager or lustful. **2.** *Chiefly Scot.* lacking any sense of propriety or restraint; reckless. ~*n., pl.* **rand·ies. 3.** *Chiefly Scot.* **a.** a rude or reckless person. **b.** a coarse rowdy woman. [C17: probably from obsolete *rand* to RANT] —'**rand·i+ly** *adv.* —'**rand·i+ness** *n.*
ra+nee ('rɑːnɪ) *n.* a variant spelling of **rani.**
rang (ræŋ) *vb.* the past tense of **ring**[2].
Usage. See at **ring**[2].
range (reɪndʒ) *n.* **1.** the limits within which a person or thing can function effectively: *the range of vision.* **2.** the limits within which any fluctuation takes place: *a range of values.* **3. a.** the maximum effective distance of a projectile fired from a weapon. **b.** the distance between a target and a weapon. **4.** an area set aside for shooting practice or rocket testing. **5.** the total distance which a ship, aircraft, or land vehicle is capable of covering without taking on fresh fuel: *the range of this car is about 160 miles.* **6.** *Physics.* the distance that a particle of ionizing radiation, such as an electron or proton, can travel through a given medium, esp. air, before ceasing to cause ionization. **7.** *Maths.* **a.** (of a function) the set of functional values. Compare **domain** (sense 6). **b.** (of a variable) the set of values that a variable can take. **8.** *Statistics.* a measure of dispersion obtained by subtracting the smallest from the largest sample values. **9.** the extent of pitch difference between the highest and lowest notes of a voice, instrument, etc. **10.** *U.S.* **a.** an extensive tract of open land on which livestock can graze. **b.** (*as modifier*): *range cattle.* **11.** the geographical region in which a species of plant or animal normally grows or lives. **12.** a rank, row, or series of items. **13.** a series or chain of mountains. **14.** a large stove with burners and one or more ovens, usually heated by solid fuel. **15.** the act or process of ranging. **16.** *Nautical.* a line of sight taken from the sea along two or more navigational aids that mark a navigable channel. **17.** the extension or direction of a survey line, established by marking two or more points. **18.** a double-faced bookcase, as in a library. ~*vb.* **19.** to establish or be situated in a line, row, or series. **20.** (*tr.; often reflexive,* foll. by *with*) to put into a specific category; classify: *she ranges herself with the angels.* **21.** (foll. by *on*) to aim or point (a telescope, gun, etc.) or (of a gun, telescope, etc.) to be pointed or aimed. **22.** to establish the distance of (a target) from (a weapon). **23.** (*intr.*) (of a gun or missile) to have a specified range. **24.** (when *intr.,* foll. by *over*) to wander about (in) an area; roam (over). **25.** (*intr.,* foll. by *over*) (of an animal or plant) to live or grow in its normal habitat. **26.** (*tr.*) to put (cattle) to graze on a range. **27.** (*intr.*) to fluctuate within specific limits: *their ages range from 18 to 21.* **28.** (*intr.*) to extend or run in a specific direction. **29.** (*tr.*) *Nautical.* to fake down (an anchor rode) so that it will pay out smoothly. **30.** (*intr.*) *Nautical.* (of a vessel) to swing back and forth while at anchor. **31.** (*tr.*) to make (lines of printers' type) level or even at the margin. [C13: from Old French: row, from *ranger* to position, from *renc* line]
range+find·er ('reɪndʒ,faɪndə) *n.* **1.** an instrument for determining the distance of an object from the observer, esp. in order to sight a gun or focus a camera. **2.** another word for **tacheometer.**
range light *n. Nautical.* **1.** one of a pattern of navigation lights, usually fixed ashore, used by vessels for manoeuvring in narrow channels at night. **2.** one of a distinctive pattern of lights shown at night on the masts of a powered vessel, such as a tugboat, to aid in identifying its size, number of barges in tow, etc.
rang+er ('reɪndʒə) *n.* **1.** *Brit.* an official in charge of a royal forest, park, estate, etc. **2.** *Originally U.S.* a person employed to patrol a State or national park or forest. Brit. equivalent: **warden. 3.** *U.S.* one of a body of armed troops employed to police a State or district: *a Texas ranger.* **4.** (in the U.S. and certain other armies) a commando specially trained in making raids. **5.** a person who wanders about large areas of country; a rover.
Rang+er[1] *or* **Rang+er Guide** ('reɪndʒə) *n. Brit.* a member of the senior branch of the Guides.
Rang+er[2] ('reɪndʒə) *n.* any of a series of nine American lunar probes launched between 1961 and 1965, three of which transmitted to earth photographs of the moon.
rang+ing pole *or* **rod** *n.* a pole for marking positions in surveying. Also called: **range pole, rod.**
Ran+goon (ræŋ'guːn) *n.* the capital and chief port of Burma: an industrial city and transport centre; dominated by the gold-covered Shwe Dagon pagoda, 112 m (368 ft.) high. Pop.: 2 055 365 (1973 est.).
rang·y ('reɪndʒɪ) *adj.* **rang·i+er, rang·i+est. 1.** (of animals or people) having long slender limbs. **2.** adapted to wandering or roaming. **3.** allowing considerable freedom of movement; spacious; roomy. —'**rang·i+ly** *adv.* —'**rang·i+ness** *n.*
ra·ni *or* **ra+nee** ('rɑːnɪ) *n.* (in oriental countries, esp. India) a queen or princess; the wife of a rajah. [C17: from Hindi: queen, from Sanskrit *rājñī,* feminine of *rājan* RAJAH]
Ran·jit Singh ('rʌndʒɪt 'sɪŋ) *n.* called *the Lion of the Punjab.* 1780–1839; founder of the Sikh kingdom in the Punjab.
rank[1] (ræŋk) *n.* **1.** a position, esp. an official one, within a social organization, esp. the armed forces: *the rank of captain.* **2.** high social or other standing; status. **3.** a line or row of people or things. **4.** a line of soldiers drawn up abreast of each other. Compare **file**[1] (sense 5). **5.** any of the eight horizontal rows of squares on a chessboard. **6.** *Music.* a set of organ pipes controlled by the same stop. **7.** *Maths.* (of a matrix) the number of rows (or columns) of the nonzero determinant of greatest order that can be extracted from the matrix. **8. break ranks.** *Military.* to fall out of line, esp. when under attack. **9. close ranks.** to maintain discipline or solidarity, esp. in anticipation of attack. **10. pull rank.** to get one's own way by virtue of one's superior position or rank. ~*vb.* **11.** (*tr.*) to arrange (people or things) in rows or lines; range. **12.** to accord or be accorded a specific position in an organization, society, or group. **13.** *U.S.* to take precedence or surpass in rank: *the colonel ranks at this camp.* [C16: from Old French *ranc* row, rank, of Germanic origin; compare Old High German *hring* circle]
rank[2] (ræŋk) *adj.* **1.** showing vigorous and profuse growth: *rank weeds.* **2.** highly offensive or disagreeable, esp. in smell or taste. **3.** (*prenominal*) complete or absolute; utter: *a rank outsider.* **4.** coarse or vulgar; gross: *his language was rank.* [Old English *ranc* straight, noble; related to Old Norse *rakkr* upright, Dutch, Swedish *rank* tall and thin, weak] —'**rank+ly** *adv.* —'**rank+ness** *n.*
Rank (*German* raŋk) *n.* **Ot·to** ('ɔto). 1884–1939, Austrian psychoanalyst, noted for his theory that the trauma of birth may be reflected in certain forms of mental illness.
rank and file *n.* **1.** the ordinary soldiers of an army, excluding the officers. **2.** the great mass or majority of any group or organization, as opposed to the leadership. **3.** (*modifier*) of, relating to, or characteristic of the rank and file: *rank-and-file opinion; rank-and-file support.*
rank+er ('ræŋkə) *n.* **1.** a soldier in the ranks. **2.** a commissioned officer who entered service as a recruit, esp. in the army. **3.** a person who ranks.
Ran·kine scale ('ræŋkɪn) *n.* an absolute scale of temperature in which the unit of temperature is equal to that on the Fahrenheit scale and the zero value of temperature is equal to −459.67°F. Compare **Kelvin scale.** [C19: named after W. J. M. *Rankine* (1820–72), Scottish physicist]
rank+ing ('ræŋkɪŋ) *adj.* **1.** *Chiefly U.S.* prominent; high ranking. ~*n.* **2.** a position on a scale; rating: *a ranking in a tennis tournament.*
ran+kle ('ræŋkᵊl) *vb.* (*intr.*) to cause severe and continuous irritation, anger, or bitterness; fester: *his failure to win still rankles.* [C14 *ranclen,* from Old French *draoncler* to fester, from *draoncle* ulcer, from Latin *dracunculus* small serpent, from *dracō* serpent; see DRAGON]
ran+sack ('rænsæk) *vb.* (*tr.*) **1.** to search through every part of (a house, box, etc.); examine thoroughly. **2.** to plunder; pillage. [C13: from Old Norse *rann* house + *saka* to search, SEEK] —'**ran+sack+er** *n.*
ran+som ('rænsəm) *n.* **1.** the release of captured prisoners, property, etc., on payment of a stipulated price. **2.** the price demanded or stipulated for such a release. **3.** rescue or redemption of any kind. **4. hold to ransom. a.** to keep (prisoners, property, etc.) in confinement until payment for their release is made or received. **b.** to attempt to force (a person or persons) to comply with one's demands. **5. a king's ransom.** a very large amount of money or valuables. ~*vb.* (*tr.*) **6.** to pay a stipulated price and so obtain the release of (prisoners, property, etc.). **7.** to set free (prisoners, property, etc.) upon receiving the payment demanded. **8.** to redeem; rescue: *Christ ransomed men from sin.* [C14: from Old French *ransoun,* from Latin *redemptiō* a buying back, REDEMPTION] —'**ran+som+er** *n.*
Ran·some ('rænsəm) *n.* **Ar·thur.** 1884–1967, English writer, best known for his books for children, including *Swallows and Amazons* (1930) and *Great Northern?* (1947).
rant (rænt) *vb.* **1.** to utter (something) in loud, violent, or bombastic tones. **2.** (*intr.*) *Chiefly Scot.* to make merry; frolic. ~*n.* **3.** loud, declamatory, or extravagant speech; bombast. **4.** *Chiefly Scot.* a wild gay revel. [C16: from Dutch *ranten* to rave; related to German *ranzen* to gambol] —'**rant+er** *n.* —'**rant+ing+ly** *adv.*
ra+nun+cu+la+ceous (rə,nʌŋkjʊ'leɪʃəs) *adj.* of, relating to, or belonging to the *Ranunculaceae,* a N temperate family of

flowering plants typically having flowers with five petals and numerous anthers and styles. The family includes the buttercup, clematis, hellebore, and columbine.

ra+nun+cu+lus (rəˈnʌŋkjʊləs) *n., pl.* **+lus·es** *or* **+li** (-ˌlaɪ). any ranunculaceous plant of the genus *Ranunculus,* having finely divided leaves and typically yellow five-petalled flowers. The genus includes buttercup, crowfoot, spearwort, and lesser celandine. [C16: from Latin: tadpole, from *rāna* a frog]

R.A.O.C. *abbrev. for* Royal Army Ordnance Corps.

rap[1] (ræp) *vb.* **raps, rap+ping, rapped. 1.** to strike (a fist, stick, etc.) against (something) with a sharp quick blow; knock: *he rapped at the door.* **2.** (*intr.*) to make a sharp loud sound, esp. by knocking. **3.** (*tr.; foll. by out*) to put (forth) in sharp rapid speech; utter in an abrupt fashion: *to rap out orders.* **4.** (*intr.*) *U.S. slang.* to talk, esp. volubly. **5. rap over the knuckles.** to reprimand. ~*n.* **6.** a sharp quick blow or the sound produced by such a blow. **7.** *U.S. slang.* voluble talk; chatter: *stop your rap.* **8. beat the rap.** *U.S. slang.* to escape punishment or be acquitted of a crime. **9. take the rap.** *Slang.* to suffer the punishment for a crime, whether guilty or not. [C14: probably of Scandinavian origin; compare Swedish *rappa* to beat]

rap[2] (ræp) *n.* (*used with a negative*) the least amount (esp. in the phrase **not to care a rap**). [C18: probably from *ropaire* counterfeit coin formerly current in Ireland]

rap[3] (ræp) *vb., n. Austral. informal.* a variant spelling of **wrap** (senses 7, 11).

ra+pa+cious (rəˈpeɪʃəs) *adj.* **1.** practising pillage or rapine. **2.** greedy or grasping. **3.** (of animals, esp. birds) subsisting by catching living prey. [C17: from Latin *rapāx* grasping, from *rapere* to seize] —**ra+ˈpa+cious+ly** *adv.* —**ra+pac+i·ty** (rəˈpæsɪtɪ) *or* **ra+ˈpa+cious+ness** *n.*

Ra·pac·ki (*Polish* raˈpatski) *n.* **Ad·am** (ˈadam). 1909–70, Polish politician. As foreign minister (1956–68), he proposed the establishment of a denuclearized zone in Europe (the **Rapacki Plan**).

Ra+pal+lo (*Italian* raˈpallo) *n.* a port and resort in NW Italy, in Liguria on the **Gulf of Rapallo** (an inlet of the Ligurian Sea): scene of the signing of two treaties after World War I. Pop.: 26 713 (1971).

Ra·pa Nu·i (ˈrɑːpɑː ˈnuːɪ) *n.* another name for **Easter Island.**

rape[1] (reɪp) *n.* **1.** *Criminal law.* the offence of forcing a woman to submit to sexual intercourse against her will. See also **statutory rape. 2.** the act of despoiling a country in warfare; rapine. **3.** any violation or abuse: *the rape of justice.* **4.** *Archaic.* abduction: *the rape of the Sabine women.* ~*vb.* (*mainly tr.*) **5.** *Criminal law.* to commit rape upon (a person). **6.** (*also intr.*) to plunder or despoil (a place) in war. **7.** *Archaic.* to carry off by force; abduct. [C14: from Latin *rapere* to seize] —**ˈrap+ist** *n.*

rape[2] (reɪp) *n.* a Eurasian cruciferous plant, *Brassica napus,* that is cultivated for its seeds, which yield a useful oil, and as a fodder plant. Also called: **colza, cole.** [C14: from Latin *rāpum* turnip]

rape[3] (reɪp) *n.* (*often pl.*) the skins and stalks of grapes left after wine-making. [C17: from French *râpe,* of Germanic origin; compare Old High German *raspōn* to scrape together]

rape oil *n.* oil extracted from rapeseed, used as a lubricant, as a constituent of soaps, etc. Also called: **rapeseed oil, colza oil.**

rape+seed (ˈreɪpˌsiːd) *n.* the seed of the rape plant.

Raph·a·el (ˈræfeɪəl) *n.* **1.** *Bible.* one of the archangels. **2.** original name *Raffaello Santi* or *Sanzio.* 1483–1520, Italian painter and architect, regarded as one of the greatest artists of the High Renaissance. His many paintings include the *Sistine Madonna* (?1513) and the *Transfiguration* (unfinished, 1520). —**ˌRaph·a·el+ˈesque** *adj.*

ra+phe (ˈreɪfɪ) *n., pl.* **+phae** (-fiː). **1.** an elongated ridge of conducting tissue along the side of certain seeds. **2.** a longitudinal groove on the valve of a diatom. **3.** *Anatomy.* a connecting ridge, as that between the two halves of the medulla oblongata. [C18: via New Latin from Greek *rhaphē* a seam, from *rhaptein* to sew together]

raph·i·a (ˈræfɪə) *n.* a variant spelling of **raffia.**

ra+phide (ˈreɪfaɪd) *or* **ra+phis** (ˈreɪfɪs) *n., pl.* **raph·i·des** (ˈræfɪˌdiːz). any of numerous needle-shaped crystals, usually of calcium oxalate, that occur in many plant cells as a metabolic product. [C18: from French, from Greek *rhaphis* needle]

rap+id (ˈræpɪd) *adj.* **1.** (of an action or movement) performed or occurring during a short interval of time; quick: *a rapid transformation.* **2.** characterized by high speed: *rapid movement.* **3.** acting or moving quickly; fast: *a rapid worker.* [C17: from Latin *rapidus* tearing away, from *rapere* to seize; see RAPE[1]] —**ˈrap+id+ly** *adv.* —**ra+pid+i·ty** (rəˈpɪdɪtɪ) *or* **ˈrap+id+ness** *n.*

rap+id eye move+ment *n.* movement of the eyeballs under closed eyelids during sleep, which occurs while the sleeper is dreaming. Abbrev.: **REM.**

rap+id fire *n.* **1.** a fast rate of gunfire. ~*adj.* **rap·id-fire. 2. a.** firing shots rapidly. **b.** denoting medium-calibre mounted guns designed for rapid fire. **3.** done, delivered, or occurring in rapid succession.

rap+ids (ˈræpɪdz) *pl. n.* part of a river where the current is very fast and turbulent.

ra+pi+er (ˈreɪpɪə) *n.* **1.** a long narrow two-edged sword with a guarded hilt, used as a thrusting weapon, popular in the 16th and 17th centuries. **2.** a smaller single-edged 18th-century sword, used principally in France. [C16: from Old French *espee rapiere,* literally: rasping sword; see RASP] —**ˈra+pi+er+ˌlike** *adj.*

rap+ine (ˈræpaɪn) *n.* the seizure of property by force; pillage. [C15: from Latin *rapīna* plundering, from *rapere* to snatch]

rap+pa+ree (ˌræpəˈriː) *n.* **1.** an Irish irregular soldier of the late 17th century. **2.** *Obsolete.* any plunderer or robber. [C17: from Irish *rapairidhe* pike, probably from English RAPIER]

rap+pee (ræˈpiː) *n.* a moist English snuff of the 18th and 19th centuries. [C18: from French *tabac râpé,* literally: scraped tobacco, from *râper* to scrape; see RAPE[3], RASP]

rap+pel (ræˈpɛl) *vb.* **+pels, +pel+ling, +pelled. 1.** (*intr.*) *Mountaineering.* to descend a steep or vertical drop by means of a rope secured above and coiled once around one's body or through karabiners attached to one's body in order to control the speed of the descent. ~*n.* **2.** Also called: **abseil.** an instance or the technique of rappelling. **3.** (formerly) a drumbeat to call soldiers to arms. [C19: from French, from *rappeler* to call back, from Latin *appellāre* to summon]

rap+per (ˈræpə) *n.* something used for rapping, such as a knocker on a door.

rap+port (ræˈpɔː) *n.* (often foll. by *with*) a sympathetic relationship or understanding. See also **en rapport.** [C15: from French, from *rapporter* to bring back, from RE- + *aporter,* from Latin *apportāre,* from *ad* to + *portāre* to carry]

rap+por+teur (ˌræpɔːˈtɜː) *n.* a person appointed by a committee to prepare reports of meetings or carry out an investigation. [French, literally: recorder, reporter]

rap+proche+ment *French.* (raprɔʃˈmã) *n.* a resumption of friendly relations, esp. between two countries.

rap+scal+lion (ræpˈskæljən) *n.* a disreputable person; rascal or rogue. [C17: from earlier *rascallion;* see RASCAL]

rapt[1] (ræpt) *adj.* **1.** totally absorbed; engrossed; spellbound, esp. through or as if through emotion: *rapt with wonder.* **2.** characterized by or proceeding from rapture: *a rapt smile.* [C14: from Latin *raptus* carried away, from *rapere* to seize; see RAPE[1]] —**ˈrapt+ly** *adv.*

rapt[2] (ræpt) *adj. Austral. informal.* a variant spelling of **wrapped** (sense 2).

rap+tor (ˈræptə) *n.* another name for **bird of prey.** [C17: from Latin: plunderer, from *rapere* to take by force]

rap+to+ri·al (ræpˈtɔːrɪəl) *adj. Zoology.* **1.** (of the feet of birds) adapted for seizing prey. **2.** (esp. of birds) feeding on prey; predatory. **3.** of or relating to birds of prey. [C19: from Latin *raptor* a robber, from *rapere* to snatch]

rap+ture (ˈræptʃə) *n.* **1.** the state of mind resulting from feelings of high emotion; joyous ecstasy. **2.** (*often pl.*) an expression of ecstatic joy. **3.** *Archaic.* the act of transporting a person from one sphere of existence to another, esp. from earth to heaven. ~*vb.* **4.** (*tr.*) *Archaic or literary.* to entrance; enrapture. [C17: from Medieval Latin *raptūra,* from Latin *raptus* RAPT]

rap+tur+ous (ˈræptʃərəs) *adj.* experiencing or manifesting ecstatic joy or delight. —**ˈrap+tur+ous+ly** *adv.* —**ˈrap+tur+ous+ness** *n.*

ra·ra a·vis (ˈrɛərə ˈeɪvɪs) *n., pl.* **ra+rae a·ves** (ˈrɛəriː ˈeɪviːz). an unusual, uncommon, or exceptional person or thing. [Latin: rare bird]

rare[1] (rɛə) *adj.* **1.** not widely known; not frequently used or experienced; uncommon or unusual: *a rare word.* **2.** occurring seldom: *a rare appearance.* **3.** not widely distributed; not generally occurring: *a rare herb.* **4.** (of a gas, esp. the atmosphere at high altitudes) having a low density; thin; rarefied. **5.** uncommonly great; extreme: *kind to a rare degree.* **6.** exhibiting uncommon excellence; superlatively good or fine: *rare skill.* **7.** highly valued because of its uncommonness: *a rare prize.* [C14: from Latin *rārus* sparse] —**ˈrare+ness** *n.*

rare[2] (rɛə) *adj.* (of meat, esp. beef) undercooked. [Old English *hrēr;* perhaps related to *hreaw* RAW]

rare+bit (ˈrɛəbɪt) *n.* another term for **Welsh rabbit.** [C18: by folk etymology from (WELSH) RABBIT; see RARE[2], BIT[1]]

rare earth *n.* **1.** any oxide of a lanthanide. **2.** Also called: **rare-earth element.** another name for **lanthanide.**

ra+ree show (ˈrɛəriː) *n.* **1.** a street show or carnival. **2.** another name for **peepshow.** [C17: *raree* from RARE[1]]

rar+e·fac+tion (ˌrɛərɪˈfækʃən) *or* **rar+e·fi+ca+tion** (ˌrɛərɪfɪˈkeɪʃən) *n.* the act or process of making less dense or the state of being less dense. —**ˌrar+e·ˈfac+tion+al, ˌrar+e·fi+ˈca+tion+al,** *or* **ˌrar+e·ˈfac+tive** *adj.*

rar+e·fied (ˈrɛərɪˌfaɪd) *adj.* **1.** exalted in nature or character; lofty: *a rarefied spiritual existence.* **2.** current within only a small group; esoteric or exclusive.

rar+e·fy (ˈrɛərɪˌfaɪ) *vb.* **+fies, +fy+ing, +fied.** to make or become rarer or less dense; thin out. [C14: from Old French *raréfier,* from Latin *rārēfacere,* from *rārus* RARE[1] + *facere* to make] —**ˈrar+e·ˌfi+a·ble** *adj.* —**ˈrar+e·ˌfi+er** *n.*

rare gas *n.* another name for **inert gas.**

rare+ly (ˈrɛəlɪ) *adv.* **1.** hardly ever; seldom: *I'm rarely in town these days.* **2.** to an unusual degree; exceptionally. **3.** *Brit. dialect.* uncommonly well; excellently: *he did rarely at market yesterday.*

rare+ripe (ˈrɛəˌraɪp) *U.S.* ~*adj.* **1.** ripening early. ~*n.* **2.** a fruit or vegetable that ripens early. [C18: *rare,* variant of RATHE + RIPE]

rar+ing (ˈrɛərɪŋ) *adj.* ready; willing; enthusiastic (esp. in the phrase **raring to go**). [C20: from *rare,* variant of REAR[2]]

rar+i·ty (ˈrɛərɪtɪ) *n., pl.* **·ties. 1.** a rare person or thing, esp. something interesting or valued because it is uncommon. **2.** the state or quality of being rare.

Ra+ro+ton+ga (ˌrɛərəˈtɒŋgə) *n.* an island in the S Pacific, in the SW Cook Islands: the chief island of the group. Chief settlement: Avarua. Pop.: 9971 (1966). Area: 67 sq. km (26 sq. miles).

R.A.S. *abbrev. for:* **1.** Royal Agricultural Society. **2.** Royal Astronomical Society.

ras+bo+ra (ræzˈbɔːrə) *n.* any of the small cyprinid fishes constituting the genus *Rasbora* of tropical Asia and East Africa. Many species are brightly coloured and are popular aquarium fishes. [from New Latin, from an East Indian language]

R.A.S.C. *abbrev. for* (the former) Royal Army Service Corps, now called Royal Corps of Transport.

ras+cal (ˈrɑːskəl) *n.* **1.** a disreputable person; villain. **2.** a mischievous or impish rogue. **3.** an affectionate or mildly reproving term for a child or old man: *you little rascal; the wicked old rascal kissed her.* **4.** *Obsolete.* a person of lowly birth. ~*adj.* **5.** (*prenominal*) *Obsolete.* **a.** belonging to the mob or rabble. **b.** dishonest; knavish. [C14: from Old French *rascaille* rabble, perhaps from Old Norman French *rasque* mud, filth]

ras+cal+i+ty (rɑːˈskælɪtɪ) *n., pl.* **·ties.** mischievous, disreputable, or dishonest character, behaviour, or action.

ras+cal+ly (ˈrɑːskəlɪ) *adj.* **1.** dishonest or mean; base. **2.** *Archaic.* (esp. of places, etc.) wretchedly unpleasant; miserable. ~*adv.* **3.** in a dishonest or mean fashion.

rase (reɪz) *vb.* a variant spelling of **raze.** —**ˈras+er** *n.*

rash[1] (ræʃ) *adj.* **1.** acting without due consideration or thought; impetuous. **2.** characterized by or resulting from excessive haste or impetuosity: *a rash word.* [C14: from Old High German *rasc* hurried, clever; related to Old Norse *roskr* brave] —**ˈrash+ly** *adv.* —**ˈrash+ness** *n.*

rash[2] (ræʃ) *n.* **1.** *Pathol.* any skin eruption. **2.** a series of unpleasant and unexpected occurrences: *a rash of forest fires.* [C18: from Old French *rasche,* from *raschier* to scratch, from Latin *rādere* to scrape] —**ˈrash+ˌlike** *adj.*

rash+er (ˈræʃə) *n.* a thin slice of bacon or ham. [C16: of unknown origin]

Rasht (ræʃt) *or* **Resht** *n.* a city in NW Iran, near the Caspian Sea: agricultural and commercial centre in a rice-growing area. Pop.: 175 000 (1973 est.).

Rask (*Danish* rasg) *n.* **Ras·mus Chris·tian** (ˈrasmus ˈkresdjan). 1787–1832, Danish philologist. He pioneered comparative philology with his work on Old Norse (1818).

Ras·mus·sen (*Danish* ˈrasmusən) *n.* **Knud Jo·han Vic·tor** (knuð joˈhan ˈviktər). 1879–1933, Danish arctic explorer and ethnologist. He led several expeditions through the Arctic in support of his theory that the North American Indians were originally migrants from Asia.

ra+so+ri·al (rəˈsɔːrɪəl) *adj.* (of birds such as domestic poultry) adapted for scratching the ground for food. [C19: from New Latin *Rasores* such birds, from Latin *rādere* to scrape]

rasp (rɑːsp) *n.* **1.** a harsh grating noise. **2.** a coarse file with rows of raised teeth. ~*vb.* **3.** (*tr.*) to scrape or rub (something) roughly, esp. with a rasp; abrade. **4.** to utter with or make a harsh grating noise. **5.** to irritate (one's nerves or senses); grate (upon). [C16: from Old French *raspe,* of Germanic origin; compare Old High German *raspōn* to scrape] —**ˈrasp+er** *n.* —**ˈrasp+ish** *adj.*

ras+pa+tor·y (ˈraspətərɪ, -trɪ) *n., pl.* **+ies.** a surgical instrument for abrading; surgeon's rasp. [C16: from Medieval Latin *raspatorium*]

rasp+ber·ry (ˈrɑːzbərɪ, -brɪ) *n., pl.* **·ries. 1.** any of the prickly shrubs of the rosaceous genus *Rubus,* such as *R. strigosus* of E North America and *R. idaeus* of Europe, that have pinkish-white flowers and typically red berry-like fruits (drupelets). See also **bramble. 2. a.** the fruit of any such plant. **b.** (*as modifier*): *raspberry jelly.* **3. black raspberry.** Popular name: **blackcap. a.** a related plant, *Rubus occidentalis,* of E North America, that has black berry-like fruits. **b.** the fruit of this plant. **4. a.** a dark purplish-red colour. **b.** (*as adj.*): *a raspberry dress.* **5.** a spluttering noise made with the tongue and lips to express contempt (esp. in the phrase **blow a raspberry**). [C17: from earlier *raspis* raspberry, of unknown origin + BERRY]

rasp+ing (ˈrɑːspɪŋ) *or* **rasp·y** *adj.* (esp. of a noise) harsh or grating; rough.

rasp+ings (ˈrɑːspɪŋz) *pl. n.* browned breadcrumbs for coating fish and other foods before frying, etc.

Ras·pu·tin (ræˈspjuːtɪn; *Russian* rasˈputin) *n.* **Gri·go·ri E·fi·mo·vich** (griˈgɔrij jɪˈfiməvitʃ). ?1871–1916, Siberian peasant monk, notorious for his debauchery, who wielded great influence over Tsarina Alexandra. He was assassinated by a group of Russian noblemen.

ras·se (ˈræsɪ, ræs) *n.* a small civet, *Viverricula indica,* of S and SE Asia. [C19: from Javanese *rase*]

Ras+ta+far+i·an (ˌræstəˈfeərɪən) *n.* **1.** a member of a Jamaican cult that regards **Ras Tafari** (the former emperor of Ethiopia, Haile Selassie) as God. ~*adj.* **2.** of, characteristic of, or relating to the Rastafarians.

ras+ter (ˈræstə) *n.* a pattern of horizontal scanning lines traced by an electron beam, esp. on a television screen. [C20: via German from Latin: rake, from *rādere* to scrape]

rat (ræt) *n.* **1.** any of numerous long-tailed murine rodents, esp. of the genus *Rattus,* that are similar to but larger than mice and are now distributed all over the world. See also **brown rat, black rat. 2.** *Informal.* a person who deserts his friends or associates, esp. in time of trouble. **3.** *Informal.* a worker who works during a strike; blackleg; scab. **4.** *Slang, chiefly U.S.* an informer; stool pigeon. **5.** *Slang.* a despicable person. **6. smell a rat.** to have suspicions of some treacherous practice. ~*vb.* **rats, rat+ting, rat+ted. 7.** (*intr.;* usually foll. by *on*) **a.** to divulge secret information (about); betray the trust (of). **b.** to default (on); abandon: *he ratted on the project at the last minute.* **8.** to hunt and kill rats. ~See also **rats.** [Old English *rætt;* related to Old Saxon *ratta,* Old High German *rato*] —**ˈrat+ˌlike** *adj.*

ra+ta (ˈrɑːtə) *n.* either of two New Zealand myrtaceous forest trees, *Metrosideros robusta* or *M. lucida,* having crimson flowers and hard wood. [C19: from Maori]

rat+a·ble *or* **rate+a·ble** (ˈreɪtəbəl) *adj.* **1.** able to be rated or evaluated. **2.** *Brit.* (of property, etc.) liable to payment of rates. —**ˌrat+a·ˈbil+i·ty, ˌrate+a·ˈbil+i·ty** *or* **ˈrat+a·ble+ness, ˈrate+a·ble+ness** *n.* —**ˈrat+a·bly** *or* **ˈrate+a·bly** *adv.*

rat+a·ble val·ue *or* **rate+a·ble val·ue** *n. Brit.* a fixed value assigned to a property by a local authority, on the basis of which variable annual rates are charged.

rat·a·fi·a (ˌrætəˈfɪə) *or* **rat·a+fee** (ˌrætəˈfiː) *n.* **1.** any liquor made from fruit or from brandy with added fruit. **2.** a flavouring essence made from almonds. **3.** *Chiefly Brit.* Also called: **ratafia biscuit.** a small macaroon flavoured with almonds. [C17: from West Indian Creole French]

ra+tal (ˈreɪtəl) *Brit.* ~*n.* **1.** the amount on which rates are assessed; ratable value. ~*adj.* **2.** of or relating to rates (local taxation). [C19: see RATE[1]]

ra+tan (ræˈtæn) *n.* a variant spelling of **rattan.**

rat·a·tat·tat (ˈrætəˌtætˈtæt) *or* **rat·a·tat** (ˈrætəˈtæt) *n.* the sound of knocking on a door.

ra+ta+touille (rætəˈtwiː) *n.* a vegetable casserole made of tomatoes, aubergines, peppers, etc., fried in oil and stewed slowly. [from French, from *touiller* to stir, from Latin *tudiculāre,* from *tudes* hammer]

rat+bag (ˈrætˌbæg) *n. Slang, chiefly Austral.* a contemptible person: used as a term of abuse or disgust.

rat+bag+ger·y (ˈrætˌbægərɪ) *n. Austral. slang.* rascally behaviour.

rat+bite fe+ver *or* **dis+ease** (ˈrætˌbaɪt) *n. Pathol.* an acute infectious febrile disease caused by the bite of a rat infected with either of two pathogenic bacteria (*Streptobacillus moniliformis* or *Spirillum minus*).

rat-catch·er *n.* a person whose job is to destroy or drive away vermin, esp. rats.

ratch+et (ˈrætʃɪt) *n.* **1.** a device in which a toothed rack or wheel is engaged by a pawl to permit motion in one direction only. **2.** the toothed rack or wheel forming part of such a device. [C17: from French *rochet,* from Old French *rocquet* blunt head of a lance, of Germanic origin: compare Old High German *rocko* distaff]

rate[1] (reɪt) *n.* **1.** a quantity or amount considered in relation to or measured against another quantity or amount: *a rate of 70 miles an hour.* **2.** a price or charge with reference to a standard or scale: *rate of interest; rate of discount.* **3.** a charge made per unit for a commodity, service, etc. **4.** See **rates. 5.** the relative speed of progress or change of something variable; pace: *he works at a great rate; the rate of production has doubled.* **6. a.** relative quality; class or grade. **b.** (*in combination*): *first-rate ideas.* **7.** *Statistics.* a measure of the frequency of occurrence of a given event, such as births and deaths, usually expressed as the number of times the event occurs for every thousand of the total population considered. **8.** a wage calculated against a unit of time. **9.** the amount of gain or loss of a timepiece. **10. at any rate.** in any case; at all events; anyway. ~*vb.* (*mainly tr.*) **11.** (*also intr.*) to assign or receive a position on a scale of relative values; rank: *he is rated fifth in the world.* **12.** to estimate the value of; evaluate: *we rate your services highly.* **13.** to be worthy of; deserve: *this hotel does not rate four stars.* **14.** to consider; regard: *I rate him among my friends.* **15.** *Brit.* to assess the value of (property) for the purpose of local taxation. **16.** *Slang.* to think highly of: *the clients do not rate the new system.* [C15: from Old French, from Medieval Latin *rata,* from Latin *prō ratā parte* according to a fixed proportion, from *ratus* fixed, from *rērī* to think, decide]

rate[2] (reɪt) *vb.* (*tr.*) to scold or criticize severely; rebuke harshly. [C14: perhaps related to Swedish *rata* to chide]

rate+a·ble (ˈreɪtəbəl) *adj.* a variant spelling of **ratable.**

ra+teen (ræˈtiːn) *n.* a variant spelling of **ratine.**

ra+tel (ˈreɪtəl) *n.* a musteline mammal, *Mellivora capensis,* inhabiting wooded regions of Africa and S Asia. It has a massive body, strong claws, and a thick coat that is paler on the back and feeds on honey and small animals. Also called: **honey badger.** [C18: from Afrikaans]

rate of ex+change *n.* See **exchange rate.**

rate+pay·er (ˈreɪtˌpeɪə) *n. Brit.* a person who pays local rates, esp. a householder.

rates (reɪts) *pl. n. Brit.* a tax on property levied by a local authority.

rat+fink (ˈrætˌfɪŋk) *n. U.S. slang.* a contemptible or undesirable person. [C20: from RAT + FINK]

rat+fish (ˈrætˌfɪʃ) *n., pl.* **+fish** *or* **+fish·es. 1.** another name for **rabbitfish** (sense 1). **2.** a chimaera, *Hydrolagus colliei,* of the North Pacific Ocean, which has a long narrow tail.

ratha (rʌt) *n.* (in India) a four-wheeled carriage drawn by horses or bullocks; chariot. [Hindi]

rathe (reɪð) *or* **rath** (rɑːθ) *adj. Archaic or literary.* **1.** blossoming or ripening early in the season. **2.** eager or prompt. [Old English *hrathe;* related to Old High German *hrado,* Old Norse *hrathr*]

Ra·the·nau (*German* ˈraːtənau) *n.* **Wal·ther** (ˈvaltər). 1867–1922, German industrialist and statesman: he organized the German war industries during World War I, became minister of reconstruction (1921) and of foreign affairs (1922), and was largely responsible for the treaty of Rapallo with Russia. His assassination by right-wing extremists caused a furore.

ra+ther (ˈrɑːðə) *adv.* (*in senses 1-4, not used with a negative*) **1.**

relatively or fairly; somewhat: *it's rather dull.* **2.** to a significant or noticeable extent; quite: *she's rather pretty.* **3.** to a limited extent or degree: *I rather thought that was the case.* **4.** with better or more just cause: *this text is rather to be deleted than rewritten.* **5.** more readily or willingly; sooner: *I would rather not see you tomorrow.* ~*sentence connector.* **6.** on the contrary: *it's not cold. Rather, it's very hot indeed.* ~*sentence substitute.* ('rɑː'ðɜː) **7.** an expression of strong affirmation, often in answer to a question: *Is it worth seeing? Rather!* [Old English *hrathor* comparative of *hræth* READY, quick; related to Old Norse *hrathr*]

Usage. Both *would* and *had* are used with *rather* in sentences such as *I would rather* (or *had rather*) *go to the film than to the play. Had rather* is less common and now widely regarded as slightly old-fashioned.

rat·i·fy ('rætɪˌfaɪ) *vb.* **-fies, -fy·ing, -fied.** (*tr.*) to give formal approval or consent to. [C14: via Old French from Latin *ratus* fixed (see RATE[1]) + *facere* to make] —'**rat·i·ˌfi·a·ble** *n.* —ˌ**rat·i·fi·'ca·tion** *n.* —'**rat·i·ˌfi·er** *n.*

ra·tine, ra·teen, rat·teen (ræ'tiːn), *or* **rat·i·né** ('rætɪˌneɪ) *n.* a coarse loosely woven cloth. [C17: from French, from *ratine*, of obscure origin]

rat·ing[1] ('reɪtɪŋ) *n.* **1.** a classification according to order or grade; ranking. **2.** (in certain navies) a sailor who holds neither commissioned nor warrant rank; an ordinary seaman. **3.** *Sailing.* a handicap assigned to a racing boat based on its dimensions, sail area, weight, draught, etc. **4.** the estimated financial or credit standing of a business enterprise or individual. **5.** *Radio, television, etc.* a figure based on statistical sampling indicating what proportion of the total listening and viewing audience tune in to a specific programme or network.

rat·ing[2] ('reɪtɪŋ) *n.* a sharp scolding or rebuke.

ra·ti·o ('reɪʃɪˌəʊ) *n., pl.* **-ti·os. 1.** a relationship that indicates the extent to which one class of objects exists compared to another: *the ratio of boys to girls.* **2.** *Maths.* a quotient of two numbers or quantities. See also **proportion** (sense 6). [C17: from Latin: a reckoning, from *rērī* to think; see REASON]

ra·ti·oc·i·nate (ˌrætɪ'ɒsɪˌneɪt) *vb.* (*intr.*) to think or argue logically and methodically; reason. [C17: from Latin *ratiōcinārī* to calculate, from *ratiō* REASON] —ˌ**ra·ti·ˌoc·i·'na·tion** *n.* —'**ra·ti·oc·i·na·tive** *adj.* —ˌ**ra·ti·'oc·i·ˌna·tor** *n.*

ra·tion ('ræʃən) *n.* **1. a.** a fixed allowance of food, provisions, etc., esp. a statutory one for civilians in time of scarcity or soldiers in time of war: *a tea ration.* **b.** (*as modifier*): *a ration book.* **2.** a sufficient or adequate amount: *you've had your ration of television for today.* ~*vb.* (*tr.*) **3.** (often foll. by *out*) to distribute (provisions), esp. to an army. **4.** to restrict the distribution or consumption of (a commodity) by (people): *the government has rationed sugar; sugar is short, so I'll have to ration you.* [C18: via French from Latin *ratiō* calculation; see REASON]

ra·tion·al ('ræʃənᵊl) *adj.* **1.** using reason or logic in thinking out a problem. **2.** in accordance with the principles of logic or reason; reasonable. **3.** of sound mind; sane: *the patient seemed quite rational.* **4.** endowed with the capacity to reason; capable of logical thought: *man is a rational being.* **5.** *Maths.* (of an expression, equation, etc.) containing no variable either in irreducible radical form or raised to a fractional power. [C14: from Latin *ratiōnālis*, from *ratiō* REASON] —'**ra·tion·al·ly** *adv.* —'**ra·tion·al·ness** *n.*

ra·tion·ale (ˌræʃə'nɑːl) *n.* a reasoned exposition, esp. one defining the fundamental reasons for a course of action, belief, etc. [C17: from New Latin, from Latin *ratiōnālis*]

ra·tion·al·ism ('ræʃənəˌlɪzəm) *n.* **1.** the doctrine that reason is the proper basis for regulating morals, conduct, etc. **2.** *Philosophy.* **a.** the doctrine that knowledge is acquired by reason without regard to experience. **b.** the Cartesian doctrine that self-evident propositions and their consequences form the basis of all knowledge. Compare **empiricism, intuitionism. 3.** *Theol.* the doctrine that human reason, rather than divine revelation, is the basis for establishing religious truth. —'**ra·tion·al·ist** *n.* —ˌ**ra·tion·al·'is·tic** *adj.* —ˌ**ra·tion·al·'is·ti·cal·ly** *adv.*

ra·tion·al·i·ty (ˌræʃə'nælɪtɪ) *n., pl.* **-ties. 1.** the state or quality of being rational or logical. **2.** the possession or utilization of reason or logic. **3.** a reasonable or logical opinion.

ra·tion·al·ize *or* **ra·tion·al·ise** ('ræʃənəˌlaɪz) *vb.* **1.** to justify (one's actions, esp. discreditable actions, or beliefs) with plausible reasons, esp. after the event. **2.** to apply logic or reason to (something). **3.** (*tr.*) to eliminate unnecessary equipment, personnel, or processes from (a factory, etc.), in order to make it more efficient. **4.** (*tr.*) *Maths.* to eliminate one or more radicals without changing the value of (an expression) or the roots of (an equation). —ˌ**ra·tion·al·i·'za·tion** *or* ˌ**ra·tion·al·i·'sa·tion** *n.* —'**ra·tion·al·ˌiz·er** *or* '**ra·tion·al·ˌis·er** *n.*

ra·tion·al num·ber *n.* any real number of the form *a*/*b* where *a* and *b* are integers and *b* is not zero, as 7 or 7/3.

ra·tions ('ræʃənz) *pl. n.* (*sometimes sing.*) a fixed daily allowance of food, esp. to military personnel or when supplies are limited. See also **iron rations.**

Rat·is·bon ('rætɪzˌbɒn) *n.* the former English name for **Regensburg.**

rat·ite ('rætaɪt) *adj.* **1.** (of flightless birds) having a breastbone that lacks a keel for the attachment of flight muscles. **2.** of or denoting the flightless birds, formerly classified as a group (the *Ratitae*), that have a flat breastbone, feathers lacking vanes, and reduced wings. ~*n.* **3.** a bird, such as an ostrich, kiwi, or rhea, that belongs to this group; a flightless bird. [C19: from Latin *ratis* raft]

rat kan·ga·roo *n.* any of several ratlike kangaroos of the genera *Bettongia, Potorous, Aepyprymnus*, etc., that occur in Australia and Tasmania.

Rat·lam (rʌt'lɑːm) *n.* a city in NW India, in Madhya Pradesh. Pop.: 106 666 (1971).

rat·line *or* **rat·lin** ('rætlɪn) *n. Nautical.* any of a series of light lines tied across the shrouds of a sailing vessel for climbing aloft. [C15: of unknown origin]

RATO ('reɪtəʊ) *acronym for* rocket-assisted takeoff.

ra·toon *or* **rat·toon** (ræ'tuːn) *n.* **1.** a new shoot that grows from near the root or crown of crop plants, esp. the sugar cane, after the old growth has been cut back. ~*vb.* **2.** to propagate or cause to propagate by such a growth. [C18: from Spanish *retoño* young shoot, from RE- + *otoñar* to sprout in autumn, from *otoño* AUTUMN]

rat race *n.* a continual routine of hectic competitive activity: *working in the City is a real rat race.*

rats (ræts) *interj.* an exclamation of rejection or disdain.

rats·bane ('rætsˌbeɪn) *n.* rat poison, esp. arsenic oxide.

Rats·kel·ler *German.* ('rɑːtsˌkɛlər) *n.* **1.** the cellar of a town hall, esp. one used as a beer hall or restaurant. **2.** any similar establishment, esp. in the U.S. [German: from *Rat(haus)* town hall + *Keller* cellar]

rat snake *n.* any of various nonvenomous rodent-eating colubrid snakes, such as *Elaphe obsoleta* of North America and *Ptyas mucosus* of Asia.

rat-tail *n.* **1.** another name for **grenadier** (the fish). **2. a.** a horse's tail that has no hairs. **b.** a horse having such a tail. **3.** a style of spoon in which the line of the handle is prolonged in a tapering moulding along the back of the bowl. **4.** a kind of woodworking or metalworking file.

rat·tan *or* **ra·tan** (ræ'tæn) *n.* **1.** any of the climbing palms of the genus *Calamus* and related genera, having tough stems used for wickerwork and canes. **2.** the stems of such plants collectively. **3.** a stick made from one of these stems. [C17: from Malay *rōtan*]

rat-tat ('rætˌtæt) *n.* variant of **ratatat-tat.**

rat·teen (ræ'tiːn) *n.* a variant spelling of **ratine.**

rat·ter ('rætə) *n.* **1.** a dog or cat that catches and kills rats. **2.** another word for **rat** (senses 3, 4).

Rat·ti·gan ('rætɪgən) *n.* Sir **Ter·ence Mer·vyn.** 1911–77, English playwright. His plays include *The Winslow Boy* (1946), *Separate Tables* (1954), and *Ross* (1960).

rat·tish ('rætɪʃ) *adj.* of, resembling, or infested with rats.

rat·tle[1] ('rætᵊl) *vb.* **1.** to make or cause to make a rapid succession of short sharp sounds, as of loose pellets colliding when shaken in a container. **2.** to shake or cause to shake with such a sound: *the explosion rattled the windows.* **3.** to send, move, drive, etc., with such a sound: *the car rattled along the country road.* **4.** (*intr.*; foll. by *on*) to chatter idly; talk, esp. at length: *he rattled on about his work.* **5.** (*tr.*, foll. by *off, out*, etc.) to recite perfunctorily or rapidly. **6.** (*tr.*) *Informal.* to disconcert; make frightened or anxious. ~*n.* **7.** a rapid succession of short sharp sounds. **8.** a baby's toy filled with small pellets that rattle when shaken. **9.** a series of loosely connected horny segments on the tail of a rattlesnake, vibrated to produce a rattling sound. **10.** any of various European scrophulariaceous plants having a capsule in which the seeds rattle, such as *Pedicularis palustris* (**red rattle**) and *Rhinanthus minor* (**yellow rattle**). **11.** idle chatter. **12.** an idle chatterer. **13.** *Pathol.* another name for **rale.** [C14: from Middle Dutch *ratelen;* related to Middle High German *razzen*, of imitative origin] —'**rat·tler** *n.*

rat·tle[2] ('rætᵊl) *vb.* (*tr.*; often foll. by *down*) to fit (a vessel or its rigging) with ratlines. [C18: back formation from *rattling*, variant of RATLINE]

rat·tle·box ('rætᵊlˌbɒks) *n.* any of various tropical and subtropical leguminous plants that have inflated pods within which the seeds rattle.

rat·tle·brain ('rætᵊlˌbreɪn), **rat·tle·head,** *or* **rat·tle·pate** *n. Slang.* a light-minded person, full of idle talk.

rat·tle·snake ('rætᵊlˌsneɪk) *n.* any of the venomous New World snakes constituting the genera *Crotalus* and *Sistrurus*, such as *C. horridus* (**black** or **timber rattlesnake**): family *Crotalidae* (pit vipers). They have a series of loose horny segments on the tail that are vibrated to produce a buzzing or whirring sound. Informal name: **rattler.**

rat·tle·snake plan·tain *n.* any of various small temperate and tropical orchids of the genus *Goodyera*, having mottled or striped leaves and spikes of yellowish-white flowers.

rat·tle·trap ('rætᵊlˌtræp) *n. Informal.* a broken-down old vehicle, esp. an old car.

rat·tling ('rætlɪŋ) *adv. Informal.* (intensifier qualifying something good, fine, pleasant, etc.): *a rattling good lunch.*

rat·tly ('rætlɪ) *adj.* **-tli·er, -tli·est.** having a rattle; rattling.

rat·toon (ræ'tuːn) *n., vb.* a variant spelling of **ratoon.**

rat·trap ('rætˌtræp) *n.* **1.** a device for catching rats. **2.** *Informal.* a type of bicycle pedal having serrated steel foot pads and a toe clip.

rat·ty ('rætɪ) *adj.* **-ti·er, -ti·est. 1.** *Brit. slang.* irritable; annoyed. **2.** *Slang.* (of the hair) straggly, unkempt, or greasy. **3.** *U.S. slang.* shabby; dilapidated. **4.** *Austral. slang.* **a.** angry. **b.** mad. **5.** of, like, or full of rats. —'**rat·ti·ly** *adv.* —'**rat·ti·ness** *n.*

rau·cous ('rɔːkəs) *adj.* (of voices, cries, etc.) harshly or hoarsely loud. [C18: from Latin *raucus* hoarse] —'**rau·cous·ly** *adv.* —'**rau·cous·ness** *or* **rau·ci·ty** ('rɔːsɪtɪ) *n.*

raun·chy ('rɔːntʃɪ) *adj.* **-chi·er, -chi·est.** *U.S. slang.* lecherous or smutty. [C20: of unknown origin] —'**raun·chi·ness** *n.*

rau·wol·fi·a (rɔː'wʊlfɪə, raʊ-) *n.* **1.** any tropical tree or shrub of the apocynaceous genus *Rauwolfia*, esp. *R. serpentina* of SE Asia. **2.** the powdered root of *R. serpentina:* a source of various drugs, esp. reserpine. [C19: New Latin, named after Leonhard *Rauwolf* (died 1596), German botanist]

rav+age ('rævɪdʒ) *vb.* **1.** to cause extensive damage to. ~*n.* **2.** (*often pl.*) destructive action: *the ravages of time.* [C17: from French, from Old French *ravir* to snatch away, RAVISH] —'**rav+age+ment** *n.* —'**rav+ag+er** *n.*

R.A.V.C. *abbrev. for* Royal Army Veterinary Corps.

rave[1] (reɪv) *vb.* **1.** to utter (something) in a wild or incoherent manner, as when mad or delirious. **2.** (*intr.*) to speak in an angry uncontrolled manner. **3.** (*intr.*) (of the sea, wind, etc.) to rage or roar. **4.** (*intr.;* foll. by *over* or *about*) *Informal.* to write or speak (about) with great enthusiasm. **5.** (*intr.*) *Brit. slang.* to enjoy oneself wildly or uninhibitedly. ~*n.* **6.** *Informal.* **a.** enthusiastic or extravagant praise. **b.** (*as modifier*)*: a rave review.* **7.** Also called: **rave-up.** *Brit. slang.* a party. **8.** *Brit. slang.* a fad or fashion: *the latest rave.* [C14 *raven,* apparently from Old French *resver* to wander]

rave[2] (reɪv) *n.* a vertical sidepiece on a wagon. [C16: modification of dialect *rathe,* of uncertain origin]

rav+el ('rævᵊl) *vb.* **+els, +el+ling, +elled** *or U.S.* **+els, +el+ing, +eled. 1.** to tangle (threads, fibres, etc.) or (of threads, etc.) to become entangled. **2.** (often foll. by *out*) to tease or draw out (the fibres of a fabric or garment) or (of a garment or fabric) to fray out in loose ends; unravel. **3.** (*tr.;* usually foll. by *out*) to disentangle or resolve: *to ravel out a complicated story.* **4.** to break up (a road surface) in patches or (of a road surface) to begin to break up; fret; scab. **5.** *Archaic.* to make or become confused or complicated. ~*n.* **6.** a tangle or complication. [C16: from Middle Dutch *ravelen*] —'**rav+el+ler** *n.* —'**rav+el+ly** *adj.*

Ra·vel (*French* ra'vɛl) *n.* **Mau·rice (Joseph)** (mɔ'ris). 1875–1937, French composer, noted for his use of unresolved dissonances and mastery of tone colour. His works include *Gaspard de la Nuit* (1908) and *Le Tombeau de Couperin* (1917) for piano, *Boléro* (1928) for orchestra, and the ballet *Daphnis et Chloé* (1912).

rave+lin ('rævlɪn) *n. Fortifications.* an outwork having two embankments at a salient angle. [C16: from Italian *ravellino* a little bank, from *riva* bank, from Latin *rīpa*]

rav+el+ment ('rævəlmənt) *n. Rare.* a ravel or tangle.

ra+ven[1] ('reɪvᵊn) *n.* **1.** a large passerine bird, *Corvus corax,* having a large straight bill, long wedge-shaped tail, and black plumage: family *Corvidae* (crows). It has a hoarse croaking cry. **2. a.** a shiny black colour. **b.** (*as adj.*)*: raven hair.* [Old English *hræfn;* related to Old High German *hraban,* Old Norse *hrafn*]

rav+en[2] ('rævᵊn) *vb.* **1.** to seize or seek (plunder, prey, etc.). **2.** to eat (something) voraciously or greedily; be ravenous in eating. [C15: from Old French *raviner* to attack impetuously; see RAVENOUS] —'**rav+en+er** *n.*

rav+en+ing ('rævənɪŋ) *adj.* (esp. of animals such as wolves) voracious; predatory. —'**rav+en+ing+ly** *adv.*

Ra+ven+na (rə'vɛnə; *Italian* ra'venna) *n.* a city and port in NE Italy, in Emilia-Romagna: capital of the Western Roman Empire from 402 to 476, of the Ostrogoths from 493 to 526, and of the Byzantine exarchate from 584 to 751; famous for its ancient mosaics. Pop.: 137 303 (1975 est.).

rav+en+ous ('rævənəs) *adj.* **1.** famished; starving. **2.** rapacious; voracious. [C16: from Old French *ravineux,* from Latin *rapīna* plunder, from *rapere* to seize] —'**rav+en+ous+ly** *adv.* —'**rav+en+ous+ness** *n.*

rav+er ('reɪvə) *n. Brit. slang.* a person who leads a wild or uninhibited social life.

rav+in ('rævɪn) *vb.* an archaic spelling of **raven**[2].

ra+vine (rə'vi:n) *n.* a deep narrow steep-sided valley, esp. one formed by the action of running water. [C15: from Old French: torrent, from Latin *rapīna* robbery, influenced by Latin *rapidus* RAPID, both from *rapere* to snatch]

rav+ing ('reɪvɪŋ) *adj.* **1. a.** delirious; frenzied. **b.** (*as adv.*)*: raving mad.* **2.** *Informal.* (intensifier): *a raving beauty.* —'**rav+ing+ly** *adv.*

ra+vi·o+li (,rævɪ'əʊlɪ) *n.* small squares of pasta containing a savoury mixture of meat, cheese, etc. [Italian dialect, literally: little turnips, from Italian *rava* turnip, from Latin *rāpa*]

rav+ish ('rævɪʃ) *vb.* (*tr.*) **1.** (*often passive*) to give great delight to; enrapture. **2.** to rape. **3.** *Archaic.* to carry off by force. [C13: from Old French *ravir,* from Latin *rapere* to seize] —'**rav+ish+er** *n.* —'**rav+ish+ment** *n.*

rav+ish+ing ('rævɪʃɪŋ) *adj.* delightful; lovely; entrancing. —'**rav+ish+ing+ly** *adv.*

raw (rɔ:) *adj.* **1.** (of food) not cooked: *raw onion.* **2.** (*prenominal*) in an unfinished, natural, or unrefined state; not treated by manufacturing or other processes: *raw materials for making steel; raw brick.* **3.** (of the skin, a wound, etc.) having the surface exposed or abraded, esp. painfully. **4.** ignorant, inexperienced, or immature: *a raw recruit.* **5.** (*prenominal*) not selected or modified: *raw statistics.* **6.** frank or realistic: *a raw picture of the breakdown of a marriage.* **7.** (of spirits) undiluted. **8.** *Chiefly U.S.* coarse, vulgar, or obscene. **9.** *Chiefly U.S.* recently done; fresh: *raw paintwork.* **10.** (of the weather) harshly cold and damp. **11.** *Informal.* unfair; unjust (esp. in the phrase **a raw deal**). ~*n.* **12. the raw.** *Brit. informal.* a sensitive point: *his criticism touched me on the raw.* **13. in the raw. a.** *Informal.* without clothes; naked. **b.** in a natural or unmodified state: *life in the raw.* [Old English *hreaw;* related to Old High German *hrao,* Old Norse *hrār* raw, Latin *cruor* thick blood, Greek *kreas* meat] —'**raw+ish** *adj.* —'**raw+ly** *adv.* —'**raw+ness** *n.*

Ra+wal+pin+di (rɔ:l'pɪndɪ) *n.* an ancient city in N Pakistan: interim capital of Pakistan (1959–67) during the building of Islamabad. Pop.: 615 392 (1972).

raw+boned ('rɔ:'bəʊnd) *adj.* having a lean bony physique.

raw+hide ('rɔ:,haɪd) *n.* **1.** untanned hide. **2.** a whip or rope made of strips cut from such a hide.

ra+win+sonde ('reɪwɪn,sɒnd) *n.* a hydrogen balloon carrying meteorological instruments and a radar target, enabling the velocity of winds in the atmosphere to be measured. [C20: blend of *radar + wind + radio sonde*]

raw ma+te·ri·al *n.* **1.** material on which a particular manufacturing process is carried out. **2.** a person or thing regarded as suitable for some particular purpose: *raw material for the army.*

raw silk *n.* **1.** untreated silk fibres reeled from the cocoon. **2.** fabric woven from such fibres.

Raws·thorne ('rɔ:s,θɔ:n) *n.* **Al·an.** 1905–71, English composer, whose works include three symphonies, several concertos, and a set of *Symphonic Studies* (1939).

ray[1] (reɪ) *n.* **1.** a narrow beam of light; gleam. **2.** a slight indication, esp. of something anticipated or hoped for: *a ray of solace.* **3.** *Maths.* a straight line extending from a point. **4.** a thin beam of electromagnetic radiation or particles. **5.** any of the bony or cartilaginous spines of the fin of a fish that form the support for the soft part of the fin. **6.** any of the arms or branches of a starfish or other radiate animal. **7.** *Astronomy.* one of a number of bright visible streaks of uncertain origin that radiate from certain lunar craters and extend for hundreds of kilometres, crossing mountain ranges and smaller craters. ~*vb.* **8.** (of an object) to emit (light) in rays or (of light) to issue in the form of rays. **9.** (*intr.*) (of lines, etc.) to extend in rays or on radiating paths. **10.** (*tr.*) to adorn (an ornament, etc.) with rays or radiating lines. [C14: from Old French *rai,* from Latin *radius* spoke, RADIUS] —'**ray+less** *adj.*

ray[2] (reɪ) *n.* any of various marine selachian fishes typically having a flattened body, greatly enlarged winglike pectoral fins, gills on the undersurface of the fins, and a long whiplike tail. They constitute the orders *Torpediniformes* (**electric rays**) and *Rajiformes.* [C14: from Old French *raie,* from Latin *raia*]

ray[3] (reɪ) *n. Music.* (in tonic solfa) the second degree of any major scale; supertonic. [C14: see GAMUT]

Ray[1] (reɪ) *n.* **Cape.** a promontory in SW Newfoundland, Canada.

Ray[2] (reɪ) *n.* **1. John.** 1627–1705, English naturalist. He originated natural botanical classification and the division of flowering plants into monocotyledons and dicotyledons. **2. Man.** 1890–1976, U.S. surrealist photographer. **3. Sat·ya·jit** ('sætjədʒɪt). born 1921, Indian film director.

ra·yah *or* **ra·ia** ('rɑ:jə, 'raɪə) *n.* a non-Muslim subject of the old Ottoman Empire. [C19: from Turkish *raiyye,* from Arabic *ra'iyah* herd, flock]

ray flow+er *or* **flo+ret** *n.* any of the small strap-shaped flowers in the flower head of certain composite plants, such as the daisy. Compare **disc flower.**

ray gun *n.* (in science fiction) a gun that emits rays to paralyse, stun, or destroy.

Ray·leigh ('reɪlɪ) *n.* **Lord,** title of *John William Strutt,* 1842–1919, English physicist. He discovered argon (1894) with Ramsay and made important contributions to the theory of sound: Nobel prize for physics 1904.

Ray·leigh disc *n.* a small light disc suspended in the path of a sound wave, used to measure the intensity of the sound by analysing the resulting deflection of the disc.

ray+on ('reɪɒn) *n.* **1.** any of a number of textile fibres made from wood pulp or other forms of cellulose. **2.** any fabric made from such a fibre. **3.** (*modifier*) consisting of or involving rayon: *a rayon shirt.* [C20: from French, from Old French *rai* RAY[1]]

raze *or* **rase** (reɪz) *vb.* (*tr.*) **1.** to demolish (buildings, etc.) completely; level (esp. in the phrase **raze to the ground**). **2.** to delete; erase. **3.** *Archaic.* to graze. [C16: from Old French *raser* from Latin *rādere* to scrape] —'**raz+er** *or* '**ras+er** *n.*

raz·ee (ræ'zi:) *History.* ~*n., pl.* **·ees. 1.** a sailing ship that has had its upper deck or decks removed. ~*vb.* **·ees, ·ee+ing, ·eed.** (*tr.*). **2.** to remove the upper deck or decks of (a sailing ship). [C19: from French *rasée* shaved close, from *raser* to RAZE]

ra+zoo (rə'zu:) *n. Austral. informal.* an imaginary coin: *not a brass razoo; they took every last razoo.*

ra+zor ('reɪzə) *n.* **1.** a sharp implement used esp. for shaving the face. **2. on a razor's edge** or **razor-edge.** in an acute dilemma. ~*vb.* **3.** (*tr.*) to cut or shave with a razor. [C13: from Old French *raseor,* from *raser* to shave; see RAZE]

ra·zor+back ('reɪzə,bæk) *n.* **1.** Also called: **finback.** another name for the **common rorqual** (see **rorqual**). **2.** a semiwild or wild pig of the southeastern U.S., having a narrow body, long legs, and a ridged back.

ra·zor+bill ('reɪzə,bɪl) *or* **ra·zor-billed auk** *n.* a common auk, *Alca torda,* of the North Atlantic, having a thick laterally compressed bill with white markings.

ra·zor-cut *vb.* **-cuts, -cut·ting, -cut. 1.** (*tr.*) to trim or shape (the hair) with a razor. ~*n.* **ra+zor cut. 2.** a fluffy hair style, usually tapering at the neck, trimmed by a razor.

ra·zor-shell *n.* any of various sand-burrowing bivalve molluscs of the genera *Ensis* and *Solen,* which have a long tubular shell. U.S. name: **razor clam.**

razz (ræz) *U.S. slang.* ~*vb.* **1.** (*tr.*) to make fun of; deride. ~*n.* **2.** short for **raspberry** (sense 5).

raz+zi·a ('ræzɪə) *n., pl.* **+zi·as.** *History.* a raid for plunder or slaves, esp. one carried out by Moors in North Africa. [C19: from French, from Arabic *ghaziah* war]

raz·zle-daz·zle ('ræzᵊl'dæzᵊl) *or* **razz+ma+tazz** ('ræzmə'tæz) *n. Slang.* **1.** noisy or showy fuss or activity. **2.** a spree or frolic (esp. in the phrase **on the razzle-dazzle**). [C19: rhyming compound based on DAZZLE]

Rb *the chemical symbol for* rubidium.

RB *international car registration for* (Republic of) Botswana.

RB- *abbrev. for* reconnaissance bomber: *RB-57.*

R.B.E. *abbrev. for* relative biological effectiveness.

r.c. *abbrev. for* reinforced concrete.

RC *international car registration for* (Nationalist Republic of) China.

R.C. *abbrev. for:* **1.** Red Cross. **2.** Reserve Corps. **3.** Roman Catholic.

RCA *international car registration for* Central African Republic.

R.C.A. *abbrev. for:* **1.** Radio Corporation of America. **2.** Royal Canadian Academy. **3.** Royal College of Art.

R.C.A.F. *abbrev. for* Royal Canadian Air Force.

RCB(CG) *international car registration for* (Republic of the) Congo.

rcd. *abbrev. for* received.

RCH *international car registration for* Republic of Chile.

R.C.M. *abbrev. for* Royal College of Music.

R.C.M.P. *abbrev. for* Royal Canadian Mounted Police.

R.C.N. *abbrev. for:* **1.** Royal Canadian Navy. **2.** Royal College of Nursing.

R.C.O. *abbrev. for* Royal College of Organists.

r-col·our *or* **r-col·our+ing** *n. Phonetics.* an (r) quality imparted to certain vowels, usually by retroflexion. —**'r-col·oured** *adj.*

R.C.P. *abbrev. for* Royal College of Physicians.

rcpt. *abbrev. for* receipt.

R.C.S. *abbrev. for:* **1.** Royal College of Science. **2.** Royal College of Surgeons. **3.** Royal Corps of Signals.

rct. *Military. abbrev. for* recruit.

R.C.T. *abbrev. for* Royal Corps of Transport.

R.C.V.S. *abbrev. for* Royal College of Veterinary Surgeons.

rd. *abbrev. for:* **1.** rendered. **2.** rod (unit of length). **3.** road. **4.** round. **5.** *Physics.* rutherford.

r.d. *or* **R.D.** (on a cheque) *abbrev. for* refer to drawer.

Rd. *abbrev. for* Road.

R.D.C. (in Britain, formerly) *abbrev. for* Rural District Council.

re[1] (reɪ, riː) *n. Music.* an alternative spelling of **ray.**

re[2] (riː) *prep.* with reference to. [C18: from Latin *rē*, dative case of *rēs* thing]

Usage. *Re,* in contexts such as *re your letter, your remarks have been noted* or *he spoke to me re your complaint,* is common in business or official correspondence. In general English *with reference to* is preferable in the former case and *about* or *concerning* in the latter. Even in business correspondence, the use of *re* is often restricted to the letter heading.

Re *the chemical symbol for* rhenium.

Re (reɪ) *n.* another name for **Ra.**

Re. *or* **re.** *abbrev. for* rupee.

R.E. *abbrev. for:* **1.** Reformed Episcopal. **2.** Right Excellent. **3.** Royal Engineers.

re- *prefix.* **1.** indicating return to a previous condition, restoration, withdrawal, etc.: *rebuild; renew; retrace; reunite.* **2.** indicating repetition of an action: *recopy; remarry.* [from Latin]

Usage. Verbs beginning with *re-* indicate repetition or restoration. It is unnecessary to add an adverb such as *back* or *again: This must not occur again* (not *recur again*); *we recounted the votes* (not *recounted the votes again,* which implies that the votes were counted three times, not two).

're *contraction of* are: *we're, you're, they're.*

reach (riːtʃ) *vb.* **1.** (*tr.*) to arrive at or get to (a place, person, etc.) in the course of movement or action: *to reach the office.* **2.** to extend as far as (a point or place): *to reach the ceiling; can you reach?* **3.** (*tr.*) to come to (a certain condition, stage, or situation): *to reach the point of starvation.* **4.** (*intr.*) to extend in influence or operation: *the Roman conquest reached throughout England.* **5.** (*tr.*) *Informal.* to pass or give (something to a person) with the outstretched hand: *to reach someone a book.* **6.** (*intr.;* foll. by *out, for,* or *after*) to make a movement (towards), as if to grasp or touch: *to reach for something on a shelf.* **7.** (*intr.;* foll. by *for* or *after*) to strive or yearn: *to reach for the impossible.* **8.** (*tr.*) to make contact or communication with (someone): *we tried to reach him all day.* **9.** (*tr.*) to strike, esp. in fencing or boxing. **10.** (*tr.*) to amount to (a certain sum): *to reach the five million mark.* **11.** (*intr.*) *Nautical.* to sail on a tack with the wind on or near abeam. ~*n.* **12.** the act of reaching. **13.** the extent or distance of reaching. **14.** the range of influence, power, jurisdiction, etc. **15.** an open stretch of water, esp. on a river. **16.** *Nautical.* the direction or distance sailed by a vessel on one tack. **17.** a bar on the rear axle of a vehicle connecting it with some part at the front end. [Old English *rǣcan;* related to Old Frisian *rēka,* Old High German *reihheu*] —**'reach+a·ble** *adj.* —**'reach+er** *n.*

reach-me-down *n.* another name for **hand-me-down.**

re+act (rɪ'ækt) *vb.* **1.** (*intr.,* foll. by *to, upon,* etc.) (of a person or thing) to act in response to another person, a stimulus, etc. or (of two people or things) to act together in a certain way. **2.** (*intr.,* foll. by *against*) to act in an opposing or contrary manner. **3.** (*intr.*) *Physics.* to exert an equal force in the opposite direction to an acting force. **4.** *Chem.* to undergo or cause to undergo a chemical reaction. [C17: from Late Latin *reagere,* from RE- + Latin *agere* to drive, do]

re-act (riː'ækt) *vb.* (*tr.*) to act or perform again.

re+ac+tance (rɪ'æktəns) *n.* **1.** the opposition to the flow of alternating current by the capacitance or inductance of an electrical circuit; the imaginary part of the impedance Z, $Z = R + iX$, where R is the resistance, $i = \sqrt{-1}$, and X is the reactance. It is expressed in ohms. Compare **resistance** (sense 3). **2.** the opposition to the flow of an acoustic or mechanical vibration, usually due to inertia or stiffness. It is the magnitude of the imaginary part of the acoustic or mechanical impedance.

re+ac+tant (rɪ'æktənt) *n.* a substance that participates in a chemical reaction, esp. a substance that is present at the start of the reaction. Compare **product** (sense 4).

re+ac+tion (rɪ'ækʃən) *n.* **1.** a response to some foregoing action or stimulus. **2.** the reciprocal action of two things acting together. **3.** opposition to change, esp. political change, or a desire to return to a former condition or system. **4. a.** a response indicating a person's feelings or emotional attitude. **b.** a group of responses characteristic of a certain mental disorder. **5.** *Med.* **a.** any effect produced by the action of a drug, esp. an adverse effect. Compare **side effect. b.** any effect produced by a substance (allergen) to which a person is allergic. **6.** the equal but opposite force produced when any force is applied to a body or system. **7.** short for **chemical reaction** or **nuclear reaction. 8.** *Stock Exchange.* a sharp fall in price interrupting a general rise. —**re+'ac+tion+al** *adj.*

re+ac+tion+ar·y (rɪ'ækʃənərɪ, -ʃənrɪ) *or* **re+ac+tion+ist** *adj.* **1.** of, relating to, or characterized by reaction, esp. against radical political or social change. ~*n.* **2.** a person opposed to radical change. —**re+'ac+tion+ism** *n.*

re+ac+tion en+gine *or* **mo+tor** *n.* an engine, such as a jet or rocket engine, that ejects gas at high velocity and develops its thrust from the ensuing reaction.

re+ac+tion for+ma+tion *n. Psychol.* a defence mechanism by which a person converts a socially unacceptable impulse into socially acceptable behaviour.

re+ac+tion tur+bine *n.* a turbine in which the working fluid is accelerated by expansion in both the static nozzles and the rotor blades. Torque is produced by the momentum changes in the rotor and by reaction from fluid accelerating out of the rotor. Compare **impulse turbine.**

re+ac+ti+vate (rɪ'æktɪ,veɪt) *vb.* (*tr.*) to make (something) active or functional again. —**re+,ac+ti+'va+tion** *n.*

re+ac+tive (rɪ'æktɪv) *adj.* **1.** readily partaking in chemical reactions: *sodium is a reactive metal; free radicals are very reactive.* **2.** of, concerned with, or having a reactance. **3.** responsive to stimulus. —**re+'ac+tive+ly** *adv.* —**re+ac+tiv+i·ty** (,riæk'tɪvɪtɪ) *or* **re+'ac+tive+ness** *n.*

re+ac+tor (rɪ'æktə) *n.* **1.** *Chem.* a substance, such as a reagent, that undergoes a reaction. **2.** short for **nuclear reactor. 3.** a vessel, esp. one in industrial use, in which a chemical reaction takes place. **4.** a coil of low resistance and high inductance that introduces reactance into a circuit. **5.** *Med.* a person sensitive to a particular drug or agent.

read[1] (riːd) *vb.* **reads, read+ing, read** (rɛd). **1.** to comprehend the meaning of (something written or printed) by looking at and interpreting the written or printed characters. **2.** to be occupied in such an activity: *he was reading all day.* **3.** (when *tr.,* often foll. by *out*) to look at, interpret, and speak aloud (something written or printed): *he read to us from the Bible.* **4.** (*tr.*) to interpret the significance or meaning of through scrutiny and recognition: *he read the sky and predicted rain; to read a map.* **5.** (*tr.*) to interpret or understand the meaning of (signs, characters, etc.) other than by visual means: *to read Braille.* **6.** (*tr.*) to have sufficient knowledge of (a language) to understand the written or printed word: *do you read German?* **7.** (*tr.*) to discover or make out the true nature or mood of: *to read someone's mind.* **8.** to interpret or understand (something read) in a specified way, or (of something read) to convey a particular meaning or impression: *I read this speech as satire; this book reads well.* **9.** (*tr.*) to adopt as a reading in a particular passage: *for "boon" read "bone".* **10.** (*intr.*) to have or contain a certain form or wording: *the sentence reads as follows.* **11.** to undertake a course of study in (a subject): *to read history; read for the bar.* **12.** to gain knowledge by reading: *he read about the war.* **13.** (*tr.*) to register, indicate, or show: *the meter reads 100.* **14.** (*tr.*) to bring or put into a specified condition by reading: *to read a child to sleep.* **15.** (*tr.*) to hear and understand, esp. when using a two-way radio: *we are reading you loud and clear.* **16.** *Computer technol.* to obtain (data) from a storage device, such as magnetic tape. Compare **write** (sense 16). **17.** (*tr.*) to understand (written or printed music) by interpretation of the notes on the staff and to be able to reproduce the musical sounds represented by these notes. **18. read a lesson** (*or* **lecture**). *Informal.* to censure or reprimand, esp. in a long-winded manner. **19. read between the lines.** *Informal.* to perceive or deduce a meaning that is hidden or implied rather than being openly stated. ~*n.* **20.** matter suitable for reading: *this new book is a very good read.* **21.** the act of reading. ~See also **read in, read into, read out, read up.** [Old English *rǣdan* to advise, explain; related to Old Frisian *rēda,* Old High German *rātan,* Gothic *garēdan*]

,re+ab+'sorb *vb.*
,re+ab+'sorp+tion *n.*
,re+ac+'cede *vb.*
,re+ac+'cent *vb.*
,re+ac+'cept *vb.*
,re+ac+'cep+tance *n.*
,re+ac+'claim *vb.*
,re+ac+'com+mo+,date *vb.*
,re+ac+'cred+it *vb.*
,re+ac+'cus+tom *vb.*
,re+a+'cid+i+,fy *vb.,* **+fies, +fy+ing, +fied.**
,re+ac+'quaint *vb.*
,re+ac+'quaint+ance *n.*
,re+ac+'quire *vb.*
,re+ac+qui+'si+tion *n.*

read[2] (rɛd) *vb.* **1.** past tense and past participle of **read**[1]. ~*adj.* **2.** having knowledge gained from books (esp. in the phrases **widely read** and **well-read**).

read·a·ble ('riːdəbᵊl) *adj.* **1.** (of handwriting, etc.) able to be read or deciphered; legible. **2.** (of style of writing) interesting, easy, or pleasant to read. —ˌ**read·a·'bil·i·ty** *or* **'read·a·ble·ness** *n.* —**'read·a·bly** *adv.*

Reade (riːd) *n.* **Charles.** 1814–84, English novelist: author of *The Cloister and the Hearth* (1861), a historical romance.

read·er ('riːdə) *n.* **1.** a person who reads. **2.** a person who is fond of reading. **3. a.** *Chiefly Brit.* a senior lecturer at a university. **b.** *U.S.* a teaching assistant in a faculty who grades papers, examinations, etc., on behalf of a professor. **4. a.** a book that is part of a planned series for those learning to read. **b.** a standard textbook, esp. for foreign-language learning. **5.** a person who reads aloud in public. **6.** a person who reads and assesses the merit of manuscripts submitted to a publisher. **7.** a person employed to read proofs and indicate errors by comparison with the original copy; proofreader. **8.** short for **lay reader.**

read·er·ship ('riːdəˌʃɪp) *n.* **1.** all the readers collectively of a particular publication or author: *a readership of five million; Dickens's readership.* **2.** *Chiefly Brit.* the office, position, or rank of university reader.

read·i·ly ('rɛdɪlɪ) *adv.* **1.** promptly; eagerly; willingly. **2.** without difficulty or delay; easily or quickly.

read in (riːd) *vb.* (*adv.*) **1.** to read (data) into a computer memory or storage device. **2. read oneself in.** *Church of England.* to assume possession of a benefice by publicly reading the Thirty-nine Articles.

read·i·ness ('rɛdɪnɪs) *n.* **1.** the state of being ready or prepared, as for use or action. **2.** willingness or eagerness to do something. **3.** ease or promptness.

read·ing ('riːdɪŋ) *n.* **1. a.** the act of a person who reads. **b.** (*as modifier*): *a reading room; a reading lamp.* **2. a.** ability to read. **b.** (*as modifier*): *the reading public; a child of reading age.* **3.** any matter that can be read; written or printed text. **4.** a public recital or rendering of a literary work. **5.** the form of a particular word or passage in a given text, esp. where more than one version exists. **6.** an interpretation, as of a piece of music, a situation, or something said or written. **7.** knowledge gained from books: *a person of little reading.* **8.** a measurement indicated by a gauge, dial, scientific instrument, etc. **9.** *Parliamentary procedure.* **a.** the formal recital of the body or title of a bill in a legislative assembly in order to begin one of the stages of its passage. **b.** one of the three stages in the passage of a bill through a legislative assembly. See **first reading, second reading, third reading.** **10.** the formal recital of something written, esp. a will.

Read·ing ('rɛdɪŋ) *n.* a town in S England, administrative centre of Berkshire, on the River Thames: university (1892). Pop.: 132 023 (1971).

read in·to (riːd) *vb.* (*tr., prep.*) to discern in or infer from a statement (meanings not intended by the speaker or writer).

re·ad·just (ˌriːə'dʒʌst) *vb.* to adjust or adapt (oneself or something) again, esp. after an initial failure. —ˌ**re·ad·'just·a·ble** *adj.* —ˌ**re·ad·'just·er** *n.* —ˌ**re·ad·'just·ment** *n.*

read out (riːd) *vb.* (*adv.*) **1.** (*tr.*) to read (something) aloud. **2.** (*tr.*) *U.S.* to expel (someone) from a political party or other society. **3.** to retrieve information from a computer memory or storage device. ~*n.* **read-out. 4. a.** the act of retrieving information from a computer memory or storage device. **b.** the information retrieved.

read up (riːd) *vb.* (*adv.;* when *intr.,* often foll. by *on*) to acquire information about (a subject) by reading intensively.

read-write head ('riːd'raɪt) *n. Computer technol.* an electromagnet that can both read and write information on a magnetic medium such as magnetic tape or disk.

read·y ('rɛdɪ) *adj.* **read·i·er, read·i·est. 1.** in a state of completion or preparedness, as for use or action. **2.** willing or eager: *ready helpers.* **3.** prompt or rapid: *a ready response.* **4.** (*prenominal*) quick in perceiving; intelligent: *a ready mind.* **5.** (*postpositive*) (foll. by *to*) on the point (of) or liable (to): *ready to collapse.* **6.** (*postpositive*) conveniently near (esp. in the phrase **ready to hand**). **7. make** *or* **get ready.** to prepare (oneself or something) for use or action. ~*n.* **8.** *Informal.* short for **ready money. 9. at** *or* **to the ready. a.** (of a rifle) in the position normally adopted immediately prior to aiming and firing. **b.** poised for use or action: *with pen at the ready.* [Old English (*ge*)*rǣde;* related to Old Frisian *rēde,* Old High German *reiti,* Old Norse *reithr* ready]

read·y-made *adj.* **1.** made for purchase and immediate use by any customer: *a ready-made jacket.* **2.** extremely convenient or ideally suited: *a ready-made solution.* **3.** unoriginal or conventional: *ready-made phrases.* ~*n.* **4.** a ready-made article, esp. a garment.

read·y-mix *n.* **1.** (*modifier*) consisting of ingredients blended in advance, esp. of food that is ready to cook or eat after addition of milk or water: *a ready-mix cake.* **2.** concrete that is mixed before or during delivery to a building site.

read·y mon·ey *n.* funds for immediate use; cash.

read·y reck·on·er *n.* a table of numbers used to facilitate simple calculations, esp. one for working out rates of discount, interest, charging, etc.

read·y-wit·ted *adj.* quick to learn or perceive.

re·af·for·est (ˌriːə'fɒrɪst) *or* **re·for·est** *vb.* (*tr.*) to replant (an area that was formerly forested). —ˌ**re·af·ˌfor·est·'a·tion** *or* ˌ**re·for·est·'a·tion** *n.*

Rea·gan ('reɪgən) *n.* **Ron·ald.** born 1911, U.S. actor; Republican politician; Governor of California (1966-74); president of the U.S. from 1981.

re·a·gent (riː'eɪdʒənt) *n.* a substance for use in a chemical reaction, esp. for use in chemical synthesis and analysis.

re·al[1] ('rɪəl) *adj.* **1.** existing or occurring in the physical world; not imaginary, fictitious, or theoretical; actual. **2.** (*prenominal*) true; actual; not false: *the real reason.* **3.** (*prenominal*) deserving the name; rightly so called: *a real friend; a real woman.* **4.** not artificial or simulated; genuine: *real sympathy; real fur.* **5.** *Philosophy.* existent or relating to actual existence (as opposed to nonexistent, potential, contingent, or apparent). **6.** (*prenominal*) *Economics.* (of prices, incomes, wages, etc.) considered in terms of purchasing power rather than nominal currency value. **7.** (*prenominal*) denoting or relating to immovable property such as land and tenements: *real property; real estate.* Compare **personal. 8.** *Physics.* See **image** (sense 2). **9.** *Maths.* involving or containing real numbers; nonimaginary. The real part of a complex number z is usually written Rez. **10.** *Music.* **a.** (of the answer in a fugue) preserving the intervals as they appear in the subject. **b.** denoting a fugue as having such an answer. Compare **tonal** (sense 3). **11.** *Informal.* (intensifier): *a real fool; a real genius.* ~*n.* **12. the real.** that which exists in fact; reality. **13. for real.** *Slang.* not as a test or trial; in earnest. [C15: from Old French *réel,* from Late Latin *reālis,* from Latin *rēs* thing] —**'re·al·ness** *n.*

re·al[2] (reɪ'ɑːl; *Spanish* re'al) *n., pl.* **re·als** *or* **re·a·les** (*Spanish* re'ales). a former small Spanish or Spanish-American silver coin. [from Spanish, literally: royal, from Latin *rēgālis;* see REGAL]

re·al[3] (*Portuguese* re'al) *n., pl.* **reis** (rəjʃ). a former coin of Portugal and Brazil. [ultimately from Latin *rēgālis* REGAL]

re·al·gar (rɪ'ælgə) *n.* a rare orange-red soft mineral consisting of arsenic sulphide in monoclinic crystalline form. It occurs in Utah and Rumania and as a deposit from hot springs. It is an important ore of arsenic and is also used as a pigment. Formula: AsS. [C14: via Medieval Latin from Arabic *rahj al-ghar* powder of the mine]

re·al·ism ('rɪəˌlɪzəm) *n.* **1.** awareness or acceptance of the physical universe, events, etc., as they are, as opposed to the abstract or ideal. **2.** awareness or acceptance of the facts and necessities of life; a practical rather than a moral or dogmatic view of things. **3.** a style of painting and sculpture that seeks to represent the familiar or typical in real life, rather than an idealized, formalized, or romantic interpretation of it. **4.** any similar school or style in other arts, esp. literature. **5.** *Philosophy.* the theory that things named by general words, including universals, have a real existence independent of their names. Compare **Platonism, nominalism, conceptualism. 6.** *Philosophy.* the theory that physical objects continue to exist whether they are perceived or not. Compare **idealism, phenomenalism.**

re·al·ist ('rɪəlɪst) *n.* **1.** a person who is aware of and accepts the physical universe, events, etc., as they are; pragmatist. **2.** an artist or writer who seeks to represent the familiar or typical in real life rather than an idealized, formalized, or romantic interpretation. **3.** *Philosophy.* a person who accepts realism. **4.** (*modifier*) of, relating to, or characteristic of realism or realists in the arts, philosophy, etc.: *a realist school.*

re·al·is·tic (ˌrɪə'lɪstɪk) *adj.* **1.** showing awareness and acceptance of reality. **2.** practical or pragmatic rather than ideal or moral. **3.** (of a book, film, etc.) depicting or emphasizing what is real and actual rather than abstract or ideal. **4.** of or relating to philosophical realism. —ˌ**re·al·'is·ti·cal·ly** *adv.*

re·al·i·ty (rɪ'ælɪtɪ) *n., pl.* **·ties. 1.** the state of things as they are or appear to be, rather than as one might wish them to be. **2.** something that is real. **3.** the state of being real. **4.** *Philosophy.* **a.** that which exists, independent of human awareness. **b.** the totality of facts. Compare **appearance** (sense 6). **5. in reality.** actually; in fact.

re·al·ize *or* **re·al·ise** ('rɪəˌlaɪz) *vb.* **1.** (when *tr., may take a clause as object*) to become conscious or aware of (something). **2.** (*tr., often passive*) to bring (a plan, ambition, etc.) to fruition; make actual or concrete. **3.** (*tr.*) to give (something, such as a drama or film) the appearance of reality. **4.** (*tr.*) (of goods, property, etc.) to sell for or make (a certain sum): *this table realized £800.* **5.** (*tr.*) to convert (property or goods) into cash. **6.** (*tr.*) (of a musicologist or performer) **a.** to expand or complete (a thorough-bass part in a piece of baroque music) by supplying the harmonies indicated in the figured bass. **b.** to reconstruct (a composition) from an incomplete set of parts. **7.** to sound or utter (a phoneme or other speech sound) in actual speech; articulate. —**'re·al·ˌiz·a·ble** *or* **'re·al·ˌis·a·ble** *adj.* —**'re·al·ˌiz·a·bly** *or* **'re·al·ˌis·a·bly** *adv.* —ˌ**re·al·i·'za·tion** *or* ˌ**re·al·i·'sa·tion** *n.* —**'re·al·ˌiz·er** *or* **'re·al·ˌis·er** *n.*

re·al·ly ('rɪəlɪ) *adv.* **1.** in reality; in actuality; assuredly: *it's really quite harmless.* **2.** truly; genuinely: *really beautiful.* ~*interj.* **3.** an exclamation of dismay, disapproval, doubt, surprise, etc. **4. not really?** an exclamation of surprise or polite doubt.

Usage. See at **very.**

ˌ**re·a·'dapt** *vb.*
ˌ**re·a·dap·'ta·tion** *n.*
re·'add *vb.*
ˌ**re·ad·'dress** *vb.*
ˌ**re·ad·'journ** *vb.*
ˌ**re·ad·'journ·ment** *n.*
ˌ**re·ad·'mis·sion** *n.*
ˌ**re·ad·'mit** *vb.,* **·mits, ·mit·ting, ·mit·ted.**
ˌ**re·ad·'mit·tance** *n.*
ˌ**re·a·'dopt** *vb.*
ˌ**re·af·'firm** *vb.*
ˌ**re·af·fir·'ma·tion** *n.*
ˌ**re·a·'lign** *vb.*
ˌ**re·a·'lign·ment** *n.*
re·'al·lo·ˌcate *vb.*

realm (rɛlm) *n.* **1.** a royal domain; kingdom (now chiefly in such phrases as **Peer of the Realm**). **2.** a field of interest, study, etc.: *the realm of the occult.* [C13: from Old French *reialme,* from Latin *regimen* rule, influenced by Old French *reial* royal, from Latin *rēgālis* REGAL]

re·al num·ber *n.* any rational or irrational number.

re·al part *n.* the term *a* in a complex number *a* + *ib,* where $i = \sqrt{-1}$.

Re·al·po·li·tik *German.* (re'alpoli,ti:k) *n.* a ruthlessly realistic and opportunist approach to statesmanship, rather than a moralistic one, esp. as exemplified by Bismarck. [C19: German: politics of realism]

re·al pres·ence *n.* the doctrine that the body of Christ is actually present in the Eucharist.

re·al prop·er·ty *n. Property Law.* immoveable property, esp. freehold land.

re·al ten·nis *n.* an ancient form of tennis played in a four-walled indoor court with various openings, a sloping-roofed corridor along three sides, and a buttress on the fourth side. Also called: **royal tennis.**

re·al-time *adj.* denoting or relating to a data-processing system in which a computer is on-line to a source of data and processes the data as it is generated.

re·al·tor ('rɪəltə, -,tɔ:) *n.* a U.S. word for an **estate agent,** esp. an accredited one. [C20: from REALTY + -OR[1]]

re·al·ty ('rɪəltɪ) *n.* another term for **real property.**

re·al wag·es *pl. n. Economics.* wages evaluated with reference to their purchasing power rather than to the money actually paid. Compare **money wages.**

ream[1] (ri:m) *n.* **1.** a number of sheets of paper, formerly 480 sheets (**short ream**), now 500 sheets (**long ream**) or 516 sheets (**printer's ream** or **perfect ream**). One ream is equal to 20 quires. **2.** (*often pl.*) *Informal.* a large quantity, esp. of written matter: *he wrote reams.* [C14: from Old French *raime,* from Spanish *rezma,* from Arabic *rizmah* bale]

ream[2] (ri:m) *vb.* (*tr.*) **1.** to enlarge (a hole) by use of a reamer. **2.** *U.S.* to extract (juice) from (a citrus fruit) using a reamer. [perhaps from C14 *remen* to open up, from Old English *rȳman* to widen]

ream·er ('ri:mə) *n.* **1.** a steel tool with a cylindrical or tapered shank around which longitudinal teeth are ground, used for smoothing the bores of holes accurately to size. **2.** *U.S.* a utensil with a conical projection used for extracting juice from citrus fruits; lemon squeezer.

reap (ri:p) *vb.* **1.** to cut or harvest (a crop), esp. corn, from (a field or tract of land). **2.** (*tr.*) to gain or get (something) as a reward for or result of some action or enterprise. [Old English *riopan;* related to Norwegian *ripa* to scratch, Middle Low German *repen* to card, ripple (flax)] —**'reap·a·ble** *adj.*

reap·er ('ri:pə) *n.* **1:** a person who reaps or a machine for reaping. **2. the grim reaper.** death.

rear[1] (rɪə) *n.* **1.** the back or hind part. **2.** the area or position that lies at the back: *a garden at the rear of the house.* **3.** the section of a military force or procession farthest from the front. **4.** an informal word for **buttocks. 5. bring up the rear.** to be at the back in a procession, race, etc. **6. in the rear.** at the back. **7.** (*modifier*) of or in the rear: *the rear legs; the rear side.* [C17: probably abstracted from REARWARD]

rear[2] (rɪə) *vb.* **1.** (*tr.*) to care for and educate (children) until maturity; bring up; raise. **2.** (*tr.*) to breed (animals) or grow (plants, etc.). **3.** (*tr.*) to place or lift (a ladder, etc.) upright. **4.** (*tr.*) to erect (a monument, building, etc.); put up. **5.** (*intr.;* often foll. by *up*) (esp. of horses) to lift the front legs in the air and stand nearly upright. **6.** (*intr.;* often foll. by *up* or *over*) (esp. of tall buildings) to rise high; tower. **7.** (*intr.*) to start with anger, resentment, etc. [Old English *rǣran;* related to Old High German *rēren* to distribute, Old Norse *reisa* to RAISE] —**'rear·er** *n.*

rear ad·mi·ral *n.* an officer holding flag rank in any of certain navies junior to a vice admiral.

rear·guard ('rɪə,gɑ:d) *n.* **1.** a detachment detailed to protect the rear of a military formation, esp. in retreat. **2.** an entrenched or conservative element, as in a political party. **3.** (*modifier*) of, relating to, or characteristic of a rearguard: *a rearguard action.* [C15: from Old French *rereguarde* (modern French *arrière-garde*), from *rer,* from Latin *retro* back + *guarde* GUARD; compare VANGUARD]

rear light *or* **lamp** *n.* a red light, usually one of a pair, attached to the rear of a motor vehicle. U.S. names: **taillight, tail lamp.**

re·arm (ri:'ɑ:m) *vb.* **1.** to arm again. **2.** (*tr.*) to equip (an army, etc.) with better weapons. —**re·'arm·a·ment** *n.*

rear·most ('rɪə,məʊst) *adj.* nearest the rear; coming last.

rear·mouse ('rɪə,maʊs) *n., pl.* **·mice.** an archaic or dialect word for **bat** (the animal). [See REREMOUSE]

re·ar·range (,ri:ə'reɪndʒ) *vb.* (*tr.*) **1.** to put (something) into a new order: *to rearrange the lighting.* **2.** to put (something) back in its original order after it has been displaced. **3.** to fix a new date or time for (something postponed): *to rearrange a match.* —**,re·ar·'rang·er** *n.* —**,re·ar·'range·ment** *n.*

rear sight *n.* the sight of a gun nearest to the breech.

rear-view mir·ror *n.* a mirror on a motor vehicle enabling the driver to see traffic behind him.

rear·ward ('rɪəwəd) *adj., adv.* **1.** Also (for adv. only): **rear·wards.** towards or in the rear. ~*n.* **2.** a position in the rear, esp. the rear division of a military formation. [C14 (as a noun: the part of an army positioned behind the main body of troops): from Anglo-French *rerewarde,* variant of *reregarde;* see REARGUARD]

rea·son ('ri:zᵊn) *n.* **1.** the faculty of rational argument, deduction, judgment, etc. **2.** sound mind; sanity. **3.** a cause or motive, as for a belief, action, etc. **4.** an argument in favour or a justification for something. **5.** *Philosophy.* intellect, as opposed to sensibility. **6.** *Logic.* a premiss of an argument, esp. the minor premiss. **7. by reason of.** because of. **8. in** *or* **within reason.** within moderate or justifiable bounds. **9. it stands to reason.** it is logical or obvious: *it stands to reason that he will lose.* **10. listen to reason.** to be persuaded peaceably. **11. reasons of State.** political justifications for an immoral act. ~*vb.* **12.** (when *tr., takes a clause as object*) to think logically or draw (logical conclusions) from facts or premisses. **13.** (*intr.,* usually foll. by *with*) to urge or seek to persuade by reasoning. **14.** (*tr.,* often foll. by *out*) to work out or resolve (a problem) by reasoning. [C13: from Old French *reisun,* from Latin *ratiō* reckoning, from *rērī* to think] —**'rea·son·er** *n.*

Usage. In both speech and writing careful users of English avoid the expression *the reason is because...* since *the reason is...* and *because* mean the same thing. The word *because* should be replaced by *that: the reason is that...*

rea·son·a·ble ('ri:zənəbᵊl) *adj.* **1.** showing reason or sound judgment. **2.** having the ability to reason. **3.** having modest or moderate expectations; not making unfair demands. **4.** moderate in price; not expensive. **5.** fair; average: *reasonable weather.* —**'rea·son·a·bly** *adv.* —**'rea·son·a·ble·ness** *n.*

rea·soned ('ri:zᵊnd) *adj.* well thought-out or well presented: *a reasoned explanation.* —**'rea·soned·ly** *adv.*

rea·son·ing ('ri:zənɪŋ) *n.* **1.** the act or process of drawing conclusions from facts, evidence, etc. **2.** the arguments, proofs, etc., so adduced.

re·as·sure (,ri:ə'ʃʊə) *vb.* (*tr.*) **1.** to relieve (someone) of anxieties; restore confidence to. **2.** another term for **reinsure.** —**,re·as·'sur·ance** *n.* —**,re·as·'sur·er** *n.* —**,re·as·'sur·ing·ly** *adv.*

reast (ri:st) *vb.* a variant spelling of **reest.**

Réaum. *abbrev. for* Réaumur (scale).

Ré·au·mur ('reɪə,mjʊə) *adj.* indicating measurement on the Réaumur scale of temperature.

Ré·au·mur scale *n.* a scale of temperature in which the freezing point of water is taken as 0° and the boiling point is 80°. [C18: named after René Antoine Ferchault de *Réaumur* (1683–1757), French physicist, who introduced it]

reave[1] (ri:v) *vb.* **reaves, reav·ing, reaved** *or* **reft.** *Archaic.* **1.** to carry off (property, prisoners, etc.) by force. **2.** (*tr.;* foll. by *of*) to deprive; strip. [Old English *reāfian;* related to Old High German *roubōn* to rob, Old Norse *raufa* to break open]

reave[2] (ri:v) *vb.* **reaves, reav·ing, reaved** *or* **reft.** *Archaic.* to break or tear (something) apart; cleave. [C13 *reven,* probably from REAVE[1] and influenced in meaning by RIVE]

reb (rɛb) *n.* (*sometimes cap.*) *U.S. informal.* a Confederate soldier in the American Civil War (1861–65). Also called: **Johnny Reb.** [short for REBEL]

re·bar·ba·tive (rɪ'bɑ:bətɪv) *adj. Rare.* fearsome; forbidding. [C19: from French *rébarbatif,* from Old French *rebarber* to repel (an enemy), to withstand (him) face to face, from RE- + *barbe* beard, from Latin *barba*]

re·bate[1] *n.* ('ri:beɪt). **1.** a refund of a fraction of the amount payable or paid, as for goods purchased in quantity; discount. ~*vb.* (rɪ'beɪt). (*tr.*) **2.** to deduct (a part) of a payment from (the total). **3.** *Archaic.* to reduce or diminish (something or the effectiveness of something). [C15: from Old French *rabattre* to beat down, hence reduce, deduct, from RE- + *abatre* to put down; see ABATE] —**re·'bat·a·ble** *or* **re·'bate·a·ble** *adj.* —**'re·bat·er** *n.*

re·bate[2] ('ri:beɪt, 'ræbɪt) *or* **rab·bet** *n.* **1.** a recess, groove, or step, usually of rectangular section, cut into a surface or along the edge of a piece of timber to receive a mating piece. **2.** a joint made between two pieces of timber using a rebate. ~*vb.* (*tr.*) **3.** to cut or form a rebate in (timber, etc.). **4.** to join (pieces of timber) using a rebate. [C15: *rabbet,* from Old French *rabattre* to beat down]

,re·al·lo·'ca·tion *n.*
,re·al·'lot *vb.,* **·lots, ·lot·ting, ·lot·ted.**
,re·al·'lot·ment *n.*
,re·'al·ter *vb.*
,re·al·ter·'a·tion *n.*
re·'an·a·,lyse *vb.*
,re·a·'nal·y·sis *n., pl.* **·ses.**
re·'an·a·,lyze *vb.*
re·'an·i·,mate *vb.*
,re·an·i·'ma·tion *n.*
,re·ap·'pear *vb.*
,re·ap·'pear·ance *n.*
,re·ap·pli·'ca·tion *n.*
,re·ap·'ply *vb.,* **·plies, ·ply·ing, ·plied.**
,re·ap·'point *vb.*
,re·ap·'point·ment *n.*
,re·ap·'por·tion *vb.*
,re·ap·'por·tion·ment *n.*
,re·ap·'prais·al *n.*
,re·ap·'praise *vb.*
re·'ar·gue *vb.,* **·gues, ·gu·ing, ·gued.**
,re·a·'rous·al *n.*
,re·a·'rouse *vb.*
,re·ar·'range *vb.*
,re·ar·'rest *vb., n.*
,re·as·'cend *vb.*
,re·as·'cent *n.*
,re·as·'sem·ble *vb.*
,re·as·'sem·bly *n., pl.* **·blies.**
,re·as·'sert *vb.*
,re·as·'ser·tion *n.*
,re·as·'sess *vb.*
,re·as·'sess·ment *n.*
,re·as·'sign *vb.*
,re·as·'sign·ment *n.*
,re·as·'sim·i·,late *vb.*
,re·as·,sim·i·'la·tion *n.*
,re·as·'sume *vb.*
,re·as·'sump·tion *n.*
,re·at·'tach *vb.*
,re·at·'tach·ment *n.*
,re·at·'tain *vb.*
,re·at·'tain·ment *n.*
,re·at·'tempt *vb.*
,re·a·'wak·en *vb.*
re·'bap·tism *n.*
re·bap·'tize *or* **re·bap·'tise** *vb.*
re·'bid *vb.,* **·bids, ·bid·ding, ·bid.**

re+ba+to (rəˈbɑːtəʊ) *n., pl.* **+tos.** a variant spelling of **rabato.**

re+bec *or* **re+beck** (ˈriːbɛk) *n.* a medieval stringed instrument resembling the violin but having a lute-shaped body. [C16: from Old French *rebebe,* from Arabic *rebāb;* perhaps also influenced by Old French *bec* beak]

Re·bec·ca (rɪˈbɛkə) *n. Old Testament.* the sister of Laban, who became the wife of Isaac and the mother of Esau and Jacob (Genesis 24–27). Douay spelling: **Re·bek·ah.**

re+bel *vb.* (rɪˈbɛl), **+bels, +bel+ling, +belled.** (*intr.*, often foll. by *against*) **1.** to resist or rise up against a government or other authority, esp. by force of arms. **2.** to dissent from an accepted moral code or convention of behaviour, dress, etc. **3.** to show repugnance (towards). ~*n.* (ˈrɛbᵊl). **4. a.** a person who rebels. **b.** (*as modifier*): *a rebel soldier; a rebel leader.* **5.** a person who dissents from some accepted moral code or convention of behaviour, dress, etc. [C13: from Old French *rebelle,* from Latin *rebellis* insurgent, from RE- + *bellum* war] —**ˈreb+el+dom** *n.*

re+bel+lion (rɪˈbɛljən) *n.* **1.** organized resistance or opposition to a government or other authority. **2.** dissent from an accepted moral code or convention of behaviour, dress, etc. [C14: via Old French from Latin *rebelliō* revolt (of those conquered); see REBEL]

re+bel+lious (rɪˈbɛljəs) *adj.* **1.** showing a tendency towards rebellion. **2.** (of a problem, etc.) difficult to overcome; refractory. —**re+ˈbel+lious+ly** *adv.* —**re+ˈbel+lious+ness** *n.*

re+bel+low (rɪˈbɛləʊ) *vb. Archaic or literary.* to re-echo loudly.

re+birth (riːˈbɜːθ) *n.* **1.** a revival or renaissance: *the rebirth of learning.* **2.** a second or new birth; reincarnation.

re+bore *n.* (ˈriːˌbɔː). **1.** the process of boring out the cylinders of a worn reciprocating engine and fitting oversize pistons. ~*vb.* (riːˈbɔː). **2.** (*tr.*) to carry out this process.

re+born (riːˈbɔːn) *adj.* born or as if born again, esp. in having undergone spiritual regeneration.

re+bound *vb.* (rɪˈbaʊnd). (*intr.*) **1.** to spring back, as from a sudden impact. **2.** to misfire, esp. so as to hurt the perpetrator: *the plan rebounded.* ~*n.* (ˈriːbaʊnd). **3.** the act or an instance of rebounding. **4. on the rebound. a.** in the act of springing back. **b.** *Informal.* in a state of recovering from rejection, disappointment, etc.: *he married her on the rebound from an unhappy love affair.* [C14: from Old French *rebondir,* from RE- + *bondir* to BOUND²]

re+bo+zo (rɪˈbəʊzəʊ; *Spanish* reˈboθo) *n., pl.* **+zos** (-zəʊz; *Spanish* -θos). a long wool or linen scarf covering the shoulders and head, worn by Latin American women. [Spanish: shawl, from *rebozar* to muffle]

re+buff (rɪˈbʌf) *vb.* (*tr.*) **1.** to snub, reject, or refuse (a person offering help or sympathy, an offer of help, etc.) abruptly or out of hand. **2.** to beat back (an attack); repel. ~*n.* **3.** a blunt refusal or rejection; snub. **4.** any sudden check to progress or action. [C16: from Old French *rebuffer,* from Italian *ribuffare,* from *ribuffo* a reprimand, from *ri-* RE- + *buffo* puff, gust, apparently of imitative origin]

re+buke (rɪˈbjuːk) *vb.* **1.** (*tr.*) to scold or reprimand (someone). ~*n.* **2.** a reprimand or scolding. [C14: from Old Norman French *rebuker,* from RE- + Old French *buchier* to hack down, from *busche* log, of Germanic origin] —**re+ˈbuk+a+ble** *adj.* —**re+ˈbuk+er** *n.* —**re+ˈbuk+ing+ly** *adv.*

re+bus (ˈriːbəs) *n., pl.* **+bus·es. 1.** a puzzle consisting of pictures representing syllables and words; in such a puzzle the word *hear* might be represented by H followed by a picture of an ear. **2.** a heraldic emblem or device that is a pictorial representation of or pun on the name of the bearer. [C17: from French *rébus,* from the Latin phrase *nōn verbīs sed rēbus* not by words but by things]

re+but (rɪˈbʌt) *vb.* **+buts, +but+ting, +but+ted.** (*tr.*) to refute or disprove, esp. by offering a contrary contention or argument. [C13: from Old French *reboter,* from RE- + *boter* to thrust, BUTT³] —**re+ˈbut+ta+ble** *adj.* —**re+ˈbut+tal** *n.*

re+but+ter (rɪˈbʌtə) *n.* **1.** *Law.* a defendant's pleading in reply to a plaintiff's surrejoinder. **2.** a person who rebuts.

rec (rɛk) *n. Informal.* short for **recreation** (ground).

rec. *abbrev. for:* **1.** receipt. **2.** recipe. **3.** record. **4.** recorder.

re+cal+ci+trant (rɪˈkælsɪtrənt) *adj.* **1.** not susceptible to control or authority; refractory. ~*n.* **2.** a recalcitrant person. [C19: via French from Latin *recalcitrāre,* from RE- + *calcitrāre* to kick, from *calx* heel] —**re+ˈcal+ci+trance** *n.*

re+cal+esce (ˌriːkəˈlɛs) *vb.* (*intr.*) to undergo recalescence.

re+ca+les+cence (ˌriːkəˈlɛsəns) *n.* a sudden spontaneous increase in the temperature of cooling iron resulting from an exothermic change in crystal structure occurring at a particular temperature. [C19: from Latin *recalēscere* to grow warm again, from RE- + *calēscere,* from *calēre* to be hot] —**ˌre+ca+ˈles+cent** *adj.*

re+call (rɪˈkɔːl) *vb.* (*tr.*) **1.** (*may take a clause as object*) to bring back to mind; recollect; remember. **2.** to order to return; call back permanently or temporarily: *to recall an ambassador.* **3.** to revoke or take back. **4.** to cause (one's thoughts, attention, etc.) to return from a reverie or digression. **5.** *Poetic.* to restore or revive. ~*n.* **6.** the act of recalling or state of being recalled. **7.** revocation or cancellation. **8.** the ability to remember things; recollection. **9.** *Military.* (esp. formerly) a signal to call back troops, etc., usually a bugle call: *to sound the recall.* **10.** *U.S.* the process by which elected officials may be deprived of office by popular vote. —**re+ˈcall+a+ble** *adj.*

re+cant (rɪˈkænt) *vb.* to repudiate or withdraw (a former belief or statement), esp. formally in public. [C16: from Latin *recantāre* to sing again, from RE- + *cantāre* to sing; see CHANT] —**re+can+ta+tion** (ˌriːkænˈteɪʃən) *n.* —**re+ˈcant+er** *n.*

re+cap *vb.* (ˈriːˌkæp, riːˈkæp), **+caps, +cap+ping, +capped,** *n.* (ˈriːˌkæp). *Informal.* short for **recapitulate** *or* **recapitulation.** —**re+ˈcap+pa+ble** *adj.*

re+ca+pit·u·late (ˌriːkəˈpɪtjʊˌleɪt) *vb.* **1.** to restate the main points of (an argument, speech, etc.); summarize. **2.** (*tr.*) (of an animal) to repeat (stages of its evolutionary development) during the embryonic stages of its life. **3.** to repeat at some point during a piece of music (material used earlier in the same work). [C16: from Late Latin *recapitulāre,* literally: to put back under headings; see CAPITULATE] —**ˌre+ca+ˈpit·u·la+tive** *or* **ˌre+ca+ˈpit·u·la+to·ry** *adj.*

re+ca+pit·u·la+tion (ˌriːkəˌpɪtjʊˈleɪʃən) *n.* **1.** the act of recapitulating, esp. summing up, as at the end of a speech. **2.** Also called: **palingenesis.** *Biology.* the apparent repetition in the embryonic development of an animal of the changes that occurred during its evolutionary history. Compare **caenogenesis. 3.** *Music.* the repeating of earlier themes, esp. when forming the final section of a movement in sonata form.

re+cap+tion (riːˈkæpʃən) *n. Law.* the process of taking back one's own wife, child, property, etc., without causing a breach of the peace. [C17: from RE- + CAPTION (in the sense: seizure)]

re+cap+ture (riːˈkæptʃə) *vb.* (*tr.*) **1.** to capture or take again. **2.** to recover, renew, or repeat (a lost or former ability, sensation, etc.): *she soon recaptured her high spirits.* **3.** *U.S.* (of the government) to take lawfully (a proportion of the profits of a public-service undertaking). ~*n.* **4.** the act of recapturing or fact of being recaptured. **5.** *U.S.* the seizure by the government of a proportion of the profits of a public-service undertaking.

rec+ce (ˈrɛkɪ) *n., vb.,* **+ces, +ce+ing, +ced** *or* **+ceed.** a slang word for **reconnaissance** or **reconnoitre.**

recd. *or* **rec'd.** *abbrev. for* received.

re+cede (rɪˈsiːd) *vb.* (*intr.*) **1.** to withdraw from a point or limit; go back: *the tide receded.* **2.** to become more distant: *hopes of rescue receded.* **3.** to slope backwards: *apes have receding foreheads.* **4. a.** (of a man's hair) to cease to grow at the temples and above the forehead. **b.** (of a man) to start to go bald in this way. **5.** to decline in value or character. **6.** (usually foll. by *from*) to draw back or retreat, as from a promise. [C15: from Latin *recēdere* to go back, from RE- + *cēdere* to yield, CEDE]

re-cede (riːˈsiːd) *vb.* (*tr.*) to restore to a former owner.

re+ceipt (rɪˈsiːt) *n.* **1.** a written acknowledgment by a receiver of money, goods, etc., that payment or delivery has been made. **2.** the act of receiving or fact of being received. **3.** (*usually pl.*) an amount or article received. **4.** *Obsolete or U.S. dialect.* another word for **recipe.** ~*vb.* **5.** (*tr.*) to acknowledge payment of (a bill), as by marking it. **6.** *Chiefly U.S.* to issue a receipt for (money, goods, etc.). [C14: from Old Norman French *receite,* from Medieval Latin *recepta,* from Latin *recipere* to RECEIVE]

re+ceipt+or (rɪˈsiːtə) *n. Chiefly U.S.* a person who receipts.

re+ceiv+a+ble (rɪˈsiːvəbᵊl) *adj.* **1.** suitable for or capable of being received, esp. as payment or legal tender. **2.** (of a bill, etc.) awaiting payment: *accounts receivable.* ~*n.* **3.** (*usually pl.*) the part of the assets of a business represented by accounts due for payment.

re+ceive (rɪˈsiːv) *vb.* (*mainly tr.*) **1.** to take (something offered) into one's hand or possession. **2.** to have (an honour, blessing, etc.) bestowed. **3.** to accept delivery or transmission of (a letter, telephone call, etc.). **4.** to be informed of (news or information). **5.** to hear and consent to or acknowledge (an oath, confession, etc.). **6.** (of a vessel or container) to take or hold (a substance, commodity, or certain amount). **7.** to support or sustain (the weight of something); bear. **8.** to apprehend or perceive (ideas, etc.). **9.** to experience, undergo, or meet with: *to receive a crack on the skull.* **10.** (*also intr.*) to be at home to (visitors). **11.** to greet or welcome (visitors or guests), esp. in formal style. **12.** to admit (a person) to a place, society, condition, etc.: *he was received into the priesthood.* **13.** to accept or acknowledge (a precept or principle) as true or valid. **14.** to convert (incoming radio signals) into sounds, pictures, etc., by means of a receiver. **15.** (*also intr.*) *Tennis.* to play at the other end from the server; be required to return (service). **16.** (*also intr.*) to partake of (the Christian Eucharist). **17.** (*intr.*) *Chiefly Brit.* to buy and sell stolen goods. [C13: from Old French *receivre,* from Latin *recipere* to take back, from RE- + *capere* to take]

Re+ceived Pro+nun+ci+a+tion *n.* the accent of standard Southern British English. Abbrev.: **RP**

re+ceiv+er (rɪˈsiːvə) *n.* **1.** a person who receives something; recipient. **2.** a person appointed by a court to manage property pending the outcome of litigation, during the infancy of the owner, or after the owner(s) has been declared bankrupt or of unsound mind. **3.** *Chiefly Brit.* a person who receives stolen goods knowing that they have been stolen. **4.** the equipment in a telephone, radio, or television that receives incoming electri-

---

re+ˈbid+dable *adj.*
re+ˈbind *vb.,* **+binds, +bind+ing, +bound.**
re+ˈboil *vb.*
re+ˈbroad+cast *vb.,* **+casts, +cast+ing, +cast.**
re+ˈbuild *vb.,* **+builds, +build+ing, +built.**
re+ˈbur+i+al *n.*
re+ˈbur·y *vb.,* **+bur·ies, +bur·y+ing, +bur+ied.**
re+ˈbut+ton *vb.*
re+ˈcal+cu+ˌlate *vb.*
re+ˌcap·i·tal·i·ˈza+tion *or* **re+ˌcap·i·tal·i·ˈsa+tion** *n.*
re+ˈcap·i·tal+ˌize *or* **re+ˈcap·i·tal+ˌise** *vb.*
re+ˈcast *vb.,* **+casts, cast+ing, +cast.**
re+ˈcau+tion *vb.*

cal signals or modulated radio waves and converts them into the original audio or video signals. **5.** the equipment in a radar system, radio telescope, etc., that converts incoming radio signals into a useful form, usually displayed on the screen of a cathode-ray oscilloscope. **6.** an obsolete word for **receptacle.** **7.** *Chem.* a vessel in which the distillate is collected during distillation. **8.** the metallic frame situated behind the breech of a gun to guide the round into the chamber.

re·ceiv·er·ship (rɪ'siːvəˌʃɪp) *n. Law.* **1.** the office or function of a receiver. **2.** the condition of being administered by a receiver.

re·ceiv·ing or·der *n. Brit.* a court order appointing a receiver to manage the property of a debtor or bankrupt.

re·cen·sion (rɪ'sɛnʃən) *n.* **1.** a critical revision of a literary work. **2.** a text revised in this way. [C17: from Latin *recēnsiō*, from *recēnsēre* to survey, from RE- + *cēnsēre* to assess]

re·cent ('riːsᵊnt) *adj.* having appeared, happened, or been made not long ago; modern, fresh, or new. [C16: from Latin *recens* fresh; related to Greek *kainos* new] —**'re·cent·ly** *adv.* —**'re·cent·ness** *or* **'re·cen·cy** *n.*

Re·cent ('riːsᵊnt) *adj., n. Geology.* another word for **Holocene.**

re·cept ('riːsɛpt) *n. Psychol.* an idea or image formed in the mind by repeated experience of a particular pattern of sensory stimulation. [C20: from RE- + (CON)CEPT]

re·cep·ta·cle (rɪ'sɛptəkᵊl) *n.* **1.** an object that holds something; container. **2.** *Botany.* **a.** the enlarged or modified tip of the flower stalk that bears the parts of the flower. **b.** the shortened flattened stem bearing the florets of the capitulum of composite flowers such as the daisy. **c.** the part of lower plants that bears the reproductive organs or spores. [C15: from Latin *receptāculum* a store-place, from *receptāre* to receive again, from *recipere* to RECEIVE]

re·cep·tion (rɪ'sɛpʃən) *n.* **1.** the act of receiving or state of being received. **2.** the manner in which something, such as a guest or a new idea, is received: *a cold reception.* **3.** a formal party for guests, such as one after a wedding. **4.** an area in an office, hotel, etc., where visitors or guests are received and appointments or reservations dealt with. **5.** short for **reception room.** **6.** the quality or fidelity of a received radio broadcast: *the reception was poor.* **7.** *Brit.* **a.** the first class in an infant school. **b.** a class in a school designed to receive new immigrants, esp. those whose knowledge of English is poor. **c.** (*as modifier*): *a reception teacher.* [C14: from Latin *receptiō* a receiving, from *recipere* to RECEIVE]

re·cep·tion·ist (rɪ'sɛpʃənɪst) *n.* a person employed in an office, hotel, doctor's surgery, etc., to receive clients, patients, or guests, answer the telephone, and arrange appointments, etc.

re·cep·tion room *n.* **1.** a room in a private house suitable for entertaining guests, esp. a lounge or dining room. **2.** a room in a hotel suitable for large parties, receptions, etc.

re·cep·tive (rɪ'sɛptɪv) *adj.* **1.** able to apprehend quickly. **2.** tending to receive new ideas or suggestions favourably. **3.** able to hold or receive. —**re'cep·tive·ly** *adv.* —**re·cep·tiv·i·ty** (ˌriːsɛp'tɪvɪtɪ) *or* **re'cep·tive·ness** *n.*

re·cep·tor (rɪ'sɛptə) *n.* **1.** *Physiol.* a sensory nerve ending that changes specific stimuli into nerve impulses. **2.** any of various devices that receive information, signals, etc.

re·cess *n.* (rɪ'sɛs, 'riːsɛs). **1.** a space, such as a niche or alcove, set back or indented. **2.** (*often pl.*) a secluded or secret place: *recesses of the mind.* **3.** a cessation of business, such as the closure of Parliament during a vacation. **4.** *Anatomy.* a small cavity or depression in a bodily organ, part, or structure. **5.** *U.S.* a break between classes at a school. ~*vb.* (rɪ'sɛs). **6.** (*tr.*) to place or set (something) in a recess. **7.** (*tr.*) to build a recess or recesses in (a wall, etc.). [C16: from Latin *recessus* a retreat, from *recēdere* to RECEDE]

re·ces·sion[1] (rɪ'sɛʃən) *n.* **1.** a temporary depression in economic activity or prosperity. **2.** the withdrawal of the clergy and choir in procession from the chancel at the conclusion of a church service. **3.** the act of receding. **4.** a part of a building, wall, etc., that recedes. [C17: from Latin *recessio;* see RECESS]

re·ces·sion[2] (riː'sɛʃən) *n.* the act of restoring possession to a former owner. [C19: from RE- + CESSION]

re·ces·sion·al (rɪ'sɛʃənᵊl) *adj.* **1.** of or relating to recession. ~*n.* **2.** a hymn sung as the clergy and choir withdraw from the chancel at the conclusion of a church service.

re·ces·sive (rɪ'sɛsɪv) *adj.* **1.** tending to recede or go back; receding. **2.** *Genetics.* **a.** (of a gene) capable of producing its characteristic phenotype in the organism only when its allele is identical. **b.** (of a character) controlled by such a gene. Compare **dominant** (sense 4). **3.** *Linguistics.* (of stress) tending to be placed on or near the initial syllable of a polysyllabic word. ~*n.* **4.** *Genetics.* **a.** a recessive gene or character. **b.** an organism having such a gene or character. —**re'ces·sive·ly** *adv.* —**re'ces·sive·ness** *n.*

Rech·a·bite ('rɛkəˌbaɪt) *n.* a total abstainer from alcoholic drink, esp. a member of the **Independent Order of Rechabites,** a society devoted to abstention. [C14: via Medieval Latin from Hebrew *Rēkābīm* descendants of *Rēkāb.* See Jeremiah 35:6]

ré·chauf·fé *French.* (reʃo'fe) *n.* **1.** warmed-up leftover food. **2.** old, stale, or reworked material. [C19: from French *réchauffer* to reheat, from RE- + *chauffer* to warm; see CHAFE]

re·cher·ché (rə'ʃɛəʃeɪ; *French* rəʃɛr'ʃe) *adj.* **1.** known only to connoisseurs; choice or rare. **2.** studiedly refined or elegant. [French: past participle of *rechercher* to make a thorough search for; see RESEARCH]

re·cid·i·vism (rɪ'sɪdɪˌvɪzəm) *n.* habitual relapse into crime. [C19: from Latin *recidīvus* falling back, from RE- + *cadere* to fall] —**re'cid·i·vist** *n., adj.* —**re·ˌcid·i'vis·tic** *or* **re'cid·i·vous** *adj.*

Re·ci·fe (rɛ'siːfə) *n.* a port at the easternmost point of Brazil on the Atlantic: capital of Pernambuco state; built partly on an island, with many waterways and bridges. Pop.: 1 046 454 (1970). Former name: **Pernambuco.**

rec·i·pe ('rɛsɪpɪ) *n.* **1.** a list of ingredients and directions for making something, esp. a food preparation. **2.** *Med.* (formerly) a medical prescription. **3.** a method for achieving some desired objective: *a recipe for success.* [C14: from Latin, literally: take (it)! from *recipere* to take, RECEIVE]

re·cip·i·ence (rɪ'sɪpɪəns) *n.* **1.** the act of receiving. **2.** the quality of being receptive; receptiveness.

re·cip·i·ent (rɪ'sɪpɪənt) *n.* **1.** a person who or thing that receives. ~*adj.* **2.** a less common word for **receptive.** [C16: via French from Latin *recipiēns,* from *recipere* to RECEIVE]

re·cip·ro·cal (rɪ'sɪprəkᵊl) *adj.* **1.** of, relating to, or designating something given by each of two people, countries, etc., to the other; mutual: *reciprocal friendship; reciprocal trade.* **2.** given or done in return: *a reciprocal favour.* **3.** (of a pronoun) indicating that action is given and received by each subject; for example, *each other* in the sentence *they started to shout at each other.* **4.** *Maths.* of or relating to a number or quantity divided into one. ~*n.* **5.** something that is reciprocal. **6.** Also called: **inverse.** *Maths.* a number or quantity that when multiplied by a given number or quantity gives a product of one: *the reciprocal of 2 is 0.5.* [C16: from Latin *reciprocus* alternating] —**re·ˌcip·ro'cal·i·ty** *or* **re'cip·ro·cal·ness** *n.* —**re'cip·ro·cal·ly** *adv.*

re·cip·ro·cate (rɪ'sɪprəˌkeɪt) *vb.* **1.** to give or feel in return. **2.** to move or cause to move backwards and forwards. **3.** (*intr.*) to be correspondent or equivalent. [C17: from Latin *reciprocāre,* from *reciprocus* RECIPROCAL] —**re·ˌcip·ro'ca·tion** *n.* —**re'cip·ro·ca·tive** *or* **re'cip·ro·ˌca·to·ry** *adj.* —**re'cip·ro·ˌca·tor** *n.*

re·cip·ro·cat·ing en·gine *n.* an engine in which one or more pistons move backwards and forwards inside a cylinder or cylinders.

rec·i·proc·i·ty (ˌrɛsɪ'prɒsɪtɪ) *n.* **1.** reciprocal action or relation. **2.** a mutual exchange of commercial or other privileges. [C18: via French from Latin *reciprocus* RECIPROCAL]

rec·i·proc·i·ty fail·ure *n. Photog.* a failure of the two exposure variables, light intensity and exposure time, to behave in a reciprocal fashion at very high or very low values.

re·ci·sion (rɪ'sɪʒən) *n.* the act of cancelling or rescinding; annulment: *the recision of a treaty.* [C17: from Latin *recīsiō,* from *recīdere* to cut back]

recit. *Music. abbrev. for* recitative.

re·cit·al (rɪ'saɪtᵊl) *n.* **1.** a musical performance by a soloist or soloists. Compare **concert** (sense 1). **2.** the act of reciting or repeating something learned or prepared. **3.** an account, narration, or description. **4.** a detailed statement of facts, figures, etc. **5.** (*often pl.*) *Law.* the preliminary statement in a deed showing the reason for its existence and leading up to and explaining the operative part. —**re'cit·al·ist** *n.*

rec·i·ta·tion (ˌrɛsɪ'teɪʃən) *n.* **1.** the act of reciting from memory, esp. a formal reading of verse before an audience. **2.** something recited.

rec·i·ta·tive[1] (ˌrɛsɪtə'tiːv) *n.* a passage in a musical composition, esp. the narrative parts in an oratorio, set for one voice with either continuo accompaniment only or full accompaniment, reflecting the natural rhythms of speech. [C17: from Italian *recitativo;* see RECITE]

re·cit·a·tive[2] (rɪ'saɪtətɪv) *adj.* of or relating to recital.

re·cite (rɪ'saɪt) *vb.* **1.** to repeat (a poem, etc.) aloud from memory before an audience, teacher, etc. **2.** (*tr.*) to give a detailed account of. **3.** (*tr.*) to enumerate (examples, etc.). [C15: from Latin *recitāre* to cite again, from RE- + *citāre* to summon; see CITE] —**re'cit·a·ble** *adj.* —**re'cit·er** *n.*

reck (rɛk) *vb. Archaic.* (*used mainly with a negative*) **1.** to mind or care about (something): *to reck nought.* **2.** (*usually impersonal*) to concern or interest (someone). [Old English *reccan;* related to Old High German *ruohhen* to take care, Old Norse *rækja,* Gothic *rakjan*]

reck·less ('rɛklɪs) *adj.* having or showing no regard for danger or consequences; heedless; rash: *a reckless driver; a reckless attempt.* [Old English *recceleās* (see RECK, -LESS); related to Middle Dutch *roekeloos,* Old High German *ruahhalōs*] —**'reck·less·ly** *adv.* —**'reck·less·ness** *n.*

Reck·ling·hau·sen (*German* ˌrɛklɪŋ'haʊzən) *n.* an industrial city in NW West Germany, in North Rhine-Westphalia on the N edge of the Ruhr. Pop.: 124 383 (1974 est.).

reck·on ('rɛkən) *vb.* **1.** to calculate or ascertain by calculating; compute. **2.** (*tr.*) to include; count as part of a set or class: *I reckon her with the angels.* **3.** (*usually passive*) to consider or regard: *he is reckoned clever.* **4.** (when *tr., takes a clause as object*) to think or suppose; be of the opinion: *I reckon you don't know where to go next.* **5.** (*intr.,* foll. by *with*) to settle accounts (with). **6.** (*intr.,* foll. by *with* or *without*) to take into account or fail to take into account: *the bully reckoned without John's big brother.* **7.** (*intr.,* foll. by *on* or *upon*) to rely or depend: *I reckon on your support in this crisis.* **8.** (*tr.*) *Slang.* to regard as good: *I don't reckon your chances of success.* **9. to be reckoned with.** of considerable importance or influence. [Old

---

re'chal·lenge *vb.*
re'charge *vb., n.*
re'chart *vb.*
re'char·ter *vb.*
re'check *vb.*
re'chris·ten *vb.*
re'cir·cu·ˌlate *vb.*
ˌre·clas·si·fi'ca·tion *n.*

English *(ge)recenian* recount; related to Old Frisian *rekenia,* Old High German *rehhanón* to count]

Usage. Some senses of *reckon* are considered informal by many writers and speakers. The usage *I reckon on your support* is sometimes avoided in formal contexts, while in the sentence *It will snow tonight, I reckon,* the words *believe, suppose, think,* or *imagine* are preferred to *reckon.*

reck·on·er ('rɛkənə) *n.* any of various devices or tables used to facilitate reckoning, esp. a ready reckoner.

reck·on·ing ('rɛkənɪŋ) *n.* **1.** the act of counting or calculating. **2.** settlement of an account or bill. **3.** a bill or account. **4.** retribution for one's actions (esp. in the phrase **day of reckoning**). **5.** *Navigation.* short for **dead reckoning.**

re·claim (rɪ'kleɪm) *vb. (tr.)* **1.** to convert (desert, marsh, waste ground, etc.) into land suitable for growing crops. **2.** to recover (useful substances) from waste products. **3.** to convert (someone) from sin, folly, vice, etc. **4.** *Falconry.* to render (a hawk or falcon) tame. *~n.* **5.** the act of reclaiming or state of being reclaimed. [C13: from Old French *réclamer,* from Latin *reclāmāre* to cry out, protest, from RE- + *clāmāre* to shout] —**re·'claim·a·ble** *adj.* —**re·'claim·ant** *or* **re·'claim·er** *n.*

rec·la·ma·tion (ˌrɛklə'meɪʃən) *n.* **1.** the conversion of desert, marsh, or other waste land into land suitable for cultivation. **2.** the recovery of useful substances from waste products. **3.** the act of reclaiming or state of being reclaimed.

ré·clame *French.* (re'klam) *n.* **1.** public acclaim or attention; publicity. **2.** the capacity for attracting publicity.

rec·li·nate ('rɛklɪˌneɪt) *adj.* (esp. of a leaf or stem) naturally curved or bent backwards so that the upper part rests on the ground. [C18: from Latin *reclīnātus* bent back]

re·cline (rɪ'klaɪn) *vb.* to rest or cause to rest in a leaning position. [C15: from Old French *recliner,* from Latin *reclīnāre* to lean back, from RE- + *clīnāre* to LEAN[1]] —**re·'clin·a·ble** *adj.* —**rec·li·na·tion** (ˌrɛklɪ'neɪʃən) *n.* —**re·'clin·er** *n.*

re·cluse (rɪ'klu:s) *n.* **1.** a person who lives in seclusion. **2.** a person who lives in solitude to devote himself to prayer and religious meditation; a hermit, anchorite, or anchoress. *~adj.* **3.** solitary; retiring. [C13: from Old French *reclus,* from Late Latin *reclūdere* to shut away, from Latin RE- + *claudere* to close] —**re·clu·sion** (rɪ'klu:ʒən) *n.* —**re·'clu·sive** *adj.*

rec·og·ni·tion (ˌrɛkəg'nɪʃən) *n.* **1.** the act of recognizing or fact of being recognized. **2.** acceptance or acknowledgment of a claim, duty, fact, truth, etc. **3.** a token of thanks or acknowledgment. **4.** formal acknowledgment of a government or of the independence of a country. **5.** *U.S.* an instance of a chairman granting a person the right to speak in a deliberative body. [C15: from Latin *recognitiō,* from *recognoscere* to know again, from RE- + *cognoscere* to know, ascertain] —**re·'cog·ni·tive** (rɪ'kɒgnɪtɪv) *or* **re·'cog·ni·to·ry** *adj.*

re·cog·ni·zance *or* **re·cog·ni·sance** (rɪ'kɒgnɪzəns) *n.* **1.** *Law.* **a.** a bond entered into before a court or magistrate by which a person binds himself to do a specified act, as to appear in court on a stated day, keep the peace, or pay a debt. **b.** a monetary sum pledged to the performance of such an act. **2.** an obsolete word for **recognition.** [C14: from Old French *reconoissance,* from *reconoistre* to RECOGNIZE] —**re·'cog·ni·zant** *or* **re·'cog·ni·sant** *adj.*

rec·og·nize *or* **rec·og·nise** ('rɛkəgˌnaɪz) *vb. (tr.)* **1.** to perceive (a person, creature, or thing) to be the same as or belong to the same class as something previously seen or known; know again. **2.** to accept or be aware of (a fact, duty, problem, etc.): *to recognize necessity.* **3.** to acknowledge formally (a government of a state) or the independence of (a country). **4.** *U.S.* to grant (a person) the right to speak in a deliberative body. **5.** to give a token of thanks for (a service rendered, etc.). **6.** to acknowledge formally (a claim, etc.). **7.** to show approval or appreciation of (something good or pleasing). **8.** to acknowledge or greet (a person), as when meeting by chance. **9.** *(intr.) Chiefly U.S.* to enter into a recognizance. [C15: from Latin *recognoscere* to know again, from RE- + *cognoscere* to know, ascertain] —'**rec·og·ˌniz·a·ble** *or* '**rec·og·ˌnis·a·ble** *adj.* —ˌ**rec·og·ˌniz·a·'bil·i·ty** *or* ˌ**rec·og·ˌnis·a·'bil·i·ty** *n.* —'**rec·og·ˌniz·a·bly** *or* '**rec·og·ˌnis·a·bly** *adv.* —'**rec·og·ˌniz·er** *or* '**rec·og·ˌnis·er** *n.*

re·cog·ni·zee *or* **re·cog·ni·see** (rɪˌkɒgnɪ'zi:) *n. Law.* the person to whom one entering into a recognizance is bound.

re·cog·ni·zor *or* **re·cog·ni·sor** (rɪˌkɒgnɪ'zɔ:) *n. Law.* a person who enters into a recognizance.

re·coil *vb.* (rɪ'kɔɪl). *(intr.)* **1.** to jerk back, as from an impact or violent thrust. **2.** (often foll. by *from*) to draw back in fear, horror, or disgust: *to recoil from the sight of blood.* **3.** (foll. by *on* or *upon*) to go wrong, esp. so as to hurt the perpetrator. **4.** (of a nucleus, atom, molecule, or elementary particle) to change momentum as a result of the emission of a photon or particle. *~n.* (rɪ'kɔɪl, 'ri:kɔɪl). **5. a.** the backward movement of a gun when fired. **b.** the distance moved. **6.** the motion acquired by a particle as a result of its emission of a photon or other particle. **7.** the act of recoiling. [C13: from Old French *reculer,* from RE- + *cul* rump, from Latin *cūlus*] —**re·'coil·er** *n.* —**re·'coil·less** *adj.*

rec·ol·lect (ˌrɛkə'lɛkt) *vb.* (when *tr., often takes a clause as object*) to recall from memory; remember. [C16: from Latin *recolligere* to gather again, from RE- + *colligere* to COLLECT] —ˌ**rec·ol·'lec·tion** *n.* —ˌ**rec·ol·'lec·tive** *adj.* —ˌ**rec·ol·'lec·tive·ly** *adv.*

re·com·bi·na·tion (ˌri:kɒmbɪ'neɪʃən) *n. Genetics.* the rearrangement of the genes in a chromosome of an organism into an order differing from that in either of its parents: usually results from crossing over at meiosis.

rec·om·mend (ˌrɛkə'mɛnd) *vb. (tr.)* **1.** *(may take a clause as object or an infinitive)* to advise as the best course or choice; counsel: *to recommend prudence.* **2.** to praise or commend: *to recommend a new book.* **3.** to make attractive or advisable: *the trip has little to recommend it.* **4.** *Archaic.* to entrust (a person or thing) to someone else's care; commend. [C14: via Medieval Latin from Latin RE- + *commendāre* to COMMEND] —ˌ**rec·om·'mend·a·ble** *adj.* —ˌ**rec·om·'mend·er** *n.*

rec·om·men·da·tion (ˌrɛkəmɛn'deɪʃən) *n.* **1.** the act of recommending. **2.** something that recommends, esp. a letter presenting someone as suitable for a job, etc. **3.** something that is recommended, such as a course of action.

rec·om·mend·a·to·ry (ˌrɛkə'mɛndətərɪ, -trɪ) *adj.* intended to or serving to recommend.

re·com·mit (ˌri:kə'mɪt) *vb.* **·mits, ·mit·ting, ·mit·ted.** *(tr.)* **1.** to send (a bill) back to a committee for further consideration. **2.** to commit again. —ˌ**re·com·'mit·ment** *or* ˌ**re·com·'mit·tal** *n.*

rec·om·pense ('rɛkəmˌpɛns) *vb.* **1.** *(tr.)* to pay or reward for service, work, etc. **2.** *(tr.)* to compensate for loss, injury, etc. *~n.* **3.** compensation for loss, injury, etc.: *to make recompense.* **4.** reward, remuneration, or repayment. [C15: from Old French *recompenser,* from Latin RE- + *compensāre* to balance in weighing; see COMPENSATE] —'**rec·om·ˌpen·sa·ble** *adj.* —'**rec·om·ˌpens·er** *n.*

re·com·pose (ˌri:kəm'pəʊz) *vb. (tr.)* **1.** to restore to composure or calmness. **2.** to arrange or compose again; reform. —**re·com·po·si·tion** (ˌri:kɒmpə'zɪʃən) *n.*

rec·on·cil·a·ble ('rɛkənˌsaɪləbᵊl, ˌrɛkən'saɪ-) *adj.* able or willing to be reconciled. —ˌ**rec·on·ˌcil·a·'bil·i·ty** *or* '**rec·on·ˌcil·a·ble·ness** *n.* —'**rec·on·ˌcil·a·bly** *adv.*

rec·on·cile ('rɛkənˌsaɪl) *vb. (tr.)* **1.** *(often passive;* usually foll. by *to)* to make (oneself or another) no longer opposed; cause to acquiesce in something unpleasant: *she reconciled herself to poverty.* **2.** to become friendly with (someone) after estrangement or to re-establish friendly relations between (two or more people). **3.** to settle (a quarrel or difference). **4.** to make (two apparently conflicting things) compatible or consistent with each other. **5.** to reconsecrate (a desecrated church, etc.). [C14: from Latin *reconciliāre* to bring together again, from RE- + *conciliāre* to make friendly, CONCILIATE] —'**rec·on·ˌcile·ment** *n.* —'**rec·on·ˌcil·er** *n.* —**rec·on·cil·i·a·tion** (ˌrɛkənˌsɪlɪ'eɪʃən) *n.* —**rec·on·cil·i·a·to·ry** (ˌrɛkən'sɪlɪətərɪ, -trɪ) *adj.*

re·con·dite (rɪ'kɒndaɪt, 'rɛkənˌdaɪt) *adj.* **1.** requiring special knowledge to be understood; abstruse. **2.** dealing with abstruse or profound subjects. [C17: from Latin *reconditus* hidden away, from RE- + *condere* to conceal] —**re·'con·dite·ly** *adv.* —**re·'con·dite·ness** *n.*

re·con·di·tion (ˌri:kən'dɪʃən) *vb. (tr.)* to restore to good condition or working order: *to recondition an engine.* —ˌ**re·con·'di·tion·er** *n.*

re·con·nais·sance *or* **re·con·nois·sance** (rɪ'kɒnɪsəns) *n.* **1.** the act of reconnoitring. **2.** the process of obtaining information about the position, activities, resources, etc., of an enemy or potential enemy. **3.** a preliminary inspection of an area of land before an engineering survey is made. [C18: from French, from Old French *reconoistre* to explore, RECOGNIZE]

rec·on·noi·tre *or U.S.* **re·con·noi·ter** (ˌrɛkə'nɔɪtə) *vb.* **1.** to survey or inspect (an enemy's position, region of land, etc.); make a reconnaissance (of). *~n.* **2.** the act or process of reconnoitring; a reconnaissance. [C18: from obsolete French *reconnoître* to inspect, explore; see RECOGNIZE] —ˌ**rec·on·'noi·trer** *or U.S.* ˌ**rec·on·'noi·ter·er** *n.*

re·con·sid·er (ˌri:kən'sɪdə) *vb.* **1.** to consider (something) again, with a view to changing one's policy or course of action. **2.** (in a legislative assembly or similar body) to consider again (a bill or other matter) that has already been voted upon. —ˌ**re·con·ˌsid·er·'a·tion** *n.*

re·con·sti·tute (ri:'kɒnstɪˌtju:t) *vb. (tr.)* **1.** to restore (food, etc.) to its former or natural state or a semblance of it, as by the addition of water to a concentrate: *reconstituted lemon juice.* **2.** to reconstruct; form again. —**re·con·stit·u·ent** (ˌri:kən'stɪtjʊənt) *adj., n.* —ˌ**re·con·sti·'tu·tion** *n.*

re·con·struct (ˌri:kən'strʌkt) *vb. (tr.)* **1.** to construct or form again; rebuild: *to reconstruct a Greek vase from fragments.* **2.** to form a picture of (a crime, past event, etc.) by piecing together evidence or acting out a version of what might have taken place. —ˌ**re·con·'struc·ti·ble** *adj.* —ˌ**re·con·'struc·tion** *n.* —ˌ**re·con·'struc·tive** *or* ˌ**re·con·'struc·tion·al** *adj.* —ˌ**re·con·'struc·tor** *n.*

Re·con·struc·tion (ˌri:kən'strʌkʃən) *n. U.S. history.* the period after the Civil War when the South was reorganized and reintegrated into the Union (1865–77).

---

re·'clas·si·fy *vb.,* **·fies, ·fy·ing, ·fied.**
re·'clothe *vb.*
re·'coin *vb.*
ˌ**re·col·o·ni·'za·tion** *or* ˌ**re·col·o·ni·'sa·tion** *n.*
re·'col·o·ˌnize *or* **re·'col·o·ˌnise** *vb.*
re·'col·our *vb.*
re·'comb *vb.*
ˌ**re·com·'mence** *vb.*
ˌ**re·com·'mence·ment** *n.*
ˌ**re·com·'par·i·son** *n.*
ˌ**re·com·'pound** *vb.*
re·'con·cen·ˌtrate *vb.*
ˌ**re·con·cen·'tra·tion** *n.*
ˌ**re·con·den·'sa·tion** *n.*
ˌ**re·con·'dense** *vb.*
ˌ**re·con·'firm** *vb.*
ˌ**re·con·fir·'ma·tion** *n.*
ˌ**re·con·'nect** *vb.*
ˌ**re·con·'nec·tion** *n.*
re·'con·quer *vb.*
re·'con·quest *n.*
re·'con·se·ˌcrate *vb.*
ˌ**re·con·se·'cra·tion** *n.*
ˌ**re·con·'sign** *vb.*
ˌ**re·con·'sign·ment** *n.*
ˌ**re·con·'sol·i·date** *vb.*
ˌ**re·con·ˌsol·i·'da·tion** *n.*
ˌ**re·con·'test** *vb.*
ˌ**re·con·'vene** *vb.*

Re+con+struc+tion+ism (ˌri:kənˈstrʌkʃəˌnɪzəm) *n. U.S.* militant Zionism. —ˌ**Re+con+ˈstruc+tion+ist** *n., adj.*

re+con+vert (ˌri:kənˈvɜ:t) *vb.* (*tr.*) **1.** to change (something) back to a previous state or form. **2.** to bring (someone) back to his former religion. **3.** *Logic.* to transpose (the subject and predicate of a proposition) for the second time. **4.** *Property law.* to convert back (property previously converted) into its original form, as land into money and vice versa. See also **conversion** (sense 5). —**re+con+ver+sion** (ˌri:kənˈvɜ:ʃən) *n.*

rec+ord *n.* (ˈrɛkɔ:d). **1.** an account in permanent form, esp. in writing, preserving knowledge or information about facts or events. **2.** a written account of some transaction that serves as legal evidence of the transaction. **3.** a written official report of the proceedings of a court of justice or legislative body, including the judgments given or enactments made. **4.** anything serving as evidence or as a memorial: *the First World War is a record of human folly.* **5.** (*often pl.*) information or data on a specific subject collected methodically over a long period: *weather records.* **6. a.** the best or most outstanding amount, rate, height, etc., ever attained, as in some field of sport: *an Olympic record; a world record; to break the record for the long jump.* **b.** (*as modifier*): *a record time.* **7.** the sum of one's recognized achievements, career, or performance: *the officer has an excellent record.* **8.** a list of crimes of which an accused person has previously been convicted, which are known to the police but may only be disclosed to a court in certain circumstances. **9. have a record.** to be a known criminal; have a previous conviction or convictions. **10.** Also called: **gramophone record, disc.** a thin disc of a plastic material upon which sound has been recorded. Each side has a spiral groove, the walls of which undulate in accordance with the frequency and amplitude of the sound. Records were formerly made from a shellac-based compound but are now usually made from vinyl plastics. **11.** the markings made by a recording instrument such as a seismograph. **12.** *Computer technol.* a group of data or piece of information preserved as a unit in machine-readable form. **13. for the record.** for the sake of strict factual accuracy. **14. go on record.** to state one's views publicly. **15. off the record.** confidential or confidentially; not for publication or disclosure. **16. on record. a.** stated in a public document. **b.** publicly known. **17. set** *or* **put the record straight.** to correct an error or misunderstanding. ~*vb.* (rɪˈkɔ:d). (*mainly tr.*) **18.** to set down in some permanent form so as to preserve the true facts of: *to record the minutes of a meeting.* **19.** to contain or serve to relate (facts, information, etc.). **20.** to indicate, show, or register: *his face recorded his disappointment.* **21.** to remain as or afford evidence of: *these ruins record the life of the Romans in Britain.* **22.** (*also intr.*) to make a recording of (music, speech, etc.) for reproduction, esp. on a record-player or tape recorder, or for later broadcasting. **23.** (*also intr.*) (of an instrument) to register or indicate (information) on a scale: *the barometer recorded a low pressure.* [C13: from Old French *recorder* to call to mind, from Latin *recordārī* to remember, from RE- + *cor* heart] —**re+ˈcord+a+ble** *adj.*

rec·ord-chang·er *n.* a device in a record player for changing records automatically.

re+cord+ed de+liv+er·y *n.* a Post Office service by which an official record of posting and delivery is obtained for a letter or package. Compare **registered post.**

re+cord+er (rɪˈkɔ:də) *n.* **1.** a person who records, such as an official or historian. **2.** something that records, esp. an apparatus that provides a permanent record of experiments, etc. **3.** short for **tape recorder. 4.** *Music.* a wind instrument of the flute family, blown through a fipple in the mouth end, having a reedlike quality of tone. There are four usual sizes: bass, tenor, treble, and descant. **5.** (in England) a barrister or solicitor of at least ten years' standing appointed to sit as a part-time judge in the crown court. —**re+ˈcord+er+ˌship** *n.*

re+cord+ing (rɪˈkɔ:dɪŋ) *n.* **1. a.** the act or process of making a record, esp. of sound on a gramophone record or magnetic tape. **b.** (*as modifier*): *recording studio; recording head.* **2.** the record or tape so produced. **3.** something that has been recorded, esp. a radio or television programme.

Re+cord+ing An+gel *n.* an angel who supposedly keeps a record of every person's good and bad acts.

rec·ord-play·er *n.* a machine, often a small or portable one, for playing gramophone records.

re+count (rɪˈkaʊnt) *vb.* (*tr.*) to tell the story or details of; narrate. [C15: from Old French *reconter,* from RE- + *conter* to tell, relate; see COUNT[1]] —**re+ˈcount+al** *n.*

re-count *vb.* (ri:ˈkaʊnt). **1.** to count (votes, etc.) again. ~*n.* (ˈri:ˌkaʊnt). **2.** a second or further count, esp. of votes in a closely contested election.

re+coup (rɪˈku:p) *vb.* **1.** to regain or make good (a financial or other loss). **2.** (*tr.*) to reimburse or compensate (someone), as for a loss. **3.** *Law.* to keep back (something due), having rightful claim to do so; withhold; deduct. ~*n.* **4.** *Rare.* the act of recouping; recoupment. [C15: from Old French *recouper* to cut back, from RE- + *couper* to cut, from *coper* to behead; see COUP] —**re+ˈcoup+a+ble** *adj.* —**re+ˈcoup+ment** *n.*

re+course (rɪˈkɔ:s) *n.* **1.** the act of resorting to a person, course of action, etc., in difficulty or danger (esp. in the phrase **have recourse to**). **2.** a person, organization, or course of action that is turned to for help, protection, etc. **3.** the right to demand payment, esp. from the drawer or endorser of a bill of exchange or other negotiable instrument when the person accepting it fails to pay. **4. without recourse.** a qualified endorsement on such a negotiable instrument, by which the endorser protects himself from liability to subsequent holders. [C14: from Old French *recours,* from Late Latin *recursus* a running back, from RE- + *currere* to run]

re+cov+er (rɪˈkʌvə) *vb.* **1.** (*tr.*) to find again or obtain the return of (something lost). **2.** to regain (loss of money, position, time, etc.); recoup. **3.** (of a person) to regain (health, spirits, composure, etc.), as after illness, a shock, or a setback. **4.** to regain (a former and usually better condition): *industry recovered after the war.* **5.** *Law.* **a.** (*tr.*) to gain (something) by the judgment of a court of law: *to recover damages.* **b.** (*intr.*) to succeed in a lawsuit. **6.** (*tr.*) to obtain (useful substances) from waste. **7.** (*intr.*) (in fencing, swimming, rowing, etc.) to make a recovery. [C14: from Old French *recoverer,* from Latin *recuperāre* RECUPERATE] —**re+ˈcov+er+a+ble** *adj.* —**re+ˌcov+er+a+ˈbil+i+ty** *n.* —**re+ˈcov+er+er** *n.*

re-cov·er (ri:ˈkʌvə) *vb.* (*tr.*) **1.** to cover again. **2.** to provide (a piece of furniture, etc.) with a new cover.

re+cov+er·y (rɪˈkʌvərɪ) *n., pl.* **+er·ies. 1.** the act or process of recovering, esp. from sickness, a shock, or a setback; recuperation. **2.** restoration to a former or better condition. **3.** the regaining of something lost. **4.** the extraction of useful substances from waste. **5.** *Law.* **a.** the obtaining of a right, title, etc., by the judgment of a court. **b.** (in the U.S.) the final judgment or verdict in a case. **6.** *Fencing.* a return to the position of guard after making an attack. **7.** *Swimming, rowing, etc.* the action of bringing the arm, oar, etc., forward for another stroke. **8.** *Golf.* a stroke played from the rough or a bunker to the fairway or green.

rec+re+ant (ˈrɛkrɪənt) *Archaic.* ~*adj.* **1.** cowardly; faint-hearted. **2.** disloyal. ~*n.* **3.** a disloyal or cowardly person. [C14: from Old French, from *recroire* to surrender, from RE- + Latin *crēdere* to believe; compare MISCREANT] —**ˈrec+re+ance** *or* **ˈrec+re+an+cy** *n.* —**ˈrec+re+ant+ly** *adv.*

rec+re+ate (ˈrɛkrɪˌeɪt) *vb. Rare.* to amuse (oneself or someone else). [C15: from Latin *recreāre* to invigorate, renew, from RE- + *creāre* to CREATE] —**ˈrec+re·a+tive** *adj.* —**ˈrec+re·a+tive+ly** *adv.* —**ˈrec+re·ˌa+tor** *n.*

re-cre·ate (ˌri:krɪˈeɪt) *vb.* to create anew; reproduce. —ˌ**re-cre·ˈa·tion** *n.* —ˌ**re-cre·ˈa·tor** *n.*

rec+re·a·tion (ˌrɛkrɪˈeɪʃən) *n.* **1.** refreshment of health or spirits by relaxation and enjoyment. **2.** an activity or pastime that promotes this. **3. a.** an interval of free time between school lessons. **b.** (*as modifier*): *recreation period.* —ˌ**rec+re·ˈa+tion+al** *adj.*

rec+re·a·tion ground *n.* an open space for public recreation, esp. one in a town with swings and slides, etc., for children.

rec+re+ment (ˈrɛkrɪmənt) *n.* **1.** *Physiol.* any substance, such as bile, that is secreted from a part of the body and later reabsorbed instead of being excreted. **2.** waste matter; refuse; dross. [C16: via Old French from Latin *recrēmentum* slag, filth, from RE- + *cernere* to sift] —ˌ**rec+re+ˈmen+tal** *adj.*

re+crim·i+nate (rɪˈkrɪmɪˌneɪt) *vb.* (*intr.*) to return an accusation against someone or engage in mutual accusations. [C17: from Medieval Latin *recrīmināre,* from Latin *crīminārī* to accuse, from *crīmen* an accusation; see CRIME] —**re+ˈcrim·i+na+tive** *or* **re+ˈcrim·i+na+to·ry** *adj.* —**re+ˈcrim·i+ˌna+tor** *n.*

re+crim·i+na+tion (rɪˌkrɪmɪˈneɪʃən) *n.* **1.** the act or an instance of recriminating. **2.** *Law.* a charge made by an accused against his accuser; countercharge.

re+cru+desce (ˌri:kru:ˈdɛs) *vb.* (*intr.*) (of a disease, trouble, etc.) to break out or appear again after a period of dormancy; recur. [C19: from Latin *recrūdēscere* to become raw again, from RE- + *crūdēscere* to grow worse, from *crūdus* bloody, raw; see CRUDE] —ˌ**re+cru+ˈdes+cence** *n.*

re+cruit (rɪˈkru:t) *vb.* **1. a.** to enlist (men) for military service. **b.** to raise or strengthen (an army, etc.) by enlistment. **2.** (*tr.*) to enrol or obtain (members, support, etc.). **3.** to furnish or be furnished with a fresh supply; renew. **4.** *Archaic.* to recover (health, strength, spirits, etc.). ~*n.* **5.** a newly joined member of a military service. **6.** any new member or supporter. [C17: from French *recrute* literally: new growth, from *recroître* to grow again, from Latin *recrēscere,* from RE- + *crēscere* to grow] —**re+ˈcruit+a+ble** *adj.* —**re+ˈcruit+er** *n.* —**re+ˈcruit+ment** *n.*

re+crys+tal+lize *or* **re+crys+tal+lise** (ri:ˈkrɪstəˌlaɪz) *vb.* **1.** *Chem.* to dissolve and subsequently crystallize (a substance) from the solution, as in purifying chemical compounds, or (of a substance) to crystallize in this way. **2.** to undergo or cause to undergo the process in which a deformed metal forms a new set of undeformed crystal grains. —**re+ˌcrys+tal+li+ˈza+tion** *or* **re+ˌcrys+tal+li+ˈsa+tion** *n.*

rect. *or* **rec't.** *abbrev. for* receipt.

Rect. *abbrev. for:* **1.** Rector. **2.** Rectory.

rec+ta (ˈrɛktə) *n.* the plural of **rectum.**

rec+tal (ˈrɛktəl) *adj.* of or relating to the rectum. —**ˈrec+tal+ly** *adv.*

rec+tan+gle (ˈrɛkˌtæŋgəl) *n.* a parallelogram having four right angles. Compare **rhombus.** [C16: from Medieval Latin *rectangulum,* from Latin *rectus* straight + *angulus* angle]

rec+tan+gu+lar (rɛkˈtæŋgjʊlə) *adj.* **1.** shaped like a rectangle. **2.** having or relating to right angles. **3.** mutually perpendicular: *rectangular coordinates.* **4.** having a base or section shaped like a rectangle. —**rec+ˌtan+gu+ˈlar+i+ty** *n.* —**rec+ˈtan+gu+lar+ly** *adv.*

ˌ**re+con+ˈvey** *vb.*
re+ˈcop·y *vb.,* **+cop+ies, +cop·y+ing, +cop+ied.**
re+ˈcross *vb.*
re+ˈcrown *vb.*
re+ˈdec·o+ˌrate *vb.*
re+ˌdec·o+ˈra+tion *n.*
re+ˈded·i+ˌcate *vb.*

rec+tan+gu+lar co+or+di+nates *pl. n.* the Cartesian coordinates in a system of mutually perpendicular axes.

rec+tan+gu+lar hy+per+bo+la *n.* a hyperbola with perpendicular asymptotes.

rec+ti ('rɛktaɪ) *n.* the plural of **rectus.**

rec+ti- *or before a vowel* **rect-** *combining form.* straight or right: *rectilinear; rectangle.* [from Latin *rectus*]

rec+ti+fi+er ('rɛktɪˌfaɪə) *n.* **1.** an electronic device, such as a semiconductor diode or valve, that converts an alternating current to a direct current by suppression or inversion of alternate half cycles. **2.** *Chem.* an apparatus for condensing a hot vapour to a liquid in distillation; condenser. **3.** a thing or person that rectifies.

rec+ti+fy ('rɛktɪˌfaɪ) *vb.* **+fies, +fy+ing, +fied.** (*tr.*) **1.** to put right; correct; remedy. **2.** to separate (a substance) from a mixture or refine (a substance) by fractional distillation. **3.** to convert (alternating current) into direct current. **4.** *Maths.* to determine the length of (a curve). **5.** to cause (an object) to assume a linear motion or characteristic. [C14: via Old French from Medieval Latin *rectificāre* to adjust, from Latin *rectus* straight + *facere* to make] —**'rec+ti+ˌfi+a+ble** *adj.* —**ˌrec+ti+fi+'ca+tion** *n.*

rec+ti+lin+e+ar (ˌrɛktɪ'lɪnɪə) *or* **rec+ti+lin+e+al** *adj.* **1.** in, moving in, or characterized by a straight line or lines: *the rectilinear propagation of light.* **2.** consisting of, bounded by, or formed by a straight line or lines. —**ˌrec+ti+'lin+e+ar+ly** *or* **ˌrec+ti+'lin+e+al+ly** *adv.*

rec+ti+tude ('rɛktɪˌtju:d) *n.* **1.** moral or religious correctness. **2.** correctness of judgment. [C15: from Late Latin *rectitūdō,* from Latin *rectus* right, straight, from *regere* to rule]

rec+to ('rɛktəʊ) *n., pl.* **+tos. 1.** the front of a sheet of printed paper. **2.** the right-hand pages of a book, bearing the odd numbers. Compare **verso** (sense 1b). [C19: from Latin *rectus* right, in *rectō foliō* on the right-hand page]

rec+to+cele ('rɛktəʊˌsi:l) *n. Pathol.* a protrusion or herniation of the rectum into the vagina.

rec+tor ('rɛktə) *n.* **1.** *Church of England.* a clergyman in charge of a parish in which, as its incumbent, he would formerly have been entitled to the whole of the tithes. Compare **vicar. 2.** *R.C. Church.* a cleric in charge of a college, religious house, or congregation. **3.** *Protestant Episcopal Church.* a clergyman in charge of a parish. **4.** *Chiefly Brit.* the head of certain schools, colleges, or universities. [C14: from Latin: director, ruler, from *regere* to rule] —**'rec+tor+ate** *n.* —**rec+tor+i+al** (rɛk'tɔ:rɪəl) *adj.* —**'rec+tor+ship** *n.*

rec+to+ry ('rɛktərɪ) *n., pl.* **-ries. 1.** the official house of a rector. **2.** *Church of England.* the office and benefice of a rector.

rec+trix ('rɛktrɪks) *n., pl.* **rec+tri+ces** ('rɛktrɪˌsi:z, rɛk'traɪsi:z). any of the large stiff feathers of a bird's tail, used in controlling the direction of flight. [C17: from Late Latin, feminine of *rector* governor, RECTOR]

rec+tum ('rɛktəm) *n., pl.* **+tums** *or* **+ta** (-tə). the lower part of the alimentary canal, between the sigmoid flexure of the colon and the anus. [C16: shortened from New Latin *rectum intestinum* the straight intestine]

rec+tus ('rɛktəs) *n., pl.* **+ti** (-taɪ). *Anatomy.* a straight muscle, esp. either of two muscles of the anterior abdominal wall (**rectus abdominis**). [C18: from New Latin *rectus musculus*]

re+cum+bent (rɪ'kʌmbənt) *adj.* **1.** lying down; reclining. **2.** (of a part or organ) leaning or resting against another organ or the ground: *a recumbent stem.* **3.** (of a fold in a rock formation) having strata nearly parallel to those of the surrounding formation. [C17: from Latin *recumbere* to lie back, from RE- + *cumbere* to lie] —**re+'cum+bence** *or* **re+'cum+ben+cy** *n.* —**re+'cum+bent+ly** *adv.*

re+cu+per+ate (rɪ'ku:pəˌreɪt, -'kju:-) *vb.* **1.** (*intr.*) to recover from illness or exhaustion. **2.** to recover (losses of money, etc.). [C16: from Latin *recuperāre* to recover, from RE- + *capere* to gain, take] —**re+ˌcu+per+'a+tion** *n.* —**re+'cu+per+a+tive** *adj.* —**re+'cu+per+ˌa+tor** *n.*

re+cu+per+a+tor (rɪ'ku:pəˌreɪtə, -'kju:-) *n.* **1.** a device employing springs or pneumatic power to return a gun to the firing position after the recoil. **2.** *Chemical engineering.* a system of flues that transfers heat from the hot gases leaving a furnace to the incoming air.

re+cur (rɪ'kɜ:) *vb.* **+curs, +cur+ring, +curred.** (*intr.*) **1.** to happen again, esp. at regular intervals. **2.** (of a thought, etc.) to come back to the mind. **3.** (of a problem, etc.) to come up again. **4.** *Maths.* (of a digit or group of digits) to be repeated an infinite number of times at the end of a decimal. [C15: from Latin *recurrere,* from RE- + *currere* to run] —**re+cur+rence** (rɪ'kʌrəns) *n.* —**re+'cur+ring+ly** *adv.*

re+cur+rent (rɪ'kʌrənt) *adj.* **1.** happening or tending to happen again or repeatedly. **2.** *Anatomy.* (of certain nerves, branches of vessels, etc.) turning back, so as to run in the opposite direction. —**re+'cur+rent+ly** *adv.*

re+cur+rent fe+ver *n.* another name for **relapsing fever.**

re+cur+ring dec+i+mal *n.* a rational number that contains a pattern of digits repeated indefinitely after the decimal point. Also called: **circulating decimal, repeating decimal.**

re+cur+sion (rɪ'kɜ:ʃən) *n.* **1.** the act or process of returning or running back. **2.** *Maths.* repetition of a mathematical operation, esp. in a repeated formula (**recursion formula**). [C17: from Latin *recursio,* from *recurrere* RECUR] —**re+'cur+sive** *adj.*

re+cur+vate (rɪ'kɜ:vɪt, -veɪt) *adj. Rare.* bent back.

re+curve (rɪ'kɜ:v) *vb.* to curve or bend (something) back or down or (of something) to be so curved or bent. [C16: from Latin *recurvāre* from RE- + *curvāre* to CURVE]

rec+u+sant ('rɛkjʊzənt) *n.* **1.** (in 16th to 18th century England) a Roman Catholic who did not attend the services of the Church of England, as was required by law. **2.** any person who refuses to submit to authority. ~*adj.* **3.** (formerly, of Catholics) refusing to attend services of the Church of England. **4.** refusing to submit to authority. [C16: from Latin *recūsāns* refusing, from *recūsāre* from RE- + *causārī* to dispute, from *causa* a CAUSE] —**'rec+u+sance** *or* **'rec+u+san+cy** *n.*

re+cy+cle (ri:'saɪkᵊl) *vb.* (*tr.*) **1.** to pass (a substance) through a system again for further treatment or use. **2.** to reclaim for further use: *to recycle water.* **3.** to institute a different cycle of processes or events in (a machine, system, etc.). **4.** to repeat (a series of operations). ~*n.* **5.** the repetition of a fixed sequence of events.

red[1] (rɛd) *n.* **1.** any of a group of colours, such as that of a ripe tomato or fresh blood, that lie at one end of the visible spectrum, next to orange, and are perceived by the eye when light in the approximate wavelength range 740–620 nanometres falls on the retina. Red is the complementary colour of cyan and forms a set of primary colours with blue and green. **2.** a pigment or dye of or producing these colours. **3.** red cloth or clothing: *dressed in red.* **4.** a red ball in snooker, etc. **5.** (in roulette and other gambling games) one of two colours on which players may place even bets, the other being black. **6.** Also called: **inner.** *Archery.* a red ring on a target, between the blue and the gold, scoring seven points. **7. in the red.** *Informal.* in debit; owing money. **8. see red.** *Informal.* to become very angry. ~*adj.* **red+der, red+dest. 9.** of the colour red. **10.** reddish in colour or having parts or marks that are reddish: *red hair; red deer.* **11.** having the face temporarily suffused with blood, being a sign of anger, shame, etc. **12.** (of the eyes) bloodshot. **13.** (of the hands) stained with blood, as after committing murder. **14.** bloody or violent: *red revolution.* **15.** (of wine) made from black grapes and coloured by their skins. ~*vb.* **reds, red+ding, red+ded. 16.** another word for **redden.** [Old English *rēad;* compare Old High German *rōt,* Gothic *rauths,* Latin *ruber,* Greek *eruthros,* Sanskrit *rohita*] —**'red+ness** *n.*

red[2] (rɛd) *vb.* **reds, red+ding, red** *or* **red+ded.** (*tr.*) a variant spelling of **redd**[1].

Red (rɛd) *Informal.* ~*adj.* **1.** Communist, Socialist, or Soviet. **2.** radical, leftist, or revolutionary. ~*n.* **3.** a member or supporter of a Communist or Socialist Party or a national of a state having such a government, esp. the Soviet Union. **4.** a radical leftist or revolutionary. [C19: from the colour chosen to symbolize revolutionary socialism]

red. *abbrev. for* reduce(d).

re+dact (rɪ'dækt) *vb.* (*tr.*) **1.** to compose or draft (an edict, proclamation, etc.). **2.** to put (a literary work, etc.) into appropriate form for publication; edit. [C15: from Latin *redigere* to bring back, from *red-* RE- + *agere* to drive] —**re+'dac+tion** *n.* —**re+'dac+tion+al** *adj.* —**re+'dac+tor** *n.*

red ad+mi+ral *n.* a nymphalid butterfly, *Vanessa atalanta,* of temperate Europe and Asia, having black wings with red and white markings. See also **white admiral.**

red al+gae *pl. n.* the numerous algae that constitute the family *Rhodophyceae,* which contain a red pigment in addition to chlorophyll. The group includes carrageen, dulse, and laver.

re+dan (rɪ'dæn) *n.* a fortification of two parapets at a salient angle. [C17: from French, from earlier *redent* notching of a saw edge, from RE- + *dent* tooth, from Latin *dēns*]

red-backed shrike *n.* a common Eurasian shrike, *Lanius collurio,* the male of which has a grey crown and rump, brown wings and back, and a black-and-white face.

red+back spi+der *n.* a small venomous Australian spider, *Latrodectus hasselti,* having long thin legs and, in the female, a red stripe on the back of its globular abdomen.

red bag *n.* (in Britain) a fabric bag for a barrister's robes, presented by a Queen's Counsel to a junior in appreciation of good work in a case. See also **blue bag.**

red bark *n.* a kind of cinchona containing a high proportion of alkaloids.

red bid+dy *n. Informal.* cheap red wine fortified with methylated spirits.

red blood cell *or* **cor+pus+cle** *n.* another name for **erythrocyte.**

red-blood+ed *adj. Informal.* vigorous; virile. —**ˌred-'blood+ed+ness** *n.*

red+breast ('rɛdˌbrɛst) *n.* any of various birds having a red breast, esp. the Old World robin (see **robin** (sense 1)).

red+brick ('rɛdˌbrɪk) *n.* (*modifier*) denoting, relating to, or characteristic of a provincial British university of relatively recent foundation, esp. as distinguished from Oxford and Cambridge.

Red+bridge ('rɛdˌbrɪdʒ) *n.* a borough of NE Greater London: includes part of Epping Forest. Pop.: 231 600 (1976 est.).

Red Bri+gades *pl. n.* **the.** a group of urban guerrillas, based in Italy, who kidnapped and murdered Aldo Moro in 1978.

red+bud ('rɛdˌbʌd) *n.* an American leguminous tree, *Cercis canadensis,* that has heart-shaped leaves and small budlike pink flowers. Also called: **American Judas tree.**

red+bug ('rɛdˌbʌg) *n. U.S.* another name for **chigger.**

red+cap ('rɛdˌkæp) *n.* **1.** *Brit. informal.* a military policeman. **2.** another name for the **European goldfinch. 3.** *U.S.* a porter at an airport or station.

red car+pet *n.* **1.** a strip of red carpeting laid for important dignitaries to walk on when arriving or departing. **2. a.** deferential treatment accorded to a person of importance. **b.** (*as modifier*): *the returning hero had a red-carpet reception.*

red ce+dar *n.* **1.** any of several North American coniferous trees, esp. *Juniperus virginiana,* a juniper that has fragrant reddish wood used for making pencils, and *Thuja plicata,* an arbor vitae. **2.** the wood of any of these trees.

red cent *n.* (*used with a negative*) *U.S. informal.* a cent considered as a trivial amount of money (esp. in the phrases **not have a red cent, not worth a red cent,** etc.).

Red Chi+na *n.* an unofficial name for (the People's Republic of) **China.**

red clo+ver *n.* a papilionaceous plant, *Trifolium pratense,* native to Europe and Asia, frequently planted as a forage crop. It has fragrant red flowers and three-lobed compound leaves.

red+coat ('rɛd,kəʊt) *n.* (formerly) a British soldier.

red cor+al *n.* any of several corals of the genus *Corallium,* the skeletons of which are pinkish red in colour and used to make ornaments, etc. Also called: **precious coral.**

red cor+pus+cle *or* **blood cell** *n.* another name for **erythrocyte.**

Red Cres+cent *n.* a national branch of or the emblem of the Red Cross Society in a Muslim country.

Red Cross *n.* **1.** an international humanitarian organization (**Red Cross Society**) formally established by the Geneva Convention of 1864. It was originally limited to providing medical care for war casualties but its services now include liaison between prisoners of war and their families, relief to victims of natural disasters, etc. **2.** any national branch of this organization. **3.** the emblem of this organization, consisting of a red cross on a white background.

red+cur+rant ('rɛd'kʌrənt) *n.* **1.** a N temperate shrub, *Ribes rubrum,* having greenish flowers and small edible rounded red berries: family *Grossulariaceae.* **2. a.** the fruit of this shrub. **b.** (*as modifier*): *redcurrant jelly.*

redd[1] *or* **red** (rɛd) *vb.* **redds, red+ding, redd** *or* **red+ded.** (*tr.;* often foll. by *up*) *Northern Brit. dialect.* to bring order to; tidy (up). [C15 *redden* to clear, perhaps a variant of RID] —**'redd+er** *n.*

redd[2] (rɛd) *n.* a hollow in sand or gravel on a river bed, scooped out as a spawning place by salmon, trout, or other fish. [C17 (originally: spawn): of obscure origin]

red deer *n.* a large deer, *Cervus elaphus,* formerly widely distributed in the woodlands of Europe and Asia. The coat is reddish brown in summer and the short tail is surrounded by a patch of light-coloured hair.

Red Deer *n.* **1.** a river in W Canada, in SW Alberta, flowing southeast into the South Saskatchewan River. Length: about 620 km (385 miles). **2.** a river in W Canada, flowing east through **Red Deer Lake** into Lake Winnipegosis. Length: about 225 km (140 miles).

red+den ('rɛdᵊn) *vb.* **1.** to make or become red. **2.** (*intr.*) to flush with embarrassment, anger, etc.; blush.

Red·ding ('rɛdɪŋ) *n.* **O·tis.** 1941–67, U.S. soul singer and songwriter. His recordings include *Otis Blue* (1964), *Dictionary of Soul* (1965), *Sittin' on the Dock of the Bay* (1967), *Live at Monterey* (1967).

red+dish ('rɛdɪʃ) *adj.* somewhat red. —**,red+dish+ly** *adv.* —**,red+dish+ness** *n.*

Red+ditch ('rɛdɪtʃ) *n.* a town in W central England, in Hereford and Worcester: designated a new town in the mid-1960s; metal-working industries. Pop.: 40 775 (1971).

red+dle ('rɛdᵊl) *n., vb.* a variant spelling of **ruddle.**

red dust+er *n. Brit.* an informal name for the **Red Ensign.**

red dwarf *n.* one of a class of small cool main-sequence stars.

rede (ri:d) *Archaic.* ~*n.* **1.** advice or counsel. **2.** an explanation. ~*vb.* (*tr.*) **3.** to advise; counsel. **4.** to explain. [Old English *rǣdan* to rule; see READ[1]]

red earth *n.* a clayey zonal soil of tropical savanna lands, formed by extensive chemical weathering, coloured by iron compounds, and less strongly leached than laterite.

re+deem (rɪ'di:m) *vb.* (*tr.*) **1.** to recover possession or ownership of by payment of a price or service; regain. **2.** to convert (bonds, shares, etc.) into cash. **3.** to pay off (a promissory note, loan, etc.). **4.** to recover (something pledged, mortgaged, or pawned). **5.** to convert (paper money) into bullion or specie. **6.** to fulfil (a promise, pledge, etc.). **7.** to exchange (trading stamps, coupons, etc.) for goods. **8.** to reinstate in someone's estimation or good opinion; restore to favour: *he redeemed himself by his altruistic action.* **9.** to make amends for. **10.** to recover from captivity, esp. by a money payment. **11.** *Christianity.* (of Christ as Saviour) to free (men) from sin by his death on the Cross. [C15: from Old French *redimer,* from Latin *redimere* to buy back, from *red-* RE- + *emere* to buy] —**re+'deem+er** *n.*

re+deem+a·ble (rɪ'di:məbᵊl) *or* **re+demp+ti·ble** (rɪ'dɛmptəbᵊl) *adj.* **1.** (of bonds, shares, etc.) subject to cancellation by repayment at a specified date or under specified conditions. **2.** (of bonds, etc.) payable in or convertible into cash. —**re+,deem+a·'bil+i·ty** *n.* —**re+'deem+a+bly** *adv.*

Re+deem+er (rɪ'di:mə) *n.* **The.** Jesus Christ as having brought redemption to mankind.

re+deem+ing (rɪ'di:mɪŋ) *adj.* serving to compensate for faults or deficiencies in quality, etc.: *one redeeming feature.*

re+demp+tion (rɪ'dɛmpʃən) *n.* **1.** the act or process of redeeming. **2.** the state of being redeemed. **3.** *Christianity.* **a.** deliverance from sin through the incarnation, sufferings, and death of Christ. **b.** atonement for guilt. **4.** conversion of paper money into bullion or specie. **5. a.** removal of a financial obligation by paying off a note, bond, etc. **b.** (*as modifier*): *redemption date.* [C14: via Old French from Latin *redemptiō* a buying back; see REDEEM] —**re+'demp+tion+al, re+'demp+tive,** *or* **re+'demp+to·ry** *adj.* —**re+'demp+tive+ly** *adv.*

re+demp+tion+er (rɪ'dɛmpʃənə) *n. History.* an emigrant to Colonial America who paid for his passage by becoming an indentured servant.

Re+demp+tor+ist (rɪ'dɛmptərɪst) *n. R.C. Church.* a member of a religious congregation founded in 1732 to do missionary work among the poor.

Red En+sign *n.* the ensign of the British Merchant Navy, having the Union Jack on a red background at the upper corner of the vertical edge alongside the hoist. Compare **White Ensign.**

re+de·ploy (,ri:dɪ'plɔɪ) *vb.* to assign new positions or tasks to (labour, troops, etc.). —**,re+de·'ploy+ment** *n.*

re+de·vel+op (,ri:dɪ'vɛləp) *vb.* (*tr.*) **1.** to rebuild or replan (a building, area, etc.). **2.** *Photog.* to develop (a negative or print) for a second time, in order to improve the contrast, colour, etc. **3.** to develop (something) again. —**,re+de·'vel+op+er** *n.* —**,re+de·'vel+op+ment** *n.*

re+de·vel+op+ment ar·e·a *n.* an urban area in which all or most of the buildings are demolished and rebuilt.

red+eye ('rɛd,aɪ) *n.* **1.** *U.S. slang.* inferior whiskey. **2.** *Canadian slang.* a drink incorporating beer and tomato juice. **3.** another name for **rudd.**

red-faced *adj.* flushed with embarrassment or anger. —**red-fac·ed+ly** (,rɛd'feɪsɪdlɪ, -'feɪstlɪ) *adv.*

red+fin ('rɛd,fɪn) *n.* any of various small cyprinid fishes of the genus *Notropis,* esp. *N. cornutus.* They have reddish fins and are popular aquarium fishes.

red fir *n.* **1.** a North American coniferous tree, *Abies magnifica,* having reddish wood valued as timber: family *Pinaceae.* **2.** any of various other pinaceous trees that have reddish wood. **3.** the wood of any of these trees.

red fire *n.* any combustible material that burns with a bright red flame: used in flares and fireworks. The colour is usually produced by strontium salts.

red+fish ('rɛd,fɪʃ) *n., pl.* **+fish** *or* **+fish·es.** **1.** a male salmon that has recently spawned. Compare **blackfish** (sense 2). **2.** any of several red European scorpaenid fishes of the genus *Sebastes,* esp. *S. marinus,* valued as a food fish.

red flag *n.* **1.** a symbol of socialism, communism, or revolution. **2.** an object or event likely to arouse anger.

Red·ford ('rɛdfəd) *n.* **Rob·ert.** born 1936, U.S. film actor: his films include *The Chase* (1966), *Butch Cassidy and the Sundance Kid* (1969), *The Sting* (1973), and *Three Days of the Condor* (1975).

red fox *n.* the common fox, *Vulpes vulpes,* which has a reddish-brown coat: family *Canidae,* order *Carnivora* (carnivores).

red gi+ant *n.* a giant star that emits red light (spectral type M).

Red·grave ('rɛd,greɪv) *n.* **1. Lynn.** born 1944, English stage and film actress. Her films include *Georgy Girl* (1966), *The Virgin Soldiers* (1969), *The National Health* (1973), and *The Happy Hooker* (1975). **2.** her father Sir **Mi·chael.** born 1908, English stage and film actor. Among his films are *The Lady Vanishes* (1938), *The Dam Busters* (1955), *The Loneliness of the Long Distance Runner* (1963), and *The Go Between* (1971). **3.** his elder daughter **Va·nes·sa.** born 1937, English stage and film actress, whose roles include performances in the films *Blow Up* (1966), *Isadora* (1968), *Mary, Queen of Scots* (1972), and *Julia* (1977): noted also for her left-wing politics.

red grouse *n.* a reddish-brown grouse, *Lagopus scoticus,* of upland moors of Great Britain: an important game bird.

Red Guard *n.* a member of a Chinese youth movement that attempted to effect the Cultural Revolution (1965–71).

red gum *n.* **1.** any of several Australian myrtaceous trees of the genus *Eucalyptus,* esp. *E. camaldulensis,* which has reddish wood. See also **blue gum.** **2.** the hard red wood from this tree, used for making railway sleepers, posts, etc.

red-hand·ed *adj.* (*postpositive*) in the act of committing a crime or doing something wrong or shameful (esp. in the phrase **catch red-handed**). [C19 (earlier, C15 *red hand*)] —**,red-'hand·ed+ly** *adv.* —**,red-'hand·ed+ness** *n.*

red hat *n.* **1.** the broad-brimmed crimson hat given to cardinals as the symbol of their rank and office. **2.** the rank and office of a cardinal.

red+head ('rɛd,hɛd) *n.* **1.** a person with red hair. **2.** a diving duck, *Aythya americana,* of North America, the male of which has a grey-and-black body and a reddish-brown head.

red-head·ed *adj.* **1.** (of a person) having red hair. **2.** (of an animal) having a red head.

red heat *n.* **1.** the temperature at which a substance is red-hot. **2.** the state or condition of being red-hot.

red her+ring *n.* **1.** anything that diverts attention from a topic or line of inquiry. **2.** a dried and smoked herring.

red-hot *adj.* **1.** (esp. of metal) heated to the temperature at which it glows red: *iron is red-hot at about 500°C.* **2.** extremely hot: *the stove is red-hot, so don't touch it.* **3.** keen, excited, or eager; enthusiastic. **4.** furious; violent: *red-hot anger.* **5.** very recent or topical: *red-hot information.*

red-hot pok+er *n.* a plant of the African liliaceous genus

---

re+,ded·i+'ca+tion *n.*
,re+de·'fine *vb.*
,re+de·'fy *vb.,* **+fies, +fy+ing, +fied.**
,re+de·,lib+er·'a+tion *n.*
,re+de·'liv+er *vb.*
,re+de·'liv+er·y *n.*
,re+de·'mand *vb.*
re+'dem+on+,strate *vb.*
re+,dem+on+'stra+tion *n.*
,re+de·'pos+it *vb., n.*
,re+de·'scend *vb.*
,re+de·'scribe *vb.*
,re+de·'sign *vb.*
,re+de·'ter+mine *vb.*
,re+de·'vel+op *vb.*
,re+de·'vel+op+er *n.*
,re+de·'vel+op+ment *n.*
re+'di+al *vb.*
,re+di+'gest *vb.*

Kniphofia: widely cultivated for its showy spikes of red or yellow flowers.

re·di·a ('riːdɪə) *n., pl.* **·di·ae** (-dɪˌiː). a parasitic larva of flukes that has simple locomotory organs, pharynx, and intestine and gives rise either to other rediae or to a different larva (the cercaria). [C19: from New Latin, named after Francesco *Redi* (1629–97), Italian naturalist]

Re·dif·fu·sion (ˌriːdɪ'fjuːʒən) *n. Brit. trademark.* a system by which radio or television programmes are relayed to subscribers from a receiver via cables.

Red In·di·an *n., adj.* another name for **American Indian.**

red·in·gote ('rɛdɪŋˌgəʊt) *n.* **1.** a man's or woman's full-skirted outer coat of the 18th and 19th centuries. **2.** a woman's light dress or coat of the 18th century, with an open-fronted skirt, revealing a decorative underskirt. [C19: from French, from English *riding coat*]

red·in·te·grate (rɛ'dɪntɪˌgreɪt) *vb.* **1.** (*tr.*) to make whole or complete again; restore to a perfect state; renew. **2.** (*intr.*) *Psychol.* to engage in the process of redintegration. [C15: from Latin *redintegrāre* to renew, from *red-* RE- + *integer* complete] —**red·'in·te·gra·tive** *adj.*

red·in·te·gra·tion (rɛˌdɪntɪ'greɪʃən) *n.* **1.** the act or process of making whole again; renewal. **2.** *Psychol.* the process of responding to a part of a situation in the same manner as one has responded to the whole situation, as in the case of a souvenir reminding one of a holiday.

red·i·vi·vus (ˌrɛdɪ'vaɪvəs) *adj. Rare.* returned to life; revived. [from Late Latin, from Latin *red-* RE- + *vīvus* alive]

red lead (lɛd) *n.* a bright-red poisonous insoluble oxide of lead usually obtained as a powder by heating litharge in air. It is used as a pigment in paints. Formula: Pb_3O_4. Also called: **minium.**

red-lead ore ('rɛd'lɛd) *n.* another name for **crocoite.**

red·leg ('rɛdˌlɛg) *n. Caribbean, derogatory.* a poor White.

red-leg·ged par·tridge *n.* a partridge, *Alectoris rufa*, having a reddish tail, red legs and bill, and flanks barred with chestnut, black, and white: common on farmlands and heaths in SW Europe, including Britain.

red-let·ter day *n.* a memorably important or happy occasion. [C18: from the red letters used in ecclesiastical calendars to indicate saints' days and feasts]

red light *n.* **1.** a signal to stop, esp. a red traffic signal in a system of traffic lights. **2.** a danger signal. **3.** an instruction to stop or discontinue. **4. a.** a red lamp hanging outside a house indicating that it is a brothel. **b.** (*as modifier*): *a red-light district.*

red man *n.* a North American Indian.

red meat *n.* any meat that is dark in colour, esp. beef and lamb. Compare **white meat.**

Red·mond ('rɛdmənd) *n.* **John Ed·ward.** 1856–1918, Irish politician. He led the Parnellites from 1891 and helped to procure the Home Rule bill of 1912, but was considered too moderate by extreme nationalists.

red mul·let *n.* any of the marine percoid fishes constituting the family *Mullidae*, esp. *Mullus surmuletus*, a food fish of European waters. They have a pair of long barbels beneath the chin and a reddish coloration. U.S. name: **goatfish.**

red·neck ('rɛdˌnɛk) *n. Disparaging.* (in the southwestern U.S.) a poor uneducated White farm worker.

red·ness ('rɛdnɪs) *n.* the quality or fact of being red.

re·do (riː'duː) *vb.* **·does, ·do·ing, ·did, ·done.** (*tr.*) **1.** to do over again. **2.** *Informal.* to redecorate, esp. thoroughly: *we redid the house last summer.*

red oak *n.* **1.** any of several deciduous oak trees, esp. *Quercus borealis*, native to North America, having bristly leaves with triangular lobes and acorns with small cups. **2.** the hard cross-grained reddish wood of this tree.

red o·chre *n.* any of various natural red earths containing ferric oxide: used as pigments.

red·o·lent ('rɛdəʊlənt) *adj.* **1.** having a pleasant smell; fragrant. **2.** (*postpositive;* foll. by *of* or *with*) having the odour or smell (of); scented (with): *a room redolent of country flowers.* **3.** (*postpositive;* foll. by *of* or *with*) reminiscent or suggestive (of): *a picture redolent of the 18th century.* [C14: from Latin *redolens* smelling (of), from *redolēre* giving off an odour, from *red-* RE- + *olēre* to smell] —**'red·o·lence** *or* **'red·o·len·cy** *n.* —**'red·o·lent·ly** *adv.*

Re·don (*French* rə'dɔ̃) *n.* **O·di·lon** (ɔdi'lɔ̃). 1840–1916, French symbolist painter and etcher. He foreshadowed the surrealists in his paintings of fantastic dream images.

red o·sier *n.* any of several willow trees that have red twigs used for basketwork.

re·dou·ble (rɪ'dʌbəl) *vb.* **1.** to make or become much greater in intensity, number, etc.: *to redouble one's efforts.* **2.** to send back (sounds) or (of sounds) to be sent back; echo or re-echo. **3.** *Bridge.* to double (an opponent's double). ~*n.* **4.** the act of redoubling.

re·doubt (rɪ'daʊt) *n.* **1.** a temporary earthwork built inside a permanent fort as a last defensive position. **2.** any isolated fortified stronghold. [C17: via French from obsolete Italian *ridotta*, from Medieval Latin *reductus* shelter, from Latin *redūcere* to withdraw, from RE- + *dūcere* to lead]

re·doubt·a·ble (rɪ'daʊtəbəl) *adj.* **1.** to be feared; formidable. **2.** worthy of respect. [C14: from Old French, from *redouter* to dread, from RE- + *douter* to be afraid, DOUBT] —**re·'doubt·a·ble·ness** *n.* —**re·'doubt·a·bly** *adv.*

re·dound (rɪ'daʊnd) *vb.* **1.** (*intr.;* foll. by *to*) to have an advantageous or disadvantageous effect (on): *brave deeds redound to your credit.* **2.** (*intr.;* foll. by *on* or *upon*) to recoil or rebound. **3.** (*intr.*) *Archaic.* to arise; accrue: *wealth redounding from wise investment.* **4.** (*tr.*) *Archaic.* to reflect; bring: *his actions redound dishonour upon him.* [C14: from Old French *redonder*, from Latin *redundāre* to stream over, from *red-* RE- + *undāre* to rise in waves, from *unda* a wave]

red·o·wa ('rɛdəvə, -wə) *n.* a Bohemian folk dance similar to the waltz. [C19: via French and German from Czech *rejdovák*, from *rejdovati* to guide around]

re·dox ('riːdɒks) *n.* (*modifier*) another term for **oxidation-reduction.** [C20: from RED(UCTION) + OX(IDATION)]

red pack·et *n.* (in Hong Kong, Malaysia, etc.) **1.** a sum of money folded inside red paper and given at the Chinese New Year to unmarried younger relatives. **2.** such a gift given at Chinese weddings by the parents to the bride and groom and by the bride and groom to unmarried younger relatives.

red-pen·cil *vb.* **·cils, ·cil·ling, ·cilled** *or U.S.* **·cils, ·cil·ing, ·ciled.** (*tr.*) to revise or correct (a book, manuscript, etc.).

red pep·per *n.* **1.** any of several varieties of the pepper plant *Capsicum frutescens*, cultivated for their hot pungent red podlike fruits. **2.** the fruit of any of these plants. **3.** the ripe red fruit of the sweet pepper. **4.** another name for **cayenne pepper.**

red pine *n.* a coniferous tree, *Dacrydium cupressinum*, of New Zealand, having narrow sharp pointed leaves: family *Taxaceae*. Also called: **rimu.**

Red Plan·et *n.* **the.** an informal name for **Mars.**

red·poll ('rɛdˌpɒl) *n.* either of two widely distributed finches, *Acanthis flammea* or *A. hornemanni* (**arctic** *or* **hoary redpoll**), having a greyish-brown plumage with a red crown and pink breast.

Red Poll *or* **Polled** *n.* a red hornless short-haired breed of beef and dairy cattle.

re·draft *n.* ('riːˌdrɑːft). **1.** a second draft. **2.** a bill of exchange drawn on the drawer or endorser of a protested bill by the holder for the amount of the protested bill plus costs and charges. **3.** a re-exported commodity. ~*vb.* (riː'drɑːft). (*tr.*) **4.** to make a second copy; draft again: *to redraft proposals for a project.*

red rag *n.* a provocation; something that infuriates. [so called because red objects supposedly infuriate bulls]

re·dress (rɪ'drɛs) *vb.* (*tr.*) **1.** to put right (a wrong), esp. by compensation; make reparation for: *to redress a grievance.* **2.** to correct or adjust (esp. in the phrase **redress the balance**). **3.** to make compensation to (a person) for a wrong. ~*n.* **4.** the act or an instance of setting right a wrong; remedy or cure: *to seek redress of grievances.* **5.** compensation, amends, or reparation for a wrong, injury, etc. **6.** relief from poverty or want. [C14: from Old French *redrecier* to set up again, from RE- + *drecier* to straighten; see DRESS] —**re·'dress·a·ble** *or* **re·'dress·i·ble** *adj.* —**re·'dress·er** *or* **re·'dres·sor** *n.*

re-dress (riː'drɛs) *vb.* (*tr.*) to dress (something) again.

Red Riv·er *n.* **1.** Also called: **Red River of the South.** a river in the S central U.S., flowing east from N Texas through Arkansas into the Mississippi in Louisiana. Length: 1639 km (1018 miles). **2.** a river in the northern U.S., flowing north as the border between North Dakota and Minnesota and into Lake Winnipeg, Canada. Length: 515 km (320 miles). **3.** a river in SE Asia, rising in SW China in Yünnan province and flowing southeast across N Vietnam to the Gulf of Tongkin: the chief river of N Vietnam, with an extensive delta. Length: 500 km (310 miles). Vietnamese name: **Song Koi.**

red·root ('rɛdˌruːt) *n.* **1.** a bog plant, *Lachnanthes tinctoria*, of E North America, having woolly yellow flowers and roots that yield a red dye: family *Haemodoraceae*. **2.** another name for **pigweed** (sense 1).

red rose *n. English history.* the emblem of the House of Lancaster. See also **Wars of the Roses, white rose.**

red salm·on *n.* **1.** any salmon having reddish flesh, esp. the sockeye salmon. **2.** the flesh of such a fish, esp. canned.

Red Sea *n.* a long narrow sea between Arabia and NE Africa, linked with the Mediterranean in the north by the Suez Canal and with the Indian Ocean in the south: occasionally reddish in appearance through algae. Area: 438 000 sq. km (169 000 sq. miles).

red set·ter *n.* a popular name for **Irish setter.**

red·shank ('rɛdˌʃæŋk) *n.* either of two large common European sandpipers, *Tringa totanus* or *T. erythropus* (**spotted redshank**), having red legs.

red shank *n.* an annual polygonaceous plant, *Polygonum persicaria*, of N temperate regions, having red stems, narrow leaves, and oblong spikes of pink flowers. Also called: **persicaria, lady's-thumb.**

red shift *n.* a shift in the spectral lines of a stellar spectrum towards the red end of the visible region relative to the wavelength of these lines in the terrestrial spectrum. It is thought to be a result of the Doppler effect caused by the recession of stars.

red·skin ('rɛdˌskɪn) *n.* an informal name for an **American Indian.**

ˌ**re·di·'ges·tion** *n.*
ˌ**re·di·'rect** *vb.*
ˌ**re·di·'rec·tion** *n.*
re·'dis·count *vb., n.*
ˌ**re·dis·'cov·er** *vb.*
ˌ**re·dis·'cov·er·y** *n., pl.* **·er·ies.**
ˌ**re·dis·'solve** *vb.*
ˌ**re·dis·'trib·ute** *vb.*
ˌ**re·dis·tri·'bu·tion** *n.*
ˌ**re·dis·'trib·u·tive** *adj.*
ˌ**re·di·'vide** *vb.*
ˌ**re·di·'vis·ion** *n.*
re·'dock *vb.*
re·'draw *vb.,* **·draws, ·draw·ing, ·drew, ·drawn.**
re·'drill *vb.*
re·'dry *vb.,* **·dries, ·dry·ing, ·dried.**
re·'dye *vb.*
re-'ed·it *vb.*

red snap·per *n.* any of various marine percoid food fishes of the genus *Lutjanus,* esp. *L. blackfordi,* having a reddish coloration, common in American coastal regions of the Atlantic: family *Lutjanidae* (snappers).

red spi·der *n.* short for **red spider mite** (see **spider mite**).

Red Spot *n.* a reddish oval spot, about 48 000 kilometres long, seen to drift around the S hemisphere of Jupiter. It varies considerably in intensity and is possibly an atmospheric phenomenon.

red squir·rel *n.* **1.** a reddish-brown squirrel, *Sciurus vulgaris,* inhabiting woodlands of Europe and parts of Asia. **2. American red squirrel.** Also called: **chickaree.** either of two reddish-brown squirrels, *Tamiasciurus hudsonicus* or *T. douglasii,* inhabiting forests of North America.

red·start (ˈrɛdˌstɑːt) *n.* **1.** any European songbird of the genus *Phoenicurus,* esp. *P. phoenicurus,* in which the male has a black throat, orange-brown tail and breast, and grey back: family *Muscicapidae* (thrushes, etc.). **2.** any North American warbler of the genus *Setophaga,* esp. *S. ruticilla.* [Old English *read* RED + *steort* tail; compare German *Rotsterz*]

red tape *n.* obstructive official routine or procedure; time-consuming bureaucracy. [C18: from the red tape used to bind official government documents]

re·duce (rɪˈdjuːs) *vb.* (*mainly tr.*) **1.** (*also intr.*) to make or become smaller in size, number, extent, degree, intensity, etc. **2.** to bring into a certain state, condition, etc.: *to reduce a forest to ashes.* **3.** (*also intr.*) to make or become slimmer; lose or cause to lose excess weight. **4.** to impoverish (esp. in the phrase **in reduced circumstances**). **5.** to bring into a state of submission to one's authority; subjugate: *the whole country was reduced after three months.* **6.** to bring down the price of (a commodity): *the shirt was reduced in the sale.* **7.** to lower the rank or status of; demote: *he was reduced from corporal to private; reduced to the ranks.* **8.** to set out systematically as an aid to understanding; simplify: *his theories have been reduced in a popular treatise.* **9.** *Maths.* to modify or simplify the form of (an expression or equation), esp. by substitution of one term by another. **10.** to thin out (paint) by adding oil, turpentine, etc.; dilute. **11.** (*also intr.*) *Chem.* **a.** to undergo or cause to undergo a chemical reaction with hydrogen or formation of a hydride. **b.** to lose or cause to lose oxygen atoms. **c.** to undergo or cause to undergo an increase in the number of electrons. Compare **oxidize. 12.** *Photog.* to lessen the density of (a negative or print) by converting some of the blackened silver in the emulsion to soluble silver compounds by an oxidation process using a photographic reducer. **13.** *Surgery.* to manipulate or reposition (a broken or displaced bone, organ, or part) back to its normal site. **14.** *Biology.* to undergo or cause to undergo meiosis. [C14: from Latin *redūcere* to bring back, from RE- + *dūcere* to lead] —**re·ˈduc·i·ble** *adj.* —**re·ˌduc·i·ˈbil·i·ty** *n.* —**re·ˈduc·i·bly** *adv.*

re·duced lev·el *n. Surveying.* calculated elevation in relation to a particular datum.

re·duc·er (rɪˈdjuːsə) *n.* **1.** *Photog.* a chemical solution used to lessen the density of a negative or print by oxidizing some of the blackened silver to soluble silver compounds. Compare **intensifier** (sense 3). **2.** a pipe fitting connecting two pipes of different diameters. **3.** a person or thing that reduces.

re·duc·ing a·gent *n. Chem.* a substance that reduces another substance in a chemical reaction, being itself oxidized in the process. Compare **oxidizing agent.**

re·duc·ing glass *n.* a lens or curved mirror that produces an image smaller than the object observed.

re·duc·tase (rɪˈdʌkteɪz) *n.* any enzyme that catalyses a biochemical reduction reaction. [C20: from REDUCTION + -ASE]

re·duc·ti·o ad ab·sur·dum *Latin.* (rɪˈdʌktɪəʊ æd æbˈsɜːdəm) *n.* **1.** a method of disproving a proposition by showing that its inevitable consequences would be absurd. **2.** a method of indirectly proving a proposition by assuming its negation to be true and showing that this leads to an absurdity. **3.** application of a principle or proposed principle to an instance in which it is absurd. [literally: reduction to the absurd]

re·duc·tion (rɪˈdʌkʃən) *n.* **1.** the act or process or an instance of reducing. **2.** the state or condition of being reduced. **3.** the amount by which something is reduced. **4.** a form of an original resulting from a reducing process, such as a copy on a smaller scale. **5.** a simplified form, such as an orchestral score arranged for piano. **6.** *Maths.* **a.** the process of converting a fraction into its decimal form. **b.** the process of dividing out the common factors in the numerator and denominator of a fraction; cancellation. —**re·ˈduc·tion·al** *or* **re·ˈduc·tive** *adj.*

re·duc·tion di·vi·sion *n.* another name for **meiosis.**

re·duc·tion for·mu·la *n. Maths.* a formula, such as sin $(90° \pm A) = \cos A$, expressing the values of a trigonometric function of any angle greater than 90° in terms of a function of an acute angle.

re·duc·tion·ism (rɪˈdʌkʃəˌnɪzəm) *n.* **1.** the analysis of complex things, data, etc., into less complex constituents. **2.** *Often disparaging.* any theory or method that holds that a complex idea, system, etc., can be completely understood in terms of its simpler parts or components. —**re·ˈduc·tion·ist** *n.* —**re·ˌduc·tion·ˈist·ic** *adj.*

re·dun·dan·cy (rɪˈdʌndənsɪ) *n., pl.* **·cies. 1. a.** the state or condition of being redundant or superfluous, esp. superfluous in one's job. **b.** (*as modifier*): *a redundancy payment.* **2.** excessive proliferation or profusion, esp. of superfluity. **3.** duplication of components in electronic or mechanical equipment so that operations can continue following failure of a part. **4.** repetition of information or inclusion of additional information to reduce errors in telecommunication transmissions and computer processing.

re·dun·dant (rɪˈdʌndənt) *adj.* **1.** surplus to requirements; unnecessary or superfluous. **2.** verbose or tautological. **3.** deprived of one's job because it is no longer necessary for efficient operation: *he has been made redundant.* **4.** (of components, information, etc.) duplicated or added as a precaution against failure, error, etc. [C17: from Latin *redundans* overflowing, from *redundāre* to run back, stream over; see REDOUND] —**re·ˈdun·dant·ly** *adv.*

redupl. *abbrev. for* reduplicate *or* reduplication.

re·du·pli·cate *vb.* (rɪˈdjuːplɪˌkeɪt). **1.** to make or become double; repeat. **2.** to repeat (a sound or syllable) in a word or (of a sound or syllable) to be repeated, esp. in forming inflections in certain languages. ~*adj.* (rɪˈdjuːplɪkɪt). **3.** doubled or repeated. **4.** (of petals or sepals) having the margins curving outwards. —**re·ˈdu·pli·ca·tive** *adj.*

re·du·pli·ca·tion (rɪˌdjuːplɪˈkeɪʃən) *n.* **1.** the process or an instance of redoubling. **2.** the state, condition, or quality of being redoubled. **3.** a thing that has been redoubled. **4.** repetition of a sound or syllable in a word, as in the formation of the Latin perfect *tetigi* from *tangere* "touch"

re·du·vi·id (rɪˈdjuːvɪɪd) *n.* **1.** any hemipterous bug of the family *Reduviidae,* which includes the assassin bugs and the wheel bug. ~*adj.* **2.** of, relating to, or belonging to the family *Reduviidae.* [C19: from New Latin *Reduviidae,* from Latin *reduvia* a hangnail]

red·ware (ˈrɛdˌwɛə) *n.* another name for **kelp** (the seaweed).

red-wa·ter *n.* a disease of cattle caused by the protozoan *Babesia* (or *Piroplasma*) *bovis,* which destroys the red blood cells, characterized by the passage of red or blackish urine.

red·wing (ˈrɛdˌwɪŋ) *n.* **1.** a small European thrush, *Turdus iliacus,* having a speckled breast, reddish flanks, and brown back. **2.** a North American oriole, *Agelaius phoeniceus,* the male of which has a black plumage with a red-and-yellow patch on each wing.

red·wood (ˈrɛdˌwʊd) *n.* a giant coniferous tree, *Sequoia sempervirens,* of coastal regions of California, having reddish fibrous bark and durable timber: family *Taxodiaceae.* The largest specimen is over 120 metres (360 feet) tall. See also **sequoia.**

ree·bok (ˈriːbʌk, -bɒk) *n., pl.* **·boks** *or* **·bok.** a variant spelling of **rhebok.**

re-ech·o (riːˈɛkəʊ) *vb.* **·oes, ·o·ing, ·oed. 1.** to echo (a sound that is already an echo); resound. **2.** (*tr.*) to repeat like an echo.

reed (riːd) *n.* **1.** any of various widely distributed tall grasses of the genus *Phragmites,* esp. *P. communis,* that grow in swamps and shallow water and have jointed hollow stalks. **2.** the stalk, or stalks collectively, of any of these plants, esp. as used for thatching. **3.** *Music.* **a.** a thin piece of cane or metal inserted into the tubes of certain wind instruments, which sets in vibration the air column inside the tube. **b.** a wind instrument or organ pipe that sounds by means of a reed. **4.** one of the several vertical parallel wires on a loom that may be moved upwards to separate the warp threads. **5.** a small semicircular architectural moulding. See also **reeding. 6.** an ancient Hebrew unit of length equal to six cubits. **7.** an archaic word for **arrow. 8. broken reed.** a weak, unreliable, or ineffectual person. ~*vb.* (*tr.*) **9.** to fashion into or supply with reeds or reeding. **10.** to thatch using reeds. [Old English *hreod;* related to Old Saxon *hriod,* Old High German *hriot*]

Reed (riːd) *n.* **1.** Sir **Car·ol.** 1906–76, English film director. His films include *The Third Man* (1949), *Outcasts of the Island* (1951), and *Our Man in Havana* (1959). **2. Wal·ter.** 1851–1902, U.S. physician, who proved that yellow fever is transmitted by mosquitoes (1900).

reed·buck (ˈriːdˌbʌk) *n., pl.* **·bucks** *or* **·buck.** any antelope of the genus *Redunca,* of Africa south of the Sahara, having a buff-coloured coat and inward-curving horns.

reed bunt·ing *n.* a common European bunting, *Emberiza schoeniclus,* that occurs near reed beds and has a brown streaked plumage with, in the male, a black head.

reed grass *n.* a tall perennial grass, *Glyceria maxima,* of rivers and ponds of Europe, Asia, and Canada.

reed·ing (ˈriːdɪŋ) *n.* **1.** a set of small semicircular architectural mouldings. **2.** the milling on the edges of a coin.

reed·ling (ˈriːdlɪŋ) *n.* a titlike Eurasian songbird, *Panurus biarmicus,* common in reed beds: family *Muscicapidae* (Old World flycatchers, etc.). It has a tawny back and tail and, in the male, a grey-and-black head. Also called: **bearded tit.**

reed mace *n.* **1.** Also called: **cat's-tail.** a tall reedlike marsh plant, *Typha latifolia,* with straplike leaves and flowers in long brown spikes: family *Typhaceae.* **2.** a related and similar plant, *Typha angustifolia.*

reed or·gan *n.* **1.** a wind instrument, such as the harmonium, accordion, or harmonica, in which the sound is produced by reeds, each reed producing one note only. **2.** a type of pipe organ, such as the regal, in which all the pipes are fitted with reeds.

reed pipe *n.* **1.** a wind instrument, such as a clarinet or oboe, whose sound is produced by a vibrating reed. **2.** an organ pipe sounded by a vibrating reed.

reed stop *n.* an organ stop controlling a rank of reed pipes.

reed war·bler *n.* any of various common Old World warblers of the genus *Acrocephalus,* esp. *A. scirpaceus,* that inhabit marshy regions and have a brown plumage.

reed·y (ˈriːdɪ) *adj.* **reed·i·er, reed·i·est. 1.** (of a place, esp. a marsh) abounding in reeds. **2.** of or like a reed. **3.** having a tone like a reed instrument; shrill or piping: *a reedy voice.* —**ˈreed·i·ness** *n.*

reef[1] (riːf) *n.* **1.** a ridge of rock, sand, coral, etc., the top of which lies close to the surface of the sea. **2.** a vein of ore, esp. one of gold-bearing quartz. [C16: from Middle Dutch *ref*, from Old Norse *rif* RIB[1], REEF[2]]

reef[2] (riːf) *Nautical.* ~*n.* **1.** the part gathered in when sail area is reduced, as in a high wind. ~*vb.* **2.** to reduce the area of (sail) by taking in a reef. **3.** (*tr.*) to shorten or bring inboard (a spar). [C14: from Middle Dutch *rif;* related to Old Norse *rif* reef, RIB[1], German *reffen* to reef; see REEF[1]]

Reef (riːf) *n.* **the.** another name for **(the) Witwatersrand.**

reef·er (ˈriːfə) *n.* **1.** *Nautical.* a person who reefs, such as a midshipman. **2.** another name for **reefing jacket. 3.** *Slang.* a hand-rolled cigarette, esp. one containing cannabis. [C19: from REEF[2]; applied to the cigarette because of its resemblance to the rolled reef of a sail]

reef·ing jack·et *n.* a man's short double-breasted jacket of sturdy wool. Also called: **reefer.**

reef knot *n.* a knot consisting of two overhand knots turned opposite ways. Also called: **square knot.**

reef point *n. Nautical.* one of several short lengths of line stitched through a sail for tying a reef.

reek (riːk) *vb.* **1.** (*intr.*) to give off or emit a strong unpleasant odour; smell or stink. **2.** (*intr.;* often foll. by *of*) to be permeated (by); be redolent (of): *the letter reeks of subservience.* **3.** (*tr.*) to treat with smoke; fumigate. **4.** (*tr.*) *Chiefly dialect.* to give off or emit (smoke, fumes, vapour, etc.). ~*n.* **5.** a strong offensive smell; stink. **6.** *Chiefly dialect.* smoke or steam; vapour. [Old English *rēocan;* related to Old Frisian *riāka* to smoke, Old High German *rouhhan,* Old Norse *rjūka* to smoke, steam] —**ˈreek·ing·ly** *adv.* —**ˈreek·y** *adj.*

reel[1] (riːl, rɪəl) *n.* **1.** any of various cylindrical objects or frames that turn on an axis and onto which film, magnetic tape, paper tape, wire, thread, etc., may be wound. U.S. equivalent: **spool. 2.** *Angling.* a device for winding, casting, etc., consisting of a revolving spool with a handle, attached to a fishing rod. **3.** a roll of celluloid exhibiting a sequence of photographs to be projected. ~*vb.* (*tr.*) **4.** to wind (cotton, thread, etc.) onto a reel. **5.** (foll. by *in, out,* etc.) to wind or draw with a reel: *to reel in a fish.* [Old English *hrēol;* related to Old Norse *hræll* weaver's rod, Greek *krekein* to weave] —**ˈreel·a·ble** *adj.* —**ˈreel·er** *n.*

reel[2] (riːl, rɪəl) *vb.* (*mainly intr.*) **1.** to sway, esp. under the shock of a blow or through dizziness or drunkenness. **2.** to whirl about or have the feeling of whirling about: *his brain reeled.* ~*n.* **3.** a staggering or swaying motion or sensation. [C14 *relen,* probably from REEL[1]]

reel[3] (riːl, rɪəl) *n.* **1.** any of various lively Scottish dances, such as the **eightsome reel** and **foursome reel,** for a fixed number of couples who combine in square and circular formations. **2.** a piece of music composed for or in the rhythm of this dance. [C18: from REEL[2]]

reel-fed *adj. Printing.* involving or printing on a web of paper: *a reel-fed press.* Compare **sheet-fed.**

reel man *n. Austral.* the member of a beach life-saving team who controls the reel on which the line is wound.

reel off *vb.* (*tr., adv.*) to recite or write fluently and without apparent effort: *to reel off items on a list.*

reel-to-reel *adj.* **1.** (of magnetic tape) wound from one reel to another in use. **2.** (of a tape recorder) using magnetic tape wound from one reel to another, as opposed to cassettes.

reen *or* **rean** (riːn) *n. Southwest Brit. dialect.* a ditch, esp. a drainage channel. [from earlier *rhine,* from Old English *ryne*]

re-en·ter·ing an·gle *n.* an interior angle of a polygon that is greater than 180°. Also called: **re-entrant angle.**

re-en·trant (riːˈɛntrənt) *adj.* **1.** pointing inwards. Compare **salient** (sense 2). ~*n.* **2.** an angle or part that points inwards.

re-en·try (riːˈɛntrɪ) *n., pl.* **·tries. 1.** the act of retaking possession of land, etc., under a right reserved in an earlier transfer of the property, such as a lease. **2.** the return of a spacecraft into the earth's atmosphere.

reest *or* **reast** (riːst) *vb.* (*intr.*) *Northern English dialect.* (esp. of horses) to be noisily uncooperative. [probably from Scottish *arreest* ARREST; perhaps related to RESTIVE]

reeve[1] (riːv) *n.* **1.** *English history.* the local representative of the king in a shire (under the ealdorman) until the early 11th century. Compare **sheriff. 2.** (in medieval England) a manorial steward who supervised the daily affairs of the manor: often a villein elected by his fellows. **3.** *Canadian government.* a president of a local council, esp. in a rural area. **4.** (formerly) a minor local official in any of several parts of England and the U.S. [Old English *gerēva;* related to Old High German *ruova* number, array]

reeve[2] (riːv) *vb.* **reeves, reev·ing; reeved** *or* **rove.** (*tr.*) *Nautical.* **1.** to pass (a rope or cable) through an eye or other narrow opening. **2.** to fasten by passing through or around something. [C17: perhaps from Dutch *rēven* REEF[2]]

reeve[3] (riːv) *n.* the female of the ruff (the bird). [C17: of uncertain origin]

re·ex·am·ine (ˌriːɪgˈzæmɪn) *vb.* (*tr.*) **1.** to examine again. **2.** *Law.* to examine (one's own witness) again upon matters arising out of his cross-examination. —**ˌre·ex·ˈam·in·a·ble** *adj.* —**ˌre·ex·ˌam·i·ˈna·tion** *n.* —**ˌre·ex·ˈam·in·er** *n.*

re·ex·port *vb.* (ˌriːɪkˈspɔːt, riːˈɛkspɔːt). **1.** to export (imported goods, esp. after processing). ~*n.* (riːˈɛkspɔːt). **2.** the act of re-exporting. **3.** a re-exported commodity. —**ˌre·ex·por·ˈta·tion** *n.* —**ˌre·ex·ˈport·er** *n.*

ref (rɛf) *n.* an informal shortening of **referee.**

ref. *abbrev. for:* **1.** referee. **2.** reference. **3.** reformed.

re·face (riːˈfeɪs) *vb.* (*tr.*) **1.** to repair or renew the facing of (a wall). **2.** to put a new facing on (a garment).

Ref. Ch. *abbrev. for* Reformed Church.

re·fec·tion (rɪˈfɛkʃən) *n.* refreshment with food and drink. [C14: from Latin *refectiō* a restoring, from *reficere* to remake, from RE- + *facere* to make]

re·fec·to·ry (rɪˈfɛktərɪ, -trɪ) *n., pl.* **·ries.** a communal dining hall in a religious, academic, or other institution. [C15: from Late Latin *refectōrium,* from Latin *refectus* refreshed]

re·fec·to·ry ta·ble *n.* a long narrow dining table supported by two trestles joined by a stretcher or set into a base.

re·fer (rɪˈfɜː) *vb.* **·fers, ·fer·ring, ·ferred.** (often foll. by *to*). **1.** (*intr.*) to make mention (of); allude (to). **2.** (*tr.*) to direct the attention of (someone) for information, facts, etc.: *the reader is referred to Chomsky, 1965.* **3.** (*intr.*) to seek information (from): *I referred to directory enquiries; he referred to his notes.* **4.** (*intr.*) to be relevant (to); pertain or relate (to): *this song refers to an incident in the Civil War.* **5.** (*tr.*) to assign or attribute: *Cromwell referred his victories to God.* **6.** (*tr.*) to hand over for consideration, reconsideration, or decision: *to refer a complaint to another department.* **7.** (*tr.*) to hand back to the originator as unacceptable or unusable. **8.** (*tr.*) *Brit.* to fail (a student) in an examination. **9.** (*tr.*) *Brit.* to send back (a thesis) to a student for improvement. **10. refer to drawer.** a request by a bank that the payee consult the drawer concerning a cheque payable by that bank (usually because the drawer has insufficient funds in his account), payment being suspended in the meantime. **11.** (*tr.*) to direct (a patient) for treatment to another doctor, usually a specialist. [C14: from Latin *referre* to carry back, from RE- + *ferre* to BEAR[1]] —**ref·er·a·ble** (ˈrɛfərəbᵊl) *or* **re·fer·ra·ble** (rɪˈfɜːrəbᵊl) *adj.* —**re·ˈfer·ral** *n.* —**re·ˈfer·rer** *n.*

Usage. The common practice of adding *back* to *refer* is tautologous, since this meaning is already contained in the *re-* of *refer: this refers to* (not *back to*) *what has already been said.* However, when *refer* is used in the sense of passing a document or question for further consideration to the person from whom it was received, it may be appropriate to say *he referred the matter back.*

ref·er·ee (ˌrɛfəˈriː) *n.* **1.** a person to whom reference is made, esp. for an opinion, information, or a decision. **2.** the umpire or judge in any of various sports, esp. football and boxing, responsible for ensuring fair play according to the rules. **3.** a person who is willing to testify to the character or capabilities of someone. **4.** *Law.* See **Official Referee.** ~*vb.* **·ees, ·ee·ing, ·eed. 5.** to act as a referee (in); preside (over).

ref·er·ence (ˈrɛfərəns, ˈrɛfrəns) *n.* **1.** the act or an instance of referring. **2.** something referred, esp. proceedings submitted to a referee in law. **3.** a direction of the attention to a passage elsewhere or to another book, document etc. **4.** a book or passage referred to. **5.** a mention or allusion: *this book contains several references to the Civil War.* **6.** the relation between a word or phrase and the object or idea to which it refers. **7. a.** a source of information or facts. **b.** (*as modifier*): *a reference book; a reference library.* **8.** a written testimonial regarding one's character or capabilities. **9.** a person referred to for such a testimonial. **10. a.** (foll. by *to*) relation or delimitation, esp. to or by membership of a specific class or group; respect or regard: *all people, without reference to sex or age.* **b.** (*as modifier*): *a reference group.* **11. terms of reference.** the specific limits of responsibility that determine the activities of an investigating body, etc. **12. point of reference.** a fact forming the basis of an evaluation or assessment; criterion. ~*vb.* (*tr.*) **13.** to furnish or compile a list of references for (an academic thesis, publication, etc.). **14.** to make a reference to; refer to: *he referenced Chomsky 1956.* ~*prep.* **15.** *Business jargon.* with reference to: *reference your letter of the 9th inst.* Abbrev.: **re** —**ˈref·er·enc·er** *n.* —**ref·er·en·tial** (ˌrɛfəˈrɛnʃəl) *adj.*

ref·er·ence book *n.* **1.** a book, such as an encyclopedia, dictionary, etc., from which information may be obtained. **2.** *S. African.* another name for **passbook.**

ref·er·en·dum (ˌrɛfəˈrɛndəm) *n., pl.* **·dums** *or* **·da** (-də). **1.** submission of an issue of public importance to the direct vote of the electorate. **2.** a vote on such a measure. **3.** a poll of the members of a club, union, or other group to determine their views on some matter. **4.** a diplomatic official's note to his government requesting instructions. ~See also (for senses 1,

---

re-ˈed·u·ˌcate *vb.*
re-ˌed·u·ˈca·tion *n.*
ˌre-e·ˈlect *vb.*
ˌre-e·ˈlec·tion *n.*
re-ˈel·i·gi·ble *adj.*
ˌre-em·ˈbark *vb.*
ˌre-em·ˈbod·y *vb.*, **·bod·ies, ·bod·y·ing, ·bod·ied.**
ˌre-e·ˈmerge *vb.*
ˌre-e·ˈmer·gence *n.*
ˌre-e·ˈmer·gent *adj.*
re-ˈem·pha·ˌsize *or* re-ˈem·pha·ˌsise *vb.*
ˌre-em·ˈploy *vb.*
ˌre-em·ˈploy·ment *n.*
ˌre-en·ˈact *vb.*
ˌre-en·ˈact·ment *n.*
ˌre-en·ˈclose *vb.*
ˌre-en·ˈdow *vb.*
ˌre-en·ˈforce *vb.*
ˌre-en·ˈforce·ment *n.*
ˌre-en·ˈforc·er *n.*
ˌre-en·ˈgage *vb.*
ˌre-en·ˈlarge *vb.*
ˌre-en·ˈlarge·ment *n.*
ˌre-en·ˈlight·en *vb.*
ˌre-en·ˈslave *vb.*
re-ˈen·ter *vb.*
re-ˈen·trance *n.*
ˌre-e·ˈquip *vb.*, **·quips, ·quip·ping, ·quipped.**
ˌre-e·ˈrect *vb.*
ˌre-es·ˈtab·lish *vb.*
ˌre-es·ˈtab·lish·ment *n.*
ˌre-e·ˈval·u·ˌate *vb.*
ˌre-e·ˌval·u·ˈa·tion *n.*
ˌre-ex·ˈhib·it *vb.*
ˌre-ex·ˈpe·ri·ence *vb.*
re·ˈfash·ion *vb.*
re·ˈfas·ten *vb.*

2) **plebiscite.** [C19: from Latin: something to be carried back, from *referre* to REFER]

ref·er·ent ('rɛfərənt) *n.* **1.** the object or idea to which a word or phrase refers. **2.** *Logic.* the term in a proposition from which a relation proceeds, as *John* in *John loves Ann.* [C19: from Latin *referens* from *referre* to REFER]

re·ferred pain *n. Psychol.* pain felt in the body at some place other than its actual place of origin.

re·fill *vb.* (riː'fɪl). **1.** to fill (something) again. ~*n.* ('riːfɪl). **2.** a replacement for a consumable substance in a permanent container. **3.** a second or subsequent filling: *a refill at the petrol station.* **4.** *Informal.* another drink to replace one already drunk. —**re·'fill·a·ble** *adj.*

re·fine (rɪ'faɪn) *vb.* **1.** to make or become free from impurities, sediment, or other foreign matter; purify. **2.** (*tr.*) to separate (a mixture) into pure constituents, as in an oil refinery. **3.** to make or become free from coarse characteristics; make or become elegant or polished. **4.** (*tr.; often foll. by out*) to remove (something impure or extraneous). **5.** (*intr.;* often foll. by *on* or *upon*) to enlarge or improve (upon) by making subtle or fine distinctions. **6.** (*tr.*) to make (language) more subtle or polished. [C16: from RE- + FINE[1]] —**re·'fin·a·ble** *adj.* —**re·'fin·er** *n.*

re·fined (rɪ'faɪnd) *adj.* **1.** not coarse or vulgar; genteel, elegant, or polite. **2.** freed from impurities; purified.

re·fine·ment (rɪ'faɪnmənt) *n.* **1.** the act of refining or the state of being refined. **2.** a fine or delicate point, distinction, or expression; a subtlety. **3.** fineness or precision of thought, expression, manners, etc.; polish or cultivation.

re·fin·er·y (rɪ'faɪnərɪ) *n., pl.* **·er·ies.** a factory for the purification of some crude material, such as ore, sugar, oil, etc.

re·fit *vb.* (riː'fɪt), **·fits, ·fit·ting, ·fit·ted. 1.** to make or be made ready for use again by repairing, re-equipping, or resupplying. ~*n.* ('riːˌfɪt). **2.** a repair or re-equipping, as of a ship, for further use. —**re·'fit·ment** *n.*

refl. *abbrev. for:* **1.** reflection. **2.** reflective. **3.** reflex(ive).

re·flate (rɪː'fleɪt) *vb.* to inflate or be inflated again. [C20: back formation from REFLATION]

re·fla·tion (rɪː'fleɪʃən) *n.* **1.** an increase in economic activity. **2.** an increase in the supply of money and credit designed to cause such an increase. ~Compare **inflation** (sense 2). [C20: from RE- + *-flation,* as in INFLATION or DEFLATION]

re·flect (rɪ'flɛkt) *vb.* **1.** to undergo or cause to undergo a process in which light, other electromagnetic radiation, sound, particles, etc., are thrown back after impinging on a surface. **2.** (of a mirror, etc.) to form an image of (something) by reflection. **3.** (*tr.*) to show or express in one's behaviour, attitude, etc.: *his tactics reflect his desire for power.* **4.** (*intr.;* usually foll. by *on*) to think, meditate, or ponder. **5.** (*intr.;* often foll. by *on* or *upon*) to cast dishonour or honour, credit or discredit, etc. (on): *his conduct reflects on his parents.* [C15: from Latin *reflectere* to bend back, from RE- + *flectere* to bend; see FLEX] —**re·'flect·ing·ly** *adv.*

re·flec·tance (rɪ'flɛktəns) *or* **re·flec·tion fac·tor** *n.* a measure of the ability of a surface to reflect light or other electromagnetic radiation, equal to the ratio of the reflected flux to the incident flux. Symbol: ρ Compare **transmittance, absorptance.**

re·flect·ing tel·e·scope *n.* a type of telescope in which the initial image is formed by a concave mirror. Also called: **reflector.** Compare **refracting telescope.**

re·flec·tion *or* **re·flex·ion** (rɪ'flɛkʃən) *n.* **1.** the act of reflecting or the state of being reflected. **2.** something reflected or the image so produced, as by a mirror. **3.** careful or long consideration or thought. **4.** implicit or explicit attribution of discredit or blame. **5.** *Maths.* a transformation in which the direction of one axis is reversed. **6.** *Anatomy.* the bending back of a structure or part upon itself. —**re·'flec·tion·al** *or* **re·'flex·ion·al** *adj.*

re·flec·tion den·si·ty *n. Physics.* a measure of the extent to which a surface reflects light or other electromagnetic radiation, equal to the logarithm to base ten of the reciprocal of the reflectance. Symbol: *D* Former name: **optical density.**

re·flec·tive (rɪ'flɛktɪv) *adj.* **1.** characterized by quiet thought or contemplation. **2.** capable of reflecting: *a reflective surface.* **3.** produced by reflection. —**re·'flec·tive·ly** *adv.*

re·flec·tiv·i·ty (ˌriːflɛk'tɪvɪtɪ) *n.* **1.** *Physics.* a measure of the ability of a surface to reflect radiation, equal to the reflectance of a layer of material sufficiently thick for the reflectance not to depend on the thickness. **2.** Also: **re·flec·tive·ness.** the quality or capability of being reflective.

re·flec·tor (rɪ'flɛktə) *n.* **1.** a person or thing that reflects. **2.** a surface or object that reflects light, sound, heat, etc. **3.** a small translucent red disc, strip, etc., with a reflecting backing on the rear of a road vehicle, which reflects the light of the headlights of a following vehicle. **4.** another name for **reflecting telescope. 5.** a part of an aerial placed so as to increase the forward radiation of the radiator and decrease the backward radiation.

re·flet (rə'fleɪ) *n.* an iridescent glow or lustre, as on ceramic ware. [C19: from French: a reflection, from Italian *riflesso,* from Latin *reflexus,* from *reflectere* to REFLECT]

re·flex *n.* ('riːflɛks). **1. a.** an immediate involuntary response, such as coughing or removal of the hand from a hot surface, evoked by a given stimulus. **b.** (*as modifier*): *a reflex action.* See also **reflex arc. 2. a.** a mechanical response to a particular situation, involving no conscious decision. **b.** (*as modifier*): *a reflex response.* **3.** a reflection; an image produced by or as if by reflection. **4.** a speech element derived from a corresponding form in an earlier state of the language: *"sorrow" is a reflex of Middle English "sorwe."* ~*adj.* ('riːflɛks). **5.** *Maths.* (of an angle) between 180° and 360°. **6.** (*prenominal*) turned, reflected, or bent backwards. ~*vb.* (rɪ'flɛks). **7.** (*tr.*) to bend, turn, or reflect backwards. [C16: from Latin *reflexus* bent back, from *reflectere* to reflect] —**re·'flex·i·ble** *adj.* —**re·ˌflex·i·'bil·i·ty** *n.*

re·flex arc *n. Physiol.* the neural pathway over which impulses travel to produce a reflex action, consisting of at least one afferent (receptor) and one efferent (effector) neuron.

re·flex cam·er·a *n.* a camera in which the image is composed and focused on a large ground-glass viewfinder screen. In a **single-lens reflex** the light enters through the camera lens and falls on the film when the viewfinder mirror is retracted. In a **twin-lens reflex** the light enters through a separate lens and is deflected onto the viewfinder screen.

re·flex·ion (rɪ'flɛkʃən) *n. Brit.* a less common spelling of **reflection.** —**re·'flex·ion·al** *adj.*

re·flex·ive (rɪ'flɛksɪv) *adj.* **1.** denoting a class of pronouns that refer back to the subject of a sentence or clause. Thus, in the sentence *that man thinks a great deal of himself,* the pronoun *himself* is reflexive. **2.** denoting a verb used transitively with the reflexive pronoun as its direct object, as the French *se lever* "to get up" (literally "to raise oneself") or English *to dress oneself.* **3.** *Physiol.* of or relating to a reflex. ~*n.* **4.** a reflexive pronoun or verb. —**re·'flex·ive·ly** *adv.* —**re·'flex·ive·ness** *or* **re·flex·iv·i·ty** (ˌriːflɛk'sɪvɪtɪ) *n.*

ref·lu·ent ('rɛfluənt) *adj. Rare.* flowing back; ebbing. [C18: from Latin *refluere* to flow back] —**'ref·lu·ence** *n.*

re·flux ('riːflʌks) *vb.* **1.** *Chem.* to boil or be boiled in a vessel attached to a condenser, so that the vapour condenses and flows back into the vessel. ~*n.* **2.** *Chem.* **a.** an act of refluxing. **b.** (*as modifier*): *a reflux condenser.* **3.** the act or an instance of flowing back; ebb. [C15: from Medieval Latin *refluxus,* from Latin *refluere* to flow back]

re·form (rɪ'fɔːm) *vb.* **1.** (*tr.*) to improve (an existing institution, law, practice, etc.) by alteration or correction of abuses. **2.** to give up or cause to give up a reprehensible habit or immoral way of life. **3.** *Chem.* to change the molecular structure of (a hydrocarbon) to make it suitable for use as petrol by heat, pressure, and the action of catalysts. ~*n.* **4.** an improvement or change for the better, esp. as a result of correction of legal or political abuses or malpractices. **5.** a principle, campaign, or measure aimed at achieving such change. **6.** improvement of morals or behaviour, esp. by giving up some vice. [C14: via Old French from Latin *reformāre* to form again] —**re·'form·a·ble** *adj.* —**re·'form·a·tive** *adj.* —**re·'form·er** *n.*

re-form (riː'fɔːm) *vb.* to form anew. —ˌ**re-for·'ma·tion** *n.*

ref·or·ma·tion (ˌrɛfə'meɪʃən) *n.* the act or an instance of reforming or the state of being reformed. —ˌ**ref·or·'ma·tion·al** *adj.*

Ref·or·ma·tion (ˌrɛfə'meɪʃən) *n.* a religious and political movement of 16th-century Europe that began as an attempt to reform the Roman Catholic Church and resulted in the establishment of the Protestant Churches.

re·form·a·to·ry (rɪ'fɔːmətərɪ, -trɪ) *n., pl.* **·ries. 1.** Also called: **re·form school.** (formerly) a place of instruction where young offenders were sent for corrective training. Compare **approved school.** ~*adj.* **2.** having the purpose or function of reforming.

Re·form Bill *or* **Act** *n. English history.* any of several bills or acts extending the franchise or redistributing parliamentary seats, esp. the acts of 1832 and 1867.

Re·formed (rɪ'fɔːmd) *adj.* **1.** of or designating a Protestant Church, esp. the Calvinist as distinct from the Lutheran. **2.** of or designating Reform Judaism.

re·form·ism (rɪ'fɔːmɪzəm) *n.* a doctrine or movement advocating reform, esp. political or religious reform rather than abolition. —**re·'form·ist** *n., adj.*

Re·form Ju·da·ism *n.* a movement in Judaism originating in the 19th century, which does not require strict observance of the law, but adapts the historical forms of Judaism to the contemporary world.

re·fract (rɪ'frækt) *vb.* **1.** to cause or undergo refraction. **2.** (*tr.*) to measure the refractive capabilities of (the eye, a lens, etc.). [C17: from Latin *refractus* broken up, from *refringere,* from RE- + *frangere* to break] —**re·'fract·a·ble** *adj.*

re·fract·ing tel·e·scope *n.* a type of telescope in which the image is formed by a set of lenses. Also called: **refractor.** Compare **reflecting telescope.**

re·frac·tion (rɪ'frækʃən) *n.* **1.** *Physics.* the change in direction of a propagating wave, such as light or sound, in passing from one medium to another in which it has a different velocity. **2.** the amount by which a wave is refracted. **3.** the ability of the eye to refract light. **4.** the determination of the refractive condition of the eye. **5.** *Astronomy.* the apparent elevation in position of a celestial body resulting from the refraction of light by the earth's atmosphere. —**re·'frac·tion·al** *adj.*

re·frac·tive (rɪ'fræktɪv) *adj.* **1.** of or concerned with refraction. **2.** (of a material or substance) capable of causing re-

---

re·'file *vb.*
re·'film *vb.*
re·'fil·ter *vb.*
re·'fi·nance *vb.*
re·'fin·ish *vb.*
re·'fin·ish·er *n.*
re·'fire *vb.*
re·'float *vb.*
re·'flow·er *vb.*
re·'fo·cus *vb.,* **·cus·es, ·cus·ing, ·cused** *or* **·cus·ses, ·cus·sing, ·cussed.**
re·'fold *vb.*
re·'for·est *vb.*
ˌ**re·for·est·'a·tion** *n.*
re·'forge *vb.*
re·'for·mu·ˌlate *vb.*
ˌ**re·for·mu·'la·tion** *n.*
re·'for·ti·ˌfy *vb.,* **·fies, ·fy·ing, ·fied.**

fraction. —re+'frac+tive+ly *adv.* —re+'frac+tive+ness *or* **re+frac+tiv+i+ty** (ˌriːfræk'tɪvɪtɪ) *n.*

re+frac+tive in+dex *n. Physics.* a measure of the extent to which a medium refracts light; the ratio of the speed of light in a vacuum to that in the medium (**absolute refractive index**) or of its speed in a reference medium to that in the medium (**relative refractive index**). Symbol: *ν*, *μ*

re+frac+tom+e+ter (ˌriːfræk'tɒmɪtə) *n.* any instrument for determining the refractive index of a substance. —**re+frac+to+met+ric** (rɪˌfræktə'mɛtrɪk) *adj.* —ˌ**re+frac+'tom+e+try** *n.*

re+frac+tor (ri'fræktə) *n.* **1.** an object or material that refracts. **2.** another name for **refracting telescope.**

re+frac+to+ry (rɪ'fræktərɪ) *adj.* **1.** unmanageable or obstinate. **2.** *Med.* not responding to treatment. **3.** *Physiol.* (of a nerve or muscle) incapable of responding to stimulation, esp. during the period (**refractory period**) immediately following a previous stimulation. **4.** (of a material) able to withstand high temperatures without fusion or decomposition. ~*n., pl.* **·ries. 5.** a material, such as fireclay or alumina, that is able to withstand high temperatures: used to line furnaces, etc. —**re+'frac+to+ri+ly** *adv.* —**re+'frac+to+ri+ness** *n.*

re+frain[1] (rɪ'freɪn) *vb.* (*intr.;* usually foll. by *from*) to abstain (from action); forbear. [C14: from Latin *refrēnāre* to check with a bridle, from RE- + *frēnum* a bridle] —**re+'frain+er** *n.* —**re+'frain+ment** *n.*

re+frain[2] (rɪ'freɪn) *n.* **1.** a regularly recurring melody, such as the chorus of a song. **2.** a much repeated saying or idea. [C14: via Old French, ultimately from Latin *refringere* to break into pieces]

re+fran+gi+ble (rɪ'frændʒɪbᵊl) *adj.* capable of being refracted. [C17: from Latin *refringere* to break up, from RE- + *frangere* to break] —**re+ˌfran+gi+'bil+i+ty** *or* **re+'fran+gi+ble+ness** *n.*

re+fresh (rɪ'frɛʃ) *vb.* **1.** (*usually tr. or reflexive*) to make or become fresh or vigorous, as through rest, drink, or food; revive or reinvigorate. **2.** (*tr.*) to enliven (something worn or faded), as by adding new decorations. **3.** (*tr.*) to stimulate (the memory, etc.). **4.** (*tr.*) to replenish, as with new equipment or stores. [C14: from Old French *refreschir;* see RE-, FRESH] —**re+'fresh+ful** *adj.*

re+fresh+er (rɪ'frɛʃə) *n.* **1.** something that refreshes, such as a cold drink. **2.** *English law.* a fee, additional to that marked on the brief, paid to counsel in a case that lasts more than a day.

re+fresh+er course *n.* a short educational course for people to review their subject and developments in it.

re+fresh+ing (rɪ'frɛʃɪŋ) *adj.* **1.** able to or tending to refresh; invigorating. **2.** pleasantly different or novel. —**re+'fresh+ing+ly** *adv.*

re+fresh+ment (rɪ'frɛʃmənt) *n.* **1.** the act of refreshing or the state of being refreshed. **2.** (*pl.*) snacks and drinks served as a light meal.

re+frig+er+ant (rɪ'frɪdʒərənt) *n.* **1.** a fluid capable of changes of phase at low temperatures: used as the working fluid of a refrigerator. **2.** a cooling substance, such as ice or solid carbon dioxide. **3.** *Med.* an agent that provides a sensation of coolness or reduces fever. ~*adj.* **4.** causing cooling or freezing.

re+frig+er+ate (rɪ'frɪdʒəˌreɪt) *vb.* to make or become frozen or cold, esp. for preservative purposes; chill or freeze. [C16: from Latin *refrīgerāre* to make cold, from RE- + *frīgus* cold] —**re+ˌfrig+er+'a+tion** *n.* —**re+'frig+er+a+tive** *or* **re+'frig+er+a+to+ry** *adj.*

re+frig+er+a+tor (rɪ'frɪdʒəˌreɪtə) *n.* a chamber in which food, drink, etc., are kept cool. Informal word: **fridge.**

re+frin+gent (rɪ'frɪndʒənt) *adj. Physics.* of, concerned with, or causing refraction; refractive. [C18: from Latin *refringere* to break up; see REFRACT] —**re+'frin+gen+cy** *or* **re+'frin+gence** *n.*

reft (rɛft) *vb.* a past tense and past participle of **reave.**

re+fu+el (riː'fjuːəl) *vb.* **+els, +el+ling, +elled** *or U.S.* **+els, +el+ing, +eled.** to supply or be supplied with fresh fuel.

ref+uge ('rɛfjuːdʒ) *n.* **1.** shelter or protection, as from the weather or danger. **2.** any place, person, action, or thing that offers or appears to offer protection, help, or relief: *accused of incompetence, he took refuge in lying.* **3.** another name for a traffic island. See **island** (sense 2). ~*vb.* **4.** *Archaic.* to take refuge or give refuge to. [C14: via Old French from Latin *refugium,* from *refugere* to flee away, from RE- + *fugere* to escape]

ref+u+gee (ˌrɛfjʊ'dʒiː) *n.* **a.** a person who has fled from some danger or problem, esp. political persecution. **b.** (*as modifier*): *a refugee camp; a refugee problem.* —ˌ**ref+u+'gee+ism** *n.*

re+fu+gi+um (rɪ'fjuːdʒɪəm) *n., pl.* **+gi+a** (-dʒɪə). a geographical region that has remained unaltered by a climatic change affecting surrounding regions and that therefore forms a haven for relict fauna and flora. [C20: Latin: refuge]

re+ful+gent (rɪ'fʌldʒənt) *adj. Literary.* shining, brilliant, or radiant. [C16: from Latin *refulgēre* to shine brightly, from RE- + *fulgēre* to shine] —**re+'ful+gence** *or* **re+'ful+gen+cy** *n.* —**re+'ful+gent+ly** *adv.*

re+fund *vb.* (rɪ'fʌnd). (*tr.*) **1.** to give back (money, etc.), as when an article purchased is unsatisfactory. **2.** to reimburse (a person). ~*n.* ('riːˌfʌnd). **3.** return of money to a purchaser or the amount so returned. [C14: from Latin *refundere* to pour back, from RE- + *fundere* to pour] —**re+'fund+a+ble** *adj.* —**re+'fund+er** *n.*

re-fund (riː'fʌnd) *vb.* (*tr.*) *Finance.* **1.** to discharge (an old or matured debt) by new borrowing, as by a new bond issue. **2.** to replace (an existing bond issue) with a new one. [C20: from RE- + FUND]

re+fur+bish (riː'fɜːbɪʃ) *vb.* (*tr.*) to make neat, clean, or complete, as by renovating, re-equipping, or restoring. —**re+'fur+bish+ment** *n.*

re+fus+al (rɪ'fjuːzᵊl) *n.* **1.** the act or an instance of refusing. **2.** the opportunity to reject or accept; option.

re+fuse[1] (rɪ'fjuːz) *vb.* **1.** (*tr.*) to decline to accept (something offered): *to refuse a present; to refuse promotion.* **2.** to decline to give or grant (something) to (a person, organization, etc.). **3.** (when *tr., takes an infinitive*) to express determination not (to do something); decline: *he refuses to talk about it.* **4.** (of a horse) to be unwilling to take (a jump), as by swerving or stopping. **5.** (*tr.*) (of a woman) to declare one's unwillingness to accept (a suitor) as a husband. [C14: from Old French *refuser,* from Latin *refundere* to pour back; see REFUND] —**re+'fus+a+ble** *adj.* —**re+'fus+er** *n.*

ref+use[2] ('rɛfjuːs) *n.* **a.** anything thrown away; waste; rubbish. **b.** (*as modifier*): *a refuse collection.* [C15: from Old French *refuser* to REFUSE[1]]

ref+u+ta+tion (ˌrɛfjʊ'teɪʃən) *n.* **1.** the act or process of refuting. **2.** something that refutes; disproof.

re+fute (rɪ'fjuːt) *vb.* (*tr.*) to prove (a statement, theory, charge, etc.) of (a person) to be false or incorrect; disprove. [C16: from Latin *refūtāre* to rebut] —**ref+u+ta+ble** ('rɛfjʊtəbᵊl, rɪ'fjuː-) *adj.* —**ref+u+ta+bil+i+ty** (ˌrɛfjʊtə'bɪlɪtɪ, rɪˌfjuː-) *n.* —**'ref+u+ta+bly** *adv.* —**re+'fut+er** *n.*

Usage. *Refute* is often used incorrectly as a synonym of *deny.* In careful usage, however, to *deny* something is to state that it is untrue; to *refute* something is to assemble evidence in order to prove it untrue: *all he could do was deny the allegations since he was unable to refute them.*

reg. *abbrev. for:* **1.** regiment. **2.** register(ed). **3.** registrar. **4.** registry. **5.** regular(ly). **6.** regulation. **7.** regulator.

Reg. *abbrev. for:* **1.** Regent. **2.** Regina.

re+gain (rɪ'geɪn) *vb.* (*tr.*) **1.** to take or get back; recover. **2.** to reach again. —**re+'gain+a+ble** *adj.* —**re+'gain+er** *n.*

re+gal[1] ('riːgᵊl) *adj.* of, relating to, or befitting a king or queen; royal. [C14: from Latin *rēgālis,* from *rēx* king] —**'re+gal+ly** *adv.*

re+gal[2] ('riːgᵊl) *n.* (*sometimes pl.*) a portable organ equipped only with small reed pipes, popular from the 15th century and recently revived for modern performance.

re+gale (rɪ'geɪl) *vb.* (*tr.,* usually foll. by *with*) **1.** to give delight or amusement to: *he regaled them with stories of his youth.* **2.** to provide with choice or abundant food or drink. ~*n.* **3.** *Archaic.* **a.** a feast. **b.** a delicacy of food or drink. [C17: from French *régaler,* from *gale* pleasure; related to Middle Dutch *wale* riches; see also GALA] —**re+'gale+ment** *n.*

re+ga+li+a (rɪ'geɪlɪə) *n.* (*pl., sometimes functioning as sing.*) **1.** the ceremonial emblems or robes of royalty, high office, an order, etc. **2.** any splendid or special clothes; finery. [C16: from Medieval Latin: royal privileges, from Latin *rēgālis* REGAL]

re+gal+i+ty (riː'gælɪtɪ) *n., pl.* **·ties. 1.** the state or condition of being royal; kingship or queenship; royalty. **2.** the rights or privileges of royalty.

re+gard (rɪ'gɑːd) *vb.* **1.** to look closely or attentively at (something or someone); observe steadily. **2.** (*tr.*) to hold (a person or thing) in respect, admiration, or affection: *we regard your work very highly.* **3.** (*tr.*) to look upon or consider in a specified way: *she regarded her brother as her responsibility.* **4.** (*tr.*) to relate to; concern; have a bearing on. **5.** to take notice of or pay attention to (something); heed: *he has never regarded the conventions.* **6. as regards.** (*prep.*) in respect of; concerning. ~*n.* **7.** a gaze; look. **8.** attention; heed: *he spends without regard to his bank balance.* **9.** esteem, affection, or respect. **10.** reference, relation, or connection (esp. in the phrases **with regard to** or **in regard to**) **11.** (*pl.*) good wishes or greetings (esp. in the phrase **with kind regards,** used at the close of a letter). [C14: from Old French *regarder* to look at, care about, from RE- + *garder* to GUARD] —**re+'gard+a+ble** *adj.*

re+gar+dant (rɪ'gɑːdᵊnt) *adj.* (*usually postpositive*) *Heraldry.* (of a beast) shown looking backwards over its shoulder. [C15: from Old French; see REGARD]

re+gard+ful (rɪ'gɑːdfʊl) *adj.* **1.** (often foll. by *of*) showing regard (for); heedful (of). **2.** showing regard, respect, or consideration. —**re+'gard+ful+ly** *adv.* —**re+'gard+ful+ness** *n.*

re+gard+ing (rɪ'gɑːdɪŋ) *prep.* in respect of; on the subject of.

re+gard+less (rɪ'gɑːdlɪs) *adj.* **1.** (usually foll. by *of*) taking no regard or heed; heedless. ~*adv.* **2.** in spite of everything; disregarding drawbacks: *to carry on regardless.* —**re+'gard+less+ly** *adv.* —**re+'gard+less+ness** *n.*

re+gat+ta (rɪ'gætə) *n.* an organized series of races of yachts, rowing boats, etc. [C17: from obsolete Italian (Venetian dialect) *rigatta* contest, of obscure origin]

regd. *abbrev. for* registered.

re+ge+late ('riːdʒɪˌleɪt) *vb. Physics.* to undergo or cause to undergo regelation.

re+ge+la+tion (ˌriːdʒɪ'leɪʃən) *n.* the rejoining together of two pieces of ice as a result of melting under pressure at the interface between them and subsequent refreezing.

re+gen+cy ('riːdʒənsɪ) *n., pl.* **+cies. 1.** government by a regent or a body of regents. **2.** the office of a regent or body of regents. **3.** a territory under the jurisdiction of a regent or body of regents. **4.** *Rare.* the use or exercise of authority; rule or government. [C15: from Medieval Latin *regentia,* from Latin *regere* to rule]

Re+gen+cy ('riːdʒənsɪ) *n.* (preceded by *the*) **1.** (in England) the

re+'frame *vb.*
re+'freeze *vb.,* +freez·es, +freez+ing, +froze, +fro+zen.
re+'fry *v.,* +fries, +fry+ing, +fried.
re+'fur+nish *vb.*
re+'gal+va+ˌnize *or* re+'gal+va+ˌnise *vb.*
re+'gath+er *vb.*

period (1811–20) during which the Prince of Wales (later George IV) acted as regent during his father's periods of insanity. **2.** (in France) the period of the regency of Philip, Duke of Orleans, during the minority of Louis XV (1715–23). ~*adj.* **3.** characteristic of or relating to the Regency periods in France or England or to the styles of architecture, furniture, art, literature, etc., produced in them.

re·gen·er·ate *vb.* (rɪˈdʒɛnəˌreɪt). **1.** to undergo or cause to undergo moral, spiritual, or physical renewal or invigoration. **2.** to form or be formed again; come or bring into existence once again. **3.** to replace (lost or damaged tissues or organs) by new growth, or to cause (such tissues) to be replaced. **4.** *Chem.* to restore or be restored to an original physical or chemical state. **5.** (*tr.*) *Electronics.* to amplify (a signal) by means of regeneration. ~*adj.* (rɪˈdʒɛnərɪt). **6.** morally, spiritually, or physically renewed or reborn; restored or refreshed. —**re·ˈgen·er·a·ble** *adj.* —**re·ˈgen·er·a·cy** *n.* —**re·ˈgen·er·a·tive** *adj.* —**re·ˈgen·er·a·tive·ly** *adv.* —**re·ˈgen·er·ˌa·tor** *n.*

re·gen·er·a·tion (rɪˌdʒɛnəˈreɪʃən) *n.* **1.** the act or process of regenerating or the state of being regenerated; rebirth or renewal. **2.** the regrowth by an animal or plant of an organ, tissue, or part that has been lost or destroyed. **3.** *Electronics.* the use of positive feedback, esp. to improve the demodulation and amplification of a receiver.

re·gen·er·a·tive cool·ing *n.* the process of cooling the walls of the combustion chamber of a rocket by circulating the propellant around the chamber before combustion.

Re·gens·burg (*German* ˈreːgənsˌbʊrk) *n.* a city in SE West Germany, in Bavaria on the River Danube: a free Imperial city from 1245 and the leading commercial city of S Germany in the 12th and 13th centuries; the Imperial Diet was held in the town hall from 1663 to 1806. Pop.: 133 800 (1974 est.). Former English name: **Ratisbon.**

re·gent (ˈriːdʒənt) *n.* **1.** the ruler or administrator of a country during the minority, absence, or incapacity of its monarch. **2.** (formerly) a senior teacher or administrator in any of certain universities. **3.** *U.S.* a member of the governing board of certain schools and colleges. **4.** *Rare.* any person who governs or rules. ~*adj.* **5.** (*usually postpositive*) acting or functioning as a regent: *a queen regent.* **6.** *Rare.* governing, ruling, or controlling. [C14: from Latin *regēns* ruling, from *regere* to rule] —**ˈre·gent·al** *adj.* —**ˈre·gent·ˌship** *n.*

Re·ger (*German* ˈreːgər) *n.* **Max** (maks). 1873–1916, German composer, noted esp. for his organ works.

reg·gae (ˈrɛgeɪ) *n.* a type of West Indian popular music having four beats to the bar, the upbeat being strongly accented. [C20: of West Indian origin]

Reg·gio di Ca·la·bria (*Italian* ˈreddʒo di kaˈlabrja) *n.* a port in S Italy, in Calabria on the Strait of Messina: founded about 720 B.C. by Greek colonists. Pop.: 155 248 (1975 est.).

Reg·gio nell'E·mi·lia (*Italian* ˈreddʒo nelleˈmiːlja) *n.* a city in N central Italy, in Emilia-Romagna: founded in the 2nd century B.C. by Marcus Aemilius Lepidus; ruled by the Este family in the 15th–18th centuries. Pop.: 129 884 (1975 est.).

reg·i·cide (ˈrɛdʒɪˌsaɪd) *n.* **1.** the killing of a king. **2.** a person who kills a king. [C16: from Latin *rēx* king + -CIDE] —**ˌreg·i·ˈcid·al** *adj.*

re·gime *or* **ré·gime** (reɪˈʒiːm) *n.* **1.** a system of government or a particular administration: *a fascist regime; the regime of Fidel Castro.* **2.** a social system or order. **3.** *Med.* another word for **regimen** (sense 1). [C18: from French, from Latin *regimen* guidance, from *regere* to rule]

reg·i·men (ˈrɛdʒɪˌmɛn) *n.* **1.** Also called: **regime.** *Med.* a systematic course of therapy, often including a recommended diet. **2.** administration or rule. [C14: from Latin: guidance]

reg·i·ment *n.* (ˈrɛdʒɪmənt). **1.** a military unit comprising two or more battalions, usually with headquarters and support units: *a tank regiment; an artillery regiment.* **2.** a large number in regular or organized groups: *regiments of beer bottles.* ~*vb.* (ˈrɛdʒɪˌmɛnt). (*tr.*) **3.** to force discipline or order on, esp. in a domineering manner. **4.** to organize into a regiment or regiments. **5.** to form into organized groups. **6.** to assign to a regiment. [C14: via Old French from Late Latin *regimentum* government, from Latin *regere* to rule] —**ˌreg·i·ˈmen·tal** *adj.* —**ˌreg·i·ˈmen·tal·ly** *adv.* —**ˌreg·i·men·ˈta·tion** *n.*

reg·i·men·tals (ˌrɛdʒɪˈmɛntᵊlz) *pl. n.* **1.** the uniform and insignia of a regiment. **2.** military dress.

Re·gin (ˈreɪgɪn) *n. Norse myth.* a dwarf smith, tutor of Sigurd, whom he encouraged to kill Fafnir for the gold he guarded.

Re·gi·na[1] (rɪˈdʒaɪnə) *n.* queen: now used chiefly in documents, inscriptions, etc. Compare **Rex.**

Re·gi·na[2] (rɪˈdʒaɪnə) *n.* a city in W Canada, capital and largest city of Saskatchewan: founded in 1822 as Pile O'Bones. Pop.: 139 469 (1971).

Re·gi·o·mon·ta·nus (ˌriːdʒɪəʊmɒnˈteɪnəs, -ˈtɑː-, -ˈtæn-) *n.* original name *Johann Müller.* 1436–76, German mathematician and astronomer, who furthered the development of trigonometry.

re·gion (ˈriːdʒən) *n.* **1.** any large, indefinite, and continuous part of a surface or space. **2.** an area considered as a unit for geographical, functional, social, or cultural reasons. **3.** an administrative division of a country: *Tuscany is one of the regions of the Italian Republic.* **4.** a realm or sphere of activity or interest. **5.** range, area, or scope: *in what region is the price likely to be?* **6.** (in Scotland since 1975) any of the eight territorial divisions into which the country is divided for purposes of local government. [C14: from Latin *regiō*, from *regere* to govern]

re·gion·al (ˈriːdʒənᵊl) *adj.* of, characteristic of, or limited to a region: *the regional dialects of English.* —**ˈre·gion·al·ly** *adv.*

re·gion·al en·ter·i·tis *n.* another name for **Crohn's disease.**

re·gion·al·ism (ˈriːdʒənəˌlɪzəm) *n.* **1.** division of a country into administrative regions having partial autonomy. **2.** advocacy of such division. **3.** loyalty to one's home region; regional patriotism. **4.** the common interests of national groups, people, etc., living in the same part of the world. **5.** a word, custom, accent, or other characteristic associated with a specific region. —**ˈre·gion·al·ist** *n., adj.*

ré·gis·seur *French.* (reʒiˈsœr) *n.* an official in a dance company with varying duties, usually including directing productions. [French, from *régir* to manage]

reg·is·ter (ˈrɛdʒɪstə) *n.* **1.** an official or formal list recording names, events, or transactions. **2.** the book in which such a list is written. **3.** an entry in such a list. **4.** a recording device that accumulates data, totals sums of money, etc.: *a cash register.* **5.** a movable plate that controls the flow of air into a furnace, chimney, room, etc. **6.** *Computer technol.* a location in a storage device that can hold one or more words, esp. one designed for a specific function. **7.** *Music.* **a.** the timbre characteristic of a certain manner of voice production. See **head voice, chest voice. b.** any of the stops on an organ as classified in respect of its tonal quality: *the flute register.* **8.** *Printing.* **a.** the correct alignment of the separate plates in colour printing. **b.** the exact correspondence of lines of type, etc., on the two sides of a printed sheet of paper. **9.** a form of a language associated with a particular social situation or subject matter, such as obscene slang, legal language, or journalese. **10.** the act or an instance of registering. ~*vb.* **11.** (*tr.*) to enter or cause someone to enter (an event, person's name, ownership, etc.) on a register; formally record. **12.** to show or be shown on a scale or other measuring instrument: *the current didn't register on the meter.* **13.** to show or be shown in a person's face, bearing, etc.: *his face registered surprise.* **14.** (*intr.*) *Informal.* to have an effect; make an impression: *her uncle's death did not register.* **15.** to send (a letter, package, etc.) by registered post. **16.** (*tr.*) *Printing.* to adjust (a printing press, forme, etc.) to ensure that the printed matter is in register. **17.** (*intr.; often foll. by with*) (of a mechanical part) to align (with another part). [C14: from Medieval Latin *registrum*, from Latin *regerere* to transcribe, from RE- + *gerere* to bear] —**ˈreg·is·ter·er** *n.* —**ˈreg·is·tra·ble** *adj.*

reg·is·tered post *n.* **1.** a Post Office service by which compensation is paid for loss or damage to mail for which a registration fee has been paid. Compare **recorded delivery. 2.** mail sent by this service.

reg·is·ter ton *n.* the full name for **ton**[1] (sense 7).

reg·is·trant (ˈrɛdʒɪstrənt) *n.* a person who registers a trademark or patent.

reg·is·trar (ˌrɛdʒɪˈstrɑː) *n.* **1.** a person who keeps official records. **2.** an administrative official responsible for student records, enrolment procedure, etc., in a school, college, or university. **3.** *Brit.* a hospital doctor senior to a houseman but junior to a consultant, specializing in either medicine (**medical registrar**) or surgery (**surgical registrar**). **4.** *Chiefly U.S.* a person employed by a company to maintain a register of its security issues. —**ˈreg·is·trar·ˌship** *n.*

reg·is·tra·tion (ˌrɛdʒɪˈstreɪʃən) *n.* **1. a.** the act of registering or state of being registered. **b.** (*as modifier*): *a registration number.* **2.** an entry in a register. **3.** a group of people, such as students, who register at a particular time. **4.** a combination of organ or harpsichord stops used in the performance of a piece of music. —**ˌreg·is·ˈtra·tion·al** *adj.*

reg·is·tra·tion num·ber *n.* a sequence of letters and numbers assigned to a motor vehicle when it is registered, usually indicating the year and place of registration, displayed on numberplates at the front and rear of the vehicle.

reg·is·try (ˈrɛdʒɪstrɪ) *n., pl.* **·tries. 1.** a place where registers are kept, such as the part of a church where the bride and groom sign a register after a wedding. **2.** the registration of a ship's country of origin: *a ship of Liberian registry.* **3.** another word for **registration.**

reg·is·try of·fice *n. Brit.* a government office where civil marriages are performed and births, marriages, and deaths are recorded.

Re·gi·us pro·fes·sor (ˈriːdʒɪəs) *n. Brit.* a person appointed by the Crown to a university chair founded by a royal patron. [C17: *regius*, from Latin: royal, from *rex* king]

reg·let (ˈrɛglɪt) *n.* **1.** a flat narrow architectural moulding. **2.** *Printing.* a strip of oiled wood used for spacing between lines. Compare **lead**[2] (sense 6). [C16: from Old French, literally: a little rule, from *régle* rule, from Latin *rēgula*]

reg·nal (ˈrɛgnəl) *adj.* **1.** of a sovereign, reign, or kingdom. **2.** designating a year of a sovereign's reign calculated from the date of his or her accession. [C17: from Medieval Latin *rēgnālis*, from Latin *rēgnum* sovereignty; see REIGN]

reg·nant (ˈrɛgnənt) *adj.* **1.** (*postpositive*) reigning. **2.** prevalent; current. [C17: from Latin *regnāre* to REIGN] —**ˈreg·nan·cy** *n.*

reg·o (ˈrɛdʒəʊ) *n. Austral. slang.* **a.** the registration of a motor vehicle. **b.** a fee paid for this.

reg·o·lith (ˈrɛgəlɪθ) *n.* another name for **mantle rock.** [C20: from Greek *rhēgos* covering, blanket + *lithos* stone]

re·gorge (rɪˈgɔːdʒ) *vb.* **1.** (*tr.*) to vomit up; disgorge. **2.** (*intr.*) (esp. of water) to flow or run back. [C17: from French *regorger*; see GORGE]

---

re·ˈgauge *vb.*
re·ˈgen·e·sis *n.*
re·ˈger·mi·ˌnate *vb.*
ˌre·ger·mi·ˈna·tion *n.*
re·ˈgild *vb.*
re·ˈglaze *vb.*
re·ˈglue *vb.*, **·glues, ·glu·ing, ·glued.**

reg·o·sol ('rɛgəˌsɒl) *n.* a type of azonal soil consisting of unconsolidated material derived from freshly deposited alluvium or sands. [C20: from Greek *rhēgos* covering, blanket + Latin *solum* soil]

Reg. prof. *abbrev. for* Regius professor.

re·grate (rɪ'greɪt) *vb.* (*tr.*) **1.** to buy up (commodities, etc.) in advance so as to raise their price for profitable resale. **2.** to resell (commodities so purchased); retail. [C15: from Old French *regrater* perhaps from RE- + *grater* to scratch] —**re·'grat·er** *n.*

re·gress *vb.* (rɪ'grɛs). **1.** (*intr.*) to return or revert, as to a former place, condition, or mode of behaviour. **2.** (*tr.*) *Statistics.* to measure the extent to which (a dependent variable) is associated with one or more independent variables. ~*n.* ('ri:grɛs). **3.** the act of regressing. **4.** movement in a backward direction; retrogression. [C14: from Latin *regressus* a retreat, from *regredī* to go back, from RE- + *gradī* to go] —**re·'gres·sor** *n.*

re·gres·sion (rɪ'grɛʃən) *n.* **1.** *Psychol.* the adoption by an adult or adolescent of behaviour more appropriate to a child, esp. as a defence mechanism to avoid anxiety. **2.** *Statistics.* **a.** the analysis or measure of the association between one variable (the dependent variable) and one or more other variables (the independent variables), usually formulated in an equation in which the independent variables have parametric coefficients, which may enable future values of the dependent variable to be predicted. **b.** (*as modifer*): *regression curve.* **3.** *Astronomy.* the slow movement around the ecliptic of the two points at which the moon's orbit intersects the ecliptic. One complete revolution occurs about every 19 years. **4.** the act of regressing.

re·gres·sive (rɪ'grɛsɪv) *adj.* **1.** regressing or tending to regress. **2.** (of a tax or tax system) levied or graduated so that the rate decreases as the amount taxed increases. Compare **progressive** (sense 5). **3.** of, relating to, or characteristic of regression. —**re·'gres·sive·ly** *adv.* —**re·'gres·sive·ness** *n.*

re·gret (rɪ'grɛt) *vb.* **·grets, ·gret·ting, ·gret·ted.** (*tr.*) **1.** (*may take a clause as object or an infinitive*) to feel sorry, repentant, or upset about. **2.** to bemoan or grieve the death or loss of. ~*n.* **3.** a sense of repentance, guilt, or sorrow, as over some wrong done or an unfulfilled ambition. **4.** a sense of loss or grief. **5.** (*pl.*) a polite expression of sadness, esp. in a formal refusal of an invitation. [C14: from Old French *regreter,* of Scandinavian origin; compare Old Norse *grāta* to weep] —**re·'gret·ful** *adj.* —**re·'gret·ful·ly** *adv.* —**re·'gret·ful·ness** *n.* —**re·'gret·ta·ble** *adj.* —**re·'gret·ta·bly** *adv.* —**re·'gret·ter** *n.*

re·group (ri:'gru:p) *vb.* **1.** to reorganize (military forces), esp. after an attack or a defeat. **2.** (*tr.*) to rearrange into a new grouping or groupings.

Regt. *abbrev. for:* **1.** Regent. **2.** Regiment.

reg·u·la·ble ('rɛgjʊləbᵊl) *adj.* able to be regulated.

reg·u·lar ('rɛgjʊlə) *adj.* **1.** normal, customary, or usual. **2.** according to a uniform principle, arrangement, or order: *trees planted at regular intervals.* **3.** occurring at fixed or prearranged intervals: *to make a regular call on a customer.* **4.** following a set rule or normal practice; methodical or orderly. **5.** symmetrical in appearance or form; even: *regular features.* **6.** (*prenominal*) organized, elected, conducted, etc., in a proper or officially prescribed manner. **7.** (*prenominal*) officially qualified or recognized: *he's not a regular doctor.* **8.** (*prenominal*) (intensifier): *a regular fool.* **9.** *U.S. informal.* likable, dependable, or nice (esp. in the phrase **a regular guy**). **10.** denoting or relating to the personnel or units of the permanent military services: *a regular soldier; the regular army.* **11.** (of flowers) having any of their parts, esp. petals, alike in size, shape, arrangement, etc.; symmetrical. **12.** (of the formation, inflections, etc., of a word) following the usual pattern of formation in a language. **13.** *Maths.* **a.** (of a polygon) equilateral and equiangular. **b.** (of a polyhedron) having identical regular polygons as faces that make identical angles with each other. **c.** (of a prism) having regular polygons as bases. **d.** (of a pyramid) having a regular polygon as a base and the altitude passing through the centre of the base. **e.** another name for **analytic** (sense 5). **14.** *Botany.* another word for **actinomorphic. 15.** (*postpositive*) subject to the rule of an established religious order or community: *canons regular.* **16.** *U.S. politics.* of, selected by, or loyal to the leadership or platform of a political party: *a regular candidate; regular policies.* **17.** *Crystallog.* another word for **cubic** (sense 4). ~*n.* **18.** a professional long-term serviceman in a military unit. **19.** *Informal.* a person who does something regularly, such as attending a theatre or patronizing a shop. **20.** a member of a religious order or congregation, as contrasted with a secular. **21.** *U.S. politics.* a party member loyal to the leadership, organization, platform, etc., of his party. [C14: from Old French *reguler,* from Latin *rēgulāris* of a bar of wood or metal, from *rēgula* ruler, model] —ˌ**reg·u·'lar·i·ty** *n.* —'**reg·u·lar·ly** *adv.*

reg·u·lar·ize *or* **reg·u·lar·ise** ('rɛgjʊləˌraɪz) *vb.* (*tr.*) to make regular; cause to conform. —ˌ**reg·u·lar·i·'za·tion** *or* ˌ**reg·u·lar·i·'sa·tion** *n.*

reg·u·late ('rɛgjʊˌleɪt) *vb.* (*tr.*) **1.** to adjust (the amount of heat, sound, etc., of something) as required; control. **2.** to adjust (an instrument or appliance) so that it operates correctly. **3.** to bring into conformity with a rule, principle, or usage. [C17: from Late Latin *rēgulāre* to control, from Latin *rēgula* a ruler] —'**reg·u·ˌla·tive** *or* '**reg·u·ˌla·to·ry** *adj.* —'**reg·u·ˌla·tive·ly** *adv.*

reg·u·la·tion (ˌrɛgjʊ'leɪʃən) *n.* **1.** the act or process of regulating. **2.** a rule, principle, or condition that governs procedure or behaviour. **3.** a governmental or ministerial order having the force of law. **4.** *Embryol.* the ability of an animal embryo to develop normally after its structure has been altered or damaged in some way. **5.** (*modifier*) as required by official rules or procedure: *regulation uniform.* **6.** (*modifier*) normal; usual; conforming to accepted standards: *a regulation haircut.*

reg·u·la·tor ('rɛgjʊˌleɪtə) *n.* **1.** a person or thing that regulates. **2.** the mechanism, including the hairspring and the balance wheel, by which the speed of a timepiece is regulated. **3.** a timepiece, known to be accurate, by which others are timed and regulated. **4.** any of various mechanisms or devices, such as a governor valve, for controlling fluid flow, pressure, temperature, etc.

reg·u·lus ('rɛgjʊləs) *n., pl.* **·lus·es** *or* **·li** (-ˌlaɪ). impure metal forming beneath the slag during the smelting of ores. [C16: from Latin: a petty king, from *rēx* king; formerly used for *antimony,* because it combines readily with gold, thought of as the king of metals] —'**reg·u·line** *adj.*

Reg·u·lus[1] ('rɛgjʊləs) *n.* **Mar·cus A·ti·li·us** ('mɑ:kəs ə'tɪlɪəs). died ?250 B.C., Roman general; consul (267; 256). Captured by the Carthaginians in the First Punic War, he was sent to Rome on parole to deliver the enemy's peace terms, advised the Senate to refuse them, and was tortured to death on his return to Carthage.

Reg·u·lus[2] ('rɛgjʊləs) *n.* the brightest star in the constellation Leo. Visual magnitude: 1.3; spectral type: B8; distance: 85 light years.

re·gur·gi·tate (rɪ'gɜ:dʒɪˌteɪt) *vb.* **1.** to vomit forth (partially digested food). **2.** (of some birds and certain other animals) to bring back to the mouth (undigested or partly digested food with which to feed the young). **3.** (*intr.*) to be cast up or out, esp. from the mouth. [C17: from Medieval Latin *regurgitāre,* from RE- + *gurgitāre* to flood, from Latin *gurges* gulf, whirlpool] —**re·'gur·gi·tant** *n., adj.* —**re·ˌgur·gi·'ta·tion** *n.*

re·ha·bil·i·tate (ˌri:ə'bɪlɪˌteɪt) *vb.* (*tr.*) **1.** to help (a person who is physically or mentally disabled or has just been released from prison) to readapt to society or a new job, as by vocational guidance, retraining, or therapy. **2.** to restore to a former position or rank. **3.** to restore the good reputation of. [C16: from Medieval Latin *rehabilitāre* to restore, from RE- + Latin *habilitās* skill, ABILITY] —ˌ**re·ha·'bil·i·ta·tive** *adj.*

re·ha·bil·i·ta·tion (ˌri:əˌbɪlɪ'teɪʃən) *n.* **1.** the act or process of rehabilitating. **2.** *Med.* the treatment of physical disabilities by massage, electrotherapy, and exercises.

re·hash (ri:'hæʃ) *vb.* **1.** (*tr.*) to rework, reuse, or make over (old or already used material). ~*n.* **2.** something consisting of old, reworked, or reused material. [C19: from RE- + HASH[1] (to chop into pieces)]

re·hears·al (rɪ'hɜ:sᵊl) *n.* **1.** a session of practising a play, concert, speech etc., in preparation for public performance. **2.** the act of going through or recounting; recital: *rehearsal of his own virtues was his usual occupation.* **3. in rehearsal.** being prepared for public performance.

re·hearse (rɪ'hɜ:s) *vb.* **1.** to practise (a play, concert, etc.), in preparation for public performance. **2.** (*tr.*) to run through; recount; recite: *the official rehearsed the grievances of the committee.* **3.** (*tr.*) to train or drill (a person or animal) for the public performance of a part in a play, show, etc. [C16: from Anglo-Norman *rehearser,* from Old French *rehercier* to harrow a second time, from RE- + *herce* harrow] —**re·'hears·er** *n.*

re·heat *vb.* (ri:'hi:t). **1.** to heat or be heated again: *to reheat yesterday's soup.* **2.** (*tr.*) to add fuel to (the exhaust gases of an aircraft jet engine) to produce additional heat and thrust. ~*n.* ('ri:hi:t), *also* **re·heat·ing. 3.** *Aeronautics.* another name (esp. Brit.) for **afterburning** (sense 1). —**re·'heat·er** *n.*

re·ho·bo·am (ˌri:ə'bəʊəm) *n.* a wine bottle holding the equivalent of six normal bottles (approximately 156 ounces). [named after *Rehoboam,* a son of King Solomon, from Hebrew, literally: the nation is enlarged]

Reich[1] (raɪk; *German* raɪç) *n.* **1.** the Holy Roman Empire (**First Reich**). **2.** the Hohenzollern empire from 1871 to 1919 (**Second Reich**). **3.** the Weimar Republic from 1919 to 1933. **4.** the Nazi dictatorship from 1933 to 1945 (**Third Reich**). [German: kingdom]

Reich[2] (raɪk; *German* raɪç) *n.* **Wil·helm** ('vɪlhɛlm). 1897–1957, Austrian psychologist, living in the U.S. An ardent socialist and advocate of sexual freedom, he proclaimed a cosmic unity of all energy and built a machine (the **orgone accumulator**) to concentrate this energy on human beings. His books include *The Function of the Orgasm* (1927).

Reich·en·berg ('raɪçənˌbɛrk) *n.* the German name for **Liberec.**

Reichs·mark ('raɪksˌmɑ:k; *German* 'raɪçsˌmark) *n., pl.* **·marks** *or* **·mark.** the standard monetary unit of Germany between 1924 and 1948, divided into 100 **Reichspfennigs.**

Reichs·rat (*German* 'raɪçsˌrat) *n.* **1.** the bicameral parliament of the Austrian half of Austria-Hungary (1867–1918). **2.** the council of representatives of state governments within Germany from 1919 to 1934.

---

re·'grade *vb.*
re·'grow *vb.,* **·grows, ·grow·ing, ·grew, ·grown.**
re·'growth *n.*
re·'han·dle *vb.*
re·'hang *vb.,* **·hangs, ·hang·ing, ·hung.**
re·'hard·en *vb.*
re·'har·ness *vb.*
re·'hear *vb.*
re·'heel *vb.*
re·'hem *vb.,* **·hems, ·hem·ming, ·hemmed.**
re·'hinge *vb.*
re·'hire *vb.*
re·'house *vb.*
re·'hu·man·ize *or* **re·'hu·man·ise** *vb.*
ˌ**re·ig·'nite** *vb.*
ˌ**re·im·'pose** *vb.*

Reichs·tag ('raɪksˌtɑːg; *German* 'raɪçsˌtak) *n.* **1.** Also called: **diet.** (in medieval Germany) the estates or a meeting of the estates. **2.** the legislative assembly representing the people in the North German Confederation (1867–71) and in the German empire (1871–1919). **3.** the sovereign assembly of the Weimar Republic (1919–33). **4.** the building in Berlin in which this assembly met: its destruction by fire on Feb. 27, 1933 (probably by agents of the Nazi government) marked the end of Weimar democracy.

Reid (riːd) *n.* **1.** Sir **George Hou·ston.** 1845–1918, Australian statesman, born in Scotland: prime minister of Australia (1904–05). **2. Thom·as.** 1710–96, Scottish philosopher and founder of what came to be known as the philosophy of common sense.

re·i·fy ('riːɪˌfaɪ) *vb.* **·fies, ·fy·ing, ·fied.** (*tr.*) to consider or make (an abstract idea or concept) real or concrete. [C19: from Latin *rēs* thing; compare DEIFY] —ˌ**re·i·fi·'ca·tion** *n.* —ˌ**re·i·fi·'ca·to·ry** *adj.* —'**re·iˌfi·er** *n.*

Rei·gate ('raɪgɪt, -geit) *n.* a town in S England, in Surrey at the foot of the North Downs. Pop.: 56 088 (1971).

reign (reɪn) *n.* **1.** the period during which a monarch is the official ruler of a country. **2.** a period during which a person or thing is dominant, influential, or powerful: *the reign of violence is over.* ~*vb.* (*intr.*) **3.** to exercise the power and authority of a sovereign. **4.** to be accorded the rank and title of a sovereign without having ruling authority, as in a constitutional monarchy. **5.** to predominate; prevail: *a land where darkness reigns.* **6.** (*usually present participle*) to be the most recent winner of a competition, contest, etc.: *the reigning heavyweight champion.* [C13: from Old French *reigne,* from Latin *rēgnum* kingdom, from *rēx* king]

Reign of Ter·ror *n.* the period of Jacobin rule during the French Revolution, during which thousands of people were executed for treason (Oct. 1793–July 1794).

re·im·burse (ˌriːɪm'bɜːs) *vb.* (*tr.*) to repay or compensate (someone) for (money already spent, losses, damages, etc.): *your fare will be reimbursed after your interview.* [C17: from RE- + *imburse,* from Medieval Latin *imbursāre* to put in a moneybag, from *bursa* PURSE] —ˌ**re·im·'burs·a·ble** *adj.* —ˌ**re·im·'burse·ment** *n.* —ˌ**re·im·'burs·er** *n.*

re·im·port *vb.* (ˌriːɪm'pɔːt, riː'ɪmpɔːt). **1.** (*tr.*) to import (goods manufactured from exported raw materials). ~*n.* (riː'ɪmpɔːt). **2.** the act of reimporting. **3.** a reimported commodity. —ˌ**re·im·por·'ta·tion** *n.*

re·im·pres·sion (ˌriːɪm'preʃən) *n.* a reprinting of a book without editorial changes or additions.

Reims *or* **Rheims** (riːmz; *French* rɛ̃s) *n.* a city in NE France: scene of the coronation of most French monarchs. Pop.: 183 610 (1975).

rein (reɪn) *n.* **1.** (*often pl.*) one of a pair of long straps, usually connected together and made of leather, used to control a horse, running from the side of the bit or the headstall to the hand of the rider, driver, or trainer. **2.** a similar device used to control a very young child. **3.** any form or means of control: *to take up the reins of government.* **4.** the direction in which a rider turns (in phrases such as **on a left** (or **right**) **rein, change the rein**). **5.** something that restrains, controls, or guides. **6. give (a) free rein.** to allow considerable freedom; remove restraints. **7. keep a tight rein on.** to control carefully; limit: *we have to keep a tight rein on expenditure.* **8. on a long rein.** with the reins held loosely so that the horse is relatively unconstrained. **9. shorten the reins.** to take up the reins so that the distance between hand and bit is lessened, in order that the horse may be more collected. ~*vb.* **10.** (*tr.*) to check, restrain, hold back, or halt with or as if with reins. **11.** to control or guide (a horse) with a rein or reins: *they reined left.* ~See also **rein in.** [C13: from Old French *resne,* from Latin *retinēre* to hold back, from RE- + *tenēre* to hold; see RESTRAIN]

re·in·car·nate *vb.* (riː'ɪnkɑːneɪt) (*tr.; often passive*) **1.** to cause to undergo reincarnation; be born again. ~*adj.* (ˌriːɪn'kɑːnɪt). **2.** born again in a new body.

re·in·car·na·tion (ˌriːɪnkɑː'neɪʃən) *n.* **1.** the belief that on the death of the body the soul transmigrates to or is born again in another body. **2.** the incarnation or embodiment of a soul in a new body after it has left the old one at physical death. **3.** embodiment again in a new form, as of a principle or idea. —ˌ**re·in·car·'na·tion·ist** *n., adj.*

rein·deer ('reɪnˌdɪə) *n., pl.* **·deer** *or* **·deers.** a large deer, *Rangifer tarandus,* having large branched antlers in the male and female and inhabiting the arctic regions of Greenland, Europe, and Asia. It also occurs in North America, where it is known as a caribou. [C14: from Old Norse *hreindȳri,* from *hreinn* reindeer + *dyr* animal; related to Dutch *rendier,* German *Renntier;* see DEER]

Rein·deer Lake *n.* a lake in W Canada, in Saskatchewan and Manitoba: drains into the Churchill River via the **Reindeer River.** Area: 6390 sq. km (2467 sq. miles).

rein·deer moss *n.* any of various lichens of the genus *Cladonia,* esp. *C. rangiferina,* which occur in arctic and subarctic regions, providing food for reindeer.

re·in·force (ˌriːɪn'fɔːs) *vb.* (*tr.*) **1.** to give added strength or support to. **2.** to give added emphasis to; stress, support, or increase: *his rudeness reinforced my determination.* **3.** to give added support to (a military force) by providing more men, supplies, etc. **4.** *Psychol.* to reward an action or response of (a human or animal) so that it becomes more likely to occur again. —ˌ**re·in·'force·ment** *n.*

re·in·forced con·crete *n.* concrete with steel bars, mesh, etc., embedded in it to enable it to withstand tensile and shear stresses.

Rein·hardt ('raɪnˌhɑːt) *n.* **1. Djan·go** ('dʒæŋgəʊ). original name *Jean Baptiste Reinhardt.* 1910–53, Belgian jazz guitarist, whose work was greatly influenced by gypsy music. With Stéphane Grappelli, he led the Quintet of the Hot Club of France between 1934 and 1939. **2. Max.** 1873–1943, Austrian theatre producer and director, in the U.S. after 1933.

rein in *vb.* (*adv.*) to stop (a horse) by pulling on the reins.

reins (reɪnz) *pl. n. Archaic.* the kidneys or loins. [C14: from Old French, from Latin *rēnēs* the kidneys]

re·in·state (ˌriːɪn'steɪt) *vb.* (*tr.*) to restore to a former rank or condition. —ˌ**re·in·'state·ment** *n.* —ˌ**re·in·'sta·tor** *n.*

re·in·sure (ˌriːɪn'ʃʊə, -'ʃɔː) *vb.* (*tr.*) **1.** to insure again. **2.** (of an insurer) to obtain partial or complete insurance coverage from another insurer for (a risk on which a policy has already been issued). —ˌ**re·in·'sur·ance** *n.* —ˌ**re·in·'sur·er** *n.*

reis (*Portuguese* rəjʃ) *n.* the plural of **real**[3] (the coin).

re·it·er·ate (riː'ɪtəˌreɪt) *vb.* (*tr.; may take a clause as object*) to say or do again or repeatedly. [C16: from Latin *reiterāre* to repeat, from RE- + *iterāre* to do again, from *iterum* again] —**re·'it·er·ant** *adj.* —**re·ˌit·er·'a·tion** *n.* —**re·'it·er·a·tive** *adj.* —**re·'it·er·a·tive·ly** *adv.*

Reith (riːθ) *n.* **John (Charles Walsham),** 1st Baron. 1889–1971, British public servant: first general manager (1922–27) and first director general (1927–38) of the B.B.C.

reive (riːv) *vb.* (*intr.*) *Northern Brit. dialect.* to go on a plundering raid. [variant of REAVE] —'**reiv·er** *n.*

re·ject *vb.* (rɪ'dʒɛkt). (*tr.*) **1.** to refuse to accept, acknowledge, use, believe, etc. **2.** to throw out as useless or worthless; discard. **3.** to rebuff (a person). **4.** (of an organism) to fail to accept (a foreign tissue graft or organ transplant) because of immunological incompatibility. ~*n.* ('riːdʒɛkt). **5.** something rejected as imperfect, unsatisfactory, or useless. [C15: from Latin *rēicere* to throw back, from RE- + *jacere* to hurl] —**re·'ject·a·ble** *adj.* —**re·'ject·er** *or* **re·'jec·tor** *n.* —**re·'jec·tion** *n.* —**re·'jec·tive** *adj.*

re·jig (riː'dʒɪg) *vb.* **·jigs, ·jig·ging, ·jigged.** (*tr.*) **1.** to re-equip (a factory or plant). **2.** *Informal.* to rearrange. —**re·'jig·ger** *n.*

re·joice (rɪ'dʒɔɪs) *vb.* **1.** (when *tr., takes a clause as object or an infinitive;* when *intr.,* often foll. by *in*) to feel or express great joy or happiness. **2.** (*tr.*) *Archaic.* to cause to feel joy. [C14: from Old French *resjoir,* from RE- + *joir* to be glad, from Latin *gaudēre* to rejoice] —**re·'joic·er** *n.*

re·join[1] (riː'dʒɔɪn) *vb.* **1.** to come again into company with (someone or something). **2.** (*tr.*) to put or join together again; reunite.

re·join[2] (rɪ'dʒɔɪn) *vb.* (*tr.*) **1.** to say (something) in reply; answer, reply, or retort. **2.** *Law.* to answer (a plaintiff's reply). [C15: from Old French *rejoign-,* stem of *rejoindre;* see RE-, JOIN]

re·join·der (rɪ'dʒɔɪndə) *n.* **1.** a reply or response to a question or remark, esp. a quick witty one; retort. **2.** *Law.* (in pleading) the answer made by a defendant to the plaintiff's reply. [C15: from Old French *rejoindre* to REJOIN[2]]

re·ju·ve·nate (rɪ'dʒuːvɪˌneɪt) *vb.* (*tr.*) **1.** to give new youth, restored vitality, or youthful appearance to. **2.** (*usually passive*) *Geography.* **a.** to cause (a river) to begin eroding more vigorously to a new lower base level, usually because of uplift of the land. **b.** to cause (a land surface) to develop youthful features. [C19: from RE- + Latin *juvenis* young] —**re·ˌju·ve·'na·tion** *n.* —**re·'ju·ve·ˌna·tor** *n.*

re·ju·ve·nesce (rɪˌdʒuːvə'nɛs) *vb.* **1.** to make or become youthful or restored to vitality. **2.** *Biology.* to convert (cells) or (of cells) to be converted into a more active form. —**re·ˌju·ve·'nes·cence** *n.* —**re·ˌju·ve·'nes·cent** *adj.*

rel. *abbrev. for:* **1.** relating. **2.** relative(ly). **3.** released. **4.** religion. **5.** religious.

re·lapse (rɪ'læps) *vb.* (*intr.*) **1.** to lapse back into a former state or condition, esp. one involving bad habits. **2.** to become ill again after apparent recovery. ~*n.* **3.** the act or an instance of relapsing. **4.** the return of ill health after an apparent or partial recovery. [C16: from Latin *relabī* to slip back, from RE- + *labī* to slip, slide] —**re·'laps·er** *n.*

re·laps·ing fe·ver *n.* any of various infectious diseases

ˌ**re·im·po·'si·tion** *n.*
ˌ**re·im·'pris·on** *vb.*
ˌ**re·in·'cor·po·ˌrate** *vb.*
ˌ**re·in·cor·po·'ra·tion** *n.*
ˌ**re·in·'cur** *vb.,* **·curs, ·cur·ring, ·curred.**
ˌ**re·in·'duce** *vb.*
ˌ**re·in·'duc·tion** *n.*
ˌ**re·in·'fect** *vb.*
ˌ**re·in·'fec·tion** *n.*
ˌ**re·in·'flame** *vb.*
ˌ**re·in·'form** *vb.*
ˌ**re·in·'fuse** *vb.*
ˌ**re·in·'fu·sion** *n.*
ˌ**re·in·'oc·u·ˌlate** *vb.*
ˌ**re·in·ˌoc·u·'la·tion** *n.*
ˌ**re·in·'sert** *vb.*
ˌ**re·in·'ser·tion** *n.*
ˌ**re·in·'spect** *vb.*
ˌ**re·in·'spec·tion** *n.*
ˌ**re·in·'stall** *vb.*
ˌ**re·in·stal·'la·tion** *n.*
ˌ**re·in·'struct** *vb.*
ˌ**re·in·'struc·tion** *n.*
re·'in·te·ˌgrate *vb.*
ˌ**re·in·te·'gra·tion** *n.*
ˌ**re·in·'ter** *vb.,* **·ters, ·ter·ring, ·terred.**
ˌ**re·in·'ter·ment** *n.*
ˌ**re·in·'ter·pret** *vb.*
ˌ**re·in·ˌter·pre·'ta·tion** *n.*
ˌ**re·in·'ter·ro·ˌgate** *vb.*
ˌ**re·in·ˌter·ro·'ga·tion** *n.*
ˌ**re·in·tro·'duce** *vb.*
ˌ**re·in·tro·'duc·tion** *n.*
ˌ**re·in·'ves·ti·ˌgate** *vb.*
ˌ**re·in·ˌves·ti·'ga·tion** *n.*
ˌ**re·in·'vig·or·ˌate** *vb.*
ˌ**re·in·ˌvig·or·'a·tion** *n.*
ˌ**re·in·'vite** *vb.*
ˌ**re·in·'voke** *vb.*
ˌ**re·in·'volve** *vb.*
ˌ**re·in·'volve·ment** *n.*
re·'judge *vb.*
re·'kin·dle *vb.*
re·'la·bel *vb.,* **·bels, ·bel·ling, ·belled** *or U.S.* **·bels, ·bel·ing, ·beled.**

characterized by recurring fever, caused by the bite of body lice or ticks infected with spirochaetes of the genus *Borrelia*. Also called: **recurrent fever.**

re+late (rɪˈleɪt) *vb.* **1.** (*tr.*) to tell or narrate (a story, etc.). **2.** (often foll. by *to*) to establish association (between two or more things) or (of something) to have relation or reference (to something else). **3.** (*intr.;* often foll. by *to*) to form a sympathetic or significant relationship (with other people, things, etc.). [C16: from Latin *relātus* brought back, from *referre* to carry back, from RE- + *ferre* to bear; see REFER] —**re+ˈlat+a·ble** *adj.* —**re+ˈlat+er** *n.*

Usage. *Relate* is frequently applied to personal relationships, as in sense 3, but this usage is vague and is avoided by careful speakers and writers.

re+lat+ed (rɪˈleɪtɪd) *adj.* **1.** connected; associated. **2.** connected by kinship or marriage. **3.** (in diatonic music) denoting or relating to a key that has notes in common with another key or keys. —**re+ˈlat+ed+ness** *n.*

re+la+tion (rɪˈleɪʃən) *n.* **1.** the state or condition of being related or the manner in which things are related. **2.** connection by blood or marriage; kinship. **3.** a person who is connected by blood or marriage; relative; kinsman. **4.** reference or regard (esp. in the phrase **in** *or* **with relation to**). **5.** the position, association, connection, or status of one person or thing with regard to another or others. **6.** the act of relating or narrating. **7.** an account or narrative. **8.** *Law.* the principle by which an act done at one time is regarded in law as having been done antecedently. **9.** *Law.* the statement of grounds of complaint made by a relator. **10.** *Maths.* an association, such as equality or inequality, between two numbers, quantities, expressions, etc. [C14: from Latin *relātiō* a narration, a relation (between philosophical concepts)]

re+la+tion+al (rɪˈleɪʃənəl) *adj.* **1.** *Grammar.* indicating or expressing syntactic relation, as for example the case endings in Latin. **2.** having relation or being related.

re+la+tions (rɪˈleɪʃənz) *pl. n.* **1.** social, political, or personal connections or dealings between or among individuals, groups, nations, etc.: *to enjoy good relations.* **2.** family or relatives. **3.** *Euphemistic.* sexual intercourse.

re+la+tion+ship (rɪˈleɪʃən,ʃɪp) *n.* **1.** the state of being connected or related. **2.** association by blood or marriage; kinship. **3.** the mutual dealings, connections, or feelings that exist between two parties, countries, people, etc.: *a business relationship.* **4.** an emotional or sexual affair or liaison. **5.** *Maths.* another name for **relation** (sense 10).

rel·a·tive (ˈrɛlətɪv) *adj.* **1.** having meaning or significance only in relation to something else; not absolute: *a relative value.* **2.** (*prenominal*) (of a scientific quantity) being measured or stated relative to some other substance or measurement: *relative humidity; relative density.* Compare **absolute** (sense 10). **3.** (*prenominal*) comparative or respective: *the relative qualities of speed and accuracy.* **4.** (*postpositive;* foll. by *to*) in proportion (to); corresponding (to): *earnings relative to production.* **5.** *Grammar.* denoting or belonging to a class of words that function as subordinating conjunctions in introducing relative clauses. In English, relative pronouns and determiners include *who, which,* and *that.* Compare **demonstrative, interrogative. 6.** *Grammar.* denoting or relating to a clause (**relative clause**) that modifies a noun or pronoun occurring earlier in the sentence. **7.** (of a musical key or scale) having the same key signature as another key or scale: *C major is the relative major of A minor.* ~*n.* **8.** a person who is related by blood or marriage; relation. **9.** a relative pronoun, clause, or grammatical construction. [C16: from Late Latin *relātīvus* referring] —**ˈrel·a+tive+ly** *adv.* —**ˈrel·a+tive+ness** *n.*

rel·a+tive ap+er+ture *n. Photog.* the ratio of the equivalent focal length of a lens to the effective aperture of the lens; written as *f/n, f:n,* or *fn,* where *n* is the numerical value of this ratio and is equivalent to the f-number.

rel·a+tive a·tom+ic mass *n.* another name for **atomic weight.** Symbol: A_r

rel·a+tive den+si·ty *n.* the ratio of the density of a substance to the density of a standard substance under specified conditions. For liquids and solids the standard is usually water at 4°C or some other specified temperature. For gases the standard is often air or hydrogen at the same temperature and pressure as the substance. Symbol: *d* See also **specific gravity, vapour density.**

rel·a+tive fre+quen+cy *n.* the ratio of the actual number of favourable events to the total possible number of events; often taken as an estimate of probability.

rel·a+tive hu+mid+i·ty *n.* the mass of water vapour present in the air expressed as a percentage of the mass that would be present in an equal volume of saturated air at the same temperature. Compare **absolute humidity.**

rel·a+tive ma+jor+i·ty *n. Brit.* the excess of votes or seats won by the winner of an election over the runner-up when no candidate or party has more than 50 per cent. Compare **absolute majority.**

rel·a+tive mo+lec·u+lar mass *n.* another name for **molecular weight.** Symbol: M_r

rel·a+tive per+me+a·bil+i·ty *n.* the ratio of the permeability of a medium to that of free space. Symbol: μ_r

rel·a+tive per+mit+tiv+i·ty *n.* the ratio of the permittivity of a substance to that of a vacuum. Symbol: ϵ_r Also called: **dielectric constant.**

rel·a+tiv+ism (ˈrɛlətɪ,vɪzəm) *n.* any theory holding that knowledge and values are not absolute but are relative to a person's nature and situation, etc. —**ˈrel·a+tiv+ist** *n., adj.*

rel·a+tiv+is+tic (,rɛlətɪˈvɪstɪk) *adj.* **1.** *Physics.* having or involving a speed close to that of light so that the behaviour is described by the theory of relativity rather than by Newtonian mechanics: *a relativistic electron; a relativistic velocity.* **2.** *Physics.* of, concerned with, or involving relativity. **3.** of or relating to relativism. —**,rel·a·tiv+ˈis+ti+cal+ly** *adv.*

rel·a+tiv+i·ty (,rɛləˈtɪvɪtɪ) *n.* **1.** either of two theories developed by Albert Einstein, the **special theory of relativity,** dealing with space, time, and uniform motion, and the **general theory of relativity,** dealing with acceleration and gravitation. **2.** *Philosophy.* the quality of being dependent upon psychological, social, economic, and other factors, as knowledge, values, etc. **3.** the state or quality of being relative.

rel·a+tiv+ize *or* **rel·a+tiv+ise** (ˈrɛlətɪvaɪz) *vb.* **1.** to make or become relative. **2.** (*tr.*) to apply the theory of relativity to. —**,rel·a·tiv·i+ˈza+tion** *or* **,rel·a·tiv·i+ˈsa+tion** *n.*

re+la+tor (rɪˈleɪtə) *n.* **1.** a person who relates a story; narrator. **2.** *English law.* a person who gives information upon which the attorney general brings an action. **3.** *U.S. law.* a person who institutes proceedings by criminal information or quo warranto.

re+la+tum (rɪˈleɪtəm) *n., pl.* **+ta** (-tə). *Logic.* one of the objects between which a relation is said to hold.

re+lax (rɪˈlæks) *vb.* **1.** to make (muscles, a grip, etc.) less tense or rigid or (of muscles and the like) to become looser or less rigid. **2.** (*intr.*) to take rest, as from work or effort. **3.** to lessen the force of (effort, concentration, etc.) or (of effort) to become diminished. **4.** to make (rules or discipline) less rigid or strict or (of rules, etc.) to diminish in severity. **5.** (*intr.*) (of a person) to become less formal; unbend. [C15: from Latin *relaxāre* to loosen, from RE- + *laxāre* to loosen, from *laxus* loose, LAX] —**re+ˈlax+a·ble** *adj.* —**re+lax+ed+ly** (rɪˈlæksɪdlɪ) *adv.* —**re+ˈlax+er** *n.*

re+lax+ant (rɪˈlæksənt) *n.* **1.** *Med.* a drug or agent that relaxes, esp. one that relaxes tense muscles. ~*adj.* **2.** of, relating to, or tending to produce relaxation.

re+lax·a+tion (,riːlækˈseɪʃən) *n.* **1.** rest or refreshment, as after work or effort; recreation. **2.** a form of rest or recreation: *his relaxation is cricket.* **3.** a partial lessening of a punishment, duty, etc. **4.** the act of relaxing or state of being relaxed. **5.** *Physics.* the return of a system to equilibrium after a displacement from this state. **6.** *Maths.* a method by which errors resulting from an approximation are reduced by using new approximations.

re+lax+in (rɪˈlæksɪn) *n.* **1.** a mammalian polypeptide hormone secreted by the corpus luteum during pregnancy, which relaxes the pelvic ligaments. **2.** a preparation of this hormone, used to facilitate childbirth. [C20: from RELAX + -IN]

re+lay *n.* (ˈriːleɪ). **1.** a person or team of people relieving others, as on a shift. **2.** a fresh team of horses, etc., posted at intervals along a route to relieve others. **3.** the act of relaying or process of being relayed. **4. a.** short for **relay race. b.** one of the sections of a relay race. **5.** an automatic device that controls the setting of a valve, switch, etc., by means of an electric motor, solenoid, or pneumatic mechanism. **6.** *Electronics.* an electrical device in which a small change in current or voltage controls the switching on or off of circuits or other devices. **7.** *Radio.* **a.** a combination of a receiver and transmitter designed to receive radio signals and retransmit them, in order to extend their range. **b.** (*as modifier*): *a relay station.* ~*vb.* (rɪˈleɪ). (*tr.*) **8.** to carry or spread (something, such as news or information) by relays. **9.** to supply or replace with relays. **10.** to retransmit (a signal) by means of a relay. **11.** *Brit.* to broadcast (a performance) by sending out signals through a transmitting station: *this concert is being relayed from the Albert Hall.* [C15 *relaien,* from Old French *relaier* to leave behind, from RE- + *laier* to leave, ultimately from Latin *laxāre* to loosen; see RELAX]

re+lay fast *n.* (esp. in India) a form of protest in which a number of persons go without food by turns. Also called: **relay hunger strike.**

re+lay race *n.* a race between two or more teams of contestants in which each contestant covers a specified portion of the distance.

re+lease (rɪˈliːs) *vb.* (*tr.*) **1.** to free (a person, animal, etc.) from captivity or imprisonment. **2.** to free (someone) from obligation or duty. **3.** to free (something) from (one's grip); let go or fall. **4.** to issue (a record, film, book, etc.) for sale or circulation. **5.** to make (news or information) known or allow (news, etc.) to be made known: *to release details of an agreement.* **6.** *Law.* to relinquish (a right, claim, title, etc.) in favour of someone else. ~*n.* **7.** the act of freeing or state of being freed, as from captivity, imprisonment, duty, pain, life, etc. **8.** the act of issuing for sale or publication. **9.** something issued for sale or public showing, esp. a film or a record: *a new release from Bob Dylan.* **10.** a news item, etc., made available for publication, broadcasting, etc. **11.** *Law.* the surrender of a claim, right, title, etc., in favour of someone else. **12.** a control mechanism for starting or stopping an engine. **13. a.** the opening of the exhaust valve of a steam engine near the end of the piston stroke. **b.** the moment at which this valve opens. [C13: from Old French *relesser,* from Latin *relaxāre* to slacken; see RELAX] —**re+ˈleas+er** *n.*

rel+e·gate (ˈrɛlɪ,geɪt) *vb.* (*tr.*) **1.** to move to a position of less authority, importance, etc.; demote. **2.** (*usually passive*) *Chiefly Brit.* to demote (a football team, etc.) to a lower division. **3.** to assign or refer (a matter) to another or others, as for action or decision. **4.** (foll. by *to*) to banish or exile. **5.** to assign (something) to a particular group or category. [C16: from Latin *relēgāre* to send away, from RE- + *lēgāre* to send] —**ˈrel+e·ga+ta·ble** *adj.* —**,rel+e·ˈga+tion** *n.*

re+lent (rɪˈlɛnt) *vb.* (*intr.*) **1.** to change one's mind about some decided course, esp. a harsh one; become more mild or amenable. **2.** (of the pace or intensity of something) to slacken. **3.** (of the weather) to become more mild. [C14: from RE- + Latin *lentāre* to bend, from *lentus* flexible, tenacious]

re+lent+less (rɪˈlɛntlɪs) *adj.* **1.** (of an enemy, hostile attitude, etc.) implacable; inflexible; inexorable. **2.** (of pace or intensity) sustained; unremitting. —**re+ˈlent+less+ly** *adv.* —**re+ˈlent+less+ness** *n.*

rel+e·vant (ˈrɛlɪvənt) *adj.* **1.** having direct bearing on the matter in hand; pertinent. **2.** *Linguistics.* another word for **distinctive** (sense 2). [C16: from Medieval Latin *relevans,* from Latin *relevāre* to lighten, from RE- + *levāre* to raise, RELIEVE] —**ˈrel+e·vance** *or* **ˈrel+e·van+cy** *n.* —**ˈrel+e·vant+ly** *adv.*

re+li·a·ble (rɪˈlaɪəbᵊl) *adj.* able to be trusted; predictable or dependable. —**re+ˌli+a·ˈbil+i·ty** *or* **re+ˈli+a·ble+ness** *n.* —**re+ˈli+a·bly** *adv.*

re+li+ance (rɪˈlaɪəns) *n.* **1.** dependence, confidence, or trust. **2.** something or someone upon which one relies. —**re+ˈli+ant** *adj.* —**re+ˈli+ant+ly** *adv.*

rel+ic (ˈrɛlɪk) *n.* **1.** something that has survived from the past, such as an object or custom. **2.** something kept as a remembrance or treasured for its past associations; keepsake. **3.** (*usually pl.*) a remaining part or fragment. **4.** *R.C. Church, Eastern Church.* part of the body of a saint or something supposedly used by or associated with a saint, venerated as holy. **5.** *Informal.* an old or old-fashioned person or thing. **6.** (*pl.*) *Archaic.* the remains of a dead person; corpse. **7.** *Ecology.* a less common term for **relict.** [C13: from Old French *relique,* from Latin *reliquiae* remains, from *relinquere* to leave behind, RELINQUISH]

rel+ict (ˈrɛlɪkt) *n.* **1.** *Ecology.* **a.** a group of animals or plants that exists as a remnant of a formerly widely distributed group in an environment different from that in which it originated. **b.** (*as modifier*): *a relict fauna.* **2.** *Geology.* **a.** a mountain, lake, glacier, etc., that is a remnant of a pre-existing formation after a destructive process has occurred. **b.** a mineral that remains unaltered after metamorphism of the rock in which it occurs. **3.** an archaic word for **widow. 4.** an archaic word for **relic.** [C16: from Latin *relictus* left behind, from *relinquere* to RELINQUISH]

re+lief (rɪˈli:f) *n.* **1.** a feeling of cheerfulness or optimism that follows the removal of anxiety, pain, or distress. **2.** deliverance from or alleviation of anxiety, pain, distress, etc. **3. a.** help or assistance, as to the poor, needy, or distressed. **b.** (*as modifier*): *relief work.* **4.** something that affords a diversion from monotony. **5.** a person who replaces or relieves another at some task or duty. **6.** a bus, shuttle plane, etc., that carries additional passengers when a scheduled service is full. **7.** a road (**relief road**) carrying traffic round an urban area; bypass. **8. a.** the act of freeing a beleaguered town, fortress, etc.: *the relief of Mafeking.* **b.** (*as modifier*): *a relief column.* **9.** Also called: **relievo, rilievo.** *Sculpture, architecture, etc.* **a.** the projection of forms or figures from a flat ground, so that they are partly or wholly free of it. **b.** a piece of work of this kind. **10.** a printing process, such as engraving, letterpress, etc., that employs raised surfaces from which ink is transferred to the paper. **11.** any vivid effect resulting from contrast: *comic relief.* **12.** variation in altitude in an area; difference between highest and lowest level: *a region of low relief.* **13.** *Law.* redress of a grievance or hardship: *to seek relief through the courts.* **14.** *European history.* a payment made to his lord by the heir to a fief: the size of the relief was determined by the lord within bounds set by custom. **15. on relief.** *U.S.* (of people) in receipt of government aid because of personal need. [C14: from Old French, from *relever* to raise up; see RELIEVE]

re+lief map *n.* a map that shows the configuration and height of the land surface, usually by means of contours.

re+lieve (rɪˈli:v) *vb.* (*tr.*) **1.** to bring alleviation of (pain, distress, etc.) to (someone). **2.** to bring aid or assistance to (someone in need, a disaster area, etc.). **3.** to take over the duties or watch of (someone). **4.** to bring aid or a relieving force to (a besieged town, etc.). **5.** to free (someone) from an obligation. **6.** to make (something) less unpleasant, arduous, or monotonous. **7.** to bring into relief or prominence, as by contrast. **8.** (foll. by *of*) *Informal.* to take from: *the thief relieved him of his watch.* **9. relieve oneself.** to urinate or defecate. [C14: from Old French *relever,* from Latin *relevāre* to lift up, relieve, from RE- + *levāre* to lighten] —**re+ˈliev+a·ble** *adj.* —**re+ˈliev+er** *n.*

re+lieved (rɪˈli:vd) *adj.* (*postpositive;* often foll. by *at, about,* etc.) experiencing relief, esp. from worry or anxiety.

re+li+gieuse *French.* (rəliˈʒjøz) *n.* a nun. [C18: feminine of RELIGIEUX]

re+li+gieux *French.* (rəliˈʒjø) *n., pl.* **+gieux** (-ˈʒjø). a member of a monastic order or clerical body. [C17: from Latin *religiōsus* religious]

re+li+gion (rɪˈlɪdʒən) *n.* **1.** belief in, worship of, or obedience to a supernatural power or powers considered to be divine or to have control of human destiny. **2.** any formal or institutionalized expression of such belief: *the Christian religion.* **3.** the attitude and feeling of one who believes in a transcendent controlling power or powers. **4.** *Chiefly R.C. Church.* the way of life determined by the vows of poverty, chastity, and obedience entered upon by monks, friars, and nuns: *to enter religion.* **5.** something of overwhelming importance to a person: *football is his religion.* **6.** *Archaic.* **a.** the practice of sacred ritual observances. **b.** sacred rites and ceremonies. [C12: via Old French from Latin *religiō* fear of the supernatural, piety, probably from *religāre* to tie up, from RE- + *ligāre* to bind]

re+li+gion+ism (rɪˈlɪdʒəˌnɪzəm) *n.* extreme religious fervour. —**reˈli+gion+ist** *n., adj.*

re+lig·i+ose (rɪˈlɪdʒɪˌəʊs) *adj.* affectedly or extremely pious; sanctimoniously religious. —**re+ˈlig·i+ˌose+ly** *adv.* —**re+lig·i+os+i·ty** (rɪˌlɪdʒɪˈɒsɪtɪ) *n.*

re+li+gious (rɪˈlɪdʒəs) *adj.* **1.** of, relating to, or concerned with religion. **2. a.** pious; devout; godly. **b.** (*as collective n.,* preceded by *the*): *the religious.* **3.** appropriate to or in accordance with the principles of a religion. **4.** scrupulous, exact, or conscientious. **5.** *Christianity.* of or relating to a way of life dedicated to religion by the vows of poverty, chastity, and obedience, and defined by a monastic rule. ~*n.* **6.** *Christianity.* a member of an order or congregation living by such a rule; a monk, friar, or nun. —**re+ˈli+gious+ly** *adv.* —**re+ˈli+gious+ness** *n.*

re+lin+quish (rɪˈlɪŋkwɪʃ) *vb.* (*tr.*) **1.** to give up (a task, struggle, etc.); abandon. **2.** to surrender or renounce (a claim, right, etc.). **3.** to release; let go. [C15: from French *relinquir,* from Latin *relinquere* to leave behind, from RE- + *linquere* to leave] —**re+ˈlin+quish+er** *n.* —**re+ˈlin+quish+ment** *n.*

rel·i+quar·y (ˈrɛlɪkwərɪ) *n., pl.* **+quar·ies.** a receptacle or repository for relics, esp. relics of saints. [C17: from Old French *reliquaire,* from *relique* RELIC]

rel+ique (rəˈli:k, ˈrɛlɪk) *n.* an archaic spelling of **relic.**

re+liq·ui·ae (rɪˈlɪkwɪˌi:) *pl. n.* fossil remains of animals or plants. [C19: from Latin: remains]

rel+ish (ˈrɛlɪʃ) *vb.* (*tr.*) **1.** to savour or enjoy (an experience) to the full. **2.** to anticipate eagerly; look forward to. **3.** to enjoy the taste or flavour of (food, etc.); savour. **4.** to give appetizing taste or flavour to (food), by or as if by the addition of pickles or spices. ~*n.* **5.** liking or enjoyment, as of something eaten or experienced (esp. in the phrase **with relish**). **6.** pleasurable anticipation: *he didn't have much relish for the idea.* **7.** an appetizing or spicy food added to a main dish to enhance its flavour. **8.** an appetizing taste or flavour. **9.** a zestful trace or touch: *there was a certain relish in all his writing.* **10.** *Music.* (in English lute, viol, and keyboard music of the 16th and 17th centuries) a trilling ornament, used esp. at cadences. [C16: from earlier *reles* aftertaste, from Old French: something remaining, from *relaisser* to leave behind; see RELEASE] —**ˈrel+ish+a·ble** *adj.*

re+live (ri:ˈlɪv) *vb.* (*tr.*) to experience (a sensation, event, etc.) again, esp. in the imagination. —**re+ˈliv+a·ble** *adj.*

re+lu+cent (rɪˈlu:sᵊnt) *adj. Archaic.* bright; shining. [C16: from Latin *relūcēre* to shine out, from RE- + *lūcēre* to shine, from *lūx* light]

re+luct (rɪˈlʌkt) *vb.* (*intr.*) *Archaic.* **1.** (often foll. by *against*) to struggle or rebel. **2.** to object; show reluctance. [C16: from Latin *reluctārī* to resist, from RE- + *luctārī* to struggle]

re+luc+tance (rɪˈlʌktəns) *or* **re+luc+tan+cy** *n.* **1.** lack of eagerness or willingness; disinclination. **2.** *Physics.* a measure of the resistance of a closed magnetic circuit to a magnetic flux, equal to the ratio of the magnetomotive force to the magnetic flux.

re+luc+tant (rɪˈlʌktənt) *adj.* **1.** not eager; unwilling; disinclined. **2.** *Archaic.* offering resistance or opposition. [C17: from Latin *reluctārī* to resist; see RELUCT] —**re+ˈluc+tant+ly** *adv.*

rel+uc+tiv+i·ty (ˌrɛlʌkˈtɪvɪtɪ) *n., pl.* **·ties.** *Physics.* a specific or relative reluctance of a magnetic material. [C19: RELUCT + *-ivity* on the model of *conductivity*]

re+lume (rɪˈlu:m) *or* **re+lu+mine** (rɪˈlu:mɪn) *vb.* (*tr.*) *Archaic.* to light or brighten again; rekindle. [C17: from Late Latin *relūmināre,* from Latin RE- + *illūmināre* to ILLUMINE]

re+ly (rɪˈlaɪ) *vb.* **+lies, +ly+ing, +lied.** (*intr.;* foll. by *on* or *upon*) **1.** to be dependent (on): *he relies on his charm.* **2.** to have trust or confidence (in): *you can rely on us.* [C14: from Old French *relier* to fasten together, repair, from Latin *religāre* to tie back, from RE- + *ligāre* to tie]

REM *abbrev. for* rapid eye movement.

REM *or* **rem** (rɛm) *n. acronym for* roentgen equivalent man.

re+main (rɪˈmeɪn) *vb.* (*mainly intr.*) **1.** to stay behind or in the same place: *to remain at home; only Tom remained.* **2.** (*copula*) to continue to be: *to remain cheerful.* **3.** to be left, as after use, consumption, the passage of time, etc.: *a little wine still remained in the bottle.* **4.** to be left to be done, said, etc.: *it remains to be pointed out.* [C14: from Old French *remanoir,* from Latin *remanēre* to be left, from RE- + *manēre* to stay]

re+main+der (rɪˈmeɪndə) *n.* **1.** a part or portion that is left, as after use, subtraction, expenditure, the passage of time, etc.: *the remainder of the milk; the remainder of the day.* **2.** *Maths.* **a.** the amount left over when one quantity cannot be exactly divided by another: *for 10 ÷ 3, the remainder is 1.* **b.** another name for **difference** (sense 6b.). **3.** *Property law.* a future interest in property; an interest in a particular estate that will pass to one at some future date, as on the death of the current possessor. Compare **particular estate. 4.** a number of copies of a book left unsold when demand slows or ceases, which are sold at a reduced price by the publisher. ~*vb.* **5.** (*tr.*) to sell (copies of a book) as a remainder.

re·main·der·man (rɪˈmeɪndəˌmæn) *n., pl.* **+men.** *Property law.* the person entitled to receive a particular estate on its determination. Compare **reversioner.**

re+mains (rɪˈmeɪnz) *pl. n.* **1.** any pieces, scraps, fragments, etc., that are left unused or still extant, as after use, consumption, the passage of time, etc.: *the remains of a meal; archaeological remains.* **2.** the body of a dead person; corpse. **3.**

---

re+ˈlay *vb.,* **-lays, -lay·ing, -laid.**
re+ˈlearn *vb.*
re+ˈlet *vb.,* **+lets, +let+ting, +let.**
re+ˈli+cense *vb.*
re+ˈlight *vb.,* **+lights, +light+ing, +light+ed** *or* **+lit.**
re+ˈline *vb.*
re+ˈlist *vb.*
re+ˈload *vb.*
re+ˈloan *n., vb.*
ˌre+lo+ˈcate *vb.*
ˌre+lo+ˈca+tion *n.*

Also called: **literary remains.** the unpublished writings of an author at the time of his death.

re+make *n.* ('riːˌmeɪk). **1.** something that is made again, esp. a new version of an old film. **2.** the act of making again or anew. ~*vb.* (riː'meɪk), **+makes, +mak+ing, +made. 3.** (*tr.*) to make again or anew.

re+mand (rɪ'mɑːnd) *vb.* (*tr.*) **1.** *Law.* (of a court or magistrate) to send (a prisoner or accused person) back into custody or admit him to bail, esp. on adjourning a case for further inquiries to be made. **2.** to send back. ~*n.* **3.** the sending of a prisoner or accused person back into custody (or sometimes admitting him to bail) to await trial or continuation of his trial. **4.** the act of remanding or state of being remanded. **5. on remand.** in custody or on bail awaiting trial or completion of one's trial. [C15: from Medieval Latin *remandāre* to send back word, from Latin RE- + *mandāre* to command, confine; see MANDATE] —**re'mand+ment** *n.*

re+mand home *or* **cen+tre** *n.* (in England) an institution to which juvenile offenders are sent for detention while awaiting appearance before a court.

rem·a+nence ('rɛmənəns) *n. Physics.* the ability of a material to retain magnetization, equal to the magnetic flux density of the material after the removal of the magnetizing field. Also called: **retentivity.** [C17: from Latin *remanēre* to stay behind, REMAIN]

rem·a+nent ('rɛmənənt) *adj. Rare.* remaining or left over.

re+mark (rɪ'mɑːk) *vb.* **1.** (when *intr.*, often foll. by *on* or *upon;* when *tr., may take a clause as object*) to pass a casual comment (about); reflect in informal speech or writing. **2.** (*tr.; may take a clause as object*) to perceive; observe; notice. ~*n.* **3.** a brief casually expressed thought or opinion; observation. **4.** notice comment, or observation: *the event passed without remark.* **5.** *Engraving.* a variant of **remarque.** [C17: from Old French *remarquer* to observe, from RE- + *marquer* to note, MARK] —**re'mark+er** *n.*

re+mark+a·ble (rɪ'mɑːkəbᵊl) *adj.* **1.** worthy of note or attention: *a remarkable achievement.* **2.** unusual, striking, or extraordinary: *a remarkable sight.* —**re'mark+a·ble+ness** *or* **reˌmark+a·'bil·i·ty** *n.* —**re'mark+a·bly** *adv.*

re+marque *or* **re+mark** (rɪ'mɑːk) *n.* **1.** a mark in the margin of an engraved plate to indicate the stage of production of the plate. It is removed before the plate is finished. **2.** a plate so marked. **3.** a print or proof from a plate so marked. [C19: from French; see REMARK]

Re·marque (rɪ'mɑːk) *n.* **E·rich Ma·ri·a** ('eːrɪç ma'riːa). 1898–1970, U.S. novelist, born in Germany, noted for his novel of World War I, *All Quiet on the Western Front* (1929).

re+match *n.* ('riːˌmætʃ). **1.** *Sport.* a second or return match between contestants. ~*vb.* (riː'mætʃ). **2.** (*tr.*) to match (two contestants) again.

rem+blai (*French* rɑ̃'ble) *n.* earth used for an embankment or rampart. [French, from *remblayer* to embank, from *emblayer* to pile up]

Rem·brandt ('rɛmbrænt) *n.* full name *Rembrandt Harmensz* (or *Harmenszoon*) *van Rijn* (or *van Ryn*). 1606–69, Dutch painter, noted for his handling of shade and light, esp. in his portraits. —ˌ**Rem+brandt+'esque** *adj.*

REME ('riːmiː) *n. acronym for* Royal Electrical and Mechanical Engineers.

re+me·di·al (rɪ'miːdɪəl) *adj.* **1.** affording a remedy; curative. **2.** denoting or relating to special teaching, teaching methods, or material for backward and slow learners: *remedial education.* —**re'me·di·al+ly** *adv.*

rem+e·dy ('rɛmɪdɪ) *n., pl.* **·dies. 1.** (usually foll. by *for* or *against*) any drug or agent that cures a disease or controls its symptoms. **2.** (usually foll. by *for* or *against*) anything that serves to put a fault to rights, cure defects, improve conditions, etc.: *a remedy for industrial disputes.* **3.** the legally permitted variation from the standard weight or quality of coins; tolerance. ~*vb.* (*tr.*) **4.** to relieve or cure (a disease, illness, etc.) by or as if by a remedy. **5.** to put to rights (a fault, error, etc.); correct. [C13: from Anglo-Norman *remedie,* from Latin *remedium* a cure, from *remedērī* to heal again, from RE- + *medērī* to heal; see MEDICAL] —**re+me·di·a·ble** (rɪ'miːdɪəbᵊl) *adj.* —**re'me·di·a·bly** *adv.* —**'rem+e·di·less** *adj.*

re+mem+ber (rɪ'mɛmbə) *vb.* **1.** to become aware of (something forgotten) again; bring back to one's consciousness; recall. **2.** to retain (an idea, intention, etc.) in one's conscious mind: *to remember Pythagoras' theorem; remember to do one's shopping.* **3.** (*tr.*) to give money, etc., to (someone), as in a will or in tipping. **4.** (*tr.;* foll. by *to*) to mention (a person's name) to another person, as by way of greeting or friendship: *remember me to your mother.* **5.** (*tr.*) to mention (a person) favourably, as in prayer. **6.** (*tr.*) to commemorate (a person, event, etc.): *to remember the dead of the wars.* **7. remember oneself.** to recover one's good manners after a lapse; stop behaving badly. [C14: from Old French *remembrer,* from Late Latin *rememorārī* to recall to mind, from Latin RE- + *memor* mindful; see MEMORY] —**re'mem+ber+er** *n.*

re+mem+brance (rɪ'mɛmbrəns) *n.* **1.** the act of remembering or state of being remembered. **2.** something that is remembered; reminiscence. **3.** a memento or keepsake. **4.** the extent in time of one's power of recollection. **5. a.** the act of honouring some past event, person, etc. **b.** (*as modifier*): *a remembrance service.*

re+mem+branc·er (rɪ'mɛmbrənsə) *n. Archaic.* a reminder, memento, or keepsake.

Re+mem+branc·er (rɪ'mɛmbrənsə) *n. Brit.* **1.** any of several officials of the Exchequer esp. one (**Queen's** *or* **King's Remembrancer**) whose duties include collecting debts due to the Crown. **2.** an official (**City Remembrancer**) appointed by the Corporation of the City of London to represent its interests to Parliament and elsewhere.

Re+mem+brance Sun+day *n. Brit.* the Sunday closest to November 11, the anniversary of the armistice of 1918 that ended World War I, on which the dead of both World Wars are commemorated. Also called: **Remembrance Day.**

re+mex ('riːmɛks) *n., pl.* **rem+i+ges** ('rɛmɪˌdʒiːz). any of the large flight feathers of a bird's wing. [C18: from Latin: a rower, from *rēmus* oar] —**re+mig+i·al** (rɪ'mɪdʒɪəl) *adj.*

re+mind (rɪ'maɪnd) *vb.* (*tr.;* usually foll. by *of; may take a clause as object or an infinitive*) to cause (a person) to remember (something or to do something); make (someone) aware (of something he may have forgotten): *remind me to phone home; flowers remind me of holidays.* —**re'mind+er** *n.*

re+mind+ful (rɪ'maɪndfʊl) *adj.* **1.** serving to remind. **2.** (*postpositive*) bearing in mind; mindful.

rem·i+nisce (ˌrɛmɪ'nɪs) *vb.* (*intr.*) to talk or write about old times, past experiences, etc.

rem·i+nis+cence (ˌrɛmɪ'nɪsəns) *n.* **1.** the act of recalling or narrating past experiences. **2.** (*often pl.*) some past experience, event, etc., that is recalled or narrated; anecdote. **3.** an event, phenomenon, or experience that reminds one of something else. **4.** (in the philosophy of Plato) the doctrine that perception and recognition of particulars is possible because the mind has seen the universal forms of all things in a previous disembodied existence.

rem·i+nis+cent (ˌrɛmɪ'nɪsᵊnt) *adj.* **1.** (*postpositive;* foll. by *of*) stimulating memories (of) or comparisons (with). **2.** characterized by reminiscence. **3.** (of a person) given to reminiscing. [C18: from Latin *reminiscī* to call to mind, from RE- + *mēns* mind] —ˌ**rem·i'nis+cent+ly** *adv.*

re+mise (rɪ'maɪz) *vb.* **1.** (*tr.*) *Law.* to give up or relinquish (a right, claim, etc.); surrender. **2.** *Fencing.* to make a renewed thrust on the same lunge after the first has missed. ~*n.* **3.** *Fencing.* a second thrust made on the same lunge after the first has missed. **4.** *Obsolete.* a hired carriage. **5.** *Obsolete.* a coach-house. [C17: from French *remettre* to put back, from Latin *remittere* to send back, from RE- + *mittere* to send]

re+miss (rɪ'mɪs) *adj.* (*postpositive*) **1.** lacking in care or attention to duty; negligent. **2.** lacking in energy; dilatory. [C15: from Latin *remissus, from remittere* to release, from RE- + *mittere* to send] —**re'miss+ly** *adv.* —**re'miss+ness** *n.*

re+mis+si·ble (rɪ'mɪsəbᵊl) *adj.* able to be remitted. [C16: from Latin *remissibilis;* see REMIT] —**reˌmis+si'bil·i·ty** *or* **re'mis+si·ble+ness** *n.*

re+mis+sion (rɪ'mɪʃən) *or* **re+mit+tal** (rɪ'mɪtᵊl) *n.* **1.** the act of remitting or state of being remitted. **2.** a reduction of the term of a sentence of imprisonment, as for good conduct: *he got three years' remission.* **3.** forgiveness for sin. **4.** discharge or release from penalty, obligation, etc. **5.** lessening of intensity; abatement, as in the severity of symptoms of a disease. **6.** *Rare.* the act of sending a remittance; payment. —**re'mis+sive** *adj.* —**re'mis+sive+ly** *adv.*

re+mit *vb.* (rɪ'mɪt). **+mits, +mit+ting, +mit+ted.** (*mainly tr.*) **1.** (*also intr.*) to send (money, payment, etc.), as for goods or service, esp. by post. **2.** *Law.* (esp. of an appeal court) to send back (a case or proceeding) to an inferior court for further consideration or action. **3.** to cancel or refrain from exacting (a penalty or punishment). **4.** (*also intr.*) to relax (pace, intensity, etc.) or (of pace or the like) to slacken or abate. **5.** to postpone; defer. **6.** *Archaic.* to pardon or forgive (crime, sins, etc.). ~*n.* ('riːmɪt, rɪ'mɪt). **7.** *Law,* the transfer of a case from one court or jurisdiction to another, esp. from an appeal court to an inferior tribunal. **8.** the act of remitting. **9.** something remitted. [C14: from Latin *remittere* to send back, release, RE- + *mittere* to send] —**re'mit+ta·ble** *adj.*

re+mit+tal (rɪ'mɪtᵊl) *n.* the act of remitting.

re+mit+tance (rɪ'mɪtəns) *n.* **1.** payment for goods or services received or as an allowance, esp. when sent by post. **2.** the act of remitting.

re+mit+tance man *n.* a man living abroad on money sent from home, esp. in the days of the British Empire.

re+mit+tee (rɪˌmɪt'iː) *n.* the recipient of a remittance; one to whom payment is sent.

re+mit+tent (rɪ'mɪtᵊnt) *adj.* (of a fever or the symptoms of a disease) characterized by periods of diminished severity. —**re'mit+tence** *or* **re'mit+ten+cy** *n.* —**re'mit+tent+ly** *adv.*

re+mit+ter (rɪ'mɪtə) *n.* **1.** Also: **re+mit+tor.** a person who remits. **2.** *Property law.* the principle by which a person out of possession of land to which he had a good title is adjudged to regain this when he again enters into possession of the land.

rem+nant ('rɛmnənt) *n.* **1.** (*often pl.*) a part left over after use, processing, etc. **2.** a surviving trace or vestige, as of a former era: *a remnant of imperialism.* **3.** a piece of material from the end of a roll, sold at a lower price. ~*adj.* **4.** remaining; left

---

re+'mail *vb.*
re+'man *vb.*, **+mans, +man+ning, +manned.**
ˌre+man+u+'fac+ture *vb.*
re+'mar+riage *n.*
re+'mar+ry *vb.*, **+ries, +ry+ing, +ried.**
re+'meas+ure *vb.*
re+'meas+ure+ment *n.*
re+'melt *vb.*
re+'mend *vb.*
re+mi+'grate *vb.*
ˌre+mil+i+ta+ri+'za+tion *or* ˌre+mil+i+ta+ri+'sa+tion *n.*
re+'mil+i+ta+ˌrize *or*
re+'mil+ta+ˌrise *vb.*
re+'mint *vb.*
re+'mix *vb.*
re+'mod+el *vb.*, **+els, +el+ling, +elled.**

over. [C14: from Old French *remenant* remaining, from *remanoir* to REMAIN]

re+mon+e·tize *or* **re+mon+e·tise** (riːˈmʌnɪˌtaɪz) *vb. (tr.)* to reinstate as legal tender: *to remonetize silver.* —**re+ˌmon+e·ti+ˈza+tion** *or* **re+ˌmon+e·ti+ˈsa+tion** *n.*

re+mon+strance (rɪˈmɒnstrəns) *n.* **1.** the act of remonstrating; protestation. **2.** a protest or reproof, esp. a petition presented in protest against something.

Re+mon+strance (rɪˈmɒnstrəns) *n. History.* **1.** See **Grand Remonstrance. 2.** the statement of Arminian principles drawn up in 1610 in Gouda in the Netherlands.

re+mon+strant (rɪˈmɒnstrənt) *n.* **1.** a person who remonstrates, esp. one who signs a remonstrance. ~*adj.* **2.** *Rare.* remonstrating or protesting.

Re+mon+strant (rɪˈmɒnstrənt) *n.* a Dutch supporter of the Arminian Remonstrance of 1610.

re+mon+strate (ˈrɛmənˌstreɪt) *vb. (intr.)* **1.** (usually foll. by *with, against,* etc.) to argue in protest or objection: *to remonstrate with the government.* **2.** *Archaic.* to show or point out. [C16: from Medieval Latin *remonstrāre* to point out (errors, etc.), from Latin RE- + *monstrāre* to show] —**ˌre+mon+ˈstra+tion** *n.* —**re+mon+stra+tive** (rɪˈmɒnstrətɪv) *adj.* —**ˈre+mon+ˌstra+tor** *n.*

re+mon+tant (rɪˈmɒntənt) *adj.* **1.** (esp. of cultivated roses) flowering more than once in a single season. ~*n.* **2.** a rose having such a growth. [C19: from French: coming up again, from *remonter;* see REMOUNT]

rem+on+toir *or* **rem+on+toire** (ˌrɛmənˈtwɑː) *n.* any of various devices used in watches, clocks, etc., to compensate for errors arising from the changes in the force driving the escapement. [C19: from French: winding mechanism, from *remonter* to wind; see REMOUNT]

rem·o+ra (ˈrɛmərə) *n.* any of the marine spiny-finned fishes constituting the family *Echeneidae.* They have a flattened elongated body and attach themselves to larger fish, rocks, etc., by a sucking disc on the top of the head. [C16: from Latin, from RE- + *mora* delay; an allusion to its alleged habit of delaying ships]

re+morse (rɪˈmɔːs) *n.* **1.** a sense of deep regret and guilt for some misdeed. **2.** compunction; pity; compassion. [C14: from Medieval Latin *remorsus* a gnawing, from Latin *remordēre* to bite again, from RE- + *mordēre* to bite] —**re+ˈmorse+ful** *adj.* —**re+ˈmorse+ful+ly** *adv.* —**re+ˈmorse+ful+ness** *n.*

re+morse+less (rɪˈmɔːslɪs) *adj.* **1.** without compunction, pity, or compassion. **2.** not abating in intensity; relentless: *a remorseless wind.* —**re+ˈmorse+less+ly** *adv.* —**re+ˈmorse+less+ness** *n.*

re+mote (rɪˈməʊt) *adj.* **1.** located far away; distant. **2.** far from any centre of population, society, or civilization; out-of-the-way. **3.** distant in time. **4.** distantly related or connected: *a remote cousin.* **5.** removed, as from the source or point of action. **6.** slight or faint (esp. in the phrases **not the remotest idea, a remote chance**). **7.** (of a person's manner) aloof or abstracted. [C15: from Latin *remōtus* far removed, from *removēre,* from RE- + *movēre* to move] —**re+ˈmote+ly** *adv.* —**re+ˈmote+ness** *n.*

re+mote con+trol *n.* control of a system or activity by a person at a different place, usually by means of radio or ultrasonic signals or by electrical signals transmitted by wire. —**re·ˈmote-con·ˈtrolled** *adj.*

ré+mou+lade (ˌrɛməˈleɪd; *French* remuˈlad) *n.* a mayonnaise sauce flavoured with herbs, mustard, and capers, served with salads, cold meat, etc. [French, from Picard dialect *ramolas* horseradish, from Latin *armoracea*]

re+mould *vb.* (ˌriːˈməʊld). **1.** *(tr.)* to mould again. ~*n.* (ˈriːˌməʊld). **2.** another name for **retread** (tyre).

re+mount *vb.* (riːˈmaʊnt). **1.** to get on (a horse, bicycle, etc.) again. **2.** *(tr.)* to mount (a picture, jewel, exhibit, etc.) again. ~*n.* (ˈriːmaʊnt). **3.** a fresh horse, esp. (formerly) to replace one killed or injured in battle.

re+mov+al (rɪˈmuːvᵊl) *n.* **1.** the act of removing or state of being removed. **2. a.** a change of residence. **b.** *(as modifier): a removal company.* **3.** dismissal from office.

re+mov+al+ist (rɪˈmuːvəlɪst) *n. Austral.* a person or company that transports household effects to a new home.

re+move (rɪˈmuːv) *vb. (mainly tr.)* **1.** to take away and place elsewhere. **2.** to displace (someone) from office; dismiss. **3.** to do away with (a grievance, cause of anxiety, etc.); abolish. **4.** to cause (dirt, stains, or anything unwanted) to disappear; get rid of. **5.** *Euphemistic.* to assassinate; kill. **6.** *(intr.) Formal.* to change the location of one's home or place of business: *the publishers have removed to Mayfair.* ~*n.* **7.** the act of removing, esp. (formal) a removal of one's residence or place of work. **8.** the degree of difference separating one person, thing, or condition from another: *only one remove from madness.* **9.** *Brit.* (in certain schools) a class or form, esp. one for children of about 14 years. [C14: from Old French *removoir,* from Latin *removēre;* see MOVE] —**re+ˈmov+a·ble** *adj.* —**re+ˌmov+a·ˈbil+i·ty** *or* **re+ˈmov+a·ble+ness** *n.* —**re+ˈmov+a·bly** *adv.* —**re+ˈmov+er** *n.*

re+moved (rɪˈmuːvd) *adj.* **1.** separated by distance or abstract distinction. **2.** *(postpositive)* separated by a degree of descent or kinship: *the child of a person's first cousin is his first cousin once removed.* —**re+mov+ed+ness** (rɪˈmuːvɪdnɪs) *n.*

Rem+scheid (*German* ˈrɛmʃaɪt) *n.* an industrial city in W West Germany, in North Rhine-Westphalia. Pop.: 135 587 (1974 est.).

re+mu+ner+ate (rɪˈmjuːnəˌreɪt) *vb. (tr.)* to reward or pay for work, service, etc. [C16: from Latin *remūnerārī* to reward, from RE- + *mūnerāre* to give, from *mūnus* a gift; see MUNIFICENT] —**re+ˌmu+ner+a·ˈbil+i·ty** *n.* —**re+ˈmu+ner+a·ble** *adj.* —**re+ˈmu+ner·a·tive** *adj.* —**re+ˈmu+ner·a·tive+ly** *adv.* —**re+ˈmu+ner·a·tive+ness** *n.* —**reˈmu+ner·ˌa+tor** *n.*

re+mu+ner·a+tion (rɪˌmjuːnəˈreɪʃən) *n.* **1.** the act of remunerating. **2.** pay; recompense.

Re+mus (riːməs) *n. Roman myth.* the brother of Romulus.

re+nais+sance (rəˈneɪsəns; *U.S. also* ˈrɛnəˌsɒns) *or* **re+nas+cence** *n.* a revival or rebirth, esp. of culture and learning. [C19: from French, from Latin RE- + *nascī* to be born]

Re+nais+sance (rəˈneɪsəns; *U.S. also* ˈrɛnəˌsɒns) *n.* **1. the.** the period of European history marking the waning of the Middle Ages and the rise of the modern world: usually considered as beginning in Italy in the 14th century. **2. a.** the spirit, culture, art, science, and thought of this period. Characteristics of the Renaissance are usually considered to include intensified classical scholarship, scientific and geographical discovery, a sense of individual human potentialities, and the assertion of the active and secular over the religious and contemplative life. **b.** *(as modifier): Renaissance writers.* See also **Early Renaissance, High Renaissance.** ~*adj.* **3.** of, characteristic of, or relating to the Renaissance, its culture, etc.

Re+nais+sance man *n.* a man of any period who has a broad range of intellectual interests.

re+nal (ˈriːnᵊl) *adj.* of, relating to, resembling, or situated near the kidney. [C17: from French, from Late Latin *rēnālis,* from Latin *rēnēs* kidneys, of obscure origin]

re+nal pel+vis *n.* a small funnel-shaped cavity of the kidney into which urine is discharged before passing into the ureter.

re+nas+cence (rɪˈnæsəns, -ˈneɪ-) *n.* a variant spelling of **renaissance.**

re+nas+cent (rɪˈnæsᵊnt, -ˈneɪ-) *adj.* becoming active or vigorous again; reviving: *renascent nationalism.* [C18: from Latin *renascī* to be born again]

ren+coun+ter (rɛnˈkaʊntə) *Archaic.* ~*n. also* **ren+con+tre** (rɛnˈkɒntə). **1.** an unexpected meeting. **2.** a hostile clash, as of two armies, adversaries, etc.; skirmish. ~*vb.* **3.** to meet (someone) unexpectedly. [C16: from French *rencontre,* from *rencontrer;* see ENCOUNTER]

rend (rɛnd) *vb.* **rends, rend+ing, rent. 1.** to tear with violent force or to be torn in this way; rip. **2.** *(tr.)* to tear or pull (one's clothes, etc.), esp. as a manifestation of rage or grief. **3.** *(tr.)* (of a noise or cry) to disturb (the air, silence, etc.) with a shrill or piercing tone. **4.** *(tr.)* to pain or distress (the heart, conscience, etc.). [Old English *rendan;* related to Old Frisian *renda*] —**ˈrend+er** *n.* —**ˈrend+i·ble** *adj.*

ren+der (ˈrɛndə) *vb. (tr.)* **1.** to present or submit (accounts, etc.) for payment, approval, or action. **2.** to give or provide (aid, charity, a service, etc.). **3.** to show (obedience), as due or expected. **4.** to give or exchange, as by way of return or requital: *to render blow for blow.* **5.** to cause to become: *grief had rendered him simple-minded.* **6.** to deliver (a verdict or opinion) formally. **7.** to portray or depict (something), as in painting, music, or acting. **8.** to translate (something) into another language or form. **9.** (sometimes foll. by *up*) to yield or give: *the tomb rendered up its secret.* **10.** (often foll. by *back*) to return (something); give back. **11.** to cover the surface of (brickwork, etc.) with a coat of plaster. **12.** (often foll. by *down*) to extract (fat) from (meat) by melting. **13.** *Nautical.* **a.** to reeve (a line). **b.** to slacken (a rope, etc.). **14.** *History.* (of a feudal tenant) to make (payment) in money, goods, or services to one's overlord. ~*n.* **15.** a first thin coat of plaster applied to a surface. **16.** *History.* a payment in money, goods, or services made by a feudal tenant to his lord. [C14: from Old French *rendre,* from Latin *reddere* to give back (influenced by Latin *prendere* to grasp), from RE- + *dare* to give] —**ˈren+der·a·ble** *adj.* —**ˈren+der+er** *n.*

ren+der+ing (ˈrɛndərɪŋ) *n.* **1.** the act or an instance of performing a play, piece of music, etc. **2.** a translation of a text from a foreign language. **3.** Also called: **rendering coat, render.** a coat of plaster or cement mortar applied to a surface. **4.** a perspective drawing showing an architect's idea of a finished building, interior, etc.

ren+dez+vous (ˈrɒndɪˌvuː) *n., pl.* **+vous** (-ˌvuːz). **1.** a meeting or appointment to meet at a specified time and place. **2.** a place where people meet. ~*vb.* **3.** to meet or cause to meet at a specified time or place. [C16: from French, from *rendez-vous!* present yourselves! from *se rendre* to present oneself; see RENDER]

ren+di+tion (rɛnˈdɪʃən) *n.* **1.** a performance of a musical composition, dramatic role, etc. **2.** a translation of a text. **3.** the act of rendering. **4.** *Archaic.* surrender. [C17: from obsolete French, from Late Latin *redditiō;* see RENDER]

ren+dzi+na (rɛnˈdziːnə) *n.* a dark interzonal type of soil found in grassy or formerly grassy areas of moderate rainfall, esp. on chalklands. [C20: from Polish]

ren+e·gade (ˈrɛnɪˌgeɪd) *n.* **1. a.** a person who deserts his cause or faith for another; apostate; traitor. **b.** *(as modifier): a renegade priest.* **2.** any outlaw or rebel. [C16: from Spanish *renegado,* from Medieval Latin *renegāre* to renounce, from Latin RE- + *negāre* to deny]

re+ne·ga+do (ˌrɛnɪˈgɑːdəʊ) *n., pl.* **+dos.** an archaic word for **renegade.**

re+nege *or* **re+negue** (rɪˈniːg, -ˈneɪg) *vb.* **1.** *(intr.;* often foll. by

---

re+ˈmod+el+ler *n.*
ˌre+mod·i·fi+ˈca+tion *n.*
re+ˈmod·i·fy *vb.,* **+fies, +fy·ing, +fied.**
re+ˈmod+u+ˌlate *vb.*
re+ˈmort+gage *vb.*
re+ˈname *vb.*
ˌre+ne·ˈgo+ti·a·ble *adj.*

on) to go back (on one's promise, etc.). ~*vb., n.* **2.** *Cards.* other words for **revoke.** [C16 (in the sense: to deny, renounce): from Medieval Latin *renegāre* to renounce; see RENEGADE] —**re'neg·er** *or* **re'negu·er** *n.*

re·new (rɪ'nju:) *vb.* (*mainly tr.*) **1.** to take up again. **2.** (*also intr.*) to begin (an activity) again; recommence: *to renew an attempt.* **3.** to restate or reaffirm (a promise, etc.). **4.** (*also intr.*) to make (a lease, licence, or contract) valid or effective for a further period. **5.** to extend the period of loan of (a library book). **6.** to regain or recover (vigour, strength, activity, etc.). **7.** to restore to a new or fresh condition. **8.** to replace (an old or worn-out part or piece). **9.** to replenish (a supply, etc.). —**re'new·a·ble** *adj.* —**re,new·a'bil·i·ty** *n.* —**re'new·er** *n.*

re·new·al (rɪ'nju:əl) *n.* **1.** the act of renewing or state of being renewed. **2.** something that is renewed.

Ren·frew ('rɛnfru:) *n.* **1.** a shipbuilding town in W central Scotland, W of Glasgow. Pop.: 18 589 (1971). **2.** Also called: **Renfrewshire.** (until 1975) a county of W central Scotland, on the Firth of Clyde: now part of Strathclyde region.

ren·i- *combining form.* kidney or kidneys: *reniform.* [from Latin *rēnēs*]

Re·ni (*Italian* 'rɛ:ni) *n.* **Gui·do** ('gwi:do). 1575–1642, Italian baroque painter and engraver.

ren·i·form ('rɛnɪ,fɔ:m) *adj.* having the shape or profile of a kidney: *a reniform leaf; a reniform mass of haematite.*

re·nin ('ri:nɪn) *n.* a proteolytic enzyme secreted by the kidneys, which plays an important part in the maintenance of blood pressure. [C20: from RENI- + -IN]

re·ni·tent (rɪ'naɪtᵊnt, 'rɛnɪtənt) *adj. Rare.* **1.** reluctant; recalcitrant. **2.** not flexible. [C18: from Latin *renītī* to strive afresh, from RE- + *nītī* to endeavour] —**re'ni·tence** *or* **re'ni·ten·cy** *n.*

Rennes (*French* rɛn) *n.* a city in NW France: the ancient capital of Brittany. Pop.: 205 733 (1975).

ren·net ('rɛnɪt) *n.* **1. a.** the membrane lining the fourth stomach (abomasum) of a young calf. **b.** the stomach of certain other young animals. **2.** a substance, containing the enzyme rennin, prepared esp. from the stomachs of calves and used for curdling milk in making cheese and junket. [C15: related to Old English *gerinnan* to curdle, RUN]

ren·nin ('rɛnɪn) *n.* an enzyme that occurs in gastric juice and is an active constituent of rennet. It coagulates milk by converting caseinogen to casein. Also called: **chymosin.** [C20: from RENNET + -IN]

Re·no ('ri:nəʊ) *n.* a city in W Nevada, at the foot of the Sierra Nevada: noted as a divorce, wedding, and gambling centre by reason of its liberal laws. Pop.: 72 863 (1970).

Re·noir ('rɛnwɑ:; *French* rə'nwa:) *n.* **1. Jean** (ʒã). 1894-1979, French film director: his films include *La Grande Illusion* (1937), *La Règle du jeu* (1939), and *Diary of a Chambermaid* (1945). **2.** his father, **Pierre Au·guste** (pjɛ:r o'gyst). 1841-1919, French painter. One of the initiators of impressionism, he broke away from the movement with his later paintings, esp. his many nude studies, which are more formal compositions.

re·nounce (rɪ'naʊns) *vb.* **1.** (*tr.*) to give up (a claim or right), esp. by formal announcement: *to renounce a title.* **2.** (*tr.*) to repudiate: *to renounce Christianity.* **3.** (*tr.*) to give up (some habit, etc.) voluntarily: *to renounce one's old ways.* **4.** (*intr.*) *Cards.* to fail to follow suit because one has no more cards of the suit led. ~*n.* **5.** *Rare.* a failure to follow suit in a card game. [C14: from Old French *renoncer,* from Latin *renuntiāre* to disclaim, from RE- + *nuntiāre* to announce, from *nuntius* messenger] —**re'nounce·ment** *n.* —**re'nounc·er** *n.*

ren·o·vate ('rɛnə,veɪt) *vb.* (*tr.*) **1.** to restore (something) to good condition: *to renovate paintings.* **2.** to revive or refresh (one's spirits, health, etc.). [C16: from Latin *renovāre,* from RE- + *novāre* to make new, from *novus* NEW] —**,ren·o'va·tion** *n.* —**'ren·o,va·tive** *adj.* —**'ren·o,va·tor** *n.*

re·nown (rɪ'naʊn) *n.* widespread reputation, esp. of a good kind; fame. [C14: from Anglo-Norman *renoun,* from Old French *renom,* from *renomer* to celebrate, from RE- + *nomer* to name, from Latin *nōmināre*] —**re'nowned** *adj.*

rens·se·laer·ite ('rɛnsələ,raɪt, ,rɛnsə'lɪəraɪt) *n.* a white or yellow compact variety of talc, used for ornaments. [C19: named after Stephen Van *Rensselaer* (1764–1839), American army officer and politician]

rent[1] (rɛnt) *n.* **1.** a payment made periodically by a tenant to a landlord or owner for the occupation or use of land, buildings, or other property, such as a telephone. **2.** *Economics.* **a.** that portion of the national income accruing to owners of land and real property. **b.** the return derived from the cultivation of land in excess of production costs. **c.** See **economic rent. 3. for rent.** *Chiefly U.S.* available for use and occupation subject to the payment of rent. ~*vb.* **4.** (*tr.*) to grant (a person) the right to use one's property in return for periodic payments. **5.** (*tr.*) to occupy or use (property) in return for periodic payments. **6.** (*intr.;* often foll. by *at*) to be let or rented (for a specified rental). [C12: from Old French *rente* revenue, from Vulgar Latin *rendere* (unattested) to yield; see RENDER] —**,rent·a'bil·i·ty** *n.* —**'rent·a·ble** *adj.*

rent[2] (rɛnt) *n.* **1.** a slit or opening made by tearing or rending; tear. **2.** a breach or division, as in relations. ~*vb.* **3.** the past tense or past participle of **rend.**

rent·al ('rɛntᵊl) *n.* **1. a.** the amount paid by a tenant as rent. **b.** an income derived from rents received. **2.** property available for renting. **3.** a less common name for **rent-roll.** ~*adj.* **4.** of or relating to rent.

rente *French.* (rãt) *n.* **1.** annual income from capital investment; annuity. **2.** government securities of certain countries, esp. France. **3.** the interest on such securities.

rent·er ('rɛntə) *n.* **1.** a person who lets his property in return for rent, esp. a landlord. **2.** a person who rents property from another; tenant. **3.** a distributor of films to cinemas for commercial showing.

rent-free *adj., adv.* without payment of rent.

ren·tier *French.* (rãtje) *n.* **a.** a person whose income consists primarily of fixed unearned amounts, such as rent or bond interest. **b.** (*as modifier*): *the rentier class.* [from *rente;* see RENT[1]]

rent-roll *n.* **1.** a register of lands and buildings owned by a person, company, etc., showing the rent due and total amount received from each tenant. **2.** the total income arising from rented property.

re·nun·ci·a·tion (rɪ,nʌnsɪ'eɪʃən) *n.* **1.** the act or an instance of renouncing. **2.** a formal declaration renouncing something. [C14: from Latin *renunciātiō* a declaration, from *renuntiāre* to report, RENOUNCE] —**re'nun·ci·a·tive** *or* **re'nun·ci·a·to·ry** *adj.*

ren·voi (rɛn'vɔɪ) *n.* the referring of a dispute or other legal question to a jurisdiction other than that in which it arose. [French: a sending back, from *renvoyer,* from RE- + *envoyer* to send; see ENVOY]

rep[1] *or* **repp** (rɛp) *n.* a silk, wool, rayon, or cotton fabric with a transversely corded surface. [C19: from French *reps,* perhaps from English *ribs;* see RIB[1]] —**repped** *adj.*

rep[2] (rɛp) *n. Theatre.* short for **repertory (company).**

rep[3] (rɛp) *n.* short for **representative** (sense 2).

rep[4] (rɛp) *n. U.S. informal.* short for **reputation.**

rep. *abbrev. for:* **1.** report. **2.** reported. **3.** reporter. **4.** representative. **5.** reprint.

Rep. *abbrev. for:* **1.** *U.S.* Representative. **2.** *U.S.* Republican. **3.** Republic.

re·pair[1] (rɪ'pɛə) *vb.* (*tr.*) **1.** to restore (something damaged or broken) to good condition or working order. **2.** to heal (a breach or division) in (something): *to repair a broken marriage.* **3.** to make good or make amends for (a mistake, injury, etc.). ~*n.* **4.** the act, task, or process of repairing. **5.** a part that has been repaired. **6.** state or condition: *in good repair.* [C14: from Old French *reparer,* from Latin *reparāre,* from RE- + *parāre* to make ready] —**re'pair·a·ble** *adj.* —**re'pair·er** *n.*

re·pair[2] (rɪ'pɛə) *vb.* (*intr.*) **1.** (usually foll. by *to*) to go (to a place): *to repair to the country.* **2.** (usually foll. by *to*) to have recourse (to) for help, etc.: *to repair to one's lawyer.* **3.** (usually foll. by *from*) *Archaic.* to come back; return. ~*n. Archaic.* **4.** the act of going or returning. **5.** a haunt or resort. [C14: from Old French *repairier,* from Late Latin *repatriāre* to return to one's native land, from Latin RE- + *patria* fatherland; compare REPATRIATE]

re·pair·man (rɪ'pɛə,mæn) *n., pl.* **-men.** a man whose job it is to repair machines, appliances, etc.

re·pand (rɪ'pænd) *adj. Botany.* having a wavy margin: *a repand leaf.* [C18: from Latin *repandus* bent backwards, from RE- + *pandus* curved] —**re'pand·ly** *adv.*

rep·a·ra·ble ('rɛpərəbᵊl, 'rɛprə-) *adj.* able to be repaired, recovered, or remedied: *a reparable loss.* [C16: from Latin *reparābilis,* from *reparāre* to REPAIR[1]] —**,rep·a·ra'bil·i·ty** *n.* —**'rep·a·ra·bly** *adv.*

rep·a·ra·tion (,rɛpə'reɪʃən) *n.* **1.** the act or process of making amends: *an injury admitting of no reparation.* **2.** (*usually pl.*) compensation exacted as an indemnity from a defeated nation by the victors: esp. the compensation demanded of Germany by the Treaty of Versailles after World War I. **3.** the act or process of repairing or state of having been repaired. [C14 *reparacioun,* ultimately from Latin *reparāre* to REPAIR[1]] —**re·par·a·tive** (rɪ'pærətɪv) *or* **re'par·a·to·ry** *adj.*

rep·ar·tee (,rɛpɑ:'ti:) *n.* **1.** a sharp, witty, or aphoristic remark made as a reply. **2.** terse rapid conversation consisting of such remarks. **3.** skill in making sharp witty replies or conversation. [C17: from French *repartie,* from *repartir* to retort, from RE- + *partir* to go away]

rep·ar·ti·tion (,ri:pɑ:'tɪʃən) *n.* **1.** distribution or allotment. **2.** the act or process of distributing afresh. ~*vb.* **3.** (*tr.*) to divide up again; reapportion or reallocate.

re·past (rɪ'pɑ:st) *n.* **1.** a meal or the food provided at a meal: *a light repast.* **2.** *Archaic.* **a.** food in general; nourishment. **b.** the act of taking food or refreshment. ~*vb.* **3.** (*intr.*) *Archaic.* to feed (on). [C14: from Old French, from *repaistre* to feed, from Late Latin *repāscere* to nourish again, from Latin RE- + *pāscere* to feed, pasture (of animals)]

re·pat·ri·ate *vb.* (ri:'pætrɪ,eɪt). **1.** (*tr.*) to send back (a refugee,

---

,re·ne'go·ti·ate *vb.*
,re·ne·go·ti·'a·tion *n.*
re'nom·i,nate *vb.*
,re·nom·i'na·tion *n.*
,re·no·ti·fi'ca·tion *n.*
re'no·ti,fy *vb.*, **-fies, -fy·ing, -fied.**
re'num·ber *vb.*
,re·ob'tain·a·ble *adj.*
,re·oc·cu'pa·tion *n.*
,re'oc·cu,py *vb.*, **-pies, -py·ing, -pied.**
re'oil *vb.*
re'o·pen *vb.*
re'or·der *vb.*
,re·or·gan·i'za·tion *or* **,re·or·gan·i'sa·tion** *n.*
re'or·gan,ize *or* **re'or·gan,ise** *vb.*
re'or·gan,iz·er *or* **re'or·gan,is·er** *n.*
re'or·i·ent *vb.*
,re·or·i·en'ta·tion *n.*
re'pack *vb.*
re'pack·age *vb.*
re'paint *vb., n.*
re'pa·per *vb.*
re'pass *vb.*

prisoner of war, etc.) to the country of his birth or citizenship. ~*n.* (riːˈpætrɪɪt). **2.** a person who has been repatriated. [C17: from Late Latin *repatriāre, from Latin* RE- + *patria* fatherland; compare REPAIR[2]] —**re₊ˌpat·ri·ˈa·tion** *n.*

re₊pay (rɪˈpeɪ) *vb.* **₊pays, ₊pay₊ing, ₊paid. 1.** to pay back (money, etc.) to (a person); refund or reimburse. **2.** to make a return for (something) by way of compensation: *to repay kindness.* —**re₊ˈpay₊a·ble** *adj.* —**re₊ˈpay₊ment** *n.*

re₊peal (rɪˈpiːl) *vb.* (*tr.*) **1.** to annul or rescind officially (something previously ordered); revoke: *these laws were repealed.* **2.** *Obsolete.* to call back (a person) from exile. ~*n.* **3.** an instance or the process of repealing; annulment. [C14: from Old French *repeler,* from RE- + *apeler* to call, APPEAL] —**re₊ˈpeal₊a·ble** *adj.* —**re₊ˈpeal₊er** *n.*

Re₊peal (rɪˈpiːl) *n.* (esp. in the 19th century) the proposed dissolution of the Union between Great Britain and Ireland.

re₊peat (rɪˈpiːt) *vb.* **1.** (when *tr., may take a clause as object*) to say or write (something) again, either once or several times; restate or reiterate. **2.** to do or experience (something) again once or several times. **3.** (*intr.*) to occur more than once: *the last figure repeats.* **4.** (*tr.; may take a clause as object*) to reproduce (the words, sounds, etc.) uttered by someone else; echo. **5.** (*tr.*) to utter (a poem, speech, etc.) from memory; recite. **6.** (*intr.*) **a.** (of food) to be tasted again after ingestion as the result of belching or slight regurgitation. **b.** to belch. **7.** (*tr.; may take a clause as object*) to tell to another person (the words, esp. secrets, imparted to one by someone else). **8.** (*intr.*) (of a clock) to strike the hour or quarter-hour just past, when a spring is pressed. **9.** (*intr.*) *U.S.* to vote (illegally) more than once in a single election. **10. repeat oneself.** to say or do the same thing more than once, esp. so as to be tedious. ~*n.* **11. a.** the act or an instance of repeating. **b.** (*as modifier*): *a repeat performance.* **12.** a word, action, etc., that is repeated. **13.** an order made out for goods, provisions, etc., that duplicates a previous order. **14.** a duplicate copy of something; reproduction. **15.** *Radio, television.* a second broadcast of a programme, film, etc., which has already been broadcast before. **16.** *Music.* a passage that is an exact restatement of the passage preceding it. [C14: from Old French *repeter,* from Latin *repetere* to seek again, from RE- + *petere* to seek] —**re₊ˌpeat₊a·ˈbil₊i·ty** *n.* —**re₊ˈpeat₊a·ble** *adj.*

re₊peat₊ed (rɪˈpiːtɪd) *adj.* done, made, or said again and again; continual or incessant. —**re₊ˈpeat₊ed₊ly** *adv.*

re₊peat₊er (rɪˈpiːtə) *n.* **1.** a person or thing that repeats. **2.** Also called: **repeating firearm.** a firearm capable of discharging several shots without reloading. **3.** a timepiece having a mechanism enabling it to strike the hour or quarter-hour just past, when a spring is pressed. **4.** *Electrical engineering.* a device that amplifies or augments incoming electrical signals and retransmits them, thus reducing power loss. **5.** Also called: **substitute.** *Nautical.* one of three signal flags hoisted with others to indicate that one of the top three is to be repeated.

re₊peat₊ing dec·i₊mal *n.* another name for **recurring decimal.**

rep₊e·chage (ˌrɛpɪˈʃɑːʒ) *n.* a heat of a competition, esp. in rowing or fencing, in which eliminated contestants have another chance to qualify for the next round or the final. [C19: from French *repêchage* literally: fishing out again, from RE- + *pêcher* to fish + -AGE]

re₊pel (rɪˈpɛl) *vb.* **₊pels, ₊pel₊ling, ₊pelled.** (*mainly tr.*) **1.** to force or drive back (something or somebody, esp. an attacker). **2.** (*also intr.*) to produce a feeling of aversion or distaste in (someone or something); be disgusting (to). **3.** to push aside; dismiss: *he repelled the rumour of their divorce.* **4.** to be effective in keeping away, controlling, or resisting: *an aerosol spray that repels flies.* **5.** to have no affinity for; fail to mix with or absorb: *water and oil repel each other.* **6.** to disdain to accept (something); turn away from or spurn: *she repelled his advances.* **7.** (*also intr.*) to exert an opposing force on (something): *an electric charge repels another charge of the same sign.* [C15: from Latin *repellere,* from RE- + *pellere* to push, drive] —**re₊ˈpel₊ler** *n.* —**re₊ˈpel₊ling₊ly** *adv.*

re₊pel₊lent (rɪˈpɛlənt) *adj.* **1.** giving rise to disgust or aversion; distasteful or repulsive. **2.** driving or forcing away or back; repelling. ~*n. also* **re₊pel₊lant. 3.** something, esp. a chemical substance, that repels: *insect repellent.* **4.** a substance with which fabrics are treated to increase their resistance to water. —**re₊ˈpel₊lence** *or* **re₊ˈpel₊len·cy** *n.* —**re₊ˈpel₊lent₊ly** *adv.*

re₊pent[1] (rɪˈpɛnt) *vb.* to feel remorse (for); be contrite (about); show penitence (for): *he repents of his extravagance; he repented his words.* [C13: from Old French *repentir,* from RE- + *pentir* to be contrite, from Latin *paenitēre* to repent] —**re₊ˈpent₊er** *n.*

re₊pent[2] (ˈriːpᵊnt) *adj. Botany.* lying or creeping along the ground; reptant: *repent stems.* [C17: from Latin *rēpere* to creep]

re₊pent₊ance (rɪˈpɛntəns) *n.* **1.** remorse or contrition for one's past actions or sins. **2.** an act or the process of being repentant; penitence.

re₊pent₊ant (rɪˈpɛntənt) *adj.* **1.** reproaching oneself for one's past actions or sins; contrite. **2.** characterized by or proceeding from a sense of contrition: *a repentant heart; his repentant words.* —**re₊ˈpent₊ant₊ly** *adv.*

re₊per₊cus₊sion (ˌriːpəˈkʌʃən) *n.* **1.** (*often pl.*) a result or consequence, esp. one that is somewhat removed from the action or event which precipitated it: *the repercussions of the war are still keenly felt.* **2.** recoil after impact; rebound. **3.** a reflection, esp. of sound; echo or reverberation. **4.** *Music.* the reappearance of a fugal subject and answer after an episode. [C16: from Latin *repercussiō,* from *repercutere* to strike back; see PERCUSSION] —**ˌre₊per₊ˈcus₊sive** *adj.*

rep₊er₊toire (ˈrɛpəˌtwɑː) *n.* **1.** all the plays, songs, operas, or other works collectively that a company, actor, singer, dancer, etc., has prepared and is competent to perform. **2.** the entire stock of things available in a field or of a kind: *the comedian's repertoire of jokes was becoming stale.* [C19: from French, from Late Latin *repertōrium* inventory; see REPERTORY]

rep₊er₊to·ry (ˈrɛpətərɪ, -trɪ) *n., pl.* **-ries. 1.** the entire stock of things available in a field or of a kind; repertoire. **2.** a building or place where a stock of things is kept; repository. **3.** short for **repertory company.** [C16: from Late Latin *repertōrium* storehouse, from Latin *reperīre* to obtain, from RE- + *parere* to bring forth] —**ˌrep₊er₊ˈto₊ri·al** *adj.*

rep₊er₊to·ry com₊pa₊ny *n.* a theatrical company that performs plays from a repertoire, esp. at its own theatre. U.S. name: **stock company.**

rep₊e·tend (ˈrɛpɪˌtɛnd, ˌrɛpɪˈtɛnd) *n.* **1.** *Maths.* the digit or series of digits in a recurring decimal that repeats itself. **2.** anything repeated. [C18: from Latin *repetendum* what is to be repeated, from *repetere* to REPEAT]

ré₊pé₊ti₊teur *French.* (repetiˈtœr) *n.* a member of an opera company who accompanies rehearsals on the piano and coaches the singers. —***ré₊pé₊ti₊teuse*** (repetiˈtøz) *fem. n.*

rep₊e·ti₊tion (ˌrɛpɪˈtɪʃən) *n.* **1.** the act or an instance of repeating; reiteration. **2.** a thing, word, action, etc., that is repeated. **3.** a replica or copy. **4.** *Civil and Scot. law.* the recovery or repayment of money paid or received by mistake, as when the same bill has been paid twice.

rep₊e·ti₊tious (ˌrɛpɪˈtɪʃəs) *adj.* characterized by unnecessary repetition. —**ˌrep₊e·ˈti₊tious₊ly** *adv.* —**ˌrep₊e·ˈti₊tious₊ness** *n.*

re₊pet·i₊tive (rɪˈpɛtɪtɪv) *adj.* characterized by or given to repetition: *a repetitive rhythm.* —**re₊ˈpet·i₊tive₊ly** *adv.* —**re₊ˈpet·i₊tive₊ness** *n.*

re₊phrase (riːˈfreɪz) *vb.* (*tr.*) to phrase again, esp. so as to express more clearly.

re₊pine (rɪˈpaɪn) *vb.* (*intr.*) to be fretful or low-spirited through discontent. [C16: from RE- + PINE[2]]

re₊place (rɪˈpleɪs) *vb.* (*tr.*) **1.** to take the place of; supersede: *the manual worker is being replaced by the machine.* **2.** to substitute a person or thing for (another which has ceased to fulfil its function); put in place of: *to replace an old pair of shoes.* **3.** to put back or return; restore to its rightful place. —**re₊ˈplace₊a·ble** *adj.* —**re₊ˌplace₊a·ˈbil₊i·ty** *n.* —**re₊ˈplac₊er** *n.*

re₊place₊ment (rɪˈpleɪsmənt) *n.* **1.** the act or process of replacing. **2.** a person or thing that replaces another. **3.** *Geology.* the growth of a mineral within another of different chemical composition by gradual simultaneous deposition and removal.

re₊play *n.* (ˈriːˌpleɪ). **1.** Also called: **action replay.** *Television.* a showing again of a sequence of action, esp. of part of a sporting contest in slow motion immediately after it happens. **2.** a rematch. ~*vb.* (riːˈpleɪ). **3.** to play again (a record, television sequence, sporting contest, etc.).

re₊plen₊ish (rɪˈplɛnɪʃ) *vb.* (*tr.*) **1.** to make full or complete again by supplying what has been used up or is lacking. **2.** to put fresh fuel on (a fire). [C14: from Old French *replenir,* from RE- + *plenir* to fill, from Latin *plēnus* full] —**re₊ˈplen₊ish₊er** *n.* —**re₊ˈplen₊ish₊ment** *n.*

re₊plete (rɪˈpliːt) *adj.* (*usually postpositive*) **1.** (often foll. by *with*) copiously supplied (with); abounding (in). **2.** having one's appetite completely or excessively satisfied by food and drink; stuffed; gorged; satiated. [C14: from Latin *replētus,* from *replēre* to refill, from RE- + *plēre* to fill] —**re₊ˈplete₊ly** *adv.* —**re₊ˈplete₊ness** *n.*

re₊ple₊tion (rɪˈpliːʃən) *n.* **1.** the state or condition of being replete; fullness, esp. excessive fullness due to overeating. **2.** the satisfaction of a need or desire.

re₊plev₊in (rɪˈplɛvɪn) *Law.* ~*n.* **1.** the recovery of goods unlawfully taken, made subject to establishing the validity of the recovery in a legal action and returning the goods if the decision is adverse. **2.** (formerly) a writ of replevin. ~*vb.* **3.** another word for **replevy.** [C15: from Anglo-French, from Old French *replevir* to give security for, from RE- + *plevir* to PLEDGE]

re₊plev·y (rɪˈplɛvɪ) *Law.* ~*vb.* **₊plev·ies, ₊plev·y₊ing, ₊plev₊ied.** (*tr.*) **1.** to recover possession of (goods) by replevin. ~*n., pl.* **₊plev·ies. 2.** another word for **replevin.** [C15: from Old French *replevir; see* REPLEVIN] —**re₊ˈplev·i₊a·ble** *or* **re₊ˈplev₊is₊a·ble** *adj.*

rep₊li₊ca (ˈrɛplɪkə) *n.* an exact copy or reproduction, esp. on a smaller scale. [C19: from Italian, literally: a reply, from *replicare* to repeat, from Latin: to bend back, repeat]

rep₊li₊cate *vb.* (ˈrɛplɪˌkeɪt). (*mainly tr.*) **1.** (*also intr.*) to make or be a copy of; reproduce. **2.** to fold (something) over on itself; bend back. **3.** to reply to. ~*adj.* (ˈrɛplɪkɪt). **4.** folded back on itself: *a replicate leaf.* [C19: from Latin *replicātus* bent back; see REPLICA] —**ˈrep₊li₊ca₊tive** *adj.*

rep₊li₊ca₊tion (ˌrɛplɪˈkeɪʃən) *n.* **1.** a reply or response. **2.** *Law.* (formerly) the plaintiff's reply to a defendant's answer or plea. **3.** *Biology.* the production of exact copies of complex molecules, such as DNA molecules, that occurs during growth of living tissue. **4.** repetition of a procedure, such as a scientific

---

re₊ˈpave *vb.*
re₊ˈpeo₊ple *vb.*
re₊ˈpin *vb.,* **₊pins, ₊pin₊ning, ₊pinned.**
re₊ˈplan *vb.,* **₊plans, ₊plan₊ning, ₊planned.**
re₊ˈplant *vb.*
re₊ˈpol₊ish *vb.*

experiment, in order to reduce errors. **5.** a less common word for **replica.** [C14: via Old French from Latin *replicātiō* a folding back, from *replicāre* to unroll; see REPLY]

re·ply (rɪˈplaɪ) *vb.* **·plies, ·ply·ing, ·plied.** (*mainly intr.*) **1.** to make answer (to) in words or writing or by an action; respond: *he replied with an unexpected move.* **2.** (*tr.; takes a clause as object*) to say (something) in answer to: *he replied that he didn't want to come.* **3.** *Law.* to answer a defendant's plea. **4.** to return (a sound); echo. ~*n., pl.* **·plies. 5.** an answer made in words or writing or through an action; response. **6.** the answer made by a plaintiff or petitioner to a defendant's case. [C14: from Old French *replier* to fold again, reply, from Latin *replicāre* to fold back, from RE- + *plicāre* to fold] —**reˈpli·er** *n.*

re·point (ˌriːˈpɔɪnt) *vb.* (*tr.*) to repair the joints of (brickwork, masonry, etc.) with mortar or cement.

re·pone (rɪˈpəʊn) *vb.* (*tr.*) *Scot. law.* to restore (someone) to his former status, office, etc.; rehabilitate. [C16: from Latin *repōnere* to put back, replace]

re·port (rɪˈpɔːt) *n.* **1.** an account prepared for the benefit of others, esp. one that provides information obtained through investigation and published in a newspaper or broadcast. **2.** a statement made widely known; rumour: *according to report, he is not dead.* **3.** an account of the deliberations of a committee, body, etc.: *a report of parliamentary proceedings.* **4.** *Brit.* a statement on the progress, academic achievement, etc., of each child in a school, written by teachers and sent to the parents or guardian annually or each term. **5.** a written account of a case decided at law, giving the main points of the argument on each side, the court's findings, and the decision reached. **6.** comment on a person's character or actions; reputation: *he is of good report here.* **7.** a sharp loud noise, esp. one made by a gun. ~*vb.* (when *tr., may take a clause as object;* when *intr.,* often foll. by *on*) **8.** to give an account (of); describe. **9.** to give an account of the results of an investigation (into): *to report on housing conditions.* **10.** (of a committee, legislative body, etc.) to make a formal report on (a bill). **11.** (*tr.*) to complain about (a person), esp. to a superior: *I'll report you to the teacher.* **12.** (*tr.*) to reveal information about (a fugitive, escaped prisoner, etc.) esp. concerning his whereabouts. **13.** to present (oneself) or be present at an appointed place or for a specific purpose: *report to the manager's office.* **14.** (*intr.*) to say or show that one is (in a certain state): *to report fit.* **15.** (*intr.*) to act as a reporter for a newspaper or for radio or television. **16.** *Law.* to take down in writing details of (the proceedings of a court of law, etc.) as a record or for publication. [C14: from Old French, from *reporter* to carry back, from Latin *reportāre,* from RE- + *portāre* to carry] —**reˈport·a·ble** *adj.*

re·port·age (rɪˈpɔːtɪdʒ, ˈrəpɔːˈtɑːʒ) *n.* **1.** the act or process of reporting news or other events of general interest. **2.** a journalist's style of reporting. **3.** a technique of documentary film or photo journalism that tells a story entirely through pictures.

re·port·ed·ly (rɪˈpɔːtɪdlɪ) *adv.* according to rumour or report: *he is reportedly living in Australia.*

re·port·ed speech *n.* another term for **indirect speech.**

re·port·er (rɪˈpɔːtə) *n.* **1.** a person who reports, esp. one employed to gather news for a newspaper, news agency, or broadcasting organization. **2.** a person, esp. a barrister, authorized to write official accounts of judicial proceedings. **3.** a person authorized to report the proceedings of a legislature.

re·por·to·ri·al (rɪpɔːˈtɔːrɪəl) *adj. Chiefly U.S.* of or relating to a newspaper reporter. [C20: from REPORTER, influenced by EDITORIAL] —**re·porˈto·ri·al·ly** *adv.*

re·port stage *n.* the stage preceding the third reading in the passage of a bill through Parliament, at which the bill, as amended in committee, is reported back to the chamber considering it.

re·pose[1] (rɪˈpəʊz) *n.* **1.** a state of quiet restfulness; peace or tranquillity. **2.** dignified calmness of manner; composure. ~*vb.* **3.** to place (oneself or one's body) in a state of quiet relaxation; lie or lay down at rest. **4.** (*intr.*) to lie when dead, as in the grave. **5.** *Formal.* (*intr.;* foll. by *on, in,* etc.) to take support (from) or be based (on): *your plan reposes on a fallacy.* [C15: from Old French *reposer,* from Late Latin *repausāre,* from RE- + *pausāre* to stop; see PAUSE] —**reˈpos·al** *n.* —**re·pos·ed·ly** (rɪˈpəʊzɪdlɪ) *adv.* —**reˈpos·er** *n.* —**reˈpose·ful** *adj.* —**reˈpose·ful·ly** *adv.* —**reˈpose·ful·ness** *n.*

re·pose[2] (rɪˈpəʊz) *vb.* (*tr.*) **1.** to put (trust or confidence) in a person or thing. **2.** to place or put (an object) somewhere. [C15: from Latin *repōnere* to store up, from RE- + *pōnere* to put] —**reˈpo·sal** *n.*

re·pos·it (rɪˈpɒzɪt) *vb.* (*tr.*) to put away, deposit, or store up. [C17: from Latin *repositus* replaced, from *repōnere;* see REPOSE[2], POSIT]

re·po·si·tion (ˌriːpəˈzɪʃən) *n.* **1.** the act or process of depositing or storing. **2.** *Surgery.* the return of a broken or displaced organ, or part to its normal site. **3.** *Archaic.* the reinstatement of a person in a post or office. ~*vb.* **4.** (*tr.*) to place in a new position.

re·pos·i·to·ry (rɪˈpɒzɪtərɪ, -trɪ) *n., pl.* **·ries. 1.** a place or container in which things can be stored for safety. **2.** a place where things are kept for exhibition; museum. **3.** a place where commodities are kept before being sold; warehouse. **4.** a place of burial; sepulchre. **5.** a receptacle containing the relics of the dead. **6.** a person to whom a secret is entrusted; confidant. [C15: from Latin *repositōrium,* from *repōnere* to place]

re·pos·sess (ˌriːpəˈzɛs) *vb.* (*tr.*) **1.** to take back possession of (property), esp. for nonpayment of money due under a hire-purchase agreement. **2.** to restore ownership of (something) to someone. —**re·pos·ses·sion** (ˌriːpəˈzɛʃən) *n.* —ˌ**re·posˈses·sor** *n.*

re·pot (riːˈpɒt) *vb.* **·pots, ·pot·ting, ·pot·ted.** (*tr.*) to put (a house plant) into a new usually larger pot.

re·pous·sé (rəˈpuːseɪ) *adj.* **1.** raised in relief, as a design on a thin piece of metal hammered through from the underside. **2.** decorated with such designs. ~*n.* **3.** a design or surface made in this way. **4.** the technique of hammering designs in this way. [C19: from French, from *repousser* to push back, from RE- + *pousser* to PUSH]

repp (rɛp) *n.* a variant spelling of **rep**[1]. —**repped** *adj.*

repr. *abbrev. for:* **1.** represented. **2.** representing. **3.** reprint(ed).

rep·re·hend (ˌrɛprɪˈhɛnd) *vb.* (*tr.*) to find fault with; criticize. [C14: from Latin *reprehendere* to hold fast, rebuke, from RE- + *prendere* to grasp] —ˌ**rep·reˈhend·a·ble** *adj.* —ˌ**rep·reˈhend·er** *n.* —**rep·re·hen·so·ry** (ˌrɛprɪˈhɛnsərɪ) *adj.*

rep·re·hen·si·ble (ˌrɛprɪˈhɛnsəbᵊl) *adj.* open to criticism or rebuke; blameworthy. [C14: from Late Latin *reprehensibilis,* from Latin *reprehendere* to hold back, reprove; see REPREHEND] —ˌ**rep·re**ˌ**hen·si·ˈbil·i·ty** *or* ˌ**rep·reˈhen·si·ble·ness** *n.* —ˌ**rep·reˈhen·si·bly** *adv.*

rep·re·hen·sion (ˌrɛprɪˈhɛnʃən) *n.* the act or an instance of reprehending; reproof or rebuke. —ˌ**rep·reˈhen·sive** *adj.* —ˌ**rep·reˈhen·sive·ly** *adv.*

rep·re·sent (ˌrɛprɪˈzɛnt) *vb.* (*tr.*) **1.** to stand as an equivalent of; correspond to: *our tent represents home to us when we go camping.* **2.** to act as a substitute or proxy (for). **3.** to act as or be the authorized delegate or agent for (a person, country, etc.): *an M.P. represents his constituency.* **4.** to serve or use as a means of expressing: *letters represent the sounds of speech.* **5.** to exhibit the characteristics of; exemplify; typify: *romanticism in music is represented by Beethoven.* **6.** to present an image of through the medium of a picture or sculpture; portray. **7.** to bring clearly before the mind. **8.** to set forth in words; state or explain. **9.** to describe as having a specified character or quality; make out to be: *he represented her as a saint.* **10.** to act out the part of on stage; portray. **11.** to perform or produce (a play); stage. [C14: from Latin *repraesentāre* to exhibit, from RE- + *praesentāre* to PRESENT[2]] —ˌ**rep·reˈsent·a·ble** *adj.* —ˌ**rep·re**ˌ**sent·a·ˈbil·i·ty** *n.*

re-pres·ent (ˌriːprɪˈzɛnt) *vb.* (*tr.*) to present again. —**re-pres·en·ta·tion** (ˌriːprɛzənˈteɪʃən) *n.*

rep·re·sen·ta·tion (ˌrɛprɪzɛnˈteɪʃən) *n.* **1.** the act or instance of representing or the state of being represented. **2.** anything that represents, such as a verbal or pictorial portrait. **3.** anything that is represented, such as an image brought clearly to mind. **4.** the principle by which delegates act for a constituency. **5.** a body of representatives. **6.** *Contract law.* an assertion of fact made by one party to induce another to enter into a contract. **7.** an instance of acting for another, on his authority, in a particular capacity, such as executor or administrator. **8.** a dramatic production or performance. **9.** (*often pl.*) a statement of facts, true or alleged, esp. one set forth by way of remonstrance or expostulation. **10.** *Linguistics.* an analysis of a word, sentence, etc., into its constituents: *phonetic representation.*

rep·re·sen·ta·tion·al (ˌrɛprɪzɛnˈteɪʃənᵊl) *adj.* **1.** *Fine art.* depicting or attempting to depict objects, scenes, figures, etc., directly as seen; naturalistic. **2.** of or relating to representation.

rep·re·sen·ta·tion·al·ism (ˌrɛprɪzɛnˈteɪʃənəˌlɪzəm) *or* **rep·re·sen·ta·tion·ism** *n.* **1.** *Philosophy.* the doctrine that objects are not identical with our perceptions of them but are either true copies of them or representations modified by the nature of the mind. Compare **presentationism. 2.** *Fine art.* the practice or advocacy of attempting to depict objects, scenes, figures, etc., directly as seen. —ˌ**rep·re·sen**ˌ**ta·tion·alˈis·tic** *adj.* —ˌ**rep·re·senˈta·tion·ist** *n., adj.*

rep·re·sent·a·tive (ˌrɛprɪˈzɛntətɪv) *n.* **1.** a person or thing that represents another or others. **2.** a person who represents and tries to sell the products or services of a firm, esp. a travelling salesman. Often shortened to **rep. 3.** a typical example. **4.** a person representing a constituency in a deliberative, legislative, or executive body, esp. (*cap.*) a member of the **House of Representatives** (the lower house of Congress). ~*adj.* **5.** serving to represent; symbolic. **6.** exemplifying a class or kind; typical. **7.** acting as deputy or proxy for another or others. **8.** acting for or representing a constituency or the whole people in the process of government: *a representative council.* **9.** of, characterized by, or relating to the political principle of representation of the people: *representative government.* **10.** of or relating to a mental picture or representation. —ˌ**rep·reˈsent·a·tive·ly** *adv.* —ˌ**rep·reˈsent·a·tive·ness** *n.*

re·press (rɪˈprɛs) *vb.* (*tr.*) **1.** to keep (feelings, etc.) under control; suppress or restrain: *to repress a desire.* **2.** to put into a state of subjugation: *to repress a people.* **3.** *Psychol.* to banish (thoughts and impulses that conflict with conventional standards of conduct) from one's conscious mind. [C14: from Latin *reprimere* to press back, from RE- + *premere* to PRESS[1]] —**reˈpress·er** *or* **reˈpres·sor** *n.* —**reˈpress·i·ble** *adj.* —**reˈpres·sion** *n.* —**reˈpres·sive** *adj.* —**reˈpres·sive·ly** *adv.* —**reˈpres·sive·ness** *n.*

re-press (riːˈprɛs) *vb.* (*tr.*) to press again, esp. to reproduce more copies of a gramophone record by a second pressing.

re·prieve (rɪˈpriːv) *vb.* (*tr.*) **1.** to postpone or remit the punishment of (a person, esp. one condemned to death). **2.** to give temporary relief to (a person or thing), esp. from otherwise irrevocable harm: *the government has reprieved the company with a huge loan.* ~*n.* **3.** a postponement or remission of punishment, esp. of a person condemned to death. **4.** a warrant granting a postponement. **5.** a temporary relief from pain or harm; respite. **6.** the act of reprieving or the state of being reprieved. [C16: from Old French *repris* (something) taken back, from *reprendre* to take back, from Latin *reprehendere;* perhaps also influenced by obsolete English *repreve* to reprove] —**re+'priev+a·ble** *adj.* —**re+'priev+er** *n.*

rep+ri+mand ('rɛprɪˌmɑːnd) *n.* **1.** a reproof or formal admonition; rebuke. ~*vb.* **2.** (*tr.*) to admonish or rebuke, esp. formally; reprove. [C17: from French *réprimande*, from Latin *reprimenda* (things) to be repressed; see REPRESS] —**'rep+ri+ˌmand+er** *n.* —**ˌrep+ri+'mand+ing+ly** *adv.*

re+print *n.* ('riːˌprɪnt). **1.** a reproduction in print of any matter already published; offprint. **2.** a reissue of a printed work using the same type, plates, etc., as the original. ~*vb.* (riː'prɪnt). **3.** (*tr.*) to print again. —**re+'print+er** *n.*

re+pris+al (rɪ'praɪzᵊl) *n.* **1.** (*often pl.*) retaliatory action against an enemy in wartime, such as the execution of prisoners of war, destruction of property, etc. **2.** the act or an instance of retaliation in any form. **3.** (formerly) the forcible seizure of the property or subjects of one nation by another. [C15: from Old French *reprisaille*, from Old Italian *ripresaglia*, from *riprendere* to recapture, from Latin *reprehendere* to hold fast; see REPREHEND]

re+prise (rɪ'priːz) *Music.* ~*n.* **1.** the repeating of an earlier theme. ~*vb.* **2.** to repeat (an earlier theme). [C14: from Old French, from *reprendre* to take back, from Latin *reprehendere;* see REPREHEND]

re+pro ('riːprəʊ) *n., pl.* **+pros.** **1.** short for **reproduction** (sense 2): *repro furniture.* **2.** short for **reproduction proof.**

re+proach (rɪ'prəʊtʃ) *vb.* (*tr.*) **1.** to impute blame to (a person) for an action or fault; rebuke. **2.** *Archaic.* to bring disgrace or shame upon. ~*n.* **3.** the act of reproaching. **4.** rebuke or censure; reproof: *words of reproach.* **5.** disgrace or shame: *to bring reproach upon one's family.* **6.** something that causes or merits blame, rebuke, or disgrace. **7. above** *or* **beyond reproach,** perfect; beyond criticism. [C15: from Old French *reprochier,* from Latin RE- + *prope* near] —**re+'proach+a·ble** *adj.* —**re+'proach+a·ble+ness** *n.* —**re+'proach+a·bly** *adv.* —**re+'proach+er** *n.* —**re+'proach+ing+ly** *adv.*

re+proach+ful (rɪ'prəʊtʃfʊl) *adj.* **1.** full of or expressing reproach. **2.** *Archaic.* deserving of reproach; disgraceful. —**re+'proach+ful+ly** *adv.* —**re+'proach+ful+ness** *n.*

rep+ro+bate ('rɛprəʊˌbeɪt) *adj.* **1.** morally unprincipled; depraved. **2.** *Christianity.* destined or condemned to eternal punishment in hell. ~*n.* **3.** an unprincipled, depraved, or damned person. **4.** a disreputable or roguish person: *the old reprobate.* ~*vb.* (*tr.*) **5.** to disapprove of; condemn. **6.** (of God) to destine, consign, or condemn to eternal punishment in hell. [C16: from Late Latin *reprobātus* held in disfavour, from Latin RE- + *probāre* to APPROVE] —**rep+ro+ba+cy** ('rɛprəbəsɪ) *n.* —**'rep+ro+ˌbat+er** *n.*

rep+ro+ba+tion (ˌrɛprəʊ'beɪʃən) *n.* **1.** disapproval, blame, or censure. **2.** *Christianity.* condemnation to eternal punishment in hell; rejection by God. —**rep+ro+ba+tive** ('rɛprəbətɪv) *or* **ˌrep+ro+'ba+tion+ar·y** *adj.* —**'rep+ro+ba+tive+ly** *adv.*

re+pro+duce (ˌriːprə'djuːs) *vb.* (*mainly tr.*) **1.** to make a copy, representation, or imitation of; duplicate. **2.** (*also intr.*) *Biology.* to undergo or cause to undergo a process of reproduction. **3.** to produce or exhibit again. **4.** to bring back into existence again; re-create. **5.** to bring before the mind again (a scene, event, etc.) through memory or imagination. **6.** (*intr.*) to come out (well, badly, etc.), when copied. **7.** to replace (damaged parts or organs) by a process of natural growth; regenerate. —**ˌre+pro+'duc+er** *n.* —**ˌre+pro+'duc+i·ble** *adj.* —**ˌre+pro+'duc+i·bly** *adv.* —**ˌre+pro+ˌduc+i·'bil+i·ty** *n.*

re+pro+duc+tion (ˌriːprə'dʌkʃən) *n.* **1.** *Biology.* any of various processes, either sexual or asexual, by which an animal or plant produces one or more individuals similar to itself. **2. a.** an imitation or facsimile of a work of art, esp. of a picture made by photoengraving. **b.** (*as modifier*): *a reproduction portrait.* **3.** the act or process of reproducing. **4.** the state of being reproduced. **5.** a revival of an earlier production, as of a play.

re+pro+duc+tion proof *n. Printing.* a proof of very good quality used for photographic reproduction to make a printing plate. Sometimes shortened to **repro** or **repro proof.**

re+pro+duc+tive (ˌriːprə'dʌktɪv) *adj.* of, relating to, characteristic of, or taking part in reproduction. —**ˌre+pro+'duc+tive+ly** *adv.* —**ˌre+pro+'duc+tive+ness** *n.*

re+prog+ra+phy (rɪ'prɒgrəfɪ) *n.* the art or process of copying, reprinting, or reproducing printed material. —**rep+ro+graph+ic** (ˌrɛprə'græfɪk) *adj.* —**ˌrep+ro+'graph·i+cal+ly** *adv.*

re+proof (rɪ'pruːf) *n.* an act or expression of rebuke or censure. Also: **re+prov+al** (rɪ'pruːvᵊl). [C14: *reproffe,* from Old French *reprove,* from Late Latin *reprobāre* to disapprove of; see REPROBATE]

re-proof (riː'pruːf) *vb.* (*tr.*) **1.** to treat (a garment, etc.) so as to renew its texture, waterproof qualities, etc. **2.** to provide a new proof of (a book, galley, etc.)

re+prove (rɪ'pruːv) *vb.* (*tr.*) to speak disapprovingly to (a person); rebuke or scold. [C14: from Old French *reprover,* from Late Latin *reprobāre,* from Latin RE- + *probāre* to examine, APPROVE] —**re+'prov+a·ble** *adj.* —**re+'prov+er** *n.* —**re+'prov+ing+ly** *adv.*

rept. *abbrev. for:* **1.** receipt. **2.** report.

rep+tant ('rɛptənt) *adj. Biology.* creeping, crawling, or lying along the ground. Also: **repent.** [C17: from Latin *reptāre* to creep]

rep+tile ('rɛptaɪl) *n.* **1.** any of the cold-blooded vertebrates constituting the class *Reptilia,* characterized by lungs, an outer covering of horny scales or plates, and young produced in amniotic eggs. The class today includes the tortoises, turtles, snakes, lizards, and crocodiles; in Mesozoic times it was the dominant group, containing the dinosaurs and related forms. **2.** a grovelling insignificant person: *you miserable little reptile!* ~*adj.* **3.** creeping, crawling, or squirming. **4.** grovelling or insignificant; mean; contemptible. [C14: from Late Latin *reptilis* creeping, from Latin *rēpere* to crawl]

rep+til+i·an (rɛp'tɪlɪən) *adj. also* **rep+ti+loid** ('rɛptɪˌlɔɪd). **1.** of, relating to, resembling, or characteristic of reptiles. **2.** mean or treacherous; contemptible: *reptilian behaviour.* ~*n.* **3.** a less common name for **reptile.**

Repub. *abbrev. for:* **1.** Republic. **2.** Republican.

re+pub+lic (rɪ'pʌblɪk) *n.* **1.** a form of government in which the people or their elected representatives possess the supreme power. **2.** a political or national unit possessing such a form of government. **3.** a constitutional form in which the head of state is an elected or nominated president. **4.** any community or group that resembles a political republic in that its members or elements exhibit a general equality, shared interests, etc.: *the republic of letters.* [C17: from French *république,* from Latin *rēspublica* literally: the public thing, from *rēs* thing + *publica* PUBLIC]

re+pub+li+can (rɪ'pʌblɪkən) *adj.* **1.** of, resembling, or relating to a republic. **2.** supporting or advocating a republic. ~*n.* **3.** a supporter or advocate of a republic.

Re+pub+li+can (rɪ'pʌblɪkən) *adj.* **1.** of, belonging to, or relating to a Republican Party. **2.** of, belonging to, or relating to the Irish Republican Army. ~*n.* **3.** a member or supporter of a Republican Party. **4.** a member or supporter of the Irish Republican Army.

re+pub+li+can+ism (rɪ'pʌblɪkəˌnɪzəm) *n.* **1.** the principles or theory of republican government. **2.** support for a republic. **3.** (*often cap.*) support for a Republican Party or for the Irish Republican Army.

re+pub+li+can+ize *or* **re+pub+li+can+ise** (rɪ'pʌblɪkəˌnaɪz) *vb.* (*tr.*) to make republican. —**re+ˌpub+li+can·i+'za+tion** *or* **re+ˌpub+li+can·i+'sa+tion** *n.*

Re+pub+li+can Par+ty *n.* **1.** one of the two major political parties in the U.S.: established around 1854. Compare **Democratic Party.** **2.** any of a number of political parties in other countries, usually so named to indicate their opposition to monarchy. **3.** *U.S. history.* another name for the **Democratic-Republican Party.**

re+pu+di+ate (rɪ'pjuːdɪˌeɪt) *vb.* (*tr.*) **1.** to reject the authority or validity of; refuse to accept or ratify: *Congress repudiated the treaty that the President had negotiated.* **2.** to refuse to acknowledge or pay (a debt). **3.** to cast off or disown (a son, lover, etc.). [C16: from Latin *repudiāre* to put away, from *repudium* a separation, divorce, from RE- + *pudēre* to be ashamed] —**re+'pu+di·a+ble** *adj.* —**re+ˌpu+di·'a+tion** *n.* —**re+'pu+di·a+tive** *or* **re+'pu+di·a+to+ry** *adj.* —**re+'pu+di·ˌa+tor** *n.*

re+pugn (rɪ'pjuːn) *vb. Archaic.* to oppose or conflict (with). [C14: from Old French *repugner,* from Latin *repugnāre* to fight against, from RE- + *pugnāre* to fight]

re+pug+nant (rɪ'pʌgnənt) *adj.* **1.** repellent to the senses; causing aversion. **2.** distasteful; offensive; disgusting. **3.** contradictory; inconsistent or incompatible. [C14: from Latin *repugnāns* resisting; see REPUGN] —**re+'pug+nance** *or* **re+'pug+nan+cy** *n.* —**re+'pug+nant+ly** *adv.*

re+pulse (rɪ'pʌls) *vb.* (*tr.*) **1.** to drive back or ward off (an attacking force); repel; rebuff. **2.** to reject with coldness or discourtesy: *she repulsed his advances.* ~*n.* **3.** the act or an instance of driving back or warding off; rebuff. **4.** a cold discourteous rejection or refusal. [C16: from Latin *repellere* to drive back, REPEL] —**re+'puls+er** *n.*

Usage. The verbs *repulse* and *repel* share a common meaning of physically driving back or away, but they can be carefully distinguished in other senses. Although the related adjective *repulsive* has the meaning of causing feelings of disgust, *repulse* does not mean to drive away by arousing disgust. Instead, *repel* is normally used in this sense, and *repulse* is used when the required meaning is to reject coldly or drive away with discourtesy.

re+pul+sion (rɪ'pʌlʃən) *n.* **1.** a feeling of disgust or aversion. **2.** *Physics.* a force tending to separate two objects, such as the force between two like electric charges or magnetic poles.

re+pul+sive (rɪ'pʌlsɪv) *adj.* **1.** causing or occasioning repugnance; loathsome; disgusting or distasteful: *a repulsive sight.* **2.** tending to repel, esp. by coldness and discourtesy. **3.** *Physics.* concerned with, producing, or being a repulsion. —**re+'pul+sive+ly** *adv.* —**re+'pul+sive+ness** *n.*

rep+u·ta+ble ('rɛpjʊtəbᵊl) *adj.* **1.** having a good reputation; honoured, trustworthy, or respectable. **2.** (of words) acceptable as good usage; standard. —**ˌrep+u·ta·'bil+i·ty** *or* **'rep+u+ta·ble+ness** *n.* —**'rep+u·ta·bly** *adv.*

rep+u·ta+tion (ˌrɛpjʊ'teɪʃən) *n.* **1.** the estimation in which a person or thing is generally held; opinion. **2.** a high opinion generally held about a person or thing; esteem. **3.** notoriety or fame, esp. for some specified characteristic. **4. have a reputation.** to be known or notorious, esp. for promiscuity, excessive drinking, or the like. [C14: from Latin *reputātiō* a reckoning, from *reputāre* to calculate, meditate; see REPUTE] —**ˌrep+u+'ta+tion+less** *adj.*

re+pute (rɪ'pjuːt) *vb.* **1.** (*tr.; usually passive*) to consider (a

---

re+'pop+u+ˌlate *vb.*
re+'price *vb.*
re+'pro+cess *vb.*
ˌre+pro+'vi+sion *vb.*
ˌre+pub+li+'ca+tion *n.*
re+'pub+lish *vb.*
re+'pub+lish+a·ble *adj.*
re+'pur+chase *vb.*

person or thing) to be as specified: *he is reputed to be intelligent.* ~*n.* **2.** public estimation; reputation: *a writer of little repute.* [C15: from Old French *reputer,* from Latin *reputāre* to think over, from RE- + *putāre* to think]

re+put+ed (rɪˈpjuːtɪd) *adj.* (*prenominal*) generally reckoned or considered; supposed or alleged: *he is the reputed writer of two epic poems.* —**re'put+ed+ly** *adv.*

req. *abbrev. for:* **1.** request. **2.** required. **3.** requisition.

re+quest (rɪˈkwɛst) *vb.* (*tr.*) **1.** to express a desire for, esp. politely; ask for or demand: *to request a bottle of wine.* ~*n.* **2. a.** the act or an instance of requesting, esp. in the form of a written statement, etc.; petition or solicitation: *a request for a song.* **b.** (*as modifier*): *a request programme.* **3. at the request of.** in accordance with the specific demand or wish of (someone). **4. by request.** in accordance with someone's desire. **5. in request.** in demand; popular: *he is in request in concert halls all over the world.* **6. on request.** on the occasion of a demand or request: *application forms are available on request.* [C14: from Old French *requeste,* from Vulgar Latin *requaerere* (unattested) to seek after; see REQUIRE, QUEST] —**re'quest+er** *n.*

re+quest stop *n.* a point on a route at which a bus, etc., will stop only if signalled to do so. U.S. equivalent: **flag stop.**

Req·ui+em (ˈrɛkwɪˌɛm) *n.* **1.** *R.C. Church.* a Mass celebrated for the dead. **2.** a musical setting of this Mass. **3.** any piece of music composed or performed as a memorial to a dead person or persons. [C14: from Latin *requiēs* rest, from the opening of the introit, *Requiem aeternam dona eis* Rest eternal grant unto them]

req·ui+em shark *n.* any shark of the family *Carcharhinidae,* occurring mostly in tropical seas and characterized by a nictitating membrane and a heterocercal tail. The family includes the tiger shark and the soupfin.

req·ui+es+cat (ˌrɛkwɪˈɛskæt) *n.* a prayer for the repose of the souls of the dead. [Latin, from *requiescat in pace* may he rest in peace]

re+quire (rɪˈkwaɪə) *vb.* (*mainly tr.; may take a clause as object or an infinitive*) **1.** to have need of; depend upon; want. **2.** to impose as a necessity; make necessary: *this work requires precision.* **3.** (*also intr.*) to make formal request (for); insist upon or demand, esp. as an obligation. **4.** to call upon or oblige (a person) authoritatively; order or command: *to require someone to account for his actions.* [C14: from Old French *requerre,* from Vulgar Latin *requaerere* (unattested) to seek after, from Latin *requīrere* to seek to know, but also influenced by *quaerere* to seek] —**re'quir+a·ble** *adj.* —**re'quir+er** *n.*

re+quire+ment (rɪˈkwaɪəmənt) *n.* **1.** something demanded or imposed as an obligation: *Latin is no longer a requirement for entry to university.* **2.** a thing desired or needed. **3.** the act or an instance of requiring.

req·ui+site (ˈrɛkwɪzɪt) *adj.* **1.** absolutely essential; indispensable. ~*n.* **2.** something indispensable; necessity. [C15: from Latin *requīsītus* sought after, from *requīrere* to seek for, REQUIRE] —**'req·ui+site+ly** *adv.* —**'req·ui+site+ness** *n.*

req·ui+si+tion (ˌrɛkwɪˈzɪʃən) *n.* **1.** a request or demand, esp. an authoritative or formal one. **2.** an official form on which such a demand is made. **3.** the act of taking something over, esp. temporarily for military or public use in time of emergency. **4.** a necessary or essential condition; requisite. **5.** a formal request by one government to another for the surrender of a fugitive from justice. ~*vb.* (*tr.*) **6.** to demand and take for use or service, esp. by military or public authority. **7.** (*may take an infinitive*) to require (someone) formally to do (something): *to requisition a soldier to drive a staff officer's car.* —**ˌreq·ui'si+tion+ar·y** *adj.* —**ˌreq·ui'si+tion+er** *or* **ˌreq·ui'si+tion+ist** *n.*

re+quit+al (rɪˈkwaɪtᵊl) *n.* **1.** the act or an instance of requiting. **2.** a return or compensation for a good or bad action.

re+quite (rɪˈkwaɪt) *vb.* (*tr.*) to make return to (a person for a kindness or injury); repay with a similar action. [C16: RE- + obsolete *quite* to discharge, repay; see QUIT] —**re'quit+a·ble** *adj.* —**re'quite+ment** *n.* —**re'quit+er** *n.*

re+ra+di+a+tion (ˌriːreɪdɪˈeɪʃən) *n.* radiation resulting from the previous absorption of primary radiation.

rere+dos (ˈrɪədɒs) *n.* **1.** a screen or wall decoration at the back of an altar, in the form of a hanging, tapestry, painting, or piece of metalwork or sculpture. **2.** another word for **fireback.** [C14: from Old French *areredos,* from *arere* behind + *dos* back, from Latin *dorsum*]

rere+mouse *or* **rear+mouse** (ˈrɪəˌmaʊs) *n., pl.* **+mice.** an archaic or dialect word for **bat** (the animal). [Old English *hrēremūs,* probably from *hrēran* to move + *mūs* MOUSE]

re+run *vb.* (riːˈrʌn), **+runs, +run+ning, +ran.** (*tr.*) **1.** to broadcast or put on (a film, play, series, etc.) again. **2.** to run (a race, etc.) again. ~*n.* (ˈriːˌrʌn). **3.** a film, play, series, etc., that is broadcast or put on again; repeat. **4.** a race that is run again.

res (reɪs) *n., pl.* **res.** *Latin.* a thing, matter, or object.

res. *abbrev. for:* **1.** research. **2.** reserve. **3.** residence. **4.** resides. **5.** resigned. **6.** resolution.

res ad+ju+di+ca+ta (ˈreɪs əˌdʒuːdɪˈkɑːtə) *n.* another term for **res judicata.**

re+sale (ˈriːˌseɪl, riːˈseɪl) *n.* the selling again of something purchased. —**re'sal+a·ble** *or* **re'sale+a·ble** *adj.*

re+sale price main+te+nance *n.* the practice by which a manufacturer establishes a fixed or minimum price for the resale of a brand product by retailers or other distributors. U.S. equivalent: **fair trade.** Abbrev.: **r.p.m.**

re+scind (rɪˈsɪnd) *vb.* (*tr.*) to annul or repeal. [C17: from Latin *rēscindere* to cut off, from *re-* (intensive) + *scindere* to cut] —**re'scind+a·ble** *adj.* —**re'scind+er** *n.* —**re'scind+ment** *n.*

re+scis+si·ble (rɪˈsɪsəbᵊl) *adj.* able to be rescinded.

re+scis+sion (rɪˈsɪʒən) *n.* the act of rescinding.

re+scis+so·ry (rɪˈsɪsərɪ) *adj.* having the power to rescind.

re+script (ˈriːˌskrɪpt) *n.* **1.** (in ancient Rome) an ordinance taking the form of a reply by the emperor to a question on a point of law. **2.** any official announcement or edict; a decree. **3.** something rewritten. **4.** the act or process of rewriting. [C16: from Latin *rēscriptum* a reply, from *rēscribere* to write back]

res+cue (ˈrɛskjuː) *vb.* **+cues, +cu+ing, +cued.** (*tr.*) **1.** to bring (someone or something) out of danger, attack, harm, etc.; deliver or save. **2.** to free (a person) from legal custody by force. **3.** *Law.* to seize (goods or property) by force. ~*n.* **4. a.** the act or an instance of rescuing. **b.** (*as modifier*): *a rescue party.* **5.** the forcible removal of a person from legal custody. **6.** *Law.* the forcible seizure of goods or property. [C14: *rescowen,* from Old French *rescourre,* from RE- + *escourre* to pull away, from Latin *excutere* to shake off, from *quatere* to shake] —**'res+cu+a·ble** *adj.* —**'res+cu+er** *n.*

re+search (rɪˈsɜːtʃ) *n.* **1.** systematic investigation to establish facts or principles or to collect information on a subject. ~*vb.* **2.** to carry out investigations into (a subject, problem, etc.). [C16: from Old French *recercher* to seek, search again, from RE- + *cercher* to SEARCH] —**re'search+a·ble** *adj.* —**re'search+er** *n.*

re+seat (riːˈsiːt) *vb.* (*tr.*) **1.** to show (a person) to a new seat. **2.** to put a new seat on (a chair, etc.). **3.** to provide new seats for (a hall, theatre, etc.). **4.** to re-form the seating of (a valve).

re+seau (ˈrɛzəʊ) *n., pl.* **+seaux** (-zəʊ, -zəʊz) *or* **+seaus. 1.** a mesh background to a lace or other pattern. **2.** *Astronomy.* a network of fine lines cut into a glass plate used as a reference grid on star photographs. **3.** *Photog.* a screen covered in a regular pattern of minute coloured dots or lines, formerly used in colour photography. [French, from Old French *resel* a little net, from *rais* net, from Latin *rēte*]

re+sect (rɪˈsɛkt) *vb. Surgery.* to cut out part of a bone, organ, or other structure or part. [C17: from Latin *resecāre* to cut away, from RE- + *secāre* to cut]

re+sec+tion (rɪˈsɛkʃən) *n.* **1.** *Surgery.* excision of part of a bone, organ, or other part. **2.** *Surveying.* a method of fixing the position of a point by making angular observations to three fixed points. —**re'sec+tion+al** *adj.*

res+e·da (ˈrɛsɪdə) *n.* **1.** any plant of the genus *Reseda,* of the Mediterranean region, including mignonette and dyer's rocket, which has small spikes of grey-green flowers. ~*adj.* **2.** of a greyish-green colour; mignonette. [C18: from New Latin, from Latin: heal! from *resēdāre* to assuage, from RE- + *sēdāre* to soothe; see SEDATE²]

re+sem+blance (rɪˈzɛmbləns) *n.* **1.** the state or quality of resembling; likeness or similarity in nature, appearance, etc. **2.** the degree or extent to which or the respect in which a likeness exists. **3.** something resembling something else; semblance; likeness. —**re'sem+blant** *adj.*

re+sem+ble (rɪˈzɛmbᵊl) *vb.* (*tr.*) to possess some similarity to; be like. [C14: from Old French *resembler,* from RE- + *sembler* to look like, from Latin *similis* like] —**re'sem+bler** *n.*

re+sent (rɪˈzɛnt) *vb.* (*tr.*) to feel bitter, indignant, or aggrieved at. [C17: from French *ressentir,* from RE- + *sentir* to feel, from Latin *sentīre* to perceive; see SENSE]

re+sent+ful (rɪˈzɛntfʊl) *adj.* feeling or characterized by resentment. —**re'sent+ful+ly** *adv.* —**re'sent+ful+ness** *n.*

re+sent+ment (rɪˈzɛntmənt) *n.* anger, bitterness, or ill will.

re+ser+pine (ˈrɛsəpɪn) *n.* an insoluble alkaloid, extracted from the roots of the plant *Rauwolfia serpentina,* used medicinally to lower blood pressure and as a sedative and tranquillizer. Formula: $C_{33}H_{40}N_2O_9$; melting pt.: 264–5°C. [C20: from German *Reserpin,* probably from the New Latin name of the plant]

res+er+va+tion (ˌrɛzəˈveɪʃən) *n.* **1.** the act or an instance of reserving. **2.** something reserved, esp. hotel accommodation, a seat on an aeroplane, in a theatre, etc. **3.** (*often pl.*) a stated or unstated qualification of opinion that prevents one's wholehearted acceptance of a proposal, claim, statement, etc. **4.** an area of land set aside, esp. (in the U.S.) for American Indian peoples. **5.** *Brit.* the strip of land between the two carriageways of a dual carriageway. **6.** the act or process of keeping back, esp. for oneself; withholding. **7.** *Law.* a right or interest retained by the grantor in property granted, conveyed, leased, etc., to another: *a reservation of rent.*

re+serve (rɪˈzɜːv) *vb.* (*tr.*) **1.** to keep back or set aside, esp. for future use or contingency; withhold. **2.** to keep for oneself; retain: *I reserve the right to question these men later.* **3.** to obtain or secure by advance arrangement: *I have reserved two tickets for tonight's show.* **4.** to delay delivery of (a judgment), esp. in order to allow time for full consideration of the issues involved. ~*n.* **5. a.** something kept back or set aside, esp. for future use or contingency. **b.** (*as modifier*): *a reserve stock.* **6.** the state or condition of being reserved: *I have plenty in reserve.* **7.** a tract of land set aside for wild animals, flowers, etc.: *a nature reserve.* **8.** *Austral.* a public park. **9.** the act of reserving; reservation. **10.** a member of a team who only plays if a playing member drops out; a substitute. **11.** (*often pl.*) **a.** a part of an army or formation not committed to immediate action in a military engagement. **b.** that part of a nation's armed services not in active service. **12.** coolness or formality

---

re+'pur+i+fy *vb.* **+fies, +fy+ing, +fied.**
re+'quick+en *vb.*
re+'read *vb.,* **+reads, +read+ing, +read.**
re+'route *vb.*
re+'sched+ule *vb.*
re+'seal *vb.*
re+'seal+a·ble *adj.*
re-'search *vb.*
re+'sell *vb.,* **+sells, +sell+ing, +sold.**

of manner; restraint, silence, or reticence. **13.** *Finance.* **a.** a portion of capital not invested (a **capital reserve**) or a portion of profits not distributed (a **revenue** or **general reserve**) by a bank or business enterprise and held to meet legal requirements, future liabilities, or contingencies. **b.** liquid assets held by an organization, government, etc., to meet expenses and liabilities. **14. without reserve.** without reservations; fully; wholeheartedly. [C14: from Old French *reserver,* from Latin *reservāre* to save up, from RE- + *servāre* to keep] —**re'serv·a·ble** *adj.* —**re'serv·er** *n.*

re-serve (riː'sɜːv) *vb. (tr.)* to serve again.

re·serve bank *n.* one of the twelve banks forming part of the U.S. Federal Reserve System.

re·serve cur·ren·cy *n.* foreign currency that is acceptable as a medium of international payments and that is therefore held in reserve by many countries.

re·served (rɪ'zɜːvd) *adj.* **1.** set aside for use by a particular person or people: *this table is reserved.* **2.** cool or formal in manner; restrained, silent, or reticent. **3.** destined; fated: *a man reserved for great things.* —**re·serv·ed·ly** (rɪ'zɜːvɪdlɪ) *adv.* —**re'serv·ed·ness** *n.*

re·served list *n. Brit.* a list of retired naval, army, or air-force officers available for recall to active service in an emergency.

re·served oc·cu·pa·tion *n. Brit.* (formerly) an occupation from which one will not be called up for military service.

re·serve price *n. Brit.* the minimum price acceptable to the owner of property being auctioned. U.S. equivalent: **upset price.**

re·serv·ist (rɪ'zɜːvɪst) *n.* one who serves in the reserve formations of a nation's armed forces.

res·er·voir ('rɛzəˌvwɑː) *n.* **1.** a natural or artificial lake or large tank used for collecting and storing water, esp. for community water supplies or irrigation. **2.** a receptacle for storing gas, esp. one attached to a stove. **3.** *Biology.* a vacuole or cavity in an organism, containing a secretion or some other fluid. **4.** *Anatomy.* another name for **cisterna. 5.** a place where a great stock of anything is accumulated. **6.** a large supply of something; reserve: *a reservoir of talent.* [C17: from French *réservoir,* from *réserver* to RESERVE]

re·set *vb.* (riː'sɛt), **·sets, ·set·ting, ·set.** *(tr.)* **1.** to set again (a broken bone, matter in type, a gemstone, etc.). **2.** to restore (a gauge, dial, etc.) to zero. ~*n.* ('riːˌsɛt). **3.** the act or an instance of setting again. **4.** a thing that is set again. **5.** a plant that has been recently transplanted. **6.** a device for resetting instruments, controls, etc. —**re'set·ter** *n.*

res ges·tae ('reɪs 'dʒɛstiː) *pl. n.* **1.** things done or accomplished; achievements. **2.** *Law.* incidental facts and circumstances that are admissible in evidence because they introduce or explain the matter in issue. [Latin]

resh (reɪʃ; *Hebrew* rɛʃ) *n.* the 20th letter in the Hebrew alphabet (ר), transliterated as *r.* [from Hebrew, from *rōsh* head]

re·shape (riː'ʃeɪp) *vb. (tr.)* to shape again or differently.

Resht (rɛʃt) *n.* a variant spelling of **Rasht.**

re·shuf·fle (riː'ʃʌfᵊl) *n.* **1.** an act of shuffling again. **2.** a reorganization, esp. of jobs within a government or cabinet. ~*vb.* **3.** *(tr.)* to carry out a reshuffle (on).

re·side (rɪ'zaɪd) *vb. (intr.) Formal.* **1.** to live permanently or for a considerable time (in a place); have one's home (in): *he now resides in London.* **2.** (of things, qualities, etc.) to be inherently present (in); be vested (in): *political power resides in military strength.* [C15: from Latin *residēre* to sit back, from RE- + *sedēre* to sit] —**re'sid·er** *n.*

res·i·dence ('rɛzɪdəns) *n.* **1.** the place in which one resides; abode or home. **2.** a large imposing house; mansion. **3.** the fact of residing in a place or a period of residing. **4.** the official house of the governor of any of various countries. **5.** the state of being officially present (esp. in the phrase **in residence**). **6.** the seat of some inherent quality, etc.

res·i·den·cy ('rɛzɪdənsɪ) *n., pl.* **·cies. 1.** a variant of **residence. 2.** *U.S.* the period, following internship, during which a physician undergoes further clinical training, usually in one medical speciality. **3.** (in India, formerly) the official house of the governor general at the court of a native prince.

res·i·dent ('rɛzɪdənt) *n.* **1.** a person who resides in a place. **2.** (esp. formerly) a representative of the British government in a British protectorate. **3.** (esp. in the 17th century) a diplomatic representative ranking below an ambassador. **4.** (in India, formerly) a representative of the British governor general at the court of a native prince. **5.** a bird or other animal that does not migrate. **6.** *U.S.* a physician who lives in the hospital where he works while undergoing specialist training after completing his internship. Compare **house physician.** ~*adj.* **7.** living in a place; residing. **8.** living or staying at a place in order to discharge a duty, etc. **9.** (of qualities, characteristics, etc.) existing or inherent (in). **10.** (of birds and other animals) not in the habit of migrating. —**'res·i·dent·ˌship** *n.*

res·i·dent com·mis·sion·er *n.* the representative of Puerto Rico in the U.S. House of Representatives. He may speak but has no vote.

res·i·den·tial (ˌrɛzɪ'dɛnʃəl) *adj.* **1.** suitable for or allocated for residence: *a residential area.* **2.** relating to or having residence. —ˌ**res·i'den·tial·ly** *adv.*

res·i·den·tiar·y (ˌrɛzɪ'dɛnʃərɪ) *adj.* **1.** residing in a place, esp. officially; resident. **2.** subject to an obligation to reside in an official residence: *a residentiary benefice.* ~*n., pl.* **·tiar·ies. 3.** a clergyman obliged to reside in the place of his official appointment.

re·sid·u·al (rɪ'zɪdjʊəl) *adj.* **1.** of, relating to, or designating a residue or remainder; remaining; left over. **2.** (of deposits, soils, etc.) formed by the weathering of pre-existing rocks and the removal of disintegrated material. **3.** *U.S.* of or relating to the payment of residuals. ~*n.* **4.** something left over as a residue; remainder. **5.** *Statistics.* **a.** the difference between the mean of a set of observations and one particular observation. **b.** the difference between the numerical value of one particular observation and the theoretical result. **6.** *(often pl.) U.S.* payment made by the sponsor of a television programme to an actor or actress for subsequent use of film in which the actor or actress appears. —**re'sid·u·al·ly** *adv.*

re·sid·u·ar·y (rɪ'zɪdjʊərɪ) *adj.* **1.** of, relating to, or constituting a residue; residual. **2.** *Law.* entitled to the residue of an estate after payment of debts and distribution of specific gifts.

res·i·due ('rɛzɪˌdjuː) *n.* **1.** matter remaining after something has been removed. **2.** *Law.* what is left of an estate after the discharge of debts and distribution of specific gifts. [C14: from Old French *residu,* from Latin *residuus* remaining over, from *residēre* to stay behind, RESIDE]

re·sid·u·um (rɪ'zɪdjʊəm) *n., pl.* **·u·a** (-jʊə). a more formal word for **residue.**

re·sign (rɪ'zaɪn) *vb.* **1.** (when *intr.,* often foll. by *from*) to give up tenure of (a job, office, etc.). **2.** *(tr.)* to reconcile (oneself) to; yield: *to resign oneself to death.* **3.** *(tr.)* to give up (a right, claim, etc.); relinquish: *he resigned his claim to the throne.* [C14: from Old French *resigner,* from Latin *resignāre* to unseal, invalidate, destroy, from RE- + *signāre* to seal; see SIGN] —**re'sign·er** *n.*

re-sign (riː'saɪn) *vb.* to sign (a document, etc.) again.

res·ig·na·tion (ˌrɛzɪg'neɪʃən) *n.* **1.** the act of resigning. **2.** a formal document stating one's intention to resign. **3.** a submissive unresisting attitude; passive acquiescence.

re·signed (rɪ'zaɪnd) *adj.* characteristic of or proceeding from an attitude of resignation; acquiescent or submissive. —**re·sign·ed·ly** (rɪ'zaɪnɪdlɪ) *adv.* —**re'sign·ed·ness** *n.*

re·sile (rɪ'zaɪl) *vb. (intr.)* to spring or shrink back; recoil or resume original shape. [C16: from Old French *resilir* from Latin *resilīre* to jump back, from RE- + *salīre* to jump] —**re'sile·ment** *n.*

re·sil·i·ent (rɪ'zɪlɪənt) *adj.* **1.** (of an object or material) capable of regaining its original shape or position after bending, stretching, compression, or other deformation; elastic. **2.** (of a person) recovering easily and quickly from shock, illness, hardship, etc.; irrepressible. —**re'sil·i·ence** *or* **re'sil·i·en·cy** *n.* —**re'sil·i·ent·ly** *adv.*

res·in ('rɛzɪn) *n.* **1.** Also called: **rosin.** any of a group of solid or semisolid amorphous compounds that are obtained directly from certain plants as exudations. They are used in medicine and in varnishes. **2.** any of a large number of synthetic, usually organic, materials that have a polymeric structure, esp. such a substance in a raw state before it is moulded or treated with plasticizer, stabilizer, filler, etc. Compare **plastic** (sense 1). ~*vb.* **3.** *(tr.)* to treat or coat with resin. [C14: from Old French *resine,* from Latin *rēsīna,* from Greek *rhētinē* resin from a pine] —**'res·in·ous** *adj.* —**'res·in·ous·ly** *adv.* —**'res·in·ous·ness** *n.*

res·in·ate ('rɛzɪˌneɪt) *vb. (tr.)* to impregnate with resin.

res·in·if·er·ous (ˌrɛzɪ'nɪfərəs) *adj.* yielding or producing resin.

res·in·oid ('rɛzɪˌnɔɪd) *adj.* **1.** resembling, characteristic of, or containing resin. ~*n.* **2.** any resinoid substance, esp. a synthetic compound.

res·i·pis·cence (ˌrɛsɪ'pɪsəns) *n. Literary.* acknowledgement that one has been mistaken. [C16: from Late Latin *resipiscentia,* from *resipiscere* to recover one's senses, from Latin *sapere* to know] —ˌ**res·i'pis·cent** *adj.*

res ip·sa loq·ui·tur *Law.* the thing or matter speaks for itself. [Latin]

re·sist (rɪ'zɪst) *vb.* **1.** to stand firm (against); not yield (to); fight (against). **2.** *(tr.)* to withstand the deleterious action of; be proof against: *to resist corrosion.* **3.** *(tr.)* to oppose; refuse to accept or comply with: *to resist arrest; resist the introduction of new technology.* **4.** *(tr.)* to refrain from, esp. in spite of temptation (esp. in the phrases **cannot** or **could not resist (something)**). ~*n.* **5.** a substance used to protect something, esp. a coating that prevents corrosion. [C14: from Latin *resistere* to stand still, oppose, from RE- + *sistere* to stand firm] —**re'sist·er** *n.* —**re'sist·i·ble** *adj.* —**re**ˌ**sist·i'bil·i·ty** *or* **re'sist·i·ble·ness** *n.* —**re'sist·i·bly** *adv.*

re·sist·ance (rɪ'zɪstəns) *n.* **1.** the act or an instance of resisting. **2.** the capacity to withstand something, esp. the body's natural capacity to withstand disease. **3. a.** the opposition to a flow of electric current through a circuit component, medium, or substance. It is the magnitude of the real part of the impedance and is measured in ohms. Symbol: *R* Compare **reactance** (sense 1). **b.** *(as modifier): resistance coupling; a resistance thermometer.* **4.** any force that tends to retard or oppose motion: *air resistance; wind resistance.* **5.** (in psychoanalytical theory) the tendency of a person to prevent the translation of repressed thoughts and ideas from the unconscious to the conscious. **6.** *Physics.* the magnitude of the real part of the acoustic or mechanical impedance. **7. line of least resistance.** the easiest, but not necessarily the best or most honourable, course of action. **8.** See **passive resistance.**

Re·sist·ance (rɪ'zɪstəns) *n.* **the.** an illegal organization fighting for national liberty in a country under enemy occupation, esp. in France during World War II.

re'set·tle *vb.*
re'set·tle·ment *n.*
re'shape *vb.*
re'sharp·en *vb.*
re'ship *vb.* **·shod.**
re'shoe *vb.,* **·shoes, ·shoe·ing,** **re'site** *vb.*

re+sist+ance ther+mom+e·ter *n.* an accurate type of thermometer in which temperature is calculated from the resistance of a coil of wire (usually of platinum) or of a semiconductor placed at the point at which the temperature is to be measured.

re+sist+ance weld+ing *n.* a welding technique in which the parts to be joined are held together under pressure and heat is produced by passing a current through the contact resistance formed between the two surfaces.

re+sist+ant (rɪˈzɪstənt) *or* **re+sis+tive** *adj.* **1.** characterized by or showing resistance; resisting. **2. a.** impervious to the action of corrosive substances, heat, etc.: *a highly resistant surface.* **b.** (*in combination*): *a heat-resistant surface.* ~*n.* **3.** a person or thing that resists. —**re+ˈsist+ant+ly** *or* **re+ˈsis+tive+ly** *adv.* —**re+ˈsis+tive+ness** *n.*

Re+sis+ten+cia (*Spanish* ˌresisˈtenθja) *n.* a city in NE Argentina, on the Paraná River. Pop.: 142 736 (1970).

re+sis+tiv+i·ty (ˌriːzɪsˈtɪvɪtɪ) *n.* **1.** the electrical resistance that a unit volume of a particular material offers to the flow of current at 0°C. It is equal to *RA/l*, where *R* is the resistance, *A* the cross-sectional area, and *l* the length, and is the reciprocal of conductivity. It is measured in ohm meters. Symbol: ρ Former name: **specific resistance. 2.** the power or capacity to resist; resistance.

re+sist+less (rɪˈzɪstlɪs) *adj. Archaic.* **1.** unresisting. **2.** irresistible. —**re+ˈsist+less+ly** *adv.*

re+sis+tor (rɪˈzɪstə) *n.* an electrical component designed to introduce a known value of resistance into a circuit.

re+sit (riːˈsɪt) *vb.* **+sits, +sit+ting, +sat.** (*tr.*) to sit (an examination) again.

res ju+di+ca+ta (ˈreɪs ˌdʒuːdɪˈkɑːtə) *or* **res ad+ju+di+ca+ta** *n. Law.* a matter already adjudicated upon that cannot be raised again. [Latin]

Res·nais (*French* rɛˈnɛ) *n.* **Al·ain** (aˈlɛ̃). born 1922, French film director, whose films include *Hiroshima mon amour* (1959) and *L'Année dernière à Marienbad* (1961).

res+na+tron (ˈrɛznəˌtrɒn) *n.* a tetrode used to generate high power at high frequencies. [C20: from RESONATOR + -TRON]

re+sol+u·ble (rɪˈzɒljʊbᵊl, ˈrɛzəl-) *or* **re+solv+a·ble** *adj.* able to be resolved or analysed. [C17: from Late Latin *resolubilis*, from Latin *resolvere* to reveal; see RESOLVE] —**re+ˌsol+u·ˈbil+i·ty, re+ˌsolv+a·ˈbil+i·ty** *or* **re+ˈsol+u·ble+ness, re+ˈsolv+a·ble+ness** *n.*

re-sol·u·ble (riːˈsɒljʊbᵊl) *adj.* capable of being dissolved again. —**re-ˈsol·u·ble+ness** *or* **re-ˌsol·u·ˈbil+i·ty** *n.* —**re-ˈsol·u·bly** *adv.*

res·o+lute (ˈrɛzəˌluːt) *adj.* **1.** firm in purpose or belief; steadfast. **2.** characterized by resolution; determined: *a resolute answer.* [C16: from Latin *resolutus*, from *resolvere* to RESOLVE] —**ˈres·o+ˌlute+ly** *adv.* —**ˈres·o+ˌlute+ness** *n.*

res·o+lu+tion (ˌrɛzəˈluːʃən) *n.* **1.** the act or an instance of resolving. **2.** the condition or quality of being resolute; firmness or determination. **3.** something resolved or determined; decision. **4.** a formal expression of opinion by a meeting, esp. one agreed by a vote. **5.** a judicial decision on some matter; verdict; judgment. **6.** the act or process of separating something into its constituent parts or elements. **7.** *Med.* **a.** return from a pathological to a normal condition. **b.** subsidence of the symptoms of a disease, esp. the disappearance of inflammation without the formation of pus. **8.** *Music.* the process in harmony whereby a dissonant note or chord is followed by a consonant one. **9.** *Physics.* another word for **resolving power.** —ˌ**res·o+ˈlu+tion+er** *or* ˌ**res·o+ˈlu+tion+ist** *n.*

re+sol+u+tive (rɪˈzɒljʊtɪv) *adj.* capable of dissolving; causing disintegration.

re+solve (rɪˈzɒlv) *vb.* (*mainly tr.*) **1.** (*takes a clause as object or an infinitive*) to decide or determine firmly. **2.** to express (an opinion) formally, esp. (of a public meeting) one agreed by a vote. **3.** (*also intr.;* usually foll. by *into*) to separate or cause to separate (into) (constituent parts or elements). **4.** (*usually reflexive*) to change, alter, or appear to change or alter: *the ghost resolved itself into a tree.* **5.** to make up the mind of; cause to decide: *the tempest resolved him to stay at home.* **6.** to find the answer or solution to; solve: *to resolve a problem.* **7.** to explain away or dispel: *to resolve a doubt.* **8.** to bring to an end; conclude: *to resolve an argument.* **9.** *Med.* to cause (a swelling or inflammation) to subside, esp. without the formation of pus. **10.** (*also intr.*) to follow (a dissonant note or chord) or (of a dissonant note or chord) to be followed by one producing a consonance. **11.** *Chem.* to separate (a racemic mixture) into its optically active constituents. **12.** *Physics.* **a.** to distinguish between (separate parts) of (an image) as in a microscope, telescope, or other optical instrument. **b.** to separate (two adjacent peaks) in a spectrum by means of a spectrometer. **13.** *Maths.* to split (a vector) into its components in specified directions. **14.** an obsolete word for **dissolve.** ~*n.* **15.** something determined or decided; resolution: *he had made a resolve to work all day.* **16.** firmness of purpose; determination: *nothing can break his resolve.* [C14: from Latin *resolvere* to unfasten, reveal, from RE- + *solvere* to loosen; see SOLVE] —**re+ˈsolv·a·ble** *adj.* —**re+ˌsolv+a·ˈbil+i·ty** *or* **re+ˈsolv+a·ble+ness** *n.* —**re+ˈsolv+er** *n.*

re+solved (rɪˈzɒlvd) *adj.* fixed in purpose or intention; determined. —**re+solv+ed+ly** (rɪˈzɒlvɪdlɪ) *adv.* —**re+ˈsolv+ed+ness** *n.*

re+sol+vent (rɪˈzɒlvənt) *adj.* **1.** serving to dissolve or separate something into its elements; resolving. ~*n.* **2.** something that resolves; solvent. **3.** a drug or agent able to reduce swelling or inflammation.

re+solv+ing pow+er *n.* **1.** Also called: **resolution.** *Physics.* **a.** the ability of a microscope, telescope, or other optical instrument to produce separate images of closely placed objects. **b.** the ability of a spectrometer to separate two adjacent peaks in a spectrum. **2.** *Photog.* the ability of an emulsion to show up fine detail in an image.

res·o+nance (ˈrɛzənəns) *n.* **1.** the condition or quality of being resonant. **2.** sound produced by a body vibrating in sympathy with a neighbouring source of sound. **3.** the condition of a body or system when it is subjected to a periodic disturbance of the same frequency as the natural frequency of the body or system. At this frequency the system displays an entranced oscillation or vibration. **4.** amplification of speech sounds by sympathetic vibration in the bone structure of the head and chest, resounding in the cavities of the nose, mouth, and pharynx. **5.** *Electronics.* the condition of an electrical circuit when the frequency is such that the capacitive reactance is just balanced by the inductive reactance, leading to relatively large alternating currents. **6.** *Med.* the sound heard when tapping a hollow bodily structure, esp. the chest or abdomen. Change in the quality of the sound often indicates an underlying disease or disorder. **7.** *Chem.* the phenomenon in which the electronic structure of a molecule can be represented by two or more hypothetical structures involving single, double, and triple chemical bonds. The true structure is considered to be an average of these theoretical structures. **8.** *Physics.* **a.** the condition of a system in which there is a sharp maximum probability for the absorption of electromagnetic radiation or capture of particles. **b.** a type of elementary particle of extremely short lifetime. Resonances are regarded as excited states of more stable particles. [C16: from Latin *resonāre* to RESOUND] —**ˈres·o+nant** *adj.* —**ˈres·o+nant+ly** *adv.*

res·o+nant cav+i·ty *n.* another name for **cavity resonator.**

res·o+nate (ˈrɛzəˌneɪt) *vb.* **1.** to resound or cause to resound; reverberate. **2.** (of a mechanical system, electrical circuit, chemical compound, etc.) to exhibit or cause to exhibit resonance. [C19: from Latin *resonāre*] —ˌ**res·o+ˈna+tion** *n.*

res·o+na+tor (ˈrɛzəˌneɪtə) *n.* any body or system that displays resonance, esp. a tuned electrical circuit or a conducting cavity in which microwaves are generated by a resonant current.

re+sorb (rɪˈsɔːb) *vb.* (*tr.*) to absorb again. [C17: from Latin *resorbēre*, from RE- + *sorbēre* to suck in; see ABSORB] —**re+ˈsorb+ent** *adj.* —**re+ˈsorp+tion** *n.* —**re+ˈsorp+tive** *adj.*

res+or+cin+ol (rɪˈzɔːsɪˌnɒl) *n.* a colourless crystalline phenol with a sweet taste, used in making dyes, drugs, resins, and adhesives. Formula: $C_6H_4(OH)_2$; relative density: 1.27; melting pt.: 111°C; boiling pt.: 178°C (16 mmHg). [C19: New Latin, from RESIN + ORCINOL] —**re+ˈsor+cin+al** *adj.*

re+sort (rɪˈzɔːt) *vb.* (*intr.*) **1.** (usually foll. by *to*) to have recourse (to) for help, use, etc.: *to resort to violence.* **2.** to go, esp. often or habitually; repair: *to resort to the beach.* ~*n.* **3.** a place to which many people go for recreation, etc.: *a holiday resort.* **4.** the use of something as a means, help, or recourse. **5.** the act of going to a place, esp. for recreation, rest, etc. **6. last resort.** the last possible course of action open to one. [C14: from Old French *resortir* to come out again, from RE- + *sortir* to emerge] —**re+ˈsort+er** *n.*

re-sort (riːˈsɔːt) *vb.* (*tr.*) to sort again.

re+sound (rɪˈzaʊnd) *vb.* (*intr.*) **1.** to ring or echo with sound; reverberate: *the hall resounded with laughter.* **2.** to make a prolonged echoing noise: *the trumpet resounded.* **3.** (of sounds) to echo or ring. **4.** to be widely famous: *his achievements resounded throughout India.* [C14: from Old French *resoner*, from Latin *resonāre* to sound again] —**re+ˈsound+ing** *adj.* —**re+ˈsound+ing+ly** *adv.*

re-sound (riːˈsaʊnd) *vb.* to sound or cause to sound again.

re+source (rɪˈzɔːs, -ˈsɔːs) *n.* **1.** capability, ingenuity, and initiative; quick-wittedness: *a man of resource.* **2.** (*often pl.*) a source of economic wealth, esp. of a country (mineral, land, labour, etc.) or business enterprise (capital, equipment, personnel, etc.). **3.** a supply or source of aid or support; something resorted to in time of need. **4.** a means of doing something; expedient. [C17: from Old French *ressourse* relief, from *resourdre* to rise again, from Latin *resurgere*, from RE- + *surgere* to rise] —**re+ˈsource+less** *adj.* —**re+ˈsource+less+ness** *n.*

re+source+ful (rɪˈzɔːsfʊl, -ˈsɔːs-) *adj.* ingenious, capable, and full of initiative, esp. in dealing with difficult situations. —**re+ˈsource+ful+ly** *adv.* —**re+ˈsource+ful+ness** *n.*

resp. *abbrev. for:* **1.** respective(ly). **2.** respondent.

re+spect (rɪˈspɛkt) *n.* **1.** an attitude of deference, admiration, or esteem; regard. **2.** the state of being honoured or esteemed. **3.** a detail, point, or characteristic; particular: *he differs in some respects from his son.* **4.** reference or relation (esp. in the phrases **in respect of, with respect to**). **5.** polite or kind regard; consideration: *respect for people's feelings.* **6.** (*often pl.*) an expression of esteem or regard (esp. in the phrase **pay one's respects**). ~*vb.* (*tr.*) **7.** to have an attitude of esteem towards; show or have respect for: *to respect one's elders.* **8.** to pay proper attention to; not violate: *to respect Swiss neutrality.* **9.** to show consideration for; treat courteously or kindly. **10.** *Archaic.* to concern or refer to. [C14: from Latin *rēspicere* to look back, pay attention to, from RE- + *specere* to look]

re+spect+a·ble (rɪˈspɛktəbᵊl) *adj.* **1.** having or deserving the respect of other people; estimable; worthy. **2.** having good social standing or reputation. **3.** having socially or conventionally acceptable morals, standards, etc.: *a respectable woman.* **4.** relatively or fairly good; considerable: *a respectable salary.* —**re+ˌspect+a·ˈbil+i·ty** *or* **re+ˈspect+a·ble+ness** *n.* —**re+ˈspect+a·bly** *adv.*

re+spect+er (rɪˈspɛktə) *n.* **1.** a person who respects someone or something. **2. no respecter of persons.** a person whose attitude and behaviour is uninfluenced by consideration of another's rank, power, wealth, etc.

re+spect+ful (rɪ'spɛktfʊl) *adj.* full of, showing, or giving respect. —**re+'spect+ful+ly** *adv.* —**re+'spect+ful+ness** *n.*
re+spect+ing (rɪ'spɛktɪŋ) *prep.* concerning; regarding.
re+spec+tive (rɪ'spɛktɪv) *adj.* **1.** belonging or relating separately to each of several people or things; several: *we took our respective ways home.* **2.** an archaic word for **respectful.** —**re+'spec+tive+ness** *n.*
re+spec+tive+ly (rɪ'spɛktɪvlɪ) *adv.* (in listing a number of items or attributes that refer to another list) separately in the order given: *he gave Janet and John a cake and a chocolate respectively.*
Re·spi·ghi (*Italian* res'pi:gi) *n.* **Ot·to·ri·no** (ˌotto'ri:no). 1879–1936, Italian composer, noted esp. for his suites *The Fountains of Rome* (1917) and *The Pines of Rome* (1924).
res+pir+a·ble ('rɛspɪrəbᵊl) *adj.* **1.** able to be breathed. **2.** suitable or fit for breathing. —ˌ**re+spir+a·'bil+i·ty** *n.*
res+pi+ra+tion (ˌrɛspə'reɪʃən) *n.* **1.** the process in living organisms of taking in oxygen from the surroundings and giving out carbon dioxide (**external respiration**). In terrestrial animals this is effected by breathing air. **2.** the chemical breakdown of complex organic substances, such as carbohydrates and fats, that takes place in the cells and tissues of animals and plants, during which energy is released and carbon dioxide produced (**internal respiration**). —**res+pir·a·to·ry** ('rɛspərətərɪ, -trɪ) *or* ˌ**res+pi+'ra+tion+al** *adj.*
res+pi+ra+tor ('rɛspəˌreɪtə) *n.* **1.** an apparatus for providing long-term artificial respiration. **2.** a device worn over the mouth and nose to prevent inhalation of noxious fumes or to warm cold air before it is breathed.
re+spir·a·to·ry quo+tient *n. Biology.* the ratio of the volume of carbon dioxide expired to the volume of oxygen consumed by an organism, tissue, or cell in a given time.
re+spire (rɪ'spaɪə) *vb.* **1.** to inhale and exhale (air); breathe. **2.** (*intr.*) to undergo the process of respiration. **3.** *Literary.* to breathe again in a relaxed or easy manner, as after stress or exertion. [C14: from Latin *rēspīrāre* to exhale, from RE- + *spīrāre* to breathe; see SPIRIT]
res+pite ('rɛspɪt, -paɪt) *n.* **1.** a pause from exertion; interval of rest. **2.** a temporary delay. **3.** a temporary stay of execution; reprieve. ~*vb.* **4.** (*tr.*) to grant a respite to; reprieve. [C13: from Old French *respit,* from Latin *respectus* a looking back; see RESPECT] —**'res+pite+less** *adj.*
re+splend+ent (rɪ'splɛndənt) *adj.* having a brilliant or splendid appearance. [C15: from *rēsplendēre* to shine brightly, from RE- + *splendēre* to shine; see SPLENDOUR] —**re+'splend+ence** *or* **re+'splend+en+cy** *n.* —**re+'splend+ent+ly** *adv.*
re+spond (rɪ'spɒnd) *vb.* **1.** to state or utter (something) in reply. **2.** (*intr.*) to act in reply; react: *to respond by issuing an invitation.* **3.** (*intr.;* foll. by *to*) to react favourably: *this patient will respond to treatment.* **4.** an archaic word for **correspond.** ~*n.* **5.** *Architect.* a pilaster or an engaged column that supports an arch or a lintel. **6.** *Christianity.* a choral anthem chanted in response to a lesson read at a church service. [C14: from Old French *respondre,* from Latin *rēspondēre* to return like for like, from RE- + *spondēre* to pledge; see SPOUSE, SPONSOR] —**re+'spond+ence** *or* **re+'spond+en+cy** *n.* —**re+'spond+er** *n.*
re+spond+ent (rɪ'spɒndənt) *n.* **1.** *Law.* a person against whom a petition, esp. in a divorce suit, or appeal is brought. ~*adj.* **2.** a less common word for **responsive.**
re+sponse (rɪ'spɒns) *n.* **1.** the act of responding; reply or reaction. **2.** *Bridge.* a bid replying to a partner's bid or double. **3.** (*usually pl.*) *Christianity.* a short sentence or phrase recited or sung by the choir or congregation in reply to the officiant at a church service. **4.** *Electronics.* the ratio of the output to the input level, at a particular frequency, of a transmission line or electrical device. **5.** any pattern of glandular, muscular, or electrical reactions that arises from stimulation of the nervous system. [C14: from Latin *rēsponsum* answer, from *rēspondēre* to RESPOND] —**re+'sponse+less** *adj.*
re+spons+er *or* **re+spon+sor** (rɪ'spɒnsə) *n.* a radio or radar receiver used in conjunction with an interrogator to receive and display signals from a transponder.
re+spon+si·bil+i·ty (rɪˌspɒnsə'bɪlɪtɪ) *n., pl.* **·ties. 1.** the state or position of being responsible. **2.** a person or thing for which one is responsible. **3.** the ability or authority to act or decide on one's own, without supervision.
re+spon+si·ble (rɪ'spɒnsəbᵊl) *adj.* **1.** (*postpositive;* usually foll. by *for*) having control or authority (over). **2.** (*postpositive;* foll. by *to*) being accountable for one's actions and decisions (to): *to be responsible to one's commanding officer.* **3.** (of a position, duty, etc.) involving decision and accountability. **4.** (often foll. by *for*) being the agent or cause (of some action): *to be responsible for a mistake.* **5.** able to take rational decisions without supervision; accountable for one's own actions: *a responsible adult.* **6.** able to meet financial obligations; of sound credit. [C16: from Latin *rēsponsus,* from *rēspondēre* to RESPOND] —**re+'spon+si·ble+ness** *n.* —**re+'spon+si·bly** *adv.*
re+spon+sive (rɪ'spɒnsɪv) *adj.* **1.** reacting or replying quickly or favourably, as to a suggestion, initiative, etc. **2.** (of an organism) reacting to a stimulus. —**re+'spon+sive+ly** *adv.* —**re+'spon+sive+ness** *n.*
re+spon+so+ry (rɪ'spɒnsərɪ) *n., pl.* **+ries.** *Christianity.* an anthem or chant consisting of versicles and responses and recited or sung after a lesson in a church service. [C15: from Late Latin *rēsponsōrium,* from Latin *rēspondēre* to answer]
re+spon+sum (rɪ'spɒnsəm) *n., pl.* **+sa** (-sə). a written answer from a rabbinic authority to a question submitted. [Latin, literally: reply, RESPONSE]
res pu+bli+ca *Latin.* ('reɪs 'pʊblɪˌkɑ:) *n.* the state, republic, or commonwealth. [literally: the public thing]
rest[1] (rɛst) *n.* **1. a.** relaxation from exertion or labour. **b.** (*as modifier*): *a rest period.* **2.** repose; sleep. **3.** any relief or refreshment, as from worry or something troublesome. **4.** calm; tranquillity. **5.** death regarded as repose: *eternal rest.* **6.** cessation from motion. **7. at rest. a.** not moving; still. **b.** calm; tranquil. **c.** dead. **d.** asleep. **8.** a pause or interval. **9.** a mark in a musical score indicating a pause of specific duration. **10.** *Prosody.* a pause in or at the end of a line; caesura. **11.** a shelter or lodging: *a seaman's rest.* **12.** a thing or place on which to put something for support or to steady it; prop. **13.** *Billiards.* any of various special sticks used as supports for difficult shots. **14. lay to rest.** to bury (a dead person). **15. set (someone's mind) at rest.** to reassure or settle. ~*vb.* **16.** to take or give rest, as by sleeping, lying down, etc. **17.** to place or position (oneself, etc.) for rest or relaxation. **18.** (*tr.*) to place or position for support or steadying: *to rest one's elbows on the table.* **19.** (*intr.*) to be at ease; be calm. **20.** to cease or cause to cease from motion or exertion; halt. **21.** (*intr.*) to remain without further attention or action: *let the matter rest.* **22.** to direct (one's eyes) or (of one's eyes) to be directed: *her eyes rested on the sleeping child.* **23.** to depend or cause to depend; base; rely: *the whole argument rests on one crucial fact.* **24.** to place or be placed, as blame, censure, etc. **25.** (*intr.;* foll. by *with, on, upon,* etc.) to be a responsibility (of): *it rests with us to apportion blame.* **26.** *Law.* to finish the introduction of evidence in (a case). **27. rest on one's laurels.** to depend on one's past achievements for power, merit, etc. **28. rest on one's oars. a.** to stop rowing for a time. **b.** to stop doing anything for a time. [Old English *ræst, reste,* of Germanic origin; related to Gothic *rasta* a mile, Old Norse *röst* mile] —**'rest+er** *n.*
rest[2] (rɛst) *n.* (usually preceded by *the*) **1.** something left or remaining; remainder. **2.** the others: *the rest of the world.* ~*vb.* **3.** (*copula*) to continue to be (as specified); remain: *rest assured.* [C15: from Old French *rester* to remain, from Latin *rēstāre,* from RE- + *stāre* to STAND]
re+state (ri:'steɪt) *vb.* (*tr.*) to state or affirm again or in a new way. —**re+'state+ment** *n.*
res+tau+rant ('rɛstəˌrɒŋ, 'rɛstrɒŋ, -rɒnt) *n.* a commercial establishment where meals are prepared and served to customers. [C19: from French, from *restaurer* to RESTORE]
res+tau+rant car *n. Brit.* a railway coach in which meals are served. Also called: **dining car.**
res+tau+ra+teur (ˌrɛstərə'tɜ:) *n.* a person who owns or runs a restaurant. [C18: via French from Late Latin *restaurātor* one who restores, from Latin *restaurāre* to RESTORE]
rest-cure *n.* a rest taken as part of a course of medical treatment, as for stress, anxiety, etc.
rest+ful ('rɛstfʊl) *adj.* **1.** giving or conducive to rest. **2.** being at rest; tranquil; calm. —**'rest+ful+ly** *adv.* —**'rest+ful+ness** *n.*
rest+har·row ('rɛstˌhærəʊ) *n.* any of several Eurasian papilionaceous plants of the genus *Ononis,* such as *O. repens* and *O. spinosa,* with tough woody stems and roots. [C16: from *rest,* variant of ARREST (to hinder, stop) + HARROW[1]]
rest-home *n.* an old people's home.
res+ti+form ('rɛstɪˌfɔ:m) *adj.* (esp. of bundles of nerve fibres) shaped like a cord or rope; cordlike. [C19: from New Latin *restiformis,* from Latin *restis* a rope + *forma* shape]
rest+ing ('rɛstɪŋ) *adj.* **1.** not moving or working; at rest. **2.** *Euphemistic.* (of an actor) out of work. **3.** (esp. of plant spores) undergoing a period of dormancy before germination. **4.** (of cells) not undergoing mitosis.
rest+ing place *n.* a place where someone or something rests, esp. (**last resting place**) the grave.
res+ti+tu+tion (ˌrɛstɪ'tju:ʃən) *n.* **1.** the act of giving back something that has been lost or stolen. **2.** *Law.* the act of compensating for loss or injury by reverting as far as possible to the position before such injury occurred. **3.** the return of an object or system to its original state, esp. a restoration of shape after elastic deformation. [C13: from Latin *rēstitūtiō,* from *rēstituere* to rebuild, from RE- + *statuere* to set up] —**'res+ti+ˌtu+tive** *or* ˌ**res+ti+'tu+to·ry** *adj.*
res+tive ('rɛstɪv) *adj.* **1.** restless, nervous, or uneasy. **2.** impatient of control or authority. [C16: from Old French *restif* balky, from *rester* to remain] —**'res+tive+ly** *adv.* —**'res+tive+ness** *n.*
rest+less ('rɛstlɪs) *adj.* **1.** unable to stay still or quiet. **2.** ceaselessly active or moving: *the restless wind.* **3.** worried; anxious; uneasy. **4.** not restful; without repose: *a restless night.* —**'rest+less+ly** *adv.* —**'rest+less+ness** *n.*
rest mass *n.* the mass of an object that is at rest relative to an observer. It is the mass used in Newtonian mechanics.
res+to+ra+tion (ˌrɛstə'reɪʃən) *n.* **1.** the act of restoring or state of being restored, as to a former or original condition, place, etc. **2.** the replacement or giving back of something lost, stolen, etc. **3.** something restored, replaced, or reconstructed. **4.** a model or representation of an extinct animal, landscape of a former geological age, etc.
Res+to+ra+tion (ˌrɛstə'reɪʃən) *n. British history.* **a.** the re-establishment of the monarchy in 1660 or the reign of Charles II (1660–85). **b.** (*as modifier*): *Restoration drama.*
res+to+ra+tion+ism (ˌrɛstə'reɪʃəˌnɪzəm) *n.* belief in a future life in which men will be restored to a state of perfection and happiness. —ˌ**res+to+'ra+tion+ist** *n., adj.*

re+'sole *vb.*
re+'spray *vb.*
re+'stack *vb.*
re+'staff *vb.*
re+'stage *vb.*
re+'start *vb., n.*
re+'stock *vb.*
re+'straight+en *vb.*

re·stor·a·tive (rɪ'stɒrətɪv) *adj.* **1.** tending to revive or renew health, spirits, etc. ~*n.* **2.** anything that restores or revives, esp. a drug or agent that promotes health or strength.

re·store (rɪ'stɔː) *vb.* (*tr.*) **1.** to return (something, esp. a work of art or building) to an original or former condition. **2.** to bring back to health, good spirits, etc. **3.** to return (something lost, stolen, etc.) to its owner. **4.** to reintroduce or re-enforce: *to restore discipline.* **5.** to reconstruct (an extinct animal, former landscape, etc.). [C13: from Old French, from Latin *restaurāre* to rebuild, from RE- + *-staurāre*, as in *instaurāre* to renew] —**re'stor·a·ble** *adj.* —**re'stor·a·ble·ness** *n.* —**re'stor·er** *n.*

re·strain (rɪ'streɪn) *vb.* (*tr.*) **1.** to hold (someone) back from some action, esp. by force. **2.** to deprive (someone) of liberty, as by imprisonment. **3.** to limit or restrict. [C14 *restreyne*, from Old French *restreindre*, from Latin *rēstringere* to draw back tightly, from RE- + *stringere* to draw, bind; see STRAIN[1]] —**re'strain·a·ble** *adj.* —**re·strain·ed·ly** (rɪ'streɪnɪdlɪ) *adv.* —**re'strain·ing·ly** *adv.*

re·strain·er (rɪ'streɪnə) *n.* **1.** a person who restrains. **2.** a chemical, such as potassium bromide, added to a photographic developer in order to reduce the amount of fog on a film and to retard the development.

re·straint (rɪ'streɪnt) *n.* **1.** the ability to control or moderate one's impulses, passions, etc.: *to show restraint.* **2.** the act of restraining or the state of being restrained. **3.** something that restrains; restriction. [C15: from Old French *restreinte*, from *restreindre* to RESTRAIN]

re·straint of trade *n.* action tending to interfere with the freedom to compete in business.

re·strict (rɪ'strɪkt) *vb.* (often foll. by *to*) to confine or keep within certain often specified limits or selected bounds: *to restrict one's drinking to the evening.* [C16: from Latin *rēstrictus* bound up, from *rēstringere*; see RESTRAIN]

re·strict·ed (rɪ'strɪktɪd) *adj.* **1.** limited or confined. **2.** not accessible to the general public or (*esp. U.S.*) out of bounds to military personnel. **3.** *Brit.* denoting or in a zone in which a speed limit or waiting restrictions for vehicles apply. —**re'strict·ed·ly** *adv.* —**re'strict·ed·ness** *n.*

re·stric·tion (rɪ'strɪkʃən) *n.* **1.** something that restricts; a restrictive measure, law, etc. **2.** the act of restricting or the state of being restricted. —**re'stric·tion·ist** *n., adj.*

re·stric·tive (rɪ'strɪktɪv) *adj.* **1.** restricting or tending to restrict. **2.** *Grammar.* denoting a relative clause or phrase that restricts the number of possible referents of its antecedent. The relative clause in *Americans who live in New York* is restrictive; the relative clause in *Americans, who are generally extrovert,* is nonrestrictive. —**re'stric·tive·ly** *adv.* —**re'stric·tive·ness** *n.*

re·stric·tive prac·tice *n. Brit.* **1.** a trading agreement against the public interest. **2.** a practice of a union or other group tending to limit the freedom of other workers or employers.

rest room *n.* a U.S. name for **public convenience.**

rest stop *n.* the U.S. name for **lay-by.**

re·sult (rɪ'zʌlt) *n.* **1.** something that ensues from an action, policy, course of events, etc.; outcome; consequence. **2.** a number, quantity, or value obtained by solving a mathematical problem. **3.** *U.S.* a decision of a legislative body. **4.** (*often pl.*) the final score or outcome of a sporting contest. ~*vb.* (*intr.*) **5.** (often foll. by *from*) to be the outcome or consequence (of). **6.** (foll. by *in*) to issue or terminate (in a specified way, state, etc.); end: *to result in tragedy.* **7.** *Property law.* (of an undisposed or partially disposed of interest in land) to revert to a former owner when the prior interests come to an end. [C15: from Latin *resultāre* to rebound, spring from, from RE- + *saltāre* to leap]

re·sult·ant (rɪ'zʌltənt) *adj.* **1.** that results; resulting. ~*n.* **2.** *Maths., physics.* a single vector that is the vector sum of two or more other vectors.

re·sume (rɪ'zjuːm) *vb.* **1.** to begin again or go on with (something adjourned or interrupted). **2.** (*tr.*) to occupy again, take back, or recover: *to resume one's seat; resume possession.* **3.** (*tr.*) to assume (a title, office, etc.) again: *to resume the presidency.* **4.** *Archaic.* to summarize; make a résumé of. [C15: from Latin *resūmere* to take up again, from RE- + *sūmere* to take up] —**re'sum·a·ble** *adj.* —**re'sum·er** *n.*

ré·su·mé ('rɛzjʊˌmeɪ) *n.* a short descriptive summary, as of events, etc. [C19: from French, from *résumer* to RESUME]

re·sump·tion (rɪ'zʌmpʃən) *n.* the act of resuming or beginning again. [C15: via Old French from Late Latin *resumptiō*, from Latin *resūmere* to RESUME] —**re'sump·tive** *adj.* —**re'sump·tive·ly** *adv.*

re·su·pi·nate (rɪ'sjuːpɪnɪt) *adj. Botany.* (of plant parts) reversed or inverted in position, so as to appear to be upside down. [C18: from Latin *resupīnātus* bent back, from *resupīnāre*, from RE- + *supīnāre* to place on the back; see SUPINE] —**reˌsu·pi'na·tion** *n.*

re·su·pine (rɪ'sjuːpaɪn) *adj. Rare.* lying on the back; supine. [C17: from Latin *resupīnus* lying on the back]

re·surge (rɪ'sɜːdʒ) *vb.* (*intr.*) *Rare.* to rise again from or as if from the dead. [C16: from Latin *resurgere* to rise again, reappear, from RE- + *surgere* to lift, arise, SURGE]

re·sur·gent (rɪ'sɜːdʒənt) *adj.* rising again, as to new life, vigour, etc.: *resurgent nationalism.* —**re'sur·gence** *n.*

res·ur·rect (ˌrɛzə'rɛkt) *vb.* **1.** to rise or raise from the dead; bring or be brought back to life. **2.** (*tr.*) to bring back into use or activity; revive: *to resurrect an ancient law.* **3.** (*tr.*) to renew (one's hopes, etc.). **4.** (*tr.*) *Facetious.* (formerly) to exhume and steal (a body) from its grave, esp. in order to sell it.

res·ur·rec·tion (ˌrɛzə'rɛkʃən) *n.* **1.** a supposed act or instance of a dead person coming back to life. **2.** belief in the possibility of this as part of a religious or mystical system. **3.** the condition of those who have risen from the dead: *we shall all live in the resurrection.* [C13: via Old French from Late Latin *resurrectiō*, from Latin *resurgere* to rise again; see RESURGE] —**ˌres·ur'rec·tion·al** *or* **ˌres·ur'rec·tion·ar·y** *adj.*

Res·ur·rec·tion (ˌrɛzə'rɛkʃən) *n. Christian theol.* **1.** the rising again of Christ from the tomb three days after his death. **2.** the rising again from the dead of all men at the Last Judgment.

res·ur·rec·tion·ism (ˌrɛzə'rɛkʃəˌnɪzəm) *n.* **1.** belief that men will rise again from the dead, esp. the Christian doctrine of the Resurrection of Christ and of all men at the Last Judgment. **2.** *Facetious.* (formerly) body-snatching.

res·ur·rec·tion·ist (ˌrɛzə'rɛkʃənɪst) *n.* **1.** *Facetious.* (formerly) a body-snatcher. **2.** a member of an Anglican religious community founded in 1892. **3.** a person who believes in the Resurrection.

res·ur·rec·tion plant *n.* any of several unrelated desert plants that form a tight ball when dry and unfold and bloom when moistened. The best-known examples are the cruciferous *Anastatica hierochuntica*, club mosses of the genus *Selaginella*, and the composite *Asteriscus pygmoeus.* Also called: **rose of Jericho.**

re·sus·ci·tate (rɪ'sʌsɪˌteɪt) *vb.* (*tr.*) to restore to consciousness; revive. [C16: from Latin *resuscitāre*, from RE- + *suscitāre* raise, from *sub-* up from below + *citāre* to rouse, from *citus* quick] —**re'sus·ci·ta·ble** *adj.* —**reˌsus·ci'ta·tion** *n.* —**re'sus·ci·ta·tive** *adj.*

re·sus·ci·ta·tor (rɪ'sʌsɪˌteɪtə) *n.* **1.** an apparatus for forcing oxygen or a mixture containing oxygen into the lungs. **2.** a person who resuscitates.

ret (rɛt) *vb.* **rets, ret·ting, ret·ted.** (*tr.*) to moisten or soak (flax, hemp, jute, etc.) to promote bacterial action in order to facilitate separation of the fibres from the woody tissue by beating. [C15: of Germanic origin; related to Middle Dutch *reeten*, Swedish *röta*, German *rösten*; see ROT]

ret. *abbrev. for:* **1.** retain. **2.** retired. **3.** return(ed).

re·ta·ble (rɪ'teɪbᵊl) *n.* an ornamental screenlike structure above and behind an altar, esp. one used as a setting for a religious picture or carving. [C19: from French, from Spanish *retablo*, from Latin *retrō* behind + *tabula* board; see REAR[1], TABLE]

re·tail ('riːteɪl) *n.* **1.** the sale of goods individually or in small quantities to consumers. Compare **wholesale.** ~*adj.* **2.** of, relating to, or engaged in such selling: *retail prices.* ~*adv.* **3.** in small amounts or at a retail price. ~*vb.* **4.** to sell or be sold in small quantities to consumers. **5.** (*tr.*) (rɪ'teɪl). to relate (gossip, scandal, etc.) in detail, esp. persistently. [C14: from Old French *retaillier* to cut off, from RE- + *taillier* to cut; see TAILOR] —**'re·tail·er** *n.*

re·tain (rɪ'teɪn) *vb.* (*tr.*) **1.** to keep in one's possession. **2.** to be able to hold or contain: *soil that retains water.* **3.** (of a person) to be able to remember (information, etc.) without difficulty. **4.** to hold in position. **5.** to keep for one's future use, as by paying a retainer or nominal charge: *to retain one's rooms for the holidays.* **6.** *Law.* to engage the services of (a barrister) by payment of a preliminary fee. **7.** (in selling races) to buy back a winner that one owns when it is auctioned after the race. **8.** (of racehorse trainers) to pay an advance fee to (a jockey) so as to have prior or exclusive claims upon his services throughout the season. [C14: from Old French *retenir*, from Latin *retinēre* to hold back, from RE- + *tenēre* to hold] —**re'tain·a·ble** *adj.* —**reˌtain·a'bil·i·ty** *or* **re'tain·a·ble·ness** *n.* —**re'tain·ment** *n.*

re·tained ob·ject *n. Grammar.* a direct or indirect object of a passive verb. The phrase *the drawings* in the sentence *Harry was given the drawings* is a retained object.

re·tain·er (rɪ'teɪnə) *n.* **1.** *History.* a supporter or dependant of a person of rank, esp. a soldier. **2.** a servant, esp. one who has been with a family for a long time. **3.** a clip, frame, or similar device that prevents a part of a machine, engine, etc., from moving. **4.** a dental appliance for holding a loose tooth or prosthetic device in position. **5.** a fee paid in advance to secure first option on the services of a barrister, jockey, etc. **6.** a reduced rent paid for a flat, room, etc., during absence to reserve it for future use.

re·tain·ing wall *n.* a wall constructed to hold back earth, loose rock, etc. Also called: **revetment.**

re·take *vb.* (riː'teɪk), **·takes, ·tak·ing, ·took, ·tak·en.** (*tr.*) **1.** to take back or capture again: *to retake a fortress.* **2.** *Films.* to shoot again (a shot or scene). **3.** to tape again (a recording). ~*n.* ('riːˌteɪk). **4.** *Films.* a rephotographed shot or scene. **5.** a retaped recording. —**re'tak·er** *n.*

re·tal·i·ate (rɪ'tælɪˌeɪt) *vb.* **1.** (*intr.*) to take retributory action, esp. by returning some injury or wrong in kind. **2.** (*tr.*) *Rare.* to avenge (an injury, wrong, etc.). [C17: from Late Latin *retāliāre*, from Latin RE- + *tālis* of such kind] —**reˌtal·i'a·tion** *n.* —**re'tal·i·a·tive** *or* **re'tal·i·a·to·ry** *adj.* —**re'tal·iˌa·tor** *n.*

re·tard (rɪ'tɑːd) *vb.* (*tr.*) to delay or slow down (the progress, speed, or development) of (something). [C15: from Old French *retarder*, from Latin *retardāre*, from RE- + *tardāre* to make slow, from *tardus* sluggish; see TARDY] —**re'tard·ing·ly** *adv.*

re·tard·ant (rɪ'tɑːdᵊnt) *n.* **1.** a substance that reduces the rate of a chemical reaction. ~*adj.* **2.** having a slowing effect.

---

re'string *vb.*, **·strings, ·string·ing, ·strung.**
re'struc·ture *vb.*
re'style *vb.*
ˌre·sub'mit *vb.*, **·mits, ·mit·ting, ·mit·ted.**
ˌre·sub'scribe *vb.*
re'sum·mon *vb.*
ˌre·sup'ply *vb.*, **·plies, ·ply·ing, ·plied.**
re'sur·face *vb.*
ˌre·sur'vey *vb.*

re+tard+ate (rɪ'tɑ:deɪt) *n. Psychol.* a person who is retarded.

re+tar+da+tion (ˌri:tɑ:'deɪʃən) *or* **re+tard+ment** (rɪ'tɑ:dmənt) *n.* **1.** the act of retarding or the state of being retarded. **2.** something that retards; hindrance. **3.** the rate of deceleration. —**re+'tard·a+tive** *or* **re+'tard·a+to·ry** *adj.*

re+tard+ed (rɪ'tɑ:dɪd) *adj.* underdeveloped, esp. mentally and esp. having an IQ of 70 to 85. Compare **subnormal.**

re+tard+er (rɪ'tɑ:də) *n.* **1.** a person or thing that retards. **2.** a substance added to slow down the rate of a chemical change, such as one added to cement to delay its setting.

retch (rɛtʃ, ri:tʃ) *vb.* **1.** (*intr.*) to undergo an involuntary spasm of ineffectual vomiting; heave. **2.** to vomit. ~*n.* **3.** an involuntary spasm of ineffectual vomiting. [Old English *hræcan;* related to Old Norse *hrækja* to spit]

retd. *abbrev. for:* **1.** retired. **2.** retained. **3.** returned.

re+te ('ri:tɪ) *n., pl.* **re+ti·a** ('ri:ʃɪə, -tɪə). *Anatomy.* any network of nerves or blood vessels; plexus. [C14 (referring to a metal network used with an astrolabe): from Latin *rēte* net] —'**re+ti·al** *adj.*

re+tene ('ri:ti:n, 'rɛt-) *n.* a yellow crystalline hydrocarbon found in tar oils from pine wood and in certain fossil resins. Formula: $C_{18}H_{18}$. [C19: from Greek *rhētinē* resin]

re+ten+tion (rɪ'tɛnʃən) *n.* **1.** the act of retaining or state of being retained. **2.** the capacity to hold or retain liquid, etc. **3.** the capacity to remember. **4.** *Pathol.* the abnormal holding within the body of urine, faeces, etc., that are normally excreted. [C14: from Latin *retentiō,* from *retinēre* to RETAIN]

re+ten+tion+ist (rɪ'tɛnʃənɪst) *n.* a person who advocates the retention of something, esp. capital punishment.

re+ten+tive (rɪ'tɛntɪv) *adj.* having the capacity to retain or remember. —**re+'ten+tive+ly** *adv.* —**re+'ten+tive+ness** *n.*

re+ten+tiv+i+ty (ˌri:tɛn'tɪvɪtɪ) *n.* **1.** the state or quality of being retentive. **2.** *Physics.* another name for **remanence.**

re+think *vb.* (ri:'θɪŋk), +**thinks,** +**think+ing,** +**thought. 1.** to think about (something) again, esp. with a view to changing one's tactics or opinions. ~*n.* ('ri:ˌθɪŋk). **2.** the act or an instance of thinking again.

re+ti+ar+i+us (ˌri:tɪ'ɛərɪəs, ˌri:ʃɪ-) *n., pl.* +**ar·i+i** (-'ɛərɪˌaɪ). (in ancient Rome) a gladiator armed with a net and trident. [Latin, from *rēte* net]

re+ti+ar·y ('ri:tɪərɪ, -ʃɪə-) *adj. Rare.* of, relating to, or resembling a net or web. [C17: from Latin RETIARIUS]

ret·i+cent ('rɛtɪsənt) *adj.* not open or communicative; not saying all that one knows; taciturn; reserved. [C19: from Latin *reticēre* to keep silent, from RE- + *tacēre* to be silent] —'**ret·i+cence** *n.* —'**ret·i+cent+ly** *adv.*

ret·i+cle ('rɛtɪkᵊl) *or* **ret·i+cule** *n.* a network of fine lines, wires, etc., placed in the focal plane of an optical instrument to assist measurement of the size or position of objects under observation. Also called: **graticule.** [C17: from Latin *rēticulum* a little net, from *rēte* net]

re+tic·u+late *adj.* (rɪ'tɪkjʊlɪt), *also* **re+tic·u+lar** (rɪ'tɪkjʊlə). **1.** in the form of a network or having a network of parts: *a reticulate leaf.* **2.** resembling, covered with, or having the form of a net. ~*vb.* (rɪ'tɪkjʊˌleɪt). **3.** to form or be formed into a net. [C17: from Late Latin *rēticulātus* made like a net] —**re+'tic·u+late+ly** *adv.* —**re+ˌtic·u+'la+tion** *n.*

ret·i+cule ('rɛtɪˌkju:l) *n.* **1.** (in the 18th and 19th centuries) a woman's small bag or purse, usually in the form of a pouch with a drawstring and made of net, beading, brocade, etc. **2.** a variant spelling of **reticle.** [C18: from French *réticule,* from Latin *rēticulum* RETICLE]

re+tic·u+lo+cyte (rɪ'tɪkjʊləˌsaɪt) *n.* an immature red blood cell containing a network of granules or filaments. [C20: from RETICULUM + -CYTE]

re+tic·u+lo+en+do+the+li·al (rɪˌtɪkjʊləʊˌɛndəʊ'θi:lɪəl) *adj. Physiol.* denoting or relating to a bodily system that consists of all the cells able to ingest bacteria, colloidal particles, etc., with the exception of the leucocytes. See also **macrophage.** [C20: from RETICULUM + ENDOTHELIAL]

re+tic·u+lum (rɪ'tɪkjʊləm) *n., pl.* +**la** (-lə). **1.** any fine network, esp. one in the body composed of cells, fibres, etc. **2.** the second compartment of the stomach of ruminants, situated between the rumen and psalterium. [C17: from Latin: little net, from *rēte* net]

Re+tic·u+lum (rɪ'tɪkjʊləm) *n., Latin genitive* **Re+tic·u+li** (rɪ'tɪkjʊˌlaɪ). a small constellation in the S hemisphere lying between Dorado and Hydrus.

re+ti+form ('ri:tɪˌfɔ:m, 'rɛt-) *adj. Rare.* netlike; reticulate. [C17: from Latin *rēte* net + *forma* shape]

ret·i+na ('rɛtɪnə) *n., pl.* +**nas** *or* +**nae** (-ˌni:). the light-sensitive membrane forming the inner lining of the posterior wall of the eyeball, composed largely of a specialized terminal expansion of the optic nerve. Images focused here by the lens of the eye are transmitted to the brain as nerve impulses. [C14: from Medieval Latin, perhaps from Latin *rēte* net] —'**ret·i+nal** *adj.*

ret·i+nac·u+lum (ˌrɛtɪ'nækjʊləm) *n., pl.* +**la** (-lə). **1.** connection or retention or something that connects or retains. **2.** *Zoology.* a small hook that joins the forewing and hind wing of a moth during flight. [C18 (a surgical instrument used in castration): Latin, from *rētinēre* to hold back] —ˌ**ret·i+'nac·u+lar** *adj.*

ret·i+nene ('rɛtɪˌni:n) *n.* a yellow pigment, the aldehyde of vitamin A, that is formed in the rods of the eye by the action of bright light on rhodopsin. Formula: $C_{19}H_{27}CHO$. Also called: **visual yellow.** [C20: from RETINA + -ENE]

ret·i+nite ('rɛtɪˌnaɪt) *n.* any of various resins of fossil origin, esp. one derived from lignite. [C19: from French *rétinite,* from Greek *rhētinē* resin + -ITE[1]]

ret·i+ni+tis (ˌrɛtɪ'naɪtɪs) *n.* inflammation of the retina. [C20: from New Latin, from RETINA + -ITIS]

ret·i+nos+co+py (ˌrɛtɪ'nɒskəpɪ) *n. Ophthalmol.* a procedure for detecting errors of refraction in the eye by means of an instrument (**retinoscope**) that reflects a beam of light from a mirror into the eye. Diagnosis is made by observing the areas of shadow and the direction in which the light moves when the mirror is rotated. Also called: **skiascopy, shadow test.** —**ret·i+no+scop+ic** (ˌrɛtɪnə'skɒpɪk) *adj.* —ˌ**ret·i+no+'scop·i+cal+ly** *adv.* —ˌ**ret·i+'nos+co+pist** *n.*

ret·i+nue ('rɛtɪˌnju:) *n.* a body of aides and retainers attending an important person, royalty, etc. [C14: from Old French *retenue,* from *retenir* to RETAIN] —'**ret·i+ˌnued** *adj.*

re+tire (rɪ'taɪə) *vb.* (*mainly intr.*) **1.** (*also tr.*) to give up or to cause (a person) to give up his work, a post, etc., esp. on reaching pensionable age (in Britain and Australia usually 65 for men, 60 for women). **2.** to go away, as into seclusion, for recuperation, etc. **3.** to go to bed. **4.** to recede or disappear: *the sun retired behind the clouds.* **5.** to withdraw from a sporting contest, esp. because of injury. **6.** (*also tr.*) to pull back (troops, etc.) from battle or an exposed position or (of troops, etc.) to fall back. **7.** (*tr.*) **a.** to remove (bills, bonds, shares, etc.) from circulation by taking them up and paying for them. **b.** to remove (money) from circulation. [C16: from French *retirer,* from Old French RE- + *tirer* to pull, draw] —**re+'tire+ment** *n.* —**re+'tir+er** *n.*

re+tire+ment pen+sion *n. Brit.* a weekly payment made by the government to a retired man over 65 or woman over 60.

re+tir+ing (rɪ'taɪərɪŋ) *adj.* shunning contact with others; shy; reserved. —**re+'tir+ing+ly** *adv.*

re+tool (ri:'tu:l) *vb.* **1.** to replace, re-equip, or rearrange the tools in (a factory, etc.). **2.** *Chiefly U.S.* to revise or reorganize.

re+tor+sion (rɪ'tɔ:ʃən) *n.* retaliatory action taken by a state whose citizens have been mistreated by a foreign power by treating the subjects of that power similarly; reprisal.

re+tort[1] (rɪ'tɔ:t) *vb.* **1.** (when *tr., takes a clause as object*) to utter (something) quickly, sharply, wittily, or angrily, in response. **2.** to use (an argument) against its originator; turn the tables by saying (something). ~*n.* **3.** a sharp, angry, or witty reply. **4.** an argument used against its originator. [C16: from Latin *retorquēre* to twist back, from RE- + *torquēre* to twist, wrench] —**re+'tort+er** *n.*

re+tort[2] (rɪ'tɔ:t) *n.* **1.** a glass vessel with a round bulb and long tapering neck that is bent down, used esp. in a laboratory for distillation. **2.** a vessel in which large quantities of material may be heated, esp. one used for heating ores in the production of metals or heating coal to produce gas. ~*vb.* **3.** (*tr.*) to heat in a retort. [C17: from French *retorte,* from Medieval Latin *retorta,* from Latin *retorquēre* to twist back; see RETORT[1]]

re+tor+tion (rɪ'tɔ:ʃən) *n.* **1.** the act of retorting. **2.** a variant spelling of **retorsion.**

re+touch (ri:'tʌtʃ) *vb.* (*tr.*) **1.** to restore, correct, or improve (a painting, make-up, etc.) with new touches. **2.** *Photog.* to alter (a negative or print) by painting over blemishes or adding details. **3.** to make small finishing improvements to. **4.** *Archaeol.* to detach small flakes from (a blank) in order to make a tool. ~*n.* **5.** the art or practice of retouching. **6.** a detail that is the result of retouching. **7.** a photograph, painting, etc., that has been retouched. **8.** *Archaeol.* fine percussion to shape flakes of stone into usable tools. —**re+'touch+a·ble** *adj.* —**re+'touch+er** *n.*

re+trace (rɪ'treɪs) *vb.* (*tr.*) **1.** to go back over (one's steps, a route, etc.) again: *we retraced the route we took last summer.* **2.** to go over (a past event) in the mind; recall. **3.** to go over (a story, account, etc.) from the beginning. —**re+'trace+a·ble** *adj.* —**re+'trace+ment** *n.*

re-trace (ri:'treɪs) *vb.* (*tr.*) to trace (a map, etc.) again.

re+tract (rɪ'trækt) *vb.* **1.** (*tr.*) to draw in (a part or appendage): *a snail can retract its horns; to retract the landing gear of an aircraft.* **2.** to withdraw (a statement, opinion, charge, etc.) as invalid or unjustified. **3.** to go back on (a promise or agreement). **4.** (*intr.*) to shrink back, as in fear. **5.** *Phonetics.* to modify the articulation of (a vowel) by bringing the tongue back away from the lips. [C16: from Latin *retractāre* to withdraw, from *tractāre* to pull, from *trahere* to drag] —**re+'tract+a·ble** *or* **re+'tract+i·ble** *adj.* —**re+ˌtract+a·'bil+i+ty** *or* **re+ˌtract+i·'bil+i+ty** *n.* —**re+trac+ta+tion** (ˌri:træk'teɪʃən) *n.* —**re+'trac+tive** *adj.*

re+trac+tile (rɪ'træktaɪl) *adj.* capable of being drawn in: *the retractile claws of a cat.* —**re+trac+til+i+ty** (ˌri:træk'tɪlɪtɪ) *n.*

re+trac+tion (rɪ'trækʃən) *n.* **1.** the act of retracting or state of being retracted. **2.** the withdrawal of a statement, etc.

re+trac+tor (rɪ'træktə) *n.* **1.** *Anatomy.* any of various muscles that retract an organ or part. **2.** *Surgery.* an instrument for holding back the edges of a surgical incision or organ or part. **3.** a person or thing that retracts.

re+tral ('ri:trəl, 'rɛtrəl) *adj. Rare.* at, near, or towards the back. [C19: from Latin *retrō* backwards] —'**re+tral+ly** *adv.*

re+tread *vb.* (ri:'trɛd), +**treads,** +**tread+ing,** +**tread+ed. 1.** (*tr.*) to remould (a used pneumatic tyre) to give it new treads. ~*n.* ('ri:ˌtrɛd). **2.** Also called: **remould.** a used pneumatic tyre that has been remoulded to give it new treads.

re+'teach *vb.,* +**teach·es,** +**teach+ing,** +**taught.**
re+'tell *vb.,* +**tells,** +**tell+ing,** +**told.**
re+'test *vb.*
re+'tes+ti+ˌfy *vb.,* +**fies,** +**fy+ing,** +**fied.**
re+'think *vb.,* +**thinks,** +**think+ing,** +**thought.**
re+'tie *vb.,* +**ties,** +**ty+ing,** +**tied.**
re+'ti+tle *vb.*
re+'train *vb.*
re+trans+'fer *vb.*
ˌ**re+trans+'late** *vb.*
ˌ**re+trans+'la+tion** *n.*
ˌ**re+trans+'mis+sion** *n.*

re·tread (riːˈtrɛd) *vb.* **-treads, -tread·ing, -trod, -trod·den** *or* **-trod.** (*tr.*) to tread or walk over (one's steps, etc.) again.

re·treat (rɪˈtriːt) *vb.* (*mainly intr.*) **1.** *Military.* to withdraw or retire in the face of or from action with an enemy, either due to defeat or in order to adopt a more favourable position. **2.** to retire or withdraw, as to seclusion or shelter. **3.** (of a person's features) to slope back; recede. **4.** (*tr.*) *Chess.* to move (a piece) back. ~*n.* **5.** the act of retreating or withdrawing. **6.** *Military.* **a.** a withdrawal or retirement in the face of the enemy. **b.** a bugle call signifying withdrawal or retirement, esp. (formerly) to within a defended fortification. **7.** retirement or seclusion. **8.** a place, such as a sanatorium or monastery, to which one may retire for refuge, quiet, etc. **9.** an institution, esp. a private one, for the care and treatment of the mentally ill, infirm, elderly, etc. [C14: from Old French *retret*, from *retraire* to withdraw, from Latin *retrahere* to pull back; see RETRACT] —**re·ˈtreat·al** *adj.*

re·trench (rɪˈtrɛntʃ) *vb.* **1.** to reduce or curtail (costs); economize. **2.** (*tr.*) to shorten, delete, or abridge. **3.** (*tr.*) to protect by a retrenchment. [C17: from Old French *retrenchier*, from RE- + *trenchier* to cut, from Latin *truncāre* to lop; see TRENCH] —**re·ˈtrench·a·ble** *adj.*

re·trench·ment (rɪˈtrɛntʃmənt) *n.* **1.** the act of reducing expenditure in order to improve financial stability. **2.** an extra interior fortification to reinforce outer walls.

re·tri·al (riːˈtraɪəl) *n.* a second or new trial, esp. of a case that has already been adjudicated upon.

ret·ri·bu·tion (ˌrɛtrɪˈbjuːʃən) *n.* **1.** the act of punishing or taking vengeance for wrongdoing, sin, or injury. **2.** punishment or vengeance. [C14: via Old French from Church Latin *retribūtiō*, from Latin *retribuere* to repay, from RE- + *tribuere* to pay; see TRIBUTE] —**re·trib·u·tive** (rɪˈtrɪbjʊtɪv) *or* **re·ˈtrib·u·to·ry** *adj.* —**re·ˈtrib·u·tive·ly** *adv.*

re·triev·al (rɪˈtriːvᵊl) *n.* **1.** the act or process of retrieving. **2.** the possibility of recovery, restoration, or rectification (esp. in the phrase **beyond retrieval**).

re·trieve (rɪˈtriːv) *vb.* (*mainly tr.*) **1.** to get or fetch back again; recover: *he retrieved his papers from various people's drawers.* **2.** to bring back to a more satisfactory state; revive. **3.** to extricate from trouble or danger; rescue or save. **4.** to recover or make newly available (stored information) from a computer system. **5.** (*also intr.*) (of dogs) to find and fetch (shot game, etc.). **6.** *Tennis, etc.* to return successfully (a shot difficult to reach). **7.** to recall; remember. ~*n.* **8.** the act of retrieving. **9.** the chance of being retrieved. [C15: from Old French *retrover*, from RE- + *trouver* to find, perhaps from Vulgar Latin *tropāre* (unattested) to compose; see TROVER, TROUBADOUR] —**re·ˈtriev·a·ble** *adj.* —**re·ˌtriev·a·ˈbil·i·ty** *n.* —**re·ˈtriev·a·bly** *adv.*

re·triev·er (rɪˈtriːvə) *n.* **1.** one of a breed of large hunting dogs that can be trained to retrieve game. **2.** any dog used to retrieve shot game. **3.** a person or thing that retrieves.

ret·ro (ˈrɛtrəʊ) *n., pl.* **·ros.** short for **retrorocket.**

ret·ro- *prefix.* **1.** back or backwards: *retroactive.* **2.** located behind: *retrolental.* [from Latin *retrō* behind, backwards]

ret·ro·act (ˈrɛtrəʊˌækt) *vb.* (*intr.*) **1.** to act in opposition. **2.** to influence or have reference to past events.

ret·ro·ac·tion (ˌrɛtrəʊˈækʃən) *n.* **1.** an action contrary or reciprocal to a preceding action. **2.** a retrospective action, esp. a law affecting events prior to its enactment.

ret·ro·ac·tive (ˌrɛtrəʊˈæktɪv) *adj.* **1.** applying or referring to the past: *retroactive legislation.* **2.** effective or operative from a date or for a period in the past. —**ˌret·ro·ˈac·tive·ly** *adv.* —**ˌret·ro·ˈac·tive·ness** *or* **ˌret·ro·ac·ˈtiv·i·ty** *n.*

ret·ro·ac·tive in·hi·bi·tion *n. Psychol.* the tendency for the results of learning to be impaired by immediately subsequent activity. Compare **proactive inhibition.**

ret·ro·cede (ˌrɛtrəʊˈsiːd) *vb.* **1.** (*tr.*) to give back; return. **2.** (*intr.*) to go back or retire; recede. —**ret·ro·ces·sion** (ˌrɛtrəʊˈsɛʃən) *or* **ˌret·ro·ˈced·ence** *n.* —**ˌret·ro·ˈces·sive** *or* **ˌret·ro·ˈced·ent** *adj.*

ret·ro·choir (ˈrɛtrəʊˌkwaɪə) *n.* the space in a large church or cathedral behind the high altar.

ret·ro·fire (ˈrɛtrəʊˌfaɪə) *n.* **1.** the act of firing a retrorocket. **2.** the moment at which it is fired.

ret·ro·fit (ˈrɛtrəʊˌfɪt) *vb.* **·fits, ·fit·ting, ·fit·ted.** (*tr.*) to equip (a car, aircraft, etc.) with new parts, safety devices, etc., after manufacture.

ret·ro·flex (ˈrɛtrəʊˌflɛks) *or* **ret·ro·flexed** *adj.* **1.** bent or curved backwards. **2.** *Phonetics.* of, relating to, or involving retroflexion. [C18: from Latin *retrōflexus*, from *retrōflectere*, from RETRO- + *flectere* to bend]

ret·ro·flex·ion *or* **ret·ro·flec·tion** (ˌrɛtrəʊˈflɛkʃən) *n.* **1.** the act or condition of bending or being bent backwards. **2.** the act of turning the tip of the tongue upwards and backwards towards the hard palate in the articulation of a vowel or a consonant.

ret·ro·grade (ˈrɛtrəʊˌgreɪd) *adj.* **1.** moving or bending backwards. **2.** (esp. of order) reverse or inverse. **3.** tending towards an earlier worse condition; declining or deteriorating. **4.** *Astronomy.* **a.** occurring or orbiting in a direction opposite to that of the earth's motion around the sun. Compare **direct** (sense 18). **b.** occurring or orbiting in a direction around a planet opposite to the planet's rotational direction: *the retrograde motion of the satellite Phoebe around Saturn.* **c.** appearing to move in a clockwise direction due to the rotational period exceeding the period of revolution around the sun: *Venus has retrograde rotation.* **5.** *Biology.* tending to retrogress; degenerate. **6.** *Music.* of, concerning, or denoting a melody or part that is played backwards. **7.** *Obsolete.* opposed, contrary, or repugnant to. ~*vb.* (*intr.*) **8.** to move in a retrograde direction; retrogress. [C14: from Latin *retrōgradī* to go backwards, from *gradi* to walk, go] —**ˌret·ro·gra·ˈda·tion** *n.* —**ˌret·ro·ˈgra·da·to·ry** *adj.* —**ˈret·ro·ˌgrade·ly** *adv.*

ret·ro·gress (ˌrɛtrəʊˈgrɛs) *vb.* (*intr.*) **1.** to go back to an earlier, esp. worse, condition; degenerate or deteriorate. **2.** to move backwards; recede. **3.** *Biology.* to develop characteristics or features of lower or simpler organisms; degenerate. [C19: from Latin *retrōgressus* having moved backwards, from *retrōgradī*; see RETROGRADE] —**ˌret·ro·ˈgres·sion** *n.* —**ˌret·ro·ˈgres·sive** *adj.* —**ˌret·ro·ˈgres·sive·ly** *adv.*

ret·ro·ject (ˌrɛtrəʊˈdʒɛkt) *vb.* (*tr.*) to throw backwards (opposed to *project*). —**ˌret·ro·ˈjec·tion** *n.*

ret·ro·len·tal (ˌrɛtrəʊˈlɛntᵊl) *adj.* behind a lens, esp. of the eye. [C20: from RETRO- + *-lental*, from New Latin: LENS]

ret·ro-op·er·a·tive *adj.* affecting or operating on past events; retroactive.

ret·ro·pack (ˈrɛtrəʊˌpæk) *n.* a system of retrorockets on a spacecraft.

ret·ro·rock·et (ˈrɛtrəʊˌrɒkɪt) *n.* a small auxiliary rocket engine on a larger rocket, missile, or spacecraft, that produces thrust in the opposite direction to the direction of flight in order to decelerate the vehicle or make it move backwards. Often shortened to **retro.**

re·trorse (rɪˈtrɔːs) *adj.* (esp. of plant parts) pointing backwards or in a direction opposite to normal. [C19: from Latin *retrōrsus*, shortened form of *retrōversus* turned back, from RETRO- + *vertere* to turn] —**re·ˈtrorse·ly** *adv.*

ret·ro·spect (ˈrɛtrəʊˌspɛkt) *n.* **1.** the act of surveying things past (often in the phrase **in retrospect**). ~*vb. Archaic.* **2.** to contemplate (anything past); look back on (something). **3.** (*intr.*; often foll. by *to*) to refer back. [C17: from Latin *retrōspicere* to look back, from RETRO- + *specere* to look]

ret·ro·spec·tion (ˌrɛtrəʊˈspɛkʃən) *n.* the act of recalling things past, esp. in one's personal experience.

ret·ro·spec·tive (ˌrɛtrəʊˈspɛktɪv) *adj.* **1.** looking or directed backwards, esp. in time; characterized by retrospection. **2.** applying to the past; retroactive. ~*n.* **3.** an exhibition of an artist's life's work or a representative selection of it. —**ˌret·ro·ˈspec·tive·ly** *adv.* —**ˌret·ro·ˈspec·tive·ness** *n.*

re·trous·sé (rəˈtruːseɪ; *French* rətruˈse) *adj.* (of a nose) turned up. [C19: from French *retrousser* to tuck up; see TRUSS]

ret·ro·ver·sion (ˌrɛtrəʊˈvɜːʃən) *n.* **1.** the act of turning or condition of being turned backwards. **2.** the condition of a part or organ, esp. the uterus, that is turned or tilted backwards. —**ˈret·ro·ˌverse** *adj.* —**ˈret·ro·ˌvert·ed** *adj.*

re·try (riːˈtraɪ) *vb.* **·tries, ·try·ing, ·tried.** (*tr.*) to try again (a case already determined); give a new trial to.

ret·si·na (rɛtˈsiːnə, ˈrɛtsɪnə) *n.* a Greek wine flavoured with resin. [Modern Greek, from Italian *resina* RESIN]

re·turn (rɪˈtɜːn) *vb.* **1.** (*intr.*) to come back to a former place or state. **2.** (*tr.*) to give, take, or carry back; replace or restore. **3.** (*tr.*) to repay or recompense, esp. with something of equivalent value: *return the compliment.* **4.** (*tr.*) to earn or yield (profit or interest) as an income from an investment or venture. **5.** (*intr.*) to come back or revert in thought or speech: *I'll return to that later.* **6.** (*intr.*) to recur or reappear: *the symptoms have returned.* **7.** to answer or reply. **8.** (*tr.*) to vote into office; elect. **9.** (*tr.*) *Law.* (of a jury) to deliver or render (a verdict). **10.** (*tr.*) to send back or reflect (light or sound): *the canyon returned my shout.* **11.** (*tr.*) to submit (a report, etc.) about (someone or something) to someone in authority. **12.** (*tr.*) *Cards.* to lead back (the suit led by one's partner). **13.** (*tr.*) *Ball games.* to hit, throw, or play (a ball) back. **14.** (*tr.*) *Architect.* to turn (a part, decorative moulding, etc.) away from its original direction. **15. return thanks.** (of Christians) to say grace before a meal. ~*n.* **16.** the act or an instance of coming back. **17.** something that is given or sent back, esp. unsatisfactory merchandise returned to the maker or supplier or a theatre ticket sent back by a purchaser for resale. **18.** the act or an instance of putting, sending, or carrying back; replacement or restoration. **19.** (*often pl.*) the yield, revenue, or profit accruing from an investment, transaction, or venture. **20.** the act or an instance of reciprocation or repayment (esp. in the phrase **in return for**). **21.** a recurrence or reappearance. **22.** an official report, esp. of the financial condition of a company. **23. a.** a form (a **tax return**) on which a statement concerning one's taxable income is made. **b.** the statement itself. **24.** (*often pl.*) a statement of the votes counted at an election or poll. **25.** an answer or reply. **26.** *Brit.* short for **return ticket. 27.** *Architect.* **a.** a part of a building that forms an angle with the façade. **b.** any part of an architectural feature that forms an angle with the main part. **28.** *Law.* a report by a bailiff or other officer on the outcome of a formal document such as a writ, summons, etc., issued by a court. **29.** *Cards.* a lead of a card in the suit that one's partner has previously led. **30.** *Ball games.* the act of playing or throwing a ball, etc., back. **31.** (*modifier*) of, relating to, or characterized by a return: *a return visit; a return performance.* **32. by return (of post).** *Brit.* by the next post. **33. many happy returns (of the day).** a conventional greeting to someone on his or her birthday. **34. the point of no return.** the point at which a person's commitment is irrevocable. [C14: from Old French *retorner*; see RE-, TURN] —**re·ˈturn·er** *n.*

ˌre·trans·ˈmit *vb.*, **·mits, ·mit·ting, ·mit·ted.**
re·ˈtrim *vb.*, **·trims, ·trim·ming, ·trimmed.**
re·ˈturf *vb.*
re·ˈtwist *vb.*
re·ˈtype *vb.*
ˌre·up·ˈhol·ster *vb.*

re+turn·a·ble (rɪ'tɜːnəbᵊl) *adj.* **1.** able to be taken, given, or sent back. **2.** required to be returned by law, as a writ to the court from which it issued. —**re+ˌturn·a·'bil·i·ty** *n.*
re·turn crease *n. Cricket.* one of two lines marked at right-angles to each bowling crease, from inside which a bowler must deliver the ball.
re+turn+ing of+fic+er *n.* (in Britain, Canada, Australia, etc.) an official in charge of conducting an election.
re·turn tick+et *n. Brit.* a ticket entitling a passenger to travel to his destination and back again. U.S. equivalent: **round-trip ticket.**
re+tuse (rɪ'tjuːs) *adj. Botany.* having a rounded apex and a central depression: *retuse leaves.* [C18: from Latin *retundere* to make blunt, from RE- + *tundere* to pound]
Reu·ben ('ruːbɪn) *n. Old Testament.* **1.** the eldest son of Jacob and Leah: one of the 12 patriarchs of Israel (Genesis 29:30). **2.** the Israelite tribe descended from him. **3.** the territory of this tribe, lying to the northeast of the Dead Sea. Douay spelling: **Ru·ben.**
Reuch·lin (*German* 'rɔɪçliːn) *n.* **Jo·hann** ('joːhan). 1455–1522, German humanist, who promoted the study of Greek and Hebrew.
re+u·ni+fy (riː'juːnɪˌfaɪ) *vb.* **+fies, +fy+ing, +fied.** (*tr.*) to bring together again (something, esp. a country previously divided). —**ˌre+u·ni+fi+'ca+tion** *n.*
re+un·ion (riː'juːnjən) *n.* **1.** the act or process of coming together again. **2.** the state or condition of having been brought together again. **3.** a gathering of relatives, friends, or former associates.
Ré·u·nion (riː'juːnjən; *French* rey'njɔ̃) *n.* an island in the Indian Ocean, in the Mascarene Islands: an overseas region of France, having been in French possession since 1642. Capital: Saint-Denis. Pop.: 481 400 (1975). Area: 2510 sq. km (970 sq. miles).
re+un·ion+ist (riː'juːnjənɪst) *n.* a person who desires or works for reunion between the Roman Catholic Church and the Church of England. —**re+'un·ion+ism** *n.* —**re+ˌun·ion+'is+tic** *adj.*
re+u·nite (ˌriːjuː'naɪt) *vb.* to bring or come together again. —**ˌre+u·'nit+a·ble** *adj.* —**ˌre+u·'nit+er** *n.*
Re·us (*Spanish* 'reus) *n.* a city in NE Spain, northwest of Tarragona: became commercially important after the establishment of an English colony (about 1750). Pop.: 59 095 (1970).
Reu·ter ('rɔɪtə) *n.* Baron **Paul Ju·lius von** (paul 'juːlius fɔn). original name *Israel Beer Josaphat.* 1816-99, German telegrapher, who founded a news agency in London (1851).
Reut+ling+en (*German* 'rɔɪtlɪŋən) *n.* a city in SW West Germany, in Baden-Württemberg: founded in the 11th century; an Imperial free city from 1240 until 1802; textile industry. Pop.: 79 700 (1970).
rev (rɛv) *Informal.* ~*n.* **1.** revolution per minute: *the engine was doing 5000 revs.* ~*vb.* **revs, rev+ving, revved. 2.** (often foll. by *up*) to increase the speed of revolution of (an engine).
rev. *abbrev. for:* **1.** revenue. **2.** reverse(d). **3.** review. **4.** revise(d). **5.** revision. **6.** revolution. **7.** revolving.
Rev. *abbrev. for:* **1.** *Bible.* Revelation. **2.** Reverend.
Re·val ('reːval) *n.* the German name for **Tallinn.**
re+val+or+ize *or* **re+val+or+ise** (riː'vælәraɪz) *vb.* (*tr.*) **1.** to change the valuation of (assets). **2.** to revalue (currency). —**re+ˌval+or·i+'za+tion** *or* **re+ˌval+or·i+'sa+tion** *n.*
re+val·ue (riː'væljuː) *or U.S.* **re+val·u·ate** *vb.* **1.** to adjust the exchange value of (a currency), esp. upwards. Compare **devalue. 2.** (*tr.*) to make a fresh valuation or appraisal of. —**re+ˌval·u·'a+tion** *n.*
re+vamp (riː'væmp) *vb.* (*tr.*) **1.** to patch up or renovate; repair or restore. ~*n.* **2.** something that has been renovated or revamped. **3.** the act or process of revamping. [C19: from RE- + VAMP²] —**re+'vamp+er** *n.* —**re+'vamp+ing** *n.*
re+vanch+ism (rɪ'væntʃɪzəm) *n.* **1.** a foreign policy aimed at revenge or the regaining of lost territories. **2.** desire or support for such a policy. [C20: from French *revanche* REVENGE] —**re+'vanch+ist** *n., adj.*
rev count+er *n. Brit.* an informal name for **tachometer.**
Revd. *abbrev. for* Reverend.
re+veal (rɪ'viːl) *vb.* (*tr.*) **1.** (*may take a clause as object or an infinitive*) to disclose (a secret); divulge. **2.** to expose to view or show (something concealed). **3.** (of God) to disclose (divine truths) either directly or through the medium of prophets, etc. ~*n.* **4.** *Architect.* the vertical side of an opening in a wall, esp. the side of a window or door between the frame and the front of the wall. [C14: from Old French *reveler,* from Latin *revēlāre* to unveil, from RE- + *vēlum* a VEIL] —**re+'veal+a·ble** *adj.* —**re+ˌveal+a·'bil·i·ty** *n.* —**re+'veal+er** *n.* —**re+'veal+ing+ly** *adv.* —**re+'veal+ing+ness** *n.* —**re+'veal+ment** *n.*
re+vealed re+li+gion *n.* religion that is based on the revelation by God to man of ideas that he would not have arrived at by his natural reason alone.
re+veg·e·tate (riː'vɛdʒɪˌteɪt) *vb.* (*intr.*) (of plants) to grow again and produce new tissue. —**re+ˌveg+e·'ta+tion** *n.*
re+veil+le (rɪ'vælɪ) *n.* **1.** a signal, given by a bugle, drum, etc., to awaken soldiers or sailors in the morning. **2.** the hour at which this takes place. [C17: from French *réveillez!* awake! from RE- + Old French *esveillier* to be wakeful, ultimately from Latin *vigilāre* to keep watch; see VIGIL]
rev+el ('rɛvᵊl) *vb.* **+els, +el+ling, +elled** *or U.S.* **+els, +el+ing, +eled.** (*intr.*) **1.** (foll. by *in*) to take pleasure or wallow: *to revel in success.* **2.** to take part in noisy festivities; make merry. ~*n.* **3.** (*often pl.*) an occasion of noisy merrymaking. **4.** a less common word for **revelry.** [C14: from Old French *reveler* to be merry, noisy, from Latin *rebellāre* to revolt, REBEL] —**'rev+el+ler** *n.* —**'rev+el+ment** *n.*
rev+e·la+tion (ˌrɛvə'leɪʃən) *n.* **1.** the act or process of disclosing something previously secret or obscure, esp. something true. **2.** a fact disclosed or revealed, esp. in a dramatic or surprising way. **3.** *Christianity.* **a.** God's disclosure of his own nature and his purpose for mankind, esp. through the words of human intermediaries. **b.** something in which such a divine disclosure is contained, such as the Bible. [C14: from Church Latin *revēlātiō,* from Latin *revēlāre* to REVEAL] —**ˌrev+e·'la+tion+al** *adj.*
Rev+e·la+tion (ˌrɛvə'leɪʃən) *n.* (*often pl.*) the last book of the New Testament, containing visionary descriptions of heaven, of conflicts between good and evil, and of the end of the world. Also called: the **Apocalypse,** the **Revelation of Saint John the Divine.**
rev+e·la+tion+ist (ˌrɛvə'leɪʃənɪst) *n.* a person who believes that God has revealed certain truths to man.
rev+el+ry ('rɛvᵊlrɪ) *n., pl.* **+ries.** noisy or unrestrained merry-making. —**'rev+el+rous** *adj.*
rev+e·nant ('rɛvɪnənt) *n.* something, esp. a ghost, that returns. [C19: from French: ghost, from *revenir* to come back, from Latin *revenīre,* from RE- + *venīre* to come]
re+venge (rɪ'vɛndʒ) *n.* **1.** the act of retaliating for wrongs or injury received; vengeance. **2.** something done as a means of vengeance. **3.** the desire to take vengeance or retaliate. **4.** a return match, regarded as a loser's opportunity to even the score. ~*vb.* (*tr.*) **5.** to inflict equivalent injury or damage for (injury received); retaliate in return for. **6.** to take vengeance for (oneself or another); avenge. [C14: from Old French *revenger,* from Late Latin *revindicāre,* from RE- + *vindicāre* to VINDICATE] —**re+'venge+less** *adj.* —**re+'veng+er** *n.* —**re+'veng+ing+ly** *adv.*
re+venge+ful (rɪ'vɛndʒfʊl) *adj.* full of or characterized by desire for vengeance; vindictive. —**re+'venge+ful+ly** *adv.* —**re+'venge+ful+ness** *n.*
rev+e·nue ('rɛvɪˌnjuː) *n.* **1.** the income accruing from taxation to a government during a specified period of time, usually a year. **2. a.** a government department responsible for the collection of government revenue. **b.** (*as modifier*): *revenue men.* **3.** the gross income from a business enterprise, investment, property, etc. **4.** a particular item of income. **5.** something that yields a regular financial return; source of income. [C16: from Old French, from *revenir* to return, from Latin *revenīre;* see REVENANT] —**'rev+e·ˌnued** *adj.*
rev+e·nue cut+ter *n.* a small lightly armed boat used to enforce customs regulations and catch smugglers.
rev+e·nu+er ('rɛvɪˌnjuːə) *n. U.S. slang.* a revenue officer or cutter.
rev+e·nue tar+iff *n.* a tariff for the purpose of producing public revenue. Compare **protective tariff.**
re+ver+ber+ate (rɪ'vɜːbəˌreɪt) *vb.* **1.** (*intr.*) to resound or re-echo: *the explosion reverberated through the castle.* **2.** to reflect or be reflected many times. **3.** (*intr.*) to rebound or recoil. **4.** (*intr.*) (of the flame or heat in a reverberatory furnace) to be deflected onto the metal or ore on the hearth. **5.** (*tr.*) to heat, melt, or refine (a metal or ore) in a reverberatory furnace. [C16: from Latin *reverberāre* to strike back, from RE- + *verberāre* to beat, from *verber* a lash] —**re+'ver+ber+ant** *or* **re+'ver+ber+a+tive** *adj.* —**re+'ver+ber+ant+ly** *adv.* —**re+'ver+ber·'a+tion** *n.*
re+ver+ber·a+tion time *n.* a measure of the acoustic properties of a room, equal to the time taken for a sound to fall in intensity by 60 decibels. It is usually measured in seconds.
re+ver+ber·a+tor (rɪ'vɜːbəˌreɪtə) *n.* **1.** anything that produces or undergoes reverberation. **2.** another name for **reverberatory furnace.**
re+ver+ber·a+to+ry (rɪ'vɜːbərətərɪ, -trɪ) *adj.* **1.** characterized by, utilizing, or produced by reverberation. ~*n., pl.* **·ries. 2.** short for **reverberatory furnace.**
re+ver+ber·a+to+ry fur+nace *n.* a metallurgical furnace having a curved roof that deflects heat onto the charge so that the fuel is not in direct contact with the ore.
re+vere (rɪ'vɪə) *vb.* (*tr.*) to be in awe of and respect deeply; venerate. [C17: from Latin *reverērī,* from RE- + *verērī* to fear, be in awe of] —**re+'ver+a·ble** *adj.* —**re+'ver+er** *n.*
Re·vere (rɪ'vɪə) *n.* **Paul.** 1735–1818, American patriot and silversmith, best known for his night ride on April 18, 1775, to warn the Massachusetts colonists of the coming of the British troops.
rev+er+ence ('rɛvərəns) *n.* **1.** a feeling or attitude of profound respect, usually reserved for the sacred or divine; devoted veneration. **2.** an outward manifestation of this feeling, esp. a bow or act of obeisance. **3.** the state of being revered or commanding profound respect. **4. saving your reverence.** *Archaic.* a form of apology for using an obscene or taboo expression. ~*vb.* **5.** (*tr.*) to revere or venerate. —**'rev+er+enc+er** *n.*
Rev+er+ence ('rɛvərəns,) *n.* (preceded by *Your* or *His*) a title sometimes used to address or refer to a Roman Catholic priest.
rev+er+end ('rɛvərənd) *adj.* **1.** worthy of reverence. **2.** relating to or designating a clergyman or the clergy. ~*n.* **3.** *Informal.* a clergyman. [C15: from Latin *reverendus* fit to be revered; see REVERE]

ˌre+us+a·'bil·i·ty *n.*
re+'us+a·ble *adj.*
re+'us+a·ble+ness *n.*
re+'us+a·bly *adv.*
re+'use *vb., n.*
ˌre+u·ti+li+'za+tion *or*
ˌre+u·ti+li+'sa+tion *n.*
re+'u·ti+ˌlize *or* **re+'u·ti+ˌlise** *vb.*

Rev+er+end ('rɛvərənd) *adj.* a title of respect for a clergyman. Abbrev.: **Rev.** or **Revd.** See also **Very Reverend, Right Reverend, Most Reverend.**
Usage. *Reverend* with a surname alone (*Reverend Smith*), as a term of address (*"Yes, Reverend"*), or in the salutation of a letter (*Dear Rev. Mr. Smith*) are all generally considered to be wrong usage. Preferred are (*the*) *Reverend John Smith* or *Reverend Mr. Smith* and *Dear Mr. Smith.*

Rev+er+end Moth+er *n.* a title of respect or form of address for the Mother Superior of a convent.

rev+er+ent ('rɛvərənt, 'rɛvrənt) *adj.* feeling, expressing, or characterized by reverence. [C14: from Latin *reverēns* respectful] —**'rev+er+ent+ly** *adv.* —**'rev+er+ent+ness** *n.*

rev+er+en+tial (ˌrɛvə'rɛnʃəl) *adj.* resulting from or showing reverence: *a pilgrimage is a reverential act, performed by reverent people.* —ˌ**rev+er+'en+tial+ly** *adv.*

rev+er+ie *or* **rev+er+y** ('rɛvərɪ) *n., pl.* **+er+ies. 1.** an act or state of absent-minded daydreaming: *to fall into a reverie.* **2.** a piece of instrumental music suggestive of a daydream. **3.** *Archaic.* a fanciful or visionary notion; daydream. [C14: from Old French *resverie* wildness, from *resver* to behave wildly, of uncertain origin; see RAVE]

re+vers (rɪ'vɪə) *n., pl.* **+vers** (-'vɪəz). (*usually pl.*) the turned-back lining of part of a garment, esp. of a lapel or cuff. [C19: from French, literally: REVERSE]

re+ver+sal (rɪ'vɜːsᵊl) *n.* **1.** the act or an instance of reversing. **2.** a change for the worse; reverse: *a reversal of fortune.* **3.** the state of being reversed. **4.** the annulment of a judicial decision, esp. by an appeal court on grounds of error or irregularity.

re+verse (rɪ'vɜːs) *vb.* (*mainly tr.*) **1.** to turn or set in an opposite direction, order, or position. **2.** to change into something different or contrary; alter completely: *reverse one's policy.* **3.** (*also intr.*) to move or cause to move backwards or in an opposite direction: *to reverse a car.* **4.** to run (machinery, etc.) in the opposite direction to normal. **5.** to turn inside out. **6.** *Law.* to revoke or set aside (a judgment, decree, etc.); annul. **7.** (often foll. by *out*) to print from plates so made that white lettering or design of (a page, text, display, etc.) appears on a black or coloured background. **8. reverse arms.** *Military.* to turn one's arms upside down, esp. as a token of mourning. **9. reverse the charge(s).** to make a telephone call at the recipient's expense. ~*n.* **10.** the opposite or contrary of something. **11.** the back or rear side of something. **12.** a change to an opposite position, state, or direction. **13.** a change for the worse; setback or defeat. **14. a.** the mechanism or gears by which machinery, a vehicle, etc., can be made to reverse its direction. **b.** (*as modifier*): *reverse gear.* **15.** the side of a coin bearing a secondary design. Compare **obverse** (sense 6). **16. a.** printed matter in which normally black or coloured areas, esp. lettering, appear white, and vice versa. **b.** (*as modifier*): *reverse plates.* **17. in reverse.** in an opposite or backward direction. **18. the reverse of.** emphatically not; not at all: *he was the reverse of polite when I called.* ~*adj.* **19.** opposite or contrary in direction, position, order, nature, etc.; turned backwards. **20.** back to front; inverted. **21.** operating or moving in a manner contrary to that which is usual. **22.** denoting or relating to a mirror image. [C14: from Old French, from Latin *reversus,* from *revertere* to turn back] —**re+'verse+ly** *adv.* —**re+'vers+er** *n.*

re·verse-charge *adj.* (*prenominal*) (of a telephone call) made at the recipient's expense.

re+verse tran+scrip+tase (træn'skrɪpteɪz) *n.* any of a group of enzymes that convert certain forms of messenger RNA to DNA, the genetic information of the RNA molecule being transcribed into DNA.

re+ver+si (rɪ'vɜːsɪ) *n.* a game played on a draughts board with 64 pieces, black on one side and white on the other. When pieces are captured they are turned over to join the capturing player's forces; the winner is the player who fills the board with pieces of his colour. [C19: from French; see REVERSE]

re+vers+i+ble (rɪ'vɜːsəbᵊl) *adj.* **1.** capable of being reversed: *a reversible decision.* **2.** capable of returning to an original condition. **3.** *Chem., physics.* capable of assuming or producing either of two possible states and changing from one to the other: *a reversible reaction.* **4.** *Thermodynamics.* (of a change, process, etc.) occurring through a number of intermediate states that are all in thermodynamic equilibrium. **5.** (of a fabric or garment) woven, printed, or finished so that either side may be used as the outer side. ~*n.* **6.** a reversible garment, esp. a coat. —**re+ˌvers+i+'bil+i+ty** *or* **re+'vers+i+ble+ness** *n.* —**re+'vers+i+bly** *adv.*

re+vers+ing light *n.* a light on the rear of a motor vehicle to provide illumination when the vehicle is being reversed.

re+ver+sion (rɪ'vɜːʃən) *n.* **1.** a return to or towards an earlier condition, practice, or belief; act of reverting. **2.** the act of reversing or the state of being reversed; reversal. **3.** *Biology.* **a.** the return of individuals, organs, etc., to a more primitive condition or type. **b.** the reappearance of primitive characteristics in an individual or group. **4.** *Property law.* **a.** an interest in an estate that reverts to the grantor or his heirs at the end of a period, esp. at the end of the life of a grantee. **b.** an estate so reverting. **c.** the right to succeed to such an estate. **5.** the benefit payable on the death of a life-insurance policyholder. —**re+'ver+sion+al+ly** *adv.* —**re+'ver+sion+ar+y** *or* **re+'ver+sion+al** *adj.*

re+ver+sion+er (rɪ'vɜːʃənə) *n. Property law.* a person entitled to an estate in reversion. Compare **remainderman.**

re+ver+so (rɪ'vɜːsəʊ) *n., pl.* **+sos.** another name for **verso.**

re+vert *vb.* (rɪ'vɜːt). (*intr.,* foll. by *to*). **1.** to go back to a former practice, condition, belief, etc.: *she reverted to her old wicked ways.* **2.** to take up again or come back to a former topic. **3.** *Biology.* (of individuals, organs, etc.) to return to a more primitive, earlier, or simpler condition or type. **4.** *Property law.* (of an estate or interest in land) to return to its former owner or his heirs when a grant, esp. a grant for the lifetime of the grantee, comes to an end. **5. revert to type.** to resume characteristics that were thought to have disappeared. ~*n.* ('riːˌvɜːt). **6.** a person who, having been converted, has returned to his former beliefs or Church. [C13: from Latin *revertere* to return, from RE- + *vertere* to turn] —**re+'vert+er** *n.* —**re+'vert+i+ble** *adj.* —**re+'ver+tive** *adj.*

re+vest (riː'vɛst) *vb.* (often foll. by *in*) to restore (former power, authority, status, etc., to a person) or (of power, etc.) to be restored. [C16: from Old French *revestir* to clothe again, from Latin RE- + *vestīre* to clothe; see VEST]

re+vet (rɪ'vɛt) *vb.* **+vets, +vet+ting, +vet+ted.** to face (a wall or embankment) with stones. [C19: from French *revêt,* from Old French *revestir* to reclothe; see REVEST]

re+vet+ment (rɪ'vɛtmənt) *n.* **1.** a facing of stones, sand bags, etc., to protect a wall, embankment, or earthworks. **2.** another name for **retaining wall.** [C18: from French *revêtement* literally, a reclothing, from *revêtir;* see REVEST]

re+view (rɪ'vjuː) *vb.* (*mainly tr.*) **1.** to look at or examine again: *to review a situation.* **2.** to look back upon (a period of time, sequence of events, etc.); remember: *he reviewed his achievements with pride.* **3.** to inspect, esp. formally or officially: *the general reviewed his troops.* **4.** to read through or go over in order to correct. **5.** *Law.* to re-examine (a decision) judicially. **6.** to write a critical assessment of (a book, film, play, concert, etc.), esp. as a profession. ~*n.* **7.** Also called: **re+view+al.** the act or an instance of reviewing. **8.** a general survey or report: *a review of the political situation.* **9.** a critical assessment of a book, film, play, concert, etc., esp. one printed in a newspaper or periodical. **10. a.** a publication containing such articles. **b.** (*cap. when part of a name*): *the Saturday Review.* **11.** a second consideration; re-examination. **12.** a retrospective survey. **13.** a formal or official inspection. **14.** a U.S. word for **revision** (sense 2). **15.** *Law.* judicial re-examination of a case, esp. by a superior court. **16.** a less common spelling of **revue.** [C16: from French, from *revoir* to see again, from Latin *re-* RE- + *vidēre* to see] —**re+'view+a+ble** *adj.* —**re+'view+er** *n.*

re+view cop·y *n.* a copy of a book sent by a publisher to a journal, newspaper, etc., to enable it to be reviewed.

re+vile (rɪ'vaɪl) *vb.* to use abusive or scornful language against (someone or something). [C14: from Old French *reviler,* from RE- + *vil* VILE] —**re+'vile+ment** *n.* —**re+'vil+er** *n.* —**re+'vil+ing+ly** *adv.*

re+vise (rɪ'vaɪz) *vb.* **1.** (*tr.*) to change, alter, or amend: *to revise one's opinion.* **2.** *Brit.* to reread (a subject or notes on it) so as to memorize it, esp. in preparation for an examination. **3.** (*tr.*) to prepare a new version or edition of (a previously printed work). ~*n.* **4.** the act, process, or result of revising; revision. [C16: from Latin *revīsere* to look back at, from RE- + *vīsere* to inspect, from *vidēre* to see; see REVIEW, VISIT] —**re+'vis+a+ble** *adj.* —**re+'vis+al** *n.* —**re+'vis+er** *n.*

Re+vised Stand+ard Ver+sion *n.* a revision by American scholars of the American Standard Version of the Bible. The New Testament was published in 1946 and the entire Bible in 1953.

Re+vised Ver+sion *n.* a revision of the Authorized Version of the Bible prepared by two committees of British scholars, the New Testament being published in 1881 and the Old in 1885.

re+vi+sion (rɪ'vɪʒən) *n.* **1.** the act or process of revising. **2.** *Brit.* the process of rereading a subject or notes on it, esp. in preparation for an examination. **3.** a corrected or new version of a book, article, etc. —**re+'vi+sion+al** *or* **re+'vi+sion+ar+y** *adj.*

re+vi+sion+ism (rɪ'vɪʒəˌnɪzəm) *n.* **1.** (*sometimes cap.*) **a.** a moderate, nonrevolutionary version of Marxism developed in Germany around 1900. **b.** (in Marxist-Leninist ideology) any dangerous departure from the true interpretation of Marx's teachings. **2.** the advocacy of revision of some political theory, religious doctrine, historical or critical interpretation, etc. —**re+'vi+sion+ist** *n., adj.*

re+vi+so+ry (rɪ'vaɪzərɪ) *adj.* of, relating to, or having the power to revise.

re+vi+tal+ize *or* **re+vi+tal+ise** (riː'vaɪtᵊˌlaɪz) *vb.* (*tr.*) to restore vitality or animation to. —**re+ˌvi+tal+i+'za+tion** *or* **re+ˌvi+tal+i+'sa+tion** *n.*

re+viv+al (rɪ'vaɪvᵊl) *n.* **1.** the act or an instance of reviving or the state of being revived. **2.** an instance of returning to life or consciousness; restoration of vigour or vitality. **3.** a renewed use, acceptance of, or interest in (past customs, styles, etc.): *a revival of learning; the Gothic revival.* **4.** a new production of a play that has not been recently performed. **5.** a reawakening of faith or renewal of commitment to religion. **6.** an evangelistic meeting or service intended to effect such a reawakening in those present. **7.** the re-establishment of legal validity, as of a judgment, contract, etc.

re+viv+al+ism (rɪ'vaɪvəˌlɪzəm) *n.* **1.** a movement, esp. an evangelical Christian one, that seeks to reawaken faith. **2.** the tendency or desire to revive former customs, styles, etc.

re+viv+al+ist (rɪ'vaɪvəlɪst) *n.* **1.** a person who holds, promotes, or presides over religious revivals. **2.** a person who revives customs, institutions, ideas, etc. ~*adj.* **3.** of, relating to, or

re+'vac+cin+ate *vb.*
re+vac+cin·'a+tion *n.*
re+'var+nish *vb.*
ˌre+ver+i+fi+'ca+tion *n.*
re+'ver+i+ˌfy *vb.,* **+fies, +fy+ing, +fied.**
re+'vict+ual *vb.*
re+'vi+o+ˌlate *vb.*

characterizing revivalism or religious revivals: *a revivalist meeting.* —**re+ˌviv+al+ˈis+tic** *adj.*

re+vive (rɪˈvaɪv) *vb.* **1.** to bring or be brought back to life, consciousness, or strength; resuscitate or be resuscitated: *revived by a drop of whisky.* **2.** to give or assume new vitality; flourish again or cause to flourish again. **3.** to make or become operative or active again: *the youth movement was revived.* **4.** to bring or come into use or currency again: *to revive a language.* **5.** (*tr.*) to take up again: *he revived his old hobby.* **6.** to bring or come back to mind. **7.** (*tr.*) *Theatre.* to mount a new production of (an old play). [C15: from Old French *revivre* to live again, from Latin *revīvere,* from RE- + *vīvere* to live; see VIVID] —**re+ˈviv+a·ble** *adj.* —**re+ˌviv+a·ˈbil+i·ty** *n.* —**re+ˈviv+a·bly** *adv.* —**re+ˈviv+er** *n.* —**re+ˈviv+ing+ly** *adv.*

re+viv·i·fy (rɪˈvɪvɪˌfaɪ) *vb.* **+fies, +fy+ing, +fied.** (*tr.*) to give new life or spirit to; revive. —**re+ˌviv+i+fi+ˈca+tion** *n.*

rev·i+vis+cence (ˌrɛvɪˈvɪsəns, rɪˈvɪvɪsəns) *n. Literary.* restoration to life or animation; revival. [C17: from Latin, from *revīviscere* come back to life, related to *vīvere* to live; see REVIVE] —**ˌrev·i+ˈvis+cent** *adj.*

rev·o+ca·ble (ˈrɛvəkəbᵊl) *or* **re+vok+a·ble** (rɪˈvəʊkəbᵊl) *adj.* capable of being revoked; able to be cancelled. —**ˌrev·o+ca·ˈbil+i·ty, re+ˌvok+a·ˈbil+i·ty** *or* **ˈrev·o+ca·ble+ness, re+ˈvok+a·ble+ness** *n.* —**ˈrev·o+ca·bly** *or* **re+ˈvok+a·bly** *adv.*

rev·o+ca+tion (ˌrɛvəˈkeɪʃən) *n.* **1.** the act of revoking or state of being revoked; cancellation. **2. a.** the cancellation or annulment of a legal instrument, esp. a will. **b.** the withdrawal of an offer, power of attorney, etc. —**re+voc·a+tive** (rɪˈvɒkətɪv) *or* **rev·o+ca+to·ry** (ˈrɛvəkətərɪ, -trɪ) *adj.*

re+voice (riːˈvɔɪs) *vb.* (*intr.*) **1.** to utter again; echo. **2.** to adjust the design of (an organ pipe or wind instrument) as after disuse or to conform with modern pitch.

re+voke (rɪˈvəʊk) *vb.* **1.** (*tr.*) to take back or withdraw; cancel; rescind: *to revoke a law.* **2.** (*intr.*) *Cards.* to break a rule of play by failing to follow suit when able to do so; renege. ~*n.* **3.** *Cards.* the act of revoking; a renege. [C14: from Latin *revocāre* to call back, withdraw, from RE- + *vocāre* to call] —**re+ˈvok+er** *n.*

re+volt (rɪˈvəʊlt) *n.* **1.** a rebellion or uprising against authority. **2. in revolt.** in the process or state of rebelling. ~*vb.* **3.** (*intr.*) to rise up in rebellion against authority. **4.** (*usually passive*) to feel or cause to feel revulsion, disgust, or abhorrence. [C16: from French *révolter* to revolt, from Old Italian *rivoltare* to overturn, ultimately from Latin *revolvere* to roll back, REVOLVE] —**re+ˈvolt+er** *n.*

re+volt+ing (rɪˈvəʊltɪŋ) *adj.* **1.** causing revulsion; nauseating, disgusting, or repulsive. **2.** *Informal.* unpleasant or nasty: *that dress is revolting.* —**re+ˈvolt+ing+ly** *adv.*

rev·o+lute (ˈrɛvəˌluːt) *adj.* (esp. of the margins of a leaf) rolled backwards and downwards. [C18: from Latin *revolūtus* rolled back; see REVOLVE]

rev·o+lu+tion (ˌrɛvəˈluːʃən) *n.* **1.** the overthrow or repudiation of a regime or political system by the governed. **2.** (in Marxist theory) the violent and historically necessary transition from one system of production in a society to the next, as from feudalism to capitalism. **3.** a far-reaching and drastic change, esp. in ideas, methods, etc. **4. a.** movement in or as if in a circle. **b.** one complete turn in such a circle: *a turntable rotating at 33 revolutions per minute.* **5. a.** the orbital motion of one body, such as a planet or satellite, around another. Compare **rotation** (sense 5a). **b.** one complete turn in such motion. **6.** a cycle of successive events or changes. **7.** *Geology.* a profound change in conditions over a large part of the earth's surface, esp. one characterized by mountain building: *an orogenic revolution.* [C14: via Old French from Late Latin *revolūtiō,* from Latin *revolvere* to REVOLVE]

rev·o+lu+tion+ar·y (ˌrɛvəˈluːʃənərɪ) *n., pl.* **+ar·ies.** **1.** a person who advocates or engages in revolution. ~*adj.* **2.** relating to or characteristic of a revolution. **3.** advocating or engaged in revolution. **4.** radically new or different: *a revolutionary method of making plastics.* **5.** rotating or revolving. —**ˌrev·o+ˈlu+tion+ar+i+ly** *adv.*

Rev·o+lu+tion+ar·y (ˌrɛvəˈluːʃənərɪ) *adj.* **1.** *Chiefly U.S.* of or relating to the conflict or period of the War of American Independence (1775–83). **2.** of or relating to any of various other Revolutions, esp. the **Russian Revolution** (1917) or the **French Revolution** (1789).

Rev·o+lu+tion+ar·y cal+en+dar *n.* the calendar adopted by the French First Republic in 1793 and abandoned in 1805. Dates were calculated from Sept. 22, 1792. The months were called Vendémiaire, Brumaire, Frimaire, Nivôse, Pluviôse, Ventôse, Germinal, Floréal, Prairial, Messidor, Thermidor, and Fructidor.

Rev·o+lu+tion+ar·y Wars *pl. n.* the series of wars (1792–1802) fought against Revolutionary France by a combination of other powers, esp. England, Austria, and Prussia.

rev·o+lu+tion+ist (ˌrɛvəˈluːʃənɪst) *n.* **1.** a less common word for a **revolutionary.** ~*adj.* **2.** of, characteristic of, or relating to revolution or revolutionaries.

rev·o+lu+tion+ize *or* **rev·o+lu+tion+ise** (ˌrɛvəˈluːʃəˌnaɪz) *vb.* (*tr.*) **1.** to bring about a radical change in: *science has revolutionized civilization.* **2.** to inspire or infect with revolutionary ideas: *they revolutionized the common soldiers.* **3.** to cause a revolution in (a country, etc.). —**ˌrev·o+ˈlu+tion+ˌiz+er** *or* **ˌrev·o+ˈlu+tion+ˌis+er** *n.*

re+volve (rɪˈvɒlv) *vb.* **1.** to move or cause to move around a centre or axis; rotate. **2.** (*intr.*) to occur periodically or in cycles. **3.** to consider or be considered. **4.** (*intr.;* foll. by *around* or *about*) to be centred or focused (upon): *Juliet's thoughts revolved around Romeo.* [C14: from Latin *revolvere,* from RE- + *volvere* to roll, wind] —**re+ˈvolv+a·ble** *adj.* —**re+ˈvolv+a·bly** *adv.*

re+volv+er (rɪˈvɒlvə) *n.* a pistol having a revolving multichambered cylinder that allows several shots to be discharged without reloading.

re+volv+ing (rɪˈvɒlvɪŋ) *adj.* denoting or relating to an engine, such as a radial aero engine, in which the cylinders revolve about a fixed shaft. —**re+ˈvolv+ing+ly** *adv.*

re+volv+ing cred+it *n.* a letter of credit for a fixed sum, specifying that the beneficiary may make repeated use of the credit provided that the fixed sum is never exceeded.

re+volv+ing door *n.* a door that rotates about a central vertical axis, esp. one with four leaves arranged at right angles to each other, thereby excluding draughts.

re+volv+ing fund *n.* a fund set up for a specific purpose and constantly added to by fresh appropriations or by income from the investments it finances.

re+vue *or* **re+view** (rɪˈvjuː) *n.* a form of light entertainment consisting of a series of topical sketches, songs, dancing, comic turns, etc. [C20: from French; see REVIEW]

re+vul+sion (rɪˈvʌlʃən) *n.* **1.** a sudden and unpleasant violent reaction in feeling, esp. one of extreme loathing. **2.** the act or an instance of drawing back or recoiling from something. **3.** the diversion of disease or congestion from one part of the body to another by cupping, counterirritants, etc. [C16: from Latin *revulsiō* a pulling away, from *revellere,* from RE- + *vellere* to pull, tear] —**re+ˈvul+sion+ar·y** *adj.*

re+vul+sive (rɪˈvʌlsɪv) *adj.* **1.** of or causing revulsion. ~*n.* **2.** *Med.* a counterirritant. —**re+ˈvul+sive+ly** *adv.*

Rev. Ver. *abbrev. for* Revised Version (of the Bible).

re+ward (rɪˈwɔːd) *n.* **1.** something given or received in return for a deed or service rendered. **2.** a sum of money offered, esp. for help in finding a criminal or for the return of lost or stolen property. **3.** profit or return. ~*vb.* **4.** (*tr.*) to give (something) to (someone), esp. in gratitude for a service rendered; recompense. [C14: from Old Norman French *rewarder* to regard, from RE- + *warder* to care for, guard, of Germanic origin; see WARD] —**re+ˈward+a·ble** *adj.* —**re+ˈward+er** *n.* —**re+ˈward+less** *adj.*

re+ward+ing (rɪˈwɔːdɪŋ) *adj.* giving personal satisfaction; gratifying: *caring for the elderly is rewarding.*

re·wa·re·wa (ˌreɪwəˈreɪwə) *n.* a tall proteacebus tree of New Zealand, *Knightia excelsa,* yielding a beautiful reddish timber. [C19: from Maori]

re+wind *vb.* (riːˈwaɪnd), **+winds, +wind+ing, +wound.** **1.** (*tr.*) to wind back, esp. a film or tape onto the original reel. ~*n.* (ˈriːˌwaɪnd, riːˈwaɪnd). **2.** something rewound. **3.** the act of rewinding. —**re+ˈwind+er** *n.*

re+wire (riːˈwaɪə) *vb.* (*tr.*) to provide (a house, engine, etc.) with new wiring. —**re+ˈwir+a·ble** *adj.*

re+word (riːˈwɜːd) *vb.* (*tr.*) to alter the wording of; express differently.

re+work (riːˈwɜːk) *vb.* (*tr.*) **1.** to use again in altered form: *the theme was reworked in countless poems.* **2.** to rewrite or revise. **3.** to reprocess for use again.

re+write *vb.* (riːˈraɪt), **+writes, +writ+ing, +wrote, +writ+ten.** (*tr.*) **1.** to write (written material) again, esp. changing the words or form. ~*n.* (ˈriːˌraɪt). **2.** something rewritten.

re+write rule *n. Generative grammar.* another name for **phrase-structure rule.**

Rex (rɛks) *n.* king: part of the official title of a king, now used chiefly in documents, legal proceedings, inscriptions on coins, etc. Compare **Regina**[1]. [Latin]

Rexine (ˈrɛksiːn) *n. Trademark.* a form of artificial leather.

Rey+kja+vik (ˈreɪkjəˌviːk) *n.* the capital and chief port of Iceland, situated in the southwest: its buildings are heated by natural hot water. Pop.: 84 589 (1974 est.).

Reyn+ard *or* **Ren+ard** (ˈrɛnəd, ˈrɛnɑːd) *n.* a name for a fox, used in children's tales, fables, etc.

Rey·naud (*French* rɛˈno) *n.* **Paul** (pɔl). 1878–1966, French statesman: premier during the defeat of France by Germany (1940); later imprisoned by the Germans.

Reyn·olds (ˈrɛnəldz) *n.* Sir **Josh·u·a.** 1723–92, English portrait painter. He was the first president of the Royal Academy (1768): the annual lectures he gave there, published as *Discourses,* are important contributions to art theory and criticism.

Rey·nolds num+ber *n.* a number, $v\rho l/\eta$, where v is the fluid velocity, ρ the density, η the viscosity and l a dimension of the system. The value of the number indicates the type of fluid flow. [C19: named after Osborne *Reynolds* (1842–1912), British physicist]

Rey+no+sa (*Spanish* reˈnosa) *n.* a city in E Mexico, in Tamaulipas state on the Rio Grande. Pop.: 193 653 (1975 est.).

rf *or* **rf.** *Music. abbrev. for* rinforzando. Also: **rfz.**

RF *abbrev. for* radio frequency.

R.F.C. *abbrev. for* Rugby Football Club.

R.G.S. *abbrev. for* Royal Geographical Society.

Rgt. *abbrev. for* regiment.

ˌre+vi·o+ˈla+tion *n.*
re+ˈvis+it *vb.*
re+ˈwake *vb.,* **+wakes, +wak+ing, +waked** *or* **+woke.**
re+ˈwak+en *vb.*
re+ˈwarm *vb.*
re+ˈwash *vb.*
re+ˈweave *vb.,* **+weaves, +weav+ing, +wove** *or* **+weaved, +wo+ven** *or* **+weaved.**
re+ˈweigh *vb.*
re+ˈweld *vb.*
re+ˈwid+en *vb.*
re+ˈwrap *vb.,* **+wraps, +wrap+ping, +wrapped.**
re+ˈzone *vb.*

Rh 1. *the chemical symbol for* rhodium. **2.** *abbrev. for* rhesus (esp. in **Rh factor**).
RH. 1. *abbrev. for* Royal Highness. **2.** *international car registration for* (Republic of) Haiti.
r.h. *or* **R.H.** *abbrev. for* right hand.
R.H.A. *abbrev. for* Royal Horse Artillery.
rhab+do+man+cy ('ræbdəˌmænsɪ) *n.* divination for water or mineral ore by means of a rod or wand; dowsing; divining. [C17: via Late Latin from Late Greek *rhabdomanteia,* from *rhabdos* a rod + *manteia* divination] —**'rhab+do+ˌman+tist** *or* **'rhab+do+ˌman+cer** *n.*
rhab+do+my+o+ma (ˌræbdəʊmaɪ'əʊmə) *n., pl.* **+mas** *or* **+ma+ta** (-mətə). *Pathol.* a benign tumour of striated muscle. [C19: from New Latin, from Greek *rhabdos* a rod + MYOMA]
rha+chis ('reɪkɪs) *n., pl.* **rha+chis+es** *or* **rha+chi+des** ('rækɪˌdi:z, 'reɪ-). a variant spelling of **rachis.**
Rhad·a·man·thus *or* **Rhad·a·man·thys** (ˌrædə'mænθəs) *n. Greek myth.* one of the judges of the dead in the underworld. —**ˌRhad·a+'man+thine** *adj.*
Rhae+ti·a ('ri:ʃɪə) *n.* an Alpine province of ancient Rome including parts of present-day Tyrol and E Switzerland.
Rhae+tian ('ri:ʃən) *n.* **1.** Also called: **Rhae·to-Ro·man·ic** ('ri:təʊrəʊ'mænɪk). a group of Romance languages or dialects spoken in certain valleys of the Alps, including Romansch, Ladin, and Friulian. ~*adj.* **2.** denoting or relating to this group of languages. **3.** of or relating to Rhaetia.
Rhae+tian Alps *pl. n.* a section of the central Alps along E Switzerland's borders with Austria and Italy. Highest peak: Piz Bernina, 4049 m (13 284 ft.).
Rhae+tic *or* **Rhe+tic** ('ri:tɪk) *adj.* **1.** of or relating to a series of rocks formed between the Triassic and Jurassic periods. ~*n.* **2.** the Rhaetic series.
rham+na+ceous (ræm'neɪʃəs) *adj.* of, relating to, or belonging to the *Rhamnaceae,* a widely distributed family of trees and shrubs having small inconspicuous flowers. The family includes the buckthorns. [C19: from New Latin *Rhamnaceae,* from Greek *rhamnos* a thorn]
rhap+sod+ic (ræp'sɒdɪk) *adj.* **1.** of or like a rhapsody. ~*n.* **2.** lyrical or romantic. —**rhap+'sod·i+cal+ly** *adv.*
rhap+so+dist ('ræpsədɪst) *n.* **1.** a person who speaks or writes rhapsodies. **2.** a person who speaks with extravagant enthusiasm. **3.** Also called: **rhap+sode** ('ræpsəʊd). (in ancient Greece) a professional reciter of poetry, esp. of Homer. —**ˌrhap+so+'dis+tic** *adj.*
rhap+so+dize *or* **rhap+so+dise** ('ræpsəˌdaɪz) *vb.* **1.** to speak or write (something) with extravagant enthusiasm. **2.** (*intr.*) to recite or write rhapsodies.
rhap+so+dy ('ræpsədɪ) *n., pl.* **+dies. 1.** *Music.* a composition, free in structure and highly emotional in character. **2.** an expression of ecstatic enthusiasm. **3.** (in ancient Greece) an epic poem or part of an epic recited by a rhapsodist. **4.** a literary work composed in an intense or exalted style. **5.** rapturous delight or ecstasy. **6.** *Obsolete.* a medley. [C16: via Latin from Greek *rhapsōidia,* from *rhaptein* to sew together + *ōidē* song]
rhat·a+ny ('rætənɪ) *n., pl.* **+nies. 1.** either of two South American leguminous shrubs, *Krameria triandra* or *K. argentea,* that have thick fleshy roots. **2.** the dried roots of such shrubs for use as an astringent. ~Also called: **krameria.** [C19: from New Latin *rhatānia,* ultimately from Quechua *ratánya*]
r.h.d. *abbrev. for* right-hand drive.
rhe·a ('rɪə) *n.* either of two large fast-running flightless birds, *Rhea americana* and *Pterocnemia pennata,* inhabiting the open plains of S South America: order *Rheiformes* (see **ratite**). They are similar to but smaller than the ostrich, having three-toed feet and a completely feathered body. [C19: New Latin; arbitrarily named after RHEA¹]
Rhe·a¹ ('rɪə) *n. Greek myth.* a Titaness, wife of Cronus and mother of several of the gods, including Zeus: a fertility goddess. Roman counterpart: **Ops.**
Rhe·a² ('rɪə) *n.* one of the ten satellites of the planet Saturn.
Rhe·a Sil·vi·a *or* **Re·a Sil·vi·a** ('sɪlvɪə) *n. Roman myth.* the mother of Romulus and Remus by Mars. See also **Ilia.**
rhe+bok *or* **ree+bok** ('ri:bʌk, -bɒk) *n., pl.* **+boks** *or* **+bok.** an antelope, *Pelea capreolus,* of southern Africa, having woolly brownish-grey hair. [C18: Afrikaans, from Dutch *reebok* ROEBUCK]
Rhee (ri:) *n.* **Syng·man** ('sɪŋmən). 1875–1965, Korean statesman, leader of the campaign for independence from Japan; first president of South Korea (1948–60). Popular unrest forced his resignation.
Rheims (ri:mz; *French* rɛ̃s) *n.* a variant spelling of **Reims.**
Rhein (raɪn) *n.* the German name for the **Rhine.**
Rhein+land ('raɪnlant) *n.* See **Rhineland.**
Rhe+mish ('ri:mɪʃ) *adj.* of, relating to, or originating in Reims.
Rhen+ish ('rɛnɪʃ, 'ri:-) *adj.* **1.** of or relating to the River Rhine or the lands adjacent to it, esp. the Rhineland-Palatinate. ~*n.* **2.** another word for **hock** (the wine).
rhe+ni·um ('ri:nɪəm) *n.* a dense silvery-white metallic element that has a high melting point. It occurs principally in gadolinite and molybdenite and is used, alloyed with tungsten or molybdenum, in high-temperature thermocouples. Symbol: Re; atomic no.: 75; atomic wt.: 186.2; valency: 1-7; relative density: 21.0; melting pt.: 3180°C; boiling pt.: 5627°C (est.). [C19: New Latin, from *Rhēnus* the Rhine]
rheo. *abbrev. for* rheostat.
rhe·o- *combining form.* indicating stream, flow, or current: *rheometer; rheoscope.* [from Greek *rheos* stream, anything flowing, from *rhein* to flow]
rhe·o+base ('ri:əʊˌbeɪs) *n. Physiol.* the minimum nerve impulse required to elicit a response from a tissue.
rhe+ol·o+gy (rɪ'ɒlədʒɪ) *n.* the branch of physics concerned with the flow and change of shape of matter, esp. the viscosity of liquids. —**rhe·o·log·i+cal** (ˌri:ə'lɒdʒɪkᵊl) *adj.* —**rhe+'ol·o+gist** *n.*
rhe+om+e·ter (ri:'ɒmɪtə) *n.* **1.** *Med.* an instrument for measuring the velocity of the blood flow. **2.** another word for **galvanometer.** —**rhe·o+met+ric** (ˌri:ə'mɛtrɪk) *adj.* —**rhe+'om+e·try** *n.*
rhe·o+stat ('rɪəˌstæt) *n.* a variable resistance, usually consisting of a coil of wire with a terminal at one end and a sliding contact that moves along the coil to tap off the current. —**ˌrhe·o+'stat+ic** *adj.*
rhe·o+tax+is (ˌrɪə'tæksɪs) *n.* movement of an organism towards or away from a current of water. —**rhe·o+tac+tic** (ˌrɪə'tæktɪk) *adj.*
rhe+ot+ro+pism (ri:'ɒtrəˌpɪzəm) *n.* growth of a plant or sessile animal in the direction of a current of water. —**rhe·o+trop+ic** (ˌrɪə'trɒpɪk) *adj.*
Rhe·sus ('ri:səs) *n. Greek myth.* a king of Thrace, who arrived in the tenth year of the Trojan War to aid Troy. Odysseus and Diomedes stole his horses because an oracle had said that if these horses drank from the River Xanthus, Troy would not fall.
rhe+sus ba+by *n.* a baby suffering from haemolytic disease at birth as its red blood cells (which are Rh positive) have been attacked in the womb by antibodies from its Rh negative mother.
rhe+sus fac+tor ('ri:səs) *n.* See **Rh factor.**
rhe+sus mon+key *n.* a macaque monkey, *Macaca mulatta,* of S Asia: used extensively in medical research. [C19: New Latin, arbitrarily from Greek *Rhesos* RHĒSUS]
rhet. *abbrev. for* rhetoric(al).
Rhe+tic ('ri:tɪk) *adj.* a variant spelling of **Rhaetic.**
rhe+tor ('ri:tə) *n.* **1.** a teacher of rhetoric. **2.** (in ancient Greece) an orator. [C14: via Latin from Greek *rhētōr;* related to *rhēma* word]
rhet·o+ric ('rɛtərɪk) *n.* **1.** the study of the technique of using language effectively. **2.** the art of using speech to persuade, influence, or please; oratory. **3.** excessive use of ornamentation and contrivance in spoken or written discourse; bombast. **4.** speech or discourse that pretends to significance but lacks true meaning: *all the politician says is mere rhetoric.* [C14: via Latin from Greek *rhētorikē* (*tekhnē*) (the art of) rhetoric, from *rhētōr* RHETOR]
rhe+tor·i+cal (rɪ'tɒrɪkᵊl) *adj.* **1.** concerned with effect or style rather than content or meaning; bombastic. **2.** of or relating to rhetoric or oratory. —**rhe+'tor·i·cal+ly** *adv.*
rhe+tor·i·cal ques+tion *n.* a question to which no answer is required: used esp. for dramatic effect. An example is *Who knows?* (with the implication *Nobody knows*).
rhe+tor·i+cian (ˌrɛtə'rɪʃən) *n.* **1.** a teacher of the art of rhetoric. **2.** a stylish or eloquent writer or speaker. **3.** a person whose speech is pompous or extravagant.
rheum (ru:m) *n.* a watery discharge from the eyes or nose. [C14: from Old French *reume,* ultimately from Greek *rheuma* bodily humour, stream, from *rheein* to flow]
rheu+mat+ic (ru:'mætɪk) *adj.* **1.** of, relating to, or afflicted with rheumatism. ~*n.* **2.** a person afflicted with rheumatism. [C14: ultimately from Greek *rheumatikos,* from *rheuma* a flow; see RHEUM] —**rheu+'mat·i·cal+ly** *adv.*
rheu+mat+ic fe+ver *n.* a disease characterized by sore throat, fever, inflammation, and pain in the joints.
rheu+mat+ics (ru:'mætɪks) *n. Informal.* rheumatism.
rheu+ma+tism ('ru:məˌtɪzəm) *n.* any painful disorder of joints, muscles, or connective tissue. Compare **arthritis, fibrositis.** [C17: from Latin *rheumatismus* catarrh, from Greek *rheumatismos;* see RHEUM]
rheu+ma+toid ('ru:məˌtɔɪd) *or* **rheu+ma+toi+dal** *adj.* (of the symptoms of a disease) resembling rheumatism. —**ˌrheu+ma+'toi+dal+ly** *adv.*
rheu+ma+toid ar+thri+tis *n.* a chronic disease of the musculoskeletal system, characterized by inflammation and swelling of joints (esp. joints in the hands, wrists, knees, and feet), muscle weakness, and fatigue.
rheu+ma+tol·o·gy (ˌru:mə'tɒlədʒɪ) *n.* the branch of medicine concerned with the study of rheumatic diseases.
rheum·y ('ru:mɪ) *adj.* **1.** of the nature of rheum. **2.** *Literary.* damp and unhealthy: *the rheumy air.*
Rheydt (*German* raɪt) *n.* an industrial town in W West Germany, in North Rhine-Westphalia. Pop.: 100 939 (1974 est.).
Rh fac+tor *n.* an agglutinogen commonly found in human blood: it may cause a haemolytic reaction, esp. during pregnancy or following transfusion of blood that does not contain this agglutinogen. Full name: **rhesus factor.** See also **Rh positive, Rh negative.** [named after the rhesus monkey, in which it was first discovered]
R.H.G. *abbrev. for* Royal Horse Guards.
rhig·o+lene ('rɪgəʊˌli:n) *n.* a volatile liquid obtained from petroleum and used as a local anaesthetic. [C19: from Greek *rhigos* cold; see -OLE, -ENE]
rhi+nal ('raɪnᵊl) *adj.* of or relating to the nose; nasal.
Rhine (raɪn) *n.* a river in central and W Europe, rising in SE Switzerland: flows through Lake Constance north through West Germany and west through the Netherlands to the North Sea. Length: about 1320 km (820 miles). Dutch name: **Rijn.** French name: **Rhin** (rɛ̃). German name: **Rhein.**

Rhine+land ('raɪnˌlænd, -lənd) *n.* the region of West Germany surrounding the Rhine. German name: **Rheinland.**

Rhine·land-Pa·lat·i·nate *n.* a state of W West Germany: formed in 1946 from the S part of the Prussian Rhine province, the Bavarian Palatinate, and parts of Rhine-Hesse and Hesse-Nassau; agriculture (with over two thirds of West Germany's vineyards) and tourism are important. Capital: Mainz. Pop.: 3 645 437 (1970). Area: 19 832 sq. km (7657 sq. miles). German name: **Rheinland-Pfalz.**

rhi+nen+ceph·a+lon (ˌraɪnɛn'sɛfəˌlɒn) *n., pl.* **+lons** *or* **+la** (-lə). *Anatomy.* the part of the brain that contains the olfactory bulb and tract and is concerned with the sense of smell. **—rhi+nen+ce·phal+ic** (ˌraɪnɛnsɪ'fælɪk) *adj.*

rhine+stone ('raɪnˌstəʊn) *n.* an imitation gem made of paste. [C19: translation of French *caillou du Rhin*, referring to Strasbourg, where such gems were made]

Rhine wine *n.* any of several wines produced along the banks of the Rhine, characteristically a white table wine such as riesling.

rhi+ni+tis (raɪ'naɪtɪs) *n.* inflammation of the mucous membrane that lines the nose.

rhi+no[1] ('raɪnəʊ) *n., pl.* **+nos** *or* **+no.** short for **rhinoceros.**

rhi+no[2] ('raɪnəʊ) *n. Brit.* a slang word for **money.** [C17: of unknown origin]

rhi·no- *or before a vowel* **rhin-** *combining form.* indicating the nose or nasal: *rhinology.* [from Greek *rhis, rhin*]

rhi+noc+er+os (raɪ'nɒsərəs, -'nɒsrəs) *n., pl.* **+os·es** *or* **+os.** any of several perissodactyl mammals constituting the family *Rhinocerotidae* of SE Asia and Africa and having either one horn, like the **Indian rhinoceros** (*Rhinoceros unicornis*), or two horns, like the African **white rhinoceros** (*Diceros simus*). They have a very thick skin, massive body, and three digits on each foot. [C13: via Latin from Greek *rhinokerōs*, from *rhis* nose + *keras* horn] **—rhi+no+ce+rot+ic** (ˌraɪnəʊsɪ'rɒtɪk) *adj.*

rhi+noc+er+os bee+tle *n.* any of various scarabaeid beetles having one or more horns on the head, esp. *Oryctes rhinoceros,* a serious pest on coconut plantations.

rhi+noc+er+os bird *n.* another name for the **oxpecker.**

rhi+nol+o·gy (raɪ'nɒlədʒɪ) *n.* the branch of medical science concerned with the nose and its diseases. **—rhi+no+log·i+cal** (ˌraɪnə'lɒdʒɪkəl) *adj.* **—rhi+'nol·o+gist** *n.*

rhi+no+plas+ty ('raɪnəʊˌplæstɪ) *n.* plastic surgery of the nose. **—ˌrhi+no+'plas+tic** *adj.*

rhi+nos+co+py (raɪ'nɒskəpɪ) *n. Med.* examination of the nasal passages, esp. with a special instrument called a **rhi+no+scope** ('raɪnəʊˌskəʊp). **—rhi+no+scop+ic** (ˌraɪnəʊ'skɒpɪk) *adj.*

rhi·zo- *or before a vowel* **rhiz-** *combining form.* root: *rhizomorphous.* [from Greek *rhiza*]

rhi+zo+bi·um (raɪ'zəʊbɪəm) *n., pl.* **+bi·a** (-bɪə). any rod-shaped bacterium of the genus *Rhizobium,* typically occurring in the root nodules of leguminous plants and able to fix atmospheric nitrogen. See also **nitrogen fixation.**

rhi+zo+car+pous (ˌraɪzəʊ'kɑːpəs) *adj.* **1.** (of plants) producing subterranean flowers and fruit. **2.** (of perennial plants) having roots that persist throughout the year but stems and leaves that wither at the end of the growing season.

rhi+zo+ceph·a+lan (ˌraɪzəʊ'sɛfələn) *n.* **1.** any parasitic crustacean of the order *Rhizocephala,* esp. *Sacculina carcini,* which has a saclike body and sends out absorptive processes into the body of its host, the crab: subclass *Cirripedia* (barnacles). *~adj. also* **rhi+zo+ceph·a+lous. 2.** of, relating to, or belonging to the order *Rhizocephala.* [C19: from New Latin *Rhizocephala* (literally: root-headed), from RHIZO- + *-cephala* from Greek *kephalē* head]

rhi+zo+gen+ic (ˌraɪzəʊ'dʒɛnɪk), **rhi+zo+ge+net+ic** (ˌraɪzəʊdʒə'nɛtɪk), *or* **rhi+zog+e+nous** (raɪ'zɒdʒənəs). *adj.* (of cells and tissues) giving rise to roots.

rhi+zoid ('raɪzɔɪd) *n.* any of various slender hairlike structures that function as roots in mosses, ferns, fungi, and related plants. **—rhi+'zoi+dal** *adj.*

rhi+zome ('raɪzəʊm) *n.* a thick horizontal underground stem of plants such as the mint and iris whose buds develop into new plants. Also called: **rootstock, rootstalk.** [C19: from New Latin *rhizoma,* from Greek, from *rhiza* a root] **—rhi+zom·a+tous** (raɪ'zɒmətəs, -'zəʊ-) *adj.*

rhi+zo+morph ('raɪzəʊˌmɔːf) *n.* a rootlike structure of certain fungi, such as the honey fungus *Armillaria mellea,* consisting of a dense mass of hyphae.

rhi+zo+mor+phous (ˌraɪzəʊ'mɔːfəs) *adj. Botany.* having the appearance of a root.

rhi+zo+pod ('raɪzəʊˌpɒd) *n.* **1.** any protozoan of the subclass *Rhizopoda,* characterized by naked protoplasmic processes (pseudopodia): class *Sarcodina.* The group includes the amoebas and foraminifers. *~adj.* **2.** of, relating to, or belonging to the *Rhizopoda.* **—rhi+zop·o+dan** (raɪ'zɒpədən) *adj., n.* **—rhi+'zop·o·dous** *adj.*

rhi+zo+pus ('raɪzəʊpəs) *n.* any phycomycetous fungus of the genus *Rhizopus,* esp. *R. nigricans,* a bread mould. [C19: New Latin, from RHIZO- + Greek *pous* foot]

rhi+zo+sphere ('raɪzəʊˌsfɪə) *n.* the region of the soil in contact with the roots of a plant. It contains many microorganisms and its composition is affected by root activities.

rhi+zot·o+my (raɪ'zɒtəmɪ) *n., pl.* **+mies.** surgical incision into the roots of spinal nerves, esp. for the relief of pain.

Rh neg·a+tive *n.* **1.** blood that does not contain the Rh factor. **2.** a person having such blood.

rho (rəʊ) *n., pl.* **rhos.** the 17th letter in the Greek alphabet (Ρ, ρ), a consonant transliterated as *r* or *rh.*

rho+da+mine ('rəʊdəˌmiːn, -mɪn) *n.* any one of a group of synthetic red or pink basic dyestuffs used for wool and silk. They are made from phthalic anhydride and aminophenols. [C20: from RHODO- + AMINE]

Rhode Is+land (rəʊd) *n.* a state of the northeastern U.S., bordering on the Atlantic: the smallest state in the U.S.; mainly low-lying and undulating, with an indented coastline in the east and uplands in the northwest. Capital: Providence. Pop.: 949 723 (1970). Area: 2717 sq. km (1049 sq. miles). Abbrevs.: **R.I.** or (with zip code) **RI**

Rhode Is+land Red *n.* a breed of domestic fowl, originating in America, characterized by a dark reddish-brown plumage and the production of brown eggs.

Rhodes[1] (rəʊdz) *n.* **1.** a Greek island in the SE Aegean Sea, about 16 km (10 miles) off the Turkish coast: the largest of the Dodecanese and the most easterly island in the Aegean. Capital: Rhodes. Pop.: 70 110 (1971). Area: 1400 sq. km (540 sq. miles). **2.** a port on this island, in the NE: founded in 408 B.C.; of great commercial and political importance in the 3rd century B.C.; suffered several earthquakes, notably in 225, when the Colossus was destroyed. Pop.: 33 100 (1971). ~Ancient Greek name: **Rhodos.** Modern Greek name: **Ródhos.**

Rhodes[2] (rəʊdz) *n.* **Cec·il John.** 1853–1902, English colonial financier and statesman in South Africa. He made a fortune in diamond and gold mining and, as prime minister of the Cape Colony (1890–96), he helped to extend British territory. He established the annual **Rhodes scholarships** to Oxford.

Rhodes grass *n.* a perennial grass, *Chloris gayana,* native to Africa but widely cultivated in dry regions for forage. [C19: named after Cecil RHODES]

Rho+de·sia (rəʊ'diːʃə, -zɪə) *n.* a former self-governing British colony in southern Africa: founded when the British South Africa Company conquered the Matabele in 1889, obtained the mineral rights, and administered the country until a self-governing colony was established in 1923; joined with Northern Rhodesia (now Zambia) and Nyasaland (now Malawi) as the Federation of Rhodesia and Nyasaland from 1953 to 1962; made a unilateral declaration of independence under the leadership of Ian Smith in 1965 on the basis of white minority rule; proclaimed a republic in 1970; in 1976 the principle of black majority rule was accepted and in 1978 a transitional government was set up, strongly opposed by some black nationalist organizations. In 1980 it became an independent republic named **Zimbabwe.** Former name (until 1964): **Southern Rhodesia.** See also **Zimbabwe.** **—Rho+'de·sian** *adj., n.*

Rho+de·sia and Ny+as·a+land *n.* **Fed+er·a+tion of.** a federation consisting of Northern Rhodesia, Southern Rhodesia, and Nyasaland, which existed from 1953 to 1963.

Rho+de·sian Front *n.* the governing party in Rhodesia since 1962, led by Ian Smith since 1964.

Rho+de·sian man *n.* a type of early man, *Homo rhodesiensis* (or *H. sapiens rhodesiensis*), occurring in Africa in late Pleistocene times and resembling Neanderthal man in many features.

Rho+de·sian ridge+back *n.* a large short-haired breed of dog characterized by a ridge of hair growing along the back in the opposite direction to the rest of the coat.

Rho+de·soid (rəʊ'diːzɔɪd) *adj.* relating to or resembling Rhodesian man.

Rhodes schol+ar+ship *n.* one of 72 scholarships founded by Cecil Rhodes, awarded annually on merit to Commonwealth and U.S. students to study for two or sometimes three years at Oxford University. **—Rhodes schol+ar** *n.*

Rho+di·an ('rəʊdɪən) *adj.* **1.** of or relating to the island of Rhodes. *~n.* **2.** a native or inhabitant of Rhodes.

rho+dic ('rəʊdɪk) *adj.* of or containing rhodium, esp. in the tetravalent state.

rho+di+nal ('rəʊdɪˌnæl) *n.* another name for **citronellal.**

rho+di·um ('rəʊdɪəm) *n.* a hard corrosion-resistant silvery-white element of the platinum metal group, occurring free with other platinum metals in alluvial deposits and in nickel ores. It is used as an alloying agent to harden platinum and palladium. Symbol: Rh; atomic no.: 45; atomic wt.: 102.90; valency: 1-6; relative density: 12.4; melting pt.: 1966°C; boiling pt.: 3727°C (approx.). [C19: New Latin, from Greek *rhodon* rose, from the pink colour of its compounds]

rho·do- *or before a vowel* **rhod-** *combining form.* rose or rose-coloured: *rhododendron; rhodolite.* [from Greek *rhodon* rose]

rho+do+chro+site (ˌrəʊdəʊ'krəʊsaɪt) *n.* a pink, grey, or brown mineral that consists of manganese carbonate in hexagonal crystalline form and occurs in ore veins. Formula: $MnCO_3$. [C19: from Greek *rhodokhrōs* of a rosy colour, from *rhodon* rose + *khrōs* colour]

rho+do+den+dron (ˌrəʊdə'dɛndrən) *n.* any ericaceous shrub of the genus *Rhododendron,* native to S Asia but widely cultivated in N temperate regions. They are mostly evergreen and have clusters of showy red, purple, pink, or white flowers. Also called (U.S.): **rosebay.** See also **azalea.** [C17: from Latin: oleander, from Greek, from *rhodon* rose + *dendron* tree]

rhod·o+lite ('rɒdəˌlaɪt) *n.* a pale violet or red variety of garnet, used as a gemstone.

rhod·o+nite ('rɒdəˌnaɪt) *n.* a brownish translucent mineral consisting of manganese silicate in triclinic crystalline form with calcium, iron, or magnesium sometimes replacing the manganese. It occurs in metamorphic rocks, esp. in New Jersey and Russia, and is used as an ornamental stone, glaze, and pigment. Formula: $MnSiO_3$. [C19: from German *Rhodonit,* from Greek *rhodon* rose + -ITE[1]]

Rhod·o+pe Moun+tains ('rɒdəpɪ, rɒ'dəʊ-) *pl. n.* a mountain range in SE Europe, in the Balkan Peninsula extending along the border between Bulgaria and Greece. Highest peak: Mount Musala (Bulgaria), 2925 m (9597 ft.).

rho·dop·sin (rəʊˈdɒpsɪn) *n.* a red pigment in the rods of the retina in vertebrates. It is dissociated by light into retinene, the light energy being converted into nerve signals, and is re-formed in the dark. Also called: **visual purple.** See also **iodopsin.** [C20: from RHODO- + OPSIN]

Rho·dos (ˈrɔðɔs) *n.* the Ancient Greek name for **Rhodes.**

-rhoe·a *combining form.* variant of **-rrhoea.**

rhomb (rɒm) *n.* another name for **rhombus.**

rhom·ben·ceph·a·lon (ˌrɒmbɛnˈsɛfəˌlɒn) *n.* the part of the brain that develops from the posterior portion of the embryonic neural tube. Compare **mesencephalon, prosencephalon.** Non-technical name: **hindbrain.** [C20: from RHOMBUS + ENCEPHALON]

rhom·bic (ˈrɒmbɪk) *or* **rhom·bi·cal** *adj.* **1.** relating to or having the shape of a rhombus. **2.** *Crystallog.* another word for **orthorhombic.**

rhom·bic ae·ri·al *n.* a directional travelling-wave aerial, usually horizontal, consisting of two conductors each forming a pair of adjacent sides of a rhombus.

rhom·bo·he·dral (ˌrɒmbəʊˈhiːdrəl) *adj.* **1.** of or relating to a rhombohedron. **2.** *Crystallog.* another term for **trigonal** (sense 2).

rhom·bo·he·dron (ˌrɒmbəʊˈhiːdrən) *n.* a six-sided prism whose sides are parallelograms. [C19: from RHOMBUS + -HEDRON] —ˌ**rhom·bo·ˈhe·dral** *adj.*

rhom·boid (ˈrɒmbɔɪd) *n.* **1.** a parallelogram having adjacent sides of unequal length. ~*adj. also* **rhom·ˈboi·dal.** **2.** having such a shape. [C16: from Late Latin *rhomboides,* from Greek *rhomboeidēs* shaped like a RHOMBUS]

rhom·bus (ˈrɒmbəs) *n., pl.* **·bus·es** *or* **·bi** (-baɪ). an oblique-angled parallelogram having four equal sides. Also called: **rhomb.** Compare **rectangle.** [C16: from Greek *rhombos* something that spins; related to *rhembein* to whirl]

rhon·chus (ˈrɒŋkəs) *n., pl.* **·chi** (-kaɪ). a rattling or whistling respiratory sound resembling snoring, caused by secretions in the trachea or bronchi. [C19: from Latin, from Greek *rhenkhos* snoring] —ˈ**rhon·chal** *or* ˈ**rhon·chi·al** *adj.*

Rhon·dda (ˈrɒndə) *n.* a town in S Wales, in Mid Glamorgan on two branches of the **Rhondda Valley**: developed into a major coal-mining centre after 1807 and grew to a population of 167 900 in 1924. Pop.: 88 924 (1971).

Rhône (rəʊn) *n.* **1.** a river in W Europe, rising in S Switzerland in the **Rhône glacier** and flowing to Lake Geneva, then into France through gorges between the Alps and Jura and south to its delta on the Gulf of Lions: important esp. for hydroelectricity and for wine production along its valley. Length: 812 km (505 miles). **2.** a department of E central France, in the Rhône-Alpes region. Capital: Lyons. Pop.: 1 449 527 (1975). Area: 3233 sq. km (1261 sq. miles).

Rhône-Alpes (*French* roːn alp) *n.* a region of E France: mainly mountainous, rising to the edge of the Massif Central in the west and the French Alps in the east; drained by the Rivers Rhône, Saône, and Isère.

rho·ta·cism (ˈrəʊtəˌsɪzəm) *n.* excessive use or idiosyncratic pronunciation of *r.* [C19: from New Latin *rhōtacismus,* from Greek *rhōtakizein* (verb) from the letter *rho*] —ˈ**rho·ta·cist** *n.* —ˌ**rho·ta·ˈcis·tic** *adj.*

rho·tic (ˈrəʊtɪk) *adj. Phonetics.* denoting or speaking a dialect of English in which preconsonantal *r*s are pronounced.

Rh pos·i·tive *n.* **1.** blood containing the Rh factor. **2.** a person having such blood.

R.H.S. *abbrev. for:* **1.** Royal Historical Society. **2.** Royal Horticultural Society. **3.** Royal Humane Society.

rhu·barb (ˈruːbɑːb) *n.* **1.** any of several temperate and subtropical plants of the polygonaceous genus *Rheum,* esp. *R. rhaponticum* (**common garden rhubarb**), which has long green and red acid-tasting edible leafstalks, usually eaten sweetened and cooked. **2.** the leafstalks of this plant. **3.** a related plant, *Rheum officinale,* of central Asia, having a bitter-tasting underground stem that can be dried and used medicinally as a laxative or astringent. **4.** *U.S. slang.* a heated discussion or quarrel. ~*interj., n., vb.* **5.** the noise made by actors to simulate conversation, esp. by repeating the word *rhubarb* at random. [C14: from Old French *reubarbe,* from Medieval Latin *reubarbum,* probably a variant of *rha barbarum* barbarian rhubarb, from *rha* rhubarb (from Greek, perhaps from *Rha* ancient name of the Volga) + Latin *barbarus* barbarian]

rhumb (rʌm) *n.* short for **rhumb line.**

rhum·ba (ˈrʌmbə, ˈrʊm-) *n., pl.* **·bas.** a variant spelling of **rumba.**

rhum·ba·tron (ˈrʌmbəˌtrɒn) *n.* another name for **cavity resonator.** [C20: from RHUMBA + -TRON, from the rhythmic variation of the waves]

rhumb line *n.* **1.** an imaginary line on the surface of a sphere, such as the earth, that intersects all meridians at the same angle. **2.** the course navigated by a vessel or aircraft that maintains a uniform compass heading. ~Often shortened to **rhumb.** [C16: from Old Spanish *rumbo,* apparently from Middle Dutch *ruum* space, ship's hold, but also influenced by Latin RHOMBUS]

rhyme *or* **rime** (raɪm) *n.* **1.** identity of the terminal sounds in lines of verse or in words. **2.** a word that is identical to another in its terminal sound: *"while" is a rhyme for "mile".* **3.** a verse or piece of poetry having corresponding sounds at the ends of the lines: *the boy made up a rhyme about his teacher.* **4.** any verse or piece of poetry. **5. rhyme or reason.** sense, logic, or meaning: *this proposal has no rhyme or reason.* ~*vb.* **6.** to use (a word) or (of a word) to be used so as to form a rhyme; be or make identical in sound. **7.** to render (a subject) into rhyme. **8.** to compose (verse) in a metrical structure. ~See also **masculine rhyme, feminine rhyme, eye rhyme.** [C12: from Old French *rime,* from *rimer* to rhyme, from Old High German *rīm* a number; spelling influenced by RHYTHM] —ˈ**rhyme·less** *or* ˈ**rime·less** *adj.*

rhyme roy·al *n. Prosody.* a stanzaic form introduced into English verse by Chaucer, consisting of seven lines of iambic pentameter rhyming a b a b b c c.

rhyme·ster, rime·ster (ˈraɪmstə), **rhym·er,** *or* **rim·er** *n.* a poet, esp. one considered to be mediocre or mechanical in diction; poetaster or versifier.

rhym·ing slang *n.* slang in which a word is replaced by another word or phrase that rhymes with it; for example, *apples and pears* meaning *stairs.*

rhyn·cho·ce·phal·i·an (ˌrɪŋkəʊsɪˈfælɪən) *adj.* **1.** of, relating to, or belonging to the *Rhyncocephalia,* an order of lizard-like reptiles common in the Mesozoic era but today represented only by the tuatara. ~*n.* **2.** any reptile belonging to the order *Rhyncocephalia.* [C19: from New Latin *Rhynchocephalia,* from Greek *rhunkhos* a snout + *kephalē* head]

rhy·o·lite (ˈraɪəˌlaɪt) *n.* a fine-grained igneous rock consisting of quartz, feldspars, and mica or amphibole. It is the volcanic equivalent of granite. [C19: *rhyo-* from Greek *rhuax* a stream of lava + -LITE] —**rhy·o·lit·ic** (ˌraɪəˈlɪtɪk) *adj.*

rhythm (ˈrɪðəm) *n.* **1. a.** the arrangement of the relative durations of and accents on the notes of a melody, usually laid out into regular groups (**bars**) of beats, the first beat of each bar carrying the stress. **b.** any specific arrangement of such groupings; time: *quadruple rhythm.* **2.** (in poetry) **a.** the arrangement of words into a more or less regular sequence of stressed and unstressed or long and short syllables. **b.** any specific such arrangement; metre. **3.** (in painting, sculpture, architecture, etc.) a harmonious sequence or pattern of masses alternating with voids, of light alternating with shade, of alternating colours, etc. **4.** any sequence of regularly recurring functions or events, such as the regular recurrence of certain physiological functions of the body. [C16: from Latin *rhythmus,* from Greek *rhuthmos;* related to *rhein* to flow] —ˈ**rhythm·less** *adj.*

rhythm-and-blues *n.* any of various kinds of popular music derived from or influenced by the blues. Abbrev.: **R & B**

rhyth·mi·cal (ˈrɪðmɪkᵊl) *or* **rhyth·mic** *adj.* of, relating to, or characterized by rhythm, as in movement or sound; metrical, periodic, or regularly recurring. —ˈ**rhyth·mi·cal·ly** *adv.* —**rhyth·mic·i·ty** (rɪðˈmɪsɪtɪ) *n.*

rhyth·mics (ˈrɪðmɪks) *n.* (*functioning as sing.*) the study of rhythmical movement.

rhyth·mist (ˈrɪðmɪst) *n. Rare.* a person who has a good sense of rhythm.

rhythm meth·od *n.* an attempted method of controlling conception without the aid of a contraceptive device, by restricting sexual intercourse to those days in a woman's menstrual cycle when conception is considered least likely to occur. See also **safe period.**

rhythm sec·tion *n.* those instruments in a band or group (usually piano, double bass, and drums) whose prime function is to supply the rhythm.

rhy·ton (ˈraɪtɒn) *n., pl.* **·ta** (-tə). (in ancient Greece) a horn-shaped drinking vessel with a hole in the pointed end through which to drink. [C19: from Greek *rhuton,* from *rhutos* flowing; related to *rhein* to flow]

RI *international car registration for* (Republic of) Indonesia.

R.I. *abbrev. for:* **1.** Regina et Imperatrix. [Latin: Queen and Empress] **2.** Rex et Imperator. [Latin: King and Emperor] **3.** Rhode Island. **4.** Royal Institution.

ri·a (ˈrɪə) *n.* a long narrow inlet of the sea coast, being a former valley that was submerged by a rise in the level of the sea. Rias are found esp. on the coasts of SW Ireland and NW Spain. [C19: from Spanish, from *rio* river]

ri·al (ˈraɪəl) *n.* **1.** the standard monetary and currency unit of Iran, divided into 100 dinars. **2.** the standard monetary and currency unit of Oman. **3.** another name for **riyal.** [C14: from Persian, from Arabic *riyāl* RIYAL]

ri·al·to (rɪˈæltəʊ) *n., pl.* **·tos.** a market or exchange. [C19: after the RIALTO]

Ri·al·to (rɪˈæltəʊ) *n.* an island in Venice, Italy, linked with San Marco Island by the **Rialto Bridge** (1590) over the Grand Canal: the business centre of medieval and renaissance Venice.

ri·ant (ˈraɪənt) *adj. Rare.* laughing; smiling; cheerful. [C16: from French, from *rire* to laugh, from Latin *rīdēre*] —ˈ**ri·ant·ly** *adv.*

ri·a·ta *or* **re·a·ta** (rɪˈɑːtə) *n. Southern and western U.S.* a lariat or lasso. [C19: from American Spanish *reata,* from Spanish *reatar* to tie together again, from RE- + *atar* to tie, from Latin *aptāre* to fit, from *aptus* fitting, suitable]

rib[1] (rɪb) *n.* **1.** any of the 24 curved elastic arches of bone that together form the chest wall in man. All are attached behind to the thoracic part of the spinal column. Technical name: **costa.** Compare **true rib, false rib, floating rib.** **2.** the corresponding bone in other vertebrates. **3.** a cut of meat including one or more ribs. **4.** a part or element similar in function or appearance to a rib, esp. a structural or supporting member or a raised strip or ridge. **5.** a structural member in an aerofoil that extends from the leading edge to the trailing edge and maintains the shape of the aerofoil surface. **6.** a projecting moulding or band on the underside of a vault or ceiling, which may be structural or ornamental. **7.** one of a series of raised rows in knitted fabric. See also **ribbing.** **8.** a raised ornamental line on the spine of a book where the stitching runs across it. **9.** any of the transverse stiffening timbers or joists forming the frame of a ship's hull. **10.** any of the larger veins of a leaf. **11.** a metal strip running along the top of the barrel of a shotgun or handgun and guiding the alignment of the sights. **12.** a vein of ore in rock. **13.** a projecting ridge of a mountain; spur. ~*vb.* **ribs, rib·bing, ribbed.** (*tr.*) **14.** to furnish or support with a rib or ribs. **15.** to mark with or form into ribs or ridges. **16.** to knit plain and purl stitches alternately in order to make raised rows in (knitting). **17.** *Archaic.* to enclose with or as if with ribs. [Old English *ribb;* related to Old High German *rippi,* Old Norse *rif* REEF[1]] —**'rib·less** *adj.* —**'rib·,like** *adj.*

rib[2] (rɪb) *Informal.* ~*vb.* **ribs, rib·bing, ribbed. 1.** (*tr.*) to tease or ridicule. ~*n.* **2.** a joke or hoax. [C20: short for *rib-tickle* (vb.)]

R.I.B.A. *abbrev. for* Royal Institute of British Architects.

rib·ald ('rɪbᵊld) *adj.* **1.** coarse, obscene, or licentious, usually in a humorous or mocking way. ~*n.* **2.** a ribald person. [C13: from Old French *ribauld,* from *riber* to live licentiously, of Germanic origin] —**'rib·ald·ly** *adv.*

rib·ald·ry ('rɪbᵊldrɪ) *n.* ribald language or behaviour.

rib·and *or* **rib·band** ('rɪbənd) *n.* **1.** a ribbon, esp. one awarded for some achievement. See also **blue ribband. 2.** a flat rail attached to posts in a palisade. [C14: variant of RIBBON]

ribbed and smoked sheet *n.* another name for **smoked rubber.** Abbrev.: **RSS.**

Rib·ben·trop (*German* 'rɪbᵊn,trɔp) *n.* **Jo·a·chim von** ('joːaxɪm fɔn). 1893–1946, German Nazi politician: foreign minister under Hitler (1938–45). He was hanged after conviction as a war criminal at Nuremberg.

rib·bing ('rɪbɪŋ) *n.* **1.** a framework or structure of ribs. **2.** ribs collectively. **3.** a raised pattern in woven or knitted material, made in knitting by doing purl and plain stitches alternately.

Rib·ble ('rɪbᵊl) *n.* a river in NW England, flowing south and west through Lancashire to the Irish Sea. Length: 121 km (75 miles).

rib·bon ('rɪbᵊn) *n.* **1.** a narrow strip of fine material, esp. silk, used for trimming, tying, etc. **2.** something resembling a ribbon; a long strip: *a ribbon of land.* **3.** a long thin flexible band of metal used as a graduated measure, spring, etc. **4.** a long narrow strip of ink-impregnated cloth for making the impression of type characters on paper in a typewriter or similar device. **5.** (*pl.*) ragged strips or shreds (esp. in the phrase **torn to ribbons**). **6.** a small strip of coloured cloth signifying membership of an order or award of military decoration, prize, or other distinction. ~*vb.* (*tr.*) **7.** to adorn with a ribbon or ribbons. **8.** to mark with narrow ribbon-like marks. **9.** to reduce to ribbons; tear into strips. [C14 *ryban,* from Old French *riban,* apparently of Germanic origin; probably related to RING, BAND[2]] —**'rib·bon-,like** *or* **'rib·bon·y** *adj.*

rib·bon de·vel·op·ment *n. Brit.* the building of houses in a continuous row along a main road: common in England between the two World Wars.

rib·bon·fish ('rɪbᵊn,fɪʃ) *n., pl.* **·fish** *or* **·fish·es.** any of various soft-finned deep-sea teleost fishes, esp. *Regalecus glesne* (see **oarfish**), that have an elongated compressed body. They are related to the opah and dealfishes.

rib·bon strip *n.* another name for **ledger board** (sense 2).

rib·bon·wood ('rɪbən,wʊd) *n.* a small evergreen malvaceous tree, *Hoheria populnea,* of New Zealand. Its wood is used in furniture-making and the tough bark for making cord.

rib·bon worm *n.* another name for a **nemertean.**

Ri·bei·rão Prê·to (*Portuguese* ,ribeɪ'rɐ̃ʊ 'pretu) *n.* a city in SE Brazil, in São Paulo state. Pop.: 190 897 (1970).

Ri·be·ra (*Spanish* ri'βera) *n.* **Jo·sé de** (xo'se ðe) also called *Jusepe de Ribera,* Italian nickname *Lo Spagnoletto* (The Little Spaniard). 1588–1652, Spanish artist, living in Italy. His religious pictures often dwell on horrible suffering, presented in realistic detail.

rib·grass ('rɪb,grɑːs) *n.* another name for **ribwort.**

ri·bo·fla·vin *or* **ri·bo·fla·vine** (,raɪbəʊ'fleɪvɪn) *n.* a yellow water-soluble vitamin of the B complex that occurs in green vegetables, germinating seeds, and in milk, fish, egg yolk, liver, and kidney. It is essential for the carbohydrate metabolism of cells. Formula: $C_{17}H_{20}N_4O_6$. Also called: **vitamin B_2, lactoflavin.** [C20: from RIBOSE + FLAVIN]

ri·bo·nu·cle·ase (,raɪbəʊ'njuːklɪ,eɪs, -,eɪz) *n.* any of a group of enzymes that catalyse the hydrolysis of RNA. [C20: from RIBONUCLE(IC ACID) + -ASE]

ri·bo·nu·cle·ic ac·id (,raɪbəʊnjuː'kliːɪk, -'kleɪ-) *n.* the full name of **RNA.** [C20: from RIBO(SE) + NUCLEIC ACID]

ri·bose ('raɪbəʊz, -bəʊs) *n. Biochem.* a pentose sugar that is an isomeric form of arabinose and that occurs in RNA and riboflavin. Formula: $CH_2OH(CHOH)_3CHO$. [C20: changed from ARABINOSE]

ri·bo·so·mal RNA *n. Biochem.* a type of RNA thought to be transcribed from DNA in the nucleoli of cell nuclei, subsequently forming the component of ribosomes on which the translation of messenger RNA into protein chains is accomplished. Sometimes shortened to **r-RNA.**

ri·bo·some ('raɪbə,səʊm) *n.* any of numerous minute particles in the cytoplasm of cells, either free or attached to the endoplasmic reticulum, that contain RNA and protein and are the site of protein synthesis. [C20: from RIBO(NUCLEIC ACID) + -SOME] —**,ri·bo·'so·mal** *adj.*

rib·wort ('rɪb,wɜːt) *n.* a Eurasian plant, *Plantago lanceolata,* that has lancelike ribbed leaves, which form a rosette close to the ground, and a dense spike of small white flowers: family *Plantaginaceae.* Also called: **ribgrass.** See also **plantain**[1].

R.I.C. *abbrev. for* Royal Institute of Chemistry.

Ri·car·do (rɪ'kɑːdəʊ) *n.* **Da·vid.** 1772–1823, English economist. His main work is *Principles of Political Economy and Taxation* (1817). —**Ri·'card·i·an** *adj., n.*

Ric·cio (*Italian* 'rittʃo) *n.* a variant of (David) **Rizzio.**

rice (raɪs) *n.* **1.** an erect grass, *Oryza sativa,* that grows in East Asia on wet ground and has drooping flower spikes and yellow oblong edible grains that become white when polished. **2.** the grain of this plant. ~*vb.* **3.** (*tr.*) *U.S.* to sieve (potatoes or other vegetables) to a coarse mashed consistency, esp. with a ricer. ~See also **Indian rice.** [C13 *rys,* via French, Italian, and Latin from Greek *orūza,* of Oriental origin]

Rice (raɪs) *n.* **El·mer,** original name *Elmer Reizenstein.* 1892–1967, U.S. dramatist. His plays include *The Adding Machine* (1923) and *Street Scene* (1929), which was made into a musical by Kurt Weill in 1947.

rice·bird ('raɪs,bɜːd) *n.* any of various birds frequenting rice fields, esp. the bobolink.

rice bowl *n.* **1.** a small bowl for eating rice out of, esp. a decorative one made of china or porcelain. **2.** a fertile rice-producing region.

rice pa·per *n.* **1.** a thin semitransparent edible paper made from the straw of rice, on which macaroons and similar cakes are baked. **2.** a thin delicate Chinese paper made from an araliaceous plant, *Tetrapanax papyriferum* (**rice-paper plant**) of Taiwan, the pith of which is pared and flattened into sheets.

ric·er ('raɪsə) *n. U.S.* a kitchen utensil with small holes through which cooked potatoes and similar soft foods are pressed to form a coarse mash.

ri·cer·ca·re (,riːtʃə'kɑːreɪ) *or* **ri·cer·car** ('riːtʃə,kɑː) *n., pl.* **·ca·ri** (-'kɑːriː) *or* **·cars.** (in music of the 16th and 17th centuries) **1.** an elaborate polyphonic composition making extensive use of contrapuntal imitation and usually very slow in tempo. **2.** an instructive composition to illustrate instrumental technique; étude. [Italian, literally: to seek again]

rich (rɪtʃ) *adj.* **1. a.** well supplied with wealth, property, etc.; owning much. **b.** (*as collective n.* preceded by *the*): *the rich.* **2.** (when *postpositive,* usually foll. by *in*) having an abundance of natural resources, minerals, etc.: *a land rich in metals.* **3.** producing abundantly; fertile: *rich soil.* **4.** (when *postpositive,* foll. by *in* or *with*) well supplied (with desirable qualities); abundant (in): *a country rich with cultural interest.* **5.** of great worth or quality; valuable: *a rich collection of antiques.* **6.** luxuriant or prolific: *a rich growth of weeds.* **7.** expensively elegant, elaborate, or fine; costly: *a rich display.* **8.** (of food) having a large proportion of flavoursome or fatty ingredients, such as spices, butter, or cream. **9.** having a full-bodied flavour: *a rich ruby port.* **10.** (of a smell) pungent or fragrant. **11.** (of colour) intense or vivid; deep: *a rich red.* **12.** (of sound or a voice) full, mellow, or resonant. **13.** (of a fuel-air mixture) containing a relatively high proportion of fuel. Compare **weak** (sense 11). **14.** very amusing, laughable, or ridiculous: *a rich joke; a rich situation.* ~*n.* **15.** See **riches.** [Old English *rīce* (originally of persons: great, mighty), of Germanic origin, ultimately from Celtic (compare Old Irish *rī* king)] —**'rich·ly** *adv.* —**'rich·ness** *n.*

Rich·ard I ('rɪtʃəd) *n.* nicknamed *Coeur de Lion* or *the Lion-Heart.* 1157–99, king of England (1189–99); a leader of the third crusade (1191). On his way home, he was captured in Austria (1192) and held to ransom. After a brief return to England, where he was crowned again (1194), he spent the rest of his life in France.

Rich·ard II *n.* 1367-1400, king of England (1377-99), whose reign was troubled by popular discontent and baronial opposition. He was forced to abdicate in favour of Henry Bolingbroke, who became Henry IV.

Rich·ard III *n.* 1452–85, king of England (1483–85), notorious as the suspected murderer of his two young nephews in the Tower of London. He proved an able administrator until his brief reign was ended by his death at the hands of Henry Tudor (later Henry VII) at the battle of Bosworth.

Rich·ards ('rɪtʃədz) *n.* **I(vor) A(rmstrong).** 1893-1979, English literary critic and linguist, who, with C. K. Ogden, wrote *The Meaning of Meaning* (1923) and devised Basic English.

Rich·ard·son ('rɪtʃədsən) *n.* **1.** Sir **Ralph (David).** born 1902, English stage and screen actor. **2.** Sir **Ow·en Wil·lans.** 1879–1959, English physicist; a pioneer in the study of atomic physics: Nobel prize for physics 1928. **3. Sam·u·el.** 1689–1761, English novelist whose psychological insight and use of the epistolary form exerted a great influence on the development of the novel. His chief novels are *Pamela* (1740) and *Clarissa* (1747).

Rich·e·lieu ('rɪʃə,ljɜː; *French* riʃᵊ'ljø) *n.* **Ar·mand Jean du Ples·sis** (armɑ̃ ʒɑ̃ dy ple'si). 1585–1642, French statesman and cardinal, principal minister to Louis XIII and virtual ruler of France (1624–42). He destroyed the power of the Huguenots and strengthened the crown in France and the role of France in Europe.

Rich·e·lieu Riv·er *n.* a river in E Canada, in S Quebec, rising in Lake Champlain and flowing north to the St. Lawrence River. Length: 338 km (210 miles).

rich·es ('rɪtʃɪz) *pl. n.* wealth; an abundance of money, valuable possessions, or property.

rich·ly ('rɪtʃlɪ) *adv.* **1.** in a rich or elaborate manner: *a richly decorated carving.* **2.** fully and appropriately: *he was richly rewarded for his service.*

Rich·mond ('rɪtʃmənd) *n.* **1.** a borough of Greater London, on the River Thames: formed in 1965 by the amalgamation of Barnes, Richmond, and Twickenham; site of Hampton Court Palace and the Royal Botanic Gardens at Kew. Pop.: 166 800 (1976 est.). Official name: **Richmond-upon-Thames. 2.** a town in N England, in North Yorkshire. Pop.: 7245 (1971). **3.** a port in E Virginia, the state capital, at the falls of the James River: developed after the establishment of a trading post (1637); scene of the Virginia Conventions of 1774 and 1775; Confederate capital in the American Civil War. Pop.: 238 087 (1973 est.). **4.** a borough of SW New York City: consists of Staten Island and several smaller islands. Pop.: 295 443 (1970).

rich rhyme *n. Prosody.* another term for **rime riche.**

Rich·ter *n.* **1.** (*German* 'riçtər). **Jo·hann Fried·rich** ('jo:han 'fri:drıç), wrote under the name *Jean Paul.* 1763–1825, German romantic novelist. His works include *Hesperus* (1795) and *Titan* (1800–03). **2.** (*Russian* 'rixtır). **Svia·to·slav** (svıta'slaf). born 1914, Soviet concert pianist.

Rich·ter scale *n.* a scale for expressing the intensity of an earthquake by the amount of energy dissipated, ranging from 0 to over 8. [C20: named after Charles *Richter* (born 1900) U.S. seismologist]

Richt·ho·fen (*German* 'riçtho:fᵊn) *n.* Baron **Man·fred von** ('manfre:t fɔn). 1892–1918, German aviator; commander during World War I of the 11th Chasing Squadron (**Richthofen's Flying Circus**). He was credited with 80 air victories before he was shot down.

ri+cin ('raısın, 'rıs-) *n. Biochem.* a toxic albumin that occurs in castor-oil seeds. [C19: from New Latin *Ricinus* genus name, from Latin: the castor-oil plant]

ric+in·o+le·ic ac·id (ˌrısınəʊ'li:ık, -'nəʊlıık) *n.* **1.** an oily unsaturated carboxylic acid found, as the glyceride, in castor oil and used in the manufacture of soap and in finishing textiles; 12-hydroxy-9-octadecanoic acid. Formula: $C_{18}H_{34}O_3$. **2.** the mixture of fatty acids obtained by hydrolysing castor oil.

rick[1] (rık) *n.* **1.** a large stack of hay, corn, peas, etc., built in the open in a regular-shaped pile, esp. one with a thatched top. ~*vb.* **2.** (*tr.*) to stack or pile into ricks. [Old English *hrēac;* related to Old Norse *hraukr*]

rick[2] (rık) *n.* **1.** a wrench or sprain, as of the back. ~*vb.* **2.** (*tr.*) to wrench or sprain (a joint, limb, the back, etc.) [C18: variant of WRICK]

rick+ets ('rıkıts) *n. Pathol.* a disease mainly of children, characterized by softening of developing bone, and hence bow legs, malnutrition, and enlargement of the liver and spleen, caused by a deficiency of vitamin D. [C17: of unknown origin]

rick+ett+si·a (rı'kɛtsıə) *n., pl.* **+si·ae** (-sıˌi:) *or* **+si·as.** any of a group of parasitic microorganisms, intermediate in structure between bacteria and viruses, that live in the tissues of ticks, mites, and other arthropods, and cause disease when transmitted to man. [C20: named after Howard T. *Ricketts* (1871–1910), U.S. pathologist] —**rick+'ett+si·al** *adj.*

rick+ett+si·al dis+ease *n.* any of several acute infectious diseases caused by ticks, mites, or body lice infected with rickettsiae. The main types include typhus, spotted fever, Q fever, trench fever, and tsutsugamushi disease.

rick+et·y ('rıkıtı) *adj.* **1.** (of a structure, piece of furniture, etc.) likely to collapse or break; shaky. **2.** feeble with age or illness; infirm. **3.** relating to, resembling, or afflicted with rickets. [C17: from RICKETS] —**'rick+et·i·ness** *n.*

rick+ey (ˌrıkı) *n.* a cocktail consisting of gin or vodka, lime juice, and soda water, served iced (esp. in the phrase **a gin rickey**).

rick+rack *or* **ric+rac** ('rıkˌræk) *n.* a zigzag braid used for trimming. [C20: dissimilated reduplication of RACK[1]]

rick+shaw ('rıkʃɔ:) *or* **rick+sha** ('rıkʃə) *n.* **1.** Also called: **jinrikisha.** a small two-wheeled passenger vehicle drawn by one or two men, used in parts of Asia. **2.** Also called: **trishaw.** a similar vehicle with three wheels, propelled by a man pedalling as on a tricycle. ~See also **autorickshaw.** [shortened from JINRIKISHA]

ric·o·chet ('rıkəˌʃeı, 'rıkəˌʃɛt) *vb.* **+chets, +chet+ing** (-ˌʃeııŋ), **+chet+ed** (-ˌʃeıd) *or* **+chets, +chet+ting** (-ˌʃɛtıŋ), **+chet+ted** (-ˌʃɛtıd). **1.** (*intr.*) (esp. of a bullet) to rebound from a surface or surfaces, usually with a characteristic whining or zipping sound. ~*n.* **2.** the motion or sound of a rebounding object, esp. a bullet. [C18: from French, of unknown origin]

ri+cot+ta (rı'kɒtə) *n.* a soft white unsalted cheese made from sheep's milk, used esp. in making ravioli and gnocchi. [Italian, from Latin *recocta* recooked, from *recoquere,* from RE- + *coquere* to COOK]

R.I.C.S. *abbrev. for* Royal Institution of Chartered Surveyors.

ric+tus ('rıktəs) *n., pl.* **+tus** *or* **+tus·es.** the gap or cleft of an open mouth or beak. [C18: from Latin, from *ringī* to gape] —**'ric+tal** *adj.*

rid (rıd) *vb.* **rids, rid+ding, rid** *or* **rid+ded.** (*tr.*) **1.** (foll. by *of*) to relieve or deliver from something disagreeable or undesirable; make free (of): *to rid a house of mice.* **2. get rid of.** to relieve or free oneself of (something or someone unpleasant or undesirable). [C13 (meaning: to clear land): from Old Norse *rythja;* related to Old High German *riutan* to clear land] —**'rid+der** *n.*

rid+dance ('rıdᵊns) *n.* the act of getting rid of something undesirable or unpleasant; deliverance or removal (esp. in the phrase **good riddance**).

rid+den ('rıdᵊn) *vb.* **1.** the past participle of **ride.** ~*adj.* **2.** (*in combination*) afflicted, affected, or dominated by something specified: *damp-ridden; disease-ridden.*

rid+dle[1] ('rıdᵊl) *n.* **1.** a question, puzzle, or verse so phrased that ingenuity is required for elucidation of the answer or meaning; conundrum. **2.** a person or thing that puzzles, perplexes, or confuses; enigma. ~*vb.* **3.** to solve, explain, or interpret (a riddle or riddles). **4.** (*intr.*) to speak in riddles. [Old English *rǣdelle, rǣdelse,* from *rǣd* counsel; related to Old Saxon *rādislo,* German *Rätsel*] —**'rid+dler** *n.*

rid+dle[2] ('rıdᵊl) *vb.* (*tr.*) **1.** (usually foll. by *with*) to pierce or perforate with numerous holes: *riddled with bullets.* **2.** to damage or impair. **3.** to put through a sieve; sift. ~*n.* **4.** a sieve, esp. a coarse one used for sand, grain, etc. [Old English *hriddel* a sieve, variant of *hridder;* related to Latin *crībrum* sieve] —**'rid+dler** *n.*

ride (raıd) *vb.* **rides, rid+ing, rode, rid+den. 1.** to sit on and control the movements of (a horse or other animal). **2.** (*tr.*) to sit on and propel (a bicycle or similar vehicle). **3.** (*intr.;* often foll. by *on* or *in*) to be carried along or travel on or in a vehicle: *she rides to work on the bus.* **4.** (*tr.*) to travel over or traverse: *they rode the countryside in search of shelter.* **5.** (*tr.*) to take part in by riding: *to ride a race.* **6.** to travel through or be carried across (sea, sky, etc.): *the small boat rode the waves; the moon was riding high.* **7.** (*tr.*) *U.S.* to cause to be carried: *to ride someone out of town.* **8.** (*intr.*) to be supported as if floating: *the candidate rode to victory on his new policies.* **9.** (*intr.*) (of a vessel) to lie at anchor. **10.** (*tr.*) (of a vessel) to be attached to (an anchor). **11.** (esp. of a bone) to overlap or lie over (another structure or part). **12.** *S. African informal.* **a.** (*intr.*) to drive a car. **b.** (*tr.*) to transport (goods, farm produce, etc.) by motor vehicle or cart. **13.** (*tr.*) (esp. of a male animal) to copulate with; mount. **14.** (*tr.; usually passive*) to tyrannize over or dominate: *ridden by fear.* **15.** (*tr.*) *Informal.* to persecute, esp. by constant or petty criticism: *don't ride me so hard over my failure.* **16.** (*intr.*) *Informal.* to continue undisturbed: *I wanted to change something, but let it ride.* **17.** (*intr.;* often foll. by *on*) (of a bet) to remain placed: *let your winnings ride on the same number.* **18.** (*intr.*) *Jazz.* to play well, esp. in freely improvising at perfect tempo. **19. ride roughshod over.** to act with complete disregard (for). **20. ride to hounds.** to hunt. **21. ride for a fall.** to act in such a way as to invite disaster. **22. ride again.** *Informal.* to return to a former activity or scene of activity. **23. riding high.** confident, popular, and successful. ~*n.* **24.** a journey or outing on horseback or in a vehicle. **25.** a path specially made for riding on horseback. **26.** transport in a vehicle, esp. when given freely to a pedestrian; lift: *can you give me a ride to the station?* **27.** a device or structure, such as a roller coaster at a fairground, in which people ride for pleasure or entertainment. **28. take for a ride.** *Informal.* **a.** to cheat, swindle, or deceive. **b.** to take (someone) away in a car and murder him. ~See also **ride down, ride out, ride up.** [Old English *rīdan,* related to Old High German *rītan,* Old Norse *rītha*] —**'rid+a·ble** *or* **'ride+a·ble** *adj.*

ride down *vb.* (*tr., adv.*) **1.** to trample under the hooves of a horse. **2.** to catch up with or overtake by riding.

ri+dent ('raıdᵊnt) *adj. Rare.* laughing, smiling, or gay. [C17: from Latin *rīdēre* to laugh; see RIANT]

ride out *vb.* (*tr., adv.*) to endure successfully; survive (esp. in the phrase **ride out the storm**).

rid+er ('raıdə) *n.* **1.** a person or thing that rides, esp. a person who rides a horse, a bicycle, or a motorcycle. **2.** an additional clause, amendment, or stipulation added to a legal or other document, esp. (in Britain) a legislative bill at its third reading. **3.** *Brit.* a statement made by a jury in addition to its verdict, such as a recommendation for mercy. **4.** *Maths.* a problem arising out of a theorem. **5.** any of various objects or devices resting on, surmounting, or strengthening something else. **6.** a small weight that can be slid along one arm of a chemical balance to make fine adjustments during weighing. **7.** *Geology.* a thin seam, esp. of coal or mineral ore, overlying a thicker seam. —**'rid+er+less** *adj.*

ride up *vb.* (*intr., adv.*) to move or work away from the proper place or position: *her new skirt rode up uncomfortably.*

ridge (rıdʒ) *n.* **1.** a long narrow raised land formation with sloping sides. **2.** any long narrow raised strip or elevation, as on a fabric or in ploughed land. **3.** *Anatomy.* any elongated raised margin or border on a bone, tooth, tissue membrane, etc. **4. a.** the top of a roof at the junction of two sloping sides. **b.** (*as modifier*): *a ridge tile.* **5.** the back or backbone of an animal, esp. a whale. **6.** *Meteorol.* an elongated area of high pressure, esp. an extension of an anticyclone. Compare **trough** (sense 4). ~*vb.* **7.** to form into a ridge or ridges. [Old English *hrycg;* related to Old High German *hrucki,* Old Norse *hryggr*] —**'ridge+ˌlike** *adj.* —**'ridg·y** *adj.*

ridge+ling, ridg+ling ('rıdʒlıŋ), *or* **rid+gel** ('rıdʒəl) *n.* a domestic male animal with undescended testicles, esp. a horse. [C16: perhaps from RIDGE, from the belief that the undescended testicles were near the animal's ridge or back]

ridge+pole ('rıdʒˌpəʊl) *n.* **1.** a timber laid along the ridge of a roof, to which the upper ends of the rafters are attached. **2.** the horizontal pole at the apex of a tent.

ridge+tree ('rıdʒˌtri:) *n.* another name for **ridgepole** (sense 1).

ridge+way ('rıdʒˌweı) *n. Brit.* a road or track along a ridge, esp. one of great antiquity.

rid·i·cule ('rıdıˌkju:l) *n.* **1.** language or behaviour intended to humiliate or mock; derision. ~*vb.* **2.** (*tr.*) to make fun of, mock, or deride. [C17: from French, from Latin *rīdiculus,* from *rīdēre* to laugh] —**'rid·i+ˌcul+er** *n.*

ri+dic·u·lous (rı'dıkjʊləs) *adj.* worthy of or exciting ridicule; absurd, preposterous, laughable, or contemptible. [C16: from Latin *rīdiculōsus,* from *rīdēre* to laugh] —**ri+'dic·u·lous+ly** *adv.* —**ri+'dic·u·lous+ness** *n.*

rid+ing[1] ('raıdıŋ) *n.* **a.** the art or practice of horsemanship. **b.** (*as modifier*): *a riding school; riding techniques.*

rid+ing[2] ('raıdıŋ) *n.* **1.** (*cap. when part of a name*) any of the three former administrative divisions of Yorkshire: **North Riding, East Riding,** and **West Riding. 2.** (in Canada) a parliamentary constituency. [from Old English *thriding,* from Old Norse *thrithjungr* a third. The *th-* was lost by assimilation to the *-t* or *-th* that preceded it, as in *west thriding,* etc.]

rid+ing breech·es *pl. n.* tough breeches with a large baggy seat and padding inside the knees, worn for riding horses.

rid+ing crop *n.* a short whip with a thong at one end and a handle for opening gates at the other.

rid+ing hab+it *n.* a woman's dress worn for riding, usually with a full or a divided skirt.

rid+ing lamp *or* **light** *n.* a light on a boat or ship showing that it is at anchor.

Rid·ley ('rɪdlɪ) *n.* **Nich·o·las.** ?1500–55, English bishop, who helped to revise the liturgy under Edward VI. He was burnt at the stake for refusing to disavow his Protestant beliefs when Mary I assumed the throne.

ri+dot+to (rɪ'dɒtəʊ) *n., pl.* **+tos.** an entertainment with music and dancing, often in masquerade: popular in 18th-century England. [C18: from Italian: retreat, from Latin *reductus,* from *redūcere* to lead back]

Rief·en·stahl (*German* 'riːfənˌʃtaːl) *n.* **Len·i.** ('leːni). born 1902, German film director, best known for her Nazi propaganda films, such as *Triumph of the Will* (1934).

ri·el ('riːəl) *n.* the standard monetary and currency unit of Cambodia, divided into 100 sen.

Rie·mann (*German* 'riːman) *n.* **Ge·org Frie·drich Bern·hard** ('geːɔrk 'friːdrɪç 'bɛrnhart). 1826–66, German mathematician whose non-Euclidean geometry was used by Einstein as a basis for his general theory of relativity. —**Rie+'mann+i·an** *adj.*

Rie·mann+i·an ge+om+e·try *n.* a branch of non-Euclidean geometry in which space is regarded as having the form of the surface of a sphere and a line is a great circle. Also called: **elliptic geometry.**

riem+pie ('rɪmpɪ) *n. S. African.* a leather thong or lace used mainly to make chair seats. [C19 (earlier *riem*): from Afrikaans, diminutive of *riem,* from Dutch: RIM]

Ri·en·zi (rɪ'ɛnzɪ; *Italian* 'rjɛntsi) *or* **Ri·en·zo** (rɪ'ɛnzəʊ; *Italian* 'rjɛntso) *n.* **Co·la di** ('kɔːla di). 1313–54, Italian radical political reformer in Rome.

ries+ling ('riːzlɪŋ, 'raɪz-) *n.* **1.** a dry white wine from the Rhine valley in Germany and from certain districts in Austria, Hungary, and Yugoslavia. **2.** the grape used to make this wine. [C19: from German, from earlier *Rüssling,* of obscure origin]

Rif, Riff (rɪf), *or* **Rif·i** ('rɪfɪ) *n.* **1.** (*pl.* **Rifs, Riffs, Rif·is** *or* **Rif, Riff, Rif·i**) a member of a Berber people, inhabiting the Atlas Mountains in Morocco. **2.** Also called: **Rifian, Riffian.** the dialect of Berber spoken by this people. **3.** See **Er Rif.**

rife (raɪf) *adj.* (*postpositive*) **1.** of widespread occurrence; prevalent or current: *rumour was rife in the village.* **2.** very plentiful; abundant. **3.** (foll. by *with*) rich or abounding (in): *a garden rife with flowers.* [Old English *rīfe;* related to Old Norse *rīfr* generous, Middle Dutch *rīve*] —**'rife+ly** *adv.* —**'rife+ness** *n.*

riff (rɪf) *Jazz.* ~*n.* **1.** an ostinato played over changing harmonies. ~*vb.* **2.** (*intr.*) to play or perform riffs. [C20: probably altered and shortened from REFRAIN]

rif+fle ('rɪfəl) *vb.* **1.** (when *intr.,* often foll. by *through*) to flick rapidly through (the pages of a book, etc.), esp. in a desultory manner. **2.** to shuffle (playing cards) by halving the pack and flicking the adjacent corners together. **3.** to make or become a riffle. ~*n.* **4.** *U.S.* **a.** a rapid in a stream. **b.** a rocky shoal causing a rapid. **c.** a ripple on water. **5.** *Mining.* a contrivance on the bottom of a sluice, containing transverse grooves for trapping particles of gold. **6.** the act or an instance of riffling. [C18: probably from RUFFLE[1], influenced by RIPPLE[1]]

rif+fler ('rɪflə) *n.* a file with a curved face for filing concave surfaces. [C18: from French *rifloir,* from *rifler* to scratch]

riff+raff ('rɪfˌræf) *n.* (*sometimes functioning as pl.*) **1.** worthless people, esp. collectively; rabble. **2.** *Dialect.* worthless rubbish. [C15 *rif and raf,* from Old French *rif et raf;* related to *rifler* to plunder, and *rafle* a sweeping up; see RIFLE[2], RAFFLE]

ri+fle[1] ('raɪfəl) *n.* **1. a.** a firearm having a long barrel with a spirally grooved interior, which imparts to the bullet spinning motion and thus greater accuracy over a longer range. **b.** (*as modifier*): *rifle fire.* **2.** (formerly) a large cannon with a rifled bore. **3.** one of the grooves in a rifled bore. **4.** (*pl.*) **a.** a unit of soldiers equipped with rifles. **b.** (*cap. as part of a name*): *the King's Own Rifles.* ~*vb.* (*tr.*) **5.** to cut or mould spiral grooves inside the barrel of (a gun). **6.** to throw or hit (a ball, etc.) with great speed. [C18: from Old French *rifler* to scratch; related to Low German *rifeln* from *riefe* groove, furrow]

ri+fle[2] ('raɪfəl) *vb.* (*tr.*) **1.** to search (a house, safe, etc.) and steal from it; ransack. **2.** to steal and carry off: *to rifle goods from a shop.* [C14: from Old French *rifler* to plunder, scratch, of Germanic origin] —**'ri+fler** *n.*

ri·fle+bird ('raɪfəlˌbɜːd) *n.* any of various birds of paradise of the genera *Ptiloris* and *Craspedophora,* such as *C. magnifica* (**magnificent riflebird**).

rif·le green *n. Brit.* **a.** a dark olive green, as in the uniforms of certain rifle regiments. **b.** (*as adj.*): *rifle-green cloth.*

ri+fle gre+nade *n.* a grenade fired from a rifle.

ri·fle+man ('raɪfəlmən) *n., pl.* **+men. 1.** a person skilled in the use of a rifle, esp. a soldier. **2.** a wren, *Acanthisitta chloris,* of New Zealand: family *Xenicidae.* See also **bush wren.**

ri+fle range *n.* an area used for target practice with rifles.

ri+fle+ry ('raɪfəlrɪ) *n. U.S.* **1.** rifle shots. **2.** the practice or skill of rifle marksmanship.

ri+fling ('raɪflɪŋ) *n.* **1.** the cutting of spiral grooves on the inside of a firearm's barrel. **2.** the series of grooves so cut.

rift[1] (rɪft) *n.* **1.** a gap or space made by cleaving or splitting; fissure. **2.** *Geology.* a fault produced by tension on either side of the fault plane. **3.** a gap between two cloud masses; break or chink: *he saw the sun through a rift in the clouds.* **4.** a break in friendly relations between people, nations, etc. ~*vb.* **5.** to burst or cause to burst open; split. [C13: from Old Norse; related to Danish *rift* cleft, Icelandic *ript* breach of contract]

rift[2] (rɪft) *n. U.S.* **1.** a shallow or rocky part in a stream. **2.** the backwash from a wave that has just broken. [C14: from Old Norse *rypta;* related to Icelandic *ropa* to belch]

rift val+ley *n.* a long narrow valley resulting from the subsidence of land between two parallel faults.

rig (rɪg) *vb.* **rigs, rig+ging, rigged.** (*tr.*) **1.** *Nautical.* to equip (a vessel, mast, etc.) with (sails, rigging, etc.). **2.** *Nautical.* to set up or prepare ready for use. **3.** to put the components of (an aircraft, etc.) into their correct positions. **4.** to manipulate in a fraudulent manner, esp. for profit: *to rig prices; to rig an election.* ~*n.* **5.** *Nautical.* the distinctive arrangement of the sails, masts, and other spars of a vessel. **6.** the installation used in drilling for and exploiting petroleum and natural gas deposits: *an oil rig.* **7.** apparatus or equipment; gear. **8.** *U.S.* a carriage together with one or more horses. **9.** *U.S.* an articulated lorry. ~See also **rig down, rig out, rig up.** [C15: from Scandinavian; related to Norwegian *rigga* to wrap]

Ri·ga ('riːgə) *n.* a port in the W Soviet Union, capital of the Latvian SSR, on the **Gulf of Riga** at the mouth of the Western Dvina: a major trading centre of the Baltic since Viking times. Pop.: 796 000 (1975 est.).

rig·a·doon (ˌrɪgə'duːn) *or* **ri+gau+don** (*French* rigo'dɔ̃) *n.* **1.** an old Provençal couple dance, light and graceful, in lively duple time. **2.** a piece of music for or in the rhythm of this dance. [C17: from French, allegedly from its inventor *Rigaud,* a dancing master at Marseille]

rig·a+ma+role ('rɪgəməˌrəʊl) *n.* a variant of **rigmarole.**

ri+ga+to+ni (ˌrɪːgə'təʊnɪ) *n.* macaroni in the form of short ridged often slightly curved pieces. [Italian, plural of *rigato,* from *rigare* to draw lines, make stripes, from *riga* a line, of Germanic origin]

rig down *vb.* (*adv.*) *Nautical.* to disassemble and stow.

Ri+gel ('raɪdʒəl, 'raɪgəl) *n.* the brightest star, Beta Orionis, in the constellation Orion: a remote blue-white giant and a visual binary. Visual magnitude: 0.2; spectral type: B8. [C16: from Arabic *rijl* foot; from its position in Orion's foot]

-rigged *adj.* (*in combination*) (of a sailing vessel) having a rig of a certain kind: *ketch-rigged; schooner-rigged.*

rig+ger ('rɪgə) *n.* **1.** a workman who rigs vessels, etc. **2.** *Rowing.* a bracket on a racing shell or other boat to support a projecting rowlock. **3.** a person skilled in the use of pulleys, lifting gear, cranes, etc.

rig+ging ('rɪgɪŋ) *n.* **1.** the shrouds, stays, halyards, etc., of a vessel. **2.** the bracing wires, struts, and lines of a biplane, balloon, etc. **3.** any form of lifting gear, tackle, etc.

rig+ging loft *n.* **1.** a loft or gallery in a boatbuilder's yard from which rigging can be fitted. **2.** a loft in a theatre from which scenery, etc., is raised and lowered.

right (raɪt) *adj.* **1.** in accordance with accepted standards of moral or legal behaviour, justice, etc.: *right conduct.* **2.** in accordance with fact, reason, or truth; correct or true: *the right answer.* **3.** appropriate, suitable, fitting, or proper: *the right man for the job.* **4.** most favourable or convenient; preferred: *the right time to act.* **5.** in a satisfactory condition; orderly: *things are right again now.* **6.** indicating or designating the correct time: *the clock is right.* **7.** correct in opinion or judgment. **8.** sound in mind or body; healthy or sane. **9.** (*usually prenominal*) of, designating, or located near the side of something or someone that faces east when the front is turned towards the north. **10.** (*usually prenominal*) worn on a right hand, foot, etc. **11.** (*sometimes cap.*) of, designating, supporting, belonging to, or relating to the political or intellectual right (see sense 37). **12.** (*sometimes cap.*) conservative or reactionary: *the right wing of the party.* **13.** *Geom.* **a.** formed by or containing a line or plane perpendicular to another line or plane. **b.** having the axis perpendicular to the base: *a right circular cone.* **c.** straight: *a right line.* **14.** relating to or designating the side of cloth worn or facing outwards. **15.** *Informal.* (intensifier): *a right idiot.* **16. in one's right mind.** sane. **17. the right side of. a.** in favour with: *you'd better stay on the right side of him.* **b.** younger than: *she's still on the right side of fifty.* ~*adv.* **18.** in accordance with correctness or truth; accurately: *to guess right.* **19.** in the appropriate manner; properly: *do it right next time!* **20.** in a straight line; directly: *right to the top.* **21.** in the direction of the east from the point of view of a person or thing facing north. **22.** absolutely or completely; utterly: *he went right through the floor.* **23.** without delay; immediately or promptly: *I'll be right over.* **24.** exactly or precisely: *right here.* **25.** in a manner consistent with a legal or moral code; justly or righteously: *do right by me.* **26.** in accordance with propriety; fittingly or suitably: *it serves you right.* **27.** to good or favourable advantage; well: *it all came out right in the end.* **28.** (esp. in religious titles) most or very: *right reverend.* **29.** *Informal or dialect.* (intensifier): *I'm right glad to see you.* **30. right, left, and centre.** on all sides; from every direction. **31. she'll be right.** *Austral. informal.* that's all right; not to worry. **32. right off the bat.** as the first in a series; to begin with. ~*n.* **33.** any claim, title, etc., that is morally just or legally granted as allowable or due to a person: *I know my rights.* **34.** anything that accords with the principles of legal or moral justice. **35.** the fact or state of being in accordance with reason, truth, or accepted standards (esp. in the phrase **in the right**). **36.** the right side, direction, position, area, or part: *the* *right of the army; look to the right.* **37.** (*often cap.* and preceded by *the*) the supporters or advocates of social, political, or economic conservatism or reaction, based generally on a belief that things are better left unchanged (opposed to *radical* or *left*). **38.** *Boxing.* **a.** a punch with the right hand. **b.** the right hand. **39.** *Finance.* **a.** (*often pl.*) the privilege of a company's shareholders to subscribe for new issues of the company's shares on advantageous terms. **b.** the negotiable certificate signifying this privilege. **40. by right** (*or* **rights**). properly; justly: *by rights you should be in bed.* **41. in one's own right.** having a claim or title oneself rather than through marriage or other connection: *a peeress in her own right.* **42. to rights.** consistent with justice, correctness, or orderly arrangement: *he put the matter to rights.* ~*vb.* (*mainly tr.*) **43.** (*also intr.*) to restore to or attain a normal, esp. an upright, position: *the raft righted in a few seconds.* **44.** to make (something) accord with truth or facts; correct. **45.** to restore to an orderly state or condition; put right. **46.** to make reparation for; compensate for or redress (esp. in the phrase **right a wrong**). ~*interj.* **47.** an expression of agreement or compliance. [Old English *riht, reoht;* related to Old High German *reht,* Gothic *raihts,* Latin *rēctus*] —ˈ**right+er** *n.*

right+a·ble (ˈraɪtəbᵊl) *adj.* capable of being righted. —ˈ**right+a·bly** *adv.* —ˈ**right+a·ble+ness** *n.*

right a·bout *n.* **1.** one's direction after making one complete clockwise turn through 180°. **2.** a turn executed through 180°. ~*adj., adv.* **3.** in the opposite direction.

right an+gle *n.* **1.** the angle between two perpendicular lines; an angle of 90°. **2. at right angles.** perpendicular or perpendicularly. —ˈ**right-ˌan·gled** *adj.*

right-an·gled tri+ang·le *n.* a triangle one angle of which is a right angle. U.S. name: **right triangle.**

right as+cen+sion *n. Astronomy.* the angular distance measured eastwards along the celestial equator from the vernal equinox to the point at which the celestial equator intersects a great circle passing through the celestial pole and the heavenly object in question. Symbol: α. Compare **declination** (sense 1).

right a·way *adv.* without delay; immediately or promptly.

right-down *adv., adj.* variant of **downright.**

right+en (ˈraɪtᵊn) *vb.* **1.** (*tr.*) to set right. **2.** to restore to or attain a normal or upright position.

right+eous (ˈraɪtʃəs) *adj.* **1. a.** characterized by, proceeding from, or in accordance with accepted standards of morality, justice, or uprightness; virtuous: *a righteous man.* **b.** (*as n.*): *the righteous.* **2.** morally justifiable or right, esp. from one's own point of view: *righteous indignation.* [Old English *rīhtwīs,* from RIGHT + WISE²] —ˈ**right+eous+ly** *adv.* —ˈ**right+eous+ness** *n.*

right-foot·er *n.* (esp. in Ireland) a Protestant.

right+ful (ˈraɪtfʊl) *adj.* **1.** in accordance with what is right; proper or just. **2.** (*prenominal*) having a legally or morally just claim: *the rightful owner.* **3.** (*prenominal*) held by virtue of a legal or just claim: *my rightful property.* —ˈ**right+ful+ly** *adv.* —ˈ**right+ful·ness** *n.*

right-hand *adj.* (*prenominal*) **1.** of, relating to, located on, or moving towards the right: *a right-hand bend; this car has right-hand drive.* **2.** for use by the right hand; right-handed. **3. right-hand man.** one's most valuable assistant or supporter.

right-hand·ed *adj.* **1.** using the right hand with greater skill or ease than the left. **2.** performed with the right hand: *right-handed writing.* **3.** made for use by the right hand. **4.** worn on the right hand. **5.** turning from left to right; clockwise. —ˌ**right-ˈhand·ed·ness** *n.*

right-hand·er *n.* **1.** a blow with the right hand. **2.** a person who is right-handed.

Right Hon+our+a·ble *adj.* **1.** (in Britain and certain Commonwealth countries) a title of respect for a Privy Councillor or an appeal-court judge. **2.** (in Britain) a title of respect for an earl, a viscount, a baron, or the Lord Mayor or Lord Provost of any of certain cities.

right+ish (ˈraɪtɪʃ) *adj.* somewhat right, esp. politically.

right+ist (ˈraɪtɪst) *adj.* **1.** of, tending towards, or relating to the political right or its principles; conservative, traditionalist, or reactionary. ~*n.* **2.** a person who supports or belongs to the political right. —ˈ**right+ism** *n.*

right+ly (ˈraɪtlɪ) *adv.* **1.** in accordance with the true facts; correctly. **2.** in accordance with principles of justice or morality. **3.** with good reason; justifiably: *he was rightly annoyed with her.* **4.** properly or suitably; appropriately: *rightly dressed for a wedding.* **5.** (*used with a negative*) *Informal.* with certainty; positively or precisely (usually in the phrases **I don't rightly know; I can't rightly say).**

right-mind·ed *adj.* holding opinions or principles that accord with what is right or with the opinions of the speaker. —ˌ**right-ˈmind·ed+ly** *adv.* —ˌ**right-ˈmind·ed+ness** *n.*

right+ness (ˈraɪtnɪs) *n.* the state or quality of being right.

right-o *or* **right oh** (ˈraɪtˈəʊ) *interj. Brit. informal.* an expression of agreement or compliance.

right off *adv.* immediately; right away.

right of search *n.* the right of a belligerent to stop and search neutral merchant ships on the high seas in wartime.

right of way *n., pl.* **rights of way. 1.** the right of one vehicle or vessel to take precedence over another, as laid down by law or custom. **2. a.** the legal right of someone to pass over another's land, acquired by grant or by long usage. **b.** the path or road used by this right. **3.** the strip of land over which a power line, railway line, road, etc., extends.

right on (*sentence substitute*) *Slang, chiefly U.S.* an exclamation of full agreement, concurrence, or compliance with the wishes, words, or actions of another.

Right Rev+er+end *adj.* a title of respect for a bishop, esp. an Anglican bishop.

rights is+sue *n. Stock exchange.* an issue of new shares offered by a company to its existing shareholders on favourable terms. Also called: **capitalization issue.**

right tri+an+gle *n.* U.S. name for **right-angled triangle.**

right+ward (ˈraɪtwəd) *adj.* **1.** situated on or directed towards the right. ~*adv.* **2.** a variant of **rightwards.**

right+wards (ˈraɪtwədz) *or* **right+ward** *adv.* towards or on the right.

right whale *n.* any large whalebone whale of the family *Balaenidae.* They are grey or black, have a large head, and, in most, no dorsal fin, and are hunted as a source of whalebone and oil. See also **bowhead.** [C19: perhaps so named because it was *right* for hunting]

right wing *n.* **1.** (*often cap.*) the conservative faction of an assembly, party, etc. **2.** the part of an army or field of battle on the right from the point of view of one facing the enemy. **3. a.** the right-hand side of the field of play from the point of view of a team facing its opponent's goal. **b.** a player positioned in this area in any of various games. **c.** the position occupied by such a player. ~*adj.* **right-wing. 4.** of, belonging to, or relating to the right wing. —ˈ**right-ˈwing·er** *n.*

Ri·gi (ˈriːgɪ) *n.* a mountain in the Alps of N central Switzerland, between Lakes Lucerne, Zug, and Lauerz.

rig+id (ˈrɪdʒɪd) *adj.* **1.** not bending; physically inflexible or stiff: *a rigid piece of plastic.* **2.** rigorously strict; severe: *rigid rules.* [C16: from Latin *rigidus,* from *rigēre* to be stiff] —ˈ**rig+id+ly** *adv.* —**ri+ˈgid+i+ty** *or* ˈ**rig+id+ness** *n.*

ri+gid·i·fy (rɪˈdʒɪdɪˌfaɪ) *vb.* **+fies, +fy+ing, +fied.** to make or become rigid.

Ri+gil Kent (ˈraɪdʒɪl ˈkɛnt) *n. Astronomy.* the star Alpha Centauri. Often shortened to **Rigil.** [from *Rigil Kentaurus,* from Arabic *al Rigil al Kentaurus* the Centaur's foot]

rig+ma+role (ˈrɪgməˌrəʊl) *or* **rig·a+ma+role** (ˈrɪgəməˌrəʊl) *n.* **1.** any long complicated procedure. **2.** a set of incoherent or pointless statements; garbled nonsense. [C18: from earlier *ragman roll* a list, probably a roll used in a medieval game, wherein various characters were described in verse, beginning with *Ragemon le bon* Ragman the good]

ri+gor (ˈraɪgɔː, ˈrɪgə) *n.* **1.** *Med.* a sudden feeling of chilliness, often accompanied by shivering: it sometimes precedes a fever. **2.** (ˈrɪgə). *Pathol.* rigidity of a muscle; muscular cramp. **3.** a state of rigidity assumed by some animals in reaction to sudden shock. **4.** the inertia assumed by some plants in conditions unfavourable to growth. [see RIGOUR]

rig+or+ism (ˈrɪgəˌrɪzəm) *n.* **1.** strictness in judgment or conduct. **2.** the religious cult of extreme self-denial. **3.** *R.C. Theol.* the doctrine that in cases of doubt in moral matters the stricter course must always be followed. —ˈ**rig+or+ist** *n.* —ˌ**rig+or+ˈis+tic** *adj.*

rig+or mor+tis (ˈrɪgə ˈmɔːtɪs) *n. Pathol.* the stiffness of joints and muscular rigidity of a dead body, caused by depletion of ATP in the tissues. It begins two to four hours after death and lasts up to about four days, after which the muscles and joints relax. [C19: Latin, literally: rigidity of death]

rig+or+ous (ˈrɪgərəs) *adj.* **1.** characterized by or proceeding from rigour; harsh, strict, or severe: *rigorous discipline.* **2.** severely accurate; scrupulous: *rigorous book-keeping.* **3.** (esp. of weather) extreme or harsh. **4.** *Maths., logic.* logically valid or correct. —ˈ**rig+or+ous+ly** *adv.* —ˈ**rig+or+ous+ness** *n.*

rig+our *or U.S.* **rig+or** (ˈrɪgə) *n.* **1.** harsh but just treatment or action. **2.** a severe or cruel circumstance; hardship: *the rigours of famine.* **3.** strictness, harshness, or severity of character. **4.** strictness in judgment or conduct; rigorism. **5.** *Maths., logic.* logical validity or accuracy. **6.** *Obsolete.* rigidity. [C14: from Latin *rigor*]

rig out *vb.* **1.** (*tr., adv.;* often foll. by *with*) to equip or fit out (with): *his car is rigged out with gadgets.* **2.** to dress or be dressed: *rigged out smartly.* ~*n.* **rig+out. 3.** *Informal.* a person's clothing or costume, esp. a bizarre outfit.

rigs+da+ler (ˈrɪgzˌdɑːlə) *n.* another word for **rix-dollar.**

rig up *vb.* (*tr., adv.*) to erect or construct, esp. as a temporary measure: *cameras were rigged up to televise the event.*

Rig-Ve·da (rɪgˈveɪdə, -ˈviːdə) *n.* a compilation of 1028 Hindu poems dating from 2000 B.C. or earlier. [C18: from Sanskrit *rigveda,* from *ric* song of praise + VEDA]

Ri+je+ka (rɪˈɛkə; *Serbo-Croatian* riˈjɛka) *n.* a port in NW Yugoslavia, in Croatia: an ancient town, changing hands many times before passing to Yugoslavia in 1947. Pop.: 132 222 (1971). Italian name: **Fiume.** Ancient name: **Tarsatica.**

rijks+daa+ler (ˈraɪksˌdɑːlə) *n.* a variant spelling of **rix-dollar.**

Rijn (rɛjn) *n.* the Dutch name for the **Rhine.**

Rijs+wijk (ˈraɪsvaɪk; *Dutch* ˈrɛjswɛjk) *n.* a town in the SW Netherlands, in South Holland province on the SE outskirts of The Hague: scene of the signing (1697) of the **Treaty of Rijswijk,** ending the War of the Grand Alliance. Pop.: 51 860 (1973 est.). English name: **Ryswick.**

Riks+dag (*Swedish* ˈriksdag) *n.* the Swedish parliament.

Riks+mål *Norwegian.* (ˈriksmɔl) *n.* a former name for **Bokmål.** [literally: language of the kingdom]

rile (raɪl) *vb.* (*tr.*) **1.** *Informal.* to annoy or anger; irritate. **2.** *U.S.* to stir up or agitate (water, etc.); roil or make turbid. [C19: variant of ROIL]

Ri·ley (ˌraɪlɪ) *n.* **the life of Riley.** a luxurious and carefree existence. [C20: origin unknown]

ri+lie+vo *Italian.* (ri'ljevo; *English* ˌrɪlɪ'eɪvəʊ) *n., pl.* ***+vi*** (-viː). another name for **relief** (sense 9).

Ril·ke ('rɪlkə) *n.* **Rai·ner Ma·ri·a** ('raɪnər ma'riːa). 1875–1926, German poet, born in Austria. Author of intense visionary lyrics, notably in the *Duino Elegies* (1922) and *Sonnets to Orpheus* (1923).

rill (rɪl) *n.* **1.** a brook or stream; rivulet. **2.** a small channel or gulley, such as one formed during soil erosion. **3.** Also **rille.** one of many winding cracks on the moon. [C15: from Low German *rille;* related to Dutch *ril*]

ril+let ('rɪlɪt) *n.* a little rill.

rim (rɪm) *n.* **1.** the raised edge of an object, esp. of something more or less circular such as a cup or crater. **2.** the peripheral part of a wheel, to which the tyre is attached. **3.** *Basketball.* the hoop from which the net is suspended. ~*vb.* **rims, rim+ming, rimmed.** (*tr.*) **4.** to put a rim on (a pot, cup, wheel, etc.). **5.** *Ball games.* (of a ball) to run around the edge of (a hole, basket, etc.). [Old English *rima;* related to Old Saxon *rimi,* Old Norse *rimi* ridge]

RIM *international car registration for* (Islamic Republic of) Mauritania.

Rim·baud (*French* rɛ̃'bo) *n.* **Ar·thur** (ar'tyr). 1854–91, French poet, whose work, culminating in the prose poetry of *Illuminations* (published 1884), greatly influenced the symbolists. *A Season in Hell* (1873) draws on his tempestuous homosexual affair with Verlaine, after which he abandoned writing (aged about 20) and spent the rest of his life travelling.

rime[1] (raɪm) *n.* **1.** frost formed by the freezing of supercooled water droplets in fog onto solid objects. ~*vb.* **2.** (*tr.*) to cover with rime or something resembling rime. [Old English, *hrīm;* related to Dutch *rijm,* Middle High German *rīmeln* to coat with frost]

rime[2] (raɪm) *n.* a variant spelling of **rhyme.**

rim+er ('raɪmə) *n.* another name for **rhymester.**

rime riche ('riːm 'riːʃ) *n., pl.* **rimes riches** ('riːm 'riːʃ). rhyme between words or syllables that are identical in sound, as in *command/demand, pair/pear.* [French, literally: rich rhyme]

rime+ster ('raɪmstə) *n.* a variant spelling of **rhymester.**

rim-fire *adj.* **1.** (of a cartridge) having the primer in the rim of the base. **2.** (of a firearm) adapted for such cartridges. ~Compare **centre-fire.**

Ri+mi+ni ('rɪmɪnɪ) *n.* a port and resort in NE Italy, on the N Adriatic coast. Pop.: 123 850 (1975 est.). Latin name: **Ariminum.**

ri+mose (raɪ'məʊs, -'məʊz) *adj.* (esp. of plant parts) having the surface marked by a network of intersecting cracks. [C18: from Latin *rīmōsus,* from *rīma* a split, crack] —**'ri+mose+ly** *adv.* —**ri+mos+i·ty** (raɪ'mɒsɪtɪ) *n.*

rim+rock ('rɪmˌrɒk) *n.* rock forming the boundaries of a sandy or gravelly alluvial deposit.

Rim·sky-Kor·sa·kov ('rɪmskɪ 'kɔːsəkɒf; *Russian* 'rimskij 'kɔrsəkəf) *n.* **Ni·ko·lai An·dre·ye·vich** (nika'laj an'drjejɪvitʃ). 1844–1908, Russian composer; noted for such works as the orchestral suite *Scheherazade* (1888) and the opera *Le Coq d'or* (first performed in 1910).

ri·mu ('riːmuː) *n.* another name for **red pine.** [from Maori]

rim·y ('raɪmɪ) *adj.* **rim·i+er, rim·i·est.** coated with rime.

rind (raɪnd) *n.* **1.** a hard outer layer or skin on bacon, cheese, etc. **2.** the outer layer of a fruit or of the spore-producing body of certain fungi. **3.** the outer layer of the bark of a tree. [Old English *rinde;* Old High German *rinta,* German *Rinde*]

rin·der+pest ('rɪndəˌpɛst) *n.* an acute contagious viral disease of cattle, characterized by severe inflammation of the intestinal tract and diarrhoea. [C19: German: cattle pest]

rin+for+zan+do (ˌriːnfɔː'tsændəʊ) a less common term for **sforzando.** [Italian, literally: reinforcing]

ring[1] (rɪŋ) *n.* **1.** a circular band of a precious metal or the like, esp. gold, often set with gems and worn upon the finger as an adornment or as a token of engagement or marriage. **2.** any object or mark that is circular in shape. **3.** a circular path or course: *to run around in a ring.* **4.** a group of people or things standing or arranged so as to form a circle: *a ring of spectators.* **5.** an enclosed space, usually circular in shape, where circus acts are performed. **6.** a square apron or raised platform, marked off by ropes, in which contestants box or wrestle. **7. the ring.** the sport of boxing. **8.** the field of competition or rivalry. **9. throw one's hat in the ring.** to announce one's intention to be a candidate or contestant. **10.** a group or organization of people, usually illegal, cooperating for the self-interested purpose of controlling the market in art treasures, antiques, etc. **11.** (esp. at county fairs) an enclosure, often circular, where horses, cattle, and other livestock are paraded and auctioned. **12.** an area reserved for betting at a racecourse. **13.** a circular strip of bark cut from a tree or branch, esp. in order to kill it. **14.** a single turn in a spiral. **15.** *Geom.* the area of space lying between two concentric circles. **16.** *Maths.* a set that is subject to two binary operations, addition and multiplication, such that the set is an Abelian group under addition and is closed under multiplication, this latter operation being associative. **17.** *Botany.* short for **annual ring. 18.** Also called: **closed chain.** *Chem.* a closed loop of atoms in a molecule. **19.** one of the system of three planar circular bands orbiting the planet Saturn. See also **Saturn**[2] (sense 1). **20. to run rings around.** *Informal.* to be greatly superior to; outclass completely. ~*vb.* **rings, ring+ing, ringed.** (*tr.*) **21.** to surround with or as if with or form a ring; encircle. **22.** to mark a bird with a ring or clip for subsequent identification. **23.** to fit a ring in the nose of (a bull, pig, etc.) so that it can be led easily. **24.** Also (Austral.): **ring+bark** ('rɪŋ-bɑːk). to cut away a circular strip of bark from (a tree or branch) in order to kill it. [Old English *hring;* related to Old Norse *hringr*]

ring[2] (rɪŋ) *vb.* **rings, ring+ing, rang, rung. 1.** to emit or cause to emit a sonorous or resonant sound, characteristic of certain metals when struck. **2.** to cause (a bell, etc.) to emit a ringing sound by striking it once or repeatedly or (of a bell) to emit such a sound. **3. a.** (*tr.*) to cause (a large bell, esp. a church bell) to emit a ringing sound by pulling on a rope that is attached to a wheel on which the bell swings back and forth, being sounded by a clapper inside it. Compare **chime**[1] (sense 6). **b.** (*intr.*) (of a bell) to sound by being swung in this way. **4.** (*intr.*) (of a building, place, etc.) to be filled with sound; echo: *the church rang with singing.* **5.** (*intr.;* foll. by *for*) to call by means of a bell, buzzer, etc.: *to ring for the butler.* **6.** Also: **ring up.** *Chiefly Brit.* to call (a person) by telephone. **7.** (*tr.*) to strike or tap (a coin) in order to assess its genuineness by the sound produced. **8.** (*intr.*) (of the ears) to have or give the sensation of humming or ringing. **9. ring a bell.** to bring something to the mind or memory; remind one of something: *that rings a bell.* **10. ring down the curtain. a.** to lower the curtain at the end of a theatrical performance. **b.** (foll. by *on*) to put an end (to). **11. ring false.** to give the impression of being false. **12. ring the bell. a.** to do, say, or be the right thing. **b.** to reach the pinnacle of success or happiness. **13. ring the changes.** to vary the manner or performance of an action that is often repeated. **14. ring true.** to give the impression of being true: *that story doesn't ring true.* ~*n.* **15.** the act of or a sound made by ringing. **16.** a sound produced by or suggestive of a bell. **17.** any resonant or metallic sound, esp. one sustained or re-echoed: *the ring of trumpets.* **18.** *Informal, chiefly Brit.* a telephone call: *he gave her a ring last night.* **19.** the complete set of bells in a tower or belfry: *a ring of eight bells.* See **peal** (sense 2). **20.** an inherent quality or characteristic: *his explanation has the ring of sincerity.* ~See also **ring back, ring in, ring off, ring out, ring up.** [Old English *hringan;* related to Old High German *hringen,* Old Norse *hringja*]

Usage. *Rang* and *sang* are the correct forms of the past tenses of *ring* and *sing,* although *rung* and *sung* are still heard informally and dialectally: *he rung* (*rang*) *the bell.*

ring back *vb.* (*adv.*) to return a telephone call (to).

ring+bolt ('rɪŋˌbəʊlt) *n.* a bolt with a ring fitted through an eye attached to the bolt head.

ring+bone ('rɪŋˌbəʊn) *n.* an abnormal bony growth affecting the pastern of a horse, often causing lameness.

ring cir+cuit *n.* an electrical system in which distribution points are connected to the main supply in a continuous closed circuit.

ring+dove ('rɪŋˌdʌv) *n.* **1.** another name for **wood pigeon. 2.** an Old World turtledove, *Streptopelia risoria,* having a greyish plumage with a black band around the neck.

ring-dyke *n.* a dyke having an approximately circular outcrop of rock.

ringed (rɪŋd) *adj.* **1.** displaying ringlike markings. **2.** having or wearing a ring. **3.** formed by rings; annular.

ringed plov+er *n.* a European shorebird, *Charadrius hiaticula,* with a greyish-brown back, white underparts with a black throat band, and orange legs: family *Charadriidae* (plovers).

rin+gent ('rɪndʒənt) *adj.* (of the corolla of plants such as the snapdragon) consisting of two distinct gaping lips. [C18: from Latin *ringī* to open the mouth wide]

ring+er ('rɪŋə) *n.* **1.** a quoit thrown so as to encircle a peg. **2.** such a throw. **3.** a contestant, esp. a horse, entered in a competition under false representations of identity, record, or ability. **4.** Also called: **dead ringer.** *Slang.* a person or thing that is almost identical to another. **5.** a person or thing that rings a bell, etc. **6.** *Austral.* the fastest shearer in a shed. **7.** *Austral. informal.* the fastest or best at anything.

Ring·er's so+lu·tion ('rɪŋəz) *n.* a solution containing the chlorides of sodium, potassium, and calcium, used to correct dehydration and, in physiological experiments, as a medium for in vitro preparations.

ring fin+ger *n.* the third finger, esp. of the left hand, on which a wedding ring is traditionally worn.

ring+git ('rɪŋgɪt) *n.* the standard monetary unit of Malaysia, divided into 100 sens. [from Malay]

ring+hals ('rɪŋhæls) *n., pl.* **+hals** *or* **+hals·es.** a venomous elapid snake, *Hemachatus hemachatus,* of southern Africa, which spits venom at its enemies from a distance. Also called: **spitting snake.** [Afrikaans, literally: ring neck]

ring in *vb.* (*adv.*) **1.** (*intr.*) *Chiefly Brit.* to report to someone by telephone. **2.** (*tr.*) to accompany the arrival of with bells (esp. in the phrase **ring in the new year**).

ring+ing tone *n. Brit.* a sequence of pairs of tones heard by the dialler on a telephone when the number dialled is ringing. Compare **engaged tone, dialling tone.**

ring+lead·er ('rɪŋˌliːdə) *n.* a person who leads a riot or mutiny.

ring+let ('rɪŋlɪt) *n.* **1.** a lock of hair hanging down in a spiral curl. **2.** any of numerous butterflies of the genus *Erebia,* most of which occur in S Europe and have dark brown wings marked with small black-and-white eyespots: family *Satyridae.* —**'ring+let+ed** *adj.*

ring main *n.* a domestic electrical supply in which outlet sockets are connected to the mains supply through a ring circuit.

ring+mas·ter ('rɪŋˌmɑːstə) *n.* the master of ceremonies in a circus.

ring-necked *adj.* (of animals, esp. certain birds and snakes) having a band of distinctive colour around the neck.

ring-necked pheas+ant *n.* a common pheasant, *Phasianus* *colchicus*, originating in Asia. The male has a bright plumage with a band of white around the neck and the female is mottled brown.

ring off *vb.* (*intr., adv.*) *Chiefly Brit.* to terminate a telephone conversation by replacing the receiver; hang up.

Ring of the Ni·bel·ung *n. Germanic myth.* a magic ring on which the dwarf Alberich placed a curse after it was stolen from him.

ring out *vb.* (*adv.*) **1.** (*tr.*) to accompany the departure of with bells (esp. in the phrase **ring out the old year**). **2.** (*intr.*) to send forth a loud resounding noise.

ring ou·zel *n.* a European thrush, *Turdus torquatus*, common in rocky areas. The male has a blackish plumage with a white band around the neck and the female is brown.

ring road *n.* a main road that bypasses a town or town centre. U.S. names: **belt, beltway.**

ring-shout *n.* a West African circle dance that has influenced jazz, surviving in the Black churches of the southern U.S.

ring·side ('rɪŋˌsaɪd) *n.* **1.** the area immediately surrounding an arena, esp. the row of seats nearest a boxing or wrestling ring. **2. a.** any place affording a close uninterrupted view. **b.** (*as modifier*): *a ringside seat.*

ring·ster ('rɪŋstə) *n.* a member of a ring controlling a market in antiques, art treasures, etc.

ring·tail ('rɪŋˌteɪl) *n.* **1.** Also called: **ring-tailed cat.** another name for **cacomistle. 2.** *Austral.* any of several possums having curling prehensile tails used to grasp branches while climbing.

ring-tailed *adj.* (of an animal) having a tail marked with rings of a distinctive colour.

ring taw *n.* a game of marbles in which players attempt to knock other players' marbles out of a ring.

ring up *vb.* (*adv.*) **1.** *Chiefly Brit.* to make a telephone call (to). **2.** (*tr.*) to record on a cash register. **3.** (*tr.*) to chronicle; record: *to ring up another success.* **4. ring up the curtain. a.** to begin a theatrical performance. **b.** (often foll. by *on*) to make a start (on).

ring·worm ('rɪŋˌwɜːm) *n.* any of various fungal infections of the skin (esp. the scalp) or nails, often appearing as itching circular patches. Also called: **tinea.**

rink (rɪŋk) *n.* **1.** an expanse of ice for skating on, esp. one that is artificially prepared and under cover. **2.** an area for roller skating on. **3.** a building or enclosure for ice skating or roller skating. **4.** *Bowls.* a strip of the green, usually about 5–7 metres wide, on which a game is played. **5.** *Curling.* the strip of ice on which the game is played, usually 41 by 4 metres. **6.** (in bowls and curling) the players on one side in a game. [C14 (Scots): from Old French *renc* row, RANK[1]]

rinse (rɪns) *vb.* (*tr.*) **1.** to remove soap from (clothes, etc.) by applying clean water in the final stage in washing. **2.** to wash lightly, esp. without using soap: *to rinse one's hands.* **3.** to give a light tint to (hair). ~*n.* **4.** the act or an instance of rinsing. **5.** *Hairdressing.* a liquid preparation put on the hair when wet to give a tint to it: *a blue rinse.* [C14: from Old French *rincer*, from Latin *recens* fresh, new] —'**rins·a·ble** *or* '**rins·i·ble** *adj.* —ˌ**rins·a·'bil·i·ty** *or* ˌ**rins·i·'bil·i·ty** *n.* —'**rins·er** *n.*

Ri·o Bran·co (*Portuguese* 'riu 'brɐŋku) *n.* **1.** a city in W Brazil, capital of Acre state. Pop.: 84 845 (1970). **2.** a river in Brazil, flowing south to the Rio Negro. Length: 644 km (400 miles).

Río Bra·vo ('rio 'βravo) *n.* the Mexican name for the **Rio Grande.**

Ri·o de Ja·nei·ro (ˌriːəʊ də dʒə'nɪərəʊ) *or* **Ri·o** *n.* **1.** a port in SE Brazil, on Guanabara Bay: the country's chief port and its capital from 1763 to 1960; backed by mountains, notably Sugar Loaf Mountain; founded by the French in 1555 and taken by the Portuguese in 1567. Pop.: 4 252 009 (1970). **2.** a state of E Brazil. Capital: Rio de Janeiro. Pop.: 8 994 802 (1970). Area: 42 911 sq. km (16 568 sq. miles).

Río de la Pla·ta ('riːəʊ də lɑː 'plɑːtə) *n.* See **Plata.**

Río de O·ro (*Spanish* 'rio ðe 'oro) *n.* a former region of W Africa: comprised the S part of the Spanish Sahara.

Ri·o Grande *n.* **1.** ('riːəʊ 'grænd, 'grændɪ). a river in North America, rising in SW Colorado and flowing southeast to the Gulf of Mexico, forming the border between the U.S. and Mexico. Length: about 3030 km (1885 miles). Mexican name: **Río Bravo. 2.** (*Portuguese* 'riu 'grɐndi). a port in SE Brazil, in SE Rio Grande do Sul state: serves as the port for Pôrto Alegre. Pop.: 116 827 (1970).

Ri·o Gran·de do Nor·te (*Portuguese* 'riu 'grɐndi du 'nɔrti) *n.* a state of NE Brazil, on the Atlantic: much of it is semiarid plateau. Capital: Natal. Pop.: 1 550 244 (1970). Area: 53 014 sq. km (20 469 sq. miles).

Ri·o Gran·de do Sul (*Portuguese* 'riu 'grɐndi du 'sul) *n.* a state of S Brazil, on the Atlantic. Capital: Pôrto Alegre. Pop.: 6 664 891 (1970). Area: 282 183 sq. km (108 951 sq. miles).

Rí·o Mu·ni (*Spanish* 'rio 'muni) *n.* one of the two provinces of Equatorial Guinea: comprises the mainland part of the country, with some offshore islands. Capital: Bata. Pop.: 203 000 (1968 est.). Area: 26 021 sq. km (10 047 sq. miles).

Rí·o Ne·gro (ˌriːəʊ 'neɪgrəʊ, 'nɛg-; *Spanish* 'rio 'neɣro) *n.* See **Negro.**

ri·ot ('raɪət) *n.* **1. a.** a disturbance made by an unruly mob or (in law) three or more persons; tumult or uproar. **b.** (*as modifier*): *a riot gun; riot police; a riot shield.* **2.** boisterous activity; unrestrained revelry. **3.** an occasion of boisterous merriment. **4.** *Slang.* a person who occasions boisterous merriment. **5.** a dazzling or arresting display: *a riot of colour.* **6.** *Hunting.* the indiscriminate following of any scent by hounds. **7.** *Archaic.* wanton lasciviousness. **8. run riot. a.** to behave wildly and without restraint. **b.** (of plants) to grow rankly or profusely. ~*vb.* **9.** (*intr.*) to take part in a riot. **10.** (*intr.*) to indulge in unrestrained revelry or merriment. **11.** (*tr.*; foll. by *away*) to spend (time or money) in wanton or loose living: *he has rioted away his life.* [C13: from Old French *riote* dispute, from *ruihoter* to quarrel, probably from *ruir* to make a commotion, from Latin *rugīre* to roar] —'**ri·ot·er** *n.*

Ri·ot Act *n.* **1.** *Criminal law.* (formerly in England) a statute of 1715 by which persons committing a riot had to disperse within an hour of the reading of the act by a magistrate. **2. read the riot act (to).** to warn or reprimand severely.

ri·ot·ous ('raɪətəs) *adj.* **1.** proceeding from or of the nature of riots or rioting. **2.** inciting to riot. **3.** characterized by wanton or lascivious revelry: *riotous living.* **4.** characterized by boisterous or unrestrained merriment: *riotous laughter.* —'**ri·ot·ous·ly** *adv.* —'**ri·ot·ous·ness** *n.*

rip[1] (rɪp) *vb.* **rips, rip·ping, ripped. 1.** to tear or be torn violently or roughly; split or be rent. **2.** (*intr.*) *Informal.* to move violently or precipitously; rush headlong. **3.** (*intr.*, foll. by *into*) *Informal.* to pour violent abuse (on); make a verbal attack (on). **4.** (*tr.*) to saw or split (wood) in the direction of the grain. **5. let rip.** to act or speak without restraint. ~*n.* **6.** the place where something is torn; a tear or split. **7.** short for **ripsaw.** ~See also **rip off, rip up.** [C15: perhaps from Flemish *rippen*; compare Middle Dutch *rippen* to pull] —'**rip·pa·ble** *adj.* —'**rip·per** *n.*

rip[2] (rɪp) *n.* short for **riptide.** [C18: perhaps from RIP[1]]

rip[3] (rɪp) *n. Informal, archaic.* **1.** something or someone of little or no value. **2.** an old worn-out horse. [C18: perhaps altered from *rep*, shortened from REPROBATE]

R.I.P. *abbrev. for* requiescat *or* requiescant in pace. [Latin: may he, she, *or* they rest in peace]

ri·par·i·an (raɪ'pɛərɪən) *adj.* **1.** of, inhabiting, or situated on the bank of a river. **2.** denoting or relating to the legal rights of the owner of land on a river bank, such as fishing or irrigation. ~*n.* **3.** *Property law.* a person who owns land on a river bank. [C19: from Latin *rīpārius*, from *rīpa* a river bank]

rip·cord ('rɪpˌkɔːd) *n.* **1.** a cord that when pulled opens a parachute from its pack. **2.** a cord on the gas bag of a balloon that when pulled opens a panel, enabling gas to escape and the balloon to descend.

ripe (raɪp) *adj.* **1.** (of fruit, grain, etc.) mature and ready to be eaten or used; fully developed. **2.** mature enough to be eaten or used: *ripe cheese.* **3.** fully developed in mind or body. **4.** resembling ripe fruit, esp. in redness or fullness: *a ripe complexion.* **5.** (*postpositive*; foll. by *for*) ready or eager (to undertake or undergo an action). **6.** (*postpositive*; foll. by *for*) suitable; right or opportune: *the time is not yet ripe.* **7.** mature in judgment or knowledge. **8.** advanced but healthy (esp. in the phrase **a ripe old age**). [Old English *rīpe*; related to Old Saxon *rīpi*, Old High German *rīfi*, German *reif*] —'**ripe·ly** *adv.* —'**ripe·ness** *n.*

rip·en ('raɪpᵊn) *vb.* to make or become ripe. —'**rip·en·er** *n.*

ri·pie·no (rɪ'pjɛnəʊ; *Italian* ri'pjeːno) *n.* (in baroque concertos and concerti grossi) the full orchestra, as opposed to the instrumental soloists. Also called: **concerto.** Compare **concertino.** [C18: from Italian: from *ri-* RE- + *pieno*, from Latin *plēnus* full]

Rip·ley ('rɪplɪ) *n.* **George.** 1802–80, U.S. social reformer and transcendentalist: founder of the Brook Farm experiment in communal living in Massachusetts (1841).

rip off *vb.* **1.** (*tr.*) to tear violently or roughly (from). **2.** (*adv.*) *Slang.* to steal from or cheat (someone). ~*n.* **rip-off. 3.** *Slang.* an article or articles stolen. **4.** *Slang.* a grossly overpriced article. **5.** *Slang.* the act of stealing or cheating.

Rip·on ('rɪpᵊn) *n.* a city in N England, in North Yorkshire: cathedral (12th–16th centuries). Pop.: 10 987 (1971).

ri·poste *or* **ri·post** (rɪ'pɒst, rɪ'pəʊst) *n.* **1.** a swift sharp reply in speech or action. **2.** *Fencing.* a counterattack made immediately after a successful parry. ~*vb.* **3.** (*intr.*) to make a riposte. [C18: from French, from Italian *risposta*, from *rispondere* to reply, RESPOND]

rip·per ('rɪpə) *n.* **1.** a person who rips. **2.** *Chiefly Austral. slang.* a fine or excellent person or thing.

rip·ping ('rɪpɪŋ) *adj. Archaic Brit. slang.* excellent; splendid. —'**rip·ping·ly** *adv.*

rip·ple[1] ('rɪpᵊl) *n.* **1.** a slight wave or undulation on the surface of water. **2.** a small wave or undulation in fabric, hair, etc. **3.** a sound reminiscent of water flowing quietly in ripples: *a ripple of laughter.* **4.** *Electronics.* an oscillation of small amplitude superimposed on a steady value. **5.** *U.S.* a small rapid. **6.** another word for **ripple mark.** ~*vb.* **7.** (*intr.*) to form ripples or flow with a rippling or undulating motion. **8.** (*tr.*) to stir up (water) so as to form ripples. **9.** (*tr.*) to make ripple marks. **10.** (*intr.*) (of sounds) to rise and fall gently: *her laughter rippled through the air.* [C17: perhaps from RIP[1]] —'**rip·pler** *n.* —'**rip·pling·ly** *adv.* —'**rip·ply** *adj.*

rip·ple[2] ('rɪpᵊl) *n.* **1.** a special kind of comb designed to separate the seed from the stalks in flax, hemp, or broomcorn. ~*vb.* **2.** (*tr.*) to comb with this tool. [C14: of Germanic origin; compare Middle Dutch *repelen*, Middle High German *reffen* to ripple] —'**rip·pler** *n.*

rip·ple mark *n.* one of a series of small wavy ridges of sand formed by waves on a beach, by a current in a sandy riverbed, or by wind on land.

rip·plet ('rɪplɪt) *n.* a tiny ripple.

rip-roar·ing *adj. Informal.* characterized by excitement, intensity, or boisterous behaviour.

rip·saw ('rɪpˌsɔː) *n.* a handsaw for cutting along the grain of timber.

rip+snort·er ('rɪpˌsnɔːtə) *n. Slang.* a person or thing noted for its intensity. —'**rip+ˌsnort+ing** *adj.*

rip+tide ('rɪpˌtaɪd) *n.* **1.** Also called: **rip, tide-rip.** a stretch of turbulent water in the sea, caused by the meeting of currents or abrupt changes in depth. **2.** Also called: **rip current.** a strong current, esp. one flowing outwards from the shore, causing disturbance on the surface.

Rip·u+ar+i·an (ˌrɪpjʊ'ɛərɪən) *adj.* **1. a.** of or relating to the group of Franks who lived during the 4th century near Cologne along the Rhine. **b.** of or designating their code of laws. ~*n.* **2.** a Ripuarian Frank. [C18: from Medieval Latin *Ripuārius,* perhaps from Latin *rīpa* a river bank]

rip up *vb. (tr., adv.)* **1.** to tear (paper, etc.) into small pieces. **2.** to annul, cancel, or unilaterally disregard. **3.** to dig up, dig into, or remove (a surface): *they are ripping up the street.*

Rip Van Win·kle ('rɪp væn 'wɪŋkᵊl) *n. Informal.* **1.** a person who is oblivious to changes, esp. in social attitudes or thought. **2.** a person who sleeps a lot. [C19: from a character who slept for 20 years, in a story (1819) by Washington Irving]

rise (raɪz) *vb.* **ris·es, ris+ing, rose, ris·en.** *(mainly intr.)* **1.** to get up from a lying, sitting, kneeling, or prone position. **2.** to get out of bed, esp. to begin one's day: *he always rises early.* **3.** to move from a lower to a higher position or place; ascend. **4.** to ascend or appear above the horizon: *the sun is rising.* **5.** to increase in height or level: *the water rose above the normal level.* **6.** to attain higher rank, status, or reputation: *he will rise in the world.* **7.** to be built or erected: *those blocks of flats are rising fast.* **8.** to become apparent; appear: *new troubles rose to afflict her.* **9.** to increase in strength, degree, intensity, etc.: *her spirits rose; the wind is rising.* **10.** to increase in amount or value: *house prices are always rising.* **11.** to swell up: *dough rises.* **12.** to become erect, stiff, or rigid: *the hairs on his neck rose in fear.* **13.** (of one's stomach or gorge) to manifest or feel nausea; retch. **14.** to become actively rebellious; revolt: *the people rose against their oppressors.* **15.** to slope upwards: *the ground rises beyond the lake.* **16.** to return from the dead; be resurrected. **17.** to originate; come into existence: *that river rises in the mountains.* **18.** (of a session of a court, legislative assembly, etc.) to come to an end; adjourn. **19.** *Angling.* (of fish) to come to the surface of the water, as when taking flies. **20.** *(tr.) Nautical.* another term for **raise** (sense 20). **21.** (often foll. by *to*) *Informal.* to respond (to teasing, etc.) or fall into a trap prepared for one. ~*n.* **22.** the act or an instance of rising; ascent. **23.** an increase in height; elevation. **24.** an increase in rank, status, or position. **25.** an increase in amount, cost, or value. **26.** an increase in degree or intensity. **27.** *Brit.* an increase in salary or wages. U.S. word: **raise. 28.** a piece of rising ground. **29.** an upward slope or incline. **30.** the appearance of the sun, moon, or other celestial body above the horizon. **31.** the vertical height of a step or of a flight of stairs. **32.** the vertical height of a roof above the walls or columns. **33.** the height of an arch above the impost level. **34.** *Angling.* the act or instance of fish coming to the surface of the water to take flies, etc. **35.** the beginning, origin, or source; derivation. **36. get a rise out of.** *Slang.* to provoke an angry or petulant reaction from. **37. give rise to.** to cause the development of; produce. [Old English *rīsan;* related to Old Saxon *rīsan,* Gothic *reisan*]

rise a·bove *vb. (intr., prep.)* to overcome or be unaffected by (something mean or contemptible).

ris+er ('raɪzə) *n.* **1.** a person who rises, esp. from bed: *an early riser.* **2.** the vertical part of a stair or step. **3.** a vertical pipe, esp. one within a building.

rise to *vb. (intr., prep.)* to respond adequately to (the demands of something, esp. a testing challenge).

ris+i·bil+i·ty (ˌrɪzɪ'bɪlɪtɪ) *n., pl.* **·ties. 1.** a tendency to laugh. **2.** hilarity; laughter.

ris+i·ble ('rɪzɪbᵊl) *adj.* **1.** having a tendency to laugh. **2.** causing laughter; ridiculous. [C16: from Late Latin *rīsibilis,* from Latin *rīdēre* to laugh] —'**ris+i+bly** *adv.*

ris+ing ('raɪzɪŋ) *n.* **1.** an insurrection or rebellion; revolt. **2.** the yeast or leaven used to make dough rise in baking. ~*adj. (prenominal)* **3.** increasing in rank, status, or reputation: *a rising young politician.* **4.** increasing in maturity; growing up to adulthood: *the rising generation.*

ris+ing trot *n.* a horse's trot in which the rider rises from the saddle every second beat. Compare **sitting trot.**

risk (rɪsk) *n.* **1.** the possibility of incurring misfortune or loss; hazard. **2.** *Insurance.* **a.** chance of a loss or other event on which a claim may be filed. **b.** the type of such an event, such as fire or theft. **c.** the amount of the claim should such an event occur. **d.** a person or thing considered with respect to the characteristics that may cause an insured event to occur. **3. no risk.** *Austral. informal.* an expression of assent. **4. take** *or* **run a risk.** to proceed in an action without regard to the possibility of danger involved in it. ~*vb. (tr.)* **5.** to expose to danger or loss; hazard. **6.** to act in spite of the possibility of (injury or loss): *to risk a fall in climbing.* [C17: from French *risque,* from Italian *risco,* from *rischiare* to be in peril, from Greek *rhiza* cliff (from the hazards of sailing along rocky coasts)] —'**risk+er** *n.*

risk cap·i·tal *n. Chiefly Brit.* capital invested in an issue of ordinary shares, esp. of a speculative enterprise. Also called (esp. U.S.): **venture capital.**

risk·y ('rɪskɪ) *adj.* **risk·i+er, risk·i+est.** involving danger; perilous. —'**risk+i+ly** *adv.* —'**risk·i+ness** *n.*

Ri+sor+gi+men+to (rɪˌsɔːdʒɪ'mɛntəʊ) *n.* the period of and the movement for the political unification of Italy in the 19th century. [Italian, from *risorgere* to rise again, from Latin *resurgere,* from RE- + *surgere* to rise]

ri+sot+to (rɪ'zɒtəʊ) *n.* a dish of rice cooked in stock and served variously with tomatoes, cheese, chicken, etc. [Italian, from *riso* RICE]

ris+qué ('rɪskeɪ) *adj.* bordering on impropriety or indecency: *a risqué joke.* [C19: from French *risquer* to hazard, RISK]

Riss (rɪs) *n.* the third major Pleistocene glaciation in Alpine Europe. See also **Günz, Mindel, Würm.** [C20: named after the river *Riss,* a tributary of the Danube in Germany]

ris+sole ('rɪsəʊl) *n.* a mixture of minced cooked meat coated in egg and breadcrumbs, often covered with pastry, and fried. Compare **croquette.** [C18: from French, probably ultimately from Latin *russus* red; see RUSSET]

ri+sus sar+do+ni+cus ('riːsəs sɑː'dɒnɪkəs) *n. Pathol.* fixed contraction of the facial muscles resulting in a peculiar distorted grin, caused esp. by tetanus. Also called: **tris+mus cyn·i·cus** ('trɪzməs 'sɪnɪkəs). [New Latin, literally: sardonic laugh]

rit. *Music. abbrev. for:* **1.** ritardando. **2.** ritenuto.

ri+tar+dan+do (ˌrɪtɑː'dændəʊ) another word for **rallentando.** Abbrev.: **rit.** [Italian, from *ritardare* to slow down]

rite (raɪt) *n.* **1.** a formal act or procedure prescribed or customary in religious ceremonies: *fertility rites; the rite of baptism.* **2.** a particular body of such acts or procedures, esp. of a particular Christian Church: *the Latin rite.* **3.** a Christian Church: *the Greek rite.* [C14: from Latin *rītus* religious ceremony]

ri+te·nu+to (ˌrɪtə'nuːtəʊ) *adj., adv. Music.* **1.** held back momentarily. **2.** Abbrev.: **rit.** another term for **rallentando.**

rite of pas+sage *n.* a ceremony performed in some cultures at times when an individual changes his status, as at puberty and marriage.

ri+tor+nel+lo (ˌrɪtə'nɛləʊ) *n. Music.* **1.** an orchestral passage between verses of an aria or song. **2.** a ripieno passage in a concerto grosso. [C17: from Italian, literally: a little return, from *ritorno* a RETURN]

rit·u+al ('rɪtjʊəl) *n.* **1.** the prescribed or established form of a religious or other ceremony. **2.** such prescribed forms in general or collectively. **3.** stereotyped activity or behaviour. **4.** *Psychol.* any repetitive behaviour, such as hand-washing, performed by a person with a compulsive personality disorder. **5.** any formal act, institution, or procedure that is followed consistently: *the ritual of the law.* ~*adj.* **6.** of, relating to, or characteristic of religious, social, or other rituals. [C16: from Latin *rītuālis,* from *rītus* RITE] —'**rit·u·al+ly** *adv.*

rit·u+al+ism ('rɪtjʊəˌlɪzəm) *n.* **1.** emphasis, esp. exaggerated emphasis, on the importance of rites and ceremonies. **2.** the study of rites and ceremonies, esp. magical or religious ones. —'**rit·u·al+ist** *n.* —ˌ**rit·u·al+'is+tic** *adj.* —ˌ**rit·u·al+'is+ti·cal+ly** *adv.*

rit·u+al+ize *or* **rit·u+al+ise** ('rɪtjʊəˌlaɪz) *vb.* **1.** *(intr.)* to engage in ritualism or devise rituals. **2.** *(tr.)* to make (something) into a ritual.

ritz·y ('rɪtsɪ) *adj.* **ritz·i+er, ritz·i+est.** *Slang.* luxurious or elegant. [C20: after the hotels established by César *Ritz* (1850–1918), Swiss hotelier] —'**ritz·i+ly** *adv.* —'**ritz·i+ness** *n.*

riv. *abbrev. for* river.

riv+age ('rɪvɪdʒ) *n. Archaic.* a bank, shore, or coast. [C14: from Old French, from *rive* river bank, from Latin *rīpa*]

ri+val ('raɪvᵊl) *n.* **1. a.** a person, organization, team, etc., that competes with another for the same object or in the same field. **b.** *(as modifier): rival suitors; a rival company.* ~*vb.* **+vals, +val+ling, +valled** *or U.S.* **+vals, +val+ing, +valed.** *(tr.)* **2.** to be the equal or near equal of: *an empire that rivalled Rome.* **3.** to try to equal or surpass; compete with in rivalry. [C16: from Latin *rīvalis,* literally: one who shares the same brook, from *rīvus* a brook]

ri+val+ry ('raɪvəlrɪ) *n., pl.* **+ries. 1.** the act of rivalling; competition. **2.** the state of being a rival or rivals. —'**ri+val+rous** *adj.*

rive (raɪv) *vb.* **rives, riv+ing, rived, rived** *or* **riv+en.** *(usually passive)* **1.** to split asunder: *a tree riven by lightning.* **2.** to tear apart: *riven to shreds.* **3.** *Archaic.* to break (the heart, etc.) or (of the heart) to be broken. [C13: from Old Norse *rīfa;* related to Old Frisian *rīva*]

riv+er ('rɪvə) *n.* **1. a.** a large natural stream of fresh water flowing along a definite course, usually into the sea, being fed by tributary streams. **b.** *(as modifier): river traffic; a river basin.* **c.** *(in combination): riverside; riverbed.* Related adj.: **fluvial. 2.** any abundant stream or flow: *a river of blood.* **3. sell down the river.** *Informal.* to deceive or betray. [C13: from Old French *riviere,* from Latin *rīpārius* of a river bank, from *rīpa* bank] —'**riv+er+less** *adj.*

Ri·ve·ra (*Spanish* ri'βera) *n.* **Die·go** ('djeɣo). 1886–1957, Mexican painter, noted for his monumental murals in public buildings, which are influenced by Aztec art and depict revolutionary themes.

riv+er horse *n.* an informal name for the **hippopotamus.**

riv+er+ine ('rɪvəˌraɪn) *adj.* **1.** of, like, relating to, or produced by a river. **2.** located or dwelling near a river; riparian.

Riv+ers ('rɪvəz) *n.* a state of S Nigeria, in the Niger River Delta on the Gulf of Guinea. Capital: Port Harcourt. Pop.: 1 544 314 (1976 est.). Area: 17 941 sq. km (6929 sq. miles).

Riv·er+side ('rɪvəˌsaɪd) *n.* a city in SW California. Pop.: 154 618 (1973 est.).

riv+et ('rɪvɪt) *n.* **1.** a short metal pin for fastening two or more pieces together, having a head at one end, the other end being hammered flat after being passed through holes in the pieces. ~*vb. (tr.)* **2.** to join by riveting. **3.** to hammer in order to form into a head. **4.** *(often passive)* to cause to be fixed or held firmly, as in fascinated attention, horror, etc.: *to be riveted to* *the spot.* [C14: from Old French, from *river* to fasten, fix, of unknown origin] —'**riv+et+er** *n.*

Riv·i+er·a (ˌrɪvɪ'ɛərə) *n.* the Mediterranean coastal region between Cannes, France, and La Spezia, Italy: contains some of Europe's most popular resorts. [Italian, literally: shore, ultimately from Latin *rīpa* bank, shore]

ri+vi+ère (ˌrɪvɪ'ɛə) *n.* a necklace the diamonds or other precious stones of which gradually increase in size up to a large centre stone. [C19: from French: brook, RIVER]

riv·u+let ('rɪvjʊlɪt) *n.* a small stream. [C16: from Italian *rivoletto*, from Latin *rīvulus*, from *rīvus* stream]

rix-dol·lar ('rɪksˌdɒlə) *n.* any of various former Scandinavian or Dutch small silver coins. Also: **rijksdaaler, rigsdaler.** [C16: partial translation of obsolete Dutch *rijksdaler; rijk* realm, kingdom]

Ri+yadh (rɪ'jɑːd) *n.* the joint capital (with Mecca) of Saudi Arabia, situated in a central oasis: the largest city in the country. Pop.: 225 000 (1965 est.).

ri+yal (rɪ'jɑːl) *n.* the standard monetary and currency unit of Saudi Arabia, Yemen, or Dubai. [from Arabic *riyāl*, from Spanish *real* REAL[2]]

Ri+zal[1] (*Spanish* ri'θal) *n.* another name for **Pasay.**

Ri·zal[2] (*Spanish* ri'θal) *n.* **Jo·se** (xo'se). 1861–96, Philippine nationalist, executed by the Spanish during the Philippine revolution of 1896.

Riz·zio (*Italian* 'rittsjo) *or* **Ric·cio** *n.* **Da·vid** ('david). ?1533–66, Italian musician and courtier who became the secretary and favourite of Mary Queen of Scots. He was murdered by her husband Darnley.

RL *international car registration for* (Republic of) Lebanon.

R.L. *abbrev. for* Rugby League.

rly. *abbrev. for* railway.

RM *international car registration for* Malagasy Republic.

R.M. *abbrev. for:* **1.** Royal Mail. **2.** Royal Marines.

rm. *abbrev. for:* **1.** ream. **2.** room.

R.M.A. *abbrev. for* Royal Military Academy (Sandhurst).

RMM *international car registration for* (Republic of) Mali.

rms *or* **r.m.s.** *abbrev. for* root mean square.

R.M.S. *abbrev. for:* **1.** Royal Mail Service. **2.** Royal Mail Steamer.

Rn *the chemical symbol for* radon.

R.N. *abbrev. for* Royal Navy.

RNA *n. Biochem.* ribonucleic acid; any of a group of nucleic acids, present in all living cells, that play an essential role in the synthesis of proteins. On hydrolysis they yield the pentose sugar ribose, the purine bases adenine and guanine, the pyrimidine bases cytosine and uracil, and phosphoric acid. See also **messenger RNA, transfer RNA, ribosomal RNA, DNA.**

R.N.A.S. *abbrev. for:* **1.** Royal Naval Air Service(s). **2.** Royal Naval Air Station.

R.N.L.I. *abbrev. for* Royal National Lifeboat Institution.

R.N.R. *abbrev. for* Royal Naval Reserve.

R.N.V.R. *abbrev. for* Royal Naval Volunteer Reserve.

R.N.W.M.P. (in Canada) *abbrev. for* Royal Northwest Mounted Police.

R.N.Z.A.F. *abbrev. for* Royal New Zealand Air Force.

R.N.Z.N. *abbrev. for* Royal New Zealand Navy.

roach[1] (rəʊtʃ) *n., pl.* **roach·es** *or* **roach. 1.** a European freshwater cyprinid food fish, *Rutilus rutilus*, having a deep compressed body and reddish ventral and tail fins. **2.** any of various similar fishes. [C14: from Old French *roche*, of obscure origin]

roach[2] (rəʊtʃ) *n.* **1.** short for **cockroach. 2.** *Slang.* the butt of a cannabis cigarette.

roach[3] (rəʊtʃ) *n. Nautical.* **1.** the amount by which the leech of a fore-and-aft sail projects beyond an imaginary straight line between the clew and the head. **2.** the curve at the foot of a square sail. [C18: of unknown origin]

road (rəʊd) *n.* **1. a.** an open way, usually surfaced with tarmac or concrete, providing passage from one place to another. **b.** (*as modifier*): *road traffic; a road map; a road sign.* **c.** (*in combination*): *the roadside.* **2. a.** a street. **b.** (*cap. as part of a name*): *London Road.* **3. a.** *U.S.* short for **railroad. b.** *Brit.* one of the tracks of a railway. **4.** a way, path, or course: *the road to fame.* **5.** (*often pl.*) Also called: **roadstead.** *Nautical.* a partly sheltered anchorage. **6.** a drift or tunnel in a mine, esp. a level one. **7. hit the road.** *Slang.* to start or resume travelling. **8. on the road. a.** travelling about; on tour. **b.** leading a wandering life. **9. take (to) the road.** to begin a journey or tour. **10. one for the road.** *Informal.* a last alcoholic drink before leaving. [Old English *rād;* related to *rīdan* to RIDE, and to Old Saxon *rēda*, Old Norse *reith*] —'**road+less** *adj.*

road a·gent *n. U.S.* (formerly) a bandit who robbed stagecoaches; highwayman.

road+bed ('rəʊdˌbɛd) *n.* **1.** the material used to make a road. **2.** a layer of ballast that supports the sleepers of a railway track.

road+block ('rəʊdˌblɒk) *n.* a barrier set up across a road by the police or military, in order to stop a fugitive, inspect traffic, etc.

road book *n.* a book of maps, sometimes including a gazetteer.

road-fund licence *n. Brit.* a licence showing that the tax payable in respect of a motor vehicle has been paid. [C20: from the former *road fund* for the maintenance of public highways]

road hog *n. Informal.* a selfish or aggressive driver.

road+hold·ing ('rəʊdˌhəʊldɪŋ) *n.* the extent to which a motor vehicle is stable and does not skid, esp. at high speeds, or on sharp bends or wet roads.

road+house ('rəʊdˌhaʊs) *n.* a pub, restaurant, etc., that is situated at the side of a road, esp. a country road.

road met+al *n.* crushed rock, broken stone, etc., used to construct a road.

road rash *n. Slang.* a bruise or cut resulting from falling off a skateboard.

road+roll·er ('rəʊdˌrəʊlə) *n.* a motor vehicle with heavy rollers for compressing road surfaces during road-making.

road+run·ner ('rəʊdˌrʌnə) *n.* a terrestrial crested bird, *Geococcyx californianus*, of Central and S North America, having a streaked plumage and long tail: family *Cuculidae* (cuckoos). Also called: **chaparral cock.**

road show *n.* a group of entertainers, esp. pop musicians, on tour.

road+stead ('rəʊdˌstɛd) *n. Nautical.* another word for **road** (sense 5).

road+ster ('rəʊdstə) *n.* **1.** *Archaic.* an open car, esp. one seating only two. **2.** a kind of bicycle.

road test *n.* **1.** a test to ensure that a vehicle is roadworthy, esp. after repair or servicing, by driving it on roads. ~*vb.* **road-test.** (*tr.*) **2.** to test a vehicle in this way.

road train *n. Austral.* a line of linked trailers pulled by a truck, used for transporting stock, etc.

road+way ('rəʊdˌweɪ) *n.* **1.** the surface of a road. **2.** the part of a road that is used by vehicles.

road+work ('rəʊdˌwɜːk) *n.* sports training by running along roads.

road works *pl. n.* repairs to a road or cable under a road, esp. when forming a hazard or obstruction to traffic.

road+wor·thy ('rəʊdˌwɜːðɪ) *adj.* (of a motor vehicle) mechanically sound; fit for use on the roads. —'**road+ˌwor·thi·ness** *n.*

roam (rəʊm) *vb.* **1.** to travel or walk about with no fixed purpose or direction; wander. ~*n.* **2.** the act of roaming. [C13: origin unknown] —'**roam+er** *n.*

roan (rəʊn) *adj.* **1.** (of a horse) having a bay (**red roan**), chestnut (**strawberry roan**), or black (**blue roan**) coat sprinkled with white hairs. ~*n.* **2.** a horse having such a coat. **3.** a soft unsplit sheepskin leather with a close tough grain, used in bookbinding, etc. [C16: from Old French, from Spanish *roano*, probably from Gothic *rauths* red]

Ro·a+noke Is+land ('rəʊəˌnəʊk) *n.* an island off the coast of North Carolina: site of the first attempted English settlement in America. Length: 19 km (12 miles). Average width: 5 km (3 miles).

roar (rɔː) *vb.* (*mainly intr.*) **1.** (of lions and other animals) to utter characteristic loud growling cries. **2.** (*also tr.*) (of people) to utter (something) with a loud deep cry, as in anger or triumph. **3.** to laugh in a loud hearty unrestrained manner. **4.** (of horses) to breathe with laboured rasping sounds. See **roaring** (sense 4). **5.** (of the wind, waves, etc.) to blow or break loudly and violently, as during a storm. **6.** (of a fire) to burn fiercely with a roaring sound. **7.** (of a machine, gun, etc.) to operate or move with a loud harsh noise. **8.** (*tr.*) to bring (oneself) into a certain condition by roaring: *to roar oneself hoarse.* ~*n.* **9.** a loud deep cry, uttered by a person or crowd, esp. in anger or triumph. **10.** a prolonged loud cry of certain animals, esp. lions. **11.** any similar noise made by a fire, the wind, waves, artillery, an engine, etc. [Old English *rārian;* related to Old High German *rērēn*, Middle Dutch *reren*] —'**roar+er** *n.*

roar+ing ('rɔːrɪŋ) *adj.* **1.** *Informal.* very brisk and profitable (esp. in the phrase **a roaring trade**). ~*adv.* **2.** noisily or boisterously (esp. in the phrase **roaring drunk**). ~*n.* **3.** a loud prolonged cry. **4.** a debilitating breathing defect of horses characterized by rasping sounds with each breath: caused by inflammation of the respiratory tract or obstruction of the larynx. Compare **whistling.** —'**roar+ing+ly** *adv.*

Roar+ing For+ties *pl. n.* **the.** *Nautical.* the areas of ocean between 40° and 50° latitude in the S Hemisphere, noted for gale-force winds.

roar up *vb.* (*tr., adv.*) *Austral. informal.* to rebuke or reprimand (a person).

roast (rəʊst) *vb.* (*mainly tr.*) **1.** to cook (meat or other food) by dry heat, usually with added fat and esp. in an oven. **2.** to brown or dry (coffee, etc.) by exposure to heat. **3.** *Metallurgy.* to heat (an ore) in order to produce a concentrate that is easier to smelt. **4.** to heat (oneself or something) to an extreme degree, as when sunbathing, sitting before the fire, etc. **5.** (*intr.*) to be excessively and uncomfortably hot. **6.** *Informal.* to criticize severely. ~*n.* **7.** something that has been roasted, esp. meat. [C13: from Old French *rostir*, of Germanic origin; compare Middle Dutch *roosten* to roast] —'**roast+er** *n.*

roast+ing ('rəʊstɪŋ) *Informal.* ~*adj.* **1.** extremely hot. ~*n.* **2.** severe criticism.

rob (rɒb) *vb.* **robs, rob+bing, robbed. 1.** to take something from (someone) illegally, as by force or threat of violence. **2.** (*tr.*) to plunder (a house, etc.). **3.** (*tr.*) to deprive unjustly: *to be robbed of an opportunity.* [C13: from Old French *rober*, of Germanic origin; compare Old High German *roubōn* to rob] —'**rob+ber** *n.*

rob·a+lo ('rɒbəˌləʊ, 'rəʊ-) *n., pl.* **+los** *or* **+lo.** any percoid fish of the family *Centropomidae*, occurring in warm and tropical (mostly marine) waters. Some of the larger species, such as the snooks, are important food fishes and many of the smaller ones are aquarium fishes. [Spanish, probably changed from *lobaro* (unattested), from *lobo* wolf, from Latin *lupus*]

rob+and ('rɒbənd, 'rəʊbənd) *or* **rob+bin** *n. Nautical.* a piece of marline used for fastening a sail to a spar. [C18: probably related to Middle Dutch *rabant*, from *ra* sailyard + *bant* band]

Robbe-Gril·let (*French* rɔbgri'jɛ) *n.* **A·lain** (a'lɛ̃). born 1922,

French novelist. Author of *The Voyeur* (1955) and *Jealousy* (1957), he is one of the leading practitioners of the anti-roman.

Rob·ben Is·land ('rɒbᵊn) *n.* a small island 11 km (7 miles) off the Cape Peninsula: used by the South African government to house political prisoners.

rob·ber crab *n.* a terrestrial crab, *Birgus latro,* of the Indo-Pacific region, known for its habit of climbing coconut palms to feed on the nuts.

rob·ber fly *n.* any of the predatory dipterous flies constituting the family *Asilidae,* which have a strong bristly body with piercing mouthparts and which prey on other insects. Also called: **bee killer.**

rob·ber·y ('rɒbərɪ) *n., pl.* **·ber·ies. 1.** *Criminal law.* the stealing of property from a person by using or threatening to use force. **2.** the act or an instance of robbing.

Rob·bia ('rəʊbɪə; *Italian* 'robbja) *n.* **1. An·dre·a del·la** (an'drɛ:a 'della). 1435–1525, Florentine sculptor, best known for his polychrome reliefs and his statues of infants in swaddling clothes. **2.** his uncle, **Lu·ca del·la** ('lu:ka 'della). ?1400–82, Florentine sculptor, who perfected a technique of enamelling terra cotta for reliefs.

rob·bin ('rɒbɪn) *n. Nautical.* another word for **roband.**

robe (rəʊb) *n.* **1.** any loose flowing garment, esp. the official vestment of a peer, judge, or academic. **2.** a dressing gown or bathrobe. **3.** *Austral. slang.* a wardrobe. ~*vb.* **4.** to put a robe, etc., on (oneself or someone else); dress. [C13: from Old French: of Germanic origin; compare Old French *rober* to ROB, Old High German *roub* booty]

robe-de-cham·bre *French.* (rɔb də 'ʃɑ̃br) *n., pl.* ***robes-de-cham·bre*** (rɔb də 'ʃɑ̃br). a dressing gown or bathrobe.

Rob·ert I ('rɒbət) *n.* known as *Robert the Bruce.* 1274–1329, king of Scotland (1306–29): he defeated the English army of Edward II at Bannockburn (1314) and gained recognition of Scotland's independence (1328).

Robe·son ('rəʊbsən) *n.* **Paul.** 1898–1976, U.S. bass singer, actor, and leader in the Black civil-rights movement.

Robes·pierre ('rəʊbzpjɛə; *French* rɔbɛs'pjɛ:r) *n.* **Max·i·mi·lien Fran·çois Ma·rie I·si·dore de** (maksimiljɛ̃ frɑ̃swa mari izi'dɔ:r də). 1758–94, French revolutionary and Jacobin leader: established the Reign of Terror as a member of the Committee of Public Safety (1793–94): executed in the coup d'état of Thermidor (1794).

rob·in ('rɒbɪn) *n.* **1.** Also called: **robin redbreast.** a small Old World songbird, *Erithacus rubecula,* related to the thrushes: family *Muscicapidae.* The male has a brown back, orange-red breast and face, and grey underparts. **2.** a North American thrush, *Turdus migratorius,* similar to but larger than the Old World robin. **3.** any of various similar birds having a reddish breast. [C16: arbitrary use of given name]

rob·ing room *n.* a room in a palace, court, legislature, etc., where official robes of office are put on.

Rob·in Hood *n.* a legendary English outlaw of the reign of Richard I, who according to tradition lived in Sherwood Forest and robbed the rich to give to the poor.

ro·bin·i·a (rə'bɪnɪə) *n.* any tree of the leguminous genus *Robinia,* esp. the locust tree (see **locust** (sense 2).

rob·in's-egg blue *n. Chiefly U.S.* **a.** a light greenish-blue colour. **b.** (*as adj.*): *a robin's-egg-blue dress.*

Ro·bin·son ('rɒbɪnsən) *n.* **1. Ed·ward G(oldenberg).** 1893–1973, U.S. film actor, famous esp. for gangster roles: his films include *Little Caesar* (1930), *Kid Galahad* (1937), *Brother Orchid* (1940), and *All My Sons* (1948). **2. Ed·win Ar·ling·ton.** 1869–1935, U.S. poet, author of narrative verse, often based on Arthurian legend. His works include *Collected Poems* (1922), *The Man Who Died Twice* (1924), and *Tristram* (1927). **3. "Sug·ar" Ray,** original name *Walker Smith.* born 1920, U.S. boxer, winner of the world middleweight championship on five separate occasions.

ro·ble ('rəʊbleɪ) *n.* **1.** Also called: **white oak.** an oak tree, *Quercus lobata,* of California, having leathery leaves and slender pointed acorns. **2.** any of several similar or related trees. [Spanish: from Latin *rōbur* oak, strength]

ro·bor·ant ('rəʊbərənt, 'rɒb-) *adj.* **1.** tending to fortify or increase strength. ~*n.* **2.** a drug or agent that increases strength. [C17: from Latin *rorborāre* strengthen, from *rōbur* an oak]

ro·bot ('rəʊbɒt) *n.* **1.** any automated machine programmed to perform specific mechanical functions in the manner of a man. **2.** (*modifier*) not controlled by man; automatic: *a robot pilot.* **3.** a person who works or behaves like a machine; automaton. **4.** *S. African.* a set of traffic lights. [C20: (used in *R.U.R.,* a play by Karel Čapek) from Czech *robota* work; related to Old Slavonic *rabota* servitude, German *Arbeit* work] —**'ro·bot·ism** *or* **'ro·bot·ry** *n.* —**'ro·bot-,like** *adj.*

ro·bot bomb *n.* another name for the **V-1.**

Rob Roy ('rɒb 'rɔɪ) *n.* original name *Robert Macgregor.* 1671–1734, Scottish outlaw.

Rob·son ('rɒbsən) *n.* **Mount.** a mountain in SW Canada, in E British Columbia: the highest peak in the Canadian Rockies. Height: 3954 m (12 972 ft.).

ro·bust (rəʊ'bʌst, 'rəʊbʌst) *adj.* **1.** strong in constitution; hardy; vigorous. **2.** sturdily built: *a robust shelter.* **3.** requiring or suited to physical strength: *a robust sport.* **4.** (esp. of wines) having a rich full-bodied flavour. **5.** rough or boisterous. **6.** (of thought, intellect, etc.) straightforward and imbued with common sense. [C16: from Latin *rōbustus,* from *rōbur* an oak, strength] —**ro·'bust·ly** *adv.* —**ro·'bust·ness** *n.*

ro·bus·tious (rəʊ'bʌstʃəs) *adj. Archaic.* **1.** rough; boisterous. **2.** strong, robust, or stout. —**ro·'bus·tious·ly** *adv.* —**ro·'bus·tious·ness** *n.*

roc (rɒk) *n.* (in Arabian legend) a bird of enormous size and power. [C16: from Arabic *rukhkh,* from Persian *rukh*]

R.O.C. *abbrev. for* Royal Observer Corps.

Ro·ca ('rəʊkə) *n.* **Cape.** a cape in SW central Portugal, near Lisbon: the westernmost point of continental Europe.

ro·caille (rɒ'kaɪ) *n.* decorative rock or shell work, esp. as ornamentation in a rococo fountain, grotto, or interior. [from French, from *roc* ROCK]

roc·am·bole ('rɒkəm,bəʊl) *n.* a variety of sand leek whose garlic-like bulb is used for seasoning. [C17: from French, from German *Rockenbolle,* literally: distaff bulb (with reference to its shape)]

Roch·dale ('rɒtʃ,deɪl) *n.* a town in NW England, in Lancashire: textile industry. Pop.: 91 344 (1971).

Ro·chelle pow·der (rɒ'ʃɛl) *n.* another name for **Seidlitz powder.** [C18: named after *La Rochelle,* French port]

Ro·chelle salt *n.* a white crystalline double salt used in Seidlitz powder. Formula: $KNaC_4H_4O_6.4H_2O$.

roche mou·ton·née ('rəʊʃ ,mu:tə'neɪ) *n., pl.* **roches mou·ton·nées** ('rəʊʃ ,mu:tə'neɪz). a rounded mass of rock smoothed and striated by ice that has flowed over it. [French, literally: fleecy rock, from *mouton* sheep]

Roch·es·ter ('rɒtʃɪstə) *n.* **1.** a city in SE England, in Kent on the River Medway: with Chatham and Gillingham forms the conurbation of the Medway towns. Pop.: 55 460 (1971). **2.** a city in NW New York State, on Lake Ontario. Pop.: 276 796 (1973 est.).

roch·et ('rɒtʃɪt) *n.* a white surplice with tight sleeves, worn by bishops, abbots, and certain other Church dignitaries. [C14: from Old French, from *roc* coat, outer garment, of Germanic origin; compare Old High German *roc* coat]

rock[1] (rɒk) *n.* **1.** *Geology.* any aggregate of minerals that makes up part of the earth's crust. It may be unconsolidated, such as a sand, clay, or mud, or consolidated, such as granite, limestone, or coal. See also **igneous, sedimentary,** and **metamorphic. 2.** any hard mass of consolidated mineral matter, such as a boulder. **3.** *U.S., Austral.* a stone. **4.** a person or thing suggesting a rock, esp. in being dependable, unchanging, or providing firm foundation. **5.** *Brit.* a hard sweet, typically a long brightly-coloured peppermint-flavoured stick, sold esp. in holiday resorts. **6.** *Slang.* a jewel, esp. a diamond. **7.** short for **rock salmon. 8.** (*pl.*) *Taboo slang.* the testicles. **9. on the rocks. a.** in a state of ruin or destitution. **b.** (of drinks, esp. whisky) served with ice. [C14: from Old French *roche,* of unknown origin]

rock[2] (rɒk) *vb.* **1.** to move or cause to move from side to side or backwards and forwards. **2.** to reel or sway or cause (someone) to reel or sway, as with a violent shock or emotion. **3.** (*tr.*) to shake or move (something) violently. **4.** (*intr.*) to dance in the rock-and-roll style. **5.** *Mining.* to wash (ore) or (of ore) to be washed in a cradle. **6.** (*tr.*) to roughen (a copper plate) with a rocker before engraving a mezzotint. **7. rock the boat.** to create a disturbance; make trouble. ~*n.* **8.** a rocking motion. **9.** short for **rock-and-roll. 10.** Also called: **rock music.** any of various styles of pop music having a heavy beat, derived from rock-and-roll. [Old English *roccian;* related to Middle Dutch, Old High German *rocken,* German *rücken*] —**'rock·ing·ly** *adv.*

Rock (rɒk) *n.* **The.** an informal name for **Gibraltar.**

rock·a·bil·ly ('rɒkə,bɪlɪ) *n.* **a.** rock music containing a strong country-and-western element. **b.** (*as modifier*): *a rockabilly number.* [C20: from ROCK(-AND-ROLL) + (HILL)BILLY]

rock-and-roll *or* **rock-'n'-roll** *n.* **1. a.** a type of pop music originating in the 1950s as a blend of rhythm-and-blues and country-and-western. It is generally based upon the twelve-bar blues, the second and fourth beats in each bar being heavily accented. **b.** (*as modifier*): *the rock-and-roll era.* **2.** dancing performed to such music, with exaggerated body movements stressing the beat. ~*vb.* **3.** (*intr.*) to perform this dance. —**'rock-and-'roll·er** *or* **'rock-'n'-'roll·er** *n.*

rock·a·way ('rɒkə,weɪ) *n. U.S.* a four-wheeled horse-drawn carriage, usually with two seats and a hard top.

rock bass (bæs) *n.* **1.** a North American freshwater percoid fish, *Ambloplites rupestris:* an important food fish; family *Centrarchidae* (sunfishes, etc.). **2.** any similar or related fish.

rock bot·tom *n.* **a.** the lowest possible level. **b.** (*as modifier*): *rock-bottom prices.*

rock-bound *adj.* hemmed in or encircled by rocks. Also (poetic): **rock-girt.**

rock brake *n.* any of various ferns of the genera *Pellaea* and *Cryptogramma,* which grow on rocky ground and have sori at the ends of the veins.

rock cake *n.* a small cake containing dried fruit and spice, with a rough surface supposed to resemble a rock.

rock can·dy *n.* the usual U.S. name for **rock**[1] (sense 5).

rock crys·tal *n.* a pure transparent colourless quartz, used in electronic and optical equipment. Formula: SiO_2.

rock dove *or* **pi·geon** *n.* a common dove, *Columba livia,* from which domestic and feral pigeons are descended. It has a pale grey plumage with black-striped wings.

Rock·e·fel·ler ('rɒkə,fɛlə) *n.* **1. John D(avison).** 1839–1937, U.S. industrialist and philanthropist. **2.** his son, **John D(avison).** 1874–1960, U.S. capitalist and philanthropist. **3.** his son, **Nel·son (Aldrich).** 1908-79, U.S. politician; governor of New York State (1958-74); vice president 1974-76.

rock·er ('rɒkə) *n.* **1.** any of various devices that transmit or operate with a rocking motion. See also **rocker arm. 2.** another word for **rocking chair.** **3.** either of two curved supports on the legs of a chair or other article of furniture on which it may rock. **4.** a steel tool with a curved toothed cage, used to roughen the copper plate in engraving a mezzotint. **5.** *Mining.* another word for **cradle** (sense 8). **6. a.** an ice skate with a curved blade. **b.** the curve itself. **7.** *Skating.* **a.** a figure consisting of three interconnecting circles. **b.** a half turn in which the skater turns through 180°, so facing about while continuing to move in the same direction. **8.** *Brit.* a member of a group of teenagers in the mid-1960s who characteristically wore leather jackets and rode powerful motorcycles. See also **mod. 9. off one's rocker.** *Slang.* crazy; demented.

rock+er arm *n.* a lever that rocks about a central pivot, esp. one in an internal-combustion engine that transmits the motion of a pushrod or cam to a valve.

rock+er·y ('rɒkərɪ) *n., pl.* **+er·ies.** a garden constructed with rocks, esp. one where alpine plants are grown. Also called: **rock garden.**

rock+et[1] ('rɒkɪt) *n.* **1.** a self-propelling device, esp. a cylinder containing a mixture of solid explosives, used as a firework, distress signal, line carrier, etc. **2. a.** any vehicle propelled by a rocket engine, esp. one used to carry a warhead, spacecraft, etc. **b.** (*as modifier*): *rocket propulsion; rocket launcher.* **3.** *Brit. informal.* a severe reprimand (esp. in the phrase **get a rocket**). ~*vb.* **4.** (*tr.*) to propel (a missile, spacecraft, etc.) by means of a rocket. **5.** (*intr.; foll. by off, away, etc.*) to move off at high speed. **6.** (*intr.*) to rise rapidly: *he rocketed to the top.* [C17: from Old French *roquette*, from Italian *rochetto* a little distaff, from *rocca* distaff, of Germanic origin]

rock+et[2] ('rɒkɪt) *n.* **1.** a Mediterranean cruciferous plant, *Eruca sativa,* having yellowish-white flowers and leaves used as a salad. **2.** any of several plants of the related genus *Sisymbrium,* esp. *S. irio* **(London rocket),** which grow on waste ground and have pale yellow flowers. **3. yellow rocket.** any of several yellow-flowered plants of the related genus *Barbarea,* esp. *B. vulgaris.* **4. sea rocket.** any of several plants of the related genus *Cakile,* esp. *C. maritima,* which grow along the seashores of Europe and North America and have mauve, pink, or white flowers. **5. dame's rocket.** another name for **dame's violet.** ~See also **dyer's rocket, wall rocket.** [C16: from French *roquette*, from Italian *rochetta*, from Latin *ērūca* a caterpillar, hairy plant]

rock+et+eer (ˌrɒkɪ'tɪə) *n.* an engineer or scientist concerned with the design, operation, or launching of rockets.

rock+et en+gine *n.* a reaction engine in which a fuel and oxidizer are burnt in a combustion chamber, the products of combustion expanding through a nozzle and producing thrust. Also called: **rocket motor.**

rock+et+ry ('rɒkɪtrɪ) *n.* the science and technology of the design, operation, maintenance, and launching of rockets.

rock+fish ('rɒkˌfɪʃ) *n., pl.* **+fish** *or* **+fish·es.** any of various fishes that live among rocks, esp. scorpaenid fishes of the genus *Sebastodes* and related genera, such as *S. caurinus* **(copper rockfish)** of North American Pacific coastal waters.

Rock+ford ('rɒkfəd) *n.* a city in N Illinois, on the Rock River. Pop.: 142 173 (1973 est.).

rock gar+den *n.* a garden featuring rocks or rockeries.

Rock+hamp+ton (rɒk'hæmptən, -'hæmtən) *n.* a port in Australia, in E Queensland on the Fitzroy River. Pop.: 51 500 (1975 est.).

rock hop+per *n.* a penguin, *Eudyptes crestatus,* of the New Zealand area, with a yellow crest on each side of its head.

Rock·ies ('rɒkɪz) *pl. n.* another name for the **Rocky Mountains.**

rock+ing chair *n.* a chair set on curving supports so that the sitter may rock backwards and forwards.

Rock·ing·ham ('rɒkɪŋəm) *n.* **Marquess of,** title of *Charles Watson-Wentworth.* 1730–82, English statesman and leader of the Whig opposition, whose members were known as the **Rockingham Whigs;** prime minister (1765–66; 1782). He opposed the war with the American colonists.

rock+ing horse *n.* a toy horse mounted on a pair of rockers on which a child can rock to and fro in a seesaw movement.

rock+ing stone *n.* a boulder so delicately poised that it can be rocked.

rock+ling ('rɒklɪŋ) *n., pl.* **+lings** *or* **+ling.** any small gadoid fish of the genera *Gaidropsarus, Ciliata,* etc. (formerly all included in *Motella*), which have an elongated body with barbels around the mouth and occur mainly in the North Atlantic Ocean. [C17: from ROCK[1] + -LING[1]]

rock lob+ster *n.* another name for the **spiny lobster.**

rock mel+on *n. U.S., Austral.* another name for **cantaloupe.**

rock-'n'-roll *n.* a variant spelling of **rock-and-roll.** —**'rock-'n'roll·er** *n..*

rock oil *n.* another name for **petroleum.**

rock+oon (rɒ'ku:n) *n.* a rocket carrying scientific equipment for studying the upper atmosphere, fired from a balloon at high altitude. [C20: from ROCKET[1] + BALLOON]

rock pi+geon *n.* another name for **rock dove.**

rock plant *n.* any plant that grows on rocks or in rocky ground.

rock+rose ('rɒkˌrəʊz) *n.* any of various cistaceous shrubs or herbaceous plants of the Mediterranean genera *Helianthemum, Tuberaria,* and *Cistus,* cultivated for their yellow-white or reddish roselike flowers.

rock salm+on *n. Brit.* any of several coarse fishes when used as food, esp. the dogfish or wolffish.

rock salt *n.* another name for **halite.**

rock+shaft ('rɒkˌʃɑ:ft) *n.* a shaft that rotates backwards and forwards rather than continuously, esp. one used in the valve gear of a steam engine.

rock snake *or* **py+thon** *n.* any large Australasian python of the genus *Liasis.*

rock+weed ('rɒkˌwi:d) *n.* any of various seaweeds that grow on rocks exposed at low tide.

rock wool *n.* another name for **mineral wool.**

rock·y[1] ('rɒkɪ) *adj.* **rock·i+er, rock·i+est. 1.** consisting of or abounding in rocks: *a rocky shore.* **2.** hard or unyielding: *rocky determination.* **3.** hard like rock: *rocky muscles.* —**'rock·i+ly** *adv.* —**'rock·i+ness** *n.*

rock·y[2] ('rɒkɪ) *adj.* **rock·i+er, rock·i+est. 1.** weak, shaky, or unstable. **2.** *Informal.* (of a person) dizzy; sickly; nauseated. —**'rock·i+ly** *adv.* —**'rock·i+ness** *n.*

Rock·y Moun+tain goat *n.* a sure-footed goat antelope, *Oreamnos americanus,* inhabiting the Rocky Mountains. It has thick white hair and black backward-curving horns.

Rock·y Moun+tains *or* **Rock·ies** *pl. n.* the chief mountain system of W North America, extending from British Columbia to New Mexico: forms the Continental Divide. Highest peak: Mount Elbert, 4399 m (14 431 ft.). Mount McKinley (6194 m (20 320 ft.)), in the Alaska Range, is not strictly part of the Rocky Mountains.

Rock·y Moun+tain spot+ted fe+ver *n.* an acute rickettsial disease characterized by high fever, chills, pain in muscles and joints, skin rash, etc. It is caused by the bite of a tick infected with the microorganism *Rickettsia rickettsii.*

ro+co+co (rə'kəʊkəʊ) *n.* (*often cap.*) **1.** a style of architecture and decoration that originated in France in the early 18th century and spread throughout Europe, characterized by elaborate but graceful ornamentation. **2.** an 18th-century style of music characterized by petite prettiness, a decline in the use of counterpoint, and extreme use of ornamentation. **3.** any florid or excessively ornamental style. ~*adj.* **4.** denoting, being in, or relating to the rococo. **5.** florid or excessively elaborate. [C19: from French, from ROCAILLE, from *roc* ROCK[1]]

rod (rɒd) *n.* **1.** a slim cylinder of metal, wood, etc.; stick or shaft. **2.** a switch or bundle of switches used to administer corporal punishment. **3.** any of various staffs of insignia or office. **4.** power, esp. of a tyrannical kind: *a dictator's iron rod.* **5.** a straight slender shoot, stem, or cane of a woody plant. **6.** See **fishing rod. 7.** Also called: **pole, perch. a.** a unit of length equal to 5½ yards. **b.** a unit of square measure equal to 30¼ square yards. **8.** a straight narrow board marked with the dimensions of a piece of joinery, as the spacing of steps on a staircase. **9.** *Surveying.* another name (esp. U.S.) for **staff**[1] (sense 8). **10.** Also called: **retinal rod.** any of the elongated cylindrical cells in the retina of the eye, containing the visual purple (rhodopsin), which are sensitive to dim light but not to colour. Compare **cone** (sense 4). **11.** any rod-shaped bacterium. **12.** a slang word for **penis. 13.** *U.S.* a slang name for **pistol. 14.** short for **hot rod.** [Old English *rodd;* related to Old Norse *rudda* club, Norwegian *rudda, rydda* twig] —**'rod+ˌlike** *adj.*

rode[1] (rəʊd) *vb.* the past tense of **ride.**

rode[2] (rəʊd) *n. Nautical.* an anchor rope or chain. [C17: of unknown origin]

ro+dent ('rəʊdᵊnt) *n.* **a.** any of the relatively small placental mammals that constitute the order *Rodentia,* having constantly growing incisor teeth specialized for gnawing. The group includes porcupines, rats, mice, squirrels, marmots, etc. **b.** (*as modifier*): *rodent characteristics.* [C19: from Latin *rōdere* to gnaw, corrode] —**'ro·dent-ˌlike** *adj.*

ro+dent·i+cide (rəʊ'dɛntɪˌsaɪd) *n.* a substance used for killing rats, mice, and other rodents.

ro+dent op+er+a·tive *or* **of+fic+er** *n.* facetious or pompous names for a **rat-catcher.**

ro+de·o ('rəʊdɪˌəʊ) *Chiefly U.S.* ~*n., pl.* **·os. 1.** a display of the skills of cowboys, including bareback riding, steer wrangling, etc. **2.** the rounding up of cattle for branding, counting, inspection, etc. **3.** an enclosure for cattle that have been rounded up. [C19: from Spanish, from *rodear* to go around, from *rueda* a wheel, from Latin *rota*]

Rodg·ers ('rɒdʒəz) *n.* **Rich·ard.** 1902–79, U.S. composer of musical comedies. He collaborated with the librettist Lorenz Hart on such musicals as *A Connecticut Yankee* (1927), *On Your Toes* (1936), and *Pal Joey* (1940). After Hart's death his librettist was Oscar Hammerstein. Two of their musicals, *Oklahoma!* (1943) and *South Pacific* (1949), received the Pulitzer Prize.

Ró+dhos ('rɔðɔs) *n.* transliteration of the Modern Greek name for **Rhodes.**

Ro·din (*French* rɔ'dɛ̃) *n.* **Au·guste** (o'gyst). 1840–1917, French sculptor, noted for his portrayal of the human form. His works include *The Kiss* (1886), *The Burghers of Calais* (1896), and *The Thinker* (1905).

Rod·ney ('rɒdnɪ) *n.* **George Brydg·es,** 1st Baron Rodney. 1718–92, English admiral.

rod·o·mon+tade (ˌrɒdəmɒn'teɪd, -'tɑ:d) *Literary.* ~*n.* **1. a.** boastful words or behaviour; bragging. **b.** (*as modifier*): *rodomontade behaviour.* ~*vb.* **2.** (*intr.*) to boast, bluster, or rant. [C17: from French, from Italian *rodomonte* a boaster, from *Rodomonte* the name of a braggart king of Algiers in epic poems by Boiardo and Ariosto]

roe[1] (rəʊ) *n.* **1.** Also called: **hard roe.** the ovary of a female fish filled with mature eggs. **2.** Also called: **soft roe.** the testis of a male fish filled with mature sperm. **3.** the ripe ovary of certain crustaceans, such as the lobster. [C15: from Middle Dutch *roge,* from Old High German *roga;* related to Old Norse *hrogn*]

roe[2] (rəʊ) *n., pl.* **roes** *or* **roe.** short for **roe deer.** [Old English *rā(ha)*, related to Old High German *rēh(o)*, Old Norse *rā*]
roe+buck (ˈrəʊˌbʌk) *n., pl.* **+bucks** *or* **+buck.** the male of the roe deer.
roe deer *n.* a small graceful deer, *Capreolus capreolus,* of woodlands of Europe and Asia. The antlers are small and the summer coat is reddish-brown.
roent+gen *or* **rönt+gen** (ˈrɒntgən, -tjən, ˈrɛnt-) *n.* a unit of dose of electromagnetic radiation equal to the dose that will produce in air a charge of 0.258 × 10^{-3} coulomb on all ions of one sign, when all the electrons of both signs liberated in a volume of air of mass one kilogram are stopped completely. Symbol: R or r
Roent·gen *or* **Rönt·gen** (ˈrɒntgən, -tjən-, ˈrɛnt-; *German* ˈrœntgᵊn) *n.* **Wil·helm Kon·rad** (ˈvɪlhɛlm ˈkɔnraːt). 1845–1923, German physicist, who in 1895 discovered x-rays: Nobel prize for physics 1901.
roent·gen e·quiv·a+lent man *n.* the dose of ionizing radiation that produces the same effect in man as one roentgen of x- or gamma-radiation. Abbrev.: **REM** *or* **rem**
roent+gen+ize, roent+gen+ise *or* **rönt+gen+ize, rönt+gen+ise** (ˈrɒntgəˌnaɪz, -tjə-, ˈrɛnt-) *vb.* (*tr.*) to bombard with x-rays. —**ˌroent+gen·i+ˈza+tion, ˌroent+gen·i+ˈsa+tion** *or* **ˌrönt+gen·i+ˈza+tion, ˌrönt+gen·i+ˈsa+tion** *n.*
roent·gen·o- *or* **rönt·gen·o-** *combining form.* indicating x-rays: *roentgenogram.* [from ROENTGEN]
roent+gen·o+gram, rönt+gen·o+gram (ˈrɒntgənəˌgræm, -tjə-, ˈrɛnt-) *or* **roent+gen·o+graph, rönt+gen·o+graph** *n. Chiefly U.S.* an x-ray.
roent+gen+ol+o·gy *or* **rönt+gen+ol+o·gy** (ˌrɒntgəˈnɒlədʒɪ, -tjə-, ˌrɛnt-) *n.* another name for **radiology.** —**roent+gen·o+log·i·cal** *or* **rönt+gen·o+log·i·cal** (ˌrɒntgənəˈlɒdʒɪkᵊl, -tjə-, ˌrɛnt-) *adj.* —**ˌroent+gen·o+ˈlog·i·cal+ly** *or* **ˌrönt+gen·o+ˈlog·i·cal+ly** *adv.* —**ˌroent+gen+ˈol·o+gist** *or* **ˌrönt+gen+ˈol·o+gist** *n.*
roent+gen+o·paque *or* **rönt+gen+o·paque** (ˌrɒntgənəʊˈpeɪk, -tjən-, ˌrɛnt-) *adj.* (of a material) not allowing the transmission of x-rays.
roent+gen·o+scope *or* **rönt+gen·o+scope** (ˈrɒntgənəʊˌskəʊp, -tjə-, ˈrɛnt-) *n.* a less common name for **fluoroscope.** —**roent+gen·o+scop+ic** *or* **rönt+gen·o+scop+ic** (ˌrɒntgənəʊˈskɒpɪk, -tjə-, ˌrɛnt-) *adj.* —**roent+gen+os+co+py** *or* **rönt+gen+os+co+py** (ˌrɒntgəˈnɒskəpɪ, -tjə-, ˌrɛnt-) *n.*
roent+gen·o+ther·a+py *or* **rönt+gen·o+ther·a+py** (ˌrɒntgənəˈθɛrəpɪ, -tjə-, ˌrɛnt-) *n.* the therapeutic use of x-rays.
roent+gen ray *n.* a former name for **x-ray.**
Roe+se+la+re (ˈruːsəlaːrə) *n.* the Flemish name for **Roulers.**
Roeth·ke (ˈrɛtkə) *n.* **The·o·dore.** 1908–63, U.S. poet, whose books include *Words for the Wind* (1957) and *The Far Field* (1964).
ro+ga+tion (rəʊˈgeɪʃən) *n.* (*usually pl.*) *Christianity.* a solemn supplication, esp. in a form of ceremony prescribed by the Church. [C14: from Latin *rogātiō*, from *rogāre* to ask, make supplication]
Ro+ga+tion Days *pl. n.* April 25 (the **Major Rogation**) and the Monday, Tuesday, and Wednesday before Ascension Day, observed by Christians as days of solemn supplication for the harvest and marked by processions, special prayers, and blessing of the crops.
rog·a·to·ry (ˈrɒgətərɪ, -trɪ) *adj.* (esp. in legal contexts) seeking or authorized to seek information. [C19: from Medieval Latin *rogātōrius,* from Latin *rogāre* to ask]
rog+er (ˈrɒdʒə) *interj.* **1.** (used in signalling, telecommunications, etc.) message received and understood. Compare **wilco. 2.** an expression of agreement. ~*vb.* **3.** *Taboo slang.* (of a man) to copulate (with). [C20: from the name *Roger,* representing *R* for *received*]
Rog·ers (ˈrɒdʒəz) *n.* **1. Gin·ger.** stage name of *Virginia McMath.* born 1911, U.S. dancer and film actress, who partnered Fred Astaire. **2. Will.** original name *William Penn Adair Rogers.* 1879–1935, U.S. actor, newspaper columnist, and humorist in the homespun tradition.
Ro·get (ˈrɒʒeɪ) *n.* **Pe·ter Mark.** 1779–1869, English physician, who on retirement devised a *Thesaurus of English Words and Phrases* (1852), a classified list of synonyms.
rogue (rəʊg) *n.* **1.** a dishonest or unprincipled person, esp. a man; rascal; scoundrel. **2.** *Often jocular.* a mischievous or wayward person, often a child; scamp. **3.** any inferior or defective specimen, esp. a defective crop plant, or one of a different, unwanted variety. **4.** *Archaic.* a vagrant. **5. a.** an animal of vicious character that has separated from the main herd and leads a solitary life. **b.** (*as modifier*): *a rogue elephant.* ~*vb.* **6.** (*tr.*) to remove (plants) from the main crop. [C16: of unknown origin; perhaps related to Latin *rogāre* to beg]
ro+guer·y (ˈrəʊgərɪ) *n., pl.* **+guer·ies. 1.** behaviour characteristic of a rogue. **2.** a roguish or mischievous act.
rogues' gal+ler·y *n.* a collection of portraits of known criminals kept by the police for identification purposes.
ro+guish (ˈrəʊgɪʃ) *adj.* **1.** dishonest or unprincipled. **2.** mischievous or arch. —**ˈro+guish+ly** *adv.* —**ˈro+guish+ness** *n.*
roil (rɔɪl) *vb.* **1.** (*tr.*) to make (a liquid) cloudy or turbid by stirring up dregs or sediment. **2.** (*intr.*) (esp. of a liquid) to be agitated or disturbed. **3.** (*intr.*) *Brit. dialect.* **a.** to be noisy or boisterous. **b.** another word for **rile.** [C16: of unknown origin; compare RILE]
roil·y (ˈrɔɪlɪ) *adj.* **roil·i·er, roil·i·est.** *Rare.* cloudy or muddy.
rois+ter (ˈrɔɪstə) *vb.* (*intr.*) **1.** to engage in noisy or unrestrained merrymaking; revel. **2.** to brag, bluster, or swagger. [C16: from Old French *rustre* lout, from *ruste* uncouth, from Latin *rusticus* rural; see RUSTIC] —**ˈroist+er+er** *n.* —**ˈroist+er+ous** *adj.* —**ˈroist+er+ous+ly** *adv.*
ro+jak (ˈrodʒa) *n.* (in Malaysia) a salad dish served in chilli sauce. [from Malay]
ROK *international car registration for* Republic of Korea.
Ro·land (ˈrəʊlənd) *n.* **1.** the greatest of the legendary 12 peers (paladins) in attendance on Charlemagne; he died in battle at Roncesvalles (778 A.D.). **2. a Roland for an Oliver.** an effective retort or retaliation.
role *or* **rôle** (rəʊl) *n.* **1.** a part or character in a play, film, etc., to be played by an actor or actress. **2.** *Psychol.* the part played by a person in a particular social setting, influenced by his expectation of what is appropriate. **3.** usual or customary function: *what is his role in the organization?* [C17: from French *rôle* ROLL, an actor's script]
role-play·ing *n. Psychol.* activity in which a person imitates, consciously or unconsciously, a role uncharacteristic of himself. See also **psychodrama.**
Rolf (rɒlf) *n.* another name for **Rollo.** Also called: **Rolf the Ganger.**
roll (rəʊl) *vb.* **1.** to move or cause to move along by turning over and over. **2.** to move or cause to move along on wheels or rollers. **3.** to flow or cause to flow onwards in an undulating movement: *billows of smoke rolled over the ground.* **4.** (*intr.*) to extend in undulations: *the hills roll down to the sea.* **5.** (*intr.;* usually foll. by *around*) to move or occur in cycles. **6.** (*intr.*) (of a planet, the moon, etc.) to revolve in an orbit. **7.** (*intr.;* foll. by *on, by,* etc.) to pass or elapse: *the years roll by.* **8.** to rotate or cause to rotate wholly or partially: *to roll one's eyes.* **9.** to curl, cause to curl, or admit of being curled, so as to form a ball, tube, or cylinder; coil. **10.** to make or form by shaping into a ball, tube, or cylinder: *to roll a cigarette.* **11.** (often foll. by *out*) to spread or cause to spread out flat or smooth under or as if under a roller: *to roll the lawn; to roll pastry.* **12.** to emit, produce, or utter with a deep prolonged reverberating sound: *the thunder rolled continuously.* **13.** to trill or cause to be trilled: *to roll one's r's.* **14.** (*intr.*) (of a vessel, aircraft, rocket, etc.) to turn from side to side around the longitudinal axis. Compare **pitch**[1] (sense 10), **yaw** (sense 1). **15.** to cause (an aircraft) to execute a roll or (of an aircraft) to execute a roll (sense 38). **16.** (*intr.*) to walk with a swaying gait, as when drunk; sway. **17.** (*tr.*) to apply ink to (type, etc.) with a roller or rollers. **18.** to throw (dice). **19.** (*intr.*) to operate or begin to operate: *the presses rolled.* **20.** *Informal.* to make progress; move or go ahead: *let the good times roll.* **21.** (*tr.*) *Slang, chiefly U.S.* to rob (a helpless person, such as someone drunk or asleep). **22.** (*tr.*) *Slang.* to have sexual intercourse or foreplay with (a person). **23. start the ball rolling.** *Informal.* to open or initiate (an action, discussion, movement, etc.). ~*n.* **24.** the act or an instance of rolling. **25.** anything rolled up in a cylindrical form: *a roll of newspaper.* **26.** an official list or register, esp. of names: *an electoral roll.* **27.** a rounded mass: *rolls of flesh.* **28.** a strip of material, esp. leather, fitted with pockets or pouches for holding tools, toilet articles, needles and thread, etc. **29.** a cylinder used to flatten something; roller. **30.** a small loaf of bread for one person: eaten plain, with butter, or with a meat, egg, salad, or other filling, as a light meal or snack or as a side dish. **31.** a flat pastry or cake rolled up with a meat (**sausage roll**), jam (**jam roll**), or other filling. See also **Swiss roll. 32.** a swell, ripple, or undulation on a surface: *the roll of the hills.* **33.** a swaying, rolling, or unsteady movement or gait. **34.** a deep prolonged reverberating sound: *the roll of thunder.* **35.** a rhythmical cadenced flow of words. **36.** a trilling sound; trill. **37.** a very rapid beating of the sticks on a drum. **38.** a flight manoeuvre in which an aircraft makes one complete rotation about its longitudinal axis without loss of height or change in direction. **39.** the angular displacement of a vessel, rocket, missile, etc., caused by rolling. **40.** a throw of dice. **41.** a bookbinder's tool having a brass wheel, used to impress a line or repeated pattern on the cover of a book. **42.** *Slang.* an act of sexual intercourse or petting (esp. in the phrase **a roll in the hay**). **43.** *U.S. slang.* an amount of money, esp. a wad of paper money. **44. strike off the roll(s). a.** to expel from membership. **b.** to debar (a solicitor) from practising, usually because of dishonesty. ~See also **roll in, roll on, roll up.** [C14 *rollen,* from Old French *roler,* from Latin *rotulus* a little wheel, from *rota* a wheel]
Rol·land (*French* rɔˈlã) *n.* **Ro·main** (rɔˈmɛ̃). 1866–1944, French novelist, dramatist, and essayist, best known for his cycle of novels about a musical genius, *Jean-Christophe,* (1904–12): Nobel prize for literature 1915.
roll+a·way (ˈrəʊləˌweɪ) *n.* (*modifier*) mounted on rollers so as to be easily moved, esp. to be stored away after use.
roll+bar (ˈrəʊlˌbaː) *n.* a bar that reinforces the frame of a car used for racing, rallying, etc., to protect the driver if the car should turn over.
roll call *n.* **1.** the reading aloud of an official list of names, those present responding when their names are read out. **2.** the time or signal for such a reading.
rolled gold *n.* a metal, such as brass, coated with a thin layer of gold, usually of above 9 carat purity. It is used in inexpensive jewellery. Also called (U.S.): **filled gold.**
rolled-steel joist *n.* a steel beam, esp. one with a cross section in the form of a letter *H* or *I.* Abbrev.: **RSJ**
roll+er (ˈrəʊlə) *n.* **1.** a cylinder having an absorbent surface and a handle, used for spreading paint. **2.** Also called: **garden roller.** a heavy cast-iron cylinder or pair of cylinders on an axle to which a handle is attached; used for flattening lawns. **3.** a long heavy wave of the sea, advancing towards the shore. Compare **breaker**[1] (sense 2). **4.** a hardened cylinder of precision-ground

steel that forms one of the rolling components of a roller bearing or of a linked driving chain. **5.** a cylinder fitted on pivots, used to enable heavy objects to be easily moved; castor. **6.** *Printing.* a cylinder, usually of hard rubber, used to ink a forme or plate before impression. **7.** a cylindrical tube or barrel onto which material is rolled for transport or storage. **8.** any of various other cylindrical devices that rotate about a cylinder, used for any of various purposes. **9.** a small cylinder, esp. one that is heated, onto which a woman's hair may be rolled to make it curl. **10.** *Med.* a bandage consisting of a long strip of muslin or cheesecloth rolled tightly into a cylindrical form before application. **11.** a band fastened around a horse's belly to keep a blanket in position. **12.** any of various Old World birds of the family *Coraciidae,* such as *Coracias garrulus* (**European roller**), that have a blue, green, and brown plumage, a slightly hooked bill, and an erratic flight: order *Coraciiformes* (kingfishers, etc.). **13.** (*often cap.*) a variety of tumbler pigeon that performs characteristic backward somersaults in flight. **14.** a person or thing that rolls. **15.** *Austral.* a man who rolls and trims fleeces after shearing. **16.** short for **roadroller** or **steamroller.**

roll+er bear+ing *n.* a bearing in which a shaft runs on a number of hardened-steel rollers held within a cage.

roll+er coast+er *n.* another term for **big dipper.**

rol+ler der+by *n.* a race on roller skates, esp. one involving aggressive tactics.

roll+er skate *n.* **1.** a device having clamps and straps for fastening to a boot or shoe and four small wheels that enable the wearer to glide swiftly over a floor or other surface. ~*vb.* **roll·er-skate. 2.** (*intr.*) to move on roller skates. —**roll+er skat+er** *n.*

roll+er tow+el *n.* a towel with the two ends sewn together, hung on a roller.

roll film *n.* a length of photographic film backed with opaque paper and rolled on a spool.

rol+lick ('rɒlɪk) *vb.* **1.** (*intr.*) to behave in a carefree, frolicsome, or boisterous manner. ~*n.* **2.** a boisterous or carefree escapade or event. [C19: of Scottish dialect origin, probably from ROMP + FROLIC] —'**rol+lick·ing** *adj.*

roll in *vb.* (*mainly intr.*) **1.** (*adv.*) to arrive in abundance or in large numbers. **2.** (*adv.*) *Informal.* to arrive at one's destination. **3. be rolling in.** (*prep.*) *Slang.* to abound or luxuriate in (wealth, money, etc.). **4.** (*adv.; also tr.*) *Hockey.* to return (the ball) to play after it has crossed the touchline.

roll+ing ('rəʊlɪŋ) *adj.* **1.** having gentle rising and falling slopes; undulating: *rolling country.* **2.** deeply resounding; reverberating: *rolling thunder.* **3.** that may be turned up or down: *a rolling hat brim.* **4.** *Slang.* extremely rich. ~*adv.* **5.** *Slang.* swaying or staggering (in the phrase **rolling drunk**).

roll+ing hitch *n.* a knot used for fastening one rope to another or to a spar, being easily released but jamming when the rope is pulled.

roll+ing mill *n.* **1.** a mill or factory where ingots of heated metal are passed between rollers to produce sheets or bars of a required cross section and form. **2.** a machine having rollers that may be shaped to reduce ingots, etc., to a required cross section and form.

roll+ing pin *n.* a cylinder with handles at both ends, often of wood, used for rolling dough, pastry, etc., out flat.

roll+ing stock *n.* the wheeled vehicles collectively used on a railway, including the locomotives, passenger coaches, freight wagons, guard's vans, etc.

roll+ing stone *n.* a restless or wandering person.

Roll+ing Stones *pl. n.* **the.** English rock group (formed 1962): comprising Mick Jagger (born 1943; lead vocals), Keith Richard (born 1943; guitar, vocals), Brian Jones (1942–69; guitar), Charlie Watts (born 1941; drums), Bill Wyman (born 1936; bass guitar), and subsequently Mick Taylor (born 1941; guitar; with the group 1969–74) and Ron Wood (born 1947; guitar; with the group from 1975). Their classic recordings include many hit singles such as *Satisfaction* (1965), *Get Off my Cloud* (1965), *Jumpin' Jack Flash* (1968), and *Honky Tonk Woman* (1969); the EP *Five by Five* (1965); and the albums *Their Satanic Majesties request* (1967), *Get yer Ya-Ya's out* (1969), *Sticky Fingers* (1971), and *Exile on Main Street* (1973). Many of their numbers were written by Jagger and Richard.

roll+mop ('rəʊl,mɒp) *n.* a herring fillet rolled, usually around onion slices, and pickled in spiced vinegar. [from German *Rollmops,* from *rollen* to ROLL + *Mops* pug dog]

roll+neck ('rəʊl,nɛk) *adj.* **1.** (of a garment) having a high neck that may be rolled over. ~*n.* **2.** a rollneck sweater or other garment.

Rol·lo ('rɒləʊ) *n.* ?860–?930 A.D., Norse war leader who received from Charles the Simple a fief that formed the basis of the duchy of Normandy. Also called: **Rolf.**

roll of hon+our *n.* a list of those who have died in war for their country, esp. those from a particular locality.

roll on *vb.* **1.** *Brit.* used to express the wish that an eagerly anticipated event or date will come quickly: *roll on Saturday.* ~*adj.* **2.** (of a deodorant, etc.) dispensed by means of a revolving ball fitted into the neck of the container. ~*n.* **3.** a woman's foundation garment, made of elasticized material and having no fastenings. **4.** a liquid cosmetic, esp. a deodorant, packed in a container having an applicator consisting of a revolving ball.

roll-on/roll-off *adj.* denoting a cargo ship or ferry designed so that lorries and trailers can be driven straight on and straight off.

roll-top desk *n.* a desk having a slatted wooden panel that can be pulled down over the writing surface when not in use. Also called: **roll-top.**

roll up *vb.* (*adv.*) **1.** to form or cause to form a cylindrical shape. **2.** (*tr.*) to wrap (an object) round on itself or on an axis: *to roll up a map.* **3.** (*intr.*) *Informal.* to arrive, esp. in a vehicle.

roll+way ('rəʊl,weɪ) *n.* **1.** an incline down which logs are rolled for transportation. **2.** a series of rollers laid parallel to each other, over which heavy loads may be moved.

ro·ly-po·ly ('rəʊlɪ'pəʊlɪ) *adj.* **1.** plump, buxom, or rotund. ~*n., pl.* **·lies. 2.** *Brit.* a strip of suet pastry spread with jam, fruit, or a savoury mixture, rolled up, and baked or steamed as a pudding. **3.** a plump, buxom, or rotund person. [C17: apparently by reduplication from *roly,* from ROLL]

Rom (rɒm) *n., pl.* **Rom·a** ('rɒmə). a male Gypsy. [Romany]

ROM (rɒm) *n. Computer technol. acronym for* read only memory.

rom. *Printing. abbrev. for* roman (type).

Rom. *abbrev. for:* **1.** Roman. **2.** Romance (languages). **3.** *Bible.* Romans.

Ro·ma ('ro:ma) *n.* the Italian name for **Rome.**

Ro+ma+gna (*Italian* ro'maɲɲa) *n.* an area of N Italy: part of the Papal States up to 1860.

Ro+ma+ic (rəʊ'meɪɪk) *Obsolete.* ~*n.* **1.** the modern Greek vernacular, esp. Demotic. ~*adj.* **2.** of or relating to Greek, esp. Demotic. [C19: from Greek *Rhōmaikos* Roman, with reference to the Eastern Roman Empire]

ro+maine (rəʊ'meɪn) *n.* the usual U.S. name for **cos**[1] (lettuce). [C20: from French, from *romain* Roman]

Ro·mains (*French* rɔ'mɛ̃) *n.* **Jules** (ʒyl). pseudonym of *Louis Farigoule.* 1885–1972, French poet, dramatist, and novelist. His works include the novel *Men of Good Will* (1932–46).

ro+ma+ji ('rəʊmɑːdʒɪ) *n.* the Roman alphabet as used to write Japanese.

ro+man[1] (rəʊmən) *adj.* **1.** of, relating to, or denoting a vertical style of printing type: the usual form of type for most printed matter. Compare **italic.** ~*n.* **2.** roman type or print. [C16: so called because the style of letters is that used in ancient Roman inscriptions]

ro+man[2] (*French* rɔ'mɑ̃) *n.* a metrical narrative in medieval French literature derived from the *chansons de geste.*

Ro+man ('rəʊmən) *adj.* **1.** of or relating to Rome or its inhabitants in ancient or modern times. **2.** of or relating to Roman Catholicism or the Roman Catholic Church. **3.** denoting, relating to, or having the style of architecture used by the ancient Romans, characterized by large-scale masonry domes, barrel vaults, and semicircular arches. ~*n.* **4.** a citizen or inhabitant of ancient or modern Rome. **5.** *Informal.* short for **Roman Catholic.**

ro+man à clef *French.* (rɔmɑ̃ a 'kle) *n., pl.* ***ro+mans à clef*** (rɔmɑ̃ a 'kle). a novel in which real people are depicted under fictitious names. [literally: novel with a key]

Ro+man al+pha+bet *n.* the alphabet evolved by the ancient Romans for the writing of Latin, based upon an Etruscan form derived from the Greeks and ultimately from the Phoenicians. The alphabet serves for writing most of the languages of W Europe and many other languages.

Ro+man arch *n.* another name for **Norman arch.**

Ro+man cal+en+dar *n.* the lunar calendar of ancient Rome, replaced in 45 B.C. by the Julian calendar. It originally consisted of 10 months, with a special month intercalated between Feb. 23 and 24.

Ro+man can+dle *n.* a firework that produces a continuous shower of sparks punctuated by coloured balls of fire. [C19: so called from its having been originated in Italy]

Ro+man Cath·o+lic *adj.* **1.** of or relating to the Roman Catholic Church. ~*n.* **2.** a member of this Church. ~Often shortened to **Catholic.**

Ro+man Cath·o+lic Church *n.* the Christian Church over which the pope presides, with administrative headquarters in the Vatican. Also called: **Catholic Church, Church of Rome.**

Ro+man Ca+thol·i+cism *n.* the beliefs, practices, and system of government of the Roman Catholic Church.

ro+mance *n.* (rə'mæns, 'rəʊmæns). **1.** a love affair, esp. an intense and happy but short-lived affair involving young people. **2.** love, esp. romantic love idealized for its purity or beauty. **3.** a spirit of or inclination for adventure, excitement, or mystery. **4.** a mysterious, exciting, sentimental, or nostalgic quality, esp. one associated with a place. **5.** a narrative in verse or prose, written in a vernacular language in the Middle Ages, dealing with strange and exciting adventures of chivalrous heroes. **6.** any similar narrative work dealing with events and characters remote from ordinary life. **7.** the literary genre represented by works of these kinds. **8.** (in Spanish literature) a short narrative poem, usually an epic or historical ballad. **9.** a story, novel, film, etc., dealing with love, usually in an idealized or sentimental way. **10.** an extravagant, absurd, or fantastic account or explanation. **11.** a lyrical song or short instrumental composition having a simple melody. ~*vb.* (rə'mæns). **12.** (*intr.*) to tell, invent, or write extravagant or romantic fictions. **13.** (*intr.*) to tell extravagant or improbable lies. [C13 *romauns,* from Old French *romans,* ultimately from Latin *Rōmānicus* Roman] —**ro+'man+cer** *n.*

Ro+mance (rə'mæns, 'rəʊmæns) *adj.* **1.** denoting, relating to, or belonging to the languages derived from Latin, including Italian, Spanish, Portuguese, French, and Rumanian. **2.** denoting a word borrowed from a Romance language: *there are many Romance words in English.* ~*n.* **3.** this group of languages; the living languages that belong to the Italic branch of the Indo-European family.

Ro+man col+lar *n.* another name for **clerical collar.**

Ro+man Em+pire *n.* **1.** the territories ruled by ancient Rome. At its height under Trajan, the Roman Empire included W and S Europe, Africa north of the Sahara, and SW Asia. In 395 A.D. it was divided by Theodosius into the **Eastern Roman Empire,** whose capital was Byzantium and which lasted until 1453, and the **Western Roman Empire,** which lasted until the sack of Rome in 476. **2.** the government of Rome and its dominions by the emperors from 27 B.C. **3.** the Byzantine Empire. **4.** the Holy Roman Empire.

Rom·a+nes ('rɒmənɪs) *n.* Romany; the language of the Gypsies. [from Romany]

Ro+man+esque (ˌrəʊmə'nɛsk) *adj.* **1.** denoting, relating to, or having the style of architecture used in W and S Europe from the 9th to the 12th century, characterized by the rounded arch, the groin vault, massive-masonry wall construction, and a restrained use of mouldings. See also **Norman** (sense 6). **2.** denoting or relating to a corresponding style in painting, sculpture, etc. [C18: see ROMAN, -ESQUE]

ro·man-fleuve *French.* (rɔmɑ̃'flœv) *n., pl.* ***ro·mans-fleuves*** (rɔmɑ̃'flœv). a novel or series of novels dealing with a family or other group over several generations. [literally: stream novel]

Ro+man hol·i·day *n.* entertainment or pleasure that depends on the suffering of others. [C19: from Byron's poem *Childe Harold* (IV, 141)]

Ro+ma·ni·a (rəʊ'meɪnɪə) *n.* a variant spelling of **Rumania.** —**Ro+'ma+ni·an** *adj., n.*

Ro+man+ic (rəʊ'mænɪk) *adj.* another word for **Roman** or **Romance.**

Ro+man+ism ('rəʊməˌnɪzəm) *n.* Roman Catholicism, esp. when regarded as excessively or superstitiously ritualistic.

Ro+man+ist ('rəʊmənɪst) *n.* **1.** a member of a Church, esp. the Church of England, who favours or is influenced by Roman Catholicism. **2.** a Roman Catholic. **3.** a student of classical Roman civilization or law. —ˌ**Ro+man+'is+tic** *adj.*

Ro+man+ize *or* **Ro+man+ise** ('rəʊməˌnaɪz) *vb.* **1.** (*tr.*) to impart a Roman Catholic character to (a ceremony, practice, etc.). **2.** (*intr.*) to be converted to Roman Catholicism. **3.** (*tr.*) to transcribe or transliterate (a language) into the Roman alphabet. **4.** to make Roman in character, allegiance, style, etc. —ˌ**Ro+man·i+'za+tion** *or* ˌ**Ro+man·i+'sa+tion** *n.*

Ro+man law *n.* **1.** the system of jurisprudence of ancient Rome, codified under Justinian and forming the basis of many modern legal systems. **2.** another term for **civil law.**

Ro+man mile *n.* a unit of length used in ancient Rome, equivalent to about 1620 yards or 1481 metres.

Ro+man nose *n.* a nose having a high prominent bridge.

Ro+man nu+mer+als *pl. n.* the letters used by the Romans for the representation of cardinal numbers, still used occasionally today. The integers are represented by the following letters: I (= 1), V (= 5), X (= 10), L (= 50), C (= 100), D (= 500), and M (= 1000). If a numeral is followed by another numeral of lower denomination, the two are added together; if it is preceded by one of lower denomination, the smaller numeral is subtracted from the greater. Thus VI = 6 (V + I), but IV = 4 (V - I). Other examples are XC (= 90), CL (= 150), XXV (= 25), XLIV (= 44).

Ro+ma+no[1] (rəʊ'mɑːnəʊ) *n.* a hard light-coloured sharp-tasting cheese, similar to Parmesan.

Ro·ma·no[2] (*Italian* ro'maːno) *n.* See **Giulio Romano.**

Ro·ma·nov ('rəʊmənɒf; *Russian* ra'manəf) *n.* any of the Russian imperial dynasty that ruled from the crowning (1613) of Mikhail Fyodorovich to the abdication (1917) of Nicholas II during the February Revolution.

Ro+man pace *n.* an ancient Roman measure of length, equal to 5 Roman feet or about 58 inches (145 centimetres). See also **geometric pace.**

Ro+mans ('rəʊmənz) *n.* (*functioning as sing.*) a book of the New Testament (in full **The Epistle of Paul the Apostle to the Romans),** containing one of the fullest expositions of the doctrines of Saint Paul, written in 58 A.D.

Ro+mansch *or* **Ro+mansh** (rəʊ'mænʃ) *n.* a group of Rhaetian dialects spoken in the Swiss canton of Grisons; an official language of Switzerland since 1938. See also **Friulian, Ladin.** [C17: from Romansch, literally: Romance language, from Latin *Rōmānicus* ROMANIC]

ro+man+tic (rəʊ'mæntɪk) *adj.* **1.** of, relating to, imbued with, or characterized by romance. **2.** evoking or given to thoughts and feelings of love, esp. idealized or sentimental love: *a romantic woman; a romantic setting.* **3.** impractical, visionary, or idealistic: *a romantic scheme.* **4.** *Often euphemistic.* imaginary or fictitious: *a romantic account of one's war service.* **5.** (*often cap.*) of or relating to a movement in European art, music, and literature in the late 18th and early 19th centuries, characterized by an emphasis on feeling and content rather than order and form, on the sublime, supernatural, and exotic, and the free expression of the passions and individuality. ~*n.* **6.** a person who is romantic, as in being idealistic, amorous, or soulful. **7.** a person whose tastes in art, literature, etc., lie mainly in romanticism; romanticist. **8.** (*often cap.*) a poet, composer, etc., of the romantic period or whose main inspiration or interest is romanticism. [C17: from French *romantique,* from obsolete *romant* story, romance, from Old French *romans* ROMANCE] —**ro+'man+ti+cal+ly** *adv.*

ro+man+ti+cism (rəʊ'mæntɪˌsɪzəm) *n.* **1.** (*often cap.*) the theory, practice, and style of the romantic art, music, and literature of the late 18th and early 19th centuries, usually opposed to classicism. **2.** romantic attitudes, ideals, or qualities. —**ro+'man+ti+cist** *n.*

ro+man+ti+cize *or* **ro+man+ti+cise** (rəʊ'mæntɪˌsaɪz) *vb.* **1.** (*intr.*) to think or act in a romantic way. **2.** (*tr.*) to interpret according to romantic precepts. **3.** to make or become romantic, as in style. —**ro+ˌman+ti+ci+'za+tion** *or* **ro+ˌman+ti+ci+'sa+tion** *n.*

Rom·a+ny *or* **Rom+ma+ny** ('rɒmənɪ, 'rəʊ-) *n., pl.* **+nies.** **1. a.** another name for a **Gypsy. b.** (*as modifier*): *Romany customs.* **2.** the language of the Gypsies, belonging to the Indic branch of the Indo-European family, but incorporating extensive borrowings from local European languages. Most of its 250 000 speakers are bilingual. It is extinct in Britain. [C19: from Romany *romani* (adj.) Gypsy, ultimately from Sanskrit *domba* man of a low caste of musicians, of Dravidian origin]

ro+maunt (rə'mɔːnt) *n. Archaic.* a verse romance. [C16: from Old French; see ROMANTIC]

Rom·berg ('rɒmbɜːg) *n.* **Sig·mund.** 1887–1951, U.S. composer of operettas, born in Hungary. He wrote *The Student Prince* (1924) and *The Desert Song* (1926).

Rom. Cath. *abbrev. for* Roman Catholic.

Rome (rəʊm) *n.* **1.** the capital of Italy, on the River Tiber: includes the independent state of the Vatican City; traditionally founded by Romulus on the Palatine Hill in 753 B.C., later spreading to six other hills east of the Tiber; capital of the Roman Empire; a great cultural and artistic centre, esp. during the Renaissance. Pop.: 2 868 248 (1975 est.). Italian name: **Roma. 2.** the Roman Empire.

Ro·me·o ('rəʊmɪəʊ) *n., pl.* **·os.** an ardent male lover. [from the hero of Shakespeare's *Romeo and Juliet*]

Ro+mish ('rəʊmɪʃ) *adj. Usually derogatory.* of, relating to, or resembling Roman Catholic beliefs or practices.

Rom·mel (*German* 'rɔməl) *n.* **Er·win** ('ɛrviːn), nicknamed *the Desert Fox.* 1891–1944, German field marshal, noted for his brilliant generalship in N Africa in World War II. Later a commander in N France, he committed suicide after the officers' plot against Hitler.

Rom·ney ('rɒmnɪ, 'rʌm-) *n.* **George.** 1734–1802, English painter, who painted more than 50 portraits of Lady Hamilton in various historical roles.

Rom+ney Marsh ('rɒmnɪ, 'rʌm-) *n.* **1.** a marshy area of SE England, on the Kent coast between New Romney and Rye: includes Dungeness. **2.** a type of hardy British sheep from this area, with long wool, bred for mutton.

romp (rɒmp) *vb.* (*intr.*) **1.** to play or run about wildly, boisterously, or joyfully. **2. romp home** (*or* **in**). to win a race, etc., easily. ~*n.* **3.** a noisy or boisterous game or prank. **4.** Also called: **romp+er.** *Archaic.* a playful or boisterous child, esp. a girl. **5.** an easy victory. [C18: probably variant of RAMP, from Old French *ramper* to crawl, climb] —**'romp+ing+ly** *adv.* —**'romp+ish** *adj.*

romp+ers ('rɒmpəz) *pl. n.* a one-piece baby garment consisting of trousers and a bib with straps.

romp through *vb.* (*intr., prep.*) *Informal.* to progress quickly and easily through something: *he romped through the work.*

Rom·u·lus ('rɒmjʊləs) *n. Roman myth.* the founder of Rome, suckled with his twin brother Remus by a she-wolf after they were abandoned in infancy. Their parents were Rhea Silvia and Mars. Romulus later killed Remus in an argument over the new city.

Ron+ces+valles ('rɒnsəˌvælz; *Spanish* rɔnθez'βaʎes) *n.* a village in N Spain, in the Pyrenees: a nearby pass was the scene of the defeat of Charlemagne and death of Roland in 778. French name: **Ronce+vaux** (rɔ̃s'vo).

ron+deau ('rɒndəʊ) *n., pl.* **+deaux** (-dəʊ, -dəʊz). a poem consisting of 13 or 10 lines with two rhymes and having the opening words of the first line used as an unrhymed refrain. See also **roundel.** [C16: from Old French, from *rondel* a little round, from *rond* ROUND]

ron+del ('rɒndəl) *n.* a rondeau consisting of three stanzas of 13 or 14 lines with a two-line refrain appearing twice or three times. Also called: **roundel.** [C14: from Old French, literally: a little circle, from *rond* ROUND]

ron·de·let ('rɒndəˌlɛt) *n.* a brief rondeau, having five or seven lines and a refrain taken from the first line. [C16: from Old French: a little RONDEL]

ron+do ('rɒndəʊ) *n., pl.* **+dos.** a piece of music in which a refrain is repeated between episodes: often constitutes the form of the last movement of a sonata or concerto. [C18: from Italian, from French RONDEAU]

Ron+dô+nia (*Portuguese* rɔn'dɔnja) *n.* a federal territory of W Brazil: consists chiefly of tropical rainforest; a centre of the Amazon rubber boom until about 1912. Capital: Pôrto Velho. Pop.: 111 064 (1970). Area: 243 043 sq. km (93 839 sq. miles). Former name (until 1956): **Guaporé.**

ron+dure ('rɒndjʊə) *n. Literary.* **1.** a circle or curve. **2.** roundness or curvature. [C17: from French *rondeur,* from *rond* ROUND]

rone (rəʊn) *n. Scot.* a drainpipe or gutter for carrying rainwater from a roof. [C19: origin unknown]

Ro+ne·o ('rəʊnɪəʊ) *Trademark.* ~*vb.* **+ne·os, +ne·o+ing, +ne·oed.** (*tr.*). **1.** to duplicate (a document) from a stencil. ~*n., pl.* **+ne·os. 2.** a document reproduced by this process.

rong+geng ('rɒŋgɛŋ) *n.* a Malay traditional dance.

ro+nin ('rəʊnɪn) *n. Japanese history.* **1.** a lordless samurai, esp. one reduced to banditry by the death of his lord. **2.** such samurai collectively.

Røn+ne (*Danish* 'rœnə) *n.* a port in Denmark, on the W coast of Bornholm Island. Pop.: 14 741 (1970).

Ron·sard (*French* rɔ̃'saːr) *n.* **Pierre de** (pjɛːr də). 1524–85, French poet, foremost of the *Pléiade.*

rönt·gen ('rɒntgən, -tjən, 'rɛnt-) *n.* a variant spelling of **roentgen.**
Rönt·gen ('rɒntgən, -tjən, 'rɛnt-; *German* 'rœntgən) *n.* a variant spelling of **(Wilhelm Konrad) Roentgen.**
roo (ru:) *n. Austral. informal.* a kangaroo.
rood (ru:d) *n.* **1. a.** a crucifix, esp. one set on a beam or screen at the entrance to the chancel of a church. **b.** (*as modifier*): *rood beam; rood arch; rood screen.* **2.** the Cross on which Christ was crucified. **3.** a unit of area equal to one quarter of an acre or 0.10117 hectares. **4.** a unit of area equal to one square rod. [Old English *rōd;* related to Old Saxon *rōda,* Old Norse *rōtha*]
Roo·de·poort-Ma·rais·burg ('ru:də,puət mə'reɪsbɜ:g) *n.* an industrial city in NE South Africa, in S Transvaal on the Witwatersrand. Pop.: 134 630 (1970).
roof (ru:f) *n., pl.* **roofs** (ru:fs, ru:vz). **1. a.** a structure that covers or forms the top of a building. **b.** (*in combination*): *the rooftop.* **c.** (*as modifier*): *a roof garden.* **2.** the top covering of a vehicle, oven, or other structure: *the roof of a car.* **3.** *Anatomy.* any structure that covers an organ or part: *the roof of the mouth.* **4.** a highest or topmost point or part: *Mount Everest is the roof of the world.* **5.** a house or other shelter: *a poor man's roof.* **6. hit** (*or* **raise** *or* **go through) the roof.** *Informal.* to get extremely angry; become furious. ~*vb.* **7.** (*tr.*) to provide or cover with a roof or rooflike part. [Old English *hrōf;* related to Middle Dutch, Old Norse *hrōf*] —**'roof·er** *n.* —**'roof·less** *adj.* —**'roof·,like** *adj.*
roof gar·den *n.* a garden on a flat roof of a building.
roof·ing ('ru:fɪŋ) *n.* **1.** material used to construct a roof. **2.** the act of constructing a roof.
roof rack *n.* a rack attached to the roof of a motor vehicle for carrying luggage, skis, etc.
roof·tree ('ru:f,tri:) *n.* another name for **ridgepole.**
roo·i·nek ('rɔɪnɛk, 'rɔɪ-) *n. S. African.* a facetious name for an Englishman. [C19: Afrikaans, literally: red neck]
rook[1] (rʊk) *n.* **1.** a large Eurasian passerine bird, *Corvus frugilegus,* with a black plumage and a whitish base to its bill: family *Corvidae* (crows). **2.** *Slang.* a swindler or cheat, esp. one who cheats at cards. ~*vb.* **3.** (*tr.*) *Slang.* to overcharge, swindle, or cheat. [Old English *hrōc;* related to Old High German *hruoh,* Old Norse *hrōkr*]
rook[2] (rʊk) *n.* a chess piece that may move any number of unoccupied squares in a straight line, horizontally or vertically. Also called: **castle.** [C14: from Old French *rok,* ultimately from Arabic *rukhkh*]
rook·er·y ('rʊkərɪ) *n., pl.* **·er·ies. 1.** a group of nesting rooks. **2.** a clump of trees containing rooks' nests. **3.** a group of breeding birds of certain other species, esp. penguins.
rook·ie ('rʊkɪ) *n. Informal.* an inexperienced person or newcomer, esp. a raw recruit in the army. [C20: changed from RECRUIT]
rook·y ('rʊkɪ) *adj.* **rook·i·er, rook·i·est.** *Literary.* abounding in rooks.
room (ru:m, rʊm) *n.* **1.** space or extent, esp. unoccupied or unobstructed space for a particular purpose: *is there room to pass?* **2.** an area within a building enclosed by a floor, a ceiling, and walls or partitions. **3.** (*functioning as sing. or pl.*) the people present in a room: *the whole room was laughing.* **4.** (foll. by *for*) opportunity or scope: *room for manoeuvre.* **5.** a euphemistic word for **lavatory.** ~*vb.* **6.** (*intr.*) to occupy or share a room or lodging: *where does he room?* [Old English *rūm;* related to Gothic, Old High German *rūm*] —**'room·er** *n.*
room·ette (ru:'mɛt, rʊ'mɛt) *n. U.S.* a compartment in a railway sleeping car.
room·ful ('ru:m,fʊl, 'rʊm-) *n., pl.* **·fuls.** a number or quantity sufficient to fill a room: *a roomful of furniture.*
room·ing house *n. U.S.* a house having self-contained furnished rooms or flats for renting.
room·mate ('ru:m,meɪt, 'rʊm-) *n.* a person with whom one shares a room or lodging.
room ser·vice *n.* service in a hotel providing meals, etc., in guests' rooms.
room tem·per·a·ture *n.* the normal temperature of a living room, usually taken as being around 20°C.
room·y ('ru:mɪ, 'rʊmɪ) *adj.* **room·i·er, room·i·est.** having ample room; spacious. —**'room·i·ly** *adv.* —**'room·i·ness** *n.*
roor·back ('rʊə,bæk) *n. U.S.* a false or distorted report or account, used to obtain political advantage. [C19: after Baron von *Roorback,* invented author of an imaginary *Tour through the Western and Southern States* (1844), which contained a passage defaming James K. Polk]
roose (ru:z) *vb.* (*tr.*) *Northern Brit. dialect.* to praise or flatter. [C13 (n.): from Scandinavian; compare Icelandic *hrōsa* to praise] —**'roos·er** *n.*
Roo·se·velt ('rəʊzə,vɛlt) *n.* **1. (Anna) El·ea·nor.** 1884–1962, U.S. writer, diplomat, and advocate of liberal causes: delegate to the United Nations (1945–52). **2.** her husband, **Frank·lin Del·a·no.** 1882–1945, 32nd president of the U.S. (1933–45); elected four times. He instituted major reforms (the **New Deal**) to counter the economic crisis of the 1930s and was a forceful leader during World War II. **3. The·o·dore.** 1858–1919, 26th president of the U.S. (1901–09). A proponent of extending military power, he won for the U.S. the right to build the Panama Canal (1903). He won the Nobel peace prize (1906), for mediating in the Russo-Japanese war.
roost (ru:st) *n.* **1.** a place, perch, branch, etc., where birds, esp. domestic fowl, rest or sleep. **2.** a temporary place to rest or stay. **3. rule the roost.** to be in charge or dominate. ~*vb.* **4.** (*intr.*) to rest or sleep on a roost. **5.** (*intr.*) to settle down or stay. **6. come home to roost.** to have unfavourable repercussions. [Old English *hrōst;* related to Old Saxon *hrost* loft, German *Rost* grid]
Roost (ru:st) *n.* **the.** a powerful current caused by conflicting tides around the Shetland and Orkney Islands. [C16: from Old Norse *röst*]
roost·er ('ru:stə) *n. Chiefly U.S.* the male of the domestic fowl; a cock.
root[1] (ru:t) *n.* **1. a.** the organ of a higher plant that anchors the rest of the plant in the ground, absorbs water and mineral salts from the soil, and does not bear leaves or buds. **b.** (loosely) any of the branches of such an organ. **2.** any plant part, such as a rhizome or tuber, that is similar to a root in structure, function, or appearance. **3.** the essential, fundamental, or primary part or nature of something: *your analysis strikes at the root of the problem.* **4.** *Anatomy.* the embedded portion of a tooth, nail, hair, etc. **5.** origin or derivation, esp. as a source of growth, vitality, or existence. **6.** (*pl.*) a person's sense of belonging in a community, place, etc., esp. the one in which he was born or brought up. **7.** an ancestor or antecedent. **8.** *Bible.* a descendant. **9.** the form of a word that remains after removal of all affixes; a morpheme with lexical meaning that is not further subdivisible into other morphemes with lexical meaning. Compare **stem**[1] (sense 9). **10.** *Maths.* a number or quantity that when multiplied by itself a certain number of times equals a given number or quantity: *3 is a cube root of 27.* **11.** Also called: **solution.** *Maths.* a number that when substituted for the variable satisfies a given equation: *2 is a root of* $x^3 - 2x - 4 = 0$. **12.** *Music.* (in harmony) the note forming the foundation of a chord. **13.** *Austral. slang.* sexual intercourse. **14. root and branch.** (*adv.*) entirely; completely; utterly. ~Related adj.: **radical.** ~*vb.* **15.** (*intr.*) Also: **take root.** to put forth or establish a root and begin to grow. **16.** (*intr.*) Also: **take root.** to become established, embedded, or effective. **17.** (*tr.*) to fix or embed with or as if with a root or roots. **18.** *Austral. slang.* to have sexual intercourse (with). ~See also **root out, root up.** [Old English *rōt,* from Old Norse; related to Old English *wyrt* WORT] —**'root·er** *n.* —**'root·,like** *adj.* —**'root·y** *adj.* —**'root·i·ness** *n.*
root[2] (ru:t) *vb.* (*intr.*) **1.** (of a pig) to burrow in or dig up the earth in search of food, using the snout. **2.** (foll. by *about, around, in,* etc.) *Informal.* to search vigorously but unsystematically. [C16: changed (through influence of ROOT[1]) from earlier *wroot,* from Old English *wrōtan;* related to Old English *wrōt* snout, Middle Dutch *wrōte* mole] —**'root·er** *n.*
root beer *U.S.* an effervescent drink made from extract of various roots and herbs.
root ca·nal *n.* the passage in the root of a tooth through which its nerves and blood vessels enter the pulp cavity.
root cap *n.* a hollow cone of loosely arranged cells that covers the growing tip of a root and protects it during its passage through the soil.
root climb·er *n.* any of various climbing plants, such as the ivy, that adhere to a supporting structure by means of small roots growing from the side of the stem.
root crop *n.* a crop, as of turnips or beets, cultivated for the food value of its roots.
root·ed ('ru:tɪd) *adj.* **1.** having roots. **2.** deeply felt: *rooted objections.* **3.** *Austral. slang.* tired or defeated. **4. get rooted!** *Austral. taboo slang.* an exclamation of contemptuous anger or annoyance, esp. against another person.
root for *vb.* (*intr., prep.*) *U.S. Informal.* to give support to (a contestant, team, etc.), as by cheering. [C19: *root* perhaps a variant of Scottish *rout* to make a loud noise, from Old Norse *rauta* to roar]
root hair *n.* any of the hollow hairlike outgrowths of the outer cells of a root, just behind the tip, that absorb water and salts from the soil.
root·le ('ru:tᵊl) *vb.* (*intr.*) *Brit.* another word for **root**[2].
root·less ('ru:tlɪs) *adj.* having no roots, esp. (of a person) having no ties with a particular place or community.
root·let ('ru:tlɪt) *n.* a small root or branch of a root.
root mean square *n.* the square root of the average of the squares of a set of numbers or quantities: *the root mean square of* 1, 2, *and* 4 *is* $\sqrt{[(1^2 + 2^2 + 4^2)/3]} = \sqrt{7}$. Abbrev: **rms**
root nod·ule *n.* a swelling on the root of a leguminous plant, such as the pea or clover, that contains bacteria of the genus *Rhizobium,* capable of nitrogen fixation.
root out *vb.* (*tr., adv.*) to remove or eliminate completely: *we must root out inefficiency.*
root po·si·tion *n. Music.* the vertical distribution of the written notes of a chord in which the root of the chord is in the bass. See **position** (sense 12a), **inversion** (sense 5a).
root·stock ('ru:t,stɒk) *n.* **1.** another name for **rhizome. 2.** another name for **stock** (sense 7). **3.** *Biology.* a basic structure from which offshoots have developed.
root up *vb.* (*tr., adv.*) to tear or dig up by the roots.
rop·a·ble *or* **rope·a·ble** ('rəʊpəbᵊl) *adj.* **1.** capable of being roped. **2.** *Austral., N.Z. informal.* **a.** angry. **b.** wild or intractable: *a ropable beast.*
rope (rəʊp) *n.* **1. a.** a fairly thick cord made of twisted and intertwined hemp or other fibres or of wire or other strong material. **b.** (*as modifier*): *a rope bridge; rope ladder.* **2.** a row of objects fastened or united to form a line: *a rope of pearls; a rope of onions.* **3.** a quantity of material twisted or wound in the form of a cord. **4.** anything in the form of a filament or strand, esp. something viscous or glutinous: *a rope of slime.* **5. the rope. a.** a rope, noose, or halter used for hanging. **b.** death by hanging, strangling, etc. **6. give (someone) enough rope to hang himself** *or* **plenty of rope.** to allow (a person) to accom-

plish his own downfall by his own foolish acts. **7. know the ropes. a.** to have a thorough understanding of a particular sphere of activity. **b.** to be experienced in the ways of the world. **8. on the ropes. a.** *Boxing.* driven against the ropes enclosing the ring by an opponent's attack. **b.** in a defenceless or hopeless position. ~*vb.* **9.** (*tr.*) to bind or fasten with or as if with a rope. **10.** (*tr.;* usually foll. by *off*) to enclose or divide by means of a rope. **11.** (*intr.*) to become extended in a long filament or thread. **12.** (when *intr.*, foll. by *up*) *Mountaineering.* to tie (climbers) together with a rope. [Old English *rāp;* related to Old Saxon *rēp,* Old High German *reif*]

rope danc+er *n.* another name for a **tightrope walker.**

rope in *vb.* (*tr., adv.*) **1.** *Brit.* to persuade to take part in some activity. **2.** *U.S.* to trick or entice into some activity.

rope's end *n.* a short piece of rope, esp. as formerly used for flogging sailors.

rope+walk ('rəʊpˌwɔːk) *n.* a long narrow usually covered path or shed where ropes are made.

rope yarn *n.* the natural or synthetic fibres out of which rope is made.

rop·y ('rəʊpɪ) *adj.* **rop·i·er, rop·i·est. 1.** Also: **rop·ey.** *Brit. informal.* inferior or inadequate. **2.** (of a viscous or sticky substance) forming strands or filaments. **3.** resembling a rope: *ropy muscles.* —'**rop·i·ly** *adv.* —'**rop·i·ness** *n.*

roque (rəʊk) *n. U.S.* a game developed from croquet, played on a hard surface with a resilient surrounding border from which the ball can rebound. [C19: variant of CROQUET]

Roque+fort ('rɒkfɔː) *n.* a blue-veined cheese with a strong flavour, made from ewe's and goat's milk: matured in caves. [C19: named after *Roquefort,* village in S France]

roq·ue+laure ('rɒkəˌlɔː) *n.* a man's hooded knee-length cloak of the 18th and 19th centuries. [C18: from French, named after the Duc de *Roquelaure* (1656–1738), French marshal]

ro+quet ('rəʊkɪ) *Croquet.* ~*vb.* **+quets** (-kɪz), **+quet+ing** (-kɪɪŋ), **+queted** (-kɪd). **1.** to drive one's ball against (another person's ball) in order to be allowed to croquet. ~*n.* **2.** the act of roqueting. [C19: variant of CROQUET]

Ro+rai+ma (*Portuguese* rɔ'raɪma) *n.* a federal territory of N Brazil: chiefly rainforest. Capital: Boa Vista. Area: 230 104 sq. km (89 740 sq. miles). Pop.: 40 885 (1970).

ror+qual ('rɔːkwəl) *n.* any of several whalebone whales of the genus *Balaenoptera,* esp. *B. physalus:* family *Balaenopteridae.* They have a dorsal fin and a series of grooves along the throat and chest. Also called: **finback.** [C19: from French, from Norwegian *rörhval,* from Old Norse *reytharhvalr,* from *reythr* (from *rauthr* red) + *hvalr* whale]

Ror·schach test ('rɔːʃɑːk; *German* 'rɔrʃax) *n. Psychol.* a personality test consisting of a number of unstructured ink blots presented for interpretation. [C20: name after Hermann *Rorschach* (1884–1922), Swiss psychiatrist]

rort (rɔːt) *n. Austral. informal.* a rowdy party or celebration. [C20: back formation from *rorty* (in the sense: good, splendid)] —'**ror·ty** *adj.*

Ro·sa[1] ('rəʊzə, *Italian* 'rɔːza) *n.* **Mon+te** ('mɒntɪ; *Italian* 'monte). a mountain between Italy and Switzerland: the highest in the Pennine Alps. Height: 4634 m (15 204 ft.).

Ro·sa[2] (*Italian* 'rɔːza) *n.* **Sal·va·tor** ('salvaˌtɔr). 1615–73, Italian artist, noted esp. for his romantic landscapes.

ros+ace ('rəʊzeɪs) *n.* **1.** another name for **rose window. 2.** another name for **rosette.** [C19: from French, from Latin *rosāceus* ROSACEOUS]

ro+sa+ceous (rəʊ'zeɪʃəs) *adj.* **1.** of, relating to, or belonging to the *Rosaceae,* a family of flowering plants typically having white, yellow, pink, or red five-petalled flowers. The family includes the rose, strawberry, blackberry, and many fruit trees such as apple, cherry, and plum. **2.** of the colour rose; rose-coloured; rosy. [C18: from Latin *rosāceus* composed of roses, from *rosa* ROSE[1]]

ro+san·i+line (rəʊ'zænɪˌliːn, -lɪn) *or* **ro+san·i+lin** *n.* a reddish-brown crystalline insoluble derivative of aniline used, in the form of its soluble hydrochloride, as a red dye. See also **fuchsin.** [C19: from ROSE[1] + ANILINE]

ro+sar·i·an (rəʊ'zɛərɪən) *n.* a person who cultivates roses, esp. professionally.

Ro+sa+rio (rəʊ'sɑːrɪəʊ; *Spanish* rɔ'sarjo) *n.* an inland port in E Argentina, on the Paraná River: the second largest city in the country; industrial centre. Pop.: 810 840 (1970).

ro+sar·i·um (rəʊ'zɛərɪəm) *n., pl.* **+sar·i·ums** *or* **+sar·i·a.** a rose garden. [C19: New Latin]

ro+sar·y ('rəʊzərɪ) *n., pl.* **+sar·ies. 1.** *R.C. Church.* **a.** a series of prayers counted on a string of beads, usually consisting of five or 15 decades of Aves, each decade beginning with a Paternoster and ending with a Gloria. **b.** a string of 55 or 165 beads used to count these prayers as they are recited. **2.** (in other religions) a similar string of beads used in praying. **3.** a bed or garden of roses. **4.** an archaic word for a **garland** (of flowers, etc.). [C14: from Latin *rosārium* rose garden, from *rosārius* of roses, from *rosa* ROSE[1]]

Ros·ci·us ('rɒskɪəs, -sɪəs) *n.* **1.** full name *Quintus Roscius Gallus.* died 62 B.C. Roman actor. **2.** any actor. —'**Ros+ci·an** *adj.*

Ros+com+mon (rɒs'kɒmən) *n.* an inland county of N central Ireland, in Connacht: economy based on cattle and sheep farming. County town: Roscommon. Pop.: 53 519 (1971). Area: 2463 sq. km (951 sq. miles).

rose[1] (rəʊz) *n.* **1. a.** any shrub or climbing plant of the rosaceous genus *Rosa,* typically having prickly stems, compound leaves, and fragrant flowers. **b.** (*in combination*): *rosebush; rosetree.* **2.** the flower of any of these plants. **3.** any of various similar plants, such as the rockrose and Christmas rose. **4. a.** a moderate purplish-red colour; purplish pink. **b.** (*as adj.*): *rose paint.* **5.** *Jewellery.* **a.** a cut for a diamond or other gemstone, having a hemispherical faceted crown and a flat base. **b.** a gem so cut. **6.** a perforated cap fitted to the spout of a watering can or the end of a hose, causing the water to issue in a spray. **7.** a design or decoration shaped like a rose; rosette. **8.** *History.* See **red rose, white rose. 9. bed of roses.** a situation of ease and luxury. **10. under the rose.** in secret; privately; sub rosa. ~*vb.* **11.** (*tr.*) to make rose-coloured; cause to blush or redden. [Old English, from Latin *rosa,* probably from Greek *rhodon* rose] —'**rose+ˌlike** *adj.*

rose[2] (rəʊz) *vb.* the past tense of **rise.**

ro·sé ('rəʊzeɪ) *n.* any pink wine, made either by removing the skins of red grapes after only a little colour has been extracted or by mixing red and white wines. [from French, literally: pink, from Latin *rosa* ROSE[1]]

rose a·ca·cia *n.* a leguminous shrub, *Robinia hispida,* of the southern U.S., having prickly branches bearing clusters of red scentless flowers. See also **locust** (sense 2).

rose ap+ple *n.* an ornamental myrtaceous tree, *Eugenia jambos,* of the East Indies, cultivated in the tropics for its edible fruit.

ro+se·ate ('rəʊzɪˌeɪt) *adj.* **1.** of the colour rose or pink. **2.** excessively or idealistically optimistic. —'**ro+se·ˌate+ly** *adv.*

rose+bay ('rəʊzˌbeɪ) *n.* **1.** *U.S.* any of several rhododendrons, esp. *Rhododendron maximum* of E North America. **2. rosebay willowherb.** a perennial onagraceous plant, *Chamaenerion* (formerly *Epilobium*) *angustifolium,* that has spikes of deep pink flowers and is widespread in open places throughout N temperate regions. **3.** another name for **oleander.**

Rose·ber·y ('rəʊzbərɪ, -brɪ) *n.* **Earl of,** title of *Archibald Philip Primrose.* 1847–1929, British statesman; Liberal prime minister (1894–95).

rose+bud ('rəʊzˌbʌd) *n.* **1.** the bud of a rose. **2.** *Literary.* a pretty young woman.

rose cam+pi+on *n.* a European caryophyllaceous plant, *Lychnis coronaria,* widely cultivated for its pink flowers. Its stems and leaves are covered with white woolly down. Also called: **dusty miller.**

rose chaf+er *or* **bee+tle** *n.* a British scarabaeid beetle, *Cetonia aurata,* that has a greenish-golden body with a metallic lustre and feeds on plants.

rose-col·oured *adj.* **1.** of the colour rose; rosy. **2.** excessively optimistic. **3. see through rose-coloured glasses** (*or* **spectacles**). to view in an excessively optimistic light.

rose-cut *adj.* (of a gemstone) cut with a hemispherical faceted crown and a flat base.

rose+fish ('rəʊzˌfɪʃ) *n., pl.* **+fish** *or* **+fish·es. 1.** a red scorpaenid food fish, *Sebastes marinus,* of North Atlantic coastal waters. **2.** any of various other red fishes.

rose ge+ra+ni·um *n.* a small geraniaceous shrub, *Pelargonium graveolens,* grown in North America for its pink flowers and fragrant leaves, used for scenting perfumes and cosmetics.

rose+hip ('rəʊzˌhɪp) *n.* the berry-like fruit of a rose plant. See **hip**[2].

ro+sel+la (rəʊ'zɛlə) *n.* any of various Australian parrots of the genus *Platycercus,* such as *P. elegans* (**crimson rosella**), often kept as cage birds. [C19: probably alteration of *Rose-hiller,* after *Rose Hill,* Parramatta, near Sydney]

ro+se+ma+ling ('rəʊzəˌmɑːlɪŋ, -sə-) *n.* a type of painted or carved decoration in Scandinavian peasant style consisting of floral motifs. [Norwegian, literally: rose painting]

rose mal+low *n.* **1.** Also called in the U.S.: **marsh mallow.** any of several malvaceous marsh plants of the genus *Hibiscus,* such as *H. moscheutos,* of E North America, having pink or white flowers and downy leaves. **2.** *U.S.* another name for the **hollyhock.**

rose+mar·y ('rəʊzmərɪ) *n., pl.* **+mar·ies.** an aromatic European shrub, *Rosmarinus officinalis,* widely cultivated for its grey-green evergreen leaves, which are used in cookery for flavouring and yield a fragrant oil used in the manufacture of perfumes: family *Labiatae* (labiates). It is the traditional flower of remembrance. [C15: earlier *rosmarine,* from Latin *rōs* dew + *marīnus* marine; modern form influenced by folk etymology, as if ROSE[1] + MARY]

rose moss *n.* a low-growing portulacaceous plant, *Portulaca grandiflora,* native to Brazil but widely cultivated as a garden plant for its brightly coloured flowers.

rose of Jer·i·cho *n.* another name for the **resurrection plant.**

rose of Shar+on *n.* **1.** Also called: **Aaron's beard.** a creeping shrub, *Hypericum calycinum,* native to SE Europe but widely cultivated, having large yellow flowers: family *Hypericaceae.* **2.** Also called: **althaea.** a Syrian malvaceous shrub, *Hibiscus syriacus* (or *Althaea frutex*), cultivated for its red or purplish flowers.

ro+se·o+la (rəʊ'ziːələ) *n. Pathol.* **1.** any red skin eruption or rash. **2.** another name for **rubeola.** [C19: from New Latin, diminutive of Latin *roseus* rosy] —**ro+'se·o+lar** *adj.*

rose quartz *n.* a rose-pink often translucent variety of quartz that is used for ornaments.

rose-root *n.* a Eurasian crassulaceous mountain plant, *Sedum rosea,* with fleshy pink-tipped leaves, a thick fleshy pinkish underground stem, and a cluster of yellow flowers. Also called: **midsummer-men.**

ro+ser·y ('rəʊzərɪ) *n., pl.* **+ser·ies.** a bed or garden of roses.

Ro+set+ta (rəʊ'zɛtə) *n.* a town in N Egypt, in the Nile delta. Pop.: 36 711 (1966).

Ro+set+ta stone *n.* a basalt slab discovered in 1799 at Rosetta, dating to the reign of Ptolemy V (196 B.C.) and carved with parallel inscriptions in Greek, demotic, and hieroglyphics, which provided the key to the decipherment of ancient Egyptian texts.

ro+sette (rəʊ'zɛt) *n.* **1.** a decoration or pattern resembling a rose, esp. an arrangement of ribbons or strips formed into a rose-shaped design and worn as a badge or presented as a prize. **2.** another name for **rose window. 3.** a rose-shaped patch of colour, such as one of the clusters of spots marking a leopard's fur. **4.** *Botany.* a circular cluster of leaves growing from the base of a stem. **5.** any of various plant diseases characterized by abnormal leaf growth. [C18: from Old French: a little ROSE[1]]

Rose·wall ('rəʊz,wɔːl) *n.* **Ken(neth).** born 1934, Australian tennis player: Australian champion 1953, 1955, and 1971–72; U.S. champion 1956 and 1970.

rose-wa·ter *n.* **1. a.** scented water used as a perfume and in cooking, made by the distillation of rose petals or by impregnation with oil of roses. **b.** (*as modifier*): *rose-water scent.* **2.** (*modifier*) elegant or delicate, esp. excessively so.

rose win+dow *n.* a circular window, esp. one that has ornamental tracery radiating from the centre to form a symmetrical roselike pattern. Also called: **wheel window, rosette.**

rose+wood ('rəʊz,wʊd) *n.* **1.** the hard dark wood of any of various tropical and subtropical leguminous trees, esp. of the genus *Dalbergia.* It has a roselike scent and is used in cabinet-work. **2.** any of the trees yielding this wood.

Rosh Ha+sha+nah *or* **Rosh Ha+sha+na** ('rɒʃ hə'ʃɑːnə; *Hebrew* 'rɔʃ haʃa'na) *n.* the Jewish New Year, celebrated on the first or first and second of Tishri and marked chiefly by the blowing of the shofar. [from Hebrew *rōsh hasshānāh,* literally: beginning of the year, from *rōsh* head + *hash-shānāh* year]

Ro+si+cru+cian (,rəʊzɪ'kruːʃən) *n.* **1.** a member of a society professing esoteric religious doctrines, venerating the emblems of the rose and Cross as symbols of Christ's Resurrection and Redemption, and claiming various occult powers. ~*adj.* **2.** of, relating to, or designating the Rosicrucians or Rosicrucianism. [C17: from Latin *Rosae Crucis* Rose of the Cross, translation of the German name Christian *Rosenkreuz,* supposed founder of the society in the 15th century] —**,Ro+si+'cru+cian+ism** *n.*

Ro+sie Lee ('rəʊzɪ 'liː) *n. Cockney rhyming slang.* tea.

ros·i+ly ('rəʊzɪlɪ) *adv.* in a rosy manner; cheerfully.

ros+in ('rɒzɪn) *n.* **1.** Also called: **colophony.** a translucent brittle amber substance produced in the distillation of crude turpentine oleoresin and used in making varnishes, printing inks, and sealing waxes and for treating the bows of stringed instruments. **2.** another name for **resin** (sense 1). ~*vb.* **3.** (*tr.*) to treat or coat with rosin. [C14: variant of RESIN] —**'ros+in·y** *adj.*

Ros+in+an+te (,rɒzɪ'næntɪ) *n.* a worn-out emaciated old horse. [from Spanish, the name of Don Quixote's horse, from *rocin* old horse]

ros+in oil *n.* a yellowish fluorescent oily liquid obtained from certain resins, used in the manufacture of carbon black, varnishes, and lacquers. Also called: **rosinol, retinol.**

ros·in+weed ('rɒzɪn,wiːd) *n.* any of several North American plants of the genus *Silphium* and related genera, esp. the compass plant, having resinous juice, sticky foliage, and a strong smell: family *Compositae* (composites).

Ros+kil+de (*Danish* 'rɔskilə) *n.* a city in Denmark, on NE Sjælland west of Copenhagen: capital of Denmark from the 10th century to 1443; scene of the signing (1658) of the **Peace of Roskilde** between Denmark and Sweden. Pop.: 39 147 (1970).

ROSPA ('rɒspə) *n.* (in Britain) *acronym for* Royal Society for the Prevention of Accidents.

Ross (rɒs) *n.* **1.** Sir **James Clark.** 1800–62, British naval officer; explorer of the Arctic and Antarctic. He located the north magnetic pole (1831) and discovered the Ross Sea during an Antarctic voyage (1839–43). **2.** his uncle, Sir **John.** 1777–1856, Scottish naval officer and Arctic explorer. **3.** Sir **Ron·ald.** 1857–1932, English bacteriologist, who discovered the transmission of malaria by mosquitoes: Nobel prize for medicine 1902.

Ross and Crom+ar+ty ('krɒmətɪ) *n.* (until 1975) a county of NW Scotland, including the island of Lewis and many islets: now part of the Highland region.

Ross De+pend+en+cy *n.* a section of Antarctica administered by New Zealand: includes the coastal regions of Victoria Land and King Edward VII Land, the Ross Sea and islands, and the Ross Ice Shelf. Area: about 414 400 sq. km (160 000 sq. miles).

Ros·set·ti (rɒ'zɛtɪ) *n.* **1. Chris·ti·na Geor·gi·na.** 1830–94, English Pre-Raphaelite poet. **2.** her brother, **Dan·te Ga·bri·el.** 1828–82, English poet and painter: a leader of the Pre-Raphaelites.

Ross Ice Shelf *n.* the ice shelf forming the S part of the Ross Sea, between Victoria Land and Byrd Land. Also called: **Ross Barrier, Ross Shelf Ice.**

Ros·si·ni (rɒ'siːni) *n.* **Gio·ac·chi·no An·to·nio** (,dʒoak'kiːno an'tɔːnjo). 1792–1868, Italian composer, esp. of operas, such as *The Barber of Seville* (1816) and *William Tell* (1829).

Ross Is+land *n.* an island in the W Ross Sea: contains the active volcano Mount Erebus.

Ros+si+ya (ra'siːjə) *n.* transliteration of the Russian name for **Russia.**

Ross Sea *n.* a large arm of the S Pacific in Antarctica, incorporating the Ross Ice Shelf and lying between Victoria Land and the Edward VII Peninsula.

Ros·tand (*French* rɔs'tã) *n.* **Ed·mond** (ɛd'mɔ̃). 1868–1918, French playwright and poet in the romantic tradition; best known for his verse drama *Cyrano de Bergerac* (1897).

ros+tel+lum (rɒ'stɛləm) *n., pl.* **+la** (-lə). *Biology.* a small beak-like process, such as the hooked projection from the top of the head in tapeworms or the outgrowth from the stigma of an orchid. [C18: from Latin: a little beak, from *rōstrum* a beak] —**ros+'tel+late** *or* **ros+'tel+lar** *adj.*

ros+ter ('rɒstə) *n.* **1.** a list or register, esp. one showing the order of people enrolled for duty. ~*vb.* **2.** (*tr.*) to place on a roster. [C18: from Dutch *rooster* grating or list (the lined paper looking like a grid)]

Ros+tock ('rɒstɒk) *n.* a port in N East Germany, on the Warnow estuary 13 km (8 miles) from the Baltic and its outport, Warnemünde: the chief port of East Germany; university (1419). Pop.: 211 723 (1975 est.).

Ros+tov *or* **Ros·tov-on-Don** ('rɒstɒv) *n.* a port in the S Soviet Union, on the River Don 48 km (30 miles) from the Sea of Azov: industrial centre. Pop.: 888 000 (1975 est.).

Ros·tro·po·vich (,rɒstrə'pəʊvɪtʃ; *Russian* rəstra'pɔvitʃ) *n.* **Ms·ti·slav Le·o·pol·do·vich** ('mɪstɪslɑːv; *Russian* msti'slaf lea'pɔldavitʃ). born 1927 in the Soviet Union, cellist, composer, and conductor.

ros+trum ('rɒstrəm) *n., pl.* **+trums** *or* **+tra** (-trə). **1.** any platform, stage, or dais on which public speakers stand to address an audience. **2.** a platform or dais in front of an orchestra on which the conductor stands. **3.** another word for **ram** (sense 5). **4.** the prow or beak of an ancient Roman ship. **5.** *Biology.* a beak or beaklike part. [C16: from Latin *rōstrum* beak, ship's prow, from *rōdere* to nibble, gnaw; in plural, *rōstra,* orator's platform, because this platform in the Roman forum was adorned with the prows of captured ships] —**'ros+tral, 'ros+trate,** *or* **ros+'trat+ed** *adj.*

ros·y ('rəʊzɪ) *adj.* **ros·i+er, ros·i+est. 1.** of the colour rose or pink. **2.** having a healthy pink complexion: *rosy cheeks.* **3.** optimistic, esp. excessively so: *a rosy view of social improvements.* **4.** full of health, happiness, or joy: *rosy slumbers.* **5.** resembling, consisting of, or abounding in roses. —**'ros·i+ly** *adv.* —**'ros·i+ness** *n.*

ros·y finch *n.* any of several finches of the genus *Leucosticte,* occurring in mountainous regions of North America and Asia. They have brown or grey plumage with pink patches on the wings, rump, and tail.

rot[1] (rɒt) *vb.* **rots, rot+ting, rot+ted. 1.** to decay or cause to decay as a result of bacterial or fungal action. **2.** (*intr.; usually foll. by off or away*) to fall or crumble (off) or break (away), as from natural decay, corrosive action, or long use. **3.** (*intr.*) to become weak, debilitated, or depressed through inertia, confinement, etc.; languish: *rotting in prison.* **4.** to become or cause to become morally corrupt or degenerate. **5.** (*tr.*) *Textiles.* another word for **ret.** ~*n.* **6.** the process of rotting or the state of being rotten. **7.** something decomposed, disintegrated, or degenerate. Related adj.: **putrid. 8.** short for **dry rot. 9.** *Pathol.* any putrefactive decomposition of tissues. **10.** a condition in plants characterized by breakdown and decay of tissues, caused by parasitic bacteria, fungi, etc. **11.** *Vet. science.* a contagious fungal disease of sheep characterized by inflammation, swelling, a foul-smelling discharge, and lameness. **12.** (*also interj.*) nonsense; rubbish. [Old English *rotian* (vb.); related to Old Norse *rotna.* C13 (n.), from Scandinavian]

rot[2] *abbrev. for* rotation (of a mathematical function).

ro·ta ('rəʊtə) *n. Chiefly Brit.* a register of names showing the order in which people take their turn to perform certain duties. [C17: from Latin: a wheel]

Ro·ta ('rəʊtə) *n. R.C. Church.* the supreme ecclesiastical tribunal for judging cases brought before the Holy See.

Ro+ta+me+ter ('rəʊtə,miːtə) *n. Trademark.* a device used for measuring the flow of a fluid. It consists of a small float supported in a tapering glass by the flow of fluid, the height of the float indicating the rate of flow.

Ro+tar+i·an (rəʊ'tɛərɪən) *n.* **1.** a member of a Rotary Club. ~*adj.* **2.** of or relating to Rotary Clubs or their members. —**Ro+'tar·i+an+ism** *n.*

ro+ta+ry ('rəʊtərɪ) *adj.* **1.** of, relating to, or operating by rotation. **2.** turning or able to turn; revolving. ~*n., pl.* **+ries. 3.** a part of a machine that rotates about an axis. **4.** *U.S. and Canadian.* another term for **roundabout** (for traffic). [C18: from Medieval Latin *rotārius,* from Latin *rota* a wheel]

Ro+ta+ry Club *n.* any of the local clubs that form **Rotary International,** an international association of professional and business men founded in the U.S. in 1905 to promote community service.

ro+ta+ry en+gine *n.* **1.** an internal-combustion engine having radial cylinders that rotate about a fixed crankshaft. **2.** an engine, such as a turbine or Wankel engine, in which power is transmitted directly to rotating components.

ro+ta+ry plough *or* **till+er** *n.* an implement with a series of blades mounted on a power-driven shaft which rotates so as to break up soil or destroy weeds.

ro+ta+ry press *n.* a machine for printing from a revolving cylindrical forme, usually onto a continuous strip of paper.

ro+tate *vb.* (rəʊ'teɪt). **1.** to turn or cause to turn around an axis, line, or point; revolve or spin. **2.** to follow or cause to follow a set order or sequence. ~*adj.* ('rəʊteɪt). **3.** *Botany.* designating a corolla the united petals of which radiate from a central point like the spokes of a wheel. —**ro+'tat+a·ble** *adj.*

ro+ta+tion (rəʊ'teɪʃən) *n.* **1.** the act of rotating; rotary motion. **2.** a regular cycle of events in a set order or sequence. **3.** a planned sequence of cropping according to which the crops grown in successive seasons on the same land are varied so as to make a balanced demand on its resources of fertility. **4.**

Maths. **a.** a circular motion of a configuration about a given point or line, without a change in shape. **b.** a transformation in which the coordinate axes are rotated by a fixed angle about the origin. **c.** another name for **curl** (sense 12). Abbrev. (for c.): **rot 5. a.** the spinning motion of a body, such as a planet, about an internal axis. Compare **revolution** (sense 5a.). **b.** one complete turn in such motion. —**ro·'ta·tion·al** *adj.*

ro·ta·tive ('rəutətɪv) *or* **ro·ta·to·ry** ('rəutətərɪ, -trɪ) *adj.* of, relating to, possessing, or causing rotation. —**'ro·ta·tive·ly** *adv.*

ro·ta·tor (rəu'teɪtə) *n.* **1.** a person, device, or part that rotates or causes rotation. **2.** *Anatomy.* any of various muscles that revolve a part on its axis.

rote[1] (rəut) *n.* **1.** a habitual or mechanical routine or procedure. **2. by rote.** by repetition; by heart (often in the phrase **learn by rote).** [C14: origin unknown]

rote[2] (rəut) *n.* an ancient violin-like musical instrument; crwth. [C13: from Old French *rote,* of Germanic origin; related to Old High German *rotta,* Middle Dutch *rotte*]

ro·te·none ('rəutɪˌnəun) *n.* a white odourless crystalline substance extracted from the roots of derris: a powerful insecticide. Formula: $C_{23}H_{22}O_6$; relative density: 1.27; melting pt.: 163°C. [C20: from Japanese *rōten* derris + -ONE]

rot·gut ('rɒtˌgʌt) *n. Facetious slang.* alcoholic drink, esp. spirits, of inferior quality.

Roth·er·ham ('rɒðərəm) *n.* an industrial town in N England, in South Yorkshire. Pop.: 84 646 (1971).

Roth·er·mere ('rɒðəˌmɪə) *n.* **Viscount.** title of *Harold Sidney Harmsworth.* 1868–1940, British newspaper magnate.

Rothe·say ('rɒθsɪ) *n.* a town in SW Scotland, in Strathclyde region, on the E coast of Bute Island. Pop.: 6524 (1971).

Roth·ko ('rɒθkəu) *n.* **Mark.** born 1903, U.S. abstract expressionist painter, born in Russia.

Roth·schild ('rɒθtʃaɪld, 'rɒθs-) *n.* a powerful family of European Jewish bankers, prominent members of which were: **1. Li·o·nel Na·than,** Baron de Rothschild. 1809–79, English banker and first Jewish member of Parliament. **2.** his grandfather **Mey·er Am·schel** ('maɪə 'amʃəl). 1743–1812, German financier and founder of the Rothschild banking firm. **3.** his son, **Na·than Mey·er,** Baron de Rothschild. 1777–1836, British banker, born in Germany.

ro·ti ('rəutɪ, 'rʊtɪ) *n.* (in the Caribbean) a type of unleavened bread. [from Hindi: bread]

ro·ti·fer ('rəutɪfə) *n.* any minute aquatic multicellular invertebrate of the phylum *Rotifera,* having a ciliated wheel-like organ used in feeding and locomotion: common constituents of freshwater plankton. Also called: **wheel animalcule.** [C18: from New Latin *Rotifera,* from Latin *rota* wheel + *ferre* to bear] —**ro·tif·er·al** (rəu'tɪfərəl) *or* **ro·'tif·er·ous** *adj.*

ro·tis·ser·ie (rəu'tɪsərɪ) *n.* **1.** a rotating spit on which meat, poultry, etc., can be cooked. **2.** a shop or restaurant where meat is roasted to order. [French, from Old French *rostir* to ROAST]

rot·l ('rɒtᵊl) *n., pl.* **rot·ls** *or* **ar·tal** ('ɑ:tɑ:l). a unit of weight used in Moslem countries, varying in value between about one and five pounds. [from Arabic *ratl,* perhaps from Greek *litra* a pound]

ro·to·gra·vure (ˌrəutəugrə'vjʊə) *n.* **1.** a printing process using copper cylinders etched photomechanically with many small holes, from which ink is transferred to a moving web of paper, plastic, etc., in a rotary press. **2.** printed material produced in this way, esp. magazines. ~Often shortened to **roto.** [C20: from Latin *rota* wheel + GRAVURE]

ro·tor ('rəutə) *n.* **1.** the rotating member of a machine or device, esp. the armature of a motor or generator or the rotating assembly of a turbine. Compare **stator. 2.** a system of rotating parts, esp. the assembly of aerofoils of a helicopter. **3.** the revolving arm of the distributor of an internal-combustion engine. [C20: shortened form of ROTATOR]

Ro·to·ru·a (ˌrəutə'ru:ə) *n.* a city in New Zealand, on N central North Island at the SW end of Lake Rotorua: health resort in a volcanic region. Pop.: 31 265 (1971).

rot·ten ('rɒtᵊn) *adj.* **1.** affected with rot; decomposing, decaying, or putrid. **2.** breaking up, esp. through age or hard use; disintegrating: *rotten ironwork.* **3.** morally despicable or corrupt. **4.** untrustworthy, disloyal, or treacherous. **5.** *Informal.* unpleasant, unfortunate, or nasty: *rotten luck; rotten weather.* **6.** *Informal.* unsatisfactory or poor: *rotten workmanship.* **7.** (of rocks, soils, etc.) soft and crumbling, esp. as a result of weathering. **8.** *Slang, chiefly Austral.* intoxicated; drunk. [C13: from Old Norse *rottin;* related to Old English *rotian* to ROT] —**'rot·ten·ly** *adv.* —**'rot·ten·ness** *n.*

rot·ten bor·ough *n.* (before the Reform Act of 1832) any of certain English parliamentary constituencies with only a very few electors. Compare **pocket borough.**

rot·ten·stone ('rɒtᵊnˌstəun) *n.* a much-weathered limestone, rich in silica: used in powdered form for polishing metal.

rot·ter ('rɒtə) *n. Slang, chiefly Brit.* a worthless, unpleasant, or despicable person.

Rot·ter·dam ('rɒtəˌdæm) *n.* a port in the SW Netherlands, in South Holland province: the second largest city of the Netherlands and one of the world's largest ports; oil refineries, shipbuilding yards, etc. Pop.: 628 389 (1974 est.).

Rott·wei·ler ('rɒtˌwaɪlə) *n.* a breed of large dog with a smooth coat, black and dark tan in colour, and usually having a docked tail. [German, named after *Rottweil,* German city where the dog was originally bred]

ro·tund (rəu'tʌnd) *adj.* **1.** rounded or spherical in shape. **2.** plump. **3.** sonorous or grandiloquent; full in tone, style of speaking, etc. [C18: from Latin *rotundus* wheel-shaped, round, from *rota* wheel] —**ro·'tun·di·ty** *or* **ro·'tund·ness** *n.* —**ro·'tund·ly** *adv.*

ro·tun·da (rəu'tʌndə) *n.* a building or room having a circular plan, esp. one that has a dome. [C17: from Italian *rotonda,* from Latin *rotundus* round, from *rota* a wheel]

Rou·ault (ru:'əu; *French* rwo) *n.* **Georges** (ʒɔrʒ). 1871–1958, French expressionist artist. His work is deeply religious; it includes much stained glass.

Rou·baix (*French* ru'bɛ) *n.* a city in N France near the Belgian border: forms, with Tourcoing, a large industrial conurbation. Pop.: 109 797 (1975).

rou·ble *or* **ru·ble** ('ru:bᵊl) *n.* the standard monetary unit of the Soviet Union, divided into 100 kopecks. [C16: from Russian *rubl* silver bar, from Old Russian *rublĭ* bar, block of wood, from *rubiti* to cut up]

rou·cou ('ru:ˌku:) *n.* another name for **annatto.** [C17: via French from Tupi *urucú*]

rou·é ('ru:eɪ) *n.* a debauched or lecherous man; rake. [C19: from French, literally: one broken on the wheel, from *rouer,* from Latin *rotāre* to revolve, from *rota* a wheel; with reference to the fate deserved by a debauchee]

Rou·en (*French* rwɑ̃) *n.* a city in N France, on the River Seine: the chief river port of France; became capital of the duchy of Normandy in 912; scene of the burning of Joan of Arc (1431); university (1964). Pop.: 118 332 (1975).

rouge (ru:ʒ) *n.* **1.** a red powder, used as a cosmetic for adding redness to the cheeks. **2.** short for **jeweller's rouge.** ~*vb.* (*tr.*) **3.** to apply rouge to. [C18: from French: red, from Latin *rubeus*]

Rouge Croix (ˌru:ʒ 'krwɑ:) *n.* a pursuivant at the English college of arms.

Rouge Drag·on (ˌru:ʒ 'drægən) *n.* a pursuivant at the English college of arms.

rouge et noir ('ru:ʒ eɪ 'nwɑ:; *French* ruʒ e 'nwar) *n.* a card game in which the players put their stakes on any of two red and two black diamond-shaped spots marked on the table. [French, literally: red and black]

Rou·get de Lisle (*French* ruʒɛ də 'lil) *n.* **Claude Jo·seph** (klo:d ʒo'zɛf). 1760–1836, French army officer: composer of the *Marseillaise* (1792), the French national anthem.

rough (rʌf) *adj.* **1.** (of a surface) not smooth; uneven or irregular. **2.** (of ground) covered with scrub, boulders, etc. **3.** denoting or taking place on uncultivated ground: *rough grazing; rough shooting.* **4.** shaggy or hairy. **5.** turbulent; agitated: *a rough sea.* **6.** (of the performance or motion of something) uneven; irregular: *a rough engine.* **7.** (of behaviour or character) rude, coarse, ill mannered, inconsiderate, or violent. **8.** harsh or sharp: *rough words.* **9.** *Informal.* severe or unpleasant: *a rough lesson.* **10.** (of work, a task, etc.) requiring physical rather than mental effort. **11.** *Informal.* ill or physically upset: *he felt rough after an evening of heavy drinking.* **12.** unfair or unjust: *rough luck.* **13.** harsh or grating to the ear. **14.** harsh to the taste. **15.** without refinement, luxury, etc. **16.** not polished or perfected in any detail; rudimentary; not elaborate: *rough workmanship; rough justice.* **17.** not prepared or dressed: *rough gemstones.* **18.** (of a guess, estimate, etc.) approximate. **19.** *Austral. informal.* (of a chance) not good. **20.** having the sound of *h;* aspirated. **21. rough on.** *Informal, chiefly Brit.* **a.** severe towards. **b.** unfortunate for (a person). **22. the rough side of one's tongue.** harsh words; a reprimand, rebuke, or verbal attack. ~*n.* **23.** rough ground. **24.** a sketch or preliminary piece of artwork. **25.** unfinished or crude state (esp. in the phrase **in the rough**). **26. the rough.** *Golf.* the part of the course bordering the fairways where the grass is untrimmed. **27.** the side of a tennis or squash racket on which the binding strings form an uneven line. **28.** *Informal.* a rough or violent person; thug. **29.** the unpleasant side of something (esp. in the phrase **take the rough with the smooth**). ~*adv.* **30.** in a rough manner; roughly. **31. sleep rough.** to spend the night in the open; be without a home or without shelter. ~*vb.* **32.** (*tr.*) to make rough; roughen. **33.** (*tr.;* foll. by *out, in,* etc.) to prepare (a sketch, report, piece of work, etc.) in preliminary form. **34. rough it.** *Informal.* to live without the usual comforts or conveniences of life. ~See also **rough up.** [Old English *rūh;* related to Old Norse *ruksa,* Middle Dutch *rūge, rūwe,* German *rauh*] —**'rough·ly** *adv.* —**'rough·ness** *n.*

rough·age ('rʌfɪdʒ) *n.* **1.** the coarse indigestible constituents of food or fodder, which provide bulk to the diet and aid digestion. **2.** any rough or coarse material.

rough-and-read·y *adj.* **1.** crude, unpolished, or hastily prepared, but sufficient for the purpose. **2.** (of a person) without formality or refinement; rudely vigorous. —**'rough-and-'read·i·ness** *n.*

rough-and-tum·ble *n.* **1.** a fight or scuffle without rules. ~*adj.* **2.** characterized by roughness, disorderliness, and disregard for rules or conventions.

rough breath·ing *n.* (in Greek) the sign (ʽ) placed over an initial vowel, indicating that (in ancient Greek) it was pronounced with an *h.* Compare **smooth breathing.**

rough·cast ('rʌfˌkɑ:st) *n.* **1.** a coarse plaster used to cover the surface of an external wall. **2.** any rough or preliminary form, model, etc. ~*adj.* **3.** covered with or denoting roughcast. ~*vb.* **-casts, -cast·ing, -cast. 4.** to apply roughcast to (a wall, etc.). **5.** to prepare in rough. **6.** (*tr.*) another word for **rough-hew.** —**'rough·ˌcast·er** *n.*

rough di·a·mond *n.* **1.** an unpolished diamond. **2.** an intrinsically trustworthy or good person with uncouth manners or dress.

rough-dry *adj.* **1.** (of clothes or linen) dried ready for pressing.

~*vb.* **-dries, -dry·ing, -dried. 2.** (*tr.*) to dry (clothes, etc.) without smoothing or pressing.

rough+en ('rʌfᵊn) *vb.* to make or become rough.

rough fish *n.* a fish that is neither a sport fish nor useful as food or bait for sport fish.

rough-hew *vb.* **-hews, -hew·ing, -hewed; -hewed** *or* **-hewn.** (*tr.*) **1.** to cut or hew (timber, stone, etc.) roughly without finishing the surface. **2.** Also: **roughcast.** to shape roughly or crudely.

rough+house ('rʌf,haʊs) *Slang.* ~*n.* **1.** rough, disorderly, or noisy behaviour. ~*vb.* **2.** to treat (someone) in a boisterous or rough way.

rough+ish ('rʌfɪʃ) *adj.* somewhat rough.

rough-leg·ged buz+zard *n.* a buzzard, *Buteo lagopus,* of Europe, Asia, and North America, having feathers covering its legs.

rough+neck ('rʌf,nɛk) *n. Slang.* **1.** a rough or violent person; thug. **2.** a worker in an oil-drilling operation.

rough pass+age *n.* **1.** a stormy sea journey. **2.** a difficult or testing time.

rough puff pas+try *n.* a rich flaky pastry made with butter and used for pie-crusts, flans, etc.

rough+rid·er ('rʌf,raɪdə) *n.* a rider of wild or unbroken horses.

rough+shod ('rʌf,ʃɒd) *adj.* **1.** (of a horse) shod with rough-bottomed shoes to prevent sliding. ~*adv.* **2. ride roughshod over.** to treat harshly and without consideration.

rough-spok·en *adj.* rude or uncouth in speech; blunt.

rough stuff *n. Informal.* violence.

rough up *vb.* (*tr., adv.*) **1.** to treat violently; beat up. **2.** to cause (feathers, hair, etc.) to stand up by rubbing against the grain.

rou+lade (ruː'lɑːd) *n.* **1.** a slice of meat rolled, esp. around a stuffing, and cooked. **2.** an elaborate run in vocal music. [C18: from French, literally: a rolling, from *rouler* to ROLL]

rou+leau ('ruːləʊ) *n., pl.* **+leaux** (-ləʊ, -ləʊz) *or* **+leaus. 1.** a roll of paper containing coins. **2.** (*often pl.*) a roll of ribbon. [C17: from French, from *role* ROLL]

Rou+lers (ruː'lɛəz; *French* ru'lɛrs) *n.* a city in NW Belgium, in West Flanders province. Pop.: 40 428 (1970). Flemish name: **Roeselare.**

rou+lette (ruː'lɛt) *n.* **1.** a gambling game in which a ball is dropped onto a spinning horizontal wheel divided into 37 or 38 coloured and numbered slots, with players betting on the slot into which the ball will fall. **2.** a toothed wheel for making a line of perforations. **3.** a curve generated by a point on one curve rolling on another. ~*vb.* (*tr.*) **4.** to use a roulette on (something), as in engraving, making stationery, etc. [C18: from French, from *rouelle* a little wheel, from *roue* a wheel, from Latin *rota*]

Rou+ma+ni·a (ruː'meɪnɪə) *n.* a variant spelling of **Rumania.** —**Rou+'ma+ni·an** *adj., n.*

Rou+me+li·a (ruː'miːlɪə) *n.* a variant spelling of **Rumelia.**

round (raʊnd) *adj.* **1.** having a flat circular shape, as a disc or hoop. **2.** having the shape of a sphere or ball. **3.** curved; not angular. **4.** involving or using circular motion. **5.** (*prenominal*) complete; entire: *a round dozen.* **6.** *Maths.* **a.** forming or expressed by an integer or whole number, with no fraction. **b.** expressed to the nearest ten, hundred, or thousand: *in round figures.* **7.** (of a sum of money) considerable; ample. **8.** fully depicted or developed, as a character in a book. **9.** (of sound) full and sonorous. **10.** (of pace) brisk; lively. **11.** (*prenominal*) (of speech) candid; straightforward; unmodified: *a round assertion.* **12.** (of a vowel) pronounced with rounded lips. ~*n.* **13.** a round shape or object. **14. in the round. a.** in full detail. **b.** *Theatre.* with the audience all round the stage. **15.** a session, as of a negotiation: *a round of talks.* **16.** a series, cycle, or sequence: *a giddy round of parties.* **17. the daily round.** the usual activities of one's day. **18.** a stage of a competition: *he was eliminated in the first round.* **19.** (*often pl.*) a series of calls, esp. in a set order: *a doctor's rounds; a milkman's round.* **20.** a playing of all the holes on a golf course. **21.** a single turn of play by each player, as in a card game. **22.** one of a number of periods constituting a boxing, wrestling, or other match, each usually lasting three minutes. **23.** *Archery.* a specified number of arrows shot from a specified distance. **24.** a single discharge by a number of guns or a single gun. **25.** a bullet, blank cartridge, or other charge of ammunition. **26.** a number of drinks bought at one time for a group of people. **27.** a single slice of bread or toast or a single sandwich. **28.** a general outburst of applause, cheering, etc. **29.** movement in a circle or around an axis. **30.** *Music.* a partsong in which the voices follow each other at equal intervals at the same pitch. **31.** a sequence of bells rung in order of treble to tenor. Compare **change** (sense 29). **32.** a dance in which the dancers move in a circle. **33.** a cut of beef from the thigh between the rump and the shank. **34. go** *or* **make the rounds. a.** to go from place to place, as in making deliveries or social calls. **b.** (of information, rumour, etc.) to be passed around, so as to be generally known. ~*prep., adv.* **35.** a less formal word for **around. 36. all year round.** throughout the year; in every month. ~*vb.* **37.** to make or become round. **38.** (*tr.*) to encircle; surround. **39.** to move or cause to move with circular motion: *to round a bend.* **40.** (*tr.*) **a.** to pronounce (a speech sound) with rounded lips. **b.** to purse (the lips). ~See also **round down, round off, round on, round out, roundup.** [C13: from Old French *ront,* from Latin *rotundus* round, from *rota* a wheel] —**'round+ness** *n.*

Usage. See **around.**

round+a·bout ('raʊndə,baʊt) *n.* **1.** *Brit.* a revolving circular platform provided with wooden animals, seats, etc., on which people ride for amusement; merry-go-round. **2.** a road junction in which traffic streams circulate around a central island. U.S. name: **traffic circle.** ~*adj.* **3.** indirect or circuitous; devious. ~*adv., prep.* **round about. 4.** on all sides: *spectators standing round about.* **5.** approximately: *at round about 5 o'clock.*

round and round *adv., prep.* following a circuitous or circular course for a comparatively long time, esp. vainly.

round an+gle *n.* another name for **perigon.**

round-arm *adj., adv. Cricket.* denoting or using bowling with the arm held more or less horizontal.

round clam *n.* another name for the **quahog.**

round dance *n.* **1.** a dance in which the dancers form a circle. **2.** a ballroom dance, such as the waltz, in which couples revolve.

round down *vb.* (*tr., adv.*) to lower (a number) to the nearest whole number or ten, hundred, or thousand below it. Compare **round up.**

round+ed ('raʊndɪd) *adj.* **1.** round or curved. **2.** having been made round or curved. **3.** full, mature, or complete. **4.** (of the lips) pursed, as in pronouncing the sound (uː). **5.** (of a speech sound) articulated with rounded lips. —**'round+ed+ly** *adv.* —**'round+ed+ness** *n.*

roun+del ('raʊndᵊl) *n.* **1.** a form of rondeau consisting of three stanzas each of three lines with a refrain after the first and the third. **2.** a circular mark of red, white, and blue on British military aircraft. **3.** a small ornamental circular window, panel, medallion, plate, disc, etc. **4.** a round plate of armour used to protect the armpit. **5.** *Heraldry.* a charge in the shape of a circle. **6.** another word for **roundelay.** [C13: from Old French *rondel* a little circle; see RONDEL]

roun+de+lay ('raʊndɪ,leɪ) *n.* **1.** Also called: **roundel.** a slow medieval dance performed in a circle. **2.** a song in which a line or phrase is repeated as a refrain. [C16: from Old French *rondelet* a little rondel, from *rondel;* also influenced by LAY[4]]

round+er ('raʊndə) *n.* **1.** a run round all four bases after one hit in rounders. **2.** a tool or machine for rounding edges or surfaces.

round+ers ('raʊndəz) *n. Brit.* a ball game resembling baseball, in which players run between bases after hitting the ball, scoring a **rounder** if they run round all four before the ball is retrieved.

round hand *n.* a style of handwriting with large rounded curves. Compare **italic, copperplate** (sense 3).

Round+head ('raʊnd,hɛd) *n. English history.* a supporter of Parliament against Charles I during the Civil War. Compare **Cavalier.** [referring to their short-cut hair]

round+house ('raʊnd,haʊs) *n.* **1.** a circular building in which railway locomotives are serviced or housed, radial tracks being fed by a central turntable. **2.** *Boxing slang.* **a.** a swinging punch or style of punching. **b.** (*as modifier*): *a roundhouse style.* **3.** *Pinochle, U.S.* a meld of all four kings and queens. **4.** an obsolete word for **jail. 5.** *Obsolete.* a cabin on the quarter-deck of a sailing ship.

round+ish ('raʊndɪʃ) *adj.* somewhat round.

round+let ('raʊndlɪt) *n. Literary.* a small circle. [C14: from Old French *rondelet,* from Old French RONDEL]

round+ly ('raʊndlɪ) *adv.* **1.** frankly, bluntly, or thoroughly: *to be roundly criticized.* **2.** in a round manner or so as to be round.

round off (*tr., adv.*) **1.** (often foll. by *with*) to bring to a satisfactory conclusion; complete, esp. agreeably: *we rounded off the evening with a brandy.* **2.** to make round or less jagged.

round on *vb.* (*intr., prep.*) to attack or reply to (someone) with sudden irritation or anger.

round out *vb.* (*tr., adv.*) **1.** to make or become bigger or plumper; fill out, esp. so as to be symmetrical. **2.** to round up (a number).

round rob+in *n.* **1.** a letter, esp. a petition or protest, having the signatures in a circle in order to disguise the order of signing. **2.** any letter or petition signed by a number of people. **3.** *U.S.* a tournament, as in a competitive game or sport, in which each player plays against every other player.

round-shoul·dered *adj.* denoting a faulty posture characterized by drooping shoulders and a slight forward bending of the back.

rounds+man ('raʊndzmən) *n., pl.* **+men.** *Brit.* a person who makes rounds, as for inspection or to deliver goods.

round ta+ble *n.* **a.** a meeting of parties or people on equal terms for discussion. **b.** (*as modifier*): *a round-table conference.*

Round Ta+ble *n.* **the. 1.** (in Arthurian legend) the table of King Arthur, shaped so that his knights could sit around it without any having precedence. **2.** Arthur and his knights collectively. **3.** one of an organization of clubs of young business and professional men who meet in order to further social and business activities and charitable work.

round-the-clock *adj.* (*or as adv.* **round the clock**) throughout the day and night.

round top *n.* a platform round the masthead of a sailing ship.

round trip *n.* a trip to a place and back again, esp. returning by a different route.

round-trip tick+et *n.* the usual U.S. word for **return ticket.**

round+up ('raʊnd,ʌp) *n.* **1.** the act of gathering together livestock, esp. cattle, so that they may be branded, counted, or sold. **2.** *Informal.* a collection of suspects or criminals by the police, esp. in a raid. **3.** *Informal.* any similar act of collecting or bringing together: *a roundup of today's news.* ~*vb.* **round up.** (*tr., adv.*) **4.** to gather (animals, suspects, etc.) together: *to round ponies up.* **5.** to raise (a number) to the nearest whole number or ten, hundred, or thousand above it. Compare **round down.**

round+worm ('raʊndˌwɜːm) *n.* any nematode worm, esp. *Ascaris lumbricoides*, a common intestinal parasite of man and pigs.

roup^{1} (ruːp) *n. Vet. science.* any of various chronic respiratory diseases of birds, esp. poultry. [C16: of unknown origin] —'**roup·y** *adj.*

roup^{2} (rəʊp) *Scot. and northern Brit. dialect.* ~*vb.* (*tr.*) **1.** to sell by auction. ~*n.* **2.** an auction. [C16 (originally: to shout): of Scandinavian origin; compare Icelandic *raupa* to boast]

rouse^{1} (raʊz) *vb.* **1.** to bring (oneself or another person) out of sleep, unconsciousness, etc., or (of a person) to come to consciousness in this way. **2.** (*tr.*) to provoke or stir: *to rouse someone's anger.* **3. rouse oneself.** to become active or energetic. **4.** *Hunting.* to start or cause to start from cover: *to rouse game birds.* **5.** (*intr.*) *Falconry.* (of hawks) to ruffle the feathers and cause them to stand briefly on end (a sign of contentment). **6.** (*intr.*; foll. by *on*) *Austral.* to speak scoldingly or rebukingly (to). [C15 (in sense 5): origin obscure] —**rous+ed·ness** ('raʊzɪdnɪs) *n.* —'**rous+er** *n.*

rouse^{2} (raʊz) *n. Archaic.* **1.** an alcoholic drink, esp. a full measure. **2.** another word for **carousal.** [C17: probably a variant of CAROUSE (as in the phrase *drink a rouse*, erroneous for *drink carouse*); compare Danish *drikke en rus* to become drunk, German *Rausch* drunkenness]

rouse+a·bout ('raʊzəˌbaʊt) *n. Austral.* an unskilled labourer.

rous+ing ('raʊzɪŋ) *adj.* tending to rouse or excite; lively, brisk, or vigorous: *a rousing chorus.* —'**rous+ing+ly** *adv.*

Rous·seau (*French* ru'so) *n.* **1. Hen·ri** (ɑ̃'ri), called *le Douanier.* 1844–1910, French painter, who created bold dreamlike pictures, often of exotic landscapes in a naive style. Among his works are *Sleeping Gypsy* (1897) and *Jungle with a Lion* (1904–06). He also worked as a customs official. **2. Jean Jacques** (ʒɑ̃ 'ʒak). 1712–78, French philosopher and writer, born in Switzerland, who strongly influenced the theories of the French Revolution and the romantics. Many of his ideas spring from his belief in the natural goodness of man, whom he felt was warped by society. His works include *Du contrat social* (1762), *Émile* (1762), and his *Confessions* (1782). **3. Thé·o·dore** (teɔ'dɔr). 1812–67, French landscape painter: leader of the Barbizon school.

Rous+sil+lon (*French* rusi'jɔ̃) *n.* a former province of S France: united with Aragon in 1172; passed to the French crown in 1659; now forms part of the region of Languedoc-Roussillon.

roust (raʊst) *vb.* (*tr.*; often foll. by *out*) to rout or stir, as out of bed. [C17: perhaps an alteration of ROUSE^{1}]

roust+a·bout ('raʊstəˌbaʊt) *n.* **1.** *Chiefly U.S.* an unskilled labourer. **2.** *Austral.* a hand hired to work in the woolsheds at sheep shearing, though not himself a shearer.

rout^{1} (raʊt) *n.* **1.** an overwhelming and disorderly defeat. **2.** a noisy rabble. **3.** *Law.* a group of three or more people proceeding to commit an illegal act. **4.** *Archaic.* a large party or social gathering. ~*vb.* **5.** (*tr.*) to defeat and cause to flee in confusion. [C13: from Anglo-Norman *rute*, from Old French: disorderly band, from Latin *ruptus* broken, from *rumpere* to burst; see ROUTE]

rout^{2} (raʊt) *vb.* **1.** to dig over or turn up (something), esp. (of an animal) with the snout; root. **2.** (*tr.*; usually foll. by *out* or *up*) to get or find by searching. **3.** (*tr.*; usually foll. by *out*) to force or drive out: *they routed him out of bed at midnight.* **4.** (*tr.*; often foll. by *out*) to hollow or gouge out. **5.** (*intr.*) to search, poke, or rummage. [C16: variant of ROOT^{2}]

route (ruːt) *n.* **1.** the choice of roads taken to get to a place. **2.** a regular journey travelled. **3.** *Med.* the means (mouth or injection) by which a drug or agent is administered or enters the body: *oral route.* ~*vb.* (*tr.*) **4.** to plan the route of; send by a particular route. [C13: from Old French *rute*, from Vulgar Latin *rupta via* (unattested), literally: a broken (established) way, from Latin *ruptus* broken, from *rumpere* to break, burst]

route+march ('ruːtˌmɑːtʃ) *n.* **1.** *Military.* a long training march. **2.** *Informal.* any long exhausting walk. ~*vb.* **3.** to go or send on a routemarch.

rout+er ('raʊtə) *n.* any of various tools or machines for hollowing out, cutting grooves, etc.

rou+tine (ruː'tiːn) *n.* **1.** a usual or regular method of procedure, esp. one that is unvarying. **2.** *Computer technol.* a program or part of a program performing a specific function: *an input routine; an output routine.* **3.** a set sequence of dance steps. **4.** *Informal.* a hackneyed or insincere speech. ~*adj.* **5.** of, relating to, or characteristic of routine. [C17: from Old French, from *route* a customary way, ROUTE] —**rou+'tine+ly** *adv.* —**rou+'tin+ism** *n.* —**rou+'tin+ist** *n.*

roux (ruː) *n.* a mixture of equal amounts of fat and flour, heated, blended, and used as a basis for sauces. [French: brownish, from Latin *russus* RUSSET]

rove^{1} (rəʊv) *vb.* **1.** to wander about (a place) with no fixed direction; roam. **2.** (*intr.*) (of the eyes) to look around; wander. **3.** (*intr.*) *Informal.* (esp. of a man) to be sexually unfaithful; have affairs. **4.** (*intr.*) *Australian Rules football.* to play as a rover. ~*n.* **5.** the act of roving. [C15 *roven* (in archery) to shoot at a target chosen at random (C16: to wander, stray), from Scandinavian; compare Icelandic *rāfa* to wander]

rove^{2} (rəʊv) *vb.* **1.** (*tr.*) to pull out and twist (fibres of wool, cotton, etc.) lightly, as before spinning or in carding. ~*n.* **2.** wool, cotton, etc., thus prepared.

rove^{3} (rəʊv) *n.* a metal plate through which a rivet is passed and then clenched over. [C15: from Scandinavian; compare Icelandic *ro*]

rove^{4} (rəʊv) *vb.* a past tense or past participle of **reeve**^{2}.

rove bee+tle *n.* any beetle of the family *Staphylinidae*, characterized by very short elytra and an elongated body: typically they are of carnivorous or scavenging habits.

rove-o·ver *adj. Prosody.* (in sprung rhythm) denoting a metrical foot left incomplete at the end of one line and completed in the next.

rov+er^{1} ('rəʊvə) *n.* **1.** a person who roves; wanderer. **2.** *Archery.* a mark selected at random for use as a target. **3.** *Croquet.* a ball that has been driven through all the hoops but has not yet hit the winning peg. **4.** *Australian Rules football.* one of the players in the ruck. [C15: from ROVE^{1}]

rov+er^{2} ('rəʊvə) *n.* a pirate or pirate ship. [C14: probably from Middle Dutch or Middle Low German, from *roven* to rob]

rov+er^{3} ('rəʊvə) *n.* a machine for roving wool, cotton, etc., or a person who operates such a machine. [C18: from ROVE^{2}]

Rov+er *or* **Rov+er Scout** ('rəʊvə) *n. Brit.* the former name for **Venture Scout.**

rov+ing com+mis+sion *n.* authority or power given in a general area, without precisely defined terms of reference.

row^{1} (rəʊ) *n.* **1.** an arrangement of persons or things in a line: *a row of chairs.* **2. a.** *Chiefly Brit.* a street, esp. a narrow one lined with identical houses. **b.** (*cap. when part of a street name*): *Church Row.* **3.** a line of seats, as in a cinema, theatre, etc. **4.** *Maths.* a horizontal linear arrangement of numbers, quantities, or terms, esp. in a determinant or matrix. **5.** a horizontal rank of squares on a chessboard or draughtsboard. **6. in a row.** in succession; one after the other: *he won two gold medals in a row.* **7. a hard row to hoe.** a difficult task or assignment. [Old English *rāw*, *rǣw*; related to Old High German *rīga* line, Lithuanian *raiwe* strip]

row^{2} (rəʊ) *vb.* **1.** to propel (a boat) by using oars. **2.** (*tr.*) to carry (people, goods, etc.) in a rowing boat. **3.** to be propelled by means of (oars or oarsmen). **4.** (*intr.*) to take part in the racing of rowing boats as a sport, esp. in eights, in which each member of the crew pulls one oar. Compare **scull** (sense 6). **5.** (*tr.*) to race against in a boat propelled by oars: *Oxford row Cambridge every year.* ~*n.* **6.** an act, instance, period, or distance of rowing. **7.** an excursion in a rowing boat. [Old English *rōwan*; related to Middle Dutch *roien*, Middle High German *rüejen*, Old Norse *rōa*, Latin *rēmus* oar] —'**row+er** *n.*

row^{3} (raʊ) *Informal.* ~*n.* **1.** a noisy quarrel or dispute. **2.** a noisy disturbance; commotion: *we couldn't hear the music for the row next door.* **3.** *Archaic.* a reprimand. ~*vb.* **4.** (*intr.*; often foll. by *with*) to quarrel noisily. **5.** (*tr.*) *Archaic.* to reprimand. [C18: origin unknown]

ro+wan ('rəʊən, 'raʊ-) *n.* another name for the (European) **mountain ash.** [C16: from Scandinavian; compare Norwegian *rogn, raun*, Old Norse *reynir*]

row+boat ('rəʊˌbəʊt) *n.* the usual U.S. word for **rowing boat.**

row+dy ('raʊdɪ) *adj.* **+di+er, +di+est. 1.** tending to create noisy disturbances; rough, loud, or disorderly: *a rowdy gang of football supporters.* ~*n., pl.* **+dies. 2.** a person who behaves in a rough disorderly fashion. [C19: originally U.S. slang, perhaps related to ROW^{3}] —'**row+di+ly** *adv.* —'**row+di+ness** *or* '**row+dy+ism** *n.*

Rowe (rəʊ) *n.* **Nich·o·las.** 1674–1718, English dramatist; poet laureate (1715–18). His plays include *Tamerlane* (1702), *The Fair Penitent* (1703), and *Jane Shore* (1714).

row+el ('raʊəl) *n.* **1.** a small spiked wheel attached to a spur. **2.** *Vet. science.* a piece of leather or other material inserted under the skin of a horse to cause a discharge. ~*vb.* **+els, +el+ling, +elled** *or U.S.* **+els, +el+ing, +eled.** (*tr.*) **3.** to goad (a horse) using a rowel. **4.** *Vet. science.* to insert a rowel in (the skin of a horse) to cause a discharge. [C14: from Old French *roel* a little wheel, from *roe* a wheel, from Latin *rota*]

row+en ('raʊən) *n.* another word for **aftermath** (sense 2). [C14 *reywayn*, corresponding to Old French *regaïn*, from RE- + *gaïn* rowen, from *gaignier* to till, earn; see GAIN^{1}]

row house (rəʊ) *n.* the U.S. term for **terraced house.**

row+ing boat ('rəʊɪŋ) *n. Chiefly Brit.* a small pleasure boat propelled by one or more pairs of oars. Usual U.S. word: **rowboat.**

row+ing ma+chine *n.* a device with oars and a sliding seat resembling a sculling boat, used to provide exercise.

Row·land·son ('rəʊləndsən) *n.* **Thom·as.** 1756–1827, English caricaturist, noted for the vigour of his attack on sordid aspects of contemporary society and on statesmen such as Napoleon.

row+lock ('rɒlək) *n.* a swivelling device attached to the gunwale of a boat that holds an oar in place and acts as a fulcrum during rowing. Usual U.S. word: **oarlock.**

row o·ver *vb.* (*intr., adv.*) **1.** to win a rowing race unopposed, by rowing the course. ~*n.* **row+o·ver. 2.** the act of doing this.

Rox·as y A·cu·ña (*Spanish* 'roxas i a'kuɲa) *n.* **Ma·nuel** (ma'nwel). 1892–1948, Philippine statesman; first president of the Republic of the Philippines (1946–48).

Rox+burgh ('rɒksbərə, -brə) *or* **Rox+burgh+shire** *n.* (until 1975) a county of SE Scotland, now part of the Borders region.

roy+al ('rɔɪəl) *adj.* **1.** of, relating to, or befitting a king, queen, or other monarch; regal. **2.** (*prenominal; often cap.*) established, chartered by, under the patronage or in the service of royalty: *the Royal Society of St. George.* **3.** being a member of a royal family. **4.** above the usual or normal in standing, size, quality, etc. **5.** *Informal.* unusually good or impressive; first-rate. **6.** *Nautical.* just above the topgallant (in the phrase **royal mast**). ~*n.* **7.** *Nautical.* a sail set next above the topgallant, on a royal mast. **8.** a size of printing paper, 20 by 25 inches. **9.** Also called: **small royal.** *Chiefly Brit.* a size of writing paper, 19 by 24 inches. **10.** any of various book sizes, esp. 6¼ by 10 inches (**royal octavo**), 6¾ by 10¼ inches (**super royal octavo**), and (chiefly Brit.) 10 by 12½ inches (**royal quarto**) and 10¼ by 13½ inches (**super royal quarto**). 11. Also: **royal stag.** a stag with antlers having 12 or more branches. [C14: from Old French *roial,* from Latin *rēgālis,* fit for a king, from *rēx* king; compare REGAL] —'**roy+al+ly** *adv.*

Roy+al A·cad+e·my *n.* a society founded by George III in 1768 to foster a national school of painting, sculpture, and design in England. Full name: **Royal Academy of Arts.**

Roy+al Air Force *n.* the airforce of Great Britain. Abbrevs.: **RAF, R.A.F.**

Roy+al Air Force List *n. Brit.* an official list of all serving commissioned officers of the RAF and reserve officers liable for recall.

roy+al as+sent *n. Brit.* the formal signing of an act of Parliament by the sovereign, by which it becomes law.

roy+al blue *n., adj.* **a.** a deep blue colour. **b.** (*as adj.*): *a royal-blue carpet.*

Roy+al Ca+na+di·an Mount+ed Po+lice *n.* the federal police force of Canada. Abbrev.: **R.C.M.P.**

Roy+al Com+mis+sion *n.* (in Britain) a body set up by the monarch on the recommendation of the prime minister to gather information about the operation of existing laws or to investigate any social, educational, or other matter. The commission has prescribed terms of reference and reports to the government on how any change might be achieved.

roy+al duke *n.* a duke who is also a royal prince, being a member of the royal family.

Roy+al En+gin+eers *pl. n.* a branch of the British army that undertakes the building of fortifications, mines, bridges, and other engineering works.

roy+al fern *n.* a fern, *Osmunda regalis,* of damp regions, having large fronds up to 2 metres (7 feet) in height, some of which are modified for bearing spores: family *Osmundaceae.*

roy+al flush *n. Poker.* a hand made up of the five top honours of a suit.

Roy+al High+ness *n.* a title of honour used in addressing or referring to a member of a royal family.

roy+al ic+ing *n. Brit.* a hard white icing made from egg whites and icing sugar, used for coating and decorating cakes, esp. fruit cakes.

Roy+al In+sti+tu+tion *n.* a British society founded in 1799 for the dissemination of scientific knowledge.

roy+al+ist ('rɔɪəlɪst) *n.* **1.** a supporter of a monarch or monarchy, esp. a supporter of the Stuarts during the English Civil War. **2.** *Informal.* an extreme reactionary or conservative: *an economic royalist.* ~*adj.* also **roy+al+is+tic. 3.** of, characteristic of, or relating to royalists. —'**roy+al+ism** *n.*

roy+al jel+ly *n.* a substance secreted by the pharyngeal glands of worker bees and fed to all larvae when very young and to larvae destined to become queens throughout their development.

Roy+al Ma+rines *pl. n. Brit.* a corps of soldiers specially trained in amphibious warfare.

Roy+al Na+vy *n.* the navy of Great Britain. Abbrev.: **R.N.**

roy+al palm *n.* any of several palm trees of the genus *Roystonea,* esp. *R. regia,* of tropical America, having a tall trunk with a tuft of feathery pinnate leaves.

roy+al poin+ci·a+na *n.* a caesalpiniaceous tree, *Delonix regia,* that is native to Madagascar but widely cultivated elsewhere, having clusters of large scarlet flowers and long pods. Also called: **flamboyant.**

roy+al pur+ple *n., adj.* **a.** a deep reddish-purple colour, sometimes approaching a strong violet. **b.** (*as adj.*): *a royal-purple dress.*

roy+al road *n.* an easy or direct way of achieving a desired end: *the royal road to success.*

Roy+al So+ci+e·ty *n.* an association founded in England by Charles II in 1660 to promote research in the sciences.

roy+al stand+ard *n.* a flag bearing the arms of the British sovereign, flown only when she (or he) is present.

roy+al ten+nis *n.* another name for **real tennis.**

roy+al+ty ('rɔɪəltɪ) *n., pl.* **+ties. 1.** the rank, power, or position of a king or queen. **2. a.** royal persons collectively. **b.** one who belongs to the royal family. **3.** any quality characteristic of a monarch; kingliness or regal dignity. **4.** a percentage of the revenue from the sale of a book, performance of a theatrical work, use of a patented invention or of land, etc., paid to the author, inventor, or proprietor.

Roy+al Vic+to+ri·an Or+der *n. Brit.* an order of chivalry founded by Queen Victoria in 1896, membership of which is conferred for special services to the sovereign.

roy+al war+rant *n.* an authorization to a tradesman to supply goods to a royal household.

Roy+al Worces+ter *n.* Worcester china made after 1862.

Royce (rɔɪs) *n.* **Jo·si·ah.** 1855–1916, U.S. philosopher of monistic idealism. In his ethical studies he emphasized the need for individual loyalty to the world community.

roz+zer ('rɒzə) *n. Cockney slang.* a policeman. [C19: of unknown origin]

RP *abbrev. for:* **1.** Received Pronunciation. **2.** Reformed Presbyterian. **3.** Regius Professor.

R.P.C. *abbrev. for* Royal Pioneer Corps.

r.p.m. *abbrev. for:* **1.** revolutions per minute. **2.** resale price maintenance.

r.p.s. *abbrev. for* revolutions per second.

R.P.S. (in Britain) *abbrev. for* Royal Photographic Society.

rpt. *abbrev. for* report.

R.Q. *abbrev. for* respiratory quotient.

R.R. *abbrev. for* Right Reverend.

-rrha·gi·a *n. combining form.* (in pathology) an abnormal discharge or flow: *menorrhagia.* [from Greek *-rrhagia* a bursting forth, from *rhēgnunai* to burst, break]

-rrhoe·a *or esp. U.S.* **-rrhe·a** *n. combining form.* (in pathology) a discharge or flow: *diarrhoea.* [from New Latin, from Greek *-rrhoia,* from *rhoia* a flowing, from *rhein* to flow]

r-RNA *abbrev. for* ribosomal RNA.

Rs. *abbrev. for* rupees.

R.S. (in Britain) *abbrev. for* Royal Society.

R.S.A. *abbrev. for:* **1.** Republic of South Africa. **2.** Royal Scottish Academy. **3.** Royal Scottish Academician. **4.** Royal Society of Arts.

RSFSR *abbrev. for* Russian Soviet Federated Socialist Republic.

R.S.G.B. *abbrev. for* Radio Society of Great Britain (amateur radio operators).

RSJ *abbrev. for* rolled-steel joist.

R.S.L. *abbrev. for:* **1.** Royal Society of Literature. **2.** (in Australia) Returned Services League.

R.S.M. *abbrev. for:* **1.** regimental sergeant major. **2.** Royal School of Mines. **3.** Royal Society of Medicine. ~**4.** *international car registration for* (Republic of) San Marino.

R.S.P.B. (in Britain) *abbrev. for* Royal Society for the Protection of Birds.

R.S.P.C.A. (in Britain) *abbrev. for* Royal Society for the Prevention of Cruelty to Animals.

RSR *international car registration for* Rhodesia (formerly Southern Rhodesia).

R.S.V. *abbrev. for* Revised Standard Version (of the Bible).

R.S.V.P. *abbrev. for* répondez s'il vous plaît. [French: please reply]

rt. *abbrev. for* right.

R.T. *abbrev. for* radio telegraphy *or* radio telephony.

R.T.C. (in India) *abbrev. for:* **1.** Road Transport Corporation. **2.** Round Table Conference.

Rt. Hon. *abbrev. for* Right Honourable.

RTL *Electronics. abbrev. for* Resistor Transistor Logic: a stage in the development of electronic logic circuits.

R.T.R. *abbrev. for* Royal Tank Regiment.

Rt. Rev. *abbrev. for* Right Reverend.

RTT *or* **RTTY** *abbrev. for* radioteletype.

Ru *the chemical symbol for* ruthenium.

RU *international car registration for* Burundi.

R.U. *abbrev. for* Rugby Union.

Ru·an·da-U·run·di (rʊ'ændə ʊ'rʊndɪ) *n.* a former territory of central Africa: part of German East Africa from 1890; a League of Nations mandate under Belgian administration from 1919; a United Nations trusteeship from 1946; divided into the independent states of Rwanda and Burundi in 1962.

rub (rʌb) *vb.* **rubs, rub+bing, rubbed. 1.** to apply pressure and friction to (something) with a circular or backward and forward motion. **2.** to move (something) with pressure along, over, or against (a surface). **3.** to chafe or fray. **4.** (*tr.*) to bring into a certain condition by rubbing: *rub it clean.* **5.** (*tr.*) to spread with pressure, esp. in order to cause to be absorbed: *she rubbed ointment into his back.* **6.** (foll. by *off, out, away,* etc.) to remove or be removed by rubbing: *the mark would not rub off the chair.* **7.** *Bowls.* (of a bowl) to be slowed or deflected by an uneven patch on the green. **8.** (*tr.;* often foll. by *together*) to move against each other with pressure and friction (esp. in the phrases **rub one's hands,** often a sign of glee, keen anticipation, or satisfaction, and **rub noses,** a greeting among Eskimos). **9. rub (someone's) nose in (something).** to harp insistently on (something distasteful or distressing to a person, esp. a failing or fault of his). **10. rub (up) the wrong way.** to arouse anger (in); annoy. **11. rub shoulders (or elbows) with.** to mix with socially. ~*n.* **12.** the act of rubbing. **13.** (preceded by *the*) an obstacle or difficulty (esp. in the phrase **there's the rub**). **14.** something that hurts the feelings or annoys; cut; rebuke. **15.** *Bowls.* an uneven patch in the green. **16.** any roughness or unevenness of surface. ~See also **rub along, rub down, rub in, rub off, rub out, rub up.** [C15: perhaps from Low German *rubben,* of obscure origin]

ru+bái+yát ('ruːbaɪˌjæt) *n. Prosody.* (in Persian poetry) a verse form consisting of four-line stanzas. See also **Omar Khayyam.** [from Arabic *rubā'īyah,* from *rubā'īy* consisting of four elements]

Rub' al Kha+li ('rʊb æl 'kɑːlɪ) *n.* a desert in S Arabia, extending southeast from Nejd to Hadramaut and northeast from Yemen to the United Arab Emirates. Area: about 777 000 sq. km (300 000 sq. miles). English names: **Great Sandy Desert, Empty Quarter.** Also called: **Ar Rimal, Dahna.**

rub a·long *vb.* (*intr., adv.*) *Brit.* **1.** to continue in spite of difficulties. **2.** to maintain an amicable relationship; not quarrel.

ru+ba+to (ruː'bɑːtəʊ) *Music.* ~*n., pl.* **+tos. 1.** flexibility of tempo in performance. ~*adj, adv.* **2.** to be played with a flexible tempo. [C19: from the Italian phrase *tempo rubato,* literally: stolen time, from *rubare* to ROB]

rub+ber[1] ('rʌbə) *n.* **1.** Also called: **India rubber, gum elastic, caoutchouc.** a cream to dark brown elastic material obtained by coagulating and drying the latex from certain plants, esp. the tree *Hevea brasiliensis.* **2.** any of a large variety of elastomers produced by improving the properties of natural rubber or by synthetic means. **3.** *Chiefly Brit.* a piece of rubber or felt used for erasing something written, typed, etc.; eraser. **4.** a coarse file. **5.** a cloth, pad, etc., used for polishing or buffing. **6.** a person who rubs something in order to smooth, polish, or massage. **7.** (*often pl.*) *Chiefly U.S.* a rubberized waterproof article, such as a mackintosh or overshoe. **8.** *Slang.* a male contraceptive; condom. **9.** (*modifier*) made of or producing rubber: *a rubber ball; a rubber factory.* [C17: from RUB + -ER[1]; the tree was so named because its product was used for rubbing out writing]

rub+ber[2] ('rʌbə) *n.* **1.** *Bridge, whist, etc.* **a.** a match of three games. **b.** the deal that wins such a match. **2.** a series of matches or games in any of various sports. [C16: origin unknown]

rub+ber band *n.* a continuous loop of thin rubber, used to hold papers, etc., together. Also called: **elastic band.**

rub+ber ce+ment *n.* any of a number of adhesives made by dissolving rubber in a solvent such as benzene.

rub+ber cheque *n. Facetious.* a cheque that bounces.

rub+ber goods *pl. n. Euphemistic.* contraceptives; condoms.

rub+ber+ize *or* **rub+ber+ise** ('rʌbəˌraɪz) *vb.* (*tr.*) to coat or impregnate with rubber.

rub·ber+neck ('rʌbəˌnɛk) *Slang.* ~*n.* **1.** a person who stares or gapes inquisitively, esp. in a naive or foolish manner. **2.** a sightseer or tourist. ~*vb.* **3.** (*intr.*) to stare in a naive or foolish manner.

rub+ber plant *n.* **1.** a moraceous plant, *Ficus elastica,* with glossy leathery leaves: grows as a tall tree in India and Malaya but is cultivated as a house plant in Europe and North America. **2.** any of several tropical trees, the sap of which yields crude rubber. See also **rubber tree.**

rub+ber shoes *pl. n.* sneakers, gymshoes, or tennis shoes.

rub+ber stamp *n.* **1.** a device used for imprinting dates or commonly used phrases on forms, invoices, etc. **2.** automatic authorization of a payment, proposal, etc., without challenge. **3.** a person who makes such automatic authorizations; a cipher or person of little account. ~*vb.* **rub·ber-stamp.** (*tr.*) **4.** to imprint (forms, invoices, etc.) with a rubber stamp. **5.** *Informal.* to approve automatically.

rub+ber tree *n.* a tropical American euphorbiaceous tree, *Hevea brasiliensis,* cultivated throughout the tropics, esp. in Malaya, for the latex of its stem, which is the major source of commercial rubber. See also **Pará rubber.**

rub+ber·y ('rʌbərɪ) *adj.* having the texture of or resembling rubber, esp. in flexibility or toughness.

rub+bing ('rʌbɪŋ) *n.* an impression taken of an incised or raised surface, such as a brass plate on a tomb, by laying paper over it and rubbing with wax, graphite, etc.

rub+bish ('rʌbɪʃ) *n.* **1.** worthless, useless, or unwanted matter. **2.** discarded or waste matter; refuse. **3.** foolish words or speech; nonsense. ~*vb.* **4.** (*tr.*) *Austral. informal.* to criticize; attack verbally. [C14 *robys,* of uncertain origin] —**'rub+bish·y** *adj.*

rub+ble ('rʌbᵊl) *n.* **1.** fragments of broken stones, bricks, etc. **2.** any fragmented solid material. **3.** *Quarrying.* the weathered surface layer of rock. **4.** Also called: **rubblework.** masonry constructed of broken pieces of rock, stone, etc. [C14 *robyl;* perhaps related to Middle English *rubben* to rub, or to RUBBISH] —**'rub+bly** *adj.*

Rub·bra ('rʌbrə) *n.* **(Charles) Ed·mund.** born 1901, English composer of works in a traditional idiom.

rub+by ('rʌbɪ) *n., pl.* **+bies.** *Canadian slang.* an old broken-down alcoholic. [origin unknown]

rub down *vb.* (*adv.*) **1.** to dry or clean (a horse, athlete, oneself, etc.) vigorously, esp. after exercise. **2.** to make or become smooth by rubbing. **3.** (*tr.*) to prepare (a surface) for painting by rubbing it with sandpaper. ~*n.* **rub+down. 4.** the act of rubbing down. **5.** the Hong Kong term for **dressing down.**

rube (ru:b) *n. U.S. slang.* an unsophisticated countryman. [C20: probably from the given name *Reuben*]

ru+be·fy ('ru:bɪˌfaɪ) *vb.* (*tr.*) to make red, esp. (of a counter-irritant) to make the skin go red. [C19: from Latin *rubefacere,* from *rubeus* red + *facere* to make] —**ru+be·fa+cient** (ˌru:bɪ'feɪʃənt) *adj., n.* —**ru+be·fac+tion** (ˌru:bɪ'fækʃən) *n.*

ru+bel+la (ru:'bɛlə) *n.* a mild contagious viral disease, somewhat similar to measles, characterized by cough, sore throat, skin rash, and occasionally vomiting. It can cause congenital defects if caught during the first three months of pregnancy. Also called: **German measles.** [C19: from New Latin, from Latin *rubellus* reddish, from *rubeus* red]

ru+bel+lite ('ru:bɪˌlaɪt, ru:'bɛl-) *n.* a red transparent variety of tourmaline, used as a gemstone. [C18: from Latin *rubellus* reddish]

Ru+bens ('ru:bɪnz) *n.* Sir **Pe·ter Paul.** 1577–1640, Flemish painter, regarded as the greatest exponent of the Baroque: appointed (1609) painter to Archduke Albert of Austria, who gave him many commissions, artistic and diplomatic. He was knighted by Charles I of England in 1629. His prolific output includes the triptych in Antwerp Cathedral, *Descent from the Cross* (1611–14), *The Rape of the Sabines* (1635), and his *Self-Portrait* (?1639).

ru+be·o+la (ru:'bi:ələ) *n.* technical name for **measles.** Compare **rubella.** [C17: from New Latin, from Latin *rubeus* reddish, from *ruber* red] —**ru+'be·o+lar** *adj.*

ru+bes+cent (ru:'bɛsᵊnt) *adj. Literary.* reddening; blushing. [C18: from Latin *rubescere* to grow red, from *ruber* red] —**ru+'bes+cence** *n.*

ru+bi·a+ceous (ˌru:bɪ'eɪʃəs) *adj.* of, relating to, or belonging to the *Rubiaceae,* a widely distributed family of trees, shrubs, and herbaceous plants that includes the coffee and cinchona trees, gardenia, madder, and bedstraws. [C19: from New Latin *Rubiaceae,* from Latin *rubia* madder, from *rubeus* red]

Ru+bi+con ('ru:bɪkən) *n.* **1.** a stream in N Italy: in ancient times the boundary between Italy and Cisalpine Gaul. By leading his army across it and marching on Rome in 49 B.C., Julius Caesar broke the law that a general might not lead an army out of the province to which he was posted and so committed himself to civil war with the senatorial party. **2.** (*sometimes not cap.*) a point of no return. **3.** a penalty in piquet by which the score of a player who fails to reach 100 points in six hands is added to his opponent's. **4. cross** (*or* **pass**) **the Rubicon.** to commit oneself irrevocably to some course of action.

ru+bi+cund ('ru:bɪkənd) *adj.* of a reddish colour; ruddy; rosy. [C16: from Latin *rubicundus,* from *rubēre* to be ruddy, from *ruber* red] —**ru+bi+cun+di·ty** (ˌru:bɪ'kʌndɪtɪ) *n.*

ru+bid+i·um (ru:'bɪdɪəm) *n.* a soft highly reactive radioactive element of the alkali metal group; the 16th most abundant element in the earth's crust (310 parts per million), occurring principally in pollucite, carnallite, and lepidolite. It is used in electronic valves, photocells, and special glass. Symbol: Rb; atomic no.: 37; atomic wt.: 85.47; half-life of ^{87}Rb: 5×10^{11} years; valency: 1, 2, 3, or 4; relative density: 1.53 (solid), 1.47 (liquid); melting pt.: 38.89°C; boiling pt.: 688°C. [C19: from New Latin, from Latin *rubidus* dark red, with reference to the two red lines in its spectrum] —**ru+'bid+ic** *adj.*

ru+bid·i·um-stron·ti+um dat+ing *n.* a technique for determining the age of minerals based on the occurrence in natural rubidium of a fixed amount of the radioisotope ^{87}Rb which decays to the stable strontium isotope ^{87}Sr with a half-life of 5×10^{11} years. Measurement of the ratio of these isotopes thus gives the age of a mineral, for ages of up to about 10^9 years.

ru+big·i+nous (ru:'bɪdʒɪnəs) *adj.* rust-coloured. [C17: from Latin *rūbīginōsus,* from *rūbīgō* rust, from *ruber* red]

rub in *vb.* (*tr., adv.*) **1.** to spread with pressure, esp. in order to cause to be absorbed. **2.** *Informal.* to harp on (something distasteful to a person, of which he does not wish to be reminded).

Ru·bin·stein ('ru:bɪnˌstaɪn) *n.* **1. An·ton Gri·go·re·vich** (an'tɔn gri'gɔrjɪvitʃ). 1829–94, Russian composer and pianist. **2. Ar·tur** ('artur). born 1886, U.S. pianist, born in Poland.

ru+bi+ous ('ru:bɪəs) *adj. Literary.* of the colour ruby; dark red.

ru+ble ('ru:bᵊl) *n.* a variant spelling of **rouble.**

rub off *vb.* **1.** to remove or be removed by rubbing. **2.** (*intr.;* often foll. by *on* or *onto*) to have an effect through close association or contact, esp. so as to make similar: *her crude manners have rubbed off on you.*

rub out *vb.* (*tr., adv.*) **1.** to remove or be removed with a rubber. **2.** *U.S. slang.* to murder. **3.** *Australian Rules football.* to suspend (a player).

ru+bric ('ru:brɪk) *n.* **1.** a title, heading, or initial letter in a book, manuscript, or section of a legal code, esp. one printed or painted in red ink or in some similarly distinguishing manner. **2.** a set of rules of conduct or procedure. **3.** a set of directions for the conduct of Christian church services, often printed in red in a prayerbook or missal. **4.** instructions to a candidate at the head of the examination paper. **5.** an obsolete name for **red ochre.** ~*adj.* **6.** written, printed, or marked in red. [C15 *rubrike* red ochre, red lettering, from Latin *rubrīca* (*terra*) red (earth), ruddle, from *ruber* red] —**'ru+bri+cal** *adj.* —**'ru+bri+cal+ly** *adv.*

ru+bri+cate ('ru:brɪˌkeɪt) *vb.* (*tr.*) **1.** to print (a book or manuscript) with red titles, headings, etc. **2.** to mark in red. **3.** to supply with or regulate by rubrics. [C16: from Latin *rubricāre* to colour red, from *rubrīca* red earth; see RUBRIC] —**ˌru+bri+'ca+tion** *n.* —**'ru+bri+ˌca+tor** *n.*

ru+bri+cian (ru:'brɪʃən) *n.* an authority on liturgical rubrics.

rub+stone ('rʌbˌstəʊn) *n.* a stone used for sharpening or smoothing, esp. a whetstone.

rub up *vb.* (*adv.*) *Chiefly Brit.* **1.** (when *intr.,* foll. by *on*) to refresh one's memory (of). **2.** (*tr.*) to smooth or polish.

ru·by ('ru:bɪ) *n., pl.* **·bies. 1.** a deep-red transparent precious variety of corundum: occurs naturally in Burma and Ceylon but is also synthesized. It is used as a gemstone, in lasers, and for bearings and rollers in watchmaking. Formula: Al_2O_3. **2. a.** the deep-red colour of a ruby. **b.** (*as adj.*): *ruby lips.* **3. a.** something resembling, made of, or containing a ruby. **b.** (*as modifier*): *ruby necklace.* **4.** (*modifier*) denoting a fortieth anniversary: *our ruby wedding.* **5.** (formerly) a size of printer's type approximately equal to 5½ point. [C14: from Old French *rubi,* from Latin *rubeus* reddish, from *ruber* red] —**'ru·by-ˌlike** *adj.*

ru·by sil+ver *n.* another name for **proustite** or **pyrargyrite.**

ru·by spi+nel *n.* a red transparent variety of spinel, used as a gemstone.

R.U.C. *abbrev. for* Royal Ulster Constabulary.

ruche *or* **rouche** (ru:ʃ) *n.* a strip of pleated or frilled lawn, lace, etc., used to decorate blouses, dresses, etc., or worn around the neck like a small ruff as in the 16th century. [C19: from French, literally: beehive, from Medieval Latin *rūsca* bark of a tree, of Celtic origin]

ruch+ing ('ru:ʃɪŋ) *n.* **1.** material used for a ruche. **2.** a ruche or ruches collectively.

ruck[1] (rʌk) *n.* **1.** a large number or quantity; mass, esp. of ordinary or undistinguished people or things. **2.** (in a race) a group of competitors who are well behind the leaders at the finish. **3.** *Rugby.* a loose scrummage or maul for the ball. **4.** *Australian Rules football.* a group of three players who follow the ball closely. ~*vb.* **5.** (*intr.*) *Rugby.* to try to win the ball by mauling and scrummaging. [C13 (meaning "heap of firewood"): perhaps from Scandinavian; compare Old Norse *hraukr* RICK]

ruck² (rʌk) *n.* **1.** a wrinkle, crease, or fold. ~*vb.* **2.** (usually foll. by *up*) to become or make wrinkled, creased, or puckered. [C18: from Scandinavian; related to Old Norse *hrukka*]

ruck³ (rʌk) *n. Prison slang.* a fight. [C20: short for RUCKUS]

ruck·sack ('rʌkˌsæk) *n.* a large bag, usually having two straps and a supporting frame, carried on the back and often used to carry camping equipment, etc. U.S. name: **backpack.** [C19: from German, literally: back sack]

ruck·us ('rʌkəs) *n., pl.* ·**us·es.** *Informal.* an uproar; ruction. [C20: from RUCTION + RUMPUS]

ruc·tion ('rʌkʃən) *Informal.* an uproar; noisy or quarrelsome disturbance. [C19: perhaps changed from INSURRECTION]

ru·da·ceous (ruːˈdeɪʃəs) *adj.* (of conglomerate, breccia, and similar rocks) composed of coarse-grained material. Compare **arenaceous** (sense 1), **argillaceous.** [C20: from Latin *rudis* coarse, rough + -ACEOUS]

rud·beck·i·a (rʌdˈbɛkɪə) *n.* any plant of the North American genus *Rudbeckia,* cultivated for their showy flowers, which have golden-yellow rays and green or black conical centres: family *Compositae* (composites). See also **coneflower, black-eyed Susan.** [C18: New Latin, named after Olaus *Rudbeck* (1630–1702), Swedish botanist]

rudd (rʌd) *n.* a European freshwater cyprinid fish, *Scardinius erythrophthalmus,* having a compressed dark greenish body and reddish ventral and tail fins. [C17: probably from dialect *rud* red colour, from Old English *rudu* redness]

rud·der ('rʌdə) *n.* **1.** *Nautical.* a pivoted vertical vane that projects into the water at the stern of a vessel and can be controlled by a tiller, wheel, or other apparatus to steer the vessel. **2.** a vertical control surface attached to the rear of the fin used to steer an aircraft, in conjunction with the ailerons. **3.** anything that guides or directs. [Old English *rōther;* related to Old French *rōther,* Old High German *ruodar,* Old Norse *rōthr.* See ROW²] —'**rud·der·less** *adj.*

rud·der·head ('rʌdəˌhɛd) *n. Nautical.* the top of the rudderpost, to which the steering apparatus may be fixed.

rud·der·post ('rʌdəˌpəʊst) *n. Nautical.* **1.** Also called: **rud·der·stock** ('rʌdəˌstɒk). a postlike member at the forward edge of a rudder. **2.** the part of the stern frame of a vessel to which a rudder is fitted.

rud·dle ('rʌdᵊl), **rad·dle,** *or* **red·dle** *n.* **1.** a red ochre, used esp. to mark sheep. ~*vb.* **2.** (*tr.*) to mark (sheep) with ruddle. [C16: diminutive formed from Old English *rudu* redness; see RUDD]

rud·dock ('rʌdək) *n.* a Brit. dialect name for the **robin.** [Old English *rudduc;* related to *rudu* redness; see RUDD]

rud·dy ('rʌdɪ) *adj.* ·**di·er,** ·**di·est.** **1.** (of the complexion) having a healthy reddish colour, usually resulting from an outdoor life. **2.** coloured red or pink: *a ruddy sky.* ~*adv., adj. Informal, chiefly Brit.* **3.** (intensifier) bloody; damned: *a ruddy fool.* [Old English *rudig,* from *rudu* redness (see RUDD); related to Old High German *rot* RED, Swedish *rod,* Old Norse *rythga* to make rusty] —'**rud·di·ly** *adv.* —'**rud·di·ness** *n.*

rud·dy duck *n.* a small duck, *Oxyura jamaicensis,* that inhabits marshes, ponds, etc., in North America and N South America and has a stiff upright tail. The male has a reddish-brown body and blue bill in the breeding season.

rude (ruːd) *adj.* **1.** insulting or uncivil; discourteous; impolite: *he was rude about her hair style.* **2.** lacking refinement; coarse or uncouth. **3.** vulgar or obscene: *a rude joke.* **4.** roughly or crudely made: *we made a rude shelter on the island.* **5.** rough or harsh in sound, appearance, or behaviour. **6.** humble or lowly. **7.** (*prenominal*) robust or sturdy: *in rude health.* **8.** (*prenominal*) approximate or imprecise: *a rude estimate.* [C14: via Old French from Latin *rudis* coarse, unformed] —'**rude·ly** *adv.* —'**rude·ness** *or* '**ru·der·y** *n.*

ru·de·ral ('ruːdərəl) *n.* **1.** a plant that grows on waste ground. ~*adj.* **2.** growing in waste places. [C19: from New Latin *rūderālis,* from Latin *rūdus* rubble]

Ru·des·heim·er ('ruːdəsˌhaɪmə) *n.* a white Rhine wine: named after the town of Rüdesheim on the Rhine.

ru·di·ment ('ruːdɪmənt) *n.* **1.** (*often pl.*) the first principles or elementary stages of a subject. **2.** (*often pl.*) a partially developed version of something. **3.** *Biology.* an organ or part in its earliest recognizable form, esp. one in an embryonic or vestigial state. [C16: from Latin *rudīmentum* a beginning, from *rudis* unformed; see RUDE]

ru·di·men·ta·ry (ˌruːdɪˈmɛntərɪ) *or* **ru·di·men·tal** *adj.* **1.** basic; fundamental; not elaborated or perfected. **2.** incompletely developed; vestigial: *rudimentary leaves.* —ˌ**ru·di'men·ta·ri·ly** *or* ˌ**ru·di'men·tal·ly** *adv.*

rud·ish ('ruːdɪʃ) *adj.* somewhat rude.

Ru·dolf ('ruːdɒlf) *n.* **Lake.** a long narrow lake in E Africa, in the Great Rift Valley. Area: 7104 sq. km (2743 sq. miles).

Ru·dolf I *or* **Ru·dolph I** ('ruːdɒlf) *n.* 1218–91, king of Germany (1273–91): founder of the Hapsburg dynasty based on the duchies of Styria and Austria.

rue¹ (ruː) *vb.* **rues, ru·ing, rued.** **1.** to feel sorrow, remorse, or regret for (one's own wrongdoing, past events with unpleasant consequences, etc.). ~*n.* **2.** *Archaic.* sorrow, pity, or regret. [Old English *hrēowan;* related to Old Saxon *hreuwan,* Old High German *hriuwan*] —'**ru·er** *n.*

rue² (ruː) *n.* any rutaceous plant of the genus *Ruta,* esp. *R. graveolens,* an aromatic Eurasian shrub with small yellow flowers and evergreen leaves which yield an acrid volatile oil, formerly used medicinally as a narcotic and stimulant. Archaic name: **herb of grace.** Compare **goat's-rue, meadow rue, wall rue.** [C14: from Old French, from Latin *rūta,* from Greek *rhutē*]

rue·ful ('ruːfʊl) *adj.* **1.** feeling or expressing sorrow or repentance: *a rueful face.* **2.** inspiring sorrow or pity. —'**rue·ful·ly** *adv.* —'**rue·ful·ness** *n.*

ru·fes·cent (ruːˈfɛsᵊnt) *adj. Botany.* tinged with red or becoming red. [C19: from Latin *rūfescere* to grow reddish, from *rūfus* red, auburn] —**ru'fes·cence** *n.*

ruff¹ (rʌf) *n.* **1.** a circular pleated, gathered, or fluted collar of lawn, muslin, etc., often starched or wired, worn by both men and women in the 16th and 17th centuries. **2.** a natural growth of long or coloured hair or feathers around the necks of certain animals or birds. **3. a.** an Old World shore bird, *Philomachus pugnax,* the male of which has a large erectile ruff of feathers in the breeding season: family *Scolopacidae* (sandpipers, etc.), order *Charadriiformes.* **b.** the male of this bird. Compare **reeve**³. [C16: back formation from RUFFLE¹] —'**ruff**ˌ**like** *adj.*

ruff² (rʌf) *n. Cards.* **1.** (*also vb.*) another word for **trump**¹. **2.** an old card game similar to whist. [C16: from Old French *roffle;* perhaps changed from Italian *trionfa* TRUMP¹]

ruffe *or* **ruff**³ (rʌf) *n.* a European freshwater teleost fish, *Acerina cernua,* having a single spiny dorsal fin: family *Percidae* (perches). Also called: **pope.** [C15: perhaps an alteration of ROUGH (referring to its scales)]

ruffed grouse *n.* a large North American grouse, *Bonasa umbellus,* having brown plumage with darker markings around the neck and a black-tipped fan-shaped tail.

ruf·fi·an ('rʌfɪən) *n.* a violent or lawless person; hoodlum or villain. [C16: from Old French *rufien,* from Italian *ruffiano,* perhaps related to Langobardic *hruf* scurf, scabbiness] —'**ruf·fi·an·ism** *n.* —'**ruf·fi·an·ly** *adj.*

ruf·fle¹ ('rʌfᵊl) *vb.* **1.** to make, be, or become irregular or rumpled: *to ruffle a child's hair; a breeze ruffling the water.* **2.** to annoy, irritate, or be annoyed or irritated. **3.** (*tr.*) to make into a ruffle; pleat. **4.** (of a bird) to erect (its feathers) in anger, display, etc. **5.** (*tr.*) to flick (cards, pages, etc.) rapidly with the fingers. ~*n.* **6.** an irregular or disturbed surface. **7.** a strip of pleated material used for decoration or as a trim. **8.** *Zoology.* another name for **ruff**¹ (sense 2). **9.** annoyance or irritation. [C13: of Germanic origin; compare Middle Low German *ruffelen* to crumple, Old Norse *hrufla* to scratch]

ruf·fle² ('rʌfᵊl) *n.* **1.** a low continuous drumbeat. ~*vb.* **2.** (*tr.*) to beat a drum with a low repetitive beat. [C18: from earlier *ruff,* of imitative origin]

ruf·fle³ ('rʌfᵊl) *vb.* (*intr.*) *Archaic.* to behave riotously or arrogantly; swagger. [C15: of obscure origin]

ruf·fler ('rʌflə) *n.* **1.** a person or thing that ruffles. **2.** an attachment on a sewing machine used for making frills.

ru·fous ('ruːfəs) *adj.* reddish brown. [C18: from Latin *rūfus*]

rug (rʌg) *n.* **1.** a floor covering, smaller than a carpet and made of thick wool or of other material, such as an animal skin. **2.** *Chiefly Brit.* a blanket, esp. one used as a wrap or lap robe for travellers. **3. pull the rug out from under.** to betray, expose, or leave defenceless. [C16: from Scandinavian; compare Norwegian *rugga,* Swedish *rugg* coarse hair. See RAG¹] —'**rug**ˌ**like** *adj.*

ru·ga ('ruːgə) *n., pl.* ·**gae** (-dʒiː). *Anatomy.* (*usually pl.*) a fold, wrinkle, or crease. [C18: Latin]

rug·by *or* **rug·by foot·ball** ('rʌgbɪ) *n.* a form of football played with an oval ball in which the handling and carrying of the ball is permitted. Also called: **rugger.** See also **rugby league, rugby union.** [named after the public school at Rugby, where it was first played]

Rug·by ('rʌgbɪ) *n.* a town in central England, in E Warwickshire: famous public school, founded in 1567. Pop.: 59 372 (1971). —'**Rug·bei·an** *adj., n.*

rug·by league *n.* a form of rugby football played between teams of 13 players, professionalism being allowed.

rug·by un·ion *n.* a form of rugby football played only by amateurs, played between teams of 15 players.

rug·ged ('rʌgɪd) *adj.* **1.** having an uneven or jagged surface. **2.** rocky or steep: *rugged scenery.* **3.** (of the face) strong-featured or furrowed. **4.** rough, severe, or stern in character. **5.** without refinement or culture; rude: *rugged manners.* **6.** involving hardship; harsh: *he leads a rugged life in the mountains.* **7.** difficult or hard: *a rugged test.* **8.** *Chiefly U.S.* sturdy or strong; robust. [C14: from Scandinavian; compare Swedish *rugga* to make rough] —'**rug·ged·ly** *adv.* —'**rug·ged·ness** *n.*

rug·ged·ize *or* **rug·ged·ise** ('rʌgɪˌdaɪz) *vb.* (*tr.*) to make durable, as for military use.

rug·ger ('rʌgə) *n. Chiefly Brit.* an informal name for **rugby.**

ru·gose ('ruːgəʊs, -gəʊz), **ru·gous,** *or* **ru·gate** ('ruːgeɪt, -gɪt) *adj.* wrinkled: *rugose leaves.* [C18: from Latin *rūgōsus,* from *rūga* a wrinkle] —'**ru·gose·ly** *adv.* —**ru·gos·i·ty** (ruːˈgɒsɪtɪ) *n.*

Ruhr (rʊə; *German* ruːr) *n.* the chief coalmining and industrial region of West Germany: in North Rhine-Westphalia around the valley of the **River Ruhr** (a tributary of the Rhine 235 km (146 miles) long). German name: **Ruhrgebiet.**

ru·in ('ruːɪn) *n.* **1.** destroyed or decayed building or town. **2.** the state or condition of being destroyed or decayed. **3.** loss of wealth, position, etc., or something that causes such loss; downfall. **4.** something that is severely damaged: *his life was a ruin.* **5.** a person who has suffered a downfall, bankruptcy, etc. **6.** loss of value or usefulness. **7.** *Archaic.* loss of her virginity by a woman outside marriage. ~*vb.* **8.** (*tr.*) to bring to ruin; destroy. **9.** (*tr.*) to injure or spoil: *the town has been ruined with tower blocks.* **10.** (*intr.*) *Archaic or poetic.* to fall into ruins; collapse. **11.** (*tr.*) *Archaic.* to seduce and abandon (a woman). [C14: from Old French *ruine,* from Latin *ruīna* a falling down, from *ruere* to fall violently] —**'ru+in+a·ble** *adj.* —**'ru+in+er** *n.*

ru+in·a+tion (ˌruːɪ'neɪʃən) *n.* **1.** the act of ruining or the state of being ruined. **2.** something that causes ruin.

ru+in+ous ('ruːɪnəs) *adj.* causing, tending to cause, or characterized by ruin or destruction: *a ruinous course of action.* —**'ru+in+ous+ly** *adv.* —**'ru+in+ous+ness** *n.*

Ruis·dael *or* **Ruys·dael** ('riːzdɑːl, -deɪl, 'raɪz-; *Dutch* 'rœɪzdaːl) *n.* **Ja·cob van** ('jaːkɔp van). ?1628–82, Dutch landscape painter.

rule (ruːl) *n.* **1.** an authoritative regulation or direction concerning method or procedure, as for a court of law, legislative body, game, or other human institution or activity: *judges' rules; play according to the rules.* **2.** the exercise of governmental authority or control: *the rule of Caesar.* **3.** the period of time in which a monarch or government has power: *his rule lasted 100 days.* **4.** a customary form or procedure; regular course of action: *he made a morning swim his rule.* **5.** (usually preceded by *the*) the common order of things; normal condition: *violence was the rule rather than the exception.* **6.** a prescribed method or procedure for solving a mathematical problem. **7.** any of various devices with a straight edge for guiding or measuring; ruler: *a carpenter's rule.* **8. a.** a printed or drawn character in the form of a long thin line. **b.** another name for **dash**[1] (sense 12): *en rule; em rule.* **c.** a strip of brass or other metal used to print such a line. **9.** *Christianity.* a systematic body of prescriptions defining the way of life to be followed by members of a religious order. **10.** *Law.* an order by a court or judge. **11. as a rule.** normally or ordinarily. ~*vb.* **12.** to exercise governing or controlling authority over (a people, political unit, individual, etc.): *he ruled for 20 years; his passion for her ruled his life.* **13.** (when *tr., often takes a clause as object*) to decide authoritatively; decree: *the chairman ruled against the proposal.* **14.** (*tr.*) to mark with straight parallel lines or make one straight line, as with a ruler: *to rule a margin.* **15.** (*tr.*) to restrain or control: *to rule one's temper.* **16.** (*intr.*) to be customary or prevalent: *chaos rules in this school.* **17.** (*intr.*) to be pre-eminent or superior: *football rules in the field of sport.* **18.** (*tr.*) *Astrology.* (of a planet) to have a strong affinity with certain human attributes, activities, etc., associated with (one or sometimes two signs of the zodiac): *Mars rules Aries.* **19. rule the roost** (*or* **roast**). to be pre-eminent; be in charge. [C13: from Old French *riule,* from Latin *rēgula* a straight edge; see REGULATE] —**'rul+a·ble** *adj.*

rule of three *n.* a mathematical rule asserting that the value of one unknown quantity in a proportion is found by multiplying the denominator of each ratio by the numerator of the other.

rule of thumb *n.* **a.** a rough and practical approach, based on experience, rather than a scientific or precise one based on theory. **b.** (*as modifier*): *a rule-of-thumb decision.*

rule out *vb.* (*tr., adv.*) **1.** to dismiss from consideration. **2.** to make impossible; preclude or prevent: *the rain ruled out outdoor games.*

rul+er ('ruːlə) *n.* **1.** a person who rules or commands. **2.** Also called: **rule.** a strip of wood, metal, or other material, having straight edges graduated usually in millimetres or inches, used for measuring and drawing straight lines.

Rules (ruːlz) *n.* **1.** short for **Australian Rules** (football). **2. the Rules.** *English history.* the neighbourhood around certain prisons (esp. the Fleet and King's Bench prison) in which trusted prisoners were allowed to live under specified restrictions.

rul+ing ('ruːlɪŋ) *n.* **1.** a decision of someone in authority, such as a judge. **2.** one or more parallel ruled lines. ~*adj.* **3.** controlling or exercising authority: *the ruling classes.* **4.** prevalent or predominant.

rum[1] (rʌm) *n.* spirit made from sugar cane, either coloured brownish-red by the addition of caramel or by maturation in oak containers, or left white. [C17: perhaps shortened from C16 *rumbullion,* of uncertain origin]

rum[2] (rʌm) *adj.* **rum+mer, rum+mest.** *Brit. slang.* strange; peculiar; odd. [C19: perhaps from Romany *rom* man] —**'rum+ly** *adv.* —**'rum+ness** *n.*

rum[3] (rʌm) *n.* short for **rummy**[1] (the card game).

Rum. *abbrev. for* Rumania(n).

Ru+ma+ni·a, Rou+ma+ni·a (ruː'meɪnɪə), *or* **Ro+ma+ni·a** *n.* a republic in SE Europe, bordering on the Black Sea: united in 1861; became independent in 1879; Communist government set up in 1945; became a socialist republic in 1965. It consists chiefly of a great central arc of the Carpathian Mountains and Transylvanian Alps, with the plains of Walachia, Moldavia, and Dobriya on the south and east and the Pannonian Plain in the west. Language: Rumanian. Currency: leu. Capital: Bucharest. Pop.: 21 178 000 (1975 UN est.). Area: 237 500 sq. km (91 699 sq. miles).

Ru+ma+ni·an, Rou+ma+ni·an (ruː'meɪnɪən), *or* **Ro+ma+ni·an** *n.* **1.** the official language of Rumania, belonging to the Romance group of the Indo-European family. **2.** a native, citizen, or inhabitant of Rumania. ~*adj.* **3.** relating to, denoting, or characteristic of Rumania, its people, or their language.

rum+ba *or* **rhum+ba** ('rʌmbə, 'rʊm-) *n.* **1.** a rhythmic and syncopated Cuban dance in duple time. **2.** a ballroom dance derived from this. **3.** a piece of music composed for or in the rhythm of this dance. [C20: from Spanish: lavish display, of uncertain origin]

rum+ble ('rʌmbᵊl) *vb.* **1.** to make or cause to make a deep resonant sound: *thunder rumbled in the sky.* **2.** to move with such a sound: *the train rumbled along.* **3.** (*tr.*) to utter with a rumbling sound: *he rumbled an order.* **4.** (*tr.*) to tumble (metal components, gemstones, etc.) in a barrel of smooth stone in order to polish them. **5.** (*tr.*) *Brit. slang.* to find out about (someone or something); discover (something): *the police rumbled their plans.* **6.** (*intr.*) *U.S. slang.* to be involved in a gang fight. ~*n.* **7.** a deep resonant sound. **8.** a widespread murmur of discontent. **9.** another name for **tumbler** (sense 4). **10.** *U.S. slang.* a gang fight. [C14: perhaps from Middle Dutch *rummelen;* related to German *rummeln, rumpeln*] —**'rum+bler** *n.* —**'rum+bling+ly** *adv.*

rum+ble seat *n. U.S.* a folding outside seat at the rear of some early cars; dicky.

rum+bus+tious (rʌm'bʌstjəs) *adj.* boisterous or unruly. [C18: probably a variant of ROBUSTIOUS] —**rum+'bus+tious+ly** *adv.* —**rum+'bus+tious+ness** *n.*

Ru+me·li·a (ruː'miːlɪə) *n. History.* the possessions of the Ottoman Empire in the Balkan peninsula: including Macedonia, Albania, Thrace, and an autonomous province (**Eastern Rumelia**) ceded in 1885 to Bulgaria.

ru+men ('ruːmɛn) *n., pl.* **+mens** *or* **+mi+na** (-mɪnə). the first compartment of the stomach of ruminants, behind the reticulum, in which food is partly digested before being regurgitated as cud. [C18: from Latin: throat, gullet]

Rum·ford ('rʌmfəd) *n.* **Count.** See (Benjamin) **Thompson.**

ru+mi+nant ('ruːmɪnənt) *n.* **1.** any artiodactyl mammal of the suborder *Ruminantia,* the members of which chew the cud and have a stomach of four compartments. The group includes deer, antelopes, cattle, sheep, and goats. **2.** any other animal that chews the cud, such as a camel. ~*adj.* **3.** of, relating to, or belonging to the suborder *Ruminantia.* **4.** (of members of this suborder and related animals, such as camels) chewing the cud; ruminating. **5.** meditating or contemplating in a slow quiet way. —**'ru+mi+nant+ly** *adv.*

ru+mi+nate ('ruːmɪˌneɪt) *vb.* **1.** (of ruminants) to chew (the cud). **2.** (when *intr.,* often foll. by *upon, on,* etc.) to meditate or ponder (upon). [C16: from Latin *rūmināre* to chew the cud, from RUMEN] —**ˌru+mi+'na+tion** *n.* —**'ru+mi+ˌnat+ing+ly** *adv.* —**'ru+mi+na+tive** *adj.* —**'ru+mi+na+tive+ly** *adv.* —**'ru+mi+ˌna+tor** *n.*

rum+mage ('rʌmɪdʒ) *vb.* **1.** (when *intr.,* often foll. by *through*) to search (through) while looking for something, often causing disorder or confusion. ~*n.* **2.** an act of rummaging. **3.** a jumble of articles. **4.** *Obsolete.* confusion or bustle. [C14 (in the sense: to pack a cargo): from Old French *arrumage,* from *arrumer* to stow in a ship's hold, probably of Germanic origin] —**'rum+mag+er** *n.*

rum+mage out *or* **up** *vb.* (*tr.*) to find by searching vigorously; turn out.

rum+mage sale *n.* **1.** the U.S. term for **jumble sale. 2.** *U.S.* a sale of unclaimed property or unsold stock.

rum+mer ('rʌmə) *n.* a drinking glass, typically having an ovoid bowl on a short stem. [C17: from Dutch *roemer* a glass for drinking toasts, from *roemen* to praise]

rum+my[1] ('rʌmɪ) *or* **rum** *n.* a card game based on collecting sets and sequences. [C20: perhaps from RUM[2]]

rum+my[2] ('rʌmɪ) *n., pl.* **+mies. 1.** *U.S.* a slang word for **drunkard.** ~*adj.* **2.** of or like rum in taste or smell.

ru+mour *or U.S.* **ru+mor** ('ruːmə) *n.* **1. a.** information, often a mixture of truth and untruth, passed around verbally. **b.** (*in combination*): *a rumour-monger.* **2.** gossip or hearsay. **3.** *Archaic.* din or clamour. **4.** *Obsolete.* fame or reputation. ~*vb.* **5.** (*tr.; usually passive*) to pass around or circulate in the form of a rumour: *it is rumoured that the Queen is coming.* **6.** *Literary.* to make or cause to make a murmuring noise. [C14: via Old French from Latin *rūmor* common talk; related to Old Norse *rymja* to roar, Sanskrit *rāuti* he cries]

rump (rʌmp) *n.* **1.** the hindquarters of a mammal, not including the legs. **2.** the rear part of a bird's back, nearest to the tail. **3.** a person's buttocks. **4.** Also called: **rump steak.** a cut of beef from behind the loin and above the round. **5.** an inferior remnant. [C15: from Scandinavian; compare Danish *rumpe,* Icelandic *rumpr,* German *Rumpf* trunk of the body] —**'rump+less** *adj.*

Rum·pel·stilts·kin (ˌrʌmpᵊl'stɪltskɪn) *n.* a dwarf in a German folktale who aids the king's bride on condition that she give him her first child or guess the dwarf's name. She guesses correctly and he is destroyed.

rum+ple ('rʌmpᵊl) *vb.* **1.** to make or become wrinkled, crumpled, ruffled, or dishevelled. ~*n.* **2.** a wrinkle, fold, or crease. [C17: from Middle Dutch *rompelen;* related to Old English *gerumpen* creased, wrinkled] —**'rum+ply** *adj.*

Rump Par+lia+ment *or* **the Rump** *n. English history.* the remainder of the Long Parliament after Pride's Purge. It sat from 1648–53 and from 1659–60.

rum+pus ('rʌmpəs) *n., pl.* **+pus·es.** a noisy, confused, or disruptive commotion. [C18: of unknown origin]

rum+pus room *n. U.S.* a room used for noisy activities, such as parties or children's games.

run (rʌn) *vb.* **runs, run+ning, ran, run. 1.** (*intr.*) **a.** (of a two-legged creature) to move on foot at a rapid pace so that both feet are off the ground together for part of each stride. **b.** (of a four-legged creature) to move at a rapid gait; gallop or canter. **2.** (*tr.*) to pass over (a distance, route, etc.) in running: *to run a mile; run a race.* **3.** (*intr.*) to run in or finish a race as specified, esp. in a particular position: *John is running third.* **4.** (*tr.*) to perform or accomplish by or as if by running: *to run an errand.* **5.** (*tr.*) to bring into a specified state or condition by running: *to run oneself to a standstill.* **6.** (*tr.*) to track down or hunt (an animal): *to run a fox to earth.* **7.** (*intr.*) to move about freely and without restraint: *the children are running in the garden.* **8.** (*intr.;* usually foll. by *to*) to go or have recourse, as for aid, assistance, etc.: *he's always running to his mother when he's in trouble.* **9.** (*tr.*) to set (animals) loose on (a field or tract of land) so as to graze freely. **10.** (*intr.;* often foll. by *over, round,* or *up*) to make a short trip or brief informal visit: *I'll run over to your house this afternoon.* **11.** to move quickly and easily on wheels by rolling, or in any of certain other ways: *a ball running along the ground; a sledge running over snow.* **12.** to move or cause to move with a specified result or in a specified manner: *to run a ship aground; to run into a tree.* **13.** (often foll. by *over*) to move or pass or cause to move or pass quickly: *to run a sweeper over the carpet; to run one's eyes over a page.* **14.** (*tr.;* foll. by *into, out of, through,* etc.) to force, thrust, or drive: *she ran a needle into her finger.* **15.** (*tr.*) to drive or maintain and operate (a vehicle). **16.** (*tr.*) to give a lift to (someone) in a vehicle; transport: *he ran her to the station.* **17.** to ply or cause to ply between places on a route: *the bus runs from Piccadilly to Golders Green.* **18.** to operate or be operated; function or cause to function: *the engine is running smoothly; to run a program on a computer.* **19.** (*tr.*) to be in charge of; manage: *to run a company.* **20.** to extend or continue or cause to extend or continue in a particular direction, for a particular duration or distance, etc.: *the road runs north; the play ran for two years; the months ran into years.* **21.** (*intr.*) *Law.* **a.** to have legal force or effect: *the lease runs for two more years.* **b.** to accompany; be an integral part of or adjunct to: *an easement runs with the land.* **22.** (*tr.*) to be subjected to, be affected by, or incur: *to run a risk; run a temperature.* **23.** (*intr.;* often foll. by *to*) to be characterized (by); tend or incline: *her taste runs to extravagant hats; to run to fat.* **24.** (*intr.*) to recur persistently or be inherent: *red hair runs in my family.* **25.** to cause or allow (liquids) to flow or (of liquids) to flow, esp. in a manner specified: *water ran from the broken pipe; the well has run dry.* **26.** (*intr.*) to melt and flow: *the wax grew hot and began to run.* **27.** *Metallurgy.* **a.** to melt or fuse. **b.** (*tr.*) to mould or cast (molten metal): *to run lead into ingots.* **28.** (*intr.*) (of waves, tides, rivers, etc.) to rise high, surge, or be at a specified height: *a high sea was running that night.* **29.** (*intr.*) to be diffused: *the colours in my dress ran when I washed it.* **30.** (*intr.*) (of stitches) to unravel or come undone or (of a garment) to have stitches unravel or come undone. **31.** to sew (an article) with continuous stitches. **32.** (*intr.*) (of growing vines, creepers, etc.) to trail, spread, or climb: *ivy running over a cottage wall.* **33.** (*intr.*) to spread or circulate quickly: *a rumour ran through the town.* **34.** (*intr.*) to be stated or reported: *his story runs as follows.* **35.** to publish or print or be published or printed in a newspaper, magazine, etc.: *they ran his story in the next issue.* **36.** (often foll. by *for*) *Chiefly U.S.* to be a candidate or present as a candidate for political or other office: *Jones is running for president.* **37.** (*tr.*) to get past or through; evade: *to run a blockade.* **38.** (*tr.*) to deal in (arms, etc.), esp. by importing illegally: *he runs guns for the rebels.* **39.** *Nautical.* to sail (a vessel, esp. a sailing vessel) or (of such a vessel) to be sailed with the wind coming from astern. **40.** (*intr.*) (of fish) **a.** to migrate upstream from the sea, esp. in order to spawn. **b.** to swim rapidly in any area of water, esp. during migration. **41.** (*tr.*) *Cricket.* to score (a run or number of runs) by hitting the ball and running between the wickets. **42.** (*tr.*) *Billiards, etc.* to make (a number of successful shots) in sequence. **43.** (*tr.*) *Golf.* to hit (the ball) so that it rolls along the ground. **44.** (*tr.*) *Bridge.* to cash (all one's winning cards in a long suit) successively. **45. run close.** to compete closely with; present a serious challenge to: *he got the job, but a younger man ran him close.* **46. run for it.** *Informal.* to attempt to escape from arrest, etc., by running. **47. be run off one's feet.** to be extremely busy. ~*n.* **48.** an act, instance, or period of running. **49.** a gait, pace, or motion faster than a walk: *she went off at a run.* **50.** a distance covered by running or a period of running: *a run of ten miles.* **51.** an act, instance, or period of travelling in a vehicle, esp. for pleasure: *to go for a run in the car.* **52.** free and unrestricted access: *we had the run of the house and garden.* **53. a.** a period of time during which a machine, computer, etc., operates. **b.** the amount of work performed in such a period. **54.** a continuous or sustained period: *a run of good luck.* **55.** a continuous sequence of performances: *the play had a good run.* **56.** *Cards.* a sequence of winning cards in one suit, usually more than five: *a run of spades.* **57.** tendency or trend: *the run of the market.* **58.** type, class, or category: *the usual run of graduates.* **59.** (usually foll. by *on*) a continuous and urgent demand: *a run on butter; a run on the dollar.* **60.** a series of unravelled stitches, esp. in stockings or tights; ladder. **61.** the characteristic pattern or direction of something: *the run of the grain on a piece of wood.* **62. a.** a continuous vein or seam of ore, coal, etc. **b.** the direction in which it lies. **63. a.** a period during which water or other liquid flows. **b.** the amount of such a flow. **64.** a pipe, channel, etc., through which water or other liquid flows. **65.** *U.S.* a small stream. **66.** a steeply inclined pathway or course, esp. a snow-covered one used for skiing and bobsleigh racing. **67.** an enclosure for domestic fowls or other animals, in which they have free movement: *a chicken run.* **68.** (esp. in Australia and New Zealand) a tract of land for grazing livestock. **69.** a track or area frequented by animals: *a deer run; a rabbit run.* **70.** a group of animals of the same species moving together. **71.** the migration of fish upstream in order to spawn. **72.** *Nautical.* **a.** the tack of a sailing vessel in which the wind comes from astern. **b.** part of the hull of a vessel near the stern where it curves upwards and inwards. **73.** *Military.* **a.** a mission in a warplane. **b.** short for **bombing run. 74.** the movement of an aircraft along the ground during takeoff or landing. **75.** *Music.* a rapid scalelike passage of notes. **76.** *Cricket.* a score of one, normally achieved by both batsmen running from one end of the wicket to the other after one of them has hit the ball. Compare **extra** (sense 6), **boundary** (sense 2c). **77.** *Baseball.* an instance of a batter touching all four bases safely, thereby scoring. **78.** *Golf.* the distance that a ball rolls after hitting the ground. **79. a run for (one's) money.** *Informal.* **a.** a strong challenge or close competition. **b.** pleasure derived from an activity. **80. in the long run.** as the eventual outcome of a sequence of events, actions, etc.; ultimately. **81. in the short run.** as the immediate outcome of a series of events, etc. **82. on the run. a.** escaping from arrest; fugitive. **b.** in rapid flight; retreating: *the enemy is on the run.* **c.** hurrying from place to place: *she's always on the run.* **83. the runs.** *Slang.* diarrhoea. ~See also **run about, run across, run along, run around, run away, run down, run in, run into, run off, run on, run out, run over, run through, run to, run up.** [Old English *runnen,* past participle of (*ge*)*rinnan;* related to Old French, Old Norse *rinna,* Old Saxon, Gothic, Old High German *rinnan*]

run·a·bout (ˈrʌnəˌbaut) *n.* **1.** a small car, esp. one for use in a town. **2.** a light aircraft. **3.** a light motorboat. **4.** a person who moves about constantly or busily. ~*vb.* **run a·bout. 5.** (*intr., adv.*) to move busily from place to place.

run a·cross *vb.* (*intr., prep.*) to meet unexpectedly; encounter by chance.

run af·ter *vb.* (*intr., prep.*) *Informal.* **1.** to pursue (a member of the opposite sex) with persistent attention. **2.** to pursue (anything) persistently.

run·a·gate (ˈrʌnəˌgeɪt) *n.* *Archaic.* **a.** a vagabond, fugitive, or renegade. **b.** (*as modifier*): *a runagate priest.* [C16: variant (influenced by RUN) of RENEGADE]

run a·long *vb.* (*intr., adv.*) (often said patronizingly) to go away; leave.

run a·round *vb.* (*intr., adv.*) *Informal.* **1.** (often foll. by *with*) to associate habitually (with). **2.** to behave in a fickle or promiscuous manner. ~*n.* **run-a·round. 3.** *Informal.* deceitful or evasive treatment of a person (esp. in the phrase **give** or **get the run-around**). **4.** *Printing.* an arrangement of printed matter in which the column width is narrowed to accommodate an illustration.

run a·way *vb.* (*intr., adv.*) **1.** to take flight; escape. **2.** to go away; depart. **3.** (of a horse) to gallop away uncontrollably. **4. run away with. a.** to abscond or elope with: *he ran away with his boss's daughter.* **b.** to make off with; steal. **c.** to escape from the control of: *his enthusiasm ran away with him.* **d.** to win easily or be assured of victory in (a competition): *he ran away with the race.* ~*n.* **run·a·way. 5. a.** a person or animal that runs away. **b.** (*as modifier*): *a runaway horse.* **6.** the act or an instance of running away. **7.** (*modifier*) occurring as a result of the act of eloping: *a runaway wedding.* **8.** (*modifier*) (of a race, victory, etc.) easily won.

runch (rʌntʃ) *n.* another name for **white charlock.** See **charlock** (sense 2).

run·ci·ble spoon (ˈrʌnsɪbᵊl) *n.* a forklike utensil with two broad prongs and one sharp curved prong. [*runcible* coined by Edward Lear in a nonsense poem (1871)]

run·ci·nate (ˈrʌnsɪnɪt, -ˌneɪt) *adj.* (of a leaf) having a saw-toothed margin with the teeth or lobes pointing backwards. [C18: from New Latin *runcīnātus,* from Latin *runcīnāre* to plane off, from *runcīna* a carpenter's plane]

Run·corn (ˈrʌŋˌkɔːn) *n.* a town in NW England, in N Cheshire on the Manchester Ship Canal: port and industrial centre; designated a new town in 1964. Pop.: 35 953 (1971).

run·dle (ˈrʌndᵊl) *n.* **1.** a rung of a ladder. **2.** a wheel, esp. of a wheelbarrow. [C14: variant of ROUNDEL]

rund·let (ˈrʌndlɪt) *n.* *Obsolete.* a liquid measure, generally about 15 gallons. [C14: see ROUNDLET]

run down *vb.* (*mainly adv.*) **1.** to cause or allow (an engine, battery, etc.) to lose power gradually and cease to function or (of an engine, battery, etc.) to do this. **2.** to decline or reduce in number or size: *the firm ran down its sales force.* **3.** (*tr., usually passive*) to tire, sap the strength of, or exhaust: *he was thoroughly run down and needed a holiday.* **4.** (*tr.*) to criticize adversely; denigrate; decry. **5.** (*tr.*) to hit and knock to the ground with a moving vehicle. **6.** *Nautical.* **a.** (*tr.*) to collide with and cause to sink. **b.** (*intr., prep.*) to navigate so as to move parallel to (a coast). **7.** (*tr.*) to pursue and find or capture: *to run down a fugitive.* **8.** (*tr.*) to read swiftly or perfunctorily: *he ran down their list of complaints.* ~*adj.* **run-down. 9.** tired; exhausted. **10.** worn-out, shabby, or dilapidated: *a run-down old house.* ~*n.* **run·down. 11.** a brief review, résumé, or summary. **12.** the process of a motor or mechanism coming gradually to a standstill after the source of power is removed. **13.** a reduction in number or size.

Rund·stedt (ˈrʊndstɛt; *German* ˈrʊntʃtɛt) *n.* **Karl Ru·dolf Gerd von** (karl ˈruːdɔlf ˈgɛrt fɔn). 1875–1953, German field marshal; directed the conquest of Poland and France in World War II; commander of the Western Front (1942–44); led the Ardennes counteroffensive (Dec. 1944).

rune (ruːn) *n.* **1.** any of the characters of an ancient Germanic alphabet, derived from the Roman alphabet, in use, esp. in Scandinavia, from the 3rd century A.D. to the end of the Middle Ages. Each character was believed to have a magical significance. **2.** any obscure piece of writing using mysterious symbols. **3.** a kind of Finnish poem or a stanza in such a poem. [Old English *rūn,* from Old Norse *rūn* secret; related to Old Saxon, Old High German, Gothic *runa*] —ˈ**ru·nic** *adj.*

rung[1] (rʌŋ) *n.* **1.** one of the bars or rods that form the steps of a ladder. **2.** a crosspiece between the legs of a chair, etc. **3.** *Nautical.* a spoke on a ship's wheel or a handle projecting from the periphery. **4.** *Brit. dialect.* a cudgel or staff. —ˈ**rung·less** *adj.*

rung[2] (rʌŋ) *vb.* the past participle of **ring**[2].

run in *vb.* (*adv.*) **1.** to run (an engine) gently, usually for a specified period when it is new, in order that the running surfaces may become polished. **2.** (*tr.*) to insert or include. **3.** (*intr.*) (of an aircraft) to approach a point or target. **4.** (*tr.*) *Slang.* to take into custody; arrest: *he was run in for assault.* ~*n.* **run-in. 5.** *Informal.* an argument or quarrel: *he had a run-in with the boss yesterday.* **6.** *Printing.* matter inserted in an existing paragraph.

run in·to *vb.* (*prep.; mainly intr.*) **1.** (*also tr.*) to collide with or cause to collide with: *her car ran into a tree.* **2.** to encounter unexpectedly. **3.** (*also tr.*) to be beset by or cause to be beset by: *the project ran into financial difficulties.* **4.** to extend to; be of the order of: *debts running into thousands.*

run·let ('rʌnlɪt) *n. Archaic.* a cask for wine, beer, etc. [C14: from Old French *rondelet* ROUNDLET]

run·nel ('rʌnᵊl) *n. Literary.* a small stream. [C16: from Old English *rynele;* related to RUN]

run·ner ('rʌnə) *n.* **1.** a person who runs, esp. an athlete. **2.** a messenger for a bank or brokerage firm. **3.** an employee of an art or antique dealer who visits auctions to bid on desired lots. **4.** a person engaged in the solicitation of business. **5.** a person on the run; fugitive. **6. a.** a person or vessel engaged in smuggling; smuggler. **b.** (*in combination*)*: a rum-runner.* **7.** a person who operates, manages, or controls something. **8. a.** either of the strips of metal or wood on which a sledge runs. **b.** the blade of an ice skate. **9.** a roller or guide for a sliding component. **10.** any of various carangid fishes of temperate and tropical seas, such as *Caranx crysos* (**blue runner**) of American Atlantic waters. **11.** *Botany.* **a.** Also called: **stolon.** a slender horizontal stem, as of the strawberry, that grows along the surface of the soil and propagates by producing roots and shoots at the nodes or tip. **b.** a plant that propagates in this way. **12.** a strip of lace, linen, etc., placed across a table or dresser for protection and decoration. **13.** a narrow rug or carpet, as for a passage. **14.** another word for **rocker** (on a rocking chair).

run·ner bean *n.* another name for **scarlet runner.**

run·ner-up *n., pl.* **run·ners-up.** a contestant finishing a race or competition in second place.

run·ning ('rʌnɪŋ) *adj.* **1.** maintained continuously; incessant: *a running battle; running commentary.* **2.** (*postpositive*) without interruption; consecutive: *he lectured for two hours running.* **3.** denoting or relating to the scheduled operation of a public vehicle: *the running time of a train.* **4.** accomplished at a run: *a running jump.* **5.** moving or slipping easily, as a rope or a knot. **6.** (of a wound, sore, etc.) discharging pus or a serous fluid. **7.** denoting or relating to operations or maintenance: *running repairs.* **8.** prevalent; current: *running prices.* **9.** repeated or continuous: *a running design.* **10.** (of certain plants, plant stems, etc.) creeping along the ground. **11.** flowing: *running water.* **12.** (of handwriting) having the letters run together. ~*n.* **13.** management or organization: *the running of a company.* **14.** operation or maintenance: *the running of a machine.* **15.** competition or competitive situation (in the phrases **in the running, out of the running**). **16. make the running.** to set the pace in a competition or race. **17.** *Rare.* the power or ability to run.

run·ning board *n.* a ledge beneath the doors of certain old cars.

run·ning head *or* **ti·tle** *n. Printing.* a heading printed at the top of every page or every other page of a book.

run·ning light *n. Nautical.* one of several white, red, or green lights displayed by vessels operating at night.

run·ning mate *n.* **1.** *U.S.* a candidate for the subordinate of two linked positions, esp. a candidate for the vice-presidency. **2.** a horse that pairs another in a team.

run·ning rig·ging *n. Nautical.* the wires and ropes used to control the operations of a sailing vessel. Compare **standing rigging.**

run·ning stitch *n.* a simple form of hand stitching, consisting of small stitches that look the same on both sides of the fabric, usually used for gathering. Sometimes called: **gathering stitch.**

run·ny ('rʌnɪ) *adj.* **·ni·er, ·ni·est. 1.** tending to flow; liquid. **2.** (of the nose or nasal passages) exuding mucus.

Run·ny·mede ('rʌnɪˌmi:d) *n.* a meadow on the S bank of the Thames near Windsor, where King John met his rebellious barons in 1215 and acceded to Magna Carta.

run off *vb.* (*adv.*) **1.** (*intr.*) to depart in haste. **2.** (*tr.*) to produce quickly, as copies on a duplicating machine. **3.** to drain (liquid) or (of liquid) to be drained. **4.** (*tr.*) to decide (a race) by a runoff. **5.** (*tr.*) to get rid of (weight, etc.) by running. **6.** (*intr.*) (of a flow of liquid) to begin to dry up; cease to run. **7. run off with. a.** to steal; purloin. **b.** to elope with. ~*n.* **run·off. 8.** an extra race to decide the winner after a tie. **9.** that portion of rainfall that runs into streams as surface water rather than being absorbed by the soil. **10.** the overflow of a liquid from a container.

run-of-pa·per *adj.* (of a story, advertisement, etc.) placed anywhere in a newspaper, at the discretion of the editor.

run-of-the-mill *adj.* ordinary, average, or undistinguished in quality, character, or nature; not special or excellent.

run on *vb.* (*adv.*) **1.** (*intr.*) to continue without interruption. **2.** to handwrite with linked-up characters. **3.** *Printing.* to compose text matter without indention or paragraphing. ~*n.* **run-on. 4.** *Printing.* **a.** text matter composed without indenting. **b.** (*as modifier*)*: run-on text matter.* **5. a.** a word added at the end of a dictionary entry whose meaning can be easily inferred from the definition of the headword. **b.** (*as modifier*)*: a run-on entry.*

run out *vb.* (*adv.*) **1.** (*intr.;* often foll. by *of*) to exhaust (a supply of something) or (of a supply) to become exhausted. **2. run out on.** *Informal.* to desert or abandon. **3.** (*tr.*) *Cricket.* to dismiss (a running batsman) by breaking the wicket with the ball, or with the ball in the hand, while he is out of his ground. ~*n.* **run-out. 4.** *Cricket.* dismissal of a batsman by running him out.

run o·ver *vb.* **1.** (*tr., adv.*) to knock down (a person) with a moving vehicle. **2.** (*intr.*) to overflow the capacity of (a container). **3.** (*intr., prep.*) to examine hastily or make a rapid survey of. **4.** (*intr., prep.*) to exceed (a limit): *we've run over our time.*

runt (rʌnt) *n.* **1.** the smallest and weakest young animal in a litter, esp. the smallest piglet in a litter. **2.** *Derogatory.* an undersized or inferior person. **3.** a large pigeon, originally bred for eating. [C16: origin unknown] —**'runt·ish** *adj.* —**'runt·ish·ly** *adv.* —**'runt·ish·ness** *n.* —**'runt·y** *adj.* —**'runt·i·ness** *n.*

run through *vb.* **1.** (*tr., adv.*) to pierce with a sword or other weapon. **2.** (*intr., prep.*) to exhaust (money) by wasteful spending; squander. **3.** (*intr., prep.*) to practise or rehearse: *let's run through the plan.* **4.** (*intr., prep.*) to examine hastily. ~*n.* **run-through. 5.** a practice or rehearsal. **6.** a brief survey.

run to *vb.* (*intr., prep.*) to be sufficient for: *my income doesn't run to luxuries.*

run up *vb.* (*tr., adv.*) **1.** to amass or accumulate; incur: *to run up debts.* **2.** to make by sewing together quickly: *to run up a dress.* **3.** to hoist: *to run up a flag.* ~*n.* **run-up. 4.** an approach run by an athlete for a long jump, pole vault, etc. **5.** a preliminary or preparatory period: *the run-up to the election.*

run·way ('rʌnˌweɪ) *n.* **1.** a hard level roadway or other surface from which aircraft take off and on which they land. **2.** an enclosure for domestic animals; run. **3.** *Forestry, North American.* a chute for sliding logs down. **4.** a narrow ramp extending from the stage into the audience in a theatre, nightclub, etc.

Run·yon ('rʌnjən) *n.* **(Alfred) Da·mon.** 1884–1946, U.S. short-story writer, best known for his humorous tales about racy Broadway characters. His story collections include *Guys and Dolls* (1932), which became the basis of a musical (1950).

ru·pee (ru:'pi:) *n.* the standard monetary unit of India, Pakistan, and Bhutan (divided into 100 paisas), Sri Lanka, the Maldive Islands, Mauritius, and the Seychelles (divided into 100 cents), and of Nepal (divided into 100 pice). [C17: from Hindi *rupaīyā,* from Sanskrit *rūpya* coined silver, from *rūpa* shape, beauty]

Ru·pert ('ru:pət) *n.* **Prince.** 1619–82, German-born nephew of Charles I: Royalist general during the Civil War (until 1646) and commander of the Royalist fleet (1648–50). After the Restoration he was an admiral of the English fleet in wars against the Dutch.

ru·pi·ah (ru:'pi:ə) *n., pl.* **·ah** *or* **·ahs.** the standard monetary unit of Indonesia, divided into 100 sen. [from Hindi: RUPEE]

rup·ture ('rʌptʃə) *n.* **1.** the act of breaking or bursting or the state of being broken or burst. **2.** a breach of peaceful or friendly relations. **3.** *Pathol.* **a.** the breaking or tearing of a bodily structure or part. **b.** another word for **hernia.** ~*vb.* **4.** to break or burst or cause to break or burst. **5.** to affect or be affected with a rupture or hernia. **6.** to undergo or cause to undergo a breach in relations or friendship. [C15: from Latin *ruptūra* a breaking, from *rumpere* to burst forth; see ERUPT] —**'rup·tur·a·ble** *adj.*

ru·ral ('rʊərəl) *adj.* **1.** of, relating to, or characteristic of the country or country life. **2.** living in or accustomed to the country. **3.** of, relating to, or associated with farming. ~Compare **urban.** [C15: via Old French from Latin *rūrālis,* from *rūs* the country] —**'ru·ral·ism** *n.* —**'ru·ral·ist** *or* **'ru·ral·ite** *n.* —**ru·'ral·i·ty** *n.* —**'ru·ral·ly** *adv.*

ru·ral dean *n. Chiefly Brit.* a clergyman having authority over a group of parishes.

ru·ral dis·trict *n.* (in England and Wales from 1888 to 1974 and Northern Ireland from 1898 to 1973) a rural division of a county.

ru·ral·ize *or* **ru·ral·ise** ('rʊərəˌlaɪz) *vb.* **1.** (*tr.*) to make rural in character, appearance, etc. **2.** (*intr.*) to go into the country to live. —**ˌru·ral·i·'za·tion** *or* **ˌru·ral·i·'sa·tion** *n.*

ru·ral sci·ence *or* **stud·ies** *n. Brit.* the study and theory of agriculture, biology, ecology, and associated fields.

Ru·rik ('rʊərɪk) *n.* died 879. Varangian (Scandinavian Viking) leader who founded the Russian monarchy. He gained control over Novgorod (?862) and his dynasty, the **Rurikids,** ruled until 1598.

Ru·ri·ta·ni·a (ˌrʊərɪ'teɪnɪə, -njə) *n.* **1.** an imaginary kingdom of central Europe: setting of several novels by Anthony Hope, esp. *The Prisoner of Zenda* (1894). **2.** any setting of adventure, romance, and intrigue. —**Ru·ri·'ta·ni·an** *adj., n.*

Rus. *abbrev. for* Russia(n).

ruse (ru:z) *n.* an action intended to mislead, deceive, or trick; stratagem. [C15: from Old French: trick, esp. to evade capture, from *ruser* to retreat, from Latin *recūsāre* to refuse]

Ru·se ('ru:seɪ) *n.* a city in NE Bulgaria, on the River Danube: the chief river port and one of the largest industrial centres in Bulgaria. Pop.: 158 240 (1971 est.).

rush[1] (rʌʃ) *vb.* **1.** to hurry or cause to hurry; hasten. **2.** to make a sudden attack upon (a fortress, position, person, etc.). **3.** (when *intr.,* often foll. by *at, in,* or *into*) to proceed or approach in a reckless manner. **4. rush one's fences.** to proceed with precipitate haste. **5.** (*intr.*) to come, flow, swell, etc., quickly or suddenly: *tears rushed to her eyes.* **6.** (*tr.*) *U.S.* to make a concerted effort to secure the agreement, participation, etc., of (a person). **7.** (*tr.*) *Rugby.* (of a pack) to move (the ball) forwards by short kicks and runs. ~*n.* **8.** the act or condition of rushing. **9.** a sudden surge towards someone or something: *a gold rush.* **10.** a sudden demand. **11.** (*usually pl.*) (in film-making) the initial prints of a scene or scenes before editing. **12.** *Rugby.* the act of rushing the ball. ~*adj.* (*prenominal*) **13.** requiring speed or urgency: *a rush job.* **14.** characterized by much movement, business, etc.: *a rush period.* [C14 *ruschen,* from Old French *ruser* to put to flight, from Latin *recūsāre* to refuse, reject] —'**rush·er** *n.*

rush[2] (rʌʃ) *n.* **1.** any annual or perennial plant of the genus *Juncus,* growing in wet places and typically having grasslike cylindrical leaves and small green or brown flowers: family *Juncaceae.* Many species are used to make baskets. **2.** any of various similar or related plants, such as the woodrush, scouring rush, and spike-rush. **3.** something valueless; a trifle; straw: *not worth a rush.* **4.** short for **rush light.** [Old English *risce, rysce;* related to Middle Dutch *risch,* Norwegian *rusk,* Old Slavonic *rozga* twig, rod] —'**rush·,like** *adj.*

rush hour *n.* a period at the beginning and end of the working day when large numbers of people are travelling to or from work.

rush light *or* **can·dle** *n.* a narrow candle, formerly in use, made of the pith of various types of rush dipped in tallow.

Rush·more ('rʌʃmɔː) *n.* **Mount.** a mountain in W South Dakota, in the Black Hills: a national memorial, with the faces of Washington, Lincoln, Jefferson, and Roosevelt carved into its side by Gutzon Borglum between 1927 and 1941. Height: 1841 m (6040 ft.).

rush·y ('rʌʃɪ) *adj.* **rush·i·er, rush·i·est.** abounding in, covered with, or made of rushes. —'**rush·i·ness** *n.*

rusk (rʌsk) *n.* **1.** a kind of light biscuit. **2.** a light bread dough, sweet or plain, baked twice until it is brown, hard, and crisp. [C16: from Spanish or Portuguese *rosca* screw, bread shaped in a twist, of unknown origin]

Rusk (rʌsk) *n.* **(David) Dean.** born 1909, U.S. politician and diplomat: secretary of state (1961–69).

Rus·kin ('rʌskɪn) *n.* **John.** 1819–1900, English art critic and social reformer. He was a champion of the Gothic Revival and the Pre-Raphaelites and saw a close connection between art and morality. From about 1860 he argued vigorously for social and economic planning. His works include *Modern Painters* (1843–60), *The Stones of Venice* (1851–53), *Unto this Last* (1862), *Time and Tide* (1867), and *Fors Clavigera* (1871–84).

Russ (rʌs) *n., pl.* **Russ** *or* **Russ·es,** *adj.* an archaic word for **Russian** (person or language).

Russ. *abbrev. for* Russia(n).

Rus·sell ('rʌsᵊl) *n.* **1. Ber·trand (Arthur William),** 3rd Earl Russell. 1872–1970, English philosopher and mathematician. His books include *Principles of Mathematics* (1903), *Principia Mathematica* (1910–13) with A. N. Whitehead, *Introduction to Mathematical Philosophy* (1919), *The Problems of Philosophy* (1912), *The Analysis of Mind* (1921), and *An Enquiry into Meaning and Truth* (1940): Nobel prize for literature 1950. **2. George Wil·liam,** penname *Æ.* 1867–1935, Irish poet and journalist. **3. John,** 1st Earl Russell. 1792–1878, English statesman; prime minister (1846–52; 1865–66). He led the campaign to carry the 1832 Reform Act. **4. Ken.** born 1927, English film director: his films include *Women in Love* (1969), *The Music Lovers* (1970), *The Boy Friend* (1971), and *Valentino* (1977).

Rus·sell di·a·gram *n.* See **Hertzsprung-Russell diagram.**

rus·set ('rʌsɪt) *n.* **1.** brown with a yellowish or reddish tinge. **2. a.** a rough homespun fabric, reddish-brown in colour, formerly in use for clothing. **b.** (*as modifier*): *a russet coat.* **3.** any of various apples with rough brownish-red skins. **4.** abnormal roughness on fruit, caused by parasites, pesticides, or frost. ~*adj.* **5.** (of tanned hide leather) dressed ready for staining. **6.** *Archaic.* simple; homely; rustic: *a russet life.* **7.** of the colour russet: *russet hair.* [C13: from Anglo-Norman, from Old French *rosset,* from *rous,* from Latin *russus;* related to Latin *ruber* red] —'**rus·set·ish** *or* '**rus·set·y** *adj.* —'**rus·set·,like** *adj.*

Rus·sia ('rʌʃə) *n.* **1.** another name for the **Russian Empire. 2.** another name for the **Soviet Union. 3.** another name for the **Russian Soviet Federated Socialist Republic.**

Rus·sia leath·er *n.* a smooth dyed leather made from calfskin and scented with birch tar oil, originally produced in Russia.

Rus·sian ('rʌʃən) *n.* **1.** the official language of the Soviet Union: an Indo-European language belonging to the East Slavonic branch. **2.** a native or inhabitant of Russia or the Soviet Union. ~*adj.* **3.** of, relating to, or characteristic of Russia or the Soviet Union, its people, or their language.

Rus·sian dress·ing *n.* mayonnaise with chilli sauce, chopped gherkins, etc.

Rus·sian Em·pire *n.* the tsarist empire in Asia and E Europe, overthrown by the Russian Revolution of 1917.

Rus·sian·ize *or* **Rus·sian·ise** ('rʌʃə,naɪz) *vb.* to make or become Russian in style, etc. —**,Rus·sian·i·'za·tion** *or* **,Rus·sian·i·'sa·tion** *n.*

Rus·sian Or·tho·dox Church *n.* the national Church of Russia, constituting a branch of the Eastern Church presided over by the Patriarch of Moscow.

Rus·sian Rev·o·lu·tion *n.* **1.** Also called: **February Revolution.** the uprising in Russia in March 1917, during which the tsar abdicated and a provisional government was set up. **2.** Also called: **October Revolution.** the seizure of power by the Bolsheviks under Lenin in November 1917, transforming the uprising into a socialist revolution. This was followed by a period of civil war against counter-revolutionary armies (1918–22), which ended in eventual victory for the Bolsheviks.

Rus·sian rou·lette *n.* **1.** a game of chance in which each player in turn spins the cylinder of a revolver loaded with only one cartridge and presses the trigger with the barrel against his own head. **2.** any foolish or potentially suicidal undertaking.

Rus·sian sal·ad *n.* a salad of cold diced cooked vegetables mixed with Russian dressing.

Rus·sian So·vi·et Fed·er·at·ed So·cial·ist Re·pub·lic *n.* the largest administrative division of the Soviet Union (over 76 per cent of the total area and 55 per cent of the population), extending from the Baltic to the Pacific and from the Arctic Ocean to the Caspian Sea: ranges from arctic to subtropical in climate and includes tundra, forests, steppes, and rich arable land; contains 20 major nationality groups and produces about 70 per cent of the agricultural and industrial output of the Soviet Union. Capital: Moscow. Pop.: 130 079 210 (1970). Area: 17 074 984 sq. km (6 592 658 sq. miles). Abbrev.: **RSFSR**

Rus·sian Tur·ke·stan *n.* See **Turkestan.**

Rus·sian wolf·hound *n.* a less common name for **borzoi.**

Rus·sian Zone *n.* another name for the **Soviet Zone.**

Russ·ky *or* **Russ·ki** ('rʌskɪ) *n., pl.* **·kies** *or* **·kis,** *adj. Chiefly U.S.* a slang word for **Russian.** [C20]

Rus·so- ('rʌsəʊ-) *combining form.* Russia or Russian: *Russo-Japanese.*

Rus·so-Jap·an·ese War *n.* a war (1904–05) between Russia and Japan, caused largely by rivalry over Korea and Manchuria. Russia suffered a series of major defeats.

Rus·so·phile ('rʌsəʊ,faɪl) *or* **Rus·so·phil** *n.* an admirer of Russia or the Soviet Union, its customs, political system, etc.

Rus·so·phobe ('rʌsəʊ,fəʊb) *n.* a person who feels intense and often irrational hatred (**Russophobia**) for the Soviet Union, its political system, etc. —**,Rus·so·'pho·bic** *adj.*

rust (rʌst) *n.* **1.** a reddish-brown oxide coating formed on iron or steel by the action of oxygen and moisture. **2.** Also called: **rust fungus.** *Plant pathol.* **a.** any basidiomycetous fungus of the order *Uredinales,* parasitic on cereal plants, conifers, etc. **b.** any of various plant diseases characterized by reddish-brown discoloration of the leaves and stem, esp. that caused by the rust fungi. **3. a.** a strong brown colour, sometimes with a reddish or yellowish tinge. **b.** (*as adj.*): *a rust carpet.* **4.** any corrosive or debilitating influence, esp. lack of use. ~*vb.* **5.** to become or cause to become coated with a layer of rust. **6.** to deteriorate or cause to deteriorate through some debilitating influence or lack of use: *he allowed his talent to rust over the years.* [Old English *rūst;* related to Old Saxon, Old High German *rost*] —'**rust·less** *adj.*

rust buck·et *n. Austral. slang.* a very badly rusted car.

rus·tic ('rʌstɪk) *adj.* **1.** of, characteristic of, or living in the country; rural. **2.** having qualities ascribed to country life or people; simple; unsophisticated: *rustic pleasures.* **3.** crude, awkward, or uncouth. **4.** made of untrimmed branches: *a rustic seat.* **5.** denoting or characteristic of a style of furniture popular in England in the 18th and 19th centuries, in which the legs and feet of chairs, tables, etc., were made to resemble roots, trunks, and branches of trees. **6.** (of masonry, etc.) having a rough or irregular surface and chamfered or recessed joints. ~*n.* **7.** a person who comes from or lives in the country. **8.** an unsophisticated, simple, or clownish person from the country. **9.** Also called: **rusticwork.** brick or stone having a rough finish. [C16: from Old French *rustique,* from Latin *rūsticus,* from *rūs* the country] —'**rus·ti·cal·ly** *adv.* —**rus·tic·i·ty** (rʌ'stɪsɪtɪ) *n.*

rus·ti·cate ('rʌstɪ,keɪt) *vb.* **1.** to banish or retire to the country. **2.** to make or become rustic in style, behaviour, etc. **3.** (*tr.*) to construct (brickwork or masonry) in a rustic manner. **4.** (*tr.*) *Brit.* to send down from university for a specified time as a punishment. [C17: from Latin *rūsticārī,* from *rūs* the country] —**,rus·ti·'ca·tion** *n.* —'**rus·ti·,ca·tor** *n.*

rus·tle[1] ('rʌsᵊl) *vb.* **1.** to make or cause to make a low crisp whispering or rubbing sound, as of dry leaves or paper. **2.** to move with such a sound. ~*n.* **3.** such a sound or sounds. [Old English *hrūxlian;* related to Gothic *hrukjan* to CROW, Old Norse *hraukr* raven, CROW] —'**rus·tling·ly** *adv.*

rus·tle[2] ('rʌsᵊl) *vb. U.S.* **1.** to steal (cattle, horses, etc.). **2.** *Informal.* to move swiftly and energetically. [C19: probably special use of RUSTLE[1] (in the sense: to move with quiet sound)]

rus·tler ('rʌslə) *n. U.S. informal.* **1.** a cattle or horse thief. **2.** an energetic or vigorous person.

rus·tle up *vb.* (*tr., adv.*) **1.** to prepare (a meal, etc.) rapidly, esp. at short notice. **2.** to forage for and obtain.

rust·proof ('rʌst,pruːf) *adj.* treated against rusting.

rust·y ('rʌstɪ) *adj.* **rust·i·er, rust·i·est.** **1.** covered with, affected by, or consisting of rust: *a rusty machine; a rusty deposit.* **2.** of the colour rust. **3.** discoloured by age: *a rusty coat.* **4.** (of the voice) tending to croak. **5.** old-fashioned in appearance; seemingly antiquated: *a rusty old gentleman.* **6.** out of practice; impaired in skill or knowledge by inaction or neglect. **7.** (of plants) affected by the rust fungus. —'**rust·i·ly** *adv.* —'**rust·i·ness** *n.*

rut[1] (rʌt) *n.* **1.** a groove or furrow in a soft road, caused by wheels. **2.** any deep mark, hole, or groove. **3.** a narrow or predictable way of life, set of attitudes, etc.; dreary or undeviating routine (esp. in the phrase **in a rut**). ~*vb.* **ruts, rut·ting, rut·ted. 4.** (*tr.*) to make a rut or ruts in. [C16: probably from French *route* road]

rut[2] (rʌt) *n.* **1.** a recurrent period of sexual excitement and reproductive activity in certain male ruminants, such as the deer, that corresponds to the period of oestrus in females. **2.** another name for **oestrus.** ~*vb.* **ruts, rut·ting, rut·ted. 3.** (*intr.*) (of male ruminants) to be in a period of sexual excitement and activity. [C15: from Old French *rut* noise, roar, from Latin *rugītus,* from *rugīre* to roar]

ru·ta·ba·ga (,ruːtə'beɪgə) *n.* the U.S. name for **swede.** [C18: from Swedish dialect *rotabagge,* literally: root bag]

ru+ta+ceous (ruːˈteɪʃəs) *adj.* of, relating to, or belonging to the *Rutaceae,* a family of tropical and temperate flowering plants many of which have aromatic leaves. The family includes rue, citrus trees, and dittany. [C19: from New Latin *Rutaceae,* from Latin *rūta* RUE[2]]

ruth (ruːθ) *n. Archaic.* **1.** pity; compassion. **2.** repentance; remorse. **3.** grief or distress. [C12: from *rewen* to RUE[1]]

Ruth (ruːθ) *n.* **1.** *Old Testament.* **a.** a Moabite woman, who left her own people to remain with her mother-in-law Naomi, and became the wife of Boaz; an ancestress of David. **b.** the book in which these events are recounted. **2. George Her·man.** nicknamed *Babe.* 1895–1948, U.S. professional baseball player from 1914 to 1935.

Ru+the+ni+a (ruːˈθiːnɪə) *n.* a region of E Europe on the south side of the Carpathian Mountains: belonged to Hungary from the 14th century, to Czechoslovakia from 1918 to 1939, and was ceded to the Soviet Union in 1945; now forms the Transcarpathian Region of the Ukrainian SSR. Also called: **Carpatho-Ukraine.**

Ru+the+ni+an (ruːˈθiːnɪən) *adj.* **1.** of or relating to Ruthenia, its people, or their dialect of Ukrainian. ~*n.* **2.** a dialect of Ukrainian. **3.** a native or inhabitant of Ruthenia.

ru+then+ic (ruːˈθɛnɪk) *adj.* of or containing ruthenium, esp. in a high valency state.

ru+the+ni·ous (ruːˈθiːnɪəs) *adj.* of or containing ruthenium in a divalent state.

ru+the+ni·um (ruːˈθiːnɪəm) *n.* a hard brittle white element of the platinum metal group. It occurs free with other platinum metals in pentlandite and other ores and is used to harden platinum and palladium. Symbol: Ru; atomic no.: 44; atomic wt.: 101.07; valency: 1-8; relative density: 12.41; melting pt.: 2310°C; boiling pt.: 3900°C. [C19: from Medieval Latin *Ruthenia* Russia, where it was first discovered]

ruth+er+ford (ˈrʌðəfəd) *n.* a unit of activity equal to the quantity of a radioactive nuclide required to produce one million disintegrations per second. Abbrev.: rd. [C20: named after Ernest RUTHERFORD]

Ruth·er·ford (ˈrʌðəfəd) *n.* **Er·nest,** 1st Baron Rutherford. 1871–1937, British physicist, born in New Zealand, who discovered the atomic nucleus (1909). Nobel prize for chemistry 1908.

ruth+er+for+di·um (ˌrʌðəˈfɔːdɪəm) *n.* the U.S. name for the element with the atomic number 104, known in the USSR as Kurchatovium. [C20: named after E. RUTHERFORD]

ruth+ful (ˈruːθfʊl) *adj. Archaic.* full of or causing sorrow or pity. —**ˈruth+ful+ly** *adv.* —**ˈruth+ful+ness** *n.*

ruth+less (ˈruːθlɪs) *adj.* feeling or showing no mercy; hardhearted. —**ˈruth+less+ly** *adv.* —**ˈruth+less+ness** *n.*

ru+ti+lant (ˈruːtɪlənt) *adj. Rare.* of a reddish colour or glow. [C15: from Latin *rutilāns* having a red glow, from *rutilāre,* from *rutilus* ruddy, red]

ru+ti+lat+ed (ˈruːtɪˌleɪtɪd) *adj.* (of minerals, esp. quartz) containing needles of rutile.

ru+tile (ˈruːtaɪl) *n.* a golden or reddish-brown to black mineral consisting of titanium dioxide in tetragonal crystalline form. It occurs in plutonic and metamorphic rocks, and is an important source of titanium and titanium dioxide. Formula: TiO_2. [C19: via French from German *Rutil,* from Latin *rutilus* red, glowing]

Rut+land (ˈrʌtlənd) *n.* a former inland county of central England: the smallest English county. It became part of Leicestershire in 1974.

rut+tish (ˈrʌtɪʃ) *adj.* **1.** (of an animal) in a condition of rut. **2.** lascivious or salacious. —**ˈrut+tish+ly** *adv.* —**ˈrut+tish+ness** *n.*

rut+ty (ˈrʌtɪ) *adj.* **+ti+er, +ti+est.** full of ruts or holes: *a rutty track.* —**ˈrut+ti+ly** *adv.* —**ˈrut+ti+ness** *n.*

Ru+wen+zo+ri (ˌruːwɛnˈzɔːrɪ) *n.* a mountain range in central Africa, on the Ugandan-Zaïrese border between Lakes Edward and Albert: generally thought to be Ptolemy's "Mountains of the Moon". Highest peak: Mount Stanley, 5109 m (16 763 ft.).

Ruys·dael (ˈriːzdɑːl, -deɪl, ˈraɪz-; *Dutch* ˈrœyzdaːl) a variant spelling of **Ruisdael.**

Ruy·ter (ˈraɪtə; *Dutch* ˈrœytər) *n.* **Mi·chel A·dri·aans·zoon de** (ˈmixəl ˌadriˈansun də). 1607–76, Dutch admiral, who distinguished himself against several foreign fleets. Twice he entered English rivers (the Medway and the Thames) in pursuit of the English fleet (1667).

R.V. *abbrev. for* Revised Version (of the Bible).

R.W. *abbrev. for:* **1.** Right Worshipful. **2.** Right Worthy.

RWA *international car registration for* Rwanda.

Rwan+da[1] (rʊˈændə) *n.* a republic in central Africa: part of German East Africa from 1899 until 1917, when Belgium took over the administration; became a republic in 1961 after the successful Hutu revolt against the Tutsi (1959). Official languages: Rwanda and French. Currency: Rwanda franc. Capital: Kigali. Pop.: 3 572 550 (1970). Area: 26 338 sq. km (10 169 sq. miles). Former name (until 1962): **Ruanda.**

Rwan+da[2] (rʊˈændə) *n.* the official language of Rwanda, belonging to the Bantu group of the Niger-Congo family and closely related to Kirundi.

r.w.d. *abbrev. for* rear-wheel drive.

Rwy. *or* **Ry.** *abbrev. for* railway.

-ry *suffix forming nouns.* variant of **-ery:** *dentistry.*

Rya+zan (*Russian* rjaˈzanj) *n.* a city in the W central Soviet Union: capital of a medieval principality; oil refineries and engineering industries. Pop.: 419 000 (1975 est.).

Ry+binsk (*Russian* ˈribinsk) *n.* a city in the W central Soviet Union, on the River Volga: an important river port, terminal of the Mariinsk Waterway (between Leningrad and the Volga) at the SE end of the **Rybinsk Reservoir** (area: 4700 sq. km (1800 sq. miles)). Pop.: 233 000 (1975 est.). Former name (from the Revolution until 1957): **Shcherbakov.**

Ry+dal (ˈraɪdᵊl) *n.* a village in NW England, in Cumbria on **Rydal Water** (a small lake): site of **Rydal Mount,** home of Wordsworth from 1813 to 1850.

rye[1] (raɪ) *n.* **1.** a tall hardy widely cultivated annual grass, *Secale cereale,* having soft bluish-green leaves, bristly flower spikes, and light brown grain. See also **wild rye. 2.** the grain of this grass, used in making flour and whiskey, and as a livestock food. **3.** Also called: **rye whiskey.** whiskey distilled from rye. U.S. whiskey must by law contain not less than 51 per cent rye. [Old English *ryge;* related to Old Norse *rugr,* Old French *rogga,* Old Saxon *roggo*]

rye[2] (raɪ) *n. Gypsy dialect.* a gentleman. [from Romany *rai,* from Sanskrit *rājan* king; see RAJAH]

rye bread *n.* any of various breads made entirely or partly from rye flour, often with caraway seeds.

rye-brome *n.* a grass, *Bromus secalinus,* native to Europe and Asia, having rough leaves and wheatlike ears. U.S. names: **cheat, chess.**

rye-grass *n.* any of various grasses of the genus *Lolium,* esp. *L. perenne,* native to Europe, N Africa, and Asia and widely cultivated as forage crops. They have a flattened flower spike and hairless leaves.

Ry+o·bu Shin+to (riːˈəʊbuː) *n.* a fusion of Shinto and Buddhism, which flourished in Japan in the 13th century. [from Japanese *ryō bu,* literally: two parts]

ry·o+kan (rɪˈəʊkən) *n.* a traditional Japanese inn.

ry·ot (ˈraɪət) *n.* (in India) a peasant or tenant farmer. [C17: from Hindi *raʿīyat,* from Arabic *raʿīyah* flock, peasants, from *raʿā* pasture]

Rys+wick (ˈrɪzwɪk) *n.* the English name for **Rijswijk.**

Ry·u+kyu Is+lands (rɪˈuːkjuː) *n.* a chain of 55 islands in the W Pacific, extending almost 650 km (400 miles) from S Japan to N Taiwan: an ancient kingdom, under Chinese rule from the late 14th century, Japanese supremacy from 1872 to 1945, and U.S. control from 1945 to 1972; now part of Japan again. They are subject to frequent typhoons. Chief town: Naha City (on Okinawa). Pop.: 945 111 (1970). Area: 2196 sq. km (849 sq. miles).

Ryu·rik (ˈrʊərɪk) *n.* a variant spelling of **Rurik.**

S

s *or* **S** (ɛs) *n., pl.* **s's, S's,** *or* **Ss. 1.** the 19th letter and 15th consonant of the modern English alphabet. **2.** a speech sound represented by this letter, usually an alveolar fricative, either voiceless, as in *sit,* or voiced, as in *dogs.* **3. a.** something shaped like an S. **b.** (*in combination*)*: an S-bend in a road.*

S *symbol for:* **1.** satisfactory. **2.** Society. **3.** small (size). **4.** South. **5.** *Chem.* sulphur. **6.** *Physics.* **a.** entropy. **b.** siemens. **7.** *Physics.* strangeness. ~ **8.** *international car registration for* Sweden.

s. *abbrev. for:* **1.** second (of time). **2.** section. **3.** see. **4.** semi-. **5.** shilling. **6.** sign(ed). **7.** singular. **8.** sire. **9.** son. **10.** substantive. **11.** succeeded.

S. *abbrev. for:* **1.** sabbath. **2.** (*pl.* **SS**) Saint. **3.** Saturday. **4.** Saxon. **5.** *Currency.* **a.** schilling. **b.** sol. **c.** sucre. **6.** school. **7.** Sea. **8.** senate. **9.** September. **10.** (in prescriptions) signā. [Latin: label] **11.** Signor. **12.** Socialist. **13.** Society. **14.** Sunday. **15.** (in titles) Fellow. [Latin *socius*]

-s[1] *or* **-es** *suffix.* forming the plural of most nouns: *boys; boxes.* [from Old English *-as,* plural nominative and accusative ending of some masculine nouns]

-s[2] *or* **-es** *suffix.* forming the third person singular present indicative tense of verbs: *he runs; she washes.* [from Old English (northern dialect) *-es, -s,* originally the ending of the second person singular]

-s[3] *suffix of nouns.* forming nicknames and names expressing affection or familiarity: *Fats; Fingers; ducks.* [special use of -s[1]]

-'s *suffix.* **1.** forming the possessive singular of nouns and some pronouns: *man's; one's.* **2.** forming the possessive plural of nouns whose plurals do not end in *-s: children's.* **3.** forming the plural of numbers, letters, or symbols: *20's; p's and q's.* **4.** *Informal.* contraction of *is* or *has: he's here; John's coming; it's gone.* **5.** *Informal.* contraction of *us* with *let: let's.* **6.** *Informal.* contraction of *does* in some questions: *where's he live? what's he do?* [senses 1, 2: assimilated contraction from Middle English *-es,* from Old English, masculine and neuter genitive singular; sense 3, equivalent to -s[1]]

-s' *suffix.* forming the possessive of plural nouns ending in the sound *s* or *z* and of some singular nouns: *girls'; beaux'; for goodness' sake.*

Sa *a former chemical symbol for* samarium.

s.a. *abbrev. for:* **1.** semiannual. **2.** sex appeal. **3.** sine anno. [Latin: without date]

S.A. *abbrev. for:* **1.** Salvation Army. **2.** South Africa. **3.** South America. **4.** South Australia. **5.** *Sturmabteilung:* the Nazi terrorist militia, organized around 1924.

Saa·di ('sɑːdiː) *n.* a variant spelling of **Sadi.**

Saar (sɑː, *German* zaːr) *n.* **1.** a river in W Europe, rising in the Vosges Mountains and flowing north to the Moselle River in West Germany. Length: 246 km (153 miles). **2. the Saar.** another name for **Saarland.**

Saar+brück+en (*German* zaːr'brykᵊn) *n.* an industrial city in W West Germany, capital of Saarland state, on the Saar River. Pop.: 389 717 (1974 est.).

Saa·ri·nen ('sɑːrɪnən) *n.* **Ee·ro** ('eɪrəʊ). 1910–61, U.S. architect, born in Finland. His works include the U.S. Embassy, London (1960).

Saar+land (*German* 'zaːrlant) *n.* a state of W West Germany: formed in 1919; under League of Nations administration until 1935; occupied by France (1945–57); contains rich coal deposits and is a major industrial region. Capital: Saarbrücken. Pop.: 1 119 742 (1970). Area: 2567 sq. km (991 sq. miles).

Sab. *abbrev. for* Sabbath.

Sa·ba ('sɑːbə) *n.* **1.** an island in the NE West Indies, in the Netherlands Antilles. Pop.: 971 (1972 est.). Area: 13 sq. km (5 sq. miles). **2.** another name for **Sheba**[1].

Sa+ba+dell (*Spanish* ˌsaβaˌðel) *n.* a town in NE Spain, near Barcelona: textile manufacturing. Pop.: 159 408 (1970).

sab·a+dil+la (ˌsæbə'dɪlə) *n.* **1.** a tropical American liliaceous plant, *Schoenocaulon officinale.* **2.** the bitter brown seeds of this plant, which contain the alkaloids veratrine and veratridine and are used in insecticides. [C19: from Spanish *cebadilla,* diminutive of *cebada* barley, from Latin *cibāre* to feed, from *cibus* food]

Sa+bae·an *or* **Sa+be·an** (sə'biːən) *n.* **1.** an inhabitant or native of ancient Saba. **2.** the ancient Semitic language of Saba. ~*adj.* **3.** of or relating to ancient Saba, its inhabitants, or their language. [C16: from Latin *Sabaeus,* from Greek *Sabaios* belonging to Saba (Sheba)]

Sa+bah ('sɑːbɑː) *n.* a state of Malaysia, occupying N Borneo and offshore islands in the South China and Sulu Seas: became a British protectorate in 1888; gained independence and joined Malaysia in 1963. Capital: Kota Kinabalu. Pop.: 655 622 (1970). Area: 76 522 sq. km (29 545 sq. miles). Former name (until 1963): **North Borneo.**

Sab·a+oth (sæ'beɪɒθ, 'sæbeɪɒθ) *n. Bible.* hosts, armies (esp. in the phrase **the Lord of Sabaoth** in Romans 9:29). [C14: via Latin and Greek from Hebrew *ç'bāōth,* from *çābā*]

Sa·ba·tier (*French* saba'tjeː) *n.* **Paul** (pɔl). 1854–1941, French chemist, who discovered a process for the hydrogenation of organic compounds: shared the Nobel prize for chemistry (1912).

sa+ba+yon (ˌsæbaɪjɒn; *French* saba'jɔ̃) *n.* a dessert very similar to zabaglione, but made with cream.

sab+bat ('sæbæt, -ət) *n.* another word for **Sabbath** (sense 3).

Sab+ba+tar+i·an (ˌsæbə'tɛərɪən) *n.* **1.** a person advocating the strict religious observance of Sunday. **2.** a person who observes Saturday as the Sabbath. ~*adj.* **3.** of or relating to the Sabbath or its observance. [C17: from Late Latin *sabbatārius* a Sabbath-keeper] —ˌ**Sab+ba+'tar+i·an+ism** *n.*

Sab+bath ('sæbəθ) *n.* **1.** the seventh day of the week, Saturday, devoted to worship and rest from work in Judaism and in certain Christian Churches. **2.** Sunday, observed by Christians as the day of worship and rest from work in commemoration of Christ's Resurrection. **3.** (*not cap.*) a period of rest. **4.** Also called: **sabbat, witches' Sabbath.** a midnight meeting or secret rendezvous for practitioners of witchcraft, sorcery, or devil worship. [Old English *sabbat,* from Latin *sabbatum,* from Greek *sabbaton,* from Hebrew *shabbāth,* from *shābath* to rest]

sab+bath school *n.* (*sometimes cap.*) *Chiefly U.S.* a school for religious instruction held on the Sabbath.

sab+bat·i+cal (sə'bætɪkᵊl) *adj.* **1.** denoting a period of leave granted to university staff, teachers, etc., esp. approximately every seventh year: *a sabbatical year; sabbatical leave.* **2.** denoting a post that renders the holder eligible for such leave. ~*n.* **3.** any sabbatical period. [C16: from Greek *sabbatikos;* see SABBATH]

Sab+bat·i+cal (sə'bætɪkᵊl) *adj. also* **Sab+bat+ic. 1.** of, relating to, or appropriate to the Sabbath as a day of rest and religious observance. ~*n.* **2.** short for **sabbatical year.**

sab+bat·i+cal year *n.* (*often cap.*) *Bible.* a year during which the land was to be left uncultivated, debts annulled, etc., supposed to be observed every seventh year by the ancient Israelites according to Leviticus 25.

S.A.B.C. *abbrev. for* South African Broadcasting Corporation.

Sa+bel+li·an (sə'belɪən) *n.* **1.** an extinct language or group of languages of ancient Italy, surviving only in a few inscriptions belonging to the Osco-Umbrian group. **2.** a member of any of the ancient peoples speaking this language, including the Sabines. ~*adj.* **3.** of or relating to this language or its speakers. [C17: from Latin *Sabellī* group of Italian tribes]

sa+ber ('seɪbə) *n., vb.* the U.S. spelling of **sabre.**

sa+bin ('sæbɪn, 'seɪ-) *n. Physics.* a unit of acoustic absorption equal to the absorption resulting from one square foot of a perfectly absorbing surface. [C20: introduced by Wallace C. *Sabine* (1868–1919), U.S. physicist]

Sa·bin ('seɪbɪn) *n.* **Al·bert Bruce.** born 1906, U.S. microbiologist, born in Poland. He developed the **Sabin vaccine** (1955), taken orally to immunize against poliomyelitis.

Sab+ine ('sæbaɪn) *n.* **1.** a member of an ancient Oscan-speaking people who lived in central Italy northeast of Rome. ~*adj.* **2.** of, characteristic of, or relating to this people or their language.

sa+ble ('seɪbᵊl) *n., pl.* **+bles** *or* **+ble. 1.** a marten, *Martes zibellina,* of N Asian forests, with dark brown luxuriant fur. **2. a.** the highly valued fur of this animal. **b.** (*as modifier*)*: a sable coat.* **3. American sable.** the brown, slightly less valuable fur of the American marten, *Martes americana.* **4.** the colour of sable fur: a dark brown to yellowish-brown colour. ~*adj.* **5.** of the colour of sable fur. **6.** black; dark; gloomy. **7.** (*usually postpositive*) *Heraldry.* of the colour black. [C15: from Old French, from Old High German *zobel,* of Slavic origin; related to Russian *sobol',* Polish *sobol*]

Sa+ble ('seɪbᵊl) *n.* **Cape. 1.** a cape at the S tip of Florida: the southernmost point of continental U.S. **2.** the southernmost point of Nova Scotia, Canada.

sa+ble an+te+lope *n.* a large black E African antelope, *Hippotragus niger,* with long backward-curving horns.

sab+ot ('sæbəʊ; *French* sa'boː) *n.* **1.** a shoe made from a single block of wood. **2.** a shoe with a wooden sole and a leather or cloth upper. **3.** a metal casing fitted around the base of a projectile in order to make it fit the rifling of a firearm better and so increase its velocity. **4.** *Austral.* a small yacht with a shortened bow. [C17: from French, probably from Old French *savate* an old shoe, also influenced by *bot* BOOT[1]; related to Italian *ciabatta* old shoe, Old Provençal *sabata*]

sab·o+tage ('sæbəˌtɑːʒ) *n.* **1.** the deliberate destruction, disruption, or damage of equipment, a public service, etc., as by enemy agents, dissatisfied employees, etc. **2.** any similar action or behaviour. ~*vb.* **3.** (*tr.*) to destroy, damage, or disrupt, esp. by secret means. [C20: from French, from *saboter* to spoil through clumsiness (literally: to clatter in sabots)]

sab·o+teur (ˌsæbə'tɜː) *n.* a person who commits sabotage. [C20: from French; see SABOTAGE]

sa+bra ('sɑːbrə) *n.* a Jew born in Israel. [from Hebrew *Sabēr* prickly pear, common plant in the coastal areas of the country]

sa+bre *or U.S.* **sa+ber** ('seɪbə) *n.* **1.** a stout single-edged cavalry sword, having a curved blade. **2.** a sword used in fencing, having a narrow V-shaped blade, a semicircular guard, and a slightly curved hand. **3.** a cavalry soldier. ~*vb.* **4.** (*tr.*) to injure or kill with a sabre. [C17: via French from German (dialect) *Sabel,* from Middle High German *sebel,* perhaps from Magyar *szablya;* compare Russian *sablya* sabre]

sa·bre·tache (ˈsæbəˌtæʃ) *n.* a leather case suspended from a cavalryman's saddle. [C19: via French from German *Säbeltasche* sabre pocket]

sa·bre-toothed ti·ger *or* **cat** *n.* any of various extinct Tertiary felines of the genus *Smilodon* and related genera, with long curved upper canine teeth.

sab·u·lous (ˈsæbjʊləs) *or* **sab·u·lose** (ˈsæbjʊləʊs) *adj.* like sand in texture; gritty. [C17: from Latin *sabulōsus,* from *sabulum* SAND] —**sab·u·los·i·ty** (ˌsæbjʊˈlɒsɪtɪ) *n.*

sac (sæk) *n.* a pouch, bag, or pouchlike part in an animal or plant. [C18: from French, from Latin *saccus;* see SACK[1]] —**sac·cate** (ˈsækɪt, -eɪt) *adj.* —ˈ**sac·ˌlike** *adj.*

sac·a·ton (ˌsækəˈtəʊn) *n.* a coarse grass, *Sporobolus wrightii,* of the southwestern U.S. and Mexico, grown for hay and pasture. [American Spanish *zacatón,* from *zacate* coarse grass, from Nahuatl *zacatl*]

sac·cha·rase (ˈsækəˌreɪs) *n.* another name for **invertase.**

sac·cha·rate (ˈsækəˌreɪt) *n.* any salt or ester of saccharic acid.

sac·char·ic ac·id (sæˈkærɪk) *n.* a white soluble solid dicarboxylic acid obtained by the oxidation of cane sugar or starch; 2,3,4,5-tetrahydroxyhexanedioic acid. Formula: $COOH(CHOH)_4COOH$.

sac·cha·ride (ˈsækəˌraɪd, -rɪd) *n.* any sugar or other carbohydrate, esp. a simple sugar.

sac·char·i·fy (sæˈkærɪˌfaɪ), **sac·cha·rize,** *or* **sac·cha·rise** (ˈsækəˌraɪz) *vb.* ·**fies,** ·**fy·ing,** ·**fied** (*tr.*) to convert (starch) into sugar. —**sac·ˌchar·i·fi·ˈca·tion, ˌsac·cha·ri·ˈza·tion,** *or* **ˌsac·cha·ri·ˈsa·tion** *n.*

sac·cha·rim·e·ter (ˌsækəˈrɪmɪtə) *n.* any instrument for measuring the strength of sugar solutions, esp. a type of polarimeter for determining the concentration from the extent to which the solution rotates the plane of polarized light. —**ˌsac·cha·ˈrim·e·try** *n.*

sac·cha·rin (ˈsækərɪn) *n.* a very sweet white crystalline slightly soluble powder used as a nonfattening sweetener. Formula: $C_7H_5NO_3S$. [C19: from SACCHARO- + -IN]

sac·cha·rine (ˈsækəˌraɪn, -ˌriːn) *adj.* **1.** excessively sweet; sugary: *a saccharine smile.* **2.** of, relating to, of the nature of, or containing sugar or saccharin. —ˈ**sac·cha·rine·ly** *adv.* —**sac·cha·rin·i·ty** (ˌsækəˈrɪnɪtɪ) *n.*

sac·cha·ro- *or before a vowel* **sac·char-** *combining form.* sugar: *saccharomycete.* [via Latin from Greek *sakkharon,* ultimately from Sanskrit *śarkarā* sugar]

sac·cha·roid (ˈsækəˌrɔɪd) *adj.* **1.** Also: **saccharoidal.** *Geology.* having or designating a texture resembling that of loaf sugar: *saccharoid marble.* ~*n.* **2.** *Biochem.* any of a group of polysaccharides that remotely resemble sugars, but are not sweet and are often insoluble.

sac·cha·rom·e·ter (ˌsækəˈrɒmɪtə) *n.* a hydrometer used to measure the strengths of sugar solutions. It is usually calibrated directly to give a reading of concentration.

sac·cha·rose (ˈsækəˌrəʊz, -ˌrəʊs) *n.* a technical name for **sugar** (sense 1).

Sac·co (ˈsækəʊ) *n.* **Ni·co·la** (niˈkɔːla). 1891–1927, U.S. radical agitator, born in Italy. With Bartolomeo Vanzetti, he was executed for murder (1927) despite suspicions that their political opinions influenced the verdict: the case caused international protests.

sac·cu·late (ˈsækjʊlɪt, -ˌleɪt), **sac·cu·lat·ed,** *or* **sac·cu·lar** *adj.* of, relating to, or possessing a saccule, saccules, or a sacculus. —**ˌsac·cu·ˈla·tion** *n.*

sac·cule (ˈsækjuːl) *or* **sac·cu·lus** (ˈsækjʊləs) *n.* **1.** a small sac. **2.** the smaller of the two parts of the membranous labyrinth of the internal ear. Compare **utricle** (sense 1). [C19: from Latin *sacculus* diminutive of *saccus* SACK[1]]

sac·er·do·tal (ˌsæsəˈdəʊtᵊl) *adj.* of, relating to, or characteristic of priests. [C14: from Latin *sacerdōtālis,* from *sacerdōs* priest, from *sacer* sacred] —**ˌsac·er·ˈdo·tal·ly** *adv.*

sac·er·do·tal·ism (ˌsæsəˈdəʊtᵊˌlɪzəm) *n.* **1.** the principles, methods, etc., of the priesthood. **2.** the belief that ordained priests are endowed with sacramental and sacrificial powers. **3.** exaggerated respect for priests. **4.** *Derogatory.* power over people's opinions and actions achieved by priests through sophistry or guile. —**ˌsac·er·ˈdo·tal·ist** *n.*

sa·chem (ˈseɪtʃəm) *n.* **1.** *U.S.* a leader of a political party or organization, esp. of Tammany Hall. **2.** another name for **sagamore.** [C17: from Narragansett *săchim* chief] —**sa·chem·ic** (seɪˈtʃɛmɪk, ˈseɪtʃə-) *adj.*

sa·chet (ˈsæʃeɪ) *n.* **1.** a small sealed envelope, usually made of plastic or waxed paper, for containing cream, shampoo, etc. **2. a.** a small soft bag containing perfumed powder, placed in drawers to scent clothing. **b.** the powder contained in such a bag. [C19: from Old French: a little bag, from *sac* bag; see SACK[1]]

Sachs (*German* zaks) *n.* **Hans** (hans). 1494–1576, German master shoemaker and Meistersinger, portrayed by Wagner in *Die Meistersinger von Nürnberg.*

Sach·sen (ˈzaksᵊn) *n.* the German name for **Saxony.**

sack[1] (sæk) *n.* **1.** a large bag made of coarse cloth, thick paper, etc., used as a container. **2.** Also called: **sackful.** the amount contained in a sack, sometimes used as a unit of measurement. **3.** Also called: **sacque** (sæk). **a.** a woman's full loose hip-length jacket, worn in the 18th and mid-20th centuries. **b.** a woman's loose tube-shaped dress. **4.** *Cricket.* the Australian word for **bye. 5.** a slang word for **bed. 6. the sack.** *Informal.* dismissal from employment. **7. hit the sack.** *Slang.* to go to bed. ~*vb.* (*tr.*) **8.** *Informal.* to dismiss from employment. **9.** to put into a sack or sacks. [Old English *sacc,* from Latin *saccus* bag, from Greek *sakkos;* related to Hebrew *saq*] —ˈ**sack·ˌlike** *adj.*

sack[2] (sæk) *n.* **1.** the plundering of a place by an army or mob, usually involving destruction, slaughter, etc. ~*vb.* **2.** (*tr.*) to plunder and partially destroy (a place). [C16: from French phrase *mettre à sac,* literally: to put (loot) in a sack, from Latin *saccus* SACK[1]] —ˈ**sack·er** *n.*

sack[3] (sæk) *n. Archaic except in trademarks.* any dry white wine from SW Europe, esp. sherry. [C16 *wyne seck,* from French *vin sec* dry wine, from Latin *siccus* dry]

sack·but (ˈsækˌbʌt) *n.* a medieval form of trombone. [C16: from French *saqueboute,* from Old French *saquer* to pull + *bouter* to push; see BUTT[3]]

sack·cloth (ˈsækˌklɒθ) *n.* **1.** coarse cloth such as sacking. **2.** garments made of such cloth, worn formerly to indicate mourning or penitence. **3. sackcloth and ashes.** a public display of extreme grief, remorse, or repentance.

sack coat *or* **sacque** (sæk) *n.* a hip-length coat with no waist seam, worn as the jacket of a suit. —ˈ**sack-ˌcoat·ed** *adj.*

sack·ing (ˈsækɪŋ) *n.* coarse cloth used for making sacks, woven from flax, hemp, jute, etc.

sack race *n.* a race in which the competitors' legs and often bodies are enclosed in sacks. —**sack rac·ing** *n.*

Sack·ville (ˈsækvɪl) *n.* **Thom·as,** 1st Earl of Dorset. 1536–1608, English poet, dramatist, and statesman. He collaborated with Thomas Norton on the early blank-verse tragedy *Gorboduc* (1561).

sa·cral[1] (ˈseɪkrəl) *adj.* of, relating to, or associated with sacred rites. [C19: from Latin *sacrum* sacred object]

sa·cral[2] (ˈseɪkrəl) *adj.* of or relating to the sacrum. [C18: from New Latin *sacrālis* of the SACRUM]

sac·ra·ment (ˈsækrəmənt) *n.* **1.** an outward sign combined with a prescribed form of words and regarded as conferring some specific grace upon those who receive it. The Protestant sacraments are baptism and the Lord's Supper. In the Roman Catholic and Eastern Churches they are baptism, penance, confirmation, the Eucharist, holy orders, matrimony, and extreme unction. **2.** (*often cap.*) the Eucharist. **3.** the consecrated elements of the Eucharist, esp. the bread. **4.** something regarded as possessing a sacred or mysterious significance. **5.** a symbol; pledge. [C12: from Church Latin *sacrāmentum* vow, from Latin *sacrāre* to consecrate]

sac·ra·men·tal (ˌsækrəˈmɛntᵊl) *adj.* **1.** of, relating to, or having the nature of a sacrament. **2.** bound by or as if by a sacrament. ~*n.* **3.** *R.C. Church.* a sacrament-like ritual action, such as the sign of the cross or the use of holy water. —**ˌsac·ra·ˈmen·tal·ly** *adv.* —**sac·ra·men·tal·i·ty** (ˌsækrəmɛnˈtælɪtɪ) *or* **ˌsac·ra·ˈmen·tal·ness** *n.*

sac·ra·men·tal·ism (ˌsækrəˈmɛntᵊˌlɪzəm) *n. Theol.* belief in or special emphasis upon the efficacy of the sacraments for conferring grace. —**ˌsac·ra·ˈmen·tal·ist** *n.*

Sac·ra·men·tar·i·an (ˌsækrəmɛnˈtɛərɪən) *n.* **1.** *Theol.* any Protestant theologian, such as Zwingli, who maintained that the bread and wine of the Eucharist were the body and blood of Christ only in a figurative sense and denied his real presence in these elements. **2.** one who believes in sacramentalism. ~*adj.* **3.** of or relating to Sacramentarians. **4.** (*not cap.*) of or relating to sacraments. —**ˌSac·ra·men·ˈtar·i·an·ism** *n.*

Sac·ra·men·to (ˌsækrəˈmɛntəʊ) *n.* **1.** an inland port in N central California, capital of the state at the confluence of the American and Sacramento Rivers: became a boom town in the gold rush of the 1850s. Pop.: 267 483 (1973 est.). **2.** a river in N California, flowing generally south to San Francisco Bay. Length: 615 km (382 miles).

sa·crar·i·um (sæˈkrɛərɪəm) *n., pl.* ·**crar·i·a** (-ˈkrɛərɪə). **1.** the sanctuary of a church. **2.** *R.C. Church.* a place near the altar of a church, similar in function to the piscina, where materials used in the sacred rites are deposited or poured away. [C18: from Latin *sacrārium,* from *sacer* SACRED]

sa·cred (ˈseɪkrɪd) *adj.* **1.** exclusively devoted to a deity or to some religious ceremony or use; holy; consecrated. **2.** worthy of or regarded with reverence, awe, or respect. **3.** protected by superstition or piety from irreligious actions. **4.** connected with or intended for religious use: *sacred music.* **5. sacred to.** dedicated to; in honour of. [C14: from Latin *sacrāre* to set apart as holy, from *sacer* holy] —ˈ**sa·cred·ly** *adv.* —ˈ**sa·cred·ness** *n.*

Sa·cred Col·lege *n.* the collective body of the cardinals of the Roman Catholic Church.

sa·cred cow *n. Informal.* a person, institution, custom, etc., unreasonably held to be beyond criticism. [alluding to the Hindu belief that cattle are sacred]

Sa·cred Heart *n. R.C. Church.* **1.** the heart of Jesus Christ, a symbol of His love and sacrifice. **2.** a representation of this, usually bleeding, as an aid to devotion.

sa·cred mush·room *n.* **1.** any of various hallucinogenic mushrooms, esp. species of *Psilocybe* and *Amanita,* that have been eaten in rituals in various parts of the world. **2.** a mescal button, used in a similar way.

sac·ri·fice (ˈsækrɪˌfaɪs) *n.* **1.** a surrender of something of value as a means of gaining something more desirable or of preventing some evil. **2.** a ritual killing of a person or animal with the intention of propitiating or pleasing a deity. **3.** a symbolic offering of something to a deity. **4.** the person, animal, or object surrendered, destroyed, killed, or offered. **5.** a religious ceremony involving one or more sacrifices. **6.** loss entailed by giving up or selling something at less than its value. **7.** *Chess.* the act or an instance of sacrificing a piece. ~*vb.* **8.** to make a sacrifice (of); give up, surrender, or destroy (a person, thing, etc.). **9.** *Chess.* to permit or force one's opponent to capture a piece freely, as in playing a combination or gambit: *he sacrificed his queen and checkmated his opponent on the next move.* [C13: via Old French from Latin *sacrificium,* from *sacer* holy + *facere* to make] —**'sac+ri+ˌfice+a·ble** *adj.* —**'sac+ri+ˌfic+er** *n.* —**'sac+ri+ˌfic+ing+ly** *adv.*

sac+ri+fi·cial (ˌsækrɪ'fɪʃəl) *adj.* used in or connected with a sacrifice. —**ˌsac+ri+'fi·cial+ly** *adv.*

sac+ri+fi·cial an+ode *n. Metallurgy.* an electropositive metal, such as zinc, that protects a more important electronegative part by corroding when attacked by electrolytic action.

sac+ri+lege ('sækrɪlɪdʒ) *n.* **1.** the misuse or desecration of anything regarded as sacred or as worthy of extreme respect: *to play Mozart's music on a kazoo is sacrilege.* **2.** the act or an instance of taking anything sacred for secular use. [C13: from Old French *sacrilège,* from Latin *sacrilegium,* from *sacrilegus* temple-robber, from *sacra* sacred things + *legere* to take] —**sac+ri+le·gist** (ˌsækrɪ'li:dʒɪst) *n.*

sac+ri+le·gious (ˌsækrɪ'lɪdʒəs) *adj.* **1.** of, relating to, or involving sacrilege; impious. **2.** guilty of sacrilege. —**ˌsac+ri+'le·gious+ly** *adv.* —**ˌsac+ri+'le·gious+ness** *n.*

sa+cring ('seɪkrɪŋ) *n. Archaic.* the act or ritual of consecration, esp. of the Eucharist or of a bishop. [C13: from obsolete *sacren* to consecrate, from Latin *sacrāre;* see SACRED]

sa+cring bell *n. Chiefly R.C. Church.* a small bell rung at the elevation of the Host and chalice during Mass.

sac+ris+tan ('sækrɪstən) *or* **sac+rist** ('sækrɪst, 'seɪ-) *n.* **1.** a person who has charge of the contents of a church, esp. the sacred vessels, vestments, etc. **2.** a less common word for **sexton.** [C14: from Medieval Latin *sacristānus,* from *sacrista,* from Latin *sacer* holy]

sac+ris+ty ('sækrɪstɪ) *n., pl.* **+ties.** a room attached to a church or chapel where the sacred vessels, etc., are kept and where priests attire themselves. [C17: from Medieval Latin *sacristia;* see SACRISTAN]

sa+cro·il·i+ac (ˌseɪkrəʊ'ɪlɪˌæk, ˌsæk-) *Anatomy.* ~*adj.* **1.** of or relating to the sacrum and ilium, their articulation, or their associated ligaments. ~*n.* **2.** the joint where these bones meet.

sac+ro+sanct ('sækrəʊˌsæŋkt) *adj.* very sacred or holy; inviolable. [C17: from Latin *sacrōsanctus* made holy by sacred rite, from *sacrō* by sacred rite, from *sacer* holy + *sanctus,* from *sancīre* to hallow] —**ˌsac+ro+'sanc+ti·ty** *or* **'sac+ro+ˌsanct+ness** *n.*

sa+crum ('seɪkrəm, 'sækrəm) *n., pl.* **+cra** (-krə). **1.** the large wedge-shaped bone, consisting of five fused vertebrae, in the lower part of the back. **2.** the corresponding part in some other vertebrates. [C18: from Latin *os sacrum* holy bone, because it was used in sacrifices, from *sacer* holy]

sad (sæd) *adj.* **sad+der, sad+dest. 1.** feeling sorrow; unhappy. **2.** causing, suggestive, or expressive of such feelings: *a sad story; a sad colour.* **3.** unfortunate; unsatisfactory; shabby; deplorable: *her clothes were in a sad state.* [Old English *sæd* weary; related to Old Norse *sathr,* Gothic *saths,* Latin *satur, satis* enough] —**'sad+ly** *adv.*

Sa·dat (sə'dæt) *n.* **(Mohammed) An·war El** ('ænwɑ: ɛl). 1918–81, Egyptian statesman: president of Egypt (1970–81); assassinated.

sad+den ('sædᵊn) *vb.* to make or become sad.

sad+dle ('sædᵊl) *n.* **1.** a seat for a rider, usually made of leather, placed on a horse's back and secured with a girth under the belly. **2.** a similar seat on a bicycle, tractor, etc., made of leather or steel. **3.** a back pad forming part of the harness of a packhorse. **4.** anything that resembles a saddle in shape, position, or function. **5.** a cut of meat, esp. mutton, consisting of part of the backbone and both loins. **6.** the part of a horse or similar animal on which a saddle is placed. **7.** the part of the back of a domestic chicken that is nearest to the tail. **8.** the nontechnical name for **clitellum. 9.** Also called: **saddleback.** a pass or ridge that slopes gently between two peaks. **10.** a raised piece of wood or metal for covering a doorsill. **11. in the saddle.** in a position of control. ~*vb.* **12.** (sometimes foll. by *up*) to put a saddle on (a horse). **13.** (*intr.*) to mount into the saddle. **14.** (*tr.*) to burden; charge: *I didn't ask to be saddled with this job.* [Old English *sadol, sædel;* related to Old Norse *sothull,* Old High German *satul*] —**'sad·dle+less** *adj.* —**'sad·dle-ˌlike** *adj.*

sad·dle+back ('sædᵊlˌbæk) *n.* **1.** a marking resembling a saddle on the backs of various animals. **2.** another name for **saddle roof. 3.** another name for **saddle** (sense 9).

sad·dle-backed *adj.* **1.** having the back curved in shape or concave like a saddle. **2.** having a saddleback.

sad·dle+bag ('sædᵊlˌbæg) *n.* a pouch or small bag attached to the saddle of a horse, bicycle, etc.

sad·dle+bill ('sædᵊlˌbɪl) *n.* a large black-and-white stork, *Ephippiorhynchus senegalensis,* of tropical Africa, having a heavy red bill with a black band around the middle and a yellow patch at the base. Also called: **jabiru.**

sad+dle block *n. Surgery.* a type of spinal anaesthesia producing sensory loss in the buttocks, inner sides of the thighs, and perineum.

sad·dle+bow ('sædᵊlˌbəʊ) *n.* the pommel of a saddle.

sad·dle+cloth ('sædᵊlˌklɒθ) *n.* a light cloth put under a horse's saddle, so as to prevent rubbing.

sad+dle horse *n.* a lightweight horse kept for riding only. Compare **carthorse.** Also called: **saddler.**

sad+dler ('sædlə) *n.* a person who makes, deals in, or repairs saddles and other leather equipment for horses.

sad+dle roof *n.* a roof that has a ridge and two gables. Also called: **saddleback.**

sad+dler·y ('sædlərɪ) *n., pl.* **+dler·ies. 1.** saddles, harness, and other leather equipment for horses collectively. **2.** the business, work, or place of work of a saddler.

sad+dle soap *n.* a soft soap containing neat's-foot oil used to preserve and clean leather.

sad·dle-sore *adj.* **1.** sore after riding a horse. **2.** (of a horse or rider) having sores caused by the chafing of the saddle. ~*n.* **sad+dle sore. 3.** such a sore.

sad·dle+tree ('sædᵊlˌtri:) *n.* the frame of a saddle.

Sad+du+cee ('sædjʊˌsi:) *n. Judaism.* a member of an ancient Jewish sect that was opposed to the Pharisees, denying the resurrection of the dead, the existence of angels, and the validity of oral tradition. [Old English *saddūcēas,* via Latin and Greek from Late Hebrew *sāddūqī,* probably from *Sadoq* Zadok, high priest and supposed founder of the sect] —**ˌSad+du+'ce·an** *adj.* —**'Sad+du+ˌcee+ism** *n.*

Sade (sɑ:d) *n.* Comte **Do·na·tien Al·phonse Fran·çois de** (dɔnasjɛ̃ alfɔ:s frɑ̃'swa də), known as the *Marquis de Sade.* 1740–1814, French soldier and writer, whose exposition of sexual perversion gave rise to the term sadism.

sa+dhe, sa·de, *or* **tsa+de** ('sɑ:di:, 'tsɑ:di:; *Hebrew* 'tsadi:) *n.* the 18th letter in the Hebrew alphabet (צ or, at the end of a word ץ), transliterated as *ṣ* or *ts* and pronounced more or less like English *s* or *ts* with pharyngeal articulation.

sa+dhu *or* **sad+dhu** ('sɑ:du:) *n.* a Hindu wandering holy man. [Sanskrit, from *sādhu* good]

Sa·di *or* **Saa·di** (sɑ:'di:) *n.* original name *Sheikh Muslih Addin.* ?1184–1292, Persian poet. His best-known works are *Gulistān* (Flower Garden) and *Būstān* (Tree Garden), long moralistic poems in prose and verse.

sad+i·ron ('sædˌaɪən) *n.* a heavy iron for pressing clothes, pointed at both ends. [C19: from SAD (in the obsolete sense: heavy) + IRON]

sad+ism ('seɪdɪzəm, 'sæ-) *n.* the gaining of pleasure or sexual gratification from the infliction of pain and mental suffering on another person. See also **algolagnia.** Compare **masochism.** [C19: from French, named after the Marquis de SADE] —**'sad+ist** *n.* —**sa+dis+tic** (sə'dɪstɪk) *adj.* —**sa+'dis+ti+cal+ly** *adv.*

sad+ness ('sædnɪs) *n.* the quality or condition of being sad.

sad·o+mas·o+chism (ˌseɪdəʊ'mæsəˌkɪzəm, ˌsædəʊ-) *n.* the combination of sadistic and masochistic elements in one person, characterized by both aggressive and submissive periods in relationships with others. Compare **sadism, masochism.** —**ˌsad·o+mas·o+'chis+tic** *adj.*

Sa+do+wa ('sɑ:dəʊvə) *n.* a village in W Czechoslovakia, in NE Bohemia: scene of the decisive battle of the Austro-Prussian war (1866) in which the Austrians were defeated by the Prussians. Czech name: **Sa+do+vá** ('sadɔva:).

sad sack *n. U.S. slang.* an inept person who makes mistakes despite good intentions.

s.a.e. *abbrev. for* stamped addressed envelope.

Sa+far *or* **Sa+phar** (sə'fɑ:) *n.* the second month of the Muslim year. [from Arabic]

sa+fa+ri (sə'fɑ:rɪ) *n., pl.* **+ris. 1.** an overland journey or hunting expedition, esp. in Africa. **2.** the people, animals, etc., that go on the expedition. [C19: from Swahili: journey, from Arabic *safarīya,* from *safara* to travel]

sa+fa+ri jack+et *n.* another name for **bush jacket.**

sa+fa+ri park *n.* an enclosed park in which lions and other wild animals are kept in the open and can be viewed by the public in cars, etc.

sa+fa+ri suit *n.* an outfit made of tough cotton, denim, etc., consisting of a bush jacket with matching trousers, shorts, or skirt.

safe (seɪf) *adj.* **1.** affording security or protection from harm: *a safe place.* **2.** (*postpositive*) free from danger, etc.: *you'll be safe here.* **3.** secure from risk; certain; sound: *a safe investment; a safe bet.* **4.** worthy of trust; prudent: *a safe companion.* **5.** tending to avoid controversy or risk: *a safe player.* **6.** unable to do harm; not dangerous: *a criminal safe behind bars; water safe to drink.* **7. on the safe side.** as a precaution. ~*adv.* **8.** in a safe condition: *the children are safe in bed now.* **9. play safe.** to act in a way least likely to cause danger, controversy, or defeat. ~*n.* **10.** a strong container, usually of metal and provided with a secure lock, for storing money or valuables. **11.** a container for storing food. **12.** *U.S.* a slang word for **condom.** [C13: from Old French *salf,* from Latin *salvus;* related to Latin *salus* safety] —**'safe+ly** *adv.* —**'safe+ness** *n.*

safe-blow·er *n.* a person who uses explosives to open safes and rob them.

safe-break·er *n.* a person who breaks open and robs safes. Also called: **safe-cracker.**

safe-con·duct *n.* **1.** a document giving official permission to travel through a region, esp. in time of war. **2.** the protection afforded by such a document. ~*vb.* (*tr.*) **3.** to conduct (a person) in safety. **4.** to give a safe-conduct to.

safe-de·pos·it *or* **safe·ty-de·pos·it** *n.* **a.** a place or building with facilities for the safe storage of money or valuables. **b.** (*as modifier*): *a safe-deposit box.*

safe+guard ('seɪfˌgɑ:d) *n.* **1.** a person or thing that ensures protection against danger, damage, injury, etc. **2.** a document authorizing safe-conduct. ~*vb.* **3.** (*tr.*) to defend or protect.

safe+keep·ing ('seɪf'ki:pɪŋ) *n.* the act of keeping or state of being kept in safety.

safe+light ('seɪfˌlaɪt) *n. Photog.* a light that can be used in a room in which photographic material is handled, transmitting only those colours to which a particular type of film, plate, or paper is relatively insensitive.

safe pe·ri·od *n. Informal.* the period during the menstrual cycle when conception is considered least likely to occur. See also **rhythm method.**

safe·ty ('seɪftɪ) *n., pl.* **·ties. 1.** the quality of being safe. **2.** freedom from danger or risk of injury. **3.** a contrivance or device designed to prevent injury. **4.** *American football.* **a.** Also called: **safetyman.** the defensive player furthest back in the field. **b.** a play in which the ball is put down by a player behind his own goal line when the ball is caused to pass the goal line by one of his own team. Compare **touchback.**

safe·ty belt *n.* **1.** another name for **seat belt. 2.** a belt or strap worn by a person working at a great height and attached to a fixed object to prevent him from falling.

safe·ty cur·tain *n.* a curtain made of fireproof material that can be lowered to separate the auditorium and stage in a theatre to prevent the spread of a fire.

safe·ty fac·tor *n.* another name for **factor of safety.**

safe·ty film *n.* photographic film consisting of a nonflammable cellulose acetate or polyester base.

safe·ty fuse *n.* **1.** a slow-burning fuse for igniting detonators from a distance. **2.** an electrical fuse that protects a circuit from overloading.

safe·ty glass *n.* glass made by sandwiching a layer of plastic or resin between two sheets of glass so that if broken the fragments will not shatter.

Safe·ty Is·lands *pl. n.* a group of three small French islands in the Atlantic, off the coast of French Guiana. French name: **Îles du Salut.**

safe·ty lamp *n.* an oil-burning miner's lamp in which the flame is surrounded by a metal gauze to prevent it from igniting combustible gas. Also called: **Davy lamp.**

safe·ty match *n.* a match that will light only when struck against a specially prepared surface.

safe·ty pin *n.* **1.** a spring wire clasp with a covering catch, made so as to shield the point when closed and to prevent accidental unfastening. **2.** another word for **pin** (sense 9).

safe·ty ra·zor *n.* a razor with a guard over the blade to prevent accidental cutting of the skin.

safe·ty valve *n.* **1.** a valve in a pressure vessel that allows fluid to escape when a predetermined level of pressure has been reached. **2.** a harmless outlet for emotion, etc.

saf·fi·an ('sæfɪən) *n.* leather tanned with sumach and usually dyed a bright colour. [C16: via Russian and Turkish from Persian *sakhtiyān* goatskin, from *sakht* hard]

saf·flow·er ('sæflaʊə) *n.* **1.** a thistle-like Eurasian annual plant, *Carthamus tinctorius,* having large heads of orange-yellow flowers and yielding a dye and an oil used in paints, medicines, etc.: family *Compositae* (composites). **2.** a red dye used for cotton and for colouring foods and cosmetics, or a drug obtained from the florets of this plant. ~Also called: **false saffron.** [C16: via Dutch *saffloer* or German *safflor* from Old French *saffleur.* See SAFFRON, FLOWER]

saf·fron ('sæfrən) *n.* **1.** an Old World crocus, *Crocus sativus,* having purple or white flowers with orange stigmas. **2.** the dried stigmas of this plant, used to flavour or colour food. **3. meadow saffron.** another name for **autumn crocus. 4. false saffron.** another name for **safflower. 5. a.** an orange to orange-yellow colour. **b.** (*as adj.*): *a saffron dress.* [C13: from Old French *safran,* from Medieval Latin *safranum,* from Arabic *za'farān*]

Sa·fi (*French* sa'fi) *n.* a port in W Morocco, 170 km (105 miles) northwest of Marrakesh, to which it is the nearest port. Pop.: 129 113 (1971).

Sa·fid Rud (sæ'fiːd 'ruːd) *n.* a river in N Iran, flowing northeast to a delta on the Caspian Sea. Length: about 785 km (490 miles).

S.Afr. *abbrev. for* South Africa(n).

saf·ra·nine *or* **saf·ra·nin** ('sæfrənɪn, -ˌniːn) *n.* any of a class of dyes devised from phenzine and used for textiles and biological stains. [C19: from French *safran* SAFFRON + -INE[2]]

saf·role ('sæfrəʊl) *n.* a colourless or yellowish oily water-insoluble liquid present in sassafras and camphor oils and used in soaps and perfumes. Formula: $C_3H_5C_6H_3O_2CH_2$. [C19: from (SAS)SAFR(AS) + -OLE[1]]

sag (sæg) *vb.* (*mainly intr.*) **sags, sag·ging, sagged. 1.** (*also tr.*) to sink or cause to sink in parts, as under weight or pressure: *the bed sags in the middle.* **2.** to fall in value: *prices sagged to a new low.* **3.** to hang unevenly; droop. **4.** (of courage, etc.) to weaken; flag. ~*n.* **5.** the act or an instance of sagging: *a sag in profits.* **6.** *Nautical.* the extent to which a vessel's keel sags at the centre. Compare **hog** (sense 6). **7. a.** a marshy depression in an area of glacial till, chiefly in the U.S. Middle West. **b.** (*as modifier*): *sag and swell topography.* [C15: from Scandinavian; compare Swedish *sacka,* Dutch *zakken,* Norwegian dialect *sakka* to subside, Danish *sakke* to lag behind]

sa·ga ('sɑːgə) *n.* **1.** any of several medieval prose narratives written in Iceland and recounting the exploits of a hero or a family. **2.** any similar heroic narrative. **3.** Also called: **saga novel.** a series of novels about several generations or members of a family. **4.** any other artistic production said to resemble a saga. **5.** *Informal.* a series of events or a story stretching over a long period. [C18: from Old Norse: a narrative; related to Old English *secgan* to SAY]

sa·ga·cious (sə'geɪʃəs) *adj.* **1.** having or showing sagacity; wise. **2.** *Obsolete.* (of hounds) having an acute sense of smell. [C17: from Latin *sagāx,* from *sāgīre* to be astute] —**sa·'ga·cious·ly** *adv.* —**sa·'ga·cious·ness** *n.*

sa·gac·i·ty (sə'gæsɪtɪ) *n.* foresight, discernment, or keen perception; ability to make good judgments.

sag·a·more ('sægəˌmɔː) *n.* (among some North American Indians) a chief or eminent man. Also called: **sachem.** [C17: from Abnaki *sāgimau,* literally: he overcomes]

sage[1] (seɪdʒ) *n.* **1.** a man revered for his profound wisdom. ~*adj.* **2.** profoundly wise or prudent. **3.** *Obsolete.* solemn. [C13: from Old French, from Latin *sapere* to be sensible; see SAPIENT] —**'sage·ly** *adv.* —**'sage·ness** *n.*

sage[2] (seɪdʒ) *n.* **1.** a perennial Mediterranean plant, *Salvia officinalis,* having grey-green leaves and purple, blue, or white flowers: family *Labiatae* (labiates). **2.** the leaves of this plant, used in cooking for flavouring. **3.** short for **sagebrush.** [C14: from Old French *saulge,* from Latin *salvia,* from *salvus* safe, in good health (from the curative properties attributed to the plant)]

sage·brush ('seɪdʒˌbrʌʃ) *n.* any of several aromatic plants of the genus *Artemisia,* esp. *A. tridentata,* a shrub of W North America, having silver-green leaves and large clusters of small white flowers: family *Compositae* (composites).

sage Der·by *n.* See **Derby**[2] (sense 3).

sage grouse *n.* a large North American grouse, *Centrocercus urophasianus,* the males of which perform elaborate courtship displays.

sag·gar *or* **sag·ger** ('sægə) *n.* a clay box in which fragile ceramic wares are placed for protection during firing. [C17: perhaps alteration of SAFEGUARD]

Sa·ghal·ien (sə'gɑːljən) *n.* a variant spelling of **Sakhalin.**

Sa·git·ta (sə'gɪtə) *n., Latin genitive* **Sa·git·tae** (sə'gɪtiː). a small constellation in the N hemisphere lying between Cygnus and Aquila and crossed by the Milky Way. [C16: from Latin, literally: an arrow]

sag·it·tal ('sædʒɪtᵊl) *adj.* **1.** resembling an arrow; straight. **2.** of or relating to the sagittal suture. **3.** situated in a plane parallel to the sagittal suture. —**'sag·it·tal·ly** *adv.*

sag·it·tal su·ture *n.* a serrated line on the top of the skull that marks the junction of the two parietal bones.

Sag·it·ta·ri·us (ˌsædʒɪ'tɛərɪəs) *n., Latin genitive* **Sag·it·ta·ri·i** (ˌsædʒɪ'tɛərɪˌaɪ). **1.** *Astronomy.* a large conspicuous zodiacal constellation in the S hemisphere lying between Scorpius and Capricornus on the ecliptic and crossed by the Milky Way. **2.** Also called: the **Archer.** *Astrology.* **a.** the ninth sign of the zodiac, symbol ♐, having a mutable fire classification and ruled by the planet Jupiter. The sun is in this sign between Nov. 22 and Dec. 21. **b.** a person born when the sun is in this sign. ~*adj.* **3.** *Astrology.* born under or characteristic of Sagittarius. ~Also (for senses 2b., 3): **Sag·it·tar·i·an** (ˌsædʒɪ'tɛərɪən). [C14: from Latin: an archer, from *sagitta* an arrow]

sag·it·tate ('sædʒɪˌteɪt) *or* **sa·git·ti·form** (sə'dʒɪtɪˌfɔːm, 'sædʒ-) *adj.* (esp. of leaves) shaped like the head of an arrow. [C18: from New Latin *sagittātus,* from Latin *sagitta* arrow]

sa·go ('seɪgəʊ) *n.* a starchy cereal obtained from the powdered pith of a sago palm, used for puddings and as a thickening agent. [C16: from Malay *sāgū*]

sa·go grass *n. Austral.* a tall tough grass, *Paspalidum globoideum,* grown as forage for cattle.

sa·go palm *n.* **1.** any of various tropical Asian palm trees, esp. any of the genera *Metroxylon, Arenga,* and *Caryota,* the trunks of which yield sago. **2.** any of several palmlike cycads that yield sago, esp. *Cycas revoluta.*

Sa·guache (sə'wætʃ) *n.* a variant spelling of **Sawatch.**

sa·gua·ro (sə'gwɑːrəʊ, sə'wɑː-) *or* **sa·hua·ro** (sə'wɑːrəʊ) *n., pl.* **·ros.** a giant cactus, *Carnegiea gigantea,* of desert regions of Arizona, S California, and Mexico, having white nocturnal flowers and edible red pulpy fruits. [Mexican Spanish, variant of *sahuaro,* an Indian name]

Sag·ue·nay (ˌsægə'neɪ) *n.* a river in SE Canada in S Quebec, rising as the Péribonca River on the central plateau and flowing south, then east to the St. Lawrence. Length: 764 km (475 miles).

Sa·gui·a el Ham·ra ('sɑːgɪə ɛl 'hæmrə) *n.* the N zone of Western Sahara.

Sa·gun·to (*Spanish* sa'ɣunto) *n.* an industrial town in E Spain, near Valencia: allied to Rome and made a heroic resistance to the Carthaginian attack led by Hannibal (219–218 B.C.). Pop.: 47 026 (1970). Ancient name: **Saguntum.**

Sa·hap·tin (sɑː'hæptɪn), **Sa·hap·tan** (sɑː'hæptən), *or* **Sa·hap·ti·an** (sɑː'hæptɪən) *n.* **1.** (*pl.* **·tins, ·tans, ·ti·ans** *or* **·tin, ·tan, ·ti·an**) a member of a North American Indian people of Oregon and Washington, including the Nez Percé. **2.** the language of this people. ~Also spelled: **Shahaptin.**

Sa·ha·ra (sə'hɑːrə) *n.* a desert in N Africa, extending from the Atlantic to the Red Sea and from the Mediterranean to central Mali, Niger, Chad, and the Sudan: the largest desert in the world, occupying over a quarter of Africa; rises to over 3300 m (11 000 ft.) in the central mountain system of the Ahaggar and Tibesti massifs; large reserves of iron ore, oil, and natural gas. Area: 9 100 000 sq. km (3 500 000 sq. miles). Average annual rainfall: less than 254 mm (10 in.). Highest recorded temperature: 58°C (136.4°F).

Sa·har·an (sə'hɑːrən) *n.* **1.** a group of languages spoken in parts of Chad and adjacent countries, now generally regarded as forming a branch of the Nilo-Saharan family. ~*adj.* **2.** relating to or belonging to this group of languages. **3.** of or relating to the Sahara.

Sa·ha·ran·pur (sə'hɑːrənˌpʊə) *n.* a town in N India, in NW Uttar Pradesh. Pop.: 225 396 (1971).

sa·hib ('sɑːhɪb) *or* **sa·heb** *n.* (in India) a form of address or title placed after a man's name or designation, used as a mark of respect. [C17: from Urdu, from Arabic *çāhib*, literally: friend]

Sa+hit+ya A·kad+e·mi (sɑː'hɪtjə ə'kɑːdəmɪ) *n.* a body set up by the Government of India for cultivating literature in Indian languages and in English.

said[1] (sɛd) *adj.* **1.** (*prenominal*) (in contracts, pleadings, etc.) named or mentioned previously; aforesaid. ~*vb.* **2.** the past tense or past participle of **say.**

sa·id[2] ('sɑːɪd) *n., adj.* a variant spelling of **sayyid.**

Sa·i+da ('sɑːɪdə) *n.* a port in SW Lebanon, on the Mediterranean: on the site of ancient Sidon; terminal of the Trans-Arabian pipeline from Saudi Arabia. Pop.: 25 000 (1973 est.).

sai+ga ('saɪgə) *n.* either of two antelopes, *Saiga tatarica* or *S. mongolica*, of the plains of central Asia, having an enlarged slightly elongated nose. [C19: from Russian, from Chagatai *saigak*]

Sai+gon (saɪ'gɒn) *n.* the former name (until 1976) of **Ho Chi Minh City.**

sail (seɪl) *n.* **1.** an area of fabric, usually Terylene or nylon (formerly canvas), with fittings for holding it in any suitable position to catch the wind, used for propelling certain kinds of vessels, esp. over water. **2.** a voyage on such a vessel: *a sail down the river.* **3.** a vessel with sails or such vessels collectively: *to travel by sail; we raised seven sail in the northeast.* **4.** a ship's sails collectively. **5.** something resembling a sail in shape, position, or function, such as the part of a windmill that is turned by the wind or the part of a Portuguese man-of-war that projects above the water. **6.** the conning tower of a submarine. **7. in sail.** having the sail set. **8. make sail. a.** to run up the sail or to run up more sail. **b.** to begin a voyage. **9. set sail. a.** to embark on a voyage by ship. **b.** to hoist sail. **10. under sail. a.** with sail hoisted. **b.** under way. ~*vb.* (*mainly intr.*) **11.** to travel in a boat or ship: *we sailed to Le Havre.* **12.** (of a vessel) to move over the water: *the liner is sailing to the Caribbean.* **13.** (*tr.*) to manoeuvre or navigate a vessel: *he sailed the schooner up the channel.* **14.** (*tr.*) to sail over: *she sailed the Atlantic single-handed.* **15.** (often foll. by *over, through,* etc.) to move fast or effortlessly: *we sailed through customs; the ball sailed over the fence.* **16.** to move along smoothly; glide. **17.** (often foll. by *in* or *into*) *Informal.* **a.** to begin (something) with vigour. **b.** to make an attack (on) violently with words or physical force. [Old English *segl;* related to Old Frisian *seil,* Old Norse *segl,* German *Segel*] —'**sail·a·ble** *adj.* —'**sail+less** *adj.*

sail+cloth ('seɪl,klɒθ) *n.* **1.** any of various fabrics from which sails are made. **2.** a lighter cloth used for clothing, etc.

sail+er ('seɪlə) *n.* a vessel, esp. one equipped with sails, with specified sailing characteristics: *a good sailer.*

sail+fish ('seɪl,fɪʃ) *n., pl.* **+fish** *or* **+fish·es.** any of several large scombroid game fishes of the genus *Istiophorus,* such as *I. albicans* (**Atlantic sailfish**), of warm and tropical seas: family *Istiophoridae.* They have an elongated upper jaw and a long sail-like dorsal fin.

sail+ing ('seɪlɪŋ) *n.* **1.** the practice, art, or technique of sailing a vessel. **2.** a method of navigating a vessel: *rhumb-line sailing.* **3.** an instance of a vessel's leaving a port: *scheduled for a midnight sailing.*

sail+ing boat *or esp. U.S.* **sail+boat** *n.* a boat propelled chiefly by sail.

sail+ing ship *n.* a large sailing vessel.

sail+or ('seɪlə) *n.* **1.** any member of a ship's crew, esp. one below the rank of officer. **2.** a person who sails, esp. with reference to the likelihood of his becoming seasick: *a good sailor.* **3.** short for **sailor hat** or **sailor suit.** —'**sail+or+ly** *adj.*

sail+or hat *n.* a hat with a flat round crown and fairly broad brim that is rolled upwards.

sail·or's-choice *n.* any of various small percoid fishes of American coastal regions of the Atlantic, esp. the grunt *Haemulon parra* and the pinfish.

sail+or suit *n.* a child's suit, usually navy and white, with a collar that is squared off at the back like a sailor's.

sail+plane ('seɪl,pleɪn) *n.* a high-performance glider.

sain (seɪn) *vb.* (*tr.*) *Archaic.* to make the sign of the cross over so as to bless or protect from evil or sin. [Old English *segnian,* from Latin *signare* to SIGN (with the cross)]

sain+foin ('sænfɔɪn) *n.* a Eurasian perennial papilionaceous plant, *Onobrychis viciifolia,* widely grown as a forage crop, having pale pink flowers and curved pods. [C17: from French, from Medieval Latin *sānum faenum* wholesome hay, referring to its former use as a medicine]

saint (seɪnt; *unstressed* sənt) *n.* **1.** a person who after death is formally recognized by a Christian Church, esp. the Roman Catholic Church, as having attained, through holy deeds or behaviour, a specially exalted place in heaven entitling him to veneration. **2.** a person of exceptional holiness or goodness. **3.** (*pl.*) *Bible.* the collective body of those who are righteous in God's sight. ~*vb.* **4.** (*tr.*) to canonize; recognize formally as a saint. [C12: from Old French, from Latin *sanctus* holy, from *sancīre* to hallow] —'**saint+dom** *n.* —'**saint+less** *adj.* —'**saint+like** *adj.*

Saint Ag·nes's Eve *n., usually abbreviated to* **St. Ag·nes's Eve.** the night of Jan. 20, when according to tradition a woman can discover the identity of her future husband by performing certain rites.

Saint Al+bans ('ɔːlbənz) *n., usually abbreviated to* **St. Al+bans.** a city in SE England, in W Hertfordshire: founded in 948 A.D. around the Benedictine abbey first built in Saxon times on the site of the martyrdom (about 303 A.D.) of St. Alban; present abbey built in 1077; Roman ruins. Pop.: 52 057 (1971). Latin name: **Verulamium.**

Saint An+drews *n., usually abbreviated to* **St. An+drews.** a city in E Scotland, in Fife region on the North Sea: the oldest university in Scotland (1411); famous golf links. Pop.: 11 468 (1971).

Saint An·drew's Cross *n., usually abbreviated to* **St. An·drew's Cross. 1.** a diagonal cross with equal arms. **2.** a white diagonal cross on a blue ground.

Saint An·tho·ny's Cross *n., usually abbreviated to* **St. An·tho·ny's Cross.** another name for **tau cross.**

Saint An·tho·ny's fire *n., usually abbreviated to* **St. An·tho·ny's fire.** *Pathol.* another name for **ergotism** or **erysipelas.**

Saint Au+gus+tine ('ɔːgəs,tiːn) *n., usually abbreviated to* **St. Au+gus+tine.** a resort in NE Florida, on the Intracoastal Waterway: the oldest town in North America (1565); the northernmost outpost of the Spanish colonial empire for over 200 years. Pop.: 12 352 (1970).

Saint Aus+tell ('ɔːstəl) *n., usually abbreviated to* **St. Aus+tell.** a town in SW England, in S Cornwall on **St. Austell Bay** (an inlet of the English Channel): china clay industry; administratively part of St. Austell with Fowey since 1968. Pop.: (with Fowey): 32 252 (1971).

Saint Bar·thol·o·mew's Day Mas+sa+cre *n., usually abbreviated to* **St. Bar·thol·o·mew's Day Mas+sa+cre.** the murder of Huguenots in Paris that began on Aug. 24, 1572 on the orders of Charles IX, acting under the influence of his mother Catherine de' Medici.

Saint Ber·nard *n., usually abbreviated to* **St. Ber·nard.** a large breed of dog with a dense red-and-white coat, often used as a rescue dog in mountainous areas.

Saint Ber+nard Pass *n., usually abbreviated to* **St. Ber+nard Pass.** either of two passes over the Alps: the **Great St. Bernard Pass,** 2472 m (8110 ft.) high, east of Mont Blanc between Italy and Switzerland, or the **Little St. Bernard Pass,** 2157 m (7077 ft.) high, south of Mont Blanc between Italy and France.

Saint-Bri·euc (*French* sɛ̃ bri'ø) *n., usually abbreviated to* **St-Bri·euc.** a market town in NW France, near the N coast of Brittany. Pop.: 56 282 (1975).

Saint Cath·a+rines *n., usually abbreviated to* **St. Cath·a+rines.** an industrial city in S central Canada, in S Ontario on the Welland Canal. Pop.: 109 722 (1971).

Saint Chris+to+pher *n., usually abbreviated to* **St. Chris+to+pher.** another name for **Saint Kitts.**

Saint Chris+to·pher-Ne·vis-An·guil+la *n., usually abbreviated to* **St. Chris+to·pher-Ne·vis-An·guil+la.** the official name of **Saint Kitts-Nevis-Anguilla.**

Saint Clair *n., usually abbreviated to* **St. Clair. Lake.** a lake between SE Michigan and Ontario: linked with Lake Huron by the **St. Clair River** and with Lake Erie by the Detroit River. Area: 1191 sq. km (460 sq. miles).

Saint-Cloud (*French* sɛ̃ 'klu) *n., usually abbreviated to* **St-Cloud.** a residential suburb of Paris: former royal palace; Sèvres porcelain factory. Pop.: 28 162 (1968).

Saint Croix (krɔɪ) *n., usually abbreviated to* **St. Croix.** an island in the West Indies, the largest of the Virgin Islands of the U.S.: purchased by the U.S. in 1917. Chief town: Christiansted. Pop.: 31 779 (1970). Area: 207 sq. km (80 sq. miles). Also called: **Santa Cruz.**

Saint Croix Riv+er *n., usually abbreviated to* **St. Croix Riv+er.** a river on the border between the northeast U.S. and SE Canada, flowing from the Chiputneticook Lakes to Passamaquoddy Bay, forming the border between Maine, U.S., and New Brunswick, Canada. Length: 121 km (75 miles).

Saint Da+vid's *n., usually abbreviated to* **St. Da+vid's.** a town in SW Wales, in Dyfed: its cathedral was a place of pilgrimage in medieval times. Pop.: 1500 (1971 est.).

Saint-De·nis (*French* sɛ̃ də'ni) *n., usually abbreviated to* **St-De·nis. 1.** a town in N France, on the Seine: 12th-century Gothic abbey church, containing the tombs of many French monarchs; an industrial suburb of Paris. Pop.: 96 759 (1975). **2.** the capital of the French overseas region of Réunion, a port on the N coast. Pop.: 86 000 (1967).

Sainte-Beuve (*French* sɛ̃t 'bœːv) *n.* **Charles Au·gus·tin** (ʃarl ogy'stɛ̃). 1804–69, French critic, best known for his collections of essays *Port Royal* (1840–59) and *Les Causeries du Lundi* (1851–62).

saint+ed ('seɪntɪd) *adj.* **1.** canonized. **2.** like a saint in character or nature. **3.** hallowed or holy.

Sainte Foy (seɪnt 'fɔɪ, sənt) *n., usually abbreviated to* **Ste. Foy.** a SW suburb of Quebec, on the St. Lawrence River. Pop.: 68 385 (1971).

Saint E·li+as Moun+tains *pl. n., usually abbreviated to* **St. E·li+as Moun+tains.** a mountain range between SE Alaska and the SW Yukon, Canada. Highest peak: Mount Logan, 6050 m (19 850 ft.).

Saint El·mo's fire *n., usually abbreviated to* **St. El·mo's fire.** (*not in technical usage*) a luminous region that sometimes appears around church spires, the masts of ships, etc. It is a corona discharge in the air caused by atmospheric electricity. Also called: **corposant.**

Saint-É·mil·ion (*French* sɛ̃ temi'ljɔ̃) *n.* a full-bodied red wine, similar to a Burgundy, produced around the town of Saint-Émilion in Bordeaux.

Saint-É·tienne (*French* sɛ̃ te'tjɛn) *n., usually abbreviated to* **St-É·tienne.** a town in E central France: a major producer of textiles and armaments. Pop.: 221 775 (1975).

Saint-Ex·u·pé·ry (*French* sɛ̃ tɛgzype'ri) *n.* **An·toine de** (ɑ̃'twan də). 1900–44, French novelist and aviator. His novels of aviation include *Vol de nuit* (1931) and *Terre des Hommes* (1939); he also wrote the fairy tale *Le petit prince* (1943).

Saint Gall (*French* sɛ̃ 'gal) *n., usually abbreviated to* **St. Gall. 1.** a canton of NE Switzerland. Capital: St. Gall. Pop.: 384 475 (1970). Area: 2012 sq. km (777 sq. miles). **2.** a town in NE Switzerland, capital of St. Gall canton: an important educational centre in the Middle Ages. Pop.: 80 852 (1970). ~German name: **Sankt Gallen** (zaŋkt 'galən).

Saint George's *n., usually abbreviated to* **St. George's.** the capital of Grenada, a port in the southwest. Pop.: 6634 (1970).

Saint George's Chan·nel *n., usually abbreviated to* **St. George's Chan·nel.** a strait between Wales and Ireland, linking the Irish Sea with the Atlantic. Length: about 160 km (100 miles). Width: up to 145 km (90 miles).

Saint George's Cross *n., usually abbreviated to* **St. George's Cross.** a red Greek cross on a white background.

Saint Gott·hard ('gɒtəd) *n., usually abbreviated to* **St. Gott·hard. 1.** a range of the Lepontine Alps in SE central Switzerland. **2.** a pass over the St. Gotthard mountains, in S Switzerland. Height: 2114 m (6935 ft.).

Saint He·le·na (hə'li:nə) *n., usually abbreviated to* **St. He·le·na.** a volcanic island in the SE Atlantic, forming (with its dependencies Tristan da Cunha and Ascension) a British colony: discovered by the Portuguese in 1502 and annexed by England in 1651; scene of Napoleon's exile and death. Capital: Jamestown. Pop.: 5056 (1971 est.). Area: 122 sq. km (47 sq. miles).

Saint Hel·ens *n., usually abbreviated to* **St. Hel·ens.** a town in NW England, in Merseyside: glass industry. Pop.: 104 173 (1971).

Saint Hel·ier ('hɛlɪə) *n., usually abbreviated to* **St. Hel·ier.** a market town and resort in the Channel Islands, on the S coast of Jersey. Pop.: 28 135 (1971).

saint·hood ('seɪnthʊd) *n.* **1.** the state or character of being a saint. **2.** saints collectively.

Saint James's Pal·ace *n., usually abbreviated to* **St. James's Pal·ace.** a palace in Pall Mall, London: residence of British monarchs from 1697 to 1837.

Saint John *n., usually abbreviated to* **St. John. 1.** a port in E Canada, at the mouth of the St. John River: the largest city in New Brunswick. Pop.: 89 039 (1971). **2.** an island in the West Indies, in the Virgin Islands of the U.S. Pop.: 1729 (1970). Area: 49 sq. km (19 sq. miles). **3. Lake.** a lake in Canada, in S Quebec: drained by the Saguenay River. Area: 971 sq. km (375 sq. miles). **4.** a river in E North America, rising in Maine, U.S., and flowing northeast to New Brunswick, Canada, then generally southeast to the Bay of Fundy. Length: 673 km (418 miles).

Saint John's *n., usually abbreviated to* **St. John's. 1.** a port in Canada, capital of Newfoundland, on the E coast of the Avalon Peninsula. Pop.: 88 102 (1971). **2.** the capital of the British Associated State of Antigua: a port on the NW coast of the island. Pop.: 14 000 (1972 est.).

Saint John's bread *n., usually abbreviated to* **St. John's bread.** another name for **carob** (sense 2).

Saint John's wort *n., usually abbreviated to* **St. John's wort.** any of numerous shrubs or herbaceous plants of the temperate genus *Hypericum,* such as *H. perforatum,* having yellow flowers and glandular leaves: family *Hypericaceae.* See also **rose of Sharon** (sense 1), **tutsan.**

Saint-Just (*French* sɛ̃ 'ʒyst) *n.* **Louis An·toine Lé·on de** (lwi ɑ̃twan le'ɔ̃ də). 1767–94, French Revolutionary leader and orator. A member of the Committee of Public Safety (1793–94), he was guillotined with Robespierre.

Saint Kil·da ('kɪldə) *n., usually abbreviated to* **St. Kil·da.** a small island in the Atlantic, in the Outer Hebrides: uninhabited since 1930; bird sanctuary.

Saint Kitts (kɪts) *n., usually abbreviated to* **St. Kitts.** an island in the E West Indies, in the Leeward Islands: part of the British Associated State of St. Kitts-Nevis-Anguilla. Capital: Basseterre. Pop.: 34 227 (1970). Area: 168 sq. km (65 sq. miles). Also called: **Saint Christopher.**

Saint Kitts-Ne·vis-An·guil·la *n., usually abbreviated to* **St. Kitts-Ne·vis-An·guil·la.** a British Associated State in the E Caribbean, in the West Indies: formed by the uniting of the three islands as a colony in 1882; granted full internal self-government in 1967. Capital: Basseterre (St. Kitts). Pop.: 50 957 (1970). Area: 365 sq. km (141 sq. miles). Official name: **Saint Christopher-Nevis-Anguilla.**

Saint Lau·rent (*French* sɛ̃ lɔ'rɑ̃) *n., usually abbreviated to* **St. Lau·rent.** a W suburb of Montreal. Pop.: 62 955 (1971).

Saint-Lau·rent (*French* sɛ̃ lɔ'rɑ̃) *n.* **Yves** (iv). born 1936, French couturier: popularized trousers for women for all occasions.

Saint Law·rence *n., usually abbreviated to* **St. Law·rence. 1.** a river in SE Canada, flowing northeast from Lake Ontario, forming part of the border between Canada and the U.S., to the Gulf of St. Lawrence: commercially one of the most important rivers in the world as the easternmost link of the St. Lawrence Seaway. Length: 1207 km (750 miles). Width at mouth: 145 km (90 miles). **2. Gulf of.** a deep arm of the Atlantic off the E coast of Canada between Newfoundland and the mainland coasts of Quebec, New Brunswick, and Nova Scotia.

Saint Law·rence Sea·way *n., usually abbreviated to* **St. Law·rence Sea·way.** an inland waterway of North America, passing through the Great Lakes, the St. Lawrence River, and connecting canals and locks: one of the most important waterways in the world. Length: 3993 km (2480 miles).

Saint Leg·er ('lɛdʒə) *n., usually abbreviated to* **St. Leg·er. the.** an annual horse race run at Doncaster since 1776: one of the classics of the flat-racing season.

Saint Leon·ard ('lɛnəd) *n., usually abbreviated to* **St. Leon·ard.** a N suburb of Montreal. Pop.: 52 040 (1971).

Saint-Lô (*French* sɛ̃ 'lo) *n., usually abbreviated to* **St-Lô.** a market town in NW France: a Calvinist stronghold in the 16th century. Pop.: 25 037 (1975).

Saint Lou·is *n., usually abbreviated to* **St. Lou·is.** a port in E Missouri, on the Mississippi River near its confluence with the Missouri: the largest city in the state; university; major industrial centre. Pop.: 558 006 (1973 est.).

Saint-Lou·is *n., usually abbreviated to* **St-Lou·is.** a port in NW Senegal, on an island at the mouth of the Senegal River: the first French settlement in W Africa (1689); capital of Senegal until 1958. Pop.: 75 000 (1970 est.).

Saint Lu·ci·a *n., usually abbreviated to* **St. Lu·ci·a.** a volcanic island in the Caribbean, in the Windward Islands, Lesser Antilles: formerly a British colony; from 1979 an independent state within the British Commonwealth. Capital: Castries. Pop.: 101 000 (1970). Area: 616 sq. km (238 sq. miles).

Saint Luke's sum·mer *n., usually abbreviated to* **St. Luke's summer.** a period of unusually warm weather in the autumn. [referring to St. Luke's feast-day, Oct. 18]

saint·ly ('seɪntlɪ) *adj.* like, relating to, or suitable for a saint. —'**saint·li·ly** *adv.* —'**saint·li·ness** *n.*

Saint Mar·tin *n., usually abbreviated to* **St. Mar·tin.** an island in the E West Indies, in the Leeward Islands: administratively divided since 1648, the north belonging to France (as a dependency of Guadeloupe) and the south belonging to the Netherlands (as part of the Netherlands Antilles); salt industry. Pop.: (French) 5061 (1967); (Dutch) 8970 (1972 est.). Areas: (French) 52 sq. km (20 sq. miles); (Dutch) 33 sq. km (13 sq. miles). Dutch name: **Sint Maarten.**

Saint Mar·tin's sum·mer *n., usually abbreviated to* **St. Mar·tin's summer.** a period of unusually warm weather in the late autumn, esp. November. [referring to St. Martin's feast-day, Nov. 11]

Saint-Maur-des-Fos·sés (*French* sɛ̃ mɔr de fo'se) *n., usually abbreviated to* **St-Maur-des-Fos·sés.** a town in N France, on the River Marne: a residential suburb of SE Paris. Pop.: 81 117 (1975).

Saint-Mi·hiel (*French* sɛ̃ mi'jɛl) *n., usually abbreviated to* **St-Mi·hiel.** a village in NE France, on the River Meuse: site of a battle in World War I, in which the American army launched its first offensive in France.

Saint Mo·ritz (mə'rɪts) *n., usually abbreviated to* **St. Mo·ritz.** a village in E Switzerland, in Graubünden canton in the Upper Engadine, at an altitude of 1856 m (6089 ft.): sports and tourist centre. Pop.: 5699 (1970).

Saint-Na·zaire (*French* sɛ̃ na'zɛ:r) *n., usually abbreviated to* **St-Na·zaire.** a port in NW France, at the mouth of the River Loire: German submarine base in World War II; shipbuilding. Pop.: 69 769 (1975).

Saint-Ouen (*French* sɛ̃ 'twɛ̃) *n., usually abbreviated to* **St-Ouen.** a town in N France, on the Seine: an industrial suburb of Paris; famous flea market. Pop.: 43 695 (1975).

Saint Paul *n., usually abbreviated to* **St. Paul.** a port in SE Minnesota, capital of the state, at the head of navigation of the Mississippi: now contiguous with Minneapolis (the Twin Cities). Pop.: 287 305 (1973 est.).

saint·pau·li·a (sənt'pɔ:lɪə) *n.* another name for **African violet.** [C20: New Latin, named after Baron W. von *Saint Paul,* German soldier (died 1910), who discovered it]

Saint Paul's *n., usually abbreviated to* **St. Paul's.** a cathedral in central London, built between 1675 and 1710 to replace an earlier cathedral destroyed during the Great Fire (1666): regarded as Wren's masterpiece.

Saint Pe·ter's *n., usually abbreviated to* **St. Pe·ter's.** the basilica of the Vatican City, built between 1506 and 1615 to replace an earlier church: the largest church in the world, 188 m (615 ft.) long, and chief pilgrimage centre of Europe; designed by many architects, notably Bramante, Raphael, Sangallo, Michelangelo, and Bernini.

Saint Pe·ters·burg ('pi:təz,bɜ:g) *n., usually abbreviated to* **St. Pe·ters·burg. 1.** the former name (1703–1914) of **Leningrad. 2.** a city and resort in W Florida, on Tampa Bay. Pop.: 234 284 (1973 est.).

Saint Pierre (*French* sɛ̃ 'pjɛ:r) *n., usually abbreviated to* **St. Pierre. 1.** a town on the SW coast of the French island of Réunion, in the Indian Ocean. Pop.: 43 186 (1970). **2.** a former town on the coast of the French island of Martinique, destroyed by the eruption of Mont Pelée in 1902.

Saint-Pierre (*French* sɛ̃ 'pjɛ:r) *n.* **Jacques Hen·ri Ber·nar·din de** (ʒak ɑ̃rɪ bɛrnar'dɛ̃ də). 1737–1814, French author; his work, which was greatly influenced by the writings of Rousseau, includes *Voyage à l'Île de France* (1773), *Études de la nature* (1784, 1788), and *La Chaumière indienne* (1791).

Saint Pierre and Miq·ue·lon (ˌmɪkə'lɒn; *French* mi'klɔ̃) *n., usually abbreviated to* **St. Pierre and Miq·ue·lon.** an archipelago in the Atlantic, just off the S coast of Newfoundland: administratively an overseas department of France and the only remaining French possession in North America; consists of the islands of St. Pierre, with most of the population, and Miquelon, about ten times as large; fishing industries. Capital: St. Pierre. Pop.: 5840 (1974). Area: 242 sq. km (94 sq. miles).

Saint Pöl·ten ('pɜ:ltən) *n.* See **Sankt Pölten.**

Saint-Quen·tin (*French* sɛ̃ kɑ̃'tɛ̃) *n., usually abbreviated to*

St.-Quen·tin. a town in N France, on the River Somme: textile industry. Pop.: 69 153 (1975).

Saint-Saëns (*French* sɛ̃ 'sɑ:s) *n.* **(Charles) Ca·mille** (ka'mij). 1835–1921, French composer, pianist, and organist. His works include the symphonic poem *Danse Macabre* (1874), the opera *Samson and Delilah* (1877), the humorous orchestral suite *Carnival of Animals* (1886), five symphonies, and five piano concertos.

Saints·bur·y ('seɪntsbərɪ, -brɪ) *n.* **George Ed·ward Bate·man.** 1845–1933, English literary critic and historian; author of many works on English and French literature.

saint's day *n. Christianity.* a day in the church calendar commemorating a saint.

Saint-Si·mon (*French* sɛ̃ si'mɔ̃) *n.* **1. Comte de** ('kɔ̃:t də), title of *Claude Henri de Rouvroy.* 1760–1825, French social philosopher, generally regarded as the founder of French socialism. He thought society should be reorganized along industrial lines and that scientists should be the new spiritual leaders. His most important work is *Nouveau Christianisme* (1825). **2. Duc de** ('dyk də), title of *Louis de Rouvroy.* 1675–1755, French soldier, statesman, and writer: his *Mémoires* are an outstanding account of the period 1694–1723, during the reigns of Louis XIV and Louis XV.

Saint-Si·mon·i·an+ism (sənt sɪ'məunɪəˌnɪzəm) *or* **Saint-Si·mon·ism** (sənt 'saɪmənɪzəm) *n.* the socialist system advocated by the Comte de Saint-Simon. —**Saint-Si·'mon·i·an** *n., adj.*

Saint Swith·in's Day *n., usually abbreviated to* **St. Swith·in's Day.** July 15, observed as a Church festival commemorating Saint Swithin. It is popularly supposed that if it rains on this day the rain will persist for the next 40 days.

Saint Thom+as *n., usually abbreviated to* **St. Thom+as. 1.** an island in the E West Indies, in the Virgin Islands of the U.S. Capital: Charlotte Amalie. Pop.: 28 960 (1970). Area: 83 sq. km (28 sq. miles). **2.** the former name (1921–37) of **Charlotte Amalie.**

Saint Val·en·tine's Day *n., usually abbreviated to* **St. Val·en·tine's Day.** Feb. 14, the day on which valentines are exchanged, originally connected with the pagan festival of Lupercalia.

Saint Vin+cent *n., usually abbreviated to* **St. Vin+cent. 1.** a British Associated State in the Caribbean, in the Windward Islands of the Lesser Antilles, with dependencies in the Grenadines: became a British possession in 1763 and gained internal self-government in 1969; became independent in 1980. Capital: Kingstown. Pop.: 89 632 (1970). Area: 390 sq. km (150 sq. miles). **2. Cape.** a headland at the SW extremity of Portugal: scene of several important naval battles, notably in 1797, when the English defeated the French and Spanish. **3. Gulf.** a shallow inlet of SE South Australia, between Yorke Peninsula and the mainland: salt industry.

Saint Vi·tus's dance ('vaɪtəsɪz) *n., usually abbreviated to* **St. Vi·tus's dance.** *Pathol.* a nontechnical name for **chorea.**

Sai+pan (saɪ'pæn) *n.* an island in the W Pacific, in the S central Mariana Islands: administrative centre of the U.S. Trust Territory of the Pacific Islands; captured by the Americans and used as a leading air base until the end of World War II; administered by the U.S. since 1946. Pop.: 10 458 (1970). Area: 180 sq. km (70 sq. miles).

Sa·ïs ('seɪɪs) *n.* (in ancient Egypt) a city in the W Nile delta; the royal capital of the 24th dynasty (about 730–715 B.C.) and the 26th dynasty (about 664–525 B.C.). —**Sa+ite** ('seɪaɪt) *n.* ~**Sa+'it+ic** *adj.*

saith (sɛθ) *vb.* (used with *he, she,* or *it*) *Archaic.* a form of the present tense (indicative mood) of **say.**

saithe (seɪθ) *n. Brit.* another name for **coalfish.**

Sai+va ('saɪvə, 'ʃaɪ-) *n.* **1.** a member of a branch of Hinduism devoted to the worship of Siva, but rejecting the notion of his incarnations. ~*adj.* **2.** of or relating to Saivism or Saivites. —**'Sai+vism** *n.* —**'Sai+vite** *n.*

sa+kai ('sakaɪ) *n.* (in Malaysia). **1.** a Malaysian aborigine. **2.** a wild or uncouth person. [from Malay]

Sa+kai (sɑ:'kaɪ) *n.* a port in S Japan, on S Honshu on Osaka Bay: a major port in the 16th century; an industrial satellite of Osaka. Pop.: 716 498 (1974 est.).

sake[1] (seɪk) *n.* **1.** benefit or interest (esp. in the phrase **for (someone's or one's own) sake**). **2.** the purpose of obtaining or achieving (esp. in the phrase **for the sake of (something)**). **3.** used in various exclamations of impatience, urgency, etc.: *for heaven's sake; for pete's sake.* [C13 (in the phrase *for the sake of,* probably from legal usage): from Old English *sacu* lawsuit (hence, a cause); related to Old Norse *sok,* German *Sache* matter]

sa·ke[2], **sa·ké,** *or* **sa·ki** ('sɑ:kɪ) *n.* a Japanese alcoholic drink made of fermented rice. [C17: from Japanese]

sa+ker ('seɪkə) *n.* a large falcon, *Falco cherrug,* of E Europe and central Asia: used in falconry. [C14 *sagre,* from Old French *sacre,* from Arabic *saqr*]

Sa+kha+lin (*Russian* səxa'lin) *or* **Sa+ghal+ien** *n.* an island in the Sea of Okhotsk, off the SE coast of the Soviet Union north of Japan: fishing, forestry, and mineral resources (coal and petroleum). Capital: Yuzhno-Sakhalinsk. Pop.: 615 652 (1970). Area: 76 000 sq. km (29 300 sq. miles). Japanese name (1905–24): **Karafuto.**

Sakh·a·rov (*Russian* 'saxərəf) *n.* **An·drei** (an'drjej). born 1921, Soviet nuclear physicist and human-rights campaigner: Nobel peace prize 1975.

sa·ki ('sɑ:kɪ) *n.* any of several small mostly arboreal New World monkeys of the genera *Pithecia* and *Chiropotes,* having long hair and a long bushy tail. [C20: French, from Tupi *saqi*]

Sa·ki ('sɑ:kɪ) *n.* pen name of (Hector Hugh) **Munro.**

Sak+tas ('sæktəs) *n.* a Hindu sect worshipping female goddesses represented by the vulva.

Sak+ti ('sæktɪ) *n. Hinduism.* **1.** the female principle or organ of reproduction and generative power in general. **2.** this principle manifested in the consorts of the gods, esp. Kali.

Sa+kya+mu+ni (ˌsɑ:kjə'mu:nɪ) *n.* one of the titles of the Buddha, deriving from the name of Sakya where he was born. [Sanskrit, literally: hermit of the *Sākya* tribe]

sal (sæl) *n.* a pharmacological term for **salt** (sense 3). [Latin: salt]

sa+laam (sə'lɑ:m) *n.* **1.** a Muslim form of salutation consisting of a deep bow with the right palm on the forehead. **2.** a salutation signifying peace, used chiefly by Muslims. ~*vb.* **3.** to make a salaam or salute (someone) with a salaam. [C17: from Arabic *salām* peace, from the phrase *assalām 'alaikum* peace be to you]

sal+a·ble ('seɪləb°l) *adj.* the U.S. spelling of **saleable.**

sa+la+cious (sə'leɪʃəs) *adj.* **1.** having an excessive interest in sex. **2.** (of books, etc.) erotic, bawdy, or lewd. [C17: from Latin *salax* fond of leaping, from *salīre* to leap] —**sa+'la+cious+ly** *adv.* —**sa+'la+cious+ness** *or* **sa+lac+i·ty** (sə'læsɪtɪ) *n.*

sal+ad ('sæləd) *n.* **1.** a dish of raw vegetables, such as lettuce, tomatoes, cucumber, etc., served as a separate course with cheese, cold meat, eggs, etc., or as part of a main course. **2.** any dish of cold vegetables or fruit served with a dressing: *potato salad; fruit salad.* **3.** any green vegetable or herb used in such a dish, esp. lettuce. [C15: from Old French *salade,* from Old Provençal *salada,* from *salar* to season with salt, from Latin *sal* salt]

sal+ad days *pl. n.* a period of youth and inexperience.

sal+ad dress+ing *n.* a sauce for salad, such as oil and vinegar or mayonnaise.

sa+lade (sə'lɑ:d) *n.* another word for **sallet.**

Sal·a·din ('sælədɪn) *n.* Arabic name *Salah-ed-Din Yusuf ibn-Ayyub.* ?1137–93, sultan of Egypt and Syria and opponent of the Crusaders. He defeated the Christians near Tiberias (1187) and captured Acre, Jerusalem, and Ashkelon. He fought against Richard I of England and Philip II of France during the Third Crusade (1189–92).

Sa+la+do (*Spanish* sa'laðo) *n.* **1.** a river in N Argentina, rising in the Andes as the Juramento and flowing southeast to the Paraná River. Length: 2012 km (1250 miles). **2.** a river in W Argentina, rising near the Chilean border as the Desaguadero and flowing south to the Colorado River. Length: about 1365 km (850 miles).

Sal·a·man+ca (*Spanish* ˌsala'maŋka) *n.* a city in W Spain: a leading cultural centre of Europe till the end of the 16th century; market town. Pop.: 125 220 (1970).

sal·a·man+der ('sæləˌmændə) *n.* **1.** any of various urodele amphibians, such as *Salamandra salamandra* (**European fire salamander**) of central and S Europe (family *Salamandridae*). They are typically terrestrial, have an elongated body, and only return to water to breed. **2.** *Chiefly U.S.* any urodele amphibian. **3.** a mythical reptilian creature supposed to live in fire. **4.** an elemental fire-inhabiting being. **5.** any person or thing able to exist in fire or great heat. **6.** *Metallurgy.* a residue of metal and slag deposited on the walls of a furnace. **7.** a portable stove used to heat or dry out a building under construction. [C14: from Old French *salamandre,* from Latin *salamandra,* from Greek] —**sal·a·man+drine** (ˌsælə'mæn-drɪn) *adj.*

Sa+lam+bri·a (sə'læmbrɪə, ˌsɑ:lɑ:m'brɪə) *n.* a river in N Greece, in Thessaly, rising in the Pindus Mountains and flowing southeast and east to the Gulf of Salonika. Length: about 200 km (125 miles). Ancient name: **Peneus.** Modern Greek name: **Piniós.**

sa+la+mi (sə'lɑ:mɪ) *n.* a highly seasoned type of sausage, usually flavoured with garlic. [C19: from Italian, plural of *salame,* from Vulgar Latin *salāre* (unattested) to salt, from Latin *sal* salt]

Sal·a+mis ('sæləmɪs) *n.* an island in the Saronic Gulf, off the SE coast of Greece: scene of the naval battle in 480 B.C., in which the Greeks under Themistocles defeated the Persians under Xerxes. Pop.: 18 364 (1971). Area: 95 sq. km (37 sq. miles).

sal am+mo+ni+ac *n.* another name for **ammonium chloride.**

sal·a+ried ('sælərɪd) *adj.* earning or yielding a salary: *a salaried worker; salaried employment.*

sal·a+ry ('sælərɪ) *n., pl.* **+ries. 1.** a fixed regular payment made by an employer, often monthly, for professional or office work as opposed to manual work. Compare **wage.** ~*vb.* **+ries, +ry+ing, +ried. 2.** (*tr.*) to pay a salary to. [C14: from Anglo-Norman *salarie,* from Latin *salārium* the sum given to Roman soldiers to buy salt, from *sal* salt]

Sal·a·zar (*Portuguese* sələ'zar) *n.* **An·to·nio de O·li·vei·ra** (ən'tɔnju də oli'vəɪrə). 1889–1970, Portuguese statesman; dictator (1932–68).

sal+chow ('sɑ:lkəu) *n. Figure skating.* a jump from the inner backward edge of one foot with a full turn in the air, returning to the outer backward edge of the opposite foot. [C20: named after Ulrich *Salchow,* 1877–1949, Swedish figure-skater, who originated it]

Sal+du+ba (sæl'du:bə, 'sældəbə) *n.* the pre-Roman (Celtiberian) name for **Zaragoza.**

sale (seɪl) *n.* **1.** the exchange of goods, property, or services for an agreed sum of money or credit. **2.** the amount sold. **3.** the opportunity to sell; market: *there was no sale for luxuries.* **4.**

the rate of selling or being sold: *a slow sale of synthetic fabrics.* **5. a.** an event at which goods are sold at reduced prices, usually to clear old stocks. **b.** (*as modifier*): *sale bargains.* **6.** an auction. [Old English *sala,* from Old Norse *sala.* See SELL]

Sale (seɪl) *n.* **1.** a town in NW England, in Greater Manchester: a residential suburb of Manchester. Pop.: 55 623 (1971). **2.** a city in SE Australia, in SE Victoria: centre of an agricultural region. Pop.: 10 400 (1971).

Sa·lé (*French* sa'le) *n.* a port in NW Morocco, on the Atlantic adjoining Rabat. Pop.: (with Rabat) 530 366 (1971).

sale·a·ble *or U.S.* **sal·a·ble** ('seɪləbᵊl) *adj.* fit for selling or capable of being sold. —ˌ**sale·a·'bil·i·ty, 'sale·a·ble·ness** *or U.S.* ˌ**sal·a·'bil·i·ty, 'sal·a·ble·ness** *n.* —'**sale·a·bly** *or U.S.* '**sal·a·bly** *adv.*

Sa·lem ('seɪləm) *n.* **1.** a city in S India, in Tamil Nadu: textile industries. Pop.: 308 716 (1971). **2.** a city in NE Massachusetts, on the Atlantic: scene of the execution of 19 witches after the witch hunts of 1692. Pop.: 40 556 (1970). **3.** an Old Testament name for **Jerusalem.** (Genesis 14:18; Psalms 76:2).

sale or re·turn *or* **sale and re·turn** *n.* an arrangement by which a retailer pays only for goods sold, returning those that are unsold to the wholesaler or manufacturer.

sal·ep ('sælɛp) *n.* the dried ground starchy tubers of various orchids, used for food and formerly as drugs. [C18: via French and Turkish from Arabic *sahlab,* shortened from *khusy ath-tha'lab,* literally: fox's testicles, name of an orchid]

sal·e·ra·tus (ˌsælə'reɪtəs) *n.* another name for **sodium bicarbonate,** esp. when used in baking powders. [C19: from New Latin *sal aerātus* aerated salt]

Sa·ler·no (*Italian* sa'lɛrno) *n.* a port in SW Italy, in Campania on the **Gulf of Salerno:** first medical school of medieval Europe. Pop.: 159 518 (1975 est.).

sale·room ('seɪlˌruːm, -ˌrʊm) *n. Chiefly Brit.* a room where objects are displayed for sale, esp. by auction.

sales·clerk ('seɪlzˌklɑːk) *n. U.S.* a shop assistant. Sometimes shortened to **clerk.**

sales·man ('seɪlzmən) *n., pl.* **·men. 1.** Also called: (*fem.*) **sales·wom·an, sales·girl, sales·la·dy,** *or* (esp. among supporters of women's lib) **sales·per·son.** a person who sells merchandise or services either in a shop or by canvassing in a designated area. **2.** short for **travelling salesman.**

sales·man·ship ('seɪlzmənˌʃɪp) *n.* **1.** the technique, skill, or ability of selling. **2.** the work of a salesman.

sales pro·mo·tion *n.* activities or techniques intended to create consumer demand for a product or service.

sales re·sist·ance *n. Chiefly U.S.* opposition of potential customers to selling, esp. aggressive selling.

sales·room ('seɪlzˌruːm, -ˌrʊm) *n.* a room in which merchandise on sale is displayed.

sales talk *or* **pitch** *n. Chiefly U.S.* an argument or other persuasion used in selling.

sales tax *n. U.S.* a tax levied on retail sales receipts and added to selling prices by retailers.

sal·et ('sælɪt) *n.* a variant spelling of **sallet.**

Sal·ford ('sɔːlfəd, 'sɒl-) *n.* a city in NW England in Greater Manchester, on the Manchester Ship Canal: a major centre of the cotton industry in the 19th century; extensive docks. Pop.: 130 641 (1971).

Sa·li·an ('seɪlɪən) *adj.* **1.** denoting or relating to a group of Franks (the **Salii**) who settled in the Netherlands in the 4th century A.D. and later conquered large areas of Gaul, esp. in the north. ~*n.* **2.** a member of this group.

sal·ic ('sælɪk, 'seɪ-) *adj.* (of rocks and minerals) having a high content of silica and alumina.

Sal·ic *or* **Sal·ique** ('sælɪk, 'seɪlɪk) *adj.* of or relating to the Salian Franks or the Salic law.

sal·i·ca·ceous (ˌsælɪ'keɪʃəs) *adj.* of, relating to, or belonging to the *Salicaceae,* a chiefly N temperate family of trees and shrubs having catkins: includes the willows and poplars. [C19: via New Latin from Latin *salix* a willow]

sa·li·cin *or* **sa·li·cine** ('sælɪsɪn) *n.* a colourless or white crystalline water-soluble glucoside obtained from the bark of poplar trees and used as a medical analgesic. Formula: $C_{13}H_{18}O_7$. [C19: from French *salicine,* from Latin *salix* willow]

sa·li·cion·al (sə'lɪʃənəl) *or* **sa·li·cet** ('sælɪˌsɛt) *n.* a soft-toned organ stop with a reedy quality. [C19: from German, from Latin *salix* willow]

Sal·ic law *n. History.* **1. a.** the code of laws of the Salic Franks and other Germanic tribes. **b.** a law within this code excluding females from inheritance. **2.** a law excluding women from succession to the throne in certain countries, such as France and Spain.

sal·i·cor·ni·a (ˌsælɪ'kɔːnɪə) *n.* any chenopodiaceous plant of the genus *Salicornia,* of seashores and salt marshes: includes glasswort. [C19: from Late Latin, perhaps from Latin *sal* salt + *cornu* a horn]

sa·lic·y·late (sə'lɪsɪˌleɪt) *n.* any salt or ester of salicylic acid.

sal·i·cyl·ic ac·id (ˌsælɪ'sɪlɪk) *n.* a white crystalline slightly water-soluble substance with a sweet taste and bitter aftertaste, used in the manufacture of aspirin, dyes, and perfumes, and as a fungicide. Formula: $C_6H_4(OH)(COOH)$.

sa·li·ent ('seɪlɪənt) *adj.* **1.** prominent, conspicuous, or striking: *a salient feature.* **2.** projecting outwards at an angle of less than 180°. Compare **re-entrant** (sense 1). **3.** (esp. of animals) leaping. ~*n.* **4.** *Military.* a projection of the forward line into enemy-held territory. **5.** a salient angle. [C16: from Latin *salīre* to leap] —'**sa·li·ence** *or* '**sa·li·en·cy** *n.* —'**sa·li·ent·ly** *adv.* —'**sa·li·ent·ness** *n.*

sa·li·en·ti·an (ˌseɪlɪ'ɛnʃɪən) *n., adj.* another word for **anuran.** [C19: from New Latin *Salientia,* literally: leapers, from Latin *salīre* to leap]

sa·lif·er·ous (sæ'lɪfərəs) *adj.* (esp. of rock strata) containing or producing salt. [C19: from Latin *sal* SALT + *ferre* to bear]

sal·i·fy ('sælɪˌfaɪ) *vb.* **·fies, ·fy·ing, ·fied.** (*tr.*) **1.** to treat, mix with, or cause to combine with a salt. **2.** to convert (a substance) into a salt: *to salify ammonia by treatment with hydrochloric acid.* [C18: from French *salifier,* from New Latin *salificāre,* from Latin *sal* salt + *facere* to make] —'**sal·i·ˌfi·a·ble** *adj.* —ˌ**sal·i·fi·'ca·tion** *n.*

sal·im·e·ter (sæ'lɪmɪtə) *n.* another word for **salinometer.** —**sal·i·met·ric** (ˌsælɪ'mɛtrɪk) *adj.* —**sal·'im·e·try** *n.*

sa·lin·a (sə'laɪnə) *n.* a salt marsh, lake, or spring. [C17: from Spanish, from Medieval Latin: salt pit, from Late Latin *salīnus* SALINE]

sa·line ('seɪlaɪn) *adj.* **1.** of, concerned with, consisting of, or containing common salt: *a saline taste.* **2.** *Med.* of or relating to a saline. **3.** of, concerned with, consisting of, or containing any chemical salt, esp. a metallic salt resembling sodium chloride. ~*n.* **4.** *Med.* an isotonic solution of sodium chloride and distilled water. [C15: from Late Latin *salīnus,* from Latin *sal* salt] —**sa·lin·i·ty** (sə'lɪnɪtɪ) *n.*

Sal·in·ger ('sælɪndʒə) *n.* **J(erome) D(avid).** born 1919, U.S. writer, noted particularly for his novel of adolescence *The Catcher in the Rye* (1951).

sal·i·nom·e·ter (ˌsælɪ'nɒmɪtə) *n.* a hydrometer for determining the amount of salt in a solution, usually calibrated to measure concentration. Also called: **salimeter.** —**sal·i·no·met·ric** (ˌsælɪnə'mɛtrɪk) *adj.* —ˌ**sal·i·'nom·e·try** *n.*

Sal·ique ('sælɪk, 'seɪ-) *adj.* a variant spelling of **Salic.**

Salis·bur·y[1] ('sɔːlzbərɪ, -brɪ) *n.* **1.** the capital of Rhodesia, in the northeast: University of Rhodesia (1957); industrial and commercial centre. Pop.: 502 000 (1973 est.). **2.** a city in S Australia: an industrial suburb of N Adelaide. Pop.: 56 290 (1971). **3.** a city in S England, in SE Wiltshire: nearby Old Sarum was the site of an Early Iron Age hill fort; its cathedral (1220–58) has the highest spire in England. Pop.: 35 271 (1971). Ancient name: **Sarum.** Official name: **New Sarum.**

Salis·bur·y[2] ('sɔːlzbərɪ, -brɪ) *n.* **Rob·ert Gas·coyne Cec·il** ('gæskɔɪn), 3rd Marquess of Salisbury. 1830–1903. British statesman; Conservative prime minister (1885–86; 1886–92; 1895–1902). His greatest interest was in foreign and imperial affairs.

Salis·bur·y Plain *n.* an open chalk plateau in S England, in Wiltshire: site of Stonehenge; military training area. Average height: 120 m (400 ft.).

Sa·lish ('seɪlɪʃ) *or* **Sa·lish·an** ('seɪlɪʃən, 'sæl-) *n.* **1.** a family of North American Indian languages spoken in the northwestern U.S. and W Canada. **2. the Salish.** (*functioning as pl.*) the peoples collectively who speak these languages.

sa·li·va (sə'laɪvə) *n.* the secretion of salivary glands, consisting of a clear usually slightly acid aqueous fluid of variable composition. It moistens the oral cavity and prepares food for swallowing. [C17: from Latin, of obscure origin] —**sal·i·var·y** (sə'laɪvərɪ, 'sælɪvərɪ) *adj.*

sal·i·var·y gland *n.* any of the glands in mammals that secrete saliva. In man the chief salivary glands are the **parotid, sublingual,** and **submaxillary glands.**

sal·i·vate ('sælɪˌveɪt) *vb.* **1.** (*intr.*) to secrete saliva, esp. an excessive amount. **2.** (*tr.*) to cause (a laboratory animal, etc.) to produce saliva, as by the administration of mercury. —ˌ**sal·i·'va·tion** *n.*

Salk (sɔːlk) *n.* **Jo·nas Ed·ward.** born 1914, U.S. virologist: developed an injected vaccine against poliomyelitis (1954).

sal·lee ('sælɪ) *n. Austral.* **1.** Also called: **snow gum.** a SE Australian eucalyptus tree, *Eucalyptus pauciflora,* with pale grey bark. **2.** any of various acacia trees. [probably of native origin]

sal·let, sal·et ('sælɪt), *or* **sa·lade** *n.* a light round helmet extending over the back of the neck; replaced the basinet in the 15th century. [C15: from French *salade,* probably from Old Italian *celata,* from *celare* to conceal, from Latin]

sal·low[1] ('sæləʊ) *adj.* **1.** (esp. of human skin) of an unhealthy pale or yellowish colour. ~*vb.* **2.** (*tr.*) to make sallow. [Old English *salu;* related to Old Norse *sol* seaweed (Icelandic *sōlr* yellowish), Old High German *salo,* French *sale* dirty] —'**sal·low·ish** *adj.* —'**sal·low·ly** *adv.* —'**sal·low·ness** *n.*

sal·low[2] ('sæləʊ) *n.* **1.** any of several small willow trees, esp. the Eurasian *Salix cinerea* (**common sallow**), which has large catkins that appear before the leaves. **2.** a twig or the wood of any of these trees. [Old English *sealh;* related to Old Norse *selja,* Old High German *salaha,* Middle Low German *salwīde,* Latin *salix*] —'**sal·low·y** *adj.*

Sal·lust ('sæləst) *n.* full name *Gaius Sallustius Crispus.* 86–?34 B.C., Roman historian and statesman, noted for his histories of the Catiline conspiracy and the Roman war against Jugurtha.

sal·ly ('sælɪ) *n., pl.* **·lies. 1.** a sudden violent excursion, esp. by troops. **2.** a sudden outburst or emergence into action, expression, or emotion. **3.** an excursion or jaunt. **4.** a jocular retort. ~*vb.* **·lies, ·ly·ing, ·lied.** (*intr.*) **5.** to make a sudden violent excursion. **6.** (often foll. by *forth*) to go out on an expedition, etc. **7.** to come, go, or set out in an energetic manner. **8.** to rush out suddenly. [C16: from Old French *saillie,* from *saillir* to dash forwards, from Latin *salīre* to leap] —'**sal·li·er** *n.*

Sal·ly Ar·my *n. Brit. informal.* short for **Salvation Army.**

Sal·ly Lunn (lʌn) *n.* a flat round cake made from a sweet yeast dough, usually served hot. [C19: said to be named after an 18th-century English baker who invented it]

sal+ma+gun+di *or* **sal+ma+gun+dy** (ˌsælməˈgʌndɪ) *n.* **1.** a mixed salad dish of cooked meats, eggs, beetroot, etc., popular in 18th-century England. **2.** a miscellany; potpourri. [C17: from French *salmigondis,* perhaps from Italian *salami conditi* pickled salami]

Sal+ma+naz+ar (ˌsælməˈnæzə) *n.* a wine bottle holding the equivalent of twelve normal bottles (approximately 312 ounces). [C19: humorous allusion to an Assyrian king mentioned in the Bible (II Kings 17:3); compare JEROBOAM]

sal+mi *or* **sal+mis** (ˈsælmɪ) *n., pl.* **+mis** (-mɪ). a ragout of game stewed in a rich brown sauce. [C18: from French, shortened form of *salmigondis* SALMAGUNDI]

salm+on (ˈsæmən) *n., pl.* **+ons** *or* **+on. 1.** any soft-finned fish of the family *Salmonidae,* esp. *Salmo salar* of the Atlantic and *Oncorhynchus* species (sockeye, Chinook, etc.) of the Pacific, which are important food fishes. They occur in cold and temperate waters and many species migrate to fresh water to spawn. **2.** *Austral.* any of several unrelated fish. **3.** short for **salmon pink.** [C13: from Old French *saumon,* from Latin *salmō;* related to Late Latin *salar* trout]

salm·on+ber·ry (ˈsæmənbərɪ, -brɪ) *n., pl.* **·ries. 1.** a spineless raspberry bush, *Rubus spectabilis,* of North America, having reddish-purple flowers and large red or yellow edible fruits. **2.** the fruit of this plant.

sal+mo+nel+la (ˌsælməˈnɛlə) *n., pl.* **+lae** (-ˌliː). any Gram-negative rod-shaped aerobic bacteria of the genus *Salmonella,* including *S. typhosa,* which causes typhoid fever, and many species causing food poisoning (**salmonellosis**): family *Enterobacteriaceae.* [C19: New Latin, named after Daniel E. *Salmon* (1850–1914), U.S. veterinary surgeon]

sal+mo+noid (ˈsælməˌnɔɪd) *adj.* **1.** of, relating to, or belonging to the *Salmonoidea,* a suborder of soft-finned teleost fishes having a fatty fin between the dorsal and tail fins: includes the salmon, whitefish, grayling, smelt, and char. **2.** of, relating to, or resembling a salmon. *~n.* **3.** any fish belonging to the suborder *Salmonoidea,* esp. any of the family *Salmonidae* (salmon, trout, char).

salm+on pink *n., adj.* **a.** a yellowish-pink colour, sometimes with an orange tinge. **b.** (*as adj.*): *a salmon-pink hat.* Sometimes shortened to **salmon.**

salm+on trout *n.* any of various large trout, esp. the brown trout or rainbow trout.

sal+ol (ˈsælɒl) *n.* a white sparingly soluble crystalline compound with a slight aromatic odour, used as a preservative and to absorb light in sun-tan lotions, plastics, etc.; phenyl salicylate. Formula: $C_6H_4(OH)COOC_6H_5$.

Sa·lo·me (səˈləʊmɪ) *n. New Testament.* the daughter of Herodias, at whose instigation she beguiled Herod by her seductive dancing into giving her the head of John the Baptist.

sa+lon (ˈsælɒn) *n.* **1.** a room in a large house in which guests are received. **2.** an assembly of guests in a fashionable household, esp. a gathering of major literary, artistic, and political figures from the 17th to the early 20th centuries. **3.** a commercial establishment in which hairdressers, beauticians, etc., carry on their businesses: *beauty salon.* **4. a.** a hall for exhibiting works of art. **b.** such an exhibition, esp. one showing the work of living artists. [C18: from French, from Italian *salone,* augmented form of *sala* hall, of Germanic origin; compare Old English *sele* hall, Old High German *sal,* Old Norse *salr* hall]

Sa+lo+ni+ka *or* **Sa+lo+ni+ca** (səˈlɒnɪkə) *n.* the English name for **Thessaloniki.**

sa+lon mu+sic *n. Sometimes derogatory.* light classical music intended esp. for domestic entertaining.

sa+loon (səˈluːn) *n.* **1.** Also called: **saloon bar.** *Brit.* another word for **lounge** (sense 5). **2.** a large public room on a passenger ship. **3.** any large public room used for a specific purpose: *a dancing saloon.* **4.** *U.S.* a place where alcoholic drink is sold and consumed. **5.** a closed two-door or four-door car with four to six seats. U.S. name: **sedan. 6.** an obsolete word for **salon** (sense 1). [C18: from French SALON]

sa+loop (səˈluːp) *n.* an infusion of aromatic herbs or other plant parts, esp. salep, formerly used as a tonic or cure. [C18: changed from SALEP]

Sal+op (ˈsæləp) *n.* **1.** a county of W central England, coextensive with the former county of Shropshire: mainly agricultural. Administrative centre: Shrewsbury. Pop.: 359 000 (1976 est.). Area: 3579 sq. km (1379 sq. miles). **2.** another name for **Shropshire.**

sal·o+pette (ˌsæləˈpɛt) *n.* a garment worn for skiing, consisting of quilted trousers reaching to the chest and held up by shoulder straps. [C20: from French]

sal+pa (ˈsælpə) *n., pl.* **+pas** *or* **+pae** (-piː). any of various minute floating animals of the genus *Salpa,* of warm oceans, having a transparent barrel-shaped body with openings at either end: class *Thaliacea,* subphylum *Tunicata* (tunicates). [C19: from New Latin, from Latin: variety of stockfish, from Greek *salpē*] **—sal+pi+form** (ˈsælpɪˌfɔːm) *adj.*

sal+pi+con (ˈsælpɪkən) *n.* a mixture of chopped fish, meat, or vegetables in a sauce, used as fillings for croquettes, etc. [C18: from French, from Spanish, from *salpicar* to sprinkle with salt]

sal+pi+glos+sis (ˌsælpɪˈglɒsɪs) *n.* any solanaceous plant of the Chilean genus *Salpiglossis,* some species of which are cultivated for their bright funnel-shaped flowers. [C19: New Latin, from Greek *salpinx* trumpet + *glōssa* tongue]

sal+pin+gec+to+my (ˌsælpɪnˈdʒɛktəmɪ) *n., pl.* **+mies.** surgical removal of a Fallopian tube. [C20: from SALPINX + -ECTOMY]

sal+pin+gi+tis (ˌsælpɪnˈdʒaɪtɪs) *n.* inflammation of a Fallopian tube or a Eustachian tube. [C19: from SALPINX + -ITIS] **—sal+pin+git+ic** (ˌsælpɪnˈdʒɪtɪk) *adj.*

sal+pinx (ˈsælpɪŋks) *n., pl.* **sal+pin+ges** (sælˈpɪndʒiːz). *Anatomy.* another name for the **Fallopian tube** or the **Eustachian tube.** [C19: from Greek: trumpet] **—sal+pin+gi·an** (sælˈpɪndʒɪən) *adj.*

sal+si+fy (ˈsælsɪfɪ) *n., pl.* **+fies. 1.** Also called: **oyster plant, vegetable oyster.** a Mediterranean plant, *Tragopogon porrifolius,* having grasslike leaves, purple flower heads, and a long white edible taproot: family *Compositae* (composites). **2.** the root of this plant, which tastes of oysters and is eaten as a vegetable. [C17: from French *salsifis,* from Italian *sassefrica,* from Late Latin *saxifrica,* from Latin *saxum* rock + *fricāre* to rub]

sal so·da *n.* the crystalline decahydrate of sodium carbonate.

SALT (sɔːlt) *n. acronym for* Strategic Arms Limitation Talks.

salt (sɔːlt) *n.* **1.** a white powder or colourless crystalline solid, consisting mainly of sodium chloride and used for seasoning and preserving food. **2.** (*modifier*) preserved in, flooded with, containing, or growing in salt or salty water: *salt pork; salt marshes.* **3.** *Chem.* any of a class of usually crystalline solid compounds that are formed from, or can be regarded as formed from, an acid and a base by replacement of one or more hydrogen atoms in the acid molecules by positive ions from the base. **4.** liveliness or pungency: *his wit added salt to the discussion.* **5.** dry or laconic wit. **6.** a sailor, esp. one who is old and experienced. **7.** short for **saltcellar. 8. rub salt into someone's wounds.** to make someone's pain, shame, etc., even worse. **9. salt of the earth.** a person or group of people regarded as the finest of their kind. **10. with a grain** (*or* **pinch**) **of salt.** with reservations; sceptically. **11. worth one's salt.** efficient; worthy of one's pay. *~vb.* (*tr.*) **12.** to season or preserve with salt. **13.** to scatter salt over (an iced road, etc.) to melt the ice. **14.** to add zest to. **15.** (often foll. by *down* or *away*) to preserve or cure with salt or saline solution. **16.** *Chem.* to treat with common salt or other chemical salt. **17.** to provide (cattle, etc.) with salt. **18.** to give a false appearance of value to, esp. to introduce valuable ore fraudulently into (a mine, sample, etc.). *~adj.* **19.** not sour, sweet, or bitter; salty. **20.** *Obsolete.* rank or lascivious (esp. in the phrase **a salt wit**). *~*See also **salt away, salt out, salts.** [Old English *sealt;* related to Old Norse, Gothic *salt,* German *Salz,* Lettish *sāls,* Latin *sāl,* Greek *hals*] **—ˈsalt+ish** *adj.* **—ˈsalt+less** *adj.* **—ˈsalt+ˌlike** *adj.* **—ˈsalt+ness** *n.*

Sal+ta (*Spanish* ˈsalta) *n.* a city in NW Argentina: thermal springs. Pop.: 176 130 (1970).

sal+tant (ˈsæltənt) *adj.* (of an organism) differing from others of its species because of a saltation. [C17: from Latin *saltāns* dancing, from *saltāre,* from *salīre* to spring]

sal+ta+rel+lo (ˌsæltəˈrɛləʊ) *n., pl.* **+li** (-lɪ) *or* **+los. 1.** a traditional Italian dance, usually in compound duple time. **2.** a piece of music composed for or in the rhythm of this dance. [C18: from Italian, from *saltare* to dance energetically, from Latin; see SALTANT]

sal+ta+tion (sælˈteɪʃən) *n.* **1.** *Biology.* an abrupt variation in the appearance of an organism, species, etc., usually caused by genetic mutation. **2.** *Geology.* the leaping movement of sand or soil particles carried in water or by the wind. **3.** a sudden abrupt movement or transition. [C17: from Latin *saltātiō* a dance, from *saltāre* to leap about]

sal+ta+to+ri·al (ˌsæltəˈtɔːrɪəl) *or* **sal+ta+to·ry** *adj.* **1.** *Biology.* specialized for or characterized by jumping: *the saltatorial legs of a grasshopper.* **2.** of or relating to saltation. [C17 *saltatory,* from Latin *saltātōrius* concerning dancing, from *saltātor* a dancer; see SALTANT]

salt a·way *or* **down** *vb.* (*tr., adv.*) to hoard or save (money, valuables, etc.).

salt+box (ˈsɔːltˌbɒks) *n.* **1.** a box for salt with a sloping lid. **2.** *U.S.* a house that has two storeys in front and one storey at the back, with a gable roof that extends downwards over the rear.

salt+bush (ˈsɔːltˌbʊʃ) *n.* any of various chenopodiaceous shrubs of the genus *Atriplex* that grow in alkaline desert regions.

salt cake *n.* an impure form of sodium sulphate obtained as a by-product in several industrial processes: used in the manufacture of detergents, glass, and ceramic glazes.

salt+cel+lar (ˈsɔːltˌsɛlə) *n.* **1.** a small container for salt used at the table. **2.** *Brit. informal.* either of the two hollows formed above the collarbones of very slim people. [changed (through influence of cellar) from C15 *salt saler; saler* from Old French *saliere* container for salt, from Latin *salārius* belonging to salt, from *sal* salt]

salt+chuck (ˈsɔːltˌtʃʌk) *n. Canadian, chiefly W coast.* any body of salt water. [C20: from SALT + CHUCK[4]]

salt+chuck+er (ˈsɔːltˌtʃʌkə) *n. Canadian W coast informal.* a saltwater angler.

salt dome *or* **plug** *n.* a domelike structure of stratified rocks containing a central core of salt: formed by the upward movement of a salt deposit.

salt+ed (ˈsɔːltɪd) *adj.* **1.** seasoned, preserved, or treated with salt. **2.** *Informal.* experienced in an occupation, etc.

salt+er (ˈsɔːltə) *n.* **1.** a person who deals in or manufactures salt. **2.** a person who treats meat, fish, etc., with salt.

salt+ern (ˈsɔːltən) *n.* **1.** another word for **saltworks. 2.** a place where salt is obtained from pools of evaporated sea water. [Old English *saltærn,* from SALT + *ærn* house. Compare BARN, RANSACK]

salt+fish (ˈsɔːltfɪʃ) *n. Caribbean.* salted cod.

salt flat *n.* a flat expanse of salt left by the total evaporation of a body of water.

sal+ti+grade (ˈsæltɪˌgreɪd) *adj.* (of animals) adapted for moving in a series of jumps. [C19: from New Latin *Saltigradae,* name formerly applied to jumping spiders, from Latin *saltus* a leap + *gradī* to move]

Sal·til·lo (*Spanish* sal'tijo) *n.* a city in N Mexico, capital of Coahuila state: resort and commercial centre of a mining region. Pop.: 211 129 (1975 est.).

sal·tire *or* **sal·tier** ('sɔːlˌtaɪə) *n. Heraldry.* an ordinary consisting of a diagonal cross on a shield. [C14 *sawturoure,* from Old French *sauteour* cross-shaped barricade, from *saulter* to jump, from Latin *saltāre*]

Salt Lake Cit·y *n.* a city in N central Utah, near the Great Salt Lake at an altitude of 1330 m (4300 ft): state capital; founded in 1847 by the Mormons as world capital of the Mormon Church; University of Utah (1850). Pop.: 169 234 (1973 est.).

salt lick *n.* **1.** a place where wild animals go to lick naturally occurring salt deposits. **2.** a block of salt or a salt preparation given to domestic animals to lick.

Sal·to (*Spanish* 'salto) *n.* a port in NW Uruguay, on the Uruguay River: Uruguay's second largest city. Pop.: 60 000 (1970 est.).

salt out *vb.* (*adv.*) Chem. to cause (a dissolved substance) to come out of solution by adding an electrolyte.

salt·pan ('sɔːltˌpæn) *n.* a shallow basin, usually in a desert region, containing salt, gypsum, etc., that was deposited from an evaporated salt lake.

salt·pe·tre *or U.S.* **salt·pe·ter** (ˌsɔːlt'piːtə) *n.* **1.** another name for **potassium nitrate.** **2.** short for **Chile saltpetre.** [C16: from Old French *salpetre,* from Latin *sal petrae* salt of rock]

salt pork *n.* pork, esp. the fat pork taken from the back, sides, and belly, that has been cured with salt.

salts (sɔːlts) *pl. n.* **1.** *Med.* any of various mineral salts, such as magnesium sulphate or sodium sulphate, for use as a cathartic. **2.** short for **smelling salts.**

sal·tus ('sæltəs) *n., pl.* **·tus·es.** a break in the continuity of a sequence, esp. the omission of a necessary step in a logical argument. [Latin: a leap]

salt·wa·ter ('sɔːltˌwɔːtə) *adj.* of, relating to, or inhabiting salt water, esp. the sea: *saltwater fishes.*

salt·works ('sɔːltˌwɜːks) *n.* (*functioning as sing.*) a place, building, or factory where salt is produced.

salt·wort ('sɔːltˌwɜːt) *n.* **1.** Also called: **glasswort, kali.** any of several chenopodiaceous plants of the genus *Salsola,* esp. *S. kali,* of beaches and salt marshes, which has prickly leaves, striped stems, and small green flowers. See also **barilla.** **2.** another name for **sea milkwort.**

salt·y ('sɔːltɪ) *adj.* **salt·i·er, salt·i·est. 1.** of, tasting of, or containing salt. **2.** (esp. of humour) sharp; piquant. **3.** relating to life at sea. —**'salt·i·ly** *adv.* —**'salt·i·ness** *n.*

sa·lu·bri·ous (sə'luːbrɪəs) *adj.* conducive or favourable to health; wholesome. [C16: from Latin *salūbris,* from *salūs* health] —**sa·'lu·bri·ous·ly** *adv.* —**sa·'lu·bri·ous·ness** *or* **sa·lu·bri·ty** (sə'luːbrɪtɪ) *n.*

Sa·lu·ki (sə'luːkɪ) *n.* a tall breed of hound with a smooth coat and long fringes on the ears and tail. [C19: from Arabic *salūqīy* of Saluq, name of an ancient Arabian city]

sal·u·tar·y ('sæljʊtərɪ, -trɪ) *adj.* **1.** promoting or intended to promote an improvement or beneficial effect: *a salutary warning.* **2.** promoting or intended to promote health. [C15: from Latin *salūtāris* wholesome, from *salūs* safety] —**'sal·u·tar·i·ly** *adv.* —**'sal·u·tar·i·ness** *n.*

sal·u·ta·tion (ˌsæljʊ'teɪʃən) *n.* **1.** an act, phrase, gesture, etc., that serves as a greeting. **2.** a form of words used as an opening to a speech or letter, such as *Dear Sir* or *Ladies and Gentlemen.* **3.** the act of saluting. [C14: from Latin *salūtātiō,* from *salūtāre* to greet; see SALUTE]

sa·lu·ta·to·ry (sə'luːtətərɪ, -trɪ) *adj.* of, relating to, or resembling a salutation. —**sa·'lu·ta·to·ri·ly** *adv.*

sa·lute (sə'luːt) *vb.* **1.** (*tr.*) to address or welcome with friendly words or gestures of respect, such as bowing or lifting the hat; greet. **2.** (*tr.*) to acknowledge with praise or honour: *we salute your gallantry.* **3.** *Military.* to pay or receive formal respect, as by presenting arms or raising the right arm. ~*n.* **4.** the act of saluting. **5.** a formal military gesture of respect. [C14: from Latin *salūtāre* to greet, from *salūs* wellbeing] —**sa·'lut·er** *n.*

salv·a·ble ('sælvəbəl) *adj.* capable of or suitable for being saved or salvaged. [C17: from Late Latin *salvāre* to save, from *salvus* safe; see SAVE[1]] —ˌ**sal·va·'bil·i·ty** *or* **'sal·va·ble·ness** *n.* —**'sal·va·bly** *adv.*

Sal·va·dor ('sælvəˌdɔː; *Portuguese* ˌsalva'dor) *n.* a port in E Brazil, capital of Bahia state: founded in 1549 as capital of the Portuguese colony, which it remained until 1763; a major centre of the African slave trade in colonial times. Pop.: 998 258 (1970). Former name: **Bahia.** Official name: **São Sal·va·dor da Ba·hi·a de To·dos os San·tos** (sãʊ ˌsalva'dor da ba'ia de 'toduz us 'sɐntus). —ˌ**Sal·va·'do·ri·an** *adj., n.*

sal·vage ('sælvɪdʒ) *n.* **1.** the act, process, or business of rescuing vessels or their cargoes from loss at sea. **2. a.** the act of saving any goods or property in danger of damage or destruction. **b.** (*as modifier*): *a salvage operation.* **3.** the goods or property so saved. **4.** compensation paid for the salvage of a vessel or its cargo. **5.** the proceeds from the sale of salvaged goods or property. ~*vb.* (*tr.*) **6.** to save or rescue (goods or property) from fire, shipwreck, etc. **7.** to gain (something beneficial) from a failure: *she salvaged little from the broken marriage.* [C17: from Old French, from Medieval Latin *salvāgium,* from *salvāre* to SAVE[1]] —**'sal·vage·a·ble** *adj.* —**'sal·vag·er** *n.*

sal·va·tion (sæl'veɪʃən) *n.* **1.** the act of preserving or the state of being preserved from harm. **2.** a person or thing that is the means of preserving from harm. **3.** *Theol.* deliverance by redemption from the power of sin and from the penalties ensuing from it. **4.** *Christian Science.* the realization that Life, Truth, and Love are supreme and that they can destroy such illusions as sin, death, etc. [C13: from Old French *sauvacion,* from Late Latin *salvātiō,* from Latin *salvātus* saved, from *salvāre* to SAVE[1]] —**sal·'va·tion·al** *adj.*

Sal·va·tion Ar·my *n.* **a.** a Christian body founded in 1865 by William Booth and organized on quasi-military lines for evangelism and social work among the poor. **b.** (*as modifier*): *the Salvation Army Hymn Book.*

sal·va·tion·ist (sæl'veɪʃənɪst) *n.* **1.** a member of an evangelical sect emphasizing the doctrine of salvation. **2.** (*often cap.*) a member of the Salvation Army. ~*adj.* **3.** stressing the doctrine of salvation. **4.** (*often cap.*) of or relating to the Salvation Army. —**sal·'va·tion·ism** *n.*

salve[1] (sælv, sɑːv) *n.* **1.** an ointment for wounds, sores, etc. **2.** anything that heals or soothes. ~*vb.* (*tr.*) **3.** to apply salve to (a wound, sore, etc.). **4.** to soothe, comfort, or appease. [Old English *sealf;* related to Old High German *salba,* Greek *elpos* oil, Sanskrit *sarpis* lard]

salve[2] (sælv) *vb.* **1.** a less common word for **salvage. 2.** an archaic word for **save**[1] (sense 3). [C18: from SALVAGE]

sal·ver ('sælvə) *n.* a tray, esp. one of silver, on which food, letters, visiting cards, etc., are presented. [C17: from French *salve,* from Spanish *salva* tray from which the king's taster sampled food, from Latin *salvāre* to SAVE[1]]

sal·ver·form ('sælvəˌfɔːm) *adj.* (of the corolla of the phlox and certain other flowers) consisting of a narrow tube with flat spreading terminal petals.

sal·vi·a ('sælvɪə) *n.* any herbaceous plant or small shrub of the genus *Salvia,* such as the sage, grown for their medicinal or culinary properties or for ornament: family *Labiatae* (labiates). [C19: from Latin: SAGE[2]]

sal·vo[1] ('sælvəʊ) *n., pl.* **·vos** *or* **·voes. 1.** a discharge of fire from weapons in unison, esp. on a ceremonial occasion. **2.** concentrated fire from many weapons, as in a naval battle. **3.** an outburst, as of applause. [C17: from Italian *salva,* from Old French *salve,* from Latin *salvē!* greetings! from *salvēre* to be in good health, from *salvus* safe]

sal·vo[2] ('sælvəʊ) *n., pl.* **·vos.** *Rare.* **1.** an excuse or evasion. **2.** an expedient to save a reputation or soothe hurt feelings. **3.** (in legal documents) a saving clause; reservation. [C17: from such Medieval Latin phrases as *salvō iurē* the right of keeping safe, from Latin *salvus* safe]

Sal·vo ('sælvəʊ) *n., pl.* **·vos.** *Austral. slang.* a member of the Salvation Army.

sal vol·a·ti·le (vɒ'lætɪlɪ) *n.* **1.** another name for **ammonium carbonate. 2.** Also called: **spirits of ammonia** *or* (archaic) **hartshorn.** a solution of ammonium carbonate in alcohol and aqueous ammonia, often containing aromatic oils, used as smelling salts. [C17: from New Latin: volatile salt]

sal·vor *or* **sal·ver** ('sælvə) *n.* a person instrumental in salvaging a vessel or its cargo. [C17: from SALVAGE + -OR[1]]

Sal·ween ('sælwiːn) *n.* a river in SW Asia, rising in the Tibetan Plateau and flowing east and south through SW China and Burma to the Gulf of Martaban. Length: 2400 km (1500 miles).

Sal·yut (sæl'juːt) *n.* either of two Soviet space stations the first of which was launched into earth orbit in April 1971 the second in April 1973. [C20: Russian: salute]

Salz·burg (*German* 'zaltsbʊrk; *English* 'sæltsbɜːg) *n.* **1.** a city in W Austria, capital of Salzburg province: 7th-century Benedictine abbey; a music centre since the Middle Ages and birthplace of Mozart; tourist centre. Pop.: 128 845 (1971). **2.** a province of W Austria. Pop.: 401 766 (1971). Area: 7154 sq. km (2762 sq. miles).

Salz·git·ter (*German* zalts'gɪtər) *n.* an industrial city in West Germany, in SE Lower Saxony. Pop.: 119 181 (1974 est.).

SAM (sæm) *n. acronym for* surface-to-air missile.

Sam. *Bible. abbrev. for* Samuel.

S.Am. *abbrev. for* South America(n).

Sa·mar ('sɑːmɑ) *n.* an island in the E central Philippines, separated from S Luzon by the San Bernardino Strait: the third largest island in the republic. Capital: Catbalogan. Pop.: 1 019 358 (1970). Area: 13 080 sq. km (5050 sq. miles).

sa·ma·ra (sə'mɑːrə) *n.* a dry indehiscent one-seeded fruit with a winglike extension to aid dispersal: occurs in the ash, maple, etc. Also called: **key fruit.** [C16: from New Latin, from Latin: seed of an elm]

Sa·ma·ra (*Russian* sa'marə) *n.* the former name (until 1935) of **Kuibyshev.**

Sa·ma·rang (sə'mɑːrɑːŋ) *n.* a variant spelling of **Semarang.**

Sa·mar·i·a (sə'mɛərɪə) *n.* **1.** the region of ancient Palestine that extended from Judaea to Galilee and from the Mediterranean to the River Jordan; the N kingdom of Israel. **2.** the capital of this kingdom; constructed northwest of Shechem in the 9th century B.C.

Sa·mar·i·tan (sə'mærɪtən) *n.* **1.** a native or inhabitant of Samaria. **2.** short for **good Samaritan. 3.** a member of a voluntary organization (**the Samaritans**) whose aim is to help people in distress or despair. **4.** the dialect of Aramaic spoken in Samaria. ~*adj.* **5.** of or relating to Samaria. —**Sa·'mar·i·tan·ism** *n.*

sa·mar·i·um (sə'mɛərɪəm) *n.* a silvery metallic element of the lanthanide series occurring chiefly in monazite and bastnaesite and used in carbon-arc lighting, as a doping agent in laser crystals, and as a neutron-absorber. Symbol: Sm; atomic no.: 62; atomic wt.: 150.35; valency: 2 or 3; relative density: 7.5; melting pt.: 1072°C; boiling pt.: 1778°C. [C19: New Latin, from SAMARSKITE + -IUM]

Sa·mar·kand ('sæməˌkænd; *Russian* səmar'kant) *n.* a city in the S central Soviet Union, in the Uzbek SSR: under Tamerlane it became the chief economic and cultural centre of central Asia, on trade routes from China and India (the "silk road"). Pop.: 299 000 (1975 est.). Ancient name: **Maracanda.**

sa+mar+skite (sə'mɑːskaɪt) *n.* a velvety black mineral of complex composition occurring in pegmatites: used as a source of uranium and certain rare earth elements. [C19: named after Colonel von *Samarski,* 19th-century Russian inspector of mines]

Sa·ma-Ve·da ('sɑːmə'veɪdə) *n. Hinduism.* the third Veda containing the rituals for sacrifices.

sam+ba ('sæmbə) *n., pl.* **+bas. 1.** a lively modern ballroom dance from Brazil in bouncy duple time. **2.** a piece of music composed for or in the rhythm of this dance. ~*vb.* **+bas, +ba+ing, +baed. 3.** (*intr.*) to perform such a dance. [Portuguese, of African origin]

sam+bar *or* **sam+bur** ('sæmbə) *n., pl.* **+bars, +bar** *or* **+burs, +bur.** a S Asian deer, *Cervus unicolor,* with three-tined antlers. [C17: from Hindi, from Sanskrit *śambarra,* of obscure origin]

sam+bo ('sæmbəʊ) *n., pl.* **+bos. 1.** *Slang.* an offensive word for **Negro:** often used as a term of address. **2.** the offspring of a Negro and a member of another race or a mulatto. [C18: from American Spanish *zambo* a person of Negro descent; perhaps related to Bantu *nzambu* monkey]

Sam+bre (*French* 'sɑ̃ːbr) *n.* a river in W Europe, rising in N France and flowing east into Belgium to join the Meuse at Namur. Length: 190 km (118 miles).

Sam Browne belt *n.* a military officer's wide belt supported by a strap passing from the left side of the belt over the right shoulder. [C20: named after Sir *Samuel J. Browne* (1824–1901), British general, who invented such a belt]

same (seɪm) *adj.* (usually preceded by *the*) **1.** being the very one: *she is wearing the same hat she wore yesterday.* **2. a.** being the one previously referred to; aforesaid. **b.** (*as n.*): *a note received about same.* **3. a.** identical in kind, quantity, etc.: *two girls of the same age.* **b.** (*as n.*): *we'd like the same, please.* **4.** unchanged in character or nature: *his attitude is the same as ever.* **5. all the same. a.** Also: **just the same.** nevertheless; yet. **b.** immaterial: *it's all the same to me.* ~*adv.* **6.** in an identical manner. [C12: from Old Norse *samr;* related to Old English adverbial phrase *swā same* likewise, Gothic *sama,* Latin *similis,* Greek *homos* same]

Usage. The use of *same* exemplified in *if you send us your order for the materials, we will deliver same tomorrow* is common in business and official English. In general English, however, this use of the word is avoided: *may I borrow your book? I'll return it* (not *same*) *tomorrow.*

sa+mekh ('sɑːmək; *Hebrew* 'samɛx) *n.* the 15th letter in the Hebrew alphabet (ס) transliterated as *s.*

same+ness ('seɪmnɪs) *n.* **1.** the state or quality of being the same. **2.** lack of change; monotony.

sam+foo ('sæmfuː) *n.* a style of casual dress worn by Chinese women, consisting of a waisted blouse and trousers. [from Chinese (Cantonese) *sam* dress + *foo* trousers]

Sa+mi·an ('seɪmɪən) *adj.* **1.** of or relating to Samos or its inhabitants. ~*n.* **2.** a native or inhabitant of Samos.

Sa+mi·an ware *n.* **1.** a fine earthenware pottery, reddish-brown or black in colour, found in large quantities on Roman sites. **2.** Also called: **Arretine ware.** the earlier pottery from which this developed, an imitation of a type of Greek pottery, made during the first century B.C. at Arretium. [C19: named after the island of SAMOS, source of a reddish-coloured earth resembling terra sigillata, similar to the earth from which the pottery was made]

sam+iel ('sæmjɛl) *n.* another word for **simoom.** [C17: from Turkish *samyeli,* from *sam* poisonous + *yel* wind]

sam·i+sen ('sæmɪ,sɛn) *n.* a Japanese plucked stringed instrument with a long neck, an unfretted fingerboard, and a rectangular soundbox. [Japanese, from Chinese *san-hsien,* from *san* three + *hsien* string]

sam+ite ('sæmaɪt, 'seɪ-) *n.* a heavy fabric of silk, often woven with gold or silver threads, used in the Middle Ages for clothing. [C13: from Old French *samit,* from Medieval Latin *examitum,* from Greek *hexamiton,* from *hexamitos* having six threads, from *hex* six + *mitos* a thread]

sa+mi+ti *or* **sa+mi+thi** ('sʌmɪtɪ) *n.* (in India) an association, esp. one formed to organize political activity. [Hindi]

sa+miz+dat (*Russian* səmiz'dat) *n.* (in the Soviet Union) **a.** a system of clandestine printing and distribution of banned or dissident literature. **b.** (*as modifier*): *a samizdat publication.* [from Russian]

sam+my ('sæmɪ) *n., pl.* **+mies.** *Informal.* (in South Africa) an Indian fruit and vegetable vendor who goes from house to house. [C20: from the Christian name *Sammy*]

Sam+nite ('sæmnaɪt) *n.* (in ancient Italy) **1.** a member of an Oscan-speaking people of the S Apennines, who clashed repeatedly with Rome between 350 B.C. and 200 B.C. ~*adj.* **2.** of or relating to this people.

Sam+ni+um ('sæmnɪəm) *n.* an ancient country of central Italy inhabited by Oscan-speaking Samnites: corresponds to the present-day region of Abruzzi e Molise and part of Campania.

Sa+mo·a *or* **Sa+mo·a Is+lands** (sə'məʊə) *pl. n.* a group of islands in the S Pacific, northeast of Fiji: an independent kingdom until the mid-19th century, when it was divided administratively into **American Samoa** (in the east) and **German Samoa** (in the west); the latter was mandated to New Zealand in 1919 and gained full independence in 1962 as **Western Samoa.** Area: 3038 sq. km (1173 sq. miles). **—Sa+'mo+an** *n., adj.*

Sa+mos ('seɪmɒs) *n.* an island in the E Aegean Sea, off the SW coast of Turkey: a leading commercial centre of ancient Greece. Pop.: 32 671 (1971). Area: 492 sq. km (190 sq. miles).

Sam·o+thrace ('sæmə,θreɪs) *n.* a Greek island in the NE Aegean Sea: mountainous. Pop.: 3012 (1971).

sam·o+var ('sæmə,vɑː, ,sæmə'vɑː) *n.* (esp. in Russia) a metal urn for making tea, in which the water is usually heated by charcoal held in an inner container. [C19: from Russian, from *samo-* self (related to SAME) + *varit'* to boil]

Sam·o+yed (,sæmə'jɛd) *n.* **1.** (*pl.* **+yed** *or* **+yeds**) a member of a people who migrated along the Soviet Arctic coast and now live chiefly in the area of the N Urals: related to the Finns. **2.** the language of this people, distantly related to the Finno-Ugric family. See also **Uralic. 3.** a white or cream breed of dog of the Spitz family, having a dense coat and a tightly curled tail. [C17: from Russian *Samoed*] **—,Sam·o+'yed+ic** *adj.*

sam+pan ('sæmpæn) *n.* any small skiff, widely used in the Orient, that is propelled by oars or a scull. [C17: from Chinese *san pan,* from *san* three + *pan* board]

sam+phire ('sæm,faɪə) *n.* **1.** Also called: **rock samphire.** an umbelliferous plant, *Crithmum maritimum,* of Eurasian coast, having fleshy divided leaves and clusters of small white flowers. **2. golden samphire.** a Eurasian coastal plant, *Inula crithmoides,* with fleshy leaves and yellow flower heads: family *Compositae* (composites). **3. marsh samphire.** another name for **glasswort** (sense 1). **4.** any of several other plants of coastal areas. [C16 *sampiere,* from French *herbe de Saint Pierre* Saint Peter's herb; perhaps influenced by *camphire* CAMPHOR]

sam+ple ('sɑːmpᵊl) *n.* **1. a.** a small part of anything, intended as representative of the whole; specimen. **b.** (*as modifier*): *a sample bottle.* **2.** Also called: **sampling.** *Statistics.* **a.** a set of individuals or items selected at random from a population and analysed to yield estimates of and test hypotheses about parameters of the population. **b.** (*as modifier*): *sample distribution.* ~*vb.* **3.** (*tr.*) to take a sample or samples of. [C13: from Old French *essample,* from Latin *exemplum* EXAMPLE]

sam+pler ('sɑːmplə) *n.* **1.** a person who takes samples. **2.** a piece of embroidery in which many different stitches are used. **3.** a collection of samples.

sam+pling ('sɑːmplɪŋ) *n.* **1.** the process of selecting a random sample. **2.** a variant of **sample** (sense 2). **3.** a process in which a continuous electrical signal is approximately represented by a series of discrete values, usually regularly spaced.

sam+sa+ra (səm'sɑːrə) *n.* **1.** *Hinduism.* the endless cycle of birth, death, and rebirth. **2.** *Buddhism.* the transmigration or rebirth of a person. [Sanskrit, literally: a passing through, from *sam* altogether + *sarati* it runs]

sam+shu ('sæmʃuː, -sjuː) *n.* an alcoholic drink from China that is made from fermented rice and resembles sake. [C17: perhaps modification of Chinese *shao chiu* spirits that will burn, from *shao* to burn + *chiu* spirits]

Sam·son ('sæmsən) *n.* **1.** a judge of Israel, who performed herculean feats of strength against the Philistine oppressors until he was betrayed to them by his mistress Delilah (Judges 13–16). **2.** any man of outstanding physical strength.

Sam+sun (*Turkish* 'samsun) *n.* a port in N Turkey, on the Black Sea. Pop.: 168 478 (1975). Ancient name: **Amisus.**

Sam·u·el ('sæmjʊəl) *n. Old Testament.* **1.** a Hebrew prophet, seer, and judge, who anointed the first two kings of the Israelites (I Samuel 1–3; 8–15). **2.** either of the two books named after him, **I** and **II Samuel.**

sam·u+rai ('sæmʊ,raɪ, 'sæmjʊ-) *n., pl.* **+rai. 1.** the Japanese warrior caste that provided the administrative and fighting aristocracy from the 11th to the 19th centuries. **2.** a member of this aristocracy. [C19: from Japanese]

San[1] (sɑːn) *n.* a group of the Khoisan languages, spoken mostly by Bushmen.

San[2] (sɑːn) *n.* a river in E central Europe, rising in the W Soviet Union and flowing northwest across SE Poland to the Vistula River. Length: about 450 km (280 miles).

Sa·n'a *or* **Sa+naa** (sɑː'nɑː) *n.* the capital of Yemen, on the central plateau at an altitude of 2350m (7700 ft.): became capital of Yemen when Turkish rule ended in 1918. Pop.: 120 000 (1970 est.).

San An+to+ni·o (sæn æn'təʊnɪ,əʊ) *n.* a city in S Texas: site of the Alamo; the leading town in Texas until about 1930. Pop.: 756 226 (1973 est.). **—San An+to+ni·an** *adj., n.*

san·a+tive ('sænətɪv) *adj.* a less common word for **curative.** [C15: from Medieval Latin *sānātīvus,* from Latin *sānāre* to heal, from *sānus* healthy]

san·a+to+ri·um (,sænə'tɔːrɪəm) *or U.S.* **san·i+ta+ri·um** *n., pl.* **+ri·ums** *or* **+ri·a** (-rɪə). **1.** an institution for the medical care and recuperation of persons who are chronically ill. **2.** a health resort. **3.** *Brit.* a room in a boarding school where sick pupils may be treated in isolation. [C19: from New Latin, from Latin *sānāre* to heal]

san+be+ni+to (,sænbə'niːtəʊ) *n., pl.* **+tos. 1.** a yellow garment bearing a red cross, worn by penitent heretics in the Inquisition. **2.** a black garment bearing flames and devils, worn by impenitent heretics at an auto-da-fé. [C16: from Spanish *San Benito* Saint Benedict, an ironical allusion to its likeness to the Benedictine scapular]

San Ber+nar+di+no (sæn ,bɜːnə'diːnəʊ) *n.* a city in SE California: founded in 1851 by Mormons from Salt Lake City. Pop.: 110 987 (1973 est.).

San Ber+nar+di+no Pass *n.* a pass over the Lepontine Alps in SE Switzerland. Highest point: 2062 m (6766 ft.).

San Blas ('sɑːn 'blɑːs) *n.* **1. Isth·mus of.** the narrowest part of the Isthmus of Panama. Width: about 50 km (30 miles). **2. Gulf of.** an inlet of the Caribbean on the N coast of Panama.

San Cris+tó+bal (*Spanish* saŋ kri'stoβal) *n.* **1.** Also called: **Chatham Island.** an island in the Pacific, in the Galápagos Islands. Area: 505 sq. km (195 sq. miles). **2.** a city in SW Venezuela: founded in 1561 by Spanish conquistadores. Pop.: 151 717 (1971).

sanc+ti+fied ('sæŋktɪˌfaɪd) *adj.* **1.** consecrated or made holy. **2.** a less common word for **sanctimonious.**

sanc+ti+fy ('sæŋktɪˌfaɪ) *vb.* **+fies, +fy+ing, +fied.** (*tr.*) **1.** to make holy. **2.** to free from sin; purify. **3.** to sanction (an action or practice) as religiously binding: *to sanctify a marriage.* **4.** to declare or render (something) productive of or conductive to holiness, blessing, or grace. **5.** *Obsolete.* to authorize to be revered. [C14: from Late Latin *sanctificāre,* from Latin *sanctus* holy + *facere* to make] —**'sanc+ti+ˌfi+a+ble** *adj.* —**ˌsanc+ti+fi+'ca+tion** *n.* —**'sanc+ti+ˌfi+er** *n.*

sanc+ti+mo+ni+ous (ˌsæŋktɪ'məʊnɪəs) *adj.* affecting piety or making a display of holiness. [C17: from Latin *sanctimonia* sanctity, from *sanctus* holy] —**ˌsanc+ti+'mo+ni+ous+ly** *adv.* —**ˌsanc+ti+'mo+ni+ous+ness** *n.* —**'sanc+ti+ˌmo+ny** *n.*

sanc+tion ('sæŋkʃən) *n.* **1.** final permission; authorization. **2.** aid or encouragement. **3.** something, such as an ethical principle, that imparts binding force to a rule, oath, etc. **4.** the penalty laid down in a law for contravention of its provisions. **5.** (*often pl.*) a coercive measure, esp. one taken by one or more states against another guilty of violating international law. ~*vb.* (*tr.*) **6.** to give authority to; permit. **7.** to make authorized; confirm. [C16: from Latin *sanctiō* the establishment of an inviolable decree, from *sancīre* to decree] —**'sanc+tion+a+ble** *adj.* —**'sanc+tion+er** *n.* —**'sanc+tion+less** *adj.*

sanc+tion mark *n.* a mark on pieces of 19th-century French furniture signifying that the piece met the quality standards required by the Parisian guild of ebonists.

sanc+ti+tude ('sæŋktɪˌtju:d) *n.* saintliness; holiness.

sanc+ti+ty ('sæŋktɪtɪ) *n., pl.* **·ties. 1.** the condition of being sanctified; holiness. **2.** anything regarded as sanctified or holy. [C14: from Old French *saincteté,* from Latin *sanctitās,* from *sanctus* holy]

sanc+tu+ar+y ('sæŋktjʊərɪ) *n., pl.* **+ar+ies. 1.** a holy place. **2.** a consecrated building or shrine. **3.** *Old Testament.* **a.** the Israelite temple at Jerusalem, esp. the holy of holies. **b.** the tabernacle in which the Ark was enshrined during the wanderings of the Israelites. **4.** the chancel, or that part of a sacred building surrounding the main altar. **5. a.** a sacred building where fugitives were formerly entitled to immunity from arrest or execution. **b.** the immunity so afforded. **6.** a place of refuge; asylum. **7.** a place, protected by law, where animals, esp. birds, can live and breed without interference. [C14: from Old French *sainctuarie,* from Late Latin *sanctuārium* repository for holy things, from Latin *sanctus* holy]

sanc+tum ('sæŋktəm) *n., pl.* **+tums** *or* **+ta** (-tə). **1.** a sacred or holy place. **2.** a room or place of total privacy or inviolability. [C16: from Latin, from *sanctus* holy]

sanc+tum sanc+to+rum (sæŋk'tɔ:rəm) *n.* **1.** *Judaism.* another term for the **holy of holies. 2.** *Often facetious.* an especially private place. [C14: from Latin, literally: holy of holies, rendering Hebrew *qōdesh haqqodāshīm*]

Sanc+tus ('sæŋktəs) *n.* **1.** *Liturgy.* the hymn that occurs immediately after the preface in the celebration of the Eucharist. **2.** a musical setting of this, usually incorporated into the Ordinary of the Roman Catholic Mass. [C14: from the first word of the hymn, *Sanctus sanctus sanctus* Holy, holy, holy, from Latin *sancīre* to consecrate]

Sanc+tus bell *n. Chiefly R.C. Church.* a bell rung as the opening words of the Sanctus are pronounced and also at other important points during Mass.

sand (sænd) *n.* **1.** loose material consisting of rock or mineral grains, esp. rounded grains of quartz, between 0.2 and 2 mm in diameter. **2.** (*often pl.*) a sandy area, esp. on the seashore or in a desert. **3. a.** a greyish-yellow colour. **b.** (*as adj.*): *sand upholstery.* **4.** the grains of sandlike material in an hourglass. **5.** *U.S. informal.* courage; grit. **6. the sands are running out.** time is passing quickly; there is not much time left. ~*vb.* **7.** (*tr.*) to smooth or polish the surface of with sandpaper or sand: *to sand a floor.* **8.** (*tr.*) to sprinkle or cover with or as if with sand; add sand to. **9.** to fill or cause to fill with sand: *the channel sanded up.* [Old English; related to Old Norse *sandr,* Old High German *sant,* Greek *hamathos*] —**'sand+ˌlike** *adj.*

Sand (*French* sã:d) *n.* **George** (ʒɔrʒ), pen name of *Amandine Aurore Lucie Dupin.* 1804–76, French novelist, best known for such pastoral novels as *La Mare au diable* (1846) and *François le Champi* (1847–48) and for her works for women's rights to independence.

San+da+kan (sɑ:n'dɑ:kɑ:n) *n.* a port in Malaysia, on the NE coast of Sabah: capital (until 1947) of North Borneo. Pop.: 42 249 (1970).

san+dal ('sændᵊl) *n.* **1.** a light shoe consisting of a sole held on the foot by thongs, straps, etc., worn in hot weather or by women for evening wear. **2.** a strap passing over the instep or around the ankle to keep a low shoe on the foot. [C14: from Latin *sandalium,* from Greek *sandalion* a small sandal, from *sandalon* sandal] —**'san+dalled** *adj.*

san·dal+wood ('sændᵊlˌwʊd) *or* **san+dal** *n.* **1.** any of several evergreen trees of the genus *Santalum,* esp. *S. album* (**white sandalwood**), of S Asia and Australia, having hard light-coloured heartwood: family *Santalaceae.* **2.** the wood of any of these trees, which is used for carving, is burned as incense, and yields an aromatic oil used in perfumery. **3.** any of various similar trees or their wood, esp. *Pterocarpus santalinus* (**red sandalwood**), a leguminous tree of SE Asia having dark red wood used as a dye. [C14 *sandal,* from Medieval Latin *sandalum,* from Late Greek *sandanon,* from Sanskrit *candana* sandalwood]

San·dal+wood Is+land *n.* the former name for **Sumba.**

san+da+rac *or* **san+da+rach** ('sændəˌræk) *n.* **1.** Also called: **sandarac tree.** a pinaceous tree, *Tetraclinis articulata* (or *Callitris quadrivalvis*), of NW Africa, having hard fragrant dark wood. **2.** a brittle pale yellow transparent resin obtained from the bark of this tree and used in making varnish and incense. **3.** Also called: **citron wood.** the wood of this tree, used in building. [C16 *sandaracha,* from Latin *sandaraca* red pigment, from Greek *sandarakē*]

sand+bag ('sændˌbæg) *n.* **1.** a sack filled with sand used for protection against gunfire, floodwater, etc., or as ballast in a balloon, ship, etc. **2.** a bag filled with sand and used as a weapon. ~*vb.* **+bags, +bag+ging, +bagged.** (*tr.*) **3.** to protect or strengthen with sandbags. **4.** to hit with or as if with a sandbag. —**'sand+ˌbag+ger** *n.*

sand+bank ('sændˌbæŋk) *n.* a submerged bank of sand in a sea or river, that may be exposed at low tide.

sand bar *n.* a ridge of sand in a river or sea, built up by the action of tides, etc., and often exposed at low tide.

sand+blast ('sændˌblɑ:st) *n.* **1.** a jet of sand or grit blown from a nozzle under air pressure or steam pressure. ~*vb.* **2.** (*tr.*) to clean, grind, or decorate (a surface) with a sandblast. —**'sand+ˌblast+er** *n.*

sand-blind *adj.* not completely blind; partially able to see. Compare **stone-blind.** [C15: changed (through influence of SAND) from Old English *samblind* (unattested), from *sam-* half, SEMI- + BLIND] —**'sand-ˌblind·ness** *n.*

sand+box ('sændˌbɒks) *n.* **1.** a container on a railway locomotive from which sand is released onto the rails to assist the traction. **2.** a box with sand shaped for moulding metal. **3.** a container of sand for small children to play in.

sand+box tree *n.* a tropical American euphorbiaceous tree, *Hura crepitans,* having small woody seed capsules, which explode when ripe to scatter the seeds: formerly used to hold sand for blotting ink.

Sand·burg ('sændbɜ:g, 'sænbɜ:g) *n.* **Carl.** 1878–1967, U.S. writer, noted esp. for his poetry, often written in free verse.

sand-cast *vb.* **-casts, -cast·ing, -cast.** (*tr.*) to produce (a casting) by pouring molten metal into a mould of sand. —**'sand-ˌcast·ing** *n.*

sand cas+tle *n.* a mass of sand moulded into a castle-like shape, esp. as made by a child on the seashore.

sand crack *n. Vet. science.* a deep crack or fissure in the wall of a horse's hoof, often causing lameness. See also **toe crack, quarter crack.**

sand dab *n.* any of various small flatfishes of the genus *Citharichthys* that occur in American Pacific coastal waters and are important food fishes.

sand dol+lar *n.* any of various flattened disclike echinoderms of the order *Clypeasteroida,* of shallow North American coastal waters: class *Echinoidea* (sea urchins).

sand eel *or* **lance** *n.* any silvery eel-like marine spiny-finned fish of the family *Ammodytidae* found burrowing in sand or shingle. Popular name: **launce.**

sand+er ('sændə) *n.* **1.** a power-driven tool for smoothing surfaces, esp. wood, plastic, etc., by rubbing with an abrasive disc. **2.** a person who uses such a device.

sand+er+ling ('sændəlɪŋ) *n.* a small sandpiper, *Crocethia alba,* that frequents sandy shores. [C17: perhaps from SAND + Old English *erthling, eorthling,* EARTHLING]

sand flea *n.* another name for the **chigoe** (sense 1) and **sand hopper.**

sand+fly ('sændˌflaɪ) *n., pl.* **+flies. 1.** any of various small mothlike dipterous flies of the genus *Phlebotomus* and related genera: the bloodsucking females transmit diseases including leishmaniasis: family *Psychodidae.* **2.** any of various similar and related flies.

sand+glass ('sændˌglɑ:s) *n.* a less common word for **hourglass.**

sand+grouse ('sændˌgraʊs) *n.* any bird of the family *Pteroclididae,* of dry regions of the Old World, having very short feet, a short bill, and long pointed wings and tail: order *Columbiformes.*

san+dhi ('sændɪ) *n., pl.* **+dhis.** *Linguistics.* modification of the form or sound of a word under the influence of an adjacent word. [from Sanskrit *samdhi* a placing together, from *sam* together + *dadhāti* he puts]

sand+hog ('sændˌhɒg) *n. Chiefly U.S.* a person who works in underground or underwater construction projects.

sand hop+per *n.* any of various small hopping amphipod crustaceans of the genus *Orchestia* and related genera, common in intertidal regions of seashores. Also called: **beach flea, sand flea.**

Sand+hurst ('sændˌhɜ:st) *n.* a village in S England, in Berkshire: seat of the Royal Military Academy for the training of officer cadets in the British Army. Pop.: 6445 (1971).

San Di+e+go (ˌsæn dɪ'eɪgəʊ) *n.* a port in S California, on the Pacific: naval base; two universities. Pop.: 757 148 (1973 est.).

sand lance *or* **launce** *n.* another name for **sand eel.**

sand leek *n.* a Eurasian alliaceous plant, *Allium scorodoprasum,* having reddish-pink flowers, purple bulbils, and a garlic-like bulb. See also **rocambole.**

sand liz+ard *n.* a small greyish-brown European lizard, *Lacerta agilis,* that has long clawed digits and, in the male, bright green underparts: family *Lacertidae.*

sand+man ('sændˌmæn) *n., pl.* **+men.** (in folklore) a magical person supposed to put children to sleep by sprinkling sand in their eyes.

sand mar·tin *n.* a small brown European songbird, *Riparia riparia*, with white underparts: it nests in tunnels bored in sand, river banks, etc.: family *Hirundinidae* (swallows and martins).

sand paint·ing *n.* a type of painting done by American Indians, esp. in the healing ceremonies of the Navaho, using fine coloured sand on a neutral ground.

sand·pa·per ('sænd,peɪpə) *n.* **1.** a strong paper coated with sand or other abrasive material for smoothing and polishing. ~*vb.* **2.** (*tr.*) to polish or grind (a surface) with or as if with sandpaper.

sand·pi·per ('sænd,paɪpə) *n.* **1.** any of numerous N hemisphere shore birds of the genera *Tringa, Calidris*, etc., typically having a long slender bill and legs and cryptic plumage: family *Scolopacidae*, order *Charadriiformes*. **2.** any other bird of the family *Scolopacidae*, which includes snipes and woodcocks.

sand·pit ('sænd,pɪt) *n.* **1.** a shallow pit or container holding sand for children to play in. **2.** a pit from which sand is extracted.

San·dring·ham ('sændrɪŋəm) *n.* a village in E England, in Norfolk near the E shore of the Wash: site of **Sandringham House,** a residence of the royal family.

San·dro·cot·tus (,sændrəʊ'kɒtəs) *n.* the Greek name of **Chandragupta.**

sand·soap ('sænd,səʊp) *n.* a gritty general purpose soap.

sand·stone ('sænd,stəʊn) *n.* any of a group of common sedimentary rocks consisting of sand grains consolidated with such materials as quartz, haematite, and clay minerals: used widely in building.

sand·storm ('sænd,stɔ:m) *n.* a strong wind that whips up clouds of sand, esp. in a desert.

sand trap *n.* (on a golf course) a shallow pit filled with sand, designed as a hazard. Also called (esp. Brit.): **bunker.**

sand vi·per *n.* **1.** a S European viper, *Vipera ammodytes*, having a yellowish-brown coloration with a zigzag pattern along the back. **2.** another name for **horned viper.**

sand·wich ('sænwɪdʒ, -wɪtʃ) *n.* **1.** two or more slices of bread, usually buttered, with a filling of meat, cheese, etc. **2.** anything that resembles a sandwich in arrangement. ~*vb.* (*tr.*) **3.** to insert tightly between two other things. **4.** to put into a sandwich. **5.** to place between two dissimilar things. [C18: named after John Montagu, 4th Earl of *Sandwich* (1718–92), who ate sandwiches rather than leave the gambling table for meals]

sand·wich board *n.* one of two connected boards, usually bearing advertisements, that are hung over the shoulders in front of and behind a person.

sand·wich cake *n.* a cake that is made up of two or more layers with a jam or other filling. Also called: **layer cake.**

sand·wich com·pound *n. Chem.* any of a class of organometallic compounds whose molecules have a metal atom or ion bound between two plane parallel organic rings. See also **metallocene.**

sand·wich course *n.* any of several courses consisting of alternate periods of study and industrial work.

Sand·wich Is·lands *pl. n.* the former name of the **Hawaiian Islands.**

sand·wich man *n.* a man who carries sandwich boards.

sand·wich tern *n.* a European tern, *Sterna sandvicensis*, that has a yellow-tipped bill, whitish plumage, and white forked tail, and nests in colonies on beaches, etc.

sand·worm ('sænd,wɜ:m) *n.* any of various polychaete worms that live in burrows on sandy shores, esp. the lugworm.

sand·wort ('sænd,wɜ:t) *n.* **1.** any of numerous caryophyllaceous plants of the genus *Arenaria*, which grow in dense tufts on sandy soil and have white or pink solitary flowers. **2.** any of various related plants.

sand·y ('sændɪ) *adj.* **sand·i·er, sand·i·est.** **1.** consisting of, containing, or covered with sand. **2.** (esp. of hair) reddish-yellow. **3.** resembling sand in texture. —**'sand·i·ness** *n.*

sand yacht *n.* a wheeled boat with sails, built to be propelled over sand, esp. beaches, by the wind.

sand·y blight *n. Austral.* a nontechnical name for any of various eye inflammations.

sane (seɪn) *adj.* **1.** sound in mind; free from mental disturbance. **2.** having or showing reason, good judgment, or sound sense. **3.** *Obsolete.* healthy. [C17: from Latin *sānus* healthy] —**'sane·ly** *adv.* —**'sane·ness** *n.*

San Fer·nan·do (*Spanish* san fer'nando) *n.* **1.** a port in SW Trinidad, on the Gulf of Paria: the second largest town in the country. Pop.: 37 313 (1970). **2.** an inland port in W Venezuela, on the Apure River. Pop.: 38 960 (1971). Official name: **San Fernando de Apure.** **3.** a port in SW Spain, on the Isla de León SE of Cádiz; site of an arsenal (founded 1790) and of the most southerly observatory in Europe. Pop.: 60 187 (1970).

San·for·ize *or* **San·for·ise** ('sænfə,raɪz) *vb.* (*tr.*) *Trademark.* to preshrink (a fabric) using a patented process.

San Fran·cis·co (,sæn fræn'sɪskəʊ) *n.* a port in W California, situated around the Golden Gate: developed rapidly during the California gold rush; a major commercial centre and one of the world's finest harbours. Pop.: 687 450 (1973 est.). —**San Fran·cis·can** *n., adj.*

San Fran·cis·co Bay *n.* an inlet of the Pacific in W California, linked with the open sea by the Golden Gate strait. Length: about 80 km (50 miles). Greatest width: 19 km (12 miles).

sang (sæŋ) *vb.* the past tense of **sing.**
Usage. See at **ring**[2].

san·ga·ree (,sæŋgə'ri:) *n.* a spiced drink similar to sangria. [C18: from Spanish *sangría* a bleeding, from *sangre* blood, from Latin *sanguis*; see SANGUINE]

Sang·er ('sæŋə) *n.* **1. Fred·er·ick.** born 1918, English biochemist, who determined the molecular structure of insulin: Nobel prize for chemistry 1958. **2. Mar·gar·et (Higgins).** 1883–1966, U.S. leader of the birth-control movement.

sang-froid (*French* sã 'frwa) *n.* composure; self-possession; calmness. [C18: from French, literally: cold blood]

Sangh (sʌŋg) *n.* (in India) an association or union, esp. a political or labour organization. [Hindi]

San·go ('sɑ:ŋgəʊ) *n.* a language used in Chad, the Central African Republic, N Zaïre, and the Congo, belonging to the Adamawa branch of the Niger-Congo family.

San·graal (sæŋ'greɪl) *or* **San·gre·al** ('sæŋgrɪəl) *n.* another name for the **Holy Grail.**

San·gre de Cris·to Moun·tains ('sæŋgrɪ də 'krɪstəʊ) *pl. n.* a mountain range in S Colorado and N New Mexico: part of the Rocky Mountains. Highest peak: Blanca Peak, 4364 m (14 317 ft.).

san·gri·a (sæŋ'gri:ə) *n.* a Spanish drink of red wine, sugar, orange or lemon juice, and iced soda, sometimes laced with brandy. [Spanish: a bleeding; see SANGAREE]

san·gui·nar·i·a (,sæŋgwɪ'nɛərɪə) *n.* **1.** the dried rhizome of the bloodroot, used as an emetic. **2.** another name for **bloodroot** (sense 1). [C19: from New Latin *herba sanguināria*, literally: the bloody herb]

san·gui·nar·y ('sæŋgwɪnərɪ) *adj.* **1.** accompanied by much bloodshed. **2.** bloodthirsty. **3.** consisting of, flowing, or stained with blood. [C17: from Latin *sanguinārius*] —**'san·gui·nar·i·ly** *adv.* —**'san·gui·nar·i·ness** *n.*

san·guine ('sæŋgwɪn) *adj.* **1.** cheerful and confident; optimistic. **2.** (esp. of the complexion) ruddy in appearance. **3.** blood-red. **4.** an obsolete word for **sanguinary** (sense 2). ~*n.* **5.** Also called: **red chalk.** a red pencil containing ferric oxide, used in drawing. [C14: from Latin *sanguineus* bloody, from *sanguis* blood] —**'san·guine·ly** *adv.* —**'san·guine·ness** *or* **san·'guin·i·ty** *n.*

san·guin·e·ous (sæŋ'gwɪnɪəs) *adj.* **1.** of, containing, relating to, or associated with blood. **2.** a less common word for **sanguine** (senses 1–3). —**san·'guin·e·ous·ness** *n.*

san·guin·o·lent (sæŋ'gwɪnələnt) *adj.* containing, tinged with, or mixed with blood. [C15: from Latin *sanguinolentus*, from *sanguis* blood] —**san·'guin·o·len·cy** *n.*

San·hed·rin ('sænɪdrɪn) *n. Judaism.* **1.** the supreme judicial, ecclesiastical, and administrative council of the Jews in New Testament times, having 71 members. **2.** a similar tribunal of 23 members having less important functions and authority. [C16: from Late Hebrew, from Greek *sunedrion* council, from *sun-* SYN- + *hedra* seat]

san·i·cle ('sænɪkᵊl) *n.* any umbelliferous plant of the genus *Sanicula*, of most regions except Australia, having clusters of small white flowers and oval fruits with hooked bristles: formerly thought to have healing powers. [C15: via Old French from Medieval Latin *sānicula*, probably from Latin *sānus* healthy]

sa·ni·es ('seɪnɪ,i:z) *n. Pathol.* a thin greenish foul-smelling discharge from a wound, ulcer, etc., containing pus and blood. [C16: from Latin, of obscure origin]

San Il·de·fon·so (*Spanish* san ,ilde'fonso) *n.* a town in central Spain, near Segovia: site of the 18th-century summer palace of the kings of Spain. Also called: **La Granja.**

san·i·tar·i·an (,sænɪ'tɛərɪən) *adj.* **1.** of or relating to sanitation. ~*n.* **2.** a sanitation expert.

san·i·ta·ri·um (,sænɪ'tɛərɪəm) *n., pl.* **·ri·ums** *or* **·ri·a** (-rɪə). the U.S. spelling of **sanatorium.** [C19: from Latin *sānitās* health]

san·i·tar·y ('sænɪtərɪ, -trɪ) *adj.* **1.** of or relating to health and measures for the protection of health. **2.** conducive to or promoting health; free from dirt, germs, etc.; hygienic. [C19: from French *sanitaire*, from Latin *sānitās* health] —**'san·i·tar·i·ly** *adv.* —**'san·i·tar·i·ness** *n.*

san·i·tar·y belt *n.* a belt for supporting a sanitary towel.

san·i·tar·y en·gi·neer·ing *n.* the branch of civil engineering associated with the supply of water, disposal of sewage, and other public health services. —**san·i·tar·y en·gi·neer** *n.*

san·i·tar·y tow·el *or esp. U.S.* **nap·kin** *n.* an absorbent pad worn externally by women during menstruation to absorb the menstrual flow.

san·i·ta·tion (,sænɪ'teɪʃən) *n.* the study and use of practical measures for the preservation of public health.

san·i·tize *or* **san·i·tise** ('sænɪ,taɪz) *vb.* (*tr.*) *Chiefly U.S.* to make sanitary or hygienic, as by sterilizing. —**,san·i·ti·'za·tion** *or* **,san·i·ti·'sa·tion** *n.*

san·i·ty ('sænɪtɪ) *n.* **1.** the state of being sane. **2.** good sense or soundness of judgment. [C15: from Latin *sānitās* health, from *sānus* healthy]

san·jak ('sændʒæk) *n.* (in the Turkish Empire) a subdivision of a vilayet. [C16: from Turkish *sancak*, literally: a flag]

San Jo·se (,sæn həʊ'zeɪ) *n.* a city in W central California: a leading world centre of the fruit drying and canning industry. Pop.: 523 116 (1973 est.).

San Jo·sé (*Spanish* ,san xo'se) *n.* the capital of Costa Rica, on the central plateau: a major centre of coffee production in the mid-19th century; University of Costa Rica (1843). Pop.: 215 441 (1973).

San Jo·se scale *n.* a small E Asian homopterous insect, *Quadraspidiotus perniciosus*, introduced into the U.S. and other countries, where it has become a serious pest of fruit trees: family *Diaspididae.* [C20: from its first being seen in the United States at *San Jose*, California]

San Juan (*Spanish* san 'xwan) *n.* **1.** the capital and chief port of Puerto Rico, on the NE coast; University of Puerto Rico; manufacturing centre. Pop.: 452 749 (1970). **2.** a city in W Argentina: almost completely destroyed by an earthquake in 1944. Pop.: 224 000 (1970).

San Juan Bau·tis·ta (*Spanish* 'san 'xwan bau'tista) *n.* the former name of **Villahermosa.**

San Juan Is·lands (sæn 'wɑːn, 'hwɑːn) *pl. n.* a group of islands between NW Washington, U.S., and SE Vancouver Island, Canada: administratively part of Washington.

San Juan Moun·tains *pl. n.* a mountain range in SW Colorado and N New Mexico: part of the Rocky Mountains. Highest peak: Uncompahgre Peak, 4363 m (14 314 ft.).

sank (sæŋk) *vb.* the past tense of **sink.**

San·key ('sæŋkɪ) *n.* **I·ra Da·vid.** 1840–1908, U.S. evangelist and hymnodist, noted for his revivalist campaigns in Britain and the U.S. with D. L. Moody.

San·khya ('sæŋkjə) *n.* one of the six orthodox schools of Hindu philosophy, teaching an eternal interaction of spirit and matter. [from Sanskrit *sāmkhya,* literally: based on calculation, from *samkhyāti* he reckons]

Sankt Pöl·ten (*German* zaŋkt 'pœltᵊn) *n., usually abbreviated to* **St. Pöl·ten.** a city in NE Austria, in Lower Austria province. Pop.: 50 144 (1971).

San Lu·is Po·to·sí (*Spanish* ˌsan ˌlwis ˌpoto'si) *n.* **1.** a state of central Mexico: mainly high plateau; economy based on mining (esp. silver) and agriculture. Capital: San Luis Potosí. Pop.: 1 281 996 (1970). Area: 62 849 sq. km (24 266 sq. miles). **2.** an industrial city in central Mexico, capital of San Luis Potosi state, at an altitude of 1850 m (6000 ft.). Pop.: 281 534 (1975 est.).

San Ma·ri·no (ˌsæn mə'riːnəʊ) *n.* a republic in S central Europe in the Apennines, forming an enclave in Italy: the smallest republic in Europe, according to tradition founded by St. Marinus in the 4th century. Language: Italian. Religion: Roman Catholic. Currency: lira. Capital: San Marino. Pop.: 19 000 (1974 est.). Area: 62 sq. km (24 sq. miles). **—San Mar·i·nese** (ˌsæn ˌmærɪ'niːz) *or* **Sam·mar·i·nese** (səˌmærɪ'niːz) *adj., n.*

San Mar·tín (*Spanish* ˌsan mar'tin) *n.* **Jo·sé de** (xo'se de). 1778–1850, South American patriot, who played an important part in gaining independence for Argentina, Chile, and Peru. He was protector of Peru (1821–22).

San·mi·che·li (*Italian* ˌsammi'kɛːli) *n.* **Mi·che·le** (mi'kɛːle). ?1484–1559, Italian mannerist architect.

sann·ya·si (sʌn'jɑːsɪ) *or* **sann·ya·sin** (sʌn'jɑːsɪn) *n.* a Brahman who having attained the fourth and last stage of life as a beggar will not be reborn, but will instead be absorbed into the Universal Soul. [from Hindi: abandoning, from Sanskrit *samnyāsin*]

San Pe·dro Su·la (*Spanish* ˌsam 'pedro 'sula) *n.* a city in NW Honduras: the country's chief industrial centre. Pop.: 200 881 (1974).

San Re·mo (*Italian* san 'rɛːmo) *n.* a port and resort in NW Italy, in Liguria on the slopes of the Maritime Alps; flower market. Pop.: 62 210 (1971).

sans (sænz) *prep.* an archaic word for **without.** [C13: from Old French *sanz,* from Latin *sine* without, but probably also influenced by Latin *absentiā* in the absence of]

Sans. *or* **Sansk.** *abbrev. for* Sanskrit.

San Sal·va·dor (sæn 'sælvəˌdɔː; *Spanish* san ˌsalβa'ðor) *n.* the capital of El Salvador, situated in the SW central part: became capital in 1841; ruined by earthquakes in 1854 and 1873; university (1841). Pop.: 337 171 (1971).

San Sal·va·dor Is·land *n.* an island in the central Bahamas: the first land in the New World seen by Christopher Columbus (1492). Area: 156 sq. km (60 sq. miles). Also called: **Watling Island.**

sans-cu·lotte (ˌsænzkjʊ'lɒt; *French* sɑ̃ky'lɔt) *n.* **1.** (during the French Revolution) **a.** (originally) a revolutionary of the poorer class. **b.** (later) any revolutionary, esp. one having extreme republican sympathies. **2.** any revolutionary extremist. [C18: from French, literally: without knee breeches, because the revolutionaries wore pantaloons or trousers rather than knee breeches] **—ˌsans-cu·'lot·tism** *n.* **—ˌsans-cu·'lot·tist** *n.*

San Se·bas·tián (ˌsæn sə'bæstjən; *Spanish* sanˌseβas'tjan) *n.* a port and resort in N Spain on the Bay of Biscay: former summer residence of the Spanish court. Pop.: 165 829 (1970).

san·se·vier·i·a (ˌsænsɪ'vɪərɪə) *n.* any herbaceous perennial plant of the liliaceous genus *Sansevieria,* of Old World tropical regions, having stiff leaves that yield a useful fibre: cultivated as a house plant. Also called: **bowstring hemp.** [New Latin, named after Raimondo di Sangro (1710–1771), Italian scholar and prince of *San Seviero*]

San·skrit ('sænskrɪt) *n.* an ancient language of India, the language of the Vedas, of Hinduism, and of an extensive philosophical and scientific literature dating from the beginning of the first millennium B.C. It is the oldest recorded member of the Indic branch of the Indo-European family of languages; recognition of the existence of the Indo-European family arose in the 18th century from a comparison of Sanskrit with Greek and Latin. Although it is used only for religious purposes, it is one of the official languages of India. [C17: from Sanskrit *samskrta* perfected, literally: put together] **—'San·skrit·ist** *n.*

San·skrit·ic (sæn'skrɪtɪk) *adj.* **1.** of or relating to Sanskrit. **2.** denoting or belonging to those Indic languages that developed directly from Sanskrit, such as Pali, Hindi, Punjabi, and Bengali. *~n.* **3.** this group of languages.

San·son-Flam·steed pro·jec·tion ('sænsən'flæmstiːd) *n.* another name for **sinusoidal projection.**

sans ser·if *or* **san·ser·if** (sæn'sɛrɪf) *n.* a style of printer's typeface in which the characters have no serifs.

San Ste·fa·no (ˌsæn stɪ'fɑːnəʊ) *n.* a village in NW Turkey, near Istanbul on the Sea of Marmara: scene of the signing (1878) of the treaty ending the Russo-Turkish War. Turkish name: **Yeşilköy.**

San·ta ('sæntə) *n. Informal.* short for **Santa Claus.**

San·ta An·a *n.* **1.** (*Spanish* 'santa 'ana). a city in NW El Salvador: the second largest city in the country; coffee-processing industry. Pop.: 172 300 (1971). **2.** ('sæntə 'ænə). a city in SW California: commercial and processing centre of a rich agricultural region. Pop.: 167 905 (1973 est.).

San·ta An·na *or* **San·ta A·na** (*Spanish* 'santa 'ana) *n.* **An·to·nio Ló·pez de** (a'tonjo 'lopeθ ðe). ?1795–1876, Mexican general, revolutionary, and president (1833–36, 1841–?45, 1847–48, 1853–55). In 1836, he captured the Alamo in an attempt to crush the Texan Revolution but was then defeated at San Jacinto.

San·ta Cat·a·li·na ('sæntə ˌkætᵊ'liːnə) *n.* an island in the Pacific, off the coast of SW California: part of Los Angeles county; resort. Area: 181 sq. km (70 sq. miles). Also called: **Catalina Island.**

San·ta Ca·ta·ri·na (*Portuguese* 'sɐnta ˌkata'rina) *n.* a state of S Brazil, on the Atlantic: consists chiefly of the Great Escarpment. Capital: Florianópolis. Pop.: 2 901 734 (1970). Area: 95 985 sq. km (37 060 sq. miles).

San·ta Cla·ra (*Spanish* 'santa 'klara) *n.* a city in W central Cuba: sugar and tobacco industries. Pop.: 130 241 (1970).

San·ta Claus ('sæntə ˌklɔːz) *n.* the legendary patron saint of children, commonly identified with Saint Nicholas, who brings presents to children on Christmas Eve or, in some European countries, on Saint Nicholas' Day. Also called: **Father Christmas.**

San·ta Cruz ('sæntə 'kruːz; *Spanish* 'santa 'kruθ) *n.* **1.** a province of S Argentina, on the Atlantic: consists of a large part of Patagonia, with the forested foothills of the Andes in the west. Capital: Río Gallegos. Pop.: 84 000 (1970). Area: (94 186 sq. miles). **2.** a city in E Bolivia: the third largest town in Bolivia. Pop.: 149 230 (1975 est.). **3.** another name for **Saint Croix.**

San·ta Cruz de Te·ne·rife ('sæntə 'kruːz də ˌtɛnə'riːf; *Spanish* 'santa 'kruθ ðe ˌtene'rife) *n.* a port and resort in the W Canary Islands, on NE Tenerife: oil refinery. Pop.: 180 666 (1968).

San·ta Fe *n.* **1.** ('sæntə 'feɪ). a city in N central New Mexico, capital of the state: one of the oldest European settlements in North America, founded in 1610 as the capital of the Kingdom of New Mexico; developed trade with the U.S. by the Santa Fe Trail in the early 19th century. Pop.: 41 167 (1970). **2.** (*Spanish* 'santa 'fe). an inland port in E Argentina, on the Salado River: University of the Littoral (1920). Pop.: 208 900 (1960). **—San·ta Fe·an** *adj., n.*

San·ta Fe Trail *n.* an important trade route in the western U.S. from about 1821 to 1880, linking Independence, Missouri to Santa Fe, New Mexico.

San·ta Ger·tru·dis ('sæntə gə'truːdɪs) *n.* a breed of red beef cattle developed in Texas.

San·ta Is·a·bel (*Spanish* 'santa ˌisa'βel) *n.* the former name (until 1973) of **Malabo.**

san·ta·la·ceous (ˌsæntə'leɪʃəs) *adj.* of, relating to, or belonging to the *Santalaceae,* a family of semiparasitic plants of Australia and Malaysia including sandalwood and quandong. [C19: via New Latin from Late Greek *santalon* sandalwood]

San·ta Ma·ri·a[1] ('sæntə mə'riːə) *n.* **the.** the flagship of Columbus on his first voyage to America (1492).

San·ta Ma·ri·a[2] (*Spanish* 'santa ma'ria) *n.* **1.** a city in S Brazil, in Rio Grande do Sul state. Pop.: 120 667 (1970). **2.** an active volcano in SW Guatemala. Height: 3768 m (12 362 ft.).

San·ta Mar·ta (*Spanish* 'santa 'marta) *n.* a port in NW Colombia, on the Caribbean: the oldest city in Colombia, founded in 1525; terminus of the Atlantic railway from Bogotá (opened 1961). Pop.: 102 484 (1973).

San·ta Mau·ra ('santa 'maʊra) *n.* the Italian name for **Levkás.**

San·tan·a (sæn'tɑːnə) *n.* **Car·los** ('karlos). born 1947, Mexican rock musician in San Francisco: formed his own band in 1969: their albums include *Santana* (1969), *Abraxas* (1970), and *Santana 3* (1973).

San·tan·der (*Spanish* ˌsantan'der) *n.* a port and resort in N Spain, on an inlet of the Bay of Biscay: noted for its prehistoric collection from nearby caves; shipyards and an oil refinery. Pop.: 149 704 (1970).

San·ta·rém (*Portuguese* ˌsɐnta'rẽj) *n.* a port in N Brazil, in Pará state where the Tapajós River flows into the Amazon. Pop.: 111 706 (1968 est.).

San·ta Ro·sa de Co·pán (*Spanish* 'santa 'rosa ðe ko'pan) *n.* a village in W Honduras: noted for the ruined Mayan city of Copán, which lies to the west.

San·ta·ya·na (ˌsæntɪ'ænə) *n.* **George.** 1863–1952, U.S. philosopher, poet, and critic, born in Spain. His works include *The Life of Reason* (1905–06) and *The Realms of Being* (1927–40).

San·tee (sæn'tiː) *n.* a river in SE central South Carolina, formed by the union of the Congaree and Wateree Rivers: flows southeast to the Atlantic; part of the **Santee-Wateree-Catawba River System,** an inland waterway 866 km (538 miles) long. Length: 230 km (143 miles).

San·ti·a·go (ˌsæntɪ'ɑːgəʊ; *Spanish* san'tjaɣo) *n.* **1.** the capital of Chile, at the foot of the Andes: commercial and industrial centre; two universities. Pop.: 3 186 000 (1975 est.). Official name: **San·ti·a·go de Chi·le** (ðe 'tʃile). **2.** a city in the N Dominican Republic. Pop.: 155 151 (1970). Official name: **San·ti·a·go de los Ca·ba·ller·os** (ðe los ˌkaβa'ʎeros).

San·ti·a·go de Com·po·ste·la (*Spanish* ðe ˌkompo'stela) *n.* a city in NW Spain: place of pilgrimage since the 9th century and the most visited (after Jerusalem and Rome) in the Middle Ages; cathedral built over the tomb of the apostle St. James. Pop.: 70 893 (1970). Latin name: **Campus Stellae.**

San·ti·a·go de Cu·ba (*Spanish* ðe 'kuβa) *n.* a port in SE Cuba, on **Santiago Bay** (a large inlet of the Caribbean): capital of Cuba until 1589; university (1947); industrial centre. Pop.: 277 600 (1970).

San·ti·a·go del Es·te·ro (*Spanish* ðel es'tero) *n.* a city in N Argentina: the oldest continuous settlement in Argentina, founded in 1553 by Spaniards from Peru. Pop.: 105 209 (1970).

San·to Do·min·go ('sæntəʊ də'mɪŋgəʊ; *Spanish* 'santo ðo'miŋgo) *n.* **1.** the capital and chief port of the Dominican Republic, on the S coast: the oldest continuous European settlement in the Americas, founded in 1496; university (1538). Pop.: 671 402 (1970). **2.** the former name (until 1844) of the **Dominican Republic. 3.** another name (esp. in colonial times) for **Hispaniola.**

san·ton·i·ca (sæn'tɒnɪkə) *n.* **1.** an oriental wormwood plant, *Artemisia cina* (or *maritima*). **2.** the dried flower heads of this plant, formerly used as a vermifuge. ~Also called: **wormseed.** [C17: New Latin, from Late Latin *herba santonica* herb of the *Santones* (probably wormwood), from Latin *Santonī* a people of Aquitania]

san·to·nin ('sæntənɪn) *n.* a white crystalline soluble substance extracted from the dried flower heads of santonica and used in medicine as an anthelmintic. Formula: $C_{15}H_{18}O_3$. [C19: from SANTONICA + -IN]

San·tos (*Portuguese* 'sɐntus) *n.* a port in S Brazil, in São Paulo state: the world's leading coffee port. Pop.: 341 317 (1970).

San·tos-Du·mont (*French* sɑ̃to dy'mɔ̃) *n.* **Al·ber·to** (al'bɛrto). 1873–1932, Brazilian aeronaut, living in France. He constructed dirigibles and aircraft, including a monoplane (1909).

São Fran·cis·co (*Portuguese* sɐ̃ʊ frɐ̃'sisku) *n.* a river in E Brazil, rising in SW Minas Gerais state and flowing northeast, then southeast to the Atlantic northeast of Aracajú. Length: 3200 km (1990 miles).

São Luís (*Portuguese* sɐ̃ʊ 'lwis) *or* **São Luíz** ('lwiz) *n.* a port in NE Brazil, capital of Maranhão state, on the W coast of São Luís Island: founded in 1612 by the French and taken by the Portuguese in 1615. Pop.: 167 529 (1970).

São Mi·guel (*Portuguese* sɐ̃ʊ mi'γɛl) *n.* an island in the E Azores: the largest of the group. Pop.: 159 000 (1970). Area: 854 sq. km (333 sq. miles).

Saône (*French* so:n) *n.* a river in E France, rising in Lorraine and flowing generally south to join the Rhône at Lyon, as its chief tributary: canalized for 375 km (233 miles) above Lyon; linked by canals with the Rhine, Marne, Seine, and Loire Rivers. Length: 480 km (298 miles).

Saône-et-Loire (*French* so:n e 'lwa:r) *n.* a department of central France, in Burgundy region. Capital: Mâcon. Pop.: 580 060 (1975). Area: 8627 sq. km (3365 sq. miles).

São Pau·lo (*Portuguese* sɐ̃ʊm 'paulu) *n.* **1.** a state of SE Brazil: consists chiefly of tableland draining west into the Paraná River. Capital: São Paulo. Pop.: 17 771 984 (1970). Area: 247 239 sq. km (95 459 sq. miles). **2.** a city in S Brazil, capital of São Paulo state: the largest city and industrial centre in Brazil, with one of the busiest airports in the world; three universities; rapidly expanding population. Pop.: 25 000 (1874); 2 017 025 (1950); 5 186 752 (1970).

Saor·stat Eir·eann ('sɛəstɑ:t 'ɛərən) *n.* the Gaelic name for the **Irish Free State.**

São Sal·va·dor (*Portuguese* sɐ̃ʊ ˌsalva'dor) *n.* short for **São Salvador da Bahia de Todos os Santos,** the official name for **Salvador.**

São To·mé e Prín·ci·pe (*Portuguese* sɐ̃ʊn tu'mɛ e 'prĩsipə) *n.* a republic in the Gulf of Guinea, off the W coast of Africa, on the Equator: consists of the islands of Príncipe and São Tomé; colonized by the Portuguese in the late 15th century; became independent in 1975. Capital: São Tomé. Pop.: 79 000 (1974 UN est.). Area: 964 sq. km (372 sq. miles).

sap[1] (sæp) *n.* **1.** a solution of mineral salts, sugars, etc., that circulates in a plant. **2.** any vital body fluid. **3.** energy; vigour. **4.** *Slang.* a gullible or foolish person. **5.** another name for **sapwood.** ~*vb.* **saps, sap·ping, sapped.** (*tr.*) **6.** to drain of sap. [Old English *sæp;* related to Old High German *sapf,* German *Saft* juice, Middle Low German *sapp,* Sanskrit *sabar* milk juice] —'**sap·less** *adj.*

sap[2] (sæp) *n.* **1.** a deep and narrow trench used to approach or undermine an enemy position, esp. in siege warfare. ~*vb.* **saps, sap·ping, sapped. 2.** to undermine (a fortification, etc.) by digging saps. **3.** (*tr.*) to weaken. [C16 *zappe,* from Italian *zappa* spade, of uncertain origin; perhaps from Old Italian (dialect) *zappo* a goat]

sap·a·jou ('sæpəˌdʒu:) *n.* another name for **capuchin** (monkey). [C17: from French, of Tupi origin]

sa·pan·wood ('sæpənˌwʊd) *n.* a variant spelling of **sappanwood.**

sa·pe·le (sə'pi:lɪ) *n.* **1.** any of several W African meliaceous trees of the genus *Entandrophragma,* esp. *E. cylindricum,* yielding a hard timber resembling mahogany. **2.** the timber obtained from such a tree, used to make furniture. [C20: West African name]

sap·head ('sæpˌhɛd) *n. Slang.* a simpleton, idiot, or fool. —'**sap·ˌhead·ed** *adj.*

sa·phe·na (sə'fi:nə) *n., pl.* **·nae** (-ni:). *Anatomy.* either of two large superficial veins of the legs. [C14: via Medieval Latin from Arabic *ṣāfīn*] —**sa·'phe·nous** *adj.*

sap·id ('sæpɪd) *adj.* **1.** having a pleasant taste. **2.** agreeable or engaging. [C17: from Latin *sapidus,* from *sapere* to taste] —**sa·pid·i·ty** (sə'pɪdɪtɪ) *or* '**sap·id·ness** *n.*

sa·pi·ent ('seɪpɪənt) *adj. Often used ironically.* wise or sagacious. [C15: from Latin *sapere* to taste] —'**sa·pi·ence** *or* '**sa·pi·en·cy** *n.* —'**sa·pi·ent·ly** *adv.*

sa·pi·en·tial (ˌseɪpɪ'ɛnʃəl, ˌsæpɪ-) *adj.* showing, having, or providing wisdom. —ˌ**sa·pi·'en·tial·ly** *adv.*

sap·in·da·ceous (ˌsæpɪn'deɪʃəs) *adj.* of, relating to, or belonging to the *Sapindaceae,* a tropical and subtropical family of trees, shrubs, and lianas including the soapberry, litchi, and supplejack. [C19: via New Latin from Latin *sāpō* soap + *Indus* Indian]

Sa·pir (sə'pɪə, 'seɪˌpɪə) *n.* **Ed·ward.** 1884–1939, U.S. anthropologist and linguist, noted for his study of the ethnology and languages of North American Indians.

sap·ling ('sæplɪŋ) *n.* **1.** a young tree. **2.** *Literary.* a youth.

sap·o·dil·la (ˌsæpə'dɪlə) *n.* **1.** a large tropical American evergreen tree, *Achras zapota,* the latex of which yields chicle. **2.** Also called: **sapodilla plum.** the edible brown rough-skinned fruit of this tree, which has a sweet yellowish pulp. ~Also called: **naseberry, sapota.** [C17: from Spanish *zapotillo,* diminutive of *zapote* sapodilla fruit, from Nahuatl *tsapotl*]

sap·o·na·ceous (ˌsæpəʊ'neɪʃəs) *adj.* resembling soap; soapy. [C18: from New Latin *sāpōnāceus,* from Latin *sāpō* SOAP] —ˌ**sap·o·'na·ceous·ness** *n.*

sa·pon·i·fy (sə'pɒnɪˌfaɪ) *vb.* **·fies, ·fy·ing, ·fied.** *Chem.* **1.** to undergo or cause to undergo a process in which a fat is converted into a soap by treatment with alkali. **2.** to undergo or cause to undergo a reaction in which an ester is hydrolysed to an acid and an alcohol as a result of treatment with an alkali. [C19: from French *saponifier,* from Latin *sāpō* SOAP] —**sa·'pon·i·ˌfi·a·ble** *adj.* —**sa·'pon·i·ˌfi·er** *n.* —**sa·ˌpon·i·fi·'ca·tion** *n.*

sap·o·nin ('sæpənɪn) *n.* any of a group of plant glycosides with a steroid structure that foam when shaken and are used in detergents. [C19: from French *saponine,* from Latin *sāpō* SOAP]

sap·o·nite ('sæpəˌnaɪt) *n.* a clay mineral consisting of hydrated magnesium aluminium silicate and occurring in metamorphic rocks such as serpentine. [C19: from Swedish *saponit* (a rendering of German *Seifenstein* soapstone), from Latin *sāpō* SOAP]

sa·por ('seɪpɔ:, -pə) *n. Rare.* the quality in a substance that is perceived by the sense of taste; flavour. [C15: from Latin: SAVOUR] —ˌ**sap·o·'rif·ic** *or* '**sap·o·rous** *adj.*

sa·po·ta (sə'pəʊtə) *n.* **1.** (in tropical America) any of various different fruits. **2.** another name for **sapodilla.** [C16: from Spanish *zapote,* from Nahuatl *tsapotl;* see SAPODILLA]

sap·o·ta·ceous (ˌsæpə'teɪʃəs) *adj.* of, relating to, or belonging to the *Sapotaceae,* a family of leathery-leaved tropical plants: includes the gutta-percha and balata trees, sapodilla, and shea. [C19: from New Latin *sapota* SAPOTA]

sap·pan·wood *or* **sap·an·wood** ('sæpənˌwʊd) *n.* **1.** a small caesalpiniaceous tree, *Caesalpinia sappan,* of S Asia producing wood that yields a red dye. **2.** the wood of this tree. [C16: *sapan,* via Dutch from Malay *sapang*]

sap·per ('sæpə) *n.* **1.** a soldier who digs trenches, etc. **2.** (in the British Army) a private of the Royal Engineers.

Sap·phic ('sæfɪk) *adj.* **1.** *Prosody.* denoting a metre associated with Sappho, consisting generally of a trochaic pentameter line with a dactyl in the third foot. **2.** of or relating to Sappho or her poetry. ~*n.* **3.** *Prosody.* a verse, line, or stanza written in the Sapphic form.

Sap·phic ode *n.* another term for **Horatian ode.**

Sap·phi·ra (sæ'faɪrə) *n. New Testament.* the wife of Ananias, who together with her husband was struck dead for fraudulently concealing their wealth from the Church (Acts 5).

sap·phire ('sæfaɪə) *n.* **1. a.** any precious corundum gemstone that is not red, esp. the highly valued transparent blue variety. A synthetic form is used in electronics and precision apparatus. Formula: Al_2O_3. **b.** (*as modifier*): *a sapphire ring.* **2. a.** the blue colour of sapphire. **b.** (*as adj.*): *sapphire eyes.* [C13 *safir,* from Old French, from Latin *sapphīrus,* from Greek *sappheiros,* perhaps from Hebrew *sappīr,* ultimately perhaps from Sanskrit *śanipriya,* literally: beloved of the planet Saturn, from *śani* Saturn + *priya* beloved]

sap·phir·ine ('sæfəˌri:n, -rɪn) *n.* **1.** a rare blue or bluish-green mineral that consists of magnesium aluminium silicate in monoclinic crystalline form and occurs as small grains in some metamorphic rocks. **2.** a blue variety of spinel. ~*adj.* **3.** relating to or resembling sapphire.

sap·phism ('sæfɪzəm) *n.* a less common word for **lesbianism.** [C19: after SAPPHO, who is believed to have been a lesbian]

Sap·pho ('sæfəʊ) *n.* 6th century B.C., Greek lyric poetess of Lesbos.

Sap·po·ro ('sɑ:pəʊˌrəʊ) *n.* a city in N Japan, on W Hokkaido: commercial centre; university (1918). Pop.: 1 240 000 (1975).

sap·py ('sæpɪ) *adj.* **·pi·er, ·pi·est. 1.** (of plants) full of sap. **2.** full of energy or vitality. **3.** *Slang.* silly or fatuous. —'**sap·pi·ly** *adv.* —'**sap·pi·ness** *n.*

sa·prae·mi·a (sæ'pri:mɪə) *n. Pathol.* blood poisoning caused by toxins of putrefactive bacteria. [C19: New Latin, from SAPRO- + -EMIA] —**sa·'prae·mic** *adj.*

sap·ro- *or before a vowel* **sapr-** *combining form.* indicating dead or decaying matter: *saprogenic; saprolite.* [from Greek *sapros* rotten]

sap·robe ('sæprəub) *n.* an organism, esp. a plant, that lives in stagnant or foul water. [C20: from Greek, from SAPRO- + *bios* life] —**sap·'ro·bic** *adj.*

sap·ro·gen·ic (ˌsæprəu'dʒɛnɪk) *or* **sap·ro·gen·ous** (sæ'prɒdʒɪnəs) *adj.* **1.** producing or resulting from decay: *saprogenic bacteria.* **2.** growing on decaying matter. —**sap·ro·ge·nic·i·ty** (ˌsæprədʒə'nɪsɪtɪ) *n.*

sap·ro·lite ('sæprəuˌlɪt) *n.* a deposit of earth, clay, silt, etc., formed by decomposition of rocks that has remained in its original site. —ˌ**sap·ro·'lit·ic** *adj.*

sap·ro·pel ('sæprəˌpɛl) *n.* an unconsolidated sludge consisting of the decomposed remains of aquatic organisms, esp. algae, that accumulates at the bottoms of lakes and oceans. [C20: from SAPRO- + *-pel* from Greek *pēlos* mud] —ˌ**sap·ro·'pel·ic** *adj.*

sa·proph·a·gous (sæ'prɒfəgəs) *adj.* (of certain animals) feeding on dead or decaying organic matter.

sap·ro·phyte ('sæprəuˌfaɪt) *n.* any plant, esp. a fungus or bacterium, that lives and feeds on dead organic matter. —**sap·ro·phyt·ic** (ˌsæprəu'fɪtɪk) *adj.* —ˌ**sap·ro·'phyt·i·cal·ly** *adv.*

sap·ro·zo·ic (ˌsæprəu'zəuɪk) *adj.* **1.** (of animals or plants) feeding on dead organic matter. **2.** of or relating to nutrition in which the nutrient substances are derived from dead organic matter.

sap·sa·go ('sæpsəˌgəu) *n.* a hard greenish Swiss cheese made with sour skim milk and coloured and flavoured with clover. [C19: changed from German *Schabziger,* from *schaben* to grate + dialect *Ziger* a kind of cheese]

sap·suck·er ('sæpˌsʌkə) *n.* either of two North American woodpeckers, *Sphyrapicus varius* or *S. thyroideus,* that have white wing patches and feed on the sap from trees.

sap·wood ('sæpˌwud) *n.* the soft wood, just beneath the bark in tree trunks, that consists of living tissue. Compare **heartwood.**

Sar. *abbrev. for* Sardinia(n).

sar·a·band *or* **sar·a·bande** ('særəˌbænd) *n.* **1.** a decorous 17th-century courtly dance. **2.** *Music.* a piece of music composed for or in the rhythm of this dance, in slow triple time, often incorporated into the classical suite. [C17: from French *sarabande,* from Spanish *zarabanda,* of uncertain origin]

Sar·a·cen ('særəsᵊn) *n.* **1.** *History.* a member of one of the nomadic Arabic tribes, esp. of the Syrian desert, that harassed the borders of the Roman Empire in that region. **2. a.** a Muslim, esp. one who opposed the crusades. **b.** (in later use) any Arab. ~*adj.* **3.** of or relating to Arabs of either of these periods, regions, or types. **4.** designating, characterizing, or relating to Muslim art or architecture. [C13: from Old French *Sarrazin,* from Late Latin *Saracēnus,* from Late Greek *Sarakēnos,* perhaps from Arabic *sharq* sunrise, from *shāraqa* to rise] —**Sar·a·cen·ic** (ˌsærə'sɛnɪk) *or* ˌ**Sar·a·'cen·i·cal** *adj.*

Sar·a·gos·sa (ˌsærə'gɒsə) *n.* the English name for **Zaragoza.**

Sa·rah ('sɛərə) *n. Old Testament.* the wife of Abraham and mother of Isaac (Genesis 17:15–22).

Sa·ra·je·vo (*Serbo-Croatian* 'sarajɛvɔ) *or* **Se·ra·je·vo** *n.* a city in central Yugoslavia, capital of Bosnia and Herzegovina: developed as a Turkish town in the 15th century; capital of the Turkish and Austro-Hungarian administrations in 1850 and 1878 respectively; scene of the assassination of Archduke Francis Ferdinand in 1914, precipitating World War I. Pop.: 243 980 (1971).

sa·ran (sə'ræn) *n.* any one of a class of thermoplastic resins based on vinylidene chloride, used in fibres, moulded articles, and coatings. [C20: after *Saran,* trademark coined by the Dow Chemical Co.]

sa·ran·gi (sɑː'rʌŋgɪ) *n. Music.* a stringed instrument of India played with a bow. [Hindi]

Sa·ransk (*Russian* sa'ransk) *n.* a city in the W central Soviet Union, capital of the Mordovian ASSR: university (1957). Pop.: 232 000 (1975 est.).

Sa·ra·tov (*Russian* sa'ratəf) *n.* an industrial city in the W Soviet Union, on the River Volga: university (1919). Pop.: 834 000 (1975 est.).

Sa·ra·wak (sə'rɑːwək) *n.* a state of Malaysia, on the NW coast of Borneo on the South China Sea: granted to Sir James Brooke by the Sultan of Brunei in 1841 as a reward for helping quell a revolt; mainly agricultural. Capital: Kuching. Pop.: 977 013 (1970). Area: about 121 400 sq. km (48 250 sq. miles).

sar·casm ('sɑːkæzəm) *n.* **1.** mocking, contemptuous, or ironic language intended to convey scorn or insult. **2.** the use or tone of such language. [C16: from Late Latin *sarcasmus,* from Greek *sarkasmos,* from *sarkazein* to rend the flesh, from *sarx* flesh]

sar·cas·tic (sɑː'kæstɪk) *adj.* **1.** characterized by sarcasm. **2.** given to the use of sarcasm. —**sar·'cas·ti·cal·ly** *adv.*

sarce·net *or* **sarse·net** ('sɑːsnɪt) *n.* a fine soft silk fabric formerly from Italy and used for clothing, ribbons, etc. [C15: from Old French *sarzinet,* from *Sarrazin* SARACEN]

sar·co- *or before a vowel* **sarc-** *combining form.* indicating flesh: *sarcoma.* [from Greek *sark-, sarx,* flesh]

sar·co·carp ('sɑːkəuˌkɑːp) *n. Botany.* **1.** the fleshy mesocarp of such fruits as the peach or plum. **2.** any fleshy fruit.

sar·coid ('sɑːkɔɪd) *adj.* **1.** of, relating to, or resembling flesh: *a sarcoid tumour.* ~*n.* **2.** a tumour resembling a sarcoma.

sar·co·ma (sɑː'kəumə) *n. Pathol.* a usually malignant tumour arising from connective tissue. [C17: via New Latin from Greek *sarkōma* fleshy growth; see SARCO-, -OMA] —**sar·'co·ma·ˌtoid** *or* **sa·'co·ma·tous** *adj.*

sar·co·ma·to·sis (sɑːˌkəumə'təusɪs) *n. Pathol.* a condition characterized by the development of several sarcomas at various bodily sites. [C19: see SARCOMA, -OSIS]

sar·coph·a·gus (sɑː'kɒfəgəs) *n., pl.* **-gi** (-ˌgaɪ) *or* **-gus·es.** a stone or marble coffin or tomb, esp. one bearing sculpture or inscriptions. [C17: via Latin from Greek *sarkophagos* flesh-devouring; from the type of stone used, which was believed to destroy the flesh of corpses]

sar·co·plasm ('sɑːkəuˌplæzəm) *n.* the protoplasm between the fibrils of muscle fibres.

sar·cous ('sɑːkəs) *adj.* (of tissue) muscular or fleshy. [C19: from Greek *sarx* flesh]

sard (sɑːd) *or* **sar·di·us** ('sɑːdɪəs) *n.* an orange, red, or brown variety of chalcedony, used as a gemstone. Formula: SiO_2. Also called: **sardine.** [C14: from Latin *sarda,* from Greek *sardios* stone from Sardis]

Sar·da·na·pa·lus (ˌsɑːdə'næpələs) *n.* the Greek name of **Ashurbanipal.**

sar·dar *or* **sir·dar** (sə'dɑː) *n.* (in India) **1.** a title used before the name of Sikh men. **2.** a leader. [Hindi, from Persian]

Sar·de·gna (sar'deɲɲa) *n.* the Italian name for **Sardinia.**

sar·dine[1] (sɑː'diːn) *n., pl.* **-dine** *or* **-dines. 1.** any of various small marine food fishes of the herring family, esp. a young pilchard. See also **sild. 2. like sardines.** very closely crowded together. [C15: via Old French from Latin *sardīna,* diminutive of *sarda* a fish suitable for pickling]

sar·dine[2] ('sɑːdiːn, -dᵊn) *n.* another name for **sard.** [C14: from Late Latin *sardinus,* from Greek *sardinos lithos* Sardian stone, from *Sardeis* Sardis]

Sar·din·i·a (sɑː'dɪnɪə) *n.* the second largest island in the Mediterranean: forms, with offshore islands, an administrative region of Italy; ceded to Savoy by Austria in 1720 in exchange for Sicily and formed the Kingdom of Sardinia with Piedmont; became part of Italy in 1861. Capital: Cagliari. Pop.: 1 468 737 (1971). Area: 24 089 sq. km (9301 sq. miles). Italian name: **Sardegna.**

Sar·din·i·an (sɑː'dɪnɪən) *adj.* **1.** of or relating to Sardinia, its inhabitants, or their language. ~*n.* **2.** a native or inhabitant of Sardinia. **3.** the spoken language of Sardinia, sometimes regarded as a dialect of Italian but containing many loan words from Spanish.

Sar·dis ('sɑːdɪs) *or* **Sar·des** ('sɑːdiːz) *n.* an ancient city of W Asia Minor: capital of Lydia.

sar·di·us ('sɑːdɪəs) *n.* **1.** *Old Testament.* a precious stone, probably a ruby, set in the breastplate of the high priest. **2.** another name for **sard.** [C14: via Late Latin from Greek *sardios,* from *Sardeis* Sardis]

sar·don·ic (sɑː'dɒnɪk) *adj.* characterized by irony, mockery, or derision. [C17: from French *sardonique,* from Latin *sardonius,* from Greek *sardonios* derisive, literally: of Sardinia, alteration of Homeric *sardanios* scornful (laughter or smile)] —**sar·'don·i·cal·ly** *adv.* —**sar·'don·i·cism** *n.*

sar·don·yx ('sɑːdənɪks) *n.* a variety of chalcedony with alternating reddish-brown and white parallel bands, used as a gemstone. Formula: SiO_2. [C14: via Latin from Greek *sardonux,* perhaps from *sardion* SARDINE[2] + *onux* nail]

Sar·dou (*French* sar'du) *n.* **Vic·to·rien** (viktɔ'rjɛ̃). 1831–1908, French dramatist. His plays include *Fédora* (1882) and *La Tosca* (1887), the source of Puccini's opera.

sar·gas·so *or* **sar·gas·so weed** (sɑː'gæsəu) *n., pl.* **-sos.** another name for **gulfweed.** [C16: from Portuguese *sargaço,* of unknown origin]

Sar·gas·so Sea *n.* a calm area of the N Atlantic, between the West Indies and the Azores, where there is an abundance of floating seaweed of the genus *Sargassum.*

sar·gas·sum (sɑː'gæsəm) *n.* any floating brown seaweed of the genus *Sargassum,* such as gulfweed, of warm seas, having ribbon-like fronds containing air sacs.

sarge (sɑːdʒ) *n. Informal.* sergeant: used esp. as a term of address.

Sar·gent ('sɑːdʒənt) *n.* **1.** Sir **(Harold) Mal·colm (Watts).** 1895–1967, English conductor. **2. John Sing·er.** 1856–1925, U.S. painter, esp. of society portraits; in London from 1885.

Sar·go·dha (sɑː'gəudə) *n.* a city in NE Pakistan: grain market. Pop.: 201 407 (1972).

Sar·gon II ('sɑːgɒn) *n.* died 705 B.C., king of Assyria (722–705). He developed a policy of transporting conquered peoples to distant parts of his empire.

sa·ri ('sɑːrɪ) *n., pl.* **-ris.** the traditional dress of women of India, Pakistan, etc., consisting of a very long narrow piece of cloth elaborately swathed around the body. [C18: from Hindi *sārī,* from Sanskrit *śāṭī*]

Sark (sɑːk) *n.* an island in the English Channel in the Channel Islands, consisting of **Great Sark** and **Little Sark,** connected by an isthmus: ruled by a hereditary seigneur or dame. Pop.: 590 (1971). Area: 5 sq. km (2 sq. miles). French name: **Sercq.**

Sar·kis ('sɑːkiːs) *n.* **E·li·as** ('iːlɪəs). born 1924, Lebanese statesman; president of Lebanon since 1976.

Sar·ma·ti·a (sɑː'meɪʃɪə) *n.* the ancient name of a region of present-day Poland and the SW Soviet Union, between the Volga and Vistula Rivers. —**Sar·'ma·ti·an** *n., adj.* —**Sar·mat·ic** (sɑː'mætɪk) *adj.*

sar·men·tose (sɑː'mɛntəus), **sar·men·tous** (sɑː'mɛntəs), *or* **sar·men·ta·ceous** (ˌsɑːmən'teɪʃəs) *adj.* (of plants such as the strawberry) having stems in the form of runners. [C18: from Latin *sarmentōsus* full of twigs, from *sarmentum* brushwood, from *sarpere* to prune]

Sar·nen (*German* 'zarnən) *n.* a town in central Switzerland, capital of Obwalden demicanton: resort. Pop.: 6952 (1970).

Sar·ni·a ('sɑːnɪə) *n.* an inland port in S central Canada, in SW

Ontario at the S end of Lake Huron: oil refineries. Pop.: 57 644 (1971).

sa·rong (sə'rɒŋ) *n.* a draped skirtlike garment worn by men and women in the Malay Archipelago, Sri Lanka, the Pacific islands, etc. [C19: from Malay, literally: sheath]

Sa·ron·ic Gulf (sə'rɒnɪk) *n.* an inlet of the Aegean on the SE coast of Greece. Length: about 80 km (50 miles). Width: about 48 km (30 miles). Also called: (Gulf of) **Aegina.**

sa·ros ('seɪrɒs) *n.* a cycle of about 18 years 11 days (6585.32 days) in which eclipses of the sun and moon occur in the same sequence and at the same intervals as in the previous such cycle. [C19: from Greek, from Babylonian *šāru* 3600 (years); modern astronomical use apparently based on mistaken interpretation of *šāru* as a period of 18½ years] **—sa·ron·ic** (sə'rɒnɪk) *adj.*

Sa·ros ('sɑːrɒs) *n.* **Gulf of.** an inlet of the Aegean in NW Turkey, north of the Gallipoli Peninsula. Length: 59 km (37 miles). Width: 35 km (22 miles).

sar·panch (sə'pʌntʃ) *n.* the head of a Panchayat. [Urdu, from *sar* head + Sanskrit *panch* five; see PANCHAYAT]

Sar·pe·don (sɑː'piːdɒn) *n. Greek myth.* a son of Zeus and Laodameia, or perhaps Europa, and king of Lycia. He was slain by Patroclus while fighting on behalf of the Trojans.

sar·ra·ce·ni·a (ˌsærə'siːnɪə) *n.* any American pitcher plant of the genus *Sarracenia,* having single nodding flowers and leaves modified as pitchers that trap and digest insects: family *Sarraceniaceae.* [C18: New Latin, named after D. *Sarrazin,* 17th-century botanist of Quebec]

sar·ra·ce·ni·a·ceous (ˌsærəˌsiːnɪ'eɪʃəs) *adj.* of, relating to, or belonging to the *Sarraceniaceae,* an American family of pitcher plants.

Sar·raute (*French* sa'roːt) *n.* **Na·tha·lie** (nata'li). born 1902, French novelist, noted as an exponent of the anti-roman. Her novels include *Portrait of a Man Unknown* (1947) and *Martereau* (1954).

Sarre (saːr) *n.* the French name for the **Saar.**

sar·rus·o·phone (sə'ruːzəˌfəʊn) *n.* a wind instrument resembling the oboe but made of brass. [C19: named after *Sarrus,* French bandmaster, who invented it (1856)]

sar·sa·pa·ril·la (ˌsɑːsəpə'rɪlə, ˌsɑːspə-) *n.* **1.** any of various prickly climbing plants of the tropical American genus *Smilax* having large aromatic roots and heart-shaped leaves: family *Smilacaceae.* **2.** the dried roots of any of these plants, formerly used in medicine to treat psoriasis, etc. **3.** a nonalcoholic drink prepared from these roots. **4.** any of various plants resembling true sarsaparilla, esp. the araliaceous plant *Aralia nudicaulis* (**wild sarsaparilla**), of North America. [C16: from Spanish *sarzaparrilla,* from *zarza* a bramble, (from Arabic *šaras*) + *-parrilla,* from Spanish *parra* a climbing plant]

sar·sen ('sɑːsᵊn) *n. Geology.* a boulder of silicified sandstone, probably of Tertiary age, found in large numbers in S England. [C17: probably a variant of SARACEN]

sarse·net ('sɑːsnɪt) *n.* a variant spelling of **sarcenet.**

Sarthe (*French* sart) *n.* a department of NW France, in Pays-de-la-Loire region. Capital: Le Mans. Pop.: 502 306 (1975). Area: 6245 sq. km (2436 sq. miles).

Sar·to (*Italian* 'sarto) *n.* **An·dre·a del** (an'drɛːa del). 1486–1531, Florentine painter. His works include *The Nativity of the Virgin* (1514) in the church of Sant' Annunziata, Florence.

sar·tor ('sɑːtə) *n.* a humorous or literary word for **tailor.** [C17: from Latin: a patcher, from *sarcīre* to patch]

sar·to·ri·al (sɑː'tɔːrɪəl) *adj.* **1.** of or relating to a tailor or to tailoring. **2.** *Anatomy.* of or relating to the sartorius. [C19: from Late Latin *sartōrius* from SARTOR] **—sar·'to·ri·al·ly** *adv.*

sar·to·ri·us (sɑː'tɔːrɪəs) *n., pl.* **·to·ri·i** (-'tɔːrɪˌaɪ). *Anatomy.* a long ribbon-shaped muscle that aids in flexing the knee. [C18: New Latin, from *sartorius musculus,* literally: tailor's muscle, because it is used when one sits in the cross-legged position in which tailors traditionally sat while sewing]

Sar·tre (*French* 'sartr) *n.* **Jean-Paul** (ʒɑ̃ 'pɔl). 1905–80, French philosopher, novelist, and dramatist; chief French exponent of atheistic existentialism. His works include the philosophical essay *Being and Nothingness* (1943), the novels *Nausea* (1938) and *Les Chemins de la liberté* (1945–49), a trilogy, and the plays *Les Mouches* (1943), *Huis clos* (1944), and *Les Mains sales* (1948).

Sar·um ('sɛərəm) *n.* the ancient name of **Salisbury**[1] (sense 3).

Sar·um use *n.* the distinctive local rite or system of rites used at Salisbury cathedral in late medieval times.

Sar·vo·da·ya (sə'vəʊdəjə) *n.* (in India) economic and social development and improvement of a community as a whole. (Hindi, from *sarva* all + *udaya* rise]

Sa·se·bo ('sɑːsəˌbəʊ) *n.* a port in SW Japan, on NW Kyushu on Omura Bay: naval base. Pop.: 261 187 (1974 est.).

sash[1] (sæʃ) *n.* a long piece of ribbon, silk, etc., worn around the waist like a belt or over one shoulder, as a symbol of rank. [C16: from Arabic *shāsh* muslin]

sash[2] (sæʃ) *n.* **1.** a frame that contains the panes of a window or door. *~vb.* **2.** (*tr.*) to furnish (a house, etc.) with a sash, sashes, or sash windows. [C17: originally plural *sashes,* variant of *shashes,* from CHASSIS]

sash cord *n.* a strong cord connecting a sash weight to a sliding sash.

sash weight *n.* a weight used to counterbalance the weight of a sliding sash in a sash window and thus hold it in position at any height.

sash win·dow *n.* a window consisting of two sashes placed one above the other so that one or each can be slid over the other to open the window.

sas·in ('sæsɪn) *n.* another name for the **black buck.** [C19: of unknown origin]

Sask. *abbrev. for* Saskatchewan.

Sas·katch·e·wan (sæs'kætʃɪˌwən) *n.* **1.** a province of W Canada: consists of the Canadian Shield in the north and open prairie in the south; economy based chiefly on agriculture and mineral resources. Capital: Regina. Pop.: 921 323 (1976). Area: 651 900 sq. km (251 700 sq. miles). **2.** a river in W Canada, formed by the confluence of the North and South Saskatchewan Rivers: flows east to Lake Winnipeg. Length: 596 km (370 miles).

sas·ka·toon (ˌsæskə'tuːn) *n.* a species of serviceberry, *Amelanchier alnifolia,* of W Canada: noted for its succulent purplish berries. [from Cree *misaskwatomin,* from *misaskwat* tree of many branches + *min* fruit]

Sas·ka·toon (ˌsæskə'tuːn) *n.* a city in W Canada, in S Saskatchewan on the South Saskatchewan River: oil refining; university (1907). Pop.: 126 449 (1971).

sass (sæs) *U.S. informal.* *~n.* **1.** insolent or impudent talk or behaviour. *~vb.* **2.** (*intr.*) to talk or answer back in such a way. [C20: back formation from SASSY[1]]

sas·sa·by ('sæsəbɪ) *n., pl.* **·bies.** an African antelope, *Damaliscus lunatus* of grasslands and semideserts, having angular curved horns and an elongated muzzle: thought to be the swiftest hoofed mammal. [C19: from Bantu *tshêsêbê*]

sas·sa·fras ('sæsəˌfræs) *n.* **1.** an aromatic deciduous lauraceous tree, *Sassafras albidum,* of North America, having three-lobed leaves and dark blue fruits. **2.** the aromatic dried root bark of this tree, used as a flavouring, and yielding sassafras oil. **3.** *Austral.* any of several unrelated trees having a similar fragrant bark. [C16: from Spanish *sasafras,* of uncertain origin]

sas·sa·fras oil *n.* a clear volatile oil that is extracted from the root of the sassafras tree and contains camphor, pinene, and safrole.

Sas·sa·nid ('sæsənɪd) *n., pl.* **·sa·nids** *or* **·san·i·dae** (-'sænɪˌdiː). any member of the native dynasty that built and ruled an empire in Persia from 224 to 636 A.D.

Sas·sa·ri (*Italian* 'sassaˌri) *n.* a city in NW Sardinia, Italy: the second largest city on the island; university (1565). Pop.: 113 875 (1975 est.).

Sas·se·nach ('sæsəˌnæk) *n. Scot. and occasionally Irish.* an English person. [C18: from Irish *Sasanach,* from Late Latin *saxonēs* Saxons]

Sas·soon (sæ'suːn) *n.* **Sieg·fried (Lorraine).** 1886–1967, English poet and novelist, best known for his poems of the horrors of war collected in *Counterattack* (1918) and *Satirical Poems* (1926). He also wrote a semi-fictitious autobiographical trilogy *The Memoirs of George Sherston* (1928–36).

sas·sy[1] ('sæsɪ) *adj.* **·si·er, ·si·est.** a dialect word for **saucy.** **—'sas·si·ly** *adv.* **—'sas·si·ness** *n.*

sas·sy[2] ('sæsɪ), **sass·wood** ('sæsˌwʊd), *or* **sas·sy wood** *n.* **1.** a W African leguminous tree, *Erythrophleum guineense,* with poisonous bark (**sassy bark**) and hard strong wood. **2.** the bark or wood of this tree or the alkaloid derived from them, which is sometimes used in medicine. [C19: probably from a language of the Kwa family: compare Twi *sese* plane tree, Ewe *sesewu* a kind of timber tree]

sa·stru·ga (sə'struːgə, sæ-) *or* **zas·tru·ga** *n.* one of a series of ridges on snow-covered plains, caused by the action of wind laden with ice particles. [from Russian *zastruga* groove, from *za* by + *struga* deep place]

sat (sæt) *vb.* the past tense or past participle of **sit.**

Sat. *abbrev. for:* **1.** Saturday. **2.** Saturn.

S.A.T. *abbrev. for* South Australian Time.

sa·tai *or* **sa·tay** ('sateɪ) *n.* (in Malaysia and Indonesia) barbecued spiced meat cooked on skewers usually made from the stems of coconut leaves. [from Malay]

Sa·tan ('seɪtᵊn) *n.* the devil, adversary of God, and tempter of mankind: sometimes identified with Lucifer (Luke 4:5–8). [Old English, from Late Latin, from Greek, from Hebrew: plotter, from *sātan* to plot against]

sa·tang (sæ'tæŋ) *n., pl.* **·tang.** a Thai monetary unit worth one hundredth of a baht. [from Thai *satān*]

sa·tan·ic (sə'tænɪk) *or* **sa·tan·i·cal** *adj.* **1.** of or relating to Satan. **2.** supremely evil or wicked; diabolic. **—sa·'tan·i·cal·ly** *adv.* **—sa·'tan·i·cal·ness** *n.*

Sa·tan·ism ('seɪtᵊˌnɪzəm) *n.* **1.** the worship of Satan. **2.** a form of such worship which includes blasphemous or obscene parodies of Christian prayers, etc. **3.** a satanic disposition or satanic practices. **—'Sa·tan·ist** *n., adj.*

S.A.T.B. *abbrev. for* soprano, alto, tenor, bass: a combination of voices in choral music.

satch·el ('sætʃəl) *n.* a rectangular bag, usually made of leather or cloth and provided with a shoulder strap, used for carrying books, esp. school books. [C14: from Old French *sachel* a little bag, from Late Latin *saccellus,* from Latin *saccus* SACK[1]] **—'satch·elled** *adj.*

sate[1] (seɪt) *vb.* (*tr.*) **1.** to satisfy (a desire or appetite) fully. **2.** to supply beyond capacity or desire. [Old English *sadian;* related to Old High German *satōn;* see SAD, SATIATE]

sate[2] (sæt, seɪt) *vb. Archaic.* a past tense or past participle of **sit.**

sa·teen (sæ'tiːn) *n.* a glossy linen or cotton fabric, woven in such a way that it resembles satin. [C19: changed from SATIN, on the model of VELVETEEN]

sat·el·lite ('sætᵊˌlaɪt) *n.* **1.** a celestial body orbiting around a planet or star: *the earth is a satellite of the sun.* **2.** Also called: **artificial satellite.** a man-made device orbiting around the earth, moon, or another planet transmitting to earth scientific information or used for communication. See also **communications satellite.** **3.** a person, esp. one who is obsequious, who follows or serves another. **4.** a country or political unit under the domination of a foreign power. **5.** a subordinate area or community that is dependent upon a larger adjacent town or city. **6.** (*modifier*) **a.** of or relating to a satellite: *satellite communications.* **b.** subordinate to or dependent upon another: *a satellite nation.* [C16: from Latin *satelles* an attendant, probably of Etruscan origin]

sat·el·lit·i·um (ˌsætəˈlɪtɪəm, -ˈlɪʃɪəm) *n. Astrology.* a group of three or more planets lying in one sign of the zodiac.

sa·tem (ˈsɑːtəm, ˈseɪ-) *adj.* denoting or belonging to the group of Indo-European languages in which original velar stops became palatalized (k > s or ʃ). These languages belong to the Indic, Iranian, Armenian, Slavonic, Baltic, and Albanian branches and are traditionally regarded as the E group. Compare **centum.** [from Avestan *satəm* hundred; chosen to exemplify the variation of initial *s* with initial *k* (as in *centum*) in Indo-European languages]

sa·ti·a·ble (ˈseɪʃɪəbəl, ˈseɪʃə-) *adj.* capable of being satiated. —ˌ**sa·ti·a·ˈbil·i·ty** *or* ˈ**sa·ti·a·ble·ness** *n.* —ˈ**sa·ti·a·bly** *adv.*

sa·ti·ate (ˈseɪʃɪˌeɪt) *vb.* (*tr.*) **1.** to fill or supply beyond capacity or desire, often arousing weariness. **2.** to supply to satisfaction or capacity. [C16: from Latin *satiāre* to satisfy, from *satis* enough] —ˌ**sa·ti·ˈa·tion** *n.*

Sa·tie (*French* saˈti) *n.* **E·rik (Alfred Leslie)** (eˈrik). 1866–1925, French composer, noted for his eccentricity, experimentalism, and his direct and economical style. His music, including numerous piano pieces and several ballets, excercised a profound influence upon other composers, such as Debussy and Ravel.

sa·ti·e·ty (səˈtaɪɪtɪ) *n.* the state of being satiated. [C16: from Latin *satietās*, from *satis* enough]

sat·in (ˈsætɪn) *n.* **1.** a fabric of silk, rayon, etc., closely woven to show much of the warp, giving a smooth glossy appearance. **2.** (*modifier*) of or like satin in texture: *a satin finish.* [C14: via Old French from Arabic *zaitūnī* of *Zaytūn*, Arabic rendering of Chinese *Tseutung* (now *Tsinkiang*), port in southern China from which the cloth was probably first exported] —ˈ**sat·in-ˌlike** *adj.* —ˈ**sat·in·y** *adj.*

sat·i·net *or* **sat·i·nette** (ˌsætɪˈnɛt) *n.* a thin or imitation satin. [C18: from French: small satin]

sat·in·flow·er (ˈsætɪnˌflaʊə) *n.* another name for **greater stitchwort** (see **stitchwort**).

sat·in·pod (ˈsætɪnˌpɒd) *n.* another name for **honesty** (the plant).

sat·in stitch *n.* an embroidery stitch consisting of rows of flat stitches placed close together.

sat·in·wood (ˈsætɪnˌwʊd) *n.* **1.** a tree, *Chloroxylon swietenia*, that occurs in the East Indies and has hard wood with a satiny texture: family *Flindersiaceae.* **2.** the wood of this tree, used in veneering, cabinetwork, marquetry, etc. **3. West Indian satinwood.** another name for **yellowwood** (sense 2).

sat·ire (ˈsætaɪə) *n.* **1.** a novel, play, entertainment, etc., in which topical issues, folly, or evil are held up to scorn by means of ridicule and irony. **2.** the genre constituted by such works. **3.** the use of ridicule, irony, etc., to create such an effect. [C16: from Latin *satira* a mixture, from *satur* sated, from *satis* enough]

sa·tir·i·cal (səˈtɪrɪkəl) *or* **sa·tir·ic** *adj.* **1.** of, relating to, or containing satire. **2.** given to the use of satire. —**sa**ˈ**tir·i·cal·ly** *adv.* —**sa**ˈ**tir·i·cal·ness** *n.*

sat·i·rist (ˈsætərɪst) *n.* **1.** a person who writes satire. **2.** a person given to the use of satire.

sat·i·rize *or* **sat·i·rise** (ˈsætəˌraɪz) *vb.* to deride (a person or thing) by means of satire. —ˌ**sat·i·ri·ˈza·tion** *or* ˌ**sat·i·ri·ˈsa·tion** *n.* —ˈ**sat·i·ˌriz·er** *or* ˈ**sat·i·ˌris·er** *n.*

sat·is·fac·tion (ˌsætɪsˈfækʃən) *n.* **1.** the act of satisfying or state of being satisfied. **2.** the fulfilment of a desire. **3.** the pleasure obtained from such fulfilment. **4.** a source of fulfilment. **5.** reparation or compensation for a wrong done or received. **6.** *R.C. Church, Church of England.* the performance by a repentant sinner of a penance. **7.** *Christianity.* the atonement for sin by the death of Christ. —ˌ**sat·is·ˈfac·tion·al** *adj.*

sat·is·fac·to·ry (ˌsætɪsˈfæktərɪ, -trɪ) *adj.* **1.** adequate or suitable; acceptable: *a satisfactory answer.* **2.** giving satisfaction. **3.** constituting or involving atonement, recompense, or expiation for sin. —ˌ**sat·is·ˈfac·to·ri·ly** *adv.* —ˌ**sat·is·ˈfac·to·ri·ness** *n.*

sat·is·fy (ˈsætɪsˌfaɪ) *vb.* **·fies, ·fy·ing, ·fied.** (*mainly tr.*) **1.** (*also intr.*) to fulfil the desires or needs of (a person). **2.** to provide amply for (a need or desire). **3.** to relieve of doubt; convince. **4.** to dispel (a doubt). **5.** to make reparation to or for. **6.** to discharge or pay off (a debt) to (a creditor). **7.** to fulfil the requirements of; comply with: *you must satisfy the terms of your lease.* **8.** *Maths.* **a.** to reduce (an equation or set of equations) to an identity, following substitution: *$x = 3$ satisfies $x^2 - 4x + 3 = 0$.* **b.** to fulfil conditions of (a theorem, inequality, set of assumptions, etc.). [C15: from Old French *satisfier*, from Latin *satisfacere*, from *satis* enough + *facere* to make, do] —ˈ**sat·is·ˌfi·a·ble** *adj.* —ˈ**sat·is·ˌfi·er** *n.* —ˈ**sat·is·ˌfy·ing·ly** *adv.*

sa·to·ri (səˈtɔːrɪ) *n. Zen Buddhism.* the state of sudden indescribable intuitive enlightenment. [from Japanese]

sa·trap (ˈsætrəp) *n.* **1.** (in ancient Persia) a provincial governor. **2.** a subordinate ruler, esp. a despotic one. [C14: from Latin *satrapa*, from Greek *satrapēs*, from Old Persian *khshathrapāvan*, literally: protector of the land]

sa·trap·y (ˈsætrəpɪ) *n., pl.* **·trap·ies.** the province, office, or period of rule of a satrap.

sat·su·ma (sætˈsuːmə) *n.* **1.** a small citrus tree, *Citrus nobilis* var. *unshiu*, cultivated, esp. in Japan, for its edible fruit. **2.** the fruit of this tree, which has a loose rind and easily separable segments.

Sa·tsu·ma (ˈsætsʊˌmɑː) *n.* a former province of SW Japan, on S Kyushu: famous for its porcelain.

Sa·tsu·ma ware *n.* porcelain ware made in Satsuma, Japan, from the late 18th century.

sat·u·ra·ble (ˈsætʃərəbəl) *adj. Chem.* capable of being saturated. —ˌ**sat·u·ra·ˈbil·i·ty** *n.*

sat·u·rant (ˈsætʃərənt) *Chem.* ~*n.* **1.** the substance that causes a solution, etc., to be saturated. ~*adj.* **2.** (of a substance) causing saturation. [C18: from Latin *saturāns*]

sat·u·rate *vb.* (ˈsætʃəˌreɪt). **1.** to fill, soak, or imbue totally. **2.** to make (a chemical compound, vapour, solution, magnetic material, etc.) saturated or (of a compound, etc.) to become saturated. **3.** (*tr.*) *Military.* to bomb or shell heavily. ~*adj.* (ˈsætʃərɪt, -ˌreɪt). **4.** a less common word for **saturated.** [C16: from Latin *saturāre*, from *satur* sated, from *satis* enough] —ˌ**sat·u·ˈrat·er** *or* ˌ**sat·u·ˈra·tor** *n.*

sat·u·rat·ed (ˈsætʃəˌreɪtɪd) *adj.* **1.** (of a solution or solvent) containing the maximum amount of solute that can normally be dissolved at a given temperature and pressure. See also **supersaturated.** **2.** (of a colour) having a large degree of saturation. **3.** (of a chemical compound) **a.** containing no multiple bonds and thus being incapable of undergoing additional reactions: *a saturated hydrocarbon.* **b.** containing no unpaired valence electrons. **4.** (of a vapour) containing the maximum amount of gaseous material at a given temperature and pressure. See also **supersaturated.** **5.** (of a magnetic material) fully magnetized.

sat·u·ra·tion (ˌsætʃəˈreɪʃən) *n.* **1.** the act of saturating or the state of being saturated. **2.** *Chem.* the state of a chemical compound, solution, or vapour when it is saturated. **3.** *Meteorol.* the state of the atmosphere when it can hold no more water vapour at its particular temperature and pressure, the relative humidity then being 100 per cent. **4.** the attribute of a colour that enables an observer to judge its proportion of pure chromatic colour. See also **colour.** **5.** *Physics.* the state of a ferromagnetic material in which it is fully magnetized. The magnetic domains are then all fully aligned.

Sat·ur·day (ˈsætədɪ) *n.* the seventh and last day of the week: the Jewish Sabbath. [Old English *sæternes dæg*, translation of Latin *Saturnī diēs* day of Saturn; compare Middle Dutch *saterdach*, Dutch *zaterdag*]

Sat·urn[1] (ˈsætɜːn) *n.* the Roman god of agriculture and vegetation. Greek counterpart: **Cronus.**

Sat·urn[2] (ˈsætɜːn) *n.* **1.** one of the **giant planets,** the sixth planet from the sun, around which revolve three planar concentric rings (**Saturn's rings**) consisting of small frozen particles. The planet has ten satellites. Mean distance from sun: 1425 million km; period of revolution around sun: 29.46 years; period of axial rotation: 10.23 hours; diameter and mass: 9.36 and 95.14 times that of the earth, respectively. See also **Titan**[2]. **2.** a large U.S. rocket used for launching various objects, such as a spaceprobe or an Apollo spacecraft, into space. **3.** the alchemical name for **lead.** —**Sa·tur·ni·an** (sæˈtɜːnɪən) *adj.*

Sat·ur·na·li·a (ˌsætəˈneɪlɪə) *n., pl.* **·li·a** *or* **·li·as.** **1.** an ancient Roman festival celebrated in December: renowned for its general merrymaking. **2.** (*sometimes not cap.*) a period or occasion of wild revelry. [C16: from Latin *Sāturnālis* relating to SATURN] —ˌ**Sat·ur·ˈna·li·an** *adj.*

Sa·tur·ni·an (sæˈtɜːnɪən) *adj.* **1.** of or connected with the Roman god Saturn, whose reign was thought of as a golden age. **2.** *Prosody.* denoting a very early verse form in Latin in which the accent was one of stress rather than quantity, there being an equal number of main stresses in each line, regardless of the number of unaccented syllables. ~*n.* **3.** a line in Saturnian metre.

sa·tur·ni·id (sæˈtɜːnɪɪd) *n.* **1.** any moth of the mainly tropical family *Saturniidae*, typically having large brightly coloured wings: includes the emperor, cecropia, and luna moths. ~*adj.* **2.** of, relating to, or belonging to the *Saturniidae.*

sat·ur·nine (ˈsætəˌnaɪn) *adj.* **1.** having a gloomy temperament; taciturn. **2.** *Archaic.* **a.** of or relating to lead. **b.** having or symptomatic of lead poisoning. [C15: from French *saturnin*, from Medieval Latin *sāturnīnus* (unattested), from Latin *Sāturnus* Saturn, with reference to the gloomy influence attributed to the planet Saturn] —ˈ**sat·ur·ˌnine·ly** *adv.* —ˈ**sat·ur·ˌnine·ness** *or* **sat·ur·nin·i·ty** (ˌsætəˈnɪnɪtɪ) *n.*

sat·ur·nism (ˈsætəˌnɪzəm) *n. Pathol.* another name for **lead poisoning.** [C19: from New Latin *sāturnismus;* properties similar to those of lead were attributed to the planet]

sat·ya·gra·ha (ˈsʌtjəˌgrʌhə) *n.* **1.** the policy of nonviolent resistance adopted by Mahatma Gandhi from about 1919 to oppose British rule in India. **2.** any movement of nonviolent resistance. [via Hindi from Sanskrit, literally: insistence on truth, from *satya* truth + *graha* grasping]

sat·ya·gra·hi (ˈsʌtjəˌgrʌhiː) *n.* an exponent of nonviolent resistance, esp. as a form of political protest.

sa·tyr (ˈsætə) *n.* **1.** *Greek myth.* one of a class of sylvan deities, represented as goatlike men who drank and danced in the train of Dionysus and chased the nymphs. **2.** a man who has strong sexual desires. **3.** a man who has satyriasis. **4.** any of various butterflies of the genus *Satyrus* and related genera, having dark wings often marked with eyespots: family *Satyridae.*

[C14: from Latin *satyrus,* from Greek *saturos*] —**sa·tyr·ic** (səˈtɪrɪk) *or* **sa·ˈtyr·i·cal** *adj.* —**ˈsa·tyr-ˌlike** *adj.*

sat·y·ri·a·sis (ˌsætɪˈraɪəsɪs) *or* **sa·tyr·o·ma·ni·a** (sæˌtɪrəʊˈmeɪnɪə) *n.* an abnormally intense and persistent desire in a man for sexual intercourse. Compare **nymphomania.** [C17: via New Latin from Greek *saturiasis;* see SATYR, -IASIS]

sa·ty·rid (səˈtɪərɪd) *n.* any butterfly of the family *Satyridae,* having typically brown or dark wings with paler markings: includes the graylings, satyrs, browns, ringlets, and gatekeepers.

sa·tyr play *n.* (in ancient Greek drama) a ribald play with a chorus of satyrs, presented at the Dionysian festival.

sauce (sɔːs) *n.* **1.** any liquid or semiliquid preparation eaten with food to enhance its flavour. **2.** anything that adds piquancy. **3.** *U.S.* stewed fruit. **4.** *U.S. dialect.* vegetables eaten with meat. **5.** *Informal.* impudent language or behaviour. ~*vb.* (*tr.*) **6.** to prepare (food) with sauce. **7.** to add zest to. **8.** to make agreeable or less severe. **9.** *Informal.* to be saucy to. [C14: via Old French from Latin *salsus* salted, from *salīre* to sprinkle with salt, from *sal* salt] —**ˈsauce·less** *adj.*

sauce·box (ˈsɔːsˌbɒks) *n. Informal.* a saucy person.

sauce·pan (ˈsɔːspən) *n.* a metal or enamel pan with a long handle and often a lid, used for cooking food.

sau·cer (ˈsɔːsə) *n.* **1.** a small round dish on which a cup is set. **2.** any similar dish. [C14: from Old French *saussier* container for SAUCE] —**ˈsau·cer·ful** *n.* —**ˈsau·cer·less** *adj.*

sauc·y (ˈsɔːsɪ) *adj.* **·ci·er, ·ci·est. 1.** impertinent. **2.** pert; sprightly: *a saucy hat.* —**ˈsau·ci·ly** *adv.* —**ˈsau·ci·ness** *n.*

Saud (saʊd) *n.* Full name *Saud ibn Abdul-Aziz.* 1902–69, king of Saudi Arabia (1953–64); son of Ibn Saud. He was deposed by his brother Faisal.

Sau·di A·ra·bi·a (ˈsɔːdɪ, ˈsaʊ-) *n.* a kingdom in SW Asia, occupying most of the Arabian peninsula between the Persian Gulf and the Red Sea: founded in 1932 by Ibn Saud, who united Hejaz and Nejd; consists mostly of desert plateau; large reserves of petroleum and natural gas. Language: Arabic. Religion: Sunni Muslim. Currency: riyal. Capital: Riyadh (royal), Jidda (administrative). Pop.: 7 965 000 (1970 UN est.). Area: 2 260 353 sq. km (872 722 sq. miles). —**Sau·di** *or* **Sau·di A·ra·bi·an** *adj., n.*

sau·er·bra·ten (ˈsaʊəˌbrɑːtᵊn; *German* ˈzaʊərˌbraːtᵊn) *n.* beef marinated in vinegar, sugar, and seasonings, and then braised. [German, from *sauer* SOUR + *Braten* roast]

sau·er·kraut (ˈsaʊəˌkraʊt) *n.* finely shredded and pickled cabbage. [German, from *sauer* SOUR + *Kraut* cabbage]

sau·ger (ˈsɔːgə) *n.* a small North American pikeperch, *Stizostedion canadense,* with a spotted dorsal fin: valued as a food and game fish. [C19: of unknown origin]

Saul (sɔːl) *n.* **1.** *Old Testament.* the first king of Israel (?1020–1000 B.C.). He led Israel successfully against the Philistines, but was in continual conflict with the high priest Samuel. He became afflicted with madness and died by his own hand; succeeded by David. **2.** *New Testament.* the name borne by Paul prior to his conversion (Acts 9:1–30).

Sault Sainte Ma·rie (ˈsuː seɪnt məˈriː) *n., usually abbreviated to* **Sault Ste. Ma·rie. 1.** an inland port in central Canada, in Ontario on the St. Mary's River, which links Lake Superior and Lake Huron, opposite Sault Ste. Marie, Michigan: canal bypassing the rapids completed in 1895. Pop.: 80 332 (1971). **2.** an inland port in NE Michigan, opposite Sault Ste. Marie, Ontario: canal around the rapids completed in 1855, enlarged and divided in 1896 and 1919 (popularly called **Soo Canals**). Pop.: 15 136 (1970).

sau·na (ˈsɔːnə) *n.* **1.** an invigorating bath originating in Finland in which the bather is subjected to hot steam, usually followed by a cold plunge or by being lightly beaten with birch twigs. **2.** the place in which such a bath is taken. [C20: from Finnish]

saun·ter (ˈsɔːntə) *vb.* **1.** (*intr.*) to walk in a casual manner; stroll. ~*n.* **2.** a leisurely pace or stroll. **3.** a leisurely old-time dance. [C17 (meaning: to wander aimlessly), C15 (to muse): of obscure origin] —**ˈsaun·ter·er** *n.*

-saur *or* **-sau·rus** *n. combining form.* lizard: *dinosaur.* [from New Latin *saurus*]

sau·rel (ˈsɔːrəl) *n.* a U.S. name for **horse mackerel** (sense 1). [C19: via French from Late Latin *saurus,* from Greek *sauros,* of obscure origin]

sau·ri·an (ˈsɔːrɪən) *adj.* **1.** of, relating to, or resembling a lizard. **2.** of, relating to, or belonging to the *Sauria,* a former suborder of reptiles (now called *Lacertilia*), which included the lizards. ~*n.* **3.** a former name for **lizard.** [C15: from New Latin *Sauria,* from Greek *sauros*]

saur·is·chi·an (sɔːˈrɪskɪən) *adj.* **1.** of, relating to, or belonging to the *Saurischia,* an order of late Triassic dinosaurs including the theropods and sauropods. ~*n.* **2.** any dinosaur belonging to the order *Saurischia.* [C19: from New Latin *Saurischia;* see SAURO-, ISCHIUM]

sau·ro·pod (ˈsɔːrəˌpɒd) *n.* any herbivorous quadrupedal saurischian dinosaur of the suborder *Sauropoda,* of Jurassic and Cretaceous times, including the brontosaurus, diplodocus, and titanosaurs. They had small heads and long necks and tails and were partly amphibious. —**sau·rop·o·dous** (sɔːˈrɒpədəs) *adj.*

sau·ry (ˈsɔːrɪ) *n., pl.* **·ries.** any teleost fish, such as the Atlantic *Scomberesox saurus* of the family *Scomberesocidae* of tropical and temperate seas, having an elongated body and long toothed jaws. Also called: **skipper.** [C18: perhaps from Late Latin *saurus;* see SAUREL]

sau·sage (ˈsɒsɪdʒ) *n.* **1.** finely minced meat, esp. pork or beef, mixed with fat, cereal or bread, and seasonings (**sausage meat**), and packed into a tube-shaped animal intestine or synthetic casing. **2.** an object shaped like a sausage. **3.** *Aeronautics, informal.* a captive balloon shaped like a sausage. **4. not a sausage.** nothing at all. [C15: from Old Norman French *saussiche,* from Late Latin *salsīcia,* from Latin *salsus* salted; see SAUCE] —**ˈsau·sage-ˌlike** *adj.*

sau·sage dog *n.* an informal word for **dachshund.**

sau·sage roll *n. Brit.* a roll of sausage meat in pastry.

Saus·sure (*French* soˈsyːr) *n.* **Fer·di·nand de** (fɛrdiˈnã də). 1857–1913, Swiss linguist. He pioneered structuralism in linguistics and the separation of scientific language description from historical philological studies. —**Saus·ˈsur·e·an** *adj., n.*

sau·té (ˈsəʊteɪ) *vb.* **·tés, ·té·ing** *or* **·tée·ing, ·téed. 1.** to fry (food) quickly in a little fat. ~*n.* **2.** a dish of sautéed food, esp. meat that is browned and then cooked in a sauce. ~*adj.* **3.** sautéed until lightly brown: *sauté potatoes.* [C19: from French: tossed, from *sauter* to jump, from Latin *saltāre* to dance, from *salīre* to spring]

Sau·ternes (səʊˈtɜːn) *n.* (*sometimes not cap.*) a sweet white wine made in the southern Bordeaux district of France. [C18: from *Sauternes,* the district where it is produced]

sauve qui peut *French.* (sov ki ˈpø) *n.* a state of panic or disorder; rout. [literally: save (himself) who can]

sav (sæv) *n. Austral. informal.* short for **saveloy.**

Sa·va (ˈsɑːvə) *or* **Save** (sɑːv) *n.* a river in N Yugoslavia, flowing east to the Danube at Belgrade: the longest river wholly in Yugoslavia. Length: 940 km (584 miles).

sav·age (ˈsævɪdʒ) *adj.* **1.** wild; untamed: *savage beasts of the jungle.* **2.** ferocious in temper; vicious: *a savage dog.* **3.** uncivilized; crude: *savage behaviour.* **4.** (of peoples) nonliterate or primitive: *a savage tribe.* **5.** (of terrain) rugged and uncultivated. **6.** *Obsolete.* far from human habitation. ~*n.* **7.** a member of a nonliterate society, esp. one regarded as primitive. **8.** a crude or uncivilized person. **9.** a fierce or vicious person or animal. ~*vb.* (*tr.*) **10.** to criticize violently. **11.** to attack ferociously and wound: *the dog savaged the child.* [C13: from Old French *sauvage,* from Latin *silvāticus* belonging to a wood, from *silva* a wood] —**ˈsav·age·dom** *n.* —**ˈsav·age·ly** *adv.* —**ˈsav·age·ness** *n.*

Sav·age (ˈsævɪdʒ) *n.* **Mi·chael Jo·seph.** 1872-1940, New Zealand statesman; prime minister of New Zealand (1935-40).

Sav·age Is·land *n.* another name for **Niue.**

sav·age·ry (ˈsævɪdʒrɪ) *n., pl.* **·ries. 1.** an uncivilized condition. **2.** a savage act or nature. **3.** savages collectively.

Sa·vai·i (sɑːˈvaɪiː) *n.* the largest island in Western Samoa: mountainous and volcanic. Pop.: 39 828 (1971). Area: 1174 sq. km (662 sq. miles).

sa·van·na *or* **sa·van·nah** (səˈvænə) *n.* open grasslands, usually with scattered bushes or trees, characteristic of much of tropical Africa. Whether this is the natural climax vegetation or the result of clearing or burning by man is disputed. [C16: from Spanish *zavana;* from Taino *zabana*]

Sa·van·nah (səˈvænə) *n.* **1.** a port in E Georgia, near the mouth of the Savannah River: port of departure of the *Savannah* for Liverpool (1819), the first steamship to cross the Atlantic. Pop.: 105 768 (1973 est.). **2.** a river in the southeastern U.S., formed by the confluence of the Tugaloo and Seneca Rivers in NW South Carolina: flows southeast to the Atlantic. Length: 505 km (314 miles).

sa·vant (ˈsævənt, *French* saˈvã) *n.* a man of great learning; sage. [C18: from French, from *savoir* to know, from Latin *sapere* to be wise; see SAPIENT] —**ˈsa·vante** *fem. n.*

sa·vate (səˈvæt) *n.* a form of boxing in which blows may be delivered with the feet as well as the hands. [C19: from French, literally: old worn-out shoe; related to SABOT]

save[1] (seɪv) *vb.* **1.** (*tr.*) to rescue, preserve, or guard (a person or thing) from danger or harm. **2.** to avoid the spending, waste, or loss of (money, possessions, etc.). **3.** (*tr.*) *Theol.* to deliver from sin; redeem. **4.** (often foll. by *up*) to set aside or reserve (money, goods, etc.) for future use. **5.** (*tr.*) to treat with care so as to avoid or lessen wear or degeneration: *use a good light to save your eyes.* **6.** (*tr.*) to prevent the necessity for; obviate the trouble of: *good work now will save future revision.* **7.** (*tr.*) *Soccer, hockey, etc.* to prevent (a goal) by stopping (a struck ball or puck). **8.** (*intr.*) *Chiefly U.S.* (of food) to admit of preservation; keep. ~*n.* **9.** *Soccer, hockey, etc.* the act of saving a goal. [C13: from Old French *salver,* via Late Latin *salvāre,* from Latin *salvus* safe] —**ˈsav·a·ble** *or* **ˈsave·a·ble** *adj.* —**ˈsav·a·ble·ness** *or* **ˈsave·a·ble·ness** *n.* —**ˈsav·er** *n.*

save[2] (seɪv) *Archaic.* ~*prep.* **1.** (often foll. by *for*) Also: **saving.** with the exception of. ~*conj.* **2.** but; except. [C13 *sauf,* from Old French, from Latin *salvō,* from *salvus* safe]

save-all *n.* **1.** a device to prevent waste or loss. **2.** *Nautical.* **a.** a net used while loading a ship. **b.** a light sail set to catch wind spilling from another sail. **3.** *Dialect.* overalls or a pinafore. **4.** *Brit.* a dialect word for **miser.**

save as you earn *n.* (in Britain) a savings scheme operated by the government, in which monthly contributions earn tax-free interest. Abbrev.: **S.A.Y.E.**

sav·e·loy (ˈsævɪˌlɔɪ) *n.* a smoked sausage made from salted pork, well seasoned and coloured red with saltpetre. [C19: probably via French from Italian *cervellato,* from *cervello* brain, from Latin *cerebellum,* diminutive of *cerebrum* brain]

sav·in *or* **sav·ine** (ˈsævɪn) *n.* **1.** a small spreading juniper bush, *Juniperus sabina,* of Europe, N Asia, and North America. **2.** the oil derived from the shoots and leaves of this plant, formerly used in medicine to treat rheumatism, etc. **3.** another name for **red cedar** (sense 1). [C14: from Old French *savine,* from Latin *herba Sabina* the Sabine plant]

sav·ing (ˈseɪvɪŋ) *adj.* **1.** tending to save or preserve. **2.**

redeeming or compensating (esp. in the phrase **saving grace**). **3.** thrifty or economical. **4.** *Law.* denoting or relating to an exception or reservation: *a saving clause in an agreement.* ~*n.* **5.** preservation or redemption, esp. from loss or danger. **6.** economy or avoidance of waste. **7.** reduction in cost or expenditure: *a saving of 20p.* **8.** anything saved. **9.** (*pl.*) money saved for future use. **10.** *Law.* an exception or reservation. ~*prep.* **11.** with the exception of. ~*conj.* **12.** except. —'**sav·ing·ly** *adv.*

sav·ings ac·count *n.* an account at a bank that accumulates interest.

sav·ings and loan as·so·ci·a·tion *n.* a U.S. name for a **building society.**

sav·ings bank *n.* **1.** a bank that accepts the savings of depositors and pays interest on them. **2.** a container, usually having a slot in the top, for saving coins.

sav·iour *or U.S.* **sav·ior** ('seɪvjə) *n.* a person who rescues another person or a thing from danger or harm. [C13 *saveour,* from Old French, from Church Latin *Salvātor* the Saviour; see SAVE[1]]

Sav·iour *or U.S.* **Sav·ior** ('seɪvjə) *n. Christianity.* Jesus Christ regarded as the saviour of men from sin.

Sa·voie (*French* sa'vwa) *n.* **1.** a department of E France, in Rhône-Alpes region. Capital: Chambéry. Pop.: 315 098 (1975). Area: 6188 sq. km (2413 sq. miles). **2.** the French name for **Savoy.**

sa·voir-faire ('sævwɑː'fɛə; *French* savwar'fɛːr) *n.* the ability to do the right thing in any situation. [French, literally: a knowing how to do]

Sa·vo·na (*Italian* sa'voːna) *n.* a port in NW Italy, in Liguria on the Mediterranean: an important centre of the Italian iron and steel industry. Pop.: 79 618 (1971).

Sav·o·na·ro·la (*Italian* ˌsavona'rɔːla) *n.* **Gi·ro·la·mo** (dʒiː'rɔlamo). 1452–98, Italian religious and political reformer. As a Dominican prior in Florence he preached against contemporary sinfulness and moral corruption. When the Medici were expelled from the city (1494) he instituted a severely puritanical republic but lost the citizens' support after being excommunicated (1497). He was hanged and burned as a heretic.

sa·vor·y ('seɪvərɪ) *n., pl.* **-vor·ies. 1.** any of numerous aromatic plants of the genus *Satureja,* esp. *S. montana* (**winter savory**) and *S. hortensis* (**summer savory**), of the Mediterranean region, having narrow leaves and white, pink, or purple flowers: family *Labiatae* (labiates). **2.** the leaves of any of these plants, used as a potherb. [C14: probably from Old English *sætherie,* from Latin *saturēia,* of obscure origin]

sa·vour *or U.S.* **sa·vor** ('seɪvə) *n.* **1.** the quality in a substance that is perceived by the sense of taste or smell. **2.** a specific taste or smell: *the savour of lime.* **3.** a slight but distinctive quality or trace. **4.** the power to excite interest: *the savour of wit has been lost.* **5.** *Archaic.* reputation. ~*vb.* **6.** (*intr.;* often foll. by *of*) to possess the taste or smell (of). **7.** (*intr.;* often foll. by *of*) to have a suggestion (of). **8.** (*tr.*) to give a taste to; season. **9.** (*tr.*) to taste or smell, esp. appreciatively. **10.** (*tr.*) to relish or enjoy. [C13: from Old French *savour,* from Latin *sapor* taste, from *sapere* to taste] —'**sa·vour·ing·ly** *or U.S.* '**sa·vor·ing·ly** *adv.* —'**sa·vour·less** *or U.S.* '**sa·vor·less** *adj.* —'**sa·vor·ous** *adj.*

sa·vour·y *or U.S.* **sa·vor·y** ('seɪvərɪ) *adj.* **1.** attractive to the sense of taste or smell. **2.** salty or spicy; not sweet: *a savoury dish.* **3.** pleasant. **4.** respectable. ~*n., pl.* **-vour·ies. 5.** *Chiefly Brit.* a savoury dish served as an hors d'oeuvre or dessert. [C13 *savure,* from Old French *savouré,* from *savourer* to SAVOUR] —'**sa·vour·i·ly** *or U.S.* '**sa·vor·i·ly** *adv.* —'**sa·vour·i·ness** *or U.S.* '**sa·vor·i·ness** *n.*

sa·voy (sə'vɔɪ) *n.* a cultivated variety of cabbage, *Brassica oleracea capitata,* having a compact head and wrinkled leaves. [C16: named after the SAVOY region]

Sa·voy[1] (sə'vɔɪ) *n.* an area of SE France, bordering on Italy, mainly in the Savoy Alps: a duchy in the late Middle Ages and part of the Kingdom of Sardinia from 1720 to 1860, when it became part of France. French name: **Savoie.**

Sa·voy[2] (sə'vɔɪ) *n.* a noble family of Italy that ruled over the duchy of Savoy and became the royal house of Italy (1861–1946): the oldest reigning dynasty in Europe before the dissolution of the Italian monarchy.

Sa·voy Alps *pl. n.* a range of the Alps in SE France. Highest peak: Mont Blanc, 4807 m (15 772 ft.).

Sa·voy·ard[1] (sə'vɔɪɑːd; *French* savwa'jaːr) *n.* **1.** a native of Savoy. **2.** the dialect of French spoken in Savoy. ~*adj.* **3.** of or relating to Savoy, its inhabitants, or their dialect.

Sa·voy·ard[2] (sə'vɔɪɑːd) *n.* **1.** a person keenly interested in the operettas of Gilbert and Sullivan. **2.** a person who takes part in these operettas. [C20: from the *Savoy* Theatre, built in London in 1881 by Richard D'Oyly Carte for the presentation of operettas by Gilbert and Sullivan]

sav·vy ('sævɪ) *Slang.* ~*vb.* **-vies, -vy·ing, -vied. 1.** to understand or get the sense of (an idea, etc.). **2. no savvy.** I don't (he doesn't, etc.) understand. ~*n.* **3.** comprehension. ~*adj.* **-vi·er, -vi·est. 4.** *Chiefly U.S.* shrewd; well-informed. [C18: corruption of Spanish *sabe* (*usted*) (you) know, from *saber* to know, from Latin *sapere* to be wise]

saw[1] (sɔː) *n.* **1.** any of various hand tools for cutting wood, metal, etc., having a blade with teeth along one edge. **2.** any of various machines or devices for cutting by use of a toothed blade, such as a power-driven circular toothed wheel or toothed band of metal. ~*vb.* **saws, saw·ing, sawed; sawed** *or* **sawn. 3.** to cut with a saw. **4.** to form by sawing. **5.** to cut as if wielding a saw: *to saw the air.* **6.** to move (an object) from side to side as if moving a saw. [Old English *sagu;* related to Old Norse *sog,* Old High German *saga,* Latin *secāre* to cut, *secūris* axe] —'**saw·er** *n.* —'**saw·ˌlike** *adj.*

saw[2] (sɔː) *vb.* the past tense of **see**[1].

saw[3] (sɔː) *n.* a wise saying, maxim, or proverb. [Old English *sagu* a saying; related to SAGA]

saw·bill ('sɔːˌbɪl) *n.* **1.** another name for **merganser** or **motmot. 2.** any of various hummingbirds of the genus *Ramphodon.*

saw·bones ('sɔːˌbəʊnz) *n., pl.* **-bones** *or* **-bones·es.** *Slang.* surgeon or doctor.

saw·buck ('sɔːˌbʌk) *n.* **1.** *U.S.* a sawhorse, esp. one having an X-shaped supporting structure. **2.** *U.S. slang.* a ten-dollar bill. [C19: (in the sense: sawhorse) translated from Dutch *zaagbok;* (in the sense: ten-dollar bill) from the legs of a sawbuck forming the Roman numeral X]

saw·der ('sɔːdə) *n. Informal.* flattery; compliments (esp. in the phrase **soft sawder**). ~*vb.* (*tr.*) **1.** to flatter. [C19: metaphorical use of variant of SOLDER]

saw·dust ('sɔːˌdʌst) *n.* particles of wood formed by sawing.

saw·fish ('sɔːˌfɪʃ) *n., pl.* **-fish** *or* **-fish·es.** any sharklike ray of the family *Pristidae* of subtropical coastal waters and estuaries, having a serrated bladelike mouth.

saw·fly ('sɔːˌflaɪ) *n., pl.* **-flies.** any of various hymenopterous insects of the family *Tenthredinidae* and related families, the females of which have a sawlike ovipositor.

saw·horse ('sɔːˌhɔːs) *n.* a stand for timber during sawing.

saw·mill ('sɔːˌmɪl) *n.* **1.** an industrial establishment where timber is sawn into planks, etc. **2.** a large sawing machine.

sawn (sɔːn) *vb.* a past participle of **saw**[1].

Saw·ney ('sɔːnɪ) *n.* **1.** a derogatory word for **Scotsman. 2.** (*also not cap.*) *Informal.* a fool. [C18: Scots variant of *Sandy,* short for *Alexander*]

sawn-off *adj.* (*prenominal*) (of a shotgun) having the barrel cut short, mainly to facilitate concealment of the weapon.

saw pal·met·to *n.* any of several dwarf prickly palms, esp. any of the genus *Sabal,* of the southeastern U.S.

saw set *n.* a tool used for setting the teeth of a saw, consisting of a type of clamp used to bend each tooth in turn at a slight angle to the plane of the saw, alternate teeth being bent in the same direction.

saw·tooth ('sɔːˌtuːθ) *adj.* **1.** (of a waveform) having an amplitude that varies linearly with time between two values, the interval in one direction being much greater than the other. **2.** having or generating such a waveform.

saw-wort ('sɔːˌwɜːt) *n.* a perennial Old World plant, *Serratula tinctoria.* having serrated leaves that yield a yellow dye: family *Compositae* (composites).

saw·yer ('sɔːjə) *n.* a person who saws timber for a living. [C14 *sawier,* from SAW[1] + *-ier,* variant of -ER[1]]

sax[1] (sæks) *n.* a tool resembling a small axe, used for cutting roofing slate. [Old English *seax* knife; related to Old Saxon *sahs,* Old Norse *sax*]

sax[2] (sæks) *n. Informal.* short for **saxophone.**

Sax. *abbrev. for:* **1.** Saxon. **2.** Saxony.

Saxe[1] (saks) *n.* the French name for **Saxony.**

Saxe[2] (*French* saks) *n.* **Her·mann Mau·rice** (ɛrman mɔ'ris) comte de Saxe. 1696–1750, French marshal born in Saxony: he distinguished himself in the War of the Austrian Succession (1740–48).

saxe blue (sæks) *n.* **a.** a light greyish-blue colour. **b.** (*as adj.*): *a saxe-blue dress.* [C19: from French *Saxe* Saxony, source of a dye of this colour]

Saxe-Co·burg-Go·tha (sæks 'kəʊbɜːg 'gəʊθə) *n.* the ruling house of the former German duchy of Saxe-Coburg-Gotha (until 1918) and the name of the British royal family (1901–17) through Prince Albert.

sax·horn ('sæksˌhɔːn) *n.* a valved brass instrument used chiefly in brass and military bands, having a tube of conical bore and a brilliant tone colour. It resembles the tuba and constitutes a family of instruments related to the flugelhorn and cornet. [C19: named after Adolphe *Sax* (see SAXOPHONE), who invented it (1845)]

sax·ic·o·lous (sæk'sɪkələs) *adj.* living on or among rocks: *saxicolous plants.* Also: **sax·a·tile** ('sæksəˌtaɪl). [C19: from New Latin *saxicolus,* from Latin *saxum* rock + *colere* to dwell]

sax·i·fra·ga·ceous (ˌsæksɪfrə'geɪʃəs) *adj.* of, relating to, or belonging to the *Saxifragaceae,* a chiefly arctic and alpine family of plants having a basal rosette of leaves and small flowers: includes saxifrage.

sax·i·frage ('sæksɪˌfreɪdʒ) *n.* any saxifragaceous plant of the genus *Saxifraga,* having small white, yellow, purple, or pink flowers. [C15: from Late Latin *saxifraga,* literally: rock-breaker, from Latin *saxum* rock + *frangere* to break]

Sax·o Gram·mat·i·cus ('sæksəʊ grə'mætɪkəs) *n.* ?1150–?1220, Danish chronicler, noted for his *Gesta Danorum,* a history of Denmark down to 1185, written in Latin, which is partly historical and partly mythological, and contains the Hamlet (Amleth) legend.

Sax·on ('sæksən) *n.* **1.** a member of a West Germanic people who in Roman times spread from Schleswig across NW Germany to the Rhine. Saxons raided and settled parts of S Britain in the fifth and sixth centuries A.D. In Germany they established a duchy and other dominions, which changed and shifted through the centuries, usually retaining the name Saxony. **2.** a native or inhabitant of Saxony. **3. a.** the Low German dialect of Saxony. **b.** any of the West Germanic dialects spoken by the ancient Saxons or their descendants. ~*adj.* **4.** of, relating to, or characteristic of the ancient Saxons, the Anglo-Saxons, or their descendants. **5.** of, relating to, or characteristic of Saxony, its inhabitants, or their Low German dialect. ~See also **West Saxon, Anglo-Saxon.** [C13 (replacing Old English *Seaxe*): via Old French from Late Latin *Saxon-, Saxo,* from Greek; of Germanic origin and perhaps related to the name of a knife used by the Saxons; compare SAW[1]]

Sax+on blue *n.* a dye made dissolving indigo in a solution of sulphuric acid. [C19: named after SAXONY, where it originated]

sax·o+ny ('sæksənɪ) *n.* **1.** a fine 3-ply yarn used for knitting and weaving. **2.** a fine woollen fabric used for coats, etc. [C19: named after SAXONY, where it was produced]

Sax·o+ny ('sæksənɪ) *n.* a region in S East Germany around the upper Elbe River: referred at various times to those places inhabited by Saxons or ruled by Saxon princes. German name: **Sachsen.** French name: **Saxe.**

sax·o+phone ('sæksəˌfəʊn) *n.* a keyed wind instrument of mellow tone colour, used mainly in jazz and dance music. It is made in various sizes, has a conical bore, and a single reed. Often shortened to **sax.** [C19: named after Adolphe *Sax* (1814–94), Belgian musical-instrument maker, who invented it (1846)] —**sax·o·phon+ic** (ˌsæksə'fɒnɪk) *adj.* —**sax+oph·o+nist** (sæk'sɒfənɪst) *n.*

say (seɪ) *vb.* **says, say+ing, said.** (*mainly tr.*) **1.** to speak, pronounce, or utter. **2.** (*also intr.*) to express (an idea, etc.) in words; tell: *we asked his opinion but he refused to say.* **3.** (*also intr.; may take a clause as object*) to state (an opinion, fact, etc.) positively; declare; affirm. **4.** to recite: *to say grace.* **5.** (*may take a clause as object*) to report or allege: *they say we shall have rain today.* **6.** (*may take a clause as object*) to take as an assumption; suppose: *let us say that he is lying.* **7.** (*may take a clause as object*) to convey by means of artistic expression: *the artist in this painting is saying that we should look for hope.* **8.** to make a case for: *there is much to be said for either course of action.* **9. go without saying.** to be so obvious as to need no explanation. **10. I say!** *Chiefly Brit. informal.* an exclamation of surprise. **11. not to say.** even; and indeed. **12. that is to say.** in other words; more explicitly. **13. to say nothing of.** even disregarding. **14. to say the least.** without the slightest exaggeration; at the very least. ~*adv.* **15.** approximately: *there were, say, 20 people present.* **16.** for example: *choose a number, say, four.* ~*n.* **17.** the right or chance to speak: *let him have his say.* **18.** authority, esp. to influence a decision: *he has a lot of say in the company's policy.* **19.** a statement of opinion: *you've had your say, now let me have mine.* ~*interj.* **20.** *U.S. informal.* an exclamation to attract attention or express surprise, etc. [Old English *secgan;* related to Old Norse *segja,* Old Saxon *seggian,* Old High German *sagēn*] —**'say+er** *n.*

say[2] (seɪ) *n. Archaic.* a type of fine woollen fabric. [C13: from Old French *saie,* from Latin *saga,* plural of *sagum* a type of woollen cloak]

Sa+yan Moun+tains (sɑː'jæn) *pl. n.* a mountain range in the SE Soviet Union, in S Siberia. Highest peak: Munku-Sardyk, 3437 m (11 457 ft.).

S.A.Y.E. *abbrev. for* save as you earn.

Say·ers ('seɪəz) *n.* **Dor·o·thy L(eigh).** 1893–1957, English detective-story writer.

say+ing ('seɪɪŋ) *n.* a maxim, adage, or proverb.

say-so *n. Informal.* **1.** an arbitrary assertion. **2.** an authoritative decision. **3.** the authority to make a final decision.

say+yid, say+id ('saɪɪd), *or* **sa·id** *n.* **1.** a Muslim claiming descent from Mohammed's grandson Husain. **2.** a Muslim honorary title. [C17: from Arabic: lord]

saz+e·rac ('sæzəˌræk) *n. U.S.* a mixed drink of whisky, pernod, syrup, bitters, and lemon. [C20: of uncertain origin]

Sb *the chemical symbol for* antimony. [from New Latin *stibium*]

sb. *abbrev. for* substantive.

Sc *the chemical symbol for* scandium.

sc. *abbrev. for:* **1.** scale. **2.** scene. **3.** science. **4.** scilicet. **5.** screw. **6.** scruple (unit of weight).

s.c. *Printing. abbrev. for* small capitals.

S.C. *abbrev. for:* **1.** Signal Corps. **2.** South Carolina.

scab (skæb) *n.* **1.** the dried crusty surface of a healing skin wound or sore. **2.** a contagious disease of sheep resembling mange, caused by a mite (*Psoroptes communis*). **3.** a fungal disease of plants characterized by crusty spots on the fruits, leaves, etc. **4.** *Derogatory.* **a.** Also called: **blackleg.** a person who refuses to support a trade union, esp. one who replaces a worker who is on strike. **b.** (*as modifier*): *scab labour.* **5.** a despicable person. ~*vb.* (*intr.*) **scabs, scab+bing, scabbed. 6.** to become covered with a scab. **7.** (of a road surface) to become loose so that potholes develop. **8.** *Chiefly U.S.* to replace a striking worker. [Old English *sceabb;* related to Old Norse *skabb,* Latin *scabiēs,* Middle Low German *schabbe* scoundrel, German *schäbig* SHABBY] —**'scab+ˌlike** *adj.*

scab+bard ('skæbəd) *n.* a holder for a bladed weapon such as a sword or bayonet; sheath. [C13 *scauberc,* from Norman French *escaubers,* (pl.) of Germanic origin; related to Old High German *skār* blade and *bergan* to protect]

scab+bard fish *n.* any of various marine spiny-finned fishes of the family *Trichiuridae,* esp. of the genus *Lepidopus,* having a long whiplike scaleless body and long sharp teeth: most common in warm waters.

scab+ble ('skæbᵊl) *vb.* (*tr.*) to shape (stone) roughly. [C17: from earlier *scapple,* from French *escapler* to shape (timber)]

scab+by ('skæbɪ) *adj.* **+bi+er, +bi+est. 1.** *Pathol.* having an area of the skin covered with scabs. **2.** *Pathol.* having scabies. **3.** *Informal.* despicable. —**'scab+bi+ly** *adv.* —**'scab+bi+ness** *n.*

sca+bies ('skeɪbiːz, -bɪˌiːz) *n.* a contagious skin infection caused by the mite *Sarcoptes scaboi,* characterized by intense itching, inflammation, and the formation of vesicles and pustules. [C15: from Latin: scurf, from *scabere* to scratch; see SHAVE] —**sca+bi+et+ic** (ˌskeɪbɪ'ɛtɪk) *adj.*

sca+bi+ous[1] ('skeɪbɪəs) *adj.* **1.** having or covered with scabs. **2.** of, relating to, or resembling scabies. [C17: from Latin *scabiōsus,* from SCABIES]

sca+bi+ous[2] ('skeɪbɪəs) *n.* **1.** any plant of the genus *Scabiosa,* esp. *S. atropurpurea,* of the Mediterranean region, having blue, red, or whitish dome-shaped flower heads: family *Dipsacaceae.* **2.** any of various similar plants of the related genus *Knautia.* **3. devil's bit scabious.** a similar and related Eurasian marsh plant, *Succisa pratensis.* [C14: from Medieval Latin *scabiōsa herba* the scabies plant, referring to its use in treating scabies]

sca+brous ('skeɪbrəs) *adj.* **1.** roughened because of small projections; scaly. **2.** indelicate, indecent, or salacious: *scabrous humour.* **3.** difficult to deal with; knotty. [C17: from Latin *scaber* rough; related to SCABIES] —**'sca+brous+ly** *adv.* —**'sca+brous+ness** *n.*

scad[1] (skæd) *n., pl.* **scad** *or* **scads.** any of various carangid fishes of the genus *Trachurus,* esp. the horse mackerel. [C17: of uncertain origin; compare Swedish *skädde* flounder]

scad[2] (skæd) *n.* (*often pl.*) *U.S. informal.* a large amount or number. [C19: of uncertain origin]

Sca+fell Pike (skɔː'fɛl) *n.* a mountain in NW England, in Cumbria in the Lake District: the highest peak in England. Height: 963 m (3210 ft.).

scaf+fold ('skæfəld, -fəʊld) *n.* **1.** a temporary metal or wooden framework that is used to support workmen and materials during the erection, repair, etc., of a building or other construction. **2.** a raised wooden platform on which plays are performed, tobacco, etc., is dried, or (esp. formerly) criminals are executed. ~*vb.* (*tr.*) **3.** to provide with a scaffold. **4.** to support by means of a scaffold. [C14: from Old French *eschaffaut,* from Vulgar Latin *catafalicum* (unattested); see CATAFALQUE] —**'scaf+fold+er** *n.*

scaf+fold+ing ('skæfəldɪŋ) *n.* **1.** a scaffold or system of scaffolds. **2.** the building materials used to make scaffolds.

scag (skæg) *South Wales and southwest English dialect.* ~*n.* **1.** a tear in a garment or piece of cloth. ~*vb.* **scags, scag+ging, scagged. 2.** (*tr.*) to make a tear in (cloth). [apparently related to Old Norse *skaga* to project]

scagl·io+la (skæl'jəʊlə) *n.* imitation marble made of glued gypsum with a polished surface of coloured stone or marble dust. [C16: from Italian, diminutive of *scaglia* chip of marble, of Germanic origin; related to SHALE, SCALE[2]]

scal+a·ble ('skeɪləbᵊl) *adj.* capable of being scaled or climbed. —**'scal+a·ble+ness** *n.* —**'scal+a·bly** *adv.*

sca+lade (skə'leɪd) *or* **sca+la+do** (skə'leɪdəʊ) *n., pl.* **+lades** *or* **+la+dos.** short for **escalade.** [C16: from Old Italian *scalada,* from *scala* a ladder; see SCALE[3]]

scal+age ('skeɪlɪdʒ) *n.* **1.** *U.S.* a percentage deducted from the price, etc., of goods liable to shrink or leak. **2.** *Forestry, U.S.* the estimated amount of usable timber in a log.

sca+lar ('skeɪlə) *n.* **1.** a variable quantity, such as time or temperature, that has magnitude but not direction. Compare **vector** (sense 1), **tensor** (sense 2). ~*adj.* **2.** having magnitude but not direction. [C17 (meaning: resembling a ladder): from Latin *scālaris,* from *scāla* ladder]

sca+lar·e (skə'lɛərɪ) *n.* another name for **angelfish** (sense 2). [C19: from Latin *scālāris* of a ladder, SCALAR, referring to the runglike pattern on its body]

sca+lar·i+form (skə'lærɪˌfɔːm) *adj. Biology.* resembling a ladder: *a scalariform cell.* [C19: from New Latin *scālāriformis* from Late Latin *scālāris* of a ladder + -FORM]

sca+lar prod+uct *n.* the product of two vectors to form a scalar, whose value is the product of the magnitudes of the vectors and the cosine of the angle between them. Written: ***A·B*** or ***AB*** Compare **vector product.** Also called: **dot product.**

scal·a+wag ('skæləˌwæg) *n.* a variant spelling of **scallywag.**

scald[1] (skɔːld) *vb.* **1.** to burn or be burnt with or as if with hot liquid or steam. **2.** (*tr.*) to subject to the action of boiling water, esp. so as to sterilize. **3.** (*tr.*) to heat (a liquid) almost to boiling point. ~*n.* **4.** the act or result of scalding. **5.** an abnormal condition in plants, characterized by discoloration and wrinkling of the skin of the fruits, caused by exposure to excessive sunlight, gases, etc. [C13: via Old Norman French from Late Latin *excaldāre* to wash in warm water, from *calida* (*aqua*) warm (water), from *calēre* to be warm] —**'scald+er** *n.*

scald[2] (skɔːld) *n.* a variant spelling of **skald.** —**'scald+ic** *adj.*

scald[3] (skɔːld) *Obsolete.* ~*adj. also* **scalled.** scabby. ~*n.* a less common word for **scab.** [C16: from SCALL]

scald+fish ('skɔːldˌfɪʃ, 'skɑːld-) *n., pl.* **+fish** *or* **+fish·es.** a small European flatfish, *Arnoglossus laterna,* covered with large fragile scales: family *Bothidae.*

scale[1] (skeɪl) *n.* **1.** any of the numerous plates, made of various substances resembling enamel or dentine, covering the bodies of fishes. **2. a.** any of the horny or chitinous plates covering a part or the entire body of certain reptiles and mammals. **b.** any of the numerous minute structures covering the wings of lepidoptera. **3.** a thin flat piece or flake. **4.** a thin flake of dead epidermis shed from the skin: excessive shedding may be the result of a skin disease. **5.** a specialized leaf or bract, esp. the protective covering of a bud or the dry membranous bract of a catkin. **6.** See **scale insect. 7.** a flaky black oxide of iron formed on the surface of iron or steel at high temperatures. **8.** any oxide formed on a metal during heat treatment. *~vb.* **9.** (*tr.*) to remove the scales or coating from. **10.** to peel off or cause to peel off in flakes or scales. **11.** (*intr.*) to shed scales. **12.** to cover or become covered with scales, incrustation, etc. **13.** (*tr.*) to throw (a disc or thin flat object) edgewise through the air or along the surface of water. **14.** (*intr.*) *Austral. informal.* to ride on public transport without paying a fare. [C14: from Old French *escale,* of Germanic origin; compare Old English *scealu* SHELL] —**'scale+,like** *adj.*

scale[2] (skeɪl) *n.* **1.** (*often pl.*) a machine or device for weighing. **2.** one of the pans of a balance. **3. tip the scales a.** to exercise a decisive influence. **b.** (foll. by *at*) to amount in weight (to). *~vb.* (*tr.*) **4.** to weigh with or as if with scales. **5.** to have a weight of. [C13: from Old Norse *skāl* bowl, related to Old High German *scāla* cup, Old English *scealu* SHELL, SCALE[1]]

scale[3] (skeɪl) *n.* **1.** a sequence of marks at regular intervals, used as a reference in making measurements. **2.** a measuring instrument having such a scale. **3. a.** the ratio between the size of something real and that of a model or representation of it: *the scale of the map was so large that we could find our house on it.* **b.** (*as modifier*): *a scale model.* **4.** a line, numerical ratio, etc., for showing this ratio. **5.** a progressive or graduated table of things, wages, etc., in order of size, value, etc.: *a wage scale for carpenters.* **6.** an established measure or standard. **7.** a relative degree or extent: *he entertained on a grand scale.* **8.** *Music.* a group of notes taken in ascending or descending order, esp. within the compass of one octave. **9.** *Maths.* the notation of a given number system: *the decimal scale.* **10.** a graded series of tests measuring mental development, etc. **11.** *Obsolete.* a ladder or staircase. *~vb.* **12.** to climb to the top of (a height) by or as if by a ladder. **13.** (*tr.*) to make or draw (a model, etc.) according to a particular ratio of proportionate reduction. **14.** (*tr.; usually foll. by up or down*) to increase or reduce proportionately in size, etc. **15.** *U.S. forestry.* **a.** to measure (logs). **b.** to calculate the number of (trees). [C15: via Italian from Latin *scāla* ladder; related to Old French *eschiele,* Spanish *escala*]

scale+board ('skeɪl,bɔːd, 'skæbəd) *n.* **1.** a very thin piece of board, used for backing a picture, as a veneer, etc. **2.** *Printing.* a thin wooden strip used in justifying type.

scale in+sect *n.* any small homopterous insect of the family *Coccidae* and related families, which typically live and feed on plants and secrete a protective scale around themselves. Many species, such as the San Jose scale, are important pests.

scale leaf *n. Botany.* a modified leaf, often small and membranous, protecting buds, etc.

scale moss *n.* any of various leafy liverworts of the order *Jungermanniales,* which resemble mosses.

sca+lene ('skeɪliːn) *adj.* **1.** *Maths.* (of a triangle) having all sides of unequal length. **2.** *Anatomy.* of or relating to any of the scalenus muscles. [C17: from Late Latin *scalēnus* with unequal sides, from Greek *skalēnos*]

sca+le·nus (skə'liːnəs, skeɪ-) *n., pl.* **·ni** (-naɪ). *Anatomy.* any one of the three muscles situated on each side of the neck extending from the cervical vertebrae to the first or second pair of ribs. [C18: from New Latin; see SCALENE]

scal+er ('skeɪlə) *n.* **1.** a person or thing that scales. **2.** Also called: **counter, scaling circuit.** an electronic device or circuit that aggregates electric pulses and gives a single output pulse for a predetermined number of input pulses.

Scales (skeɪlz) *n.* **the.** the constellation Libra, the seventh sign of the zodiac.

Scal·i·ger ('skælɪdʒə) *n.* **1. Jo·seph Jus·tus** ('dʒʌstəs). 1540–1609, French scholar, who revolutionized the study of ancient chronology by his work *De Emendatione temporum* (1583). **2.** his father, **Ju·li·us Cae·sar.** 1484–1558, Italian classical scholar, and writer on biology and medicine.

scal+ing lad+der *n.* a ladder used to climb high walls, esp. one used formerly to enter a besieged town, fortress, etc.

scall (skɔːl) *n. Pathol.* a former term for any of various diseases of the scalp characterized by itching and scab formation. [C14: from Old Norse *skalli* bald head. See SKULL] —**scalled** *adj.*

scal+lion ('skæljən) *n.* any of various onions or similar plants, such as the spring onion, that have a small bulb and long leaves and are eaten in salads. Also called: **green onion.** [C14: from Anglo-French *scalun,* from Latin *Ascalōnia* (*caepa*) Ascalonian (onion), from *Ascalo* Ascalon, a Palestinian port]

scal+lop ('skɒləp, 'skæl-) *n.* **1.** any of various marine bivalves of the family *Pectinidae,* having a fluted fan-shaped shell: includes free-swimming species (genus *Pecten*) and species attached to a substratum (genus *Chlamys*). See also **pecten** (sense 3). **2.** the edible adductor muscle of certain of these molluscs. **3.** either of the shell valves of any of these molluscs. **4.** a scallop shell or similarly shaped dish, in which fish, esp. shellfish, is cooked and served. **5.** one of a series of curves along an edge, esp. an edge of cloth. **6.** the shape of a scallop shell used as the badge of a pilgrim, esp. in the Middle Ages. **7.** *Austral.* a potato cake fried in batter. *~vb.* **8.** (*tr.*) to decorate (an edge) with scallops. **9.** to bake (food) in a scallop shell or similar dish. **10.** (*intr.*) to collect scallops. [C14: from Old French *escalope* shell, of Germanic origin; see SCALP] —**'scal+lop+er** *n.* —**'scal+lop+ing** *n.*

scal+ly+wag ('skælɪ,wæg) *n.* **1.** *Informal.* a scamp; rascal. **2.** (after the U.S. Civil War) a White Southerner who supported the Republican Party and its policy of Black emancipation. Scallywags were viewed as traitors by their fellow Southerners. *~*Also: **scalawag, scallawag.** [C19: (originally undersized animal): of uncertain origin]

sca+lop+pi+ne *or* **sca+lop+pi+ni** (,skælə'piːnɪ) *n.* escalopes of meat, esp. veal, cooked in a rich sauce, usually of wine with seasonings. [Italian: from *scaloppa* a fillet, probably from Old French *escalope* SCALLOP]

scalp (skælp) *n.* **1.** *Anatomy.* the skin and subcutaneous tissue covering the top of the head. **2.** (among North American Indians) a part of this removed as a trophy from a slain enemy. **3.** a trophy or token signifying conquest. **4.** *Hunting, chiefly U.S.* a piece of hide cut from the head of a victim as a trophy or as proof of killing in order to collect a bounty. **5.** *Informal, chiefly U.S.* a small speculative profit taken in quick transactions. **6.** *Scottish dialect.* a projection of bare rock from vegetation, etc. *~vb.* (*tr.*) **7.** to cut the scalp from. **8.** *Informal, chiefly U.S.* to purchase and resell (securities) quickly so as to make several small profits. **9.** *Informal.* to buy (tickets) cheaply and resell at an inflated price. [C13: probably from Scandinavian; compare Old Norse *skalpr* sheath, Middle Dutch *schelpe,* Danish *skalp* husk] —**'scalp+er** *n.*

scal+pel ('skælpᵊl) *n.* a surgical knife with a short thin blade. [C18: from Latin *scalpellum,* from *scalper* a knife, from *scalpere* to scrape] —**scal+pel+lic** (skæl'pɛlɪk) *adj.*

scalp+ing ('skælpɪŋ) *n.* a process in which the top portion of a metal ingot is machined away before use, thus removing the layer containing defects and impurities.

scalp lock *n.* a small tuft or plait of hair left on the shaven scalp by American Indian warriors as a challenge to enemies.

scal·y ('skeɪlɪ) *adj.* **scal·i·er, scal·i·est. 1.** resembling or covered in scales. **2.** peeling off in scales. —**'scal·i·ness** *n.*

scal·y ant+eat·er *n.* another name for **pangolin.**

Sca+man+der (skə'mændə) *n.* the ancient name for the **Menderes** (sense 2).

scam+mo+ny ('skæmənɪ) *n., pl.* **+nies. 1.** a twining Asian convolvulus plant, *Convolvulus scammonia,* having arrow-shaped leaves, white or purple flowers, and tuberous roots. **2.** a resinous juice obtained from the roots of this plant and having purgative properties. **3.** any of various similar medicinal resins or the plants that yield them. [Old English, via Latin from Greek *skammōnia,*] —**scam+mo+ni+ate** (skæ'məunɪɪt) *adj.*

scamp[1] (skæmp) *n.* **1.** an idle mischievous person; rascal. **2.** a mischievous child. [C18: from *scamp* (vb.) to be a highway robber, probably from Middle Dutch *schampen* to decamp, from Old French *escamper,* from *es-* EX-[1] + *-camper,* from Latin *campus* field] —**'scamp+ish** *adj.*

scamp[2] (skæmp) *vb.* a less common word for **skimp.** —**'scamp+er** *n.*

scamp+er ('skæmpə) *vb.* **1.** (*intr.*) to run about playfully. *~n.* **2.** the act of scampering. [C17: probably from *scamp* (vb.); see SCAMP[1]] —**'scam+per+er** *n.*

scam+pi ('skæmpɪ) *n.* large prawns, usually eaten fried in batter. [Italian: plural of *scampo* shrimp, of obscure origin]

scan (skæn) *vb.* **scans, scan+ning, scanned. 1.** (*tr.*) to scrutinize minutely. **2.** (*tr.*) to glance over quickly. **3.** (*tr.*) *Prosody.* to read or analyse (verse) according to the rules of metre and versification. **4.** (*intr.*) *Prosody.* to conform to the rules of metre and versification. **5.** (*tr.*) *Electronics.* to move a beam of light, electrons, etc., in a predetermined pattern over (a surface or region) to obtain information, esp. either to sense and transmit or to reproduce a television image. **6.** (*tr.*) to examine data stored on (magnetic tape, etc.), usually in order to retrieve information. **7.** to examine or search (a prescribed region) by systematically varying the direction of a radar or sonar beam. **8.** *Physics.* to examine or produce or be examined or produced by a continuous charge of some variable: *to scan a spectrum.* *~n.* **9.** the act or an instance of scanning. [C14: from Late Latin *scandere* to scan (verse), from Latin: to climb] —**'scan+na·ble** *adj.*

Scand. *or* **Scan.** *abbrev. for* Scandinavia(n).

scan+dal ('skændᵊl) *n.* **1.** a disgraceful action or event: *his negligence was a scandal.* **2.** censure or outrage arising from an action or event. **3.** a person whose conduct causes reproach or disgrace. **4.** malicious talk, esp. gossip about the private lives of other people. **5.** *Law.* a libellous action or statement. *~vb.* (*tr.*) *Obsolete.* **6.** to disgrace. **7.** to scandalize. [C16: from Late Latin *scandalum* stumbling block, from Greek *skandalon* a trap] —**'scan+dal+ous** *adj.* —**'scan+dal+ous+ly** *adv.* —**'scan+dal+ous+ness** *n.*

scan+dal+ize *or* **scan+dal+ise** ('skændə,laɪz) *vb.* (*tr.*) to shock, as by improper behaviour. —**,scan+dal·i+'za+tion** *or* **,scan+dal·i+'sa+tion** *n.* —**'scan+dal+,iz+er** *or* **'scan+dal+,is+er** *n.*

scan·dal+mon·ger ('skændᵊl,mʌŋgə) *n.* a person who spreads or enjoys scandal, gossip, etc.

Scan+da+roon (,skændə'ruːn) *n.* a large variety of fancy pigeon having a long thin body and an elongated neck and head. [from *Scandaroon* the former name of *Ishenderon* a seaport in Turkey]

scan+dent ('skændənt) *adj.* (of plants) having a climbing habit. [C17: from Latin *scandere* to climb]

Scan·der·beg ('skændə,bɛg) *n.* original name *George Castriota;* Turkish name *Iskender Bey.* ?1403–68, Albanian patriot. He was an army commander for the sultan of Turkey until 1443, when he changed sides and drove the Turks from Albania.

Scan+di+an ('skændɪən) *n.* another name for a **Scandinavian.** [C17: from Latin *Scandia* Scandinavia]

scan+dic ('skændɪk) *adj.* of or containing scandium.

Scan+di+na+vi·a (,skændɪ'neɪvɪə) *n.* **1.** Also called: **the Scandinavian Peninsula.** the peninsula of N Europe occupied by Norway and Sweden. **2.** the countries of N Europe, esp.

considered as a cultural unit and including Norway, Sweden, Denmark, and often Finland, Iceland, and the Faeroe Islands.

Scan+di+na+vi·an (ˌskændɪˈneɪvɪən) *adj.* **1.** of, relating to, or characteristic of Scandinavia, its inhabitants, or their languages. ~*n.* **2.** a native or inhabitant of Scandinavia. **3.** Also called: **Norse.** the northern group of Germanic languages, consisting of Swedish, Danish, Norwegian, Icelandic, and Faeroese.

Scan+di+na+vi·an Shield *n.* another name for **Baltic Shield.**

scan+di·um (ˈskændɪəm) *n.* a rare light silvery-white metallic element occurring in minute quantities in numerous minerals. Symbol: Sc; atomic no.: 21; atomic wt.: 44.96; valency: 3; relative density: 2.99; melting pt.: 1539°C; boiling pt.: 2832°C. [C19: from New Latin, from Latin *Scandia* Scandinavia, where it was discovered]

scan+ner (ˈskænə) *n.* **1.** a person or thing that scans. **2.** a device, usually electronic, used to measure or sample the distribution of some quantity or condition in a particular system, region, or area. **3.** an aerial or similar device designed to transmit or receive signals, esp. radar signals, inside a given solid angle of space, thus allowing a particular region to be scanned.

scan+sion (ˈskænʃən) *n.* the analysis of the metrical structure of verse. See **quantity** (sense 7), **stress** (sense 3). [C17: from Latin: climbing up, from *scandere* to climb, SCAN]

scan+so+ri·al (skænˈsɔːrɪəl) *adj. Zoology.* specialized for, characterized by, or relating to climbing: *a scansorial bird.* [C19: from Latin *scānsōrius,* from *scandere* to climb]

scant (skænt) *adj.* **1.** scarcely sufficient; limited: *he paid her scant attention.* **2.** (*prenominal*) slightly short of the amount indicated; bare: *a scant ten inches.* **3.** (*postpositive;* foll. by *of*) having a short supply (of). ~*vb.* (*tr.*) **4.** to limit in size or quantity. **5.** to provide with a limited or inadequate supply of. **6.** to treat in a slighting or inadequate manner. ~*adv.* **7.** scarcely; barely. [C14: from Old Norse *skamt,* from *skammr* short; related to Old High German *scam*] —ˈ**scant+ly** *adv.* —ˈ**scant+ness** *n.*

scant+ling (ˈskæntlɪŋ) *n.* **1.** a piece of sawn timber, such as a rafter, that has a small cross section. **2.** the dimensions of a piece of building material or the structural parts of a ship, esp. those in cross section. **3.** a building stone, esp. one that is more than 6 feet in length. **4.** a small quantity or amount. [C16: changed (through influence of SCANT and -LING[1]) from earlier *scantillon,* a carpenter's gauge, from Old Norman French *escantillon,* ultimately from Latin *scandere* to climb; see SCAN]

scant·y (ˈskæntɪ) *adj.* **scant·i+er, scant·i+est. 1.** limited; barely enough; meagre. **2.** insufficient; inadequate. **3.** lacking fullness; small. —ˈ**scant·i·ly** *adv.* —ˈ**scant·i+ness** *n.*

Scap·a Flow (ˈskæpə) *n.* an extensive landlocked anchorage off the N coast of Scotland, in the Orkney Islands: major British naval base in both World Wars. Length: about 24 km (15 miles). Width: 13 km (8 miles).

scape[1] (skeɪp) *n.* **1.** a leafless stalk in plants that arises from a rosette of leaves and bears one or more flowers. **2.** *Zoology.* a stalklike part, such as the first segment of an insect's antenna. [C17: from Latin *scāpus* stem, from (Doric) Greek *skapos;* see SHAFT] —ˈ**scap+ose** *adj.*

scape[2] *or* **'scape** (skeɪp) *vb., n.* an archaic word for **escape.**

-scape *suffix forming nouns.* indicating a scene or view of something, esp. a pictorial representation: *seascape.* [abstracted from LANDSCAPE]

scape+goat (ˈskeɪpˌgəʊt) *n.* **1.** a person made to bear the blame for others. **2.** *Old Testament.* a goat used in the ritual of Yom Kippur (Leviticus 16); it was symbolically laden with the sins of the Israelites and sent into the wilderness to be destroyed. [C16: from ESCAPE + GOAT, coined by William Tyndale to translate Biblical Hebrew *azāzēl* (probably) goat for Azazel, mistakenly thought to mean "goat that escapes"]

scape+grace (ˈskeɪpˌgreɪs) *n.* an idle mischievous person. [C19: from SCAPE[2] + GRACE, alluding to a person who lacks God's grace]

scape+wheel (ˈskeɪpˌwiːl) *n.* a less common name for **escape wheel.**

scaph+oid (ˈskæfɔɪd) *adj. Anatomy.* an obsolete word for **navicular.** [C18: via New Latin from Greek *skaphoeidēs,* from *skaphē* boat]

scaph·o·pod (ˈskæfəˌpɒd) *n.* any marine mollusc of the class *Scaphopoda,* which includes the tusk (or tooth) shells.

scap·o+lite (ˈskæpəˌlaɪt) *n.* any of a group of colourless, white, grey, or violet fluorescent minerals consisting of sodium or calcium aluminium silicate, carbonate, and chloride in tetragonal crystalline form. They occur mainly in impure limestones and pegmatites. Also called: **wernerite.** [C19: from German *Skapolith,* from Greek *skapos* rod + -LITE]

scap·u+la (ˈskæpjʊlə) *n., pl.* **+lae** (-liː) *or* **+las. 1.** either of two large flat triangular bones, one on each side of the back part of the shoulder in man. Nontechnical name: **shoulder blade. 2.** the corresponding bone in most vertebrates. [C16: from Late Latin: shoulder]

scap·u+lar (ˈskæpjʊlə) *adj.* **1.** *Anatomy.* of or relating to the scapula. ~*n.* **2.** part of the monastic habit worn by members of many Christian, esp. Roman Catholic, religious orders, consisting of a piece of woollen cloth worn over the shoulders, and hanging down in front and behind to the ankles. **3.** two small rectangular pieces of woollen cloth joined by tapes passing over the shoulders and worn under secular clothes in token of affiliation to a religious order. **4.** any of the small feathers that are attached to the humerus of a bird and lie along the shoulder. ~Also called (for senses 2 and 3): **scapulary.**

scar[1] (skɑː) *n.* **1.** any mark left on the skin or other tissue following the healing of a wound, etc. **2.** a permanent change in a person's character resulting from emotional distress: *his wife's death left its scars on him.* **3.** the mark on a plant indicating the former point of attachment of a part, esp. the attachment of a leaf to a stem. **4.** a mark of damage; blemish. ~*vb.* **scars, scar+ring, scarred. 5.** to mark or become marked with a scar. **6.** (*intr.*) to heal leaving a scar. [C14: via Late Latin from Greek *eskhara* scab]

scar[2] (skɑː) *n.* **1.** a bare craggy rock formation. **2.** a similar formation in a river or sea. [C14: from Old Norse *sker* low reef, SKERRY]

scar+ab (ˈskærəb) *n.* **1.** any scarabaeid beetle, esp. *Scarabaeus sacer* (**sacred scarab**), regarded by the ancient Egyptians as divine. **2.** the scarab as represented on amulets, etc., of ancient Egypt, or in hieroglyphics as a symbol of the solar deity. [C16: from Latin *scarabaeus;* probably related to Greek *karabos* horned beetle]

scar·a+bae+id (ˌskærəˈbiːɪd) *or* **scar·a+bae·an** (ˌskærəˈbiːən) *n.* **1.** any beetle of the family *Scarabaeidae,* including the sacred scarab and other dung beetles, the chafers, goliath beetles, and rhinoceros beetles. ~*adj.* **2.** of, relating to, or belonging to the family *Scarabaeidae.* [C19: from New Latin]

scar·a+bae+oid (ˌskærəˈbiːɔɪd) *adj.* **1.** Also: **scar·a+boid** (ˈskærəˌbɔɪd). of, relating to, or resembling a scarabaeid. **2.** a former word for **lamellicorn** (sense 1).

scar·a+bae+us (ˌskærəˈbiːəs) *n., pl.* **+bae+us·es** *or* **+bae·i** (-ˈbiːaɪ). a less common name for **scarab.**

Scar·a+mouch *or* **Scar·a+mouche** (ˈskærəˌmaʊtʃ, -ˌmuːtʃ) *n.* a stock character who appears as a boastful coward in commedia dell'arte and farce. [C17: via French from Italian *Scaramuccia,* from *scaramuccia* a SKIRMISH]

Scar+borough (ˈskɑːbrə) *n.* a fishing port and resort in NE England, in North Yorkshire on the North Sea: developed as a spa after 1660; ruined 12th-century castle. Pop.: 44 370 (1971).

scarce (skɛəs) *adj.* **1.** rarely encountered. **2.** insufficient to meet the demand. **3. make oneself scarce.** *Informal.* to go away, esp. suddenly. ~*adv.* **4.** *Archaic or literary.* scarcely. [C13: from Old Norman French *scars,* from Vulgar Latin *excarpsus* (unattested) plucked out, from Latin *excerpere* to select; see EXCERPT] —ˈ**scarce+ness** *n.*

scarce+ly (ˈskɛəslɪ) *adv.* **1.** hardly at all; only just. **2.** *Often used ironically.* probably not or definitely not: *that is scarcely justification for your actions.*

Usage. See at **hardly.**

scarce+ment (ˈskɛəsmənt) *n.* a ledge in a wall. [C16: probably from obsolete sense of SCARCE to reduce + -MENT]

scar+ci·ty (ˈskɛəsɪtɪ) *n., pl.* **·ties. 1.** inadequate supply; dearth; paucity. **2.** rarity or infrequent occurrence.

scare (skɛə) *vb.* **1.** to fill or be filled with fear or alarm. **2.** (*tr.;* often foll. by *away* or *off*) to drive (away) by frightening. **3.** *U.S. informal.* (foll by *up*) to produce (a meal, etc.) quickly from what is available. ~*n.* **4.** a sudden attack of fear or alarm. **5.** a period of general fear or alarm. [C12: from Old Norse *skirra;* related to Norwegian *skjerra,* Swedish dialect *skjarra*] —ˈ**scar+er** *n.* —ˈ**scar+ing+ly** *adv.*

scare+crow (ˈskɛəˌkrəʊ) *n.* **1.** an object, usually in the shape of a man, made out of sticks and old clothes to scare birds away from seeds, etc. **2.** a person or thing that appears frightening but is not actually harmful. **3.** *Informal.* **a.** an untidy-looking person. **b.** a very thin person.

scare+mon·ger (ˈskɛəˌmʌŋgə) *n.* a person who delights in spreading rumours of disaster. —ˈ**scare+ˌmon·ger+ing** *n.*

scarf[1] (skɑːf) *n., pl.* **scarfs** *or* **scarves** (skɑːvz). **1.** a rectangular, triangular, or long narrow piece of cloth worn around the head, neck, or shoulders for warmth or decoration. ~*vb.* (*tr.*) *Rare.* **2.** to wrap with or as if with a scarf. **3.** to use as or in the manner of a scarf. [C16: of uncertain origin; compare Old Norman French *escarpe,* Medieval Latin *scrippum* pilgrim's pack; see SCRIP[2]]

scarf[2] (skɑːf) *n., pl.* **scarfs. 1.** Also called: **scarf joint, scarfed joint.** a lapped joint between two pieces of timber made by notching or grooving the ends and strapping, bolting, or gluing the two pieces together. **2.** the end of a piece of timber shaped to form such a joint. **3.** *Whaling.* an incision made along a whale's body before stripping off the blubber. ~*vb.* (*tr.*) **4.** to join (two pieces of timber) by means of a scarf. **5.** to make a scarf on (a piece of timber). **6.** to cut a scarf in (a whale). [C14: probably from Scandinavian; compare Norwegian *skarv,* Swedish *skarf,* Low German, Dutch *scherf* SCARF[1]]

scarf+skin (ˈskɑːfˌskɪn) *n.* the outermost layer of the skin; epidermis or cuticle. [C17: from SCARF[1] (in the sense: an outer covering)]

scar·i+fi+ca+tor (ˈskɛərɪfɪˌkeɪtə, ˈskærɪ-) *n.* a surgical instrument for use in puncturing the skin or other tissue.

scar·i+fy (ˈskɛərɪˌfaɪ, ˈskærɪ-) *vb.* **+fies, +fy+ing, +fied.** (*tr.*) **1.** *Surgery.* to make tiny punctures or superficial incisions in (the skin or other tissue), as for inoculating. **2.** *Agriculture.* **a.** to break up and loosen (soil) to a shallow depth. **b.** to scratch or abrade the outer surface of (seeds) to increase water absorption or hasten germination. **3.** to wound with harsh criticism. [C15: via Old French from Latin *scarīfāre* to scratch open, from Greek *skariphasthai* to draw, from *skariphos* a pencil] —ˌ**scar·i+fi+ˈca+tion** *n.* —ˈ**scar·i+ˌfi+er** *n.*

scar·i·ous (ˈskɛərɪəs) *or* **scar·i+ose** (ˈskɛərɪˌəʊs) *adj.* (of plant parts) membranous, dry, and brownish in colour: *scarious bracts.* [C19: from New Latin *scariōsus,* of uncertain origin]

scar+la+ti+na (ˌskɑːləˈtiːnə) *n.* the technical name for **scarlet fever.** [C19: from New Latin, from Italian *scarlattina,* diminutive of *scarlatto* SCARLET] —ˌ**scar+la+ˈti+nal** *or* **scar+la+ti+nous** (ˌskɑːləˈtiːnəs, skɑːˈlætɪnəs) *adj.*

Scar·lat·ti (skɑːˈlætɪ) *n.* **1. A·les·san·dro** (ˌalesˈsandro). ?1659–1725, Italian composer; regarded as the founder of modern opera. **2.** his son, **(Giuseppe) Do·me·ni·co** (doˈmeːniko). 1685–1757, Italian composer and harpsichordist, in Portugal and Spain from 1720. He wrote over 550 single-movement sonatas for harpsichord, many of them exercises in virtuoso technique.

scar+let (ˈskɑːlɪt) *n.* **1.** a vivid red colour, sometimes with an orange tinge. **2.** cloth or clothing of this colour. ~*adj.* **3.** of the colour scarlet. **4.** sinful or immoral, esp. unchaste. [C13: from Old French *escarlate,* of unknown origin]

scar+let fe+ver *n.* an acute communicable disease characterized by fever, strawberry-coloured tongue, and a typical rash starting on the neck and chest and spreading to the abdomen and limbs, caused by the bacterium *Streptococcus scarlatinae.* Technical name: **scarlatina.**

scar+let hat *n.* another term for **red hat.**

scar+let let+ter *n.* (esp. among U.S. Puritans) a scarlet letter *A* formerly worn by a person convicted of adultery.

scar+let pim+per+nel *n.* a primulaceous plant, *Anagallis arvensis,* of temperate regions, having small red, purple, or white star-shaped flowers that close in bad weather. Also called: **shepherd's** (or **poor man's**) **weatherglass.**

scar+let run+ner *n.* a climbing perennial bean plant, *Phaseolus multiflorus* (or *P. coccineus*), of tropical America, having scarlet flowers: widely cultivated for its long green edible pods containing edible seeds. Also called: **runner bean, string bean.**

scar+let tan·a·ger *n.* an E North American tanager, *Piranga olivacea,* the male of which has a bright red head and body with black wings and tail.

scar+let wom+an *n.* **1.** *New Testament.* a sinful woman described in Revelation 17, interpreted as a figure either of pagan Rome or of the Roman Catholic Church regarded as typifying vice overlaid with gaudy pageantry. **2.** any sexually promiscuous woman, esp. a prostitute.

scarp (skɑːp) *n.* **1.** a steep slope, esp. one formed by erosion or faulting; escarpment. See also **cuesta. 2.** *Fortifications.* the side of a ditch cut nearest to and immediately below a rampart. ~*vb.* **3.** (*tr.; often passive*) to wear or cut so as to form a steep slope. [C16: from Italian *scarpa*]

scarp+er (ˈskɑːpə) *Brit. slang.* ~*vb.* **1.** (*intr.*) to depart in haste. ~*n.* **2.** a hasty departure. [of uncertain origin]

Scar·ron (*French* skaˈrɔ̃) *n.* **Paul** (pɔl). 1610–60, French comic dramatist and novelist, noted particularly for his picaresque novel *Le Roman comique* (1651–57).

scarves (skɑːvz) *n.* a plural of **scarf.**

scar·y (ˈskɛərɪ) *adj.* **scar·i+er, scar·i+est.** *Informal.* **1.** causing fear or alarm; frightening. **2.** easily roused to fear; timid.

scat[1] (skæt) *vb.* **scats, scat+ting, scat+ted.** (*intr.; usually imperative*) *Informal.* to go away in haste. [C19: perhaps from a hiss + the word *cat,* used to frighten away cats]

scat[2] (skæt) *n.* **1.** a type of jazz singing characterized by improvised vocal sounds instead of words. ~*vb.* **scats, scat+ting, scat+ted. 2.** (*intr.*) to sing jazz in this way. [C20: perhaps imitative]

scat[3] (skæt) *n.* any marine and freshwater percoid fish of the Asian family *Scatophagidae,* esp. *Scatophagus argus,* which has a beautiful coloration. [C20: shortened from *Scatophagus;* see SCATO-]

scathe (skeɪð) *vb.* (*tr.*) **1.** *Rare.* to attack with severe criticism. **2.** *Archaic or dialect.* to injure. ~*n.* **3.** *Archaic or dialect.* harm. [Old English *sceatha;* related to Old Norse *skathi,* Old Saxon *scatho*] —**ˈscathe+ful** *adj.*

scath+ing (ˈskeɪðɪŋ) *adj.* **1.** harshly critical; scornful: *a scathing remark.* **2.** damaging; painful. —**ˈscath+ing+ly** *adv.*

scat·o- *or before a vowel* **scat-** *combining form.* dung or excrement: *scatophagous.* [from Greek *skōr, skat-*]

sca+tol+o·gy (skæˈtɒlədʒɪ) *n.* **1.** the scientific study of excrement, esp. in medicine for diagnostic purposes, and in palaeontology of fossilized excrement. **2.** obscenity or preoccupation with obscenity, esp. in the form of references to excrement. —**scat·o·log·i·cal** (ˌskætəˈlɒdʒɪkᵊl) *or* ˌ**scat·o·ˈlog·ic** *adj.* —**sca·ˈtol·o·gist** *n.*

scat+ter (ˈskætə) *vb.* **1.** (*tr.*) to throw about in various directions; strew. **2.** to separate and move or cause to move in various directions; disperse. **3.** to deviate or cause to deviate in many directions, as in the diffuse reflection or refraction of light. ~*n.* **4.** the act of scattering. **5.** a substance or a number of objects scattered about. [C13: probably a variant of SHATTER] —**ˈscat+ter+a·ble** *adj.* —**ˈscat+ter+er** *n.* —**ˈscat+ter+ing+ly** *adv.*

scat·ter+brain (ˈskætəˌbreɪn) *n.* a person who is incapable of serious thought or concentration. —**ˈscat·ter·ˌbrained** *adj.*

scat·ter-gun *n.* a shotgun.

scat+ter+ing (ˈskætərɪŋ) *n.* **1.** a small amount. **2.** *Physics.* the process in which particles, atoms, etc., are deflected as a result of collision.

scat+ter pin *n.* a small decorative pin usually worn in groups of two or three.

scat+ter rug *n.* a small rug used to cover a limited area.

scat+ty (ˈskætɪ) *adj.* **+ti+er, +ti+est.** *Brit. informal.* empty-headed, frivolous, or thoughtless. [C20: from SCATTER-BRAINED] —**ˈscat+ti+ly** *adv.* —**ˈscat+ti+ness** *n.*

scaup *or* **scaup duck** (skɔːp) *n.* either of two diving ducks, *Aythya marila* (**greater scaup**) or *A. affinis* (**lesser scaup**), of Europe and America, having a black-and-white plumage in the male. Also called (U.S.): **bluebill, broadbill.** [C16: Scottish variant of SCALP]

scau+per (ˈskɔːpə) *n.* a variant spelling of **scorper.**

scav+enge (ˈskævɪndʒ) *vb.* **1.** to search for (anything usable) among discarded material. **2.** (*tr.*) to purify (a molten metal) by bubbling a suitable gas through it. The gas may be inert or may react with the impurities. **3.** to clean up filth from (streets, etc.). **4.** *Chem.* to act as a scavenger for (atoms, molecules, ions, radicals, etc.).

scav+en+ger (ˈskævɪndʒə) *n.* **1.** a person who collects things discarded by others. **2.** any animal that feeds on decaying organic matter, esp. on refuse. **3.** a substance added to a chemical reaction or mixture to counteract the effect of impurities. **4.** a person employed to clean the streets. [C16: from Anglo-Norman *scawager,* from Old Norman French *escauwage* examination, from *escauwer* to scrutinize, of Germanic origin; related to Flemish *scauwen*] —**ˈscav+en+ger·y** *n.*

Sc.D. *abbrev. for* Doctor of Science.

S.C.E. *abbrev. for* Scottish Certificate of Education.

sce+nar·i·o (sɪˈnɑːrɪˌəʊ) *n., pl.* **+nar·i·os.** a summary of the plot of a play, etc., including information about its characters, scenes, etc. [C19: via Italian from Latin *scēnārium,* from *scēna;* see SCENE] —**sce+nar+ist** (ˈsiːnərɪst, sɪˈnaː-) *n.*

scend *or* **send** (sɛnd) *Nautical.* ~*vb.* **scends, scend+ing, scend+ed** *or* **sends, send+ing, sent. 1.** (*intr.*) (of a vessel) to surge upwards in a heavy sea. ~*n.* **2.** the upward heaving of a vessel pitching. **3.** the forward lift given a vessel by the sea. [C17: perhaps from DESCEND or ASCEND]

scene (siːn) *n.* **1.** the place where an action or event, real or imaginary, occurs. **2.** the setting for the action of a play, novel, etc. **3.** an incident or situation, real or imaginary, esp. as described or represented. **4. a.** a subdivision of an act of a play, in which the time is continuous and the setting fixed. **b.** a single event, esp. a significant one, in a play. **5.** *Films.* a shot or series of shots that constitutes a unit of the action. **6.** the backcloths, stage setting, etc., for a play or film set; scenery. **7.** the prospect of a place, landscape, etc. **8.** a display of emotion, esp. an embarrassing one to the onlookers. **9.** *Informal.* the environment for a specific activity: *the fashion scene.* **10.** *Informal.* interest or chosen occupation: *classical music is not my scene.* **11.** *Rare.* the stage, esp. of a theatre in ancient Greece or Rome. **12. behind the scenes.** out of public view. [C16: from Latin *scēna* theatrical stage, from Greek *skēnē* tent, stage]

scene dock *or* **bay** *n.* a place in a theatre where scenery is stored, usually near the stage.

scen+er·y (ˈsiːnərɪ) *n., pl.* **+er·ies. 1.** the natural features of a landscape. **2.** *Theatre.* the painted backcloths, stage structures, etc., used to represent a location in a theatre or studio. [C18: from Italian SCENARIO]

sce+nic (ˈsiːnɪk, ˈsɛn-) *adj.* **1.** of or relating to natural scenery. **2.** having beautiful natural scenery: *a scenic drive.* **3.** of or relating to the stage or stage scenery. **4.** (in painting, etc.) representing a scene, such as a scene of action or a historical event. —**ˈsce+ni+cal+ly** *adv.*

sce+nic rail+way *n.* **1.** a miniature railway used for amusement in a park, zoo, etc. **2.** a roller coaster.

sce+nog+ra+phy (siːˈnɒgrəfɪ) *n.* **1.** the art of portraying objects or scenes in perspective. **2.** scene painting, esp. in ancient Greece. [C17: via Latin from Greek *skēnographia* a drawing in perspective, from *skēnē* SCENE] —**sce+ˈnog+raph+er** *n.* —**sce+no+graph+ic** (ˌsiːnəʊˈgræfɪk) *or* ˌ**sce+no+ˈgraph·i·cal** *adj.* —ˌ**sce+no+ˈgraph·i·cal+ly** *adv.*

scent (sɛnt) *n.* **1.** a distinctive smell, esp. a pleasant one. **2.** a smell left in passing, by which a person or animal may be traced. **3.** a trail, clue, or guide. **4.** an instinctive ability for finding out or detecting. **5.** another word (esp. Brit.) for **perfume.** ~*vb.* **6.** (*tr.*) to recognize or be aware of by or as if by the smell. **7.** (*tr.*) to have a suspicion of; detect: *I scent foul play.* **8.** (*tr.*) to fill with odour or fragrance. **9.** (*intr.*) (of hounds, etc.) to hunt by the sense of smell. **10.** to smell (at): *the dog scented the air.* [*C14: from Old French sentir* to sense, from Latin *sentīre* to feel; see SENSE] —**ˈscent+less** *adj.*

scep+tic *or U.S.* **skep+tic** (ˈskɛptɪk) *n.* **1.** a person who habitually doubts the authenticity of accepted beliefs. **2.** a person who mistrusts people, ideas, etc., in general. **3.** a person who doubts the truth of religion, esp. Christianity. ~*adj.* **4.** of or relating to sceptics; sceptical. [C16: from Latin *scepticus,* from Greek *skeptikos* one who reflects upon, from *skeptesthai* to consider] —**ˈscep+ti+cal** *or U.S* **ˈskep+ti+cal** *adj.* —**ˈscep+ti+cal+ly** *or U.S.* **ˈskep+ti+cal+ly** *adv.* —**ˈscep+ti+cal+ness** *or U.S.* **ˈskep+ti+cal+ness** *n.* —**ˈscep+ti+cism** *or U.S.* **ˈskep+ti+cism** *n.*

Scep+tic *or U.S.* **Skep+tic** (ˈskɛptɪk) *n.* **1.** a member of one of the ancient Greek schools of philosophy, esp. that of Pyrrho, who believed that real knowledge of things is impossible. ~*adj.* **2.** of or relating to the Sceptics. —**ˈScep+ti+cism** *or U.S.* **ˈSkep+ti+cism** *n.*

scep+tre *or U.S.* **scep+ter** (ˈsɛptə) *n.* **1.** a ceremonial staff held by a monarch as the symbol of authority. **2.** imperial authority; sovereignty. ~*vb.* **3.** (*tr.*) to invest with authority. [C13: from Old French *sceptre,* from Latin *scēptrum,* from Greek *skeptron* staff] —**ˈscep+tred** *or U.S.* **ˈscep+tered** *adj.*

sch. *abbrev. for* school.

Scha+den+freude *German.* (ˈʃaːdᵊnˌfrɔɪdə) *n.* delight in another's misfortune. [German: from *Schaden* harm + *Freude joy*]

Schaer+beek (*Flemish* ˈsxaːrbeːk) *n.* a city in central Belgium, in Brabant province: an industrial suburb of Brussels. Pop.: 118 950 (1970).

Schaff+hau+sen (*German* ʃafˈhaʊzᵊn) *n.* **1.** a small canton of N Switzerland. Pop.: 72 854 (1970). Area: 298 sq. km (115 sq. miles). **2.** a town in N Switzerland, capital of Schaffhausen canton, on the Rhine. Pop.: 37 035 (1970). French name: **Schaffhouse.**

schap·pe ('ʃæpə) *n.* a yarn or fabric made from waste silk. [from German]

schat·chen *Yiddish.* ('ʃatxən) *n., pl.* ***schat·cho·nim*** (ʃat'xɔnɪm) *or* ***schat·chens.*** a variant spelling of **shadchan.**

Schaum·burg-Lip·pe (*German* 'ʃaumbʊrk 'lɪpə) *n.* a former state of NW Germany, between Westphalia and Hanover: part of Lower Saxony since 1946.

sched·ule ('ʃɛdju:l; *also, esp. U.S.* 'skɛdʒʊəl) *n.* **1.** a plan of procedure for a project, allotting the work to be done and the time for it. **2.** a list of items: *a schedule of fixed prices.* **3.** a list of times, esp. of arrivals and departures; timetable. **4.** a list of tasks to be performed, esp. within a set period. **5.** *Law.* a list or inventory, usually supplementary to a contract, will, etc. **6. on schedule.** at the expected or planned time. ~*vb.* (*tr.*) **7.** to make a schedule of or place in a schedule. **8.** to plan to occur at a certain time. [C14: earlier *cedule, sedule* via Old French from Late Latin *schedula* small piece of paper, from Latin *scheda* sheet of paper] —**'sched·u·lar** *adj.*

sched·uled castes *pl. n.* certain classes in Indian society offically granted special concessions. See **Harijan.**

sched·uled ter·ri·to·ries *pl. n.* **the.** another name for **sterling area.**

Scheel (*German* ʃe:l) *n.* **Wal·ter** ('valtər). born 1919, West German statesman; president of West Germany since 1974.

Schee·le (*Swedish* 'ʃe:lə) *n.* **Karl Wil·helm** (kɑ:rl 'vilhɛlm). 1742–86, Swedish chemist. He discovered oxygen, independently of Priestley, and many other substances.

scheel·ite ('ʃi:laɪt) *n.* a white, brownish, or greenish mineral, usually fluorescent, consisting of calcium tungstate in tetragonal crystalline form with some tungsten often replaced by molybdenum: occurs principally in contact metamorphic rocks and quartz veins, and is an important source of tungsten and purified calcium tungstate. Formula: $CaWO_4$. [C19: from German *Scheelit,* named after K. W. SCHEELE]

Scheldt (ʃɛlt, skɛlt) *n.* a river in W Europe, rising in NE France and flowing north and northeast through W Belgium to Antwerp, then northwest to the North Sea in the SW Netherlands. Length: 435 km (270 miles). Flemish and Dutch name: **Schel·de** ('sxɛldɛ). French name: **Escaut.**

Schel·ling (*German* 'ʃɛlɪŋ) *n.* **Frie·drich Wil·helm Jo·seph von** ('fri:drɪç 'vɪlhɛlm 'jo:zɛf fɔn). 1775–1854, German philosopher. He expanded Fichte's idea that there is one reality, the infinite and absolute Ego, by regarding nature as an absolute being working towards self-consciousness. His works include *Ideas towards a Philosophy of Nature* (1797) and *System of Transcendental Idealism* (1800). —**Schel·lin·gi·an** (ʃɛ'lɪŋɪən) *adj.*

sche·ma ('ski:mə) *n., pl.* **·ma·ta** (-mətə). **1.** a plan, diagram, or scheme. **2.** (in the philosophy of Kant) a rule or principle that enables the understanding to apply its categories and unify experience: *universal succession is the schema of causality.* **3.** *Psychol.* the internal representation of the external world, consisting of an organized set of concepts or internalized actions, which is constantly compared with information from the external world during perception of cognition. See also **cognitive theory.** [C19: from Greek: form]

sche·mat·ic (skɪ'mætɪk, ski:-) *adj.* **1.** of or relating to the nature of a diagram, plan, or schema. ~*n.* **2.** a schematic diagram, esp. of an electrical circuit, etc. —**sche·'mat·i·cal·ly** *adv.*

sche·ma·tism ('ski:mə,tɪzəm) *n.* the general form, arrangement, or classification of something.

sche·ma·tize *or* **sche·ma·tise** ('ski:mə,taɪz) *vb.* (*tr.*) to form into or arrange in a scheme. —**,sche·ma·ti·'za·tion** *or* **,sche·ma·ti·'sa·tion** *n.*

scheme (ski:m) *n.* **1.** a systematic plan for a course of action. **2.** a systematic arrangement of correlated parts; system. **3.** a secret plot. **4.** a visionary or unrealizable project. **5.** a chart, diagram, or outline. **6.** an astrological diagram giving the aspects of celestial bodies at a particular time. **7.** *Chiefly Brit.* a plan formally adopted by a commercial enterprise or governmental body, as for pensions, etc. ~*vb.* **8.** (*tr.*) to devise a system for. **9.** to form intrigues (for) in an underhand manner. [C16: from Latin *schema,* from Greek *skhēma* form] —**'schem·er** *n.*

schem·ing ('ski:mɪŋ) *adj.* **1.** given to making plots; cunning. ~*n.* **2.** intrigues. —**'schem·ing·ly** *adv.*

scher·zan·do (skɛə'tsændəʊ) *Music.* ~*adj., adv.* **1.** to be performed in a light-hearted manner. ~*n., pl.* **·di** (-di:) *or* **·dos. 2.** a movement, passage, etc., directed to be performed in this way. [Italian, literally: joking. See SCHERZO]

scher·zo ('skɛətsəʊ) *n., pl.* **·zos** *or* **·zi** (-tsi:). a brisk lively movement, developed from the minuet, with a contrastive middle section (a trio). See **minuet** (sense 2). [Italian: joke, of Germanic origin; compare Middle High German *scherzen* to jest]

Schia·pa·rel·li (*Italian* ,skjapa'rɛlli) *n.* **1. El·sa** ('elsa). 1896–1973, Italian couturière, noted esp. for the dramatic colours of her designs. **2. Gio·van·ni Vir·gin·io** (dʒo'vanni vir'dʒi:njo). 1835–1910, Italian astronomer, who discovered the asteroid Hesperia (1861) and the canals of Mars (1877).

Schick·ard ('ʃɪkəd) *n.* a large crater in the SE quadrant of the moon, about 215 kilometres (134 miles) in diameter.

Schick test (ʃɪk) *n. Med.* a skin test to determine immunity to diphtheria: a dilute diphtheria toxin is injected into the skin; within two or three days a red inflamed area will develop if no antibodies are present. [C20: named after Bela *Schick* (1877–1967), U.S. paediatrician]

Schie·dam (*Dutch* sxi:'dɑm) *n.* a port in the SW Netherlands, in South Holland province west of Rotterdam: gin distilleries. Pop.: 81 202 (1973 est.).

schil·ler ('ʃɪlə) *n.* an unusual metallic lustre in some minerals caused by internal reflection from certain inclusions such as gas cavities. [C19: from German *Schiller* iridescence, from Old High German *scilihen* to blink]

Schil·ler (*German* 'ʃɪlər) *n.* **Jo·hann Chris·toph Frie·drich von** ('jo:han 'krɪstɔf 'fri:drɪç fɔn). 1759–1805, German poet, dramatist, historian, and critic. His concern with the ideal freedom of the human spirit to rise above the constraints placed upon it is reflected in his great trilogy *Wallenstein* (1800) and in *Maria Stuart* (1800).

schil·ling ('ʃɪlɪŋ) *n.* **1.** the standard monetary unit of Austria, divided into 100 groschen. **2.** an old German coin of low denomination. [C18: from German: SHILLING]

schip·per·ke ('ʃɪpəkɪ, 'skɪp-) *n.* a small breed of dog with a foxy head, pricked ears, and usually a black coat. [C19: from Dutch, literally: little boatman. See SKIPPER[1]]

schism ('sɪzəm, 'skɪz-) *n.* **1.** the division of a group into opposing factions. **2.** the factions so formed. **3.** division within or separation from an established Church, esp. the Roman Catholic Church, not necessarily involving differences in doctrine. [C14: from Church Latin *schisma,* from Greek *skhisma* a cleft, from *skhizein* to split]

schis·mat·ic (sɪz'mætɪk, skɪz-) *or* **schis·mat·i·cal** *adj.* **1.** of, relating to, or promoting, schism. ~*n.* **2.** a person who causes schism or belongs to a schismatic faction. —**schis·'mat·i·cal·ly** *adv.* —**schis·'mat·i·cal·ness** *n.*

schist (ʃɪst) *n.* any metamorphic rock that can be split into thin layers because its micaceous minerals have become aligned in thin parallel bands. [C18: from French *schiste,* from Latin *lapis schistos* stone that may be split, from Greek *skhizein* to split]

schis·to·some (,ʃɪstə'səʊm) *n.* any of various blood flukes of the chiefly tropical genus *Schistosoma,* which cause disease in man and domestic animals. Also called: **bilharzia.** [C19: from New Latin *Schistosoma*; see SCHIST, -SOME[3]] —**'schis·tose** *adj.* —**schis·tos·i·ty** (ʃɪ'stɒsɪtɪ) *n.*

schis·to·so·mi·a·sis (,ʃɪstəsəʊ'maɪəsɪs) *n.* a disease caused by infestation of the body with blood flukes of the genus *Schistosoma.* Also called: **bilharziasis.**

schiz·o ('skɪtsəʊ) *Informal.* ~*adj.* **1.** schizophrenic. ~*n., pl.* **·os. 2.** a schizophrenic person.

schiz·o- *or before a vowel* **schiz-** *combining form.* indicating a cleavage, split, or division: *schizocarp; schizophrenia.* [from Greek *skhizein* to split]

schiz·o·carp ('skɪzə,kɑ:p) *n. Botany.* a dry fruit that splits into two or more one-seeded portions at maturity. —**,schiz·o·'car·pous** *or* **,schiz·o·'car·pic** *adj.*

schiz·o·gen·e·sis (,skɪtsəʊ'dʒɛnɪsɪs) *n.* asexual reproduction by fission of the parent organism or part. —**schiz·o·ge·net·ic** (,skɪtsəʊdʒɪ'nɛtɪk) *adj.*

schi·zog·o·ny (skɪt'sɒgənɪ) *n.* asexual reproduction in protozoans that is characterized by multiple fission.

schiz·oid ('skɪtsɔɪd) *adj.* **1.** of, relating to, or characteristic of schizophrenia. **2.** of, relating to, or characteristic of a personality that is inwardly directed. ~*n.* **3.** a person who has a schizoid personality.

schiz·o·my·cete (,skɪtsəʊmaɪ'si:t) *n.* any microscopic organism of the class *Schizomycetes,* which includes the bacteria. —**schiz·o·my·cet·ic** (,skɪtsəʊmaɪ'sɛtɪk) *or* **,schiz·o·my·'ce·tous** *adj.*

schi·zont ('skɪtsɒnt) *n.* a cell formed from a trophozoite during the asexual stage of the life cycle of protozoans of the class *Sporozoa,* such as the malaria parasite. [C19: from SCHIZO- + -*ont* a being, from Greek *einai* to be]

schiz·o·phre·ni·a (,skɪtsəʊ'fri:nɪə) *n.* any of a group of psychotic disorders characterized by progressive deterioration of the personality, withdrawal from reality, hallucinations, delusions, social apathy, emotional instability, etc. See **catatonia, hebephrenia, paranoia.** —**,schiz·o·'phren·ic** *adj., n.*

schiz·o·phy·ceous (,skɪtsəʊ'fɪʃəs) *adj.* of, relating to, or belonging to the *Schizophyceae,* a group of blue-green algae that grow in salt and fresh water and often pollute drinking water. [C19: from New Latin *Schizophyceae,* from SCHIZO- + Greek *phukos* seaweed]

schiz·o·phyte ('skɪtsəʊ,faɪt) *n.* any of various plants, such as certain fungi and bacteria, that reproduce only by multiple fission. —**schiz·o·phyt·ic** (,skɪtsəʊ'fɪtɪk) *adj.*

schiz·o·pod ('skɪtsəʊ,pɒd) *n.* any of various shrimplike crustaceans of the former order *Schizopoda,* now separated into the orders *Mysidacea* (opossum shrimps) and *Euphausiacea.*

schiz·o·thy·mi·a (,skɪtsəʊ'θaɪmɪə) *n. Psychiatry.* the condition of being schizoid or introverted. It encompasses elements of schizophrenia but does not involve the same depth of psychological disturbance. [C20: New Latin, from SCHIZO- + -*thymia,* from Greek *thumos* spirit] —**,schiz·o·'thy·mic** *adj.*

Schle·gel (*German* 'ʃle:gᵊl) *n.* **1. Au·gust Wil·helm von** ('aʊgust 'vɪlhɛlm fɔn). 1767–1845, German romantic critic and scholar, noted particularly for his translations of Shakespeare. **2.** his brother, **Frie·drich von** ('fri:drɪç fɔn). 1772–1829, German philosopher and critic; a founder of the romantic movement in Germany.

Schlei·er·ma·cher (*German* 'ʃlaɪər,maxər) *n.* **Frie·drich Ernst Da·niel** ('fri:drɪç ɛrnst 'da:nje:l). 1768–1834, German Protestant theologian and philosopher. His works include *The Christian Faith* (1821–22).

schle·miel, schle·mihl, *or* **shle·miel** (ʃlə'mi:l) *n. U.S. slang.* a clumsy or unlucky person. [Yiddish, from German, after the hero of a novel by Chamisso (1781–1838)]

schlep (ʃlɛp) *U.S. slang.* ~*vb.* **schleps, schlep+ping, schlepped. 1.** to drag or lug (oneself or an object) with difficulty. ~*n.* **2.** a stupid or clumsy person. **3.** an arduous journey or procedure. [Yiddish, from German *schleppen*]

Schle+si+en (ˈʃleːzɪən) *n.* the German name for **Silesia.**

Schles•wig (*German* ˈʃleːsvɪç) *n.* **1.** a fishing port in N West Germany, in Schleswig-Holstein state: on an inlet of the Baltic. Pop.: 32 100 (1970). **2.** a former duchy, in the S Jutland Peninsula: annexed by Prussia in 1864; N part returned to Denmark after a plebiscite in 1920; S part forms part of the West German state of Schleswig-Holstein. Danish name: **Slesvig.**

Schles•wig-Hol•stein (*German* ˈʃleːsvɪç ˈhɔlʃtaɪn) *n.* a state of N West Germany: drained chiefly by the River Elbe; mainly agricultural. Capital: Kiel. Pop.: 2 494 104 (1970). Area: 15 658 sq. km (6045 sq. miles).

Schlie•ffen (*German* ˈʃliːfᵊn) *n.* **Al•fred** (ˈalfreːt), Count von Schlieffen. 1833–1913, German field marshal, who devised the **Schlieffen Plan** (1905): it was intended to ensure German victory over a Franco-Russian alliance by holding off Russia with minimal strength and swiftly defeating France by a massive flanking movement through the Low Countries. In a modified form, it was unsuccessfully employed in World War I.

Schlie•mann (*German* ˈʃliːman) *n.* **Hein•rich** (ˈhaɪnrɪç). 1822–90, German archaeologist, who discovered nine superimposed city sites of Troy (1871–90). He also excavated the site of Mycenae (1876).

schlie+ren (ˈʃlɪərən) *n.* **1.** *Physics.* visible streaks produced in a transparent fluid as a result of variations in the fluid's density leading to variations in refractive index. They can be recorded by flash photography (**schlieren photography**). **2.** streaks or platelike masses of mineral in a rock mass, that differ in texture or composition from the main mass. [German, plural of *Schliere* streak] —**ˈschlie+ric** *adj.*

schlock (ʃlɒk) *U.S. slang.* ~*n.* **1.** goods or produce of cheap or inferior quality; trash. ~*adj.* **2.** cheap, inferior, or trashy. [Yiddish: damaged merchandise, probably from German *Schlag* a blow; related to SLAY]

schlock rock *n. Slang.* uninspired pop music.

schmaltz *or* **schmalz** (ʃmælts, ʃmɔːlts) *n.* **1.** *U.S.* animal fat used in cooking. **2.** *Slang.* excessive sentimentality, esp. in music. [C20: from German (*Schmalz*) and Yiddish: melted fat, from Old High German *smalz*] —**ˈschmaltz•y** *adj.*

Schmidt (*German* ʃmɪt) *n.* **Hel•mut** (**Heinrich Waldemar**) (ˈhɛlmuːt). born 1918, German statesman; chancellor of West Germany 1974–82.

Schmidt tel+e•scope *or* **cam+er•a** (ʃmɪt) *n.* a type of reflecting telescope incorporating a camera and consisting of a thin convex glass plate placed at the centre of curvature of a spherical mirror, thus correcting for spherical aberration, coma, and astigmatism. Wide areas of the sky can be photographed in one exposure. [C20: named after B. *Schmidt* (1879–1935), Swedish-born German inventor]

schmo *or* **shmo** (ʃməʊ) *n., pl.* **schmoes** *or* **shmoes.** *Yiddish.* a dull, stupid, or boring person. [from Yiddish *shmok*]

schmooze (ʃmuːz) *U.S. slang.* ~*vb.* **1.** (*intr.*) to chat or gossip. ~*n.* **2.** a trivial conversation; chat. [Yiddish, from *schmues* a chat, from Hebrew *shemuoth* reports]

schmuck (ʃmʌk) *n. U.S. slang.* a stupid or contemptible person; oaf. [from Yiddish *schmuck* penis, from German *Schmuck* decoration, from Middle High German *smucken* to press into]

Schna•bel (ˈʃnɑːbᵊl) *n.* **Ar•tur** (ˈartʊr). 1882–1951, U.S. pianist and composer, born in Austria.

schnapps *or* **schnaps** (ʃnæps) *n.* **1.** a Dutch spirit distilled from potatoes. **2.** (in Germany) any strong spirit. [C19: from German *Schnaps,* from *schnappen* to SNAP]

schnau+zer (ˈʃnaʊtsə) *n.* a wire-haired breed of dog, originally from Germany, of the terrier type with a greyish coat. [C19: from German *Schnauze* SNOUT]

schneck+en (ˈʃnɛkən) *pl. n., sing.* **schneck•e** (ˈʃnɛkə). *Chiefly U.S.* a sweet spiral-shaped bread roll flavoured with cinnamon and nuts. [German, plural of *Schnecke* SNAIL]

schnit+zel (ˈʃnɪtsəl) *n.* a thin slice of meat, esp. veal. See also **Wiener schnitzel.** [German: cutlet, from *schnitzen* to carve, *schnitzeln* to whittle]

Schnitz•ler (*German* ˈʃnɪtslər) *n.* **Ar•thur** (ˈartʊr). 1862–1931, Austrian dramatist and novelist. His best-known work is *Anatol* (1893), a series of one-act plays that reveal his psychological insight and preoccupation with sexuality.

schnook (ʃnʊk) *n. U.S. slang.* a stupid or gullible person. [from Yiddish *shnok,* variant of *shmok* SCHMO]

schnor+kle (ˈʃnɔːkᵊl) *n.* a less common spelling of **snorkel.**

schnor+rer (ˈʃnɔːrə) *n. U.S. slang.* a person who lives off the charity of others; professional beggar. [Yiddish, from German *Schnurrer* beggar (who played an instrument), from Middle High German *snurren* to hum]

schnoz+zle (ˈʃnɒzᵊl) *n. U.S.* a slang word for **nose.** [alteration of Yiddish *shnoitsl,* diminutive of *shnoits,* from German *Schnauze* SNOUT]

Schoen•berg *or* **Schön•berg** (ˈʃɜːnbɜːg; *German* ˈʃøːnbɛrk) *n.* **Ar•nold** (ˈarnɔlt). 1874–1951, Austrian composer and musical theorist, in the U.S. after 1933. The harmonic idiom of such early works as the string sextet *Verklärte Nacht* (1899) gave way to his development of atonality, as in the song cycle *Pierrot Lunaire* (1912), and later of the twelve-tone technique. He wrote many choral, orchestral, and chamber works and the unfinished opera *Moses and Aaron.*

scho+la can+to+rum (ˈskəʊlə kænˈtɔːrəm) *n., pl.* **scho+lae can+to+rum** (ˈskəʊliː). a choir or choir school maintained by a church. [Medieval Latin: school of singers]

schol+ar (ˈskɒlə) *n.* **1.** a learned person, esp. in the humanities. **2.** a person, esp. a child, who studies; pupil. **3.** a student of merit at an educational establishment who receives financial aid, esp. from an endowment given for such a purpose. [C14: from Old French *escoler,* via Late Latin from Latin *schola* SCHOOL] —**ˈschol+ar+less** *adj.* —**ˈschol+ar+ly** *adj.* —**ˈschol+ar+li+ness** *n.*

schol+ar+ship (ˈskɒləˌʃɪp) *n.* **1.** academic achievement; erudition; learning. **2. a.** financial aid provided for a scholar because of academic merit. **b.** the position of a student who gains this financial aid. **c.** (*as modifier*): *a scholarship student.* **3.** the qualities of a scholar.

scho+las+tic (skəˈlæstɪk) *adj. also* **scho+las+ti+cal. 1.** of, relating to, or befitting schools, scholars, or education. **2.** pedantic or precise. **3.** (*often cap.*) characteristic of or relating to the medieval Schoolmen. ~*n.* **4.** a student or pupil. **5.** a person who is given to quibbling or logical subtleties; pedant. **6.** (*often cap.*) a disciple or adherent of scholasticism; Schoolman. **7. a.** a Jesuit student who is undergoing a period of probation prior to commencing his theological studies. **b.** the status and position of such a student. **8.** a formalist in art. [C16: via Latin from Greek *skholastikos* devoted to learning, ultimately from *skholē* SCHOOL] —**scho+ˈlas+ti+cal+ly** *adv.*

scho+las+ti+cate (skəˈlæstɪˌkeɪt, -kɪt) *n. R.C. Church.* the state of being a scholastic, the period during which a Jesuit student is a scholastic, or an institution where scholastics pass this period. [C19: from New Latin *scholasticātus,* from Latin *scholasticus* SCHOLASTIC]

scho+las+ti+cism (skəˈlæstɪˌsɪzəm) *n.* **1.** (*sometimes cap.*) the system of philosophy, theology, and teaching that dominated medieval western Europe and was based on the writings of the Church Fathers and (from the 12th century) Aristotle. **2.** strict adherence to traditional doctrines.

scho+li+ast (ˈskəʊlɪˌæst) *n.* a medieval annotator, esp. of classical texts. [C16: from Late Greek *skholiastēs,* from *skholiazein* to write a SCHOLIUM] —**ˌscho+li+ˈas+tic** *adj.*

scho+li+um (ˈskəʊlɪəm) *n., pl.* **+li•a** (-lɪə). a commentary or annotation, esp. on a classical text. [C16: from New Latin, from Greek *skholion* exposition, from *skholē* SCHOOL]

Schön•berg (ˈʃɜːnbɜːg; *German* ˈʃøːnbɛrk) *n.* See (Arnold) **Schoenberg.**

Schon•gau•er (*German* ˈʃoːngaʊər) *n.* **Mar•tin** (ˈmartiːn). ?1445–91, German painter and engraver.

school[1] (skuːl) *n.* **1. a.** an institution or building at which children and young people usually under 19 receive education. **b.** (*as modifier*): *school bus; school day.* **c.** (*in combination*): *schoolroom; schoolwork.* **2.** any educational institution or building. **3.** a faculty, institution, or department specializing in a particular subject: *a law school.* **4.** the staff and pupils of a school. **5.** the period of instruction in a school or one session of this: *he stayed after school to do extra work.* **6.** meetings held occasionally for members of a profession, etc. **7.** a place or sphere of activity that instructs: *the school of hard knocks.* **8.** a body of people or pupils adhering to a certain set of principles, doctrines, or methods. **9.** a group of artists, writers, etc., linked by the same style, teachers, or aims: *the Venetian school of painting.* **10.** a style of life: *a gentleman of the old school.* **11.** *Austral.* a group assembled for a common purpose, esp. gambling or drinking. ~*vb.* (*tr.*) **12.** to train or educate in or as in a school. **13.** to discipline or control. **14.** an archaic word for **reprimand.** [Old English *scōl,* from Latin *schola* school, from Greek *skholē* leisure spent in the pursuit of knowledge]

school[2] (skuːl) *n.* **1.** a group of porpoises or similar aquatic animals that swim together. ~*vb.* **2.** (*intr.*) to form such a group. [Old English *scolu* SHOAL[2]]

school board *n.* **1.** (formerly in Britain) an elected board of ratepayers who provided local elementary schools between 1870 and 1902. **2.** (in the U.S.) a local board of education.

school+boy (ˈskuːlˌbɔɪ) *or* (*fem.*) **school+girl** *n.* a child attending school.

school+house (ˈskuːlˌhaʊs) *n.* **1.** a building used as a school, esp. a rural school. **2.** a house attached to a school.

school•ie (ˈskuːlɪ) *n. Austral. slang.* a schoolteacher.

school+ing (ˈskuːlɪŋ) *n.* **1.** education, esp. when received at school. **2.** the process of teaching or being taught in a school. **3.** the training of an animal, esp. of a horse for dressage. **4.** an archaic word for **reprimand.**

school+man (ˈskuːlmən) *n., pl.* **+men. 1.** (*sometimes cap.*) a scholar versed in the learning of the Schoolmen. **2.** *Rare, chiefly U.S.* a professional educator or teacher.

School+man (ˈskuːlmən) *n., pl.* **+men.** (*sometimes not cap.*) a master in one of the schools or universities of the Middle Ages who was versed in scholasticism; scholastic.

school+marm (ˈskuːlˌmɑːm) *n. Informal.* **1.** a woman schoolteacher, esp. when considered to be prim, prudish, or old-fashioned. **2.** *Brit.* any woman considered to be prim, prudish, or old-fashioned. —**ˈschool+ˌmarm+ish** *adj.*

school+mas•ter (ˈskuːlˌmɑːstə) *n.* **1.** a man who teaches in or runs a school. **2.** a person or thing that acts as an instructor. **3.** a food fish, *Lutjanus apodus,* of the warm waters of the Caribbean and Atlantic: family *Lutjanidae* (snappers). ~vb. (*intr.*) **4.** to be a schoolmaster. —**ˈschool+ˌmas•ter+ˌship** *n.*

school+mate (ˈskuːlˌmeɪt) *or* **school+fel•low** *n.* a companion at school; fellow pupil.

school+mis•tress (ˈskuːlˌmɪstrɪs) *n.* a woman who teaches in or runs a school. —**ˈschool+ˌmis•tress•y** *adj.*

Schools (skuːlz) *pl. n.* **1. the.** the medieval Schoolmen collectively. **2.** (at Oxford University) **a.** the Examination Schools, the University building in which examinations are held. **b.** *Informal.* the Second Public Examination for the degree of Bachelor of Arts; finals.

school ship *n.* a ship for training young men in seamanship, for a career in the regular or merchant navy.

school+teach·er ('sku:l,ti:tʃə) *n.* a person who teaches in a school.

school wel+fare of+fic+er *n. Brit.* a social worker concerned with school attendance and the issue of free school dinners, clothes, and transport for children in need.

school year *n.* **1.** a twelve-month period, usually of three terms, during which pupils remain in the same class. **2.** the time during this period when the school is open.

schoon+er ('sku:nə) *n.* **1.** a sailing vessel with at least two masts, with all lower sails rigged fore-and-aft. **2.** *Brit.* a large glass for sherry. **3.** *U.S., Austral.* a large glass for beer. [C18: origin uncertain]

Scho·pen·hau·er (*German* 'ʃo:pənˌhauər) *n.* **Ar·thur** ('artur). 1788–1860, German pessimist philosopher. In his chief work, *The World as Will and Idea* (1819), he expounded the view that will is the creative primary factor and idea the secondary receptive factor. —**Scho+pen+hau+er+i·an** (ˌʃəupən'hauərıən) *adj.* —**'Scho+pen+ˌhau+er+ˌism** *n.*

schorl (ʃɔ:l) *n.* a black tourmaline consisting of a borosilicate of sodium, iron, and aluminium. Formula: $NaFe_3B_3Al_3(Al_3Si_6O_{27})(OH)_4$. [C18: from German *Schörl*, origin unknown] —**schor+'la+ceous** *adj.*

schot+tische (ʃɒ'ti:ʃ) *n.* **1.** a 19th-century German dance resembling a slow polka. **2.** a piece of music composed for or in the manner of this dance. [C19: from German *der schottische Tanz* the Scottish dance]

Schott·ky noise ('ʃɒtkı) *n.* another name for **shot noise.** [after Walter *Schottky* (born 1886), German physicist]

Schou+ten Is+lands ('ʃautən) *pl. n.* a group of islands in the Pacific, off the N coast of West Irian. Pop.: 25 487 (1966). Area: 3185 sq. km (1230 sq. miles).

Schrö·ding·er (*German* 'ʃrø:dıŋər) *n.* **Er·win** ('ɛrvi:n). 1887–1961, Austrian physicist, who discovered the wave equation: shared the Nobel prize for physics (1933).

Schrö·ding·er e·qua·tion *n.* an equation used in wave mechanics to describe a physical system. For a particle of mass *m* and potential energy *V* it is written $(ih/2\pi).(\partial\psi/\partial t) = (-h/8\pi^2m^2)\nabla^2\psi + V\psi$, where $i = \sqrt{-1}$, *h* is the Planck constant, *t* the time, ∇^2 the Laplace operator, and ψ the wave function. Also called: **wave equation.**

Schu·bert ('ʃu:bət) *n.* **Franz (Peter)** (frants). 1797–1828, Austrian composer; the originator and supreme exponent of the modern German lied. His many songs include the cycles *Die Schöne Müllerin* (1823) and *Die Winterreise* (1827). His other works include symphonies and much piano and chamber music including string quartets and the *Trout* piano quintet (1819).

schul (ʃu:l) *n.* a variant spelling of **shul.**

Schu·mach·er (*German* 'ʃu:maxər) *n.* **Ernst Frie·drich** (ɛrnst 'fri:drıç). 1911–77, British economist, born in Germany. He is best known for his book *Small is Beautiful* (1973).

Schu·man *n.* **1.** (*French* ʃu'man). **Ro·bert** (rɔ'bɛ:r). 1886–1963, French statesman; prime minister (1947–48). He proposed (1950) pooling the coal and steel resources of W Europe. **2.** ('ʃu:mən). **Wil·liam (Howard).** born 1910, U.S. composer.

Schu·mann ('ʃu:mən) *n.* **1. E·liz·a·beth** (e'li:zabɛt). 1885–1952, German soprano, noted esp. for her interpretations of lieder. **2. Ro·bert A·le·xan·der** ('ro:bɛrt alɛ'ksandər). 1810–56, German romantic composer, noted esp. for his piano music, such as *Carnaval* (1835) and *Kreisleriana* (1838), his songs, and four symphonies.

schuss (ʃʊs) *Skiing.* ~*n.* **1.** a straight high-speed downhill run. ~*vb.* **2.** (*intr.*) to perform a schuss. [German: SHOT[1]]

Schütz (*German* ʃyts) *n.* **Hein·rich** ('haınrıç). 1585–1672, German composer, esp. of church music and madrigals.

Schutz+staf+fel *German.* ('ʃutsˌʃtafəl) *n., pl.* **+feln** (-fəln). See **SS.**

schwa *or* **shwa** (ʃwɑ:) *n.* **1.** a central vowel represented in the International Phonetic Alphabet by (ə). The sound occurs in unstressed syllables in English, as in *around, mother,* and *sofa.* **2.** the symbol (ə) used to represent this sound. [C19: via German from Hebrew *shewā*, a diacritic indicating lack of a vowel sound]

Schwa+ben ('ʃva:bən) *n.* the German name for **Swabia.**

Schwann (*German* ʃvan) *n.* **The·o·dor** ('te:oˌdo:r). 1810–82, German physiologist, who founded the theory that all animals consist of cells or cell products.

Schwarz·kopf (*German* 'ʃvartsˌkɔpf) *n.* **E·liz·a·beth** (e'li:zabɛt). born 1915, German operatic soprano.

Schwarz+wald ('ʃvartsˌvalt) *n.* the German name for the **Black Forest.**

Schwein+furt (*German* 'ʃvaınfʊrt) *n.* a city in central West Germany, in N Bavaria on the River Main. Pop.: 58 200 (1970).

Schweit·zer ('ʃwaıtsə, 'ʃvaıt-) *n.* **Al·bert.** 1875–1965, Franco-German medical missionary, philosopher, theologian, and organist, born in Alsace. He took up medicine in 1905 and devoted most of his life after 1913 to a medical mission at Lambaréné, Gabon: Nobel peace prize 1952.

Schweiz (ʃvaıts) *n.* the German name for **Switzerland.**

Schwe+rin (*German* ʃve'ri:n) *n.* a city in N East Germany, on **Lake Schwerin:** capital of the former state of Mecklenburg. Pop.: 105 951 (1975 est.).

Schwit·ters (*German* 'ʃvıtərs) *n.* **Kurt** (kʊrt). 1887–1948, German dadaist painter and poet, noted for his collages composed of discarded materials.

Schwyz (*German* ʃvi:ts) *n.* **1.** a canton of central Switzerland: played an important part in the formation of the Swiss confederation, to which it gave its name. Capital: Schwyz. Pop.: 92 072 (1970). Area: 908 sq. km (351 sq. miles). **2.** a town in E central Switzerland, capital of Schwyz canton: tourism. Pop.: 12 194 (1970).

sci. *abbrev. for:* **1.** science. **2.** scientific.

sci+ae·nid (saı'i:nıd) *or* **sci+ae·noid** *adj.* **1.** of, relating to, or belonging to the *Sciaenidae*, a family of mainly tropical and subtropical marine percoid fishes that includes the drums, grunts, and croakers. ~*n.* **2.** any sciaenid fish. [C19: from Latin *sciaena* a type of fish, from Greek *skiaina*]

sci+am·a+chy (saı'æməkı), **sci+om·a+chy,** *or* **ski+am·a+chy** (skaı'æməkı) *n., pl.* **+chies.** *Rare.* a fight with an imaginary enemy. [C17: from Greek *skiamakhia* a mock fight, from *skia* a shadow + *makhesthai* to fight]

sci+at+ic (saı'ætık) *adj.* **1.** *Anatomy.* of or relating to the hip or the hipbone. **2.** of, relating to, or afflicted with sciatica. [C16: from French *sciatique*, from Late Latin *sciaticus*, from Latin *ischiadicus* relating to pain in the hip, from Greek *iskhiadikos*, from *iskhia* hip-joint]

sci+at·i·ca (saı'ætıkə) *n.* a form of neuralgia characterized by intense pain and tenderness along the course of the body's longest nerve (**sciatic nerve**), extending from the back of the thigh down to the calf of the leg. [C15: from Late Latin *sciatica;* see SCIATIC]

sci+ence ('saıəns) *n.* **1.** the systematic study of the nature and behaviour of the material and physical universe, based on observation, experiment, and measurement, and the formulation of laws to describe these facts in general terms. **2.** the knowledge so obtained or the practice of obtaining it. **3.** any particular branch of this knowledge: *the pure and applied sciences.* **4.** any body of knowledge organized in a systematic manner. **5.** skill or technique. **6.** *Archaic.* knowledge. [C14: via Old French from Latin *scientia* knowledge, from *scīre* to know]

sci+ence fic+tion *n.* **a.** a literary genre that makes imaginative use of scientific knowledge or conjecture. **b.** (*as modifier*): *a science fiction writer.*

sci+en+ter (saı'ɛntə) *adv. Law.* knowingly; wilfully. [from Latin]

sci+en+tial (saı'ɛnʃəl) *adj.* **1.** of or relating to science. **2.** skilful or knowledgeable.

sci+en+tif+ic (ˌsaıən'tıfık) *adj.* **1.** (*prenominal*) of, relating to, derived from, or used in science: *scientific equipment.* **2.** (*prenominal*) occupied in science: *scientific manpower.* **3.** conforming with the principles or methods used in science: *a scientific approach.* —**ˌsci+en+'tif·i·cal+ly** *adv.*

sci+en+tif+ic meth+od *n.* a method of investigation in which a problem is first identified and observations, experiments, or other relevant data are then used to construct or test hypotheses that purport to solve it.

sci+en+tif+ic so+cial+ism *n.* Marxist socialism. Compare **utopian socialism.**

sci+en+tism ('saıənˌtızəm) *n.* **1.** the application of, or belief in, the scientific method. **2.** the uncritical application of scientific or quasi-scientific methods to inappropriate fields of study or investigation. —**ˌsci+en+'tis+tic** *adj.*

sci+en+tist ('saıəntıst) *n.* a person who studies or practises any of the sciences or who uses scientific methods.

Sci+en+tist ('saıəntıst) *n.* **1.** *Christian Science.* Christ as supreme spiritual healer. **2.** short for **Christian Scientist.**

Sci+en+tol+o·gy (ˌsaıən'tɒlədʒı) *n.* a cult, founded in the early 1950s, based on the belief that self-awareness is paramount, that rejects the notion of a supreme being, and that believes in reincarnation. [C20: from Latin *scient(ia)* SCIENCE + -OLOGY] —**ˌSci+en+'tol·o·gist** *n.*

sci-fi ('saı'faı) *n.* short for **science fiction.**

scil·i+cet ('sılıˌsɛt) *n.* namely; that is: used esp. in explaining a text that is obscure or supplying a missing word. [Latin: shortened from *scīre licet* it is permitted to know]

scil+la ('sılə) *n.* any liliaceous plant of the genus *Scilla*, of Old World temperate regions, having small bell-shaped flowers. See also **squill** (sense 3). [C19: via Latin from Greek *skilla;* compare SQUILL]

Scil+ly Isles, Scil+ly Is+lands ('sılı), *or* **Scil+lies** ('sılız) *pl. n.* a group of about 140 small islands (only five inhabited) off the extreme SW coast of England: administratively part of the county of Cornwall; tourist centre. Capital: Hugh Town. Pop.: 2428 (1971). Area: 16 sq. km (6 sq. miles). —**Scil+lo+ni·an** (sı'ləunıən) *adj., n.*

scim·i·tar *or* **sim·i·tar** ('sımıtə) *n.* an oriental sword with a curved blade. [C16: from Old Italian *scimitarra*, probably from Persian *shimshīr*, of obscure origin]

scin+coid ('sıŋkɔıd) *or* **scin+coid+i·an** *adj.* **1.** of, relating to, or resembling a skink. ~*n.* **2.** any animal, esp. a lizard, resembling a skink. [C18: from New Latin *scincoidēs*, from Latin *scincus* a SKINK]

scin+tig+ra+phy (ˌsın'tıgrəfı) *n. Med.* a diagnostic technique using a radioactive tracer and scintillation counter for producing pictures (**scintigrams**) of internal parts of the body. [C20: from SCINTI(LLATION) + -GRAPHY]

scin+til+la (sın'tılə) *n. Rare.* a minute amount; hint, trace, or particle. [C17: from Latin: a spark]

scin+til+late ('sıntıˌleıt) *vb.* (*mainly intr.*) **1.** (*also tr.*) to give off (sparks); sparkle; twinkle. **2.** to be animated or brilliant. **3.** *Physics.* to give off flashes of light as a result of the impact of particles or photons. [C17: from Latin *scintillāre*, from *scintilla* a spark] —'**scin·til·lant** *adj.* —'**scin·til·lant·ly** *adv.* —'**scin·til·ˌlat·ing·ly** *adv.*

scin·til·la·tion (ˌsɪntɪ'leɪʃən) *n.* **1.** the act of scintillating. **2.** a spark or flash. **3.** the twinkling of stars, caused by rapid changes in the density of the earth's atmosphere producing uneven refraction of starlight. **4.** *Physics.* a flash of light produced when a material scintillates.

scin·til·la·tion count·er *n.* an instrument for detecting and measuring the intensity of high-energy radiation. It consists of a phosphor with which particles collide producing flashes of light that are detected by a photomultiplier and converted into pulses of electric current that are counted by electronic equipment.

scin·til·la·tor ('sɪntɪˌleɪtə) *n.* *Physics.* a phosphor that produces scintillations.

scin·til·lom·e·ter (ˌsɪntɪ'lɒmɪtə) *n.* *Physics.* a device for observing ionizing radiation by the scintillations it produces in a suitable material.

sci·o·lism ('saɪəˌlɪzəm) *n.* *Rare.* the practice of opinionating on subjects of which one has only superficial knowledge. [C19: from Late Latin *sciolus* someone with a smattering of knowledge, from Latin *scīre* to know] —'**sci·o·list** *n.* —ˌ**sci·o·'lis·tic** *adj.*

sci·om·a·chy (saɪ'ɒməkɪ) *n., pl.* **·chies.** a variant spelling of **sciamachy.**

sci·o·man·cy ('saɪəˌmænsɪ) *n.* divination with the help of ghosts. [C17: via Latin from Greek *skia* ghost + -MANCY] —'**sci·o·man·cer** *n.* —ˌ**sci·o·'man·tic** *adj.*

sci·on ('saɪən) *n.* **1.** a descendant, heir, or young member of a family. **2.** a shoot or twig of a plant used to form a graft. [C14: from Old French *cion*, of Germanic origin; compare Old High German *chīnan* to sprout]

Scip·i·o ('sɪpɪˌəʊ) *n.* **1.** full name *Publius Cornelius Scipio Africanus Major.* 237–183 B.C., Roman general. He commanded the Roman invasion of Carthage in the Second Punic War, defeating Hannibal at Zama (202). **2.** full name *Publius Cornelius Scipio Aemilianus Africanus Minor.* ?185–129 B.C., Roman statesman and general; the grandson by adoption of Scipio Africanus Major. He commanded an army against Carthage in the last Punic War and razed the city to the ground (146). He became the leader (132) of the opposition in Rome to popular reforms.

sci·re fa·ci·as ('saɪərɪ 'feɪʃɪˌæs) *n.* *Law, rare.* **1.** a judicial writ founded upon some record, such as a judgment, letters patent, etc., requiring the person against whom it is brought to show cause why the record should not be enforced or annulled. **2.** a proceeding begun by the issue of such a writ. [C15: from legal Latin, literally: cause (him) to know]

scir·rhous ('sɪrəs) *adj.* *Pathol.* of or resembling a scirrhus; hard. —**scir·rhos·i·ty** (sɪ'rɒsɪtɪ) *n.*

scir·rhus ('sɪrəs) *n., pl.* **·rhi** (-raɪ) *or* **·rhus·es.** *Pathol.* a firm cancerous growth composed of fibrous tissues. [C17: from New Latin, from Latin *scirros*, from Greek *skirros*, from *skiros* hard] —**scir·rhoid** ('sɪrɔɪd) *n.*

scis·sel ('skɪsᵊl) *n.* the waste metal left over from sheet metal after discs have been punched out of it. [C19: from French *cisaille*, from *cisailler* to clip]

scis·sile ('sɪsaɪl) *adj.* capable of being cut or divided. [C17: from Latin *scissilis* that can be split, from *scindere* to cut]

scis·sion ('sɪʃən) *n.* the act or an instance of cutting, splitting, or dividing. [C15: from Late Latin *scissiō*, from *scindere* to split]

scis·sor ('sɪzə) *vb.* to cut (an object) with scissors.

scis·sors ('sɪzəz) *pl. n.* **1.** Also called: **pair of scissors.** a cutting instrument used for cloth, hair, etc., having two crossed pivoted blades that cut by a shearing action, with ring-shaped handles at one end. **2.** a wrestling hold in which a wrestler wraps his legs round his opponent's body or head, locks his feet together, and squeezes. **3.** any gymnastic or athletic feat in which the legs cross and uncross in a scissor-like movement. **4.** *Athletics.* a technique in high-jumping, now little used, in which the legs perform a scissor-like movement in clearing the bar. [C14 *sisoures*, from Old French *cisoires*, from Vulgar Latin *cīsōria* (unattested), ultimately from Latin *caedere* to cut; see CHISEL] —'**scis·sor·ˌlike** *adj.*

scis·sors kick *n.* **1.** a type of swimming kick used esp. in the sidestroke, in which one leg is moved forward and the other bent back and they are then brought together again in a scissor-like action. **2.** *Football.* a kick in which the player leaps into the air raising one leg and brings up his other leg to kick the ball.

scis·sure ('sɪʒə, 'sɪʃə) *n.* *Rare.* a longitudinal cleft. [C15: from Latin *scissūra* a rending, from Latin *scindere* to split]

sci·u·rine ('saɪjʊrɪn, -ˌraɪn) *adj.* **1.** of, relating to, or belonging to the *Sciuridae*, a family of rodents inhabiting most parts of the world except Australia and southern South America: includes squirrels, marmots, and chipmunks. ~*n.* **2.** any sciurine animal. [C19: from Latin *sciūrus*, from Greek *skiouros* squirrel, from *skia* a shadow + *oura* a tail]

sci·u·roid ('saɪjʊrɔɪd, saɪ'jʊərɔɪd) *adj.* **1.** (of an animal) resembling a squirrel. **2.** (esp. of the spikes of barley) shaped like a squirrel's tail. [C19: from Latin *sciūrus* squirrel + -OID]

sclaff (sklæf) *Golf.* ~*vb.* **1.** to cause (the club) to hit (the ground) when making a stroke. ~*n.* **2.** a sclaffing stroke or shot. ~Also: **duff**[2]. [C19: from Scottish *sclaf* to shuffle] —'**sclaff·er** *n.*

scle·ra ('sklɪərə) *n.* the firm white fibrous membrane that forms the outer covering of the eyeball. Also called: **sclerotic.** [C19: from New Latin, from Greek *sklēros* hard]

scle·ren·chy·ma (sklɪə'rɛŋkɪmə) *n.* a supporting tissue in plants consisting of dead cells with very thick lignified walls. [C19: from SCLERO- + PARENCHYMA] —**scle·ren·chym·a·tous** (ˌsklɪərɛŋ'kɪmətəs) *adj.*

scle·rite ('sklɪəraɪt) *n.* *Zoology.* **1.** any of the hard chitinous plates that make up the exoskeleton of an arthropod. **2.** any calcareous or chitinous part, such as a spicule or plate. [C19: from SCLERO- + -ITE[1]] —**scle·rit·ic** (sklɪə'rɪtɪk) *adj.*

scle·ri·tis (sklɪə'raɪtɪs) *or* **scle·ro·ti·tis** (ˌsklɪərəʊ'taɪtɪs) *n.* *Pathol.* inflammation of the sclera.

scle·ro- *or before a vowel* **scler-** *combining form.* **1.** indicating hardness: *sclerosis.* **2.** of or relating to the sclera: *sclerotomy.* [from Greek *sklēros* hard]

scle·ro·der·ma (ˌsklɪərəʊ'dɜːmə), **scle·ro·der·mi·a** (ˌsklɪərəʊ'dɜːmɪə), *or* **scle·ri·a·sis** (sklɪ'raɪəsɪs) *n.* a chronic progressive disease most common among women, characterized by a local or diffuse thickening and hardening of the skin.

scle·ro·der·ma·tous (ˌsklɪərəʊ'dɜːmətəs) *adj.* **1.** (of animals) possessing a hard external covering of scales or plates. **2.** of or relating to scleroderma.

scle·roid ('sklɪərɔɪd) *adj.* (of organisms and their parts) hard or hardened.

scle·ro·ma (sklɪə'rəʊmə) *n., pl.* **·ma·ta** (-mətə). *Pathol.* any small area of abnormally hard tissue, esp. in a mucous membrane. [C17: from New Latin, from Greek, from *sklēroun* to harden, from *sklēros* hard]

scle·rom·e·ter (sklɪə'rɒmɪtə) *n.* an instrument that determines the hardness of a mineral or metal by means of a diamond point. —**scler·o·met·ric** (ˌsklɪərə'mɛtrɪk) *adj.*

scle·ro·phyll ('sklɛrəʊˌfɪl) *n.* a woody plant with small leathery evergreen leaves that is the dominant plant form in certain hot dry areas, esp. the Mediterranean region. —**scle·roph·yl·lous** (sklɛ'rɒfɪləs) *adj.*

scle·ro·pro·tein (ˌsklɪərəʊ'prəʊtiːn) *n.* any of a group of insoluble stable proteins such as keratin, elastin, and collagen that occur in skeletal and connective tissues. Also called: **albuminoid.**

scle·rosed ('sklɪərəʊst) *adj.* *Pathol.* hardened; sclerotic.

scle·ro·sis (sklɪə'rəʊsɪs) *n., pl.* **·ses** (-siːz). **1.** *Pathol.* a hardening or thickening of organs, tissues, or vessels from chronic inflammation, abnormal growth of fibrous tissue, or degeneration of the myelin sheath of nerve fibres, or (esp. on the inner walls of arteries) deposition of fatty plaques. Compare **arteriosclerosis, atherosclerosis, multiple sclerosis. 2.** the hardening of a plant cell wall or tissue by the deposition of lignin. [C14: via Medieval Latin from Greek *sklērōsis* a hardening] —**scle·'ro·sal** *adj.*

scle·rot·ic (sklɪə'rɒtɪk) *adj.* **1.** of or relating to the sclera. **2.** of, relating to, or having sclerosis. **3.** *Botany.* characterized by the hardening and strengthening of cell walls. ~*n.* **4.** another name for **sclera.** [C16: from Medieval Latin *sclērōticus*, from Greek; see SCLEROMA]

scle·ro·ti·um (sklɪə'rəʊʃɪəm) *n., pl.* **·ti·a** (-ʃɪə). a compact mass of hyphae, that is formed by certain fungi and gives rise to new fungal growth or spore-producing structures. [C18: from New Latin, from Greek *sklēros* hard] —**scle·'ro·ti·oid** *or* **scle·'ro·tial** *adj.*

scle·rot·o·my (sklɪə'rɒtəmɪ) *n., pl.* **·mies.** surgical incision into the sclera.

scle·rous ('sklɪərəs) *adj.* *Anatomy, pathol.* hard; bony; indurated. [C19: from Greek *sklēros* hard]

S.C.M. (in Britain) *abbrev. for:* **1.** State Certified Midwife. **2.** Student Christian Movement.

scoff[1] (skɒf) *vb.* **1.** (*intr.;* often foll. by *at*) to speak contemptuously (about); express derision (for); mock. **2.** (*tr.*) *Obsolete.* to regard with derision. ~*n.* **3.** an expression of derision. **4.** an object of derision. [C14: probably from Scandinavian; compare Old Frisian *skof* mockery, Danish *skof, skuf* jest] —'**scoff·er** *n.* —'**scoff·ing·ly** *adv.*

scoff[2] (skɒf) *Slang, chiefly Brit.* ~*vb.* **1.** to eat (food) fast and greedily; devour. ~*n.* **2.** food or rations. [C19: variant of *scaff* food; related to Afrikaans, Dutch *schoft* quarter of the day, one of the four daily meals]

scoff·law ('skɒflɔː) *n.* *U.S. informal.* a person who habitually flouts or violates the law, esp. one who fails to pay debts or answer summonses.

Sco·field ('skəʊfiːld) *n.* **Paul.** born 1922, English stage and film actor.

scold (skəʊld) *vb.* **1.** to find fault with or reprimand (a person) harshly; chide. **2.** (*intr.*) to use harsh or abusive language. ~*n.* **3.** a person, esp. a woman, who constantly finds fault. [C13: from Old Norse SKALD] —'**scold·a·ble** *adj.* —'**scold·er** *n.* —'**scold·ing** *n.* —'**scold·ing·ly** *adv.*

scol·e·cite ('skɒlɪˌsaɪt, 'skəʊl-) *n.* a white zeolite mineral consisting of hydrated calcium aluminium silicate in groups of radiating monoclinic crystals. Formula: $CaAl_2Si_3O_{10}.3H_2O$. [C19: *scolec-* from Greek *skōlēx* SCOLEX + -ITE[1]]

sco·lex ('skəʊlɛks) *n., pl.* **sco·le·ces** (skəʊ'liːsiːz) *or* **scol·i·ces** ('skɒlɪˌsiːz, 'skəʊ-). the headlike part of a tapeworm, bearing hooks and suckers by which the animal is attached to the tissues of its host. [C19: from New Latin, from Greek *skōlēx* worm]

sco·li·o·sis (ˌskɒlɪ'əʊsɪs) *or* **sco·li·o·ma** *n.* *Pathol.* an abnormal lateral curvature of the spine, of congenital origin or caused by trauma or disease of the vertebrae or hipbones. Compare **kyphosis, lordosis.** [C18: from New Latin, from Greek: a curving, from *skolios* bent] —**sco·li·ot·ic** (ˌskɒlɪ'ɒtɪk) *adj.*

scol·lop ('skɒləp) *n., vb.* a variant spelling of **scallop.**

scol·o+pen+drid (ˌskɒlə'pɛndrɪd) *n.* any centipede of the family *Scolopendridae,* including some large and poisonous species. [C19: from New Latin *Scolopendridae,* from Latin *scolopendra,* from Greek *skolopendra* legendary sea-fish] **—scol·o+pen+drine** (ˌskɒlə'pɛndraɪn, -drɪn) *adj.*

scom+broid ('skɒmbrɔɪd) *adj.* **1.** of, relating to, or belonging to the *Scombroidea,* a suborder of marine spiny-finned fishes having a spindle-shaped body and a forked powerful tail: includes the mackerels, tunnies, bonitos, swordfish, and sailfish. *~n.* **2.** any fish belonging to the suborder *Scombroidea.* [C19: from Greek *skombros* a mackerel; see -OID]

sconce[1] (skɒns) *n.* **1.** a bracket fixed to a wall for holding candles or lights. **2.** a flat candlestick with a handle. [C14: from Old French *esconse* hiding place, lantern, or from Late Latin *sconsa,* from *absconsa* dark lantern]

sconce[2] (skɒns) *n.* a small protective fortification, such as an earthwork. [C16: from Dutch *schans,* from Middle High German *schanze* bundle of brushwood]

sconce[3] (skɒns) (at Oxford and Cambridge Universities, esp. formerly) *~vb.* (*tr.*) **1.** to challenge (a fellow student) on the grounds of a social misdemeanour to drink a large quantity of beer without stopping. **2.** *Obsolete.* to fine (a student) for some minor misdemeanour. *~n.* **3.** the act of sconcing. **4.** a mug or tankard used in sconcing. [C17: of obscure origin]

sconce[4] (skɒns) *n. Archaic.* **1.** the head or skull. **2.** sense, brain, or wit. [C16: probably jocular use of SCONCE[1]]

scone (skəʊn, skɒn) *n.* a light plain doughy cake made from flour with very little fat, cooked in an oven or (esp. originally) on a griddle, usually split open and buttered. [C16: Scottish, perhaps from Middle Low German *schonbrot,* Middle Dutch *schoonbrot* fine bread]

Scone (skuːn) *n.* a parish in E Scotland near Perth, consisting of the two villages of New Scone and Old Scone, which was the Pictish capital: original site of the stone upon which medieval Scottish kings were crowned. The stone was removed to Westminster Abbey by Edward I in 1296.

scoop (skuːp) *n.* **1.** a utensil used as a shovel or ladle, esp. a small shovel with deep sides and a short handle, used for taking up flour, etc. **2.** a utensil with a long handle and round bowl used for dispensing liquids, etc. **3.** anything that resembles a scoop in action, such as the bucket on a dredge. **4.** a spoonlike surgical instrument for scraping or extracting foreign matter, etc., from the body. **5.** the quantity taken up by a scoop. **6.** the act of scooping, dredging, etc. **7.** a hollow cavity. **8.** *Slang.* a large quick gain, as of money. **9.** a news story reported in one newspaper, etc., before all the others; an exclusive. **10.** any sensational piece of news. *~vb.* (*mainly tr.*) **11.** (often foll. by *up*) to take up and remove (an object or substance) with or as if with a scoop. **12.** (often foll. by *out*) to hollow out with or as if with a scoop: *to scoop a hole in a hillside.* **13.** to make (a large sudden profit). **14.** to beat (rival newspapers, etc.) in uncovering a news item. **15.** *Hockey, golf, etc.* to hit (the ball) on its underside so that it rises into the air. [C14: via Middle Dutch *schōpe* from Germanic; compare Old High German *scephan* to ladle, German *schöpfen, Schaufel* SHOVEL, Dutch *schoep* vessel for baling] **—'scoop+er** *n.* **—'scoopˌful** *n.*

scoop neck *n.* a rounded low-cut neckline on a woman's garment.

scoot (skuːt) *vb.* **1.** to go or cause to go quickly or hastily; dart or cause to dart off or away. *~n.* **2.** the act of scooting. [C19 (U.S.): of unknown origin]

scoot+er ('skuːtə) *n.* **1.** a child's vehicle consisting of a low footboard mounted between two small wheels with a handlebar. It is propelled by pushing one foot against the ground. **2.** See **motor scooter. 3.** (in the U.S. and Canada) another term for **iceyacht. 'scoot+er+ist** *n.*

scop (skɒp) *n.* (in Anglo-Saxon England) a bard or minstrel. [Old English: related to Old Norse *skop, skaup,* Old High German *scof, scopf* poem]

Sco·pas ('skəʊpəs) *n.* 4th century B.C., Greek sculptor and architect.

scope (skəʊp) *n.* **1.** opportunity for exercising the faculties or abilities; capacity for action. **2.** range of view, perception, or grasp; outlook. **3.** the area covered by an activity, topic, etc.; range: *the scope of his thesis was vast.* **4.** *Nautical.* slack left in an anchor cable. **5.** *Logic.* the part of a formula that follows a quantifier or an operator. **6.** *Informal.* short for **telescope, microscope, oscilloscope,** etc. **7.** *Archaic.* purpose or aim. [C16: from Italian *scopo* goal, from Latin *scopus,* from Greek *skopos* target; related to Greek *skopein* to watch]

-scope *n. combining form.* indicating an instrument for observing, viewing, or detecting: *microscope; stethoscope.* [from New Latin *-scopium,* from Greek *-skopion,* from *skopein* to look at] **—-scop·ic** *adj. combining form.*

sco+pol·a+mine (skə'pɒləˌmiːn, -mɪn; ˌskəʊpə'læmɪn) *n.* a colourless viscous liquid alkaloid extracted from certain plants, such as henbane: used in preventing travel sickness and as an anticholinergic, sedative, and truth serum. Formula: $C_{17}H_{21}NO_4$. Also called: **hyoscine.** See also **atropine.** [C20: *scopol-* from New Latin *scopolia Japonica* Japanese belladonna (from which the alkaloid is extracted), named after G. A. *Scopoli* (1723–88), Italian naturalist, + AMINE]

sco+po+line ('skəʊpəˌliːn, -lɪn) *n.* a soluble crystalline alkaloid obtained from the decomposition of scopolamine and used as a sedative. Formula: $C_8H_{13}NO_2$. Also called: **oscine.** [C19: from *scopol-* (as in SCOPOLAMINE) + -INE[2]]

scop·u+la ('skɒpjʊlə) *n., pl.* **+las** *or* **+lae** (-ˌliː). a small tuft of dense hairs on the legs and chelicerae of some spiders. [C19: from Late Latin: a broom-twig, from *scōpa* thin twigs] **—scop·u+late** ('skɒpjʊˌleɪt, -lɪt) *adj.*

Sco+pus ('skəʊpəs) *n.* **Mount.** a mountain in central Israel, east of Jerusalem: a N extension of the Mount of Olives; site of the Hebrew University (1925). Height: 834 m (2736 ft.).

-sco·py *combining form.* indicating a viewing or observation: *microscopy.* [from Greek *-skopia,* from *skopein* to look at]

scor+bu+tic (skɔː'bjuːtɪk) *or* **scor+bu+ti+cal** *adj.* of, relating to, or having scurvy. [C17: from New Latin *scorbūticus,* from Medieval Latin *scorbūtus,* probably of Germanic origin; compare Old English *sceorf* scurf, Middle Low German *scorbuk* scurvy] **—scor+'bu+ti+cal+ly** *adv.*

scorch (skɔːtʃ) *vb.* **1.** to burn or become burnt, so as to affect the colour, taste, etc., or to cause or feel pain. **2.** to wither or parch or cause to wither from exposure to heat. **3.** (*intr.*) *Informal.* to be very hot: *it is scorching outside.* **4.** (*tr.*) *Informal.* to criticize harshly. **5.** (*intr.*) *Brit. slang.* to drive or ride very fast. *~n.* **6.** a slight burn. **7.** a mark caused by the application of too great heat. **8.** *Horticulture.* a mark or series of marks on fruit, etc., caused by pests or insecticides. [C15: probably from Old Norse *skorpna* to shrivel up] **—'scorch+ing** *adj.*

scorched earth pol·i+cy *n.* the policy in warfare of removing or destroying everything that might be useful to an invading enemy, esp. by fire.

scorch+er ('skɔːtʃə) *n.* **1.** a person or thing that scorches. **2.** something severe or caustic. **3.** *Informal.* a very hot day. **4.** *Brit. informal.* something remarkable.

score (skɔː) *n.* **1.** an evaluative usually numerical record of a competitive game or match. **2.** the total number of points made by a side or individual in a game or match. **3.** the act of scoring, esp. a point or points. **4. the score.** *Informal.* the actual situation; the true facts: *to know the score.* **5.** *U.S.* the result of a test or exam. **6.** a group or set of twenty: *three score years and ten.* **7.** (*usually pl.;* foll. by *of*) a great number; lots: *I have scores of things to do.* **8.** *Music.* **a.** the written or printed form of a composition in which the instrumental or vocal parts appear on separate staves vertically arranged on large pages (**full score**) or in a condensed version, usually for piano (**short score**) or voices and piano (**vocal score**). **b.** the incidental music for a film or play. **c.** the songs, music, etc., for a stage or film musical. **9.** a mark or notch, esp. one made in keeping a tally. **10.** an account of amounts due. **11.** an amount recorded as due. **12.** a reason or account: *the book was rejected on the score of length.* **13.** a grievance. **14. a.** a line marking a division or boundary. **b.** (*as modifier*): *score line.* **15.** *Informal.* the victim of a theft or swindle. **16.** *Dancing.* notation indicating a dancer's moves. **17. settle** *or* **pay off a score. a.** to avenge a wrong. **b.** to repay a debt. *~vb.* **18.** to gain (a point or points) in a game or contest. **19.** (*tr.*) to make a total score of: *to score twelve.* **20.** to keep a record of the score (of). **21.** (*tr.*) to be worth (a certain amount) in a game. **22.** (*tr.*) *U.S.* to evaluate (a test, etc.) numerically; mark. **23.** (*tr.*) to record by making notches in. **24.** to make (cuts, lines, etc.) in or on. **25.** (*intr.*) *Slang.* to obtain something desired, esp. to purchase an illegal drug. **26.** (*intr.*) *Slang.* (of men) to be successful in seducing a person. **27.** (*tr.*) **a.** to set or arrange (a piece of music) for specific instruments or voices. **b.** to write the music for (a film, play, etc.). **28.** to achieve (success or an advantage): *your idea really scored with the boss.* **29.** (*tr.*) *Chiefly U.S.* to criticize harshly; berate. **30.** to accumulate or keep a record of (a debt). [Old English *scora;* related to Old Norse *skor* notch, tally, twenty] **—'scor+er** *n.*

score+board ('skɔːˌbɔːd) *n. Sport, etc.* a board for displaying the score of a game or match.

score+card ('skɔːˌkɑːd) *n.* **1.** a card on which scores are recorded in various games, esp. golf. **2.** a card identifying the players in a sports match, esp. cricket or baseball.

score off *vb.* (*intr., prep.*) to gain an advantage at someone else's expense.

sco+ri·a ('skɔːrɪə) *n., pl.* **+ri·ae** (-rɪˌiː). **1.** a rough heavy mass of solidified lava containing many cavities. **2.** refuse obtained from smelted ore; slag. [C17: from Latin: dross, from Greek *skōria,* from *skōr* excrement] **—sco+ri·a+ceous** (ˌskɔːrɪ'eɪʃəs) *adj.*

sco+ri+fy ('skɔːrɪˌfaɪ) *vb.* **+fies, +fy+ing, +fied.** to remove (impurities) from metals by forming scoria. **—ˌsco+ri+fi+'ca+tion** *n.* **—'sco+ri+ˌfi+er** *n.*

scorn (skɔːn) *n.* **1.** open contempt or disdain for a person or thing; derision. **2.** an object of contempt or derision. **3.** *Archaic.* an act or expression signifying contempt. *~vb.* **4.** to treat with contempt or derision. **5.** (*tr.*) to reject with contempt. [C12 *schornen,* from Old French *escharnir,* of Germanic origin; compare Old High German *scerōn* to behave rowdily, obsolete Dutch *schern* mockery] **—'scorn+er** *n.* **—'scorn+ful** *adj.* **—'scorn+ful+ly** *adv.* **—'scorn+ful+ness** *n.*

scor+pae+nid (skɔː'piːnɪd) *n.* **1.** any spiny-finned marine fish of the family *Scorpaenidae,* having sharp spines on the fins and a heavy armoured head: includes the scorpion fishes, rockfishes, and redfishes. *~adj.* **2.** of, relating to, or belonging to the family *Scorpaenidae.* [via New Latin from Latin *scorpaena* a sea-scorpion; see SCORPION]

scor+pae+noid (skɔː'piːnɔɪd) *adj.* **1.** of, relating to, or belonging to the *Scorpaenoidea,* a suborder of spiny-finned fishes having bony plates covering the head: includes the sculpins, scorpion fishes, gurnards, etc. *~n.* **2.** any fish belonging to the suborder *Scorpaenoidea.*

scor+per *or* **scau+per** ('skɔːpə) *n.* a kind of fine chisel with a square or curved tip used in wood engraving for clearing away large areas of the block or clearing away lines. [C19: erroneously for *scauper* scalper, from Latin *scalper* knife]

Scor·pi·o ('skɔːpɪˌəʊ) *n.* **1.** Also called: the **Scorpion.** *Astrology.* **a.** the eighth sign of the zodiac, symbol ♏, having a fixed water classification and ruled by the planets Mars and Pluto. The sun is in this sign between about Oct. 23 and Nov. 21. **b.** a person born during a period when the sun is in this sign. **2.** *Astronomy.* another name for **Scorpius.** ~*adj.* **3.** *Astrology.* born under or characteristic of Scorpio. ~Also (for senses 1b., 3): **Scor·pi·on·ic** (ˌskɔːpɪ'ɒnɪk). [Latin: SCORPION]

scor·pi·oid ('skɔːpɪˌɔɪd) *adj.* **1.** of, relating to, or resembling scorpions or the order (*Scorpionida*) to which they belong. **2.** *Botany.* (esp. of a cymose inflorescence) having the main stem coiled during development.

scor·pi·on ('skɔːpɪən) *n.* **1.** any arachnid of the order *Scorpionida,* of warm dry regions, having a segmented body with a long tail terminating in a venomous sting. **2. false scorpion.** any small nonvenomous arachnid of the order *Pseudoscorpionida* (or *Chelonethida*), which superficially resemble scorpions but lack the long tail. See **book scorpion. 3.** any of various other similar arachnids, such as the whip scorpion, or other arthropods, such as the water scorpion. **4.** *Old Testament.* a barbed scourge (I Kings 12:11). **5.** *History.* a war engine for hurling stones; ballista. [C13: via Old French from Latin *scorpiō,* from Greek *skorpios,* of obscure origin]

Scor·pi·on ('skɔːpɪən) *n.* **the.** the constellation Scorpio, the eighth sign of the zodiac.

scor·pi·on fish *n.* any of various scorpaenid fishes of the genus *Scorpaena* and related genera, of temperate and tropical seas, having venomous spines on the dorsal and anal fins.

scor·pi·on fly *n.* any of various insects of the family *Panorpidae,* of the N hemisphere, having a scorpion-like but nonvenomous tail in the males, long antennae, and a beaklike snout: order *Mecoptera.*

scor·pi·on grass *n.* another name for **forget-me-not.**

Scor·pi·us ('skɔːpɪəs) *n., Latin genitive* **Scor·pi·i** ('skɔːpɪˌaɪ). a large zodiacal constellation lying between Libra and Sagittarius and crossed by the Milky Way. It contains the first magnitude star Antares. Also called: **Scorpio.**

Scot (skɒt) *n.* **1.** a native or inhabitant of Scotland. **2.** a member of a tribe of Celtic raiders from northern Ireland who carried out periodic attacks against the British mainland coast from the 3rd century A.D., eventually settling in N Britain during the 5th and 6th centuries.

Scot. *abbrev. for:* **1.** Scotch (whisky). **2.** Scotland. **3.** Scottish.

scot and lot *n. British history.* a municipal tax paid by burgesses and others that came to be regarded as a qualification for the borough franchise in parliamentary elections (until the Reform Act of 1832). [C13 *scot* tax, from Germanic; compare Old Norse *skot;* related to Old French *escot* (French *écot*)]

scotch[1] (skɒtʃ) *vb.* (*tr.*) **1.** to put an end to; crush: *bad weather scotched our plans.* **2.** *Archaic.* to injure so as to render harmless. **3.** *Obsolete.* to cut or score. ~*n.* **4.** *Archaic.* a gash; scratch. **5.** a line marked down, as for hopscotch. [C15: of obscure origin]

scotch[2] (skɒtʃ) *vb.* **1.** (*tr.*) to block, prop, or prevent from moving with or as if with a wedge. ~*n.* **2.** a block or wedge to prevent motion. [C17: of obscure origin]

Scotch[1] (skɒtʃ) *adj.* **1.** another word for **Scottish.** ~*n.* **2.** the Scots or their language.

Usage. In the north of England and in Scotland, *Scotch* is not used outside fixed expressions such as *Scotch whisky.* The use of *Scotch* for *Scots* or *Scottish* is otherwise felt to be incorrect, esp. when applied to persons.

Scotch[2] (skɒtʃ) *n.* **1.** Also called: **Scotch whisky.** whisky distilled from fermented malted barley and made in Scotland. **2.** *Northeast Brit.* a type of relatively mild beer.

Scotch broth *n. Brit.* a thick soup made from beef stock, vegetables, and pearl barley.

Scotch egg *n. Brit.* a hard-boiled egg enclosed in a layer of sausage meat, covered in egg and crumbs, and fried.

Scotch·man ('skɒtʃmən) *n., pl.* **·men.** (*regarded as bad usage by the Scots*) another word for **Scotsman.** —**'Scotch·wom·an** *fem. n.*

Scotch mist *n.* **1.** a heavy wet mist. **2.** drizzle.

Scotch pan·cake *n.* another name for **drop scone.**

Scotch snap *n. Music.* a rhythmical pattern consisting of a short note followed by a long one. Also called: **Scotch catch.**

Scotch tape *n. Trademark.* a transparent or coloured adhesive tape made of cellulose or a similar substance.

Scotch ter·ri·er *n.* another name for **Scottish terrier.**

Scotch wood·cock *n.* hot toast spread with anchovies or anchovy paste and topped with creamy scrambled eggs.

sco·ter ('skəʊtə) *n., pl.* **·ters** *or* **·ter.** any sea duck of the genus *Melanitta,* such as *M. nigra* (**common scoter**), of northern regions. The male plumage is black with white patches around the head and eyes. [C17: origin unknown]

scot-free *adv., adj.* (*predicative*) without harm, loss, or penalty. [C16: see SCOT AND LOT]

sco·tia ('skəʊʃə) *n.* a deep concave moulding, esp. one used on the base of an Ionic column between the two torus mouldings. [C16: via Latin from Greek *skotia,* from *skotos* darkness (from the shadow in the cavity)]

Sco·tism ('skəʊtɪzəm) *n.* the doctrines of Duns Scotus, esp. those holding that philosophy and theology are independent. See **haecceity.** —**'Sco·tist** *n., adj.* —**Sco·'tis·tic** *adj.*

Scot·land ('skɒtlənd) *n.* a country that is part of the United Kingdom, occupying the north of Great Britain: the English and Scottish thrones were united under one monarch in 1603 and the parliaments in 1707. It consists of the Highlands in the north, the central Lowlands, and hilly uplands in the south; has a deeply indented coastline, about 800 offshore islands (mostly in the west), and many lochs. Capital: Edinburgh. Pop.: 5 205 100 (1976 est.). Area: 78 768 sq. km (30 412 sq. miles). Related adj.: **Caledonian.**

Scot·land Yard *n.* the headquarters of the police force of metropolitan London, controlled directly by the British Home Office and hence having certain national responsibilities. Official name: **New Scotland Yard.**

sco·to·ma (skɒ'təʊmə) *n., pl.* **·mas** *or* **·ma·ta** (-mətə). **1.** *Pathol.* a blind spot; a permanent or temporary area of depressed or absent vision caused by lesions of the optic nerve, viewing the sun directly (**eclipse scotoma**), squinting, etc. **2.** *Psychol.* a mental blind spot; inability to understand or perceive certain matters. [C16: via Medieval Latin from Greek *skotōma* giddiness, from *skotoun* to make dark, from *skotos* darkness] —**sco·tom·a·tous** (skɒ'tɒmətəs) *adj.*

sco·to·pi·a (skə'təʊpɪə, skəʊ-) *n.* the ability of the eye to adjust for night vision. [New Latin, from Greek *skotos* darkness + -OPIA] —**sco·top·ic** (skə'tɒpɪk, skəʊ-) *adj.*

Scots (skɒts) *adj.* **1.** of, relating to, or characteristic of Scotland, its people, their English dialect, or their Gaelic language. ~*n.* **2.** any of the English dialects spoken or written in Scotland.. See also **Lallans.**

Scots·man ('skɒtsmən) *n., pl.* **·men.** a native or inhabitant of Scotland. —**'Scots·wom·an** *fem. n.*

Scots pine *or* **Scotch pine** *n.* **1.** a coniferous tree, *Pinus sylvestris,* of Europe and W and N Asia, having blue-green needle-like leaves and brown cones with a small prickle on each scale: a valuable timber tree. **2.** the wood of this tree. ~Also called: **Scots** (or **Scotch**) **fir.**

Scott (skɒt) *n.* **1.** Sir **George Gil·bert.** 1811–78, English architect, prominent in the Gothic revival. He restored many churches and cathedrals and designed the Albert Memorial (1863) and St Pancras Station (1865). **2. Rob·ert Fal·con.** 1868–1912, English naval officer and explorer of the Antarctic. He commanded two Antarctic expeditions (1901–04; 1910–12) and reached the South Pole on Jan. 18, 1912, shortly after Amundsen; he and the rest of his party died on the return journey. **3.** Sir **Wal·ter.** 1771–1832, Scottish romantic novelist and poet. He is remembered chiefly for his tales inspired by Scottish history and folklore, esp. the "Waverley" novels, including *Waverley* (1814), *Rob Roy* (1817), *The Heart of Midlothian* (1818), *Ivanhoe* (1819), *Kenilworth* (1821), *Quentin Durward* (1823), and *Redgauntlet* (1824). His narrative poems include *The Lay of the Last Minstrel* (1805), *Marmion* (1808), and *The Lady of the Lake* (1810).

Scot·ti·cism ('skɒtɪˌsɪzəm) *n.* a Scottish idiom, word, etc.

Scot·tie *or* **Scot·ty** ('skɒtɪ) *n., pl.* **·ties. 1.** See **Scottish terrier. 2.** *Informal.* a Scotsman.

Scot·tish ('skɒtɪʃ) *adj.* **1.** of, relating to, or characteristic of Scotland, its people, their Gaelic language, or their English dialect. ~*n.* **2. the.** (*functioning as pl.*) the Scots collectively.

Scot·tish Cer·tif·i·cate of Ed·u·ca·tion *n.* the Scottish examination equivalent to the General Certificate of Education in England.

Scot·tish Gael·ic *n.* the Goidelic language of the Celts of Scotland, still spoken in the Highlands and Western Isles.

Scot·tish ter·ri·er *n.* a small long-haired breed of terrier, usually with a black coat, having erect ears and tail. Often shortened to **Scottie.**

Sco·tus ('skəʊtəs) *n.* See (John) **Duns Scotus.**

scoun·drel ('skaʊndrəl) *n.* a worthless or villainous person. [C16: of unknown origin] —**'scoun·drel·ly** *adj.*

scour[1] (skaʊə) *vb.* **1.** to clean or polish (a surface) by washing and rubbing, as with an abrasive cloth. **2.** to remove dirt from or have the dirt removed from. **3.** (*tr.*) to clear (a channel) by the force of water; flush. **4.** (*tr.*) to remove by or as if by rubbing. **5.** (*intr.*) (of livestock, esp. cattle) to have diarrhoea. **6.** (*tr.*) to cause (livestock) to purge their bowels. ~*n.* **7.** the act of scouring. **8.** the place scoured, esp. by running water. **9.** something that scours, such as a cleansing agent. **10.** (*often pl.*) prolonged diarrhoea in livestock, esp. cattle. [C13: via Middle Low German *schūren,* from Old French *escurer,* from Late Latin *excūrāre* to cleanse, from *cūrāre;* see CURE] —**'scour·er** *n.*

scour[2] (skaʊə) *vb.* **1.** to range over (territory), as in making a search. **2.** to move swiftly or energetically over (territory). [C14: from Old Norse *skūr*]

scourge (skɜːdʒ) *n.* **1.** a whip used for inflicting punishment or torture. **2.** a means of inflicting punishment or suffering. **3.** a person who harasses, punishes, or causes destruction. ~*vb.* (*tr.*) **4.** to whip; flog. **5.** to punish severely. [C13: from Anglo-French *escorge,* from Old French *escorgier* (unattested) to lash, from *es-* EX-[1] + Latin *corrigia* whip] —**'scourg·er** *n.* —**'scourg·ing·ly** *adv.*

scour·ing rush *n.* any of several horsetails, esp. *Equisetum hyemale,* that have rough-ridged stems and were formerly used for scouring and polishing.

scour·ings ('skaʊərɪŋz) *pl. n.* **1.** the residue left after cleaning grain. **2.** residue that remains after scouring.

scouse (skaʊs) *n. Liverpool dialect.* a stew made from left-over meat. [C19: shortened from LOBSCOUSE]

Scouse (skaʊs) *Brit. informal.* ~*n.* **1.** a person who lives in or comes from Liverpool. **2.** the dialect spoken by such a person. ~*adj.* **3.** of or from Liverpool; Liverpudlian.

scout[1] (skaʊt) *n.* **1.** a person, ship, or aircraft sent out to gain information. **2.** *Military.* a person or unit despatched to reconnoitre the position of the enemy, etc. **3.** *Sport.* a person employed by a club to seek new players, etc. **4.** the act or an instance of scouting. **5.** (esp. at Oxford University) a college servant. **6.** (in Britain) a patrolman of a motoring organization. **7.** *Informal.* a fellow or companion. ~*vb.* **8.** to examine or observe (anything) in order to obtain information. **9.** (*tr.;* sometimes foll. by *out* or *up*) to seek. **10.** (*intr.*) to act as a scout for a sports club. **11.** (*intr.,*foll. by *about* or *around*) to go in search (for). [C14: from Old French *ascouter* to listen to, from Latin *auscultāre* to AUSCULTATE] —**'scout·er** *n.*

scout² (skaʊt) *vb. Archaic.* to reject (a person or thing) with contempt. [C17: from Old Norse *skūta* derision]

Scout (skaʊt) *n.* (*sometimes not cap.*) a boy or (in the U.S.) a girl who is a member of a worldwide movement (the **Scout Association**) founded as the Boy Scouts in England in 1908 by Lord Baden-Powell with the aim of developing character and responsibility. British female counterpart: **Guide.** See also **Air Scout, Sea Scout.**

scout car *n.* a fast lightly armoured vehicle used for reconnaissance.

Scout·ing ('skaʊtɪŋ) *n.* **a.** the activities, programmes, principles, etc., of the Scout Association. **b.** (*as modifier*)*: the international Scouting movement.*

scout·mas·ter ('skaʊtˌmɑːstə) *n.* the leader of a troop of Scouts.

scow (skaʊ) *n.* **1.** an unpowered barge used for freight, etc.; lighter. **2.** (esp. in the midwestern U.S.) a sailing yacht with a flat bottom, designed to plane. [C18: via Dutch *schouw* from Low German *schalde,* related to Old Saxon *skaldan* to push (a boat) into the sea]

scowl (skaʊl) *vb.* **1.** (*intr.*) to contract the brows in a threatening or angry manner. ~*n.* **2.** a gloomy or threatening expression. [C14: probably from Scandinavian; compare Danish *skule* to look down, Old English *scūlēgede* squint-eyed] —**'scowl·er** *n.* —**'scowl·ing·ly** *adv.*

S.C.R. (in British universities) *abbrev. for* senior common room.

scr. *abbrev. for* scruple (unit of weight).

scrab·ble ('skræbᵊl) *vb.* **1.** (*intr.;* often foll. by *about* or *at*) to scrape (at) or grope (for), as with hands or claws. **2.** to struggle (with). **3.** (*intr.;* often foll. by *for*) to struggle to gain possession, esp. in a disorderly manner. **4.** to scribble. ~*n.* **5.** the act or an instance of scrabbling. **6.** scribble. **7.** a disorderly struggle. [C16: from Middle Dutch *shrabbelen,* frequentative of *shrabben* to scrape] —**'scrab·bler** *n.*

Scrab·ble ('skræbᵊl) *n. Trademark.* a game in which words are formed in a pattern similar to a crossword puzzle.

scrag (skræg) *n.* **1.** a thin or scrawny person or animal. **2.** the lean end of a neck of veal or mutton. **3.** *Informal.* the neck of a human being. ~*vb.* **scrags, scrag·ging, scragged. 4.** (*tr.*) *Informal.* to wring the neck of; throttle. [C16: perhaps variant of CRAG; related to Norwegian *skragg,* German *Kragen* collar]

scrag·gly ('skræglɪ) *adj.* **·gli·er, ·gli·est.** untidy or irregular.

scrag·gy ('skrægɪ) *adj.* **·gi·er, ·gi·est. 1.** lean or scrawny. **2.** rough; unkempt. —**'scrag·gi·ly** *adv.* —**'scrag·gi·ness** *n.*

scram (skræm) *vb.* **scrams, scram·ming, scrammed.** (*intr.; often imperative*) *Informal.* to go away hastily; get out. [C20: shortened from SCRAMBLE]

scramb *or* **scram** (skræm) *vb.* (*tr.*) *Brit. dialect.* to scratch with nails or claws. [from Dutch *schrammen*]

scram·ble ('skræmbᵊl) *vb.* **1.** (*intr.*) to climb, crawl, or proceed hurriedly, esp. by using the hands to aid movement. **2.** (*intr.;* often foll. by *for*) to compete with others, esp. in a disordered manner: *to scramble for a prize.* **3.** (*intr.;* foll. by *through*) to deal with hurriedly and unsystematically. **4.** (*tr.*) to throw together in a haphazard manner; jumble. **5.** (*tr.*) to collect in a hurried or disorganized manner. **6.** (*tr.*) to cook (eggs that have been whisked up with milk and seasoning) in a pan containing a little melted butter. **7.** *Military.* to order (a crew or aircraft) to take off immediately or (of a crew or aircraft) to take off immediately. **8.** (*tr.*) to render (speech) unintelligible during transmission by means of an electronic scrambler. ~*n.* **9.** the act of scrambling. **10.** a climb or trek over difficult ground, esp. with the help of the hands. **11.** a disorderly struggle, esp. to gain possession. **12.** *Military.* an immediate preparation for action, as of crew, aircraft, etc. **13.** *Brit.* a motorcycle rally in which competitors race across rough open ground. [C16: blend of SCRABBLE and RAMP]

scram·bled eggs *pl. n. Slang.* gold embroidery on the peak of a high-ranking military officer's cap.

scram·bler ('skræmblə) *n.* **1.** a plant that produces long weak shoots by which it grows over other plants. **2.** an electronic device that renders speech unintelligible during transmission, normal speech being restored at the receiving system.

scran (skræn) *n.* **1.** *Slang.* food; provisions. **2. bad scran to.** *Irish dialect.* bad luck to. [C18: of unknown origin]

scran·nel ('skrænᵊl) *adj. Archaic.* **1.** thin. **2.** harsh. [C17: probably from Norwegian *skran* lean. See SCRAWNY]

Scran·ton ('skræntən) *n.* an industrial city in NE Pennsylvania: university (1888). Pop.: 103 564 (1970).

scrap¹ (skræp) *n.* **1.** a small piece of something larger; fragment. **2.** an extract from something written. **3. a.** waste material or used articles, esp. metal, often collected and reprocessed. **b.** (*as modifier*)*: scrap iron.* **4.** (*pl.*) pieces of discarded food. ~*vb.* **scraps, scrap·ping, scrapped.** (*tr.*) **5.** to make into scrap. **6.** to discard as useless. [C14: from Old Norse *skrap;* see SCRAPE]

scrap² (skræp) *Informal.* ~*n.* **1.** a fight or argument. ~*vb.* **scraps, scrap·ping, scrapped. 2.** (*intr.*) to quarrel or fight. [C17: perhaps from SCRAPE]

scrap·book ('skræpˌbʊk) *n.* a book or album of blank pages in which to mount newspaper cuttings, pictures, etc.

scrape (skreɪp) *vb.* **1.** to move (a rough or sharp object) across (a surface), esp. to smooth or clean. **2.** (*tr.,* often foll. by *away* or *off*) to remove (a layer) by rubbing. **3.** to produce a harsh or grating sound by rubbing against (an instrument, surface, etc.). **4.** (*tr.*) to injure or damage by rough contact: *to scrape one's knee.* **5.** (*intr.*) to be very economical (esp. in the phrase **scrimp and scrape). 6.** (*intr.*) to draw the foot backwards in making a bow. **7.** (*tr.*) to finish (a surface) by use of a scraper. **8.** (*tr.*) to make (a bearing, etc.) fit by scraping. **9. bow and scrape.** to behave with excessive humility. **10. scrape acquaintance with.** to contrive an acquaintance with. ~*n.* **11.** the act of scraping. **12.** a scraped place. **13.** a harsh or grating sound. **14.** *Informal.* an awkward or embarrassing predicament. **15.** *Informal.* a conflict or struggle. [Old English *scrapian;* related to Old Norse *skrapa,* Middle Dutch *schrapen,* Middle High German *schraffen*] —**'scrap·a·ble** *adj.* —**'scrap·er** *n.*

scrape in *vb.* (*intr., adv.*) to succeed in entering with difficulty or by a narrow margin: *he only just scraped into university.* Also: **scrape into.**

scrap·er·board ('skreɪpəˌbɔːd) *n.* **1.** thin card covered with a layer of white china clay and a black top layer of Indian ink, which can be scraped away with a special tool to leave a white line. **2.** a picture or design produced in this way.

scrape through *vb.* (*adv.*) **1.** (*intr.*) to manage or survive with difficulty. **2.** to succeed in with difficulty or by a narrow margin: *he scraped through by one mark.*

scrape to·geth·er *or* **up** *vb.* (*tr., adv.*) to collect with difficulty: *to scrape together money for a new car.*

scrap·heap ('skræpˌhiːp) *n.* a pile of discarded material.

scrap·py¹ ('skræpɪ) *adj.* **·pi·er, ·pi·est.** fragmentary; disjointed. —**'scrap·pi·ly** *adv.* —**'scrap·pi·ness** *n.*

scrap·py² ('skræpɪ) *adj.* **·pi·er, ·pi·est.** *Informal.* pugnacious.

scratch (skrætʃ) *vb.* **1.** to mark or cut (the surface of something) with a rough or sharp instrument. **2.** (often foll. by *at, out, off,* etc.) to scrape (the surface of something), as with claws, nails, etc. **3.** to scrape (the surface of the skin) with the nails, as to relieve itching. **4.** to chafe or irritate (a surface, esp. the skin). **5.** to make or cause to make a grating sound; scrape. **6.** (*tr.;* sometimes foll. by *out*) to erase by or as if by scraping. **7.** (*tr.*) to write or draw awkwardly. **8.** (*intr.;* sometimes foll. by *along*) to earn a living, manage, etc., with difficulty. **9.** to withdraw (an entry) from a race, match, etc. **10.** (*intr.*) *Billiards, etc.,* **a.** to make a shot resulting in a penalty. **b.** to make a lucky shot. **11.** (*tr.*) *U.S.* to cancel (the name of a candidate) from a party ticket in an election. **12.** (*intr.,* often foll. by *for*) *Austral. informal.* to be struggling or in difficulty, esp. in earning a living. **13. you scratch my back and I will scratch yours.** if you will help me, I will help you. ~*n.* **14.** the act of scratching. **15.** a slight injury. **16.** a mark made by scratching. **17.** a slight grating sound. **18.** (in a handicap sport) **a.** a competitor or the status of a competitor who has no allowance or receives a penalty. **b.** (*as modifier*)*: a scratch player.* **19.** the time, initial score, etc., of such a competitor. **20. a.** the line from which competitors start in a race. **b.** (formerly) a line drawn on the floor of a prize ring at which the contestants stood to begin or continue fighting. **21.** a withdrawn competitor in a race, etc. **22.** *Billiards, etc.* **a.** a shot that results in a penalty, as when the cue ball enters the pocket. **b.** a lucky shot. **23.** poultry food. **24. from scratch.** *Informal.* from the very beginning. **25. up to scratch.** (*usually used with a negative*) *Informal.* up to standard. ~*adj.* **26.** *Sport.* (of a team) assembled hastily. **27.** (in a handicap sport) with no allowance or penalty. **28.** *Informal.* rough or haphazard. [C15: via Old French *escrater* from Germanic; compare Old High German *krazzōn* (German *kratzen*)*;* related to Old French *gratter* to GRATE] —**'scratch·er** *n.* —**'scratch·y** *adj.* —**'scratch·i·ly** *adv.* —**'scratch·i·ness** *n.*

scratch·es ('skrætʃɪz) *n.* (*functioning as sing.*) a disease of horses characterized by eczematous weeping lesions in the region of the fetlock.

scratch pad *n.* a notebook, esp. one with detachable leaves.

scratch sheet *n. U.S. informal.* another term for a **dope sheet.**

scratch test *n. Med.* a skin test to determine allergic sensitivity to various substances by placing the allergen to be tested over an area of lightly scratched skin. A positive reaction is typically indicated by the formation of a weal.

scratch to·geth·er *or* **up** *vb.* (*tr., adv.*) to assemble with difficulty: *he scratched up a team for the football match.*

scrawl (skrɔːl) *vb.* **1.** to write or draw (signs, words, etc.) carelessly or hastily; scribble. ~*n.* **2.** careless or scribbled writing, drawing, or marks. [C17: perhaps a blend of SPRAWL and CRAWL] —**'scrawl·er** *n.* —**'scrawl·y** *adj.*

scrawn·y ('skrɔːnɪ) *adj.* **scrawn·i·er, scrawn·i·est. 1.** very thin and bony; scraggy. **2.** meagre or stunted: *scrawny vegetation.* [C19: variant of dialect *scranny;* see SCRANNEL] —**'scrawn·i·ly** *adv.* —**'scrawn·i·ness** *n.*

screak (skriːk) *Dialect, chiefly U.S.* ~*vb.* **1.** (*intr.*) to screech or creak. ~*n.* **2.** a screech or creak. [C16: from Old Norse *skrækja.* See SCREECH, SHRIEK] —**'screak·y** *adj.*

scream (skriːm) *vb.* **1.** to utter or emit (a sharp piercing cry or similar sound or sounds), esp. as of fear, pain, etc. **2.** (*intr.*) to laugh wildly. **3.** (*intr.*) to speak, shout, or behave in a wild or impassioned manner. **4.** (*tr.*) to bring (oneself) into a specified state by screaming: *she screamed herself hoarse.* **5.** (*intr.*) to be extremely conspicuous: *the colours in the room screamed as*

I walked in. ~*n.* **6.** a sharp piercing cry or sound, esp. one denoting fear or pain. **7.** *Informal.* a person or thing that causes great amusement. [C13: from Germanic; compare Middle Dutch *schreem,* West Frisian *skrieme* to weep]

scream·er ('skri:mə) *n.* **1.** a person or thing that screams. **2.** any goose-like aquatic bird, such as *Chauna torquata* (**crested screamer**), of the family *Anhimidae* of tropical and subtropical South America: order *Anseriformes* (ducks, geese, etc.). **3.** *Informal.* (in printing) an exclamation mark. **4.** someone or something that raises screams of laughter or astonishment. **5.** *U.S. slang.* a sensational headline. **6.** *Austral. slang.* **a.** a person or thing that is excellent of its kind. **b.** See **two-pot screamer.**

scree (skri:) *n.* an accumulation of weathered rock fragments at the foot of a cliff or hillside, often forming a sloping heap. Also called: **talus.** [Old English *scrīthan* to slip; related to Old Norse *skrītha* to slide, German *schreiten* to walk]

screech[1] (skri:tʃ) *n.* **1.** a shrill, harsh, or high-pitched sound or cry. ~*vb.* **2.** to utter with or produce a screech. [C16: Variant of earlier *scritch,* of imitative origin] —'**screech·er** *n.* —'**screech·y** *adj.*

screech[2] (skri:tʃ) *n. Canadian slang.* **1.** a dark rum. **2.** any strong cheap drink. [perhaps special use of SCREECH[1]]

screech owl *n.* **1.** a small North American owl, *Otus asio,* having ear tufts and a reddish-brown or grey plumage. **2.** *Brit.* any owl that utters a screeching cry.

screed (skri:d) *n.* **1.** a long or prolonged speech or piece of writing. **2.** a strip of wood, plaster, or metal placed on a surface to act as a guide to the thickness of the cement or plaster coat to be applied. **3.** a mixture of cement, sand, and water applied to a concrete slab, etc., to give a smooth surface finish. **4.** *Scot.* a rent or tear or the sound produced by this. [C14: probably variant of Old English *scrēade* SHRED]

screen (skri:n) *n.* **1.** a light movable frame, panel, or partition serving to shelter, divide, hide, etc. **2.** anything that serves to shelter, protect, or conceal. **3.** a frame containing a mesh that is placed over a window or opening to keep out insects. **4.** a decorated partition, esp. in a church around the choir. See also **rood screen. 5.** a sieve. **6.** a system for selecting people, such as candidates for a job. **7.** the wide end of a cathode-ray tube, esp. in a television set, on which a visible image is formed. **8.** a white or silvered surface, usually fabric, placed in front of a projector to receive the enlarged image of a film or of slides. **9. the screen.** the film industry or films collectively. **10.** *Photog.* a plate of ground glass in some types of camera on which the image of a subject is focussed before being photographed. **11.** *Printing.* a glass marked with fine intersecting lines, used in a camera for making half-tone reproductions. **12.** men or ships deployed around and ahead of a larger military formation to warn of attack or protect from a specific threat. **13.** *Sport, chiefly U.S.* a tactical ploy in which players block an opponent, etc. **14.** *Psychoanal.* anything that prevents a person from realizing his true feelings about someone or something. **15.** *Electronics.* See **screen grid.** ~*vb.* (*tr.*) **16.** (sometimes foll. by *off*) to shelter, protect, or conceal. **17.** to sieve or sort. **18.** to test or check (an individual or group) so as to determine suitability for a task, etc. **19.** to examine for the presence of a disease, weapons, etc.: *the authorities screened five hundred cholera suspects.* **20.** to provide with a screen or screens. **21.** to project (a film) onto a screen, esp. for public viewing. **22.** *Printing.* to photograph (a picture, etc.) through a screen to render it suitable for half-tone reproduction. [C15: from Old French *escren* (French *écran*); related to Old High German *skrank,* German *Schrank* cupboard] —'**screen·a·ble** *adj.* —'**screen·er** *n.* —'**screen·,like** *adj.*

screen grid *n. Electronics.* an electrode placed between the control grid and anode of a valve and having a fixed positive potential relative to the grid. It acts as an electrostatic shield preventing capacitive coupling between grid and anode, thus increasing the stability of the device. Sometimes shortened to **screen.** See also **suppressor grid.**

screen·ings ('skri:nɪŋz) *pl. n.* refuse separated by sifting.

screen mem·o·ry *n. Psychoanal.* a memory that is tolerable but allied to a distressing event and which is unconsciously used to hide the distressing memory.

screen·play ('skri:n,pleɪ) *n.* the script for a film, including instructions for sets and camera work.

screen pro·cess *n.* a method of printing using a fine mesh of silk, nylon, etc., treated with an impermeable coating except in the areas through which ink is subsequently forced onto the paper behind. Also called: **silk-screen printing.**

screen test *n.* **1.** a filmed audition of a prospective actor or actress to test suitability. **2.** the test film so made.

screw (skru:) *n.* **1.** a device used for fastening materials together, consisting of a threaded and usually tapered shank that has a slotted head by which it may be rotated so as to cut its own thread as it bores through the material. **2.** a threaded cylindrical rod that engages with a similarly threaded cylindrical hole; bolt. **3.** a thread in a cylindrical hole corresponding with that on the bolt or screw with which it is designed to engage. **4.** anything resembling a screw in shape or spiral form. **5.** a twisting movement of or resembling that of a screw. **6.** Also called: **screw-back.** *Billiards, etc.* **a.** a stroke in which the cue ball recoils or moves backward after striking the object ball, made by striking the cue ball below its centre. **b.** the motion resulting from this stroke. **7.** another name for **propeller** (sense 1). **8.** *Slang.* a prison guard. **9.** *Brit. slang.* salary, wages, or earnings. **10.** *Brit.* a small amount of salt, tobacco, etc., in a twist of paper. **11.** *Slang.* a person who is mean with money. **12.** *Slang.* an old, unsound, or worthless horse. **13.** (*often pl.*) *Slang.* force or compulsion (esp. in the phrase **put the screws on**). **14.** *Taboo slang.* sexual intercourse. **15. have a screw loose.** *Slang.* to be insane. ~*vb.* **16.** (*tr.*) to rotate (a screw or bolt) so as to drive it into or draw it out of a material. **17.** (*tr.*) to cut a screw thread in (a rod or hole) with a tap or die or on a lathe. **18.** to turn or cause to turn in the manner of a screw. **19.** (*tr.*) to attach or fasten with a screw or screws. **20.** (*tr.*) *Informal.* to take advantage of; cheat. **21.** (*tr.*; often foll. by *up*) *Informal.* to distort or contort: *he screwed his face into a scowl.* **22.** Also: **screw back.** to impart a screw to (a ball). **23.** (*tr.*) *Informal.* to coerce or force. **24.** *Taboo slang.* to have sexual intercourse (with). **25.** (*tr.*) *Informal.* to burgle. **26. have one's head screwed on the right way.** *Informal.* to be wise or sensible. ~See also **screw up.** [C15: from French *escroe,* from Medieval Latin *scrōfa* screw, from Latin: sow, presumably because the thread of the screw is like the spiral of the sow's tail] —'**screw·er** *n.* —'**screw·,like** *adj.*

screw·ball ('skru:,bɔ:l) *U.S. slang.* ~*n.* **1.** an odd or eccentric person. ~*adj.* **2.** odd; zany; eccentric.

screw·driv·er ('skru:,draɪvə) *n.* **1.** a tool used for turning screws, usually having a handle of wood, plastic, etc., and a steel shank with a flattened square-cut tip that fits into a slot in the head of the screw. **2.** an alcoholic beverage consisting of orange juice and vodka.

screwed (skru:d) *adj.* **1.** fastened by a screw or screws. **2.** having spiral grooves like a screw; threaded. **3.** twisted or distorted. **4.** *Brit.* a slang word for **drunk.**

screw eye *n.* a wood screw with its shank bent into a ring.

screw jack *n.* a lifting device utilizing the mechanical advantage of a screw thread, the effort being applied through a bevel drive. Also called: **jackscrew, jack.**

screw pine *n.* any of various pandanaceous plants of the Old World tropical genus *Pandanus,* having a spiral mass of pineapple-like leaves and heavy conelike fruits.

screw pro·pel·ler *n.* an early form of ship's propeller in which an Archimedes screw is used to produce thrust by accelerating a flow of water. —'**screw-pro·'pelled** *adj.*

screw up *vb.* (*tr., adv.*) **1.** to twist out of shape or distort. **2.** to summon up or call upon: *to screw up one's courage.* **3.** *Informal.* to mishandle or bungle. **4.** (*often passive*) *Informal.* to cause to become very anxious, confused, or nervous: *he is really screwed up about his exams.*

screw·worm ('skru:,wɜ:m) *n.* **1.** the larva of a dipterous fly, *Callitroga macellaria,* that develops beneath the skin of living mammals often causing illness or death. **2. screwworm fly.** the fly producing this larva: family *Calliphoridae.*

screw·y ('skru:ɪ) *adj.* **screw·i·er, screw·i·est.** *Informal.* odd, crazy, or eccentric.

Scria·bin ('skrɪəbɪn; *Russian* 'skrjabin) *n.* **A·le·ksan·dr Ni·ko·la·ye·vich** (alɪ'ksandᵊr nika'lajivitʃ). 1872–1915, Russian composer, whose works came increasingly to express his theosophic beliefs. He wrote many piano works; his orchestral compositions include *Prometheus* (1911).

scrib·ble[1] ('skrɪbᵊl) *vb.* **1.** to write or draw in a hasty or illegible manner. **2.** to make meaningless or illegible marks (on). **3.** *Derogatory or facetious.* to write poetry, novels, etc. ~*n.* **4.** hasty careless writing or drawing. **5.** writing, esp. literary matter, of poor quality. **6.** meaningless or illegible marks. [C15: from Medieval Latin *scrībillāre* to write hastily, from Latin *scrībere* to write] —'**scrib·bler** *n.* —'**scrib·bly** *adj.*

scrib·ble[2] ('skrɪbᵊl) *vb.* (*tr.*) to card (wool, etc.). [C17: probably from Low German; compare *schrubben* SCRUB[1]]

scribe (skraɪb) *n.* **1.** a person who copies documents, esp. a person who made handwritten copies before the invention of printing. **2.** a clerk or public copyist. **3.** *Old Testament.* a recognized scholar and teacher of the Jewish Law. **4.** an author or journalist: used humorously. **5.** another name for **scriber.** ~*vb.* **6.** to score a line on (a surface) with a pointed instrument, as in metalworking. [(in the senses: writer, etc.) C14: from Latin *scrība* clerk, from *scribere* to write; C17 (vb.): perhaps from INSCRIBE] —'**scrib·al** *adj.*

Scribe (*French* skrib) *n.* **Au·gus·tin Eu·gène** (ogystɛ̃ ø'ʒɛn). 1791–1861, French author or coauthor of over 350 vaudevilles, comedies, and libretti for light opera.

scrib·er ('skraɪbə) *n.* a pointed steel tool used to score materials as a guide to cutting, etc. Also called: **scribe.**

scrim (skrɪm) *n.* a fine open-weave fabric, used in the theatre to create the illusion of a solid wall or to suggest haziness, etc., according to the lighting. [C18: origin unknown]

scrim·mage ('skrɪmɪdʒ) *n.* **1.** a rough or disorderly struggle. **2.** *American football.* the period of a game from the time the ball goes into play to the time it is declared dead. ~*vb.* **3.** (*intr.*) to engage in a scrimmage. **4.** (*tr.*) to put (the ball) into a scrimmage. [C15: from earlier *scrimish,* variant of SKIRMISH] —'**scrim·mag·er** *n.*

scrimp (skrɪmp) *vb.* **1.** (when *intr.*, sometimes foll. by *on*) to be very sparing in the use (of) (esp. in the phrase **scrimp and scrape**). **2.** (*tr.*) to treat meanly: *he is scrimping his children.* **3.** (*tr.*) to cut too small. ~*adj.* **4.** a less common word for **scant.** [C18: Scottish, origin unknown] —'**scrimp·y** *adj.* —'**scrimp·i·ly** *adv.* —'**scrimp·i·ness** *n.*

scrim·shank ('skrɪm,ʃæŋk) *vb.* (*intr.*) *Brit. military slang.* to shirk work. [C19: of unknown origin]

scrim·shaw ('skrɪm,ʃɔ:) *n.* **1.** the art of decorating or carving shells, ivory, etc., done by sailors as a leisure activity. **2. a.** an article made in this manner. **b.** such articles collectively. ~*vb.* **3.** to produce scrimshaw (from). [C19: origin uncertain, perhaps after a surname]

scrip[1] (skrɪp) *n.* **1.** a written certificate, list, etc. **2.** a small scrap, esp. of paper with writing on it. **3.** *Finance.* **a.** a certificate representing a claim to part of a share of stock. **b.** the shares allocated in a bonus issue. [C18: in some senses, probably from SCRIPT; otherwise, short for *subscription receipt*]

scrip[2] (skrɪp) *n. Archaic.* a small bag or wallet, as carried by pilgrims. [C14: from Old French *escreppe*, variant of *escarpe* SCARF[1]]

scrip is+sue *n.* another name for **bonus issue.**

script (skrɪpt) *n.* **1.** handwriting as distinguished from print, esp. cursive writing. **2.** the letters, characters, or figures used in writing by hand. **3.** any system or style of writing. **4.** written copy for the use of performers in films and plays. **5.** *Law.* **a.** an original or principal document. **b.** (esp. in England) a will or codicil or the draft for one. **6.** any of various typefaces that imitate handwriting. **7.** an answer paper in an examination. ~*vb.* **8.** (*tr.*) to write a script (for). [C14: from Latin *scriptum* something written, from *scrībere* to write]

Script. *abbrev. for:* **1.** scriptural. **2.** Scripture(s).

scrip+to+ri·um (skrɪp'tɔːrɪəm) *n., pl.* **+ri·ums** *or* **+ri·a** (-rɪə). a room, esp. in a monastery, set apart for the writing or copying of manuscripts. [from Medieval Latin]

scrip+tur+al ('skrɪptʃərəl) *adj.* **1.** (*often cap.*) of, in accordance with, or based on Scripture. **2.** of or relating to writing. —**'scrip+tur+al+ly** *adv.* —**'scrip+tur+al+ness** *n.*

scrip+ture ('skrɪptʃə) *n.* **1.** a sacred, solemn, or authoritative book or piece of writing. [C13: from Latin *scriptūra* written material, from *scrībere* to write]

Scrip+ture ('skrɪptʃə) *n.* **1.** Also called: **Holy Scripture, Holy Writ, the Scriptures.** *Christianity.* the Old and New Testaments. **2.** any book or body of writings, esp. when regarded as sacred by a particular religious group.

script+writ·er ('skrɪpt,raɪtə) *n.* a person who prepares scripts, esp. for a film. —**'script+,writ·ing** *n.*

scrive+ner ('skrɪvnə) *n. Archaic.* **1.** a person who writes out deeds, letters, etc.; copyist. **2.** a notary. [C14: from *scrivein* clerk, from Old French *escrivain,* ultimately from Latin *scrība* SCRIBE]

scro+bic·u+late (skrəʊ'bɪkjʊlɪt, -,leɪt) *or* **scro+bic·u+lat+ed** *adj. Biology.* having a surface covered with small round pits or grooves. [C19: from Latin *scrobiculus* diminutive of *scrobis* a ditch]

scrod (skrɒd) *n. U.S.* a young cod or haddock, esp. one split and prepared for cooking. [C19: perhaps from obsolete Dutch *schrood,* from Middle Dutch *schrode* SHRED (n.); the name perhaps refers to the method of preparing the fish for cooking]

scrof·u+la ('skrɒfjʊlə) *n. Pathol.* (*no longer in technical use*) tuberculosis of the lymphatic glands. Also called (formerly): (the) **king's evil.** [C14: from Medieval Latin, from Late Latin *scrōfulae* swollen glands in the neck, literally: little sows (sows were thought to be particularly prone to the disease), from Latin *scrōfa* sow]

scrof·u+lous ('skrɒfjʊləs) *adj.* **1.** of, relating to, resembling, or having scrofula. **2.** morally degraded. —**'scrof·u+lous+ly** *adv.* —**'scrof·u+lous+ness** *n.*

scroll (skrəʊl) *n.* **1.** a roll of parchment, paper, etc., usually inscribed with writing. **2.** an ancient book in the form of a roll of parchment, papyrus, etc. **3. a.** a decorative carving or moulding resembling a scroll. **b.** (*as modifier*): *a scroll saw.* **c.** (*in combination*): *scrollwork.* ~*vb.* **4.** (*tr.*) to saw into scrolls. **5.** to roll up like a scroll. [C15 *scrowle,* from *scrowe,* from Old French *escroe* scrap of parchment, but also influenced by ROLL]

scroll saw *n.* a saw with a narrow blade for cutting intricate ornamental curves in wood.

scroll+work ('skrəʊl,wɜːk) *n.* ornamental work in scroll-like patterns, esp. when done with a scroll saw.

Scrooge (skruːdʒ) *n.* a mean or miserly person. [C19: after a character in Dickens' story *A Christmas Carol* (1843)]

scroop (skruːp) *Dialect.* ~*vb.* **1.** (*intr.*) to emit a grating or creaking sound. ~*n.* **2.** such a sound. [C18: of imitative origin]

scroph·u+lar·i·a+ceous (,skrɒfjʊ,lɛərɪ'eɪʃəs) *adj.* of, relating to, or belonging to the *Scrophulariaceae,* a family of plants including figwort, snapdragon, foxglove, toadflax, speedwell, and mullein. [C19: from New Latin (*herba*) *scrophularia* scrofula (plant), from the use of such plants in treating scrofula]

scro+tum ('skrəʊtəm) *n., pl.* **+ta** (-tə) *or* **+tums.** the pouch of skin containing the testes in most mammals. [C16: from Latin] —**'scro+tal** *adj.*

scrouge (skraʊdʒ, skruːdʒ) *vb.* (*tr.*) *Dialect.* to crowd or press. [C18: alteration of C16 *scruze* to squeeze, perhaps blend of SCREW + SQUEEZE]

scrounge (skraʊndʒ) *vb. Informal.* **1.** (when *intr.,* sometimes foll. by *around*) to search in order to acquire (something) without cost. **2.** to obtain or seek to obtain (something) by cadging or begging. [C20: variant of dialect *scrunge* to steal, of obscure origin] —**'scroung+er** *n.*

scrub[1] (skrʌb) *vb.* **scrubs, scrub+bing, scrubbed. 1.** to rub (a surface, etc.) hard, with or as if with a brush, soap, and water, in order to clean it. **2.** to remove (dirt) by rubbing with a brush, etc., and water. **3.** (*intr.;* foll. by *up*) (of a surgeon) to wash the hands and arms thoroughly before operating. **4.** (*tr.*) to purify (a vapour or gas) by removing impurities. **5.** (*tr.*) *Informal.* to delete or cancel. **6.** (*intr.*) *Horse racing slang.* (of jockeys) to urge a horse forwards by moving the arms and whip rhythmically forwards and backwards alongside its neck. ~*n.* **7.** the act of or an instance of scrubbing. [C14: from Middle Low German *schrubben,* or Middle Dutch *schrobben*]

scrub[2] (skrʌb) *n.* **1. a.** vegetation consisting of stunted trees, bushes, and other plants growing in an arid area. **b.** (*as modifier*): *scrub vegetation.* **2.** an area of arid land covered with such vegetation. **3. a.** an animal of inferior breeding or condition. **b.** (*as modifier*): *a scrub bull.* **4.** a small or insignificant person. **5.** anything stunted or inferior. **6.** *Sport, U.S.* **a.** a player not in the first team. **b.** a team composed of such players. **c.** a contest between scratch or incomplete teams. **7. the scrub.** *Austral. informal.* a remote place, esp. one where contact with people can be avoided. ~*adj.* (*prenominal*) **8.** small, stunted, or inferior. **9.** *Sport, U.S.* **a.** (of a player) not in the first team. **b.** (of a team) composed of such players. **c.** (of a contest) between scratch or incomplete teams. [C16: variation of SHRUB]

scrub+ber[1] ('skrʌbə) *n.* **1.** a person or thing that scrubs. **2.** an apparatus for purifying a gas. **3.** *Derogatory Brit. and Austral. slang.* a promiscuous girl.

scrub+ber[2] ('skrʌbə) *n. Austral.* a domestic animal, esp. a bullock, that has run wild in the bush. [C19: from SCRUB[2]]

scrub bird *n.* either of two fast-running wren-like passerine birds, *Atrichornis clamosus* and *A. rufescens,* that constitute the Australian family *Atrichornithidae.*

scrub+by ('skrʌbɪ) *adj.* **+bi+er, +bi+est. 1.** covered with or consisting of scrub. **2.** (of trees or vegetation) stunted in growth. **3.** *Brit. informal.* messy. —**'scrub+bi+ness** *n.*

scrub fowl *or* **tur+key** *n.* another name for **megapode.**

scrub+land ('skrʌb,lænd) *n.* an area of scrub vegetation.

scrub round *vb.* (*intr., prep.*) *Informal.* to waive; avoid or ignore: *we can scrub round the rules.*

scrub ty+phus *n.* an acute febrile disease characterized by severe headache, skin rash, chills, and swelling of the lymph nodes, caused by the bite of mites infected with the microorganism *Rickettsia tsutsugamushi:* occurs mainly in Asia, Australia, and the islands of the western Pacific.

scruff[1] (skrʌf) *n.* the nape of the neck (esp. in the phrase **by the scruff of the neck**). [C18: variant of *scuft,* perhaps from Old Norse *skoft* hair; related to Old High German *scuft*]

scruff[2] (skrʌf) *n.* another name for **scum** (sense 3).

scruff·y ('skrʌfɪ) *adj.* **scruff·i·er, scruff·i·est.** unkempt or shabby.

scrum (skrʌm) *n.* **1.** *Rugby.* the act or method of restarting play after an infringement, etc., when the two opposing packs of forwards group together with heads down and arms interlocked and push to gain ground while the scrum half throws the ball in and the hookers attempt to scoop it out to their own team. A scrum is usually called by the referee (**set scrum**) but may be formed spontaneously (**loose scrum**). 2. *Informal.* a disorderly struggle. ~*vb.* **scrums, scrum+ming, scrummed. 3.** (*intr.;* usually foll. by *down*) *Rugby.* to form a scrum. [C19: shortened from SCRUMMAGE]

scrum half *n. Rugby.* **1.** a player who puts in the ball at scrums and tries to get it away to his three-quarter backs. **2.** this position in a team.

scrum+mage ('skrʌmɪdʒ) *n., vb.* **1.** *Rugby.* another word for **scrum. 2.** a variant of **scrimmage.** [C19: variant of SCRIMMAGE] —**'scrum+mag+er** *n.*

scrump (skrʌmp) *vb. Brit. dialect.* to steal (apples) from an orchard or garden. [dialect variant of SCRIMP]

scrump+tious ('skrʌmpʃəs) *adj. Informal.* very pleasing; delicious. [C19: probably changed from SUMPTUOUS] —**'scrump+tious+ly** *adv.* —**'scrump+tious+ness** *n.*

scrump·y ('skrʌmpɪ) *n.* a rough dry cider, brewed esp. in the West Country. [from *scrump,* variant of SCRIMP (in obsolete sense: withered), referring to the apples used]

scrunch (skrʌntʃ) *vb.* **1.** to crumple, crush, or crunch or to be crumpled, crushed, or crunched. ~*n.* **2.** the act or sound of scrunching. [C19: variant of CRUNCH]

scru+ple ('skruːpᵊl) *n.* **1.** a doubt or hesitation as to what is morally right in a certain situation. **2.** *Archaic.* a very small amount. **3.** a unit of weight equal to 20 grains (1.296 grams). **4.** an ancient Roman unit of weight equivalent to approximately one twenty-fourth of an ounce. ~*vb.* **5.** (*obsolete when tr.*) to have doubts (about), esp. from a moral compunction. [C16: from Latin *scrūpulus* a small weight, from *scrūpus* rough stone] —**'scru+ple+less** *adj.*

scru+pu+lous ('skruːpjʊləs) *adj.* **1.** characterized by careful observation of what is morally right. **2.** very careful or precise. [C15: from Latin *scrūpulōsus punctilious*] —**'scru+pu+lous+ly** *adv.* —**'scru+pu+lous+ness** *n.*

scru+ta·ble ('skruːtəbᵊl) *adj. Rare.* open to or able to be understood by scrutiny. [C17: from Latin *scrūtārī* to inspect closely; see SCRUTINY] —**,scru+ta·'bil+i·ty** *n.*

scru+ta+tor (skruː'teɪtə) *n.* a person who examines or scrutinizes. [from Latin, from *scrūtārī* to search]

scru+ti+neer (,skruːtɪ'nɪə) *n.* a person who examines, esp. one who scrutinizes the conduct of an election poll.

scru+ti+nize *or* **scru+ti+nise** ('skruːtɪ,naɪz) *vb.* (*tr.*) to examine carefully or in minute detail. —**'scru+ti+,niz+er** *or* **'scru+ti+,nis+er** *n.* —**'scru+ti+,niz+ing+ly** *or* **'scru+ti+,nis+ing+ly** *adv.*

scru+ti+ny ('skruːtɪnɪ) *n., pl.* **+nies. 1.** close or minute examination. **2.** a searching look. **3. a.** (in the early Christian Church) a formal testing that catechumens had to undergo before being baptized. **b.** a similar examination of candidates for holy orders. [C15: from Late Latin *scrūtinium* an investigation, from *scrūtārī* to search (originally referring to ragpickers), from *scrūta* rubbish]

scry (skraɪ) *vb.* **scries, scry+ing, scried.** (*intr.*) to divine, esp. by crystal-gazing. [C16: from DESCRY]

scu+ba ('skjuːbə) *n.* **a.** an apparatus used in skindiving, consisting of a cylinder or cylinders containing compressed air attached to a breathing apparatus. **b.** (*as modifier*): *scuba diving.* [C20: from the initials of *self-contained underwater breathing apparatus*]

scud (skʌd) *vb.* **scuds, scud·ding, scud·ded.** (*intr.*) **1.** (esp. of clouds) to move along swiftly and smoothly. **2.** *Nautical.* to run before a gale. ~*n.* **3.** the act of scudding. **4.** *Meteorol.* **a.** a formation of low fractostratus clouds driven by a strong wind beneath rain-bearing clouds. **b.** a sudden shower or gust of wind. [C16: probably of Scandinavian origin; related to Norwegian *skudda* to thrust, Swedish *skudda* to shake]

scu·do ('sku:dəʊ) *n., pl.* **·di** (-di:). any of several former Italian coins. [C17: from Italian: shield, from Latin *scūtum*]

scuff (skʌf) *vb.* **1.** to scrape or drag (the feet) while walking. **2.** to rub or scratch (a surface) or (of a surface) to become rubbed or scratched. **3.** (*tr.*) *U.S.* to poke at (something) with the foot. ~*n.* **4.** the act or sound of scuffing. **5.** a rubbed place caused by scuffing. **6.** a backless slipper. [C19: probably of imitative origin]

scuf·fle[1] ('skʌfᵊl) *vb.* (*intr.*) **1.** to fight in a disorderly manner. **2.** to move by shuffling. **3.** to move in a hurried or confused manner. ~*n.* **4.** a disorderly struggle. **5.** the sound made by scuffling or shuffling. [C16: from Scandinavian; compare Swedish *skuff, skuffa* to push]

scuf·fle[2] ('skʌfᵊl) *n. U.S.* a type of hoe operated by pushing rather than pulling. [C18: from Dutch *schoffel* SHOVEL]

scull (skʌl) *n.* **1.** a single oar moved from side to side over the stern of a boat to propel it. **2.** one of a pair of short-handled oars, both of which are pulled by one oarsman, esp. in a racing shell. **3.** a racing shell propelled by a single oarsman pulling two oars. **4.** (*pl.*) a race between racing shells, each propelled by one oarsman pulling two oars. **5.** an act, instance, period, or distance of sculling. ~*vb.* **6.** to propel (a boat) with a scull. [C14: of unknown origin] —**'scull·er** *n.*

scul·ler·y ('skʌlərɪ) *n., pl.* **·ler·ies.** *Chiefly Brit.* a small room or part of a kitchen where kitchen utensils are kept and rough household work is done. [C15: from Anglo-Norman *squillerie*, from Old French *escuelerie*, from *escuele* a bowl, from Latin *scutella*, from *scutra* a flat tray]

Scul·lin ('skʌlɪn) *n.* **James Hen·ry.** 1876–1953, Australian statesman; prime minister of Australia (1929–31).

scul·lion ('skʌljən) *n.* **1.** a mean or despicable person. **2.** *Archaic.* a servant employed to do rough household work in a kitchen. [C15: from Old French *escouillon* cleaning cloth, from *escouve* a broom, from Latin *scōpa*]

sculp. *abbrev. for:* **1.** Also: **sculpt.** sculpsit. **2.** sculptor, sculptress, or sculpture.

scul·pin ('skʌlpɪn) *n., pl.* **·pin** *or* **·pins.** *U.S.* any of various fishes of the family *Cottidae* (bullheads and sea scorpions). [C17: of unknown origin]

sculp·sit ('skʌlpsɪt) he (or she) sculptured it: an inscription following the artist's name on a sculpture. [Latin]

sculpt (skʌlpt) *vb.* **1.** a variant of **sculpture** (senses 5–8). **2.** (*intr.*) to practise sculpture. ~Also: **sculp.** [C19: from French *sculpter*, from Latin *sculpere* to carve]

sculp·tor ('skʌlptə) *or* (*fem.*) **sculp·tress** *n.* a person who practises sculpture.

Sculp·tor ('skʌlptə) *n., Latin genitive* **Sculp·to·ris** (skʌlp'tɔ:rɪs). a faint constellation in the S hemisphere lying between Phoenix and Cetus.

sculp·ture ('skʌlptʃə) *n.* **1.** the art of making figures or designs in relief or the round by carving wood, moulding plaster, etc., or casting metals, etc. **2.** works or a work made in this way. **3.** ridges or indentations as on a shell, formed by natural processes. **4.** the gradual formation of the landscape by erosion. ~*vb.* (*mainly tr.*) **5.** (*also intr.*) to carve, cast, or fashion (stone, bronze, etc.) three-dimensionally. **6.** to portray (a person, etc.) by means of sculpture. **7.** to form in the manner of sculpture, esp. to shape (landscape) by erosion. **8.** to decorate with sculpture. ~Also (for senses 5–8): **sculpt.** [C14: from Latin *sculptūra* a carving; see SCULPT] —**'sculp·tur·al** *adj.* —**'sculp·tur·al·ly** *adv.*

sculp·tur·esque (ˌskʌlptʃə'rɛsk) *adj.* resembling sculpture. —ˌ**sculp·tur·'esque·ly** *adv.* —ˌ**sculp·tur·'esque·ness** *n.*

scum (skʌm) *n.* **1.** a layer of impure matter that forms on the surface of a liquid, often as the result of boiling or fermentation. **2.** the greenish film of algae and similar vegetation surface of a stagnant pond. **3.** Also called: **dross, scruff.** the skin of oxides or impurities on the surface of a molten metal. **4.** waste matter. **5.** a worthless person or group of people. ~*vb.* **scums, scum·ming, scummed. 6.** (*tr.*) to remove scum from. **7.** (*intr.*) *Rare.* to form a layer of or become covered with scum. [C13: of Germanic origin; related to Old High German *scūm*, Middle Dutch *schūm*, Old French *escume*; see SKIM] —**'scum·**ˌ**like** *adj.* —**'scum·mer** *n.* —**'scum·my** *adj.*

scum·ble ('skʌmbᵊl) *vb.* **1.** (in painting and drawing) to soften or blend (an outline or colour) with an upper coat of opaque colour, applied very thinly. ~*n.* **2.** the upper layer of colour applied in this way. **3.** the technique or effects of scumbling. [C18: probably from SCUM]

scun·cheon ('skʌntʃən) *n.* the inner part of a door jamb or window frame. [C15: from Old French *escoinson*, from *coin* angle]

scunge (skʌndʒ) *Austral. slang.* ~*vb.* **1.** to borrow. ~*n.* **2.** a dirty or worthless person. **3.** a person who borrows, esp. habitually. [C20: of unknown origin]

scung·y ('skʌndʒɪ) *adj.* **scung·i·er, scung·i·est.** *Austral. informal.* miserable; sordid. [C20: of uncertain origin]

scun·ner ('skʌnə) *Dialect, chiefly Scot.* ~*vb.* **1.** (*intr.*) to feel aversion. ~*n.* **2.** a strong aversion (often in the phrase **take a scunner**). 3. an object of dislike. [C14: from Scottish *skunner*, of unknown origin]

Scun·thorpe ('skʌnˌθɔ:p) *n.* a town in E England, in Humberside: developed rapidly after the discovery of local iron ore (1871); iron and steel centre. Pop.: 70 880 (1971).

scup (skʌp) *n.* a common sparid fish, *Stenotomus chrysops*, of American coastal regions of the Atlantic. Also called: **northern porgy.** [C19: from Narragansett *mishcup*, from *mishe* big + *kuppe* close together; from the form of the scales]

scup·per[1] ('skʌpə) *n.* **1.** *Nautical.* a drain or spout allowing water on the deck of a vessel to flow overboard. **2.** an opening in the side of a building for draining off water. **3.** a drain in a factory floor for running off the water from a sprinkler system. [C15 *skopper*, of uncertain origin; perhaps related to SCOOP]

scup·per[2] ('skʌpə) *vb.* (*tr.*) *Brit. slang.* to overwhelm, ruin, or disable. [C19: of unknown origin]

scup·per·nong ('skʌpəˌnɒŋ) *n.* **1.** a sweet American wine, slightly golden, made from a variety of muscadine grape. **2.** another name for **muscadine** (sense 2), esp. the variety from which this wine is made. [C19: named after *Scuppernong* River in North Carolina where the grape grows]

scurf (skɜ:f) *n.* **1.** another name for **dandruff. 2.** flaky or scaly matter adhering to or peeling off a surface. [Old English *scurf*; related to Old Norse *skurfóttr* scurfy, Old High German *scorf*, Danish *skurv*] —**'scurf·y** *adj.*

scur·ril·ous ('skʌrɪləs) *adj.* **1.** grossly or obscenely abusive or defamatory. **2.** characterized by gross or obscene humour. [C16: from Latin *scurrīlis* derisive, from *scurra* buffoon] —**scur·ril·i·ty** (skə'rɪlɪtɪ) *n.* —**'scur·ri·lous·ly** *adv.* —**'scur·ri·lous·ness** *n.*

scur·ry ('skʌrɪ) *vb.* **·ries, ·ry·ing, ·ried. 1.** to move about or proceed hurriedly. **2.** (*intr.*) to whirl about. ~*n., pl.* **·ries. 3.** the act or sound of scurrying. **4.** a brisk light whirling movement, as of snow. **5.** *Horse racing.* a short race or sprint. [C19: probably shortened from HURRY-SCURRY]

scur·vy ('skɜ:vɪ) *n.* **1.** a disease caused by a lack of vitamin C, characterized by anaemia, spongy gums, bleeding beneath the skin, and (in infants) malformation of bones and teeth. ~*adj.* **·vi·er, ·vi·est. 2.** mean or despicable. [C16: see SCURF] —**'scur·vi·ly** *adv.* —**'scur·vi·ness** *n.*

scur·vy grass *n.* any of various cruciferous plants of the genus *Cochlearia*, esp. *C. officinalis*, of Europe and North America, formerly used to treat scurvy.

scut (skʌt) *n.* the short tail of animals such as the deer and rabbit. [C15: probably of Scandinavian origin; compare Old Norse *skutr* end of a vessel, Icelandic *skott* tail]

scu·ta ('skju:tə) *n.* the plural of **scutum.**

scu·tage ('skju:tɪdʒ) *n.* (in feudal society) a payment sometimes exacted by a lord from his vassal in lieu of military service. [C15: from Medieval Latin *scūtāgium*, literally: shield dues, from Latin *scūtum* a shield]

Scu·ta·ri *n.* **1.** ('sku:tərɪ, sku:'tɑ:rɪ). the former name of **Üsküdar. 2.** (sku'ta:ri). the Italian name for **Shkodër.**

scu·tate ('skju:teɪt) *adj.* **1.** (of animals) having or covered with large bony or horny plates. **2.** *Botany.* shaped like a round shield or buckler: *a scutate leaf.* [C19: from Latin *scūtātus* armed with a shield, from *scūtum* a shield] —**scu·'ta·tion** *n.*

scutch (skʌtʃ) *vb.* **1.** (*tr.*) to separate the fibres from the woody part of (flax, etc.) by pounding. ~*n.* **2.** Also called **scutcher.** the tool used for this. [C18: from obsolete French *escoucher*, from Vulgar Latin *excuticāre* (unattested) to beat out, from Latin EX-[1] + *quatere* to shake]

scutch·eon ('skʌtʃən) *n.* **1.** a variant of **escutcheon. 2.** any rounded or shield-shaped structure, esp. a scute. —**'scutch·eon·less** *adj.* —**'scutch·eon·**ˌ**like** *adj.*

scutch grass *n.* another name for **bermuda grass** and **couch grass.** Sometimes shortened to **scutch.** [variant of COUCH]

scute (skju:t) *n. Zoology.* a horny or chitinous plate that makes up part of the exoskeleton in armadillos, turtles, fishes, etc. [C14 (the name of a French coin; C19 in zoological sense): from Latin *scūtum* shield]

scu·tel·la·tion (ˌskju:tɪ'leɪʃən) *n. Zoology.* **1.** the way in which scales or plates are arranged in an animal. **2.** a covering of scales or scutella, as on a bird's leg.

scu·tel·lum (skju:'tɛləm) *n., pl.* **·la** (-lə). *Biology.* **1.** the last of three plates into which the notum of an insect's thorax is divided. **2.** one of the scales on the tarsus of a bird's leg. **3.** the cotyledon of a developing grass seed. **4.** any other small shield-shaped part or structure. [C18: from New Latin: a little shield, from Latin *scūtum* a shield] —**scu·'tel·lar** *adj.* —**scu·tel·late** ('skju:tɪˌleɪt, -lɪt) *adj.*

scu·ti·form ('skju:tɪˌfɔ:m) *adj.* (esp. of plant parts) shaped like a shield. [C17: from New Latin *scūtiformis*, from Latin *scūtum* a shield + *forma* shape]

scut·ter ('skʌtə) *vb., n. Brit.* an informal word for **scurry.** [C18: probably from SCUTTLE[2], with -ER[1] as in SCATTER]

scut·tle[1] ('skʌtᵊl) *n.* **1.** See **coal scuttle. 2.** *Dialect, chiefly Brit.* a shallow basket for carrying vegetables, etc. **3.** the part of a motor-car body lying immediately behind the bonnet. [Old English *scutel* trencher, from Latin *scutella* bowl, diminutive of *scutra* platter; related to Old Norse *skutill*, Old High German *scuzzila*, perhaps to Latin *scūtum* shield]

scut·tle[2] ('skʌtᵊl) *vb.* **1.** (*intr.*) to run or move about with short hasty steps. ~*n.* **2.** a hurried pace or run. [C15: perhaps from SCUD[1], influenced by SHUTTLE]

scut·tle[3] ('skʌtᵊl) *vb.* **1.** (*tr.*) *Nautical.* to cause (a vessel) to sink by opening the seacocks or making holes in the bottom. **2.** (*tr.*) to give up (hopes, plans, etc.). ~*n.* **3.** *Nautical.* a small hatch or its cover. [C15 (n.): via Old French from Spanish *escotilla* a small opening, from *escote* opening in a piece of cloth, from *escotar* to cut out]

scut·tle+butt ('skʌtᵊl,bʌt) *n. Nautical.* **1.** a drinking fountain. **2.** (formerly) a cask of drinking water aboard a ship.

scu+tum ('skju:təm) *n., pl.* **+ta** (-tə). **1.** the middle of three plates into which the notum of an insect's thorax is divided. **2.** another word for **scute. 3.** a large Roman shield. [Latin: shield]

Scu+tum ('skju:təm) *n., Latin genitive* **Scu+ti** ('skju:taɪ). a small faint constellation in the S hemisphere lying between Sagittarius and Aquila and crossed by the Milky Way. Also called: **Scutum Sobieskii.**

Scyl·la ('sɪlə) *n.* **1.** *Greek myth.* a sea nymph transformed into a sea monster believed to drown sailors navigating the Straits of Messina. She was identified with a rock off the Italian coast. Compare **Charybdis. 2. between Scylla and Charybdis.** in a predicament in which avoidance of either of two dangers means exposure to the other.

scy+phi+form ('saɪfɪ,fɔ:m) *adj.* shaped like a cup or goblet: *a scyphiform cell.* [C19: from Greek *skuphos* cup + -FORM]

scy+phis+to+ma (saɪ'fɪstəmə) *n., pl.* **+mae** (-,mi:) *or* **+mas.** a sessile hydra-like individual representing the polyp stage of scyphozoans. It produces forms which become free-swimming jellyfish. [C19: from Greek *skuphos cup* + STOMA]

scy+pho+zo+an (,saɪfə'zəʊən) *n.* **1.** any marine medusoid coelenterate of the class *Scyphozoa;* a jellyfish. ~*adj.* **2.** of, relating to, or belonging to the *Scyphozoa.* [C19: via New Latin from Greek *skuphos* bowl + *zōion* animal]

scy+phus ('saɪfəs) *n., pl.* **+phi** (-faɪ). **1.** an ancient Greek two-handled drinking cup without a footed base. **2.** *Botany.* a cuplike body formed at the end of the thallus in certain lichens. [C18: from Latin: goblet, from Greek *skuphos*]

Scy+ros ('ski:rɒs) *n.* a variant spelling of **Skyros.**

scythe (saɪð) *n.* **1.** a manual implement for cutting grass, etc., having a long handle held with both hands and a curved sharpened blade that moves in a plane parallel to the ground. ~*vb.* **2.** (*tr.*) to cut (grass, etc.) with a scythe. [Old English *sigthe;* related to Old Norse *sigthr,* Old High German *segansa*] —**'scythe+,like** *adj.*

Scyth·i·a ('sɪðɪə) *n.* an ancient region of SE Europe and Asia, north of the Black Sea: now part of the Soviet Union.

Scyth+i·an ('sɪðɪən) *adj.* **1.** of or relating to ancient Scythia, its inhabitants, or their language. ~*n.* **2.** a member of an ancient nomadic people of Scythia. **3.** the extinct language of this people, belonging to the East Iranian branch of the Indo-European family.

SD *international car registration for* Swaziland.

s.d. *abbrev. for* sine die.

S.D. *abbrev. for:* **1.** South Dakota. **2.** Also: **s.d.** *Statistics.* standard deviation.

S. Dak. *abbrev. for* South Dakota.

SDP (in Britain) *abbrev. for* Social Democratic Party.

SDRs *abbrev. for* special drawing rights.

Se *the chemical symbol for* selenium.

SE *abbrev. for* southeast(ern).

sea (si:) *n.* **1. a.** (usually preceded by *the*) the mass of salt water on the earth's surface as differentiated from the land. Related adjs.: **marine, maritime. b.** (*as modifier*): *sea air.* **2.** (*cap. when part of place name*) **a.** one of the smaller areas of ocean: *the Irish Sea.* **b.** a large inland area of water: *the Caspian Sea.* **3.** turbulence or swell, esp. of considerable size: *heavy seas.* **4.** (*cap. when part of a name*) *Astronomy.* any of many huge dry plains on the surface of the moon: *Sea of Serenity.* See also **mare**[2]. **5.** anything resembling the sea in size or apparent limitlessness. **6.** the life or career of a sailor (esp. in the phrase **follow the sea**). **7. at sea. a.** on the ocean. **b.** in a state of confusion. **8. go to sea.** to become a sailor. **9. put (out) to sea.** to embark on a sea voyage. [Old English *sǣ;* related to Old Norse *sǣr,* Old Frisian *sē,* Gothic *saiws,* Old High German *sēo*]

sea an+chor *n. Nautical.* any device, such as a bucket or canvas funnel, dragged in the water to slow a vessel.

sea a·nem·o·ne *n.* any of various anthozoan coelenterates, esp. of the order *Actiniaria,* having a polypoid body with oral rings of tentacles. See also **actinia.**

sea bag *n.* a canvas bag, closed by a line rove through grommets at the top, used by a seaman for his belongings.

sea bass (bæs) *n.* any of various American coastal percoid fishes of the genus *Centropristes* and related genera, such as *C. striatus* (**black sea bass**), having an elongated body with a long spiny dorsal fin almost divided into two: family *Serranidae.*

Sea+bee ('si:,bi:) *n.* a member of the U.S. Navy's Construction Battalions established to build airstrips. [C20: from pronunciation of *CB,* for *Construction Battalion*]

sea bird *n.* a bird such as a gull, that lives on the sea.

sea bis+cuit *n.* another term for **hardtack.**

sea+board ('si:,bɔ:d) *n. Chiefly U.S.* **a.** land bordering on the sea; the seashore. **b.** (*as modifier*): *seaboard towns.*

Sea·borg ('si:bɔ:g) *n.* **Glenn The·o·dore.** born 1912, U.S. chemist and nuclear physicist. With E. M. McMillan, he discovered several transuranic elements, including plutonium (1940), curium, and americium (1944), and shared a Nobel prize for chemistry 1951.

sea+borne ('si:,bɔ:n) *adj.* **1.** carried on or by the sea. **2.** transported by ship.

sea bream *n.* any sparid fish, esp. *Pagellus centrodontus,* of European seas, valued as a food fish.

sea breeze *n.* a wind blowing from the sea to the land, esp. during the day when the land surface is warmer.

sea but·ter+fly *n.* another name for **pteropod.**

sea cap+tain *n.* the master of a ship, usually a merchant ship.

sea chest *n.* a usually large firm chest used by a sailor for storing personal property.

sea+coast ('si:,kəʊst) *n.* land bordering on the sea; a coast.

sea+cock ('si:,kɒk) *n. Nautical.* a valve in the hull of a vessel below the water line for admitting sea water or for pumping out bilge water.

sea cow *n.* **1.** any sirenian mammal, such as a dugong or manatee. **2.** an archaic name for **walrus.**

sea cu+cum+ber *n.* any echinoderm of the class *Holothuroidea,* having an elongated body covered with a leathery skin and bearing a cluster of tentacles at the oral end. They usually creep on the sea bed or burrow in sand.

sea+dog ('si:,dɒg) *n.* another word for **fogbow** or **fogdog.**

sea dog *n.* an experienced or old sailor.

sea duck *n.* any of various large diving ducks, such as the eider and the scoter, that occur along coasts.

sea ea·gle *n.* any of various fish-eating eagles that live near the sea, esp. *Haliaetus albicilla* (**European sea eagle** *or* **white-tailed eagle**) having a brown plumage and white tail.

sea-ear *n.* another name for the **ormer.**

sea el+e·phant *n.* another name for **elephant seal.**

sea fan *n.* any of various corals of the genus *Gorgonia* and related genera, having a treelike or fan-shaped horny skeleton: order *Gorgonacea* (gorgonians).

sea+far·er ('si:,fɛərə) *n.* **1.** a traveller who goes by sea. **2.** a less common word for **sailor.**

sea+far·ing ('si:,fɛərɪŋ) *adj.* (*prenominal*) **1.** travelling by sea. **2.** working as a sailor. ~*n.* **3.** the act of travelling by sea. **4.** the career or work of a sailor.

sea foam *n.* **1.** foam formed on the surface of the sea. **2.** a former name for **meerschaum** (sense 1).

sea+food ('si:,fu:d) *n.* edible saltwater fish or shellfish.

sea+front ('si:,frʌnt) *n.* a built-up area facing the sea.

sea+girt ('si:,gɜ:t) *adj. Literary.* surrounded by the sea.

sea+go·ing ('si:,gəʊɪŋ) *adj.* intended for or used at sea.

sea goose+ber·ry *n.* any of various ctenophores of the genus *Pleurobrachia* and related genera, having a rounded body with longitudinal rows of cilia and hairlike tentacles.

sea green *n.* **a.** a moderate green colour, sometimes with a bluish or yellowish tinge. **b.** (*as adj.*): *a sea-green carpet.*

sea gull *n.* a popular name for the **gull** (the bird).

sea hare *n.* any of various marine gastropods of the order *Aplysiomorpha* (or *Anaspidea*), esp. *Aplysia punctata,* having a soft body with an internal shell and two pairs of earlike tentacles.

sea heath *n.* a small tough perennial plant, *Frankenia laevis,* of Eurasian salt marshes, having minute leaves and pink flowers: family *Frankeniaceae.*

sea hol+ly *n.* a European umbelliferous plant, *Eryngium maritimum,* of sandy shores, having spiny bluish-green stems and blue flowers.

sea horse *n.* **1.** any marine teleost fish of the temperate and tropical genus *Hippocampus,* having a bony-plated body, a prehensile tail, and a horselike head and swimming in an upright position: family *Syngnathidae* (pipefishes). **2.** an archaic name for the **walrus. 3.** a fabled sea creature with the tail of a fish and the front parts of a horse.

sea-is·land cot+ton *n.* **1.** a cotton plant, *Gossypium barbadense,* of the Sea Islands, widely cultivated for its fine long fibres. **2.** the fibre of this plant or the material woven from it.

Sea Is+lands *pl. n.* a chain of islands in the Atlantic off the coasts of South Carolina, Georgia, and Florida.

sea kale *n.* a European coastal cruciferous plant, *Crambe maritima,* with broad fleshy leaves and white flowers: cultivated for its edible asparagus-like shoots. Compare **kale.**

sea+kale beet *n.* another name for **chard.**

sea king *n.* any of the greater Viking pirate chiefs who led raids on the coasts of early medieval Europe.

seal[1] (si:l) *n.* **1.** a device impressed on a piece of wax, etc., fixed to a letter, etc., as a mark of authentication. **2.** a stamp, ring, etc., engraved with a device to form such an impression. **3.** a substance, esp. wax, so placed over an envelope, etc., that it must be broken before the object can be opened or used. **4.** any substance or device used to close or fasten tightly. **5.** a material, such as putty or cement, that is used to close an opening to prevent the passage of air, water, etc. **6.** a small amount of water contained in the trap of a drain to prevent the passage of foul smells. **7.** an agent or device for keeping something hidden or secret. **8.** anything that gives a pledge or confirmation. **9.** a decorative stamp often sold in aid of charity. **10.** *R.C. Church.* Also called: **seal of confession.** the obligation never to reveal anything said by a penitent in confession. **11. set one's seal on** (*or* **to**). **a.** to mark with one's sign or seal. **b.** to endorse. ~*vb.* (*tr.*) **12.** to affix a seal to, as proof of authenticity, etc. **13.** to stamp with or as if with a seal. **14.** to approve or authorize. **15.** (sometimes foll. by *up*) to close or secure with or as if with a seal: *to seal one's lips; seal up a letter.* **16.** (foll. by *off*) to enclose (a place) with a fence, etc. **17.** to decide irrevocably. **18.** *Mormon Church.* to make (a marriage or adoption) perpetually binding. **19.** to close tightly so as to render airtight or watertight. **20.** to paint (a porous material) with a nonporous coating. [C13 *seel,* from Old French, from Latin *sigillum* little figure, from *signum* a sign] —**'seal+a·ble** *adj.*

seal[2] (si:l) *n.* **1.** any pinniped mammal of the families *Otariidae* (see **eared seal**) and *Phocidae* (see **earless seal**) that are aquatic but come on shore to breed. **2.** any earless seal (family *Phocidae*), esp. the common or harbour seal or the grey seal

(*Halichoerus grypus*). **3.** sealskin. ~*vb.* **4.** (*intr.*) to hunt for seals. [Old English *seolh;* related to Old Norse *selr,* Old High German *selah,* Old Irish *selige* tortoise] —'**seal-,like** *adj.*
sea lad+der *n.* a rope ladder, set of steps, etc., by which a boat may be boarded at sea.
sea lam+prey *n.* a common anadromous lamprey, *Petromyzon marinus,* a form of which occurs in the Great Lakes and causes great losses of fish.
sea-lane *n.* an established route for ships.
seal+ant ('si:lənt) *n.* **1.** any substance, such as wax, used for sealing documents, bottles, or the like. **2.** any of a number of substances used for waterproofing wood, etc.
sea lav+en+der *n.* any of numerous perennial plants of the plumbaginaceous genus *Limonium,* of temperate salt marshes, having spikes of white, pink, or mauve flowers.
sea law+yer *n. Nautical slang.* a contentious seaman.
seal brown *n.* **a.** a dark brown colour often with a yellowish or greyish tinge. **b.** (*as adj.*)*: a seal-brown dress.*
sealed (si:ld) *vb.* **1.** the past participle of **seal.** ~*adj. Austral.* **2.** (of a road) having a hard surface; made-up.
sealed-beam *adj.* (esp. of a car headlight) having a lens and prefocused reflector sealed in the lamp vacuum.
sealed book *n.* another term for **closed book.**
sealed move *n. Chess.* the last move before an adjournment, which is written down by the player making it, sealed in an envelope, and kept secret from his opponent until play is resumed.
sealed or+ders *pl. n.* written instructions that are not to be read until a specified time.
sea legs *pl. n. Informal.* **1.** the ability to maintain one's balance on board ship, esp. in rough weather. **2.** the ability to resist seasickness, esp. in rough weather.
seal+er[1] ('si:lə) *n.* **1.** a person or thing that seals. **2.** *U.S.* an official who examines the accuracy of weights, etc. **3.** a coating of paint, varnish, etc., applied to a surface to prevent the absorption of subsequent coats.
seal+er[2] ('si:lə) *n.* a person or ship occupied in sealing.
seal+er·y ('si:lərɪ) *n., pl.* **+er·ies. 1.** the occupation of hunting seals. **2.** any place where seals are regularly to be found, esp. a seal rookery.
sea let+ter *n.* **1.** Also called: **passport.** a document issued to a merchant vessel, esp. in wartime, authorizing it to leave a port or proceed freely. **2.** (formerly) a document issued to a vessel in port, describing its cargo, etc.
sea let+tuce *n.* any of various green seaweeds of the genus *Ulva,* which have edible wavy translucent fronds.
sea lev+el *n.* the level of the surface of the sea with respect to the land, taken to be the mean level between high and low tide, and used as a standard base for measuring heights and depths.
sea lil·y *n.* any of various sessile echinoderms, esp. of the genus *Ptilocrinus,* in which the body consists of a long stalk attached to a hard surface and bearing a central disc with delicate radiating arms: class *Crinoidea* (crinoids).
seal+ing wax *n.* a hard material made of shellac, turpentine, and pigment that softens when heated. It is used for sealing documents, parcels, letters, etc.
sea li·on *n.* any of various large eared seals, such as *Zalophus californianus* (**Californian sea lion**), of the N Pacific, often used as a performing animal.
Sea Lord *n.* (in Britain) either of the two serving naval officers (**First** and **Second Sea Lords**) who sit on the admiralty board of the Ministry of Defence.
seal-point *n.* a popular variety of the Siamese cat, having a dark brown mask, paws, and tail, and a cream body.
seal ring *n.* another term for **signet ring.**
seal+skin ('si:l,skɪn) *n.* **1. a.** the skin or pelt of a fur seal, esp. when dressed with the outer hair removed and the underfur dyed dark brown. **b.** (*as modifier*)*: a sealskin coat.* **2.** a garment made of this skin.
Seal·y+ham ter+ri+er ('si:lɪəm) *n.* a small wire-haired breed of terrier with a medium-length coat, usually white. Often shortened to **Sealyham.**
seam (si:m) *n.* **1.** the line along which pieces of fabric, etc., are joined, esp. by stitching. **2.** a ridge or line made by joining two edges. **3.** a stratum of coal, ore, etc. **4. in a good seam.** *Northern Brit. dialect.* doing well, esp. financially. **5.** a linear indentation, such as a wrinkle or scar. **6.** *Surgery.* another name for **suture** (sense 1b.). **7.** *Anatomy.* another name for **raphe. 8.** (*modifier*) *Cricket.* of or relating to a style of bowling in which the bowler utilizes the stitched seam round the ball in order to make it swing in flight and after touching the ground: *a seam bowler.* **9. bursting at the seams.** full to overflowing. ~*vb.* **10.** (*tr.*) to join or sew together by or as if by a seam. **11.** *U.S.* to make ridges in (knitting) using purl stitch. **12.** to mark or become marked with or as if with a seam or wrinkle. [Old English; related to Old Norse *saumr,* Old High German *soum*] —'**seam+er** *n.* —'**seam+less** *adj.* —'**seam+less+ness** *n.*
sea+man ('si:mən) *n., pl.* **+men. 1.** a rating trained in seamanship as opposed to electrical engineering, etc. **2.** a man who serves as a sailor. **3.** a person skilled in seamanship. —'**sea·man-,like** *adj.* —'**sea+man+ly** *adj., adv.*
sea+man+ship ('si:mən,ʃɪp) *n.* skill in and knowledge of the work of navigating, maintaining, and operating a vessel.
sea+mark ('si:,mɑ:k) *n. Nautical.* an aid to navigation, such as a conspicuous object on a shore used as a guide.
sea mat *n.* a popular name for a **bryozoan.**
sea mew *n.* another name for **mew** (the bird).
Se·a·mi (si:'ɑ:mɪ) *n.* **Mo·to·ki·yo** (,məʊtəʊ'ki:əʊ). a variant spelling of **Zeami.**
sea mile *n.* an Imperial unit of length, formerly used in navigation, equal to 6000 feet or 1000 fathoms. It is equivalent to 1828.8 metres. Compare **nautical mile.**
sea milk+wort *n.* a primulaceous plant, *Glaux maritima,* of estuary mud and seaside rocks of N temperate coasts, having trailing stems and small pink flowers. Also called: **saltwort, black saltwort.** Compare **milkwort.**
sea+mount ('si:,maʊnt) *n.* a submarine mountain rising more than 920 metres (3000 feet) above the ocean floor.
sea mouse *n.* any of several large polychaete worms of the genus *Aphrodite* and related genera, having a broad flattened body covered dorsally with a dense mat of iridescent hairlike chaetae.
seam+stress ('sɛmstrɪs) *or* **semp+stress** ('sɛmpstrɪs) *n.* a woman who sews and makes clothes, esp. professionally.
seam·y ('si:mɪ) *adj.* **seam·i+er, seam·i+est. 1.** showing the least pleasant aspect; sordid. **2.** (esp. of the inner side of a garment) showing many seams. —'**seam·i·ness** *n.*
Sean+ad Éire+ann ('sænɑ:d 'ɛərən) *n.* (in the Republic of Ireland) the upper chamber of parliament; the Senate. [from Irish, literally: senate of Ireland]
se+ance ('seɪɒns) *n.* **1.** a meeting at which spiritualists attempt to receive messages from the spirits of the dead. **2.** a meeting of a society. [C19: from French, literally: a sitting, from Old French *seoir* to sit, from Latin *sedēre*]
sea on+ion *n.* another name for **sea squill.**
sea ot+ter *n.* a large marine otter, *Enhydra lutris,* of N Pacific coasts, formerly hunted for its thick dark brown fur.
sea pen *n.* any of various anthozoan coelenterates of the genus *Pennatula* and related genera, forming fleshy feather-like colonies in warm seas: order *Pennatulacea.*
sea perch *n.* **1.** any of various marine serranid fishes, such as the bass and stone bass, that have an elongated body with a very spiny dorsal fin and occur in all except polar seas. **2.** another name for **surfperch.**
sea pink *n.* another name for **thrift** (the plant).
sea+plane ('si:,pleɪn) *n.* any aircraft that lands on and takes off from water. Also called (esp. U.S.): **hydroplane.**
sea+port ('si:,pɔ:t) *n.* **1.** a port or harbour accessible to seagoing vessels. **2.** a town or city located at such a place.
sea pow+er *n.* **1.** a nation that possesses great naval strength. **2.** the naval strength of a country or nation.
sea purse *n.* a tough horny envelope containing fertilized eggs, produced by the female of certain sharks and skates. Also called: **mermaid's purse.**
sea purs+lane *n.* a small chenopodiaceous shrub, *Halimione portulacoides,* of salt marshes in Eurasia and parts of Africa, having oval leaves and inconspicuous flowers.
sea+quake ('si:,kweɪk) *n.* an agitation and disturbance of the sea caused by an earthquake at the sea bed.
sear[1] (sɪə) *vb.* (*tr.*) **1.** to scorch or burn the surface of. **2.** to brand with a hot iron. **3.** to cause to wither or dry up. **4.** *Rare.* to make callous or unfeeling. ~*n.* **5.** a mark caused by searing. ~*adj.* **6.** *Poetic.* dried up. [Old English *sēarian* to become withered, from *sēar* withered; related to Old High German *sōrēn, Greek hauos* dry, Sanskrit *sōsa* drought]
sear[2] (sɪə) *n.* the catch in the lock of a small firearm that holds the hammer cocked. [C16: probably from Old French *serre* a clasp, from *serrer* to hold firmly, from Late Latin *sērāre* to bolt, from Latin *sera* a bar]
sea rang+er *n. Brit.* a senior Guide training in seamanship. U.S. equivalent: **mariner.**
sea ra+ven *n.* a large fish, *Hemitripterus americanus,* of North American Atlantic coastal waters that inflates itself with air when caught: family *Cottidae* (bullheads and sea scorpions).
search (sɜ:tʃ) *vb.* **1.** to look through (a place, etc.) thoroughly in order to find someone or something. **2.** (*tr.*) to examine (a person) for concealed objects by running one's hands over the clothing, etc. **3.** to look at or examine (something) closely: *to search one's conscience.* **4.** (*tr.*; foll. by *out*) to discover by investigation. **5.** *Surgery.* **a.** to explore (a bodily cavity, etc.) during a surgical procedure. **b.** to probe (a wound, etc.). **6.** (*tr.*) *Military.* to fire all over (an area). **7.** *Archaic.* to penetrate. **8. search me.** *Informal.* I don't know. ~*n.* **9.** the act or an instance of searching. **10.** the examination of a vessel by the right of search. **11. right of search.** *International law.* the right possessed by the warships of a belligerent state in time of war to board and search merchant vessels to ascertain whether ship or cargo is liable to seizure. [C14: from Old French *cerchier,* from Late Latin *circāre* to go around, from Latin *circus* CIRCLE] —'**search+a·ble** *adj.* —'**search+a·ble+ness** *n.* —'**search+er** *n.*
search+ing ('sɜ:tʃɪŋ) *adj.* keenly penetrating: *a searching look.* —'**search+ing+ly** *adv.* —'**search+ing+ness** *n.*
search+light ('sɜ:tʃ,laɪt) *n.* **1.** a device, consisting of a light source and a reflecting surface behind it, that projects a powerful beam of light in a particular direction. **2.** the beam of light produced by such a device.
search par+ty *n.* a group of people taking part in an organized search, as for a lost, missing, or wanted person.
search war+rant *n.* a written order issued by a justice of the peace authorizing a constable or other officer to enter and search premises for stolen goods, etc.
sea rob+in *n.* any of various American gurnards of the genus *Prionotus* and related genera, such as *P. carolinus* (**northern sea robin**).
sea room *n.* sufficient space to manoeuvre a vessel.
sea+scape ('si:,skeɪp) *n.* a sketch, picture, etc., of the sea.
sea scor+pi+on *n.* any of various northern marine scorpaenoid

fishes of the family *Cottidae,* esp. *Taurulus bubalis* (**long-spined sea scorpion**). They have a tapering body and a large head covered with bony plates and spines.

Sea Scout *n.* a Scout belonging to any of a number of Scout troops whose main activities are canoeing, sailing, etc., and who wear sailors' caps as part of their uniform.

sea ser+pent *n.* a huge legendary creature of the sea resembling a snake or dragon.

sea+shell ('siːˌʃɛl) *n.* the empty shell of a marine mollusc.

sea+shore ('siːˌʃɔː) *n.* **1.** land bordering on the sea. **2.** *Law.* the land between the marks of high and low water.

sea+sick ('siːˌsɪk) *adj.* suffering from nausea and dizziness caused by the motion of a ship at sea. —**'sea+ˌsick+ness** *n.*

sea+side ('siːˌsaɪd) *n.* **a.** any area bordering on the sea, esp. one regarded as a resort. **b.** (*as modifier*): *a seaside hotel.*

sea slug *n.* any of various shell-less marine gastropod molluscs, esp. those of the order *Nudibranchia.* See **nudibranch.**

sea snail *n.* any small spiny-finned fish of the family *Liparidae,* esp. *Liparis liparis,* of cold seas, having a soft scaleless tadpole-shaped body with the pelvic fins fused into a sucker. Also called: **snailfish.**

sea snake *n.* any venomous snake of the family *Hydrophiidae,* of tropical seas, that swims by means of a laterally compressed oarlike tail.

sea+son ('siːzᵊn) *n.* **1.** one of the four equal periods into which the year is divided by the equinoxes and solstices, resulting from the apparent movement of the sun north and south of the equator during the course of the earth's orbit around it. These periods (spring, summer, autumn, and winter) have their characteristic weather conditions in different regions, and occur at opposite times of the year in the N and S hemispheres. **2.** a period of the year characterized by particular conditions or activities: *the rainy season.* **3.** the period during which any particular species of animal, bird, or fish is legally permitted to be caught or killed: *open season on red deer.* **4.** any definite or indefinite period. **5.** any of the major periods into which the ecclesiastical calendar is divided, such as Lent, Advent, or Easter. **6. in good season.** early enough. **7. in season. a.** (of game) permitted to be caught or killed. **b.** (of fresh food) readily available. **c.** (of some female mammals) sexually receptive. **d.** appropriate. ~*vb.* **8.** (*tr.*) to add herbs, salt, pepper, or spice to (food). **9.** (*tr.*) to add zest to. **10.** (in the preparation of timber) to undergo or cause to undergo seasoning. **11.** (*tr.; usually passive*) to make or become mature or experienced: *seasoned troops.* **12.** (*tr.*) to mitigate or temper: *to season one's admiration with reticence.* [C13: from Old French *seson,* from Latin *satiō* a sowing, from *serere* to sow] —**'sea+soned+ly** *adv.* —**'sea+son+er** *n.* —**'sea+son+less** *adj.*

sea+son+a+ble ('siːzənəbᵊl) *adj.* **1.** suitable for the season. **2.** taking place at the appropriate time. —**'sea+son+a+ble+ness** *n.* —**'sea+son+a+bly** *adv.*

sea+son+al ('siːzənᵊl) *adj.* of, relating to, or occurring at a certain season or certain seasons of the year: *seasonal labour.* —**'sea+son+al+ly** *adv.* —**'sea+son+al+ness** *n.*

sea+son+ing ('siːzənɪŋ) *n.* **1.** something that enhances the flavour of food, such as salt or herbs. **2.** the processing of timber until it has a moisture content suitable for the purposes for which it is to be used.

sea+son tick+et *n.* a ticket for a series of events, number of journeys, etc., within a limited time, usually obtained at a reduced rate.

sea squill *or* **on+ion** *n.* a Mediterranean liliaceous plant, *Urginea maritima,* having dense spikes of small white flowers, and yielding a bulb with medicinal properties.

sea squirt *n.* any minute primitive marine animal of the class *Ascidiacea,* most of which are sedentary, having a saclike body with openings through which water enters and leaves. See also **ascidian.**

sea steps *pl. n.* projecting metal bars attached to a ship's side, used for boarding.

sea swal+low *n.* a popular name for **tern** (the bird).

seat (siːt) *n.* **1.** a piece of furniture designed for sitting on, such as a chair or sofa. **2.** the part of a chair, bench, etc., on which one sits. **3.** a place to sit, esp. one that requires a ticket: *I have two seats for the film tonight.* **4.** another name for **buttocks. 5.** the part of a garment covering the buttocks. **6.** the part or area serving as the base of an object. **7.** the part or surface on which the base of an object rests. **8.** the place or centre in which something is located: *a seat of government.* **9.** a place of abode, esp. a country mansion that is or was originally the chief residence of a family. **10.** a membership or the right to membership in a legislative or similar body. **11.** *Chiefly Brit.* a parliamentary constituency. **12.** membership in a stock exchange. **13.** the manner in which a rider sits on a horse. **14. on seat.** *West African informal.* (of officials) in the office rather than on tour or on leave: *the agricultural advisor will be on seat tomorrow.* ~*vb.* **15.** (*tr.*) to bring to or place on a seat; cause to sit down. **16.** (*tr.*) to provide with seats. **17.** (*tr.; often passive*) to place or centre: *the ministry is seated in the capital.* **18.** (*tr.*) to set firmly in place. **19.** (*tr.*) to fix or install in a position of power. **20.** (*tr.*) to put a seat on or in (an item of furniture, garment, etc.). **21.** (*intr.*) (of garments) to sag in the area covering the buttocks: *your thin skirt has seated badly.* [Old English *gesete;* related to Old Norse *sæti,* Old High German *gasāzi,* Middle Dutch *gesaete*] —**'seat+er** *n.* —**'seat+less** *adj.*

sea tan+gle *n.* any of various brown seaweeds, esp. any of the genus *Laminaria.*

seat belt *n.* **1.** Also called: **safety belt.** a belt or strap worn in a car to restrain forward motion in the event of a collision. **2.** a similar belt or strap worn in an aircraft at takeoff and landing and in rough weather.

seat+ing ('siːtɪŋ) *n.* **1.** the act of providing with a seat or seats. **2. a.** the provision of seats, as in a theatre, etc. **b.** (*as modifier*): *seating arrangements.* **3.** material used for covering or making seats.

SEATO ('siːtəʊ) *n. acronym for* Southeast Asian Treaty Organization; a former anti-Communist defence association for the Far East and the W Pacific (1954–77), consisting of the U.S., Britain, France, Australia, New Zealand, Pakistan, the Philippines, and Thailand.

Sea+ton Val+ley ('siːtᵊn) *n.* a region in NE England, in SE Northumberland: consists of a group of coal-mining villages. Pop.: 32 011 (1971).

sea trout *n.* **1.** a silvery marine variety of the brown trout that migrates to fresh water to spawn. Compare **brown trout. 2.** any of several marine sciaenid fishes of the genus *Cynoscion,* such as *C. nebulosus* (**spotted sea trout**) and the weakfish, of North American coastal waters.

Se+at+tle (sɪ'ætᵊl) *n.* a port in W Washington, on the isthmus between Lake Washington and Puget Sound: the largest city in the state and chief commercial centre of the Northwest; two universities. Pop.: 503 073 (1973 est.).

sea ur+chin *n.* any echinoderm of the class *Echinoidea,* such as *Echinus esculentus* (**edible sea urchin**), typically having a globular body enclosed in a rigid spiny test and occurring in shallow marine waters.

sea wall *n.* a wall or embankment built to prevent encroachment or erosion by the sea or to serve as a breakwater. —**'sea-ˌwalled** *adj.*

sea+wan *or* **se+wan** ('siːwən) *n.* shell beads, usually unstrung, used by certain North American Indians as money; wampum. [C18: from Narragansett *seawohn* loose]

sea+ward ('siːwəd) *adv.* **1.** a variant of **seawards.** ~*adj.* **2.** directed or moving towards the sea. **3.** (esp. of a wind) coming from the sea.

sea+wards ('siːwədz) *or* **sea+ward** *adv.* towards the sea.

sea+ware ('siːˌwɛə) *n.* any of numerous large coarse seaweeds, esp. when cast ashore and used as fertilizer. [Old English *sǣwār,* from *sǣ* SEA + *wār* sea weed]

sea+way ('siːˌweɪ) *n.* **1.** a waterway giving access to an inland port, navigable by ocean-going ships. **2.** a vessel's progress. **3.** a rough or heavy sea. **4.** a route across the sea.

sea+weed ('siːˌwiːd) *n.* **1.** any of numerous multicellular marine algae that grow on the seashore, in salt marshes, in brackish water, or submerged in the ocean. **2.** any of certain other plants that grow in or close to the sea.

sea+wor+thy ('siːˌwɜːðɪ) *adj.* in a fit condition or ready for a sea voyage. —**'sea+ˌwor+thi+ness** *n.*

sea wrack *n.* any of various seaweeds found on the shore, esp. any of the larger species.

se+ba+ceous (sɪ'beɪʃəs) *adj.* **1.** of or resembling sebum, fat, or tallow; fatty. **2.** secreting fat or a greasy lubricating substance. [C18: from Late Latin *sēbāceus,* from SĒBUM]

se+ba+ceous glands *pl. n.* the small glands in the skin that secrete sebum into hair follicles and onto most of the body surface except the soles of the feet and the palms of the hands.

se+bac+ic ac+id (sɪ'bæsɪk, -'beɪ-) *n.* another name for **decanedioic acid.**

Se+bas+tian (sɪ'bæstjən) *n.* **Saint.** died ?288 A.D., Christian martyr. According to tradition, he was first shot with arrows and then beaten to death. Feast day: Jan. 20.

Se+bas+to+pol (sɪ'bæstəpəl) *n.* the English name for **Sevastopol.**

seb+i- *or* **seb+o-** *combining form.* fat or fatty matter: *sebiferous.* [from Latin *sēbum* tallow]

se+bif+er+ous (sɪ'bɪfərəs) *adj. Biology.* producing or carrying a fatty, oily, or waxlike substance.

seb+or+rhoe+a *or esp. U.S.* **seb+or+rhe+a** (ˌsɛbə'rɪə) *n.* a disease of the sebaceous glands characterized by excessive secretion of sebum and its accumulation on the skin surface. —**ˌseb+or+'rhoe+al, ˌseb+or+'rhoe+ic** *or esp. U.S.* **ˌseb+or+'rhe+al, ˌseb+or+'rhe+ic** *adj.*

se+bum ('siːbəm) *n.* the oily secretion of the sebaceous glands that acts as a lubricant for the hair and skin and provides some protection against bacteria. [C19: from New Latin, from Latin: tallow]

sec[1] (sɛk) *adj.* **1.** (of wines) dry. **2.** (of champagne) of medium sweetness. [C19: from French, from Latin *siccus*]

sec[2] (sɛk) *n. Informal.* short for **second**[2]: *wait a sec.*

sec[3] (sɛk) *abbrev. for* secant.

sec. *abbrev. for:* **1.** second (of time). **2.** secondary. **3.** secretary. **4.** section. **5.** sector.

SECAM ('siːˌkæm) *n. acronym for* système électronique couleur avec mémoire: a colour-television broadcasting system adopted in France.

se+cant ('siːkənt) *n.* **1.** (of an angle) a trigonometric function that in a right-angled triangle is the ratio of the length of the hypotenuse to that of the adjacent side; the reciprocal of cosine. Abbrev.: **sec 2.** a line that intersects a curve. [C16: from Latin *secāre* to cut] —**'se+cant+ly** *adv.*

sec+a+teurs ('sɛkətəz, ˌsɛkə'tɜːz) *pl. n. Chiefly Brit.* a small pair of shears for pruning, having a pair of pivoted handles, sprung so that they are normally open, and a single cutting blade that closes against a flat surface. [C19: plural of French *sécateur,* from Latin *secāre* to cut]

sec+co ('sɛkəʊ) *n., pl.* **+cos. 1.** wall painting done on dried plaster with tempera or pigments ground in limewater.

Compare **fresco. 2.** any wall painting other than true fresco. [C19: from Italian: dry, from Latin *siccus*]

se·cede (sɪ'siːd) *vb.* (*intr.*; often foll. by *from*) (of a person, section, etc.) to make a formal withdrawal of membership, as from a political alliance, organization, etc. [C18: from Latin *sēcēdere* to withdraw, from *sē-* apart + *cēdere* to go] —**se'ced·er** *n.*

se·cern (sɪ'sɜːn) *vb.* (*tr.*) *Rare.* **1.** (of a gland or follicle) to secrete. **2.** to distinguish or discriminate. [C17: from Latin *sēcernere* to separate, from *sē-* apart + *cernere* to distinguish] —**se'cern·ment** *n.*

se·ces·sion (sɪ'sɛʃən) *n.* **1.** the act of seceding. **2.** (*often cap.*) *Chiefly U.S.* the withdrawal in 1860–61 of 11 Southern states from the Union to form the Confederacy, precipitating the American Civil War. [C17: from Latin *sēcessiō* a withdrawing, from *sēcēdere* to SECEDE] —**se'ces·sion·al** *adj.* —**se'ces·sion·ˌism** *n.* —**se'ces·sion·ist** *n.*

sech (ʃɛk, sɛtʃ) hyperbolic secant; a hyperbolic function that is the reciprocal of cosh.

se·clude (sɪ'kluːd) *vb.* (*tr.*) **1.** to remove from contact with others. **2.** to shut off or screen from view. [C15: from Latin *sēclūdere* to shut off, from *sē-* + *claudere* to imprison]

se·clud·ed (sɪ'kluːdɪd) *adj.* **1.** kept apart from the company of others: *a secluded life.* **2.** sheltered; private. —**se'clud·ed·ly** *adv.* —**se'clud·ed·ness** *n.*

se·clu·sion (sɪ'kluːʒən) *n.* **1.** the act of secluding or the state of being secluded. **2.** a secluded place. [C17: from Medieval Latin *sēclūsiō*; see SECLUDE]

se·clu·sive (sɪ'kluːsɪv) *adj.* **1.** tending to seclude. **2.** fond of seclusion. —**se'clu·sive·ly** *adv.* —**se'clu·sive·ness** *n.*

sec·ond[1] ('sɛkənd) *adj.* (*usually prenominal*) **1. a.** coming directly after the first in numbering or counting order, position, time, etc.; being the ordinal number of *two:* often written 2nd. **b.** (*as n.*): *the second in line.* **2.** rated, graded, or ranked between the first and third levels. **3.** alternate: *every second Thursday.* **4.** additional; extra: *a second opportunity.* **5.** resembling a person or event from an earlier period of history; unoriginal: *a second Wagner.* **6.** of lower quality; inferior: *belonging to the second class.* **7.** denoting the lowest but one forward ratio of a gearbox in a motor vehicle. **8.** *Music.* **a.** relating to or denoting a musical part, voice, or instrument lower in pitch than another part, voice, or instrument (the first): *the second violins.* **b.** of or relating to a part, instrument, or instrumentalist regarded as subordinate to another (the first): *the second flute.* **9. at second hand.** by hearsay. ~*n.* **10.** *Brit. education.* an honours degree of the second class, usually further divided into an upper and lower designation. Full term: **second-class honours degree. 11.** the lowest but one forward ratio of a gearbox in a motor vehicle: *he changed into second on the bend.* **12.** (in boxing, duelling, etc.) an attendant who looks after a competitor. **13.** a speech seconding a motion or the person making it. **14.** *Music.* **a.** the interval between one note and another lying next above or below it in the diatonic scale. **b.** one of two notes constituting such an interval in relation to the other. See also **minor** (sense 4), **major** (sense 11), **interval. 15.** (*pl.*) goods of inferior quality. **16.** (*pl.*) *Informal.* a second helping of food. **17.** (*pl.*) the second course of a meal. ~*vb.* (*tr.*) **18.** to give aid or backing to. **19.** (in boxing, etc.) to act as second to (a competitor). **20.** to make a speech or otherwise express formal support for (a motion already proposed). ~*adv.* **21.** Also **secondly.** in the second place. ~ **22.** *sentence connector.* Also: **secondly.** as the second point: linking what follows with the previous statement. [C13: via Old French from Latin *secundus* coming next in order, from *sequī* to follow] —'**sec·ond·er** *n.*

sec·ond[2] ('sɛkənd) *n.* **1. a.** 1/60 of a minute of time. **b.** the basic SI unit of time: the duration of 9 192 631 770 periods of radiation corresponding to the transition between two hyperfine levels of the ground state of caesium-133. Symbol: s **2.** 1/60 of a minute of angle. Symbol: ″ **3.** a very short period of time; moment. [C14: from Old French, from Medieval Latin *pars minūta secunda* the second small part (a minute being the first small part of an hour); see SECOND[1]]

se·cond[3] (sɪ'kɒnd) ~*vb.* (*tr.*) *Brit.* **1.** to transfer (an employee) temporarily to another branch, etc. **2.** *Military.* to transfer (an officer) to another post, often retiring him to a staff or nonregimental position. [C19: from French *en second* in second rank (or position)] —**se'cond·ment** *n.*

Sec·ond Ad·vent *n.* another term for the **Second Coming.**

sec·ond·ar·y ('sɛkəndərɪ, -drɪ) *adj.* **1.** one grade or step after the first; not primary. **2.** derived from or depending on what is primary, original, or first: *a secondary source.* **3.** below the first in rank, importance, etc.; not of major importance. **4.** (*prenominal*) of or relating to the education of young people between the ages of 11 and 18: *secondary education.* **5.** (of the flight feathers of a bird's wing) growing from the ulna. **6. a.** being the part of an electric circuit, such as a transformer or induction coil, in which a current is induced by a changing current in a neighbouring coil: *a secondary coil.* **b.** (of a current) flowing in such a circuit. Compare **primary** (sense 7). **7.** (of an industry) involving the manufacture of goods from raw materials. Compare **primary** (sense 8b), **tertiary** (sense 2). **8.** *Geology.* (of minerals) formed by the alteration of pre-existing minerals. **9.** *Chem.* **a.** (of an organic compound) having a functional group attached to a carbon atom that is attached to one hydrogen atom and two other groups. **b.** (of an amine) having only two organic groups attached to a nitrogen atom; containing the group NH. **c.** (of a salt) derived from a tribasic acid by replacement of two acidic hydrogen atoms with metal atoms or electropositive groups. **10.** *Linguistics.* **a.** derived from a word that is itself a derivation from another word. Thus, *lovably* comes from *lovable* and is a secondary derivative from *love.* **b.** (of a tense in Latin, Greek, or Sanskrit) another word for **historic** (sense 3). ~*n., pl.* **-ar·ies. 11.** a person or thing that is secondary. **12.** a subordinate, deputy, or inferior. **13.** a secondary coil, winding, inductance, or current in an electric circuit. **14.** *Ornithol.* any of the flight feathers that grow from the ulna of a bird's wing. See **primary** (sense 6). **15.** *Astronomy.* a celestial body that orbits around a specified primary body: *the moon is the secondary of the earth.* **16.** short for **secondary colour.** —'**sec·ond·ar·i·ly** *adv.* —'**sec·ond·ar·i·ness** *n.*

sec·ond·ar·y ac·cent *or* **stress** *n. Phonetics.* (in a system of transcribing utterances recognizing three levels of stress) the accent on a syllable of a word or breath group that is weaker than the primary accent but stronger than the lack of stress: *in the word "agriculture" the secondary accent falls on the third syllable.* Compare **primary accent.**

sec·ond·ar·y cell *n.* an electric cell that can be recharged and can therefore be used to store electrical energy in the form of chemical energy. See also **accumulator.** Compare **primary cell.**

sec·ond·ar·y col·our *n.* a colour formed by mixing two primary colours. Sometimes shortened to **secondary.**

sec·ond·ar·y e·mis·sion *n. Physics.* the emission of electrons (**secondary electrons**) from a solid as a result of bombardment with a beam of electrons, ions, or metastable atoms: used in electron multipliers.

sec·ond·ar·y mod·ern school *n. Brit.* (formerly) a secondary school offering a more technical or practical and less academic education than a grammar school.

sec·ond·ar·y pro·cess·es *pl. n. Psychoanal.* the logical conscious type of mental functioning, guided by external reality. Compare **primary processes.**

sec·ond·ar·y school *n.* a school for young people, usually between the ages of 11 and 18.

sec·ond·ar·y sex·u·al char·ac·ter·is·tic *n.* any of various features distinguishing individuals of different sex but not directly concerned in reproduction. Examples are the antlers of a stag and the beard of a man.

sec·ond·ar·y stress *n.* another term for **secondary accent.**

sec·ond bal·lot *n.* an electoral procedure in which if no candidate emerges as a clear winner in a first ballot, candidates at the bottom of the poll are eliminated and another ballot is held among the remaining candidates.

sec·ond ba·na·na *n. Slang, chiefly U.S.* **1.** a performer in vaudeville, etc., who plays a role subordinate to another. **2.** any person in a or secondary position to another.

sec·ond-best *adj.* **1.** next to the best. **2. come off second best.** *Informal.* to be defeated in competition.

sec·ond cham·ber *n.* the upper house of a bicameral legislative assembly.

sec·ond child·hood *n.* dotage; senility (esp. in the phrases **in his, her, etc., second childhood**).

sec·ond class *n.* **1.** the class or grade next in value, quality, etc., to the first. ~*adj.* (**sec·ond-class** *when prenominal*). **2.** of the class or grade next to the best in quality, etc.: *a second-class citizen.* **3.** shoddy or inferior. **4.** of or denoting the class of accommodation in a hotel or on an aircraft, etc., next in quality and price to first class. **5. a.** (in Britain) of or relating to letters that are handled more slowly than first-class letters. **b.** (in the U.S. and Canada) of or relating to mail that consists mainly of newspapers, etc. **6.** *Education.* See **second**[1] (sense 10). ~*adv.* **7.** by second-class mail, transport, etc.

Sec·ond Com·ing *or* **Ad·vent** *n. Theol.* the prophesied return of Christ to earth at the Last Judgment.

sec·ond cous·in *n.* the child of a first cousin of either of one's parents.

sec·ond-de·gree burn *n. Pathol.* See **burn**[1] (sense 19).

se·conde (sɪ'kɒnd; *French* sə'gɔ̃d) *n.* the second of eight positions from which a parry or attack can be made in fencing. [C18: from French *seconde parade* the second parry]

Sec·ond Em·pire *n.* **1. a.** the imperial government of France under Napoleon III. **b.** the period during which this government functioned (1852–70). **2.** the style of furniture and decoration of the Second Empire, reviving the Empire style, but with fussier ornamentation.

sec·ond es·tate *n. Rare.* the nobility collectively.

sec·ond fid·dle *n. Informal.* **1. a.** the second violin in a string quartet or one of the second violins in an orchestra. **b.** the musical part assigned to such an instrument. **2.** a secondary status. **3.** a person who has a secondary status.

sec·ond floor *n.* **1.** *Brit.* the storey of a building immediately above the first and two floors up from the ground. U.S. term: **third floor. 2.** the U.S. term for **first floor.**

sec·ond growth *n.* natural regrowth of a forest after fire, cutting, or some other disturbance.

sec·ond-guess *vb. Informal, chiefly U.S.* **1.** to criticize or evaluate with hindsight. **2.** to attempt to anticipate or predict (a person or thing). —'**sec·ond-'guess·er** *n.*

sec·ond hand *n.* a pointer on the face of a timepiece that indicates the seconds. Compare **hour hand, minute hand.**

sec·ond-hand *adj.* **1.** previously owned or used. **2.** not from an original source or experience. **3.** dealing in or selling goods that are not new: *a second-hand car dealer.* ~*adv.* **4.** from a source of previously owned or used goods: *he prefers to buy second-hand.* **5.** not directly: *he got the news second-hand.*

Sec·ond In·ter·na·tion·al *n.* **1. the.** an international association of socialist parties and trade unions that began in

Paris in 1889 and collapsed during World War I. The right-wing elements reassembled at Berne in 1919. See also **Labour and Socialist International.** **2.** another name for the **Labour and Socialist International.**

sec+ond lieu+ten+ant *n.* an officer holding the lowest commissioned rank in the armed forces of certain nations.

sec+ond+ly ('sɛkəndlɪ) *adv.* another word for **second,** usually used to precede the second item in a list of topics.

sec+ond man *n.* a person who assists the driver in crewing a locomotive.

sec+ond mate *n.* the next in command of a merchant vessel after the first mate.

sec+ond mort+gage *n.* a mortgage incurred after a first mortgage and having second claim against the security.

sec+ond na+ture *n.* a habit, characteristic, etc., not innate but so long practised or acquired as to seem so.

se+con+do (sɛ'kɒndəʊ) *n., pl.* **+di** (-di:). the left-hand part in a piano duet. Compare **primo.** [Italian: SECOND[1]]

sec+ond per+son *n.* a grammatical category of pronouns and verbs used when referring to or describing the individual or individuals being addressed.

sec·ond-rate *adj.* **1.** not of the highest quality; mediocre. **2.** second in importance, etc. —**'sec·ond-'rat·er** *n.*

sec+ond read+ing *n.* the second presentation of a bill in a legislative assembly, as to approve its general principles (in Britain), or to discuss a committee's report on it (in the U.S.).

Sec+ond Re+pub+lic *n.* **1.** the republican government of France from the deposition of Louis Philippe (1848) until the Second Empire (1852). **2.** the period during which this form of government existed (1848–52).

sec+ond sight *n.* the alleged ability to foresee the future, see actions taking place elsewhere, etc.; clairvoyance. —**'sec·ond-'sight·ed** *adj.* —**'sec·ond-'sight·ed+ness** *n.*

sec+ond string *n.* **1.** *Chiefly U.S.* a substitute or reserve player or team. **2.** *Chiefly Brit.* an alternative course of action, etc., intended to come into use should the first fail (esp. in the phrase **a second string to one's bow**). —*adj.* **sec·ond-string.** *Chiefly U.S.* **3.** *Sport.* **a.** being a substitute player. **b.** being the second-ranked player of a team in an individual sport. **4.** second-rate or inferior.

sec+ond thought *n.* (*usually pl.*) a revised opinion or idea on a matter already considered.

sec+ond wind (wɪnd) *n.* **1.** the return of the ability to breathe at a normal rate, esp. following a period of exertion. **2.** renewed ability to continue in an effort.

Sec+ond World War *n.* another name for **World War II.**

se+cre+cy ('si:krɪsɪ) *n., pl.* **+cies. 1.** the state or quality of being secret. **2.** the state of keeping something secret. **3.** the ability or tendency to keep things secret.

se+cret ('si:krɪt) *adj.* **1.** kept hidden or separate from the knowledge of others. Related adj.: **cryptic. 2.** known only to initiates: *a secret password.* **3.** hidden from general view or use: *a secret garden.* **4.** able or tending to keep things private or to oneself. **5.** operating without the knowledge of outsiders: *a secret society.* **6.** outside the normal range of knowledge. ~*n.* **7.** something kept or to be kept hidden. **8.** something unrevealed; mystery. **9.** an underlying explanation, reason, etc., that is not apparent: *the secret of success.* **10.** a method, plan, etc., known only to initiates. **11.** *Liturgy.* a variable prayer, part of the Mass, said by the celebrant after the offertory and before the preface. **12. in the secret.** among the people who know a secret. [C14: via Old French from Latin *sēcrētus* concealed, from *sēcernere* to sift; see SECERN] —**'se+cret+ly** *adv.*

se+cret a·gent *n.* a person employed in espionage.

sec+re+tar+i+at (ˌsɛkrɪ'tɛərɪət) *n.* **1. a.** an office responsible for the secretarial, clerical, and administrative affairs of a legislative body, executive council, or international organization. **b.** the staff of such an office. **c.** the building or rooms in which such an office is housed. **2.** a body of secretaries. **3.** a secretary's place of work; office. **4.** the position of a secretary. [C19: via French from Medieval Latin *sēcrētāriātus,* from *sēcrētārius* SECRETARY]

sec+re+tar·y ('sɛkrətrɪ) *n., pl.* **+tar·ies. 1.** a person who handles correspondence, keeps records, and does general clerical work for an individual, organization, etc. **2.** (in the U.S.) the head of a government administrative department. **3.** (in Britain) See **secretary of state. 4.** (in Australia) the head of a public service department. **5.** *Diplomacy.* the assistant to an ambassador or diplomatic minister of certain countries. **6.** Also called (esp. Brit.): **sec+re+taire** (ˌsɛkrɪ'tɛə). an enclosed writing desk, usually having an upper cabinet section. [C14: from Medieval Latin *sēcrētārius, from Latin sēcrētum* something hidden; see SECRET] —**sec+re+tar+i·al** (ˌsɛkrɪ'tɛərɪəl) *adj.* —**'sec+re+tar·y+ˌship** *n.*

sec+re+tar·y bird *n.* a large African long-legged diurnal bird of prey, *Sagittarius serpentarius,* having a crest and tail of long feathers and feeding chiefly on snakes: family *Sagittariidae,* order *Falconiformes* (hawks, falcons, etc.).

sec+re·tar·y-gen·er·al *n., pl.* **sec+re+tar·ies-gen·er·al.** a chief administrative official, as of the United Nations.

sec+re+tar·y of state *n.* **1.** (in Britain) the head of any of several government departments. **2.** (in the U.S.) the head of the government department in charge of foreign affairs (**State Department**). 3. (in certain U.S. states) an official with various duties, such as keeping records.

se+crete[1] (sɪ'kri:t) *vb.* (of a cell, organ, etc.) to synthesize and release (a secretion). [C18: back formation from SECRETION] —**se+'cre+tor** *n.*

se+crete[2] (sɪ'kri:t) *vb.* (*tr.*) to put in a hiding place. [C18: variant of obsolete *secret* to hide away; see SECRET (n.)]

se+cre+tin (sɪ'kri:tɪn) *n.* a peptic hormone secreted by the mucosae of the duodenum and jejunum when food passes from the stomach. [C20: from SECRETION + -IN]

se+cre+tion (sɪ'kri:ʃən) *n.* **1.** a substance that is released from a cell, esp. a glandular cell, and is synthesized in the cell from simple substances extracted from the blood or a similar fluid. **2.** the process involved in producing and releasing such a substance from the cell. [C17: from Medieval Latin *sēcrētiō,* from Latin: a separation; see SECERN] —**se+'cre+tion+ar·y** *adj.*

se+cre+tive ('si:krɪtɪv, sɪ'kri:tɪv) *adj.* **1.** inclined to secrecy; reticent. **2.** another word for **secretory.** —**'se+cre+tive+ly** *adv.* —**'se+cre+tive+ness** *n.*

se+cre+to·ry (sɪ'kri:tərɪ) *adj.* of, relating to, or producing a secretion: *a secretory cell; secretory function.*

se+cret po+lice *n.* a police force that operates relatively secretly to check subversion.

se+cret ser+vice *n.* **1.** a government agency or department that conducts intelligence or counterintelligence operations. **2.** such operations.

Se+cret Ser+vice *n.* a U.S. government agency responsible for the protection of the president, the suppression of counterfeiting, and certain other police activities.

se+cret so+ci+e·ty *n.* a society or organization that conceals its rites, activities, etc., from those who are not members.

sect (sɛkt) *n.* **1.** a subdivision of a larger religious group (esp. the Christian Church as a whole) the members of which have to some extent diverged from the rest by developing deviating beliefs, practices, etc. **2.** *Often disparaging.* **a.** a schismatic religious body characterized by an attitude of exclusiveness in contrast to the more inclusive religious groups called denominations or Churches. **b.** a religious group regarded as extreme or heretical. **3.** a group of people with a common interest, doctrine, etc.; faction. [C14: from Latin *secta* faction, following, from the stem of *sequī* to follow]

sect. *abbrev. for* section.

-sect *vb. combining form.* to cut or divide, esp. into a specified number of parts: *trisect.* [from Latin *sectus* cut, from *secāre* to cut; see SAW[1]]

sec+tar+i·an (sɛk'tɛərɪən) *adj.* **1.** of, belonging or relating to, or characteristic of sects or sectaries. **2.** adhering to a particular sect, faction, or doctrine. **3.** narrow-minded, esp. as a result of rigid adherence to a particular sect. ~*n.* **4.** a member of a sect or faction, esp. one who is bigoted in his adherence to its doctrines or in his intolerance towards other sects, etc. —**sec+'tar·i·an+ˌism** *n.* —**sec+'tar·i·an+ly** *adv.*

sec+tar·i·an+ize *or* **sec+tar·i·an+ise** (sɛk'tɛərɪəˌnaɪz) *vb.* (*tr.*) to render sectarian.

sec+tar·y ('sɛktərɪ) *n., pl.* **+tar·ies. 1.** a member of a sect, esp. a person who belongs to a religious sect that is regarded as heretical or schismatic. **2.** a person excessively devoted to a particular sect. **3.** a member of a Nonconformist denomination, esp. one that is small. [C16: from Medieval Latin *sectārius,* from Latin *secta* SECT]

sec+tile ('sɛktaɪl) *adj.* able to be cut smoothly. [C18: from Latin *sectilis, from secāre* to cut] —**sec+til+i·ty** (sɛk'tɪlɪtɪ) *n.*

sec+tion ('sɛkʃən) *n.* **1.** a part cut off or separated from the main body of something. **2.** a part or subdivision of a piece of writing, book, etc.: *the sports section of the newspaper.* **3.** one of several component parts. **4.** a distinct part or subdivision of a country, community, etc. **5.** *U.S.* an area one mile square (640 acres) in a public survey, esp. in the western parts of the U.S. and Canada. **6.** the section of a railway track that is maintained by a single crew or is controlled by a particular signal box. **7.** the act or process of cutting or separating by cutting. **8.** *Geom.* **a.** a plane surface formed by cutting through a solid. **b.** the shape or area of such a plane surface. **c.** a drawing or photograph of this shape. Compare **cross section** (sense 1). **9.** *Surgery.* any procedure involving the cutting or division of an organ, structure, or part. **10.** a thin slice of biological tissue, mineral, etc., prepared for examination by microscope. **11.** a segment of an orange or other citrus fruit. **12.** a small military formation, typically comprising two or more squads or aircraft. **13.** *Austral.* a fare stage on a bus, tram, etc. **14.** *Music.* **a.** an extended division of a composition or movement that forms a coherent part of the structure: *the development section.* **b.** a division in an orchestra, band, etc., containing instruments belonging to the same class: *the brass section.* **15.** Also called: **signature, gathering, gather, quire.** a folded printing sheet or sheets ready for gathering and binding. ~*vb.* (*tr.*) **16.** to cut or divide into sections. **17.** to cut through so as to reveal a section. **18.** (in drawing, esp. mechanical drawing) to shade so as to indicate sections. **19.** *Surgery.* to cut or divide (an organ, structure, or part). [C16: from Latin *sectiō,* from *secāre* to cut]

sec+tion+al ('sɛkʃənəl) *adj.* **1.** composed of several sections. **2.** of or relating to a section. —**'sec+tion+al+ly** *adv.*

sec+tion+al+ism ('sɛkʃənəˌlɪzəm) *n.* excessive or narrow-minded concern for local or regional interests as opposed to the interests of the whole. —**'sec+tion+al+ist** *n.*

sec+tion+al+ize *or* **sec+tion+al+ise** ('sɛkʃənəˌlaɪz) *vb.* (*tr.*) **1.** to render sectional. **2.** to divide into sections, esp. geographically. —**ˌsec+tion+al·i+'za+tion** *or* **ˌsec+tion+al·i+'sa+tion** *n.*

sec+tion mark *n. Printing.* a mark (§) inserted into text matter to draw attention to a footnote or to indicate a section of a book, etc. Also called: **section.**

sec+tor ('sɛktə) *n.* **1.** a part or subdivision, esp. of a society or an economy: *the private sector.* **2.** *Geom.* either portion of a circle included between two radii and an arc. Area: $\frac{1}{2}r^2\theta$, where *r* is the radius and θ is the central angle subtended by the arc (in radians). **3.** a measuring instrument consisting of two graduated arms hinged at one end. **4.** a part or subdivision of an area of military operations. [C16: from Late Latin: sector, from Latin: a cutter, from *secāre* to cut] —**'sec·tor·al** *adj.*

sec·to·ri·al (sɛk'tɔːrɪəl) *adj.* **1.** of or relating to a sector. **2.** *Zoology.* **a.** adapted for cutting: *the sectorial teeth of carnivores.* **b.** designating a vein in the wing of an insect that links certain branches of the radius vein.

sec·u·lar ('sɛkjʊlə) *adj.* **1.** of or relating to worldly as opposed to sacred things; temporal. **2.** not concerned with or related to religion. **3.** not within the control of the Church. **4.** (of an education, etc.) **a.** having no particular religious affinities. **b.** not including compulsory religious studies or services. **5.** (of clerics) not bound by religious vows to a monastic or other order. **6.** occurring or appearing once in an age or century. **7.** lasting for a long time. **8.** *Astronomy.* occurring slowly over a long period of time: *the secular perturbation of a planet's orbit.* ~*n.* **9.** a member of the secular clergy. **10.** another word for **layman.** [C13: from Old French *seculer,* from Late Latin *saeculāris* temporal, from Latin: concerning an age, from *saeculum* an age] —**'sec·u·lar·ly** *adv.*

sec·u·lar·ism ('sɛkjʊlə,rɪzəm) *n.* **1.** *Philosophy.* a doctrine that rejects religion, esp. in ethics. **2.** the attitude that religion should have no place in civil affairs. **3.** the state of being secular. —**'sec·u·lar·ist** *n.* —**,sec·u·lar·'is·tic** *adj.*

sec·u·lar·i·ty (,sɛkjʊ'lærɪtɪ) *n., pl.* **·ties. 1.** the state or condition of being secular. **2.** interest in or adherence to secular things. **3.** a secular concern or matter.

sec·u·lar·ize *or* **sec·u·lar·ise** ('sɛkjʊlə,raɪz) *vb.* (*tr.*) **1.** to change from religious or sacred to secular functions, etc. **2.** to dispense from allegiance to a religious order. **3.** *Law.* to transfer (property) from ecclesiastical to civil possession or use. **4.** *English legal history.* to transfer (an offender) from the jurisdiction of the ecclesiastical courts to that of the civil courts for the imposition of a more severe punishment. —**,sec·u·lar·i·'za·tion** *or* **,sec·u·lar·i·'sa·tion** *n.* —**'sec·u·lar·,iz·er** *or* **'sec·u·lar·,is·er** *n.*

se·cund (sɪ'kʌnd) *adj. Botany.* having or designating parts arranged on or turned to one side of the axis. [C18: from Latin *secundus* following, from *sequī* to follow; see SECOND[1]] —**se·'cund·ly** *adv.*

Se·cun·der·a·bad (sə'kʌndərə,bæd, -,bɑːd) *n.* a former town in S central India, in N Andra Pradesh: one of the largest British military stations in India: now part of Hyderabad city.

sec·un·dine ('sɛkən,daɪn, -dɪn) *n. Botany.* the inner of two integuments surrounding the ovule of a plant.

sec·un·dines ('sɛkən,daɪnz, sɪ'kʌndɪnz) *pl. n. Physiol.* a technical word for **afterbirth.** [C14: from Late Latin *secundīnae,* from Latin *secundus* following; see SECOND[1]]

se·cure (sɪ'kjʊə) *adj.* **1.** free from danger, damage, etc. **2.** free from fear, care, etc. **3.** in safe custody. **4.** not likely to fail, become loose, etc. **5.** able to be relied on; certain: *a secure investment.* **6.** *Nautical.* stowed away or made inoperative. **7.** *Archaic.* careless or overconfident. ~*vb.* **8.** (*tr.*) to obtain or get possession of: *I will secure some good seats.* **9.** (when *intr.,* often foll. by *against*) to make or become free from danger, fear, etc. **10.** (*tr.*) to make fast or firm; fasten. **11.** (when *intr.,* often foll. by *against*) to make or become certain; guarantee: *this plan will secure your happiness.* **12.** (*tr.*) to assure (a creditor) of payment, as by giving security. **13.** (*tr.*) to make (a military position) safe from attack. **14.** *Nautical.* to make (a vessel or its contents) safe or ready by battening down hatches, stowing gear, etc. **15.** (*tr.*) *Nautical.* to stow or make inoperative: *to secure the radio.* [C16: from Latin *sēcūrus* free from care, from *sē-* without + *cūra* care] —**se·'cur·a·ble** *adj.* —**se·'cure·ly** *adv.* —**se·'cure·ment** *n.* —**se·'cure·ness** *n.* —**se·'cur·er** *n.*

Se·cu·ri·ties and Ex·change Com·mis·sion *n.* a U.S. federal agency established in 1934 to supervise and regulate issues of and transactions in securities and to prosecute illegal stock manipulations.

se·cu·ri·ty (sɪ'kjʊərɪtɪ) *n., pl.* **·ties. 1.** the state of being secure. **2.** assured freedom from poverty or want: *he needs the security of a permanent job.* **3.** a person or thing that secures, guarantees, etc. **4.** precautions taken to ensure against theft, espionage, etc.: *the security in the government offices was not very good.* **5.** (*often pl.*) **a.** a certificate of creditorship or property carrying the right to receive interest or dividend, such as shares or bonds. **b.** the financial asset represented by such a certificate. **6.** the specific asset that a creditor can claim title to in the event of default on an obligation. **7.** something given or pledged to secure the fulfilment of a promise or obligation. **8.** a person who undertakes to fulfil another person's obligation. **9.** *Archaic.* carelessness or overconfidence.

Se·cu·ri·ty Coun·cil *n.* a permanent organ of the United Nations established to maintain world peace.

se·cu·ri·ty risk *n.* a person deemed to be a threat to state security in that he could be open to pressure, have subversive political beliefs, etc.

secy. *or* **sec'y.** *abbrev. for* secretary.

se·dan (sɪ'dæn) *n.* **1.** the U.S. name for a **saloon** (sense 5). **2.** short for **sedan chair.** [C17: of uncertain origin; compare Latin *sēdēs* seat]

Se·dan (*French* sə'dã; *English* sɪ'dæn) *n.* a town in NE France, on the River Meuse: passed to France in 1642; a Protestant stronghold (16th–17th centuries); scene of a French defeat (1870) during the Franco-Prussian War and of a battle (1940) in World War II, which began the German invasion of France. Pop.: 25 430 (1975).

se·dan chair *n.* a closed chair for one passenger, carried on poles by two bearers. It was commonly used in the 17th and 18th centuries. Sometimes shortened to **sedan.**

se·date[1] (sɪ'deɪt) *adj.* **1.** habitually calm and composed in manner; serene. **2.** staid, sober, or decorous. [C17: from Latin *sēdāre* to soothe; related to *sedēre* to sit] —**se·'date·ly** *adv.* —**se·'date·ness** *n.*

se·date[2] (sɪ'deɪt) *vb.* (*tr.*) to administer a sedative to. [C20: back formation from SEDATIVE]

se·da·tion (sɪ'deɪʃən) *n.* **1.** a state of calm or reduced nervous activity. **2.** the administration of a sedative.

sed·a·tive ('sɛdətɪv) *adj.* **1.** having a soothing or calming effect. **2.** of or relating to sedation. ~*n.* **3.** *Med.* a sedative drug or agent. [C15: from Medieval Latin *sēdātīvus,* from Latin *sēdātus* assuaged; see SEDATE[1]]

Sed·don ('sɛdᵊn) *n.* **Rich·ard John,** known as *King Dick.* 1845–1906, New Zealand statesman, born in England; prime minister of New Zealand (1893–1906).

sed·en·tar·y ('sɛdᵊntərɪ, -trɪ) *adj.* **1.** characterized by or requiring a sitting position: *sedentary work.* **2.** tending to sit about without taking much exercise. **3.** (of animals) moving about very little, usually because of attachment to a rock or other surface. **4.** (of birds) not migratory. [C16: from Latin *sedentārius,* from *sedēre* to sit] —**'sed·en·tar·i·ly** *adv.* —**'sed·en·tar·i·ness** *n.*

Se·der ('seɪdə) *n. Judaism.* a ceremonial meal with prescribed ritual reading of the Haggadah observed in Jewish homes on the first night or first two nights of Passover. [from Hebrew *sēdher* order]

sedge (sɛdʒ) *n.* **1.** any grasslike cyperaceous plant of the genus *Carex,* typically growing on wet ground and having rhizomes, triangular stems, and minute flowers in spikelets. **2.** any other plant of the family *Cyperaceae.* [Old English *secg;* related to Middle High German *segge* sedge, Old English *sagu* SAW[1]] —**'sedg·y** *adj.*

Sedge·moor ('sɛdʒ,mʊə) *n.* a plain in SW England, in central Somerset: scene of the defeat (1685) of the Duke of Monmouth.

sedge war·bler *n.* a European songbird, *Acrocephalus schoenobaenus,* of reed beds and swampy areas, having a streaked brownish plumage with white eye stripes: family *Muscicapidae* (Old World flycatchers, etc.).

se·di·li·a (sɛ'daɪlɪə) *n.* (*functioning as sing.*) the group of three seats, each called a **se·di·le** (sɛ'daɪlɪ), often recessed, on the south side of a sanctuary where the celebrant and ministers sit at certain points during High Mass. [C18: from Latin, from *sedīle* a chair, from *sedēre* to sit]

sed·i·ment ('sɛdɪmənt) *n.* **1.** matter that settles to the bottom of a liquid. **2.** material that has been deposited from water, ice, or wind. [C16: from Latin *sedimentum* a settling, from *sedēre* to sit] —**sed·i·men·tous** (,sɛdɪ'mɛntəs) *adj.*

sed·i·men·ta·ry (,sɛdɪ'mɛntərɪ) *or* **sed·i·men·tal** (,sɛdɪ'mɛntᵊl) *adj.* **1.** characterized by, resembling, or containing sediment. **2.** (of rocks) formed by the accumulation and consolidation of mineral and organic fragments that have been deposited by water, ice, or wind. Compare **igneous, metamorphic.** —**,sed·i·'men·tar·i·ly** *adv.*

sed·i·men·ta·tion (,sɛdɪmɛn'teɪʃən) *n.* **1.** the process of formation of sedimentary rocks. **2.** the deposition or production of sediment.

sed·i·men·tol·o·gy (,sɛdɪmɛn'tɒlədʒɪ) *n.* the branch of geology concerned with sedimentary rocks and deposits.

se·di·tion (sɪ'dɪʃən) *n.* **1.** speech or behaviour directed against the peace of a state. **2.** an offence that tends to undermine the authority of a state. **3.** an incitement to public disorder. **4.** *Archaic.* revolt. [C14: from Latin *sēditiō* discord, from *sēd-* apart + *itiō* a going, from *īre* to go] —**se·'di·tion·ar·y** *n., adj.*

se·di·tious (sɪ'dɪʃəs) *adj.* **1.** of, like, or causing sedition. **2.** inclined to or taking part in sedition. —**se·'di·tious·ly** *adv.* —**se·'di·tious·ness** *n.*

se·duce (sɪ'djuːs) *vb.* (*tr.*) **1.** to persuade to engage in sexual intercourse. **2.** to lead astray, as from the right action. **3.** to win over, attract, or lure. [C15: from Latin *sēdūcere* to lead apart, from *sē-* apart + *dūcere* to lead] —**se·'duc·i·ble** *or* **se·'duce·a·ble** *adj.* —**se·'duc·ing·ly** *adv.*

se·duc·er (sɪ'djuːsə) *or* (*fem.*) **se·duc·tress** (sɪ'dʌktrɪs) *n.* a person who entices, allures, or seduces, esp. one who entices another to engage in sexual intercourse.

se·duc·tion (sɪ'dʌkʃən) *n.* **1.** the act of seducing or the state of being seduced. **2.** a means of seduction.

se·duc·tive (sɪ'dʌktɪv) *adj.* tending to seduce or capable of seducing; enticing; alluring. —**se·'duc·tive·ly** *adv.* —**se·'duc·tive·ness** *n.*

sed·u·lous ('sɛdjʊləs) *adj.* constant or persistent in use or attention; assiduous; diligent. [C16: from Latin *sēdulus,* of uncertain origin] —**se·du·li·ty** (sɪ'djuːlɪtɪ) *n.* —**'sed·u·lous·ly** *adv.* —**'sed·u·lous·ness** *n.*

se·dum ('siːdəm) *n.* any crassulaceous rock plant of the genus *Sedum,* having thick fleshy leaves and clusters of white, yellow, or pink flowers. See also **stonecrop, rose-root, orpine.** [C15: from Latin: houseleek]

see[1] (siː) *vb.* **sees, see·ing, saw, seen. 1.** to perceive with the eyes. **2.** (when *tr., may take a clause as object*) to perceive (an idea) mentally; understand: *I explained the problem but he could not see it.* **3.** (*tr.*) to perceive with any or all of the senses: *I hate to see you so unhappy.* **4.** (*tr.; may take a clause as object*) to be aware of in advance; foresee: *I can see what will happen if you don't help.* **5.** (when *tr., may take a clause as object*) to ascertain or find out (a fact); learn: *see who is at the door.* **6.** (when *tr., takes a clause as object;* when *intr.,* foll. by *to*) to make sure (of something) or take care (of something): *see that he gets to bed early.* **7.** (when *tr., may take a clause as object*) to consider, deliberate, or decide: *see if you can come next week.* **8.** (*tr.*) to have experience of; undergo: *he had seen much unhappiness in his life.* **9.** (*tr.*) to allow to be in a specified condition: *I cannot stand by and see a child in pain.* **10.** (*tr.*) to be characterized by: *this period of history has seen much unrest.* **11.** (*tr.*) to meet or pay a visit to: *to see one's solicitor.* **12.** (*tr.*) to receive, esp. as a guest or visitor: *the Prime Minister will see the deputation now.* **13.** (*tr.*) to frequent the company of: *she is seeing a married man.* **14.** (*tr.*) to accompany or escort: *I saw her to the door.* **15.** (*tr.*) to refer to or look up: *for further information see the appendix.* **16.** (in gambling, esp. in poker) to match (another player's bet) or match the bet of (another player) by staking an equal sum. **17. as far as I can see.** to the best of my judgment or understanding. **18. see fit.** (*takes an infinitive*) to consider proper, desirable, etc.: *I don't see fit to allow her to come here.* **19. see (someone) hanged** *or* **damned first.** *Informal.* to refuse absolutely to do what one has been asked. **20. see (someone) right.** *Brit. informal.* to ensure fair treatment of: *if he has cheated you, I'll see you right.* **21. see the light (of day).** See **light**[1] (sense 22). **22. see you, see you later,** *or* **be seeing you.** an expression of farewell. **23. you see.** *Informal.* a parenthetical filler phrase used to make a pause in speaking or add slight emphasis. ~See also **see about, see into, see of, see off, see out, see over, see through.** [Old English *sēon;* related to Old Norse *sjā,* Gothic *saihwan,* Old Saxon *sehan*] —'**see+a·ble** *adj.*

see[2] (si:) *n.* the diocese of a bishop, or the place within it where his cathedral or procathedral is situated. See also **Holy See.** [C13: from Old French *sed,* from Latin *sēdēs* a seat; related to *sedēre* to sit]

see a·bout *vb.* (*intr., prep.*) **1.** to take care of; look after: *he couldn't see about the matter because he was ill.* **2.** to investigate; enquire into: *to see about a new car.*

See+beck ('si:bɛk) *n. Philately.* **1.** any of a set of stamps issued (1890–99) in Nicaragua, Honduras, Ecuador, and El Salvador and named after Nicholas Frederick Seebeck, who provided them free to the respective governments. **2.** any of the reprints issued later for personal gain by Seebeck.

See·beck ef+fect ('si:bɛk; *German* 'ze:bɛk) *n.* the phenomenon in which a current is produced in a circuit containing two or more different metals when the junctions between the metals are maintained at different temperatures. Also called: **thermoelectric effect.** Compare **Peltier effect.** [C19: named after Thomas *Seebeck* (1770–1831), German physicist]

seed (si:d) *n.* **1.** *Botany.* a mature fertilized plant ovule, consisting of an embryo and its food store surrounded by a protective seed coat (testa). Related adj.: **seminal. 2.** the small hard seedlike fruit of plants such as wheat. **3.** any propagative part of a plant, such as a tuber, spore, or bulb. **4.** such parts collectively. **5.** the source, beginning, or germ of anything: *the seeds of revolt.* **6.** *Chiefly Bible.* offspring or descendants: *the seed of Abraham.* **7.** an archaic or dialect term for **sperm** or **semen. 8.** *Sport.* a seeded player. **9.** the egg cell or cells of the lobster and certain other animals. **10.** See **seed oyster. 11.** *Chem.* a small crystal added to a supersaturated solution or supercooled liquid to induce crystallization. **12. go** *or* **run to seed. a.** (of plants) to produce and shed seeds. **b.** to lose vigour, usefulness, etc. ~*vb.* **13.** to plant (seeds, grain, etc.) in (soil): *we seeded this field with oats.* **14.** (*intr.*) (of plants) to form or shed seeds. **15.** (*tr.*) to remove the seeds from (fruit, etc.). **16.** (*tr.*) *Chem.* to add a small crystal to (a supersaturated solution or supercooled liquid) in order to cause crystallization. **17.** (*tr.*) to scatter certain substances, such as silver iodide, in (clouds) in order to cause rain. **18.** (*tr.*) **a.** to arrange (the draw of a tournament) so that outstanding teams or players will not meet in the early rounds. **b.** to distribute (players or teams) in this manner. [Old English *sǣd;* related to Old Norse *sāth,* Gothic *sēths,* Old High German *sāt*] —'**seed+,like** *adj.* —'**seed+less** *adj.*

seed+bed ('si:d,bɛd) *n.* **1.** a plot of land in which seeds or seedlings are grown before being transplanted. **2.** the place where something develops: *the seedbed of discontent.*

seed+cake ('si:d,keɪk) *n.* a sweet cake flavoured with caraway seeds and lemon rind or essence.

seed cap+sule *or* **seed+case** ('si:d,keɪs) *n.* the part of a fruit enclosing the seeds; pericarp.

seed coat *n.* the nontechnical name for **testa.**

seed cor+al *n.* small pieces of coral used in jewellery, etc.

seed corn *n.* the good quality ears or kernels of corn that are used as seed.

seed+er ('si:də) *n.* **1.** a person or thing that seeds. **2.** a device used to remove seeds, as from fruit, etc. **3.** any of various devices for sowing grass seed or grain on the surface of the ground.

seed fern *n.* another name for **pteridosperm.**

seed leaf *n.* the nontechnical name for **cotyledon.**

seed+ling ('si:dlɪŋ) *n.* a plant produced from a seed, esp. a very young plant.

seed mon+ey *n.* money used for the establishment of an enterprise.

seed oy+ster *n.* a young oyster, esp. a cultivated oyster, ready for transplantation.

seed pearl *n.* a tiny pearl weighing less than a quarter of a grain.

seed plant *n.* the nontechnical name for **spermatophyte.**

seed po+ta+to *n.* a potato tuber used for planting.

seed ves+sel *n. Botany.* a dry fruit, such as a capsule.

seed·y ('si:dɪ) *adj.* **seed·i·er, seed·i·est. 1.** shabby or unseemly in appearance: *seedy clothes.* **2.** (of a plant) at the stage of producing seeds. **3.** *Informal.* not physically fit; sickly. —'**seed·i+ly** *adv.* —'**seed·i+ness** *n.*

See·ger ('si:gə) *n.* **Pete.** born 1919. U.S. folk singer and songwriter, noted for his protest songs, which include *We shall overcome* (1960), *Where have all the Flowers gone?* (1961), *If I had a Hammer* (1962), and *Little Boxes* (1962).

see+ing ('si:ɪŋ) *n.* **1.** the sense or faculty of sight; vision. **2.** *Astronomy.* the condition of the atmosphere with respect to observation of stars, planets, etc: *the bad seeing was due to turbulent air.* ~*conj.* **3.** (*subordinating;* often foll. by *that*) in light of the fact (that); inasmuch as; since.

see in·to *vb.* (*intr., prep.*) **1.** to examine or investigate. **2.** to discover the true nature of: *I can't see into your thoughts.*

seek (si:k) *vb.* **seeks, seek+ing, sought.** (*mainly tr.*) **1.** (when *intr.,* often foll. by *for* or *after*) to try to find by searching; look for: *to seek a solution.* **2.** (*also intr.*) to try to obtain or acquire: *to seek happiness.* **3.** to attempt (to do something); try: *I'm only seeking to help.* **4.** (*also intr.*) to enquire about or request (something): *to seek help.* **5.** to go or resort to: *to seek the garden for peace.* **6.** an archaic word for **explore.** [Old English *sēcan;* related to Old Norse *sōkja,* Gothic *sōkjan,* Old High German *suohhen,* Latin *sāgīre* to perceive by scent; see BESEECH] —'**seek+er** *n.*

seek out *vb.* (*tr., adv.*) to search hard for a specific person or thing and find: *she sought out her friend from amongst the crowd.*

seel (si:l) *vb.* (*tr.*) **1.** to sew up the eyelids of (a hawk or falcon) so as to render it quiet and tame. **2.** *Obsolete.* to close up the eyes of, esp. by blinding. [C15 *silen,* from Old French *ciller,* from Medieval Latin *ciliāre,* from Latin *cilium* an eyelid]

See+land ('ze:lant) *n.* the German name for **Sjælland.**

seem (si:m) *vb.* (may take an infinitive) **1.** (*copula*) to appear to the mind or eye; look: *this seems nice; the car seems to be running well.* **2.** to give the impression of existing; appear to be: *there seems no need for all this nonsense.* **3.** used to diminish the force of a following infinitive to be polite, more noncommittal, etc.: *I can't seem to get through to you.* [C12: perhaps from Old Norse *soma* to beseem, from *sœmr* befitting; related to Old English *sēman* to reconcile; see SAME] —'**seem+er** *n.*

seem+ing ('si:mɪŋ) *adj.* **1.** (*prenominal*) apparent but not actual or genuine: *seeming honesty.* ~*n.* **2.** outward or false appearance. —'**seem+ing+ly** *adv.* —'**seem+ing+ness** *n.*

seem+ly ('si:mlɪ) *adj.* **+li+er, +li+est. 1.** proper or fitting. **2.** *Obsolete.* pleasing or handsome in appearance. ~*adv.* **3.** *Archaic.* properly or decorously. [C13: from Old Norse *sœmiligr,* from *sœmr* befitting] —'**seem+li+ness** *n.*

seen (si:n) *vb.* the past participle of **see**[1].

see of *vb.* (*tr., prep.*) to meet; be in contact with: *we haven't seen much of him since he got married.*

see off *vb.* (*tr., adv.*) **1.** to be present at the departure of (a person making a journey). **2.** *Informal.* to cause to leave or depart, esp. by force.

see out *vb.* (*tr., adv.*) **1.** to remain or endure until the end of: *we'll see the first half of the game out and then leave.* **2.** to be present at the departure of (a person from a house, room, etc.).

see o·ver *or* **round** *vb.* (*intr., prep.*) to inspect by making a tour of: *she said she'd like to see over the house.*

seep (si:p) *vb.* **1.** (*intr.*) to pass gradually or leak through or as if through small openings; ooze. ~*n.* **2.** a small spring or place where water, oil, etc., has oozed through the ground. **3.** another word for **seepage.** [Old English *sīpian;* related to Middle High German *sīfen,* Swedish dialect *sipa*]

seep+age ('si:pɪdʒ) *n.* **1.** the act or process of seeping. **2.** liquid or moisture that has seeped.

seer[1] (sɪə) *n.* **1.** a person who can supposedly see into the future; prophet. **2.** a person who professes supernatural powers. **3.** a person who sees. —'**seer+ess** *fem. n.*

seer[2] (sɪə) *n.* a variant spelling of **ser.**

seer+suck·er ('sɪə,sʌkə) *n.* a light cotton, linen, or other fabric with a crinkled surface and often striped. [C18: from Hindi *śīrśakar,* from Persian *shīr o shakkar,* literally: milk and sugar]

see+saw ('si:,sɔ:) *n.* **1.** a plank balanced in the middle so that two people seated on the ends can ride up and down by pushing on the ground with their feet. **2.** the pastime of riding up and down on a seesaw. **3. a.** an up-and-down or back-and-forth movement. **b.** (*as modifier*): *a seesaw movement.* ~*vb.* **4.** (*intr.*) to move up and down or back and forth in such a manner; oscillate. [C17: reduplication of SAW[1], alluding to the movement from side to side, as in sawing]

seethe (si:ð) *vb.* **1.** (*intr.*) to boil or to foam as if boiling. **2.** (*intr.*) to be in a state of extreme agitation. **3.** (*tr.*) to soak in liquid. **4.** (*tr.*) *Archaic.* to cook or extract the essence of (a food) by boiling. ~*n.* **5.** the act or state of seething. [Old English *sēothan;* related to Old Norse *sjōtha,* Old High German *siodan* to seethe] —'**seeth+ing+ly** *adv.*

see through *vb.* **1.** (*tr.*) to help out in time of need or trouble: *I know you're short of money, but I'll see you through.* **2.** (*tr., adv.*) to remain with until the end or completion: *let's see the job through.* **3.** (*intr., prep.*) to perceive the true nature of: *I can see through your evasion.* ~*adj.* **see+through. 4.** partly or wholly transparent or translucent, esp. (of clothes) in a titillating way: *a seethrough nightie.*

Se·fer·is (sə'fɛərɪs) *n.* **George.** pen name of *Georgios Seferiades.* 1900–71, Greek poet and diplomat: Nobel prize for literature 1963.

seg+ment ('sɛgmənt) *n.* **1.** *Maths.* **a.** a part of a line or curve between two points. **b.** a part of a plane or solid figure cut off by an intersecting line, plane, or planes, esp. one between a chord and an arc of a circle. **2.** one of several parts or sections into which an object is divided; portion. **3.** *Zoology.* any of the parts into which the body or appendages of an annelid or arthropod are divided. **4.** *Linguistics.* a speech sound considered in isolation. ~*vb.* **5.** to cut or divide (a whole object) into segments. [C16: from Latin *segmentum,* from *secāre* to cut] —**seg·men·tar·y** ('sɛgməntərɪ, -trɪ) *adj.*

seg·men·tal (sɛg'mɛntᵊl) *adj.* **1.** of, like, or having the form of a segment. **2.** divided into segments. **3.** *Linguistics.* of, relating to, or constituting an isolable speech sound. —**seg·'men·tal·ly** *adv.*

seg·men·ta·tion (ˌsɛgmɛn'teɪʃən) *n.* **1.** the act or an instance of dividing into segments. **2.** *Embryol.* another name for **cleavage** (sense 4). **3.** *Zoology.* another name for **metamerism** (sense 1).

seg·men·ta·tion cav·i·ty *n.* another name for **blastocoel.**

se·gno ('sɛnjəʊ; *Italian* 'seɲɲo) *n., pl.* **·gni** (-njiː; *Italian* -ɲɲi). *Music.* a sign at the beginning or end of a section directed to be repeated. Symbol: 𝄋 or :S: [Italian: a sign, from Latin *signum*]

Se·go·vi·a[1] (sɪ'gəʊvɪə; *Spanish* se'ɣoβja) *n.* a town in central Spain: site of a Roman aqueduct, still in use, and the fortified palace of the kings of Castile (the Alcázar). Pop.: 41 880 (1970).

Se·go·vi·a[2] (sɪ'gəʊvɪə; *Spanish* se'ɣoβja) *n.* **An·drés** (an'dres). born 1893, Spanish classical guitarist.

seg·re·gate ('sɛgrɪˌgeɪt) *vb.* **1.** to set or be set apart from others or from the main group. **2.** (*tr.*) to impose segregation on (a racial or minority group). **3.** *Genetics, metallurgy.* to undergo or cause to undergo segregation. [C16: from Latin *sēgregāre,* from *sē-* apart + *grex* a flock] —**seg·re·ga·ble** ('sɛgrɪgəbᵊl) *adj.* —**'seg·re·ˌga·tive** *adj.* —**'seg·re·ˌga·tor** *n.*

seg·re·ga·tion (ˌsɛgrɪ'geɪʃən) *n.* **1.** the act of segregating or state of being segregated. **2.** *Sociol.* the practice or policy of creating separate facilities within the same society for the use of a minority group. **3.** *Genetics.* the separation at meiosis of the two members of any pair of alleles into separate gametes. See also **Mendel's laws. 4.** *Metallurgy.* the process in which a component of an alloy or solid solution separates in small regions within the solid or on the solid's surface. —ˌ**seg·re·'ga·tion·al** *adj.*

seg·re·ga·tion·ist (ˌsɛgrɪ'geɪʃənɪst) *n.* a person who favours, advocates, or practises racial segregation.

se·gui·dil·la (ˌsɛgɪ'diːljə) *n.* **1.** a Spanish dance in a fast triple rhythm. **2.** a piece of music composed for or in the rhythm of this dance. **3.** *Prosody.* a stanzaic form consisting of four to seven lines and marked by a characteristic rhythm. [Spanish: a little dance, from *seguida* a dance, from *seguir* to follow, from Latin *sequī*]

sei·cen·to (*Italian* seɪ'tʃɛnto) *n.* the 17th century with reference to Italian art and literature. [Italian, shortened from *mille seicento* one thousand six hundred]

seiche (seɪʃ) *n.* a periodic rhythmical movement of a body of water caused by variations in the level of the water. [C19: from Swiss French, of obscure origin]

Seid·litz pow·der *or* **pow·ders** ('sɛdlɪts) *n.* a laxative consisting of two powders, tartaric acid and a mixture of sodium bicarbonate and Rochelle salt. Also called: **Rochelle powder.** [C19: named after *Seidlitz,* a village in Bohemia with mineral springs having similar laxative effects]

seif dune (seɪf) *n.* (in deserts, esp. the Sahara) a long ridge of blown sand, often several miles long. [*seif,* from Arabic: sword, from the shape of the dune]

sei·gneur (sɛ'njɜː; *French* sɛ'ɲœːr) *n.* **1.** a feudal lord, esp. in France. **2.** (in French Canada) the landlord of an estate that was subdivided among peasants who held their plots by a form of feudal tenure until 1854. [C16: from Old French, from Vulgar Latin *senior,* from Latin: an elderly man; see SENIOR] —**sei·'gneu·ri·al** *adj.*

sei·gneur·y ('seɪnjərɪ) *n., pl.* **·gneur·ies.** the estate of a seigneur.

sei·gnior ('seɪnjə) *n.* **1.** a less common name for a **seigneur. 2.** (in England) the lord of a seigniory. [C14: from Anglo-French *segnour;* see SEIGNEUR] —**sei·gnio·ri·al** (seɪ'njɔːrɪəl) *adj.*

sei·gnior·age ('seɪnjərɪdʒ) *n.* **1.** something claimed by a sovereign or superior as a prerogative, right, or due. **2.** a fee payable to a government for coining bullion. **3.** the difference in value between the cost of bullion and the face value of the coin made from it.

sei·gnior·y ('seɪnjərɪ) *or* **si·gnor·y** ('siːnjərɪ) *n., pl.* **·gnior·ies** *or* **·gnor·ies. 1.** less common names for a **seigneury. 2.** (in England) the fee or manor of a seignior; a feudal domain. **3.** the authority of a seignior or the relationship between him and his tenants. **4.** a body of lords.

seine (seɪn) *n.* **1.** a large fishing net that hangs vertically in the water by means of floats at the top and weights at the bottom. ~*vb.* **2.** to catch (fish) using this net. [Old English *segne,* from Latin *sagēna,* from Greek *sagēnē;* related to Old High German *segina,* Old French *saïne*]

Seine (seɪn; *French* sɛn) *n.* a river in N France, rising on the Plateau de Langres and flowing northwest through Paris to the English Channel: the second longest river in France, linked by canal with the Rivers Somme, Scheldt, Meuse, Rhine, Saône, and Loire. Length: 776 km (482 miles).

Seine-et-Marne (*French* sɛn e 'marn) *n.* a department of N central France, in Île-de-France region. Capital: Melun. Pop.: 770 854 (1975). Area: 5931 sq. km (2313 sq. miles).

Seine-Ma·ri·time (*French* sɛn mari'tim) *n.* a department of N France, in Haute-Normandie region. Capital: Rouen. Pop.: 1 187 919 (1975). Area: 6342 sq. km (2473 sq. miles).

Seine-Saint-De·nis (*French* sɛn sɛ̃ də'ni) *n.* a department of N central France, in Île-de-France region. Capital: Bobigny. Pop.: 1 326 240 (1975). Area: 236 sq. km (92 sq. miles).

seise *or U.S.* **seize** (siːz) *vb.* to put into legal possession of (property, etc.). —**'seis·a·ble** *adj.* —**'seis·er** *n.*

sei·sin *or U.S.* **sei·zin** ('siːzɪn) *n. Property law.* feudal possession of an estate in land. [C13: from Old French *seisine,* from *seisir* to SEIZE]

seism ('saɪzəm) *n.* a less common name for **earthquake.** [C19: from Greek *seismos,* from *seiein* to shake]

seis·mic ('saɪzmɪk), **seis·mal,** *or* **seis·mi·cal** ('saɪzmɪkᵊl) *adj.* relating to or caused by earthquakes or artificially produced earth tremors. —**'seis·mi·cal·ly** *adv.*

seis·mism ('saɪzˌmɪzəm) *n.* the processes and phenomena associated with earthquakes, collectively.

seis·mo- *or before a vowel* **seism-** *combining form.* earthquake: *seismology.* [from Greek *seismos*]

seis·mo·graph ('saɪzməˌgrɑːf, -ˌgræf) *n.* an instrument that registers and records the features of earthquakes. A **seismogram** is the record from such an instrument. Also called: **seismometer.** —**seis·mo·graph·ic** (ˌsaɪzmə'græfɪk) *adj.* —**seis·mog·ra·pher** (saɪz'mɒgrəfə) *n.* —**seis·'mog·ra·phy** *n.*

seis·mol·o·gy (saɪz'mɒlədʒɪ) *n.* the branch of geology concerned with the study of earthquakes. —**seis·mo·log·ic** (ˌsaɪzmə'lɒdʒɪk) *or* ˌ**seis·mo·'log·i·cal** *adj.* —ˌ**seis·mo·'log·i·cal·ly** *adv.* —**seis·'mol·o·gist** *n.*

seis·mo·scope ('saɪzməˌskəʊp) *n.* an instrument that indicates the occurrence of an earthquake. Compare **seismograph.** —**seis·mo·scop·ic** (ˌsaɪzmə'skɒpɪk) *adj.*

sei whale (seɪ) *n.* a rorqual, *Balaenoptera borealis,* hunted for its fine whalebone.

seize (siːz) *vb.* (*mainly tr.*) **1.** (also *intr.,* foll. by *on*) to take hold of quickly; grab: *she seized her hat and ran for the bus.* **2.** to grasp mentally, esp. rapidly: *she immediately seized his idea.* **3.** to take mental possession of: *alarm seized the crowd.* **4.** to take possession of rapidly and forcibly: *the thief seized the woman's purse.* **5.** to take legal possession of; take into custody. **6.** to take by force or capture: *the army seized the undefended town.* **7.** to take immediate advantage of: *to seize an opportunity.* **8.** *Nautical.* to bind (two ropes together or a piece of gear to a rope). See also **serve** (sense 19). **9.** (*intr.;* often foll. by *up*) (of mechanical parts) to become jammed, esp. because of excessive heat. [C13 *saisen,* from Old French *saisir,* from Medieval Latin *sacīre* to position, of Germanic origin; related to Gothic *satjan* to SET] —**'seiz·a·ble** *adj.*

seiz·ing ('siːzɪŋ) *n. Nautical.* a binding used for holding together two ropes, two spars, etc., esp. by lashing with a separate rope.

sei·zure ('siːʒə) *n.* **1.** the act or an instance of seizing or the state of being seized. **2.** *Pathol.* a sudden manifestation or recurrence of a disease, such as an epileptic convulsion.

se·jant *or* **se·jeant** ('siːdʒənt) *adj.* (*usually postpositive*) *Heraldry.* (of a beast) shown seated. [C16: variant of *seant,* from Old French, from *seoir* to sit, from Latin *sedēre*]

Sejm (seɪm) *n.* the unicameral legislature of Poland. [Polish: assembly]

Sek·on·di (ˌsɛkən'diː) *n.* a port in SW Ghana, 8 km (5 miles) northeast of Takoradi: linked administratively with Takoradi in 1946. Pop. (with Takoradi): 91 874 (1970).

se·la·chi·an (sɪ'leɪkɪən) *adj.* **1.** of, relating to, or belonging to the *Selachii* (or *Elasmobranchii*), a large subclass of cartilaginous fishes including the sharks, rays, dogfish, and skates. ~*n.* **2.** any fish belonging to the subclass *Selachii.* ~Also: **elasmobranch.** [C19: from New Latin *Selachii,* from Greek *selakhē* a shark; related to Greek *selas* brightness]

sel·a·gi·nel·la (ˌsɛlədʒɪ'nɛlə) *n.* any club moss of the genus *Selaginella,* having stems covered in small pointed leaves and small spore-bearing cones: family *Selaginellaceae.* See also **resurrection plant.** [C19: from New Latin, diminutive of Latin *selāgō* plant similar to the savin]

se·lah ('siːlə) *n.* a Hebrew word of unknown meaning occurring in the Old Testament psalms, and thought to be a musical direction. [C16: from Hebrew]

Se·lan·gor (sə'læŋə) *n.* a state of West Malaysia, on the Strait of Malacca: established as a British protectorate in 1874; tin producer. Capital: Shah Alam. Pop.: 1 625 625 (1970). Area: 8203 sq. km (3167 sq. miles).

Sel·den ('sɛldən) *n.* **John.** 1584–1654, English antiquary and politician. As a member of Parliament, he was twice imprisoned for opposing the king.

sel·dom ('sɛldəm) *adv.* not often; rarely. [Old English *seldon;* related to Old Norse *sjāldan,* Old High German *seltan*]

se·lect (sɪ'lɛkt) *vb.* **1.** to choose (someone or something) in preference to another or others. ~*adj. also* **se·lect·ed. 2.** chosen in preference to another or others. **3.** of particular quality or excellence. **4.** limited as to membership or entry: *a select gathering.* **5.** careful in making a choice. [C16: from Latin *sēligere* to sort, from SE- apart + *legere* to choose] —**se·'lect·ly** *adv.* —**se·'lect·ness** *n.*

se·lect·ee (sɪˌlɛk'tiː) *n. U.S.* a person who is selected, esp. for military service.

se·lec·tion (sɪ'lɛkʃən) *n.* **1.** the act or an instance of selecting or the state of being selected. **2.** a thing or number of things that have been selected. **3.** a range from which something may be selected: *this shop has a good selection of clothes.* **4.** *Biology.* the natural or artificial process by which certain organisms or characters are reproduced and perpetuated in the species in preference to others. See also **natural selection. 5.** a contestant in a race chosen as likely to win or come second or third.

se+lec+tive (sɪˈlɛktɪv) *adj.* **1.** of or characterized by selection. **2.** tending to choose carefully or characterized by careful choice. **3.** *Electronics.* occurring at, operating at, or capable of separating out a particular frequency or band of frequencies. —**se+ˈlec+tive+ly** *adv.* —**se+ˈlec+tive+ness** *n.*

se+lec+tive at+ten+tion *n. Psychol.* the process by which a person can selectively pick out one message from a mixture of messages occurring simultaneously.

se+lec+tive serv+ice *n. U.S.* (formerly) compulsory military service under which men were conscripted selectively.

se+lec+tiv+i+ty (sɪˌlɛkˈtɪvɪtɪ) *n.* **1.** the state or quality of being selective. **2.** the degree to which a radio receiver or other circuit can respond to and separate the frequency of a desired signal from other frequencies by tuning.

se·lect+man (sɪˈlɛktmən) *n., pl.* **+men.** any of the members of the local boards of most New England towns.

se+lec+tor (sɪˈlɛktə) *n.* **1.** a person or thing that selects. **2.** a device used in automatic telephone switching that connects one circuit with any one of a number of other circuits. **3.** *Brit.* a person who chooses the members of a sports team.

sel+e·nate (ˈsɛlɪˌneɪt) *n.* any salt or ester formed by replacing one or both of the hydrogens of selenic acid with metal ions or organic groups. [C19: from SELENIUM + -ATE[1]]

Se·le·ne (sɪˈliːnɪ) *n.* the Greek goddess of the moon. Roman counterpart: **Luna.**

se+le·nic (sɪˈliːnɪk) *adj.* of or containing selenium, esp. in the hexavalent state.

se+le·nic ac·id *n.* a colourless crystalline soluble strong dibasic acid analogous to sulphuric acid. Formula: H_2SeO_4.

se+le·ni+ous (sɪˈliːnɪəs) *or* **se+le·nous** (sɪˈliːnəs) *adj.* of or containing selenium in the divalent or tetravalent state.

se+le·ni+ous ac·id *n.* a white soluble crystalline strong dibasic acid analogous to sulphurous acid. Formula: H_2SeO_3.

sel+e·nite (ˈsɛlɪˌnaɪt) *n.* a colourless glassy variety of gypsum.

se+le·ni·um (sɪˈliːnɪəm) *n.* a nonmetallic element that exists in several allotropic forms. It occurs free in volcanic areas and in sulphide ores, esp. pyrite. The common form is a grey crystalline solid that is photoconductive, photovoltaic, and semiconducting: used in photocells, solar cells, and in xerography. Symbol: Se; atomic no.: 34; atomic wt.: 78.96; valency: 2,4, or 6; relative density: 4.79 (grey); melting pt.: 217°C (grey); boiling pt.: 684.9°C (grey). [C19: from New Latin, from Greek *selēnē* moon; named by analogy to TELLURIUM (from Latin *tellus* earth)]

se+le·ni·um cell *n.* a photoelectric cell containing a strip of selenium between two metal electrodes.

se·le·no- *or before a vowel* **se·len-** *combining form.* denoting the moon: *selenology.* [from Greek *selēnē* moon]

se+le·no·dont (sɪˈliːnəˌdɒnt) **1.** *adj.* (of the teeth of certain mammals) having crescent-shaped ridges on the crowns, as in deer. **2.** *n.* a mammal with selenodont teeth. [C19: from SELENO- (moon-shaped) + -ODONT]

se·le·nog+ra·phy (ˌsiːlɪˈnɒgrəfɪ) *n.* the branch of astronomy concerned with the description and mapping of the surface features of the moon. —**se+le·no+graph** (sɪˈliːnəʊˌgrɑːf, -ˌgræf) *n.* —**ˌse+le·ˈnog+ra·pher** *or* **ˌsel+le·ˈnog+ra·phist** *n.* —**se+le·no+graph+ic** (sɪˌliːnəʊˈgræfɪk) *or* **se+ˌle·no+ˈgraph·i·cal** *adj.* —**se+ˌle·no+ˈgraph·i·cal+ly** *adv.*

se+le·nol+o·gy (ˌsiːlɪˈnɒlədʒɪ) *n.* the branch of astronomy concerned with the moon, its physical characteristics, nature, origin, etc. —**ˌse+le·ˈnol·o·gist** *n.*

se+le·no+mor+phol+o·gy (sɪˌliːnəʊmɔːˈfɒlədʒɪ) *n.* the study of the lunar surface and landscape.

Se+leu+ci·a (sɪˈluːʃɪə) *n.* **1.** an ancient city in Mesopotamia, on the River Tigris: founded by Seleucus Nicator in 312 B.C.; became the chief city of the Seleucid empire; sacked by the Romans around 162 A.D. **2.** an ancient city in SE Asia Minor, on the River Calycadnus (modern Goksu Nehri): captured by the Turks in the 13th century; site of present-day Silifke (Turkey). Official name: **Se+leu+ci·a Tra+che·o·tis** (ˌtrakɪˈəʊtɪs) or **Tra+che·a** (trəˈkɪə). **3.** an ancient port in Syria, on the River Orontes: the port of Antioch, of military importance during the wars between the Ptolemies and Seleucids; largely destroyed by earthquake in 526; site of present-day Samandağ (Turkey). Official name: **Se+leu+ci·a Pi+er·i·a** (paɪˈɪrɪə).

Se+leu+cid (sɪˈluːsɪd) *n., pl.* **+cids** *or* **+ci·dae** (-sɪˌdiː). **1.** a member of a royal dynasty (312–64 B.C.) that at the zenith of its power ruled over an area extending from Thrace to India. ~*adj.* **2.** of, relating to, or supporting the Seleucids or their dynasty. —**Se+leu+ci+dan** (sɪˈluːsɪdᵊn) *adj.*

Se·leu·cus I (sɪˈluːkəs) *n.* surname *Nicator.* ?358–280 B.C., Macedonian general under Alexander the Great, who founded the Seleucid kingdom.

self (sɛlf) *n., pl.* **selves** (sɛlvz). **1.** distinct identity or character. **2.** one's bodily make-up or personal characteristics: *her usual self.* **3. good self** *or* **selves.** *Rare.* a polite way of referring to or addressing a person, used following *your, his, her,* or *their.* **4.** one's own welfare or interests: *he only thinks of self.* **5.** an individual's consciousness of his own identity or being. **6.** a bird, animal, etc., that is a single colour throughout, esp. a self-coloured pigeon. ~*pron.* **7.** *Not standard.* myself, yourself, etc.: *seats for self and wife.* ~*adj.* **8.** the same in colour or material as the rest; matching. See also **self-coloured. 9.** *Obsolete.* the same. [Old English *seolf;* related to Old Norse *sjálfr,* Gothic *silba,* Old High German *selb*]

self- *combining form.* **1.** of oneself or itself: *self-defence; self-rule.* **2.** by, to, in, due to, for, or from the self: *self-employed; self-inflicted; self-respect.* **3.** automatic or automatically: *self-propelled.*

self-ab·ne·ga+tion *n.* the denial of one's own interests in favour of the interests of others. —**ˌself-ˈab·ne·ˌgat·ing** *adj.*

self-ab·sorp+tion *n.* **1.** preoccupation with oneself to the exclusion of others or the outside world. **2.** *Physics.* the process in which some of the radiation emitted by a material is absorbed by the material itself.

self-a·buse *n.* **1.** disparagement or misuse of one's own abilities, etc. **2.** a censorious term for **masturbation.**

self-act·ing *adj.* not requiring an external influence or control to function; automatic. —**ˌself-ˈac·tion** *n.*

self-ac·tu·al·i·za+tion *n. Psychol.* the process of establishing oneself as a whole person, able to develop one's abilities and to understand oneself.

self-ad·dressed *adj.* **1.** addressed for return to the sender. **2.** directed to oneself: *a self-addressed remark.*

self-ag·gran+dize+ment *n.* the act of increasing one's own power, importance, etc., esp. in an aggressive or ruthless manner. —**ˌself-ag·ˈgran+ˌdiz+ing** *adj.*

self-a·nal·y+sis *n.* the unaided analysis of one's own personality, etc. —**ˌself-ˌan·a·ˈlyt·i·cal** *adj.*

self-an·neal+ing *adj. Metallurgy.* denoting certain metals, such as lead, tin, and zinc, that recrystallize at air temperatures and so may be cold-worked without strain-hardening.

self-an·ni·hi+la+tion *n.* the surrender of the self in mystical contemplation, union with God, etc.

self-ap·point+ed *adj.* having assumed authority without the agreement of others: *a self-appointed critic.*

self-as·ser·tion *n.* the act or an instance of putting forward one's own opinions, etc., esp. in an aggressive or conceited manner. —**ˌself-as·ˈsert·ing** *adj.* —**ˌself-as·ˈsert·ing+ly** *adv.* —**ˌself-as·ˈser·tive** *adj.* —**ˌself-as·ˈser·tive+ly** *adv.* —**ˌself-as·ˈser·tive+ness** *n.*

self-as·sur·ance *n.* confidence in the validity, value, etc., of one's own ideas, opinions, etc.

self-as·sured *adj.* confident of one's own worth. —**ˌself-as·ˈsur·ed·ness** *n.*

self-cat·er+ing *adj.* denoting accommodation in which the tenant or visitor provides his own food.

self-cen·tred *adj.* totally preoccupied with one's own concerns. —**ˌself-ˈcen·tred+ly** *adv.* —**ˌself-ˈcen·tred+ness** *n.*

self-col·oured *adj.* **1.** having only a single and uniform colour: *self-coloured flowers; a self-coloured dress.* **2.** (of cloth, material, etc.) **a.** having the natural or original colour. **b.** retaining the colour of the thread before weaving.

self-com·mand *n.* another term for **self-control.**

self-con·cept *n. Psychol.* the whole set of attitudes, opinions, and cognitions that a person has of himself.

self-con·fessed *adj.* according to one's own testimony or admission: *a self-confessed liar.*

self-con·fi·dence *n.* confidence in one's own powers, judgment, etc. —**ˌself-ˈcon·fi·dent** *adj.* —**ˌself-ˈcon·fi·dent+ly** *adv.*

self-con·scious *adj.* **1.** unduly aware of oneself as the object of the attention of others; embarrassed. **2.** conscious of one's existence. —**ˌself-ˈcon·scious+ly** *adv.* —**ˌself-ˈcon·scious+ness** *n.*

self-con·tained *adj.* **1.** containing within itself all parts necessary for completeness. **2.** (of a flat) having its own kitchen, bathroom, and lavatory not shared by others and usually having its own entrance. **3.** able or tending to keep one's feelings, thoughts, etc., to oneself; reserved. **4.** able to control one's feelings or emotions in the presence of others. —**ˌself-con·ˈtain+ed+ly** *adv.* —**ˌself-con·ˈtain·ed+ness** *n.*

self-con·trol *n.* the ability to exercise restraint or control over one's feelings, emotions, reactions, etc. —**ˌself-con·ˈtrolled** *adj.* —**ˌself-con·ˈtrol+ling** *adj.*

self-de·cep·tion *or* **self-de·ceit** *n.* the act or an instance of deceiving oneself, esp. as to the true nature of one's feelings or motives. —**ˌself-de·ˈcep·tive** *adj.*

self-de·fence *n.* **1.** the act of defending oneself, one's actions, ideas, etc. **2.** boxing as a means of defending the person (esp. in the phrase **noble art of self-defence**). **3.** *Law.* the right to

ˌself-a·ˈban·don+ment *n.*
ˌself-a·ˈbase·ment *n.*
ˌself-ab·ˈhor+rence *n.*
ˌself-ab·ˈsorbed *adj.*
ˌself-ac·cu·ˈsa·tion *n.*
ˌself-ac·ˈcu·sat·or·y *adj.*
ˌself-ad·ˈhes·ive *adj.*
ˌself-ad·ˈjust·ing *adj.*
ˌself-ad·ˈmin·is+tered *adj.*
ˌself-ad·mi·ˈra+tion *n.*
ˌself-ad·ˈvance+ment *n.*
ˌself-ad·ˈver·tise+ment *n.*
ˌself-a·ˈlign+ing *adj.*
ˌself-ap·ˌpre·ci·ˈa+tion *n.*
ˌself-ap·ˈprov+al *n.*
ˌself-as·ˈsumed *adj.*
ˌself-a·ˈware *adj.*
ˌself-be·ˈtray+al *n.*
ˌself-ˈclean·ing *adj.*
ˌself-ˈclos·ing *adj.*
ˌself-com·ˈmit+ment *n.*
ˌself-com·ˈpla+cent *adj.*
ˌself-con·ˈcern *n.*
ˌself-con·dem+ˈna+tion *n.*
ˌself-con·ˈdemned *adj.*
ˌself-con·ˌgrat·u·ˈla+tion *n.*
ˌself-con·ˈsis+ten+cy *n.*
ˌself-con·ˈsis+tent *adj.*
ˌself-ˈcon·sti+ˌtut+ed *adj.*
ˌself-con·ˈtempt *n.*
ˌself-con·ˈtent *n., adj.*
ˌself-con·ˈtent·ed *adj.*
ˌself-con·ˈtent+ed+ly *adv.*
ˌself-ˌcon·tra+ˈdict+ing *adj.*
ˌself-ˌcon·tra+ˈdic+tion *n.*
ˌself-ˌcon·tra+ˈdic+to·ry *adj.*
ˌself-con·ˈvict+ed *adj.*
ˌself-cor·ˈrect+ing *adj.*
ˌself-cre·ˈat·ed *adj.*
ˌself-ˈcrit·i·cal *adj.*
ˌself-ˈcrit·i·cism *n.*
ˌself-de·ˈfeat+ing *adj.*
ˌself-ˌdeg·ra·ˈda+tion *n.*
ˌself-de·ˈlu·sion *n.*

defend one's person or property against attack or threat of attack by the use of no more force than is reasonable. —ˌ**self-de·ˈfen·sive** *adj.*

self-de·ni·al *n.* the denial or sacrifice of one's own desires. —ˌ**self-de·ˈny·ing** *adj.* —ˌ**self-de·ˈny·ing·ly** *adv.*

self-de·ter·mi·na·tion *n.* **1.** the power or ability to make a decision for oneself without influence from outside. **2.** the right of a nation or people to determine its own form of government without influence from outside. —ˌ**self-de·ˈter·mined** *adj.* —ˌ**self-de·ˈter·min·ing** *adj.*

self-dis·ci·pline *n.* the act of disciplining or power to discipline one's own feelings, desires, etc., esp. with the intention of improving oneself. —ˌ**self-ˈdis·ci·plined** *adj.*

self-drive *adj.* denoting or relating to a hired car that is driven by the hirer.

self-ed·u·cat·ed *adj.* **1.** educated through one's own efforts without formal instruction. **2.** educated at one's own expense, without financial aid. —ˌ**self-ˌed·u·ˈca·tion** *n.*

self-ef·face·ment *n.* the act of making oneself, one's actions, etc., inconspicuous, esp. because of humility or timidity. —ˌ**self-ef·ˈfac·ing** *adj.* —ˌ**self-ef·ˈfac·ing·ly** *adv.*

self-em·ployed *adj.* earning one's living in one's own business or through freelance work, rather than as the employee of another. —ˌ**self-em·ˈploy·ment** *n.*

self-es·teem *n.* a good, esp. unduly high, opinion of oneself.

self-ev·i·dent *adj.* containing its own evidence or proof without need of further demonstration. —ˌ**self-ˈev·i·dence** *n.* —ˌ**self-ˈev·i·dent·ly** *adv.*

self-ex·am·i·na·tion *n.* scrutiny of one's own conduct, motives, desires, etc. —ˌ**self-ex·ˈam·in·ing** *adj.*

self-ex·cit·ed *adj.* **1.** (of an electrical machine) having the current for the magnetic field system generated by the machine itself or by an auxiliary machine coupled to it. **2.** (of an oscillator) generating its own energy and depending on resonant circuits for frequency determination.

self-ex·e·cut·ing *adj.* (of a law, treaty, or clause in a deed or contract, etc.) coming into effect automatically at a specified time, no legislation being needed for enforcement.

self-ex·ist·ent *adj. Philosophy.* existing independently of any other being or cause. —ˌ**self-ex·ˈist·ence** *n.*

self-ex·plan·a·to·ry *or* **self-ex·plain·ing** *adj.* understandable without explanation; self-evident.

self-ex·pres·sion *n.* the expression of one's own personality, feelings, etc., as in painting, poetry, or other creative activity. —ˌ**self-ex·ˈpress·ive** *adj.*

self-feed·er *n.* any machine or device capable of automatically supplying materials when and where they are needed, esp. one for making measured quantities of food constantly available to farm livestock.

self-fer·ti·li·za·tion *n.* fertilization in a plant or animal by the fusion of male and female gametes produced by the same individual. Compare **cross-fertilization** (sense 1). —ˌ**self-ˈfer·ti·ˌlized** *adj.* —ˌ**self-ˈfer·ti·ˌliz·ing** *or* ˌ**self-ˈfer·tile** *adj.*

self-for·get·ful *adj.* forgetful of one's own interests. —ˌ**self-for·ˈget·ful·ly** *adv.* —ˌ**self-for·ˈget·ful·ness** *n.*

self-gov·ern·ment *n.* **1.** the government of a country, nation, etc., by its own people. **2.** the state of being self-controlled. **3.** an archaic term for **self-control.** —ˌ**self-ˈgov·erned** *adj.* —ˌ**self-ˈgov·ern·ing** *adj.*

self·heal (ˈsɛlfˌhiːl) *n.* **1.** a low-growing European herbaceous plant, *Prunella vulgaris,* with tightly clustered violet-blue flowers and reputedly having healing powers: family *Labiatae* (labiates). **2.** any of several other plants thought to have healing powers. ~Also called: **allheal, heal-all.**

self-help *n.* the act or state of providing the means to help oneself without relying on the assistance of others.

self·hood (ˈsɛlfhʊd) *n.* **1.** *Philosophy.* **a.** the state of having a distinct identity. **b.** the individuality so possessed. **2.** a person's character. **3.** the quality of being egocentric.

self-i·den·ti·ty *n.* the conscious recognition of the self as having a unique identity.

self-im·port·ant *adj.* having or showing an unduly high opinion of one's own abilities, importance, etc. —ˌ**self-im·ˈport·ant·ly** *adv.* —ˌ**self-im·ˈport·ance** *n.*

self-im·prove·ment *n.* the improvement of one's status, position, education, etc., by one's own efforts.

self-in·duced *adj.* **1.** induced or brought on by oneself or itself. **2.** *Electronics.* produced by self-induction.

self-in·duct·ance *n.* the inherent inductance of a circuit, given by the ratio of the electromotive force produced in the circuit by self-induction to the rate of change of current producing it. It is usually expressed in henries. Symbol: *L* Also called: **coefficient of self-induction.**

self-in·duc·tion *n.* the production of an electromotive force in a circuit when the magnetic flux linked with the circuit changes as a result of a change in current in the same circuit. See also **self-inductance.** Compare **mutual induction.** —ˌ**self-in·ˈduc·tive** *adj.*

self-in·dul·gent *adj.* tending to indulge or gratify one's own desires, etc. —ˌ**self-in·ˈdul·gence** *n.* —ˌ**self-in·ˈdul·gent·ly** *adv.*

self-in·sur·ance *n.* the practice of insuring oneself or one's property by accumulating a reserve out of one's income or funds rather than by purchase of an insurance policy.

self-in·ter·est *n.* **1.** one's personal interest or advantage. **2.** the act or an instance of pursuing one's own interest. —ˌ**self-ˈin·ter·est·ed** *adj.* —ˌ**self-ˈin·ter·est·ed·ness** *n.*

self·ish (ˈsɛlfɪʃ) *adj.* **1.** chiefly concerned with one's own interest, advantage, etc., esp. to the total exclusion of the interests of others. **2.** relating to or characterized by selfishness. —ˈ**self·ish·ly** *adv.* —ˈ**self·ish·ness** *n.*

self-jus·ti·fi·ca·tion *n.* the act or an instance of justifying or providing excuses for one's own behaviour, etc.

self-jus·ti·fy·ing *adj.* **1.** *Printing.* (of a typesetting machine) automatically adjusting the lengths of lines of type. **2.** offering excuses for one's behaviour, often when they are not called for.

self-know·ledge *n.* knowledge of one's own character, etc.

self·less (ˈsɛlflɪs) *adj.* having little concern for one's own interests. —ˈ**self·less·ly** *adv.* —ˈ**self·less·ness** *n.*

self-liq·ui·dat·ing *adj.* **1.** (of a loan, bill of exchange, etc.) used to finance transactions whose proceeds are expected to accrue before the date of redemption or repayment. **2.** (of a business transaction, project, investment, etc.) yielding proceeds sufficient to cover the initial outlay or to finance any recurrent outlays.

self-load·ing *adj.* (of a firearm) utilizing some of the force of the explosion to eject the empty shell and replace it with a new one. Also: **autoloading.** See also **automatic** (sense 5), **semiautomatic** (sense 2).

self-love *n.* the instinct or tendency to seek one's own well-being or to further one's own interest.

self-made *adj.* **1.** having achieved wealth, status, etc., by one's own efforts. **2.** made by oneself.

self-o·pin·ion·at·ed *or* **self-o·pin·ioned** *adj.* **1.** having an unduly high regard for oneself or one's own opinions. **2.** clinging stubbornly to one's own opinions.

self-pit·y *n.* the act or state of pitying oneself, esp. in an exaggerated or self-indulgent manner. —ˌ**self-ˈpit·y·ing** *adj.* —ˌ**self-ˈpit·y·ing·ly** *adv.*

self-pol·li·na·tion *n.* the transfer of pollen from the anthers to the stigma of the same flower. Compare **cross-pollination.** —ˌ**self-ˈpol·li·ˌnat·ed** *adj.*

self-pos·sessed *adj.* having control of one's emotions, etc. —ˌ**self-pos·ˈsess·ed·ly** *adv.* —ˌ**self-pos·ˈses·sion** *n.*

self-pre·ser·va·tion *n.* the preservation of oneself from danger or injury, esp. as a basic instinct.

self-pro·nounc·ing *adj.* (in a phonetic transcription) of, relating to, or denoting a word that, except for additional diacritic marks of stress, may keep the letters of its ordinary orthography to represent its pronunciation.

self-pro·pelled *adj.* (of a vehicle) provided with its own source of tractive power rather than requiring an external means of propulsion. —ˌ**self-pro·ˈpel·ling** *adj.*

self-rais·ing *adj.* (of flour) having a raising agent, such as bicarbonate of soda, already added.

self-re·al·i·za·tion *n.* the realization or fulfilment of one's own potential or abilities.

self-re·gard *n.* **1.** concern for one's own interest. **2.** proper esteem for oneself. —ˌ**self-re·ˈgard·ing** *adj.*

self-re·li·ance *n.* reliance on one's own abilities, decisions, etc. —ˌ**self-re·ˈli·ant** *adj.* —ˌ**self-re·ˈli·ant·ly** *adv.*

self-re·nun·ci·a·tion *n.* the renunciation of one's own rights, claims, interest, etc., esp. in favour of those of others. —ˌ**self-re·ˈnun·ci·a·to·ry** *adj.*

self-re·proach *n.* the act of finding fault with or blaming oneself. —ˌ**self-re·ˈproach·ful** *adj.* —ˌ**self-re·ˈproach·ful·ly** *adv.*

self-re·spect *n.* a proper sense of one's own dignity and integrity. —ˌ**self-re·ˈspect·ful** *or* ˌ**self-re·ˈspect·ing** *adj.*

ˌ**self-de·ˈpend·ence** *n.*
ˌ**self-de·ˈpend·ent** *adj.*
ˌ**self-de·ˈspair** *n.*
ˌ**self-de·ˈstroy·ing** *adj.*
ˌ**self-de·ˈstruc·tion** *n.*
ˌ**self-de·ˈvel·op·ment** *n.*
ˌ**self-de·ˈvo·tion** *n.*
ˌ**self-di·ˈrect·ed** *adj.*
ˌ**self-dis·ˈtrust** *n.*
ˌ**self-ˈdoubt** *n.*
ˌ**self-ˈdriv·en** *adj.*
ˌ**self-e·ˈlect·ed** *adj.*
ˌ**self-en·ˈclosed** *adj.*
ˌ**self-en·ˈjoy·ment** *n.*
ˌ**self-en·ˈrich·ment** *n.*
ˌ**self-e·ˈvolved** *adj.*
ˌ**self-ex·ˈer·tion** *n.*
ˌ**self-ex·ˈpand·ing** *adj.*
ˌ**self-ˈflat·ter·y** *n.*
ˌ**self-ˈfo·cus·ing** *adj.*
ˌ**self-ful·ˈfill·ing** *adj.*
ˌ**self-ful·ˈfil·ment** *n.*
ˌ**self-ˈgen·er·ˌat·ing** *adj.*
ˌ**self-ˈgiv·ing** *adj.*
ˌ**self-ˈhate** *n.*
ˌ**self-ˈha·tred** *n.*
ˌ**self-ˈheal·ing** *n.*
ˌ**self-hu·ˌmil·i·ˈa·tion** *n.*
ˌ**self-hyp·ˈno·sis** *n.*
ˌ**self-hyp·ˈnot·ic** *adj.*
ˌ**self-ˈhyp·no·tism** *n.*
ˌ**self-ˈim·age** *n.*
ˌ**self-ˌim·mo·ˈla·tion** *n.*
ˌ**self-im·ˈposed** *adj.*
ˌ**self-in·ˈflict·ed** *adj.*
ˌ**self-in·ˈi·ti·ˌat·ed** *adj.*
ˌ**self-ˈjudg·ment** *n.*
ˌ**self-ˈlock·ing** *adj.*
ˌ**self-ˈmas·ter·y** *n.*
ˌ**self-ˈmov·ing** *adj.*
ˌ**self-ˈmur·der** *n.*
ˌ**self-neg·ˈlect** *n.*
ˌ**self-ˈoc·cu·ˌpied** *adj.*
ˌ**self-ˈop·er·ˌat·ing** *adj.*
ˌ**self-o·ˈpin·ion** *n.*
ˌ**self-or·ˈdained** *adj.*
ˌ**self-per·ˈpet·u·at·ing** *adj.*
ˌ**self-ˈpor·trait** *n.*
ˌ**self-ˈpow·ered** *adj.*
ˌ**self-ˈpraise** *n.*
ˌ**self-ˌprep·a·ˈra·tion** *n.*
ˌ**self-pre·ˈpared** *adj.*
ˌ**self-pro·ˈclaimed** *adj.*
ˌ**self-pro·ˈduced** *adj.*
ˌ**self-pro·ˈfessed** *adj.*
ˌ**self-ˈprop·a·gat·ing** *adj.*
ˌ**self-pro·ˈpelled** *adj.*
ˌ**self-pro·ˈpul·sion** *n.*
ˌ**self-pro·ˈtect·ing** *adj.*
ˌ**self-pro·ˈtec·tion** *n.*
ˌ**self-pro·ˈtec·tive** *adj.*
ˌ**self-ˈpun·ish·ment** *n.*
ˌ**self-ˈques·tion·ing** *adj.*
ˌ**self-re·ˈflec·tion** *n.*
ˌ**self-ˈre·gis·ter·ing** *adj.*
ˌ**self-ˈreg·u·ˌlat·ing** *adj.*
ˌ**self-re·ˈpeat·ing** *adj.*
ˌ**self-re·ˈpel·lent** *adj.*
ˌ**self-re·ˈpose** *n.*
ˌ**self-re·ˈpres·sion** *n.*
ˌ**self-re·ˈproof** *n.*
ˌ**self-re·ˈsent·ment** *n.*

self-re·straint *n.* restraint imposed by oneself on one's own feelings, desires, etc.
self-right·eous *adj.* having or showing an exaggerated awareness of one's own virtuousness or rights. —ˌ**self-'right·eous·ly** *adv.* —ˌ**self-'right·eous·ness** *n.*
self-rule *n.* another term for **self-government.**
self-sac·ri·fice *n.* the sacrifice of one's own desires, interest, etc., for the sake of duty or for the well-being of others. —ˌ**self-'sac·ri·ˌfic·ing** *adj.* —ˌ**self-'sac·ri·ˌfic·ing·ly** *adv.*
self·same ('sɛlfˌseɪm) *adj.* (*prenominal*) the very same.
self-sat·is·fied *adj.* having or showing a complacent satisfaction with oneself, one's own actions, behaviour, etc. —ˌ**self-ˌsat·is·'fac·tion** *n.*
self-seal·ing *adj.* (esp. of an envelope) designed to become sealed with the application of pressure only.
self-seek·ing *n.* **1.** the act or an instance of seeking one's own profit or interest, esp. exclusively. ~*adj.* **2.** having or showing an exclusive preoccupation with one's own profit or interest: *a self-seeking attitude.* —ˌ**self-'seek·er** *n.*
self-serv·ice *adj.* **1.** of or denoting a shop, restaurant, etc., where the customer serves himself. ~*n.* **2.** the practice of serving oneself, as in a shop, etc.
self-sown *adj.* (of plants) growing from seed dispersed by any means other than by the agency of man or animals. Also: **self-seeded.**
self-start·er *n.* **1.** an electric motor used to start an internal-combustion engine. **2.** the switch that operates this motor.
self-styled *adj.* (*prenominal*) claiming to be of a specified nature, quality, profession, etc.: *a self-styled expert.*
self-suf·fi·cient *or* **self-suf·fic·ing** *adj.* **1.** able to provide for or support oneself without the help of others. **2.** *Rare.* having undue confidence in oneself, one's own abilities, etc. —ˌ**self-suf·'fi·cien·cy** *n.* —ˌ**self-suf·'fi·cient·ly** *adv.*
self-sug·ges·tion *n.* another term for **autosuggestion.**
self-sup·port·ing *adj.* **1.** able to support or maintain oneself without the help of others. **2.** able to stand up or hold firm without support, props, attachments, etc.
self-will *n.* stubborn adherence to one's own will, desires, etc., esp. at the expense of others. —ˌ**self-'willed** *adj.*
self-wind·ing *adj.* (of a wrist watch) having a mechanism, activated by the movements of the wearer, in which a rotating or oscillating weight rewinds the mainspring.
Sel·juk (sɛl'dʒuːk) *or* **Sel·ju·ki·an** (sɛl'dʒuːkɪən) *n.* **1.** a member of any of the pre-Ottoman Turkish dynasties ruling over large parts of Asia in the 11th, 12th, and 13th centuries A.D. ~*adj.* **2.** of or relating to these dynasties or to their subjects. [C19: from Turkish]
Sel·kirk[1] ('sɛlkɜːk) *n.* (until 1975) a county of SE Scotland, now part of the Borders region.
Sel·kirk[2] ('sɛlkɜːk) *n.* **Al·ex·an·der.** original name *Alexander Selcraig.* 1676–1721, Scottish sailor, who was marooned on one of the islets of Juan Fernández and is regarded as the prototype of Defoe's *Robinson Crusoe.*
Sel·kirk Moun·tains *pl. n.* a mountain range in SW Canada, in SE British Columbia. Highest peak: Mount Sir Sandford, 3533 m (11 590 ft.).
sell (sɛl) *vb.* **sells, sell·ing, sold.** **1.** to dispose of or transfer or be disposed of or transferred to a purchaser in exchange for money or other consideration; put or be on sale. **2.** to deal in (objects, property, etc.): *he sells used cars for a living.* **3.** (*tr.*) to give up or surrender for a price or reward: *to sell one's honour.* **4.** to promote or facilitate the sale of (objects, property, etc.): *publicity sells many products.* **5.** to induce or gain acceptance of: *to sell an idea.* **6.** (*intr.*) to be in demand on the market: *these dresses sell well in the spring.* **7.** (*tr.*) *Informal.* to deceive or cheat. **8.** (*tr.*; foll. by *on*) *Chiefly U.S.* to persuade to accept or approve (of): *to sell a buyer on a purchase.* **9. sell down the river.** *Informal.* to betray. **10. sell oneself. a.** to convince someone else of one's potential or worth. **b.** to give up one's moral or spiritual standards, etc. **11. sell short. a.** *Informal.* to disparage or belittle. **b.** *Finance.* to sell securities or goods without owning them in anticipation of buying them before delivery at a lower price. ~*n.* **12.** the act or an instance of selling. Compare **hard sell, soft sell.** **13.** *Informal.* a trick, hoax, or deception. [Old English *sellan* to lend, deliver; related to Old Norse *selja* to sell, Gothic *saljan* to offer sacrifice, Old High German *sellen* to sell, Latin *cōnsilium* advice]
sell·er ('sɛlə) *n.* **1.** a person who sells. **2.** an article to be sold: *this item is always a good seller.* **3.** short for **selling race.**
Sel·lers ('sɛləz) *n.* **Pe·ter.** 1925-80, English radio, stage, and film actor and comedian: noted for his gift of precise vocal mimicry, esp. in *The Goon Show* (with Spike Milligan and Harry Secombe; BBC Radio, 1952–60). His films include *The Lady Killers* (1955), *The Millionairess* (1961), *The Pink Panther* (1963), *Dr Strangelove* (1964), *Soft Beds and Hard Battles* (1973), and *The Pink Panther strikes again* (1977).
sell·ers' mar·ket *n.* a market in which demand exceeds supply and sellers can influence prices.
sell·ing-plat·er *n.* **1.** a horse that competes, or is only good enough to compete, in a selling race. **2.** a person or thing of limited ability or value.
sell·ing race *or* **plate** *n.* a horse race in which the winner must be offered for sale at auction.
sell off *vb.* (*tr., adv.*) to sell (remaining or unprofitable items), esp. at low prices.
Sel·lo·tape ('sɛləˌteɪp) *n.* **1.** *Trademark.* a type of adhesive tape. ~*vb.* (*tr.*) **2.** to seal or stick using adhesive tape.
sell out *vb.* (*adv.*) **1.** Also (*chiefly Brit.*): **sell up.** to dispose of (supplies of something) completely by selling. **2.** (*tr.*) *Informal.* to betray, esp. through a secret agreement. ~*n.* **sell·out. 3.** *Informal.* a performance for which all tickets are sold. **4.** a commercial success. **5.** *Informal.* a betrayal.
sell up *vb.* (*adv.*) *Chiefly Brit.* **1.** (*tr.*) to sell all (the possessions or assets) of (a bankrupt debtor) in order to discharge his debts as far as possible. **2.** (*intr.*) to sell a business.
sel·syn ('sɛlsɪn) *n.* another name for **synchro.**
Selt·zer ('sɛltsə) *n.* **1.** a natural effervescent water with a high content of minerals. **2.** a similar synthetic water, used as a beverage. ~Also called: **Seltzer water.** [C18: changed from German *Selterser Wasser* water from (*Nieder*) *Selters,* district where mineral springs are located, near Wiesbaden, Germany]
sel·va ('sɛlvə) *n.* **1.** dense equatorial forest, esp. in the Amazon basin, characterized by tall broad-leaved evergreen trees, epiphytes, lianas, etc. **2.** a tract of such forest. [C19: from Spanish and Portuguese, from Latin *silva* forest]
sel·vage *or* **sel·vedge** ('sɛlvɪdʒ) *n.* **1.** the finished nonfraying edge of a length of woven fabric. **2.** a similar strip of material allowed in fabricating a metal or plastic article, used esp. for handling components during manufacture. [C15: from SELF + EDGE; related to Dutch *selfegghe,* German *Selbende*] —'**sel·vaged** *adj.*
selves (sɛlvz) *n.* **a.** the plural of **self. b.** (*in combination*): *ourselves, yourselves, themselves.*
sem. *abbrev. for:* **1.** semester. **2.** semicolon.
Sem. *abbrev. for:* **1.** Seminary. **2.** Semitic.
se·man·teme (sɪ'mæntiːm) *n.* another word for **sememe** (sense 2).
se·man·tic (sɪ'mæntɪk) *adj.* **1.** of or relating to meaning or arising from distinctions between the meanings of different words or symbols. **2.** of or relating to semantics. [C19: from Greek *sēmantikos* having significance, from *sēmainein* to signify, from *sēma* a sign] —**se·'man·ti·cal·ly** *adv.*
se·man·tics (sɪ'mæntɪks) *n.* (*functioning as sing.*) **1.** the branch of linguistics that deals with the study of meaning, changes in meaning, and the principles that govern the relationship between sentences or words and their meanings. **2.** the study of the relationships between signs and symbols and what they represent. **3.** *Logic.* the principles that determine the truth-values of the formulas in a logical system. —**se·'man·ti·cist** *n.*
sem·a·phore ('sɛməˌfɔː) *n.* **1.** an apparatus for conveying information by means of visual signals, as with movable arms or railway signals, flags, etc. **2.** a system of signalling by holding a flag in each hand and moving the arms to designated positions to denote each letter of the alphabet. ~*vb.* **3.** to signal (information) by means of semaphore. [C19: via French, from Greek *sēma* a signal + -PHORE] —**sem·a·phor·ic** (ˌsɛmə'fɒrɪk) *or* ˌ**sem·a·'phor·i·cal** *adj.* —ˌ**sem·a·'phor·i·cal·ly** *adv.*
Se·ma·rang *or* **Sa·ma·rang** (sə'mɑːrɑːŋ) *n.* a port in S Indonesia, in N Java on the Java Sea. Pop.: 646 590 (1971).
se·ma·si·ol·o·gy (sɪˌmeɪsɪ'ɒlədʒɪ) *n.* another name for **semantics.** [C19: from Greek *sēmasia* meaning, from *sēmainein* to signify + -LOGY] —**se·ma·si·o·log·i·cal** (sɪˌmeɪsɪə'lɒdʒɪkᵊl) *adj.* —**seˌma·si·o·'log·i·cal·ly** *adv.* —**seˌma·si·'ol·o·gist** *n.*
se·mat·ic (sɪ'mætɪk) *adj.* (of the conspicuous coloration of certain animals) acting as a warning, esp. to potential predators. [C19: from Greek *sēma* a sign]
sem·a·tol·o·gy (ˌsɛmə'tɒlədʒɪ) *n.* another name for **semantics.** [C19: from Greek *sēmat-, sēma* sign + -LOGY]
sem·bla·ble ('sɛmbləbᵊl) *Archaic.* ~*adj.* **1.** resembling or similar. **2.** apparent rather than real. ~*n.* **3.** something that resembles another thing. **4.** a resemblance. [C14: from Old French, from *sembler* to seem; see SEMBLANCE] —'**sem·bla·bly** *adv.*
sem·blance ('sɛmbləns) *n.* **1.** outward appearance, esp. without any inner substance or reality. **2.** a resemblance or copy. [C13: from Old French, from *sembler* to seem, from Latin *simulāre* to imitate, from *similis* like]
se·mé *or* **se·mée** ('sɛmeɪ; *French* sə'me) *adj.* (*postpositive*) (usually foll. by *of*) *Heraldry.* dotted (with): *semé of fleurs-de-lis gules.* [C16: from French, literally: sown, from *semer* to sow, from Latin *sēmināre,* from *sēmen* seed]
se·mei- for words beginning thus, see the more common spelling in **semi-.**
Sem·e·le ('sɛmɪlɪ) *n. Greek myth.* mother of Dionysus by Zeus.
sem·eme ('siːmiːm) *n. Linguistics.* **1.** the meaning of a morpheme. **2.** Also called: **semanteme.** a minimum unit of meaning in terms of which it is sometimes proposed that meaning in general might be analysed. [C20 (coined in 1933 by L. BLOOMFIELD): from Greek *sēma* a sign + -EME]
se·men ('siːmɛn) *n.* **1.** the thick whitish fluid containing spermatozoa that is ejaculated from the male genital tract. **2.** another name for **sperm.** [C14: from Latin: seed]
Se·me·ru *or* **Se·me·roe** (sə'mɛruː) *n.* a volcano in Indonesia: the highest peak in Java. Height: 3676 m (12 060 ft.).
se·mes·ter (sɪ'mɛstə) *n.* **1.** *Chiefly U.S.* either of two divisions

ˌ**self-re·'strict·ed** *adj.*
ˌ**self-re·'veal·ing** *n.*
ˌ**self-'right·ing** *adj.*
ˌ**self-'schooled** *adj.*
ˌ**self-sur·'ren·der** *n.*
ˌ**self-'taught** *adj.*
ˌ**self-'tor·ment** *n.*
ˌ**self-tor·'ment·ing** *adj.*
ˌ**self-'tor·ture** *n.*
ˌ**self-'trained** *adj.*
ˌ**self-ˌtrans·for·'ma·tion** *n.*
ˌ**self-'treat·ment** *n.*
ˌ**self-'trust** *n.*
ˌ**self-ˌun·der·'stand·ing** *n.*
ˌ**self-ˌvin·di·'ca·tion** *n.*
ˌ**self-'wor·ship** *n.*

of the academic year, ranging from 15 to 18 weeks. **2.** (in German universities) a session of six months. [C19: via German from Latin *sēmestris* half-yearly, from *sex* six + *mensis* a month] —**se+'mes+tral** *adj.*

sem·i ('sɛmɪ) *n. Informal.* **1.** *Brit.* short for **semidetached (house)**. **2.** short for **semifinal**. **3.** *U.S., Austral.* short for **semitrailer**.

sem·i- *prefix.* **1.** half: *semicircle.* Compare **demi-** (sense 1), **hemi-**. **2.** partially, partly, not completely, or almost: *semiprofessional; semifinal.* **3.** occurring twice in a specified period of time: *semiannual; semiweekly.* [from Latin; compare Old English *sōm-, sām-* half, Greek *hēmi-*]

sem·i+an+nu·al (ˌsɛmɪ'ænjʊəl) *adj.* **1.** occurring every half-year. **2.** lasting for half a year. —ˌ**sem·i+'an+nu+al+ly** *adv.*

sem·i+a·quat+ic (ˌsɛmɪə'kwætɪk) *adj.* (of organisms, esp. plants) occurring close to the water and sometimes within it.

sem·i+ar+id (ˌsɛmɪ'ærɪd) *adj.* characterized by scanty rainfall and scrubby vegetation, often occurring in continental interiors. —ˌ**sem·i+a·'rid+i·ty** *n.*

sem·i+au·to+mat+ic (ˌsɛmɪˌɔːtə'mætɪk) *adj.* **1.** partly automatic. **2.** (of a firearm) self-loading but firing only one shot at each pull of the trigger. Compare **automatic** (sense 5). ~*n.* **3.** a semiautomatic firearm. —ˌ**sem·i+ˌau·to+'mat·i·cal+ly** *adv.*

Sem·i-Ban·tu *n.* **1.** a group of languages of W Africa, mainly SE Nigeria and Cameroon, that were not traditionally classed as Bantu but that show certain essential Bantu characteristics. They are now classed with Bantu in the Benue-Congo branch of the Niger-Congo family. ~*adj.* **2.** relating to or belonging to this group of languages.

sem·i+bold (ˌsɛmɪ'bəʊld) *Printing.* ~*adj.* **1.** denoting a weight of typeface between medium and bold face. **2.** denoting matter printed in this. ~*n.* **3.** semibold type.

sem·i+breve ('sɛmɪˌbriːv) *n. Music.* a note, now the longest in common use, having a time value that may be divided by any power of 2 to give all other notes. Usual U.S. name: **whole note.** See also **breve** (sense 2).

sem·i+cen+ten+ni·al (ˌsɛmɪsɛn'tɛnɪəl) *adj.* **1.** (*prenominal*) of or relating to the 50th anniversary of some event. **2.** occurring once every 50 years. ~*n.* **3.** a 50th anniversary.

sem·i+cir+cle ('sɛmɪˌsɜːkᵊl) *n.* **1. a.** one half of a circle. **b.** half the circumference of a circle. **2.** anything having the shape or form of half a circle. —**sem·i+cir+cu+lar** (ˌsɛmɪ'sɜːkjʊlə) *adj.* —ˌ**sem·i+'cir+cu+lar+ly** *adv.*

sem·i+cir+cu+lar ca+nal *n. Anatomy.* any of the three looped fluid-filled membranous tubes, at right angles to one another, that comprise the labyrinth of the ear: concerned with the sense of orientation and equilibrium.

sem·i+co+lon (ˌsɛmɪ'kəʊlən) *n.* the punctuation mark (;) used to indicate a pause intermediate in value or length between that of a comma and that of a full stop.

sem·i+con+duc+tor (ˌsɛmɪkən'dʌktə) *n.* **1.** a substance, such as germanium or silicon, that has an electrical conductivity that increases with temperature and is intermediate between that of a metal and an insulator. The behaviour may be exhibited by the pure substance (**intrinsic semiconductor**) or as a result of impurities (**extrinsic semiconductor**). **2. a.** a device, such as a transistor or integrated circuit, that depends on the properties of such a substance. **b.** (*as modifier*): *a semiconductor diode.* —ˌ**sem·i+con+'duc+tion** *n.*

sem·i+con+scious (ˌsɛmɪ'kɒnʃəs) *adj.* not fully conscious. —ˌ**sem·i+'con+scious+ly** *adv.* —ˌ**sem·i+'con+scious+ness** *n.*

sem·i+de+tached (ˌsɛmɪdɪ'tætʃt) *adj.* **a.** (of a building) joined to another on one side by a common wall. **b.** (*as n.*): *they live in a suburban semidetached.*

sem·i+di+ur+nal (ˌsɛmɪdaɪ'ɜːnᵊl) *adj.* **1.** of or continuing during half a day. **2.** occurring every 12 hours.

sem·i+dome ('sɛmɪˌdəʊm) *n.* a half-dome, esp. one used to cover a semicircular apse.

sem·i+el+lip+ti+cal (ˌsɛmɪɪ'lɪptɪkᵊl) *adj.* shaped like one half of an ellipse, esp. one divided along the major axis.

sem·i+fi+nal (ˌsɛmɪ'faɪnᵊl) *n.* **a.** the round before the final in a competition. **b.** (*as modifier*): *the semifinal draw.*

sem·i+fi+nal+ist (ˌsɛmɪ'faɪnᵊlɪst) *n.* a player or team taking part in a semifinal.

sem·i+flu+id (ˌsɛmɪ'fluːɪd) *adj.* also **sem·i+flu+id+ic** (ˌsɛmɪfluː'ɪdɪk). **1.** having properties between those of a liquid and those of a solid. ~*n.* **2.** a substance that has such properties because of high viscosity: *tar is a semifluid.* ~Also: **semiliquid.** —ˌ**sem·i+flu+'id+i·ty** *n.*

sem·i+lit+er+ate (ˌsɛmɪ'lɪtərɪt) *adj.* **1.** hardly able to read or write. **2.** able to read but not to write.

sem·i+lu+nar (ˌsɛmɪ'luːnə) *adj.* shaped like a crescent or half-moon.

sem·i+lu+nar valve *n. Anatomy.* either of two crescent-shaped valves, one in the aorta and one in the pulmonary artery, that prevent regurgitation of blood into the heart.

sem·i+nal ('sɛmɪnəl) *adj.* **1.** potentially capable of development. **2.** highly original, influential and important. **3.** rudimentary or unformed. **4.** of or relating to semen: *seminal fluid.* **5.** *Biology.* of or relating to seed. [C14: from Late Latin *sēminālis* belonging to seed, from Latin *sēmen* seed] —ˌ**sem·i+'nal+i·ty** *n.* —'**sem·i+nal+ly** *adv.*

sem·i+nar ('sɛmɪˌnɑː) *n.* **1.** a small group of students meeting regularly under the guidance of a tutor, professor, etc., to exchange information, discuss theories, etc. **2.** one such meeting or the place in which it is held. **3.** a higher course for postgraduates. **4.** any group or meeting for holding discussions or exchanging information. [C19: via German from Latin *sēminārium* SEMINARY]

sem·i+nar+i·an (ˌsɛmɪ'nɛərɪən) *n.* a student at a seminary.

sem·i+nar·y ('sɛmɪnərɪ) *n., pl.* **+nar·ies.** **1.** an academy for the training of priests, rabbis, etc. **2.** *Rare.* a private secondary school, esp. for girls. **3.** *U.S.* another word for **seminar** (sense 1). **4.** a place where something is grown. ~*adj.* **5.** another word for **seminal.** [C15: from Latin *sēminārium* a nursery garden, from *sēmen* seed] —ˌ**sem·i+'nar+i·al** *adj.*

sem·i+na·tion (ˌsɛmɪ'neɪʃən) *n. Rare.* the production, dispersal, or sowing of seed. [C16: from Late Latin *sēminātiō*, from Latin *sēmināre* to sow, from *sēmen* seed]

sem·i+nif+er+ous (ˌsɛmɪ'nɪfərəs) *adj.* **1.** containing, conveying, or producing semen: *the seminiferous tubules of the testes.* **2.** (of plants) bearing or producing seeds.

Sem·i+nole ('sɛmɪˌnəʊl) *n.* **1.** (*pl.* **+noles** *or* **+nole**) a member of a North American Indian people consisting of Creeks who moved into Florida in the 18th century. **2.** the language of this people, belonging to the Muskhogean family. [from Creek *simanó-li* fugitive, from American Spanish *cimarrón* runaway]

se+mi+ol+o·gy *or* **se+mei+ol+o·gy** (ˌsɛmɪ'ɒlədʒɪ, ˌsiːmɪ-) *n.* another word for **semiotics.** [C17 (in the sense "sign language"): from Greek *sēmeion* sign + -LOGY] —**se+mi·o+log+ic** (ˌsɛmɪə'lɒdʒɪk, ˌsiːmɪ-), ˌ**se+mi·o·'log·i·cal** *or* ˌ**se+mei·o·'log+ic,** ˌ**se+mei·o+'log·i·cal** *adj.* —ˌ**se+mi+'ol·o·gist** *or* ˌ**se+mei+'ol·o·gist** *n.*

se+mi+ot+ic *or* **se+mei+ot+ic** (ˌsɛmɪ'ɒtɪk, ˌsiːmɪ-) *adj.* **1.** relating to signs and symbols, esp. spoken or written signs. **2.** relating to semiotics. **3.** of, relating to, or resembling the symptoms of disease; symptomatic. [C17: from Greek *sēmeiōtikos* taking note of signs, from *sēmeion* a sign]

se+mi+ot+ics *or* **se+mei+ot+ics** (ˌsɛmɪ'ɒtɪks, ˌsiːmɪ-) *n.* (*functioning as sing.*) **1.** the study of signs and symbols, esp. the relations between written or spoken signs and their referents in the physical world or the world of ideas. See also **semantics, syntactics, pragmatics.** **2.** the scientific study of the symptoms of disease; symptomatology. ~Also called: **semiology, semeiology.**

Se+mi+pa+la+tinsk (*Russian* sɪmipa'latinsk) *n.* a city in the S Soviet Union, in the NE Kazakh SSR on the Irtysh River. Pop.: 271 000 (1975 est.).

sem·i+pal+mate (ˌsɛmɪ'pɑːlmɪt) *or* **sem·i+pal+mat+ed** *adj.* (of the feet of some birds) having the front three toes partly webbed.

sem·i+par·a+sit+ic (ˌsɛmɪˌpærə'sɪtɪk) *adj.* **1.** (of plants) obtaining shelter and some food from a host but undergoing photosynthesis at the same time. **2.** (of plants or animals, esp. fungi) usually parasitic but capable of living as a saprophyte. —**sem·i+par·a+site** (ˌsɛmɪ'pærəsaɪt) *n.* —**sem·i+par·a·sit+ism** (ˌsɛmɪ'pærəsɪˌtɪzəm) *n.*

sem·i+per+me·a·ble (ˌsɛmɪ'pɜːmɪəbᵊl) *adj.* (esp. of a cell membrane) selectively permeable. —ˌ**sem·i+ˌper+me·a·'bil·i·ty** *n.*

sem·i+porce+lain (ˌsɛmɪ'pɔːslɪn) *n.* a durable porcellaneous stoneware; stone china.

sem·i+post+al (ˌsɛmɪ'pəʊstᵊl) *adj. Philately, chiefly U.S.* denoting stamps where all or part of the receipts from sale are given to some charitable cause.

sem·i+pre·cious (ˌsɛmɪ'prɛʃəs) *adj.* (of certain stones) having less value than a precious stone.

sem·i+pro ('sɛmɪˌprəʊ) *adj., n., pl.* **+pros.** short for **semiprofessional.**

ˌsem·i+'ac+tive *adj.*
ˌsem·i+ˌag+ri+'cul+tur+al *adj.*
ˌsem·i+'an+gu+lar *adj.*
ˌsem·i+'an·i+ˌmat+ed *adj.*
ˌsem·i+au·'ton·o+mous *adj.*
ˌsem·i+ˌbi·o+'graph·i·cal *adj.*
ˌsem·i+'blind *adj.*
ˌsem·i+'civ·i+ˌlized *or* ˌsem·i+'civ·i+ˌlised *adj.*
ˌsem·i+'clas+si·cal *adj.*
ˌsem·i+'clas+si+cal+ly *adv.*
'sem·i+ˌco+ma *n.*
ˌsem·i+'com·i·cal *adj.*
ˌsem·i+'dai+ly *adj., adv.*
ˌsem·i+'dark+ness *n.*
ˌsem·i+'deaf *adj.*
ˌsem·i·de+'pend+ence *n.*
ˌsem·i·de·'pend+ent *adj.*
ˌsem·i·di+'am+e+ter *n.*
ˌsem·i·di+'rect *adj.*
ˌsem·i·di+'vine *adj.*
ˌsem·i+ˌdoc·u·'men+ta+ry *n., adj.*
ˌsem·i·do+'mes+ti+ˌcat+ed *adj.*
ˌsem·i·do+ˌmes+ti+'ca+tion *n.*
ˌsem·i+'dry *adj.*
ˌsem·i+e·'rect *adj.*
ˌsem·i+ex+'posed *adj.*
ˌsem·i+'fic+tion+al *adj.*
ˌsem·i+'fin+ished *adj.*
ˌsem·i+'formed *adj.*
ˌsem·i+'fri+a·ble *adj.*
ˌsem·i+'glob+u+lar *adj.*
ˌsem·i+'hard *adj.*
ˌsem·i-il·'lit+er+ate *adj.*
ˌsem·i-ˌin·de·'pend+ence *n.*
ˌsem·i-ˌin·de·'pend+ent *adj.*
ˌsem·i-in·'dus·tri+al *adj.*
ˌsem·i-in·'dus·tri+al+ˌized *or* ˌsem·i-in·'dus·tri +al+ˌised *adj.*
ˌsem·i-in·'stinc+tive *adj.*
ˌsem·i-in·'stinc+tive+ly *adv.*
ˌsem·i-in·'tox·i+ˌcat+ed *adj.*
ˌsem·i·'in·va·lid *n.*
ˌsem·i·'leg+end+ˌar·y *adj.*
ˌsem·i·ma+'ture *adj.*
ˌsem·i+'month+ly *adj., adv.*
ˌsem·i+'moun+tain+ous *adj.*
ˌsem·i+'mys+ti·cal *adj.*
ˌsem·i+'myth·i+cal *adj.*
ˌsem·i+'nor+mal *adj.*
ˌsem·i+'nude *adj.*
ˌsem·i+'nu+di+ty *n.*
ˌsem·i+of+'fi+cial *adj.*
ˌsem·i+o·'paque *adj.*
ˌsem·i+'or+gan+ˌized *or* ˌsem·i+'or+gan+ised *adj.*
ˌsem·i+ˌo+ri+'en+tal *adj.*
ˌsem·i+'pa+gan *n., adj.*
ˌsem·i+pa+'ral+y+sis *n.*
ˌsem·i+ˌpar·a+'lyt+ic *n., adj.*
ˌsem·i+'perm+a+nent *adj.*
ˌsem·i+'pet+ri+ˌfied *adj.*
ˌsem·i+'plas+tic *adj.*
ˌsem·i+po+'lit·i·cal *adj.*
ˌsem·i+'po+rous *adj.*
ˌsem·i+'prim·i+tive *adj.*
ˌsem·i+'pri+vate *adj.*
ˌsem·i+'pub+lic *adj.*

sem·i+pro+fes+sion+al (ˌsɛmɪprəˈfɛʃənᵊl) *adj.* **1.** (of a person) engaged in an activity or sport part-time but for pay. **2.** (of an activity or sport) engaged in by semiprofessional people. **3.** of or relating to a person whose activities are professional in some respects: *a semiprofessional pianist.* ~*n.* **4.** a semi-professional person. —ˌ**sem·i+pro+ˈfes+sion+al+ly** *adv.*

sem·i+qua+ver (ˈsɛmɪˌkweɪvə) *n. Music.* a note having the time value of one-sixteenth of a semibreve. Usual U.S. name: **sixteenth note.**

Se+mir·a+mis (sɛˈmɪrəmɪs) *n.* the legendary founder of Babylon and wife of Ninus, king of Assyria, which she ruled with great skill after his death.

sem·i+rig+id (ˌsɛmɪˈrɪdʒɪd) *adj.* **1.** partly but not wholly rigid. **2.** (of an airship) maintaining shape by means of a main supporting keel and internal gas pressure.

sem·i+skilled (ˌsɛmɪˈskɪld) *adj.* partly skilled or trained but not sufficiently so to perform specialized work.

sem·i+sol+id (ˌsɛmɪˈsɒlɪd) *adj.* **1. a.** having a viscosity and rigidity intermediate between that of a solid and a liquid. **b.** partly solid. ~*n.* **2.** a substance in this state.

Se+mite (ˈsiːmaɪt) *or* **Shem+ite** *n.* **1.** a member of the group of Caucasoid peoples who speak a Semitic language, including the Jews and Arabs as well as the ancient Babylonians, Assyrians, and Phoenicians. **2.** another word for a **Jew.** [C19: from New Latin *sēmīta* descendant of Shem, via Greek *Sēm,* from Hebrew SHEM]

Se+mit+ic (sɪˈmɪtɪk) *or* **She+mit+ic** *n.* **1.** a branch or subfamily of the Afro-Asiatic family of languages that includes Arabic, Hebrew, Aramaic, Amharic, and such ancient languages as Akkadian and Phoenician. ~*adj.* **2.** denoting, relating to, or belonging to this group of languages. **3.** denoting, belonging to, or characteristic of any of the peoples speaking a Semitic language, esp. the Jews or the Arabs. **4.** another word for **Jewish.**

Se+mit+ics (sɪˈmɪtɪks) *n.* (*functioning as sing.*) the study of Semitic languages and culture. —**Sem·i+tist** (ˈsɛmɪtɪst) *n.*

Sem·i·to-Ha·mit·ic (ˈsɛmɪtəʊhæˈmɪtɪk) *n.* **1.** a former name for the **Afro-Asiatic** family of languages. ~*adj.* **2.** denoting or belonging to this family of languages.

sem·i+tone (ˈsɛmɪˌtəʊn) *n.* an interval corresponding to a frequency difference of 100 cents as measured in the system of equal temperament, and denoting the pitch difference between certain adjacent degrees of the diatonic scale (**diatonic semitone**) or between one note and its sharpened or flattened equivalent (**chromatic semitone**); minor second. Also called (U.S.): **half step.** Compare **whole tone.** —**sem·i+ton+ic** (ˌsɛmɪˈtɒnɪk) *adj.* —ˌ**sem·i+ˈton+al+ly** *adv.*

sem·i+trail+er (ˌsɛmɪˈtreɪlə) *n.* a type of trailer or articulated lorry that has wheels only at the rear, the front end being supported by the towing vehicle.

sem·i+trop·i+cal (ˌsɛmɪˈtrɒpɪkᵊl) *adj.* **1.** partly tropical. **2.** another word for **subtropical.** —ˌ**sem·i+ˈtrop+ics** *pl. n.*

sem·i+vit+re·ous (ˌsɛmɪˈvɪtrɪəs) *adj.* **1.** partially vitreous. **2.** *Ceramics.* not wholly impervious to liquid.

sem·i+vo+cal (ˌsɛmɪˈvəʊkᵊl) *or* **sem·i+vo+cal+ic** (ˌsɛmɪvəʊˈkælɪk) *adj.* of or relating to a semivowel.

sem·i+vow+el (ˈsɛmɪˌvaʊəl) *n. Phonetics.* **1.** a vowel-like sound that acts like a consonant, in that it serves the same function in a syllable carrying the same amount of prominence as a consonant relative to a true vowel, the nucleus of the syllable. In English and many other languages the chief semivowels are (w) in *well* and (j), represented as *y,* in *yell.* **2.** a frictionless continuant classified as one of the liquids; (l) or (r). ~Also called: **glide.**

sem·i+year+ly (ˌsɛmɪˈjɪəlɪ) *adj.* another word for **semiannual.**

sem·o+li+na (ˌsɛməˈliːnə) *n.* the large hard grains of wheat left after flour has been bolted, used for puddings, soups, etc. [C18: from Italian *semolino,* diminutive of *semola* bran, from Latin *simila* very fine wheat flour]

Sem+pach (*German* ˈzɛmpax) *n.* a village in central Switzerland, in Lucerne canton on **Lake Sempach:** scene of the victory (1386) of the Swiss over the Hapsburgs.

sem+per fi+de+lis *Latin.* (ˈsɛmpə fɪˈdeɪlɪs) always faithful.

sem+per pa+ra+tus *Latin.* (ˈsɛmpə pəˈrɑːtəs) always prepared.

sem+pi+ter+nal (ˌsɛmpɪˈtɜːnᵊl) *adj. Literary.* everlasting; eternal. [C15: from Old French *sempiternel,* from Late Latin *sempiternālis,* from Latin *sempiternus,* from *semper* always + *aeternus* ETERNAL] —ˌ**sem+pi+ˈter+nal+ly** *adv.* —**sem+pi+ter+ni·ty** (ˌsɛmpɪˈtɜːnɪtɪ) *n.*

sem+pli+ce (ˈsɛmplɪtʃɪ) *adj., adv. Music.* to be performed in a simple manner. [Italian: simple, from Latin *simplex*]

sem+pre (ˈsɛmprɪ) *adv. Music.* (preceding a tempo or dynamic marking) always; consistently. It is used to indicate that a specified volume, tempo, etc., is to be sustained throughout a piece or passage. [Italian: always, from Latin *semper*]

semp+stress (ˈsɛmpstrɪs) *n.* a rare word for **seamstress.**

sen (sɛn) *n., pl.* **sen.** a monetary unit of Indonesia and Cambodia, worth one hundredth of the rupiah and the riel respectively. [C19: ultimately from Chinese *ch'ien* coin]

SEN *or* **S.E.N.** (in Britain) *abbrev. for* State Enrolled Nurse.

Sen. *or* **sen.** *abbrev. for:* **1.** senate. **2.** senator. **3.** senior.

se·na (ˈseɪnɑː) *n.* (in India) the army: used in the names of certain paramilitary political organizations. [Hindi]

sen+ar+mon+tite (ˌsɛnɑːˈmɒntaɪt) *n.* a white or grey mineral consisting of antimony trioxide in cubic crystalline form. Formula: Sb_2O_3. [C19: named after Henri de *Sénarmont* (died 1862), French mineralogist]

sen+a·ry (ˈsiːnərɪ) *adj.* of or relating to the number six; having six parts or units. [C17: from Latin *sēnārius,* from *sēnī* six each, from *sex* SIX]

sen+ate (ˈsɛnɪt) *n.* **1.** any legislative or governing body considered to resemble a Senate. **2.** the main governing body at some colleges and universities. [C13: from Latin *senātus* council of the elders, from *senex* an old man]

Sen+ate (ˈsɛnɪt) *n.* (*sometimes not cap.*) **1.** the upper chamber of the legislatures of the U.S., Canada, Australia, and many other countries. **2.** the legislative council of ancient Rome. Originally the council of the kings, the Senate became the highest legislative, judicial, and religious authority in republican Rome. **3.** the ruling body of certain free cities in medieval and modern Europe.

sen·a+tor (ˈsɛnətə) *n.* **1.** (*often cap.*) a member of a Senate or senate. **2.** any legislator or statesman.

sen·a+to+ri·al (ˌsɛnəˈtɔːrɪəl) *adj.* **1.** of, relating to, befitting, or characteristic of a senator. **2.** composed of senators. **3.** *Chiefly U.S.* electing or entitled to representation by a senator: *senatorial districts.* —ˌ**sen·a+ˈto+ri+al+ly** *adv.*

se+na+tus con+sul+tum *Latin.* (səˈnɑːtəs kənˈsʊltəm) *n., pl.* ***se+na+tus con+sul+ta*** (kənˈsʊltə). a decree of the Senate of ancient Rome, taking the form of advice to a magistrate.

send[1] (sɛnd) *vb.* **sends, send+ing, sent. 1.** (*tr.*) to cause or order (a person or thing) to be taken, directed, or transmitted to another place: *to send a letter; she sent the salesman away.* **2.** (when *intr.,* foll. by *for;* when *tr., takes an infinitive*) to dispatch a request or command (for something or to do something): *he sent for a bottle of wine; he sent to his son to come home.* **3.** (*tr.*) to direct or cause to go to a place or point: *his blow sent the champion to the floor.* **4.** (*tr.*) to bring to a state or condition: *this noise will send me mad.* **5.** (*tr.;* often foll. by *forth, out,* etc.) to cause to issue; emit: *his cooking sent forth a lovely smell from the kitchen.* **6.** (*tr.*) to cause to happen or come: *misery sent by fate.* **7.** to transmit (a message) by radio, esp. in the form of pulses. **8.** (*tr.*) *Slang.* to move to excitement or rapture: *this music really sends me.* **9. send (someone) about his** *or* **her business.** Also: **send (someone) packing.** to dismiss or get rid of (someone). ~*n.* **10.** another word for **swash** (sense 4). [Old English *sendan;* related to Old Norse *senda,* Gothic *sandjan,* Old High German *senten*] —ˈ**send+a·ble** *adj.* —ˈ**send+er** *n.*

send[2] (sɛnd) *vb.* **sends, send+ing, sent.** *n.* a variant spelling of **scend.**

Sen+dai (sɛnˈdaɪ) *n.* a city in central Japan, on NE Honshu: university (1907). Pop.: 575 603 (1974 est.).

sen+dal (ˈsɛndᵊl) *n.* **1.** a fine silk fabric used, esp. in the Middle Ages, for ceremonial clothing, etc. **2.** a garment of such fabric. [C13: from Old French *cendal,* from Medieval Latin *cendalum;* probably related to Greek *sindon* fine linen]

send down *vb.* (*tr., adv.*) **1.** *Brit.* to expel from a university, esp. permanently. **2.** to send to prison.

send+off (ˈsɛndˌɒf) *n. Informal.* **1.** a demonstration of good wishes to a person about to set off on a journey, new career, etc. **2.** a start, esp. an auspicious one, to a venture. ~*vb.* **send off.** (*tr., adv.*) **3.** to cause to depart; despatch. **4.** *Soccer, rugby, etc.* (of the referee) to dismiss (a player) from the field of play for some offence. **5.** *Informal.* to give a sendoff to.

send up *Slang.* ~*vb.* (*tr., adv.*) **1.** to send to prison. **2.** *Brit.* to make fun of, esp. by doing an imitation or parody of: *he sent up the teacher marvellously.* ~*n.* **send-up. 3.** *Brit.* a parody or imitation.

Sen+e·ca[1] (ˈsɛnɪkə) *n.* **1.** (*pl.* **·cas** *or* **·ca**) a member of a North American Indian people formerly living south of Lake Ontario; one of the Iroquois peoples. **2.** the language of this people, belonging to the Iroquoian family. [C19: from Dutch *Sennecaas* (plural), probably of Algonquian origin]

Sen·e·ca[2] (ˈsɛnɪkə) *n.* **1. Lu·ci·us An·nae·us** (əˈniːəs), called *the Younger.* ?4 B.C.–65 A.D., Roman philosopher, statesman, and dramatist; tutor and adviser to Nero. He was implicated in a plot to murder Nero and committed suicide. His works include Stoical essays on ethical subjects and tragedies that had a considerable influence on Elizabethan drama. **2.** his father, **Mar·cus** (ˈmɑːkəs) *or* **Lu·ci·us An·nae·us,** called *the Elder* or *the Rhetorician.* ?55 B.C.–?39 A.D., Roman writer on oratory and history.

sen+e·ga (ˈsɛnɪgə) *n.* **1.** a milkwort plant, *Polygala senega,* of the eastern U.S., with small white flowers. **2.** the root of this plant, used as an expectorant. ~Also called: **senega snakeroot, seneca snakeroot.** [C18: variant of *Seneca* (the Indian tribe)]

Sen+e·gal (ˌsɛnɪˈgɔːl) *n.* a republic in West Africa, on the Atlantic: made part of French West Africa in 1895; became

---

ˌ**sem·i+ˈpur+pos+ive** *adj.*
ˌ**sem·i+re+ˈbel+lious** *adj.*
ˌ**sem·i+re+ˈfined** *adj.*
ˌ**sem·i+ˈres+o+ˌlute** *adj.*
ˌ**sem·i+re+ˌspect+a+ˈbil·i+ty** *n.*
ˌ**sem·i+re+ˌspect+a·ble** *adj.*
ˌ**sem·i+re+ˈtired** *adj.*
ˌ**sem·i+re+ˈtire+ment** *n.*
ˌ**sem·i+ˈround** *adj.*
ˌ**sem·i+ˈru+ral** *adj.*
ˌ**sem·i+ˈsa+cred** *adj.*
ˌ**sem·i+sa+ˈtir·i+cal** *adj.*
ˌ**sem·i+sa+ˈtir·i+cal+ly** *adv.*
ˌ**sem·i+ˈse+ri+ous** *adj.*
ˌ**sem·i+ˌso+cial+ˈis+tic** *adj.*
ˌ**sem·i+ˈsoft** *adj.*
ˌ**sem·i+ˈspec+u+ˌla+tive** *adj.*
ˌ**sem·i+sub+ˈur+ban** *adj.*
ˌ**sem·i+suc+ˈcess+ful** *adj.*
ˌ**sem·i+ˈsweet** *adj.*
ˌ**sem·i+tra+ˈdi+tion+al** *adj.*
ˌ**sem·i+ˈtrained** *adj.*
ˌ**sem·i+trans+ˈlu+cent** *adj.*
ˌ**sem·i+trans+ˈpar+ent** *adj.*
ˌ**sem·i+ˈtruth+ful** *adj.*
ˌ**sem·i+ˈur+ban** *adj.*
ˌ**sem·i+ˈvol+un+ˌtar·y** *adj.*
ˌ**sem·i+ˈweek+ly** *adj., adv.*

fully independent in 1960; mostly low-lying, with semidesert in the north and tropical forest in the southwest. Official language: French. Religion: Muslim majority. Currency: franc. Capital: Dakar. Pop.: 4 315 000 (1974 UN est.). Area: 197 160 sq. km (76 124 sq. miles). —**Sen·e·ga·lese** (ˌsɛnɪgəˈliːz) *adj., n.*

Sen·e·gam·bi·a (ˌsɛnəˈgæmbɪə) *n.* a region of W Africa, between the Senegal and Gambia Rivers: now mostly in Senegal.

se·nes·cent (sɪˈnɛsᵊnt) *adj.* **1.** growing old. **2.** characteristic of old age. [C17: from Latin *senēscere* to grow old, from *senex* old] —**seˈnes·cence** *n.*

sen·e·schal (ˈsɛnɪʃəl) *n.* **1.** a steward of the household of a medieval prince or nobleman who took charge of domestic arrangements, etc. **2.** *Brit.* a cathedral official. [C14: from Old French, from Medieval Latin *siniscalcus,* of Germanic origin; related to Old High German *senescalh* oldest servant, from *sene-* old + *scalh* a servant]

Sen·ghor (*French* sɛ̃ˈgɔːr) *n.* **Lé·o·pold Sé·dar** (leɔpɔl seˈdaːr). born 1906, Senegalese statesman and writer; president of Senegal since 1960.

se·nile (ˈsiːnaɪl) *adj.* **1.** of, relating to, or characteristic of old age. **2.** mentally or physically weak or infirm on account of old age. **3.** (of land forms or rivers) at an advanced stage in the cycle of erosion. See **old** (sense 18). [C17: from Latin *senīlis,* from *senex* an old man] —**ˈse·nile·ly** *adv.* —**se·nil·i·ty** (sɪˈnɪlɪtɪ) *n.*

sen·ior (ˈsiːnjə) *adj.* **1.** higher in rank or length of service. **2.** older in years: *senior citizens.* **3.** of or relating to adulthood, maturity, or old age: *senior privileges.* **4.** *Education.* **a.** of, relating to, or designating more advanced or older pupils. **b.** of or relating to a secondary school. ~*n.* **5.** a senior person. **6. a.** a senior pupil, student, etc. **b.** a fellow of senior rank in an English university. [C14: from Latin: older, from *senex* old]

Sen·ior (ˈsiːnjə) *adj. Chiefly U.S.* being the older: used to distinguish the father from the son with the same first name or names: *Charles Parker, Senior.* Abbrev.: **Sr., Sen.**

sen·ior cit·i·zen *n. Brit., euphemistic.* an elderly person.

sen·ior com·mon room *n.* (in British universities, colleges, etc.) a common room for the use of academic staff. Compare **junior common room.**

sen·ior·i·ty (ˌsiːnɪˈɒrɪtɪ) *n., pl.* **-ties. 1.** the state of being senior. **2.** precedence in rank, etc., due to senior status.

Sen·lac (ˈsɛnlæk) *n.* a hill in Sussex: site of the Battle of Hastings in 1066.

sen·na (ˈsɛnə) *n.* **1.** any of various tropical plants of the caesalpiniaceous genus *Cassia,* esp. *C. angustifolia* (**Arabian senna**) and *C. acutifolia* (**Alexandrian senna**), having typically yellow flowers and long pods. **2. senna leaf.** the dried leaflets of any of these plants, used as a cathartic and laxative. **3. senna pods.** the dried fruits of any of these plants, used as a cathartic and laxative. ~See also **bladder senna.** [C16: via New Latin from Arabic *sanā*]

Sen·nach·er·ib (sɛˈnækərɪb) *n.* died 681 B.C., king of Assyria (705–681); son of Sargon II. He invaded Judah twice, defeated Babylon, and rebuilt Nineveh.

Sen·nar (ˈsɛnɑː, sɛˈnɑː) *n.* **1.** a region of the E Sudan, between the White Nile and the Blue Nile: a kingdom from the 16th to 19th centuries. **2.** a town in this region, on the Blue Nile: the nearby **Sennar Dam** (1925) supplies irrigation water to Gezira. Pop.: 10 000 (1972 est.).

sen·net (ˈsɛnɪt) *n.* a fanfare: used as a stage direction in Elizabethan drama. [C16: probably variant of SIGNET (meaning "a sign")]

sen·night *or* **se'n·night** (ˈsɛnaɪt) *n.* an archaic word for **week.** [Old English *seofan nihte;* see SEVEN, NIGHT]

sen·nit (ˈsɛnɪt) *n.* **1.** a flat braided cordage used on ships. **2.** plaited straw, grass, palm leaves, etc., as for making hats. [C17: of unknown origin]

se·ñor (sɛˈnjɔː; *Spanish* seˈɲor) *n., pl.* **·ñors** *or* **·ñor·es** (*Spanish* -ˈɲores). a Spaniard: a title of address equivalent to *Mr.* when placed before a name or *sir* when used alone. [Spanish, from Latin *senior* an older man, SENIOR]

se·ño·ra (sɛˈnjɔːrə; *Spanish* seˈɲora) *n., pl.* **·ras** (-rəz; *Spanish* -ras). a married Spanish or Spanish-speaking woman: a title of address equivalent to *Mrs.* when placed before a name or *madam* when used alone.

se·ño·ri·ta (ˌsɛnjɔːˈriːtə; *Spanish* ˌseɲoˈrita) *n., pl.* **·tas** (-təz; *Spanish* -tas). an unmarried Spanish or Spanish-speaking woman: a title of address equivalent to *Miss* when placed before a name or *madam* or *miss* when used alone.

sen·sate (ˈsɛnseɪt) *or* **sen·sat·ed** *adj.* **1.** perceived by the senses. **2.** *Obsolete.* having the power of sensation. [C16: from Late Latin *sensātus* endowed with sense, from Latin *sensus* SENSE] —**ˈsen·sate·ly** *adv.*

sen·sa·tion (sɛnˈseɪʃən) *n.* **1.** the power of perceiving through the senses. **2.** a physical condition or experience resulting from the stimulation of one of the sense organs: *a sensation of warmth.* **3.** a general feeling or awareness: *a sensation of fear.* **4.** a state of widespread public excitement: *his announcement caused a sensation.* **5.** anything that causes such a state: *your speech was a sensation.* [C17: from Medieval Latin *sensātiō,* from Late Latin *sensātus* SENSATE] —**senˈsa·tion·less** *adj.*

sen·sa·tion·al (sɛnˈseɪʃənᵊl) *adj.* **1.** causing or intended to cause intense feelings, esp. of curiosity, horror, etc.: *sensational disclosures in the press.* **2.** *Informal.* extremely good: *a sensational skater.* **3.** of or relating to the faculty of sensation. **4.** *Philosophy.* of or relating to sensationalism. —**senˈsa·tion·al·ly** *adv.*

sen·sa·tion·al·ism (sɛnˈseɪʃənᵊˌlɪzəm) *n.* **1.** the use of sensational language, etc., to arouse an intense emotional response. **2.** such sensational matter itself. **3. a.** *Philosophy.* the theory that all knowledge derives from the senses. **b.** *Ethics.* the doctrine that the ability to gratify the senses is the only criterion of goodness. **4.** *Psychol.* the theory that all experience and mental life may be explained in terms of sensations and remembered images. **5.** *Aesthetics.* the theory of the beauty of sensuality in the arts. Also called (for senses 3, 4): **sen·sa·tion·ism.** —**senˈsa·tion·al·ist** *n.* —**senˌsa·tion·alˈis·tic** *adj.*

sense (sɛns) *n.* **1.** any of the five faculties of sight, hearing, smell, taste, and touch through which humans and animals perceive the external world. **2.** such faculties collectively; the ability to perceive. **3.** a feeling perceived through one of the senses: *a sense of warmth.* **4.** a mental perception or awareness: *a sense of happiness.* **5.** moral discernment; understanding: *a sense of right and wrong.* **6.** (*sometimes pl.*) sound practical judgment or intelligence: *he is a man without any sense.* **7.** reason or purpose: *what is the sense of going out in the rain?* **8.** substance or gist; meaning: *what is the sense of this proverb?* **9.** an opinion or consensus. **10.** *Maths.* one of two opposite directions in which a vector can operate. **11. make sense.** to be reasonable or understandable. **12. take leave of one's senses.** *Informal.* to go mad. ~*vb.* (*tr.*) **13.** to perceive through one or more of the senses. **14.** to apprehend or detect without or in advance of the evidence of the senses. **15.** to understand. **16.** *Computer technol.* **a.** to test or locate the position of (a part of computer hardware). **b.** to read (data). [C14: from Latin *sēnsus,* from *sentīre* to feel]

sense da·tum *n.* a unit of sensation or empirical knowledge, such as a sharp pain or an after-image, detached from the information it may convey about reality.

sense·less (ˈsɛnslɪs) *adj.* **1.** lacking in sense; foolish: *a senseless plan.* **2.** lacking in feeling; unconscious. **3.** lacking in perception; stupid. —**ˈsense·less·ly** *adv.* —**ˈsense·less·ness** *n.*

sense or·gan *n.* a structure in animals that is specialized for receiving external stimuli and transmitting them in the form of nervous impulses to the brain.

sense per·cep·tion *n.* awareness or perception gained through the senses rather than the intellect.

sen·si·bil·i·a (ˌsɛnsɪˈbɪlɪə) *n.* that which can be sensed. [Latin, neuter plural of *sensibilis* SENSIBLE]

sen·si·bil·i·ty (ˌsɛnsɪˈbɪlɪtɪ) *n., pl.* **·ties. 1.** the ability to perceive or feel. **2.** (*often pl.*) the capacity for responding to emotion, impression, etc. **3.** (*often pl.*) the capacity for responding to aesthetic stimuli. **4.** mental responsiveness; discernment; awareness. **5.** (*usually pl.*) emotional or moral feelings: *cruelty offends most people's sensibilities.* **6.** the condition of a plant of being susceptible to external influences, esp. attack by parasites.

sen·si·ble (ˈsɛnsɪbᵊl) *adj.* **1.** having or showing good sense or judgment; practical. **2.** having the capacity for sensation; sensitive. **3.** capable of being apprehended by the senses. **4.** perceptible to the mind. **5.** having perception; aware. **6.** readily perceived; considerable. ~*n.* **7.** Also called: **sensible note.** a less common term for **leading note.** [C14: from Old French, from Late Latin *sēnsibilis,* from Latin *sentīre* to sense] —**ˈsen·si·ble·ness** *n.* —**ˈsen·si·bly** *adv.*

sen·si·ble ho·ri·zon *n.* See under **horizon** (sense 2a.).

sen·sil·lum (sɛnˈsɪləm) *n., pl.* **·la** (-lə). a sense organ in insects, typically consisting of a receptor organ in the integument connected to sensory neurons. [New Latin, diminutive of Latin *sensus* sense (Middle Latin: sense organ)]

sen·si·tive (ˈsɛnsɪtɪv) *adj.* **1.** having the power of sensation. **2.** easily irritated; delicate: *sensitive skin.* **3.** affected by external conditions or stimuli. **4.** easily offended. **5.** of or relating to the senses or the power of sensation. **6.** capable of registering small differences or changes in amounts, quality, etc.: *a sensitive instrument.* **7.** *Photog.* having a high sensitivity: *a sensitive emulsion.* **8.** *Chiefly U.S.* connected with matters affecting national security, esp. through access to classified information. **9.** (of a stock market or prices) quickly responsive to external influences and thus fluctuating or tending to fluctuate. [C14: from Medieval Latin *sēnsitīvus,* from Latin *sentīre* to feel] —**ˈsen·si·tive·ly** *adv.* —**ˈsen·si·tive·ness** *n.*

sen·si·tive plant *n.* **1.** a tropical American mimosa plant, *Mimosa pudica,* the leaflets and stems of which fold if touched. **2.** any of several similar plants, such as the caesalpiniaceous plant *Cassia nictitans* of E North America.

sen·si·tiv·i·ty (ˌsɛnsɪˈtɪvɪtɪ) *n., pl.* **·ties. 1.** the state or quality of being sensitive. **2.** *Physiol.* the state, condition, or quality of reacting or being sensitive to an external stimulus, drug, allergen, etc. **3.** *Electronics.* the magnitude or time of response of an instrument, circuit, etc., to an input signal, such as a current. **4.** *Photog.* the degree of response of an emulsion to light or other actinic radiation, esp. to light of a particular colour, expressed in terms of its speed.

sen·si·tize *or* **sen·si·tise** (ˈsɛnsɪˌtaɪz) *vb.* **1.** to make or become sensitive. **2.** (*tr.*) to render (an individual) sensitive to a drug, allergen, etc. **3.** (*tr.*) *Photog.* to make (a material) sensitive to light or to other actinic radiation, esp. to light of a particular colour, by coating it with a photographic emulsion often containing special chemicals, such as dyes. —**ˌsen·si·tiˈza·tion** *or* **ˌsen·si·tiˈsa·tion** *n.* —**ˈsen·si·tiz·er** *or* **ˈsen·si·ˌtis·er** *n.*

sen·si·tom·e·ter (ˌsɛnsɪˈtɒmɪtə) *n.* an instrument for measuring the sensitivity to light of a photographic material over a range of exposures. —**ˌsen·si·ˈtom·e·try** *n.*

sen·sor (ˈsɛnsə) *n.* anything, such as a photoelectric cell, that receives a signal or stimulus and responds to it. [C19: from Latin *sēnsus* perceived, from *sentīre* to observe]

sen·so·ri·mo·tor (ˌsɛnsərɪˈməʊtə) *or* **sen·so·mo·tor** (ˌsɛnsəˈməʊtə) *adj.* of or relating to both the sensory and motor functions of an organism or to the nerves controlling them.

sen·so·ri·um (sɛnˈsɔːrɪəm) *n.* **1.** the area of the brain considered responsible for receiving and integrating sensations from the outside world. **2.** *Physiol.* the entire sensory and intellectual apparatus of the body. [C17: from Late Latin, from Latin *sēnsus* felt, from *sentīre* to perceive]

sen·so·ry (ˈsɛnsərɪ) *or* **sen·so·ri·al** (sɛnˈsɔːrɪəl) *adj.* **1.** of or relating to the senses or the power of sensation. **2.** of or relating to those processes and structures within an organism that receive stimuli from the environment and convey them to the brain.

sen·so·ry dep·ri·va·tion *n. Psychol.* an experimental situation in which all stimulation is cut off from the sensory receptors.

sen·su·al (ˈsɛnsjʊəl) *adj.* **1.** of or relating to any of the senses or sense organs; bodily. **2.** strongly or unduly inclined to gratification of the senses. **3.** tending to arouse the bodily appetites, esp. the sexual appetite. **4.** of or relating to sensualism. —**ˈsen·su·al·ly** *adv.* —**ˈsen·su·al·ness** *n.*

sen·su·al·ism (ˈsɛnsjʊəˌlɪzəm) *n.* **1.** the quality or state of being sensual. **2.** another word for **sensationalism** (senses 3a, b).

sen·su·al·i·ty (ˌsɛnsjʊˈælɪtɪ) *n., pl.* **·ties. 1.** the quality or state of being sensual. **2.** excessive indulgence in sensual pleasures. —**sen·su·al·ist** (ˈsɛnsjʊəlɪst) *n.*

sen·su·ous (ˈsɛnsjʊəs) *adj.* **1.** aesthetically pleasing to the senses. **2.** appreciative of or moved by qualities perceived by the senses. **3.** of, relating to, or derived from the senses. —**ˈsen·su·ous·ly** *adv.* —**ˈsen·su·ous·ness** *n.*

sent (sɛnt) *vb.* the past tense or past participle of **send.**

sen·tence (ˈsɛntəns) *n.* **1.** a sequence of words capable of standing alone to make an assertion, ask a question, or give a command, usually consisting of a subject and a predicate containing a finite verb. **2.** the judgment formally pronounced upon a person convicted in criminal proceedings, esp. the decision as to what punishment is to be imposed. **3.** an opinion, judgment, or decision. **4.** *Music.* another word for **period** (sense 11). **5.** any short passage of scripture employed in liturgical use: *the funeral sentences.* **6.** *Archaic.* a proverb, maxim, or aphorism. ~*vb.* **7.** (*tr.*) to pronounce sentence on (a convicted person) in a court of law: *the judge sentenced the murderer to life imprisonment.* [C13: via Old French from Latin *sententia* a way of thinking, from *sentīre* to feel] —**sen·ten·tial** (sɛnˈtɛnʃəl) *adj.* —**sen·ˈten·tial·ly** *adv.*

sen·tence con·nec·tor *n.* a word or phrase that introduces a clause or sentence and serves as a transition between it and a previous clause or sentence, as for example *also* in *I'm buying eggs and also I'm looking for a dessert for tonight.* It may be preceded by a coordinating conjunction.

sen·tence stress *n.* the stress given to a word or words in a sentence, often conveying nuances of meaning or emphasis.

sen·tence sub·sti·tute *n.* a word or phrase, esp. one traditionally classified as an adverb, that is used in place of a finite sentence, such as *yes, no, certainly,* and *never.*

sen·ten·tial func·tion *n.* an expression containing one or more variables and becoming a declarative sentence when the variables are substituted by constants.

sen·ten·tious (sɛnˈtɛnʃəs) *adj.* **1.** characterized by or full of aphorisms, terse pithy sayings, or axioms. **2.** constantly using aphorisms, etc. **3.** tending to indulge in pompous moralizing. [C15: from Latin *sententiōsus* full of meaning, from *sententia;* see SENTENCE] —**sen·ˈten·tious·ly** *adv.* —**sen·ˈten·tious·ness** *n.*

sen·tience (ˈsɛnʃəns) *or* **sen·tien·cy** *n.* **1.** the state or quality of being sentient; awareness. **2.** sense perception not involving intelligence or mental perception; feeling.

sen·ti·ent (ˈsɛntɪənt) *adj.* **1.** having the power of sense perception or sensation; conscious. ~*n.* **2.** *Rare.* a sentient person or thing. [C17: from Latin *sentiēns* feeling, from *sentīre* to perceive] —**ˈsen·ti·ent·ly** *adv.*

sen·ti·ment (ˈsɛntɪmənt) *n.* **1.** susceptibility to tender, delicate, or romantic emotion: *she has too much sentiment to be successful.* **2.** (*often pl.*) a thought, opinion, or attitude. **3.** exaggerated, overindulged, or mawkish feeling or emotion. **4.** an expression of response to deep feeling, esp. in art or literature. **5.** a feeling, emotion, or awareness: *a sentiment of pity.* **6.** a mental attitude modified or determined by feeling: *there is a strong revolutionary sentiment in his country.* [C17: from Medieval Latin *sentīmentum,* from Latin *sentīre* to feel]

sen·ti·ment·al (ˌsɛntɪˈmɛntᵊl) *adj.* **1.** tending to indulge the emotions excessively. **2.** making a direct appeal to the emotions, esp. to romantic feelings. **3.** relating to or characterized by sentiment. —**ˌsen·ti·ˈmen·tal·ly** *adv.*

sen·ti·men·tal·ism (ˌsɛntɪˈmɛntᵊˌlɪzəm) *n.* **1.** the state or quality of being sentimental. **2.** an act, statement, etc., that is sentimental. —**ˌsen·ti·ˈmen·tal·ist** *n.*

sen·ti·men·tal·i·ty (ˌsɛntɪmɛnˈtælɪtɪ) *n., pl.* **·ties. 1.** the state, quality, or an instance of being sentimental. **2.** an act, statement, etc., that is sentimental.

sen·ti·men·tal·ize *or* **sen·ti·men·tal·ise** (ˌsɛntɪˈmɛntᵊˌlaɪz) *vb.* to make sentimental or behave sentimentally. —**ˌsen·ti·ˌmen·tal·i·ˈza·tion** *or* **ˌsen·ti·ˌmen·tal·i·ˈsa·tion** *n.*

sen·ti·ment·al val·ue *n.* the value of an article in terms of its sentimental associations for a particular person.

sen·ti·nel (ˈsɛntɪnᵊl) *n.* **1.** a person, such as a sentry, assigned to keep guard. **2.** *Computer technol.* a character used to indicate the beginning or end of a particular block of information. ~*vb.* (*tr.*) **3.** to guard as a sentinel. **4.** to post as a sentinel. **5.** to provide with a sentinel. [C16: from Old French *sentinelle,* from Old Italian *sentinella,* from *sentina* watchfulness, from *sentire* to notice, from Latin]

sen·try (ˈsɛntrɪ) *n., pl.* **·tries. 1.** a soldier who guards or prevents unauthorized access to a place, keeps watch for danger, etc. **2.** the watch kept by a sentry. [C17: perhaps shortened from obsolete *centrinel,* C16 variant of SENTINEL]

sen·try box *n.* a small shelter with an open front in which a sentry may stand to be sheltered from the weather.

Se·nus·si *or* **Se·nu·si** (sɛˈnuːsɪ) *n., pl.* **·sis.** a member of a zealous and aggressive Muslim sect of North Africa and Arabia, founded in 1837 A.D. by **Sidi Mohammed ibn Ali al Senussi** (?1787–1859). —**Se·ˈnus·si·an** *or* **Se·ˈnu·si·an** *adj.*

sen·za (ˈsɛntsɑː) *prep. Music.* without; omitting. [Italian]

Seoul (səʊl) *n.* the capital of South Korea, in the west on the Han River: capital of Korea from 1392 to 1910, then seat of the Japanese administration until 1945; became capital of South Korea in 1948; cultural centre, with four universities. Pop.: 6 879 149 (1975). Also called: **Kyongsong.** Japanese name: **Keijo.**

sep. *abbrev. for:* **1.** sepal. **2.** separate.

Sep. *abbrev. for:* **1.** September. **2.** Septuagint.

sep·al (ˈsɛpᵊl) *n.* any of the separate parts of the calyx of a flower. [C19: from New Latin *sepalum: sep-* from Greek *skepē* a covering + *-alum,* from New Latin *petalum* PETAL] —**ˈsep·alled** *or* **sep·al·ous** (ˈsɛpələs) *adj.*

se·pa·loid (ˈsiːpəˌlɔɪd) *or* **se·pa·line** *adj.* (esp. of petals) resembling a sepal in structure and function.

-sep·a·lous *adj. combining form.* having sepals of a specified type or number: *polysepalous.* —**-sep·a·ly** *n. combining form.*

sep·a·ra·ble (ˈsɛpərəbᵊl, ˈsɛprəbᵊl) *adj.* able to be separated, divided, or parted. —**ˌsep·a·ra·ˈbil·i·ty** *or* **ˈsep·a·ra·ble·ness** *n.* —**ˈsep·a·ra·bly** *adv.*

sep·a·rate *vb.* (ˈsɛpəˌreɪt). **1.** (*tr.*) to act as a barrier between: *a range of mountains separates the two countries.* **2.** to put or force or be put or forced apart. **3.** to part or be parted from a mass or group. **4.** (*tr.*) to discriminate between: *to separate the men and the boys.* **5.** to divide or be divided into component parts; sort or be sorted. **6.** to sever or be severed. **7.** (*intr.*) (of a married couple) to cease living together by mutual agreement or after obtaining a decree of judicial separation. ~*adj.* (ˈsɛprɪt, ˈsɛpərɪt). **8.** existing or considered independently: *a separate problem.* **9.** disunited or apart. **10.** set apart from the main body or mass. **11.** distinct, individual, or particular. **12.** solitary or withdrawn. **13.** (*sometimes cap.*) designating or relating to a Church or similar institution that has ceased to have associations with an original parent organization. [C15: from Latin *sēparāre,* from *sē* apart + *parāre* to obtain] —**ˈsep·a·rate·ly** *adv.* —**ˈsep·a·rate·ness** *n.*

sep·a·rates (ˈsɛprɪts, ˈsɛpərɪts) *n.* women's outer garments that only cover part of the body and so are worn in combination with others, usually unmatching; skirts, blouses, jackets, trousers, etc. Compare **coordinates.**

sep·a·rate school *n.* (in Canada) a school for a large religious minority financed by its rates and administered by its own school board but under the authority of the provincial department of education.

sep·a·ra·tion (ˌsɛpəˈreɪʃən) *n.* **1.** the act of separating or state of being separated. **2.** the place or line where a separation is made. **3.** a gap that separates. **4.** *Family law.* the cessation of cohabitation between a man and wife, either by mutual agreement or under a decree of a court. See **judicial separation.** Compare **divorce. 5. a.** the act of jettisoning a burnt-out stage of a multistage rocket. **b.** the instant at which such a stage is jettisoned.

sep·a·ra·tist (ˈsɛpərətɪst, ˈsɛprə-) *or* **sep·a·ra·tion·ist** *n.* **a.** a person who advocates or practises secession from an organization or group. **b.** (*as modifier*): *a separatist movement.* —**ˈsep·a·ra·ˌtism** *n.* —**ˌsep·a·ra·ˈtis·tic** *adj.*

Sep·a·rat·ist (ˈsɛpərətɪst, ˈsɛprə-) *n.* (*sometimes not cap.*) a person, esp. a Québecois, who advocates the secession of Quebec from Canada. —**ˈSep·a·ra·ˌtism** *n.*

sep·a·ra·tive (ˈsɛpərətɪv, ˈsɛprə-) *adj.* tending to separate or causing separation. —**ˈsep·a·ra·tive·ly** *adv.* —**ˈsep·a·ra·tive·ness** *n.*

sep·a·ra·tor (ˈsɛpəˌreɪtə) *n.* **1.** a person or thing that separates. **2.** a device for separating things into constituent parts, as milk into cream, etc. —**ˈsep·a·ra·to·ry** *adj.*

sep·a·ra·trix (ˈsɛpəˌreɪtrɪks) *n., pl.* **sep·a·ra·tri·ces** (ˌsɛpəˈreɪtrɪˌsiːz). another name for **solidus** (sense 1). [via New Latin from Late Latin, feminine of *sēparātor* one that separates]

Se·phar·di (sɪˈfɑːdiː) *n., pl.* **·dim** (-dɪm). *Judaism.* **1.** a Jew of Spanish, Portuguese, or North African descent. **2.** the pronunciation of Hebrew used by these Jews, and of Modern Hebrew as spoken in Israel. **3.** (*modifier*) of or pertaining to the Sephardim, esp. to their liturgy and ritual. ~Compare **Ashkenazi.** [C19: from Late Hebrew, from Hebrew *sepharad* a region mentioned in Obadiah 20, thought to have been Spain] —**Se·ˈphar·dic** *adj.*

se·pi·a (ˈsiːpɪə) *n.* **1.** a dark reddish-brown pigment obtained from the inky secretion of the cuttlefish. **2.** any cuttlefish of the genus *Sepia.* **3.** a brownish tone imparted to a photograph, esp. an early one such as a calotype. It can be produced by first bleaching a print (after fixing) and then immersing it for a short time in a solution of sodium sulphide or of alkaline thiourea. **4.** a brownish-grey to dark yellowish-brown colour. **5.** a drawing or photograph in sepia. ~*adj.* **6.** of the

colour sepia or done in sepia: *a sepia print.* [C16: from Latin: a cuttlefish, from Greek; related to Greek *sēpein* to make rotten]
se+pi·o+lite ('si:pɪəˌlaɪt) *n.* another name for **meerschaum** (sense 1). [C19: from German *Sepiolith,* from Greek *sēpion* bone of a cuttlefish; see SEPIA, -LITE]
se+poy ('si:pɔɪ) *n.* (formerly) an Indian soldier in the service of the British. [C18: from Portuguese *sipaio,* from Urdu *sipāhī,* from Persian: horseman, from *sipāh* army]
Se+poy Re+bel+lion *or* **Mu+ti+ny** *n.* the Indian Mutiny of 1857–58.
sep+pu+ku (sɛ'pu:ku:) *n.* another word for **harakiri.** [from Japanese, from Chinese *ch'ieh* to cut + *fu* bowels]
sep+sis ('sɛpsɪs) *n.* the presence of pus-forming bacteria in the body. [C19: via New Latin from Greek *sēpsis* a rotting; related to Greek *sēpein* to cause to decay]
sept (sɛpt) *n.* **1.** *Anthropol.* a clan or group that believes itself to be descended from a common ancestor. **2.** a branch of a tribe or nation, esp. in medieval Ireland or Scotland. [C16: perhaps a variant of SECT]
Sept. *abbrev. for:* **1.** September. **2.** Septuagint.
sep+ta ('sɛptə) *n.* the plural of **septum.**
sep+tal ('sɛptəl) *adj.* of or relating to a septum.
sep+tar+i·um (sɛp'tɛərɪəm) *n., pl.* **·i·a** (-ɪə). a mass of mineral substance having cracks filled with another mineral, esp. calcite. [C18: from New Latin, from Latin SEPTUM] —**sep+'tar+i·an** *adj.*
sep+tate ('sɛpteɪt) *adj.* divided by septa: *a septate plant ovary.* [C19: from New Latin *septātus* having a SEPTUM]
sep+ta+va+lent (ˌsɛptə'veɪlənt) *adj. Chem.* another word for **heptavalent.** [C19: from SEPT(IVALENT) + (HEPT)AVALENT]
Sep+tem+ber (sɛp'tɛmbə) *n.* the ninth month of the year, consisting of 30 days. [Old English, from Latin: the seventh (month) according to the calendar of ancient Rome, from *septem* seven]
Sep+tem+ber Mas+sa+cre *n.* (during the French Revolution) the massacre of royalist prisoners and others in Paris between Sept. 2 and 6, 1792.
Sep+tem+brist (sɛp'tɛmbrɪst) *n. French history.* a person who took part in the September Massacre.
sep+te+nar·y ('sɛptɪnərɪ) *adj.* **1.** of or relating to the number seven. **2.** forming a group of seven. **3.** another word for **septennial.** ~*n., pl.* **+nar·ies. 4.** the number seven. **5.** a group of seven things. **6.** a period of seven years. **7.** *Prosody.* a line of seven metrical feet. [C16: from Latin *septēnārius,* from *septēnī* seven each, from *septem* seven]
sep+ten+ni+al (sɛp'tɛnɪəl) *adj.* **1.** occurring every seven years. **2.** relating to or lasting seven years. [C17: from Latin *septennis,* from *septem* seven + *annus* a year] —**sep+'ten+ni+al+ly** *adv.*
sep+ten+ni·um (sɛp'tɛnɪəm) *n., pl.* **+ni·ums** *or* **+ni·a** (-nɪə). a period or cycle of seven years. [C19: from Latin, from *septem* seven + *-ennium,* from *annus* year]
sep+ten+tri+on (sɛp'tɛntrɪˌɒn) *n. Archaic.* the northern regions or the north. [C14: from Latin *septentriōnēs,* literally: the seven ploughing oxen (the constellation of the Great Bear), from *septem* seven + *triōnēs* ploughing oxen] —**sep+'ten+tri·o+nal** *adj.*
sep+tet *or* **sep+tette** (sɛp'tɛt) *n.* **1.** *Music.* a group of seven singers or instrumentalists or a piece of music composed for such a group. **2.** a group of seven people or things. [C19: from German, from Latin *septem* seven]
sep·ti-[1] *or before a vowel* **sept-** *combining form.* seven: *septivalent.* [from Latin *septem*]
sep·ti-[2] *combining form.* septum: *septicidal.*
sep+tic ('sɛptɪk) *adj.* **1.** of, relating to, or caused by sepsis. **2.** of, relating to, or caused by putrefaction. ~*n.* **3.** *Austral. informal.* See **septic tank.** [C17: from Latin *sēpticus,* from Greek *sēptikos,* from *sēptos* decayed, from *sēpein* to make rotten] —**'sep+ti+cal+ly** *adv.* —**sep+tic+i+ty** (sɛp'tɪsɪtɪ) *n.*
sep+ti+cae+mi·a *or* **sep+ti+ce·mi·a** (ˌsɛptɪ'si:mɪə) *n.* any of various diseases caused by microorganisms in the blood. Nontechnical name: **blood poisoning.** See also **bacteremia, pyaemia.** [C19: from New Latin, from Greek *sēptik(os)* SEPTIC + -AEMIA] —ˌ**sep+ti+'cae+mic** *or* ˌ**sep+ti+'ce·mic** *adj.*
sep+ti+ci+dal (ˌsɛptɪ'saɪdᵊl) *adj. Botany.* (of a dehiscence) characterized by splitting along the partitions of the seed capsule. [C19: from SEPTI-[2] + -CIDAL] —ˌ**sep+ti+'ci+dal+ly** *adv.*
sep+tic tank *n.* a tank, usually below ground, for containing sewage to be decomposed by anaerobic bacteria.
sep+tif+ra+gal (sɛp'tɪfrəgᵊl) *adj.* (of a dehiscence) characterized by breaking apart from a natural line of division in the fruit. [C19: from SEPTI-[2] + *-fragal,* from Latin *frangere* to break]
sep+ti+lat+er+al (ˌsɛptɪ'lætərəl) *adj.* having seven sides.
sep+til+lion (sɛp'tɪljən) *n., pl.* **+lions** *or* **+lion. 1.** (in Britain and Germany) the number represented as one followed by 42 zeros (10^{42}). **2.** (in the U.S. and France) the number represented as one followed by 24 zeros (10^{24}). Brit. word: **quadrillion.** [C17: from French, from *sept* seven + *-illion,* on the model of *million*] —**sep+'til+lionth** *adj., n.*
sep+time ('sɛpti:m) *n.* the seventh of eight basic positions from which a parry or attack can be made in fencing. [C19: from Latin *septimus* seventh, from *septem* seven]
sep+ti+va+lent (ˌsɛptɪ'veɪlənt) *or* **sep+ta+va+lent** (ˌsɛptə'veɪlənt) *adj. Chem.* another word for **heptavalent.**
sep+tu·a+ge·nar+i·an (ˌsɛptjʊədʒɪ'nɛərɪən) *n.* **1.** a person who is from 70 to 79 years old. ~*adj.* **2.** being between 70 and 79 years old. **3.** of or relating to a septuagenarian. [C18: from Latin *septuāgēnārius* from *septuāgēnī* seventy each, from *septuāgintā* seventy]
Sep+tu·a+ges·i+ma (ˌsɛptjʊə'dʒɛsɪmə) *n.* the third Sunday before Lent. [C14: from Church Latin *septuāgēsima* (*dies*) the seventieth (day); compare QUINQUAGESIMA]
Sep+tu·a+gint ('sɛptjʊəˌdʒɪnt) *n.* the principal Greek version of the Old Testament, including the Apocrypha, believed to have been translated by 70 or 72 scholars. [C16: from Latin *septuāgintā* seventy]
sep+tum ('sɛptəm) *n., pl.* **+ta** (-tə). *Biology, anatomy.* a dividing partition between two tissues or cavities. [C18: from Latin *saeptum* wall, from *saepīre* to enclose; related to Latin *saepēs* a fence]
sep+tu+ple ('sɛptjʊpᵊl) *adj.* **1.** seven times as much or many; sevenfold. **2.** consisting of seven parts or members. ~*vb.* **3.** (*tr.*) to multiply by seven. [C17: from Late Latin *septuplus,* from *septem* seven; compare QUADRUPLE]
sep+tup+let (sɛp'tju:plɪt, 'sɛptjʊplɪt) *n.* **1.** *Music.* a group of seven notes played in a time value of six, eight, etc. **2.** one of seven offspring produced at one birth. **3.** a group of seven things.
sep+tu+pli+cate (sɛp'tju:plɪkət) *n.* **1.** a group or set of seven things. ~*adj.* **2.** having or being in seven parts; sevenfold.
se+pul+chral (sɪ'pʌlkrəl) *adj.* **1.** suggestive of a tomb; gloomy. **2.** of or relating to a sepulchre. —**se+'pul+chral+ly** *adv.*
sep+ul+chre *or U.S.* **sep+ul+cher** ('sɛpəlkə) *n.* **1.** a burial vault, tomb, or grave. **2.** Also called: **Easter sepulchre.** a separate alcove in some medieval churches in which the Eucharistic elements were kept from Good Friday until the Easter ceremonies. ~*vb.* **3.** (*tr.*) to bury in a sepulchre. [C12: from Old French *sépulcre,* from Latin *sepulcrum,* from *sepelīre* to bury]
sep+ul+ture ('sɛpəltʃə) *n.* **1.** the act of placing in a sepulchre. **2.** an archaic word for **sepulchre.** [C13: via Old French from Latin *sepultūra,* from *sepultus* buried, from *sepelīre* to bury]
seq. *abbrev. for:* **1.** sequel. **2.** sequens. [Latin: the following (one)]
seqq. *abbrev. for* sequentia. [Latin: the following (ones)]
se+qua+cious (sɪ'kweɪʃəs) *adj.* **1.** logically following in regular sequence. **2.** ready to follow any leader; pliant. [C17: from Latin *sequāx* pursuing, from *sequī* to follow] —**se+'qua+cious+ly** *adv.* —**se+quac+i+ty** (sɪ'kwæsɪtɪ) *n.*
se+quel ('si:kwəl) *n.* **1.** anything that follows from something else; development. **2.** a consequence or result. **3.** a novel, play, etc., that continues a previously related story. [C15: from Late Latin *sequēla,* from Latin *sequī* to follow]
se+que·la (sɪ'kwi:lə) *n., pl.* **·lae** (-li:). (*often pl.*) *Med.* **1.** any abnormal bodily condition or disease related to or arising from a pre-existing disease. **2.** any complication of a disease. [C18: from Latin: SEQUEL]
se+quence ('si:kwəns) *n.* **1.** an arrangement of two or more things in a successive order. **2.** the successive order of two or more things: *chronological sequence.* **3.** a sequentially ordered set of related things or ideas. **4.** an action or event that follows another or others. **5. a.** *Cards.* a set of three or more consecutive cards, usually of the same suit. **b.** *Bridge.* a set of two or more consecutive cards. **6.** *Music.* an arrangement of notes or chords repeated several times at different pitches. **7.** *Maths.* **a.** an ordered set of numbers or other mathematical entities in one-to-one correspondence with the integers 1 to *n.* **b.** an ordered infinite set of mathematical entities in one-to-one correspondence with the natural numbers. **8.** a section of a film constituting a single continuous uninterrupted episode. **9.** *R.C. Church.* another word for **prose** (sense 3). [C14: from Medieval Latin *sequentia* that which follows, from Latin *sequī* to follow]
se+quence of tens·es *n. Grammar.* the sequence according to which the tense of a subordinate verb in a sentence is determined by the tense of the principal verb, as in *I believe he is lying, I believed he was lying,* etc.
se+quenc+er ('si:kwənsə) *n.* **1.** an electronic device that determines the order in which a number of operations occur. **2.** an electronic device that sorts information into the required order for data processing.
se+quent ('si:kwənt) *adj.* **1.** following in order or succession. **2.** following as a result; consequent. ~*n.* **3.** something that follows; consequence. [C16: from Latin *sequēns,* from *sequī* to follow] —**'se+quent+ly** *adv.*
se+quen+tial (sɪ'kwɛnʃəl) *adj.* **1.** characterized by or having a regular sequence. **2.** another word for **sequent.** —**se+quen+ti+al+i·ty** (sɪˌkwɛnʃɪ'ælɪtɪ) *n.* —**se+'quen+tial+ly** *adv.*
se+quen+tial ac+cess *n.* a method of reaching and reading data from a computer file by reading through the file from the beginning. Compare **direct access.**
se+ques+ter (sɪ'kwɛstə) *vb.* (*tr.*) **1.** to remove or separate. **2.** (*usually passive*) to retire into seclusion. **3.** *Law.* to take (property) temporarily out of the possession of its owner, esp. to hold a debtor's goods until the claims of his creditors are satisfied. **4.** *International law.* to requisition or appropriate (enemy property). [C14: from Late Latin *sequestrāre* to surrender for safe keeping, from *sequester* a trustee] —**se+'ques+tra·ble** *adj.*
se+ques+trant (sɪ'kwɛstrənt) *n. Chem.* any substance used to bring about sequestration, often by chelation. They are used in horticulture to counteract lime in the soil.
se+ques+trate (sɪ'kwɛstreɪt) *vb.* (*tr.*) **1.** *Law.* a variant of **sequester** (sense 3). **2.** *Chiefly Scot. law.* **a.** to place (the property of a bankrupt) in the hands of a trustee for the benefit of his creditors. **b.** to render (a person) bankrupt. **3.** *Archaic.*

to seclude or separate. [C16: from Late Latin *sequestrāre* to SEQUESTER] —**se+ques+tra+tor** ('siːkwɛsˌtreɪtə, sɪ'kwɛstreɪtə) *n.*

se+ques+tra+tion (ˌsiːkwɛ'streɪʃən) *n.* **1.** the act of sequestering or state of being sequestered. **2.** *Law.* the sequestering of property. **3.** *Chem.* the effective removal of ions from a solution by coordination with another type of ion or molecule to form complexes that do not have the same chemical behaviour as the original ions. See also **sequestrant.**

se+ques+trum (sɪ'kwɛstrəm) *n., pl.* **+tra** (-trə). *Pathol.* a detached piece of necrotic bone that often migrates to a wound, abscess, etc. [C19: from New Latin, from Latin: something deposited; see SEQUESTER] —**se+'ques+tral** *adj.*

se+quin ('siːkwɪn) *n.* **1.** a small piece of shiny coloured metal foil or plastic, usually round, used to decorate garments, etc. **2.** Also called: **zecchino.** any of various gold coins formerly minted in Italy, Turkey, and Malta. [C17: via French from Italian *zecchino,* from *zecca* mint, from Arabic *sikkah* die for striking coins] —**'se+quined** *adj.*

se+quoi·a (sɪ'kwɔɪə) *n.* either of two giant Californian coniferous trees, *Sequoia sempervirens* (**redwood**) or *Sequoiadendron giganteum* (formerly *Sequoia gigantea*) (**big tree** or **giant sequoia**): family *Taxodiaceae.* [C19: New Latin, named after *Sequoya,* known also as George Guess, (?1770–1843), American Indian scholar and leader]

Se+quoi·a Na+tion+al Park *n.* a national park in central California, in the Sierra Nevada Mountains: established in 1890 to protect groves of giant sequoias, some of which are about 4000 years old. Area: 1556 sq. km (601 sq. miles).

ser *or* **seer** (sɪə) *n.* a unit of weight used in India, usually taken as one fortieth of a maund. [from Hindi]

ser. *abbrev. for:* **1.** serial. **2.** series. **3.** sermon.

se·ra ('sɪərə) *n.* a plural of **serum.**

sé+rac ('sɛræk) *n.* a pinnacle of ice among crevasses on a glacier, usually on a steep slope. [C19: from Swiss French: a variety of white cheese (hence the ice that it resembles) from Medieval Latin *serācium,* from Latin *serum* whey]

se+ra+gli·o (sɛ'rɑːlɪˌəʊ) *or* **se+rail** (sə'raɪ, -'raɪl, -'reɪl) *n., pl.* **+ra+gli·os** *or* **+rails. 1.** the harem of a Muslim house or palace. **2.** a sultan's palace, esp. in the former Turkish empire. **3.** the wives and concubines of a Muslim. [C16: from Italian *serraglio* animal cage, from Medieval Latin *serrāculum* bolt, from Latin *sera* a door bar; associated also with Turkish *seray* palace]

se+rai (sɛ'raɪ) *n.* (in the East) a caravanserai or inn. [C17: from Turkish *saray* palace, from Persian *sarāī* palace; see CARAVANSERAI]

Se+ra+je·vo (*Serbo-Croatian* 'sɛrajɛvɔ) *n.* a variant spelling of **Sarajevo.**

Se+ram (sɪ'ræm) *n.* a variant spelling of **Ceram.**

Se+rang (sə'ræŋ) *n.* another name for **Ceram.**

ser+aph ('sɛrəf) *n., pl.* **+aphs** *or* **+a·phim** (-əfɪm). **1.** *Theol.* a member of the highest order of angels in the celestial hierarchies, often depicted as the winged head of a child. **2.** *Old Testament.* one of the fiery six-winged beings attendant upon Jehovah in Isaiah's vision (Isaiah 6). [C17: back formation from plural *seraphim,* via Late Latin from Hebrew] —**se+raph+ic** (sɪ'ræfɪk) *or* **se+'raph·i+cal** *adj.*

Ser+a·pis ('sɛrəpɪs) *n.* a Graeco-Egyptian god combining attributes of Apis and Osiris.

Serb (sɜːb) *n., adj.* another word for **Serbian.** [C19: from Serbian *Srb*]

Serb. *abbrev. for* Serbia(n).

Ser+bi·a ('sɜːbɪə) *n.* a constituent republic of SE Yugoslavia: includes the autonomous regions of Vojvodina and Kosovo-Metohija; precipitated World War I by the conflict with Austria; became part of the Kingdom of the Serbs, Croats, and Slovenes (later called Yugoslavia) in 1918. Capital: Belgrade. Pop.: 8 446 591 (1971). Area: 128 278 sq. km (49 528 sq. miles). Former name: **Servia.** Serbian name: **Srbija.**

Ser+bi·an ('sɜːbɪən) *adj.* **1.** of, relating to, or characteristic of Serbia, its people, or their dialect of Serbo-Croatian. ~*n.* **2.** the dialect of Serbo-Croatian spoken in Serbia. **3. a.** a native or inhabitant of Serbia. **b.** (esp. in other parts of Yugoslavia) a speaker of the Serbian dialect.

Ser·bo-Cro·a·tian *or* **Ser·bo-Cro·at** *n.* **1.** the chief official language of Yugoslavia, belonging to the South Slavonic branch of the Indo-European family. The Serbian dialect is usually written in the Cyrillic alphabet, the Croatian in Roman. ~*adj.* **2.** of or relating to this language.

Sercq (sɛrk) *n.* the French name for **Sark.**

ser+dab ('sɜːdæb, sə'dæb) *n.* a secret chamber in an ancient Egyptian tomb. [C19 (earlier, in the sense: cellar): from Arabic: cellar, from Persian *sardāb* ice cellar, from *sard* cold + *āb* water]

sere[1] *or* **sear** (sɪə) *adj.* **1.** *Archaic.* dried up or withered. ~*vb., n.* **2.** a rare spelling of **sear**[1]. [Old English *sēar;* see SEAR[1]]

sere[2] (sɪə) *n.* the series of changes occurring in the ecological succession of a particular community. [C20: from SERIES]

se+rein (sə'reɪn) *n.* fine rain falling from a clear sky after sunset, esp. in the tropics. [C19: via French, from Old French *serain* dusk, from Latin *sērus* late]

Ser+em+ban (sə'rɛmbən) *n.* a town in West Malaysia, capital of Negri Sembilan state. Pop.: 80 921 (1970).

ser+e·nade (ˌsɛrɪ'neɪd) *n.* **1.** a piece of music appropriate to the evening, characteristically played outside the house of a woman. **2.** a piece of music indicative or suggestive of this. **3.** an extended composition in several movements similar to the modern suite or divertimento. ~*vb.* **4.** (*tr.*) to play a serenade for (someone). **5.** (*intr.*) to play a serenade. ~Compare **aubade.** [C17: from French *sérénade,* from Italian *serenata,* from *sereno* peaceful, from Latin *serēnus* calm; also influenced in meaning by Italian *sera* evening, from Latin *sērus* late] —ˌ**ser+e+'nad+er** *n.*

se+re·na+ta (ˌsɛrɪ'nɑːtə) *n.* **1.** an 18th-century cantata, often dramatic in form. **2.** another word for **serenade.** [C18: from Italian; see SERENADE]

ser+en+dip+i·ty (ˌsɛrən'dɪpɪtɪ) *n.* the faculty of making fortunate discoveries by accident. [C18: coined by Horace Walpole, from the Persian fairytale *The Three Princes of Serendip,* in which the heroes possess this gift]

se+rene (sɪ'riːn) *adj.* **1.** peaceful or tranquil; calm. **2.** clear or bright: *a serene sky.* **3.** (*often cap.*) honoured: used as part of certain royal titles: *His Serene Highness.* [C16: from Latin *serēnus*] —**se+'rene+ly** *adv.* —**se+'rene+ness** *n.*

se+ren+i·ty (sɪ'rɛnɪtɪ) *n., pl.* **·ties. 1.** the state or quality of being serene. **2.** (*often cap.*) a title of honour used of certain royal personages: preceded by *his, her,* etc.

serf (sɜːf) *n.* (esp. in medieval Europe) an unfree person, esp. one bound to the land. If his lord sold the land, the serf was passed on to the new landlord. [C15: from Old French, from Latin *servus* a slave; see SERVE] —**'serf+dom** *or* **'serf+hood** *n.* —**'serf+ˌlike** *adj.*

serge (sɜːdʒ) *n.* **1.** a twill-weave woollen or worsted fabric used for clothing. **2.** a similar twilled cotton, silk, or rayon fabric. [C14: from Old French *sarge,* from Vulgar Latin *sārica* (unattested), from Latin *sēricum,* from Greek *sērikon* silk, from *sērikos* silken, from *sēr* silkworm]

ser+geant ('sɑːdʒənt) *n.* **1.** a noncommissioned officer in certain armies, air forces, and marine corps, usually ranking immediately above a corporal. **2. a.** (in Britain) a police officer ranking between constable and inspector. **b.** (in the U.S.) a police officer ranking below a captain. **3.** See **sergeant at arms. 4.** a court or municipal officer who has ceremonial duties. **5.** (formerly) a tenant by military service, not of knightly rank. **6.** See **serjeant at law.** ~Also: **serjeant.** [C12: from Old French *sergent,* from Latin *serviēns,* literally: serving, from *servīre* to SERVE] —**ser+gean+cy** ('sɑːdʒənsɪ) *or* **'ser+geant+ˌship** *n.*

ser+geant at arms *n.* **1.** an officer of a legislative or fraternal body responsible for maintaining internal order. **2.** (formerly) an officer who served a monarch or noble, esp. as an armed attendant. ~Also: **sergeant, serjeant at arms, serjeant.**

ser+geant at law *n.* a variant spelling of **serjeant at law.**

ser+geant ma+jor *n.* **1.** a noncommissioned officer of the highest rank or having specific administrative tasks in branches of the armed forces of various countries. **2.** a large damselfish, *Abudefduf saxatilis,* having a bluish-grey body marked with black stripes.

Ser+gi+pe (*Portuguese* ser'ʒipi) *n.* a state of NE Brazil: the smallest Brazilian state; a centre of resistance to Dutch conquest (17th century). Capital: Aracajú. Pop.: 900 744 (1970). Area: 13 672 sq. km (8492 sq. miles).

se+ri·al ('sɪərɪəl) *n.* **1.** a novel, play, etc., presented in separate instalments at regular intervals. **2.** *Library science.* a publication, usually regularly issued and consecutively numbered. ~*adj.* **3.** of, relating to, or resembling a series. **4.** published or presented as a serial. **5.** of or relating to such publication or presentation. **6.** *Computer technol.* of or operating on items of information, instructions, etc., in the order in which they occur. Compare **parallel** (sense 5). **7.** of, relating to, or using the techniques of serialism. [C19: from New Latin *seriālis,* from Latin *seriēs* SERIES] —**'se+ri·al+ly** *adv.*

se+ri·al cor+re+la+tion *n. Statistics.* another name for **autocorrelation.**

se+ri·al+ism ('sɪərɪəˌlɪzəm) *n.* (in 20th-century music) the use of a sequence of notes in a definite order as a thematic basis for a composition and a source from which the musical material is derived. See also: **twelve-tone.**

se+ri·al+ize *or* **se+ri·al+ise** ('sɪərɪəˌlaɪz) *vb.* (*tr.*) to publish or present in the form of a serial. —ˌ**se+ri·al·i+'za+tion** *or* ˌ**se+ri·al·i+'sa+tion** *n.*

se+ri·al num+ber *n.* any of the consecutive numbers assigned to machines, tools, books, etc.

se+ri+ate ('sɪərɪɪt) *adj.* forming a series. —**'se+ri+ate+ly** *adv.*

se+ri·a+tim (ˌsɪərɪ'ætɪm, ˌsɛr-) *adv.* in a series; one after another in regular order. [C17: from Medieval Latin, from Latin *seriēs* SERIES]

se+ri+ceous (sɪ'rɪʃəs) *adj. Botany.* **1.** covered with a layer of small silky hairs: *a sericeous leaf.* **2.** silky. [C18: from Late Latin *sēriceus* silken, from Latin *sēricus;* see SERGE]

ser·i·cin ('sɛrɪsɪn) *n.* a gelatinous protein found on the fibres of raw silk. [C19: from Latin *sēricum* silk + -IN]

ser·i·cul+ture ('sɛrɪˌkʌltʃə) *n.* the rearing of silkworms for the production of raw silk. [C19: via French; *seri-* from Latin *sēricum* silk, from Greek *sērikos* silken, from *sēr* a silkworm] —ˌ**ser·i+'cul+tur+al** *adj.* —ˌ**ser·i+'cul+tur+ist** *n.*

ser·i·e·ma (ˌsɛrɪ'iːmə) *n.* either of two cranelike South American birds, *Cariama cristata* or *Chunga burmeisteri,* having a crest just above the bill, rounded wings, and a long tail: family *Cariamidae,* order *Gruiformes* (cranes, rails, etc.). [C19: from New Latin, from Tupi *çariama* crested]

se+ries ('sɪəriːz, -rɪz) *n., pl.* **+ries. 1.** a group or connected succession of similar or related things, usually arranged in order. **2.** a set of radio or television programmes having the same characters and setting but different stories. **3.** a set of books having the same format, related content, etc., published by one firm. **4.** a set of stamps, coins, etc., issued at a particular time. **5.** *Maths.* the sum of a finite or infinite sequence of numbers or quantities. See also **geometric series.** **6.** *Electronics.* **a.** a configuration of two or more components connected in a circuit so that the same current flows in turn through each of them (esp. in the phrase **in series**). Compare **parallel** (sense 10). **b.** (*as modifier*): *a series circuit.* **7.** *Rhetoric.* a succession of coordinate elements in a sentence. **8.** *Geology.* a stratigraphical unit that is a subdivision of a system and represents the rocks formed during an epoch. [C17: from Latin: a row, from *serere* to link]

se·ries-wound ('sɪəri:z,waʊnd, -rɪz-) *n.* (of a motor or generator) having the field and armature circuits connected in series. Compare **shunt-wound.**

ser+if *or* **ser+iph** ('sɛrɪf) *n. Printing.* a small line at the extremities of a main stroke in a type character. [C19: perhaps from Dutch *schreef* dash, probably of Germanic origin, compare Old High German *screvōn* to engrave]

ser·i·graph ('sɛrɪ,græf, -,grɑ:f) *n.* a colour print made by an adaptation of the silk-screen process. [C19: from *seri-*, from Latin *sēricum* silk + -GRAPH] —**se+rig+ra+phy** (sə'rɪgrəfɪ) *n.*

ser+in ('sɛrɪn) *n.* any of various small yellow-and-brown finches of the genus *Serinus,* esp. *S. serinus,* of parts of Europe. See also **canary.** [C16: from French, perhaps from Old Provençal *sirena* a bee-eater, from Latin *sīrēn,* a kind of bird, from SIREN]

ser+ine ('sɛri:n, 'sɪəri:n, -rɪn) *n.* a sweet-tasting amino acid that is synthesized in the body and is involved in the synthesis of cysteine; 2-amino-3-hydroxypropanoic acid. Formula: $CH_2(OH)CH(NH_2)COOH$. [C19: from SERICIN + -INE[2]]

se+rin+ga (sə'rɪŋgə) *n.* **1.** any of several euphorbiaceous trees of the Brazilian genus *Hevea,* that yield rubber. **2.** a deciduous simaroubaceous tree, *Kirkia acuminata,* of southern Africa with a graceful shape. [C18: from Portuguese, variant of SYRINGA]

Se+rin+ga+pa+tam (sə,rɪŋgəpə'tæm) *n.* a small town in S India, in Karnataka on **Seringapatam Island** in the Cauvery River: capital of Mysore from 1610 to 1799, when it was besieged and captured by the British. Pop.: 14 100 (1971).

se+ri·o+com+ic (,sɪərɪəʊ'kɒmɪk) *or* **se+ri·o+com·i+cal** *adj.* mixing serious and comic elements. —,**se+ri·o+'com·i·cal+ly** *adv.*

se+ri+ous ('sɪərɪəs) *adj.* **1.** grave in nature or disposition; thoughtful: *a serious person.* **2.** marked by deep feeling; in earnest; sincere: *is he serious or joking?* **3.** concerned with important matters: *a serious conversation.* **4.** requiring effort or concentration: *a serious book.* **5.** giving rise to fear or anxiety; critical: *a serious illness.* [C15: from Late Latin *sēriōsus,* from Latin *sērius;* probably related to Old English *swǣr* gloomy, Gothic *swers* esteemed] —'**se+ri+ous+ly** *adv.* —'**se+ri+ous+ness** *n.*

ser+jeant ('sɑ:dʒənt) *n.* a variant spelling of **sergeant.**

ser+jeant at arms *n.* a variant spelling of **sergeant at arms.**

ser+jeant at law *n.* (formerly in England) a barrister of a special rank, to which he was raised by a writ under the Great Seal. Also: **serjeant, sergeant at law, sergeant.**

ser+mon ('sɜ:mən) *n.* **1. a.** an address of religious instruction or exhortation, often based on a passage from the Bible, esp. one delivered during a church service. **b.** a written version of such an address. **2.** a serious speech, esp. one administering reproof. [C12: via Old French from Latin *sermō* discourse, probably from *serere* to join together] —**ser+mon+ic** (sɜ:'mɒnɪk) *or* **ser+'mon·i·cal** *adj.*

ser+mon+ize *or* **ser+mon+ise** ('sɜ:mə,naɪz) *vb.* to talk to or address (a person or audience) as if delivering a sermon. —'**ser+mon+,iz+er** *or* '**ser+mon+,is+er** *n.*

Ser+mon on the Mount *n. New Testament.* the first major discourse delivered by Christ (Matthew 5–7).

se+ro- *combining form.* indicating a serum: *serotherapy.*

se+rol+o+gy (sɪ'rɒlədʒɪ) *n.* the branch of science concerned with serums. —**se+ro+log+ic** (,sɪərə'lɒdʒɪk) *or* ,**se+ro+'log·i·cal** *adj.* —**se+'rol·o·gist** *n.*

se+ro+sa (sɪ'rəʊsə) *n.* **1.** another name for **serous membrane.** **2.** one of the thin membranes surrounding the embryo in an insect's egg. [C19: from New Latin, from *serōsus* relating to SERUM]

ser·o+tine ('sɛrə,taɪn) *adj.* **1.** Also: **se+rot·i+nal** (sɪ'rɒtɪnᵊl), **se+rot·i·nous.** *Biology.* produced, flowering, or developing late in the season. ~*n.* **2.** either of two insectivorous bats, *Eptesicus serotinus* or *Vespertilio serotinus:* family *Vespertilionidae.* [C16: from Latin *sērōtinus* late, from *sērus* late; applied to the bat because it flies late in the evening]

ser·o+to+nin (,sɛrə'təʊnɪn) *n.* a compound that occurs in the brain, intestines, and blood platelets and induces vasodilation and muscular contraction; 5-hydroxytryptamine (5HT). Formula: $C_{10}H_{12}N_2O$.

se+rous ('sɪərəs) *adj.* of, resembling, producing, or containing serum. [C16: from Latin *serōsus,* from SERUM] —**se+ros·i·ty** (sɪ'rɒsɪtɪ) *or* '**se+rous+ness** *n.*

se+rous flu+id *n.* a thin watery fluid found in many body cavities, esp. those lined with serous membrane.

se+rous mem+brane *n.* any of the smooth moist delicate membranes, such as the pleura or peritoneum, that line the closed cavities of the body.

ser+ow ('sɛrəʊ) *n.* either of two antelopes, *Capricornis sumatraensis* and *C. crispus,* of mountainous regions of S and SE Asia, having a dark coat and conical backward-pointing horns. [C19: from Lepcha *sǎ-ro* Tibetan goat]

Ser+pens ('sɜ:pənz) *n., Latin genitive* **Ser+pen+tis** (sə'pɛntɪs). a faint extensive constellation situated in the N and S equatorial regions and divided into two parts, **Serpens Caput** (the head) lying between Ophiuchus and Boötes and **Serpens Cauda** (the tail) between Ophiuchus and Aquila. [Latin: SERPENT]

ser+pent ('sɜ:pənt) *n.* **1.** a literary or dialect word for **snake.** **2.** *Old Testament.* a manifestation of Satan as a guileful tempter (Genesis 3:1–5). **3.** a sly, deceitful, or unscrupulous person. **4.** an obsolete wind instrument resembling a snake in shape, the bass form of the cornet. **5.** a firework that moves about with a serpentine motion when ignited. [C14: via Old French from Latin *serpēns* a creeping thing, from *serpere* to creep; related to Greek *herpein* to crawl]

ser+pen+tine[1] ('sɜ:pən,taɪn) *adj.* **1.** of, relating to, or resembling a serpent. **2.** twisting; winding. [C14: from Late Latin *serpentīmus,* from *serpēns* SERPENT]

ser+pen+tine[2] ('sɜ:pən,taɪn) *n.* any of several secondary minerals, consisting of hydrated magnesium silicate, that are green to black in colour and greasy to the touch: common in ultrabasic igneous rocks and used chiefly in ornamental decoration. Formula: $Mg_3Si_2O_5.2H_2O$. [C15 *serpentyn,* from Medieval Latin *serpentīnum* SERPENTINE[1]; referring to the snakelike patterns of these minerals]

ser+pi+go (sɜ:'paɪgəʊ) *n. Pathol.* any progressive skin eruption, such as ringworm or herpes. [C14: from Medieval Latin, from Latin *serpere* to creep] —**ser+pig·i+nous** (sɜ:'pɪdʒɪnəs) *adj.*

ser+pu+lid ('sɜ:pjʊlɪd) *n.* a marine polychaete worm of the family *Serpulidae,* which constructs and lives in a calcareous tube attached to stones or seaweed and has a crown of ciliated tentacles. [C19: Latin, from *serpula* a little serpent]

ser+ra+nid (sə'rænɪd, 'sɛrə-) *or* **ser+ra+noid** ('sɛrə,nɔɪd) *n.* **1.** any of numerous mostly marine percoid fishes of the family *Serranidae:* includes the sea basses, sea perches, groupers, and jewfish. ~*adj.* **2.** of, relating to, or belonging to the family *Serranidae.* [C19: from New Latin *Serranidae,* from *serrānus* genus name from Latin *serra* sawfish]

ser+rate *adj.* ('sɛrɪt, -eɪt). **1.** (of leaves) having a margin of forward pointing teeth. **2.** having a notched or sawlike edge. ~*vb.* (sɛ'reɪt). **3.** (*tr.*) to make serrate. [C17: from Latin *serrātus* saw-shaped, from *serra* a saw] —**ser+'rat+ed** *adj.*

ser+ra+tion (sɛ'reɪʃən) *or* **ser+ra+ture** ('sɛrətʃə) *n.* **1.** the state or condition of being serrated. **2.** a row of notches or toothlike projections on an edge. **3.** a single notch.

ser+ried ('sɛrɪ:d) *adj.* in close or compact formation: *serried ranks of troops.* [C17: from Old French *serré* close-packed, from *serrer* to shut up; see SEAR[2]]

ser+ri+form ('sɛrɪ,fɔ:m) *adj. Biology.* resembling a notched or sawlike edge. [*serri-,* from Latin *serra* saw]

ser+ru+late ('sɛrʊ,leɪt, -lɪt) *or* **ser+ru+lat+ed** *adj.* (esp. of leaves) minutely serrate. [C18: from New Latin *serrulātus,* from Latin *serrula* diminutive of *serra* a saw]

ser+ru+la+tion (,sɛrʊ'leɪʃən) *n.* **1.** any of the notches in a serrulate object. **2.** the condition of being serrulate.

Ser·to·ri·us (sɜ:'tɔ:rɪəs) *n.* **Quin·tus** ('kwɪntəs). ?123–72 B.C., Roman soldier who fought with Marius in Gaul (102) and led an insurrection in Spain against Sulla until he was assassinated.

ser+tu+lar·i·an (,sɜ:tjʊ'lɛərɪən) *n.* any of various hydroid coelenterates of the genus *Sertularia,* forming feathery colonies of long branched stems bearing stalkless paired polyps. [C18: from New Latin *Sertulāria,* from Latin *sertula* diminutive of *serta* a garland, from *serere* to wreathe]

se+rum ('sɪərəm) *n., pl.* **+rums** *or* **+ra** (-rə). **1.** See **blood serum.** **2.** antitoxin obtained from the blood serum of immunized animals. **3.** *Physiol., zoology.* clear watery fluid, esp. that exuded by serous membranes. **4.** a less common word for **whey.** [C17: from Latin: whey] —'**se+rum+al** *adj.*

se+rum al+bu+min *n.* the principal protein of the blood. See also **albumin.**

se+rum glob·u+lin *n.* the blood serum component consisting of proteins with a larger molecular weight than serum albumin. See also **immunoglobulin.**

se+rum hep·a·ti+tis *n.* an acute infectious viral disease characterized by inflammation and enlargement of the liver, fever, gastrointestinal discomfort, and jaundice: transmitted by means of injection with a contaminated needle or transfusion of contaminated blood. See also **hepatitis, infectious hepatitis.**

se+rum sick+ness *n.* an allergic reaction, such as vomiting, skin rash, etc., that sometimes follows injection of a foreign serum.

serv. *abbrev. for:* **1.** servant. **2.** service.

ser+val ('sɜ:vᵊl) *n., pl.* **+vals** *or* **+val.** a slender feline mammal, *Felis serval,* of the African bush, having an orange-brown coat with black spots, large ears, and long legs. [C18: via French from Late Latin *cervālis* staglike, from Latin *cervus* a stag]

serv+ant ('sɜ:vᵊnt) *n.* **1.** a person employed to work for another, esp. one who performs household duties. **2.** See **public servant.** [C13: via Old French, from *servant* serving, from *servir* to SERVE] —'**serv·ant·,like** *adj.*

serve (sɜ:v) *vb.* **1.** to be in the service of (a person). **2.** to render or be of service to (a person, cause, etc.); help. **3.** to attend to (customers) in a shop, restaurant, etc. **4.** (*tr.*) to provide (guests, customers, etc.) with food, drink, etc.: *she served her guests with cocktails.* **5.** to distribute or provide (food, drink, etc.) for guests, customers, etc.: *do you serve coffee?* **6.** (*tr.,* sometimes foll. by *up*) to present (food, drink, etc.) in a specified manner: *cauliflower served with cheese sauce.* **7.** (*tr.*) to provide with a regular supply of. **8.** (*tr.*) to work actively for: *to serve the government.* **9.** (*tr.*) to pay homage to: *to serve God.* **10.** to answer the requirements of; suit: *this will serve my purpose.* **11.** (*intr.; may take an infinitive*) to have a use; function: *this wood will serve to build* *a fire.* **12.** to go through (a period of service, enlistment, imprisonment, etc.). **13.** (*intr.*) (of weather, conditions, etc.) to be favourable or suitable. **14.** (*tr.*) Also: **service.** (of a male animal) to copulate with (a female animal). **15.** *Tennis, squash, etc.* to put (the ball) into play. **16.** (*intr.*) *R.C. Church.* to act as server at Mass or other services. **17.** (*tr.*) to deliver (a legal document, esp. a writ or summons) to (a person). **18.** to provide (a machine, etc.) with an impulse or signal for control purposes or with a continuous supply of fuel, working material, etc. **19.** (*tr.*) *Nautical.* to bind (a rope, spar, etc.) with wire or fine cord to protect it from chafing, etc. See also **seize** (sense 8). **20. serve (a person) right.** *Informal.* to pay back, esp. for wrongful or foolish treatment or behaviour. ~*n.* **21.** *Tennis, squash, etc.* short for **service** (sense 17). [C13: from Old French *servir,* from Latin *servīre,* from *servus* a slave] —**'serv·a·ble** *or* **'serve·a·ble** *adj.*

serv·er ('sɜːvə) *n.* **1.** a person who serves. **2.** *Chiefly R.C. Church.* a person who acts as acolyte or assists the priest at Mass. **3.** something that is used in serving food and drink. **4.** the player who serves in racket games.

Ser·ve·tus (sɜː'viːtəs) *n.* **Mi·chael,** Spanish name *Miguel Serveto.* 1511–53, Spanish theologian and physician. He was burnt at the stake by order of Calvin for denying the doctrine of the Trinity and the divinity of Christ.

Ser·vi·a ('sɜːvɪə) *n.* the former name of **Serbia.** —**'Ser·vi·an** *adj., n.*

ser·vice ('sɜːvɪs) *n.* **1.** an act of help or assistance. **2.** an organized system of labour and material aids used to supply the needs of the public: *telephone service; bus service.* **3.** the supply, installation, or maintenance of goods carried out by a dealer. **4.** the state of availability for use by the public (esp. in the phrases **into** *or* **out of service**). **5.** a periodic overhaul made on a car, machine, etc. **6.** the act or manner of serving guests, customers, etc., in a shop, hotel, restaurant, etc. **7.** a department of public employment and its employees: *civil service.* **8.** employment in or performance of work for another: *he has been in the service of our firm for ten years.* **9.** the work of a public servant. **10. a.** one of the branches of the armed forces. **b.** (*as modifier*): *service life.* **11.** the state, position, or duties of a domestic servant (esp. in the phrase **in service**). **12.** the act or manner of serving food. **13.** a complete set of dishes for use at table. **14.** public worship carried out according to certain prescribed forms: *divine service.* **15.** the prescribed form according to which a specific kind of religious ceremony is to be carried out: *the burial service.* **16.** a unified collection of musical settings of the canticles and other liturgical items prescribed by the Book of Common Prayer as used in the Church of England. **17.** *Tennis, squash, etc.* **a.** the act, manner, or right of serving a ball. **b.** the game in which a particular player serves: *he has lost his service.* Often shortened to **serve. 18.** (in feudal law) the duty owed by a tenant to his lord. **19.** the serving of a writ, summons, etc., upon a person. **20.** *Nautical.* a length of tarred marline or small stuff used in serving. **21.** (of male animals) the act of mating. **22.** (*modifier*) of, relating to, or for the use of servants or employees. ~*vb.* (*tr.*) **23.** to make fit for use. **24.** to supply with assistance. **25.** to overhaul (a car, machine, etc.). **26.** (of a male animal) to mate with (a female). **27.** *Brit.* to meet interest and capital payments on (debt). [C12 *servise,* from Old French, from Latin *servitium* condition of a slave, from *servus* a slave]

ser·vice·a·ble ('sɜːvɪsəbᵊl) *adj.* **1.** capable of or ready for service; usable. **2.** capable of giving good service; durable. **3.** *Archaic.* diligent in service. —ˌ**ser·vice·a·'bil·i·ty** *or* **'ser·vice·a·ble·ness** *n.* —**'ser·vice·a·bly** *adv.*

ser·vice ar·e·a *n.* a place on a motorway providing garage services, restaurants, toilet facilities, etc.

ser·vice·ber·ry ('sɜːvɪsˌbɛrɪ) *n., pl.* **·ries. 1.** Also called: **shadbush.** any of various North American rosaceous trees or shrubs of the genus *Amelanchier,* esp. *A. canadensis,* which has white flowers and edible purplish berries. **2.** the fruit of any of these plants. **3.** the fruit of the service tree. ~Also called (for senses 1, 2): **shadberry, Juneberry.**

ser·vice ceil·ing *n.* the height above sea level, measured under standard conditions, at which the rate of climb of an aircraft has fallen to a specified amount. Compare **absolute ceiling.**

ser·vice charge *n.* a percentage of a bill, as at a restaurant or hotel, added to the total to pay for service.

ser·vice in·dus·try *n.* an industry that provides services, such as transport or entertainment, rather than goods.

ser·vice line *n.* (in certain racket games) **1.** the line at the back of the court behind which the server must stand when serving. **2.** a line indicating the boundary of a permissible service, as on the backwall of a squash court.

ser·vice·man ('sɜːvɪsˌmæn, -mən) *n., pl.* **·men. 1.** a person who serves in the armed services of a country. **2.** a man employed to service and maintain equipment.

ser·vice mod·ule *n.* a section of an Apollo spacecraft housing the rocket engine, radar, fuel cells, etc., and jettisoned on re-entry into the earth's atmosphere. See also **lunar module, command module.**

ser·vice road *n. Brit.* a relatively narrow road running parallel to a main road and providing access to houses, shops, offices, factories, etc., situated along its length.

ser·vic·es ('sɜːvɪsɪz) *n.* **1.** work performed for remuneration. **2.** (usually preceded by *the*) the armed forces. **3.** (*sometimes sing.*) *Economics.* commodities, such as banking, that are mainly intangible and usually consumed concurrently with their production. Compare **goods** (sense 2).

ser·vice sta·tion *n.* **1.** a place that supplies fuel, oil, etc., for motor vehicles and often carries out repairs, servicing, etc. **2.** a place that repairs and sometimes supplies mechanical or electrical equipment.

ser·vice tree *n.* **1.** Also called: **sorb.** a Eurasian rosaceous tree, *Sorbus domestica,* cultivated for its white flowers and brown edible apple-like fruits. **2. wild service tree.** a similar and related Eurasian tree, *Sorbus torminalis.* [*service,* from Old English *syrfe,* from Vulgar Latin *sorbea* (unattested), from Latin *sorbus* SORB]

ser·vi·ent ten·e·ment ('sɜːvɪənt) *n. Property Law.* the land or tenement over which an easement or other servitude is exercised. Compare **dominant tenement.**

ser·vi·ette (ˌsɜːvɪ'ɛt) *n. Chiefly Brit.* a small square of cloth or paper used while eating to protect the clothes, wipe the mouth and hands, etc. [C15: from Old French, from *servir* to SERVE; formed on the model of OUBLIETTE]

ser·vile ('sɜːvaɪl) *adj.* **1.** obsequious or fawning in attitude or behaviour; submissive. **2.** of or suitable for a slave. **3.** existing in or relating to a state of slavery. **4.** (when *postpositive,* foll. by *to*) submitting or obedient. [C14: from Latin *servīlis,* from *servus* slave] —**'ser·vile·ly** *adv.* —**ser·vil·i·ty** (sɜː'vɪlɪtɪ) *or* **'ser·vile·ness** *n.*

ser·vile work *n. R.C. Church.* work of a physical nature that is forbidden on Sundays and on certain holidays.

serv·ing ('sɜːvɪŋ) *n.* a portion or helping of food or drink.

ser·vi·tor ('sɜːvɪtə) *n. Archaic.* a person who serves another. [C14: from Old French *servitour,* from Late Latin *servītor,* from Latin *servīre* to SERVE]

ser·vi·tude ('sɜːvɪˌtjuːd) *n.* **1.** the state or condition of a slave; bondage. **2.** the state or condition of being subjected to or dominated by a person or thing: *servitude to drink.* **3.** *Law.* a burden attaching to an estate for the benefit of an adjoining estate or of some definite person. See also **easement. 4.** short for **penal servitude.** [C15: via Old French from Latin *servitūdō,* from *servus* a slave]

ser·vo ('sɜːvəʊ) *adj.* **1.** (*prenominal*) of, relating to, forming part of, or activated by a servomechanism: *servo brakes.* ~*n., pl.* **·vos. 2.** *Informal.* short for **servomechanism.**

ser·vo·mech·a·nism ('sɜːvəʊˌmɛkəˌnɪzəm, ˌsɜːvəʊ'mɛk-) *n.* a mechanism for converting a small mechanical force into a larger force, esp. for control purposes. The output power is proportional to the input power and the system may include an electronic negative feedback device. —**ser·vo·me·chan·i·cal** (ˌsɜːvəʊmɪ'kænɪkᵊl) *adj.*

ser·vo·mo·tor ('sɜːvəʊˌməʊtə) *n.* any motor that supplies power to a servomechanism.

ses·a·me ('sɛsəmɪ) *n.* **1.** a tropical herbaceous plant, *Sesamum indicum,* of the East Indies, cultivated, esp. in India, for its small oval seeds: family *Pedaliaceae.* **2.** the seeds of this plant, used in flavouring bread and yielding an edible oil (**benne oil** or **gingili**). ~Also called: **benne, gingili, til.** [C15: from Latin *sēsamum,* from Greek *sēsamon, sēsamē,* of Semitic origin; related to Arabic *simsim*]

ses·a·moid ('sɛsəˌmɔɪd) *adj. Anatomy.* **1.** of or relating to various small bones formed in tendons, such as the patella. **2.** of or relating to any of various small cartilages, esp. those of the nose. [C17: from Latin *sēsamoīdēs* like sesame (seed), from Greek]

Se·so·tho (sɪ'suːtʊ) *n.* the dialect of Sotho spoken by the Basotho: an official language of Lesotho. Also called: **Southern Sotho.** Former name: **Basuto.**

ses·qui- *prefix.* indicating one and a half: *sesquicentennial.* [from Latin, contraction of SEMI- + *as* AS² + *-que* and]

ses·qui·al·te·ra (ˌsɛskwɪ'æltərə) *n. Music.* **1.** a mixture stop on an organ. **2.** another term for **hemiola.** [C16: from Latin *sesqui-* half + *alter* second, other]

ses·qui·car·bon·ate (ˌsɛskwɪ'kɑːbəˌneɪt, -nɪt) *n.* a mixed salt consisting of a carbonate and a hydrogen carbonate, such as sodium sesquicarbonate, $Na_2CO_3.NaHCO_3.2H_2O$.

ses·qui·cen·ten·ni·al (ˌsɛskwɪsɛn'tɛnɪəl) *adj.* **1.** of or relating to a period of 150 years. ~*n.* **2.** a period or cycle of 150 years. **3.** a 150th anniversary or its celebration. —ˌ**ses·qui·cen·'ten·ni·al·ly** *adv.*

ses·qui·ox·ide (ˌsɛskwɪ'ɒksaɪd) *n.* any of certain oxides whose molecules contain three atoms of oxygen for every two atoms of the element: *chromium sesquioxide,* Cr_2O_3.

ses·qui·pe·da·li·an (ˌsɛskwɪpɪ'deɪlɪən) *or* **ses·quip·e·dal** (sɛs'kwɪpədᵊl) *adj.* **1.** tending to use very long words. **2.** (of words or expressions) long and ponderous; polysyllabic. ~*n.* **3.** a polysyllabic word. [C17: from Latin *sēsquipedālis* of a foot and a half, from SESQUI- + *pedālis* of the foot, from *pēs* foot] —ˌ**ses·qui·pe·'da·li·an·ism** *n.*

ses·sile ('sɛsaɪl) *adj.* **1.** (of flowers or leaves) having no stalk; growing directly from the stem. **2.** (of animals such as the barnacle) permanently attached to a substratum. [C18: from Latin *sēssilis* concerning sitting, from *sedēre* to sit] —**ses·sil·i·ty** (sɛ'sɪlɪtɪ) *n.*

ses·sile oak *n.* another name for the **durmast.**

ses·sion ('sɛʃən) *n.* **1.** the meeting of a court, legislature, judicial body, etc., for the execution of its function or the transaction of business. **2.** a single continuous meeting of such a body. **3.** a series or period of such meetings. **4.** *Education.* **a.** the time during which classes are held. **b.** a school or university term or year. **5.** *Presbyterian Church.* the judicial and administrative body presiding over a local congregation and consisting of the minister and elders. **6.** a meeting of a group of people to pursue an activity. **7.** any period devoted to an activity. **8.** See **Court of Session.** [C14: from Latin *sessiō* a sitting, from *sedēre* to sit] —'**ses·sion·al** *adj.* —'**ses·sion·al·ly** *adv.*

ses·sions ('sɛʃənz) *pl. n.* the sittings or a sitting of justice in court. See **magistrates' court, quarter sessions.**

Ses·sions ('sɛʃənz) *n.* **Rog·er (Huntington).** born 1896, U.S. composer.

ses·terce ('sɛstəs) *or* **ses·ter·ti·us** (sɛ'stɜːtɪəs) *n.* a silver or, later, bronze coin of ancient Rome worth a quarter of a denarius. [C16: from Latin *sēstertius* a coin worth two and a half asses, from *sēmis* half + *tertius* a third]

ses·ter·ti·um (sɛ'stɜːtɪəm) *n., pl.* **·ti·a** (-tɪə). an ancient Roman money of account equal to 1000 sesterces. [C16: from Latin, from the phrase *mille sestertium* a thousand of sesterces; see SESTERCE]

ses·tet (sɛ'stɛt) *n.* **1.** *Prosody.* the last six lines of a Petrarchan sonnet. **2.** *Prosody.* any six-line stanza. **3.** another word for **sextet** (sense 1). [C19: from Italian *sestetto,* from *sesto* sixth, from Latin *sextus,* from *sex* six]

ses·ti·na (sɛ'stiːnə) *n.* an elaborate verse form of Italian origin, normally unrhymed, consisting of six stanzas of six lines each and a concluding tercet. The six final words of the lines in the first stanza are repeated in a different order in each of the remaining five stanzas and also in the concluding tercet. Also called: **sextain.** [C19: from Italian, from *sesto* sixth, from Latin *sextus*]

Ses·tos ('sɛstɒs) *n.* a ruined town in NW Turkey, at the narrowest point of the Dardanelles: N terminus of the bridge of boats built by Xerxes in 481 B.C. for the crossing of his armies of invasion.

set[1] (sɛt) *vb.* **sets, set·ting, set.** (*mainly tr.*) **1.** to put or place in position or into a specified state or condition: *to set a book on the table; to set someone free.* **2.** (*also intr.;* foll. by *to* or *on*) to put or be put (to); apply or be applied: *he set fire to the house; they set the dogs on the scent.* **3.** to put into order or readiness for use; prepare: *to set a trap; to set the table for dinner.* **4.** (*also intr.*) to put, form, or be formed into a jelled, firm, fixed, or rigid state: *the jelly set in three hours.* **5.** (*also intr.*) to put or be put into a position that will restore a normal state: *to set a broken bone.* **6.** to adjust (a clock or other instrument) to a position. **7.** to determine or establish: *we have set the date for our wedding.* **8.** to prescribe or allot (an undertaking, course of study, etc.): *the examiners have set "Paradise Lost."* **9.** to arrange in a particular fashion, esp. an attractive one: *she set her hair; the jeweller set the diamonds in silver.* **10.** (of clothes) to hang or fit (well or badly) when worn. **11.** Also: **set to music.** to provide music for (a poem or other text to be sung). **12.** Also: **set up.** *Printing.* to arrange or produce (type, film, etc.) from (text or copy); compose. **13.** to arrange (a stage, television studio, etc.) with scenery and props. **14.** to describe or present (a scene or the background to a literary work, story, etc.) in words: *his novel is set in Russia.* **15.** to present as a model of good or bad behaviour (esp. in the phrases **set an example, set a good example, set a bad example**). **16.** (foll. by *on* or *by*) to value (something) at a specified price or estimation of worth: *he set a high price on his services.* **17.** (foll. by *at*) to price (the value of something) at a specified sum: *he set his services at £300.* **18.** (*also intr.*) to give or be given a particular direction: *his course was set to the East.* **19.** (*also intr.*) to rig (a sail) or (of a sail) to be rigged so as to catch the wind. **20.** (*intr.*) (of the sun, moon, etc.) to disappear beneath the horizon. **21.** to leave (dough, etc.) in one place so that it may prove. **22.** to sharpen (a cutting blade) by grinding or honing the angle adjacent to the cutting edge. **23.** to displace alternate teeth of (a saw) to opposite sides of the blade in order to increase the cutting efficiency. **24.** to sink (the head of a nail) below the surface surrounding it by using a nail set. **25.** *Computer technol.* to give (a binary circuit) the value 1, so that it can be operated when required. Compare **reset** (sense 2). **26.** (of plants) to produce (fruits, seeds, etc.) after pollination or (of fruits or seeds) to develop after pollination. **27.** to plant (seeds, seedlings, etc.). **28.** to place (a hen) on (eggs) for the purpose of incubation. **29.** (*intr.*) (of a gun dog) to turn in the direction of game, indicating its presence. **30.** *Bridge.* to defeat (one's opponents) in their attempt to make a contract. **31.** a dialect word for **sit. 32. set eyes on.** to see. *~n.* **33.** the act of setting or the state of being set. **34.** a condition of firmness or hardness. **35.** bearing, carriage, or posture: *the set of a gun dog when pointing.* **36.** the fit or hang of a garment, esp. when worn. **37.** the scenery and other props used in and identifying the location of a dramatic production. **38.** Also called: **set width.** *Printing.* **a.** the width of the body of a piece of type. **b.** the width of the lines of type in a page or column. **39.** *Nautical.* **a.** the cut of the sails or the arrangement of the sails, spars, rigging, etc., of a vessel. **b.** the direction from which a wind is blowing or towards which a tide or current is moving. **40.** *Psychol.* a temporary bias disposing an organism to react to a stimulus in one way rather than in others. **41.** a seedling, cutting, or similar part that is ready for planting: *onion sets.* **42.** a blacksmith's tool with a short head similar to a cold chisel set transversely onto a handle and used, when struck with a hammer, for cutting off lengths of iron bars. **43.** See **nail set. 44.** a variant spelling of **sett.** *~adj.* **45.** fixed or established by authority or agreement: *set hours of work.* **46.** (*usually postpositive*) rigid or inflexible: *she is set in her ways.* **47.** conventional, artificial, or stereotyped, rather than spontaneous: *she made her apology in set phrases.* **48.** (*postpositive;* foll. by *on* or *upon*) resolute in intention: *he is set upon marrying.* **49.** (of a book, etc.) prescribed for students' preparation for an examination. ~See also **set about, set against, set aside, set back, set down, set forth, set in, set off, set on, set out, set to, set up.** [Old English *settan,* causative of *sittan* to SIT; related to Old Frisian *setta,* Old High German *sezzan*]

set[2] (sɛt) *n.* **1.** a number of objects or people grouped or belonging together, often forming a unit or having certain features or characteristics in common: *a set of coins; John is in the top set for maths.* **2.** a group of people who associate together, etc., esp. a clique: *he's part of the jet set.* **3.** Also called: **class.** *Maths.* a collection of numbers, quantities, objects, etc., that have at least one common property or characteristic: *the set of positive integers.* **4.** any apparatus that receives or transmits television or radio signals. **5.** *Tennis, squash, etc.* one of the units of a match, in tennis one in which one player or pair of players must win at least six games. **6. a.** the number of couples required for a formation dance such as a quadrille. **b.** a series of figures that made up a formation dance. **7. make a dead set at. a.** to attack by arguing or ridiculing. **b.** (of a woman) to try to gain the attention and affections of (a man). *~vb.* **sets, set·ting, set. 8.** (*intr.*) (in square dancing and country dancing) to perform a sequence of steps while facing towards another dancer: *set to your partners.* **9.** (*usually tr.*) to divide into sets: *in this school we set our older pupils for English.* [C14 (in the obsolete sense: a religious sect): from Old French *sette,* from Latin *secta* SECT; later sense development influenced by the verb SET[1]]

SET *or* **S.E.T.** (in Britain) *abbrev. for* selective employment tax: an employment payroll tax, first levied in 1966 and replaced by VAT in 1973.

se·ta ('siːtə) *n., pl.* **·tae** (-tiː). (in invertebrates and some plants) any bristle or bristle-like appendage. [C18: from Latin] —**se·ta·ceous** (sɪ'teɪʃəs) *adj.* —**se·'ta·ceous·ly** *adv.* —'**se·tal** *adj.*

set a·bout *vb.* (*intr., prep.*) **1.** to start or begin. **2.** to attack physically or verbally.

set a·gainst *vb.* (*tr., prep.*) **1.** to balance or compare: *to set a person's faults against his virtues.* **2.** to cause to be hostile or unfriendly to.

set a·side *vb.* (*tr., adv.*) **1.** to reserve for a special purpose; put to one side. **2.** to discard, dismiss, or quash.

set back *vb.* (*tr., adv.*) **1.** to hinder; impede. **2.** *Informal.* to cost (a person) a specified amount. *~n.* **set·back. 3.** anything that serves to hinder or impede. **4.** a recession in the upper part of a high building, esp. one that increases the daylight at lower levels. **5.** Also called: **offset, setoff.** a steplike shelf where a wall is reduced in thickness.

set chis·el *n.* another name for **cold chisel.**

set down *vb.* (*tr., adv.*) **1.** to write down or record. **2.** to judge, consider, or regard: *he set him down as an idiot.* **3.** (foll. by *to*) to ascribe; attribute: *his attitude was set down to his illness.* **4.** to reprove; rebuke. **5.** to snub; dismiss. **6.** *Brit.* to allow (passengers) to alight from a bus, taxi, etc.

se ten·ant *French.* (sə tə'nɑ̃) *adj.* **1.** denoting two postage stamps of different face values and sometimes of different designs in an unseparated pair. *~n.* **2.** such a pair of stamps. [literally: holding together]

set forth *vb.* (*adv.*) *Formal or archaic.* **1.** (*tr.*) to state, express, or utter: *he set forth his objections.* **2.** (*intr.*) to start out on a journey: *the expedition set forth on the first of July.*

Seth (sɛθ) *n. Old Testament.* Adam's third son, given by God in place of the murdered Abel (Genesis 4:25).

se·tif·er·ous (sɪ'tɪfərəs) or **se·tig·er·ous** (sɪ'tɪdʒərəs) *adj. Biology.* bearing bristles. [C19: see SETA, -FEROUS, -GEROUS]

se·ti·form ('siːtɪˌfɔːm) *adj. Biology.* shaped like a seta.

set in *vb.* (*intr., adv.*) **1.** to become established: *the winter has set in.* **2.** (of wind) to blow or (of current) to move towards shore. *~adj.* **set-in. 3.** (of a part) made separately and then added to a larger whole: *a set-in sleeve.*

set·line ('sɛtˌlaɪn) *n.* any of various types of fishing line that consist of a long line suspended across a stream, between buoys, etc., and having shorter hooked and baited lines attached. See **trawl** (sense 2), **trotline.**

set off *vb.* (*adv.*) **1.** (*intr.*) to embark on a journey. **2.** (*tr.*) to cause (a person) to act or do something, such as laugh or tell stories. **3.** (*tr.*) to cause to explode. **4.** (*tr.*) to act as a foil or contrast to, esp. so as to improve: *that brooch sets your dress off well.* **5.** (*tr.*) *Accounting.* to cancel a credit on (one account) against a debit on another, both of which are in the name of the same person, enterprise, etc. **6.** (*intr.*) to bring a claim by way of setoff. *~n.* **set·off. 7.** anything that serves as a counterbalance. **8.** anything that serves to contrast with or enhance something else; foil. **9.** another name for **setback** (sense 5). **10.** *Chiefly U.S.* a counterbalancing debt or claim offered by a debtor against a creditor. **11.** a cross claim brought by a debtor that partly offsets the creditor's claim. See also **counterclaim.**

set-off *n. Printing.* a fault in which ink is transferred from a heavily inked or undried printed sheet to the sheet next to it in a pile. Also called (esp. Brit.): **offset.**

Se·ton ('siːtᵊn) *n.* **Er·nest Thomp·son.** 1860–1946, U.S. author and illustrator of animal books, born in England.

set on *vb.* **1.** (*prep.*) to attack or cause to attack: *they set the dogs on him; three thugs set on him.* **2.** (*tr., adv.*) to instigate or incite; urge: *he set the child on to demand food.*

Se·to Nai·kai ('sɛtəʊ 'naɪkaɪ) *n.* transliteration of the Japanese name for the **Inland Sea.**

se·tose ('siːtəʊs) *adj. Biology.* covered with setae; bristly. [C17: from Latin *saetōsus,* from *saeta* a bristle]

set out *vb.* (*adv., mainly tr.*) **1.** to present, arrange, or display: *he set the flowers out in the vase.* **2.** to give a full account of; explain exactly: *he set out the matter in full.* **3.** to plan or lay out (a garden, etc.). **4.** (*intr.*) to begin or embark on an undertaking, esp. a journey.

set piece *n.* **1.** a work of literature, music, etc., often having a conventional or prescribed theme, intended to create an impressive effect. **2.** a piece of scenery built to stand independently as part of a stage set. **3.** a display of fireworks.

set point *n. Tennis, etc.* a point that would enable one side to win a set.

set+screw ('sɛt,skru:) *n.* a screw that fits into the boss or hub of a wheel, coupling, cam, etc., and prevents motion of the part relative to the shaft on which it is mounted.

set square *n.* a thin flat piece of plastic, metal, etc., in the shape of a right-angled triangle, used in technical drawing.

sett *or* **set** (sɛt) *n.* **1.** a small rectangular paving block made of stone, such as granite, used to provide a durable road surface. Compare **cobblestone. 2.** the burrow of a badger. [C19: variant of SET[1] (n.)]

set+tee (sɛ'ti:) *n.* a seat, for two or more people, with a back and usually with arms. [C18: changed from SETTLE[2]]

set+ter ('sɛtə) *n.* any of various breeds of large gundog. See **English setter, Gordon setter, Irish setter.**

set the·o·ry *n. Maths.* the branch of mathematics concerned with the properties and interrelationships of sets.

set+ting ('sɛtɪŋ) *n.* **1.** the surroundings in which something is set; scene. **2.** the scenery, properties, or background, used to create the location for a stage play, film, etc. **3.** *Music.* a composition consisting of a certain text and music provided or arranged for it. **4.** the metal mounting and surround of a gem: *diamonds in an antique gold setting.* **5.** the tableware, cutlery, etc., for a single place at table. **6.** a clutch of eggs in a bird's nest, esp. a clutch of hen's eggs.

set+ting lo+tion *n.* a perfumed solution of gum or a synthetic resin in a solvent, used in hairdressing to make a set last longer.

set+ting rule *n. Printing.* a metal strip used in the hand composition of type in a stick to separate the line being set from the previous one.

set+tle[1] ('sɛtᵊl) *vb.* **1.** (*tr.*) to put in order; arrange in a desired state or condition: *he settled his affairs before he died.* **2.** to arrange or be arranged in a fixed or comfortable position: *he settled himself by the fire.* **3.** (*intr.*) to come to rest or a halt: *a bird settled on the hedge.* **4.** to take up or cause to take up residence: *the family settled in the country.* **5.** to establish or become established in a way of life, job, residence, etc. **6.** (*tr.*) to migrate to and form a community; colonize. **7.** to make or become quiet, calm, or stable. **8.** (*intr.*) to be cast or spread; come down: *fog settled over a wide area.* **9.** to make (a liquid) clear or (of a liquid) to become clear; clarify. **10.** to cause (sediment) to sink to the bottom, as in a liquid, or (of sediment) to sink thus. **11.** to subside or cause to subside and become firm or compact: *the dust settled.* **12.** (sometimes foll. by *up*) to pay off or account for (a bill, debt, etc.). **13.** (*tr.*) to decide, conclude, or dispose of: *to settle an argument.* **14.** (*intr.;* often foll. by *on* or *upon*) to agree or fix: *to settle upon a plan.* **15.** (*tr.;* usually foll. by *on* or *upon*) to secure (title, property, etc.) to a person, as by making a deed of settlement, will, etc.: *he settled his property on his wife.* **16.** to determine (a legal dispute, etc.) by agreement of the parties without resort to court action (esp. in the phrase **settle out of court**). [Old English *setlan;* related to Dutch *zetelen;* see SETTLE[2]] —'**set+tle+a·ble** *adj.*

set+tle[2] ('sɛtᵊl) *n.* a seat, for two or more people, usually made of wood with a high back and arms, and sometimes having a storage space in the boxlike seat. [Old English *setl;* related to Old Saxon, Old High German *sezzal*]

set+tle down *vb.* (*adv., mainly intr.*) **1.** (*also tr.*) to make or become quiet and orderly. **2.** (often foll. by *to*) to apply oneself diligently: *please settle down to work.* **3.** to adopt an orderly and routine way of life, take up a permanent post, etc., esp. after marriage.

set+tle for *vb.* (*intr., prep.*) to accept or agree to in spite of dispute or dissatisfaction.

set+tle in *vb.* (*adv.*) to become or help to become adapted to and at ease in a new home, environment, etc.

set+tle+ment ('sɛtᵊlmənt) *n.* **1.** the act or state of settling or being settled. **2.** the establishment of a new region; colonization. **3.** a place newly settled; colony. **4.** a collection of dwellings forming a community, esp. on a frontier. **5.** a community formed by members of a group, esp. of a religious sect. **6.** a public building used to provide educational and general welfare facilities for persons living in deprived areas. **7.** a subsidence of all or part of a structure. **8.** an adjustment or agreement reached in matters of finance, business, etc. **9.** *Law.* **a.** a conveyance, usually to trustees, of property to be enjoyed by several persons in succession. **b.** the deed or other instrument conveying such property. **c.** the determination of a dispute, etc., by mutual agreement without resorting to legal proceedings.

set+tler ('sɛtlə) *n.* a person who settles in a new country or a colony.

set+tle with *vb.* (*prep.*) **1.** (*intr.*) to pay a debt or bill to. **2.** (*intr.*) to make an agreement with. **3.** to get one's revenge for (a wrong or injury) with (a person).

set+tlings ('sɛtlɪŋz) *pl. n.* any matter or substance that has settled at the bottom of a liquid; sediment; dregs.

set+tlor ('sɛtlə) *n. Law.* a person who settles property on someone.

set to *vb.* (*intr., adv.*) **1.** to begin working. **2.** to start fighting. ~*n.* **set-to. 3.** *Informal.* a brief disagreement or fight.

Se+tú+bal (*Portuguese* sə'tuβal) *n.* a port in SW Portugal, on **Setúbal Bay** south of Lisbon: an earthquake in 1755 destroyed most of the old town. Pop.: 64 531 (1970).

set up *vb.* (*adv., mainly tr.*) **1.** (*also intr.*) to put into a position of power, etc. **2.** (*also intr.*) to begin or enable (someone) to begin (a new venture), as by acquiring or providing means, equipment, etc. **3.** to build or construct: *to set up a shed.* **4.** to raise, cause, or produce: *to set up a wail.* **5.** to advance or propose: *to set up a theory.* **6.** to restore the health of: *the sea air will set you up again.* **7.** to establish (a record). **8.** *Austral. informal.* to cause (a person) to be blamed, accused, etc. **9.** *Informal.* **a.** to provide (drinks, etc.) for: *set 'em up, Joe!* **b.** to pay for the drinks of: *I'll set up the next round.* **10.** *Printing.* another term for **set**[1] (sense 38). ~*n.* **set+up. 11.** *Informal.* the way in which anything is organized or arranged. **12.** *Slang, chiefly U.S.* an event the result of which is prearranged: *it's a setup.* **13.** a prepared arrangement of materials, machines, etc., for a job or undertaking. **14.** a station at which a surveying instrument, esp. a theodolite, is set up. **15.** *Films.* the position of the camera, microphones, and performers at the beginning of a scene. ~*adj.* **set-up. 16.** physically well-built.

set width *n.* another name for **set**[1] (sense 38).

Seu·rat (*French* sœ'ra) *n.* **Georges** (ʒɔrʒ). 1859–91, French neoimpressionist painter. He developed the pointillist technique of painting, characterized by brilliant luminosity, as in *Dimanche à la Grande-Jatte* (1886).

Se+van (sɛ'vɑ:n) *n.* **Lake.** a lake in the SW Soviet Union, in the N Armenian SSR at an altitude of 1914 m (6279 ft.). Area: 1417 sq. km (547 sq. miles).

Se+vas+to+pol (*Russian* sɪvas'tɔpəlj) *n.* a port and resort in the SW Soviet Union, in the S Ukrainian SSR on the Black Sea: captured and destroyed by British, French, and Turkish forces after a siege of 11 months (1854–55) during the Crimean War; taken by the Germans after a siege of 8 months (1942) during World War II; a major naval base. Pop.: 267 000 (1975 est.). English name: **Sebastopol.**

sev+en ('sɛvᵊn) *n.* **1.** the cardinal number that is the sum of six and one and is a prime number. See also **number** (sense 1). **2.** a numeral 7, VII, etc., representing this number. **3.** the amount or quantity that is one greater than six. **4.** anything representing, represented by, or consisting of seven units, such as a playing card with seven symbols on it. **5.** Also called: **seven o'clock.** seven hours after noon or midnight. ~*determiner.* **6. a.** amounting to seven: *seven swans a-swimming.* **b.** (*as pronoun*): *you've eaten seven already.* ~Related prefixes: **hepta-, septi-.** [Old English *seofon;* related to Gothic *sibun,* German *sieben,* Old Norse *sjau,* Latin *septem,* Greek *hepta,* Sanskrit *saptá*]

Sev+en a·gainst Thebes *pl. n. Greek myth.* the seven members of an expedition undertaken to regain for Polynices, a son of Oedipus, his share in the throne of Thebes from his usurping brother Eteocles. The seven are usually listed as Polynices, Adrastus, Amphiaraus, Capaneus, Hippomedon, Tydeus, and Parthenopaeus. The campaign failed and the warring brothers killed each other in single combat before the Theban walls. See also **Adrastus.**

sev+en dead+ly sins *pl. n.* a fuller name for the **deadly sins.**

sev+en+fold ('sɛvᵊn,fəʊld) *adj.* **1.** equal to or having seven times as many or as much. **2.** composed of seven parts. ~*adv.* **3.** by or up to seven times as many or as much.

Sev+en Hills of Rome *pl. n.* the hills on which the ancient city of Rome was built: the Palatine, Capitoline, Quirinal, Caelian, Aventine, Esquiline, and Viminal.

sev+ens ('sɛvᵊnz) *n.* a Rugby Union match played with seven players on each side.

sev+en seas *pl. n.* the oceans of the world considered as the N and S Pacific, the N and S Atlantic, and the Arctic, Antarctic, and Indian Oceans.

sev+en+teen ('sɛvᵊn'ti:n) *n.* **1.** the cardinal number that is the sum of ten and seven and is a prime number. See also **number** (sense 1). **2.** a numeral 17, XVII, etc., representing this number. **3.** the amount or quantity that is seven more than ten. **4.** something represented by, representing, or consisting of 17 units. ~*determiner.* **5. a.** amounting to seventeen: *seventeen attempts.* **b.** (*as pronoun*): *seventeen were sold.* [Old English *seofontīene;* see SEVEN, -TEEN]

sev+en+teenth ('sɛvᵊn'ti:nθ) *adj.* **1.** (*usually prenominal*) **a.** coming after the sixteenth in numbering or counting order, position, time, etc.; being the ordinal number of *seventeen:* often written 17th. **b.** (*as n.*): *the ship docks on the seventeenth.* ~*n.* **2. a.** one of 17 approximately equal parts of something. **b.** (*as modifier*): *a seventeenth part.* **3.** the fraction equal to one divided by 17 (1/17).

sev+en·teen-year lo+cust *n.* an E North American cicada, *Magicicada septendecim,* appearing in great numbers at infrequent intervals because its nymphs take 13 or 17 years to mature. Also called: **periodical cicada.**

sev+enth ('sɛvᵊnθ) *adj.* **1.** (*usually prenominal*) **a.** coming after the sixth and before the eighth in numbering or counting order, position, time, etc.; being the ordinal number of *seven:* often written 7th. **b.** (*as n.*): *she left on the seventh; he was the seventh to arrive.* ~*n.* **2. a.** one of seven equal or nearly equal parts of an object, quantity, measurement, etc. **b.** (*as modifier*): *a seventh part.* **3.** the fraction equal to one divided by seven (1/7). **4.** *Music.* **a.** the interval between one note and another seven notes away from it counting inclusively along the diatonic scale. **b.** one of two notes constituting such an interval in relation to the other. See also **major** (sense 11), **minor** (sense 4), **interval** (sense 5). **c.** short for **seventh chord.** ~*adv.* **5.** Also: **seventhly.** after the sixth person, position, event, etc. ~ **6.** *sentence connector.* Also: **seventhly.** as the seventh point: linking what follows to the previous statements, as in a speech or argument.

sev+enth chord *n. Music.* a chord consisting of a triad with a seventh added above the root. See **dominant seventh, diminished seventh, major seventh.**

Sev·enth-Day Ad+ven+tist *n. Protestant.* a member of that branch of the Adventists which constituted itself as a separate body after the expected Second Coming of Christ failed to be realized in 1844. They are strongly Protestant, believe that Christ's coming is imminent, and observe Saturday instead of Sunday as their Sabbath.

sev+enth heav+en *n.* **1.** the final state of eternal bliss, esp. according to Talmudic and Muslim eschatology. **2.** a state of supreme happiness.

sev+en+ti+eth ('sɛvᵊntɪɪθ) *adj.* **1.** (*usually prenominal*) **a.** being the ordinal number of *seventy* in numbering or counting order, position, time, etc.: often written 70th. **b.** (*as n.*): *the seventieth in line.* ~*n.* **2. a.** one of 70 approximately equal parts of something. **b.** (*as modifier*): *a seventieth part.* **3.** the fraction equal to one divided by 70 (1/70).

sev+en+ty ('sɛvᵊntɪ) *n., pl.* **+ties. 1.** the cardinal number that is the product of ten and seven. See also **number** (sense 1). **2.** a numeral 70, LXX, etc., representing this number. **3.** (*pl.*) the numbers 70–79, esp. the 70th to the 79th year of a person's life or of a particular century. **4.** the amount or quantity that is seven times as big as ten. **5.** something represented by, representing, or consisting of 70 units. ~*determiner.* **6. a.** amounting to seventy: *the seventy varieties of fabric.* **b.** (*as pronoun*): *to invite seventy to the wedding.*

sev·en-up *n.* a card game in which the lead to each round determines the trump suit. Also called: **all fours, pitch.**

Sev+en Won+ders of the World *pl. n.* the seven structures considered by ancient and medieval scholars to be the most wondrous of the ancient world. The list varies, but generally consists of the Pyramids of Egypt, the Hanging Gardens of Babylon, Phidias' statue of Zeus at Olympia, the temple of Artemis at Ephesus, the mausoleum of Halicarnassus, the Colossus of Rhodes, and the Pharos (or lighthouse) of Alexandria.

sev·en-year itch *n.* **1.** *Pathol.* an informal name for **scabies. 2.** *Informal.* a tendency towards infidelity, traditionally said to begin after about seven years of marriage.

Sev+en Years' War *n.* the war (1756–63) of Britain and Prussia, who emerged in the ascendant, against France and Austria, resulting from commercial and colonial rivalry between Britain and France and from the conflict in Germany between Prussia and Austria.

sev+er ('sɛvə) *vb.* **1.** to put or be put apart; separate. **2.** to divide or be divided into parts. **3.** (*tr.*) to break off or dissolve (a tie, relationship, etc.). [C14 *severen,* from Old French *severer,* from Latin *sēparāre* to SEPARATE]

sev+er+a·ble ('sɛvərəbᵊl) *adj.* **1.** able to be severed. **2.** *Law.* capable of being separated, as a clause in an agreement: *a severable contract.*

sev+er+al ('sɛvrəl) *determiner.* **1. a.** more than a few; an indefinite small number: *several people objected.* **b.** (*as pronoun; functioning as pl.*): *several of them know.* ~*adj.* **2.** (*prenominal*) various; separate: *the members with their several occupations.* **3.** (*prenominal*) distinct; different: *three several times.* **4.** *Law.* capable of being dealt with separately; not shared. Compare **joint** (sense 14). [C15: via Anglo-French from Medieval Latin *sēparālis,* from Latin *sēpār,* from *sēparāre* to SEPARATE]

sev+er+al+ly ('sɛvrəlɪ) *adv. Archaic or literary.* **1.** separately, individually, or distinctly. **2.** each in turn; respectively.

sev+er+al+ty ('sɛvrəltɪ) *n., pl.* **+ties. 1.** the state of being several or separate. **2.** (usually preceded by *in*) *Property law.* the tenure of property, esp. land, in a person's own right and not jointly with another or others.

sev+er+ance ('sɛvərəns) *n.* **1.** the act of severing or state of being severed. **2.** a separation. **3.** *Law.* the division into separate parts of a joint estate, contract, etc.

sev+er+ance pay *n.* compensation paid by a firm to employees for loss of employment.

se+vere (sɪ'vɪə) *adj.* **1.** rigorous or harsh in the treatment of others; strict: *a severe parent.* **2.** serious in appearance or manner; stern. **3.** critical or dangerous: *a severe illness.* **4.** causing misery or discomfort by its harshness: *severe weather.* **5.** strictly restrained in appearance; austere: *a severe way of dressing.* **6.** hard to endure, perform, or accomplish: *a severe test.* **7.** rigidly precise or exact. [C16: from Latin *sevērus*] —**se+'vere+ly** *adv.* —**se+'vere+ness** *or* **se+ver+i·ty** (sɪ'vɛrɪtɪ) *n.*

Sev+ern ('sɛvᵊn) *n.* **1.** a river in E Wales and W England, rising in Powys and flowing northeast and east into England, then south to the Bristol Channel: the longest river in Great Britain. Length: about 290 km (180 miles). **2.** a river in SE central Canada, in Ontario, flowing northeast to Hudson Bay. Length: about 676 km (420 miles).

Se+ver+na+ya Zem+lya (*Russian* 'sjevɪrnəjə zɪm'lja) *n.* an archipelago in the Arctic Ocean off the coast of the N central Soviet Union.

Se·ve·rus (sɪ'vɪərəs) *n.* **Lu·ci·us Sep·ti·mi·us** (sɛp'tɪmɪəs). 146–211 A.D., Roman soldier and emperor (193–211). He waged war successfully against the Parthians (197–202) and spent his last years in Britain (208–11).

Sé·vi·gné (*French* sevi'ɲe) *n.* **Mar·quise de,** title of *Marie de Rabutin-Ghantal.* 1626–96, French letter writer. Her correspondence with her daughter and others provides a vivid account of society during the reign of Louis XIV.

Se+ville (sə'vɪl) *n.* a port in SW Spain, on the Guadalquivir River: chief town of S Spain under the Vandals and Visigoths (5th–8th centuries); centre of Spanish colonial trade (16th–17th centuries); tourist centre. Pop.: 548 072 (1970). Ancient name: **Hispalis.** Spanish name: **Se+vi+lla** (se'βiʎa).

Se+ville or+ange *n.* **1.** an orange tree, *Citrus aurantium,* of tropical and semitropical regions: grown for its bitter fruit, which is used to make marmalade. **2.** the fruit of this tree. ~Also called: **bitter orange.**

Sèvres (*French* 'sɛ:vr) *n.* porcelain ware manufactured at Sèvres, near Paris, from 1756, characterized by the use of clear colours and elaborate decorative detail.

sew (səʊ) *vb.* **sews, sew+ing, sewed; sewn** *or* **sewed. 1.** to join or decorate (pieces of fabric, etc.) by means of a thread repeatedly passed through with a needle or similar implement. **2.** (*tr.;* often foll. by *on* or *up*) to attach, fasten, or close by sewing. **3.** (*tr.*) to make (a garment, etc.) by sewing. ~See also **sew up.** [Old English *sēowan;* related to Old Norse *sȳja,* Gothic *siujan,* Old High German *siuwen,* Latin *suere* to sew, Sanskrit *sīvjati* he sews]

sew+age ('su:ɪdʒ) *n.* waste matter from domestic or industrial establishments that is carried away in sewers or drains for dumping or conversion into a form that is not toxic. [C19: back formation from SEWER[1]]

sew+age farm *n.* a place where sewage is treated, esp. for use as manure.

se+wan ('si:wən) *n.* a variant spelling of **seawan.**

Sew·ard ('sju:əd) *n.* **Wil·liam Hen·ry.** 1801–72, U.S. statesman; secretary of state (1861–69). He was a leading opponent of slavery and was responsible for the purchase of Alaska (1867).

Sew+ard Pen+in+su+la *n.* a peninsula of W Alaska, on the Bering Strait. Length: about 290 km (180 miles).

Sew·ell ('su:əl) *n.* **Hen·ry.** 1807–79, New Zealand statesman, born in England: first prime minister of New Zealand (1856).

se+wel+lel (sɪ'wɛləl) *n.* another name for **mountain beaver** (see **beaver**[1] (sense 3)). [C19: probably from Chinook]

sew+er[1] ('su:ə) *n.* **1.** a drain or pipe, esp. one that is underground, used to carry away surface water or sewage. ~*vb.* **2.** (*tr.*) to provide with sewers. [C15: from Old French *esseveur,* from *essever* to drain, from Vulgar Latin *exaquāre* (unattested), from Latin EX- *aqua* water]

sew+er[2] ('səʊə) *n.* a person or thing that sews.

sew+er[3] ('su:ə) *n.* (in medieval England) a servant of high rank in charge of the serving of meals and the seating of guests. [C14: shortened from Anglo-French *asseour,* from Old French *asseoir* to cause to sit, from Latin *assidēre,* from *sedēre* to sit]

sew+er+age ('su:ərɪdʒ) *n.* **1.** an arrangement of sewers. **2.** the removal of surface water or sewage by means of sewers. **3.** another word for **sewage.**

sew+ing ('səʊɪŋ) *n.* **a.** a piece of cloth, etc., that is sewn or to be sewn. **b.** (*as modifier*): *sewing basket.*

sew+ing ma+chine *n.* any machine designed to sew material. It is now usually driven by electric motor but is sometimes operated by a foot treadle or by hand.

sewn (səʊn) *vb.* a past participle of **sew.**

sew up *vb.* (*tr., adv.*) **1.** to fasten or mend completely by sewing. **2.** *U.S.* to acquire sole use or control of. **3.** *Informal.* to complete or negotiate successfully: *to sew up a deal.*

sex (sɛks) *n.* **1.** the sum of the characteristics that distinguish organisms on the basis of their reproductive function. **2.** either of the two categories, male or female, into which organisms are placed on this basis. **3.** *Informal.* short for **sexual intercourse. 4.** feelings or behaviour resulting from the urge to gratify the sexual instinct. **5.** sexual matters in general. ~*modifier.* **6.** of or concerning sexual matters: *sex education; sex hygiene.* **7.** based on or arising from the difference between the sexes: *sex discrimination.* ~*vb.* **8.** (*tr.*) to ascertain the sex of. [C14: from Latin *sexus;* compare *secāre* to divide]

sex- *combining form.* six: *sexcentennial.* [from Latin]

sex·a+ge·nar+i·an (ˌsɛksədʒɪ'nɛərɪən) *n.* **1.** a person from 60 to 69 years old. ~*adj.* **2.** being from 60 to 69 years old. **3.** of or relating to a sexagenarian. [C18: from Latin *sexāgēnārius,* from *sexāgēnī* sixty each, from *sexāgintā* sixty] —**sex+ag+e·nar·y** (sɛk'sædʒɪnərɪ) *adj., n.*

Sex·a+ges·i·ma (ˌsɛksə'dʒɛsɪmə) *n.* the second Sunday before Lent. [C16: from Latin: sixtieth, from *sexāgintā* sixty]

sex·a+ges·i·mal (ˌsɛksə'dʒɛsɪməl) *adj.* **1.** relating to or based on the number 60: *sexagesimal measurement of angles.* ~*n.* **2.** a fraction in which the denominator is some power of 60; a sixtieth.

sex+an+gu·lar (sɛks'æŋgjʊlə) *adj.* another name for **hexagonal.** —**sex+'an+gu·lar+ly** *adv.*

sex ap+peal *n.* the quality or power of attracting the opposite sex.

sex+cen+te·nar·y (ˌsɛksɛn'ti:nərɪ) *adj.* **1.** of or relating to 600 or a period of 600 years. **2.** of, relating to, or celebrating a 600th anniversary. ~*n., pl.* **+nar·ies. 3.** a 600th anniversary or its celebration. [C18: from Latin *sexcentēnī* six hundred each]

sex chro+mo+some *n.* either of the chromosomes determining the sex of animals. See also **X-chromosome, Y-chromosome.**

sexed (sɛkst) *adj.* **1.** (*in combination*) having a specified degree of sexuality: *under-sexed.* **2.** of, relating to, or having sexual differentiation.

sex+en+ni·al (sɛk'sɛnɪəl) *adj.* **1.** occurring once every six years or over a period of six years. ~*n.* **2.** a sixth anniversary. [C17: from Latin *sexennis* of six years, from *sex* six + *annus* a year] —**sex+'en+ni·al·ly** *adv.*

sex hor+mone *n.* an animal hormone affecting development and growth of reproductive organs and related parts.
sex+ism ('sɛksɪzəm) *n.* discrimination on the basis of sex, esp. the oppression of women by men. —'**sex+ist** *n., adj.*
sex·i+va+lent *or* **sex·a+va+lent** (ˌsɛksɪ'veɪlənt) *adj. Chem.* another word for **hexavalent.**
sex+less ('sɛkslɪs) *adj.* **1.** having or showing no sexual differentiation. **2.** having no sexual desires. **3.** sexually unattractive. —'**sex+less+ly** *adv.* —'**sex+less+ness** *n.*
sex-lim·i·ted *adj. Genetics.* of or designating a character or the gene producing it that appears in one sex only.
sex link+age *n. Genetics.* the condition in which a particular gene is located on a sex chromosome, esp. on the X-chromosome, so that the character controlled by the gene is associated with either of the sexes. —'**sex+ˌlinked** *adj.*
sex+ol+o·gy (sɛk'sɒlədʒɪ) *n.* the study of sexual behaviour in human beings. —**sex+'ol·o+gist** *n.* —**sex·o+log·i+cal** (ˌsɛksə'lɒdʒɪkᵊl) *adj.*
sex+par+tite (sɛks'pɑːtaɪt) *adj.* **1.** (esp. of vaults, arches, etc.) divided into or composed of six parts. **2.** maintained by or involving six participants or groups of participants.
sex+pot ('sɛksˌpɒt) *n. Slang.* a person, esp. a young woman, considered as being sexually very attractive.
sext (sɛkst) *n. Chiefly R.C. Church.* the fourth of the seven canonical hours of the divine office or the prayers prescribed for it: originally the sixth hour of the day (noon). [C15: from Church Latin *sexta hōra* the sixth hour]
sex+tain ('sɛksteɪn) *n.* another word for **sestina.** [C17: from obsolete French *sestine* SESTINA, but also influenced by obsolete *sixain* stanza of six lines]
sex+tan ('sɛkstən) *adj.* (of a fever) marked by paroxysms that recur every fifth day. [C17: from Medieval Latin *sextana* (*febris*) (fever) of the sixth (day)]
Sex+tans ('sɛkstənz) *n., Latin genitive* **Sex+tan+tis** (sɛks'tæntɪs). a faint constellation lying on the celestial equator close to Leo and Hydra. [New Latin: SEXTANT]
sex+tant ('sɛkstənt) *n.* **1.** an optical instrument used in navigation and consisting of a telescope through which a sighting of a heavenly body is taken, with protractors for determining its angular distance above the horizon or from another heavenly body. **2.** a sixth part of a circle having an arc which subtends an angle of 60°. [C17: from Latin *sextāns* one sixth of a unit]
sex+tet *or* **sex+tette** (sɛks'tɛt) *n.* **1.** *Music.* a group of six singers or instrumentalists or a piece of music composed for such a group. **2.** a group of six people or things. [C19: variant of SESTET, with Latinization of *ses-*]
sex+tile ('sɛkstaɪl) *n.* **1.** *Statistics.* one of five actual or notional values of a variable dividing its distribution into six groups with equal frequencies. **2.** *Astrology, astronomy.* an aspect or position of 60° between two planets or other celestial bodies. [C16: from Latin *sextīlis* one sixth (of a circle), from *sextus* sixth]
sex+til+lion (sɛks'tɪljən) *n., pl.* **+lions** *or* **+lion. 1.** (in Britain and Germany) the number represented as one followed by 36 zeros (10^{36}). **2.** (in the U.S. and France) the number represented as one followed by 21 zeros (10^{21}). [C17: from French, from SEX- + *-illion,* on the model of SEPTILLION] —**sex+'til+lionth** *adj., n.*
sex+to ('sɛkstəʊ) *n., pl.* **+tos.** *Bookbinding.* another word for **sixmo.** [C19: from Latin *sextus* sixth]
sex+to+dec·i+mo (ˌsɛkstəʊ'dɛsɪˌməʊ) *n., pl.* **+mos.** *Bookbinding.* another word for **sixteenmo.** [C17: from Latin *sextusdecimus* sixteenth]
sex+ton ('sɛkstən) *n.* **1.** a man employed to act as caretaker of a church and its contents and graveyard, and often also as bell-ringer, gravedigger, etc. **2.** another name for the **burying beetle.** [C14: from Old French *secrestein,* from Medieval Latin *sacristānus* SACRISTAN]
sex+tu+ple ('sɛkstjʊpᵊl) *n.* **1.** a quantity or number six times as great as another. ~*adj.* **2.** six times as much or many; sixfold. **3.** consisting of six parts or members. **4.** (of musical time or rhythm) having six beats per bar. [C17: Latin *sextus* sixth + *-uple,* as in QUADRUPLE]
sex+tup+let ('sɛkstjʊplɪt) *n.* **1.** one of six offspring born at one birth. **2.** a group of six things. **3.** *Music.* a group of six notes played in a time value of four.
sex+tu+pli+cate *n.* (sɛks'tuːpləkɪt, -ˌkeɪt, -'tjuː-, -'tʌp-). **1.** a group or set of six things, esp. identical copies. ~*adj.* (sɛks'tuːpləkɪt, -ˌkeɪt, -'tjuː-, -'tʌp-). **2.** six times as many, much, or often. **3.** *Maths.* raised to the sixth power. ~*vb.* (sɛks'tuːpləˌkeɪt, -'tjuː-, -'tʌp-). **4.** to multiply or become multiplied by six. [C20: from SEXTU(PLE + DU)PLICATE]
sex+u·al ('sɛksjʊəl) *adj.* **1.** of, relating to, or characterized by sex or sexuality. **2.** (of reproduction) characterized by the union of male and female gametes. Compare **asexual** (sense 2). [C17: from Late Latin *sexuālis;* see SEX] —'**sex+u·al+ly** *adv.*
sex+u·al in·ter+course *n.* the act of sexual procreation in which the insertion of the male's erect penis into the female's vagina is followed by rhythmic thrusting usually culminating in orgasm; copulation; coitus.
sex·u·al+i·ty (ˌsɛksjʊ'ælɪtɪ) *n.* **1.** the state or quality of being sexual. **2.** preoccupation with or involvement in sexual matters. **3.** the possession of sexual potency.
sex+u·al re+pro+duc+tion *n.* reproduction involving the fusion of a male and female haploid gamete.
sex+u·al se+lec+tion *n.* an evolutionary process in animals, in which selection by females of males with certain characters, such as large antlers or bright plumage, results in the preservation of these characters in the species.
sex·y ('sɛksɪ) *adj.* **sex·i+er, sex·i+est.** *Informal.* provoking or intended to provoke sexual interest: *a sexy dress; a sexy book.* —'**sex·i+ly** *adv.* —'**sex·i+ness** *n.*
Sey+chelles (seɪ'ʃɛl, -'ʃɛlz) *pl. n.* a group of volcanic islands in the W Indian Ocean: taken by the British from the French in 1744: became an independent republic within the Commonwealth in 1976, incorporating the British Indian Ocean Territory islands of Aldabra, Farquhar and Desroches. Official languages: English and French. Currency: rupee. Capital: Victoria. Pop.: 58 000 (1974 UN est.). Area: 375 sq. km (145 sq. miles).
Sey·fert gal+ax·y ('saɪfət) *n.* any of a class of small spiral galaxies having a very bright nucleus and inconspicuous arms. [C20: named after Carl K. *Seyfert* (died 1960) U.S. astronomer]
Sey+han (seɪ'hɑːn) *n.* another name for **Adana.**
Sey·mour ('siːmɔː) *n.* **Jane.** ?1509–37, third wife of Henry VIII of England; mother of Edward VI.
sf, sf., sfz, *or* **sfz.** *Music. abbrev. for* sforzando.
SF 1. Also: **sf** *abbrev. for* science fiction. ~ **2.** *international car registration for* Finland. [from Finnish *Suomi*]
Sfax (sfæks) *n.* a port in E Tunisia, on the Gulf of Gabès: the second largest town in Tunisia; commercial centre of a phosphate region. Pop.: 215 836 (1966).
sfer+ics ('sfɛrɪks) *n.* the usual U.S. spelling of **spherics**².
Sfor+za (*Italian* 'sfɔrtsa) *n.* **1.** Count **Car·lo** ('karlo). 1873–1952, Italian statesman; leader of the anti-Fascist opposition. **2. Fran·ces·co** (fran'tʃesko). 1401–66, duke of Milan (1450–66). **3.** his father **Gia·co·muz·zo** (ˌdʒako'muttso) or **Mu·zio** ('muttsjo), original name *Attendolo.* 1369–1424, Italian condottiere and founder of the dynasty that ruled Milan (1450–1535). **4. Lo·do·vi·co** (ˌlodo'viːko), called *the Moor.* 1451–1508, duke of Milan (1494–1500), but effective ruler from 1480; patron of Leonardo da Vinci.
sfor+zan+do (sfɔː'tsɑːndəʊ) *or* **sfor+za+to** (sfɔː'tsɑːtəʊ) *Music.* ~*adj., adv.* **1.** to be played with strong initial attack. Abbrev: **sf** ~*n.* **2.** a symbol, mark, etc., such as >, written above a note, indicating this. [C19: from Italian, from *sforzare* to force, from EX-¹ + *forzare,* from Vulgar Latin *fortiāre* (unattested) to FORCE]
sfu+ma+to (sfuː'mɑːtəʊ) *n.* (in painting) a gradual transition between areas of different colour, avoiding sharp outlines. [from Italian, from *sfumato* shaded off, from *sfumare* to shade off, from Latin EX- + *fūmāre* to smoke]
SG (in transformational grammar) *abbrev. for* singular.
SG *or* **S.G.** *abbrev. for* solicitor general.
s.g. *abbrev. for* specific gravity.
sgd. *abbrev. for* signed.
SGP *international car registration for* Singapore.
sgraf+fi+to (sgræ'fiːtəʊ) *n., pl.* **+ti** (-tɪ). **1.** a technique in mural or ceramic decoration in which the top layer of glaze, plaster, etc., is incised with a design to reveal parts of the ground. **2.** such a decoration. **3.** an object decorated in such a way. [C18: from Italian, from *sgraffire* to scratch; see GRAFFITO]
's Gra+ven+ha+ge (ˌsxraːvən'haːxə) *n.* the Dutch name for **The Hague.**
Sgt. *abbrev. for* Sergeant.
Sgt. Maj. *abbrev. for* Sergeant Major.
sh (*spelling pron.* ʃʃʃ) *interj.* an exclamation to request silence or quiet.
sh. *abbrev. for:* **1.** *Stock exchange.* share. **2.** sheep. **3.** *Bookbinding.* sheet.
SHA *Navigation. abbrev. for* sidereal hour angle.
Sha+ba ('ʃɑːbə) *n.* a province of SE Zaire: important for hydroelectric power and rich mineral resources (copper and tin ore). Capital: Lubumbashi. Pop.: 2 753 714 (1970). Area: 496 964 sq. km (191 878 sq. miles). Former name (until 1972): **Katanga.**
Sha+ban *or* **Shaa+ban** (ʃə'bɑːn, ʃɑː-) *n.* the eighth month of the Muslim year. [from Arabic *sha'bān*]
Shab+bat *or* **Shab+bas** (ʃɑː'bɑːt, 'ʃɑːbəs) *n., pl.* **+bat+im** *or* **+ba+sim** (-'bɑːtɪm, -'bɔːsɪm). *Judaism.* another word for the **Sabbath.** [from Hebrew *shabbāth;* see SABBATH]
shab+by ('ʃæbɪ) *adj.* **+bi+er, +bi+est. 1.** threadbare or dilapidated in appearance. **2.** wearing worn and dirty clothes; seedy. **3.** mean, despicable, or unworthy: *shabby treatment.* **4.** dirty or squalid. [C17: from Old English *sceabb* SCAB + -Y¹] —'**shab+bi+ly** *adv.* —'**shab+bi+ness** *n.*
Sha+bu+oth *or* **Sha+vu+ot** (ʃə'vuːəs, -əʊs; *Hebrew* ʃavuː'ɔt) *n.* a Jewish festival, celebrated on the sixth or sixth and seventh days of Sivan to commemorate the revelation of the Law and the giving of the Ten Commandments to Moses. Also called: **Feast of Weeks, Pentecost.** [from Hebrew *shābhū'ōth,* plural of *shābhūā'* week]
shack (ʃæk) *n.* **1.** a roughly built hut. ~*vb.* **2.** See **shack up.** [C19: perhaps from dialect *shackly* ramshackle, from dialect *shack* to shake]
shack+le ('ʃækᵊl) *n.* **1.** (*often pl.*) a metal ring or fastening, usually part of a pair used to secure a person's wrists or ankles; fetter. **2.** (*often pl.*) anything that confines or restricts freedom. **3.** a rope, tether, or hobble for an animal. **4.** a U-shaped bracket, the open end of which is closed by a bolt (**shackle pin**), used for securing ropes, chains, etc. ~*vb.* (*tr.*) **5.** to confine with or as if with shackles. **6.** to fasten or connect with a shackle. [Old English *sceacel;* related to Dutch *schakel,* Old Norse *skokull* wagon pole, Latin *cingere* to surround] —'**shack+ler** *n.*
Shack·le·ton ('ʃækəltən) *n.* Sir **Er·nest Hen·ry.** 1874–1922,

British explorer. He commanded three expeditions to the Antarctic (1907–09; 1914–17; 1921–22), during which the south magnetic pole was located (1909).

shack up *vb.* (*intr., adv.*; usually foll. by *with*) *Slang.* to live or take up residence, esp. with a mistress or lover.

shad (ʃæd) *n., pl.* **shad** *or* **shads.** **1.** any of various herring-like food fishes of the genus *Alosa* and related genera, such as *A. alosa* (**allis shad**) of Europe, that migrate from the sea to freshwater to spawn: family *Clupeidae* (herrings). **2.** any of various similar but unrelated fishes. [Old English *sceadd;* related to Norwegian *skadd,* German *Schade* shad, Old Irish *scatān* herring, Latin *scatēre* to well up]

shad+ber·ry (ˈʃædbərɪ, -brɪ) *n., pl.* **·ries.** another name for **serviceberry** (senses 1, 2).

shad+bush (ˈʃædˌbʊʃ) *n.* another name for **serviceberry** (sense 1).

shad+chan *or* ***schat+chen*** *Yiddish.* (ˈʃatxən) *n., pl.* ***shad+cha+nim, schat+cho+nim*** (ʃatˈxɔnɪm) *or* ***shad+chans, schat+chens.*** a Jewish marriage broker. [from Hebrew *shadhkhān,* from *shiddēkh* to arrange a marriage]

shad+dock (ˈʃædək) *n.* **1.** a tropical rutaceous tree, *Citrus maxima* (or *C. decumana*), grown widely in oriental regions for its yellow grapefruit-like edible fruit. **2.** the fruit of this tree. ~Also called (esp. U.S.): **pomelo.** [C17: named after Captain *Shaddock,* who brought its seed from the East Indies to Jamaica in 1696]

shade (ʃeɪd) *n.* **1.** relative darkness produced by the blocking out of light. **2.** a place made relatively darker or cooler than other areas by the blocking of light, esp. sunlight. **3.** a position of relative obscurity. **4.** something used to provide a shield or protection from a direct source of light, such as a lampshade. **5.** a darker area indicated in a painting, drawing, etc., by shading. **6.** a colour that varies slightly from a standard colour due to a difference in hue, saturation, or luminosity: *a darker shade of green.* **7.** a slight amount: *a shade of difference.* **8.** *Literary.* a ghost. **9.** an archaic word for **shadow.** ~*vb.* (*mainly tr.*) **10.** to screen or protect from heat, light, view, etc. **11.** to make darker or dimmer. **12.** to represent (a darker area) in (a painting, drawing, etc.), by means of hatching, using a darker colour, etc. **13.** (*also intr.*) to change or cause to change slightly. **14.** to lower (a price). [Old English *sceadu;* related to Gothic *skadus,* Old High German *skato,* Old Irish *scāth* shadow, Greek *skotos* darkness, Swedish *skädda* fog] —ˈ**shade+less** *adj.*

shades (ʃeɪdz) *pl. n.* **1.** gathering darkness at nightfall. **2.** a slang word for **sunglasses.** **3.** (*often cap;* preceded by *the*) a literary term for **Hades.** **4.** (foll. by *of*) undertones or suggestions: *shades of my father!*

shad+ing (ˈʃeɪdɪŋ) *n.* the graded areas of tone, lines, dots, etc., indicating light and dark in a painting or drawing.

sha+doof *or* **sha+duf** (ʃəˈduːf) *n.* a mechanism for raising water, consisting of a pivoted pole with a bucket at one end and a counterweight at the other, esp. as used in Egypt and the Near East. [C19: from Egyptian Arabic]

shad+ow (ˈʃædəʊ) *n.* **1.** a dark image or shape cast on a surface by the interception of light rays by an opaque body. **2.** an area of relative darkness. **3.** the dark portions of a picture. **4.** a hint, image, or faint semblance: *beyond a shadow of a doubt.* **5.** a remnant or vestige: *a shadow of one's past self.* **6.** a reflection. **7.** a threatening influence; blight: *a shadow over one's happiness.* **8.** a spectre. **9.** an inseparable companion. **10.** a person who trails another in secret, such as a detective. **11.** *Med.* a dark area on an x-ray film representing an opaque structure or part. **12.** *Archaic or rare.* protection or shelter. **13.** (*modifier*) *Brit.* designating a member or members of the main opposition party in Parliament who would hold ministerial office if their party were in power: *shadow Chancellor; shadow cabinet.* ~*vb.* (*tr.*) **14.** to cast a shadow over. **15.** to make dark or gloomy; blight. **16.** to shade from light. **17.** to follow or trail secretly. **18.** (often foll. by *forth*) to represent vaguely. **19.** *Painting, drawing, etc.* another word for **shade** (sense 12). [Old English *sceadwe,* oblique case of *sceadu* SHADE; related to Dutch *schaduw*] —ˈ**shad+ow+er** *n.* —ˈ**shad+ow+less** *adj.*

shad·ow-box *vb.* (*intr.*) **1.** *Boxing.* to practise blows and footwork against an imaginary opponent. **2.** to act or speak unconvincingly, without saying what one means, etc.: *he's just shadow-boxing.* —ˈ**shad·ow-ˌbox·ing** *n.*

shad+ow+graph (ˈʃædəʊˌgrɑːf, -ˌgræf) *n.* **1.** a silhouette made by casting a shadow, usually of the hands, on a lighted surface. **2.** another name for **radiograph.**

shad+ow mask *n. Television.* a perforated metal sheet mounted close to the phosphor-dotted screen in some colour television tubes. The holes are positioned so that each of the three electron beams strikes the correct phosphor dot producing the required colour mixture in the image.

shad+ow play *n.* a theatrical entertainment using shadows thrown by puppets or actors onto a lighted screen.

shad+ow test *n. Med.* another name for **retinoscopy.**

shad+ow·y (ˈʃædəʊɪ) *adj.* **1.** full of shadows; dark; shady. **2.** resembling a shadow in faintness; vague. **3.** illusory or imaginary. —ˈ**shad+ow+i+ness** *n.*

Shad·rach (ˈʃædræk, ˈʃeɪ-) *n. Old Testament.* one of Daniel's three companions, who, together with Meshach and Abednego, was miraculously saved from destruction in Nebuchadnezzar's fiery furnace (Daniel 3:12–30).

sha+duf (ʃəˈduːf) *n.* a variant spelling of **shadoof.**

Shad·well (ˈʃædwəl) *n.* **Thom·as.** ?1642–92, English dramatist; poet laureate (1688–92). He was satirized by Dryden.

shad·y (ˈʃeɪdɪ) *adj.* **shad·i·er, shad·i·est.** **1.** full of shade; shaded. **2.** affording or casting a shade. **3.** dim, quiet, or concealed. **4.** *Informal.* dubious or questionable as to honesty or legality. —ˈ**shad·i·ly** *adv.* —ˈ**shad·i·ness** *n.*

SHAEF (ʃeɪf) *n. acronym for* Supreme Headquarters Allied Expeditionary Forces.

shaft (ʃɑːft) *n.* **1.** the long narrow pole that forms the body of a spear, arrow, etc. **2.** something directed at a person in the manner of a missile: *shafts of sarcasm.* **3.** a ray, beam, or streak, esp. of light. **4.** a rod or pole forming the handle of a hammer, axe, golf club, etc. **5.** a revolving rod that transmits motion or power. **6.** one of the two wooden poles by which an animal is harnessed to a vehicle. **7.** *Anatomy.* **a.** the middle part (diaphysis) of a long bone. **b.** the main portion of any elongated structure or part. **8.** the middle part of a column or pier, between the base and the capital. **9.** a column, obelisk, etc., esp. one that forms a monument. **10.** *Architecture.* a column that supports a vaulting rib, sometimes one of a set. **11.** a vertical passageway through a building, as for a lift. **12.** a vertical passageway into a mine. **13.** *Ornithol.* the central rib of a feather. **14.** an archaic or literary word for **arrow.** **15.** *Taboo, U.S.* a slang word for **penis.** **16.** **get the shaft.** *U.S. slang.* to be tricked or cheated. ~*vb.* **17.** *U.S. slang.* to trick or cheat. [Old English *sceaft;* related to Old Norse *skapt,* German *Schaft,* Latin *scāpus* shaft, Greek *skeptron* SCEPTRE, Lettish *skeps* javelin]

Shaftes·bur·y (ˈʃɑːftsbərɪ, -brɪ) *n.* **1.** **1st Earl of,** title of *Anthony Ashley Cooper.* 1621–83, English statesman, a major figure in the Whig opposition to Charles II. **2.** **7th Earl of,** title of *Anthony Ashley Cooper.* 1801–85, English evangelical churchman and social reformer. He promoted measures to improve conditions in mines (1842), factories (1833; 1847; 1850), and schools.

shaft feath+er *n. Archery.* one of the two fletchings on an arrow. Compare **cock feather.**

shaft+ing (ˈʃɑːftɪŋ) *n.* **1.** an assembly of shafts for transmitting power. **2.** the stock from which shafts are made. **3.** *Architecture.* a set of shafts.

shag[1] (ʃæg) *n.* **1.** a matted tangle, esp. of hair, wool, etc. **2.** a napped fabric, usually a rough wool. **3.** shredded coarse tobacco. ~*vb.* **shags, shag+ging, shagged.** **4.** (*tr.*) to make shaggy. [Old English *sceacga;* related to *sceaga* SHAW, Old Norse *skegg* beard, *skagi* tip, *skōgr* forest]

shag[2] (ʃæg) *n.* another name for **cormorant,** esp. (in Britain) the **green cormorant** (*Phalacrocorax aristotelis*). [C16: special use of SHAG[1], with reference to its crest]

shag[3] (ʃæg) *Brit. slang.* ~*vb.* **shags, shag+ging, shagged.** **1.** *Taboo.* to have sexual intercourse with (a person). **2.** (*tr.;* often foll. by *out; usually passive*) to exhaust; tire. ~*n.* **3.** *Taboo.* an act of sexual intercourse. [C20: of unknown origin]

shag+bark (ˈʃægˌbɑːk) *or* **shell+bark** *n.* **1.** a North American hickory tree, *Carya ovata,* having loose rough bark and edible nuts. **2.** the wood of this tree, used for tool handles, fuel, etc. **3.** the light-coloured hard-shelled nut of this tree.

shag+gy (ˈʃægɪ) *adj.* **+gi+er, +gi+est.** **1.** having or covered with rough unkempt fur, hair, wool, etc.: *a shaggy dog.* **2.** rough or unkempt. **3.** (in textiles) having a nap of long rough strands. —ˈ**shag+gi+ly** *adv.* —ˈ**shag+gi+ness** *n.*

shag+gy cap *n.* an edible saprophytic agaricaceous fungus, *Coprinus comatus,* having a white cap covered with shaggy scales.

shag+gy dog sto+ry *n. Informal.* a long rambling joke ending in an anticlimax, such as a pointless punch line.

sha+green (ʃæˈgriːn) *n.* **1.** the rough skin of from certain sharks and rays, used as an abrasive. **2.** a rough grainy leather made from certain animal hides. [C17: from French *chagrin,* from Turkish *çagri* rump; also associated through folk etymology with SHAG[1], GREEN]

shah (ʃɑː) *n.* a ruler of certain Middle Eastern countries, esp. (formerly) Iran. [C16: from Persian: king] —ˈ**shah+dom** *n.*

Sha+hap+tin (ʃəˈhæptɪn), **Sha+hap+tan** (ʃəˈhæptən), *or* **Sha+hap+ti+an** (ʃəˈhæptɪən) *n.* variant spellings of **Sahaptin.**

Shah Ja·han (dʒəˈhɑːn) *n.* 1592–1666, Mogul emperor (1628–58). During his reign the finest monuments of Mogul architecture in India were built, including the Taj Mahal and the Pearl Mosque at Agra.

Shah+ja+han+pur (ˌʃɑːdʒəˌhɑːnˈpʊə) *n.* a city in N India, in central Uttar Pradesh: founded in 1647 in the reign of Shah Jahan. Pop.: 135 604 (1971).

Shai+tan (ʃaɪˈtɑːn) *n.* (in Muslim countries) **a.** Satan. **b.** any evil spirit. **c.** a vicious person or animal. [C17: from Arabic *shaytān,* from Hebrew *śātān;* see SATAN]

Sha+ka (ˈʃaka) *n.* died 1828, Zulu military leader, who founded the Zulu Empire in southern Africa.

shake (ʃeɪk) *vb.* **shakes, shak+ing, shook, shak+en.** **1.** to move or cause to move up and down or back and forth with short quick movements; vibrate. **2.** to sway or totter or cause to sway or totter. **3.** to clasp or grasp (the hand) of (a person) in greeting, agreement, etc.: *he shook John by the hand; he shook John's hand; they shook and were friends.* **4.** **shake hands.** to clasp hands in greeting, agreement, etc. **5.** **shake on it.** *Informal.* to shake hands in agreement, reconciliation, etc. **6.** to bring or come to a specified condition by or as if by shaking: *he shook free and ran.* **7.** (*tr.*) to wave or brandish: *he shook his sword.* **8.** (*tr.;* often foll. by *up*) to rouse, stir, or agitate. **9.** (*tr.*) to undermine or weaken: *the crisis shook his faith.* **10.** to mix (dice) by rattling in a cup or the hand before throwing. **11.** (*tr.*) *Austral. slang.* to steal. **12.** (*tr.*) *U.S. informal.* to escape from: *can you shake that detective?* **13.** *Music.* to perform a trill on a (note). **14.** **shake a leg.** *Informal.* to hurry or hasten. **15.** **shake in one's shoes.** to tremble with fear or apprehension. **16.** **shake one's head.** to indicate disagreement or disapproval by moving the head from side to side. **17. shake the dust from one's feet.** to depart gladly or with the intention not to return. ~*n.* **18.** the act or an instance of shaking. **19.** a tremor or vibration. **20. the shakes.** *Informal.* a state of uncontrollable trembling or a condition that causes it, such as a fever. **21.** *Informal.* a very short period of time; jiffy: *in half a shake.* **22.** a shingle or clapboard made from a short log by splitting it radially. **23.** a fissure or crack in timber or rock. **24.** an instance of shaking dice before casting. **25.** *Music.* another word for **trill**[1] (sense 1). **26.** a modern dance in which the body is shaken convulsively in time to the beat. **27.** an informal name for **earthquake. 28.** short for **milk shake. 29. no great shakes.** *Informal.* of no great merit or value; ordinary. ~See also **shake down, shake off, shake up.** [Old English *sceacan;* related to Old Norse *skaka* to shake, Old High German *untscachōn* to be driven] —**'shak+a·ble** *or* **'shake+a·ble** *adj.*

shake down *vb.* (*adv.*) **1.** to fall or settle or cause to fall or settle by shaking. **2.** (*tr.*) *U.S. slang.* to extort money from, esp. by blackmail or threats of violence. **3.** (*tr.*) *U.S. slang.* to search thoroughly. **4.** (*tr.*) *Informal, chiefly U.S.* to submit (a vessel, etc.) to a shakedown test. **5.** (*intr.*) to go to bed, esp. to a makeshift bed. **6.** (*intr.*) (of a person, animal, etc.) to settle down. ~*n.* **shake+down. 7.** *U.S. slang.* a swindle or act of extortion. **8.** *U.S. slang.* a thorough search. **9.** a makeshift bed, esp. of straw, blankets, etc. **10.** *Informal, chiefly U.S.* **a.** a voyage to test the performance of a ship or aircraft or to familiarize the crew with their duties. **b.** (*as modifier*): *a shakedown run.*

shake off *vb.* (*adv.*) **1.** to remove or be removed with or as if with a quick movement: *she shook off her depression.* **2.** (*tr.*) to escape from; elude: *they shook off the police.*

shak+er ('ʃeɪkə) *n.* **1.** a person or thing that shakes. **2.** a container, often having a perforated top, from which something, such as a condiment, is shaken. **3.** a container in which the ingredients of alcoholic drinks are shaken together.

Shak+ers ('ʃeɪkəz) *pl. n.* **the.** an American millenarian sect, founded in 1747 as an offshoot of the Quakers, given to ecstatic shaking, advocating celibacy for its members, and practising common ownership of property.

Shake·speare ('ʃeɪkspɪə) *n.* **Wil·liam.** 1564–1616, English dramatist and poet. He was born and died at Stratford-upon-Avon but spent most of his life as an actor and playwright in London. His plays with approximate dates of composition are: *Henry VI, Parts I–III* (1590); *Richard III* (1592); *The Comedy of Errors* (1592); *Titus Andronicus* (1593); *The Taming of the Shrew* (1593); *The Two Gentlemen of Verona* (1594); *Love's Labours Lost* (1594); *Romeo and Juliet* (1594); *Richard II* (1595); *A Midsummer Night's Dream* (1595); *King John* (1596); *The Merchant of Venice* (1596); *Henry IV, Parts I–II* (1597); *Much Ado about Nothing* (1598); *Henry V* (1598); *Julius Caesar* (1599); *As You Like It* (1599); *Twelfth Night* (1599); *Hamlet* (1600); *The Merry Wives of Windsor* (1600); *Troilus and Cressida* (1601); *All's Well that ends Well* (1602); *Measure for Measure* (1604); *Othello* (1604); *King Lear* (1605); *Macbeth* (1605); *Antony and Cleopatra* (1606); *Coriolanus* (1607); *Timon of Athens* (1607); *Pericles* (1608); *Cymbeline* (1609); *The Winter's Tale* (1610); and *The Tempest* (1611). His *Sonnets,* variously addressed to a fair young man and a dark lady, were published in 1609.

Shake+spear+e·an *or* **Shake+spear+i·an** (ʃeɪk'spɪərɪən) *adj.* **1.** of, relating to, or characteristic of Shakespeare or his works. ~*n.* **2.** a student of or specialist in Shakespeare's works.

Shake+spear+e·an son+net *n.* a sonnet form developed in 16th-century England and employed by Shakespeare, having the rhyme scheme a b a b c d c d e f e f g g. Also called: **Elizabethan sonnet, English sonnet.**

shake up *vb.* (*tr., adv.*) **1.** to shake or agitate in order to mix. **2.** to reorganize drastically. **3.** to stir or rouse. **4.** to restore the shape of (a pillow, cushion, etc.). **5.** *Informal.* to disturb or shock mentally or physically. ~*n.* **shake-up. 6.** *Informal.* a radical or drastic reorganization.

Shakh+ty (*Russian* 'ʃaxtɪ) *n.* an industrial city in the SW Soviet Union, in Rostov Region: the chief town of the E Donets Basin. Pop.: 219 000 (1975 est.).

shak+ing pal+sy *n.* another name for **Parkinson's disease.**

shak·o *or* **shack·o** ('ʃækəʊ) *n., pl.* **shak·os, shak·oes** *or* **shack·os, shack·oes.** a tall usually cylindrical military headdress, having a plume and often a peak, popular esp. in the 19th century. [C19: via French from Hungarian *csákó,* from Middle High German *zacke* a sharp point]

Shak+ta ('ʃʌktə) *n. Hinduism.* a devotee of Sakti, the wife of Siva. [from Sanskrit *śākta* concerning Shakti] —**'Shak+tism** *n.* —**'Shak+tist** *n.*

Shak+ti ('ʃʌktɪ) *n.* a variant spelling of **Sakti.**

shak·y ('ʃeɪkɪ) *adj.* **shak·i+er, shak·i+est. 1.** tending to shake or tremble. **2.** liable to prove defective; unreliable. **3.** uncertain or questionable: *your arguments are very shaky.* —**'shak·i+ly** *adv.* —**'shak·i+ness** *n.*

shale (ʃeɪl) *n.* a dark fine-grained laminated sedimentary rock formed by compression of successive layers of clay. [Old English *scealu* SHELL; compare German *Schalstein* laminated limestone; see SCALE[1], SCALE[2]] —**'shal·y** *adj.*

shale oil *n.* an oil distilled from shales and used as fuel.

shall (ʃæl; *unstressed* ʃəl) *vb. past* **should.** (takes an infinitive without *to* or an implied infinitive) used as an auxiliary: **1.** (esp. with *I* or *we* as subject) to make the future tense: *we shall see you tomorrow.* Compare **will**[1] (sense 1). **2.** (with *you, he, she, it, they,* or a noun as subject) **a.** to indicate determination on the part of the speaker, as in issuing a threat: *you shall pay for this!* **b.** to indicate compulsion, now esp. in official documents: *the Tenant shall return the keys to the Landlord.* **c.** to indicate certainty or inevitability: *our day shall come.* **3.** (*with any noun or pronoun as subject, esp. in conditional clauses or clauses expressing doubt*) to indicate nonspecific futurity: *I don't think I shall ever see her again; he doubts whether he shall be in tomorrow.* [Old English *sceal;* related to Old Norse *skal,* Old High German *scal,* Dutch *zal*]

Usage. The usual rule given for the use of *shall* and *will* is that where the meaning is one of simple futurity, *shall* is used for the first person of the verb and *will* for the second and third: *I shall go tomorrow; they will be there now.* Where the meaning involves command, obligation, or determination, the positions are reversed: *it shall be done; I will definitely go.* However, *shall* has come to be largely neglected in favour of *will,* which has become the commonest form of the future in all three persons.

shal+loon (ʃæ'lu:n) *n.* a light twill-weave woollen fabric used chiefly for coat linings, etc. [C17: from Old French *chalon,* from the name of *Châlons-sur-Marne,* France, where it originated]

shal+lop ('ʃæləp) *n.* **1.** a light boat used for rowing in shallow water. **2.** (formerly) a two-masted gaff-rigged vessel. [C16: from French *chaloupe,* from Dutch *sloep* SLOOP]

shal+lot (ʃə'lɒt) *n.* **1.** Also called: **scallion.** an alliaceous plant, *Allium ascalonicum,* cultivated for its edible bulb. **2.** the bulb of this plant, which divides into small sections and is used in cooking for flavouring and as a vegetable. [C17: from Old French *eschalotte,* from Old French *eschaloigne,* from Latin *Ascalōnia caepa* Ascalonian onion, from *Ascalon,* a Palestinian town]

shal+low ('ʃæləʊ) *adj.* **1.** having little depth. **2.** lacking intellectual or mental depth or subtlety; superficial. ~*n.* **3.** (*often pl.*) a shallow place in a body of water; shoal. ~*vb.* **4.** to make or become shallow. [C15: related to Old English *sceald* shallow; see SHOAL[1]] —**'shal+low+ly** *adv.* —**'shal+low+ness** *n.*

sha+lom a·lei+chem *Hebrew.* (ʃa'lɔm a'lexɛm; *English* ʃə'lɒm ə'leɪxəm) *interj.* peace be to you: used by Jews as a greeting or farewell. Often shortened to **shalom.**

shalt (ʃælt) *vb. Archaic or dialect.* (used with the pronoun *thou* or its relative equivalent) a singular form of the present tense (indicative mood) of **shall.**

sham (ʃæm) *n.* **1.** anything that is not what it purports or appears to be. **2.** something false, fake, or fictitious that purports to be genuine. **3.** a person who pretends to be something other than he is. ~*adj.* **4.** counterfeit or false; simulated. ~*vb.* **shams, sham+ming, shammed. 5.** to falsely assume the appearance of (something); counterfeit: *to sham illness.* [C17: perhaps a Northern English dialect variant of SHAME] —**'sham+mer** *n.*

sham+an ('ʃæmən) *n.* **1.** a priest of shamanism. **2.** a medicine man of a similar religion, esp. among certain tribes of North American Indians. [C17: from Russian *shaman,* from Tungusian *sāman,* from Pali *samana* Buddhist monk, ultimately from Sanskrit *śrama* religious exercise. —**sha+man+ic** (ʃə'mænɪk) *adj.*

sham+an+ism ('ʃæməˌnɪzəm) *n.* **1.** the religion of certain peoples of northern Asia, based on the belief that the world is pervaded by good and evil spirits who can be influenced or controlled only by the shamans. **2.** any similar religion involving forms of spiritualism. —**'sham+an+ist** *n., adj.* —**ˌsham+an+'is+tic** *adj.*

Sha+mash ('ʃɑ:mæʃ) *n.* the sun god of Assyria and Babylonia. [from Akkadian: sun]

sham+ba ('ʃamba) *n.* (in E Africa) a plantation. [Swahili]

sham+ble ('ʃæmbᵊl) *vb.* **1.** (*intr.*) to walk or move along in an awkward or unsteady way. ~*n.* **2.** an awkward or unsteady walk. [C17: from *shamble* (adj.) ungainly, perhaps from the phrase *shamble legs* legs resembling those of a meat vendor's table; see SHAMBLES]

sham+bles ('ʃæmbᵊlz) *n.* (*functioning as sing. or pl.*) **1.** a place of great disorder: *the room was a shambles after the party.* **2.** a place where animals are brought to be slaughtered. **3.** any place of slaughter or execution. **4.** *Brit. dialect.* a row of covered stalls or shops where goods, originally meat, are sold. [C14 *shamble* table used by meat vendors, from Old English *sceamel* stool, from Late Latin *scamellum* a small bench, from Latin *scamnum* stool]

shame (ʃeɪm) *n.* **1.** a painful emotion resulting from an awareness of having done something dishonourable, unworthy, degrading, etc. **2.** capacity to feel such an emotion. **3.** ignominy or disgrace. **4.** a person or thing that causes this. **5.** an occasion for regret, disappointment, etc.: *it's a shame you can't come with us.* **6. put to shame. a.** to disgrace. **b.** to surpass totally. ~*vb.* (*tr.*) **7.** to cause to feel shame. **8.** to bring shame on; disgrace. **9.** (often foll. by *into*) to compel through a sense of shame: *he shamed her into making an apology.* [Old English *scamu;* related to Old Norse *skömm,* Old High German *skama*] —**'sham+a·ble** *or* **'shame+a·ble** *adj.*

shame+faced ('ʃeɪmˌfeɪst) *adj.* **1.** bashful or modest. **2.** showing a sense of shame. [C16: alteration of earlier *shamefast,* from Old English *sceamfaest;* see SHAME, FAST[1]] —**shame+fac+ed+ly** (ʃeɪm'feɪsɪdlɪ, 'ʃeɪmˌfeɪstlɪ) *adv.* —**shame+'fac+ed+ness** *n.*

shame+ful ('ʃeɪmfʊl) *adj.* causing or deserving shame; scandalous. —**'shame+ful+ly** *adv.* —**'shame+ful+ness** *n.*

shame+less ('ʃeɪmlɪs) *adj.* **1.** having no sense of shame; brazen. **2.** done without shame; without decency or modesty. —**'shame+less+ly** *adv.* —**'shame+less+ness** *n.*

sham+mes or **sham+mas** ('ʃɑːməs; Hebrew ʃa'maʃ) n., pl. **sham+mo+sim** (Hebrew ʃa'mɔsɪm). *Judaism.* **1.** an official acting as the beadle, sexton, and caretaker of a synagogue. **2.** the extra candle used on the Feast of Hanukkah to kindle the lamps or candles of the menorah. [from Hebrew *shāmmāsh,* from Aramaic *shěmāsh* to serve]

sham+my ('ʃæmɪ) n., pl. **+mies.** *Informal.* another word for **chamois** (sense 3). Also called: **shammy leather.**

Sha+mo ('ʃɑː'məʊ) n. transliteration of the Chinese name for the **Gobi.**

sham+poo (ʃæm'puː) n. **1.** a liquid or cream preparation of soap or detergent to wash the hair. **2.** a similar preparation for washing carpets, etc. **3.** the process of shampooing. ~*vb.* **+poos, +poo+ing, +pooed. 4.** (*tr.*) to wash (the hair, etc.) with such a preparation. [C18: from Hindi *chāmpo,* from *chāmpnā* to knead] —**sham+'poo+er** n.

sham+rock ('ʃæmˌrɒk) n. a plant having leaves divided into three leaflets, variously identified as the wood sorrel, red clover, white clover, and black medick: the national emblem of Ireland. [C16: from Irish Gaelic *seamrōg,* diminutive of *seamar* clover]

sha+mus ('ʃɑːməs, 'ʃeɪ-) n., pl. **+mus·es.** *U.S. slang.* a police or private detective. [probably from SHAMMES, influenced by Irish *Séamas* James]

Shan (ʃɑːn) n. **1.** (*pl.* **Shans** or **Shan**) a member of a Mongoloid people living in Burma, Thailand, and SW China. **2.** the language or group of dialects spoken by the Shan, belonging to the Sino-Tibetan family and closely related to Thai.

shan+dry+dan ('ʃændrɪˌdæn) n. **1.** a two-wheeled cart or chaise, esp. one with a hood. **2.** any decrepit old-fashioned conveyance. [C19: of unknown origin]

shan+dy ('ʃændɪ) or *U.S.* **shan+dy+gaff** ('ʃændɪˌgæf) n., pl. **+dies** or **+gaffs.** an alcoholic drink made of beer and ginger beer or lemonade. [C19: of unknown origin]

Shang (ʃæŋ) n. **1.** the dynasty ruling in China from about the 18th to the 12th centuries B.C. ~*adj.* **2.** of or relating to the pottery produced during the Shang dynasty.

Shan+gaan ('ʃaŋgɑːn) n. a member of any of the Tsonga-speaking Bantu peoples settled in Mozambique and NE Transvaal, esp. one who works in a gold mine.

shang+hai ('ʃæŋhaɪ, ʃæŋ'haɪ) *Slang.* ~*vb.* **+hais, +hai+ing, +haied.** (*tr.*) **1.** to kidnap (a man or seaman) for enforced service at sea, esp. on a merchant ship. **2.** to force or trick (someone) into doing something, going somewhere, etc. **3.** *Austral.* to shoot with a catapult. ~*n.* **4.** *Austral.* a catapult. [C19: from the city of SHANGHAI; from the forceful methods formerly used to collect crews for voyages to the Orient]

Shang+hai ('ʃæŋ'haɪ) n. a port in E China, in SE Kiangsu near the estuary of the Yangtze: the largest city in China and one of the largest ports in the world; a major cultural and industrial centre, with two universities. Pop.: 10 000 000 (1976 est.).

Shan+go ('ʃæŋgəʊ) n. **a.** a W African religious cult surviving in some parts of the Caribbean. **b.** (*as modifier*): *Shango ritual.* [Yoruba]

Shan·gri-la (ˌʃæŋgrɪ'lɑː) n. a remote or imaginary utopia. [C20: from the name of an imaginary valley in the Himalayas, from *Lost Horizon* (1933), a novel by James Hilton]

shank (ʃæŋk) n. **1.** *Anatomy.* the shin. **2.** the corresponding part of the leg in other vertebrates. **3.** a cut of meat from the top part of an animal's shank. **4.** the main part of a tool, between the working part and the handle. **5.** the part of a bolt between the thread and the head. **6.** the cylindrical part of a bit by which it is held in the drill. **7.** the ring or stem on the back of some buttons. **8.** the stem or long narrow part of a key, anchor, hook, spoon handle, nail, pin, etc. **9.** the band of a ring as distinguished from the setting. **10. a.** the part of a shoe connecting the wide part of the sole with the heel. **b.** the metal or leather piece used for this. **11.** *Printing.* the body of a piece of type, between the shoulder and the foot. **12.** *Music.* another word for **crook** (sense 6). **13.** *Rare.* the latter or remaining part of anything. ~*vb.* **14.** (*intr.*) (of fruits, roots, etc.) to show disease symptoms, esp. discoloration. [Old English *scanca;* related to Old Frisian *schanke,* Middle Low German *schenke,* Danish, Swedish *skank* leg]

Shan·kar ('ʃæŋkɑː) n. **Ra·vi** ('rɑːviː). born 1920, Indian sitarist.

Shan·ka·ra·char·ya ('ʃʌŋkərɑː'tʃɑːrjə) or **Shan·ka·ra** ('ʃʌŋkərə) n. 9th century A.D., Hindu philosopher and teacher; chief exponent of Vedanta philosophy.

shanks's po·ny or *U.S.* **shanks's mare** n. *Informal.* one's own legs as a means of transportation.

Shan+non ('ʃænən) n. a river in the Republic of Ireland, rising in NW Co. Cavan and flowing south to the Atlantic by an estuary 113 km (70 miles) long: the longest river in the Republic of Ireland. Length: 260 km (161 miles).

shan+ny ('ʃænɪ) n., pl. **+nies.** a European blenny, *Blennius pholis,* of rocky coastal waters. [C19: of obscure origin]

Shan+si ('ʃæn'siː) n. a province of N China: China's richest coal reserves and much heavy industry. Capital: Taiyuan. Pop.: 23 000 000 (1971 est.). Area: 157 099 sq. km (60 656 sq. miles).

Shan State (ʃɑːn, ʃæn) n. an administrative division of E Burma: formed in 1947 from the joining of the Federation of Shan States with the Wa States; consists of the **Shan plateau,** crossed by forested mountain ranges reaching over 2100 m (7000 ft.). Pop.: 2 785 000 (1970 est.). Area: 149 743 sq. km (57 816 sq. miles).

shan't (ʃɑːnt) *contraction of* **shall not.**

Shan+tow or **Shan-t'ou** ('ʃæn'taʊ) n. another name for **Swatow.**

shan+tung (ʃæn'tʌŋ) n. **1.** a heavy silk fabric with a knobbly surface. **2.** a cotton or rayon imitation of this.

Shan+tung (ʃæn'tʌŋ) n. a province of NE China, on the Yellow Sea and the Gulf of Chihli: part of the earliest organized state of China (1520–1030 B.C.); consists chiefly of the fertile plain of the lower Yellow River, with mountains over 1500 m (5000 ft.) high in the centre. Capital: Tsinan. Pop.: 68 000 000 (1976 est.). Area: 153 300 sq. km (59 189 sq. miles).

shan+ty[1] ('ʃæntɪ) n., pl. **+ties. 1.** a ramshackle hut; crude dwelling. **2.** *Austral.* a public house, esp. an unlicensed one. [C19: from Canadian French *chantier* cabin built in a lumber camp, from Old French *gantier* GANTRY]

shan+ty[2], **shan+tey** ('ʃæntɪ), **chan+ty,** or *U.S.* **chan+tey** ('ʃæntɪ, 'tʃæn-) n., pl. **+ties** or **+teys.** a song originally sung by sailors, esp. a rhythmical one forming an accompaniment to work. [C19: from French *chanter* to sing; see CHANT]

shan·ty+town ('ʃæntɪˌtaʊn) n. a town or section of a town or city inhabited by very poor people living in shanties.

shape (ʃeɪp) n. **1.** the outward form of an object defined by outline. **2.** the figure or outline of the body of a person. **3.** a phantom. **4.** organized or definite form: *my plans are taking shape.* **5.** the form that anything assumes; guise. **6.** something used to provide or define form; pattern; mould. **7.** *Informal.* condition or state of efficiency: *to be in good shape.* **8. out of shape. a.** in bad physical condition. **b.** bent, twisted, or deformed. **9. take shape.** to assume a definite form. ~*vb.* **10.** (when *intr.,* often foll. by *into* or *up*) to receive or cause to receive shape or form. **11.** (*tr.*) to mould into a particular pattern or form; modify. **12.** (*tr.*) to plan, devise, or prepare: *to shape a plan of action.* **13.** an obsolete word for **appoint.** [Old English *gesceap,* literally: that which is created, from *scieppan* to create; related to *sceap* sexual organs, Old Norse *skap* destiny, Old High German *scaf* form] —**'shap+a·ble** or **'shape+a·ble** *adj.* —**'shap+er** n.

SHAPE (ʃeɪp) n. *acronym for* Supreme Headquarters Allied Powers Europe.

-shaped (ʃeɪpt) *adj. combining form.* having the shape of: *an L-shaped room; a pearshaped figure.*

shape+less ('ʃeɪplɪs) *adj.* **1.** having no definite shape or form: *a shapeless mass; a shapeless argument.* **2.** lacking a symmetrical or aesthetically pleasing shape: *a shapeless figure.* —**'shape+less+ly** *adv.* —**'shape+less+ness** n.

shape+ly ('ʃeɪplɪ) *adj.* **+li+er, +li+est.** (esp. of a woman's body or legs) pleasing or attractive in shape. —**'shape+li+ness** n.

shape up *vb.* (*intr., adv.*) **1.** *Informal.* to proceed or develop satisfactorily. **2.** *Informal.* to develop a definite or proper form. ~*n.* **shape+up. 3.** *U.S.* (formerly) a method of hiring dockers for a day or shift by having a union hiring boss select them from a gathering of applicants.

shard (ʃɑːd) or **sherd** n. **1.** a broken piece or fragment of a brittle substance, esp. of pottery. **2.** *Zoology.* a tough sheath, scale, or shell, esp. the elytra of a beetle. [Old English *sceard;* related to Old Norse *skarth* notch, Middle High German *scharte* notch]

share[1] (ʃɛə) n. **1.** a part or portion of something owned, allotted to, or contributed by a person or group. **2.** (*often pl.*) any of the equal parts, usually of low par value, into which is divided the capital stock of a company. **3. go shares.** *Informal.* to share (something) with another or others. ~*vb.* **4.** (*tr.;* often foll. by *out*) to divide or apportion, esp. equally. **5.** (when *intr.,* often foll. by *in*) to receive or contribute a portion of: *we can share the cost of the petrol; six people shared in the inheritance.* **6.** to join with another or others in the use of (something): *can I share your umbrella?* [*Old English scearu;* related to Old Norse *skor* amount, Old High German *scara* crowd; see SHEAR] —**'shar+a·ble** or **'share+a·ble** *adj.* —**'shar+er** n.

share[2] (ʃɛə) n. short for **ploughshare.** [Old English *scear;* related to Old Norse *skeri,* Old High German *scaro*]

share cer+tif·i+cate n. a document issued by a company certifying ownership of one or more of its shares. U.S. equivalent: **stock certificate.**

share+crop ('ʃɛəˌkrɒp) *vb.* **+crops, +crop+ping, +cropped.** *Chiefly U.S.* to cultivate (farmland) as a sharecropper.

share+crop+per ('ʃɛəˌkrɒpə) n. *Chiefly U.S.* a farmer, esp. a tenant farmer, who pays over a proportion of a crop or crops as rent.

share+farm+er ('ʃɛəˌfɑːmə) n. *Austral.* a farmer who shares his profits with his farm workers.

share+hold·er ('ʃɛəˌhəʊldə) n. the owner of one or more shares in a company.

share pre+mi·um n. *Brit.* the excess of the amount actually subscribed for an issue of corporate capital over its par value. Also called (esp. U.S.): **capital surplus.**

Sha+ri ('ʃɑːrɪ) n. a variant spelling of **Chari** (the river).

sha+ri·a or **she+ri·a** (ʃə'riːə) n. the body of doctrines that regulate the lives of those who profess Islam. [Arabic]

shark[1] (ʃɑːk) n. any of various usually ferocious selachian fishes, typically marine with a long body, two dorsal fins, rows of sharp teeth, and between five and seven gill slits on each side of the head. [C16: of uncertain origin] —**'shark+ˌlike** *adj.*

shark[2] (ʃɑːk) n. **1.** a person who preys on or victimizes others, esp. by swindling or extortion. ~*vb.* **2.** *Archaic.* to obtain (something) by cheating or deception. [C18: probably from German *Schurke* rogue]

shark bell n. *Chiefly Austral.* a bell sounded to warn swimmers of the presence of sharks.

shark net n. *Chiefly Austral.* **1.** a net for catching sharks. **2.** a long piece of netting strung across a bay, inlet, etc., to exclude sharks.

shark pa·trol *n. Chiefly Austral.* a watch for sharks kept by an aircraft flying over beaches used by swimmers.

shark si·ren *n. Chiefly Austral.* a siren sounded to warn swimmers of the presence of sharks.

shark·skin ('ʃɑːkˌskɪn) *n.* a smooth glossy fabric of acetate rayon, used for sportswear, etc.

shark·suck·er ('ʃɑːkˌsʌkə) *n.* an informal name for a **remora.**

Sha·ron ('ʃærən) *n.* **Plain of.** a plain in W Israel, between the Mediterranean and the hills of Samaria, extending from Haifa to Tel Aviv.

sharp (ʃɑːp) *adj.* **1.** having a keen edge suitable for cutting. **2.** having an edge or point; not rounded or blunt. **3.** involving a sudden change, esp. in direction: *a sharp bend.* **4.** moving, acting, or reacting quickly, efficiently, etc.: *sharp reflexes.* **5.** clearly defined. **6.** mentally acute; clever; astute. **7.** sly or artful; clever in an underhand way: *sharp practice.* **8.** bitter or harsh: *sharp words.* **9.** shrill or penetrating: *a sharp cry.* **10.** having an acrid taste. **11.** keen; biting: *a sharp wind; sharp pain.* **12.** *Music.* **a.** (*immediately postpositive*) denoting a note that has been raised in pitch by one chromatic semitone: *B sharp.* **b.** (of an instrument, voice, etc.) out of tune by being or tending to be too high in pitch. Compare **flat**[1] (sense 22). **13.** *Phonetics.* a less common word for **fortis.** ~*adv.* **14.** in a sharp manner. **15.** exactly: *six o'clock sharp.* **16.** *Music.* **a.** higher than a standard pitch. **b.** out of tune by being or tending to be too high in pitch: *she sings sharp.* Compare **flat**[1] (sense 27). ~*n.* **17.** *Music.* **a.** an accidental that raises the pitch of the following note by one chromatic semitone. Usual symbol: **#** **b.** a note affected by this accidental. Compare **flat**[1] (sense 33). **18.** a thin needle with a sharp point. **19.** *Informal.* a sharper. ~*vb.* **20.** (*tr.*) *Music.* the usual U.S. word for **sharpen.** [Old English *scearp;* related to Old Norse *skarpr,* Old High German *scarpf,* Old Irish *cerb,* Lettish *skarbs*] —**'sharp·ly** *adv.* —**'sharp·ness** *n.*

sharp·en ('ʃɑːpᵊn) *vb.* **1.** to make or become sharp or sharper. **2.** *Music.* to raise the pitch of (a note), esp. by one chromatic semitone. Usual U.S. word: **sharp.** —**'sharp·en·er** *n.*

sharp·er ('ʃɑːpə) *n.* a person who cheats or swindles; fraud.

sharp-eyed *adj.* **1.** having very good eyesight. **2.** observant or alert.

sharp·ie ('ʃɑːpɪ) *n. Austral.* a member of a teenage group having short hair and distinctive clothes. Compare **skinhead.**

sharp-set *adj.* **1.** set to give an acute cutting angle. **2.** keenly hungry. **3.** keen or eager.

sharp·shoot·er ('ʃɑːpˌʃuːtə) *n.* an expert marksman, esp. with a rifle. —**'sharp·ˌshoot·ing** *n.*

sharp-sight·ed *adj.* having keen vision; sharp-eyed. —**ˌsharp-'sight·ed·ly** *adv.* —**ˌsharp-'sight·ed·ness** *n.*

sharp-tongued *adj.* bitter or critical in speech; sarcastic.

sharp-wit·ted *adj.* having or showing a keen intelligence; alert; perceptive. —**ˌsharp-'wit·ted·ly** *adv.* —**ˌsharp-'wit·ted·ness** *n.*

shash·lik *or* **shash·lick** (ʃɑːʃ'lɪk, 'ʃɑːʃlɪk) *n.* a type of kebab. [from Russian, of Turkic origin; compare *shish kebab*]

Shas·ta dai·sy ('ʃæstə) *n.* a Pyrenean plant, *Chrysanthemum maximum,* widely cultivated for its large white daisy-like flowers: family *Compositae* (composites).

Shatt-al-Ar·ab ('ʃæt æl 'ærəb) *n.* a river in SE Iraq, formed by the confluence of the Tigris and Euphrates Rivers: flows southeast as part of the border between Iraq and Iran to the Persian Gulf. Length: 193 km (120 miles).

shat·ter ('ʃætə) *vb.* **1.** to break or be broken into many small pieces. **2.** (*tr.*) to impair or destroy: *his nerves were shattered by the torture.* **3.** (*tr.*) to dumbfound or thoroughly upset: *she was shattered by the news.* **4.** an obsolete word for **scatter.** ~*n.* **5.** (*usually pl.*) *Obsolete or dialect.* a fragment. [C12: perhaps obscurely related to SCATTER] —**'shat·ter·er** *n.* —**'shat·ter·ing·ly** *adv.*

shat·ter·proof ('ʃætəˌpruːf) *adj.* designed to resist shattering.

shave (ʃeɪv) *vb.* **shaves, shav·ing, shaved; shaved** *or* **shav·en.** (*mainly tr.*) **1.** (*also intr.*) to remove (the beard, hair, etc.) from (the face, head, or body) by scraping the skin with a razor. **2.** to cut or trim very closely. **3.** to reduce to shavings. **4.** to remove thin slices from (wood, etc.) with a sharp cutting tool; plane or pare. **5.** to touch or graze in passing. **6.** *Informal.* to reduce (a price) by a slight amount. **7.** *U.S. commerce.* to purchase (a commercial paper) at a greater rate of discount than is customary or legal. ~*n.* **8.** the act or an instance of shaving. **9.** any tool for scraping. **10.** a thin slice or shaving. **11.** an instance of barely touching something. **12.** **close shave.** *Informal.* a narrow escape. [Old English *sceafan;* related to Old Norse *skafa,* Gothic *skaban* to shave, Latin *scabere* to scrape] —**'shav·a·ble** *or* **'shave·a·ble** *adj.*

shave·ling ('ʃeɪvlɪŋ) *n. Archaic.* **1.** *Derogatory.* a priest or clergyman with a shaven head. **2.** a young fellow; youth.

shav·en ('ʃeɪvᵊn) *adj.* **a.** closely shaved or tonsured. **b.** (*in combination*): *clean-shaven.*

shav·er ('ʃeɪvə) *n.* **1.** a person or thing that shaves. **2.** Also called: **electric razor, electric shaver.** an electrically powered implement for shaving, having reciprocating or rotating blades behind a fine metal comb or pierced foil. **3.** *Informal.* a youngster, esp. a young boy. **4.** *Obsolete.* a person who makes hard or extortionate bargains.

Sha·vi·an ('ʃeɪvɪən) *adj.* **1.** of, relating to, or like George Bernard Shaw, his works, ideas, etc. ~*n.* **2.** an admirer of Shaw or his works. —**'Sha·vi·an·ism** *n.*

shav·ing ('ʃeɪvɪŋ) *n.* **1.** a thin paring or slice, esp. of wood, that has been shaved from something. ~*modifier.* **2.** used when shaving the face, etc.: *shaving cream.*

Sha·vu·ot (ʃə'vuːəs, -əʊs; *Hebrew* ʃavuː'ɔt) *n.* a variant spelling of **Shabuoth.**

shaw (ʃɔː) *n. Archaic or dialect.* a small wood; thicket; copse. [Old English *sceaga;* related to Old Norse *skagi* tip, *skaga* to jut out, *skōgr* forest, *skegg* beard]

Shaw (ʃɔː) *n.* **1. George Ber·nard,** often known as *GBS.* 1856–1950, Irish dramatist and critic, in England from 1876. He was an active socialist and became a member of the Fabian Society but his major works are effective as satiric attacks rather than political tracts. These include *Arms and the Man* (1894), *Candida* (1894), *Man and Superman* (1903), *Major Barbara* (1905), *Pygmalion* (1913), *Back to Methuselah* (1921), and *St. Joan* (1923): Nobel prize for literature 1925. **2. Hen·ry Wheel·er.** the original name of (Josh) **Billings. 3. Rich·ard Nor·man.** 1831–1912, English architect. **4. Thom·as Ed·ward.** the name assumed by (T. E.) **Lawrence** after 1927.

shawl (ʃɔːl) *n.* a piece of fabric or knitted or crocheted material worn around the shoulders by women or wrapped around a baby. [C17: from Persian *shāl*]

shawl col·lar *n.* a collar rolled back in a continuous and tapering line along the surplice neckline of a garment.

shawm (ʃɔːm) *n. Music.* a medieval form of the oboe with a conical bore and flaring bell, blown through a double reed. [C14 *shalmye,* from Old French *chalemie,* ultimately from Latin *calamus* a reed, from Greek *kalamos*]

Shaw·nee (ʃɔː'niː) *n.* **1.** (*pl.* **·nees** *or* **·nee**) a member of a North American Indian people formerly living along the Tennessee River. **2.** the language of this people, belonging to the Algonquian family. [C20: back formation from obsolete *Shawnese,* from Shawnee *Shaawanwaaki* people of the south, from *shaawanawa* south]

Shaw·wal (ʃə'wɑːl) *n.* the tenth month of the Muslim year. [from Arabic]

shay (ʃeɪ) *n.* a dialect word for **chaise.** [C18: back formation from CHAISE, mistakenly thought to be plural]

Shays (ʃeɪz) *n.* **Dan·iel.** ?1747–1825, American soldier and revolutionary leader of a rebellion of Massachusetts farmers against the U.S. government (1786–87).

Shcheg·lovsk (*Russian* ʃtʃɪg'lɔfsk) *n.* the former name (until 1932) of **Kemerovo.**

Shcher·ba·kov (*Russian* ʃtʃɪrba'kɔf) *n.* the former name (from the Revolution until 1957) of **Rybinsk.**

she (ʃiː) *pron.* (*subjective*) **1.** refers to a female person or animal: *she is an actress; she's a fine mare.* **2.** refers to things personified as feminine, such as cars, ships, and nations. ~*n.* **3.** a female person or animal. [Old English *sīe,* accusative of *sēo,* feminine demonstrative pronoun]

she·a ('ʃɪə) *n.* **1.** a tropical African sapotaceous tree, *Butyrospermum parkii,* with oily seeds. **2. shea butter.** the white butter-like fat obtained from the seeds of this plant and used as food, to make soaps, etc. [C18: from Bambara *si*]

shead·ing ('ʃiːdɪŋ) *n.* any of the six subdivisions of the Isle of Man. [variant of *shedding;* see SHED]

sheaf (ʃiːf) *n., pl.* **sheaves** (ʃiːvz). **1.** a bundle of reaped but unthreshed corn tied with one or two bonds. **2.** a bundle of objects tied together. **3.** the arrows contained in a quiver. ~*vb.* **4.** (*tr.*) to bind or tie into a sheaf. [Old English *sceaf,* related to Old High German *skoub* sheaf, Old Norse *skauf* tail, Gothic *skuft* tuft of hair]

shear (ʃɪə) *vb.* **shears, shear·ing, sheared; sheared** *or* **shorn. 1.** (*tr.*) to remove (the fleece or hair) of (sheep, etc.) by cutting or clipping. **2.** to cut or cut through (something) with shears or a sharp instrument. **3.** *Engineering.* to cause (a part, member, shaft, etc.) to deform or fracture or (of a part, etc.) to deform or fracture as a result of excess torsion or transverse load. **4.** (*tr.;* often foll. by *of*) to strip or divest: *to shear someone of his power.* **5.** (when *intr.,* foll. by *through*) to move through (something) by or as if by cutting. **6.** *Scot. or dialect.* to reap (corn, etc.) with a scythe or sickle. ~*n.* **7.** the act, process, or an instance of shearing. **8.** a shearing of a sheep or flock of sheep, esp. when referred to as an indication of age: *a sheep of two shears.* **9.** a form of deformation or fracture in which parallel planes in a body or assembly slide over one another. **10.** *Physics.* the deformation of a body, part, etc., expressed as the lateral displacement between two points in parallel planes divided by the distance between the planes. **11.** either one of the blades of a pair of shears, scissors, etc. **12.** a machine that cuts sheet material by passing a knife blade through it. **13.** a device for lifting heavy loads consisting of a tackle supported by a framework held steady by guy ropes. ~See also **shore**[3]. [Old English *sceran;* related to Old Norse *skera* to cut, Old Saxon, Old High German *skeran* to shear; see SHARE[2]] —**'shear·er** *n.*

shear·legs ('ʃɪəˌlɛgz) *n.* a variant spelling of **sheerlegs.**

shear·ling ('ʃɪəlɪŋ) *n.* **1.** a young sheep after its first shearing. **2.** the skin of such an animal.

shear pin *n.* an easily replaceable pin inserted in a machine at a critical point and designed to break and stop the machine if the stress becomes too great.

shears (ʃɪəz) *pl. n.* **1. a.** large scissors, as for cutting cloth, jointing poultry, etc. **b.** a large scissor-like and usually hand-held cutting tool with flat blades, as for cutting hedges. **2.** any of various analogous cutting or clipping implements or machines. **3.** short for **sheerlegs.**

shear·wa·ter ('ʃɪəˌwɔːtə) *n.* any of several oceanic birds of the genera *Puffinus,* such as *P. puffinus* (**Manx shearwater**), *Procellaria,* etc., specialized for an aerial or aquatic existence: family *Procellariidae,* order *Procellariiformes* (petrels).

sheat+fish ('ʃi:t,fɪʃ) *n., pl.* **+fish** *or* **+fish·es.** another name for **European catfish** (see **silurid** (sense 1)). [C16: variant of *sheathfish;* perhaps influenced by German *Schaid* sheatfish; see SHEATH, FISH]

sheath (ʃi:θ) *n., pl.* **sheaths** (ʃi:ðz). **1.** a case or covering for the blade of a knife, sword, etc. **2.** any similar close-fitting case. **3.** *Biology.* an enclosing or protective structure, such as a leaf base encasing the stem of a plant. **4.** the protective covering on an electric cable. **5.** a figure-hugging dress with a narrow tapering skirt. **6.** another name for **condom.** ~*vb.* **7.** (*tr.*) another word for **sheathe.** [Old English *scēath;* related to Old Norse *skeithir,* Old High German *sceida* a dividing; compare Old English *scādan* to divide]

sheath+bill ('ʃi:θ,bɪl) *n.* either of two pigeon-like shore birds, *Chionis alba* or *C. minor,* of antarctic and subantarctic regions, constituting the family *Chionididae:* order *Charadriiformes.* They have a white plumage and a horny sheath at the base of the bill.

sheathe (ʃi:ð) *vb.* (*tr.*) **1.** to insert (a knife, sword, etc.) into a sheath. **2.** (esp. of cats) to retract (the claws). **3.** to surface with or encase in a sheath or sheathing.

sheath+ing ('ʃi:ðɪŋ) *n.* **1.** any material used as an outer layer, as on a ship's hull. **2.** boarding, etc., used to cover the wall studding or roof joists of a timber frame.

sheath knife *n.* a knife carried in or protected by a sheath.

sheave[1] (ʃi:v) *vb.* (*tr.*) to gather or bind into sheaves.

sheave[2] (ʃi:v) *n.* a wheel with a grooved rim, esp. one used as a pulley. [C14: of Germanic origin; compare Old High German *scība* disc]

sheaves (ʃi:vz) *n.* the plural of **sheaf.**

She+ba[1] ('ʃi:bə) *n.* **1.** Also called: **Saba.** the ancient kingdom of the Sabeans: a rich trading nation dealing in gold, spices, and precious stones (I Kings 10). **2.** the region inhabited by this nation, located in the SW corner of the Arabian peninsula: modern Yemen.

She·ba[2] ('ʃi:bə) *n.* **Queen of.** *Old Testament.* a queen of the Sabeans, who visited Solomon (I Kings 10:1–13).

she+bang (ʃɪ'bæŋ) *n. Slang, chiefly U.S.* **1.** a situation, matter, or affair (esp. in the phrase **the whole shebang**). **2.** a hut or shack. [C19: of uncertain origin]

She+bat *or* ***She+vat*** *Hebrew.* (ʃɛ'vat) *n.* the fifth month of the civil year and the eleventh of the ecclesiastical year in the Jewish calendar, falling approximately in January and February. [from Hebrew *shĕbhāt,* from Assyrian-Babylonish *shabātu*]

she+been *or* **she+bean** (ʃə'bi:n) *n.* **1.** *Irish, Scot., S. African.* a place where alcoholic drink is sold illegally. **2.** (in South Africa) a place where Black African men engage in social drinking. **3.** (in the U.S. and Ireland) weak beer. [C18: from Irish Gaelic *sībīn* beer of poor quality]

She+chem ('ʃɛkəm, -ɛm) *n.* the ancient name of **Nablus.**

She+chi+na (ʃɛ'kaɪnə; *Hebrew* ʃəxi:'na) *n.* a variant spelling of **Shekina.**

shed[1] (ʃɛd) *n.* **1.** a small building or lean-to of light construction, used for storage, shelter, etc. **2.** a large roofed structure, esp. one with open sides, used for storage, repairing locomotives, sheepshearing, etc. [Old English *sced;* probably variant of *scead* shelter, SHADE] **—'shed+,like** *adj.*

shed[2] (ʃɛd) *vb.* **sheds, shed+ding, shed.** (*mainly tr.*) **1.** to pour forth or cause to pour forth: *to shed tears; shed blood.* **2. shed light on** *or* **upon.** to clarify (a problem, etc.). **3.** to cast off or lose: *the snake shed its skin; trees shed their leaves.* **4.** to repel: *this coat sheds water.* **5.** (*also intr.*) (in weaving) to form an opening between (the warp threads) in order to permit the passage of the shuttle. ~*n.* **6.** (in weaving) the space made by shedding. **7.** short for **watershed.** [Old English *sceadan;* related to Gothic *skaidan,* Old High German *skeidan* to separate; see SHEATH] **—'shed+a·ble** *or* **'shed+da·ble** *adj.*

she'd (ʃi:d) *contraction of* she had *or* she would.

shed+der ('ʃɛdə) *n.* **1.** a person or thing that sheds. **2.** an animal, such as a llama, snake, or lobster, that moults.

shed hand *n. Chiefly Austral.* a worker in a sheepshearing shed.

sheen (ʃi:n) *n.* **1.** a gleaming or glistening brightness; lustre. **2.** *Poetic.* splendid clothing. ~*adj.* **3.** *Rare.* shining and beautiful; radiant. ~*vb.* **4.** (*intr.*) *Northern Brit. dialect.* to gleam. [Old English *sciene;* related to Old Norse *skjōni* white horse, Gothic *skauns* beautiful, Old High German *scōni* bright] **—'sheen·y** *adj.*

Sheene (ʃi:n) *n.* **Bar·ry.** born 1950, English racing motorcyclist: won the 500 cc. world championship in 1976.

sheen·y ('ʃi:nɪ) *n., pl.* **sheen·ies.** *Slang.* a derogatory word for a **Jew.** [C19: of unknown origin]

sheep (ʃi:p) *n., pl.* **sheep.** **1.** any of various bovid mammals of the genus *Ovis* and related genera, esp. *O. aries* (**domestic sheep**), having transversely ribbed horns and a narrow face. **2. Barbary sheep.** another name for **aoudad.** **3.** a meek or timid person, esp. one without initiative. **4. separate the sheep from the goats.** to pick out the people who are superior in some respects. [Old English *sceap;* related to Old Frisian *skēp,* Old Saxon *scāp,* Old High German *scāf*] **—'sheep+,like** *adj.*

sheep+cote ('ʃi:p,kəʊt) *n. Chiefly Brit.* another word for **sheepfold.**

sheep-dip *n.* **1.** any of several liquid disinfectants and insecticides in which sheep are immersed to kill vermin and germs in their fleece. **2.** a deep trough containing such a liquid.

sheep+dog ('ʃi:p,dɒg) *n.* any of various breeds of dog reared originally for herding sheep. See **Old English sheepdog, Shetland sheepdog.**

sheep+dog tri+al *n.* (*often pl.*) a competition in which sheepdogs are tested in their tasks.

sheep+fold ('ʃi:p,fəʊld) *n.* a pen or enclosure for sheep.

sheep+ish ('ʃi:pɪʃ) *adj.* **1.** abashed or embarrassed, esp. through looking foolish or being in the wrong. **2.** resembling a sheep in timidity or lack of initiative. **—'sheep+ish+ly** *adv.* **—'sheep+ish+ness** *n.*

sheep ked *or* **tick** *n.* a wingless dipterous fly, *Melophagus ovinus,* that is an external parasite of sheep: family *Hippoboscidae.*

sheep's eyes *pl. n. Informal.* amorous or inviting glances.

sheep's fes+cue *n.* a temperate perennial tufted grass, *Festuca ovina,* with narrow inwardly rolled leaves.

sheep+shank ('ʃi:p,ʃæŋk) *n.* a knot, hitch, or bend made in a rope to shorten it temporarily.

sheeps+head ('ʃi:ps,hɛd) *n., pl.* **+head** *or* **+heads.** any of several sparid fishes with strong crushing teeth, esp. *Archosargus rhomboidalis,* of the American Atlantic, which is marked with dark bands.

sheep+shear·ing ('ʃi:p,ʃɪərɪŋ) *n.* **1.** the act or process of shearing sheep. **2.** the season or an occasion of shearing sheep. **3.** a feast held on such an occasion. **—'sheep+,shear·er** *n.*

sheep+skin ('ʃi:p,skɪn) *n.* **a.** the skin of a sheep, esp. when used for clothing, etc., or with the fleece removed and used for parchment. **b.** (*as modifier*): *a sheepskin coat.*

sheep sor+rel *or* **sheep's sor+rel** *n.* a polygonaceous plant, *Rumex acetosella,* of the N hemisphere, having slightly bitter-tasting leaves and small reddish flowers.

sheep sta+tion *or* **run** *n. Austral.* a large sheep farm.

sheep tick *n.* **1.** a tick, *Ixodes ricinus,* that is parasitic on sheep, cattle, and man and transmits the disease louping ill in sheep. **2.** another name for **sheep ked.**

sheep+walk ('ʃi:p,wɔ:k) *n. Chiefly Brit.* a tract of land for grazing sheep.

sheer[1] (ʃɪə) *adj.* **1.** perpendicular; very steep: *a sheer cliff.* **2.** (of textiles) so fine as to be transparent. **3.** (*prenominal*) absolute; unmitigated: *sheer folly.* **4.** *Obsolete.* bright or shining. ~*adv.* **5.** steeply or perpendicularly. **6.** completely or absolutely. ~*n.* **7.** any transparent fabric used for making garments. [Old English *scīr;* related to Old Norse *skīrr* bright, Gothic *skeirs* clear, Middle High German *schīr*] **—'sheer+ly** *adv.* **—'sheer+ness** *n.*

sheer[2] (ʃɪə) *vb.* (foll. by *off* or *away* (*from*)) **1.** to deviate or cause to deviate from a course. **2.** (*intr.*) to avoid an unpleasant person, thing, topic, etc. ~*n.* **3.** the upward sweep of the deck or bulwarks of a vessel. **4.** *Nautical.* the position of a vessel relative to its mooring. [C17: perhaps variant of SHEAR]

sheer+legs *or* **shear+legs** ('ʃɪə,lɛgz) *n.* (*functioning as sing.*) a device for lifting heavy weights consisting of two or more spars lashed together at the upper ends from which a lifting tackle is suspended. Also called: **shears.** [C19: variant of *shear legs*]

Sheer+ness (,ʃɪə'nɛs) *n.* a port and resort in SE England, in N Kent at the junction of the Medway estuary and the Thames: administratively part of Queenborough in Sheppey since 1968.

sheet[1] (ʃi:t) *n.* **1.** a large rectangular piece of cotton, linen, etc., generally one of a pair used as inner bedclothes. **2. a.** a thin piece of a substance such as paper, glass, or metal, usually rectangular in form. **b.** (*as modifier*): *sheet iron.* **3.** a broad continuous surface; expanse or stretch: *a sheet of rain.* **4.** a newspaper, esp. a tabloid. **5.** a piece of printed paper to be folded into a section for a book. **6.** a page of stamps, usually of one denomination and already perforated. **7.** any thin tabular mass of rock covering a large area. ~*vb.* **8.** (*tr.*) to provide with, cover, or wrap in a sheet. [Old English *sciete;* related to *sceat* corner, lap, Old Norse *skaut,* Old High German *scōz* lap]

sheet[2] (ʃi:t) *n. Nautical.* a line or rope for controlling the position of a sail relative to the wind. [Old English *scēata* corner of a sail; related to Middle Low German *schōte* rope attached to a sail; see SHEET[1]]

sheet an+chor *n. Nautical.* a large strong anchor for use in emergency.

sheet bend *n.* a knot used esp. for joining ropes of different sizes. Also called: **becket bend, weaver's hitch.**

sheet down *vb.* (*intr., adv.*) (of rain) to fall heavily in sheets.

sheet-fed *adj. Printing.* involving or printing on separate sheets of paper. Compare **reel-fed.**

sheet+ing ('ʃi:tɪŋ) *n.* fabric from which sheets are made.

sheet light+ning *n.* lightning that appears as a broad sheet, caused by the reflection of more distant lightning.

sheet met+al *n.* metal in the form of a sheet, the thickness being intermediate between that of plate and that of foil.

sheet mu+sic *n.* **1.** the printed or written copy of a short composition or piece, esp. in the form of unbound leaves. **2.** music in its written or printed form.

Shef+field ('ʃɛfi:ld) *n.* a city in N England, on the River Don: important centre of steel manufacture and of the cutlery industry; university (1905); 15th-century church now cathedral. Pop.: 519 703 (1971).

sheik *or* **sheikh** (ʃeɪk) *n.* **1.** (in Muslim countries) **a.** the head of an Arab tribe, village, etc. **b.** a venerable old man. **c.** a religious leader; high priest. **2.** *Informal.* an attractive man. [C16: from Arabic *shaykh* old man]

sheik+dom *or* **sheikh+dom** ('ʃeɪkdəm) *n.* the territory ruled by a sheik.

shei+la ('ʃi:lə) *n. Austral.* a slang word for **girl** or **woman.** [C19: from the girl's name *Sheila*]

shek+el ('ʃɛkəl) *n.* **1.** any of several former coins and units of weight of the Near East. **2.** (*often pl.*) *Informal.* any coin or money. [C16: from Hebrew *sheqel*]

She·ki·nah *or* **She·chi·na** (ʃɛˈkaɪnə; *Hebrew* ʃəxiːˈna) *n. Judaism.* **1.** the radiance in which God's immanent presence in the midst of his people, esp. in the temple, is visibly manifested. **2.** the divine presence itself as contrasted with the divine transcendence. [C17: from Hebrew *shĕkhīnāh,* from *shākhan* to dwell]

shel·duck (ˈʃɛlˌdʌk) *or* (*masc.*) **shel·drake** (ˈʃɛlˌdreɪk) *n., pl.* **·ducks, ·duck** *or* **·drakes, ·drake.** any of various large usually brightly coloured gooselike ducks, such as *Tadorna tadorna* (**common shelduck**), of the Old World. [C14: *shel,* probably from dialect *sheld* pied; related to Middle Dutch *schillede* variegated]

shelf (ʃɛlf) *n., pl.* **shelves** (ʃɛlvz). **1.** a thin flat plank of wood, metal, etc., fixed horizontally against a wall, etc., for the purpose of supporting objects. **2.** something resembling this in shape or function. **3.** the objects placed on a shelf, regarded collectively: *a shelf of books.* **4.** a projecting layer of ice, rock, etc., on land or in the sea. See also **continental shelf. 5.** *Mining.* a layer of bedrock hit when sinking a shaft. **6.** *Archery.* the part of the hand on which an arrow rests when the bow is grasped. **7. on the shelf.** put aside or abandoned, used esp. of unmarried women considered to be past the age of marriage. [Old English *scylfe* ship's deck; related to Middle Low German *schelf* shelf, Old English *scylf* crag] —ˈ**shelf·ˌlike** *adj.*

shelf ice *n.* a less common term for **ice shelf.**

shelf life *n.* the length of time a packaged food, chemical, etc., will last without deteriorating.

shell (ʃɛl) *n.* **1.** the protective calcareous or membranous outer layer of an egg, esp. a bird's egg. **2.** the hard outer covering of many molluscs that is secreted by the mantle. **3.** any other hard outer layer, such as the exoskeleton of many arthropods. **4.** the hard outer layer of some fruits, esp. of nuts. **5.** any hard outer case. **6.** a hollow artillery projectile filled with explosive primed to explode either during flight, on impact, or after penetration. Compare **ball**[1] (sense 7a). **7.** a small-arms cartridge comprising a hollow casing inside which is the primer, charge, and bullet. **8.** a pyrotechnic cartridge designed to explode in the air. **9.** *Rowing.* a very light narrow racing boat. **10.** the external structure of a building, esp. one that is unfinished or one that has been gutted by fire. **11.** the basic structural case of a machine or vehicle. **12.** *Physics.* a class of electron orbits in an atom in which the electrons have the same principal quantum number and differences in their energy are small compared with differences in energy between shells. **13.** the pastry case of a pie, flan, etc. **14.** a thin slab of concrete or a skeletal framework made of wood or metal that forms a shell-like roof. **15.** *Brit.* (in some schools) a class or form. **16. come** (*or* **bring**) **out of one's shell.** to become (or help a person to become) less shy and reserved. ~*vb.* **17.** to divest or be divested of a shell, husk, pod, etc. **18.** to separate or be separated from the ear, husk, cob, etc. **19.** (*tr.*) to bombard with artillery shells. ~See also **shell out.** [Old English *sciell;* related to Old Norse *skel* shell, Gothic *skalja* tile, Middle Low German *schelle* shell; see SCALE, SHALE] —ˈ**shell-less** *adj.* —ˈ**shell-ˌlike** *adj.* —ˈ**shell·y** *adj.*

she'll (ʃiːl; *unstressed* ʃɪl) *contraction of* she will *or* she shall.

shel·lac (ʃəˈlæk, ˈʃɛlæk) *n.* **1.** a yellowish resin secreted by the lac insect, esp. a commercial preparation of this used in varnishes, polishes, and leather dressings. **2.** Also called: **shellac varnish.** a varnish made by dissolving shellac in ethanol or a similar solvent. **3.** a gramophone record based on shellac. ~*vb.* **·lacs, ·lack·ing, ·lacked.** (*tr.*) **4.** to coat or treat (an article, etc.) with a shellac varnish. [C18: SHELL + LAC[1], translation of French *laque en écailles,* literally: lac in scales, that is, in thin plates] —**shel·ˈlack·er** *n.*

shell·back (ˈʃɛlˌbæk) *n.* **1.** *Informal.* a sailor who has crossed the equator. Compare **polliwog. 2.** an experienced or old sailor.

shell·bark (ˈʃɛlˌbɑːk) *n.* another name for **shagbark.**

shell bean *n. U.S.* any of various bean plants that are cultivated for their edible seeds rather than for their pods.

Shel·ley (ˈʃɛlɪ) *n.* **1. Mar·y Woll·stone·craft (Godwin)** (ˈwʊlstənˌkrɑːft). 1797–1851, English writer; author of *Frankenstein* (1818); eloped with Percy Bysshe Shelley. **2. Per·cy Bysshe** (bɪʃ). 1792–1822, English Romantic poet. His major works include *Queen Mab* (1813), *The Revolt of Islam* (1817), and the verse drama *Prometheus Unbound* (1820). He wrote an elegy on the death of Keats, *Adonais* (1821), and shorter lyrics, including the odes *To the West Wind* and *To a Skylark* (both 1820). He was drowned in the Ligurian Sea while sailing from Leghorn to La Spezia.

shell·fire (ˈʃɛlˌfaɪə) *n.* the firing of artillery shells.

shell·fish (ˈʃɛlˌfɪʃ) *n., pl.* **·fish** *or* **·fish·es.** any aquatic invertebrate having a shell or shell-like carapace, esp. such an animal used as human food. Examples are crustaceans such as crabs and lobsters and molluscs such as oysters.

shell jack·et *n.* a rare name for **mess jacket.**

shell out *vb.* (*adv.*) *Informal.* to pay out or hand over (money).

shell·proof (ˈʃɛlˌpruːf) *adj.* designed, intended, or able to resist shellfire.

shell shock *n.* loss of sight, memory, etc., resulting from psychological strain during prolonged engagement in warfare. Also called: **combat neurosis.** —ˈ**shell-ˌshocked** *adj.*

Shel·ta (ˈʃɛltə) *n.* a secret language used by some itinerant tinkers in Ireland and parts of Britain, based on systematically altered Gaelic. [C19: from earlier *sheldrū,* perhaps an arbitrary alteration of Old Irish *bēlre* speech]

shel·ter (ˈʃɛltə) *n.* **1.** something that provides cover or protection, as from weather or danger; place of refuge. **2.** the protection afforded by such a cover; refuge. **3.** the state of being sheltered. ~*vb.* **4.** (*tr.*) to provide with or protect by a shelter. **5.** (*intr.*) to take cover, as from rain; find refuge. **6.** (*tr.*) to act as a shelter for; take under one's protection. [C16: of uncertain origin] —ˈ**shel·ter·er** *n.* —ˈ**shel·ter·less** *adj.*

shel·ter tent *n. U.S.* a military tent for two men.

shel·tie *or* **shel·ty** (ˈʃɛltɪ) *n., pl.* **·ties.** another name for **Shetland pony** or **Shetland sheepdog.** [C17: probably from Orkney dialect *sjalti,* from Old Norse *Hjalti* Shetlander, from *Hjaltland* Shetland]

shelve[1] (ʃɛlv) *vb.* (*tr.*) **1.** to place on a shelf. **2.** to provide with shelves. **3.** to put aside or postpone from consideration. **4.** to dismiss or cause to retire. —ˈ**shelv·er** *n.*

shelve[2] (ʃɛlv) *vb.* (*intr.*) to slope away gradually; incline.

shelves (ʃɛlvz) *n.* the plural of **shelf.**

shelv·ing (ˈʃɛlvɪŋ) *n.* **1.** material for making shelves. **2.** a set of shelves; shelves collectively.

Shem (ʃɛm) *n. Old Testament.* the eldest of Noah's three sons (Genesis 10:21). Douay spelling: **Sem** (sɛm).

She·ma (ʃəˈmɑː) *n.* the declaration of the basic principles of the Jewish faith, proclaiming the absolute unity of God, comprising Deuteronomy 6:4–9 and 11:13–21 and Numbers 15:37–41. [Hebrew, literally: hear]

Shem·be (ˈʃɛmbɛ) *n.* (in South Africa) an African sect that combines Christianity with aspects of Bantu religion.

Shem·ite (ˈʃɛmaɪt) *n.* another word for **Semite.**

She·mit·ic (ʃəˈmɪtɪk) *n., adj.* another word for **Semitic.**

Shen·an·do·ah Na·tion·al Park (ˌʃɛnənˈdəʊə) *n.* a national park in N Virginia: established in 1935 to protect part of the Blue Ridge Mountains. Area: 782 sq. km (302 sq. miles).

she·nan·i·gan (ʃɪˈnænɪgən) *n. Informal.* **1.** (*usually pl.*) roguishness; mischief. **2.** an act of treachery; deception. [C19: of unknown origin]

shend (ʃɛnd) *vb.* **shends, shend·ing, shent.** (*tr.*) *Archaic.* **1.** to put to shame. **2.** to chide or reproach. **3.** to injure or destroy. [Old English *gescendan,* from *scand* SHAME]

Shen·si (ˈʃɛnˈsiː) *n.* a province of NW China: one of the earliest centres of Chinese civilization; largely mountainous. Capital: Sian. Pop.: 26 000 000 (1976 est.). Area: 195 800 sq. km (75 598 sq. miles).

Shen·yang (ˈʃɛnˈjæŋ) *n.* a walled city in NE China in S Manchuria, capital of Liaoning province: capital of the Manchu dynasty from 1644–1912; seized by the Japanese in 1931. Pop.: 2 800 000 (1970 est.). Former name: **Mukden.**

she-oak *n.* any of various Australian trees of the genus *Casuarina.* See **casuarina.** [C18: *she* (in the sense: inferior) + OAK]

She·ol (ˈʃiːəʊl, -ɒl) *n. Old Testament.* **1.** the abode of the dead. **2.** (*often not cap.*) hell. [C16: from Hebrew *shĕʾōl*]

Shep·ard (ˈʃɛpəd) *n.* **Al·an Bart·lett, Jr.** born 1923, U.S. naval officer; first U.S. astronaut in space (1961).

shep·herd (ˈʃɛpəd) *n.* **1.** a person employed to tend sheep. Fem. equivalent: **shep·herd·ess. 2.** a person, such as a clergyman, who watches over or guides a group of people. **3.** *Austral.* a miner who retains the rights to a mining claim without working it. ~*vb.* (*tr.*) **4.** to guide or watch over in the manner of a shepherd. **5.** *Austral.* to retain (a mining claim) without working it. **6.** *Australian Rules football.* to prevent opponents from tackling (a member of one's own team) by blocking their path.

shep·herd dog *n.* another term for **sheepdog.**

shep·herd's nee·dle *n.* a European umbelliferous plant, *Scandix pecten-veneris,* with long needle-like fruits.

shep·herd's pie *n. Chiefly Brit.* a baked dish of minced meat covered with mashed potato. Also called: **cottage pie.**

shep·herd's-purse *n.* a cruciferous plant, *Capsella bursa-pastoris,* having small white flowers and flattened triangular seed pods.

shep·herd's weath·er·glass *n. Brit.* another name for the **scarlet pimpernel.**

sher·ard·ize *or* **sher·ard·ise** (ˈʃɛrəˌdaɪz) *vb. Metallurgy.* to coat (iron or steel) with zinc by heating in a container with zinc dust or (of iron or steel) to be coated in this way. [C20: process named after *Sherard* Cowper-Coles (died 1936), English inventor] —ˌ**sher·ard·i·ˈza·tion** *or* ˌ**sher·ard·i·ˈsa·tion** *n.*

Sher·a·ton[1] (ˈʃɛrətən) *n.* **Thom·as.** 1751–1806, English furniture maker, author of the influential *Cabinet-Maker and Upholsterer's Drawing Book* (1791).

Sher·a·ton[2] (ˈʃɛrətən) *adj.* denoting furniture made by or in the style of Thomas Sheraton, characterized by lightness, elegance, and the extensive use of inlay.

sher·bet (ˈʃɜːbət) *n.* **1.** a fruit-flavoured slightly effervescent powder, eaten as a sweet or used to make a drink: *lemon sherbet.* **2.** another word (esp. U.S.) for **sorbet** (sense 1). **3.** *Austral. slang.* beer. [C17: from Turkish *şerbet,* from Persian *sharbat,* from Arabic *sharbah* drink, from *shariba* to drink]

Sher·brooke (ˈʃɜːˌbrʊk) *n.* a city in E Canada, in S Quebec: industrial and commercial centre. Pop.: 80 711 (1971).

sherd (ʃɜːd) *n.* another word for **shard.**

she·ri·a (ʃəˈriːə) *n.* a variant spelling of **sharia.**

Sher·i·dan (ˈʃɛrɪdən) *n.* **1. Phil·ip Hen·ry.** 1831–88, American Union cavalry commander in the Civil War. He forced Lee's surrender to Grant (1865). **2. Rich·ard Brins·ley** (ˈbrɪnzlɪ). 1751–1816, Irish dramatist, politician, and orator, noted for his comedies of manners *The Rivals* (1775), *School for Scandal* (1777), and *The Critic* (1779).

she·rif *or* **she·reef** (ʃɛˈriːf) *n. Islam.* **1.** a descendant of Mohammed through his daughter Fatima. **2.** the governor of

Mecca. **3.** an honorific title accorded to any Muslim ruler. [C16: from Arabic *sharīf* noble]

sher·iff ('ʃɛrɪf) *n.* **1.** (in the U.S.) the chief law-enforcement officer in a county: popularly elected, except in Rhode Island. **2.** (in England and Wales) the chief executive officer of the Crown in a county, having chiefly ceremonial duties. **3.** (in Scotland) a judge in any of the sheriff courts. [Old English *scīrgerēfa,* from *scīr* SHIRE + *gerēfa* REEVE]

sher·iff court *n.* (in Scotland) a court having jurisdiction to try summarily or on indictment all but the most serious crimes and to deal with most civil actions.

Sher·man ('ʃɜːmən) *n.* **Wil·liam Te·cum·seh** (tɪ'kʌmsə). 1820–91, American Union commander during the Civil War. He led the victorious march through Georgia (1864), becoming commander of the army in 1869.

Sher·pa ('ʃɜːpə) *n., pl.* **·pas** *or* **·pa.** a member of a Tibetan people living on the southern slopes of the Himalayas in Nepal, noted as mountaineers.

Sher·ring·ton ('ʃɛrɪŋtən) *n.* Sir **Charles Scott.** 1857–1952, English physiologist, noted for his work on reflex action, published in *The Integrative Action of the Nervous System* (1906): shared the Nobel prize for medicine with Adrian (1932).

sher·ry ('ʃɛrɪ) *n., pl.* **·ries.** a fortified wine, originally only from the Jerez region of southern Spain, usually drunk as an aperitif. [C16: from earlier *sherris* (assumed to be plural), from Spanish *Xeres,* now *Jerez*]

's Her·to·gen·bosch (*Dutch* ˌshɛrtoːxən'bɔs) *n.* a city in the S Netherlands, capital of North Brabant province: birthplace of Hieronymus Bosch. Pop.: 84 914 (1973 est.). Also called: **Den Bosch.** French name: **Bois-le-Duc.**

sher·wa·ni (ʃɛə'wɑːnɪ) *n.* a long coat closed up to the neck, worn by men in India. [Hindi]

Sher·wood ('ʃɜːˌwʊd) *n.* **Ro·bert Em·met.** 1896–1955, U.S. dramatist. His plays include *The Petrified Forest* (1935), *Idiot's Delight* (1936), and *There shall be no Night* (1940).

Sher·wood For·est *n.* an ancient forest in central England, in Nottinghamshire: formerly a royal hunting ground and much more extensive; famous as the home of Robin Hood.

she's (ʃiːz) *contraction of* she is *or* she has.

Shet·land *or* **Shet·land Is·lands** ('ʃɛtlənd) *pl. n.* a group of about 100 islands (fewer than 20 inhabited), off the N coast of Scotland, which constitute an island authority of Scotland: a Norse dependency from the 8th century until 1472; noted for the breeding of Shetland ponies, knitwear manufacturing, and fishing. Administrative centre: Lerwick. Pop.: 18 962 (1976 est.). Area: 1426 sq. km (550 sq. miles). Official name (until 1974): **Zetland.**

Shet·land po·ny *n.* a very small sturdy breed of pony with a long shaggy mane and tail.

Shet·land sheep·dog *n.* a small sheepdog similar in appearance to a collie.

Shet·land wool *n.* a fine loosely twisted wool yarn obtained from Shetland sheep and used esp. for sweaters.

sheugh (ʃʌx) *n. Scot. dialect.* a ditch or trough. [dialect variant of SOUGH²]

She·vat *Hebrew.* (ʃɛ'vat) *n. Judaism.* a variant spelling of **Shebat.**

shew (ʃəʊ) *vb.* **shews, shew·ing, shewed; shewn** *or* **shewed.** an archaic spelling of **show.** —**'shew·er** *n.*

shew·bread *or* **show·bread** ('ʃəʊˌbrɛd) *n. Old Testament.* the loaves of bread placed every Sabbath on the table beside the altar of incense in the tabernacle or temple of ancient Israel (Exodus 25:30; Leviticus 24:5–9).

SHF, S.H.F., *or* **s.h.f.** *Radio. abbrev. for* superhigh frequency.

Shi·ah ('ʃiːə) *n.* **1.** one of the two main branches of orthodox Islam, now mainly in Persia, which regards Mohammed's cousin Ali and his successors as the true imams. **2.** another name for **Shiite.** ~*adj.* **3.** designating or characteristic of this sect or its beliefs and practices. [C17: from Arabic *shī'ah* sect, from *shā'a* to follow]

shi·ai ('ʃiːaɪ) *n.* a judo contest. [Japanese]

shib·bo·leth ('ʃɪbəˌlɛθ) *n.* a custom, phrase, or use of language that distinguishes members of a particular social class, profession, etc., from other people. [C14: from Hebrew, literally: ear of grain; the word is used in the Old Testament by the Gileadites as a test word for the Ephraimites, who could not pronounce the sound *sh*]

shick·er ('ʃɪkə) *n. Austral. slang.* alcoholic drink; liquor. [via Yiddish from Hebrew]

shick·ered ('ʃɪkəd) *adj. Austral. slang.* drunk; intoxicated.

shied (ʃaɪd) *vb.* the past tense or past participle of **shy.**

shield (ʃiːld) *n.* **1.** any protection used to intercept blows, missiles, etc., such as a tough piece of armour carried on the arm. **2.** any similar protective device. **3.** Also called: **scutcheon, escutcheon.** *Heraldry.* a pointed stylized shield used for displaying armorial bearings. **4.** anything that resembles a shield in shape, such as a prize in a sports competition. **5.** the protective outer covering of an animal, such as the shell of a turtle. **6.** *Physics.* a structure of concrete, lead, etc., placed around a nuclear reactor or other source of radiation in order to prevent the escape of radiation. **7.** a broad stable plateau of ancient Precambrian rocks forming the rigid nucleus of a particular continent. See **Baltic Shield, Canadian Shield. 8.** short for **dress shield.** ~*vb.* (*tr.*) **9.** to protect, hide, or conceal (something) from danger or harm. [Old English *scield;* related to Old Norse *skjöldr,* Gothic *skildus,* Old High German *scilt* shield, Old English *sciell* SHELL] —**'shield·er** *n.* —**'shield·ˌlike** *adj.*

shield bug *n.* any shield-shaped herbivorous heteropterous insect of the superfamily *Pentamoidea,* esp. any of the family *Pentatomidae.* Also called: **stink bug.**

shield-fern *n.* any temperate woodland fern of the genus *Polystichum* having shield-shaped flaps covering the spore-producing bodies.

Shield of Da·vid *n.* another term for the **Star of David.**

shiel·ing ('ʃiːlɪŋ) *n. Chiefly Scot.* **1.** a temporary shelter used by people tending cattle on high ground. **2.** a hut in the hills or in a remote spot. **3.** pasture land for the grazing of cattle in summer. [C16: from earlier *shiel,* from Middle English *shale* hut, of unknown origin]

shi·er¹ ('ʃaɪə) *adj.* a comparative of **shy**¹.

shi·er² *or* **shy·er** ('ʃaɪə) *n.* a horse that shies habitually.

shi·est ('ʃaɪɪst) *adj.* a superlative of **shy**¹.

shift (ʃɪft) *vb.* **1.** to move or cause to move from one place or position to another. **2.** (*tr.*) to change for another or others. **3.** to change (gear) in a motor vehicle. **4.** (*intr.*) (of a sound or set of sounds) to alter in a systematic way. **5.** (*intr.*) to provide for one's needs (esp. in the phrase **shift for oneself**). **6.** (*intr.*) to proceed by indirect or evasive methods. **7.** to remove or be removed, esp. with difficulty: *no detergent can shift these stains.* **8.** *Slang.* to move quickly. ~*n.* **9.** the act or an instance of shifting. **10.** a group of workers who work for a specific period. **11.** the period of time worked by such a group. **12.** an expedient, contrivance, or artifice. **13.** the displacement of rocks, esp. layers or seams in mining, at a geological fault. **14.** an underskirt or dress with little shaping. [Old English *sciftan;* related to Old Norse *skipta* to divide, Middle Low German *schiften,* to separate] —**'shift·er** *n.* —**'shift·ing·ly** *adv.* —**'shift·ing·ness** *n.*

shift·ing cul·ti·va·tion *n.* a land-use system, esp. in tropical Africa, in which a tract of land is cleared and the land cultivated until its fertility diminishes, when the area is abandoned until this is restored naturally.

shift·ing span·ner *n. Austral.* an adjustable spanner. Also called: **shifter.**

shift key *n.* a key on a typewriter used to adjust the action of the machine so that it types capital letters.

shift·less ('ʃɪftlɪs) *adj.* lacking in ambition or initiative. —**'shift·less·ly** *adv.* —**'shift·less·ness** *n.*

shift·y ('ʃɪftɪ) *adj.* **shift·i·er, shift·i·est. 1.** given to evasions; artful. **2.** furtive in character or appearance. **3.** full of expedients; resourceful. —**'shift·i·ly** *adv.* —**'shift·i·ness** *n.*

shi·gel·la (ʃɪ'gɛlə) *n.* any rod-shaped Gram-negative bacterium of the genus *Shigella,* some species of which cause dysentery. [C20: named after K. *Shiga* (1870–1957), Japanese bacteriologist, who discovered it]

Shih·chia·chuang *or* **Shih·kia·chwang** (ˌʃiːtʃjɑː'tʃwæŋ) *n.* a city in NE China, capital of Hopeh province: textile manufacturing. Pop.: 800 000 (1970 est.).

shih-tzu (ʃiː'tsuː) *n.* a Chinese breed of small dog similar to a Pekingese. [from Chinese, literally: lion]

Shi·ism ('ʃiːɪzəm) *n. Islam.* the beliefs and practices of Shiah.

Shi·ite ('ʃiːaɪt) *or* **Shi·ah** *Islam.* ~*n.* **1.** an adherent of Shiah. ~*adj.* **2.** of, relating to Shiah. —**Shi·it·ic** (ʃiː'ɪtɪk) *adj.*

shi·kar (ʃɪ'kɑː) (in India) ~*n.* **1.** hunting, esp. big-game hunting. ~*vb.* **·kars, ·kar·ring, ·karred. 2.** to hunt (game, esp. big game). [C17: via Urdu from Persian]

shi·ka·ri *or* **shi·ka·ree** (ʃɪ'kɑːrɪ) *n., pl.* **·ris** *or* **·rees.** (in India) a hunter.

Shi·ko·ku ('ʃiːkəʊˌkuː) *n.* the smallest of the four main islands of Japan, separated from Honshu by the Inland Sea: mostly forested and mountainous. Pop.: 3 904 014 (1970). Area: 17 759 sq. km (6857 sq. miles).

shik·sa ('ʃɪksə) *n. Often derogatory.* (used by Jews) **1.** a non-Jewish girl. **2.** a Jewish girl who fails to live up to traditional Jewish standards. [Yiddish *shikse,* feminine of *sheygets* non-Jewish youth, from Hebrew *sheqes* defect]

shil·le·lagh *or* **shil·la·la** (ʃə'leɪlə, -lɪ) *n.* (in Ireland) a stout club or cudgel, esp. one made of oak or blackthorn. [C18: from *Shillelagh,* town in County Wicklow, Ireland, whose trees formerly furnished the wood for such cudgels]

shil·ling ('ʃɪlɪŋ) *n.* **1.** a British silver or (later) cupronickel coin worth one twentieth of a pound, replaced by the 5p piece in 1970. Abbrev.: **s., sh. 2.** the standard monetary unit of Kenya, Uganda, the Somali Republic, and Tanzania: divided into 100 cents. **3.** an old monetary unit of the U.S. varying in value in different states. [Old English *scilling;* related to Old Norse *skillingr,* Gothic *skilliggs,* Old High German *skilling*]

shil·ling mark *n.* another name for **solidus** (sense 1).

Shil·long (ʃɪ'lɒŋ) *n.* a city in NE India, capital of the states of Assam and Meghalaya and of the Union Territory of Arunachal Pradesh: situated on the **Shillong Plateau** at an altitude of 1520 m (4987 ft.); destroyed by earthquake in 1897 and rebuilt. Pop.: 87 659 (1971).

shil·ly·shal·ly ('ʃɪlɪˌʃælɪ) *Informal.* ~*vb.* **·lies, ·ly·ing, ·lied. 1.** (*intr.*) to be indecisive, esp. over unimportant matters; hesitate. ~*adv.* **2.** in an indecisive manner. ~*adj.* **3.** indecisive or hesitant. ~*n., pl.* **·lies. 4.** indecision or hesitation; vacillation. —**'shil·ly·ˌshal·li·er** *n.*

Shi·loh ('ʃaɪləʊ) *n.* a town in central ancient Palestine, in Canaan on the E slope of Mount Ephraim: keeping place of the tabernacle and the ark; destroyed by the Philistines.

shi·ly ('ʃaɪlɪ) *adv.* a less common spelling of **shyly.**

shim (ʃɪm) *n.* **1.** a thin packing strip or washer often used with a number of similar washers or strips to adjust a clearance for gears, etc. ~*vb.* **shims, shim·ming, shimmed. 2.** (*tr.*) to modify a load or clearance on (a gear, etc.) by use of shims. [C18: of unknown origin]

shim·mer ('ʃɪmə) *vb.* **1.** (*intr.*) to shine with a glistening or tremulous light. ~*n.* **2.** a faint, glistening, or tremulous light. [Old English *scimerian;* related to Middle Low German *schēmeren* to grow dark, Old Norse *skimi* brightness] —'**shim·mer·ing·ly** *adv.* —'**shim·mer·y** *adj.*

shim·my ('ʃɪmɪ) *n., pl.* **·mies. 1.** an American ragtime dance with much shaking of the hips and shoulders. **2.** abnormal wobbling motion in a motor vehicle, esp. in the front wheels or steering. **3.** an informal word for **chemise.** ~*vb.* **·mies, ·my·ing, ·mied.** (*intr.*) **4.** to dance the shimmy. **5.** to vibrate or wobble. [C19: changed from CHEMISE, mistakenly assumed to be plural]

Shi·mo·no·se·ki (ˌʃɪmənəʊ'sɛkɪ) *n.* a port in SW Japan, on SW Honshu: scene of the peace treaty (1895) ending the Sino-Japanese War; a heavy industrial centre. Pop.: 266 233 (1974 est.).

shin[1] (ʃɪn) *n.* **1.** the front part of the lower leg. **2.** the front edge of the tibia. **3.** *Chiefly Brit.* a cut of beef, the lower foreleg. ~*vb.* **shins, shin·ning, shinned. 4.** (when *intr.*, often foll. by *up*) to climb (a pole, tree, etc.) by gripping with the hands or arms and the legs and hauling oneself up. **5.** (*tr.*) to kick (a person) in the shins. [Old English *scinu;* related to Old High German *scina* needle, Norwegian dialect *skina* small disc]

shin[2] (ʃɪn) *n.* the 22nd letter in the Hebrew alphabet (ש), transliterated as *sh.* [from Hebrew *shīn,* literally: tooth]

Shi·nar ('ʃaɪnə) *n. Old Testament.* the southern part of the valley of the Tigris and Euphrates, often identified with Sumer; Babylonia.

shin·bone ('ʃɪnˌbəʊn) *n.* the nontechnical name for **tibia** (sense 1).

shin·dig ('ʃɪnˌdɪg) *or* **shin·dy** ('ʃɪndɪ) *n., pl.* **·digs** *or* **·dies.** *Slang.* **1.** a noisy party, dance, etc. **2.** a quarrel or commotion. [C19: variant of SHINTY]

shine (ʃaɪn) *vb.* **shines, shin·ing, shone. 1.** (*intr.*) to emit light. **2.** (*intr.*) to glow or be bright with reflected light. **3.** (*tr.*) to direct the light of (a lamp, etc.): *he shone the torch in my eyes.* **4.** (*tr.; past tense and past participle* **shined**) to cause to gleam by polishing: *to shine shoes.* **5.** (*intr.*) to be conspicuously competent; excel: *she shines at tennis.* **6.** (*intr.*) to appear clearly; be conspicuous: *the truth shone out of his words.* ~*n.* **7.** the state or quality of shining; sheen; lustre. **8. come rain or shine.** whatever the weather. **9.** *Informal.* short for **moonshine** (whisky). **10.** *Informal.* a liking or fancy (esp. in the phrase **take a shine to**). [Old English *scīnan;* related to Old Norse *skīna,* Gothic *skeinan,* Old High German *scīnan* to shine, Greek *skia* shadow]

shin·er ('ʃaɪnə) *n.* **1.** something that shines, such as a polishing device. **2.** any of numerous small North American freshwater cyprinid fishes of the genus *Notropis* and related genera, such as *N. cornutus* (**common shiner**) and *Notemigonus crysoleucas* (**golden shiner**). **3.** a popular name for the **mackerel. 4.** *Informal.* a black eye.

shin·gle[1] ('ʃɪŋgᵊl) *n.* **1.** a thin rectangular tile, esp. one made of wood, that is laid with others in overlapping rows to cover a roof or a wall. **2.** a woman's short-cropped hair style. **3.** *U.S. informal.* a small signboard or name plate fixed outside the office of a doctor, lawyer, etc. **4. a shingle short.** *Austral. informal.* unintelligent or mentally subnormal. ~*vb.* (*tr.*) **5.** to cover (a roof or a wall) with shingles. **6.** to cut (the hair) in a short-cropped style. [C12 *scingle,* from Late Latin *scindula* a split piece of wood, from Latin *scindere* to split] —'**shin·gler** *n.*

shin·gle[2] ('ʃɪŋgᵊl) *n.* **1.** coarse gravel, esp. the pebbles found on beaches. **2.** a place or area strewn with shingle. [C16: of Scandinavian origin; compare Norwegian *singl* pebbles, Frisian *singel* gravel] —'**shin·gly** *adj.*

shin·gle[3] ('ʃɪŋgᵊl) *vb.* (*tr.*) *Metallurgy.* to hammer or squeeze the slag out of (iron) after puddling in the production of wrought iron. [C17: from Old French dialect *chingler* to whip, from *chingle* belt, from Latin *cingula* girdle; see CINGULUM]

shin·gles ('ʃɪŋgᵊlz) *n.* an acute viral disease affecting the ganglia of certain nerves, characterized by inflammation, pain, and skin eruptions along the course of the affected nerve. Technical names: **herpes zoster, zoster.** [C14: from Medieval Latin *cingulum* girdle, rendering Greek *zōnē* ZONE]

shin·kin ('ʃɪŋkɪn) *n. South Wales dialect.* a worthless person. [Welsh, from the surname *Jenkin,* of Dutch origin]

shin·leaf ('ʃɪnˌliːf) *n., pl.* **·leaves.** the usual U.S. name for **wintergreen** (sense 3).

shin·plas·ter ('ʃɪnˌplɑːstə) *n. U.S., Austral.* a promissory note on brittle paper, issued by an individual.

Shin·to ('ʃɪntəʊ) *n.* the indigenous religion of Japan, polytheistic in character and incorporating the worship of a number of ethnic divinities, from the chief of which the emperor is believed to be descended. [C18: from Japanese: the way of the gods, from Chinese *shên* gods + *tao* way] —'**Shin·to·ism** *n.* —'**Shin·to·ist** *n., adj.*

shin·ty ('ʃɪntɪ) *or U.S.* **shin·ny** ('ʃɪnɪ) *n., pl.* **·ties. 1.** a simple form of hockey played with a ball and sticks curved at the lower end. **2.** the stick used in this game. ~*vb.* **·ties, ·ty·ing, ·tied** *or U.S.* **·nies, ·ny·ing, ·nied.** (*intr.*) **3.** to play shinty. [C17: probably from the cry *shin ye* in the game]

shin·y ('ʃaɪnɪ) *adj.* **shin·i·er, shin·i·est. 1.** glossy or polished; bright. **2.** (of clothes or material) worn to a smooth and glossy state, as by continual rubbing. —'**shin·i·ness** *n.*

ship (ʃɪp) *n.* **1.** a vessel propelled by engines or sails for navigating on the water, esp. a large vessel that cannot be carried aboard another, as distinguished from a boat. **2.** *Nautical.* a large sailing vessel with three or more square-rigged masts. **3.** the crew of a ship. **4.** short for **airship** or **spaceship. 5.** *Informal.* any vehicle or conveyance. **6. when one's ship comes in** (*or* **home**). when one has become successful or wealthy. ~*vb.* **ships, ship·ping, shipped. 7.** to place, transport, or travel on any conveyance, esp. aboard a ship: *ship the microscopes by aeroplane; can we ship tomorrow?* **8.** (*tr.*) *Nautical.* to take (water) over the side. **9.** to bring or go aboard a vessel: *to ship oars.* **10.** (*tr.;* often foll. by *off*) *Informal.* to send away, often in order to be rid of: *they shipped the children off to boarding school.* **11.** (*intr.*) to engage to serve aboard a ship: *I shipped aboard a Liverpool liner.* ~See also **ship out.** [Old English *scip;* related to Old Norse *skip,* Old High German *skif* ship, *scipfi* cup] —'**ship·pa·ble** *adj.*

-ship *suffix forming nouns.* **1.** indicating state or condition: *fellowship.* **2.** indicating rank, office, or position: *lordship.* **3.** indicating craft or skill: *horsemanship; workmanship; scholarship.* [Old English *-scipe;* compare SHAPE]

ship·board ('ʃɪpˌbɔːd) *n.* **1.** (*modifier*) taking place, used, or intended for use aboard a ship: *a shipboard encounter.* **2. on shipboard.** on board a ship.

ship·build·er ('ʃɪpˌbɪldə) *n.* a person or business engaged in the building of ships. —'**ship·ˌbuild·ing** *n.*

ship chan·dler *n.* a person or business dealing in supplies for ships. —**ship chan·dler·y** *n.*

Ship·ka Pass ('ʃɪpkə) *n.* a pass over the Balkan Mountains in central Bulgaria: scene of fierce fighting in the Russo-Turkish War (1877–78). Height: 1334 m (4376 ft.).

ship·load ('ʃɪpˌləʊd) *n.* the quantity carried by a ship.

ship·mas·ter ('ʃɪpˌmɑːstə) *or* **ship·man** ('ʃɪpmən) *n., pl.* **·mas·ters** *or* **·men.** the master or captain of a ship.

ship·mate ('ʃɪpˌmeɪt) *n.* a sailor who serves on the same ship as another.

ship·ment ('ʃɪpmənt) *n.* **1. a.** goods shipped together as part of the same lot: *a shipment of grain.* **b.** (*as modifier*): *a shipment schedule.* **2.** the act of shipping cargo.

ship mon·ey *n. English history.* a tax levied to finance the fitting out of warships: abolished 1640.

ship of the line *n. Nautical.* (formerly) a warship large enough to fight in the first line of battle.

ship out *vb.* (*adv.*) to depart or cause to depart by ship: *we shipped out at dawn; they shipped out the new recruits.*

ship·own·er ('ʃɪpˌəʊnə) *n.* a person who owns or has shares in a ship or ships.

ship·per ('ʃɪpə) *n.* a person or company in the business of shipping freight.

ship·ping ('ʃɪpɪŋ) *n.* **1. a.** the business of transporting freight, esp. by ship. **b.** (*as modifier*): *a shipping magnate; shipping office.* **2. a.** ships collectively: *there is a lot of shipping in the Channel.* **b.** the tonnage of a number of ships: *shipping for this year exceeded that of last.*

ship·ping clerk *n.* a person employed by a company to receive, unpack, pack, and send shipments of goods.

ship·ping ton *n.* the full name for **ton**[1] (sense 5).

ship-rigged *adj.* rigged as a full-rigged ship.

ship's bis·cuit *n.* another name for **hardtack.**

ship's boy *n.* a young man or boy employed to attend the needs of passengers or officers aboard ship.

ship·shape ('ʃɪpˌʃeɪp) *adj.* **1.** neat; orderly. ~*adv.* **2.** in a neat and orderly manner.

ship's pa·pers *pl. n.* the documents that are required by law to be carried by a ship for the purpose of ascertaining details of her ownership, nationality, destination, and cargo or to prove her neutrality.

ship·way ('ʃɪpˌweɪ) *n.* **1.** the structure on which a vessel is built, then launched. **2.** a canal used by ships.

ship·worm ('ʃɪpˌwɜːm) *n.* any wormlike marine bivalve mollusc of the genus *Teredo* and related genera and family *Teredinidae.* They bore into wooden piers, ships, etc., by means of drill-like shell valves. See also **piddock.**

ship·wreck ('ʃɪpˌrɛk) *n.* **1.** the partial or total destruction of a ship at sea. **2.** a wrecked ship or part of such a ship. **3.** ruin or destruction: *the shipwreck of all my hopes.* ~*vb.* (*tr.*) **4.** to wreck or destroy (a ship). **5.** to bring to ruin or destruction. [Old English *scipwræc,* from SHIP + *wræc* something driven by the sea; see WRACK]

ship·wright ('ʃɪpˌraɪt) *n.* an artisan skilled in one or more of the tasks required to build vessels.

ship·yard ('ʃɪpˌjɑːd) *n.* a place or facility for the building, maintenance, and repair of ships.

shi·ra·lee (ˌʃɪrə'liː) *n. Austral. informal.* a swag; swagman's bundle. [C19: of unknown origin]

Shi·raz (ʃɪə'rɑːz) *n.* a city in SW Iran, at an altitude of 1585 m (5200 ft.): an important Muslim cultural centre in the 14th century; university (1948); noted for fine carpets. Pop.: 373 000 (1973 est.).

shire[1] (ʃaɪə) *n.* **1. a.** one of the British counties. **b.** (*in combination*): *Yorkshire.* **2.** (in Australia) a rural district having its own local council. **3.** See **shire horse. 4. the Shires.** the Midland counties of England, esp. Northamptonshire and Leicestershire, famous for hunting, etc. [Old English *scīr* office; related to Old High German *scīra* business]

shire[2] (ʃaɪə) *vb.* (*tr.*) *Ulster dialect.* to refresh or rest: *let me get my head shired.* [from Old English *scīr* clear]

Shi·ré ('ʃɪəreɪ) *n.* a river in E central Africa, flowing from Lake Malawi through Malawi and Mozambique to the Zambezi. Length: 596 km (370 miles).

Shi·ré High·lands *pl. n.* an upland area of S Malawi. Average height: 900 m (3000 ft.).

shire horse *n.* a large heavy breed of carthorse with long hair on the fetlocks. Often shortened to **shire.**

shirk (ʃɜːk) *vb.* **1.** to avoid discharging (work, a duty, etc.); evade. ~*n. also* **shirk·er. 2.** a person who shirks. [C17: probably from German *Schurke* rogue; see SHARK²]

shirr (ʃɜː) *vb.* **1.** to gather (fabric) into two or more parallel rows to decorate a dress, blouse, etc., often using elastic thread. **2.** (*tr.*) to bake (eggs) out of their shells. ~*n. also* **shirr·ing. 3.** a series of gathered rows decorating a dress, blouse, etc. [C19: of unknown origin]

shirt (ʃɜːt) *n.* **1.** a garment worn on the upper part of the body, esp. by men, usually of light material and typically having a collar and sleeves and buttoning up the front. **2.** short for **nightshirt** or **undershirt. 3. keep your shirt on.** *Informal.* to refrain from losing one's temper (often used as an exhortation to another). **4. put** *or* **lose one's shirt on.** *Informal.* to bet or lose all one has on (a horse, etc.). [Old English *scyrte; related* to Old English *sceort* SHORT, Old Norse *skyrta* skirt, Middle High German *schurz* apron]

shirt·ing ('ʃɜːtɪŋ) *n.* fabric used in making men's shirts.

shirt·sleeve ('ʃɜːtˌsliːv) *n.* **1.** the sleeve of a shirt. **2. in one's shirtsleeves.** not wearing a jacket.

shirt-tail *n.* the part of a shirt that extends below the waist.

shirt·waist·er ('ʃɜːtˌweɪstə) *or U.S.* **shirt·waist** *n.* a woman's dress with a tailored bodice resembling a shirt.

shirt·y ('ʃɜːtɪ) *adj.* **shirt·i·er, shirt·i·est.** *Slang, chiefly Brit.* bad-tempered or annoyed. [C19: perhaps based on such phrases as *to get someone's shirt out* to annoy someone]

shish ke·bab ('ʃiːʃ kəˈbæb) *n.* the full term for **kebab.** [from Turkish *şiş kebab,* from *şiş* skewer; see KEBAB]

shit (ʃɪt) *vb.* **shits, shit·ting; shit·ted** *or* **shit. 1.** to defecate. ~*n.* **2.** faeces; excrement. **3.** *Slang.* rubbish; nonsense. **4.** *Slang.* cannabis resin. **5. in the shit.** *Slang.* in trouble. ~*interj.* **6.** *Slang.* an exclamation expressing anger, disgust, etc. [Old English *scite* (unattested) dung, *scītan* to defecate, of Germanic origin; related to Old English *scēadan* to separate, Old Norse *skīta* to defecate, Middle Dutch *schitte* excrement] —'**shit·ty** *adj.*

shit·head ('ʃɪtˌhɛd) *n.* **1.** *Taboo slang.* a fool; idiot: used as a term of abuse. **2.** *Brit. slang.* a habitual smoker of marijuana or hashish.

shit·tah ('ʃɪtə) *n., pl.* **shit·tim** ('ʃɪtɪm) *or* **shit·tahs.** a tree mentioned in the Old Testament, thought to be either of two Asian acacias, *Acacia seyal* or *A. tortilis,* having close-grained yellow-brown wood. [C17: from Hebrew *shittāh;* related to Egyptian *sout* acacia]

Shit·tim ('ʃɪtɪm) *n. Old Testament.* the site to the east of the Jordan and northeast of the Dead Sea where the Israelites encamped before crossing the Jordan (Numbers 25:1–9).

shit·tim wood ('ʃɪtɪm) *n. Old Testament.* a kind of wood, probably acacia, from which the Ark of the Covenant and parts of the tabernacle were made. [C14: from Hebrew *shittīm,* plural of SHITTAH]

shiv (ʃɪv) *n.* a slang word for **knife.** [perhaps from Romany *chiv* blade]

Shi·va ('ʃiːvə, 'ʃɪvə) *n.* a variant spelling of **Siva.** —'**Shi·va·ism** *n.* —'**Shi·va·ist** *n.*

shiv·a·ree (ˌʃɪvəˈriː) *n.* a variant spelling (esp. U.S.) of **charivari.**

shive (ʃaɪv) *n.* **1.** a flat cork or bung for wide-mouthed bottles. **2.** an archaic word for **slice.** [C13: from Middle Dutch or Middle Low German *schīve;* see SHEAVE]

shiv·er¹ ('ʃɪvə) *vb.* (*intr.*) **1.** to shake or tremble, as from cold or fear. **2. a.** (of a sail) to luff; flap or shake. **b.** (of a sailing vessel) to sail close enough to the wind to make the sails luff. ~*n.* **3.** the act of shivering; a tremulous motion. **4. the shivers.** an attack of shivering, esp. through fear or illness. [C13 *chiveren,* perhaps variant of *chevelen* to chatter (used of teeth), from Old English *ceafl* JOWL] —'**shiv·er·er** *n.* —'**shiv·er·ing·ly** *adv.*

shiv·er² ('ʃɪvə) *vb.* **1.** to break or cause to break into fragments. ~*n.* **2.** a splintered piece. [C13: of Germanic origin; compare Old High German *scivaro,* Middle Dutch *scheveren* to shiver, Old Norse *skīfa* to split]

shiv·er·y¹ ('ʃɪvərɪ) *adj.* **1.** inclined to shiver or tremble. **2.** causing shivering, esp. through cold or fear.

shiv·er·y² ('ʃɪvərɪ) *adj. Rare.* easily shattered; brittle.

Shi·zu·o·ka (ˌʃiːzuːˈəʊkə) *n.* a city in central Japan, on S Honshu: a centre for green tea; university (1949). Pop.: 443 851 (1974 est.).

Shko·dër (*Albanian* 'ʃkodər) *n.* a market town in NW Albania, on **Lake Shkodër:** an Illyrian capital in the first millennium B.C. Pop.: 55 300 (1970 est.). Italian name: **Scutari.**

Shluh (ʃəˈluː, ʃluː) *n.* **1.** (*pl.* **Shluhs** *or* **Shluh**) a member of a Berber people inhabiting the Atlas Mountains in Morocco and Algeria. **2.** the dialect of Berber spoken by this people.

S.H.M. *abbrev. for* simple harmonic motion.

Sho·a ('ʃəʊə) *n.* a province of central Ethiopia: high plateau country, with the Great Rift Valley in the east and southeast. Capital: Addis Ababa. Pop.: 5 209 700 (1971 est.). Area: 65 483 sq. km (25 283 sq. miles).

shoal¹ (ʃəʊl) *n.* **1.** a stretch of shallow water. **2.** a sandbank or rocky area in a stretch of water, esp. one that is visible at low water. ~*vb.* **3.** to make or become shallow. **4.** (*intr.*) *Nautical.* to sail into shallower water. ~*adj. also* **shoal·y. 5.** a less common word for **shallow. 6.** *Nautical.* (of the draught of a vessel) drawing little water. [Old English *sceald* SHALLOW] —'**shoal·i·ness** *n.*

shoal² (ʃəʊl) *n.* **1.** a large group of fish. **2.** a large group of people or things. ~*vb.* **3.** (*intr.*) to collect together in such a group. [Old English *scolu;* related to Middle Low German, Middle Dutch *schōle* SCHOOL²]

shoat *or* **shote** (ʃəʊt) *n.* a piglet that has recently been weaned. [C15: related to West Flemish *schote*]

shock¹ (ʃɒk) *vb.* **1.** to experience or cause to experience extreme horror, disgust, surprise, etc.: *the atrocities shocked us; she shocks easily.* **2.** to cause a state of shock in (a person). **3.** to come or cause to come into violent contact; jar. ~*n.* **4.** a sudden and violent jarring blow or impact. **5.** something that causes a sudden and violent disturbance in the emotions: *the shock of her father's death made her ill.* **6.** *Pathol.* a state of bodily collapse or near collapse caused by circulatory failure or sudden lowering of the blood pressure, as from severe bleeding, burns, fright, etc.: *people close to the bomb blast were treated for shock.* **7.** See **electric shock.** [C16: from Old French *choc,* from *choquier* to make violent contact with, of Germanic origin; related to Middle High German *schoc*] —'**shock·a·ble** *adj.* —ˌ**shock·a·'bil·i·ty** *n.*

shock² (ʃɒk) *n.* **1.** a number of sheaves set on end in a field to dry. **2.** a pile or stack of unthreshed corn. ~*vb.* **3.** (*tr.*) to set up (sheaves) in shocks. [C14: probably of Germanic origin; compare Middle Low German, Middle Dutch *schok* shock of corn, group of sixty]

shock³ (ʃɒk) *n.* **1.** a thick bushy mass, esp. of hair. ~*adj.* **2.** *Rare.* bushy; shaggy. [C19: perhaps from SHOCK²]

shock ab·sorb·er *n.* any device designed to absorb mechanical shock, esp. one fitted to a motor vehicle to damp the recoil of the road springs.

shock·er ('ʃɒkə) *n. Informal.* **1.** a person or thing that shocks or horrifies. **2.** a sensational novel, film, or play.

shock·head·ed ('ʃɒkˌhɛdɪd) *adj.* having a head of bushy or tousled hair.

shock·ing ('ʃɒkɪŋ) *adj.* **1.** causing shock, horror, or disgust. **2. shocking pink.** a vivid or garish shade of pink. **3.** *Informal.* very bad or terrible: *shocking weather.* —'**shock·ing·ly** *adv.* —'**shock·ing·ness** *n.*

shock·proof ('ʃɒkˌpruːf) *adj.* capable of absorbing shock without damage: *a shockproof watch.*

shock·stall ('ʃɒkˌstɔːl) *n.* the strain put on an aircraft when its speed is close to that of sound: caused by air resistance.

shock ther·a·py *or* **treat·ment** *n.* the treatment of certain psychotic conditions by injecting drugs or by passing an electric current through the brain **(electroconvulsive therapy)** to produce convulsions and coma.

shock troops *pl. n.* soldiers specially trained and equipped to carry out an assault.

shock tube *n.* an apparatus in which a gas is heated to very high temperatures by means of a shock wave, usually for spectroscopic investigation of the natures and reactions of the resulting radicals and excited molecules.

shock wave *n.* a narrow region of high pressure and temperature travelling through a gas at high velocity, caused by supersonic flow of a body through the gas or by a detonation. See also **sonic boom, shock tube.**

shod (ʃɒd) *vb.* a past participle of **shoe.**

shod·dy ('ʃɒdɪ) *adj.* **·di·er, ·di·est. 1.** imitating something of better quality. **2.** of poor quality; trashy. **3.** made of shoddy material. ~*n.* **4.** a yarn or fabric made from wool waste or clippings. **5.** anything of inferior quality that is designed to simulate superior quality. [C19: of unknown origin] —'**shod·di·ly** *adv.* —'**shod·di·ness** *n.*

shoe (ʃuː) *n.* **1. a.** one of a matching pair of coverings shaped to fit the foot, esp. one ending below the ankle, having an upper of leather, plastic, etc., on a sole and heel of heavier leather, rubber, or synthetic material. **b.** (*as modifier*): *shoe cleaner.* **2.** anything resembling a shoe in shape, function, position, etc., such as a horseshoe. **3.** a band of metal or wood on the bottom of the runner of a sledge. **4.** (in baccarat, etc.) a boxlike device for holding several packs of cards and allowing the cards to be dispensed singly. **5.** a base for the supports of a superstructure of a bridge, roof, etc. **6.** a metal collector attached to an electric train that slides along the third rail and picks up power for the motor. **7.** See **brake shoe, pile shoe. 8. be in (a person's) shoes.** *Informal.* to be in another person's situation. ~*vb.* **shoes, shoe·ing, shod.** (*tr.*) **9.** to furnish with shoes. **10.** to fit (a horse) with horseshoes. **11.** to furnish with a hard cover, such as a metal plate, for protection against friction or bruising. [Old English *scōh;* related to Old Norse *skōr,* Gothic *skōhs,* Old High German *scuoh*]

shoe·bill ('ʃuːˌbɪl) *n.* a large wading bird, *Balaeniceps rex,* of tropical E African swamps, having a dark plumage, a large head, and a large broad bill: family *Balaenicipitidae,* order *Ciconiiformes.*

shoe·black ('ʃuːˌblæk) *n.* another word for **bootblack.**

shoe·horn ('ʃuːˌhɔːn) *n.* a smooth curved implement of horn, metal, plastic, etc., inserted at the heel of a shoe to ease the foot into it.

shoe·lace ('ʃuːˌleɪs) *n.* a cord or lace for fastening shoes.

shoe leath·er *n.* **1.** leather used to make shoes. **2. save shoe leather.** to avoid wearing out shoes, as by taking a bus rather than walking.

shoe·mak·er ('ʃuːˌmeɪkə) *n.* a person who makes or repairs shoes or boots. —'**shoe**ˌ**mak·ing** *n.*

sho·er ('ʃuːə) *n. Rare.* a person who shoes horses.

shoe·shine ('ʃuːˌʃaɪn) *n.* **1.** the act or an instance of polishing a pair of shoes. **2.** the appearance or shiny surface of polished shoes.

shoe·string ('ʃuːˌstrɪŋ) *n.* **1.** another word for **shoelace. 2.**

Informal. **a.** a very small or petty amount of money (esp. in the phrase **on a shoestring**). **b.** (*as modifier*): *a shoestring budget.*

shoe+tree ('ʃuː,triː) *n.* a wooden or metal form inserted into a shoe or boot to stretch it or preserve its shape.

sho+far *or* **sho+phar** ('ʃəʊfɑː; *Hebrew* ʃɔ'far) *n., pl.* **+fars, +phars** *or* **+froth, +phroth** (*Hebrew* -'frɔt). *Judaism.* an ancient type of musical horn, made from a ram's horn, sounded by the ancient Israelites as a warning, summons, etc., and in modern times used in the synagogue on certain occasions. [from Hebrew *shōphār* ram's horn]

sho+gun ('ʃəʊ,guːn) *n. Japanese history.* **1.** (from 794 A.D.) a chief military commander. **2.** (from about 1192 to 1867) any of a line of hereditary military dictators who relegated the emperors to a position of purely theoretical supremacy. [C17: from Japanese, from Chinese *chiang chün* general, from *chiang* to lead + *chün* army] —'**sho+,gun+al** *adj.*

sho+gun+ate ('ʃəʊgʊnɪt, -,neɪt) *n. Japanese history.* the office or rule of a shogun.

sho+ji ('ʃəʊʒiː, -dʒiː) *n., pl.* **+ji** *or* **+jis.** **1.** a rice-paper screen in a sliding wooden frame, used in Japanese houses as a partition. **2.** any similar screen. [from Japanese]

Sho+la+pur ('ʃəʊlə,pʊə) *n.* a city in SW India, in S Maharashtra: major textile centre. Pop.: 398 361 (1971).

Sho·lo·khov (*Russian* 'ʃɔləxəf) *n.* **Mi·kha·il A·le·ksan·dro·vich** (mixa'il alɪ'ksandrəvitʃ). born 1905, Soviet author, noted particularly for *And Quiet flows the Don* (1934) and *The Don flows Home to the Sea* (1940), describing the effect of the Revolution and civil war on the life of the Cossacks: Nobel prize for literature 1965.

Sho+na ('ʃɒnə) *n.* **1.** (*pl.* **+na** *or* **+nas**) a member of a Sotho people of S central Africa, living chiefly in Rhodesia and Mozambique. **2.** the language of this people, belonging to the Bantu group of the Niger-Congo family.

shone (ʃɒn; *U.S.* ʃəʊn) *vb.* the past tense or past participle of **shine.**

shoo (ʃuː) *interj.* **1.** go away!: used to drive away unwanted or annoying people, animals, etc. ~*vb.* **shoos, shoo+ing, shooed.** **2.** (*tr.*) to drive away by or as if by crying "shoo." **3.** (*intr.*) to cry "shoo." [C15: imitative; related to Middle High German *schū*, French *shou*, Italian *scio*]

shoo+fly pie ('ʃuː,flaɪ) *n. U.S.* a dessert similar to treacle tart.

shoo+gle ('ʃʊgᵊl) *Brit. dialect, chiefly Scot.* ~*vb.* **1.** (*tr.*) to shake or rock back and forth. ~*n.* **2.** a rocking motion; shake. [from dialectal *shog, shug;* apparently related to German *schaukeln* to shake] —'**shoo+gly** *adj.*

shoo-in *n. U.S.* a person or thing that is certain to win or succeed.

shook[1] (ʃʊk) *n.* **1.** a set of parts ready for assembly, esp. of a barrel. **2.** a group of sheaves piled together on end; shock. [C18: of unknown origin]

shook[2] (ʃʊk) *vb.* **1.** the past tense of **shake.** **2. shook on.** *Austral. informal.* keen on; enthusiastic about.

shool (ʃuːl) *n.* a dialect word for **shovel.**

shoon (ʃuːn) *n. Dialect, chiefly Scot.* a plural of **shoe.**

shoot (ʃuːt) *vb.* **shoots, shoot+ing, shot.** **1.** (*tr.*) to hit, wound, damage, or kill with a missile fired from a weapon. **2.** to discharge (a missile or missiles) from a weapon. **3.** to fire (a weapon) or (of a weapon) to be fired. **4.** to send out or be sent out as if from a weapon: *he shot questions at her.* **5.** (*intr.*) to move very rapidly; dart. **6.** (*tr.*) to slide or push into or out of a fastening: *to shoot a bolt.* **7.** to emit (a ray of light) or (of a ray of light) to be emitted. **8.** (*tr.*) to go or pass quickly over or through: *to shoot rapids.* **9.** (*intr.*) to hunt game with a gun for sport. **10.** (*tr.*) to pass over (an area) in hunting game. **11.** to extend or cause to extend; project. **12.** (*tr.*) to discharge down or as if down a chute. **13.** (*intr.*) (of a plant) to produce (buds, branches, etc.). **14.** (*intr.*) (of a seed) to germinate. **15.** to photograph or record (a sequence, subject, etc.). **16.** (*tr.; usually passive*) to variegate or streak, as with colour. **17.** *Soccer, hockey, etc.* to hit or propel (the ball, etc.) towards the goal. **18.** (*tr.*) *Sport, chiefly U.S.* to score (points, strokes, etc.): *he shot 72 on the first round.* **19.** (*tr.*) to plane (a board) to produce a straight edge. **20.** (*tr.*) *Mining.* to detonate. **21.** (*tr.*) to measure the altitude of (a celestial body). **22.** (often foll. by *up*) *Slang.* to inject (someone, esp. oneself) with (a drug, esp. heroin). **23. shoot a line.** *Slang.* **a.** to boast or exaggerate. **b.** to tell a lie. **24. shoot off one's mouth.** *Slang, chiefly U.S.* **a.** to talk indiscreetly. **b.** to boast or exaggerate. **25. shoot one's bolt.** *Slang.* to put in every possible effort. ~*n.* **26.** the act of shooting. **27.** the action or motion of something that is shot. **28.** the first aerial part of a plant to develop from a germinating seed. **29.** any new growth of a plant, such as a bud, young branch, etc. **30.** *Chiefly Brit.* a meeting or party organized for hunting game with guns. **31.** an area or series of coverts and woods where game can be hunted with guns. **32.** a steep descent in a stream; rapid. **33.** *Geology, mining.* a narrow workable vein of ore. **34.** *Obsolete.* the reach of a shot. **35. the whole shoot.** *Slang.* everything. ~*interj.* **36.** *U.S.* an exclamation expressing disbelief, scepticism, etc. ~See also **shoot down, shoot out, shoot through, shoot up.** [Old English *sceōtan;* related to Old Norse *skjōta*, Old High German *skiozan* to shoot, Old Slavonic *iskydati* to throw out] —'**shoot+er** *n.*

shoot down *vb.* (*tr., adv.*) **1.** to shoot callously. **2.** to cause to fall to earth by hitting with a missile. **3.** to defeat or disprove: *he shot down her argument.*

shoot+ing box *n.* a small country house providing accommodation for a shooting party during the shooting season. Also called: **shooting lodge.**

shoot+ing brake *n. Brit.* another name for **estate car.**

shoot+ing gal+ler·y *n.* an area, often enclosed, designed for target practice, shooting, etc.

shoot+ing i·ron *n. U.S. slang.* a firearm, esp. a pistol.

shoot+ing script *n. Films.* written instructions indicating to the cameraman the order of shooting.

shoot+ing star *n.* an informal name for **meteor.**

shoot+ing stick *n.* a device that resembles a walking stick, having a spike at one end and a folding seat at the other.

shoot out *vb.* (*tr., adv.*) **1.** to fight to the finish by shooting (esp. in the phrase **shoot it out**). ~*n.* **shoot-out. 2.** a conclusive gun fight.

shoot through *vb.* (*intr., adv.*) *Austral.* to leave; depart.

shoot up *vb.* (*adv.*) **1.** (*intr.*) to grow or become taller very fast. **2.** (*tr.*) to hit with a number of shots. **3.** (*tr.*) to spread terror throughout (a place) by lawless and wanton shooting. **4.** (*tr.*) *Slang.* to inject (someone, esp. oneself) with (a drug, esp. heroin).

shop (ʃɒp) *n.* **1.** a place, esp. a small building, for the retail sale of goods and services. **2.** a place for the performance of a specified type of work; workshop. **3. all over the shop.** *Informal.* **a.** in disarray: *his papers were all over the shop.* **b.** in every direction: *I've searched for it all over the shop.* **4. shut up shop.** to close business at the end of the day or permanently. **5. talk shop.** *Informal.* to discuss one's business, profession, etc., esp. so as to exclude those not similarly employed. ~*vb.* **shops, shop+ping, shopped.** **6.** (*intr.;* often foll. by *for*) to visit a shop or shops in search of (goods) with the intention of buying them. **7.** (*tr.*) *Slang, chiefly Brit.* to inform on or betray to the police. [Old English *sceoppa* stall, booth; related to Old High German *scopf* shed, Middle Dutch *schoppe* stall]

shop a·round *vb.* (*intr., adv.*) *Informal.* **1.** to visit a number of shops or stores to compare goods and prices. **2.** to consider a number of possibilities before making a choice.

shop as+sis+tant *n.* a person who serves in a shop.

shop floor *n.* **1.** the part of a factory housing the machines and men directly involved in production. **2. a.** workers, esp. factory workers organized in a union. **b.** (*as modifier*): *shop-floor protest.*

sho+phar ('ʃəʊfɑː; *Hebrew* ʃɔ'far) *n., pl.* **+phars** *or* **+phroth** (*Hebrew* -'frɔt). a variant spelling of **shofar.**

shop+keep·er ('ʃɒp,kiːpə) *n.* a person who owns or manages a shop or small store. —'**shop+,keep·ing** *n.*

shop+lift·er ('ʃɒp,lɪftə) *n.* a person who steals goods from a shop during shopping hours. —'**shop+,lift·ing** *n.*

shop+per ('ʃɒpə) *n.* a person who buys goods in a shop.

shop+ping ('ʃɒpɪŋ) *n.* **1.** a number or collection of articles purchased. **2.** the act or an instance of making purchases.

shop+ping cen+tre *n.* the area of a town where most of the shops are situated.

shop+ping pre+cinct *n.* a pedestrian area containing shops, restaurants, etc., forming a single architectural unit and usually providing car-parking facilities.

shop+soiled ('ʃɒp,sɔɪld) *adj.* **1.** worn, faded, tarnished, etc., from being displayed in a shop or store. U.S. word: **shop-worn.** **2.** no longer new or fresh.

shop stew+ard *n.* an elected representative of the union workers in a shop, factory, etc.

shop+talk ('ʃɒp,tɔːk) *n.* conversation concerning one's work, esp. when carried on outside business hours.

shop+walk·er ('ʃɒp,wɔːkə) *n. Brit.* a person employed by a departmental store to supervise sales personnel, assist customers, etc. U.S. equivalent: **floorwalker.**

shop+worn ('ʃɒp,wɔːn) *adj.* the U.S. word for **shopsoiled.**

shor+an ('ʃɔːræn) *n.* a short-range radar system by which an aircraft, ship, etc., can accurately determine its position by the time taken for a signal to be sent to two radar beacons at known locations and be returned. [C20: *sho(rt) ra(nge) n(avigation)*]

shore[1] (ʃɔː) *n.* **1.** the land along the edge of a sea, lake, or wide river. Related adj.: **littoral.** **2. a.** land, as opposed to water (esp. in the phrase **on shore**). **b.** (*as modifier*): *shore duty.* **3.** *Law.* the tract of coastland lying between the ordinary marks of high and low water. **4.** (*often pl.*) a country: *his native shores.* ~*vb.* **5.** (*tr.*) to move or drag (a boat) onto a shore. [C14: probably from Middle Low German, Middle Dutch *schōre;* compare Old High German *scorra* cliff; see SHEAR]

shore[2] (ʃɔː) *n.* **1.** a prop, post, or beam used to support a wall, building, ship in dry dock, etc. ~*vb.* **2.** (*tr.;* often foll. by *up*) to prop or make safe with or as if with a shore. [C15: from Middle Dutch *schōre;* related to Old Norse *skortha* prop] —'**shor+ing** *n.*

shore[3] (ʃɔː) *vb. Archaic or Austral.* a past tense or past participle of **shear.**

shore bird *n.* any of various birds that live close to water, esp. any bird of the families *Charadriidae* or *Scolopacidae* (plovers, sandpipers, etc.). Also called (Brit.): **wader.**

shore leave *n. Naval.* **1.** permission to go ashore, esp. when granted to an officer. Compare **liberty** (sense 5). **2.** time spent ashore during leave.

shore+less ('ʃɔːlɪs) *adj.* **1.** without a shore suitable for landing. **2.** *Poetic.* boundless; vast: *the shoreless wastes.*

shore+line ('ʃɔː,laɪn) *n.* the edge of a body of water.

shore pa+trol *n. U.S.* a naval unit serving the same function as the military police.

shore+ward ('ʃɔːwəd) *adj.* **1.** near or facing the shore. ~*adv.* *also* **shore+wards.** **2.** towards the shore.

shorn (ʃɔːn) *vb.* a past participle of **shear.**

short (ʃɔːt) *adj.* **1.** of little length; not long. **2.** of little height; not tall. **3.** of limited duration. **4.** not meeting a requirement;

deficient: *the number of places laid at the table was short by four.* **5.** (*postpositive;* often foll. by *of* or *on*) lacking (in) or needful (of): *I'm always short of money.* **6.** concise; succinct. **7.** lacking in the power of retentiveness: *a short memory.* **8.** abrupt to the point of rudeness: *the salesgirl was very short with him.* **9.** *Finance.* **a.** not possessing the securities or commodities that have been sold under contract and therefore obliged to make a purchase before the delivery date. **b.** of or relating to such sales, which depend on falling prices for profit. **10.** *Phonetics.* **a.** denoting a vowel of relatively brief temporal duration. **b.** classified as short, as distinguished from other vowels. Thus in English (ɪ) in *bin,* though of longer duration than (iː) in *beat,* is nevertheless regarded as a short vowel. **c.** (in popular usage) denoting the qualities of the five English vowels represented orthographically in the words *pat, pet, pit, pot, put,* and *putt.* **11.** *Prosody.* **a.** denoting a vowel that is phonetically short or a syllable containing such a vowel. In classical verse short vowels are followed by one consonant only or sometimes one consonant plus a following *l* or *r.* **b.** (of a vowel or syllable in verse that is not quantitative) not carrying emphasis or accent; unstressed. **12.** (of pastry) crumbly in texture. **13. caught** *or* **taken short.** having a sudden need to urinate or defecate. **14. short for.** an abbreviation for. **15. short and sweet.** unexpectedly brief. **16. in short supply.** scarce. *~adv.* **17.** abruptly: *to stop short.* **18.** briefly or concisely. **19.** rudely or curtly. **20. fall short.** not to reach the required mark or standard. **21.** *Finance.* without possessing the securities or commodities at the time of their contractual sale: *to sell short.* **22. go short.** not to have a sufficient amount, etc. **23. short of.** except: *nothing short of a miracle can save him now.* *~n.* **24.** anything that is short. **25.** a drink consisting of a spirit, often with lime, soda, etc., added, as opposed to a long drink such as beer. **26.** *Phonetics, prosody.* a short vowel or syllable. **27.** *Finance.* **a.** a short contract or sale. **b.** a short seller. **28.** a short film, usually of a factual nature. **29.** See **short circuit. 30. for short.** *Informal.* as an abbreviation: *he is called Jim for short.* **31. in short. a.** as a summary. **b.** in a few words. *~vb.* **32.** See **short-circuit.** [Old English *scort;* related to Old Norse *skortr* a lack, *skera* to cut, Old High German *scurz* short] —ˈ**short+ness** *n.*

short ac+count *n.* **1.** the aggregate of short sales on an open market, esp. a stock market. **2.** the account of a stock-market speculator who sells short.

short+age (ˈʃɔːtɪdʒ) *n.* a deficiency or lack in the amount needed, expected, or due; deficit.

short+bread (ˈʃɔːtˌbrɛd) *n.* a rich crumbly biscuit made from dough with a large proportion of butter.

short+cake (ˈʃɔːtˌkeɪk) *n.* **1.** a kind of shortbread made from a rich biscuit dough. **2.** a dessert made of layers of short pastry filled with fruit and cream.

short-change *vb.* (*tr.*) **1.** to give less than correct change to. **2.** *Slang.* to cheat or swindle. —ˌ**short-ˈchang·er** *n.*

short cir+cuit *n.* **1.** a faulty or accidental connection between two points of different potential in an electric circuit, bypassing the load and establishing a path of low resistance through which an excessive current can flow. It can cause damage to the components if the circuit is not protected by a fuse. *~vb.* **short-cir·cuit. 2.** to develop or cause to develop a short circuit. **3.** (*tr.*) to bypass (a procedure, etc.). **4.** (*tr.*) to hinder or frustrate (plans, etc.). ~Sometimes (for senses 1, 2) shortened to **short.**

short+com·ing (ˈʃɔːtˌkʌmɪŋ) *n.* a failing, defect, or deficiency.

short cov+er+ing *n.* **1.** the purchase of securities or commodities by a short seller to meet delivery requirements. **2.** the securities or commodities purchased.

short cut *n.* **1.** a route that is shorter than the usual one. **2.** a means of saving time or effort. *~vb.* **short-cut. -cut, -cut·ting, -cut. 3.** to use a short cut.

short-dat·ed *adj.* (of a gilt-edged security) having less than five years to run before redemption. Compare **medium-dated, long-dated.**

short-day *adj.* (of plants) able to flower only if exposed to short periods of daylight (less than 12 hours), each followed by a long dark period. Compare **long-day.**

short di+vi+sion *n.* the division of numbers, usually integers, that can be worked out mentally rather than on paper.

short+en (ˈʃɔːtᵊn) *vb.* **1.** to make or become short or shorter. **2.** (*tr.*) *Nautical.* to reduce the area of (sail). **3.** (*tr.*) to make (pastry, bread, etc.) short, by adding butter or another fat to the dough. **4.** *Gambling.* to cause (the odds) to lessen or (of odds) to become less. —ˈ**short+en+er** *n.*

short+en+ing (ˈʃɔːtᵊnɪŋ) *n.* butter, lard, or other fat, used in a dough, cake mixture, etc., to make the mixture short.

Short+er Cat+e·chism *n. Chiefly Presbyterian Church.* the more widely used and influential of two catechisms of religious instruction drawn up in 1647.

short+fall (ˈʃɔːtˌfɔːl) *n.* **1.** failure to meet a goal or a requirement. **2.** the amount of such a failure; deficiency.

short+hand (ˈʃɔːtˌhænd) *n.* **a.** a system of rapid handwriting employing simple strokes and other symbols to represent words or phrases. **b.** (*as modifier*): *a shorthand typist.*

short-hand·ed *adj.* lacking the usual or necessary number of assistants, workers, etc. —ˌ**short-ˈhand·ed·ness** *n.*

short+hand typ+ist *n. Brit.* a person skilled in the use of shorthand and in typing. U.S. name: **stenographer.**

short+horn (ˈʃɔːtˌhɔːn) *n.* a short-horned breed of cattle with several regional varieties. Also called: **Durham.**

short hun·dred+weight *n.* the full name for **hundredweight** (sense 2).

short·ie *or* **short·y** (ˈʃɔːtɪ) *n., pl.* **short·ies.** *Informal.* **a.** a person or thing that is extremely short. **b.** (*as modifier*): *a shortie nightdress.*

short jen+ny *n. Billiards.* an in-off into a middle pocket. Compare **long jenny.** [from *Jenny,* pet form of *Janet*]

short list *Chiefly Brit.* *~n.* **1.** a list of suitable applicants for a job, post, etc., from which the successful candidate will be selected. *~vb.* (*tr.*) **short-list. 2.** to put (someone) on a short list.

short-lived *adj.* living or lasting only for a short time.

short+ly (ˈʃɔːtlɪ) *adv.* **1.** in a short time; soon. **2.** in a few words; briefly. **3.** in a curt or rude manner.

short-range *adj.* of small or limited extent in time or distance: *a short-range forecast; a short-range gun.*

shorts (ʃɔːts) *pl. n.* **1.** trousers reaching the top of the thigh, worn by both sexes for sport, relaxing in summer, etc. **2.** *Chiefly U.S.* men's underpants that usually reach mid-thigh. Usual Brit. word: **pants. 3.** short-dated gilt-edged securities. **4.** short-term bonds. **5.** timber cut shorter than standard lengths. **6.** a livestock feed containing a large proportion of bran and wheat germ. **7.** items needed to make up a deficiency.

short shrift *n.* **1.** brief and unsympathetic treatment. **2.** (formerly) a brief period allowed to a condemned prisoner to make confession. **3. make short shrift of.** to dispose of quickly and unsympathetically.

short-sight·ed *adj.* **1.** relating to or suffering from myopia. **2.** lacking foresight: *a short-sighted plan.* —ˌ**short-ˈsight·ed+ly** *adv.* —ˌ**short-ˈsight·ed+ness** *n.*

short-spo·ken *adj.* tending to be abrupt in speech.

short-staffed *adj.* lacking an adequate number of staff, assistants, etc.

short+stop (ˈʃɔːtˌstɒp) *n. Baseball.* **a.** the fielding position to the left of second base viewed from home plate. **b.** the player at this position.

short sto+ry *n.* a prose narrative of shorter length than the novel, esp. one that concentrates on a single theme.

short sub+ject *n. Chiefly U.S.* a short film, esp. one presented between screenings of a feature film.

short-tem·pered *adj.* easily moved to anger; irascible.

short-term *adj.* **1.** of, for, or extending over a limited period. **2.** *Finance.* extending over or maturing within a short period of time, usually twelve months: *short-term credit.*

short-term mem·o+ry *n. Psychol.* that section of the memory storage system of limited capacity (approximately seven items) that is capable of storing material for a brief period of time. Compare **long-term memory.**

short ton *n.* the full name for **ton**[1] (sense 2).

short-waist·ed *adj.* unusually short from the shoulders to the waist.

short wave *n.* **a.** a radio wave with a wavelength in the range 10–100 metres. **b.** (*as modifier*): *a short-wave broadcast.*

short-wind·ed *adj.* **1.** tending to run out of breath, esp. after exertion. **2.** (of speech or writing) terse or abrupt.

Sho+sho+ne *or* **Sho+sho+ni** (ʃəʊˈʃəʊnɪ) *n.* **1.** (*pl.* **+nes, +ne** *or* **+nis, +ni**) a member of a North American Indian people of the southwestern U.S., related to the Aztecs. **2.** the language of this people, belonging to the Uto-Aztecan family.

Sho+sho+ne·an *or* **Sho+sho+ni·an** (ʃəʊˈʃəʊnɪən, ˌʃəʊʃəˈniːən) *n.* a subfamily of North American Indian languages belonging to the Uto-Aztecan family, spoken mainly in the southwestern U.S.

Shos·ta·ko·vich (ˌʃɒstəˈkəʊvɪtʃ; *Russian* ʃəstaˈkɔvitʃ) *n.* **Dmi·tri Dmi·tri·ye·vich** (ˈdmitrij ˈdmitrijɪvitʃ). 1906–75, Soviet composer, noted esp. for his 15 symphonies and his chamber music.

shot[1] (ʃɒt) *n.* **1.** the act or an instance of firing a projectile. **2.** (*pl.* **shot**) a solid missile, such as an iron ball or a lead pellet, discharged from a firearm. **3. a.** small round pellets of lead collectively, as used in cartridges. **b.** metal in the form of coarse powder or small pellets. **4.** the distance that a discharged projectile travels or is capable of travelling. **5.** a person who shoots, esp. with regard to his ability: *he is a good shot.* **6.** *Informal.* an attempt; effort. **7.** *Informal.* a guess or conjecture. **8.** any act of throwing or hitting something, as in certain sports. **9.** the launching of a rocket, missile, etc., esp. to a specified destination: *a moon shot.* **10. a.** a single photograph: *I took 16 shots of the wedding.* **b.** a series of frames on cine film concerned with a single event. **c.** a length of film taken by a single camera without breaks, used with others to build up a full motion picture. **11.** *Informal.* an injection, as of a vaccine or narcotic drug. **12.** *Informal.* a glass of alcoholic drink, esp. spirits. **13.** *Sport.* a heavy metal ball used in the shot put. **14.** an explosive charge used in blasting. **15.** globules of metal occurring in the body of a casting that are harder than the rest of the casting. **16.** a unit of chain length equal to 75 feet (Brit.) or 90 feet (U.S.). **17. call the shots.** *Slang.* to have control over an organization, course of action, etc. **18. have a shot at.** *Informal.* **a.** to attempt. **b.** *Austral.* to jibe at or vex. **19. like a shot.** very quickly, esp. willingly. **20. shot in the arm.** *Informal.* anything that regenerates, increases confidence or efficiency, etc.: *his arrival was a shot in the arm for the company.* **21. shot in the dark.** a wild guess. **22. that's the shot.** *Austral. informal.* that is the right thing to do. *~vb.* **shots, shot+ting, shot+ted. 23.** (*tr.*) to weight or load with shot. [Old English *scot;* related to Old Norse *skot,* Old High German *scoz* missile; see SHOOT]

shot[2] (ʃɒt) *vb.* **1.** the past tense or past participle of **shoot.** *~adj.* **2.** (of textiles) woven to give a changing colour effect. **3.** streaked with colour.

shot-blast·ing *n.* the cleaning of metal, etc., by a stream of shot.

shote (ʃəʊt) *n.* a variant spelling of **shoat.**

shot+gun (ˈʃɒtˌgʌn) *n.* **1. a.** a shoulder firearm with unrifled bore designed for the discharge of small shot at short range and used mainly for hunting small game. **b.** (*as modifier*): *shotgun fire.* ~*adj.* **2.** *Chiefly U.S.* involving coercion or duress: *a shotgun merger.* **3.** *Chiefly U.S.* involving or relying on speculative suggestions, etc.: *a shotgun therapy.* ~*vb.* **+guns, +gun+ning, +gunned. 4.** (*tr.*) *U.S.* to shoot or threaten with or as if with a shotgun.

shot+gun wed+ding *n. Informal.* a wedding into which one or both partners are coerced, usually because the woman is pregnant.

shot hole *n.* a drilled hole into which explosive is put for blasting.

shot noise *or* **ef+fect** *n.* the inherent electronic noise arising in the anode circuit of a valve as a result of the random motion of the electrons emitted by the heated cathode. Also called: **Schottky noise.**

shot put *n.* **1.** an athletic event in which contestants hurl or put a heavy metal ball or shot as far as possible. **2.** a single put of the shot. —ˈ**shot-ˌput·ter** *n.*

shott *or* **chott** (ʃɒt) *n.* **1.** a shallow temporary salt lake or marsh in the North African desert. **2.** the hollow in which it lies. [C19: via French *chott* from Arabic *shatt*]

shot+ten (ˈʃɒtᵊn) *adj.* **1.** (of fish, esp. herring) having recently spawned. **2.** *Archaic.* worthless or undesirable.

shot tow+er *n.* a building formerly used in the production of shot, in which molten lead was graded and dropped into water, thus cooling it and forming the shot.

should (ʃʊd) *vb.* the past of **shall:** used as an auxiliary verb to indicate that an action is considered by the speaker to be obligatory (*you should go*) or to form the subjunctive mood with *I* or *we* (*I should like to see you; if I should be late, go without me*). [Old English *sceold;* see SHALL]

Usage. *Should* has, as its most common meaning in modern English, the sense *ought* as in *I should go to the graduation, but I don't see how I can.* However, the older sense of the subjunctive of *shall* is often used with *I* or *we* to indicate a more polite form than *would: I should like to go, but I can't.* In much speech and writing, *should* has been replaced by *would* in contexts of this kind, but it remains in conditional subjunctives: *should* (never *would*) *I go, I should* (or *would*) *wear my black dress.*

shoul+der (ˈʃəʊldə) *n.* **1.** the part of the vertebrate body where the arm or a corresponding forelimb joins the trunk: the pectoral girdle and associated structures. **2.** the joint at the junction of the forelimb with the pectoral girdle. **3.** a cut of meat including the upper part of the foreleg. **4.** *Printing.* the flat surface of a piece of type from which the face rises. **5.** *Tanning.* the portion of a hide covering the shoulders and neck of the animal, usually including the cheeks. **6.** the part of a garment that covers the shoulder. **7.** anything that resembles a shoulder in shape or position. **8.** the strip of unpaved land that borders a road. **9.** *Photog.* the portion of the characteristic curve of a photographic material indicating the maximum density that can be produced on the material. **10.** *Jewellery.* the part of a ring where the shank joins the setting. **11. give (someone) the cold shoulder.** *Informal.* **a.** to treat in a cold manner; snub. **b.** to ignore or shun. **12. put one's shoulder to the wheel.** *Informal.* to work very hard. **13. rub shoulders with.** *Informal.* to associate with. **14. shoulder to shoulder. a.** side by side or close together. **b.** in a corporate effort. ~*vb.* **15.** (*tr.*) to bear or carry (a burden, responsibility, etc.) as if on one's shoulders. **16.** to push (something) with or as if with the shoulder. **17.** (*tr.*) to lift or carry on the shoulders. **18. shoulder arms.** *Military.* to bring the rifle vertically close to the right side with the muzzle uppermost and held at the trigger guard. [Old English *sculdor;* related to Old High German *sculterra*]

shoul+der blade *n.* the nontechnical name for **scapula.**

shoul+der pad *n.* a small pad inserted to raise or give shape to the shoulder of a garment.

shoul+der patch *n. Military.* an emblem worn high on the arm as an insignia. Also called: **shoulder flash.**

shoul+der strap *n.* a strap over one or both of the shoulders, as to hold up a garment or to support a bag, etc.

should·n't (ˈʃʊdᵊnt) *contraction of* should not.

shouldst (ʃʊdst) *or* **should+est** (ˈʃʊdɪst) *vb. Archaic or dialect.* (used with the pronoun *thou* or its relative equivalent) a form of the past tense of **shall.**

shouse (ʃaʊs) *Austral. slang.* ~*n.* **1.** a toilet; lavatory. ~*adj.* **2.** unwell or in poor spirits. [C20: shortening of *shithouse*]

shout (ʃaʊt) *n.* **1.** a loud cry, esp. to convey emotion or a command. **2.** *Informal, Brit. or Austral.* a round, esp. of drinks. ~*vb.* **3.** to utter (something) in a loud cry; yell. **4.** (*intr.*) to make a loud noise. **5.** (*tr.*) *Austral. informal.* to treat (someone) to (something), esp. a round of drinks. [C14: probably from Old Norse *skūta* taunt; related to Old Norse *skjōta* to SHOOT] —ˈ**shout+er** *n.*

shout down *vb.* (*tr., adv.*) to drown, overwhelm, or silence by shouting or talking loudly.

shove (ʃʌv) *vb.* **1.** to give a thrust or push to (a person or thing). **2.** (*tr.*) to give a violent push to; jostle. **3.** (*tr.*) *Informal.* to put (something) somewhere, esp. hurriedly or carelessly: *shove it in the bin.* **4.** (*tr.*) *Slang.* to instil (knowledge, etc.) into a person, esp. by repetition (esp. in the phrase **shove (something) down someone's throat**). ~*n.* **5.** the act or an instance of shoving. ~See also **shove off.** [Old English *scūfan;* related to Old Norse *skūfa* to push, Gothic *afskiuban* to push away, Old High German *skioban* to shove] —ˈ**shov+er** *n.*

shove-half·pen·ny *n. Brit.* a game in which players try to propel old halfpennies or polished discs with the hand into lined sections of a wooden board.

shov+el (ˈʃʌvᵊl) *n.* **1.** an instrument for lifting or scooping loose material, such as earth, coal, etc., consisting of a curved blade or a scoop attached to a handle. **2.** any machine or part resembling a shovel in action. **3.** Also called: **shovelful.** the amount that can be contained in a shovel. **4.** short for **shovel hat.** ~*vb.* **+els, +el+ling, +elled** *or U.S.* **+els, +el+ing, +eled. 5.** to lift (earth, etc.) with a shovel. **6.** (*tr.*) to clear or dig (a path) with or as if with a shovel. **7.** (*tr.*) to gather, load, or unload in a hurried or careless way: *he shovelled the food into his mouth and rushed away.* [Old English *scofl;* related to Old High German *scūfla* shovel, Dutch *schoffel* hoe; see SHOVE] —ˈ**shov+el+ler** *or U.S.* ˈ**shov+el+er** *n.*

shov+el+er (ˈʃʌvələ) *n.* a duck, *Anas* (or *Spatula*) *clypeata,* of ponds and marshes, having a spoon-shaped bill, a blue patch on each wing, and in the male a green head, white breast, and reddish-brown body.

shov+el hat *n.* a black felt hat worn by some clergymen, with a brim rolled up to resemble a shovel in shape.

shov·el+head (ˈʃʌvᵊlˌhɛd) *n.* a common shark, *Sphyrna tiburo,* of the Atlantic and Pacific Oceans, having a shovel-shaped head: family *Sphyrnidae* (hammerheads).

shov·el+nose (ˈʃʌvᵊlˌnəʊz) *n.* an American freshwater sturgeon, *Scaphirhynchus platorynchus,* having a broad shovel-like snout.

shove off *vb.* (*intr., adv.; often imperative*) **1.** to move from the shore in a boat. **2.** *Informal.* to go away; depart.

show (ʃəʊ) *vb.* **shows, show+ing, showed; shown** *or* **showed. 1.** to make, be, or become visible or noticeable: *to show one's dislike.* **2.** (*tr.*) to present to view; exhibit: *he showed me a picture.* **3.** (*tr.*) to indicate or explain; prove: *to show that the earth moves round the sun.* **4.** (*tr.*) to exhibit or present (oneself or itself) in a specific character: *to show oneself to be trustworthy.* **5.** (*tr.;* foll. by *how* and an infinitive) to instruct by demonstration: *show me how to swim.* **6.** (*tr.*) to indicate or register: *a barometer shows changes in the weather.* **7.** (*tr.*) to grant or bestow: *to show favour to someone.* **8.** (*intr.*) to appear: *to show to advantage.* **9.** to exhibit, display, or offer (goods, etc.) for sale: *three artists were showing at the gallery.* **10.** (*tr.*) to allege, as in a legal document: *to show cause.* **11.** to present (a play, film, etc.) or (of a play, etc.) to be presented, as at a theatre or cinema. **12.** (*tr.*) to guide or escort: *please show me to my room.* **13. show in** *or* **out.** to conduct a person into or out of a room or building by opening the door for him. **14.** (*intr.*) to win a place in a horse race, etc. **15.** to give a performance of riding and handling (a horse) to display its best points. **16.** (*intr.*) *Slang.* to put in an appearance; arrive. ~*n.* **17.** a display or exhibition. **18.** a public spectacle. **19.** an ostentatious or pretentious display. **20.** a theatrical or other entertainment. **21.** a trace or indication. **22.** *Obstetrics.* a discharge of blood at the onset of labour. **23.** *Informal.* a chance; opportunity (esp. in the phrase **give someone a show**). **24.** a sporting event consisting of contests in which riders perform different exercises to show their skill and their horses' ability and breeding. **25.** *Slang, chiefly Brit.* a thing or affair (esp. in the phrases **good show, bad show,** etc.). **26. for show.** in order to attract attention. **27. run the show.** *Informal.* to take charge of or manage an affair, business, etc. **28. steal the show.** *Informal.* to draw the most attention or admiration. **29. stop the show.** *Informal.* **a.** (of a stage act, etc.) to receive so much applause as to interrupt the performance. **b.** to be received with great enthusiasm. ~See also **show off, show up.** [Old English *scēawian;* related to Old High German *scouwōn* to look, Old Norse *örskār* careful, Greek *thuoskoos* seer]

show bill *n.* a poster advertising a play or show. Also called: **show card.**

show+boat (ˈʃəʊˌbəʊt) *n.* a paddle-wheel river steamer with a theatre and a repertory company.

show+bread (ˈʃəʊˌbrɛd) *n.* a variant spelling of **shewbread.**

show busi+ness *n.* the entertainment industry, including theatres, films, television, and radio. Informal term: **show biz.**

show+case (ˈʃəʊˌkeɪs) *n.* **1.** a glass case used to display objects in a museum or shop. **2.** a setting in which anything may be displayed to best advantage. ~*vb.* **3.** (*tr.*) *U.S.* to exhibit or display.

show cop·y *n. Films.* a positive print of a film for use at an important presentation such as a premiere.

showd (ʃaʊd) *Northeast Scot. dialect.* ~*vb.* **1.** (*tr.*) to rock (a baby in one's arms or in a pram). ~*n.* **2.** a rocking motion. [from Old English *scūdan* to shake]

show+down (ˈʃəʊˌdaʊn) *n.* **1.** *Informal.* an action that brings matters to a head or acts as a conclusion or point of decision. **2.** *Poker.* the exposing of the cards in the player's hands on the table at the end of the game.

show+er[1] (ˈʃaʊə) *n.* **1.** a brief period of rain, hail, sleet, or snow. **2.** a sudden abundant fall or downpour, as of tears, sparks, or light. **3.** a rush; outpouring: *a shower of praise.* **4. a.** a kind of bath in which a person stands upright and is sprayed with water from a nozzle. **b.** the room, booth, etc., containing such a bath. Full name: **shower bath. 5.** *Brit. slang.* a derogatory term applied to a person or group, esp. to a group considered as being slack, untidy, etc. **6.** *U.S.* a party held to honour and present gifts to a person, as to a prospective bride. **7.** a large number of particles formed by the collision of a cosmic-ray particle with a particle in the atmosphere. ~*vb.* **8.** (*tr.*) to sprinkle or spray with or as if with a shower: *shower the powder into the milk.* **9.** (often with *it* as subject) to fall or cause to fall in the form of a shower. **10.** (*tr.*) to give (gifts, etc.) in abundance or present (a person) with (gifts, etc.): *they showered gifts on him.* **11.** (*intr.*) to take a shower. [Old English *scūr;* related to Old Norse *skūr,* Old High German *skūr* shower, Latin *caurus* north-west wind] —**ˈshow+er·y** *adj.*

show+er[2] (ˈʃəʊə) *n.* a person or thing that shows.

show·er+proof (ˈʃaʊəˌpruːf) *adj.* (of a garment, etc.) resistant to or partly impervious to rain. —**ˈshow·er+ˌproof·ing** *n.*

show+girl (ˈʃəʊˌgɜːl) *n.* a girl who appears in variety shows, nightclub acts, etc., esp. as a singer or dancer.

show+ing (ˈʃəʊɪŋ) *n.* **1.** a presentation, exhibition, or display. **2.** manner of presentation; performance.

show+jump·ing (ˈʃəʊˌdʒʌmpɪŋ) *n.* the riding of horses in competitions to demonstrate skill in jumping over or between various obstacles. —**ˈshow-ˌjump·er** *n.*

show+man (ˈʃəʊmən) *n., pl.* **+men. 1.** a person who presents or produces a theatrical show, etc. **2.** a person skilled at presenting anything in an effective manner. —**ˈshow+man+ship** *n.*

shown (ʃəʊn) *vb.* a past participle of **show.**

show off *vb.* (*adv.*) **1.** (*tr.*) to exhibit or display so as to invite admiration. **2.** (*intr.*) *Informal.* to behave in such a manner as to make an impression. ~*n.* **show-off. 3.** *Informal.* a person who makes a vain display of himself.

show of hands *n.* the raising of hands to indicate voting for or against a proposition.

show+piece (ˈʃəʊˌpiːs) *n.* **1.** anything displayed or exhibited. **2.** anything prized as a very fine example of its type.

show+place (ˈʃəʊˌpleɪs) *n.* a place exhibited or visited for its beauty, historic interest, etc.

show+room (ˈʃəʊˌruːm, -ˌrʊm) *n.* a room in which goods, such as cars, are on display.

show stop+per *n. Informal.* a stage act, etc., that receives so much applause as to interrupt the performance.

show tri+al *n.* a trial conducted primarily to make a particular impression on the public or on other nations, esp. one that demonstrates the power of the state over the individual.

show up *vb.* (*adv.*) **1.** to reveal or be revealed clearly. **2.** (*tr.*) to expose or reveal the faults or defects of by comparison. **3.** (*tr.*) *Informal.* to put to shame; embarrass: *he showed me up in front of my friends.* **4.** (*intr.*) *Informal.* to appear or arrive.

show·y (ˈʃəʊɪ) *adj.* **show·i·er, show·i·est. 1.** gaudy, flashy, or ostentatious. **2.** making a brilliant or imposing display. —**ˈshow·i+ly** *adv.* —**ˈshow·i+ness** *n.*

shpt. *abbrev. for* shipment.

shr. *Stock exchange. abbrev. for* share.

shrank (ʃræŋk) *vb.* a past tense of **shrink.**

shrap+nel (ˈʃræpnᵊl) *n.* **1. a.** a projectile containing a number of small pellets or bullets exploded before impact. **b.** such projectiles collectively. **2.** fragments from this or any other type of shell. [C19: named after H. *Shrapnel* (1761–1842), English army officer, who invented it]

shred (ʃrɛd) *n.* **1.** a long narrow strip or fragment torn or cut off. **2.** a very small piece or amount; scrap. ~*vb.* **shreds, shred+ding, shred+ded** *or* **shred. 3.** (*tr.*) to tear or cut into shreds. [Old English *scread;* related to Old Norse *skrjōthr* torn-up book, Old High German *scrōt* cut-off piece; see SCROLL, SHROUD, SCREED] —**ˈshred+der** *n.*

Shreve+port (ˈʃriːvˌpɔːt) *n.* a city in NW Louisiana, on the Red River: centre of an oil and natural-gas region. Pop.: 184 030 (1973 est.).

shrew (ʃruː) *n.* **1.** Also called: **shrewmouse.** any small mouse-like long-snouted mammal, such as *Sorex araneus* (**common shrew**), of the family *Soricidae:* order *Insectivora* (insectivores). See also **water shrew. 2.** a bad-tempered or mean-spirited woman. [Old English *scrēawa;* related to Old High German *scrawaz* dwarf, Icelandic *skröggr* old man, Norwegian *skrugg* dwarf]

shrewd (ʃruːd) *adj.* **1.** astute and penetrating, often with regard to business. **2.** artful and crafty: *a shrewd politician.* **3.** *Obsolete.* **a.** piercing: *a shrewd wind.* **b.** spiteful. [C14: from *shrew* (obsolete vb.) to curse, from SHREW] —**ˈshrewd+ly** *adv.* —**ˈshrewd+ness** *n.*

shrewd·ie (ˈʃruːdɪ) *n. Austral. informal.* a shrewd person. [C20: from SHREWD + -IE]

shrew+ish (ˈʃruːɪʃ) *adj.* (esp. of a woman) bad-tempered and nagging. —**ˈshrew+ish+ly** *adv.* —**ˈshrew+ish+ness** *n.*

shrew mole *n.* any of several moles, such as *Uropsilus soricipes* of E Asia or *Neurotrichus gibbsi* of E North America, having a long snout and long tail.

shrew+mouse (ˈʃruːˌmaʊs) *n., pl.* **+mice.** another name for **shrew,** esp. the common shrew.

Shrews+bur·y (ˈʃrəʊzbərɪ, -brɪ, ˈʃruːz-) *n.* a city in W central England, administrative centre of Salop, on the River Severn: strategically situated near the Welsh border; market town. Pop.: 56 140 (1971).

shriek (ʃriːk) *n.* **1.** a shrill and piercing cry. ~*vb.* **2.** to produce or utter (words, sounds, etc.) in a shrill piercing tone. [C16: probably from Old Norse *skrækja* to SCREECH] —**ˈshriek+er** *n.*

shrie+val (ˈʃriːvᵊl) *adj.* of or relating to a sheriff.

shriev+al+ty (ˈʃriːvəltɪ) *n., pl.* **+ties. 1.** the office or term of office of a sheriff. **2.** the jurisdiction of a sheriff. [C16: from SHRIEVE, on the model of *mayoralty*]

shrieve (ʃriːv) *n.* an archaic word for **sheriff.**

shrift (ʃrɪft) *n. Archaic.* the act or an instance of shriving or being shriven. ~See also **short shrift.** [Old English *scrift,* from Latin *scriptum* SCRIPT]

shrike (ʃraɪk) *n.* **1.** Also called: **butcherbird.** any songbird of the chiefly Old World family *Laniidae,* having a heavy hooked bill and feeding on smaller animals which they sometimes impale on thorns, barbed wire, etc. See also **bush shrike** (sense 1). **2.** any of various similar but unrelated birds, such as the cuckoo shrikes. **3. shrike thrush** *or* **tit.** another name for **thickhead** (the bird). [Old English *scrīc* thrush; related to Middle Dutch *schrīk* corncrake; see SCREECH, SHRIEK]

shrill (ʃrɪl) *adj.* **1.** sharp and high-pitched in quality. **2.** emitting a sharp high-pitched sound. ~*vb.* **3.** to utter (words, sounds, etc.) in a shrill tone. **4.** *Rare.* to cause to produce a shrill sound. [C14: probably from Old English *scralletan;* related to German *schrill* shrill, Dutch *schrallen* to shriek] —**ˈshrill+ness** *n.* —**ˈshril+ly** *adv.*

shrimp (ʃrɪmp) *n.* **1.** any of various chiefly marine decapod crustaceans of the genus *Crangon* and related genera, having a slender flattened body with a long tail and a single pair of pincers. **2.** any of various similar but unrelated crustaceans, such as the opossum shrimp and mantis shrimp. **3.** *Informal.* a diminutive person, esp. a child. ~*vb.* **4.** (*intr.*) to fish for shrimps. [C14: probably of Germanic origin; compare Middle Low German *schrempen* to shrink; see SCRIMP, CRIMP] —**ˈshrimp+er** *n.*

shrine (ʃraɪn) *n.* **1.** a place of worship hallowed by association with a sacred person or object. **2.** a container for sacred relics. **3.** the tomb of a saint or other holy person. **4.** a place or site venerated for its association with a famous person or event. **5.** *R.C. Church.* a building, alcove, or shelf arranged as a setting for a statue, picture, or other representation of Christ, the Virgin Mary, or a saint. ~*vb.* **6.** short for **enshrine.** [Old English *scrīn,* from Latin *scrīnium* bookcase; related to Old Norse *skrín,* Old High German *skrīni*] —**ˈshrine+ˌlike** *adj.*

shrink (ʃrɪŋk) *vb.* **shrinks, shrink+ing; shrank** *or* **shrunk; shrunk** *or* **shrunk+en. 1.** to contract or cause to contract as from wetness, heat, cold, etc. **2.** to become or cause to become smaller in size. **3.** (*intr.;* often foll. by *from*) **a.** to recoil or withdraw: *to shrink from the sight of blood.* **b.** to feel great reluctance (at): *to shrink from killing an animal.* ~*n.* **4.** the act or an instance of shrinking. **5. shrinking violet.** *Informal.* a shy person. **6.** a slang word for **psychiatrist.** [Old English *scrincan;* related to Old Norse *skrokkr* torso, Old Swedish *skrunkin* wrinkled, Old Norse *hrukka* a crease, Icelandic *skrukka* wrinkled woman] —**ˈshrink+a·ble** *adj.* —**ˈshrink+er** *n.* —**ˈshrink+ing+ly** *adv.*

shrink+age (ˈʃrɪŋkɪdʒ) *n.* **1.** the act or fact of shrinking. **2.** the amount by which anything decreases in size, value, weight, etc. **3.** the loss in body weight during shipment and preparation of livestock for marketing as meat.

shrink-wrap *vb.* **-wraps, -wrap·ping, -wrapped.** (*tr.*) to package a product in a flexible plastic wrapping designed to shrink about its contours to protect and seal it.

shrive (ʃraɪv) *vb.* **shrives, shriv+ing; shrove** *or* **shrived; shriv+en** *or* **shrived.** *Chiefly R.C. Church.* **1.** to hear the confession of (a penitent). **2.** (*tr.*) to impose a penance upon (a penitent) and grant him sacramental absolution. **3.** (*intr.*) to confess one's sins to a priest in order to obtain sacramental forgiveness. [Old English *scrīfan,* from Latin *scrībere* to write] —**ˈshriv+er** *n.*

shriv+el (ˈʃrɪvᵊl) *vb.* **+els, +el+ling, +elled** *or U.S.* **+els, +el+ing, +eled. 1.** to make or become shrunken and withered. **2.** to lose or cause to lose vitality. [C16: probably of Scandinavian origin; compare Swedish *skryvla* wrinkle]

shroff (ʃrɒf) *n.* **1.** (in China, Japan, etc., esp. formerly) an expert employed to separate counterfeit money or base coin from the genuine. **2.** (in India) a moneychanger or banker. ~*vb.* **3.** (*tr.*) to test (money) and separate out the counterfeit and base. [C17: from Portuguese *xarrafo,* from Hindi *sarrāf* moneychanger, from Arabic]

Shrop+shire (ˈʃrɒpʃɪə, -ʃə) *n.* the former name (until 1974) of **Salop.**

shroud (ʃraʊd) *n.* **1.** a garment or piece of cloth used to wrap a dead body. **2.** anything that envelops like a garment: *a shroud of mist.* **3.** a protective covering for a piece of equipment. **4.** *Nautical.* one of a pattern of ropes or cables used to stay a mast. **5.** any of a set of wire cables stretched between a smokestack or similar structure and the ground, to prevent side sway. **6.** Also called: **shroud line.** any of a set of lines running from the canopy of a parachute to the harness. ~*vb.* **7.** (*tr.*) to wrap in a shroud. **8.** (*tr.*) to cover, envelop, or hide. **9.** *Archaic.* to seek or give shelter. [Old English *scrūd* garment; related to Old Norse *skrūth* gear] —**ˈshroud+less** *adj.*

shroud-laid *adj.* (of a rope) made with four strands twisted to the right, usually around a core.

shrove (ʃrəʊv) *vb.* a past tense of **shrive.**

Shrove+tide (ˈʃrəʊvˌtaɪd) *n.* the Sunday, Monday, and Tuesday before Ash Wednesday, formerly a time when confessions were made in preparation for Lent.

Shrove Tues+day *n.* the last day of Shrovetide; Pancake Day.

shrub[1] (ʃrʌb) *n.* a woody perennial plant, smaller than a tree, with several major branches arising from near the base of the main stem. [Old English *scrybb;* related to Middle Low German *schrubben* coarse, uneven, Old Swedish *skrubba* to SCRUB[1]] —**ˈshrub+ˌlike** *adj.*

shrub[2] (ʃrʌb) *n.* **1.** a mixed drink of rum, fruit juice, sugar, and spice. **2.** mixed fruit juice, sugar, and spice made commercially to be mixed with rum or other spirits. [C18: from Arabic *sharāb,* variant of *shurb* drink; see SHERBET]

shrub+ber·y (ˈʃrʌbərɪ) *n., pl.* **+ber·ies. 1.** a place where a number of shrubs are planted. **2.** shrubs collectively.

shrub+by (ˈʃrʌbɪ) *adj.* **+bi·er, +bi+est. 1.** consisting of, planted with, or abounding in shrubs. **2.** resembling a shrub. —**'shrub+bi+ness** *n.*

shrug (ʃrʌg) *vb.* **shrugs, shrug+ging, shrugged. 1.** to draw up and drop (the shoulders) abruptly in a gesture expressing indifference, contempt, ignorance, etc. ~*n.* **2.** the gesture so made. **3.** a woman's short jacket. [C14: of uncertain origin]

shrug off *vb.* (*tr., adv.*) **1.** to minimize the importance of; dismiss. **2.** to get rid of. **3.** to wriggle out of or push off (clothing).

shrunk (ʃrʌŋk) *vb.* a past participle or past tense of **shrink.**

shrunk+en ('ʃrʌŋkᵊn) *vb.* **1.** a past participle of **shrink.** ~*adj.* **2.** (*usually prenominal*) reduced in size.

shtg. *abbrev. for* shortage.

shuck (ʃʌk) *n.* **1.** the outer covering of something, such as the husk of a grain of maize, a pea pod, or an oyster shell. ~*vb.* (*tr.*) **2.** to remove the shucks from. **3.** *Informal, chiefly U.S.* to throw off or remove (clothes, etc.). [C17: American dialect, of unknown origin] —**'shuck+er** *n.*

shucks (ʃʌks) *U.S. informal.* ~*n.* **1.** something of little value (esp. in the phrase **not worth shucks**). ~*interj.* **2.** an exclamation of disappointment, annoyance, etc.

shud+der ('ʃʌdə) *vb.* **1.** (*intr.*) to shake or tremble suddenly and violently, as from horror, fear, aversion, etc. ~*n.* **2.** the act of shuddering; convulsive shiver. [C18: from Middle Low German *schōderen;* related to Old Frisian *skedda* to shake, Old High German *skutten* to shake] —**'shud+der+ing+ly** *adv.* —**'shud+der·y** *adj.*

shuf+fle ('ʃʌfᵊl) *vb.* **1.** to walk or move (the feet) with a slow dragging motion. **2.** to change the position of (something), esp. quickly or in order to deceive others. **3.** (*tr.*) to mix together in a careless manner: *he shuffled the papers nervously.* **4.** to mix up (cards in a pack) to change their order. **5.** (*intr.*) to behave in an awkward, evasive, or underhand manner; equivocate. **6.** (when *intr.*, often foll. by *into* or *out of*) to move or cause to move clumsily: *he shuffled out of the door.* **7.** (*intr.*) to dance the shuffle. ~*n.* **8.** the act or an instance of shuffling. **9.** a dance or dance step with short dragging movements of the feet. [C16: probably from Low German *schüffeln;* see SHOVE] —**'shuf+fler** *n.*

shuf·fle+board ('ʃʌfᵊl,bɔ:d) *n.* **1.** a game in which players push wooden or plastic discs with a long cue towards numbered scoring sections marked on a floor, esp. a ship's deck. **2.** the marked area on which this game is played.

shuf·fle off *vb.* (*tr., adv.*) to thrust off or put aside.

shuf+ty ('ʃʊftɪ, 'ʃʌftɪ) *n., pl.* **+ties.** *Brit. slang.* a look; peep. [C20: from Arabic]

Shu+fu *or* **Su·fu** ('ʃu:'fu:) *n.* the transliteration of the Chinese name for **Kashgar.**

shug+gy ('ʃʌgɪ) *n., pl.* **+gies.** *Northeastern English dialect.* a swing, as at a fairground. [from *shog, shug* to shake; see SHOOGLE]

shul *or* **schul** (ʃu:l) *n., pl.* **shuln** *or* **schuln** (ʃu:ln). *Judaism.* another word for **synagogue.** [Yiddish: synagogue, from Old High German *scuola* SCHOOL[1]]

Shu+la+mite ('ʃu:lə,maɪt) *n. Old Testament.* an epithet of uncertain meaning applied to the bride in the Song of Solomon 6:13.

shun (ʃʌn) *vb.* **shuns, shun+ning, shunned.** (*tr.*) to avoid deliberately; keep away from. [Old English *scunian,* of obscure origin] —**'shun+na·ble** *adj.* —**'shun+ner** *n.*

shunt (ʃʌnt) *vb.* **1.** to turn or cause to turn to one side; move or be moved aside. **2.** *Railways.* to transfer (rolling stock) from track to track. **3.** *Electronics.* to divert or be diverted through a shunt. **4.** (*tr.*) to evade by putting off onto someone else. **5.** (*tr.*) *Motor racing slang.* to crash (a car). ~*n.* **6.** the act or an instance of shunting. **7.** a railway point. **8.** *Electronics.* a low-resistance conductor connected in parallel across a device, circuit, or part of a circuit to provide an alternative path for a known fraction of the current. **9.** *Med.* a channel that bypasses the normal circulation of the blood: a congenital abnormality or surgically induced. **10.** *Slang.* a car crash. [C13: perhaps from *shunen* to SHUN] —**'shunt+er** *n.*

shunt+er ('ʃʌntə) *n.* a small railway locomotive used for manoeuvring coaches rather than for making journeys.

shunt-wound ('ʃʌnt,waʊnd) *adj. Electrical engineering.* (of a motor or generator) having the field and armature circuits connected in parallel. Compare **series-wound.**

shush (ʃʊʃ) *interj.* **1.** be quiet! hush! ~*vb.* **2.** to silence or calm (someone) by or as if by saying "shush". [C20: reduplication of SH, influenced by HUSH]

Shu+shan ('ʃu:ʃæn) *n.* the Biblical name for **Susa.**

shut (ʃʌt) *vb.* **shuts, shut+ting, shut. 1.** to move (something) so as to cover an aperture; close: *to shut a door.* **2.** to close (something) by bringing together the parts: *to shut a book.* **3.** (*tr.;* often foll. by *up*) to close or lock the doors of: *to shut up a house.* **4.** (*tr.;* foll. by *in, out,* etc.) to confine, enclose, or exclude: *to shut a child in a room.* **5.** (*tr.*) to prevent (a business, etc.) from operating. **6. shut one's eyes to.** to ignore deliberately. **7. shut the door on. a.** to refuse to think about. **b.** to render impossible. ~*adj.* **8.** closed or fastened. ~*n.* **9.** the act or time of shutting. **10.** the line along which pieces of metal are welded. ~See also **shutdown, shut-off, shutout, shut up.** [Old English *scyttan;* related to Old Frisian *sketta* to shut in, Middle Dutch *schutten* to obstruct]

shut+down ('ʃʌt,daʊn) *n.* **1.** the closing of a factory, shop, etc. ~*vb.* **shut down.** (*adv.*) **2.** to cease or cause to cease operation. **3.** (*tr.*) to close by lowering. **4.** (*tr.*) (of fog, etc.) to descend and envelop. **5.** (*intr.;* foll. by *on* or *upon*) *Informal.* to put a stop to; clamp down on.

Shute (ʃu:t) *n.* **Nev·il,** pen name of *Nevil Shute Norway.* 1899–1960, English novelist, noted for his novels set in Australia, esp. *A Town like Alice* (1950) and *On the Beach* (1957).

shut+eye ('ʃʌt,aɪ) *n.* a slang term for **sleep.**

shut-in *n.* **1. a.** *Chiefly U.S.* a person confined indoors by illness. **b.** (*as modifier*): *a shut-in patient.* **2.** *Psychiatry.* a condition in which the person is highly withdrawn and unable to express his own feelings. See also **schizoid.**

shut-off *n.* **1.** a device that shuts something off, esp. a machine control. **2.** a stoppage or cessation. ~*vb.* **shut off.** (*tr., adv.*) **3.** to stem the flow of. **4.** to block off the passage through. **5.** to isolate or separate.

shut+out ('ʃʌt,aʊt) *n.* **1.** a less common word for a **lockout.** ~*vb.* **shut out.** (*tr., adv.*) **2.** to keep out or exclude. **3.** to conceal from sight: *we planted trees to shut out the view of the road.* **4.** *U.S.* to prevent (an opponent) from scoring.

shut-out bid *n. Bridge.* a pre-emptive bid.

shut+ter ('ʃʌtə) *n.* **1.** a hinged doorlike cover, often louvred and usually one of a pair, for closing off a window. **2. put up the shutters.** to close business at the end of the day or permanently. **3.** *Photog.* an opaque shield in a camera that, when tripped, admits light to expose the film or plate for a predetermined period, usually a fraction of a second. It is either built into the lens system or lies in the focal plane of the lens (**focal-plane shutter**). **4.** *Photog.* a rotating device in a film projector that permits an image to be projected onto the screen only when the film is momentarily stationary. **5.** *Music.* one of the louvred covers over the mouths of organ pipes, operated by the swell pedal. **6.** a person or thing that shuts. ~*vb.* (*tr.*) **7.** to close with a shutter or shutters. **8.** to equip with a shutter or shutters.

shut+ter+ing ('ʃʌtərɪŋ) *n.* another word (esp. Brit.) for **formwork.**

shut+tle ('ʃʌtᵊl) *n.* **1.** a bobbin-like device used in weaving for passing the weft thread between the warp threads. **2.** a small bobbin-like device used to hold the thread in a sewing machine or in tatting, knitting, etc. **3.** a bus, train, aircraft, etc., that plies between two points. **4.** *Badminton, etc.* short for **shuttlecock.** ~*vb.* **5.** to move or cause to move by or as if by a shuttle. [Old English *scytel* bolt; related to Middle High German *schüzzel* Swedish *skyttel.* See SHOOT, SHOT]

shut+tle arm·a+ture *n.* a simple H-shaped armature used in small direct-current motors.

shut·tle+cock ('ʃʌtᵊl,kɒk) *n.* **1.** a light cone consisting of a cork stub with feathered flights, struck to and fro in badminton and battledore. Often shortened to **shuttle. 2.** anything moved to and fro, as in an argument. ~*vb.* **3.** to move or cause to move to and fro, like a shuttlecock.

shut up *vb.* (*adv.*) **1.** (*tr.*) to prevent all access to. **2.** (*tr.*) to confine or imprison. **3.** *Informal.* to cease to talk or make a noise or cause to cease to talk or make a noise: often used in commands. **4.** (*intr.*) (of horses in a race) to cease through exhaustion from maintaining a racing pace.

shwa (ʃwɑ:) *n.* a variant spelling of **schwa.**

shy[1] (ʃaɪ) *adj.* **shy+er, shy+est** *or* **shi+er, shi+est. 1.** not at ease in the company of others. **2.** easily frightened; timid. **3.** (often foll. by *of*) watchful or wary. **4.** *Poker.* (of a player) without enough money to back his bet. **5.** (of plants and animals) not breeding or producing offspring freely. **6.** *U.S. informal.* short of. **7.** (*in combination*) showing reluctance or disinclination: *work-shy.* ~*vb.* **shies, shy+ing, shied.** (*intr.*) **8.** to move suddenly, as from fear: *the horse shied at the snake in the road.* **9.** (usually foll. by *off* or *away*) to draw back; recoil. ~*n., pl.* **shies. 10.** a sudden movement, as from fear. [Old English *sceoh;* related to Old High German *sciuhen* to frighten away, Dutch *schuw* shy, Swedish *skygg*] —**'shy+er** *n.* —**'shy+ly** *adv.* —**'shy+ness** *n.*

shy[2] (ʃaɪ) *vb.* **shies, shy+ing, shied. 1.** to throw (something) with a sideways motion. ~*n., pl.* **shies. 2.** a quick throw. **3.** *Informal.* a gibe. **4.** *Informal.* an attempt; experiment. **5.** short for **cockshy.** [C18: of Germanic origin; compare Old High German *sciuhen* to make timid, Middle Dutch *schüchteren* to chase away] —**'shy+er** *n.*

Shy+lock ('ʃaɪ,lɒk) *n.* a heartless or demanding creditor. [C19: after *Shylock,* the name of the heartless usurer in Shakespeare's *Merchant of Venice* (1595)]

shy+poo (ʃaɪ'pu:) *n. Austral. informal.* **a.** liquor of poor quality. **b.** a place where this is sold. **c.** (*as modifier*): *a shypoo shanty.* [C20: of uncertain origin]

shy+ster ('ʃaɪstə) *n. Slang, chiefly U.S.* a person, esp. a lawyer or politician, who uses discreditable or unethical methods. [C19: probably based on *Scheuster,* name of a disreputable 19th-century New York lawyer]

si (si:) *n. Music.* a variant of **ti.**

Si *the chemical symbol for* silicon.

Si, Hsi (ʃi:), *or* **Si Kiang** ('ʃi: 'kjæŋ, kaɪ'æŋ) *n.* a river in S China, rising in Yünnan province and flowing east to the Canton delta on the South China Sea: the main river system of S China. Length: about 1900 km (1200 miles).

SI *abbrev. for* Système International (d'Unités).

si·al ('saɪəl) *n.* the discontinuous outermost part of the earth's crust, consisting of a granitic material rich in silica and aluminium, occurring in continental masses. [C20: *si*(*licon*) + *al*(*uminium*)] —**si+al+ic** (saɪ'ælɪk) *adj.*

si+al·a+gogue *or* **si+al·o+gogue** ('saɪələ,gɒg, saɪ'ælə,gɒg) *n. Med.* any drug or agent that can stimulate the flow of saliva. [C18: from New Latin *sialagōgus,* from Greek *sialon* saliva + -AGOGUE] —**si+al·a+gog+ic** *or* **si+al·o+gog+ic** (,saɪələ'gɒdʒɪk) *adj.*

Si·al·kot (sɪ'ælkɒt) *n.* a city in NE Pakistan: shrine of Guru Nanak. Pop.: 203 779 (1972).
si·a·loid ('saɪə,lɔɪd) *adj.* resembling saliva.
Si·am (saɪ'æm, 'saɪæm) *n.* **1.** the former name (until 1939 and 1945–49) of **Thailand. 2. Gulf of.** an arm of the South China Sea between the Malay Peninsula and Indochina.
si·a·mang ('saɪə,mæŋ) *n.* a large black gibbon, *Hylobates* (or *Symphalangus*) *syndactylus,* of Sumatra and the Malay Peninsula, having a large reddish-brown vocal sac beneath the chin and the second and third toes united. [C19: from Malay]
Si·a·mese (,saɪə'mi:z) *n., pl.* **-mese. 1.** See **Siamese cat.** ~*adj.* **2.** characteristic of, relating to, or being a Siamese twin. ~*adj., n.* **3.** another word for **Thai.**
Si·a·mese cat *n.* a short-haired breed of cat with a tapering tail, blue eyes, and dark ears, mask, tail, and paws.
Si·a·mese fight·ing fish *n.* a brightly coloured labyrinth fish, *Betta splendens,* of Thailand and Malaysia, having large sail-like fins: the males are very pugnacious.
Si·a·mese twins *pl. n.* twin babies born joined together at some point, such as at the hips. Some have lived for many years without being surgically separated.
Sian *or* **Hsian** (ʃjɑ:n) *n.* an industrial city in central China, capital of Shensi province: capital of China for 970 years at various times between the 3rd century B.C. and the 10th century A.D.; seat of the Northwestern University (1937). Pop.: 1 600 000 (1970 est.).
Siang *or* **Hsiang** (ʃjɑ:ŋ) *n.* **1.** a river in SE central China, rising in NE Kwangsi and flowing northeast and north to Tung Ting Lake. Length: about 1150 km (715 miles). **2.** a river in S China, rising in SE Yunnan and flowing generally east to the Hungshui (the upper course of the Si River). Length: about 800 km (500 miles).
Siang·tan ('ʃjɑ:ŋ'tɑ:n) *n.* a city in S central China, in NE Hunan on the Siang River: centre of a region noted for tea production. Pop.: 183 600 (1953).
sib *or* **sibb** (sɪb) *n.* **1.** a blood relative. **2.** kinsmen collectively; kindred. **3.** any social unit that is bonded by kinship through one line of descent only. [Old English *sibb;* related to Old Norse *sifjar* relatives, Old High German *sippa* kinship, Latin *suus* one's own; see GOSSIP]
Sib. *abbrev. for* Siberia(n).
Si·be·li·us (sɪ'beɪlɪəs) *n.* **Jean** (ʒan). 1865–1957, Finnish composer, noted for the nationalism of his music, as in his symphonies, his symphonic poems, such as *Finlandia* (1900), and his violin concerto (1905).
Si·be·ri·a (saɪ'bɪərɪə) *n.* a vast region of the Soviet Union: extends from the Ural Mountains to the Pacific and from the Arctic Ocean to the borders with China and the Mongolian People's Republic; colonized rapidly after the building of the Trans-Siberian Railway. Area: 13 807 037 sq. km (5 330 896 sq. miles). —**Si'be·ri·an** *n., adj.*
sib·i·lant ('sɪbɪlənt) *adj.* **1.** *Phonetics.* relating to or denoting the consonants (s, z, ʃ, ʒ), all pronounced with a characteristic hissing sound. **2.** having a hissing sound: *the sibilant sound of wind among the leaves.* ~*n.* **3.** a sibilant consonant. [C17: from Latin *sībilāre* to hiss, of imitative origin; compare Greek *sizein* to hiss] —**'sib·i·lance** *or* **'sib·i·lan·cy** *n.* —**'sib·i·lant·ly** *adv.*
sib·i·late ('sɪbɪ,leɪt) *vb.* to pronounce or utter (words or speech) with a hissing sound. —**,sib·i'la·tion** *n.*
Si·bi·u (*Rumanian* si'biu) *n.* an industrial town in W central Rumania: originally a Roman city, refounded by German colonists in the 12th century. Pop.: 129 985 (1974 est.). German name: **Hermannstadt.** Hungarian name: **Nagyszeben.**
sib·ling ('sɪblɪŋ) *n.* **1. a.** a person's brother or sister. **b.** (*as modifier*): *sibling rivalry.* **2.** any fellow member of a sib. [C19: specialized modern use of Old English *sibling* relative, from SIB; see -LING[1]]
sib·yl ('sɪbɪl) *n.* **1.** (in ancient Greece and Rome) any of a number of women believed to be oracles or prophetesses, one of the most famous being the sibyl of Cumae, who guided Aeneas through the underworld. See also **Amalthea** (sense 2). **2.** a witch, fortune-teller, or sorceress. [C13: ultimately from Greek *Sibulla,* of obscure origin] —**sib·yl·line** ('sɪbɪ,laɪn, sɪ'bɪlaɪn) *or* **si·byl·ic** (sɪ'bɪlɪk) *adj.*
Sib·yl·line Books *pl. n.* (in ancient Rome) a collection of prophetic sayings, supposedly bought from the Cumaean sibyl, bearing upon Roman policy and religion.
sic[1] (sɪk) *adv.* so or thus: inserted in brackets in a written or printed text to indicate that an odd or questionable reading is in fact accurate. [Latin]
sic[2] (sɪk) *vb.* **sics, sick·ing, sicked.** (*tr.*) **1.** to turn on or attack: used only in commands, as to a dog. **2.** to urge (a dog) to attack. [C19: dialect variant of SEEK]
sic[3] (sɪk) *adj.* a Scot. word for **such.**
Sic. *abbrev. for:* **1.** Sicilian. **2.** Sicily.
Si·ca·ni·an (sɪ'keɪnɪən) *adj.* another word for **Sicilian.**
sic·ca·tive ('sɪkətɪv) *n.* a substance added to a liquid to promote drying: used in paints and some medicines. [C16: from Late Latin *siccātīvus,* from Latin *siccāre* to dry up, from *siccus* dry]
Si·ci·lia (si'tʃi:lja) *n.* the Latin and Italian name for **Sicily.**
Si·cil·i·an Ves·pers *n.* a revolt in 1282 against French rule in Sicily, in which the ringing of the vesper bells on Easter Monday served as the signal to massacre and drive out the French.
Sic·i·ly ('sɪsɪlɪ) *n.* the largest island in the Mediterranean, separated from the tip of SW Italy by the Strait of Messina: administratively an autonomous region of Italy; settled by Phoenicians, Greeks, and Carthaginians before the Roman conquest of 241 B.C.; under Normans (12th–13th centuries); formed the **Kingdom of the Two Sicilies** with Naples in 1815; mountainous and volcanic. Capital: Palermo. Pop.: 4 667 316 (1971). Area: 25 460 sq. km (9830 sq. miles). Latin names: **Sicilia, Trinacria.** Italian name: **Sicilia.** —**Si·cil·i·an** (sɪ'sɪlɪən) *adj., n.*
sick[1] (sɪk) *adj.* **1.** inclined or likely to vomit. **2. a.** suffering from ill health. **b.** (*as n.*): *the sick.* **3. a.** of, relating to, or used by people who are unwell: *sick benefits.* **b.** (*in combination*): *a sickroom; sickbed.* **4.** deeply affected with a mental or spiritual feeling akin to physical sickness: *sick at heart.* **5.** mentally, psychologically, or spiritually disturbed. **6.** *Informal.* delighting in or catering for the macabre or sadistic; morbid: *sick humour.* **7.** (often foll. by *of*) *Informal.* disgusted or weary, esp. because satiated: *I am sick of his everlasting laughter.* **8.** (often foll. by *for*) weary with longing; pining: *I am sick for my own country.* **9.** pallid or sickly. **10.** not in working order. **11.** (of land) unfit for the adequate production of certain crops. ~*n., vb.* **12.** an informal word for **vomit.** [Old English *sēoc;* related to Old Norse *skjūkr,* Gothic *siuks,* Old High German *sioh*] —**'sick·ish** *adj.*
sick[2] (sɪk) *vb.* a variant spelling of **sic**[2].
sick·bay ('sɪk,beɪ) *n.* a room or area for the treatment of the sick or injured, as on board a ship.
sick·en ('sɪkən) *vb.* **1.** to make or become sick, nauseated, or disgusted. **2.** (*intr.;* often foll. by *for*) to show symptoms (of an illness). —**'sick·en·er** *n.*
sick·en·ing ('sɪkənɪŋ) *adj.* **1.** causing sickness or revulsion. **2.** *Informal.* extremely annoying. —**'sick·en·ing·ly** *adv.*
Sick·ert ('sɪkət) *n.* **Wal·ter Rich·ard.** 1860–1942, British impressionist painter, esp. of scenes of London music halls.
sick head·ache *n.* **1.** a headache accompanied by nausea. **2.** a nontechnical name for **migraine.**
sick·ie ('sɪkɪ) *n. Austral. informal.* a day of sick leave from work, whether for genuine sickness or not. [C20: from SICK[1] + -IE]
sick·le ('sɪk^{ə}l) *n.* an implement for cutting grass, corn, etc., having a curved blade and a short handle. [Old English *sicol,* from Latin *sēcula;* related to *secāre* to cut]
sick leave *n.* leave of absence from work through illness.
sick·le·bill ('sɪk^{ə}l,bɪl) *n.* any of various birds having a markedly curved bill, such as *Falculea palliata,* a Madagascan bird of the family *Vangidae, Hemignathus procerus,* a Hawaiian honey-creeper, and certain hummingbirds and birds of paradise.
sick·le cell a·nae·mi·a *n.* an inherited form of anaemia occurring mainly in Negroes, in which a large number of red blood cells become sickle-shaped. It is characterized by fever, abdominal pain, jaundice, leg ulcers, etc.
sick·le feath·er *n.* (*often pl.*) any of the elongated tail feathers of certain birds, esp. the domestic cock.
sick·le med·ick *n.* a small Eurasian papilionaceous plant, *Medicago falcata,* having trifoliate leaves, yellow flowers, and sickle-shaped pods. Also called: **yellow medick.**
sick·ly ('sɪklɪ) *adj.* **-li·er, -li·est. 1.** disposed to frequent ailments; not healthy; weak. **2.** of, relating to, or caused by sickness. **3.** (of a smell, taste, etc.) causing revulsion or nausea. **4.** (of light or colour) faint or feeble. **5.** mawkish; insipid: *sickly affectation.* ~*adv.* **6.** in a sick or sickly manner. —**'sick·li·ness** *n.*
sick·ness ('sɪknɪs) *n.* **1.** an illness or disease. **2.** nausea or queasiness. **3.** the state or an instance of being sick.
sick·ness ben·e·fit *n.* (in the British National Insurance scheme) a weekly payment to a person who has been off work through illness for more than three days and less than six months.
sick-out *Caribbean.* ~*n.* **1.** a form of industrial action in which all workers in a factory, etc. report sick simultaneously. ~*vb.* **2.** (*intr.*) to take part in such action.
sic pas·sim *Latin.* ('sɪk 'pæsɪm) a phrase used in printed works to indicate that a word, spelling, etc., occurs in the same form throughout. [literally: thus everywhere]
sick pay *n.* wages paid to an employee while he is on sick leave.
sic tran·sit glo·ri·a mun·di *Latin.* ('sɪk 'trænsɪt 'glɔ:rɪ,ɑ: 'mʊndi:) thus passes the glory of the world.
Sic·y·on ('sɪsɪ,ɒn, 'sɪsɪən) *n.* an ancient city in S Greece, in the NE Peloponnese near Corinth: declined after 146 B.C.
Sid·dhar·tha (sɪ'dɑ:tə) *n.* the personal name of the Buddha.
Sid·dons ('sɪd^{ə}nz) *n.* **Sar·ah.** 1755–1831, English tragedienne.
sid·dur *Hebrew.* (si:'du:r; *English* 'sɪdʊə) *n., pl.* ***-du·rim*** (-du:'ri:m) *or* ***-durs.*** *Judaism.* the Jewish prayer book. [literally: order]
side (saɪd) *n.* **1.** a line or surface that borders anything. **2.** *Geom.* **a.** any line segment forming part of the perimeter of a plane geometric figure. **b.** another name for **face** (sense 13). **3.** either of two parts into which an object, surface, area, etc., can be divided, esp. by a line, median, space, etc.: *the right side and the left side.* **4.** either of the two surfaces of a flat object: *the right and wrong side of the cloth.* **5.** a surface or part of an object that extends vertically: *the side of a cliff.* **6.** either half of a human or animal body, esp. the area around the waist, as divided by the median plane: *I have a pain in my side.* **7.** the area immediately next to a person or thing: *he stood at her side.* **8.** a district, point, or direction within an area identified by reference to a central point: *the south side of the city.* **9.** the area at the edge of a room, road, etc., as distinguished from the middle. **10.** aspect or part: *look on the bright side; his cruel side.* **11.** one of two or more contesting factions, teams, etc. **12.** a page in an essay, book, etc. **13.** a position, opinion, etc., held

in opposition to another in a dispute. **14.** line of descent: *he gets his brains from his mother's side.* **15.** *Informal.* a television channel. **16.** *Billiards, etc.* spin imparted to a ball by striking it off-centre with the cue. U.S. equivalent: **English. 17.** *Brit. slang.* insolence, arrogance, or pretentiousness: *to put on side.* **18. on one side.** set apart from the rest, as provision for emergencies, etc., or to avoid muddling. **19. on the side. a.** apart from or in addition to the main object. **b.** as a sideline. **20. side by side. a.** close together. **b.** (foll. by *with*) beside or near to. **21. take sides.** to support one group, opinion, etc., as against another. **22. on the weak, heavy,** *etc.,* **side.** tending to be too weak, heavy, etc. ~*adj.* **23.** being on one side; lateral. **24.** from or viewed as if from one side. **25.** directed towards one side. **26.** not main; subordinate or incidental: *side door; side road.* ~*vb.* **27.** (*intr.;* usually foll. by *with*) to support or associate oneself with a faction, interest, etc. **28.** (*tr.*) to provide with siding or sides. **29.** (*tr.;* often foll. by *away* or *up*) *Northern English dialect.* to tidy up or clear (dishes, a table, etc.). [Old English *sīde;* related to *sīd* wide, Old Norse *sītha* side, Old High German *sīta*]

side arms *pl. n.* weapons carried on the person, by sling, belt, or holster, such as a sword, pistol, etc.

side+band (ˈsaɪdˌbænd) *n.* the frequency band either above (**upper sideband**) or below (**lower sideband**) the carrier frequency, within which fall the spectral components produced by modulation of a carrier wave. See also **single sideband transmission.**

side+board (ˈsaɪdˌbɔːd) *n.* a piece of furniture intended to stand at the side of a dining room, with drawers, cupboards, and shelves to hold silver, china, linen, etc.

side+boards (ˈsaɪdˌbɔːdz) *pl. n. Brit.* a man's whiskers grown down either side of the face in front of the ears. Also called: **side whiskers.** U.S. term: **sideburns.**

side+burns (ˈsaɪdˌbɜːnz) *pl. n.* another term (esp. U.S.) for **sideboards.** [C19: variant of BURNSIDES]

side+car (ˈsaɪdˌkɑː) *n.* **1.** a small car attached on one side to a motorcycle, usually for one passenger, the other side being supported by a single wheel. **2.** a cocktail containing brandy with equal parts of cointreau and lemon juice.

side chain *n. Chem.* a group of atoms bound to an atom, usually a carbon, that forms part of a larger chain or ring in a molecule.

-sid·ed *adj.* (*in combination*) having a side or sides as specified: *three-sided; many-sided.*

side dish *n.* a portion of food served in addition to the main dish.

side-dress *vb.* (*tr.*) to place fertilizers on or in the soil near the roots of (growing plants).

side drum *n.* a small double-headed drum carried at the side with snares that produce a rattling effect.

side ef+fect *n.* **1.** any unwanted nontherapeutic effect caused by a drug. Compare **aftereffect** (sense 2). **2.** any secondary effect, esp. an undesirable one.

side+kick (ˈsaɪdˌkɪk) *n. Slang, chiefly U.S.* a close friend or follower who accompanies another on adventures, etc.

side+light (ˈsaɪdˌlaɪt) *n.* **1.** light coming from the side. **2.** a side window. **3.** either of the two navigational running lights used by vessels at night, a red light on the port and a green on the starboard. **4.** *Brit.* either of two small lights on the front of a motor vehicle, used to indicate the presence of the vehicle at night rather than to assist the driver. **5.** additional or incidental information.

side+line (ˈsaɪdˌlaɪn) *n.* **1.** *Sport.* a line that marks the side boundary of a playing area. **2.** a subsidiary interest or source of income. **3.** an auxiliary business activity or line of merchandise. ~*vb.* (*tr.*) *Chiefly U.S.* **4.** to prevent (a player) from taking part in a game. **5.** to prevent (a person) from taking part in any activity.

side+lines (ˈsaɪdˌlaɪnz) *pl. n.* **1.** *Sport.* the area immediately outside the playing area, where substitute players sit. **2.** the peripheral areas of any region, organization, etc.

side+long (ˈsaɪdˌlɒŋ) *adj.* (*prenominal*) **1.** directed or inclining to one side. **2.** indirect or oblique. ~*adv.* **3.** from the side; obliquely.

side+man (ˈsaɪdmən) *n., pl.* **+men.** a member of a dance band or a jazz group other than the leader.

side meat *n. U.S. informal.* salt pork or bacon.

si+de·re·al (saɪˈdɪərɪəl) *adj.* **1.** of, relating to, or involving the stars. **2.** determined with reference to one or more stars: *the sidereal day.* [C17: from Latin *sīdereus,* from *sīdus* a star, a constellation] —**si+ˈde·re·al·ly** *adv.*

si+de·re·al day *n.* See under **day** (sense 5).

si+de·re·al hour *n.* a 24th part of a sidereal day.

si+de·re·al month *n.* See under **month** (sense 5).

si+de·re·al time *n.* time based upon the rotation of the earth with respect to a particular star, the **sidereal day** being the unit of measurement.

si+de·re·al year *n.* See under **year** (sense 5).

si+der+ite (ˈsaɪdəˌraɪt) *n.* **1.** Also called: **chalybite.** a pale yellow to brownish-black mineral consisting chiefly of iron carbonate in hexagonal crystalline form. It occurs mainly in ore veins and sedimentary rocks and is an important source of iron. Formula: $FeCO_3$. **2.** a meteorite consisting principally of metallic iron. —**si+der+it+ic** (ˌsaɪdəˈrɪtɪk) *adj.*

si·der·o- *or before a vowel* **si·der-** *combining form.* indicating iron: *siderolite.* [from Greek *sidēros*]

si+der·o+lite (ˈsaɪdərəˌlaɪt) *n.* a meteorite consisting of a mixture of iron, nickel, and such ferromagnesian minerals as olivine and pyroxene.

si+der·o+phil+in (ˌsɪdəˈrɒfəlɪn) *n.* another name for **transferrin.**

si+der+o·sis (ˌsaɪdəˈrəʊsɪs) *n.* **1.** a lung disease caused by breathing in fine particles of iron or other metallic dust. **2.** an excessive amount of iron in the blood or tissues. —**sid+er+ot+ic** (ˌsɪdəˈrɒtɪk) *adj.*

si+der·o+stat (ˈsaɪdərəʊˌstæt) *n.* an astronomical instrument consisting essentially of a plane mirror rotated by a clock mechanism about two axes so that light from a celestial body, esp. the sun, is reflected along a constant direction for a long period of time. See also **heliostat.** Compare **coelostat.** —ˌ**si+der·o+ˈstat+ic** *adj.*

side-sad·dle *n.* **1.** a riding saddle originally designed for women riders in skirts who sit with both legs on the near side of the horse. ~*adv.* **2.** on or as if on a side-saddle: *to be riding side-saddle.*

side+show (ˈsaɪdˌʃəʊ) *n.* **1.** a small show or entertainment offered in conjunction with a larger attraction, as at a circus or fair. **2.** a subordinate event or incident.

side+slip (ˈsaɪdˌslɪp) *n.* **1.** a sideways skid, as of a motor vehicle. ~*vb.* **+slips, +slip+ping, +slipped. 2.** another name for **slip**[1] (sense 12).

sides+man (ˈsaɪdzmən) *n., pl.* **+men.** *Church of England.* a man elected to help the parish church warden.

side-split·ting *adj.* **1.** producing great mirth. **2.** (of laughter) uproarious or very hearty.

side+step (ˈsaɪdˌstɛp) *vb.* **+steps, +step+ping, +stepped. 1.** to step aside from or out of the way of (something). **2.** (*tr.*) to dodge or circumvent. ~*n.* **side step. 3.** a movement to one side, as in dancing, boxing, etc. —**ˈside+ˌstep+per** *n.*

side street *n.* a minor or unimportant street, esp. one leading off a main thoroughfare.

side+stroke (ˈsaɪdˌstrəʊk) *n.* a type of swimming stroke in which the swimmer lies sideways in the water paddling with his arms and making a scissors kick with his legs.

side+swipe (ˈsaɪdˌswaɪp) *n.* **1.** a glancing blow or hit along or from the side. ~*vb.* **2.** to strike (someone) with such a blow. —**ˈside+ˌswip+er** *n.*

side+track (ˈsaɪdˌtræk) *vb.* **1.** to distract or be distracted from a main subject or topic. ~*n.* **2.** *U.S.* a railway siding. **3.** the act or an instance of sidetracking; digression.

side-valve en+gine *n.* a type of internal-combustion engine in which the inlet and exhaust valves are in the cylinder block at the side of the pistons. Compare **overhead-valve engine.**

side+walk (ˈsaɪdˌwɔːk) *n.* the U.S. word for **pavement.**

side+wall (saɪdˈwɔːl) *n.* either of the sides of a pneumatic tyre between the tread and the rim.

side+ward (ˈsaɪdwəd) *adj.* **1.** directed or moving towards one side. ~*adv. also* **side+wards. 2.** towards one side.

side+ways (ˈsaɪdˌweɪz) *adv.* **1.** moving, facing, or inclining towards one side. **2.** from one side; obliquely. **3.** with one side forward. ~*adj.* (*prenominal*) **4.** moving or directed to or from one side. **5.** towards or from one side.

side+wheel (ˈsaɪdˌwiːl) *n.* one of the paddle wheels of a side-wheeler.

side+wheel·er (ˈsaɪdˌwiːlə) *n.* a vessel, esp. a riverboat, propelled by two large paddle wheels, one on each side. Compare **sternwheeler.**

side whis+kers *pl. n.* another name for **sideboards.**

side+wind·er (ˈsaɪdˌwaɪndə) *n.* **1.** a North American rattlesnake, *Crotalus cerastes,* that moves forwards by a sideways looping motion. **2.** *Boxing, U.S.* a heavy swinging blow from the side. **3.** a U.S. air-to-air missile using infrared homing aids in seeking its target.

Si·di-bel-Ab·bès (*French* sidi bɛl aˈbɛs) *n.* a city in NW Algeria: headquarters of the Foreign Legion until Algerian independence (1962). Pop.: 105 000 (1966 est.).

Si·di If·ni (*Spanish* ˈsiði ˈifni) *n.* the capital of the former Spanish province of Ifni in S Morocco. Pop.: 12 751 (1960).

sid+ing (ˈsaɪdɪŋ) *n.* **1.** a short stretch of railway track connected to a main line, used for storing rolling stock or to enable trains on the same line to pass. **2.** a short railway line giving access to the main line for freight from a factory, mine, quarry, etc. **3.** *U.S.* material attached to the outside of a building to make it weatherproof.

si+dle (ˈsaɪdᵊl) *vb.* (*intr.*) **1.** to move in a furtive or stealthy manner; edge along. **2.** to move along sideways. ~*n.* **3.** a sideways movement. [C17: back formation from SIDELING and SIDELONG] —**ˈsi+dler** *n.*

Sid·ney *or* **Syd·ney** (ˈsɪdnɪ) *n.* Sir **Phil·ip.** 1554–86, English poet, courtier, and soldier. His works include the pastoral romance *Arcadia* (1590), the sonnet sequence *Astrophel and Stella* (1591), and *The Defence of Poesie* (1595), one of the earliest works of literary criticism in English.

Si+don (ˈsaɪdᵊn) *n.* the chief city of ancient Phoenicia: founded in the third millennium B.C.; wealthy through trade and the making of glass and purple dyes; now the Lebanese city of Saïda. —**Si+do·ni·an** (saɪˈdəʊnɪən) *adj., n.*

Sid+ra (ˈsɪdrə) *n.* **Gulf of.** a wide inlet of the Mediterranean on the N coast of Libya.

siè+cle *French.* (ˈsjɛkl) *n.* a century, period, or era.

Sieg·bahn (ˈsiːgbɑːn) *n.* **Karl Man·ne Ge·org** (kɑːrl ˈmanə ˈjeːɔrj). 1886–1978, Swedish physicist, who discovered the M series in x-ray spectroscopy: Nobel prize for physics 1924.

siege (siːdʒ) *n.* **1. a.** the offensive operations carried out to capture a fortified place by surrounding it, severing its communications and supply lines, and deploying weapons against it. **b.** (*as modifier*): *siege warfare.* **2.** a persistent attempt to gain something. **3.** a long tedious period, as of illness, etc. **4.** *Obsolete.* a seat or throne. **5. lay siege to.** to besiege. ~*vb.* **6.** (*tr.*) to besiege or assail. [C13: from Old French *sege* a seat, from Vulgar Latin *sēdicāre* (unattested) to sit down, from Latin *sedēre*]

Siege Per·i·lous *n.* (in Arthurian legend) the seat at the Round Table that could be filled only by the knight destined to find the Holy Grail and that was fatal to anyone else.

Sieg·fried ('si:gfri:d; *German* 'zi:kfri:t) *n. German myth.* a German prince, the son of Sigmund and husband of Kriemhild, who, in the *Nibelungenlied,* assumes possession of the treasure of the Nibelungs by slaying the dragon that guards it, wins Brunhild for King Gunther, and is eventually killed by Hagen. Norse equivalent: **Sigurd.**

Sieg·fried line *n.* the line of fortifications built by the Germans prior to and during World War II opposite the Maginot line in France.

Sieg Heil *German.* ('zi:k 'haɪl) hail to victory: a Nazi salute, often accompanied by the raising of the right arm.

sie+mens ('si:mənz) *n., pl.* **sie+mens.** the derived SI unit of electrical conductance equal to 1 reciprocal ohm. Symbol: S Formerly called: **mho.**

Sie·mens ('si:mənz) *n.* **1. Ernst Wer·ner von** (ɛrnst 'vɛrnər fɔn). 1816–92, German engineer, inventor, and pioneer in telegraphy. Among his inventions are the self-excited dynamo and an electrolytic refining process. **2.** his brother, Sir **Wil·liam,** original name *Karl Wilhelm Siemens.* 1823–83, British engineer, born in Germany, who invented the open-hearth process for making steel.

Si·en·a (sɪ'ɛnə; *Italian* 'sjɛ:na) *n.* a walled city in central Italy, in Tuscany: founded by the Etruscans; important artistic centre (13th–14th centuries); university (13th century). Pop.: 65 347 (1971).

Sien·kie·wicz (*Polish* ʃɛŋ'kjɛvitʃ) *n.* **Hen·ryk** ('xɛnrɪk). 1846–1916, Polish novelist. His best-known works are *Quo Vadis* (1896), set in Nero's Rome, and the war trilogy *With Fire and Sword* (1884), *The Deluge* (1886), and *Pan Michael* (1888), set in 17th-century Poland: Nobel prize for literature (1905).

si+en+na (sɪ'ɛnə) *n.* **1.** a natural earth containing ferric oxide used as a yellowish-brown pigment when untreated (**raw sienna**) or a reddish-brown pigment when roasted (**burnt sienna**). **2.** the colour of this pigment. See also **burnt sienna.** [C18: from Italian *terra di Siena* earth of SIENA]

si+er+ra (sɪ'ɛərə) *n.* a range of mountains with jagged peaks, esp. in Spain or America. [C17: from Spanish, literally: saw, from Latin *serra;* see SERRATE] —**si+'er+ran** *adj.*

Si+er+ra Le·o+ne (sɪ'ɛərə lɪ'əʊnɪ, lɪ'əʊn) *n.* a republic in West Africa, on the Atlantic: became a British colony in 1808 and gained independence (within the Commonwealth) in 1961; declared a republic in 1971; consists of coastal swamps rising to a plateau in the east. Official language: English. Religion: animist majority and Muslim. Currency: leone. Capital: Freetown. Pop.: 2 730 000 (1974). Area: 72 326 sq. km (27 925 sq. miles). —**Si+er+ra Le+on+e·an** *adj., n.*

Si+er+ra Ma+dre (*Spanish* 'sjera 'maðre) *pl. n.* the main mountain system of Mexico, extending for 2500 km (1500 miles) southeast from the N border: consists of the **Sierra Madre Oriental** in the east, the **Sierra Madre Occidental** in the west, and the **Sierra Madre del Sur** in the south. Highest peak: Citlaltépetl, 5699 m (18 134 ft.).

Si+er+ra Mo+re+na (*Spanish* 'sjera mo'rena) *pl. n.* a mountain range in SW Spain, between the Guadiana and Guadalquivir Rivers. Highest peak: Estrella, 1299 m (4262 ft.).

Si+er+ra Ne+va+da *pl. n.* **1.** (sɪ'ɛərə nɪ'vɑ:də). a mountain range in E California, parallel to the Coast Ranges. Highest peak: Mount Whitney, 4418 m (14 495 ft.). **2.** (*Spanish* 'sjera ne'βaða). a mountain range in SE Spain, mostly in Granada and Almería provinces. Highest peak: Cerro de Mulhacén, 3478 m (11 411 ft.).

si+es+ta (sɪ'ɛstə) *n.* a rest or nap, usually taken in the early afternoon, as in hot countries. [C17: from Spanish, from Latin *sexta hōra* the sixth hour, that is, noon]

sieve (sɪv) *n.* **1.** a device for separating lumps from powdered material, straining liquids, grading particles, etc., consisting of a container with a mesh or perforated bottom through which the material is shaken or poured. **2.** *Informal.* a person who gossips and spreads secrets. ~*vb.* **3.** to pass or cause to pass through a sieve. **4.** (*tr.;* often foll. by *out*) to separate or remove (lumps, materials, etc.) by use of a sieve. [Old English *sife;* related to Old Norse *sef* reed with hollow stalk, Old High German *sib* sieve, Dutch *zeef*] —**'sieve+,like** *adj.*

sieve tube *n. Botany.* an element of phloem tissue consisting of a longitudinal row of thin-walled elongated cells with perforations in their connecting walls through which food materials pass.

Sie·yès (*French* sje'jɛs) *n.* **Em·ma·nu·el Jo·seph** (ɛmanɥɛl ʒo'zɛf), called *Abbé Sieyès.* 1748–1836, French statesman, political theorist, and churchman, who became prominent during the Revolution following the publication of his pamphlet *Qu'est-ce que le tiers état?* (1789). He was instrumental in bringing Napoleon I to power (1799).

si+fa+ka (sɪ'fɑ:kə) *n.* either of two large rare arboreal lemuroid primates, *Propithecus diadema* or *P. verreauxi,* of Madagascar, having long strikingly patterned or coloured fur: family *Indriidae.* [from Malagasy]

sift (sɪft) *vb.* **1.** (*tr.*) to sieve (sand, flour, etc.) in order to remove the coarser particles. **2.** to scatter (something) over a surface through a sieve. **3.** (*tr.*) to separate with or as if with a sieve; distinguish between. **4.** (*tr.*) to examine minutely: *to sift evidence.* **5.** (*intr.*) to move as if through a sieve. [Old English *siftan;* related to Middle Low German *siften* to sift, Dutch *ziften;* see SIEVE] —**'sift+er** *n.*

sift+ings ('sɪftɪŋz) *pl. n.* material or particles separated out by or as if by a sieve.

sig. *abbrev. for:* **1.** signature. **2.** signor. **3.** signore.

Sig. *abbrev. for:* **1.** (in prescriptions) signā. [Latin: sign] **2.** (in prescriptions) signature. **3.** signor. **4.** signore.

sigh (saɪ) *vb.* **1.** (*intr.*) to draw in and exhale audibly a deep breath as an expression of weariness, despair, relief, etc. **2.** (*intr.*) to make a sound resembling this: *trees sighing in the wind.* **3.** (*intr.;* often foll. by *for*) to yearn, long, or pine. **4.** (*tr.*) to utter or express with sighing. ~*n.* **5.** the act or sound of sighing. [Old English *sīcan,* of obscure origin] —**'sigh+er** *n.*

sight (saɪt) *n.* **1.** the power or faculty of seeing; perception by the eyes; vision. Related adj.: **visual. 2.** the act or an instance of seeing. **3.** the range of vision: *within sight of land.* **4.** range of mental vision; point of view; judgment: *in his sight she could do nothing wrong.* **5.** a glimpse or view (esp. in the phrase **to catch sight of**). **6.** anything that is seen. **7.** (*often pl.*) anything worth seeing; spectacle: *the sights of London.* **8.** *Informal.* anything unpleasant or undesirable to see: *his room was a sight!* **9.** any of various devices or instruments used to assist the eye in making alignments or directional observations, esp. such a device used in aiming a gun. **10.** an observation or alignment made with such a device. **11.** an opportunity for observation. **12.** *Obsolete.* insight or skill. **13. a sight.** *Informal.* a great deal: *she's a sight too good for him.* **14. a sight for sore eyes.** a person or thing that one is pleased or relieved to see. **15. at** (or **on**) **sight. a.** as soon as seen. **b.** on presentation: *a bill payable at sight.* **16. know by sight.** to be familiar with the appearance of without having personal acquaintance: *I know Mr. Brown by sight but we have never spoken.* **17. not by a long sight.** *Informal.* on no account; not at all. **18. out of sight.** *Slang.* **a.** extreme or very unusual. **b.** (as *interj.*) that's marvellous! **19. set one's sights on.** to have (a specified goal) in mind; aim for. **20. sight unseen.** without having seen the object at issue: *to buy a car sight unseen.* ~*vb.* **21.** (*tr.*) to see, view, or glimpse. **22.** (*tr.*) **a.** to furnish with a sight or sights. **b.** to adjust the sight of. **23.** to aim (a firearm) using the sight. [Old English *sihth;* related to Old High German *siht;* see SEE] —**'sight+a·ble** *adj.* —**'sight+er** *n.*

sight bill *or esp. U.S.* **draft** *n.* variants of **demand bill.**

sight+ed ('saɪtɪd) *adj.* **1.** not blind. **2.** (*in combination*) having sight of a specified kind: *short-sighted.*

sight+er ('saɪtə) *n. Shooting, archery.* any of six practice shots allowed to each competitor in a tournament.

sight+less ('saɪtlɪs) *adj.* **1.** blind. **2.** invisible. —**'sight+less+ly** *adv.* —**'sight+less+ness** *n.*

sight+ly ('saɪtlɪ) *adj.* **+li+er, +li+est. 1.** pleasing or attractive to see. **2.** *U.S.* providing a pleasant view. —**'sight+li+ness** *n.*

sight-read ('saɪt,ri:d) *vb.* **-reads, -read·ing, -read** (-,rɛd). to sing or play (music in a printed or written form) without previous preparation. —**'sight-,read·er** *n.* —**sight-read·ing** *n.*

sight+screen ('saɪt,skri:n) *n. Cricket.* a large white screen placed near the boundary behind the bowler to help the batsman see the ball.

sight+see ('saɪt,si:) *vb.* **+sees, +see+ing, +saw, +seen.** *Informal.* to visit the famous or interesting sights of (a place). —**'sight+,seer** *n.* —**'sight+,see+ing** *n.*

sig+il ('sɪdʒɪl) *n. Rare.* **1.** a seal or signet. **2.** a sign or image supposedly having magical power. [C17: from Latin *sigillum* a little sign, from *signum* a SIGN] —**sig+il+lar·y** ('sɪdʒɪlərɪ) *adj.*

Si·gis·mund ('sɪgɪsmənd) *n.* 1368–1437, king of Hungary (1387–1437) and of Bohemia (1419–37); Holy Roman Emperor (1411–37). He helped to end the Great Schism in the Church; implicated in the death of Huss.

sig+la ('sɪglə) *n.* the list of symbols used in a book, usually collected together as part of the preliminaries. [Latin: plural of *siglum,* diminutive of *signum* sign]

sig+los ('sɪglɒs) *n., pl.* **+loi** (-lɔɪ). a silver coin of ancient Persia worth one twentieth of a daric.

sig+ma ('sɪgmə) *n.* **1.** the 18th letter in the Greek alphabet (Σ, σ or, when final, ς), a consonant, transliterated as *S.* **2.** *Maths.* the symbol Σ, indicating summation of the numbers or quantities indicated.

sig+mate ('sɪgmɪt, -meɪt) *adj.* shaped like the Greek letter sigma or the Roman *S.* —**sig+ma+tion** (sɪg'meɪʃən) *n.*

sig+moid ('sɪgmɔɪd) *adj. also* **sig+moi+dal. 1.** shaped like the letter S. **2.** of or relating to the sigmoid flexure of the large intestine. ~*n.* **3.** See **sigmoid flexure.** [C17: from Greek *sigmoeidēs* sigma-shaped]

sig+moid flex+ure *n.* **1.** the S-shaped bend in the final portion of the large intestine. **2.** *Zoology.* an S-shaped curve, as in the necks of certain birds.

sig+moid·o·scope (sɪg'mɔɪdə,skəʊp) *n.* an instrument incorporating a light for the direct observation of the colon, rectum, and sigmoid flexure. —**sig+moid·o·scop+ic** (sɪg,mɔɪdə'skɒpɪk) *adj.* —**sig+moid+os+co+py** (,sɪgmɔɪd'ɒskəpɪ) *n.*

Sig·mund ('sɪgmənd, 'si:gmʊnd; *German* 'zi:kmʊnt) *n.* **1.** *Norse myth.* the father of the hero Sigurd. **2.** Also called: **Sieg·mund** (*German* 'zi:kmʊnt). *German myth.* king of the Netherlands, father of Siegfried.

sign (saɪn) *n.* **1.** something that indicates or acts as a token of a fact, condition, etc., that is not immediately or outwardly observable. **2.** an action or gesture intended to convey information, a command, etc. **3. a.** a board, placard, etc., displayed in public and inscribed with words or designs intended to inform, warn, etc. **b.** (*as modifier*): *a sign painter.* **4.** an arbitrary or conventional mark or device that stands for a word, phrase, etc. **5.** a symbol used to indicate a mathematical operation: *a plus sign.* **6.** an indication or vestige: *the house* *showed no signs of being occupied.* **7.** a portentous or significant event. **8.** an indication, such as a scent or spoor, of the presence of an animal. **9.** *Med.* any objective evidence of the presence of a disease or disorder. Compare **symptom** (sense 1). **10.** *Astrology.* See **sign of the zodiac.** ~*vb.* **11.** to write (one's name) as a signature to (a document, etc.) in attestation, confirmation, ratification, etc. **12.** (*intr.; often foll. by to*) to make a sign; signal. **13.** to engage or be engaged by written agreement, as a player for a team, etc. **14.** (*tr.*) to outline in gestures a sign over, esp. the sign of the cross. **15.** (*tr.*) to indicate by or as if by a sign; betoken. ~See also **sign away, sign in, sign off, sign on, sign out, sign up.** [C13: from Old French *signe,* from Latin *signum* a sign] —**'sign+a·ble** *adj.* —**'sign+er** *n.*

Si·gnac (*French* siˈɲak) *n.* **Paul** (pɔl). 1863–1935, French neo-impressionist painter, influenced by Seurat.

sig+nal (ˈsɪgnᵊl) *n.* **1.** any sign, gesture, token, etc., that serves to communicate information. **2.** anything that acts as an incitement to action: *the rise in prices was a signal for rebellion.* **3. a.** a variable parameter, such as a current or electromagnetic wave, by which information is conveyed through an electronic circuit, communications system, etc. **b.** the information so conveyed. **c.** (*as modifier*): *signal strength; a signal generator.* ~*adj.* **4.** distinguished or conspicuous. **5.** used to give or act as a signal. ~*vb.* **+nals, +nal+ling, +nalled** *or U.S.* **+nals, +nal+ing, +naled. 6.** to communicate (a message, etc.) to (a person). [C16: from Old French *seignal,* from Medieval Latin *signāle,* from Latin *signum* SIGN] —**'sig+nal+ler** *n.*

sig+nal box *n.* **1.** a building containing manually operated signal levers for all the railway lines in its section. **2.** a control point for a large area of a railway system, operated electrically and semiautomatically.

sig+nal+ize *or* **sig+nal+ise** (ˈsɪgnəˌlaɪz) *vb.* (*tr.*) **1.** to make noteworthy or conspicuous. **2.** to point out carefully.

sig+nal+ly (ˈsɪgnəlɪ) *adv.* conspicuously or especially.

sig·nal+man (ˈsɪgnᵊlmən) *n., pl.* **+men. 1.** a railway employee in charge of the signals and points within a section. **2.** a man who sends and receives signals, esp. in the navy.

sig+nal+ment (ˈsɪgnᵊlmənt) *n. U.S.* a detailed description of a person, for identification or use in police records. [from French *signalement,* from *signaler* to distinguish]

sig·nal-to-noise ra+ti·o *n.* the ratio of one parameter, such as power of a wanted signal to the same parameter of the noise at a specified point in an electronic circuit, etc.

sig+na+to·ry (ˈsɪgnətərɪ, -trɪ) *n., pl.* **·ries. 1.** a person who has signed a document such as a treaty or contract or an organization, state, etc., on whose behalf such a document has been signed. ~*adj.* **2.** having signed a document, treaty, etc. [C17: from Latin *signātōrius* concerning sealing, from *signāre* to mark out, seal, from *signum* a mark]

sig+na+ture (ˈsɪgnɪtʃə) *n.* **1.** the name of a person or a mark or sign representing his name, marked by himself or by an authorized deputy. **2.** the act of signing one's name. **3.** a distinctive mark, characteristic, etc., that identifies a person or thing. **4.** *Music.* See **key signature, time signature. 5.** the part of a medical prescription that instructs a patient how frequently and in what amounts he should take a drug or agent. Abbrevs.: **sig., S. 6.** *Printing.* **a.** a sheet of paper printed with several pages that upon folding will become a section or sections of a book. **b.** such a sheet so folded. **c.** a mark, esp. a letter, printed on the first page of a signature. [C16: from Old French, from Medieval Latin *signātura,* from Latin *signāre* to sign]

sig+na+ture tune *n. Brit.* a melody used to introduce or identify a television or radio programme, a dance band, a performer, etc. Also called (esp. U.S.): **theme song.**

sign a·way *vb.* (*tr., adv.*) to dispose of or lose by or as if by signing a document: *he signed away all his rights.*

sign+board (ˈsaɪnˌbɔːd) *n.* a board carrying a sign or notice, esp. one used to advertise a product, event, etc.

sig+net (ˈsɪgnɪt) *n.* **1.** a small seal, esp. one as part of a finger ring. **2.** a seal used to stamp or authenticate documents. **3.** the impression made by such a seal. ~*vb.* **4.** (*tr.*) to stamp or authenticate with a signet. [C14: from Medieval Latin *signētum* a little seal, from Latin *signum* a SIGN]

sig+net ring *n.* a finger ring bearing a signet.

sig+nif·i+cance (sɪgˈnɪfɪkəns) *n.* **1.** consequence or importance. **2.** something signified, expressed, or intended. **3.** the state or quality of being significant.

sig+nif·i+cant (sɪgˈnɪfɪkənt) *adj.* **1.** having or expressing a meaning; indicative. **2.** having a covert or implied meaning; suggestive. **3.** important, notable, or momentous. **4.** *Statistics.* of or relating to a difference between a result derived from a hypothesis and its observed value that is too large to be attributed to chance and that therefore tends to refute the hypothesis. [C16: from Latin *significāre* to SIGNIFY] —**sig+'nif·i+cant+ly** *adv.*

sig+nif·i+cant fig+ures *or esp. U.S.* **sig+nif·i+cant dig+its** *pl. n.* **1.** the figures of a number that express a magnitude to a specified degree of accuracy, rounding up or down the final figure: *3.141 59 to four significant figures is 3.142.* **2.** the number of such figures: *3.142 has four significant figures.* Compare **decimal place** (sense 2).

sig+ni+fi+ca+tion (ˌsɪgnɪfɪˈkeɪʃən) *n.* **1.** something that is signified; meaning or sense. **2.** the act of signifying.

sig+nif·i+ca+tive (sɪgˈnɪfɪkətɪv) *adj.* **1.** (of a sign, mark, etc.) symbolic. **2.** another word for **significant.** —**sig+'nif·i+ca+tive+ly** *adv.* —**sig+'nif·i+ca+tive+ness** *n.*

sig+ni+fy (ˈsɪgnɪˌfaɪ) *vb.* **+fies, +fy+ing, +fied.** (when *tr., may take a clause as object*) **1.** (*tr.*) to indicate, show, or suggest. **2.** (*tr.*) to imply or portend: *the clouds signified the coming storm.* **3.** (*tr.*) to stand as a symbol, sign, etc. (for). **4.** (*intr.*) *Informal.* to be significant or important. [C13: from Old French *signifier,* from Latin *significāre,* from *signum* a sign, mark + *facere* to make] —**'sig+ni+ˌfi+a·ble** *adj.* —**'sig+ni+ˌfi+er** *n.*

sign in *vb.* (*adv.*) **1.** to sign or cause to sign a register, as at a hotel, club, etc. **2.** to make or become a member, as of a club.

sign lan+guage *n.* any system of communication by manual signs or gestures, such as one used by the deaf.

sign man+u·al *n. Law.* a person's signature in his own hand, esp. that of a sovereign on an official document.

sign off *vb.* (*adv.*) **1.** (*intr.*) to announce the end of a radio or television programme, esp. at the end of a day. **2.** *Bridge.* to make a conventional bid indicating to one's partner that one wishes the bidding to stop. **3.** (*tr.*) to withdraw or retire from (an activity). **4.** (*tr.*) (of a doctor) to declare unfit for work, because of illness.

sign of the cross *n. Chiefly R.C. Church.* a gesture in which the right hand is moved from the forehead to the breast and from the left shoulder to the right to describe the form of a cross in order to invoke the grace of Christ.

sign of the zo+di+ac *n.* any of the 12 equal areas, 30° wide, into which the zodiac can be divided, named after the 12 zodiacal constellations. In astrology, it is thought that a person's psychological type and attitudes to life can be correlated with the sign in which the sun lay at the moment of his birth and to a lesser extent with the signs in which other planets lay at this time. Also called: **sign.** See also **planet** (sense 3), **house** (sense 9).

sign on *vb.* (*adv.*) **1.** (*tr.*) to hire or employ. **2.** (*intr.*) to commit oneself to a job, activity, etc. **3.** (*intr.*) *Brit.* to register at a labour exchange.

si+gnor *or* **si+gnior** (ˈsiːnjɔː; *Italian* siɲˈɲoːr) *n., pl.* **+gnors** *or* **+gnor·i** (*Italian* -ˈɲoːri). an Italian man: usually used before a name as a title equivalent to *Mr.*

si+gno+ra (sɪːnˈjɔːrə; *Italian* siɲˈɲoːra) *n., pl.* **+ras** *or* **+re** (*Italian* -re). a married Italian woman: a title of address equivalent to *Mrs.* when placed before a name or *madam* when used alone. [Italian, feminine of SIGNORE]

si+gno+re (siːnˈjɔːriː; *Italian* siɲˈɲoːre) *n., pl.* **+ri** (-rɪ; *Italian* -ri). an Italian man: a title of respect equivalent to *sir* when used alone. [Italian, ultimately from Latin *senior* an elder, from *senex* an old man]

Si·gno·rel·li (*Italian* ˌsiɲɲoˈrɛlli) *n.* **Lu·ca** (ˈluːka). ?1441–1523, Italian painter, noted for his frescoes.

si+gnor·i+na (ˌsiːnjɔːˈriːnə; *Italian* ˌsiɲɲoˈriːna) *n., pl.* **+nas** *or* **+ne** (*Italian* -ne). an unmarried Italian woman: a title of address equivalent to *Miss* when placed before a name or *madam* or *miss* when used alone. [Italian, diminutive of SIGNORA]

si+gnor·y (ˈsiːnjərɪ) *n., pl.* **+gnor·ies.** a variant spelling of **seigniory.**

sign out *vb.* (*adv.*) to sign (one's name) to indicate that one is leaving a place: *he signed out for the evening.*

sign+post (ˈsaɪnˌpəʊst) *n.* **1.** a post bearing a sign that shows the way, as at a roadside. **2.** something that serves as a clue or indication; sign. ~*vb.* (*tr.; usually passive*) **3.** to mark with signposts. **4.** to indicate direction towards: *the campsite is signposted from the road.*

sign up *vb.* (*adv.*) to enlist or cause to enlist, as for military service.

Sig+urd (ˈsɪgʊəd; *German* ˈziːgʊrt) *n. Norse myth.* a hero who killed the dragon Fafnir to gain the treasure of Andvari, won Brynhild for Gunnar by deception, and then was killed by her when she discovered the fraud. His wife was Gudrun. German counterpart: **Siegfried.**

Si·han·ouk (ˈsɪənʊk) *n.* Prince **No·ro·dom** (ˌnɒrəˈdɒm). born 1922, Cambodian statesman; king (1941–55); prime minister (1955–60), after which he became head of state. He was deposed in 1970 but reinstated (1975–76) following the victory of the Khmer Rouge in the civil war.

si·ka (ˈsiːkə) *n.* a Japanese forest-dwelling deer, *Cervus nippon,* having a brown coat, spotted with white in summer, and a large white patch on the rump. [from Japanese *shika*]

Si+kang (ˈʃiːˈkæŋ) *n.* a former province of W China: established in 1928 from part of W Szechwan and E Tibet; dissolved in 1955.

sike (saɪk, sɪk) *n. Northern Brit. dialect.* a small stream or gulley. [Old English *sīc;* related to Old Norse *sīk* ditch, Middle Low German *sīk* puddle]

Sikh (siːk) *n.* **1.** a member of a reformed Hindu sect, founded in the 16th century, that teaches monotheism and that has the Granth as its chief religious document, rejecting the authority of the Vedas. ~*adj.* **2.** of or relating to the Sikhs or their religious beliefs and customs. [C18: from Hindi, literally: disciple, from Sanskrit *śiksati* he studies] —**'Sikh+ˌism** *n.*

Si Kiang (ˈsiː ˈkjæŋ, kaɪˈæŋ) *n.* See **Si.**

Si+king (ˈsiːˈkɪŋ) *n.* a former name for **Sian.**

Sik+kim (ˈsɪkɪm) *n.* a state of NE India: under British control (1861–1947); became an Indian protectorate in 1950 and an Indian state in 1975; lies in the Himalayas, rising to over 8600 m (28 200 ft.) in Kanchenjunga in the north. Capital: Gangtok. Pop.: 208 609 (1971). Area: 7325 sq. km (2828 sq. miles). —**ˌSik+ki+'mese** *adj., n.*

Si·kor·sky (sɪˈkɔːskɪ) *n.* **I·gor.** 1889–1972, U.S. aeronautical engineer, born in Russia. He designed and flew the first four-engined aircraft (1913) and designed the first successful helicopter (1939).

si+lage (ˈsaɪlɪdʒ) *n.* any crop harvested while green for fodder and kept succulent by partial fermentation in a silo. Also called: **ensilage.** [C19: alteration (influenced by SILO) of ENSILAGE]

Si·las·tic (sɪ'læstɪk) *n. Trademark.* a flexible inert silicone rubber, used esp. in prosthetic medicine.

sild (sɪld) *n.* any of various small young herrings, esp. when prepared and canned in Norway. [Norwegian]

sile (saɪl) *vb. Northern English dialect.* to pour with rain. [probably from Old Norse; compare Swedish and Norwegian dialect *sila* to pass through a strainer]

si·lence ('saɪləns) *n.* **1.** the state or quality of being silent. **2.** the absence of sound or noise; stillness. **3.** refusal or failure to speak, communicate, etc., when expected: *his silence on the subject of their promotion was alarming.* **4.** a period of time without noise. **5.** oblivion or obscurity. ~*vb.* (*tr.*) **6.** to bring to silence. **7.** to put a stop to; extinguish: *to silence all complaint.*

si·lenc·er ('saɪlənsə) *n.* **1.** any device designed to reduce noise, esp. the tubular device containing baffle plates in the exhaust system of a motor vehicle. U.S. name: **muffler. 2.** a tubular device fitted to the muzzle of a firearm to deaden the report. **3.** a person or thing that silences.

si·lent ('saɪlənt) *adj.* **1.** characterized by an absence or near absence of noise or sound: *a silent house.* **2.** tending to speak very little or not at all. **3.** unable to speak. **4.** failing to speak, communicate, etc., when expected: *the witness chose to remain silent.* **5.** not spoken or expressed: *silent assent.* **6.** not active or in operation: *a silent volcano.* **7.** (of a letter) used in the conventional orthography of a word but no longer pronounced in that word: *the "k" in "know" is silent.* **8.** denoting a film that has no accompanying soundtrack, esp. one made before 1927, when such soundtracks were developed. ~*n.* **9.** a silent film. [C16: from Latin *silēns*, from *silēre* to be quiet] —'**si·lent·ly** *adv.* —'**si·lent·ness** *n.*

si·lent ma·jor·i·ty *n.* a presumed moderate majority of the citizens who are too passive to make their views known.

si·lent part·ner *n.* another name (esp. U.S.) for **sleeping partner.**

Si·le·nus (saɪ'li:nəs) *n. Greek myth.* **1.** chief of the satyrs and foster father to Dionysus: often depicted riding drunkenly on a donkey. **2.** (*often not cap.*) one of a class of woodland deities, closely similar to the satyrs.

si·le·si·a (saɪ'li:ʃɪə) *n.* a twill-weave fabric of cotton or other fibre, used esp. for pockets, linings, etc. [C17: Latinized form of German *Schlesien*]

Si·le·si·a (saɪ'li:ʃɪə) *n.* a region of central Europe around the upper and middle Oder valley: mostly annexed by Prussia in 1742 but became almost wholly Polish in 1945; rich coal and iron ore deposits. Polish name: **Śląsk.** Czech name: **Slezsko.** German name: **Schlesien.** —**Si'le·si·an** *adj., n.*

si·lex ('saɪlɛks) *n.* a type of heat-resistant glass made from fused quartz. [C16: from Latin: hard stone, flint]

sil·hou·ette (ˌsɪlu:'ɛt) *n.* **1.** the outline of a solid figure as cast by its shadow. **2.** an outline drawing filled in with black, often a profile portrait cut out of black paper and mounted on a light ground. ~*vb.* **3.** (*tr.*) to cause to appear in silhouette. [C18: named after Étienne de *Silhouette* (1709–67), French politician, perhaps referring to silhouettes as partial portraits, with a satirical allusion to Silhouette's brief career as controller-general (1759)]

sil·i·ca ('sɪlɪkə) *n.* **1.** the dioxide of silicon, occurring naturally as quartz, cristobalite, and tridymite. It is a refractory insoluble material used in the manufacture of glass, ceramics, and abrasives. **2.** short for **silica glass.** [C19: New Latin, from Latin: SILEX]

sil·i·ca gel *n.* an amorphous form of silica capable of absorbing large quantities of water: used in drying gases and oils, as a carrier for catalysts and an anticaking agent for cosmetics.

sil·i·ca glass *n.* another name for **quartz glass.**

sil·i·cate ('sɪlɪkɪt, -ˌkeɪt) *n.* a salt or ester of silicic acid, esp. one of a large number of usually insoluble salts with polymeric negative ions having a structure formed of tetrahedrons of SiO_4 groups linked in rings, chains, sheets, or three dimensional frameworks. Silicates constitute a large proportion of the earth's minerals and are present in cement and glass.

si·li·ceous *or* **si·li·cious** (sɪ'lɪʃəs) *adj.* **1.** of, relating to, or containing silica: *siliceous deposits; a siliceous clay.* **2.** (of plants) growing in or needing soil rich in silica.

si·lic·i- *or before a vowel* **si·lic-** *combining form.* indicating silica or silicon: *silicify.*

si·lic·ic (sɪ'lɪsɪk) *adj.* of, concerned with, or containing silicon or an acid obtained from silicon.

si·lic·ic ac·id *n.* a white gelatinous substance obtained by adding an acid to a solution of sodium silicate. It has an ill-defined composition and is best regarded as hydrated silica, $SiO_2.nH_2O$.

sil·i·cide ('sɪlɪˌsaɪd) *n.* any one of a class of binary compounds formed between silicon and certain metals.

sil·i·cif·er·ous (ˌsɪlɪ'sɪfərəs) *n.* containing or yielding silicon or silica.

si·lic·i·fy (sɪ'lɪsɪˌfaɪ) *vb.* **·fies, ·fy·ing, ·fied.** to convert or be converted into silica: *silicified wood.* —**si·ˌlic·i·fi·'ca·tion** *n.*

si·lic·i·um (sɪ'lɪsɪəm) *n.* a rare name for **silicon.**

sil·i·cle ('sɪlɪkᵊl), **si·lic·u·la** (sɪ'lɪkjʊlə), *or* **sil·i·cule** ('sɪlɪˌkju:l) *n. Botany.* a short broad siliqua, occurring in such cruciferous plants as honesty and shepherd's purse. [C18: from Latin *silicula* a small pod; see SILIQUA]

sil·i·con ('sɪlɪkən) *n.* a brittle metalloid element that exists in two allotropic forms; occurs principally in sand, quartz, granite, feldspar, and clay. It is usually a grey crystalline solid but is also found as a brown amorphous powder. It is used in transistors, rectifiers, solar cells, and in alloys. Its compounds are widely used in glass manufacture, the building industry, and in the form of silicones. Symbol: Si; atomic no.: 14; atomic wt.: 28.09; valency: 4; relative density: 2.33; melting pt.: 1410°C; boiling pt.: 2355°C. [C19: from SILICA, on the model of *boron, carbon*]

sil·i·con car·bide *n.* an extremely hard bluish-black insoluble crystalline substance produced by heating carbon with sand at a high temperature and used as an abrasive and refractory material. Silicon carbide whiskers have a high tensile strength and are used in composites; very pure crystals are used as semiconductors. Formula: SiC.

sil·i·con con·trolled rec·ti·fi·er *n.* a semiconductor rectifier whose forward current between two electrodes, the anode and cathode, is initiated by means of a signal applied to a third electrode, the gate. The current subsequently becomes independent of the signal; the solid-state equivalent of the thyratron. Abbrev.: **SCR.** Also called: **thyristor.**

sil·i·cone ('sɪlɪˌkəʊn) *n. Chem.* **a.** any of a large class of polymeric synthetic materials that usually have resistance to temperature, water, and chemicals, and good insulating and lubricating properties, making them suitable for wide use as oils, water-repellents, resins, etc. Chemically they have alternate silicon and oxygen atoms with the silicon atoms bound to organic groups. **b.** (*as modifier*): *silicone rubber.* See also **siloxane.**

sil·i·co·sis (ˌsɪlɪ'kəʊsɪs) *n. Pathol.* a form of pneumoconiosis caused by breathing in tiny particles of silica, quartz, or slate, and characterized by shortness of breath and fibrotic changes in the tissues of the lungs.

si·lic·u·lose (sɪ'lɪkjʊˌləʊs, -ˌləʊz) *adj.* (of certain cruciferous plants such as honesty) producing silicles.

si·li·qua (sɪ'li:kwə, 'sɪlɪkwə) *or* **si·lique** (sɪ'li:k, 'sɪlɪk) *n., pl.* **·li·quae** (-'li:kwi:), **·li·quas,** *or* **·liques.** the long dry dehiscent fruit of cruciferous plants, such as the wallflower, consisting of two compartments separated by a central septum to which the seeds are attached. [C18: via French from Latin *siliqua* a pod] —**sil·i·qua·ceous** (ˌsɪlɪ'kweɪʃəs) *adj.* —**sil·i·quose** ('sɪlɪˌkwəʊs) *or* **sil·i·quous** ('sɪlɪkwəs) *adj.*

silk (sɪlk) *n.* **1.** the very fine soft lustrous fibre produced by a silkworm to make its cocoon. **2. a.** thread or fabric made from this fibre. **b.** (*as modifier*): *a silk dress.* **3.** a garment made of this. **4.** a very fine fibre produced by a spider to build its web, nest, or cocoon. **5.** the tuft of long fine styles on an ear of maize. **6.** *Brit.* **a.** the gown worn by a Queen's (or King's) Counsel. **b.** *Informal.* a Queen's (or King's) Counsel. **c. take silk.** to become a Queen's (or King's) Counsel. ~*vb.* **7.** (*intr.*) *U.S.* (of maize) to develop long hairlike styles. [Old English *sioluc;* compare Old Norse *silki*, Greek *sērikon*, Korean *sir;* all ultimately from Chinese *ssŭ* silk] —'**silk·ˌlike** *adj.*

silk·a·line *or* **silk·a·lene** (ˌsɪlkə'li:n) *n.* a fine smooth cotton fabric used for linings, etc. [C20: from SILK + *-aline*, from *-oline* as in CRINOLINE]

silk cot·ton *n.* another name for **kapok.**

silk-cot·ton tree *n.* any of several tropical bombacaceous trees of the genus *Ceiba*, esp. *Ceiba pentandra*, having seeds covered with silky hairs from which kapok is obtained. Also called: **kapok tree.**

silk·en ('sɪlkən) *adj.* **1.** made of silk. **2.** resembling silk in smoothness or gloss. **3.** dressed in silk. **4.** soft and delicate. **5.** *Rare.* luxurious or elegant.

silk hat *n.* a man's top hat covered with silk.

silk-screen print·ing *n.* another name for **screen process.**

silk·weed ('sɪlkˌwi:d) *n.* another name for **milkweed** (sense 1).

silk·worm ('sɪlkˌwɜ:m) *n.* **1.** the larva of the Chinese moth *Bombyx mori*, that feeds on the leaves of the mulberry tree: widely cultivated as a source of silk. **2.** any of various similar or related larvae. **3. silkworm moth.** the moth of any of these larvae.

silk·y ('sɪlkɪ) *adj.* **silk·i·er, silk·i·est. 1.** resembling silk in texture; glossy. **2.** made of silk. **3.** (of a voice, manner, etc.) suave; smooth. **4.** *Botany.* covered with long fine soft hairs: *silky leaves.* —'**silk·i·ly** *adv.* —'**silk·i·ness** *n.*

silk·y oak *n.* any of several trees of the Australian genus *Grevillea*, esp. *G. robusta*, having divided leaves and showy clusters of orange, red, or white flowers: cultivated in the tropics as shade trees: family *Proteaceae.*

sill (sɪl) *n.* **1.** a shelf at the bottom of a window inside a room. **2.** a horizontal piece along the outside lower member of a window, that throws water clear of the wall below. **3.** the lower horizontal member of a window or door frame. **4.** a continuous horizontal member placed on top of a foundation wall in order to carry a timber framework. **5.** a flat usually horizontal mass of igneous rock, situated between two layers of older sedimentary rock, that was formed by an intrusion of magma. [Old English *syll;* related to Old Norse *svill* sill, Icelandic *svoli* tree trunk, Old High German *swella* sill, Latin *solum* ground]

sil·la·bub ('sɪləˌbʌb) *n.* a variant spelling of **syllabub.**

Sil·lan·pää (*Finnish* 'sillɑmpæ:) *n.* **Frans Ee·mil** (frans 'e:mil). 1888–1964, Finnish writer, noted for his novels *Meek Heritage* (1919) and *The Maid Silja* (1931): Nobel prize for literature 1939.

sil·li·ma·nite ('sɪlɪməˌnaɪt) *n.* a white, brown, or green fibrous mineral that consists of aluminium silicate in orthorhombic crystalline form and occurs in metamorphic rocks. Formula: Al_2SiO_5. [C19: named after Benjamin *Silliman* (1779–1864), U.S. chemist]

sil·ly ('sɪlɪ) *adj.* **·li·er, ·li·est. 1.** lacking in good sense;

absurd. **2.** frivolous, trivial, or superficial. **3.** feeble-minded. **4.** *Informal.* dazed, as from a blow. **5.** *Obsolete.* homely or humble. ~*n.* **6.** (*modifier*) *Cricket.* (of a fielding position) near the batsman's wicket: *silly mid-on.* **7.** Also called **sil·ly·bil·ly.** *Informal.* a foolish person. [C15 (in the sense: pitiable, hence the later senses: foolish): from Old English *sǣlig* (unattested) happy, from *sǣl* happiness; related to Gothic *sēls* good] —'**sil+li+ness** *n.*

sil+ly sea+son *n. Brit.* a period, usually during the hot summer months, when journalists fill space reporting on frivolous events and activities.

si·lo ('saɪləʊ) *n., pl.* **·los.** **1.** a pit, trench, horizontal container, or tower, often cylindrical in shape, in which silage is made and stored. **2.** a strengthened underground position in which missile systems are sited for protection against attack. [C19: from Spanish, perhaps from Celtic]

Si+lo+am (saɪ'ləʊəm, sɪ-) *n. Bible.* a pool in Jerusalem where Jesus cured a man of his blindness (John 9).

Si·lo·ne (*Italian* si'lo:ne) *n.* **I·gna·zio** (iɲ'ɲattsjo). 1900–78, Italian writer, noted for his humanitarian socialistic novels, *Fontamara* (1933) and *Bread and Wine* (1937).

si+lox+ane (sɪ'lɒkseɪn) *n.* any of a class of compounds containing alternate silicon and oxygen atoms with the silicon atoms bound to hydrogen atoms or organic groups. Many are highly complex polymers. See also **silicone.** [C20: from SIL(ICON) + OX(YGEN) + (METH)ANE]

silt (sɪlt) *n.* **1.** a fine deposit of mud, clay, etc., esp. one in a river or lake. ~*vb.* **2.** (usually foll. by *up*) to fill or become filled with silt; choke. [C15: of Scandinavian origin; compare Norwegian, Danish *sylt* salt marsh; related to Old High German *sulza* salt marsh; see SALT] —**sil+'ta+tion** *n.* —'**silt·y** *adj.*

silt+stone ('sɪlt,stəʊn) *n.* a variety of fine sandstone formed from consolidated silt.

Si+lu+res (saɪ'lʊəri:z) *pl. n.* a powerful and warlike tribe of ancient Britain, living chiefly in SE Wales, who fiercely resisted Roman invaders in the 1st century A.D.

Si+lu+ri·an (saɪ'lʊərɪən) *adj.* **1.** of, denoting, or formed in the third period of the Palaeozoic era, between the Ordovician and Devonian periods, which lasted for 40 million years, during which fishes first appeared. **2.** of or relating to the Silures. ~*n.* **3. the.** the Silurian period or rock system.

si+lu+rid (saɪ'lʊərɪd) *n.* **1.** any freshwater teleost fish of the Eurasian family *Siluridae,* including catfish, such as *Silurus glanis* (**European catfish**), that have an elongated body, naked skin, and a long anal fin. ~*adj.* **2.** of, relating to, or belonging to the family *Siluridae.* [C19: from Latin *silūrus,* from Greek *silouros* a river-fish]

sil+va ('sɪlvə) *n.* a variant spelling of **sylva.**

sil+van ('sɪlvən) *adj.* a variant spelling of **sylvan.**

Sil·va·nus *or* **Syl·va·nus** (sɪl'veɪnəs) *n. Roman myth.* the Roman god of woodlands, fields, and flocks. Greek counterpart: **Pan.** [Latin: from *silva* woodland]

sil+ver ('sɪlvə) *n.* **1. a.** a very ductile malleable brilliant greyish-white element having the highest electrical and thermal conductivity of any metal. It occurs free and in argentite and other ores: used in jewellery, tableware, coinage, electrical contacts, and in electroplating. Its compounds are used in photography. Symbol: Ag; atomic no.: 47; atomic wt.: 107.870; valency: 1 or 2; relative density: 10.5; melting pt.: 961.93°C; boiling pt.: 2212°C. **b.** (*as modifier*): *a silver coin.* Related adj.: **argent.** **2.** coin made of this metal. **3.** cutlery, whether made of silver or not. **4.** any household articles made of silver. **5.** *Photog.* any of a number of silver compounds used either as photosensitive substances in emulsions or as sensitizers. **6. a.** a brilliant or light greyish-white colour. **b.** (*as adj.*): *silver hair.* ~*adj.* **7.** well-articulated: *silver speech.* **8.** (*prenominal*) denoting the 25th in a series, esp. an annual series: *a silver wedding anniversary.* ~*vb.* **9.** (*tr.*) to coat with silver or a silvery substance: *to silver a spoon.* **10.** to become or cause to become silvery in colour. [Old English *siolfor;* related to Old Norse *silfr,* Gothic *silubr,* Old High German *silabar,* Old Slavonic *sirebro*] —'**sil+ver+er** *n.* —'**sil+ver+ing** *n.*

sil+ver age *n.* **1.** (in Greek and Roman mythology) the second of the world's major epochs, inferior to the preceding Golden Age and characterized by opulence and irreligion. **2.** the postclassical period of Latin literature, occupying the early part of the Roman imperial era, characterized by an over-indulgence in elegance for its own sake and empty scholarly rhetoric.

sil+ver bell *n.* any of various deciduous trees of the styracaceous genus *Halesia,* esp. *H. carolina,* of North America and China, having white bell-shaped flowers. Also called: **snowdrop tree.**

sil+ver birch *n.* a betulaceous tree, *Betula pendula,* of N temperate regions of the Old World, having silvery-white peeling bark. See also **birch** (sense 1).

sil+ver bro+mide *n.* a yellowish insoluble powder that darkens when exposed to light: used in making photographic emulsions. Formula: AgBr.

sil+ver cer+tif·i+cate *n.* (formerly) a bank note issued by the U.S. Treasury to the public and redeemable in silver.

sil+ver chlo+ride *n.* a white insoluble powder that darkens on exposure to light because of the production of metallic silver: used in making photographic emulsions and papers. Formula: AgCl.

sil·ver-eye *n. Austral.* another name for **white-eye.**

sil+ver fir *n.* any of various fir trees the leaves of which have a silvery undersurface, esp. *Abies alba,* an important timber tree of central and S Europe.

sil·ver+fish ('sɪlvə,fɪʃ) *n., pl.* **+fish** *or* **+fish·es.** **1.** a silver variety of the goldfish *Carassius auratus.* **2.** any of various other silvery fishes, such as the moonfish *Monodactylus argenteus.* **3.** any of various small primitive wingless insects of the genus *Lepisma,* esp. *L. saccharina,* that have long antennae and tail appendages and occur in buildings, feeding on food scraps, book bindings, etc.: order *Thysanura* (bristletails).

sil+ver fox *n.* **1.** an American red fox in a colour phase in which the fur is black with long silver-tipped hairs. **2.** the valuable fur or pelt of this animal.

sil+ver frost *n.* another name for **glaze ice.**

sil+ver i·o·dide *n.* a yellow insoluble powder that darkens on exposure to light: used in photography and artificial rain-making. Formula: AgI.

sil+ver lin+ing *n.* a comforting or hopeful aspect of an otherwise desperate or unhappy situation.

sil+ver ma+ple *n.* a North American maple tree, *Acer saccharinum,* having five-lobed leaves that are green above and silvery-white beneath.

sil+ver med+al *n.* a medal of silver awarded to a competitor who comes second in a contest or race. Compare **gold medal, bronze medal.**

sil+vern ('sɪlvən) *adj. Archaic or poetic.* silver.

sil+ver ni+trate *n.* a white crystalline soluble poisonous substance used in making photographic emulsions, other silver salts, and as a medical antiseptic and astringent. Formula: $AgNO_3$. See also **lunar caustic.**

sil+ver plate *n.* **1.** a thin layer of silver deposited on a base metal. **2.** articles, esp. tableware, made of silver plate. ~*vb.* **sil·ver-plate.** **3.** (*tr.*) to coat (a metal, object, etc.) with silver, as by electroplating.

sil·ver+point ('sɪlvə,pɔɪnt) *n.* a drawing technique popular esp. in the 15th and 16th centuries, using an instrument with a silver wire tip on specially prepared paper.

sil+ver screen *n.* **the.** *Informal.* **1.** films collectively or the film industry. **2.** the screen onto which films are projected.

sil·ver+side ('sɪlvə,saɪd) *n.* **1.** *Brit.* a coarse cut of beef below the aitchbone and above the leg. **2.** Also called: **silversides.** any small marine or freshwater teleost fish of the family *Atherinidae,* related to the grey mullets: includes the jacksmelt.

sil·ver+smith ('sɪlvə,smɪθ) *n.* a craftsman who makes or repairs articles of silver. —'**sil·ver+,smith·ing** *n.*

sil+ver stand+ard *n.* a monetary system in which the legal unit of currency is defined with reference to silver of a specified fineness and weight and sometimes (esp. formerly) freely redeemable for it.

sil+ver+tail ('sɪlvə,teɪl) *n. Austral. informal.* a rich and influential person.

sil+ver thaw *n. Canadian.* **1.** a freezing rainstorm. **2.** another name for **glitter ice.**

sil·ver-tongued *adj.* persuasive; eloquent.

sil·ver+ware ('sɪlvə,wɛə) *n.* articles, esp. tableware, made of or plated with silver.

sil·ver+weed ('sɪlvə,wi:d) *n.* **1.** a rosaceous perennial creeping plant, *Potentilla anserina,* with silvery pinnate leaves and yellow flowers. **2.** any of various convolvulaceous twining shrubs of the genus *Argyreia,* of SE Asia and Australia, having silvery leaves and showy purple flowers.

sil+ver·y ('sɪlvərɪ) *adj.* **1.** of or having the appearance of silver: *the silvery moon.* **2.** containing or covered with silver. **3.** having a clear ringing sound. —'**sil+ver·i+ness** *n.*

sil+vi+cul+ture ('sɪlvɪ,kʌltʃə) *n.* the branch of forestry that is concerned with the cultivation of trees. [C20: *silvi-,* from Latin *silva* woodland + CULTURE] —,**sil+vi+'cul+tur+al** *adj.* —,**sil+vi+'cul+tur+ist** *n.*

s'il vous plaît *French.* (sil vu 'plɛ) if you please; please.

si·ma ('saɪmə) *n.* the continuous lower layer of the earth's crust, consisting of basic rock material rich in silica and magnesia. [C20: from SI(LICA) + MA(GNESIA)]

si+mar (sɪ'mɑ:) *n.* a variant spelling of **cymar.**

sim·a+rou+ba *or* **sim·a+ru+ba** (,sɪmə'ru:bə) *n.* **1.** any tropical American tree of the genus *Simarouba,* esp. *S. amara,* having divided leaves and fleshy fruits: family *Simaroubaceae.* **2.** the medicinal bark of any of these trees. [C18: from New Latin, from Carib *simaruba*]

sim·a+rou+ba+ceous *or* **sim·a+ru+ba+ceous** (,sɪməru:'beɪʃəs) *adj.* of, relating to, or belonging to the *Simaroubaceae,* a mainly tropical family of trees and shrubs that includes ailanthus, seringa, and quassia.

sim+ba ('sɪmbə) *n.* an E African word for **lion.**

Sim+birsk (*Russian* sim'birsk) *n.* the former name (until 1924) of **Ulyanovsk.**

Sim+chath To+rah *or* **Sim+hath To+rah** ('sɪmkɑ:s; *Hebrew* sim'xat, 'sɪmxas) *n.* a Jewish holiday celebrated on Tishri 23 (in Israel Tishri 22) to mark the completion of the yearly cycle of Torah readings at the synagogue. [from Hebrew *śimhath tōrāh,* literally: celebration of the Torah]

Sim·e·on ('sɪmɪən) *n.* **1. a.** *Old Testament.* the second son of Jacob and Leah. **b.** the tribe descended from him. **c.** the territory once occupied by this tribe in the extreme south of the land of Canaan. **2.** *New Testament.* a devout Jew, who recognized the infant Jesus as the Messiah and uttered the canticle *Nunc Dimittis* over him in the Temple (Luke 2:25–35).

Sim·e·on Sty·li·tes (staɪ'laɪti:z) *n.* **Saint.** ?390–459 A.D., Syrian monk, first of the ascetics who lived on pillars. Feast day: Jan. 5.

Sim+fe·ro+pol (*Russian* simfɪ'rɔpəlj) *n.* a city in the SW Soviet Union, in the S Ukrainian SSR on the S Crimean Peninsula: a

Scythian town in the 1st century B.C.; seized by the Russians in 1736. Pop.: 280 000 (1975 est.).
sim·i·an ('sɪmɪən) *adj.* **1.** Also: **sim·i·ous.** of, relating to, or resembling a monkey or ape. ~*n.* **2.** a monkey or ape. [C17: from Latin *sīmia* an ape, probably from *sīmus* flat-nosed, from Greek *sīmos*]
sim·i·lar ('sɪmɪlə) *adj.* **1.** showing resemblance in qualities, characteristics, or appearance; alike but not identical. **2.** *Geom.* (of two or more figures) having corresponding angles equal and all corresponding sides in the same ratio. Compare **congruent** (sense 2). [C17: from Old French *similaire,* from Latin *similis*] —**sim·i·lar·i·ty** (ˌsɪmɪ'lærɪtɪ) *n.* —'**sim·i·lar·ly** *adv.*
Usage. Careful writers prefer not to use *similarly* where *correspondingly* would be appropriate: *if our competitors raise their prices, we must correspondingly* (not *similarly*) *make increases in ours.*
sim·i·le ('sɪmɪlɪ) *n.* a figure of speech that expresses the resemblance of one thing to another of a different category, usually introduced by *as* or *like.* Compare **metaphor.** [C14: from Latin *simile* something similar, from *similis* like]
si·mil·i·tude (sɪ'mɪlɪˌtju:d) *n.* **1.** likeness; similarity. **2.** a thing or sometimes a person that is like or the counterpart of another. **3.** *Archaic.* a simile, allegory, or parable. [C14: from Latin *similitūdō,* from *similis* like]
sim·i·tar ('sɪmɪtə) *n.* a rare spelling of **scimitar.**
Sim·la ('sɪmlə) *n.* a city in N India, capital of Himachal Pradesh state: summer capital of India (1865–1939); hill resort and health centre. Pop.: 55 368 (1971).
sim·mer ('sɪmə) *vb.* **1.** to cook (food) gently at or just below the boiling point. **2.** (*intr.*) to be about to break out in rage or excitement. ~*n.* **3.** the act, sound, or state of simmering. [C17: perhaps of imitative origin; compare German *summen* to hum] —'**sim·mer·ing·ly** *adv.*
sim·mer down *vb.* (*adv.*) **1.** (*intr.*) *Informal.* to grow calmer or quieter, as after intense rage or excitement. **2.** (*tr.*) to reduce the volume of (a liquid) by boiling slowly.
sim·nel cake ('sɪmnᵊl) *n. Brit.* a fruit cake, often coloured with saffron and covered with a layer of marzipan, traditionally eaten in Lent or at Easter. [C13 *simenel,* from Old French, from Latin *simila* fine flour, probably of Semitic origin; related to Greek *semidalis* fine flour]
Si·mon ('saɪmən) *n.* **1.** the original name of (Saint) **Peter. 2.** *New Testament.* **a.** See **Simon Zelotes. b.** a relative of Jesus, who may have been identical with Simon Zelotes (Matthew 13:55). **c.** Also called: **Simon the Tanner.** a Christian of Joppa with whom Peter stayed (Acts of the Apostles 9:43). **3. John (Allsebrook),** 1st Viscount Simon. 1873–1954, English statesman and lawyer. He was Liberal home secretary (1915–16) and, as a leader of the National Liberals, foreign secretary (1931–35), home secretary (1935–37), chancellor of the Exchequer (1937–40), Lord Chancellor (1940–45). **4. Paul.** born 1941, U.S. rock singer and songwriter. His recordings include: with Art Garfunkel (born 1941), *Sounds of Silence* (1966), *The Graduate* (film soundtrack, 1968), and *Bridge over Troubled Water* (1970); and, solo, *There Goes Rhymin' Simon* (1973) and *Still Crazy after All these Years* (1975).
si·mo·ni·ac (sɪ'məʊnɪˌæk) *n.* a person who is guilty of practising simony. —**si·mo·ni·a·cal** (ˌsaɪmə'naɪəkᵊl) *adj.* —ˌ**si·mo·'ni·a·cal·ly** *adv.*
Si·mon·i·des (saɪ'mɒnɪˌdi:z) *n.* ?556–?468 B.C., Greek lyric poet and epigrammatist, noted for his odes to victory.
Si·mon Ma·gus *n. New Testament.* a Samaritan sorcerer, probably from Gitta, of the 1st century A.D. After being converted to Christianity, he tried to buy miraculous powers from the apostles (Acts of the Apostles 8:9–24). He is also identified as the founder of a Gnostic sect.
Si·mon Pe·ter *n. New Testament.* the full name of the apostle Peter, a combination of his original name and the name given him by Christ (Matthew 16:17–18).
si·mon-pure *adj. Rare.* real; genuine; authentic. [C19: from the phrase *the real Simon Pure,* name of a character in the play *A Bold Stroke for a Wife* (1717) who is impersonated by another character in some scenes]
si·mo·ny ('saɪmənɪ) *n. Ecclesiast.* the practice, now usually regarded as a sin, of buying or selling spiritual or Church benefits such as pardons, relics, etc., or preferments. [C13: from Old French *simonie,* from Late Latin *sīmōnia,* from the name of SIMON MAGUS] —'**si·mon·ist** *n.*
Si·mon Ze·lo·tes (zɪ'ləʊti:z) *n.* one of the 12 apostles, who had probably belonged to the Zealot party before becoming a Christian (Luke 6:15). Owing to a misinterpretation of two similar Aramaic words he is also, but mistakenly, called *the Canaanite* (Matthew 10:4).
si·moom (sɪ'mu:m) *or* **si·moon** (sɪ'mu:n) *n.* a strong suffocating sand-laden wind of the deserts of Arabia and North Africa. Also called: **samiel.** [from Arabic *samūm* poisonous, from *sam* poison, from Aramaic *sammā* poison]
simp (sɪmp) *n. U.S. slang.* short for **simpleton.**
sim·pa·ti·co (sɪm'pɑ:tɪˌkəʊ, -'pæt-) *adj. Informal.* **1.** pleasant or congenial. **2.** of similar mind or temperament; compatible. [Italian: from *simpatia* SYMPATHY]
sim·per ('sɪmpə) *vb.* **1.** (*intr.*) to smile coyly, affectedly, or in a silly self-conscious way. **2.** (*tr.*) to utter (something) in a simpering manner. ~*n.* **3.** a simpering smile; smirk. [C16: probably from Dutch *simper* affected] —'**sim·per·er** *n.* —'**sim·per·ing·ly** *adv.*
sim·ple ('sɪmpᵊl) *adj.* **1.** not involved or complicated; easy to understand or do: *a simple problem.* **2.** plain; unadorned: *a simple dress.* **3.** consisting of one element or part only; not combined or complex: *a simple mechanism.* **4.** unaffected or unpretentious: *although he became famous, he remained a simple and well-liked man.* **5.** not guileful; sincere; frank: *her simple explanation was readily accepted.* **6.** of humble condition or rank: *the peasant was of simple birth.* **7.** weak in intelligence; feeble-minded. **8.** (*prenominal*) without additions or modifications; mere: *the witness told the simple truth.* **9.** (*prenominal*) ordinary or straightforward: *a simple case of mumps.* **10.** *Chem.* (of a substance or material) consisting of only one chemical compound rather than a mixture of compounds. **11.** *Maths.* **a.** (of a fraction) containing only integers. **b.** (of an equation) containing variables to the first power only; linear. **12.** *Biology.* not divided into parts: *a simple leaf; a simple eye.* **13.** *Music.* relating to or denoting a time where the number of beats per bar may be two, three, or four. ~*n. Archaic.* **14.** a simpleton; fool. **15.** a plant, esp. a herbaceous plant, having medicinal properties. [C13: via Old French from Latin *simplex* plain] —'**sim·ple·ness** *or* **sim·plic·i·ty** (sɪm'plɪsɪtɪ) *n.*
sim·ple frac·tion *n.* a fraction in which the numerator and denominator are both integers. Also called: **common fraction, vulgar fraction.**
sim·ple frac·ture *n.* a fracture in which the broken bone does not pierce the skin. Also called: **closed fracture.** Compare **compound fracture.**
sim·ple fruit *n.* a fruit, such as a grape or cherry, that is formed from only one ovary.
sim·ple har·mon·ic mo·tion *n.* a form of periodic motion of a particle, etc., in which the acceleration is always directed towards some equilibrium point and is proportional to the displacement from this point. Abbrev.: **S.H.M.**
sim·ple-heart·ed *adj.* free from deceit; open; frank; sincere.
sim·ple in·ter·est *n.* interest calculated or paid on the principal alone. Compare **compound interest.**
sim·ple ma·chine *n.* a simple device for altering the magnitude or direction of a force. The six basic types are the lever, wheel and axle, pulley, screw, wedge, and inclined plane.
sim·ple mi·cro·scope *n.* a microscope having a single lens; magnifying glass. Compare **compound microscope.**
sim·ple-mind·ed *adj.* **1.** stupid; foolish; feeble-minded. **2.** mentally defective. **3.** unsophisticated; artless. —ˌ**sim·ple-'mind·ed·ly** *adv.* —ˌ**sim·ple-'mind·ed·ness** *n.*
sim·ple sen·tence *n.* a sentence consisting of a single main clause. Compare **compound sentence, complex sentence.**
Sim·ple Si·mon *n.* a foolish man or boy; simpleton. [C20: after the name of a character in a nursery rhyme]
sim·ple tense *n. Grammar.* a tense of verbs, in English and other languages, not involving the use of an auxiliary verb in addition to the main verb, as for example the past *He drowned* as opposed to the future *He will drown.*
sim·ple·ton ('sɪmpᵊltən) *n.* a foolish or ignorant person.
sim·plex ('sɪmplɛks) *adj.* **1.** permitting the transmission of signals in either direction in a radio circuit, etc., but not simultaneously. Compare **duplex** (sense 4), **diplex.** ~*n.* **2.** *Geom.* the most elementary geometric figure in Euclidean space of a given dimension; a line in one-dimensional space or a triangle in two-dimensional space. [C16: from Latin: simple, literally: one-fold, from *sim-* one + *-plex,* from *plicāre* to fold; compare DUPLEX]
sim·pli·ci·den·tate (ˌsɪmplɪsɪ'dɛnteɪt) *adj.* **1.** of, relating to, or belonging to the *Simplicidentata,* a former suborder including all the mammals now classified as rodents: used when Lagomorphs were included in the order *Rodentia.* ~*n.* **2.** any animal of this type.
sim·pli·fy ('sɪmplɪˌfaɪ) *vb.* **-fies, -fy·ing, -fied.** (*tr.*) **1.** to make less complicated, clearer, or easier. **2.** *Maths.* to reduce (an equation, fraction, etc.) to its simplest form. [C17: via French from Medieval Latin *simplificāre,* from Latin *simplus* simple + *facere* to make] —ˌ**sim·pli·fi·'ca·tion** *n.* —'**sim·pli·fi·ca·tive** *adj.* —'**sim·pli·ˌfi·er** *n.*
sim·plis·tic (sɪm'plɪstɪk) *adj.* **1.** characterized by extreme simplicity; naive. **2.** oversimplifying complex problems; making unrealistically simple judgments or analyses. —'**sim·plism** *n.* —**sim·'plis·ti·cal·ly** *adv.*
Sim·plon Pass ('sɪmplɒn) *n.* a pass over the Lepontine Alps in S Switzerland, between Brig (Switzerland) and Iselle (Italy). Height: 2009 m (6590 ft.).
simp·ly ('sɪmplɪ) *adv.* **1.** in a simple manner. **2.** merely; only. **3.** absolutely; altogether; really: *a simply wonderful holiday.* **4.** (*sentence modifier*) frankly; candidly.
Simp·son Des·ert ('sɪmpsən) *n.* an uninhabited arid region in central Australia, mainly in the Northern Territory. Area: about 145 000 sq. km (56 000 sq. miles).
sim·sim ('sɪmsɪm) *n.* an E African word for **sesame.**
sim·u·la·crum (ˌsɪmjʊ'leɪkrəm) *n., pl.* **-cra** (-krə). *Archaic.* **1.** any image or representation of something. **2.** a slight, unreal, or vague semblance of something; superficial likeness. [C16: from Latin: likeness, from *simulāre* to imitate, from *similis* like]
sim·u·lant ('sɪmjʊlənt) *adj.* **1.** simulating. **2.** (esp. of plant parts) resembling another part in structure or function.
sim·u·lar ('sɪmjʊlə) *Archaic.* ~*n.* **1.** a person or thing that simulates or imitates; sham. ~*adj.* **2.** fake; simulated.
sim·u·late *vb.* ('sɪmjʊˌleɪt). (*tr.*) **1.** to make a pretence of; feign: *to simulate anxiety.* **2.** to reproduce the conditions of (a situation, etc.), as in carrying out an experiment: *to simulate weightlessness.* **3.** to assume or have the appearance of; imitate. ~*adj.* ('sɪmjʊlɪt, -ˌleɪt). **4.** *Archaic.* assumed or

simulated. [C17: from Latin *simulāre* to copy, from *similis* like] —**'sim·u·la·tive** *adj.* —**'sim·u·la·tive·ly** *adv.*

sim·u·lat·ed ('sɪmjʊˌleɪtɪd) *adj.* **1.** (of fur, leather, pearls, etc.) being an imitation of the genuine article, usually made from cheaper material. **2.** (of actions, qualities, emotions, etc.) imitated; feigned.

sim·u·la·tion (ˌsɪmjʊ'leɪʃən) *n.* **1.** the act or an instance of simulating. **2.** the assumption of a false appearance or form. **3.** a representation of a problem, situation, etc., in mathematical terms, esp. using a computer. **4.** *Psychiatry.* the conscious process of feigning illness in order to gain some particular end; malingering.

sim·u·la·tor ('sɪmjʊˌleɪtə) *n.* **1.** any device or system that simulates specific conditions or the characteristics of a real process for the purposes of research or operator training: *space simulator.* **2.** a person who simulates.

sim·ul·cast ('sɪməlˌkɑːst) *vb.* **1.** (*tr.*) to broadcast (a programme, etc.) simultaneously on radio and television. ~*n.* **2.** a programme, etc., so broadcast. [C20: from SIMULTANEOUS + BROADCAST]

sim·ul·ta·ne·ous (ˌsɪməl'teɪnɪəs; *U.S.* ˌsaɪməl'teɪnɪəs) *adj.* occurring, existing, or operating at the same time; concurrent. [C17: formed on the model of INSTANTANEOUS from Latin *simul* at the same time, together] —**ˌsim·ul·'ta·ne·ous·ly** *adv.* —**ˌsim·ul·'ta·ne·ous·ness** *or* **sim·ul·ta·ne·i·ty** (ˌsɪməltə'niːɪtɪ; *U.S.* ˌsaɪməltə'niːɪtɪ) *n.*

Usage. See at **unique.**

sim·ul·ta·ne·ous e·qua·tions *pl. n.* a set of equations that are all satisfied by the same values of the variables, the number of variables being equal to the number of equations.

sin[1] (sɪn) *n.* **1.** *Theol.* **a.** transgression of God's known will or any principle or law regarded as embodying this. **b.** the condition of estrangement from God arising from such transgression. See also **actual sin, mortal sin, original sin, venial sin. 2.** any serious offence, as against a religious or moral principle. **3.** any offence against a principle or standard. **4. live in sin.** *Informal.* (of an unmarried couple) to live together. ~*vb.* (*intr.*) **sins, sin·ning, sinned. 5.** *Theol.* to commit a sin. **6.** (usually foll. by *against*) to commit an offence (against a person, principle, etc.). [Old English *synn;* related to Old Norse *synth,* Old High German *suntea* sin, Latin *sons* guilty] —**'sin·ner** *n.*

sin[2] (sɪn) *n.* a Scot. dialect word for **since.**

sin[3] (siːn) *n.* the 21st letter in the Hebrew alphabet (ש), transliterated as *S.*

sin[4] *Maths. abbrev. for* sine.

Si·nai ('saɪnaɪ) *n.* **1.** a mountainous peninsula of NE Egypt at the N end of the Red Sea, between the Gulf of Suez and the Gulf of Aqaba: occupied by Israel in 1967; partly restored in 1975. **2. Mount.** the mountain where Moses received the Law from God (Exodus 19–20): often identified as Jebel Musa, sometimes as Jebel Serbal, both on the S Sinai Peninsula. —**Si·na·it·ic** (ˌsaɪnɪ'ɪtɪk) *or* **Si·na·ic** (sɪ'neɪɪk) *adj.*

Si·na·lo·a (ˌsiːnə'ləʊə, ˌsɪn-; *Spanish* ˌsina'loa) *n.* a state of W Mexico. Capital: Culiacán. Pop.: 1 266 528 (1970). Area: 58 092 sq. km (22 429 sq. miles).

sin·an·thro·pus (sɪn'ænθrəpəs) *n.* a primitive apelike man of the genus *Sinanthropus,* now considered a subspecies of *Homo erectus.* See also **Java man, Peking man.** [C20: from New Latin, from Late Latin *Sīnae* the Chinese + *-anthropus,* from Greek *anthrōpos* man]

sin·a·pism ('sɪnəˌpɪzəm) *n.* a technical name for **mustard plaster.** [C17: from Late Latin *sināpismus,* from Greek *sinapismos* application of mustard plaster, from *sinapi* mustard, of Egyptian origin]

Sin·ar·quist ('sɪnɑːkɪst, -kwɪst) *n.* (in Mexico) a member of a fascist movement in the 1930s and 1940s having links with the Nazis and the Falangists: hostile towards the U.S., Communism, Jews, organized labour, etc. [C20: Mexican Spanish *sinarquista,* from Spanish *sin* without + *anarquista* anarchist] —**'Sin·ar·quism** *n.*

Si·na·tra (sɪ'nɑːtrə) *n.* **Fran·cis Al·bert,** called *Frank.* born 1917, U.S. singer.

since (sɪns) *prep.* **1.** during or throughout the period of time after: *since May it has only rained once.* ~*conj.* (*subordinating*) **2.** (sometimes preceded by *ever*) continuously from or starting from the time when: *since we last met, important things have happened.* **3.** seeing that; because: *since you have no money, you can't come.* ~*adv.* **4.** since that time: *he left yesterday and I haven't seen him since.* [Old English *sīththan,* literally: after that; related to Old High German *sīd* since, Latin *sērus* late]

Usage. See at **ago.**

sin·cere (sɪn'sɪə) *adj.* **1.** not hypocritical or deceitful; open; genuine: *a sincere person; sincere regret.* **2.** *Archaic.* pure; unadulterated; unmixed. **3.** *Obsolete.* sound; whole. [C16: from Latin *sincērus*] —**sin'cere·ly** *adv.* —**sin'cere·ness** *or* **sin·cer·i·ty** (sɪn'sɛrɪtɪ) *n.*

sin·ci·put ('sɪnsɪˌpʌt) *n., pl.* **sin·ci·puts** *or* **sin·cip·i·ta** (sɪn'sɪpɪtə). *Anatomy.* the forward upper part of the skull. [C16: from Latin: half a head, from SEMI- + *caput* head] —**sin·'cip·i·tal** *adj.*

Sin·clair (sɪŋ'klɛə, 'sɪŋklɛə) *n.* **Up·ton (Beall).** 1878–1968, U.S. novelist, whose *The Jungle* (1906) exposed the working and sanitary conditions of the Chicago meat-packing industry and prompted the passage of food inspection laws.

Sind (sɪnd) *n.* a region of SE Pakistan, mainly in the lower Indus valley: formerly a province of British India; became a province of Pakistan in 1947; divided in 1955 between Hyderabad and Khairpur.

Sin·dhi ('sɪndɪ) *n.* **1.** (*pl.* **·dhi** *or* **·dhis**) a former inhabitant of Sind. The Muslim majority now lives in Pakistan while the Hindu minority has mostly moved to India. **2.** the language of this people, belonging to the Indic branch of the Indo-European family.

sine[1] (saɪn) *n.* (of an angle) **a.** a trigonometric function that in a right-angled triangle is the ratio of the length of the opposite side to that of the hypotenuse. **b.** a function that in a circle centred at the origin of a Cartesian coordinate system is the ratio of the ordinate of a point on the circumference to the radius of the circle. Abbrev.: **sin.** [C16: from Latin *sinus* a bend; in New Latin, *sinus* was mistaken as a translation of Arabic *jiba* sine (from Sanskrit *jīva,* literally: bowstring) because of confusion with Arabic *jaib* curve]

si·ne[2] ('saɪnɪ) *prep.* (esp. in Latin phrases or legal terms) lacking; without.

si·ne·cure ('saɪnɪˌkjʊə) *n.* **1.** a paid office or post involving minimal duties. **2.** a Church benefice to which no spiritual or pastoral charge is attached. [C17: from Medieval Latin phrase (*beneficium*) *sine cūrā* (benefice) without cure (of souls), from Latin *sine* without + *cūra* cure, care] —**'si·ne·ˌcur·ism** *n.* —**'si·ne·ˌcur·ist** *n.*

sine curve *n.* a curve of the equation $y = \sin x$. Also called: **sinusoid.**

si·ne di·e *Latin.* ('saɪnɪ 'daɪɪ) *adv., adj.* without a day fixed: *an adjournment sine die.* [literally: without a day]

si·ne pro·le *Latin.* ('saɪnɪ 'prəʊlɪ) *adj., adv. Law.* without issue (esp. in the phrase ***demisit sine prole*** (died without issue)).

si·ne qua non *Latin.* ('saɪnɪ kweɪ 'nɒn) *n.* an essential condition or requirement. [literally: without which not]

sin·ew ('sɪnjuː) *n.* **1.** *Anatomy.* another name for **tendon. 2.** (*often pl.*) **a.** a source of strength or power. **b.** a literary word for **muscle.** [Old English *sionu;* related to Old Norse *sin,* Old Saxon *sinewa,* Old High German *senawa* sinew, Lettish *pasainis* string] —**'sin·ew·less** *adj.*

sine wave *n.* any oscillation, such as a sound wave or alternating current, whose waveform is that of a sine curve.

sin·ew·y ('sɪnjʊɪ) *adj.* **1.** consisting of or resembling a tendon or tendons. **2.** muscular; brawny. **3.** (esp. of language, style, etc.) vigorous; forceful. **4.** (of meat, etc.) tough; stringy. —**'sin·ew·i·ness** *n.*

sin·fo·ni·a (ˌsɪnfə'nɪə) *n., pl.* **·ni·e** (-'niːeɪ). **1.** another word for **symphony** (senses 2, 3). **2.** (*cap. when part of a name*) a symphony orchestra. [Italian]

sin·fo·niet·ta (ˌsɪnfən'jɛtə, -fəʊn-) *n.* **1.** a short or light symphony. **2.** (*cap. when part of name*) a small symphony orchestra. [Italian: a little symphony, from SINFONIA]

sin·ful ('sɪnfʊl) *adj.* **1.** having committed or tending to commit sin: *a sinful person.* **2.** characterized by or being a sin: *a sinful act.* —**'sin·ful·ly** *adv.* —**'sin·ful·ness** *n.*

sing (sɪŋ) *vb.* **sings, sing·ing, sang, sung. 1.** to produce or articulate (sounds, words, a song, etc.) with definite and usually specific musical intonation. **2.** (when *intr.,* often foll. by *to*) to perform (a song) to the accompaniment (of): *to sing to a guitar.* **3.** (*intr.;* foll. by *of*) to tell a story or tale in song (about): *I sing of a maiden.* **4.** (*intr.;* foll. by *to*) to address a song (to) or perform a song (for). **5.** (*intr.*) to perform songs for a living, as a professional singer. **6.** (*intr.*) (esp. of certain birds and insects) to utter calls or sounds reminiscent of music. **7.** (when *intr.,* usually foll. by *of*) to tell (something) or give praise (to someone), esp. in verse: *the poet who sings of the Trojan dead.* **8.** (*intr.*) to make a whining, ringing, or whistling sound: *the kettle is singing; the arrow sang past his ear.* **9.** (*intr.*) (of the ears) to experience a continuous ringing or humming sound. **10.** (*tr.*) (esp. in church services) to chant or intone (a prayer, psalm, etc.). **11.** (*tr.*) to bring to a given state by singing: *to sing a child to sleep.* **12.** (*intr.*) *Slang, chiefly U.S.* to confess or act as an informer. ~*n.* **13.** *Informal.* an act or performance of singing. **14.** a ringing or whizzing sound, as of bullets. ~See also **sing out.** [Old English *singan;* related to Old Norse *syngja* to sing, Gothic *siggwan,* Old High German *singan*] —**'sing·a·ble** *adj.* —**'sing·ing·ly** *adv.*

Usage. See at **ring**[2].

sing. *abbrev. for* singular.

Sin·ga·pore (ˌsɪŋə'pɔː, ˌsɪŋgə-) *n.* **1.** a republic in SE Asia, occupying one main island and about 40 small islands at the S end of the Malay Peninsula: established as a British trading post in 1819 and made a British colony in 1946; part of Malaysia from 1962 to 1965, when it became an independent republic (within the Commonwealth). Languages: Malay, English, Chinese, and Tamil. Currency: Singapore dollar. Capital: Singapore. Pop.: 2 250 000 (1975 est.). Area: 580 sq. km (224 sq. miles). **2.** the capital of the republic of Singapore: a major international port. Pop.: 2 249 900 (1975 est.). —**ˌSin·ga·'po·re·an** *adj., n.*

singe (sɪndʒ) *vb.* **1.** to burn or be burnt superficially; scorch: *to singe one's clothes.* **2.** (*tr.*) to burn the ends of (hair, etc.). **3.** (*tr.*) to expose (a carcass) to flame to remove bristles or hair. ~*n.* **4.** a superficial burn. [Old English *sengan;* related to Middle High German *sengen* to singe, Dutch *sengel* spark, Norwegian *sengla* to smell of burning, Swedish *sjängla* to singe, Icelandic *sāngr*]

sing·er ('sɪŋə) *n.* **1.** a person who sings, esp. one who earns a living by singing. **2.** a singing bird. **3.** an obsolete word for **poet.**

Sing·er ('sɪŋə) *n.* **1. I·saac Bash·e·vis.** born 1904, U.S. writer of Yiddish novels and short stories; born in Poland. His works include *Satan in Goray* (1935), *The Family Moskrat* (1950), and the autobiographical *In my Father's Court* (1966): Nobel prize for literature 1978. **2. I·saac Mer·rit.** 1811–75, U.S. inventor, who originated and developed an improved chain-stitch sewing machine (1852).

Sin·gha·lese (ˌsɪŋə'li:z) *n., pl.* **·lese,** *adj.* a variant spelling of **Sinhalese.**

sin·gle ('sɪŋgᵊl) *adj.* (*usually prenominal*) **1.** existing alone; solitary: *upon the hill stood a single tower.* **2.** distinct from other things; unique or individual. **3.** composed of one part. **4.** designed for one user: *a single room; a single bed.* **5.** (*also postpositive*) unmarried. **6.** connected with the condition of being unmarried: *he led a single life.* **7.** (esp. of combat) involving two individuals; one against one. **8.** sufficient for one person or thing only: *a single portion of food.* **9.** even one: *there wasn't a single person on the beach.* **10.** (of a flower) having only one set or whorl of petals. **11.** determined; single-minded: *a single devotion to duty.* **12.** (of the eye) seeing correctly: *to consider something with a single eye.* **13.** *Rare.* honest or sincere; genuine. **14.** *Archaic.* (of ale, beer, etc.) mild in strength. ~*n.* **15.** something forming one individual unit. **16.** a gramophone record with a short recording, usually of pop music, on each side: now usually 7 inches (18 centimetres) in diameter and played at 45 revolutions per minute. Compare **EP. 17.** *Golf.* a game between two players. **18.** *Cricket.* a hit from which one run is scored. **19. a.** *Brit.* a pound note. **b.** *U.S.* a dollar note. **20.** See **single ticket.** ~*vb.* **21.** (*tr.;* usually foll. by *out*) to select from a group of people or things; distinguish by separation: *he singled him out for special mention.* **22.** short for **single-foot.** [C14: from Old French *sengle,* from Latin *singulus* individual] —'**sin·gle·ness** *n.*

sin·gle-act·ing *adj.* (of a reciprocating engine or pump) having a piston or pistons that are pressurized on one side only. Compare **double-acting** (sense 1).

sin·gle-ac·tion *n.* (*modifier*) (of a firearm) requiring the hammer to be cocked by hand before firing each shot.

sin·gle-blind *adj.* of or relating to an experiment, esp. one to discover people's reactions to certain commodities, drugs, etc., in which the experimenters but not the subjects know the particulars of the test items during the experiment. Compare **double-blind.**

sin·gle bond *n. Chem.* a covalent bond formed between two atoms by the sharing of one pair of electrons.

sin·gle-breast·ed *adj.* (of a garment) having the fronts overlapping only slightly and with one row of fastenings.

sin·gle-cross *n. Genetics.* a hybrid of the first generation between two inbred lines.

sin·gle-deck·er *n. Brit. informal.* a bus with only one passenger deck.

sin·gle-end *n. Scot. dialect.* accommodation consisting of a single room.

sin·gle en·try *n.* **a.** a simple book-keeping system in which transactions are entered in one account only. Compare **double entry. b.** (*as modifier*): *a single-entry account.*

sin·gle file *n.* a line of persons, animals, or things ranged one behind the other, either stationary or moving.

sin·gle-foot *n.* **1.** a rapid showy gait of a horse in which each foot strikes the ground separately, as in a walk. ~*vb.* **2.** to move or cause to move at this gait.

sin·gle-hand·ed *adj., adv.* **1.** unaided or working alone: *a single-handed crossing of the Atlantic.* **2.** having or operated by one hand or one person only. —ˌ**sin·gle-'hand·ed·ly** *adv.* —ˌ**sin·gle-'hand·ed·ness** *n.*

sin·gle-lens re·flex *n.* See **reflex camera.**

sin·gle-mind·ed *adj.* having but one aim or purpose; dedicated. —ˌ**sin·gle-'mind·ed·ly** *adv.* —ˌ**sin·gle-'mind·ed·ness** *n.*

sin·gle-phase *adj.* (of a system, circuit, or device) having, generating, or using a single alternating voltage.

sin·gles ('sɪŋgᵊlz) *pl. n. Tennis, etc.* a match played with one person on each side.

sin·gle side·band trans·mis·sion *n.* a method of transmitting radio waves in which either the upper or the lower sideband is transmitted, the carrier being either wholly or partially suppressed. This reduces the required bandwidth and improves the signal-to-noise ratio. Abbrev.: **S.S.B.**

sin·gle-space *vb.* (*tr.*) to type (copy) without leaving a space between the lines.

sin·gle-step *vb.* **-steps, -step·ping, -stepped.** (*tr.*) *Computer technol.* to perform a single instruction on (a program), generally under the control of a debug program.

sin·gle·stick ('sɪŋgᵊlˌstɪk) *n.* **1.** a wooden stick used instead of a sword for fencing. **2.** fencing with such a stick. **3.** any short heavy stick.

sin·glet ('sɪŋglɪt) *n.* **1.** *Chiefly Brit.* a man's sleeveless vest. **2.** *Austral.* any vest. **3.** *Chiefly Brit.* a garment worn with shorts by athletes, boxers, etc. **4.** *Physics.* a multiplet that has only one member. **5.** *Chem.* a chemical bond consisting of one electron. [C18: from SINGLE, on the model of *doublet*]

sin·gle tax *n. U.S.* **1.** a taxation system in which a tax on one commodity, usually land, is the only source of revenue. **2.** such a tax.

sin·gle tick·et *n. Brit.* a ticket entitling a passenger to travel only to his destination, without returning. U.S. equivalent: **one-way ticket.** Compare **return ticket.**

sin·gle·ton ('sɪŋgᵊltən) *n.* **1.** *Bridge, etc.* an original holding of one card only in a suit. **2.** a single object, individual, etc., separated or distinguished from a pair or group. **3.** *Maths.* a set containing only one member. [C19: from SINGLE, on the model of SIMPLETON]

sin·gle-tongue *vb. Music.* to play (any nonlegato passage) on a wind instrument by obstructing and uncovering the air passage through the lips with the tongue. Compare **double-tongue, triple-tongue.** —**sin·gle tongu·ing** *n.*

sin·gle-track *adj.* **1.** (of a railway) having only a single pair of lines, so that trains can travel in only one direction at a time. **2.** (of a road) only wide enough for one vehicle. **3.** able to think about only one thing; one-track.

sin·gle·tree ('sɪŋgᵊlˌtri:) *n.* another word for **whiffletree.**

sin·gly ('sɪŋglɪ) *adv.* **1.** one at a time; one by one. **2.** apart from others; separately; alone.

sing out *vb.* (*tr., adv.*) to call out in a loud voice; shout.

Sing Sing *n.* a prison in New York State, in Ossining.

sing·song ('sɪŋˌsɒŋ) *n.* **1.** an accent, metre, or intonation that is characterized by an alternately rising and falling rhythm, as in a person's voice, piece of verse, etc. **2.** *Brit.* an informal session of singing, esp. of popular or traditional songs. ~*adj.* **3.** having a regular or monotonous rising and falling rhythm: *a singsong accent.*

Sing·spiel *German.* ('zɪŋˌʃpi:l) *n.* a type of comic opera in German with spoken dialogue, popular during the late 18th and early 19th centuries. [literally: singing play]

sin·gu·lar ('sɪŋgjʊlə) *adj.* **1.** remarkable; exceptional; extraordinary: *a singular feat.* **2.** unusual; odd: *a singular character.* **3.** unique. **4.** denoting a word or an inflected form of a word indicating that not more than one referent is being referred to or described. **5.** *Logic.* of or referring to a specific thing or person as opposed to something general. ~*n.* **6.** *Grammar.* **a.** the singular number. **b.** a singular form of a word. [C14: from Latin *singulāris* SINGLE] —'**sin·gu·lar·ly** *adv.* —'**sin·gu·lar·ness** *n.*

sin·gu·lar·i·ty (ˌsɪŋgjʊ'lærɪtɪ) *n., pl.* **·ties. 1.** the state, fact, or quality of being singular. **2.** something distinguishing a person or thing from others. **3.** something remarkable or unusual.

sin·gu·lar·ize *or* **sin·gu·lar·ise** ('sɪŋgjʊləˌraɪz) *vb.* (*tr.*) **1.** to make (a word, etc.) singular. **2.** to make conspicuous. —ˌ**sin·gu·lar·i·'za·tion** *or* ˌ**sin·gu·lar·i·'sa·tion** *n.*

sin·gul·tus (sɪŋ'gʌltəs) *n.* a technical name for **hiccup.** [C18: from Latin, literally: a sob]

sinh (ʃaɪn, sɪnʃ) hyperbolic sine; a hyperbolic function, sinh $z = \frac{1}{2}(e^z - e^{-z})$, related to sine by the expression sinh $iz = i$ sin z, where $i = \sqrt{-1}$. [C20: from SIN(E) + H(YPERBOLIC)]

Sin·hai·lien *or* **Hsin-hai-lien** ('ʃɪn'haɪ'ljɛn) *n.* a city in E China, near the coast of Kiangsu. Pop.: 207 600 (1953).

Sin·ha·lese (ˌsɪnhə'li:z) *or* **Sin·gha·lese** *n.* **1.** (*pl.* **·leses** *or* **·lese**) a member of a people living chiefly in Ceylon, where they constitute the majority of the population. **2.** the language of this people, belonging to the Indic branch of the Indo-European family: the official language of Ceylon. It is written in a script of Indian origin. ~*adj.* **3.** of or relating to this people or their language.

Si·ni·cism ('saɪnɪˌsɪzəm, 'sɪn-) *n. Rare.* a Chinese custom or idiom. [C19: from Medieval Latin *Sinicus* Chinese, from Late Latin *Sīnae* the Chinese, from Greek *Sinai,* from Arabic *Sīn* China]

Si·ning *or* **Hsi·ning** ('ʃi:'nɪŋ) *n.* a city in W China, capital of Tsinghai province, at an altitude of 2300 m (7500 ft.). Pop.: 500 000 (1970 est.).

sin·is·ter ('sɪnɪstə) *adj.* **1.** threatening or suggesting evil or harm; ominous: *a sinister glance.* **2.** evil or treacherous, esp. in a mysterious way. **3.** (*usually postpositive*) *Heraldry.* of, on, or starting from the left side from the bearer's point of view and therefore on the spectator's right. **4.** *Archaic.* located on the left side. **5.** *Archaic.* (of signs, omens, etc.) unfavourable. ~Compare **dexter.** [C15: from Latin *sinister* on the left-hand side, considered by Roman augurers to be the unlucky one] —'**sin·is·ter·ly** *adv.* —'**sin·is·ter·ness** *n.*

sin·is·tral ('sɪnɪstrəl) *adj.* **1.** of, relating to, or located on the left side, esp. the left side of the body. **2.** a technical term for **left-handed. 3.** (of the shells of certain gastropod molluscs) coiling in a clockwise direction from the apex. ~Compare **dextral.** —'**sin·is·tral·ly** *adv.*

sin·is·tro·dex·tral (ˌsɪnɪstrəʊ'dɛkstrəl) *adj.* going or directed from left to right: *a sinistrodextral script.*

sin·is·trorse ('sɪnɪˌstrɔ:s, ˌsɪnɪ'strɔ:s) *adj.* (of some climbing plants) growing upwards in a spiral from right to left. Compare **dextrorse.** [C19: from Latin *sinistrōrsus* turned towards the left, from *sinister* on the left + *vertere* to turn] —ˌ**sin·is·'tror·sal** *adj.* —'**sin·is·ˌtrorse·ly** *adv.*

sin·is·trous ('sɪnɪstrəs) *adj. Archaic.* **1.** sinister or ill-omened. **2.** sinistral. —'**sin·is·trous·ly** *adv.*

Si·nit·ic (sɪ'nɪtɪk) *n.* **1.** a branch of the Sino-Tibetan family of languages, consisting of the various languages or dialects of Chinese. Compare **Tibeto-Burman.** ~*adj.* **2.** belonging or relating to this group of languages.

sink (sɪŋk) *vb.* **sinks, sink·ing, sank** *or* **sunk; sunk** *or* **sunk·en. 1.** to descend or cause to descend, esp. beneath the surface of a liquid or soft substance. **2.** (*intr.*) to appear to move down towards or descend below the horizon. **3.** (*intr.*) to slope downwards; dip. **4.** (*intr.;* often foll. by *in* or *into*) to pass into or gradually enter a specified lower state or condition: *to sink into apathy.* **5.** to make or become lower in volume, pitch, etc. **6.** to make or become lower in value, price, etc. **7.** (*intr.*) to become weaker in health, strength, etc. **8.** to decline or cause to decline in moral value, worth, etc. **9.** (*intr.*) to seep or penetrate. **10.** (*tr.*) to suppress or conceal: *he sank his worries in drink.* **11.** (*tr.*) to dig, cut, drill, bore, or excavate (a hole, shaft, etc.). **12.** (*tr.*) to drive into the ground: *to sink a stake.* **13.** (*tr.;* usually foll. by *in* or *into*) **a.** to invest (money). **b.** to lose (money) in an unwise or unfortunate investment. **14.** (*tr.*) to pay (a debt). **15.** (*intr.*) to become hollow; cave in: *his cheeks* *had sunk during his illness.* **16.** (*tr.*) to hit, throw, or propel (a ball) into a hole, basket, pocket, etc.: *he sank a 15-foot putt.* **17. sink or swim.** to take risks where the alternatives are loss and failure or security and success. ~*n.* **18.** a fixed basin, esp. in a kitchen, made of stone, earthenware, metal, etc., used for washing. **19.** See **sinkhole. 20.** another word for **cesspool. 21.** a place of vice or corruption. **22.** an area of ground below that of the surrounding land, where water collects. **23.** *Physics.* a device or part of a system at which energy is removed from the system: *a heat sink.* [Old English *sincan;* related to Old Norse *sökkva* to sink, Gothic *siggan,* Old High German *sincan,* Swedish *sjunka*] —**'sink·a·ble** *adj.*

sink·age ('sɪŋkɪdʒ) *n. Rare.* the act of sinking or degree to which something sinks or has sunk.

sink·er ('sɪŋkə) *n.* **1.** a weight attached to a fishing line, net, etc., to cause it to sink in water. **2.** a person who sinks shafts, etc. **3.** *U.S.* an informal word for **doughnut. 4. hook, line, and sinker.** See **hook** (sense 17).

sink·hole ('sɪŋk,həʊl) *n.* **1.** Also called (esp. in Britain): **swallow hole.** a depression in the ground surface, esp. in limestone, where a surface stream disappears underground. **2.** a place into which foul matter runs.

Sin·kiang-Ui·ghur Au·ton·o·mous Re·gion ('sɪn'kjæŋ 'wi:gʊə) *n.* an administrative division of NW China: established in 1955 for the Uighur ethnic minority, with autonomous subdivisions for other small minorities; produces over half China's wool and contains valuable mineral resources. Capital: Urumchi. Pop.: 8 000 000 (1967–71). Area: 1 646 799 sq. km (635 829 sq. miles).

sink in *vb.* (*intr., adv.*) to enter or penetrate the mind: *eventually the news sank in.*

sink·ing ('sɪŋkɪŋ) *n.* **a.** a feeling in the stomach caused by hunger or uneasiness. **b.** (*as modifier*): *a sinking feeling.*

sink·ing fund *n.* a fund accumulated out of a business enterprise's earnings or a government's revenue and invested to repay a long-term debt or meet a depreciation charge.

sin·less ('sɪnlɪs) *adj.* free from sin or guilt; innocent; pure. —**'sin·less·ly** *adv.* —**'sin·less·ness** *n.*

Sinn Fein ('ʃɪn 'feɪn) *n.* an Irish republican political movement founded about 1905 and linked to the revolutionary Irish Republican Army: divided into a Provisional and an Official movement since a similar split in the IRA in late 1969. [C20: from Irish: we ourselves] —**Sinn Fein·er** *n.* —**Sinn Fein·ism** *n.*

Si·no- ('saɪnəʊ-) *combining form.* Chinese: *Sino-Tibetan; Sinology.* [from French, from Late Latin *Sīnae* the Chinese, from Late Greek *Sinai,* from Arabic *Sīn* China, probably from Chinese *Ch'in*]

Si·nol·o·gy (saɪ'nɒlədʒɪ, sɪ-) *n.* the study of Chinese history, language, culture, etc. —**Si·no·log·i·cal** (,saɪnə'lɒdʒɪkᵊl, ,sɪn-) *adj.* —**Si·'nol·o·gist** *n.* —**Si·no·logue** ('saɪnə,lɒg) *n.*

Si·no-Ti·bet·an *n.* **1.** a family of languages that includes most of the languages of China, as well as Tibetan, Burmese, and Thai. Their most noticeable phonological characteristic is the phonemic use of tones. ~*adj.* **2.** belonging or relating to this family of languages.

sin·ter ('sɪntə) *n.* **1.** a whitish porous incrustation, usually consisting of silica, that is deposited from hot springs. **2.** the product of a sintering process. **3.** another name for **cinder** (sense 3). ~*vb.* **4.** (*tr.*) to form large particles, lumps, or masses from (metal powders or powdery ores) by heating or pressure or both. [C18: German: CINDER]

Sint Maar·ten (sɪnt 'ma:rtə) *n.* the Dutch name for **Saint Martin.**

sin·u·ate ('sɪnjʊɪt, -,eɪt) *or* **sin·u·at·ed** *adj.* **1.** Also: **sinuous.** (of leaves) having a strongly waved margin. **2.** another word for **sinuous.** [C17: from Latin *sinuātus* curved; see SINUS, -ATE[1]] —**'sin·u·ate·ly** *adv.*

Si·nŭ·i·ju (sɪ,nu:ɪ'dʒu:) *n.* a port in North Korea, on the Yalu River opposite Antung, China: developed by the Japanese during their occupation (1910–45); industrial centre. Pop.: 165 000 (1967 est.).

sin·u·os·i·ty (,sɪnjʊ'ɒsɪtɪ) *or* **sin·u·a·tion** *n., pl.* **·os·i·ties** *or* **·a·tions. 1.** the quality of being sinuous. **2.** a turn, curve, or intricacy.

sin·u·ous ('sɪnjʊəs) *adj.* **1.** full of turns or curves; intricate. **2.** devious; not straightforward. **3.** supple; lithe. ~Also: **sinuate.** [C16: from Latin *sinuōsus* winding, from *sinus* a curve] —**'sin·u·ous·ly** *adv.* —**'sin·u·ous·ness** *n.*

si·nus ('saɪnəs) *n., pl.* **·nus·es. 1.** *Anatomy.* **a.** any bodily cavity or hollow space. **b.** a large channel for venous blood, esp. between the brain and the skull. **c.** any of the air cavities in the cranial bones. **2.** *Pathol.* a passage leading to a cavity containing pus. **3.** *Botany.* a small rounded notch between two lobes of a leaf, petal, etc. **4.** an irregularly shaped cavity. [C16: from Latin: a curve, bay]

si·nus·i·tis (,saɪnə'saɪtɪs) *n.* inflammation of the membrane lining a sinus, esp. a nasal sinus.

si·nus·oid ('saɪnə,sɔɪd) *n.* another name for **sine curve.**

si·nus·oi·dal (,saɪnə'sɔɪdᵊl) *adj.* **1.** *Maths.* of or relating to a sine curve. **2.** *Physics.* having a magnitude that varies as a sine curve. —**,si·nus·'oi·dal·ly** *adv.*

si·nus·oi·dal pro·jec·tion *n.* an equal-area map projection on which all parallels are straight lines and all except the prime meridian are sine curves, often used to show tropical latitudes. Also called: **Sanson-Flamsteed projection.**

Si·on *n.* **1.** (*French* sjɔ̃). a town in SW Switzerland, capital of Valais canton, on the River Rhone. Pop.: 21 925 (1970). Latin name: **Sedunum. 2.** ('saɪən). a variant spelling of **Zion.**

Siou·an ('su:ən) *n.* a family of North American Indian languages spoken by the Sioux.

Sioux (su:) *n.* **1.** (*pl.* **Sioux** (su:, su:z) a member of a group of North American Indian peoples formerly ranging over a wide area of the Plains from Lake Michigan to the Rocky Mountains. **2.** any of the Siouan languages. [from French, shortened from *Nadowessioux,* from Chippewa *Nadoweisiw*] —**'Siou·an** *adj.*

sip (sɪp) *vb.* **sips, sip·ping, sipped. 1.** to drink (a liquid) by taking small mouthfuls; drink gingerly or delicately. ~*n.* **2.** a small quantity of a liquid taken into the mouth and swallowed. **3.** an act of sipping. [C14: probably from Low German *sippen*] —**'sip·per** *n.*

si·phon *or* **sy·phon** ('saɪfᵊn) *n.* **1.** a tube placed with one end at a certain level in a vessel of liquid and the other end outside the vessel below this level, so that atmospheric pressure forces the liquid through the tube and out of the vessel. **2.** See **soda siphon. 3.** *Zoology.* any of various tubular organs in different aquatic animals, such as molluscs and elasmobranch fishes, through which a fluid, esp. water, passes. ~*vb.* **4.** (often foll. by *off*) to pass or draw off through or as if through a siphon. [C17: from Latin *sīphō,* from Greek *siphōn* siphon] —**'si·phon·age** *n.* —**'si·phon·al** *or* **si·phon·ic** (saɪ'fɒnɪk) *adj.*

si·phon bot·tle *n.* another name (esp. U.S.) for **soda siphon.**

si·pho·no·phore ('saɪfənə,fɔ:, saɪ'fɒnə-) *n.* any marine colonial hydrozoan of the order *Siphonophora,* including the Portuguese man-of-war. [C19: from New Latin *siphonophora,* from Greek *siphōnophoros* tube-bearing] —**si·pho·noph·o·rous** (,saɪfə'nɒfərəs) *adj.*

si·phon·o·stele ('saɪfənə,sti:l) *n. Botany.* the cylinder of conducting tissue surrounding a central core of pith in certain stems. See also **stele** (sense 3). [C19: from SIPHON + STELE] —**si·pho·no·ste·lic** (,saɪfənə'sti:lɪk) *adj.*

Si·ple ('saɪpᵊl) *n.* **Mount.** a mountain in Antarctica, on the coast of Marie Byrd Land. Height: 3100 m (10 171 ft.).

sip·per ('sɪpə) *n. U.S. informal.* a drinking straw.

sip·pet ('sɪpɪt) *n.* a small piece of something, esp. a piece of toast or fried bread eaten with soup or gravy. [C16: used as diminutive of SOP; see -ET]

Si·quei·ros (*Spanish* si'kejros) *n.* **Da·vid Al·fa·ro** (da'βið al'faro). 1896–1974, Mexican painter, noted for his murals expressing a revolutionary message.

sir (sɜ:) *n.* **1.** a polite term of address for a man. **2.** *Archaic.* a gentleman of high social status. [C13: variant of SIRE]

Sir (sɜ:) *n.* **1.** a title of honour placed before the name of a knight or baronet: *Sir Walter Raleigh.* **2.** *Archaic.* a title placed before the name of a figure from ancient history.

Si·ra·cu·sa (,sira'ku:za) *n.* the Italian name for **Syracuse.**

Si·raj-ud-dau·la (sɪ'rɑ:dʒʊd'daʊlə) *n.* ?1728–57, Indian leader who became the Great Mogul's deputy in Bengal (1756); opponent of English colonization. He captured Calcutta (1756) from the English and many of his prisoners suffocated in a crowded room that became known as the Black Hole of Calcutta. He was defeated (1757) by a group of Indian nobles in alliance with Robert Clive.

sir·dar ('sɜ:dɑ:) *n.* **1.** a general or military leader in Pakistan and India. **2.** (formerly) the title of the British commander in chief of the Egyptian Army. **3.** a variant spelling of **sardar.** [from Hindi *sardār,* from Persian, from *sar* head + *dār* possession]

sire (saɪə) *n.* **1.** a male parent, esp. of a horse or other domestic animal. **2.** a respectful term of address, now used only in addressing a male monarch. **3.** *Obsolete.* a man of high rank. ~*vb.* **4.** (*tr.*) (esp. of a domestic animal) to father; beget. [C13: from Old French, from Latin *senior* an elder, from *senex* an old man]

si·ren ('saɪərən) *n.* **1.** a device for emitting a loud wailing sound, esp. as a warning or signal, typically consisting of a rotating perforated metal drum through which air or steam is passed under pressure. **2.** (*sometimes cap.*) *Greek myth.* one of several sea nymphs whose seductive singing was believed to lure sailors to destruction on the rocks the nymphs inhabited. **3. a.** a woman considered to be dangerously alluring or seductive. **b.** (*as modifier*): *her siren charms.* **4.** any aquatic eel-like salamander of the North American family *Sirenidae,* having external gills, no hind limbs, and reduced forelimbs. [C14: from Old French *sereine,* from Latin *sīrēn,* from Greek *seirēn*]

si·re·ni·an (saɪ'ri:nɪən) *adj.* **1.** of, relating to, or belonging to the *Sirenia,* an order of aquatic herbivorous placental mammals having forelimbs modified as paddles, no hind limbs, and a horizontally flattened tail: contains only the dugong and manatees. ~*n.* **2.** any animal belonging to the order *Sirenia;* a sea cow.

Si·ret (sɪ'rɛt) *n.* a river in SE Europe, rising in the Ukrainian SSR of the Soviet Union and flowing southeast through E Rumania to the Danube. Length: about 450 km (280 miles).

Sir·i·us ('sɪrɪəs) *n.* the brightest star in the sky, lying in the constellation Canis Major. It is a binary star whose companion, **Sirius B,** is a very faint white dwarf. Distance: 8.7 light years. Also called: the **Dog Star, Canicula, Sothis.** [C14: via Latin from Greek *Seirios,* of obscure origin]

sir·loin ('sɜ:,lɔɪn) *n.* a prime cut of beef from the loin, esp. the upper part. [C16 *surloyn,* from Old French *surlonge,* from *sur* above + *longe,* from *loigne* LOIN]

si·roc·co (sɪ'rɒkəʊ) *n., pl.* **·cos. 1.** a hot oppressive and often dusty wind usually occurring in spring, beginning in N Africa and reaching S Europe. **2.** any hot southerly wind, esp. one moving to a low pressure centre. [C17: from Italian, from Arabic *sharq* east wind]

sir·rah ('sɪrə) *n. Archaic.* a contemptuous term used in addressing a man or boy. [C16: probably variant of SIRE]
sir·ree (sə'ri:) *interj.* (*sometimes cap.*) *U.S. informal.* an emphatic exclamation used with *yes* or *no.*
sir-rev·er·ence *interj. Obsolete.* an expression of apology used esp. to introduce taboo or vulgar words or phrases. [C16: short for *save your reverence*]
Sir Rog·er de Cov·er·ley *n.* an English country dance similar to the Virginia reel and danced to a traditional tune. [C18: alteration of *Roger of Coverley* influenced by *Sir Roger de Coverley,* a fictitious character appearing in the *Spectator* essays by Addison and Steele]
sir·up ('sɪrəp) *n. U.S.* a less common spelling of **syrup.**
sir·vente (sə'vɛnt) *n.* a verse form employed by the troubadours of Provence to satirize moral or political themes. [C19: via French from Provençal *sirventes* song of a servant (that is, of a lover serving his mistress), from *sirvent* a servant, from Latin *servīre* to SERVE]
sis (sɪs) *n. Informal.* short for **sister.**
si·sal ('saɪsᵊl) *n.* **1.** a Mexican agave plant, *Agave sisalana,* cultivated for its large fleshy leaves, which yield a stiff fibre used for making rope. **2.** the fibre of this plant. **3.** any of the fibres of certain similar or related plants. ~Also called: **sisal hemp.** [C19: from Mexican Spanish, named after *Sisal,* a port in Yucatán, Mexico]
Sis·er·a ('sɪsərə) *n.* a defeated leader of the Canaanites, who was assassinated by Jael (Judges 5:21).
sis·kin ('sɪskɪn) *n.* **1.** a yellow-and-black Eurasian finch, *Carduelis spinus.* **2. pine siskin.** a North American finch, *Spinus pinus,* having a streaked yellowish-brown plumage. [C16: from Middle Dutch *sīseken,* from Middle Low German *sīsek;* related to Czech *čížek,* Russian *chizh*]
Sis·ley ('sɪslɪ; *French* si'slɛ) *n.* **Al·fred** (al'frɛd). 1839–99, French painter, esp. of landscapes; one of the originators of impressionism.
Sis·mon·di (sɪs'mɒndɪ; *French* sismɔ̃'di) *n.* **Jean Charles Lé·o·nard Si·monde de** (ʒɑ̃ ʃarl leɔna:r si'mɔ̃:d də). 1773–1842, Swiss historian and economist. His *Histoire des républiques italiennes du moyen âge* (1807–18) contributed to the movement for Italian unification.
sis·sy ('sɪsɪ) *n., pl.* **·sies. 1.** an effeminate, weak, or cowardly boy or man. ~*adj.* **2.** Also (informal or dialect): **sissified.** effeminate, weak, or cowardly. —**'sis·sy·ish** *adj.*
sis·ter ('sɪstə) *n.* **1.** a female person having the same parents as another person. **2.** See **half-sister, stepsister. 3.** a female person who belongs to the same group, trade union, etc., as another or others. **4.** *Informal.* a form of address to a woman or girl, used esp. by Blacks in the U.S. **5.** a senior nurse. **6.** *Chiefly R.C. Church.* a nun or a title given to a nun. **7.** a woman fellow member of a Church or religious body. **8.** (*modifier*) belonging to the same class, fleet, etc., as another or others: *a sister ship.* [Old English *sweostor;* related to Old Norse *systir,* Old High German *swester,* Gothic *swistar*]
sis·ter·hood ('sɪstə,hʊd) *n.* **1.** the state of being related as a sister or sisters. **2.** a religious body or society of sisters, esp. a community, order, or congregation of nuns.
sis·ter-in-law *n., pl.* **sis·ters-in-law. 1.** the sister of one's husband or wife. **2.** the wife of one's brother. **3.** the wife of the brother of one's husband or wife.
sis·ter·ly ('sɪstəlɪ) *adj.* of, resembling, or suitable to a sister, esp. in showing kindness and affection. —**'sis·ter·li·ness** *n.*
Sis·tine Chap·el ('sɪstaɪn, -ti:n) *n.* the chapel of the pope in the Vatican at Rome, built for Sixtus IV and decorated with frescoes by Michelangelo and others. [Sistine, from Italian *Sistino* relating to *Sisto* Sixtus (Pope Sixtus IV)]
sis·troid ('sɪstrɔɪd) *adj.* contained between the convex sides of two intersecting curves. Compare **cissoid** (sense 2). [C20: from SISTRUM + -OID]
sis·trum ('sɪstrəm) *n., pl.* **·tra** (-trə). a musical instrument of ancient Egypt consisting of a metal rattle. [C14: via Latin from Greek *seistron,* from *seiein* to shake]
Sis·y·phe·an (,sɪsɪ'fi:ən) *adj.* **1.** relating to Sisyphus. **2.** actually or seemingly endless and futile.
Sis·y·phus ('sɪsɪfəs) *n. Greek myth.* a king of Corinth, punished in Hades for his misdeeds by eternally having to roll a heavy stone up a hill: every time he approached the top, the stone escaped his grasp and rolled to the bottom.
sit (sɪt) *vb.* **sits, sit·ting, sat.** (*mainly intr.*) **1.** (*also tr.;* when *intr.,* often foll. by *down, in,* or *on*) to adopt or rest in a posture in which the body is supported on the buttocks and thighs and the torso is more or less upright: *to sit on a chair; sit a horse.* **2.** (*tr.*) to cause to adopt such a posture. **3.** (of an animal) to adopt or rest in a posture with the hindquarters lowered to the ground. **4.** (of a bird) to perch or roost. **5.** (of a hen or other bird) to cover eggs to hatch them; brood. **6.** to be situated or located. **7.** (of the wind) to blow from the direction specified. **8.** to adopt and maintain a posture for one's portrait to be painted, etc. **9.** to occupy or be entitled to a seat in some official capacity, as a judge, elected representative, etc. **10.** (of a deliberative body) to be convened or in session. **11.** to remain inactive or unused: *his car sat in the garage for a year.* **12.** to rest or lie as specified: *the nut was sitting so awkwardly that he couldn't turn it.* **13.** (of a garment) to fit or hang as specified: *that dress sits well on you.* **14.** to weigh, rest, or lie as specified: *greatness sits easily on him.* **15.** (*tr.*) *Chiefly Brit.* to take (an examination): *he's sitting his bar finals.* **16.** (usually foll. by *for*) *Chiefly Brit.* to be a candidate (for a qualification): *he's sitting for a B.A.* **17.** to keep watch over an invalid, a baby, etc. **18.** (*tr.*) to have seating capacity for. **19. sitting pretty.** *Informal.* well placed or established financially, socially, etc. **20. sit tight.** *Informal.* to wait patiently; bide one's time. ~See also **sit back, sit down, sit-in, sit on, sit out, sit over, sit under, sit up.** [Old English *sittan;* related to Old Norse *sitja,* Gothic *sitan,* Old High German *sizzen,* Latin *sedēre* to sit, Sanskrit *sīdati* he sits]
si·tar (sɪ'tɑ:, 'sɪtɑ:) *n.* a stringed musical instrument, esp. of India, having a long neck, a rounded body, and movable frets. The main strings, three to seven in number, overlay other sympathetic strings, the tuning depending on the raga being performed. [from Hindi *sitār,* literally: three-stringed] —**si'tar·ist** *n.*
sit back *vb.* (*intr., adv.*) to relax, as when action should be taken: *many people just sit back and ignore the problems of today.*
sit·com ('sɪt,kɒm) *n.* an informal term for **situation comedy.**
sit down *vb.* (*adv.*) **1.** to adopt or cause (oneself or another) to adopt a sitting posture. **2.** (*intr.;* foll. by *under*) to suffer (insults, etc.) without protests or resistance. ~*n.* **sit-down. 3.** a form of civil disobedience in which demonstrators sit down in a public place as a protest or to draw attention to a cause. **4.** See **sit-down strike.** ~*adj.* **sit-down. 5.** (of a meal, etc.) eaten while sitting down at a table.
sit-down strike *n.* a strike in which workers refuse to leave their place of employment until a settlement is reached.
site (saɪt) *n.* **1. a.** the piece of land where something was, is, or is intended to be located: *a building site; archaeological site.* **b.** (*as modifier*): *site office.* ~*vb.* **2.** (*tr.*) to locate, place, or install (something) in a specific place. [C14: from Latin *situs* situation, from *sinere* to be placed]
si·tel·la (sɪ'tɛlə) *n. Austral.* any of various small generally black and white birds of the genus *Neositta,* having a straight sharp beak and strong claws used to run up trees in search of insects: family *Sittidae* (nuthatches). Also called: **tree-runner.**
sit·fast ('sɪt,fɑ:st) *n.* a sore on a horse's back caused by rubbing of the saddle.
sith (sɪθ) *adv., conj., prep.* an archaic word for **since.** [Old English *siththa,* short for *siththan* SINCE]
Sit·ho·le (sɪ'təʊlɪ) *n.* **Nda·ban·in·gi** (ᵊndaba'nɪŋgɪ). born 1920, Rhodesian clergyman and politician; leader of the Zimbabwe African National Union since 1963. He was one of the negotiators of the internal settlement (1978) to pave the way for black majority rule in Rhodesia.
sit-in *n.* **1.** a form of civil disobedience in which demonstrators occupy seats in a public place and refuse to move as a protest. ~*vb.* **sit in.** (*intr., adv.*) **2.** (often foll. by *for*) to deputize (for). **3.** (foll. by *on*) to take part (in) as a visitor or guest: *we sat in on Professor Johnson's seminar.* **4.** to organize or take part in a sit-in.
Sit·ka ('sɪtkə) *n.* a town in SE Alaska, in the Alexander Archipelago on W Baranof Island: capital of Russian America (1804–67) and of Alaska (1867–1906). Pop.: 3370 (1970).
sit·ka spruce ('sɪtkə) *n.* a tall North American spruce tree, *Picea sitchensis,* having yellowish-green needle-like leaves: yields valuable timber.
si·tol·o·gy (saɪ'tɒlədʒɪ) *n.* the scientific study of food, diet, and nutrition. [C19: from Greek *sitos* food, grain + -LOGY]
sit on *vb.* (*intr., prep.*) **1.** to be a member of (a committee, etc.). **2.** *Informal.* to suppress. **3.** *Informal.* to check or rebuke.
si·tos·ter·ol (saɪ'tɒstə,rɒl) *n.* a white powder or waxy white solid extracted from soya beans, consisting of a mixture of isomers of the formula $C_{29}H_{50}O$ with other sterols: used in cosmetics and medicine. [C20: from Greek *sitos* food, grain + STEROL]
sit out *vb.* (*adv.*) **1.** (*tr.*) to endure to the end: *I sat out the play although it was terrible.* **2.** (*tr.*) to remain seated throughout (a dance, etc.). **3.** (*intr.*) *Chiefly Brit.* to lean backwards over the side of a light sailing boat in order to carry the centre of gravity as far to windward as possible to reduce heeling. U.S. term: **hike out.**
sit o·ver *vb.* (*intr., prep.*) *Cards.* to be seated in an advantageous position on the left of (the player).
Si·tsang ('si:'tsæŋ) *n.* the Chinese name for **Tibet.**
sit·ter ('sɪtə) *n.* **1.** a person or animal that sits. **2.** a person who is posing for his or her portrait to be painted, carved, etc. **3.** a broody hen or other bird that is sitting on its eggs to hatch them. **4.** Also called: **sitter-in.** See **baby-sitter.**
Sit·ter ('sɪtə) *n.* **Wil·lem de** ('wɪləm də). 1872–1934, Dutch astronomer, who calculated the size of the universe and conceived of it as expanding.
sit·ting ('sɪtɪŋ) *n.* **1.** a continuous period of being seated: *I read his novel at one sitting.* **2.** such a period in a restaurant, canteen, etc., where space and other facilities are limited: *dinner will be served in two sittings.* **3.** the act or period of posing for one's portrait to be painted, carved, etc. **4.** a meeting, esp. of an official body, to conduct business. **5.** the incubation period of a bird's eggs during which the mother sits on them to keep them warm.
Sit·ting Bull *n.* ?1831–90, American Indian chief of the Teton Dakota Sioux. Resisting white encroachment on his people's hunting grounds, he led the Sioux tribes against the U.S. Army in the Sioux War (1876–77) in which Custer was killed. The hunger of the Sioux, whose food came from the diminishing buffalo, forced his surrender (1881). He was killed during renewed strife.
sit·ting duck *n. Informal.* a person or thing in a defenceless or precarious position.
sit·ting room *n.* a room in a private house or flat used for relaxation and entertainment of guests.
sit·ting ten·ant *n.* a tenant occupying a house, flat, etc.

sit·ting trot *n.* a horse's trot during which the rider sits still in the saddle. Compare **rising trot.**

sit·u·ate ('sɪtjʊˌeɪt) *vb.* **1.** (*tr.; often passive*) to allot a site to; place; locate. ~*adj.* **2.** (now used esp. in legal contexts) situated; located. [C16: from Late Latin *situāre* to position, from Latin *situs* a SITE]

sit·u·a·tion (ˌsɪtjʊ'eɪʃən) *n.* **1.** physical placement, esp. with regard to the surroundings. **2. a.** state of affairs; combination of circumstances. **b.** a complex or critical state of affairs in a novel, play, etc. **3.** social or financial status, position, or circumstances. **4.** a position of employment; post. —ˌ**sit·u·'a·tion·al** *adj.*

sit·u·a·tion com·e·dy *n.* comedy based on the humorous situations that could arise in day-to-day life.

sit·u·la ('sɪtjʊlə) *n., pl.* **·lae** (-liː). **1.** a bucket-shaped container, usually of metal or pottery and often richly decorated: typical of the N Italian Iron Age. ~*adj.* **2.** of or relating to the type of designs usually associated with these containers. [from Latin]

sit un·der *vb.* (*intr., prep.*) *Cards.* to be seated on the right of (the player).

sit up *vb.* (*adv.*) **1.** to raise (oneself or another) from a recumbent to an upright or alert sitting posture. **2.** (*intr.*) to remain out of bed and awake, esp. until a late hour. **3.** (*intr.*) *Informal.* to become suddenly interested or alert: *devaluation of the dollar made the money market sit up.* ~*n.* **sit-up. 4.** *Gymnastics.* another name for **trunk curl.**

si·tus ('saɪtəs) *n., pl.* **·tus.** position or location, esp. the usual or right position of an organ or part of the body. [C18: from Latin: site, situation, position]

Sit·well ('sɪtwəl) *n.* **1.** Dame **E·dith.** 1887–1964, English poet and critic, noted esp. for her collection *Façade* (1922). **2.** her brother, Sir **Os·bert.** 1892–1969, English writer, best known for his five autobiographical books (1944–50). **3.** his brother, **Sa·chev·er·ell** (sə'ʃɛvərəl). born 1897, English poet and writer of books on art, architecture, music, and travel.

sitz bath (sɪts, zɪts) *n.* a bath in which the buttocks and hips are immersed in hot water, esp. for therapeutic effects, as after perineal or pelvic surgery. [half translation of German *Sitzbad,* from *Sitz* SEAT + *Bad* BATH]

sitz·krieg ('sɪtsˌkriːg, 'zɪts-) *n.* a period during a war in which both sides change positions very slowly or not at all. [C20: from German, from *sitzen* to sit + *Krieg* war]

sitz·mark ('sɪtsˌmɑːk, 'zɪts-) *n. Skiing.* a depression in the snow where a skier has fallen. [German, literally: seat mark]

SI u·nit *n.* any of the units adopted for international use under the Système International d'Unités, now employed for all scientific and most technical purposes. There are seven fundamental units: the metre, kilogram, second, ampere, kelvin, candela, and mole; and two supplementary units: the radian and the steradian. All other units are derived by multiplication or division of these units without the use of numerical factors.

Si·va ('siːvə, 'sɪvə) *or* **Shi·va** *n. Hinduism.* the destroyer, one of the three chief divinities of the later Hindu pantheon, the other two being Brahma and Vishnu. Siva is also the god presiding over personal destinies. [from Sanskrit *Śiva,* literally: the auspicious (one)]

Si·va·ism ('siːvəˌɪzəm, 'sɪvə-) *n.* the cult of Siva. —**'Si·va·ist** *n.* —ˌ**Si·va·'is·tic** *adj.*

Si·van (siː'vɑːn) *n.* the ninth month of the civil year and the third of the ecclesiastical year in the Jewish calendar, falling approximately in May and June. [from Hebrew *sīwān*]

Si·vas (*Turkish* 'sɪvɑs) *n.* a city in central Turkey, at an altitude of 1347m (4420 ft.): one of the chief cities in Asia Minor in ancient times; scene of the national congress (1919) leading to the revolution that established modern Turkey. Pop.: 149 201 (1975).

si·wash ('saɪwɒʃ) *n.* **1.** another name for **Cowichan sweater.** ~*vb.* **2.** (*intr.*) (in the Pacific Northwest) to camp out with only natural shelter. [see SIWASH]

Si·wash ('saɪwɒʃ) (*sometimes not cap.*) *Slang, derogatory.* (in the Pacific Northwest) ~*n.* **1.** a North American Indian. ~*adj.* **2.** of, characteristic of, or relating to Indians. **3.** worthless, stingy, or bad: *he's siwash.* [C19: from Chinook Jargon, from French *sauvage* SAVAGE]

six (sɪks) *n.* **1.** the cardinal number that is the sum of five and one. See also **number** (sense 1). **2.** a numeral, 6, VI, etc., representing this number. **3.** something representing, represented by, or consisting of six units, such as a playing card with six symbols on it. **4.** Also: **six o'clock.** six hours after noon or midnight. **5.** Also called: **sixer.** *Cricket.* **a.** a shot that crosses the boundary without bouncing. **b.** the six runs scored for such a shot. **6.** a division of a Brownie Guide or Cub Scout pack. **7. at sixes and sevens. a.** in disagreement. **b.** in a state of confusion. **8. knock (someone) for six.** *Informal.* to upset or overwhelm completely; stun. **9. six of one and half a dozen of the other.** Also: **six and two threes.** a situation in which the alternatives are considered equivalent. ~*determiner.* **10. a.** amounting to six: *six nations.* **b.** (*as pronoun*): *set the table for six.* ~Related prefixes: **hexa-, sexi-.** [Old English *siex;* related to Old Norse *sex,* Gothic *saihs,* Old High German *sehs,* Latin *sex,* Greek *hex,* Sanskrit *sastha*]

Six (*French* sis) *n.* **Les** (le). a group of six young composers in France, who from about 1916 formed a temporary association as a result of interest in neoclassicism and in the music of Satie and the poetry of Cocteau. Its members were Darius Milhaud, Arthur Honegger, Francis Poulenc, Georges Auric, Louis Durey, and Germaine Tailleferre.

six·ain ('sɪkseɪn) *n.* a stanza or poem of six lines.

Six Coun·ties *pl. n.* the counties of Northern Ireland.

Six Day War *n.* a war fought in the Middle East in June 1967, lasting six days. In it Israel defeated Egypt, Jordan, and Syria, occupying the Gaza Strip, the Sinai, Jerusalem, the West Bank of the Jordan, and the Golan Heights.

six-eight time *n. Music.* a form of compound duple time in which there are six quaver beats to the bar, indicated by the time signature $\frac{6}{8}$. Often shortened to **six-eight.**

six·fold ('sɪksˌfəʊld) *adj.* **1.** equal to or having six times as many or as much. **2.** composed of six parts. ~*adv.* **3.** by or up to six times as many or as much.

six-foot·er *n.* a person who is at least six feet tall.

six-gun *n. U.S. informal.* another word for **six-shooter.**

six·mo ('sɪksməʊ) *n., pl.* **·mos. 1.** Also called: **sexto.** a book size resulting from folding a sheet of paper into six leaves or twelve pages, each one sixth the size of the sheet. Often written: **6mo, 6°. 2.** a book of this size.

Six Na·tions *pl. n.* (in North America) the Indian confederacy of the Cayugas, Mohawks, Oneidas, Onondagas, Senecas, and Tuscaroras. Also called: **Iroquois.** See also **Five Nations.**

six-pack *n. Informal.* a package containing six units, esp. six cans of beer.

six·pence ('sɪkspəns) *n.* a small British cupronickel coin with a face value of six pennies, worth 2½ (new) pence, not minted since 1970.

six·pen·ny ('sɪkspənɪ) *adj.* (*prenominal*) (of a nail) two inches in length.

six-shoot·er *n. U.S. informal.* a revolver with six chambers. Also called: **six-gun.**

sixte (sɪkst) *n.* the sixth of eight basic positions from which a parry or attack can be made in fencing. [from French: (the) sixth (parrying position), from Latin *sextus* sixth]

six·teen ('sɪks'tiːn) *n.* **1.** the cardinal number that is the sum of ten and six. See also **number** (sense 1). **2.** a numeral, 16, XVI, etc., representing this number. **3.** *Music.* the numeral 16 used as the lower figure of a time signature to indicate that the beat is measured in semiquavers. **4.** something represented by, representing, or consisting of 16 units. ~*determiner.* **5. a.** amounting to sixteen: *sixteen tons.* **b.** (*as pronoun*): *sixteen are known to the police.*

six·teen·mo ('sɪks'tiːnməʊ) *n., pl.* **·mos. 1.** Also called: **sextodecimo.** a book size resulting from folding a sheet of paper into 16 leaves or 32 pages, each one sixteenth the size of the sheet. Often written: **16mo, 16°. 2.** a book of this size.

six·teenth ('sɪks'tiːnθ) *adj.* **1.** (*usually prenominal*) **a.** coming after the fifteenth in numbering or counting order, position, time, etc.; being the ordinal number of *sixteen:* often written 16th. **b.** (*as n.*): *the sixteenth of the month.* ~*n.* **2. a.** one of 16 equal or nearly equal parts of something. **b.** (*as modifier*): *a sixteenth part.* **3.** the fraction that is equal to one divided by 16 (1/16).

six·teenth note *n.* the usual U.S. name for **semiquaver.**

sixth (sɪksθ) *adj.* **1.** (*usually prenominal*) **a.** coming after the fifth and before the seventh in numbering or counting order, position, time, etc.; being the ordinal number of *six:* often written 6th. **b.** (*as n.*): *the sixth to go.* ~*n.* **2. a.** one of six equal or nearly equal parts of an object, quantity, measurement, etc. **b.** (*as modifier*): *a sixth part.* **3.** the fraction equal to one divided by six (1/6). **4.** *Music.* **a.** the interval between one note and another note six notes away from it counting inclusively along the diatonic scale. **b.** one of two notes constituting such an interval in relation to the other. See also **major** (sense 11), **minor** (sense 4), **interval** (sense 5). **c.** short for **sixth chord.** ~*adv.* **5.** Also: **sixthly.** after the fifth person, position, etc. ~ **6.** *sentence connector.* Also: **sixthly.** as the sixth point: linking what follows to the previous statements.

sixth chord *n.* (in classical harmony) the first inversion of the triad, in which the note next above the root appears in the bass. See also **added sixth.**

sixth form *n.* **a.** the most senior class in a secondary school to which pupils, usually above the legal leaving age, may proceed to take A levels, retake O levels, etc. **b.** (*as modifier*): *a sixth-form college.* —**'sixth-ˌform·er** *n.*

sixth sense *n.* any supposed sense or means of perception, such as intuition or clairvoyance, other than the five senses of sight, hearing, touch, taste, and smell.

six·ti·eth ('sɪkstɪəθ) *adj.* **1.** (*usually prenominal*) **a.** being the ordinal number of *sixty* in numbering or counting order, position, time, etc.: often written 60th. **b.** (*as n.*): *the sixtieth in a row.* ~*n.* **2. a.** one of 60 approximately equal parts of something. **b.** (*as modifier*): *a sixtieth part.* **3.** the fraction equal to one divided by 60 (1/60).

Six·tus V ('sɪkstəs) *n.* original name *Felice Peretti.* 1520–90, Italian ecclesiastic; pope (1585–90). He is noted for vigorous administrative reforms that contributed to the Counter-Reformation.

six·ty ('sɪkstɪ) *n., pl.* **·ties. 1.** the cardinal number that is the product of ten and six. See also **number** (sense 1). **2.** a numeral, 60, LX, etc., representing sixty. **3.** something represented by, representing, or consisting of 60 units. ~*determiner.* **4. a.** amounting to sixty: *sixty soldiers.* **b.** (*as pronoun*): *sixty are dead.* [Old English *sixtig*]

six·ty-four·mo (ˌsɪkstɪ'fɔːməʊ) *n., pl.* **·mos. 1.** a book size resulting from folding a sheet of paper into 64 leaves or 128 pages, each one sixty-fourth the size of the sheet. Often written **64mo, 64°. 2.** a book of this size.

six·ty-fourth note *n.* the usual U.S. name for **hemidemisemiquaver.**

six·ty-four thou·sand dol·lar ques·tion *n.* a crucial question or issue. [C20: from the top prize in a U.S. television quiz]

six·ty-nine *n.* another term for **soixante-neuf.**

six-yard line *n. Soccer.* the line marking the limits of the goal area.

siz+a·ble *or* **size+a·ble** ('saɪzəbᵊl) *adj.* quite large. —'**siz+a·ble+ness** *or* '**size+a·ble+ness** *n.* —'**siz+a·bly** *or* '**size+a·bly** *adv.*

siz+ar ('saɪzə) *n. Brit.* (at Peterhouse, Cambridge, and Trinity College, Dublin) an undergraduate receiving a maintenance grant from the college. [C16: from earlier *sizer,* from SIZE[1] (meaning "an allowance of food, etc.")] —'**si+zar+,ship** *n.*

size[1] (saɪz) *n.* **1.** the dimensions, proportions, amount, or extent of something. **2.** large or great dimensions, etc. **3.** one of a series of graduated measurements, as of clothing: *she takes size 4 shoes.* **4.** *Informal.* state of affairs as summarized: *he's bankrupt, that's the size of it.* ~*vb.* **5.** to sort according to size. **6.** (*tr.*) to make or cut to a particular size or sizes. [C13: from Old French *sise,* shortened from *assise* ASSIZE] —'**siz+er** *n.*

size[2] (saɪz) *n.* **1.** Also called: **siz+ing.** a thin gelatinous mixture, made from glue, clay, or wax, that is used as a sealer or filler on paper, cloth, or plaster surfaces. ~*vb.* **2.** (*tr.*) to treat or coat (a surface) with size. [C15: perhaps from Old French *sise;* see SIZE[1]] —'**siz·y** *adj.*

sized (saɪzd) *adj.* of a specified size: *medium-sized.*

size up *vb.* (*adv.*) **1.** (*tr.*) *Informal.* to make an assessment of (a person, problem, etc.). **2.** to conform to or make so as to conform to certain specifications of dimension.

siz+zle ('sɪzᵊl) *vb.* (*intr.*) **1.** to make the hissing sound characteristic of frying fat. **2.** *Informal.* to be very hot. **3.** *Informal.* to be very angry. ~*n.* **4.** a hissing sound.

siz+zler ('sɪzlə) *n.* **1.** something that sizzles. **2.** *Informal.* a very hot day.

S.J. *abbrev. for* Society of Jesus.

Sjæl+land (*Danish* 'sjɛlan) *n.* the largest island of Denmark, separated from the island of Fyn by the Great Belt and from S Sweden by the Sound. Chief town: Copenhagen. Pop.: 2 129 846 (1970). Area: 7016 sq. km (2709 sq. miles). English name: **Zealand.** German name: **Seeland.**

sjam+bok ('ʃæmbʌk, -bɒk) (in South Africa) ~*n.* **1.** a heavy whip of rhinoceros or hippopotamus hide. ~*vb.* **2.** (*tr.*) to strike or beat with such a whip.

S.J.C. (in the U.S.) *abbrev. for* Supreme Judicial Court.

S.J.D. *abbrev. for* Doctor of Juridical Science. [from Latin *Scientiae Juridicae Doctor*]

sk. *abbrev. for* sack.

Ska+gen ('skɑːgən) *n.* **Cape.** another name for the **Skaw.**

Skag+er+rak ('skægə,ræk) *n.* an arm of the North Sea between Denmark and Norway, merging with the Kattegat in the southeast.

skald *or* **scald** (skɔːld) *n.* (in ancient Scandinavia) a bard or minstrel. [from Old Norse, of unknown origin] —'**skald+ic** *or* '**scald+ic** *adj.*

Ska·ra Brae ('skærə) *n.* a neolithic village in NE Scotland, in the Orkney Islands: one of Europe's most perfectly preserved Stone Age villages, buried by a sand dune until uncovered by a storm in 1850.

skat (skæt) *n.* a three-handed card game using 32 cards, popular in German-speaking communities. [C19: from German, from Italian *scarto* played cards, from *scartare* to discard, from *s-* EX-[1] + *carta,* from Latin *charta* CARD[1]]

skate[1] (skeɪt) *n.* **1.** See **roller skate, ice skate. 2.** the steel blade or runner of an ice skate. **3.** such a blade fitted with straps for fastening to a shoe. **4.** a current collector on an electric railway train that collects its current from a third rail. Compare **bow collector. 5. get one's skates on.** to hurry. ~*vb.* (*intr.*) **6.** to glide swiftly on skates. **7.** to slide smoothly over a surface. **8. skate on thin ice.** to place oneself in a dangerous or delicate situation. [C17: via Dutch from Old French *éschasse* stilt, probably of Germanic origin]

skate[2] (skeɪt) *n., pl.* **skate** *or* **skates.** any large ray of the family *Rajidae,* of temperate and tropical seas, having flat pectoral fins continuous with the head, two dorsal fins, a short spineless tail, and a long snout. [C14: from Old Norse *skata*]

skate[3] (skeɪt) *n. U.S. slang.* a person; fellow. [from Scottish and northern English dialect *skate,* a derogatory term of uncertain origin]

skate+board ('skeɪt,bɔːd) *n.* **1.** a plank mounted on roller-skate wheels, usually ridden while standing up. ~*vb.* **2.** (*intr.*) to ride on a skateboard. —'**skate+,board+er** *n.*

skate o·ver *vb.* (*intr., prep.*) **1.** to cross on or as if on skates. **2.** to avoid dealing with (a matter) fully.

skate+park ('skeɪt,pɑːk) *n.* an area for skateboarding, esp. one provided with bowls, pipes, and ramps.

skat+er ('skeɪtə) *n.* **1.** a person who skates. **2.** See **pond-skater.**

skat+ole ('skætəʊl) *n.* a white or brownish crystalline solid with a strong faecal odour, found in faeces, beetroot, and coal tar; B-methylindole. Formula: C_9H_9N. [C19: from Greek *skat-,* stem of *skōr* excrement + -OLE[1]]

Skaw (skɔː) *n.* **the.** a cape at the N tip of Denmark. Also called: (Cape) **Skagen.**

skean (skiːn) *n.* a kind of double-edged dagger formerly used in Ireland and Scotland. [from Irish Gaelic *scian*]

ske+dad+dle (skɪ'dædᵊl) *Informal.* ~*vb.* **1.** (*intr.*) to run off hastily. ~*n.* **2.** a hasty retreat. [C19: of unknown origin]

skeet (skiːt) *n.* a form of clay-pigeon shooting in which targets are hurled from two traps at varying speeds and angles. Also called: **skeet shooting.** [C20: changed from Old Norse *skeyti* a thrown object, from *skjōta* to shoot]

skeg (skɛg) *n. Nautical.* **1.** a reinforcing brace between the after end of a keel and the rudderport. **2.** a support at the bottom of a rudder. **3.** a projection from the forefoot of a vessel for towing paravanes. **4.** any short keel-like projection at the stern of a boat. **5.** *Austral.* a rear fin on the underside of a surfboard. [C16: of Scandinavian origin; compare Icelandic *skegg* cutwater]

skein (skeɪn) *n.* **1.** a length of yarn, etc., wound in a long coil. **2.** something resembling this, such as a lock of hair. **3.** a flock of geese flying. Compare **gaggle** (sense 2). [C15: from Old French *escaigne,* of unknown origin]

skel+e·ton ('skɛlɪtən) *n.* **1.** a hard framework consisting of inorganic material that supports and protects the soft parts of an animal's body and provides attachment for muscles: may be internal, as in vertebrates (see **endoskeleton**), or external, as in arthropods (see **exoskeleton**). **2.** *Informal.* a very thin emaciated person or animal. **3.** the essential framework of any structure, such as a building or leaf, that supports or determines the shape of the rest of the structure. **4.** an outline consisting of bare essentials: *the skeleton of a novel.* **5.** (*modifier*) reduced to a minimum: *a skeleton staff.* **6. skeleton in the cupboard** *or* (*U.S.*) **closet.** a scandalous fact or event in the past that is kept secret. [C16: via New Latin from Greek: something desiccated, from *skellein* to dry up] —'**skel+e·tal** *adj.* —'**skel+e·tal+ly** *adv.* —'**skel·e·ton-,like** *adj.*

skel+e·ton+ize *or* **skel+e·ton+ise** ('skɛlɪtə,naɪz) *vb.* **1.** (*tr.*) to reduce to a minimum framework, number, or outline. **2.** to create the essential framework of.

skel+e·ton key *n.* a key with the serrated edge filed down so that it can open numerous locks. Also called: **passkey.**

skelf (skɛlf) *n. Northern Brit. dialect.* **1.** a splinter of wood. **2.** a thin or diminutive person. [from Scottish; see SHELF]

skel+lum ('skɛləm) *n. Archaic and Brit. dialect.* a rogue. [C17: via Dutch from Old High German *skelmo* devil]

skel+ly[1] ('skɛlɪ) *n., pl.* **+lies.** a whitefish, *Coregonus stigmaticus,* of certain lakes in the Lake District.

skel+ly[2] ('skɛlɪ) *Northern Brit. dialect.* ~*vb.* **+lies, +ly+ing, +lied. 1.** to look sideways or squint. ~*n., pl.* **+lies. 2.** a quick look; glance. [probably from Old Norse, from *skjalgr* wry; related to Old English *sceolh* a squint]

Skel+mers+dale ('skɛlməz,deɪl) *n.* a town in NW England, in Merseyside: designated a new town in 1962. Pop.: 26 686 (1971).

skelp[1] (skɛlp) *Northern Brit. dialect.* ~*vb.* **1.** (*tr.*) to slap. ~*n.* **2.** a slap. [C15: probably of imitative origin]

skelp[2] (skɛlp) *n.* sheet or plate metal that has been curved and welded to form a tube. [C19: perhaps from Scottish Gaelic *sgealb* thin strip of wood]

Skel·ton ('skɛltən) *n.* **John.** ?1460–1529, English poet celebrated for his short rhyming lines using the rhythms of colloquial speech.

sken (skɛn) *vb.* **skens, sken+ning, skenned.** (*intr.*) *Northern English dialect.* to squint or stare. [of obscure origin]

skep (skɛp) *n.* **1.** a beehive, esp. one constructed of straw. **2.** *Now chiefly dialect.* a large basket of wickerwork or straw. [Old English *sceppe,* from Old Norse *skeppa* bushel; related to Old High German *sceffil* bushel]

skep+tic ('skɛptɪk) *n., adj.* the usual U.S. spelling of **sceptic.** —'**skep+ti+cal** *adj.* —'**skep·ti+cal+ly** *adv.* —'**skep+ti+cal+ness** *n.* —'**skep+ti+cism** *n.*

sker+rick ('skɛrɪk) *n. U.S. and Austral. informal.* a small fragment or amount (esp. in the phrase **not a skerrick**). [C20: northern English dialect, probably of Scandinavian origin]

sker+ry ('skɛrɪ) *n., pl.* **+ries.** *Chiefly Scot.* a small rocky island. [C17: Orkney dialect, from Old Norse *sker* SCAR[2]]

sket (skɛt) *vb.* **skets, sket+ting, sket+ted.** (*tr.*) *South Wales dialect.* **1.** to splash (water). **2.** to splash (someone with water). [perhaps from Old Norse *skjóta* to shoot]

sketch (skɛtʃ) *n.* **1.** a rapid drawing or painting, often a study for subsequent elaboration. **2.** a brief usually descriptive and informal essay or other literary composition. **3.** a short play, often comic, forming part of a revue. **4.** a short evocative piece of instrumental music, esp. for piano. **5.** any brief outline. ~*vb.* **6.** to make (a rough drawing, etc.) (of). **7.** (*tr.;* often foll. by *out*) to make a brief description of. [C17: from Dutch *schets,* via Italian from Latin *schedius* hastily made, from Greek *skhedios* unprepared] —'**sketch+a·ble** *adj.* —'**sketch+er** *n.*

sketch+book ('skɛtʃ,bʊk) *n.* **1.** a book of plain paper containing sketches or for making sketches in. **2.** a book of literary sketches.

sketch·y ('skɛtʃɪ) *adj.* **sketch·i+er, sketch·i+est. 1.** characteristic of a sketch; existing only in outline. **2.** superficial or slight. —'**sketch·i·ly** *adv.* —'**sketch·i+ness** *n.*

skew (skjuː) *adj.* **1.** placed in or turning into an oblique position or course. **2.** *Machinery.* having a component that is at an angle to the main axis of an assembly or is in some other way asymmetrical: *a skew bevel gear.* **3.** *Maths.* composed of or being elements that are neither parallel nor intersecting. **4.** (of a statistical distribution) not having equal probabilities above and below the mean; non-normal. **5.** distorted or biased. ~*n.* **6.** an oblique, slanting, or indirect course or position. **7.** *Psychol.* the system of relationships in a family in which one parent is extremely dominating while the other parent tends to be meekly compliant. ~*vb.* **8.** to take or cause to take an oblique course or direction. **9.** (*intr.*) to look sideways; squint. **10.** (*tr.*) to place at an angle. **11.** (*tr.*) to distort or bias. [C14: from Old Norman French *escuer* to shun, of Germanic origin; compare Middle Dutch *schuwen* to avoid] —'**skew+ness** *n.*

skew arch *n.* an arch or vault, esp. one used in a bridge or tunnel, that is set at an oblique angle to the span.

skew+back ('skju:ˌbæk) *n.* **1.** the sloping surface on both sides of a segmental arch that takes the thrust. **2.** one or more stones that provide such a surface. —'**skew+ˌbacked** *adj.*

skew+bald ('skju:ˌbɔ:ld) *adj.* **1.** marked or spotted in white and any colour except black. ~*n.* **2.** a horse with this marking. [C17: see SKEW, PIEBALD]

skew+er ('skjʊə) *n.* **1.** a long pin for holding meat in position while being cooked, etc. **2.** a similar pin having some other function. ~*vb.* **3.** (*tr.*) to drive a skewer through or fasten with a skewer. [C17: probably from dialect *skiver*]

skew+whiff ('skju:'wɪf) *adj.* (*postpositive*) *Brit. informal.* not straight; askew. [C18: probably influenced by ASKEW]

ski (ski:) *n., pl.* **skis** *or* **ski.** **1. a.** one of a pair of wood, metal, or plastic runners that are used for gliding over snow. Skis are commonly attached to shoes for sport, but may also be used as landing gear for aircraft, etc. **b.** (*as modifier*): *a ski boot.* **2.** a water-ski. ~*vb.* **skis, ski+ing; skied** *or* **ski'd. 3.** (*intr.*) to travel on skis. [C19: from Norwegian, from Old Norse *skith* snow-shoes; related to Old English *scīd* SHIDE] —'**ski+a+ble** *adj.* —'**ski+er** *n.*

ski+am+a+chy (skaɪ'æməkɪ) *n., pl.* **+chies.** a variant of **sciamachy.**

ski+a+scope ('skaɪəˌskəʊp) *n. Med.* a medical instrument for examining the eye to detect errors of refraction. Also called: **retinoscope.** See also **retinoscopy.** [C19: from Greek *skia* a shadow + -SCOPE]

ski+as+co+py (skaɪ'æskəpɪ) *n. Med.* another name for **retinoscopy.**

ski+bob ('ski:bɒb) *n.* a vehicle made of two short skis, the forward one having a steering handle and the rear one supporting a low seat, for gliding down snow slopes. —'**ski+bob+ber** *n.* —'**ski+bob+bing** *n.*

skid (skɪd) *vb.* **skids, skid+ding, skid+ded. 1.** to cause (a vehicle) to slide sideways or (of a vehicle) to slide sideways while in motion, esp. out of control. **2.** (*intr.*) to slide without revolving, as the wheel of a moving vehicle after sudden braking. **3.** (*tr.*) *U.S.* to put or haul on a skid, esp. along a special track. **4.** to cause (an aircraft) to slide sideways away from the centre of a turn when insufficiently banked or (of an aircraft) to slide in this manner. ~*n.* **5.** an instance of sliding, esp. sideways. **6.** *Chiefly U.S.* one of the legs forming a skidway. **7.** a support on which heavy objects may be stored and moved short distances by sliding. **8.** a shoe or drag used to apply pressure to the metal rim of a wheel to act as a brake. [C17: perhaps of Scandinavian origin; compare SHIDE, SKI]

skid+lid ('skɪdˌlɪd) *n.* a slang word for **crash helmet.**

skid+pan ('skɪdˌpæn) *n. Chiefly Brit.* an area made slippery so that vehicle drivers can practise controlling skids.

skid+proof ('skɪdˌpru:f) *adj.* (of a road surface, tyre, etc.) preventing or resistant to skidding.

skid road *n. North American.* **1.** a track made of a set of logs laid transversely on which freshly cut timber can be hauled. **2. a.** (in W North America) the part of a town frequented by loggers. **b.** another term for **skid row.**

skid row (rəʊ) *or* **skid road** *n. Slang, chiefly U.S.* a dilapidated section of a city inhabited by vagrants, etc.

skid+way ('skɪdˌweɪ) *n. Chiefly U.S.* **1.** a platform on which logs ready for sawing are piled. **2.** a track made of logs for rolling objects along.

skied[1] (skaɪd) *vb.* the past tense or past participle of **sky.**

skied[2] (ski:d) *vb.* a past tense or past participle of **ski.**

Ski+en (*Norwegian* 'ʃe:ən) *n.* a port in S Norway, on the **Skien River:** one of the oldest towns in Norway; lumber industry. Pop.: 45 471 (1970).

skiff (skɪf) *n.* any of various small boats propelled by oars, sail, or motor. [C18: from French *esquif*, from Old Italian *schifo* a boat, of Germanic origin; related to Old High German *schif* SHIP]

skif+fle[1] ('skɪfᵊl) *n.* a style of popular music of the 1950s, played chiefly on guitars and improvised percussion instruments. [C20: of unknown origin]

skif+fle[2] ('skɪfᵊl) *n. Ulster dialect.* a drizzle: *a skiffle of rain.* [from Scottish *skiff*, from *skiff* to move lightly, probably changed from *skift*, from Old Norse *skipta* SHIFT]

ski+jor+ing (ski:'dʒɔ:rɪŋ) *n.* a sport in which a skier is pulled over snow or ice, usually by a horse. [Norwegian *skikjöring*, literally: ski-driving] —**ski+'jor+er** *n.*

ski jump *n.* **1.** a high ramp overhanging a slope from which skiers compete to make the longest jump. ~*vb.* **ski-jump. 2.** (*intr.*) to perform a ski jump. —**ski jum+per** *n.*

Skik+da ('skɪkdɑ:) *n.* a port in NE Algeria, on an inlet of the Mediterranean: founded by the French in 1838 on the site of a Roman city. Pop.: 88 000 (1966 est.). Former name: **Philippeville.**

skil+ful *or U.S.* **skill+ful** ('skɪlfʊl) *adj.* **1.** possessing or displaying accomplishment or skill. **2.** involving or requiring accomplishment or skill. —'**skil+ful+ly** *or U.S.* '**skill+ful+ly** *adv.* —'**skil+ful+ness** *or U.S.* '**skill+ful+ness** *n.*

ski lift *n.* a device for carrying skiers up a slope, usually consisting of seats suspended from a moving cable.

skill (skɪl) *n.* **1.** special ability in a task, sport, etc., esp. ability acquired by training. **2.** something, esp. a trade or technique, requiring special training or manual proficiency. **3.** *Obsolete.* understanding. [C12: from Old Norse *skil* distinction; related to Middle Low German *schēle*, Middle Dutch *geschil* difference] —'**skill-less** *or* '**skil+less** *adj.*

skilled (skɪld) *adj.* **1.** possessing or demonstrating accomplishment, skill, or special training. **2.** (*prenominal*) involving skill or special training: *a skilled job.*

skil+let ('skɪlɪt) *n.* **1.** *Chiefly U.S.* a small frying pan. **2.** *Chiefly Brit.* a saucepan. [C15: probably from *skele* bucket, of Scandinavian origin; related to Old Norse *skjōla* bucket]

skil+ling ('skɪlɪŋ) *n.* a former Scandinavian coin of low denomination. [C18: from Danish and Swedish; see SHILLING]

skil+li+on ('skɪlɪən) *n. Austral.* **a.** a part of a building having a lower, esp. sloping, roof; lean-to. **b.** (*as modifier*): *a skillion roof.* [C19: from English dialect *skilling* outhouse]

skil+ly ('skɪlɪ) *n. Chiefly Brit.* a thin soup or gruel.

skim (skɪm) *vb.* **skims, skim+ming, skimmed. 1.** (*tr.*) to remove floating material from the surface of (a liquid), as with a spoon: *to skim milk.* **2.** to glide smoothly or lightly over (a surface). **3.** (*tr.*) to throw (something) in a path over a surface, so as to bounce or ricochet: *to skim stones over water.* **4.** (when *intr.*, usually foll. by *through*) to read (a book) in a superficial or cursory manner. **5.** to cover (a liquid) with a thin layer or (of liquid) to become coated in this way, as with ice, scum, etc. ~*n.* **6.** the act or process of skimming. **7.** material skimmed off a liquid, esp. off milk. **8.** the liquid left after skimming. **9.** any thin layer covering a surface. [C15 *skimmen*, probably from *scumen* to skim; see SCUM]

skim+ble-scam+ble ('skɪmbᵊl'skæmbᵊl) *Archaic.* ~*adj.* **1.** rambling; confused. ~*n.* **2.** meaningless discourse. [C16: whimsical formation based on dialect *scamble* to struggle]

skim+mer ('skɪmə) *n.* **1.** a person or thing that skims. **2.** any of several mainly tropical coastal aquatic birds of the genus *Rynchops*, having long narrow wings and a bill with an elongated lower mandible for skimming food from the surface of the water: family *Rhychopidae*, order *Charadriiformes*. **3.** a flat perforated spoon used for skimming fat from liquids.

skim+mi+a ('skɪmɪə) *n.* any rutaceous shrub of the S and SE Asian genus *Skimmia*, grown for their ornamental red berries and evergreen foliage. [C18: New Latin from Japanese (*mijama-*) *skimmi*, a native name of the plant]

skim milk *n.* milk from which the cream has been removed. Also called: **skimmed milk.** Compare **whole milk.**

skim+mings ('skɪmɪŋz) *pl. n.* **1.** material that is skimmed off a liquid. **2.** the froth containing concentrated ore removed during a flotation process. **3.** slag, scum, or impurities removed from molten metals.

skim off *vb.* (*tr., adv.*) to take the best part of: *the teacher skimmed off the able pupils for his class.*

skimp (skɪmp) *vb.* **1.** to be extremely sparing or supply (someone) sparingly; stint. **2.** to perform (work, etc.) carelessly, hastily, or with inadequate materials. [C17: perhaps a combination of SCANT and SCRIMP]

skimp+y ('skɪmpɪ) *adj.* **skimp+i+er, skimp+i+est. 1.** made of too little material; scanty. **2.** excessively thrifty; mean; stingy. —'**skimp+i+ly** *adv.* —'**skimp+i+ness** *n.*

skin (skɪn) *n.* **1. a.** the tissue forming the outer covering of the vertebrate body: it consists of two layers (see **dermis, epidermis**), the outermost of which may be covered with hair, scales, feathers, etc. It is mainly protective and sensory in function. **b.** (*as modifier*): *a skin disease.* **2.** any similar covering in a plant or lower animal. **3.** any coating or film, such as one that forms on the surface of a liquid. **4.** unsplit leather made from the outer covering of various mammals, reptiles, etc. Compare **hide**[2] (sense 1). **5.** the outer covering of a fur-bearing animal, dressed and finished with the hair on. **6.** a container made from animal skin. **7.** the outer covering surface of a vessel, rocket, etc. **8.** a person's skin regarded as his life: *to save one's skin.* **9.** (*often pl.*) *Informal.* (in jazz or pop use) a drum. **10.** *Slang.* a cigarette paper used for rolling a cannabis cigarette. **11. by the skin of one's teeth.** by a narrow margin; only just. **12. get under one's skin.** *Informal.* to irritate. **13. jump out of one's skin.** to be very startled. **14. no skin off one's nose.** *Informal.* not a matter that affects one adversely. **15. thick** (*or* **thin**) **skin.** an insensitive (*or* sensitive) nature. ~*vb.* **skins, skin+ning, skinned. 16.** (*tr.*) to remove (the outer covering) from (fruit, etc.). **17.** (*tr.*) to scrape a small piece of skin from (a part of oneself) in falling, etc.: *he skinned his knee.* **18.** (often foll. by *over*) to cover (something) with skin or a skinlike substance or (of something) to become covered in this way. **19.** (*tr.*) *Slang.* to strip of money; swindle. [Old English *scinn*, from Old Norse *skinn*] —'**skin+less** *adj.* —'**skin+ˌlike** *adj.*

skin-deep *adj.* **1.** superficial; shallow. ~*adv.* **2.** superficially.

skin div+ing *n.* the sport or activity of underwater swimming using breathing apparatus. —'**skin-ˌdiv+er** *n.*

skin ef+fect *n.* the tendency of alternating current to concentrate in the surface layer of a conductor, esp. at high frequencies, thus increasing its effective resistance.

skin flick *n.* a film containing much nudity and explicit sex for sensational purposes.

skin+flint ('skɪnˌflɪnt) *n.* an ungenerous or niggardly person; miser. [C18: referring to a person so avaricious that he would skin (swindle) a flint] —'**skin+ˌflint+y** *adj.*

skin food *n.* a cosmetic cream for keeping the skin in good condition.

skin fric+tion *n.* the friction acting on a solid body when it is moving through a fluid.

skin+ful ('skɪnˌfʊl) *n., pl.* **+fuls.** *Slang.* sufficient alcoholic drink to make one drunk (esp. in the phrase **have a skinful**).

skin graft *n.* a piece of skin removed from one part of the body and surgically grafted at the site of a severe burn or similar injury.

skin+head ('skɪnˌhɛd) *n. Brit.* one of a gang of boys characterized by closely cropped hair and distinctive clothes.

skink (skɪŋk) *n.* any lizard of the family *Scincidae*, commonest in tropical Africa and Asia, having reduced limbs and an elongated body covered with smooth scales. [C16: from Latin *scincus* a lizard, from Greek *skinkos*]

skinned (skɪnd) *adj.* **1.** stripped of the skin. **2. a.** having a skin as specified. **b.** (*in combination*): *thick-skinned.* **3. keep one's eyes skinned** (*or* **peeled**). to watch carefully.

skin+ner ('skɪnə) *n.* a person who prepares or deals in animal skins.

Skin·ner ('skɪnə) *n.* **B(urrhus) F(rederic).** born 1904, U.S. behavioural psychologist. His "laws of learning", derived from experiments with animals, have been widely applied to education and behaviour therapy. See also **Skinner box, instrumental conditioning.**

Skin·ner box *n.* a device for studying the learning behaviour of animals, esp. rats, consisting of a box in which the animal can move a lever to obtain a reward, such as a food pellet, or a punishment, such as an electric shock. [C20: named after B. F. SKINNER]

skin+ny ('skɪnɪ) *adj.* **+ni+er, +ni+est. 1.** lacking in flesh; thin. **2.** consisting of or resembling skin. **—'skin+ni+ness** *n.*

skin·ny-dip *vb.* **-dips, -dip·ping, -dipped.** (*intr.*) to swim in the nude. **—skin+ny dip+ping** *n.*

skin-pop *Slang.* *~n.* **1.** the subcutaneous or intramuscular injection of a narcotic. *~vb.* **-pops, -pop·ping, -popped. 2.** (*intr.*) to take drugs in such a way.

skint (skɪnt) *adj.* (*usually postpositive*) *Brit. slang.* without money. [variant of *skinned,* past tense of SKIN]

skin test *n. Med.* any test to determine immunity to a disease or hypersensitivity by introducing a small amount of the test substance beneath the skin or rubbing it into a fresh scratch. See **scratch test.**

skin+tight ('skɪn'taɪt) *adj.* (of garments) fitting tightly over the body; clinging.

skip[1] (skɪp) *vb.* **skips, skip+ping, skipped. 1.** (when *intr.*, often foll. by *over, along, into,* etc.) to spring or move lightly, esp. to move by hopping from one foot to the other. **2.** (*intr.*) to jump over a skipping-rope. **3.** to cause (a stone, etc.) to bounce or skim over a surface or (of a stone) to move in this way. **4.** to omit (intervening matter), as in passing from one part or subject to another: *he skipped a chapter of the book.* **5.** (*intr.*; foll. by *through*) *Informal.* to read or deal with quickly or superficially: *he skipped through the accounts before dinner.* **6. skip it!** *Informal.* it doesn't matter! **7.** (*tr.*) *Informal.* to miss deliberately: *to skip school.* **8.** (*tr.*) *Informal, chiefly U.S.* to leave (a place) in haste or secrecy: *to skip town.* *~n.* **9.** a skipping movement or gait. **10.** the act of passing over or omitting. **11.** *Music, U.S.* another word for **leap** (sense 10). [C13: probably of Scandinavian origin; related to Old Norse *skopa* to take a run, obsolete Swedish *skuppa* to skip]

skip[2] (skɪp) *n., vb.* **skips, skip+ping, skipped.** *Informal.* short for **skipper**[1].

skip[3] (skɪp) *n.* **1.** a large open container for transporting building materials, etc. **2.** a cage used as a lift in mines, etc. [C19: variant of SKEP]

skip[4] (skɪp) *n.* a college servant, esp. of Trinity College, Dublin.

ski pants *pl. n.* trousers worn for skiing, usually of stretch material and kept taut by a strap under the foot.

skip dis+tance *n.* the shortest distance between a transmitter and a receiver that will permit reception of radio waves of a specified frequency by one reflection from the ionosphere.

skip+jack ('skɪp,dʒæk) *n., pl.* **+jack** *or* **+jacks. 1.** Also called: **skipjack tuna.** an important food fish, *Katsuwonus pelamis,* that has a striped abdomen and occurs in all tropical seas: family *Scombridae* (mackerels and tunas). **2. black skipjack.** a small spotted tuna, *Euthynnus yaito,* of Indo-Pacific seas. **3.** any of several other unrelated fishes, such as the alewife and bonito. **4.** *Nautical.* an American sloop used for oystering and as a yacht. **5.** another name for a **click beetle.**

ski+plane ('ski:,pleɪn) *n.* an aircraft fitted with skis to enable it to land on and take off from snow.

skip off *vb.* (*intr., adv.*) *Brit. informal.* to leave work, school, etc., early or without authorization.

skip+per[1] ('skɪpə) *n.* **1.** the captain of any vessel. **2.** the captain of an aircraft. **3.** a manager or leader, as of a sporting team. *~vb.* **4.** to act as skipper (of). [C14: from Middle Low German, Middle Dutch *schipper* shipper]

skip+per[2] ('skɪpə) *n.* **1.** a person or thing that skips. **2.** any small butterfly of the family *Hesperiidae,* having a hairy mothlike body and erratic darting flight. **3.** another name for the **saury** (a fish).

skip+pet ('skɪpɪt) *n.* a small round box for preserving a document or seal. [C14: perhaps from *skeppe* SKEP]

skip·ping-rope *n. Brit.* a cord, usually having handles at each end, that is held in the hands and swung round and down so that the holder or others can jump over it.

Skip+ton ('skɪptən) *n.* a market town in N England, in North Yorkshire: 11th-century castle. Pop.: 12 422 (1971).

skip zone *n.* a region surrounding a broadcasting station that cannot receive transmissions either directly or by reflection off the ionosphere.

skirl (skɜ:l) *vb.* **1.** *Northern Brit. dialect.* (esp. of a bagpipe) to emit a shrill sound. **2.** to play the bagpipes. *~n.* **3.** the sound of a bagpipe. [C14: probably of Scandinavian origin; see SHRILL]

skir+mish ('skɜ:mɪʃ) *n.* **1.** a minor short-lived military engagement. **2.** any brisk clash or encounter, usually of a minor nature. *~vb.* **3.** (*intr.*; often foll. by *with*) to engage in a skirmish. [C14: from Old French *eskirmir,* of Germanic origin; related to Old High German *skirmen* to defend] **—'skir+mish+er** *n.*

Ski+ros ('skirɔs) *n.* transliteration of the Modern Greek name for **Skyros.**

skirr (skɜ:) *vb.* **1.** (*intr.*; usually foll. by *off, away,* etc.) to move, run, or fly rapidly. **2.** (*tr.*) *Archaic or literary.* to move rapidly over (an area, etc.), esp. in order to find or apprehend. *~n.* **3.** a whirring or grating sound, as of the wings of birds in flight. [C16: variant of SCOUR[2]]

skir+ret ('skɪrɪt) *n.* an umbelliferous Old World plant, *Sium sisarum,* cultivated in parts of Europe for its edible tuberous roots. [C14 *skirwhite,* perhaps from obsolete *skir* bright (see SHEER[1]) + WHITE]

skirt (skɜ:t) *n.* **1.** a garment hanging from the waist, worn chiefly by women and girls. **2.** the part of a dress below the waist. **3.** Also called: **apron.** a frieze or circular flap, as round the base of a hovercraft. **4.** the flaps on a saddle that protect a rider's legs. **5.** *Brit.* a cut of beef from the flank. **6.** (*often pl.*) a margin or outlying area. **7. bit of skirt.** *Slang.* a girl or woman. *~vb.* **8.** (*tr.*) to form the edge of. **9.** (*tr.*) to provide with a border. **10.** (when *intr.*, foll. by *around, along,* etc.) to pass (by) or be situated (near) the outer edge of (an area, etc.). **11.** (*tr.*) to avoid (a difficulty, etc.): *he skirted the issue.* **12.** *Chiefly Austral.* to remove the trimmings or inferior wool from (a fleece). [C13: from Old Norse *skyrta* SHIRT] **—'skirt+ed** *adj.*

skirt+er ('skɜ:tə) *n. Austral.* a man who skirts fleeces. See **skirt** (sense 12).

skirt+ing ('skɜ:tɪŋ) *n.* **1.** a border, esp. of wood or tiles, fixed round the base of an interior wall to protect it from kicks, dirt, etc. **2.** material used or suitable for skirts.

skirt+ing board *n.* a skirting made of wood. U.S. names: **baseboard, mopboard.**

ski run *n.* a trail, slope, or course for skiing.

ski stick *or* **pole** *n.* a stick, usually with a metal point and a disc to prevent it from sinking into the snow, used by skiers to gain momentum and maintain balance.

skit (skɪt) *n.* **1.** a brief satirical theatrical sketch. **2.** a short satirical piece of writing. **3.** a trick or hoax. [C18: related to earlier verb *skit* to move rapidly, hence to score a satirical hit, probably of Scandinavian origin; related to Old Norse *skjóta* to shoot]

skite (skaɪt) *Austral. informal.* *~vb.* (*intr.*) **1.** to boast. *~n.* **2.** boastful talk. **3.** a person who boasts. [C19: from Scottish and northern English dialect; see SKATE[3]]

ski tow *n.* a device for pulling skiers uphill, usually a motor-driven rope grasped by the skier while riding on his skis.

skit+ter ('skɪtə) *vb.* **1.** (*intr.*; often foll. by *off*) to move or run rapidly or lightly; scamper. **2.** to skim or cause to skim lightly and rapidly, as across the surface of water. **3.** (*intr.*) *Angling.* to draw a bait lightly over the surface of water. [C19: probably from dialect *skite* to dash about; related to Old Norse *skjōta* to SHOOT]

skit+tish ('skɪtɪʃ) *adj.* **1.** playful, lively, or frivolous. **2.** difficult to handle or predict. **3.** *Now rare.* coy. [C15: probably of Scandinavian origin; compare Old Norse *skjōta* to SHOOT; see -ISH] **—'skit+tish+ly** *adv.* **—'skit+tish+ness** *n.*

skit+tle ('skɪtᵊl) *n.* **1.** a wooden or plastic pin, typically widest just above the base. **2.** (*pl., functioning as sing.*) Also called (esp. U.S.): **ninepins.** a bowling game in which players knock over as many skittles as possible by rolling a wooden ball at them. **3. beer and skittles.** *Slang.* an easy time; amusement. [C17: of obscure origin; perhaps related to Swedish, Danish *skyttel* shuttle]

skit+tle out *vb.* (*tr., adv.*) *Cricket.* to dismiss (batsmen) quickly.

skive[1] (skaɪv) *vb.* (*tr.*) to shave or remove the surface of (leather). [C19: from Old Norse *skifa;* related to English dialect *shive* a slice of bread]

skive[2] (skaɪv) *vb.* (when *intr.*, often foll. by *off*) *Brit. slang.* to evade (work or responsibility). [C20: of unknown origin]

skiv+er[1] ('skaɪvə) *n.* **1.** the tanned outer layer split from a skin. **2.** a person, tool, or machine used in skiving.

skiv+er[2] ('skaɪvə) *n. Brit. slang.* a person who persistently avoids work or responsibility.

skiv+vy ('skɪvɪ) *n., pl.* **+vies. 1.** *Chiefly Brit., often contemptuous.* a servant, esp. a female, who does menial work of all kinds; drudge. *~vb.* **+vies, +vy+ing, +vied. 2.** (*intr.*) *Brit.* to work as a skivvy. [C20: of unknown origin]

skoal (skəʊl) *interj.* good health! (a drinking toast). [C16: from Danish *skaal* bowl, from Old Norse *skal;* see SCALE[2]]

skok·i+aan ('skɔ:kɪ,ɑ:n) *n.* (in South Africa) a potent alcoholic beverage drunk by Black Africans in shebeens. [C20: from Afrikaans, of unknown origin]

skol+ly *or* **skol+lie** ('skɒlɪ) *n., pl.* **+lies.** *S. African.* a Coloured hooligan, usually one of a gang. [C20: of unknown origin]

Skop+je ('skɔ:pjɛ) *n.* a city in S Yugoslavia, capital of Macedonia, on the Vardar River: became capital of Serbia in 1346 and of Macedonia in 1945; suffered a severe earthquake in 1963. Pop.: 312 980 (1971). Serbo-Croatian name: **Skop+lje** ('skɔplje). Turkish name (1392–1913): **Üsküb.**

Skt, Skt., Skr, *or* **Skr.** *abbrev. for* Sanskrit.

sku·a ('skju:ə) *n.* any predatory aquatic gull-like bird, such as *Stercorarius parasiticus* (**arctic skua**), of the family *Stercorariidae,* order *Charadriiformes,* having a dark plumage and long tail. [C17: from New Latin, from Faeroese *skūgvur,* from Old Norse *skūfr*]

skul+dug+ger·y *or U.S.* **skull+dug+ger·y** (skʌl'dʌgərɪ) *n. Informal.* underhand dealing; trickery.

skulk (skʌlk) *vb.* (*intr.*) **1.** to move stealthily so as to avoid notice. **2.** to lie in hiding; lurk. **3.** to shirk duty or evade responsibilities; malinger. ~*n.* **4.** a person who skulks. **5.** *Obsolete.* a pack of foxes or other animals that creep about stealthily. [C13: of Scandinavian origin; compare Norwegian *skulka* to lurk, Swedish *skolka*, Danish *skulke* to shirk] —**'skulk·er** *n.*

skull (skʌl) *n.* **1.** the bony skeleton of the head of vertebrates. See **cranium. 2.** *Often derogatory.* the head regarded as the mind or intelligence: *to have a dense skull.* **3.** a picture of a skull used to represent death or danger. [C13: of Scandinavian origin; compare Old Norse *skoltr*, Norwegian *skult*, Swedish dialect *skulle*]

skull and cross·bones *n.* a picture of the human skull above two crossed thigh bones, formerly on the pirate flag, now used as a warning of danger or death.

skull·cap ('skʌlˌkæp) *n.* **1.** a rounded brimless hat fitting the crown of the head. **2.** the nontechnical name for **calvaria. 3.** any of various perennial plants of the genus *Scutellaria*, esp. *S. galericulata*, that typically have helmet-shaped flowers: family *Labiatae* (labiates).

skunk (skʌŋk) *n., pl.* **skunk** *or* **skunks. 1.** any of various American musteline mammals of the subfamily *Mephitinae*, esp. *Mephitis mephitis* (**striped skunk**), typically having a black and white coat and bushy tail: they eject an unpleasant-smelling fluid from the anal gland when attacked. **2.** *Informal.* a despicable person. ~*vb.* **3.** (*tr.*) *U.S. slang.* to defeat overwhelmingly in a game. [C17: from Algonquian; compare Abnaki *segākw* skunk]

skunk cab·bage *n.* **1.** a low-growing fetid aroid swamp plant, *Symplocarpus foetidus* of E North America, having broad leaves and minute flowers enclosed in a mottled greenish or purple spathe. **2.** a similar aroid plant, *Lysichitum americanum*, of the W coast of North America and N Asia. ~Also called: **skunk·weed.**

sky (skaɪ) *n., pl.* **skies. 1.** (*sometimes pl.*) the apparently dome-shaped expanse extending upwards from the horizon that is characteristically blue or grey during the day, red in the evening, and black at night. **2.** outer space, as seen from the earth. **3.** (*often pl.*) weather, as described by the appearance of the upper air: *sunny skies.* **4.** the source of divine power; heaven. **5.** *Informal.* the highest level of attainment: *the sky's the limit.* **6. to the skies.** highly; extravagantly. ~*vb.* **skies, sky·ing, skied. 7.** *Rowing.* to lift (the blade of an oar) too high before a stroke. **8.** (*tr.*) *Informal.* to hit (a ball) high in the air. [C13: from Old Norse *ský*; related to Old English *scio* cloud, Old Saxon *skio*, Old Norse *skjār* transparent skin] —**'sky·ˌlike** *adj.*

sky blue *n., adj.* **a.** a light or pale blue colour. **b.** (*as adj.*): *a sky-blue jumper.*

sky-blue pink *n., adj.* a jocular name for a nonexistent, unknown, or unimportant colour.

sky·dive ('skaɪˌdaɪv) *vb.* **·dives, ·div·ing, ·dived** *or U.S.* **·dove; ·dived.** (*intr.*) to take part in skydiving. —**'sky·ˌdiv·er** *n.*

sky·div·ing ('skaɪˌdaɪvɪŋ) *n.* the sport of parachute jumping, in which participants perform manoeuvres before opening the parachute and attempt to land accurately.

Skye (skaɪ) *n.* a mountainous island off the NW coast of Scotland, the largest island of the Inner Hebrides: tourist centre. Chief town: Portree. Pop.: 7372 (1971). Area: 1735 sq. km (670 sq. miles).

Skye ter·ri·er *n.* a short-legged breed of terrier with long wiry hair and erect ears.

sky-high *adj., adv.* **1.** at or to an unprecedented or excessive level: *prices rocketed sky-high.* ~*adv.* **2.** high into the air. **3. blow sky-high.** to destroy completely.

sky·jack ('skaɪˌdʒæk) *vb.* (*tr.*) to commandeer an aircraft, usually with a gun during flight, forcing the pilot to fly somewhere other than to its scheduled destination. [C20: from SKY + HIJACK] —**'sky·ˌjack·er** *n.*

Sky·lab ('skaɪˌlæb) *n.* a U.S. space station launched in May 1973 into an orbit inclined at 50° to the equatorial plane at a mean altitude of 430 kilometres (270 miles), the astronauts working there under conditions of zero gravity.

sky·lark ('skaɪˌlɑːk) *n.* **1.** an Old World lark, *Alauda arvensis*, noted for singing while hovering at a great height. ~*vb.* **2.** (*intr.*) *Informal.* to romp or play jokes. —**'sky·ˌlark·er** *n.*

sky·light ('skaɪˌlaɪt) *n.* a window placed in a roof or ceiling to admit daylight. Also called: **fanlight.**

sky·line ('skaɪˌlaɪn) *n.* **1.** the line at which the earth and sky appear to meet; horizon. **2.** the outline of buildings, mountains, trees, etc., seen against the sky.

sky mark·er *n.* a parachute flare dropped to mark a target area.

sky pi·lot *n. Slang.* a chaplain in one of the military services.

sky·rock·et ('skaɪˌrɒkɪt) *n.* **1.** another word for **rocket**[1] (sense 1). ~*vb.* **2.** (*intr.*) *Informal* to rise rapidly, as in price.

Sky·ros *or* **Scy·ros** ('skiːrɒs) *n.* a Greek island in the Aegean, the largest island in the N Sporades. Pop.: 2352 (1971). Area: 199 sq. km (77 sq. miles). Modern Greek name: **Skíros.**

sky·sail ('skaɪˌseɪl) *n. Nautical.* **1.** a square sail set above the royal on a square-rigger. **2.** a triangular sail set between the trucks of a racing schooner.

sky·scape ('skaɪˌskeɪp) *n.* a painting, drawing, photograph, etc., representing or depicting the sky.

sky·scrap·er ('skaɪˌskreɪpə) *n.* a very tall multistorey building.

sky·ward ('skaɪwəd) *adj.* **1.** directed or moving towards the sky. ~*adv.* **2.** Also: **skywards.** towards the sky.

sky wave *n.* a radio wave reflected back to the earth by the ionosphere (**ionospheric wave**) or by a communications satellite, permitting transmission around the curved surface of the earth. Compare **ground wave.**

sky·writ·ing ('skaɪˌraɪtɪŋ) *n.* **1.** the forming of words in the sky by the release of smoke or vapour from an aircraft. **2.** the words so formed. —**'sky·ˌwrit·er** *n.*

s.l. *Bibliog. abbrev. for* sine loco. [Latin: without place (of publication)]

S.L. *abbrev. for* Solicitor at Law.

slab (slæb) *n.* **1.** a broad flat thick piece of wood, stone, or other material. **2.** a thick slice of cake, etc. **3.** any of the outside parts of a log that are sawn off while the log is being made into planks. **4.** a printer's ink table. **5.** (*modifier*) *Austral.* made or constructed of coarse wooden planks: *a slab hut.* **6.** *Informal, chiefly Brit.* an operating or mortuary table. ~*vb.* **slabs, slab·bing, slabbed.** (*tr.*) **7.** to cut or make into a slab or slabs. **8.** to cover or lay with slabs. **9.** to saw slabs from (a log). [C13: of unknown origin]

slab·ber ('slæbə) *vb., n.* a dialect word for **slobber.** [C16: variant of SLOBBER]

slack[1] (slæk) *adj.* **1.** not tight, tense, or taut. **2.** negligent or careless. **3.** (esp. of water, etc.) moving slowly. **4.** (of trade, etc.) not busy. **5.** *Phonetics.* another term for **lax** (sense 4). ~*adv.* **6.** in a slack manner. ~*n.* **7.** a part of a rope, etc., that is slack: *take in the slack.* **8.** a period of decreased activity. **9. a.** a patch of water without current. **b.** a slackening of a current. **10.** *Prosody.* (in sprung rhythm) the unstressed syllable or syllables. ~*vb.* **11.** to neglect (one's duty, etc.). **12.** (often foll. by *off*) to loosen; to make slack. **13.** *Chem.* a less common word for **slake** (sense 3). [Old English *slæc, sleac;* related to Old High German *slah*, Old Norse *slākr* bad, Latin *laxus* LAX] —**'slack·ly** *adv.* —**'slack·ness** *n.*

slack[2] (slæk) *n.* small pieces of coal with a high ash content. [C15: probably from Middle Low German *slecke;* related to Dutch *slak*, German *Schlacke* dross]

slack[3] (slæk) *n. Northern Brit. dialect.* **1.** a small valley or depression. **2.** a boggy hollow. [C14 (Scottish and northern English): from Old Norse *slakki*, of obscure origin]

slack·en ('slækən) *vb.* (often foll. by *off*) **1.** to make or become looser. **2.** to make or become slower, less intense, etc.

slack·er ('slækə) *n.* a person who evades work or duty; shirker.

slacks (slæks) *pl. n.* informal trousers worn by both sexes.

slack suit *n. U.S.* casual male dress consisting of slacks and a matching shirt or jacket.

slack wa·ter *n.* the period of still water around the turn of the tide, esp. at low tide.

SLADE (sleɪd) *n.* (in Britain) *acronym for* Society of Lithographic Artists, Designers, Engravers, and Process Workers (a trade union).

slag (slæg) *n.* **1.** Also called: **cinder.** the fused material formed during the smelting or refining of metals by combining the flux with gangue, impurities in the metal, etc. It usually consists of a mixture of silicates with calcium, phosphorus, sulphur, etc. See also **basic slag. 2.** the mass of rough fragments of rock derived from volcanic lava; scoria. **3.** a mixture of shale, clay, coal dust, and other mineral waste produced during coal-mining. **4.** *Brit. slang.* a coarse or dissipated girl or woman. ~*vb.* **slags, slag·ging, slagged. 5.** to convert into or become slag. **6.** *Austral. slang.* to spit. [C16: from Middle Low German *slagge*, perhaps from *slagen* to SLAY] —**'slag·gy** *adj.*

slag down *vb.* (*tr., adv.*) *Prison slang.* to give a verbal lashing to.

slag heap *n.* a hillock of waste matter from coal-mining, etc.

slain (sleɪn) *vb.* the past participle of **slay.**

slàinte-mhath (ˌslɑːndʒə'vɑː) *or* **slàinte** *interj. Chiefly Scot.* a drinking toast; cheers. [Scots Gaelic: good health]

slais·ter ('sleɪstə) *n. Scot. and northern Brit. dialect.* a confused mess. [C18: of obscure origin]

slake (sleɪk) *vb.* **1.** (*tr.*) *Literary.* to satisfy (thirst, desire, etc.). **2.** (*tr.*) *Poetic.* to cool or refresh. **3.** Also: **slack.** to undergo or cause to undergo the process in which lime reacts with water or moist air to produce calcium hydroxide. **4.** *Archaic.* to make or become less active or intense. [Old English *slacian*, from *slæc* SLACK[1]; related to Dutch *slaken* to diminish, Icelandic *slaka*] —**'slak·a·ble** *or* **'slake·a·ble** *adj.* —**'slak·er** *n.*

slaked lime *n.* another name for **calcium hydroxide,** esp. when made by adding water to calcium oxide.

sla·lom ('slɑːləm) *n.* **1.** *Skiing, skateboarding, etc.* a race, esp. one downhill, over a winding course marked by artificial obstacles. ~*vb.* **2.** (*intr.*) to take part in a slalom. [Norwegian, from *slad* sloping + *lom* path]

slam[1] (slæm) *vb.* **slams, slam·ming, slammed. 1.** to cause (a door or window) to close noisily and with force or (of a door, etc.) to close in this way. **2.** (*tr.*) to throw (something) down noisily and violently. **3.** (*tr.*) *Slang.* to criticize harshly. **4.** (*intr.;* usually foll. by *into* or *out of*) *Informal.* to go (into or out of a room, etc.) in violent haste or anger. **5.** (*tr.*) to strike with violent force. **6.** (*tr.*) *Informal.* to defeat easily. ~*n.* **7.** the act or noise of slamming. **8.** *Slang.* harsh criticism or abuse. [C17: of Scandinavian origin; compare Old Norse *slamra*, Norwegian *slemma*, Swedish dialect *slämma*]

slam[2] (slæm) *n.* **1. a.** the winning of all (**grand slam**) or all but one (**little** or **small slam**) of the 13 tricks at bridge or whist. **b.** the bid to do so in bridge. **2.** an old card game. [C17: of uncertain origin]

slam-bang *adv.* **1.** another word (esp. U.S.) for **slap-bang. 2.** *U.S. informal.* carelessly; recklessly.

slan·der ('slɑːndə) *n.* **1.** *Law.* **a.** defamation in some transient form, as by spoken words, gestures, etc. **b.** a slanderous statement, etc. **2.** any false or defamatory words spoken about a person; calumny. *~vb.* **3.** to utter or circulate slander (about). [C13: via Anglo-French from Old French *escandle*, from Late Latin *scandalum* a cause of offence; see SCANDAL] —**'slan+der+er** *n.* —**'slan+der+ous** *adj.* —**'slan+der+ous+ly** *adv.* —**'slan+der+ous+ness** *n.*

slang (slæŋ) *n.* **1. a.** vocabulary, idiom, etc., that is not appropriate to the standard form of a language or to formal contexts, may be restricted as to social status or distribution, and is characteristically more metaphorical and transitory than standard language. **b.** (*as modifier*): *a slang word.* **2.** another word for **jargon.** *~vb.* **3.** to abuse (someone) with vituperative language; insult. [C18: of unknown origin] —**'slang·y** *adj.* —**'slang·i·ly** *adv.* —**'slang·i+ness** *n.*

slang+ing match *n. Brit.* a dispute in which insults and accusations are made by each party against the other.

slant (slɑːnt) *vb.* **1.** to incline or be inclined at an oblique or sloping angle. **2.** to write or present (news, etc.) with a bias. **3.** (*intr.*; foll. by *towards*) (of a person's opinions) to be biased. *~n.* **4.** an inclined or oblique line or direction; slope. **5.** a way of looking at something. **6.** a bias or opinion, as in an article. **7.** a less technical name for **solidus. 8. on a** (*or* **the**) **slant.** sloping. *~adj.* **9.** oblique, sloping. [C17: short for ASLANT, probably of Scandinavian origin] —**'slant+ing** *adj.* —**'slant+ing+ly** *or* **'slant+ly** *adv.*

slant rhyme *n. Prosody.* another term for **half-rhyme.**

slant+wise ('slɑːntˌwaɪz) *or* **slant+ways** ('slɑːntˌweɪz) *adv., adj.* (*prenominal*) in a slanting or oblique direction.

slap (slæp) *n.* **1.** a sharp blow or smack, as with the open hand, something flat, etc. **2.** the sound made by or as if by such a blow. **3.** a sharp rebuke; reprimand. **4. (a bit of) slap and tickle.** *Brit. informal.* sexual play. **5. a slap in the face.** an insult or rebuff. **6. a slap on the back.** congratulation. *~vb.* **slaps, slap+ping, slapped. 7.** (*tr.*) to strike (a person or thing) sharply, as with the open hand or something flat. **8.** (*tr.*) to bring down (the hand, something flat, etc.) sharply. **9.** (when *intr.*, usually foll. by *against*) to strike (something) with or as if with a slap. **10.** (*tr.*) *Informal, chiefly Brit.* to apply in large quantities, haphazardly, etc.: *she slapped butter on the bread.* **11. slap on the back.** to congratulate. *~adv. Informal.* **12.** exactly; directly: *slap on time.* **13.** forcibly or abruptly: *to fall slap on the floor.* [C17: from Low German *slapp*, German *Schlappe*, of imitative origin] —**'slap+per** *n.*

slap-bang *adv. Informal, chiefly Brit.* **1.** in a violent, sudden, or noisy manner. U.S. equivalent: **slam-bang. 2.** directly or immediately: *slap-bang in the middle.*

slap+dash ('slæpˌdæʃ) *adv., adj.* **1.** in a careless, hasty, or haphazard manner. *~n.* **2.** slapdash activity or work. **3.** another name for **roughcast** (sense 1).

slap down *vb.* (*tr., adv.*) *Informal.* to rebuke sharply, as for impertinence.

slap+hap·py ('slæpˌhæpɪ) *adj.* **·pi·er, ·pi·est.** *Informal.* **1.** cheerfully irresponsible or careless. **2.** dazed or giddy from or as if from repeated blows; punch-drunk.

slap+jack ('slæpˌdʒæk) *n.* **1.** a simple card game. **2.** *U.S.* another word for **pancake.**

slap+shot ('slæpˌʃɒt) *n. Ice hockey.* a fast shot impelled by a short but powerful swing of the stick.

slap+stick ('slæpˌstɪk) *n.* **1. a.** comedy characterized by horseplay and physical action. **b.** (*as modifier*): *slapstick humour.* **2.** a flexible pair of paddles bound together at one end, formerly used in pantomime to strike a blow to a person with a loud clapping sound but without injury.

slap-up *adj.* (*prenominal*) *Brit. informal.* (esp. of meals) lavish; excellent; first-class.

slash (slæʃ) *vb.* (*tr.*) **1.** to cut or lay about (a person or thing) with sharp sweeping strokes, as with a sword, knife, etc. **2.** to lash with a whip. **3.** to make large gashes in: *to slash tyres.* **4.** to reduce (prices, etc.) drastically. **5.** *Chiefly U.S.* to criticize harshly. **6.** to slit (the outer fabric of a garment) so that the lining material is revealed. *~n.* **7.** a sharp, sweeping stroke, as with a sword or whip. **8.** a cut or rent made by such a stroke. **9.** a decorative slit in a garment revealing the lining material. **10.** *North American.* **a.** littered wood chips and broken branches that remain after trees have been cut down. **b.** an area so littered. **11.** another name for **solidus. 12.** *Brit. slang.* the act of urinating (esp. in the phrase **have a slash**). [C14 *slaschen*, perhaps from Old French *esclachier* to break] —**'slash+er** *n.*

slash+ing ('slæʃɪŋ) *adj.* aggressively or harshly critical (esp. in the phrase **slashing attack**). —**'slash+ing+ly** *adv.*

slash pock+et *n.* a pocket in which the opening is a slit in the seam of a garment.

Śląsk (ʃlɔ̃sk) *n.* the Polish name for **Silesia.**

slat[1] (slæt) *n.* **1.** a narrow thin strip of wood or metal, as used in a Venetian blind, etc. **2.** a movable or fixed auxiliary aerofoil attached to the leading edge of an aircraft wing to increase lift, esp. during landing and takeoff. *~vb.* **slats, slat+ting, slat+ted. 3.** (*tr.*) to provide with slats. [C14: from Old French *esclat* splinter, from *esclater* to shatter]

slat[2] (slæt) *Dialect, chiefly northern Brit.* *~vb.* **slats, slat+ting, slat+ted. 1.** to throw violently; fling carelessly. **2.** to flap violently. *~n.* **3.** a sudden blow. [C13: of Scandinavian origin; related to Old Norse, Icelandic *sletta* to slap]

slate[1] (sleɪt) *n.* **1. a.** a smooth fine-grained metamorphic rock that can be split into thin layers and is used as a roofing and paving material. **b.** (*as modifier*): *a slate tile.* **2.** a roofing tile of slate. **3.** (formerly) a writing tablet of slate. **4.** a dark grey colour, often with a purplish or bluish tinge. **5.** *U.S.* a list of candidates in an election. **6. clean slate.** a record without dishonour. **7. on the slate.** *Brit. informal.* on credit. **8. wipe the slate clean.** *Informal.* to make a fresh start, esp. by forgetting past differences. *~vb.* (*tr.*) **9.** to cover (a roof) with slates. **10.** *Chiefly U.S.* to enter (a person's name) on a list, esp. on a political slate. **11.** *U.S.* to choose or destine: *he was slated to go far.* *~adj.* **12.** of the colour slate. [C14: from Old French *esclate*, from *esclat* a fragment; see SLAT[1]]

slate[2] (sleɪt) *vb.* (*tr.*) *Informal, chiefly Brit.* **1.** to criticize harshly; censure. **2.** to punish or defeat severely. [C19: probably from SLATE[1]]

slat+er ('sleɪtə) *n.* **1.** a person trained in laying roof slates. **2.** *Austral.* an informal name for **woodlouse.**

slath+er ('slɑːðə) *n.* **1.** (*usually pl.*) *Informal.* a large quantity. **2. open slather.** *Austral. and N.Z. slang.* a situation in which there are no restrictions; free-for-all. *~vb.* (*tr.*) *U.S. slang.* **3.** to squander or waste. **4.** to spread thickly or lavishly. [C19: of unknown origin]

slat+ing[1] ('sleɪtɪŋ) *n.* **1.** the act or process of laying slates. **2.** slates collectively, or material for making slates.

slat+ing[2] ('sleɪtɪŋ) *n. Informal, chiefly Brit.* a severe reprimand or critical attack.

slat+tern ('slætən) *n.* a slovenly woman or girl; slut. [C17: probably from *slattering*, from dialect *slatter* to slop; perhaps from Scandinavian; compare Old Norse *sletta* to slap] —**'slat+tern+ly** *adj.* —**'slat+tern+li+ness** *n.*

slat·y ('sleɪtɪ) *adj.* **slat·i·er, slat·i·est. 1.** consisting of or resembling slate. **2.** having the colour of slate. —**'slat·i+ness** *n.*

slaugh+ter ('slɔːtə) *n.* **1.** the killing of animals, esp. for food. **2.** the savage killing of a person. **3.** the indiscriminate or brutal killing of large numbers of people, as in war; massacre. **4.** *Informal.* a resounding defeat. *~vb.* (*tr.*) **5.** to kill (animals), esp. for food. **6.** to kill in a brutal manner. **7.** to kill indiscriminately or in large numbers. **8.** *Informal.* to defeat resoundingly. [Old English *sleaht*; related to Old Norse *slāttr* hammering, *slātr* butchered meat, Old High German *slahta*, Gothic *slauhts*, German *Schlacht* battle] —**'slaugh+ter+er** *n.* —**'slaugh+ter+ous** *adj.*

slaugh·ter+house ('slɔːtəˌhaʊs) *n.* a place where animals are butchered for food; abattoir.

slaugh·ter+man ('slɔːtəˌmæn) *n., pl.* **+men.** a person employed to kill animals in a slaughterhouse.

Slav (slɑːv) *n.* a member of any of the peoples of E Europe or Soviet Asia who speak a Slavonic language. [C14: from Medieval Latin *Sclāvus* a captive Slav; see SLAVE]

Slav. *abbrev. for* Slavonic *or* Slavic.

slave (sleɪv) *n.* **1.** a person legally owned by another and having no freedom of action or right to property. **2.** a person who is forced to work for another against his will. **3.** a person under the domination of another person or some habit or influence: *a slave to television.* **4.** a person who works in harsh conditions for low pay. **5. a.** a device that is controlled by or that duplicates the action of another similar device (the master device). **b.** (*as modifier*): *slave cylinder.* *~vb.* **6.** (*intr.*) to work like a slave. **7.** an archaic word for **enslave.** [C13: via Old French from Medieval Latin *Sclāvus* a Slav, one held in bondage (from the fact that the Slavonic races were frequently conquered in the Middle Ages), from Late Greek *Sklabos* a Slav]

slave ant *n.* any of various ants, esp. *Formica fusca*, captured and forced to do the work of a colony of ants of another species (**slave-making ants**). See also **Amazon ant.**

Slave Coast *n.* the coast of W Africa between the Volta River and Mount Cameroon, chiefly along the Bight of Benin: the main source of African slaves (16th–19th centuries).

slave cyl+in+der *n.* a small cylinder containing a piston that operates the brake shoes or pads in hydraulic brakes or the working part in any other hydraulically operated system. Compare **master cylinder.**

slave-driv·er *n.* **1.** (esp. formerly) a person forcing slaves to work. **2.** an employer who demands excessively hard work from his employees.

slave+hold·er ('sleɪvˌhəʊldə) *n.* a person who owns slaves. —**'slave+ˌhold·ing** *n.*

slav+er[1] ('sleɪvə) *n.* **1.** an owner of or dealer in slaves. **2.** another name for **slave ship.**

slav+er[2] ('slævə) *vb.* (*intr.*) **1.** to dribble saliva. **2.** (often foll. by *over*) **a.** to fawn or drool (over someone). **b.** to show great desire (for); lust (after). *~n.* **3.** saliva dribbling from the mouth. **4.** *Informal.* drivel. [C14: probably of Low Dutch origin; related to SLOBBER] —**'slav+er+er** *n.*

Slave Riv+er *n.* a river in W Canada, in the Northwest Territories and NE Alberta, flowing from Lake Athabaska northwest to Great Slave Lake. Length: about 420 km (260 miles). Also called: **Great Slave River.**

slav+er·y ('sleɪvərɪ) *n.* **1.** the state or condition of being a slave; a civil relationship whereby one person has absolute power over another and controls his life, liberty, and fortune. **2.** the subjection of a person to another person, esp. in being forced into work. **3.** the condition of being subject to some influence or habit. **4.** work done in harsh conditions for low pay.

slave ship *n.* a ship used to transport slaves, esp. formerly from Africa to the New World.

Slave State *n. U.S. history.* any of the 15 Southern states in which slavery was legal until the Civil War.

slave trade *n.* the business of trading in slaves, esp. the transportation of Black Africans to America from the 16th to 19th centuries. —**'slave-ˌtrad·er** *n.* —**'slave-ˌtrad·ing** *n.*

slav+ey ('sleɪvɪ) *n. Brit. informal.* a female servant.

Slav+ic ('slɑːvɪk) *n., adj.* another word for **Slavonic.**
slav+ish ('sleɪvɪʃ) *adj.* **1.** of or befitting a slave. **2.** being or resembling a slave; servile. **3.** unoriginal; imitative. **4.** *Archaic.* ignoble. —'**slav+ish+ly** *adv.* —'**slav+ish+ness** *n.*
Slav+ism ('slɑːvɪzəm) *n.* anything characteristic of, peculiar to, or associated with the Slavs or the Slavonic languages.
Slav+kov ('slafkɔf) *n.* the Czech name for **Austerlitz.**
slav+oc+ra+cy (sleɪ'vɒkrəsɪ) *n., pl.* **+cies.** (esp. in the U.S. before the Civil War) **1.** slaveholders as a dominant class. **2.** domination by slaveholders.
Sla+vo+ni+a (slə'vəʊnɪə) *n.* a region of N Yugoslavia, in Croatia, mainly between the Drava and Sava Rivers. —**Sla+'vo+ni+an** *adj., n.*
Sla+von+ic (slə'vɒnɪk) *or* **Slav+ic** *n.* **1.** a branch of the Indo-European family of languages, usually divided into three subbranches: **South Slavonic** (including Old Church Slavonic, Serbo-Croatian, Bulgarian, etc.), **East Slavonic** (including Ukrainian, Russian, etc.), and **West Slavonic** (including Polish, Czech, Slovak, etc.). **2.** the unrecorded ancient language from which all of these languages developed. *~adj.* **3.** of, denoting, or relating to this group of languages. **4.** of, denoting, or relating to the people who speak these languages. —**Sla+'von+i+cal+ly** *adv.*
Slav·o·phile *or* **Slav·o·phil** ('slɑːvəʊˌfɪl) *n.* **1.** a person who admires the Slavs or their cultures. **2.** (*sometimes not cap.*) (in 19th-century Russia) a person who believed in the superiority and advocated the supremacy of the Slavs. *~adj.* **3.** admiring the Slavs and Slavonic culture, etc. **4.** (*sometimes not cap.*) (in 19th-century Russia) of, characteristic of, or relating to the Slavophiles. —**Sla+voph·i+lism** (slə'vɒfɪˌlɪzəm, 'slɑːvəʊfɪˌlɪzəm) *n.*
slaw (slɔː) *n. Chiefly U.S.* short for **coleslaw.** [C19: from Danish *sla*, short for *salade* SALAD]
slay (sleɪ) *vb.* **slays, slay+ing, slew, slain.** (*tr.*) **1.** *Archaic or literary.* to kill, esp. violently. **2.** *Informal.* to impress (someone of the opposite sex). **3.** *Obsolete.* to strike. [Old English *slēan*; related to Old Norse *slā*, Gothic, Old High German *slahan* to strike, Old Irish *slacaim* I beat] —'**slay+er** *n.*
S.L.B.M. *abbrev. for* submarine-launched ballistic missile.
sld. *abbrev. for:* **1.** sailed. **2.** sealed.
sleave (sliːv) *n.* **1.** a tangled thread. **2.** a thin filament unravelled from a thicker thread. **3.** *Chiefly poetic.* anything matted or complicated. *~vb.* **4.** to disentangle (twisted thread, etc.). [Old English *slǣfan* to divide; related to Middle Low German *slēf*, Norwegian *sleiv* big spoon]
slea+zy ('sliːzɪ) *adj.* **+zi+er, +zi+est. 1.** sordid; disreputable: *a sleazy nightclub.* **2.** thin or flimsy, as cloth. [C17: origin uncertain] —'**slea+zi+ly** *adv.* —'**slea+zi+ness** *n.*
sledge[1] (slɛdʒ) *or* (*esp. U.S.*) **sled** (slɛd) *n.* **1.** Also called: **sleigh.** a vehicle mounted on runners, drawn by horses or dogs, for transporting people or goods, esp. over snow. **2.** a light wooden frame used, esp. by children, for sliding over snow; toboggan. *~vb.* **3.** to convey or travel by sledge. [C17: from Middle Dutch *sleedse*; C14 *sled*, from Middle Low German, from Old Norse *slethi*, related to SLIDE]
sledge[2] (slɛdʒ) *n.* short for **sledgehammer.**
sledge+ham·mer ('slɛdʒˌhæmə) *n.* **1.** a large heavy hammer with a long handle used with both hands for heavy work such as forging iron, breaking rocks, etc. **2.** (*modifier*) resembling the action of a sledgehammer in power, ruthlessness, etc.: *a sledgehammer blow.* *~vb.* **3.** (*tr.*) to strike (something) with or as if with a sledgehammer. [C15: *sledge*, from Old English *slecg* a large hammer; related to Old Norse *sleggja*, Middle Dutch *slegge*]
sleek (sliːk) *adj.* **1.** smooth and shiny; polished. **2.** polished in speech or behaviour; unctuous. **3.** (of an animal or bird) having a shiny healthy coat or feathers. **4.** (of a person) having a prosperous appearance. *~vb.* (*tr.*) **5.** to make smooth and glossy, as by grooming, etc. **6.** (usually foll. by *over*) to cover (up), as by making more agreeable; gloss (over). [C16: variant of SLICK] —'**sleek+ly** *adv.* —'**sleek+ness** *n.* —'**sleek·y** *adj.*
sleek+it ('sliːkɪt) *adj. Scot.* deceitful; crafty; sly. [Scottish, from past participle of SLEEK]
sleep (sliːp) *n.* **1.** a periodic state of physiological rest during which consciousness is suspended and metabolic rate is decreased. **2.** *Botany.* the nontechnical name for **nyctitropism.** **3.** a period spent sleeping. **4.** a state of quiescence or dormancy. **5.** a poetic or euphemistic word for **death.** **6.** *Informal.* the dried mucoid particles often found in the corners of the eyes after sleeping. *~vb.* **sleeps, sleep+ing, slept. 7.** (*intr.*) to be in or as in the state of sleep. **8.** (*intr.*) (of plants) to show nyctitropism. **9.** (*intr.*) to be inactive or quiescent. **10.** (*tr.*) to have sleeping accommodation for (a certain number): *the boat could sleep six.* **11.** (*tr.*; foll. by *away*) to pass (time) sleeping. **12.** (*intr.*) to fail to pay attention. **13.** (*intr.*) *Poetic or euphemistic.* to be dead. **14. sleep on it.** to give (something) extended consideration, esp. overnight. *~*See also **sleep around, sleep in, sleep off, sleep out, sleep with.** [Old English *slǣpan*; related to Old Frisian *slēpa*, Old Saxon *slāpan*, Old High German *slāfan*, German *schlaff* limp]
sleep a·round *vb.* (*intr., adv.*) *Informal.* to be sexually promiscuous.
sleep+er ('sliːpə) *n.* **1.** a person, animal, or thing that sleeps. **2.** a railway sleeping car or compartment. **3.** *Brit.* one of the blocks supporting the rails on a railway track. U.S. equivalent: **tie.** **4.** a heavy timber beam, esp. one that is laid horizontally on the ground. **5.** *Chiefly Brit.* a small plain gold circle worn in a pierced ear lobe to prevent the hole from closing up. **6.** a wrestling hold in which a wrestler presses the sides of his opponent's neck, causing him to pass out. **7.** *U.S.* an unbranded calf. **8.** Also called: **sleeper goby.** any gobioid fish of the family *Eleotridae*, of brackish or fresh tropical waters, resembling the gobies but lacking a ventral sucker. **9.** *Informal, chiefly U.S.* a person or thing that achieves unexpected success. **10.** a spy planted in advance for future use, but not currently active.
sleep in *vb.* (*intr., adv.*) **1.** *Brit.* to sleep longer than usual. **2.** to sleep at the place of one's employment.
sleep+ing bag *n.* a large well-padded bag designed for sleeping in, esp. outdoors.
sleep+ing car *n.* a railway car fitted with compartments containing bunks for people to sleep in.
sleep+ing draught *n.* any drink containing a drug or agent that induces sleep.
sleep+ing part+ner *n.* a partner in a business who does not play an active role, esp. one who supplies capital.
sleep+ing pill *n.* a pill or tablet containing a sedative drug, such as a barbiturate, used to induce sleep.
sleep+ing po·lice+man *n.* a bump built across roads, esp. in housing estates, to deter motorists from speeding.
sleep+ing sick+ness *n.* **1.** Also called: **African sleeping sickness.** an African disease caused by infection with protozoans of the genus *Trypanosoma*, characterized by fever, wasting, and sluggishness. **2.** an epidemic viral form of encephalitis characterized by extreme drowsiness. Technical name: **encephalitis lethargica.**
sleep+less ('sliːplɪs) *adj.* **1.** without sleep or rest: *a sleepless journey.* **2.** unable to sleep. **3.** always watchful or alert. **4.** *Chiefly poetic.* always active or moving: *the sleepless tides.* —'**sleep+less+ly** *adv.* —'**sleep+less+ness** *n.*
sleep move+ment *n.* the folding together of leaflets, petals, etc., that occurs at night in certain plants.
sleep off *vb.* (*tr., adv.*) *Informal.* to lose by sleeping: *to sleep off a hangover.*
sleep out *vb.* (*intr., adv.*) **1.** (esp. of a tramp) to sleep in the open air. **2.** to sleep away from the place of work. *~n.* **sleep-out. 3.** *Austral.* an area of a verandah that has been glassed in or partitioned off so that it may be used as a bedroom.
sleep+walk ('sliːpˌwɔːk) *vb.* (*intr.*) to walk while asleep. See also **somnambulism.** —'**sleep+ˌwalk+er** *n.* —'**sleep+ˌwalk+ing** *n., adj.*
sleep with *vb.* (*intr., prep.*) to have sexual intercourse and (usually) spend the night with. Also: **sleep together.**
sleep·y ('sliːpɪ) *adj.* **sleep·i+er, sleep·i+est. 1.** inclined to or needing sleep; drowsy. **2.** characterized by or exhibiting drowsiness, sluggishness, etc. **3.** conducive to sleep; soporific. **4.** without activity or bustle: *a sleepy town.* —'**sleep·i+ly** *adv.* —'**sleep·i+ness** *n.*
sleep·y+head ('sliːpɪˌhɛd) *n. Informal.* a sleepy or lazy person. —'**sleep·y+ˌhead+ed** *adj.*
sleet (sliːt) *n.* **1.** partly melted falling snow or hail or (esp. U.S.) partly frozen rain. **2.** *Chiefly U.S.* the thin coat of ice that forms when sleet or rain freezes on cold surfaces. *~vb.* **3.** (*intr.*) to fall as sleet. [C13: from Germanic; compare Middle Low German *slōten* hail, Middle High German *slōze*, German *Schlossen* hail stones] —'**sleet·y** *adj.*
sleeve (sliːv) *n.* **1.** the part of a garment covering the arm. **2.** a tubular piece that is forced or shrunk into a cylindrical bore to reduce the diameter of the bore or to line it with a different material; liner. **3.** a tube fitted externally over two cylindrical parts in order to join them; bush. **4.** a wrapping for a gramophone record. **5.** (**have a few tricks**) **up one's sleeve.** (to have options, etc.) secretly ready. *~vb.* **6.** (*tr.*) to provide with a sleeve or sleeves. [Old English *slīf*, *slēf*; related to Dutch *sloof* apron] —'**sleeve+less** *adj.* —'**sleeve+ˌlike** *adj.*
sleeve board *n.* a small ironing board for pressing sleeves, fitted onto an ironing board or table.
sleev+ing ('sliːvɪŋ) *n. Electronics, chiefly Brit.* tubular flexible insulation into which bare wire can be inserted. U.S. name: **spaghetti.**
sleigh (sleɪ) *n.* **1.** another name for **sledge** (sense 1). *~vb.* **2.** (*intr.*) to travel by sleigh. [C18: from Dutch *slee*, variant of *slede* SLEDGE[1]] —'**sleigh+er** *n.*
sleight (slaɪt) *n. Archaic.* **1.** skill; dexterity. See also **sleight of hand.** **2.** a trick or stratagem. **3.** cunning; trickery. [C14: from Old Norse *slægth*, from *slægr* SLY]
sleight of hand *n.* **1.** manual dexterity used in performing conjuring tricks. **2.** the performance of such tricks.
slen+der ('slɛndə) *adj.* **1.** of small width relative to length or height. **2.** (esp. of a person's figure) slim and well-formed. **3.** small or inadequate in amount, size, etc.: *slender resources.* **4.** (of hopes, etc.) having little foundation; feeble. **5.** very small: *a slender margin.* **6.** (of a sound) lacking volume. **7.** *Phonetics.* (now only in Irish phonology) relating to or denoting a close front vowel, such as *i* or *e*. [C14 *slendre*, of unknown origin] —'**slen+der+ly** *adv.* —'**slen+der+ness** *n.*
slen+der+ize *or* **slen+der+ise** ('slɛndəˌraɪz) *vb. Chiefly U.S.* to make or become slender.
slept (slɛpt) *vb.* the past tense or past participle of **sleep.**
Sles+vig ('sleːsvi) *n.* the Danish name for **Schleswig.**
sleuth (sluːθ) *n.* **1.** an informal word for **detective.** **2.** short for **sleuthhound** (sense 1). *~vb.* **3.** (*tr.*) to track or follow. [C19: short for *sleuthhound*, from C12 *sleuth* trail, from Old Norse *sloth*; see SLOT]
sleuth+hound ('sluːθˌhaʊnd) *n.* **1.** a dog trained to track people. **2.** an informal word for **detective.**
S lev+el *n. Brit.* the Special level of a subject taken for the General Certificate of Education: usually taken at the same time as A levels as an additional qualification.

slew[1] (slu:) *vb.* the past tense of **slay.**
slew[2] *or* **slue** (slu:) *vb.* **1.** to twist or be twisted sideways, esp. awkwardly: *he slewed around in his chair.* **2.** *Nautical.* to cause (a mast) to rotate in its step or (of a mast) to rotate in its step. ~*n.* **3.** the act of slewing. [C18: of unknown origin]
slew[3] (slu:) *n.* a variant spelling (esp. U.S.) of **slough**[1] (sense 2).
slew[4] *or* **slue** (slu:) *n. U.S. informal.* a great number or amount; a lot. [C20: from Irish Gaelic *sluagh;* related to Old Irish *slōg* army]
slewed (slu:d) *adj.* (*postpositive*) *Brit. slang.* intoxicated; drunk. [C19: from SLEW[2]]
Slezs+ko ('slɛskɔ) *n.* the Czech name for **Silesia.**
slice (slaɪs) *n.* **1.** a thin flat piece cut from something having bulk: *a slice of pork.* **2.** a share or portion: *a slice of the company's revenue.* **3.** any of various utensils having a broad flat blade and resembling a spatula. **4.** (in golf, tennis, etc.) **a.** the flight of a ball that travels obliquely because it has been struck off centre. **b.** the action of hitting such a shot. **c.** the shot so hit. ~*vb.* **5.** to divide or cut (something) into parts or slices. **6.** (when *intr.,* usually foll. by *through*) to cut in a clean and effortless manner. **7.** (when *intr.,* foll. by *into* or *through*) to move or go (through something) like a knife: *the car sliced into a field.* **8.** (usually foll. by *off, from, away,* etc.) to cut or be cut (from) a larger piece. **9.** (*tr.*) to remove by use of a slicing implement. **10.** to hit (a ball) with a slice. **11.** (*tr.*) *Rowing.* to put the blade of the oar into (the water) slantwise. [C14: from Old French *esclice* a piece split off, from *esclicier* to splinter] —'**slice+a·ble** *adj.* —'**slic+er** *n.*
slice bar *n.* an iron bar used for raking out furnaces.
slic+er ('slaɪsə) *n.* a machine that slices bread, etc., usually with an electrically driven band knife or circular knife.
slick (slɪk) *adj.* **1.** flattering and glib: *a slick salesman.* **2.** adroitly devised or executed: *a slick show.* **3.** *Informal, chiefly U.S.* shrewd; sly. **4.** *Informal.* superficially attractive: *a slick publication.* **5.** *Chiefly U.S.* smooth and glossy; slippery. ~*n.* **6.** a slippery area, esp. a patch of oil floating on water. **7.** a chisel or other tool used for smoothing or polishing a surface. **8.** the tyre of a racing car that has worn treads. ~*vb.* (*tr.*) **9.** *Chiefly U.S.* to make smooth or sleek. **10.** *U.S. informal.* (usually foll. by *up*) to smarten or tidy (oneself). **11.** (often foll. by *up*) to make smooth or glossy. [C14: probably of Scandinavian origin; compare Icelandic, Norwegian *slikja* to be or make smooth] —'**slick+ly** *adv.* —'**slick+ness** *n.*
slick+en+side ('slɪkən,saɪd) *n.* a rock surface with a polished appearance and fine parallel scratches caused by displacement of the rock during a fault. [C18: from dialect *slicken,* variant of SLICK + SIDE]
slick+er ('slɪkə) *n.* **1.** *U.S.* a shiny raincoat, esp. an oilskin. **2.** *U.S. informal.* a sly or untrustworthy person (esp. in the phrase **city slicker**). **3.** a small trowel used for smoothing the surfaces of a mould. —'**slick+ered** *adj.*
slide (slaɪd) *vb.* **slides, slid+ing, slid; slid** *or* **slid+den. 1.** to move or cause to move smoothly along a surface in continual contact with it: *doors that slide open; children sliding on the ice.* **2.** (*intr.*) to lose grip or balance: *he slid on his back.* **3.** (*intr.;* usually foll. by *into, out of, away from,* etc.) to pass or move gradually and unobtrusively: *she slid into the room.* **4.** (*intr.;* usually foll. by *into*) to go (into a specified condition) by degrees, unnoticeably, etc.: *he slid into loose living.* **5.** (foll. by *in, into,* etc.) to move (an object) unobtrusively or (of an object) to move in this way: *he slid the gun into his pocket.* **6. let slide.** to allow to follow a natural course, esp. one leading to deterioration: *to let things slide.* **7.** (*intr.*) *Music.* to execute a portamento. ~*n.* **8.** the act or an instance of sliding. **9.** a smooth surface, as of ice or mud, for sliding on. **10.** a construction incorporating an inclined smooth slope for sliding down in playgrounds, etc. **11.** *Rowing.* a sliding seat in a boat or its runners. **12.** a small glass plate on which specimens are mounted for microscopical study. **13.** Also called: **transparency.** a positive photograph on a transparent base, mounted in a cardboard or plastic frame or between glass plates, that can be viewed by means of a slide projector. **14.** Also called: **hair slide.** *Chiefly Brit.* an ornamental clip to hold hair in place. U.S. name: **barrette. 15.** *Machinery.* **a.** a sliding part or member. **b.** the track, guide, or channel on or in which such a part slides. **16.** *Music.* **a.** the sliding curved tube of a trombone that is moved in or out to allow the production of different harmonic series and a wider range of notes. **b.** a portamento. **17.** *Geology.* **a.** the downward movement of a large mass of earth, rocks, etc., caused by erosion, faulting, etc. **b.** the mass of material involved in this descent. See also **landslide.** [Old English *slīdan;* related to *slidor* slippery, *sliderian* to SLITHER, Middle High German *slīten*] —'**slid+a·ble** *adj.* —'**slid+er** *n.*
slide-ac·tion *adj.* (of a shoulder firearm) ejecting the empty case and reloading by means of a sliding lever.
slide fas+ten+er *n. Chiefly U.S.* another name for **zip** (sense 1).
slide o·ver *vb.* (*intr., prep.*) **1.** to cross by or as if by sliding. **2.** to avoid dealing with (a matter) fully.
slide rule *n.* a mechanical calculating device consisting of two strips, one sliding along a central groove in the other, each strip graduated in two or more logarithmic scales of numbers, trigonometric functions, etc. It employs the same principles as logarithm tables.
slide trom+bone *n.* See **trombone.**
slide valve *n.* **1.** a valve that slides across an aperture to expose the port or opening. **2.** (*modifier*) fitted with slide valves: *a slide-valve engine.*
slid+ing ('slaɪdɪŋ) *adj.* **1.** rising or falling in accordance with given specifications: *fees were charged as a sliding percentage of income.* **2.** regulated or moved by sliding.
slid+ing scale *n.* a variable scale according to which specified wages, tariffs, prices, etc., fluctuate in response to changes in some other factor, standard, or conditions.
slid+ing seat *n. Rowing.* a seat that slides forwards and backwards with the oarsman, lengthening his stroke.
sli+er ('slaɪə) *adj.* the comparative of **sly.**
sli+est ('slaɪɪst) *adj.* the superlative of **sly.**
slight (slaɪt) *adj.* **1.** small in quantity or extent. **2.** of small importance; trifling. **3.** slim and delicate. **4.** lacking in strength or substance. ~*vb.* (*tr.*) **5.** to show indifference or disregard for (someone); snub. **6.** to devote inadequate attention to (work, duties, etc.). **7.** to treat as unimportant or trifling. ~*n.* **8.** an act or omission indicating supercilious neglect or indifference. [C13: from Old Norse *slēttr* smooth; related to Old High German *slehtr,* Gothic *slaihts,* Middle Dutch *slecht* simple] —'**slight+ness** *n.*
slight+ing ('slaɪtɪŋ) *adj.* characteristic of a slight; disparaging; disdainful: *in a slighting manner.* —'**slight+ing+ly** *adv.*
slight+ly ('slaɪtlɪ) *adv.* in small measure or degree.
Sli+go ('slaɪgəʊ) *n.* **1.** a county of NW Ireland, on the Atlantic: has a deeply indented low-lying coast; livestock and dairy farming. County town: Sligo. Pop.: 50 275 (1971). Area: 1795 sq. km (693 sq. miles). **2.** a port in NW Ireland, county town of Co. Sligo on **Sligo Bay.** Pop.: 14 080 (1971).
sli+ly ('slaɪlɪ) *adv.* a variant spelling of **slyly.**
slim (slɪm) *adj.* **slim+mer, slim+mest. 1.** small in width relative to height or length. **2.** small in amount or quality: *slim chances of success.* ~*vb.* **3.** to make or become slim, esp. by diets and exercise. [C17: from Dutch: crafty, from Middle Dutch *slimp* slanting; compare Old High German *slimbi* obliquity] —'**slim+ly** *adv.* —'**slim+mer** *n.* —'**slim+ness** *n.*
Slim (slɪm) *n.* **Wil·liam Jo·seph,** 1st Viscount. 1891–1970, British field marshal, who commanded (1943–45) the 14th Army in the reconquest of Burma from the Japanese; governor-general of Australia (1953–60).
slime (slaɪm) *n.* **1.** soft thin runny mud or filth. **2.** any moist viscous fluid, esp. when noxious or unpleasant. **3.** a mucous substance produced by various organisms, such as fish, slugs, and fungi. ~*vb.* (*tr.*) **4.** to cover with slime. **5.** to remove slime from (fish) before canning. [Old English *slīm;* related to Old Norse *slīm,* Old High German *slīmen* to smooth, Russian *slimák* snail, Latin *līmax* snail]
slime mould *n.* another name for **myxomycete.**
slim+sy ('slɪmzɪ) *adj.* **+si+er, +si+est.** *U.S. informal.* frail.
slim·y ('slaɪmɪ) *adj.* **slim·i+er, slim·i+est. 1.** characterized by, covered with, containing, secreting, or resembling slime. **2.** offensive or repulsive. **3.** *Chiefly Brit.* characterized by servility. —'**slim·i+ly** *adv.* —'**slim·i+ness** *n.*
sling[1] (slɪŋ) *n.* **1.** a simple weapon consisting of a loop of leather, etc., in which a stone is whirled and then let fly. **2.** a rope or strap by which something may be secured or lifted. **3.** *Nautical.* **a.** a halyard for a yard. **b.** (*often pl.*) the part of a yard where the sling is attached. **4.** *Med.* a wide piece of cloth suspended from the neck for supporting an injured hand or arm across the front of the body. **5.** a loop or band attached to an object for carrying. **6.** the act of slinging. ~*vb.* **slings, sling+ing, slung. 7.** (*tr.*) to hurl with or as if with a sling. **8.** to attach a sling or slings to (a load, etc.). **9.** (*tr.*) to carry or hang loosely from or as if from a sling: *to sling washing from the line.* **10.** (*intr.*) *Austral. informal.* to pay a part of one's wages or profits as a bribe or tip. [C13: perhaps of Scandinavian origin; compare Old Norse *slyngva* to hurl, Old High German *slingan*] —'**sling+er** *n.*
sling[2] (slɪŋ) *n.* a mixed drink with a spirit base, usually sweetened. [C19: of uncertain origin]
sling+back ('slɪŋ,bæk) *n.* **a.** a shoe with a strap instead of a full covering for the heel. **b.** (*as modifier*): *slingback shoes.*
sling+er ring *n.* a tubular ring around the hub of an aircraft propeller through which antifreeze solution is spread over the propeller blades by centrifugal force.
sling off *vb.* (*intr., adv.;* often foll. by *at*) *Austral. informal.* to laugh or jeer (at).
sling+shot ('slɪŋ,ʃɒt) *n.* **1.** the U.S. name for **catapult** (sense 1). **2.** another name for **sling**[1] (sense 1).
slink (slɪŋk) *vb.* **slinks, slink+ing, slunk. 1.** (*intr.*) to move or act in a furtive or cringing manner from or as if from fear, guilt, etc. **2.** (*intr.*) to move in a sinuous alluring manner. **3.** (*tr.*) (of animals, esp. cows) to give birth to prematurely. ~*n.* **4. a.** an animal, esp. a calf, born prematurely. **b.** (*as modifier*): *slink veal.* [Old English *slincan;* related to Middle Low German *slinken* to shrink, Old Swedish *slinka* to creep, Danish *slunken* limp] —'**slink+ing+ly** *adv.*
slink·y ('slɪŋkɪ) *adj.* **slink·i+er, slink·i+est.** *Informal.* **1.** moving in a sinuously graceful or provocative way. **2.** (of clothes, etc.) figure-hugging; clinging. **3.** characterized by furtive movements. —'**slink·i+ly** *adv.* —'**slink·i+ness** *n.*
slip[1] (slɪp) *vb.* **slips, slip+ping, slipped. 1.** to move or cause to move smoothly and easily. **2.** (*tr.*) to place, insert, or convey quickly or stealthily. **3.** (*tr.*) to put on or take off easily or quickly: *to slip on a sweater.* **4.** (*intr.*) to lose balance and slide unexpectedly: *he slipped on the ice.* **5.** to let loose or be let loose. **6.** to be released from (something); escape. **7.** (*tr.*) to let go (mooring or anchor lines) over the side. **8.** (when *intr.,* often foll. by *from* or *out of*) to pass out of (the mind or memory). **9.** (*tr.*) to overlook, neglect, or miss: *to slip an opportunity.* **10.** (*intr.*) to move or pass swiftly or unperceived: *to slip quietly out of the room.* **11.** (*intr.;* sometimes foll. by *up*) to make a mistake. **12.** Also: **sideslip.** to cause (an aircraft) to slide sideways or (of an aircraft) to slide sideways. **13.** (*intr.*) to

decline in health, mental ability, etc. **14.** (*intr.*) (of an intervertebral disc) to become displaced from the normal position. **15.** (*tr.*) to dislocate (a bone). **16.** (of animals) to give birth to (offspring) prematurely. **17.** (*tr.*) to pass (a stitch) from one needle to another without knitting it. **18. a.** (*tr.*) to operate (the clutch of a motor vehicle) so that it partially disengages. **b.** (*intr.*) (of the clutch of a motor vehicle) to fail to engage, esp. as a result of wear. **19. let slip. a.** to allow to escape. **b.** to say unintentionally. **20. slip one over on.** *Slang, chiefly U.S.* to hoodwink or trick. ~*n.* **21.** the act or an instance of slipping. **22.** a mistake or oversight: *a slip of the pen.* **23.** a moral lapse or failing. **24.** a woman's sleeveless undergarment, worn as a lining for and to give support to a dress. **25.** *U.S.* a narrow space between two piers in which vessels may dock. **26.** See **slipway. 27.** a kind of dog lead that allows for the quick release of the dog. **28.** a small whetstone, esp. one having curved edges and a tapering thickness, used for honing the interior edges of gauges, tools, etc. **29.** a small block of hard steel of known thickness used for measurement, usually forming one of a set. **30.** the ratio between output speed and input speed of a transmission device when subtracted from unity, esp. of a drive belt or clutch that is not transmitting full power. **31.** *Cricket.* **a.** the position of the fielder who stands a little way behind and to the offside of the wicketkeeper. **b.** the fielder himself. **32.** the relative movement of rocks along a fault plane. **33.** *Metallurgy, crystallog.* the deformation of a metallic crystal caused when one part glides over another part along a plane. **34.** the deviation of a propeller from its helical path through a fluid, expressed as the difference between its actual forward motion and its theoretical forward motion in one revolution. **35.** another name for **sideslip** (sense 1). **36. give someone the slip.** to elude or escape from someone. ~See also **slip up.** [C13: from Middle Low German or Dutch *slippen*] —ˈ**slip·less** *adj.* —ˈ**slip·ping·ly** *adv.*

slip^{2} (slɪp) *n.* **1.** a narrow piece; strip. **2.** a small piece of paper: *a receipt slip.* **3.** a part of a plant that, when detached from the parent, will grow into a new plant; cutting; scion. **4.** a young slender person: *a slip of a child.* **5.** *Printing.* **a.** a long galley. **b.** a less common name for a **galley proof. 6.** *Chiefly U.S.* a pew or similar long narrow seat. **7.** a small piece of abrasive material of tapering section used in honing. ~*vb.* **slips, slip·ping, slipped. 8.** (*tr.*) to detach (portions of stem, etc.) from (a plant) for propagation. [C15: probably from Middle Low German, Middle Dutch *slippe* to cut, strip]

slip^{3} (slɪp) *n.* clay mixed with water to a creamy consistency, used for decorating or patching a ceramic piece. [Old English *slyppe* slime; related to Norwegian *slipa* slime on fish; see SLOP^{1}]

slip·case (ˈslɪpˌkeɪs) *n.* a protective case for a book or set of books that is open at one end so that only the spines of the books are visible.

slip·cov·er (ˈslɪpˌkʌvə) *n.* **1.** the U.S. word for a **loose cover. 2.** *U.S.* a book jacket; dust cover.

slip·knot (ˈslɪpˌnɒt) *n.* **1.** Also called: **running knot.** a nooselike knot tied so that it will slip along the rope round which it is made. **2.** a knot that can be easily untied by pulling one free end.

slip·noose (ˈslɪpˌnuːs) *n.* a noose made with a slipknot, so that it tightens when pulled.

slip-on *adj.* **1.** (of a garment or shoe) made so as to be easily and quickly put on or off. ~*n.* **2.** a slip-on garment or shoe.

slip·o·ver (ˈslɪpˌəʊvə) *adj., n.* another word for **pullover.**

slip·page (ˈslɪpɪdʒ) *n.* **1.** the act or an instance of slipping. **2.** the amount of slipping or the extent to which slipping occurs. **3. a.** an instance of not reaching a norm, target, etc. **b.** the extent of this. **4.** the power lost in a mechanical device or system as a result of slipping.

slipped disc *n. Pathol.* a herniated intervertebral disc, often resulting in pain because of pressure on the spinal nerves.

slip·per (ˈslɪpə) *n.* **1.** a light shoe of some soft material, for wearing around the house. **2.** a woman's evening or dancing shoe. ~*vb.* **3.** (*tr.*) *Informal.* to hit or beat with a slipper. —ˈ**slip·pered** *adj.* —ˈ**slip·per-ˌlike** *adj.*

slip·per bath *n.* **1.** a bath in the shape of a slipper, with a covered end. **2.** (*pl.*) an establishment where members of the public pay to have a bath.

slip·per sat·in *n.* a fine satin fabric with a mat finish.

slip·per·wort (ˈslɪpəˌwɜːt) *n.* another name for **calceolaria.**

slip·per·y (ˈslɪpərɪ, -prɪ) *adj.* **1.** causing or tending to cause objects to slip: *a slippery road.* **2.** liable to slip from the grasp, a position, etc. **3.** not to be relied upon; cunning and untrustworthy: *a slippery character.* **4.** (esp. of a situation) liable to change; unstable. [C16: probably coined by Coverdale to translate German *schlipfferig* in Luther's Bible (Psalm 35:6); related to Old English *slipor* slippery] —ˈ**slip·per·i·ness** *n.*

slip·per·y dip *n. Austral. informal.* a long slide at a playground or funfair.

slip·per·y elm *n.* **1.** a tree, *Ulmus fulva,* of E North America, having oblong serrated leaves, notched winged fruits, and a mucilaginous inner bark. **2.** the bark of this tree, used medicinally as a demulcent. ~Also called: **red elm.**

slip·py (ˈslɪpɪ) *adj.* ·**pi·er,** ·**pi·est. 1.** *Informal or dialect.* another word for **slippery** (senses 1, 2). **2.** *Brit. informal.* alert; quick. —ˈ**slip·pi·ness** *n.*

slip rail *n. Austral.* a rail in a fence that can be slipped out of place to make an opening.

slip ring *n. Electrical engineering.* a metal ring, mounted on but insulated from a rotating shaft of a motor or generator, by means of which current can be led through stationary brushes into or out of a winding on the shaft.

slip road *n. Brit.* a relatively narrow road giving access to a motorway, etc.

slip·sheet (ˈslɪpˌʃiːt) *n.* **1.** a sheet of paper that is interleaved between freshly printed sheets to prevent set-off. ~*vb.* **2.** to interleave (printed sheets) with slipsheets.

slip·shod (ˈslɪpˌʃɒd) *adj.* **1.** (of an action) negligent; careless. **2.** (of a person's appearance) slovenly; down-at-heel. [C16: from SLIP^{1} + SHOD] —ˈ**slip·ˌshod·di·ness** *or* ˈ**slip·ˌshod·ness** *n.*

slip·slop (ˈslɪpˌslɒp) *n.* **1.** *Archaic.* weak or unappetizing food or drink. **2.** *Informal.* maudlin or trivial talk or writing.

slip stitch *n.* **1.** a sewing stitch for securing hems, etc., in which only two or three threads of the material are caught up by the needle each time, so that the stitches are nearly invisible from the right side. ~*vb.* **2.** (*tr.*) to join (two edges) using slip stiches.

slip·stream (ˈslɪpˌstriːm) *n.* **1.** Also called: **airstream, race. a.** the stream of air forced backwards by an aircraft propeller. **b.** a stream of air behind any moving object. ~*vb.* **2.** *Motor racing.* to follow (another car, etc.) closely in order to take advantage of the decreased wind resistance immediately behind it.

slip up *vb.* (*intr., adv.*) **1.** *Informal.* to make a blunder or mistake; err. **2.** to fall over: *he slipped up in the street.* ~*n.* **slip-up. 3.** *Informal.* a mistake, blunder, or mishap.

slip·way (ˈslɪpˌweɪ) *n.* **1.** the sloping area in a shipyard, containing the ways. **2.** Also called: **marine railway.** the ways on which a vessel is launched. **3.** the ramp of a whaling factory ship. **4.** a pillow case; pillow slip.

slit (slɪt) *vb.* **slits, slit·ting, slit.** (*tr.*) **1.** to make a straight long incision in; split open. **2.** to cut into strips lengthwise. **3.** to sever. ~*n.* **4.** a long narrow cut. **5.** a long narrow opening. [Old English *slītan* to slice; related to Old Norse *slita,* Old High German *slīzen*] —ˈ**slit·ter** *n.*

slith·er (ˈslɪðə) *vb.* **1.** to move or slide or cause to move or slide unsteadily, as on a slippery surface. **2.** (*intr.*) to travel with a sliding motion. ~*n.* **3.** a slithering motion. [Old English *slidrian,* from *slīdan* to SLIDE] —ˈ**slith·er·y** *adj.*

slit pock·et *n.* a pocket on the underside of a garment, reached through a vertical opening.

slit trench *n. Military.* a narrow trench dug for the protection of a small number of people.

sliv·er (ˈslɪvə) *n.* **1.** a thin piece that is cut or broken off lengthwise; splinter. **2.** a loose strand or fibre obtained by carding. ~*vb.* **3.** to divide or be divided into splinters; split. **4.** (*tr.*) to form (wool, etc.) into slivers. [C14: from *sliven* to split] —ˈ**sliv·er·er** *n.* —ˈ**sliv·er-ˌlike** *adj.*

sliv·o·vitz (ˈslɪvəvɪts, ˈsliːvə-) *n.* a plum brandy from E Europe. [from Serbo-Croatian *šljivovica,* from *sljiva* plum]

Sloan (sləʊn) *n.* **John.** 1871–1951, U.S. painter and etcher, a leading member of the group of realistic painters known as the Ashcan School. His pictures of city scenes include *McSorley's Bar* (1912) and *Backyards, Greenwich Village* (1914).

slob (slɒb) *n.* **1.** *Slang.* a stupid or coarse person. **2.** *Irish.* mire. [C19: from Irish *slab* mud; compare SLAB]

slob·ber (ˈslɒbə) *or* **slab·ber** *vb.* **1.** to dribble (saliva, food, etc.) from the mouth. **2.** (*intr.*) to speak or write mawkishly. **3.** (*tr.*) to smear with matter dribbling from the mouth. ~*n.* **4.** liquid or saliva spilt from the mouth. **5.** maudlin language or behaviour. [C15: from Middle Low German, Middle Dutch *slubberen;* see SLAVER^{2}] —ˈ**slob·ber·er** *or* ˈ**slab·ber·er** *n.* —ˈ**slob·ber·y** *or* ˈ**slab·ber·y** *adj.*

slob ice *n. Canadian.* sludgy masses of floating ice.

sloe (sləʊ) *n.* **1.** the small sour blue-black fruit of the blackthorn. **2.** another name for **blackthorn.** [Old English *slāh;* related to Old High German *slēha,* Middle Dutch *sleuuwe*]

sloe-eyed *adj.* having dark slanted or almond-shaped eyes.

sloe gin *n.* gin flavoured with sloe juice.

slog (slɒg) *vb.* **slogs, slog·ging, slogged. 1.** to hit with heavy blows, as in boxing. **2.** (*intr.*) to work hard; toil. **3.** (*intr.;* foll. by *down, up, along,* etc.) to move with difficulty; plod. **4.** *Cricket.* to score freely by taking large swipes at the ball. ~*n.* **5.** a tiring hike or walk. **6.** long exhausting work. **7.** a heavy blow or swipe. [C19: of unknown origin] —ˈ**slog·ger** *n.*

slo·gan (ˈsləʊgən) *n.* **1.** a distinctive or topical phrase used in politics, advertising, etc. **2.** *Scottish history.* a Highland battle cry. [C16: from Gaelic *sluagh-ghairm* war cry, from *sluagh* army + *gairm* cry]

slo·gan·eer (ˌsləʊgəˈnɪə) *n.* **1.** *Chiefly U.S.* a person who coins or employs slogans frequently. ~*vb.* **2.** (*intr.*) *U.S.* to coin or employ slogans so as to sway opinion.

sloop (sluːp) *n.* a single-masted sailing vessel, rigged fore-and-aft, with the mast stepped about one third of the overall length aft of the bow. Compare **cutter** (sense 2). [C17: from Dutch *sloep;* related to French *chaloupe* launch, Old English *slūpan* to glide]

sloop of war *n.* (formerly) a small fast sailing warship mounting some 10 to 30 small calibre guns on one deck.

sloop-rigged *adj. Nautical.* rigged as a sloop, typically with a jib and a mainsail.

sloot (sluːt) *n. S. African.* a ditch for irrigation or drainage. [from Afrikaans, from Dutch *sluit, sluis* SLUICE]

slop^{1} (slɒp) *vb.* **slops, slop·ping, slopped. 1.** (when *intr.,* often foll. by *about*) to cause (liquid) to splash or spill or (of liquid) to splash or spill. **2.** (*tr.*) to splash liquid upon. **3.** (*intr.;* foll. by *along, through,* etc.) to tramp (through) mud or slush. **4.** (*tr.*) to feed slop or swill to: *to slop the pigs.* **5.** (*tr.*) to ladle or serve, esp. clumsily. **6.** (*intr.;* foll. by *over*) *Informal, chiefly U.S.* to be unpleasantly effusive. ~*n.* **7.** a puddle of spilled liquid. **8.** (*pl.*) wet feed, esp. for pigs, made from kitchen waste, etc. **9.**

(*pl.*) waste food or liquid refuse. **10.** (*pl.*) the beer, cider, etc., spilt from a barrel while being drawn. **11.** (*often pl.*) the residue left after spirits have been distilled. **12.** (*often pl.*) *Informal.* liquid or semiliquid food of low quality. **13.** soft mud, snow, etc. **14.** *Informal.* gushing speech or writing. [C14: probably from Old English *-sloppe* in *cūsloppe* COWSLIP; see SLIP[3]]

slop[2] (slɒp) *n.* **1.** (*pl.*) sailors' clothing and bedding issued from a ship's stores. **2.** any loose article of clothing, esp. a smock. **3.** (*pl.*) men's wide knee breeches worn in the 16th century. **4.** (*pl.*) shoddy manufactured clothing. [Old English *oferslop* surplice; related to Old Norse *slopps* gown, Middle Dutch *slop*]

slop a·round *vb.* (*intr.*) Also: **slop about.** to move around in a casual and idle way: *he slops around the house in old slippers.*

slop chest *n.* a stock of merchandise, such as clothing, tobacco, etc., maintained aboard merchant ships for sale to the crew. Compare **small stores.**

slope (sləʊp) *vb.* **1.** to lie or cause to lie at a slanting or oblique angle. **2.** (*intr.*) (esp. of natural features) to follow an inclined course: *many paths sloped down the hillside.* **3.** (*intr.*; foll. by *off, away,* etc.) to go furtively. **4.** (*tr.*) *Military.* to hold (a rifle) in the slope position (esp. in the command **slope arms**). ~*n.* **5.** an inclined portion of ground. **6.** (*pl.*) hills or foothills. **7.** any inclined surface or line. **8.** the degree or amount of such inclination. **9.** *Maths.* **a.** (of a line) the tangent of the angle between the line and another line parallel to the *x*-axis. **b.** the first derivative of the equation of a curve at a given point. **10.** the position adopted for military drill when the rifle is rested on the shoulder. [C15: short for *aslope,* perhaps from the past participle of Old English *āslūpan* to slip away, from *slūpan* to slip] —**'slop+er** *n.* —**'slop+ing** *adj.* —**'slop+ing+ly** *adv.* —**'slop+ing+ness** *n.*

slop out *vb.* (*intr., adv.*) (of prisoners) to empty chamber pots and collect water for washing.

slop+py ('slɒpɪ) *adj.* **+pi+er, pi+est. 1.** (esp. of ground conditions, etc.) wet; slushy. **2.** *Informal.* careless; untidy. **3.** *Informal.* mawkishly sentimental. **4.** (of food or drink) watery and unappetizing. **5.** splashed with slops. **6.** (of clothes) loose; baggy. —**'slop+pi+ly** *adv.* —**'slop+pi+ness** *n.*

slop+py joe *n. Informal.* a long baggy thick sweater.

slop+work ('slɒpˌwɜːk) *n.* **1.** the manufacture of cheap shoddy clothing or the clothes so produced. **2.** any work of low quality. —**'slop+ˌwork·er** *n.*

slosh (slɒʃ) *n.* **1.** watery mud, snow, etc. **2.** *Brit. slang.* a heavy blow. **3.** the sound of splashing liquid. ~*vb.* **4.** (*tr.*; foll. by *around, on, in,* etc.) *Informal.* to throw or pour (liquid). **5.** (when *intr.*, often foll. by *about* or *around*) *Informal.* **a.** to shake or stir (something) in a liquid. **b.** (of a person) to splash (around) in water, etc. **6.** (*tr.*) *Brit. slang.* to deal a heavy blow to. **7.** (usually foll. by *about* or *around*) *Informal.* to shake (a container of liquid) or (of liquid within a container) to be shaken. [C19: variant of SLUSH, influenced by SLOP[1]] —**'slosh·y** *adj.*

sloshed (slɒʃt) *adj. Chiefly Brit.* a slang word for **drunk.**

slot[1] (slɒt) *n.* **1.** an elongated aperture or groove, such as one in a vending machine for inserting a coin. **2.** an air passage in an aerofoil to direct air from the lower to the upper surface, esp. the gap formed behind a slat. **3.** a vertical opening between the leech of a foresail and a mast or the luff of another sail through which air spills from one against the other to impart forward motion. **4.** *Informal.* a place in a series or scheme. ~*vb.* **slots, slot+ting, slot+ted. 5.** (*tr.*) to furnish with a slot or slots. **6.** (usually foll. by *in* or *into*) to fit or adjust in a slot. **7.** *Informal.* to situate or be situated in a series or scheme. [C13: from Old French *esclot* the depression of the breastbone, of unknown origin] —**'slot+ter** *n.*

slot[2] (slɒt) *n.* the trail of an animal, esp. a deer. [C16: from Old French *esclot* horse's hoof-print, probably of Scandinavian origin; compare Old Norse *sloth* track; see SLEUTH]

sloth (sləʊθ) *n.* **1.** any of several shaggy-coated arboreal edentate mammals of the family *Bradypodidae,* esp. *Bradypus tridactylus* (**three-toed sloth** or **ai**) or *Choloepus didactylus* (**two-toed sloth** or **unau**), of Central and South America. They are slow-moving, hanging upside down by their long arms and feeding on vegetation. **2.** reluctance to work or exert oneself. [Old English *slǣwth;* from *slǣw,* variant of *slāw* SLOW]

sloth bear *n.* a bear, *Melursus ursinus,* of forests of S India and Sri Lanka, having a shaggy coat and an elongated snout specialized for feeding on termites.

sloth+ful ('sləʊθfʊl) *adj.* lazy; indolent. —**'sloth+ful+ly** *adv.* —**'sloth+ful+ness** *n.*

slot ma+chine *n.* a machine, esp. one for selling small articles or for gambling, activated by placing a coin or metal disc into a slot.

slouch (slaʊtʃ) *vb.* **1.** (*intr.*) to sit or stand with a drooping bearing. **2.** (*intr.*) to walk or move with an awkward slovenly gait. **3.** (*tr.*) to cause (the shoulders) to droop. ~*n.* **4.** a drooping carriage. **5.** (*usually used in negative constructions*) *Informal, chiefly U.S.* an incompetent or slovenly person: *he's no slouch at football.* [C16: of unknown origin] —**'slouch+er** *n.* —**'slouch·y** *adj.* —**'slouch·i+ly** *adv.* —**'slouch·i+ness** *n.* —**'slouch+ing+ly** *adv.*

slouch hat *n.* any soft hat with a brim that can be pulled down over the ears.

slough[1] (slaʊ) *n.* **1.** a hollow filled with mud; bog. **2.** (sluː) *North American.* **a.** (in the prairies) a large hole where water collects or the water in such a hole. **b.** (in the northwest) a sluggish side channel of a river. **c.** (on the Pacific coast) a marshy saltwater inlet. **3.** despair or degradation. [Old English *slōh;* related to Middle High German *sluoche* ditch, Swedish *slaga* swamp] —**'slough·y** *adj.*

slough[2] (slʌf) *n.* **1.** any outer covering that is shed, such as the dead outer layer of the skin of a snake, the cellular debris in a wound, etc. **2.** Also: **sluff.** *Bridge.* a discarded card. ~*vb.* **3.** (often foll. by *off*) to shed (a skin, etc.) or (of a skin, etc.) to be shed. **4.** Also: **sluff.** *Bridge.* to discard (a card or cards). [C13: of Germanic origin; compare Middle Low German *slū* husk, German *Schlauch* hose, Norwegian *slō* fleshy part of a horn] —**'slough·y** *adj.*

Slough (slaʊ) *n.* an industrial town in SE central England, in NE Berkshire. Pop.: 86 757 (1971).

slough off (slʌf) *vb.* (*tr., adv.*) to cast off (cares, etc.).

Slo+vak ('sləʊvæk) *adj.* **1.** of, relating to, or characteristic of Slovakia, its people, or their language. ~*n.* **2.** one of the two official languages of Czechoslovakia, belonging to the West Slavonic branch of the Indo-European family. Czech and Slovak are closely related and mutually intelligible. **3.** a native or inhabitant of Slovakia.

Slo+vak·i·a (sləʊ'vækɪə) *n.* a region of E Czechoslovakia: part of Hungary from the 11th century until 1918, when it united with Bohemia and Moravia to form Czechoslovakia. Area: 49 009 sq. km (18 922 sq. miles). —**Slo+'vak+i·an** *adj., n.*

slov+en ('slʌvᵊn) *n.* a person who is habitually negligent in appearance, hygiene, or work. [C15: probably related to Flemish *sloef* dirty, Dutch *slof* negligent]

Slo+vene (sləʊ'viːn) *adj.* **1.** of, relating to, or characteristic of Slovenia, its people, or their language. ~*n.* **2.** a South Slavonic language spoken in Slovenia, closely related to Serbo-Croatian. **3. a.** a native or inhabitant of Slovenia. **b.** (esp. in other parts of Yugoslavia) a speaker of Slovene.

Slo+ve·ni·a (sləʊ'viːnɪə) *n.* a constituent republic of NW Yugoslavia: settled by the Slovenes in the 6th century; joined Yugoslavia in 1918 and became an autonomous republic in 1946; rises over 2800 m (9000 ft.) in the Julian Alps. Capital: Ljubljana. Pop.: 1 727 137 (1971). Area: 20 251 sq. km (7819 sq. miles). —**Slo+'ve·ni·an** *adj., n.*

slov+en+ly ('slʌvənlɪ) *adj.* **1.** frequently or habitually unclean or untidy. **2.** negligent and careless; slipshod: *slovenly manners.* ~*adv.* **3.** in a negligent or slovenly manner. —**'slov+en+li+ness** *n.*

slow (sləʊ) *adj.* **1.** performed or occurring during a comparatively long interval of time. **2.** lasting a comparatively long time: *a slow journey.* **3.** characterized by lack of speed: *a slow walker.* **4.** (*prenominal*) adapted to or productive of slow movement: *the slow lane of a motorway.* **5.** (of a clock, etc.) indicating a time earlier than the correct time. **6.** given to or characterized by a leisurely or lazy existence: *a slow town.* **7.** not readily responsive to stimulation; intellectually unreceptive: *a slow mind.* **8.** dull or uninteresting: *the play was very slow.* **9.** not easily aroused: *a slow temperament.* **10.** lacking promptness or immediacy: *a slow answer.* **11.** unwilling to perform an action or enter into a state: *slow to anger.* **12.** unpunctual or late: *don't be slow or you'll miss the train.* **13.** behind the times. **14.** (of trade, etc.) unproductive; slack. **15.** lacking skill or nimbleness: *slow fingers.* **16.** (of a fire) burning weakly. **17.** (of an oven) cool. **18.** *Photog.* requiring a relatively long time of exposure to produce a given density: *a slow lens.* **19.** *Sport.* (of a track, etc.) tending to reduce the speed of the ball or the competitors. **20.** *Cricket.* (of a bowler, etc.) delivering the ball slowly, usually with spin. ~*adv.* **21.** in a manner characterized by lack of speed; slowly. ~*vb.* **22.** (often foll. by *up, down,* etc.) to decrease or cause to decrease in speed, efficiency, etc. [Old English *slāw* sluggish; related to Old High German *slēo* dull, Old Norse *slǣr,* Dutch *sleeuw* slow] —**'slow+ly** *adv.* —**'slow+ness** *n.*

slow burn *n.* a steadily penetrating show of anger or contempt.

slow+coach ('sləʊˌkəʊtʃ) *n. Brit. informal.* a person who moves, acts, or works slowly. U.S. equivalent: **slowpoke.**

slow+down ('sləʊˌdaʊn) *n.* **1.** the usual U.S. word for **go-slow. 2.** any slackening of pace.

slow hand+clap *n. Brit.* slow rhythmic clapping, esp. used by an audience to indicate dissatisfaction or impatience.

slow march *n. Military.* a march in slow time.

slow match *n.* a match or fuse that burns slowly without flame, esp. a wick impregnated with potassium nitrate.

slow mo+tion *n.* **1.** *Films, television, etc.* action that appears to have occurred at a slower speed than normal, usually achieved by cranking the film at a faster rate. ~*adj.* **slow-mo·tion. 2.** of or relating to such action. **3.** moving or functioning at considerably less than usual speed.

slow+poke ('sləʊˌpəʊk) *n. Informal.* the usual U.S. word for **slowcoach.**

slow time *n. Military.* a slow marching pace, usually 65 paces to the minute.

slow-wit·ted *adj.* slow in comprehension; unintelligent.

slow+worm ('sləʊˌwɜːm) *n.* a Eurasian legless lizard, *Anguis fragilis,* with a brownish-grey snakelike body: family *Anguidae.* Also called: **blindworm.**

SLR *abbrev. for* single lens reflex: denoting a type of camera.

slub (slʌb) *n.* **1.** a lump in yarn or fabric, often made intentionally to give a knobbly effect. **2.** a loosely twisted roll of fibre prepared for spinning. ~*vb.* **slubs, slub+bing, slubbed. 3.** (*tr.*) to draw out and twist (a sliver of fibre) preparatory to spinning. ~*adj.* **4.** (of material) having an irregular appearance. [C18: of unknown origin]

slub+ber+de+gul+li·on (ˌslʌbədɪ'gʌlɪən) *n. Archaic.* a slovenly or worthless person.

sludge (slʌdʒ) *n.* **1.** soft mud, snow, etc. **2.** any deposit or sediment. **3.** a surface layer of ice that is not frozen solid but has a slushy appearance. **4.** (in sewage disposal) the solid constituents of sewage that precipitate during treatment and are removed for subsequent purification. [C17: probably related to SLUSH] —**'sludg·y** *adj.*

slue[1] (slu:) *n., vb.* a variant spelling (esp. U.S.) of **slew**[2].

slue[2] (slu:) *n.* a variant spelling of **slough**[1] (sense 2).

slue[3] (slu:) *n. U.S. informal.* a variant spelling of **slew**[4].

sluff (slʌf) *n., vb. Bridge.* a variant spelling of **slough**[2].

slug[1] (slʌg) *n.* **1.** any of various terrestrial gastropod molluscs of the genera *Limax, Arion,* etc., in which the body is elongated and the shell is absent or very much reduced. Compare **sea slug. 2.** any of various other invertebrates having a soft slimy body, esp. the larvae of certain sawflies. **3.** *Informal, chiefly U.S.* a slow-moving or lazy person or animal. [C15 (in the sense: a slow person or animal): probably of Scandinavian origin; compare Norwegian (dialect) *sluggje*]

slug[2] (slʌg) *n.* **1.** an fps unit of mass; the mass that will acquire an acceleration of 1 foot per second per second when acted upon by a force of 1 pound. 1 slug is approximately equal to 32.17 pounds. **2.** *Metallurgy.* a metal blank from which small forgings are worked. **3.** a bullet or pellet larger than a pellet of buckshot. **4.** *Chiefly U.S.* a metal token for use in slot machines, etc. **5.** *Printing.* **a.** a thick strip of type metal that is less than type-high and is used for spacing. **b.** a similar strip carrying a type-high letter, used as a temporary mark by compositors. **c.** a metal strip containing a line of characters as produced by a linotype machine. **6.** a draught of alcoholic drink, esp. spirits. [C17 (bullet), C19 (printing): perhaps from SLUG[1], with allusion to the shape of the animal]

slug[3] (slʌg) *Chiefly U.S.* ~*vb.* **slugs, slug·ging, slugged. 1.** to hit very hard and solidly, as in boxing or baseball. **2.** (*intr.*) to plod as if through snow. **3.** (*tr.*) *Austral. informal.* to charge (someone) an exorbitant price. ~*n.* **4.** an act of slugging; heavy blow. **5.** *Austral. informal.* an exorbitant charge or price. [C19: perhaps from SLUG[2] (bullet)]

slug·a·bed ('slʌgəˌbɛd) *n.* a person who remains in bed through laziness. [C16: from SLUG(GARD) + ABED]

slug·gard ('slʌgəd) *n.* **1.** a person who is habitually indolent. ~*adj.* **2.** lazy. [C14 *slogarde;* related to SLUG[1]] —**'slug·gard·ly** *adj.* —**'slug·gard·li·ness** *n.* —**'slug·gard·ness** *n.*

slug·ger ('slʌgə) *n. Informal, chiefly U.S.* (esp. in boxing, baseball, etc.) a person who strikes hard.

slug·gish ('slʌgɪʃ) *adj.* **1.** lacking energy; inactive; slow-moving. **2.** functioning at below normal rate or level. **3.** exhibiting poor response to stimulation. —**'slug·gish·ly** *adv.* —**'slug·gish·ness** *n.*

sluice (slu:s) *n.* **1.** Also called: **sluiceway.** a channel that carries a rapid current of water, esp. one that has a sluicegate to control the flow. **2.** the body of water controlled by a sluicegate. **3.** See **sluicegate. 4.** *Mining.* an inclined trough for washing ore, esp. one having riffles on the bottom to trap particles. **5.** an artificial channel through which logs can be floated. **6.** *Informal.* a brief wash in running water. ~*vb.* **7.** (*tr.*) to draw out or drain (water, etc.) from (a pond, etc.) by means of a sluice. **8.** (*tr.*) to wash or irrigate with a stream of water. **9.** (*tr.*) *Mining.* to wash in a sluice. **10.** (*tr.*) to send (logs, etc.) down a sluice. **11.** (*intr.;* often foll. by *away* or *out*) (of water, etc.) to run or flow from or as if from a sluice. **12.** (*tr.*) to provide with a sluice. [C14: from Old French *escluse,* from Late Latin *exclūsa aqua* water shut out, from Latin *exclūdere* to shut out, EXCLUDE] —**'sluice·ˌlike** *adj.*

sluice·gate ('slu:sˌgeɪt) *n.* a valve or gate fitted to a sluice to control the rate of flow of water. Sometimes shortened to **sluice.** See also **floodgate** (sense 1).

slum (slʌm) *n.* **1.** a squalid overcrowded house, etc. **2.** (*often pl.*) a squalid section of a city, characterized by inferior living conditions and usually by overcrowding. **3.** (*modifier*) of, relating to, or characteristic of slums: *slum conditions.* ~*vb.* **slums, slum·ming, slummed.** (*intr.*) **4.** to visit slums, esp. for curiosity. **5.** Also: **slum it.** to suffer conditions below those to which one is accustomed. [C19: originally slang, of obscure origin] —**'slum·mer** *n.* —**'slum·my** *adj.*

slum·ber ('slʌmbə) *vb.* **1.** (*intr.*) to sleep, esp. peacefully. **2.** (*intr.*) to be quiescent or dormant. **3.** (*tr.;* foll. by *away*) to spend (time) sleeping. ~*n.* **4.** (*sometimes pl.*) sleep. **5.** a dormant or quiescent state. [Old English *slūma* sleep (n.); related to Middle High German *slummeren,* Dutch *sluimeren*] —**'slum·ber·er** *n.* —**'slum·ber·ing·ly** *adv.* —**'slum·ber·less** *adj.*

slum·ber·ous ('slʌmbərəs, -brəs) *adj. Chiefly poetic.* **1.** sleepy; drowsy. **2.** inducing sleep. **3.** characteristic of slumber. —**'slum·ber·ous·ly** *adv.* —**'slum·ber·ous·ness** *n.*

slum·ber par·ty *n. U.S.* a party attended by girls who dress in night clothes and pass the night eating, talking, etc.

slum·gul·lion (slʌm'gʌljən, 'slʌmˌgʌl-) *n. U.S.* **1.** *Slang.* an inexpensive stew. **2.** offal, esp. the refuse from whale blubber. **3.** a reddish mud deposited in mine sluices. [C19: from SLUM + *gullion,* perhaps a variant of CULLION]

slum·lord ('slʌmˌlɔ:d) *n. Informal, chiefly U.S.* an absentee landlord of slum property, esp. one who profiteers.

slump (slʌmp) *vb.* (*intr.*) **1.** to sink or fall heavily and suddenly. **2.** to relax ungracefully. **3.** (of business activity, etc.) to decline suddenly; collapse. **4.** (of health, interest, etc.) to deteriorate or decline suddenly or markedly. **5.** (of soil or rock) to slip down a slope, esp. a cliff, usually with a rotational movement. ~*n.* **6.** a sudden or marked decline or failure, as in progress or achievement; collapse. **7.** a decline in commercial activity, prices, etc. **8.** *Economics.* another word for **depression. 9.** the act of slumping. **10.** a slipping of earth or rock; landslide. [C17: probably of Scandinavian origin; compare Low German *slump* bog, Norwegian *slumpa* to fall]

Slump (slʌmp) *n.* **the.** another name for the **Depression.**

slump test *n. Brit.* a test to determine the relative water content of concrete, depending on the loss in height (slump) of a sample obtained from a cone-shaped mould.

slung (slʌŋ) *adj.* the past tense or past participle of **sling.**

slung shot *n.* a weight attached to the end of a cord and used as a weapon.

slunk (slʌŋk) *vb.* the past tense or past participle of **slink.**

slur (slɜ:) *vb.* **slurs, slur·ring, slurred.** (*mainly tr.*) **1.** (often foll. by *over*) to treat superficially, hastily, or without due deliberation; gloss. **2.** (*also intr.*) to pronounce or utter (words, etc.) indistinctly. **3.** to speak disparagingly of or cast aspersions on. **4.** *Music.* to execute (a melodic interval of two or more notes) smoothly, as in legato performance. **5.** (*also intr.*) to blur or smear. **6.** *Archaic.* to stain or smear; sully. ~*n.* **7.** an indistinct sound or utterance. **8.** a slighting remark; aspersion. **9.** a stain or disgrace, as upon one's reputation; stigma. **10.** *Music.* **a.** a performance or execution of a melodic interval of two or more notes in a part. **b.** the curved line (⌒ or ‿) indicating this. **11.** a blur or smear. [C15: probably from Middle Low German; compare Middle Low German *slūren* to drag, trail, Middle Dutch *sloren,* Dutch *sleuren*]

slurp (slɜ:p) *Informal.* ~*vb.* **1.** to eat or drink (something) noisily. ~*n.* **2.** a sound produced in this way. [C17: from Middle Dutch *slorpen* to sip; related to German *schlürfen*]

slur·ry ('slʌrɪ) *n., pl.* **·ries.** a suspension of solid particles in a liquid, as in a mixture of cement, clay, or coal dust with water. [C15 *slory;* see SLUR]

slush (slʌʃ) *n.* **1.** any watery muddy substance, esp. melting snow. **2.** *Informal.* sloppily sentimental language. **3.** *Nautical.* waste fat from the galley of a ship. ~*vb.* **4.** (*intr.;* often foll. by *along*) to make one's way through or as if through slush. **5.** (*intr.*) to make a slushing sound. [C17: related to Danish *slus* sleet, Norwegian *slusk* slops; see SLUDGE, SLOSH] —**'slush·i·ness** *n.*

slush fund *n. U.S.* **1.** a fund for financing political corruption, such as buying votes. **2.** *Nautical.* a fund accumulated from the sale of slush from the galley.

slush·y ('slʌʃɪ) *adj.* **1.** of, resembling, or consisting of slush. ~*n. Austral. slang.* **2.** an unskilled kitchen assistant.

slut (slʌt) *n.* **1.** a dirty slatternly woman. **2.** an immoral woman. **3.** *Archaic.* a female dog. [C14: of unknown origin] —**'slut·tish** *adj.* —**'slut·tish·ly** *adv.* —**'slut·tish·ness** *n.*

sly (slaɪ) *adj.* **sly·er, sly·est** *or* **sli·er, sli·est. 1.** crafty; artful: *a sly dodge.* **2.** insidious; furtive: *a sly manner.* **3.** playfully mischievous; roguish: *sly humour.* ~*n.* **4. on the sly.** in a secretive manner. [C12: from Old Norse *slǣgr* clever, literally: able to strike, from *slā* to SLAY] —**'sly·ly** *or* **'sli·ly** *adv.* —**'sly·ness** *n.*

sly grog *n. Austral.* illicitly sold liquor.

slype (slaɪp) *n.* a covered passageway in a cathedral or church that connects the transept to the chapter house. [C19: probably from Middle Flemish *slijpen* to slip]

Sm *the chemical symbol for* samarium.

S.M. *abbrev. for* sergeant major.

smack[1] (smæk) *n.* **1.** a smell or flavour that is distinctive though faint. **2.** a distinctive trace or touch: *the smack of corruption.* **3.** a small quantity, esp. a mouthful or taste. **4.** a slang word for **heroin.** ~*vb.* (*intr.;* foll. by *of*) **5.** to have the characteristic smell or flavour (of something): *to smack of the sea.* **6.** to have an element suggestive (of something): *his speeches smacked of bigotry.* [Old English *smæc;* related to Old High German *smoc,* Icelandic *smekkr* a taste, Dutch *smaak*]

smack[2] (smæk) *vb.* **1.** (*tr.*) to strike or slap smartly, with or as if with the open hand. **2.** to strike or send forcibly or loudly or to be struck or sent forcibly or loudly. **3.** to open and close (the lips) loudly, esp. to show pleasure. **4.** (*tr.*) to kiss noisily. ~*n.* **5.** a sharp resounding slap or blow with something flat, or the sound of such a blow. **6.** a loud kiss. **7.** a sharp sound made by the lips, as in enjoyment. **8. have a smack at.** *Informal, chiefly Brit.* to attempt. **9. smack in the eye.** *Informal, chiefly Brit.* a snub or setback. ~*adv.* **10.** *Informal.* directly; squarely. **11.** *Informal.* with a smack; sharply and unexpectedly. [C16: from Middle Low German or Middle Dutch *smacken,* probably of imitative origin]

smack[3] (smæk) *n.* **1.** a sailing vessel, usually sloop-rigged, used in coasting and fishing along the British coast. **2.** a fishing vessel equipped with a well for keeping the catch alive. [C17: from Low German *smack* or Dutch *smak,* of unknown origin]

smack·er ('smækə) *n. Slang.* **1.** a loud kiss; smack. **2.** a pound note or dollar bill.

smack·ing ('smækɪŋ) *adj.* brisk; lively: *a smacking breeze.*

small (smɔ:l) *adj.* **1.** comparatively little; limited in size, number, importance, etc. **2.** of little importance or on a minor scale: *a small business.* **3.** lacking in moral or mental breadth or depth: *a small mind.* **4.** modest or humble: *small beginnings.* **5.** of low or inferior status, esp. socially. **6.** (of a child or animal) young; not mature. **7.** not outstanding: *a small actor.* **8.** of, relating to, or designating the ordinary modern minuscule letter used in printing and cursive writing. Compare **capital**[1] (sense 13). See also **lower case. 9.** lacking great strength or force: *a small effort.* **10.** in fine particles: *small gravel.* **11.** *Obsolete.* (of beer, etc.) of low alcoholic strength. ~*adv.* **12.** into small pieces: *cut it small.* **13.** in a small or soft manner. **14. feel small.** to be humiliated or inferior. **15. sing small.** *Rare.* to behave humbly. ~*n.* **16.** (often preceded by *the*) an object, person, or group considered to be small: *the small or the* *large?* **17.** a small slender part, esp. of the back. **18.** (*pl.*) *Informal, chiefly Brit.* items of personal laundry, such as underwear. [Old English *smæl;* related to Old High German *smal,* Old Norse *smali* small cattle] —**'small·ish** *adj.* —**'small·ness** *n.*

smal·lage ('smɔːlɪdʒ) *n.* an archaic name for **wild celery.** [C13: from earlier *smalache,* from *smal* SMALL + *ache* wild celery, from Old French, from Latin *apium*]

small arms *n.* portable firearms of relatively small calibre.

small beer *n.* **1.** *Informal, chiefly Brit.* people or things of no importance. **2.** *Now rare.* weak or inferior beer.

small·boy ('smɔːlˌbɔɪ) *n.* the steward's assistant or deputy steward in European households in W Africa.

small burgh *n.* (in Scotland from 1929 to 1975) an incorporated town, usually of less than 20 000 inhabitants, with a lesser degree of self-government than a large burgh.

small cal·o·rie *n.* another name for **calorie.**

small cap·i·tal *n.* a letter having the form of an upper-case letter but the same height as a lower-case letter.

small change *n.* **1.** coins, esp. those of low value. **2.** *Rare.* a person or thing that is not outstanding or important.

small chop *n. W. African.* cocktail snacks.

small cir·cle *n.* a circular section of a sphere that does not contain the centre of the sphere. Compare **great circle.**

small claims court *n. Brit.* a local court administered by the county court with jurisdiction to try civil actions involving small claims.

small·clothes ('smɔːlˌkləʊz, -ˌkləʊðz) *pl. n.* men's close-fitting knee breeches of the 18th and 19th centuries.

small fry *pl. n.* **1.** people or things regarded as unimportant. **2.** young children. **3.** young or small fishes.

small goods *pl. n. Austral.* meats bought from a delicatessen, such as sausages.

small·hold·ing ('smɔːlˌhəʊldɪŋ) *n.* a holding of agricultural land smaller than a small farm. —**'small·ˌhold·er** *n.*

small hours *pl. n.* **the.** the early hours of the morning, after midnight and before dawn.

small in·tes·tine *n.* the longest part of the alimentary canal, consisting of the duodenum, jejunum, and ileum, in which digestion is completed. Compare **large intestine.**

small let·ter *n.* a lower-case letter.

small-mind·ed *adj.* narrow-minded; petty; intolerant; mean. —ˌ**small-'mind·ed·ly** *adv.* —ˌ**small-'mind·ed·ness** *n.*

small·mouth bass ('smɔːlˌmaʊθ 'bæs) *n.* a North American freshwater black bass, *Micropterus dolomieu,* that is a popular game fish.

small pi·ca *n.* (formerly) a size of printer's type approximately equal to 11 point.

small po·ta·toes *n. U.S. informal.* someone or something of little significance or value, esp. a small amount of money.

small·pox ('smɔːlˌpɒks) *n.* an acute highly contagious viral disease characterized by high fever, severe prostration, and a pinkish rash changing in form from papules to pustules, which dry up and form scabs that are cast off, leaving pitted depressions. Technical name: **variola.**

small print *n.* matter in a contract, etc., printed in small type, esp. when considered to be a trap for the unwary.

small-scale *adj.* **1.** of limited size or scope. **2.** (of a map, model, etc.) giving a relatively small representation of something, usually missing out details.

small screen *n.* an informal name for **television.**

small slam *n. Bridge.* another name for **little slam.**

small stores *n. Navy.* personal items, such as clothing, sold aboard ship or at a naval base. Compare **slop chest.**

small stuff *n. Nautical.* any light twine or yarn used aboard ship for serving lines, etc.

small·sword ('smɔːlˌsɔːd) *n.* a light sword used in the 17th and 18th centuries: formerly a fencing weapon.

small talk *n.* light conversation for social occasions.

small-time *adj. Informal.* insignificant; minor: *a small-time criminal.* —**'small-'tim·er** *n.*

smalt (smɔːlt) *n.* **1.** a type of silica glass coloured deep blue with cobalt oxide. **2.** a pigment made by crushing this glass, used in colouring enamels. **3.** the blue colour of this pigment. [C16: via French from Italian SMALTO, of Germanic origin; related to SMELT[1]]

smalt·ite ('smɔːltaɪt) *n.* a silver-white to greyish mineral consisting chiefly of cobalt arsenide with nickel in cubic crystalline form. It occurs in veins associated with silver, nickel, and copper minerals, and is an important ore of cobalt and nickel. Formula: $(Co,Ni)As_2$.

smal·to ('smɑːltəʊ) *n., pl.* **·tos** *or* **·ti** (-tiː). coloured glass, etc., used in mosaics. [C18: from Italian; see SMALT]

smar·agd ('smærægd) *n. Archaic.* any green gemstone, such as the emerald. [C13: via Latin from Greek *smaragdos;* see EMERALD] —**sma·rag·dine** (smə'rægdɪn) *adj.*

sma·rag·dite (smə'rægdaɪt) *n.* a green fibrous amphibole mineral.

smarm (smɑːm) *Brit. informal.* ~*vb.* **1.** (*tr.;* often foll. by *down*) to flatten (the hair, etc.) with cream or grease. **2.** (when *intr.,* foll. by *up to*) to ingratiate oneself (with). ~*n.* **3.** obsequious flattery. [C19: of unknown origin]

smarm·y ('smɑːmɪ) *adj.* **smarm·i·er, smarm·i·est.** *Brit. informal.* obsequiously flattering or unpleasantly suave.

smart (smɑːt) *adj.* **1.** astute, as in business; clever or bright. **2.** quick, witty, and often impertinent in speech: *a smart talker.* **3.** fashionable; chic: *a smart hotel.* **4.** well-kept; neat. **5.** causing a sharp stinging pain. **6.** vigorous or brisk. **7.** *Dialect.* considerable or numerous: *a smart price.* ~*vb.* (*mainly intr.*) **8.** to feel, cause, or be the source of a sharp stinging physical pain or keen mental distress: *a nettle sting smarts; he smarted under their abuse.* **9.** (often foll. by *for*) to suffer a harsh penalty. ~*n.* **10.** a stinging pain or feeling. ~*adv.* **11.** in a smart manner. [Old English *smeortan;* related to Old High German *smerzan,* Latin *mordēre* to bite, Greek *smerdnos* terrible] —**'smart·ing·ly** *adv.* —**'smart·ish** *adj.* —**'smart·ly** *adv.* —**'smart·ness** *n.*

smart al·eck ('ælɪk) *or* **smart·y** ('smɑːtɪ) *n., pl.* **smart al·ecks** *or* **smart·ies.** *Informal.* a conceited person. [C19: from *Aleck, Alec,* short for *Alexander*] —**'smart-ˌal·eck·y** *adj.*

smart·en ('smɑːtᵊn) *vb.* (usually foll. by *up*) **1.** (*intr.*) to make oneself neater. **2.** (*tr.*) to make quicker or livelier.

smart·ie ('smɑːtɪ) *n. Austral. informal.* a clever person.

smart mon·ey *n. U.S.* **1.** *Law.* damages awarded to a plaintiff where the wrong was aggravated by fraud, malice, etc. **2.** money paid in order to extricate oneself from an unpleasant situation or agreement, esp. from military service. **3. a.** money bet or invested by experienced gamblers or investors, esp. with inside information. **b.** the gamblers or investors themselves. **4.** money paid by an employer to someone injured while working for him.

smart set *n.* (*functioning as sing. or pl.*) fashionable sophisticated people considered as a group.

smash (smæʃ) *vb.* **1.** to break into pieces violently and usually noisily. **2.** (when *intr.,* foll. by *against, through, into,* etc.) to throw or crash (against) vigorously, causing shattering: *he smashed the equipment; it smashed against the wall.* **3.** (*tr.*) to hit forcefully and suddenly. **4.** (*tr.*) *Tennis, etc.* to hit (the ball) fast and powerfully, esp. with an overhead stroke. **5.** (*tr.*) to defeat or wreck (persons, theories, etc.). **6.** (*tr.*) to make bankrupt. **7.** (*intr.*) to collide violently; crash. **8.** (*intr.;* often foll. by *up*) to go bankrupt. **9. smash someone's face in.** *Informal.* to beat (a person) severely. ~*n.* **10.** an act, instance, or sound of smashing or the state of being smashed. **11.** a violent collision, esp. of vehicles. **12.** a total failure or collapse, as of a business. **13.** *Tennis, etc.* a fast and powerful overhead stroke. **14.** *Informal.* **a.** something having popular success. **b.** (*in combination*): *smash-hit.* ~*adv.* **15.** with a smash. [C18: probably from SM(ACK[2] + M)ASH] —**'smash·a·ble** *adj.*

smash-and-grab *adj. Informal.* of or relating to a robbery in which a shop window is broken and the contents removed.

smashed (smæʃt) *adj. Slang.* **1.** completely intoxicated with alcohol. **2.** noticeably under the influence of a drug.

smash·er ('smæʃə) *n. Informal, chiefly Brit.* a person or thing that is very attractive or outstanding.

smash·ing ('smæʃɪŋ) *adj. Informal, chiefly Brit.* excellent or first-rate; wonderful: *we had a smashing time.*

smash-up *Informal.* ~*n.* **1.** a bad collision, esp of cars. ~*vb.* **smash up. 2.** (*tr., adv.*) to damage to the point of complete destruction: *they smashed the place up.*

smatch (smætʃ) *n.* a less common word for **smack**[1].

smat·ter ('smætə) *n.* **1.** a smattering. ~*vb.* **2.** (*intr.*) *Rare.* to prattle. **3.** (*tr.*) *Archaic.* to dabble in. [C14 (in the sense: to prattle): of uncertain origin; compare Middle High German *smetern* to gossip] —**'smat·ter·er** *n.*

smat·ter·ing ('smætərɪŋ) *n.* **1.** a slight or superficial knowledge. **2.** a small amount. —**'smat·ter·ing·ly** *adv.*

smaze (smeɪz) *n. U.S.* a smoky haze, less damp than fog. [C20: from SM(OKE + H)AZE[1]]

SME *international car registration for* Surinam.

smear (smɪə) *vb.* (*mainly tr.*) **1.** to bedaub or cover with oil, grease, etc. **2.** to rub over or apply thickly. **3.** to rub so as to produce a smudge. **4.** to slander. **5.** *U.S. slang.* to defeat completely. **6.** (*intr.*) to be or become smeared or dirtied. ~*n.* **7.** a dirty mark or smudge. **8. a.** a slanderous attack. **b.** (*as modifier*): *smear tactics.* **9.** a preparation of blood, secretions, etc., smeared onto a glass slide for examination under a microscope. [Old English *smeoru* (n.); related to Old Norse *smjör* fat, Old High German *smero,* Greek *muron* ointment] —**'smear·er** *n.* —**'smear·y** *adj.* —**'smear·i·ness** *n.*

smear test *n. Med.* another name for **Pap test.**

smec·tic ('smɛktɪk) *adj. Chem.* (of a substance) existing in or having a mesomorphic state in which the molecules are orientated in layers. Compare **nematic.** See also **liquid crystal.** [C17: via Latin from Greek *smēktikos,* from *smēkhein* to wash; from the soaplike consistency of a smectic substance]

smeg·ma ('smɛgmə) *n. Physiol.* sebum. [C19: via Latin from Greek *smēgma* detergent, from *smekhein* to wash]

smell (smɛl) *vb.* **smells, smell·ing, smelt** *or* **smelled. 1.** (*tr.*) to perceive the scent or odour of (a substance) by means of the olfactory nerves. **2.** (*copula*) to have a specified smell; appear to the sense of smell to be: *the beaches smell of seaweed; some tobacco smells very sweet.* **3.** (*intr.;* often foll. by *of*) to emit an odour (of): *the park smells of flowers.* **4.** (*intr.*) to emit an unpleasant odour; stink. **5.** (*tr.;* often foll. by *out*) to detect through shrewdness or instinct. **6.** (*intr.*) to have or use the sense of smell. **7.** (*intr.;* foll. by *of*) to give indications (of): *he smells of money.* **8.** (*intr.;* foll. by *around, about,* etc.) to search, investigate, or pry. **9.** (*copula*) to be or seem to be untrustworthy or corrupt. **10. smell a rat.** *Informal.* to detect something suspicious. ~*n.* **11.** that sense (olfaction) by which scents or odours are perceived. Related adj.: **olfactory. 12.** anything detected by the sense of smell; odour; scent. **13.** a trace or indication. **14.** the act or an instance of smelling. [C12: of uncertain origin; compare Middle Dutch *smölen* to scorch] —**'smell·er** *n.*

Usage. *Smell* in its neutral sense of emitting an odour is followed by an adjective rather than by an adverb: *this flower smells good* (rather than *well*). *Smell* in the sense of emitting

S

an unpleasant odour is followed by an adverb: *this chemical smells unbelievably.*

smell·ing salts *pl. n.* a pungent preparation containing crystals of ammonium carbonate that has a stimulant action when sniffed in cases of faintness, headache, etc.

smell·y ('smɛlɪ) *adj.* **smell·i·er, smell·i·est.** having a strong or nasty smell. —**'smell·i·ness** *n.*

smelt[1] (smɛlt) *vb.* (*tr.*) to extract (a metal) from (an ore) by heating. [C15: from Middle Low German, Middle Dutch *smelten;* related to Old High German *smelzan* to melt]

smelt[2] (smɛlt) *n., pl.* **smelt** *or* **smelts.** any marine or freshwater salmonoid food fish of the family *Osmeridae,* such as *Osmerus eperlanus* of Europe, having a long silvery body and occurring in temperate and cold northern waters. [Old English *smylt;* related to Dutch, Danish *smelt,* Norwegian *smelta,* German *Schmelz*]

smelt[3] (smɛlt) *vb.* a past tense or past participle of **smell.**

smel·ter ('smɛltə) *n.* **1.** a person engaged in smelting. **2.** Also called: **smeltery.** an industrial plant in which smelting is carried out.

Sme·ta·na (*Czech* 'smɛtana) *n.* **Bed·řich** ('bɛdrʒix). 1824–84, Czech composer, founder of his country's national school of music. His works include *My Fatherland* (1874–79), a cycle of six symphonic poems, and the opera *The Bartered Bride* (1866).

smew (smjuː) *n.* a merganser, *Mergus albellus,* of N Europe and Asia, having a male plumage of white with black markings. [C17: of uncertain origin]

smid·gen *or* **smid·gin** ('smɪdʒən) *n. Informal, chiefly U.S.* a very small amount or part. [C20: of obscure origin]

smi·la·ca·ceous (ˌsmaɪlə'keɪʃəs) *adj.* of, relating to, or belonging to the *Smilacaceae,* a temperate and tropical family of monocotyledonous flowering plants, most of which are climbing shrubs with prickly stems: includes smilax. [C19: via New Latin from Latin SMILAX]

smi·lax ('smaɪlæks) *n.* **1.** any typically climbing shrub of the smilacaceous genus *Smilax,* of warm and tropical regions, having slightly lobed leaves, small greenish or yellow flowers, and berry-like fruits: includes the sarsaparilla plant and greenbrier. **2.** a fragile, much branched liliaceous vine, *Asparagus asparagoides,* of southern Africa: cultivated by florists for its glossy bright green foliage. [C17: via Latin from Greek: bindweed]

smile (smaɪl) *n.* **1.** a facial expression characterized by an upturning of the corners of the mouth, usually showing amusement, friendliness, etc., but sometimes scorn, etc. **2.** favour or blessing: *the smile of fortune.* **3.** an agreeable appearance. ~*vb.* **4.** (*intr.*) to wear or assume a smile. **5.** (*intr.;* foll. by *at*) **a.** to look (at) with a kindly or amused expression. **b.** to look derisively (at) instead of being annoyed. **c.** to bear (troubles, etc.) patiently. **6.** (*intr.;* foll. by *on* or *upon*) to show approval; bestow a blessing. **7.** (*tr.*) to express by means of a smile: *she smiled a welcome.* **8.** (*tr.;* often foll. by *away*) to drive away or change by smiling: *smile away one's tears.* **9. come up smiling.** to recover cheerfully from misfortune. [C13: probably of Scandinavian origin; compare Swedish *smila,* Danish *smile;* related to Middle High German *smielen*] —**'smil·er** *n.* —**'smil·ing·ly** *adv.* —**'smil·ing·ness** *n.*

smirch (smɜːtʃ) *vb.* (*tr.*) **1.** to dirty; soil. ~*n.* **2.** the act of smirching or state of being smirched. **3.** a smear or stain. [C15 *smorchen,* of unknown origin] —**'smirch·er** *n.*

smirk (smɜːk) *n.* **1.** a smile expressing scorn, smugness, etc., rather than pleasure. ~*vb.* **2.** (*intr.*) to give such a smile. **3.** (*tr.*) to express with such a smile. [Old English *smearcian;* related to *smer* derision, Old High German *bismer* contempt, *bismerōn* to scorn] —**'smirk·er** *n.* —**'smirk·ing·ly** *adv.*

smit (smɪt) *or* **smit·tle** ('smɪtᵊl) *n.* **the.** *Northern English dialect.* an infection: *he's got the smit.* [Old English *smitte* a spot, and *smittian* to smear; related to Old High German *smiz,* whence Middle High German *smitz*]

smite (smaɪt) *vb.* **smites, smit·ing, smote; smit·ten** *or* **smit.** (*mainly tr.*) *Now archaic in most senses.* **1.** to strike with a heavy blow or blows. **2.** to damage with or as if with blows. **3.** to afflict or affect severely: *smitten with flu.* **4.** to afflict in order to punish. **5.** (*intr.;* foll. by *on*) to strike forcibly or abruptly: *the sun smote down on him.* [Old English *smītan;* related to Old High German *smīzan* to smear, Gothic *bismeitan,* Old Swedish *smēta* to daub] —**'smit·er** *n.*

smith (smɪθ) *n.* **1. a.** a person who works in metal, esp. one who shapes metal by hammering. **b.** (*in combination*): *a silversmith.* **2.** See **blacksmith.** [Old English; related to Old Norse *smithr,* Old High German *smid,* Middle Low German *smīde* jewellery, Greek *smilē* carving knife]

Smith (smɪθ) *n.* **1. Ad·am.** 1723–90, Scottish economist and philosopher, whose influential book *The Wealth of Nations* (1776) advocated free trade and private enterprise and opposed state interference. **2. Bes·sie.** 1894–1937, U.S. blues singer. **3. F. E.** See (1st Earl of) **Birkenhead. 4. I·an Doug·las.** born 1919, Rhodesian statesman; prime minister (1964–79). He declared independence from Britain unilaterally (1965). **5. John.** ?1580–1631, English explorer and writer, who helped found the North American colony of Jamestown, Virginia. He was reputedly saved by the Indian chief's daughter Pocahontas from execution by her tribe. Among his works is a *Description of New England* (1616). **6. Jo·seph.** 1805–44, U.S. religious leader; founder of the Mormon Church. **7. Syd·ney.** 1771–1845, English clergyman and writer, noted for *The Letters of Peter Plymley* (1807–08), in which he advocated Catholic emancipation. **8. Wil·liam.** 1769–1839, English geologist, who founded the science of stratigraphy by proving that rock strata could be dated by the fossils they contained.

smith·er·eens (ˌsmɪðə'riːnz) *pl. n.* little shattered pieces or fragments. [C19: from Irish Gaelic *smidirīn,* from *smiodar*]

smith·er·y ('smɪθərɪ) *n., pl.* **·er·ies. 1.** the trade or craft of a blacksmith. **2.** a rare word for **smithy.**

Smith·son ('smɪθsən) *n.* **James.** original name *James Lewes Macie.* 1765–1829, English chemist and mineralogist, who left a bequest to found the Smithsonian Institution.

Smith·so·ni·an In·sti·tu·tion (smɪθ'səʊnɪən) *n.* a national museum and institution in Washington, D.C., founded in 1846 from a bequest by James Smithson, primarily concerned with ethnology, zoology, and astrophysics.

smith·son·ite ('smɪθsəˌnaɪt) *n.* **1.** a white mineral consisting of zinc carbonate in hexagonal crystalline form: occurs chiefly in dry limestone regions and is a source of zinc. Formula: $ZnCO_3$. Former Brit. name: **calamine. 2.** the former Brit. name for **hemimorphite.** [C19: named after James SMITHSON]

smith·y ('smɪðɪ) *n., pl.* **smith·ies.** a place in which metal, usually iron or steel, is worked by heating and hammering; forge. [Old English *smiththe;* related to Old Norse *smithja,* Old High German *smidda,* Middle Dutch *smisse*]

smit·ten ('smɪtᵊn) *vb.* the past participle of **smite.**

smock (smɒk) *n.* **1.** any loose protective garment, worn by artists, laboratory technicians, etc. **2.** a woman's loose blouse-like garment, reaching to below the waist, worn over slacks, etc. **3.** Also called: **smock frock.** a loose protective overgarment decorated with smocking, worn formerly esp. by farm workers. **4.** *Archaic.* a woman's loose undergarment, worn from the 16th to the 18th centuries. ~*vb.* **5.** to ornament (a garment) with smocking. [Old English *smocc;* related to Old High German *smocco,* Old Norse *smokkr* blouse, Middle High German *gesmuc* decoration] —**'smock·ˌlike** *adj.*

smock·ing ('smɒkɪŋ) *n.* ornamental needlework used to gather and stitch material in a honeycomb pattern so that the part below the gathers hangs in even folds.

smock mill *n.* a type of windmill having a revolving top.

smog (smɒg) *n.* a mixture of smoke and fog. [C20: from SM(OKE + F)OG[1]] —**'smog·gy** *adj.*

smoke (sməʊk) *n.* **1.** the product of combustion, consisting of fine particles of carbon carried by hot gases and air. **2.** any cloud of fine particles suspended in a gas. **3. a.** the act of smoking tobacco or other substances, esp. in a pipe or as a cigarette or cigar. **b.** the duration of smoking such substances. **4.** *Informal.* **a.** a cigarette or cigar. **b.** a substance for smoking, such as pipe tobacco or marijuana. **5.** something with no concrete or lasting substance: *everything turned to smoke.* **6.** a thing or condition that obscures. **7.** any of various colours similar to that of smoke, esp. a dark grey with a bluish, yellowish, or greenish tinge. **8. go** *or* **end up in smoke. a.** to come to nothing. **b.** to burn up vigorously. **c.** to flare up in anger. ~*vb.* **9.** (*intr.*) to emit smoke or the like, sometimes excessively or in the wrong place. **10.** to draw in on (a burning cigarette, etc.) and exhale the smoke. **11.** (*intr.*) *Slang.* to use marijuana for smoking. **12.** (*tr.*) to bring (oneself) into a specified state by smoking. **13.** (*tr.*) to subject or expose to smoke. **14.** (*tr.*) to cure (meat, fish, cheese, etc.) by treating with smoke. **15.** (*tr.*) to fumigate or purify the air of (rooms, etc.). **16.** (*tr.*) to darken (glass, etc.) by exposure to smoke. **17.** (*tr.*) *Obsolete.* to tease or mock. **18.** (*tr.*) *Archaic.* to suspect or detect. ~See also **smoke out.** [Old English *smoca* (n.); related to Middle Dutch *smieken* to emit smoke] —**'smok·a·ble** *or* **'smoke·a·ble** *adj.*

Smoke (sməʊk) *n.* **the. 1.** *Brit.* a slang name for **London. 2.** (*also not cap.*) Also called: **the big smoke.** *Austral.* a slang name for the city or a specific city, esp. Melbourne and Sydney.

smoke bomb *n.* a device that emits large quantities of smoke when ignited.

smoke-dried *adj.* (of fish, meat, etc.) cured in smoke.

smoked rub·ber *n.* a type of crude natural rubber in the form of brown sheets obtained by coagulating latex with an acid, rolling it into sheets, and drying over open wood fires. It is the main raw material for natural rubber products. Also called: **ribbed and smoked sheet.** Compare **crepe rubber.**

smoke·ho ('sməʊkəʊ) *n.* a variant spelling of **smoko.**

smoke·house ('sməʊkˌhaʊs) *n.* a building or special construction for curing meat, fish, etc., by smoking.

smoke·jack ('sməʊkˌdʒæk) *n.* a device formerly used for turning a roasting spit, operated by the movement of ascending gases in a chimney.

smoke·less ('sməʊklɪs) *adj.* having or producing little or no smoke: *smokeless fuel.*

smoke·less pow·der *n.* any one of a number of explosives that burn with relatively little smoke. They consist mainly of nitrocellulose and are used as propellants.

smoke·less zone *n.* an area designated by the local authority where only smokeless fuels are permitted.

smoke out *vb.* (*tr., adv.*) **1.** to subject to smoke in order to drive out of hiding. **2.** to bring into the open; expose to the public: *they smoked out the plot.*

smok·er ('sməʊkə) *n.* **1.** a person who habitually smokes tobacco. **2.** Also called: **smoking compartment.** a compartment of a train where smoking is permitted. **3.** an informal social gathering, as at a club.

smoke screen *n.* **1.** *Military.* a cloud of smoke produced by artificial means to obscure movements or positions. **2.** something said or done in order to hide the truth.

smoke·stack ('sməʊkˌstæk) *n.* a tall chimney that conveys smoke into the air. Sometimes shortened to **stack.**

smoke tree *n.* **1.** an anacardiaceous shrub, *Cotinus coggygria,* of S Europe and Asia, having clusters of yellowish feathery flowers. **2.** a related tree, *Cotinus americanus,* of the southern U.S.

smok·ing jack·et *n.* a man's comfortable jacket of velvet, etc., closed by a tie belt or fastenings, worn at home.

smok·ing room *or (esp. Brit.)* **smoke room** *n.* a room, esp. in a hotel or club, for those who wish to smoke.

smo·ko *or* **smoke·ho** ('sməʊkəʊ) *n. Austral. and N.Z. informal.* a short break from work for tea, a cigarette, etc.

smok·y ('sməʊkɪ) *adj.* **smok·i·er, smok·i·est. 1.** emitting, containing, or resembling smoke. **2.** emitting smoke excessively or in the wrong place: *a smoky fireplace.* **3.** of or tinged with the colour smoke. **4.** having the flavour or having been cured by smoking. **5.** made dark, dirty, or hazy by smoke. —'**smok·i·ly** *adv.* —'**smok·i·ness** *n.*

Smok·y Moun·tains *n.* See **Great Smoky Mountains.**

smok·y quartz *n.* another name for **cairngorm.**

smol·der ('sməʊldə) *vb., n.* the U.S. spelling of **smoulder.**

Smo·lensk (*Russian* sma'ljɛnsk; *English* 'smɒlɛnsk) *n.* a city in the W Soviet Union, on the Dnieper River: a major commercial centre in medieval times; scene of severe fighting (1941 and 1943) in World War II. Pop.: 250 000 (1975 est.).

Smol·lett ('smɒlɪt) *n.* **To·bi·as George.** 1721–71, Scottish novelist, whose picaresque satires include *Roderick Random* (1748), *Peregrine Pickle* (1751), and *Humphry Clinker* (1771).

smolt (sməʊlt) *n.* a young salmon at the stage when it migrates from fresh water to the sea. [C14: Scottish, of uncertain origin; perhaps related to SMELT[2]]

smooch (smu:tʃ) *Slang.* ~*vb.* (*intr.*) **1.** Also (Austral.): **smoodge.** (of two people) to kiss and cuddle. **2.** *Brit.* to dance very slowly and amorously with one's arms around another person, or (of two people) to dance together in such a way. ~*n.* **3.** the act of smooching. **4.** *Brit.* a piece of music played for dancing to slowly and amorously. [C20: variant of dialect *smouch,* of imitative origin]

smoodge (smu:dʒ) *vb.* an Austral. word for **smooch** (sense 1).

smooth (smu:ð) *adj.* **1.** resting in the same plane; without bends or irregularities. **2.** silky to the touch: *smooth velvet.* **3.** lacking roughness of surface; flat. **4.** tranquil or unruffled: *smooth temper.* **5.** lacking obstructions or difficulties. **6. a.** suave or persuasive, esp. as suggestive of insincerity. **b.** (*in combination*): *smooth-tongued.* **7.** (of the skin) free from hair. **8.** of uniform consistency: *smooth batter.* **9.** not erratic; free from jolts: *smooth driving.* **10.** not harsh or astringent: *a smooth wine.* **11.** having all projections worn away: *smooth tyres.* **12.** *Phonetics.* without preliminary or simultaneous aspiration. **13.** gentle to the ear; flowing. **14.** *Physics.* (of a plane, surface, etc.) regarded as being frictionless. ~*adv.* **15.** in a calm or even manner; smoothly. ~*vb.* (*mainly tr.*) **16.** (*also intr.;* often foll. by *down*) to make or become flattened or without roughness or obstructions. **17.** (often foll. by *out* or *away*) to take or rub (away) in order to make smooth: *she smoothed out the creases in her dress.* **18.** to make calm; soothe. **19.** to make easier: *smooth his path.* **20.** *Obsolete.* to make more polished or refined. ~*n.* **21.** the smooth part of something. **22.** the act of smoothing. **23.** *Tennis, etc.* the side of a racket on which the binding strings form a continuous line. Compare **rough** (sense 27). [Old English *smōth;* related to Old Saxon *māthmundi* gentle-minded, *smōthi* smooth] —'**smooth·a·ble** *adj.* —'**smooth·er** *n.* —'**smooth·ly** *adv.* —'**smooth·ness** *n.*

smooth·bore ('smu:ð,bɔ:) *n.* **1.** (*modifier*) (of a firearm) having an unrifled bore: *a smoothbore shotgun.* **2.** such a firearm. —'**smooth·,bored** *adj.*

smooth breath·ing *n.* (in Greek) the sign (') placed over an initial vowel, indicating that (in ancient Greek) it was not pronounced with an *h.* Compare **rough breathing.**

smooth·en ('smu:ðən) *vb.* to make or become smooth.

smooth hound *n.* any of several small sharks of the genus *Mustelus,* esp. *M. mustelus,* a species of North Atlantic coastal regions: family *Triakidae.* See also **dogfish** (sense 3).

smooth·ie *or* **smooth·y** ('smu:ðɪ) *n., pl.* **smooth·ies.** *Slang, usually derogatory.* a person, esp. a man, who is suave or slick, esp. in speech, dress, or manner.

smooth·ing i·ron *n.* a former name for **iron** (senses 2, 3).

smooth mus·cle *n.* muscle that is capable of slow rhythmic involuntary contractions: occurs in the walls of the blood vessels, alimentary canal, etc.

smooth o·ver *vb.* (*tr.*) to ease or gloss over: *to smooth over a situation.*

smooth snake *n.* any of several slender nonvenomous colubrid snakes of the European genus *Coronella,* esp. *C. austriaca,* having very smooth scales and a reddish-brown coloration.

smooth-spok·en *adj.* speaking or spoken in a gently persuasive or competent manner.

smooth-tongued *adj.* suave or persuasive in speech.

smor·gas·bord ('smɔ:gəs,bɔ:d, 'smɜ:-) *n.* a variety of cold or hot savoury dishes, such as pâté, smoked salmon, etc., served in Scandinavia as hors d'oeuvres or as a buffet meal. [Swedish, from *smörgås* sandwich + *bord* table]

smør·re·brød (*Danish* 'smœrə,brœð) *n.* small open savoury sandwiches, served esp. in Denmark as hors d'oeuvres, etc. [Danish, from *smør* butter + *brød* bread]

smote (sməʊt) *vb.* the past tense of **smite.**

smoth·er ('smʌðə) *vb.* **1.** to suffocate or stifle by cutting off or being cut off from the air. **2.** (*tr.*) to surround (with) or envelop (in): *he smothered her with love.* **3.** (*tr.*) to extinguish (a fire) by covering so as to cut it off from the air. **4.** to be or cause to be suppressed or stifled: *smother a giggle.* **5.** (*tr.*) to cook or serve (food) thickly covered with sauce, etc. ~*n.* **6.** anything, such as a cloud of smoke, that stifles. **7.** a profusion or turmoil. **8.** *Archaic.* a state of smouldering or a smouldering fire. [Old English *smorian* to suffocate; related to Middle Low German *smōren*] —'**smoth·er·y** *adj.*

smoth·ered mate *n. Chess.* checkmate occurring when the king cannot move to a vacant square and is checkmated by a knight.

smoul·der *or U.S.* **smol·der** ('sməʊldə) *vb.* (*intr.*) **1.** to burn slowly without flame, usually emitting smoke. **2.** (esp. of anger, etc.) to exist in a suppressed or half-suppressed state. **3.** to have strong repressed or half repressed feelings, esp. anger. ~*n.* **4.** dense smoke, as from a smouldering fire. **5.** a smouldering fire. [C14: from *smolder* (n.), of obscure origin]

smri·ti ('smrɪtɪ) *n.* a class of Hindu sacred literature derived from the Vedas, containing social, domestic, and religious teaching.

smudge (smʌdʒ) *vb.* **1.** to smear, blur, or soil or cause to do so. **2.** (*tr.*) *Chiefly U.S.* to fill (an area) with smoke in order to drive insects away or guard against frost. ~*n.* **3.** a smear or dirty mark. **4.** a blurred form or area: *that smudge in the distance is a quarry.* **5.** *Chiefly U.S.* a smoky fire for driving insects away or protecting fruit trees or plants from frost. [C15: of uncertain origin] —'**smudge·less** *adj.* —'**smudg·y** *adj.* —'**smudg·i·ly** *or* '**smudg·ed·ly** *adv.* —'**smudg·i·ness** *n.*

smug (smʌg) *adj.* **smug·ger, smug·gest. 1.** excessively self-satisfied or complacent. **2.** *Archaic.* trim or neat. [C16: of Germanic origin; compare Low German *smuck* neat] —'**smug·ly** *adv.* —'**smug·ness** *n.*

smug·gle ('smʌgᵊl) *vb.* **1.** to import or export (prohibited or dutiable goods) secretly. **2.** (*tr.;* often foll. by *into* or *out of*) to bring or take secretly, as against the law or rules. **3.** (*tr.;* foll. by *away*) to conceal; hide. [C17: from Low German *smukkelen* and Dutch *smokkelen,* perhaps from Old English *smūgen* to creep; related to Old Norse *smjūga*] —'**smug·gler** *n.* —'**smug·gling** *n.*

smut (smʌt) *n.* **1.** a small dark smudge or stain, esp. one caused by soot. **2.** a speck of soot or dirt. **3.** something obscene or indecent. **4. a.** any of various fungal diseases of flowering plants, esp. cereals, in which black sooty masses of spores cover the affected parts. **b.** any parasitic basidiomycetous fungus of the order *Ustilaginales* that causes such a disease. ~*vb.* **smuts, smut·ting, smut·ted. 5.** to mark or become marked or smudged, as with soot. **6.** to affect (grain, etc.) or (of grain) to be affected with smut. **7.** (*tr.*) to remove smut from (grain). **8.** (*tr.*) to make obscene. **9.** (*intr.*) to emit soot or smut. [Old English *smitte;* related to Middle High German *smitze;* associated with SMUDGE, SMUTCH] —'**smut·ty** *adj.* —'**smut·ti·ly** *adv.* —'**smut·ti·ness** *n.*

smutch (smʌtʃ) *vb.* **1.** (*tr.*) to smudge; mark. ~*n.* **2.** a mark; smudge. **3.** soot; dirt. [C16: probably from Middle High German *smutzen* to soil; see SMUT] —'**smutch·y** *adj.*

Smuts (smʌts) *n.* **Jan Chris·ti·aan** (jɑn 'kristi,an). 1870–1950, South African statesman; prime minister (1919–24; 1939–48). He fought for the Boers during the Boer War, then worked for Anglo-Boer reconciliation and served the Allies during World Wars I and II.

Smyr·na ('smɜ:nə) *n.* an ancient city on the W coast of Asia Minor: a major trading centre in the ancient world; a centre of early Christianity. Modern name: **Izmir.**

Sn *the chemical symbol for* tin. [from New Latin *stannum*]

SN *international car registration for* Senegal.

snack (snæk) *n.* **1.** a light quick meal eaten between or in place of main meals. **2.** a sip or bite. **3.** *Rare.* a share. **4.** *Austral. informal.* a very easy task. ~*vb.* **5.** (*intr.*) to eat a snack. [C15: probably from Middle Dutch *snacken,* variant of *snappen* to SNAP]

snack bar *n.* a place where light meals or snacks can be obtained, often with a self-service system.

snack·ette ('snækɛt) *n.* a Caribbean name for **snack bar.**

snaf·fle ('snæfᵊl) *n.* **1.** Also called: **snaffle bit.** a simple jointed bit for a horse. ~*vb.* (*tr.*) **2.** *Brit. informal.* to steal or take for oneself. **3.** to equip or control with a snaffle. [C16: of uncertain origin; compare Old Frisian *snavel* mouth, Old High German *snabul* beak]

sna·fu (snæ'fu:) *U.S. slang, chiefly military.* ~*n.* **1.** confusion or chaos regarded as the normal state. ~*adj.* **2.** (*postpositive*) confused or muddled up, as usual. ~*vb.* **·fues, ·fu·ing, ·fued. 3.** (*tr.*) to throw into chaos. [C20: from *s*(*ituation*) *n*(*ormal*): *a*(*ll*) *f*(*ucked*) *u*(*p*)]

snag (snæg) *n.* **1.** a difficulty or disadvantage: *the snag is that I have nothing suitable to wear.* **2.** a sharp protuberance, such as a tree stump. **3.** a small loop or hole in a fabric caused by a sharp object. **4.** *Chiefly U.S.* a tree stump in a riverbed that is dangerous to navigation. **5.** (*pl.*) *Austral. slang.* sausages. ~*vb.* **snags, snag·ging, snagged. 6.** (*tr.*) to hinder or impede. **7.** (*tr.*) to tear or catch (fabric). **8.** (*intr.*) to develop a snag. **9.** (*intr.*) *Chiefly U.S.* (of a boat) to strike or be damaged by a snag. **10.** (*tr.*) to clear (a stretch of water) of snags. **11.** (*tr.*) *U.S.* to seize (an opportunity, benefit, etc.). [C16: of Scandinavian origin; compare Old Norse *snaghyrndr* sharp-pointed, Norwegian *snage* spike, Icelandic *snagi* peg] —'**snag·gy** *adj.* —'**snag·,like** *adj.*

snag·gle·tooth ('snægᵊl,tu:θ) *n., pl.* **·teeth.** a tooth that is broken or projecting. —'**snag·gle·,toothed** *adj.*

snail (sneɪl) *n.* **1.** any of numerous terrestrial or freshwater gastropod molluscs with a spirally coiled shell, esp. any of the family *Helicidae,* such as *Helix aspersa* (**garden snail**). **2.** any other gastropod with a spirally coiled shell, such as a whelk. **3.**

a slow-moving or lazy person or animal. [Old English *snægl;* related to Old Norse *snigill,* Old High German *snecko*] —'snail-,like *adj.*

snail·fish *n., pl.* ·**fish** *or* ·**fish·es.** another name for **sea snail.**

snail's pace *n.* a very slow or sluggish speed or rate.

snake (sneɪk) *n.* **1.** any reptile of the suborder *Ophidia* (or *Serpentes*), typically having a scaly cylindrical limbless body, fused eyelids, and a jaw modified for swallowing large prey: includes venomous forms such as cobras and rattlesnakes, large nonvenomous constrictors (boas and pythons), and small harmless types such as the grass snake. **2.** Also: **snake in the grass.** a deceitful or treacherous person. **3.** anything resembling a snake in appearance or action. **4.** a tool in the form of a long flexible wire for unblocking drains. ~*vb.* **5.** (*intr.*) to glide or move like a snake. **6.** (*tr.*) *U.S.* to haul (a heavy object, esp. a log) by fastening a rope around one end of it. **7.** (*tr.*) *U.S.* (often foll. by *out*) to pull jerkily. **8.** (*tr.*) to move in or follow (a sinuous course). [Old English *snaca;* related to Old Norse *snākr* snake, Old High German *snahhan* to crawl, Norwegian *snōk* snail] —'**snake**·,**like** *adj.*

snake·bird ('sneɪk,bɜːd) *n.* another name for **darter** (the bird).

snake·bite ('sneɪk,baɪt) *n.* **1.** a bite inflicted by a snake, esp. a venomous one. **2.** the state or condition resulting from being bitten by a poisonous snake.

snake charm·er *n.* an entertainer, esp. in Asia, who charms or appears to charm snakes by playing music and by rhythmical body movements.

snake dance *n.* **1.** a ceremonial dance, performed by the priests of the American Hopi Indians, in which live snakes are held in the mouth. **2. a.** the swaying movements of snakes responding to a snake charmer. **b.** a Hindu dance in which performers imitate such snake movements.

snake fly *n.* any of various neuropterous insects of the family *Raphidiidae,* having an elongated thorax: order *Megaloptera.*

snake juice *n. Austral. slang.* any strong alcoholic drink, esp. when home-made.

snake·mouth ('sneɪk,maʊθ) *n.* a terrestrial orchid, *Pogonia ophioglossoides,* of E North America, having solitary fragrant pinkish-purple flowers.

Snake Riv·er *n.* a river in the northwestern U.S., rising in NW Wyoming and flowing west through Idaho, turning north as part of the border between Idaho and Oregon, and flowing west to the Columbia River near Pasco, Washington. Length: 1670 km (1038 miles).

snake·root ('sneɪk,ruːt) *n.* **1.** any of various North American plants, such as *Aristolochia serpentaria* (**Virginia snakeroot**) and *Eupatorium urticaefolium* (**white snakeroot**), the roots or rhizomes of which have been used as a remedy for snakebite. **2.** the rhizome or root of any such plant. **3.** another name for **bistort** (senses 1, 2). ~Also called: **snakeweed.**

snakes and lad·ders *n.* (*functioning as sing.*) a board game in which players move counters along a series of squares by means of dice. A ladder provides a short cut to a square nearer the finish and a snake obliges a player to return to a square nearer the start.

snake's head *n.* a European fritillary plant, *Fritillaria meleagris,* of damp meadows, having purple-and-white chequered flowers.

snake·skin ('sneɪk,skɪn) *n.* the skin of a snake, esp. when made into a leather valued for handbags, shoes, etc.

snak·y ('sneɪkɪ) *adj.* **snak·i·er, snak·i·est. 1.** of or like a snake; sinuous. **2.** treacherous or insidious. **3.** infested with snakes. **4.** *Austral. informal.* angry or bad-tempered. —'**snak·i·ly** *adv.* —'**snak·i·ness** *n.*

snap (snæp) *vb.* **snaps, snap·ping, snapped. 1.** to break or cause to break suddenly, esp. with a sharp sound. **2.** to make or cause to make a sudden sharp cracking sound. **3.** (*intr.*) to give way or collapse suddenly, esp. from strain. **4.** to move, close, etc., or cause to move, close, etc., with a sudden sharp sound. **5.** to move or cause to move in a sudden or abrupt way. **6.** (*intr.;* often foll. by *at* or *up*) to seize something suddenly or quickly. **7.** (when *intr.,* often foll. by *at*) to bite at (something) bringing the jaws rapidly together. **8.** to speak (words) sharply or abruptly. **9.** (*intr.*) (of eyes) to flash or sparkle. **10.** to take a snapshot of (something). **11.** (*intr.*) *Hunting.* to fire a quick shot without taking deliberate aim. **12.** (*tr.*) *American football.* to put (the ball) into play by sending it back from the line of scrimmage to a teammate. **13. snap one's fingers at.** *Informal.* **a.** to dismiss with contempt. **b.** to defy. **14. snap out of it.** *Informal.* to recover quickly, esp. from depression, anger, or illness. ~*n.* **15.** the act of breaking suddenly or the sound produced by a sudden breakage. **16.** a sudden sharp sound, esp. of bursting, popping, or cracking. **17.** a catch, clasp, or fastener that operates with a snapping sound. **18.** a sudden grab or bite. **19.** the sudden release of something such as elastic thread. **20.** a brisk movement of the thumb against one or more fingers. **21.** a thin crisp biscuit: *ginger snaps.* **22.** *Informal.* See **snapshot. 23.** *Informal.* vigour, liveliness, or energy. **24.** *Informal.* a task or job that is easy or profitable to do. **25.** a short spell or period, esp. of cold weather. **26.** *Brit. dialect.* food, esp. a packed lunch taken to work. **27.** *Brit.* a card game in which the word *snap* is called when two cards of equal value are turned up on the separate piles dealt by each player. **28.** (*modifier*) done on the spur of the moment, without consideration: *a snap decision.* **29.** (*modifier*) closed or fastened with a snap. ~*adv.* **30.** with a snap. ~*interj.* **31. a.** *Cards.* the word called while playing snap. **b.** an exclamation used to draw attention to the similarity of two things. ~See also **snap up.** [C15: from Middle Low German or Middle Dutch *snappen* to seize; related to Old Norse *snapa* to snuffle] —'**snap·less** *adj.* —'**snap·pa·ble** *adj.* —'**snap·ping·ly** *adv.*

snap·back ('snæp,bæk) *n.* a sudden rebound or change in direction.

snap bean *n. U.S.* **1.** any of various bean plants that are cultivated in the U.S. for their crisp edible unripe pods. **2.** the pod of such a plant. ~See also **string bean.**

snap·drag·on ('snæp,drægən) *n.* any of several scrophulariaceous chiefly Old World plants of the genus *Antirrhinum,* esp. *A. majus,* of the Mediterranean region, having spikes of showy white, yellow, pink, red, or purplish flowers. Also called: **antirrhinum.**

snap fas·ten·er *n.* another name for **press stud.**

snap·per ('snæpə) *n., pl.* ·**per** *or* ·**pers. 1.** any large sharp-toothed percoid food fish of the family *Lutjanidae* of warm and tropical coastal regions. See also **red snapper. 2.** an Australian sparid food fish, *Chrysophrys auratus,* that has a pinkish body covered with blue spots. **3.** another name for the **bluefish** or the **snapping turtle. 4.** a person or thing that snaps.

snap·per up *n.* a person who snaps up bargains, etc.

snap·ping bee·tle *n.* another name for the **click beetle.**

snap·ping tur·tle *n.* any large aggressive North American river turtle of the family *Chelydridae,* esp. *Chelydra serpentina* (**common snapping turtle**), having powerful hooked jaws and a rough shell. Also called: **snapper.**

snap·py ('snæpɪ) *adj.* ·**pi·er,** ·**pi·est. 1.** Also: **snappish.** apt to speak sharply or irritably. **2.** Also: **snappish.** apt to snap or bite. **3.** crackling in sound: *a snappy fire.* **4.** brisk, sharp, or chilly: *a snappy pace; snappy weather.* **5.** smart and fashionable: *a snappy dresser.* **6. make it snappy.** *Slang.* be quick! hurry up! —'**snap·pi·ly** *adv.* —'**snap·pi·ness** *n.*

snap ring *n. Mountaineering.* another name for **karabiner.**

snap roll *n.* a manoeuvre in which an aircraft makes a fast roll.

snap·shot ('snæp,ʃɒt) *n.* an informal photograph taken with a simple camera. Often shortened to **snap.**

snap up *vb.* (*tr., adv.*) **1.** to avail oneself of eagerly and quickly: *she snapped up the bargains.* **2.** to interrupt abruptly.

snare[1] (snɛə) *n.* **1.** a device for trapping birds or small animals, esp. a flexible loop that is drawn tight around the prey. **2.** a surgical instrument for removing certain tumours, consisting of a wire loop that may be drawn tight around their base to sever or uproot them. **3.** anything that traps or entangles someone or something unawares. ~*vb.* (*tr.*) **4.** to catch birds or small animals with a snare. **5.** to catch or trap in or as if in a snare; capture by trickery. [Old English *sneare,* from Old Norse *snara;* related to Old High German *snaraha*] —'**snare·less** *adj.* —'**snar·er** *n.* —'**snar·ing·ly** *adv.*

snare[2] (snɛə) *n. Music.* a set of gut strings wound with wire fitted against the lower drumhead of a snare drum. They produce a rattling sound when the drum is beaten. See **snare drum.** [C17: from Middle Dutch *snaer* or Middle Low German *snare* string; related to Gothic *snōrjō* basket]

snare drum *n. Music.* a cylindrical drum with two drumheads, the upper of which is struck and the lower fitted with a snare. See **snare**[2].

snarl[1] (snɑːl) *vb.* **1.** (*intr.*) (of an animal) to growl viciously, baring the teeth. **2.** to speak or express (something) viciously or angrily. ~*n.* **3.** a vicious growl, utterance, or facial expression. **4.** the act of snarling. [C16: of Germanic origin; compare Middle Low German *snarren,* Middle Dutch *snarren* to drone] —'**snarl·er** *n.* —'**snarl·ing·ly** *adv.* —'**snarl·y** *adj.*

snarl[2] (snɑːl) *n.* **1.** a tangled mass of thread, hair, etc. **2.** a complicated or confused state or situation. **3.** a knot in wood. ~*vb.* **4.** (often foll. by *up*) to be, become, or make tangled or complicated. **5.** (*tr.;* often foll. by *up*) to confuse mentally. **6.** (*tr.*) to flute or emboss (metal) by hammering on a tool held against the under surface. [C14: of Scandinavian origin; compare Old Swedish *snarel* noose, Old Norse *snara* SNARE[1]] —'**snarl·er** *n.* —'**snarl·y** *adj.*

snarl-up *n. Informal, chiefly Brit.* a confusion, obstruction, or tangle, esp. a traffic jam.

snatch (snætʃ) *vb.* **1.** (*tr.*) to seize or grasp (something) suddenly or peremptorily: *he snatched the chocolate out of my hand.* **2.** (*intr.;* usually foll. by *at*) to seize or attempt to seize suddenly. **3.** (*tr.*) to take hurriedly: *to snatch some sleep.* **4.** (*tr.*) to remove suddenly: *she snatched her hand away.* **5.** (*tr.*) to gain, win, or rescue, esp. narrowly: *they snatched victory in the closing seconds.* **6.** (*tr.*) (in weightlifting) to lift (a weight) with a snatch. **7. snatch one's time.** *Austral. informal.* to leave a job, taking whatever pay is due. ~*n.* **8.** an act of snatching. **9.** a fragment or small incomplete part: *snatches of conversation.* **10.** a brief spell: *snatches of time off.* **11.** *Weightlifting.* a lift in which the weight is raised in one quick motion from the floor to an overhead position. **12.** *Slang, chiefly U.S.* an act of kidnapping. **13.** *Brit. slang.* a robbery: *a diamond snatch.* [C13 *snacchen;* related to Middle Dutch *snakken* to gasp, Old Norse *snaka* to sniff around] —'**snatch·er** *n.*

snatch block *n. Nautical.* a block that can be opened so that a rope can be inserted from the side, without threading it through from the end.

snatch·y ('snætʃɪ) *adj.* **snatch·i·er, snatch·i·est.** disconnected or spasmodic. —'**snatch·i·ly** *adv.*

snath (snæθ) *or* **snathe** (sneɪð) *n.* the handle of a scythe. [C16: variant of earlier *snead,* from Old English *snǣd,* of obscure origin]

snaz·zy ('snæzɪ) *adj.* ·**zi·er,** ·**zi·est.** *Informal.* (esp. of clothes) stylishly and often flashily attractive. [C20: perhaps from SN(APPY + J)AZZY] —'**snaz·zi·ly** *adv.* —'**snaz·zi·ness** *n.*

SNCC (snɪk) *n.* (in the U.S.) *acronym for* Student Nonviolent Coordinating Committee (1960–69) and Student National Coordinating Committee (from 1969); a civil-rights organization, formed originally to organize voter registration among Southern Negroes. SNCC has become increasingly militant and has adopted Black power as its goal.

SNCF *abbrev. for* Société Nationale des Chemins de Fer: the French national railway system.

sneak (sni:k) *vb.* **1.** (*intr.*; often foll. by *along, off, in,* etc.) to move furtively. **2.** (*intr.*) to behave in a cowardly or underhand manner. **3.** (*tr.*) to bring, take, or put stealthily. **4.** (*intr.*) *Informal, chiefly Brit.* to tell tales (esp. in schools). **5.** (*tr.*) *Informal.* to steal. **6.** (*intr.*; foll. by *off, out, away,* etc.) *Informal.* to leave unobtrusively. ~*n.* **7.** a person who acts in an underhand or cowardly manner, esp. as an informer. **8. a.** a stealthy act or movement. **b.** (*as modifier*): *a sneak attack.* **9.** *Brit. informal.* an unobtrusive departure. [Old English *snīcan* to creep; from Old Norse *snīkja* to hanker after] —**'sneak·y** *adj.* —**'sneak·i·ly** *adv.* —**'sneak·i·ness** *n.*

sneak·ers ('sni:kəz) *pl. n. Chiefly U.S.* canvas shoes with rubber soles worn for sports or informally.

sneak·ing ('sni:kɪŋ) *adj.* **1.** acting in a furtive or cowardly way. **2.** secret: *a sneaking desire to marry a millionaire.* **3.** slight but nagging (esp. in the phrase **a sneaking suspicion**). —**'sneak·ing·ly** *adv.* —**'sneak·ing·ness** *n.*

sneak pre·view *n. U.S.* a screening of a film at an unexpected time to test audience reaction before its release.

sneak thief *n.* a person who steals paltry articles from premises, which he enters through open doors, windows, etc.

sneck (snɛk) *n.* **1.** a small squared stone used in a rubble wall to fill spaces between stones of different height. **2.** *Dialect, chiefly northern Brit.* the latch or catch of a door or gate. ~*vb.* **3.** *Dialect, chiefly northern Brit.* to fasten (a latch). [C15 *snekk,* of uncertain origin]

sned (snɛd) *vb.* **sneds, sned·ding, sned·ded.** (*tr.*) *Northern Brit. dialect.* to lop off or prune. [Old English *snǣdan*]

sneer (snɪə) *n.* **1.** a facial expression of scorn or contempt, typically with the upper lip curled. **2.** a scornful or contemptuous remark or utterance. ~*vb.* **3.** (*intr.*) to assume a facial expression of scorn or contempt. **4.** to say or utter (something) in a scornful or contemptuous manner. [C16: perhaps from Low Dutch; compare North Frisian *sneere* contempt] —**'sneer·er** *n.* —**'sneer·ful** *adj.* —**'sneer·ing** *adj., n.* —**'sneer·ing·ly** *adv.*

sneeze (sni:z) *vb.* **1.** (*intr.*) to expel air from the nose involuntarily, esp. as the result of irritation of the nasal mucous membrane. ~*n.* **2.** the act or sound of sneezing. [Old English *fnēosan* (unattested); related to Old Norse *fnȳsa,* Middle High German *fnūsen,* Greek *pneuma* breath] —**'sneeze·less** *adj.* —**'sneez·er** *n.* —**'sneez·y** *adj.*

sneeze at *vb.* (*intr., prep.*; usually with a negative) *Informal.* to dismiss lightly: *his offer is not to be sneezed at.*

sneeze·wort ('sni:z,wɜ:t) *n.* a Eurasian plant, *Achillea ptarmica,* having daisy-like flowers and long grey-green leaves, which cause sneezing when powdered: family *Compositae* (composites). See also **yarrow.**

Snell's law (snɛlz) *n. Physics.* the principle that the ratio of the sine of the angle of incidence to the sine of the angle of refraction is constant when a light ray passes from one medium to another. [C17: named after Willebrord *Snell* (1591–1626), Dutch physicist]

snib (snɪb) *n. Scot.* **1.** the bolt or fastening of a door, window, etc. ~*vb.* (*tr.*) **snibs, snib·bing, snibbed. 2.** to bolt or fasten (a door).

snick (snɪk) *n.* **1.** a small cut; notch. **2.** a knot in thread, etc. **3.** *Cricket.* **a.** a glancing blow off the edge of the bat. **b.** the ball so hit. ~*vb.* (*tr.*) **4.** to cut a small corner or notch in (material, etc.). **5.** *Cricket.* to hit (the ball) with a snick. [C18: probably of Scandinavian origin; compare Old Norse *snikka* to whittle, Swedish *snicka*]

snick·er ('snɪkə) *n., vb.* **1.** another word, esp. U.S., for **snigger.** ~*vb.* **2.** (of a horse) to whinny. [C17: probably of imitative origin] —**'snick·er·ing·ly** *adv.*

snick·er·snee ('snɪkə,sni:) *n. Archaic.* **1.** a knife for cutting or thrusting. **2.** a fight with knives. [C17 *stick or snee,* from Dutch *steken* to STICK² + *snijen* to cut]

snick·et ('snɪkɪt) *n. Northern Brit. dialect.* a passageway between walls or fences. [of obscure origin]

snide (snaɪd) *adj.* **1.** (of a remark, etc.) maliciously derogatory; supercilious. **2.** counterfeit; sham. ~*n.* **3.** *Slang.* sham jewellery. [C19: of unknown origin] —**'snide·ness** *n.*

sniff (snɪf) *vb.* **1.** to inhale through the nose, usually in short rapid audible inspirations, as for the purpose of identifying a scent or for clearing a congested nasal passage. **2.** (when *intr.,* often foll. by *at*) to perceive or attempt to perceive (a smell) by inhaling through the nose. ~*n.* **3.** the act or sound of sniffing. **4.** a smell perceived by sniffing, esp. a faint scent. [C14: probably related to *snivelen* to SNIVEL] —**'sniff·er** *n.* —**'sniff·ing·ly** *adv.*

sniff at *vb.* (*intr., prep.*) to express contempt or dislike for.

snif·fle ('snɪfᵊl) *vb.* **1.** (*intr.*) to breathe audibly through the nose, as when the nasal passages are congested. ~*n.* **2.** the act, sound, or an instance of sniffling. —**'snif·fler** *n.*

snif·fles ('snɪfᵊlz) *or* **snuf·fles** *n. Informal.* **1. the.** a cold in the head. **2.** the sniffling that sometimes accompanies weeping or prolonged crying.

sniff out *vb.* (*tr., adv.*) to detect through shrewdness or instinct.

snif·fy ('snɪfɪ) *adj.* **·fi·er, ·fi·est.** *Informal.* contemptuous or disdainful. —**'sniff·i·ly** *adv.* —**'sniff·i·ness** *n.*

snif·ter ('snɪftə) *n.* **1.** a pear-shaped glass with a short stem and a bowl that narrows towards the top so that the aroma of brandy or some other liqueur is retained. **2.** *Informal.* a small quantity of alcoholic drink. [C19: perhaps from dialect *snifter* to sniff, perhaps of Scandinavian origin; compare Danish *snifta* (obsolete) to sniff]

snig·ger ('snɪgə) *or U.S.* **snick·er** ('snɪkə) *n.* **1.** a sly or disrespectful laugh, esp. one partly stifled. ~*vb.* (*intr.*) **2.** to utter such a laugh. [C18: variant of SNICKER] —**'snig·ger·ing·ly** *or U.S.* **'snick·er·ing·ly** *adv.*

snig·gle ('snɪgᵊl) *vb.* **1.** (*intr.*) to fish for eels by dangling or thrusting a baited hook into cavities. **2.** (*tr.*) to catch (eels) by sniggling. ~*n.* **3.** the baited hook used for sniggling eels. [C17: from C15 *snig* young eel] —**'snig·gler** *n.*

snip (snɪp) *vb.* **snips, snip·ping, snipped. 1.** to cut or clip with a small quick stroke or a succession of small quick strokes, esp. with scissors or shears. ~*n.* **2.** the act of snipping. **3.** the sound of scissors or shears closing. **4.** Also called: **snipping.** a small piece of anything, esp. one that has been snipped off. **5.** a small cut made by snipping.. **6.** *Chiefly Brit.* an informal word for **bargain. 7.** *Informal.* something easily done; cinch. **8.** *U.S. informal.* a small or insignificant person or thing, esp. an irritating or insolent one. ~*interj.* **9.** (*often reiterated*) a representation of the sound of scissors or shears closing. [C16: from Low German, Dutch *snippen;* related to Middle High German *snipfen* to snap the fingers]

snipe (snaɪp) *n., pl.* **snipe** *or* **snipes. 1.** any of various birds of the genus *Gallinago* (or *Capella*) and related genera, such as *G. gallinago* (**common** or **Wilson's snipe**), of marshes and river banks, having a long straight bill: family *Scolopacidae* (sandpipers, etc.), order *Charadriiformes.* **2.** any of various similar related birds, such as certain sandpipers and curlews. **3.** a shot, esp. a gunshot, fired from a place of concealment. ~*vb.* **4.** (when *intr.,* often foll. by *at*) to attack (a person or persons) with a rifle from a place of concealment. **5.** (*intr.*; often foll. by *at*) to criticize adversely a person or persons from a position of security. **6.** (*intr.*) to hunt or shoot snipe. [C14: from Old Norse *snīpa;* related to Old High German *snepfa* Middle Dutch *snippe*] —**'snipe·,like** *adj.*

snipe·fish ('snaɪp,fɪʃ) *n., pl.* **·fish** *or* **·fish·es.** any teleost fish of the family *Macrorhamphosidae,* of tropical and temperate seas, having a deep body, long snout, and a single long dorsal fin: order *Solenichthyes* (sea horses, etc.). Also called: **bellows fish.**

snipe fly *n.* any of various predatory dipterous flies of the family *Leptidae* (or *Rhagionidae*), such as *Rhagio scolopacea* of Europe, having an elongated body and long legs. [named after the snipe because its flight resembles that of the bird]

snip·er ('snaɪpə) *n.* a rifleman who fires from a concealed place, esp. a military marksman assigned to single out and shoot enemy soldiers from a concealed position.

snip·er·scope ('snaɪpə,skəʊp) *n.* a snooperscope designed to be attached to a rifle or other weapon.

snip·pet ('snɪpɪt) *n.* a small scrap or fragment. —**'snip·py** *adj.* —**'snip·pi·ly** *adv.* —**'snip·pi·ness** *or* **'snip·pet·i·ness** *n.*

snips (snɪps) *pl. n.* a small pair of shears used for cutting sheet metal. Also called: **tin snips.**

snitch (snɪtʃ) *Slang.* ~*vb.* **1.** (*tr.*) to steal; take, esp. in an underhand way. **2.** (*intr.*) to act as an informer. ~*n.* **3.** an informer; telltale. [C17: of unknown origin] —**'snitch·er** *n.*

sniv·el ('snɪvᵊl) *vb.* **·els, ·el·ling, ·elled** *or U.S.* **·els, ·el·ing, ·eled. 1.** (*intr.*) to sniffle as a sign of distress, esp. contemptibly. **2.** to utter (something) tearfully; whine. **3.** (*intr.*) to have a runny nose. ~*n.* **4.** an instance of snivelling. [C14 *snivelen;* related to Old English *snyflung* mucus, Dutch *snuffelen* to smell out, Old Norse *snoppa* snout] —**'sniv·el·ler** *n.* —**'sniv·el·ling** *adj., n.* —**'sniv·el·ly** *adj.*

snob (snɒb) *n.* **1.** a person who strives to associate with those of higher social status and who behaves condescendingly to others. Compare **inverted snob. 2.** a person having similar pretensions with regard to his tastes, etc.: *an intellectual snob.* [C18 (in the sense: shoemaker; hence, C19: a person who flatters those of higher station, etc.): of unknown origin] —**'snob·ber·y** *n.* —**'snob·bish** *adj.* —**'snob·bish·ly** *adv.* —**'snob·bish·ness** *or* **'snob·bism** *n.*

SNOBOL ('snəʊbɒl) *n.* String Oriented Symbolic Language: a computer-programming language for handling strings of symbols.

Sno-Cat ('snəʊ,kæt) *n. Trademark.* a type of snowmobile.

snog (snɒg) *Brit. slang.* ~*vb.* **snogs, snog·ging, snogged. 1.** (*intr.*) to kiss and cuddle. ~*n.* **2.** the act of kissing and cuddling. [of obscure origin]

snood (snu:d) *n.* **1.** a pouchlike hat, often of net, loosely holding a woman's hair at the back. **2.** a headband, esp. one formerly worn by young unmarried women in Scotland. ~*vb.* **3.** (*tr.*) to confine (the hair) in a snood. [Old English *snōd;* of obscure origin]

snook[1] (snu:k) *n., pl.* **snook** *or* **snooks.** any of several large game fishes of the genus *Centropomus,* esp. *C. undecimalis* of tropical American marine and fresh waters: family *Centropomidae* (robalos). [C17: from Dutch *snoek* pike]

snook[2] (snu:k) *n. Brit.* a rude gesture, made by putting one thumb to the nose with the fingers of the hand outstretched (esp. in the phrase **cock a snook**). [C19: of obscure origin]

snook·er ('snu:kə) *n.* **1.** a game played on a billiard table with 15 red balls, six balls of other colours, and a white cue ball. The object is to pot the balls in a certain order. **2.** a shot in which the cue ball is left in a position such that another ball blocks the object ball. The opponent is then usually forced to play the cue ball off a cushion. ~*vb.* (*tr.*) **3.** to leave (an opponent) in an unfavourable position by playing a snooker. **4.** to place (someone) in a difficult situation. [C19: of unknown origin]

snoop (snu:p) *Informal.* ~*vb.* **1.** (*intr.;* often foll. by *about* or *around*) to pry into the private business of others. ~*n.* **2.** a person who pries into the business of others. **3.** an act or instance of snooping. [C19: from Dutch *snoepen* to eat furtively] —**'snoop+er** *n.* —**'snoop·y** *adj.*

snoop·er+scope ('snu:pəˌskəʊp) *n. Military, U.S.* an instrument that enables the user to see objects in the dark by illuminating the object with infrared radiation and converting the reflected radiation to a visual image.

snoot (snu:t) *n. Slang.* the nose. [C20: variant of SNOUT]

snoot·y ('snu:tɪ) *adj.* **snoot·i+er, snoot·i+est.** *Informal.* **1.** aloof or supercilious. **2.** snobbish or exclusive: *a snooty restaurant.* —**'snoot·i+ly** *adv.* —**'snoot·i+ness** *n.*

snooze (snu:z) *Informal.* ~*vb.* **1.** (*intr.*) to take a brief light sleep. ~*n.* **2.** a nap. [C18: of unknown origin] —**'snooz+er** *n.* —**'snooz·y** *adj.*

snore (snɔ:) *vb.* **1.** (*intr.*) to breathe through the mouth and nose while asleep with snorting sounds caused by the soft palate vibrating. ~*n.* **2.** the act or sound of snoring. [C14: of imitative origin; related to Middle Low German, Middle Dutch *snorken;* see SNORT] —**'snor+er** *n.*

snor+kel ('snɔ:kᵊl) *n.* **1.** a device allowing a swimmer to breathe while face down on the surface of the water, consisting of a bent tube fitting into the mouth and projecting above the surface. **2.** (on a submarine) a retractable vertical device containing air-intake and exhaust pipes for the engines and general ventilation: its use permits extended periods of submergence at periscope depth. ~*vb.* **3.** (*intr.*) to swim with a snorkel. [C20: from German *Schnorchel;* related to German *schnarchen* to SNORE]

Snor·ri Stur·lu·son ('snɔ:rɪ 'stɜ:ləsᵊn) *n.* 1179–1241, Icelandic historian and poet; author of *Younger* or *Prose Edda* (?1222), containing a collection of Norse myths and a treatise on poetry, and the *Heimskringla* sagas of the Norwegian kings from their mythological origins to the 12th century.

snort (snɔ:t) *vb.* **1.** (*intr.*) to exhale forcibly through the nostrils, making a characteristic noise. **2.** (*intr.*) (of a person) to express contempt or annoyance by such an exhalation. **3.** (*tr.*) to utter in a contemptuous or annoyed manner. ~*n.* **4.** a forcible exhalation of air through the nostrils, esp. (of persons) as a noise of contempt or annoyance. **5.** Also called: **snorter.** *Slang.* a short drink, esp. an alcoholic one. [C14 *snorten;* probably related to *snoren* to SNORE] —**'snort+ing+ly** *adv.*

snort+er ('snɔ:tə) *n.* **1.** a person or animal that snorts. **2.** *Brit. slang.* something outstandingly impressive or difficult. **3.** *Brit. slang.* something or someone ridiculous.

snot (snɒt) *n.* (*usually considered vulgar*) **1.** nasal mucus or discharge. **2.** *Slang.* a contemptible person. [Old English *gesnot;* related to Old High German *snuzza,* Norwegian, Danish *snot,* German *schneuzen* to blow one's nose]

snot+ty ('snɒtɪ) (*considered vulgar*) ~*adj.* **+ti+er, +ti+est. 1.** dirty with nasal discharge. **2.** *Slang.* contemptible; nasty. **3.** snobbish; conceited. ~*n., pl.* **+ties. 4.** a slang word for **midshipman.** —**'snot+ti+ly** *adv.* —**'snot+ti+ness** *n.*

snout (snaʊt) *n.* **1.** the part of the head of a vertebrate, esp. a mammal, consisting of the nose, jaws, and surrounding region, esp. when elongated. **2.** the corresponding part of the head of such insects as weevils. **3.** anything projecting like a snout, such as a nozzle. **4.** *Slang.* a person's nose. **5.** *Brit. slang.* a cigarette or tobacco. **6. have (got) a snout on.** *Austral. slang.* to have a grudge against (someone). [C13: of Germanic origin; compare Old Norse *snyta,* Middle Low German, Middle Dutch *snūte*] —**'snout+ed** *adj.* —**'snout+less** *adj.* —**'snout+ˌlike** *adj.*

snout bee+tle *n.* another name for **weevil** (sense 1).

snow (snəʊ) *n.* **1.** precipitation from clouds in the form of flakes of ice crystals formed in the upper atmosphere. **2.** a layer of snowflakes on the ground. **3.** a fall of such precipitation. **4.** anything resembling snow in whiteness, softness, etc. **5.** the random pattern of white spots on a television or radar screen, produced by noise in the receiver and occurring when the signal is weak or absent. **6.** *Slang.* **a.** cocaine crystals. **b.** heroin in powder form. **7.** See **carbon dioxide snow.** ~*vb.* **8.** (*intr.,* with *it* as subject) to be the case that snow is falling. **9.** (*tr.;* usually passive, foll. by *over, under, in,* or *up*) to cover or confine with a heavy fall of snow. **10.** (often with *it* as subject) to fall or cause to fall as or like snow. **11.** (*tr.*) *U.S. slang.* to deceive or overwhelm with elaborate often insincere talk. See **snow job. 12. be snowed under.** to be overwhelmed, esp. with paperwork. [Old English *snāw;* related to Old Norse *snjōr,* Gothic *snaiws,* Old High German *snēo,* Greek *nipha*] —**'snow+less** *adj.* —**'snow+ˌlike** *adj.*

Snow (snəʊ) *n.* **C(harles) P(ercy),** Baron Snow. 1905-80, English novelist and physicist. His novels include the series *Strangers and Brothers* (1949-70).

snow+ball ('snəʊˌbɔ:l) *n.* **1.** snow pressed into a ball for throwing, as in play. **2.** a drink made of advocaat and lemonade. **3.** a dance started by one couple who separate and choose different partners. The process continues until all present are dancing. ~*vb.* **4.** (*intr.*) to increase rapidly in size, importance, etc. **5.** (*tr.*) to throw snowballs at.

snow+ball tree *n.* any of several caprifoliaceous shrubs of the genus *Viburnum,* esp. *V. opulus* var. *roseum,* a sterile cultivated variety with spherical clusters of white or pinkish flowers.

snow+ber·ry ('snəʊbərɪ, -brɪ) *n., pl.* **·ries. 1.** any of several caprifoliaceous shrubs of the genus *Symphoricarpos,* esp. *S. albus,* cultivated for their small pink flowers and white berries. **2.** Also called: **waxberry.** any of the berries of such a plant. **3.** any of various other white-berried plants.

snow+bird ('snəʊˌbɜ:d) *n.* **1.** a person with very white skin, esp. a tourist in a sunny climate. **2.** *U.S. slang.* a person addicted to cocaine, or sometimes heroin.

snow-blind *adj.* temporarily unable to see or having impaired vision because of the intense reflection of sunlight from snow. —**snow blind+ness** *n.*

snow+blink ('snəʊˌblɪŋk) *n.* a whitish glare in the sky reflected from snow. Compare **iceblink.**

snow+bound ('snəʊˌbaʊnd) *adj.* confined to one place by heavy falls or drifts of snow; snowed-in.

snow bunt+ing *n.* a bunting, *Plectrophenax nivalis,* of northern and arctic regions, having a white plumage with dark markings on the wings, back, and tail.

snow+cap ('snəʊˌkæp) *n.* a cap of snow, as on top of a mountain. —**'snow+ˌcapped** *adj.*

snow dev+il *n. Canadian.* a whirling column of snow.

Snow+don ('snəʊdᵊn) *n.* a mountain in NW Wales, in Gwynedd: the highest peak in Wales. Height: 1085 m (3560 ft.).

Snow+don·i·a (snəʊ'dəʊnɪə) *n.* **1.** a massif in NW Wales, in Gwynedd, the highest peak being Snowdon. **2.** a national park in NW Wales, in Gwynedd and Clwyd: includes the Snowdonia massif in the north. Area: 2189 sq. km (845 sq. miles).

snow+drift ('snəʊˌdrɪft) *n.* a bank of deep snow driven together by the wind.

snow+drop ('snəʊˌdrɒp) *n.* any of several amaryllidaceous plants of the Eurasian genus *Galanthus,* esp. *G. nivalis,* having drooping white bell-shaped flowers that bloom in early spring.

snow+drop tree *n.* another name for **silver bell.**

snow+fall ('snəʊˌfɔ:l) *n.* **1.** a fall of snow. **2.** *Meteorol.* the amount of snow received in a specified place and time.

snow+field ('snəʊˌfi:ld) *n.* a large area of permanent snow.

snow+flake ('snəʊˌfleɪk) *n.* **1.** one of the mass of small thin delicate arrangements of ice crystals that fall as snow. **2.** any of various European amaryllidaceous plants of the genus *Leucojum,* such as *L. vernum* (**spring snowflake**), that have white nodding bell-shaped flowers.

snow goose *n.* a North American goose, *Anser hyperboreus* (or *Chen hyperborea* or *A. caerulescens*), having a white plumage with black wing tips.

snow grass *n. Austral.* any of various grey-green grasses of the genus *Poa,* of SE Australian mountain regions.

snow gum *n.* another name for **sallee.**

snow-in-sum·mer *n.* another name for **dusty miller** (sense 1).

snow job *n. U.S. slang.* an instance of deceiving or overwhelming someone with elaborate often insincere talk.

snow leop+ard *n.* a large feline mammal, *Panthera uncia,* of mountainous regions of central Asia, closely related to the leopard but having a long pale brown coat marked with black rosettes. Also called: **ounce.**

snow line *n.* the altitudinal or latitudinal limit of permanent snow.

snow+man ('snəʊˌmæn) *n., pl.* **+men.** a figure resembling a man, made of packed snow.

snow+mo·bile ('snəʊməˌbi:l) *n.* a motor vehicle for travelling on snow, esp. one with caterpillar tracks and front skis.

snow-on-the-moun·tain *n.* a North American euphorbiaceous plant, *Euphorbia marginata,* having white-edged leaves and showy white bracts surrounding small flowers.

snow plant *n.* a saprophytic plant, *Sarcodes sanguinea,* of mountain pine forests of W North America, having a fleshy scaly reddish stalk, no leaves, and pendulous scarlet flowers that are often produced before the snow melts: family *Monotropaceae.*

snow+plough ('snəʊˌplaʊ) *n.* **1.** an implement or vehicle for clearing away snow. **2.** *Skiing.* a technique of turning the points of the skis inwards to turn or stop.

snow+shed ('snəʊˌʃɛd) *n.* a shelter built over an exposed section of railway track to prevent its blockage by snow.

snow+shoe ('snəʊˌʃu:) *n.* **1.** a device to facilitate walking on snow, esp. a racket-shaped frame with a network of thongs stretched across it. ~*vb.* **+shoes, +shoe+ing, +shoed. 2.** (*intr.*) to walk or go using snowshoes. —**'snow+ˌsho+er** *n.*

snow+shoe hare *or* **rab+bit** *n.* a N North American hare, *Lepus americanus,* having brown fur in summer, white fur in winter, and heavily furred feet.

snow+storm ('snəʊˌstɔ:m) *n.* a storm with heavy snow.

snow tyre *n.* a motor vehicle tyre with deep treads and ridges to give improved grip on snow and ice.

snow-white *adj.* **1.** white as snow. **2.** pure as white snow.

snow·y ('snəʊɪ) *adj.* **snow·i+er, snow·i+est. 1.** covered with or abounding in snow: *snowy hills.* **2.** characterized by snow: *snowy weather.* **3.** resembling snow in whiteness, purity, etc. —**'snow·i+ly** *adv.* —**'snow·i+ness** *n.*

snow·y eg+ret *n.* a small American egret, *Egretta thula,* having a white plumage, yellow legs, and a black bill.

Snow·y Moun+tains *pl. n.* a mountain range in SE Australia, part of the Australian Alps: famous hydroelectric scheme. Also called (Austral. informal): **the Snowy, the Snowies.** —**Snow·y Moun+tain** *adj.*

snow·y owl *n.* a large owl, *Nyctea scandiaca,* of tundra regions, having a white plumage flecked with brown.

Snow·y Riv+er *n.* a river in SE Australia, rising in SE New South Wales: waters diverted through a system of dams and tunnels across the watershed into the Murray and Murrumbidgee Rivers for hydroelectric power and to provide water for irrigation. Length: 426 km (265 miles).

SNP *abbrev. for* Scottish National Party.

Snr. *or* **snr.** *abbrev. for* senior.

snub (snʌb) *vb.* **snubs, snub·bing, snubbed.** (*tr.*) **1.** to insult (someone) deliberately. **2.** to stop or check the motion of (a boat, horse, etc.) by taking turns of a rope or cable around a post or other fixed object. **3.** *Archaic.* to reprimand. ~*n.* **4.** a deliberately insulting act or remark. **5. a.** *Nautical.* an elastic shock absorber attached to a mooring line. **b.** (*as modifier*): *a snub rope.* ~*adj.* **6.** short and blunt. See also **snub-nosed.** [C14: from Old Norse *snubba* to scold; related to Norwegian, Swedish dialect *snubba* to cut short, Danish *snubbe*] —**'snub·ber** *n.* —**'snub·bing·ly** *adv.* —**'snub·by** *adj.*

snub-nosed *adj.* **1.** having a short turned-up nose. **2.** (of a pistol) having an extremely short barrel.

snuck (snʌk) *vb. U.S., not standard.* a past tense or past participle of **sneak.**

snuff[1] (snʌf) *vb.* **1.** (*tr.*) to inhale through the nose. **2.** (when *intr.*, often foll. by *at*) (esp. of an animal) to examine by sniffing. ~*n.* **3.** an act or the sound of snuffing. [C16: probably from Middle Dutch *snuffen* to snuffle, ultimately of imitative origin] —**'snuff·er** *n.* —**'snuff·ing·ly** *adv.*

snuff[2] (snʌf) *n.* **1.** finely powdered tobacco for sniffing up the nostrils or less commonly for chewing. **2.** a small amount of this. **3.** any powdered substance, esp. one for sniffing up the nostrils. **4. up to snuff.** *Informal.* **a.** in good health or in good condition. **b.** *Chiefly Brit.* not easily deceived. ~*vb.* **5.** (*intr.*) to use or inhale snuff. [C17: from Dutch *snuf*, shortened from *snuftabale*, literally: tobacco for snuffing; see SNUFF[1]] —**'snuff·er** *n.*

snuff[3] (snʌf) *vb.* (*tr.*) **1.** (often foll. by *out*) to extinguish (a light from a naked flame, esp. a candle). **2.** to cut off the charred part of (the wick of a candle, etc.). **3.** (usually foll. by *out*) *Informal.* to suppress; put an end to. **4. snuff it.** *Brit. informal.* to die. ~*n.* **5.** the burned portion of the wick of a candle. [C14 *snoffe*, of obscure origin]

snuff·box ('snʌf,bɒks) *n.* a container, often of elaborate ornamental design, for holding small quantities of snuff.

snuf·fer ('snʌfə) *n.* **1.** a cone-shaped implement for extinguishing candles. **2.** (*pl.*) an instrument resembling a pair of scissors for trimming the wick or extinguishing the flame of a candle. **3.** *Rare.* a person who takes snuff.

snuf·fle ('snʌfᵊl) *vb.* **1.** (*intr.*) to breathe noisily or with difficulty. **2.** to say or speak in a nasal tone. **3.** (*intr.*) to snivel. ~*n.* **4.** an act or the sound of snuffling. **5.** a nasal tone or voice. **6. the snuffles.** a condition characterized by snuffling. [C16: from Low German or Dutch *snuffelen;* see SNUFF[1], SNIVEL] —**'snuf·fler** *n.* —**'snuf·fly** *adj.*

snuff·y ('snʌfɪ) *adj.* **snuff·i·er, snuff·i·est.** **1.** of, relating to, or resembling snuff. **2.** covered with or smelling of snuff. **3.** unpleasant; disagreeable. —**'snuff·i·ness** *n.*

snug (snʌg) *adj.* **snug·ger, snug·gest.** **1.** comfortably warm and well-protected; cosy: *the children were snug in bed during the blizzard.* **2.** small but comfortable: *a snug cottage.* **3.** well-ordered; compact: *a snug boat.* **4.** sheltered and secure: *a snug anchorage.* **5.** fitting closely and comfortably. **6.** offering safe concealment. ~*n.* **7.** (in Britain and Ireland) one of the bars in certain pubs, offering intimate seating for only a few persons. ~*vb.* **snugs, snug·ging, snugged.** **8.** to make or become comfortable and warm. **9.** (*tr.*) *Nautical.* to make (a vessel) ready for a storm by lashing down gear. [C16 (in the sense: prepared for storms (used of a ship)): related to Old Icelandic *snöggr* short-haired, Swedish *snygg* tidy, Low German *snögger* smart] —**'snug·ly** *adv.* —**'snug·ness** *n.*

snug·ger·y ('snʌgərɪ) *n., pl.* **·ger·ies.** **1.** a cosy and comfortable place or room. **2.** another name for **snug** (sense 7).

snug·gle ('snʌgᵊl) *vb.* **1.** (*usually intr.;* usually foll. by *down, up,* or *together*) to nestle into or draw close to (somebody or something) for warmth or from affection. ~*n.* **2.** the act of snuggling. [C17: frequentative SNUG (vb.)]

snye (snaɪ) *n. Canadian.* a side channel of a river. [from Canadian French *chenail*, from French *chenal* CHANNEL]

so[1] (səʊ) *adv.* **1.** (foll. by an adjective or adverb and a correlative clause often introduced by *that*) to such an extent: *the river is so dirty that it smells.* **2.** (*used with a negative;* it replaces the first *as* in an equative comparison) to the same extent as: *she is not so old as you.* **3.** (intensifier): *it's so lovely; I love you so.* **4.** in the state or manner expressed or implied: *they're happy and will remain so.* **5.** (*not used with a negative;* foll. by an auxiliary verb or *do, have,* or *be* used as main verbs) also; likewise: *I can speak Spanish and so can you.* **6.** *Archaic.* provided that. **7. and so on** *or* **forth.** and continuing similarly. **8. just so.** arranged with precision. **9. or so.** approximately: *fifty or so people came to see me.* **10. quite so.** I agree; exactly. **11. so be it.** used to express agreement or resignation. **12. so much. a.** a certain degree or amount (of). **b.** a lot (of): *it's just so much nonsense.* **13. so much for. a.** no more can or need be said about. **b.** used to express contempt for something that has failed: *so much for your bright idea.* ~*conj.* (subordinating; often foll. by *that*) **14.** in order (that): *to die so that you might live.* **15.** with the consequence (that): *he was late home, so that there was trouble.* **16. so as.** (*takes an infinitive*) in order (to): *to slim so as to lose weight.* ~*sentence connector.* **17.** in consequence; hence: *she wasn't needed, so she left.* **18.** used to introduce a sentence expressing resignation, amazement, or sarcasm: *so you're publishing a book!* **19.** thereupon; and then: *and so we ended up in France.* **20.** used to introduce a sentence or clause to add emphasis: *he's crazy, so he is.* **21. so what!** *Informal.* what importance does that have? ~*pron.* **22.** used to substitute for a clause or sentence, which may be understood: *you'll stop because I said so.* ~*adj.* **23.** (used with *is, was,* etc.) factual; true: *it can't be so.* ~*interj.* **24.** an exclamation of agreement, surprise, etc. [Old English *swā;* related to Old Norse *svā*, Old High German *sō*, Dutch *zoo*]

Usage. Careful writers of formal English consider it poor style to use *so* as a conjunction, to indicate either purpose (*he did it so he could feel happier*) or result (*he could not do it so he did not try*). In the former case *in order to* should be used instead and in the latter case *and so* or *and therefore* would be more acceptable.

so[2] (səʊ) *n. Music.* a variant spelling of **soh.**

So. *abbrev. for* south(ern).

s.o. *abbrev. for:* **1.** seller's option. **2.** shipping order.

S.O. (in Britain) *abbrev. for* Stationery Office.

soak (səʊk) *vb.* **1.** to make, become, or be thoroughly wet or saturated, esp. by immersion in a liquid. **2.** (when *intr.*, usually foll. by *in* or *into*) (of a liquid) to penetrate or permeate. **3.** (*tr.;* usually foll. by *in* or *up*) (of a permeable solid) to take in (a liquid) by absorption: *the earth soaks up rainwater.* **4.** (*tr.;* foll. by *out* or *out of*) to remove by immersion in a liquid: *she soaked the stains out of the dress.* **5.** (*tr.*) *Metallurgy.* to heat (a metal) prior to working. **6.** *Informal.* to drink excessively or make or become drunk. **7.** (*tr.*) *U.S. slang.* to overcharge. **8.** (*tr.*) *Brit. slang.* to put in pawn. ~*n.* **9.** the act of immersing in a liquid or the period of immersion. **10.** the liquid in which something may be soaked, esp. a solution containing detergent. **11.** *Austral.* another name for **soakage** (sense 3). **12.** *Brit. informal.* a heavy rainfall. **13.** *Slang.* a person who drinks to excess. [Old English *sōcian* to cook; see SUCK] —**'soak·er** *n.* —**'soak·ing·ly** *adv.*

soak·age ('səʊkɪdʒ) *n.* **1.** the process or a period in which a permeable substance is soaked in a liquid. **2.** liquid that has been soaked up or has seeped out. **3.** Also called: **soak.** *Austral.* a small pool of water or swampy patch.

soak·a·way ('səʊkə,weɪ) *n.* a pit filled with rubble, etc., into which rain or waste water drains.

so-and-so *n., pl.* **so-and-sos.** *Informal.* **1.** a person whose name is forgotten or ignored: *so-and-so came to see me.* **2.** *Euphemistic.* a person or thing regarded as unpleasant or difficult: *which so-and-so broke my razor?*

soap (səʊp) *n.* **1.** a cleaning or emulsifying agent made by reacting animal or vegetable fats or oils with potassium or sodium hydroxide. Soaps often contain colouring matter and perfume and act by emulsifying grease and lowering the surface tension of water, so that it more readily penetrates open materials such as textiles. See also **detergent.** **2.** any metallic salt of a fatty acid, such as palmitic or stearic acid. See also **metallic soap.** **3.** *Slang.* flattery or persuasive talk (esp. in the phrase **soft soap**). **4.** *U.S. slang.* money, esp. for bribery. **5. no soap.** *U.S. slang.* not possible or successful. ~*vb.* **6.** (*tr.*) to apply soap to. **7.** (*intr.;* usually foll. by *out*) *Slang.* to diminish in size, strength, etc., as a cake of soap does with use. **8.** (*tr.;* often foll. by *up*) *Slang.* **a.** to flatter or talk persuasively to. **b.** *U.S.* to bribe. [Old English *sāpe;* related to Old High German *seipfa*, Old French *savon*, Latin *sāpō*] —**'soap·less** *adj.* —**'soap·,like** *adj.*

soap·bark ('səʊp,bɑːk) *n.* **1.** Also called: **quillai.** a W South American rosaceous tree, *Quillaja saponaria*, with undivided evergreen leaves and small white flowers. **2.** Also called: **quillai bark.** the inner bark of this tree, formerly used as soap and as a source of saponin. **3.** any of several trees or shrubs that have a bark similar to this.

soap·ber·ry ('səʊp,bɛrɪ) *n., pl.* **·ries.** **1.** any of various chiefly tropical American sapindaceous trees of the genus *Sapindus*, esp. *S. saponaria* (or *S. marginatus*), having pulpy fruit containing saponin. **2.** a related plant, *S. drummondii*, of the southwestern U.S. **3.** the fruit of any of these trees. ~Also called: **chinaberry.**

soap·box ('səʊp,bɒks) *n.* **1.** a box or crate for packing soap. **2.** a crate used as a platform for speech-making. **3.** a child's homemade racing cart consisting of a wooden box set on a wooden frame with wheels and a steerable front axle.

soap bub·ble *n.* **1.** a bubble formed from soapy water. **2.** something that is ephemeral but attractive.

soap·o·lal·lie ('səʊpə,lælɪ) *n. Canadian.* a drink made by crushing soapberries. [from SOAP(BERRY) + *lallie* (compare *-lolly* as in LOBLOLLY)]

soap op·er·a *n.* a serialized drama, usually dealing with domestic themes and characterized by sentimentality, broadcast on radio or television. [C20: so called because manufacturers of soap were typical sponsors]

soap·stone ('səʊp,stəʊn) *or* **soap·rock** *n.* a massive compact variety of talc, used for making tabletops, hearths, ornaments, etc. Also called: **steatite.**

soap·suds ('səʊp,sʌdz) *pl. n.* foam or lather made from soap. —**'soap·,suds·y** *adj.*

soap·wort ('səʊp,wɜːt) *n.* a Eurasian caryophyllaceous plant, *Saponaria officinalis*, having rounded clusters of fragrant pink or white flowers and leaves that were formerly used as a soap substitute. Also called: **bouncing Bet.**

soap·y ('səʊpɪ) *adj.* **soap·i·er, soap·i·est.** **1.** containing or covered with soap: *soapy water.* **2.** resembling or characteristic of soap. **3.** *Slang.* flattering or persuasive. —**'soap·i·ly** *adv.* —**'soap·i·ness** *n.*

soar (sɔː) *vb.* (*intr.*) **1.** to rise or fly upwards into the air. **2.** (of a bird, aircraft, etc.) to glide while maintaining altitude by the use of ascending air currents. **3.** to rise or increase in volume, size, etc.: *soaring prices.* ~*n.* **4.** the act of soaring. **5.** the altitude attained by soaring. [C14: from Old French *essorer*, from Vulgar Latin *exaurāre* (unattested) to expose to the breezes, from Latin EX-[1] + *aura* a breeze] —'**soar+er** *n.* —'**soar+ing+ly** *adv.*

Soa·res (*Portuguese* 'swarɪʃ) *n.* **Má·ri·o** ('mariu). born 1924, Portuguese statesman; prime minister of Portugal (1976–77; 1978).

sob (sɒb) *vb.* **sobs, sob+bing, sobbed. 1.** (*intr.*) to weep with convulsive gasps. **2.** (*tr.*) to utter with sobs. **3.** to cause (oneself) to be in a specified state by sobbing: *to sob oneself to sleep.* ~*n.* **4.** a convulsive gasp made in weeping. [C12: probably from Low German; compare Dutch *sabben* to suck] —'**sob+ber** *n.* —'**sob+bing+ly** *adv.* —'**sob+ful** *adj.*

so+be·it (səʊ'bi:ɪt) *conj. Archaic.* provided that.

so+ber ('səʊbə) *adj.* **1.** not drunk. **2.** not given to excessive indulgence in drink or any other activity. **3.** sedate and rational: *a sober attitude to a problem.* **4.** (of colours) plain and dull or subdued. **5.** free from exaggeration or speculation: *he told us the sober truth.* ~*vb.* **6.** (usually foll. by *up*) to make or become less intoxicated, reckless, etc. [C14 *sobre,* from Old French, from Latin *sōbrius*] —'**so+ber+ing+ly** *adv.* —'**so+ber+ly** *adv.* —'**so+ber+ness** *n.*

So·bers ('səʊbəz) *n.* **Gar·field St. Au·brun.** born 1936, West Indian cricketer; one of the finest all-rounders of all time.

So+bran+je (səʊ'brɑ:njɪ) *n.* the legislature of Bulgaria.

so+bri+e·ty (səʊ'braɪətɪ) *n.* **1.** the state or quality of being sober. **2.** the quality of refraining from excess. **3.** the quality of being serious or sedate.

so+bri+quet *or* **sou+bri+quet** ('səʊbrɪˌkeɪ) *n.* a humorous epithet, assumed name, or nickname. [C17: from French *soubriquet,* of uncertain origin]

sob sis+ter *n.* a journalist, esp. a woman, on a newspaper or magazine who gives advice in reply to readers' letters and writes articles of sentimental appeal.

sob sto+ry *n.* a tale of personal distress intended to arouse sympathy, esp. one offered as an excuse or apology.

Soc. *or* **soc.** *abbrev. for:* **1.** socialist. **2.** society.

soc+age ('sɒkɪdʒ) *n.* **1.** *English legal history.* the tenure of land by certain services, esp. of an agricultural nature. **2.** *English law.* the freehold tenure of land. [C14: from Anglo-French, from *soc* SOKE] —'**soc+ag+er** *n.*

so-called *adj.* **a.** (*prenominal*) designated or styled by the name or word mentioned, esp. (in the speaker's opinion) incorrectly: *a so-called genius.* **b.** (also used parenthetically after a noun): *these experts, so-called, are no help.*

soc+cer ('sɒkə) *n.* **a.** a game in which two teams of eleven players try to kick or head a ball into their opponent's goal, only the goalkeeper on either side being allowed to touch the ball with his hands and arms. **b.** (*as modifier*): *a soccer player.* Also called: **Association Football.**

So+che *or* **So-ch'e** ('səʊ'tʃɛ) *n.* a town in W China, in the W Sinkiang-Uighur AR: a centre of the caravan trade between China, India, and Transcaspian Soviet areas. Also called: **Yarkand.**

So+chi (*Russian* 'sɔtʃi) *n.* a city and resort in the SW Soviet Union, in the Krasnodar Territory on the Black Sea: hot mineral springs. Pop.: 247 000 (1975 est.).

so+cia+ble ('səʊʃəbᵊl) *adj.* **1.** friendly or companionable. **2.** (of an occasion) providing the opportunity for friendliness and conviviality. ~*n.* **3.** *Chiefly U.S.* another name for **social** (sense 9). **4.** a type of open carriage with two seats facing each other. [C16: via French from Latin *sociābilis,* from *sociāre* to unite, from *socius* an associate] —ˌ**so+cia+'bil+i·ty** *or* '**so+cia+ble+ness** *n.* —'**so+cia+bly** *adv.*

so+cial ('səʊʃəl) *adj.* **1.** living or preferring to live in a community rather than alone. **2.** denoting or relating to human society or any of its subdivisions. **3.** of, relating to, or characteristic of the experience, behaviour, and interaction of persons forming groups. **4.** relating to or having the purpose of promoting companionship, communal activities, etc.: *a social club.* **5.** relating to or engaged in social services: *a social worker.* **6.** relating to or considered appropriate to a certain class of society, esp. one thought superior. **7.** (esp. of certain species of insects) living together in organized colonies: *social bees.* Compare **solitary** (sense 6). **8.** (of plant species) growing in clumps, usually over a wide area. ~*n.* **9.** an informal gathering, esp. of an organized group, to promote companionship, communal activity, etc. [C16: from Latin *sociālis* companionable, from *socius* a comrade] —'**so+cial+ly** *adv.* —'**so+cial+ness** *n.*

so+cial ac+count+ing *n.* the analysis of the economy by sectors leading to the calculation and publication of economic statistics, such as gross national product and national income. Also called: **national accounting.**

so+cial an+thro+pol+o·gy *n.* the branch of anthropology that deals with cultural and social phenomena such as kinship systems or beliefs, esp. of nonliterate peoples.

so+cial as+sis+tance *n.* **1.** a monetary allowance paid to various groups of people by the state to supplement their income or their national insurance benefits; welfare; relief. See also **social security, supplementary benefit. 2.** a government programme that provides for such benefits.

so+cial climb+er *n.* a person who seeks advancement to a higher social class, esp. by obsequious behaviour. Sometimes shortened to **climber.** —**so+cial climb+ing** *n.*

so+cial con+tract *or* **com+pact** *n.* (in the theories of Rousseau and others) an agreement, entered into by individuals, that results in the formation of the state or of organized society, the prime motive being the desire for protection, which entails the surrender of some or all personal liberties.

So+cial Cred+it *n.* (esp. in Canada) a right-wing Populist political party, movement, or doctrine based on the socio-economic theories of Major Clifford H. Douglas (1879–1952), an English engineer. —**So+cial Cred+it+er** *n.*

so+cial de+moc+ra+cy *n.* (*sometimes cap.*) the beliefs, principles, practices, or programme of a Social Democratic Party or of social democrats. —**so+cial dem·o+crat+ic** *adj.*

so+cial dem·o+crat *n.* **1.** any socialist who believes in the gradual transformation of capitalism into democratic socialism. **2.** (*usually cap.*) a member of a Social Democratic Party.

So+cial Dem·o+crat+ic Par+ty *n.* **1.** one of the two major political parties in West Germany: founded 1875. It was originally Marxist but now strives for democratic socialism by gradual reform within the parliamentary system. **2.** any of the similar parties in many other countries. **3.** a centrist political party founded (1981) in Britain.

so+cial ev+o+lu+tion *n. Sociol.* the process of social development from an early simple type of social organization to one that is complex and highly specialized.

so+cial in+sur+ance *n.* government insurance providing coverage for the unemployed, the injured, the old, etc.: usually financed by contributions from employers and employees, as well as general government revenue. See also **social security, national insurance, social assistance.**

so+cial+ism ('səʊʃəˌlɪzəm) *n.* **1.** an economic theory or system in which the means of production, distribution, and exchange are owned by the community collectively, usually through the state. It is characterized by production for use rather than profit, by equality of individual wealth, by the absence of competitive economic activity, and, usually, by government determination of investment, prices, and production levels. Compare **capitalism. 2.** any of various social or political theories or movements in which the common welfare is to be achieved through the establishment of a socialist economic system. **3.** (in Marxist theory) a transitional stage after the proletarian revolution in the development of a society from capitalism to communism: characterized by the distribution of income according to work rather than need.

so+cial+ist ('səʊʃəlɪst) *n.* **1.** a supporter or advocate of socialism or any party promoting socialism (**socialist party**). ~*adj.* **2.** of, characteristic of, implementing, or relating to socialism. **3.** (*sometimes cap.*) of, characteristic of, or relating to socialists or a socialist party.

so+cial+is+tic (ˌsəʊʃə'lɪstɪk) *adj.* resembling or sympathizing with socialism. —ˌ**so+cial+'is+ti+cal+ly** *adv.*

So+cial+ist In+ter+na+tion+al *n.* an international association of largely anti-Communist Social Democratic Parties founded in Frankfurt in 1951.

So+cia+list La+bor Par+ty *n.* (in the U.S.) a minor Marxist party founded in 1876.

so+cial+ite ('səʊʃəˌlaɪt) *n.* a person who is or seeks to be prominent in fashionable society.

so+ci+al+i+ty (ˌsəʊʃɪ'ælɪtɪ) *n., pl.* **·ties. 1.** the tendency of groups and persons to develop social links and live in communities. **2.** the quality or state of being social.

so+cial·i+za+tion *or* **so+cial·i+sa+tion** (ˌsəʊʃəlaɪ'zeɪʃən) *n.* **1.** *Psychol.* the modification from infancy of an individual's behaviour to conform with the demands of social life. **2.** the act of socializing or the state of being socialized.

so+cial+ize *or* **so+cial+ise** ('səʊʃəˌlaɪz) *vb.* **1.** (*intr.*) to behave in a friendly or sociable manner. **2.** (*tr.*) to prepare for life in society. **3.** (*tr.*) *Chiefly U.S.* to alter or create so as to be in accordance with socialist principles, as by nationalization. —'**so+cial+ˌiz+er** *or* '**so+cial+ˌis+er** *n.*

so+cial or+gan+i+za+tion *n. Sociol.* the formation of a stable structure of relations inside a group, which provides a basis for order and patterns relationships for new members.

so+cial psy+chol+o·gy *n. Psychol.* the area of psychology concerned with the interaction between individuals and groups and the effect of society on behaviour.

so+cial sci+ence *n.* the study of society and of the relationship of individual members within society, including economics, history, political science, psychology, anthropology, and sociology. —**so+cial sci+en+tist** *n.*

so+cial sec+re+tar·y *n.* **1.** a member of an organization who arranges its social events. **2.** a personal secretary who deals with private correspondence, etc.

so+cial se+cu+ri+ty *n.* **1.** public provision for the economic, and sometimes social, welfare of the aged, unemployed, etc., esp. through pensions and other monetary assistance. **2.** (*often cap.*) a government programme designed to provide such assistance.

so+cial ser+vic+es *pl. n.* welfare activities organized by the state and carried out by trained personnel.

so+cial work *n.* any of various social services designed to alleviate the conditions of the poor and aged and to increase the welfare of children. —**so+cial work+er** *n.*

so+ci+e+tal (sə'saɪətᵊl) *adj.* of or relating to society, esp. human society or social relations. —**so+'ci+e+tal+ly** *adv.*

so+ci+e+ty (sə'saɪətɪ) *n., pl.* **·ties. 1.** the totality of social relationships among organized groups of human beings or animals. **2.** a system of human organizations generating distinctive cultural patterns and institutions and usually providing protection, security, continuity, and a national identity for its members. **3.** such a system with reference to its mode of social and economic organization or its dominant class: *middle-class society.* **4.** those with whom one has companionship. **5.** an organized group of people associated for some specific purpose or on account of some common interest: *a learned society.* **6. a.** the privileged class of people in a community, esp. as considered superior or fashionable. **b.** (*as modifier*): *a society woman.* **7.** the social life and intercourse of such people: *to enter society as a debutante.* **8.** companionship; the fact or state of being together with someone else: *I enjoy her society.* **9.** *Ecology.* a small community of plants within a larger association. [C16: via Old French *societé* from Latin *societās,* from *socius* a comrade]

So+ci+e·ty Is+lands *pl. n.* a group of islands in the S Pacific: administratively part of French Polynesia; consists of the Windward Islands and the Leeward Islands; became a French protectorate in 1843 and a colony in 1880. Pop.: 81 424 (1967 est.). Area: 1595 sq. km (616 sq. miles).

So+ci+e·ty of Friends *n.* the official name for the **Quakers.**

So+ci+e·ty of Je·sus *n.* the religious order of the Jesuits, founded by Ignatius Loyola.

So+cin+i·an (səʊ'sɪnɪən) *n.* **1.** a supporter of the beliefs of Faustus and Laelius Socinus, who rejected such traditional Christian doctrines as the divinity of Christ, the Trinity, and original sin, and held that those who follow Christ's virtues will be granted salvation. *~adj.* **2.** of or relating to the Socinians or their beliefs. —**So+'cin·i+an+ism** *n.*

So·ci·nus (səʊ'saɪnəs) *n.* **Faus·tus** ('fɔːstəs), Italian name *Fausto Sozzini,* 1539–1604, and his uncle, **Lae·li·us** ('liːlɪəs), Italian name *Lelio Sozzini,* 1525–62, Italian Protestant theologians and reformers.

so·ci·o- *combining form.* denoting social or society: *socioeconomic; sociopolitical; sociology.*

so+ci+o+bi·ol·o+gy (ˌsəʊsɪəʊbaɪ'ɒlədʒɪ) *n.* the study of social behaviour in animals and humans.

so+ci·o+ec·o+nom+ic (ˌsəʊsɪəʊˌiːkə'nɒmɪk, -ˌɛkə-) *adj.* of, relating to, or involving both economic and social factors. —**ˌso+ci·o+ˌec·o+'nom·i+cal+ly** *adv.*

sociol. *abbrev. for* sociology.

so+ci·o+lin+guis+tics (ˌsəʊsɪəʊlɪŋ'gwɪstɪks) *n.* (*functioning as sing.*) the study of language in relation to its social context. —**ˌso+ci·o+'lin+guist** *n.* —**ˌso+ci·o+lin+'guis+tic** *adj.*

so+ci+ol·o+gy (ˌsəʊsɪ'ɒlədʒɪ) *n.* the study of the development, organization, functioning, and classification of human societies. —**so+ci·o+log·i·cal** (ˌsəʊsɪə'lɒdʒɪkəl) *adj.* —**ˌso+ci·o+'log·i+cal+ly** *adv.* —**ˌso+ci+'ol·o+gist** *n.*

so+ci+om+e·try (ˌsəʊsɪ'ɒmɪtrɪ) *n.* the study of sociological relationships, esp. of preferences, within social groups. —**so+ci·o+met+ric** (ˌsəʊsɪə'mɛtrɪk) *adj.* —**ˌso+ci+'om+e+trist** *n.*

so+ci·o+path ('səʊsɪəˌpæθ) *n.* *Psychiatry.* a person who is likely to perform antisocial actions or crimes. Compare **psychopathic personality.** —**ˌso+ci·o+'path+ic** *adj.* —**so+ci+op·a+thy** (ˌsəʊsɪ'ɒpəθɪ) *n.*

so+ci·o+po+lit·i·cal (ˌsəʊsɪəʊpə'lɪtɪkəl) *adj.* of, relating to, or involving both political and social factors.

sock[1] (sɒk) *n.* **1.** a cloth covering for the foot, reaching to between the ankle and knee and worn inside a shoe. **2.** an insole put in a shoe, as to make it fit better. **3.** a light shoe worn by actors in ancient Greek and Roman comedy, sometimes taken to allude to comic drama in general (as in the phrase **sock and buskin**). See **buskin. 4.** another name for **windsock. 5. pull one's socks up.** *Brit. informal.* to make a determined effort, esp. in order to regain control of a situation. **6. put a sock in it.** *Brit. slang.* be quiet! *~vb.* **7.** (*tr.*) to provide with socks. **8. socked in.** *U.S. slang.* (of an airport) closed by adverse weather conditions. [Old English *socc* a light shoe, from Latin *soccus,* from Greek *sukkhos*]

sock[2] (sɒk) *Slang.* *~vb.* **1.** (*usually tr.*) to hit with force. **2. sock it to.** *Slang.* to make a forceful impression on. *~n.* **3.** a forceful blow. [C17: of obscure origin]

sock a·way *vb.* (*tr.*) *U.S. informal.* to save up.

sock+dol·o+ger *or* **sock+dol·a+ger** (sɒk'dɒlədʒə) *n. Slang, chiefly U.S.* **1.** a decisive blow or remark. **2.** an outstanding person or thing.

sock+et ('sɒkɪt) *n.* **1.** a device into which an electric plug can be inserted in order to make a connection in a circuit. **2.** *Chiefly Brit.* such a device mounted on a wall and connected to the electricity supply. Informal Brit. names: **point, plug.** U.S. name: **outlet. 3.** a part with an opening or hollow into which some other part, such as a pipe, probe, etc., can be fitted. **4.** a spanner head having a recess suitable to be fitted over the head of a bolt. **5.** *Anatomy.* **a.** a bony hollow into which a part or structure fits: *a tooth socket; an eye socket.* **b.** the receptacle of a ball-and-socket joint. *~vb.* **6.** (*tr.*) to furnish with or place into a socket. [C13: from Anglo-Norman *soket* a little ploughshare, from *soc,* of Celtic origin; compare Cornish *soch* ploughshare]

sock+et wrench *n.* a wrench having a handle onto which socketed heads of various sizes can be fitted.

sock+eye ('sɒkˌaɪ) *n.* a Pacific salmon, *Oncorhynchus nerka,* having red flesh and valued as a food fish. Also called: **red salmon.** [by folk etymology from Salishan *sukkegh*]

so+cle ('səʊkəl) *n.* another name for **plinth** (sense 1). [C18: via French from Italian *zoccolo,* from Latin *socculus* a little shoe, from *soccus* a SOCK[1]]

soc+man ('sɒkmən, 'səʊk-) *or* **soke+man** ('səʊkmən) *n., pl.* **+men.** *English history.* a tenant holding land by socage. [C16: from Anglo-Latin *socmannus;* see SOKE]

So+co+tra, So+ko+tra, *or* **Su+qu+tra** (sə'kəʊtrə) *n.* an island in the Indian Ocean, about 240 km (150 miles) off Cape Guardafui, Somali Republic: administratively part of Southern Yemen. Capital: Tamrida. Area: 3100 sq. km (1200 sq. miles).

Soc·ra·tes ('sɒkrəˌtiːz) *n.* ?470–399 B.C., Athenian philosopher, whose beliefs are known only through the writings of his pupils Plato and Xenophon. He taught that virtue was based on knowledge, which was attained by a dialectical process that took into account many aspects of a stated hypothesis. He was indicted for impiety and corruption of youth (399) and was condemned to death. He refused to flee and died by drinking hemlock.

So+crat+ic (sɒ'krætɪk) *adj. also* **So+crat·i+cal. 1.** of or relating to Socrates, his methods, etc. *~n.* **2.** a person who follows the teachings of Socrates. —**So+'crat·i·cal+ly** *adv.* —**So+'crat·i+ˌcism** *n.* —**Soc+ra+tist** ('sɒkrətɪst) *n.*

So+crat+ic i·ro+ny *n. Philosophy.* a means of exposing inconsistencies in a person's opinions by close questioning and the admission of one's own ignorance.

So+crat+ic meth+od *n. Philosophy.* the method of instruction by question and answer used by Socrates in order to elicit from his pupils truths he considered to be implicitly known by all rational beings. Compare **maieutic.**

So+cred ('səʊkrɛd) *Canadian.* *~n.* **1.** a supporter or member of a Social Credit movement or party. *~adj.* **2.** of or relating to Social Credit.

sod[1] (sɒd) *n.* **1.** a piece of grass-covered surface soil held together by the roots of the grass; turf. **2.** *Poetic.* the ground. *~vb.* **sods, sod+ding, sod+ded. 3.** (*tr.*) to cover with sods. [C15: from Low German; compare Middle Low German, Middle Dutch *sode;* related to Old Frisian *sātha*]

sod[2] (sɒd) *n. Slang, chiefly Brit.* **1.** a person considered to be obnoxious. **2.** a jocular word for a person. *~interj.* **3.** a strong exclamation of annoyance. *~*See also **sod off.** [C19: shortened from SODOMITE] —**'sod+ding** *adj.*

so·da ('səʊdə) *n.* **1.** any of a number of simple inorganic compounds of sodium, such as sodium carbonate (**washing soda**), sodium bicarbonate (**baking soda**), and sodium hydroxide (**caustic soda**). **2.** See **soda water. 3.** *U.S.* a fizzy drink. **4.** the top card of the pack in faro. [C16: from Medieval Latin, from *sodanum* barilla, a plant that was burned to obtain a type of sodium carbonate, perhaps of Arabic origin]

so·da ash *n.* the anhydrous commercial form of sodium carbonate.

so·da bis+cuit *n.* a biscuit leavened with sodium bicarbonate.

so·da bread *n.* a doughy bread leavened with sodium bicarbonate combined with milk and cream of tartar.

so·da foun+tain *n. U.S.* **1.** a counter that serves drinks, snacks, etc. **2.** an apparatus dispensing soda water.

so·da jerk *n. U.S. slang.* a person who serves at a soda fountain.

so·da lime *n.* a solid mixture of sodium and calcium hydroxides used to absorb carbon dioxide and to dry gases.

so+da+lite ('səʊdəˌlaɪt) *n.* a blue, grey, yellow, or colourless mineral consisting of sodium aluminium silicate and sodium chloride in cubic crystalline form. It occurs in basic igneous rocks. Formula: $Na_4Al_3Si_3O_{12}Cl$.

so+dal+i·ty (səʊ'dælɪtɪ) *n., pl.* **·ties. 1.** *R.C. Church.* a religious or charitable society. **2.** fraternity; fellowship. [C16: from Latin *sodālitās* fellowship, from *sodālis* a comrade]

so+da+mide ('səʊdəˌmaɪd) *n.* a white crystalline compound used as a dehydrating agent, as a chemical reagent, and in making sodium cyanide. Formula: $NaNH_2$. Also called: **sodium amide.**

so·da ni+tre *n.* another name for **Chile saltpetre.**

so·da pop *n. U.S. informal.* a fizzy drink.

so·da si+phon *n.* a sealed bottle containing and dispensing soda water. The water is forced up a tube reaching to the bottom of the bottle by the pressure of gas above the water. Also called (esp. U.S.): **siphon bottle.**

so·da wa+ter *n.* an effervescent beverage made by charging water with carbon dioxide under pressure. Sometimes shortened to **soda.**

sod+den ('sɒdən) *adj.* **1.** completely saturated. **2. a.** dulled, esp. by excessive drinking. **b.** (*in combination*): *a drink-sodden mind.* **3.** heavy or doughy, as bread is when improperly cooked. **4.** *Archaic.* cooked by boiling. *~vb.* **5.** to make or become sodden. [C13 *soden,* past participle of SEETHE] —**'sod+den+ly** *adv.* —**'sod+den+ness** *n.*

Sod·dy ('sɒdɪ) *n.* **Fred·er·ick.** 1877–1956, English chemist, whose work on radioactive disintegration led to the discovery of isotopes: Nobel prize for chemistry 1921.

so+di·um ('səʊdɪəm) *n.* **a.** a very reactive soft silvery-white element of the alkali metal group occurring principally in common salt, Chile saltpetre, and cryolite. Sodium and potassium ions maintain the essential electrolytic balance in living cells. It is used in the production of chemicals, in metallurgy, and, alloyed with potassium, as a cooling medium in nuclear reactors. Symbol: Na; atomic no.: 11; atomic wt.: 22.99; valency: 1; relative density: 0.97; melting pt.: 97.81°C; boiling pt.: 892°C. **b.** (*as modifier*): *sodium light.* [C19: New Latin, from SODA + -IUM]

so+di·um ben+zo+ate *n.* a white crystalline soluble compound used in preserving food, as an antiseptic, and in making dyes and pharmaceuticals. Formula: $Na(C_6H_5COO)$. Also called: **benzoate of soda.**

so+di·um bi+car+bon+ate *n.* a white crystalline soluble compound usually obtained by the Solvay process and used in effervescent drinks, baking powders, fire extinguishers, and in medicine as an antacid; sodium hydrogen carbonate. Formula: $NaHCO_3$. Also called: **bicarbonate of soda, baking soda.**

so+di·um car+bon+ate *n.* a colourless or white odourless soluble crystalline compound existing in several hydrated forms and used in the manufacture of glass, ceramics, soap, and paper and as an industrial and domestic cleansing agent. It is made by the Solvay process and commonly obtained as the decahydrate (**washing soda** or **sal soda**) or a white anhydrous powder (**soda ash**). Formula: Na_2CO_3.

so+di·um chlo+rate *n.* a colourless crystalline soluble compound used as a bleaching agent, weak antiseptic, and weedkiller. Formula: $NaClO_3$.

so+di·um chlo+ride *n.* common table salt; a soluble colourless crystalline compound occurring naturally as halite and in sea water: widely used as a seasoning and preservative for food and in the manufacture of chemicals, glass, and soap. Formula: NaCl. Also called: **salt.**

so+di·um cy·a+nide *n.* a white odourless crystalline soluble poisonous compound with an odour of hydrogen cyanide when damp. It is used for extracting gold and silver from their ores and for case-hardening steel. Formula: NaCN.

so+di·um di+chro+mate *n.* a soluble crystalline solid compound, usually obtained as red or orange crystals and used as an oxidizing agent, corrosion inhibitor, and mordant. Formula $Na_2Cr_2O_7$. Also called (not in technical usage): **sodium bichromate.**

so+di·um flu·o+ro+ac+e·tate (ˌfluərəʊˈæsɪˌteɪt) *n.* a white crystalline odourless poisonous compound, used as a rodenticide. Formula: $Na(CH_2FCOO)$. Also called: **1080.**

so+di·um glu+ta+mate (ˈgluːtəˌmeɪt) *n.* another name for **monosodium glutamate.**

so+di·um hy+drox+ide *n.* a white deliquescent strongly alkaline solid used in the manufacture of rayon, paper, aluminium, soap, and sodium compounds. Formula: NaOH. Also called: **caustic soda.** See also **lye.**

so+di·um hy·po+sul+phite *n.* another name (not in technical usage) for **sodium thiosulphate.**

so+di·um lamp *n.* another name for **sodium-vapour lamp.**

so+di·um ni+trate *n.* a white crystalline soluble solid compound occurring naturally as Chile saltpetre and caliche and used in matches, explosives, and rocket propellants, and as a fertilizer. Formula: $NaNO_3$.

So+di·um Pen+to+thal *n. Trademark.* another name for **thiopentone sodium.**

so+di·um per+bo+rate *n.* a white odourless crystalline compound used as an antiseptic and deodorant. It is sodium metaborate with both water and hydrogen peroxide of crystallization. Formula: $NaBO_2.H_2O_2.3H_2O$.

so+di·um per+ox+ide *n.* a yellowish-white odourless soluble powder formed when sodium reacts with an excess of oxygen: used as an oxidizing agent in chemical preparations, a bleaching agent, an antiseptic, and in removing carbon dioxide from air in submarines, etc. Formula: Na_2O_2.

so+di·um phos+phate *n.* any sodium salt of any phosphoric acid, esp. one of three salts of orthophosphoric acid having formulas NaH_2PO_4 (**monosodium dihydrogen orthophosphate**), Na_2HPO_4 (**disodium monohydrogen orthophosphate**), and Na_3PO_4 (**trisodium orthophosphate**).

so+di·um pro+pi·o+nate *n.* a transparent crystalline soluble substance used as a medical fungicide and to prevent the growth of moulds, esp. to retard spoilage in packed foods. Formula: $Na(C_2H_5COO)$.

so+di·um sil·i+cate *n.* **1.** Also called: **soluble glass.** a substance having the general formula, $Na_2O.xSiO_2$, where *x* varies between 3 and 5, existing as an amorphous powder or present in a usually viscous aqueous solution. See **water glass. 2.** any sodium salt of orthosilicic acid or metasilicic acid.

so+di·um sul+phate *n.* a solid white substance that occurs naturally as thenardite and is usually used as the white anhydrous compound (**salt cake**) or the white crystalline decahydrate (**Glauber's salt**) in making glass, detergents, and pulp. Formula: Na_2SO_4.

so+di·um thi·o+sul+phate *n.* a white soluble substance used, in the pentahydrate form, in photography as a fixer to dissolve unchanged silver halides and also to remove excess chlorine from chlorinated water. Formula: $Na_2S_2O_3$. Also called (not in technical usage): **sodium hyposulphite, hypo.**

so·di·um-va·pour lamp *n.* a type of electric lamp consisting of a glass tube containing neon and sodium vapour at low pressure through which an electric current is passed to give an orange light. They are used in street lighting.

sod off *vb.* (*intr., adv.*) *Taboo slang, chiefly Brit.* to go away; depart.

Sod+om (ˈsɒdəm) *n.* **1.** *Old Testament.* a city destroyed by God for its wickedness that, with Gomorrah, traditionally typifies depravity (Genesis 19:24). **2.** this city as representing homosexuality. **3.** any place notorious for depravity.

sod·o+mite (ˈsɒdəˌmaɪt) *n.* a person who practises sodomy.

sod·o+my (ˈsɒdəmɪ) *n.* anal intercourse committed by a man with another man or a woman. ~Compare **buggery.** [C13: via Old French *sodomie* from Latin (Vulgate) *Sodoma* Sodom]

Soe·kar·no (suːˈkɑːnəʊ) *n.* a variant spelling of **Sukarno.**

Soem+ba (ˈsuːmbə) *n.* a variant spelling of **Sumba.**

Soem+ba+wa (suːmˈbɑːwə) *n.* a variant spelling of **Sumbawa.**

Soen+da Is+lands (ˈsuːndə) *n.* a variant spelling of **Sunda Islands.**

Soen+da Strait *n.* a variant spelling of **Sunda Strait.**

Soe+ra+ba+ja (ˌsʊərəˈbaɪə) *n.* a variant spelling of **Surabaya.**

so+ev·er (səʊˈɛvə) *adv.* in any way at all: used to emphasize or make less precise a word or phrase, usually in combination with *what, where, when, how,* etc., or else separated by intervening words. Compare **whatsoever.**

so·fa (ˈsəʊfə) *n.* an upholstered seat with back and arms for two or more people. [C17 (in the sense: dais upholstered as a seat): from Arabic *suffah*]

so·fa bed *n.* a sofa that can be converted into a bed.

so+far (ˈsəʊfɑː) *n.* a system for determining a position at sea, esp. that of survivors of a disaster, by exploding a charge underwater at that point. The times taken for the shock waves to travel through the water to three widely separated shore stations are used to calculate their position. [C20: from *so(und) f(ixing) a(nd) r(anging)*]

sof+fit (ˈsɒfɪt) *n.* **1.** the underside of a part of a building or a structural component, such as an arch, beam, stair, etc. **2.** the upper inner surface of a drain or sewer. Compare **invert** (sense 6a). [C17: via French from Italian *soffitto,* from Latin *suffixus* something fixed underneath, from *suffigere,* from *sub-* under + *figere* to fasten]

So+fi·a (ˈsəʊfɪə) *n.* the capital of Bulgaria, in the west: colonized by the Romans in 29 A.D.; became capital of Bulgaria in 1879; university (1880). Pop.: 962 500 (1974 est.). Ancient name: **Serdica.** Bulgarian name: **So+fi+ya** (ˈsɔfiˌja).

S. of Sol. *Bible. abbrev. for* Song of Solomon.

soft (sɒft) *adj.* **1.** easy to dent, work, or cut without shattering; malleable. **2.** not hard; giving little or no resistance to pressure or weight. **3.** fine, light, smooth, or fluffy to the touch. **4.** gentle; tranquil. **5.** (of music, sounds, etc.) low and pleasing. **6.** (of light, colour, etc.) not excessively bright or harsh. **7.** (of a breeze, climate, etc.) temperate, mild, or pleasant. **8.** slightly blurred; not sharply outlined: *soft focus.* **9.** (of a diet) consisting of easily digestible foods. **10.** kind or lenient, often excessively so. **11.** easy to influence or impose upon. **12.** *Informal.* feeble or silly; simple (often in the phrase **soft in the head**). **13.** unable to endure hardship, esp. through too much pampering. **14.** physically out of condition; flabby: *soft muscles.* **15.** loving; tender: *soft words.* **16.** *Informal.* requiring little exertion; easy: *a soft job.* **17.** *Chem.* (of water) relatively free of mineral salts and therefore easily able to make soap lather. **18.** (of a drug such as cannabis) nonaddictive or only mildly addictive. Compare **hard** (sense 19). **19.** *Phonetics.* **a.** an older word for **lenis. b.** (not in technical usage) denoting the consonants *c* and *g* in English when they are pronounced as palatal or alveolar fricatives or affricates (s, dʒ, ʃ, ð, tʃ) before *e* and *i,* rather than as velar stops (k, g). **c.** (in the Slavonic languages) palatalized before a front vowel or a special character (**soft sign**) written as ь **20.** *Military.* unarmoured, esp. as applied to a truck by comparison with a tank: *a soft target.* **21.** *Finance, chiefly U.S.* (of prices, a market, etc.) unstable and tending to decline. **22.** (of money or currency) **a.** relatively unstable in exchange value. **b.** in paper rather than coin. **23.** (of radiation, such as x-rays and ultraviolet radiation) having low energy and not capable of deep penetration of materials. **24. soft on** *or* **about. a.** gentle, sympathetic, or lenient towards. **b.** feeling affection or infatuation for. ~*adv.* **25.** in a soft manner: *to speak soft.* ~*n.* **26.** a soft object, part, or piece. **27.** *Informal.* See **softy.** ~*interj. Archaic.* **28.** quiet! **29.** wait! [Old English *sōfte;* related to Old Saxon *sāfti,* Old High German *semfti* gentle] —ˈ**soft+ly** *adv.* —ˈ**soft+ness** *n.*

sof+ta (ˈsɒftə) *n.* a Muslim student of divinity and jurisprudence, esp. in Turkey. [C17: from Turkish, from Persian *sōkhtah* aflame (with love of learning)]

soft+ball (ˈsɒftˌbɔːl) *n.* **1.** a variation of baseball using a larger softer ball, pitched underhand. **2.** the ball used.

soft-boiled *adj.* **1.** (of an egg) boiled for a short time so that the yolk is still soft. **2.** *Informal.* soft-hearted.

soft-cen·tred *adj.* (of a chocolate or boiled sweet) having a centre consisting of cream, jelly, etc.

soft chan+cre *n. Pathol.* a venereal ulcer caused by an infection that is not syphilitic. Also called: **chancroid.**

soft clam *n.* another name for the **soft-shell clam.**

soft coal *n.* another name for **bituminous coal.**

soft-cov·er *adj.* a less common word for **paperback.**

soft drink *n.* a nonalcoholic drink, usually cold.

sof+ten (ˈsɒfᵊn) *vb.* to make or become soft or softer.

sof+ten+er (ˈsɒfᵊnə) *n.* **1.** a substance added to another substance to increase its softness, pliability, or plasticity. **2.** a substance, such as a zeolite, for softening water.

sof+ten+ing of the brain *n.* an abnormal softening of the tissues of the cerebrum characterized by various degrees of mental impairment.

sof+ten up *vb.* (*adv.*) **1.** to make or become soft. **2.** (*tr.*) to weaken (an enemy's defences) by shelling, bombing, etc. **3.** (*tr.*) to weaken the resistance of (a person) by persuasive talk, advances, etc.

soft-finned *adj.* (of certain teleost fishes) having fins that are supported by flexible cartilaginous rays. See also **malacopterygian.** Compare **spiny-finned.**

soft fur+nish+ings *pl. n. Brit.* curtains, hangings, rugs, etc.

soft goods *pl. n.* another name for **dry goods.**

soft-head·ed *adj. Informal.* feeble-minded; stupid; simple. —ˌ**soft-ˈhead·ed+ness** *n.*

soft+heart·ed (ˌsɒftˈhɑːtɪd) *adj.* easily moved to pity. —ˌ**soft+ˈheart·ed·ly** *adv.* —ˌ**soft+ˈheart·ed+ness** *n.*

soft land+ing *n.* a landing by a spacecraft on the moon or a planet at a sufficiently low velocity for the equipment or occupants to remain unharmed. Compare **hard landing.**

soft pal+ate *n.* the posterior fleshy portion of the roof of the mouth. It forms a movable muscular flap that seals off the nasopharynx during swallowing and speech.

soft paste *n.* **a.** artificial porcelain made from clay, bone ash, etc. **b.** (*as modifier*): *softpaste porcelain.*

soft-ped·al *vb.* **·als, ·al·ling, ·alled** *or U.S.* **·als, ·al·ing, ·aled.** (*tr.*) **1.** to mute the tone of (a piano) by depressing the soft pedal. **2.** *Informal.* to make (something, esp. something unpleasant) less obvious by deliberately failing to emphasize or allude to it. ~*n.* **soft ped·al.** **3.** a foot-operated lever on a piano, the left one of two, that either moves the whole action closer to the strings so that the hammers strike with less force or causes fewer of the strings to sound. Compare **sustaining pedal.** See **piano**[1].

soft rot *n.* any of various bacterial or fungal plant diseases characterized by watery disintegration of fruits, roots, etc.

soft sell *n. Chiefly U.S.* a method of selling based on indirect suggestion or inducement. Compare **hard sell.**

soft-shell clam *n.* any of several marine clams of the genus *Mya,* esp. *M. arenaria,* an edible species of coastal regions of the U.S. and Europe, having a thin brittle shell. Sometimes shortened to **soft-shell.** Compare **quahog.**

soft-shell crab *n.* a crab, esp. of the edible species *Cancer pagurus,* that has recently moulted and has not yet formed its new shell. Compare **hard-shell crab.**

soft-shelled tur+tle *n.* any freshwater turtle of the family *Trionychidae,* having a flattened soft shell consisting of bony plates covered by a leathery skin.

soft-shoe *n.* (*modifier*) relating to a type of tap dancing performed wearing soft-soled shoes: *the soft-shoe shuffle.*

soft shoul+der *or* **verge** *n.* a soft edge along the side of a road that is unsuitable for vehicles to drive on.

soft soap *n.* **1.** *Med.* another name for **green soap.** **2.** *Informal.* flattering, persuasive, or cajoling talk. ~*vb.* **soft-soap.** **3.** to use such talk on (a person).

soft-spo·ken *adj.* **1.** speaking or said with a soft gentle voice. **2.** able to persuade or impress by glibness of tongue.

soft spot *n.* a sentimental fondness (esp. in the phrase **have a soft spot for**).

soft touch *n. Informal.* a person easily persuaded or imposed on, esp. to lend money.

soft+ware ('sɒft,wɛə) *n. Computer technol.* the programs that can be used with a particular computer system, esp. those supplied by the manufacturers. Compare **hardware** (sense 2).

soft wheat *n.* a type of wheat with soft kernels and a high starch content.

soft+wood ('sɒft,wʊd) *n.* **1.** the open-grained wood of any of numerous coniferous trees, such as pine and cedar, as distinguished from that of a dicotyledonous tree. **2.** any tree yielding this wood. ~Compare **hardwood.**

soft·y *or* **soft·ie** ('sɒftɪ) *n., pl.* **soft·ies.** *Informal.* a person who is sentimental, weakly foolish, or lacking in physical endurance.

SOGAT ('səʊgæt) *n.* (in Britain) *acronym for* Society of Graphical and Allied Trades.

Sog+di·an ('sɒgdɪən) *n.* **1.** a member of the people who lived in Sogdiana. **2.** the language of this people, now almost extinct, belonging to the East Iranian branch of the Indo-European family. ~*adj.* **3.** of or relating to Sogdiana, its people, or their language.

Sog+di·a·na (,sɒgdɪ'ɑːnə) *n.* a region of ancient central Asia. Its chief city was Samarkand.

sog+gy ('sɒgɪ) *adj.* **+gi+er, +gi+est. 1.** soaked with liquid. **2.** (of bread, pastry, etc.) moist and heavy. **3.** *Informal.* lacking in spirit or positiveness. [C18: probably from dialect *sog* marsh, of obscure origin] —**'sog+gi+ly** *adv.* —**'sog+gi+ness** *n.*

soh *or* **so** (səʊ) *n. Music.* (in tonic sol-fa) the name used for the fifth note or dominant of any scale. [C13: see GAMUT]

so·ho (səʊ'həʊ) *interj.* **1.** *Hunting.* an exclamation announcing the sighting of a hare. **2.** an exclamation announcing the discovery of something unexpected.

So·ho ('səʊhəʊ) *n.* a district of central London, in the City of Westminster: a foreign quarter since the late 17th century, now chiefly known for restaurants, nightclubs, striptease clubs, etc.

soi-di·sant *French.* (swadi'zɑ̃) *adj.* so-called; self-styled. [literally: calling oneself]

soi+gné *or* (*fem.*) **soi+gnée** ('swɑːnjeɪ; *French* swa'ɲe) *adj.* well-groomed; elegant. [French, from *soigner* to take good care of, of Germanic origin; compare Old Saxon *sunnea* care]

soil[1] (sɔɪl) *n.* **1.** the top layer of the land surface of the earth that is composed of disintegrated rock particles, humus, water, and air. See **zonal soil, azonal soil, intrazonal soil, horizon** (senses 4, 5). **2.** a type of this material having specific characteristics: *loamy soil.* **3.** land, country, or region: *one's native soil.* **4. the soil.** life and work on a farm; land: *he belonged to the soil, as his forefathers had.* **5.** any place or thing encouraging growth or development. [C14: from Anglo-Norman, from Latin *solium* a seat, but confused with Latin *solum* the ground]

soil[2] (sɔɪl) *vb.* **1.** to make or become dirty or stained. **2.** (*tr.*) to pollute with sin or disgrace; sully; defile: *he soiled the family honour by his cowardice.* ~*n.* **3.** the state or result of soiling. **4.** refuse, manure, or excrement. [C13: from Old French *soillier* to defile, from *soil* pigsty, probably from Latin *sūs* a swine]

soil[3] (sɔɪl) *vb.* (*tr.*) to feed (livestock) freshly cut green fodder either to fatten or purge them. [C17: perhaps from obsolete vb. (C16) *soil* to manure, from SOIL[2] (n.)]

soil+age ('sɔɪlɪdʒ) *n.* green fodder, esp. when freshly cut and fed to livestock in a confined area.

soil bank *n.* (in the U.S.) a federal programme by which farmers are paid to divert land to soil-enriching crops.

soil con+ser+va+tion *n.* the preservation of soil against deterioration or erosion, and the maintenance of the fertilizing elements for crop production.

soil pipe *n.* a pipe that conveys sewage or waste water from a toilet, etc., to a soil drain or sewer.

soil+ure ('sɔɪljə) *n. Archaic.* **1.** the act of soiling or the state of being soiled. **2.** a stain or blot.

soi+ree ('swɑːreɪ) *n.* an evening party or other gathering given usually at a private house, esp. where guests are invited to listen to, play, or dance to music. [C19: from French, from Old French *soir* evening, from Latin *sērum* a late time, from *sērus* late]

Sois+sons (*French* swa'sɔ̃) *n.* a city in N France, on the Aisne River: has Roman remains and an 11th-century abbey. Pop.: 32 112 (1975).

soix·ante-neuf *French.* (swasɑ̃t'nøf) *n.* a sexual activity in which two people simultaneously stimulate each other's genitalia with their mouths. Also called: **sixty-nine.** [literally: sixty-nine, from the position adopted by the participants]

so+journ ('sɒdʒɜːn, 'sʌdʒ-) *n.* **1.** a temporary stay. ~*vb.* **2.** (*intr.*) to stay or reside temporarily. [C13: from Old French *sojorner,* from Vulgar Latin *subdiurnāre* (unattested) to spend a day, from Latin *sub-* during + Late Latin *diurnum* day] —**'so+journ+er** *n.*

soke (səʊk) *n. English legal history.* **1.** the right to hold a local court. **2.** the territory under the jurisdiction of a particular court. [C14: from Medieval Latin *sōca,* from Old English *sōcn* a seeking; see SEEK]

soke+man ('səʊkmən) *n., pl.* **+men.** (in the Danelaw) a freeman enjoying extensive rights, esp. over his land.

So+ko+to ('səʊkə,təʊ) *n.* **1.** a state of NW Nigeria: the country's largest state, formed in 1976 from part of North-Western State. Capital: Sokoto. Pop.: 2 873 296 (1976 est.). Area: 149 066 sq. km (57 542 sq. miles). **2.** a town in NW Nigeria, capital of Sokoto state: capital of the Fulah Empire in the 19th century; Muslim place of pilgrimage. Pop.: 89 817 (1963).

So+ko+tra (sə'kəʊtrə) *n.* a variant spelling of **Socotra.**

sol[1] (sɒl) *Music.* another name for **soh.** [C14: see GAMUT]

sol[2] (sɒl) *n.* a former French copper or silver coin, usually worth 12 deniers. [C16: from Old French, from Late Latin: SOLIDUS]

sol[3] (sɒl; *Spanish* sol) *n., pl.* **sols** *or* **so+les** (*Spanish* 'soles). the standard monetary unit of Peru, divided into 100 centavos. [C19: from American Spanish, from Spanish: sun, from Latin *sōl;* referring to the design on the coin]

sol[4] (sɒl) *n.* a colloid that has a continuous liquid phase, esp. one in which a solid is suspended in a liquid. [C20: shortened from HYDROSOL]

Sol (sɒl) *n.* **1.** the Roman god personifying the sun. Greek counterpart: **Helios. 2.** a poetic word for the **sun.**

sol. *abbrev. for:* **1.** soluble. **2.** solution.

Sol. *abbrev. for:* **1.** Also: **Solr.** solicitor. **2.** *Bible.* Solomon.

so·la *Latin.* ('səʊlə) *adj.* the feminine form of **solus.**

sol+ace ('sɒlɪs) *n.* **1.** comfort in misery, disappointment, etc. **2.** something that gives comfort or consolation. ~*vb.* (*tr.*) **3.** to give comfort or cheer to (a person) in time of sorrow, distress, etc. **4.** to alleviate (sorrow, misery, etc.). [C13: from Old French *solas,* from Latin *sōlātium* comfort, from *sōlārī* to console] —**'sol+ac+er** *n.*

so+lan *or* **so+lan goose** ('səʊlən) *n.* an archaic name for the **gannet.** [C15 *soland,* of Scandinavian origin; compare Old Norse *sūla* gannet, *ǫnd* duck]

sol·a+na+ceous (,sɒlə'neɪʃəs) *adj.* of, relating to, or belonging to the *Solanaceae,* a family of plants having typically tubular flowers with reflexed petals, protruding anthers, and often poisonous or narcotic properties: includes the potato, tobacco, henbane, mandrake, and several nightshades. [C19: from New Latin *Sōlānāceae,* from Latin *sōlānum* nightshade]

so+lan+der (sə'lændə) *n.* a box for botanical specimens, maps, colour plates, etc., made in the form of a book, the front cover being the lid. [C18: named after D. D. *Solander* (1736–82), Swedish botanist]

so+la+num (səʊ'leɪnəm) *n.* any tree, shrub, or herbaceous plant of the mainly tropical solanaceous genus *Solanum:* includes the potato, aubergine, and certain nightshades. [C16: from Latin: nightshade]

so+lar ('səʊlə) *adj.* **1.** of or relating to the sun: *solar eclipse.* **2.** operating by or utilizing the energy of the sun: *solar cell.* **3.** *Astronomy.* determined from the motion of the earth relative to the sun: *solar year.* **4.** *Astrology.* subject to the influence of the sun. [C15: from Latin *sōlāris,* from *sōl* the sun]

so+lar a·pex *n.* another name for **apex** (sense 4).

so+lar cell *n.* a photovoltaic cell that produces electricity from the sun's rays, used esp. in spacecraft.

so+lar con+stant *n.* the rate at which the sun's energy is received per unit area on the earth's surface when the sun is at its mean distance from the earth and atmospheric absorption has been corrected for. Its value is 1388 watts per square metre.

so+lar day *n.* See under **day** (sense 6).

so+lar e·clipse *n.* See under **eclipse** (sense 1).

so+lar flare *n.* a brief powerful eruption of intense high-energy radiation from the sun's surface, associated with sunspots and causing radio and magnetic disturbances on earth. Sometimes shortened to **flare.** See also **solar wind.**

so+lar fur+nace *n.* a furnace utilizing the sun as a heat source, sunlight being concentrated at the focus of a system of concave mirrors.

so+lar+im+e·ter (,səʊlə'rɪmɪtə) *n.* any of various instruments for measuring solar radiation, as by use of a bolometer or thermopile. Also called: **pyranometer.**

so+lar+ism ('səʊlə,rɪzəm) *n.* the explanation of myths in terms of the movements and influence of the sun. —**'so+lar+ist** *n.*

so+lar+i·um (səʊ'lɛərɪəm) *n., pl.* **-lar·i·a** (-'lɛərɪə) *or* **-lar+i·ums.** a room built largely of glass to afford exposure to the sun. [C19: from Latin: a terrace, from *sōl* sun]

so+lar+ize *or* **so+lar+ise** ('səʊlə,raɪz) *vb.* (*tr.*) **1.** to treat by exposure to the sun's rays. **2.** *Photog.* to reverse some of the tones of (a negative or print) and introduce pronounced outlines of highlights, by exposing it briefly to light after developing and washing, and then redeveloping. **3.** to expose (a patient) to the therapeutic effects of solar or ultraviolet light. —**,so+lar·i·'za+tion** *or* **,so+lar·i+'sa+tion** *n.*

so+lar month *n.* See under **month** (sense 4).

so+lar myth *n.* a myth explaining or allegorizing the origin or movement of the sun.

so+lar plex+us *n.* **1.** *Anatomy.* the network of sympathetic nerves situated behind the stomach that supply the abdominal organs. **2.** (*not in technical usage*) the part of the stomach beneath the diaphragm; pit of the stomach. [C18: referring to resemblance between the radial network of nerves and ganglia and the rays of the sun]

so+lar sys+tem *n.* the system containing the sun and the bodies held in its gravitational field, including the planets (Mercury, Venus, earth, Mars, Jupiter, Saturn, Uranus, Neptune, Pluto), the asteroids, and comets.

so+lar wind (wɪnd) *n.* the stream of charged particles, such as protons, emitted by the sun at high velocities, its intensity increasing during periods of solar activity. It affects terrestial magnetism, some of the particles being trapped by the magnetic lines of force, and causes auroral displays. See also **Van Allen belt, magnetosphere.**

so+lar year *n.* See under **year** (sense 4).

so+la+ti·um (səʊ'leɪʃɪəm) *n., pl.* **+ti·a** (-ʃɪə). *Law, chiefly U.S.* compensation awarded to a party for injury to the feelings as distinct from physical suffering and pecuniary loss. [C19: from Latin: see SOLACE]

sold (səʊld) *vb.* **1.** the past tense or past participle of **sell.** ~*adj.* **2. sold on.** *Slang.* uncritically attached to or enthusiastic about.

sol+dan ('səʊldən, 'sɒl-) *n.* an archaic word for **sultan.** [C13: via Old French from Arabic: SULTAN]

sol+der ('sɒldə; *U.S.* 'sɒdər) *n.* **1.** an alloy for joining two metal surfaces by melting the alloy so that it forms a thin layer between the surfaces. **Soft solders** are alloys of lead and tin; **brazing solders** are alloys of copper and zinc. **2.** something that joins things together firmly; a bond. ~*vb.* **3.** to join or mend or be joined or mended with or as if with solder. [C14: via Old French from Latin *solidāre* to strengthen, from *solidus* SOLID] —**'sol+der+a·ble** *adj.* —**'sol+der+er** *n.*

sol+der+ing i·ron *n.* a hand tool consisting of a handle fixed to an iron or copper tip that is heated, electrically or in a flame, and used to melt and apply solder.

sol+dier ('səʊldʒə) *n.* **1. a.** a person who serves in an army. **b.** Also called: **common soldier.** a noncommissioned member of an army as opposed to a commissioned officer. **2.** a man with military skill or experience, but no longer serving in an army: *an old soldier.* **3.** a person who works diligently for a cause. **4.** *Zoology.* an individual in a colony of social insects, esp. ants, that has powerful jaws adapted for defending the colony, crushing large food particles, etc. ~*vb.* (*intr.*) **5.** to serve as a soldier. **6.** to malinger or shirk. [C13: from Old French *soudier,* from *soude* (army) pay, from Late Latin *solidus* a gold coin, from Latin: firm] —**'sol+dier+,ship** *n.*

sol+dier+ly ('səʊldʒəlɪ) *adj.* of or befitting a good soldier. —**'sol+dier+li+ness** *n.*

sol+dier of for+tune *n.* a man who seeks money or adventure as a soldier; mercenary.

sol+dier on *vb.* (*intr., adv.*) to persist in one's efforts in spite of difficulties, pressure, etc.

sol+dier or+chid *n.* a European orchid, *Orchis militaris,* having pale purple flowers with a four-lobed lower lip. Also called: **military orchid.** [from an imagined resemblance to a soldier]

sol+dier·y ('səʊldʒərɪ) *n., pl.* **+dier·ies. 1.** soldiers collectively. **2.** a group of soldiers. **3.** the profession of being a soldier.

sol+do ('sɒldəʊ; *Italian* 'soldo) *n., pl.* **+di** (-di:). a former Italian copper coin worth one twentieth of a lira. [C16: from Italian, from Late Latin *solidum* a gold coin; see SOLDIER]

sole[1] (səʊl) *adj.* **1.** (*prenominal*) being the only one; only. **2.** (*prenominal*) of or relating to one individual or group and no other: *sole rights on a patent.* **3.** *Law.* having no wife or husband. See also **feme sole. 4.** an archaic word for **solitary.** [C14: from Old French *soule,* from Latin *sōlus* alone] —**'sole+ness** *n.*

sole[2] (səʊl) *n.* **1.** the underside of the foot. **2.** the underside of a shoe. **3. a.** the bottom of a furrow. **b.** the bottom of a plough. **4.** the underside of a golf club head. **5.** the bottom of an oven, furnace, etc. ~*vb.* (*tr.*) **6.** to provide (a shoe) with a sole. **7.** *Golf.* to rest (the club) on the ground, as when preparing to make a stroke. [C14: via Old French from Latin *solea* sandal; probably related to *solum* the ground] —**'sole+less** *adj.*

sole[3] (səʊl) *n., pl.* **sole** *or* **soles. 1.** any tongue-shaped flatfish of the family *Soleidae,* esp. *Solea solea* (**European sole**): most common in warm seas and highly valued as food fishes. **2.** any of certain other similar fishes. [C14: via Old French from Vulgar Latin *sola* (unattested), from Latin *solea* a sandal (from the fish's shape)]

sol+e·cism ('sɒlɪ,sɪzəm) *n.* **1. a.** the nonstandard use of a grammatical construction. **b.** any mistake, incongruity, or absurdity. **2.** a violation of good manners. [C16: from Latin *soloecismus,* from Greek *soloikismos,* from *soloikos* speaking incorrectly, from *Soloi* an Athenian colony of Cilicia where the inhabitants spoke a corrupt form of Greek] —**'sol+e·cist** *n.* —**,sol+e·'cis+tic** *or* **,sol+e·'cis+ti+cal** *adj.* —**,sol+e·'cis+ti+cal+ly** *adv.*

sole+ly ('səʊllɪ) *adv.* **1.** only; completely; entirely. **2.** without another or others; singly; alone. **3.** for one thing only.

sol+emn ('sɒləm) *adj.* **1.** characterized or marked by seriousness or sincerity: *a solemn vow.* **2.** characterized by pomp, ceremony, or formality. **3.** serious, glum, or pompous. **4.** inspiring awe: *a solemn occasion.* **5.** performed with religious ceremony. **6.** gloomy or sombre: *solemn colours.* [C14: from Old French *solempne,* from Latin *sōllemnis* appointed, perhaps from *sollus* whole] —**'sol+emn+ly** *adv.* —**'sol+emn+ness** *or* **'sol+em+ness** *n.*

so+lem+ni+fy (sə'lɛmnɪ,faɪ) *vb.* **+fies, +fy+ing, +fied.** (*tr.*) to make serious or grave. —**so+,lem+ni+fi+'ca+tion** *n.*

so+lem+ni·ty (sə'lɛmnɪtɪ) *n., pl.* **·ties. 1.** the state or quality of being solemn. **2.** (*often pl.*) solemn ceremony, observance, celebration, etc. **3.** *Law.* a formality necessary to validate a deed, act, contract, etc.

sol+em+nize *or* **sol+em+nise** ('sɒləm,naɪz) *vb.* (*tr.*) **1.** to celebrate or observe with rites or formal ceremonies, as a religious occasion. **2.** to celebrate or perform the ceremony of (marriage). **3.** to make solemn or serious. **4.** to perform or hold (ceremonies, etc.) in due manner. —**,sol+em+ni+'za+tion** *or* **,sol+em+ni+'sa+tion** *n.* —**'sol+em+,niz+er** *or* **'sol+em+,nis+er** *n.*

Sol+emn League and Cov+e·nant *n.* See **Covenant.**

so+len·o+don (sə'lɛnədən) *n.* either of two rare shrew-like nocturnal mammals of the West Indies, *Atopogale cubana* (**Cuban solenodon**) or *Solenodon paradoxus* (**Haitian solenodon**), having a long hairless tail and an elongated snout: family *Solenodontidae,* order *Insectivora* (insectivores). [C19: from New Latin, from Latin *sōlēn* sea mussel, razor fish (from Greek: pipe) + Greek *odōn* tooth]

so+le·noid ('səʊlɪ,nɔɪd) *n.* **1.** a coil of wire, usually cylindrical, in which a magnetic field is set up by passing a current through it. **2.** a coil of wire, partially surrounding an iron core, that is made to move inside the coil by the magnetic field set up by a current: used to convert electrical to mechanical energy, as in the operation of a switch. **3.** such a device used as a relay, as in a motor vehicle for connecting the battery directly to the starter motor when activated by the ignition switch. [C19: from French *solénoïde,* from Greek *sōlēn* a pipe, tube] —**,so+le·'noi+dal** *adj.* —**,so+le·'noi+dal+ly** *adv.*

So+lent ('səʊlənt) *n.* **the.** a strait of the English Channel between the mainland coast of Hampshire, England and the Isle of Wight. Width: up to 6 km (4 miles).

So+leure (sɔ'lœ:r) *n.* the French name for **Solothurn.**

sol-fa ('sɒl'fɑ:) *n.* **1.** short for **tonic sol-fa.** ~*vb.* **-fas, -fa·ing, -faed. 2.** *U.S.* to use tonic sol-fa syllables in singing (a tune). [C16: see GAMUT]

sol+fa+ta+ra (,sɒlfə'tɑ:rə) *n.* a volcanic vent emitting only sulphurous gases and water vapour or sometimes hot mud. [C18: from Italian: a sulphurous volcano near Naples, from *solfo* SULPHUR] —**,sol+fa+'ta+ric** *adj.*

sol+feg+gi·o (sɒl'fɛdʒɪəʊ) *or* **sol+fège** (sɒl'fɛʒ) *n., pl.* **+feg+gi** (-'fɛdʒi:), **+feg+gi·os,** *or* **+fèg·es.** *Music.* **1.** a voice exercise in which runs, scales, etc., are sung to the same syllable or syllables. **2.** solmization, esp. the French or Italian system, in which the names correspond to the notes of the scale of C major. [C18: from Italian *solfeggiare* to use the syllables sol-fa; see GAMUT]

sol+fe+ri+no (,sɒlfə'ri:nəʊ) *n.* **a.** a moderate purplish-red colour. **b.** (*as adj.*): *a solferino suit.* [C19: from a dye discovered in 1859, the year a battle was fought at *Solferino,* a town in Italy]

so·li ('səʊlɪ) *adj., adv. Music.* (of a piece or passage) to be performed by or with soloists. ~Compare **tutti.**

so+lic+it (sə'lɪsɪt) *vb.* **1.** (when *intr.,* foll. by *for*) to make a request, application, or entreaty to (a person for business, support, etc.). **2.** to accost (a person) with an offer of sexual relations in return for money. **3.** to provoke or incite (a person) to do something wrong or illegal. [C15: from Old French *solliciter* to disturb, from Latin *sollicitāre* to harass, from *sollicitus* agitated, from *sollus* whole + *citus,* from *ciēre* to excite] —**so+,lic·i·'ta+tion** *n.*

so+lic·i+tor (sə'lɪsɪtə) *n.* **1.** (in Britain) a lawyer who advises clients on matters of law, draws up legal documents, prepares cases for barristers, etc. Compare **barrister. 2.** (in the U.S.) an officer responsible for the legal affairs of a town, city, etc. **3.** a person who solicits. —**so+'lic·i·tor+,ship** *n.*

So+lic·i·tor Gen+er+al *n., pl.* **So+lic·i·tors Gen+er+al.** (in Britain) the law officer of the Crown ranking next to the Attorney General (in Scotland to the Lord Advocate) and acting as his assistant.

so+lic·i·tous (sə'lɪsɪtəs) *adj.* **1.** showing consideration, concern, attention, etc. **2.** keenly anxious or willing; eager. [C16: from Latin *sollicitus* anxious; see SOLICIT] —**so+'lic·i·tous+ly** *adv.* —**so+'lic·i·tous+ness** *n.*

so+lic·i+tude (sə'lɪsɪ,tju:d) *n.* **1.** the state or quality of being solicitous. **2.** (*often pl.*) something that causes anxiety or concern. **3.** anxiety or concern.

sol+id ('sɒlɪd) *adj.* **1.** of, concerned with, or being a substance in a physical state in which the force of attraction between its molecules or atoms is large enough to hold them in fixed positions and cause the substance to resist changes in size and shape. Compare **liquid** (sense 1), **gas** (sense 1). **2.** consisting of matter all through. **3.** of the same substance all through: *solid rock.* **4.** sound; proved or provable: *solid facts.* **5.** reliable or sensible; upstanding: *a solid citizen.* **6.** firm, strong, compact, or substantial: *a solid table; solid ground.* **7.** (of a meal or food) substantial. **8.** (*often postpositive*) without interruption or respite; continuous: *solid bombardment.* **9.** financially sound or solvent: *a solid institution.* **10.** strongly linked or consolidated: *a solid relationship.* **11.** *Geom.* having three dimensions: *a solid object.* **12.** (of a word composed of two or more other words or elements) written or printed as a single word without a hyphen. **13.** *Geom.* of or relating to three-dimensional bodies or objects. **14.** *Printing.* with no space or leads between lines of type. **15.** **solid for.** unanimously in favour of. **16.** (of a writer, work, performance, etc.) adequate; sensible. **17.** of or having a single uniform colour or tone. ~*n.* **18.** *Geom.* **a.** a closed surface in three-dimensional space. **b.** such a surface together with the volume enclosed by it. **19.** a solid substance, such as wood, iron, or diamond. [C14: from Old French *solide,* from Latin *solidus* firm; related to Latin *sollus* whole] —**so+lid+i·ty** (səˈlɪdɪtɪ) *n.* —**ˈsol+id+ly** *adv.* —**ˈsol+id+ness** *n.*

sol·i·da·go (ˌsɒlɪˈdeɪgəʊ) *n., pl.* **+gos.** any plant of the chiefly American genus *Solidago,* which includes the goldenrods: family *Compositae* (composites). [C18: via New Latin from Medieval Latin *soldago* a plant reputed to have healing properties, from *soldāre* to strengthen, from Latin *solidāre,* from *solidus* SOLID]

sol+id an+gle *n.* a geometric surface consisting of lines originating from a common point (the vertex) and passing through a closed curve or polygon.

sol·i·dar·i·ty (ˌsɒlɪˈdærɪtɪ) *n., pl.* **·ties.** unity of interests, sympathies, etc., as among members of the same class.

sol·i·dar·y (ˈsɒlɪdərɪ, -drɪ) *adj.* marked by unity of interests, responsibilities, etc. [C19: from French *solidaire,* from *solide* SOLID]

sol+id fu·el *n.* **1.** a domestic or industrial fuel, such as coal or coke, that is a solid rather than an oil or gas. **2.** Also called: **solid propellant.** a rocket fuel that is a solid rather than a liquid or a gas.

sol+id ge+om+e·try *n.* the branch of geometry concerned with the properties of solid geometric figures.

so+lid·i·fy (səˈlɪdɪˌfaɪ) *vb.* **+fies, +fy+ing, +fied.** **1.** to make or become solid or hard. **2.** to make or become strong, united, determined, etc. —**so+ˈlid·i+ˌfi·a·ble** *adj.* —**so+ˌlid·i·fi+ˈca+tion** *n.* —**so+ˈlid·i+ˌfi+er** *n.*

sol·id-state *n.* **1.** (*modifier*) (of an electronic component or device) consisting chiefly or exclusively of semiconductor materials or components and operating or controlled by means of their electrical properties. **2.** (*modifier*) of, concerned with, characteristic of, or consisting of solid matter.

sol·id-state phys+ics *n.* the branch of physics concerned with experimental and theoretical investigations of the properties of solids, such as superconductivity, photoconductivity, and ferromagnetism.

sol·i·dus (ˈsɒlɪdəs) *n., pl.* **+di** (-ˌdaɪ). **1.** Also called: **diagonal, separatrix, shilling mark, slash, stroke, virgule.** a short oblique stroke used in text to separate items of information, such as days, months, and years in dates (*18/7/80*), alternative words (*and/or*), numerator from denominator in fractions (*55/103*), etc. **2.** a gold coin of the Byzantine empire. [C14: from Late Latin *solidus* (*nummus*) a gold coin (from *solidus* solid); in Medieval Latin, *solidus* referred to a shilling and was indicated by a long *s,* which ultimately became the virgule]

sol·i·fid·i·an (ˌsɒlɪˈfɪdɪən) *n. Christianity.* a person who maintains that man is justified by faith alone. [C16: from New Latin *sōlifidius,* from Latin *sōlus* sole + *fides* faith] —**ˌsol·i·ˈfid·i·an+ˌism** *n.*

sol·i·fluc+tion or **sol·i·flux+ion** (ˈsɒlɪˌflʌkʃən, ˈsəʊlɪ-) *n.* slow downhill movement of soil, saturated with meltwater, over a permanently frozen subsoil in tundra regions. [C20: from Latin *solum* soil + *fluctio* act of flowing]

So+li+hull (ˈsəʊlɪˌhʌl) *n.* a town in central England, in the S West Midlands near Birmingham: mainly residential. Pop.: 106 968 (1971).

so+lil·o+quize or **so+lil·o+quise** (səˈlɪləˌkwaɪz) *vb.* to utter (something) in soliloquy. —**so+lil·o+quist** (səˈlɪləkwɪst) or **so+ˈlil·o+ˌquiz+er, so+ˈlil·o+ˌquis+er** *n.*

so+lil·o+quy (səˈlɪləkwɪ) *n., pl.* **+quies.** **1.** the act of speaking alone or to oneself, esp. as a theatrical device. **2.** a speech in a play that is spoken in soliloquy: *Hamlet's first soliloquy.* [C17: via Late Latin *sōliloquium,* from Latin *sōlus* sole + *loquī* to speak]

Sol·i·man (ˈsɒlɪmən) *n.* a variant spelling of **Suleiman I.**

So+li+mões (ˌsɔliˈmɔ̃ʊs) *n.* **the.** the Brazilian name for the Amazon from the Peruvian border to the Rio Negro.

So+ling+en (*German* ˈzoːlɪŋən) *n.* a city in West Germany, in North Rhine-Westphalia: a major European centre of the cutlery industry. Pop.: 175 923 (1974 est.).

sol+ip+sism (ˈsɒlɪpˌsɪzəm) *n. Philosophy.* the theory that the self is the only thing that can be known to exist. [C19: from Latin *sōlus* alone + *ipse* self] —**ˈsol+ip+sist** *n., adj.* —**ˌsol+ip+ˈsis+tic** *adj.*

sol·i·taire (ˈsɒlɪˌtɛə, ˌsɒlɪˈtɛə) *n.* **1.** Also called: **pegboard.** a game played by one person, esp. one involving moving and taking pegs in a pegboard with the object of being left with only one. **2.** the U.S. name for **patience** (the card game). **3.** a gem, esp. a diamond, set alone in a ring. **4.** any of several extinct birds of the genus *Pezophaps,* related to the dodo. **5.** any of several dull grey North American songbirds of the genus *Myadestes:* subfamily *Turdinae* (thrushes). [C18: from Old French: SOLITARY]

sol·i·tar·y (ˈsɒlɪtərɪ, -trɪ) *adj.* **1.** following or enjoying a life of solitude: *a solitary disposition.* **2.** experienced or performed alone: *a solitary walk.* **3.** (of a place) unfrequented. **4.** (*prenominal*) single; sole: *a solitary speck in the sky.* **5.** having few companions; lonely. **6.** (of animals) not living in organized colonies or large groups: *solitary bees; a solitary elephant.* Compare **social** (sense 7), **gregarious** (sense 2). **7.** (of flowers) growing singly. ~*n., pl.* **+tar·ies.** **8.** a person who lives in seclusion; hermit; recluse. **9.** *Informal.* short for **solitary confinement.** [C14: from Latin *sōlitārius,* from *sōlus* SOLE[1]] —**ˈsol·i·tar·i+ly** *adv.* —**ˈsol·i·tar·i+ness** *n.*

sol·i·tar·y con+fine+ment *n.* isolation imposed on a prisoner, as by confinement in a special cell.

sol·i·tude (ˈsɒlɪˌtjuːd) *n.* **1.** the state of being solitary or secluded. **2.** *Poetic.* a solitary place. [C14: from Latin *sōlitūdō,* from *sōlus* alone, SOLE[1]] —**ˌsol·i·ˈtu+di+nous** *adj.*

sol+ler+et (ˌsɒləˈrɛt) *n.* a protective covering for the foot consisting of riveted plates of armour. [C19: from French, diminutive of Old French *soller* shoe, from Late Latin *subtēl* arch beneath the foot, from SUB- + *tālus* ankle]

sol+lick+er (ˈsɒlɪkə) *n. Austral. slang.* something very large. [C19: from English dialect]

sol+mi+za+tion or **sol+mi+sa+tion** (ˌsɒlmɪˈzeɪʃən) *n. Music.* a system of naming the notes of a scale by syllables instead of letters derived from the 11th-century hexachord system of Guido d'Arezzo, which assigns the names *ut* (or *do*), *re, mi, fa, sol, la, si* (or *ti*) to the degrees of the major scale of C (**fixed system**) or (excluding the syllables *ut* and *si*) to the major scale in any key (**movable system**). See also **tonic sol-fa.** [C18: from French *solmisation,* from *solmiser* to use the sol-fa syllables, from SOL[1] + MI]

so·lo (ˈsəʊləʊ) *n., pl.* **·los.** **1.** (*pl.* **·los** or **·li** (-liː)). a musical composition for one performer with or without accompaniment. **2.** any of various card games in which each person plays on his own instead of in partnership with another, such as solo whist. **3.** a flight in which an aircraft pilot is unaccompanied. **4. a.** any performance carried out by an individual without assistance from others. **b.** (*as modifier*): *a solo attempt.* ~*adj.* **5.** *Music.* unaccompanied: *a sonata for cello solo.* ~*adv.* **6.** by oneself; alone: *to fly solo.* ~*vb.* **7.** (*intr.*) to operate an aircraft alone. [C17: via Italian from Latin *sōlus* alone, SOLE[1]]

so+lo+ist (ˈsəʊləʊɪst) *n.* a person who performs a solo.

So·lo man *n.* a type of early man, *Homo soloensis,* of late Pleistocene times, having a skull resembling that of Neanderthal man but with a smaller cranial capacity. [C20: after *Solo,* site in central Java where remains were found]

Sol·o·mon (ˈsɒləmən) *n.* 10th-century B.C. king of Israel, son of David and Bathsheba, credited with great wisdom. —**Sol·o+mon+ic** (ˌsɒləˈmɒnɪk) or **Sol·o+mo+ni·an** (ˌsɒləˈməʊnɪən) *adj.*

Sol·o·mon Is+lands *pl. n.* an archipelago in the SW Pacific, extending for almost 1450 km (900 miles) in a northwest-southeast direction: the northernmost islands (Buka and Bougainville) form part of Papua New Guinea; the remainder, including Guadalcanal, form an independent state, within the Commonwealth. Pop.: 196 823 (1976). Area: 29 785 sq. km (11 500 sq. miles); (Papua New Guinea) 10 619 sq. km (4100 sq. miles).

Sol·o·mon Is+lands Pidg+in *n.* the variety of Neo-Melanesian spoken in the British Solomon Islands Protectorate and neighbouring islands.

Sol·o·mon's seal *n.* **1.** another name for **Star of David.** **2.** any of several liliaceous plants of the genus *Polygonatum* of N temperate regions, having greenish or yellow paired flowers, long narrow waxy leaves, and a thick underground stem with prominent leaf scars. [C16: translation of Medieval Latin *sigillum Solomonis,* perhaps referring to the resemblance of the leaf scars to seals]

So·lon (ˈsəʊlɒn) *n.* ?638–?559 B.C., Athenian statesman, who introduced economic, political, and legal reforms. —**So+lo+ni·an** (səʊˈləʊnɪən) or **So+lon+ic** (səʊˈlɒnɪk) *adj.*

sol+on+chak (ˌsɒlənˈtʃæk) *n.* a type of intrazonal soil of arid regions with a greyish surface crust: contains large quantities of soluble salts. [Russian, literally: salt marsh]

sol+o+netz or **sol+o+nets** (ˌsɒləˈnɛts) *n.* a type of intrazonal soil with a high saline content characterized by leaching. [Russian *solonets* salt not obtained through decoction]

so long *sentence substitute. Informal.* farewell; goodbye.

so·lo stop *n.* any of various organ stops designed to imitate a solo performance on a particular musical instrument.

So+lo+thurn (*German* ˈzoːloturn) *n.* **1.** a canton of NW Switzerland. Capital: Solothurn. Pop.: 224 133 (1970). Area: 793 sq. km (306 sq. miles). **2.** a town in NW Switzerland, capital of Solothurn canton, on the Aare River. Pop.: 17 708 (1970). ~French name: **Soleure.**

so·lo whist *n.* a version of whist for four players acting independently, each of whom may bid to win or lose a fixed number of tricks before play starts, trumps having usually been decided by cutting.

sol+stice (ˈsɒlstɪs) *n.* **1.** either the shortest day of the year (**winter solstice**), marking the beginning of the astronomical winter, or the longest day of the year (**summer solstice**), marking the beginning of the astronomical summer. **2.** either of the two points on the ecliptic at which the sun is overhead at the tropic of Cancer or Capricorn at the summer and winter solstices. [C13: via Old French from Latin *sōlstitium* literally: the (apparent) standing still of the sun, from *sōl* sun + *sistere* to stand still] —**sol+sti+tial** (sɒlˈstɪʃəl) *adj.*

Sol·ti (ˈʃɒltɪ) *n.* Sir **Ge·org** (ˈgeːɔrk). born 1912, British conductor, born in Hungary.

sol+u·bil·i·ty (ˌsɒljʊˈbɪlɪtɪ) *n., pl.* **·ties.** **1.** the ability of a substance to dissolve; the quality of being soluble. **2.** a measure of this ability for a particular substance in a particular solvent, equal to the quantity of substance dissolving in a fixed quantity of solvent to form a saturated solution under specified temperature and pressure. It is expressed in grams per cubic decametre, grams per hundred grams of solvent, moles per mole, etc.

sol·u·bil·ize *or* **sol·u·bil·ise** ('sɒljʊbɪˌlaɪz) *vb.* to make or become soluble, as in the addition of detergents to fats to make them dissolve in water.

sol·u·ble ('sɒljʊbᵊl) *adj.* **1.** (of a substance) capable of being dissolved, esp. easily dissolved in some solvent, usually water. **2.** capable of being solved or answered. [C14: from Late Latin *solūbilis,* from Latin *solvere* to dissolve] —'**sol·u·ble·ness** *n.* —'**sol·u·bly** *adv.*

sol·u·ble glass *n.* another name for **sodium silicate** (sense 1).

sol·u·ble RNA *n.* another name for **transfer RNA.**

so·lum ('səʊləm) *n., pl.* **·lums** *or* **·la** (-lə). the upper layers of the soil profile, affected by climate and vegetation. [C19: New Latin from Latin: the ground]

so·lus *Latin.* ('səʊlʊs) *or (fem.)* ***so·la*** *adj.* alone; by oneself (formerly used in stage directions).

so·lute (sɒ'lju:t) *n.* **1.** the component of a solution that changes its state in forming the solution or the component that is not present in excess; the substance that is dissolved in another substance. Compare **solvent.** ~*adj.* **2.** *Botany.* loose or unattached; free. [C16: from Latin *solūtus* free, unfettered, from *solvere* to release]

so·lu·tion (sə'lu:ʃən) *n.* **1.** a homogeneous mixture of two or more substances in which the molecules or atoms of the substances are completely dispersed. The constituents can be solids, liquids, or gases. **2.** the act or process of forming a solution. **3.** the state of being dissolved (esp. in the phrase **in solution**). **4.** a mixture of two or more substances in which one or more components are present as small particles with colloidal dimension; colloid: *a colloidal solution.* **5.** a specific answer to or way of answering a problem. **6.** the act or process of solving a problem. **7.** *Maths.* the unique set of values that yield a true statement when substituted for the variables in an equation. **8.** the stage of a disease, following a crisis, resulting in its termination. **9.** *Law.* the payment, discharge, or satisfaction of a claim, debt, etc. [C14: from Latin *solūtiō* an unloosing, from *solūtus;* see SOLUTE]

so·lu·tion set *n.* another name for **truth set.**

So·lu·tre·an (sə'lu:trɪən) *adj.* of or relating to an Upper Palaeolithic culture of Europe that was characterized by leaf-shaped flint blades. [C19: named after *Solutré,* village in central France where traces of this culture were originally found]

solv·a·ble ('sɒlvəbᵊl) *adj.* another word for **soluble.** —ˌ**solv·a·'bil·i·ty** *or* '**solv·a·ble·ness** *n.*

solv·ate ('sɒlveɪt) *vb. Chem.* to undergo, cause, or partake in solvation. [C20: from SOLVENT]

solv·a·tion (sɒl'veɪʃən) *n.* the process in which there is some chemical association between the molecules of a solute and those of the solvent. An example is an aqueous solution of copper sulphate which contains complex ions of the type $[Cu(H_2O)_4]^{2+}$.

Sol·vay pro·cess ('sɒlveɪ) *n.* an industrial process for manufacturing sodium carbonate. Carbon dioxide is passed into a solution of sodium chloride saturated with ammonia. Sodium bicarbonate is precipitated and heated to form the carbonate. [C19: named after Ernest *Solvay* (1838–1922), Belgian chemist who invented it]

solve (sɒlv) *vb. (tr.)* **1.** to find the explanation for or solution to (a mystery, problem, etc.). **2.** *Maths.* **a.** to work out the answer to (a mathematical problem). **b.** to obtain the roots of (an equation). [C15: from Latin *solvere* to loosen, release, free from debt] —'**solv·er** *n.*

sol·ven·cy ('sɒlvənsɪ) *n.* ability to pay all debts.

sol·vent ('sɒlvənt) *adj.* **1.** capable of meeting financial obligations. **2.** (of a substance, esp. a liquid) capable of dissolving another substance. ~*n.* **3.** a liquid capable of dissolving another substance: *water is a solvent for salt.* **4.** the component of a solution that does not change its state in forming the solution or the component that is present in excess. Compare **solute. 5.** something that solves. [C17: from Latin *solvēns* releasing, from *solvere* to free, SOLVE] —'**sol·vent·ly** *adv.*

sol·vol·y·sis (sɒl'vɒlɪsɪs) *n.* a chemical reaction occurring between a dissolved substance and its solvent. See also **hydrolysis.**

Sol·way Firth ('sɒlweɪ) *n.* an inlet of the Irish Sea between SW Scotland and NW England. Length: about 56 km (35 miles).

Sol·y·man ('sɒlɪmən) *n.* a variant spelling of **Suleiman I.**

Sol·zhe·ni·tsyn (*Russian* səlʒə'nitsɪn) *n.* **A·le·xan·der I·sa·ye·vich** (alɪ'ksandᵊr i'sajɪvitʃ). born 1918, exiled Soviet novelist. His books include *One Day in the Life of Ivan Denisovich* (1962), *The First Circle* (1968), *Cancer Ward* (1968), *August 1914* (1971), and *The Gulag Archipelago* (1974). His works are critical of the injustices of the Soviet regime and he was imprisoned (1945–53) and exiled to Siberia (1953–56). He was deported to the West from the Soviet Union in 1974: Nobel prize for literature 1970.

Som. *abbrev. for* Somerset.

so·ma[1] ('səʊmə) *n., pl.* **·ma·ta** (-mətə) *or* **·mas.** the body of an organism, esp. an animal, as distinct from the germ cells. [C19: via New Latin from Greek *sōma* the body]

so·ma[2] ('səʊmə) *n.* an intoxicating plant juice drink used in Vedic rituals. [from Sanskrit]

So·ma·li (səʊ'mɑ:lɪ) *n.* **1.** *(pl.* **·lis** *or* **·li)** a member of a tall dark-skinned people inhabiting Somalia. **2.** the language of this people, belonging to the Cushitic subfamily of the Afro-Asiatic family of languages. ~*adj.* **3.** of, relating to, or characteristic of Somalia, the Somalis, or their language.

So·ma·li·a (səʊ'mɑ:lɪə) *n.* a republic in NE Africa, on the Indian Ocean and the Gulf of Aden: the north became a British protectorate in 1884; the east and south were established as an Italian protectorate in 1889; gained independence and united as the Somali Republic in 1960. Languages: Arabic, Italian, English, and Somali. Religion: chiefly Sunni Muslim. Currency: Somali shilling. Capital: Mogadiscio. Pop.: 3 170 000 (1975 UN est.). Area: 637 541 sq. km (246 154 sq. miles). Official name: **Somali Democratic Republic.** —**So·'ma·li·an** *adj., n.*

So·ma·li·land (səʊ'mɑ:lɪˌlænd) *n.* a former region of E Africa, between the equator and the Gulf of Aden: includes the Somali Republic, Djibouti, and SE Ethiopia.

so·mat·ic (səʊ'mætɪk) *adj.* **1.** of or relating to the soma: *somatic cells.* **2.** of or relating to an animal body or body wall as distinct from the viscera, limbs, and head. **3.** of or relating to the human body as distinct from the mind: *a somatic disease.* [C18: from Greek *sōmatikos* concerning the body, from *sōma* the body] —**so·'mat·i·cal·ly** *adv.*

so·mat·ic cell *n.* any of the cells of a plant or animal except the reproductive cells. Compare **germ cell.**

so·ma·to- *or before a vowel* **so·mat-** *combining form.* body: *somatoplasm.* [from Greek *sōma, sōmat-,* body]

so·ma·tol·o·gy (ˌsəʊmə'tɒlədʒɪ) *n.* **1.** the branch of biology concerned with the structure and function of the body. **2.** the branch of anthropology dealing with the physical characteristics of man. —**so·ma·to·log·ic** (ˌsəʊmətə'lɒdʒɪk) *or* ˌ**so·ma·to·'log·i·cal** *adj.* —ˌ**so·ma·to·'log·i·cal·ly** *adv.* —ˌ**so·ma·'tol·o·gist** *n.*

so·ma·to·plasm ('səʊmətəˌplæzəm) *n. Biology.* **a.** the protoplasm of a somatic cell. **b.** the somatic cells collectively. Compare **germ plasm** (sense 1). —ˌ**so·ma·to·'plas·tic** *adj.*

so·ma·to·pleure ('səʊmətəˌpluə, -ˌplɜ:) *n.* a mass of tissue in embryo vertebrates that is formed by fusion of the ectoderm with the outer layer of mesoderm: develops into the amnion, chorion, and part of the body wall. [C19: from New Latin *somatopleura,* from SOMATO- + Greek *pleura* a side] —ˌ**so·ma·to·'pleu·ral** *or* ˌ**so·ma·to·'pleu·ric** *adj.*

so·ma·to·type ('səʊmətəˌtaɪp) *n.* a type or classification of physique or body build. See **endomorph, mesomorph, ectomorph.**

som·bre *or U.S.* **som·ber** ('sɒmbə) *adj.* **1.** dismal; melancholy: *a sombre mood.* **2.** dim, gloomy, or shadowy. **3.** (of colour, clothes, etc.) sober, dull, or dark. [C18: from French, from Vulgar Latin *subumbrāre* (unattested) to shade, from Latin *sub* beneath + *umbra* shade] —'**som·bre·ly** *or U.S.* '**som·ber·ly** *adv.* —'**som·bre·ness** *or U.S.* '**som·ber·ness** *n.* —**som·brous** ('sɒmbrəs) *adj.*

som·bre·ro (sɒm'brɛərəʊ) *n., pl.* **·ros.** a felt or straw hat with a wide brim, as worn by men in Mexico. [C16: from Spanish, from *sombrero de sol* shade from the sun]

some (sʌm; *unstressed* səm) *determiner.* **1. a.** (a) certain unknown or unspecified: *some lunatic drove into my car; some people never learn.* **b.** *(as pronoun; functioning as sing. or pl.): some can teach and others can't.* **2. a.** an unknown or unspecified quantity or amount of: *there's some rice on the table; he owns some horses.* **b.** *(as pronoun; functioning as sing. or pl.): we'll buy some.* **3. a.** a considerable number or amount of: *he lived some years afterwards.* **b.** a little: *show him some respect.* **4.** *(usually stressed) Informal.* an impressive or remarkable: *that was some game!* **5.** about; approximately: *he owes me some thirty pounds.* ~*adv.* **6.** a certain amount (more) (in the phrases **some more** and **and then some**). **7.** *U.S., not standard.* to a certain degree or extent: *I guess I like him some.* [Old English *sum;* related to Old Norse *sumr,* Gothic *sums,* Old High German *sum* some, Sanskrit *samá* any, Greek *hamē* somehow]

-some[1] *suffix forming adjectives.* characterized by; tending to: *awesome; tiresome.* [Old English *-sum;* related to Gothic *-sama,* German *-sam*]

-some[2] *suffix forming nouns.* indicating a group of a specified number of members: *threesome.* [Old English *sum,* special use of SOME (determiner)]

-some[3] *n. combining form.* a body: *chromosome.* [from Greek *sōma* body]

some·bod·y ('sʌmbədɪ) *pron.* **1.** some person; someone. ~*n., pl.* **·bod·ies. 2.** a person of greater importance than others: *he is somebody in this town.*

Usage. See at **everyone.**

some·day ('sʌmˌdeɪ) *adv.* at some unspecified time in the (distant) future.

some·how ('sʌmˌhaʊ) *adv.* **1.** in some unspecified way. **2.** Also: **somehow or other.** by any means that are necessary.

some·one ('sʌmˌwʌn, -wən) *pron.* some person; somebody.

Usage. See at **everyone.**

some·place ('sʌmˌpleɪs) *adv. U.S. informal.* in, at, or to some unspecified place or region.

som·er·sault *or* **sum·mer·sault** ('sʌməˌsɔ:lt) *n.* **1. a.** a forward roll in which the head is placed on the ground and the trunk and legs are turned over it. **b.** a similar roll in a backward direction. **2.** an acrobatic feat in which either of these rolls are performed in midair, as in diving or gymnastics. **3.** a complete reversal of opinion, policy, etc. ~*vb.* **4.** *(intr.)* to perform a somersault. [C16: from Old French *soubresault,* probably from Old Provençal *sobresaut,* from *sobre* over (from Latin *super*) + *saut* a jump, leap (from Latin *saltus*)]

Som·er·set ('sʌməsɪt, -ˌsɛt) *n.* a county of SW England, on the Bristol Channel: the Mendip Hills lie in the north and Exmoor in the west; mainly agricultural (esp. dairying and fruit).

Administrative centre: Taunton. Pop.: 404 400 (1976 est.). Area: 3540 sq. km (1367 sq. miles).

some+thing ('sʌmˌθɪŋ) *pron.* **1.** an unspecified or unknown thing; some thing: *he knows something you don't; take something warm with you.* **2. something or other.** one unspecified thing or an alternative thing. **3.** an unspecified or unknown amount; bit: *something less than a hundred.* **4.** an impressive or important person, thing, or event: *isn't that something?* ~*adv.* **5.** to some degree; a little; somewhat: *to look something like me.* **6.** (*foll. by an adj.*) *Informal.* (intensifier): *it hurts something awful.*

some+time ('sʌmˌtaɪm) *adv.* **1.** at some unspecified point of time. ~*adj.* **2.** (*prenominal*) having been at one time; former: *the sometime President.* **3.** (*prenominal*) *Archaic or U.S.* occasional; infrequent.

some+times ('sʌmˌtaɪmz) *adv.* **1.** now and then; from time to time; occasionally. **2.** *Obsolete.* formerly; sometime.

some+way ('sʌmˌweɪ) *adv.* in some unspecified manner.

some+what ('sʌmˌwɒt) *adv.* (*not used with a negative*) rather; a bit: *she found it somewhat less easy than he.*

some+where ('sʌmˌwɛə) *adv.* **1.** in, to, or at some unknown or unspecified place or point: *somewhere in England; somewhere between 3 and 4 o'clock.* **2. get somewhere.** *Informal.* to make progress.

some+wise ('sʌmˌwaɪz) *adv.* in some way or to some degree; somehow (archaic, except in the phrase **in somewise**).

so+mite ('səʊmaɪt) *n.* **1.** *Embryol.* any of a series of dorsal paired segments of mesoderm occurring along the notochord in vertebrate embryos. It develops into muscle and bone in the adult animal. **2.** *Zoology.* another name for **metamere.** [C19: from Greek *sōma* a body] **—so+mi+tal** ('səʊmɪtᵊl) *or* **so+mit+ic** (səʊ'mɪtɪk) *adj.*

Somme (*French* sɔm) *n.* **1.** a department of N France, in Picardy region. Capital: Amiens. Pop.: 549 164 (1975). Area: 6277 sq. km (2448 sq. miles). **2.** a river in N France, rising in Aisne department and flowing west to Amiens, then northwest to the English Channel: scene of heavy fighting in World War I. Length: 245 km (152 miles).

som+me·lier ('sʌməlˌjeɪ) *n.* a wine steward in a restaurant or hotel. [French: butler, via Old French from Old Provençal *saumalier* pack-animal driver, from Late Latin *sagma* a pack-saddle, from Greek]

som+nam+bu+late (sɒm'næmbjʊˌleɪt) *vb.* (*intr.*) to walk while asleep. [C19: from Latin *somnus* sleep + *ambulāre* to walk] **—som+'nam+bu+lance** *n.* **—som+'nam+bu+lant** *adj., n.* **—som+ˌnam+bu+'la+tion** *n.* **—som+'nam+bu+ˌla+tor** *n.*

som+nam+bu+lism (sɒm'næmbjʊˌlɪzəm) *n.* a condition characterized by walking while asleep or in a hypnotic trance. Also called: **noctambulism.** **—som+'nam+bu+list** *n.* **—som+ˌnam+bu+'lis+tic** *adj.*

som·ni- *or before a vowel* **somn-** *combining form.* sleep: *somniferous.* [from Latin *somnus*]

som+nif+er+ous (sɒm'nɪfərəs) *or* **som+nif+ic** *adj.*. *Rare.* tending to induce sleep. **—som+'nif+er+ous+ly** *adv.*

som+nil·o·quy (sɒm'nɪləkwɪ) *n., pl.* **+quies.** *Rare.* the act of talking in one's sleep. [C19: from Latin *somnus* sleep + *loqui* to speak; compare SOLILOQUY] **—som+'nil·o+quist** *n.* **—som+'nil·o+quous** *adj.*

som+no+lent ('sɒmnələnt) *adj.* **1.** drowsy; sleepy. **2.** causing drowsiness. [C15: from Latin *somnus* sleep] **—'som+no+lence** *or* **'som+no+len+cy** *n.* **—'som+no+lent+ly** *adv.*

Som·nus ('sɒmnəs) *n.* the Roman god of sleep. Greek counterpart: **Hypnos.**

son (sʌn) *n.* **1.** a male offspring; a boy or man in relation to his parents. **2.** a male descendant. **3.** (*often cap.*) a familiar term of address for a boy or man. **4.** a male from a certain country, etc., or one closely connected with a certain environment: *a son of the circus.* Related adj.: **filial.** [Old English *sunu;* related to Old Norse *sunr,* Gothic *sunus,* Old High German *sunu,* Lithuanian *sūnus,* Sanskrit *sūnu*] **—'son+less** *adj.* **—'son+ˌlike** *adj.*

Son (sʌn) *n. Christianity.* the second person of the Trinity, Jesus Christ.

so+nant ('səʊnənt) *adj.* **1.** *Phonetics.* denoting a voiced sound capable of forming a syllable or syllable nucleus. **2.** inherently possessing, exhibiting, or producing a sound. **3.** *Rare.* resonant; sounding. ~*n.* **4.** *Phonetics.* a voiced sound belonging to the class of frictionless continuants or nasals (l, r, m, n, ŋ) considered from the point of view of being a vowel and, in this capacity, able to form a syllable or syllable nucleus. [C19: from Latin *sonāns* sounding, from *sonāre* to make a noise, resound] **—'so+nance** *n.* **—so+nan+tal** (səʊ'næntᵊl) *or* **so+'nan+tic** *adj.*

so+nar ('səʊnɑː) *n.* another name for an **echo sounder.** [C20: from *so(und) na(vigation) r(anging)*]

so+na+ta (sə'nɑːtə) *n.* **1.** an instrumental composition, usually in three or more movements, for piano alone (**piano sonata**) or for any other instrument with or without piano accompaniment (**violin sonata, cello sonata,** etc.). See also **sonata form, symphony** (sense 1), **concerto** (sense 1). **2.** a one-movement keyboard composition of the baroque period. [C17: from Italian, from *sonare* to sound, from Latin]

so+na+ta form *n.* a musical structure consisting of an expanded ternary form whose three sections (exposition, development, and recapitulation), followed by a coda, are characteristic of the first movement in a sonata, symphony, string quartet, concerto, etc.

son·a·ti·na (ˌsɒnə'tiːnə) *n.* a short sonata. [C19: from Italian]

son+dage (sɒn'dɑːʒ) *n., pl.* **+dag·es** (-'dɑːʒɪz, -'dɑːʒ). *Archaeology.* a deep trial trench for inspecting stratigraphy. [C20: from French: a sounding, from *sonder* to sound]

sonde (sɒnd) *n.* a rocket, balloon, or probe used for observing in the upper atmosphere. [C20: from French: plummet, plumb line; see SOUND³]

Sond·heim ('sɒndhaɪm) *n.* **Ste·phen (Joshua).** born 1930, U.S. songwriter. He wrote the lyrics for *West Side Story* (1957) and the score for *Company* (1971) and *Follies of 1971.*

sone (səʊn) *n.* a unit of loudness equal to 40 phons. [C20: from Latin *sonus* a sound]

son et lu+mi+ère ('sɒn eɪ 'luːmɪˌɛə; *French* sɔ̃ ne ly'mjɛːr) *n.* an entertainment staged at night at a famous building, historical site, etc., whereby the history of the location is presented by means of lighting effects, sound effects, and narration. [literally: sound and light]

song (sɒŋ) *n.* **1. a.** a piece of music, usually employing a verbal text, composed for the voice, esp. one intended for performance by a soloist. **b.** the whole repertory of such pieces. **c.** (*as modifier*): *a song book.* **2.** poetical composition; poetry. **3.** the characteristic tuneful call or sound made by certain birds or insects. **4.** the act or process of singing: *they raised their voices in song.* **5. for a song.** at a bargain price. **6. on song.** *Brit. informal.* performing at peak efficiency or ability. [Old English *sang;* related to Gothic *saggws,* Old High German *sang;* see SING] **—'song+ˌlike** *adj.*

song and dance *n.* **1.** *Brit. informal.* a fuss, esp. one that is unnecessary. **2.** *U.S. informal.* a long or elaborate story or explanation, esp. one that is evasive.

song+bird ('sɒŋˌbɜːd) *n.* **1.** any passerine bird of the suborder *Oscines,* having highly developed vocal organs and, in most, a musical call. **2.** any bird having a musical call.

song cy+cle *n.* any of several groups of songs written by composers during and after the Romantic period, each series employing texts, usually by one poet, relating a story or grouped around a central motif.

song form *n.* another name for **ternary form.**

song+ful ('sɒŋfʊl) *adj.* tuneful; melodious. **—'song+ful+ly** *adv.* **—'song+ful+ness** *n.*

Son+ghai (sɒŋ'gaɪ) *n.* **1.** (*pl.* **+ghai** *or* **+ghais**) a member of a Nilotic people of W Africa, living chiefly in Mali and Niger in the central Niger valley. **2.** the language or group of dialects spoken by this people, now generally regarded as forming a branch of the Nilo-Saharan family.

Song Koi *or* **Song Coi** ('sɒŋ 'kɔɪ) *n.* transliteration of the Vietnamese name for the **Red River.**

song+kok ('sɒŋkɒ) *n.* (in Malaysia and Indonesia) a kind of oval brimless hat, resembling a skull. [from Malay]

Song of Sol·o·mon *n.* **the.** a book of the Old Testament consisting of a collection of dramatic love poems traditionally ascribed to Solomon. Also called: **Song of Songs, Canticle of Canticles.**

song+ster ('sɒŋstə) *n.* **1.** a singer or poet. **2.** a singing bird; songbird. **—'song+stress** *fem. n.*

song thrush *n.* a common Old World thrush, *Turdus philomelos,* that has a brown back and spotted breast and is noted for its song.

song+writ·er ('sɒŋˌraɪtə) *n.* a person who composes the words or music for songs in a popular idiom.

son+ic ('sɒnɪk) *adj.* **1.** of, involving, or producing sound. **2.** having a speed about equal to that of sound in air: 332 metres per second (743 miles per hour). [C20: from Latin *sonus* sound]

son+ic bar+ri+er *n.* another name for **sound barrier.**

son+ic boom *n.* a loud explosive sound caused by the shock wave of an aircraft, etc., travelling at supersonic speed.

son+ic depth find+er *n.* an instrument for detecting the depth of water or of a submerged object by means of sound waves; fathometer. See also **sonar.**

so+nif+er+ous (sɒ'nɪfərəs) *adj.* carrying or producing sound.

son-in-law *n., pl.* **sons-in-law.** the husband of one's daughter.

son+net ('sɒnɪt) *Prosody.* ~*n.* **1.** a verse form of Italian origin consisting of 14 lines in iambic pentameter with rhymes arranged according to a fixed scheme, usually divided either into octave and sestet or, in the English form, into three quatrains and a couplet. ~*vb.* **2.** (*intr.*) to compose sonnets. **3.** (*tr.*) to celebrate in a sonnet. [C16: via Italian from Old Provençal *sonet* a little poem, from *son* song, from Latin *sonus* a sound]

son+net+eer (ˌsɒnɪ'tɪə) *n.* a writer of sonnets.

son+ny ('sʌnɪ) *n., pl.* **+nies.** *Often patronizing.* a familiar term of address to a boy or man.

so+no+buoy ('səʊnəˌbɔɪ) *n.* a buoy equipped to detect underwater noises and transmit them by radio.

son of a bitch *n., pl.* **sons of bitch·es.** *U.S. slang.* a worthless or contemptible person: used as an insult.

son of a gun *n., pl.* **sons of guns.** *Slang, chiefly U.S.* a rogue or rascal: used as a jocular form of address.

son of God *n. Bible.* **1.** an angelic being. **2.** a Christian believer.

Son of Man *n. Bible.* a title of Jesus Christ.

So+no+ra (*Spanish* so'nora) *n.* a state of NW Mexico, on the Gulf of California: consists of a narrow coastal plain rising inland to the Sierra Madre Occidental; an important mining area in colonial times. Capital: Hermosillo. Pop.: 1 098 720 (1970). Area: 184 934 sq. km (71 403 sq. miles).

son+or+ant ('sɒnərənt) *Phonetics.* *n.* **1.** one of the frictionless continuants or nasals (l, r, m, n, ŋ) having consonantal or vocalic functions depending on its situation within the syllable. **2.** either of the two consonants represented in English orthography by *w* or *y* and regarded as either consonantal or vocalic articulations of the vowels (iː) and (uː).

so+no+rous (sə'nɔːrəs, 'sɒnərəs) *adj.* **1.** producing or capable of producing sound. **2.** (of language, sound, etc.) deep or resonant. **3.** (esp. of speech) high-flown; grandiloquent. [C17: from Latin *sonōrus* loud, from *sonor* a noise] **—so+nor+i·ty** (sə'nɒrɪtɪ) *n.* **—so+'no+rous+ly** *adv.* **—so+'no+rous+ness** *n.*

Sons of Free+dom *pl. n.* a Doukhobor sect, located largely in British Columbia: notorious for its acts of terrorism in opposition to the government in the 1950s and 1960s. Also called: **Freedomites.**

son+sy *or* **son+sie** ('sɒnsɪ) *adj.* **+si+er, +si+est.** *Irish, Scot., and English dialect.* **1.** plump; buxom. **2.** cheerful. [C16: from Gaelic *sonas* good fortune]

Soo Ca+nals (su:) *n.* **the.** the two ship canals linking Lakes Superior and Huron. There is a canal on the Canadian and on the U.S. side of the rapids of the St. Mary's River. See also **Sault Sainte Marie.**

Soo+chow *or* **Su-chou** ('su:'tʃaʊ) *n.* a city in E China, in S Kiangsu on the Grand Canal: noted for its gardens; produces chiefly silk. Pop.: 633 000 (1957 est.). Also called: **Wuhsien.**

sook (sʊk) *n.* **1.** *Southwest Brit. dialect.* a baby. **2.** *Derogatory.* a coward. [perhaps from Old English *sūcan* to suck, influenced by Welsh *swci swead* tame]

soon (su:n) *adv.* **1.** in or after a short time; in a little while; before long: *the doctor will soon be here.* **2. as soon as.** at the very moment that: *she burst into tears as soon as she saw him.* **3. as soon...as.** used to indicate that the second alternative mentioned is not preferable to the first: *I'd just as soon go by train as drive.* [Old English *sōna;* related to Old High German *sāno,* Gothic *suns*]

soon+er ('su:nə) *adv.* **1.** the comparative of **soon:** *he came sooner than I thought.* **2.** rather; in preference: *I'd sooner die than give up.* **3. no sooner...than.** immediately after or when: *no sooner had he got home than the rain stopped; no sooner said than done.* **4. sooner or later.** eventually; inevitably.

Soong (sʊŋ) *n.* an influential Chinese family, notably **Soong Ch'ing-ling** (born 1890), who married **Sun Yat-sen** and became a vice chairman of the People's Republic of China (1959); and **Soong Mei-ling** (born 1898), who married **Chiang Kai-shek.**

soot (sʊt) *n.* **1.** finely divided carbon deposited from flames during the incomplete combustion of organic substances such as coal. ~*vb.* **2.** (*tr.*) to cover with soot. [Old English *sōt;* related to Old Norse, Middle Low German *sōt,* Lithuanian *sódis,* Old Slavonic *sažda,* Old Irish *sūide*]

sooth (su:θ) *Archaic or poetic.* ~*n.* **1.** truth or reality (esp. in the phrase **in sooth**). ~*adj.* **2.** true or real. **3.** smooth. [Old English *sōth;* related to Old Norse *sathr* true, Old High German *sand,* Gothic *sunja* truth, Latin *sōns* guilty, *sonticus* critical] **—'sooth+ly** *adv.*

soothe (su:ð) *vb.* **1.** (*tr.*) to make calm or tranquil. **2.** (*tr.*) to relieve or assuage (pain, longing, etc.). **3.** (*intr.*) to bring tranquillity or relief. [C16 (in the sense: to mollify): from Old English *sōthian* to prove; related to Old Norse *sanna* to assert; see SOOTH] **—'sooth+er** *n.* **—'sooth+ing+ly** *adv.* **—'sooth+ing+ness** *n.*

sooth+fast ('su:θ,fɑ:st) *adj. Archaic.* **1.** truthful. **2.** loyal; true. [from Old English *sōthfæst;* see SOOTH, FAST[1]]

sooth+say ('su:θ,seɪ) *vb.* **+says, +say+ing, +said.** (*intr.*) to predict the future. **—'sooth+,say+ing** *n.*

sooth+say+er ('su:θ,seɪə) *n.* a seer or prophet.

soot·y ('sʊtɪ) *adj.* **soot·i·er, soot·i·est.** **1.** covered with soot. **2.** resembling or consisting of soot. **—'soot·i·ly** *adv.* **—'soot·i·ness** *n.*

soot·y mould *n.* **1.** a fungal plant disease characterized by a blackish growth covering the surface of leaves, fruits, etc. **2.** any of various fungi, such as species of *Meliola* or *Capnodium,* that cause this disease.

sop (sɒp) *n.* **1.** (*often pl.*) food soaked in a liquid before being eaten. **2.** a concession, bribe, etc., given to placate or mollify: *a sop to one's feelings.* **3.** *Informal.* a stupid or weak person. ~*vb.* **sops, sop+ping, sopped.** **4.** (*tr.*) to dip or soak (food) in liquid. **5.** (when *intr.,* often foll. by *in*) to soak or be soaked. ~See also **sop up.** [Old English *sopp;* related to Old Norse *soppa* SOUP, Old High German *sopfa* milk with bread; see SUP[2]]

SOP *abbrev. for* standard operating procedure.

sop. *abbrev. for* soprano.

soph+ism ('sɒfɪzəm) *n. Logic.* an argument that is deliberately invalid, specious or misleading. Compare **paralogism.** [C14: from Latin *sophisma,* from Greek: ingenious trick, from *sophizesthai* to use clever deceit, from *sophos* wise, clever]

soph+ist ('sɒfɪst) *n.* **1.** (*often cap.*) **a.** any of a group of pre-Socratic professional philosophers. **b.** any of a group of later philosophers who made an art of effective but misleading argument. **2.** a person who uses clever or quibbling arguments that are fundamentally unsound. [C16: from Latin *sophista,* from Greek *sophistēs* a wise man, from *sophizesthai* to act craftily]

soph+ist+er ('sɒfɪstə) *n.* **1.** (esp. formerly) a second-year undergraduate at certain British universities. **2.** *Rare.* another word for **sophist.**

so+phis+tic (sə'fɪstɪk) *or* **so+phis+ti+cal** *adj.* **1.** of or relating to sophists or sophistry. **2.** of or relating to sophisms. **—so+'phis+ti+cal+ly** *adv.*

so+phis+ti+cate *vb.* (sə'fɪstɪ,keɪt). **1.** (*tr.*) to make (someone) less natural or innocent, as by education. **2.** to pervert or corrupt (an argument, etc.) by sophistry. **3.** (*tr.*) to make more complex or refined. **4.** *Rare.* to falsify (a text, etc.) by alterations. ~*n.* (sə'fɪstɪ,keɪt, -kɪt). **5.** a sophisticated person. [C14: from Medieval Latin *sophisticāre,* from Latin *sophisticus* sophistic] **—so+,phis+ti+'ca+tion** *n.* **—so+'phis+ti+,ca+tor** *n.*

so+phis+ti+cat+ed (sə'fɪstɪ,keɪtɪd) *adj.* **1.** having refined or cultured tastes and habits. **2.** appealing to sophisticates: *a sophisticated restaurant.* **3.** unduly refined or cultured. **4.** pretentiously or superficially wise. **5.** (of machines, methods, etc.) complex and refined. **—so+'phis+ti+,cat+ed+ly** *adv.*

soph+ist+ry ('sɒfɪstrɪ) *n., pl.* **+ries.** **1. a.** a method of argument that is seemingly plausible though actually invalid and misleading. **b.** the art of using such arguments. **2.** subtle but unsound or fallacious reasoning. **3.** an instance of this; sophism.

Soph·o·cles ('sɒfə,kli:z) *n.* ?496–406 B.C., Greek dramatist; author of seven extant tragedies: *Ajax, Antigone, Oedipus Rex, Trachiniae, Electra, Philoctetes,* and *Oedipus at Colonus.* **—Soph·o+cle·an** (,sɒfə'kli:ən) *adj.*

soph·o+more ('sɒfə,mɔ:) *n. Chiefly U.S.* a second year student in an educational establishment. [C17: perhaps from earlier *sophumer,* from *sophum,* variant of SOPHISM, + -ER[1]]

So+phy *or* **So+phi** ('səʊfɪ) *n., pl.* **+phies.** (formerly) a title of the Persian monarchs. [C16: from Latin *sophī* wise men, from Greek *sophos* wise]

-so+phy *n. combining form.* indicating knowledge or an intellectual system: *philosophy; theosophy.* [from Greek *-sophia,* from *sophia* wisdom, from *sophos* wise] **—-soph·ic** *or* **-soph·i·cal** *adj. combining form.*

so+por ('səʊpə) *n.* an abnormally deep sleep; stupor. [C17: from Latin: a deep sleep, death; related to *somnus* sleep]

sop·o+rif+ic (,sɒpə'rɪfɪk) *adj. also* **sop·o+rif+er+ous.** **1.** inducing sleep. **2.** drowsy; sleepy. ~*n.* **3.** a drug or other agent that induces sleep. **—,sop·o+'rif·i+cal+ly** *adv.*

sop+ping ('sɒpɪŋ) *adj.* completely soaked; wet through. Also: **sopping wet.**

sop+py ('sɒpɪ) *adj.* **+pi+er, +pi+est.** **1.** wet or soggy. **2.** *Brit. informal.* silly or sentimental. **3. soppy on.** *Brit. informal.* foolishly charmed or affected by. **—'sop+pi+ly** *adv.* **—'sop+pi+ness** *n.*

so+pra+ni+no (,sɒprə'ni:nəʊ) *n., pl.* **+nos.** **a.** the instrument with the highest possible pitch in a family of instruments. **b.** (*as modifier*): *a sopranino recorder.* [Italian, diminutive of SOPRANO]

so+pra+no (sə'prɑ:nəʊ) *n., pl.* **+pra+nos** *or* **+pra+ni** (-'prɑ:ni:). **1.** the highest adult female voice, having a range approximately from middle C to the A a thirteenth above it. **2.** the voice of a young boy before puberty. **3.** a singer with such a voice. **4.** the highest part of a piece of harmony. **5. a.** the highest or second highest instrument in a family of instruments. **b.** (*as modifier*): *a soprano saxophone.* ~See also **treble.** [C18: from Italian, from *sopra* above, from Latin *suprā*]

so+pra+no clef *n.* the clef that establishes middle C as being on the bottom line of the staff. See also **C clef.**

sop up *vb.* (*tr., adv.*) to mop or take up (spilt water, etc.) with or as if with a sponge.

so·ra ('sɔ:rə) *n.* a North American rail, *Porzana carolina,* with a greyish-brown plumage and yellow bill. [C18: of unknown origin]

So+ra+ta (*Spanish* so'rata) *n.* **Mount.** a mountain in W Bolivia, in the Andes: the highest mountain in the Cordillera Real, with two peaks, Ancohuma, 6550 m (21 490 ft.), and Illampu, 6485 m (21 276 ft.).

sorb (sɔ:b) *n.* **1.** another name for **service tree** (sense 1). **2.** any of various related trees, esp. the mountain ash. **3.** Also called: **sorb apple.** the fruit of any of these trees. [C16: from Latin *sorbus* the sorb, service tree] **—'sorb+ic** *adj.*

Sorb (sɔ:b) *n.* a member of a Slavonic people living chiefly in the rural areas of SE East Germany (Lusatia). Also called: **Wend, Lusatian.**

sor+be·fa+cient (,sɔ:bɪ'feɪʃənt) *adj.* **1.** inducing absorption. ~*n.* **2.** a sorbefacient drug. [C19: from Latin *sorbē(re)* to absorb + -FACIENT]

sor+bet ('sɔ:bɪt, -beɪ) *n.* **1.** a water ice made from fruit juice, egg whites, milk, etc. **2.** a U.S. word for **sherbet** (sense 1). [C16: from French, from Old Italian *sorbetto,* from Turkish *şerbet,* from Arabic *sharbah* a drink]

Sorb+i·an ('sɔ:bɪən) *n.* **1.** a West Slavonic language spoken in the rural areas of SE East Germany; modern Wendish. **2.** a speaker of this language. ~*adj.* **3.** of or relating to these people or their language.

sorb+ic ac·id *n.* a white crystalline unsaturated carboxylic acid found in berries of the mountain ash and used to inhibit the growth of moulds and as an additive for certain synthetic coatings; 2,4-hexadienoic acid. It exists as *cis-* and *trans-*isomers, the latter being the one usually obtained. Formula: $CH_3CH{:}CHCH{:}CHCOOH$. [C19: from SORB (the tree), from its discovery in the berries of the mountain ash]

sor+bi+tol ('sɔ:bɪ,tɒl) *n.* a white water-soluble crystalline alcohol with a sweet taste, found in certain fruits and berries and manufactured by the catalytic hydrogenation of sucrose: used as a sweetener and in the manufacture of ascorbic acid and synthetic resins. Formula: $C_6H_8(OH)_6$. [C19: from SORB + -ITOL]

Sor+bonne (*French* sɔr'bɔn) *n.* **the.** a part of the University of Paris containing the faculties of science and literature: founded in 1253 by Robert de Sorbon as a theological college; given to the university in 1808.

sor+bo rub+ber ('sɔ:bəʊ) *n. Brit.* a spongy form of rubber. [C20: from ABSORB]

sor+bose ('sɔ:bəʊs) *n. Biochem.* a sweet-tasting hexose sugar derived from the berries of the mountain ash by bacterial action: used in the synthesis of ascorbic acid. Formula: $CH_2OH(CHOH)_3COCH_2OH$. [C19: from SORB + -OSE[2]]

sor+cer+er ('sɔ:sərə) *or* (*fem.*) **sor+cer+ess** ('sɔ:sərɪs) *n.* a person who seeks to control and use magic powers; a wizard or magician. [C16: from Old French *sorcier*, from Vulgar Latin *sortiārius* (unattested) caster of lots, from Latin *sors* lot]

sor·cer·y ('sɔːsərɪ) *n., pl.* **·cer·ies.** the art, practices, or spells of magic, esp. black magic, by which it is sought to harness occult forces or evil spirits in order to produce preternatural effects in the world. [C13: from Old French *sorcerie*, from *sorcier* SORCERER] —**'sor·cer·ous** *adj.* —**'sor·cer·ous·ly** *adv.*

Sor·del·lo (*Italian* sor'dɛllo) *n.* born ?1200, Italian troubadour.

sor·did ('sɔːdɪd) *adj.* **1.** dirty, foul, or squalid. **2.** degraded; vile; base: *a sordid affair.* **3.** selfish and grasping: *sordid avarice.* [C16: from Latin *sordidus*, from *sordēre* to be dirty] —**'sor·did·ly** *adv.* —**'sor·did·ness** *n.*

sor·di·no (sɔː'diːnəʊ) *n., pl.* **·ni** (-niː). **1.** a mute for a stringed or brass musical instrument. **2.** any of the dampers that arrest the vibrations of piano strings. **3. con sordino** *or* **sordini.** a musical direction to play with a mute. **4. senza sordino** *or* **sordini.** a musical direction to remove or play without the mute or (on the piano) with the sustaining pedal pressed down. ~See also **sourdine.** [Italian: from *sordo* deaf, from Latin *surdus*]

sore (sɔː) *adj.* **1.** (esp. of a wound, injury, etc.) painfully sensitive; tender. **2.** causing annoyance: *a sore point.* **3.** urgent; pressing: *in sore need.* **4.** (*postpositive*) grieved; distressed. **5.** causing grief or sorrow. ~*n.* **6.** a painful or sensitive wound, injury, etc. **7.** any cause of distress or vexation. ~*adv.* **8.** *Archaic.* direly; sorely (now only in such phrases as **sore pressed, sore afraid**). [Old English *sār*; related to Old Norse *sārr*, Old High German *sēr*, Gothic *sair* sore, Latin *saevus* angry] —**'sore·ness** *n.*

so·re·di·um (sɔː'riːdɪəm) *n.* an organ of vegetative reproduction in lichens consisting of a cluster of algal cells enclosed in fungal hyphae: dispersed by wind, insects, or other means. [C19: New Latin, from Greek *sōros* a heap]

sore·head ('sɔːˌhɛd) *n. Informal, chiefly U.S.* a peevish or disgruntled person. —**ˌsore'head·ed·ly** *adv.* —**ˌsore'head·ed·ness** *n.*

sore·ly ('sɔːlɪ) *adv.* **1.** painfully or grievously: *sorely wounded.* **2.** pressingly or greatly: *to be sorely taxed.*

sor·ghum ('sɔːgəm) *n.* any grass of the Old World genus *Sorghum*, having solid stems, large flower heads, and glossy seeds: cultivated for grain, hay, and as a source of syrup. See also **kaffir corn, durra.** [C16: from New Latin, from Italian *sorgo*, probably from Vulgar Latin *Syricum grānum* (unattested) Syrian grain]

sor·go *or* **sor·gho** ('sɔːgəʊ) *n., pl.* **·gos** *or* **·ghos.** any of several varieties of sorghum that have watery sweet juice and are grown for fodder, silage, or syrup. [Italian]

so·ri ('sɔːraɪ) *n.* the plural of **sorus.**

sor·i·cine ('sɒrɪˌsaɪn) *adj.* of, relating to, or resembling the shrews or the family (*Soricidae*) to which they belong. [C18: from Latin *sōricīnus*, from *sōrex* a shrew]

so·ri·tes (sɒ'raɪtiːz) *n. Logic.* a polysyllogism in which the premisses are arranged so that intermediate conclusions are omitted, being understood, and only the final conclusion is stated. [C16: via Latin from Greek *sōreitēs*, literally: heaped, from *sōros* a heap] —**so·rit·i·cal** (sɒ'rɪtɪk°l) *or* **so·'rit·ic** *adj.*

sorn (sɔːn) *vb.* (*intr.*, often foll. by *on* or *upon*) *Scot.* to obtain food, lodging, etc., from another person by presuming on his generosity. [C16: from earlier *sorren* a feudal obligation requiring vassals to offer free hospitality to their lord and his men, from obsolete Irish *sorthan* free quarters]

So·ro·ca·ba (*Portuguese* ˌsoro'kaba) *n.* a city in S Brazil, in São Paulo state: industrial centre. Pop.: 165 990 (1970).

so·ror·ate ('sɒrəˌreɪt) *n.* the custom in some societies of a widower marrying his deceased wife's younger sister. [C20: from Latin *soror* a sister]

so·ror·i·cide (sə'rɒrɪˌsaɪd) *n.* **1.** the act of killing one's own sister. **2.** a person who murders his or her sister. [C17: from Latin *sorōricīda* one who murders his sister, from *soror* sister + *caedere* to slay] —**so·ˌror·i·'cid·al** *adj.*

so·ror·i·ty (sə'rɒrɪtɪ) *n., pl.* **·ties.** *Chiefly U.S.* a social club or society for university women. [C16: from Medieval Latin *sorōritās*, from Latin *soror* sister]

so·ro·sis (sə'rəʊsɪs) *n., pl.* **·ses** (-siːz). a fleshy multiple fruit, such as that of the pineapple and mulberry, formed from flowers that are crowded together on a fleshy stem. [C19: from New Latin, from Greek *sōros* a heap]

sorp·tion ('sɔːpʃən) *n.* the process in which one substance takes up or holds another; adsorption or absorption. [C20: back formation from ABSORPTION, ADSORPTION]

sor·rel[1] ('sɒrəl) *n.* **1. a.** a light brown to brownish-orange colour. **b.** (*as adj.*): *a sorrel carpet.* **2.** a horse of this colour. [C15: from Old French *sorel*, from *sor* a reddish brown, of Germanic origin; related to Middle Dutch *soor* desiccated]

sor·rel[2] ('sɒrəl) *n.* **1.** any of several polygonaceous plants of the genus *Rumex*, esp. *R. acetosa*, of Eurasia and North America, having acid-tasting leaves used in salads and sauces. See also **dock**[4], **sheep sorrel. 2.** short for **wood sorrel.** [C14: from Old French *surele*, from *sur* sour, of Germanic origin; related to Old High German *sūr* SOUR]

sor·rel tree *n.* a deciduous ericaceous tree, *Oxydendrum arboreum*, of E North America, having deeply fissured bark, sour-tasting leaves, and small white flowers. Also called: **sourwood.**

Sor·ren·to (sə'rɛntəʊ; *Italian* sor'rɛnto) *n.* a port in SW Italy, in Campania on a mountainous peninsula between the Bay of Naples and the Gulf of Salerno: a resort since Roman times. Pop.: 15 040 (1971).

sor·row ('sɒrəʊ) *n.* **1.** the characteristic feeling of sadness, grief, or regret associated with loss, bereavement, sympathy for another's suffering, for an injury done, etc. **2.** a particular cause or source of regret, grief, etc. **3.** Also called: **sorrowing.** the outward expression of grief or sadness. ~*vb.* **4.** (*intr.*) to mourn or grieve. [Old English *sorg*; related to Old Norse *sorg*, Gothic *saurga*, Old High German *sworga*] —**'sor·row·er** *n.* —**'sor·row·ful** *adj.* —**'sor·row·ful·ly** *adv.* —**'sor·row·ful·ness** *n.*

sor·ry ('sɒrɪ) *adj.* **·ri·er, ·ri·est. 1.** (*usually postpositive*; often foll. by *for*) feeling or expressing pity, sympathy, remorse, grief, or regret: *I feel sorry for him.* **2.** pitiful, wretched, or deplorable: *a sorry sight.* **3.** poor; paltry: *a sorry excuse.* **4.** affected by sorrow; sad. **5.** causing sorrow or sadness. ~*interj.* **6.** an exclamation expressing apology, used esp. at the time of the misdemeanour, offence, etc. [Old English *sārig*; related to Old High German *sērag*; see SORE] —**'sor·ri·ly** *adv.* —**'sor·ri·ness** *n.*

sort (sɔːt) *n.* **1.** a class, group, kind, etc., as distinguished by some common quality or characteristic. **2.** type of character, nature, etc.: *he's a good sort.* **3.** a more or less definable or adequate example of: *it's a sort of review.* **4.** (*often pl.*) *Printing.* any of the individual characters making up a fount of type. **5.** *Archaic.* manner; way: *in this sort we struggled home.* **6. after a sort.** to some extent. **7. of sorts** *or* **of a sort. a.** of an inferior kind. **b.** of an indefinite kind. **8. out of sorts.** not in normal good health, temper, etc. **9. sort of.** in some way or other; as it were; rather. ~*vb.* **10.** (*tr.*) to arrange according to class, type, etc. **11.** (*tr.*) *Slang, chiefly Brit.* to put (a car, etc.) into working order. **12.** (*intr.*; foll. by *with, together*, etc.) *Archaic or dialect.* to associate, as on friendly terms. **13.** (*intr.*) *Archaic.* to agree; accord. [C14: from Old French, from Medieval Latin *sors* kind, from Latin: fate] —**'sort·a·ble** *adj.* —**'sort·a·bly** *adv.* —**'sort·er** *n.*

sor·tie ('sɔːtɪ) *n.* **1. a.** (of troops, etc.) the act of emerging from a contained or besieged position. **b.** the troops doing this. **2.** an operational flight made by one aircraft. ~*vb.* **·ties, ·tie·ing, ·tied. 3.** (*intr.*) to make a sortie. [C17: from French: a going out, from *sortir* to go out]

sor·ti·lege ('sɔːtɪlɪdʒ) *n.* **1.** the act or practice of divination by drawing lots. **2.** magic or sorcery. [C14: via Old French from Medieval Latin *sortilegium*, from Latin *sortilegus* a soothsayer, from *sors* fate + *legere* to select]

sor·ti·tion (sɔː'tɪʃən) *n.* the act of casting lots. [C16: from Latin *sortitio*, from *sortiri* to cast lots]

sort out *vb.* (*tr., adv.*) **1.** to take or separate, as from a larger group: *he sorted out the most likely ones.* **2.** *Informal.* to find a solution to (a problem, etc.), esp. to make clear or tidy: *it took a long time to sort out the mess.* **3.** *Informal.* to organize into an orderly and disciplined group. **4.** *Informal.* to beat or punish.

so·rus ('sɔːrəs) *n., pl.* **·ri** (-raɪ). **1.** a cluster of sporangia on the undersurface of certain fern leaves. **2.** any of various similar spore-producing structures in some lichens and fungi. [C19: via New Latin from Greek *sōros* a heap]

SOS *n.* **1.** an internationally recognized distress signal in which the letters SOS are repeatedly spelt out, as by radio telegraphy: used esp. by ships and aircraft. **2.** *Informal.* a call for help.

Sos·no·wiec (*Polish* sɔs'nɔvjɛts) *n.* an industrial town in S Poland. Pop.: 149 200 (1974 est.).

so-so *Informal.* ~*adj.* **1.** (*postpositive*) neither good nor bad. ~*adv.* **2.** in an average or indifferent manner.

sos·te·nu·to (ˌsɒstə'nuːtəʊ) *adj., adv. Music.* (preceded by a tempo marking) to be performed in a smooth sustained manner. [C18: from Italian, from *sostenere* to sustain, from Latin *sustinēre* to uphold]

sos·te·nu·to ped·al *n.* another word for **sustaining pedal.**

sot (sɒt) *n.* **1.** a habitual or chronic drunkard. **2.** a person stupefied by or as if by drink. [Old English, from Medieval Latin *sottus*; compare French *sot* a fool] —**'sot·tish** *adj.*

so·te·ri·ol·o·gy (sɒˌtɪərɪ'ɒlədʒɪ) *n. Theol.* the doctrine of salvation. [C19: from Greek *sōtēria* deliverance (from *sōtēr* a saviour) + -LOGY] —**so·te·ri·o·log·ic** (sɒˌtɪərɪə'lɒdʒɪk) *or* **so·ˌte·ri·o·'log·i·cal** *adj.*

So·thic ('səʊθɪk, 'sɒθ-) *adj.* relating to the star Sirius or to the rising of this star. [C19: from Greek *Sōthis*, from Egyptian, name of Sirius]

So·thic year *n.* the fixed year of the ancient Egyptians, 365 days 6 hours long, beginning with the appearance of the star Sirius on the eastern horizon at dawn, which heralded the yearly flooding of the Nile. A **Sothic cycle** contained 1460 such years.

So·this ('səʊθɪs) *n.* another name for **Sirius.** [Greek; see SOTHIC]

So·tho ('suːtʊ, 'səʊtəʊ) *n.* **1.** (*pl.* **·tho** *or* **·thos**) a member of a large grouping of Negroid peoples of southern Africa, living chiefly in Botswana, South Africa, and Lesotho. **2.** the group of mutually intelligible languages of this people, including Lesotho, Tswana, and Pedi. It belongs to the Bantu group of the Niger-Congo family. **3.** (*pl.* **·tho** *or* **·thos**) *S. African.* a member of the Basotho people; a Mosotho. **4.** *S. African.* the dialect of Sotho spoken by the Basotho; Sesotho. It is an official language of Lesotho along with English. ~Former name (for senses 3, 4): **Basuto.**

sot·to vo·ce ('sɒtəʊ 'vəʊtʃɪ) *adv.* in an undertone. [C18: from Italian: under (one's) voice]

sou (suː) *n.* **1.** a former French coin of low denomination. **2.** a very small amount of money: *I haven't a sou to my name.* [C19: from French, from Old French *sol*, from Latin: SOLIDUS]

sou·bise (suː'biːz) *n.* a purée of onions mixed into a thick white sauce and served over eggs, fish, etc. Also called: **soubise**

sauce. [C18: named after Charles de Rohan *Soubise* (1715–1787), marshal of France]

sou·brette (suːˈbrɛt) *n.* **1.** a minor female role in comedy, often that of a pert lady's maid. **2.** any pert or flirtatious girl. [C18: from French: maidservant, from Provençal *soubreto,* from *soubret* conceited, from *soubra* to exceed, from Latin *superāre* to surmount, from *super* above] —**sou·ˈbret·tish** *adj.*

sou·bri·quet (ˈsəʊbrɪˌkeɪ) *n.* a variant spelling of **sobriquet.**

sou·chong (ˈsuːˈʃɒŋ, -ˈtʃɒŋ) *n.* a black tea with large leaves. [C18: from Chinese *hsiao-chung* small kind]

Sou·dan (suˈdã) *n.* the French name for the **Sudan.**

souf·fle (ˈsuːfᵊl) *n. Med.* a blowing sound or murmur heard in auscultation. [C19: from French, from *souffler* to blow]

souf·flé (ˈsuːfleɪ) *n.* **1.** a very light fluffy dish made with egg yolks and stiffly beaten egg whites combined with cheese, fish, etc. **2.** a similar sweet or savoury cold dish, set with gelatine. ~*adj., also* **souf·fléed. 3.** made light and puffy, as by beating and cooking. [C19: from French, from *souffler* to blow, from Latin *sufflāre*]

Sou·frière (*French* suˈfrjɛːr) *n.* **1.** a volcano on N St. Vincent: erupted in 1902, killing about 2000 people. Height: 1234 m (4048 ft.). **2.** a volcano in the West Indies, on S Montserrat: the highest point on the island. Height: 915 m (3002 ft.). **3.** a volcano in the French West Indies, on Guadeloupe. Height: 1484 m (4869 ft.).

sough[1] (saʊ) *vb.* **1.** (*intr.*) (esp. of the wind) to make a characteristic sighing sound. ~*n.* **2.** a soft continuous murmuring sound. [Old English *swōgan* to resound; related to Gothic *gaswogjan* to groan, Lithuanian *svageti* to sound, Latin *vāgīre* to lament] —**ˈsough·ful·ly** *adv.*

sough[2] (sʌf) *n. Northern English dialect.* a sewer or drain or an outlet channel. [of obscure origin]

sought (sɔːt) *vb.* the past tense or past participle of **seek.**

sought-af·ter *adj.* in demand; wanted.

soul (səʊl) *n.* **1.** the spirit or immaterial part of man, the seat of human personality, intellect, will, and emotions: regarded as an entity that survives the body after death. **2.** *Christianity.* the spiritual part of a person, capable of redemption from the power of sin through divine grace. **3.** the essential part or fundamental nature of anything. **4.** a person's feelings or moral nature as distinct from other faculties. **5. a.** Also called: **soul music.** a type of Black music resulting from the addition of jazz, gospel, and pop elements to the urban blues style. **b.** (*as modifier*): *a soul singer.* **6.** nobility of spirit or temperament: *a man of great soul and courage.* **7.** an inspiring spirit or leading figure, as of a cause or movement. **8. the life and soul.** *Informal.* a person regarded as the main source of gaiety, merriment, etc.: *the life and soul of the party.* **9.** a person regarded as typifying some characteristic or quality: *the soul of discretion.* **10.** a person; individual: *an honest soul.* **11. upon my soul!** an exclamation of surprise. [Old English *sāwol;* related to Old Frisian *sēle,* Old Saxon *sēola,* Old High German *sēula* soul] —**ˈsoul-ˌlike** *adj.*

Soul (səʊl) *n. Christian Science.* another word for **God.**

soul-de·stroy·ing *adj.* (of an occupation, situation, etc.) unremittingly monotonous.

soul food *n. Informal.* food, such as chitterlings, yams, traditionally eaten by southern U.S. Negroes.

soul·ful (ˈsəʊlfʊl) *adj. Sometimes ironic.* expressing profound thoughts or feelings: *soulful music.* —**ˈsoul·ful·ly** *adv.* —**ˈsoul·ful·ness** *n.*

soul·less (ˈsəʊllɪs) *adj.* **1.** lacking any humanizing qualities or influences; dead; mechanical: *soulless work.* **2.** (of a person) lacking in sensitivity or nobility. **3.** heartless; cruel. —**ˈsoul·less·ly** *adv.* —**ˈsoul·less·ness** *n.*

soul mate *n.* a person for whom one has a deep affinity, esp. a lover, wife, husband, etc.

soul-search·ing *n.* **1.** deep or critical examination of one's motives, actions, beliefs, etc. ~*adj.* **2.** displaying the characteristics of deep or painful self-analysis.

Soult (*French* sult) *n.* **Nic·o·las Jean de Dieu** (nikɔlɑ ʒã də ˈdjø). 1769–1851, French marshal under Napoleon I. Under Louis-Philippe he was minister of war (1830–34; 1840–44).

sou mar·qué (ˈsuː mɑːˈkeɪ; *French* su marˈke) *n., pl.* **sous mar·qués** (ˈsu mɑːˈkeɪz; *French* su marˈke). a French copper coin of the 18th century. [French, literally: a marked sou]

sound[1] (saʊnd) *n.* **1. a.** a periodic disturbance in the pressure or density of a fluid or in the elastic strain of a solid, produced by a vibrating object. It has a velocity in air at sea level at 0°C of 332 metres per second (743 miles per hour) and travels as longitudinal waves. **b.** (*as modifier*): *a sound wave.* **2.** (*modifier*): of or relating to radio as distinguished from television: *sound broadcasting; sound radio.* **3.** the sensation produced by such a periodic disturbance in the organs of hearing. **4.** anything that can be heard. **5.** a particular instance, quality, or type of sound: *the sound of running water.* **6.** volume or quality of sound: *a radio with poor sound.* **7.** the area or distance over which something can be heard: *to be born within the sound of Big Ben.* **8.** the impression or implication of something: *I don't like the sound of that.* **9.** *Phonetics.* the auditory effect produced by a specific articulation or set of related articulations. **10.** (*often pl.*) *Slang.* music, esp. rock, jazz, or pop. **11.** *Rare.* report, news, or information, as about a person, event, etc. ~*vb.* **12.** to cause (something, such as an instrument) to make a sound or (of an instrument, etc.) to emit a sound. **13.** to announce or be announced, by a sound: *to sound the alarm.* **14.** (*intr.*) (of a sound) to be heard. **15.** (*intr.*) to resonate with a certain quality or intensity: *to sound loud.* **16.** (*copula*) to give the impression of being as specified when read, heard, etc.: *to sound reasonable.* **17.** (*tr.*) to pronounce distinctly or audibly: *to sound one's consonants.* **18.** (*intr.;* usually foll. by *in*) *Law.* to have the essential quality or nature of: *an action sounding in damages.* ~See also **sound off.** [C13: from Old French *soner* to make a sound, from Latin *sonāre,* from *sonus* a sound] —**ˈsound·a·ble** *adj.*

sound[2] (saʊnd) *adj.* **1.** free from damage, injury, decay, etc. **2.** firm; solid; substantial: *a sound basis.* **3.** financially safe or stable: *a sound investment.* **4.** showing good judgment or reasoning; sensible; wise: *sound advice.* **5.** valid, logical, or justifiable: *a sound argument.* **6.** *Now rare.* ethically correct; upright; honest. **7.** (of sleep) deep; peaceful; unbroken. **8.** thorough; complete: *a sound examination.* **9.** *Law.* (of a title, etc.) free from defect; legally valid. **10.** constituting a valid and justifiable application of correct principles; orthodox: *sound theology.* ~*adv.* **11.** soundly; deeply: now archaic except when applied to sleep. [Old English *sund;* related to Old Saxon *gisund,* Old High German *gisunt*] —**ˈsound·ly** *adv.* —**ˈsound·ness** *n.*

sound[3] (saʊnd) *vb.* **1.** to measure the depth of (a well, the sea, etc.) by lowering a plumb line, by sonar, etc. **2.** to seek to discover (someone's views, etc.), as by questioning. **3.** (*intr.*) (of a whale, etc.) to dive downwards swiftly and deeply. **4.** *Med.* **a.** to probe or explore (a bodily cavity or passage) by means of a sound. **b.** to examine (a patient) by means of percussion and auscultation. ~*n.* **5.** *Med.* an instrument for insertion into a bodily cavity or passage to dilate strictures, dislodge foreign material, etc. ~See also **sound out.** [C14: from Old French *sonder,* from *sonde* sounding line, probably of Germanic origin; related to Old English *sundgyrd* sounding pole, Old Norse *sund* strait, SOUND[4]; see SWIM]

sound[4] (saʊnd) *n.* **1.** a relatively narrow channel between two larger areas of sea or between an island and the mainland. **2.** an inlet or deep bay of the sea. **3.** the air bladder of a fish. [Old English *sund* swimming, narrow sea; related to Middle Low German *sunt* strait; see SOUND[3]]

Sound (saʊnd) *n.* **the.** a strait between SW Sweden and Zealand (Denmark), linking the Kattegat with the Baltic: busy shipping lane. Length: 113 km (70 miles). Narrowest point: 5 km (3 miles). Swedish and Danish name: **Øresund.**

sound bar·ri·er *n.* (*not in technical usage*) a hypothetical barrier to flight at or above the speed of sound, when a sudden large increase in drag occurs. Also called: **sonic barrier, transonic barrier.**

sound bow (bəʊ) *n.* the thick part of a bell against which the hammer strikes.

sound·box (ˈsaʊndˌbɒks) *n.* the resonating chamber of the hollow body of a violin, guitar, etc.

sound ef·fect *n.* any sound artificially produced, reproduced from a recording, etc., to create a theatrical effect, such as the bringing together of two halves of a hollow coconut shell to simulate a horse's gallop; used in plays, films, etc.

sound·er[1] (ˈsaʊndə) *n.* an electromagnetic device formerly used in telegraphy to convert electric signals sent over wires into audible sounds.

sound·er[2] (ˈsaʊndə) *n.* a person or device that measures the depth of water, etc.

sound hole *n.* any of variously shaped apertures in the sounding board of certain stringed instruments, such as the '*f*' shaped holes of a violin.

sound·ing[1] (ˈsaʊndɪŋ) *adj.* **1.** resounding; resonant. **2.** having an imposing sound and little content; pompous: *sounding phrases.* —**ˈsound·ing·ly** *adv.*

sound·ing[2] (ˈsaʊndɪŋ) *n.* **1.** (*sometimes pl.*) the act or process of measuring depth of water or examining the bottom of a river, lake, etc., as with a sounding line. **2.** an observation or measurement of atmospheric conditions, as made using a radiosonde or rocketsonde. **3.** (*often pl.*) measurements taken by sounding. **4.** (*pl.*) a place where a sounding line will reach the bottom, esp. less than 100 fathoms in depth. **5. on** (*or* **off**) **soundings.** in waters less than (or more than) 100 fathoms in depth.

sound·ing board *n.* **1.** Also called: **soundboard.** a thin wooden board comprising the upper surface of a resonating chamber in a violin, piano, etc., serving to amplify the vibrations produced by the strings passing across it. See also **belly** (sense 6). **2.** Also called: **soundboard.** a thin screen suspended over a pulpit, stage, etc., to reflect sound towards an audience. **3.** a person, group, experiment, etc., used to test a new idea, policy, etc., for acceptance or applicability.

sound·ing lead (lɛd) *n.* a lead weight, usually conical and having a depression in the base for a dab of grease so that, when dropped to the bottom on a sounding line, a sample of sand, gravel, etc., can be retrieved.

sound·ing line *n.* a line marked off to indicate its length and having a sounding lead at one end. It is dropped over the side of a vessel to determine the depth of the water.

sound·less[1] (ˈsaʊndlɪs) *adj.* extremely still or silent. —**ˈsound·less·ly** *adv.* —**ˈsound·less·ness** *n.*

sound·less[2] (ˈsaʊndlɪs) *adj. Chiefly poetic.* extremely deep.

sound mix·er *n. Films, radio, etc.* **1.** the person who mixes various sound sources into a composite programme. **2.** a piece of equipment designed for mixing sound.

sound off *vb.* (*intr., adv.*) **1.** to proclaim loudly, as in venting one's opinions, grievances, etc. **2.** to speak angrily.

sound out *vb.* (*tr., adv.*) to question (someone) in order to discover (opinions, facts, etc.).

sound·post (ˈsaʊndˌpəʊst) *n. Music.* a small post, usually of pine, on guitars, violins, etc., that joins the front surface to the back, helps to support the bridge, and allows the whole body of the instrument to vibrate.

sound+proof ('saʊnd,pru:f) *adj.* **1.** not penetrable by sound. *~vb.* **2.** (*tr.*) to render soundproof.

sound rang+ing *n.* the determination of the location of a source of sound waves by measuring the time lapse between their transmission and their reception at microphones situated at three or more known positions.

sound shift *n.* a systematic alteration or series of alterations in the pronunciation of a set of sounds, esp. of vowels. See also **Great Vowel Shift.**

sound spec+tro+graph *n.* an electronic instrument that produces a record (**sound spectrogram**) of the way in which the frequencies and intensities of the components of a sound, such as a spoken word, vary with time.

sound+track ('saʊnd,træk) *n.* **1.** the recorded sound accompaniment to a film. Compare **commentary** (sense 2). **2.** a narrow strip along the side of a spool of film, which carries the sound accompaniment.

sound truck *n.* the U.S. name for a **loudspeaker van.**

sound wave *n.* a wave that propagates sound.

soup (su:p) *n.* **1.** a liquid food made by boiling or simmering meat, fish, vegetables, etc., usually served hot at the beginning of a meal. **2.** *Informal.* a photographic developer. **3.** *Informal.* anything resembling soup in appearance or consistency, esp. thick fog. See also **peasouper. 4.** a slang name for **nitroglycerin. 5. in the soup.** *Slang.* in trouble or difficulties. [C17: from Old French *soupe,* from Late Latin *suppa,* of Germanic origin; compare Middle High German *suppe,* Old Norse *soppa* soup]

soup+çon *French.* (sup'sɔ̃) *n.* a slight amount; dash. [C18: from French, ultimately from Latin *suspicio* SUSPICION]

soup+fin *or* **soup+fin shark** ('su:p,fɪn) *n.* a Pacific requiem shark, *Galeorhinus zyopterus,* valued for its fins, which are used to make soup.

Sou·phan·ou·rong (,su:fænu:'rɒŋ) *n.* **Prince.** born 1902, Laotian statesman; president of Laos since 1975.

soup kitch+en *n.* **1.** a place or mobile stall where food and drink, esp. soup, is served to destitute people. **2.** *Military.* a mobile kitchen.

soup plate *n.* a deep plate with a wide rim, used esp. for drinking soup.

soup up *vb.* (*tr., adv.*) *Slang.* another term for **hot up** (sense 2).

soup·y ('su:pɪ) *adj.* **soup·i·er, soup·i·est. 1.** having the appearance or consistency of soup. **2.** *Informal, chiefly U.S.* emotional or sentimental.

sour (saʊə) *adj.* **1.** having or denoting a sharp biting taste like that of lemon juice or vinegar. Compare **bitter** (sense 1). **2.** made acid or bad, as in the case of milk or alcohol by the action of microorganisms. **3.** having a rancid or unwholesome smell. **4.** (of a person's temperament) sullen, morose, or disagreeable. **5.** (esp. of the weather or climate) harsh and unpleasant. **6.** disagreeable; distasteful: *a sour experience.* **7.** (of land, etc.) lacking in fertility, esp. due to excessive acidity. **8.** (of petrol) containing a relatively large amount of sulphur compounds. **9. go** *or* **turn sour.** to become unfavourable or inharmonious: *his marriage went sour.* *~n.* **10.** something sour. **11.** *Chiefly U.S.* any of several iced drinks usually made with spirits, lemon juice, and ice: *a whiskey sour.* **12.** an acid used in laundering and bleaching clothes or in curing animal skins. *~vb.* **13.** to make or become sour. [Old English *sūr;* related to Old Norse *sūrr,* Lithuanian *suras* salty, Old Slavonic *syrŭ* wet, raw, *surovu* green, raw, Sanskrit *surā* brandy] **—'sour+ish** *adj.* **—'sour+ly** *adv.* **—'sour+ness** *n.*

Sour (sʊə) *n.* a variant spelling of **Sur.**

source (sɔ:s) *n.* **1.** the point or place from which something originates. **2. a.** a spring that forms the starting point of a stream; headspring. **b.** the area where the headwaters of a river rise: *the source of the Nile.* **3.** a person, group, etc., that creates, issues, or originates something: *the source of a complaint.* **4. a.** any person, book, organization, etc., from which information, evidence, etc., is obtained. **b.** (*as modifier*): *source material.* **5.** anything, such as a story or work of art, that provides a model or inspiration for a later work. **6.** *Electronics.* the electrode region in a field-effect transistor from which majority carriers flow into the interelectrode conductivity channel. **7. at source.** at the point of origin. [C14: from Old French *sors,* from *sourdre* to spring forth, from Latin *surgere* to rise]

source pro+gram *n.* an original computer program written in FORTRAN, COBOL, etc., that is converted into the equivalent object program, written in machine language, by the compiler or assembler.

sour cher+ry *n.* **1.** a Eurasian rosaceous tree, *Prunus cerasus,* with white flowers: cultivated for its tart red fruits. **2.** the fruit of this tree. Compare **sweet cherry.** See also **morello, amarelle.**

sour cream *n.* cream soured by lactic acid bacteria, used in making salads, dips, etc. Also called: **soured cream.**

sour+dine (sʊə'di:n) *n. Music.* **1.** a soft stop on an organ or harmonium. **2.** another word for **sordino.** [C17 (meaning: a muted trumpet): from French: a mute, from Italian; see SORDINO]

sour+dough ('saʊə,dəʊ) *Western U.S., Canada, and Alaska.* *~adj.* **1.** (of bread) made with fermented dough used as a leaven. *~n.* **2.** an old-time prospector or pioneer.

sour gourd *n.* **1.** a large bombacaceous tree, *Adansonia gregorii,* of N Australia having gourdlike fruit. **2.** the acid-tasting fruit of this tree, which has a woody rind and large seeds. **3.** the fruit of the baobab tree.

sour grapes *n.* the attitude of despising something because one cannot or does not have it oneself.

sour gum *n.* a cornaceous tree, *Nyssa sylvatica,* of the eastern U.S., having glossy leaves, soft wood, and sour purplish fruits. Also called: **black gum, pepperidge.** See also **tupelo.** Compare **sweet gum.**

sour mash *n. U.S.* **1.** a grain mash for use in distilling certain whiskeys, consisting of a mixture of new and old mash. **2.** any whiskey distilled from such a mash.

sour+puss ('saʊə,pʊs) *n. Informal.* a person whose facial expression or nature is habitually gloomy or sullen.

sour+sop ('saʊə,sɒp) *n.* **1.** a small West Indian tree, *Annona muricata,* having large spiny fruit: family *Annonaceae.* **2.** the fruit of this tree, which has a tart edible pulp. Compare **sweetsop.**

sour+wood ('saʊə,wʊd) *n.* another name for **sorrel tree.**

Sou·sa ('su:zə) *n.* **John Phil·ip.** 1854–1932, U.S. bandmaster and composer of military marches, such as *The Stars and Stripes Forever* (1897) and *The Liberty Bell* (1893).

sou+sa+phone ('su:zə,fəʊn) *n. Music.* a large tuba that encircles the player's body and has a bell facing forwards. [C20: named after J. P. SOUSA] **—'sou+sa+,phon+ist** *n.*

souse[1] (saʊs) *vb.* **1.** to plunge (something, oneself, etc.) into water or other liquid. **2.** to drench or be drenched. **3.** (*tr.*) to pour or dash (liquid) over (a person or thing). **4.** to steep or cook (food) in a marinade. **5.** *Slang.* to make or become drunk. *~n.* **6.** the liquid or brine used in pickling. **7.** the act or process of sousing. **8.** *Slang.* a habitual drunkard. [C14: from Old French *sous,* of Germanic origin; related to Old High German *sulza* brine]

souse[2] (saʊs) *Falconry.* (of hawks or falcons) *~vb.* **1.** (often foll. by *on* or *upon*) to swoop suddenly downwards (on a prey). *~n.* **2.** a sudden downward swoop. [C16: perhaps a variant of obsolete vb. sense of SOURCE]

sous+lik ('su:slɪk) *n.* a variant spelling of **suslik.**

sou-sou *or* **su·su** ('su:su:) *n. Caribbean.* an arrangement made among friends whereby each person makes regular contributions to a fund, the money being drawn out periodically by each individual in turn. [probably of W African origin, influenced by French *sou* small coin, via Creole]

Sousse (su:s), **Su·sa,** *or* **Su+sah** *n.* a port in E Tunisia, on the Mediterranean: founded by the Phoenicians in the 9th century B.C. Pop.: 82 666 (1966). Ancient name: **Hadrumetum.**

sou+tache (su:'tæʃ) *n.* a narrow braid used as a decorative trimming. [C19: from French, from Hungarian *sujtas*]

sou+tane (su:'tæn) *n. R.C. Church.* a priest's cassock. [C19: from French, from Old Italian *sottana,* from Medieval Latin *subtanus* (adj.) (worn) beneath, from Latin *subtus* below]

sout+er ('su:tə) *n. Scot. and northern English.* a shoemaker or cobbler. [Old English *sūtere,* from Latin *sutor,* from *suere* to sew]

sou+ter+rain ('su:tə,reɪn) *n. Archaeol.* an underground chamber or passage. [C18: from French]

south (saʊθ) *n.* **1.** one of the four cardinal points of the compass, at 180° from north and 90° clockwise from east and anticlockwise from west. **2.** the direction along a meridian towards the South Pole. **3. the south.** (*often cap.*) any area lying in or towards the south. Related adjs.: **meridional, austral.** *~adj.* **4.** situated in, moving towards, or facing the south. **5.** (esp. of the wind) from the south. *~adv.* **6.** in, to, towards, or (esp. of the wind) from the south. *~*Abbrev.: **S** [Old English *sūth;* related to Old Norse *suthr* southward, Old High German *sundan* from the south]

South (saʊθ) *n.* **the. 1.** the southern part of England, generally regarded as lying to the south of an imaginary line between the Wash and the Severn. **2.** (in the U.S.) **a.** the area approximately south of Pennsylvania and the Ohio River, esp. those states south of the Mason-Dixon line that formed the Confederacy during the Civil War. **b.** the Confederacy itself. *~adj.* **3. a.** of or denoting the southern part of a specified country, area, etc. **b.** (*cap. as part of a name*): *the South Pacific.*

South Af+ri+ca *n.* **Re+pub+lic of.** a republic occupying the southernmost part of the African continent: the Dutch Cape Colony (1652) was acquired by Britain in 1806 and British victory in the Boer War resulted in the formation of the Union of South Africa in 1910, which left the Commonwealth and became a republic in 1961; implementation of the apartheid system began in 1948; mainly plateau with mountains in the south and east. Mineral production includes gold, diamonds, coal, and copper. Official languages: Afrikaans and English. Religion: chiefly Christian. Currency: rand. Capitals: Cape Town (legislative) and Pretoria (administrative). Pop.: 21 448 169 (1970), including 3 751 328 Whites and 15 057 952 Bantus. Area: 1 221 044 sq. km (471 445 sq. miles). Former name (1910–61): **Union of South Africa.**

South Af+ri+can *adj.* **1.** of or relating to the Republic of South Africa, its inhabitants, or any of their languages. *~n.* **2.** a native or inhabitant of the Republic of South Africa, esp. a White.

South Af+ri+can Dutch *n.* (not used in South Africa) another name for **Afrikaans.**

South A·mer·i·ca *n.* the fourth largest of the continents, bordering on the Caribbean in the north, the Pacific in the west, and the Atlantic in the east and joined to Central America by the Isthmus of Panama. It is dominated by the Andes Mountains, which extend over 7250 km (4500 miles) and include many volcanoes; ranges from dense tropical jungle, desert, and temperate plains to the cold wet windswept region of Tierra del Fuego. It comprises chiefly developing countries undergoing great changes. Pop.: 188 628 000 (1971 est.). Area: 17 816 600 sq. km (6 879 000 sq. miles). **—South A·mer·i·can** *adj., n.*

South A·mer·i·can tryp·a·no·so·mi·a·sis *n. Pathol.* another name for **Chagas' disease.**

South·amp·ton (ˌsaʊθ'æmptən, -'hæmp-) *n.* a port in S England, in Hampshire on **Southampton Water** (an inlet of the English Channel): chief English passenger port; university (1952); shipyards and oil refinery. Pop.: 214 826 (1971).

South·amp·ton Is·land *n.* an island in N Canada, in the Northwest Territories at the entrance to Hudson Bay: inhabited chiefly by Eskimos. Area: 49 470 sq. km (19 100 sq. miles).

South A·ra·bi·a *n.* **Fed·er·a·tion of.** the former name (1959–67) of **Southern Yemen.** —**South A·ra·bi·an** *adj., n.*

South Aus·tral·i·a *n.* a state of S central Australia, on the Great Australian Bight: generally arid, with the Great Victoria Desert in the west central part, the Lake Eyre basin in the northeast, and the Flinders Range, Murray River basin, and salt lakes in the southeast. Capital: Adelaide. Pop.: 1 244 600 (1976). Area: 984 395 sq. km (380 070 sq. miles). —**South Aus·tral·i·an** *adj., n.*

South Bend *n.* a city in N Indiana: university (1842). Pop.: 122 004 (1973 est.).

south·bound ('saʊθˌbaʊnd) *adj.* going or leading towards the south.

south by east *n.* **1.** one point on the compass east of south; 168° 45′ clockwise from north. ~*adj., adv.* **2.** in, from, or towards this direction.

south by west *n.* **1.** one point on the compass west of south; 201° 15′ clockwise from north. ~*adj., adv.* **2.** in, from, or towards this direction.

South Car·o·li·na *n.* a state of the southeastern U.S., on the Atlantic: the first state to secede from the Union in 1860; consists largely of low-lying coastal plains, rising in the northwest to the Blue Ridge Mountains; the largest U.S. textile producer. Capital: Columbia. Pop.: 2 590 516 (1970). Area: 78 282 sq. km (30 225 sq. miles). Abbrevs.: **S.C.** or (with zip code) **SC** —**South Car·o·lin·i·an** *adj., n.*

South Chi·na Sea *n.* part of the Pacific surrounded by SE China, Vietnam, the Malay Peninsula, Borneo, and the Philippines.

South Da·ko·ta *n.* a state of the western U.S.: lies mostly in the Great Plains; the chief U.S. producer of gold and beryl. Capital: Pierre. Pop.: 666 257 (1970). Area: 196 723 sq. km (75 955 sq. miles). Abbrevs.: **S.D., S. Dak.,** or (with zip code) **SD** —**South Da·ko·tan** *n., adj.*

South·down ('saʊθˌdaʊn) *n.* an English breed of sheep with short wool and a greyish-brown face and legs.

South Downs *pl. n.* a range of low hills in S England, extending from W Dorset to E Sussex.

south·east (ˌsaʊθ'i:st; *Nautical* ˌsaʊ'i:st) *n.* **1.** the point of the compass or the direction midway between south and east, 135° clockwise from north. ~*adj. also* **south·east·ern. 2.** (*sometimes cap.*) of or denoting the southeastern part of a specified country, area, etc. **3.** situated in, proceeding towards, or facing the southeast. **4.** (esp. of the wind) from the southeast. ~*adv.* **5.** in, to, towards, or (esp. of the wind) from the southeast. ~Abbrev.: **SE** —ˌ**south·'east·ern·most** *adj.*

South·east (ˌsaʊθ'i:st) *n.* (usually preceded by *the*) the southeastern part of Britain, esp. the London area.

South·east A·sia *n.* a region including Brunei, Burma, Indonesia, Cambodia, Laos, Malaysia, the Philippines, Thailand, and Vietnam. —**South·east A·sian** *adj., n.*

South·east A·sia Trea·ty Or·gan·i·za·tion *n.* the full name of **SEATO.**

south·east by east *n.* **1.** one point on the compass north of southeast; 123° 45′ clockwise from north. ~*adj., adv.* **2.** in, from, or towards this direction.

south·east by south *n.* **1.** one point on the compass south of southeast; 146° 15′ clockwise from north. ~*adj., adv.* **2.** in, from, or towards this direction.

south·east·er (ˌsaʊθ'i:stə; *Nautical* ˌsaʊ'i:stə) *n.* a strong wind or storm from the southeast.

south·east·er·ly (ˌsaʊθ'i:stəlɪ; *Nautical* ˌsaʊ'i:stəlɪ) *adj., adv.* **1.** in, towards, or (esp. of a wind) from the southeast. ~*n., pl.* **·lies. 2.** a strong wind or storm from the southeast.

south·east·ward (ˌsaʊθ'i:stwəd; *Nautical* ˌsaʊ'i:stwəd) *adj.* **1.** towards or (esp. of a wind) from the southeast. ~*n.* **2.** a direction towards or area in the southeast. ~*adv.* **3.** a variant of **southeastwards.**

south·east·wards (ˌsaʊθ'i:stwədz; *Nautical* ˌsaʊ'i:stwədz) *or* **south·east·ward** *adv.* to the southeast.

South·end-on-Sea ('saʊθˌɛnd) *n.* a town in SE England, in SE Essex on the Thames estuary: one of England's largest resorts, extending for about 11 km (7 miles) along the coast. Pop.: 162 326 (1971).

south·er ('saʊðə) *n.* a strong wind or storm from the south.

south·er·ly ('sʌðəlɪ) *adj.* **1.** of, relating to, or situated in the south. ~*adv.* **2.** towards or in the direction of the south. **3.** from the south: *a southerly wind.* ~*n., pl.* **·lies. 4.** a wind from the south. —**'south·er·li·ness** *n.*

south·er·ly bust·er *n.* (*sometimes caps.*) a sudden violent cold wind on the SE coast of Australia causing a rapid drop in temperature. Sometimes shortened to **southerly.**

south·ern ('sʌðən) *adj.* **1.** situated in or towards the south. **2.** (of a wind, etc.) coming from the south. **3.** native to, inhabiting, or growing in the south. **4.** (*sometimes cap.*) *Astronomy.* south of the celestial equator.

South·ern ('sʌðən) *adj.* of, relating to, or characteristic of the south of a particular region or country.

South·ern Alps *pl. n.* a mountain range in New Zealand, on South Island: the highest range in Australasia. Highest peak: Mount Cook, 3764 m (12 349 ft.).

South·ern Brit·ish Eng·lish *n.* the dialect of spoken English regarded as standard in England and considered as having high social status in comparison with other British English dialects. Historically, it is derived from the S East Midland dialect of Middle English. Abbrev.: **SBE.** See also **Received Pronunciation.**

South·ern Cross *n.* a small conspicuous constellation in the S hemisphere lying in the Milky Way near Centaurus. The four brightest stars form a cross the longer arm of which points to the south celestial pole. Formal names: **Crux, Crux Australis.**

South·ern·er ('sʌðənə) *n.* (*sometimes not cap.*) a native or inhabitant of the south of any specified region, esp. the South of England or the Southern states of the U.S.

south·ern hem·i·sphere *n.* (*often caps.*) **1.** that half of the earth lying south of the equator. **2.** *Astronomy.* that half of the celestial sphere lying south of the celestial equator. ~Abbrev.: **S hemisphere.**

South·ern Lights *n.* another name for **aurora australis.**

south·ern·ly ('sʌðənlɪ) *adj., adv.* a less common word for **southerly.**

south·ern·most ('sʌðənˌməʊst) *adj.* situated or occurring farthest south.

South·ern Rho·de·si·a *n.* the former name (until 1964) of **Rhodesia.** —**South·ern Rho·de·si·an** *adj., n.*

South·ern So·tho *n.* another name for **Sesotho.**

South·ern Up·lands *pl. n.* a hilly region extending across S Scotland: includes the Lowther, Moorfoot, and Lammermuir hills.

south·ern·wood ('sʌðənˌwʊd) *n.* an aromatic shrubby wormwood, *Artemisia abrotanum,* of S Europe, having finely dissected leaves and small drooping heads of yellowish flowers. Also called: **old man, lad's love.**

South·ern Yem·en *n.* a republic in SW Asia, on the Gulf of Aden: Southern Yemen separated from Turkish-occupied Yemen in 1914; became a republic in 1967. Official language: Arabic. Religion: mostly Sunni Muslim. Currency: dinar. Capital: Madinat ash Sha'b (administrative) and Aden (national). Pop.: 1 590 275 (1973). Area: about 290 275 sq. km (112 075 sq. miles). Former name (1959–67): (Federation of) **South Arabia.** Official name: **People's Democratic Republic of Yemen.** —**South·ern Yem·en·ite** *or* **Yem·e·ni** *adj., n.*

Sou·they ('saʊðɪ, 'sʌðɪ) *n.* **Rob·ert.** 1774–1843, English poet, a friend of Wordsworth and Coleridge, attacked by Byron; poet laureate (1813–43).

South Geor·gia *n.* an island in the S Atlantic, about 1300 km (800 miles) southeast of the Falkland Islands, of which it is a dependency. Area: 3755 sq. km (1450 sq. miles). —**South Geor·gian** *adj., n.*

South Gla·mor·gan *n.* a county in S Wales, formed in 1974 from part of Glamorgan, two parishes from Monmouthshire, and the county borough of Cardiff. Administrative centre: Cardiff. Pop.: 389 200 (1976 est.). Area: 422 sq. km (163 sq. miles).

South Hol·land *n.* a province of the SW Netherlands, on the North Sea: lying mostly below sea level, it has a coastal strip of dunes and is drained chiefly by distributaries of the Rhine, with large areas of reclaimed land; the most densely populated province in the country, intensively cultivated and industrialized. Capital: The Hague. Pop.: 3 018 900 (1973 est.). Area: 3196 sq. km (1234 sq. miles). Dutch name: **Zuidholland.**

south·ing ('saʊðɪŋ) *n.* **1.** *Navigation.* movement, deviation, or distance covered in a southerly direction. **2.** *Astronomy.* a south or negative declination.

South Is·land *n.* the largest island of New Zealand, separated from North Island by Cook Strait. Pop.: 810 267 (1971). Area: 153 947 sq. km (59 439 sq. miles).

South Ko·re·a *n.* a republic in NE Asia: established as a republic in 1948; invaded by North Korea and Chinese Communists in 1950 but division remained unchanged at the end of the war (1953); includes over 3000 islands; rapid industrialization. Language: Korean. Religions: Buddhist, Confucianist, Shamanist, and Chondokyo. Currency: won. Capital: Seoul. Pop.: 34 688 000 (1975). Area: 98 477 sq. km (38 022 sq. miles). —**South Ko·re·an** *adj., n.*

South Ork·ney Is·lands *pl. n.* a group of islands in the S Atlantic, southeast of Cape Horn: formerly a dependency of the Falkland Islands; part of British Antarctic Territory since 1962. Area: 621 sq. km (240 sq. miles).

South Os·se·tian Au·ton·o·mous Re·gion (ə'si:ʃən) *n.* an administrative division of the S Soviet Union, in the Georgian SSR on the S slopes of the Caucasus Mountains. Capital: Tskhinvali. Pop.: 99 421 (1970). Area: 3900 sq. km (1500 sq. miles).

south·paw ('saʊθˌpɔ:) *Informal.* ~*n.* **1.** a boxer who leads with his right hand and off his right foot as opposed to the orthodox style of leading with the left. **2.** any left-handed person. ~*adj.* **3.** of or relating to a southpaw.

South Pole *n.* **1.** the southernmost point on the earth's axis, at the latitude of 90°S. **2.** *Astronomy.* the point of intersection, in the constellation Octans, of the earth's extended axis and the southern half of the celestial sphere.

South·port ('saʊθˌpɔ:t) *n.* **1.** a town and resort in NW England, in Merseyside on the Irish Sea. Pop.: 84 349 (1971). **2.** a city and resort in E Australia, extending for 32 km (20 miles) along the S coast of Queensland. Pop.: 80 250 (1975 est.). Former name: **Gold Coast.**

South·ron ('sʌðrən) *n.* **1.** *Chiefly Scot.* a Southerner, esp. an

Englishman. **2.** *Dialect, chiefly southern U.S.* an inhabitant of the South, esp. at the time of the Civil War. ~*adj.* **3.** *Chiefly Scot.* of or relating to the South or to England. [C15: Scottish variant of SOUTHERN]

South Sas·katch·e·wan *n.* a river in S central Canada, rising in S Alberta and flowing east and northeast to join the North Saskatchewan River, forming the Saskatchewan River. Length: 1392 km (865 miles).

South Sea Bub·ble *n. British history.* the financial crash that occurred in 1720 after the **South Sea Company** had taken over the national debt in return for a monopoly of trade with the South Seas, causing feverish speculation in their stocks.

South Sea Is·lands *pl. n.* the islands in the S Pacific that constitute Oceania.

South Seas *pl. n.* the seas south of the equator.

South Shet·land Is·lands *pl. n.* a group of islands in the S Atlantic, north of the Antarctic Peninsula: formerly a dependency of the Falkland Islands; part of British Antarctic Territory since 1962. Area: 4662 sq. km (1800 sq. miles).

South Shields *n.* a port in NE England, in Tyne and Wear on the Tyne estuary opposite North Shields: shipbuilding and marine engineering industries. Pop.: 100 513 (1971).

south-south·east *n.* **1.** the point on the compass or the direction midway between southeast and south; 157° 30′ clockwise from north. ~*adj., adv.* **2.** in, from, or towards this direction. ~Abbrev.: **SSE**

south-south·west *n.* **1.** the point on the compass or the direction midway between south and southwest; 202° 30′ clockwise from north. ~*adj., adv.* **2.** in, from, or towards this direction. ~Abbrev.: **SSW**

South Ty·rol *or* **Ti·rol** *n.* a former part of the Austrian state of Tyrol: ceded to Italy in 1919, becoming the Bolzano and Trento provinces of the Trentino-Alto Adige Autonomous Region. Area: 14 037 sq. km (5420 sq. miles).

South Vi·et·nam *n.* a region of S Vietnam, on the South China Sea and the Gulf of Siam: an independent republic (1955–76). —**South Vi·et·nam·ese** *adj., n.*

south·ward ('saʊθwəd; *Nautical* 'sʌðəd) *adj.* **1.** situated, directed, or moving towards the south. ~*n.* **2.** the southward part, direction, etc.; the south. ~*adv.* **3.** a variant of **southwards.** —'**south·ward·ly** *adj., adv.*

south·wards ('saʊθwədz; *Nautical* 'sʌðədz) *or* **south·ward** *adv.* towards the south.

South·wark ('sʌðək) *n.* a borough of S central Greater London, on the River Thames: site of the Globe Theatre; docks and warehouses. Pop.: 224 900 (1976 est.).

south·west (ˌsaʊθ'wɛst; *Nautical* ˌsaʊ'wɛst) *n.* **1.** the point of the compass or the direction midway between west and south, 225° clockwise from north. ~*adj. also* **south·west·ern. 2.** (*sometimes cap.*) of or denoting the southwestern part of a specified country, area, etc.: *southwest Italy.* **3.** situated in or towards the southwest. **4.** (esp. of the wind) from the southwest. ~*adv.* **5.** in, to, towards, or (esp. of the wind) from the southwest. ~Abbrev.: **SW** —ˌ**south·'west·ern·most** *adj.*

South·west (ˌsaʊθ'wɛst) *n.* (usually preceded by *the*) the southwestern part of Britain, esp. Cornwall, Devon, and Somerset.

South West Af·ri·ca *n.* a disputed territory in southern Africa bordering on South Africa: annexed by Germany in 1884 and mandated by the League of Nations to South Africa in 1920; the mandate was terminated by the UN in 1966 but this was ignored by South Africa, as was the 1971 ruling by the International Court of Justice that the territory be surrendered. Official languages: Afrikaans and English. Religion: mostly animist, with some Christians. Currency: rand. Capital: Windhoek. Pop.: 762 184 (1970). Area: 823 328 sq. km (317 887 sq. miles). Name recognized by the UN (since 1968): **Namibia.** Former name (1885–1919): **German Southwest Africa.** —**South West Af·ri·can** *adj., n.*

south·west by south *n.* **1.** one point on the compass south of southwest; 213° 45′ clockwise from north. ~*adj., adv.* **2.** in, from, or towards this direction.

south·west by west *n.* **1.** one point on the compass north of southwest, 236° 15′ clockwise from north. ~*adj., adv.* **2.** in, from, or towards this direction.

south·west·er (ˌsaʊθ'wɛstə; *Nautical* ˌsaʊ'wɛstə) *n.* a strong wind or storm from the southwest.

south·west·er·ly (ˌsaʊθ'wɛstəlɪ; *Nautical* ˌsaʊ'wɛstəlɪ) *adj., adv.* **1.** in, towards, or (esp. of a wind) from the southwest. ~*n., pl.* **·lies. 2.** a wind or storm from the southwest.

south·west·ward (ˌsaʊθ'wɛstwəd; *Nautical* ˌsaʊ'wɛstwəd) *adj.* **1.** from or towards the southwest. ~*adv.* **2.** a variant of **southwestwards.** ~*n.* **3.** a direction towards or area in the southwest. —ˌ**south·'west·ward·ly** *adj., adv.*

south·west·wards (ˌsaʊθ'wɛstwədz; *Nautical* ˌsaʊ'wɛstwədz) *or* **south·west·ward** *adv.* to the southwest.

South York·shire *n.* a metropolitan county of N England, comprising the districts of Barnsley, Doncaster, Sheffield, and Rotherham. Administrative centre: Barnsley. Pop.: 1 318 300 (1976 est.). Area: 1562 sq. km (603 sq. miles).

Sou·tine (*French* su'tin) *n.* **Cha·im** ('xaɪɪm). 1893–1943, French expressionist painter, born in Russia; noted for his portraits and still lifes, esp. of animal carcasses.

sou·ve·nir (ˌsu:və'nɪə, 'su:vəˌnɪə) *n.* **1.** an object that recalls a certain place, occasion, or person; memento. **2.** *Rare.* a thing recalled. ~*vb.* (*tr.*) *Austral., euphemistic.* to steal or keep (something, esp. a small article) for one's own use; purloin. [C18: from French, from (*se*) *souvenir* to remember, from Latin *subvenīre* to come to mind, from *sub-* up to + *venīre* to come]

sou'·west·er (ˌsaʊ'wɛstə) *n.* a waterproof hat having a very broad rim behind, worn esp. by seamen.

sov·er·eign ('sɒvrɪn) *n.* **1.** a person exercising supreme authority, esp. a monarch. **2.** a former English gold coin worth one pound sterling. ~*adj.* **3.** supreme in rank or authority: *a sovereign lord.* **4.** excellent or outstanding: *a sovereign remedy.* **5.** of, relating to, or characteristic of a sovereign. **6.** independent of outside authority: *a sovereign state.* [C13: from Old French *soverain,* from Vulgar Latin *superānus* (unattested), from Latin *super* above; also influenced by REIGN] —'**sov·er·eign·ly** *adv.*

sov·er·eign·ty ('sɒvrəntɪ) *n., pl.* **·ties. 1.** supreme and unrestricted power, as of a state. **2.** the position, dominion, or authority of a sovereign. **3.** an independent state.

So·vetsk (*Russian* sa'vjɛtsk) *n.* a town in the W Soviet Union, in the Kaliningrad Region on the Neman River: scene of the signing of the treaty (1807) between Napoleon I and Tsar Alexander I; passed from East Prussia to the Soviet Union in 1945. Former name (until 1945): **Tilsit.**

so·vi·et ('səʊvɪət, 'sɒv-) *n.* **1.** (in the Soviet Union) an elected government council at the local, regional, and national levels, culminating in the Supreme Soviet. **2.** (in pre-revolutionary Russia) a local revolutionary council. ~*adj.* **3.** of or relating to a soviet. [C20: from Russian *sovyet* council, from Old Russian *sŭvětŭ*]

So·vi·et ('səʊvɪət, 'sɒv-) *adj.* of, characteristic of, or relating to the Soviet Union, its people, or its government.

So·vi·et Cen·tral A·sia *n.* the region of the Soviet Union occupied by the Kazakh, Kirghiz, Tadzhik, Turkmen, and Uzbek SSRs. Also called: **Russian Turkestan, West Turkestan.**

so·vi·et·ism ('səʊvɪɪˌtɪzəm, 'sɒv-) *n.* (*sometimes cap.*) **1.** the principle or practice of government through soviets, esp. as practised in the Soviet Union. **2.** any characteristic deemed representative of Soviet ideology. —'**so·vi·et·ist** *n., adj.* —ˌ**so·vi·et·'is·tic** *adj.*

so·vi·et·ize *or* **so·vi·et·ise** ('səʊvɪɪˌtaɪz, 'sɒv-) *vb.* (*often cap.*) (*tr.*) **1.** to bring (a country, person, etc.) under Soviet control or influence. **2.** to cause (a country) to conform to the Soviet model in its social, political, and economic structure. —ˌ**so·vi·et·i·'za·tion** *or* ˌ**so·vi·et·i·'sa·tion** *n.*

So·vi·et Rus·sia *n.* another name for the **Russian Soviet Federated Socialist Republic** or the **Soviet Union.**

So·vi·ets ('səʊvɪəts, 'sɒv-) *n.* the people or government of the Soviet Union.

So·vi·et Un·ion *n.* a federal republic in E Europe and central and N Asia: the revolution of 1917 achieved the overthrow of the monarchy and the USSR was established in 1922. It is the largest country in the world, occupying a seventh of the total land surface, and consists chiefly of plains, crossed by the Ural Mountains, with the Caucasus to the south and mountains rising over 7350 m (24 500 ft.) in the extreme southwest. Languages: Russian and many national minority languages. Currency: ruble. Capital: Moscow. Pop.: 257 900 000 (1977 est.). Area: 22 402 202 sq. km (8 649 489 sq. miles). Official name: **Union of Soviet Socialist Republics.** Also called: **Russia, Soviet Russia.**

So·vi·et Zone *n.* that part of Germany occupied by the Soviet forces from 1945: transformed into the German Democratic Republic in 1949–50. Also called: **Russian Zone.**

sov·khoz (sɒf'kɒz; *Russian* saf'xɔs) *n., pl.* **sov·kho·zy** (sɒf'kɒzɪ; *Russian* saf'xɔzi). (in the Soviet Union) a large mechanized farm owned by the state. [C20: Russian, from *sovetskoe khozyaistvo* soviet economy]

sov·ran ('sɒvrən) *n., adj.* a literary word for **sovereign.** —'**sov·ran·ly** *adv.* —'**sov·ran·ty** *n.*

sow[1] (səʊ) *vb.* **sows, sow·ing, sowed; sown** *or* **sowed. 1.** to scatter or place (seed, a crop, etc.) in or on (a piece of ground, field, etc.) so that it may grow: *to sow wheat; to sow a strip of land.* **2.** (*tr.*) to implant or introduce: *to sow a doubt in someone's mind.* [Old English *sāwan;* related to Old Norse *sá,* Old High German *sāen,* Old Slavonic *seja,* Latin *serere* to sow] —'**sow·a·ble** *adj.* —'**sow·er** *n.*

sow[2] (saʊ) *n.* **1.** a female adult pig. **2.** the female of certain other animals, such as the mink. **3.** *Metallurgy.* **a.** the channels for leading molten metal to the moulds in casting pig iron. **b.** iron that has solidified in these channels. [Old English *sugu;* related to Old Norse *sýr,* Old High German *sū,* Latin *sūs,* Norwegian *sugga,* Dutch *zeug:* see SWINE]

sow·back ('saʊˌbæk) *n.* another name for **hog back** (sense 1).

sow·bread ('saʊˌbrɛd) *n.* a S European primulaceous plant, *Cyclamen hederifolium,* with heart-shaped leaves and pink nodding flowers. See also **cyclamen** (sense 1). [C16: from SOW[2] + BREAD, based on Medieval Latin *panis porcinus;* the tuberous roots are eaten by swine]

sow bug (saʊ) *n. U.S.* any of various woodlice, esp. any of the genera *Oniscus* and *Porcellio.* [C18: from its resemblance to a pig in shape]

sow·ens ('səʊənz, 'su:-) *n. Scot.* a porridge made from oatmeal husks. [C16: from Scottish Gaelic *sūghan,* from *sūgh* sap; related to Old High German *sūgan* to SUCK]

So·we·to (sɔ:'wɛtəʊ) *n.* a contiguous group of Black African townships southwest of Johannesburg, South Africa: the largest purely Black African urban settlement in southern Africa: scene of riots (1976) following protests against the use of Afrikaans in schools for black African children. Area: 62 sq. km (24 sq. miles). Pop.: over 500 000. [C20: from *so*(*uth*) *we*(*st*) *to*(*wnship*)]

sown (səʊn) *vb.* a past participle of **sow**[1].

sow this+tle (saʊ) *n.* any of various plants of the Old World genus *Sonchus*, esp. *S. oleraceus*, having milky juice, prickly leaves, and heads of yellow flowers: family *Compositae* (composites). Also called: **milk thistle.**

soy·a bean (ˈsɔɪə) *or U.S.* **soy+bean** (ˈsɔɪˌbiːn) *n.* **1.** an Asian bean plant, *Glycine max* (or *G. soja*), cultivated for its nutritious seeds, for forage, and to improve the soil. **2.** the seed of this plant, used as food, forage, and as the source of an oil. [C17 *soya*, via Dutch *soya* from Japanese *shōyū*, from Chinese *chiang yu*, from *chiang* paste + *yu* sauce]

Soy·in·ka (sɔˈjɪŋkə) *n.* **Wo·le** (ˈwoːle). born 1934, Nigerian dramatist, novelist, and literary critic. His works include the plays *The Strong Breed* (1963), *The Road* (1965), and *Kongi's Harvest* (1966), and the novel *The Interpreters* (1965).

soy sauce (sɔɪ) *n.* a salty pungent dark brown sauce made from fermented soya beans, used esp. in Chinese cookery. Also called: **soya sauce.**

So+yuz (sɔɪˈjʊz) *n.* any of a series of manned Soviet spacecraft launched into earth orbit for the purpose of studying docking procedures and other manoeuvres relevant to the building and operation of an orbiting space station. See also **Salyut.** [C20: Russian: union]

soz+zled (ˈsɒzəld) *adj.* an informal word for **drunk.** [C19: perhaps from obsolete *sozzle* stupor; related to SOUSE[1]]

sp. *abbrev. for:* **1.** special. **2.** (*pl.* **spp.**) species. **3.** specific. **4.** specimen. **5.** spelling.

Sp. *abbrev. for:* **1.** Spain. **2.** Spaniard. **3.** Spanish.

s.p. *abbrev. for* without issue. [from Latin *sine prole*]

S.P. *abbrev. for* starting price.

spa (spɑː) *n.* a mineral spring or a place or resort where such a spring is found. [C17: named after SPA, a watering place in Belgium]

Spa (spɑː) *n.* a town in E Belgium, in Liège province: a resort with medicinal mineral springs (discovered in the 14th century). Pop.: 9504 (1970).

Spaak (spɑːk) *n.* **Paul Hen·ri** (pɔl ãˈri). 1899–1972, Belgian statesman, first socialist premier of Belgium (1937–38); a leading advocate of European unity, he was president of the consultative assembly of the Council of Europe (1949–51) and secretary-general of NATO (1957–61).

space (speɪs) *n.* **1.** the unlimited three-dimensional expanse in which all material objects are located. Related adj.: **spatial. 2.** an interval of distance or time between two points, objects, or events. **3.** a blank portion or area. **4. a.** unoccupied area or room: *there is no space for a table.* **b.** (*in combination*): *space-saving.* Related adj.: **spacious. 5. a.** the region beyond the earth's atmosphere containing the other planets of the solar system, stars, galaxies, etc.; universe. **b.** (*as modifier*): *a space probe; space navigation.* **6. a.** the region beyond the earth's atmosphere occurring between the celestial bodies of the universe. The density is normally negligible although cosmic rays, meteorites, gas clouds, etc., can occur. It can be divided into **cislunar space** (between the earth and moon), **interplanetary space, interstellar space,** and **intergalactic space. b.** (*as modifier*): *a space station; a space simulator.* **7.** a seat or place, as on a train, aircraft, etc. **8.** *Printing.* a piece of metal, less than type-high, used to separate letters or words. **9.** *Music.* any of the gaps between the lines that make up the staff. **10.** *Maths.* a collection of unspecified points having properties that obey a specified set of axioms: *Euclidean space.* **11.** Also called: **spacing.** *Telegraphy.* the period of time that separates complete letters, digits, and other characters in Morse code. ~*vb.* (*tr.*) **12.** to place or arrange at intervals or with spaces between. **13.** to divide into or by spaces: *to space one's time evenly.* **14.** *Printing.* to separate (letters, words, or lines) by the insertion of spaces. [C13: from Old French *espace*, from Latin *spatium*] —**ˈspac+er** *n.*

space age *n.* **1.** the period in which the exploration of space has become possible. ~*adj.* **space-age. 2.** (*usually prenominal*) futuristic or ultra-modern, esp. when suggestive of space technology.

space+band (ˈspeɪsˌbænd) *n. Printing.* a device on a linecaster for evening up the spaces between words.

space-bar *n.* a horizontal bar on a type-writer that is depressed in order to leave a space between words, letters, etc.

space cap+sule *n.* a vehicle, sometimes carrying men or animals, designed to obtain scientific information from space, planets, etc., and be recovered on returning to earth.

space+craft (ˈspeɪsˌkrɑːft) *n.* a manned or unmanned vehicle designed to orbit the earth or travel to celestial objects for the purpose of research, exploration, etc.

spaced out *adj. Slang.* intoxicated through taking a drug.

space heat+er *n.* a heater used to warm the air in an enclosed area, such as a room or office.

space lat+tice *n. Crystallog.* the more formal name for **lattice** (sense 4).

space+less (ˈspeɪslɪs) *adj. Chiefly literary.* **1.** having no limits in space; infinite or boundless. **2.** occupying no space.

space+man (ˈspeɪsˌmæn) *or* (*fem.*) **space+wom·an** *n., pl.* **+men** *or* (*fem.*) **+wom·en.** a person who travels in outer space, esp. one trained to participate in a space flight.

space med·i·cine *n.* the branch of medicine concerned with the effects on man of flight outside the earth's atmosphere. Compare **aviation medicine.**

space op·er·a *n.* a science fiction drama, such as a film or television programme, esp. one dealing with interplanetary flight.

space plat+form *n.* another name for **space station.**

space+port (ˈspeɪsˌpɔːt) *n.* a base equipped to launch, maintain, and test spacecraft.

space probe *n.* a vehicle, such as a satellite, equipped to obtain scientific information, normally transmitted back to earth by radio, about the atmosphere, surface, and temperature of a planet, conditions in space, etc.

space+ship (ˈspeɪsˌʃɪp) *n.* a manned spacecraft.

space shut+tle *n.* a vehicle, such as a two-stage rocket and aircraft, designed to be used for at least 100 space flights, carrying men and materials to space stations in orbit around the earth or to bases on the moon, etc.

space sta+tion *n.* any large manned artificial satellite designed to orbit the earth during a long period of time thus providing a base for scientific and medical research in space and a construction site, launching pad, and docking arrangements for spacecraft. Also called: **space platform, space laboratory.** See also **Skylab, Salyut.**

space+suit (ˈspeɪsˌsuːt, -ˌsjuːt) *n.* any of various types of sealed and pressurized suits worn by astronauts or cosmonauts that provide an artificial atmosphere, acceptable temperature, radio-communication link, and protection from radiation for work outside a spacecraft.

space-time *or* **space-time con+tin+u·um** *n. Physics.* the four-dimensional continuum having three spatial coordinates and one time coordinate that together completely specify the location of a particle or an event.

space+walk (ˈspeɪsˌwɔːk) *n.* **1.** the act or an instance of floating and manoeuvring in space, outside but attached by a lifeline to a spacecraft. Technical name: **extravehicular activity.** ~*vb.* **2.** (*intr.*) to float and manoeuvre in space while outside but attached to a spacecraft.

space writ+er *n.* a writer paid by the area of his copy.

spa+cial (ˈspeɪʃəl) *adj.* a variant spelling of **spatial.**

spac+ing (ˈspeɪsɪŋ) *n.* **1.** the arrangment of letters, words, etc., on a page in order to achieve legibility or aesthetic appeal. **2.** the arrangement of objects in a space.

spa+cious (ˈspeɪʃəs) *adj.* having a large capacity or area. —**ˈspa+cious+ly** *adv.* —**ˈspa+cious+ness** *n.*

spade[1] (speɪd) *n.* **1.** a tool for digging, typically consisting of a flat rectangular steel blade attached to a long wooden handle. **2. a.** an object or part resembling a spade in shape. **b.** (*as modifier*): *a spade beard.* **3.** a heavy metallic projection attached to the trail of a gun carriage that embeds itself into the ground and so reduces recoil. **4.** a type of oar blade that is comparatively broad and short. Compare **spoon** (sense 6). **5.** a cutting tool for stripping the blubber from a whale or skin from a carcass. **6. call a spade a spade.** to speak plainly and frankly. ~*vb.* **7.** (*tr.*) to use a spade on. [Old English *spadu;* related to Old Norse *spathi*, Old High German *spato*, Greek *spathē* blade] —**ˈspad+er** *n.*

spade[2] (speɪd) *n.* **1. a.** the black symbol on a playing card resembling a heart-shaped leaf with a stem. **b.** a card with one or more of these symbols or (*when pl.*) the suit of cards so marked, usually the highest ranking of the four. **2.** a derogatory word for a Negro. **3. in spades.** *U.S. informal.* in an extreme or emphatic way. [C16: from Italian *spada* sword, used as an emblem on playing cards, from Latin *spatha*, from Greek *spathē* blade, broadsword]

spade+fish (ˈspeɪdˌfɪʃ) *n., pl.* **+fish** *or* **+fish·es.** any spiny-finned food fish of the family *Ephippidae*, esp. *Chaetodipterus faber* of American Atlantic coastal waters, having a deeply compressed body.

spade foot *n.* a spadelike projection at the end of a chair leg.

spade guin·ea *n. Brit. history.* a guinea decorated with a spade-shaped shield, coined during the reign of George III.

spade+work (ˈspeɪdˌwɜːk) *n.* dull or routine preparatory work.

spa+di+ceous (speɪˈdɪʃəs) *adj. Botany.* **1.** producing or resembling a spadix. **2.** of a bright brown colour. [C17: from New Latin *spādīceus*, from Latin *spādix* palm branch; see SPADIX]

spa+dix (ˈspeɪdɪks) *n., pl.* **spa+di+ces** (speɪˈdaɪsiːz). a racemose inflorescence having many small sessile flowers borne on a fleshy stem, the whole being enclosed in spathe: occurs in aroid plants. [C18: from Latin: pulled-off branch of a palm, with its fruit, from Greek: torn-off frond; related to Greek *span* to pull off]

spae (speɪ) *vb. Scot.* to foretell (the future). [C14: from Old Norse]

spag (spæg) *vb.* **spags, spag+ging, spagged.** (*tr.*) *South Wales dialect.* (of a cat) to scratch (a person) with the claws. [of uncertain origin]

spa+ghet+ti (spəˈgɛtɪ) *n.* pasta in the form of long strings. [C19: from Italian: little cords, from *spago* a cord]

spa+ghet+ti west+ern *n.* a cowboy film about the American West made by an Italian director, in Europe.

spa+gyr+ic (spəˈdʒɪrɪk) *or* **spa+gyr·i+cal** *adj. Rare.* of or relating to alchemy. [C16: from New Latin *spagiricus*, probably coined by Paracelsus, of obscure origin] —**spa+ˈgyr·i+cal+ly** *adv.*

spa+hi *or* **spa+hee** (ˈspɑːhiː, ˈspɑːiː) *n., pl.* **+his** *or* **+hees. 1.** (formerly) an irregular cavalryman in the Turkish armed forces. **2.** a member of a body of native Algerian cavalrymen in the French armed forces: disbanded after 1962. [C16: from Old French, from Turkish *sipahi*, from Persian *sipāhī* soldier; see SEPOY]

Spain (speɪn) *n.* a kingdom of SW Europe, occupying the Iberian peninsula between the Mediterranean and the Atlantic: a leading European power in the 16th century, with many overseas possessions, esp. in the New World; became a republic in 1931; under the fascist dictatorship of Franco following the Civil War (1936–39) until his death in 1975. It consists chiefly of a central plateau (the Meseta), with the Pyrenees and the Cantabrian Mountains in the north and the Sierra Nevada in the south. Language: Spanish, with Catalan, Galician, and Basque regional minority languages. Religion: Roman Catholic. Currency: peseta. Capital: Madrid. Pop.: 34 032 801 (1970). Area: 504 748 sq. km (194 883 sq. miles). Spanish name: **España.**

spake (speɪk) *vb. Archaic or dialect.* a past tense of **speak.**

Spa+la+to ('spaːlato) *n.* the Italian name for **Split.**

spall (spɔːl) *n.* **1.** a splinter or chip of ore, rock, or stone. *~vb.* **2.** to split or cause to split into such fragments. [C15: of unknown origin]

spall·a+tion (spɔ'leɪʃən) *n. Physics.* a type of nuclear reaction in which a photon or particle hits a nucleus and causes it to emit other particles or photons.

spal+peen (spæl'piːn, 'spælpiːn) *n. Irish.* a rascal or layabout. [C18: from Irish Gaelic *spailpīn* itinerant labourer]

Spam (spæm) *n. Trademark.* a kind of tinned luncheon meat, made largely from pork.

span[1] (spæn) *n.* **1.** the interval, space, or distance between two points, such as the ends of a bridge or arch. **2.** the complete duration or extent: *the span of his life.* **3.** short for **wingspan. 4.** a unit of length based on the width of an expanded hand, usually taken as nine inches. *~vb.* **spans, span+ning, spanned.** (*tr.*) **5.** to stretch or extend across, over, or around. **6.** to provide with something that extends across or around: *to span a river with a bridge.* **7.** to measure or cover, esp. with the extended hand. [Old English *spann;* related to Old Norse *sponn,* Old High German *spanna*]

span[2] (spæn) *n.* a team of horses or oxen, esp. two matched animals. [C16 (in the sense: yoke): from Middle Dutch: something stretched, from *spannen* to stretch; see SPAN[1]]

span[3] (spæn) *vb. Archaic or dialect.* a past tense of **spin.**

Span. *abbrev. for* Spanish.

span+cel ('spænsəl) *n.* **1.** a length of rope for hobbling an animal, esp. a horse or cow. *~vb.* **+cels, +cel+ling, +celled** *or U.S.* **+cels, +cel+ing, +celed. 2.** (*tr.*) to hobble (an animal) with a loose rope. [C17: from Low German *spansel,* from *spannen* to stretch; see SPAN[2]]

span+drel *or* **span+dril** ('spændrəl) *n. Architect.* **1.** an approximately triangular surface bounded by the outer curve of an arch and the adjacent wall. **2.** the surface area between two adjacent arches and the horizontal cornice above them. [C15 *spaundrell,* from Anglo-French *spaundre* spandrel, from Old French *spandre* to spread, EXPAND]

spang (spæŋ) *adv. U.S. informal.* exactly, firmly, or straight: *spang on target.* [C19: of unknown origin]

span+gle ('spæŋgəl) *n.* **1.** a small thin piece of metal or other shiny material used as a decoration, esp. on clothes; sequin. **2.** any glittering or shiny spot or object. *~vb.* **3.** to glitter or shine with or like spangles. **4.** (*tr.*) to decorate or cover with spangles. [C15: diminutive of *spange,* perhaps from Middle Dutch: clasp; compare Old Norse *spöng*] **—'span+gly** *adv.*

Span+iard ('spænjəd) *n.* a native or inhabitant of Spain.

span+iel ('spænjəl) *n.* **1.** a breed of gundog with long frilled ears, a silky coat, and the tail usually docked. **2.** an obsequiously devoted person. [C14: from Old French *espaigneul* Spanish (dog), from Old Provençal *espanhol,* ultimately from Latin *Hispāniolus* Spanish]

Span+ish ('spænɪʃ) *n.* **1.** the official language of Spain, Mexico, and most countries of South and Central America except Brazil: also spoken in Africa, the Far East, and elsewhere. It is the native language of approximately 200 million people throughout the world. Spanish is an Indo-European language belonging to the Romance group. **2. the Spanish.** (*functioning as pl.*) Spaniards collectively. *~adj.* **3.** of or relating to the Spanish language or its speakers. **4.** of or relating to Spain or Spaniards.

Span+ish A·mer·i+ca *n.* the parts of America colonized by Spaniards from the 16th century onwards and now chiefly Spanish-speaking: includes all of South America (except Brazil, Guyana, French Guiana, and Surinam), Central America (except British Honduras), Mexico, Cuba, Puerto Rico, the Dominican Republic, and a number of small West Indian islands.

Span·ish-A·mer·i·can *adj.* **1.** of or relating to any of the Spanish-speaking countries or peoples of the Americas. *~n.* **2.** a native or inhabitant of Spanish America. **3.** a Spanish-speaking person in the U.S.

Span·ish-A·mer·i·can War *n.* the war between the U.S. and Spain (1898) resulting in Spain's withdrawal from Cuba and its cession of Guam, the Philippines, and Puerto Rico.

Span+ish Ar+ma+da *n.* the great fleet sent by Philip II of Spain against England in 1588: defeated in the Channel by the English fleets and almost completely destroyed by storms off the Hebrides. Also called: (the) **Armada.**

Span+ish bay·o·net *n.* any of several American liliaceous plants of the genus *Yucca,* esp. *Y. aloifolia,* that have a tall woody stem, stiff pointed leaves, and large clusters of white flowers: cultivated for ornament. See also **Adam's-needle.**

Span+ish ce+dar *n.* a tall meliaceous tree, *Cedrela odorata,* of tropical America, the East Indies, and Australia, having smooth bark, pinnate leaves, yellow flowers, and light-coloured aromatic wood.

Span+ish Civ+il War *n.* the civil war in Spain from 1936 to 1939 in which insurgent nationalists, led by General Franco, succeeded in overthrowing the republican government. During the war Spain became an ideological battleground for fascists and socialists from all countries.

Span+ish fly *n.* **1.** a European blister beetle, *Lytta* (or *Cantharis*) *vesicatoria,* the dried bodies of which yield the pharmaceutical product cantharides. **2.** another name for **cantharides.**

Span+ish Guin+ea *n.* the former name (until 1964) of **Equatorial Guinea.**

Span+ish gui+tar *n.* the classic form of the guitar; a six-stringed instrument with a waisted body and a central sound hole.

Span+ish In+qui+si+tion *n.* the institution that guarded the orthodoxy of Catholicism in Spain, chiefly by the persecution of heretics, Jews, etc., esp. from the 15th to 17th centuries. See also **Inquisition.**

Span+ish macke+rel *n.* **1.** Also called: **kingfish.** any scombroid food fish of the genus *Scomberomorus,* esp. *S. maculatus,* of American coastal regions of the Atlantic: family *Scombridae* (mackerels, tunnies, etc.). **2.** a mackerel, *Scomber colias,* of European and E North American coasts that is similar to the common Atlantic mackerel.

Span+ish Main *n.* **1.** the mainland of Spanish America, esp. the N coast of South America from the Isthmus of Panama to the mouth of the Orinoco River, Venezuela. **2.** the Caribbean Sea, the S part of which in colonial times was the route of Spanish treasure galleons and the haunt of pirates.

Span+ish Mo+roc+co *n.* a former Spanish colony on the N coast of Morocco: part of the kingdom of Morocco since 1956. **—Span+ish Mo+roc+can** *adj., n.*

Span+ish moss *n.* **1.** an epiphytic bromeliaceous plant, *Tillandsia usneoides,* growing in tropical and subtropical regions as long bluish-grey strands suspended from the branches of trees. **2.** a tropical lichen, *Usnea longissima,* growing as long trailing green threads from the branches of trees. *~*Also called: **long moss.**

Span+ish ome+lette *n.* an omelette made by adding green peppers, onions, tomato, etc., to the eggs.

Span+ish on+ion *n.* any of several varieties of large mild-flavoured onions that are usually eaten raw.

Span+ish pap+ri+ka *n.* a mild seasoning made from a variety of red pepper grown in Spain.

Span+ish rice *n.* rice cooked with tomatoes, onions, green peppers, etc., and often flavoured with saffron.

Span+ish Sa+ha+ra *n.* the former name (until 1975) of **Western Sahara.**

Span+ish West Af+ri+ca *n.* a former overseas territory of Spain in NW Africa: divided in 1958 into the overseas provinces of Ifni and Spanish Sahara. **—Span+ish West Af+ri+can** *adj., n.*

Span+ish wind+lass *n.* a stick used as a device for twisting and tightening a rope or cable.

spank[1] (spæŋk) *vb.* **1.** (*tr.*) to slap or smack with the open hand, esp. on the buttocks. *~n.* **2.** a slap or series of slaps with the flat of the hand. [C18: probably of imitative origin]

spank[2] (spæŋk) *vb.* (*intr.*) to go at a quick and lively pace. [C19: back formation from SPANKING[2]]

spank+er ('spæŋkə) *n.* **1.** *Nautical.* a fore-and-aft sail or a mast that is aftermost in a sailing vessel. **2.** *Informal.* a person or animal that moves at a quick smart pace. **3.** *Informal.* something outstandingly fine or large.

spank+ing[1] ('spæŋkɪŋ) *n.* a series of spanks, esp. on the buttocks, usually as a punishment for children.

spank+ing[2] ('spæŋkɪŋ) *adj.* (*prenominal*) **1.** *Informal.* outstandingly fine, smart, large, etc. **2.** quick and energetic; lively. **3.** (esp. of a breeze) fresh and brisk.

span+ner ('spænə) *n.* **1.** a steel hand tool with a handle carrying jaws or a hole of particular shape designed to grip a nut or bolt head. **2. spanner in the works.** *Brit. informal.* a source of impediment or annoyance. [C17: from German, from *spannen* to stretch, SPAN[1]]

span-new *adj. Archaic or dialect.* absolutely new. [C14: from Old Norse *spānnȳr,* from *spānn* chip + *nȳr* NEW]

span of ap+pre+hen+sion *n. Psychol.* the maximum number of objects that can be correctly assessed after a brief presentation.

span roof *n.* a roof consisting of two equal sloping sides.

spans (spænz) *pl. n.* (often foll. by *of*) *S. African slang.* a large number (esp. of people): *spans of people are coming to the party.*

spar[1] (spɑː) *n.* **1. a.** any piece of nautical gear resembling a pole and used as a mast, boom, gaff, etc. **b.** (*as modifier*): *a spar buoy.* **2.** a principal supporting structural member of an aerofoil that runs from tip to tip or root to tip. [C13: from Old Norse *sperra* beam; related to Old High German *sparro,* Old French *esparre*]

spar[2] (spɑː) *vb.* **spars, spar+ring, sparred.** (*intr.*) **1.** *Boxing.* to box using light blows, as in training. **2.** to dispute or argue. **3.** (of gamecocks, etc.) to fight with the feet or spurs. *~n.* **4.** an unaggressive fight. **5.** an argument or wrangle. [Old English, perhaps from SPUR]

spar[3] (spɑː) *n.* any of various minerals, such as feldspar or calcite, that are light coloured, microcrystalline, transparent to translucent, and easily cleavable. [C16: from Middle Low German *spar;* related to Old English *spærstān;* see FELDSPAR]

spar+a+ble ('spærəbəl) *n.* a small nail with no head, used for fixing the soles and heels of shoes. [C17: changed from *sparrow-bill,* referring to the nail's shape]

spar buoy *n. Nautical.* a buoy resembling a vertical log.

spare (spɛə) *vb.* **1.** (*tr.*) to refrain from punishing, harming, or injuring. **2.** (*tr.*) to release or relieve, as from pain, suffering, etc. **3.** (*tr.*) to refrain from using: *spare the rod, spoil the child.* **4.** (*tr.*) to be able to afford or give: *I can't spare the time.* **5.** (*usually passive*) (esp. of Providence) to allow to survive: *I'll see you again next year if we are spared.* **6.** (*intr.*) *Now rare.* to act or live frugally. **7.** (*intr.*) *Rare.* to show mercy. **8. not spare oneself.** to exert oneself to the full. **9. to spare.** more than is required: *two minutes to spare.* ~*adj.* **10.** (*often immediately postpositive*) in excess of what is needed; additional: *are there any seats spare?* **11.** able to be used when needed: *a spare part.* **12.** (of a person) thin and lean. **13.** scanty or meagre. **14.** (*postpositive*) *Brit. slang.* upset, angry, or distracted (esp. in the phrase **go spare**). ~*n.* **15.** a duplicate kept as a replacement in case of damage or loss. **16.** a spare tyre. **17.** *Tenpin bowling.* **a.** the act of knocking down all the pins with the two bowls of a single frame. **b.** the score thus made. Compare **strike** (sense 39). [Old English *sparian* to refrain from injuring; related to Old Norse *spara,* Old High German *sparōn*] —**'spare+ly** *adv.* —**'spare+ness** *n.* —**'spar+er** *n.*

spare+rib ('spɛəˌrɪb) *n.* a cut of pork ribs with most of the meat trimmed off.

spare tyre *n.* **1.** an additional tyre, usually mounted on a wheel, carried by a motor vehicle in case of puncture. **2.** *Brit. slang, jocular.* a deposit of fat just above the waist.

sparge (spɑːdʒ) *vb. Rare.* to sprinkle or scatter (something). [C16: from Latin *spargere* to sprinkle] —**'sparg+er** *n.*

spar+id ('spærɪd) *or* **spar+oid** *n.* **1.** any marine percoid fish of the chiefly tropical and subtropical family *Sparidae,* having a deep compressed body and well-developed teeth: includes the sea breams and porgies. ~*adj.* **2.** of, relating to, or belonging to the family *Sparidae.* [C20: from New Latin *Sparidae,* from Latin *sparus* a sea bream, from Greek *sparos*]

spar+ing ('spɛərɪŋ) *adj.* **1.** (sometimes foll. by *of*) economical or frugal (with). **2.** scanty; meagre. **3.** merciful or lenient. —**'spar+ing+ly** *adv.* —**'spar+ing+ness** *n.*

spark[1] (spɑːk) *n.* **1.** a fiery particle thrown out or left by burning material or caused by the friction of two hard surfaces. **2. a.** a momentary flash of light accompanied by a sharp crackling noise, produced by a sudden electrical discharge through the air or some other insulating medium between two points. **b.** the electrical discharge itself. **c.** (*as modifier*): *a spark gap.* **3.** anything that serves to animate, kindle, or excite. **4.** a trace or hint: *she doesn't show a spark of interest.* **5.** vivacity, enthusiasm, or humour. **6.** a small piece of diamond, as used in the cutting of glass. ~*vb.* **7.** (*intr.*) to give off sparks. **8.** (of the sparking plug or ignition system of an internal-combustion engine) to produce a spark. **9.** (*tr.*; often foll. by *off*) to kindle, excite, or animate. [Old English *spearca;* related to Middle Low German *sparke,* Middle Dutch *spranke,* Lettish *spirgsti* cinders, Latin *spargere* to strew]

spark[2] (spɑːk) *Rare* (*except for sense 2*). ~*n.* **1.** a fashionable or gallant young man. **2. bright spark.** *Brit, usually ironic.* a person who appears clever or witty: *some bright spark left the papers next to the open window.* ~*vb.* **3.** to woo (a person). [C16 (in the sense: beautiful or witty woman): perhaps of Scandinavian origin; compare Old Norse *sparkr* vivacious] —**'spark+ish** *adj.*

Spark (spɑːk) *n.* **Mur·i·el.** born 1918, Scottish novelist; her works include *Memento Mori* (1959), *The Prime of Miss Jean Brodie* (1961), and *The Abbess of Crewe* (1974).

spark cham+ber *n. Physics.* a device for detecting ionizing radiation, consisting of two oppositely charged metal plates in a chamber containing inert gas, so that a particle passing through the chamber ionizes the gas and causes a spark to jump between the electrodes.

spark coil *n.* an induction coil used to produce spark discharges.

spark gap *n.* the space between two electrodes across which a spark can jump. Sometimes shortened to **gap.**

spark+ing plug *n.* a device screwed into the cylinder head of an internal-combustion engine to ignite the explosive mixture by means of an electric spark which jumps across a gap between a point earthed to the body of the plug and the tip of a central insulated rod. Also called: **spark plug.**

spar+kle ('spɑːkᵊl) *vb.* **1.** to issue or reflect or cause to issue or reflect bright points of light. **2.** (*intr.*) (of wine, mineral water, etc.) to effervesce. **3.** (*intr.*) to be vivacious or witty. ~*n.* **4.** a point of light, spark, or gleam. [C12 *sparklen,* frequentative of *sparken* to SPARK[1]]

spar+kler ('spɑːklə) *n.* **1.** a type of firework that throws out showers of sparks. **2.** *Informal.* a sparkling gem.

spar+kling wine *n.* a wine made effervescent by added carbon dioxide gas, introduced artificially or produced naturally by secondary fermentation.

spark off *vb.* (*tr., adv.*) to bring into being or action; activate or initiate: *to spark off an argument.*

spark plug *n.* another name for **sparking plug.**

sparks (spɑːks) *n. Informal.* **1.** an electrician. **2.** a radio officer, esp. on a ship.

spark trans+mit+ter *n.* an early type of radio transmitter in which power is generated by discharging a capacitor through an inductor in series with a spark gap.

spar+ling ('spɑːlɪŋ) *n., pl.* **+lings** *or* **+ling.** **1.** another name for the **European smelt** (see **smelt** (the fish)). **2.** a young herring. [C14: *sperlynge,* from Old French *esperling,* from Middle Dutch *spierlinc,* from *spier* young shoot]

spar+oid ('spærɔɪd) *adj., n.* another word for **sparid.** [C19: from New Latin *Sparoīdēs;* see SPARID]

spar+ring part+ner ('spɑːrɪŋ) *n.* a person who practises with a boxer during training.

spar+row ('spærəʊ) *n.* **1.** any weaverbird of the genus *Passer* and related genera, esp. the house sparrow, having a brown or grey plumage and feeding on seeds or insects. **2.** *U.S.* any of various North American finches, such as the chipping sparrow (*Spizella passerina*) and the song sparrow (*Melospiza melodia*), that have a dullish streaked plumage. ~See also **hedge sparrow, tree sparrow.** [Old English *spearwa;* related to Old Norse *spörr,* Old High German *sparo*] —**'spar·row-ˌlike** *adj.*

spar·row+grass ('spærəʊˌgrɑːs) *n.* a dialect or popular name for **asparagus.**

spar+row hawk *n.* a very small North American falcon, *Falco sparverius,* that is closely related to the kestrels.

spar·row+hawk ('spærəʊˌhɔːk) *n.* any of several small hawks, esp. *Accipiter nisus,* of Eurasia and N Africa that prey on smaller birds.

spar+ry ('spɑːrɪ) *adj. Geology.* containing, relating to, or resembling spar: *sparry coal.*

sparse (spɑːs) *adj.* scattered or scanty; not dense. [C18: from Latin *sparsus,* from *spargere* to scatter] —**'sparse+ly** *adv.* —**'sparse+ness** *or* **'spar+si·ty** *n.*

Spar+ta ('spɑːtə) *n.* an ancient Greek city in the S Peloponnese, famous for the discipline and military prowess of its citizens and for their austere way of life.

Spar·ta·cus ('spɑːtəkəs) *n.* died 71 B.C., Thracian slave, who led an ultimately unsuccessful revolt of gladiators against Rome (73–71 B.C.).

Spar+tan ('spɑːtᵊn) *adj.* **1.** of or relating to Sparta or its citizens. **2.** (*sometimes not cap.*) very strict or austere: *a Spartan upbringing.* **3.** (*sometimes not cap.*) possessing courage and resolve. ~*n.* **4.** a citizen of Sparta. **5.** (*sometimes not cap.*) a disciplined or brave person. —**'Spar+tan+ism** *n.*

spar+te·ine ('spɑːtɪˌiːn, -ɪn) *n.* a viscous oily alkaloid extracted from the broom plant and lupin seeds. It has been used in medicine to treat heart arrhythmias. [C19: from New Latin *Spartium,* from Greek *spartos* broom]

spasm ('spæzəm) *n.* **1.** an involuntary muscular contraction, esp. one resulting in cramp or convulsion. **2.** a sudden burst of activity, emotion, etc. [C14: from Latin *spasmus,* from Greek *spasmos* a cramp, from *span* to tear]

spas+mod+ic (spæz'mɒdɪk) *or* **spas+mod·i+cal** *adj.* **1.** taking place in sudden brief spells. **2.** of or characterized by spasms. [C17: New Latin, from Greek *spasmos* SPASM] —**spas+'mod·i+cal+ly** *adv.*

Spas·sky ('spæskɪ; *Russian* 'spaskij) *n.* **Bo·ris** (ba'ris). born 1937, Soviet chess player; world champion (1969–72).

spas+tic ('spæstɪk) *adj.* **1.** affected by or resembling spasms. **2.** *Derogatory slang.* clumsy, incapable or incompetent. ~*n.* **3.** a person who is affected by spasms or convulsions, esp. one who has cerebral palsy. **4.** *Derogatory slang.* a clumsy, incapable, or incompetent person. [C18: from Latin *spasticus,* from Greek *spastikos,* from *spasmos* SPASM] —**'spas+ti+cal+ly** *adv.*

spat[1] (spæt) *n.* **1.** *Now rare.* a slap or smack. **2.** *U.S.* a slight quarrel. ~*vb.* **spats, spat+ting, spat+ted.** **3.** *Now rare.* to slap (someone). **4.** (*intr.*) *U.S.* to have a slight quarrel. [C19: probably imitative of the sound of quarrelling]

spat[2] (spæt) *vb.* a past tense or past participle of **spit**[1].

spat[3] (spæt) *n.* another name for **gaiter** (sense 2). [C19: short for SPATTERDASH]

spat[4] (spæt) *n.* **1.** a larval oyster or similar bivalve mollusc, esp. when it settles to the sea bottom and starts to develop a shell. **2.** such oysters or other molluscs collectively. [C17: from Anglo-Norman *spat;* perhaps related to SPIT[1]]

spatch+cock ('spætʃˌkɒk) *n.* **1.** a chicken or game bird split down the back and grilled. Compare **spitchcock.** ~*vb.* (*tr.*) **2.** to interpolate (words, a story, etc.) into a sentence, narrative, etc., esp. inappropriately. [C18: perhaps variant of *spitchcock* eel when prepared and cooked]

spate (speɪt) *n.* **1.** a fast flow, rush, or outpouring: *a spate of words.* **2.** *Chiefly Brit.* a sudden flood: *the rivers were in spate.* **3.** *Chiefly Brit.* a sudden heavy downpour. [C15 (Northern and Scottish): of unknown origin]

spathe (speɪð) *n.* a large bract, often coloured, that encloses the inflorescence of any of several members of the lily family. [C18: from Latin *spatha,* from Greek *spathē* a blade] —**spa+tha+ceous** (spə'θeɪʃəs) *adj.* —**'spathed** *adj.*

spath+ic ('spæθɪk) *or* **spath+ose** ('spæθəʊs) *adj.* (of minerals) resembling spar, esp. in having good cleavage.

spa+tial *or* **spa+cial** ('speɪʃəl) *adj.* **1.** of or relating to space. **2.** existing or happening in space. —**spa+ti+al+i·ty** (ˌspeɪʃɪ'ælɪtɪ) *n.* —**'spa+tial+ly** *adv.*

spa+ti·o+tem+por+al (ˌspeɪʃɪəʊ'tɛmpərəl, -'tɛmprəl) *adj.* **1.** of or existing in both space and time. **2.** of or concerned with space-time. —ˌ**spa+ti·o+'tem+po+ral+ly** *adv.*

spat+ter ('spætə) *vb.* **1.** to scatter or splash (a substance, esp. a liquid) or (of a substance) to splash (something) in scattered drops: *to spatter mud on the car; mud spattered in her face.* **2.** (*tr.*) to sprinkle, cover, or spot (with a liquid). **3.** (*tr.*) to slander or defame. **4.** (*intr.*) to shower or rain down: *bullets spattered around them.* ~*n.* **5.** the sound of something spattering. **6.** something spattered, such as a spot or splash. **7.** the act or an instance of spattering. [C16: of imitative origin; related to Low German, Dutch *spatten* to spout, Frisian *spatteren* to splash]

spat·ter+dash ('spætəˌdæʃ) *n.* **1.** *U.S.* another name for **rough-cast.** **2.** (*pl.*) long leather leggings worn in the 18th century, as to protect from mud when riding. [C17: see SPATTER, DASH]

spat·u·la (ˈspætjʊlə) *n.* a utensil with a broad flat, often flexible blade, used for lifting, spreading, or stirring foods, etc. [C16: from Latin: a broad piece, from *spatha* a flat wooden implement; see SPATHE] —ˈ**spat·u·lar** *adj.*

spat·u·late (ˈspætjʊlɪt) *adj.* **1.** shaped like a spatula. **2.** *Botany.* having a narrow base and a broad rounded apex: *a spatulate leaf.*

spav·in (ˈspævɪn) *n. Vet. science.* enlargement of the hock of a horse by a bony growth (**bony spavin**) or distension of the ligament (**bog spavin**), usually caused by inflammation or injury, and often resulting in lameness. [C15: from Old French *espavin,* of unknown origin]

spav·ined (ˈspævɪnd) *adj.* **1.** *Vet. science.* affected with spavin; lame. **2.** decrepit or worn out.

spawn (spɔːn) *n.* **1.** the mass of eggs deposited by fish, amphibians, or molluscs. **2.** *Often derogatory.* offspring, product, or yield. **3.** *Botany.* the nontechnical name for **mycelium.** ~*vb.* **4.** (of fish, amphibians, etc.) to produce or deposit (eggs). **5.** *Often derogatory.* (of people) to produce (offspring). **6.** to produce or engender. [C14: from Anglo-Norman *espaundre,* from Old French *spandre* to spread out, EXPAND] —ˈ**spawn·er** *n.*

spay (speɪ) *vb.* (*tr.*) to remove the ovaries from (a female animal). [C15: from Old French *espeer* to cut with the sword, from *espee* sword, from Latin *spatha*]

S.P.C.K. (in Britain) *abbrev. for* Society for Promoting Christian Knowledge.

speak (spiːk) *vb.* **speaks, speak·ing, spoke, spo·ken. 1.** to make (verbal utterances); utter (words). **2.** to communicate or express (something) in or as if in words: *I speak the truth.* **3.** (*intr.*) to deliver a speech, discourse, etc. **4.** (*tr.*) to know how to talk in (a language or dialect): *he does not speak German.* **5.** (*intr.*) to make a characteristic sound: *the clock spoke.* **6.** (*intr.*) (of dogs, esp. hounds used in hunting) to give tongue; bark. **7.** (*tr.*) *Nautical.* to hail and converse or communicate with (another vessel) at sea. **8.** (*intr.*) (of a musical instrument) to produce a sound. **9.** (*intr.*; foll. by *for*) to be representative or advocate (of): *he speaks for all the members.* **10. on speaking terms.** on good terms; friendly. **11. so to speak.** in a manner of speaking; as it were. **12. speak one's mind.** to express one's opinions frankly and plainly. **13. to speak of.** of a significant or worthwhile nature: *we have had no support to speak of.* ~See also **speak for, speak out, speak to, speak up.** [Old English *specan;* related to Old High German *spehhan,* Middle High German *spechten* to gossip, Middle Dutch *speken;* see SPEECH] —ˈ**speak·a·ble** *adj.*

speak·eas·y (ˈspiːkˌiːzɪ) *n., pl.* **·eas·ies.** *U.S.* a place where alcoholic drink was sold illicitly during Prohibition.

speak·er (ˈspiːkə) *n.* **1.** a person who speaks, esp. at a formal occasion. **2.** See **loudspeaker.** —ˈ**speak·er·ˌship** *n.*

Speak·er (ˈspiːkə) *n.* the presiding officer in any of numerous legislative bodies, including the House of Commons in Britain and Canada and the House of Representatives in the U.S. and Australia.

speak for *vb.* (*intr., prep.*) **1.** to speak as a representative of (other people). **2. speak for itself.** to be so evident that no further comment is necessary. **3. speak for yourself.** *Informal.* (used as an imperative) do not presume that other people agree with you.

speak·ing (ˈspiːkɪŋ) *adj.* **1.** (*prenominal*) eloquent, impressive, or striking. **2. a.** able to speak. **b.** (*in combination*) able to speak a particular language: *French-speaking.*

speak·ing clock *n. Brit.* a telephone service that gives a precise verbal statement of the correct time.

speak·ing in tongues *n.* another term for **gift of tongues.**

speak·ing trum·pet *n.* a trumpet-shaped instrument used to carry the voice a great distance or held to the ear by a deaf person to aid his hearing.

speak·ing tube *n.* a tube or pipe for conveying a person's voice from one room, area, or building to another.

speak out *vb.* (*intr., adv.*) **1.** to state one's beliefs, objections, etc., bravely and firmly. **2.** to speak more loudly and clearly.

speak to *vb.* (*intr., prep.*) **1.** to address (a person). **2.** to reprimand: *your father will speak to you later.* **3.** *Formal.* to give evidence of or comments on (a subject): *who will speak to this item?*

speak up *vb.* (*intr., adv.*) **1.** to speak more loudly. **2.** to state one's beliefs, objections, etc., bravely and firmly.

spear[1] (spɪə) *n.* **1.** a weapon consisting of a long shaft with a sharp pointed end of metal, stone, or wood that may be thrown or thrusted. **2.** a similar implement used to catch fish. **3.** another name for **spearman.** ~*vb.* **4.** to pierce (something) with or as if with a spear. [Old English *spere;* related to Old Norse *spjör* spears, Greek *sparos* gilthead] —ˈ**spear·er** *n.*

spear[2] (spɪə) *n.* a shoot, slender stalk or blade, as of grass, asparagus, or broccoli. [C16: probably variant of SPIRE[1], influenced by SPEAR[1]]

spear·fish (ˈspɪəˌfɪʃ) *n., pl.* **·fish** *or* **·fish·es.** another name for **marlin.**

spear gun *n.* a device for firing spears underwater.

spear·head (ˈspɪəˌhɛd) *n.* **1.** the pointed head of a spear. **2.** the leading force in a military attack. **3.** any person or thing that leads or initiates an attack, campaign, etc. ~*vb.* **4.** (*tr.*) to lead or initiate (an attack, campaign, etc.).

spear·man (ˈspɪəmən) *n., pl.* **·men.** a soldier armed with a spear.

spear·mint (ˈspɪəˌmɪnt) *n.* a purple-flowered mint plant, *Mentha spicata,* of S and central Europe, cultivated for its leaves, which yield an oil used for flavouring.

spear side *n.* the male side or branch of a family. Compare **distaff side.**

spear·wort (ˈspɪəˌwɜːt) *n.* any of several Eurasian ranunculaceous plants of the genus *Ranunculus,* such as *R. flammula* (**lesser spearwort**) and *R. lingua* (**great spearwort**), which grow in wet places and have long narrow leaves and yellow flowers. See also **buttercup.**

spec (spɛk) *n.* **1. on spec.** *Informal.* as a speculation or gamble: *all the tickets were sold so I went to the theatre on spec.* ~*adj. Austral. informal.* **2.** (*prenominal*) speculative: *a spec developer.*

spec. *abbrev. for:* **1.** special. **2.** specification. **3.** speculation.

spe·cial (ˈspɛʃəl) *adj.* **1.** distinguished, set apart from, or excelling others of its kind. **2.** (*prenominal*) designed or reserved for a particular purpose: *a special tool for working leather.* **3.** not usual or commonplace. **4.** (*prenominal*) particular or primary: *his special interest was music.* **5.** denoting or relating to the education of physically or mentally handicapped children: *a special school.* ~*n.* **6.** a special person or thing, such as an extra edition of a newspaper or a train reserved for a particular purpose. **7.** a dish or meal given prominence, esp. at a low price, in a cafe, etc. **8.** *Austral. slang.* a convict given special treatment on account of his education, social class, etc. **9.** short for **special constable.** [C13: from Old French *especial,* from Latin *speciālis* individual, special, from *speciēs* appearance, SPECIES] —ˈ**spe·cial·ly** *adv.* —ˈ**spe·cial·ness** *n.*

Usage. See at **especial.**

spe·cial as·sess·ment *n.* (in the U.S.) a special charge levied on property-owners by a county or municipality to help pay the costs of a civic improvement that increases the value of their property.

Spe·cial Branch *n.* (in Britain) the department of the police force that is concerned with political security.

spe·cial case *n. Law.* an agreed written statement of facts submitted by litigants to a court for a decision on a point of law.

spe·cial con·sta·ble *n.* a person recruited for temporary or occasional police duties, esp. in time of emergency.

spe·cial de·liv·er·y *n.* the delivery of a piece of mail outside the time of a scheduled delivery.

spe·cial draw·ing rights *pl. n.* (*sometimes caps.*) the reserve assets of the International Monetary Fund on which member nations may draw in proportion to their contribution to the Fund. Abbrev.: **SDRs.**

spe·cial ef·fects *pl. n. Films.* techniques used in the production of scenes that cannot be achieved by normal techniques.

spe·cial·ism (ˈspɛʃəˌlɪzəm) *n.* the act or process of specializing in something, or the thing itself.

spe·cial·ist (ˈspɛʃəlɪst) *n.* **1.** a person who specializes in or devotes himself to a particular area of activity, field of research, etc. **2.** an enlisted rank in the U.S. Army denoting technical qualifications that entitle the holder to a noncommissioned officer's pay. —ˌ**spe·cial·ˈis·tic** *adj.*

spe·ci·al·i·ty (ˌspɛʃɪˈælɪtɪ) *or U.S.* **spe·cial·ty** (ˈspɛʃəltɪ) *n., pl.* **·ties. 1.** a special interest or skill. **2. a.** a service or product specialized in, as at a restaurant: *roast beef was a speciality of the house.* **b.** (*as modifier*): *a speciality dish.* **3.** a special or distinguishing feature or characteristic.

spe·cial·ize *or* **spe·cial·ise** (ˈspɛʃəˌlaɪz) *vb.* **1.** (*intr.*) to train in or devote oneself to a particular area of study, occupation, or activity. **2.** (*usually passive*) to cause (organisms or their parts) to develop in a way most suited to a particular environment or way of life or (of organisms, etc.) to develop in this way. **3.** (*tr.*) to modify or make suitable for a special use or purpose. **4.** (*tr.*) to mention specifically; specify. **5.** (*tr.*) to endorse (a commercial paper) to a specific payee. —ˌ**spe·cial·i·ˈza·tion** *or* ˌ**spe·cial·i·ˈsa·tion** *n.*

spe·cial ju·ry *n.* (formerly) a jury whose members were drawn from some profession or rank of society as well as possessing the usual qualifications for jury service.

spe·cial li·cence *n. Brit.* a licence permitting a marriage to take place by dispensing with the usual legal conditions.

spe·cial plead·ing *n. Law.* **1.** a pleading that alleges new facts that offset those put forward by the other side rather than directly admitting or denying those facts. **2.** a pleading that emphasizes the favourable aspects of a case while omitting the unfavourable.

spe·cial priv·i·lege *n.* a legally endorsed privilege granted exclusively to some individual or group.

spe·cial sort *n. Printing.* a character, such as an accented letter, that is not a usual member of any fount. Also called: **peculiar, arbitrary.**

spe·cial the·o·ry of rel·a·tiv·i·ty *n.* the theory proposed in 1905 by Einstein, which assumes that the laws of physics are equally valid in all nonaccelerated frames of reference and that the velocity of light is independent of an observer's velocity. It leads to the idea of a space-time continuum, the equivalence of mass and energy, and the Lorentz-Fitzgerald contraction. Also called: **special relativity.** See also **general theory of relativity, Einstein's law** (sense 1).

spe·cial·ty (ˈspɛʃəltɪ) *n., pl.* **·ties. 1.** *Law.* a formal contract or obligation expressed in a deed. **2.** the usual U.S. spelling of **speciality.**

spe·ci·a·tion (ˌspiːʃɪˈeɪʃən) *n.* the evolutionary development of a biological species, as by geographical isolation of a group of individuals from the main stock.

spe·cie (ˈspiːʃiː) *n.* **1.** coin money, as distinguished from bullion or paper money. **2. in specie. a.** (of money) in coin. **b.** in kind. **c.** *Law.* in the actual form specified. [C16: from the Latin phrase *in speciē* in kind]

spe+cie point *n.* another name for **gold point.**

spe+cies ('spiːʃiːz; *Latin* 'spiːʃɪˌiːz) *n., pl.* **+cies. 1.** *Biology.* **a.** any of the taxonomic groups into which a genus is divided, the members of which are capable of interbreeding: often contain subspecies, varieties, or races. A species is designated in italics by the genus name followed by the specific name, for example *Felis domesticus* (the domestic cat). **b.** the animals of such a group. **c.** any group of related animals or plants not necessarily of this taxonomic rank. **2.** *Logic.* a group of objects or individuals, all sharing at least one common attribute, that forms a subdivision of a genus. **3.** a kind, sort, or variety: *a species of treachery.* **4.** *Chiefly R.C. Church.* the outward form of the bread and wine in the Eucharist. **5.** *Obsolete.* an outward appearance or form. **6.** *Obsolete.* specie. [C16: from Latin: appearance, from *specere* to look]

specif. *abbrev. for* specifically.

spec·i+fi+a·ble ('spɛsɪˌfaɪəbᵊl) *adj.* able to be specified.

spe+cif+ic (spɪ'sɪfɪk) *adj.* **1.** explicit, particular, or definite: *please be more specific.* **2.** relating to a specified or particular thing: *a specific treatment for arthritis.* **3.** of or relating to a biological species: *specific differences.* **4.** (of a disease) caused by a particular pathogenic agent. **5.** *Physics.* **a.** characteristic of a property of a particular substance, esp. in relation to the same property of a standard reference substance: *specific gravity.* **b.** characteristic of a property of a particular substance per unit mass, length, area, volume, etc.: *specific heat.* **c.** (of an extensive physical quantity) divided by mass: *specific heat capacity; specific volume.* **6.** Also (rare): **spe+cif·i+cal.** *International trade.* denoting a tariff levied at a fixed sum per unit of weight, quantity, volume, etc., irrespective of value. ~*n.* **7.** (*sometimes pl.*) a designated quality, thing, etc. **8.** *Med.* any drug used to treat a particular disease. [C17: from Medieval Latin *specificus,* from Latin SPECIES] —**spe+'cif·i+cal+ly** *adv.* —**spec·i+fic+i·ty** (ˌspɛsɪ'fɪsɪtɪ) *n.*

spec·i+fi+ca+tion (ˌspɛsɪfɪ'keɪʃən) *n.* **1.** the act or an instance of specifying. **2.** (in patent law) a written statement accompanying an application for a patent that describes the nature of an invention. **3.** a detailed description of the criteria for the constituents, construction, appearance, performance, etc., of a material, apparatus, etc., or of the standard of workmanship required in its manufacture. **4.** an item, detail, etc., specified.

spe+cif+ic grav+i·ty *n.* the ratio of the density of a substance to that of water. See **relative density.**

spe+cif+ic heat ca+pac+i·ty *n.* the heat required to raise unit mass of a substance by unit temperature interval under specified conditions, such as constant pressure: usually measured in joules per kelvin per kilogram. Symbol: c_p (for constant pressure). Also called: **specific heat.**

spe+cif+ic im+pulse *n.* the ratio of the thrust produced by a rocket engine to the rate of fuel consumption: it has units of time and is the length of time one pound of propellant would last if used to produce one pound of thrust continuously.

spe+cif+ic per+for+mance *n. Law.* a remedy awarded by a court where damages are an insufficient remedy.

spe+cif+ic re+sist+ance *n.* the former name for **resistivity.**

spe+cif+ic vis+cos+i·ty *n. Physics.* a measure of the resistance to flow of a fluid, expressed as the ratio of the absolute viscosity of the fluid to that of a reference fluid (usually water in the case of liquids).

spe+cif+ic vol+ume *n. Physics.* the volume of matter per unit mass; the reciprocal of the density. Symbol: ν

spec·i+fy ('spɛsɪˌfaɪ) *vb.* **+fies, +fy+ing, +fied.** (*tr.; may take a clause as object*) **1.** to refer to or state specifically. **2.** to state as a condition. **3.** to state or include in the specification of. [C13: from Medieval Latin *specificāre* to describe] —**spec·i+fi+ca+tive** ('spɛsɪfɪˌkeɪtɪv) *adj.* —**'spec·i+ˌfi+er** *n.*

spec·i+men ('spɛsɪmɪn) *n.* **1. a.** an individual, object, or part regarded as typical of the group or class to which it belongs. **b.** (*as modifier*): *a specimen signature; a specimen page.* **2.** *Med.* a sample of tissue, blood, urine, etc., taken for diagnostic examination or evaluation. **3.** the whole or a part of an organism, plant, rock, etc., collected and preserved as an example of its class, species, etc. **4.** *Informal, often derogatory.* a person. [C17: from Latin: mark, evidence, proof, from *specere* to look at]

spe+ci+os+i·ty (ˌspiːʃɪ'ɒsɪtɪ) *n., pl.* **·ties. 1.** a thing or person that is deceptively attractive or plausible. **2.** the state of being specious. **3.** *Obsolete.* the state of being beautiful.

spe+cious ('spiːʃəs) *adj.* **1.** apparently correct or true, but actually wrong or false. **2.** deceptively attractive in appearance. [C14 (originally: fair): from Latin *speciōsus* plausible, from *speciēs* outward appearance, from *specere* to look at] —**'spe+cious+ly** *adv.* —**'spe+cious+ness** *n.*

speck (spɛk) *n.* **1.** a very small mark or spot. **2.** a small or tiny piece of something. ~*vb.* **3.** (*tr.*) to mark with specks or spots. [Old English *specca;* related to Middle Dutch *spekelen* to sprinkle]

speck+le ('spɛkᵊl) *n.* **1.** a small or slight mark usually of a contrasting colour, as on the skin, a bird's plumage, or eggs. ~*vb.* **2.** (*tr.*) to mark with or as if with speckles. [C15: from Middle Dutch *spekkel;* see SPECK]

speck+led trout *n.* another name for **brook trout.**

specs (spɛks) *pl. n. Informal.* **1.** short for **spectacles. 2.** short for **specifications.**

spec+ta+cle ('spɛktəkᵊl) *n.* **1.** a public display or performance, esp. a showy or ceremonial one. **2.** a thing or person seen, esp. an unusual or ridiculous one: *he makes a spectacle of himself.* **3.** a strange or interesting object or phenomenon. [C14: via Old French from Latin *spectaculum* a show, from *spectāre* to watch, from *specere* to look at]

spec+ta+cled ('spɛktəkᵊld) *adj.* **1.** wearing glasses. **2.** (of an animal) having markings around the eyes resembling a pair of glasses.

spec+ta+cles ('spɛktəkᵊlz) *pl. n.* **1.** a pair of glasses for correcting defective vision. Often (informal) shortened to **specs. 2. pair of spectacles.** *Cricket.* a score of 0 in each innings of a match.

spec+tac·u+lar (spɛk'tækjʊlə) *adj.* **1.** of or resembling a spectacle; impressive, grand, or dramatic. **2.** unusually marked or great: *a spectacular increase in spending.* ~*n.* **3.** a lavishly produced performance. —**spec+'tac·u·lar+ly** *adv.*

spec+ta+tor (spɛk'teɪtə) *n.* a person viewing anything; onlooker; observer. [C16: from Latin, from *spectāre* to watch; see SPECTACLE]

spec+ta+tor sport *n.* a sport that attracts people as spectators rather than as participants.

spec+tra ('spɛktrə) *n.* the plural of **spectrum.**

spec+tral ('spɛktrəl) *adj.* **1.** of or like a spectre. **2.** of or relating to a spectrum: *spectral colours.* **3.** *Physics.* (of a physical quantity) relating to a single wavelength of radiation: *spectral luminous efficiency.* —**spec+tral+i·ty** (spɛk'trælɪtɪ) *or* **'spec+tral+ness** *n.* —**'spec+tral+ly** *adv.*

spec+tral lu+mi+nous ef+fi+cien+cy *n.* a measure of the efficiency of radiation of a given wavelength in producing a visual sensation. It is equal to the ratio of the radiant flux at a standard wavelength to that at the given wavelength when the standard wavelength is chosen so that the maximum value of this ratio is unity. Symbol: $V(\lambda)$ (for photopic vision) or $V'(\lambda)$ (for scotopic vision).

spec+tral type *or* **class** *n.* any of various groups into which stars are classified according to characteristic spectral lines and bands. The most important classification (**Harvard classification**) has a series of classes W, O, B, A, F, G, K, M, R, N, S, the series also being a scale of diminishing surface temperature.

spec+tre *or U.S.* **spec+ter** ('spɛktə) *n.* **1.** a ghost; phantom; apparition. **2.** a mental image of something unpleasant or menacing: *the spectre of redundancy.* [C17: from Latin *spectrum,* from *specere* to look at]

spec·tro- *combining form.* indicating a spectrum: *spectrogram.*

spec+tro+bo+lom+e·ter (ˌspɛktrəʊbəʊ'lɒmɪtə) *n.* a combined spectroscope and bolometer for determining the wavelength distribution of radiant energy emitted by a source. —**spec+tro+bol·o+met+ric** (ˌspɛktrəˌbəʊlə'mɛtrɪk) *adj.*

spec+tro+graph ('spɛktrəʊˌgræf, -ˌgrɑːf) *n.* a spectroscope or spectrometer that produces a photographic record (**spectrogram**) of a spectrum. See also **sound spectrograph.** —ˌ**spec+tro+'graph+ic** *adj.* —ˌ**spec+tro+'graph·i+cal+ly** *adv.* —**spec+'trog+ra+phy** *n.*

spec+tro+he+li·o+graph (ˌspɛktrəʊ'hiːlɪəˌgræf, -ˌgrɑːf) *n.* an instrument used to photograph the sun in light of a particular wavelength, usually that of calcium or hydrogen, to show the distribution of the element over the surface and in the atmosphere. The photograph obtained is a **spectroheliogram.** —ˌ**spec+tro+ˌhe+li·o+'graph+ic** *adj.*

spec+tro+he+li·o+scope (ˌspɛktrəʊ'hiːlɪəʊˌskəʊp) *n.* an instrument, similar to the spectroheliograph, used for observing solar radiation at one particular wavelength. —**spec+tro+he+li·o+scop+ic** (ˌspɛktrəʊˌhiːlɪəʊ'skɒpɪk) *adj.*

spec+trom+e·ter (spɛk'trɒmɪtə) *n.* any instrument for producing a spectrum, esp. one in which wavelength, energy, intensity, etc., can be measured. See also **mass spectrometer.** —**spec+tro+met+ric** (ˌspɛktrəʊ'mɛtrɪk) *adj.* —**spec+'trom+e·try** *n.*

spec+tro+pho+tom+e·ter (ˌspɛktrəʊfəʊ'tɒmɪtə) *n.* an instrument for producing or recording a spectrum and measuring the photometric intensity of each wavelength present, esp. such an instrument used for infrared, visible, and ultraviolet radiation. See also **spectrometer.** —**spec+tro+pho·to+met+ric** (ˌspɛctrəʊˌfəʊtə'mɛtrɪk) *adj.* —ˌ**spec+tro+pho+'tom+e·try** *n.*

spec+tro+scope ('spɛktrəˌskəʊp) *n.* any of a number of instruments for dispersing electromagnetic radiation and thus forming or recording a spectrum. See also **spectrometer.** —**spec+tro+scop+ic** (ˌspɛktrə'skɒpɪk) *or* ˌ**spec+tro+'scop·i+cal** *adj.* —ˌ**spec+tro+'scop·i+cal+ly** *adv.*

spec+tro+scop+ic a·nal·y·sis *n.* the use of spectroscopy in determining the chemical or physical constitution of substances.

spec+tros+co+py (spɛk'trɒskəpɪ) *n.* the science and practice of using spectrometers and spectroscopes and of analysing spectra, the methods employed depending on the radiation being examined. The techniques are widely used in chemical analysis and in studies of the properties of atoms, molecules, ions, etc. —**spec+'tros+co+pist** *n.*

spec+trum ('spɛktrəm) *n., pl* **+tra** (-trə). **1.** the distribution of colours produced when white light is dispersed by a prism or diffraction grating. There is a continuous change in wavelength from red, the longest wavelength, to violet, the shortest. Seven colours are usually distinguished: violet, indigo, blue, green, yellow, orange, and red. **2.** the whole range of electromagnetic radiation with respect to its wavelength or frequency. **3.** any particular distribution of electromagnetic radiation often showing lines or bands characteristic of the substance emitting the radiation or absorbing it. See also **absorption spectrum, emission spectrum. 4.** any similar distribution or record of the energies, velocities, masses, etc., of atoms, ions, electrons, etc.: *a mass spectrum.* **5.** any range or scale, as of capabilities, emotions, or moods. **6.** another name for an **afterimage.** [C17:

from Latin: appearance, image, from *spectāre* to observe, from *specere* to look at]

spec·trum a·nal·y·sis *n.* the analysis of a spectrum to determine the properties of its source, such as the analysis of the emission spectrum of a substance to determine the electron distribution in its molecules.

spec·u·lar ('spɛkjʊlə) *adj.* **1.** of, relating to, or having the properties of a mirror: *specular reflection.* **2.** of or relating to a speculum. [C16: from Latin *speculāris,* from *speculum* a mirror, from *specere* to look at] —'**spec·u·lar·ly** *adv.*

spec·u·late ('spɛkjʊˌleɪt) *vb.* **1.** (when *tr., takes a clause as object*) to conjecture without knowing the complete facts. **2.** (*intr.*) to buy or sell securities, property, etc., in the hope of deriving capital gains. **3.** (*intr.*) to risk loss for the possibility of considerable gain. [C16: from Latin *speculārī* to spy out, from *specula* a watchtower, from *specere* to look at] —'**spec·u·ˌla·tor** *n.*

spec·u·la·tion (ˌspɛkjʊ'leɪʃən) *n.* **1.** the act or an instance of speculating. **2.** a supposition, theory, or opinion arrived at through speculating. **3.** investment involving high risk but also the possibility of high profits.

spec·u·la·tive ('spɛkjʊlətɪv) *adj.* relating to or characterized by speculation, esp. financial speculation. —'**spec·u·la·tive·ly** *adv.* —'**spec·u·la·tive·ness** *n.*

spec·u·lum ('spɛkjʊləm) *n., pl.* **-la** (-lə) *or* **-lums. 1.** a mirror, esp. one made of polished metal for use in a telescope, etc. **2.** *Med.* an instrument for dilating a bodily cavity or passage to permit examination of its interior. **3.** a patch of distinctive colour on the wing of a bird, esp. in certain ducks. [C16: from Latin: mirror, from *specere* to look at]

spec·u·lum met·al *n.* a white hard brittle corrosion-resistant alloy of copper (55–70 per cent) and tin with smaller amounts of other metals. It takes a high polish and is used for mirrors, lamp reflectors, ornamental ware, etc.

sped (spɛd) *vb.* a past tense or past participle of **speed.**

speech (spiːtʃ) *n.* **1. a.** the act or faculty of speaking, esp. as possessed by persons: *to have speech with somebody.* **b.** (*as modifier*): *speech therapy.* **2.** that which is spoken; utterance. **3.** a talk or address delivered to an audience. **4.** a person's characteristic manner of speaking. **5.** a national or regional language or dialect. **6.** *Linguistics.* another word for **parole** (sense 5). [Old English *spēc;* related to *specan* to SPEAK]

speech com·mun·i·ty *n.* a community consisting of all the speakers of a particular language or dialect.

speech day *n. Brit.* (in schools) an annual day at which prizes are presented, speeches are made by guest speakers, etc.

speech from the throne *n.* (in Britain and the dominions of the Commonwealth) the speech at the opening of each session of Parliament in which the Government outlines its legislative programme. It is read by the sovereign or his or her representative. Also called (esp. in Britain): **Queen's** (*or* **King's**) **speech.**

speech·i·fy ('spiːtʃɪˌfaɪ) *vb.* **-fies, -fy·ing, -fied.** (*intr.*) **1.** to make a speech or speeches. **2.** to talk pompously and boringly. —ˌ**speech·i·fi·'ca·tion** *n.* —'**speech·i·ˌfi·er** *n.*

speech·less ('spiːtʃlɪs) *adj.* **1.** not able to speak. **2.** temporarily deprived of speech. **3.** not expressed or able to be expressed in words: *speechless fear.* —'**speech·less·ly** *adv.* —'**speech·less·ness** *n.*

speech-read·ing *n.* another name for **lip-reading.**

speed (spiːd) *n.* **1.** the act or quality of acting or moving fast; rapidity. **2.** the rate at which something moves, is done, or acts. **3.** *Physics.* **a.** a scalar measure of the rate of movement of a body expressed either as the distance travelled divided by the time taken (**average speed**) or the rate of change of position with respect to time at a particular point (**instantaneous speed**). It is measured in metres per second, miles per hour, etc. **b.** another word for **velocity** (sense 2). **4.** a rate of rotation, usually expressed in revolutions per unit time. **5. a.** a gear ratio in a motor vehicle, bicycle, etc. **b.** (*in combination*): *a three-speed gear.* **6.** *Photog.* a numerical expression of the sensitivity to light of a particular type of film, paper, or plate. See also **ASA/BS, DIN. 7.** *Photog.* a measure of the ability of a lens to pass light from an object to the image position, determined by the aperture and also the transmitting power of the lens. It increases as the f-number is decreased and vice versa. **8.** a slang word for **amphetamine. 9.** *Archaic.* prosperity or success. ~*vb.* **speeds, speed·ing; sped** *or* **speed·ed. 10.** to move or go or cause to move or go quickly. **11.** (*intr.*) to drive (a motor vehicle) at a high speed, esp. above legal limits. **12.** (*tr.*) to help further the success or completion of. **13.** (*intr.*) *Slang.* to take or be under the influence of amphetamines. **14.** (*intr.*) to operate or run at a high speed. **15.** *Archaic.* **a.** (*intr.*) to prosper or succeed. **b.** (*tr.*) to wish success to. [Old English *spēd* (originally in the sense: success); related to *spōwan* to succeed, Latin *spēs* hope, Old Slavonic *spěti* to be lucky] —'**speed·er** *n.*

speed·ball *n. Slang.* a mixture of cocaine with morphine or heroin.

speed·boat ('spiːdˌbəʊt) *n.* a high-speed motorboat having either an inboard or outboard motor.

speed lim·it *n.* the maximum permitted speed at which a vehicle may travel on certain roads.

speed·o ('spiːdəʊ) *n., pl.* **-os.** an informal name for **speedometer.**

speed·om·e·ter (spɪ'dɒmɪtə) *n.* a device fitted to a vehicle to measure and display the speed of travel. See also **mileometer.**

speed·ster ('spiːdstə) *n.* a fast car, esp. a sports model.

speed trap *n.* a section of road on which the police check the speed of vehicles, often using radar.

speed up *vb.* (*adv.*) **1.** to increase or cause to increase in speed or rate; accelerate. ~*n.* **speed-up. 2.** an instance of this; acceleration.

speed·way ('spiːdˌweɪ) *n.* **1. a.** the sport of racing on light powerful motorcycles round cinder tracks. **b.** (*as modifier*): *a speedway track.* **2.** the track or stadium where such races are held. **3.** *U.S.* **a.** a racetrack for cars. **b.** a road on which fast driving is allowed.

speed·well ('spiːdˌwɛl) *n.* any of various temperate scrophulariaceous plants of the genus *Veronica,* such as *V. officinalis* (**common speedwell**) and *V. chamaedrys* (**germander speedwell**), having small blue or pinkish-white flowers.

Speed·writ·ing ('spiːdˌraɪtɪŋ) *n. Trademark.* a form of shorthand in which alphabetic combinations are used to represent groups of sounds or short common words.

speed·y ('spiːdɪ) *adj.* **speed·i·er, speed·i·est. 1.** characterized by speed of motion. **2.** done or decided without delay; quick. —'**speed·i·ly** *adv.* —'**speed·i·ness** *n.*

speel (spiːl) *n. Manchester dialect.* a splinter of wood. [probably from Old Norse; compare Norwegian *spela, spila,* Swedish *spjela, spjele* SPILL[2]]

speiss (spaɪs) *n.* the arsenides and antimonides that form when ores containing arsenic or antimony are smelted. [C18: from German *Speise* food]

spe·lae·an *or* **spe·le·an** (spɪ'liːən) *adj.* of, found in, or inhabiting caves: *spelaean animals.* [C19: via New Latin, from Latin *spēlaeum* a cave, from Greek *spēlaion*]

spe·le·ol·o·gy *or* **spe·lae·ol·o·gy** (ˌspiːlɪ'ɒlədʒɪ) *n.* **1.** the scientific study of caves, esp. in respect of their geological formation, flora and fauna, etc. **2.** the sport or pastime of exploring caves. [C19: from Latin *spēlaeum* cave] —**spe·le·o·log·i·cal** *or* **spe·lae·o·log·i·cal** (ˌspiːlɪə'lɒdʒɪkᵊl) *adj.* —ˌ**spe·le·'ol·o·gist** *or* ˌ**spe·lae·'ol·o·gist** *n.*

spelk (spɛlk) *n. Northern English dialect.* a splinter of wood. [from Old English *spelc, spilc* surgical splint; related to Old Norse *spelkur* splints]

spell[1] (spɛl) *vb.* **spells, spell·ing; spelt** *or* **spelled. 1.** to write or name in correct order the letters that comprise the conventionally accepted form of (a word or part of a word). **2.** (*tr.*) (of letters) to go to make up the conventionally established form of (a word) when arranged correctly: *d-o-g spells dog.* **3.** (*tr.*) to indicate or signify: *such actions spell disaster for our cause.* ~See also **spell out.** [C13: from Old French *espeller,* of Germanic origin; related to Old Norse *spialla* to talk, Middle High German *spellen*] —'**spell·a·ble** *adj.*

spell[2] (spɛl) *n.* **1.** a verbal formula considered as having magical force. **2.** any influence that can control the mind or character; fascination. **3.** a state induced by or as if by the pronouncing of a spell; trance: *to break the spell.* **4. under a spell.** held in or as if in a spell. ~*vb.* **5.** (*tr.*) *Rare.* to place under a spell. [Old English *spell* speech; related to Old Norse *spjall* tale, Gothic *spill,* Old High German *spel*]

spell[3] (spɛl) *n.* **1.** an indeterminate, usually short, period of time: *a spell of cold weather.* **2.** a period or tour of duty after which one person or group relieves another. **3.** *Austral.* a period or interval of rest. ~*vb.* **4.** (*tr.*) *Northern Brit. dialect and U.S.* to take over from (a person) for an interval of time; relieve temporarily. [Old English *spelian* to take the place of, of obscure origin]

spell·bind ('spɛlˌbaɪnd) *vb.* **-binds, -bind·ing, -bound.** (*tr.*) to cause to be spellbound; entrance or enthral.

spell·bind·er ('spɛlˌbaɪndə) *n.* **1.** a person capable of holding others spellbound, esp. a political speaker. **2.** a novel, play, etc., that holds one enthralled.

spell·bound ('spɛlˌbaʊnd) *adj.* having one's attention held as though one is bound by a spell: *a spellbound audience.*

spell·er ('spɛlə) *n.* **1.** a person who spells words in the manner specified: *a bad speller.* **2.** a book designed to teach or improve spelling.

spel·li·can ('spɛlɪkən) *n.* a variant spelling of **spillikin.**

spell·ing ('spɛlɪŋ) *n.* **1.** the act or process of writing words by using the letters conventionally accepted for their formation; orthography. **2.** the art or study of orthography. **3.** the actual way in which a word is spelt. **4.** the ability of a person to spell: *John's spelling is good.*

spell·ing bee *n.* a contest in which players are required to spell words according to orthographic conventions.

spell·ing pro·nun·ci·a·tion *n.* a pronunciation of a word that is influenced by the word's orthography and often comes about as the modification of an earlier or original rendering, such as the pronunciation of the British name *Mainwaring,* usually ('mænərɪŋ), as ('meɪnˌwɛərɪŋ).

spell out *vb.* (*tr., adv.*) **1.** to make clear, distinct, or explicit; clarify in detail: *let me spell out the implications.* **2.** to read laboriously or with difficulty, working out each word letter by letter. **3.** to discern by study; puzzle out.

spelt[1] (spɛlt) *vb.* a past tense or past participle of **spell**[1].

spelt[2] (spɛlt) *n.* a species of wheat, *Triticum spelta,* that was formerly much cultivated and was used to develop present-day cultivated wheats. [Old English; related to Old Saxon *spelta,* Old High German *spelza*]

spel·ter ('spɛltə) *n.* impure zinc, usually containing about 3 per cent of lead and other impurities. [C17: probably from Middle Dutch *speauter,* of obscure origin; compare Old French *peautre* pewter, Italian *peltro* PEWTER]

spe·lunk·er (spɪ'lʌŋkə) *n.* a person whose hobby is the exploration and study of caves. [C20: from Latin *spēlunca,* from Greek *spēlunx* a cave] —**spe·'lunk·ing** *n.*

Spen·bor·ough ('spɛnbərə, -brə) *n.* a town in N England, in West Yorkshire: textile centre. Pop.: 40 693 (1971).

spence (spɛns) *n. Brit. dialect.* **a.** a larder or pantry. **b.** any monetary allowance. **c.** a parlour, esp. in a cottage. [C14: from Old French *despense,* from Latin *dispendere* to distribute; see DISPENSE]

Spence (spɛns) *n.* Sir **Bas·il (Unwin).** 1907–76, Scottish architect, born in India; designed Coventry Cathedral (1951).

spen+cer[1] ('spɛnsə) *n.* **1.** a short fitted coat or jacket. **2.** a woman's knitted vest.

spen+cer[2] ('spɛnsə) *n. Nautical.* a large loose-footed gaff sail on a square-rigger or barque.

Spen·cer ('spɛnsə) *n.* **1. Her·bert.** 1820–1903, English philosopher, who applied evolutionary theory to the study of society, favouring laissez-faire doctrines. **2.** Sir **Stan·ley.** 1891–1959, English painter, noted esp. for his paintings of Christ in a contemporary English setting.

Spen+cer Gulf *n.* an inlet of the Indian Ocean in S Australia, between the Eyre and Yorke Peninsulas. Length: about 320 km (200 miles). Greatest width: about 145 km (90 miles).

spend (spɛnd) *vb.* **spends, spend+ing, spent. 1.** to pay out (money, wealth, etc.). **2.** (*tr.*) to concentrate (time, effort, thought, etc.) upon an object, activity, etc. **3.** (*tr.*) to pass (time) in a specific way, activity, place, etc. **4.** (*tr.*) to use up completely: *the hurricane spent its force.* **5.** (*tr.*) to give up (one's blood, life, etc.) in a cause. **6.** (*intr.*) *Obsolete.* to be used up or exhausted. **7. spend a penny.** *Brit. informal.* to urinate. [Old English *spendan,* from Latin *expendere;* influenced also by Old French *despendre* to spend, from Latin *dispendere;* see EXPEND, DISPENSE] —**'spend+a·ble** *adj.*

spend+er ('spɛndə) *n.* a person who spends money in a manner specified: *a big spender.*

Spen·der ('spɛndə) *n.* **Ste·phen.** born 1909, English poet and critic, who played an important part in the left-wing literary movement of the 1930s: coeditor of *Horizon* (1939–41) and of *Encounter* (1953–67).

spend+ing mon+ey *n.* an allowance for small personal expenses; pocket money.

spends (spɛndz) *pl. n. Lancashire dialect.* a child's pocket money.

spend+thrift ('spɛnd,θrɪft) *n.* **1.** a person who spends money in an extravagant manner. ~*adj.* **2.** (*usually prenominal*) of or like a spendthrift: *spendthrift economies.*

Speng·ler ('spɛŋlə; *German* 'ʃpɛŋglər) *n.* **Os·wald** ('ɔsvalt). 1880–1936, German philosopher of history, noted for *The Decline of the West* (1918–22), which argues that civilizations go through natural cycles of growth and decay.

Spen·ser ('spɛnsə) *n.* **Ed·mund.** ?1552–99, English poet celebrated for *The Faerie Queene* (1590; 1596), an allegorical romance. His other verse includes the collection of eclogues *The Shepherd's Calendar* (1579) and the marriage poem *Epithalamion* (1594).

Spen+se·ri·an (spɛn'sɪərɪən) *adj.* **1.** relating to or characteristic of Edmund Spenser or his poetry. ~*n.* **2.** a student or imitator of Edmund Spenser.

Spen+se·ri·an son+net *n. Prosody.* a sonnet form used by the poet Spenser having the rhyme scheme a b a b b c b c c d c d e e.

Spen+se·ri·an stan+za *n. Prosody.* the stanza form used by the poet Spenser in his poem *The Faerie Queene,* consisting of eight lines in iambic pentameter and a concluding Alexandrine, rhyming a b a b b c b c c.

spent (spɛnt) *vb.* **1.** the past tense or past participle of **spend.** ~*adj.* **2.** used up or exhausted; consumed.

spe+os ('spi:ɒs) *n.* (esp. in ancient Egypt) a temple or tomb cut into a rock face. [C19: Greek, literally: a cave, grotto]

sperm[1] (spɜ:m) *n.* **1.** another name for **semen. 2.** a male reproductive cell; male gamete. [C14: from Late Latin *sperma,* from Greek; related to Greek *speirein* to sow]

sperm[2] (spɜ:m) *n.* short for **sperm whale, spermaceti,** or **sperm oil.**

-sperm *n. combining form.* (in botany) a seed: *gymnosperm.* —**-sper·mous** *or* **-sper·mal** *adj. combining form.*

sper+ma+cet·i (,spɜ:mə'sɛtɪ, -'si:tɪ) *n.* a white waxy substance obtained from oil from the head of the sperm whale: used in cosmetics, candles, ointments, etc. [C15: from Medieval Latin *sperma cētī* whale's sperm, from *sperma* SPERM[1] + Latin *cētus* whale, from Greek *kētos*]

sper+mar·y ('spɜ:mərɪ) *n., pl.* **+mar·ies.** any organ in which spermatozoa are produced, esp. a testis.

sper+ma+the+ca (,spɜ:mə'θi:kə) *n.* a sac or cavity within the body of many female invertebrates, esp. insects, used for storing spermatozoa before fertilization takes place. [C19: see SPERM, THECA] —**,sper+ma+'the+cal** *adj.*

sper+mat+ic (spɜ:'mætɪk), **sper+mic** ('spɜ:mɪk), *or* **sper+mous** ('spɜ:məs) *adj.* **1.** of or relating to spermatozoa: *spermatic fluid.* **2.** of or relating to the testis: *the spermatic artery.* **3.** of or relating to a spermary. [C16: from Late Latin *spermaticus,* from Greek *spermatikos* concerning seed, from *sperma* seed, SPERM[1]] —**sper+'mat·i·cal+ly** *adv.*

sper+mat+ic cord *n.* a cord in many male mammals that passes from each testis to the abdominal cavity and contains the spermatic artery and vein, vas deferens, and lymphatics.

sper+mat+ic flu+id *n.* another name for **semen.**

sper+ma+tid ('spɜ:mətɪd) *n. Zoology.* any of four immature male gametes that are formed from a spermatocyte, each of which develops into a spermatozoon.

sper+ma+ti·um (spɜ:'meɪtɪəm) *n., pl.* **+ti·a** (-tɪə). a nonmotile male reproductive cell in red algae and some fungi. [C19: New Latin, from Greek *spermation* a little seed; see SPERM[1]]

sper·ma·to-, sper·mo- *or before a vowel* **sper·mat-, sperm-** *combining form.* **1.** indicating sperm: *spermatogenesis.* **2.** indicating seed: *spermatophyte.* [from Greek *sperma, spermat-,* seed; see SPERM[1]]

sper+mat·o+cyte ('spɜ:mətəʊ,saɪt) *n.* **1.** *Zoology.* an immature male germ cell, developed from a spermatogonium, that gives rise, by meiosis, to four spermatids. **2.** *Botany.* a male germ cell that develops into an antherozoid.

sper+mat·o+gen+e·sis (,spɜ:mətəʊ'dʒɛnɪsɪs) *n.* the formation and maturation of spermatozoa in the testis. See also **spermatocyte** (sense 1). —**sper+ma+to+ge·net+ic** (,spɜ:mətəʊdʒə'nɛtɪk) *adj.*

sper+mat·o+go+ni·um (,spɜ:mətə'gəʊnɪəm) *n., pl.* **+ni·a** (-nɪə). *Zoology.* an immature male germ cell that divides to form many spermatocytes. —**,sper+mat·o+'go+ni·al** *adj.*

sper+mat·o+phore ('spɜ:mətəʊ,fɔ:) *n.* a capsule of spermatozoa extruded by some molluscs, crustaceans, annelids, and amphibians. —**sper+ma+toph·o·ral** (,spɜ:mə'tɒfərəl) *adj.*

sper+ma+to+phyte ('spɜ:mətəʊ,faɪt) *or* **sper+mo+phyte** *n.* any plant of the major division *Spermatophyta,* which includes all seed-bearing plants: divided into the *Angiospermae* (see **angiosperm**) and the *Gymnospermae* (see **gymnosperm**). Former name: **phanerogam.** —**sper+ma+to+phyt+ic** (,spɜ:mətəʊ'fɪtɪk) *adj.*

sper+ma+tor+rhoe·a *or esp. U.S.* **sper+ma+tor+rhe·a** (,spɜ:mətəʊ'rɪə) *n.* involuntary emission of semen.

sper+ma+to+zo+id (,spɜ:mətəʊ'zəʊɪd) *n. Botany.* another name for **antherozoid.**

sper+ma+to+zo+on (,spɜ:mətəʊ'zəʊɒn) *n., pl.* **+zo·a** (-zəʊə). any of the male reproductive cells released in the semen during ejaculation, consisting of a flattened egg-shaped head, a long neck, and a whiplike tail by which it moves to fertilize the female ovum. Also called: **sperm, zoosperm.** —**,sper+ma+to+'zo+al, ,sper+ma+to+'zo+an,** *or* **,sper+ma+to+'zo+ic** *adj.*

sper+mic ('spɜ:mɪk) *adj.* another word for **spermatic.**

sper+mi+cide ('spɜ:mɪ,saɪd) *n.* any drug or other agent that kills spermatozoa. —**,sper+mi+'ci+dal** *adj.*

sperm+ine ('spɜ:mi:n, -mɪn) *n.* a white or colourless basic water-soluble amine that is found in semen, sputum, and animal tissues; diaminopropyltetramethylenediamine. Formula: $C_{10}H_{26}N_4$.

sper+mi·o+gen+e·sis (,spɜ:mɪəʊ'dʒɛnɪsɪs) *n.* the stage in spermatogenesis in which spermatozoa are formed from spermatids. —**sper+mi·o+ge·net+ic** (,spɜ:mɪəʊdʒə'nɛtɪk) *adj.*

sper+mo+go+ni·um (,spɜ:mə'gəʊnɪəm) *n., pl.* **+ni·a** (-nɪə). a reproductive body in some fungi and lichens, in which spermatia are formed.

sperm oil *n.* an oil obtained from the head of the sperm whale, used as a lubricant.

sper+mo+phile ('spɜ:məʊ,faɪl) *n.* any of various North American ground squirrels of the genera *Citellus, Spermophilopsis,* etc., regarded as pests in many regions.

sper+mo+phyte ('spɜ:məʊ,faɪt) *n.* a variant spelling of **spermatophyte.**

sper+mous ('spɜ:məs) *adj.* **1.** of or relating to the sperm whale or its products. **2.** another word for **spermatic.**

sperm whale *n.* a large toothed whale, *Physeter catodon,* having a square-shaped head and hunted for sperm oil, spermaceti, and ambergris: family *Physeteridae.* Also called: **cachalot.**

sper·ry+lite ('spɛrɪ,laɪt) *n.* a white metallic mineral consisting of platinum arsenide in cubic crystalline form. Formula: $PtAs_2$. [C19: named after F. L. *Sperry,* Canadian chemist]

spes+sar+tite ('spɛsə,taɪt) *n.* a brownish-red garnet that consists of manganese aluminium silicate and is used as a gemstone. Formula: $Mn_3Al_2(SiO_4)_3$. [C19: named after *Spessart,* mountain range in Germany]

spew (spju:) *vb.* **1.** to eject (the contents of the stomach) involuntarily through the mouth; vomit. **2.** to spit (spittle, phlegm, etc.) out of the mouth. **3.** (usually foll. by *out*) to send or be sent out in a stream: *flames spewed out.* ~*n.* **4.** something ejected from the mouth. ~Also (archaic): **spue.** [Old English *spīwan;* related to Old Norse *spȳja,* Gothic *speiwan,* Old High German *spīwan,* Latin *spuere,* Lithuanian *spiauti*] —**'spew+er** *n.*

Spey (speɪ) *n.* a river in E Scotland, flowing generally northeast through the Grampian Mountains to the Moray Firth: salmon-fishing. Length: 172 km (107 miles).

Spey+er (*German* 'ʃpaɪər) *n.* a port in SW West Germany, in Rhineland-Palatinate on the Rhine: the scene of 50 imperial diets. Pop.: 42 800 (1970). English name: **Spires.**

sp. gr. *abbrev. for* specific gravity.

sphag+num ('sfægnəm) *n.* any moss of the genus *Sphagnum,* of temperate bogs, having leaves capable of holding much water: layers of these mosses decay to form peat. Also called: **peat moss, bog moss.** [C18: from New Latin, from Greek *sphagnos* a variety of moss] —**'sphag+nous** *adj.*

sphal+er+ite ('sfælə,raɪt, 'sfeɪlə-) *n.* a yellow to brownish-black mineral consisting of zinc sulphide in cubic crystalline form with varying amounts of iron, manganese, cadmium, gallium, and indium: the chief source of zinc. Formula: ZnS. Also called: **zinc blende.** [C19: from Greek *sphaleros* deceitful, from *sphallein* to cause to stumble]

sphene (sfi:n) *n.* a brown, yellow, green, or grey lustrous mineral consisting of calcium titanium silicate in monoclinic crystalline form. It occurs in metamorphic and acid igneous rocks and is used as a gemstone. Formula: $CaTiSiO_5$. Also called: **titanite.** [C19: from French *sphène,* from Greek *sphēn* a wedge, alluding to its crystals]

sphe+nic ('sfi:nɪk) *adj.* having the shape of a wedge.

sphe·no- *or before a vowel* **sphen-** *combining form.* having the shape of a wedge: *sphenogram.* [from Greek *sphēn* wedge]

sphe+no+don ('sfi:nəˌdɒn) *n.* the technical name for the **tuatara.**

sphe+no+gram ('sfi:nəˌgræm) *n.* a character used in cuneiform script.

sphe+noid ('sfi:nɔɪd) *adj. also* **sphe+noi+dal. 1.** wedge-shaped. **2.** of or relating to the sphenoid bone. ~*n.* **3.** See **sphenoid bone.**

sphe+noid bone *n.* the large butterfly-shaped compound bone at the base of the skull, containing a protective depression for the pituitary gland.

spher+al ('sfɪərəl) *adj.* **1.** of or shaped like a sphere; spherical. **2.** perfectly rounded; symmetrical.

sphere (sfɪə) *n.* **1.** *Maths.* **a.** a three-dimensional closed surface such that every point on the surface is equidistant from a given point, the centre. **b.** the solid figure bounded by this surface or the space enclosed by it. Equation: $(x-a)^2 + (y-b)^2 + (z-c)^2 = r^2$, where r is the radius and (a, b, c) are the coordinates of the centre; surface area: $4\pi r^2$; volume: $4/3\pi r^3$. **2.** any object having approximately this shape; globe. **3.** the night sky considered as a vaulted roof; firmament. **4.** any heavenly object such as a planet, natural satellite, or star. **5.** (in the Ptolemaic or Copernican systems of astronomy) one of a series of revolving hollow globes, arranged concentrically, on whose transparent surfaces the sun (or in the Copernican system the earth), the moon, the planets, and fixed stars were thought to be set, revolving around the earth (or in the Copernican system the sun). **6.** particular field of activity environment: *that's out of my sphere.* **7.** a social class or stratum of society. ~*vb.* (*tr.*) *Chiefly poetic.* **8.** to surround or encircle. **9.** to place aloft or in the heavens. [C14: from Late Latin *sphēra,* from Latin *sphaera* globe, from Greek *sphaira*]

-sphere *n. combining form.* **1.** having the shape or form of a sphere: *bathysphere.* **2.** indicating a spherelike enveloping mass: *atmosphere.* —**-spher·ic** *adj. combining form.*

sphere of in+flu+ence *n.* a region of the world in which one state is dominant.

spher·i·cal ('sfɛrɪkᵊl) *or* **spher+ic** *adj.* **1.** shaped like a sphere. **2.** of or relating to a sphere: *spherical geometry.* **3.** *Geom.* formed on the surface of or inside a sphere: *a spherical triangle.* **4. a.** of or relating to heavenly bodies. **b.** of or relating to the spheres of the Ptolemaic or the Copernican system. —**'spher·i·cal+ly** *adv.* —**'spher·i·cal+ness** *n.*

spher·i·cal ab+er+ra+tion *n. Physics.* a defect of optical systems that arises when light striking a mirror or lens near its edge is focused at different points on the axis to the light striking near the centre. The effect occurs when the mirror or lens has spherical surfaces. See also **aberration** (sense 4).

spher·i·cal an+gle *n.* an angle formed at the intersection of two great circles of a sphere.

spher·i·cal co+or+di+nates *pl. n.* three coordinates that define the location of a point in three-dimensional space in terms of its radius vector, r, the angle, θ, which this vector makes with one axis, and the angle, ϕ, which the plane of this vector makes with a mutually perpendicular axis. Usually written (r, θ, ϕ).

spher·i·cal ge+om+e+try *n.* the branch of geometry concerned with the properties of figures, esp. spherical triangles, formed on the surface of a sphere.

spher·i·cal pol·y+gon *n.* a closed geometric figure formed on the surface of a sphere that is bounded by three or more arcs of great circles.

spher·i·cal tri+an+gle *n.* a closed geometric figure formed on the surface of a sphere that is bounded by arcs of three great circles.

spher·i·cal trig·o+nom+e·try *n.* the branch of trigonometry concerned with the measurement of the angles and sides of spherical triangles.

sphe+ric·i·ty (sfɪ'rɪsɪtɪ) *n.* the state or form of being spherical.

spher+ics[1] ('sfɛrɪks) *n.* (*functioning as sing.*) the geometry and trigonometry of figures on the surface of a sphere.

spher+ics[2] *or U.S.* **sfer+ics** ('sfɛrɪks, 'sfɪər-) *n.* (*functioning as sing.*) short for **atmospherics.**

sphe+roid ('sfɪərɔɪd) *n.* another name for **ellipsoid of revolution.**

sphe+roi+dal (sfɪə'rɔɪdᵊl) *adj.* **1.** shaped like an ellipsoid of revolution; approximately spherical. **2.** of or relating to an ellipsoid of revolution. —**sphe+'roi+dal+ly** *or* **sphe+'roi+di+cal+ly** *adv.*

sphe+roi+dic+i·ty (ˌsfɪərɔɪ'dɪsɪtɪ) *n.* the state or form of being spheroidal.

sphe+rom+e·ter (sfɪə'rɒmɪtə) *n.* an instrument for measuring the curvature of a surface.

spher+ule ('sfɛru:l) *n.* a very small sphere or globule. [C17: from Late Latin *sphaerula* a little SPHERE] —**'spher·u+lar** *adj.*

spher·u+lite ('sfɛrʊˌlaɪt) *n.* any of several spherical masses of radiating needle-like crystals of one or more minerals occurring in rocks such as obsidian. —**spher·u+lit+ic** (ˌsfɛrʊ'lɪtɪk) *adj.*

spher·y ('sfɪərɪ) *adj. Poetic.* **1.** resembling a sphere. **2.** resembling a celestial body or bodies; starlike.

sphinc·ter ('sfɪŋktə) *n. Anatomy.* a ring of muscle surrounding the opening of a hollow organ or body and contracting to close it. [C16: from Late Latin, from Greek *sphinktēr,* from *sphingein* to grip tightly] —**'sphinc+ter+al** *adj.*

sphin+go+my+e·lin (ˌsfɪŋgəʊ'maɪəlɪn) *n. Biochem.* any of a group of phospholipids containing sphingosine, choline, fatty acids, and phosphoric acid. [from *sphingo-,* from Greek *sphingein* to bind + MYELIN]

sphin+go+sine ('sfɪŋgəˌsɪn, -ˌsi:n) *n. Biochem.* a long-chain compound occurring in sphingomyelins and cerebrosides, and from which it can be released by hydrolysis. Formula: $CH_3(CH_2)_{12}CH{:}CHCH(OH)CH(NH_2)CH_2OH$. [from *sphingos-,* from Greek *sphingein* to hold fast + -INE[2]]

sphinx (sfɪŋks) *n., pl.* **sphinx·es** *or* **sphin+ges** ('sfɪndʒi:z). **1.** any of a number of huge stone statues built by the ancient Egyptians, having the body of a lion and the head of a man. **2.** an inscrutable person.

Sphinx (sfɪŋks) *n.* **the. 1.** *Greek myth.* a monster with a woman's head and a lion's body. She lay outside Thebes, asking travellers a riddle and killing them when they failed to answer it. Oedipus answered the riddle and the Sphinx then killed herself. **2.** the huge statue of a sphinx near the pyramids at Gisa in Egypt, of which the head is a carved portrait of the fourth-dynasty Pharaoh, Chephrēn. [C16: via Latin from Greek, apparently from *sphingein* to hold fast]

sphinx moth *n. U.S.* another name for the **hawk moth.**

sphra+gis+tics (sfrə'dʒɪstɪks) *n.* (*functioning as sing.*) the study of seals and signet rings. [C19: from Greek *sphragistikos,* from *sphragizein* to seal, from *sphragis* a seal] —**sphra+'gis+tic** *adj.*

sp. ht. *abbrev. for* specific heat.

sphyg+mic ('sfɪgmɪk) *adj. Physiol.* of or relating to the pulse.

sphyg·mo- *or before a vowel* **sphygm-** *combining form.* indicating the pulse: *sphygmometer.* [from Greek *sphugmos* pulsation, from *sphuzein* to throb]

sphyg+mo+graph ('sfɪgməʊˌgræf, -ˌgrɑ:f) *n. Med.* an instrument for making a recording (**sphygmogram**) of variations in blood pressure and pulse. —**sphyg+mo+graph+ic** (ˌsfɪgməʊ'græfɪk) *adj.* —**sphyg+mog+ra+phy** (sfɪg'mɒgrəfɪ) *n.*

sphyg+moid ('sfɪgmɔɪd) *adj. Physiol.* resembling the pulse.

sphyg+mo+ma+nom+e·ter (ˌsfɪgməʊmə'nɒmɪtə) *n. Med.* an instrument for measuring arterial blood pressure.

spic, spick, *or* **spik** (spɪk) *n. U.S. slang.* a derogatory word for a person from a Spanish-speaking country in South or Central America or a Spanish-speaking community in the U.S. [C20: perhaps alluding to a foreigner's mispronunciation of *speak*]

spi+ca ('spaɪkə) *n., pl.* **+cae** (-si:) *or* **+cas.** *Med.* a spiral bandage formed by a series of overlapping figure-of-eight turns. [C15: from Latin: ear of corn]

Spi+ca ('spi:kə) *n.* the brightest star in the constellation Virgo. Distance: 120 light years.

spi+cate ('spaɪkeɪt) *adj. Botany.* having, arranged in, or relating to spikes: *a spicate inflorescence.* [C17: from Latin *spīcātus* having spikes, from *spīca* a point]

spic+ca+to (spɪ'kɑ:təʊ) *Music.* ~*n.* **1.** a style of playing a bowed stringed instrument in which the bow bounces lightly off the strings. ~*adj., adv.* **2.** to be played in this manner. [Italian: detached, from *spiccare* to make distinct]

spice (spaɪs) *n.* **1. a.** any of a variety of aromatic vegetable substances, such as ginger, cinnamon, nutmeg, used as flavourings. **b.** these substances collectively. **2.** something that represents or introduces zest, charm, or gusto. **3.** *Rare.* a small amount. **4.** *Yorkshire dialect.* confectionery. ~*vb.* (*tr.*) **5.** to prepare or flavour (food) with spices. **6.** to introduce charm or zest into. [C13: from Old French *espice,* from Late Latin *speciēs* (pl.) spices, from Latin *speciēs* (sing.) kind; also associated with Late Latin *spīcea* (unattested) fragrant herb, from Latin *spīceus* having spikes of foliage; see SPICA] —**'spic+er** *n.*

spice+ber·ry ('spaɪsbərɪ, -brɪ) *n., pl.* **·ries. 1.** a myrtaceous tree, *Eugenia rhombea,* of the Caribbean and Florida, with orange or black edible fruits. **2.** the fruit of this tree. **3.** any of various other aromatic plants or shrubs having spicy edible berries, such as wintergreen.

spice+bush ('spaɪsˌbʊʃ) *n.* a North American lauraceous shrub, *Lindera benzoin,* having yellow flowers and aromatic leaves and bark.

Spice Is+lands *pl. n.* the former name of the **Moluccas.**

spic+er·y ('spaɪsərɪ) *n., pl.* **+er·ies. 1.** spices collectively. **2.** the piquant or fragrant quality associated with spices. **3.** *Obsolete.* a place to store spices.

spick-and-span *or* **spic-and-span** ('spɪkən'spæn) *adj.* **1.** extremely neat and clean. **2.** new and fresh. [C17: shortened from *spick-and-span-new,* from obsolete *spick* spike, nail + SPAN-NEW]

spic+ule ('spɪkju:l) *n.* **1.** Also called: **spiculum.** a small slender pointed structure or crystal, esp. any of the calcareous or siliceous elements of the skeleton of sponges, corals, etc. **2.** *Astronomy.* a spiked ejection of hot gas occurring over 5000 kilometres above the sun's surface (in its atmosphere) and having a diameter of about 1100 kilometres. [C18: from Latin: SPICULUM] —**spic·u+late** ('spɪkjʊˌleɪt, -lɪt) *adj.*

spic·u+lum ('spɪkjʊləm) *n., pl.* **+la** (-lə). another word for **spicule** (sense 1). [C18: from Latin: small sharp point, from SPICA]

spic·y ('spaɪsɪ) *adj.* **spic·i+er, spic·i+est. 1.** seasoned with or containing spice. **2.** highly flavoured; pungent. **3.** *Informal.* suggestive of scandal or sensation. **4.** producing or yielding spices. —**'spic·i+ly** *adv.* —**'spic·i+ness** *n.*

spi+der ('spaɪdə) *n.* **1.** any predatory silk-producing arachnid of the order *Araneae,* having four pairs of legs and a rounded unsegmented body consisting of abdomen and cephalothorax. See also **wolf spider, trap-door spider, tarantula, black widow. 2.** any of various similar or related arachnids. **3.** a hub fitted with radiating spokes or arms that serve to transmit power or support a load. **4.** *Agriculture.* an instrument used with a cultivator to pulverize soil. **5.** any implement or tool having the shape of a spider. **6.** *Nautical.* a metal frame fitted at the base of a mast to which halyards are tied when not in use. **7.** any part of a machine having a number of radiating spokes, tines, or arms. **8.** Also called: **octopus.** *Brit.* a cluster of elastic straps fastened at a central point and used to hold a load on a car rack, motorcycle, etc. **9.** *Snooker, etc.* a rest having long legs, used to raise the cue above the level of the height of the ball. **10.** *Austral. informal.* another name for **ice-cream soda. 11.** short for **spider phaeton.** [Old English *spīthra;* related to Danish *spinder,* German *Spinne;* see SPIN]

spi·der crab *n.* any of various crabs of the genera *Macropodia, Libinia,* etc., having a small triangular body and very long legs.

spi·der-hunt·ing wasp *n.* any solitary wasp of the superfamily *Pompiloidea,* having a slender elongated body: the female stores her nest with spiders, on which the larvae feed.

spi·der·man ('spaɪdəˌmæn) *n., pl.* **·men.** *Informal.* **1.** *Chiefly Brit.* a person who erects the steel structure of a building. **2.** another name for a **steeplejack.**

spi·der mite *n.* any of various plant-feeding mites of the family *Tetranychidae,* esp. *Panonychus ulmi* (**red spider mite**), which is a serious orchard pest.

spi·der mon·key *n.* **1.** any of several arboreal New World monkeys of the genus *Ateles,* of Central and South America, having very long legs, a long prehensile tail, and a small head. **2. woolly spider monkey.** a rare related monkey, *Brachyteles arachnoides,* of SE Brazil.

spi·der or·chid *n.* any of several European orchids of the genus *Ophrys,* esp. *O. sphegodes,* having a flower with yellow, green, or pink sepals and a broad brown velvety lip.

spi·der phae·ton *n.* (formerly) a light horse-drawn carriage with a high body and large slender wheels. Sometimes shortened to **spider.**

spi·der·wort ('spaɪdəˌwɜːt) *n.* **1.** any of various plants of the American genus *Tradescantia,* esp. *T. virginiana,* having blue, purplish, or pink flowers and widely grown as house plants: family *Commelinaceae.* See also **tradescantia. 2.** any of various similar or related plants.

spi·der·y ('spaɪdərɪ) *adj.* thin and angular like a spider's legs: *spidery handwriting.*

spie·gel·ei·sen ('spiːgəlˌaɪzən) *n.* a type of pig iron that is rich in manganese and carbon. [C19: German, from *Spiegel* mirror + *Eisen* IRON]

spiel (ʃpiːl) *Slang, chiefly U.S.* ~*n.* **1.** glib plausible talk, associated esp. with salesmen. ~*vb.* **2.** (*intr.*) to deliver a prepared spiel. **3.** (*tr.;* usually foll. by *off*) to recite (a prepared oration). [C19: from German *Spiel* play]

spiel·er ('ʃpiːlə) *n. Slang, chiefly U.S.* **1.** a person who is proficient at talking in a glib manner. **2.** a cheat.

spi·er ('spaɪə) *n. Archaic.* a person who spies or scouts.

spif (spɪf) *n. Informal, chiefly Brit.* a postage stamp perforated with the initials of a firm to avoid theft by employees. Former name: **perfin.** [C20: from *s(tamp) p(erforated with) i(nitials of) f(irm)*]

spif·fing ('spɪfɪŋ) *adj. Brit. slang, old-fashioned.* excellent; splendid. [C19: probably from dialect *spiff* spruce, smartly dressed]

spif·fy ('spɪfɪ) *adj.* **·fi·er, ·fi·est.** *U.S. slang.* smart; stylish. [C19: from dialect *spiff*] —**'spiff·i·ly** *adv.* —**'spiff·i·ness** *n.*

spif·li·cate *or* **spif·fli·cate** ('spɪflɪˌkeɪt) *vb.* (*tr.*) *Brit. school slang.* to destroy; annihilate. [C18: a humorous coinage]

spig·nel ('spɪgnəl) *n.* a European umbelliferous plant, *Meum athamanticum,* of mountain regions, having white flowers and finely divided aromatic leaves. Also called: **baldmoney, meu.**

spig·ot ('spɪgət) *n.* **1.** a stopper for the vent hole of a cask. **2.** a tap, usually of wood, fitted to a cask. **3.** a U.S. name for **tap**[2] (sense 1). **4.** a short cylindrical projection on one component designed to fit into a hole on another, esp. the male part of a joint between two pipes. [C14: probably from Old Provençal *espiga* a head of grain, from Latin *spīca* a point]

spike[1] (spaɪk) *n.* **1.** a sharp point. **2.** any sharp-pointed object, esp. one made of metal. **3.** a long metal nail. **4.** *Physics.* **a.** a transient variation in voltage or current in an electric circuit. **b.** a graphical recording of this, such as one of the peaks on an electroencephalogram. **5.** (*pl.*) shoes with metal projections on the sole and heel for greater traction, as used by athletes. **6.** the straight unbranched antler of a young deer. ~*vb.* (*tr.*) **7.** to secure or supply with or as with spikes. **8.** to render ineffective or block the intentions of; thwart. **9.** to impale on a spike. **10.** to add (alcohol) to a drink. **11.** *Journalism.* to reject (a news story). **12.** *Volleyball.* to hit (a ball) sharply downwards with an overarm motion from the front of one's own court into the opposing court. **13.** (formerly) to render (a cannon) ineffective by blocking its vent with a spike. **14. spike someone's guns.** to thwart (someone's) purpose. [C13 *spyk;* related to Old English *spīcing* nail, Old Norse *spīk* splinter, Middle Low German *spīker* spike, Norwegian *spīk* SPOKE, Latin *spīca* sharp point; see SPIKE[2]]

spike[2] (spaɪk) *n. Botany.* **1.** an inflorescence consisting of a raceme of sessile flowers, as in the gladiolus. **2.** an ear of wheat, barley, etc. [C14: from Latin *spīca* ear of corn]

spike heel *n.* a very high heel on a woman's shoe, tapering to a very narrow tip. Often shortened to: **spike.** Also called (esp. Brit.): **stiletto, stiletto heel.**

spike lav·en·der *n.* a Mediterranean lavender plant, *Lavandula latifolia,* having pale purple flowers and yielding an oil used in paints.

spike·let ('spaɪklɪt) *n. Botany.* a small spike, esp. the inflorescence characteristic of most grasses and sedges.

spike·nard ('spaɪknɑːd, 'spaɪkəˌnɑːd) *n.* **1.** an aromatic Indian valerianaceous plant, *Nardostachys jatamans,* having rose-purple flowers. **2.** an aromatic ointment obtained from this plant. **3.** any of various similar or related plants. **4.** a North American araliaceous plant, *Aralia racemosa,* having small green flowers and an aromatic root. ~Also called (for senses 1, 2): **nard.** [C14: from Medieval Latin *spīca nardī;* see SPIKE[2], NARD]

spike-rush *n.* any perennial plant of the temperate cyperaceous genus *Eleocharis,* occurring esp. by pond, and having underground stems, narrow leaves, and small flowers.

spik·y ('spaɪkɪ) *adj.* **spik·i·er, spik·i·est. 1.** resembling a spike. **2.** having a spike or spikes. **3.** *Brit. informal.* ill-tempered. —**'spik·i·ly** *adv.* —**'spik·i·ness** *n.*

spile (spaɪl) *n.* **1.** a heavy timber stake or pile. **2.** *U.S.* a spout for tapping sap from the sugar maple tree. **3.** a plug or spigot. ~*vb.* (*tr.*) **4.** to provide or support with a spile. **5.** *U.S.* to tap (a tree) with a spile. [C16: probably from Middle Dutch *spile* peg; related to Icelandic *spila* skewer, Latin *spīna* thorn]

spill[1] (spɪl) *vb.* **spills, spill·ing; spilt** *or* **spilled.** (*mainly tr.*) **1.** (when *intr.,* usually foll. by *from, out of,* etc.) to fall or cause to fall from or as from a container, esp. unintentionally. **2.** to disgorge (contents, occupants, etc.) or (of contents, occupants, etc.) to be disgorged: *the car spilt its passengers onto the road; the crowd spilt out of the theatre.* **3.** to shed (blood). **4.** Also: **spill the beans.** *Informal.* to reveal (a secret). **5.** *Nautical.* to let (wind) escape from a sail or (of the wind) to escape from a sail. ~*n.* **6.** *Informal.* a fall or tumble. **7.** short for **spillway. 8.** a spilling of liquid, etc., or the amount spilt. **9.** *Austral.* the declaring of several political jobs vacant when one higher up becomes so: *the Prime Minister's resignation could mean a Cabinet spill.* [Old English *spillan* to destroy; related to *spildan* Old High German *spaltan* to split; see SPOIL] —**'spill·er** *n.*

spill[2] (spɪl) *n.* **1.** a splinter of wood or strip of twisted paper with which pipes, fires, etc., are lit. **2.** a small peg or rod made of metal. [C13: of Germanic origin; compare Old High German *spilla,* Middle Dutch *spile* stake]

spill·age ('spɪlɪdʒ) *n.* **1.** an instance or the process of spilling. **2.** something spilt or the amount spilt.

spil·li·kin, spil·i·kin ('spɪlɪkɪn), *or* **spel·li·can** ('spɛlɪkən) *n.* a thin strip of wood, cardboard, or plastic, esp. one used in spillikins.

spil·li·kins ('spɪlɪkɪnz) *n. Brit.* a game in which players try to pick each spillikin from a heap without moving any of the others. Also called (esp. U.S.): **jackstraws.**

spill o·ver *vb.* **1.** (*intr., adv.*) to overflow or be forced out of an area, container, etc. ~*n.* **spill·o·ver. 2.** *Chiefly U.S.* the act of spilling over. **3.** *Chiefly U.S.* the excess part of something. **4.** *Economics.* any indirect effect of public expenditure.

spill·way ('spɪlˌweɪ) *n.* a channel that carries away surplus water, as from a dam. Also called: **wasteweir, spill.**

spilt (spɪlt) *vb.* a past tense or past participle of **spill**[1].

spin (spɪn) *vb.* **spins, spin·ning, spun. 1.** to rotate or cause to rotate rapidly, as on an axis. **2. a.** to draw out and twist (natural fibres, as of silk or cotton) into a long continuous thread. **b.** to make such a thread or filament from (synthetic resins, etc.), usually by forcing through a nozzle. **3.** (of spiders, silkworms, etc.) to form (webs, cocoons, etc.) from a silky fibre exuded from the body. **4.** (*tr.*) to shape (metal) into a rounded form on a lathe. **5.** (*tr.*) *Informal.* to tell (a tale, story, etc.) by drawing it out at great length (esp. in the phrase **spin a yarn**). **6.** to bowl, pitch, hit, or kick (a ball) so that it rotates in the air and changes direction or speed on bouncing, or (of a ball) to be projected in this way. **7.** (*intr.*) (of wheels) to revolve rapidly without causing propulsion. **8.** to cause (an aircraft) to dive in a spiral descent or (of an aircraft) to dive in a spiral descent. **9.** (*intr.;* foll. by *along*) to drive or travel swiftly. **10.** (*tr.*) Also: **spin-dry.** to rotate (clothes) in a washing machine in order to extract surplus water. **11.** (*intr.*) to reel or grow dizzy, as from turning around: *my head is spinning.* **12.** (*intr.*) to fish by drawing a revolving lure through the water. ~*n.* **13.** a swift rotating motion; instance of spinning. **14.** *Physics.* **a.** the intrinsic angular momentum of an elementary particle or atomic nucleus, as distinguished from any angular momentum resulting from its motion. **b.** a quantum number determining values of this angular momentum in units of the Dirac constant, having integral or half-integral values. Symbol: *S* or *s.* **15.** a condition of loss of control of an aircraft or an intentional flight manoeuvre in which the aircraft performs a continuous spiral descent because the angle of maximum lift is less than the angle of incidence. **16.** a spinning motion imparted to a ball, etc. **17.** *Informal.* a short or fast drive, ride, etc., esp. in a car, for pleasure. **18.** *Informal, chiefly Brit.* a state of agitation or confusion. **19.** *Austral. informal.* chance or luck; fortune: *bad spin.* **20.** *Commerce, informal.* a sudden downward trend in prices, values, etc. ~See also **spin out.** [Old English *spinnan;* related to Old Norse *spinna,* Old High German *spinnan* to spin, Lithuanian *pinu* to braid]

spi·na bi·fi·da ('spaɪnə 'bɪfɪdə) *n.* a congenital condition in which the meninges of the spinal cord protrude through a gap in the backbone, sometimes causing enlargement of the skull (due to accumulation of cerebrospinal fluid) and paralysis. [New Latin; see SPINE, BIFID]

spin·ach ('spɪnɪdʒ, -ɪtʃ) *n.* **1.** a chenopodiaceous annual plant, *Spinacia oleracea,* cultivated for its dark green edible leaves. **2.** the leaves of this plant, eaten boiled as a vegetable. [C16: from Old French *espinache,* from Old Spanish *espinaca,* from Arabic *isfānākh,* from Persian]

spi·nal ('spaɪnəl) *adj.* **1.** of or relating to the spine or the spinal cord. **2.** denoting a laboratory animal in which the spinal cord has been severed: *a spinal rat.* ~*n.* **3.** short for **spinal anaesthesia.** —**'spi·nal·ly** *adv.*

spi·nal an·aes·the·sia *n.* **1.** *Surgery.* anaesthesia of the lower half of the body produced by injecting an anaesthetic beneath the arachnoid membrane surrounding the spinal cord. **2.**

Pathol. loss of sensation in some part of the body as the result of injury of the spinal cord.

spi+nal ca+nal *n.* the natural passage through the centre of the spinal column that contains the spinal cord.

spi+nal col+umn *n.* a series of contiguous or interconnecting bony or cartilaginous segments that surround and protect the spinal cord. Also called: **spine, vertebral column.** Nontechnical name: **backbone.**

spi+nal cord *n.* the thick cord of nerve tissue within the spinal canal, which in man gives rise to 31 pairs of spinal nerves, and together with the brain forms the central nervous system.

spin bowl+er *n. Cricket.* a bowler who specializes in bowling balls with a spinning motion.

spin+dle (ˈspɪndᵊl) *n.* **1.** a rod or stick that has a notch in the top, used to draw out natural fibres for spinning into thread, and a long narrow body around which the thread is wound when spun. **2.** one of the thin rods or pins bearing bobbins upon which spun thread is wound in a spinning machine. **3.** any of various parts in the form of a rod, esp. a rotating rod that acts as an axle, mandrel, or arbor. **4.** a piece of wood that has been turned, such as a baluster or table leg. **5.** a small square metal shaft that passes through the lock of a door and to which the door knobs or handles are fixed. **6.** a measure of length of yarn equal to 18 hanks (15 120 yards) for cotton or 14 400 yards for linen. **7.** *Biology.* a spindle-shaped bundle of nuclear fibres that is formed in a cell during the metaphase stage of mitosis and the corresponding stage of meiosis and along which chromosomes migrate to opposite ends of the cell. **8.** a less common name for a **hydrometer. 9.** a tall pole with a marker at the top, fixed to an underwater obstruction as an aid to navigation. **10.** a device consisting of a sharp upright spike on a pedestal on which bills, order forms, etc., are impaled. ~*vb.* **11.** (*tr.*) to form into a spindle or equip with spindles. **12.** (*intr.*) *Rare.* (of a plant, stem, shoot, etc.) to grow rapidly and become elongated and thin. [Old English *spinel;* related to *spinnan* to SPIN, Old Saxon *spinnila* spindle, Old High German *spinnala*]

spin·dle-leg·ged *or* **spin·dle-shanked** *adj.* having long thin legs.

spin·dle+legs (ˈspɪndᵊlˌlɛgz) *or* **spin·dle+shanks** *pl. n.* **1.** long thin legs. **2.** (*functioning as sing.*) a person who has long thin legs.

spin+dle tree *n.* any of various shrubs or trees of the genus *Euonymus,* esp. *E. europaeus,* of Europe and W Asia, typically having red fruits and yielding a hard wood formerly used in making spindles: family *Celastraceae.*

spin+dling (ˈspɪndlɪŋ) *adj.* **1.** long and slender, esp. disproportionately so. **2.** (of stalks, shoots, etc.) becoming long and slender. ~*n.* **3.** a spindling person or thing.

spin+dly (ˈspɪndlɪ) *adj.* **+dli+er, +dli+est.** tall, slender, and frail; attenuated.

spin+drift (ˈspɪnˌdrɪft) *or* **spoon+drift** *n.* spray blown up from the surface of the sea. [C16: Scottish variant of SPOONDRIFT]

spin-dry *vb.* **-dries, -dry·ing, -dried.** (*tr.*) to dry (clothes, etc.) in a spin-dryer.

spin-dry·er *n.* a device that extracts water from clothes, etc., by spinning them in a perforated drum.

spine (spaɪn) *n.* **1.** the spinal column. **2.** the sharply pointed tip or outgrowth of a leaf, stem, etc. **3.** *Zoology.* a hard pointed process or structure, such as the ray of a fin, the quill of a porcupine, or the ridge on a bone. **4.** Also called: **backbone.** a bound edge or back of a book. **5.** a ridge, esp. of a hill. **6.** strength of endurance, will, etc. **7.** anything resembling the spinal column in function or importance; main support or feature. [C14: from Old French *espine* spine, from Latin *spīna* thorn, backbone] —**spined** *adj.*

spine-bash·ing *n. Austral. informal.* loafing or resting. —**ˈspine-ˌbash·er** *n.*

spine-chill·er *n.* a book, film, etc., that arouses terror. —**ˈspine-ˌchill·ing** *adj.*

spi+nel (spɪˈnɛl) *n.* any of a group of hard glassy minerals of variable colour consisting of oxides of aluminium, magnesium, iron, zinc, or manganese and occurring in the form of octahedral crystals: used as gemstones. Formula: $MgAl_2O_4$. [C16: from French *spinelle,* from Italian *spinella,* diminutive of *spina* a thorn, from Latin; so called from the shape of the crystals]

spine+less (ˈspaɪnlɪs) *adj.* **1.** lacking a backbone; invertebrate. **2.** having no spiny processes: *spineless stems.* **3.** lacking strength of character, resolution, or courage. —**ˈspine+less+ly** *adv.* —**ˈspine+less+ness** *n.*

spi+nes+cent (spaɪˈnɛsᵊnt) *adj. Biology.* **1.** having or resembling a spine or spines. **2.** becoming spiny. [C18: from Late Latin *spīnēscere* to become thorny, from Latin *spīna* a thorn] —**spi+ˈnes+cence** *n.*

spin+et (ˈspɪnɪt) *n.* a small type of harpsichord having one manual. [C17: from Italian *spinetta,* perhaps from Giovanni *Spinetti,* 16th-century Italian maker of musical instruments and its supposed inventor]

spi+nif+er+ous (spaɪˈnɪfərəs) *or* **spi+nig+er+ous** (spaɪˈnɪdʒərəs) *adj.* (esp. of plants) bearing spines or thorns. [C17: from Late Latin *spīnifer* having spines, from Latin *spīna* a thorn, spine + *ferre* to bear]

spin·i+fex (ˈspɪnɪˌfɛks) *n.* **1.** any Australian grass of the genus *Spinifex,* having pointed leaves and spiny seed heads: often planted to bind loose sand. **2.** Also called: **porcupine grass.** *Austral.* any of various coarse spiny-leaved inland grasses of the genus *Triodia.* [C19: from New Latin, from Latin *spīna* a thorn + *-fex* maker, from *facere* to make]

spin+na+ker (ˈspɪnəkə; *Nautical* ˈspæŋkə) *n.* a large light triangular racing sail set from the foremast of a yacht when running or on a broad reach. [C19: probably from SPIN + (MO)NIKER, but traditionally derived from *Sphinx,* the yacht that first adopted this type of sail]

spin+ner (ˈspɪnə) *n.* **1.** a person or thing that spins. **2.** *Cricket.* **a.** a ball that is bowled with a spinning motion. **b.** a bowler who specializes in bowling such balls. **3.** a streamlined fairing that fits over and revolves with the hub of an aircraft propeller. **4.** a fishing lure with a fin or wing that revolves when drawn through the water.

spin+ner+et (ˈspɪnəˌrɛt) *n.* **1.** any of several organs in spiders and certain insects through which silk threads are exuded. **2.** a finely perforated dispenser through which a viscous liquid is extruded in the production of synthetic fibres.

spin+ney (ˈspɪnɪ) *n. Chiefly Brit.* a small wood or copse. [C16: from Old French *espinei,* from *espine* thorn, from Latin *spīna*]

spin+ning (ˈspɪnɪŋ) *n.* **1. a.** the act or process of spinning. **b.** (*as modifier*): *spinning yarn.* **2.** the act or technique of casting and drawing a revolving lure through the water so as to imitate the movement of a live fish, etc.

spin+ning jen+ny *n.* an early type of spinning frame with several spindles, invented by James Hargreaves in 1764.

spin+ning mule *n. Textiles.* See **mule**[1] (sense 3).

spin+ning top *n.* another name for **top**[2] (the toy).

spin+ning wheel *n.* a wheel-like machine for spinning at home, having one hand- or foot-operated spindle.

spi+node (ˈspaɪnəʊd) *n. Maths.* another name for **cusp** (sense 4).

spin-off *n.* any product or development derived incidentally from the application of existing knowledge or enterprise.

spi+nose (ˈspaɪnəʊs, spaɪˈnəʊs) *adj.* (esp. of plants) bearing many spines. [C17: from Latin *spīnōsus* prickly, from *spīna* a thorn] —**ˈspi+nose+ly** *adv.* —**spi+nos+i·ty** (spaɪˈnɒsɪtɪ) *n.*

spi+nous (ˈspaɪnəs) *adj. Biology.* **1.** resembling a spine or thorn: *the spinous process of a bone.* **2.** having spines or spiny projections. **3.** another word for **spinose.**

spin out *vb.* (*tr., adv.*) **1.** to extend or protract (a story, etc.) by including superfluous detail; prolong. **2.** to spend or pass (time). **3.** to contrive to cause (money, etc.) to last as long as possible.

Spi·no·za (spɪˈnəʊzə) *n.* **Ba·ruch** (bəˈruːk). 1632–77, Dutch philosopher who constructed a metaphysical system derived from a series of hypotheses that he judged self-evident. His chief work is *Ethics* (1677).

Spi+no+zism (spɪˈnəʊzɪzəm) *n.* the philosophical system of Spinoza, esp. the concept of God as the unique reality possessing an infinite number of attributes of which we can know at least thought and extension. —**Spi+ˈno+zist** *n.*

spin sta+bi+li+za+tion *n.* a technique by which spin is imparted to a bullet, rocket, etc., to assist it in maintaining a steady flight path.

spin+ster (ˈspɪnstə) *n.* **1.** an unmarried woman regarded as being beyond the age of marriage. **2.** *Law.* (in legal documents) a woman who has never married. Compare **feme sole. 3.** (formerly) a woman who spins thread for her living. [C14 (in the sense: a person, esp. a woman, whose occupation is spinning; C17: a woman still unmarried): from SPIN + -STER] —**ˈspin+ster+ˌhood** *n.* —**ˈspin+ster+ish** *adj.*

spin+tha+ri+scope (spɪnˈθærɪˌskəʊp) *n.* a device for observing ionizing radiation, consisting of a tube with a magnifying lens at one end and a phosphorescent screen at the other. A particle hitting the screen produces a scintillation. [C20: from Greek *spintharis* a little spark + -SCOPE]

spi+nule (ˈspaɪnjuːl) *n. Biology.* a very small spine, thorn, or prickle. [C18: from Late Latin *spīnula*] —**spi+nu+lose** (ˈspaɪnjʊˌləʊs) *adj.*

spin·y (ˈspaɪnɪ) *adj.* **spin·i+er, spin·i+est. 1.** (of animals) having or covered with quills or spines. **2.** (of plants) covered with spines; thorny. **3.** troublesome to handle; puzzling. **4.** shaped like a spine. —**ˈspin·i+ness** *n.*

spin·y ant+eat·er *n.* another name for **echidna.**

spin·y-finned *adj.* (of certain fishes) having fins that are supported by stiff bony spines. See also **acanthopterygian.** Compare **soft-finned.**

spin·y lob+ster *n.* any of various large edible marine decapod crustaceans of the genus *Palinurus* and related genera, having a very tough spiny carapace. Also called: **rock lobster, crawfish, langouste.**

spir·a·cle (ˈspaɪərəkᵊl, ˈspaɪrə-) *n.* **1.** any of several paired apertures in the cuticle of an insect, by which air enters and leaves the trachea. **2.** a small paired rudimentary gill slit just behind the head in skates, rays, and related fishes. **3.** any similar respiratory aperture, such as the blowhole in whales. **4.** *Geology.* a small vent in a lava flow, formed by escaping gases. [C14 (originally: breath): from Latin *spīrāculum* vent, from *spīrāre* to breathe] —**spi+rac·u+lar** (spɪˈrækjʊlə) *adj.* —**spi+ˈrac·u+late** *adj.*

spi+rae·a *or esp. U.S.* **spi+re·a** (spaɪˈrɪə) *n.* any rosaceous plant of the genus *Spiraea,* having sprays of small white or pink flowers. See also **meadowsweet** (sense 2), **hardhack.** [C17: via Latin from Greek *speiraia,* from *speira* SPIRE[2]]

spi+ral (ˈspaɪərəl) *n.* **1.** *Geom.* one of several plane curves formed by a point winding about a fixed point at an ever-increasing distance from it. Polar equation of **Archimedes spiral:** $r = a\theta$; of **logarithmic spiral:** $\log r = a\theta$; of **hyperbolic spiral:** $r\theta = a$, (where *a* is a constant). **2.** another name for **helix** (sense 1). **3.** something that pursues a winding, usually upward, course or that displays a twisting form or shape. **4.** a flight manoeuvre in which an aircraft descends describing a helix of comparatively large radius with the angle of attack within the normal flight range. Compare **spin** (sense 15). **5.** *Economics.* a continuous upward or downward movement in economic activity or prices, caused by interaction between prices, wages, demand and production. ~*adj.* **6.** having the shape of a spiral. ~*vb.* **+rals, +ral+ling, +ralled** *or U.S.* **+rals, +ral+ing, +raled. 7.** to assume or cause to assume a spiral course or shape. **8.** (*intr.*) to increase or decrease with steady acceleration: *wages and prices continue to spiral.* [C16: via French from Medieval Latin *spīrālis,* from Latin *spīra* a coil; see SPIRE[2]] **—'spi+ral+ly** *adv.*

spi+ral gal+ax·y *n.* a galaxy consisting of an ellipsoidal nucleus of old stars from opposite sides of which arms, containing younger stars, spiral outwards around the nucleus. In a **barred spiral** the arms originate at the ends of a bar-shaped nucleus.

spi+ral of Ar·chi·me·des *n. Maths.* a spiral having the equation $r = a\theta$, where a is a constant. It is the locus of a point moving to or from the origin at a constant speed along a line rotating around that origin at a constant speed.

spi+ral stair+case *n.* a staircase constructed around a central axis.

spi+rant ('spaɪrənt) *adj.* **1.** *Phonetics.* another word for **fricative.** ~*n.* **2.** a fricative consonant. [C19: from Latin *spīrāns* breathing, from *spīrāre* to breathe]

spire[1] (spaɪə) *n.* **1.** Also called: **steeple.** a tall structure that tapers upwards to a point, esp. one on a tower or roof or one that forms the upper part of a steeple. **2.** a slender tapering shoot or stem, such as a blade of grass. **3.** the apical part of any tapering formation; summit. ~*vb.* **4.** (*intr.*) to assume the shape of a spire; point up. **5.** (*tr.*) to furnish with a spire or spires. [Old English *spīr* blade; related to Old Norse *spīra* stalk, Middle Low German *spīr* shoot, Latin *spīna* thorn] **—'spir·y** *adj.*

spire[2] (spaɪə) *n.* **1.** any of the coils or turns in a spiral structure. **2.** the apical part of a spiral shell. [C16: from Latin *spīra* a coil, from Greek *speira*] **—spi+rif+er+ous** (spaɪə'rɪfərəs) *adj.*

spire+let ('spaɪəlɪt) *n.* another name for **flèche** (sense 1).

spi+reme ('spaɪriːm) *n. Cytology.* the tangled mass of chromatin threads into which the nucleus of a cell is resolved at the start of mitosis. [C19: from Greek *speirēma* a coil, from *speira* a coil, SPIRE[2]]

Spires (spaɪəz) *n.* the English name for **Speyer.**

spi+ril+lum (spaɪ'rɪləm) *n., pl.* **+la** (-lə). **1.** any bacterium having a curved or spirally twisted rodlike body. Compare **coccus** (sense 1), **bacillus** (sense 1). **2.** any bacterium of the genus *Spirillum,* such as *S. minus,* which causes ratbite fever. [C19: from New Latin, literally: a little coil, from *spīra* a coil] **—spi+'ril+lar** *adj.*

spir+it[1] ('spɪrɪt) *n.* **1.** the force or principle of life that animates the body of living things. **2.** temperament or disposition: *truculent in spirit.* **3.** liveliness; mettle: *they set to it with spirit.* **4.** the fundamental, emotional, and activating principle of a person; will: *the experience broke his spirit.* **5.** a sense of loyalty or dedication: *team spirit.* **6.** the prevailing element; feeling: *a spirit of joy pervaded the atmosphere.* **7.** state of mind or mood; attitude: *he did it in the wrong spirit.* **8.** (*pl.*) an emotional state, esp. with regard to exaltation or dejection: *in high spirits.* **9.** a person characterized by some activity, quality, or disposition: *a leading spirit of the movement.* **10.** the deeper more significant meaning as opposed to a pedantic interpretation: *the spirit of the law.* **11.** that which constitutes a person's intangible being as contrasted with his physical presence: *I shall be with you in spirit.* **12. a.** an incorporeal being, esp. the soul of a dead person. **b.** (*as modifier*): *spirit world.* ~*vb.* (*tr.*) **13.** (usually foll. by *away* or *off*) to carry off mysteriously or secretly. **14.** (often foll. by *up*) to impart animation or determination to. [C13: from Old French *esperit,* from Latin *spīritus* breath, spirit; related to *spīrāre* to breathe]

spir+it[2] ('spɪrɪt) *n.* **1.** (*often pl.*) any distilled alcoholic liquor such as brandy, rum, whisky, or gin. **2.** *Chem.* **a.** an aqueous solution of ethanol, esp. one obtained by distillation. **b.** the active principle or essence of a substance, extracted as a liquid, esp. by distillation. **3.** *Pharmacol.* **a.** a solution of a volatile substance, esp. a volatile oil, in alcohol. **b.** (*as modifier*): *a spirit burner.* **4.** *Alchemy.* any of the four substances sulphur, mercury, sal ammoniac, or arsenic. [C14: special use of SPIRIT[1], name applied to alchemical substances (as in sense 4), hence extended to distilled liquids]

Spir+it ('spɪrɪt) *n.* **the. 1. a.** another name for the **Holy Ghost. b.** God, esp. when regarded as transcending material limitations. **2.** the influence of God or divine things upon the soul. **3.** *Christian Science.* God or divine substance.

spir+it+ed ('spɪrɪtɪd) *adj.* **1.** displaying animation, vigour, or liveliness. **2.** (*in combination*) characterized by mood, temper, or disposition as specified: *high-spirited; public-spirited.* **—'spir+it+ed+ly** *adv.* **—'spir+it+ed+ness** *n.*

spir+it gum *n.* a glue made from gum dissolved in ether used to stick a false beard, etc., onto the face.

spir+it+ism ('spɪrɪˌtɪzəm) *n.* a less common word for **spiritualism. —'spir+it+ist** *n.* **—ˌspir+it+'is+tic** *adj.*

spir+it lamp *n.* a lamp that burns methylated or other spirits instead of oil.

spir+it+less ('spɪrɪtlɪs) *adj.* lacking courage or liveliness; melancholic. **—'spir+it+less+ly** *adv.* **—'spir+it+less+ness** *n.*

spir+it lev+el *n.* a device for setting horizontal surfaces, consisting of an accurate block of material in which a sealed slightly curved tube partially filled with liquid is set so that the air bubble rests between two marks on the tube when the block is horizontal.

spi+ri+to+so (ˌspɪrɪ'təʊsəʊ) *adv. Music.* (often preceded by a tempo marking) in a spirited or animated manner: *allegro spiritoso.* [Italian, from *spirito* spirit, from Latin *spīritus* breath; see SPIRIT[1]]

spir·i+tous ('spɪrɪtəs) *adj.* **1.** a variant spelling of **spirituous. 2.** *Archaic.* high-spirited. **3.** *Archaic.* ethereal; pure.

spir+its of am+mo+nia *n.* another name for **sal volatile** (sense 2).

spir+its of harts+horn *n.* another name for **aqueous ammonia.** See **ammonium hydroxide.**

spir+its of salt *n.* a solution of hydrochloric acid in water.

spir+its of tur+pen+tine *n.* another name for **turpentine** (sense 3).

spir+its of wine *n.* another name for **alcohol** (sense 1).

spir+it·u+al ('spɪrɪtʃʊəl) *adj.* **1.** relating to the spirit or soul and not to physical nature or matter; intangible. **2.** of, relating to, or characteristic of sacred things, the Church, religion, etc. **3.** standing in a relationship based on communication between the souls or minds of the persons involved: *a spiritual father.* **4.** having a mind or emotions of a high and delicately refined quality. ~*n.* **5.** See **negro spiritual. 6.** (*often pl.*) the sphere of religious, spiritual, or ecclesiastical matters, or such matters in themselves. **7. the.** the realm of spirits. **—'spir+it·u+al+ist** *n.* **—'spir+it·u+al+ly** *adv.* **—'spir+it·u+al+ness** *n.*

spir+it·u+al bou+quet *n. R.C. Church.* a collection of private devotional acts and prayers chosen and performed by one person for the benefit of another.

spir+it·u+al in+cest *n. R.C. Church.* **1.** marriage or a sexual relationship between persons related by spiritual affinity or with a person under a solemn vow of chastity. **2.** the holding of two benefices by the same priest or bishop.

spir+it·u+al+ism ('spɪrɪtʃʊəˌlɪzəm) *n.* **1.** the belief that the disembodied spirits of the dead, surviving in another world, can communicate with the living in this world, esp. through mediums. **2.** the doctrines and practices associated with this belief. **3.** *Philosophy.* the belief that because reality is to some extent immaterial it is therefore spiritual. **4.** *Philosophy.* any doctrine that asserts the separate but related existence of God. **5.** any doctrine (in philosophy, religion, etc.) that prefers the spiritual to the material. **6.** the condition or quality of being spiritual.

spir+it·u+al+i+ty (ˌspɪrɪtʃʊ'ælɪtɪ) *n., pl.* **·ties. 1.** the state or quality of being dedicated to God, religion, or spiritual things or values, esp. as contrasted with material or temporal ones. **2.** the condition or quality of being spiritual. **3.** a distinctive approach to religion or prayer: *the spirituality of the desert Fathers.* **4.** (*often pl.*) Church property or revenue or a Church benefice.

spir+it·u+al+ize *or* **spir+it·u+al+ise** ('spɪrɪtʃʊəˌlaɪz) *vb.* (*tr.*) to make spiritual or infuse with spiritual content. **—ˌspir+it·u+al·i+'za+tion** *or* **ˌspir+it·u+al·i+'sa+tion** *n.* **—'spir+it·u+al+ˌiz+er** *or* **'spir+it·u+al+ˌis+er** *n.*

spir+it·u+al+ty ('spɪrɪtʃʊəltɪ) *n., pl.* **+ties.** *Archaic.* **1.** the clergy collectively. **2.** another word for **spirituality.**

spir+it·u+el (ˌspɪrɪtʃʊ'ɛl) *adj.* having a refined and lively mind or wit. Also (fem.): **spirituelle.**

spir+it·u+ous ('spɪrɪtʃʊəs) *adj.* **1.** characterized by or containing alcohol. **2.** (of a drink) being a spirit. **—spir+it·u+os·i·ty** (ˌspɪrɪtʃʊ'ɒsɪtɪ) *or* **'spir+it·u·ous+ness** *n.*

spir·i+tus as+per ('spɪrɪtəs 'æspə) *n.* another term for **rough breathing.** [Latin: rough breath]

spir·i+tus le+nis *n.* another term for **smooth breathing.** [Latin: gentle breath]

spir+it var+nish *n.* a varnish consisting of a gum or resin, such as shellac or copal, dissolved in alcohol.

spir+ket+ting ('spɜːkɪtɪŋ) *n. Nautical.* **1.** deck planking near the bulwarks. **2.** the interior lining between ports and the overhead interior surface of the cabin. [C18: from obsolete *spirket* space between floor timbers in a ship]

spi·ro-[1] *combining form.* indicating breath or respiration: *spirograph.* [from Latin *spīrāre* to breathe]

spi·ro-[2] *combining form.* spiral; coil: *spirochaete.* [from Latin *spīra,* from Greek *speira* a coil]

spi+ro+chaete *or U.S.* **spi+ro+chete** ('spaɪrəʊˌkiːt) *n.* any of a group of spirally coiled rodlike bacteria that includes the causative agent of syphilis. See **treponema.** [C19: from New Latin *spīrochaeta;* see SPIRO-[2], CHAETA]

spi+ro+chae+to+sis *or U.S.* **spi+ro+che+to+sis** (ˌspaɪrəʊkɪ'təʊsɪs) *n.* any disease caused by a spirochaete.

spi+ro+graph ('spaɪrəˌgræf, -ˌgrɑːf) *n. Med.* an instrument for recording the movements of breathing. **—ˌspi+ro+'graph+ic** *adj.*

spi+ro+gy+ra (ˌspaɪrə'dʒaɪərə) *n.* any green freshwater multicellular alga of the genus *Spirogyra,* consisting of minute filaments containing spirally coiled chloroplasts. [C20: from New Latin, from SPIRO-[2] + Greek *guros* a circle]

spi+roid ('spaɪrɔɪd) *adj.* resembling a spiral or displaying a spiral form. [C19: from New Latin *spīroīdēs,* from Greek *speiroeidēs,* from *speira* a coil]

spi+rom+e+ter (spaɪ'rɒmɪtə) *n.* an instrument for measuring the air capacity of the lungs. Compare **pneumatometer. —spi+ro+met+ric** (ˌspaɪrə'mɛtrɪk) *adj.* **—spi+'rom+e+try** *n.*

spi+ro+no+lac+tone (ˌspaɪrənəʊ'læktəʊn) *n.* a diuretic that increases water loss from the kidneys and is much used to treat oedema in heart and kidney failure.

spirt (spɜːt) *n.* a variant spelling of **spurt.**

spir+u+la ('spaɪrʊlə) *n.* a tropical cephalopod mollusc, *Spirula peronii,* having prominent eyes, short arms, and a small flattened spirally coiled internal shell: order *Decapoda* (cuttlefish and squids). [C19: via New Latin from Late Latin: a small twisted cake, from Latin *spīra* a coil]

spir·y ('spaɪərɪ) *adj. Poetic.* of spiral form; helical.

spit[1] (spɪt) *vb.* **spits, spit·ting, spat** *or* **spit. 1.** (*intr.*) to expel saliva from the mouth; expectorate. **2.** (*intr.*) *Informal.* to show disdain or hatred by spitting. **3.** (of a fire, hot fat, etc.) to eject (fragments of coal, sparks, etc.) violently and with an explosive sound; splutter. **4.** (*intr.*) to rain very lightly. **5.** (*tr.*; often foll. by *out*) to eject or discharge (something) from the mouth: *he spat the food out; to spit blood.* **6.** (*tr.*; often foll. by *out*) to utter (short sharp words or syllables), esp. in a violent manner. **7. spit chips.** *Austral. slang.* to be very angry. **8. spit it out!** *Brit. slang.* a command given to someone that he should speak forthwith. ~*n.* **9.** another name for **spittle. 10.** a light or brief fall of rain, snow, etc. **11.** the act or an instance of spitting. **12.** *Informal, chiefly Brit.* another word for **spitting image.** [Old English *spittan;* related to *spǣtan* to spit, German dialect *spitzen*] —'**spit·ter** *n.*

spit[2] (spɪt) *n.* **1.** a pointed rod on which meat is skewered and roasted before or over an open fire. **2.** Also called: **rotisserie, rotating spit.** a similar device rotated by electricity or clockwork, fitted onto a cooker. **3.** an elongated often hooked strip of sand or shingle projecting from the shore, deposited by longshore drift, and usually above water. ~*vb.* **spits, spit·ting, spit·ted. 4.** (*tr.*) to impale on or transfix with or as if with a spit. [Old English *spitu;* related to Old High German *spiz* spit, Norwegian *spit* tip]

spit·al ('spɪtᵊl) *n. Obsolete.* **1.** a hospital, esp. for the needy sick. **2.** a highway shelter. [C13 *spitel,* changed from Medieval Latin *hospitāle* HOSPITAL]

spit and pol·ish *n. Informal.* punctilious attention to neatness, discipline, etc. esp. in the armed forces.

spitch·cock ('spɪtʃˌkɒk) *n.* an eel split and grilled or fried. Compare **spatchcock.** [C16: of unknown origin; see SPATCHCOCK]

spit curl *n.* the U.S. name for **kiss curl.**

spite (spaɪt) *n.* **1.** maliciousness involving the desire to harm another; venomous ill will. **2.** an instance of such malice; grudge. **3.** *Archaic.* something that induces vexation. **4. in spite of.** (*prep.*) in defiance of; regardless of; notwithstanding. ~*vb.* (*tr.*) **5.** to annoy in order to vent spite. **6.** *Archaic.* to offend. [C13: variant of DESPITE]

spite·ful ('spaɪtfʊl) *adj.* full of or motivated by spite; vindictive. —'**spite·ful·ly** *adv.* —'**spite·ful·ness** *n.*

spit·fire ('spɪtˌfaɪə) *n.* a person given to outbursts of spiteful temper and anger, esp. a woman or girl.

Spit·head (ˈspɪtˈhɛd) *n.* an extensive anchorage between the mainland of England and the Isle of Wight, off Portsmouth.

Spits·ber·gen ('spɪtsˌbɜːgən) *n.* another name for **Svalbard.**

spit·stick·er ('spɪtˌstɪkə) *n.* a wood-engraving tool with a fine prow-shaped point for cutting curved lines.

spit·ting dis·tance *n.* a short space or distance.

spit·ting im·age *n. Informal.* a person who bears a strong physical resemblance to another, esp. to a relative. Also called: **spit, spit and image.** [C19: modification of *spit and image,* from SPIT[1] (as in the phrase *the very spit of,* the exact likeness of (someone))]

spit·ting snake *n.* another name for the **ringhals.**

spit·tle ('spɪtᵊl) *n.* **1.** the fluid secreted in the mouth; saliva or spit. **2.** Also called: **cuckoo spit, frog spit.** the frothy substance secreted on plants by the larvae of certain froghoppers. [Old English *spǣtl* saliva; see SPIT[1]]

spit·tle in·sect *or* **spit·tle·bug** ('spɪtᵊlˌbʌg) *n.* other names for the **froghopper.**

spit·toon (spɪ'tuːn) *n.* a receptacle for spit, usually in a public place.

spitz (spɪts) *n.* any of various breeds of dog characterized by very dense hair, a stocky build, a pointed muzzle, and erect ears. [C19: from German, from *spitz* pointed]

Spitz (spɪts) *n.* **Mark.** born 1950, U.S. swimmer, who won seven gold medals at the 1972 Olympic Games.

spiv (spɪv) *n. Brit. slang.* a man or boy who makes a living by underhand dealings or swindling; black-marketeer. [C20: back formation from dialect *spiving* smart; compare SPIFFY, SPIFFING] —'**spiv·vy** *adj.*

splake (spleɪk) *n.* a type of hybrid trout bred by Canadian zoologists. [from *sp(eckled)* + *lake (trout)*]

splanch·nic ('splæŋknɪk) *adj.* of or relating to the viscera; visceral: *a splanchnic nerve.* [C17: from New Latin *splanchnicus,* from Greek *splankhnikos* concerning the entrails, from *splankhna* the entrails]

splash (splæʃ) *vb.* **1.** to scatter (liquid) about in blobs; spatter. **2.** to descend or cause to descend upon in scattered blobs: *he splashed his jacket; rain splashed against the window.* **3.** to make (one's way) by or as if by splashing: *he splashed through the puddle.* **4.** (*tr.*) to print (a story or photograph) prominently in a newspaper. ~*n.* **5.** an instance or sound of splashing. **6.** an amount splashed. **7.** a mark or patch created by or as if by splashing: *a splash of colour.* **8.** *Informal.* an extravagant display, usually for effect (esp. in the phrase **make a splash**). **9.** a small amount of soda water, water, etc., added to an alcoholic drink. [C18: alteration of PLASH[1]]

splash·back ('splæʃˌbæk) *n.* a sheet of glass, plastic, etc., attached to a wall above a basin to protect the wall against splashing.

splash·board ('splæʃˌbɔːd) *n.* **1.** a guard on a vehicle to protect people from splashing water, mud, etc. **2.** *Nautical.* another word for **washboard** (sense 4).

splash·down ('splæʃˌdaʊn) *n.* **1.** the controlled landing of a spacecraft on water at the end of a space flight. **2.** the time scheduled for this event. ~*vb.* **splash down. 3.** (*intr., adv.*) (of a spacecraft) to make a splashdown.

splash·er ('splæʃə) *n.* anything used for protection against splashes.

splash out *vb.* (*adv.*; often foll. by *on*) *Informal, chiefly Brit.* to spend (money) freely or extravagantly (on something).

splash·y ('splæʃɪ) *adj.* **splash·i·er, splash·i·est. 1.** having irregular marks. **2.** *Informal.* done to attract attention or make a sensation; showy. **3.** making a splash or splashes. —'**splash·i·ly** *adv.* —'**splash·i·ness** *n.*

splat[1] (splæt) *n.* a wet slapping sound. [C19: of imitative origin]

splat[2] (splæt) *n.* a wide flat piece of wood, esp. one that is the upright central part of a chairback. [C19: perhaps related to Old English *splātan* to SPLIT]

splat·ter ('splætə) *vb.* **1.** to splash with small blobs; spatter. ~*n.* **2.** a splash of liquid, mud, etc.

splay (spleɪ) *adj.* **1.** spread out; broad and flat. **2.** turned outwards in an awkward manner. ~*vb.* **3.** to spread out; turn out or expand. **4.** (*tr.*) *Vet. science.* to dislocate (a bone). ~*n.* **5.** a surface of a wall that forms an oblique angle to the main flat surfaces, esp. at a doorway or window opening. **6.** enlargement. [C14: short for DISPLAY]

splay·foot ('spleɪˌfʊt) *n., pl.* **·feet.** *Pathol.* another word for **flatfoot.** —'**splay·ˌfoot·ed** *adj.* —'**splay·ˌfoot·ed·ly** *adv.*

spleen (spliːn) *n.* **1.** a spongy highly vascular organ near the stomach in mammals. It forms lymphocytes, produces antibodies, aids in destroying worn-out red blood cells, and filters bacteria and foreign particles from the blood. **2.** the corresponding organ in other animals. **3.** spitefulness or ill humour; peevishness: *to vent one's spleen.* **4.** *Archaic.* the organ in the human body considered to be the seat of the emotions. **5.** *Archaic.* another word for **melancholy. 6.** *Obsolete.* whim; mood. [C13: from Old French *esplen,* from Latin *splēn,* from Greek] —'**spleen·ish** *or* '**spleen·y** *adj.*

spleen·ful ('spliːnfʊl) *adj.* affected by spleen; bad-tempered or irritable. —'**spleen·ful·ly** *adv.*

spleen·wort ('spliːnˌwɜːt) *n.* any of various ferns of the genus *Asplenium,* that often grow on walls, having linear or oblong sori on the undersurface of the fronds.

splen·dent ('splɛndənt) *adj. Archaic.* **1.** shining brightly; lustrous: *a splendent sun.* **2.** famous; illustrious. [C15: from Latin *splendēns* brilliant, from *splendēre* to shine]

splen·did ('splɛndɪd) *adj.* **1.** brilliant or fine, esp. in appearance. **2.** characterized by magnificence; imposing. **3.** glorious or illustrious: *a splendid reputation.* **4.** brightly gleaming; radiant: *her splendid face; splendid colours.* **5.** very good or satisfactory: *a splendid time.* [C17: from Latin *splendidus,* from *splendēre* to shine] —'**splen·did·ly** *adv.* —'**splen·did·ness** *n.*

splen·dif·er·ous (splɛn'dɪfərəs) *adj. Facetious.* grand; splendid: *a really splendiferous meal.* [C15: from Medieval Latin *splendiferus,* from Latin *splendor* radiance + *ferre* to bring] —**splen·'dif·er·ous·ly** *adv.* —**splen·'dif·er·ous·ness** *n.*

splen·dour *or U.S.* **splen·dor** ('splɛndə) *n.* **1.** the state or quality of being splendid. **2. sun in splendour.** *Heraldry.* a representation of the sun with rays and a human face. —'**splen·dor·ous** *or* **splen·drous** ('splɛndrəs) *adj.*

sple·nec·to·my (splɪ'nɛktəmɪ) *n., pl.* **·mies.** surgical removal of the spleen.

sple·net·ic (splɪ'nɛtɪk) *adj. also* **sple·net·i·cal. 1.** of or relating to the spleen. **2.** spiteful or irritable; peevish. **3.** *Obsolete.* full of melancholy. ~*n.* **4.** a spiteful or irritable person. —**sple·'net·i·cal·ly** *adv.*

splen·ic ('splɛnɪk, 'spliː-) *adj.* **1.** of, relating to, or in the spleen. **2.** having a disease or disorder of the spleen.

sple·ni·tis (splɪ'naɪtɪs) *n.* inflammation of the spleen.

sple·ni·us ('spliːnɪəs) *n., pl.* **·ni·i** (-nɪˌaɪ). *Anatomy.* either of two flat muscles situated at the back of the neck that rotate, flex, and extend the head and neck. [C18: via New Latin from Greek *splēnion* a plaster] —'**sple·ni·al** *adj.*

sple·no·meg·a·ly (ˌspliːnəʊ'mɛgəlɪ) *n. Pathol.* abnormal enlargement of the spleen.

splice (splaɪs) *vb.* (*tr.*) **1.** to join (two ropes) by intertwining the strands. **2.** to join up the trimmed ends of (two pieces of wire, film, magnetic tape, etc.) with solder or an adhesive material. **3.** to join (timbers) by overlapping and binding or bolting the ends together. **4.** (*usually passive*) *Informal.* to enter into marriage: *the couple got spliced last Saturday.* **5. splice the mainbrace.** *Nautical.* to issue and partake of alcoholic spirits. ~*n.* **6.** a join made by splicing. **7.** the place where such a join occurs. **8.** the wedge-shaped end of a cricket bat handle or similar instrument that fits into the blade. [C16: probably from Middle Dutch *splissen;* related to German *spleissen,* Swedish *splitsa;* see SPLIT] —'**splic·er** *n.*

spline (splaɪn) *n.* **1.** any one of a series of narrow keys (**external splines**) formed longitudinally around the circumference of a shaft that fit into corresponding grooves (**internal splines**) in a mating part: used to prevent movement between two parts, esp. in transmitting torque. **2.** a long narrow strip of wood, metal, etc.; slat. **3.** a thin narrow strip made of wood, metal, or plastic fitted into a groove in the edge of a board, tile, etc., to connect it to another. ~*vb.* **4.** (*tr.*) to provide (a shaft, part, etc.) with splines. [C18: East Anglian dialect; perhaps related to Old English *splin* spindle; see SPLINT]

splint (splɪnt) *n.* **1.** a rigid support for restricting movement of an injured part, esp. a broken bone. **2.** a thin sliver of wood, esp. one that is used to light cigars, a fire, etc. **3.** a thin strip of wood woven with others to form a chair seat, basket, etc. **4.** *Vet. science.* a bony enlargement of the cannon bone of a horse. **5.** one of the overlapping metal plates used in armour after about 1330. **6.** another word for **splinter.** ~*vb.* **7.** to apply a splint to (a broken arm, etc.). [C13: from Middle Low German *splinte;* related to Middle Dutch *splinte* splint, Old High German *spaltan* to split] —**'splint₊ˌlike** *adj.*

splint bone *n.* one of the rudimentary metacarpal or metatarsal bones in horses and similar animals, occurring on each side of the cannon bone.

splin₊ter ('splɪntə) *n.* **1.** a very small sharp piece of wood, glass, metal, etc., characteristically long and thin, broken off from a whole. **2.** a metal fragment, from the container of a shell, bomb, etc., thrown out during an explosion; piece of shrapnel. ~*vb.* **3.** to reduce or be reduced to sharp fragments; shatter. **4.** to break or be broken off in small sharp fragments. [C14: from Middle Dutch *splinter;* see SPLINT] —**'splin₊ter·y** *adj.*

splin₊ter group *n.* a number of members of an organization, political party, etc., who split from the main body and form an independent association of their own, usually as the result of dissension.

split (splɪt) *vb.* **splits, split₊ting, split. 1.** to break or cause to break, esp. forcibly, by cleaving into separate pieces, often into two roughly equal pieces: *to split a brick.* **2.** to separate or be separated from a whole: *he split a piece of wood from the block.* **3.** to separate or be separated into factions, usually through discord. **4.** (often foll. by *up*) to separate or cause to separate through a disagreement. **5.** (when *tr.*, often foll. by *up*) to divide or be divided among two or more persons: *split up the pie among the three of us.* **6.** *Slang.* to depart; leave: *let's split; we split the scene.* **7.** (*tr.*) to separate (something) into its components by interposing something else: *to split a word with hyphens.* **8.** (*intr.;* usually foll. by *on*) *Slang.* to betray the trust, plans, etc. (of); inform: *he split on me to the cops.* **9.** (*tr.*) *U.S. politics.* to mark (a ballot, etc.) so as to vote for the candidates of more than one party: *he split the ticket.* **10.** (*tr.*) to separate (an animal hide or skin) into layers. **11. split hairs.** to make a fine but needless distinction. **12. split one's sides.** to laugh very heartily. **13. split the difference.** to settle a dispute by effecting a compromise in which both sides give way to the same extent. ~*n.* **14.** the act or process of splitting. **15.** a gap or rift caused or a piece removed by the process of splitting. **16.** a breach or schism in a group or the faction resulting from such a breach. **17.** a dessert of sliced fruit and ice cream, covered with whipped cream, nuts, etc.: *banana split.* **18.** See **Devonshire split. 19. a.** a separated layer of an animal hide or skin other than the outer layer. **b.** leather made from such a layer. **20.** *Tenpin bowling.* a formation of the pins after the first bowl in which there is a large gap between two pins or groups of pins. **21.** *Informal.* an arrangement or process of dividing up loot or money. See also **split up.** [C16: from Middle Dutch *splitten* to cleave; related to Middle High German *splīzen;* see SPLICE] —**'split₊ter** *n.*

Split (*Serbo-Croatian* split) *n.* a port and resort in W Yugoslavia, in Croatia on the Adriatic: became part of Yugoslavia in 1918 after Austrian rule since 1797: shipbuilding; remains of the palace of Diocletian (295–305). Pop.: 152 905 (1971). Italian name: **Spalato.**

split de₊ci₊sion *n. Boxing.* the award of a fight on a majority verdict of the judges as opposed to a unanimous decision.

split in₊fin·i·tive *n.* (in English grammar) an infinitive used with another word between *to* (the infinitive marker) and the verb itself, as in *I want to really finish it this time.*

Usage. The traditional rule against placing an adverb between *to* and its verb is gradually disappearing. Although it is true that a split infinitive may result in a clumsy sentence (*he decided to firmly and definitively deal with the problem*), this is not enough to justify the absolute condemnation that this practice has attracted. Indeed, very often the most natural position of the adverb is between *to* and the verb (*he decided to really try next time*) and to change it would result in an artificial and awkward construction (*he really decided to try next time*). The current view is therefore that the split infinitive is not a grammatical error. Nevertheless, many writers prefer to avoid splitting infinitives in formal written English, since readers with a more traditional point of view are likely to interpret this type of construction as incorrect.

split-lev·el *adj.* (of a house, room, etc.) having the floor level of one part about half a storey above or below the floor level of an adjoining part.

split pea *n.* a pea dried and split and used in soups, pease pudding, or as a vegetable.

split per₊son₊al·i·ty *n.* **1.** the tendency to change rapidly in mood or temperament. **2.** a nontechnical term for **multiple personality** or **schizophrenia.**

splits (splɪts) *n.* (in gymnastics, etc.) the act of sinking to the floor to achieve a sitting position in which both legs are straight, pointing in opposite directions, and at right angles to the body.

split-screen tech₊nique *n.* a cinematic device by which two or more complete images are projected simultaneously onto separate parts of the screen. Also called: **split screen.**

split sec₊ond *n.* **1.** an infinitely small period of time; instant. ~*adj.* **split-sec·ond.** (*prenominal*) **2.** made or arrived at in an infinitely short time: *a split-second decision.* **3.** depending upon minute precision: *split-second timing.*

split shift *n.* a work period divided into two parts that are separated by an interval longer than a normal rest period.

split tick₊et *n.* See **split** (sense 9). See also **straight ticket.**

split tin *n. Brit.* a long loaf of bread split on top, giving a greater crust area.

split₊ting ('splɪtɪŋ) *adj.* **1.** (of a headache) intolerably painful; acute. **2.** (of the head) assailed by an overpowering unbearable pain. ~*n.* **3.** *Psychoanal.* the Freudian defence mechanism in which an object or idea (or, alternatively, the ego) is separated into two or more parts in order to remove its threatening meaning.

split up *vb.* (*adv.*) **1.** (*tr.*) to separate out into parts; divide. **2.** (*intr.*) to become separated or parted through disagreement: *they split up after years of marriage.* **3.** to break down or be capable of being broken down into constituent parts: *I have split up the question into three parts.* ~*n.* **split-up. 4.** an act or the instance of separating.

splodge (splɒdʒ) *n.* **1.** a large irregular spot or blot. ~*vb.* **2.** (*tr.*) to mark (something) with such a blot or blots. [C19: alteration of earlier SPLOTCH] —**'splodg·y** *adj.*

splore (splɔː) *n. Scot.* a revel; binge. [C18: of obscure origin]

splotch (splɒtʃ) *n., vb.* the usual U.S. word for **splodge.** [C17: perhaps a blend of SPOT + BLOTCH] —**'splotch·y** *adj.*

splurge (splɜːdʒ) *n.* **1.** an ostentatious display, esp. of wealth. **2.** a bout of unrestrained extravagance. ~*vb.* **3.** (often foll. by *on*) to spend (money) unrestrainedly or extravagantly. [C19: of uncertain origin]

splut₊ter ('splʌtə) *vb.* **1.** to spit out (saliva, food particles, etc.) from the mouth in an explosive manner, as through choking or laughing. **2.** to utter (words) with spitting sounds, as through rage or choking. **3.** to eject or be ejected in an explosive manner: *sparks spluttered from the fire.* **4.** (*tr.*) to bespatter (a person) with tiny particles explosively ejected: *he spluttered the boy next to him with ink.* ~*n.* **5.** the process or noise of spluttering. **6.** spluttering incoherent speech, esp. in argument. **7.** anything ejected through spluttering. [C17: variant of SPUTTER, influenced by SPLASH] —**'splut₊ter₊er** *n.*

Spock (spɒk) *n.* **Ben·ja·min.** born 1903, U.S. paediatrician, whose *The Common Sense Book of Baby and Child Care* (1946) has influenced the upbringing of children throughout the world.

spode (spəʊd) *n.* (*sometimes cap.*) china or porcelain manufactured by Josiah Spode, English potter (1754–1827), or his company.

spod·u₊mene ('spɒdjʊˌmiːn) *n.* a greyish-white, green, or lilac pyroxene mineral consisting of lithium aluminium silicate in monoclinic crystalline form. It is an important ore of lithium and is used in the manufacture of glass and ceramics and as a gemstone. Formula: $LiAlSi_2O_6$. [C19: from French *spodumène,* from German *Spodumen,* from Greek *spodoumenos,* from *spodousthai* to be burnt to ashes, from *spodos* wood ash]

spoil (spɔɪl) *vb.* **spoils, spoil₊ing, spoilt** *or* **spoiled. 1.** (*tr.*) to cause damage to (something), in regard to its value, beauty, usefulness, etc. **2.** (*tr.*) to weaken the character of (a child) by complying unrestrainedly with its desires. **3.** (*intr.*) (of perishable substances) to become unfit for consumption or use: *the fruit must be eaten before it spoils.* **4.** (*intr.*) *Sport.* to disrupt the play or style of an opponent, as to prevent him from settling into a rhythm. **5.** *Archaic.* to strip (a person or place) of (property or goods) by force or violence. **6. be spoiling for.** to have an aggressive desire for (a fight, etc). ~*n.* **7.** waste material thrown up by an excavation. **8.** any treasure accumulated by a person: *this gold ring was part of the spoil.* **9.** *Obsolete.* **a.** the act of plundering. **b.** a strategically placed building, city, etc., captured as plunder. [C13: from Old French *espoillier,* from Latin *spoliāre* to strip, from *spolium* booty]

spoil₊age ('spɔɪlɪdʒ) *n.* **1.** the act or an instance of spoiling or the state or condition of being spoilt. **2.** an amount of material that has been wasted by being spoilt: *the spoilage of corn was considerable.*

spoil₊er ('spɔɪlə) *n.* **1.** plunderer or robber. **2.** a person or thing that causes spoilage or corruption. **3.** a device fitted to an aircraft wing to increase drag and reduce lift. It is usually extended into the airflow to assist descent and banking. Compare **air brake** (sense 2). **4.** a similar device fitted to a car. **5.** *Sport.* a competitor who adopts spoiling tactics, as in boxing.

spoil₊five ('spɔɪlˌfaɪv) *n.* a card game for two or more players with five cards each.

spoils (spɔɪlz) *pl. n.* **1.** (*sometimes sing.*) valuables seized by violence, esp. in war. **2.** *Chiefly U.S.* the rewards and benefits of public office regarded as plunder for the winning party or candidate. See also **spoils system.**

spoils₊man ('spɔɪlzmən) *n., pl.* **₊men.** *U.S. politics.* a person who shares in the spoils of office or advocates the spoils system.

spoil₊sport ('spɔɪlˌspɔːt) *n. Informal.* a person who spoils the pleasure of other people by his actions or attitudes.

spoils sys₊tem *n. Chiefly U.S.* the practice of filling appointive public offices with friends and supporters of the ruling political party. Compare **merit system.**

spoilt (spɔɪlt) *vb.* a past tense or past participle of **spoil.**

Spo₊kane (spəʊ'kæn) *n.* a city in E Washington: commercial centre of an agricultural region. Pop.: 173 971 (1973 est.).

spoke[1] (spəʊk) *vb.* **1.** the past tense of **speak. 2.** *Archaic or dialect.* a past participle of **speak.**

spoke[2] (spəʊk) *n.* **1.** a radial member of a wheel, joining the hub to the rim. **2.** a radial projection from the rim of a wheel, as in a ship's wheel. **3.** a rung of a ladder. **4. put a spoke in someone's wheel.** *Brit.* to interfere with the plans of a person. ~*vb.* **5.** (*tr.*) to equip with or as if with spokes.

spo₊ken ('spəʊkən) *vb.* **1.** the past participle of **speak.** ~*adj.* **2.** uttered through the medium of speech. Compare written. **3.** (*in combination*) having speech as specified: *soft-spoken.* **4. spoken for.** engaged, reserved, or allocated.

spoke+shave ('spəʊkˌʃeɪv) *n.* a small plane with two handles, one on each side of its blade, used for shaping or smoothing cylindrical wooden surfaces, such as spokes.

spokes+man ('spəʊksmən) *n., pl.* **+men.** a person authorized to speak on behalf of another person, group of people, or organization. —**'spokes+ˌwom·an** *fem. n.*

spo+li+ate ('spəʊlɪˌeɪt) *vb.* a less common word for **despoil.**

spo+li·a+tion (ˌspəʊlɪ'eɪʃən) *n.* **1.** the act or an instance of despoiling or plundering. **2.** the authorized seizure or plundering of neutral vessels on the seas by a belligerent state in time of war. **3.** *Law.* the material alteration of a document so as to render it invalid. **4.** *English ecclesiastical law.* the taking of the fruits of a benefice by a person not entitled to them. [C14: from Latin *spoliātiō*, from *spoliāre* to SPOIL] —**'spo+li·a+to·ry** *adj.*

spon+da+ic (spɒn'deɪɪk) *or* **spon+da·i·cal** *adj. Prosody.* of, relating to, or consisting of spondees.

spon+dee ('spɒndi:) *n. Prosody.* a metrical foot consisting of two long syllables (¯ ¯). [C14: from Old French *spondée*, from Latin *spondēus*, from Greek *spondeios*, from *spondē* a ritual libation; from the use of spondee in the music that characteristically accompanied such ceremonies]

spon+du+lix *or* **spon+du+licks** (spɒn'dju:lɪks) *n. Slang.* money. [C19: of obscure origin]

spon+dy+li+tis (ˌspɒndɪ'laɪtɪs) *n.* inflammation of the vertebrae. [C19: from New Latin, from Greek *spondulos* vertebra; see -ITIS]

sponge (spʌndʒ) *n.* **1.** any multicellular typically marine animal of the phylum *Porifera*, usually occurring in complex sessile colonies in which the porous body is supported by a fibrous, calcareous, or siliceous skeletal framework. **2.** a piece of the light porous highly absorbent elastic skeleton of certain sponges, used in bathing, cleaning, etc. See also **spongin. 3.** any of a number of light porous elastic materials resembling a sponge. **4.** another word for **sponger. 5.** *Informal.* a person who indulges in heavy drinking. **6.** leavened dough, esp. before kneading. **7.** See **sponge cake. 8.** Also called: **sponge pudding.** *Brit.* a light steamed or baked pudding, spongy in texture, made with various flavourings or fruit. **9.** porous metal produced by electrolysis or by reducing a metal compound without fusion or sintering and capable of absorbing large quantities of gas: *platinum sponge.* **10.** a rub with a sponge. **11. throw in** (*or* **up**) **the sponge** (*or* **towel**). **a.** (in boxing) to concede defeat by the throwing of a sponge or towel into the ring by a second. **b.** to give up after considerable effort. ~*vb.* **12.** (*tr.*; often foll. by *off* or *down*) to clean (something) by wiping or rubbing with a damp or wet sponge. **13.** (*tr.*; usually foll. by *off, away, out,* etc.) to remove (marks, etc.) by rubbing with a damp or wet sponge or cloth. **14.** (when *tr.*, often foll. by *up*) to absorb (liquids, esp. when spilt) in the manner of a sponge. **15.** (*intr.*) to go collecting sponges. [Old English, from Latin *spongia*, from Greek] —**'sponge+ˌlike** *adj.*

sponge bag *n.* a small bag made of plastic or sponge rubber that holds toilet articles, used esp. when travelling.

sponge bath *n.* a washing of the body with a wet sponge or cloth, but without immersion in water.

sponge cake *n.* a light porous cake, made of eggs, sugar, flour, and flavourings without any shortening.

sponge cloth *n.* any of various porous fabrics, usually made in a loose honeycomb weave.

sponge down *vb.* (*tr., adv.*) **1.** to wipe clean with a damp sponge or cloth. ~*n.* **sponge-down. 2.** the act or instance of sponging down.

sponge off *vb.* (*prep.*) **1.** to get (something) from (someone) by presuming on his generosity: *to sponge a meal off someone.* **2.** (*intr.*) Also: **sponge on.** to obtain one's subsistence, welfare, etc., unjustifiably from: *he sponges off his friends.*

spong+er ('spʌndʒə) *n.* **1.** *Informal.* a person who lives off other people by continually taking advantage of their generosity; parasite or scrounger. **2.** a person or ship employed in collecting sponges.

spon+gin ('spʌndʒɪn) *n.* a fibrous horny protein that forms the skeletal framework of the bath sponge and related sponges. [C19: from German, from Latin *spongia* SPONGE + -IN]

spon+gi·o+blast ('spʌndʒɪəʊˌblɑ:st) *n.* any of numerous columnar epithelial cells in the brain and spinal cord that develop into neuroglia. [C20: from Greek *spongia* SPONGE + -BLAST] —**spon+gi·o+blas+tic** (ˌspʌndʒɪəʊ'blæstɪk) *adj.*

spon+gy ('spʌndʒɪ) *adj.* **+gi·er, +gi·est. 1.** of or resembling a sponge, esp. in texture, porosity, elasticity, or compressibility: *spongy bread; spongy bone.* **2.** of or like a sponge in respect of its capacity to absorb fluid and yield it when compressed. —**'spon+gi+ly** *adv.* —**'spon+gi+ness** *n.*

spon+sion ('spɒnʃən) *n.* **1.** the act or process of becoming surety; sponsorship. **2.** (*often pl.*) *International law.* an unauthorized agreement made by a public officer, esp. an admiral or general in time of war, requiring ratification by the government of the state concerned. **3.** any act or promise, esp. one made on behalf of someone else. [C17: from Latin *sponsiō, from spondēre* to pledge]

spon+son ('spɒnsən) *n.* **1.** an outboard support for a gun, etc. **2.** a float or flotation chamber along the gunwale of a canoe. **3.** a structural projection from the side of a paddle steamer for supporting a paddle wheel. [C19: perhaps from EXPANSION]

spon+sor ('spɒnsə) *n.* **1.** a person or group that promotes either another person or group in an activity or the activity itself, either for profit or charity. **2.** *Chiefly U.S.* a person or business firm that pays the costs of a radio or television programme in return for advertising time. **3.** a legislator who presents and supports a bill, motion, etc. **4.** Also called: **godparent. a.** an authorized witness who makes the required promises on behalf of a person to be baptized and thereafter assumes responsibility for his Christian upbringing. **b.** a person who presents a candidate for confirmation. **5.** *Chiefly U.S.* a person who undertakes responsibility for the actions, statements, obligations, etc., of another, as during a period of apprenticeship; guarantor. ~*vb.* **6.** (*tr.*) to act as a sponsor for. [C17: from Latin, from *spondēre* to promise solemnly] —**spon+so+ri·al** (spɒn'sɔ:rɪəl) *adj.* —**'spon+sor+ˌship** *n.*

spon+ta+ne·i·ty (ˌspɒntə'ni:ɪtɪ, -'neɪ-) *n., pl.* **·ties. 1.** the state or quality of being spontaneous. **2.** (*often pl.*) the exhibiting of actions, impulses, or behaviour that are stimulated by internal processes.

spon+ta+ne·ous (spɒn'teɪnɪəs) *adj.* **1.** occurring, produced, or performed through natural processes without external influence: *spontaneous movement.* **2.** arising from an unforced personal impulse; voluntary; unpremeditated: *a spontaneous comment.* **3.** (of plants) growing naturally; indigenous. [C17: from Late Latin *spontāneus*, from Latin *sponte* voluntarily] —**spon+'ta+ne·ous+ly** *adv.* —**spon+'ta+ne·ous+ness** *n.*

spon+ta+ne·ous com+bus+tion *n.* the ignition of a substance or body as a result of internal oxidation processes, without the application of an external source of heat, occurring in finely powdered ores, coal, straw, etc.

spon+ta+ne·ous gen+er+a+tion *n.* another name for **abiogenesis.**

spon+ta+ne·ous re+cov+er·y *n. Psychol.* the reappearance of a response after its extinction has been followed by a period of rest.

spon+toon (spɒn'tu:n) *n.* a shafted weapon similar to a pike, carried by subordinate infantry officers in the 18th and 19th centuries. [C18: from French *esponton*, from Italian *spuntone*, from *punto* POINT]

spoof (spu:f) *Informal.* ~*n.* **1.** a mildly satirical mockery or parody; lampoon: *a spoof on party politics.* **2.** a good-humoured deception or trick; prank. ~*vb.* **3.** to indulge in a spoof of (a person or thing). [C19: coined by A. Roberts (1852–1933), English comedian, to designate a game of his own invention] —**'spoof+er** *n.*

spook (spu:k) *Informal.* ~*n.* **1.** a ghost or a person suggestive of this. **2.** *U.S. slang.* a spy. ~*vb.* (*tr.*) **3.** *U.S.* to frighten: *to spook horses; to spook a person.* **4.** *U.S.* (of a ghost) to haunt. [C19: Dutch *spook*, from Middle Low German *spōk* ghost] —**'spook+ish** *adj.*

spook·y ('spu:kɪ) *adj.* **spook·i·er, spook·i·est.** *Informal.* **1.** ghostly or eerie: *a spooky house.* **2.** resembling or appropriate to a ghost. **3.** *U.S.* easily frightened; highly strung. —**'spook·i+ly** *adv.* —**'spook·i+ness** *n.*

spool (spu:l) *n.* **1.** a device around which magnetic tape, film, cotton, etc., can be automatically wound, with plates at top and bottom to prevent it from slipping off. **2.** anything round which other materials, esp. thread, are wound. ~*vb.* **3.** (sometimes foll. by *up*) to wind or be wound onto a spool or reel. [C14: of Germanic origin; compare Old High German *spuolo*, Middle Dutch *spoele*]

spoon (spu:n) *n.* **1.** a metal, wooden, or plastic utensil having a shallow concave part, usually elliptical in shape, attached to a handle, used in eating or serving food, stirring, etc. **2.** Also called: **spoon+bait.** an angling lure for spinning or trolling, consisting of a bright piece of metal which swivels on a trace to which are attached a hook or hooks. **3.** a golf club: a No. 3 wood with a shorter shaft and shallower face than a brassie, giving more lift. **4. be born with a silver spoon in one's mouth.** to inherit wealth or social standing. **5. wooden spoon.** *Brit.* another name for **booby prize. 6.** *Rowing.* a type of oar blade that is curved at the edges and tip to gain a firm grip on the water. Compare **spade**[1] (sense 4). ~*vb.* **7.** (*tr.*) to scoop up or transfer (food, liquid, etc.) from one container to another with or as if with a spoon. **8.** (*intr.*) *Slang.* to kiss and cuddle. **9.** to hollow out (a cavity or spoon-shaped bowl) (in something). **10.** *Sport.* to hit (a ball) with a weak lifting motion, as in golf, cricket, etc. [Old English *spōn* splinter; related to Old Norse *spōnn* spoon, chip, Old High German *spān*]

spoon+bill ('spu:nˌbɪl) *n.* any of several wading birds of warm regions, such as *Platalea leucorodia* (**common spoonbill**) and *Ajaia ajaja* (**roseate spoonbill**), having a long horizontally flattened bill: family *Threskiornithidae*, order *Ciconiiformes.*

spoon+drift ('spu:nˌdrɪft) *n.* a less common spelling of **spindrift.**

spoon+er+ism ('spu:nəˌrɪzəm) *n.* the transposition of the initial consonants or consonant clusters of a pair of words, often resulting in an amusing ambiguity of meaning, such as *hush my brat* for *brush my hat.* [C20: named after W. A. *Spooner* (1844–1930), English clergyman renowned for slips of this kind]

spoon-feed *vb.* **-feeds, -feed·ing, -fed.** (*tr.*) **1.** to feed with a spoon. **2.** to overindulge or spoil. **3.** to provide (a person) with ready-made opinions, judgments, etc., depriving him of original thought or action.

spoon+ful ('spu:nˌfʊl) *n., pl.* **+fuls. 1.** the amount that a spoon is able to hold. **2.** a small quantity.

spoon·y *or* **spoon+ey** ('spu:nɪ) *Slang, rare.* ~*adj.* **spoon·i+er, spoon·i+est. 1.** foolishly or stupidly amorous. ~*n., pl.* **spoon·ies. 2.** a fool or silly person, esp. one in love.

spoor (spʊə, spɔ:) *n.* **1.** the trail of an animal or person, esp. as discernible to the human eye. ~*vb.* **2.** to track (an animal) by following its trail. [C19: from Afrikaans, from Middle Dutch *spor;* related to Old English *spor* track, Old High German *spor;* see SPUR] —'**spoor+er** *n.*

Spor·a+des ('spɒrə,diːz) *pl. n.* two groups of Greek islands in the Aegean: the **Northern Sporades,** lying northeast of Euboea, and the **Southern Sporades,** which include the Dodecanese and lie off the SW coast of Turkey.

spo+rad+ic (spə'rædɪk) *or* **spo+rad·i+cal** *adj.* **1.** occurring at irregular points in time; intermittent: *sporadic firing.* **2.** scattered; isolated: *a sporadic disease.* [C17: from Medieval Latin *sporadicus,* from Greek *sporadikos,* from *sporas* scattered; related to Greek *speirein* to sow; see SPORE] —**spo+'rad·i·cal+ly** *adv.* —**spo+'rad·i·cal+ness** *n.*

spo+ran+gi·um (spə'rændʒɪəm) *n., pl.* **+gi·a** (-dʒɪə). any organ, esp. in fungi, in which asexual spores are produced. [C19: from New Latin, from SPORO- + Greek *angeion* receptacle] —**spo+'ran+gi·al** *adj.*

spore (spɔː) *n.* **1.** a reproductive body, produced by some protozoans and many plants, that develops into a new individual. A **sexual spore** is formed after the fusion of gametes and an **asexual spore** is the result of asexual reproduction. **2.** a germ cell, seed, dormant bacterium, or similar body. ~*vb.* **3.** (*intr.*) to produce, carry, or release spores. [C19: from New Latin *spora,* from Greek: a sowing; related to Greek *speirein* to sow]

spore case *n.* the nontechnical name for **sporangium.**

spo·ro- *or before a vowel* **spor-** *combining form.* (in botany) spore: *sporophyte.* [from New Latin *spora*]

spo+ro+carp ('spɔːrəʊ,kɑːp, 'spɒ-) *n.* **1.** a specialized leaf branch in certain aquatic ferns that encloses the sori. **2.** the spore-producing structure in certain algae, lichens, and fungi.

spo+ro+cyst ('spɔːrəʊ,sɪst, 'spɒ-) *n.* **1.** a thick-walled rounded structure produced by protozoans of the class *Sporozoa,* in which sporozoites are formed. **2.** the saclike larva of a trematode worm that produces redia larvae by asexual reproduction. **3.** any similar structure containing spores.

spo+ro+cyte ('spɔːrəʊ,saɪt, 'spɒ-) *n.* a diploid cell that divides by meiosis to produce four haploid spores.

spo+ro+gen+e·sis (,spɔːrəʊ'dʒɛnɪsɪs, ,spɒ-) *n.* the process of spore formation in plants and animals. —**spo+rog+e·nous** (spɔː'rɒdʒɪnəs, spɒ-)

spo+ro+go+ni·um (,spɔːrəʊ'gəʊnɪəm, ,spɒ-) *n., pl.* **+ni·a** (-nɪə). a structure in mosses and liverworts consisting of a spore-bearing capsule on a short stalk that arises from the parent plant (the sporophyte). —**,spo+ro+'go+ni·al** *adj.*

spo+rog·o·ny (spɔː'rɒgənɪ, -'rɒdʒ-, spɒ-) *n.* the process in sporozoans by which sporozoites are formed from an encysted zygote by multiple fission.

spo+ro+phore ('spɔːrəʊ,fɔː, 'spɒ-) *n.* an organ in fungi that produces or carries spores, esp. the massive spore-bearing body of mushrooms, etc.

spo+ro+phyll *or* **spo+ro+phyl** ('spɔːrəʊfɪl, 'spɒ-) *n.* a leaf in mosses, ferns, and related plants that bears the sporangia. See also **megasporophyll, microsporophyll.**

spo+ro+phyte ('spɔːrəʊ,faɪt, 'spɒ-) *n.* the diploid form of plants that have alternation of generations. It develops from a zygote and produces asexual spores. Compare **gametophyte.** —**spo+ro+phyt+ic** (,spɔːrə'fɪtɪk, ,spɒ-) *adj.*

-spor·ous *adj. combining form.* (in botany) having a specified type or number of spores: *homosporous.*

spo+ro+zo+an (,spɔːrə'zəʊən, ,spɒ-) *n.* **1.** any parasitic protozoan of the class *Sporozoa,* characterized by a complex life cycle, part of which is passed in the cells of the host, and the production of asexual spores: includes the malaria parasite. See **plasmodium** (sense 2). ~*adj.* **2.** of, relating to, or belonging to the *Sporozoa.*

spo+ro+zo+ite (,spɔːrə'zəʊaɪt, ,spɒ-) *n.* any of numerous small mobile usually infective individuals produced in sporozoans by sporogony.

spor+ran ('spɒrən) *n.* a large pouch, usually of fur, worn hanging from a belt in front in Scottish Highland dress. [C19: from Scottish Gaelic *sporan* purse; compare Irish Gaelic *sparān* purse, Late Latin *bursa* bag]

sport (spɔːt) *n.* **1.** an individual or group activity pursued for exercise or pleasure, often involving the testing of physical capabilities and taking the form of a competitive game such as football, tennis, etc. **2.** such activities considered collectively. **3.** any particular pastime indulged in for pleasure. **4.** the pleasure derived from a pastime, esp. hunting, shooting, or fishing: *we had good sport today.* **5.** playful or good-humoured joking: *to say a thing in sport.* **6.** derisive mockery or the object of such mockery: *to make sport of someone.* **7.** someone or something that is controlled by external influences: *the sport of fate.* **8.** *Informal.* (sometimes qualified by *good, bad,* etc.) a person who reacts cheerfully in the face of adversity, esp. a good loser. **9.** *Informal.* a person noted for being scrupulously fair and abiding by the rules of a game. **10.** *Informal.* a person who leads a merry existence, esp. a gambler: *he's a bit of a sport.* **11.** *Austral. informal.* a form of address used esp. between males. **12.** *Biology.* **a.** an animal or plant that differs conspicuously in one or more aspects from other organisms of the same species, usually because of a mutation. **b.** an anomalous characteristic of such an organism. ~*vb.* **13.** (*tr.*) *Informal.* to wear or display in an ostentatious or proud manner: *she was sporting a new hat.* **14.** (*intr.*) to skip about or frolic happily. **15.** to amuse (oneself), esp. in outdoor physical recreation. **16.** (*tr.;* often foll. by *away*) to squander (time or money): *sporting one's life away.* **17.** (*intr.;* often foll. by *with*) *Archaic.* to make fun (of). **18.** (*intr.*) *Biology.* to produce or undergo a mutation. [C15 *sporten,* variant of *disporten* to DISPORT] —'**sport+er** *n.* —'**sport+ful** *adj.* —'**sport+ful+ly** *adv.* —'**sport+ful+ness** *n.*

sport+ing ('spɔːtɪŋ) *adj.* **1.** (*prenominal*) of, relating to, or used or engaged in a sport or sports: *several sporting interests.* **2.** relating or conforming to sportsmanship; fair. **3.** of, relating to, or characterized by an interest in gambling. **4.** willing to take a risk. —'**sport+ing+ly** *adv.*

sport+ing house *n.* **1.** *U.S., rare.* a euphemistic word for **brothel. 2.** *Archaic.* a tavern or inn frequented by gamblers or other sportsmen.

spor+tive ('spɔːtɪv) *adj.* **1.** playful or joyous. **2.** done in jest rather than seriously. **3.** of, relating to, or interested in sports. **4.** *Obsolete.* wanton or amorous: *a sportive wench.* —'**spor+tive+ly** *adv.* —'**spor+tive+ness** *n.*

sports (spɔːts) *n.* **1.** (*modifier*) relating to, concerned with, or used in sports: *sports equipment.* **2.** Also called: **sports day.** *Brit.* a meeting held at a school or college for competitions in various athletic events.

sports car *n.* a production car designed for speed, high acceleration, and manoeuvrability, having a low body and usually adequate seating for only two persons.

sports+cast ('spɔːts,kɑːst) *n. U.S.* a radio or television broadcast consisting of sports news. —'**sports+,cast·er** *n.*

sports jack+et *n.* a man's informal jacket, made esp. of tweed: worn with trousers of different material.

sports+man ('spɔːtsmən) *n., pl.* **+men. 1.** a man who takes part in sports, esp. of the outdoor type. **2.** a person who exhibits qualities highly regarded in sport, such as fairness, generosity, observance of the rules, and good humour when losing. —'**sports·man-,like** *or* '**sports+man+ly** *adj.* —'**sports+man+,ship** *n.*

sports shirt *n.* a man's informal shirt, sometimes of knitted wool or cotton, which may be worn outside the trousers.

sports+wear ('spɔːts,wɛə) *n.* clothes worn for sport or outdoor leisure wear.

sports+wom·an ('spɔːts,wʊmən) *n., pl.* **+wom·en.** a woman who takes part in sports, esp. of the outdoor type.

sport·y ('spɔːtɪ) *adj.* **sport·i·er, sport·i·est. 1.** vulgarly ostentatious or flashy; stylish, loud, or gay. **2.** relating to or appropriate to a sportsman or sportswoman. **3.** (of women) amorous or wanton; lusty. —'**sport·i·ly** *adv.* —'**sport·i·ness** *n.*

spor·u+late ('spɒrjʊ,leɪt) *vb.* (*intr.*) to produce spores, esp. by multiple fission. —**,spor·u+'la+tion** *n.*

spor+ule ('spɒruːl) *n.* a spore, esp. a very small spore. [C19: from New Latin *sporula* a little SPORE]

spot (spɒt) *n.* **1.** a small mark on a surface, such as a circular patch or stain, differing in colour or texture from its surroundings. **2.** a geographical area that is restricted in extent: *a beauty spot.* **3.** a location: *this is the exact spot on which he died.* **4.** a blemish of the skin, esp. a pimple or one occurring through some disease. **5.** a blemish on the character of a person; moral flaw. **6.** *Informal.* a place of entertainment: *we hit all the night spots.* **7.** *Informal, chiefly Brit.* a small quantity or amount: *a spot of lunch.* **8.** *Informal.* an awkward situation: *that puts me in a bit of a spot.* **9.** a short period between regular television or radio programmes that is used for advertising. **10.** a position or length of time in a show assigned to a specific performer. **11.** short for **spotlight. 12.** (in billiards) **a.** Also called: **spot ball.** the white ball that is distinguished from the plain by a mark or spot. **b.** the player using this ball. **13.** (*modifier*) **a.** to be paid or delivered immediately: *spot cash.* **b.** involving immediate cash payment: *spot sales.* **c.** concerned with or designed for cash transactions only: *the spot market.* **14. change one's spots.** (*used mainly in negative constructions*) to reform one's character. **15. high spot.** an outstanding event: *the high spot of the holiday was the visit to the winery.* **16. knock spots off.** to outstrip or outdo with ease. **17. on the spot. a.** immediately. **b.** at the place in question. **c.** in the best possible position to deal with a situation. **d.** in an awkward predicament. **e.** without moving from the place of one's location, etc. **f.** (*as modifier*): *our on-the-spot reporter.* **18. soft spot.** a special sympathetic affection or weakness for a person or thing. **19. tight spot.** a serious, difficult, or dangerous situation. **20. weak spot. a.** some aspect of a character or situation that is susceptible to criticism. **b.** a flaw in a person's knowledge: *classics is my weak spot.* ~*vb.* **spots, spot+ting, spot+ted. 21.** (*tr.*) to observe or perceive suddenly, esp. under difficult circumstances; discern. **22.** to put stains or spots upon (something). **23.** (*intr.*) (of some fabrics) to be susceptible to spotting by or as if by water: *silk spots easily.* **24.** (*tr.*) to place here and there: *they spotted observers along the border.* **25.** (*tr.*) *Billiards.* to place (a ball) on one of the table spots. **26.** *Military.* to adjust fire in order to correct deviations from (the target) by observation. **27.** (*tr.*) *U.S. informal.* to yield (an advantage or concession) to (one's opponent): *to spot someone a piece in chess.* [C12 (in the sense: moral blemish): of German origin; compare Middle Dutch *spotte,* Old Norse *spotti*] —'**spot+ta·ble** *adj.*

spot check *n.* **1.** a quick random examination. ~*vb.* **spot-check. 2.** (*tr.*) to perform a spot check on.

spot height *n.* a mark on a map indicating the height of a hill, mountain, etc.

spot+less ('spɒtlɪs) *adj.* **1.** free from stains; immaculate. **2.** free from moral impurity; unsullied: *a spotless character.* —'**spot+less+ly** *adv.* —'**spot+less+ness** *n.*

spot+light ('spɒt,laɪt) *n.* **1.** a powerful light focused so as to illuminate a small area, usually mounted so it can be directed at will. **2. the.** the focus of attention. ~*vb.* **+lights, +light+ing, +lit** *or* **+light+ed.** (*tr.*) **3.** to direct a spotlight on. **4.** to focus attention on.

spot-on *adj. Brit. informal.* absolutely correct; very accurate.

spot+ted ('spɒtɪd) *adj.* **1.** characterized by spots or marks, esp. in having a pattern of spots. **2.** stained or blemished; soiled or bespattered.

spot+ted crake *n.* a Eurasian rail, *Porzana porzana,* of swamps and marshes, having a buff speckled plumage and dark brown wings.

spot+ted dick *or* **dog** *n. Brit.* a steamed or boiled suet pudding containing dried fruit, and shaped into a roll.

spot+ted fe+ver *n.* **1.** any of various severe febrile diseases characterized by small irregular spots on the skin, as in Rocky Mountain spotted fever or tick fever.

spot+ted fly+catch·er *n.* a European woodland songbird, *Muscicapa striata,* with a greyish-brown streaked plumage: family *Muscicapidae* (Old World flycatchers).

spot+ted sand+pip·er *n.* a North American sandpiper, *Actitis macularia,* having a spotted breast in its breeding plumage. Also called (U.S.): **peetweet.**

spot+ter ('spɒtə) *n.* **1. a.** a person or thing that watches or observes. **b.** (*as modifier*): *a spotter plane.* **2.** a person who makes a hobby of watching for and noting numbers or types of trains, buses, etc.: *a train spotter.* **3.** *Military.* a person who orders or advises adjustment of fire on a target by observations. **4.** a person, esp. one engaged in civil defence, who watches for enemy aircraft. **5.** *U.S. informal.* an employee assigned to spy on his colleagues in order to check on their honesty. **6.** *Films.* **a.** a person who checks against irregularities and inconsistencies. **b.** a person who searches for new material, performers, etc.

spot+ty ('spɒtɪ) *adj.* **+ti+er, +ti+est. 1.** abounding in or characterized by spots or marks, esp. on the skin: *a spotty face.* **2.** not consistent or uniform; irregular or uneven, often in quality. **—'spot+ti+ly** *adv.* **—'spot+ti+ness** *n.*

spot-weld *vb.* **1.** (*tr.*) to join (two pieces of metal, esp. in the form of wire or sheet) by one or more small circular welds by means of heat, usually electrically generated, and pressure. *~n.* **2.** a weld so formed. **—'spot-,weld·er** *n.*

spous+al ('spaʊzᵊl) *n.* **1.** (*often pl.*) **a.** the marriage ceremony. **b.** a wedding. *~adj.* **2.** of or relating to marriage. **—'spous+al+ly** *adv.*

spouse *n.* (spaʊs, spaʊz). **1.** a person's partner in marriage. Related adj.: **spousal.** *~vb.* (spaʊz, spaʊs). **2.** (*tr.*) *Obsolete.* to marry. [C12: from Old French *spus* (masculine), *spuse* (feminine), from Latin *sponsus, sponsa* betrothed man or woman, from *spondēre* to promise solemnly]

spout (spaʊt) *vb.* **1.** to discharge (a liquid) in a continuous jet or in spurts, esp. through a narrow gap or under pressure, or (of a liquid) to gush thus. **2.** (of a whale, etc.) to discharge air through the blowhole, so that it forms a spray at the surface of the water. **3.** *Informal.* to utter (a stream of words) on a subject, often at length. *~n.* **4.** a tube, pipe, chute, etc., allowing the passage or pouring of liquids, grain, etc. **5.** a continuous stream or jet of liquid. **6.** short for **waterspout. 7. up the spout.** *Slang.* **a.** ruined or lost: *any hope of rescue is right up the spout.* **b.** pregnant. [C14: perhaps from Middle Dutch *spouten,* from Old Norse *spyta* to spit] **—'spout+er** *n.*

spp. *abbrev. for* species (plural).

SPQR *abbrev. for* Senatus Populusque Romanus. [Latin: the Senate and People of Rome].

S.P.R. *abbrev. for* Society for Psychical Research.

sprag (spræg) *n.* **1.** a chock or steel bar used to prevent a vehicle from running backwards on an incline. **2.** a support or post used in mining. [C19: of uncertain origin]

sprain (spreɪn) *vb.* **1.** (*tr.*) to injure (a joint) by a sudden twisting or wrenching of its ligaments. *~n.* **2.** the resulting injury to such a joint, characterized by swelling and temporary disability. [C17: of uncertain origin]

sprang (spræŋ) *vb.* the past tense of **spring.**

sprat (spræt) *n.* **1.** a small marine food fish, *Clupea sprattus,* of the NE Atlantic Ocean and North Sea: family *Clupeidae* (herrings). See also **brisling. 2.** any of various small or young herrings. [C16: variant of Old English *sprott;* related to Middle Low German *sprot,* Norwegian *sprot* small rod]

sprawl (sprɔːl) *vb.* **1.** (*intr.*) to sit or lie in an ungainly manner with one's limbs spread out. **2.** to fall down or knock down with the limbs spread out in an ungainly way. **3.** to spread out or cause to spread out in a straggling fashion: *his handwriting sprawled all over the paper.* *~n.* **4.** the act or an instance of sprawling. **5.** a sprawling posture or arrangement of items. [Old English *spreawlian;* related to Old English *spryttan* to sprout, SPURT, Greek *speirein* to scatter] **—'sprawl+er** *n.* **—'sprawl·y** *adj.*

spray[1] (spreɪ) *n.* **1.** fine particles of a liquid. **2. a.** a liquid, such as perfume, paint, etc., designed to be discharged from an aerosol or atomizer: *hair spray.* **b.** the aerosol or atomizer itself. **3.** a quantity of small objects flying through the air: *a spray of bullets.* *~vb.* **4.** to scatter (liquid) in the form of fine particles. **5.** to discharge (a liquid) from an aerosol or atomizer. **6.** (*tr.*) to treat or bombard with a spray: *to spray the lawn.* [C17: from Middle Dutch *spraien;* related to Middle High German *spræjen*] **—'spray+er** *n.*

spray[2] (spreɪ) *n.* a single slender shoot, twig, or branch that bears buds, leaves, flowers, or berries, either growing on or detached from a plant. [C13: of Germanic origin; compare Old English *spræc* young shoot, Old Norse *sprek* brittle wood, Old High German *sprahhula* splinter]

spray gun *n.* a device that sprays a fluid in a finely divided form by atomizing the fluid in an air jet.

spread (sprɛd) *vb.* **spreads, spread+ing, spread. 1.** to extend or unfold or be extended or unfolded to the fullest width: *she spread the map on the table.* **2.** to extend or cause to extend over a larger expanse of space or time: *the milk spread all over the floor; the economic unrest spread over several years.* **3.** to apply or be applied in a coating: *butter does not spread very well when cold.* **4.** to distribute or be distributed over an area or region. **5.** to display or be displayed in its fullest extent: *the landscape spread before us.* **6.** (*tr.*) to prepare (a table) for a meal. **7.** (*tr.*) to lay out (a meal) on a table. **8.** to send or be sent out in all directions; disseminate or be disseminated: *someone has been spreading rumours; the disease spread quickly.* **9.** (of rails, wires, etc.) to force or be forced apart. **10.** to increase the breadth of (a part), esp. to flatten the head of a rivet by pressing, hammering, or forging. **11.** (*tr.*) *Agriculture.* **a.** to lay out (hay) in a relatively thin layer to dry. **b.** to scatter (seed, manure, etc.) over a relatively wide area. **12.** (*tr.;* often foll. by *around*) *Informal.* to make (oneself) agreeable to a large number of people, often of the opposite sex. **13.** *Phonetics.* to narrow and lengthen the aperture of (the lips) as for the articulation of a front vowel, such as (iː) in English *see* (siː). *~n.* **14.** the act or process of spreading; diffusion, dispersion, expansion, etc.: *the spread of the Christian religion.* **15.** *Informal.* the wingspan of an aircraft. **16.** an extent of space or time; stretch: *a spread of 50 years.* **17.** *Informal, chiefly U.S.* a ranch or relatively large tract of land. **18.** the limit of something fully extended: *the spread of a bird's wings.* **19.** a covering for a table or bed. **20.** *Informal.* a large meal or feast, esp. when it is laid out on a table. **21.** a food which can be spread on bread, etc.: *salmon spread.* **22.** two facing pages in a book or other publication. **23.** a widening of the hips and waist: *middle-age spread.* **24.** *Stock exchange.* **a.** the difference between the bid and offer prices quoted by a stockjobber. **b.** the excess of the price at which stock is offered for public sale over the price paid for the same stock by an underwriter. **c.** *Chiefly U.S.* a double option. Compare **straddle** (sense 9). **25.** *Jewellery.* the apparent size of a gemstone when viewed from above expressed in carats: *a diamond with a spread of four carats.* *~adj.* **26.** extended or stretched out, esp. to the fullest extent. **27.** (of a gem) shallow and flat. **28.** *Phonetics.* **a.** (of the lips) forming a long narrow aperture. **b.** (of speech sounds) articulated with spread lips: *(iː) in English "feel" is a spread vowel.* [Old English *sprædan;* related to Old High German *spreiten* to spread, Old Lithuanian *sprainas* stiff] **—'spread+a·ble** *adj.*

spread ea·gle *n.* **1.** the representation of an eagle with outstretched wings, used as an emblem of the U.S. **2.** an acrobatic skating figure.

spread-ea·gle *adj. also* **spread-ea·gled. 1.** lying or standing with arms and legs outstretched. *~vb.* **2.** to assume or cause to assume the shape of a spread eagle. **3.** (*intr.*) *Skating.* to execute a spread eagle.

spread+er ('sprɛdə) *n.* **1.** a machine or device used for scattering bulk materials, esp. manure or fertilizer, over a relatively wide area. **2.** a device for keeping apart or spacing parallel objects, such as electric wires, etc.

spreathed (spriːðd) *adj. Southwestern English and south Wales dialect.* sore; chapped. [from *spreathe* to make sore: of obscure origin]

sprech+ge+sang (*German* 'ʃprɛçgəˌzaŋ) *n. Music.* a type of vocalization between singing and recitation in which the voice sings the beginning of each note and then falls rapidly from the notated pitch. It was originated by Arnold Schoenberg, who used it in *Pierrot Lunaire* (1912). [C20: from German, literally: speaking-song]

sprech+stim·me (*German* 'ʃprɛçˌʃtɪmə) *n. Music.* a vocal part employing sprechgesang. [C20: from German: speaking voice]

spree (spriː) *n.* **1.** a session of considerable overindulgence, esp. in drinking, squandering money, etc. **2.** a romp. [C19: perhaps changed from Scottish *spreath* plundered cattle, ultimately from Latin *praeda* booty]

sprig (sprɪg) *n.* **1.** a shoot, twig, or sprout of a tree, shrub, etc.; spray. **2.** an ornamental device resembling a spray of leaves or flowers. **3.** Also called: **dowel pin.** a small wire nail without a head. **4.** *Informal, rare.* a youth. **5.** *Informal, rare.* a person considered as the descendant of an established family, social class, etc. *~vb.* **sprigs, sprig+ging, sprigged.** (*tr.*) **6.** to fasten or secure with sprigs. **7.** to ornament (fabric, etc.) with a design of sprigs. **8.** to make sprays from (twigs and branches). [C15: probably of Germanic origin; compare Low German *sprick,* Swedish *sprygg*] **—'sprig+ger** *n.* **—'sprig+gy** *adj.*

spright+ly ('spraɪtlɪ) *adj.* **+li+er, +li+est. 1.** full of vitality; lively and gay. *~adv.* **2.** *Obsolete.* in a gay or lively manner. **—'spright+li+ness** *n.*

spring (sprɪŋ) *vb.* **springs, spring+ing, sprang** *or* **sprung; sprung. 1.** to move or cause to move suddenly upwards or forwards in a single motion. **2.** to release or be released from a forced position by elastic force: *the bolt sprang back.* **3.** (*tr.*) to leap or jump over. **4.** (*intr.*) to come, issue, or arise suddenly. **5.** (*intr.*) (of a part of a mechanism, etc.) to jump out of place. **6.** to make (wood, etc.) warped or split or (of wood, etc.) to become warped or split. **7.** to happen or cause to happen unexpectedly: *to spring a surprise; the boat sprung a leak.* **8.** (*intr.*) to develop or originate: *the idea sprang from a chance meeting.* **9.** (*intr.;* usually foll. by *from*) to be descended: *he sprang from peasant stock.* **10.** (*intr.;* often foll. by *up*) to come into being or appear suddenly: *factories springing up.* **11.** (*intr.*) (of game or quarry) to start or rise suddenly from cover. **12.** (*intr.*) to appear to have a strong upward movement: *the beam springs away from the pillar.* **13.** to explode (a mine) or (of a mine) to explode. **14.** (*tr.*) to provide with a spring or springs. **15.** (*tr.*) *Informal.* to arrange the release or escape of (someone) from prison. **16.** (*intr.*) *Archaic or poetic.* (of daylight or dawn) to begin to appear. ~*n.* **17.** the act or an instance of springing. **18.** a leap, jump, or bound. **19. a.** the quality of resilience; elasticity. **b.** (*as modifier*): *spring steel.* **20.** the act or an instance of moving rapidly back from a position of tension. **21. a.** a natural outflow of ground water, as forming the source of a stream. **b.** (*as modifier*): *spring water.* **22. a.** a device, such as a coil or strip of steel, that stores potential energy when it is compressed, stretched, or bent and releases it when the restraining force is removed. **b.** (*as modifier*): *a spring mattress.* **23.** a structural defect such as a warp or bend. **24. a.** (*sometimes cap.*) the season of the year between winter and summer, astronomically from the March equinox to the June solstice in the N hemisphere and from the September equinox to the December solstice in the S hemisphere. **b.** (*as modifier*): *spring showers.* Related adj.: **vernal. 25.** the earliest or freshest time of something. **26.** a source or origin. **27.** one of a set of strips of rubber, steel, etc., running down the inside of the handle of a cricket bat, hockey stick, etc. **28.** Also called: **spring line.** *Nautical.* a mooring line, usually one of a pair that cross amidships. **29.** a flock of teal. **30.** *Architect.* another name for **springing.** [Old English *springan;* related to Old Norse *springa,* Old High German *springan,* Sanskrit *sprhayati* he desires, Old Slavonic *pragu* grasshopper] —**'spring·less** *adj.* —**'spring·,like** *adj.*

spring bal·ance *or esp. U.S.* **spring scale** *n.* a device in which an object to be weighed is attached to the end of a helical spring, the extension of which indicates the weight of the object on a calibrated scale.

spring·board ('sprɪŋ,bɔːd) *n.* **1.** a flexible board, usually projecting low over the water, used for diving. **2.** a similar board used for gaining height or momentum in gymnastics. **3.** *Austral.* a board inserted into the trunk of a tree at some height above the ground on which a lumberjack stands to chop down the tree. **4.** anything that serves as a point of departure or initiation.

spring·bok *or* **spring·buck** ('sprɪŋ,bʌk) *n., pl.* **·bok, ·boks** *or* **·buck, ·bucks.** an antelope, *Antidorcas marsupialis,* of semidesert regions of southern Africa, which moves in leaps exposing a patch of white erectile hairs on the rump that are usually covered by a fold of skin. [C18: from Afrikaans, from Dutch *springen* to SPRING + *bok* goat, BUCK[1]]

Spring·bok ('sprɪŋ,bʌk, -,bɒk) *n.* an amateur athlete who has represented South Africa in international competitions, esp. in cricket or rugby.

spring chick·en *n.* **1.** Also called: **springer.** *Chiefly U.S.* a young chicken, tender for cooking, esp. one from two to ten months old. **2.** *Informal.* (*usually used with a negative*) a young, inexperienced, or unsophisticated person.

spring-clean *vb.* **1.** to clean (a house) thoroughly: traditionally at the end of the winter. ~*n.* **2.** an instance of spring-cleaning. —**,spring-'clean·ing** *n.*

springe (sprɪndʒ) *n.* **1.** a snare set to catch small wild animals or birds and consisting of a loop attached to a bent twig or branch under tension. ~*vb.* **2.** (*intr.*) to set such a snare. **3.** (*tr.*) to catch (small wild animals or birds) with such a snare. [C13: related to Old English *springan* to SPRING]

spring·er ('sprɪŋə) *n.* **1.** Also called: **springing cow.** a cow about to give birth. **2.** a person or thing that springs. **3.** *Architect.* **a.** the first and lowest stone of an arch. **b.** the impost of an arch.

spring·er span·iel *n.* a breed of large spaniel with a wavy silky coat, usually black or liver and white in colour.

spring fe·ver *n.* the feeling of listlessness or liveliness experienced by many people at the onset of spring.

Spring·field ('sprɪŋ,fiːld) *n.* **1.** a city in S Massachusetts, on the Connecticut River: the site of the U.S. arsenal and armoury (1794–1968), which developed the Springfield and Garand rifles. Pop.: 160 358 (1973 est.). **2.** a city in SW Missouri. Pop.: 128 310 (1973 est.). **3.** a city in central Illinois, capital of the state: the home and burial place of Abraham Lincoln. Pop.: 91 753 (1970).

Spring·field ri·fle *n.* a magazine-fed bolt-action breech-loading .30 calibre rifle formerly used by the U.S. Army.

spring·haas ('sprɪŋ,hɑːs) *n., pl.* **·haas** *or* **·ha·se** (-,hɑːzə). a S and E African nocturnal rodent, *Pedetes capensis,* resembling a small kangaroo: family *Pedetidae.* [from Afrikaans: spring hare]

spring·halt ('sprɪŋ,hɔːlt) *n. Vet. science.* another name for **stringhalt.**

spring·head ('sprɪŋ,hɛd) *n.* the source of a stream; spring.

spring·house ('sprɪŋ,haʊs) *n.* a storehouse built over a spring for keeping dairy products and meat cool and fresh.

spring·ing ('sprɪŋɪŋ) *n.* the level where an arch or vault rises from a support. Also called: **spring, springing line, springing point.**

spring·let ('sprɪŋlɪt) *n.* a small spring; brooklet or rill.

spring lock *n.* a type of lock having a spring-loaded bolt, a key being required only to unlock it.

spring on·ion *n.* an immature form of the onion (*Allium cepa*), widely cultivated for its tiny bulb and long green leaves which are eaten in salads, etc. Also called: **green onion, scallion.**

Springs (sprɪŋz) *n.* a city in E South Africa, in the Transvaal: developed around a coal mine established in 1885 and later became a major world gold-mining centre, now with uranium extraction. Pop.: 104 090 (1970).

spring·tail ('sprɪŋ,teɪl) *n.* any primitive wingless insect of the order *Collembola,* having a forked springing organ with which it projects itself forward.

spring tide *n.* **1.** either of the two tides that occur at or just after new moon and full moon when the gravitational attraction of the sun acts in the same direction as that of the moon, reinforcing it and causing the greatest rise in tidal level. The highest spring tides (**equinoctial springs**) occur at the equinoxes. Compare **neap tide. 2.** any great rush or flood.

spring·time ('sprɪŋ,taɪm) *n.* **1.** Also called: **spring·tide** ('sprɪŋ,taɪd). the season of spring. **2.** the earliest, usually the most attractive, period of the existence of something.

spring·wood ('sprɪŋ,wʊd) *n.* the wood that is produced by a plant in the spring and early summer and consists of large thin-walled xylem cells. Compare **summerwood.**

spring·y ('sprɪŋɪ) *adj.* **spring·i·er, spring·i·est. 1.** possessing or characterized by resilience or bounce. **2.** (of a place) having many wells or springs of water. —**'spring·i·ly** *adv.* —**'spring·i·ness** *n.*

sprin·kle ('sprɪŋkᵊl) *vb.* **1.** to scatter (liquid, powder, etc.) in tiny particles or droplets over (something). **2.** (*tr.*) to distribute over (something): *the field was sprinkled with flowers.* **3.** (*intr.*) to drizzle slightly. ~*n.* **4.** the act or an instance of sprinkling or a quantity that is sprinkled. **5.** a slight drizzle. [C14: probably from Middle Dutch *sprenkelen;* related to Old English *spearca* SPARK[1]]

sprin·kler ('sprɪŋklə) *n.* **1.** a device perforated with small holes that is attached to a garden hose or watering can and used to spray plants, lawns, etc., with water. **2.** a person or thing that sprinkles. **3.** See **sprinkler system.**

sprin·kler sys·tem *n.* a fire-extinguishing system that releases water from overhead pipes through nozzles opened automatically by a rise in temperature.

sprin·kling ('sprɪŋklɪŋ) *n.* a small quantity or amount: *a sprinkling of commonsense.*

sprint (sprɪnt) *n.* **1.** *Athletics.* **a.** a short race run at top speed, such as the 100 metres. **b.** a fast finishing run at the end of a longer race. **2.** any quick run. ~*vb.* (*intr.*) **3.** to go at top speed, as in running, cycling, etc. [C16: from Scandinavian; related to Old English *gesprintan* to emit, Old Norse *spretta* to jump up, Old High German *sprinzan* to jump up, Swedish *sprata* to kick] —**'sprint·er** *n.*

sprit (sprɪt) *n. Nautical.* a light spar pivoted at the mast and crossing a fore-and-aft quadrilateral sail diagonally to the peak. [Old English *spreot;* related to Old High German *spriuzen* to support, Dutch *spriet* sprit, Norwegian *sprȳta*]

sprite (spraɪt) *n.* **1.** (in folklore) a nimble elflike creature, esp. one associated with water. **2.** a small dainty person. [C13: from Old French *esprit,* from Latin *spīritus* SPIRIT[1]]

sprit·sail ('sprɪt,seɪl; *Nautical* 'sprɪtsəl) *n. Nautical.* a sail extended by a sprit.

sprock·et ('sprɒkɪt) *n.* **1.** Also called: **sprocket wheel.** a relatively thin wheel having teeth projecting radially from the rim, esp. one that drives or is driven by a chain. **2.** an individual tooth on such a wheel. **3.** a cylindrical wheel with teeth on one or both rims for pulling film through a camera or projector. **4.** a small wedge-shaped piece of wood used to extend a roof over the eaves. [C16: of unknown origin]

sprout (spraʊt) *vb.* **1.** (of a plant, seed, etc.) to produce (new leaves, shoots, etc.). **2.** (*intr.;* often foll. by *up*) to begin to grow or develop: *new office blocks are sprouting up all over the city.* ~*n.* **3.** a newly grown shoot or bud. **4.** something that grows like a sprout. **5.** See **Brussels sprout.** [Old English *sprūtan;* related to Middle High German *sprūzen* to sprout, Lettish *sprausties* to jostle]

spruce[1] (spruːs) *n.* **1.** any coniferous tree of the N temperate genus *Picea,* cultivated for timber and for ornament: family *Pinaceae.* They grow in a pyramidal shape and have needle-like leaves and light-coloured wood. See also **Norway spruce, blue spruce, white spruce, black spruce. 2.** the wood of any of these trees. [C17: short for *Spruce fir,* from C14 *Spruce* Prussia, changed from *Pruce,* via Old French from Latin *Prussia*]

spruce[2] (spruːs) *adj.* neat, smart, and trim. [C16: perhaps from *Spruce leather* a fashionable leather imported from Prussia; see SPRUCE[1]] —**'spruce·ly** *adv.* —**'spruce·ness** *n.*

spruce beer *n.* an alcoholic drink made of fermented molasses flavoured with spruce twigs and cones.

spruce pine *n.* **1.** a large pine tree, *Pinus glabra,* of the southeastern U.S. **2.** any of several similar plants, such as certain pines, hemlocks, and spruces.

spruce up *vb.* (*adv.*) to make (oneself, a person, or thing) smart and neat.

sprue[1] (spruː) *n.* **1.** a vertical channel in a mould through which plastic or molten metal is introduced or out of which it flows when the mould is filled. **2.** plastic or metal that solidifies in a sprue. [C19: of unknown origin]

sprue[2] (spruː) *n.* a chronic disease, esp. of tropical climates, characterized by flatulence, diarrhoea, frothy foul-smelling stools, and emaciation. [C19: from Dutch *spruw;* related to Middle Low German *sprüwe* tumour]

sprue[3] (spruː) *n. London dialect.* an inferior type of asparagus. [C19: of unknown origin]

spru·ik ('spruːɪk) *vb.* (*intr.*) *Austral. slang.* to speak in public (used esp. of a showman or salesman). [C20: of unknown origin] —**'spru·ik·er** *n.*

sprung (sprʌŋ) *vb.* the past participle or a past tense of **spring.**

sprung rhythm *n. Prosody.* a type of poetic rhythm characterized by metrical feet of irregular composition, each having one strongly stressed syllable, often the first, and an indefinite number of unstressed syllables.

spry (spraɪ) *adj.* **spri·er, spri·est.** active and brisk; nimble.

[C18: perhaps of Scandinavian origin; compare Swedish dialect *spragg* SPRIG] —'**spry·ly** *adv.* —'**spry·ness** *n.*

spt. *abbrev. for* seaport.

spud (spʌd) *n.* **1.** an informal word for **potato. 2.** a narrow-bladed spade for cutting roots, digging up weeds, etc. **3.** Also called: **spudder.** a tool, resembling a chisel, for removing bark from trees. ~*vb.* **spuds, spud·ding, spud·ded. 4.** (*tr.*) to remove (bark) or eradicate (weeds) with a spud. **5.** (*intr.*) to drill the first foot of an oil-well. [C15 *spudde* short knife, of unknown origin; applied later to a digging tool, and hence to a potato]

spud-bash·ing *n. Brit. slang, chiefly military.* the task of peeling potatoes, given as a punishment.

Spud Is·land *n.* a slang name for **Prince Edward Island.**

spue (spju:) *vb.* **spues, spu·ing, spued.** an archaic spelling of **spew.** —'**spu·er** *n.*

spug·gy ('spʊgɪ) *or* **spug** (spʊg) *n., pl.* **spug·gies** *or* **spugs.** *Northeast English dialect.* a house sparrow. [variant of Scottish *sprug,* of obscure origin]

spume (spju:m) *n.* **1.** foam or surf, esp. on the sea; froth. ~*vb.* **2.** (*intr.*) to foam or froth. [C14: from Old French *espume,* from Latin *spūma;* related to *spuere* to SPEW] —'**spu·mous** *or* '**spum·y** *adj.*

spu·mes·cent (spju:'mɛsᵊnt) *adj.* producing or resembling foam or froth. —**spu·'mes·cence** *n.*

spu·mo·ne *or* **spu·mo·ni** (spu:'məʊnɪ; *Italian* spu'mo:ne) *n., pl.* **·ni** (-nɪ). a creamy Italian ice cream, made in sections of different colouring, usually containing candied fruit and nuts. [Italian, from *spuma* foam, SPUME]

spun (spʌn) *vb.* **1.** the past tense or past participle of **spin.** ~*adj.* **2.** formed or manufactured by spinning: *spun gold; spun glass.*

spunk (spʌŋk) *n.* **1.** *Informal.* courage or spirit. **2.** *Taboo, Brit.* a slang word for **semen. 3.** touchwood or tinder. [C16 (in the sense: a spark): from Scottish Gaelic *spong* tinder, from Latin *spongia*] —'**spunk·y** *adj.* —'**spunk·i·ly** *adv.*

spun silk *n.* yarn or fabric made from silk waste.

spun sug·ar *n. U.S.* another term for **candy floss.**

spun yarn *n. Nautical.* small stuff made from rope yarns twisted together.

spur (spɜ:) *n.* **1.** a pointed device or sharp spiked wheel fixed to the heel of a rider's boot to enable him to urge his horse on. **2.** anything serving to urge or encourage: *the increase in salary was a spur to their production.* **3.** a sharp horny projection from the leg just above the claws in male birds, such as the domestic cock. **4.** a pointed process in any of various animals; calcar. **5.** a tubular extension at the base of the corolla in flowers such as larkspur. **6.** a short or stunted branch of a tree. **7.** a ridge projecting laterally from a mountain or mountain range. **8.** a wooden prop or a masonry reinforcing pier. **9.** another name for **groyne. 10.** Also called: **spur track.** a railway branch line or siding. **11.** a sharp cutting instrument attached to the leg of a gamecock. **12. on the spur of the moment.** on impulse. ~*vb.* **spurs, spur·ring, spurred. 13.** (*tr.*) to goad or urge with or as if with spurs. **14.** (*intr.*) to go or ride quickly; press on. **15.** (*tr.*) to injure or strike with a spur. **16.** (*tr.*) to provide with a spur or spurs. [Old English *spura;* related to Old Norse *spori,* Old High German *sporo*]

spurge (spɜ:dʒ) *n.* any of various euphorbiaceous plants of the genus *Euphorbia* that have milky sap and small flowers typically surrounded by conspicuous bracts. Some species have purgative properties. [C14: from Old French *espurge,* from *espurgier* to purge, from Latin *expurgāre* to cleanse, from EX-[1] + *purgāre* to PURGE]

spur gear *or* **wheel** *n.* a gear having involuted teeth either straight or helically cut on a cylindrical surface. Two such gears are used to transmit power between parallel shafts.

spurge lau·rel *n.* See **laurel** (sense 4).

spu·ri·ous ('spjʊərɪəs) *adj.* **1.** not genuine or real. **2.** (of a plant part or organ) having the appearance of another part but differing from it in origin, development, or function; false: *a spurious fruit.* **3.** (of radiation) produced at an undesired frequency by a transmitter, causing interference, etc. **4.** *Rare.* illegitimate. [C17: from Latin *spurius* of illegitimate birth] —'**spu·ri·ous·ly** *adv.* —'**spu·ri·ous·ness** *n.*

spurn (spɜ:n) *vb.* **1.** to reject (a person or thing) with contempt. **2.** (when *intr.,* often foll. by *against*) *Archaic.* to kick (at). ~*n.* **3.** an instance of spurning. **4.** *Archaic.* a kick or thrust. [Old English *spurnan;* related to Old Norse *sporna,* Old High German *spurnan,* Latin *spernere* to despise, Lithuanian *spiriu* to kick] —'**spurn·er** *n.*

spur·ri·er ('spʌrɪə) *n.* a maker of spurs.

spur·ry *or* **spur·rey** ('spʌrɪ) *n., pl.* **·ries.** any of several low-growing caryophyllaceous plants of the European genus *Spergula,* esp. *S. arvensis,* having whorled leaves and small white flowers. [C16: from Dutch *spurrie,* perhaps from Medieval Latin *spergula;* related to German *Spergel*]

spurt *or* **spirt** (spɜ:t) *vb.* **1.** to gush or cause to gush forth in a sudden stream or jet. **2.** to make a sudden effort. ~*n.* **3.** a sudden forceful stream or jet. **4.** a short burst of activity, speed, or energy. [C16: perhaps related to Middle High German *sprützen* to squirt]

sput·nik ('spʊtnɪk, 'spʌt-) *n.* any of a series of Soviet artificial satellites, **Sputnik 1** (launched in 1957) being the first man-made satellite to orbit the earth. [C20: from Russian, literally: fellow traveller, from *s-* with + *put* path + *-nik* suffix indicating agent]

sput·ter ('spʌtə) *vb.* **1.** another word for **splutter** (senses 1-3). **2.** *Physics.* **a.** to undergo or cause to undergo a process in which atoms of a solid are removed from its surface by the impact of high-energy ions, as in a discharge tube. **b.** to coat (a film of a metal) onto (a solid surface) by using this process. ~*n.* **3.** the process or noise of sputtering. **4.** incoherent stammering speech. **5.** something that is ejected while sputtering. [C16: from Dutch *sputteren,* of imitative origin] —'**sput·ter·er** *n.*

spu·tum ('spju:təm) *n., pl.* **·ta** (-tə). **1.** a mass of salivary matter ejected from the mouth. **2.** saliva ejected from the mouth mixed with mucus or pus exuded from the respiratory passages, as in bronchitis or bronchiectasis. [C17: from Latin: spittle, from *spuere* to spit out]

spy (spaɪ) *n., pl.* **spies. 1.** a person employed by a state or institution to obtain secret information from rival countries, organizations, companies, etc. **2.** a person who keeps secret watch on others. **3.** *Obsolete.* a close view. **4. spy in the cab.** an informal name for **tachograph.** ~*vb.* **spies, spy·ing, spied. 5.** (*intr.;* usually foll. by *on*) to keep a secret or furtive watch (on). **6.** (*intr.*) to engage in espionage. **7.** (*tr.*) to catch sight of; descry. [C13 *spien,* from Old French *espier,* of Germanic origin; related to Old High German *spehōn,* Middle Dutch *spien*]

spy·glass ('spaɪˌglɑ:s) *n.* a small telescope.

spy out *vb.* (*tr., adv.*) **1.** to discover by careful observation: *to spy out a route.* **2.** to make a close scrutiny of: *to spy out the land.*

sq. *abbrev. for:* **1.** sequence. **2.** square. **3.** (*pl.* **sqq.**) the following one. [from Latin *sequens*]

Sq. *abbrev. for:* **1.** Squadron. **2.** (in place names) Square.

Sqn. Ldr. *abbrev. for* squadron leader.

sqq. *abbrev. for* the following ones. [from Latin *sequentia*]

squab (skwɒb) *n., pl.* **squabs** *or* **squab. 1.** a young unfledged bird, esp. a pigeon. **2.** a short fat person. **3. a.** a well-stuffed bolster or cushion. **b.** a sofa. ~*adj.* **4.** (of birds) recently hatched and still unfledged. **5.** short and fat. [C17: probably of Germanic origin; compare Swedish dialect *sqvabb* flabby skin, *sqvabba* fat woman, German *Quabbe* soft mass, Norwegian *kvabb* mud] —'**squab·by** *adj.*

squab·ble ('skwɒbᵊl) *vb.* **1.** (*intr.*) to quarrel over a small matter. **2.** (*tr.*) *Printing.* to disarrange (composed type). ~*n.* **3.** a petty quarrel. **4.** a printing fault in which a letter or letters are misplaced into an adjacent line. [C17: probably of Scandinavian origin; related to Swedish dialect *sqvabbel* to quarrel] —'**squab·bler** *n.*

squac·co ('skwækəʊ) *n., pl.* **·cos.** a S European heron, *Ardeola ralloides,* with a short thick neck and a buff-coloured plumage with white wings. [C17: Italian dialect]

squad (skwɒd) *n.* **1.** the smallest military formation, typically comprising a dozen soldiers, used esp. as a drill formation. **2.** any small group of people engaged in a common pursuit. **3.** *Sport.* a number of players from which a team is to be selected. [C17: from Old French *esquade,* from Old Spanish *escuadra,* from *escuadrar* to SQUARE, from the square formations used]

squad·ron ('skwɒdrən) *n.* **1. a.** a subdivision of a naval fleet detached for a particular task. **b.** a number of naval units usually of similar type and consisting of two or more divisions. **2.** a cavalry unit comprising two or more troops, headquarters, and supporting arms. **3.** the basic tactical and administrative air force unit comprising two or more flights. [C16: from Italian *squadrone* soldiers drawn up in square formation, from *squadro* SQUARE]

squad·ron lead·er *n.* an officer holding commissioned rank, between flight lieutenant and wing commander in the air forces of Britain and certain other countries.

squa·lene ('skweɪˌli:n) *n. Biochem.* a terpene first found in the liver of sharks but also present in the livers of most higher animals: an important precursor of cholesterol. [C20: from New Latin *squalus* genus name of the shark]

squal·id ('skwɒlɪd) *adj.* **1.** dirty and repulsive, esp. as a result of neglect or poverty. **2.** sordid. [C16: from Latin *squālidus,* from *squālēre* to be stiff with dirt] —**squa·lid·i·ty** (skwɒ'lɪdɪtɪ) *or* '**squal·id·ness** *n.* —'**squal·id·ly** *adv.*

squall[1] (skwɔ:l) *n.* **1.** a sudden strong wind or brief turbulent storm. **2.** any sudden commotion or show of temper. ~*vb.* **3.** (*intr.*) to blow in a squall. [C18: perhaps a special use of SQUALL[2]] —'**squall·ish** *adj.* —'**squal·ly** *adj.*

squall[2] (skwɔ:l) *vb.* **1.** (*intr.*) to cry noisily; yell. ~*n.* **2.** a shrill or noisy yell or howl. [C17: probably of Scandinavian origin; compare Icelandic *skvala* to shout; see SQUEAL] —'**squall·er** *n.*

squall line *n.* a narrow zone along a cold front along which squalls occur. See also **line squall.**

squal·or ('skwɒlə) *n.* the condition or quality of being squalid; disgusting dirt and filth. [C17: from Latin]

squa·ma ('skweɪmə) *n., pl.* **·mae** (-mi:). *Biology.* a scale or scalelike structure. [C18: from Latin] —**squa·mate** ('skweɪmeɪt) *adj.*

squa·ma·tion (skweɪ'meɪʃən) *n.* **1.** the condition of having or forming scales or squamae. **2.** the arrangement of scales in fishes or reptiles.

squa·mo·sal (skwə'məʊsᵊl) *n.* **1.** a thin platelike paired bone in the skull of vertebrates: in mammals it forms part of the temporal bone. ~*adj.* **2.** of or relating to this bone. **3.** a less common word for **squamous.**

squa·mous ('skweɪməs) *or* **squa·mose** ('skweɪməʊs) *adj. Biology.* **1.** (of epithelium) consisting of a single layer of flat platelike cells. **2.** covered with, formed of, or resembling scales. [C16: from Latin *squāmōsus,* from *squāma* a scale]

—'**squa+mous+ly** *or* '**squa+mose+ly** *adv.* —'**squa+mous+ness** *or* '**squa+mose+ness** *n.*

squam·u+lose ('skwæmjʊ,ləʊs, -,ləʊz, 'skweɪ-) *adj.* (esp. of plants or their parts) covered with minute scales. [C19: from Latin *squāmula* diminutive of *squāma* a scale]

squan+der ('skwɒndə) *vb.* (*tr.*) **1.** to spend wastefully or extravagantly; dissipate. **2.** an obsolete word for **scatter.** ~*n.* **3.** *Rare.* extravagance or dissipation. [C16: of unknown origin] —'**squan+der+er** *n.* —'**squan+der+ing+ly** *adv.*

square (skwɛə) *n.* **1.** a plane geometric figure having four equal sides and four right angles. **2.** any object, part, or arrangement having this or a similar shape: *a square of carpet; a square on a chess board.* **3.** (*cap. when part of name*) an open area in a town, sometimes including the surrounding buildings, which may form a square. **4.** *Maths.* the product of two equal factors; the second power: *the square of 2 is written* 2^2. **5.** an instrument having two strips of wood, metal, etc., set in the shape of a T or L, used for constructing or testing right angles. **6.** *Rowing.* the position of the blade of an oar perpendicular to the surface of the water just before and during a stroke. **7.** *Informal.* a person who is old-fashioned in views, customs, appearance, etc. **8.** *Astrology.* an aspect of about 90° between two planets, etc. Compare **conjunction** (sense 5), **opposition** (sense 9), **trine** (sense 1). **9.** *Obsolete.* a standard, pattern, or rule. **10. back to square one.** indicating a return to the starting-point of an investigation, experiment, etc., because of failure, lack of progress, etc. **11. on the square. a.** at right angles. **b.** on equal terms. **c.** *Informal.* honestly and openly. **12. out of square. a.** not at right angles or not having a right angle. **b.** not in order or agreement. ~*adj.* **13.** being a square in shape. **14.** having or forming one or more right angles or being at right angles to something. **15.** square or rectangular in section: *a square bar.* **16. a.** (*prenominal*) denoting a measure of area of any shape: *a circle of four square feet.* **b.** (*immediately postpositive*) denoting a square having a specified length on each side: *a board four feet square contains 16 square feet.* **17.** fair and honest (esp. in the phrase **a square deal**). **18.** straight, even, or level: *a square surface.* **19.** *Cricket.* at right angles to the wicket: *square leg.* **20.** *Soccer, hockey, etc.* in a straight line across the pitch: *a square pass.* **21.** *Nautical.* (of the sails of a square-rigger) set at right angles to the keel. **22.** *Informal.* old-fashioned in views, customs, appearance, etc. **23.** stocky or sturdy: *square shoulders.* **24.** (*postpositive*) having no remaining debts or accounts to be settled. **25.** (of a horse's gait) sound, steady, or regular. **26.** (*prenominal*) unequivocal or straightforward: *a square contradiction.* **27.** (*postpositive*) neat and tidy. **28. square meal.** a balanced meal consisting of enough food to satisfy. **29. square peg (in a round hole).** a person or thing that is a misfit, such as an employee in a job for which he is unsuited. ~*vb.* (*mainly tr.*) **30.** to make into a square or similar shape. **31.** *Maths.* to raise (a number or quantity) to the second power. **32.** to test or adjust for deviation with respect to a right angle, plane surface, etc. **33.** (sometimes foll. by *off*) to divide into squares. **34.** to position so as to be rectangular, straight, or level: *square the shoulders.* **35.** (sometimes foll. by *up*) to settle (debts, accounts, etc.). **36.** to level (the score) in a game, etc. **37.** (*also intr.*; often foll. by *with*) to agree or cause to agree: *your ideas don't square with mine.* **38.** *Rowing.* to turn (an oar) perpendicular to the surface of the water just before commencing a stroke. **39.** (in canoeing) to turn (a paddle) perpendicular to the direction of the canoe at the commencement of a stroke. Compare **feather** (sense 15). **40.** to arrange (something), esp. by a corrupt method or come to an arrangement with (someone), as by bribery: *he squared the speeding summons.* **41. square the circle.** to attempt the impossible (in reference to the insoluble problem of constructing a square having exactly the same area as a given circle). ~*adv.* **42.** in order to be square. **43.** at right angles. **44.** *Soccer, hockey, etc.* in a straight line across the pitch: *pass the ball square.* **45.** *Informal.* squarely. ~See also **square away, square off, square up.** [C13: from Old French *esquare*, from Vulgar Latin *exquadra* (unattested), from Latin EX-[1] + *quadrāre* to make square; see QUADRANT] —'**square+ness** *n.* —'**squar+er** *n.* —'**squar+ish** *adj.*

square a·way *vb.* (*adv.*) **1.** to set the sails of (a square-rigger) at right angles to the keel. **2.** *U.S.* to make neat and tidy.

square-bash·ing *n. Brit. military slang.* drill on a barrack square.

square brack+et *n.* **1.** either of a pair of characters [], used to enclose a section of writing or printing to separate it from the main text. **2.** Also called: **bracket.** either of these characters used as a sign of aggregation in mathematical or logical expressions.

square dance *n.* **1.** *Chiefly U.S.* any of various formation dances, such as a quadrille, in which the couples form squares. ~*vb.* **square-dance. 2.** (*intr.*) to perform such a dance. —'**square-,danc·er** *n.*

square knot *n.* another name for **reef knot.**

square leg *n. Cricket.* **1.** a fielding position on the on side approximately at right angles to the batsman. **2.** a person who fields in this position.

square+ly ('skwɛəlɪ) *adv.* **1.** in a direct way; straight: *he hit me squarely on the nose.* **2.** in an honest, frank, and just manner. **3.** at right angles.

square ma+trix *n. Maths.* a matrix in which the number of rows is equal to the number of columns.

square meas+ure *n.* a unit or system of units for measuring areas.

square num+ber *n.* an integer, such as 1, 4, 9, or 16, that is the square of an integer.

square off *vb.* (*intr., adv.*) to assume a posture of offence or defence, as in boxing.

square pi+an·o *n. Music.* an obsolete form of piano, horizontally strung and with an oblong frame.

square-rigged *adj. Nautical.* rigged with square sails.

square-rig·ger *n. Nautical.* a square-rigged ship.

square root *n.* a number or quantity that when multiplied by itself gives a given number or quantity: *2 is the square root of 4, usually written* $\surd 4$, $\sqrt{4}$, $4^{1/2}$.

square sail *n. Nautical.* a rectangular or square sail set on a horizontal yard rigged more or less athwartships.

square shoot+er *n. Informal, chiefly U.S.* an honest or frank person. —**square shoot+ing** *n.*

square tin *n. Brit.* a medium-sized loaf having a crusty top, baked in a tin with a square base.

square up *vb.* (*adv.*) **1.** to pay or settle (bills, debts, etc.). **2.** *Informal.* to arrange or be arranged satisfactorily. **3.** (*intr.*; foll. by *to*) to prepare to be confronted (with), esp. courageously. **4.** (*tr.*) to transfer (a drawing) by aid of a network of squares.

squar+rose ('skwærəʊz, 'skwɒ-) *adj.* **1.** *Biology.* having a rough surface, caused by the presence of projecting hairs, scales, etc. **2.** *Botany.* having or relating to overlapping parts that are pointed or recurved: *squarrose bracts.* [C18: from Latin *squarrōsus* scabby]

squash[1] (skwɒʃ) *vb.* **1.** to press or squeeze or be pressed or squeezed in or down so as to crush, distort, or pulp. **2.** (*tr.*) to suppress or overcome. **3.** (*tr.*) to humiliate or crush (a person), esp. with a disconcerting retort. **4.** (*intr.*) to make a sucking, splashing, or squelching sound. **5.** (often foll. by *in* or *into*) to enter or insert in a confined space. ~*n.* **6.** *Brit.* a still drink made from fruit juice or fruit syrup diluted with water. **7.** a crush, esp. of people in a confined space. **8.** something that is squashed. **9.** the act or sound of squashing or the state of being squashed. **10.** Also called: **squash rackets, squash racquets.** a game for two or four players played in an enclosed court with a small rubber ball and light long-handled rackets. The ball may be hit against any of the walls but must hit the facing wall at a point above a horizontal line. See also **rackets. 11.** Also called: **squash tennis.** a similar game played with larger rackets and a larger pneumatic ball. [C16: from Old French *esquasser*, from Vulgar Latin *exquassāre* (unattested), from Latin EX-[1] + *quassāre* to shatter] —'**squash+er** *n.*

squash[2] (skwɒʃ) *n., pl.* **squash·es** *or* **squash. 1.** *U.S.* any of various marrow-like cucurbitaceous plants of the genus *Cucurbita*, esp. *C. pepo* and *C. moschata*, the fruits of which have a hard rind surrounding edible flesh. **2.** the fruit of any of these plants, eaten as a vegetable. [C17: from Narragansett *askutasquash*, literally: green vegetable eaten green]

squash bug *n.* any of various heteropterous insects of the family *Coreidae*, esp. a North American species, *Anasa tristis*, which is a pest of squash, pumpkin, and related plants.

squash·y ('skwɒʃɪ) *adj.* **squash·i+er, squash·i+est. 1.** easily squashed; pulpy: *a squashy peach.* **2.** soft and wet; marshy: *squashy ground.* **3.** having a squashed appearance: *a squashy face.* —'**squash·i·ly** *adv.* —'**squash·i+ness** *n.*

squat (skwɒt) *vb.* **squats, squat+ting, squat+ted.** (*intr.*) **1.** to rest in a crouching position with the knees bent and the weight on the feet. **2.** to crouch down, esp. in order to hide. **3.** *Law.* to occupy land to which the occupant has no legal title. ~*adj.* **4.** Also: **squat+ty** ('skwɒtɪ). short and broad: *a squat chair.* ~*n.* **5.** a squatting position. **6.** a house occupied by squatters. [C13: from Old French *esquater*, from *es-* EX-[1] + *catir* to press together, from Vulgar Latin *coactīre* (unattested), from Latin *cōgere* to compress, from CO- + *agere* to drive] —'**squat+ly** *adv.* —'**squat+ness** *n.*

squat+ter ('skwɒtə) *n.* **1.** (in Britain) a person who occupies land wrongfully. **2.** (in Australia) **a.** a person who occupies a tract of land, esp. pastoral land, as tenant of the Crown. **b.** a farmer of sheep or cattle on a large scale.

squat+ter sov+er+eign+ty *n.* a contemptuous term for **popular sovereignty,** used by its critics.

squat+toc+ra+cy (skwɒ'tɒkrəsɪ) *n. Austral.* squatters (see sense 2b.) collectively, regarded as rich and influential. [C19: from SQUATTER + -CRACY]

squaw (skwɔː) *n.* **1.** a North American Indian woman. **2.** *Slang, usually facetious.* a woman or wife. [C17: of Algonquian origin; compare Natick *squa* female creature]

squawk (skwɔːk) *n.* **1.** a loud raucous cry; screech. **2.** *Informal.* a loud complaint or protest. ~*vb.* **3.** to utter a squawk or with a squawk. **4.** (*intr.*) *Informal.* to complain loudly. [C19: of imitative origin] —'**squawk+er** *n.*

squaw man *n.* a White or other non-Indian married to a North American Indian woman.

squeak (skwiːk) *n.* **1.** a short shrill cry or high-pitched sound. **2.** *Informal.* an escape (esp. in the phrases **narrow squeak, near squeak**). ~*vb.* **3.** to make or cause to make a squeak. **4.** *U.S.* to pass with only a narrow margin: *to squeak through an examination.* **5.** (*intr.*) *Informal.* to confess information about oneself or another. **6.** (*tr.*) to utter with a squeak. [C17: probably of Scandinavian origin; compare Swedish *skväka* to croak] —'**squeak+er** *n.* —'**squeak·y** *adj.*

squeal (skwiːl) *n.* **1.** a high shrill yelp, as of pain. **2.** a screaming sound, as of tyres when a car brakes suddenly. ~*vb.* **3.** to utter a squeal or with a squeal. **4.** (*intr.*) *Slang.* to confess information about another. **5.** (*intr.*) *Informal, chiefly Brit.* to complain or protest loudly. [C13 *squelen*, of imitative origin] —'**squeal+er** *n.*

squeam+ish ('skwiːmɪʃ) *adj.* **1.** easily sickened or nauseated, as by the sight of blood. **2.** easily shocked; fastidious or prudish. **3.** easily frightened: *squeamish about spiders.* [C15: from Anglo-French *escoymous,* of unknown origin] **—'squeam+ish+ly** *adv.* **—'squeam+ish+ness** *n.*

squee+gee ('skwi:dʒi:) *or* **squil+gee** *n.* **1.** an implement with a rubber blade used for wiping away surplus water from a surface, such as a windowpane. **2.** any of various similar devices used in photography for pressing the water out of wet prints or negatives or for squeezing prints onto a glazing surface. *~vb.* **+gees, +gee+ing, +geed. 3.** to remove (water or other liquid) from (something) by use of a squeegee. **4.** (*tr.*) to press down (a photographic print, etc.) with a squeegee. [C19: probably of imitative origin, influenced by SQUEEZE]

squeeze (skwi:z) *vb.* (*mainly tr.*) **1.** to grip or press firmly, esp. so as to crush or distort; compress. **2.** to crush or press (something) so as to extract (a liquid): *to squeeze the juice from an orange; to squeeze an orange.* **3.** to apply gentle pressure to, as in affection or reassurance: *he squeezed her hand.* **4.** to push or force in a confined space: *to squeeze six lettuces into one box; to squeeze through a crowd.* **5.** to hug closely. **6.** to oppress with exacting demands, such as excessive taxes. **7.** to exert pressure on (someone) in order to extort (something): *to squeeze money out of a victim by blackmail.* **8.** (*intr.*) to yield under pressure. **9.** (*tr.*) to make an impression of (a coin, etc.) in a soft substance. **10.** (*tr.*) *Bridge, whist.* to lead a card that forces (opponents) to discard potentially winning cards. *~n.* **11.** the act or an instance of squeezing or of being squeezed. **12.** a hug or handclasp. **13.** a crush of people in a confined space. **14.** *Chiefly Brit.* a condition of restricted credit imposed by a government to counteract price inflation. **15.** an impression, esp. of a coin, etc., made in a soft substance. **16.** an amount extracted by squeezing: *add a squeeze of lemon juice.* **17.** *Informal.* pressure brought to bear in order to extort something (esp. in the phrase **put the squeeze on**). **18.** Also called: **squeeze play.** *Bridge, whist.* a manoeuvre that forces opponents to discard potentially winning cards. [C16: from Middle English *queysen* to press, from Old English *cwȳsan*] **—'squeez+a+ble** *adj.* **—'squeez+er** *n.*

squeeze-box *n.* an informal name for **concertina, accordion.**

squelch (skwɛltʃ) *vb.* **1.** (*intr.*) to walk laboriously through soft wet material or with wet shoes, making a sucking noise. **2.** (*intr.*) to make such a noise. **3.** (*tr.*) to crush completely; squash. **4.** (*tr.*) *Informal.* to silence, as by a crushing retort. *~n.* **5.** a squelching sound. **6.** something that has been squelched. **7.** *Electronics.* a circuit that cuts off the audio-frequency amplifier of a radio receiver in the absence of an input signal, in order to suppress background noise. **8.** *Informal.* a crushing remark. [C17: of imitative origin] **—'squelch+er** *n.* **—'squelch+ing+ly** *adv.*

sque+teague (skwɪ'ti:g) *n., pl.* **+teague** *or* **+teagues.** any of various sciaenid food fishes of the genus *Cynoscion,* esp. *C. regalis,* of the North American coast of the Atlantic Ocean. [C19: from Narragansett *pesukwiteag,* literally: they give glue; so called because glue is made from them]

squib (skwɪb) *n.* **1.** a firework, usually having a tube filled with gunpowder, that burns with a hissing noise and culminates in a small explosion. **2.** a firework that does not explode because of a fault; dud. **3.** a short witty attack; lampoon. **4.** an electric device for firing a rocket engine. **5.** *Obsolete.* an insignificant person. **6.** *Austral. slang.* a coward. **7. damp squib.** something intended but failing to impress. *~vb.* **squibs, squib+bing, squibbed. 8.** (*intr.*) to sound, move, or explode like a squib. **9.** (*intr.*) to let off or shoot a squib. **10.** to write a squib against (someone). **11.** (*intr.*) to move in a quick irregular fashion. **12.** (*intr.*) *Austral. slang.* to behave in a cowardly fashion. [C16: probably imitative of a quick light explosion]

squid (skwɪd) *n., pl.* **squid** *or* **squids. 1.** any of various fast-moving pelagic cephalopod molluscs of the genera *Loligo, Ommastrephes,* etc., of most seas, having a torpedo-shaped body ranging from about 10 centimetres to 16.5 metres long and a pair of triangular tail fins: order *Decapoda* (decapods). See also **cuttlefish.** *~vb.* **squids, squid+ding, squid+ded. 2.** (*intr.*) (of a parachute) to assume an elongated squidlike shape due to excess air pressure. [C17: of unkown origin]

squif+fy ('skwɪfɪ) *adj.* **+fi+er, +fi+est.** *Brit. informal.* slightly drunk. [C19: of unknown origin]

squig+gle ('skwɪgᵊl) *n.* **1.** a mark or movement in the form of a wavy line; curlicue. **2.** an illegible scrawl. *~vb.* **3.** (*intr.*) to wriggle. **4.** (*intr.*) to form or draw squiggles. **5.** (*tr.*) to make into squiggles. [C19: perhaps a blend of SQUIRM + WIGGLE] **—'squig+gler** *n.* **—'squig+gly** *adj.*

squil+gee ('skwɪldʒi:) *n.* a variant spelling of **squeegee.** [C19: perhaps from SQUEEGEE, influenced by SQUELCH]

squill (skwɪl) *n.* **1.** See **sea squill. 2.** the bulb of the sea squill, which is sliced, dried, and used medicinally, as an expectorant. **3.** any Old World liliaceous plant of the genus *Scilla,* such as *S. verna* (**spring squill**) of Europe, having small blue or purple flowers. [C14: from Latin *squilla* sea onion, from Greek *skilla,* of obscure origin]

squil+la ('skwɪlə) *n., pl.* **+las** *or* **+lae** (-li:). any mantis shrimp of the genus *Squilla.* [C16: from Latin *squilla* shrimp, of obscure origin]

squinch (skwɪntʃ) *n.* a small arch, corbelling, etc., across an internal corner of a tower, used to support a superstructure such as a spire. Also called: **squinch arch.** [C15: from obsolete *scunch,* from Middle English *sconcheon,* from Old French *escoinson,* from *es-* EX-[1] + *coin* corner]

squint (skwɪnt) *vb.* **1.** (*usually intr.*) to cross or partly close (the eyes). **2.** (*intr.*) to have a squint. **3.** (*intr.*) to look or glance sideways or askance. *~n.* **4.** the nontechnical name for **strabismus. 5.** the act or an instance of squinting; glimpse. **6.** Also called: **hagioscope.** a narrow oblique opening in a wall or pillar of a church to permit a view of the main altar from a side aisle or transept. *~adj.* **7.** having a squint. [C14: short for ASQUINT] **—'squint+er** *n.* **—'squint·y** *adj.*

squint-eyed *adj.* **1.** having a squint. **2.** looking sidelong.

squire (skwaɪə) *n.* **1.** a country gentleman in England, esp. the main landowner in a rural community. **2.** *Feudal history.* a young man of noble birth, who attended upon a knight. **3.** *Rare.* a man who courts or escorts a woman. **4.** *Informal, chiefly Brit.* a term of address used by one man to another, esp., unless ironic, to a member of a higher social class. *~vb.* **5.** (*tr.*) (of a man) to escort a woman. [C13: from Old French *esquier;* see ESQUIRE]

squire+ar+chy *or* **squir+ar+chy** ('skwaɪəˌrɑ:kɪ) *n., pl.* **+chies. 1.** government by squires. **2.** squires collectively, esp. as a political or social force. **—squire+'ar+chal, squir+'ar+chal** *or* **squire+'ar+chi+cal, squir+'ar+chi+cal** *adj.*

squi+reen (skwaɪ'ri:n) *or* **squire+ling** ('skwaɪəlɪŋ) *n. Rare.* a petty squire. [C19: from SQUIRE + *-een,* Irish diminutive suffix]

squirm (skwɜ:m) *vb.* (*intr.*) **1.** to move with a wriggling motion; writhe. **2.** to feel deep mental discomfort, guilt, embarrassment, etc. *~n.* **3.** a squirming movement. [C17: of imitative origin (perhaps influenced by WORM)] **—'squirm+er** *n.* **—'squirm+ing+ly** *adv.* **—'squirm·y** *adj.*

squir+rel ('skwɪrəl; *U.S.* 'skwɜ:rəl, 'skwʌr-) *n., pl.* **+rels** *or* **+rel. 1.** any arboreal sciurine rodent of the genus *Sciurus,* such as *S. vulgaris* (**red squirrel**) or *S. carolinensis* (**grey squirrel**), having a bushy tail and feeding on nuts, seeds, etc. **2.** any other rodent of the family *Sciuridae,* such as a ground squirrel or a marmot. **3.** the fur of such an animal. **4.** *Informal.* a person who hoards things. [C14: from Old French *esquireul,* from Late Latin *sciūrus,* from Greek *skiouros,* from *skia* shadow + *oura* tail] **—'squir·rel-ˌlike** *adj.*

squir+rel cage *n.* **1.** a cage consisting of a cylindrical framework that is made to rotate by a small animal running inside the framework. **2.** a repetitive purposeless task, way of life, etc. **3.** Also called: **squirrel-cage motor.** *Electrical engineering.* the rotor of an induction motor with a cylindrical winding having copper bars around the periphery parallel to the axis. **4.** an electric fan with many long narrow blades arranged in parallel so as to form a cylinder about an axis around which they spin.

squir+rel corn *n.* a North American plant, *Dicentra canadensis,* having yellow flowers and tubers resembling grains of corn: family *Fumariaceae.* Also called: **colicweed.**

squir·rel+fish ('skwɪrəlˌfɪʃ) *n., pl.* **+fish** *or* **+fish·es.** any tropical marine brightly coloured teleost fish of the family *Holocentridae.*

squir+rel mon+key *n.* **1.** a small New World monkey, *Saimiri sciureus,* of N South American forests, having a yellowish-green coat and orange feet and limbs. **2. red-backed squirrel monkey.** a related species, *Saimiri oerstedi,* of Central America, having a reddish coat and dark brown limbs.

squir·rel-tail grass *n.* an annual grass, *Hordeum marinum,* of salt marsh margins of Europe, having bushy awns.

squirt (skwɜ:t) *vb.* **1.** to force (a liquid) or (of a liquid) to be forced out of a narrow opening. **2.** to cover or spatter with liquid so ejected. *~n.* **3.** a jet or amount of liquid so ejected. **4.** the act or an instance of squirting. **5.** an instrument used for squirting. **6.** *Informal.* **a.** a person regarded as insignificant or contemptible. **b.** a short person. [C15: of imitative origin] **—'squirt+er** *n.*

squirt gun *n. U.S.* another name for **water pistol.**

squirt+ing cu+cum+ber *n.* a hairy cucurbitaceous plant, *Ecballium elaterium,* of the Mediterranean region, having a fruit that discharges its seeds explosively when ripe.

squish (skwɪʃ) *vb.* **1.** (*tr.*) to crush, esp. so as to make a soft splashing noise. **2.** (*intr.*) (of mud, etc.) to make a splashing noise: *the ground squishes as you tread.* *~n.* **3.** a soft squashing sound: *the ripe peach fell with a squish.* [C17: of imitative origin] **—'squish·y** *adj.*

squit (skwɪt) *n. Brit. slang.* **1.** an insignificant person. **2.** nonsense; rubbish. [C19: dialectal variant of SQUIRT]

squiz (skwɪz) *n., pl.* **squiz·zes.** *Austral. slang.* a look or glance, esp. an inquisitive one. [C20: perhaps a blend of SQUINT and QUIZ]

sr *Maths. abbrev. for* steradian.

Sr *the chemical symbol for* strontium.

Sr. *or* **Sr** *abbrev. for:* **1.** (after a name) senior. **2.** Señor. **3.** Sir. **4.** Sister (religious).

Sra. *or* **Sra** *abbrev. for* Señora.

Sr+bi+ja ('sᵊrbija) *n.* the Serbian name for **Serbia.**

S.R.C. *Brit. abbrev. for* Science Research Council.

S.R.C.N. (in Britain) *abbrev. for* State Registered Children's Nurse.

S-R con+nec+tion *n. Psychol.* stimulus-response connection; the basic unit of learning according to behaviourist learning theory. See also **reflex arc.**

sri (ʃri:) *n. Hinduism.* **1.** the consort of Vishnu. **2.** a title of honour used when addressing a distinguished Hindu. [literally: majesty, holiness]

Sri Lan+ka ('srɪ 'læŋkə) *n.* a republic in S Asia, occupying the island of Ceylon: settled by the Sinhalese from S India in about 550 B.C.; became a British colony 1802; gained independence in 1948, becoming a republic within the Commonwealth in 1970. Exports include tea, cocoa, cinnamon, and copra. Languages: Sinhalese, Tamil, and English. Religion: Hinayana Buddhist majority. Currency: Sri Lanka rupee. Capital: Colombo. Pop.:

13 986 000 (1975 UN est.). Area: 65 610 sq. km (25 332 sq. miles). Official name (since 1978): **Democratic Socialist Republic of Sri Lanka.** Former name (until 1970): **Ceylon.**

Sri+na+gar (sriːˈnʌgə) *n.* a city in N India, the summer capital of the state of Jammu and Kashmir, at an altitude of 1600 m (5250 ft.) on the Jhelum River: seat of the University of Jammu and Kashmir (1948). Pop.: 403 413 (1971).

S.R.N. (in Britain) *abbrev. for* State Registered Nurse.

S.R.O. *abbrev. for:* **1.** standing room only. **2.** *Brit.* Statutory Rules and Orders.

Srta. *or* **Srta** *abbrev. for* Señorita.

SS *abbrev. for:* **1.** Saints. **2.** a paramilitary organization within the Nazi party that provided Hitler's bodyguard, security forces, concentration camp guards, etc. [German *Schutzstaffel* protection squad] **3.** steamship.

ss. *abbrev. for:* sections.

S.S. *abbrev. for:* **1.** steamship. **2.** Sunday school.

S.S.B. *abbrev. for* single sideband (transmission).

S.S.C. *abbrev. for:* **1.** (in India) Secondary School Certificate. **2.** (in Scotland) solicitor to the Supreme Court.

SSE *abbrev. for* south-southeast.

SSM *abbrev. for* surface-to-surface missile.

SSN *abbrev. for* severely subnormal; used of a person of very limited intelligence who needs special schooling.

SSR *abbrev. for* Soviet Socialist Republic.

SST *abbrev. for* supersonic transport.

SSW *abbrev. for* south-southwest.

st. *abbrev. for:* **1.** stanza. **2.** statute. **3.** *Cricket.* stumped by.

St. *or* **St** *abbrev. for:* **1.** Saint (all entries that are usually preceded by *St.* are in this dictionary listed alphabetically under **Saint**). **2.** statute. **3.** Strait. **4.** Street.

s.t. *abbrev. for* short ton.

-st *suffix.* variant of **-est**[2].

sta. *abbrev. for:* **1.** station. **2.** stationary.

stab (stæb) *vb.* **stabs, stab+bing, stabbed. 1.** (*tr.*) to pierce or injure with a sharp pointed instrument. **2.** (*tr.*) (of a sharp pointed instrument) to pierce or wound: *the knife stabbed her hand.* **3.** (when *intr.*, often foll. by *at*) to make a thrust; jab: *he stabbed at the doorway.* **4.** (*tr.*) to inflict with a sharp pain. **5. stab in the back. a.** (*vb.*) to do damage to (the reputation, etc., of a person, esp. a friend) in a surreptitious way. **b.** (*n.*) a treacherous action or remark that causes the downfall of or injury to a person. ~*n.* **6.** the act or an instance of stabbing. **7.** an injury or rift made by stabbing. **8.** a sudden sensation, esp. an unpleasant one: *a stab of pity.* **9.** an attempt (esp. in the phrase **make a stab at**). [C14: from *stabbe* stab wound; probably related to Middle English *stob* stick] —ˈ**stab+ber** *n.*

Sta+bat Ma+ter (ˈstɑːbæt ˈmɑːtə) *n.* **1.** *R.C. Church.* a Latin hymn, probably of the 13th century, commemorating the sorrows of the Virgin Mary at the crucifixion and used in the Mass and various other services. **2.** a musical setting of this hymn. [from the opening words, literally: the mother was standing]

sta+bile (ˈsteɪbaɪl) *n.* **1.** *Arts.* a stationary abstract construction, usually of wire, metal, wood, etc. Compare **mobile** (sense 6a.). ~*adj.* **2.** fixed; stable. **3.** resistant to chemical change. [C18: from Latin *stabilis*]

sta+bil+i·ty (stəˈbɪlɪtɪ) *n., pl.* **·ties. 1.** the quality of being stable. **2.** the ability of an aircraft to resume its original flight path after inadvertent displacement. **3.** *Meteorol.* **a.** the condition of an air mass characterized by no upward movement. **b.** the degree of susceptibility of an air mass to disturbance by convection currents. **4.** a vow taken by every Benedictine monk attaching him perpetually to the monastery where he is professed.

sta+bi+lize *or* **sta+bi+lise** (ˈsteɪbɪˌlaɪz) *vb.* **1.** to make or become stable or more stable. **2.** to keep or be kept stable. **3.** (*tr.*) to put or keep (an aircraft, vessel, etc.) in equilibrium by one or more special devices, or (of an aircraft, etc.) to become stable. —ˌ**sta+bi+li+ˈza+tion** *or* ˌ**sta+bi+li+ˈsa+tion** *n.*

sta+bi+li+zer *or* **sta+bi+li+ser** (ˈsteɪbɪˌlaɪzə) *n.* **1.** any device for stabilizing an aircraft. See also **horizontal stabilizer, vertical stabilizer. 2.** a substance added to something to maintain it in a stable or unchanging state. **3.** *Nautical.* **a.** a system of one or more pairs of fins projecting from the hull of a ship and controllable to counteract roll. **b.** See **gyrostabilizer. 4.** a person or thing that stabilizes.

stab kick *n. Australian Rules football.* a rapid kick of the ball from one player to another member of his team. Also called: **stab pass.**

sta+ble[1] (ˈsteɪbᵊl) *n.* **1.** a building, usually consisting of stalls, for the lodging of horses or other livestock. **2.** the animals lodged in such a building, collectively. **3. a.** the racehorses belonging to a particular establishment or owner. **b.** the establishment itself. **c.** (*as modifier*): *stable companion.* **4.** *Informal.* a source of training, such as a school, theatre, etc.: *the two athletes were out of the same stable.* **5.** a number of people considered as a source of a particular talent: *a stable of writers.* **6.** (*modifier*) of, relating to, or suitable for a stable: *stable manners.* ~*vb.* **7.** to put, keep, or be kept in a stable. [C13: from Old French *estable* cowshed, from Latin *stabulum* shed, from *stāre* to stand]

sta+ble[2] (ˈsteɪbᵊl) *adj.* **1.** steady in position or balance; firm. **2.** lasting or permanent: *a stable relationship.* **3.** steadfast or firm of purpose. **4.** (of an elementary particle, atomic nucleus, etc.) not undergoing decay; not radioactive: *a stable nuclide.* **5.** (of a chemical compound) not readily partaking in a chemical change. [C13: from Old French *estable,* from Latin *stabilis* steady, from *stāre* to stand] —ˈ**sta+ble+ness** *n.* —ˈ**sta+bly** *adv.*

sta·ble+boy (ˈsteɪbᵊlˌbɔɪ) *or* **sta·ble+man** (ˈsteɪbᵊlˌmæn, -mən) *n., pl.* **+boys** *or* **+men.** a boy or man who works in a stable.

sta+ble door *n.* a door with an upper and lower leaf that may be opened separately. U.S. equivalent: **Dutch door.**

sta+ble fly *n.* a blood-sucking muscid fly, *Stomoxys calcitrans,* that attacks man and domestic animals.

sta+bling (ˈsteɪblɪŋ) *n.* stable buildings or accommodation.

stab+lish (ˈstæblɪʃ) *vb.* an archaic variant of **establish.**

Sta+broek (*Dutch* ˈstaːˌbruːk) *n.* the former name (until 1812) of **Georgetown.**

stacc. *Music. abbrev. for* staccato.

stac+ca+to (stəˈkɑːtəʊ) *adj.* **1.** *Music.* (of notes) short, clipped, and separate. **2.** characterized by short abrupt sounds, as in speech: *a staccato command.* ~*adv.* **3.** (esp. used as a musical direction) in a staccato manner. [C18: from Italian, from *staccare* to detach, shortened from *distaccare*]

stack (stæk) *n.* **1.** an ordered pile or heap. **2.** a large orderly pile of hay, straw, etc., for storage in the open air. **3.** (*often pl.*) *Library science.* compactly spaced bookshelves, used to house collections of books in an area usually prohibited to library users. **4.** a number of aircraft circling an airport at different altitudes, awaiting their signal to land. **5.** a large amount: *a stack of work.* **6.** *Military.* a pile of rifles or muskets in the shape of a cone. **7.** *Brit.* a measure of coal or wood equal to 108 cubic feet. **8.** See **chimney stack, smokestack. 9.** a vertical pipe, such as the funnel of a ship or the soil pipe attached to the side of a building. **10.** a high column of rock, esp. one isolated from the mainland by the erosive action of the sea. **11.** an area in a computer memory for temporary storage. ~*vb.* (*tr.*) **12.** to place in a stack; pile: *to stack bricks on a lorry.* **13.** to load or fill up with piles of something: *to stack a lorry with bricks.* **14.** to control a number of aircraft waiting to land at an airport so that each flies at a different altitude. **15. stack the cards.** to prearrange the order of a pack of cards secretly so that the deal will benefit someone. [C13: from Old Norse *stakkr* haystack, of Germanic origin; related to Russian *stog*] —ˈ**stack+er** *n.*

stack a·gainst *vb.* (*tr., prep.*) to ensure a prearranged advantage or disadvantage: *the odds are stacked against us.*

stacked (stækt) *adj. Informal.* a variant of **well-stacked.**

stac+te (ˈstæktiː) *n. Old Testament.* one of several sweet-smelling spices used in incense (Exodus 30:34). [C14: via Latin from Greek *staktē* oil of myrrh, from *staktos* distilling a drop at a time, from *stazein* to flow, drip]

stad+dle (ˈstædᵊl) *n.* **1.** a support or prop, esp. a low flat-topped stone structure for supporting hay or corn stacks about two feet above ground level. **2.** a supporting frame for such a stack. **3.** the lower part of a hay or corn stack. [Old English *stathol* base; related to Old Norse *stothull* cow pen, Old High German *stadal* barn]

stad·dle+stone (ˈstædᵊlˌstəʊn) *n.* (formerly) one of several supports for a hayrick, consisting of a truncated conical stone surmounted by a flat circular stone.

stad+hold+er *or* **stadt+hold+er** (ˈstædˌhəʊldə) *n.* **1.** the chief magistrate of the former Dutch republic or of any of its provinces (from about 1580 to 1802). **2.** a viceroy or governor of a province. [C16: partial translation of Dutch *stad houder,* from *stad* city (see STEAD) + *houder* holder] —ˈ**stad+ˌhold+er+ˌate,** ˈ**stad+ˌhold+er+ˌship** *or* ˈ**stadt+ˌhold+er+ˌate,** ˈ**stadt+ˌhold+er+ˌship** *n.*

sta+di·a[1] (ˈsteɪdɪə) *n.* **1. a.** tacheometry that makes use of a telescopic surveying instrument and a graduated staff calibrated to correspond with the distance from the observer. **b.** (*as modifier*): *stadia surveying.* **2.** the two parallel crosshairs or **stadia hairs** in the eyepiece of the instrument used. **3.** the staff used. [C19: probably from STADIA[2]]

sta+di·a[2] (ˈsteɪdɪə) *n.* the plural of **stadium.**

sta+di+om+e·ter (ˌsteɪdɪˈɒmɪtə) *n.* an instrument that measures the length of curves, dashes, etc., by running a toothed wheel along them. [C19: from *stadio-,* from STADIUM + -METER]

sta+di·um (ˈsteɪdɪəm) *n., pl.* **+di·ums** *or* **+di·a** (-dɪə). **1.** a sports arena with tiered seats for spectators. **2.** (in ancient Greece) a course for races, usually located between two hills providing natural slopes for tiers of seats. **3.** an ancient Greek measure of length equivalent to about 607 feet or 184 metres. **4.** (in many arthropods) the interval between two consecutive moultings. **5.** a particular period or stage in the development of a disease. [C16: via Latin from Greek *stadion,* changed from *spadion* a racecourse, from *spān* to pull; also influenced by Greek *stadios* steady]

Staël (*French* stal) *n.* **Ma·dame de.** full name *Baronne Anne Louise Germaine* (née *Necker*) *de Staël-Holstein.* 1766–1817, French writer and salonist, whose works, esp. *De l'Allemagne* (1810), anticipated French romanticism.

staff[1] (stɑːf) *n., pl.* **staffs** *for senses 1–3;* **staffs** *or* **staves** (steɪvz) *for senses 4–9.* **1. a.** a group of people employed by a company, individual, etc., for executive, clerical, sales work, etc. **b.** (*as modifier*): *a staff doctor.* **2.** the body of teachers or lecturers of an educational institution, as distinct from the students. **3.** the officers appointed to assist a commander, service, or central headquarters organization in establishing policy, plans, etc. **4.** a stick with some special use, such as a walking stick or an emblem of authority. **5.** something that sustains or supports: *bread is the staff of life.* **6.** a pole on which a flag is hung. **7.** a pole used as a handle. **8.** *Chiefly Brit.* a graduated rod used in surveying, esp. for sighting to with a levelling instrument. Usual U.S. name: **rod. 9.** Also called: **stave.** *Music.* **a.** the system of horizontal lines grouped into sets of five (four in the case of plainsong) upon which music is written. The spaces between them are also used, being employed in conjunction with a clef in order to give a graphic indication of pitch. **b.** any set of five lines in this system together with its clef: *the treble staff.* ~*vb.* **10.** (*tr.*) to employ or provide with a staff. [Old English *stæf;* related to Old Frisian *stef,* Old Saxon *staf,* German *Stab,* Old Norse *stafr,* Gothic *Stafs;* see STAVE]

staff² (stɑːf) *n. U.S.* a mixture of plaster and hair used to cover the external surface of temporary structures and for decoration. [C19: of unknown origin]

Staf·fa ('stæfə) *n.* an island in W Scotland, in the Inner Hebrides west of Mull: site of Fingal's Cave.

staff col·lege *n.* a training centre for executive military personnel.

staff·er ('stɑːfə) *n. Informal.* a member of staff, esp., in journalism, of editorial staff.

staff·man ('stɑːf,mæn) *n., pl.* **·men.** *Brit.* a person who holds the levelling staff when a survey is being made.

staff nurse *n.* a qualified nurse ranking immediately below a sister.

staff of Aes·cu·la·pi·us *n.* an emblem consisting of a staff with a serpent entwined around it, used by the Royal Medical Corps, the Royal Canadian Medical Corps, and the American Medical Association. Compare **caduceus** (sense 2).

staff of·fic·er *n.* a commissioned officer serving on the staff of a commander, service, or central headquarters.

Staf·ford¹ ('stæfəd) *n.* a market town in central England, administrative centre of Staffordshire. Pop.: 54 890 (1971).

Staf·ford² ('stæfəd) *n.* Sir **Ed·ward Wil·liam.** 1819–1901, New Zealand statesman, born in Scotland: prime minister of New Zealand (1856–61; 1865–69; 1872).

Staf·ford·shire ('stæfəd,ʃɪə, -ʃə) *n.* a county of central England: coalfields lie in the east and south and the Pennine uplands in the north; important in the history of industry, coal and iron having been worked at least since the 13th century. Administrative centre: Stafford. Pop.: 997 600 (1976 est.). Area: 2245 sq. km (1049 sq. miles).

Staf·ford·shire ter·ri·er *or* **bull ter·ri·er** *n.* a breed of smooth-coated terrier with a stocky frame and generally a pied or brindled coat.

Staffs. (stæfs) *abbrev. for* Staffordshire.

staff ser·geant *n. Military.* **1.** *Brit.* a noncommissioned officer holding sergeant's rank and carrying out certain special duties. **2.** *U.S.* a noncommissioned officer who ranks: **a.** (in the Army) above sergeant and below sergeant first class. **b.** (in the Air Force) above airman first class and below technical sergeant. **c.** (in the Marine Corps) above sergeant and below gunnery sergeant.

stag (stæg) *n.* **1.** the adult male of a deer, esp. a red deer. **2.** a man unaccompanied by a woman at a social gathering. **3.** *Stock exchange, Brit.* **a.** a speculator who buys heavily on a new share issue in anticipation of a rise in its price when trading commences and thus an opportunity for quick profit on resale. **b.** (*as modifier*): *stag operations.* **4.** (*modifier*) (of a social gathering) attended by men only. **5.** (*modifier*) pornographic in content: *a stag show.* ~*adv.* **6.** without a female escort. [Old English *stagga* (unattested); related to Old Norse *steggr* male bird]

stag bee·tle *n.* any lamellicorn beetle of the family *Lucanidae,* the males of which have large branched mandibles.

stage (steɪdʒ) *n.* **1.** a distinct step or period of development, growth, or progress: *a child at the toddling stage.* **2.** a raised area or platform. **3.** the platform in a theatre where actors perform. **4. the.** the theatre as a profession. **5.** any scene regarded as a setting for an event or action. **6.** a portion of a journey or a stopping-place after such a portion. **7.** short for **stagecoach.** **8.** *Brit.* a division of a bus route for which there is a fixed fare. **9.** one of the separate propulsion units of a rocket that can be jettisoned when it has burnt out. See also **multistage** (sense 1). **10.** any of the various distinct periods of growth or development in the life of an organism, esp. an insect: *a larval stage; pupal stage.* **11.** the organism itself at such a period of growth. **12.** a small stratigraphical unit; a subdivision of a rock series or system. **13.** the platform on a microscope on which the specimen is mounted for examination. **14.** *Electronics.* a part of a complex circuit, esp. one of a number of transistors with the associated elements required to amplify a signal in an amplifier. **15. by** *or* **in easy stages.** not hurriedly: *he learnt French by easy stages.* ~*vb.* **16.** (*tr.*) to perform (a play), esp. on a stage: *we are going to stage "Hamlet".* **17.** (*tr.*) to set the action of a play in a particular time or place. **18.** (*tr.*) to plan, organize, and carry out (an event). **19.** (*intr.*) *Obsolete.* to travel by stagecoach. [C13: from Old French *estage* position, from Vulgar Latin *staticum* (unattested), from Latin *stāre* to stand]

stage·coach ('steɪdʒ,kəʊtʃ) *n.* a large four-wheeled horse-drawn vehicle formerly used to carry passengers, mail, etc., on a regular route between towns and cities.

stage·craft ('steɪdʒ,krɑːft) *n.* skill in or the art of writing or staging plays.

stage di·rec·tion *n. Theatre.* an instruction to an actor or director, written into the script of a play.

stage door *n.* a door at a theatre leading backstage.

stage ef·fect *n.* a special effect created on the stage by lighting, sound, etc.

stage fright *n.* nervousness or panic that may beset a person about to appear in front of an audience.

stage·hand ('steɪdʒ,hænd) *n.* a person who sets the stage, moves props, etc., in a theatrical production.

stage left *n.* the part of the stage to the left of a performer facing the audience.

stage-man·age *vb.* **1.** to work as stage manager for (a play, etc.). **2.** (*tr.*) to arrange, present, or supervise from behind the scenes: *to stage-manage a campaign.*

stage man·ag·er *n.* a person who supervises the stage arrangements of a theatrical production.

stag·er ('steɪdʒə) *n.* **1.** a person of experience; veteran (esp. in the phrase **old stager**). **2.** an archaic word for **actor.**

stage right *n.* the part of the stage to the right of a performer facing the audience.

stage-struck *adj.* infatuated with the glamour of theatrical life, esp. with the desire to act.

stage whis·per *n.* **1.** a loud whisper from one actor to another onstage intended to be heard by the audience. **2.** any loud whisper that is intended to be overheard.

stag·ey ('steɪdʒɪ) *adj.* **stag·i·er, stag·i·est.** a variant spelling (in the U.S.) of **stagy.** —'**stag·i·ly** *adv.* —'**stag·i·ness** *n.*

stag·fla·tion (stæg'fleɪʃən) *n.* an inflationary economic situation characterized by a decline in industrial output. [C20: blend of STAGNATION + INFLATION]

stag·gard ('stægəd) *n.* a male red deer in the fourth year of life. [C15: see STAG, -ARD]

stag·ger ('stægə) *vb.* **1.** (*usually intr.*) to walk or cause to walk unsteadily as if about to fall. **2.** (*tr.*) to astound or overwhelm, as with shock: *I am staggered by his ruthlessness.* **3.** (*tr.*) to place or arrange in alternating or overlapping positions or time periods to prevent confusion or congestion: *a staggered junction; to stagger holidays.* **4.** (*intr.*) to falter or hesitate: *his courage staggered in the face of the battle.* **5.** (*tr.*) to set (the wings of a biplane) so that the leading edge of one extends beyond that of the other. ~*n.* **6.** the act or an instance of staggering. **7.** a staggered arrangement on a biplane, etc. [C13 dialect *stacker,* from Old Norse *staka* to push] —'**stag·ger·er** *n.* —'**stag·ger·ing** *adj.* —'**stag·ger·ing·ly** *adv.*

stag·ger·bush ('stægə,bʊʃ) *n.* an ericaceous deciduous shrub, *Lyonia mariana,* of E North America, having white or pinkish flowers: it is poisonous to livestock.

stag·gers ('stægəz) *n.* **1.** a form of vertigo associated with decompression sickness. **2.** Also called: **blind staggers.** a disease of horses and some other domestic animals characterized by a swaying unsteady gait, caused by infection or lesions of the central nervous system.

stag·hound ('stæg,haʊnd) *n.* a breed of hound similar in appearance to the foxhound but larger.

stag·ing ('steɪdʒɪŋ) *n.* any temporary structure used in the process of building, esp. the horizontal platforms supported by scaffolding.

stag·ing ar·e·a *n.* a general locality used as a checkpoint or regrouping area for military formations in transit.

Sta·gi·ra (stə'dʒaɪrə) *n.* an ancient city on the coast of Chalcidice in Macedonia: the birthplace of Aristotle.

Sta·gi·rite ('stædʒɪ,raɪt) *n.* **1.** an inhabitant or native of Stagira. **2.** an epithet of Aristotle.

stag·nant ('stægnənt) *adj.* **1.** (of water, etc.) standing still; without flow or current. **2.** brackish and foul from standing still. **3.** stale, sluggish, or dull from inaction. **4.** not growing or developing; static. [C17: from Latin *stagnāns,* from *stagnāre* to be stagnant, from *stagnum* a pool] —'**stag·nan·cy** *or* '**stag·nance** *n.* —'**stag·nant·ly** *adv.*

stag·nate ('stægneɪt, stæg'neɪt) *vb.* (*intr.*) to be or become stagnant.

stag par·ty *n.* a party for men only, esp. one held for a bachelor before he is married. Compare **hen party.**

stag·y *or U.S.* **stag·ey** ('steɪdʒɪ) *adj.* **stag·i·er, stag·i·est.** theatrical or dramatic. —'**stag·i·ly** *adv.* —'**stag·i·ness** *n.*

staid (steɪd) *adj.* **1.** of a settled, sedate, and steady character. **2.** *Now rare.* permanent. [C16: obsolete past participle of STAY¹] —'**staid·ly** *adv.* —'**staid·ness** *n.*

stain (steɪn) *vb.* (*mainly tr.*) **1.** to mark or discolour with patches of something that dirties: *the dress was stained with coffee.* **2.** to dye with a penetrating dyestuff or pigment. **3.** to bring disgrace or shame on: *to stain someone's honour.* **4.** to colour (specimens) for microscopic study by treatment with a dye or similar reagent. **5.** (*intr.*) to produce indelible marks or discoloration: *does ink stain?* ~*n.* **6.** a spot, mark, or discoloration. **7.** a moral taint; blemish or slur. **8.** a dye or similar reagent, used to colour specimens for microscopic study. **9.** a solution or liquid used to penetrate the surface of a material, esp. wood, and impart a rich colour without covering up the surface or grain. **10.** any dye that is made into a solution and used to colour textiles and hides. [C14 *steynen* (vb.), shortened from *disteynen* to remove colour from, from Old French *desteindre* to discolour, from *des-* DIS-¹ + *teindre,* from Latin *tingere* to TINGE] —'**stain·a·ble** *adj.* —,**stain·a·'bil·i·ty** *n.* —'**stain·er** *n.*

stained glass *n.* **a.** glass that has been coloured in any of various ways, as by fusing with a film of metallic oxide or burning pigment into the surface, used esp. for church windows. **b.** (*as modifier*): *a stained-glass window.*

Staines (steɪnz) *n.* a town in SE England, in N Surrey on the River Thames. Pop.: 56 386 (1971).

stain·less ('steɪnlɪs) *adj.* **1.** resistant to discoloration, esp. discoloration resulting from corrosion; rust-resistant: *stainless steel.* **2.** having no blemish: *a stainless reputation.* ~*n.* **3.** stainless steel. —'**stain·less·ly** *adv.*

stain·less steel *n.* **a.** a type of steel resistant to corrosion as a result of the presence of large amounts of chromium (12–15 per cent). The carbon content depends on the application, being 0.2–0.4 per cent for steel used in cutlery, etc., and about 1 per cent for use in scalpels and razor blades. **b.** (*as modifier*): *stainless-steel cutlery.*

stair (stɛə) *n.* **1.** one of a flight of stairs. **2.** a series of steps: *a narrow stair.* [Old English *stæger;* related to *stīg* narrow path, *stīgan* to ascend, descend, Old Norse *steigurligr* upright, Middle Dutch *steiger* ladder]

stair·case ('stɛə,keɪs) *n.* a flight of stairs, its supporting framework, and, usually, a handrail or banisters.

stair·head ('stɛə,hɛd) *n.* the top of a flight of stairs.

stair rod *n.* any of a series of rods placed in the angles between the steps of a carpeted staircase, used to hold the carpet in position.

stairs (stɛəz) *pl. n.* **1.** a flight of steps leading from one storey or level to another, esp. indoors. **2. below stairs.** *Brit.* in the servants' quarters; in domestic service.

stair·way ('stɛə,weɪ) *n.* a means of access consisting of stairs; staircase or flight of steps.

stair·well ('stɛə,wɛl) *n.* a vertical shaft or opening that contains a staircase.

stake[1] (steɪk) *n.* **1.** a stick or metal bar driven into the ground as a marker, part of a fence, support for a plant, etc. **2.** one of a number of vertical posts that fit into sockets around a flat truck or railway wagon to hold the load in place. **3.** a method or the practice of executing a person by binding him to a stake in the centre of a pile of wood that is then set on fire. **4.** *Mormon Church.* an administrative district consisting of a group of wards under the jurisdiction of a president. **5. pull up stakes.** to leave one's home or temporary resting-place and move on. ~*vb.* (*tr.*) **6.** to tie, fasten, or tether with or to a stake. **7.** (often foll. by *out* or *off*) to fence or surround with stakes. **8.** (often foll. by *out*) to lay (a claim) to land, rights, etc. **9.** to support with a stake. [Old English *staca* pin; related to Old Frisian *staka,* Old High German *stehho,* Old Norse *stjaki;* see STICK]

stake[2] (steɪk) *n.* **1.** the money or valuables that a player must hazard in order to buy into a gambling game or make a bet. **2.** an interest, often financial, held in something: *a stake in the company's future.* **3.** (*often pl.*) the money that a player has available for gambling. **4.** (*often pl.*) a prize in a race, etc., esp. one made up of contributions from contestants or owners. **5.** (*pl.*) *Horse racing.* a race in which all owners of competing horses contribute to the prize money. **6.** *U.S. informal.* short for **grubstake** (sense 1). **7. at stake.** at risk: *two lives are at stake.* ~*vb.* (*tr.*) **8.** to hazard (money, etc.) on a result. **9.** to invest in or support by supplying with money, etc.: *to stake a business enterprise.* [C16: of uncertain origin]

Staked Plain *n.* another name for the **Llano Estacado.**

stake·out ('steɪkaʊt) *Slang, U.S.* ~*n.* **1.** a police surveillance of an area, house, or criminal suspect. **2.** an area or house kept under such surveillance. ~*vb.* **stake out. 3.** (*tr., adv.*) to keep under surveillance.

Sta·kha·nov·ism (stæ'kænə,vɪzəm) *n.* (in the Soviet Union) a system designed to raise production by offering incentives to efficient workers. [C20: named after A. G. *Stakhanov* (1906–77), Soviet coal miner, the worker first awarded benefits under the system in 1935] —**Sta·'kha·nov·,ite** *n.*

stal·ac·tite ('stælək,taɪt) *n.* a cylindrical mass of calcium carbonate hanging from the roof of a limestone cave: formed by precipitation from continually dripping water. Compare **stalagmite.** [C17: from New Latin *stalactites,* from Greek *stalaktos* dripping, from *stalassein* to drip] —**sta·lac·ti·form** (stə'læktɪ,fɔ:m) *adj.* —**stal·ac·tit·ic** (,stælək'tɪtɪk) *or* **,stal·ac·'tit·i·cal** *adj.*

sta·lag ('stælæg; *German* 'ʃtalak) *n.* a German prisoner-of-war camp in World War II, esp. for enlisted men or other ranks. [short for *Stammlager* base camp, from *Stamm* base (related to STEM[1]) + *Lager* camp]

stal·ag·mite ('stæləg,maɪt) *n.* a cylindrical mass of calcium carbonate projecting upwards from the floor of a limestone cave: formed by precipitation from continually dripping water. Compare **stalactite.** [C17: from New Latin *stalagmites,* from Greek *stalagmos* dripping; related to Greek *stalassein* to drip; compare STALACTITE] —**stal·ag·mit·ic** (,stæləg'mɪtɪk) *or* **,stal·ag·'mit·i·cal** *adj.*

stale[1] (steɪl) *adj.* **1.** (esp. of food) hard, musty, or dry from being kept too long. **2.** (of beer, etc.) flat and tasteless from being kept open too long. **3.** (of air) stagnant; foul. **4.** uninteresting from overuse; hackneyed: *stale clichés.* **5.** no longer new: *stale news.* **6.** lacking in energy or ideas through overwork or lack of variety. **7.** *Law.* (of a claim, etc.) having lost its effectiveness or force, as by failure to act or by the lapse of time. ~*vb.* **8.** to make or become stale. [C13 (originally applied to liquor in the sense: well matured): probably via Norman French from Old French *estale* (unattested) motionless, of Frankish origin; related to STALL[1], INSTALL] —**'stale·ly** *adv.* —**'stale·ness** *n.*

stale[2] (steɪl) *vb.* **1.** (*intr.*) (of livestock) to urinate. ~*n.* **2.** the urine of horses or cattle. [C15: perhaps from Old French *estaler* to stand in one position; see STALL[1]; compare Middle Low German *stallen* to urinate, Greek *stalassein* to drip]

stale·mate ('steɪl,meɪt) *n.* **1.** a chess position in which any of a player's possible moves would place his king in check: in this position the game ends in a draw. **2.** a situation in which two opposing forces find that further action is impossible or futile; deadlock. ~*vb.* **3.** (*tr.*) to subject to a stalemate. [C18: from obsolete *stale,* from Old French *estal* STALL[1] + MATE[2]]

Sta·lin[1] ('stɑ:lɪn) *n.* **1.** Also: **Stalino.** a former name of **Donetsk. 2.** the former name (1950–61) of **Braşov. 3.** the former name (1949–56) of **Varna.**

Sta·lin[2] ('stɑ:lɪn) *n.* **Jo·seph.** original name *Iosif Vissarionovich Dzhugashvili.* 1879–1953, Soviet leader; general secretary of the Communist Party of the Soviet Union (1922–53). He succeeded Lenin as head of the party and created a totalitarian state, crushing all opposition, esp. in the great purges of 1934–37. He instigated rapid industrialization and the collectivization of agriculture and established the Soviet Union as a world power.

Sta·li·na·bad (*Russian* stəlina'bat) *n.* the former name (1929–61) of **Dushanbe.**

Sta·lin·grad ('stɑ:lɪn,græd; *Russian* stəlin'grat) *n.* the former name (1925–61) of **Volgograd.**

Sta·lin·ism ('stɑ:lɪ,nɪzəm) *n.* the theory and form of government associated with Stalin: a variant of Marxism-Leninism characterized by totalitarianism, rigid bureaucracy, and loyalty to the Soviet state. —**'Sta·lin·ist** *n., adj.*

Sta·li·no·grod (*Polish* stali'nɔgrɔt) *n.* the former name (1953–56) for **Katowice.**

Sta·lin Peak *n.* a former name for **Kommunizma Peak.**

Sta·linsk (*Russian* 'stalinsk) *n.* the former name (1932–61) of **Novokuznetsk.**

stalk[1] (stɔ:k) *n.* **1.** the main stem of a herbaceous plant. **2.** any of various subsidiary plant stems, such as a leafstalk (petiole) or flower stalk (peduncle). **3.** a slender supporting structure in animals such as crinoids and certain protozoans, coelenterates, and barnacles. **4.** any long slender supporting shaft or column. [C14: probably a diminutive formed from Old English *stalu* upright piece of wood; related to Old Frisian *staal* handle] —**stalked** *adj.* —**'stalk·,less** *adj.* —**'stalk·,like** *adj.*

stalk[2] (stɔ:k) *vb.* **1.** to follow or approach (game, prey, etc.) stealthily and quietly. **2.** to spread over (a place) in a menacing or grim manner: *fever stalked the camp.* **3.** (*intr.*) to walk in a haughty, stiff, or threatening way: *he stalked out in disgust.* **4.** to search or draw (a piece of land) for prey. ~*n.* **5.** the act of stalking. **6.** a stiff or threatening stride. [Old English *bestealcian* to walk stealthily; related to Middle Low German *stolkeren,* Danish *stalke*] —**'stalk·er** *n.*

stalk·ing-horse *n.* **1.** a horse or an imitation one used by a hunter to hide behind while stalking his quarry. **2.** something serving as a means of concealing plans; pretext. **3.** *Chiefly U.S.* a candidate put forward by one group to divide the opposition or mask the candidacy of another person for whom the stalking-horse would then withdraw.

stalk·y ('stɔ:kɪ) *adj.* **stalk·i·er, stalk·i·est. 1.** like a stalk; slender and tall. **2.** having or abounding in stalks. —**'stalk·i·ly** *adv.* —**'stalk·i·ness** *n.*

stall[1] (stɔ:l) *n.* **1. a.** a compartment in a stable or shed for confining or feeding a single animal. **b.** another name for **stable. 2.** a small often temporary stand or booth for the display and sale of goods. **3.** (in a church) **a.** one of a row of seats, usually divided from the others by armrests or a small screen, for the use of the choir or clergy. **b.** a pen. **4.** an instance of an engine stalling. **5.** a condition of an aircraft in flight in which a reduction in speed or an increase in the aircraft's angle of attack causes a sudden loss of lift resulting in a downward plunge. **6.** any small room or compartment. **7.** *Brit.* **a.** a seat in a theatre that resembles a chair, usually fixed to the floor. **b.** (*pl.*) the area of seats on the ground floor of a theatre nearest to the orchestra pit. **8.** a tubelike covering for a finger, as in a glove. ~*vb.* **9.** to cause (a motor vehicle or its engine) to stop, usually by incorrect use of the clutch or incorrect adjustment of the fuel mixture, or (of an engine or motor vehicle) to stop, usually for these reasons. **10.** to cause (an aircraft) to go into a stall or (of an aircraft) to go into a stall. **11.** to stick or cause to stick fast, as in mud or snow. **12.** (*tr.*) to confine (an animal) in a stall. [Old English *steall* a place for standing; related to Old High German *stall,* and *stellen* to set]

stall[2] (stɔ:l) *vb.* **1.** to employ delaying tactics towards (someone); be evasive. **2.** (*intr.*) *Sport, chiefly U.S.* to play or fight below one's best in order to deceive. ~*n.* **3.** an evasive move; pretext. [C16: from Anglo-French *estale* bird used as a decoy, influenced by STALL[1]]

stall-feed *vb.* **-feeds, -feed·ing, -fed.** (*tr.*) to keep and feed (an animal) in a stall, esp. as an intensive method of fattening it for slaughter.

stall·ing an·gle *n.* the angle between the chord line of an aerofoil and the undisturbed relative airflow at which stalling occurs. Also called: **stall angle, critical angle.**

stal·lion ('stæljən) *n.* an uncastrated male horse, esp. one used for breeding. [C14: *staloun,* from Old French *estalon,* of Germanic origin; related to Old High German *stal* STALL[1]]

stal·wart ('stɔ:lwət) *adj.* **1.** strong and sturdy; robust. **2.** solid, dependable, and courageous: *stalwart citizens.* **3.** resolute and firm. ~*n.* **4.** a stalwart person, esp. a supporter. [Old English *stælwirthe* serviceable, from *stæl,* shortened from *stathol* support + *wierthe* WORTH] —**'stal·wart·ly** *adv.* —**'stal·wart·ness** *n.*

Stam·bul *or* **Stam·boul** (stæm'bu:l) *n.* the old part of Istanbul, Turkey, south of the Golden Horn: the site of ancient Byzantium; sometimes used as a name for the whole city.

sta·men ('steɪmɛn) *n., pl.* **sta·mens** *or* **stam·i·na** ('stæmɪnə). the male reproductive organ of a flower, consisting of a stalk (filament) bearing an anther in which pollen is produced. [C17: from Latin: the warp in an upright loom, from *stāre* to stand] —**stam·i·nif·er·ous** (,stæmɪ'nɪfərəs) *adj.* —**stam·i·nal** ('stæmɪnəl) *adj.*

Stam·ford ('stæmfəd) *n.* a city in SW Connecticut, on Long Island Sound: major chemical research laboratories. Pop.: 104 651 (1973 est.).

Stam·ford Bridge *n.* a village in N England, east of York: site of a battle (1066) in which King Harold of England defeated his brother Tostig and King Harald Hardrada of Norway, three weeks before the Battle of Hastings.

stam·i·na[1] ('stæmɪnə) *n.* enduring energy, strength, and resilience. [C19: identical with STAMINA[2], from Latin *stāmen* thread, hence the threads of life spun out by the Fates, hence energy, etc.] —**'stam·i·nal** *adj.*

stam·i·na[2] ('stæmɪnə) *n.* a plural of **stamen.**

stam·i·nate ('stæmɪnɪt, -ˌneɪt) *adj.* (of plants) having stamens, esp. having stamens but no carpels; male.

stam·i·node ('stæmɪˌnəʊd) *or* **stam·i·no·di·um** (ˌstæmɪ'nəʊdɪəm) *n., pl.* **·nodes** *or* **·no·di·a** (-'nəʊdɪə). a vestigial stamen that produces no pollen.

stam·i·no·dy ('stæmɪˌnəʊdɪ) *n.* the development of any of various plant organs, such as petals or sepals, into stamens.

stam·mel ('stæməl) *n.* **1.** a coarse woollen cloth in former use for undergarments, etc., and usually dyed red. **2.** the bright red colour of this cloth. [C16: from Old French *estamin*, from Latin *stāmineus* made of threads, from *stāmen* a thread; see STAMEN]

stam·mer ('stæmə) *vb.* **1.** to speak or say (something) in a hesitant way, esp. as a result of a speech disorder or through fear, stress, etc. ~*n.* **2.** a speech disorder characterized by involuntary repetitions and hesitations. [Old English *stamerian;* related to Old Saxon *stamarōn*, Old High German *stamm*] —**'stam·mer·er** *n.* —**'stam·mer·ing·ly** *adv.*

stamp (stæmp) *vb.* **1.** (when *intr.*, often foll. by *on*) to bring (the foot) down heavily (on the ground, etc.). **2.** (*intr.*) to walk with heavy or noisy footsteps. **3.** (*intr.;* foll. by *on*) to repress, extinguish, or eradicate: *he stamped on any criticism.* **4.** (*tr.*) to impress or mark (a particular device or sign) on (something). **5.** to mark (something) with an official impress, seal, or device: *to stamp a passport.* **6.** (*tr.*) to fix or impress permanently: *the date was stamped on her memory.* **7.** (*tr.*) to affix a postage stamp to. **8.** (*tr.*) to distinguish or reveal: *that behaviour stamps him as a cheat.* **9.** to pound or crush (ores, etc.). ~*n.* **10.** the act or an instance of stamping. **11. a.** See **postage stamp. b.** a mark applied to postage stamps for cancellation purposes. **12.** a similar piece of gummed paper used for commercial or trading purposes. **13.** a block, die, etc., used for imprinting a design or device. **14.** a design, device, or mark that has been stamped. **15.** a characteristic feature or trait; hallmark: *the story had the stamp of authenticity.* **16.** a piece of gummed paper or other mark applied to official documents to indicate payment of a fee, validity, ownership, etc. **17.** *Brit. informal.* a national insurance contribution, formerly recorded by means of a stamp on an official card. **18.** type or class: *we want to employ men of his stamp.* **19.** an instrument or machine for crushing or pounding ores, etc., or the pestle in such a device. [Old English *stampe;* related to Old High German *stampfōn* to stamp, Old Norse *stappa*] —**'stamp·er** *n.*

Stamp Act *n.* a law passed by the British Parliament requiring all publications and legal and commercial documents in the American colonies to bear a tax stamp (1765): a cause of unrest in the colonies.

stamp du·ty *or* **tax** *n.* a tax on legal documents, publications, etc., the payment of which is certified by the attaching or impressing of official stamps.

stam·pede (stæm'piːd) *n.* **1.** an impulsive headlong rush of startled cattle or horses. **2.** headlong rush of a crowd: *a stampede of shoppers.* **3.** any sudden large-scale movement or other action, such as a rush of people to support a candidate. ~*vb.* **4.** to run away or cause to run away in a stampede. [C19: from American Spanish *estampida*, from Spanish: a din, from *estampar* to stamp, of Germanic origin; see STAMP] —**stam'ped·er** *n.*

stamp·ing ground *n.* a habitual or favourite meeting or gathering place.

stamp mill *n. Metallurgy.* a machine for crushing ore.

stamp out *vb.* (*tr., adv.*) **1.** to put out or extinguish by stamping: *to stamp out a fire.* **2.** to crush or suppress by force: *to stamp out a rebellion.*

stance (stæns, stɑːns) *n.* **1.** the manner and position in which a person or animal stands. **2.** *Sport.* the posture assumed when about to play the ball, as in golf, cricket, etc. **3.** general emotional or intellectual attitude: *a leftist stance.* [C16: via French from Italian *stanza* place for standing, from Latin *stāns*, from *stāre* to stand]

stanch (stɑːntʃ) *or* **staunch** (stɔːntʃ) *vb.* **1.** to stem the flow of (a liquid, esp. blood) or (of a liquid) to stop flowing. **2.** to prevent the flow of a liquid, esp. blood, from (a hole, wound, etc.). **3.** an archaic word for **assuage.** ~*n.* **4.** a primitive form of lock in which boats are carried over shallow parts of a river in a rush of water released by the lock. [C14: from Old French *estanchier*, from Vulgar Latin *stanticāre* (unattested) to cause to stand, from Latin *stāre* to stand, halt] —**'stanch·a·ble** *or* **'staunch·a·ble** *adj.* —**'stanch·er** *or* **'staunch·er** *n.*

stan·chion ('stɑːnʃən) *n.* **1.** any vertical pole, beam, rod, etc., used as a support. ~*vb.* **2.** (*tr.*) to provide or support with a stanchion or stanchions. [C15: from Old French *estanchon*, from *estance*, from Vulgar Latin *stantia* (unattested) a standing, from Latin *stāre* to stand]

stand (stænd) *vb.* **stands, stand·ing, stood.** (*mainly intr.*) **1.** (*also tr.*) to be or cause to be in an erect or upright position. **2.** to rise to, assume, or maintain an upright position. **3.** (*copula*) to have a specified height when standing: *to stand six feet.* **4.** to be situated or located: *the house stands in the square.* **5.** to be or exist in a specified state or condition: *to stand in awe of someone.* **6.** to adopt or remain in a resolute position or attitude. **7.** (*may take an infinitive*) to be in a specified position: *I stand to lose money in this venture; he stands high in the president's favour.* **8.** to remain in force or continue in effect: *whatever the difficulties, my orders stand.* **9.** to come to a stop or halt, esp. temporarily. **10.** (of water, etc.) to collect and remain without flowing. **11.** (often foll. by *at*) (of a score, account, etc.) to indicate the specified position of the parties involved: *the score stands at 20 to 1.* **12.** (*also tr.;* when *intr.*, foll. by *for*) tolerate or bear: *I won't stand for your nonsense any longer; I can't stand spiders.* **13.** (*tr.*) to resist; survive: *to stand the test of time.* **14.** (*tr.*) to submit to: *to stand trial.* **15.** (often foll. by *for*) *Chiefly Brit.* to be or become a candidate: *will he stand for Parliament?* **16.** to navigate in a specified direction: *we were standing for Madeira when the storm broke.* **17.** (of a gun dog) to point at game. **18.** to halt, esp. to give action, repel attack, or disrupt an enemy advance when retreating. **19.** (of a male domestic animal, esp. a stallion) to be available as a stud. **20.** (*also tr.*) *Printing.* to keep (type that has been set) or (of such type) to be kept, for possible use in future printings. **21.** (*tr.*) *Informal.* to bear the cost of; pay for: *to stand someone a drink.* **22. stand a chance.** to have a hope or likelihood of winning, succeeding, etc. **23. stand fast.** to maintain one's position firmly. **24. stand one's ground.** to maintain a stance or position in the face of opposition. **25. stand still. a.** to remain motionless. **b.** (foll. by *for*) *U.S.* to tolerate: *I won't stand still for your threats.* ~*n.* **26.** the act or an instance of standing. **27.** an opinion, esp. a resolutely held one: *he took a stand on capital punishment.* **28.** a halt or standstill. **29.** a place where a person or thing stands. **30.** *Austral.* **a.** a position on the floor of a shearing shed allocated to one shearer. **b.** the shearing equipment belonging to such a position. **31.** a structure, usually of wood, on which people can sit or stand. **32.** a frame or rack on which such articles as coats and hats may be hung. **33.** a small table or piece of furniture where articles may be placed or stored: *a music stand.* **34.** a supporting framework, esp. for a tool or instrument. **35.** a stall, booth, or counter from which goods may be sold. **36.** a halt to give action, etc., esp. one taken during a retreat and having some duration or some success. **37.** *Cricket.* an extended period at the wicket by two batsmen. **38.** a growth of plants in a particular area, esp. trees in a forest or a crop in a field. **39.** a stop made by a touring theatrical company, pop group, etc., to give a performance (esp. in the phrase **one-night stand**). **40.** *S. African.* a plot or site earmarked for the erection of a building. **41.** (of a gun dog) the act of pointing at game. ~See also **stand by, stand down, stand for, stand in, standoff, stand on, stand out, stand over, stand pat, stand to, stand up.** [Old English *standan;* related to Old Norse *standa*, Old High German *stantan*, Latin *stāre* to stand; see STEAD] —**'stand·er** *n.*

stand·ard ('stændəd) *n.* **1.** an accepted or approved example of something against which others are judged or measured. **2.** (*often pl.*) a principle of propriety, honesty, and integrity: *she has no standards.* **3.** a level of excellence or quality: *a low standard of living.* **4.** any distinctive flag, device, etc., as of a nation, sovereign, or special cause. **5. a.** any of a variety of naval or military flags. **b.** the colours of a cavalry regiment. **6.** a flag or emblem formerly used to show the central or rallying point of an army in battle. **7.** a large tapering flag ending in two points, originally borne by a sovereign or high-ranking noble. **8.** the commodity or commodities in which is stated the value of a basic monetary unit: *the gold standard.* **9.** an authorized model of a unit of measure or weight. **10.** a unit of board measure equal to 1980 board feet. **11.** (in coinage) the prescribed proportion by weight of precious metal and base metal that each coin must contain. **12.** an upright pole or beam, esp. one used as a support. **13. a.** a piece of furniture consisting of an upright pole or beam on a base or support. **b.** (*as modifier*): *a standard lamp.* **14. a.** a plant, esp. a fruit tree, that is trained so that it has an upright stem free of branches. **b.** (*as modifier*): *a standard cherry.* **15.** the largest petal of a papilionaceous flower, such as a sweetpea. ~*adj.* **16.** of the usual, regularized, medium, or accepted kind: *a standard size.* **17.** of recognized authority, competence, or excellence: *the standard work on Greece.* **18.** denoting or characterized by idiom, vocabulary, etc., that is regarded as correct and acceptable by educated native speakers. Compare **nonstandard, informal. 19.** *Brit.* (formerly) (of eggs) of a size that is smaller than *large* and larger than *medium.* [C12: from Old French *estandart* gathering place, flag to mark such a place, probably of Germanic origin; compare Old High German *stantan* to stand, Old High German *ort* place]

stand·ard-bear·er *n.* **1.** an officer or man who carries a standard. **2.** a leader of a cause or party.

stand·ard-bred *n.* a U.S. breed of trotting and pacing horse, used esp. for harness-racing.

stand·ard can·dle *n.* another name for **candela:** not in scientific usage because of possible confusion with the former **international candle.**

stand·ard cell *n.* a voltaic cell producing a constant and accurately known electromotive force that can be used to calibrate voltage-measuring instruments.

stand·ard cost *n. Accounting.* the predetermined budgeted cost of a regular manufacturing process against which actual costs are compared.

stand·ard de·vi·a·tion *n. Statistics.* a measure of dispersion obtained by extracting the square root of the mean of the squared deviations of the observed values from their mean in a frequency distribution.

stand·ard gauge *n.* **1.** a railway track with a distance of 56½ inches between the lines; used on most railways. See also **narrow gauge, broad gauge.** ~*adj.* **stand·ard-gauge** *or* **stand·ard-gauged.** **2.** of, relating to, or denoting a railway with a standard gauge.

stand+ard+ize *or* **stand+ard+ise** ('stændəˌdaɪz) *vb.* **1.** to make or become standard. **2.** (*tr.*) to test by or make a comparison with a standard. —ˌ**stand+ard+i+'za+tion** *or* ˌ**stand+ard+i+'sa+tion** *n.* —'**stand+ard+**ˌ**iz+er** *or* '**stand+ard+**ˌ**is+er** *n.*

stand+ard of liv+ing *n.* a level of subsistence or material welfare of a community, class, or person.

stand+ard time *n.* the official local time of a region or country determined by the distance from Greenwich of a line of longitude passing through the area.

stand by *vb.* **1.** (*intr., adv.*) to be available and ready to act if needed or called upon. **2.** (*intr., adv.*) to be present as an onlooker or without taking any action: *he stood by at the accident.* **3.** (*intr., prep.*) to be faithful to: *to stand by one's principles.* **4.** (*tr., adv.*) *English law.* (of the Crown) to challenge (a juror) without needing to show cause. ~*n.* **stand-by.** **5. a.** a person or thing that is ready for use or can be relied on in an emergency. **b.** (*as modifier*): *stand-by provisions.*

stand down *vb.* (*adv.*) **1.** (*intr.*) to resign or withdraw, esp. in favour of another. **2.** (*intr.*) to leave the witness box in a court of law after giving evidence. **3.** *Chiefly Brit.* to go or be taken off duty.

stand·ee (stæn'diː) *n.* a person who stands, esp. when there are no vacant seats.

stand+fast ('stændˌfɑːst) *n. Rare.* a fixed position.

stand for *vb.* (*intr., prep.*) **1.** to represent or mean. **2.** *Chiefly Brit.* to be or become a candidate for. **3.** to support or recommend. **4.** *Informal.* to tolerate or bear: *he won't stand for any disobedience.*

stand in *vb.* **1.** (*intr., adv.*; usually foll. by *for*) to act as a substitute. **2. stand (someone) in good stead.** to be of benefit or advantage to. ~*n.* **stand-in.** **3. a.** a person or thing that serves as a substitute. **b.** (*as modifier*): *a stand-in teacher.* **4.** a person who substitutes for an actor during intervals of waiting or in dangerous stunts.

stand+ing ('stændɪŋ) *n.* **1.** social or financial position, status, or reputation: *a man of some standing.* **2.** length of existence, experience, etc. **3.** (*modifier*) used to stand in or on: *standing room.* ~*adj.* **4.** *Athletics.* **a.** (of the start of a race) begun from a standing position without the use of starting blocks. **b.** (of a jump, leap, etc.) performed from a stationary position without a run-up. **5.** (*prenominal*) permanent, fixed, or lasting. **6.** (*prenominal*) still or stagnant: *a standing pond.* **7.** *Printing.* (of type) set and stored for future use. Compare **dead** (sense 16).

stand+ing ar·my *n.* a permanent army of paid soldiers maintained by a nation.

stand+ing com+mit+tee *n.* a permanent committee appointed to deal with a specified subject.

stand+ing or+der *n.* **1.** Also called: **banker's order.** an instruction to a bank by a depositor to pay a stated sum at regular intervals. **2.** a rule or order governing the procedure, conduct, etc., of a legislative body. **3.** *Military.* one of a number of orders which have or are likely to have long-term validity.

stand+ing rig+ging *n.* the stays, shrouds, and other more or less fixed, though adjustable, wires and ropes that support the masts of a sailing vessel. Compare **running rigging.**

stand+ing wave *n. Physics.* a wave that has unchanging amplitude at each point along its axis, the amplitude being zero at its nodes and a maximum at its antinodes. It is produced by the interference between a transmitted wave and a reflected wave. Also called: **stationary wave.**

stand+ish ('stændɪʃ) *n.* a stand, usually of metal, for pens, ink bottles, etc. [C15: of unknown origin]

Stan·dish ('stændɪʃ) *n.* **Myles** (or **Miles**). ?1584–1656, English military leader of the Pilgrim Fathers at Plymouth, New England.

stand+off ('stændˌɒf) *n.* **1.** *U.S.* the act or an instance of standing off or apart. **2.** a deadlock or stalemate. **3.** any situation or disposition of forces that counterbalances or neutralizes. **4.** *Rugby.* short for **stand-off half.** ~*vb.* **stand off** (*adv.*). **5.** (*intr.*) to navigate a vessel so as to avoid the shore, an obstruction, etc. **6.** (*tr.*) to keep or cause to keep at a distance. **7.** (*intr.*) to reach a deadlock or stalemate. **8.** (*tr.*) to dismiss (workers), esp. temporarily.

stand-off half *n. Rugby.* **1.** a player who acts as a link between his scrum half and three-quarter backs and who marks the opposing scrum half. **2.** this position in a team. ~Also called: **fly half.**

stand+off·ish (ˌstænd'ɒfɪʃ) *adj.* reserved, haughty, or aloof.

stand oil *n.* a thick drying oil made by heating linseed, tung, or soya to over 300°C: used in oil enamel paints.

stand on *vb.* (*intr.*) **1.** (*adv.*) to continue to navigate a vessel on the same heading. **2.** (*prep.*) to insist on: *to stand on ceremony.* **3. stand on one's own (two) feet.** *Informal.* to be independent or self-reliant.

stand out *vb.* (*intr., adv.*) **1.** to be distinctive or conspicuous. **2.** to refuse to agree, consent, or comply: *they stood out for a better price.* **3.** to protrude or project. **4.** to navigate a vessel away from a port, harbour, anchorage, etc. ~*n.* **stand+out.** **5.** *U.S. informal.* a person or thing that is distinctive or outstanding. **6.** *U.S. informal.* a person who refuses to agree or consent.

stand o·ver *vb.* **1.** (*intr., prep.*) to watch closely; keep tight control over. **2.** (*adv.*) to postpone or be postponed. **3.** (*intr., prep.*) *Austral. informal.* to threaten or intimidate (a person). ~*n.* **standover.** *Austral. informal.* **4. a.** a threatening or intimidating act. **b.** (*as modifier*): *a standover man.*

stand pat *vb.* (*intr.*) **1.** *Poker.* to refuse the right to change any of one's cards; keep one's hand unchanged. **2.** to resist change or remain unchanged. —'**stand+'pat+ter** *n.*

stand+pipe ('stændˌpaɪp) *n.* a vertical pipe, open at the upper end, attached to a pipeline or tank serving to limit the pressure head to that of the height of the pipe.

stand+point ('stændˌpɔɪnt) *n.* a physical or mental position from which things are viewed.

stand+still ('stændˌstɪl) *n.* a complete cessation of movement; stop; halt: *the car came to a standstill.*

stand to *vb.* **1.** (*adv.*) *Military.* to assume positions or cause to assume positions to resist a possible attack. **2. stand to reason.** to conform with the dictates of reason: *it stands to reason that pigs can't fly.*

stand up *vb.* (*adv.*) **1.** (*intr.*) to rise to the feet. **2.** (*intr.*) to resist or withstand wear, criticism, etc. **3.** (*tr.*) *Informal.* to fail to keep an appointment with, esp. intentionally. **4. stand up for. a.** to support, side with, or defend. **b.** *U.S.* to serve as best man for (the groom) at a wedding. **5. stand up to. a.** to confront or resist courageously. **b.** to withstand or endure (wear, criticism, etc.). ~*adj.* **stand-up.** (*prenominal*) **6.** having or being in an erect position: *a stand-up collar.* **7.** done, performed, taken, etc., while standing: *a stand-up meal.* **8.** (of a comedian) performing solo, while standing before an audience. **9.** *Informal.* (of a boxer) having an aggressive style without much leg movement: *a stand-up fighter.*

stane (steɪn) *n.* a Scot. spelling of **stone.**

Stan·ford-Bi·net test ('stænfəd bɪ'neɪ) *n. Psychol.* a revision, esp. for U.S. use, of the Binet-Simon scale designed to measure mental ability by comparing the performance of an individual with the average performance for his age group. See also **Binet-Simon scale, intelligence test.** [C20: named after *Stanford University,* California, and Alfred *Binet* (1857–1911), French psychologist]

stang[1] (stæŋ) *vb. Archaic or dialect.* a past tense of **sting.**

stang[2] (stæŋ) *Northern Brit. dialect.* ~*vb.* **1.** to throb or cause to throb with pain. ~*n.* **2.** a throbbing pain.

stan+hope ('stænəp) *n.* a light one-seater carriage with two or four wheels. [C18: named after Fitzroy *Stanhope* (1787–1864), English clergyman for whom it was first built]

Stan·i·slav·sky *or* **Stan·i·slav·ski** (ˌstænɪ'slævskɪ; *Russian* stəni'slafskij) *n.* **Kon·stan·tin** (kənstan'tin). 1863–1938, Russian actor and director, cofounder of the Moscow Art Theatre (1897). He is famous for his theory of acting, known as the Method, which directs the actor to find the truth within himself about the role he is playing.

stank[1] (stæŋk) *vb.* a past tense of **stink.**

stank[2] (stæŋk) *n.* **1.** a small cofferdam, esp. one of timber made watertight with clay. **2.** *Northern Brit. dialect.* a pond or pool. ~*vb.* **3.** (*tr.*) to make (a stream, cofferdam, etc.) watertight, esp. with clay. [C13: from Old French *estanc,* probably from *estancher* to stanch]

stank[3] (stæŋk) *n. Brit. dialect.* **1.** a drain, as in a roadway. **2.** a draining board adjacent to a sink unit. [special use of STANK[2] (in the sense: pool, pond)]

Stan+ley[1] ('stænlɪ) *n.* **1.** a town in NE England, in N Durham. Pop.: 41 940 (1971). **2. Mount.** a mountain in central Africa, between Uganda and Zaïre: the highest peak of the Rumenzori range. Height: 5109 m (16 763 ft.). Zaïre name: **Ngaliema Mountain.**

Stan·ley[2] ('stænlɪ) *n.* Sir **Hen·ry Mor·ton.** 1841–1904, British explorer and journalist, who led an expedition to Africa in search of Livingstone, whom he found on Nov. 10, 1871. He led three further expeditions in Africa (1874–77; 1879–84; 1887–89) and was instrumental in securing Belgian sovereignty over the Congo Free State.

Stan+ley Falls *pl. n.* the former name of **Boyoma Falls.**

Stan+ley Pool *n.* a lake between Zaïre and the Congo, formed by a widening of the River Congo. Area: 829 sq. km (320 sq. miles). Zaïrese name: **Pool Malebo.**

Stan+ley+ville ('stænlɪˌvɪl) *n.* the former name (until 1966) of **Kisangani.**

stann- *combining form.* denoting tin: *stannite.* [from Late Latin *stannum* tin]

Stan+na+ries ('stænərɪz) *n.* **the.** a tin-mining district of Devon and Cornwall, under the jurisdiction of special courts.

stan+na+ry ('stænərɪ) *n., pl.* **+ries.** a place or region where tin is mined or worked. [C15: from Medieval Latin *stannāria,* from Late Latin: STANNUM, tin]

stan+nic ('stænɪk) *adj.* of or containing tin, esp. in the tetravalent state. [C18: from Late Latin *stannum* tin]

stan+nic sul+phide *n.* an insoluble solid compound of tin usually existing as golden crystals or as a yellowish-brown powder: used as a pigment. Formula: SnS_2. See also **mosaic gold.**

stan+nif+er+ous (stə'nɪfərəs) *adj.* containing tin; tin-bearing.

stan+nite ('stænaɪt) *n.* a grey metallic mineral that consists of a sulphide of tin, copper, and iron and is a source of tin. Formula: Cu_2FeSnS_4. [C19: from STANNUM + -ITE[1]]

stan+nous ('stænəs) *adj.* of or containing tin, esp. in the divalent state.

stan+num ('stænəm) *n.* an obsolete name for **tin** (the metal). [C18: from Late Latin: tin, from Latin: alloy of silver and lead, perhaps of Celtic origin; compare Welsh *ystaen* tin]

Sta+no+voi Range *or* **Sta+no+voy Range** (*Russian* stəna'vɔj) *n.* a mountain range in the SE Soviet Union: forms part of the watershed between rivers flowing to the Arctic and the Pacific. Highest peak: Mount Skalisty, 2482 m (8143 ft.).

Stans (*German* ʃtans) *n.* a town in central Switzerland, capital of Nidwalden demicanton, 11 km (7 miles) southeast of Lucerne: tourist centre. Pop.: 5180 (1970).

stan+za ('stænzə) *n. Prosody.* a fixed number of verse lines arranged in a definite metrical pattern, forming a unit of a poem. [C16: from Italian: halting place, from Vulgar Latin *stantia* (unattested) station, from Latin *stāre* to stand] —**'stan+zaed** *adj.* —**stan+za+ic** (stæn'zeɪɪk) *adj.*

sta+pe·li·a (stə'piːlɪə) *n.* any fleshy cactus-like leafless African plant of the asclepiadaceous genus *Stapelia,* having thick four-angled stems and large typically foetid mottled flowers. [C18: from New Latin, named after J. B. van *Stapel,* (died 1636), Dutch botanist]

sta+pes ('steɪpiːz) *n., pl.* **sta+pes** *or* **sta+pe·des** (stæ'piːdiːz). the stirrup-shaped bone that is the innermost of three small bones in the middle ear of mammals. Nontechnical name: **stirrup bone.** Compare **incus, malleus.** [C17: via New Latin from Medieval Latin, perhaps a variant of *staffa, stapeda* stirrup, influenced in form by Latin *stāre* to stand + *pēs* a foot] —**sta+pe·di·al** (stæ'piːdɪəl) *adj.*

staph·y·lo- *combining form.* **1.** uvula: *staphyloplasty.* **2.** resembling a bunch of grapes: *staphylococcus.* [from Greek *staphulē* bunch of grapes, uvula]

staph·y+lo+coc+cus (ˌstæfɪləʊ'kɒkəs) *n., pl.* **+coc+ci** (-'kɒksaɪ). any spherical Gram-positive bacterium of the genus *Staphylococcus,* typically occurring in clusters and including many pathogenic species, causing boils, infection in wounds, and septicaemia: family *Micrococcaceae.* Often shortened to **staph.** —**staph·y+lo+coc+cal** (ˌstæfɪləʊ'kɒkəl) *or* **staph·y+lo+coc+cic** (ˌstæfɪləʊ'kɒksɪk) *adj.*

staph·y+lo+plas+ty ('stæfɪləʊˌplæstɪ) *n.* plastic surgery or surgical repair involving the soft palate or the uvula. —**ˌstaph·y+lo+'plas+tic** *adj.*

staph·y+lor+rha+phy (ˌstæfɪ'lɒrəfɪ) *n.* repair of a cleft palate by means of staphyloplasty and suturing. —**staph·y+lor+rhaph+ic** (ˌstæfɪlɒ'ræfɪk) *adj.*

sta+ple[1] ('steɪpəl) *n.* **1.** a short length of thin wire bent into a square U-shape, used to fasten papers, cloth, etc. **2.** a short length of stiff wire formed into a U-shape with pointed ends, used for holding a hasp to a post, securing electric cables, etc. ~*vb.* **3.** (*tr.*) to secure (papers, wire, etc.) with a staple or staples. [Old English *stapol* prop, of Germanic origin; related to Middle Dutch *stapel* step, Old High German *staffal*]

sta+ple[2] ('steɪpəl) *adj.* **1.** of prime importance; principal: *staple foods.* **2.** (of a commodity) forming a predominant element in the product, consumption, or trade of a specified nation, region, etc. ~*n.* **3.** a staple commodity. **4.** a main constituent; integral part. **5.** *Chiefly U.S.* a principal raw material produced or grown in a region. **6.** the fibre of wool, cotton, etc., graded as to length and degree of fineness. **7.** (in medieval Europe) a town specially appointed to be the exclusive market for one or more major exports of the land. ~*vb.* **8.** (*tr.*) to arrange or sort (wool, cotton, etc.) according to length and fineness. [C15: from Middle Dutch *stapel* warehouse; see STAPLE[1]] —**'sta+pler** *n.*

sta+pler ('steɪplə) *n.* a machine that inserts staples into sheets of paper, etc., to hold them together.

star (stɑː) *n.* **1.** any of a vast number of celestial objects that are visible in the clear night sky as points of light. **2. a.** a hot gaseous mass, such as the sun, that radiates energy, esp. as heat and light, usually derived from thermonuclear reactions in the interior, and in some cases as radio waves and x-rays. The surface temperature can range from about 1500 to 100 000°C. See also **Hertzsprung-Russell diagram, giant star, white dwarf, neutron star, black hole. b.** (*as modifier*): *a star catalogue.* Related adjs.: **astral, sidereal, stellar. 3.** *Astrology.* **a.** a celestial body, esp. a planet, supposed to influence events, personalities, etc. **b.** (*pl.*) another name for **horoscope** (sense 1). **4.** an emblem shaped like a conventionalized star, usually with five or more points, often used as a symbol of rank, an award, etc. **5.** a small white blaze on the forehead of an animal, esp. a horse. **6.** Also called: **star facet.** any of the eight triangular facets cut in the crown of a brilliant. **7. a.** a distinguished or glamorous celebrity, often from the entertainment world. **b.** (*as modifier*): *star quality.* **8.** another word for **asterisk. 9. see stars.** to see or seem to see bright moving pinpoints of light, as from a blow on the head, increased blood pressure, etc. **10.** *Prison slang.* a convict serving his first prison sentence. ~*vb.* **stars, star+ring, starred. 11.** (*tr.*) to mark or decorate with a star or stars. **12.** to feature or be featured as a star: "*Greed*" *starred Erich von Stroheim; Olivier starred in* "*Hamlet*". [Old English *steorra;* related to Old Frisian *stēra,* Old Norse *stjarna,* German *Stern,* Latin *stella*] —**'star+less** *adj.* —**'star+ˌlike** *adj.*

star-ap·ple *n.* **1.** a West Indian sapotaceous tree, *Chrysophyllum cainito,* with smooth-skinned edible greenish-purple fruit. **2.** the fruit of this tree which, when cut across, reveals a star-shaped arrangement of seeds.

Sta+ra Za+go+ra (*Bulgarian* 'stara za'gɔra) *n.* a city in central Bulgaria: ceded to Bulgaria by Turkey in 1877. Pop.: 121 505 (1974 est.).

star+board ('stɑːbəd, -ˌbɔːd) *n.* **1.** the right side of an aeroplane or vessel when facing the nose or bow. Compare **port**[2]. ~*adj.* **2.** relating to or on the starboard. ~*vb.* **3.** to turn or be turned towards the starboard. [Old English *stēorbord,* literally: steering side, from *stēor* steering paddle + *bord* side; see STEER[1], BOARD; from the fact that boats were formerly steered by a paddle held over the right-hand side]

starch (stɑːtʃ) *n.* **1.** a polysaccharide composed of glucose units that occurs widely in plant tissues in the form of storage granules, consisting of amylose and amylopectin. **2.** Also called: **amylum.** a starch obtained from potatoes and some grain: it is fine white powder that forms a translucent viscous solution on boiling with water and is used to stiffen fabric and in many industrial processes. **3.** any food containing a large amount of starch, such as rice and potatoes. **4.** stiff or pompous formality of manner or conduct. ~*vb.* **5.** (*tr.*) to stiffen with or soak in starch. [Old English *stercan* (unattested except by the past participle *sterced*) to stiffen; related to Old Saxon *sterkian,* Old High German *sterken* to strengthen, Dutch *sterken;* see STARK] —**'starch+er** *n.* —**'starch+ˌlike** *adj.*

Star Cham+ber *n. English history.* the Privy Council sitting as a court of equity, esp. powerful under the Tudor monarchs; abolished 1641.

starch-re·duced *adj.* (of food, esp. bread) having the starch content reduced, as in proprietary slimming products.

starch·y ('stɑːtʃɪ) *adj.* **starch·i·er, starch·i+est. 1.** of, relating to, or containing starch: *starchy foods.* **2.** *Informal.* extremely formal, stiff, or conventional: *a starchy manner.* **3.** stiffened with starch. —**'starch·i·ly** *adv.* —**'starch·i·ness** *n.*

star con+nec+tion *n.* a connection used in a polyphase electrical device or system of devices in which the windings each have one end connected to a common junction, the **star point,** and the other end to a separate terminal. See also **Y connection.** Compare **delta connection.**

star-crossed *adj.* dogged by ill luck; destined to misfortune.

star+dom ('stɑːdəm) *n.* **1.** the fame and prestige of being a star in films, sport, etc. **2.** the world of celebrities.

star+dust ('stɑːˌdʌst) *n.* **1.** a large number of distant stars appearing to the observer as a cloud of dust. **2.** a dreamy romantic or sentimental quality or feeling.

stare (stɛə) *vb.* (*intr.*) **1.** (often foll. by *at*) to look or gaze fixedly, often with hostility or rudeness. **2.** (of an animal's fur, bird's feathers, etc.) to stand on end because of fear, ill health, etc. **3.** to stand out as obvious; glare. **4. stare one in the face.** to be glaringly obvious or imminent. ~*n.* **5.** the act or an instance of staring. [Old English *starian;* related to Old Norse *stara,* Old High German *starēn* to stare, Greek *stereos* stiff, Latin *consternāre* to confuse] —**'star+er** *n.*

stare out *or* **down** *vb.* (*tr., adv.*) to look at (a person or animal) fixedly until his gaze is turned away.

star+fish ('stɑːˌfɪʃ) *n., pl.* **+fish** *or* **+fish·es.** any echinoderm of the class *Asteroidea,* such as *Asterias rubens,* typically having a flattened body covered with a flexible test and five arms radiating from a central disc.

star+flow·er ('stɑːˌflaʊə) *n.* any of several plants with starlike flowers, esp. the star-of-Bethlehem.

star+gaze ('stɑːˌgeɪz) *vb.* (*intr.*) **1.** to observe the stars. **2.** to daydream. —**'star+ˌgaz+er** *n.* —**'star+ˌgaz+ing** *n., adj.*

star grass *n.* any of various temperate and tropical plants of the amaryllidaceous genus *Hypoxis,* having long grasslike leaves and yellow star-shaped flowers.

stark (stɑːk) *adj.* **1.** (*usually prenominal*) devoid of any elaboration; blunt: *the stark facts.* **2.** grim; desolate: *a stark landscape.* **3.** (*usually prenominal*) utter; absolute: *stark folly.* **4.** *Archaic.* severe; violent. **5.** *Archaic or poetic.* rigid, as in death (esp. in the phrases **stiff and stark, stark dead**). **6.** short for **stark-naked.** ~*adv.* **7.** completely: *stark mad.* **8.** *Rare.* starkly. [Old English *stearc* stiff; related to Old Norse *sterkr,* Gothic *gastaurknan* to stiffen] —**'stark+ly** *adv.* —**'stark+ness** *n.*

Stark (stɑːk; *German* ʃtark) *n.* **Jo·han·nes** (jo'hanəs). 1874–1957, German physicist, who discovered the splitting of the lines of a spectrum when the source of light is subjected to a strong electrostatic field (**Stark effect,** 1913): Nobel prize for physics 1919.

stark-na·ked *adj.* completely naked. Informal word (*postpositive*): **stark+ers** ('stɑːkəz). [C13 *stert naket,* literally: tail naked; *stert,* from Old English *steort* tail; related to Old Norse *stertr* tail + NAKED]

star+let ('stɑːlɪt) *n.* **1.** a young and inexperienced actress who is projected as a potential star. **2.** a small star.

star+light ('stɑːˌlaɪt) *n.* **1.** the light emanating from the stars. ~*adj.* also **star+light·ed. 2.** of or like starlight. **3.** Also: **star+lit** ('stɑːlɪt). illuminated by starlight.

star+ling[1] ('stɑːlɪŋ) *n.* any gregarious passerine songbird of the Old World family *Sturnidae,* esp. *Sturnus vulgaris,* which has a blackish plumage and a short tail. [Old English *stærlinc,* from *stær* starling (related to Icelandic *stari*) + *-line* -LING[1]]

star+ling[2] ('stɑːlɪŋ) *n.* an arrangement of piles that surround a pier of a bridge to protect it from debris, etc. [C17: probably changed from *staddling,* from STADDLE]

star-nosed mole *n.* an E North American amphibious mole, *Condylura cristata,* having a ring of pink fleshy tentacles around the nose.

star-of-Beth·le·hem *n.* **1.** Also called: **starflower.** a Eurasian liliaceous plant, *Ornithogalum umbellatum,* naturalized in the eastern U.S., having narrow leaves and starlike white flowers. **2.** any of several similar and related plants.

Star of Beth+le·hem *n.* the star that is supposed to have appeared above Bethlehem at the birth of Christ.

Star of Da·vid *n.* an emblem symbolizing Judaism and consisting of a six-pointed star formed by superimposing one equilateral triangle upon another of equal size.

Starr (stɑː) *n.* **Rin·go** ('rɪŋgəʊ). original name *Richard Starkey.* born 1940, English rock musician: drummer for the Beatles (1962–70).

starred (stɑːd) *adj.* **1. a.** having luck or fortune as specified. **b.** (*in combination*): *ill-starred.*
star+ry (ˈstɑːrɪ) *adj.* **+ri+er, +ri+est. 1.** filled, covered with, or illuminated by stars. **2.** of, like, or relating to a star or stars. —ˈ**star+ri+ly** *adv.* —ˈ**star+ri+ness** *n.*
star·ry-eyed *adj.* given to naive wishes, judgments, etc.; full of unsophisticated optimism; gullible.
Stars and Bars *n.* the flag of the Confederate States of America.
Stars and Stripes *n.* **the.** the national flag of the United States of America, consisting of 50 white stars representing the present states on a blue field and seven red and six white horizontal stripes representing the original states. Also called: the **Star-Spangled Banner.**
star sap+phire *n.* a sapphire showing a starlike figure in reflected light because of its crystalline structure.
star shell *n.* an artillery shell containing a flare or other illuminant.
star-span·gled *adj.* marked or decorated with stars.
Star-Span·gled Ban+ner *n.* **the. 1.** the national anthem of the United States of America. **2.** another term for the **Stars and Stripes.**
star stream *n.* one of two main streams of stars that, because of the rotation of the Milky Way, appear to move in opposite directions, one towards Orion, the other towards Ara.
star-stud·ded *adj.* featuring a large proportion of well-known actors or other performers: *a star-studded cast.*
start (stɑːt) *vb.* **1.** to begin or cause to begin (something or to do something); come or cause to come into being, operation, etc.: *he started a quarrel; they started to work.* **2.** (when *intr.*, sometimes foll. by *on*) to make or cause to make a beginning of (a process, series of actions, etc.): *they started on the project.* **3.** (sometimes foll. by *up*) to set or be set in motion: *he started up the machine.* **4.** (*intr.*) to make a sudden involuntary movement of one's body, from or as if from fright; jump. **5.** (*intr.*; sometimes foll. by *up, away,* etc.) to spring or jump suddenly from a position or place. **6.** to establish or be established; set up: *to start a business.* **7.** (*tr.*) to support (someone) in the first part of a venture, career, etc. **8.** to work or cause to work loose. **9.** to enter or be entered in a race. **10.** (*intr.*) to flow violently from a source: *wine started from a hole in the cask.* **11.** (*tr.*) to rouse (game) from a hiding place, lair, etc. **12.** an archaic word for **startle. 13.** (*intr.*) *Brit. informal.* to commence quarrelling or causing a disturbance. **14. to start with.** in the first place. ~*n.* **15.** the first or first part of a series of actions or operations, a journey, etc. **16.** the place or time of starting, as of a race or performance. **17.** a signal to proceed, as in a race. **18.** a lead or advantage, either in time or distance and usually of specified extent, in a competitive activity: *he had an hour's start on me.* **19.** a slight involuntary movement of the body, as through fright, surprise, etc.: *she gave a start as I entered.* **20.** an opportunity to enter a career, undertake a project, etc. **21.** *Informal.* a surprising incident. **22.** a part that has come loose or been disengaged. **23. by fits and starts.** spasmodically; without concerted effort. **24. for a start.** in the first place. ~See also **start in, start off, start on, start out, start up.** [Old English *styrtan;* related to Old Norse *sterta* to crease, Old High German *sturzen* to rush]
start+er (ˈstɑːtə) *n.* **1.** Also called: **self-starter.** a device for starting an internal-combustion engine, usually consisting of a powerful electric motor that engages with the flywheel. **2.** *U.S.* a person who organizes the timely departure of buses, trains, etc. **3.** a person who supervises and signals the start of a race. **4.** a competitor who starts in a race or contest. **5.** *Austral. informal.* an acceptable or practicable proposition, plan, idea, etc. **6.** *Austral. informal.* a person who is willing to engage in a particular activity. **7.** a culture of bacteria used to start fermentation, as in making cheese or bread. **8.** *Chiefly Brit.* the first course of a meal. **9. for starters.** *Slang.* in the first place.
star this+tle *n.* any of several plants of the genus *Centaurea,* esp. *C. calcitrapa,* of Eurasia, which has spiny purplish flower heads: family *Compositae* (composites). See also **centaury** (sense 2).
start in *vb.* (*adv.*) to undertake (something or doing something); commence or begin.
start+ing block *n.* one of a pair of adjustable devices with pads or blocks against which a sprinter braces his feet in crouch starts.
start+ing gate *n.* **1.** a movable barrier so placed on the starting line of a race course that the raising of it releases all the contestants simultaneously. **2.** the U.S. name for **starting stalls.**
start+ing grid *n. Motor racing.* a marked section of the track at the start where the cars line up according to their times in practice, the fastest occupying the front position.
start+ing price *n.* (esp. in horse racing) the latest odds offered by bookmakers at the start of a race.
start+ing stalls *pl. n. Brit.* a line of stalls in which horses are enclosed at the start of a race and from which they are released by the simultaneous springing open of retaining barriers at the front of each stall.
star+tle (ˈstɑːtᵊl) *vb.* to be or cause to be surprised or frightened, esp. so as to start involuntarily. [Old English *steartlian* to stumble; related to Middle High German *starzen,* to strut, Norwegian *sterta* to strain oneself] —ˈ**star+tler** *n.* —ˈ**star+tling** *adj.* —ˈ**star+tling+ly** *adv.*
start off *vb.* (*adv.*) **1.** (*intr.*) to set out on a journey. **2.** to be or make the first step in an activity; initiate: *he started the show off with a lively song.* **3.** (*tr.*) to cause (a person) to act or do something, such as to laugh, to tell stories, etc.
start on *vb.* (*intr., prep.*) *Brit. informal.* to pick a quarrel with (someone).
start out *vb.* (*intr., adv.*) **1.** to set out on a journey. **2.** to take the first steps, as in life, one's career, etc.: *he started out as a salesman.* **3.** to take the first actions in an activity in a particular way or specified aim: *they started out wanting a house, but eventually bought a flat.*
start up *vb.* (*adv.*) **1.** to come or cause to come into being for the first time; originate. **2.** (*intr.*) to spring or jump suddenly from a position or place. **3.** to set in motion, activity, etc.: *he started up the engine; the orchestra started up.*
star+va+tion (stɑːˈveɪʃən) *n.* **a.** the act or an instance of starving or state of being starved. **b.** (*as modifier*): *a starvation diet; starvation wages.*
starve (stɑːv) *vb.* **1.** to die or cause to die from lack of food. **2.** to deprive (a person or animal) or (of a person, etc.) to be deprived of food. **3.** (*intr.*) *Informal.* to be very hungry. **4.** (foll. by *of* or *for*) to deprive or be deprived (of something necessary), esp. so as to cause suffering or malfunctioning: *the engine was starved of fuel.* **5.** (*tr.*; foll. by *into*) to bring (to) a specified condition by starving: *to starve someone into submission.* **6.** *Archaic or Brit. dialect.* to be or cause to be extremely cold. [Old English *steorfan* to die; related to Old Frisian *sterva* to die, Old High German *sterban* to die] —ˈ**starv+er** *n.*
starve+ling (ˈstɑːvlɪŋ) *Archaic.* ~*n.* **1. a.** a starving or poorly fed person, animal, etc. **b.** (*as modifier*): *a starveling child.* ~*adj.* **2.** insufficient; meagre; scant.
star+wort (ˈstɑːˌwɜːt) *n.* **1.** any of several plants with star-shaped flowers, esp. the stitchwort. **2.** any of several aquatic plants of the genus *Callitriche,* having a star-shaped rosette of floating leaves: family *Callitrichaceae.*
stash (stæʃ) *Informal.* ~*vb.* **1.** (*tr.*; often foll. by *away*) to put or store (money, valuables, etc.) in a secret place, as for safekeeping. ~*n.* **2.** *Chiefly U.S.* a secret store or the place where this is hidden. [C20: origin unknown]
sta+sis (ˈsteɪsɪs) *n.* **1.** *Pathol.* a stagnation in the normal flow of bodily fluids, such as the blood or urine. **2.** *Literature.* a state or condition in which there is no action or progress; static situation: *dramatic stasis.* [C18: via New Latin from Greek: a standing, from *histanai* to cause to stand; related to Latin *stāre* to stand]
stat. *abbrev. for:* **1.** (in prescriptions) immediately. [from Latin *statim*] **2.** stationary. **3.** statue. **4.** statutary. **5.** statute.
-stat *n. combining form.* indicating a device that causes something to remain stationary or constant: *thermostat.* [from Greek *-statēs,* from *histanai* to cause to stand]
sta+tant (ˈsteɪtᵊnt) *adj. Heraldry.* (of an animal) in profile with all four feet on the ground. [C15: from Latin, apparently from irregularly formed present participle of *stāre* to stand]
state (steɪt) *n.* **1.** the condition of a person, thing, etc., with regard to main attributes. **2.** the structure, form, or constitution of something: *a solid state.* **3.** any mode of existence. **4.** position in life or society; estate. **5.** ceremonious style, as befitting wealth or dignity: *to live in state.* **6.** a sovereign political power or community. **7.** the territory occupied by such a community. **8.** the sphere of power in such a community: *affairs of state.* **9.** (*often cap.*) one of a number of areas or communities having their own governments and forming a federation under a sovereign government, as in the U.S. **10.** (*often cap.*) the body politic of a particular sovereign power, esp. as contrasted with a rival authority such as the Church. **11.** *Obsolete.* a class or order; estate. **12.** *Informal.* a nervous, upset, or excited condition (esp. in the phrase **in a state**). **13. lie in state.** (of a body) to be placed on public view before burial. **14. state of affairs.** a situation; present circumstances or condition. ~*modifier.* **15.** controlled or financed by a state: *state university.* **16.** of, relating to, or concerning the State: *State trial.* **17.** involving ceremony or concerned with a ceremonious occasion: *state visit.* ~*vb.* (*tr.*; *may take a clause as object*) **18.** to articulate in words; utter. **19.** to declare formally or publicly: *to state one's innocence.* **20.** to resolve. [C13: from Old French *estat,* from Latin *status* a standing, from *stāre* to stand] —ˈ**stat+a+ble** *or* ˈ**state+a+ble** *adj.* —ˈ**state+hood** *n.*
state bank *n.* (in the U.S.) a commercial bank incorporated under a State charter and not required to be a member of the Federal Reserve System. Compare **national bank.**
state cap·i+tal+ism *n.* a form of capitalism in which the state owns or controls most of the means of production and other capital: often very similar to state socialism.
state+craft (ˈsteɪtˌkrɑːft) *n.* the art of conducting public affairs; statesmanship.
stat+ed (ˈsteɪtɪd) *adj.* **1.** (esp. of a sum) determined by agreement; fixed. **2.** explicitly formulated or narrated: *a stated argument.* **3.** *Rare.* (of an official, etc.) appointed.
State+house (ˈsteɪtˌhaʊs) *n.* **1.** (in the U.S.) the building which houses a state legislature; State capitol. **2.** a building in which public affairs or state ceremonies are conducted.
state+less (ˈsteɪtlɪs) *adj.* **1.** without nationality: *stateless persons.* **2.** without a state or states. **3.** *Chiefly Brit.* without ceremonial or dignity. —ˈ**state+less+ness** *n.*
state+ly (ˈsteɪtlɪ) *adj.* **+li+er, +li+est. 1.** characterized by a graceful, dignified, and imposing appearance or manner. ~*adv.* **2.** in a stately manner. —ˈ**state+li+ness** *n.*
state+ly home *n. Brit.* a large mansion, esp. one open to the public.
state+ment (ˈsteɪtmənt) *n.* **1.** the act of stating. **2.** something that is stated, esp. a formal prepared announcement or reply. **3.** *Law.* a declaration of matters of fact, esp. in a pleading. **4.** an account containing a summary of bills or invoices and display-

ing the total amount due. **5.** an account prepared by a bank for each of its clients, usually at regular intervals, to show all credits and debits since the last account and the balance at the end of the period. **6.** *Music.* the presentation of a musical theme or idea, such as the subject of a fugue or sonata. **7.** a computer instruction written in a source language, such as FORTRAN, which is converted into one or more machine code instructions by a compiler.

state+ment of claim *n. Law.* (in England) the first pleading made by the plaintiff in a High Court action showing the facts upon which he relies in support of his claim and the relief asked for.

Stat+en Is+land ('stætᵊn) *n.* an island in SE New York State, in New York Harbor: forms the Richmond borough of New York city; heavy industry. Pop.: 295 443 (1970). Area: 155 sq. km (60 sq. miles).

state-of-the-art *adj.* (*prenominal*) (of hi-fi equipment, recordings, etc.) the most recent and therefore considered the best; up-to-the minute: *a state-of-the-art amplifier.*

state of war *n.* **1.** a period of armed conflict between states, regardless of whether or not war has been officially declared. **2.** a legal condition begun by a declaration of war and ended formally, during which the rules of international law applicable to warfare may be invoked.

state prayers *pl. n. Church of England.* prayers for the Sovereign, the royal family, the clergy, and Parliament said at matins and evensong.

State pris+on *n.* (in the U.S.) a prison where persons convicted of serious crimes are confined.

sta+ter ('steɪtə) *n.* any of various usually silver coins of ancient Greece. [C14: via Late Latin from Greek *statēr* a standard of weight, from *histanai* to stand]

state+room ('steɪtˌruːm, -ˌrʊm) *n.* **1.** a private cabin or room on a ship, train, etc. **2.** *Chiefly Brit.* a large room in a palace or other building for use on state occasions.

States *n.* **the.** an informal name for the **United States of America.**

state school *n.* any school maintained by the state, in which education is free.

state ser+vic·es *pl. n. Church of England.* services appointed to commemorate days of national celebration or deliverance such as the accession of a sovereign.

state's ev·i+dence *n.* (in the U.S.) **1.** the evidence for the prosecution given on behalf of a state in a criminal prosecution. **2.** evidence given for the state by an accomplice against his former associates in crime (esp. in the phrase **turn state's evidence**). Brit. equivalent: **queen's** (or **king's**) **evidence.**

States Gen+er+al *n.* **1.** the bicameral legislature of the Netherlands. **2.** *History.* **a.** an assembly of the estates of an entire country in contrast to those of a single province. **b.** Also called: **Estates General.** the assembly of the estates of all France, last meeting in 1789. **c.** the sovereign body of the Dutch republic from the 16th to 18th centuries.

state+side ('steɪtˌsaɪd) *adj., adv. U.S.* of, in, to, or towards the U.S.

states+man ('steɪtsmən) *n., pl.* **+men.** **1.** a political leader whose wisdom, integrity, etc., win great respect. **2.** a person active and influential in the formulation of high government policy, such as a cabinet member. **3.** a politician. **—'states·man-ˌlike** *or* **'states+man+ly** *adj.* **—'states+man+ship** *n.* **—'states+ˌwom·an** *fem. n.*

state so+cial+ism *n.* a variant of socialism in which the power of the state is employed for the purpose of creating an egalitarian society by means of public control of major industries, banks, etc., coupled with economic planning and a social security system. **—state so+cial+ist** *n.*

States of the Church *n.* another name for the **Papal States.**

states' rights *n.* (*often caps.*) (in the U.S.) **1.** the rights and powers generally conceded to the states, or all those powers claimed for the states under some interpretations of the Constitution. **2.** a doctrine advocating the severe curtailment of Federal powers by such an interpretation of the Constitution. **—states' right+er** *n.*

state troop+er *n. U.S.* a state policeman.

stat+ic ('stætɪk) *adj. also* **stat·i+cal.** **1.** not active or moving; stationary. **2.** (of a weight, force, or pressure) acting but causing no movement. **3.** of or concerned with forces that do not produce movement. Compare **dynamic** (sense 1). **4.** relating to or causing stationary electric charges; electrostatic. **5.** of or relating to interference in the reception of radio or television transmissions. **6.** of or concerned with statics. **7.** *Sociol.* characteristic of or relating to a society that has reached a state of equilibrium so that no changes are taking place. **8.** *Computer technol.* (of a memory) not needing its contents refreshed periodically. Compare **dynamic** (sense 5). *~n.* **9.** random hissing or crackling or a speckled picture caused by the interference of electrical disturbances in the reception of radio or television transmissions. **10.** electric sparks or crackling produced by friction. [C16: from New Latin *staticus,* from Greek *statikos* causing to stand, from *histanai* to stand, put on the scales] **—'stat·i·cal+ly** *adv.*

stat+ic line *n.* a line attaching the pack of a parachute to an aircraft, so that the parachute is opened when it has fallen clear of the aircraft.

stat+ics ('stætɪks) *n.* (*functioning as sing.*) the branch of mechanics concerned with the forces that produce a state of equilibrium in a system of bodies. Compare **dynamics** (sense 1).

stat+ic tube *n.* an open-ended tube used to measure the static pressure at a point in a moving fluid and positioned in such a way that it is unaffected by the fluid's motion.

sta+tion ('steɪʃən) *n.* **1.** the place or position at which a thing or person stands or is supposed to stand. **2. a.** a place along a route or line at which a bus, train, etc., stops for fuel or to pick up or let off passengers or goods, esp. one with ancillary buildings and services: *railway station.* **b.** (*as modifier*): *a station buffet.* **3. a.** the headquarters or local offices of an official organization such as the police or fire services. **b.** (*as modifier*): *a station sergeant.* See **police station, fire station.** **4.** a building, depot, etc., with special equipment for some particular purpose: *power station; petrol station; television station.* **5.** *Military.* a place of duty: *an action station.* **6.** *Navy.* **a.** a location to which a ship or fleet is assigned for duty. **b.** an assigned location for a member of a ship's crew. **7.** *Informal.* a television channel. **8.** a position or standing, as in a particular society or organization. **9.** the type of one's occupation; calling. **10.** (in British India) a place where the British district officials or garrison officers resided. **11.** *Biology.* the type of habitat occupied by a particular animal or plant. **12.** *Austral.* a large sheep or cattle farm. **13.** *Surveying.* a point at which a reading is made or which is used as a point of reference. **14.** (*sometimes cap.*) *R.C. Church.* **a.** one of the stations of the Cross. **b.** any of the churches (**station churches**) in Rome that have been used from ancient times as points of assembly for religious processions and ceremonies on particular days (**station days**). *~vb.* **15.** (*tr.*) to place in or assign to a station. [C14: via Old French from Latin *statiō* a standing still, from *stāre* to stand]

sta+tion+ar·y ('steɪʃənərɪ) *adj.* **1.** not moving; standing still. **2.** not able to be moved. **3.** showing no change: *the doctors said his condition was stationary.* **4.** tending to remain in one place. [C15: from Latin *statiōnārius,* from *statiō* STATION] **—'sta+tion+ar·i·ly** *adv.* **—'sta+tion+ar·i+ness** *n.*

sta+tion+ar·y en+gine *n.* an engine that remains in a fixed position, esp. one in a building that drives generators or other machinery. **—sta+tion+ar·y en+gi+neer** *n.*

sta+tion+ar·y or+bit *n. Astronautics.* a synchronous orbit lying in or approximately in the plane of the equator.

sta+tion+ar·y point *n.* a point on a curve at which the tangent is either horizontal or vertical, such as a maximum, a minimum, or a point of inflection.

sta+tion+ar·y wave *n.* another name for **standing wave.**

sta+tion+er ('steɪʃənə) *n.* **1.** a person who sells stationery or a shop where stationery is sold. **2.** *Obsolete.* a publisher or bookseller. [C14: from Medieval Latin *stationarius* a person having a regular station, hence a shopkeeper (esp. a bookseller) as distinguished from an itinerant tradesman; see STATION]

Sta+tion+ers' Com+pa+ny *n.* a guild, established by Royal Charter from Queen Mary in 1557, composed of booksellers, printers, etc.

sta+tion+er·y ('steɪʃənərɪ) *n.* any writing materials, such as paper, envelopes, pens, ink, rulers, etc.

sta·tion house *n. Chiefly U.S.* a house that is situated by or serves as a station, esp. as a police or fire station.

sta·tion+mas·ter ('steɪʃənˌmɑːstə) *n.* the senior official in charge of a railway station.

sta+tions of the Cross *n. R.C. Church.* **1.** a series of 14 crosses, often accompanied by 14 pictures or carvings, arranged in order around the walls of a church, to commemorate 14 supposed stages in Christ's journey to Calvary. **2.** a devotion consisting of 14 prayers relating to each of these stages.

sta+tion wag+on *n.* a U.S. name for **estate car.**

stat+ism ('steɪtɪzəm) *n.* the theory or practice of concentrating economic and political power in the state, resulting in a weak position for the individual or community with respect to the government.

stat+ist ('steɪtɪst) *n.* **1.** an advocate of statism. **2.** a less common name for a **statistician.** **3.** *Archaic.* a politician or statesman. *~adj.* **4.** of, characteristic of, advocating, or relating to statism.

sta+tis+tic (stə'tɪstɪk) *n.* a datum capable of exact numerical representation, such as the correlation coefficient of two series or the standard deviation of a sample. **—sta+'tis+ti+cal** *adj.* **—sta+'tis+ti+cal+ly** *adv.* **—stat+is+ti+cian** (ˌstætɪ'stɪʃən) *n.*

sta+tis+ti+cal me+chan+ics *n.* (*functioning as sing.*) the study of the properties of physical systems as predicted by the statistical behaviour of their constituent particles.

sta+tis+tics (stə'tɪstɪks) *n.* **1.** (*functioning as sing.*) a science concerned with the collection, classification, and interpretation of quantitative data and with the application of probability theory to the analysis and estimation of population parameters. **2.** the quantitative data themselves. [C18 (originally "science dealing with facts of a state"): via German *Statistik,* from New Latin *statisticus* concerning state affairs, from Latin *status* STATE]

Sta·ti·us ('steɪʃɪəs) *n.* **Pub·li·us Pa·pin·i·us** ('pʌblɪəs pə'pɪnɪəs). ?45–96 A.D., Roman poet; author of the collection *Silvae* and of two epics, *Thebais* and the unfinished *Achilleis.*

sta+tive ('steɪtɪv). *Grammar.* *~adj.* **1.** denoting a verb describing a state rather than an activity, act, or event, such as *know* and *want* as opposed to *leave* and *throw.* Compare **nonstative.** *~n.* **2.** a stative verb.

stat·o+blast ('stætəʊˌblɑːst) *n. Zoology.* an encapsulated bud produced asexually by certain bryozoans that can survive adverse conditions and that gives rise to a new colony.

stat·o+cyst ('stætəʊsɪst) *n.* an organ of balance in some invertebrates, such as crustaceans, that consists of a sensory vesicle containing small granules (see **statolith**).

stat·ol·a·try (steɪˈtɒlətrɪ) *n. Rare.* the act or practice of idolizing the state.

stat·o·lith (ˈstætəʊlɪθ) *n.* **1.** Also called: **otolith.** any of the granules of calcium carbonate occurring in a statocyst: movement of statoliths, caused by a change in position of the animal, stimulates hair cells, which convey the information to the brain by nerve fibres. **2.** any of various movable inclusions, such as starch grains, that occur in plant cells and are thought to function in geotropic responses. —ˌ**stat·o·ˈlith·ic** *adj.*

sta·tor (ˈsteɪtə) *n.* **1.** the stationary part of a rotary machine or device, esp. of a motor or generator. **2.** a system of nonrotating radially arranged parts within a rotating assembly, esp. the fixed blades of an axial flow compressor in a gas turbine. ~Compare **rotor** (sense 1). [C20: from Latin: one who stands (by), from *stāre* to stand]

stat·o·scope (ˈstætəˌskəʊp) *n.* a very sensitive form of aneroid barometer used to detect and measure small variations in atmospheric pressure, such as one used in an aircraft to indicate small changes in altitude.

stat·u·ar·y (ˈstætjʊərɪ) *n., pl.* **·ar·ies. 1.** statues collectively. **2.** the art of making statues. ~*adj.* **3.** of, relating to, or suitable for statues. [C16: from Latin *statuārius*]

stat·ue (ˈstætjuː) *n.* a wooden, stone, metal, plaster, or other kind of sculpture of a human or animal figure, usually life-size or larger. [C14: via Old French from Latin *statua,* from *statuere* to set up; compare STATUTE]

stat·ued (ˈstætjuːd) *adj.* decorated with or portrayed in a statue or statues.

Stat·ue of Lib·er·ty *n.* a monumental statue personifying liberty, in New York Harbor, on Liberty Island: a gift from France, erected in 1885. Official name: **Liberty Enlightening the World.**

stat·u·esque (ˌstætjʊˈɛsk) *adj.* like a statue, esp. in possessing great formal beauty or dignity. —ˌ**stat·u·ˈesque·ly** *adv.* —ˌ**stat·u·ˈesque·ness** *n.*

stat·u·ette (ˌstætjʊˈɛt) *n.* a small statue.

stat·ure (ˈstætʃə) *n.* **1.** the height of something, esp. a person or animal when standing. **2.** the degree of development of a person: *the stature of a champion.* **3.** intellectual or moral greatness: *a man of stature.* [C13: via Old French from Latin *statūra,* from *stāre* to stand]

sta·tus (ˈsteɪtəs) *n., pl.* **·tus·es. 1.** a social or professional position, condition, or standing to which varying degrees of responsibility, privilege, and esteem are attached. **2.** the relative position or standing of a person or thing. **3.** a high position or standing; prestige: *he has acquired a new status since he has been in that job.* **4.** the legal standing or condition of a person. **5.** a state of affairs. [C17: from Latin: posture, from *stāre* to stand]

sta·tus quo (kwəʊ) *n.* (usually preceded by *the*) the existing state of affairs. [literally: the state in which]

sta·tus sym·bol *n.* a possession which is regarded as proof of the owner's social position, wealth, prestige, etc.

stat·u·ta·ble (ˈstætjʊtəbᵊl) *adj.* a variant of **statutory** (senses 2, 3). —ˈ**stat·u·ta·bly** *adv.*

stat·ute (ˈstætjuːt) *n.* **1. a.** an enactment of a legislative body expressed in a formal document. **b.** this document. **2.** a permanent rule made by a body or institution for the government of its internal affairs. [C13: from Old French *estatut,* from Late Latin *statūtum,* from Latin *statuere* to set up, decree, ultimately from *stāre* to stand]

stat·ute book *n. Chiefly Brit.* a register of enactments passed by the legislative body of a state, usually made up of a series of volumes that form a complete official record: *not on the statute book.*

stat·ute law *n.* **1.** a law enacted by a legislative body. **2.** a particular example of this. ~Compare **common law, equity.**

stat·ute mile *n.* a legal or formal name for **mile** (sense 1).

stat·ute of lim·i·ta·tions *n.* a legislative enactment prescribing the period of time within which proceedings must be instituted to enforce a right or bring an action at law. See also **laches.**

Stat·ute of West·min·ster *n.* the act of Parliament that formally recognized the independence of the dominions within the Empire.

stat·u·to·ry (ˈstætjʊtərɪ, -trɪ) *adj.* **1.** of, relating to, or having the nature of a statute. **2.** prescribed or authorized by statute. **3.** (of an offence, etc.) **a.** recognized by statute. **b.** subject to a punishment or penalty prescribed by statute. —ˈ**stat·u·to·ri·ly** *adv.*

stat·u·to·ry dec·la·ra·tion *n. Law.* a declaration made under statutory authority before a justice of the peace or commissioner for oaths which may in certain cases be substituted for a statement on oath.

stat·u·to·ry rape *n.* (in the U.S.) the criminal offence of having sexual intercourse with a girl who has not reached the age of consent.

staunch[1] (stɔːntʃ) *adj.* **1.** loyal, firm, and dependable: *a staunch supporter.* **2.** solid or substantial in construction. **3.** *Rare.* (of a ship, etc.) watertight; seaworthy. [C15: (originally: watertight): from Old French *estanche,* from *estanchier* to STANCH] —ˈ**staunch·ly** *adv.* —ˈ**staunch·ness** *n.*

staunch[2] (stɔːntʃ) *vb., n.* a variant spelling of **stanch.**

stau·ro·lite (ˈstɔːrəˌlaɪt) *n.* a brown glassy mineral consisting of iron aluminium silicate in the form of prismatic crystals: used as a gemstone. Formula: $FeAl_4Si_2O_{10}(OH)_2$. [C19: from Greek *stauros* a cross + -LITE] —**stau·ro·lit·ic** (ˌstɔːrəˈlɪtɪk) *adj.*

stau·ro·scope (ˈstɔːrəˌskəʊp) *n.* an optical instrument for studying the crystal structure of minerals under polarized light. —**stau·ro·scop·ic** (ˌstɔːrəˈskɒpɪk) *adj.* —ˌ**stau·ro·ˈscop·i·cal·ly** *adv.*

Sta·vang·er (*Norwegian* staˈvaŋər) *n.* a port in SW Norway: canning and shipbuilding industries. Pop.: 81 847 (1970).

stave (steɪv) *n.* **1.** any one of a number of long strips of wood joined together to form a barrel, bucket, boat hull, etc. **2.** any of various bars, slats, or rods, usually of wood, such as a rung of a ladder or a crosspiece bracing the legs of a chair. **3.** any stick, staff, etc. **4.** a stanza or verse of a poem. **5.** *Music.* **a.** *Brit.* an individual group of five lines and four spaces used in staff notation. **b.** another word for **staff**[1] (sense 9). ~*vb.* **staves, stav·ing, staved** *or* **stove. 6.** (often foll. by *in*) to break or crush (the staves of a boat, barrel, etc.) or (of the staves of a boat) to be broken or crushed. **7.** (*tr.;* usually foll. by *in*) to burst or force (a hole in something). **8.** (*tr.*) to provide (a ladder, chair, etc.) with a stave or staves. [C14: back formation from *staves,* plural of STAFF[1]]

stave off *vb.* (*tr., adv.*) to avert or hold off (something undesirable or harmful), esp. temporarily: *to stave off hunger.*

staves (steɪvz) *n.* the plural of **staff** or **stave.**

staves·a·cre (ˈsteɪvzˌeɪkə) *n.* **1.** a Eurasian ranunculaceous plant, *Delphinium staphisagria,* having purple flowers and poisonous seeds. **2.** the seeds of this plant, which have strong emetic and cathartic properties. [C14 *staphisagre,* from Latin *staphis agria,* from Greek, from *staphis* raisin + *agria* wild]

Stav·ro·pol (*Russian* ˈstavrəpəlj) *n.* **1.** a city in the SW Soviet Union: founded as a fortress in 1777. Pop.: 233 000 (1975 est.). **2.** the former name (until 1964) of **Togliatti.**

stay[1] (steɪ) *vb.* **1.** (*intr.*) to continue or remain in a certain place, position, etc.: *to stay outside.* **2.** (*copula*) to continue to be; remain: *to stay awake.* **3.** (*intr.;* often foll. by *at*) to reside temporarily, esp. as a guest: *to stay at a hotel.* **4.** (*tr.*) to remain for a specified period: *to stay the weekend.* **5.** (*intr.*) *Central Scot. dialect.* to reside permanently or habitually: *she stays on a housing scheme.* **6.** to stop or cause to stop. **7.** (*intr.*) to wait, pause, or tarry. **8.** (*tr.*) to delay or hinder. **9.** (*tr.*) **a.** to discontinue or suspend (a judicial proceeding). **b.** to hold in abeyance or restrain from enforcing (an order, decree, etc.). **10.** to endure (something testing or difficult, such as a race): *a horse that stays the course.* **11.** (*intr.;* often foll. by *at*) *S. African.* to reside permanently or normally. **12.** (*intr.;* usually foll. by *with*) to keep pace (with a competitor in a race, etc.). **13.** (*intr.*) *Poker.* to raise one's stakes enough to stay in a round. **14.** (*tr.*) to hold back or restrain: *to stay one's anger.* **15.** (*tr.*) to satisfy or appease (an appetite, etc.) temporarily. **16.** (*tr.*) *Archaic.* to quell or suppress. **17.** (*intr.*) *Archaic.* to stand firm. **18. stay put.** See **put** (sense 18). ~*n.* **19.** the act of staying or sojourning in a place or the period during which one stays. **20.** the act of stopping or restraining or state of being stopped, etc. **21.** the suspension of a judicial proceeding, etc.: *stay of execution.* [C15 *staien,* from Anglo-French *estaier* to stay, from Old French *ester* to stay, from Latin *stāre* to stand]

stay[2] (steɪ) *n.* **1.** anything that supports or steadies, such as a prop or buttress. **2.** a thin strip of metal, plastic, bone, etc., used to stiffen corsets, etc. ~*vb.* (*tr.*) *Archaic.* **3.** (often foll. by *up*) to prop or hold. **4.** (often foll. by *up*) to comfort or sustain. **5.** (foll. by *on* or *upon*) to cause to rely or depend. [C16: from Old French *estaye,* of Germanic origin; compare STAY[3]]

stay[3] (steɪ) *n.* a rope, cable, or chain, usually one of a set, used for bracing uprights, such as masts, funnels, flagpoles, chimneys, etc.; guy. [Old English *stæg;* related to Old Norse *stag,* Middle Low German *stach,* Norwegian *stagle* wooden post]

stay-at-home *adj.* **1.** (of a person) enjoying a quiet, settled, and unadventurous use of leisure. ~*n.* **2.** a stay-at-home person.

stay·er (ˈsteɪə) *n.* **1.** a person or thing that stays. **2.** *Informal.* a persistent or tenacious person.

stay·ing pow·er *n.* endurance; stamina.

stay out *vb.* (*adv.*) **1.** (*intr.*) to remain away from home: *the cat stayed out all night.* **2.** (*tr.*) to remain beyond the end of: *to stay out a welcome.* **3.** (*tr.*) to remain throughout: *to stay the night out.*

stays (steɪz) *pl. n.* **1.** *Now rare.* corsets with bones in them. **2.** a position of a sailing vessel relative to the wind so that the sails are luffing or aback. Compare **irons** (sense 2). **3. miss stays.** Also: **refuse stays.** (of a sailing vessel) to fail to come about.

stay·sail (ˈsteɪˌseɪl; *Nautical* ˈsteɪsᵊl) *n.* an auxiliary sail, often triangular, set to catch the wind, as between the masts of a yawl (**mizzen staysail**), aft of a spinnaker (**spinnaker staysail**), etc.

stay stitch·ing *n.* a line of stitches made in the seam allowance to prevent the edges from stretching.

stbd. *abbrev. for* starboard.

S.T.C. (in India) *abbrev. for* State Trading Corporation.

std. *abbrev. for* standard.

S.T.D. *abbrev. for* Doctor of Sacred Theology.

STD code *n. Brit.* a code of two or more digits, other than those comprising a subscriber's local telephone number, that determines the routing of a call. [C20: *s*(*ubscriber*) *t*(*runk*) *d*(*ialling*)]

Ste. *or* **Ste** *abbrev. for* Saint (female). [French *Sainte*]

stead (stɛd) *n.* **1.** (preceded by *in*) *Rare.* the place, function, or position that should be taken by another: *to come in someone's stead.* **2. stand (someone) in good stead.** to be useful or of good service to (someone). ~*vb.* **3.** (*tr.*) *Archaic.* to help or benefit. [Old English *stede;* related to Old Norse *stathr* place, Old

High German *stat* place, Latin *statiō* a standing, *statim* immediately]

stead+fast *or* **sted+fast** ('stɛdfəst, -ˌfɑːst) *adj.* **1.** (esp. of a person's gaze) fixed in intensity or direction; steady. **2.** unwavering or determined in purpose, loyalty, etc.: *steadfast resolve.* —**'stead+fast+ly** *or* **'sted+fast+ly** *adv.* —**'stead+fast+ness** *or* **'sted+fast+ness** *n.*

stead·y ('stɛdɪ) *adj.* **stead·i·er, stead·i·est. 1.** not able to be moved or disturbed easily; stable. **2.** free from fluctuation: *the level stayed steady.* **3.** not easily excited; imperturbable. **4.** staid; sober. **5.** regular; habitual: *a steady drinker.* **6.** continuous: *a steady flow.* **7.** *Nautical.* (of a vessel) keeping upright, as in heavy seas. ~*vb.* **stead·ies, stead·y·ing, stead·ied. 8.** to make or become steady. ~*adv.* **9.** in a steady manner. **10. go steady.** *Informal.* to date one person regularly. ~*n., pl.* **stead·ies. 11.** *Informal.* one's regular boyfriend or girlfriend. ~*interj.* **12.** *Nautical.* an order to the helmsman to stay on a steady course. **13.** a warning to keep calm, be careful, etc. **14.** *Brit.* a command to get set to start, as in a race: *ready, steady, go!* [C16: from STEAD + -Y[1]; related to Old High German *stātīg*, Middle Dutch *stēdig*] —**'stead·i·er** *n.* —**'stead·i·ly** *adv.* —**'stead·i·ness** *n.* —**'stead·y·ing·ly** *adv.*

stead·y state *n. Physics.* the condition of a system when some or all of the quantities describing it are independent of time but not necessarily in thermodynamic or chemical equilibrium. See also **equilibrium** (sense 5).

stead·y-state the·o·ry *n.* a cosmological theory postulating that the universe exists throughout time in a steady state such that the average density of matter does not vary with distance or time. Matter is continuously created in the space left by the receding stars and galaxies of the expanding universe. Compare **big-bang theory.**

steak (steɪk) *n.* **1.** See **beefsteak. 2.** any of various cuts of beef of varying quality, used for braising, stewing, etc. **3.** a thick slice of pork, veal, etc., or of a large fish, esp. cod or salmon. **4.** minced meat prepared in the same way as steak: *hamburger steak.* [C15: from Old Norse *steik* roast; related to *steikja* to roast on a spit; see STICK[1]]

steak+house ('steɪkˌhaʊs) *n.* a restaurant that has steaks as its speciality.

steak tar+tare *or* **tar+tar** *n.* raw minced steak, mixed with onion, seasonings, and raw egg. Also called: **tartare steak, tartar steak.**

steal (stiːl) *vb.* **steals, steal+ing, stole, sto+len. 1.** to take (something) from (someone, etc.) without permission or unlawfully, esp. in a secret manner. **2.** (*tr.*) to obtain surreptitiously. **3.** (*tr.*) to appropriate (ideas, etc.) without acknowledgment, as in plagiarism. **4.** to move or convey stealthily: *they stole along the corridor.* **5.** (*intr.*) to pass unnoticed: *the hours stole by.* **6.** (*tr.*) to win or gain by strategy or luck, as in various sports: *to steal a few yards.* **7. steal a march on.** to obtain an advantage over, esp. by a trick. **8. steal someone's thunder.** to detract from the attention due to another. **9. steal the show.** to be looked upon as the most interesting, popular, etc., esp. unexpectedly. ~*n.* **10.** *Informal.* the act of stealing. **11.** *U.S. informal.* something stolen or acquired easily or at little cost. [Old English *stelan;* related to Old Frisian, Old Norse *stela,* Gothic *stilan,* German *stehlen*] —**'steal+er** *n.*

stealth (stɛlθ) *n.* **1.** the act or characteristic of moving with extreme care and quietness, esp. so as to avoid detection: *the stealth of a cat.* **2.** cunning or underhand procedure or dealing. **3.** *Archaic.* the act of stealing. [C13 *stelthe;* see STEAL, -TH[1]] —**'stealth+ful** *adj.*

stealth·y ('stɛlθɪ) *adj.* **stealth·i·er, stealth·i·est.** characterized by great caution, secrecy, etc.; furtive. —**'stealth·i·ly** *adv.* —**'stealth·i·ness** *n.*

steam (stiːm) *n.* **1.** the gas or vapour into which water is changed when boiled. **2.** the mist formed when such gas or vapour condenses in the atmosphere. **3.** any vaporous exhalation. **4.** *Informal.* power, energy, or speed. **5. get up steam. a.** (of a ship, etc.) to work up a sufficient head of steam in a boiler to drive an engine. **b.** *Informal.* to go quickly. **6. let** (*or* **blow**) **off steam.** *Informal.* to release pent-up energy, feelings, etc., esp. when angry. **7. under one's own steam.** without the assistance of others. **8.** (*modifier*) driven, operated, heated, powered, etc., by steam: *a steam radiator.* **9.** (*modifier*) treated by steam: *steam ironed.* ~*vb.* **10.** to emit or be emitted as steam. **11.** (*intr.*) to generate steam, as a boiler, etc. **12.** (*intr.*) to move or travel by steam power, as a ship, etc. **13.** (*intr.*) *Informal.* to proceed quickly and sometimes forcefully. **14.** to cook or be cooked in steam. **15.** (*tr.*) to treat with steam or apply steam to, as in cleaning, pressing clothes, etc. ~See also **steam up.** [Old English; related to Dutch *stoom* steam, perhaps to Old High German *stioban* to raise dust, Gothic *stubjus* dust]

steam bath *n.* **1.** a room or enclosure that can be filled with steam in which people bathe to induce sweating and refresh or cleanse themselves. **2.** an act of taking such a bath. **3.** an enclosure through which steam can be passed continuously, used in laboratories for sterilizing equipment, maintaining a constant temperature, etc.

steam+boat ('stiːmˌbaʊt) *n.* a boat powered by a steam engine.

steam-boil·er *n.* a vessel in which water is boiled to generate steam. An industrial boiler usually consists of a system of parallel tubes through which water passes, suspended above a furnace.

steam-chest *n.* a chamber that encloses the slide valve of a steam engine and forms a manifold for the steam supply to the valve.

steam-en·gine *n.* an engine that uses the thermal energy of steam to produce mechanical work, esp. one in which steam from a boiler is expanded in a cylinder to drive a reciprocating piston.

steam+er ('stiːmə) *n.* **1.** a boat or ship driven by steam engines. **2.** Also called: **steam box.** an apparatus for steaming wooden beams and planks to make them pliable for shipbuilding. **3.** a vessel used to cook food by steam.

steam·ie ('stiːmɪ) *n. Scot. urban dialect.* a public wash house.

steam i·ron *n.* an electric iron that emits steam from channels in the iron face to facilitate the pressing and ironing of clothes, etc., the steam being produced from water contained within the iron.

steam jack+et *n. Engineering.* a jacket containing steam that surrounds and heats a cylinder.

steam or+gan *n.* a type of organ powered by steam, once common at fairgrounds, in which the pipes are sounded either by a keyboard or in a sequence determined by a moving punched card. U.S. name: **calliope.**

steam point *n.* the temperature at which the maximum vapour pressure of water is equal to one atmosphere (1.01325×10^5 N/m^2). It has the value of 100° on the Celsius scale. Compare **ice point.**

steam+roll·er ('stiːmˌrəʊlə) *n.* **1. a.** a steam-powered vehicle with heavy rollers at the front and rear used for compressing road surfaces during road-making. **b.** another word for **roadroller. 2. a.** an overpowering force or a person with such force that overcomes all opposition. **b.** (*as modifier*): *steamroller tactics.* ~*vb.* **3.** (*tr.*) to crush (opposition, etc.) by overpowering force.

steam room *n.* a room that can be filled with steam for use as a steam bath.

steam+ship ('stiːmˌʃɪp) *n.* a ship powered by one or more steam engines.

steam-shov·el *n.* a steam-driven mechanical excavator, esp. one having a large bucket or grab on a beam slung from a revolving jib.

steam+tight ('stiːmˌtaɪt) *adj.* (of joints, cylinders, etc.) being sealed in such a way that steam cannot leak out. —**'steam+ˌtight+ness** *n.*

steam tur+bine *n.* a turbine driven by steam.

steam up *vb.* (*adv.*) **1.** to cover (windows, etc.) or (of windows, etc.) to become covered with a film of condensed steam. **2.** (*tr.; usually passive*) *Slang.* to excite or make angry: *he's all steamed up about the delay.*

steam whis+tle *n.* a type of whistle sounded by a blast of steam, as used formerly in factories, on locomotives, etc.

steam·y ('stiːmɪ) *adj.* **steam·i·er, steam·i·est. 1.** of, resembling, full of, or covered with steam. **2.** *Informal.* lustful or erotic: *steamy nightlife.* —**'steam·i·ly** *adv.* —**'steam·i·ness** *n.*

ste+ap+sin (stɪ'æpsɪn) *n. Biochem.* a pancreatic lipase. [C19: from Greek *stear* fat + PEPSIN]

stea+rate ('stɪəˌreɪt) *n.* any salt or ester of stearic acid.

ste+ar·ic (stɪ'ærɪk) *adj.* **1.** of or relating to suet or fat. **2.** of, consisting of, containing, or derived from stearic acid.

ste+ar·ic ac·id *n.* a colourless odourless insoluble waxy carboxylic acid used for making candles and suppositories; octadecanoic acid. Formula: $CH_3(CH_2)_{16}COOH$. See also **stearin** (sense 2).

stea+rin *or* **stea+rine** ('stɪərɪn) *n.* **1.** Also called: **tristearin.** a colourless crystalline ester of glycerol and stearic acid, present in fats and used in soap and candles; glycerol tristearate; glycerol trioctadecanoate. Formula: $(C_{17}H_{35}COO)_3C_3H_5$. **2.** another name for **stearic acid,** esp. a commercial grade containing other fatty acids. **3.** fat in its solid form. [C19: from French *stéarine,* from Greek *stear* fat, tallow + -IN]

ste·a+rop+tene (ˌstɪə'rɒptiːn) *n.* the part of an essential oil that separates out as a solid on cooling or standing. [C19: from Latin *stearoptenum,* from Greek *stear* fat +ˌ*-ptenum,* from Greek *ptēnos* winged (volatile)]

ste·a·tite ('stɪəˌtaɪt) *n.* another name for **soapstone.** [C18: from Latin *steatītes,* from Greek *stear* fat + -ITE[1]] —**ste·a·tit·ic** (ˌstɪə'tɪtɪk) *adj.*

ste·a·to- *combining form.* denoting fat. [from Greek *stear, steat-,* fat, tallow]

ste·a·tol·y·sis (ˌstɪə'tɒlɪsɪs) *n. Physiol.* **1.** the digestive process whereby fats are emulsified and then hydrolysed to fatty acids and glycerin. **2.** the breaking down of fat.

ste·a+to+py·gi·a (ˌstɪətəʊ'pɪdʒɪə, -'paɪ-) *or* **ste·a+to+py+ga** (ˌstɪətəʊ'paɪgə) *n.* excessive fatness of the buttocks. [C19: from New Latin, from STEATO- + Greek *pugē* the buttocks] —**ste·a+to+pyg+ic** (ˌstɪətəʊ'pɪdʒɪk) *or* **ste·a·to+py·gous** (-'tɒpɪgəs) *adj.*

ste·a+tor+rhoe·a *or esp. U.S.* **ste·a+tor+rhe·a** (ˌstɪətə'rɪə) *n. Pathol.* **1.** a condition in which the stools are abnormally fatty. **2.** another word for **seborrhoea.**

Stę+bark ('stɛmbark) *n.* the Polish name for **Tannenberg.**

Stech·er (*German* 'ʃtɛçər). *n.* **Re·na·te** (re'naːtə). née *Meissner.* born 1950, East German sprinter: won the women's 100 metres and 200 metres in the 1972 Olympic Games.

sted+fast ('stɛdfəst, -ˌfɑːst) *adj.* a less common spelling of **steadfast.**

steed (stiːd) *n. Archaic or literary.* a horse, esp. one that is spirited or swift. [Old English *stēda* stallion; related to German *Stute* female horse; see STUD[2]]

steel (stiːl) *n.* **1. a.** any of various alloys based on iron containing carbon (usually 0.1–1.7 per cent) and often small quantities of other elements such as phosphorus, sulphur, manganese, chromium, and nickel. Steels exhibit a variety of properties, such as strength, machinability, malleability, etc., depending on their composition and the way they have been treated. **b.**

(*as modifier*): *steel girders.* See also **stainless steel. 2.** something that is made of steel. **3.** a steel stiffener in a corset, etc. **4.** a ridged steel rod with a handle used for sharpening knives. **5.** the quality of hardness, esp. with regard to a person's character or attitudes. **6.** *Stock exchange.* the quotation for steel shares. **7.** (*modifier*) resembling steel: *steel determination.* ~*vb.* (*tr.*) **8.** to fit, plate, edge, or point with steel. **9.** to make hard and unfeeling: *he steeled his heart against her sorrow; he steeled himself for the blow.* [Old English *stēli;* related to Old High German *stehli,* Middle Dutch *stael*] —**'steel·y** *adj.* —**'steel·i·ness** *n.*

Steel (sti:l) *n.* **Da·vid (Martin Scott).** born 1938, British politician; leader (since 1976) of the Liberal Party. In 1977, he entered into a controversial agreement with the Labour government, which undertook to consult the Liberals in return for their support.

steel band *n. Music.* a type of instrumental band, popular in the Caribbean Islands, consisting mainly of tuned percussion instruments made chiefly from the heads of oildrums, hammered or embossed to obtain different notes.

steel blue *n., adj.* **a.** a dark bluish-grey colour. **b.** (*as adj.*): *steel-blue eyes.*

steel-die print+ing *n.* any form of intaglio printing, such as engraving.

Steele (sti:l) *n.* Sir **Rich·ard.** 1672–1729, British essayist and dramatist, born in Ireland; with Joseph Addison he was the chief contributor to the periodicals *The Tatler* (1709–11) and *The Spectator* (1711–12).

steel en+grav+ing *n.* **a.** a method or art of engraving (letters, etc.) on a steel plate. **b.** a print made from such a plate.

steel grey *n., adj.* **a.** a dark grey colour, usually slightly purple. **b.** (*as adj.*): *a steel-grey suit.*

steel gui+tar *n.* another name for **Hawaiian guitar.**

steel+head ('sti:l,hɛd) *n., pl.* **+heads** *or* **+head.** a silvery North Pacific variety of the rainbow trout (*Salmo gairdneri*).

steels (sti:lz) *pl. n. Stock exchange.* shares and bonds of steel companies.

steel wool *n.* a tangled or woven mass of fine steel fibres, used for cleaning or polishing.

steel+work ('sti:l,wɜ:k) *n.* a frame, foundation, building, or article made of steel: *the steelwork of a skyscraper.* —**'steel+,work·ing** *n.*

steel+works ('sti:l,wɜ:ks) *n.* a plant in which steel is made from iron ore and rolled or forged into blooms, billets, bars, or sheets. —**'steel+,work·er** *n.*

steel+yard ('sti:l,jɑ:d) *n.* a portable balance consisting of a pivoted bar with two unequal arms. The load is suspended from the longer one and the bar is returned to the horizontal by adding weights to the shorter one.

Steen (steɪn) *n.* **Jan** (jɑn). 1626–1679, Dutch genre painter.

steen+bok ('sti:n,bɒk) *n., pl.* **+boks** *or* **+bok.** another name for **steinbok.**

steep[1] (sti:p) *adj.* **1. a.** having or being a slope or gradient approaching the perpendicular. **b.** (*as n.*): *the steep.* **2.** *Informal.* (of a fee, price, demand, etc.) unduly high; unreasonable (esp. in the phrase **that's a bit steep**). **3.** *Informal.* excessively demanding or ambitious: *a steep task.* **4.** *Brit. informal.* (of a statement) extreme or far-fetched. **5.** *Obsolete.* elevated. [Old English *steap;* related to Old Frisian *stāp,* Old High German *stouf* cliff, Old Norse *staup*] —**'steep·ly** *adv.* —**'steep+ness** *n.*

steep[2] (sti:p) *vb.* **1.** to soak or be soaked in a liquid in order to soften, cleanse, extract an element, etc. **2.** (*tr.; usually passive*) to saturate; imbue: *steeped in ideology.* ~*n.* **3.** an instance or the process of steeping or the condition of being steeped. **4.** a liquid or solution used for the purpose of steeping something. [Old English *stēpan;* related to *steap* vessel, cup, Old High German *stouf,* Old Norse *staup,* Middle Dutch *stōp*] —**'steep+er** *n.*

steep+en ('sti:pᵊn) *vb.* to become or cause to become steep or steeper.

stee+ple ('sti:pᵊl) *n.* **1.** a tall ornamental tower that forms the superstructure of a church, temple, etc. **2.** such a tower with the spire above it. **3.** any spire or pointed structure. [Old English *stēpel;* see STEEP[1]] —**'stee+pled** *adj.*

stee·ple+bush ('sti:pᵊl,bʊʃ) *n.* another name for **hardhack.**

stee·ple+chase ('sti:pᵊl,tʃeɪs) *n.* **1.** a horse race over a course equipped with obstacles to be jumped, esp. artificial hedges, ditches, water jumps, etc. **2.** a track race, usually of 3000 metres, in which the runners have to leap hurdles, a water jump, etc. **3.** *Archaic.* **a.** a horse race across a stretch of open countryside including obstacles to be jumped. **b.** a rare word for **point-to-point.** ~*vb.* **4.** (*intr.*) to take part in a steeplechase. —**'stee·ple+,chas+ing** *n.* —**'stee·ple+,chas+er** *n.*

stee·ple+jack ('sti:pᵊl,dʒæk) *n.* a person trained and skilled in the construction and repair of steeples, chimneys, etc.

steer[1] (stɪə) *vb.* **1.** to direct the course of (a vehicle or vessel) with a steering wheel, rudder, etc. **2.** (*tr.*) to guide with tuition: *his teachers steered him through his exams.* **3.** (*tr.*) to direct the movements or course of (a person, conversation, etc.). **4.** to pursue (a specified course). **5.** (*intr.*) (of a vessel, vehicle, etc.) to admit of being guided in a specified fashion: *this boat does not steer properly.* **6. steer clear of.** to keep away from; shun. [Old English *stieran;* related to Old Frisian *stiūra,* Old Norse *stȳra,* German *stevern;* see STARBOARD, STERN[2]] —**'steer+a·ble** *adj.* —**'steer+er** *n.*

steer[2] (stɪə) *n.* a castrated male ox or bull; bullock. [Old English *stēor;* related to Old Norse *stjōrr,* Gothic *stiur,* Old High German *stior,* Middle Dutch *stēr*]

steer+age ('stɪərɪdʒ) *n.* **1.** the cheapest accommodation on a passenger ship, originally the compartments containing the steering apparatus. **2.** an instance or the practice of steering and the effect of this on a vessel or vehicle.

steer+age+way ('stɪərɪdʒ,weɪ) *n. Nautical.* enough forward movement to allow a vessel to be steered.

steer+ing com+mit+tee *n.* a committee set up to prepare and arrange topics to be discussed, the order of business, etc., for a legislative assembly or other body.

steer+ing gear *n.* any mechanism used for steering a vehicle, ship, aircraft, etc.

steer+ing wheel *n.* a wheel turned by the driver of a motor vehicle, ship, etc., when he wishes to change direction. It is connected to the front wheels, rudder, etc.

steers+man ('stɪəzmən) *n., pl.* **+men.** the helmsman of a vessel.

steeve[1] (sti:v) *n.* **1.** a spar having a pulley block at one end, used for stowing cargo on a ship. ~*vb.* **2.** (*tr.*) to stow (cargo) securely in the hold of a ship. [C15 *steven,* probably from Spanish *estibar* to pack tightly, from Latin *stīpāre* to cram full]

steeve[2] (sti:v) *Nautical.* ~*vb.* **1.** to incline (a bowsprit or other spar) upwards or (of a bowsprit) to incline upwards at an angle from the horizontal. ~*n.* **2.** such an angle. [C17: of uncertain origin]

Stef·ans·son ('stɛfənsən) *n.* **Vil·hjal·mur** ('vɪl,hjaʊmɛr) 1879–1962, Canadian explorer, noted for his books on the Eskimos.

Stef·fens ('stɛfənz) *n.* (**Joseph**) **Lin·coln.** 1866–1936, U.S. political analyst, known for his exposure of political corruption.

steg·o·don ('stɛgə,dɒn) *or* **steg·o·dont** ('stɛgə,dɒnt) *n.* any proboscidean mammal of the genus *Stegodon,* of Pliocene to Pleistocene times, similar to the mastodons. [C19: New Latin (literally: ridge-toothed), from Greek *stegos* roof, from *stegein* to cover + *odōn* tooth]

steg·o+my·ia (,stɛgə'maɪə) *n.* a former name for **aedes.** [C19: from STEGO- + *-myia,* from Greek *muia* a fly]

steg·o+saur ('stɛgə,sɔ:) *or* **steg·o+saur+us** (,stɛgə'sɔ:rəs) *n.* any quadrupedal herbivorous ornithischian dinosaur of the suborder *Stegosauria,* esp. any of the genus *Stegosaurus,* of Jurassic and early Cretaceous times, having an armour of bony plates. [C19: from Greek *stegos* roof + -SAUR]

Stei+er (*German* 'ʃtaɪər) *n.* a variant spelling of **Steyr.**

Stei+er+mark ('ʃtaɪər,mark) *n.* the German name for **Styria.**

stein (staɪn) *n.* **1.** an earthenware beer mug, esp. of a German design. **2.** the quantity contained in such a mug. [German, literally: STONE]

Stein *n.* **1.** (staɪn). **Ger·trude.** 1874–1946, U.S. writer, resident in Paris (1903–1946). Her works include *Three Lives* (1908) and *The Autobiography of Alice B. Toklas* (1933). **2.** (*German* ʃtaɪn). **Hein·rich Frie·drich Carl** ('haɪnrɪç 'fri:drɪç karl), Baron Stein. 1757–1831, Prussian statesman, who contributed greatly to the modernization of Prussia and played a major role in the European coalition against Napoleon (1813–15).

Stein·beck ('staɪnbɛk) *n.* **John (Ernst).** 1902–68, U.S. writer, noted for his novels about agricultural workers, esp. *The Grapes of Wrath* (1939): Nobel prize for literature 1962.

Stein·berg (*German* 'ʃtaɪnbɛrk) *n.* **Jo·seph von** ('jo:zɛf fɔn). 1894–1969, Austrian film director, whose films include *The Blue Angel* (1930) and the unfinished *I, Claudius* (1937).

stein+bok ('staɪn,bɒk) *or* **steen+bok** *n., pl.* **+boks** *or* **+bok. 1.** a small antelope, *Raphicercus campestris,* of central and southern Africa, having a reddish-brown coat and straight smooth horns. **2.** another name for **ibex.** [C18: from Afrikaans, from Dutch *steen* stone + *bok* BUCK[1]; compare German *Steinbock*]

Stei·ner ('staɪnə; *German* 'ʃtaɪnər) *n.* **Ru·dolf** ('ru:dɔlf). 1861–1925, Austrian philosopher, founder of anthroposophy. He was particularly influential in education.

Stei·nitz ('staɪnɪts; *German* 'ʃtaɪnɪts) *n.* **Wil·helm** ('vɪlhɛlm). 1836–1900, U.S. chess player, born in Prague; world champion (1866–94).

ste+le ('sti:lɪ, sti:l) *n., pl.* **ste+lae** ('sti:li:) *or* **ste+les** ('sti:lɪz, sti:lz). **1.** an upright stone slab or column decorated with figures or inscriptions, common in prehistoric times. **2.** a prepared vertical surface that has a commemorative inscription or design, esp. one on the face of a building. **3.** the conducting tissue of the stems and roots of plants, which is in the form of a cylinder, principally containing xylem, phloem, and pericycle. See also **protostele, siphonostele.** ~Also called (for senses 1, 2): **ste+la** ('sti:lə). [C19: from Greek *stēlē;* related to Greek *histanai* to stand, Latin *stāre*] —**ste+lar** ('sti:lə) *adj.*

stel+lar ('stɛlə) *adj.* **1.** of, relating to, involving, or resembling a star or stars. **2.** of or relating to star entertainers. [C17: from Late Latin *stellāris,* from Latin *stella* star]

stel+lar·a·tor ('stɛlə,reɪtə) *n. Physics.* an apparatus used in research into thermonuclear reactions, consisting of a toroidal vessel designed so that a plasma may be contained within it by a magnetic field.

stel+late ('stɛlɪt, -eɪt) *or* **stel+lat+ed** *adj.* resembling a star in shape; radiating from the centre: *a stellate arrangement of petals.* [C16: from Latin *stellātus* starry, from *stellāre* to stud with stars, from *stella* a star] —**'stel+late+ly** *adv.*

stel+lif+er+ous (stɛ'lɪfərəs) *adj.* full of stars.

stel+li+form ('stɛlɪ,fɔ:m) *adj.* star-shaped. [C18: from New Latin *stelliformis,* from Latin *stella* star + *forma* shape]

stel+li+fy ('stɛlɪ,faɪ) *vb.* **+fies, +fy+ing, +fied.** to change or be changed into a star. [C14: from Latin *stella* a star]

Stel+lite ('stɛlaɪt) *n. Trademark.* any of various alloys containing cobalt, chromium, carbon, tungsten, and molybdenum: characteristically very hard and wear resistant, they are used as castings or hard surface-coatings.

stel·lu·lar ('stɛljʊlə) *adj.* **1.** displaying or abounding in small stars: *a stellular pattern.* **2.** resembling a little star or little stars. [C18: from Late Latin *stellula,* diminutive of Latin *stella* star] —'**stel·lu·lar·ly** *adv.*

stem[1] (stɛm) *n.* **1.** the main axis of a plant, which bears the leaves, axillary buds, and flowers and contains a hollow cylinder of vascular tissue. **2.** any similar subsidiary structure in such plants that bears a flower, fruit, or leaf. **3.** a corresponding structure in algae and fungi. **4.** any long slender part, such as the hollow part of a tobacco pipe that lies between the bit and the bowl, or the support between the base and the bowl of a wineglass, goblet, etc. **5.** a banana stalk with several bunches attached. **6.** the main line of descent or branch of a family. **7.** a round pin in some locks on which a socket in the end of a key fits and about which it rotates. **8.** any shank or cylindrical pin or rod, such as the pin that carries the winding knob on a watch. **9.** *Linguistics.* the form of a word that remains after removal of all inflectional affixes; the root of a word, esp. as occurring together with a thematic element. Compare **root**[1] (sense 9). **10.** the main, usually vertical, stroke of a letter or of a musical note such as a minim. **11.** *Electronics.* the tubular glass section projecting from the base of a light bulb or electronic valve, on which the filament or electrodes are mounted. **12. a.** the main upright timber or structure at the bow of a vessel. **b.** the very forward end of a vessel (esp. in the phrase **from stem to stern**). ~*vb.* **stems, stem·ming, stemmed. 13.** (*intr.;* usually foll. by *from*) to be derived; originate. **14.** (*tr.*) to make headway against (a tide, wind, etc.). **15.** (*tr.*) to remove or disengage the stem or stems from. **16.** (*tr.*) to supply (something) with a stem or stems. [Old English *stemn;* related to Old Norse *stafn* stem of a ship, German *Stamm* tribe, Gothic *stōma* basis, Latin *stāmen* thread] —'**stem·,like** *adj.* —'**stem·mer** *n.*

stem[2] (stɛm) *vb.* **stems, stem·ming, stemmed. 1.** (*tr.*) to restrain or stop (the flow of something) by or as if by damming up. **2.** (*tr.*) to pack tightly or stop up. **3.** *Skiing.* to manoeuvre (a ski or skis), as in performing a stem. ~*n.* **4.** *Skiing.* a technique in which the heel of one ski or both skis is forced outwards from the direction of movement in order to slow down or turn. [C15 *stemmen,* from Old Norse *stemma;* related to Old Norse *stamr* blocked, stammering, German *stemmen* to prop; see STAMMER] —'**stem·mer** *n.*

stem cell *n. Histology.* an undifferentiated cell that gives rise to specialized cells, such as blood cells.

stem·head ('stɛm,hɛd) *n. Nautical.* the head of the stem of a vessel.

stem·ma ('stɛmə) *n.* a family tree; pedigree.

stemmed (stɛmd) *adj.* **1. a.** having a stem. **b.** (*in combination*): *a thin-stemmed plant; a long-stemmed glass.* **2.** having had the stem or stems removed.

stem·son ('stɛmsən) *n. Nautical.* a curved timber scarfed into or bolted to the stem and keelson at the bow of a wooden vessel. Compare **sternson.** [C18: from STEM[1] + (KEEL)SON]

stem turn *n. Skiing.* a turn in which the heel of one ski is forced outwards from the direction of movement and the other ski is brought parallel. Also called: **stem.**

stem·ware ('stɛm,wɛə) *n.* a collective term for glasses, goblets, etc., with stems.

stem-wind·er *n.* a watch wound by an expanded crown on the bar projecting outside the case, as opposed to one wound by a separate key. Also called: **stem-winding watch.**

stench (stɛntʃ) *n.* a strong and extremely offensive odour; stink. [Old English *stenc;* related to Old Saxon, Old High German *stank;* see STINK]

stench trap *n.* a trap in a sewer that prevents the passage of foul-smelling gases. Also called: **stink trap.**

sten·cil ('stɛnsəl) *n.* **1.** a device for applying a design, characters, etc., to a surface, consisting of a thin sheet of plastic, metal, cardboard, etc. in which the design or characters have been cut so that ink or paint can be applied through the incisions onto the surface. **2.** a decoration, design, or characters produced in this way. ~*vb.* **·cils, ·cil·ling, ·cilled** *or U.S.* **·cils, ·cil·ing, ·ciled.** (*tr.*) **3.** to mark (a surface) with a stencil. **4.** to produce (characters or a design) with a stencil. [C14 *stanselen* to decorate with bright colours, from Old French *estenceler,* from *estencele* a spark, from Latin *scintilla*] —'**sten·cil·ler** *n.*

Sten·dhal (*French* stɛ̃'dal) *n.* original name *Marie Henri Beyle.* 1783–1842, French writer, who anticipated later novelists in his psychological analysis of character. His two chief novels are *Le Rouge et le noir* (1830) and *La Chartreuse de Parme* (1839).

Sten gun (stɛn) *n.* a light sub-machine-gun formerly used in the British Army. [C20: from *s* and *t* (initials of Shepherd and Turpin, the inventors) + *-en,* as in BREN GUN]

sten·o ('stɛnəʊ) *n., pl* **sten·os.** *U.S. informal.* short for **stenographer.**

sten·o- *or before a vowel* **sten-** *combining form.* indicating narrowness or contraction: *stenography; stenosis.* [from Greek *stenos* narrow]

sten·o·graph ('stɛnə,græf, -,grɑːf) *n.* **1.** any of various keyboard machines for writing in shorthand. **2.** any character used in shorthand. ~*vb.* **3.** (*tr.*) to record (speeches, minutes, letters, etc.) in shorthand.

ste·nog·ra·pher (stə'nɒgrəfə) *n.* the U.S. name for **shorthand typist.**

ste·nog·ra·phy (stə'nɒgrəfɪ) *n.* **1.** the act or process of writing in shorthand by hand or machine. **2.** matter written in shorthand. —**sten·o·graph·ic** (,stɛnə'græfɪk) *or* ,**sten·o·'graph·i·cal** *adj.* —,**sten·o·'graph·i·cal·ly** *adv.*

sten·o·ha·line (,stɛnəʊ'heɪliːn, -laɪn) *adj.* (of certain aquatic animals) able to exist only within a narrow range of salinity. [C20: from STENO- + *haline,* from Greek *hals* salt + -INE[1]]

sten·o·pet·al·ous (,stɛnəʊ'pɛtələs) *adj.* (of flowers) having narrow petals.

ste·noph·a·gous (stə'nɒfəgəs) *adj.* (of animals) feeding on a single type or limited variety of food.

sten·o·phyl·lous (,stɛnəʊ'fɪləs) *adj.* (of plants) having narrow leaves.

ste·no·sis (stɪ'nəʊsɪs) *n., pl.* **·ses** (-siːz). *Pathol.* an abnormal narrowing of a bodily canal or passage. [C19: via New Latin from Greek *stenōsis,* from *stenoun* to constrict, from *stenos* narrow] —**ste·not·ic** (stɪ'nɒtɪk) *adj.*

sten·o·ther·mal (,stɛnə'θɜːməl) *adj.* (of animals or plants) able to exist only within a narrow range of temperature.

sten·o·trop·ic (,stɛnəʊ'trɒpɪk) *or* **sten·o·top·ic** *adj. Ecology.* (of a species, or group, etc.) able to tolerate only a narrow range of environmental changes. Compare **eurytropic.**

Sten·o·type ('stɛnə,taɪp) *n.* **1.** *Trademark.* a machine with a keyboard for recording speeches, etc., in a phonetic shorthand. **2.** any machine resembling this. **3.** the phonetic symbol typed in one stroke of such a machine.

sten·o·typ·y ('stɛnə,taɪpɪ) *n.* a form of shorthand in which alphabetic combinations are used to represent groups of sounds or short common words. —**sten·o·typ·ic** (,stɛnə'tɪpɪk) *adj.* —'**sten·o·,typ·ist** *n.*

sten·tor ('stɛntɔː) *n.* **1.** a person with an unusually loud voice. **2.** any trumpet-shaped protozoan of the genus *Stentor,* having a ciliated spiral feeding funnel at the wider end: class *Ciliata* (ciliates). [C19: after STENTOR]

Sten·tor ('stɛntɔː) *n. Greek myth.* a Greek herald with a powerful voice who died after he lost a shouting contest with Hermes, herald of the gods.

sten·to·ri·an (stɛn'tɔːrɪən) *adj.* (of the voice, etc.) uncommonly loud: *stentorian tones.*

step (stɛp) *n.* **1.** the act of motion brought about by raising the foot and setting it down again in coordination with the transference of the weight of the body. **2.** the distance or space covered by such a motion. **3.** the sound made by such a movement. **4.** the impression made by such movement of the foot; footprint. **5.** the manner of walking or moving the feet; gait: *he received his prize with a proud step.* **6.** a sequence of foot movements that make up a particular dance or part of a dance: *I have mastered the steps of the waltz.* **7.** any of several paces or rhythmic movements in marching, dancing, etc.: *the goose step.* **8.** (*pl.*) a course followed by a person in walking or as walking: *they followed in their leader's steps.* **9.** one of a sequence of separate consecutive stages in the progression towards some goal: *another step towards socialism.* **10.** a rank or grade in a series or scale: *he was always a step behind.* **11.** an object or device that offers support for the foot when ascending or descending. **12.** (*pl.*) a flight of stairs, esp. out of doors. **13.** (*pl.*) another name for **stepladder. 14.** a very short easily travelled distance: *it is only a step to my place.* **15.** *Music.* a melodic interval of a second. See **whole tone, half-step. 16.** an offset or change in the level of a surface similar to the step of a stair. **17.** a strong block or frame bolted on the keel of a vessel and fitted to receive the base of a mast. **18.** a ledge cut in mining or quarrying excavations. **19. break step.** to cease to march in step. **20. keep step.** to remain walking, marching, dancing, etc., in unison or in a specified rhythm. **21. in step. a.** marching, dancing, etc., in conformity with a specified pace or moving in unison with others. **b.** *Informal.* in agreement or harmony. **22. out of step. a.** not moving in conformity with a specified pace or in accordance with others. **b.** *Informal.* not in agreement; out of harmony. **23. step by step.** with care and deliberation; gradually. **24. take steps.** to undertake measures (to do something) with a view to the attainment of some end. **25. watch one's step. a.** *Informal.* to conduct oneself with caution and good behaviour. **b.** to walk or move carefully. ~*vb.* **steps, step·ping, stepped. 26.** (*intr.*) to move by raising the foot and then setting it down in a different position, transferring the weight of the body to this foot and repeating the process with the other foot. **27.** (*intr.;* often foll. by *in, out,* etc.) to move or go on foot, esp. for a short distance: *step this way, ladies.* **28.** (*intr.*) *Informal, chiefly U.S.* to move, often in an attractive graceful manner, as in dancing: *he can really step around.* **29.** (*intr.;* usually foll. by *on* or *upon*) to place or press the foot; tread: *to step on the accelerator.* **30.** (*intr.;* usually foll. by *into*) to enter (into a situation) apparently with ease: *she stepped into a life of luxury.* **31.** (*tr.*) to walk or take (a number of paces, etc.): *to step ten paces.* **32.** (*tr.*) to perform the steps of: *they step the tango well.* **33.** (*tr.*) to set or place (the foot). **34.** (*tr.;* usually foll. by *off* or *out*) to measure (some distance of ground) by stepping. **35.** (*tr.*) to arrange in or supply with a series of steps so as to avoid coincidence or symmetry. **36.** (*tr.*) to raise (a mast) and fit it into its step. ~See also **step down, step on, step out, step up.** [Old English *stepe, stæpe;* related to Old Frisian *stap, stepe,* Old High German *stapfo* (German *Stapfe* footprint), Old Norse *stapi* high rock] —'**step·,like** *adj.* —'**step·per** *n.*

step- *combining form.* indicating relationship through the previous marriage of a spouse or parent rather than by blood: *stepson; stepfather.* [Old English *stēop-;* compare *āstȳpan* to bereave]

step·broth·er ('stɛp,brʌðə) *n.* a son of one's stepmother or stepfather by a union with someone other than one's father or mother respectively.

step·child ('stɛp,tʃaɪld) *n., pl.* **·chil·dren.** a stepson or stepdaughter.

step·dame ('stɛpˌdeɪm) *n.* an archaic word for **stepmother.**

step dance *n.* a dance in which a display of steps is more important than gesture or posture, esp. a solo dance.

step·daugh·ter ('stɛpˌdɔːtə) *n.* a daughter of one's husband or wife by a former union.

step down *vb.* (*adv.*) **1.** (*tr.*) to reduce gradually. **2.** (*intr.*) *Informal.* to resign or abdicate (from a position). **3.** (*intr.*) *Informal.* to assume an inferior or less senior position. ~*adj.* **step-down.** (*prenominal*) **4.** (of a transformer) reducing a high voltage applied to the primary winding to a lower voltage on the secondary winding. Compare **step-up** (sense 3). **5.** decreasing or falling by stages. ~*n.* **step-down. 6.** *Informal.* a decrease in quantity or size.

step·fa·ther ('stɛpˌfɑːðə) *n.* a man who has married one's mother after the death or divorce of one's father.

steph·a·no·tis (ˌstɛfə'nəʊtɪs) *n.* any climbing asclepiadaceous shrub of the genus *Stephanotis,* esp. *S. floribunda,* of Malagasy Republic and Malaya: cultivated for their fragrant white waxy flowers. [C19: via New Latin from Greek: fit for a crown, from *stephanos* a crown]

Ste·phen ('stiːvᵊn) *n.* **1.** ?1097–1154, king of England (1135–54); grandson of William the Conqueror. He seized the throne on the death of Henry I, causing civil war with Henry's daughter Maltilda. He eventually recognized her son (later Henry II) as his successor. **2. Saint.** died ?35 A.D., the first Christian martyr. Feast day: Dec. 26. **3. Saint,** Hungarian name *István.* ?975–1038 A.D., first king of Hungary as Stephen I (997–1038). Feast day: Sept. 2. **4.** called *Saint Stephen I.* died 257 A.D.; pope (254–57). Feast day: Aug. 2. **5.** Sir **Les·lie.** 1832–1904, English biographer, critic, and first editor of the *Dictionary of National Biography;* father of the novelist Virginia Woolf.

Ste·phen·son ('stiːvənsən) *n.* **1. George.** 1781–1848, English inventor of the first successful steam locomotive (1814); constructed the first railway line to carry passengers, the Stockton and Darlington Railway (opened 1825). **2.** his son, **Rob·ert.** 1803–59, English engineer, noted for his construction of railway bridges and viaducts, esp. the tubular bridge over the Menai Straits.

step in *vb.* **1.** (*intr., adv.*) *Informal.* to intervene or involve oneself, esp. dramatically or at a senior level. ~*adj.* **step-in. 2.** (*prenominal*) (of garments, etc.) put on by being stepped into; without fastenings. **3.** (of a ski binding) engaging automatically when the boot is positioned on the ski. ~*n.* **step-in. 4.** (*often pl.*) a step-in garment, esp. underwear.

step·lad·der ('stɛpˌlædə) *n.* a folding portable ladder that is made of broad flat steps fixed to a supporting frame hinged at the top to another supporting frame.

step·moth·er ('stɛpˌmʌðə) *n.* a woman who has married one's father after the death or divorce of one's mother.

step on *vb.* (*intr., prep.*) **1.** to place or press the foot on. **2.** *Informal.* to behave harshly or contemptuously towards. **3. step on it.** *Informal.* to go more quickly, hurry up.

step out *vb.* (*intr., adv.*) **1.** to go outside or leave a room, building, etc., esp. briefly. **2.** to begin to walk more quickly and take longer strides. **3.** *U.S. informal.* to withdraw from involvement; bow out.

step-par·ent ('stɛpˌpɛərənt) *n.* a stepfather or stepmother.

steppe (stɛp) *n.* (*often pl.*) an extensive grassy plain usually without trees. Compare **prairie, pampas.** [C17: from Old Russian *step* lowland]

step·per ('stɛpə) *n.* a person who or animal that steps, esp. a horse or a dancer.

Steppes (stɛps) *n.* **the. 1.** the huge grasslands of Eurasia, chiefly in the Soviet Union. **2.** another name for **Kirghiz Steppe.**

step·ping stone *n.* **1.** one of a series of stones acting as footrests for crossing streams, marshes, etc. **2.** a circumstance that assists progress towards some goal.

step·sis·ter ('stɛpˌsɪstə) *n.* a daughter of one's stepmother or stepfather by a union with someone other than one's father or mother respectively.

step·son ('stɛpˌsʌn) *n.* a son of one's husband or wife by a former union.

step up *vb.* (*adv.*) Informal. **1.** (*tr.*) to increase or raise by stages; accelerate. **2.** (*intr.*) to make progress or effect an advancement; be promoted. ~*adj.* **step-up.** (*prenominal*) **3.** (of a transformer) increasing a low voltage applied to the primary winding to a higher voltage on the secondary winding. Compare **step-down** (sense 4). **4.** involving a rise by stages. ~*n.* **step-up. 5.** *Informal.* an increment in quantity, size, etc.

step·wise ('stɛpˌwaɪz) *adj.* **1.** arranged in the manner of or resembling steps. **2.** *Music, U.S.* proceeding by melodic intervals of a second. ~*adv.* **3.** with the form or appearance of steps; step by step. **4.** *Music, U.S.* in a stepwise motion.

ster. *abbrev. for* sterling.

-ster *suffix forming nouns.* **1.** indicating a person who is engaged in a certain activity: *prankster; songster.* Compare **-stress. 2.** indicating a person associated with or being something specified: *mobster; youngster.* [Old English *-estre*]

ste·ra·di·an (stə'reɪdɪən) *n.* an SI unit of solid angle; the angle that, having its vertex in the centre of a sphere, cuts off an area of the surface of the sphere equal to the square of the length of the radius. Symbol: sr [C19: from STEREO- + RADIAN]

ster·co·ra·ceous (ˌstɜːkə'reɪʃəs) *adj.* of, relating to, or consisting of dung or excrement. [C18: from Latin *stercus* dung + -ACEOUS]

ster·co·ric·o·lous (ˌstɜːkə'rɪkələs) *adj.* (of organisms) living in dung. [C19: from Latin *stercus* dung + *colere* to live]

ster·cu·li·a·ceous (stɜːˌkjuːlɪ'eɪʃəs) *adj.* of, relating to, or belonging to the *Sterculiaceae,* a chiefly tropical family of plants that includes cacao and cola. [C18: via New Latin from Latin *Sterculius* god of manuring, from *stercus* dung, alluding to the odour of some species]

stere (stɪə) *n.* a unit used to measure volumes of stacked timber equal to one cubic metre (35.315 cubic feet). [C18: from French *stère,* from Greek *stereos* solid]

ste·re·o ('stɛrɪəʊ, 'stɪər) *adj.* **1.** short for **stereophonic** or **stereoscopic.** ~*n., pl.* **ste·re·os. 2.** stereophonic sound: *to broadcast in stereo.* **3.** *Informal.* a stereophonic gramophone, tape recorder, etc. **4.** *Photog.* **a.** stereoscopic photography. **b.** a stereoscopic photograph. **5.** *Printing.* short for **stereotype.** [C20: shortened form]

ste·re·o- *or sometimes before a vowel* **ste·re-** *combining form.* indicating three-dimensional quality or solidity: *stereoscope.* [from Greek *stereos* solid]

ste·re·o·bate ('stɛrɪəʊˌbeɪt, 'stɪər-) *n.* **1.** another name for **stylobate. 2.** a foundation of a building in the form of a platform of masonry. [C19: via Latin, from Greek *stereobatēs* from *stereos* solid + *-batēs* base, from *bainein* to walk]

ste·re·o·chem·is·try (ˌstɛrɪəʊ'kɛmɪstrɪ, ˌstɪər-) *n.* the study of the spatial arrangement of atoms in molecules and the effect of spatial arrangement on chemical properties.

ste·re·o·chrome ('stɛrɪəʊˌkrəʊm, 'stɪər-) *n.* **1.** a picture made by stereochromy. ~*vb.* **2.** (*tr.*) to produce (a picture) by the process of stereochromy.

ste·re·o·chro·my ('stɛrɪəˌkrəʊmɪ, 'stɪər-) *n.* a method of wall painting in which water glass is used either as a painting medium or as a final fixative coat. [C19: via German *Stereochromie,* from STEREO- + Greek *khrōma* colour]

ste·re·o·gram ('stɛrɪəˌgræm, 'stɪər-) *n.* **1.** *Brit.* a stereo radiogram. **2.** another name for **stereograph.**

ste·re·o·graph ('stɛrɪəˌgræf, -ˌgrɑːf, 'stɪər-) *n.* two almost identical pictures, or one special picture, that when viewed through special glasses or a stereoscope form a single three-dimensional image. Also called: **stereogram.**

ste·re·og·ra·phy (ˌstɛrɪ'ɒgrəfɪ, ˌstɪər-) *n.* **1.** the study and construction of geometrical solids. **2.** the art of drawing a solid figure on a flat surface. —**ste·re·o·graph·ic** (ˌstɛrɪə'græfɪk, ˌstɪər-) *or* ˌ**ste·re·o·'graph·i·cal** *adj.* —ˌ**ste·re·o·'graph·i·cal·ly** *adv.*

ste·re·o·i·so·mer (ˌstɛrɪəʊ'aɪsəmə, ˌstɪər-) *n. Chem.* one of the isomers of a compound that exhibits stereoisomerism.

ste·re·o·i·som·er·ism (ˌstɛrɪəʊaɪ'sɒməˌrɪzəm, ˌstɪər-) *n. Chem.* isomerism caused by differences in the spatial arrangement of atoms in molecules. —**ste·re·o·i·so·met·ric** (ˌstɛrɪəʊˌaɪsə'mɛtrɪk, ˌstɪər-) *adj.*

ste·re·om·e·try (ˌstɛrɪ'ɒmɪtrɪ, ˌstɪər-) *n.* the measurement of volume. —**ste·re·o·met·ric** (ˌstɛrɪəʊ'mɛtrɪk, ˌstɪər-) *or* ˌ**ste·re·o·'met·ri·cal** *adj.*

ste·re·o·phon·ic (ˌstɛrɪə'fɒnɪk, ˌstɪər-) *adj.* (of a system for recording, reproducing, or broadcasting sound) using two or more separate microphones to feed two or more loudspeakers through separate channels in order to give a spatial effect to the sound. Sometimes shortened to **stereo.** Compare **monophonic, quadraphonic.** —ˌ**ste·re·o·'phon·i·cal·ly** *adv.* —**ste·re·oph·o·ny** (ˌstɛrɪ'ɒfənɪ, ˌstɪər-) *n.*

ste·re·op·sis (ˌstɛrɪ'ɒpsɪs, ˌstɪər-) *n.* stereoscopic vision.

ste·re·op·ti·con (ˌstɛrɪ'ɒptɪkᵊn, ˌstɪər-) *n.* a type of projector with two complete units arranged so that one picture dissolves as the next is forming.

ste·re·o·scope ('stɛrɪəˌskəʊp, 'stɪər-) *n.* an optical instrument for viewing two-dimensional pictures and giving them an illusion of depth and relief. It has a binocular eyepiece through which two slightly different pictures of the same object are viewed, one with each eye.

ste·re·o·scop·ic (ˌstɛrɪə'skɒpɪk, ˌstɪər-) *or* **ste·re·o·scop·i·cal** *adj.* **1.** of, concerned with, or relating to optical images that appear to be three-dimensional: *stereoscopic vision.* **2.** of, relating to, or formed by a stereoscope. —ˌ**ste·re·o·'scop·i·cal·ly** *adv.*

ste·re·os·co·py (ˌstɛrɪ'ɒskəpɪ, ˌstɪər-) *n.* **1.** the viewing or appearance of objects in or as if in three dimensions. **2.** the study and use of the stereoscope. —ˌ**ste·re·'os·co·pist** *n.*

ste·re·o·spe·cif·ic (ˌstɛrɪˌəʊspɪ'sɪfɪk, ˌstɪər-) *adj. Chem.* relating to or having fixed position in space, as in the spatial arrangements of atoms in certain polymers.

ste·re·o·spe·cif·ic cat·a·lyst *n. Chem.* a catalyst for stereospecific chemical reactions. See also **Ziegler catalyst.**

ste·re·o·spe·cif·ic pol·y·mer *n.* an organic polymer in which the steric arrangements of groups on assymetric carbon atoms occur in a regular sequence. Many natural and synthetic rubbers are stereospecific polymers.

ste·re·o·tax·is (ˌstɛrɪə'tæksɪs, ˌstɪər-) *n.* the movement of an organism in response to the stimulus of contact with a solid object. —**ste·re·o·tac·tic** (ˌstɛrɪə'tæktɪk, ˌstɪər-) *or* ˌ**ste·re·o·'tac·ti·cal** *adj.* —ˌ**ste·re·o·'tac·ti·cal·ly** *adv.*

ste·re·ot·o·my (ˌstɛrɪ'ɒtəmɪ, ˌstɪər-) *n.* the art of cutting three-dimensional solids into particular shapes.

ste·re·ot·ro·pism (ˌstɛrɪ'ɒtrəˌpɪzəm, ˌstɪər-) *n.* another name for **thigmotropism.** —**ste·re·o·trop·ic** (ˌstɛrɪə'trɒpɪk, ˌstɪər-) *adj.*

ste·re·o·type ('stɛrɪəˌtaɪp, 'stɪər-) *n.* **1. a.** a method of producing cast-metal printing plates from a mould made from a forme of type matter in papier-mâché or some other material. **b.** the plate so made. **2.** another word for **stereotypy. 3.** an idea, trait, convention, etc., that has grown stale through fixed usage. **4.** *Sociol.* a standardized image or conception shared by all members of a social group. ~*vb.* (*tr.*) **5. a.** to make a stereotype of. **b.** to print from a stereotype. **6.** to impart a fixed usage or convention to. —'**ste·re·o·ˌtyp·er** *or* '**ste·re·o·ˌtyp·ist** *n.* —**ste·re·o·typ·ic** (ˌstɛrɪəˈtɪpɪk, ˌstɪər-) *or* ˌ**ste·re·o·'typ·i·cal** *adj.*

ste·re·o·typed ('stɛrɪəˌtaɪpt, 'stɪər-) *adj.* **1.** lacking originality or individuality; conventional; trite. **2.** reproduced from or on a stereotype printing plate.

ste·re·o·typ·y ('stɛrɪəˌtaɪpɪ, 'stɪər-) *n.* **1.** the act or process of making stereotype printing plates. **2.** a tendency to think or act in rigid, repetitive, and often meaningless patterns.

ste·re·o·vi·sion ('stɛrɪəʊˌvɪʒən, 'stɪər-) *n.* the perception or exhibition of three-dimensional objects in three dimensions.

ste·ric ('stɛrɪk, 'stɪər-) *or* **ste·ri·cal** *adj. Chem.* of, concerned with, or caused by the spatial arrangement of atoms in a molecule. [C19: from STEREO- + -IC] —'**ste·ri·cal·ly** *adv.*

ster·ig·ma (stəˈrɪgmə) *n. Botany.* a minute stalk bearing a spore or chain of spores in certain fungi. [C19: New Latin from Greek *stērigma* support, from *stērizein* to sustain]

ster·i·lant ('stɛrɪlənt) *n.* any substance or agent used in sterilization.

ster·ile ('stɛraɪl) *adj.* **1.** unable to produce offspring; infertile. **2.** free from living, esp. pathogenic, microorganisms; aseptic. **3.** (of plants or their parts) not producing or bearing seeds, fruit, spores, stamens, or pistils. **4.** lacking inspiration or vitality; fruitless. **5.** *Economics, U.S.* (of gold) not being used to support credit creation or an increased money supply. [C16: from Latin *sterilis*] —'**ster·ile·ly** *adv.* —**ste·ril·i·ty** (stɛˈrɪlɪtɪ) *n.*

ster·i·li·za·tion *or* **ster·i·li·sa·tion** (ˌstɛrɪlaɪˈzeɪʃən) *n.* **1.** the act or procedure of sterilizing or making sterile. **2.** the state of being sterile; sterilized condition.

ster·i·lize *or* **ster·i·lise** ('stɛrɪˌlaɪz) *vb. (tr.)* to render sterile; make infertile or barren. —'**ster·i·ˌliz·a·ble** *or* '**ster·i·ˌlis·a·ble** *adj.* —'**ster·i·ˌliz·er** *or* '**ster·i·ˌlis·er** *n.*

ster·let ('stɜːlɪt) *n.* a small sturgeon, *Acipenser ruthenus,* of seas and rivers in N Asia and E Europe: used as a food fish and a source of caviar. [C16: from Russian *sterlyad,* of Germanic origin; compare Old High German *sturio* sturgeon]

ster·ling ('stɜːlɪŋ) *n.* **1. a.** British money: *pound sterling.* **b.** (*as modifier*): *sterling reserves.* **2.** the official standard of fineness of British coins: for gold 0.91666 and for silver 0.50. **3. a.** short for **sterling silver. b.** (*as modifier*): *a sterling bracelet.* **4.** an article or articles manufactured from sterling silver. **5.** a former British silver penny. ~*adj.* **6.** (*prenominal*) of excellent quality; first-class: *sterling bravery.* [C13: probably from Old English *steorra* STAR + -LING[1]; referring to a small star on early Norman pennies; related to Old French *esterlin*]

ster·ling ar·e·a *n.* a group of countries that use sterling as a medium of international payments and sometimes as an informal peg for their own currencies. For these purposes they deposit sterling balances and hold gold and dollar reserves in the Bank of England. Also called: **sterling bloc, scheduled territories.**

ster·ling sil·ver *n.* **1.** an alloy containing not less than 92.5 per cent of silver, the remainder usually being copper. **2.** sterling-silver articles collectively.

Ster·li·ta·mak (*Russian* stjerlitaˈmak) *n.* an industrial city in the W central Soviet Union, in the Bashkir ASSR. Pop.: 209 000 (1975 est.).

stern[1] (stɜːn) *adj.* **1.** showing uncompromising or inflexible resolve; firm, strict, or authoritarian. **2.** lacking leniency or clemency; harsh or severe. **3.** relentless; unyielding: *the stern demands of parenthood.* **4.** having an austere or forbidding appearance or nature. [Old English *styrne;* related to Old High German *stornēn* to alarm, Latin *sternāx* stubborn, Greek *stereos* hard] —'**stern·ly** *adv.* —'**stern·ness** *n.*

stern[2] (stɜːn) *n.* **1.** the rear or after part of a vessel, opposite the bow or stem. **2.** the rear part of any object. ~*adj.* **3.** relating to or located at the stern. [C13: from Old Norse *stjōrn* steering; see STEER[1]]

Stern (stɜːn) *n.* **I·saac.** born 1920, U.S. concert violinist, born in Russia.

stern-chas·er *n.* a gun mounted at the stern of a vessel for firing aft at a pursuing vessel.

Sterne (stɜːn) *n.* **Lau·rence.** 1713–68, English novelist, born in Ireland, author of *The Life and Opinions of Tristram Shandy, Gentleman* (1759–67) and *A Sentimental Journey through France and Italy* (1768).

stern·fore·most (stɜːnˈfɔːməʊst) *adv. Nautical.* backwards.

stern·most ('stɜːnˌməʊst) *adj. Nautical.* **1.** farthest to the stern; aftmost. **2.** nearest the stern.

stern·post ('stɜːnˌpəʊst) *n. Nautical.* the main upright timber or structure at the stern of a vessel.

stern sheets *pl. n. Nautical.* the part of an open boat near the stern.

stern·son ('stɜːnsᵊn) *n. Nautical.* a timber scarfed into or bolted to the sternpost and keelson at the stern of a wooden vessel. Compare **stemson.** [C19: from STERN[2] + *-son,* on the model of KEELSON]

ster·num ('stɜːnəm) *n., pl.* **·na** (-nə) *or* **·nums. 1.** (in man) a long flat vertical bone, situated in front of the thorax, to which are attached the collarbone and the first seven pairs of ribs. Nontechnical name: **breastbone. 2.** the corresponding part in many other vertebrates. **3.** a cuticular plate covering the ventral surface of a body segment of an arthropod. Compare **tergum.** [C17: via New Latin from Greek *sternon* breastbone] —'**ster·nal** *adj.*

ster·nu·ta·tion (ˌstɜːnjʊˈteɪʃən) *n.* a sneeze or the act of sneezing. [C16: from Late Latin *sternūtāre* to sneeze, from *sternuere* to sputter (of a light)]

ster·nu·ta·tor ('stɜːnjʊˌteɪtə) *n.* a substance that causes sneezing, coughing, and tears; used in chemical warfare.

ster·nu·ta·to·ry (stɜːˈnjuːtətərɪ, -trɪ) *adj.* also **ster·nu·ta·tive. 1.** causing or having the effect of sneezing. ~*n., pl.* **·to·ries. 2.** an agent or substance that causes sneezing.

stern·wards ('stɜːnwədz) *or* **stern·ward** *adv. Nautical.* towards the stern; astern.

stern·way ('stɜːnˌweɪ) *n. Nautical.* movement of a vessel sternforemost.

stern-wheel·er *n.* a vessel, esp. a riverboat, propelled by a large paddle wheel at the stern. Compare **sidewheeler.**

ster·oid ('stɛrɔɪd) *n. Biochem.* any of a large group of fat-soluble organic compounds containing a characteristic chemical ring system. The majority, including the sterols, bile acids, many hormones, and the D vitamins, have important physiological action. [C20: from STEROL + -OID] —**ste·'roi·dal** *adj.*

ster·ol ('stɛrɒl) *n. Biochem.* any of a group of natural steroid alcohols, such as cholesterol and ergosterol, that are waxy insoluble substances. [C20: shortened from CHOLESTEROL, ERGOSTEROL, etc.]

ster·tor ('stɜːtə) *n.* laborious or noisy breathing caused by obstructed air passages. [C17: from New Latin, from Latin *stertere* to snore]

ster·to·rous ('stɜːtərəs) *adj.* **1.** marked or accompanied by heavy snoring. **2.** breathing in this way. —'**ster·to·rous·ly** *adv.* —'**ster·to·rous·ness** *n.*

stet (stɛt) *n.* **1.** a word or mark indicating that certain deleted typeset or written matter is to be retained. Compare **dele.** ~*vb.* **stets, stet·ting, stet·ted. 2.** (*tr.*) to mark (matter to be retained) with a stet. [Latin, literally: let it stand]

steth·o·scope ('stɛθəˌskəʊp) *n. Med.* an instrument for listening to the sounds made within the body, typically consisting of a hollow disc that transmits the sound through hollow tubes to earpieces. [C19: from French, from Greek *stēthos* breast + -SCOPE] —**steth·o·scop·ic** (ˌstɛθəˈskɒpɪk) *adj.* —**ste·thos·co·py** (stɛˈθɒskəpɪ) *n.*

stet·son ('stɛtsᵊn) *n.* a man's felt slouch hat with a broad brim and high crown. [C20: named after John *Stetson* (1830–1906), American hatmaker who designed it]

Stet·tin (ʃtɛˈtiːn) *n.* the German name for **Szczecin.**

ste·ve·dore ('stiːvɪˌdɔː) *n.* **1.** a person employed to load or unload ships. ~*vb.* **2.** to load or unload (a ship, ship's cargo, etc.). [C18: from Spanish *estibador* a packer, from *estibar* to load (a ship), from Latin *stīpāre* to pack full]

ste·ve·dore's knot *n.* a knot forming a lump in a line, used by stevedores to secure ropes passing through holes.

Ste·ven·age ('stiːvənɪdʒ) *n.* a town in SE England, in N Hertfordshire on the Great North Road: developed chiefly as the first of the new towns (1946). Pop.: 66 918 (1971).

Ste·ven·graph ('stiːvᵊnˌgrɑːf) *or* **Ste·vens·graph** *n.* a picture, usually small, woven in silk. [named after Thomas *Stevens* (1828-88), English weaver]

Ste·vens ('stiːvᵊnz) *n.* **1. Thad·de·us** ('θædɪəs). 1792–1868, U.S. Radical Republican politician. An opponent of slavery, he supported Reconstruction and entered the resolution calling for the impeachment of President Andrew Johnson. **2. Wal·lace.** 1879–1955, U.S. poet, whose books include the collections *Harmonium* (1923), *The Man with the Blue Guitar* (1937), and *Transport to Summer* (1947).

Ste·ven·son ('stiːvənsən) *n.* **1. Ad·lai Ew·ing** ('ædleɪ 'juːɪŋ). 1900–68, U.S. statesman: twice defeated as Democratic presidential candidate (1952; 1956); U.S. delegate at the United Nations (1961–65). **2. Rob·ert Lou·is (Balfour).** 1850–94, Scottish writer: his novels include *Treasure Island* (1883) and *Kidnapped* (1886).

stew[1] (stjuː) *n.* **1. a.** a dish of meat, fish, or other food, cooked by stewing. **b.** (*as modifier*): *stew pot.* **2.** *Informal.* a difficult or worrying situation or a troubled state (esp. in the phrase **in a stew**). **3.** a heterogeneous mixture: *a stew of people of every race.* **4.** (*usually pl.*) *Archaic.* a brothel. **5.** *Obsolete.* a public room for hot steam baths. ~*vb.* **6.** to cook or cause to cook by long slow simmering. **7.** (*intr.*) *Informal.* to be troubled or agitated. **8.** (*intr.*) *Informal.* to be oppressed with heat or crowding. **9.** to cause (tea) to become bitter or (of tea) to become bitter through infusing for too long. **10. stew in one's own juice.** to suffer unaided the consequences of one's actions. [C14 *stuen* to take a very hot bath, from Old French *estuver,* from Vulgar Latin *extūfāre* (unattested), from EX-[1] + (unattested) *tūfus* vapour, from Greek *tuphos*]

stew[2] (stjuː) *n. Brit., archaic.* **1.** a fishpond or fishtank. **2.** an artificial oyster bed. [C14: from Old French *estui,* from *estoier* to shut up, confine, ultimately from Latin *studium* STUDY]

stew·ard ('stjʊəd) *n.* **1.** a person who administers the property, house, finances, etc., of another. **2.** a person who manages the eating arrangements, staff, or service at a club, hotel, etc. **3.** a waiter on a ship or aircraft. **4.** a mess attendant in a naval mess afloat or ashore. **5.** a person who helps to supervise some event or proceedings in an official capacity. **6.** short for **shop steward.** ~*vb.* **7.** to act or serve as a steward (of something). [Old English *stigweard,* from *stig* hall (see STY[1]) + *weard* WARD] —'**stew·ard·ˌship** *n.*

stew·ard·ess ('stjʊədɪs, ˌstjʊəˈdɛs) *n.* a woman who performs a steward's job on an aircraft or ship.

Stew·art ('stjʊət) *n.* **1.** the usual spelling for the royal house of **Stuart** before the reign of Mary Queen of Scots (Mary Stuart). **2. Jack·ie.** born 1939, Scottish motor-racing driver: world champion 1969, 1971, and 1973. **3. Rod.** born 1945, English rock singer: vocalist with The Faces (1969-75). His albums include *Never a Dull Moment* (1972) and *A Night on the Town* (1976).

Stew+art Is+land *n.* the third largest island of New Zealand, in the SW Pacific off the S tip of South Island. Pop.: 414 (1971). Area: 1735 sq. km (670 sq. miles).

stewed (stjuːd) *adj.* **1.** *Brit.* (of tea) having a bitter taste through having been left to infuse for too long. **2.** a slang word for **drunk.**

St. Ex. *abbrev. for* stock exchange.

Steyr *or* **Stei+er** (*German* 'ʃtaɪər) *n.* an industrial city in N central Austria, in Upper Austria. Pop.: 40 578 (1971).

stg. *abbrev. for* sterling.

stge. *abbrev. for* storage.

Sth. *abbrev. for* South.

sthen+ic ('sθɛnɪk) *adj.* abounding in energy or bodily strength; active or strong. [C18: from New Latin *sthenicus* from Greek *sthenos* force, on the model of *asthenic*]

Sthe·no ('sθiːnəʊ, 'sθɛnəʊ) *n. Greek myth.* one of the three Gorgons.

stib+ine ('stɪbaɪn) *n.* **1.** a colourless slightly soluble poisonous gas with an offensive odour: made by the action of hydrochloric acid on an alloy of antimony and zinc. Formula: SbH_3. **2.** any one of a class of stibine derivatives in which one or more hydrogen atoms have been replaced by organic groups. [C19: from Latin STIBIUM + -INE[2]]

stib+i·um ('stɪbɪəm) *n.* an obsolete name for **antimony.** [C14: from Latin: antimony (used as a cosmetic in ancient Rome), via Greek from Egyptian *stm*] —'**stib+i·al** *adj.*

stib+nite ('stɪbnaɪt) *n.* a soft greyish mineral consisting of antimony sulphide in orthorhombic crystalline form. It occurs in quartz veins and is the chief ore of antimony. Formula: Sb_2S_3. [C19: from obsolete *stibine* stibnite + -ITE[1]]

stich (stɪk) *n.* a line of poetry; verse. [C18: from Greek *stikhos* row, verse; related to *steikhein* to walk] —'**stich+ic** *adj.* —'**stich·i+cal+ly** *adv.*

sti+chom+e·try (stɪ'kɒmɪtrɪ) *n. Prosody.* the practice of writing out a prose text in lines that correspond to the sense units and indicate the phrasal rhythms. —**stich·o+met+ric** (ˌstɪkəʊ'mɛtrɪk) *or* ˌ**stich·o+'met+ri+cal** *adj.*

stich·o+myth·i·a (ˌstɪkəʊ'mɪθɪə) *or* **sti+chom·y+thy** (stɪ'kɒmɪθɪ) *n.* a form of dialogue originating in Greek drama in which single lines are uttered by alternate speakers. [C19: from Greek *stikhomuthein* to speak alternate lines, from *stikhos* line + *muthos* speech; see MYTH] —ˌ**stich·o+'myth+ic** *adj.*

-stich·ous *adj. combining form.* having a certain number of rows: *distichous.* [from Late Latin *-stichus,* from Greek *-stikhos,* from *stikhos* line, row; see STICH]

stick[1] (stɪk) *n.* **1.** a small thin branch of a tree. **2. a.** any long thin piece of wood. **b.** such a piece of wood having a characteristic shape for a special purpose: *a walking stick; a hockey stick.* **c.** a baton, wand, staff, or rod. **3.** an object or piece shaped like a stick: *a stick of celery; a stick of dynamite.* **4.** See **control stick. 5.** *Informal.* the lever used to change gear in a motor vehicle. **6.** *Nautical.* a mast or yard. **7. a.** a group of bombs arranged to fall at intervals across a target. **b.** a number of paratroops jumping in sequence. **8.** (*usually pl.*) a piece of furniture: *these few sticks are all I have.* **9.** (*pl.*) *Informal.* a rural area considered remote or backward (esp. in the phrase **in the sticks**). **10.** (*pl.*) *W and NW Canadian informal.* the wooded interior part of the country. **11.** (*pl.*) *Hockey.* a declaration made by the umpire if a player's stick is above the shoulders. **12.** *Slang.* a cannabis cigarette. **13.** a means of coercion. **14.** *Informal.* a dull boring person. **15.** (usually preceded by *old*) *Informal.* a familiar name for a person: *not a bad old stick.* **16.** *Slang.* a style of life or way of doing things. **17. in a cleft stick.** in a difficult position. **18. wrong end of the stick.** a complete misunderstanding of a situation, explanation, etc. ~*vb.* **sticks, stick+ing, sticked. 19.** to support (a plant) with sticks; stake. **20.** *Printing.* to set (type) in a composing stick. [Old English *sticca;* related to Old Norse *stikka,* Old High German *stecca*]

stick[2] (stɪk) *vb.* **sticks, stick+ing, stuck. 1.** (*tr.*) to pierce or stab with or as if with something pointed. **2.** to thrust or push (a sharp or pointed object) or (of a sharp or pointed object) to be pushed into or through another object. **3.** (*tr.*) to fasten in position by pushing or forcing a point into something: *to stick a peg in a hole.* **4.** (*tr.*) to fasten in position by or as if by pins, nails, etc.: *to stick a picture on the wall.* **5.** (*tr.*) to transfix or impale on a pointed object. **6.** (*tr.*) to cover with objects piercing or set in the surface. **7.** (when *intr.,* foll. by *out, up, through,* etc.) to put forward or be put forward; protrude or cause to protrude: *to stick one's head out of the window.* **8.** (*tr.*) *Informal.* to place or put in a specified position: *stick your coat on this chair.* **9.** to fasten or be fastened by or as if by an adhesive substance: *stick the pages together; they won't stick.* **10.** (*tr.*) *Informal.* to cause to become sticky. **11.** (when *tr., usually passive*) to come or cause to come to a standstill: *we were stuck for hours in a traffic jam; the wheels stuck.* **12.** (*intr.*) to remain for a long time: *the memory sticks in my mind.* **13.** *Slang, chiefly Brit.* to tolerate; abide: *I can't stick that man.* **14.** (*intr.*) to be reluctant. **15.** (*tr.; usually passive*) *Informal.* to cause to be at a loss; baffle, puzzle, or confuse: *I was totally stuck for an answer.* **16.** (*tr.*) *Slang.* to force or impose something unpleasant on: *they stuck me with the bill for lunch.* **17.** (*tr.*) to kill by piercing or stabbing. **18. stick in one's throat.** *Informal.* to be difficult or impossible for one to accept. **19. stick to the ribs.** *Informal.* (of food) to be hearty and satisfying. ~*n.* **20.** the state or condition of adhering. **21.** *Informal.* a substance causing adhesion. **22.** *Obsolete.* something that causes delay or stoppage. ~See also **stick around, stick at, stick by, stick down, stick out, stick to, stick together, stick-up, stick with, stuck.** [Old English *stician;* related to Old High German *stehhan* to sting, Old Norse *steikja* to roast on a spit]

stick a·round *or* **a·bout** *vb.* (*intr., adv.*) *Informal.* to remain in a place, esp. awaiting something.

stick at *vb.* (*intr., prep.*) **1.** to continue constantly at: *to stick at one's work.* **2. stick at nothing.** to allow no feelings of doubt or scruples to hinder one.

stick by *vb.* (*intr., prep.*) to remain faithful to; adhere to.

stick down *vb.* (*tr., adv.*) *Informal.* to write: *stick your name down here.*

stick+er ('stɪkə) *n.* **1.** an adhesive label, poster, or paper. **2.** a person or thing that sticks. **3.** a persevering or industrious person. **4.** something prickly, such as a thorn, that clings to one's clothing, etc. **5.** *Informal.* something that perplexes. **6.** *Informal.* a knife used for stabbing or piercing.

stick+ful ('stɪkˌfʊl) *n., pl.* **+fuls.** *Printing.* the amount of type required to fill a composing stick.

stick+ing plas+ter *n.* a thin cloth with an adhesive substance on one side, used for covering slight or superficial wounds. Usual U.S. term: **adhesive tape.**

stick in+sect *n.* any of various mostly tropical insects of the family *Phasmidae* that have an elongated cylindrical body and long legs and resemble twigs: order *Phasmida.* Usual U.S. name: **walking stick.** See also **leaf insect.**

stick-in-the-mud *n. Informal.* a staid or predictably conservative person who lacks initiative or imagination.

stick+le ('stɪk[ə]l) *vb.* (*intr.*) **1.** to dispute stubbornly, esp. about minor points. **2.** to refuse to agree or concur, esp. by making petty stipulations. [C16 *stightle* (in the sense: to arbitrate): frequentative of Old English *stihtan* to arrange; related to Old Norse *stētta* to support]

stick·le+back ('stɪk[ə]lˌbæk) *n.* any small teleost fish of the family *Gasterosteidae,* such as *Gasterosteus aculeatus* (**three-spined stickleback**) of rivers and coastal regions and *G. pungitius* (**ten-spined stickleback**) confined to rivers. They have a series of spines along the back and occur in cold and temperate northern regions.

stick+ler ('stɪklə) *n.* **1.** (usually foll. by *for*) a person who makes insistent demands: *a stickler for accuracy.* **2.** a problem or puzzle: *the investigation proved to be a stickler.*

stick out *vb.* (*adv.*) **1.** to project or cause to project. **2.** (*tr.*) *Informal.* to endure (something disagreeable) (esp. in the phrase **stick it out**). **3. stick out a mile** *or* **like a sore thumb.** *Informal.* to be extremely obvious. **4. stick out for** (*intr.*) to insist on (a demand), refusing to yield until it is met: *the unions stuck out for a ten per cent wage rise.*

stick pin *n.* the U.S. name for **tie pin.**

stick+seed ('stɪkˌsiːd) *n.* any of various Eurasian and North American plants of the boraginaceous genus *Lappula,* having red-and-blue flowers and small prickly fruits. Also called: **beggar's-lice.**

stick+tight ('stɪkˌtaɪt) *n.* any of various plants, esp. the bur marigold, that have barbed clinging fruits.

stick to *vb.* (*prep., mainly intr.*) **1.** (*also tr.*) to adhere or cause to adhere to. **2.** to continue constantly at. **3.** to remain faithful to. **4.** not to move or digress from: *the speaker stuck closely to his subject.* **5. stick to someone's fingers.** *Informal.* to be stolen by someone.

stick to+geth+er *vb.* (*intr., adv.*) *Informal.* to remain loyal or friendly to one another.

stick-up *n.* **1.** *Slang, chiefly U.S.* a robbery at gunpoint; hold-up. ~*vb.* **stick up.** (*adv.*) **2.** (*tr.*) *Slang, chiefly U.S.* to rob, esp. at gunpoint. **3. stick up for.** (*intr.*) *Informal.* to support or defend: *stick up for oneself.*

stick+weed ('stɪkˌwiːd) *n.* any of several plants that have clinging fruits or seeds, esp. the ragweed.

stick with *vb.* (*intr., prep.*) *Informal.* to persevere with; remain faithful to.

stick·y ('stɪkɪ) *adj.* **stick·i+er, stick·i+est. 1.** covered or daubed with an adhesive or viscous substance: *sticky fingers.* **2.** having the property of sticking to a surface. **3.** (of weather or atmosphere) warm and humid; muggy. **4.** (of prices) tending not to fall in deflationary conditions. **5.** *Informal.* difficult, awkward, or painful: *a sticky business.* **6.** *U.S. informal.* sentimental. ~*vb.* **7.** (*tr.*) *Informal.* to make sticky. ~*n. Austral. informal.* **8.** short for **stickybeak. 9.** an inquisitive look or stare (esp. in the phrase **have a sticky at**). —'**stick·i+ly** *adv.* —'**stick·i+ness** *n.*

stick·y+beak ('stɪkɪˌbiːk) *Austral. informal.* ~*n.* **1.** an inquisitive person. ~*vb.* **2.** (*intr.*) to pry.

stick·y end *n. Informal.* an unpleasant finish or death (esp. in the phrase **come to** *or* **meet a sticky end**).

stick·y wick+et *n.* **1.** a cricket pitch that is rapidly being dried by the sun after rain and is particularly conducive to spin. **2.** *Informal.* a difficult or awkward situation.

stick·y wil+lie *n.* another name for **cleavers.**

stiff (stɪf) *adj.* **1.** not easily bent; rigid; inflexible. **2.** not working or moving easily or smoothly: *a stiff handle.* **3.** difficult to accept in its severity or harshness: *a stiff punishment.* **4.** moving with pain or difficulty; not supple: *a stiff neck.* **5.** difficult; arduous: *a stiff climb.* **6.** unrelaxed or awkward; formal. **7.** firmer than liquid in consistency; thick or viscous. **8.** powerful; strong: *a stiff breeze; a stiff drink.* **9.** excessively high: *a stiff price.* **10.** *Nautical.* (of a sailing vessel) relatively resistant to heeling or rolling. Compare **tender**[1] (sense 11). **11.** lacking grace or attractiveness. **12.** stubborn or stubbornly maintained: *a stiff fight.* **13.** *Obsolete.* tightly stretched;

taut. **14.** *Dialect, chiefly Scot. and northern Brit.* sturdy and stocky. **15.** *Austral. slang.* unlucky. **16.** *Slang.* intoxicated. **17. stiff upper lip.** See **lip** (sense 9). **18. stiff with.** *Informal.* amply provided with. ~*n.* **19.** *Slang.* a corpse. **20.** *Horse racing slang.* a horse that is believed to be a certain loser. ~*adv.* **21.** completely or utterly: *bored stiff; frozen stiff.* [Old English *stīf;* related to Old Norse *stīfla* to dam up, Middle Low German *stīf* stiff, Latin *stīpēs* wooden post, *stīpāre* to press] —**'stiff·ish** *adj.* —**'stiff·ly** *adv.* —**'stiff·ness** *n.*

stiff·en ('stɪfᵊn) *vb.* **1.** to make or become stiff or stiffer. **2.** (*intr.*) to become suddenly tense or unyielding. —**'stiff·en·er** *n.*

stiff-necked *adj.* haughtily stubborn or obstinate.

sti·fle¹ ('staɪfᵊl) *vb.* **1.** (*tr.*) to smother or suppress: *stifle a cough.* **2.** to feel or cause to feel discomfort and difficulty in breathing. **3.** to prevent or be prevented from breathing so as to cause death. **4.** (*tr.*) to crush or stamp out. [C14: variant of *stuflen,* probably from Old French *estouffer* to smother] —**'sti·fler** *n.*

sti·fle² ('staɪfᵊl) *n.* the joint in the hind leg of a horse, dog, etc., between the femur and tibia. [C14: of unknown origin]

sti·fling ('staɪflɪŋ) *adj.* oppressively hot or stuffy: *a stifling atmosphere.* —**'sti·fling·ly** *adv.*

stig·ma ('stɪgmə) *n., pl.* **stig·mas** *or* **stig·ma·ta** ('stɪgmətə, stɪg'mɑːtə). **1.** a distinguishing mark of social disgrace: *the stigma of having been in prison.* **2.** a small scar or mark such as a birthmark. **3.** *Pathol.* **a.** any mark on the skin, such as one characteristic of a specific disease. **b.** any sign of a mental deficiency or emotional upset. **4.** *Botany.* the terminal part of the ovary, at the end of the style, where deposited pollen enters the gynoecium. **5.** *Zoology.* **a.** a pigmented eyespot in some protozoans and other invertebrates. **b.** the spiracle of an insect. **6.** *Archaic.* a mark branded on the skin. **7.** (*pl.*) *Christianity.* marks resembling the wounds of the crucified Christ, believed to appear on the bodies of certain individuals. [C16: via Latin from Greek: brand, from *stizein* to tattoo]

stig·mas·ter·ol (stɪg'mæstəˌrɒl) *n. Biochem.* a sterol obtained from Calabar beans and soya beans and used in the manufacture of progesterone. Formula: $C_{29}H_{47}OH$. [C20: from New Latin *(physo)stigma* genus name of the Calabar bean + STEROL; see PHYSOSTIGMINE]

stig·mat·ic (stɪg'mætɪk) *adj. also* **stig·mat·i·cal. 1.** relating to or having a stigma or stigmata. **2.** another word for **anastigmatic.** ~*n. also* **stig·ma·tist** ('stɪgmətɪst). **3.** *Chiefly R.C. Church.* a person marked with the stigmata.

stig·ma·tism ('stɪgməˌtɪzəm) *n.* **1.** *Physics.* the state or condition of being anastigmatic. **2.** *Pathol.* the condition resulting from or characterized by stigmata.

stig·ma·tize *or* **stig·ma·tise** ('stɪgməˌtaɪz) *vb.* (*tr.*) to mark with a stigma or stigmata. —ˌ**stig·ma·ti·'za·tion** *or* ˌ**stig·ma·ti·'sa·tion** *n.* —**'stig·maˌtiz·er** *or* **'stig·maˌtis·er** *n.*

Stijl (staɪl) *n.* **De.** See **De Stijl.**

stil·bene ('stɪlbiːn) *n.* a colourless or slightly yellow crystalline water-insoluble unsaturated hydrocarbon used in the manufacture of dyes; *trans-1,2*-diphenylethene. Formula: C_6H_5CH: CHC_6H_5. [C19: from Greek *stilbos* glittering + -ENE]

stil·bite ('stɪlbaɪt) *n.* a white or yellow zeolite mineral consisting of hydrated calcium sodium aluminium silicate, often in the form of sheaves of monoclinic crystals. Formula: $(Na_2Ca)Al_2Si_6O_{16}.6H_2O$. [C19: from Greek *stilbos* glittering (from *stilbein* to shine) + -ITE¹]

stil·boes·trol *or U.S.* **stil·bes·trol** (stɪl'biːstrəl) *n.* a synthetic hormone having derivatives with oestrogenic properties. Formula: $OHC_6H_4CH{:}CHC_6H_4OH$. Also called: **diethylstilboestrol.** [C20: from STILBENE + OESTRUS + -OL¹]

stile¹ (staɪl) *n.* **1.** a set of steps or rungs in a wall or fence to allow people, but not animals, to pass over. **2.** short for **turnstile.** [Old English *stigel;* related to *stīgan* to climb, Old High German *stigilla;* see STAIR]

stile² (staɪl) *n.* a vertical board that forms part of a panel of a door, window frame, ladder, etc. [C17: probably from Dutch *stijl* pillar, ultimately from Latin *stilus* writing instrument; see STYLE]

sti·let·to (stɪ'lɛtəʊ) *n., pl.* **·tos. 1.** a small dagger with a slender tapered blade. **2.** a sharply pointed tool used to make holes in leather, cloth, etc. **3.** Also called: **spike heel, stiletto heel.** *Brit.* a very high heel on a woman's shoe, tapering to a very narrow tip. ~*vb.* **·toes, ·toe·ing, ·toed. 4.** (*tr.*) to stab with a stiletto. [C17: from Italian, from *stilo* a dagger, from Latin *stilus* a stake, pen; see STYLUS]

Stil·i·cho ('stɪlɪkəʊ) *n.* **Fla·vi·us** ('fleɪvɪəs). ?365–408 A.D., Roman general and statesman, born a Vandal. As the guardian of Emperor Theodosius' son Honorius, he was effective ruler of the Western Roman Empire (395–408), which he defended against the Visigoths.

still¹ (stɪl) *adj.* **1.** (*usually predicative*) motionless; stationary. **2.** undisturbed or tranquil; silent and calm. **3.** not sparkling or effervescent: *a still wine.* **4.** gentle or quiet; subdued. **5.** *Obsolete.* (of a child) dead at birth. ~*adv.* **6.** continuing now or in the future as in the past: *do you still love me?* **7.** up to this or that time; yet: *I still don't know your name.* **8.** (often used with a comparative) even or yet: *still more insults.* **9.** quiet or without movement: *sit still.* **10.** *Poetic and dialect.* always. ~*n.* **11.** *Poetic.* silence or tranquillity: *the still of the night.* **12. a.** a still photograph, esp. of a scene from a motion-picture film. **b.** (*as modifier*): *a still camera.* ~*vb.* **13.** to make or become still, quiet, or calm. **14.** (*tr.*) to allay or relieve: *her fears were stilled.* ~*sentence connector.* **15.** even then; nevertheless: *the child has some new toys and still cries.* [Old English *stille;* related to Old Saxon, Old High German *stilli,* Dutch *stollen* to curdle, Sanskrit *sthānús* immobile] —**'still·ness** *n.*

still² (stɪl) *n.* **1.** an apparatus for carrying out distillation, consisting of a vessel in which a mixture is heated, a condenser to turn the vapour back to liquid, and a receiver to hold the distilled liquid, used esp. in the manufacture of spirits. **2.** a place where spirits are made; distillery. [C16: from Old French *stiller* to drip, from Latin *stillāre,* from *stilla* a drip; see DISTIL]

stil·lage ('stɪlɪdʒ) *n.* a frame or stand for keeping things off the ground, such as casks in a brewery. [C16: probably from Dutch *stillagie* frame, scaffold, from *stellen* to stand; see -AGE]

still·birth ('stɪlˌbɜːθ) *n.* **1.** birth of a dead fetus or baby. **2.** a stillborn fetus or baby.

still·born ('stɪlˌbɔːn) *adj.* **1.** (of a fetus) dead at birth. **2.** (of an idea, plan, etc.) fruitless; abortive; unsuccessful. ~*n.* **3.** a stillborn fetus or baby.

still hunt *n.* **1.** the hunting of game by stalking or ambushing. ~*vb.* **still-hunt. 2.** to hunt (quarry) in this way.

stil·li·cide ('stɪlɪˌsaɪd) *n. Law.* a right or duty relating to the drainage of water from the eaves of a roof onto adjacent land. [C17: from Latin *stillicidium,* from *stilla* drop + *-cidium,* from *cadere* to fall]

stil·li·form ('stɪlɪˌfɔːm) *adj. Rare.* having the shape of a drop or globule. [C20: from Latin *stilla* a drop + -FORM]

still life *n., pl.* **still lifes. 1. a.** a painting or drawing of inanimate objects, such as fruit, flowers, etc. **b.** (*as modifier*): *a still-life painting.* **2.** the genre of such paintings.

still room *n. Brit.* **1.** a room in which distilling is carried out. **2.** a pantry or storeroom, as in a large house.

Still·son wrench ('stɪlsᵊn) *n. Trademark.* a large wrench having jaws that tighten as the pressure on the handle is increased.

stil·ly *adv.* ('stɪllɪ). **1.** *Archaic or literary.* quietly or calmly. ~*adj.* ('stɪlɪ). **2.** *Poetic.* still, quiet, or calm.

stilt (stɪlt) *n.* **1.** either of a pair of two long poles with footrests on which a person stands and walks, as used by circus clowns. **2.** a long post or column that is used with others to support a building above ground level. **3.** any of several shore birds of the genera *Himantopus* and *Cladorhynchus,* similar to the avocets but having a straight bill. ~*vb.* **4.** (*tr.*) to raise or place on or as if on stilts. [C14 (in the sense: crutch, handle of a plough): related to Low German *stilte* pole, Norwegian *stilta*]

stilt·ed ('stɪltɪd) *adj.* **1.** (of speech, writing, etc.) formal, pompous, or bombastic. **2.** not flowing continuously or naturally: *stilted conversation.* **3.** *Architect.* (of an arch) having vertical piers between the impost and the springing. —**'stilt·ed·ly** *adv.* —**'stilt·ed·ness** *n.*

Stil·ton ('stɪltən) *n.* either of two rich cheeses made from whole milk, blue-veined **(blue Stilton)** or white **(white Stilton),** both very strong in flavour.

stim·u·lant ('stɪmjʊlənt) *n.* **1.** a drug or similar substance that increases physiological activity, esp. of a particular organ. **2.** any stimulating agent or thing. ~*adj.* **3.** a less common word for **stimulating.** [C18: from Latin *stimulāns* goading, from *stimulāre* to urge on; see STIMULUS]

stim·u·late ('stɪmjʊˌleɪt) *vb.* **1.** (*tr.*) to arouse or quicken the activity or senses of. **2.** (*tr.*) *Physiol.* to excite (a nerve, organ, etc.) with a stimulus. **3.** (*intr.*) to act as a stimulant or stimulus. [C16: from Latin *stimulāre;* see STIMULANT] —**'stim·u·la·ble** *adj.* —**'stim·uˌlat·ing·ly** *adv.* —ˌ**stim·u·'la·tion** *n.* —**'stim·u·la·tive** *adj., n.* —**'stim·uˌla·tor** *or* **'stim·uˌlat·er** *n.*

stim·u·lus ('stɪmjʊləs) *n., pl.* **·li** (-ˌlaɪ, -ˌliː). **1.** something that stimulates or acts as an incentive. **2.** any drug, agent, electrical impulse, or other factor able to cause a response in an organism. **3.** an object or event that is apprehended by the senses. **4.** *Med.* another word for a **stimulant.** [C17: from Latin: a cattle goad]

sting (stɪŋ) *vb.* **stings, sting·ing, stung. 1.** (of certain animals and plants) to inflict a wound on (an organism) by the injection of poison. **2.** to feel or cause to feel a sharp mental or physical pain. **3.** (*tr.*) to goad or incite (esp. in the phrase **sting into action**). **4.** (*tr.*) *Informal.* to cheat, esp. by overcharging. ~*n.* **5.** a skin wound caused by the poison injected by certain insects or plants. **6.** pain caused by or as if by the sting of a plant or animal. **7.** a mental pain or pang: *a sting of conscience.* **8.** a sharp pointed organ, such as the ovipositor of a wasp, by which poison can be injected into the prey. **9.** the ability to sting: *a sharp sting in his criticism.* **10.** something as painful or swift of action as a sting: *the sting of death.* **11.** a sharp stimulus or incitement. **12.** *Botany.* another name for **stinging hair.** [Old English *stingan;* related to Old Norse *stinga* to pierce, Gothic *usstangan* to pluck out, Greek *stakhus* ear of corn] —**'sting·ing·ly** *adv.* —**'sting·ing·ness** *n.*

sting·a·ree ('stɪŋəˌriː, ˌstɪŋə'riː) *n. U.S., Austral.* a popular name for the **stingray.**

sting·er ('stɪŋə) *n.* **1.** a person, plant, animal, etc., that stings or hurts. **2.** a whisky and soda with crushed ice.

sting·ing hair *n.* a multicellular hair in plants, such as the stinging nettle, that injects an irritant fluid when in contact with an animal.

sting·ing net·tle *n.* See **nettle** (sense 1).

stin·go ('stɪŋgəʊ) *n.* a strong English beer, originally made in Yorkshire.

sting·ray ('stɪŋˌreɪ) *n.* any ray of the family *Dasyatidae,* having a whiplike tail bearing a serrated venomous spine capable of inflicting painful weals on man.

stin·gy¹ ('stɪndʒɪ) *adj.* **·gi·er, ·gi·est. 1.** unwilling to spend or give. **2.** insufficient or scanty. [C17 (perhaps in the sense: ill-tempered): perhaps from *stinge,* dialect variant of STING] —'**stin·gi·ly** *adv.* —'**stin·gi·ness** *n.*

sting·y² ('stɪŋɪ) *adj.* **sting·i·er, sting·i·est. 1.** *Informal.* stinging or capable of stinging. ~*n., pl.* **sting·ies. 2.** *South Wales dialect.* a stinging nettle: *I put my hand on a stingy.*

stink (stɪŋk) *n.* **1.** a strong foul smell; stench. **2.** *Slang.* a great deal of trouble (esp. in the phrase **to make** *or* **raise a stink**). **3. like stink.** intensely; furiously. ~*vb.* **stinks, stink·ing, stank** *or* **stunk; stunk.** (*mainly intr.*) **4.** to emit a foul smell. **5.** *Slang.* to be thoroughly bad or abhorrent: *this town stinks.* **6.** *Informal.* to have a very bad reputation: *his name stinks.* **7.** to be of poor quality. **8.** (foll. by *of* or *with*) *Slang.* to have or appear to have an excessive amount (of money). **9.** (*tr.;* usually foll. by *up*) *Informal.* to cause to stink. ~See also **stink out.** [Old English *stincan;* related to Old Saxon *stinkan,* German *stinken,* Old Norse *stökkva* to burst; see STENCH]

stink ball *n.* another name for **stink pot** (sense 4).

stink bomb *n.* a small bomb, used by practical jokers, containing a liquid with an offensive smell.

stink·er ('stɪŋkə) *n.* **1.** a person or thing that stinks. **2.** *Slang.* a difficult or very unpleasant person or thing. **3.** *Slang.* something of very poor quality. **4.** *Informal.* any of several fulmars or related birds that feed on carrion.

stink·horn ('stɪŋkˌhɔːn) *n.* any of various basidiomycetous saprophytic fungi of the genus *Phallus,* such as *P. impudicus,* having an offensive odour.

stink·ing ('stɪŋkɪŋ) *adj.* **1.** having a foul smell. **2.** *Informal.* unpleasant or disgusting. **3.** (*postpositive*) *Slang.* very drunk. **4. cry stinking fish.** to decry or defame something, esp. one's own products. ~*adv.* **5.** *Informal.* (intensifier, expressing contempt for the person referred to): *stinking rich.* —'**stink·ing·ly** *adv.* —'**stink·ing·ness** *n.*

stink·ing badg·er *n.* another name for **teledu.**

stink·ing i·ris *n.* an iris plant, *Iris foetidissima,* of W Europe and N Africa, having purplish flowers and a strong unpleasant smell when bruised. Also called: **gladdon.**

stink·ing smut *n.* a smut that affects wheat and is caused by the fungus *Tilletia caries.* Also called: **bunt.**

stink·o ('stɪŋkəʊ) *adj.* (*postpositive*) a slang word for **drunk.**

stink out *vb.* (*tr., adv.*) **1.** to drive out or away by a foul smell. **2.** *Brit.* to cause to stink: *the smell of orange peel stinks out the room.*

stink·pot ('stɪŋkˌpɒt) *n.* **1.** *Slang.* a person or thing that stinks. **2.** *Slang.* a person considered to be unpleasant. **3.** another name for **musk turtle. 4.** Also called: **stink ball.** *Military.* (formerly) a container filled with material that gives off noxious or suffocating vapours. **5.** *Disparaging.* a slang word (used by yachtsmen) for a **powerboat.**

stink·stone ('stɪŋkˌstəʊn) *n.* any of various rocks producing a fetid odour when struck, esp. certain limestones.

stink trap *n.* another name for **stench trap.**

stink·weed ('stɪŋkˌwiːd) *n.* **1.** Also called: **wall mustard.** a cruciferous plant, *Diplotaxis muralis,* naturalized in Britain and S and central Europe, having pale yellow flowers, cylindrical seed pods, and a disagreeable smell when bruised. **2.** any of various other ill-smelling plants, such as mayweed.

stink·wood ('stɪŋkˌwʊd) *n.* **1.** any of various trees having offensive-smelling wood, esp. *Ocotea bullata,* a southern African lauraceous tree yielding a hard wood used for furniture. **2.** the heavy durable wood of any of these trees.

stint¹ (stɪnt) *vb.* **1.** to be frugal or miserly towards (someone) with (something). **2.** *Archaic.* to stop or check (something). ~*n.* **3.** an allotted or fixed amount of work. **4.** a limitation or check. **5.** *Obsolete.* a pause or stoppage. [Old English *styntan* to blunt; related to Old Norse *stytta* to cut short; see STUNT¹] —'**stint·er** *n.*

stint² (stɪnt) *n.* any of various small sandpipers of the chiefly northern genus *Calidris* (or *Erolia*), such as *C. minuta* (**little stint**). [Old English; related to Middle High German *stinz* small salmon, Swedish dialect *stinta* teenager; see STUNT¹]

stipe (staɪp) *n.* **1.** a stalk in plants that bears reproductive structures, esp. the stalk bearing the cap of a mushroom. **2.** the stalk that bears the leaflets of a fern or the thallus of a seaweed. **3.** *Zoology.* any stalklike part; stipes. [C18: via French from Latin *stīpes* tree trunk; related to Latin *stīpāre* to pack closely; see STIFF]

sti·pel ('staɪpᵊl) *n.* a small paired leaflike structure at the base of certain leaflets; secondary stipule. [C19: via New Latin from Latin *stipula,* diminutive of *stīpes* a log] —**sti·pel·late** (staɪ'pelɪt, -eɪt) *adj.*

sti·pend ('staɪpɛnd) *n.* a fixed or regular amount of money paid as a salary or allowance, as to a clergyman. [C15: from Old French *stipende,* from Latin *stīpendium* tax, from *stips* a contribution + *pendere* to pay out]

sti·pen·di·ar·y (staɪ'pɛndɪərɪ) *adj.* **1.** receiving or working for regular pay: *a stipendiary magistrate.* **2.** paid for by a stipend. ~*n., pl.* **·ar·ies. 3.** a person who receives regular payment. [C16: from Latin *stīpendiārius* concerning tribute, from *stīpendium* STIPEND]

sti·pes ('staɪpiːz) *n., pl.* **stip·i·tes** ('stɪpɪˌtiːz). *Zoology.* **1.** the second maxillary segment in insects and crustaceans. **2.** the eyestalk of a crab or similar crustacean. **3.** any similar stemlike structure. [C18: from Latin; see STIPE] —**sti·pi·form** ('staɪpɪˌfɔːm) *or* **stip·i·ti·form** ('stɪpɪtɪˌfɔːm) *adj.*

stip·i·tate ('stɪpɪˌteɪt) *adj. Botany.* possessing or borne on the end of a stipe. [C18: from New Latin *stīpitātus* having a stalk, from Latin *stipes;* see STIPE]

stip·ple ('stɪpᵊl) *vb.* **1.** (*tr.*) to draw, engrave, or paint using dots or flecks. ~*n. also* **stip·pling. 2.** the technique of stippling or a picture produced by or using stippling. [C18: from Dutch *stippelen,* from *stippen* to prick, from *stip* point] —'**stip·pler** *n.*

stip·u·late¹ ('stɪpjʊˌleɪt) *vb.* **1.** (*tr.; may take a clause as object*) to specify, often as a condition of an agreement. **2.** (*intr.;* foll. by *for*) to insist (on) as a term of an agreement. **3.** *Roman law.* to make (an oral contract) in the form of question and answer necessary to render it legally valid. **4.** (*tr.; may take a clause as object*) to guarantee or promise. [C17: from Latin *stipulārī,* probably from Old Latin *stipulus* firm, but perhaps from *stipula* a stalk, from the convention of breaking a straw to ratify a promise] —**stip·u·la·ble** ('stɪpjʊləbᵊl) *adj.* —ˌ**stip·u·'la·tion** *n.* —'**stip·u·ˌla·tor** *n.* —**stip·u·la·to·ry** ('stɪpjʊlətərɪ, -trɪ) *adj.*

stip·u·late² ('stɪpjʊlɪt, -ˌleɪt) *adj.* (of a plant) having stipules.

stip·ule ('stɪpjuːl) *n.* a small paired usually leaflike outgrowth occurring at the base of a leaf or its stalk. [C18: from Latin; see STIPE, STIPES] —**stip·u·lar** ('stɪpjʊlə) *adj.*

stir¹ (stɜː) *vb.* **stirs, stir·ring, stirred. 1.** to move an implement such as a spoon around in (a liquid) so as to mix up the constituents: *she stirred the porridge.* **2.** to change or cause to change position; disturb or be disturbed: *he stirred in his sleep.* **3.** (*intr.;* often foll. by *from*) to venture or depart (from one's usual or preferred place): *he won't stir from the fireside.* **4.** (*intr.*) to be active after a rest; be up and about. **5.** (*tr.*) to excite or stimulate, esp. emotionally. **6.** to move (oneself) briskly or vigorously; exert (oneself). **7.** (*tr.*) to rouse or awaken: *to stir someone from sleep; to stir memories.* **8.** (when *tr.,* foll. by *up*) to cause or incite others to cause (trouble, arguments, etc.). **9. stir one's stumps.** to move or become active. ~*n.* **10.** the act or an instance of stirring or the state of being stirred. **11.** a strong reaction, esp. of excitement: *his publication caused a stir.* **12.** a slight movement. ~See also **stir up.** [Old English *styrian;* related to Middle High German *stürn* to poke, stir, Norwegian *styrja* to cause a commotion; see STORM, STURGEON] —'**stir·ra·ble** *adj.* —'**stir·rer** *n.*

stir² (stɜː) *n.* **1.** a slang word for **prison:** *in stir.* **2. stir-crazy.** *U.S. slang.* mentally disturbed as a result of being in prison. [C19: of unknown origin]

Stir. *abbrev. for* Stirlingshire.

stir·a·bout ('stɜːrəˌbaʊt) *n.* **1.** a kind of porridge orginally made in Ireland. **2.** a bustling person.

stirk (stɜːk) *n.* **1.** a heifer of 6 to 12 months old. **2.** a yearling heifer or bullock. [Old English *stierc;* related to Middle Low German *sterke,* Old High German *stero* ram, Latin *sterilis* sterile, Greek *steira;* see STEER]

Stir·ling ('stɜːlɪŋ) *n.* **1.** a town in central Scotland, administrative centre of the Central region, on the River Forth: its castle was a regular residence of many Scottish monarchs between the 12th century and 1603. Pop.: 29 769 (1971). **2.** (until 1975) a county of central Scotland, now part of the Central region.

Stir·ling's for·mu·la *n.* a formula giving the approximate value of the factorial of a large number *n,* as $n! \simeq (n/e)^n\sqrt{2\pi n}$. [named after James *Stirling* (1692–1770), Scottish mathematician]

stirps (stɜːps) *n., pl.* **stir·pes** ('stɜːpiːz). **1.** *Genealogy.* a line of descendants from an ancestor; stock or strain. **2.** *Botany.* a race or variety, esp. one in which the characters are maintained by cultivation. [C17: from Latin: root, family origin]

stir·ring ('stɜːrɪŋ) *adj.* **1.** exciting the emotions; stimulating. **2.** active, lively, or busy. —'**stir·ring·ly** *adv.*

stir·rup ('stɪrəp) *n.* **1.** Also called: **stirrup iron.** either of two metal loops on a riding saddle, with a flat footpiece through which a rider puts his foot for support. They are attached to the saddle by **stirrup leathers. 2.** a U-shaped support or clamp made of metal, wood, leather, etc. **3.** *Nautical.* one of a set of ropes fastened to a yard at one end and having a thimble at the other through which a footrope is rove for support. [Old English *stigrāp,* from *stīg* path, step (related to Old High German *stīgan* to move up) + *rāp* ROPE; related to Old Norse *stigreip,* Old High German *stegareif*]

stir·rup bone *n.* the nontechnical name for **stapes.**

stir·rup cup *n.* a cup containing an alcoholic drink offered to a horseman ready to ride away.

stir·rup pump *n.* a hand-operated reciprocating pump, the base of the cylinder of which is placed in a bucket of water: used in fighting fires.

stir up *vb.* (*adv.*) to set or be set in motion; instigate or be instigated: *he stirred up trouble.*

stitch (stɪtʃ) *n.* **1.** a link made by drawing a thread through material by means of a needle. **2.** a loop of yarn formed around an implement used in knitting, crocheting, etc. **3.** a particular method of stitching or shape of stitch. **4.** a sharp spasmodic pain in the side resulting from running or exercising. **5.** (*usually used with a negative*) *Informal.* the least fragment of clothing: *he wasn't wearing a stitch.* **6.** *Agriculture.* the ridge between two furrows. **7. in stitches.** laughing uncontrollably. **8. drop a stitch.** to allow a loop of wool to fall off a knitting needle accidentally while knitting. ~*vb.* **9.** (*tr.*) to sew, fasten, etc., with stitches. **10.** (*intr.*) to be engaged in sewing. **11.** (*tr.*) to bind together (the leaves of a book, pamphlet, etc.) with wire staples or thread. ~*n., vb.* **12.** an informal word for **suture** (senses 1b., 6). [Old English *stice* sting; related to Old Frisian *steke,* Old High German *stih,* Gothic *stiks,* Old Norse *tikta* sharp] —'**stitch·er** *n.*

stitch wheel *n.* a notched wheel used by a harness maker to mark out the spacing for stitching.

stitch·wort ('stɪtʃˌwɜːt) *n.* any of several low-growing N temperate herbaceous plants of the caryophyllaceous genus *Stellaria,* having small white star-shaped flowers.

stith·y ('stɪðɪ) *n., pl.* **stith·ies. 1.** *Archaic or Brit. dialect.* a forge. *~vb.* **stith·ies, stith·y·ing, stith·ied. 2.** (*tr.*) *Obsolete.* to forge on an anvil. [C13: from Old Norse *stedhi*]

sti·ver ('staɪvə) *n.* **1.** a former Dutch coin worth one twentieth of a guilder. **2.** a small amount, esp. of money. [C16: from Dutch *stuiver;* related to Middle Low German *stüver,* Danish *styver*]

St. John ('sɪndʒən) *n.* **Hen·ry.** See (1st Viscount) **Bolingbroke.**

stk. *abbrev. for* stock.

sto·a ('stəʊə) *n., pl.* **sto·ae** ('stəʊiː) *or* **sto·as.** a covered walk that has a colonnade on one or both sides, esp. as used in ancient Greece. [C17: from Greek]

stoat (stəʊt) *n.* a small Eurasian musteline mammal, *Mustela erminea,* closely related to the weasels, having a brown coat and a black-tipped tail: in the northern parts of its range it has a white winter coat and is then known as an ermine. [C15: of unknown origin]

stob (stɒb) *n. Northern Brit. and U.S. dialect.* a post or stump.

sto·chas·tic (stɒ'kæstɪk) *adj.* **1.** *Statistics.* **a.** (of a variable) random with zero mean and finite variance. **b.** (of a process) involving a random variable the successive values of which are not independent. **c.** (of a matrix) square with non-negative elements that add to unity in each row. **2.** *Rare.* involving conjecture. [C17: from Greek *stokhastikos* capable of guessing, from *stokhazesthai* to aim at, conjecture, from *stokhos* a target] —**sto·'chas·ti·cal·ly** *adv.*

stock (stɒk) *n.* **1. a.** (*sometimes pl.*) the total goods or raw material kept on the premises of a shop or business. **b.** (*as modifier*): *a stock clerk; stock book.* **2.** a supply of something stored for future use: *he keeps a good stock of whisky.* **3.** *Finance.* **a.** the capital raised by a company through the issue and subscription of shares entitling their holders to dividends, partial ownership, and usually voting rights. **b.** the proportion of such capital held by an individual shareholder. **c.** the shares of a specified company or industry. **d.** (formerly) the part of an account or tally given to a creditor. **e.** the debt represented by this. **4.** standing or status. **5. a.** farm animals, such as cattle and sheep, bred and kept for their meat, skins, etc. **b.** (*as modifier*): *stock farming.* **6.** the trunk or main stem of a tree or other plant. **7.** *Horticulture.* **a.** a rooted plant into which a scion is inserted during grafting. **b.** a plant or stem from which cuttings are taken. See also **rootstock. 8.** the original type from which a particular race, family, group, etc., is derived. **9.** a race, breed, or variety of animals or plants. **10.** (*often pl.*) a small pen in which a single animal can be confined. **11.** a line of descent. **12.** any of the major subdivisions of the human species; race or ethnic group. **13. a.** the handle of a handgun. **b.** the part of a machine gun that connects the slide to the shoulder piece. **c.** the part of an artillery gun carriage consisting of a long beam resting on the ground for stability during firing. **14.** the handle of something, such as a whip or fishing rod. **15.** the main body of a tool, such as the block of a plane. **16.** short for **diestock, gunstock, linguistic stock,** or **rolling stock. 17.** (formerly) the part of a plough to which the irons and handles were attached. **18.** the main upright part of a supporting structure. **19.** a liquid or broth in which meat, fish, bones, or vegetables have been simmered for a long time. **20.** film material before exposure and processing. **21.** *Metallurgy.* **a.** a portion of metal cut from a bar upon which a specific process, such as forging, is to be carried out. **b.** the material that is smelted in a blast furnace. **22.** Also called: **gillyflower.** any of several cruciferous plants of the genus *Matthiola,* such as *M. incana* and *M. bicornis* (**evening** or **night-scented stock**), of the Mediterranean region: cultivated for their brightly coloured flowers. **23. Virginian stock.** a similar and related North American plant, *Malcomia maritima.* **24.** a long usually white neckcloth wrapped around the neck, worn in the 18th century and as part of modern riding dress. **25.** *Cards.* a pile of cards left after the deal in certain games, from which players draw. **26. a.** the repertoire of plays available to a repertory company. **b.** (*as modifier*): *a stock play.* **27.** (on some types of anchors) a crosspiece at the top of the shank under the ring. **28.** the centre of a wheel. **29.** an exposed mass of igneous rock that is the uppermost part of an underlying batholith. **30.** a log or block of wood. **31.** See **laughing stock. 32.** an archaic word for **stocking. 33. in stock. a.** stored on the premises or available for sale or use. **b.** supplied with goods of a specified kind. **34. out of stock. a.** not immediately available for sale or use. **b.** not having goods of a specified kind immediately available. **35. take stock. a.** to make an inventory. **b.** to make a general appraisal, esp. of prospects, resources, etc. **36. take stock in.** to attach importance to. **37. lock, stock, and barrel.** See **lock**[1] (sense 7). *~adj.* **38.** staple standard: *stock sizes in clothes.* **39.** (*prenominal*) being a cliché; hackneyed: *a stock phrase.* *~vb.* **40.** (*tr.*) to keep (goods) for sale. **41.** (*intr.;* usually foll. by *up* or *up on*) to obtain a store of (something) for future use or sale: *to stock up on beer.* **42.** (*tr.*) to supply with live animals, fish, etc.: *to stock a farm.* **43.** (*tr.*) to fasten or supply with a stock. **44.** (*intr.*) (of a plant) to put forth new shoots. **45.** (*tr.*) *Obsolete.* to punish by putting in the stocks. [Old English *stocc* trunk (of a tree), stem, stick (the various senses developed from these meanings, as trunk of a tree, hence line of descent; structures made of timber; a store of timber or other goods for future use, hence an aggregate of goods, animals, etc.); related to Old Saxon, Old High German *stock* stick, stump] —**'stock·er** *n.*

stock·ade (stɒ'keɪd) *n.* **1.** an enclosure or barrier of stakes and timbers. **2.** *U.S.* a military prison or detention area. *~vb.* **3.** (*tr.*) to surround with a stockade. [C17: from Spanish *estacada,* from *estaca* a stake, post, of Germanic origin; see STAKE[1]]

stock·breed·er ('stɒk,briːdə) *n.* a person who breeds or rears livestock as an occupation. —**'stock·,breed·ing** *n.*

stock·brok·er ('stɒk,brəʊkə) *n.* a person who buys and sells securities on a commission basis for customers. Often shortened to **broker.** Compare **stockjobber.** —**stock·bro·ker·age** ('stɒk,brəʊkərɪdʒ) *or* **'stock·,brok·ing** *n.*

stock·brok·er belt *n. Brit. informal.* the area outside a city, esp. London, in which rich commuters live. U.S. name: **exurbia.**

stock car *n.* **1. a.** a car, usually a production saloon, strengthened and modified for a form of racing in which the cars often collide. **b.** (*as modifier*): *stock-car racing.* **2.** the U.S. term for **cattle truck.**

stock cer·tif·i·cate *n.* the U.S. equivalent of **share certificate.**

stock com·pa·ny *n.* **1.** *U.S.* a business enterprise the capital of which is divided into transferable shares. **2.** a U.S. term for **repertory company.**

stock dove *n.* a European dove, *Columba oenas,* smaller than the wood pigeon and having a uniformly grey plumage.

stock ex·change *n.* **1.** Also called: **stock market. a.** a highly organized market facilitating the purchase and sale of securities and operated by professional stockbrokers and stockjobbers according to fixed rules. **b.** a place where securities are regularly traded. **c.** (*as modifier*): *a stock-exchange operator; stock-exchange prices.* **2.** the prices or trading activity of a stock exchange: *the stock exchange fell heavily today.*

stock farm *n.* a farm on which livestock is bred. —**stock farm·er** *n.* —**stock farm·ing** *n.*

stock·fish ('stɒk,fɪʃ) *n., pl.* **·fish** *or* **·fish·es.** fish, such as cod or haddock, cured by splitting and drying in the air.

Stock·haus·en (*German* 'ʃtɔk,haʊzᵊn) *n.* **Karl·heinz** (karl-'haɪnts). born 1928, German composer, whose avant-garde music exploits advanced serialization, electronic sounds, group improvization, and vocal and instrumental timbres and techniques. Works include *Gruppen* (1959) for three orchestras, *Stimmung* (1968) for six vocalists, and *Ylem* (1972) for instrumental ensemble and tape.

stock·hold·er ('stɒk,həʊldə) *n.* **1.** an owner of corporate capital stock. **2.** *Austral.* a person who keeps livestock. —**'stock·,hold·ing** *n.*

Stock·holm ('stɒkhəʊm; *Swedish* 'stɔkhɔlm) *n.* the capital of Sweden, a port in the E central part at the outflow of Lake Mälar into the Baltic: situated partly on the mainland and partly on islands; traditionally founded about 1250; university (1877). Pop.: 671 226 (1974 est.).

stock·i·net (,stɒkɪ'nɛt) *n.* a machine-knitted elastic fabric used, esp. formerly, for stockings, undergarments, etc. [C19: perhaps changed from earlier *stocking-net*]

stock·ing ('stɒkɪŋ) *n.* **1.** one of a pair of close-fitting garments made of knitted yarn to cover the foot and part or all of the leg. **2.** something resembling this in position, function, appearance, etc. **3. in (one's) stocking feet.** wearing stockings or socks but no shoes. [C16: from dialect *stock* stocking + -ING[1]] —**'stock·inged** *adj.*

stock·ing cap *n.* a conical knitted cap, often with a tassel.

stock·ing fill·er *n. Brit.* a present, esp. a toy, of a size suitable for inclusion in a child's Christmas stocking.

stock·ing frame *n.* a type of knitting machine. Also called: **stocking loom, stocking machine.**

stock·ing mask *n.* a nylon stocking worn over the face by a criminal to disguise the features.

stock·ing stitch *n.* a pattern of stitches in knitting consisting of alternate rows of plain and purl stitch.

stock in trade *n.* **1.** goods in stock necessary for carrying on a business. **2.** anything constantly used by someone as a part of his profession, occupation, or trade: *friendliness is the salesman's stock in trade.*

stock·ish ('stɒkɪʃ) *adj.* stupid or dull. —**'stock·ish·ly** *adv.* —**'stock·ish·ness** *n.*

stock·ist ('stɒkɪst) *n. Commerce, Brit.* a dealer who undertakes to maintain stocks of a specified product at or above a certain minimum in return for favourable buying terms granted by the manufacturer of the product.

stock·job·ber ('stɒk,dʒɒbə) *n.* **1.** *Brit.* a wholesale dealer on a stock exchange who operates as an intermediary between brokers without transacting directly with the public and derives his income from the spread between the bid and offered prices. Often shortened to **jobber.** Compare **stockbroker. 2.** *U.S., disparaging.* a stockbroker, esp. one dealing in worthless securities. —**'stock·,job·ber·y** *or* **'stock·,job·bing** *n.*

stock lock *n.* a lock that is enclosed in a wooden case.

stock·man ('stɒkmən, -,mæn) *n., pl.* **·men. 1. a.** a man engaged in the rearing or care of farm livestock, esp. cattle. **b.** an owner of cattle or other livestock. **2.** *U.S.* a man employed in a warehouse or stockroom.

stock mar·ket *n.* **1.** another name for **stock exchange** (sense 1). **2.** the usual U.S. name for **stock exchange** (sense 2).

stock·pile ('stɒk,paɪl) *vb.* **1.** to acquire and store a large quantity of (something). *~n.* **2.** a large store or supply accumulated for future use. —**'stock·,pil·er** *n.*

Stock·port ('stɒk,pɔːt) *n.* a town in NW England, in Greater Manchester: an early textile centre and scene of several labour disturbances in the early 19th century. Pop.: 139 633 (1971).

stock·pot ('stɒk,pɒt) *n. Chiefly Brit.* a pot in which stock for soup, etc., is made continually.

stock·room ('stɒk,ruːm, -,rʊm) *n.* a room in which a stock of goods is kept, as in a shop or factory.

stocks (stɒks) *pl. n.* **1.** *History.* an instrument of punishment consisting of a heavy wooden frame with holes in which the feet, hands, or head of an offender were locked. **2.** a frame in which an animal is held while receiving veterinary attention or while being shod. **3.** a frame used to support a boat while under construction. **4.** *Nautical.* a vertical post or shaft at the forward edge of a rudder, extended upwards for attachment to the steering controls. **5. on the stocks.** in preparation or under construction. **6. stocks and stones.** inanimate objects.

stock sad+dle *n. Chiefly U.S.* a cowboy's saddle, esp. an ornamental one.

stock-still *adv.* absolutely still; motionless.

stock+tak·ing (ˈstɒkˌteɪkɪŋ) *n.* **1.** the examination, counting, and valuing of goods on hand in a shop, etc. **2.** a reassessment of one's current situation, progress, prospects, etc.

Stock+ton (ˈstɒktən) *n.* an inland port in central California, on the San Joaquin River: seat of the University of the Pacific (1851). Pop.: 114 159 (1973 est.).

Stock-ton-on-Tees *n.* a port in NE England, in Cleveland on the River Tees: industrial centre, famous for the **Stockton-Darlington Railway** (1825), the first passenger-carrying railway in the world.

stock whip *n.* a whip with a long lash and a short handle, as used to herd cattle.

Stock·wood (ˈstɒkwʊd) *n.* **(Arthur) Mer·vyn.** born 1913, English Anglican prelate; bishop of Southwark since 1959.

stock·y (ˈstɒkɪ) *adj.* **stock·i+er, stock·i+est.** (usually of a person) thickset; sturdy. **—ˈstock·i+ly** *adv.* **—ˈstock·i·ness** *n.*

stock+yard (ˈstɒkˌjɑːd) *n.* a large yard with pens or covered buildings where farm animals are assembled, sold, etc.

stodge (stɒdʒ) *Informal.* ~*n.* **1.** heavy filling starchy food. **2.** *Brit. dialect, chiefly southern English.* baked or steamed pudding. **3.** a dull person or subject. ~*vb.* **4.** to stuff (oneself or another) with food. [C17: perhaps a blend of STUFF + PODGE]

stodg·y (ˈstɒdʒɪ) *adj.* **stodg·i+er, stodg·i+est. 1.** (of food) heavy or uninteresting. **2.** excessively formal and conventional. [C19: from STODGE] **—ˈstodg·i+ly** *adv.* **—ˈstodg·i·ness** *n.*

sto+gy *or* **sto+gey** (ˈstəʊgɪ) *n., pl.* **+gies.** *U.S.* any long cylindrical inexpensive cigar. [C19: from *stoga,* short for *Conestoga,* a town in Pennsylvania]

sto+ic (ˈstəʊɪk) *n.* **1.** a person who maintains stoical qualities. ~*adj.* **2.** variant of **stoical.**

Sto+ic (ˈstəʊɪk) *n.* **1.** a member of the ancient Greek school of philosophy founded by Zeno, holding that virtue and happiness can be attained only by submission to destiny and the natural law. ~*adj.* **2.** of or relating to the doctrines of the Stoics. [C16: via Latin from Greek *stōikos,* from *stoa* the porch in Athens where Zeno taught]

sto·i·cal (ˈstəʊɪkᵊl) *adj.* characterized by impassivity or resignation. **—ˈsto·i·cal+ly** *adv.* **—ˈsto·i·cal+ness** *n.*

stoi+chi·ol·o·gy, stoi+chei·ol·o·gy, *or* **stoe+chi+ol·o·gy** (ˌstɔɪkɪˈɒlədʒɪ) *n.* the branch of biology concerned with the study of the cellular components of animal tissues. [C19: from Greek *stoikheion* element + -LOGY] **—stoi+chi·o·log·i·cal, stoi·chei·o·log·i·cal,** *or* **stoe+chi·o·log·i·cal** (ˌstɔɪkɪəˈlɒdʒɪkᵊl) *adj.*

stoi+chi·o·met+ric, stoi+chei·o+met+ric, *or* **stoe+chi·o·met+ric** (ˌstɔɪkɪəˈmɛtrɪk) *adj. Chem.* **1.** concerned with, involving, or having the exact proportions for a particular chemical reaction: *a stoichiometric mixture.* **2.** (of a compound) having its component elements present in the exact proportions indicated by its formula. **3.** of or concerned with stoichiometry. [C19: see STOICHIOMETRY]

stoi+chi·om+e·try, stoi+chei·om+e·try, *or* **stoe+chi·om+e·try** (ˌstɔɪkɪˈɒmɪtrɪ) *n.* the branch of chemistry concerned with the proportions in which elements are combined in compounds and the quantitative relationships between reactants and products in chemical reactions. [C19: from Greek *stoikheion* element + -METRY]

sto·i·cism (ˈstəʊɪˌsɪzəm) *n.* **1.** indifference to pleasure and pain. **2.** (*cap.*) the philosophy of the Stoics.

stoke (stəʊk) *vb.* **1.** to feed, stir, and tend (a fire, furnace, etc.). **2.** (*tr.*) to tend the furnace of; act as a stoker for. [C17: back formation from STOKER]

stoke+hold (ˈstəʊkˌhəʊld) *n. Nautical.* **1.** a coal bunker for a ship's furnace. **2.** the hold for a ship's boilers; fire room.

stoke+hole (ˈstəʊkˌhəʊl) *n.* **1.** another word for **stokehold. 2.** a hole in a furnace through which it is stoked.

Stoke-on-Trent *n.* a city in central England, in N Staffordshire on the River Trent: a major centre of the pottery industry. Pop.: 265 153 (1971).

stok+er (ˈstəʊkə) *n.* a person employed to tend a furnace, as on a steamship. [C17: from Dutch, from *stoken* to STOKE]

stokes (stəʊks) *or* **stoke** *n.* the cgs unit of kinematic viscosity, equal to the viscosity of a fluid in poise divided by its density in grams per cubic centimetre. 1 stokes is equivalent to 10^{-4} square metre per second. Symbol: St. [C20: named after Sir George *Stokes* (1819–1903), British physicist]

stoke up *vb.* (*adv.*) **1.** to feed and tend (a fire, etc.) with fuel. **2.** (*intr.*) to fill oneself with food.

Sto·kow·ski (stəˈkɒfskɪ) *n.* **Le·o·pold.** 1887–1977, U.S. conductor, born in Britain. He did much to popularize classical music with orchestral transcriptions and film appearances, esp. in *Fantasia* (1940).

STOL (stɒl) *n.* **1.** a system in which an aircraft can take off and land in a short distance. **2.** an aircraft using this system. Compare **VTOL.** [C20: *s*(*hort*) *t*(*ake*) *o*(*ff and*) *l*(*anding*)]

stole[1] (stəʊl) *vb.* the past tense of **steal.**

stole[2] (stəʊl) *n.* a long scarf or shawl, worn by women. [Old English *stole,* from Latin *stola,* Greek *stolē* clothing; related to *stellein* to array]

stol+en (ˈstəʊlən) *vb.* the past participle of **steal.**

stol+id (ˈstɒlɪd) *adj.* showing little or no emotion or interest. [C17: from Latin *stolidus* dull; compare Latin *stultus* stupid; see STILL[1]] **—sto+lid+i·ty** (stɒˈlɪdɪtɪ) *or* **ˈstol+id+ness** *n.* **—ˈstol+id+ly** *adv.*

stol+len (ˈstəʊlən; *German* ˈʃtɔlən) *n.* a rich sweet bread containing nuts, raisins, etc. [German, from *Stollen* wooden post, prop; so called from its shape; see STALL[1]]

sto+lon (ˈstəʊlən) *n.* **1.** another name for **runner** (sense 11). **2.** a branching structure in lower animals, esp. the anchoring rootlike part of colonial organisms, such as hydroids, on which the polyps are borne. [C17: from Latin *stolō* shoot] **—sto+lon·if+er+ous** (ˌstəʊləˈnɪfərəs) *adj.*

sto+ma (ˈstəʊmə) *n., pl.* **sto+ma+ta** (ˈstəʊmətə, ˈstɒm-, stəʊˈmɑːtə). **1.** *Botany.* an epidermal pore, present in large numbers in plant leaves, that controls the passage of gases into and out of a plant. **2.** *Zoology, anatomy.* a mouth or mouthlike part. [C17: via New Latin from Greek: mouth]

stom+ach (ˈstʌmək) *n.* **1.** (in vertebrates) the enlarged muscular saclike part of the alimentary canal in which food is stored until it has been partially digested and rendered into chyme. Related adj.: **gastric. 2.** the corresponding digestive organ in invertebrates. **3.** the abdominal region. **4.** desire, appetite, or inclination: *I have no stomach for arguments.* **5.** an archaic word for **temper. 6.** an obsolete word for **pride.** ~*vb.* (*tr.; used mainly in negative constructions*) **7.** to tolerate; bear: *I can't stomach his bragging.* **8.** to eat or digest: *he cannot stomach oysters.* [C14: from Old French *stomaque,* from Latin *stomachus* (believed to be the seat of the emotions), from Greek *stomakhos,* from *stoma* mouth]

stom·ach+ache (ˈstʌməkˌeɪk) *n.* pain in the stomach or abdominal region, as from acute indigestion. Technical name: **gastralgia.** Also called: **stomach upset, upset stomach.**

stom+ach+er (ˈstʌməkə) *n.* a decorative V-shaped panel of stiff material worn over the chest and stomach by men and women in the 16th century, later only by women.

sto+mach+ic (stəˈmækɪk) *adj. also* **sto+mach·i·cal. 1.** stimulating gastric activity. **2.** of or relating to the stomach. ~*n.* **3.** a stomachic medicine.

stom+ach pump *n. Med.* a suction device for removing stomach contents via an orally-inserted tube.

stom+ach worm *n.* any of various nematode worms that are parasitic in the stomach of mammals, esp. *Haemonchus contortus,* which infests sheep: family *Trichostrongylidae.*

stom+ach·y (ˈstʌməkɪ) *adj.* **1.** having a large belly; paunchy. **2.** *Brit. dialect.* easily angered; irritable.

stom+ack (ˈstʌmək) *n.* **have a stomack.** *East African informal.* to be pregnant.

sto+ma+ta (ˈstəʊmətə, ˈstɒm-, stəʊˈmɑːtə) *n.* the plural of **stoma.**

sto+ma+tal (ˈstəʊmətᵊl, ˈstɒm-) *or* **stom·a+tous** (ˈstɒmətəs, ˈstəʊ-) *adj.* of, relating to, or possessing stomata or a stoma.

sto+mat+ic (stəʊˈmætɪk) *adj.* of or relating to a mouth or mouthlike part.

sto+ma+ti+tis (ˌstəʊməˈtaɪtɪs, ˌstɒm-) *n.* inflammation of the mouth. **—sto+ma+tit+ic** (ˌstəʊməˈtɪtɪk, ˌstɒm-) *adj.*

sto·ma·to- *or before a vowel* **sto·mat-** *combining form.* indicating the mouth or a mouthlike part: *stomatology.* [from Greek *stoma, stomat-*]

sto+ma+tol+o·gy (ˌstəʊməˈtɒlədʒɪ) *n.* the branch of medicine or dentistry concerned with the structures, functions, and diseases of the mouth. **—sto+ma+to+log+i·cal** (ˌstəʊmətəˈlɒdʒɪkᵊl) *adj.*

stom·a+to+plas+ty (ˈstɒmətəˌplæstɪ, ˈstəʊ-) *n.* plastic surgery or surgical repair involving the mouth.

stom·a+to+pod (ˈstɒmətəˌpɒd, ˈstəʊ-) *n.* any marine crustacean of the order *Stomatopoda,* having abdominal gills: subclass *Malacostraca.* The group includes the mantis shrimp.

-stome *n. combining form.* indicating a mouth or opening resembling a mouth: *peristome.* [from Greek *stoma* mouth, and *stomion* little mouth]

sto+mo+dae+um *or* **sto+mo+de+um** (ˌstəʊməˈdiːəm, ˈstɒm-) *n., pl.* **+dae·a** *or* **+de·a** (-ˈdiːə). the oral cavity of a vertebrate embryo, which is formed from an invagination of the ectoderm and develops into the part of the alimentary canal between the mouth and stomach. [C19: from New Latin, from Greek *stoma* mouth + *hodaios* on the way, from *hodos* way] **—ˌsto+mo+ˈdae·al** *or* **ˌsto+mo+ˈde·al** *adj.*

-sto·mous *adj. combining form.* having a specified type of mouth: *monostomous.*

stomp (stɒmp) *vb.* (*intr.*) **1.** *Informal.* to tread or stamp heavily. ~*n.* **2.** a rhythmical stamping jazz dance. **—ˈstomp+er** *n.*

-sto·my *n. combining form.* indicating a surgical operation performed to make an artificial opening into or for a specified part: *cytostomy.* [from Greek *-stomia,* from *stoma* mouth]

stone (stəʊn) *n.* **1.** the hard compact nonmetallic material of which rocks are made. **2.** a small lump of rock; pebble. **3.** *Jewellery.* short for **gemstone. 4. a.** a piece of rock designed or shaped for some particular purpose. **b.** (*in combination*): *gravestone; millstone.* **5. a.** something that resembles a stone. **b.** (*in combination*): *hailstone.* **6.** the woody central part of such fruits as the peach and plum, that contains the seed; endocarp. **7.** any similar hard part of a fruit, such as the stony seed of a date. **8.** (*pl.* **stone**) *Brit.* a unit of weight, used esp. to express human body weight, equal to 14 pounds or 6.350 kilograms. **9.** Also called: **granite.** the rounded heavy mass of granite or iron used in the game of curling. **10.** *Pathol.* a nontechnical name for **calculus. 11.** *Printing.* a table with a very flat iron or stone surface upon which pages are composed into formes; imposition table. **12.** *Rare.* (in certain games) a piece or man. **13.** (*usually pl.*) a rare word for **testicle.** **14. a.** any of various dull grey colours. **b.** (*as adj.*): *stone paint.* **15.** (*modifier*) relating to or made of stone: *a stone house.* **16.** (*modifier*) made of stoneware: *a stone jar.* **17. cast a stone (at).** cast aspersions (upon). **18. heart of stone.** an obdurate or unemotional nature. **19. leave no stone unturned.** to do everything possible to achieve an end. ~*adv.* **20.** (intensifier): *stone cold; stone deaf.* ~*vb.* (*tr.*) **21.** to throw stones at, esp. to kill. **22.** to remove the stones from. **23.** to furnish or provide with stones. **24.** *Vet. science.* to castrate. **25. stone the crows.** *Brit. informal.* an expression of surprise or dismay. [Old English *stān;* related to Old Saxon *stēn,* German *Stein,* Old Norse *steinn,* Gothic *stains,* Greek *stion* pebble] —**'ston·a·ble** *or* **'stone·a·ble** *adj.* —**'stone·less** *adj.* —**'stone·less·ness** *n.* —**'stone·,like** *adj.* —**'ston·er** *n.*

Stone Age *n.* a period in human culture identified by the use of stone implements and usually divided into the Palaeolithic, Mesolithic, and Neolithic stages.

stone axe *n.* a blunt axe used for cutting stone.

stone bass (bæs) *n.* a large sea perch, *Polyprion americanus,* of the Atlantic and Mediterranean. Also called: **wreckfish.**

stone-blind *adj.* completely blind. Compare **sand-blind.**

stone·boat ('stəʊn,bəʊt) *n. U.S.* a type of sleigh used for moving rocks from fields, for hauling milk cans, etc.

stone boil·ing *n.* a primitive method of boiling liquid with heated stones.

stone bram·ble *n.* a herbaceous Eurasian rosaceous plant, *Rubus saxatilis,* of stony places, having white flowers and berry-like scarlet fruits (drupelets). See also **bramble** (sense 1).

stone·cast ('stəʊn,kɑːst) *n.* a less common name for **stone's throw.**

stone·chat ('stəʊn,tʃæt) *n.* an Old World songbird, *Saxicola torquata,* having a black plumage with a reddish-brown breast: subfamily *Turdinae* (thrushes). [C18: so called from its cry, which sounds like clattering pebbles]

stone·crop ('stəʊn,krɒp) *n.* **1.** any of various N temperate crassulaceous plants of the genus *Sedum,* having fleshy leaves and typically red, yellow, or white flowers. **2.** any of various similar or related plants.

stone cur·lew *n.* any of several brownish shore birds of the family *Burhinidae,* esp. *Burhinus oedicnemus,* having a large head and eyes: order *Charadriiformes.* Also called: **thick-knee.**

stone·cut·ter ('stəʊn,kʌtə) *n.* **1.** a person who is skilled in cutting and carving stone. **2.** a machine used to dress stone. —**'stone·,cut·ting** *n.*

stoned (stəʊnd) *adj. Slang.* in a state of intoxication, stupor, or euphoria induced by drugs or alcohol.

stone·fish ('stəʊn,fɪʃ) *n., pl.* **·fish** *or* **·fish·es.** a venomous tropical marine scorpaenid fish, *Synanceja verrucosa,* that resembles a piece of rock on the seabed.

stone·fly ('stəʊn,flaɪ) *n., pl.* **·flies.** any insect of the order *Plecoptera,* in which the larvae are aquatic, living beneath stones, and the adults have long antennae and two pairs of large wings and occur near water.

stone fruit *n.* the nontechnical name for **drupe.**

stone·ground ('stəʊn,graʊnd) *adj.* (of flour) ground with millstones.

Stone·henge (,stəʊn'hɛndʒ) *n.* a prehistoric ruin in S England, in Wiltshire on Salisbury Plain: one of the most important megalithic monuments in Europe; believed to have had religious and astronomical purposes.

stone-lil·y *n.* the fossil of any of several species of sea lily or other crinoid.

stone mar·ten *n.* **1.** a marten, *Martes foina,* of Eurasian woods and forests, having a brown coat with a pale underfur. **2.** the highly valued fur of this animal.

stone·ma·son ('stəʊn,meɪsᵊn) *n.* a person who is skilled in preparing stone for building. —**'stone·,ma·son·ry** *n.*

stone pars·ley *n.* a roadside umbelliferous plant, *Sison amomum,* of W Europe and the Mediterranean region, having clusters of small white flowers and aromatic seeds.

stone pit *n.* a less common name for **quarry.**

stone roll·er *n.* a small silvery freshwater cyprinid fish, *Campostoma anomalum,* of the eastern U.S., having a narrow black stripe on the dorsal and anal fins.

Stones (stəʊnz) *pl. n.* **the.** See **Rolling Stones.**

stone saw *n.* an untoothed iron saw used to cut stone.

stone's throw *n.* a short distance. Also called: **stonecast.**

stone·wall (,stəʊn'wɔːl) *vb.* **1.** (*intr.*) *Cricket.* (of a batsman) to play defensively. **2.** to obstruct or hinder (parliamentary business). —**,stone·'wall·er** *n.*

stone·ware ('stəʊn,wɛə) *n.* **1.** a hard opaque pottery, fired at a very high temperature. ~*adj.* **2.** made of stoneware.

stone·work ('stəʊn,wɜːk) *n.* **1.** any construction made of stone. **2.** the process of dressing or setting stones. —**'stone·,work·er** *n.*

stone·wort ('stəʊn,wɜːt) *n.* any of various green algae of the genus *Chara,* which grow in brackish or fresh water and have jointed fronds encrusted with lime.

stonk (stɒŋk) *vb.* (*tr.*) **1.** to bombard (soldiers, buildings, etc.) with artillery. ~*n.* **2.** a bombardment by artillery. [C20: perhaps of imitative origin]

stonk·ered ('stɒŋkəd) *adj. Austral. slang.* completely exhausted or beaten; whacked. [C20: from *stonker* to beat, of unknown origin]

ston·y *or* **ston·ey** ('stəʊnɪ) *adj.* **ston·i·er, ston·i·est. 1.** of or resembling stone. **2.** abounding in stone or stones. **3.** unfeeling, heartless, or obdurate. **4.** short for **stony-broke.** —**'ston·i·ly** *adv.* —**'ston·i·ness** *n.*

ston·y-broke *adj. Brit. slang.* completely without money; penniless. U.S. term: **stone-broke.**

ston·y cor·al *n.* any coral of the order *Madreporaria,* having a calcareous skeleton, aggregations of which form reefs and islands.

ston·y-heart·ed *adj.* unfeeling; hardhearted. —**,ston·y-'heart·ed·ness** *n.*

stood (stʊd) *vb.* the past tense or past participle of **stand.**

stooge (stuːdʒ) *n.* **1.** an actor who feeds lines to a comedian or acts as his foil or butt. **2.** *Slang.* someone who is taken advantage of by another. ~*vb.* **3.** (*intr.*) *Slang.* to act as a stooge. [C20: of unknown origin]

stook (stuːk) *n.* **1.** a number of sheaves set upright in a field to dry with their heads together. ~*vb.* **2.** (*tr.*) to set up (sheaves) in stooks. [C15: variant of *stouk,* of Germanic origin; compare Middle Low German *stūke,* Old High German *stūhha* sleeve] —**'stook·er** *n.*

stool (stuːl) *n.* **1.** a simple seat or footrest consisting of a small flat piece of wood, etc., resting on three or four legs, a pedestal, etc. **2.** a rootstock or base of a plant from which shoots, etc., are produced. **3.** a cluster of shoots growing from such a base. **4.** *Chiefly U.S.* a decoy used in hunting. **5.** waste matter evacuated from the bowels. **6.** a lavatory seat. **7.** (in W Africa, esp. Ghana) a chief's throne. **8. fall between two stools.** to fail through vacillation between two alternatives. ~*vb.* (*intr.*) **9.** (of a plant) to send up shoots from the base of the stem, rootstock, etc. **10.** to lure wildfowl with a decoy. [Old English *stōl;* related to Old Norse *stōll,* Gothic *stōls,* Old High German *stuol* chair, Greek *stulos* pillar]

stool ball *n.* a game resembling cricket, still played by girls and women in Sussex, England.

stool pi·geon *n.* **1.** a living or dummy pigeon used to decoy others. **2.** an informer for the police; nark. **3.** *U.S. slang.* a person acting as a decoy.

stoop[1] (stuːp) *vb.* (*mainly intr.*) **1.** (*also tr.*) to bend (the body or the top half of the body) forward and downward. **2.** to carry oneself with head and shoulders habitually bent forward. **3.** (often foll. by *to*) to abase or degrade oneself. **4.** (often foll. by *to*) to condescend; deign. **5.** (of a bird of prey) to swoop down. **6.** *Archaic.* to give in. ~*n.* **7.** the act, position, or characteristic of stooping. **8.** a lowering from a position of dignity or superiority. **9.** a downward swoop, esp. of a bird of prey. [Old English *stūpan;* related to Middle Dutch *stupen* to bow, Old Norse *stūpa,* Norwegian *stupa* to fall; see STEEP[1]] —**'stoop·er** *n.* —**'stoop·ing·ly** *adv.*

stoop[2] (stuːp) *n. U.S.* a small platform with steps up to it at the entrance to a building. [C18: from Dutch *stoep,* of Germanic origin; compare Old High German *stuofa* stair, Old English *stōpel* footprint; see STEP]

stoop[3] (stuːp) *n. Archaic or northern Brit. dialect.* a pillar or post. [C15: variant of dialect *stulpe,* probably from Old Norse *stolpe;* see STELE]

stoop[4] (stuːp) *n.* a less common spelling of **stoup.**

stop (stɒp) *vb.* **stops, stop·ping, stopped. 1.** to cease from doing or being (something); discontinue: *stop talking.* **2.** to cause (something moving) to halt or (of something moving) to come to a halt: *to stop a car; the car stopped.* **3.** (*tr.*) to prevent the continuance or completion of: *to stop a show.* **4.** (*tr.;* often foll. by *from*) to prevent or restrain: *to stop George from fighting.* **5.** (*tr.*) to keep back: *to stop supplies to the navy.* **6.** (*tr.*) to intercept or hinder in transit: *to stop a letter.* **7.** (*tr.;* often foll. by *up*) to block or plug, esp. so as to close: *to stop up a pipe.* **8.** (*tr.;* often foll. by *up*) to fill a hole or opening in: *to stop up a wall.* **9.** (*tr.*) to staunch or stem: *to stop a wound.* **10.** (*tr.*) to instruct a bank not to honour (a cheque). **11.** (*tr.*) to deduct (money) from pay. **12.** (*tr.*) *Brit.* to provide with punctuation. **13.** (*tr.*) *Boxing.* to beat (an opponent) either by a knockout or a technical knockout. **14.** (*tr.*) *Informal.* to receive (a blow, hit, etc.). **15.** (*intr.*) to stay or rest: *we stopped at the Robinsons' for three nights.* **16.** (*tr.*) *Rare.* to defeat, beat, or kill. **17.** (*tr.*) *Music.* **a.** to alter the vibrating length of (a string on a violin, guitar, etc.) by pressing down on it at some point with the finger. **b.** to alter the vibrating length of an air column in a wind instrument by closing (a finger hole, etc.). **c.** to produce (a note) in this manner. **18.** (*tr.*) to place a hand inside (the bell of a French horn) to alter the tone colour and pitch or play (a note) on a French horn in such a manner. **19.** *Bridge.* to have a protecting card or winner in (a suit in which one's opponents are strong). **20. stop at nothing.** to allow no feelings of doubt or scruples to hinder one. ~*n.* **21.** an arrest of movement or progress. **22.** the act of stopping or the state of being stopped. **23.** a place where something halts or pauses: *a bus stop.* **24.** a stay in or as if in the course of a journey. **25.** the act or an instance of blocking or obstructing. **26.** a plug or stopper. **27.** a block, screw, or other device or object that prevents, limits, or terminates the motion of a mechanism or moving part. **28.** *Brit.* a punctuation mark, esp. a full stop. **29.** Also called: **stop thrust.** *Fencing.* a counterthrust made without a parry in the hope that one's blade will touch before one's opponent's blade. **30.** short for **stop payment** or **stop order. 31.** *Music.* **a.** the act of stopping the string, finger hole, etc., of an instrument. **b.** a set of organ pipes or harpsichord strings that may be allowed to sound as a group by muffling or silencing all other such sets. **c.** a knob, lever, or handle on an organ, etc., that is operated to allow sets of pipes to sound. **d.** an analogous device on a harpsichord or other instrument with variable registers, such as an electrophonic instrument. **32. pull out all**

the stops. a. to play at full volume. **b.** to spare no effort. **33.** *Austral.* a stud on a football boot. **34.** the angle between the forehead and muzzle of a dog or cat, regarded as a point in breeding. **35.** *Nautical.* a short length of line or small stuff used as a tie, esp. for a furled sail. **36.** Also called: **stop consonant.** *Phonetics.* any of a class of consonants articulated by first making a complete closure at some point of the vocal tract and then releasing it abruptly with audible plosion. Stops include the labials (p, b), the alveolars or dentals (t, d), the velars (k, g). Compare **continuant. 37.** Also called: **f-stop.** *Photog.* **a.** a setting of the aperture of a camera lens, calibrated to the corresponding f-number. **b.** another name for **diaphragm** (sense 4). **38.** a block or carving used to complete the end of a moulding. **39.** Also called: **stopper.** *Bridge.* a protecting card or winner in a suit in which one's opponents are strong. ~See also **stop down, stop off, stop out, stopover, stops.** [C14: from Old English *stoppian* (unattested), as in *forstoppian* to plug the ear, ultimately from Late Latin *stuppāre* to stop with a tow, from Latin *stuppa* tow, from Greek *stuppē*] —'**stop·pa·ble** *adj.*

stop bath *n.* a weakly acidic solution used in photographic processing to stop the action of a developer on a film, plate, or paper before the material is immersed in fixer.

stop chor·us *n. Jazz.* a solo during which the rhythm section plays only the first beat of each phrase of music.

stop·cock ('stɒp,kɒk) *n.* a valve used to control or stop the flow of a fluid in a pipe.

stop down *vb.* (*adv.*) to reduce the size of the aperture of (a camera lens).

stope (stəʊp) *n.* **1.** a steplike excavation made in a mine to extract ore. ~*vb.* **2.** to mine (ore, etc.) by cutting stopes. [C18: probably from Low German *stope;* see STOOP[2]]

Stopes (stəʊps) *n.* **Ma·rie Car·mi·chael.** 1880–1958, English pioneer of birth control, who established the first birth-control clinic in Britain (1921).

stop·gap ('stɒp,gæp) *n.* **a.** a temporary substitute for something else. **b.** (*as modifier*): *a stopgap programme.*

stop-go *adj. Brit.* (of economic policy) characterized by deliberate alternate expansion and contraction of aggregate demand in an effort to curb inflation and eliminate balance of payments deficits, and yet maintain full employment.

stop·ing ('stəʊpɪŋ) *n. Geology.* the process by which country rock is broken up and engulfed by the upward movement of magma. Also called: **magmatic stoping.** See also **stope.**

stop·light ('stɒp,laɪt) *n.* **1.** a red light on a traffic signal indicating that vehicles or pedestrians coming towards it should stop. **2.** another word for **brake light.**

stop off, stop in, *or esp. U.S.* **stop by** *vb.* (*intr., adv.;* often foll. by *at*) to halt and call somewhere, as on a visit or errand, esp. en route to another place.

stop or·der *n. Stock exchange.* an instruction to a broker to sell one or more shares when the price offered for them falls below a stipulated level. Also called: **stop-loss order.**

stop out *vb.* (*tr., adv.*) to cover (part of the area) of a piece of cloth, printing plate, etc., to prevent it from being dyed, etched, etc.

stop·o·ver ('stɒp,əʊvə) *n.* **1.** a stopping place on a journey. ~*vb.* **stop o·ver. 2.** (*intr., adv.*) to make a stopover.

stop·page ('stɒpɪdʒ) *n.* **1.** the act of stopping or the state of being stopped. **2.** something that stops or blocks. **3.** a deduction of money, as from pay. **4.** an organized cessation of work, as during a strike.

Stop·pard ('stɒpɑːd) *n.* **Tom.** born 1937, British playwright, born in Czechoslovakia: his works include *Rosencrantz and Guildenstern are Dead* (1967), *Jumpers* (1972), *Travesties* (1975), and *Dirty Linen* (1976).

stop pay·ment *n.* an instruction to a bank by the drawer of a cheque to refuse payment on it.

stopped (stɒpt) *adj.* (of a pipe or tube, esp. an organ pipe) closed at one end and thus sounding an octave lower than an open pipe of the same length.

stop·per ('stɒpə) *n.* **1.** Also called: **stopple.** a plug or bung for closing a bottle, pipe, duct, etc. **2.** a person or thing that stops or puts an end to something. **3.** *Bridge.* another name for **stop** (sense 39). ~*vb.* **4.** (*tr.*) Also: **stopple.** to close or fit with a stopper.

stop·ping ('stɒpɪŋ) *n.* **1.** *Brit. informal.* a dental filling. **2.** a solid barrier in a mine tunnel to seal off harmful gases, fire, fresh air from used air, etc. ~*adj.* **3.** *Chiefly Brit.* making many stops in a journey: *a stopping train.*

stop press *n. Brit.* **1.** news items inserted into a newspaper after the printing has been started. **2.** the space regularly left blank for this.

stops (stɒps) *n.* any one of several card games in which players must play their cards in certain sequences.

stop thrust *n. Fencing.* another name for **stop** (sense 29).

stop time *n. Jazz.* a passage where the beat stops temporarily.

stop·watch ('stɒp,wɒtʃ) *n.* a type of watch used for timing events, such as sporting events, accurately, having a device for stopping the hand or hands instantly.

stor·age ('stɔːrɪdʒ) *n.* **1.** the act of storing or the state of being stored. **2.** space or area reserved for storing. **3.** a charge made for storing. **4.** *Computer technol.* **a.** the act or process of storing information in a computer memory or on a magnetic tape, disk, etc. **b.** (*as modifier*): *a storage device; storage capacity.*

stor·age bat·ter·y *n.* another name (esp. U.S.) for **accumulator** (sense 1).

stor·age ca·pac·i·ty *n.* the maximum number of bits, bytes, or words that can be held in a computer storage device.

stor·age de·vice *n.* a piece of computer equipment, such as a magnetic tape, disk, drum, etc., in or on which data and instructions can be stored, usually in binary form.

stor·age heat·er *n.* an electric device capable of accumulating and radiating heat generated by off-peak electricity.

sto·rax ('stɔːræks) *n.* **1.** any of numerous styracaceous trees or shrubs of the genus *Styrax,* of tropical and subtropical regions, having drooping showy white flowers. **2.** a vanilla-scented solid resin obtained from one of these trees, *Styrax officinalis* of the Mediterranean region and SW Asia, formerly used as incense and in perfumery and medicine. **3.** a liquid aromatic balsam obtained from liquidambar trees, esp. *Liquidambar orientalis* of SW Asia, and used in perfumery and medicine. [C14: via Late Latin from Greek, variant of STYRAX]

store (stɔː) *vb.* **1.** (*tr.*) to keep, set aside, or accumulate for future use. **2.** (*tr.*) to place in a warehouse, depository, etc., for safekeeping. **3.** (*tr.*) to supply, provide, or stock. **4.** (*intr.*) to be put into storage. **5.** *Computer technol.* to enter or retain (information) in a storage device. ~*n.* **6. a.** an establishment for the retail sale of goods and services. **b.** (*in combination*): *storefront.* **7. a.** a large supply or stock kept for future use. **b.** (*as modifier*): *store ship.* **8.** short for **department store. 9. a.** a storage place such as a warehouse or depository. **b.** (*in combination*): *storeman.* **10.** the state of being stored (esp. in the phrase **in store**). **11.** a large amount or quantity. **12.** *Computer technol., chiefly Brit.* another name for **memory** (sense 7). **13.** Also called: **store pig.** a pig that has not yet been weaned and weighs less than 40 kg. **14. in store.** forthcoming or imminent. **15. lay, put,** *or* **set store by.** to value or reckon as important. [C13: from Old French *estor,* from *estorer* to restore, from Latin *instaurāre* to refresh; related to Greek *stauros* stake] —'**stor·a·ble** *adj.*

Sto·re Bælt ('sdoːrə 'bɛld) *n.* the Danish name for the **Great Belt.**

store·house ('stɔː,haus) *n.* a place where things are stored.

store·keep·er ('stɔː,kiːpə) *n.* a manager, owner, or keeper of a store. —'**store,keep·ing** *n.*

store·room ('stɔː,ruːm, -,rʊm) *n.* **1.** a room in which things are stored. **2.** room for storing.

stores (stɔːz) *pl. n.* supply or stock of something, esp. essentials, for a specific purpose: *the ship's stores.*

sto·rey *or U.S.* **sto·ry** ('stɔːrɪ) *n., pl.* **·reys** *or* **·ries. 1.** a floor or level of a building. **2.** a set of rooms on one level. [C14: from Anglo-Latin *historia,* picture, from Latin: narrative, probably arising from the pictures on medieval windows]

sto·reyed *or U.S.* **sto·ried** ('stɔːrɪd) *adj.* **a.** having a storey or storeys. **b.** (*in combination*): *a two-storeyed house.*

sto·rey house *n.* (in W Africa) a house having more than one storey.

stor·i·at·ed ('stɔːrɪ,eɪtɪd) *adj.* another word for **historiated** or **storied** (sense 2).

sto·ried ('stɔːrɪd) *adj.* **1.** recorded in history or in a story; fabled. **2.** decorated with narrative scenes or pictures.

stork (stɔːk) *n.* **1.** any large wading bird of the family *Ciconiidae,* chiefly of warm regions of the Old World, having very long legs and a long stout pointed bill, and typically having a white-and-black plumage: order *Ciconiiformes.* **2.** (*sometimes cap.*) a variety of domestic fancy pigeon resembling the fairy swallow. [Old English *storc;* related to Old High German *storah,* Old Norse *storkr,* Old English *stearc* stiff; from the stiff appearance of its legs; see STARK]

storks·bill ('stɔːks,bɪl) *n.* any of various geraniaceous plants of the genus *Erodium,* esp. *E. cicutarium* **(common storksbill),** having pink or reddish-purple flowers and fruits with a beak-like process.

storm (stɔːm) *n.* **1. a.** a violent weather condition of strong winds, rain, hail, thunder, lightning, blowing sand, snow, etc. **b.** (*as modifier*): *storm signal; storm sail.* **c.** (*in combination*): *stormproof.* **2.** *Meteorol.* a violent gale of force 11 on the Beaufort scale. **3.** a violent disturbance or quarrel. **4.** a direct assault on a stronghold. **5.** a heavy discharge or rain, as of bullets or missiles. **6.** short for **storm window. 7. storm in a teacup.** *Brit.* a violent fuss or disturbance over a trivial matter. U.S. equivalent: **tempest in a teapot. 8. take by storm. a.** to capture or overrun by a violent assault. **b.** to overwhelm and enthral. ~*vb.* **9.** to attack or assault (something) suddenly and violently. **10.** (*intr.*) to be vociferously angry. **11.** (*intr.*) to move or rush violently or angrily. **12.** (*intr.;* with *it* as subject) to rain, hail, or snow hard and be very windy, often with thunder or lightning. [Old English, related to Old Norse *stormr,* German *Sturm;* see STIR[1]] —'**storm,like** *adj.*

storm belt *n.* an area of the earth's surface in which storms are frequent.

storm·bound ('stɔːm,baʊnd) *adj.* detained or harassed by storms.

storm cen·tre *n.* **1.** the centre of a cyclonic storm, etc., where pressure is lowest. **2.** the centre of any disturbance or trouble.

storm cloud *n.* **1.** a heavy dark cloud presaging rain or a storm. **2.** a herald of disturbance, anger, or violence: *the storm clouds of war.*

storm-cock *n.* another name for **missel thrush.**

storm col·lar *n.* a high collar on a coat.

storm cone *n. Brit.* a canvas cone hoisted as a warning of high winds.

storm glass *n.* a sealed tube containing a solution supposed to change in appearance according to the weather.

storm lan·tern *n.* another name for **hurricane lamp.**

storm pet+rel *n.* any small petrel, such as the northern *Hydrobates pelagicus,* of the family *Hydrobatidae,* typically having a dark plumage with paler underparts. Also called: **Mother Carey's chicken, stormy petrel.**

storm+proof ('stɔːm,pruːf) *adj.* withstanding or giving protection against storms.

storm-troop·er *n.* **1.** a member of the Nazi S.A. **2.** a member of a force of shock troops.

storm warn+ing *n.* **1.** a pattern of lights, flags, etc., displayed at certain ports as a warning to shipping of an approaching storm. **2.** an announcement on radio or television of an approaching storm. **3.** any warning of approaching danger or trouble.

storm win+dow *n.* an additional window fitted to the outside of an ordinary window to provide insulation against wind, cold, rain, etc.

storm·y ('stɔːmɪ) *adj.* **storm·i+er, storm·i+est. 1.** characterized by storms. **2.** subject to, involving, or characterized by violent disturbance or emotional outburst. **—'storm·i+ly** *adv.* **—'storm·i+ness** *n.*

storm·y pet+rel *n.* **1.** another name for **storm petrel. 2.** a person who brings or portends trouble.

Stor+no+way ('stɔːnə,weɪ) *n.* a port in NW Scotland, on the E coast of Lewis in the Outer Hebrides, administrative centre of the Western Isles. Pop.: 5266 (1971).

Stor+ting *or* **Stor+thing** ('stɔːtɪŋ) *n.* the parliament of Norway. See also **Lagting, Odelsting.** [C19: Norwegian, from *stor* great + *thing* assembly]

sto+ry[1] ('stɔːrɪ) *n., pl.* **+ries. 1.** a narration of a chain of events told or written in prose or verse. **2.** Also called: **short story.** a piece of fiction, briefer and usually less detailed than a novel. **3.** Also called: **story line.** the plot of a book, film, etc. **4.** an event that could be the subject of a narrative. **5.** a report or statement on a matter or event. **6.** the event or material for such a report. **7.** *Informal.* a lie, fib, or untruth. **8. cut** (*or* **make**) **a long story short.** to leave out details in a narration. **9. quite another story now.** things or circumstances have changed. **10. the same old story.** the familiar or regular course of events. **11. the story goes.** it is commonly said or believed. *~vb.* **+ries, +ry+ing, +ried.** (*tr.*) **12.** to decorate (a pot, wall, etc.) with scenes from history or legends. **13.** *Archaic.* to tell the story of. [C13: from Anglo-French *estorie,* from Latin *historia;* see HISTORY]

sto+ry[2] ('stɔːrɪ) *n., pl.* **+ries.** another spelling (esp. U.S.) of **storey.**

sto·ry+book ('stɔːrɪ,bʊk) *n.* **1.** a book containing stories, esp. for children. *~adj.* **2.** unreal or fantastic: *a storybook world.*

sto+ry line *n.* the plot of a book, film, play, etc.

sto·ry+tell·er ('stɔːrɪ,tɛlə) *n.* **1.** a person who tells stories. **2.** *Informal.* a liar. **—'sto·ry+,tell·ing** *n., adj.*

stoss (stɒs; *German* ʃtoːs) *adj.* (of the side of a hill, crag, etc.) facing the onward flow of a glacier or the direction in which a former glacier flowed. [German, from *stossen* to thrust]

stot (stɒt) *vb.* **stots, stot+ting, stot+ted.** *Northern Brit. dialect, chiefly Scot.* **1.** to bounce or cause to bounce. **2.** (*intr.*) to stagger. [of obscure origin]

sto+tin+ka (stɒ'tɪŋkə) *n., pl.* **+ki** (-kɪ). a Bulgarian monetary unit worth one hundredth of a lev. [from Bulgarian; related to *suto* hundred]

sto+tious ('stəʊʃəs) *adj. Irish dialect.* drunk; inebriated. [of obscure origin; perhaps from STOT]

stot+ter ('stɒtə) *n. Scot. dialect, chiefly Glasgow.* a good-looking fashionably dressed young woman. [from STOT]

stound (staʊnd) *n. Obsolete or Brit. dialect.* **1.** a short while; instant. **2.** a pang or pain. [Old English *stund;* related to Old High German *stunta* period of time, hour]

stoup *or* **stoop** (stuːp) *n.* **1.** a small basin for holy water. **2.** *Northern Brit. dialect.* a bucket or cup. [C14 (in the sense: bucket): of Scandinavian origin; compare Old Norse *staup* beaker, Old English *stēap* flagon; see STEEP[1]]

stour (stuːə) *n. Archaic or Scot. and northern Brit. dialect.* **1.** turmoil or conflict. **2.** dust, esp. a cloud of dust raised by the rapid movement of a person or thing. [C14: from Old French *estour* armed combat, of Germanic origin; related to Old High German *sturm* STORM]

Stour+bridge ('staʊə,brɪdʒ) *n.* an industrial town in W central England, in the West Midlands. Pop.: 54 331 (1971).

stoush (staʊʃ) *Austral. slang.* *~vb.* **1.** (*tr.*) to hit or punch. *~n.* **2.** fighting, violence, or a fight. [C19: of uncertain origin]

stout (staʊt) *adj.* **1.** solidly built or corpulent. **2.** (*prenominal*) resolute or valiant: *stout fellow.* **3.** strong, substantial, and robust. **4. a stout heart.** courage; resolution. *~n.* **5.** strong porter highly flavoured with malt. [C14: from Old French *estout* bold, of Germanic origin; related to Middle High German *stolz* proud, Middle Dutch *stolt* brave] **—'stout+ish** *adj.* **—'stout+ly** *adv.* **—'stout+ness** *n.*

Stout (staʊt) *n.* Sir **Rob·ert.** 1844–1930, New Zealand statesman, born in Scotland: prime minister of New Zealand (1884–87).

stout+heart·ed (,staʊt'hɑːtɪd) *adj.* valiant; brave. **—,stout+'heart·ed·ly** *adv.* **—,stout+'heart·ed·ness** *n.*

stove[1] (stəʊv) *n.* **1.** another word for **cooker** (sense 1). **2.** any heating apparatus, such as a kiln. *~vb.* **3.** (*tr.*) to process (ceramics, metalwork, etc.) by heating in a stove. [Old English *stofa* bathroom; related to Old High German *stuba* steam room, Greek *tuphos* smoke]

stove[2] (stəʊv) *vb.* a past tense or past participle of **stave.**

stove e·nam+el *n.* a type of enamel made heatproof by treatment in a stove.

stove+pipe ('stəʊv,paɪp) *n.* **1.** a pipe that serves as a flue to a stove. **2.** Also called: **stovepipe hat.** a man's tall silk hat.

stove+pipes ('stəʊv,paɪps) *pl. n. Informal.* tight trousers with narrow legs.

stov+er ('stəʊvə) *n.* **1.** *Chiefly Brit.* fodder. **2.** *U.S.* cornstalks used as fodder. [C14: shortened from ESTOVER]

stow (stəʊ) *vb.* (*tr.*) **1.** (often foll. by *away*) to pack or store. **2.** to fill by packing. **3.** *Nautical.* to pack or put away (cargo, sails and other gear, etc.). **4.** to have enough room for. **5.** (*usually imperative*) *Brit. slang.* to cease from: *stow your noise! stow it!* [Old English *stōwian* to keep, hold back, from *stōw* a place; related to Old High German *stouwen* to accuse, Gothic *stōjan* to judge, Old Slavonic *staviti* to place]

Stow (stəʊ) *n.* **John.** 1525–1605, English antiquary, noted for his *Survey of London and Westminster* (1598; 1603).

stow+age ('stəʊɪdʒ) *n.* **1.** space, room, or a charge for stowing goods. **2.** the act or an instance of stowing or the state of being stowed. **3.** something that is stowed.

stow+a·way ('stəʊə,weɪ) *n.* **1.** a person who hides aboard a vehicle, ship, or aircraft in order to gain free passage. *~vb.* **stow a·way. 2.** (*intr., adv.*) to travel in such a way.

Stowe (stəʊ) *n.* **Har·ri·et E·liz·a·beth Beech·er.** 1811–96, U.S. writer, whose best-selling novel *Uncle Tom's Cabin* (1852) contributed to the antislavery cause.

S.T.P. *abbrev. for:* **1.** *Trademark.* scientifically treated petroleum: an oil substitute promising renewed power for an internal-combustion engine. **2.** Also: **NTP** standard temperature and pressure: standard conditions of 0°C temperature and 101.325 kPa (760 mmHg) pressure. **3.** Professor of Sacred Theology. [from Latin: *Sanctae Theologiae Professor*] *~n.* **4.** a synthetic hallucinogenic drug related to mescaline. [from humorous reference to the extra power resulting from scientifically treated petroleum]

str. *abbrev. for:* **1.** steamer. **2.** straight. **3.** *Music.* **a.** strings. **b.** stringed. **4.** strait. **5.** street. **6.** stroke oar.

stra+bis+mus (strə'bɪzməs) *n.* abnormal parallel alignment of one or both eyes, characterized by a turning inwards or outwards from the nose: caused by paralysis of an eye muscle, etc. Also called: **squint.** [C17: via New Latin from Greek *strabismos,* from *strabizein* to squint, from *strabos* cross-eyed] **—stra+'bis+mal, stra+'bis+mic,** *or* **stra+'bis+mi+cal** *adj.*

Stra·bo ('streɪbəʊ) *n.* ?63 B.C.–?23 A.D., Greek geographer and historian, noted for his *Geographica.*

stra+bot·o+my (strə'bɒtəmɪ) *n., pl.* **+mies.** a former method of treating strabismus by surgical division of one or more muscles of the eye. [C19: from French *strabotomie,* from Greek *strabos* squinting + -TOMY]

Stra·chey ('streɪtʃɪ) *n.* **(Giles) Lyt·ton.** 1880–1932, English biographer and critic, best known for *Eminent Victorians* (1918) and *Queen Victoria* (1921).

strad+dle ('strædᵊl) *vb.* **1.** (*tr.*) to have one leg, part, or support on each side of. **2.** (*tr.*) *U.S. informal.* to be in favour of both sides of (something). **3.** (*intr.*) to stand, walk, or sit with the legs apart. **4.** (*tr.*) to spread (the legs) apart. **5.** *Gunnery.* to fire a number of shots slightly beyond and slightly short of (a target) to determine the correct range. **6.** (*intr.*) (in poker, of the second player after the dealer) to double the ante before looking at one's cards. *~n.* **7.** the act or position of straddling. **8.** a noncommittal attitude or stand. **9.** *Stock exchange.* a contract or option permitting its purchaser either to sell securities to or buy securities from the maker of the contract within a specified period of time. It is a combination of a put and a call option. Compare **spread** (sense 24c.). **10.** *Athletics.* a high-jumping technique in which the body is parallel with the bar and the legs straddle it at the highest point of the jump. **11.** (in poker) the stake put up after the ante in poker by the second player after the dealer. [C16: frequentative formed from obsolete *strad-* (Old English *strode*), past stem of STRIDE] **—'strad+dler** *n.* **—'strad+dling+ly** *adv.*

Stra·di·va·ri (,strædɪ'vɑːrɪ) *n.* **An·to·nio** (an'tɔːnjo). ?1644–1737, Italian violin maker.

Strad·i+var+i·us (,strædɪ'vɑːrɪəs) *n.* any of a number of violins manufactured by Antonio Stradivari or his family. Often shortened to (informal) **Strad.**

strafe (streɪf, strɑːf) *vb.* (*tr.*) **1.** to bombard (troops, etc.) from the air. **2.** *Slang.* to punish harshly. *~n.* **3.** an act or instance of strafing. [C20: from German *strafen* to punish] **—'straf+er** *n.*

Straf·ford ('stræfəd) *n.* **Thom·as Went·worth,** Earl of. 1593–1641, English statesman. As lord deputy of Ireland (1632–39) and a chief adviser to Charles I, he was a leading proponent of the king's absolutist rule. He was impeached by Parliament and executed.

strag+gle ('strægᵊl) *vb.* (*intr.*) **1.** to go, come, or spread in a rambling or irregular way; stray. **2.** to linger behind or wander from a main line or part. [C14: of uncertain origin; perhaps related to STRAKE and STRETCH] **—'strag+gler** *n.* **—'strag+gling+ly** *adv.* **—'strag+gly** *adj.*

straight (streɪt) *adj.* **1.** not curved or crooked; continuing in the same direction without deviating. **2.** straightforward, outright, or candid: *a straight rejection.* **3.** even, level, or upright in shape or position. **4.** in keeping with the facts; accurate. **5.** honest, respectable, or reliable. **6.** accurate or logical: *straight reasoning.* **7.** continuous; uninterrupted. **8.** (esp. of an alcoholic drink) undiluted; neat. **9.** not crisp, kinked, or curly: *straight hair.* **10.** correctly arranged; orderly. **11.** (of a play, acting style, etc.) straightforward or serious. **12.** *Journalism.* (of a story, article, etc.) giving the facts without unnecessary embellishment. **13.** *U.S.* sold at a fixed unit price irrespective of the quantity sold. **14.** *Boxing.* (of a blow, etc.)

delivered with an unbent arm: *a straight left.* **15.** (of the cylinders of an internal-combustion engine) in line, rather than in a V-formation or in some other arrangement: *a straight eight.* **16.** a slang word for **heterosexual. 17.** *Informal.* no longer owing or being owed something: *if you buy the next round we'll be straight.* **18.** *Slang.* conventional in views, customs, appearance, etc. *~adv.* **19.** in a straight line or direct course. **20.** immediately; at once: *he came straight back.* **21.** in an even, level, or upright position. **22.** without cheating, lying, or unreliability: *tell it to me straight.* **23.** continuously; uninterruptedly. **24.** *U.S.* without discount regardless of the quantity sold. **25.** (often foll. by *out*) frankly; candidly: *he told me straight out.* **26. go straight.** *Informal.* to reform after having been dishonest or a criminal. *~n.* **27.** the state of being straight. **28.** a straight line, form, part, or position. **29.** *Brit.* a straight part of a racetrack. U.S. name: **straightaway. 30.** *Poker.* **a.** five cards that are in sequence irrespective of suit. **b.** a hand containing such a sequence. **c.** (*as modifier*): *a straight flush.* **31.** *Slang.* a conventional person. **32.** *Slang.* a cigarette containing only tobacco, without drugs. [C14: from the past participle of *streccan* to STRETCH] —**'straight+ly** *adv.* —**'straight+ness** *n.*

straight and nar+row *n. Informal.* the proper, honest, and moral path of behaviour.

straight an+gle *n.* an angle of 180°.

straight-arm *adj.* **1.** *Rugby.* (of a tackle) performed with the arm fully extended. *~vb.* **2.** (*tr.*) to ward off (an opponent) with the arm outstretched.

straight arm lift *n.* a wrestling attack, in which a wrestler twists his opponent's arm against the joint and lifts him by it, often using his shoulder as a fulcrum.

straight+a·way (ˌstreɪtəˈweɪ) *adv. also* **straight a·way. 1.** at once. *~n.* **2.** the U.S. word for **straight** (sense 29).

straight bat *n.* **1.** *Cricket.* a bat held vertically. **2.** *Brit. informal.* honest or honourable behaviour.

straight chain *n.* an open chain of atoms in a molecule with no attached side chains. Compare **branched chain.**

straight chair *n.* a straight-backed side chair.

straight+edge (ˈstreɪtˌɛdʒ) *n.* a stiff strip of wood or metal with one edge straight and true, used for ruling straight lines. —**'straight+ˌedged** *adj.*

straight+en (ˈstreɪtᵊn) *vb.* (sometimes foll. by *up* or *out*) **1.** to make or become straight. **2.** to make neat or tidy: *straighten your desk.* —**'straight+en+er** *n.*

straight+en out *vb.* (*adv.*) **1.** to make or become less complicated or confused: *the situation will straighten out.* **2.** *U.S.* to reform or become reformed.

straight+en up *vb.* (*adv.*) **1.** to become or cause to become erect. **2.** *Chiefly U.S.* to reform or become reformed.

straight face *n.* a serious facial expression, esp. one that conceals the impulse to laugh. —**'straight-'faced** *adj.*

straight fight *n.* a contest between two candidates only.

straight flush *n.* (in poker) five consecutive cards of the same suit.

straight+for·ward (ˌstreɪtˈfɔːwəd) *adj.* **1.** (of a person) honest, frank, or simple. **2.** *Chiefly Brit.* (of a task, etc.) simple; easy. *~adv., adj.* **3.** in a straight course. —**ˌstraight+'for·ward+ly** *adv.* —**ˌstraight+'for·ward+ness** *n.*

straight+jack·et (ˈstreɪtˌdʒækɪt) *n.* a less common spelling of **straitjacket.**

straight joint *n.* a vertical joint in brickwork that is directly above a vertical joint in the course below.

straight-laced *adj.* a variant spelling of **strait-laced.**

straight-line *n.* (*modifier*) **1.** (of a machine) having components that are arranged in a row or that move in a straight line when in operation. **2.** of or relating to a method of depreciation whereby equal charges are made against gross profit for each year of an asset's expected life.

straight man *n.* a subsidiary actor who acts as stooge to a comedian.

straight off *adv. Informal.* without deliberation or hesitation: *tell me the answer straight off.*

straight-out *adj. U.S. informal.* **1.** complete; thoroughgoing. **2.** frank or honest.

straight ra+zor *n.* another name for **cutthroat** (sense 2).

straight tick+et *n. U.S.* a ballot for all the candidates of one and only one political party. Compare **split ticket.**

straight+way (ˈstreɪtˌweɪ) *adv. Archaic.* at once.

strain[1] (streɪn) *vb.* **1.** to draw or be drawn taut; stretch tight. **2.** to exert, tax, or use (resources) to the utmost extent. **3.** to injure or damage or be injured or damaged by overexertion: *he strained himself.* **4.** to deform or be deformed as a result of a stress. **5.** (*intr.*) to make intense or violent efforts; strive. **6.** to subject or be subjected to mental tension or stress. **7.** to pour or pass (a substance) or (of a substance) to be poured or passed through a sieve, filter, or strainer. **8.** (*tr.*) to draw off or remove (one part of a substance or mixture from another) by or as if by filtering. **9.** (*tr.*) to clasp tightly; hug. **10.** (*tr.*) *Obsolete.* to force or constrain. **11.** (*intr.;* foll. by *at*) **a.** to push, pull, or work with violent exertion (upon). **b.** to strive (for). **c.** to balk or scruple (from). *~n.* **12.** the act or an instance of straining. **13.** the damage resulting from excessive exertion. **14.** an intense physical or mental effort. **15.** *Music.* (*often pl.*) a theme, melody, or tune. **16.** a great demand on the emotions, resources, etc. **17.** *Physics.* the change in dimension of a body under load expressed as the ratio of the total deflection or change in dimension to the original unloaded dimension. It may be a ratio of lengths, areas, or volumes. [C13: from Old French *estreindre* to press together, from Latin *stringere* to bind tightly] —**'strain+ing+ly** *adv.*

strain[2] (streɪn) *n.* **1.** the main body of descendants from one ancestor. **2.** a group of organisms within a species or variety, distinguished by one or more minor characteristics. **3.** a variety of bacterium or fungus, esp. one used for a culture. **4.** a streak; trace. **5.** *Archaic.* a kind, type, or sort. [Old English *strēon;* related to Old High German *gistriuni* gain, Latin *struere* to CONSTRUCT]

strained (streɪnd) *adj.* **1.** (of an action, performance, etc.) not natural or spontaneous. **2.** (of an atmosphere, relationship, etc.) not relaxed; tense. —**'strained+ness** *n.*

strain+er (ˈstreɪnə) *n.* **1.** a sieve used for straining sauces, vegetables, tea, etc. **2.** a gauze or simple filter used to strain liquids.

strain hard+en+ing *n.* a process in which a metal is permanently deformed in order to increase its resistance to further deformation.

strain+ing piece *or* **beam** *n.* a horizontal tie beam that connects the top of two queen posts of a roof truss.

strait (streɪt) *n.* **1.** (*often pl.*) **a.** a narrow channel of the sea linking two larger areas of sea. **b.** (*cap. as part of a name*): *the Strait of Gibraltar.* **2.** (*often pl.*) a position of acute difficulty (often in the phrase **in dire** *or* **desperate straits**). **3.** *Archaic.* a narrow place or passage. *~adj. Archaic.* **4.** (of spaces, etc.) affording little room. **5.** (of circumstances, etc.) limiting or difficult. **6.** severe, strict, or scrupulous. [C13: from Old French *estreit* narrow, from Latin *strictus* constricted, from *stringere* to bind tightly] —**'strait+ly** *adv.* —**'strait+ness** *n.*

strait+en (ˈstreɪtᵊn) *vb.* **1.** (*tr.; usually passive*) to embarrass or distress, esp. financially. **2.** (*tr.*) to limit, confine, or restrict. **3.** *Archaic.* to make or become narrow.

strait+jack·et *or* **straight+jack·et** (ˈstreɪtˌdʒækɪt) *n.* a jacket made of strong canvas material with long sleeves for binding the arms of violent prisoners or mental patients.

strait-laced *or* **straight-laced** *adj.* prudish or puritanical.

Straits Set+tle+ments *n.* (formerly) a British crown colony of SE Asia that included Singapore, Penang, Malacca, Labuan, and some smaller islands.

strake (streɪk) *n.* **1. a.** a curved metal plate forming part of the metal rim on a wooden wheel. **b.** any metal plate let into a rubber tyre. **2.** Also called: **streak.** *Nautical.* one of a continuous range of planks or plates forming the side of a vessel. [C14: related to Old English *streccan* to STRETCH]

Stral+sund (*German* ˈʃtraːlzʊnt) *n.* a port in N East Germany, on a strait of the Baltic: one of the leading towns of the Hanseatic League. Pop.: 72 138 (1972 est.).

stra+mo+ni·um (strəˈməʊnɪəm) *n.* **1.** a preparation of the dried leaves and flowers of the thorn apple, containing hyoscyamine and used as a drug to treat nervous disorders. **2.** another name for **thorn apple** (sense 1). [C17: from New Latin, of uncertain origin]

strand[1] (strænd) *vb.* **1.** to leave or drive (ships, fish, etc.) aground or ashore or (of ships or the like) to be left or driven ashore. **2.** (*tr.; usually passive*) to leave helpless, as without transport or money, etc. *~n. Chiefly poetic.* **3.** a shore or beach. **4.** a foreign country. [Old English; related to Old Norse *strönd* side, Middle High German *strant* beach, Latin *sternere* to spread]

strand[2] (strænd) *n.* **1.** a set of or one of the individual fibres or threads of string, wire, etc., that form a rope, cable, etc. **2.** a single length of string, hair, wool, wire, etc. **3.** a string of pearls or beads. *~vb.* **4.** (*tr.*) to form (a rope, cable, etc.) by winding strands together. [C15: of uncertain origin]

Strand (strænd) *n.* **the.** a street in W central London, parallel to the Thames: famous for its hotels and theatres.

Strand+lop+er (ˈstrantˌlʊəpə) *n.* a member of an extinct tribe of Hottentots or Bushmen who lived on sea food gathered on the beaches of southern Africa. [C19: from Afrikaans *strand* beach + *loper* walker]

strange (streɪndʒ) *adj.* **1.** odd, unusual, or extraordinary in appearance, effect, manner, etc.; peculiar. **2.** not known, seen, or experienced before; unfamiliar: *a strange land.* **3.** not easily explained: *a strange phenomenon.* **4.** (usually foll. by *to*) inexperienced (in) or unaccustomed (to): *strange to a task.* **5.** not of one's own kind, locality, etc.; alien; foreign. **6.** shy; distant; reserved. **7. strange to say.** it is unusual or suprising that. *~adv.* **8.** *Not standard.* in a strange manner. [C13: from Old French *estrange,* from Latin *extrāneus* foreign; see EXTRANEOUS] —**'strange+ly** *adv.*

strange+ness (ˈstreɪndʒnɪs) *n.* **1.** the state or quality of being strange. **2.** *Physics.* a property of certain elementary particles, characterized by a quantum number **(strangeness number)** conserved in strong but not in weak interactions.

strange par+ti+cle *n. Physics.* an elementary particle having a nonzero strangeness number.

stran+ger (ˈstreɪndʒə) *n.* **1.** any person whom one does not know. **2.** a person who is new to a particular locality, from another region, town, etc. **3.** a guest or visitor. **4.** (foll. by *to*) a person who is unfamiliar (with) or new (to) something: *he is no stranger to computers.* **5.** *Law.* a person who is neither party nor privy to a transaction. **6. little stranger.** *Jocular.* a newborn child.

stran+ger's gal+ler·y *n.* another name for **public gallery.**

stran+gle (ˈstræŋgᵊl) *vb.* **1.** (*tr.*) to kill by compressing the windpipe; throttle. **2.** (*tr.*) to prevent or inhibit the growth or development of: *to strangle originality.* **3.** (*tr.*) to suppress (an utterance) by or as if by swallowing suddenly: *to strangle a* *cry.* [C13: via Old French, ultimately from Greek *strangalē* a halter] —**'stran+gler** *n.*

stran·gle+hold ('stræŋgᵊlˌhəʊld) *n.* **1.** a wrestling hold in which a wrestler's arms are pressed against his opponent's windpipe. See also **Japanese stranglehold. 2.** complete power or control over a person or situation.

stran+gles ('stræŋgᵊlz) *n.* an acute bacterial disease of horses caused by infection with *Streptococcus equi,* characterized by inflammation of the mucous membranes of the respiratory tract. Also called: **equine distemper.**

stran+gu+late ('stræŋgjʊˌleɪt) *vb.* (*tr.*) **1.** to constrict (a hollow organ, vessel, etc.) so as to stop the natural flow of air, blood, etc., through it. **2.** another word for **strangle.** —**ˌstran+gu+'la+tion** *n.*

stran+gu+ry ('stræŋgjʊrɪ) *n. Pathol.* painful excretion of urine, drop by drop, caused by muscular spasms of the urinary tract. [C14: from Latin *strangūria,* from Greek, from *stranx* a drop squeezed out + *ouron* urine]

Stran+raer (stræn'rɑː) *n.* a market town in SW Scotland, in W Dumfries and Galloway region: fishing port with a steamer service to Northern Ireland. Pop.: 9853 (1971).

strap (stræp) *n.* **1.** a long strip of leather or similar material, for binding trunks, baggage, or other objects. **2.** a strip of leather or similar material used for carrying, lifting, or holding. **3.** a loop of leather, rubber, etc., suspended from the roof in a bus or train for standing passengers to hold on to. **4.** a razor strop. **5. the strap.** a beating with a strap as a punishment. **6.** short for **shoulder strap.** ~*vb.* **straps, strap+ping, strapped.** (*tr.*) **7.** to tie or bind with a strap. **8.** to beat with a strap. **9.** to sharpen with a strap or strop. [C16: variant of STROP]

strap+hang·er ('stræpˌhæŋə) *n. Informal.* a passenger in a bus, train, etc., who has to travel standing, esp. by holding on to a strap. —**'strap+ˌhang·ing** *n.*

strap hinge *n.* a hinge with a long leaf or flap attached to the face of a door, gate, etc.

strap+less ('stræplɪs) *adj.* (of a woman's formal dress, brassiere, etc.) without straps over the shoulders.

strap-oil *n. Slang.* a beating.

strap+pa+do (strə'peɪdəʊ, -'pɑː-) *n., pl.* **+does.** a system of torture in which a victim was hoisted by a rope tied to his wrists and then allowed to drop until his fall was suddenly checked by the rope. [C16: from French *strapade,* from Italian *strappare* to tug sharply, probably of Germanic origin; related to German (dialect) *strapfen* to make taut]

strapped (stræpt) *adj.* (*postpositive;* often foll. by *for*) *U.S. slang.* badly in need (of money); penniless.

strap+per ('stræpə) *n. Informal, chiefly U.S.* a strapping person.

strap+ping ('stræpɪŋ) *adj.* (*prenominal*) tall and sturdy.

strap work *n. Architecture.* decorative work resembling interlacing straps.

Stras+bourg (*French* stras'buːr; *English* 'stræzbɜːg) *n.* a city in NE France, on the Rhine: the chief French inland port; under German rule (1870–1918); university (1567); seat of the Council of Europe and of the European Parliament. Pop.: 257 303 (1975). German name: **Strass+burg** ('ʃtraːsbʊrk).

strass (stræs) *n. Jewellery.* another word for **paste** (sense 6). [C19: German, named after J. *Strasser,* 18th-century German jeweller who invented it]

stra+ta ('strɑːtə) *n.* the plural of **stratum.**

Usage. In careful usage, *strata* is the standard plural of *stratum* and is not treated as a singular noun.

strat·a+gem ('strætɪdʒəm) *n.* a plan or trick, esp. one to deceive an enemy. [C15: ultimately from Greek *stratēgos* a general, from *stratos* an army + *agein* to lead]

stra+te·gic (strə'tiːdʒɪk) *or* **stra+te·gi+cal** *adj.* **1.** of, relating to, or characteristic of strategy. **2.** important to a strategy or to strategy in general. —**stra+'te·gi+cal+ly** *adv.*

stra+te·gics (strə'tiːdʒɪks) *n.* strategy, esp. in a military sense.

strat+e·gist ('strætɪdʒɪst) *n.* a specialist or expert in strategy.

strat+e·gy ('strætɪdʒɪ) *n., pl.* **·gies. 1.** the art or science of the planning and conduct of a war. **2.** the practice or art of using stratagems, as in politics, business, etc. **3.** a plan or stratagem. [C17: from French *stratégie,* from Greek *stratēgia* function of a general; see STRATAGEM]

Strat·ford-on-A·von *or* **Strat·ford-up·on-A·von** ('strætfəd) *n.* a market town in central England, in SW Warwickshire on the River Avon: the birthplace and burial place of William Shakespeare and home of the Royal Shakespeare Company; tourist centre. Pop.: 19 449 (1971).

strath (stræθ) *n. Scot.* a broad valley or glen. [C16: from Gaelic; compare Irish *srath,* Welsh *ystrad*]

Strath+clyde (ˌstræθ'klaɪd) *n.* a local government region in W Scotland, formed in 1975 from Renfrew, Lanark, Bute, Dunbarton, and parts of Argyll, Ayr, and Stirling. Administrative centre: Glasgow. Pop.: 2 488 643 (1976 est.). Area: 13 727 sq. km (5300 sq. miles).

strath+spey (ˌstræθ'speɪ) *n.* a slow Scottish reel with gliding steps.

strat·i- *combining form.* indicating stratum or strata: *stratiform; stratigraphy.*

stra+tic·u·late (strə'tɪkjʊlɪt, -ˌleɪt) *adj.* (of a rock formation) composed of very thin even strata. [C19: from New Latin *strāticulum* (unattested), diminutive of Latin *strātum* something strewn; see STRATUS] —**stra+ˌtic·u+'la+tion** *n.*

strat·i+fi+ca+tion (ˌstrætɪfɪ'keɪʃən) *n.* **1.** the arrangement of sedimentary rocks in distinct layers (strata), each layer representing the sediment deposited over a specific period. **2.** the act of stratifying or state of being stratified. —**strat·i·fi+'ca+tion+al** *adj.*

strat·i+fi+ca+tion+al gram+mar *n. Linguistics.* a theory of grammar analysing language in terms of several structural strata or layers with different syntactic rules.

strat·i+form ('strætɪˌfɔːm) *adj.* **1.** (of rocks) occurring as or arranged in strata. **2.** *Meteorol.* resembling a stratus cloud.

strat·i+fy ('strætɪˌfaɪ) *vb.* **+fies, +fy+ing, +fied. 1.** to form or be formed in layers or strata. **2.** (*tr.*) to preserve or render fertile (seeds) by storing between layers of sand or earth. **3.** *Sociol.* to divide (a society) into horizontal status groups or (of a society) to develop such groups. [C17: from French *stratifier,* from New Latin *stratificāre,* from Latin STRATUM]

stra+tig+ra+phy (strə'tɪgrəfɪ) *n.* **1.** the study of the composition, relative positions, etc., of rock strata in order to determine their geological history. Abbrev.: **stratig. 2.** *Archaeol.* a vertical section through the earth showing the relative positions of the human artefacts and therefore the chronology of successive levels of occupation. —**stra+tig+ra+pher** (strə'tɪgrəfə) *or* **stra+tig+ra+phist** (strə'tɪgrəfɪst) *n.* —**strat·i+graph+ic** (ˌstrætɪ'græfɪk) *or* **ˌstrat·i+'graph·i·cal** *adj.*

strat·o- *combining form.* **1.** denoting stratus: *stratocumulus.* **2.** denoting the stratosphere: *stratopause.*

stra+toc+ra+cy (strə'tɒkrəsɪ). *n., pl.* **+cies.** military rule. [C17: from Greek *stratos* an army + -CRACY] —**strat·o+crat** ('strætəˌkræt) *n.* —**strat·o+crat+ic** (ˌstrætə'krætɪk) *adj.*

strat·o+cu+mu+lus (ˌstreɪtəʊ'kjuːmjʊləs) *n., pl.* **+li** (-ˌlaɪ). *Meteorol.* a uniform stretch of cloud containing dark grey globular masses.

strat·o+pause ('strætəˌpɔːz) *n. Meteorol.* the transitional zone of maximum temperature between the stratosphere and the mesosphere.

strat·o+sphere ('strætəˌsfɪə) *n.* the atmospheric layer lying between the troposphere and the mesosphere, in which temperature generally increases with height. —**strat·o+spher+ic** (ˌstrætə'sfɛrɪk) *or* **ˌstrat·o+'spher·i+cal** *adj.*

stra+tum ('strɑːtəm) *n., pl.* **+ta** (-tə) *or* **+tums. 1.** (*usually pl.*) any of the distinct layers into which sedimentary rocks are divided. **2.** *Biology.* a single layer of tissue or cells. **3.** a layer of any material, esp. one of several parallel layers. **4.** a layer of ocean or atmosphere either naturally or arbitrarily demarcated. **5.** a level of a social hierarchy that is distinguished according to such criteria as educational achievement or caste status. [C16: via New Latin from Latin: something strewn, from *sternere* to scatter] —**'stra+tal** *adj.*

stra+tus ('streɪtəs) *n., pl.* **+ti** (-taɪ). a grey layer cloud. Compare **cirrus** (sense 1), **cumulus.** [C19: via New Latin from Latin: strewn, from *sternere* to extend]

Straus (straʊs) *n.* **Os·car** (ɔs'kaːr). 1870–1954, French composer, born in Austria, noted for such operettas as *Waltz Dream* (1907) and *The Chocolate Soldier* (1908).

Strauss (straʊs; *German* ʃtraʊs) *n.* **1. Da·vid Frie·drich** ('daːfɪt 'friːdrɪç). 1808–74, German Protestant theologian: in his *Life of Jesus* (1835–36) he treated the supernatural elements of the story as myth. **2. Jo·hann** ('joːhan). 1804–49, Austrian composer, noted for his waltzes. **3.** his son, **Jo·hann,** called the *Waltz King.* 1825–99, Austrian composer, whose works include *The Blue Danube Waltz* (1867) and the operetta *Die Fledermaus* (1874). **4. Ri·chard** ('rɪçart). 1864–1949, German composer, noted esp. for his symphonic poems, including *Don Juan* (1889) and *Till Eulenspiegel* (1895), his operas, such as *Elektra* (1909) and *Der Rosenkavalier* (1911), and his *Four Last Songs* (1948).

stra+vaig (strə'veɪg) *vb.* (*intr.*) *Scot. and northern Brit. dialect.* to wander aimlessly. [C19: perhaps a variant of obsolete *extravage,* from Medieval Latin *extrāvagārī,* from *vagārī* to wander]

Stra·vin·sky (*Russian* stra'vinskij) *n.* **I·gor Fyo·do·ro·vich** ('igərj 'fjɔdərəvitʃ). 1882–1971, U.S. composer, born in Russia. He created ballet scores, such as *The Firebird* (1910), *Petrushka* (1911), and *The Rite of Spring* (1913), for Diaghilev. These were followed by neoclassical works, including *Oedipus Rex* (1927) and the *Symphony of Psalms* (1930). The 1950s saw him reconciled to serial techniques, which he employed in such works as the *Canticum Sacrum* (1955), the ballet *Agon* (1957), and *Requiem Canticles* (1966).

straw[1] (strɔː) *n.* **1. a.** stalks of threshed grain, esp. of wheat, rye, oats, or barley, used in plaiting hats, baskets, etc., or as fodder. **b.** (*as modifier*)*: a straw hat.* **2.** a single dry or ripened stalk, esp. of a grass. **3.** a long thin hollow paper or plastic tube or stem of a plant, used for sucking up liquids into the mouth. **4.** (*usually used with a negative*) anything of little value or importance: *I wouldn't give a straw for our chances.* **5.** a measure or remedy that one turns to in desperation (esp. in the phrases **clutch** *or* **grasp at a straw** *or* **straws**). **6. a.** a pale yellow colour. **b.** (*as adj.*)*: straw hair.* **7. the last straw.** a final blow or calamity. **8. straw in the wind.** a hint or indication. ~*adj.* **9.** *Chiefly U.S.* having little value or substance. ~ See also **man of straw.** [Old English *streaw;* related to Old Norse *strā,* Old Frisian *strē,* Old High German *strō;* see STREW] —**'straw+ˌlike** *adj.* —**'straw·y** *adj.*

straw[2] (strɔː) *vb.* (*tr.*) *Archaic.* another word for **strew.**

straw+ber·ry ('strɔːbərɪ, -brɪ) *n., pl.* **·ries. 1. a.** any of various low-growing rosaceous plants of the genus *Fragaria,* such as *F. vesca* (**wild strawberry**) and *F. ananassa* (**garden strawberry**), which have white flowers and red edible fruits and spread by runners. **b.** (*as modifier*)*: a strawberry patch.* **2. a.** the fruit of any of these plants, consisting of a sweet fleshy receptacle bearing small seedlike parts (the true fruits). **b.** (*as modifier*)*: strawberry ice cream.* **3. barren strawberry.** a related Eurasian plant, *Potentilla sterilis,* that does not produce edible fruit. **4. a.** a purplish-red colour. **b.** (*as adj.*)*: strawberry shoes.* [Old

English *streawberige;* perhaps from the strawlike appearance of the runners]

straw+ber·ry blonde *adj.* **1.** (of hair) reddish blonde. ~*n.* **2.** a woman with such hair.

straw+ber·ry bush *n.* **1.** an E North American shrub or small tree, *Euonymus americanus,* having pendulous capsules that split when ripe to reveal scarlet seeds: family *Celastraceae.* **2.** any of various similar or related plants.

straw+ber·ry mark *n.* a soft vascular red birthmark. Technical name: **hemangioma simplex.** Also called: **strawberry.**

straw+ber·ry to+ma+to *n.* **1.** a tropical solanaceous annual plant, *Physalis peruviana,* having bell-shaped whitish-yellow flowers and small edible round yellow berries. **2.** a similar and related plant, *Physalis pubescens.* **3.** the fruit of either of these plants, eaten fresh or made into preserves and pickles. ~Also called: **Cape gooseberry.**

straw+ber·ry tree *n.* a S European evergreen tree, *Arbutus unedo,* having white or pink flowers and red strawberry-like berries. See also **arbutus.**

straw+board ('strɔːˌbɔːd) *n.* a board made of compressed straw and adhesive, used esp. in book covers.

straw+flow·er ('strɔːˌflaʊə) *n.* an Australian plant, *Helichrysum bracteatum,* in which the coloured bracts retain their colour when the plant is dried: family *Compositae* (composites). See also **immortelle.**

straw man *n. Chiefly U.S.* **1.** a figure of a man made from straw. **2.** another term for **man of straw.**

straw vote *or* **poll** *n. Chiefly U.S.* an unofficial poll or vote taken to determine the opinion of a group or the public on some issue.

straw wine *n.* any of several wines made from grapes dried on straw mats to increase their sugar strength.

straw+worm ('strɔːˌwɜːm) *n.* another name for a **caddis worm.**

stray (streɪ) *vb.* (*intr.*) **1.** to wander away, as from the correct path or from a given area. **2.** to wander haphazardly. **3.** to digress from the point, lose concentration, etc. **4.** to deviate from certain moral standards. ~*n.* **5. a.** a domestic animal, fowl, etc., that has wandered away from its place of keeping and is lost. **b.** (*as modifier*): *stray dogs.* **6.** a lost or homeless person, esp. a child: *waifs and strays.* **7.** an isolated or random occurrence, specimen, etc., that is out of place or outside the usual pattern. ~*adj.* **8.** scattered, random, or haphazard: *a stray bullet grazed his thigh.* [C14: from Old French *estraier,* from Vulgar Latin *estragāre* (unattested), from Latin *extrā* outside + *vagārī* to roam; see ASTRAY, EXTRAVAGANT] —**'stray+er** *n.*

strays (streɪz) *pl. n.* **1.** Also called: **stray capacitance.** *Electronics.* undesired capacitance in equipment, occurring between the wiring, between the wiring and the chassis, or between components and the chassis. **2.** *Telecomm.* another word for **static** (sense 9).

streak[1] (striːk) *n.* **1.** a long thin mark, stripe, or trace of some contrasting colour. **2. a.** (of lightning) a sudden flash. **b.** (*as modifier*): *streak lightning.* **3.** an element or trace, as of some quality or characteristic. **4.** a strip, vein, or layer: *fatty streaks.* **5.** a short stretch or run, esp. of good or bad luck. **6.** *Mineralogy.* the powdery mark made by a mineral when rubbed on a hard or rough surface: its colour is an important distinguishing characteristic. **7.** *Bacteriol.* the inoculation of a culture medium by drawing a wire contaminated with the microorganisms across the surface of the medium. **8.** *Informal.* an act or the practice of running naked through a public place. ~*vb.* **9.** (*tr.*) to mark or daub with a streak or streaks. **10.** (*intr.*) to form streaks or become streaked. **11.** (*intr.*) to move rapidly in a straight line. **12.** (*intr.*) *Informal.* to run naked through a crowd of people in a public place in order to shock or amuse them. [Old English *strica,* related to Old Frisian *strike,* Old High German *strih,* Norwegian, Swedish *strika*] —**streaked** *adj.* —**'streak+er** *n.* —**'streak+ˌlike** *adj.*

streak[2] (striːk) *n.* a variant spelling of **strake** (sense 2).

streak·y ('striːkɪ) *adj.* **streak·i+er, streak·i·est. 1.** marked with streaks. **2.** occurring in streaks. **3.** (of bacon) having alternate layers of meat and fat. **4.** of varying or uneven quality. —**'streak·i+ly** *adv.* —**'streak·i+ness** *n.*

stream (striːm) *n.* **1.** a small river; brook. **2.** any steady flow of water or other fluid. **3.** something that resembles a stream in moving continuously in a line or particular direction. **4.** a rapid or unbroken flow of speech, etc.: *a stream of abuse.* **5.** *Brit.* any of several parallel classes of schoolchildren, or divisions of children within a class, grouped together because of similar ability. **6. go** (*or* **drift**) **with the stream.** to conform to the accepted standards. ~*vb.* **7.** to emit or be emitted in a continuous flow: *his nose streamed blood.* **8.** (*intr.*) to move in unbroken succession, as a crowd of people, vehicles, etc. **9.** (*intr.*) to float freely or with a waving motion: *bunting streamed in the wind.* **10.** (*tr.*) to unfurl (a flag, etc.). **11.** (*intr.*) to move causing a trail of light, condensed gas, etc., as a jet aircraft. **12.** (when *intr.,* often foll. by *for*) *Mining.* to wash (earth, gravel, etc.) in running water in prospecting (for gold, etc.), to expose the particles of ore or metal. **13.** *Brit. education.* to group or divide (children) in streams. [Old English; related to Old Frisian *strām,* Old Norse *straumr,* Old High German *stroum,* Greek *rheuma*] —**'stream+ˌlike** *adj.*

stream+er ('striːmə) *n.* **1.** a long narrow flag or part of a flag. **2.** a long narrow coiled ribbon of coloured paper that becomes unrolled when tossed. **3.** a stream of light, esp. one appearing in some forms of the aurora. **4.** *Journalism.* a large heavy headline printed across the width of a page of a newspaper.

stream+line ('striːmˌlaɪn) *n.* **1.** a contour on a body that offers the minimum resistance to a gas or liquid flowing around it. **2.** a line in a fluid such that the tangent at any point indicates the direction of the velocity of a particle of the fluid at that point. ~*vb.* (*tr.*) **3.** to make streamlined.

stream+lined ('striːmˌlaɪnd) *adj.* **1.** offering or designed to offer the minimum resistance to the flow of a gas or liquid. **2.** made more efficient, esp. by simplifying.

stream+line flow *n.* flow of a fluid in which its velocity at any point is constant or varies in a regular manner. Compare **turbulent flow.** See also **laminar flow.**

stream of con+scious+ness *n.* **1.** *Psychol.* the continuous flow of ideas, thoughts, and feelings forming the content of an individual's consciousness. The term was originated by William James. **2. a.** a literary technique that reveals the flow of thoughts and feelings of characters through long passages of soliloquy. **b.** (*as modifier*): *a stream-of-consciousness novel.*

stream·y ('striːmɪ) *adj.* **stream·i+er, stream·i+est.** *Chiefly poetic.* **1.** (of an area, land, etc.) having many streams. **2.** flowing or streaming. —**'stream·i+ness** *n.*

street (striːt) *n.* **1. a.** (*cap. when part of a name*) a public road that is usually lined with buildings, esp. in a town: *Oxford Street.* **b.** (*as modifier*): *a street directory.* **2.** the buildings lining a street. **3.** the part of the road between the pavements, used by vehicles. **4.** the people living, working, etc., in a particular street. **5. man in the street.** an ordinary or average citizen. **6. on the streets.** earning a living as a prostitute. **7. (right) up one's street.** (just) what one knows or likes best. **8. streets ahead of.** superior to, more advanced than, etc. **9. streets apart.** markedly different. [Old English *strǣt,* from Latin *via strāta* paved way (*strāta,* from *strātus,* past participle of *sternere* to stretch out); compare Old Frisian *strēte,* Old High German *strāza;* see STRATUS]

street Ar·ab *n.* a homeless child, esp. one who survives by begging and stealing; urchin.

street+car ('striːtˌkɑː) *n.* the usual U.S. name for **tram**[1] (sense 1).

street cry *n.* (*often pl.*) the cry of a street hawker.

street door *n.* the door of a house that opens onto the street.

street+light ('striːtˌlaɪt) *or* **street+lamp** *n.* a light, esp. one carried on a lamppost, that illuminates a road, etc.

street pi+an·o *n.* another name for **barrel organ.**

street+walk·er ('striːtˌwɔːkə) *n.* a prostitute who solicits on the streets. —**'street+ˌwalk·ing** *n., adj.*

Strei·sand ('straɪsænd) *n.* **Bar·bra.** born 1942, U.S. singer and film actress: her films include *Funny Girl* (1968) and *A Star is born* (1976).

stre+lit+zi·a (strɛ'lɪtsɪə) *n.* any southern African perennial herbaceous plant of the musaceous genus *Strelitzia,* cultivated for its showy flowers: includes the bird-of-paradise flower. [C18: named after Charlotte of Mecklenburg-*Strelitz* (1744–1818), queen of England]

strength (strɛŋθ) *n.* **1.** the state or quality of being physically or mentally strong. **2.** the ability to withstand or exert great force, stress, or pressure. **3.** something that is regarded as being beneficial or a source of power: *their chief strength is technology.* **4.** potency, as of a drink, drug, etc. **5.** power to convince; cogency: *the strength of an argument.* **6.** degree of intensity or concentration of colour, light, sound, flavour, etc. **7.** *Finance.* firmness of or a rising tendency in prices, esp. security prices. **8.** *Archaic or poetic.* a stronghold or fortress. **9. from strength to strength.** with ever-increasing success. **10. in strength.** in large numbers. **11. on the strength of.** on the basis of or relying upon. [Old English *strengthu;* related to Old High German *strengida;* see STRONG]

strength+en ('strɛŋθən) *vb.* to make or become stronger. —**'strength+en+er** *n.*

stren·u·ous ('strɛnjʊəs) *adj.* **1.** requiring or involving the use of great energy or effort. **2.** characterized by great activity, effort, or endeavour. [C16: from Latin *strēnuus* brisk, vigorous] —**stren·u+os+i·ty** (ˌstrɛnjʊ'ɒsɪtɪ) *or* **'stren·u·ous+ness** *n.* —**'stren·u·ous+ly** *adv.*

strep (strɛp) *n. Informal.* short for **streptococcus.**

strep·i+tous ('strɛpɪtəs) *or* **strep·i·tant** *adj. Rare.* noisy; boisterous. [C17: from Latin *strepitus* a din]

strep·to- *combining form.* **1.** indicating a shape resembling a twisted chain: *streptococcus.* **2.** indicating streptococcus: *streptolysin.* [from Greek *streptos* twisted, from *strephein* to twist]

strep+to+coc+cus (ˌstrɛptəʊ'kɒkəs) *n., pl.* **+coc+ci** (-'kɒksaɪ). any Gram-positive spherical bacterium of the genus *Streptococcus,* typically occurring in chains and including many pathogenic species, such as *S. pyogenes,* which causes scarlet fever, sore throat, etc.: family *Lactobacillaceae.* Often shortened to **strep.** —**strep+to+coc+cal** (ˌstrɛptəʊ'kɒkᵊl) *or* **strep+to+coc+cic** (ˌstrɛptəʊ'kɒksɪk) *adj.*

strep+to+ki+nase (ˌstrɛptəʊ'kaɪneɪs) *n.* an enzyme produced by streptococci that causes the fibrin of certain animal species to undergo lysis. See also **fibrinolysin.**

strep+to+my+cin (ˌstrɛptəʊ'maɪsɪn) *n.* an antibiotic obtained from the bacterium *Streptomyces griseus:* used in the treatment of tuberculosis and Gram-negative bacterial infections. Formula: $C_{21}H_{39}N_7O_{12}$.

strep+to+thri+cin (ˌstrɛptəʊ'θraɪsɪn) *n.* an antibiotic active against bacteria and some fungi, produced by the bacterium *Streptomyces lavendulae.*

stress (strɛs) *n.* **1.** special emphasis or significance attached to something. **2.** emphasis placed upon a syllable by pronouncing it more loudly than those that surround it. **3.** such emphasis as part of a regular rhythmic beat in music or poetry. **4.** a syllable so emphasized. **5.** *Physics.* **a.** force or a system of forces producing deformation or strain. **b.** the force acting per unit area. **6.** mental, emotional, or physical strain or tension. ~*vb.* (*tr.*) **7.** to give emphasis or prominence to. **8.** to pronounce (a word or syllable) more loudly than those that surround it. **9.** to subject to stress or strain. [C14: *stresse,* shortened from DISTRESS] —**'stress+ful** *adj.*

-stress *suffix forming nouns.* indicating a woman who performs or is engaged in a certain activity: *songstress; seamstress.* Compare **-ster** (sense 1). [from -ST(E)R + -ESS]

stretch (strɛtʃ) *vb.* **1.** to draw out or extend or be drawn out or extended in length, area, etc. **2.** to extend or be extended to an undue degree, esp. so as to distort or lengthen permanently. **3.** to extend (the limbs, body, etc.). **4.** (*tr.*) to reach or suspend (a rope, etc.) from one place to another. **5.** (*tr.*) to draw tight; tighten. **6.** (often foll. by *out, forward,* etc.) to reach or hold (out); extend. **7.** (*intr.;* usually foll. by *over*) to extend in time: *the course stretched over three months.* **8.** (*intr.;* foll. by *for, over,* etc.) (of a region, etc.) to extend in length or area. **9.** (*intr.*) (esp. of a garment) to be capable of expanding, as to a larger size: *socks that will stretch.* **10.** (*tr.*) to put a great strain upon or extend to the limit. **11.** to injure (a muscle, tendon, ligament, etc.) by means of a strain or sprain. **12.** (*tr.;* often foll. by *out*) to make do with (limited resources): *to stretch one's budget.* **13.** (*tr.*) *Informal.* to expand or elaborate (a story, etc.) beyond what is credible or acceptable: *that's stretching it a bit.* **14.** (*tr.; often passive*) to extend, as to the limit of one's abilities or talents. **15.** *Archaic or slang.* to hang or be hanged by the neck. **16. stretch a point. a.** to make a concession or exception not usually made. **b.** to exaggerate. **17. stretch one's legs.** to take a walk, esp. after a period of inactivity. ~*n.* **18.** the act of stretching or state of being stretched. **19.** a large or continuous expanse or distance: *a stretch of water.* **20.** extent in time, length, area, etc. **21. a.** capacity for being stretched, as in some garments. **b.** (*as modifier*): *stretch pants.* **22.** *Horse racing.* the section or sections of a racecourse that are straight, esp. the final straight section leading to the finishing line. **23.** *Slang.* a term of imprisonment. **24. at a stretch.** *Chiefly Brit.* **a.** with some difficulty; by making a special effort. **b.** if really necessary or in extreme circumstances. [Old English *streccan;* related to Old Frisian *strekka,* Old High German *strecken;* see STRAIGHT, STRAKE] —**'stretch+a·ble** *adj.* —**ˌstretch+a·'bil+i·ty** *n.*

stretch+er ('strɛtʃə) *n.* **1.** a device for transporting the ill, wounded, or dead, consisting of a sheet of canvas stretched between two poles. **2.** a strengthening often decorative member joining the legs of a chair, table, etc. **3.** the wooden frame on which canvas is stretched and fixed for oil painting. **4.** a tie beam or brace used in a structural framework. **5.** a brick or stone laid horizontally with its length parallel to the length of a wall. Compare **header** (sense 4). **6.** *Rowing.* a fixed board across a boat on which an oarsman braces his feet. **7.** *Austral.* a camp bed.

stretch·er-bear·er *n.* an attendant who helps to carry a stretcher or litter, esp. in wartime.

stretch·y ('strɛtʃɪ) *adj.* **stretch·i+er, stretch·i+est.** characterized by elasticity. —**'stretch·i+ness** *n.*

Stret+ford ('strɛtfəd) *n.* an industrial town in NW England, in Greater Manchester. Pop.: 54 011 (1971).

stret+to ('strɛtəʊ) *n., pl.* **+tos** *or* **+ti** (-tiː). **1.** (in a fugue) the close overlapping of two parts or voices, the second one entering before the first has completed its statement of the subject. **2.** Also called: **stret+ta** ('strɛtə). a concluding passage in a composition, played at a faster speed than the earlier material. [C17: from Italian, from Latin *strictus* tightly bound; see STRICT]

streu+sel ('struːsᵊl, 'strɔɪ-; *German* 'ʃtrɔɪzᵊl) *n. Chiefly U.S.* a crumbly topping for rich pastries. [German, from *streuen* to STREW]

strew (struː) *vb.* **strews, strew+ing, strewed; strewn** *or* **strewed.** to spread or scatter or be spread or scattered, as over a surface or area. [Old English *streowian;* related to Old Norse *strā,* Old High German *streuwen,* Latin *struere* to spread] —**'strew+er** *n.*

strewth (struːθ) *interj.* an expression of surprise or dismay. [C19: alteration of *God's truth*]

stri·a ('straɪə) *n., pl.* **stri·ae** ('straɪiː). (*often pl.*) **1.** Also called: **striation.** *Geology.* any of the parallel scratches or grooves on the surface of a rock over which a glacier has flowed or on the surface of a crystal. **2.** *Biology, anatomy.* a narrow band of colour or a ridge, groove, or similar linear mark, usually occurring in a parallel series. **3.** *Architect.* a narrow channel, such as a flute on the shaft of a column. [C16: from Latin: a groove]

stri+ate *adj.* ('straɪɪt), *also* **stri+at+ed. 1.** marked with striae; striped. ~*vb.* ('straɪeɪt). **2.** (*tr.*) to mark with striae. [C17: from Latin *striāre* to make grooves, from STRIA]

stri·a·tion (straɪ'eɪʃən) *n.* **1.** an arrangement or pattern of striae. **2.** the condition of being striate. **3.** another word for **stria** (sense 1).

strick (strɪk) *n. Textiles.* any bast fibres preparatory to being made into slivers. [C15 *stric,* perhaps of Low German origin; compare Middle Dutch *stric,* Middle Low German *strik* rope]

strick+en ('strɪkən) *adj.* **1.** laid low, as by disease or sickness. **2.** deeply affected, as by grief, love, etc. **3.** *Archaic.* wounded or injured. **4. stricken in years.** made feeble by age. [C14: past participle of STRIKE] —**'strick+en+ly** *adv.*

strick+le ('strɪkᵊl) *n.* **1.** Also called: **strike.** a board used for sweeping off excess material in a container. **2.** a template used for shaping a mould. **3.** a bar of abrasive material for sharpening a scythe. ~*vb.* **4.** (*tr.*) to level, form, or sharpen with a strickle. [Old English *stricel;* related to Latin *strigilis* scraper, German *Striegel;* see STRIKE]

strict (strɪkt) *adj.* **1.** adhering closely to specified rules, ordinances, etc.: *a strict faith.* **2.** complied with or enforced stringently; rigorous: *a strict code of conduct.* **3.** severely correct in attention to rules of conduct or morality: *a strict teacher.* **4.** (of a punishment, etc.) harsh; severe. **5.** (*prenominal*) complete; absolute: *in strict secrecy.* **6.** *Botany, rare.* very straight, narrow, and upright: *strict panicles.* [C16: from Latin *strictus,* from *stringere* to draw tight] —**'strict+ly** *adv.* —**'strict+ness** *n.*

stric+tion ('strɪkʃən) *n. Rare.* the act of constricting. [C19: from Late Latin *strictiō;* see STRICT]

stric+ture ('strɪktʃə) *n.* **1.** a severe criticism; censure. **2.** *Pathol.* an abnormal constriction of a tubular organ, structure, or part. **3.** *Obsolete.* severity. [C14: from Latin *strictūra* contraction; see STRICT] —**'stric+tured** *adj.*

stride (straɪd) *n.* **1.** a long step or pace. **2.** the space measured by such a step. **3.** a striding gait. **4.** an act of forward movement by a horse, etc., completed when the legs have returned to their initial relative positions. **5.** progress or development (esp. in the phrase **make rapid strides**). **6.** a regular pace or rate of progress: *to get into one's stride; to be put off one's stride.* **7.** *Rowing.* the distance covered between strokes. **8.** (*pl.*) *Austral. informal.* men's trousers. **9. take (something) in one's stride.** to do (something) without difficulty or effort. ~*vb.* **strides, strid+ing, strode, strid+den. 10.** (*intr.*) to walk with long regular or measured paces, as in haste, etc. **11.** (*tr.*) to cover or traverse by striding: *he strode thirty miles.* **12.** (often foll. by *over, across,* etc.) to cross (over a space, obstacle, etc.) with a stride. **13.** (*intr.*) *Rowing.* to achieve the desired rhythm in a racing shell. **14.** *Archaic or poetic.* to straddle or bestride. [Old English *strīdan;* related to Old High German *strītan* to quarrel; see STRADDLE] —**'strid+er** *n.*

stri+dent ('straɪdᵊnt) *adj.* **1.** (of a shout, voice, etc.) having or making a loud or harsh sound. **2.** urgent, clamorous, or vociferous: *strident demands.* [C17: from Latin *strīdēns,* from *strīdēre* to make a grating sound] —**'stri+dence** *or* **'stri+den+cy** *n.* —**'stri+dent+ly** *adv.*

stri+dor ('straɪdɔː) *n.* **1.** *Pathol.* a high-pitched whistling sound made during respiration, caused by obstruction of the air passages. **2.** *Chiefly literary.* a harsh or shrill sound. [C17: from Latin; see STRIDENT]

strid·u+late ('strɪdjʊˌleɪt) *vb.* (*intr.*) (of insects such as the cricket) to produce sounds by rubbing one part of the body against another. [C19: back formation from *stridulation,* from Latin *strīdulus* creaking, hissing, from *strīdēre* to make a harsh noise] —**ˌstrid·u+'la+tion** *n.* —**'strid·u+ˌla+tor** *n.* —**strid·u+la+to·ry** ('strɪdjʊˌleɪtərɪ) *adj.*

strid·u·lous ('strɪdjʊləs) *or* **strid·u+lant** *adj.* **1.** making a harsh, shrill, or grating noise. **2.** *Pathol.* of, relating to, or characterized by stridor. —**'strid·u·lous+ly** *or* **'strid·u·lant+ly** *adv.* —**'strid·u·lous+ness** *or* **'strid·u·lance** *n.*

strife (straɪf) *n.* **1.** angry or violent struggle; conflict. **2.** rivalry or contention, esp. of a bitter kind. **3.** *Austral.* trouble or discord of any kind. **4.** *Archaic.* striving. [C13: from Old French *estrif,* probably from *estriver* to STRIVE]

strig·i+form ('strɪdʒɪˌfɔːm) *adj.* of, relating to, or belonging to the *Strigiformes,* an order of birds comprising the owls. [via New Latin from Latin *strix* a screech owl]

strig+il ('strɪdʒɪl) *n.* **1.** a curved blade used by the ancient Romans and Greeks to scrape the body after bathing. **2.** *Architect.* a decorative fluting, esp. one in the shape of the letter *S* as used in Roman architecture. [C16: from Latin *strigilis,* from *stringere* to graze]

stri+gose ('straɪgəʊs) *adj.* **1.** *Botany.* bearing stiff hairs or bristles: *strigose leaves.* **2.** *Zoology.* marked with fine closely set grooves or ridges. [C18: via New Latin *strigōsus,* from *striga* a bristle, from Latin: grain cut down]

strike (straɪk) *vb.* **strikes, strik+ing, struck. 1.** to deliver (a blow or stroke) to (a person). **2.** to come or cause to come into sudden or violent contact (with). **3.** (*tr.*) to make an attack on. **4.** to produce (fire, sparks, etc.) or (of fire, sparks, etc.) to be produced by ignition. **5.** to cause (a match) to light by friction or (of a match) to be lighted. **6.** to press (the key of a piano, organ, etc.) or to sound (a specific note) in this or a similar way. **7.** to indicate (a specific time) by the sound of a hammer striking a bell or by any other percussive sound. **8.** (of a venomous snake) to cause injury by biting. **9.** (*tr.*) to affect or cause to affect deeply, suddenly, or radically, as if by dealing a blow: *her appearance struck him as strange; I was struck on his art.* **10.** (*past participle* **struck** *or* **strick+en**) (*tr.; passive;* usually foll. by *with*) to render incapable or nearly so: *she was stricken with grief.* **11.** (*tr.*) to enter the mind of: *it struck me that he had become very quiet.* **12.** (*past participle* **struck** *or* **strick+en**) to render: *I was struck dumb.* **13.** (*tr.*) to be perceived by; catch: *the glint of metal struck his eye.* **14.** to arrive at or come upon (something), esp. suddenly or unexpectedly: *to strike the path for home; to strike upon a solution.* **15.** (*intr.;* sometimes foll. by *out*) to set (out) or proceed, esp. upon a new course: *to strike for the coast.* **16.** (*tr.; usually passive*) to afflict with a disease, esp. unexpectedly: *he was struck with polio when he was six.* **17.** (*tr.*) to discover or come upon a source of (ore, petroleum, etc.). **18.** (*tr.*) (of a plant) to produce or send down (a root or roots). **19.** (*tr.*) to take apart or pack up; break (esp. in the phrase **strike camp**). **20.** (*tr.*) to take down or dismantle (a stage set). **21.** (*tr.*) *Nautical.* **a.** to lower or remove (a specified piece of gear). **b.** to haul down or dip (a flag, sail, etc.) in salute or in surrender. **c.** to lower (cargo, etc.)

into the hold of a ship. **22.** to attack (an objective) with the intention of causing damage to, seizing, or destroying it. **23.** to impale the hook in the mouth of (a fish) by suddenly tightening or jerking the line after the bait has been taken. **24.** (*tr.*) to form or impress (a coin, metal, etc.) by or as if by stamping. **25.** to level (a surface) by use of a flat board. **26.** (*tr.*) to assume or take up (an attitude, posture, etc.). **27.** (*intr.*) (of workers in a factory, etc.) to cease work collectively as a protest against working conditions, low pay, etc. **28.** (*tr.*) to reach by agreement: *to strike a bargain.* **29.** (*tr.*) to form (a jury, esp. a special jury) by cancelling certain names among those nominated for jury service until only the requisite number remains. See also **special jury. 30.** (*tr.*) *Rowing.* to make (a certain number of strokes) per minute: *Oxford were striking 38.* **31.** to make a stroke or kick in swimming. **32.** (*tr.*) (in Malaysia) to win (a lottery or raffle). **33. strike home. a.** to deliver an effective blow. **b.** to achieve the intended effect. **34. strike it rich.** *Informal.* **a.** to discover an extensive deposit of a mineral, petroleum, etc. **b.** to have an unexpected financial success. ~*n.* **35.** an act or instance of striking. **36.** a cessation of work by workers in a factory, industry, etc., as a protest against working conditions or low pay: *the workers are on strike again.* **37.** a military attack, esp. an air attack on a surface target: *air strike.* **38.** *Baseball.* a pitched ball judged good but missed or not swung at, three of which cause a batter to be out. **39.** Also called: **ten-strike.** *Tenpin bowling.* **a.** the act or an instance of knocking down all the pins with the first bowl of a single frame. **b.** the score thus made. Compare **spare** (sense 17). **40.** a sound made by striking. **41.** the mechanism that makes a clock strike. **42.** the discovery of a source of ore, petroleum, etc. **43.** the horizontal direction of a fault, rock stratum, etc., which is perpendicular to the direction of the dip. **44.** *Angling.* the act or an instance of striking. **45.** the number of coins or medals made at one time. **46.** another name for **strickle** (sense 1). **47.** *Informal.* an unexpected or complete success, esp. one that brings financial gain. **48. take strike.** *Cricket.* (of a batsman) to prepare to play a ball delivered by the bowler. ~See also **strike down, strike off, strike out, strike through, strike up.** [Old English *strīcan;* related to Old Frisian *strīka* to stroke, Old High German *strīhhan* to smooth, Latin *stria* furrow] —**'strike·less** *adj.*

strike·bound ('straɪk,baʊnd) *adj.* (of a factory, etc.) closed or made inoperative by a strike.

strike·break·er ('straɪk,breɪkə) *n.* a person who tries to make a strike ineffectual by working or by taking the place of those on strike. —**'strike·,break·ing** *n., adj.*

strike down *vb.* (*tr., adv.*) to die or cause to die, esp. suddenly: *he was struck down in his prime.*

strike fault *n.* a fault that runs parallel to the direction of the strike of the affected rocks.

strike note *or esp. U.S.* **strike tone** *n.* the note produced by a bell when struck, defining its musical pitch.

strike off *vb.* (*tr.*) **1.** to remove or erase from (a list, record, etc.) by or as if by a stroke of the pen. **2.** (*adv.*) to cut off or separate by or as if by a blow: *she was struck off from the inheritance.* **3.** (*adv.*) *Printing.* **a.** to take (a proof) from a relief forme by beating paper with a brush against the inked forme. **b.** to print: *they will strike off 3000 copies.* ~*n.* **strike-off. 4.** *Printing.* a proof obtained in this manner.

strike out *vb.* (*adv.*) **1.** (*tr.*) to remove or erase. **2.** (*intr.*) to start out or begin: *to strike out on one's own.* **3.** *Baseball.* to put out or be put out on strikes. **4.** (*intr.*) *U.S. informal.* to fail utterly.

strike pay *n.* money paid to strikers from the funds of a trade union.

strik·er ('straɪkə) *n.* **1.** a person who is on strike. **2.** the hammer in a timepiece that rings a bell or alarm. **3.** any part in a mechanical device that strikes something, such as the firing pin of a gun. **4.** *Soccer, informal.* an attacking player, esp. one who generally positions himself near his opponent's goal in the hope of scoring. **5.** *Cricket.* the batsman who is about to play a ball. **6. a.** a person who harpoons whales or fish. **b.** the harpoon itself.

strike through *vb.* (*tr.*) to draw (a line) through (something) to delete it.

strike up *vb.* (*adv.*) **1.** (of a band, orchestra, etc.) to begin to play or sing. **2.** (*tr.*) to bring about; cause to begin: *to strike up a friendship.* **3.** (*tr.*) to emboss (patterns, etc.) on (metal).

strik·ing ('straɪkɪŋ) *adj.* **1.** attracting attention; fine; impressive: *a striking beauty.* **2.** conspicuous; noticeable: *a striking difference.* —**'strik·ing·ly** *adv.* —**'strik·ing·ness** *n.*

strik·ing cir·cle *n. Hockey.* the semicircular area in front of each goal, which an attacking player must have entered before scoring a goal.

Stri·mon *or* **Stry·mon** ('strimɔn) *n.* a transliteration of the Greek name for the **Struma.**

Strind·berg ('strɪndbɜːg; *Swedish* 'strɪndbærj) *n.* **Au·gust** ('aʊgʊst). 1849–1912, Swedish dramatist and novelist, whose plays include *The Father* (1887), *Miss Julie* (1888), and *The Ghost Sonata* (1907).

Strine (straɪn) *n.* a humorous transliteration of Australian pronunciation, as in *Gloria Soame* for *glorious home.* [C20: a jocular rendering, coined by Alastair Morrison, of the Australian pronunciation of *Australian*]

string (strɪŋ) *n.* **1.** a thin length of cord, twine, fibre, or similar material used for tying, hanging, binding, etc. **2.** a group of objects threaded on a single strand: *a string of beads.* **3.** a series or succession of things, events, acts, utterances, etc.: *a string of oaths.* **4.** a number, chain, or group of similar things, animals, etc., owned by or associated with one person or body: *a string of girlfriends.* **5.** a tough fibre or cord in a plant: *the string of an orange; the string of a bean.* **6.** *Music.* a tightly stretched wire, cord, etc., found on stringed instruments, such as the violin, guitar, and piano. **7.** short for **bowstring. 8.** *Architect.* short for **string-course** or **stringer** (sense 1). **9.** *Mathematics, linguistics.* a sequence of symbols or words. **10.** *Linguistics.* a linear sequence, such as a sentence as it is spoken. **11.** *Billiards.* another word for **lag**[1] (sense 6). **12.** (*pl.;* usually preceded by *the*) **a.** violins, violas, cellos, and double basses collectively. **b.** the section of a symphony orchestra constituted by such instruments. **13.** (*pl.*) complications or conditions (esp. in the phrase **strings attached**). **14.** (*modifier*) composed of string-like strands woven in a large mesh: *a string bag; string vest.* **15. first (second, *etc.*) string.** a person or thing regarded as a primary (secondary, etc.) source of strength. **16. keep on a string.** to have control or a hold over (a person), esp. emotionally. **17. pull strings.** *Informal.* to exert power or influence, esp. secretly or unofficially. **18. pull the strings.** to have real or ultimate control of something. ~*vb.* **strings, string·ing, strung. 19.** (*tr.*) to provide with a string or strings. **20.** (*tr.*) to suspend or stretch from one point to another. **21.** (*tr.*) to thread on a string. **22.** (*tr.*) to form or extend in a line or series. **23.** (foll. by *out*) to space or spread out at intervals. **24.** (*tr.;* usually foll. by *up*) *Informal.* to kill (a person) by hanging. **25.** (*tr.*) to remove the stringy parts from (vegetables, esp. beans). **26.** (*intr.*) (esp. of viscous liquids) to become stringy or ropy. **27.** (*tr.;* often foll. by *up*) to cause to be tense or nervous. **28.** *Billiards.* another word for **lag**[1] (sense 3). [Old English *streng;* related to Old High German *strang,* Old Norse *strengr;* see STRONG] —**'string·,like** *adj.*

string a·long *vb.* (*adv.*) *Informal.* **1.** (*intr.;* often foll. by *with*) to agree or appear to be in agreement (with). **2.** (*tr.*) Also: **string on.** to deceive, fool, or hoax, esp. in order to gain time.

string band *n.* **1.** a band consisting of stringed instruments. **2.** an informal name for **string orchestra.**

string bass (beɪs) *n.* another name for **double bass.**

string bean *n.* **1.** any of several bean plants, such as the scarlet runner, cultivated for their edible unripe pods. See also **green bean, wax bean. 2.** *Informal.* a tall thin person.

string·board ('strɪŋ,bɔːd) *n.* a skirting that covers the ends of the steps in a staircase. Also called: **stringer.**

string course *n.* another name for **cordon** (sense 4).

stringed (strɪŋd) *adj.* (of musical instruments) having or provided with strings.

stringed in·stru·ment *n.* any musical instrument in which sound is produced by the vibration of a string across a soundboard or soundbox. Also called: **chordophone.**

strin·gen·do (strɪn'dʒɛndəʊ) *adj., adv. Music.* to be performed with increasing speed. [Italian, from *stringere* to compress, from Latin: to draw tight; see STRINGENT]

strin·gent ('strɪndʒənt) *adj.* **1.** requiring strict attention to rules, procedure, detail, etc. **2.** *Finance.* characterized by or causing a shortage of credit, loan capital, etc. **3.** *Rare.* convincing; forcible. [C17: from Latin *stringere* to bind] —**'strin·gen·cy** *n.* —**'strin·gent·ly** *adv.*

string·er ('strɪŋə) *n.* **1.** *Architect.* **a.** a long horizontal timber beam that is used for structural purposes. **b.** another name for **stringboard. 2.** *Nautical.* a longitudinal structural brace for strengthening the hull of a vessel. **3.** a journalist retained by a newspaper or news service on a part-time basis to cover a particular town or area.

string·halt ('strɪŋ,hɔːlt) *n. Vet. science.* a sudden spasmodic lifting of the hind leg of a horse, resulting from abnormal contraction of the flexor muscles of the hock. Also called: **springhalt.** [C16: probably STRING + HALT]

string line *n. Billiards.* another name for **baulkline.**

string or·ches·tra *n.* an orchestra consisting only of violins, violas, cellos, and double basses.

string·piece ('strɪŋ,piːs) *n.* a long horizontal timber beam used to strengthen or support a framework.

string quar·tet *n. Music.* **1.** an instrumental ensemble consisting of two violins, one viola, and one cello. **2.** a piece of music written for such a group, usually having the form and commonest features of a sonata.

string tie *n.* a very narrow tie, usually tied in a bow.

string·y ('strɪŋɪ) *adj.* **string·i·er, string·i·est. 1.** made of strings or resembling strings. **2.** (of meat, etc.) fibrous. **3.** (of a person's build) wiry; sinewy. **4.** (of liquids) forming in strings. —**'string·i·ly** *adv.* —**'string·i·ness** *n.*

string·y-bark *n. Austral.* any of several eucalyptus trees having a fibrous bark.

strip[1] (strɪp) *vb.* **strips, strip·ping, stripped. 1.** to take or pull (the covering, clothes, etc.) off (oneself, another person, or thing): *to strip a wall; to strip a bed.* **2.** (*intr.*) **a.** to remove all one's clothes. **b.** to perform a striptease. **3.** (*tr.*) to denude or empty completely. **4.** (*tr.*) to deprive of: *he was stripped of his pride.* **5.** (*tr.*) to rob or plunder. **6. a.** to remove the leaves from the stalks of (tobacco, etc.). **b.** to separate the two sides of a leaf from the stem of (tobacco, etc.). **7.** (*tr.*) *Agriculture.* to draw the last milk from each of the teats of (a cow). **8.** to dismantle (an engine, mechanism, etc.). **9.** to tear off or break (the thread) from (a screw, bolt, etc.) or (the teeth) from (a gear). **10.** (often foll. by *down*) to remove the accessories from (a motor vehicle): *his car was stripped down.* **11.** to remove (the most volatile constituent) from (a mixture of liquids) by boiling, evaporation, or distillation. **12.** *Printing.* (usually foll. by *in*) to combine (pieces of film or paper) to form a composite sheet from which a plate can be made. **13.** (*tr.*) (in freight transport) to unpack (a container). See also **stuffing and stripping.** ~*n.* **14.** the act or an instance of undressing or of performing a striptease. [Old English *bestriepan* to plunder; related to Old High German *stroufen* to plunder, strip]

strip[2] (strɪp) *n.* **1.** a relatively long, flat, narrow piece of something. **2.** short for **airstrip. 3.** *Philately.* a horizontal or vertical row of three or more unseparated postage stamps. **4.** *Informal.* the clothes worn by the members of a team, esp. a football team. **5. tear (someone) off a strip.** to rebuke (someone) angrily. ~*vb.* **strips, strip+ping, stripped. 6.** to cut or divide into strips. [C15: from Middle Dutch *strīpe* STRIPE[1]]

strip car+toon *n.* a sequence of drawings in a newspaper, magazine, etc., relating a humorous story or an adventure. Also called: **comic strip.**

strip club *n.* a small club in which striptease performances take place.

strip crop+ping *n.* a method of growing crops in strips or bands arranged to serve as barriers against erosion.

stripe[1] (straɪp) *n.* **1.** a relatively long band of distinctive colour or texture that differs from the surrounding material or background. **2.** a fabric having such bands. **3.** a strip, band, or chevron of fabric worn on a military uniform, etc., esp. one that indicates rank. **4.** *Chiefly U.S.* kind; sort; type: *a man of a certain stripe.* ~*vb.* **5.** (*tr.*) to mark with a stripe or stripes. [C17: probably from Middle Dutch *strīpe;* related to Middle High German *strīfe,* of obscure origin]

stripe[2] (straɪp) *n.* a stroke from a whip, rod, cane, etc. [C15: perhaps from Middle Low German *strippe;* related to STRIPE[1]]

striped (straɪpt) *adj.* marked or decorated with stripes.

strip+er ('straɪpə) *n. Military slang.* an officer who has a stripe or stripes on his uniform, esp. in the navy: *a two-striper* (lieutenant).

strip light+ing *n.* electric lighting by means of long glass tubes that are fluorescent lamps or that contain long filaments.

strip+ling ('strɪplɪŋ) *n.* a lad. [C13: from STRIP[2] + -LING[1]]

strip mill *n.* a mill in which steel slabs are rolled into strips.

strip min+ing *n.* another term (esp. U.S.) for **opencast mining.**

strip+per ('strɪpə) *n.* **1.** a striptease artist. **2.** a person or thing that strips. **3.** a device or substance for removing paint, varnish, etc.

strip pok+er *n.* a card game in which a player's losses are paid by removing an article of clothing.

strip+tease ('strɪpˌtiːz) *n.* **a.** a form of erotic entertainment in which a person gradually undresses to music. **b.** (*as modifier*): *a striptease club.* —**'strip+ˌteas·er** *n.*

strip·y ('straɪpɪ) *adj.* **strip·i+er, strip·i+est.** marked by or with stripes; striped.

strive (straɪv) *vb.* **strives, striv+ing, strove, striv+en. 1.** (*may take a clause as object or an infinitive*) to make a great and tenacious effort: *to strive to get promotion.* **2.** (*intr.*) to fight; contend. [C13: from Old French *estriver,* of Germanic origin; related to Middle High German *streben* to strive, Old Norse *strītha* to fight] —**'striv+er** *n.*

strobe (strəʊb) *n.* short for **strobe lighting** or **stroboscope.**

strobe light+ing *n.* **1.** a high-intensity flashing beam of light produced by rapid electrical discharges in a tube or by a perforated disc rotating in front of an intense light source: used in discotheques, etc. **2.** the use of or the apparatus for producing such light. Sometimes shortened to **strobe.**

stro+bic ('strəʊbɪk) *adj.* spinning or appearing to spin. [C19: from Greek *strobos* act of spinning]

stro+bi+la (strə'baɪlə) *n.* **1.** the body of a tapeworm, consisting of a string of similar segments (proglottides). **2.** a less common name for **scyphistoma.** [C19: from New Latin, from Greek *strobilē* plug of lint twisted into a cone shape, from *strobilos* a fir cone]

stro+bi+la+ceous (ˌstrəʊbɪ'leɪʃəs) *adj. Botany.* relating to or resembling a cone or cones.

stro+bi+la+tion (ˌstrəʊbɪ'leɪʃən) *n.* asexual reproduction by division into segments, as in tapeworms and jellyfishes.

stro+bi+lus ('strəʊbɪləs) *or* **stro+bile** ('strəʊbaɪl) *n., pl.* **+bi+lus·es, +bi+li** (-bɪlaɪ), *or* **+biles.** *Botany.* the technical name for **cone** (sense 3). [C18: via Late Latin from Greek *strobilos* a fir cone; see STROBILA]

stro+bo+scope ('strəʊbəˌskəʊp) *n.* **1.** an instrument producing an intense flashing light, the frequency of which can be synchronized with some multiple of the frequency of rotation, vibration, or operation of an object, etc., making it appear stationary. It is used to determine speeds of rotation or vibration, or to adjust objects or parts. Sometimes shortened to **strobe. 2.** a similar device synchronized with the opening of the shutter of a camera so that a series of still photographs can be taken of a moving object. [C19: from *strobo-,* from Greek *strobos* a twisting, whirling + -SCOPE] —**stro+bo+scop+ic** (ˌstrəʊbə'skɒpɪk) *or* **ˌstro+bo+'scop·i+cal** *adj.* —**ˌstro+bo+'scop·i+cal+ly** *adv.*

strode (strəʊd) *vb.* the past tense of **stride.**

strog·a+noff ('strɒgəˌnɒf) *n.* short for **beef stroganoff.**

Stro·heim (*German* 'ʃtroːhaɪm) *n.* **E·rich von** ('eːrɪç fɔn). 1885–1957, Austrian film director, whose films include *Foolish Wives* (1922) and *Greed* (1924).

stroke (strəʊk) *n.* **1.** the act or an instance of striking; a blow, knock, or hit. **2.** a sudden action, movement, or occurrence: *a stroke of luck.* **3.** a brilliant or inspired act or feat: *a stroke of genius.* **4.** *Pathol.* apoplexy; rupture of a blood vessel in the brain resulting in loss of consciousness, often followed by paralysis, or embolism or thrombosis affecting a cerebral vessel. **5. a.** the striking of a clock. **b.** the hour registered by the striking of a clock: *on the stroke of three.* **6.** a mark, flourish, or line made by a writing implement. **7.** another name for **solidus,** used esp. when dictating or reading aloud. **8.** a light touch or caress, as with the fingers. **9.** a pulsation, esp. of the heart. **10.** a single complete movement or one of a series of complete movements. **11.** *Sport.* the act or manner of striking the ball with a racket, club, bat, etc. **12.** any one of the repeated movements used by a swimmer to propel himself through the water. **13.** a manner of swimming, esp. one of several named styles such as the crawl or butterfly. **14. a.** any one of a series of linear movements of a reciprocating part, such as a piston. **b.** the distance travelled by such a part from one end of its movement to the other. **15.** a single pull on an oar or oars in rowing. **16.** manner or style of rowing. **17.** the oarsman who sits nearest the stern of a shell, facing the cox, and sets the rate of striking for the rest of the crew. **18. a stroke (of work).** (*usually used with a negative*) a small amount of work. **19. off one's stroke.** performing or working less well than usual. **20. on the stroke.** punctually. ~*vb.* **21.** (*tr.*) to touch, brush, or caress lightly or gently. **22.** (*tr.*) to mark a line or a stroke on or through. **23.** to act as the stroke of (a racing shell). **24.** (*tr.*) *Sport.* to strike (a ball) with a smooth swinging blow. **25.** (*tr.*) *U.S. informal.* to handle or influence (someone) with care, using persuasion, flattery, etc. [Old English *strācian;* related to Middle Low German *strēken;* see STRIKE]

stroke play *n. Golf.* **a.** scoring by counting the number of strokes taken. **b.** (*as modifier*): *a strokeplay tournament.* ~Also called: **medal play.** Compare **match play.**

stroll (strəʊl) *vb.* **1.** to walk about in a leisurely manner. **2.** (*intr.*) to wander from place to place. ~*n.* **3.** a leisurely walk. [C17: probably from dialect German *strollen,* of obscure origin; compare German *Strolch* tramp]

stroll+er ('strəʊlə) *n. Chiefly U.S.* the usual word for **pushchair.**

stro+ma ('strəʊmə) *n., pl.* **+ma+ta** (-mətə). *Biology.* **1.** the dense colourless framework of a chloroplast and certain cells. **2.** the fibrous connective tissue forming the matrix of the mammalian ovary and testis. **3.** a dense mass of hyphae that is produced by certain fungi and gives rise to spore-producing bodies. [C19: via New Latin from Late Latin: a mattress, from Greek; related to Latin *sternere* to strew] —**stro+mat+ic** (strəʊ'mætɪk) *or* **'stro+ma+tous** *adj.*

stro+mat·o+lite (strəʊ'mætəˌlaɪt) *n.* a sedimentary rock consisting of layers of fossilized algae, esp. blue-green algae. [C20: from Greek, from *strōma* covering + -LITE] —**stro+mat·o+lit+ic** (strəʊˌmætə'lɪtɪk) *adj.*

Strom+bo+li ('strɒmbəlɪ) *n.* an island in the Tyrrhenian Sea, in the Lipari Islands off the N coast of Sicily: famous for its active volcano, 927 m (3040 ft.) high.

strong (strɒŋ) *adj.* **strong+er** ('strɒŋgə), **strong+est** ('strɒŋgɪst). **1.** involving or possessing physical or mental strength. **2.** solid or robust in construction; not easily broken or injured. **3.** having a resolute will or morally firm and incorruptible character. **4.** intense in quality; not faint or feeble: *a strong voice; a strong smell.* **5.** easily defensible; incontestable or formidable. **6.** concentrated; not weak or diluted. **7. a.** (*postpositive*) containing or having a specified number: *a navy 40 000 strong.* **b.** (*in combination*): *a 40 000-strong navy.* **8.** having an unpleasantly powerful taste or smell. **9.** having an extreme or drastic effect: *strong discipline.* **10.** emphatic or immoderate: *strong language.* **11.** convincing, effective, or cogent. **12.** (of a colour) having a high degree of saturation or purity; being less saturated than a vivid colour but more so than a moderate colour; produced by a concentrated quantity of colouring agent. **13.** *Grammar.* **a.** denoting or belonging to a class of verbs, in certain languages including the Germanic languages, whose conjugation shows vowel gradation, as *sing, sang, sung.* **b.** belonging to any part-of-speech class, in any of various languages, whose inflections follow the less regular of two possible patterns. Compare **weak** (sense 9). **14.** (of a wind, current, etc.) moving fast. **15.** (of a syllable) accented or stressed. **16.** (of an industry, market, securities, etc.) firm in price or characterized by firm or increasing prices. **17.** (of certain acids and bases) producing high concentrations of hydrogen or hydroxide ions in aqueous solution. **18. have a strong stomach.** not to be prone to nausea. ~*adv.* **19.** *Informal.* in a strong way; effectively: *going strong.* **20. come on strong.** to speak or act forcefully or persuasively. [Old English *strang;* related to Old Norse *strangr,* Middle High German *strange,* Lettish *strans* courageous] —**'strong+ish** *adj.* —**'strong+ly** *adv.* —**'strong+ness** *n.*

strong-arm *Informal.* ~*n.* **1.** (*modifier*) relating to or involving physical force or violence: *strong-arm tactics.* ~*vb.* **2.** (*tr.*) to show violence towards.

strong+box ('strɒŋˌbɒks) *n.* a specially designed box or safe in which valuables are locked for safety.

strong breeze *n. Meteorol.* a considerable wind of force six on the Beaufort scale

strong drink *n.* alcoholic drink.

strong gale *n. Meteorol.* a strong wind of force nine on the Beaufort scale, capable of causing minor structural damage to buildings.

strong+hold ('strɒŋˌhəʊld) *n.* **1.** a defensible place; fortress. **2.** a major centre or area of predominance.

strong in+ter+ac+tion *n. Physics.* an interaction between elementary particles responsible for the forces between nucleons in the nucleus. It operates at distances less than about 10^{-15} metres, and is about a hundred times more powerful than the electromagnetic interaction. Compare **electromagnetic interaction, weak interaction, gravitational interaction.**

strong+man ('strɒŋˌmæn) *n., pl.* **+men. 1.** a performer, esp. one in a circus, who performs feats of strength. **2.** any person regarded as a source of power, capability, initiative, etc.

strong meat *n.* anything arousing fear, anger, repulsion, etc., except among a tolerant or receptive minority: *some scenes in the film were strong meat.*

strong-mind·ed *adj.* having strength of mind; firm, resolute, and determined. —,**strong-'mind·ed+ly** *adv.* —,**strong-'mind·ed+ness** *n.*

strong point *n.* something at which one excels; forte: *tactfulness was never his strong point.*

strong+room ('strɒŋ,ru:m, -,rʊm) *n.* a specially designed room in which valuables are locked for safety.

strong wa+ters *pl. n.* an archaic name for alcoholic drink.

strong-willed *adj.* having strength of will.

stron+gyle ('strɒndʒɪl) *or* **stron+gyl** ('strɒndʒəl) *n.* any parasitic nematode worm of the family *Strongylidae,* chiefly occurring in the intestines of horses. [C19: via New Latin *Strongylus,* from Greek *strongulos* round]

stron+ti·a ('strɒntɪə) *n.* another name for **strontium monoxide.** [C19: changed from STRONTIAN]

stron+ti·an ('strɒntɪən) *n.* **1.** another name for **strontianite. 2.** another name for **strontium** or **strontium monoxide.** [C18: named after a parish in Highland Region where discovered]

stron+ti+an+ite ('strɒntɪə,naɪt) *n.* a white, lightly coloured, or colourless mineral consisting of strontium carbonate in orthorhombic crystalline form: it is a source of strontium compounds. Formula: $SrCO_3$.

stron+ti·um ('strɒntɪəm) *n.* a soft silvery-white element of the alkaline earth group of metals, occurring chiefly in celestite and strontianite. Its compounds burn with a crimson flame and are used in fireworks. The radioisotope **strontium-90,** with a half-life of 28.1 years, is used in nuclear power sources and is a hazardous nuclear fall-out product. Symbol: Sr; atomic no.: 38; atomic wt.: 87.62; valency: 2; relative density: 2.54; melting pt.: 769°C; boiling pt.: 1384°C. [C19: from New Latin, from STRONTIAN]

stron+ti·um mon+ox+ide *n.* a white insoluble solid substance used in making strontium salts and purifying sugar. Formula: SrO. Also called: **strontium oxide, strontia.**

stron+ti·um u·nit *n.* a unit expressing the concentration of strontium-90 in an organic medium, such as soil, milk, bone, etc., relative to the concentration of calcium in the same medium. Abbrev.: **SU**

strop (strɒp) *n.* **1.** a leather strap or an abrasive strip for sharpening razors. **2.** a rope or metal band around a block or deadeye for support. ~*vb.* **strops, strop+ping, stropped. 3.** (*tr.*) to sharpen (a razor, etc.) on a strop. [C14 (in nautical use: a strip of rope): via Middle Low German or Middle Dutch *strop,* ultimately from Latin *stroppus,* from Greek *strophos* cord; see STROPHE]

stro+phan+thin (strəʊ'fænθɪn) *n.* a toxic glycoside or mixture of glycosides obtained from the ripe seeds of certain species of strophanthus: used as a cardiac stimulant.

stro+phan+thus (strəʊ'fænθəs) *n.* **1.** any small tree or shrub of the apocynaceous genus *Strophanthus,* of tropical Africa and Asia, having strap-shaped twisted petals. The seeds of certain species yield the drug strophanthin. **2.** the seeds of any of these plants.

stro+phe ('strəʊfɪ) *n. Prosody.* **1.** (in ancient Greek drama) **a.** the first of two movements made by a chorus during the performance of a choral ode. **b.** the first part of a choral ode sung during this movement. **2.** (in classical verse) the first division of the threefold structure of a Pindaric ode. **3.** the first of two metrical systems used alternately within a poem. ~See **antistrophe, epode.** [C17: from Greek: a verse, literally: a turning, from *strephein* to twist]

stroph+ic ('strɒfɪk, 'strəʊ-) *or* **stroph·i+cal** *adj.* **1.** of, relating to, or employing a strophe or strophes. **2.** (of a song) having identical or related music in each verse. Compare **through-composed.**

strop+py ('strɒpɪ) *adj.* **+pi+er, +pi+est.** *Brit. slang.* angry or awkward. [C20: changed and shortened from OBSTREPEROUS]

stroud (straʊd) *n.* a coarse woollen fabric. [C17: perhaps named after *Stroud,* textile centre in Gloucestershire]

strove (strəʊv) *vb.* the past tense of **strive.**

strow (strəʊ) *vb.* **strows, strow+ing, strowed; strown** *or* **strowed.** an archaic variant of **strew.**

stroy (strɔɪ) *vb.* an archaic variant of **destroy.** —'**stroy+er** *n.*

struck (strʌk) *vb.* **1.** the past tense or past participle of **strike.** ~*adj.* **2.** *Chiefly U.S.* (of an industry, factory, etc.) shut down or otherwise affected by a labour strike.

struck meas+ure *n.* a measure of grain, etc., in which the contents are made level with the top of the container rather than being heaped.

struc+tur+al ('strʌktʃərəl) *adj.* **1.** of, relating to, or having structure or a structure. **2.** of or relating to the structure of rocks and other features of the earth's crust. **3.** of or relating to the structure of organisms; morphological. **4.** *Chem.* of, concerned with, caused by, or involving the arrangement of atoms in molecules. —'**struc+tur+al+ly** *adv.*

struc+tur+al for+mu+la *n.* a chemical formula showing the composition and structure of a molecule. The atoms are represented by symbols and the structure is indicated by showing the relative positions of the atoms in space and the bonds between them: *H-C≡C-H is the structural formula of acetylene.* See also **empirical formula, molecular formula.**

struc+tur+al+ism ('strʌktʃərə,lɪzəm) *n.* **1.** an approach to anthropology and other social sciences and to literature that interprets and analyses its material in terms of oppositions, contrasts, and hierarchical structures, esp. as they might reflect universal mental characteristics or organizing principles. Compare **functionalism. 2.** an approach to linguistics that analyses and describes the structure of language, as distinguished from its comparative and historical aspects. —'**struc+tur+al+ist** *n., adj.*

struc+tur+al lin+guis+tics *n.* a descriptive approach to a synchronic or diachronic analysis of language on the basis of its structure as reflected by irreducible units of phonological, morphological, and semantic features.

struc+tur+al psy+chol+o·gy *n.* (formerly) a school of psychology using introspection to analyse experience into basic units.

struc+tur+al steel *n.* a strong mild steel used in construction work.

struc+ture ('strʌktʃə) *n.* **1.** a complex construction or entity. **2.** the arrangement and interrelationship of parts in a construction. **3.** the manner of construction or organization: *the structure of society.* **4.** *Biology.* morphology; form. **5.** *Chem.* the arrangement of atoms in a molecule of a chemical compound: *the structure of benzene.* **6.** *Geology.* the way in which a mineral, rock, rock mass or stratum, etc., is made up of its component parts. **7.** *Now rare.* the act of constructing. ~*vb.* **8.** to impart a structure to. [C15: from Latin *structūra,* from *struere* to build]

stru+del ('stru:dᵊl; *German* 'ʃtru:dᵊl) *n.* a thin sheet of filled dough rolled up and baked: *apple strudel.* [German, from Middle High German *strodel* eddy, whirlpool, so called from the way the pastry is rolled]

strug+gle ('strʌgᵊl) *vb.* **1.** (*intr.; usually foll. by for or against; may take an infinitive*) to exert strength, energy, and force; work or strive: *to struggle to obtain freedom.* **2.** (*intr.*) to move about strenuously so as to escape from something confining. **3.** (*intr.*) to contend, battle, or fight. **4.** (*intr.*) to go or progress with difficulty. ~*n.* **5.** a laboured or strenuous exertion or effort. **6.** a fight or battle. **7.** the act of struggling. [C14: of obscure origin] —'**strug+gler** *n.* —'**strug+gling+ly** *adv.*

strug+gle for ex+ist+ence *n.* (*not in technical usage*) competition between organisms of a population, esp. as a factor in the evolution of plants and animals. See also **natural selection.**

strum (strʌm) *vb.* **strums, strum+ming, strummed. 1.** to sound (the strings of a guitar, banjo, etc.) with a downward or upward sweep of the thumb or of a plectrum. **2.** to play (chords, a tune, etc.) in this way. —'**strum+mer** *n.*

stru+ma ('stru:mə) *n., pl.* **+mae** (-mi:). **1.** *Pathol.* an abnormal enlargement of the thyroid gland; goitre. **2.** *Botany.* a swelling, esp. one at the base of a moss capsule. **3.** another word for **scrofula.** [C16: from Latin: a scrofulous tumour, from *struere* to heap up] —**stru+mat+ic** (stru:'mætɪk), **stru+mous** ('stru:məs), *or* **stru+mose** ('stru:məʊs) *adj.*

Stru+ma ('stru:mə) *n.* a river in S Europe, rising in SW Bulgaria near Sofia and flowing generally southeast through Greece to the Aegean. Length: 362 km (225 miles). Greek names: **Strimon, Strymon.**

strum+pet ('strʌmpɪt) *n.* a prostitute or promiscuous woman. [C14: of unknown origin]

strung (strʌŋ) *vb.* **1.** a past tense and past participle of **string.** ~*adj.* **2. a.** (of a piano, etc.) provided with strings, esp. of a specified kind or in a specified manner. **b.** (*in combination*): *gut-strung.* **3. highly strung.** very nervous or volatile in character. Usual U.S. phrase: **high-strung.**

strung out *adj. Slang.* **1.** addicted to a drug. **2.** (of a drug addict) suffering or distressed because of the lack of a drug.

strung up *adj.* (*postpositive*) *Informal.* tense or nervous.

strut (strʌt) *vb.* **struts, strut+ting, strut+ted. 1.** (*intr.*) to walk in a pompous manner; swagger. **2.** (*tr.*) to support or provide with struts. ~*n.* **3.** a structural member used mainly in compression, esp. as part of a framework. **4.** an affected, proud, or stiff walk. [C14 *strouten* (in the sense: swell, stand out; C16: to walk stiffly), from Old English *strūtian* to stand stiffly; related to Low German *strutt* stiff] —'**strut+ter** *n.* —'**strut+ting+ly** *adv.*

stru+thi+ous ('stru:θɪəs) *adj.* **1.** (of birds) related to or resembling the ostrich. **2.** of, relating to, or designating all flightless (ratite) birds. [C18: from Late Latin *strūthiō,* from Greek *strouthiōn,* from *strouthos* an ostrich]

strych+nic ('strɪknɪk) *adj.* of, relating to, or derived from strychnine.

strych+nine ('strɪkni:n) *n.* a white crystalline very poisonous alkaloid, obtained from the plant nux vomica: used in small quantities as a stimulant of the central nervous system and the appetite. Formula: $C_{21}H_{22}O_2N_2$. [C19: via French from New Latin *Strychnos,* from Greek *strukhnos* nightshade]

strych+nin+ism ('strɪknɪ,nɪzəm) *n. Pathol.* poisoning caused by the excessive or prolonged use of strychnine.

Stry+mon ('straɪmən) *n.* the Greek name for the **Struma.**

Stu·art ('stjʊət) *n.* **1.** the royal house that ruled in Scotland from 1371 to 1714 and in England from 1603 to 1714. See also **Stewart** (sense 1). **2. Charles Ed·ward,** called *the Young Pretender* or *Bonnie Prince Charlie.* 1720–88, pretender to the British throne. He led the Jacobite Rebellion (1745–46) in an attempt to re-establish the Stuart succession. **3.** his father, **James Fran·cis Ed·ward,** called *the Old Pretender.* 1688–1766, pretender to the British throne; son of James II (James VII of Scotland) and his second wife, Mary of Modena. He made two unsuccessful attempts to realize his claim to the throne (1708; 1715). **4. Mar·y.** See **Mary Queen of Scots.**

stub (stʌb) *n.* **1.** a short piece remaining after something has been cut, removed, etc.: *a cigar stub.* **2.** the residual piece or section of a receipt, ticket, cheque, etc. **3.** the usual U.S. word for **counterfoil. 4.** any short projection or blunted end. **5.** the stump of a tree or plant. ~*vb.* **stubs, stub+bing, stubbed.** (*tr.*) **6.** to strike (one's toe, foot, etc.) painfully against a hard surface. **7.** (usually foll. by *out*) to put (out a cigarette or cigar) by pressing the end against a surface. **8.** to clear (land) of stubs. **9.** to dig up (the roots) of (a tree or bush). [Old English *stubb;* related to Old Norse *stubbi,* Middle Dutch *stubbe,* Greek *stupos* stem, stump]

stub ax·le *n.* a short axle that carries one of the front steered wheels of a motor vehicle and is capable of limited angular movement about a kingpin.

stub·ble ('stʌbəl) *n.* **1. a.** the stubs of stalks left in a field where a crop has been cut and harvested. **b.** (*as modifier*): *a stubble field.* **2.** any bristly growth or surface. [C13: from Old French *estuble,* from Latin *stupula,* variant of *stipula* stalk, stem, stubble] —'**stub·bled** *or* '**stub·bly** *adj.*

stub·born ('stʌbən) *adj.* **1.** refusing to comply, agree, or give in; obstinate. **2.** difficult to handle, treat, or overcome. **3.** persistent and dogged: *a stubborn crusade.* [C14 *stoborne,* of obscure origin] —'**stub·born·ly** *adv.* —'**stub·born·ness** *n.*

Stubbs (stʌbz) *n.* **George.** 1724–1806, English painter, noted esp. for his pictures of horses.

stub·by ('stʌbɪ) *adj.* **·bi·er, ·bi·est. 1.** short and broad; stumpy or thickset. **2.** bristling and stiff. ~*n. Austral. slang.* **3.** a small bottle of beer. —'**stub·bi·ly** *adv.* —'**stub·bi·ness** *n.*

stub nail *n.* **1.** a short thick nail. **2.** a worn nail in a horseshoe.

stuc·co ('stʌkəʊ) *n., pl.* **·coes** *or* **·cos. 1.** a weather-resistant mixture of dehydrated lime, powdered marble, and glue, used in decorative mouldings on buildings. **2.** any of various types of cement or plaster used for coating outside walls. **3.** Also called: **stuccowork.** decorative work moulded in stucco. ~*vb.* **·coes** *or* **·cos, ·co·ing, ·coed. 4.** (*tr.*) to apply stucco to. [C16: from Italian, of Germanic origin; compare Old High German *stukki* a fragment, crust, Old English *stycce*] —'**stuc·co·er** *n.*

stuck (stʌk) *vb.* **1.** the past tense or past participle of **stick**[2]. ~*adj.* **2.** *Informal.* baffled or nonplussed. **3.** (foll. by *on*) *Slang.* keen (on) or infatuated (with). **4. get stuck in** *or* **into.** *Informal.* **a.** to perform (a task) with determination. **b.** *Austral.* to attack (a person) verbally or physically.

stuck-up *adj. Informal.* conceited, arrogant, or snobbish. —'**stuck-'up·ness** *n.*

stud[1] (stʌd) *n.* **1.** a large-headed nail or other projection protruding from a surface, usually as decoration. **2.** a type of fastener consisting of two discs at either end of a short shank, used to fasten shirtfronts, collars, etc. **3.** *Building.* a vertical member made of timber, steel, etc., that is used with others to construct the framework of a wall. **4.** a headless bolt that is threaded at both ends, the centre portion being unthreaded. **5.** any short projection on a machine, such as the metal cylinder that forms a journal for the gears on a screw-cutting lathe. **6.** the cross bar in the centre of a link of a heavy chain. **7.** one of a number of rounded projections on the sole of a boot or shoe to give better grip, as on a football boot. ~*vb.* **studs, stud·ding, stud·ded.** (*tr.*) **8.** to provide, ornament, or make with studs. **9.** to dot or cover with: *the park was studded with daisies.* **10.** *Building.* to provide or support (a wall, partition, etc.) with studs. [Old English *studu;* related to Old Norse *stoth* post, Middle High German *stud* post]

stud[2] (stʌd) *n.* **1.** a group of pedigree animals, esp. horses, kept for breeding purposes. **2.** any male animal kept principally for breeding purposes, esp. a stallion. **3.** a farm or stable where a stud is kept. **4.** the state or condition of being kept for breeding purposes: *at stud; put to stud.* **5.** (*modifier*) of or relating to such animals or the place where they are kept: *a stud farm; a stud horse.* **6.** *Slang.* a virile or sexually active man. **7.** short for **stud poker.** [Old English *stōd;* related to Old Norse *stōth,* Old High German *stuot*]

stud·book ('stʌdˌbʊk) *n.* a written record of the pedigree of a purebred stock, esp. of racehorses.

stud·ding ('stʌdɪŋ) *n.* **1.** building studs collectively, esp. as used to form a wall or partition. See also **stud**[1] (sense 3). **2.** material that is used to form studs or serve as studs.

stud·ding·sail ('stʌdɪŋˌseɪl; *Nautical* 'stʌnsəl) *n. Nautical.* a light auxiliary sail set outboard on spars on either side of a square sail. Also called: **stunsail, stuns'l.** [C16: *studding,* perhaps from Middle Low German, Middle Dutch *stōtinge,* from *stōten* to thrust; related to German *stossen*]

stu·dent ('stjuːdənt) *n.* **1.** a person following a course of study, as in a school, college, university, etc. **2.** a person who makes a thorough study of a subject. **3.** *Rare.* a person who likes to study. [C15: from Latin *studēns* diligent, from *studēre* to be zealous; see STUDY]

stu·dent ad·vis·er *n.* another word for **counsellor** (sense 5).

stu·dent·ship ('stjuːdəntˌʃɪp) *n.* **1.** the role or position of a student. **2.** another word for **scholarship** (sense 3).

Stu·dent's t dis·tri·bu·tion *n. Statistics.* a continuous distribution obtained from a ratio of a normal and a chi-square variable approximating to the normal distribution for a small population. Also called: **t distribution.**

stud·horse ('stʌdˌhɔːs) *n.* another word for **stallion.**

stud·ied ('stʌdɪd) *adj.* **1.** carefully practised, designed, or premeditated: *a studied reply.* **2.** an archaic word for **learned.** —'**stud·ied·ly** *adv.* —'**stud·ied·ness** *n.*

stu·di·o ('stjuːdɪˌəʊ) *n., pl.* **·di·os. 1.** a room in which an artist, photographer, or musician works. **2.** a room used to record television or radio programmes, make films, etc. **3.** (*pl.*) the premises of a radio, television, or film company. [C19: from Italian, literally: study, from Latin *studium* diligence]

stu·di·o couch *n.* an upholstered couch, usually backless, convertible into a double bed.

stu·di·ous ('stjuːdɪəs) *adj.* **1.** given to study. **2.** of a serious, thoughtful, and hard-working character. **3.** showing deliberation, care, or precision. [C14: from Latin *studiōsus* devoted to, from *studium* assiduity] —'**stu·di·ous·ly** *adv.* —'**stu·di·ous·ness** *n.*

stud pok·er *n.* a variety of poker in which the first card is dealt face down before each player and the next four are dealt face up (**five-card stud**) or in which the first two cards and the last card are dealt face down and the intervening four cards are dealt face up (**seven-card stud**), with bets made after each round. Often shortened to **stud.**

stud·work ('stʌdˌwɜːk) *n.* **1.** work decorated with studs. **2.** the supporting framework of a wall or partition.

stud·y ('stʌdɪ) *vb.* **stud·ies, stud·y·ing, stud·ied. 1.** to apply the mind to the learning or understanding of (a subject), esp. by reading: *to study languages; to study all night.* **2.** (*tr.*) to investigate or examine, as by observation, research, etc.: *to study the effects of heat on metal.* **3.** (*tr.*) to look at minutely; scrutinize. **4.** (*tr.*) to give much careful or critical thought to. **5.** to take a course in (a subject), as at a college. **6.** (*tr.*) to try to memorize: *to study a part for a play.* **7.** (*intr.*) to meditate or contemplate; reflect. ~*n., pl.* **stud·ies. 8. a.** the act or process of studying **b.** (*as modifier*): *study group.* **9.** a room used for studying, reading, writing, etc. **10.** (*often pl.*) work relating to a particular discipline: *environmental studies.* **11.** a product of studying, such as a written paper or book. **12.** a drawing, sculpture, etc., executed for practice or in preparation for another work. **13.** a musical composition intended to develop one aspect of performing technique: *a study in spiccato bowing.* **14. in a brown study.** in a reverie or daydream. [C13: from Old French *estudie,* from Latin *studium* zeal, inclination, from *studēre* to be diligent]

stuff (stʌf) *vb.* (*mainly tr.*) **1.** to pack or fill completely; cram. **2.** (*intr.*) to eat large quantities. **3.** to force, shove, or squeeze: *to stuff money into a pocket.* **4.** to fill (food such as poultry or tomatoes) with a stuffing. **5.** to fill (an animal's skin) with material so as to restore the shape of the live animal. **6.** *Taboo slang.* to have sexual intercourse with (a woman). **7.** *Tanning.* to treat (an animal skin or hide) with grease. **8.** *U.S.* to fill (a ballot box) with a large number of fraudulent votes. **9.** (in marine transport) to pack (a container). See also **stuffing and stripping.** ~*n.* **10.** the raw material or fabric of something. **11.** woollen cloth or fabric. **12.** any general or unspecified substance or accumulation of objects. **13.** stupid or worthless actions, speech, ideas, etc. **14.** a slang word for **money. 15.** *Slang.* a drug, esp. cannabis. **16.** *Informal.* **do one's stuff.** to do what is expected of one. **17. that's the stuff.** that is what is needed. **18.** *Taboo slang, offensive.* a girl or woman considered sexually (esp. in the phrase **bit of stuff**). [C14: from Old French *estoffe,* from *estoffer* to furnish, provide, of Germanic origin; related to Middle High German *stopfen* to cram full] —'**stuff·er** *n.*

stuffed (stʌft) *adj.* **1.** filled with something, esp. (of poultry and other food) filled with stuffing. **2.** (foll. by *up*) (of the nasal passages) blocked with mucus. **3. get stuffed!** *Brit. taboo slang.* an exclamation of contemptuous anger or annoyance, esp. against another person.

stuffed shirt *n. Informal.* a pompous or formal person.

stuff gown *n. Brit.* a woollen gown worn by a barrister who has not taken silk.

stuff·ing ('stʌfɪŋ) *n.* **1.** the material with which something is stuffed. **2.** a mixture of chopped and seasoned ingredients with which poultry, meat, etc., is stuffed before cooking. **3. knock the stuffing out of** (**someone**). to defeat (someone) utterly.

stuff·ing and strip·ping *n.* (in marine transport) the packing and unpacking of containers.

stuff·ing box *n.* a small chamber in which an annular packing is compressed around a reciprocating or rotating rod or shaft to form a seal. Also called: **packing box.**

stuff·ing nut *n.* a large nut that is tightened to compress the packing in a stuffing box.

stuff·y ('stʌfɪ) *adj.* **stuff·i·er, stuff·i·est. 1.** lacking fresh air. **2.** excessively dull, staid, or conventional. **3.** (of the nasal passages) blocked with mucus. —'**stuff·i·ly** *adv.* —'**stuff·i·ness** *n.*

stull (stʌl) *n. Mining.* a timber prop or platform in a stope. [C18: perhaps from German *Stollen,* from Old High German *stollo*]

stul·ti·fy ('stʌltɪˌfaɪ) *vb.* **·fies, ·fy·ing, ·fied.** (*tr.*) **1.** to make useless, futile, or ineffectual, esp. by routine. **2.** to cause to appear absurd or inconsistent. **3.** to prove (someone) to be of unsound mind and thus not legally responsible. [C18: from Latin *stultus* stupid + *facere* to make] —ˌ**stul·ti·fi·'ca·tion** *n.* —'**stul·ti·ˌfi·er** *n.*

stum (stʌm) (in wine-making) ~*n.* **1.** a less common word for **must**[2]. **2.** partly fermented wine added to fermented wine as a preservative. ~*vb.* **stums, stum·ming, stummed. 3.** to preserve (wine) by adding stum. [C17: from Dutch *stom* dumb; related to German *stumm*]

stum·ble ('stʌmbəl) *vb.* (*intr.*) **1.** to trip or fall while walking or running. **2.** to walk in an awkward, unsteady, or unsure way. **3.** to make mistakes or hesitate in speech or actions. **4.** (foll. by *across* or *upon*) to come (across) by accident. **5.** to commit a grave mistake or sin. ~*n.* **6.** a false step, trip, or blunder. **7.** the act of stumbling. [C14: related to Norwegian *stumla,* Danish dialect *stumle;* see STAMMER] —'**stum·bler** *n.* —'**stum·bling·ly** *adv.*

stum·bling block *n.* any impediment or obstacle.

stu·mer ('stjuːmə) *n.* **1.** *Slang.* a forgery or cheat. **2.** *Irish dialect.* a poor bargain. [of unknown origin]

stump (stʌmp) *n.* **1.** the base part of a tree trunk left standing after the tree has been felled or has fallen. **2.** the part of something, such as a tooth, limb, or blade, that remains after a larger part has been removed. **3.** (*often pl.*) *Informal.* a leg (esp. in the phrase **stir one's stumps**). **4.** *Cricket.* any of three upright wooden sticks that, with two bails laid across them, form a wicket (the **stumps**). **5.** Also called: **tortillon.** a short sharply-pointed stick of cork or rolled paper or leather, used in drawing and shading. **6.** a heavy tread or the sound of heavy footsteps. **7.** a platform used by an orator when addressing a meeting. **8.** (*often pl.*) *Austral.* a pile used to support a house. ~*vb.* **9.** (*tr.*) to stop, confuse, or puzzle. **10.** (*intr.*) to plod or trudge heavily. **11.** (*tr.*) *Cricket.* (of a fielder, esp. a wicketkeeper) to dismiss (a batsman) by breaking his wicket with the ball or with the ball in the hand while he is out of his crease. **12.** *Chiefly U.S.* to campaign or canvass (an area), esp. by political speech-making. **13.** (*tr.*) to reduce to a stump; lop. **14.** (*tr.*) to clear (land) of stumps. [C14: from Middle Low German *stump;* related to Dutch *stomp,* German *Stumpf;* see STAMP] —**'stump·er** *n.*

stump·age ('stʌmpɪdʒ) *n. U.S.* **1.** standing timber or its value. **2.** the right to fell timber on another person's land.

stump ranch *or* **farm** *n. Canadian informal.* (in British Columbia) an undeveloped ranch in the bush where grass is grown among the stumps of felled trees.

stump up *vb.* (*adv.*) *Brit. informal.* to give (the money required).

stump·y ('stʌmpɪ) *adj.* **stump·i·er, stump·i·est. 1.** like a stump. **2.** abounding in or full of stumps. —**'stump·i·ness** *n.*

stun (stʌn) *vb.* **stuns, stun·ning, stunned.** (*tr.*) **1.** to render unconscious, as by a heavy blow or fall. **2.** to shock or overwhelm. **3.** to surprise or astound. ~*n.* **4.** the state or effect of being stunned. [C13 *stunen,* from Old French *estoner* to daze, stupefy, from Vulgar Latin *extonāre* (unattested), from Latin EX-[1] + *tonāre* to thunder]

stung (stʌŋ) *vb.* **1.** the past tense or past participle of **sting.** ~*adj.* **2.** *Austral. slang.* drunk; intoxicated.

stunk (stʌŋk) *vb.* a past tense or past participle of **stink.**

stun·ner ('stʌnə) *n. Informal.* a person or thing of great beauty, quality, size, etc.

stun·ning ('stʌnɪŋ) *adj. Informal.* very attractive, impressive, astonishing, etc. —**'stun·ning·ly** *adv.*

stun·sail *or* **stun·s'l** ('stʌnsᵊl) *n.* another word for **studdingsail.** [C18: variant of STUDDINGSAIL]

stunt[1] (stʌnt) *vb.* **1.** (*tr.*) to prevent or impede (the growth or development) of (a plant, animal, etc.). ~*n.* **2.** the act or an instance of stunting. **3.** a person, animal, or plant that has been stunted. [C17 (as vb.: to check the growth of): perhaps from C15 *stont* of short duration, from Old English *stunt* simple, foolish; sense probably influenced by Old Norse *stuttr* short in stature, dwarfed] —**'stunt·ed** *adj.* —**'stunt·ed·ness** *n.*

stunt[2] (stʌnt) *n.* **1. a.** a feat of daring or skill. **b.** (*as modifier*): *a stunt man; stunt flying.* **2.** anything spectacular or unusual done for attention. ~*vb.* **3.** (*intr.*) to perform a stunt or stunts. [C19: U.S. student slang, of unknown origin]

stu·pa ('stu:pə) *n.* a domed edifice housing Buddhist or Jain relics. Also called: **tope.** [C19: from Sanskrit: dome]

stupe[1] (stju:p) *n. Med.* a hot damp cloth, usually sprinkled with an irritant, applied to the body to relieve pain by counter-irritation. [C14: from Latin *stuppa* flax, from Greek *stuppē*]

stupe[2] (stju:p) *n. U.S. slang.* a stupid person; clot.

stu·pe·fa·ci·ent (ˌstju:pɪ'feɪʃɪənt) *or* **stu·pe·fac·tive** (ˌstju:pɪ'fæktɪv) *n.* **1.** a drug that causes stupor. ~*adj.* **2.** of, relating to, or designating this type of drug. [C17: from Latin *stupefaciēns* to make senseless, from *stupēre* to be stunned + *facere* to make]

stu·pe·fac·tion (ˌstju:pɪ'fækʃən) *n.* **1.** astonishment. **2.** the act of stupefying or the state of being stupefied.

stu·pe·fy ('stju:pɪˌfaɪ) *vb.* **·fies, ·fy·ing, ·fied.** (*tr.*) **1.** to render insensitive or lethargic. **2.** to confuse or astound. [C16: from Old French *stupefier,* from Latin *stupefacere;* see STUPEFACIENT] —**'stu·pe·ˌfi·er** *n.* —**'stu·pe·ˌfy·ing·ly** *adv.*

stu·pen·dous (stju:'pɛndəs) *adj.* astounding, wonderful, huge, etc. [C17: from Latin *stupēre* to be amazed] —**stu·'pen·dous·ly** *adv.* —**stu·'pen·dous·ness** *n.*

stu·pid ('stju:pɪd) *adj.* **1.** lacking in common sense, perception, or normal intelligence. **2.** (*usually postpositive*) stunned, dazed, or stupefied: *stupid from lack of sleep.* **3.** having dull mental responses; slow-witted. **4.** trivial, silly, or frivolous. [C16: from French *stupide,* from Latin *stupidus* silly, from *stupēre* to be amazed] —**'stu·pid·ly** *adv.* —**'stu·pid·ness** *n.*

stu·pid·i·ty (stju:'pɪdɪtɪ) *n., pl.* **·ties. 1.** the quality or state of being stupid. **2.** a stupid act, remark, etc.

stu·por ('stju:pə) *n.* **1.** a state of unconsciousness. **2.** mental dullness; torpor. [C17: from Latin, from *stupēre* to be aghast] —**'stu·por·ous** *adj.*

stur·dy[1] ('stɜ:dɪ) *adj.* **·di·er, ·di·est. 1.** healthy, strong, and vigorous. **2.** strongly built; stalwart. [C13 (in the sense: rash, harsh): from Old French *estordi* dazed, from *estordir* to stun, perhaps ultimately related to Latin *turdus* a thrush (taken as representing drunkenness)] —**'stur·di·ly** *adv.* —**'stur·di·ness** *n.*

stur·dy[2] ('stɜ:dɪ) *n. Vet. science.* another name for **staggers** (sense 2). —**'stur·died** *adj.*

stur·geon ('stɜ:dʒən) *n.* any primitive bony fish of the family *Acipenseridae,* of temperate waters of the N hemisphere, having an elongated snout and rows of spines along the body: valued as a source of caviar and isinglass. [C13: from Old French *estourgeon,* of Germanic origin; related to Old English *styria,* Old High German *sturio*]

Sturm·ab·tei·lung *German.* ('ʃturm'aptaɪluŋ) *n.* the full name of the Nazi **S.A.** [literally: storm division]

Stur·mer ('stɜ:mə) *n.* a variety of eating apple having a pale green skin and crisp sweet flesh. [C19: named after *Sturmer,* Suffolk]

Sturm und Drang *German.* ('ʃturm unt 'draŋ) *n.* a German literary movement of the latter half of the 18th century, characterized by a reaction against rationalism. [literally: storm and stress, from the title of a play by F. M. von Klinger (1752–1831), German dramatist]

Sturt (stɜ:t) *n.* **Charles.** 1795–1869, English explorer, who led three expeditions (1828–29; 1829; 1844–45) into the Australian interior, discovering the Darling River (1828).

stut·ter ('stʌtə) *vb.* **1.** to speak (a word, phrase, etc.) with recurring repetition of consonants, esp. initial ones. **2.** to make (an abrupt sound) repeatedly: *the gun stuttered.* ~*n.* **3.** the act or habit of stuttering. **4.** a stuttering sound. [C16: related to Middle Low German *stötern,* Old High German *stōzan* to push against, Latin *tundere* to beat] —**'stut·ter·er** *n.* —**'stut·ter·ing** *n., adj.* —**'stut·ter·ing·ly** *adv.*

Stutt·gart (*German* 'ʃtʊtgart) *n.* an industrial city in W West Germany, capital of Baden-Württemberg state, on the River Neckar: developed around a stud farm (*Stuotgarten*) of the Counts of Württemberg. Pop.: 624 835 (1974 est.).

Stuy·ve·sant ('staɪvɪsᵊnt) *n.* **Pe·ter.** ?1610–72, Dutch colonial administrator of New Netherland (later New York) (1646–64).

sty[1] (staɪ) *n., pl.* **sties. 1.** a pen in which pigs are housed and fed. **2.** any filthy or corrupt place. ~*vb.* **sties, sty·ing, stied. 3.** to enclose or be enclosed in a sty. [Old English *stig;* related to Old Norse *stīa* pen, fold, Old High German *stīga,* Middle Dutch *stije*]

sty[2] *or* **stye** (staɪ) *n., pl.* **sties** *or* **styes.** inflammation of a sebaceous gland of the eyelid, usually caused by bacteria. [C15 *styanye* (mistakenly taken as *sty on eye*), from Old English *stīgend* rising, hence swelling, sty + *ye* eye]

Styg·i·an ('stɪdʒɪən) *adj.* **1.** of or relating to the river Styx. **2.** *Chiefly literary.* **a.** dark, gloomy, or hellish. **b.** completely inviolable, as a vow sworn by the river Styx. [C16: from Latin *Stygius,* from Greek *Stugios,* from *Stux* STYX; related to *stugein* to hate]

style (staɪl) *n.* **1.** a form of appearance, design, or production; type or make: *a new style of house.* **2.** the way in which something is done: *good or bad style.* **3.** the manner in which something is expressed or performed, considered as separate from its intrinsic content, meaning, etc. **4.** a distinctive, formal, or characteristic manner of expression in words, music, painting, etc. **5.** elegance or refinement of manners, dress, etc. **6.** prevailing fashion in dress, looks, etc. **7.** a fashionable or ostentatious mode of existence: *to live in style.* **8.** the particular mode of orthography, punctuation, design, etc., followed in a book, journal, etc., or in a printing or publishing house. **9.** *Chiefly Brit.* the distinguishing title or form of address of a person or firm. **10.** *Botany.* the long slender extension of the ovary, bearing the stigma. **11.** *Zoology.* a slender pointed structure, such as the piercing mouthparts of certain insects. **12.** a method of expressing or calculating dates. See **Old Style, New Style. 13.** another word for **stylus** (sense 1). **14.** the arm of a sundial. ~*vb.* (*mainly tr.*) **15.** to design, shape, or tailor: *to style hair.* **16.** to adapt or make suitable for. **17.** to make consistent or correct according to a printing or publishing style. **18.** to name or call; designate: *to style a man a fool.* **19.** (*intr.*) to decorate objects using a style or stylus. [C13: from Latin *stylus, stilus* writing implement, hence characteristics of the writing, style] —**'sty·lar** *adj.* —**'styl·er** *n.*

style·book ('staɪlˌbʊk) *n.* a book containing rules and examples of punctuation, typography, etc., for the use of writers, editors, and printers.

sty·let ('staɪlɪt) *n. Surgery.* **1.** a wire for insertion into a flexible cannula or catheter to maintain its rigidity or patency during passage. **2.** a slender probe. [C17: from French *stilet,* from Old Italian STILETTO; influenced in spelling by Latin *stylus* STYLE]

sty·li·form ('staɪlɪˌfɔ:m) *adj. Zoology.* shaped like a stylus or bristle: *a styliform antenna.* [C16: from New Latin *stiliformis,* from Latin STYLUS]

styl·ish ('staɪlɪʃ) *adj.* having style; smart; fashionable. —**'styl·ish·ly** *adv.* —**'styl·ish·ness** *n.*

styl·ist ('staɪlɪst) *n.* **1.** a person who performs, writes, or acts with attention to style. **2.** a designer of clothes, décor, etc. **3.** a hairdresser who styles hair.

sty·lis·tic (staɪ'lɪstɪk) *adj.* of or relating to style, esp. artistic or literary style. —**sty·'lis·ti·cal·ly** *adv.*

sty·lite ('staɪlaɪt) *n. Christianity.* one of a class of recluses who in ancient times lived on the top of high pillars. [C17: from Late Greek *stulitēs,* from Greek *stulos* a pillar] —**sty·lit·ic** (staɪ'lɪtɪk) *adj.*

styl·ize *or* **styl·ise** ('staɪlaɪz) *vb.* (*tr.*) to give a conventional or established stylistic form to. —ˌ**styl·i·'za·tion** *or* ˌ**styl·i·'sa·tion** *n.* —**'styl·iz·er** *or* **'styl·is·er** *n.*

sty·lo- *or before a vowel* **styl-** *combining form.* **1.** (in biology) a style: *stylopodium.* **2.** indicating a column or point: *stylobate; stylograph.* [from Greek *stulos* column]

sty·lo·bate ('staɪləˌbeɪt) *n.* a continuous horizontal course of masonry that supports a colonnade. [C17: from Latin *stylobatēs,* from Greek *stulos* pillar + *-batēs,* from *bainein* to tread, walk]

sty·lo·graph ('staɪləˌgræf, -ˌgrɑ:f) *n.* a fountain pen having a fine hollow tube as the writing point instead of a nib. [C19: from STYL(US) + -GRAPH]

sty·lo·graph·ic (ˌstaɪlə'græfɪk) *or* **sty·lo·graph·i·cal** *adj.* of or relating to a stylograph or stylography. —ˌ**sty·lo·'graph·i·cal·ly** *adv.*

sty+log+ra+phy (staɪˈlɒgrəfɪ) *n.* the art or method of writing, drawing, or engraving with a stylus or style.

sty+loid (ˈstaɪlɔɪd) *adj.* **1.** resembling a stylus. **2.** *Anatomy.* of or relating to a projecting process of the temporal bone. [C18: from New Latin *styloides,* from Greek *stuloeidēs* like a STYLUS; influenced also by Greek *stulos* pillar]

sty+lo+lite (ˈstaɪləˌlaɪt) *n.* any of the small striated columnar structures within the strata of some limestones. [C19: from Greek *stulos* pillar + -LITE] **—sty+lo+lit+ic** (ˌstaɪləˈlɪtɪk) *adj.*

sty+lo+pize *or* **sty+lo+pise** (ˈstaɪləˌpaɪz) *vb.* (*tr.*) (of a stylops) to parasitize (a host): *the bee was stylopized.*

sty+lo+po+di·um (ˌstaɪləˈpəʊdɪəm) *n., pl.* **+di·a** (-dɪə). *Botany.* a swelling at the base of the style in umbelliferous plants. [C19: New Latin, from Greek *stulos* pillar + -PODIUM]

sty+lops (ˈstaɪlɒps) *n., pl.* **+lo+pes** (-ləˌpiːz). any insect of the order *Strepsiptera,* including the genus *Stylops,* living as a parasite in other insects, esp. bees and wasps: the females remain in the body of the host but the males move between hosts. [C19: New Latin, from Greek, from *stulos* a pillar + *ōps* an eye, from the fact that the male insect has stalked compound eyes]

sty+lo+stix+is (ˌstaɪləʊˈstɪksɪs) *n. Med.* another name for **acupuncture.** [C20: New Latin, from Greek *stulos* style (pointed instrument) + *stixis* mark, spot]

sty+lus (ˈstaɪləs) *n., pl.* **+li** (-laɪ) *or* **+lus·es. 1.** Also called: **style.** a pointed instrument for engraving, drawing or writing. **2.** a tool used in ancient times for writing on wax tablets, which was pointed at one end and blunt at the other for erasing mistakes. **3.** a device attached to the cartridge in the pickup arm of a gramophone that rests in the groove in the record, transmitting the vibrations to the sensing device in the cartridge. It consists of or is tipped with a hard material, such as diamond or sapphire. [C18: from Latin, variant of *stilus* writing implement; see STYLE] **—ˈsty+lar** *adj.*

sty+mie *or* **sty+my** (ˈstaɪmɪ) *vb.* **+mies, +mie+ing, +mied** *or* **+mies, +my+ing, +mied.** (*tr.; often passive*) **1.** to hinder or thwart. **2.** *Golf.* to impede with a stymie. *~n., pl.* **+mies. 3.** *Golf.* a situation in which an opponent's ball is blocking the line between the hole and the ball about to be played. **4.** a situation of obstruction. [C19: of uncertain origin]

styp+sis (ˈstɪpsɪs) *n.* the action, application, or use of a styptic. [C19: via New Latin from Late Latin: astringency, from Greek *stupsis,* from *stuphein* to contract]

styp+tic (ˈstɪptɪk) *adj. also* **styp+ti·cal. 1.** contracting the blood vessels or tissues. *~n.* **2.** a styptic drug. [C14: via Late Latin, from Greek *stuptikos* capable of contracting; see STYPSIS] **—styp+tic+i·ty** (stɪpˈtɪsɪtɪ) *n.*

styp+tic pen+cil *n.* a styptic agent in the form of a small stick, for application to razor nicks, etc.

sty+ra+ca+ceous (ˌstaɪrəˈkeɪʃəs) *adj.* of, relating to, or belonging to the *Styracaceae,* a family of Asian and American trees and shrubs having leathery leaves: includes storax and silver bell. [C19: *styrac-,* from STYRAX]

sty+rax (ˈstaɪræks) *n.* any tropical or subtropical tree of the genus *Styrax,* which includes the storaxes. [C16: via Latin from Greek *sturax*]

sty+rene (ˈstaɪriːn) *n.* a colourless oily volatile flammable water-insoluble liquid made from ethylene and benzene. It is an unsaturated compound and readily polymerizes: used in making synthetic plastics and rubbers. Formula: $C_6H_5CH{:}CH_2$. See also **polystyrene.** [C20: from STYR(AX) + -ENE]

Styr·i·a (ˈstɪrɪə) *n.* a mountainous province of SE Austria: rich mineral resources. Capital: Graz. Pop.: 1 191 960 (1971). Area: 16 384 sq. km (6326 sq. miles). German name: **Steiermark.**

Styx (stɪks) *n. Greek myth.* a river in Hades across which Charon ferried the souls of the dead. [from Greek *Stux;* related to *stugein* to hate]

SU *abbrev. for:* **1.** strontium unit. *~* **2.** *international car registration for* Soviet Union.

su+a·ble (ˈsjuːəbᵊl) *adj.* liable to be sued in a court. **—ˌsu+a·ˈbil+i·ty** *n.*

Su+a+kin (ˈsuːɑːkɪn) *n.* a port in the NE Sudan, on the Red Sea: formerly the chief port of the African Red Sea; now obstructed by a coral reef. Pop.: 5511 (1973).

Suár·ez (*Spanish* ˈswareθ) *n.* **A·dol·fo** (aˈðolfo). born 1932, Spanish statesman; prime minister (1976-78; 1979-81).

sua+sion (ˈsweɪʒən) *n.* a rare word for **persuasion.** [C14: from Latin *suāsiō,* from *suādēre* to PERSUADE] **—ˈsua+sive** *adj.*

suave (swɑːv) *adj.* (esp. of a man) displaying smoothness and sophistication in manner or attitude; urbane. [C16: from Latin *suāvis* sweet] **—ˈsuave+ly** *adv.* **—suav+i·ty** (ˈswɑːvɪtɪ) *or* **ˈsuave+ness** *n.*

sub (sʌb) *n.* **1.** short for several words beginning with *sub-,* such as **subaltern, subeditor, submarine, subordinate, subscription, substandard, substitute,** and **substratum** (in photography). **2.** *Brit. informal.* an advance payment of wages or salary. *~vb.* **subs, sub+bing, subbed. 3.** (*intr.*) to serve as a substitute. **4.** *Brit. informal.* to grant or receive (an advance payment of wages or salary). **5.** (*tr.*) *Informal.* short for **subedit. 6.** (*tr.*) *Photog.* to apply a substratum to (a film or plate base).

sub. *abbrev. for:* **1.** subeditor. **2.** subito (in music). **3.** subscription. **4.** substitute. **5.** suburb(an). **6.** subway.

sub- *prefix.* **1.** situated under or beneath: *subterranean.* **2.** secondary in rank; subordinate: *subeditor.* **3.** falling short of; less than or imperfectly: *subarctic; subhuman.* **4.** forming a subdivision or subordinate part of a whole: *subcommittee.* **5.** (in chemistry) **a.** indicating that a compound contains a relatively small proportion of a specified element: *suboxide.* **b.** indicating that a salt is basic salt: *subacetate.* [from Latin *sub*]

sub+ac+e+tate (sʌbˈæsɪˌteɪt) *n.* any one of certain crystalline basic acetates containing hydroxide ions in addition to acetate ions. For example, the subacetate of aluminium is probably $Al_3(OH)_2(CH_3COO)$.

sub+ac·id (sʌbˈæsɪd) *adj.* (esp. of some fruits) moderately acid or sour. **—sub+a·cid+i·ty** (ˌsʌbəˈsɪdɪtɪ) *or* **sub+ˈac·id+ness** *n.* **—sub+ˈac·id+ly** *adv.*

sub+a·cute (ˌsʌbəˈkjuːt) *adj.* intermediate between acute and chronic. **—ˌsub+a·ˈcute+ly** *adv.*

su+ba+dar *or* **su+bah+dar** (ˈsuːbəˌdɑː) *n.* (formerly) the chief native officer of a company of Indian soldiers in the British service. [C17: via Urdu from Persian, from *sūba* province + *-dār* holding]

su+bah (ˈsuːbɑː) *n.* (in India) **1.** a province in the Mogul empire. **2.** another word for **subadar.**

sub+al+pine (sʌbˈælpaɪn) *adj.* **1.** situated in or relating to the regions at the foot of mountains. **2.** (of plants) growing below the treeline in mountainous regions.

sub+al+tern (ˈsʌbᵊltən) *n.* **1.** a commissioned officer below the rank of captain in certain armies, esp. the British. **2.** a person of inferior rank or position. **3.** *Logic.* **a.** the relation of one proposition to another when the first is implied by the second, esp. the relation of a particular to a universal proposition. **b.** (*as modifier*): *a subaltern relation.* *~adj.* **4.** of inferior position or rank. [C16: from Late Latin *subalternus,* from Latin SUB- + *alternus* alternate, from *alter* the other]

sub+al+ter+nate (sʌbˈɔːltənɪt) *adj.* **1.** (of leaves) having an arrangement intermediate between alternate and opposite. **2.** following in turn. **3.** of lesser quality or status. **—sub+al+ter+na+tion** (sʌbˌɔːltəˈneɪʃən) *n.*

sub+ant+arc+tic (ˌsʌbæntˈɑːktɪk) *adj.* of or relating to latitudes immediately north of the Antarctic Circle.

sub+ap·o+stol+ic (ˌsʌbæpəˈstɒlɪk) *adj.* *Christianity.* of or relating to the era after that of the Apostles.

sub+aq·ua (ˌsʌbˈækwə) *adj.* of or relating to underwater sport: *subaqua swimming; a subaqua club.*

sub+a·quat+ic (ˌsʌbəˈkwætɪk, -ˈkwɒt-) *adj.* **1.** living or growing partly in water and partly on land. **2.** of or relating to conditions, existence, or activities under water.

sub+a·que+ous (sʌbˈeɪkwɪəs, -ˈækwɪ-) *adj.* occurring, appearing, formed, or used under water.

sub+arc+tic (sʌbˈɑːktɪk) *adj.* of or relating to latitudes immediately south of the Arctic Circle.

sub+ar+id (sʌbˈærɪd) *adj.* receiving slightly more rainfall than arid regions; moderately dry.

sub+as+sem+bly (ˌsʌbəˈsɛmblɪ) *n., pl.* **+blies.** a number of machine components integrated into a unit forming part of a larger assembly.

sub+as+tral (sʌbˈæstrəl) *adj.* a rare word for **terrestrial.**

sub+a·tom+ic (ˌsʌbəˈtɒmɪk) *adj.* **1.** of, relating to or being a particle making up an atom or a process occurring within atoms: *the electron is a subatomic particle.* **2.** having dimensions smaller than atomic dimensions.

sub+au·di·tion (ˌsʌbɔːˈdɪʃən) *n.* **1.** something that is not directly stated but implied. **2.** the ability or act of understanding that which is only implied.

sub+au·ric·u·lar (ˌsʌbɔːˈrɪkjʊlə) *adj.* *Anatomy.* situated below the auricle of the ear.

sub+ax+il+la+ry (ˌsʌbˈæksɪlərɪ) *adj.* **1.** situated or growing beneath the axil of a plant: *subaxillary bracts.* **2.** situated beneath the armpit.

sub+base (ˈsʌbˌbeɪs) *n.* the lowest part of a pedestal, base, or skirting. Compare **surbase.**

sub+base+ment (ˈsʌbˌbeɪsmənt) *n.* an underground storey of a building beneath the main basement.

sub+bass *or* **sub+base** (ˈsʌbˌbeɪs) *n.* another name for **bourdon.**

sub+cal·i+bre *or U.S.* **sub+cal·i·ber** (sʌbˈkælɪbə) *adj.* **1.** (of a projectile) having a calibre less than that of the firearm from which it is discharged and therefore either fitted with a disc or fired through a tube inserted into the barrel. **2.** of, relating to, or firing subcalibre projectiles.

sub+car+ti+lag·i+nous (sʌbˌkɑːtɪˈlædʒɪnəs) *adj.* **1.** composed partly of cartilage: *a subcartilaginous skeleton.* **2.** situated beneath a cartilage or a cartilaginous structure.

sub+ce+les+ti·al (ˌsʌbsɪˈlɛstɪəl) *adj.* **1.** beneath the heavens; terrestrial. *~n.* **2.** a subcelestial object.

sub+cep+tion (səbˈsɛpʃən) *n.* *Psychol.* another word for **subliminal perception.**

sub+chlo+ride (sʌbˈklɔːraɪd) *n.* a chloride of an element that contains less chlorine than its common chloride.

sub+class (ˈsʌbˌklɑːs) *n.* **1.** a principal subdivision of a class. **2.** *Biology.* a taxonomic group that is a subdivision of a class. **3.**

---

sub+ˈab+bot *n.*
ˌsub+ab+ˈdo+min+al *adj.*
ˌsub+ad+ˈmin+is+ˌtra+tive *adj.*
ˌsub+ad+ˈmin+is+ˌtra+tor *n.*
sub+ˈa·gent *n.*
ˌsub+al+ˈli+ance *n.*
ˈsub+ˌar+e·a *n.*
ˈsub+ˌar+ti+cle *n.*
ˌsub+as+ˌso+ci+ˈa+tion *n.*
ˌsub+at+ˈtor+ney *n.*
sub+ˈav+er+age *adj.*
ˈsub+ˌbranch *n.*
ˈsub+ˌbreed *n.*
ˈsub+ˌbu+reau *n., pl.* **+reaus** *or* **+reaux.**
sub+ˈcat+e+ˌgo+ry *n., pl.* **+ries.**
ˈsub+ˌcell *n.*
ˈsub+ˌcel+lar *n.*
ˈsub+ˌchap+ter *n.*
ˈsub+ˌchief *n.*
ˈsub+ˌclan *n.*
ˌsub+clas+si+fi+ˈca+tion *n.*
sub+ˈclas+si+ˌfy *vb.,* **+fies, +fy+ing, +fied.**

Maths. another name for **subset** (sense 1). ~*vb.* **4.** (*tr.*) to assign to a subclass.
sub·cla·vi·an (sʌbˈkleɪvɪən) *adj. Anatomy.* (of an artery, vein, area, etc.) situated below the clavicle. [C17: from New Latin *subclāvius,* from Latin SUB- + *clavis* key]
sub·cli·max (sʌbˈklaɪmæks) *n. Ecology.* a community in which development has been arrested before climax has been attained. —**sub·cli·mac·tic** (ˌsʌbklaɪˈmæktɪk) *adj.*
sub·clin·i·cal (sʌbˈklɪnɪkᵊl) *adj. Med.* of or relating to the stage in the course of a disease before the symptoms are first noted. —**sub·ˈclin·i·cal·ly** *adv.*
sub·con·scious (sʌbˈkɒnʃəs) *adj.* **1.** acting or existing without one's awareness: *subconscious motive.* ~*n.* **2.** *Psychol.* that part of the mind considered to be outside or only partly within one's conscious awareness. Compare **unconscious, preconscious.** —**sub·ˈcon·scious·ly** *adv.* —**sub·ˈcon·scious·ness** *n.*
sub·con·ti·nent (sʌbˈkɒntɪnənt) *n.* a large land mass that is a distinct part of a continent, such as India is of Asia. —**sub·con·ti·nen·tal** (ˌsʌbkɒntɪˈnɛntᵊl) *adj.*
sub·con·tract *n.* (sʌbˈkɒntrækt). **1.** a subordinate contract under which the supply of materials, services, or labour is let out to someone other than a party to the main contract. ~*vb.* (ˌsʌbkənˈtrækt). **2.** (*intr.;* often foll. by *for*) to enter into or make a subcontract. **3.** (*tr.*) to let out (work) on a subcontract.
sub·con·trac·tor (ˌsʌbkənˈtræktə) *n.* a person, company, etc., that enters into a subcontract, esp. a firm that undertakes to complete part of another's contract.
sub·con·tra·ry (sʌbˈkɒntrərɪ) *Logic.* ~*adj.* **1.** (of a pair of propositions) related such that they cannot both be false at once, although they may be true together. Compare **contrary** (sense 5), **contradictory** (sense 3). ~*n., pl.* **·ries. 2.** either of the two propositions of this type.
sub·cor·tex (sʌbˈkɔːtɛks) *n., pl.* **·ti·ces** (-tɪˌsiːz). *Anatomy.* the matter of the brain situated beneath the cerebral cortex. —**sub·cor·ti·cal** (sʌbˈkɔːtɪkᵊl) *adj.*
sub·crit·i·cal (sʌbˈkrɪtɪkᵊl) *adj. Physics.* (of a nuclear reaction, power station, etc.) having or involving a chain reaction that is not self-sustaining; not yet critical.
sub·cul·ture *n.* (ˈsʌbˌkʌltʃə). **1.** a subdivision of a national culture or an enclave within it with a distinct integrated network of behaviour, beliefs, and attitudes. **2.** a culture of microorganisms derived from another culture. ~*vb.* (sʌbˈkʌltʃə). **3.** (*tr.*) to inoculate (bacteria from one culture medium) onto another medium. —**sub·ˈcul·tur·al** *adj.*
sub·cu·ta·ne·ous (ˌsʌbkjuːˈteɪnɪəs) *adj. Med.* situated, used, or introduced beneath the skin: *a subcutaneous injection.* —ˌ**sub·cu·ˈta·ne·ous·ly** *adv.*
sub·dea·con (ˌsʌbˈdiːkən) *n. Chiefly R.C. Church.* **1.** a cleric who assists at High Mass. **2.** (formerly) a person ordained to the lowest of the major orders. —**sub·dea·con·ate** (sʌbˈdiːkənɪt) *n.*
sub·de·lir·i·um (ˌsʌbdəˈlɪrɪəm) *n., pl.* **·lir·i·ums** *or* **·lir·i·a** (-ˈlɪrɪə). mild or intermittent delirium.
sub·di·ac·o·nate (ˌsʌbdaɪˈækənɪt, -ˌneɪt) *n.* the rank or office of a subdeacon. —ˌ**sub·di·ˈac·o·nal** *adj.*
sub·di·vide (ˌsʌbdɪˈvaɪd, ˈsʌbdɪˌvaɪd) *vb.* **1.** to divide (something) resulting from an earlier division. **2.** (*tr.*) *U.S.* to divide (land) into lots for sale. —ˌ**sub·di·ˈvid·er** *n.*
sub·di·vi·sion (ˈsʌbdɪˌvɪʒən) *n.* **1.** the process, instance, or state of being divided again following upon an earlier division. **2.** a portion that is the result of subdividing. **3.** *U.S.* a lot resulting from subdividing land. —ˌ**sub·di·ˈvi·sion·al** *adj.*
sub·dom·i·nant (sʌbˈdɒmɪnənt) *Music.* ~*n.* **1.** the fourth degree of a major or minor scale. **2.** a key or chord based on this. ~*adj.* **3.** of or relating to the subdominant.
sub·duct (səbˈdʌkt) *vb.* (*tr.*) **1.** *Physiol.* to draw or turn (the eye, etc.) downwards. **2.** *Rare.* to take away; deduct. —**sub·ˈduc·tion** *n.*
sub·due (səbˈdjuː) *vb.* **·dues, ·du·ing, ·dued.** (*tr.*) **1.** to establish ascendancy over by force. **2.** to overcome and bring under control, as by intimidation or persuasion. **3.** to hold in check or repress (feelings, emotions, etc.). **4.** to render less intense or less conspicuous. [C14 *sobdue,* from Old French *soduire* to mislead, from Latin *subdūcere* to remove; English sense influenced by Latin *subdere* to subject] —**sub·ˈdu·a·ble** *adj.* —**sub·ˈdu·a·bly** *adv.* —**sub·ˈdu·al** *n.*
sub·dued (səbˈdjuːd) *adj.* **1.** cowed, passive, or shy. **2.** gentle or quiet: *a subdued whisper.* **3.** (of colours, etc.) not harsh or bright: *subdued lighting.* —**sub·ˈdued·ly** *adv.* —**sub·ˈdued·ness** *n.*
sub·ed·it (sʌbˈɛdɪt) *vb.* to edit and correct (written or printed material).
sub·ed·i·tor (sʌbˈɛdɪtə) *n.* a person who checks and edits copy, esp. on a newspaper.
sub·e·qua·to·ri·al (sʌbˌɛkwəˈtɔːrɪəl) *adj.* situated in or characteristic of regions immediately north or south of equatorial regions.
su·ber·ic ac·id (sjuːˈbɛrɪk) *n.* another name for **octanedioic acid.** [C18: from French *subérique,* from Latin *sūber* cork (from which the acid is obtained)]
su·ber·in (ˈsjuːbərɪn) *n.* a fatty or waxy substance that is present in the walls of cork cells, making them impermeable to water and resistant to decay. [C19: from Latin *sūber* cork + -IN]
su·ber·ize *or* **su·ber·ise** (ˈsjuːbəˌraɪz) *vb.* (*tr.*) *Botany.* to impregnate (cell walls) with suberin during the formation of corky tissue. —ˌ**su·ber·i·ˈza·tion** *or* ˌ**su·ber·i·ˈsa·tion** *n.*
su·ber·ose (ˈsjuːbəˌrəʊs), **su·be·re·ous** (sjuːˈbɛrɪəs), *or* **su·ber·ic** (sjuːˈbɛrɪk) *adj. Botany.* relating to, resembling, or consisting of cork; corky.
sub·fam·i·ly (ˈsʌbˌfæmɪlɪ) *n., pl.* **·lies. 1.** *Biology.* a taxonomic group that is a subdivision of a family. **2.** any analogous subdivision, as of a family of languages.
sub·floor (ˈsʌbˌflɔː) *n.* a rough floor that forms a base for a finished floor.
sub·fusc (ˈsʌbfʌsk) *adj.* **1.** devoid of brightness or appeal; drab, dull, or dark. ~*n.* **2.** (at Oxford University) formal academic dress. [C18: from Latin *subfuscus* dusky, from *fuscus* dark]
sub·ge·nus (sʌbˈdʒiːnəs, -ˈdʒɛn-; ˈsʌbˌdʒiːnəs, -ˌdʒɛn-) *n., pl.* **·gen·er·a** (-ˈdʒɛnərə) *or* **·ge·nus·es.** *Biology.* a taxonomic group that is a subdivision of a genus but of higher rank than a species. —**sub·ge·ner·ic** (ˌsʌbdʒəˈnɛrɪk) *adj.*
sub·gla·ci·al (sʌbˈgleɪsɪəl) *adj.* formed or occurring at the bottom of a glacier. —**sub·ˈgla·ci·al·ly** *adv.*
sub·group (ˈsʌbˌgruːp) *n.* **1.** a distinct and often subordinate division of a group. **2.** a mathematical group whose members are members of another group, both groups being subject to the same rule of combination.
sub·head·ing (ˈsʌbˌhɛdɪŋ) *or* **sub·head** *n.* **1.** the heading or title of a subdivision or subsection of a printed work. **2.** a division subordinate to a main heading or title.
sub·hu·man (sʌbˈhjuːmən) *adj.* **1.** of, relating to, or designating animals that are below man (*Homo sapiens*) in evolutionary development. **2.** less than human.
sub·in·dex (sʌbˈɪndɛks) *n., pl.* **·dic·es** (-dɪˌsiːz) *or* **·dex·es. 1.** another word for **subscript** (sense 2). **2.** *U.S.* an index to a subcategory.
sub·in·feu·date (ˌsʌbɪnˈfjuːdeɪt) *vb.* to grant (lands) by subinfeudation.
sub·in·feu·da·tion (ˌsʌbɪnfjʊˈdeɪʃən) *n.* **1.** (in feudal society) the granting of land by a vassal to another man who became his vassal. **2.** the tenure or relationship so established.
sub·in·feu·da·to·ry (ˌsʌbɪnˈfjuːdətərɪ, -trɪ) (in feudal society) ~*n., pl.* **·ries. 1.** a man who held his fief by a subinfeudation. ~*adj.* **2.** of or relating to subinfeudation.
sub·ir·ri·gate (sʌbˈɪrɪˌgeɪt) *vb.* to irrigate (land) by means of an underground system of pipe lines or by natural moisture in the subsoil. —ˌ**sub·ir·ri·ˈga·tion** *n.*
su·bi·to (ˈsuːbɪˌtəʊ) *adv. Music.* (preceding or following a dynamic marking, etc.) suddenly; immediately. Abbrev.: **sub.** [C18: via Italian from Latin: suddenly, from *subitus* sudden, from *subīre* to approach, from SUB- (indicating stealth) + *īre* to go]
subj. *abbrev. for:* **1.** subject. **2.** subjective(ly). **3.** subjunctive.
sub·ja·cent (sʌbˈdʒeɪsᵊnt) *adj.* **1.** forming a foundation; underlying. **2.** lower than though not directly below: *tall peaks and their subjacent valley.* [C16: from Latin *subjacēre* to lie close, adjoin, be under, from SUB- + *jacēre* to lie] —**sub·ˈja·cen·cy** *n.* —**sub·ˈja·cent·ly** *adv.*
sub·ject *n.* (ˈsʌbdʒɪkt). **1. a.** the predominant theme or topic, as of a book, discussion, etc. **b.** (*in combination*): *subject-heading.* **2.** any branch of learning considered as a course of study. **3.** *Grammar.* a word or phrase about which something is predicated or stated in a sentence; for example, *the cat* in the sentence *The cat catches mice.* **4.** a person or thing that undergoes experiment, analysis, treatment, etc. **5.** a person who lives under the rule of a monarch, government, etc. **6.** an object, figure, scene, etc., as selected by an artist or photographer for representation. **7.** *Philosophy.* **a.** that which thinks or feels as opposed to the object of thinking and feeling; the self or the mind. **b.** the essential nature or substance of something as opposed to its attributes. **8.** Also called: **theme.** *Music.* a melodic or thematic phrase used as the principal motif of a fugue, the basis from which the musical material is derived in a sonata-form movement, or the recurrent figure in a rondo. **9.** *Logic.* the term of a proposition about which something is asserted. **10.** an originating motive. **11. change the subject.** to select a new topic of conversation. ~*adj.* (ˈsʌbdʒɪkt). (*usually postpositive* and foll. by *to*) **12.** being under the power or sovereignty of a ruler, government, etc.: *subject peoples.* **13.** showing a tendency (towards): *a child subject to indiscipline.* **14.** exposed or vulnerable: *subject to ribaldry.* **15.** conditional upon: *the results are subject to correction.* ~*adv.* **16. subject to.** (*prep.*) under the condition that: *we accept, subject to her agreement.* ~*vb.* (səbˈdʒɛkt). (*tr.*) **17.**

ˈ**sub·**ˌ**clause** *n.*
ˈ**sub·**ˌ**clerk** *n.*
sub·ˈ**cli·mate** *n.*
ˌ**sub·com·**ˈ**mand·er** *n.*
ˈ**sub·com·**ˌ**mis·sion** *n.*
ˌ**sub·com·**ˈ**mis·sion·er** *n.*
ˈ**sub·com·**ˌ**mit·tee** *n.*
ˌ**sub·con·stel·**ˈ**la·tion** *n.*
sub·ˈ**coun·cil** *n.*
sub·ˈ**cra·ni·al** *adj.*
ˌ**sub·cu·**ˈ**ra·tor** *n.*
ˌ**sub·def·i·**ˈ**ni·tion** *n.*
ˌ**sub·de·**ˈ**part·ment** *n.*
ˌ**sub·de·part·**ˈ**men·tal** *adj.*
ˈ**sub·**ˌ**de·pot** *n.*
sub·ˈ**di·a·**ˌ**lect** *n.*
ˌ**sub·di·**ˈ**rec·tor** *n.*
ˌ**sub·dis·**ˈ**tinc·tion** *n.*
ˈ**sub·**ˌ**dis·trict** *n.*
sub·ˈ**dor·sal** *adj.*
sub·ˈ**ech·o** *n., pl.* **·oes.**
sub·ˈ**el·e·ment** *n.*
ˌ**sub·el·e·**ˈ**men·tal** *adj.*
sub·ˈ**en·try** *n., pl.* **·tries.**
sub·ˈ**ep·och** *n.*
sub·ˈ**fore·man** *n., pl.* **·men.**
sub·ˈ**frac·tion** *n.*
sub·ˈ**frac·tion·al** *adj.*
sub·ˈ**freez·ing** *adj.*
ˈ**sub·**ˌ**func·tion** *n.*
sub·ˈ**gen·i·tal** *adj.*
sub·ˈ**glot·tal** *adj.*
ˈ**sub·**ˌ**head·ing** *n.*
ˈ**sub·**ˌ**i·tem** *n.*
sub·ˈ**mem·ber** *n.*
ˌ**sub·mo·**ˈ**lec·u·lar** *adj.*

(foll. by *to*) to cause to undergo the application (of): *they subjected him to torture.* **18.** (*often passive;* foll. by *to*) to expose or render vulnerable or liable (to some experience): *he was subjected to great danger.* **19.** (foll. by *to*) to bring under the control or authority (of): *to subject a soldier to discipline.* **20.** *Now rare.* to subdue or subjugate. **21.** *Rare.* to present for consideration; submit. **22.** *Obsolete.* to place below. ~Abbrev.: **subj.** [C14: from Latin *subjectus* brought under, from *subicere* to place under, from SUB- + *jacere* to throw] —**sub+'ject+a·ble** *adj.* —**sub+ˌject+a·'bil+i·ty** *n.* —**'sub+ject+less** *adj.* —**'sub·ject-ˌlike** *adj.*

sub+ject cat·a+logue *n. Library science.* a catalogue with entries arranged by subject in a classified sequence.

sub+jec+ti+fy (səb'dʒɛktɪˌfaɪ) *vb.* **+fies, +fy+ing, +fied.** (*tr.*) to make subjective or interpret subjectively. —**sub+ˌjec+ti+fi+'ca+tion** *n.*

sub+jec+tion (səb'dʒɛkʃən) *n.* the act or process of subjecting or the state of being subjected.

sub+jec+tive (səb'dʒɛktɪv) *adj.* **1.** belonging to, proceeding from, or relating to the mind of the thinking subject and not the nature of the object being considered. **2.** of, relating to, or emanating from a person's emotions, prejudices, etc.: *subjective views.* **3.** relating to the inherent nature of a person or thing; essential. **4.** existing only as perceived and not as a thing in itself. **5.** *Med.* (of a symptom, condition, etc.) experienced only by the patient and incapable of being recognized or studied by anyone else. **6.** *Grammar.* denoting a case of nouns and pronouns, esp. in languages having only two cases, that identifies the subject of a finite verb and (in formal use in English) is selected for predicate complements, as in *It is I.* See also **nominative** (sense 1). ~*n.* **7.** *Grammar.* **a.** the subjective case. **b.** a subjective word or speech element. ~Abbrev.: **subj.** Compare **objective.** —**sub+'jec+tive+ly** *adv.* —**ˌsub+jec+'tiv+i·ty** *or* **sub+'jec+tive+ness** *n.*

sub+jec+tive i·de·al+ism *n. Philosophy.* the theory that all experience is of ideas in the mind.

sub+jec+tiv+ism (səb'dʒɛktɪˌvɪzəm) *n.* **1.** *Philosophy.* the doctrine that knowledge, perception, values, etc., are limited by and relative to the self. **2.** any theological theory that attaches primary importance to religious experience. **3.** the quality or condition of being subjective. —**sub+'jec+tiv+ist** *n.* —**sub+ˌjec+ti+'vis+tic** *adj.* —**sub+ˌjec+ti+'vis+ti+cal+ly** *adv.*

sub+ject mat+ter *n.* the substance or main theme of a book, discussion, debate, etc.

sub·ject-rais·ing *n. Transformational grammar.* a rule that moves the subject of a complement clause into the clause in which it is embedded, as in the derivation of *He is likely to be late* from *It is likely that he will be late.*

sub+join (sʌb'dʒɔɪn) *vb.* (*tr.*) to add or attach at the end of something spoken, written, etc. [C16: from French *subjoindre,* from Latin *subjungere* to add to, from *sub-* in addition + *jungere* to JOIN] —**sub+'join+der** *n.* —**sub+junc+tion** (sʌb'dʒʌŋkʃən) *n.*

sub ju+di+ce ('dʒu:dɪsɪ) *adj.* (*usually postpositive*) before a court of law or a judge; under judicial consideration.

sub+ju+gate ('sʌbdʒʊˌgeɪt) *vb.* (*tr.*) **1.** to bring into subjection. **2.** to make subservient or submissive. [C15: from Late Latin *subjugāre* to subdue, from Latin SUB- + *jugum* yoke] —**sub+ju+ga·ble** ('sʌbdʒəgəbᵊl) *adj.* —**ˌsub+ju+'ga+tion** *n.* —**'sub+ju+ˌga+tor** *n.*

sub+junc+tive (səb'dʒʌŋktɪv) *adj.* **1.** *Grammar.* denoting a mood of verbs used when the content of the clause is being doubted, supposed, feared true, etc., rather than being asserted. The rules for its use and the range of meanings it may possess vary considerably from language to language. In the following sentence, *were* is in the subjunctive: *I'd think very seriously about that if I were you.* Compare **indicative.** ~*n.* **2.** *Grammar.* **a.** the subjunctive mood. **b.** a verb in this mood. ~Abbrev.: **subj.** [C16: via Late Latin *subjunctīvus,* from Latin *subjungere* to SUBJOIN] —**sub+'junc+tive+ly** *adv.*

sub+king+dom (sʌb'kɪŋdəm) *n. Biology.* a taxonomic group that is a subdivision of a kingdom.

sub+lap+sar+i+an+ism (ˌsʌblæp'sɛərɪəˌnɪzəm) *n.* another word for **infralapsarianism.** [C17 *sublapsarian,* via New Latin, from Latin SUB- + *lāpsus* a fall] —**ˌsub+lap+'sar+i·an** *n., adj.*

sub+lease *n.* ('sʌbˌli:s). **1.** a lease of property made by a person who is himself a lessee or tenant of that property. ~*vb.* (sʌb'li:s). **2.** to grant a sublease of (property); sublet. **3.** (*tr.*) to take, obtain, or hold by sublease. —**sub+les+see** (ˌsʌblɛ'si:) *n.* —**sub+les+sor** (ˌsʌblɛ'sɔ:) *n.*

sub+let *vb.* (sʌb'lɛt), **+lets, +let+ting, +let. 1.** to grant a sublease of (property). **2.** to let out (work, etc.) under a subcontract. ~*n.* ('sʌbˌlɛt). **3.** *Informal, chiefly U.S.* a sublease.

sub+lieu+ten+ant (ˌsʌblə'tɛnənt) *n.* the most junior commissioned officer in the Royal Navy and certain other navies. —**ˌsub+lieu+'ten+an+cy** *n.*

sub+li+mate ('sʌblɪˌmeɪt) *vb.* **1.** *Psychol.* to direct the energy of (a primitive impulse, esp. a sexual one) into activities that are considered to be socially more acceptable. **2.** (*tr.*) to make purer; refine **3.** *Chem.* a less common word for **sublime** (senses 8, 9). ~*n.* **4.** *Chem.* the material obtained when a substance is sublimed. ~*adj.* **5.** exalted or purified. [C16: from Latin *subblīmāre* to elevate, from *sublīmis* lofty; see SUBLIME] —**sub+li+ma·ble** ('sʌbləməbᵊl) *adj.*

sub+li+ma+tion (ˌsʌblɪ'meɪʃən) *n.* **1.** (in Freudian psychology) the diversion of psychic energy derived from sexual impulses into nonsexual activity, esp. of a creative nature. **2.** the process or an instance of sublimating. **3.** something sublimated.

sub+lime (sə'blaɪm) *adj.* **1.** of high moral, intellectual, or spiritual value; noble; exalted. **2.** inspiring deep veneration or awe: *sublime beauty.* **3.** *Poetic.* of proud bearing or aspect. **4.** *Archaic.* raised up. ~*n.* **the sublime. 5.** something that is sublime. **6.** the ultimate degree or perfect example: *the sublime of folly.* ~*vb.* **7.** (*tr.*) to make higher or purer. **8.** to change or cause to change directly from a solid to a vapour or gas without first melting: *to sublime iodine; many mercury salts sublime when heated.* **9.** to undergo or cause to undergo this process followed by a reverse change directly from a vapour to a solid: *to sublime iodine onto glass.* [C14: from Latin *sublīmis* lofty, perhaps from *sub-* up to + *līmen* lintel] —**sub+'lime+ly** *adv.* —**sub+lim+i+ty** (sə'blɪmɪtɪ) *n.*

Sub+lime Porte *n.* the full name of the **Porte.**

sub+lim·i+nal (sʌb'lɪmɪnᵊl) *adj.* **1.** resulting from processes of which the individual is not aware. **2.** (of stimuli) less than the minimum intensity or duration required to elicit a response. [C19: from Latin SUB- below + *līmen* threshold] —**sub+'lim·i+nal+ly** *adv.*

sub+lim·i+nal ad+ver+tis+ing *n.* a form of advertising on film or television that employs subliminal images to influence the viewer unconsciously.

sub+lim·i+nal per+cep+tion *n. Psychol.* perception of or reaction to a stimulus that occurs without awareness or consciousness. Also called: **subception.**

sub+lin+gual (sʌb'lɪŋgwəl) *adj. Anatomy.* situated beneath the tongue.

sub+lit+to+ral (sʌb'lɪtərəl) *adj.* **1.** (of marine organisms) growing, living, or situated close to the seashore: *a sublittoral plant.* **2.** of or relating to the zone between the seashore and the edge of the continental shelf.

sub+lu+nar·y (sʌb'lu:nərɪ) *adj.* **1.** situated between the moon and the earth. **2.** of or relating to the earth or world. [C16: via Late Latin, from Latin SUB- + *lūna* moon]

sub-ma·chine-gun *n.* a portable automatic or semiautomatic gun with a short barrel, designed to be fired from the hip or shoulder.

sub+mar+gin+al (sʌb'mɑ:dʒɪnᵊl) *adj.* **1.** below the minimum requirements. **2.** situated close to the margin of an organ or part. **3.** (of land) infertile and unprofitable for cultivation. —**sub+'mar+gin+al+ly** *adv.*

sub+ma+rine ('sʌbməˌri:n, ˌsʌbmə'ri:n) *n.* **1.** a vessel, esp. one designed for warfare, capable of operating for protracted periods below the surface of the sea. Often shortened to **sub. 2.** (*modifier*) **a.** of or relating to a submarine: *a submarine captain.* **b.** occurring or situated below the surface of the sea: *a submarine cable.*

sub+ma+rin+er (sʌb'mærɪnə) *n.* a crewman in a submarine.

sub+max+il+lar·y (ˌsʌbmæk'sɪlərɪ) *adj.* of, relating to, or situated close to the lower jaw.

sub+max+il+lar·y gland *n.* (in mammals) either of a pair of salivary glands situated on each side behind the lower jaw.

sub+me+di+ant (sʌb'mi:dɪənt) *Music.* ~*n.* **1.** the sixth degree of a major or minor scale. **2.** a key or chord based on this. ~*adj.* **3.** of or relating to the submediant. ~Also (U.S.): **superdominant.**

sub+men+tal (sʌb'mɛntᵊl) *adj. Anatomy.* situated beneath the chin.

sub+merge (səb'mɜ:dʒ) *or* **sub+merse** (səb'mɜ:s) *vb.* **1.** to plunge, sink, or dive or cause to plunge, sink, or dive below the surface of water, etc. **2.** (*tr.*) to cover with water or some other liquid. **3.** (*tr.*) to hide; suppress. **4.** (*tr.*) to overwhelm, as with work, difficulties, etc. [C17: from Latin *submergere,* from SUB- + *mergere* to immerse] —**sub+'merg+ence** *or* **sub+mer+sion** (səb'mɜ:ʃᵊn) *n.*

sub+merged (səb'mɜ:dʒd) *or* **sub+mersed** (səb'mɜ:st) *adj.* **1.** (of plants or plant parts) growing beneath the surface of the water. **2.** hidden; obscured. **3.** overwhelmed or overburdened.

sub+mers+i·ble (səb'mɜ:səbᵊl) *or* **sub+merg+i·ble** (səb'mɜ:dʒɪbᵊl) *adj.* **1.** able to be submerged. **2.** capable of operating under water, etc. ~*n.* **3.** a warship designed to operate under water for short periods. —**sub+ˌmers+i·'bil+i·ty** *or* **sub+ˌmerg+i·'bil+i·ty** *n.*

sub+mi·cro+scop+ic (ˌsʌbmaɪkrə'skɒpɪk) *adj.* too small to be seen through an optical microscope. —**ˌsub+mi·cro+'scop·i+cal+ly** *adv.*

sub+min·i·a+ture (sʌb'mɪnɪətʃə) *adj.* smaller than miniature.

sub+min·i·a+ture cam+er·a *n.* a pocket-sized camera, usually using 16 millimetre film with a very fine grain so that negatives can produce considerably enlarged prints.

sub+min·i·a+tur+ize *or* **sub+min·i·a+tur+ise** (sʌb'mɪnɪətʃəˌraɪz) *vb.* (*tr.*) to make subminiature, as in the manufacture of electronic equipment, etc. —**sub+ˌmin·i·a+tur·i+'za+tion** *or* **sub+ˌmin·i·a+tur·i+'sa+tion** *n.*

sub+miss (səb'mɪs) *adj. Archaic or poetic.* **1.** docile; submissive. **2.** soft in tone. [C16: from Latin *submissus* lowered, gentle, from *submittere* to reduce, from SUB- + *mittere* to send]

sub+mis+sion (səb'mɪʃən) *n.* **1.** an act or instance of submitting. **2.** something submitted; a proposal, argument, etc. **3.** the quality or condition of being submissive to another. **4.** the act of referring a document, etc., for the consideration of someone else. **5.** *Law.* **a.** an agreement by the parties to a dispute to refer the matter to arbitration. **b.** the instrument referring a disputed matter to arbitration. **6.** (in wrestling) the act of causing such pain to one's opponent that he submits. Compare **fall** (sense 48). **7.** *Archaic.* a confession of error.

sub+mis+sive (səb'mɪsɪv) *adj.* of, tending towards, or indicating submission, humility, or servility. —**sub+'mis+sive+ly** *adv.* —**sub+'mis+sive+ness** *n.*

sub+mit (səb'mɪt) *vb.* **+mits, +mit+ting, +mit+ted. 1.** (often foll.

by *to*) to yield (oneself), as to the will of another person, a superior force, etc. **2.** (foll. by *to*) to subject or be voluntarily subjected (to analysis, treatment, etc.). **3.** (*tr.*; often foll. by *to*) to refer (something to someone) for judgment or consideration: *to submit a claim.* **4.** (*tr.*; *may take a clause as object*) to state, contend, or propose deferentially. **5.** (*intr.*; often foll. by *to*) to defer or accede (to the decision, opinion, etc., of another). [C14: from Latin *submittere* to place under, from SUB- + *mittere* to send] **—sub·'mit·ta·ble** *or* **sub·'mis·si·ble** *adj.* **—sub·'mit·tal** *n.* **—sub·'mit·ter** *n.* **—sub·'mit·ting·ly** *adv.*

sub·mon·tane (sʌb'mɒnteɪn) *adj.* **1.** situated on or characteristic of the lower slopes of a mountain. **2.** beneath a mountain or mountain range. [C19: from Latin SUB- + *mōns* mountain] **—sub·'mon·tane·ly** *adv.*

sub·mu·co·sa (ˌsʌbmjuː'kəʊsə) *n., pl.* **·co·sae** (-'kəʊsiː). *Anatomy.* the connective tissue beneath a mucous membrane.

sub·mul·ti·ple (sʌb'mʌltɪpᵊl) *n.* **1.** a number that can be divided into another number an integral number of times without a remainder: *three is a submultiple of nine.* ~*adj.* **2.** being a submultiple of a quantity or number.

sub·nor·mal (sʌb'nɔːməl) *adj.* **1.** less than the normal. **2.** having a low intelligence, esp. having an IQ of less than 70. ~*n.* **3.** a subnormal person. **—sub·nor·mal·i·ty** (ˌsʌbnɔː'mælɪtɪ) *n.* **—sub·'nor·mal·ly** *adv.*

sub·o·ce·an·ic (sʌbˌəʊʃɪ'ænɪk) *adj.* formed or situated beneath the ocean or ocean floor.

sub·or·bi·tal (sʌb'ɔːbɪtᵊl) *adj.* **1.** (of a rocket, missile, etc.) having a flight path that is less than one complete orbit of the earth or other celestial body. **2.** *Anatomy.* situated beneath the orbit of the eye.

sub·or·der ('sʌbˌɔːdə) *n. Biology.* a taxonomic group that is a subdivision of an order. **—sub·'or·di·nal** *adj.*

sub·or·di·nar·y (sʌb'ɔːdɪnərɪ, -dɪnrɪ) *n., pl.* **·nar·ies.** any of several heraldic bearings of secondary importance to the ordinary, such as the lozenge, the orle, and the fret.

sub·or·di·nate *adj.* (sə'bɔːdɪnɪt). **1.** of lesser order or importance. **2.** under the authority or control of another: *a subordinate functionary.* ~*n.* (sə'bɔːdɪnɪt). **3.** a person or thing that is subordinate. ~*vb.* (sə'bɔːdɪˌneɪt). (*tr.*; usually foll. by *to*) **4.** to put in a lower rank or position (than). **5.** to make subservient: *to subordinate mind to heart.* [C15: from Medieval Latin *subordināre,* from Latin SUB- + *ordō* rank] **—sub·'or·di·nate·ly** *adv.* **—sub·or·di·'na·tion** *or* **sub·'or·di·nate·ness** *n.* **—sub·'or·di·na·tive** *adj.*

sub·or·di·nate clause *n. Grammar.* a clause with an adjectival, adverbial, or nominal function, rather than one that functions as a separate sentence in its own right. Compare **coordinate clause, main clause.**

sub·or·di·nat·ing con·junc·tion *n.* a conjunction that introduces subordinate clauses, such as *if, because, although,* and *until.* Compare **coordinating conjunction.**

sub·or·di·na·tion·ism (səˌbɔːdɪ'neɪʃəˌnɪzəm) *n.* either of two interpretations of the doctrine of the Trinity, often regarded as heretical, according to which the Son is subordinate to the Father or the Holy Ghost is subordinate to both. **—sub·ˌor·di·'na·tion·ist** *n.*

sub·orn (sə'bɔːn) *vb.* (*tr.*) **1.** to bribe, incite, or instigate (a person) to commit a wrongful act. **2.** *Criminal law.* to induce (a witness) to commit perjury. [C16: from Latin *subornāre,* from *sub-* secretly + *ornāre* to furnish] **—sub·or·na·tion** (ˌsʌbɔː'neɪʃən) *n.* **—sub·or·na·tive** (sʌ'bɔːnətɪv) *adj.* **—sub·'orn·er** *n.*

Su·bo·ti·ca (*Serbo-Croatian* 'subɔtitsa) *n.* a town in NE Yugoslavia, in Serbia near the border with Hungary: agricultural and industrial centre. Pop.: 88 787 (1971). Hungarian name: **Szabadka.**

sub·ox·ide (sʌb'ɒksaɪd) *n.* an oxide of an element containing less oxygen than the common oxide formed by the element: *carbon suboxide,* C_2O_3.

sub·phy·lum (sʌb'faɪləm) *n., pl.* **·la** (-lə). *Biology.* a taxonomic group that is a subdivision of a phylum. **—sub·'phy·lar** *adj.*

sub·plot ('sʌbˌplɒt) *n.* a subordinate or auxiliary plot in a novel, play, film, etc.

sub·poe·na (səb'piːnə) *n.* **1.** a writ issued by a court of justice requiring a person to appear before the court at a specified time. ~*vb.* **·nas, ·na·ing, ·naed. 2.** (*tr.*) to serve with a subpoena. [C15: from Latin: under penalty]

sub·pop·u·la·tion (ˌsʌbpɒpjʊ'leɪʃən) *n. Statistics.* a subgroup of a statistical population.

sub·prin·ci·pal (sʌb'prɪnsɪpᵊl) *n.* a vice-principal in a college, etc.

sub·re·gion (sʌb'riːdʒən) *n.* a subdivision of a region, esp. a zoogeographical or ecological region. **—sub·'re·gion·al** *adj.*

sub·rep·tion (səb'rɛpʃən) *n.* **1.** the concealment of facts in order to obtain an ecclesiastical dispensation. Compare **obreption. 2.** any deceitful misrepresentation or concealment of facts. [C17: from Latin *subreptiō* theft, from *subripere,* from *sub-* secretly + *rapere* to seize] **—sub·rep·ti·tious** (ˌsʌbrɛp'tɪʃəs) *adj.*

sub·ro·gate ('sʌbrəˌgeɪt) *vb.* (*tr.*) *Law.* to put (one person or thing) in the place of another in respect of a right or claim. [C16: from Latin *subrogāre,* from *sub-* in place of + *rogāre* to ask]

sub·ro·ga·tion (ˌsʌbrə'geɪʃən) *n. Law.* the substitution of one person or thing for another, esp. the placing of a surety who has paid the debt in the place of the creditor, entitling him to payment from the original debtor.

sub ro·sa ('rəʊzə) *adv.* in secret. [Latin, literally: under the rose; from the rose that, in ancient times, was hung over the council table, as a token of secrecy]

sub·rou·tine ('sʌbruːˌtiːn) *n.* a section of a computer program that is stored only once but can be used when required at several different points in the program, thus saving space. Also called: **procedure.**

sub·scap·u·lar (sʌb'skæpjʊlə) *adj.* **1.** (of a muscle or artery) situated beneath the scapula. ~*n.* **2.** any subscapular muscle or artery.

sub·scribe (səb'skraɪb) *vb.* **1.** (usually foll. by *to*) to pay or promise to pay (a sum of money) as a contribution (to a fund or charity, for a magazine, etc.), esp. at regular intervals. **2.** to inscribe or sign (one's name, etc.) at the end of a contract, will, or other document. **3.** (*intr.*; foll. by *to*) to give support or approval: *to subscribe to the theory of transubstantiation.* [C15: from Latin *subscrībere* to write underneath, from SUB- + *scrībere* to write] **—sub·'scrib·er** *n.*

sub·scrib·er trunk di·al·ling *n. Brit.* a service by which telephone subscribers can obtain trunk calls by dialling direct without the aid of an operator. Abbrev.: **STD.** U.S. equivalent: **direct distance dialing.**

sub·script ('sʌbskrɪpt) *adj.* **1.** *Printing.* (of a character) written or printed below the base line. Compare **superscript.** ~*n.* **2.** Also called: **subindex.** a subscript character.

sub·scrip·tion (səb'skrɪpʃən) *n.* **1.** a payment or promise of payment for consecutive issues of a magazine, newspaper, book, etc., over a specified period of time. **2.** an amount of money paid or promised, as to a charity, or the fund raised in this way. **3.** an offer to buy shares or bonds issued by a company. **4.** the act of signing one's name to a document, etc. **5.** a signature or other appendage attached to the bottom of a document, etc. **6.** agreement, consent, or acceptance expressed by or as if by signing one's name. **7.** a signed document, statement, etc. **8.** *Chiefly Brit.* the membership dues or fees paid to a society or club. **9.** *Ecclesiast.* acceptance of a fixed body of articles of faith, doctrines, or principles laid down as universally binding upon all the members of a Church. **10.** *Med.* that part of a written prescription directing the pharmacist how to mix and prepare the ingredients: rarely seen today as modern drugs are mostly prepackaged by the manufacturers. **11.** an advance order for a new product. **12. a.** the sale of books, etc., prior to printing. **b.** (*as modifier*): *a subscription edition.* **13.** *Archaic.* allegiance; submission. Abbrev.: **sub. —sub·'scrip·tive** *adj.* **—sub·'scrip·tive·ly** *adv.*

sub·scrip·tion con·cert *n.* (esp. in the U.S.) one of a series of concerts for which a subscription ticket is sold in advance for the entire series.

sub·scrip·tion li·brar·y *n.* a commercial lending library.

sub·sel·li·um (sʌb'sɛlɪəm) *n.* a rare word for **misericord** (sense 1). [C19: from Latin, from SUB- + *sella* seat]

sub·se·quence ('sʌbsɪkwəns) *n.* **1.** the fact or state of being subsequent. **2.** a subsequent incident or occurrence.

sub·se·quent ('sʌbsɪkwənt) *adj.* occurring after; succeeding. [C15: from Latin *subsequēns* following on, from *subsequī,* from *sub-* near + *sequī* to follow] **—'sub·se·quent·ly** *adv.* **—'sub·se·quent·ness** *n.*

sub·serve (səb'sɜːv) *vb.* (*tr.*) **1.** to be helpful or useful to. **2.** *Obsolete.* to be subordinate to. [C17: from Latin *subservīre* to be subject to, from SUB- + *servīre* to serve]

sub·ser·vi·ent (səb'sɜːvɪənt) *adj.* **1.** obsequious in behaviour or attitude. **2.** serving as a means to an end. **3.** a less common word for **subordinate** (sense 2). [C17: from Latin *subserviēns* complying with, from *subservīre* to SUBSERVE] **—sub·'ser·vi·ent·ly** *adv.* **—sub·'ser·vi·ence, sub·'ser·vi·en·cy,** *or* **sub·'ser·vi·ent·ness** *n.*

sub·set ('sʌbˌsɛt) *n.* **1.** a mathematical set contained within a larger set: *A is a subset of B, usually written* $A \supset B$. **2.** a set within a larger set.

sub·shrub ('sʌbˌʃrʌb) *n.* a small bushy plant that is woody except for the tips of the branches. **—'sub·ˌshrub·by** *adj.*

sub·side (səb'saɪd) *vb.* (*intr.*) **1.** to become less loud, excited, violent, etc.; abate. **2.** to sink or fall to a lower level. **3.** (of the surface of the earth, etc.) to cave in; collapse. **4.** (of sediment, etc.) to sink or descend to the bottom; settle. [C17: from Latin *subsīdere* to settle down, from *sub-* down + *sīdere* to settle] **—sub·'sid·er** *n.*

sub·sid·ence (səb'saɪdᵊns, 'sʌbsɪdᵊns) *n.* **1.** the act or process of subsiding or the condition of having subsided. **2.** *Geology.* the gradual sinking of landforms to a lower level as a result of earth movements, mining operations, etc.

sub·sid·i·ar·ies (səb'sɪdɪərɪz) *pl. n. Printing, Brit.* a less common name for **back matter.**

sub·sid·i·ar·y (səb'sɪdɪərɪ) *adj.* **1.** serving to aid or supplement; auxiliary. **2.** of lesser importance; subordinate in function. ~*n., pl.* **·ar·ies. 3.** a person who or thing that is subsidiary. **4.** short for **subsidiary company.** [C16: from Latin *subsidiārius* supporting, from *subsidium* SUBSIDY] **—sub·'sid·i·ar·i·ly** *adv.* **—sub·'sid·i·ar·i·ness** *n.*

sub·sid·i·ar·y coin *n.* a coin of denomination smaller than that of the standard monetary unit.

---

sub·'of·fice *n.*
sub·'of·fi·cer *n.*
ˌsub·of·'fi·cial *n.*
sub·'o·ral *adj.*
sub·'par·a·ˌgraph *n.*
'sub·ˌpart *n.*
ˌsub·par·'ti·tion *n.*
sub·'pat·tern *n.*
sub·'po·lar *adj.*
sub·'prov·ince *n.*
'sub·ˌrace *n.*
'sub·ˌrule *n.*
'sub·ˌsale *n.*
ˌsub·sat·u·'ra·tion *n.*
sub·'sched·ule *n.*
'sub·ˌsect *n.*

sub+sid·i+ar·y com+pa+ny *n.* a company with at least half of its capital stock owned by another company.

sub+si+dize *or* **sub+si+dise** ('sʌbsɪˌdaɪz) *vb.* (*tr.*) **1.** to aid or support with a subsidy. **2.** to obtain the aid of by means of a subsidy. —**ˌsub+si+'diz+a·ble** *or* **ˌsub+si+'dis+a·ble** *adj.* —**ˌsub+si+di+'za+tion** *or* **ˌsub+si+di+'sa+tion** *n.* —**'sub+si+ˌdiz+er** *or* **'sub+si+ˌdis+er** *n.*

sub+si+dy ('sʌbsɪdɪ) *n., pl.* **+dies.** **1.** a financial aid supplied by a government, as to industry, for reasons of public welfare, the balance of payments, etc. **2.** *English history.* a financial grant made originally for special purposes by Parliament to the Crown. **3.** any monetary aid, grant, or contribution. [C14: from Anglo-Norman *subsidie,* from Latin *subsidium* assistance, from *subsidēre* to remain, from *sub-* down + *sedēre* to sit]

sub+sist (səb'sɪst) *vb.* (*mainly intr.*) **1.** (often foll. by *on*) to be sustained; manage to live: *to subsist on milk.* **2.** to continue in existence. **3.** (foll. by *in*) to lie or reside by virtue (of); consist. **4.** *Philosophy.* **a.** to exist as a concept or relation rather than a fact. **b.** to be conceivable. **5.** (*tr.*) *Obsolete.* to provide with support. [C16: from Latin *subsistere* to stand firm, from *sub-* up + *sistere* to make a stand] —**sub+'sist+ent** *adj.* —**sub+'sist+er** *n.* —**sub+'sist+ing+ly** *adv.*

sub+sist+ence (səb'sɪstəns) *n.* **1.** the means by which one maintains life. **2.** the act or condition of subsisting. **3.** a thing that has real existence. **4.** the state of being inherent. **5.** *Philosophy.* the quality of having abstract, real, or timeless existence.

sub+sist+ence al+low+ance *n. Chiefly Brit.* **1.** an advance paid to an employee before his first regular payday. **2.** a payment to an employee made in order to reimburse expenses, as while on assignments.

sub+sist+ence farm+ing *n.* a type of farming in which most of the produce is consumed by the farmer and his family, leaving little or nothing to be marketed.

sub+sist+ence lev+el *n.* a standard of living barely adequate to support life.

sub+so+cial (sʌb'səʊʃəl) *adj.* lacking a complex or definite social structure. —**sub+'so+cial+ly** *adv.*

sub+soil ('sʌbˌsɔɪl) *n.* **1. a.** Also called: **undersoil.** the layer of soil beneath the surface soil and overlying the bedrock. **b.** (*as modifier*): *a subsoil plough.* ~*vb.* **2.** (*tr.*) to plough (land) to a depth below the normal ploughing level and so break up the subsoil. —**'sub+ˌsoil+er** *n.*

sub+so+lar (sʌb'səʊlə) *adj.* **1.** (of a point on the earth's surface) located directly below the sun. **2.** situated between the tropics; equatorial.

sub+son+ic (sʌb'sɒnɪk) *adj.* being, having, or travelling at a velocity below that of sound: *a subsonic aircraft.*

sub+spe+cies ('sʌbˌspi:ʃi:z) *n., pl.* **+cies.** *Biology.* a taxonomic group that is a subdivision of a species: usually occurs because of isolation within a species. —**sub+spe+cif+ic** (ˌsʌbspɪ'sɪfɪk) *adj.* —**ˌsub+spe+'cif·i+cal+ly** *adv.*

subst. *abbrev. for:* **1.** substantive. **2.** substitute.

sub+stage ('sʌbˌsteɪdʒ) *n.* the part of a microscope below the stage, usually consisting of an adjustable assembly holding a condenser lens for illuminating the specimen.

sub+stance ('sʌbstəns) *n.* **1.** the tangible basic matter of which a thing consists. **2.** a specific type of matter, esp. a homogeneous material with definite or fairly definite chemical composition. **3.** the essence, meaning, etc., of a discourse, thought, or written article. **4.** solid or meaningful quality: *an education of substance.* **5.** material density or body: *a vacuum has no substance.* **6.** material possessions or wealth: *a man of substance.* **7.** *Philosophy.* **a.** the essence of anything. **b.** the basic element of anything that can receive modifications and in which attributes and accidents inhere. **c.** a thing considered as a continuing whole. **8.** *Christian Science.* that which is eternal. **9. in substance.** with regard to the salient points. [C13: via Old French from Latin *substantia,* from *substāre,* from SUB- + *stāre* to stand] —**'sub+stance+less** *adj.*

sub+stand+ard (sʌb'stændəd) *adj.* **1.** below an established or required standard. **2.** another word for **nonstandard.**

sub+stan+tial (səb'stænʃəl) *adj.* **1.** of a considerable size or value: *substantial funds.* **2.** worthwhile; important; of telling effect: *a substantial reform.* **3.** having wealth or importance: *a substantial member of the community.* **4.** (of food or a meal) sufficient and nourishing. **5.** solid or strong in construction, quality, or character: *a substantial door.* **6.** real; actual; true: *such evidence cannot be considered substantial.* **7.** of or relating to the basic or fundamental substance or aspects of a thing. **8.** *Philosophy.* of or relating to substance rather than to attributes, accidents, or modifications. ~*n.* **9.** (*often pl.*) *Rare.* an essential or important element. —**sub+stan+ti+al+i+ty** (səbˌstænʃɪ'ælɪtɪ) *or* **sub+'stan+tial+ness** *n.* —**sub+'stan+tial+ly** *adv.*

sub+stan+tial+ism (səb'stænʃəˌlɪzəm) *n. Philosophy.* **1.** the doctrine that a substantial reality underlies phenomena. **2.** the doctrine that matter is a real substance. —**sub+'stan+tial+ist** *n.*

sub+stan+tial+ize *or* **sub+stan+tial+ise** (səb'stænʃəˌlaɪz) *vb.* to make or become substantial or actual.

sub+stan+ti+ate (səb'stænʃɪˌeɪt) *vb.* (*tr.*) **1.** to establish as valid or genuine. **2.** to give form or real existence to. [C17: from New Latin *substantiāre,* from Latin *substantia* SUBSTANCE] —**sub+ˌstan+ti+'a+tion** *n.* —**sub+'stan+ti·a+tive** *adj.* —**sub+'stan+ti·ˌa+tor** *n.*

sub+stan+tive ('sʌbstəntɪv) *n.* **1.** *Grammar.* a noun or pronoun used in place of a noun. ~*adj.* **2.** of, relating to, containing, or being the essential element of a thing. **3.** having independent function, resources, or existence. **4.** of substantial quantity. **5.** solid in foundation or basis. **6.** *Grammar.* denoting, relating to, or standing in place of a noun. **7.** relating to the essential legal principles administered by the courts, as opposed to practice and procedure. Compare **adjective** (sense 3). **8.** (of a dye or colour) staining the material directly without use of a mordant. ~Abbrev.: **s., sb., subst.** [C15: from Late Latin *substantīvus,* from Latin *substāre* to stand beneath; see SUBSTANCE] —**sub+stan+ti+val** (ˌsʌbstən'taɪvᵊl) *adj.* —**ˌsub+stan+'ti+val+ly** *adv.* —**'sub+stan+tive+ly** *adv.* —**'sub+stan+tive+ness** *n.*

sub+stan+tive rank *n.* a permanent rank in the armed services obtained by length of service, selection, etc.

sub+stan+tiv+ize *or* **sub+stan+tiv+ise** ('sʌbstəntɪˌvaɪz) *vb.* (*tr.*) to make (a word other than a noun) play the grammatical role of a noun in a sentence. —**ˌsub+stan+ti+vi+'za+tion** *or* **ˌsub+stan+ti+vi+'sa+tion** *n.*

sub+sta+tion ('sʌbˌsteɪʃən) *n.* **1.** a subsidiary station. **2.** an installation at which electrical energy is received from one or more power stations for conversion from alternating to direct current, stepping down the voltage, or switching before distribution by a low-tension network.

sub+stit·u+ent (sʌb'stɪtjʊənt) *n.* **1.** *Chem.* an atom or group that replaces another atom or group in a molecule or can be regarded as replacing an atom in a parent compound. ~*adj.* **2.** substituted or substitutable. [C19: from Latin *substituere* to SUBSTITUTE]

sub+sti+tute ('sʌbstɪˌtju:t) *vb.* **1.** (often foll. by *for*) to serve or cause to serve in place of another person or thing. **2.** *Chem.* to replace (an atom or group in a molecule) with (another atom or group). ~*n.* **3. a.** a person or thing that serves in place of another, such as a player in a game who takes the place of an injured colleague. **b.** (*as modifier*): *a substitute goalkeeper.* Often shortened to **sub.** **4.** *Grammar.* another name for **pro-form.** **5.** *Nautical.* another word for **repeater** (sense 5). **6.** (formerly) a person paid to replace another due for military service. [C16: from Latin *substituere,* from *sub-* in place of + *statuere* to set up] —**ˌsub+sti+'tut+a·ble** *adj.* —**ˌsub+sti+ˌtut·a+'bil+i·ty** *n.*

sub+sti+tu+tion (ˌsʌbstɪ'tju:ʃən) *n.* **1.** the act of substituting or state of being substituted. **2.** something or someone substituted.

sub+sti+tu+tive ('sʌbstɪˌtju:tɪv) *adj.* **1.** acting or able to act as a substitute. **2.** of, relating to, or involving substitution. —**'sub+sti+ˌtu+tive+ly** *adv.*

sub+strate ('sʌbstreɪt) *n.* **1.** *Biochem.* the substance upon which an enzyme acts. **2.** another word for **substratum.**

sub+stra+tum (sʌb'strɑ:təm, -'streɪ-) *n., pl.* **+stra+ta** (-'strɑ:tə, -'streɪtə). **1.** any layer or stratum lying underneath another. **2.** a basis or foundation; groundwork. **3.** the nonliving material on which an animal or plant grows or lives. **4.** *Geology.* **a.** the solid rock underlying soils, gravels, etc.; bedrock. **b.** the layer of soil beneath the surface layer; subsoil. **5.** *Sociol.* any of several subdivisions or grades within a stratum. **6.** *Photog.* a binding layer by which an emulsion is made to adhere to a glass or film base. Sometimes shortened to **sub.** **7.** *Philosophy.* substance considered as that in which attributes and accidents inhere. **8.** *Linguistics.* the language of an indigenous population when replaced by the language of a conquering or colonizing population, esp. as it influences the form of the dominant language or of any mixed languages arising from their contact. Compare **superstratum.** [C17: from New Latin, from Latin *substrātus* strewn beneath, from *substernere* to spread under, from SUB- + *sternere* to spread] —**sub+'stra+tive** *or* **sub+'stra+tal** *adj.*

sub+struc+ture ('sʌbˌstrʌktʃə) *or* **sub+struc+tion** (sʌb'strʌkʃən) *n.* **1.** a structure, pattern, etc., that forms the basis of anything. **2.** a structure forming a foundation or framework for a building or other construction. —**sub+'struc+tur+al** *or* **sub+'struc+tion+al** *adj.*

sub+sume (səb'sju:m) *vb.* (*tr.*) **1.** to incorporate (an idea, proposition, case, etc.) under a comprehensive or inclusive classification or heading. **2.** to consider (an instance of something) as part of a general rule or principle. [C16: from New Latin *subsumere,* from Latin SUB- + *sumere* to take] —**sub+'sum+a·ble** *adj.*

sub+sump+tion (səb'sʌmpʃən) *n.* **1.** the act of subsuming or the state of being subsumed. **2.** *Logic.* an idea, concept, etc., subsumed under another, esp. the minor premiss of a syllogism. —**sub+'sump+tive** *adj.*

sub+tan+gent (sʌb'tændʒənt) *n. Geom.* a segment of the *x*-axis between the *x*-coordinate of the point of contact of a tangent to a curve and the intercept of the tangent on the axis.

sub+teen (ˌsʌb'ti:n) *n. U.S. informal.* a young person who has not yet become a teenager.

sub+tem+per+ate (sʌb'tɛmpərɪt) *adj.* of or relating to the colder temperate regions.

sub+ten+ant (sʌb'tɛnənt) *n.* a person who rents or leases property from a tenant. —**sub+'ten+an+cy** *n.*

sub+tend (səb'tɛnd) *vb.* (*tr.*) **1.** *Geom.* to be opposite to and delimit (an angle or side). **2.** (of a bract, stem, etc.) to have (a bud or similar part) growing in its axil. **3.** to mark off. **4.** to underlie; be inherent in. [C16: from Latin *subtendere* to extend beneath, from SUB- + *tendere* to stretch out]

---

sub+'sec+tion *n.*
sub+'seg+ment *n.*
sub+'se+ries *n., pl.* +ries.
sub+'sur+face *adj.*
'sub+ˌsys+tem *n.*
'sub+ˌtribe *n.*
'sub+ˌu+nit *n.*
ˌsub+va+'ri+e+ty *n., pl.* ·ties.

sub+ter+fuge ('sʌbtəˌfjuːdʒ) *n.* a stratagem employed to conceal something, evade an argument, etc. [C16: from Late Latin *subterfugium,* from Latin *subterfugere* to escape by stealth, from *subter* secretly + *fugere* to flee]

sub+term·i+nal (sʌb'tɜːmɪnᵊl) *adj.* almost at an end.

sub+ter+nat·u+ral (ˌsʌbtə'nætʃərəl, -'nætʃrəl) *adj. Rare.* falling below what is accepted as natural; less than natural.

sub+ter+ra+ne·an (ˌsʌbtə'reɪnɪən) *adj.* **1.** Also: **sub+ter+res+tri·al.** situated, living, or operating below the surface of the earth. **2.** existing or operating in concealment. [C17: from Latin *subterrāneus,* from SUB- + *terra* earth] —**ˌsub+ter+'ra+ne·an+ly** *or* **ˌsub+ter+'ra+ne·ous+ly** *adv.*

sub+tile ('sʌtᵊl) *adj.* a rare spelling of **subtle.** —**'sub+tile+ly** *adv.* —**sub+til+i·ty** (sʌb'tɪlɪtɪ) *or* **'sub+tile+ness** *n.* —**'sub+til+ty** *n.*

sub+til+ize *or* **sub+til+ise** ('sʌtɪˌlaɪz) *vb.* **1.** (*tr.*) to bring to a purer state; refine. **2.** to debate subtly. **3.** (*tr.*) to make (the mind, etc.) keener. —**ˌsub+til·i+'za+tion** *or* **ˌsub+til·i+'sa+tion** *n.* —**'sub+til+ˌiz+er** *or* **'sub+til+ˌis+er** *n.*

sub+ti+tle ('sʌbˌtaɪtᵊl) *n.* **1.** an additional subordinate title given to a literary or other work. **2.** (*often pl.*) Also called: **caption.** *Films.* **a.** a written translation superimposed on a film that has foreign dialogue. **b.** explanatory text on a silent film. ~*vb.* **3.** (*tr.; usually passive*) to provide a subtitle for. —**sub+tit·u+lar** (sʌb'tɪtjulə, -'tɪtʃə-) *adj.*

sub+tle ('sʌtᵊl) *adj.* **1.** not immediately obvious or comprehensible. **2.** difficult to detect or analyse, often through being delicate or highly refined: *a subtle scent.* **3.** showing or making or capable of showing or making fine distinctions of meaning. **4.** marked by or requiring mental acuteness or ingenuity; discriminating. **5.** delicate or faint: *a subtle shade.* **6.** cunning or wily: *a subtle rogue.* **7.** operating or executed in secret: *a subtle intrigue.* [C14: from Old French *soutil,* from Latin *subtīlis* finely woven] —**'sub+tle+ness** *n.* —**'sub+tly** *adv.*

sub+tle+ty ('sʌtᵊltɪ) *n., pl.* **+ties. 1.** the state or quality of being subtle; delicacy. **2.** a fine distinction or the ability to make such a distinction. **3.** something subtle.

sub+ton+ic (sʌb'tɒnɪk) *n. Music.* the seventh degree of a major or minor scale. Also called: **leading note.**

sub+tor+rid (sʌb'tɒrɪd) *adj.* a less common word for **subtropical.**

sub+to+tal (sʌb'təutᵊl, 'sʌbˌtəutᵊl) *n.* **1.** the total made up by a column of figures, etc., forming part of the total made up by a larger column or group. ~*vb.* **+tals, +tal+ling, +talled** *or U.S.* **+tals, +tal+ing, +taled. 2.** to establish or work out a subtotal for (a column, group, etc.).

sub+tract (səb'trækt) *vb.* **1.** to calculate the difference between (two numbers or quantities) by subtraction. **2.** to remove (a part of a thing, quantity, etc.) from the whole. [C16: from Latin *subtractus* withdrawn, from *subtrahere* to draw away from beneath, from SUB- + *trahere* to draw] —**sub+'tract+er** *n.*

sub+trac+tion (səb'trækʃən) *n.* **1.** the act or process of subtracting. **2.** a mathematical operation in which the difference between two numbers or quantities is calculated. Usually indicated by the symbol (−).

sub+trac+tive (səb'træktɪv) *adj.* **1.** able or tending to remove or subtract. **2.** indicating or requiring subtraction; having a minus sign: *−x is a subtractive quantity.*

sub+trac+tive pro+cess *n.* a photographic process in which colours are reproduced on a transparency or print by a mixture of the three subtractive colours, yellow, magenta, and cyan.

sub+tra+hend ('sʌbtrəˌhɛnd) *n.* the number to be subtracted from another number (the **minuend**). [C17: from Latin *subtrahendus,* from *subtrahere* to SUBTRACT]

sub+treas+ur·y (sʌb'trɛʒərɪ) *n. pl.* **+ur·ies.** *U.S.* a branch treasury. —**sub+'treas+ur+er** *n.* —**sub+'treas+ur+er+ˌship** *n.*

sub+trop+ics (sʌb'trɒpɪks) *pl. n.* the region lying between the tropics and temperate lands. —**sub+'trop·i+cal** *adj.*

sub+type ('sʌbˌtaɪp) *n.* a secondary or subordinate type or genre, esp. a specific one considered as falling under a general classification. —**sub+typ·i+cal** (sʌb'tɪpɪkᵊl) *adj.*

su+bu+late ('suːbjəlɪt, -ˌleɪt) *adj.* (esp. of plant parts) tapering to a point; awl-shaped. [C18: from New Latin *subulatus* like an awl, from Latin *sūbula* awl]

sub+urb ('sʌbɜːb) *n.* a residential district situated on the outskirts of a city or town. [C14: from Latin *suburbium,* from *sub-* close to + *urbs* a city] —**'sub+urbed** *adj.*

sub+ur+ban (sə'bɜːbᵊn) *adj.* **1.** of, relating to, situated in, or inhabiting a suburb or the suburbs. **2.** characteristic of or typifying a suburb or the suburbs. **3.** *Mildly derogatory.* narrow or unadventurous in outlook. ~*n.* **4.** another word for **suburbanite.**

sub+ur+ban+ite (sə'bɜːbəˌnaɪt) *n.* a person who lives in a suburb.

sub+ur+ban+ize *or* **sub+ur+ban+ise** (sʌ'bɜːbəˌnaɪz) *vb.* (*tr.*) to make suburban.

sub+ur+bi·a (sə'bɜːbɪə) *n.* **1.** suburbs or the people living in them considered as an identifiable community or class in society. **2.** the life, customs, etc., of suburbanites.

sub+ur+bi+car+i·an (səˌbɜːbɪ'kɛərɪən) *adj. R.C. Church.* situated near the city of Rome: used esp. of the dioceses surrounding Rome. [C17: from Late Latin *suburbicārius,* from *suburbium* SUBURB]

sub+vene (səb'viːn) *vb.* (*intr.*) *Rare.* to happen in such a way as to be of assistance, esp. in preventing something. [C18: from Latin *subvenīre,* from *venīre* to come]

sub+ven+tion (səb'vɛnʃən) *n.* **1.** a grant, aid, or subsidy, as from a government to an educational institution. **2.** the act or process of providing aid or help of any sort. [C15: from Late Latin *subventiō* assistance, from Latin *subvenīre* to SUBVENE] —**sub+'ven+tion+ar·y** *adj.*

sub+ver+sion (səb'vɜːʃən) *n.* **1.** the act or an instance of subverting or overthrowing a legally constituted government, institution, etc. **2.** the state of being subverted; destruction or ruin. **3.** something that brings about an overthrow. [C14: from Late Latin *subversiō* destruction, from Latin *subvertere* to SUBVERT]

sub+ver+sive (səb'vɜːsɪv) *adj.* **1.** liable to subvert or overthrow a government, legally constituted institution, etc. ~*n.* **2.** a person engaged in subversive activities, etc. —**sub+'ver+sive+ly** *adv.* —**sub+'ver+sive+ness** *n.*

sub+vert (səb'vɜːt) *vb.* (*tr.*) **1.** to bring about the complete downfall or ruin of (something existing or established by a system of law, etc.). **2.** to undermine the moral principles of (a person, etc.); corrupt. [C14: from Latin *subvertere* to overturn, from *sub-* from below + *vertere* to turn] —**sub+'vert+er** *n.*

sub+way ('sʌbˌweɪ) *n.* **1.** *Brit.* an underground passage or tunnel enabling pedestrians to cross a road, railway, etc. **2.** an underground passage or tunnel for traffic, electric power supplies, etc. **3.** *U.S.* an underground railway.

sub+zer·o (sʌb'zɪərəu) *adj.* (esp. of temperature) lower or less than zero.

suc+ce+da+ne·um (ˌsʌksɪ'deɪnɪəm) *n., pl.* **+ne·a** (-nɪə). something that is used as a substitute, esp. any medical drug or agent that may be taken or prescribed in place of another. [C17: from Latin *succēdāneus* following after, from *succēdere* to SUCCEED] —**ˌsuc+ce+'da+ne·ous** *adj.*

suc+ceed (sək'siːd) *vb.* **1.** (*intr.*) to accomplish an aim, esp. in the manner desired: *he succeeded in winning.* **2.** (*intr.*) to happen in the manner desired: *the plan succeeded.* **3.** (*intr.*) to acquit oneself satisfactorily or do well, as in a specified field: *to succeed in publishing.* **4.** (when *intr.,* often foll. by *to*) to come next in order (after someone or something). **5.** (when *intr.,* often foll. by *to*) to take over an office, post, etc. (from a person): *he succeeded to the vice presidency.* **6.** (*intr.;* usually foll. by *to*) to come into possession (of property, etc.); inherit. **7.** (*intr.*) to have a result according to a specified manner: *the plan succeeded badly.* **8.** (*intr.*) to devolve upon: *the estate succeeded to his son.* [C15: from Latin *succēdere* to follow after, from *sub-* after + *cēdere* to go] —**suc+'ceed·a·ble** *adj.* —**suc+'ceed+er** *n.* —**suc+'ceed+ing+ly** *adv.*

suc+cen+tor (sək'sɛntə) *n.* the deputy of the precentor of a cathedral that has retained its statutes from pre-Reformation days. [C17: from Late Latin: one who accompanies singing, from *succinere* to accompany, from Latin *canere* to sing] —**suc+'cen+tor+ship** *n.*

suc+cess (sək'sɛs) *n.* **1.** the favourable outcome of something attempted. **2.** the attainment of wealth, fame, etc. **3.** an action, performance, etc., that is characterized by success. **4.** a person or thing that is successful. **5.** *Obsolete.* any outcome. [C16: from Latin *successus* an outcome, from *succēdere* to SUCCEED] —**suc+'cess+less** *adj.*

suc+cess+ful (sək'sɛsfʊl) *adj.* **1.** having succeeded in one's endeavours. **2.** marked by a favourable outcome. **3.** having obtained fame, wealth, etc. —**suc+'cess+ful+ly** *adv.* —**suc+'cess+ful+ness** *n.*

suc+ces+sion (sək'sɛʃən) *n.* **1.** the act or an instance of one person or thing following another. **2.** a number of people or things following one another in order. **3.** the act, process, or right by which one person succeeds to the office, etc., of another. **4.** the order that determines how one person or thing follows another. **5.** a line of descent to a title, etc. **6.** *Ecology.* the sum of the changes in the composition of a community that occur during its development towards a stable climax community. **7. in succession.** in a manner such that one thing is followed uninterruptedly by another. [C14: from Latin *successio,* from *succēdere* to SUCCEED] —**suc+'ces+sion+al** *adj.* —**suc+'ces+sion+al+ly** *adv.*

suc+ces+sion state *n.* any of a number of usually new states that are established in or expand over the territory formerly ruled by one large state: *Czechoslovakia is a succession state of the Austro-Hungarian monarchy.*

suc+ces+sive (sək'sɛsɪv) *adj.* **1.** following another without interruption. **2.** of or involving succession: *a successive process.* —**suc+'ces+sive+ly** *adv.* —**suc+'ces+sive+ness** *n.*

suc+ces+sor (sək'sɛsə) *n.* a person or thing that follows, esp. a person who succeeds another in an office. —**suc+'ces+sor+al** *adj.*

suc+cin+ate ('sʌksɪˌneɪt) *n.* any salt or ester of succinic acid. [C18: from SUCCIN(IC) + -ATE[2]]

suc+cinct (sək'sɪŋkt) *adj.* **1.** marked by brevity and clarity; concise. **2.** compressed into a small area. **3.** *Archaic.* **a.** encircled by or as if by a girdle. **b.** drawn up tightly; closely fitting. [C15: from Latin *succinctus* girt about, from *succingere* to gird from below, from *sub-* from below + *cingere* to gird] —**suc+'cinct+ly** *adv.* —**suc+'cinct+ness** *n.*

suc+cin+ic (sʌk'sɪnɪk) *adj.* **1.** of, relating to, or obtained from amber. **2.** of, consisting of, containing, or derived from succinic acid. [C18: from French *succinique,* from Latin *succinum* amber]

suc+cin+ic ac·id *n.* a colourless odourless water-soluble dicarboxylic acid found in plant and animal tissues: used in making lacquers, dyes, perfumes, etc.; 1,4-butanedioic acid. Formula: $HOOCCH_2{:}CH_2COOH$.

suc+cor·y ('sʌkərɪ) *n., pl.* **+cor·ies.** another name for **chicory.** [C16: variant of *cicoree* CHICORY; related to Middle Low German *suckerie,* Dutch *suikerei*]

suc+co+tash ('sʌkəˌtæʃ) *n. U.S.* a mixture of cooked sweet corn kernels and lima beans, served as a vegetable. [C18: from Narragansett *msiquatash*, literally: broken pieces]

Suc+coth ('sukəut, -kəuθ; *Hebrew* suː'kɔt) *n.* a variant spelling of **Sukkoth.**

suc+cour *or U.S.* **suc+cor** ('sʌkə) *n.* **1.** help or assistance, esp. in time of difficulty. **2.** a person or thing that provides help. ~*vb.* **3.** (*tr.*) to give aid to. [C13: from Old French *sucurir*, from Latin *succurrere* to hurry to help, from *sub-* under + *currere* to run] —**'suc+cour+a·ble** *or U.S.* **'suc+cor+a·ble** *adj.* —**'suc+cour+er** *or U.S.* **'suc+cor+er** *n.* —**'suc+cour+less** *or U.S.* **'suc+cor+less** *adj.*

suc+cu+bus ('sʌkjubəs) *n., pl.* **+bi** (-ˌbaɪ). **1.** Also: **succuba.** a female demon fabled to have sexual intercourse with sleeping men. Compare **incubus. 2.** any evil demon. [C16: from Medieval Latin, from Late Latin *succuba* harlot, from Latin *succubāre* to lie beneath, from SUB- + *cubāre* to lie]

suc+cu+lent ('sʌkjulənt) *adj.* **1.** abundant in juices; juicy. **2.** (of plants) having thick fleshy leaves or stems. **3.** *Informal.* stimulating interest, desire, etc. ~*n.* **4.** a plant that is able to exist in arid conditions by using water stored in its fleshy tissues. [C17: from Latin *succulentus*, from *sūcus* juice] —**'suc+cu+lence** *or* **'suc+cu+len+cy** *n.* —**'suc+cu+lent+ly** *adv.*

suc+cumb (sə'kʌm) *vb.* (*intr.*; often foll. by *to*) **1.** to give way in face of the overwhelming force (of) or desire (for). **2.** to be fatally overwhelmed (by disease, old age, etc.); die (of). [C15: from Latin *succumbere* to be overcome, from SUB- + *-cumbere* from *cubāre* to lie down] —**suc+'cumb+er** *n.*

suc+cur+sal (sʌ'kɜːsəl) *adj.* **1.** (esp. of a religious establishment) subsidiary. ~*n.* **2.** a subsidiary establishment. [C19: from French, from Medieval Latin *succursus*, from Latin *succurrere* to SUCCOUR]

suc+cuss (sʌ'kʌs) *vb.* **1.** *Med.* to shake (a patient) to detect the sound of fluid in the thoracic or another bodily cavity. **2.** *Rare.* to shake, esp. with sudden force. [C17: from Latin *succussus* flung aloft, from *succutere* to toss up, from *sub-* from below + *quatere* to shake] —**suc+cus+sion** (sʌ'kʌʃən) *n.* —**suc+'cus+sive** *adj.*

such (sʌtʃ) (often foll. by a corresponding subordinate clause introduced by *that* or *as*) ~*determiner.* **1. a.** of the sort specified or understood: *such books shouldn't be sold here.* **b.** (*as pronoun*): *such is life; robbers, rapists, and such.* **2.** so great; so much: *such a help; I've never seen such weeping.* **3. a. as such.** in the capacity previously specified or understood: *a judge as such hasn't so much power.* **b.** in itself or themselves: *intelligence as such can't guarantee success.* **4. such and such.** specific, but not known or named: *at such and such a time.* **5. such as. a.** for example: *animals, such as elephants and tigers.* **b.** of a similar kind as; like: *people such as your friend John make me angry.* **c.** of the (usually small) amount, etc.: *the food, such as there was, was excellent.* **6. such that.** so that: used to express purpose or result: *power such that it was effortless.* ~*adv.* **7.** (intensifier): *such nice people; such a nice person that I gave him a present.* [Old English *swilc;* related to Old Frisian *sālik*, Old Norse *slīkr*, Gothic *swaleiks*, Old High German *sulih*]

such+like ('sʌtʃˌlaɪk) *adj.* **1.** (*prenominal*) of such a kind; similar: *John, Ken, and other suchlike idiots.* ~*n.* **2.** such or similar persons or things: *hyenas, jackals, and suchlike.*

Su-chou ('suː'tʃau) *n.* a variant spelling of **Soochow.**

Sü+chow *or* **Hsü-chou** ('ʃuː'tʃau) *n.* a city in N central China, in NW Kiangsu province: scene of a decisive battle (1949) in which the Communists defeated the Nationalists. Pop.: 700 000 (1970 est.).

suck (sʌk) *vb.* **1.** to draw (a liquid or other substance) into the mouth by creating a partial vacuum in the mouth. **2.** to draw in (fluid, etc.) by or as if by a similar action: *plants suck moisture from the soil.* **3.** to drink milk from (a mother's breast); suckle. **4.** (*tr.*) to extract fluid content from (a solid food): *to suck a lemon.* **5.** (*tr.*) to take into the mouth and moisten, dissolve, or roll around with the tongue: *to suck one's thumb.* **6.** (*tr.*; often foll. by *down, in,* etc.) to draw by using irresistible force: *the whirlpool sucked him down.* **7.** (*intr.*) (of a pump) to draw in air because of a low supply level or leaking valves, pipes, etc. **8.** (*tr.*) to assimilate or acquire (knowledge, comfort, etc.). ~*n.* **9.** the act or an instance of sucking. **10.** something that is sucked, esp. milk from the mother's breast. **11. give suck to.** to give (a baby or young animal) milk from the breast or udder. **12.** an attracting or sucking force: *the suck of the whirlpool was very strong.* **13.** a sound caused by sucking. ~See also **suck in, suck off, suck up to.** [Old English *sūcan;* related to Old Norse *súga*, Middle Dutch *sūgen*, Latin *sūgere* to suck, exhaust; see SOAK] —**'suck+less** *adj.*

suck+er ('sʌkə) *n.* **1.** a person or thing that sucks. **2.** *Slang.* a person who is easily deceived or swindled. **3.** *Slang.* a person who cannot resist the attractions of a particular type of person or thing: *he's a sucker for blondes.* **4.** a young animal that is not yet weaned, esp. a suckling pig. **5.** *Zoology.* an organ that is specialized for sucking or adhering. **6.** a cup-shaped device, generally made of rubber, that may be attached to articles allowing them to adhere to a surface by suction. **7.** *Botany.* **a.** a strong shoot that arises in a mature plant from a root, rhizome, or the base of the main stem. **b.** a short branch of a parasitic plant that absorbs nutrients from the host. **8.** a pipe or tube through which a fluid is drawn by suction. **9.** any small mainly North American cyprinoid fish of the family *Catostomidae*, having toothless jaws and a large sucking mouth. **10.** any of certain fishes that have sucking discs, esp. the clingfish or sea snail. **11.** a piston in a suction pump or the valve in such a piston. ~*vb.* **12.** (*tr.*) to strip off the suckers from (a plant). **13.** (*intr.*) (of a plant) to produce suckers.

suck·er+fish ('sʌkəˌfɪʃ) *or* **suck+fish** *n., pl.* **+fish** *or* **+fish·es.** other names for **remora.**

suck in *vb.* (*adv.*) **1.** (*tr.*) to attract by using an inexorable force, inducement, etc.: *the current sucked him in.* **2.** to draw in (one's breath) sharply. **3.** (*tr.*) *Slang.* to deceive or defraud.

suck+ing ('sʌkɪŋ) *adj.* **1.** not yet weaned: *sucking pig.* **2.** not yet fledged: *sucking dove.*

suck+ing louse *n.* any insect of the order *Anoplura.* See **louse** (sense 1).

suck+le ('sʌkəl) *vb.* **1.** to give (a baby or young animal) milk from the breast or (of a baby, etc.) to suck milk from the breast. **2.** (*tr.*) to bring up; nurture. [C15: probably back formation from SUCKLING] —**'suck+ler** *n.*

suck+ling ('sʌklɪŋ) *n.* **1.** an infant or young animal that is still taking milk from the mother. **2.** a very young child. [C15: see SUCK, -LING[1]; related to Middle Dutch *sūgeling*, Middle High German *sögelinc*]

Suck·ling ('sʌklɪŋ) *n.* Sir **John.** 1609–42, English Cavalier poet and dramatist.

suck off *vb.* (*tr., adv.*) *Taboo slang.* to perform the act of fellatio or cunnilingus on.

sucks (sʌks) *interj. Slang.* **1.** an expression of disappointment. **2.** an exclamation of defiance or derision (esp. in the phrase **yah boo sucks to you**).

suck up to *vb.* (*intr., adv.* + *prep.*) *Informal.* to flatter for one's own profit; toady.

su+crase ('sjuːkreɪz) *n.* another name for **invertase.** [C19: from SUCRO- + -ASE]

su+cre (*Spanish* 'sukre) *n.* the standard monetary unit of Ecuador, divided into 100 centavos. [C19: after Antonio José de SUCRE]

Su+cre[1] (*Spanish* 'sukre) *n.* the legal capital of Bolivia, in the south central part of the country in the E Andes: university (1624). Pop.: 106 590 (1973 est.). Former name (until 1839): **Chuquisaca.**

Su+cre[2] (*Spanish* 'sukre) *n.* **An·to·nio Jo·sé de** (an'tonjo xo'se ðe). 1795–1830, South American liberator, born in Venezuela, who assisted Bolivar in the colonial revolt against Spain; first president of Bolivia (1826–28).

su+crose ('sjuːkrəuz, -krəus) *n.* the technical name for **sugar** (sense 1). [C19: SUCRO- + -OSE[2]]

suc+tion ('sʌkʃən) *n.* **1.** the act or process of sucking. **2.** the force or condition produced by a pressure difference, as the force holding a suction cap onto a surface. **3.** the act or process of producing such a force or condition. [C17: from Late Latin *suctiō* a sucking, from Latin *sūgere* to suck] —**'suc+tion+al** *adj.*

suc+tion pump *n.* a pump for raising water or a similar fluid by suction. It usually consists of a cylinder containing a piston fitted with a flap valve.

suc+tion stop *n. Phonetics.* another word for **click** (sense 3).

suc+to+ri+al (sʌk'tɔːrɪəl) *adj.* **1.** specialized for sucking or adhering: *the suctorial mouthparts of certain insects.* **2.** relating to or possessing suckers or suction. [C19: from New Latin *suctōrius*, from Latin *sūgere* to suck]

Su+dan (suː'dɑːn, -'dæn) *n.* **the. 1.** a republic in NE Africa, on the Red Sea: the largest country in Africa; conquered by Mehemet Ali of Egypt (1820–22) and made an Anglo-Egyptian condominium in 1899 after joint forces defeated the Mahdist revolt; became a republic in 1956. It consists mainly of a plateau, with the Nubian Desert in the north. Official language: Arabic. Religion: Muslim majority. Currency: Sudanese pound. Capital: Khartoum. Pop.: 14 171 732 (1973). Area: 2 505 805 sq. km (967 491 sq. miles). Former name (1899–1956): **Anglo-Egyptian Sudan.** French name: **Soudan. 2.** a region stretching across Africa south of the Sahara and north of the tropical zone: inhabited chiefly by Negro tribes rather than Arabs. —**Su+da+nese** (ˌsuːdəˈniːz) *adj., n.*

Su+dan+ic (suː'dænɪk) *n.* **1.** a group of languages spoken in scattered areas of the Sudan, most of which are now generally assigned to the Chari-Nile branch of the Nilo-Saharan family. ~*adj.* **2.** relating to or belonging to this group of languages. **3.** of or relating to the Sudan.

su+dar+i·um (sju'dɛərɪəm) *n., pl.* **+dar·i·a** (-'dɛərɪə). another word for **sudatorium** or **veronica**[2]. [C17: from Latin, from *sūdāre* to sweat]

su+da+to+ri+um (ˌsjuːdə'tɔːrɪəm) *or* **su+da+to·ry** *n. pl.* **+to·ri·a** (-'tɔːrɪə) *or* **+to·ries.** a room, esp. in a Roman bath house, where sweating is induced by heat. [C18: from Latin, from *sūdāre* to sweat]

su+da+to·ry ('sjuːdətərɪ, -trɪ) *adj.* **1.** relating to or producing sweating; sudorific. ~*n., pl.* **·ries. 2.** *Med.* a sudatory agent. **3.** another word for **sudatorium.**

Sud+bur·y ('sʌdbərɪ, -brɪ) *n.* a city in central Canada, in Ontario: a major nickel-mining centre. Pop.: 90 535 (1971).

sudd (sʌd) *n.* floating masses of reeds and weeds that occur on the White Nile and obstruct navigation. [C19: from Arabic, literally: obstruction]

sud+den ('sʌdən) *adj.* **1.** occurring or performed quickly and without warning. **2.** marked by haste; abrupt. **3.** *Rare.* rash; precipitate. ~*n.* **4.** *Archaic.* an abrupt occurrence or the occasion of such an occurrence (in the phrase **on a sudden**). **5. all of a sudden.** without warning; unexpectedly. ~*adv.* **6.** *Chiefly poetic.* without warning; suddenly. [C13: via French from Late Latin *subitāneus*, from Latin *subitus* unexpected, from *subīre* to happen unexpectedly, from *sub-* secretly + *īre* to go] —**'sud+den+ly** *adv.* —**'sud+den+ness** *n.*

sud+den death *n.* **1.** (in sports, etc.) an extra game or contest to decide the winner of a tied competition. **2.** an unexpected or quick death.

Su·de·ten·land (suːˈdeɪtᵊn,lænd) *n.* a mountainous region of N and NW Czechoslovakia: annexed by Germany in 1938; returned to Czechoslovakia in 1945. Also called: **the Sudeten.**

Su·de·tes (suːˈdiːtiːz) *or* **Su·de·ten Moun·tains** *pl. n.* a mountain range in E central Europe, along the N border of Czechoslovakia, extending into East Germany and Poland: rich in minerals, esp. coal. Highest peak: Schneekoppe, 1603 m (5259 ft.).

su·dor (ˈsjuːdɔː) *n.* a technical name for **sweat.** [Latin] —**su·dor·al** (ˈsjuːdərəl) *adj.*

su·dor·if·er·ous (,sjuːdəˈrɪfərəs) *adj.* producing or conveying sweat. [C16: via New Latin from SUDOR + Latin *ferre* to bear] —**,su·dor·ˈif·er·ous·ness** *n.*

su·dor·if·ic (,sjuːdəˈrɪfɪk) *adj.* **1.** producing or causing sweating; sudatory. ~*n.* **2.** a sudorific agent. [C17: from New Latin *sūdōrificus,* from SUDOR + Latin *facere* to make]

Su·dra (ˈsjuːdrə) *n.* the lowest of the four main Hindu castes, the workers. [C17: from Sanskrit]

suds (sʌdz) *pl. n.* **1.** the bubbles on the surface of water in which soap, detergents, etc., have been dissolved; lather. **2.** soapy water. **3.** *Slang, chiefly U.S.* beer or the bubbles floating on it. [C16: probably from Middle Dutch *sudse* marsh; related to Middle Low German *sudde* swamp; see SEETHE] —**ˈsuds·y** *adj.*

sue (sjuː, suː) *vb.* **sues, su·ing, sued. 1.** to institute legal proceedings (against). **2.** to make suppliant requests of (someone for something). **3.** *Archaic.* to pay court (to). [C13: via Anglo-Norman from Old French *sivre,* from Latin *sequī* to follow] —**ˈsu·er** *n.*

Sue (*French* sy) *n.* **Eu·gène** (øˈʒɛn). original name *Marie-Joseph Sue.* 1804–57, French novelist, whose works, notably *Les Mystères de Paris* (1842–43) and *Le Juif errant* (1844–45), were among the first to reflect the impact of the industrial revolution on France.

suede (sweɪd) *n.* **a.** a leather finished with a fine velvet-like nap, usually on the flesh side of the skin or hide, produced by abrasive action. **b.** (*as modifier*): *a suede coat.* [C19: from French *gants de Suède,* literally: gloves from Sweden]

su·et (ˈsuːɪt, ˈsjuːɪt) *n.* a hard waxy fat around the kidneys and loins in sheep, cattle, etc., used in cooking and making tallow. [C14: from Old French *seu,* from Latin *sēbum*] —**ˈsu·et·y** *adj.*

Sue·to·ni·us (swiːˈtəʊnɪəs) *n.* full name *Gaius Suetonius Tranquillus.* 75–150 A.D., Roman biographer and historian, whose chief works were *Concerning Illustrious Men* and *The Lives of the Caesars* (from Julius Caesar to Domitian).

su·et pud·ding *n. Brit.* any of a variety of sweet or savoury puddings made with suet and steamed or boiled.

Su·ez (ˈsuːɪz) *n.* **1.** a port in NE Egypt, at the head of the Gulf of Suez at the S end of the Suez Canal: an ancient trading site and a major naval station under the Ottoman Empire; port of departure for pilgrims to Mecca; oil-refining centre. It suffered severely in the Arab–Israeli conflicts of 1967 and 1973. Pop.: 368 000 (1974 est.). **2. Isthmus of.** a strip of land in NE Egypt, between the Mediterranean and the Red Sea: links Africa and Asia and is crossed by the Suez Canal. **3. Gulf of.** the NW arm of the Red Sea: linked with the Mediterranean by the Suez Canal.

Su·ez Ca·nal *n.* a sea-level canal in NE Egypt, crossing the Isthmus of Suez and linking the Mediterranean with the Red Sea: built (1854–69) by de Lesseps with French and Egyptian capital; nationalized in 1956 by the Egyptians. Length: 163 km (101 miles).

suf. *abbrev. for* suffix.

suff. *abbrev. for:* **1.** sufficient. **2.** suffix.

Suff. *abbrev. for:* **1.** Suffolk. **2.** Suffragan.

suf·fer (ˈsʌfə) *vb.* **1.** to undergo or be subjected to (pain, punishment, etc.). **2.** (*tr.*) to undergo or experience (anything): *to suffer a change of management.* **3.** (*intr.*) to be set at a disadvantage: *this author suffers in translation.* **4.** to be prepared to endure (pain, death, etc.): *he suffers for the cause of freedom.* **5.** (*tr.*) *Archaic.* to permit (someone to do something): *suffer the little children to come unto me.* **6. suffer from. a.** to be ill with, esp. recurrently. **b.** to be given to: *he suffers from a tendency to exaggerate.* [C13: from Old French *soffrir,* from Latin *sufferre,* from SUB- + *ferre* to bear] —**ˈsuf·fer·er** *n.*

suf·fer·a·ble (ˈsʌfərəbᵊl, ˈsʌfrə-) *adj.* able to be tolerated or suffered; endurable. —**ˈsuf·fer·a·bly** *adv.*

suf·fer·ance (ˈsʌfərəns, ˈsʌfrəns) *n.* **1.** tolerance arising from failure to prohibit; tacit permission. **2.** capacity to endure pain, injury, etc. **3.** the state or condition of suffering. **4.** *Archaic.* patient endurance. **5. on sufferance.** with reluctance. [C13: via Old French from Late Latin *sufferentia* endurance, from Latin *sufferre* to SUFFER]

suf·fer·ing (ˈsʌfərɪŋ, ˈsʌfrɪŋ) *n.* **1.** the pain, misery, or loss experienced by a person who suffers. **2.** the state or an instance of enduring pain, etc. —**ˈsuf·fer·ing·ly** *adv.*

suf·fice (səˈfaɪs) *vb.* **1.** to be adequate or satisfactory for (something). **2. suffice it to say that.** (*takes a clause as object*) let us say no more than that; I shall just say that. [C14: from Old French *suffire,* from Latin *sufficere* from *sub-* below + *facere* to make] —**sufˈfic·er** *n.*

suf·fi·cien·cy (səˈfɪʃənsɪ) *n., pl.* **·cies. 1.** the quality or condition of being sufficient. **2.** an adequate amount or quantity, as of income. **3.** *Archaic.* efficiency.

suf·fi·cient (səˈfɪʃənt) *adj.* **1.** enough to meet a need or purpose; adequate. **2.** *Logic.* (of a condition) assuring the truth of a statement, fact, etc., logically following from the condition once that condition has been fulfilled. Compare **necessary** (sense 3c.). **3.** *Archaic.* competent; capable. ~*n.* **4.** a sufficient quantity. [C14: from Latin *sufficiens* supplying the needs of, from *sufficere* to SUFFICE] —**sufˈfi·cient·ly** *adv.*

suf·fix *n.* (ˈsʌfɪks). **1.** *Grammar.* an affix that follows the stem to which it is attached, as for example *-s* and *-ness* in *dogs* and *softness.* Compare **prefix** (sense 1). **2.** anything that is added at the end of something else. ~*vb.* (ˈsʌfɪks, səˈfɪks). **3.** (*tr.*) *Grammar.* to add (a morpheme) as a suffix to the end of a word. [C18: from New Latin *suffixum,* from Latin *suffixus* fastened below, from *suffigere,* from SUB- + *figere* to fasten] —**ˈsuf·fix·al** (ˈsʌfɪksəl) *adj.* —**suf·fix·ion** (sʌˈfɪkʃən) *n.*

suf·flate (sʌˈfleɪt) *vb.* an archaic word for **inflate.** [C17: from Latin *sufflāre* from SUB- + *flāre* blow] —**sufˈfla·tion** *n.*

suf·fo·cate (ˈsʌfə,keɪt) *vb.* **1.** to kill or be killed by the deprivation of oxygen, as by obstruction of the air passage or inhalation of noxious gases. **2.** to block the air passages or have the air passages blocked. **3.** to feel or cause to feel discomfort from heat and lack of air. [C16: from Latin *suffōcāre,* from SUB- + *faucēs* throat] —**ˈsuf·fo·,cat·ing·ly** *adv.* —**,suf·foˈca·tion** *n.* —**ˈsuf·fo·,ca·tive** *adj.*

Suf·folk[1] (ˈsʌfək) *n.* a county of SE England, on the North Sea: its coast is flat and marshy, indented by broad tidal estuaries. Administrative centre: Ipswich. Pop.: 577 600 (1976 est.). Area: 3802 sq. km (1468 sq. miles).

Suf·folk[2] (ˈsʌfək) *n.* a black-faced breed of sheep.

Suf·folk punch *n.* a breed of draught horse with a chestnut coat and short legs.

Suffr. *abbrev. for* Suffragan.

suf·fra·gan (ˈsʌfrəgən) *adj.* **1. a.** (of any bishop of a diocese) subordinate to and assisting his superior archbishop or metropolitan. **b.** (of any assistant bishop) having the duty of assisting the bishop of the diocese to which he is appointed but having no ordinary jurisdiction in that diocese. ~*n.* **2.** a suffragan bishop. [C14: from Medieval Latin *suffragāneus,* from *suffrāgium* assistance, from Latin: SUFFRAGE] —**ˈsuf·fra·gan·,ship** *n.*

suf·frage (ˈsʌfrɪdʒ) *n.* **1.** the right to vote, esp. in public elections; franchise. **2.** the exercise of such a right; casting a vote. **3.** a supporting vote. **4.** a prayer, esp. a short intercessory prayer. [C14: from Latin *suffrāgium*]

suf·fra·gette (,sʌfrəˈdʒɛt) *n.* a female advocate of the extension of the franchise to women, esp. a militant one, as in Britain at the beginning of the 20th century. [C20: from SUFFRAG(E) + -ETTE] —**,suf·fraˈget·tism** *n.*

suf·fra·gist (ˈsʌfrədʒɪst) *n.* an advocate of the extension of the franchise, esp. to women. —**ˈsuf·frag·ism** *n.*

suf·fru·ti·cose (səˈfruːtɪ,kəʊz) *adj.* (of a plant) having a permanent woody base and herbaceous branches. [C18: from New Latin *suffruticōsus,* from Latin SUB- + *frutex* a shrub]

suf·fu·mi·gate (səˈfjuːmɪ,geɪt) *vb.* (*tr.*) to fumigate from or as if from beneath. [C16: from Latin *suffūmigāre,* from SUB- + *fūmigāre* to FUMIGATE] —**suf·,fu·miˈga·tion** *n.*

suf·fuse (səˈfjuːz) *vb.* (*tr.; usually passive*) to spread or flood through or over (something): *the evening sky was suffused with red.* [C16: from Latin *suffūsus* overspread with, from *suffundere,* from SUB- + *fundere* to pour] —**suf·fu·sion** (səˈfjuːʒən) *n.* —**sufˈfu·sive** *adj.*

Su·fi (ˈsuːfɪ) *n., pl.* **·fis.** an adherent of a Muslim mystical and pantheist sect, mainly in Persia. [C17: from Arabic *sūfīy,* literally: (man) of wool, from *sūf* wool; probably from the ascetic's woollen garments] —**ˈSu·fic** *adj.*

Su·fism (ˈsuːfɪzəm) *n.* the mystical doctrines of the Sufis. —**Su·fis·tic** (suːˈfɪstɪk) *adj.*

Su·fu (ˈʃuːˈfuː) *n.* a variant spelling of **Shufu.**

sug·ar (ˈʃʊgə) *n.* **1.** Also called: **sucrose, saccharose.** a white crystalline sweet carbohydrate, a disaccharide, found in many plants and extracted from sugar cane and sugar beet: it is used esp. as a sweetening agent in food and drinks. Formula: $C_{12}H_{22}O_{11}$. Related adj.: **saccharine. 2.** any of a class of simple water-soluble carbohydrates, such as sucrose, lactose, and fructose. **3.** *Informal, chiefly U.S.* a term of affection, esp. for one's sweetheart. **4.** *Rare.* a slang word for **money. 5.** a slang name for **LSD.** ~*vb.* **6.** (*tr.*) to add sugar to; make sweet. **7.** (*tr.*) to cover or sprinkle with sugar. **8.** (*intr.*) to produce sugar. **9. sugar the pill** *or* **medicine.** to make something unpleasant more agreeable by adding something pleasant: *the government stopped wage increases but sugared the pill by reducing taxes.* [C13 *suker,* from Old French *çucre,* from Medieval Latin *zuccārum,* from Italian *zucchero,* from Arabic *sukkar,* from Persian *shakar,* from Sanskrit *śarkarā*] —**ˈsug·ar·less** *adj.* —**ˈsug·ar-,like** *adj.*

sug·ar ap·ple *n.* another name for **sweetsop.**

sug·ar beet *n.* a variety of the plant *Beta vulgaris* that is cultivated for its white roots from which sugar is obtained. Compare **sugar cane.**

sug·ar bird *n.* a South African nectar-eating bird, *Promerops cafer,* with a long curved bill and long tail: family *Meliphagidae* (honey-eaters).

sug·ar bush *n.* an anacardiaceous evergreen shrub, *Rhus ovata,* of S California and Arizona, having pale oval leaves, spikes of yellow-tinged red flowers, and deep red fruits.

sug·ar can·dy *n.* **1.** Also called: **rock candy.** large crystals of sugar formed by suspending strings in a strong sugar solution that hardens on the strings, used chiefly for sweetening coffee. **2.** *Chiefly U.S.* confectionery; sweets.

sug·ar cane *n.* a coarse perennial grass, *Saccharum officinarum,* of Old World tropical regions, having tall stout canes that yield sugar: cultivated chiefly in the West Indies and the southern U.S. Compare **sugar beet.**

sug·ar-coat *vb.* (*tr.*) **1.** to coat or cover with sugar. **2.** to cause to appear more attractive; make agreeable.

sug+ar corn *n.* another name for **sweet corn** (sense 1).

su+gar dad+dy *n. Slang.* a rich usually middle-aged or old man who bestows expensive gifts on a young person in return for companionship or sexual favours.

su+gar di·a+be·tes *n.* an informal name for **diabetes mellitus** (see **diabetes**).

sug+ared ('ʃʊgəd) *adj.* made sweeter or more appealing with or as with sugar.

sug+ar gli+der *n.* a common Australian possum, *Petaurus breviceps,* that glides from tree to tree feeding on insects and nectar.

sug+ar gum *n. Austral.* a small eucalyptus tree, *Eucalyptus cladocalyx,* having smooth bark and barrel-shaped fruits and grown for timber and ornament.

sug+ar loaf *n.* **1.** a large conical mass of hard refined sugar. **2.** something resembling this in shape.

Sug+ar Loaf Moun+tain *n.* a mountain in SE Brazil, in Rio de Janeiro on Guanabara Bay. Height: 390 m (1280 ft.). Portuguese name: **Pão de Açúcar.**

sug+ar ma+ple *n.* a North American maple tree, *Acer saccharum,* that is grown as a source of sugar, which is extracted from the sap, and for its hard wood.

sug+ar of lead (lɛd) *n.* another name for **lead acetate.**

sug+ar of milk *n.* another name for **lactose.**

sug+ar pine *n.* a pine tree, *Pinus lambertiana,* of California and Oregon, having spreading pendulous branches, light brown cones, and sugary resin.

sug·ar+plum ('ʃʊgə,plʌm) *n.* a crystallized plum.

sug+ar·y ('ʃʊgərɪ) *adj.* **1.** of, like, or containing sugar. **2.** containing too much sugar; excessively sweet. **3.** deceptively pleasant; insincere. —**'sug+ar·i+ness** *n.*

sug+gest (sə'dʒɛst, *U.S.* səg'dʒɛst) *vb.* (*tr.; may take a clause as object*) **1.** to put forward (a plan, idea, etc.) for consideration: *I suggest Smith for the post; a plan suggested itself.* **2.** to evoke (a person, thing, etc.) in the mind of someone by the association of ideas: *that painting suggests home to me.* **3.** to give an indirect or vague hint of: *his face always suggests his peace of mind.* [C16: from Latin *suggerere* to bring up, from SUB- + *gerere* to bring] —**sug+'gest+er** *n.* —**sug+'gest+ing+ly** *adv.*

sug+gest+i·bil+i·ty (sə,dʒɛstɪ'bɪlɪtɪ) *n. Psychol.* a state, esp. under hypnosis, in which a person will accept the suggestions of another person and act accordingly.

sug+gest+i·ble (sə'dʒɛstɪbᵊl) *adj.* **1.** easily influenced by ideas provided by other persons. **2.** characteristic of something that can be suggested. —**sug+'gest+i·ble+ness** *n.* —**sug+'gest+i·bly** *adv.*

sug+ges+tion (sə'dʒɛstʃən) *n.* **1.** something that is suggested. **2.** a hint or indication: *a suggestion of the odour of violets.* **3.** *Psychol.* the process whereby the mere presentation of an idea to a receptive individual leads to the acceptance of that idea. See also **autosuggestion.**

sug+ges+tive (sə'dʒɛstɪv) *adj.* **1.** (*postpositive;* foll. by *of*) conveying a hint (of something): *this painting is suggestive of a hot summer day.* **2.** tending to suggest something improper or indecent. **3.** able or liable to suggest an idea, plan, etc. —**sug+'ges+tive+ly** *adv.* —**sug+'ges+tive+ness** *n.*

Su·har·to (sʊ'hɑːtəʊ) *n.* born 1921, Indonesian general and statesman; president since 1968.

su·i+cid+al (,suːɪ'saɪdᵊl, ,sjuː-) *adj.* **1.** involving, indicating, or tending towards suicide. **2.** liable to result in suicide: *a suicidal attempt.* **3.** liable to destroy one's own interests or prospects; dangerously rash. —**,su·i+'cid+al+ly** *adv.*

su·i+cide ('suːɪ,saɪd, 'sjuː-) *n.* **1.** the act or an instance of killing oneself intentionally. **2.** the self-inflicted ruin of one's own prospects or interests: *a merger would be financial suicide.* **3.** a person who kills himself intentionally. **4.** (*modifier*) reckless; extremely dangerous: *a suicide mission.* [C17: from New Latin *suīcīdium,* from Latin *suī* of oneself + *-cīdium,* from *caedere* to kill]

su·i gen+e·ris (,suːaɪ 'dʒɛnərɪs) *adj.* unique. [Latin, literally: of its own kind]

su·i ju+ris ('suːaɪ 'dʒʊərɪs) *adj.* (*usually postpositive*) *Law.* of full age and not under disability; legally competent to manage one's own affairs; independent. [C17: from Latin, literally: of one's own right]

su+int ('suːɪnt, swɪnt) *n.* a water-soluble substance found in the fleece of sheep, consisting of peptides, organic acids, metal ions, and inorganic cations and formed from dried perspiration. [C18: from French *suer* to sweat, from Latin *sūdāre*]

Suisse (sɥis) *n.* the French name for **Switzerland.**

suit (suːt, sjuːt) *n.* **1.** any set of clothes of the same or similar material designed to be worn together, now usually (for men) a jacket with matching trousers or (for women) a jacket with matching or contrasting skirt or trousers. **2.** (*in combination*) any outfit worn for a specific purpose: *a spacesuit.* **3.** any set of items, such as the full complement of sails of a vessel or parts of personal armour. **4.** any of the four sets of 13 cards in a pack of playing cards, being spades, hearts, diamonds, and clubs. The cards in each suit are two to ten, jack, queen, and king in the usual order of ascending value, with ace counting as either the highest or lowest according to the game. **5.** a civil proceeding; lawsuit. **6.** the act or process of suing in a court of law. **7.** a petition or appeal made to a person of superior rank or status or the act of making such a petition. **8.** a man's courting of a woman. **9. follow suit. a.** to play a card of the same suit as the card played immediately before it. **b.** to act in the same way as someone else. **10. strong** *or* **strongest suit.** something that one excels in. ~*vb.* **11.** to make or be fit or appropriate for: *that dress suits your figure.* **12.** to meet the requirements or standards (of). **13.** to be agreeable or acceptable to (someone). **14.** (*tr.*) *Archaic.* to supply with clothing. **15. suit oneself.** to pursue one's own intentions without reference to others. [C13: from Old French *sieute* set of things, from *sivre* to follow; compare SUE] —**'suit+,like** *adj.*

suit+a·ble ('suːtəbᵊl, 'sjuːt-) *adj.* appropriate; proper; fit. —**,suit+a·'bil+i·ty** *or* **'suit+a·ble+ness** *n.* —**'suit+a·bly** *adv.*

suit+case ('suːt,keɪs, 'sjuːt-) *n.* a portable rectangular travelling case, usually stiffened, for carrying clothing, etc.

suite (swiːt) *n.* **1.** a series of items intended to be used together; set. **2.** a number of connected rooms in a hotel forming one living unit: *the presidential suite.* **3.** a matching set of furniture, esp. of two armchairs and a settee. **4.** a number of attendants or followers. **5.** *Music.* **a.** an instrumental composition consisting of several movements in the same key based on or derived from dance rhythms, esp. in the baroque period. **b.** an instrumental composition in several movements less closely connected than a sonata. **c.** a piece of music containing movements based on or extracted from music already used in an opera, ballet, play, etc. [C17: from French, from Old French *sieute;* see SUIT]

suit+ing ('suːtɪŋ, 'sjuːt-) *n.* a fabric used for suits.

suit+or ('suːtə, 'sjuːt-) *n.* **1.** a man who courts a woman; wooer. **2.** *Law.* a person who brings a suit in a court of law; plaintiff. **3.** *Rare.* a person who makes a request or appeal for anything. [C13: from Anglo-Norman *suter,* from Latin *secūtor* follower, from *sequī* to follow]

Sui+yüan ('swiː'yɑːn) *n.* a former province in N China: now part of the Inner Mongolian Autonomous Region.

Su+kar+na+pu+ra (sʊ,kɑːnə'pʊərə) *n.* a former name of **Djajapura.**

Su·kar·no (suː'kɑːnəʊ) *n.* **Ach·med** ('ɑːkmɛd). 1901–70, Indonesian statesman; first president of the Republic of Indonesia (1945–67).

Su+kar+no Peak *n.* a former name of (Mount) **Djaja.**

Su+khu+mi (*Russian* su'xumi) *n.* a port and resort in the SW Soviet Union, in the Georgian SSR on the Black Sea: site of an ancient Greek colony. Pop.: 115 000 (1975 est.).

su+ki+ya+ki (,suːkɪ'jɑːkɪ) *n.* a Japanese dish consisting of thinly sliced beef or other meat, vegetables, and seasonings cooked together, usually at the table. [from Japanese]

Suk+koth *or* **Suc+coth** ('sʊkəʊt, -kəʊθ; *Hebrew* suː'kɔt) *n.* an eight-day Jewish harvest festival beginning on Tishri 15, which commemorates the period when the Israelites lived in the wilderness. [from Hebrew, literally: tabernacles]

Su+la+we+si (,suːlə'weɪsɪ) *n.* the Indonesian name for the **Celebes.**

sul+cate ('sʌlkeɪt) *adj. Biology.* marked with longitudinal parallel grooves: *sulcate stems.* [C18: via Latin *sulcātus* from *sulcāre* to plough, from *sulcus* a furrow] —**sul+'ca+tion** *n.*

sul+cus ('sʌlkəs) *n., pl.* **+ci** (-saɪ). **1.** a linear groove, furrow, or slight depression. **2.** any of the narrow grooves on the surface of the brain that mark the cerebral convolutions. Compare **fissure.** [C17: from Latin]

Sul·lei·man I (,suːlɪ'mɑːn, -leɪ-), **So·li·man,** *or* **So·ly·man** *n.* called *the Magnificent.* ?1495–1566, sultan of the Ottoman Empire (1520–66), whose reign was noted for its military power and cultural achievements.

sulf- *combining form.* U.S. variant of **sulph-.**

sul+fur ('sʌlfə) *n.* the U.S. preferred spelling of **sulphur.**

sulk (sʌlk) *vb.* **1.** (*intr.*) to be silent and resentful because of a wrong done to one, esp. in order to gain sympathy; brood sullenly: *the child sulked in a corner after being slapped.* ~*n.* **2.** (*often pl.*) a state or mood of feeling resentful or sullen: *he's in a sulk because he lost the game; he's got the sulks.* **3.** Also: **sulk+er.** a person who sulks. [C18: perhaps a back formation from SULKY[1]]

sulk·y[1] ('sʌlkɪ) *adj.* **sulk·i+er, sulk·i+est. 1.** sullen, withdrawn, or moody, through or as if through resentment. **2.** dull or dismal: *sulky weather.* [C18: perhaps from obsolete *sulke* sluggish, probably related to Old English *āseolcan* to be lazy] —**'sulk·i+ly** *adv.* —**'sulk·i+ness** *n.*

sulk·y[2] ('sʌlkɪ) *n., pl.* **sulk·ies.** a light two-wheeled vehicle for one person, usually drawn by one horse. [C18: from SULKY[1], because it can carry only one person]

Sul·la ('sʌlə) *n.* full name *Lucius Cornelius Sulla Felix.* 138–78 B.C., Roman general and dictator (82–79). He introduced reforms to strengthen the power of the Senate.

sul+lage ('sʌlɪdʒ) *n.* **1.** filth or waste, esp. sewage. **2.** sediment deposited by running water. [C16: perhaps from French *souiller* to sully; compare Old English *sol* mud]

sul+len ('sʌlən) *adj.* **1.** unwilling to talk or be sociable; sulky; morose. **2.** sombre; gloomy: *a sullen day.* **3.** *Literary.* sluggish; slow: *a sullen stream.* **4.** *Obsolete.* threatening. ~*n.* **5.** (*pl.*) *Archaic.* a sullen mood. [C16: perhaps from Anglo-French *solain* (unattested), ultimately related to Latin *sōlus* alone] —**'sul+len+ly** *adv.* —**'sul+len+ness** *n.*

Sul·li·van ('sʌlɪvᵊn) *n.* **1.** Sir **Ar·thur (Seymour).** 1842–1900, English composer who wrote operettas, such as *H.M.S. Pinafore* (1878) and *The Mikado* (1885), with W. S. Gilbert as librettist. **2. Lou·is (Henri).** 1856–1924, U.S. pioneer of modern architecture: he coined the slogan "form follows function".

sul+ly ('sʌlɪ) *vb.* **+lies, +ly+ing, +lied. 1.** (*tr.*) to stain or tarnish (a reputation, etc.) or (of a reputation) to become stained or tarnished. ~*n., pl.* **+lies. 2.** a stain. **3.** the act of sullying.

[C16: probably from French *souiller* to soil] —'**sul+li+a·ble** *adj.*

Sul·ly ('sʌlɪ; *French* syl'li) *n.* **Ma·xi·mi·lien de Bé·thune** (maksimiljɛ̃ də be'tyn), Duc de Sully. 1559–1641, French statesman; minister of Henry IV. He helped restore the finances of France after the Wars of Religion.

Sul·ly-Pru·dhomme (*French* sylli pry'dɔm) *n.* **Re·né Fran·çois Ar·mand** (rə'ne frãswa ar'mã). 1839–1907, French poet: Nobel prize for literature 1901.

sulph- *or U.S.* **sulf-** *combining form.* containing sulphur: *sulphate; sulphonic acid.*

sul+pha+di·a+zine (ˌsʌlfə'daɪəˌziːn) *n.* an important sulpha drug used chiefly in combination with an antibiotic. Formula: $C_{10}H_{10}N_4O_2S$.

sul+pha drug ('sʌlfə) *n.* any of a group of sulphonamide compounds that inhibit the activity of bacteria and are used in medicine to treat bacterial infections.

sul+pha+nil·a+mide (ˌsʌlfə'nɪləˌmaɪd) *n.* a white odourless crystalline compound formerly used in medicine in the treatment of bacterial infections. Formula: $NH_2C_6H_4SO_2NH_2$. See also **sulpha drug.**

sul+phate ('sʌlfeɪt) *n.* **1.** any salt or ester of sulphuric acid, such as sodium sulphate, Na_2SO_4, sodium hydrogen sulphate, or diethyl sulphate, $(C_2H_5)_2SO_4$. ~*vb.* **2.** (*tr.*) to treat with a sulphate or convert into a sulphate. **3.** to undergo or cause to undergo the formation of a layer of lead sulphate on the plates of an accumulator. [C18: from New Latin *sulfātum*; see SULPHUR] —**sul+'pha+tion** *n.*

sul+pha+thi·a+zole (ˌsʌlfə'θaɪəˌzəʊl) *n.* a sulpha drug used in veterinary medicine and formerly in clinical medicine. Formula: $C_9H_9N_3O_2S_2$.

sul+phide ('sʌlfaɪd) *n.* **1.** a compound of sulphur with a more electropositive element. **2.** another name for **thio-ether.**

sul+phi+nyl ('sʌlfənɪl) *n.* (*modifier*) another term (no longer in technical usage) for **thionyl.** [C20: from SULF- + -IN + -YL]

sul+phi+sox·a+zole (ˌsʌlfɪ'sɒksəˌzəʊl) *n.* a sulpha drug used in the treatment of meningitis and certain diseases of the eye, such as trachoma. Formula: $C_{11}H_{13}N_3O_3S$.

sul+phite ('sʌlfaɪt) *n.* any salt or ester of sulphurous acid, containing the ions SO_3^{2-} or HSO_3^- (**hydrogen sulphite**) or the groups SO_3 or HSO_3. The salts are usually soluble crystalline compounds. —**sul+phit+ic** (sʌl'fɪtɪk) *adj.*

sul+phon·a+mide (sʌl'fɒnəˌmaɪd) *n.* any of a class of organic compounds that are amides of sulphonic acids containing the group $-SO_2NH_2$ or a group derived from this. An important class of sulphonamides are the sulpha drugs.

sul+pho+nate ('sʌlfəˌneɪt) *Chem.* ~*n.* **1.** a salt or ester of any sulphonic acid containing the ion RSO_2O^- or the group RSO_2O-, R being an organic group. ~*vb.* **2.** (*tr.*) to introduce a sulphonic acid group, SO_2OH, into (a molecule).

sul+phone ('sʌlfəʊn) *n.* any of a class of organic compounds containing the divalent group SO_2 linked to two other organic groups. Certain sulphones are used in the treatment of leprosy and tuberculosis.

sul+phon+ic ac·id (sʌl'fɒnɪk) *n.* any of a large group of strong organic acids that contain the group $-SO_2OH$ and are used in the manufacture of dyes and drugs.

sul+pho+ni·um com+pound *or* **salt** (sʌl'fəʊnɪəm) *n.* any one of a class of salts derived by the addition of a proton to the sulphur atom of a thiol or thio-ether thus producing a positive ion (**sulphonium ion**).

sul+phon+me+thane (ˌsʌlfɒn'miːθeɪn) *n.* a colourless crystalline compound used medicinally as a hypnotic. Formula: $C_7H_{16}O_4S_2$.

sul+pho+nyl ('sʌlfənɪl) *n.* (*modifier*) another term for **sulphuryl.**

sul+phur *or U.S.* **sul+fur** ('sʌlfə) *n.* **a.** an allotropic nonmetallic element, occurring free in volcanic regions and in combined state in gypsum, pyrite, and galena. The stable yellow rhombic form converts on heating to monoclinic needles. It is used in the production of sulphuric acid, in the vulcanization of rubber, and in fungicides. Symbol: S; atomic no.: 16; atomic wt.: 32.064; valency: 2, 4, or 6; relative density: 2.07 (rhombic), 1.96 (monoclinic); melting pt.: 112.8°C (rhombic), 119.0°C (monoclinic); boiling pt.: 444.6°C. **b.** (*as modifier*): *sulphur springs.* [C14 *soufre*, from Old French, from Latin *sulfur*] —**sul+phu+ric** *or U.S.* **sul+fu+ric** (sʌl'fjʊərɪk) *adj.*

sul+phur+ate ('sʌlfjʊˌreɪt) *vb.* to combine or treat with sulphur or a sulphur compound. —ˌ**sul+phu+'ra+tion** *n.*

sul·phur-bot·tom *n.* another name for **blue whale.**

sul+phur di+ox+ide *n.* a colourless soluble pungent gas produced by burning sulphur. It is both an oxidizing and a reducing agent and is used in the manufacture of sulphuric acid, the preservation of foodstuffs, bleaching, and disinfecting. Formula: SO_2.

sul+phu+re·ous (sʌl'fjʊərɪəs) *n.* **1.** another word for **sulphurous** (sense 1). ~*adj.* **2.** of the yellow colour of sulphur. —**sul+'phu+re·ous+ly** *adv.* —**sul+'phu+re·ous+ness** *n.*

sul+phu+ret ('sʌlfjʊˌrɛt) *vb.* **+rets, +ret+ting, +ret+ted** *or U.S.* **+rets, +ret+ing, +ret+ed.** to treat or combine with sulphur.

sul+phu+ret+ted hy+dro+gen *n.* another name for **hydrogen sulphide.**

sul+phu+ric ac·id *n.* a colourless dense oily corrosive liquid produced by the reaction of sulphur trioxide with water and used in accumulators and in the manufacture of fertilizers, dyes, and explosives. Formula: H_2SO_4.

sul+phu+rize *or* **sul+phu+rise** ('sʌlfjʊˌraɪz) *vb.* (*tr.*) to combine or treat with sulphur or a sulphur compound. —ˌ**sul+phu+ri+'za+tion** *or* ˌ**sul+fu+ri+'sa+tion** *n.*

sul+phur+ous ('sʌlfərəs) *adj.* **1.** Also: **sulphureous.** of, relating to, or resembling sulphur: *a sulphurous colour.* **2.** of or containing sulphur in the divalent state: *sulphurous acid.* **3.** of or relating to hellfire. **4.** hot-tempered. —'**sul+phur+ous+ly** *adv.* —'**sul+phur+ous+ness** *n.*

sul+phur+ous ac·id *n.* an unstable acid produced when sulphur dioxide dissolves in water: used as a preservative for food and a bleaching agent. Formula: H_2SO_3.

sul+phur tri+ox+ide *n.* a white corrosive substance existing in three crystalline forms of which the stable (*alpha-*) form is usually obtained as silky needles. It is produced by the oxidation of sulphur dioxide, and is used in the sulphonation of organic compounds. Formula: SO_3.

sul+phur+yl ('sʌlfjʊrɪl, -fərɪl) *n.* (*modifier*) of, consisting of, or containing the divalent group, $=SO_2$: *sulphuryl chloride.* Also: **sulphonyl.**

sul+tan ('sʌltən) *n.* **1.** the sovereign of a Muslim country, esp. of the former Ottoman Empire. **2.** an arbitrary ruler; despot. **3.** a small domestic fowl with a white crest and heavily feathered legs and feet: originated in Turkey. [C16: from Medieval Latin *sultānus*, from Arabic *sultān* rule, from Aramaic *salita* to rule] —**sul+tan+ic** (sʌl'tænɪk) *adj.* —'**sul·tan-**ˌ**like** *adj.* —'**sul+tan+**ˌ**ship** *n.*

sul+tan·a (sʌl'tɑːnə) *n.* **1. a.** the dried fruit of a small white seedless grape, originally produced in SW Asia: used in cakes, curries, etc.; seedless raisin. **b.** the grape itself. **2.** Also called: **sultaness.** a wife, concubine, or female relative of a sultan. **3.** a mistress; concubine. [C16: from Italian, feminine of *sultano* SULTAN]

Sul+tan·a+bad (sʌlˌtɑːnə'bæd) *n.* the former name of **Arak.**

sul+tan+ate ('sʌltəˌneɪt) *n.* **1.** the territory or a country ruled by a sultan. **2.** the office, rank, or jurisdiction of a sultan.

sul+try ('sʌltrɪ) *adj.* **+tri+er, +tri+est. 1.** (of weather or climate) oppressively hot and humid. **2.** characterized by or emitting oppressive heat. **3.** displaying or suggesting passion; sensual: *sultry eyes.* [C16: from obsolete *sulter* to SWELTER + -Y[1]] —'**sul+tri+ly** *adv.* —'**sul+tri+ness** *n.*

Su·lu Ar+chi+pel·a+go ('suːluː) *pl. n.* a chain of over 500 islands in the SW Philippines, separating the Sulu Sea from the Celebes Sea: formerly a sultanate, ceded to the Philippines in 1940. Capital: Jolo. Pop.: 425 617 (1970). Area: 2686 sq. km (1037 sq. miles).

Su·lu Sea *n.* part of the W Pacific between Borneo and the central Philippines.

sum (sʌm) *n.* **1. a.** the result of the addition of numbers, quantities, objects, etc. **b.** the single number obtained by combining two or more other numbers in such a way that the units making up this single number can be paired with those making up the other numbers without remainder. **2.** one or more columns or rows of numbers to be added, subtracted, multiplied, or divided. **3.** *Maths.* the limit of the first *n* terms of a converging infinite series as *n* tends to infinity. **4.** (*pl.*) another name for **number work. 5.** a quantity, esp. of money: *he borrows enormous sums.* **6.** the essence or gist of a matter (esp. in the phrases **in sum, in sum and substance**). **7.** a less common word for **summary. 8.** *Archaic.* the summit or maximum. **9.** (*modifier*) complete or final (esp. in the phrase **sum total**). ~*vb.* **sums, sum+ming, summed. 10.** (often foll. by *up*) to add or form a total of (something). **11.** (*tr.*) to calculate the sum of (the terms in a sequence). ~See also **sum up.** [C13 *summe*, from Old French, from Latin *summa* the top, sum, from *summus* highest, from *superus* in a higher position; see SUPER]

su+mach *or U.S.* **su+mac** ('suːmæk, 'ʃuː-) *n.* **1.** any temperate or subtropical shrub or small tree of the anacardiaceous genus *Rhus*, having compound leaves, clusters of green flowers, and red hairy fruits. See also **poison sumach. 2.** a preparation of powdered leaves of certain species of *Rhus*, esp. *R. coriaria*, used in dyeing and tanning. **3.** the wood of any of these plants. [C14: via Old French from Arabic *summāq*]

Su+ma+tra (sʊ'mɑːtrə) *n.* a mountainous island in W Indonesia, in the Greater Sunda Islands, separated from the Malay Peninsula by the Strait of Malacca: Dutch control began in the 16th century; joined Indonesia in 1945. Pop.: 20 812 682 (1971). Area: 473 606 sq. km (182 859 sq. miles). —**Su+'ma+tran** *adj., n.*

Sum+ba *or* **Soem+ba** ('suːmbə) *n.* an island in Indonesia, in the Lesser Sunda Islands, separated from Flores by the **Sumba Strait:** formerly important for sandalwood exports. Pop.: 251 126 (1961). Area: 11 153 sq. km (4306 sq. miles). Former name: **Sandalwood Island.**

Sum+ba+wa *or* **Soem+ba+wa** (suːm'bɑːwə) *n.* a mountainous island in Indonesia, in the Lesser Sunda Islands, between Lombok and Flores Islands. Pop.: 407 596 (1961). Area: 14 750 sq. km (5695 sq. miles).

Su+mer ('suːmə) *n.* the S region of Babylonia; seat of a civilization of city-states that reached its height in the 3rd millennium B.C.

Su+me+ri·an (suː'mɪərɪən, -'mɛər-) *n.* **1.** a member of a people who established a civilization in Sumer during the 4th millennium B.C. **2.** the extinct language of this people, of no known relationship to any other language. ~*adj.* **3.** of or relating to ancient Sumer, its inhabitants, or their language or civilization.

sum+ma ('sʊmɑː) *n., pl.* **+mae** (-miː). **1.** *Medieval theol.* **a.** a compendium of theology, philosophy, or canon law, or sometimes of all three together. The **Summa Theologica** of St. Thomas Aquinas, written between 1265 and 1274, was the most famous of all such compendia. **2.** *Rare.* a comprehensive work or survey. [C15: from Latin: SUM]

sum+ma cum lau+de ('sʊmɑː kʊm 'laʊdeɪ) *Chiefly U.S.* with the utmost praise: the highest of three designations for above-average achievement in examinations. In Britain it is sometimes used to designate a first-class honours degree. [from Latin]

sum·mand ('sʌmænd, sʌ'mænd) *n.* a number or quantity forming part of a sum. [C19: from Medieval Latin *summandus,* from Latin *summa* SUM]

sum·ma·rize *or* **sum·ma·rise** ('sʌməˌraɪz) *vb.* (*tr.*) to make or be a summary of; express concisely. —**'sum·maˌriz·a·ble** *or* **'sum·maˌris·a·ble** *adj.* —**ˌsum·ma·ri·'za·tion** *or* **ˌsum·ma·ri·'sa·tion** *n.* —**'sum·maˌriz·er, 'sum·maˌris·er,** *or* **'sum·ma·rist** *n.*

sum·mar·y ('sʌmərɪ) *n., pl.* **·mar·ies. 1.** a brief account giving the main points of something. ~*adj.* (*usually prenominal*). **2.** performed arbitrarily and quickly, without formality: *a summary execution.* **3.** (of legal proceedings) short and free from the complexities and delays of a full trial. **4. summary jurisdiction.** the right a court has to adjudicate immediately upon some matter arising during its proceedings. **5.** giving the gist or essence. [C15: from Latin *summārium,* from *summa* SUM] —**'sum·mar·i·ly** *adv.* —**'sum·mar·i·ness** *n.*

sum·mar·y of·fence *n.* an offence that is triable in a magistrates' court.

sum·ma·tion (sʌ'meɪʃən) *n.* **1.** the act or process of determining a sum. **2.** the result of such an act or process. **3.** *U.S. law.* the concluding statements made by opposing counsel in a case before a court. [C18: from Medieval Latin *summātiō,* from *summāre* to total, from Latin *summa* SUM] —**sum·'ma·tion·al** *adj.*

sum·mer[1] ('sʌmə) *n.* **1.** (*sometimes cap.*) **a.** the warmest season of the year, between spring and autumn, astronomically from the June solstice to the September equinox in the N hemisphere and at the opposite time of year in the S hemisphere. **b.** (*as modifier*): *summer flowers; a summer dress.* Related adj.: **aestival. 2.** the period of hot weather associated with the summer. **3.** a time of blossoming, greatest happiness, etc. **4.** *Chiefly poetic.* a year represented by this season: *a child of nine summers.* ~*vb.* **5.** (*intr.*) to spend the summer (at a place). **6.** (*tr.*) to keep or feed (farm animals) during the summer: *they summered their cattle on the mountain slopes.* [Old English *sumor;* related to Old Frisian *sumur,* Old Norse *sumar,* Old High German *sumar,* Sanskrit *samā* season] —**'sum·mer·less** *adj.* —**'sum·mer-ˌlike** *adj.* —**'sum·mer·ly** *adj., adv.* —**'sum·mer·y** *adj.* —**'sum·mer·i·ness** *n.*

sum·mer[2] ('sʌmə) *n.* **1.** Also called: **summer tree.** a large horizontal beam or girder, esp. one that supports floor joists. **2.** another name for **lintel. 3.** a stone on the top of a column, pier, or wall that supports an arch or lintel. [C14: from Anglo-Norman *somer,* from Old French *somier* beam, packhorse, from Late Latin *sagmārius* (*equus*) pack(horse), from *sagma* a packsaddle, from Greek]

sum·mer cy·press *n.* a Eurasian plant, *Kochia scoparia* (or *trichophylla*), having dense foliage that turns bright red in autumn: family *Chenopodiaceae* (chenopods). Also called: **burning bush.**

sum·mer·house ('sʌməˌhaʊs) *n.* a small building in a garden or park, used for shade or recreation in the summer.

sum·mer pud·ding *n. Brit.* a pudding made by filling a bread-lined basin with a purée of fruit, leaving it to soak, and then turning it out.

sum·mer·sault ('sʌməˌsɔːlt) *n., vb.* a variant spelling of **somersault.**

sum·mer school *n.* a school, academic course, etc., held during the summer.

sum·mer sol·stice *n.* **1.** the time at which the sun is at its northernmost point in the sky (southernmost point in the S hemisphere), appearing at noon at its highest altitude above the horizon. It occurs about June 21 (December 22 in the S hemisphere). **2.** *Astronomy.* the point on the celestial sphere, opposite the **winter solstice,** at which the ecliptic is furthest north from the celestial equator. Right ascension: 6 hours; declination: 23.5°.

sum·mer·time ('sʌməˌtaɪm) *n.* **1.** the period or season of summer. **2.** *Brit.* any daylight-saving time, esp. British Summer Time.

sum·mer·weight ('sʌməˌweɪt) *adj.* (of clothes) suitable in weight for wear in the summer; relatively light.

sum·mer·wood ('sʌməˌwʊd) *n.* the wood that is produced by a plant near the end of the growing season: consists of small thick-walled xylem cells. Compare **springwood.**

sum·ming-up *n.* **1.** a review or summary of the main points of an argument, speech, etc. **2.** a direction regarding the law and a summary of the evidence, given by a judge in his address to the jury before they retire to consider their verdict.

sum·mit ('sʌmɪt) *n.* **1.** the highest point or part, esp. of a mountain or line of communication; top. **2.** the highest possible degree or state; peak or climax: *the summit of ambition.* **3.** the highest level, importance, or rank: *a meeting at the summit.* **4. a.** a meeting of chiefs of governments or other high officials. **b.** (*as modifier*): *a summit conference.* [C15: from Old French *somet,* diminutive of *som,* from Latin *summum;* see SUM] —**'sum·mit·al** *adj.* —**'sum·mit·less** *adj.*

sum·mit·ry ('sʌmɪtrɪ) *n. Chiefly U.S.* the practice of conducting international negotiations by summit conferences.

sum·mon ('sʌmən) *vb.* (*tr.*) **1.** to order to come; send for, esp. to attend court, by issuing a summons. **2.** to order or instruct (to do something) or call (to something): *the bell summoned them to their work.* **3.** to call upon to meet or convene. **4.** (often foll. by *up*) to muster or gather (one's strength, courage, etc.). **5.** *Archaic.* to call upon to surrender. [C13: from Latin *summonēre* to give a discreet reminder, from *monēre* to advise] —**'sum·mon·a·ble** *adj.*

sum·mons ('sʌmənz) *n., pl.* **·mons·es. 1.** a call, signal, or order to do something, esp. to appear in person or attend at a specified place or time. **2. a.** an official order requiring a person to attend court, either to answer a charge or to give evidence. **b.** the writ making such an order. Compare **warrant. 3.** a call or command given to the members of an assembly to convene a meeting. ~*vb.* **4.** to take out a summons against (a person). [C13: from Old French *somonse,* from *somondre* to SUMMON]

sum·mum bo·num *Latin.* ('sʊmʊm 'bɒnʊm) *n.* the principle of goodness in which all moral values are included or from which they are derived; highest or supreme good.

Su·mo ('sjuːməʊ) *n.* the national style of wrestling of Japan, the object of which is to force one's opponent to touch the ground with any part of his body except the soles of his feet or to step out of the ring. [from Japanese *sumō*]

sump (sʌmp) *n.* **1.** a receptacle, such as the lower part of the crankcase of an internal-combustion engine, into which liquids, esp. lubricants, can drain to form a reservoir. **2.** another name for **cesspool. 3.** *Mining.* **a.** a depression at the bottom of a shaft where water collects before it is pumped away. **b.** the front portion of a shaft or tunnel, ahead of the main bore. **4.** *Brit. dialect.* a muddy pool or swamp. [C17: from Middle Dutch *somp* marsh; see SWAMP]

sump·ter ('sʌmptə) *n. Archaic.* a packhorse, mule, or other beast of burden. [C14: from Old French *sometier* driver of a baggage horse, from Vulgar Latin *sagmatārius* (unattested), from Late Latin *sagma* packsaddle]

sump·tu·a·ry ('sʌmptjʊərɪ) *adj.* relating to or controlling expenditure or extravagance. [C17: from Latin *sumptuārius* concerning expense, from *sumptus* expense, from *sūmere* to spend]

sump·tu·a·ry law *n.* (formerly) a law imposing restraint on luxury, esp. by limiting personal expenditure or by regulating personal conduct in religious and moral spheres.

sump·tu·ous ('sʌmptjʊəs) *adj.* **1.** expensive or extravagant: *sumptuous costumes.* **2.** magnificent; splendid: *a sumptuous scene.* [C16: from Old French *somptueux,* from Latin *sumptuōsus* costly, from *sumptus;* see SUMPTUARY] —**'sump·tu·ous·ly** *adv.* —**'sump·tu·ous·ness** *or* **sump·tu·os·i·ty** (ˌsʌmptjʊ'ɒsɪtɪ) *n.*

Sum·ter ('sʌmtə) *n.* See **Fort Sumter.**

sum up *vb.* (*adv.*) **1.** to summarize (feelings, the main points of an argument, etc.): *the judge began to sum up.* **2.** (*tr.*) to form a quick opinion of: *I summed him up in five minutes.*

Su·my (*Russian* 'sumɪ) *n.* a city in the SW Soviet Union, in the NE Ukrainian SSR: site of early Slav settlements. Pop.: 194 000 (1975 est.).

sun (sʌn) *n.* **1.** the star that is the source of heat and light for the planets in the solar system. It is a gaseous body having a highly compressed core, in which energy is generated by thermonuclear reactions (at about 20 million °C), surrounded by a less dense convective zone serving to transport the energy to the surface (the **photosphere**). The atmospheric layers (the **chromosphere** and **corona**) are normally invisible except during a total eclipse. Mass and diameter: 333 000 and 109 times that of earth respectively; mean distance from earth: 149.6 million km (1 astronomical unit). Related adjs.: **heliacal, solar. 2.** any star around which a planetary system revolves. **3.** the sun as it appears at a particular time or place: *the winter sun.* **4.** the radiant energy, esp. heat and light, received from the sun; sunshine. **5.** a person or thing considered as a source of radiant warmth, glory, etc. **6.** a pictorial representation of the sun, often depicted with a human face. **7.** *Poetic.* a year or a day. **8.** *Poetic.* a climate. **9.** *Archaic.* sunrise or sunset (esp. in the phrase **from sun to sun**). **10. catch the sun.** to become slightly sunburnt. **11. place in the sun.** a prominent or favourable position. **12. take** *or* **shoot the sun.** *Nautical.* to measure the altitude of the sun in order to determine latitude. **13. touch of the sun.** slight sunstroke. **14. under** *or* **beneath the sun.** on earth; at all: *nobody under the sun eats more than you do.* ~*vb.* **suns, sun·ning, sunned. 15.** to expose (oneself) to the sunshine. **16.** (*tr.*) to expose to the sunshine in order to warm, tan, etc. [Old English *sunne;* related to Old High German *sunna,* Old Frisian *senne,* Gothic *sunno*] —**'sunˌlike** *adj.*

Sun. *abbrev. for* Sunday.

sun·bake ('sʌnˌbeɪk) *n. Austral. informal.* a period of time spent sunbathing.

sun·baked ('sʌnˌbeɪkt) *adj.* **1.** (esp. of roads, etc.) dried or cracked by the sun's heat. **2.** baked hard by the heat of the sun: *sunbaked bricks.*

sun bath *n.* the exposure of the body to the rays of the sun or a sun lamp, esp. in order to get a suntan.

sun·bathe ('sʌnˌbeɪð) *vb.* (*intr.*) to bask in the sunshine, esp. in order to get a suntan. —**'sunˌbath·er** *n.*

sun·beam ('sʌnˌbiːm) *n.* **1.** a beam, ray, or stream of sunlight. **2.** *Austral. slang.* a piece of crockery or cutlery laid for a meal but remaining unused. —**'sunˌbeamed** *or* **'sunˌbeam·y** *adj.*

sun bear *n.* a small bear, *Helarctos malayanus,* of tropical forests in S and SE Asia, having a black coat and a yellowish snout and feeding mostly on honey and insects. Also called: **honey bear.**

sun·bird ('sʌnˌbɜːd) *n.* any small songbird of the family *Nectariniidae,* of tropical regions of the Old World, esp. Africa, having a long slender curved bill and a bright plumage in the males.

sun bit·tern *n.* a cranelike bird, *Eurypyga helias,* of tropical

American forests, having a greyish plumage with orange and brown wings: family *Eurypygidae*, order *Gruiformes* (cranes, rails, etc.).

sun blind *n. Chiefly Brit.* a blind, such as a Venetian blind, that shades a room from the sun's glare.

sun·bon·net ('sʌnˌbɒnɪt) *n.* a baby's hat that shades the face and neck from the sun, esp. one of cotton with a projecting brim. —'**sun·ˌbon·net·ed** *adj.*

sun·bow ('sʌnˌbəʊ) *n.* a bow of prismatic colours similar to a rainbow, produced when sunlight shines through spray.

sun·burn ('sʌnˌbɜːn) *n.* **1.** inflammation of the skin caused by overexposure to the sun. Technical name: **erythema solare. 2.** another word for **suntan.** —'**sun·ˌburnt** *or* '**sun·ˌburned** *adj.*

sun·burst ('sʌnˌbɜːst) *n.* **1.** a burst of sunshine, as through a break in the clouds. **2.** a pattern or design resembling that of the sun. **3.** a jewelled brooch with this pattern.

sun·burst pleats *pl. n.* the U.S. term for **sunray pleats.**

Sun·bur·y-on-Thames ('sʌnbərɪ, -brɪ) *n.* a town in SE England, in N Surrey. Pop.: 40 035 (1971).

sun-cured *adj.* cured or preserved by exposure to the sun.

sun·dae ('sʌndiː, -deɪ) *n.* ice cream topped with a sweet sauce, nuts, whipped cream, etc. [C20: of uncertain origin]

Sun·da Is·lands ('sʌndə) *or* **Soen·da Is·lands** *pl. n.* a chain of islands in the Malay Archipelago, consisting of the **Greater Sunda Islands** (chiefly Sumatra, Java, Borneo, and Celebes) and the **Lesser Sunda Islands** (chiefly Bali, Lombok, Sumbawa, Sumba, Flores, Timor, Alor, and Wetar): includes most of the land area of Indonesia.

sun dance *n.* a North American Indian ceremony associated with the sun, performed at the summer solstice.

Sun·da Strait *or* **Soen·da Strait** *n.* a strait between Sumatra and Java, linking the Java Sea with the Indian Ocean. Narrowest point: about 26 km (16 miles).

Sun·day ('sʌndɪ) *n.* the first day of the week and the Christian day of worship. [Old English *sunnandæg*, translation of Latin *diēs sōlis* day of the sun, translation of Greek *hēmera hēliou;* related to Old Norse *sunnu dagr*, German *Sonntag*]

Sun·day best *n.* one's best clothes, esp. regarded as those most suitable for churchgoing.

Sun·day paint·er *n.* a person who paints pictures as a hobby.

Sun·day punch *n. Informal, chiefly U.S.* **1.** *Boxing.* a heavy blow intended to knock out one's opponent. **2.** any manoeuvre or action intended to crush an opponent.

Sun·day school *n.* **1. a.** a school for the religious instruction of children on Sundays, usually held in a church and formerly also providing secular education. **b.** (*as modifier*): *a Sunday-school outing.* **2.** the members of such a school.

sun deck *n.* an upper open deck on a passenger ship.

sun·der ('sʌndə) *Archaic or literary.* ~*vb.* **1.** to break or cause to break apart or in pieces. ~*n.* **2. in sunder.** into pieces; apart. [Old English *sundrian;* related to Old Norse *sundr* asunder, Gothic *sundrō* apart, Old High German *suntar,* Latin *sine* without] —'**sun·der·a·ble** *adj.* —'**sun·der·ance** *n.* —'**sun·der·er** *n.*

Sun·der·land ('sʌndələnd) *n.* a port in NE England, in Tyne and Wear at the mouth of the River Wear: shipbuilding and marine engineering. Pop.: 216 892 (1971).

sun·dew ('sʌnˌdjuː) *n.* any of several bog plants of the genus *Drosera,* having leaves covered with sticky hairs that trap and digest insects: family *Droseraceae.* [C16: translation of Latin *ros solis*]

sun·di·al ('sʌnˌdaɪəl) *n.* a device indicating the time during the hours of sunlight by means of a stationary arm (the **gnomon**) that casts a shadow onto a plate or surface marked in hours at right angles to the gnomon.

sun disc *n.* a disc symbolizing the sun, esp. one flanked by two serpents and the extended wings of a vulture, used as a religious figure in ancient Egypt.

sun·dog ('sʌnˌdɒg) *n.* **1.** another word for **parhelion. 2.** a small rainbow or halo near the horizon.

sun·down ('sʌnˌdaʊn) *n.* another name for **sunset.**

sun·down·er ('sʌnˌdaʊnə) *n.* **1.** *Austral. slang.* a tramp, esp. one who seeks food and lodging at sundown when it is too late to work. **2.** *Nautical.* a strict ship's officer. **3.** *Informal, chiefly Brit.* an alcoholic drink taken at sunset.

sun·dress ('sʌnˌdrɛs) *n.* a dress for hot weather that exposes the shoulders, arms, and back, esp. one with straps over the shoulders.

sun-dried *adj.* dried or preserved by exposure to the sun.

sun·dry ('sʌndrɪ) *determiner.* **1.** several or various; miscellaneous. ~*pron.* **2. all and sundry.** all the various people. ~*n., pl.* **-dries. 3.** (*pl.*) miscellaneous unspecified items. **4.** *Austral. slang.* (in cricket) an extra player. [Old English *syndrig* separate; related to Old High German *suntarīg;* see SUNDER, -Y[1]]

sun·dry shop *n.* (in Malaysia) a shop, similar to a delicatessen, that sells predominantly Chinese foodstuffs.

Sunds·vall (*Swedish* 'sundsval) *n.* a port in E Sweden, on the Gulf of Bothnia: icebound in winter; cellulose industries. Pop.: 64 920 (1970).

sun·fast ('sʌnˌfɑːst) *adj. Chiefly U.S.* not fading in sunlight.

sun·fish ('sʌnˌfɪʃ) *n., pl.* **·fish** *or* **·fish·es. 1.** any large plectognath fish of the family *Molidae,* of temperate and tropical seas, esp. *Mola mola,* which has a large rounded compressed body, long pointed dorsal and anal fins, and a fringelike tail fin. **2.** any of various small predatory North American freshwater percoid fishes of the family *Centrarchidae,* typically having a compressed brightly coloured body.

sun·flow·er ('sʌnˌflaʊə) *n.* **1.** any of several American plants of the genus *Helianthus,* esp. *H. annuus,* having very tall thick stems, large flower heads with yellow rays, and seeds used as food, esp. for poultry: family *Compositae* (composites). See also **Jerusalem artichoke. 2. sunflower seed oil.** the oil extracted from sunflower seeds, used as a salad oil, in the manufacture of margarine, etc.

sung (sʌŋ) *vb.* **1.** the past participle of **sing.** ~*adj.* **2.** produced by singing: *a sung syllable.*
Usage. See at **ring**[2].

Sung (sʊŋ) *n.* an imperial dynasty of China (960–1279 A.D.), notable for its art, literature, and philosophy.

Sun·ga·ri ('sʊŋgərɪ) *n.* a river in NE China, rising in SE Kirin province and flowing north and northeast to the Amur River near Tungkiang: the chief river of Manchuria and largest tributary of the Amur; frozen from November to April. Length: over 1300 km (800 miles). Also called: **Sung-hua** ('sʌŋ'wɑː).

Sung·kiang ('sʊŋ'kjæŋ, -kaɪ'æŋ) *n.* a former province of NE China: now part of the Inner Mongolian AR.

sun·glass ('sʌnˌglɑːs) *n.* a convex lens used to focus the sun's rays and thus produce heat or ignition; burning glass.

sun·glass·es ('sʌnˌglɑːsɪz) *pl. n.* glasses with darkened or polarizing lenses that protect the eyes from the sun's glare.

sun·glow ('sʌnˌgləʊ) *n.* a pinkish glow often seen in the sky before sunrise or after sunset. It is caused by scattering or diffraction of sunlight by particles in the atmosphere.

sun-god *n.* **1.** the sun considered as a personal deity. **2.** a deity associated with the sun or controlling its movements.

sun·grebe ('sʌnˌgriːb) *n.* another name for **finfoot.**

sun·hat ('sʌnˌhæt) *n.* a hat that shades the face and neck from the sun, worn esp. by women and children.

sunk (sʌŋk) *vb.* **1.** a past tense or past participle of **sink.** ~*adj.* **2.** *Informal.* with all hopes dashed; ruined: *if the police come while we're opening the safe, we'll be sunk.* ~*n.* **3.** *Scot. dialect.* a cellar or basement.

sunk·en ('sʌŋkən) *vb.* **1.** a past participle of **sink.** ~*adj.* **2.** unhealthily hollow: *sunken cheeks.* **3.** situated at a lower level than the surrounding or usual one. **4.** situated under water; submerged. **5.** depressed; low: *sunken spirits.*

sunk fence *n.* a ditch, one side of which is made into a retaining wall so as to enclose an area of land while remaining hidden in the total landscape. Also called: **ha-ha.**

Sun King *n.* **the.** an epithet of **Louis XIV.**

sun lamp *n.* **1.** a lamp that generates ultraviolet rays, used for obtaining an artificial suntan, for muscular therapy, etc. **2.** a lamp used in film studios, etc., to give an intense beam of light by means of parabolic mirrors.

sun·less ('sʌnlɪs) *adj.* **1.** without sun or sunshine. **2.** gloomy; depressing. —'**sun·less·ly** *adv.* —'**sun·less·ness** *n.*

sun·light ('sʌnlaɪt) *n.* **1.** the light emanating from the sun. **2.** an area or the time characterized by sunshine. —'**sun·lit** *adj.*

sun lounge *or U.S.* **sun par·lor** *n.* a room with large windows positioned to receive as much sunlight as possible.

sunn (sʌn) *n.* **1.** a leguminous plant, *Crotalaria juncea,* of the East Indies, having yellow flowers. **2.** the hemplike fibre obtained from the inner bark of this plant, used in making rope, sacking, etc. [C18: from Hindi *san,* from Sanskrit *śāṇá* hempen]

Sun·na ('sʌnə) *n.* the body of traditional Islamic law accepted by most orthodox Muslims as based on the words and acts of Mohammed. [C18: from Arabic *sunnah* rule]

Sun·ni ('sʌnɪ) *n., pl.* **·ni. 1.** one of the two main branches of orthodox Islam (the other being the Shiah), consisting of those who acknowledge the authority of the Sunna. **2.** a less common word for **Sunnite.**

Sun·nite ('sʌnaɪt) *n. Islam.* an adherent of the Sunni.

sun·ny ('sʌnɪ) *adj.* **·ni·er, ·ni·est. 1.** full of or exposed to sunlight. **2.** radiating good humour. **3.** of or resembling the sun. —'**sun·ni·ly** *adv.* —'**sun·ni·ness** *n.*

sun·ny side *n.* **1.** the cheerful aspect or point of view: *look on the sunny side of things.* **2. on the sunny side of.** *Informal.* younger than (a specified age).

sun·ny-side up *adj.* (of eggs) fried on one side only.

sun·ray pleats ('sʌnˌreɪ) *pl. n. Brit.* bias-cut knife pleats that are narrower at the top than at the bottom, producing a flared effect, used esp. for skirts. U.S. term: **sunburst pleats.**

sun·rise ('sʌnˌraɪz) *n.* **1.** the daily appearance of the sun above the horizon. **2.** the atmospheric phenomena accompanying this appearance. **3.** Also called (esp. U.S.): **sunup.** the time at which the sun rises at a particular locality.

sun·set ('sʌnˌsɛt) *n.* **1.** the daily disappearance of the sun below the horizon. **2.** the atmospheric phenomena accompanying this disappearance. **3.** Also called: **sundown.** the time at which the sun sets at a particular locality. **4.** the final stage or closing period, as of a person's life.

sun·shade ('sʌnˌʃeɪd) *n.* a device, esp. a parasol or awning, serving to shade from the sun.

sun·shine ('sʌnˌʃaɪn) *n.* **1.** the light received directly from the sun. **2.** the warmth from the sun. **3.** a sunny area. **4.** a light-hearted term of affection. —'**sun·shin·y** *adj.*

sun·shine roof *or* **sun·roof** ('sʌnˌruːf) *n.* a panel in the roof of a car that may be opened by sliding it back.

sun·spot ('sʌnˌspɒt) *n.* any of the dark cool patches, with a diameter of up to several thousand kilometres, that appear on the surface of the sun and last about a week. They occur in approximately 11-year cycles and possess a strong magnetic field. —'**sun·ˌspot·ted** *adj.*

sun·star ('sʌnˌstɑː) *n.* any starfish of the genus *Solaster,* having up to 13 arms radiating from a central disc.

sun+stone ('sʌnˌstəʊn) *n.* another name for **aventurine** (sense 2).

sun+stroke ('sʌnˌstrəʊk) *n.* heatstroke caused by prolonged exposure to intensely hot sunlight.

sun+suit ('sʌnˌsu:t, -ˌsju:t) *n.* a child's outfit consisting of a brief top and shorts or a short skirt.

sun+tan ('sʌnˌtæn) *n.* **a.** a brownish colouring of the skin caused by the formation of the pigment melanin within the skin on exposure to the ultraviolet rays of the sun or a sunlamp. Often shortened to **tan. b.** (*as modifier*): *suntan oil.* —**'sun+ˌtanned** *adj.*

sun+trap ('sʌnˌtræp) *n.* a very sunny sheltered place.

sun+ward ('sʌnwəd) *adj.* **1.** directed or moving towards the sun. ~*adv.* **2.** a variant of **sunwards.**

sun+wards ('sʌnwədz) *or* **sun+ward** *adv.* towards the sun.

sun+wise ('sʌnˌwaɪz) *adv.* moving in the same direction as the sun; clockwise.

Sun Yat-sen ('sʊn 'jɑ:t'sɛn) *n.* 1866–1925, Chinese statesman, who was instrumental in the overthrow of the Manchu dynasty and was the first president of the Republic of China (1911). He reorganized the Kuomintang.

su·o ju·re ('su:əʊ 'dʒʊərɪ) *adv. Chiefly law.* in one's own right. [Latin]

su·o lo·co ('su:əʊ 'lɒkəʊ) *adv. Chiefly law.* in a person or thing's own or rightful place. [Latin]

Su·o+mi ('suɔmi) *n.* the Finnish name for **Finland.**

sup[1] (sʌp) *vb.* **sups, sup+ping, supped. 1.** (*intr.*) *Archaic.* to have supper. **2.** (*tr.*) *Obsolete.* to provide with supper. [C13: from Old French *soper;* see SUP[2]]

sup[2] (sʌp) *vb.* **sups, sup+ping, supped. 1.** to partake of (liquid) by swallowing a little at a time. **2.** *Northern Brit. dialect.* to drink. ~*n.* **3.** a sip. [Old English *sūpan;* related to Old High German *sūfan,* German *saufen;* see also SUP[1]]

sup. *abbrev. for:* **1.** above. [from Latin *supra*] **2.** superior. **3.** *Grammar.* superlative. **4.** supine (noun). **5.** supplement. **6.** supplementary. **7.** supply.

su+per ('su:pə, 'sju:pə) *adj.* **1.** *Informal.* **a.** outstanding; superfine; superb. **b.** (*in combination*): *superstar.* ~*n.* **2. a.** a product of superior quality, size, etc. **b.** such quality, etc. ~*interj.* **3.** *Chiefly Brit.* good! excellent! [from Latin: above]

super. *abbrev. for:* **1.** superintendent. **2.** superfine. **3.** superior. **4.** supernumerary. **5.** supervisor. **6.** *Austral.* **a.** superphosphate. **b.** superannuation benefits.

su·per- *prefix.* **1.** placed above or over: *superscript.* **2.** of greater size, extent, quality, etc.: *supermarket.* **3.** beyond a standard or norm; exceeding or exceedingly: *supersonic.* **4.** indicating that a chemical compound contains a specified element in a higher proportion than usual: *superoxide.* [from Latin *super* above]

su·per+a·ble ('su:pərəbᵊl, -prəbᵊl, 'sju:-) *adj.* able to be surmounted or overcome. [C17: from Latin *superābilis,* from *superāre* to overcome] —**ˌsu·per+a·'bil+i·ty** *or* **'su·per+a·ble+ness** *n.* —**'su·per+a·bly** *adv.*

su·per+a·bound (ˌsu:pərə'baʊnd, ˌsju:-) *vb.* **1.** (*intr.*) to abound abnormally; be in surplus. **2.** *Rare.* to be more abundant than (something else). —**su·per·a+bun+dant** (ˌsu:pərə'bʌndənt, ˌsju:-) *adj.*

su·per+add (ˌsu:pər'æd, ˌsju:-) *vb.* (*tr.*) to add (something) to something that has already been added; add as extra. —**ˌsu·per+ad+'di+tion** *n.* —**ˌsu·per+ad+'di+tion+al** *adj.*

sup·er+al·tar ('su:pəˌɔ:ltə, 'sju:-) *n. Ecclesiast.* a consecrated portable stone slab for use on an unconsecrated altar.

su·per+an+nu+ate (ˌsu:pər'ænjʊˌeɪt, ˌsju:-) *vb.* (*tr.*) **1.** to pension off. **2.** to discard as obsolete or old-fashioned.

su·per+an+nu+at+ed (ˌsu:pər'ænjʊˌeɪtɪd, ˌsju:-) *adj.* **1.** discharged, esp. with a pension, owing to age or illness. **2.** too old to serve usefully. **3.** obsolete. [C17: from Medieval Latin *superannātus* aged more than one year, from Latin SUPER- + *annus* a year]

su·per+an+nu·a+tion (ˌsu:pərˌænjʊ'eɪʃən, ˌsju:-) *n.* **1. a.** the amount deducted regularly from employees' incomes in a contributory pension scheme. **b.** the pension finally paid to such employees. **2.** the act or process of superannuating or the condition of being superannuated.

su+perb (sʊ'pɜ:b, sjʊ-) *adj.* **1.** surpassingly good; excellent: *a superb actor.* **2.** majestic or imposing: *a superb mansion.* **3.** magnificently rich; luxurious: *the jubilee was celebrated with a superb banquet.* [C16: from Old French *superbe,* from Latin *superbus* distinguished, from *super* above] —**su+'perb+ly** *adv.* —**su+'perb+ness** *n.*

su·per+ba+zaar *or* **su·per+ba+zar** ('su:pəbə'zɑ:) *n.* (in India) a large department store or supermarket, esp. one set up as a cooperative store by the government.

su·per+cal+en+der (ˌsu:pə'kæləndə, ˌsju:-) *n.* **1.** a calender with a number of rollers that gives a high gloss to paper. ~*vb.* **2.** (*tr.*) to produce a glossy finish on (paper) by pressing in a supercalender. —**ˌsu·per+'cal+en+dered** *adj.*

su·per+car+go (ˌsu:pə'kɑ:gəʊ, 'sju:) *n., pl.* **+goes.** an officer on a merchant ship who supervises commercial matters and is in charge of the cargo. [C17: changed from Spanish *sobrecargo,* from *sobre* over (from Latin SUPER) + *cargo* CARGO]

su·per+charge ('su:pəˌtʃɑ:dʒ, 'sju:-) *vb.* (*tr.*) **1.** to increase the intake pressure of (an internal-combustion engine) with a supercharger; boost. **2.** to charge (the atmosphere, a remark, etc.) with an excess amount of (tension, emotion, etc.). **3.** to apply pressure to (a fluid); pressurize.

su·per+char+ger ('su:pəˌtʃɑ:dʒə, 'sju:-) *n.* a device, usually a fan or compressor, that increases the mass of air drawn into an internal-combustion engine by raising the intake pressure. Also called: **blower, booster.**

su·per+cil·i+ar·y (ˌsu:pə'sɪlɪərɪ, ˌsju:-) *adj.* relating to or situated over the eyebrow or a corresponding region in lower animals. [C18: from New Latin *superciliaris,* from Latin *supercilium,* from SUPER- + *cilium* eyelid]

su·per+cil·i+ous (ˌsu:pə'sɪlɪəs, ˌsju:-) *adj.* displaying arrogant pride, scorn, or indifference. [C16: from Latin *superciliōsus,* from *supercilium* eyebrow; see SUPERCILIARY] —**ˌsu·per+'cil·i+ous+ly** *adv.* —**ˌsu·per+'cil·i+ous+ness** *n.*

su·per+class ('su:pəˌklɑ:s, 'sju:-) *n.* a taxonomic group that is a subdivision of a subphylum.

su·per+co+lum+nar (ˌsu:pəkə'lʌmnə, ˌsju:-) *adj. Architect.* **1.** having one colonnade above another. **2.** placed above a colonnade or a column. —**ˌsup·er+col+ˌum+ni·'a+tion** *n.*

su·per+con+duc+tiv+i·ty (ˌsu:pəˌkɒndʌk'tɪvɪtɪ, ˌsju:-) *n. Physics.* the property of certain substances that have almost no electrical resistance at temperatures close to absolute zero. The effect has been used in making powerful electromagnets. —**su·per+con+duc+tion** (ˌsu:pəkən'dʌkʃən, ˌsju:-) *n.* —**ˌsu·per+con+'duc+tive** *or* **ˌsu·per+con+'duct+ing** *adj.* —**ˌsu·per+con+'duc+tor** *n.*

su·per+cool (ˌsu:pə'ku:l, ˌsju:-) *vb. Chem.* to cool or be cooled without freezing or crystallization to a temperature below that at which freezing or crystallization should occur. Supercooled liquids are not in equilibrium.

su·per+dense the·o+ry (ˌsu:pə'dɛns, ˌsju:-) *n. Astronomy.* another name for the **big bang theory.**

su·per+dom·i+nant (ˌsu:pə'dɒmɪnənt, ˌsju:-) *n. U.S.* another word for **submediant.**

su·per+du·per ('su:pə'du:pə, 'sju:-) *adj. Informal.* extremely pleasing, impressive, etc.: often used as an exclamation.

su·per+e·go (ˌsu:pə'i:gəʊ, -'ɛgəʊ, ˌsju:-) *n., pl.* **·gos.** *Psychoanal.* that part of the unconscious mind that acts as a conscience for the ego, developing mainly from the relationship between a child and his parents. See also **id, ego.**

su·per+el·e·va+tion (ˌsu:pəˌɛlɪ'veɪʃən, ˌsju:-) *n.* **1.** another name for **bank**[2] (sense 7). **2.** the difference between the heights of the sides of a road or railway track on a bend.

su·per+em·i+nent (ˌsu:pər'ɛmɪnənt, ˌsju:-) *adj.* of distinction, dignity, or rank superior to that of others; pre-eminent. —**ˌsu·per+'em·i+nence** *n.* —**ˌsu·per+'em·i+nent+ly** *adv.*

su·per+er·o·gate (ˌsu:pər'ɛrəˌgeɪt, ˌsju:-) *vb.* (*intr.*) *Obsolete.* to do or perform more than is required. [C16: from Late Latin *superērogāre* to spend over and above, from Latin SUPER- + *ērogāre* to pay out] —**ˌsu·per+'er·o+ˌga+tor** *n.*

su·per+er·o·ga+tion (ˌsu:pərˌɛrə'geɪʃən, ˌsju:-) *n.* **1.** the performance of work in excess of that required or expected. **2.** *R.C. Church.* supererogatory prayers, devotions, etc.

su·per+e·rog·a·to·ry (ˌsu:pərɛ'rɒgətərɪ, -trɪ, ˌsju:-) *adj.* **1.** performed to an extent exceeding that required or expected. **2.** exceeding what is needed; superfluous. **3.** *R.C. Church.* of, characterizing, or relating to prayers, good works, etc., performed over and above those prescribed as obligatory. [C16: from Medieval Latin *superērogātōrius;* see SUPEREROGATE] —**ˌsu·per+e·'rog·a·to·ri+ly** *adv.*

su·per+fam·i+ly ('su:pəˌfæmɪlɪ, 'sju:-) *n., pl.* **+lies.** *Biology.* a taxonomic group that is a subdivision of a suborder.

su·per+fe+cun+da+tion (ˌsu:pəˌfi:kən'deɪʃən, ˌsju:-) *n. Physiol.* the fertilization of two or more ova, produced during the same menstrual cycle, by sperm ejaculated during two or more acts of sexual intercourse.

su·per+fe+male ('su:pəˌfi:meɪl, 'sju:-) *n.* a former name for **metafemale.**

su·per+fe+ta+tion (ˌsu:pəfi:'teɪʃən, ˌsju:-) *n. Physiol.* the presence in the uterus of two fetuses developing from ova fertilized at different times. [C17 *superfetate,* from Latin *superfētāre* to fertilize when already pregnant, from SUPER- + *fētāre* to impregnate, from *fētus* offspring] —**su·per+fe+tate** (ˌsu:pə'fi:teɪt, ˌsju:-) *adj.*

su·per+fi+cial (ˌsu:pə'fɪʃəl, ˌsju:-) *adj.* **1.** of, relating to, being near, or forming the surface: *superficial bruising.* **2.** displaying a lack of thoroughness or care: *a superficial inspection.* **3.** only outwardly apparent rather than genuine or actual: *the similarity was merely superficial.* **4.** of little substance or significance; trivial: *superficial differences.* **5.** lacking originality or profundity: *the film's plot was quite superficial.* **6.** (of measurements) involving only the surface area. [C14: from Late Latin *superficiālis* of the surface, from Latin SUPERFICIES] —**su·per+fi+ci+al+i·ty** (ˌsu:pəˌfɪʃɪ'ælɪtɪ) *or* **ˌsu·per+'fi+cial+ness** *n.* —**ˌsu·per+'fi+cial+ly** *adv.*

su·per+fi+cies (ˌsu:pə'fɪʃi:z, ˌsju:-) *n., pl.* **+cies.** *Rare.* **1.** a surface or outer face. **2.** the outward form of a thing. [C16: from Latin: upper side, from SUPER- + *faciēs* face]

su·per+fine (ˌsu:pə'faɪn, ˌsju:-) *adj.* **1.** of exceptional fineness or quality. **2.** excessively refined. —**ˌsu·per+'fine+ness** *n.*

ˌsu·per+ac+'com+mo+dat+ing *adj.*
ˌsu·per+ac+'com+plished *adj.*
ˌsu·per+'ac+tive *adj.*
ˌsu·per+am+'bi+tious *adj.*
ˌsu·per+'bold *adj.*
ˌsu·per+co+'los+sal *adj.*
ˌsu·per+'com+plex *adj.*
ˌsu·per+'con+fi+dent *adj.*
ˌsu·per+con+'form+i+ty *n.*
ˌsu·per+con+'gest+ed *adj.*
ˌsu·per+con+'serv+a+tive *adj.*
ˌsu·per+'crim·i+nal *n., adj.*
ˌsu·per+'cri+ti+cal *adj.*
ˌsu·per+'cu+ri+ous *adj.*
ˌsu·per+'cyn·i+cal *adj.*
ˌsu·per+'def·i+cit *n.*
ˌsu·per+de+'vo+tion *n.*
ˌsu·per+'dif+fi+cult *adj.*
ˌsu·per+di+'plo+ma+cy *n.*
ˌsu·per+'dose *n.*
ˌsu·per+ef+'fec+tive *adj.*
ˌsu·per+ex+'cit+ed *adj.*
ˌsu·per+ex+'pres+sive *adj.*
ˌsu·per+'fi+nite *adj.*

su·per+fix ('su:pəˌfɪks, 'sju:-) *n. Linguistics.* a suprasegmental feature distinguishing the meaning or grammatical function of one word or phrase from that of another, as stress does for example between the noun *conduct* and the verb *conduct.*

su·per+flu·id (ˌsu:pə'flu:ɪd, ˌsju:-) *n.* **1.** *Physics.* a fluid in a state characterized by a very low viscosity, high thermal conductivity, high capillarity, etc. The only known example is that of liquid helium at temperatures close to absolute zero. *~adj.* **2.** being or relating to a superfluid.

su·per+flu·id+i·ty (ˌsu:pəflu:'ɪdɪtɪ, ˌsju:-) *n. Physics.* the state of being or property of becoming a superfluid.

su·per+flu+i·ty (ˌsu:pə'flu:ɪtɪ, ˌsju:-) *n.* **1.** the condition of being superfluous. **2.** a quantity or thing that is in excess of what is needed. **3.** a thing that is not needed. [C14: from Old French *superfluité,* via Late Latin from Latin *superfluus* SUPERFLUOUS]

su·per+flu+ous (su:'pɜ:fluəs, sju:-) *adj.* **1.** exceeding what is sufficient or required. **2.** not necessary or relevant; uncalled for. **3.** *Obsolete.* extravagant in expenditure or oversupplied with possessions. [C15: from Latin *superfluus* overflowing, from SUPER- + *fluere* to flow] **—su·'per+flu+ous+ly** *adv.* **—su·'per+flu+ous+ness** *n.*

su·per+fuse (ˌsu:pə'fju:z, ˌsju:-) *vb. Obsolete.* to pour or be poured so as to cover something. [C17: from Latin *superfūsus* poured over, from *superfundere,* from SUPER- + *fundere* to pour] **—ˌsu·per+'fu+sion** *n.*

su·per+gi+ant ('su:pəˌdʒaɪənt, 'sju:-) *n.* any of a class of extremely bright stars, such as Betelgeuse, which have expanded to a diameter hundreds or thousands of times greater than that of the sun and have an extremely low mean density. Compare **giant star, white dwarf.**

su·per+gla+ci·al (ˌsu:pə'gleɪsɪəl, ˌsju:-) *adj.* on or originating from the surface of a glacier.

su·per+heat (ˌsu:pə'hi:t, ˌsju:-) *vb. (tr.)* **1.** to heat (a vapour, esp. steam) to a temperature above its saturation point for a given pressure. **2.** to heat (a liquid) to a temperature above its boiling point without boiling occurring. **3.** to heat excessively; overheat. **—ˌsu·per+'heat+er** *n.*

su·per+he+ro ('su:pəˌhɪərəʊ, 'sju:-) *n., pl.* **+roes.** any of various comic-strip characters with superhuman abilities or magical powers, wearing a distinctive costume, and fighting against evil.

su·per+het ('su:pəˌhɛt, 'sju:-) *n.* See **superheterodyne receiver.**

su·per+het+er+o·dyne re+ceiv+er (ˌsu:pə'hɛtərəˌdaɪn, ˌsju:-) *n.* a radio receiver that combines two radio-frequency signals by heterodyne action, to produce a signal above the audible frequency limit. This signal is amplified and demodulated to give the desired audio-frequency signal. Sometimes shortened to **superhet.** [C20: from SUPER(SONIC) + HETERODYNE]

su·per+high fre+quen+cy ('su:pəˌhaɪ, 'sju:-) *n.* a radio-frequency band or radio frequency lying between 30 000 and 3000 megahertz. Abbrev.: **SHF.**

su·per+high+way ('su:pəˌhaɪweɪ, 'sju:-) *n. Chiefly U.S.* a fast dual-carriageway road.

su·per+hu+man (ˌsu:pə'hju:mən, ˌsju:-) *adj.* **1.** having powers above and beyond those of mankind. **2.** exceeding normal human ability or experience. **—ˌsu·per+hu+'man+i·ty** *or* **ˌsu·per+'hu+man+ness** *n.* **—ˌsu·per+'hu+man+ly** *adv.*

su·per+hum+e·ral (ˌsu:pə'hju:mərəl, ˌsju:-) *n.* an ecclesiastical vestment worn over the shoulders. [C17: from Late Latin *superhumerāle;* see SUPER-, HUMERAL]

su·per+im+pose (ˌsu:pərɪm'pəʊz, ˌsju:-) *vb. (tr.)* **1.** to set or place on or over something else. **2.** (usually foll. by *on* or *upon*) to add (to). **—ˌsu·per+ˌim+po+'si+tion** *n.*

su·per+in+cum+bent (ˌsu:pərɪn'kʌmbənt, ˌsju:-) *adj.* **1.** lying or being on top of something else. **2.** situated or suspended above; overhanging. **—ˌsu·per+in+'cum+bence** *or* **ˌsu·per+in+'cum+ben+cy** *n.* **—ˌsu·per+in+'cum+bent+ly** *adv.*

su·per+in+duce (ˌsu:pərɪn'dju:s, ˌsju:-) *vb. (tr.)* to introduce as an additional feature, factor, etc. **—ˌsu·per+in+'duce+ment** *n.* **—su·per+in+duc+tion** (ˌsu:pərɪn'dʌkʃən, ˌsju:-) *n.*

su·per+in+tend (ˌsu:pərɪn'tɛnd, ˌsu:prɪn-, ˌsju:-) *vb.* to undertake the direction or supervision (of); manage. [C17: from Church Latin *superintendere,* from Latin SUPER- + *intendere* to give attention to] **—ˌsu·per+in+'tend+ence** *n.*

su·per+in+tend+en+cy (ˌsu:pərɪn'tɛndənsɪ, ˌsu:prɪn-, ˌsju:-) *n., pl.* **+cies. 1.** the office or jurisdiction of a superintendent. **2.** a district under the jurisdiction of a superintendent.

su·per+in+ten+dent (ˌsu:pərɪn'tɛndənt, ˌsu:prɪn-, ˌsju:-) *n.* **1.** a person who directs and manages an organization, office, etc. **2.** (in England) a senior police officer higher in rank than an inspector but lower than a chief superintendent. **3.** (in the U.S.) the head of a police department. **4.** *Chiefly U.S.* a caretaker. *~adj.* **5.** of or relating to supervision; superintending. [C16: from Church Latin *superintendens* overseeing]

su+pe+ri+or (su:'pɪərɪə, sju:-) *adj.* **1.** greater in quality, quantity, etc. **2.** of high or extraordinary worth, merit, etc. **3.** higher in rank or status: *a superior tribunal.* **4.** displaying a conscious sense of being above or better than others; supercilious. **5.** (*often postpositive;* foll. by *to*) not susceptible (to) or influenced (by). **6.** placed higher up; situated further from the base. **7.** *Astronomy.* **a.** (of a planet) having an orbit further from the sun than the orbit of the earth. **b.** (of a conjunction) occurring when the sun lies between the earth and an inferior planet. **8.** (of a plant ovary) situated above the calyx and other floral parts. **9.** *Anatomy.* (of one part in relation to another) situated above or higher. **10.** *Printing.* (of a character) written or printed above the line; superscript. *~n.* **11.** a person or thing of greater rank or quality. **12.** *Printing.* a character set in a superior position. **13.** (*often cap.*) the head of a community in a religious order. [C14: from Latin, from *superus* placed above, from *super* above] **—su+'pe·ri+or+ess** *fem. n.* **—su+pe·ri+or+i·ty** (su:ˌpɪərɪ'ɒrɪtɪ, sju:-) *n.* **—su+'pe·ri+or+ly** *adv.*

Su+pe·ri+or (su:'pɪərɪə, sju:-) *n.* **Lake.** a lake in the N central U.S. and S Canada: one of the largest freshwater lakes in the world and westernmost of the Great Lakes. Area: 82 362 sq. km (31 800 sq. miles).

su+pe·ri+or court *n.* **1.** (in England) a higher court not subject to control by any other court except by way of appeal. See also **Supreme Court of Judicature. 2.** *U.S.* (in several states) a court of general jurisdiction ranking above the inferior courts and below courts of last resort.

su+pe·ri+or+i·ty com+plex *n. Informal.* an inflated estimate of one's own merit, usually manifested in arrogance.

su+pe·ri+or plan+et *n.* any of the six planets (Mars, Jupiter, Saturn, Uranus, Neptune, and Pluto) whose orbit lies outside that of the earth.

su·per+ja+cent (ˌsu:pə'dʒeɪsᵊnt, ˌsju:-) *adj.* lying immediately above or upon. [C17: from Late Latin *superjacēre,* from Latin SUPER- + *jacēre* to lie]

superl. *abbrev. for* superlative.

su·per+la+tive (su:'pɜ:lətɪv, sju:-) *adj.* **1.** of outstanding quality, degree, etc.; supreme. **2.** *Grammar.* denoting the form of an adjective or adverb that expresses the highest or a very high degree of quality. In English the superlative degree is usually marked by the suffix *-est* or the word *most,* as in *loudest* or *most loudly.* Compare **positive** (sense 10), **comparative** (sense 3). **3.** (of language or style) excessive; exaggerated. *~n.* **4.** a thing that excels all others or is of the highest quality. **5.** *Grammar.* the superlative form of an adjective. **6.** the highest degree; peak. [C14: from Old French *superlatif,* via Late Latin from Latin *superlātus* extravagant, from *superferre* to carry beyond, from SUPER- + *ferre* to bear] **—su·'per+la+tive+ly** *adv.* **—su·'per+la+tive+ness** *n.*

su·per+load ('su:pəˌləʊd, 'sju:-) *n.* another name for **live load.**

su·per+lun+ar (ˌsu:pə'lu:nə, ˌsju:-) *adj.* situated beyond the moon; celestial. **—ˌsuper+'lun+ar·y** *adj.*

su·per+male ('su:pəˌmeɪl, 'sju:-) *n.* a former name for **metamale.**

su·per+man ('su:pəˌmæn, 'sju:-) *n., pl.* **+men. 1.** (in the philosophy of Nietzsche) an ideal man who through personal integrity and creative ability would rise above good and evil and who represents the goal of human evolution. **2.** any man of apparently superhuman powers.

su·per+mar+ket ('su:pəˌmɑ:kɪt, 'sju:-) *n.* a large self-service store retailing food and household supplies.

su·per+mun+dane (ˌsu:pə'mʌndeɪn, ˌsju:-) *adj.* of or relating to what is elevated above earthly things.

su·per+nal (su:'pɜ:nᵊl, sju:-) *adj. Literary.* **1.** of or from the world of the divine; celestial. **2.** of or emanating from above or from the sky. [C15: from Medieval Latin *supernālis,* from Latin *supernus* that is on high, from *super* above] **—su·'per+nal+ly** *adv.*

su·per+na+tant (ˌsu:pə'neɪtᵊnt, ˌsju:-) *adj.* **1.** floating on the surface or over something. **2.** *Chem.* (of a liquid) lying above a sediment or settled precipitate. [C17: from Latin *supernatāre* to float, from SUPER- + *natāre* to swim] **—ˌsu·per+na+'ta+tion** *n.*

su·per+na+tion+al (ˌsu:pə'næʃənᵊl, ˌsju:-) *adj.* a less common word for **supranational. —ˌsu·per+'na+tion+al+ism** *n.* **—ˌsu·per+'na+tion+al+ist** *n.* **—ˌsu·per+'na+tion+al+ly** *adv.*

su·per+nat·u+ral (ˌsu:pə'nætʃrəl, -'nætʃərəl, ˌsju:-) *adj.* **1.** of or relating to things that cannot be explained according to natural laws. **2.** characteristic of or caused by or as if by a god; miraculous. **3.** of, involving, or ascribed to occult beings. **4.** exceeding the ordinary; abnormal. *~n.* **5. the.** supernatural forces, occurrences, and beings collectively or their realm. **—ˌsu·per+'nat·u+ral+ly** *adv.* **—ˌsu·per+'nat·u+ral+ness** *n.*

su·per+nat·u+ral+ism (ˌsu:pə'nætʃrəlɪzəm, -'nætʃərə-, ˌsju:-) *n.* **1.** the quality or condition of being supernatural. **2.** a supernatural agency, the effects of which are felt to be apparent in this world. **3.** belief in supernatural forces or agencies as producing effects in this world. **—ˌsu·per+'nat·u+ral+ist** *n., adj.* **—ˌsu·per+ˌnat·u+ral+'is+tic** *adj.*

su·per+nor+mal (ˌsu:pə'nɔ:məl, ˌsju:-) *adj.* greatly exceeding the normal. **—su·per+nor+mal+i·ty** (ˌsu:pənɔ:'mælɪtɪ, ˌsju:-) *or* **ˌsu·per+'nor+mal+ness** *n.* **—ˌsu·per+'nor+mal+ly** *adv.*

su·per+no+va (ˌsu:pə'nəʊvə, ˌsju:-) *n., pl.* **+vae** (-vi:) *or* **+vas.** a star that explodes catastrophically due to instabilities following the exhaustion of its nuclear fuel, becoming for a few days up to one hundred million times brighter than the sun. The expanding shell of debris (the **supernova remnant**) creates a nebula that radiates radio waves, x-rays, and light, for hundreds or thousands of years. Compare **nova.**

su·per+nu+mer+ar·y (ˌsu:pə'nju:mərərɪ, -'nju:mrərɪ, ˌsju:-) *adj.* **1.** exceeding a regular or proper number; extra. **2.** functioning as a substitute or assistant with regard to a regular body or staff. *~n., pl.* **+ar+ies. 3.** a person or thing that exceeds the normal, required, or regular number. **4.** a person who functions as a substitute or assistant. **5.** an actor who has no lines, esp. a nonprofessional one. [C17: from Late Latin *supernumerārius,* from Latin SUPER- + *numerus* number]

ˌsu·per+'gen+er+ous *adj.*
ˌsu·per+'ig+no+rant *adj.*
ˌsu·per+im+'por+tant *adj.*
ˌsu·per+in+'dif+fer+ence *adj.*
ˌsu·per+in+di+'vid·u+al+ist *n.*
ˌsu·per+in+'sist *vb.*
ˌsu·per+ˌin+tel+'lec+tu+al *adj.*
ˌsu·per+'log+i+cal *adj.*
ˌsu·per+'luck·y *adj.*
ˌsu·per+lux·'u+ri+ous *adj.*
ˌsu·per+'neg+li+gent *adj.*
ˌsu·per+ˌob+li+'ga+tion *n.*

su·per·or·der ('suːpəˌɔːdə, 'sjuː-) *n. Biology.* a taxonomic group that is a subdivision of a subclass.

su·per·or·di·nate *adj.* (ˌsuːpər'ɔːdənɪt, ˌsjuː-). **1.** of higher status or condition. **2.** *Logic.* bearing the relation of a universal proposition to a particular proposition in which the terms are the same. ~*n.* (ˌsuːpər'ɔːdɪnɪt, ˌsjuː-). **3.** a person or thing that is superordinate. ~*vb.* (ˌsuːpər'ɔːdɪˌneɪt, ˌsjuː-). **4.** (*tr.*) *Rare.* to make superordinate.

su·per·or·gan·ic (ˌsuːpərɔː'gænɪk, ˌsjuː-) *adj. Sociol.* (no longer widely used) relating to those aspects of a culture that are conceived as being superior to the individual members of the society. —ˌ**su·per·or·'gan·i·cism** *n.* —ˌ**su·per·or·'gan·i·cist** *n.*

su·per·ox·ide (ˌsuːpər'ɒksaɪd, ˌsjuː-) *n.* any of certain metal oxides that contain the O_2^- ion: *potassium superoxide, KO_2.*

su·per·phos·phate (ˌsuːpə'fɒsfeɪt, ˌsjuː-) *n.* **1.** a mixture of the diacid calcium salt of orthophosphoric acid $Ca(H_2PO_4)_2$ with calcium sulphate and small quantities of other phosphates: used as a fertilizer. **2.** a salt of phosphoric acid formed by incompletely replacing its acidic hydrogen atoms; acid phosphate; hydrogen phosphate.

su·per·phys·i·cal (ˌsuːpə'fɪzɪkᵊl, ˌsjuː-) *adj.* not explained by the known physical laws and phenomena; supernatural.

su·per·pose (ˌsuːpə'pəʊz, ˌsjuː-) *vb.* (*tr.*) **1.** *Geom.* to place (one figure) upon another so that their perimeters coincide. **2.** a rare word for **superimpose** (sense 1). [C19: from French *superposer,* from Latin *superpōnere,* from SUPER- + *pōnere* to place] —ˌ**su·per'pos·a·ble** *adj.*

su·per·po·si·tion (ˌsuːpəpə'zɪʃən, ˌsjuː-) *n.* **1.** the act of superposing or state of being superposed. **2.** *Geology.* the principle that in a series of stratified sedimentary rocks the lowest strata are the oldest.

su·per·pow·er ('suːpəˌpaʊə, 'sjuː-) *n.* **1.** an extremely powerful state, such as the U.S. **2.** extremely high power, esp. electrical or mechanical. —'**su·per·ˌpow·ered** *adj.*

su·per·sat·u·rat·ed (ˌsuːpə'sætʃəˌreɪtɪd, ˌsjuː-) *adj.* **1.** (of a solution) containing more solute than a saturated solution and therefore not in equilibrium. **2.** (of a vapour) containing more material than a saturated vapour and therefore not in equilibrium. —ˌ**su·per·ˌsat·u·'ra·tion** *n.*

su·per·scribe (ˌsuːpə'skraɪb, ˌsjuː-) *vb.* (*tr.*) to write (an inscription, name, etc.) above, on top of, or outside. [C16: from Latin *superscrībere,* from SUPER- + *scrībere* to write]

su·per·script ('suːpəˌskrɪpt, 'sjuː-) *adj.* **1.** *Printing.* (of a character) written or printed above the line; superior. Compare **subscript.** ~*n.* **2.** a superscript or superior character. **3.** *Obsolete.* a superscription on a document, letter, etc. [C16: from Latin *superscriptus;* see SUPERSCRIBE]

su·per·scrip·tion (ˌsuːpə'skrɪpʃən, ˌsjuː-) *n.* **1.** the act of superscribing. **2.** a superscribed title, address, etc. **3.** the symbol (℞) at the head of a medical prescription, which stands for the Latin word *recipe* (take).

su·per·sede (ˌsuːpə'siːd, ˌsjuː-) *vb.* (*tr.*) **1.** to take the place of (something old-fashioned or less appropriate); supplant. **2.** to replace in function, office, etc.; succeed. **3.** to discard or set aside or cause to be set aside as obsolete or inferior. [C15: via Old French from Latin *supersedēre* to sit above, from SUPER- + *sedēre* to sit] —ˌ**su·per'sed·a·ble** *adj.* —ˌ**su·per'sed·ence** *n.* —ˌ**su·per'sed·er** *n.* —**su·per·se·dure** (ˌsuːpə'siːdʒə, ˌsjuː-) *n.* —**su·per·ses·sion** (ˌsuːpə'sɛʃən, ˌsjuː-) *n.*

su·per·sen·si·ble (ˌsuːpə'sɛnsɪbᵊl, ˌsjuː-) *or* **su·per·sen·so·ry** (ˌsuːpə'sɛnsərɪ, ˌsjuː-) *adj.* imperceptible to or beyond reach of the senses. —ˌ**su·per'sen·si·bly** *adv.*

su·per·sex ('suːpəˌsɛks, 'sjuː-) *n. Genetics.* a sterile organism in which the ratio between the sex chromosomes is disturbed. See **metafemale, metamale.**

su·per·son·ic (ˌsuːpə'sɒnɪk, ˌsjuː-) *adj.* being, having, or capable of reaching a velocity in excess of the velocity of sound: *supersonic aircraft.* —ˌ**su·per'son·i·cal·ly** *adv.*

su·per·son·ics (ˌsuːpə'sɒnɪks, ˌsjuː-) *n.* (*functioning as sing.*) **1.** the study of supersonic motion. **2.** a less common name for **ultrasonics.**

su·per·star ('suːpəˌstɑː, 'sjuː-) *n.* a popular singer, film star, etc., who is idolized by fans and elevated to a position of importance in the entertainment industry.

su·per·sti·tion (ˌsuːpə'stɪʃən, ˌsjuː-) *n.* **1.** irrational belief usually founded on ignorance or fear and characterized by obsessive reverence for omens, charms, etc. **2.** a notion, act or ritual that derives from such belief. **3.** any irrational belief, esp. with regard to the unknown. [C15: from Latin *superstitiō* dread of the supernatural, from *superstāre* to stand still by something (as in amazement)]

su·per·sti·tious (ˌsuːpə'stɪʃəs, ˌsjuː-) *adj.* **1.** disposed to believe in superstition. **2.** of or relating to superstition. —ˌ**su·per'sti·tious·ly** *adv.* —ˌ**su·per'sti·tious·ness** *n.*

su·per·stra·tum (ˌsuːpə'strɑːtəm, -'streɪ-, ˌsjuː-) *n., pl.* **·ta** (-tə) *or* **·tums. 1.** *Geology.* a layer or stratum overlying another layer or similar structure. **2.** *Linguistics.* the language of a conquering or colonizing population as it supplants that of an indigenous population, as for example French and English in the West Indies. Compare **substratum** (sense 8).

su·per·struct (ˌsuːpə'strʌkt, ˌsjuː-) *vb.* (*tr.*) to erect upon a foundation or on top of another building or part.

su·per·struc·ture ('suːpəˌstrʌktʃə, 'sjuː-) *n.* **1.** the part of a building above its foundation. **2.** any structure or concept erected on something else. **3.** *Nautical.* any structure above the main deck of a ship with sides flush with the sides of the hull. **4.** the part of a bridge supported by the piers and abutments. **5.** (in Marxist theory) an edifice of interdependent agencies of the state, including legal and political institutions and ideologies, each possessing some autonomy but remaining products of the dominant mode of economic production. —'**su·per·ˌstruc·tur·al** *adj.*

su·per·tank·er ('suːpəˌtæŋkə, 'sjuː-) *n.* a large fast tanker of more than 275 000 tons capacity.

su·per·tax ('suːpəˌtæks, 'sjuː-) *n.* a tax levied in addition to the basic or normal tax, esp. a graduated surtax on incomes above a certain level.

su·per·ton·ic (ˌsuːpə'tɒnɪk, ˌsjuː-) *n. Music.* **1.** the second degree of a major or minor scale. **2.** a key or chord based on this.

su·per·vene (ˌsuːpə'viːn, ˌsjuː-) *vb.* (*intr.*) **1.** to follow closely; ensue. **2.** to occur as an unexpected or extraneous development. [C17: from Latin *supervenīre* to come upon, from SUPER- + *venīre* to come] —ˌ**su·per'ven·i·ence** *or* **su·per·ven·tion** (ˌsuːpə'vɛnʃən, ˌsjuː-) *n.* —ˌ**su·per'ven·i·ent** *adj.*

su·per·vise ('suːpəˌvaɪz, 'sjuː-) *vb.* (*tr.*) **1.** to direct or oversee the performance or operation of. **2.** to watch over so as to maintain order, etc. [C16: from Medieval Latin *supervidēre,* from Latin SUPER- + *vidēre* to see] —**su·per·vi·sion** (ˌsuːpə'vɪʒən, ˌsjuː-) *n.*

su·per·vi·sor ('suːpəˌvaɪzə, 'sjuː-) *n.* **1.** a person who manages or supervises. **2.** (in some British universities) a tutor supervising the work, esp. research work, of a student. **3.** (in some U.S. schools) an administrator running a department of teachers. **4.** (in some U.S. states) the elected chief official of a township or other subdivision of a county. **5.** *Obsolete.* a spectator. —'**su·per·ˌvi·sor·ˌship** *n.*

su·per·vi·so·ry ('suːpəˌvaɪzərɪ, 'sjuː-) *adj.* of, involving, or limited to supervision: *a supervisory capacity.*

su·pi·nate ('suːpɪˌneɪt, 'sjuː-) *vb.* to turn (the hand and forearm) so that the palm faces up or forwards. [C19: from Latin *supīnāre* to lay on the back, from *supīnus* SUPINE] —ˌ**su·pi'na·tion** *n.*

su·pi·na·tor ('suːpɪˌneɪtə, 'sjuː-) *n. Anatomy.* the muscle of the forearm that can produce the motion of supination.

su·pine *adj.* (suː'paɪn, sjuː-; 'suːpaɪn, 'sjuː-). **1.** lying or resting on the back with the face, palm, etc., upwards. **2.** displaying no interest or animation; lethargic. ~*n.* ('suːpaɪn, 'sjuː-). **3.** *Grammar.* a noun form derived from a verb in Latin, often used to express purpose with verbs of motion. Abbrev.: **sup.** [C15: from Latin *supīnus* related to *sub* under, up; (in grammatical sense) from Latin *verbum supīnum* supine word (the reason for this use is unknown)] —**su'pine·ly** *adv.* —**su'pine·ness** *n.*

su·plex ('suːplɛks) *n.* a wrestling hold in which a wrestler grasps his opponent round the waist from behind and carries him backwards. [C20: of uncertain origin]

supp. *or* **suppl.** *abbrev. for* supplement(ary).

sup·per ('sʌpə) *n.* **1.** an evening meal, esp. a light one. **2.** an evening social event featuring a supper. **3. sing for one's supper.** to obtain something by performing a service. ~*vb.* **4.** (*tr.*) *Rare.* to give supper to. **5.** (*intr.*) *Rare.* to eat supper. [C13: from Old French *soper;* see SUP[1]] —'**sup·per·less** *adj.*

sup·per club *n. U.S.* a small expensive nightclub.

sup·plant (sə'plɑːnt) *vb.* (*tr.*) to take the place of, often by trickery or force: *he easily supplanted his rival.* [C13: via Old French from Latin *supplantāre* to trip up, from *sub-* from below + *planta* sole of the foot] —**sup·plan·ta·tion** (ˌsʌplɑːn'teɪʃən) *n.* —**sup'plant·er** *n.*

sup·ple ('sʌpᵊl) *adj.* **1.** bending easily without damage. **2.** capable of or showing easy or graceful movement; lithe. **3.** mentally flexible; responding readily. **4.** disposed to agree, sometimes to the point of servility. ~*vb.* **5.** *Rare.* to make or become supple. [C13: from Old French *souple,* from Latin *supplex* bowed] —'**sup·ple·ness** *n.*

sup·ple·jack ('sʌpᵊlˌdʒæk) *n.* **1.** a North American twining rhamnaceous woody vine, *Berchemia scandens,* that has greenish-white flowers and purple fruits. **2.** a tropical American woody sapindaceous vine, *Paullinia curassavica,* having strong supple wood. **3.** any of various other vines with strong supple stems. **4.** *U.S.* a walking stick made from the wood of *Paullinia curassavica.*

sup·ple·ment *n.* ('sʌplɪmənt). **1.** an addition designed to complete, make up for a deficiency, etc. **2.** a section appended to a publication to supply further information, correct errors, etc. **3.** a magazine or section inserted into a newspaper or periodical, such as one with colour photographs issued every week. **4.** *Geom.* **a.** either of a pair of angles whose sum is 180°. **b.** an arc of a circle that when added to another arc forms a semicircle. ~Abbrev.: **sup., supp.** ~*vb.* ('sʌplɪˌmɛnt). **5.** (*tr.*) to provide a supplement to, esp. in order to remedy a

ˌsu·per·of·'fi·cious *adj.*
ˌsu·per'op·ti·mist *n.*
ˌsu·per·po·'lite *n.*
ˌsu·per'pol·y·mer *n.*
ˌsu·per·pre'cise *adj.*
ˌsu·per·pre'pared *adj.*
ˌsu·per'pure *adj.*
ˌsu·per·re'fine *vb.*
ˌsu·per·re'li·ance *n.*
ˌsu·per·re'spect·a·ble *adj.*
ˌsu·per·re'strict·ion *n.*
ˌsu·per'right·eous *adj.*
ˌsu·per'sa·cred *adj.*
ˌsu·per·sar'cas·tic *adj.*
ˌsu·per'se·cret *adj.*
ˌsu·per'sen·si·tive *adj.*
ˌsu·per·se'vere *adj.*
ˌsu·per·sim'plic·i·ty *n.*
ˌsu·per'spe·cial·ize *or*
ˌsu·per'spe·cial·ise *vb.*
ˌsu·per'strict *adj.*
ˌsu·per'styl·ish *adj.*
ˌsu·per·suf'fi·cien·cy *n.*
ˌsu·per'sweet *adj.*
ˌsu·per'ten·sion *n.*
ˌsu·per'thor·ough *adj.*
ˌsu·per'vig·i·lant *adj.*
ˌsu·per'vir·u·lent *adj.*

deficiency. [C14: from Latin *supplēmentum*, from *supplēre* to SUPPLY] —ˌ**sup+ple·men+ˈta+tion** *n.* —ˈ**sup+ple·ˌment+er** *n.*

sup+ple·men+ta+ry (ˌsʌplɪˈmɛntərɪ, -trɪ) *adj.* **1.** Also: **supplemental.** forming or acting as a supplement. ~*n., pl.* **+ries. 2.** a person or thing that is a supplement. —ˌ**sup+ple+ˈmen+ta+ri+ly** *or* ˌ**sup+ple·ˈmen+tal+ly** *adv.*

sup+ple·men+ta+ry an+gle *n.* either of two angles whose sum is 180°.

sup+ple·men+ta+ry ben+e·fit *n.* (in Britain) a weekly allowance paid to various groups of people by the state to bring their incomes up to minimum levels established by law; social assistance. Former name: **national assistance.** See also **social security, national insurance.**

sup+ple·tion (səˈpliːʃən) *n.* the use of an unrelated word to complete the otherwise defective paradigm of a given word, as for example the use of *went* for the past tense of *go.* [C14: from Medieval Latin *supplētiō* a completing, from Latin *supplēre* to SUPPLY[1]] —**sup+ˈple·tive** *n., adj.*

sup+ple·to·ry (ˈsʌplɪtərɪ, -trɪ) *adj. Archaic.* remedying deficiencies; supplementary. —ˈ**sup+ple·to+ri+ly** *adv.*

sup+pli+ant (ˈsʌplɪənt) *adj.* **1.** expressing entreaty or supplication. ~*n., adj.* **2.** another word for **supplicant.** [C15: from French *supplier* to beseech, from Latin *supplicāre* to kneel in entreaty; see SUPPLE] —ˈ**sup+pli+ant+ly** *adv.* —ˈ**sup+pli+ance, ˈsup+pli+an+cy,** *or* ˈ**sup+pli+ant+ness** *n.*

sup+pli+cant (ˈsʌplɪkənt) *or* **sup+pli+ant** *n.* **1.** a person who supplicates. ~*adj.* **2.** entreating humbly; supplicating. [C16: from Latin *supplicāns* beseeching; see SUPPLE]

sup+pli+cate (ˈsʌplɪˌkeɪt) *vb.* **1.** to make a humble request to (someone); plead. **2.** (*tr.*) to ask for or seek humbly. [C15: from Latin *supplicāre* to beg on one's knees; see SUPPLE] —ˈ**sup+pli+ˌca+to·ry** *adj.*

sup+pli+ca+tion (ˌsʌplɪˈkeɪʃən) *n.* **1.** the act of supplicating. **2.** a humble entreaty or petition; prayer.

sup+ply[1] (səˈplaɪ) *vb.* **+plies, +ply+ing, +plied. 1.** (*tr.;* often foll. by *with*) to furnish with something that is required: *to supply the community with good government.* **2.** (*tr.;* often foll. by *to* or *for*) to make available or provide (something that is desired or lacking): *to supply books to the library.* **3.** (*tr.*) to provide for adequately; make good; satisfy: *who will supply their needs?* **4.** to serve as a substitute, usually temporary, in (another's position, etc.): *there are no clergymen to supply the pulpit.* **5.** (*tr.*) *Brit.* to fill (a vacancy, position, etc.). ~*n., pl.* **+plies. 6. a.** the act of providing or something that is provided. **b.** (*as modifier*): *a supply dump.* **7.** (*often pl.*) an amount available for use; stock. **8.** (*pl.*) food, equipment, etc., needed for a campaign or trip. **9.** *Economics.* **a.** willingness and ability to offer goods and services for sale. **b.** the amount of a commodity that producers are willing and able to offer for sale at a specified price. Compare **demand** (sense 9). **10.** *Military.* **a.** the management and disposal of food and equipment. **b.** (*as modifier*): *supply routes.* **11.** (*often pl.*) a grant of money voted by a legislature for government expenses, esp. those not covered by other revenues. **12.** (in Parliament and similar legislatures) the money voted annually for the expenses of the civil service and armed forces. **13. a.** a person who acts as a temporary substitute, esp. a clergyman. **b.** (*as modifier*): *a supply teacher.* **14.** a source of electrical energy, gas, etc. **15.** *Obsolete.* aid or assistance. [C14: from Old French *souppleier*, from Latin *supplēre* to complete, from *sub-* up + *plēre* to fill] —**sup+ˈpli+a·ble** *adj.* —**sup+ˈpli+er** *n.*

sup+ply[2] (ˈsʌplɪ) *or* **sup+ple+ly** (ˈsʌpəlɪ) *adv.* in a supple manner.

sup+port (səˈpɔːt) *vb.* (*tr.*) **1.** to carry the weight of. **2.** to bear or withstand (pressure, weight, etc.). **3.** to provide the necessities of life for (a family, person, etc.). **4.** to tend to establish (a theory, statement, etc.) by providing new facts; substantiate. **5.** to speak in favour of (a motion). **6.** to give aid or courage to. **7.** to give approval to (a cause, principle, etc.); subscribe to: *to support a political candidature.* **8.** to endure with forbearance: *I will no longer support bad behaviour.* **9.** to give strength to; maintain: *to support a business.* **10.** *Films, theatre.* **a.** to play a subordinate role to. **b.** to accompany (the feature) in a film programme. **11.** to act or perform (a role or character). ~*n.* **12.** the act of supporting or the condition of being supported. **13.** a thing that bears the weight or part of the weight of a construction. **14.** a person who or thing that furnishes aid. **15.** the means of maintenance of a family, person, etc. **16.** (often preceded by *the*) an actor or group of actors playing subordinate roles. **17.** *Med.* an appliance worn to ease the strain on an injured bodily structure or part. **18.** the solid material on which a painting is executed, such as canvas. **19.** See **athletic support.** [C14: from Old French *supporter*, from Latin *supportāre* to bring, from *sub-* up + *portāre* to carry] —**sup+ˈport+ive** *adj.* —**sup+ˈport+less** *adj.*

sup+port+a·ble (səˈpɔːtəbəl) *adj.* able to be supported or endured; bearable. —**sup+ˌport+a·ˈbil+i·ty** *or* **sup+ˈport+a·ble+ness** *n.* —**sup+ˈport+a·bly** *adv.*

sup+port+er (səˈpɔːtə) *n.* **1.** a person who or thing that acts as a support. **2.** a person who backs a sports team, politician, etc. **3.** a garment or device worn to ease the strain on or restrict the movement of a bodily structure or part. **4.** *Heraldry.* a figure or beast in a coat of arms depicted as holding up the shield.

sup+port+ing (səˈpɔːtɪŋ) *adj.* **1.** (of a role) being a fairly important but not leading part, esp. in a play or film. **2.** (of an actor or actress) playing a supporting role.

sup+port+ive ther+a·py *n.* **1.** *Med.* any treatment, such as the intravenous administration of certain fluids, designed to reinforce or sustain the physiological well-being of a patient. **2.** *Psychol.* a form of therapy for mental disturbances employing guidance and encouragement to develop the patient's own resources.

sup+pose (səˈpəʊz) *vb.* (*tr.; may take a clause as object*) **1.** to presume (something) to be true without certain knowledge: *I suppose he meant to kill her.* **2.** to consider as a possible suggestion for the sake of discussion, elucidation, etc.; postulate: *suppose that he wins the election.* **3.** (of theories, propositions, etc.) to imply the inference or assumption (of): *your policy supposes full employment.* [C14: from Old French *supposer*, from Medieval Latin *suppōnere*, from Latin: to substitute, from SUB- + *pōnere* to put] —**sup+ˈpos+a·ble** *adj.* —**sup+ˈpos+er** *n.*

sup+posed (səˈpəʊzd, -ˈpəʊzɪd) *adj.* **1.** (*prenominal*) presumed to be true without certain knowledge: *his supposed date of birth.* **2.** (*prenominal*) believed to be true on slight grounds; highly doubtful: *the supposed existence of ghosts.* **3.** (səˈpəʊzd). (*postpositive;* foll. by *to*) expected or obliged (to): *I'm supposed to be there at nine.* **4.** (*postpositive; used in negative;* foll. by *to*) expected or obliged not (to): *you're not supposed to walk on the grass.* —**sup+pos+ed+ly** (səˈpəʊzɪdlɪ) *adv.*

sup+po·si+tion (ˌsʌpəˈzɪʃən) *n.* **1.** the act of supposing. **2.** a fact, theory, etc., that is supposed. —ˌ**sup+po+ˈsi+tion+al** *adj.* —ˌ**sup+po+ˈsi+tion+al+ly** *adv.* —ˌ**sup+po+ˈsi+tion+less** *adj.*

sup+po·si+tious (ˌsʌpəˈzɪʃəs) *or* **sup+pos·i+ti+tious** (səˌpɒzɪˈtɪʃəs) *adj.* **1.** deduced from supposition; hypothetical. **2.** substituted with intent to mislead or deceive. —ˌ**sup+po+ˈsi+tious+ly** *or* **sup+ˌpos·i+ˈti+tious+ly** *adv.* —ˌ**sup+po+ˈsi+tious+ness** *or* **sup+ˌpos·i+ˈti+tious+ness** *n.*

sup+pos·i+tive (səˈpɒzɪtɪv) *adj.* **1.** of, involving, or arising out of supposition. **2.** *Grammar.* denoting a conjunction introducing a clause expressing a supposition, as for example *if, supposing,* or *provided that.* ~*n.* **3.** *Grammar.* a suppositive conjunction. —**sup+ˈpos·i+tive+ly** *adv.*

sup+pos·i+to·ry (səˈpɒzɪtərɪ, -trɪ) *n., pl.* **·ries.** *Med.* an encapsulated or solid medication for insertion into the vagina, rectum, or urethra, where it melts and releases the active substance. [C14: from Medieval Latin *suppositōrium*, from Latin *suppositus* placed beneath, from *suppōnere;* see SUPPOSE]

sup+press (səˈprɛs) *vb.* (*tr.*) **1.** to put an end to; prohibit. **2.** to hold in check; restrain: *I was obliged to suppress a smile.* **3.** to withhold from circulation or publication: *to suppress seditious pamphlets.* **4.** to stop the activities of; crush: *to suppress a rebellion.* **5.** *Electronics.* **a.** to reduce or eliminate (unwanted oscillations) in a circuit. **b.** to eliminate (a particular frequency or group of frequencies) in a signal. **6.** *Psychiatry.* **a.** to resist consciously an idea or a desire entering one's mind. **b.** to exercise self-control by preventing the expression of certain desires. Compare **repress** (sense 3). [C14: from Latin *suppressus* held down, from *supprimere* to restrain, from *sub-* down + *premere* to press] —**sup+ˈpress+i·ble** *adj.* —**sup+ˈpres+sor** *or* **sup+ˈpress+er** *n.*

sup+pres+sion (səˈprɛʃən) *n.* **1.** the act or process of suppressing or the condition of being suppressed. **2.** *Psychiatry.* the conscious avoidance of unpleasant thoughts. Compare **repression. 3.** *Electronics.* the act or process of suppressing a frequency, oscillation, etc. **4.** *Botany.* the failure of an organ or part to develop.

sup+pres+sive (səˈprɛsɪv) *adj.* **1.** tending or acting to suppress; involving suppression. **2.** *Psychiatry.* tending to prevent the expression of certain of one's desires or to resist the emergence of mental symptoms.

sup+pres+sor grid *n.* an electrode placed between the screen grid and anode of a valve. Its negative potential, relative to both screen and anode, prevents secondary electrons from the anode reaching the screen.

sup+pu+rate (ˈsʌpjʊˌreɪt) *vb.* (*intr.*) *Pathol.* (of a wound, sore, etc.) to discharge pus; fester. [C16: from Latin *suppūrāre*, from SUB- + *pūs* PUS]

sup+pu+ra+tion (ˌsʌpjʊˈreɪʃən) *n.* **1.** the discharging of pus from a wound, sore, etc. **2.** the discharge itself.

sup+pu+ra+tive (ˈsʌpjʊrətɪv) *adj.* **1.** causing suppuration. ~*n.* **2.** any suppurative drug.

supr. *abbrev. for* supreme.

su+pra (ˈsuːprə, ˈsjuː-) *adv.* above, esp. referring to earlier parts of a book etc. [C15: from Latin; related to SUPER-]

su·pra- *prefix.* over, above, beyond, or greater than: *supranational; supramolecular.* [from Latin *suprā* above]

su·pra+glot+tal (ˌsuːprəˈglɒtəl, ˌsjuː-) *adj. Anatomy.* situated above the glottis: *supraglottal obstruction.*

su·pra+lap+sar+i·an (ˌsuːprəlæpˈsɛərɪən, ˌsjuː-) *n. Theol., chiefly Calvanist.* a person who believes that God decreed the election or nonelection of individuals to salvation even before the fall. Compare **infralapsarian.** [C17: from New Latin *suprālapsārius*, from Latin SUPRA- + *lapsus* a fall] —ˌ**su·pra+lap+ˈsar·i·an+ism** *n.*

su·pra+lim·i+nal (ˌsuːprəˈlɪmɪnəl, ˌsjuː-) *adj.* of or relating to any stimulus that is above the threshold of sensory awareness. Compare **subliminal.** —ˌ**su·pra+ˈlim·i·nal+ly** *adv.*

su·pra+mo+lec·u·lar (ˌsuːprəməˈlɛkjʊlə, ˌsjuː-) *adj.* **1.** more complex than a molecule. **2.** consisting of more than one molecule.

su·pra+na·tion+al (ˌsuːprəˈnæʃnəl, ˌsjuː-) *adj.* involving or relating to more than one nation. —ˌ**su·pra+ˈna·tion·al+ism** *n.* —ˌ**su·pra+ˈna·tion+al+ly** *adv.*

su·pra+or·bit+al (ˌsuːprəˈɔːbɪtəl, ˌsjuː-) *adj. Anatomy.* situated above the orbit.

su·pra+re·nal (ˌsuːprəˈriːnəl, ˌsjuː-) *adj. Anatomy.* situated above a kidney.

su·pra·re·nal gland *n.* another name for **adrenal gland.**

su·pra·seg·men·tal (ˌsuːprəsɛgˈmɛntəl, ˌsjuː-) *adj. Linguistics.* denoting those features of a sound or sequence of sounds that accompany rather than form part of the consecutive segments of a word or sentence, as for example stress and pitch in English. —ˌ**su·pra·seg·ˈmen·tal·ly** *adv.*

su·prem·a·cist (sʊˈprɛməsɪst, sjʊ-) *n.* **1.** a person who promotes or advocates the supremacy of any particular group. ~*adj.* **2.** characterized by belief in the supremacy of any particular group. —**su·ˈprem·a·tism** *n.*

su·prem·a·cy (sʊˈprɛməsɪ, sjʊ-) *n.* **1.** supreme power; authority. **2.** the quality or condition of being supreme.

Su·prem·a·tism (sʊˈprɛməˌtɪzəm, sjʊ-) *n.* a form of pure cubist art, launched in Russia in 1913, and based on the principle that paintings should be composed only of rectangles, circles, triangles, or crosses. [C20: from *suprematist* a supporter of this theory, from French *suprématie* SUPREMACY] —**Su·ˈprem·a·ˌtist** *n., adj.*

su·preme (sʊˈpriːm, sjʊ-) *adj.* **1.** of highest status or power: *a supreme tribunal.* **2.** (*usually prenominal*) of highest quality, importance, etc.: *supreme endeavour.* **3.** greatest in degree; extreme: *supreme folly.* **4.** (*prenominal*) final or last, esp. being last in one's life or progress; ultimate: *the supreme judgment.* [C16: from Latin *suprēmus* highest, from *superus* that is above, from *super* above] —**su·ˈpreme·ly** *adv.* —**su·ˈpreme·ness** *n.*

su·prême (sʊˈpriːm, -ˈprɛm, sjʊ-) *n.* **1.** Also called: **suprême sauce.** a rich velouté sauce made with a base of veal or chicken stock, with cream or egg yolks added. **2.** the best or most delicate part of meat, esp. the breast and wing of chicken, cooked in suprême sauce. [French: SUPREME]

Su·preme Be·ing *n.* the most exalted being; God.

su·preme com·mand·er *n.* the military officer in overall command of all forces in one theatre of operations.

Su·preme Court *n.* (in the U.S.) **1.** the highest Federal court, possessing final appellate jurisdiction and exercising supervisory jurisdiction over the lower courts. **2.** (in many states) the highest state court.

Su·preme Court of Ju·di·ca·ture *n.* (in England) a court formed in 1873 by the amalgamation of several superior courts into two divisions, the High Court of Justice and the Court of Appeal.

su·preme sac·ri·fice *n.* **the.** the sacrifice of one's life.

Su·preme So·vi·et *n.* (in the Soviet Union) **1.** the bicameral legislature, comprising the **Soviet of the Union** and the **Soviet of the Nationalities;** officially the highest organ of state power. **2.** a similar legislature in each republic.

su·pre·mo (sʊˈpriːməʊ, sjʊ-) *n., pl.* **·mos.** *Brit. informal.* a person in overall authority. [C20: from SUPREME]

Supt. *or* **supt.** *abbrev. for* superintendent.

Su·qu·tra (səˈkəʊtrə) *n.* a variant spelling of **Socotra.**

Sur *or* **Sour** (sʊə) *n.* transliteration of the Arabic name for **Tyre.**

sur-[1] *prefix.* over; above; beyond: *surcharge; surrealism.* Compare **super-.** [from Old French, from Latin SUPER-]

sur-[2] *prefix.* variant of **sub-** before *r: surrogate.*

su·ra (ˈsʊərə) *n.* any of the 114 chapters of the Koran. [C17: from Arabic *sūrah,* section]

Su·ra·ba·ya, Su·ra·ba·ja, *or* **Soe·ra·ba·ja** (ˌsʊərəˈbaɪə) *n.* a port in Indonesia, on E Java on the **Surabaya Strait:** the country's second port and chief naval base; university (1954); fishing and ship-building industries; oil refinery. Pop.: 1 556 255 (1971).

su·rah (ˈsʊərə) *n.* a twill-weave fabric of silk or rayon, used for dresses, blouses, etc. [C19: from the French pronunciation of SURAT]

Su·ra·kar·ta (ˌsʊərəˈkɑːtə) *n.* a town in Indonesia, on central Java: textile manufacturing. Pop.: 414 285 (1971).

su·ral (ˈsjʊərəl) *adj. Anatomy.* of or relating to the calf of the leg. [C17: via New Latin from Latin *sūra* calf]

su·rat (sjuːˈræt) *n.* (formerly) a cotton fabric from the Surat area of India.

Su·rat (sʊˈræt, ˈsʊərət) *n.* a port in W India, in W Gujarat: a major port in the 17th century; textile manufacturing. Pop.: 471 656 (1971).

sur·base (ˈsɜːˌbeɪs) *n.* the uppermost part, such as a moulding, of a pedestal, base, or skirting. Compare **subbase.** —**sur·ˈbase·ment** *n.*

sur·based (ˈsɜːˌbeɪst) *adj. Architect.* **1.** having a surbase. **2.** (of an arch) having a rise of less than half the span. [C18: from French *surbaisser* to depress, from *sur-* (intensive) + *baisser* to lower, from *bas* low; see BASE[1]]

sur·cease (sɜːˈsiːs) *Archaic.* ~*n.* **1.** cessation or intermission. ~*vb.* **2.** to desist from (some action). **3.** to cease or cause to cease. [C16: from earlier *sursesen,* from Old French *surseoir,* from Latin *supersedēre;* see SUPERSEDE]

sur·charge *n.* (ˈsɜːˌtʃɑːdʒ). **1.** a charge in addition to the usual payment, tax, etc. **2.** an excessive sum charged, esp. when unlawful. **3.** an extra and usually excessive burden or supply. **4.** *Law.* the act or an instance of surcharging. **5.** an overprint that alters the face value of a postage stamp. ~*vb.* (sɜːˈtʃɑːdʒ, ˈsɜːˌtʃɑːdʒ). (*tr.*) **6.** to charge an additional sum, tax, etc. **7.** to overcharge (a person) for something. **8.** to put an extra physical burden upon; overload. **9.** to fill to excess; overwhelm. **10.** *Law.* to insert credits that have been omitted in (an account). **11.** to overprint a surcharge on (a stamp). —**sur·ˈcharg·er** *n.*

sur·cin·gle (ˈsɜːˌsɪŋgəl) *n.* **1.** a girth for a horse which goes around the body, used esp. with a racing saddle. **2.** the belt worn with a cassock. ~*vb.* **3.** to put a surcingle on or over (a horse). [C14: from Old French *surcengle,* from *sur-* over + *cengle* a belt, from Latin *cingulum*]

sur·coat (ˈsɜːˌkəʊt) *n.* **1.** a tunic, often embroidered with heraldic arms, worn by a knight over his armour during the Middle Ages. **2.** an outer coat or other garment.

sur·cu·lose (ˈsɜːkjʊˌləʊs) *adj.* (of a plant) bearing suckers. [C19: from Latin *surculōsus* woody, from *surculus* twig, from *sūrus* a branch]

surd (sɜːd) *n.* **1.** *Maths.* a sum containing one or more irrational roots of numbers, such as $2\sqrt{3} + 3\sqrt{2} + 6$. **2.** *Phonetics.* a voiceless consonant, such as (t). ~*adj.* **3.** of or relating to a surd. [C16: from Latin *surdus* muffled]

sure (ʃʊə, ʃɔː) *adj.* **1.** (sometimes foll. by *of*) free from hesitancy or uncertainty (with regard to a belief, conviction, etc.): *we are sure of the accuracy of the data; I am sure that he is lying.* **2.** (foll. by *of*) having no doubt, as of the occurrence of a future state or event: *sure of success.* **3.** always effective; unfailing: *a sure remedy.* **4.** reliable in indication or accuracy: *a sure criterion.* **5.** (of persons) worthy of trust or confidence: *a sure friend.* **6.** not open to doubt: *sure proof.* **7.** admitting of no vacillation or doubt: *he is very sure in his beliefs.* **8.** bound to be or occur; inevitable: *victory is sure.* **9.** (*postpositive*) bound inevitably (to be or do something); certain: *she is sure to be there tonight.* **10.** physically secure or dependable: *a sure footing.* **11.** *Obsolete.* free from exposure to harm or danger. **12. be sure.** (*usually imperative or dependent imperative; takes a clause as object or an infinitive,* sometimes with *to* replaced by *and*) to be careful or certain: *be sure and shut the door; I told him to be sure to shut the door.* **13. for sure.** without a doubt; surely. **14. make sure. a.** (*takes a clause as object*) to make certain; ensure. **b.** (foll. by *of*) to establish or confirm power or possession (over). **15. sure enough.** *Informal.* as might have been confidently expected; definitely: often used as a sentence substitute. **16. to be sure. a.** without doubt; certainly. **b.** it has to be acknowledged; admittedly. ~*adv.* **17.** (*sentence modifier*) *U.S. informal.* without question; certainly. **18.** (*sentence substitute*) *U.S. informal.* willingly; yes. [C14: from Old French *seur,* from Latin *sēcūrus* SECURE] —**ˈsure·ness** *n.*

sure-fire *adj.* (*usually prenominal*) *Informal.* certain to succeed or meet expectations; assured.

sure-foot·ed *adj.* **1.** unlikely to fall, slip, or stumble. **2.** not likely to err or fail, as in judgment. —ˌ**sure-ˈfoot·ed·ly** *adv.* —ˌ**sure-ˈfoot·ed·ness** *n.*

sure·ly (ˈʃʊəlɪ, ˈʃɔː-) *adv.* **1.** without doubt; assuredly: *things could surely not have been worse.* **2.** without fail; inexorably (esp. in the phrase **slowly but surely**). **3.** (*sentence modifier*) am I not right in thinking that?; I am sure that: *surely you don't mean it?* **4.** *Rare.* in a sure manner. **5.** *Archaic.* safely; securely. **6.** (*sentence substitute*) *Chiefly U.S.* willingly; of course; yes.

sure thing *Informal.* **1.** (*sentence substitute*) *Chiefly U.S.* all right! yes indeed! used to express enthusiastic assent. ~*n.* **2.** something guaranteed to be successful.

sure·ty (ˈʃʊətɪ, ˈʃʊərɪtɪ) *n., pl.* **·ties. 1.** a person who assumes legal responsibility for the fulfilment of another's debt or obligation and himself becomes liable if the other defaults. **2.** security given against loss or damage or as a guarantee that an obligation will be met. **3.** *Obsolete.* the quality or condition of being sure. **4.** *Obsolete.* a means of assurance or safety. **5. stand surety.** to act as a surety. [C14: from Old French *seurte,* from Latin *sēcūritās* SECURITY] —**ˈsure·ty·ˌship** *n.*

surf (sɜːf) *n.* **1.** waves breaking on the shore or on a reef. **2.** foam caused by the breaking of waves. ~*vb.* **3.** (*intr.*) to take part in surfing. [C17: probably variant of SOUGH[1]] —**ˈsurf·a·ble** *adj.* —**ˈsurf·ˌlike** *adj.* —**ˈsurf·y** *adj.*

sur·face (ˈsɜːfɪs) *n.* **1. a.** the exterior face of an object or one such face. **b.** (*as modifier*): *surface gloss.* **2. a.** the area or size of such a face. **b.** (*as modifier*): *surface measurements.* **3.** material resembling such a face, with length and width but without depth. **4. a.** the superficial appearance as opposed to the real nature. **b.** (*as modifier*): *a surface resemblance.* **5.** *Geom.* **a.** the complete boundary of a solid figure. **b.** a continuous two-dimensional configuration. **6. a.** the uppermost level of the land or sea. **b.** (*as modifier*): *surface transportation.* **7. come to the surface.** to emerge; become apparent. **8. on the surface.** to all appearances. ~*vb.* **9.** to rise or cause to rise to or as if to the surface (of water, etc.). **10.** (*tr.*) to treat the surface of, as by polishing, smoothing, etc. **11.** (*tr.*) to furnish with a surface. **12.** (*intr.*) *Mining.* **a.** to work at or near the ground surface. **b.** to wash surface ore deposits. **13.** (*intr.*) to become apparent; emerge. [C17: from French, from *sur* on + *face* FACE, probably on the model of Latin SUPERFICIES] —**ˈsur·face·less** *adj.* —**ˈsur·fac·er** *n.*

sur·face-ac·tive *adj.* (of a substance, esp. a detergent) capable of lowering the surface tension of a liquid, usually water. See also **surfactant.**

sur·face fric·tion drag *n.* the part of the drag on a body moving through a fluid that is dependent on the nature of the surface of the body. Also called: **skin friction.**

sur·face mail *n.* mail transported by land or sea. Compare **air mail.**

sur·face noise *n.* noise produced by the friction of the needle or stylus of a record player with the rotating record.

sur·face plate *n.* another name for **faceplate** (sense 2).

sur·face struc·ture *n. Generative grammar.* a representation of a string of elements as they occur in a sentence, together with labels and brackets that represent its syntactic structure. Compare **deep structure.**

sur·face ten·sion *n.* **1.** a property of liquids caused by intermolecular forces near the surface leading to the apparent presence of a surface film and to capillarity, etc. **2.** a measure of this property expressed as the force acting normal to one side of a line of unit length on the surface: measured in newtons per metre. Symbol: T, γ, or σ.

sur·face-to-air *adj.* of or relating to a missile launched from the surface of the earth against airborne targets.

sur·face-to-sur·face *adj.* of or relating to a missile launched from the surface of the earth against surface targets.

sur+fac+tant (sɜːˈfæktənt) *n.* a substance, such as a detergent, that can reduce the surface tension of a liquid and thus allow it to foam or penetrate solids; a wetting agent. Also called: **surface-active agent.** [C20: *surf(ace)-act(ive) a(ge)nt*]

surf+bird (ˈsɜːfˌbɜːd) *n.* an American shore bird, *Aphriza virgata,* having a spotted plumage, with a black and white tail: family *Scolopacidae* (sandpipers, etc.), order *Charadriiformes.*

surf+board (ˈsɜːfˌbɔːd) *n.* **1.** a long narrow board used in surfing. **2.** a wrestling hold in which a wrestler sits on the floor and locks his feet round his opponent's ankles, seizes the arms or head, and bends his opponent's body backwards, placing his knees against his opponent's back.

surf+boat (ˈsɜːfˌbəʊt) *n.* a boat with a high bow and stern and flotation chambers, equipped for use in rough surf.

surf+cast·ing (ˈsɜːfˌkɑːstɪŋ) *n.* fishing from the shore by casting into the surf. —**ˈsurf+ˌcast·er** *n.*

sur+feit (ˈsɜːfɪt) *n.* **1.** (usually foll. by *of*) an excessive or immoderate amount. **2.** overindulgence, esp. in eating or drinking. **3.** disgust, nausea, etc., caused by such overindulgence. ~*vb.* **4.** (*tr.*) to supply or feed excessively; satiate. **5.** (*intr.*) *Archaic.* to eat, drink, or be supplied to excess. **6.** (*intr.*) *Obsolete.* to feel uncomfortable as a consequence of overindulgence. [C13: from French *sourfait,* from *sourfaire* to overdo, from SUR-[1] + *faire,* from Latin *facere* to do] —**ˈsur+feit+er** *n.*

surf·ie (ˈsɜːfɪ) *n. Austral. slang.* a young man whose main interest is in surfing, esp. when considered as a cult figure.

surf+ing (ˈsɜːfɪŋ) *n.* the sport of riding towards shore on the crest of a wave by standing or lying on a surfboard. —**ˈsurf+er** *or* **ˈsurf+ˌrid·er** *n.*

surf+perch (ˈsɜːfˌpɜːtʃ) *n.* any viviparous marine percoid fish of the family *Embiotocidae,* of North American Pacific coastal waters. Also called: **sea perch.**

surf sco·ter *or* **duck** *n.* a North American scoter, *Melanitta perspicillata,* having white patches on the head.

surg. *abbrev. for:* **1.** surgeon. **2.** surgery. **3.** surgical.

surge (sɜːdʒ) *n.* **1.** a strong rush or sweep; sudden increase: *a surge of anger.* **2.** the rolling swell of the sea, esp. after the passage of a large wave. **3.** a heavy rolling motion or sound: *the surge of the trumpets.* **4.** an undulating rolling surface, as of hills. **5.** a billowing cloud or volume. **6.** *Nautical.* a temporary release or slackening of a rope or cable. **7.** a large momentary increase in the voltage or current in an electric circuit. **8.** an instability or unevenness in the power output of an engine. **9.** *Astronomy.* a short-lived disturbance, occurring during the eruption of a solar flare. ~*vb.* **10.** (*intr.*) (of waves, the sea, etc.) to rise or roll with a heavy swelling motion. **11.** (*intr.*) to move like a heavy sea. **12.** *Nautical.* to slacken or temporarily release (a rope or cable) from a capstan or (of a rope, etc.) to be slackened or released and slip back. **13.** (*intr.*) (of an electric current or voltage) to undergo a large momentary increase. **14.** (*tr.*) *Rare.* to cause to move in or as if in a wave or waves. [C15: from Latin *surgere* to rise, from *sub-* up + *regere* to lead] —**ˈsurge+less** *adj.* —**ˈsurg+er** *n.*

sur+geon (ˈsɜːdʒən) *n.* **1.** a medical practioner who specializes in surgery. **2.** a medical officer in the Royal Navy. [C14: from Anglo-Norman *surgien,* from Old French *cirurgien;* see SURGERY]

sur+geon+cy (ˈsɜːdʒənsɪ) *n., pl.* **+cies.** *Chiefly Brit.* the office, duties, or position of a surgeon, esp. in the army or navy.

sur·geon+fish (ˈsɜːdʒənˌfɪʃ) *n., pl.* **+fish** *or* **+fish·es.** any tropical marine spiny-finned fish of the family *Acanthuridae,* having a compressed brightly coloured body with one or more knifelike spines at the base of the tail.

sur+geon gen+er+al *n., pl.* **sur+geons gen+er+al. 1.** (in the British, U.S., and certain other armies and navies) the senior officer of the medical service. **2.** the head of the public health service in the U.S.

sur+geon's knot *n.* a knot used by surgeons in tying ligatures, etc.

sur+ger·y (ˈsɜːdʒərɪ) *n., pl.* **+ger·ies. 1.** the branch of medicine concerned with treating disease, injuries, etc., by means of manual or operative procedures, esp. by incision into the body. **2.** the performance of such procedures by a surgeon. **3.** *Brit.* a place where a doctor, dentist, etc., can be consulted. **4.** *U.S.* an operating theatre where surgical operations are performed. [C14: via Old French from Latin *chirurgia,* from Greek *kheirurgia,* from *kheir* hand + *ergon* work]

sur+gi+cal (ˈsɜːdʒɪkəl) *adj.* of, relating to, involving, or used in surgery. —**ˈsur+gi+cal+ly** *adv.*

sur+gi+cal boot *n.* a specially designed boot or shoe that compensates for deformities of the foot or leg.

sur+gi+cal spir+it *n.* methylated spirit containing small amounts of oil of wintergreen and castor oil: used medically for sterilizing.

Su+ri+ba+chi (ˌsʊərɪˈbɑːtʃɪ) *n.* **Mount.** a volcanic hill in the Volcano Islands, on Iwo Jima: site of a U.S. victory (1945) over the Japanese in World War II.

su+ri+cate (ˈsjʊərɪˌkeɪt) *n.* another name for **slender-tailed meerkat** (see **meerkat**). [C18: from French *surikate,* probably from a native South African word]

Su+ri+nam (ˌsʊərɪˈnæm) *n.* a republic in NE South America, on the Atlantic: became a self-governing part of the Netherlands in 1954 and fully independent in 1975; a leading exporter of bauxite. Languages: Dutch and English. Currency: guilder. Capital: Paramaribo. Pop.: 411 000 (1974 UN est.). Area: 163 820 sq. km (63 251 sq. miles). Former names: **Dutch Guiana, Netherlands Guiana.**

Su+ri+nam toad *n.* another name for **pipa.**

sur+jec+tion (sɜːˈdʒɛkʃən) *n.* a mathematical function or mapping for which every element of the image space is a value for some members of the domain. See also **injection** (sense 5), **bijection.** —**sur+ˈjec+tive** *adj.*

sur+ly (ˈsɜːlɪ) *adj.* **+li+er, +li+est. 1.** sullenly ill-tempered or rude. **2.** (of an animal) ill-tempered or refractory. **3.** dismal. **4.** *Obsolete.* arrogant. [C16: from obsolete *sirly* haughty; see SIR] —**ˈsur+li+ly** *adv.* —**ˈsur+li+ness** *n.*

sur+mise *vb.* (sɜːˈmaɪz). **1.** (when *tr., may take a clause as object*) to infer (something) from incomplete or uncertain evidence. ~*n.* (sɜːˈmaɪz, ˈsɜːmaɪz). **2.** an idea inferred from inconclusive evidence. [C15: from Old French, from *surmettre* to accuse, from Latin *supermittere* to throw over, from SUPER- + *mittere* to send] —**sur+ˈmis+a·ble** *adj.* —**sur+mis+ed+ly** (sɜːˈmaɪzɪdlɪ) *adv.* —**sur+ˈmis+er** *n.*

sur+mount (sɜːˈmaʊnt) *vb.* (*tr.*) **1.** to prevail over; overcome: *to surmount tremendous difficulties.* **2.** to ascend and cross to the opposite side of. **3.** to lie on top of or rise above. **4.** to put something on top of or above. **5.** *Obsolete.* to surpass or exceed. [C14: from Old French *surmonter,* from SUR-[1] + *monter* to MOUNT[1]] —**sur+ˈmount+a·ble** *adj.* —**sur+ˈmount+a·ble+ness** *n.* —**sur+ˈmount+er** *n.*

sur+mul+let (sɜːˈmʌlɪt) *n.* a U.S. name for the **red mullet.** [C17: from French *sormulet,* from *sor* brown + MULLET]

sur+name (ˈsɜːˌneɪm) *n.* **1.** a family name as opposed to a Christian name. **2.** (formerly) a descriptive epithet attached to a person's name to denote a personal characteristic, profession, etc.; nickname. ~*vb.* **3.** (*tr.*) to furnish with or call by a surname. —**ˈsur+ˌnam+er** *n.*

sur+pass (sɜːˈpɑːs) *vb.* (*tr.*) **1.** to be greater than in degree, extent, etc. **2.** to be superior to in achievement or excellence. **3.** to overstep the limit or range of: *the theory surpasses my comprehension.* [C16: from French *surpasser,* from SUR-[1] + *passer* to PASS] —**sur+ˈpass+a·ble** *adj.*

sur+pas+sing (sɜːˈpɑːsɪŋ) *adj.* **1.** exceptional; extraordinary. ~*adv.* **2.** *Obsolete or poetic.* (intensifier): *surpassing fair.* —**sur+ˈpass+ing+ly** *adv.* —**sur+ˈpass+ing+ness** *n.*

sur+plice (ˈsɜːplɪs) *n.* a loose wide-sleeved liturgical vestment of linen, reaching to the knees, worn over the cassock by clergymen, choristers, and acolytes. [C13: via Anglo-French from Old French *sourpelis,* from Medieval Latin *superpellīcium,* from SUPER- + *pellīcium* coat made of skins, from Latin *pellis* a skin] —**ˈsur+pliced** *adj.*

sur+plus (ˈsɜːpləs) *n., pl.* **+plus·es. 1.** a quantity or amount in excess of what is required. **2.** *Accounting.* **a.** an excess of total assets over total liabilities. **b.** an excess of actual net assets over the nominal value of capital stock. **c.** an excess of revenues over expenditures during a certain period of time. **3.** *Economics.* **a.** an excess of government revenues over expenditures during a certain financial year. **b.** an excess of receipts over payments on the balance of payments. ~*adj.* **4.** being in excess; extra. [C14: from Old French, from Medieval Latin *superplūs,* from Latin SUPER- + *plūs* more]

sur+plus+age (ˈsɜːpləsɪdʒ) *n.* **1.** *Law.* (in pleading, etc.) irrelevant matter, such as a superfluous allegation. **2.** an excess of words. **3.** a less common word for **surplus.**

sur+print (ˈsɜːˌprɪnt) *vb.* **1.** (*tr.*) to print (additional matter) over something already printed; overprint. ~*n.* **2.** marks, printed matter, etc., that have been surprinted.

sur+prise (səˈpraɪz) *vb.* (*tr.*) **1.** to cause to feel amazement or wonder. **2.** to encounter or discover unexpectedly or suddenly. **3.** to capture or assault suddenly and without warning. **4.** to present with something unexpected, such as a gift. **5.** (foll. by *into*) to provoke (someone) to unintended action by a trick, etc.: *to surprise a person into an indiscretion.* **6.** (often foll. by *from*) to elicit by unexpected behaviour or by a trick: *to surprise information from a prisoner.* ~*n.* **7.** the act or an instance of surprising; the act of taking unawares. **8.** a sudden or unexpected event, gift, etc. **9.** the feeling or condition of being surprised; astonishment. **10.** (*modifier*) causing, characterized by, or relying upon surprise: *a surprise move.* **11. take by surprise. a.** to come upon suddenly and without warning. **b.** to capture unexpectedly or catch unprepared. **c.** to astonish; amaze. [C15: from Old French, from *surprendre* to overtake, from SUR-[1] + *prendre* from Latin *prehendere* to grasp; see PREHENSILE] —**sur+ˈpris+al** *n.* —**sur+pris+ed+ly** (səˈpraɪzɪdlɪ) *adv.* —**sur+ˈpris+er** *n.*

sur+pris+ing (səˈpraɪzɪŋ) *adj.* causing surprise; unexpected or amazing. —**sur+ˈpris+ing+ly** *adv.* —**sur+ˈpris+ing+ness** *n.*

sur+ra (ˈsʊərə) *n.* a tropical febrile disease of cattle, horses, camels, and dogs, characterized by severe emaciation: caused by the protozoan *Trypanosoma evansi* and transmitted by fleas. [from Marathi]

sur+re+al (səˈrɪəl) *adj.* **1.** suggestive of surrealism; dreamlike. ~*n.* **2. the.** the atmosphere or qualities evoked by surrealism.

sur+re+al+ism (səˈrɪəˌlɪzəm) *n.* (*sometimes cap.*) a movement in art and literature in the 1920s, which developed esp. from dada, characterized by the evocative juxtaposition of incongruous images in order to include unconscious and dream elements. [C20: from French *surréalisme,* from SUR-[1] + *réalisme* REALISM] —**sur+ˈre+al+ist** *n., adj.* —**sur+ˌre+al+ˈis+tic** *adj.* —**sur+ˌre+al+ˈis+ti+cal+ly** *adv.*

sur+re+but+tal (ˌsɜːrɪˈbʌtᵊl) *n. Law.* (in pleading) the giving of evidence in support of a surrebutter.

sur+re+but+ter (ˌsɜːrɪˈbʌtə) *n. Law.* (in pleading) the plaintiff's reply to the defendant's rebutter.

sur+re+join+der (ˌsɜːrɪˈdʒɔɪndə) *n. Law.* (in pleading) the plaintiff's reply to the defendant's rejoinder.

sur+ren+der (səˈrɛndə) *vb.* **1.** (*tr.*) to relinquish to the control or possession of another under duress or on demand: *to surrender a city.* **2.** (*tr.*) to relinquish or forego (an office, position, etc.), esp. as a voluntary concession to another: *he surrendered his place to a lady.* **3.** to give (oneself) up physically, as or as if to an enemy. **4.** to allow (oneself) to yield, as to a temptation, influence, etc. **5.** (*tr.*) to give up (hope, etc.) **6.** (*tr.*) *Law.* to give up or restore (an estate), esp. to give up a lease before expiration of the term. **7.** (*tr.*) *Obsolete.* to return or render (thanks, etc.). **8. surrender to bail.** to present oneself at court at the appointed time after having been on bail. ~*n.* **9.** the act or instance of surrendering. **10.** *Insurance.* the voluntary discontinuation of a life policy by its holder in return for a consideration (the **surrender value**). **11.** *Law.* **a.** the yielding up or restoring of an estate, esp. the giving up of a lease before its term has expired. **b.** the giving up to the appropriate authority of a fugitive from justice. **c.** the act of surrendering or being surrendered to bail. **d.** the deed by which a legal surrender is effected. [C15: from Old French *surrendre* to yield, from SUR-¹ + *rendre* to RENDER] —**sur+ˈren+der+er** *n.*

sur+rep+ti+tious (ˌsʌrəpˈtɪʃəs) *adj.* **1.** done, acquired, etc., in secret or by improper means. **2.** operating by stealth. **3.** characterized by fraud or misrepresentation of the truth. [C15: from Latin *surreptīcius* furtive, from *surripere* to steal, from *sub-* secretly + *rapere* to snatch] —ˌ**sur+rep+ˈti+tious+ly** *adv.* —ˌ**sur+rep+ˈti+tious+ness** *n.*

sur+rey (ˈsʌrɪ) *n.* a light four-wheeled horse-drawn carriage having two or four seats. [C19: shortened from *Surrey cart,* after SURREY¹, where it was originally made]

Sur+rey¹ (ˈsʌrɪ) *n.* a county of SE England, on the River Thames: urban in the northeast; crossed from east to west by the North Downs and drained by tributaries of the Thames. Administrative centre: Kingston-upon-Thames. Pop.: 1 002 900 (1976 est.). Area: 1678 sq. km (648 sq. miles).

Sur+rey² (ˈsʌrɪ) *n.* **Earl of,** title of *Henry Howard.* ?1517–47, English courtier and poet; one of the first in England to write sonnets. He was beheaded for high treason.

sur+ro+gate *n.* (ˈsʌrəgɪt). **1.** a person or thing acting as a substitute. **2.** *Chiefly Brit.* a deputy, such as a clergyman appointed to deputize for a bishop in granting marriage licences. **3.** *Psychiatry.* a person who is a substitute for someone else, esp. in childhood when different persons, such as a brother or teacher, can act as substitutes for the parents. **4.** (in some U.S. states) a judge with jurisdiction over the probate of wills, etc. **5.** (*modifier*) of, relating to, or acting as a surrogate: *a surrogate pleasure.* ~*vb.* (ˈsʌrəˌgeɪt). (*tr.*) **6.** to put in another's position as a deputy, substitute, etc. **7.** to appoint as a successor to oneself. [C17: from Latin *surrogāre* to substitute; see SUBROGATE] —**ˈsur+ro+gate+ˌship** *n.* —ˌ**sur+ro+ˈga+tion** *n.*

sur+round (səˈraʊnd) *vb.* (*tr.*) **1.** to encircle or enclose or cause to be encircled or enclosed. **2.** to deploy forces on all sides of (a place or military formation), so preventing access or retreat. **3.** to exist around: *I dislike the people who surround her.* ~*n.* **4.** *Chiefly Brit.* a border, esp. the area of uncovered floor between the walls of a room and the carpet or around an opening or panel. **5.** *Chiefly U.S.* **a.** a method of capturing wild beasts by encircling the area in which they are believed to be. **b.** the area so encircled. [C15 *surrounden* to overflow, from Old French *suronder,* from Late Latin *superundāre,* from Latin SUPER- + *undāre* to abound, from *unda* a wave] —**sur+ˈround+ed+ly** *adv.* —**sur+ˈround+ing** *adj.*

sur+round+ings (səˈraʊndɪŋz) *pl. n.* the conditions, scenery, etc., around a person, place, or thing; environment.

sur+sum cor+da (ˈsɜːsəm ˈkɔːdə) *n.* **1.** *R.C. Church.* a Latin versicle meaning *Lift up your hearts,* said by the priest at Mass. **2.** a cry of exhortation, hope, etc.

sur+tax (ˈsɜːˌtæks) *n.* **1.** a tax, usually highly progressive, levied on the amount by which a person's income exceeds a specific level. **2.** an additional tax on something that has already been taxed. ~*vb.* **3.** (*tr.*) to assess for liability to surtax; charge with an extra tax.

sur+tout (ˈsɜːtuː; *French* syrˈtu) *n.* a man's overcoat resembling a frock coat, popular in the late 19th century. [C17: from French, from *sur* over + *tout* all]

surv. *abbrev. for:* **1.** Also: **survey.** surveying. **2.** surveyor.

sur+veil+lance (sɜːˈveɪləns) *n.* close observation or supervision maintained over a person, group, etc., esp. one in custody or under suspicion. [C19: from French, from *surveiller* to watch over, from SUR-¹ + *veiller* to keep watch (from Latin *vigilāre;* see VIGIL)] —**sur+ˈveil+lant** *adj., n.*

sur+vey *vb.* (sɜːˈveɪ, ˈsɜːveɪ). **1.** (*tr.*) to view or consider in a comprehensive or general way: *to survey the situation.* **2.** (*tr.*) to examine carefully, as or as if to appraise value: *to survey oneself in a mirror.* **3.** to plot a detailed map of (an area of land) by measuring or calculating distances and height. **4.** *Brit.* to inspect a building to determine its condition and value. **5.** to examine a vessel thoroughly in order to determine its seaworthiness. **6.** (*tr.*) to run a statistical survey on (incomes, opinions, etc.). ~*n.* (ˈsɜːveɪ). **7.** a comprehensive or general view: *a survey of English literature.* **8.** a critical, detailed, and formal inspection: *a survey of the nation's hospitals.* **9.** *Brit.* an inspection of a building to determine its condition and value. **10.** a report incorporating the results of such an inspection. **11. a.** a body of surveyors. **b.** an area surveyed. **12.** *Statistics.* a random sample. [C15: from French *surveoir,* from SUR-¹ + *veoir* to see, from Latin *vidēre*] —**sur+ˈvey+a+ble** *adj.*

sur+vey+ing (sɜːˈveɪɪŋ) *n.* **1.** the study or practice of measuring altitudes, angles, and distances on the land surface so that they can be accurately plotted on a map. **2.** the setting out on the ground of the positions of proposed construction or engineering works.

sur+vey+or (sɜːˈveɪə) *n.* **1.** a person whose occupation is to survey land or buildings. See also **quantity surveyor. 2.** *Chiefly Brit.* a person concerned with the official inspection of something for purposes of measurement and valuation. **3.** a person who carries out surveys, esp. of ships (**marine surveyor**) to determine seaworthiness, etc. **4.** (formerly in the U.S.) a customs official. **5.** *Archaic.* a supervisor. —**sur+ˈvey+or+ˌship** *n.*

sur+vey+or's chain *n.* a measuring chain 22 yards in length; Gunter's chain. See **chain** (sense 7).

sur+vey+or's lev+el *n.* another term for **level** (sense 20).

sur+vey+or's meas+ure *n.* the system of measurement based on the chain (66 feet) as a unit.

sur+viv+al (səˈvaɪvᵊl) *n.* **1.** a person or thing that survives, such as a custom. **2. a.** the act or fact of surviving or condition of having survived. **b.** (*as modifier*): *survival kit.*

sur+viv+al of the fit+test *n.* a popular term for **natural selection.**

sur+vive (səˈvaɪv) *vb.* **1.** (*tr.*) to live after the death of (another): *he survived his wife by 12 years.* **2.** to continue in existence or use after (a passage of time, an adversity, etc.). **3.** *Informal.* to endure (something): *I don't know how I survive such an awful job.* [C15: from Old French *sourvivre,* from Latin *supervīvere,* from SUPER- + *vīvere* to live] —**sur+ˈviv+a+ble** *adj.* —**sur+ˌviv+a+ˈbil+i+ty** *n.*

sur+vi+vor (səˈvaɪvə) *n.* **1.** a person or thing that survives. **2.** *Property law.* one of two or more specified persons having joint interests in property who lives longer than the other or others and thereby becomes entitled to the whole property. —**sur+ˈvi+vor+ˌship** *n.*

Su+sa (ˈsuːsə) *n.* an ancient city north of the Persian Gulf: capital of Elam and of the Persian Empire; flourished as a Greek polis under the Seleucids and Parthians.

Su+sah *or* **Su+sa** (ˈsuːzə) *n.* other names for **Sousse.**

Su+san+na (suːˈzænə) *n. Apocrypha.* **1.** the wife of Joachim, who was condemned to death for adultery because of a false accusation, but saved by Daniel's sagacity. **2.** the book of the Apocrypha containing this story.

sus+cep+tance (səˈsɛptəns) *n. Physics.* the imaginary component of the admittance. [C19: from SUSCEPT(IBILITY) + -ANCE]

sus+cep+ti+bil+i+ty (səˌsɛptəˈbɪlɪtɪ) *n., pl.* **·ties. 1.** the quality or condition of being susceptible. **2.** the ability or tendency to be impressed by emotional feelings; sensitivity. **3.** (*pl.*) emotional sensibilities; feelings. **4.** *Physics.* **a.** Also called: **electric susceptibility.** (of a dielectric) the amount by which the relative permittivity differs from unity. Symbol: Χ. **b.** Also called: **magnetic susceptibility.** (of a magnetic medium) the amount by which the relative permeability differs from unity. Symbol: Κ.

sus+cep+ti+ble (səˈsɛptəbᵊl) *adj.* **1.** (*postpositive;* foll. by *of* or *to*) yielding readily (to); capable (of): *hypotheses susceptible of refutation; susceptible to control.* **2.** (*postpositive;* foll. by *to*) liable to be afflicted (by): *susceptible to colds.* **3.** easily impressed emotionally. [C17: from Late Latin *susceptibilis,* from Latin *suscipere* to take up, from SUB- + *capere* to take] —**sus+ˈcep+ti+ble+ness** *n.* —**sus+ˈcep+ti+bly** *adv.*

sus+cep+tive (səˈsɛptɪv) *adj.* **1.** another word for **receptive. 2.** a variant of **susceptible.** —**sus+cep+tiv+i+ty** (ˌsʌsɛpˈtɪvɪtɪ) *or* **sus+ˈcep+tive+ness** *n.*

su+shi (ˈsuːʃɪ) *n.* a Japanese dish consisting of cold rice and raw fish. [from Japanese]

Su+si+an (ˈsuːzɪən) *n., adj.* another word for **Elamite.**

sus+lik (ˈsʌslɪk) *or* **sous+lik** *n.* a central Eurasian ground squirrel, *Citellus citellus,* of dry open areas, having large eyes and small ears. [from Russian]

sus+pect *vb.* (səˈspɛkt). **1.** (*tr.*) to believe guilty of a specified offence without proof. **2.** (*tr.*) to think false, questionable, etc.: *she suspected his sincerity.* **3.** (*tr.; may take a clause as object*) to surmise to be the case; think probable: *to suspect fraud.* **4.** (*intr.*) to have suspicion. ~*n.* (ˈsʌspɛkt). **5.** a person who is under suspicion. ~*adj.* (ˈsʌspɛkt). **6.** causing or open to suspicion. [C14: from Latin *suspicere* to mistrust, from SUB- + *specere* to look] —**sus+ˈpect+er** *n.* —**ˈsus+pect+less** *adj.*

sus+pend (səˈspɛnd) *vb.* **1.** (*tr.*) to hang from above so as to permit free movement. **2.** (*tr.; passive*) to cause to remain floating or hanging: *a cloud of smoke was suspended over the town.* **3.** (*tr.*) to render inoperative or cause to cease, esp. temporarily: *to suspend interest payments.* **4.** (*tr.*) to hold in abeyance; postpone action on: *to suspend a decision.* **5.** (*tr.*) to debar temporarily from privilege, office, etc., as a punishment. **6.** (*tr.*) *Chem.* to cause (particles) to be held in suspension in a fluid. **7.** (*tr.*) *Music.* to continue (a note) until the next chord is sounded, with which it usually forms a dissonance. See **suspension** (sense 11). **8.** (*intr.*) to cease payment, as from incapacity to meet financial obligations. **9.** (*tr.*) *Obsolete.* to put or keep in a state of anxiety or wonder. **10.** (*intr.*) *Rare.* to come to a stop, esp. temporarily. **11.** (*intr.*) *Obsolete.* to be attached from above. [C13: from Latin *suspendere* from SUB- + *pendere* to hang] —**sus+ˈpend+i+ble** *or* **sus+ˈpens+i+ble** *adj.* —**sus+ˌpend+i+ˈbil+i+ty** *n.*

sus+pend+ed an+i+ma+tion *n.* a temporary cessation of the vital functions, as by freezing an organism.

sus+pend+ed sen+tence *n.* a sentence of imprisonment that is not served by an offender unless he commits a further offence during its currency. Compare **deferred sentence.**

sus+pend+er (sə'spɛndə) *n.* **1.** (*often pl.*) *Brit.* **a.** an elastic strap attached to a belt or corset having a fastener at the end, for holding up women's stockings. **b.** a similar fastener attached to a garter worn by men in order to support socks. U.S. equivalent: **garter. 2.** (*pl.*) the U.S. name for **braces. 3.** a person or thing that suspends, such as one of the vertical cables in a suspension bridge.

sus+pend+er belt *n.* a belt with suspenders hanging from it to hold up women's stockings. U.S. name: **garter belt.**

sus+pense (sə'spɛns) *n.* **1.** the condition of being insecure or uncertain: *the matter of the succession remained in suspense for many years.* **2.** mental uncertainty; anxiety: *their father's illness kept them in a state of suspense.* **3.** excitement felt at the approach of the climax: *a play of terrifying suspense.* **4.** the condition of being suspended. [C15: from Medieval Latin *suspensum* delay, from Latin *suspendere* to hang up; see SUSPEND] —**sus+'pense+ful** *adj.*

sus+pense ac+count *n.* an account in which entries are made until determination of their proper disposition.

sus+pen+sion (sə'spɛnʃən) *n.* **1.** an interruption or temporary revocation: *the suspension of a law.* **2.** a temporary debarment, as from position, privilege, etc. **3.** a deferment, esp. of a decision, judgment, etc. **4.** *Law.* **a.** a postponement of execution of a sentence or the deferring of a judgment, etc. **b.** a temporary extinguishment of a right or title. **5.** cessation of payment of business debts, esp. as a result of insolvency. **6.** the act of suspending or the state of being suspended. **7.** a system of springs, shock absorbers, etc., that supports the body of a wheeled vehicle and insulates it and its occupants from shocks transmitted by the wheels. See also **hydraulic suspension. 8.** a device or structure, usually a wire or spring, that serves to suspend or support something, such as the pendulum of a clock. **9.** *Chem.* a dispersion of fine solid or liquid particles in a fluid, the particles being supported by buoyancy. See also **colloid. 10.** the process by which eroded particles of rock are transported in a river. **11.** *Music.* one or more notes of a chord that are prolonged until a subsequent chord is sounded, usually to form a dissonance.

sus+pen+sion bridge *n.* a bridge that has a deck suspended by cables or rods from other cables or chains that hang between two towers and are anchored at both ends.

sus+pen+sion point *n. Chiefly U.S.* one of a group of dots, usually three, used in written material to indicate the omission of a word or words.

sus+pen+sive (sə'spɛnsɪv) *adj.* **1.** having the power of deferment; effecting suspension. **2.** causing, characterized by, or relating to suspense. **3.** inclined to defer judgment; undecided. **4.** *Rare.* characterized by physical suspension. —**sus+'pen+sive+ly** *adv.* —**sus+'pen+sive+ness** *n.*

sus+pen+soid (sə'spɛnsɔɪd) *n. Chem.* a system consisting of a suspension of solid particles in a liquid.

sus+pen+sor (sə'spɛnsə) *n.* **1.** another name for **suspensory** (sense 1). **2.** *Botany.* (in a seed) a row of cells attached to the embryo plant, by means of which it is pushed into the endosperm.

sus+pen+so+ry (sə'spɛnsərɪ) *n., pl.* **·ries. 1.** Also called: **suspensor.** *Anatomy.* a ligament or muscle that holds a structure or part in position. **2.** *Med.* a bandage, sling, etc., for supporting a dependent part. **3.** another name (esp. U.S.) for **athletic support.** ~*adj.* **4.** suspending or supporting. **5.** *Anatomy.* (of a ligament or muscle) supporting or holding a structure or part in position.

sus+pi+cion (sə'spɪʃən) *n.* **1.** the act or an instance of suspecting; belief without sure proof, esp. that something is wrong. **2.** the feeling of mistrust of a person who suspects. **3.** the state of being suspected: *to be shielded from suspicion.* **4.** a slight trace. **5. above suspicion.** in such a position that no guilt may be thought or implied, esp. through having an unblemished reputation. **6. on suspicion.** as a suspect. **7. under suspicion.** regarded with distrust. [C14: from Old French *sospeçon,* from Latin *suspīciō* distrust, from *suspicere* to mistrust; see SUSPECT] —**sus+'pi+cion+al** *adj.* —**sus+'pi+cion+less** *adj.*

sus+pi+cious (sə'spɪʃəs) *adj.* **1.** exciting or liable to excite suspicion; questionable. **2.** disposed to suspect something wrong. **3.** indicative or expressive of suspicion. —**sus+'pi+cious+ly** *adv.* —**sus+'pi+cious+ness** *n.*

sus+pire (sə'spaɪə) *vb. Archaic or poetic.* **1.** to sigh or utter with a sigh; yearn. **2.** (*intr.*) to breathe; respire. [C15: from Latin *suspīrāre* to take a deep breath, from SUB- + *spīrāre* to breathe] —**sus+pi+ra+tion** (ˌsʌspɪ'reɪʃən) *n.*

Sus+que+han+na (ˌsʌskwɪ'hænə) *n.* a river in the eastern U.S., rising in Otsego Lake and flowing generally south to Chesapeake Bay at Havre de Grace: the longest river in the eastern U.S. Length: 714 km (444 miles).

suss (sʌs) *vb.* (*tr.*) *Brit. slang.* **1.** (often foll. by *out*) to attempt to work out (a situation, person's character, etc.), esp. using one's intuition. **2.** to become aware of; suspect (esp. in the phrase **suss it**). [C20: shortened from SUSPECT]

Sus+sex ('sʌsɪks) *n.* **1.** (until 1974) a county of SE England, now divided into the separate counties of East Sussex and West Sussex. **2.** (in Anglo-Saxon England) the kingdom of the South Saxons, which became a shire of the kingdom of Wessex in the early 9th century A.D. **3.** a breed of red beef cattle originally from Sussex. **4.** a heavy and long-established breed of domestic fowl used principally as a table bird.

Sus+sex span+iel *n.* a short-legged breed of spaniel with a golden-brown coat.

sus+so ('sʌsəʊ) *n., pl.* **+sos.** *Austral. slang.* **a.** money paid by the government to an unemployed person. **b.** an unemployed person receiving such money. [C20: from SUSTENANCE]

sus+tain (sə'steɪn) *vb.* (*tr.*) **1.** to hold up under; withstand: *to sustain great provocation.* **2.** to undergo (an injury, loss, etc.); suffer: *to sustain a broken arm.* **3.** to maintain or prolong: *to sustain a discussion.* **4.** to support physically from below. **5.** to provide for or give support to, esp. by supplying necessities: *to sustain one's family; to sustain a charity.* **6.** to keep up the vitality or courage of. **7.** to uphold or affirm the justice or validity of: *to sustain a decision.* **8.** to establish the truth of; confirm. [C13: via Old French from Latin *sustinēre* to hold up, from SUB- + *tenēre* to hold] —**sus+'tain+a+ble** *adj.* —**sus+tain+ed+ly** (sə'steɪnɪdlɪ) *adv.* —**sus+'tain+ing+ly** *adv.* —**sus+'tain+ment** *n.*

sus+tain+er (sə'steɪnə) *n.* a rocket engine that maintains the velocity of a space vehicle after the booster has been jettisoned.

sus+tain+ing ped+al *n. Music.* a foot-operated lever on a piano, usually the right one of two, that keeps the dampers raised from the strings when keys are released, allowing them to continue to vibrate. Compare **soft pedal.**

sus+tain+ing pro+gram *n. U.S.* a television or radio programme promoted by the broadcasting network or station itself and not by a commercial sponsor.

sus+te+nance ('sʌstənəns) *n.* **1.** means of sustaining health or life; nourishment. **2.** means of maintenance; livelihood. **3.** Also: **sus+ten+tion** (sə'stenʃən). the act or process of sustaining or the quality of being sustained. [C13: from Old French *sostenance,* from *sustenir* to SUSTAIN]

sus+ten+tac+u+lar (ˌsʌstɛn'tækjʊlə) *adj. Anatomy.* (of fibres, cells, etc.) supporting or forming a support. [C19: from Latin *sustentāculum* a stay, from *sustentāre* to support, from *sustinēre* to SUSTAIN]

sus+ten+ta+tion (ˌsʌstɛn'teɪʃən) *n.* a less common word for **sustenance.** [C14: from Latin *sustentātio,* from *sustentāre,* frequentative of *sustinēre* to SUSTAIN]

Su·su ('su:su:) *n.* **1.** (*pl.* **·su** *or* **·sus**) a member of a Negroid people of W Africa, living chiefly in Guinea, the Sudan, and Sierra Leone. **2.** the language of this people, belonging to the Mande branch of the Niger-Congo family.

su+sur+rate ('sju:səˌreɪt) *vb.* (*intr.*) *Literary.* to make a soft rustling sound; whisper; murmur. [C17: from Latin *susurrāre* to whisper] —**su+sur+rant** (sju:'sʌrənt) *adj.* —**ˌsu+sur+'ra+tion** *or* **'su+sur+rus** *n.*

Sut·cliffe ('sʌtˌklɪf) *n.* **Her·bert.** 1894–1978, English cricketer, who played for Yorkshire; scorer of 149 centuries and 1000 runs in a season 24 times.

Suth. *abbrev. for* Sutherland.

Suth+er+land[1] ('sʌðələnd) *n.* (until 1975) a county of N Scotland, now part of the Highland region.

Suth·er·land[2] ('sʌðələnd) *n.* **1. Gra·ham.** 1903–80, English artist, noted for his work as an official war artist (1941–44) and for his tapestry *Christ in Majesty* (1962) in Coventry Cathedral. **2. Joan.** born 1926, Australian operatic soprano.

Suth+er+land Falls *n.* a waterfall in New Zealand, on SW South Island. Height: 580 m (1904 ft.).

Sut+lej ('sʌtlɪdʒ) *n.* a river in S Asia, rising in SW Tibet and flowing west through the Himalayas: crosses Himachal Pradesh and the Punjab (India), enters Pakistan, and joins the Chenab west of Bahawalpur: the longest of the five rivers of the Punjab. Length: 1368 m (850 miles).

sut+ler ('sʌtlə) *n.* (formerly) a merchant who accompanied an army in order to sell provisions to the soldiers. [C16: from obsolete Dutch *soeteler,* from Middle Low German *suteler,* from Middle High German *sudelen* to do dirty work; related to SOOT, SEETHE] —**'sut+ler+ˌship** *n.*

su+tra ('su:trə) *n.* **1.** *Hinduism.* Sanskrit sayings or collections of sayings on Vedic doctrine dating from about 200 A.D. onwards. **2.** (*modifier*) *Hinduism.* **a.** of or relating to the last of the Vedic literary periods, from about 500 to 100 B.C.: *the sutra period.* **b.** of or relating to the sutras or compilations of sutras of about 200 A.D. onwards. **3.** *Buddhism.* collections of dialogues and discourses of classic Mahayana Buddhism dating from the 2nd to the 6th centuries A.D. [C19: from Sanskrit: list of rules]

sut+tee (sʌ'ti:, 'sʌti:) *n.* **1.** the former Hindu custom whereby a widow burnt herself to death on her husband's funeral pyre. **2.** a Hindu widow who immolated herself in this way. [C18: from Sanskrit *satī* virtuous woman, from *sat* good] —**sut+'tee+ism** *n.*

Sut+ton ('sʌtᵊn) *n.* a borough of S Greater London. Pop.: 166 700 (1976 est.).

Sut+ton Cold+field ('kəʊldˌfi:ld) *n.* a town in central England, in the N West Midlands. Pop.: 83 130 (1971).

Sut+ton Hoo (hu:) *n.* a 7th-century site in Suffolk where a Saxon long boat containing rich grave goods, probably for an East Anglian king, was found in 1939.

Sut·ton-in-Ash·field ('æʃˌfi:ld) *n.* a market town in N central England, in W Nottinghamshire. Pop.: 40 725 (1971).

su+ture ('su:tʃə) *n.* **1.** *Surgery.* **a.** catgut, silk thread, or wire used to stitch together two bodily surfaces. **b.** the surgical seam formed after joining two surfaces. **2.** *Anatomy.* a type of immovable joint, esp. between the bones of the skull (**cranial suture**). **3.** a seam or joining, as in sewing. **4.** *Zoology.* a line of junction in a mollusc shell, esp. the line between adjacent chambers of a nautiloid shell. **5.** *Botany.* a line marking the point of dehiscence in a seed pod or capsule. ~*vb.* **6.** (*tr.*) *Surgery.* to join (the edges of a wound, etc.) by means of sutures. [C16: from Latin *sūtūra,* from *suere* to SEW] —ˈ**su+tur+al** *adj.* —ˈ**su+tur+al+ly** *adv.*

Su·va (ˈsuːvə) *n.* the capital and chief port of Fiji, on the SE coast of Viti Levu. Pop.: 63 200 (1976).

Su·vo·rov (*Russian* suˈvɔrəf) *n.* **A·le·ksan·dr Va·si·lye·vich** (alɪˈksandᵊr vaˈsiljɪvɪtʃ). 1729–1800, Russian field marshal, who fought successfully against the Turks (1787–91), the Poles (1794), and the French in Italy (1798–99).

Su+wan+nee (sʊˈwɒnɪ) *or* **Swa+nee** *n.* a river in the southeastern U.S., rising in SE Georgia and flowing across Florida to the Gulf of Mexico at **Suwannee Sound.** Length: about 400 km (250 miles).

su+ze+rain (ˈsuːzəˌreɪn) *n.* **1. a.** a state or sovereign exercising some degree of dominion over a dependent state, usually controlling its foreign affairs. **b.** (*as modifier*): *a suzerain power.* **2. a.** a feudal overlord. **b.** (*as modifier*): *suzerain lord.* [C19: from French, from *sus* above (from Latin *sursum* turned upwards, from *sub-* up + *vertere* to turn) + *-erain,* as in *souverain* SOVEREIGN]

su+ze+rain+ty (ˈsuːzərəntɪ) *n., pl.* **+ties. 1.** the position, power, or dignity of a suzerain. **2.** the relationship between suzerain and subject.

s.v. *abbrev. for:* **1.** sailing vessel. **2.** side valve. **3.** sub verbo *or* voce. [Latin: under the word]

S.V. *abbrev. for:* **1.** Sancta Virgo. [Latin: Holy Virgin] **2.** Sanctitas Vestra. [Latin: Your Holiness]

Sval+bard (*Norwegian* ˈsvaːlbar) *pl. n.* a Norwegian archipelago in the Arctic Ocean, about 650 km (400 miles) north of Norway: consists of the main group (West Spitsbergen, North East Land, Edge Island, Barents Island, and Prince Charles Foreland) and a number of outlying islands; sovereignty long disputed but granted to Norway in 1920; coal-mining. Administrative centre: Longyearben. Area: 62 050 sq. km (23 958 sq. miles). Also called: **Spitsbergen.**

svelte (svɛlt, sfɛlt) *adj.* **1.** attractively or gracefully slim; slender. **2.** urbane or sophisticated. [C19: from French, from Italian *svelto,* from *svellere* to pull out, from Latin *ēvellere,* from EX- + *vellere* to pull]

Sverd+lovsk (*Russian* svɪrˈdlɔfsk) *n.* a city in the W central Soviet Union, in the Ural Mountains: scene of the execution (1918) of Nicholas II and his family; university (1920); one of the largest centres of heavy engineering in the Soviet Union. Pop.: 1 147 000 (1975 est.). Former name (until 1924): **Yekaterinburg.**

Sve+ri+ge (ˈsværjə) *n.* the Swedish name for **Sweden.**

Sviz+ze+ra (ˈzvittsera) *n.* the Italian name for **Switzerland.**

SW *or* **S.W.** *abbrev. for* short wave.

SW *abbrev. for* southwest(ern).

Sw. *abbrev. for:* **1.** Sweden. **2.** Swedish.

SWA *international car registration for* South West Africa.

S.W.A. *abbrev. for* South West Africa.

swab (swɒb) *n.* **1.** *Med.* **a.** a small piece of cotton, gauze, etc., for use in applying medication, cleansing a wound, or obtaining a specimen of a secretion, etc. **b.** the specimen so obtained. **2.** a mop for cleaning floors, decks, etc. **3.** a brush used to clean a firearm's bore. **4.** *Slang.* an uncouth or worthless fellow. ~*vb.* **swabs, swab+bing, swabbed. 5.** (*tr.*) to clean or medicate with or as if with a swab. **6.** (*tr.;* foll. by *up*) to take up with a swab. [C16: probably from Middle Dutch *swabbe* mop; related to Norwegian *svabba* to splash, Dutch *zwabberen* to mop, German *schwappen* to slop over]

swab+ber (ˈswɒbə) *n.* **1.** a person who uses a swab. **2.** a device designed for swabbing. **3.** *Slang.* an uncouth fellow.

Swa+bi·a (ˈsweɪbɪə) *n.* a region and former duchy (from the 10th century to 1313) of SW West Germany: now part of Baden-Württemberg and Bavaria. German name: **Schwa+ben** (ˈʃvaːbᵊn). —ˈ**Swa+bi·an** *adj., n.*

swacked (swækt) *adj. Slang.* in a state of intoxication, stupor, or euphoria induced by drugs or alcohol. [C20: perhaps from Scottish *swack* a heavy blow, of imitative origin]

swad+dle (ˈswɒdᵊl) *vb.* (*tr.*) **1.** to wind a bandage round. **2.** to wrap (a baby) in swaddling clothes. **3.** to restrain as if by wrapping with bandages; smother. ~*n.* **4.** *Chiefly U.S.* swaddling clothes. [C15: from Old English *swæthel* swaddling clothes; related to *swathian* to SWATHE]

swad+dling clothes *pl. n.* **1.** long strips of linen or other cloth formerly wrapped round a newly born baby. **2.** restrictions or supervision imposed on the immature.

Swa+de·shi (swəˈdeɪʃɪ) *adj.* **1.** (in present-day India) produced within the country; not imported. ~*n.* **2.** (in British India) the encouragement of domestic production and boycott of foreign goods as part of the campaign for independence. [C20: from Bengali *svadesī,* from Sanskrit *svadeśin,* from *sva* one's own + *deśa* country]

swag (swæg) *n.* **1.** *Slang.* property obtained by theft or other illicit means. **2.** *Slang.* goods; valuables. **3.** an ornamental festoon of fruit, flowers, or drapery or a representation of this. **4.** a swaying movement; lurch. **5.** *Midland England dialect.* a depression filled with water, resulting from mining subsidence. **6.** *Austral. informal.* a swagman's pack containing personal belongings, etc. ~*vb.* **swags, swag+ging, swagged. 7.** *Chiefly Brit.* to lurch or sag or cause to lurch or sag. **8.** (*tr.*) to adorn or arrange with swags. **9.** (*intr.*) *Austral. informal.* to tramp about carrying a pack of personal belongings. [C17: perhaps of Scandinavian origin; compare Norwegian *svagga* to SWAY]

swage (sweɪdʒ) *n.* **1.** a shaped tool or die used in forming cold metal by hammering, pressing, etc. **2.** a decorative moulding. ~*vb.* **3.** (*tr.*) to form (metal) with a swage. [C19: from French *souage,* of unknown origin] —ˈ**swag+er** *n.*

swage block *n.* an iron block cut with holes, recesses, and grooves to assist in the cold-working of metal.

swag+ger (ˈswægə) *vb.* **1.** (*intr.*) to walk or behave in an arrogant manner. **2.** (*intr.;* often foll. by *about*) to brag loudly. **3.** (*tr.*) *Rare.* to force, influence, etc., by blustering. ~*n.* **4.** arrogant gait, conduct, or manner. ~*adj.* **5.** *Brit. informal, rare.* elegantly fashionable. [C16: probably from SWAG] —ˈ**swag+ger+er** *n.* —ˈ**swag+ger+ing+ly** *adv.*

swag+ger stick *or esp. Brit.* **swag+ger cane** *n.* a short cane or stick carried on occasion mainly by army officers.

swag+man (ˈswægˌmæn, -mən) *n., pl.* **+men.** *Austral. informal.* a labourer who carries his personal possessions in a pack or swag while travelling about in search of work; vagrant worker. Also called **swagger, swaggie.**

Swa+hi+li (swɑːˈhiːlɪ) *n.* **1.** a language of E Africa that is an official language of Kenya and Tanzania and is widely used as a lingua franca throughout E and central Africa. It is a member of the Bantu group of the Niger-Congo family, originally spoken in Zanzibar, and has a large number of loan words taken from Arabic and other languages. **2.** (*pl.* **+lis** *or* **+li**) a member of a people speaking this language, living chiefly in Zanzibar. [C19: from Arabic *sawāhil* coasts] —**Swa+ˈhi+li·an** *adj.*

swain (sweɪn) *n. Archaic or poetic.* **1.** a male lover or admirer. **2.** a country youth. [Old English *swān* swineherd; related to Old High German *swein,* Old Norse *sveinn* boy; see SWINE] —ˈ**swain+ish** *adj.* —ˈ**swain+ish+ness** *n.*

swale (sweɪl) *n. Chiefly U.S.* **a.** a moist depression in a tract of land, usually with rank vegetation. **b.** (*as modifier*): *swell and swale topography.* [C16: probably of Scandinavian origin; compare Old Norse *svala* to chill]

swal+low[1] (ˈswɒləʊ) *vb.* (*mainly tr.*) **1.** to pass (food, drink, etc.) through the mouth to the stomach by means of the muscular action of the oesophagus. **2.** (often foll. by *up*) to engulf or destroy as if by ingestion: *Nazi Germany swallowed up several small countries.* **3.** *Informal.* to believe gullibly: *he will never swallow such an excuse.* **4.** to refrain from uttering or manifesting: *to swallow one's disappointment.* **5.** to endure without retaliation. **6.** to enunciate (words, etc.) indistinctly; mutter. **7.** (often foll. by *down*) to eat or drink reluctantly. **8.** (*intr.*) to perform or simulate the act of swallowing, as in gulping. **9. swallow one's words.** to retract a statement, argument, etc., often in humiliating circumstances. ~*n.* **10.** the act of swallowing. **11.** the amount swallowed at any single time; mouthful. **12.** Also: **crown, throat.** *Nautical.* the opening between the shell and the groove of the sheave of a block, through which the rope is passed. **13.** *Rare.* another word for **throat** or **gullet. 14.** *Rare.* a capacity for swallowing; appetite. [Old English *swelgan;* related to Old Norse *svelga,* Old High German *swelgan* to swallow, Swedish *svalg* gullet] —ˈ**swal+low+a·ble** *adj.* —ˈ**swal+low+er** *n.*

swal+low[2] (ˈswɒləʊ) *n.* **1.** any passerine songbird of the family *Hirundinidae,* esp. *Hirundo rustica* (**common** or **barn swallow**), having long pointed wings, a forked tail, short legs, and a rapid flight. **2.** See **fairy swallow.** [Old English *swealwe;* related to Old Frisian *swale,* Old Norse *svala,* Old High German *swalwa*] —ˈ**swal·low-ˌlike** *adj.*

swal+low dive *n.* a type of dive in which the diver arches back while in the air, keeping his legs straight and together and his arms outstretched, finally entering the water headfirst. U.S. equivalent: **swan dive.**

swal+low hole *n. Chiefly Brit.* another word for **sinkhole** (sense 1).

swal·low+tail (ˈswɒləʊˌteɪl) *n.* **1.** any of various butterflies of the genus *Papilio* and related genera, esp. *P. machaon* of Europe, having a tail-like extension of each hind wing: family *Papilionidae.* **2.** the forked tail of a swallow or similar bird. **3.** short for **swallow-tailed coat.**

swal·low-tailed *adj.* **1.** (of a bird) having a deeply forked tail. **2.** having a part resembling a swallow's tail.

swal·low-tailed coat *n.* another name for **tail coat.**

swal·low+wort (ˈswɒləʊˌwɜːt) *n.* **1.** any of several Eurasian vines of the genus *Cynanchum,* esp. *C. nigrum,* having small brownish-purple flowers: family *Asclepiadaceae.* **2.** a related European herbaceous plant, *Vincetoxicum officinale* (or *Cynanchum vincetoxicum*), having an emetic root. **3.** another name for **greater celandine.**

swam (swæm) *vb.* the past tense of **swim.**

swa+mi (ˈswɑːmɪ) *n., pl.* **+mies** *or* **+mis.** (in India) a title of respect for a Hindu saint or religious teacher. [C18: from Hindi *svāmī,* from Sanskrit *svāmin* master, from *sva* one's own]

swamp (swɒmp) *n.* **1. a.** permanently waterlogged ground that is usually overgrown and sometimes partly forested. Compare **marsh. b.** (*as modifier*): *swamp fever.* ~*vb.* **2.** to drench or submerge or be drenched or submerged. **3.** *Nautical.* to cause (a boat) to sink or fill with water or (of a boat) to sink or fill with water. **4.** to overburden or overwhelm or be overburdened or overwhelmed, as by excess work or great numbers: *we have been swamped with applications.* **5.** to sink or stick or cause to sink or stick in or as if in a swamp. **6.** (*tr.*) to render helpless. Related adj.: **paludial.** [C17: probably from Middle Dutch *somp;* compare Middle High German *sumpf,* Old Norse *svöppr* sponge, Greek *somphos* spongy] —ˈ**swamp+ish** *adj.* —ˈ**swamp+less** *adj.* —ˈ**swamp·y** *adj.*

swamp boat *n.* a shallow-draught boat powered by an æroplane engine mounted on a raised structure for use in swamps. Also called: **airboat.**

swamp bug+gy *n.* (esp. in the U.S.) a light aerofoil conveyance for use in regions with swamps, lakes, etc.
swamp cy+press *n.* a North American deciduous coniferous tree, *Taxodium distichum,* that grows in swamps and sends up aerial roots from its base. Also called: **bald cypress.**
swamp+er ('swɒmpə) *n.* **1.** *U.S.* **a.** a person who lives or works in a swampy region, esp. in the southern U.S. **b.** a person who clears a swamp of trees and undergrowth or who clears a path in a forest for transporting logs. **2.** *Austral.* **a.** a bullock driver's assistant. **b.** a person getting a lift in return for a small service.
swamp fe+ver *n.* **1.** Also called: **equine infectious anaemia.** a viral disease of horses characterized by recurring fever, staggering gait, and general debility. **2.** *U.S.* another name for **malaria.**
swamp+land ('swɒmp,lænd) *n.* a permanently waterlogged area; marshland.
swan (swɒn) *n.* **1.** any large aquatic bird of the genera *Cygnus* and *Coscoroba,* having a long neck and usually a white plumage: family *Anatidae,* order *Anseriformes.* **2.** *Rare, literary.* **a.** a poet. **b.** *(cap. when part of a title or epithet): the Swan of Avon* (Shakespeare). ~*vb.* **swans, swan+ning, swanned. 3.** *(intr.; usually foll. by around or about) Informal.* to wander idly. [Old English; related to Old Norse *svanr,* Middle Low German *swōn*] —'**swan+,like** *adj.*
Swan[1] (swɒn) *n.* a river in SW Western Australia, rising as the Avon northeast of Narrogin and flowing northwest and west to the Indian Ocean below Perth. Length: about 240 km (150 miles).
Swan[2] (swɒn) *n.* Sir **Jo·seph Wil·son.** 1828–1914, English physicist and chemist, who developed the incandescent electric light (1880) independently of Edison.
swan dive *n.* the U.S. name for **swallow dive.**
Swa+nee ('swɒnɪ) *n.* a variant spelling of **Suwanee.**
swan+herd ('swɒn,hɜːd) *n.* a person who herds swans.
swank (swæŋk) *Informal.* ~*vb.* **1.** *(intr.)* to show off or swagger. ~*n.* **2.** Also called: **swankpot.** *Brit.* a swaggering or conceited person. **3.** *Chiefly U.S.* elegance or style, esp. of a showy kind. **4.** swagger; ostentation. ~*adj.* **5.** another word (esp. U.S.) for **swanky.** [C19: perhaps from Middle High German *swanken* to sway; see SWAG]
swank·y ('swæŋkɪ) *adj.* **swank·i+er, swank·i·est.** *Informal.* **1.** expensive and showy; stylish: *a swanky hotel.* **2.** boastful or conceited. —'**swank·i+ly** *adv.* —'**swank·i+ness** *n.*
swan maid+en *n.* any of a group of maidens in folklore who by magic are transformed into swans.
swan neck *n.* a tube, rail, etc., curved like a swan's neck.
swan+ner·y ('swɒnərɪ) *n., pl.* **+ner·ies.** a place where swans are kept and bred.
swan's-down *n.* **1.** the fine soft down feathers of a swan, used to trim powder puffs, clothes, etc. **2.** a thick soft fabric of wool with silk, cotton, or rayon, used for infants' clothing, etc. **3.** a cotton fabric with a heavy nap.
Swan+sea ('swɒnzɪ) *n.* a port in S Wales, in West Glamorgan on an inlet of the Bristol Channel (**Swansea Bay**); a metallurgical and oil-refining centre; university (1920). Pop.: 172 566 (1971).
swan+skin ('swɒn,skɪn) *n.* **1.** the skin of a swan with the feathers attached. **2.** a fine twill-weave flannel fabric.
swan song *n.* **1.** the last act, appearance, publication, or utterance of a person before retirement or death. **2.** the song that a dying swan is said to sing.
swan-up·ping *n. Brit.* **1.** the practice or action of marking nicks in swans' beaks as a sign of ownership. **2.** the annual swan-upping of royal cygnets on the River Thames.
swap *or* **swop** (swɒp) *Informal.* ~*vb.* **swaps, swap+ping, swapped** *or* **swops, swop+ping, swopped. 1.** to trade or exchange (something or someone) for another. ~*n.* **2.** an exchange. **3.** something that is exchanged. [C14 (in the sense: to shake hands on a bargain, strike): probably of imitative origin] —'**swap+per** *or* '**swop+per** *n.*
swa+raj (swə'rɑːdʒ) *n.* (in British India) self-government; independence. [C20: from Sanskrit *svarāj,* from *sva* self + *rājya* rule] —**swa+'raj+ism** *n.* —**swa+'raj+ist** *n., adj.*
sward (swɔːd) *or* **swarth** (swɔːθ) *n.* **1.** turf or grass or a stretch of turf or grass. ~*vb.* **2.** to cover or become covered with grass. [Old English *sweard* skin; related to Old Frisian *swarde* scalp, Middle High German *swart* hide]
swarf (swɔːf, swɑːf) *n.* material removed by cutting tools in the machining of metals or cutting of gramophone records. [C16: of Scandinavian origin; related to Old Norse *svarf* metallic dust]
swarm[1] (swɔːm) *n.* **1.** a group of social insects, esp. bees led by a queen, that has left the parent hive in order to start a new colony. **2.** a large mass of small animals, esp. insects. **3.** a throng or mass, esp. when moving or in turmoil. ~*vb.* **4.** *(intr.)* (of small animals, esp. bees) to move in or form a swarm. **5.** *(intr.)* to congregate, move about or proceed in large numbers. **6.** (when *intr.,* often foll. by *with*) to overrun or be overrun (with): *the house swarmed with rats.* **7.** *(tr.)* to cause to swarm. [Old English *swearm;* related to Old Norse *svarmr* uproar, Old High German *swaram* swarm]
swarm[2] (swɔːm) *vb.* (when *intr.,* usually foll. by *up*) to climb (a ladder, etc.) by gripping with the hands and feet: *the boys swarmed up the rigging.* [C16: of unknown origin]
swarm cell *or* **spore** *n.* another name for **zoospore.**
swart (swɔːt) *or* **swarth** (swɔːθ) *adj. Archaic or dialect.* swarthy. [Old English *sweart;* related to Old Frisian *swart,* Old Norse *svartr,* Old High German *swarz* black, Latin *sordēs* dirt; see SORDID] —'**swart+ness** *or* '**swarth+ness** *n.*
swarth·y ('swɔːðɪ) *adj.* **swarth·i+er, swarth·i·est.** dark-hued or dark-complexioned. [C16: from obsolete *swarty,* from SWART + -Y[1]] —'**swarth·i+ly** *adv.* —'**swarth·i+ness** *n.*
swash (swɒʃ) *vb.* **1.** *(intr.)* (esp. of water or things in water) to wash or move with noisy splashing. **2.** *(tr.)* to dash (a liquid, esp. water) against or upon. **3.** *(intr.) Archaic.* to swagger or bluster. ~*n.* **4.** Also called: **send.** the dashing movement or sound of water, such as that of waves on a beach. Compare **backwash. 5.** any other swashing movement or sound. **6.** a sandbar washed by the waves. **7.** Also called: **swash channel.** a channel of moving water cutting through or running behind a sandbank. **8.** *Archaic.* **a.** swagger or bluster. **b.** a swashbuckler. [C16: probably of imitative origin] —'**swash+ing+ly** *adv.*
swash+buck+ler ('swɒʃ,bʌklə) *n.* a swaggering or daredevil adventurer or bully. [C16: see SWASH, BUCKLE, -ER[1]]
swash+buck+ling ('swɒʃ,bʌklɪŋ) *adj.* *(usually prenominal)* **1.** of or characteristic of a swashbuckler, esp. in being daredevil, swaggering, or bullying. **2.** (esp. of films in period costume) full of adventure and excitement.
swash let+ter *n. Printing.* a decorative letter, esp. an ornamental italic capital.
swas+ti+ka ('swɒstɪkə) *n.* **1.** a primitive religious symbol or ornament in the shape of a Greek cross, usually having the ends of the arms bent at right angles in either a clockwise or anticlockwise direction. **2.** this symbol with clockwise arms, officially adopted in 1935 as the emblem of Nazi Germany. [C19: from Sanskrit *svastika,* from *svasti* prosperity; from the belief that it brings good luck]
swat (swɒt) *vb.* **swats, swat+ting, swat+ted.** *(tr.)* **1.** to strike or hit sharply: *to swat a fly.* ~*n.* **2.** another word (esp. Brit.) for **swatter** (sense 1). **3.** a sharp or violent blow. [C17: northern English dialect and U.S. variant of SQUAT] —'**swat+ter** *n.*
Swat (swɒt) *n.* **1.** a former princely state of NW India: passed to Pakistan in 1947. **2.** a river in Pakistan, rising in the north and flowing south to the Kabul River north of Peshawar. Length: about 640 km (400 miles).
swatch (swɒtʃ) *n.* **1.** a sample of cloth. **2.** a number of such samples, usually fastened together in book form. [C16: Scottish and northern English, of uncertain origin]
swath (swɔːθ) *or* **swathe** (sweɪð) *n., pl.* **swaths** (swɔːðz) *or* **swathes. 1.** the width of one sweep of a scythe or of the blade of a mowing machine. **2.** the strip cut by either of these in one course. **3.** the quantity of cut grass, hay, or similar crop left in one course of such mowing. **4.** a long narrow strip or belt. [Old English *swæth;* related to Old Norse *svath* smooth patch]
swathe (sweɪð) *vb.* *(tr.)* **1.** to bandage (a wound, limb, etc.), esp. completely. **2.** to wrap a band, garment, etc., around, esp. so as to cover completely; swaddle. **3.** to envelop. ~*n.* **4.** a bandage or wrapping. **5.** a variant spelling of **swath.** [Old English *swathian;* related to *swæthel* swaddling clothes, Old High German *swedil,* Dutch *zwadel;* see SWADDLE] —'**swath+a·ble** *or* '**swathe+a·ble** *adj.*
Swa+tow ('swɒ'taʊ) *n.* a port in SE China, in E Kwantung near the mouth of the Han River: became a treaty port in 1869. Pop.: 280 400 (1953). Also called: **Shantow.**
swats (swæts) *pl. n. Northern Brit. dialect.* newly brewed ale or beer. [Old English *swātan* (plural) beer]
swat+ter ('swɒtə) *n.* **1.** a device for killing insects, esp. a meshed flat attached to a handle. **2.** a person who swats.
sway (sweɪ) *vb.* **1.** *(usually intr.)* to swing or cause to swing to and fro: *the door swayed in the wind.* **2.** *(usually intr.)* to lean or incline or cause to lean or incline to one side or in different directions in turn. **3.** *(usually intr.)* to vacillate or cause to vacillate between two or more opinions. **4.** to be influenced or swerve or influence or cause to swerve to or from a purpose or opinion. **5.** *(tr.) Nautical.* to hoist (a yard, mast, or other spar). **6.** *Archaic or poetic.* to rule or wield power (over). **7.** *(tr.) Archaic.* to wield (a weapon). ~*n.* **8.** control; power. **9.** a swinging or leaning movement. **10.** *Archaic.* dominion; governing authority. **11. hold sway.** to be master; reign. [C16: probably from Old Norse *sveigja* to bend; related to Dutch *zwaaien,* Low German *swājen*] —'**sway+a·ble** *adj.* —'**sway+er** *n.* —'**sway+ful** *adj.* —'**sway+ing+ly** *adv.*
sway-back *n. Vet. science.* an abnormal sagging or concavity of the spine in horses. —'**sway-,backed** *adj.*
Swa+zi ('swɑːzɪ) *n.* **1.** *(pl.* **+zis** *or* **+zi)** a member of a racially mixed people of southern Africa living chiefly in Swaziland, who first formed into a strong political group in the late 19th century. **2.** the language of this people: an official language of Swaziland along with English. It belongs to the Nabtu group of the Niger-Congo family and is closely related to Xhosa and Zulu.
Swa+zi+land ('swɑːzɪ,lænd) *n.* a kingdom in southern Africa: made a protectorate of the Transvaal by Britain in 1894; gained independence in 1968; a member of the Commonwealth. Official languages: English and Swazi. Currency: rand. Capital: Mbabane. Pop.: 374 697 (1966). Area: 17 363 sq. km (6704 sq. miles).
Swa+zi Ter+ri+to·ry *n.* the former name of **KaNgwane.**
swear (swɛə) *vb.* **swears, swear+ing, swore, sworn. 1.** to declare or affirm (a statement) as true, esp. by invoking a deity, etc., as witness. **2.** (foll. by *by*) **a.** to invoke (a deity, etc.) by name as a witness or guarantee to an oath. **b.** to trust implicitly; have complete confidence (in). **3.** *(intr.; often foll. by at)* to curse, blaspheme, or use swearwords. **4.** (when *tr., may take a clause as object or an infinitive*) to promise solemnly on oath; vow. **5.** *(tr.)* to assert or affirm with great emphasis or earnestness. **6.** *(intr.)* to give evidence or make any statement or solemn declaration on oath. **7.** to take an oath in order to add force or solemnity to (a statement or declaration). ~*n.* **8.** a period of

swearing. [Old English *swerian;* related to Old Norse *sverja,* Gothic *swaran,* Old Frisian *swera,* German *schwören*] —'**swear+er** *n.* —'**swear+ing+ly** *adv.*

swear in *vb. (tr., adv.)* to administer an oath to (a person) on his assuming office, entering the witness box to give evidence, etc.

swear off *vb. (intr., prep.)* to promise to abstain from something: *to swear off drink.*

swear out *vb. (tr., adv.) U.S.* to secure the issue of (a warrant for an arrest) by making a charge under oath.

swear+word ('swɛə,wɜ:d) *n.* a socially taboo word or phrase of a profane, obscene, or insulting character.

sweat (swɛt) *n.* **1.** the secretion from the sweat glands, esp. when profuse and visible, as during strenuous activity, from excessive heat, etc.; perspiration. **2.** the act or process of secreting this fluid. **3.** the act of inducing the exudation of moisture. **4.** drops of moisture given forth or gathered on the surface of something. **5.** *Informal.* a state or condition of worry or eagerness (esp. in the phrase **in a sweat**). **6.** *Informal.* drudgery or hard labour: *mowing lawns is a real sweat!* **7.** *Chiefly U.S.* an exercise gallop given to a horse, esp. on the day of a race. **8. no sweat!** *(interj.) Slang, chiefly U.S.* easily accomplished. ~*vb.* **sweats, sweat+ing; sweat** *or* **sweat+ed. 9.** to secrete (sweat) through the pores of the skin, esp. profusely; perspire. **10.** *(tr.)* to make wet or stain with perspiration. **11.** to give forth or cause to give forth (moisture) in droplets: *a sweating cheese; the maple sweats sap.* **12.** *(intr.)* to collect and condense moisture on an outer surface: *a glass of beer sweating in the sun.* **13.** *(intr.)* (of a liquid) to pass through a porous surface in droplets. **14.** (of tobacco leaves, cut and dried hay, etc.) to exude moisture and, sometimes, begin to ferment or to cause (tobacco leaves, etc.) to exude moisture. **15.** *(tr.)* to heat (food, esp. vegetables) slowly in butter in a tightly closed saucepan. **16.** *(tr.)* to join (pieces of metal) by pressing together and heating. **17.** *(tr.)* to heat (solder) until it melts. **18.** *(tr.)* to heat (a partially fused metal) to extract an easily fusible constituent. **19.** to shake together (coins, esp. gold coins) so as to remove particles for illegal use. **20.** *Informal.* to suffer anxiety, impatience, or distress. **21.** *Informal.* to overwork or be overworked. **22.** *(tr.) Informal.* to employ at very low wages and under bad conditions. **23.** *(tr.) Informal.* to extort, esp. by torture: *to sweat information out of a captive.* **24.** *(intr.) Informal.* to suffer punishment: *you'll sweat for this!* **25. sweat blood.** *Slang.* **a.** to work very hard. **b.** to be filled with anxiety or impatience. [Old English *swǣtan* to sweat, from *swāt* sweat; related to Old Saxon *swēt,* Old Norse *sveiti,* Old High German *sweiz,* Latin *sūdor,* Sanskrit *svedas*] —'**sweat+less** *adj.*

sweat+band ('swɛt,bænd) *n.* **1.** a band of material set in a hat or cap to protect it from sweat. **2.** a piece of cloth tied around the forehead to keep sweat out of the eyes or around the wrist to keep the hands dry, as in sports.

sweat+box ('swɛt,bɒks) *n.* **1.** a device for causing tobacco leaves, fruit, or hides to sweat. **2.** a very small pen or cubicle where a pig is fattened intensively. **3.** *Informal, chiefly U.S.* a narrow room or cell for a prisoner. **4.** *Informal.* any place where a person sweats on account of confinement, heat, etc.

sweat+ed ('swɛtɪd) *adj.* **1.** made by exploited labour: *sweated goods.* **2.** (of workers, etc.) forced to work in poor conditions for low pay.

sweat+er ('swɛtə) *n.* **1. a.** a garment made of knitted or crocheted material covering the upper part of the body, esp. a heavy one worn for warmth. **b.** *(as modifier): a sweater dress.* **2.** a person or thing that sweats. **3.** an employer who overworks and underpays his employees.

sweat+er girl *n. Slang, now rare.* a young woman or girl with large breasts who wears tight sweaters.

sweat gland *n.* any of the coiled tubular subcutaneous glands that secrete sweat by means of a duct that opens on to the surface of the skin.

sweat+ing sick+ness *n.* **1.** the nontechnical name for **miliary fever. 2.** an acute infectious febrile disease that was widespread in Europe during the late 15th century, characterized by profuse sweating. **3.** a disease of cattle, esp. calves, prevalent in southern Africa and transmitted by ticks.

sweat off *or* **a·way** *vb. (tr., adv.) Informal.* to get rid of (weight) by strenuous exercise or sweating.

sweat out *vb. (tr., adv.)* **1.** to cure or lessen the effects of (a cold, respiratory infection, etc.) by sweating. **2.** *Informal.* to endure (hardships) for a time (often in the phrase **sweat it out**). **3. sweat one's guts out.** *Informal.* to work extremely hard.

sweat shirt *n. Chiefly U.S.* a long-sleeved knitted cotton sweater worn by athletes, etc.

sweat+shop ('swɛt,ʃɒp) *n.* a workshop where employees work long hours under bad conditions for low wages.

sweat suit *n. Chiefly U.S.* a suit worn by athletes for training comprising knitted cotton trousers fitting closely at the ankle and a light cotton sweater.

sweat·y ('swɛtɪ) *adj.* **sweat·i+er, sweat·i+est. 1.** covered with perspiration; sweating. **2.** smelling of or like sweat. **3.** causing sweat. —'**sweat·i+ly** *adv.* —'**sweat·i+ness** *n.*

swede (swi:d) *n.* **1.** a Eurasian cruciferous plant, *Brassica napobrassica,* cultivated for its bulbous edible root, which is used as a vegetable and as cattle fodder. **2.** the root of this plant. ~Also called: **Swedish turnip.** U.S. name: **rutabaga.** [C19: so called after being introduced into Scotland from Sweden in the 18th century]

Swede (swi:d) *n.* a native, citizen, or inhabitant of Sweden.

Swe+den ('swi:dᵊn) *n.* a kingdom in NW Europe, occupying the E part of the Scandinavian Peninsula, on the Gulf of Bothnia and the Baltic: first united during the Viking period (8th–11th centuries). About 50 per cent of the total area is forest and 9 per cent lakes. Exports include timber, pulp, paper, iron ore, and steel. Language: Swedish. Religion: mostly Lutheran. Currency: krona. Capital: Stockholm. Pop.: 8 161 000 (1974 est.). Area: 449 793 sq. km (173 665 sq. miles). Swedish name: **Sverige.**

Swe·den·borg ('swi:dᵊn,bɔ:g; *Swedish* 'sve:dən,bɔrj) *n.* **E·ma·nu·el** (e'manuel). original surname *Svedberg.* 1688–1772, Swedish scientist and theologian, whose mystical ideas became the basis of a religious movement.

Swe+den+bor+gi+an+ism (,swi:dᵊn'bɔ:dʒɪə,nɪzəm, -gɪ-) *or* **Swe+den+bor+gism** ('swi:dᵊn,bɔ:dʒɪzəm, -gɪz-) *n.* the system of philosophical and religious doctrines of Emanuel Swedenborg, emphasizing the spiritual structure of the universe, the possibility of direct contact with spirits, and the divinity of Christ. This provided the basis for the **New Jerusalem Church** (or **New Church**) founded by Swedenborg's followers. —,**Swe+den+'bor+gi·an** *n., adj.*

Swe+dish ('swi:dɪʃ) *adj.* **1.** of, relating to, or characteristic of Sweden, its people, or their language. ~*n.* **2.** the official language of Sweden, belonging to the North Germanic branch of the Indo-European family: one of the two official languages of Finland. **3. the Swedish.** *(functioning as pl.)* the people of Sweden collectively.

Swe+dish mas+sage *n.* massage combined with a system (**Swedish movements** or **gymnastics**) of passive and active exercising of muscles and joints.

Swe+dish mile *n.* a unit of length used in Sweden, equal to 10 kilometres.

Swee·linck (*Dutch* 'swe:lɪŋk) *n.* **Jan Pie·ters·zoon** (jɑn 'pi:tər-,zo:n). 1562–1621, Dutch composer and organist, whose organ works are important for being the first to incorporate independent parts for the pedals.

swee+ny ('swi:nɪ) *n. Vet. science.* a wasting of the shoulder muscles of a horse, esp. as the result of a nerve injury.

sweep (swi:p) *vb.* **sweeps, sweep+ing, swept. 1.** to clean or clear (a space, chimney, etc.) with a brush, broom, etc. **2.** (often foll. by *up*) to remove or collect (dirt, rubbish, etc.) with a brush, broom, etc. **3.** to move in a smooth or continuous manner, esp. quickly or forcibly: *cars swept along the road.* **4.** to move in a proud or dignified fashion: *she swept past.* **5.** *(tr.)* to spread or pass rapidly across, through, or along (a region, area, etc.): *the news swept through the town.* **6.** *(tr.)* to direct (the gaze, line of fire, etc.) over; survey. **7.** *(tr.;* foll. by *away* or *off)* to overwhelm emotionally: *she was swept away by his charm.* **8.** *(tr.)* to brush or lightly touch (a surface, etc.): *the dress swept along the ground.* **9.** *(tr.;* often foll. by *away)* to convey, clear, or abolish, esp. with strong or continuous movements: *the sea swept the sandcastle away; secondary modern schools were swept away.* **10.** *(intr.)* to extend gracefully or majestically, esp. in a wide circle: *the plains sweep down to the sea.* **11.** to search (a body of water) for mines, etc., by dragging. **12.** *(tr.)* to win overwhelmingly, esp. in an election: *Labour swept the country.* **13.** *Cricket.* to play (a ball) with a sweep. **14.** *(tr.)* to propel (a boat) with sweeps. **15. sweep the board. a.** (in gambling) to win all the cards or money. **b.** to achieve a triumphant success. **16. sweep (something) under the carpet.** to conceal (something, esp. a problem) in the hope that it will be overlooked by others. ~*n.* **17.** the act or an instance of sweeping; removal by or as if by a brush or broom. **18.** a swift or steady movement, esp. in an arc: *with a sweep of his arms.* **19.** the distance, arc, etc., through which something, such as a pendulum, moves. **20.** a wide expanse or scope: *the sweep of the plains.* **21.** any curving line or contour. **22.** *Cards.* **a.** the winning of every trick in a hand of whist. **b.** the taking, by pairing, of all exposed cards in cassino. **23.** short for **sweepstake. 24.** *Cricket.* a shot in which the ball is hit more or less square on the leg side from a half-kneeling position with the bat held nearly horizontal. **25. a.** a long oar used on an open boat. **b.** *Austral.* a person steering a surf boat with such an oar. **26.** any of the sails of a windmill. **27.** *Electronics.* a steady horizontal or circular movement of an electron beam across or around the fluorescent screen of a cathode-ray tube. **28.** *Agriculture.* **a.** a rakelike attachment for the front of a motor vehicle for pushing hay into piles. **b.** a triangular blade on a cultivator used to cut through roots below the surface of the soil. **29.** a curving driveway. **30.** *Chiefly Brit.* See **chimney sweep. 31.** another name for **swipe** (sense 4). **32. clean sweep. a.** an overwhelming victory or success. **b.** a complete change; purge: *to make a clean sweep.* [C13 *swepen;* related to Old English *swāpan, Old Norse sveipa;* see SWIPE, SWOOP] —'**sweep·y** *adj.*

sweep+back ('swi:p,bæk) *n.* the rearward inclination of a component or surface, such as an aircraft wing, fin, etc.

sweep+er ('swi:pə) *n.* **1.** a person employed to sweep, such as a roadsweeper. **2.** any device for sweeping: *a carpet sweeper.* **3.** *Informal, soccer.* a player who supports the main defenders, as by intercepting loose balls, etc.

sweep hand *n. Horology.* a long hand that registers seconds or fractions of seconds on the perimeter of the dial.

sweep+ing ('swi:pɪŋ) *adj.* **1.** comprehensive and wide-ranging: *sweeping reforms.* **2.** indiscriminate or without reservations: *sweeping statements.* **3.** decisive or overwhelming: *a sweeping victory.* **4.** taking in a wide area: *a sweeping glance.* **5.** driving steadily onwards, esp. over a large area: *a sweeping attack.* —'**sweep+ing+ly** *adv.* —'**sweep+ing+ness** *n.*

sweep+ings ('swi:pɪŋz) *pl. n.* debris, litter, or refuse.

sweep+stake ('swi:p,steɪk) *or esp. U.S.* **sweep+stakes** *n.* **1.**

a. a lottery in which the stakes of the participants constitute the prize. **b.** the prize itself. **2.** any event involving a lottery, esp. a horse race in which the prize is the competitors' stakes. ~Often shortened to **sweep.** [C15: originally referring to someone who *sweeps* or takes all the stakes in a game]

sweet (swi:t) *adj.* **1.** having or denoting a pleasant taste like that of sugar. **2.** agreeable to the senses or the mind: *sweet music.* **3.** having pleasant manners; gentle: *a sweet child.* **4.** (of wine, etc.) having a relatively high sugar content; not dry. **5.** (of foods) not decaying or rancid: *sweet milk.* **6.** not salty: *sweet water.* **7.** free from unpleasant odours: *sweet air.* **8.** containing no corrosive substances: *sweet soil.* **9.** (of petrol) containing no sulphur compounds. **10.** sentimental or unrealistic. **11.** *Jazz.* performed with a regular beat, with the emphasis on clearly outlined melody and little improvisation. **12.** *Austral. slang.* satisfactory or in order; all right. **13.** *Archaic.* respected; dear (used in polite forms of address): *sweet sir.* **14.** effortlessly done: *a sweet shot.* **15.** **sweet on.** fond of or infatuated with. **16.** **at one's own sweet will.** as it suits oneself alone. **17.** **keep (someone) sweet.** to ingratiate oneself in order to ensure cooperation. ~*adv.* **18.** *Informal.* in a sweet manner. ~*n.* **19.** a sweet taste or smell; sweetness in general. **20.** (*often pl.*) *Brit.* any of numerous kinds of confectionery consisting wholly or partly of sugar, esp. of sugar boiled and crystallized (**boiled sweets**). **21.** *Brit.* a pudding, fruit, or any sweet dish served as a dessert. **22.** dear; sweetheart (used as a form of address). **23.** anything that is sweet. **24.** (*often pl.*) a pleasurable experience, state, etc.: *the sweets of success.* **25.** *U.S.* See **sweet potato.** [Old English *swēte;* related to Old Saxon *swōti,* Old High German *suozi,* Old Norse *sœtr,* Latin *suādus* persuasive, *suāvis* sweet, Greek *hēdus,* Sanskrit *svādu;* see PERSUADE, SUAVE] —**'sweet+ish** *adj.* —**'sweet+ly** *adv.* —**'sweet+ness** *n.*

Sweet *n.* **Hen·ry.** 1845–1912, English philologist; a pioneer of modern phonetics. His books include *A History of English Sounds* (1874).

sweet a·lys+sum *n.* a Mediterranean cruciferous plant, *Lobularia maritima,* having clusters of small fragrant white or violet flowers: widely grown in gardens. See also **alyssum.**

sweet-and-sour *adj.* (of food) cooked in a sauce made from sugar and vinegar and other ingredients.

sweet bas+il *n.* See **basil** (sense 1).

sweet bay *n.* **1.** a small tree, *Magnolia virginiana,* of SE North America, having large fragrant white flowers: family *Magnoliaceae* (magnolias). Sometimes shortened to **bay.** **2.** another name for **bay**[4] (sense 1).

sweet+bread ('swi:tˌbrɛd) *n.* the pancreas (**stomach sweetbread**) or the thymus gland (**neck** or **throat sweetbread**) of an animal, used for food. [C16: SWEET + BREAD, perhaps from Old English *brǣd* meat; related to Old Saxon *brādo* ham, Old High German *brāt,* Old Norse *brāth*]

sweet+bri·er ('swi:tˌbraɪə) *n.* a Eurasian rose, *Rosa rubiginosa,* having a tall bristly stem, fragrant leaves, and single pink flowers. Also called: **eglantine.**

sweet cher+ry *n.* **1.** a white-flowered rosaceous tree, *Prunus avium,* of Europe, W Asia, and N Africa, cultivated for its edible bright or dark red sweet spherical fruit. **2.** the fruit of this tree. See also **heart cherry.** ~Also called: **gean, wild cherry.** Compare **sour cherry.**

sweet chest+nut *n.* See **chestnut** (sense 1).

sweet cic+e·ly *n.* **1.** Also called: **myrrh.** an aromatic umbelliferous European plant, *Myrrhis odorata,* having compound leaves and clusters of small white flowers. **2.** the leaves of this plant, formerly used in cookery for their flavour of aniseed. **3.** any of various plants of the umbelliferous genus *Osmorhiza,* of Asia and America, having aromatic roots and clusters of small white flowers.

sweet ci+der *n.* **1.** *Brit.* cider having a high sugar content. **2.** *U.S.* unfermented apple juice. Compare **hard cider.**

sweet clo+ver *n.* another name for **melilot.**

sweet corn *n.* **1.** Also called: **sugar corn, green corn.** a variety of maize, *Zea mays saccharata,* whose kernels are rich in sugar and eaten as a vegetable when young. **2.** the unripe ears of maize, esp. the sweet kernels removed from the cob, cooked as a vegetable.

sweet+en ('swi:tᵊn) *vb.* (*mainly tr.*) **1.** (*also intr.*) to make or become sweet or sweeter. **2.** to mollify or soften (a person). **3.** to make more agreeable. **4.** (*also intr.*) *Chem.* to free or be freed from unpleasant odours, acidic or corrosive substances, or the like. **5.** *Finance, chiefly U.S.* to raise the value of (loan collateral) by adding more securities. **6.** *Informal, poker.* to enlarge (the pot) by adding chips.

sweet+en+er ('swi:tᵊnə) *n.* **1.** a sweetening agent, esp. one that does not contain sugar. **2.** a slang word for **bribe.**

sweet+en+ing ('swi:tᵊnɪŋ) *n.* something that sweetens.

sweet fern *n.* a North American shrub, *Comptonia* (or *Myrica*) *asplenifolia,* having scented fernlike leaves and heads of brownish flowers: family *Myricaceae.*

sweet flag *n.* an aroid marsh plant, *Acorus calamus,* having swordlike leaves, small greenish flowers, and aromatic roots. Also called: **calamus.**

sweet gale *n.* a shrub, *Myrica gale,* of northern swamp regions, having yellow catkin-like flowers and aromatic leaves: family *Myricaceae.* Also called: **bog myrtle.** Often shortened to **gale.**

sweet gum *n.* **1.** a North American liquidambar tree, *Liquidambar styraciflua,* having prickly spherical fruit clusters and fragrant sap: the wood is used to make furniture. Compare **sour gum.** **2.** the wood or sap of this tree.

sweet+heart ('swi:tˌhɑ:t) *n.* **1.** a person loved by another. **2.** *Informal.* a lovable, generous, or obliging person. **3.** a term of endearment for a beloved or lovable person.

sweet+heart a·gree+ment *n. Austral.* an industrial agreement negotiated directly between employers and employees, without resort to arbitration.

sweet·ie ('swi:tɪ) *n. Informal.* **1.** sweetheart; darling: used as a term of endearment. **2.** *Brit.* a child's word for **sweet** (sense 20). **3.** *Chiefly Brit.* an endearing person.

sweet·ie+wife ('swi:tɪˌwaɪf) *n., pl.* **+wives.** *Scot. dialect.* **1.** a garrulous woman. **2.** (formerly) a woman who sells sweets.

sweet+ing ('swi:tɪŋ) *n.* **1.** a variety of sweet apple. **2.** an archaic word for **sweetheart.**

sweet+man ('swi:tˌmæn) *n., pl.* **+men.** (in the Caribbean) a man kept by a woman.

sweet mar+jo+ram *n.* another name for **marjoram** (sense 1).

sweet+meal ('swi:tˌmi:l) *adj.* (of biscuits) sweet and wholemeal.

sweet+meat ('swi:tˌmi:t) *n.* a sweetened delicacy, such as a preserve, sweet, or, formerly, a cake or pastry.

sweet oil *n.* another name for **olive oil.**

sweet pea *n.* a climbing papilionaceous plant, *Lathyrus odoratus,* of S Europe, widely cultivated for its butterfly-shaped fragrant flowers of delicate pastel colours.

sweet pep+per *n.* **1.** a pepper plant, *Capsicum frutescens grossum,* with large bell-shaped fruits that are eaten unripe (**green pepper**) or ripe (**red pepper**). **2.** the fruit of this plant.

sweet po+ta+to *n.* **1.** a convolvulaceous twining plant, *Ipomoea batatas,* of tropical America, cultivated in the tropics for its edible fleshy yellow root. **2.** the root of this plant.

sweet shop *n. Chiefly Brit.* a shop solely or largely selling sweets, esp. boiled sweets.

sweet+sop ('swi:tˌsɒp) *n.* **1.** a small West Indian tree, *Annona squamosa,* having yellowish green fruit: family *Annonaceae.* **2.** the fruit of this tree, which has a sweet edible pulp. ~Also called: **sugar apple, custard apple.** Compare **soursop.**

sweet-talk *U.S. informal.* ~*vb.* **1.** to coax, flatter, or cajole (someone). ~*n.* **sweet talk.** **2.** cajolery; coaxing.

sweet tooth *n.* a strong liking for sweet foods.

sweet wil+liam *n.* a widely cultivated Eurasian caryophyllaceous plant, *Dianthus barbatus,* with flat clusters of white, pink, red, or purple flowers.

sweet wood+ruff *n.* a Eurasian and North African rubiaceous plant, *Galium odoratum* (or *Asperula odorata*), having whorls of leaves and clusters of fragrant white flowers.

swell (swɛl) *vb.* **swells, swell+ing, swelled; swol+len** *or* **swelled.** **1.** to grow or cause to grow in size, esp. as a result of internal pressure. Compare **contract** (senses 1,3). **2.** to expand or cause to expand at a particular point or above the surrounding level; protrude. **3.** to grow or cause to grow in size, amount, intensity, or degree: *the party is swelling with new recruits.* **4.** to puff or be puffed up with pride or another emotion. **5.** (*intr.*) (of seas or lakes) to rise in waves. **6.** (*intr.*) to well up or overflow. **7.** (*tr.*) to make (a musical phrase) increase gradually in volume and then diminish. ~*n.* **8.** **a.** the undulating movement of the surface of the open sea. **b.** a succession of waves or a single large wave. **9.** a swelling or being swollen; expansion. **10.** an increase in quantity or degree; inflation. **11.** a bulge; protuberance. **12.** a gentle hill. **13.** *Informal.* a person very fashionably dressed. **14.** *Informal.* a man of high social or political standing. **15.** *Music.* a crescendo followed by an immediate diminuendo. **16.** Also called: **swell organ.** *Music.* **a.** a set of pipes on an organ housed in a box (**swell box**) fitted with a shutter operated by a pedal, which can be opened or closed to control the volume. **b.** the manual on an organ controlling this. Compare **choir** (sense 4), **great** (sense 20). ~*adj.* **17.** *Informal.* stylish or grand. **18.** *Slang.* excellent; first-class. [Old English *swellan;* related to Old Norse *svella,* Old Frisian *swella,* German *schwellen*]

swelled head *or* **swol+len head** *n. Informal.* an inflated view of one's own worth, often caused by sudden success.

swell+fish ('swɛlˌfɪʃ) *n., pl.* **+fish** *or* **+fish·es.** a popular name for **puffer** (sense 2).

swell+ing ('swɛlɪŋ) *n.* **1.** the act of expansion or inflation. **2.** the state of being or becoming swollen. **3.** a swollen or inflated part or area. **4.** an abnormal enlargement of a bodily structure or part, esp. as the result of injury. Related adj.: **tumescent.**

swel+ter ('swɛltə) *vb.* **1.** (*intr.*) to suffer under oppressive heat, esp. to perspire and feel faint. **2.** (*tr.*) *Archaic.* to exude (venom). **3.** (*tr.*) *Rare.* to cause to suffer under oppressive heat. ~*n.* **4.** a sweltering condition (esp. in the phrase **in a swelter**). **5.** oppressive humid heat. [C15: *swelten,* from Old English *sweltan* to die; related to Old Norse *svelta* to starve, Old High German *swelzan* to burn with passion; see SULTRY]

swel+ter+ing ('swɛltərɪŋ) *adj.* oppressively hot and humid: *a sweltering day.* —**'swel+ter+ing+ly** *adv.*

swept (swɛpt) *vb.* the past tense of **sweep.**

swept+back ('swɛptˌbæk) *adj.* (of an aircraft wing) having leading edge and trailing edges inclined backwards towards the rear of the fuselage.

swept+wing ('swɛptˌwɪŋ) *adj.* (of an aircraft, winged missile, etc.) having wings swept backwards.

swerve (swɜ:v) *vb.* **1.** to turn or cause to turn aside, usually sharply or suddenly, from a course. ~*n.* **2.** the act, instance, or degree of swerving. [Old English *sweorfan* to scour; related to Old High German *swerban* to wipe off, Gothic *afswairban* to wipe off, Old Norse *sverfa* to file] —**'swerv+a·ble** *adj.* —**'swerv+er** *n.* —**'swerv+ing+ly** *adv.*

swev+en ('swɛvᵊn) *n. Archaic.* a vision or dream. [Old English *swefn;* related to Old Norse *svefn* dream, sleep, Lithuanian *sāpnas,* Old Slavonic *sunu,* Latin *somnus*]

Sweyn (sweɪn) *n.* known as *Sweyn Forkbeard.* died 1014, king of Denmark (?986–1014). He conquered England, forcing Ethelred II to flee (1013), father of Canute.

S.W.G. Standard Wire Gauge; a notation for the diameters of metal rods or thickness of metal sheet ranging from 16 mm to 0.02 mm or from 0.5 inch to 0.001 inch.

swift (swɪft) *adj.* **1.** moving or able to move quickly; fast. **2.** occurring or performed quickly or suddenly; instant: *a swift response.* **3.** (*postpositive;* foll. by *to*) prompt to act or respond: *swift to take revenge.* ~*adv.* **4. a.** swiftly or quickly. **b.** (*in combination*): *swift-moving.* ~*n.* **5.** any bird of the families *Apodidae* and *Hemiprocnidae,* such as *Apus apus* (**common swift**) of the Old World: order *Apodiformes.* They have long narrow wings and spend most of the time on the wing. **6.** (*sometimes cap.*) a variety of domestic fancy pigeon originating in Egypt and Syria and having a somewhat similar appearance to a swift. **7.** any of certain North American lizards of the genera *Sceloporus* and *Uta* that can run very rapidly: family *Iguanidae* (iguanas). **8.** the main cylinder in a carding machine. **9.** an expanding reel used to hold skeins of silk. [Old English, from *swīfan* to turn; related to Old Norse *svifa* to rove, Old Frisian *swīvia* to waver, Old High German *sweib* a reversal; see SWIVEL] —**'swift·ly** *adv.* —**'swift·ness** *n.*

Swift (swɪft) *n.* **Jon·a·than.** 1667–1745, Anglo-Irish satirist and churchman, who became dean of St. Patrick's, Dublin, in 1713. His works include *A Tale of a Tub* (1704) and *Gulliver's Travels* (1726).

swift·er ('swɪftə) *n. Nautical.* a line run around the ends of capstan bars to prevent their falling out of their sockets.

swift fox *n.* a small fox, *Vulpes velox,* of the plains of W North America. Also called: **kit fox.**

swift·ie *or* **swift·y** ('swɪftɪ) *n. Austral. slang.* a trick, ruse, or deception.

swift·let ('swɪftˌlɪt) *n.* any of various small swifts of the Asian genus *Collocalia* that often live in caves and use echolocation: the nests, which are made of hardened saliva, are used in oriental cookery to make birds' nest soup.

swig (swɪg) *Informal.* ~*n.* **1.** a large swallow or deep drink, esp. from a bottle. ~*vb.* **swigs, swig·ging, swigged.** **2.** to drink (some liquid) deeply, esp. from a bottle. [C16: of unknown origin] —**'swig·ger** *n.*

swill (swɪl) *vb.* **1.** to drink large quantities of (liquid, esp. alcoholic drink); guzzle. **2.** (*tr.;* often foll. by *out*) *Chiefly Brit.* to drench or rinse in large amounts of water. **3.** (*tr.*) to feed swill to (pigs, etc.). ~*n.* **4.** wet feed, esp. for pigs, consisting of kitchen waste, skim milk, etc. **5.** garbage or refuse, esp. from a kitchen. **6.** a deep draught of drink, esp. beer. **7.** any liquid mess. **8.** the act of swilling. [Old English *swilian* to wash out] —**'swill·er** *n.*

swim (swɪm) *vb.* **swims, swim·ming, swam, swum.** **1.** (*intr.*) to move along in water, etc., by means of movements of the body or parts of the body, esp. the arms and legs, or (in the case of fish) tail and fins. **2.** (*tr.*) to cover (a distance or stretch of water) in this way. **3.** (*tr.*) to compete in (a race) in this way. **4.** (*intr.*) to be supported by and on a liquid; float. **5.** (*tr.*) to use (a particular stroke) in swimming. **6.** (*intr.*) to move smoothly, usually through air or over a surface. **7.** (*intr.*) to reel or seem to reel: *my head swam; the room swam around me.* **8.** (*intr.;* often foll. by *in* or *with*) to be covered or flooded with water or other liquid. **9.** (*intr.;* often foll. by *in*) to be liberally supplied (with): *he's swimming in money.* **10.** (*tr.*) to cause to float or swim. **11.** (*tr.*) to provide (something) with water deep enough to float in. **12. swim with** (*or* **against**) **the stream** *or* **tide.** to conform to (or resist) prevailing opinion. ~*n.* **13.** the act, an instance, or period of swimming. **14.** any graceful gliding motion. **15.** a condition of dizziness; swoon. **16.** a pool in a river good for fishing. **17. in the swim.** *Informal.* fashionable or active in social or political activities. [Old English *swimman;* related to Old Norse *svima,* German *schwimmen,* Gothic *swumsl* pond, Norwegian *svamla* to paddle] —**'swim·ma·ble** *adj.* —**'swim·mer** *n.*

swim blad·der *n. Ichthyol.* another name for **air bladder** (sense 1).

swim·mer·et ('swɪməˌrɛt) *n.* any of the small paired appendages on the abdomen of crustaceans, used chiefly in locomotion and reproduction. Also called: **pleopod.**

swim·ming bath *n.* (*often pl.*) an indoor swimming pool.

swim·ming cos·tume *or* **bath·ing cos·tume** *n. Chiefly Brit.* any apparel worn for swimming or sunbathing, such as a woman's one-piece garment covering most of the torso but not the limbs. Usual U.S. term: **bathing suit.**

swim·ming·ly ('swɪmɪŋlɪ) *adv.* successfully, effortlessly, or well (esp. in the phrase **go swimmingly**).

swim·ming pool *n.* an artificial pool for swimming.

swim·suit ('swɪmˌsuːt, -ˌsjuːt) *n.* a woman's one-piece swimming garment that leaves the arms and legs bare.

Swin·burne ('swɪnˌbɜːn) *n.* **Al·ger·non Charles.** 1837–1909, English lyric poet and critic.

swin·dle ('swɪndᵊl) *vb.* **1.** to cheat (someone) of money, etc.; defraud. **2.** (*tr.*) to obtain (money, etc.) by fraud. ~*n.* **3.** a fraudulent scheme or transaction. [C18: back formation from German *Schwindler,* from *schwindeln,* from Old High German *swintilōn,* frequentative of *swintan* to disappear] —**'swin·dler** *n.* —**'swin·dling·ly** *adv.*

swin·dle sheet *n.* a slang term for **expense account.**

Swin·don ('swɪndən) *n.* a town in S England, in NE Wiltshire: railway workshops. Pop.: 90 830 (1971).

swine (swaɪn) *n.* **1.** (*pl.* **swines**) a coarse or contemptible person. **2.** (*pl.* **swine**) another name for a **pig.** [Old English *swīn;* related to Old Norse *svīn,* Gothic *swein,* Latin *suīnus* relating to swine] —**'swine·ˌlike** *adj.* —**'swin·ish** *adj.* —**'swin·ish·ly** *adv.* —**'swin·ish·ness** *n.*

swine fe·ver *n.* an infectious viral disease of pigs, characterized by fever, refusal to eat, weight loss, and diarrhoea. U.S. term: **hog cholera.**

swine·herd ('swaɪnˌhɜːd) *n.* a person who looks after pigs.

swine·pox ('swaɪnˌpɒks) *n.* **1.** Also called: **variola porcina.** an acute infectious viral disease of pigs characterized by skin eruptions. **2.** a form of chickenpox in which the skin eruptions are not pitted.

swine ve·sic·u·lar dis·ease *n.* a viral disease of swine characterized by vesicular lesions on the feet, legs, snout, and tongue.

swing (swɪŋ) *vb.* **swings, swing·ing, swung.** **1.** to move or cause to move rhythmically to and fro, as a free-hanging object; sway. **2.** (*intr.*) to move, walk, etc., with a relaxed and swaying motion. **3.** to pivot or cause to pivot, as on a hinge. **4.** to move or cause to move in a curve: *the car swung around the bend.* **5.** to move or cause to move by suspending or being suspended. **6.** to hang or be hung so as to be able to turn freely. **7.** (*intr.*) *Slang.* to be hanged: *he'll swing for it.* **8.** to alter or cause to alter habits, a course, etc. **9.** (*tr.*) *Informal.* to influence or manipulate successfully: *I hope he can swing the deal.* **10.** (*tr.;* foll. by *up*) to raise or hoist, esp. in a sweeping motion. **11.** (*intr.;* often foll. by *at*) to hit out or strike (at), esp. with a sweeping motion. **12.** (*tr.*) to wave (a weapon, etc.) in a sweeping motion; flourish. **13.** to arrange or play (music) with the rhythmically flexible and compulsive quality associated with jazz. **14.** (*intr.*) (of popular music, esp. jazz, or of the musicians who play it) to have this quality. **15.** *Slang.* to be lively and modern. **16.** (*intr.*) *Cricket.* to bowl (a ball) with swing or (of a ball) to move with a swing. **17.** to turn (a ship or aircraft) in order to test compass error. **18. swing the lead.** to malinger or make up excuses. ~*n.* **19.** the act or manner of swinging or the distance covered while swinging: *a wide swing.* **20.** a sweeping stroke or blow. **21.** *Boxing.* a wide punch from the side similar to but longer than a hook. **22.** *Cricket.* the lateral movement of a bowled ball through the air. **23.** any free swaying motion. **24.** any curving movement; sweep. **25.** something that swings or is swung, esp. a suspended seat on which a person may sit and swing back and forth. **26. a.** a kind of popular dance music influenced by jazz, usually played by big bands and originating in the 1930s. **b.** (*as modifier*): *swing music.* **27.** *Prosody.* a steady distinct rhythm or cadence in prose or verse. **28.** *Informal.* the normal round or pace: *get into the swing of things.* **29.** a fluctuation, as in some business activity, voting pattern etc. **30.** *U.S. informal.* free scope; freedom of activity. **31.** *Chiefly U.S.* a circular tour. **32. in full swing.** operating with full vigour. [Old English *swingan;* related to Old Frisian *swinga,* Old High German *swingan*]

swing·boat ('swɪŋˌbəʊt) *n.* a piece of fairground equipment consisting of a boat-shaped carriage for swinging in.

swing bridge *n.* a low bridge that can be rotated about a vertical axis to permit the passage of ships, etc. Also called: **pivot bridge, turn bridge.** Compare **drawbridge.**

swing door *or* **swing·ing door** *n.* a door pivoted or hung on double-sided hinges so that it can open either way.

swinge (swɪndʒ) *vb.* **swing·es, swinge·ing** *or* **swing·ing, swinged.** (*tr.*) *Archaic.* to beat, flog, or punish. [Old English *swengan;* related to Old Frisian *swenga* to drench, Gothic *afswaggwjan* to cause to sway; see SWING]

swinge·ing ('swɪndʒɪŋ) *adj. Chiefly Brit.* punishing; severe.

swing·er ('swɪŋə) *n. Slang.* a person regarded as being modern and lively. —**'swing·ing** *adj.* —**'swing·ing·ly** *adv.*

swing·ing vot·er *n. Austral. informal.* a person who does not vote consistently for any single political party.

swin·gle ('swɪŋgᵊl) *n.* **1.** a flat-bladed wooden instrument used for beating and scraping flax or hemp to remove coarse matter from it. ~*vb.* **2.** to use a swingle on. [Old English *swingel* stroke; related to Middle High German *swüngel,* Middle Dutch *swinghel;* see SWING, -LE]

swin·gle·tree ('swɪŋgᵊlˌtriː) *n.* another name for **whiffletree.**

swing·om·e·ter (swɪŋ'ɒmɪtə) *n.* a device used in television broadcasting during a general election to indicate the swing of votes from one political party to another.

swing shift *n. U.S. informal.* **1.** the evening work shift, usually from the middle of the afternoon until midnight. **2.** the employees working such a shift. —**swing shift·er** *n.*

swing-wing *adj.* **1.** of or relating to an aircraft equipped with wings that are automatically swept back close to the fuselage when flying at high speed and are brought forward for landing and takeoff. ~*n.* **2. a.** an aircraft fitted with such wings. **b.** either of the two wings of such an aircraft.

swink (swɪŋk) *Archaic or Brit. dialect.* ~*vb.* **1.** (*intr.*) to toil or drudge. ~*n.* **2.** toil or drudgery. [Old English *swinc,* from *swincan*] —**'swink·er** *n.*

swipe (swaɪp) *vb.* **1.** (when *intr.,* usually foll. by *at*) to hit hard with a sweeping blow. **2.** (*tr.*) *Slang.* to steal. ~*n.* **3.** *Informal.* a hard blow. **4.** Also called: **sweep.** a type of lever for raising and lowering a weight, such as a bucket in a well. [C19: perhaps related to SWEEP]

swipes (swaɪps) *pl. n. Brit. slang.* beer, esp. when poor or weak. [C18: probably related to SWEEP]

swip·ple *or* **swi·ple** ('swɪpᵊl) *n.* the part of a flail that strikes the grain. [C15 *swipyl,* variant of *swepyl,* from *swep(en)* to SWEEP + *-yl,* suffix denoting an instrument]

swirl (swɜːl) *vb.* **1.** to turn or cause to turn in a twisting spinning fashion. **2.** (*intr.*) to be dizzy; swim: *my head was swirling.* ~*n.* **3.** a whirling or spinning motion, esp. in water. **4.** a whorl; curl. **5.** the act of swirling or stirring. **6.** dizzy confusion or disorder. [C15: probably from Dutch *zwirrelen;* related to Norwegian *svirla,* German *schwirren*] —**'swirl+ing** *adj.* —**'swirl+ing+ly** *adv.* —**'swirl·y** *adj.*

swish (swɪʃ) *vb.* **1.** to move with or make or cause to move with or make a whistling or hissing sound. **2.** (*intr.*) (esp. of fabrics) to rustle. **3.** (*tr.*) *Slang, now rare.* to whip; flog. **4.** (*tr.;* foll. by *off*) to cut with a swishing blow. ~*n.* **5.** a hissing or rustling sound or movement. **6.** a rod for flogging or a blow from such a rod. **7.** *U.S. slang.* an effeminate male homosexual. **8.** a W African building material composed of mortar and mud or laterite, or more recently of cement and earth. ~*adj.* **9.** *Informal, chiefly Brit.* fashionable; smart. **10.** *U.S. slang.* effeminate and homosexual. [C18: of imitative origin] —**'swish+er** *n.* —**'swish+ing+ly** *adv.* —**'swish·y** *adj.*

Swiss (swɪs) *adj.* **1.** of, relating to, or characteristic of Switzerland, its inhabitants, or their dialects of German, French, and Italian. ~*n.* **2.** a native, inhabitant, or citizen of Switzerland.

Swiss chard *n.* another name for **chard.**

Swiss cheese *n.* a hard white or pale yellow cheese with holes, such as Gruyère or Emmenthal.

Swiss Guard *n.* **1.** the bodyguard of the pope, recruited from Swiss nationals. **2.** a member of this bodyguard.

swiss mus+lin *n.* a fine muslin dress fabric, usually having a raised or woven pattern of dolls or figures.

swiss roll *n.* a sponge cake spread with jam, cream, or some other filling, and rolled up.

switch (swɪtʃ) *n.* **1.** a mechanical, electrical, or electronic device for opening or closing a circuit or for diverting a current from one part of a circuit to another. **2.** a swift and usually sudden shift or change. **3.** an exchange or swap. **4.** a flexible rod or twig, used esp. for punishment. **5.** the sharp movement or blow of such an instrument. **6.** a tress of false hair used to give added length or bulk to a woman's own hair style. **7.** the tassel-like tip of the tail of cattle and certain other animals. **8.** any of various card games in which the suit is changed during play. **9.** *U.S.* a railway siding. **10.** *U.S.* a railway point. **11.** *Austral. informal.* See **switchboard.** ~*vb.* **12.** to shift, change, turn aside, or change the direction of (something). **13.** to exchange (places); replace (something by something else): *the battalions switched fronts.* **14.** *Chiefly U.S.* to transfer or be transferred from one railway track to another. **15.** (*tr.*) to cause (an electric current) to start or stop flowing or to change its path by operating a switch. **16.** to swing or cause to swing, esp. back and forth. **17.** (*tr.*) to lash or whip with or as if with a switch. [C16: perhaps from Middle Dutch *swijch* branch, twig] —**'switch+er** *n.* —**'switch+,like** *adj.*

switch+back ('swɪtʃ,bæk) *n.* **1.** a steep mountain road, railway, or track with hairpin bends or a hairpin bend on such a road, etc. **2.** another word (esp. Brit.) for **roller coaster.**

switch+blade *or* **switch+blade knife** ('swɪtʃ,bleɪd) *n.* another name (esp. U.S.) for **flick knife.**

switch+board ('swɪtʃ,bɔ:d) *n.* **1.** an installation in a telephone exchange, office, hotel, etc., at which the interconnection of telephone lines is manually controlled. **2.** a similar installation of switches, terminals, etc., by which certain electrical equipment is operated.

switch+er·oo (,swɪtʃə'ru:) *n. U.S. slang.* a surprising or unexpected change or variation. [C20: from SWITCH]

switch+girl ('swɪtʃ,gɜ:l) *n. Austral. informal.* a girl or woman who operates a telephone switchboard.

switch+man ('swɪtʃmən) *n., pl.* **+men.** the U.S. name for **pointsman.**

switch off *vb.* (*adv.*) **1.** to cause (a device) to stop operating by or as if by moving a switch, knob, or lever; turn off. **2.** *Informal.* to cease to interest or be interested; make or become bored, alienated, etc.

switch on *vb.* (*adv.*) **1.** to cause (a device) to operate by or as if by moving a switch, knob, or lever; turn on. **2.** (*tr.*) *Informal.* to produce (charm, tears, etc.) suddenly or automatically. **3.** (*tr.*) *Informal.* (now slightly dated) to make up-to-date, esp. regarding outlook, dress, etc. **4.** (*tr.*) *Slang.* to arouse emotionally or sexually. **5.** (*intr.*) *Slang.* to take or become intoxicated by drugs. **6.** (*tr.*) *Slang.* to introduce (someone) to drugs.

switch yard *n. U.S.* an area in a railway system where rolling stock is shunted, as in forming trains.

swith+er ('swɪðə) *Scot. dialect.* *vb.* (*intr.*) **1.** to hesitate; be perplexed. ~*n.* **2.** hesitation; perplexity; agitation. [C16: of unknown origin]

Swith·in *or* **Swith·un** ('swɪðɪn, 'swɪθ-) *n.* **Saint.** died 862 A.D., English ecclesiastic: bishop of Winchester (?852–862). Feast day: July 15.

Switz. *or* **Swit.** *abbrev. for* Switzerland.

Switz+er ('swɪtsə) *n.* **1.** a less common word for **Swiss.** **2.** a member of the Swiss Guard. [C16: from Middle High German, from *Swīz* Switzerland]

Swit+zer+land ('swɪtsələnd) *n.* a federal republic in W central Europe: the cantons of Schwyz, Uri, and Unterwalden formed a defensive league against the Hapsburgs in 1291, later joined by other cantons; gained independence in 1499; adopted a policy of permanent neutrality from 1516; a leading centre of the Reformation in the 16th century. It lies in the Jura Mountains and the Alps, with a plateau between the two ranges. Languages: German, French, Italian, and Romansch. Religion: mostly Protestant and Roman Catholic. Currency: Swiss franc. Capital: Bern. Pop.: 6 443 000 (1974 est.). Area: 41 288 sq. km (15 941 sq. miles). German name: **Schweiz.** French name: **Suisse.** Italian name: **Svizzera.** Related adj.: **Helvetic.**

swive (swaɪv) *vb. Archaic.* to have sexual intercourse with (a person). [Old English *swīfan* to revolve, SWIVEL]

swiv+el ('swɪvᵊl) *n.* **1.** a coupling device which allows an attached object to turn freely. **2.** such a device made of two parts which turn independently, such as a compound link of a chain. **3. a.** a pivot on which is mounted a gun that may be swung from side to side in a horizontal plane. **b.** Also called: **swivel gun.** the gun itself. ~*vb.* **+els, +el+ling, +elled** *or U.S.* **+els, +el+ing, +eled.** **4.** to turn or swing on or as if on a pivot. **5.** (*tr.*) to provide with, secure by, or support with a swivel. [C14: from Old English *swīfan* to turn; see SWIFT] —**'swiv·el-,like** *adj.*

swiv+el chair *n.* a chair, the seat of which is joined to the legs by a swivel and which thus may be spun round.

swiv+el pin *n.* another name for **kingpin** (sense 1).

swiv+et ('swɪvɪt) *n. Dialect.* a condition of nervous excitement or exasperation. [C20: of unknown origin]

swiz+zle ('swɪzᵊl) *n.* **1.** *U.S.* an unshaken cocktail. **2.** a Caribbean drink of milk and rum. **3.** Also called: **swizz.** *Brit. informal.* a swindle or disappointment. ~*vb.* **4.** (*tr.*) to stir a swizzle stick in (a drink). [C19: of unknown origin]

swiz+zle stick *n.* a small rod used to agitate an effervescent drink to facilitate the escape of carbon dioxide.

swob (swɒb) *n., vb.,* **swobs, swob+bing, swobbed.** a less common word for **swab.**

swol+len ('swəulən) *vb.* **1.** the past participle of **swell.** ~*adj.* **2.** tumid or enlarged by or as if by swelling. **3.** turgid or bombastic. —**'swol+len+ly** *adv.* —**'swol+len+ness** *n.*

swoon (swu:n) *vb.* (*intr.*) **1.** a literary word for **faint.** **2.** to become ecstatic. ~*n.* **3.** an instance of fainting. ~Also (archaic or dialect): **swound** (swaʊnd). [Old English *geswōgen* insensible, past participle of *swōgan* (unattested except in compounds) to suffocate] —**'swoon+ing+ly** *adv.*

swoop (swu:p) *vb.* **1.** (*intr.;* usually foll. by *down, on,* or *upon*) to sweep or pounce suddenly. **2.** (*tr.;* often foll. by *up, away,* or *off*) to seize or scoop suddenly. ~*n.* **3.** the act of swooping. **4.** a swift descent. [Old English *swāpan* to sweep; related to Old High German *sweifan* to swing around, Old Norse *sveipa* to throw]

swoosh (swʊʃ) *vb.* **1.** to make or cause to make a rustling or swirling sound, esp. when moving or pouring out. ~*n.* **2.** a swirling or rustling sound or movement. [C20: of imitative origin (probably influenced by SWISH and SWOOP)]

swop (swɒp) *n., vb.,* **swops, swop+ping, swopped.** a variant spelling of **swap.**

sword (sɔ:d) *n.* **1.** a thrusting, striking, or cutting weapon with a long blade having one or two cutting edges, a hilt, and usually a crosspiece or guard. **2.** such a weapon worn on ceremonial occasions as a symbol of authority. **3.** something resembling a sword, such as the snout of a swordfish. **4. cross swords.** to argue or fight. **5. the sword. a.** violence or power, esp. military power. **b.** death; destruction: *to put to the sword.* [Old English *sweord;* related to Old Saxon *swerd,* Old Norse *sverth,* Old High German *swert*] —**'sword+less** *adj.* —**'sword+,like** *adj.*

sword bay·o·net *n.* a bayonet with a swordlike blade.

sword+bear·er *n.* an official who carries a ceremonial sword.

sword belt *n.* a belt with a sling or strap for a sword.

sword+bill ('sɔ:d,bɪl) *n.* a South American hummingbird, *Ensifera ensifera,* having a bill as long as its body.

sword cane *n.* another name for **swordstick.**

sword+craft ('sɔ:d,krɑ:ft) *n.* the art of using a sword.

sword dance *n.* a dance in which the performers dance nimbly over swords on the ground or brandish them in the air. —**sword danc+er** *n.* —**sword danc+ing** *n.*

sword fern *n.* any of numerous ferns having sword-shaped fronds.

sword+fish ('sɔ:d,fɪʃ) *n., pl.* **+fish** *or* **+fish·es.** a large scombroid fish, *Xiphias gladius,* with a very long upper jaw: valued as a food and game fish: family *Xiphiidae.*

sword grass *n.* any of various grasses and other plants having sword-shaped sharp leaves.

sword knot *n.* a loop on the hilt of a sword by which it was attached to the wrist, now purely decorative.

sword lil·y *n.* another name for **gladiolus** (sense 1).

Sword of Dam·o·cles *n.* a closely impending disaster.

sword+play ('sɔ:d,pleɪ) *n.* **1.** the action or art of fighting with a sword. **2.** verbal sparring. —**'sword+,play·er** *n.*

swords+man ('sɔ:dzmən) *n., pl.* **+men.** one who uses or is skilled in the use of a sword. —**'swords+man+,ship** *n.*

sword+stick ('sɔ:d,stɪk) *n.* a hollow walking stick used as a sheath for a short sword or dagger.

sword+tail ('sɔ:d,teɪl) *n.* any of several small freshwater cyprinodont fishes of the genus *Xiphophorus,* esp. *X. helleri,* of Central America, having a long swordlike tail.

swore (swɔ:) *vb.* the past tense of **swear.**

sworn (swɔ:n) *vb.* **1.** the past participle of **swear.** ~*adj.* **2.** bound, pledged, or made inveterate, by or as if by an oath: *a sworn statement; he was sworn to God.*

swot¹ (swɒt) *Brit. informal.* ~*vb.* **swots, swot+ting, swot+ted.** **1.** (often foll. by *up*) to study (a subject) intensively, as for an examination; cram. ~*n.* **2.** Also called: **swotter** ('swɒtə). a person who works or studies hard. **3.** hard work or grind. [C19: dialect variant of SWEAT (n.)]

swot² (swɒt) *vb.* **swots, swot+ting, swot+ted,** *n.* a variant of **swat.**

swound (swaʊnd) *n., vb.* an archaic or dialect word for **swoon.**

swounds *or* **'swounds** (zwaʊndz, zaʊndz) *interj. Archaic.* less common spellings of **zounds.**

swum (swʌm) *vb.* the past participle of **swim.**

swung (swʌŋ) *vb.* the past tense or past participle of **swing.**
swung dash *n.* a mark, ~, used in text to indicate the omission of a word or part of a word.
swy (swaɪ) *n. Austral.* another name for **two-up.** [C20: from German *zwei* two]
SY *international car registration for* Seychelles.
Syb·a·ris (ˈsɪbərɪs) *n.* a Greek colony in S Italy, on the Gulf of Taranto: notorious for its luxurious living, founded about 720 B.C. and sacked in 510. —**ˈSyb·a·rite** *n.* —**Syb·a·rit·ic** (ˌsɪbəˈrɪtɪk) *or* **ˌSyb·aˈrit·i·cal** *adj.* —**ˌSyb·aˈrit·i·cal·ly** *adv.*
syb·a·rite (ˈsɪbəˌraɪt) *n.* **1.** (*sometimes cap.*) a devotee of luxury and the sensual vices. ~*adj.* **2.** luxurious; sensuous. [C16: from Latin *Sybarīta*, from Greek *Subaritēs* inhabitant of SYBARIS] —**syb·a·rit·ic** (ˌsɪbəˈrɪtɪk) *or* **ˌsyb·aˈrit·i·cal** *adj.* —**ˌsyb·aˈrit·i·cal·ly** *adv.* —**ˈsyb·a·rit·ism** *n.*
syc·a·mine (ˈsɪkəˌmaɪn) *n.* a mulberry tree mentioned in the Bible, thought to be the black mulberry, *Morus nigra.* [C16: from Latin *sȳcamīnus*, from Greek *sukaminon*, from Hebrew *shiqmāh*]
syc·a·more (ˈsɪkəˌmɔː) *n.* **1.** a Eurasian maple tree, *Acer pseudoplatanus*, naturalized in Britain and North America, having five-lobed leaves, yellow flowers, and two-winged fruits. **2.** *U.S.* an American plane tree, *Platanus occidentalis.* See **plane tree. 3.** a moraceous tree, *Ficus sycomorus*, of N Africa and W Asia, having an edible figlike fruit. [C14: from Old French *sicamor*, from Latin *sȳcomorus*, from Greek *sukomoros*, from *sukon* fig + *moron* mulberry]
syce, sice, *or* **saice** (saɪs) *n.* (formerly, in India) a servant employed to look after horses, drive carriages, etc. [C17: from Urdu *sā'is*, from Arabic, from *sāsa* to administer]
sy·cee *or* **sy·cee sil·ver** (saɪˈsiː) *n.* silver ingots formerly used as a medium of exchange in China. [C18: from Chinese *sai sz* fine silk; so called because the silver can be made into threads as fine as silk]
sy·co·ni·um (saɪˈkəʊnɪəm) *n., pl.* **·ni·a** (-nɪə). *Botany.* the fleshy fruit of the fig, consisting of a greatly enlarged receptacle. [C19: from New Latin, from Greek *sukon* fig]
syc·o·phant (ˈsɪkəfənt) *n.* a person who uses flattery to win favour from individuals wielding influence; toady. [C16: from Latin *sȳcophanta*, from Greek *sukophantēs*, literally: the person showing a fig, apparently referring to the fig sign used in making an accusation, from *sukon* fig + *phainein* to show; sense probably developed from "accuser" to "informer, flatterer"] —**ˈsyc·o·phan·cy** *n.* —**syc·o·phan·tic** (ˌsɪkəˈfæntɪk), **ˌsyc·oˈphan·ti·cal,** *or* **ˌsyc·oˈphant·ish** *adj.* —**ˌsyc·oˈphan·ti·cal·ly** *or* **ˌsyc·oˈphant·ish·ly** *adv.*
sy·co·sis (saɪˈkəʊsɪs) *n.* chronic inflammation of the hair follicles, esp. those of the beard, caused by a staphylococcal infection. [C16: via New Latin from Greek *sukōsis*, from *sukon* fig]
Syd·ney[1] (ˈsɪdnɪ) *n.* **1.** a port in SE Australia, capital of New South Wales, on an inlet of the S Pacific: the largest city in Australia and the first British settlement, established as a penal colony in 1788; developed rapidly after 1820 with the discovery of gold in its hinterland; large wool market; three universities. Pop.: 2 922 760 (1975 est.). **2.** a port in SE Canada, in Nova Scotia on NE Cape Breton Island: capital of Cape Breton Island until 1820, when the island united administratively with Nova Scotia. Pop.: 33 230 (1971).
Syd·ney[2] (ˈsɪdnɪ) *n.* a variant spelling of (Sir Philip) **Sidney.**
Syd·ney·sid·er (ˈsɪdnɪˌsaɪdə) *n. Austral.* a resident of Sydney.
Syd·ney silk·y *n.* a small silky-coated breed of terrier, originally from Australia.
Sy·e·ne (saɪˈiːnɪ) *n.* transliteration of the Ancient Greek name for **Aswan.**
sy·e·nite (ˈsaɪəˌnaɪt) *n.* a light-coloured coarse-grained plutonic igneous rock consisting of feldspars with hornblende or biotite. [C18: from French *syénite*, from Latin *syēnītēs lapis* stone from *Syene* (Aswan), where it was originally quarried] —**sy·e·nit·ic** (ˌsaɪəˈnɪtɪk) *adj.*
Syk·tyv·kar (*Russian* sɪktɪfˈkar) *n.* a city in the NW Soviet Union, capital of the Komi ASSR: timber industry. Pop.: 152 000 (1975 est.).
syl. *or* **syll.** *abbrev. for:* **1.** syllable. **2.** syllabus.
syl·la·bar·y (ˈsɪləbərɪ) *n., pl.* **·bar·ies. 1.** a table or list of syllables. **2.** a set of symbols used in certain writing systems, such as one used for Japanese, in which each symbol represents a spoken syllable. [C16: from New Latin *syllabārium*, from Latin *syllaba* SYLLABLE]
syl·la·bi (ˈsɪləˌbaɪ) *n.* a plural of **syllabus.**
syl·lab·ic (sɪˈlæbɪk) *adj.* **1.** of or relating to syllables or the division of a word into syllables. **2.** denoting a kind of verse line based on a specific number of syllables rather than being regulated by stresses or quantities. **3.** (of a consonant) constituting a syllable. **4.** (of plainsong and similar chanting) having each syllable sung to a different note. ~*n.* **5.** a syllabic consonant. —**sylˈlab·i·cal·ly** *adv.*
syl·lab·i·fy (sɪˈlæbɪˌfaɪ) *or* **syl·lab·i·cate** *vb.* **·fies, ·fy·ing, ·fied** *or* **·cates, ·cat·ing, ·cat·ed.** (*tr.*) to divide (a word) into its constituent syllables. —**sylˌlab·i·fiˈca·tion** *or* **sylˌlab·iˈca·tion** *n.*
syl·la·bism (ˈsɪləˌbɪzəm) *n.* use of a writing system consisting of characters for syllables rather than for individual sounds or whole words. Also called: **syllabography.**
syl·la·ble (ˈsɪləbᵊl) *n.* **1.** a combination or set of one or more units of sound in a language that must consist of a sonorous element (a sonant or vowel) and may or may not contain less sonorous elements (consonants or semivowels) flanking it on either or both sides: for example "paper" has two syllables. See also: **open** (sense 33), **closed** (sense 6a). **2.** (in the writing systems of certain languages, esp. ancient ones) a symbol or set of symbols standing for a syllable. **3.** the least mention in speech or print: *don't breathe a syllable of it.* **4. in words of one syllable.** simply; bluntly. ~*vb.* **5.** to pronounce syllables of (a text); articulate. **6.** (*tr.*) to write down in syllables. [C14: via Old French from Latin *syllaba*, from Greek *sullabē*, from *sullambanein* to collect together, from *sul-* SYN- + *lambanein* to take]
syl·lab·o·gram (sɪˈlæbəʊˌgræm) *n.* a written symbol representing a single syllable.
syl·lab·og·ra·phy (ˌsɪləˈbɒgrəfɪ) *n.* another word for **syllabism.** Compare **logography, phonography.**
syl·la·bub *or* **sil·la·bub** (ˈsɪləˌbʌb) *n.* **1.** a spiced drink made of milk with rum, port, brandy, or wine, often hot. **2.** *Brit.* a cold dessert made from milk or cream beaten with sugar, wine, and lemon juice. [C16: of unknown origin]
syl·la·bus (ˈsɪləbəs) *n., pl.* **·bus·es** *or* **·bi** (-ˌbaɪ). **1.** an outline of a course of studies, text, etc. **2.** *Brit.* **a.** the subjects studied for a particular course. **b.** a list of these subjects. [C17: from Late Latin, erroneously from Latin *sittybus* parchment strip giving title and author, from Greek *sittuba*]
Syl·la·bus (ˈsɪləbəs) *n. R.C. Church.* **1.** Also called: **Syllabus of Errors.** a list of 80 doctrinal theses condemned as erroneous by Pius IX in 1864. **2.** a list of 65 Modernist propositions condemned as erroneous by Pius X in 1907.
syl·lep·sis (sɪˈlɛpsɪs) *n., pl.* **·ses** (-siːz). **1.** (in grammar or rhetoric) the use of a single sentence construction in which a verb, adjective, etc. is made to cover two syntactical functions, as the verb form *have* in *she and they have promised to come.* **2.** another word for **zeugma.** [C16: from Late Latin, from Greek *sullēpsis*, from *sul-* SYN- + *lēpsis* a taking, from *lambanein* to take] —**sylˈlep·tic** *adj.* —**sylˈlep·ti·cal·ly** *adv.*
syl·lo·gism (ˈsɪləˌdʒɪzəm) *n.* **1.** a deductive inference by which a conclusion is derived from two propositions, the **major premiss** and the **minor premiss.** The subject of the conclusion, the **minor term** (F), appears in the minor premiss, the predicate of the conclusion, the **major term** (H), appears in the major premiss, and the **middle term** (G), appears only in both premisses, not the conclusion. The most common type of syllogism consists of categorical statements, such as *all* F *are* G, *all* H *are* F, *therefore all* H *are* G. **2.** a piece of deductive reasoning from the general to the particular. **3.** a subtle or deceptive piece of reasoning. [C14: via Latin from Greek *sullogismos*, from *sullogizesthai* to reckon together, from *sul-* SYN- + *logizesthai* to calculate, from *logos* a discourse]
syl·lo·gis·tic (ˌsɪləˈdʒɪstɪk) *adj.* also **syl·lo·gis·ti·cal. 1.** of, relating to or consisting of syllogisms. ~*n.* (*often pl.*) **2.** the branch of logic concerned with syllogisms. **3.** reasoning by means of syllogisms. —**ˌsyl·loˈgis·ti·cal·ly** *adv.*
syl·lo·gize *or* **syl·lo·gise** (ˈsɪləˌdʒaɪz) *vb.* to reason or infer by using syllogisms. [C15: via Old French from Late Latin *syllogizāre*, from Greek *sullogizesthai*; see SYLLOGISM] —**ˌsyl·lo·giˈza·tion** *or* **ˌsyl·lo·giˈsa·tion** *n.* —**ˈsyl·loˌgiz·er** *or* **ˈsyl·loˌgis·er** *n.*
sylph (sɪlf) *n.* **1.** a slender graceful girl or young woman. **2.** any of a class of imaginary beings assumed to inhabit the air. [C17: from New Latin *sylphus*, probably coined from Latin *silva* wood + Greek *numphē* NYMPH] —**ˈsylph·ic, ˈsylph·id, ˈsylph·ˌlike, ˈsylph·ish,** *or* **ˈsylph·y** *adj.*
syl·va *or* **sil·va** (ˈsɪlvə) *n., pl.* **·vas** *or* **·vae** (-viː). the trees growing in a particular region. [C17: Latin *silva* a wood]
syl·van *or* **sil·van** (ˈsɪlvən) *Chiefly poetic.* ~*adj.* **1.** of, characteristic of, or consisting of woods or forests. **2.** living or located in woods or forests. **3.** idyllically rural or rustic. ~*n.* **4.** an inhabitant of the woods, esp. a spirit. [C16: from Latin *silvānus*, from *silva* forest]
syl·van·ite (ˈsɪlvəˌnaɪt) *n.* a silver-white mineral consisting of a telluride of gold and silver in the form of elongated striated crystals: a source of gold in Australia and North America. Formula: $(Au,Ag)Te_2$. [C18: from (TRAN)SYLVAN(IA) + -ITE[1], with reference to the region where it was first found]
Syl·va·nus (sɪlˈveɪnəs) *n.* a variant spelling of **Silvanus.**
syl·vat·ic (sɪlˈvætɪk) *adj.* growing, living, or occurring in a wood or beneath a tree. Also: **syl·ves·tral** (sɪlˈvɛstrəl).
syl·vi·cul·ture (ˈsɪlvɪˌkʌltʃə) *n.* a variant spelling of **silviculture.**
syl·vite (ˈsɪlvaɪt) *or* **syl·vine** (ˈsɪlviːn) *n.* a soluble colourless, white, or coloured mineral consisting of potassium chloride in cubic crystalline form with sodium impurities: it occurs chiefly in sedimentary beds and is an important ore of potassium. Formula: KCl. [C19: *sylvite*, alteration of *sylvine*, from New Latin *sal digestiva Sylvii* digestive salt of Sylvius, after Franciscus *Sylvius* (died 1672), German anatomist. See -ITE[1], -INE[2]]
sym. *abbrev. for:* **1.** symbol. **2.** *Chem.* symmetrical. **3.** symphony. **4.** symptom.
sym- *prefix.* variant of **syn-** before *b*, *p*, and *m*.
sym·bi·ont (ˈsɪmbɪˌɒnt) *n.* an organism living in a state of symbiosis. [C19: from Greek *sumbioun* to live together, from *bioun* to live] —**ˌsym·biˈon·tic** *adj.* —**ˌsym·biˈon·ti·cal·ly** *adv.*
sym·bi·o·sis (ˌsɪmbɪˈəʊsɪs) *n.* **1.** a close association of two animal or plant species that are dependent on one another. **2.** a similar relationship between interdependent persons or groups. [C19: via New Latin from Greek: a living together; see SYMBIONT] —**ˌsym·biˈot·ic** *or* **ˌsym·biˈot·i·cal** *adj.*
sym·bol (ˈsɪmbᵊl) *n.* **1.** something that represents or stands for something else, usually by convention or association, esp. a

material object used to represent something abstract. **2.** an object, person, idea, etc., used in a literary work, film, etc., to stand for or suggest something else with which it is associated either explicitly or in some more subtle way. **3.** a letter, figure, or sign used in mathematics, science, music, etc. to represent a quantity, phenomenon, operation, function, etc. **4.** *Psychoanal.* the end product, in the form of an object or act, of a conflict in the unconscious between repression processes and the actions and thoughts being repressed: *the symbols of dreams.* **5.** *Psychol.* any mental process that represents some feature of external reality. ~*vb.* **+bols, +bol+ling, +bolled** *or U.S.* **+bols, +bol+ing, +boled. 6.** (*tr.*) another word for **symbolize.** [C15: from Church Latin *symbolum,* from Greek *sumbolon* sign, from *sumballein* to throw together, from SYN- + *ballein* to throw]

sym+bol+ic (sɪm'bɒlɪk) *or* **sym+bol·i+cal** *adj.* **1.** of or relating to a symbol or symbols. **2.** serving as a symbol. **3.** characterized by the use of symbols or symbolism. **—sym+'bol·i+cal+ly** *adv.* **—sym+'bol·i+cal+ness** *n.*

sym+bol·i+cal books *pl. n. Christianity.* the books containing the creeds, beliefs, or doctrine of religious groups that have emerged since the Reformation.

sym+bol+ic log+ic *n.* a treatment of formal logic in which terms and their relationships are represented by specific symbols to simplify the analysis of propositions, etc. Also called: **mathematical logic.**

sym+bol+ism ('sɪmbəˌlɪzəm) *n.* **1.** the representation of something in symbolic form or the attribution of symbolic meaning or character to something. **2.** a system of symbols or symbolic representation. **3.** a symbolic significance or quality. **4.** (*often cap.*) a late 19th-century movement in art that sought to express mystical or abstract ideas through the symbolic use of images. See also **synthetism. 5.** *Theol.* any symbolist interpretation of the Eucharist.

sym+bol+ist ('sɪmbəlɪst) *n.* **1.** a person who uses or can interpret symbols, esp. as a means to revealing aspects of truth and reality. **2.** an artist or writer who practises symbolism in his work. **3.** (*usually cap.*) a writer associated with the symbolist movement. **4.** (*often cap.*) an artist associated with the movement of symbolism. **5.** *Theol.* a person who rejects any interpretation of the Eucharist that suggests that Christ is really present in it, and who maintains that the bread and wine are only symbols of his body and blood. ~*adj.* **6.** of, relating to, or characterizing symbolism or symbolists. **—ˌsym+bol+'is+tic** *or* **ˌsym+bol+'is+ti+cal** *adj.* **—ˌsym+bol+'is+ti+cal+ly** *adv.*

sym+bol+ist move+ment *n.* (*usually cap.*) a movement beginning in French and Belgian poetry towards the end of the 19th century with the verse of Mallarmé, Valéry, Verlaine, Rimbaud, Maeterlinck, and others, and seeking to express states of mind rather than objective reality by making use of the power of words and images to suggest as well as denote.

sym+bol+ize *or* **sym+bol+ise** ('sɪmbəˌlaɪz) *vb.* **1.** (*tr.*) to serve as or be a symbol of. **2.** (*tr.;* usually foll. by *by*) to represent by a symbol or symbols. **3.** (*intr.*) to use symbols. **4.** (*tr.*) to treat or regard as symbolic or figurative. **—ˌsym+bol·i+'za+tion** *or* **ˌsym+bol·i+'sa+tion** *n.*

sym+bol·o·gy (sɪm'bɒlədʒɪ) *n.* the use, study, or interpretation of symbols. **—sym+bo+log·i·cal** (ˌsɪmbə'lɒdʒɪkəl) *adj.* **—sym+'bol·o·gist** *n.*

sym+met+al+lism *or U.S.* **sym+met+al+ism** (sɪ'mɛtəˌlɪzəm) *n.* **1.** the use of an alloy of two or more metals in fixed relative value as the standard of value and currency. **2.** the economic policies and doctrine supporting a symmetallic standard.

sym+met+ri+cal (sɪ'mɛtrɪkəl) *adj.* **1.** possessing or displaying symmetry. Compare **asymmetric. 2.** *Maths.* **a.** (of two points) capable of being joined by a line that is bisected by a given point or bisected perpendicularly by a given line or plane: *the points* (*x, y*) *and* (*−x, −y*) *are symmetrical about the origin.* **b.** (of a configuration) having pairs of points that are symmetrical about a given point, line, or plane: *a circle is symmetrical about a diameter.* **c.** (of an equation or function of two or more variables) remaining unchanged in form after an interchange of two variables: *x + y = z is a symmetrical equation.* **3.** *Logic, maths.* (of a relation) unchanged in meaning or value if the related terms are interchanged, as in *Anne is a sister of Jill.* **4.** *Chem.* (of a compound) having a molecular structure in which substituents are symmetrical about the molecule. **5.** *Botany.* another word for **actinomorphic. 6.** Also: **symmetric.** (of a disease, infection, etc.) affecting both sides of the body or corresponding parts, such as both legs. **—sym+'met+ri+cal+ly** *adv.* **—sym+'met+ri+cal+ness** *n.*

sym+met+ric ma+trix *n. Maths.* a square matrix that is equal to its transpose, being symmetrical about its main diagonal. A **skew symmetric matrix** is equal to the negation of its transpose. Compare **orthogonal matrix.**

sym+me+trize *or* **sym+me+trise** ('sɪmɪˌtraɪz) *vb.* (*tr.*) to render symmetrical or perfectly balanced. **—ˌsym+me+tri+'za+tion** *or* **ˌsym+me+tri+'sa+tion** *n.*

sym+me+try ('sɪmɪtrɪ) *n., pl.* **+tries. 1.** similarity, correspondence, or balance among systems or parts of a system. **2.** *Maths.* an exact correspondence in position or form about a given point, line, or plane. See **symmetrical** (sense 2). **3.** beauty or harmony of form based on a proportionate arrangement of parts. **4.** *Physics.* the independence of a property with respect to direction; isotropy. [C16: from Latin *symmetria,* from Greek *summetria* proportion, from SYN- + *metron* measure]

Sym·onds ('sɪməndz) *n.* **John Ad·ding·ton** ('ædɪŋtən). 1840–93, English writer, noted for his *Renaissance in Italy* (1875–86) and for studies of homosexuality.

Sy·mons ('saɪmənz) *n.* **Ar·thur.** 1865–1945, English poet and critic, who helped to introduce the French symbolists to England.

sym+pa+thec+to+my (ˌsɪmpə'θɛktəmɪ) *n., pl.* **+mies.** the surgical excision or chemical destruction (**chemical sympathectomy**) of one or more parts of the sympathetic nervous system. [C20: from SYMPATHETIC + -ECTOMY]

sym+pa+thet+ic (ˌsɪmpə'θɛtɪk) *or* **sym+pa+thet·i+cal** *adj.* **1.** characterized by, feeling, or showing sympathy; understanding. **2.** in accord with the subject's personality or mood; congenial: *a sympathetic atmosphere.* **3.** (when *postpositive,* often foll. by *to* or *towards*) showing agreement (with) or favour (towards): *sympathetic to the proposals.* **4.** *Anatomy, physiol.* of or relating to the division of the autonomic nervous system that acts in opposition to the parasympathetic system accelerating the heartbeat, dilating the bronchi, inhibiting the smooth muscles of the digestive tract, etc. Compare **parasympathetic. 5.** relating to vibrations occurring as a result of similar vibrations in a neighbouring body: *sympathetic strings on a sitar.* **—ˌsym+pa+'thet·i+cal+ly** *adv.*

sym+pa+thet+ic ink *n.* another term for **invisible ink.**

sym+pa+thet+ic mag+ic *n.* a type of magic in which it is sought to produce a large-scale effect, often at a distance, by performing some small-scale ceremony resembling it, such as the pouring of water on an altar to induce rainfall.

sym+pa+thin ('sɪmpəθɪn) *n.* a substance released at certain sympathetic nerve endings: thought to be identical with adrenaline. [C20: from SYMPATH(ETIC) + -IN]

sym+pa+thize *or* **sym+pa+thise** ('sɪmpəˌθaɪz) *vb.* (*intr.;* often foll. by *with*) **1.** to feel or express compassion or sympathy (for); commiserate: *he sympathized with my troubles.* **2.** to share or understand the sentiments or ideas (of); be in sympathy (with). **—'sym+pa+ˌthiz+er** *or* **'sym+pa+ˌthis+er** *n.* **—'sym+pa+ˌthiz+ing+ly** *or* **'sym+pa+ˌthis+ing+ly** *adv.*

sym+pa+tho+lyt+ic (ˌsɪmpəθəʊ'lɪtɪk) *Med.* ~*adj.* **1. a.** inhibiting or antagonistic to nerve impulses of the sympathetic nervous system. **b.** of or relating to such inhibition. ~*n.* **2.** a sympatholytic drug. Compare **sympathomimetic.** [C20: from SYMPATH(ETIC) + -LYTIC]

sym+pa+tho+mi+met+ic (ˌsɪmpəθəʊmɪ'mɛtɪk) *Med.* ~*adj.* **1.** causing a physiological effect similar to that produced by stimulation of the sympathetic nervous system. ~*n.* **2.** a sympathomimetic drug. Compare **sympatholytic.** [C20: from SYMPATH(ETIC) + MIMETIC]

sym+pa+thy ('sɪmpəθɪ) *n., pl.* **+thies. 1.** the sharing of another's emotions, esp. of sorrow or anguish; pity; compassion. **2.** an affinity or harmony, usually of feelings or interests, between persons or things: *to be in sympathy with someone.* **3.** mutual affection or understanding arising from such a relationship; congeniality. **4.** the condition of a physical system or body when its behaviour is similar or corresponds to that of a different system that influences it, such as the vibration of sympathetic strings. **5.** (*sometimes pl.*) a feeling of loyalty, support, or accord, as for an idea, cause, etc. **6.** *Physiol.* the mutual relationship between two organs or parts whereby a change in one has an effect on the other. [C16: from Latin *sympathīa,* from Greek *sumpatheia,* from *sumpathēs,* from SYN- + *pathos* suffering]

sym+pa+thy strike *n.* a strike organized in support of another section of workers or a cause and not because of direct grievances. Also called: **sympathetic strike.**

sym+pat+ric (sɪm'pætrɪk) *adj.* (of biological speciation or species) taking place or existing in the same or overlapping geographical areas. Compare **allopatric.** [C20: from SYN- + *-patric,* from Greek *patra* native land, from *patēr* father] **—sym+'pat+ri+cal+ly** *adv.*

sym+pet+al+ous (sɪm'pɛtələs) *adj. Botany.* another word for **gamopetalous.**

sym+phile ('sɪmfaɪl) *n.* an insect or other organism that lives in the nests of social insects, esp. ants and termites, and is fed and reared by the inmates. Compare **synoekete.** [C20: from Greek *sumphilein* to love mutually; see SYN-, -PHILE]

sym+phon+ic po·em *n. Music.* an extended orchestral composition, originated by Liszt, based on nonmusical material, such as a work of literature or folk tale. Also called: **tone poem.**

sym+pho+ni+ous (sɪm'fəʊnɪəs) *adj. Literary.* harmonious or concordant. **—sym+'pho+ni+ous+ly** *adv.*

sym+pho+nist ('sɪmfənɪst) *n.* a person who composes symphonies.

sym+pho+ny ('sɪmfənɪ) *n., pl.* **+nies. 1.** an extended large-scale orchestral composition, usually with several movements, at least one of which is in sonata form. The classical form of the symphony was fixed by Haydn and Mozart, but the innovations of subsequent composers have freed it entirely from classical constraints. It continues to be a vehicle for serious, large-scale orchestral music. **2.** a piece of instrumental music in up to three very short movements, used as an overture to or interlude in a baroque opera. **3.** any purely orchestral movement in a vocal work, such as a cantata or oratorio. **4.** short for **symphony orchestra. 5.** (in musical theory, esp. of classical Greece) **a.** another word for **consonance** (sense 3). Compare **diaphony** (sense 2). **b.** the interval of unison. **6.** anything distinguished by a harmonious composition: *the picture was a symphony of green.* **7.** *Archaic.* harmony in general; concord. [C13: from Old French *symphonie,* from Latin *symphōnia* concord, concert, from Greek *sumphōnia,* from SYN- + *phōnē* sound] **—sym+phon+ic** (sɪm'fɒnɪk) *adj.* **—sym+'phon·i+cal+ly** *adv.*

sym+pho+ny or+ches+tra *n. Music.* an orchestra capable of performing symphonies, esp. the large orchestra comprising strings, brass, woodwind, harp and percussion, used in the performance of romantic and postromantic works.

sym+phy+sis (ˈsɪmfɪsɪs) *n., pl.* **+ses** (-ˌsiːz). **1.** *Anatomy, botany.* a growing together of parts or structures, such as two bony surfaces joined by an intermediate layer of fibrous cartilage. **2.** a line marking this growing together. **3.** *Pathol.* an abnormal adhesion of two or more parts or structures. [C16: via New Latin from Greek *sumphusis,* from *sumphuein,* from SYN- + *phuein* to grow] —**sym+phys+i·al** *or* **sym+phys+e·al** (sɪmˈfɪzɪəl) *adj.* —**sym+phys+tic** (sɪmˈfɪstɪk) *or* **sym+ˈphyt+ic** *adj.*

sym+po+di·um (sɪmˈpəʊdɪəm) *n., pl.* **+di·a** (-dɪə). the main axis of growth in the grapevine and similar plants: a number of lateral branches that arise from just behind the apex of the main stem, which ceases to grow. Compare **monopodium.** [C19: from New Latin, from SYN- + Greek *podion* a little foot, from *pous* foot] —**sym+ˈpo+di·al** *adj.* —**sym+ˈpo+di+al+ly** *adv.*

sym+po+si+ac (sɪmˈpəʊzɪˌæk) *adj.* **1.** of, suitable for, or occurring at a symposium. ~*n.* **2.** an archaic word for **symposium.** [C17: from Latin *symposiacus;* see SYMPOSIUM]

sym+po+si+arch (sɪmˈpəʊzɪˌɑːk) *n.* **1.** the president of a symposium, esp. in classical Greece. **2.** a rare word for **toastmaster.** [C17: from Greek; see SYMPOSIUM, -ARCH]

sym+po+si·um (sɪmˈpəʊzɪəm) *n., pl.* **+si·ums** *or* **+si·a** (-zɪə). **1.** a conference or meeting for the discussion of some subject, esp. an academic topic or social problem. **2.** a collection of scholarly contributions, usually published together, on a given subject. **3.** (in classical Greece) a drinking party with intellectual conversation, music, etc. [C16: via Latin from Greek *sumposion,* from *sumpinein* to drink together, from *sum-* SYN- + *pinein* to drink]

symp+tom (ˈsɪmptəm) *n.* **1.** *Med.* any sensation or change in bodily function experienced by a patient that is associated with a particular disease. Compare **sign** (sense 9). **2.** any phenomenon or circumstance accompanying something and regarded as evidence of its existence; indication. [C16: from Late Latin *symptōma,* from Greek *sumptōma* chance, from *sumpiptein* to occur, from SYN- + *piptein* to fall] —**ˈsymp+tom+less** *adj.*

symp+to+mat+ic (ˌsɪmptəˈmætɪk) *or* **symp+to+mat·i+cal** *adj.* **1.** (often foll. by *of*) being a symptom; indicative: *symptomatic of insanity.* **2.** of or relating to a symptom or symptoms. **3.** according to symptoms: *a symptomatic analysis of a case.* —ˌ**symp+to+ˈmat·i+cal+ly** *adv.*

symp+tom·a+tol+o·gy (ˌsɪmptəməˈtɒlədʒɪ) *n.* the branch of medicine concerned with the study and classification of the symptoms of disease.

syn. *abbrev. for* synonym(ous).

syn- *prefix.* **1.** with or together: *synecology.* **2.** fusion: *syngamy.* [from Greek *sun* together, with]

syn+aer+e·sis (sɪˈnɪərɪsɪs) *n.* a variant spelling of **syneresis.**

syn+aes+the+si·a *or U.S.* **syn+es+the+si·a** (ˌsɪniːsˈθiːzɪə) *n.* **1.** *Physiol.* a sensation experienced in a part of the body other than the part stimulated. **2.** *Psychol.* the subjective sensation of a sense other than the one being stimulated. For example, a sound may evoke sensations of colour. [from New Latin, from SYN- + *-esthesia,* from Greek *aisthēsis* sensation] —**syn+aes+thet+ic** *or U.S.* **syn+es+thet+ic** (ˌsɪniːsˈθetɪk) *adj.*

syn·a+gogue (ˈsɪnəˌgɒg) *n.* **1. a.** a building for Jewish religious services and usually also for religious instruction. **b.** (*as modifier*): *synagogue services.* **2.** a congregation of Jews who assemble for worship or religious study. **3.** the religion of Judaism as organized in such congregations. [C12: from Old French *sinagogue,* from Late Latin *synagōga,* from Greek *sunagōgē* a gathering, from *sunagein* to bring together, from SYN- + *agein* to lead] —**syn·a+gog·i+cal** (ˌsɪnəˈgɒdʒɪkᵊl) *or* **syn·a+gog+al** (ˈsɪnəˌgɒgᵊl) *adj.*

syn·a+le·pha *or* **syn·a+loe·pha** (ˌsɪnəˈliːfə) *n. Linguistics.* vowel elision, esp. as it arises when one word ends in a vowel and the following word begins with one. [C16: from Late Latin *synaloepha,* from Greek *sunaliphē,* from SYN- + *aleiphein* to melt, smear]

syn+apse (ˈsaɪnæps) *n.* the point at which a nerve impulse is relayed from the terminal portion of an axon to the dendrites of an adjacent neuron.

syn+ap+sis (sɪˈnæpsɪs) *n., pl.* **+ses** (-siːz). **1.** *Cytology.* the association in pairs of homologous chromosomes at the start of meiosis. **2.** another word for **synapse.** [C19: from New Latin, from Greek *sunapsis* junction, from *sunaptein* to join together, from SYN- + *haptein* to connect] —**syn+ap+tic** (sɪˈnæptɪk) *or* **syn+ˈap+ti+cal** *adj.* —**syn+ˈap+ti·cal+ly** *adv.*

syn+ar+chy (ˈsɪnəkɪ) *n., pl.* **+chies.** joint rule. [C18: from Greek *sunarchia,* from *sunarchein* to rule jointly]

syn+ar+thro+sis (ˌsɪnɑːˈθrəʊsɪs) *n., pl.* **+ses** (-siːz). *Anatomy.* any of various joints which lack a synovial cavity and are virtually immovable; a fixed joint. [via New Latin from Greek *sunarthrōsis,* from *sunarthrousthai* to be connected by joints, from *sun-* SYN- + *arthron* a joint] —ˌ**syn+ar+ˈthro+di·al** *adj.* —ˌ**syn+ar+ˈthro+di+al+ly** *adv.*

sync (sɪŋk) *Films, television, computers.* ~*vb.* **1.** an informal word for **synchronize.** ~*n.* **2.** an informal word for **synchronization.**

syn+carp (ˈsɪnkɑːp) *n. Botany.* a fleshy multiple fruit, formed from two or more carpels of one flower or the aggregated fruits of several flowers. [C19: from New Latin *syncarpium,* from SYN- + Greek *karpos* fruit]

syn+car+pous (sɪnˈkɑːpəs) *adj.* **1.** (of the ovaries of certain flowering plants) consisting of united carpels. Compare **apocarpous. 2.** of or relating to a syncarp. —**syn+car+py** (ˈsɪnkɑːpɪ) *n.*

syn+chro (ˈsɪŋkrəʊ) *n., pl.* **+chros.** any of a number of electrical devices in which the angular position of a rotating part is transformed into a voltage, or vice versa. Also called: **selsyn.**

syn·chro- *combining form.* indicating synchronization: *synchroflash.*

syn+chro+cy+clo+tron (ˌsɪŋkrəʊˈsaɪkləˌtrɒn) *n.* a type of cyclotron in which the frequency of the electric field is modulated to allow for relativistic effects at high velocities and thus produce higher energies.

syn+chro+flash (ˈsɪŋkrəʊˌflæʃ) *n.* a mechanism in a camera that enables the shutter to be fully open while the light from a flashbulb or electronic flash is at its brightest.

syn+chro+mesh (ˈsɪŋkrəʊˌmɛʃ) *adj.* **1.** (of a gearbox, etc.) having a system of clutches that synchronizes the speeds of the driving and driven members before engagement to avoid shock in gear changing and to reduce noise and wear. ~*n.* **2.** a gear system having these features. [C20: shortened from *synchronized mesh*]

syn+chron+ic (sɪnˈkrɒnɪk) *adj.* **1.** concerned with the events or phenomena at a particular period without considering historical antecedents: *synchronic linguistics.* Compare **diachronic. 2.** synchronous. —**syn+ˈchron·i+cal+ly** *adv.*

syn+chro+nism (ˈsɪŋkrəˌnɪzəm) *n.* **1.** the quality or condition of being synchronous. **2.** a chronological usually tabular list of historical persons and events, arranged to show parallel or synchronous occurrence. **3.** the representation in a work of art of one or more incidents that occurred at separate times. [C16: from Greek *sunkhronismos;* see SYNCHRONOUS, -ISM] —ˌ**syn+chro+ˈnis+tic** *or* ˌ**syn+chro+ˈnis+ti+cal** *adj.* —ˌ**syn+chro+ˈnis+ti+cal+ly** *adv.*

syn+chro+nize *or* **syn+chro+nise** (ˈsɪŋkrəˌnaɪz) *vb.* **1.** (when *intr.,* usually foll. by *with*) to occur or recur or cause to occur or recur at the same time or in unison. **2.** to indicate or cause to indicate the same time: *synchronize your watches.* **3.** (*tr.*) *Film.* to establish (the picture and soundtrack records) in their correct relative position. **4.** (*tr.*) to designate events as simultaneous. —ˌ**syn+chro+ni+ˈza+tion** *or* ˌ**syn+chro+ni+ˈsa+tion** *n.* —**ˈsyn+chro+ˌniz+er** *or* **ˈsyn+chro+ˌnis+er** *n.*

syn+chro+nous (ˈsɪŋkrənəs) *adj.* **1.** occurring at the same time; contemporaneous. **2.** *Physics.* (of periodic phenomena, such as voltages) having the same frequency and phase. **3.** occurring or recurring exactly together and at the same rate: *the synchronous flapping of a bird's wings.* [C17: from Late Latin *synchronus,* from Greek *sunkhronos,* from SYN- + *khronos* time] —**ˈsyn+chro+nous+ly** *adv.* —**ˈsyn+chro+nous+ness** *n.*

syn+chro+nous con+vert+er *n.* a synchronous machine that converts alternating current to direct current, or vice versa.

syn+chro+nous ma+chine *n.* an electrical machine, whose rotating speed is proportional to the frequency of the alternating-current supply and independent of the load.

syn+chro+nous mo+tor *n.* an alternating-current motor that runs at a speed that is equal to or is a multiple of the frequency of the supply.

syn+chro+nous or+bit *n. Astronautics.* an earth orbit in which a satellite makes one complete revolution in the period taken for the earth to rotate about its axis.

syn+chro+scope (ˈsɪŋkrəˌskəʊp) *or* **syn+chron·o+scope** (sɪŋˈkrɒnəˌskəʊp) *n.* an instrument used to indicate whether two periodic quantities or motions are synchronous.

syn+chro+tron (ˈsɪŋkrəˌtrɒn) *n.* a type of particle accelerator similar to a betatron but having an electric field of fixed frequency as well as a changing magnetic field. It is capable of producing very high energies in the GeV range. [C20: from SYNCHRO- + (ELEC)TRON]

syn+chro+tron ra+di·a+tion *n.* electromagnetic radiation emitted in narrow beams tangential to the orbit of very high energy charged particles, such as electrons, spiralling along the lines of force in a strong magnetic field. It occurs in synchrotron accelerators and in supernova remnants such as the Crab Nebula.

syn+clas+tic (sɪŋˈklæstɪk) *adj. Maths.* (of a surface) having a curvature at a given point and in a particular direction that is of the same sign as the curvature at that point in perpendicular direction. Compare **anticlastic.** [C19: from SYN- (alike) + Greek *klastos* bent, from *klan* to bend]

syn+cline (ˈsɪŋklaɪn) *n.* a downward fold of stratified rock in which the strata slope towards a vertical axis. Compare **anticline.** —**syn+ˈcli+nal** *adj.*

syn+cli+no+ri+um (ˌsɪŋklɪˈnɔːrɪəm) *n., pl.* **+ri·a** (-rɪə). a vast elongated syncline with its strata further folded into anticlines and synclines. [C19: New Latin, from SYNCLINE + *-orium,* suffix indicating a place]

Syn+com (ˈsɪnˌkɒm) *n.* a communications satellite in stationary orbit. [C20: from *syn(chronous) com(munication)*]

syn+co+pate (ˈsɪŋkəˌpeɪt) *vb.* (*tr.*) **1.** *Music.* to modify or treat (a beat, rhythm, note, etc.) by syncopation. **2.** to shorten (a word) by omitting sounds or letters from the middle. [C17: from Medieval Latin *syncopāre* to omit a letter or syllable, from Late Latin *syncopa* SYNCOPE] —**ˈsyn+co+ˌpa+tor** *n.*

syn+co+pa+tion (ˌsɪŋkəˈpeɪʃən) *n.* **1.** *Music.* **a.** the displacement of the usual rhythmical accent away from a strong beat onto a weak beat. **b.** a note, beat, rhythm, etc., produced by syncopation. **2.** another word for **syncope** (sense 2).

syn+co+pe (ˈsɪŋkəpɪ) *n.* **1.** *Pathol.* a technical word for a **faint. 2.** the omission of one or more sounds or letters from the middle of a word. [C16: from Late Latin *syncopa,* from Greek *sunkopē* a cutting off, from SYN- + *koptein* to cut] —**syn+cop+ic** (sɪŋˈkɒpɪk) *or* **ˈsyn+co+pal** *adj.*

syn+cre+tism (ˈsɪŋkrɪˌtɪzəm) *n.* **1.** the tendency to syncretize. **2.** the historical tendency of languages to reduce their use of inflection, as in the development of Old English with all its case endings into Modern English. [C17: from New Latin *syncrētismus*, from Greek *sunkrētismos* alliance of Cretans, from *sunkrētizein* to join forces (in the manner of the Cretan towns), from SYN- + *Krēs* a Cretan] —**syn+cret+ic** (sɪŋ'krɛtɪk), **syn+'cret·i+cal**, **ˌsyn+cre+'tis+tic**, *or* **ˌsyn+cre+'tis+ti+cal** *adj.* —**'syn+cre+ˌtist** *n.*

syn+cre+tize *or* **syn+cre+tise** ('sɪŋkrɪˌtaɪz) *vb.* to combine or attempt to combine the characteristic teachings, beliefs, or practices of (differing systems of religion or philosophy). —**ˌsyn+cre+ti+'za+tion** *or* **ˌsyn+cre+ti+'sa+tion** *n.*

syn+cri+sis ('sɪŋkrɪsɪs) *n. Rare.* a rhetorical device by which opposites are compared. [via Late Latin from Greek *sunkrisis* comparison, from SYN- + *krinein* to assess]

syn+cyt+i+um (sɪn'sɪtɪəm) *n., pl.* **+cyt·i·a** (-'sɪtɪə). *Zoology.* a mass of cytoplasm containing many nuclei and enclosed in a cell membrane. [C19: New Latin; see SYN-, CYTO-, -IUM] —**syn+'cyt+i+al** *adj.*

synd. *abbrev. for* syndicate.

syn+dac+tyl (sɪn'dæktɪl) *adj.* **1.** (of certain animals) having two or more digits growing fused together. ~*n.* **2.** an animal with this arrangement of digits. —**syn+'dac+tyl+ism** *n.*

syn+de+sis (sɪn'di:sɪs) *n. Grammar.* **1.** the use of syndetic constructions. **2.** another name for **polysyndeton** (sense 2). [C20: from Greek, from *sundein* to bind together, from SYN- + *dein* to bind]

syn+des+mo+sis (ˌsɪndɛs'məʊsɪs) *n., pl.* **+ses** (-si:z). *Anatomy.* a type of joint in which the articulating bones are held together by a ligament of connective tissue. [New Latin, from Greek *sundein* to bind together; see SYNDESIS] —**syn+des+mot+ic** (ˌsɪndɛs'mɒtɪk) *adj.*

syn+det+ic (sɪn'dɛtɪk) *or* **syn+det·i+cal** *adj.* denoting a grammatical construction in which two clauses are connected by a conjunction. Compare **asyndetic** (sense 2). [C17: from Greek *sundetikos*, from *sundetos* bound together; see SYNDESIS] —**syn+'det·i+cal+ly** *adv.*

syn+de+ton (sɪn'di:tᵊn) *n. Grammar.* a syndetic construction. Compare **asyndeton** (sense 2). [C20: from Greek *sundeton* a bond, from *sundein* to bind together; see SYNDESIS]

syn+dic ('sɪndɪk) *n.* **1.** *Brit.* a business agent of some universities or other bodies. **2.** (in several countries) a government administrator or magistrate with varying powers. [C17: via Old French from Late Latin *syndicus*, from Greek *sundikos* defendant's advocate, from SYN- + *dikē* justice] —**'syn+dic+ˌship** *n.* —**'syn+di+cal** *adj.*

syn+di+cal+ism ('sɪndɪkəˌlɪzəm) *n.* **1.** a revolutionary movement and theory advocating the seizure of the means of production and distribution by syndicates of workers through direct action, esp. a general strike. **2.** an economic system resulting from such action. —**'syn+di+cal** *adj.* —**'syn+di+cal+ist** *adj., n.* —**ˌsyn+di+cal+'is+tic** *adj.*

syn+di+cate *n.* ('sɪndɪkɪt). **1.** an association of business enterprises or individuals organized to undertake a joint project requiring considerable capital. **2.** a news agency that sells articles, photographs, etc., to a number of newspapers for simultaneous publication. **3.** any association formed to carry out an enterprise or enterprises of common interest to its members. **4.** a board of syndics or the office of a syndic. **5.** (in Italy under the Fascists) a local organization of employers or employees. ~*vb.* ('sɪndɪˌkeɪt). **6.** (*tr.*) to sell (articles, photographs, etc.) to several newspapers for simultaneous publication. **7.** to form a syndicate of (people). [C17: from Old French *syndicat* office of a SYNDIC] —**ˌsyn+di+'ca+tion** *n.*

syn+di·o+tac+tic (ˌsɪndɪəʊ'tæktɪk) *adj. Chem.* (of a stereospecific polymer) having alternating stereochemical configurations of the groups on successive carbon atoms in the chain. Compare **isotactic.** [C20: from *syndyo*, from Greek *sunduo* two together + -TACTIC]

syn+drome ('sɪndrəʊm) *n.* **1.** *Med.* any combination of signs and symptoms that are indicative of a particular disease or disorder. **2.** a symptom, characteristic, or set of symptoms or characteristics indicating the existence of a condition, problem, etc. [C16: via New Latin from Greek *sundromē*, literally: a running together, from SYN- + *dramein* to run] —**syn+drom+ic** (sɪn'drɒmɪk) *adj.*

syne *or* **syn** (saɪn) *adv., prep., conj.* a Scot. word for **since.** [C14: probably related to Old English *sīth* since]

syn+ec+do+che (sɪn'ɛkdəkɪ) *n.* a figure of speech in which a part is substituted for a whole or a whole for a part, as in *50 head of cattle* for *50 cows*, or *the army* for *a soldier.* [C14: via Latin from Greek *sunekdokhē*, from SYN- + *ekdokhē* interpretation, from *dekhesthai* to accept] —**syn+ec+doch+ic** (ˌsɪnɛk'dɒkɪk) *or* **ˌsyn+ec+'doch·i+cal** *adj.* —**ˌsyn+ec+'doch·i+cal+ly** *adv.*

syn+e·cious (sɪ'ni:ʃəs) *adj.* a variant spelling of **synoecious.**

syn+e·col+o·gy (ˌsɪnɪ'kɒlədʒɪ) *n.* the ecological study of communities of plants and animals. Compare **autecology.** —**syn+ec·o+log+ic** (sɪnˌɛkə'lɒdʒɪk) *or* **syn+ˌec·o+'log·i+cal** *adj.* —**syn+ˌec·o+'log·i+cal+ly** *adv.*

syn+ec+tics (sɪ'nɛktɪks) *n.* (*functioning as sing.*) a method of identifying and solving problems that depends on creative thinking, the use of analogy, and informal conversation among a small group of individuals with diverse experience and expertise. [C20: from SYN- + ECTO- + -ICS, in the sense: working together from outside]

syn+er+e·sis *or* **syn+aer+e·sis** (sɪ'nɪərɪsɪs) *n.* **1.** *Chem.* the process in which a gel contracts on standing and exudes liquid, as in the separation of whey in cheese-making. **2.** the contraction of two vowels into a diphthong. **3.** another word for **synizesis.** [C16: via Late Latin from Greek *sunairesis* a shortening, from *sunairein* to draw together, from SYN- + *hairein* to take]

syn+er+get+ic (ˌsɪnə'dʒɛtɪk) *or* **syn+er+gis+tic** (ˌsɪnə'dʒɪstɪk) *adj.* acting together. [C17: from Greek *sunergētikos*, from SYN- + *-ergētikos*, from *ergon* work; see ENERGY] —**ˌsyn+er+'get·i+cal+ly** *or* **ˌsyn+er+'gis+ti+cal+ly** *adv.*

syn+er+gism ('sɪnəˌdʒɪzəm, sɪ'nɜ:-) *n.* **1.** Also called: **synergy.** the working together of two or more drugs, muscles, etc., to produce an effect greater than the sum of their individual effects. **2.** *Theol.* the doctrine or belief that the human will cooperates with the Holy Spirit and with divine grace, esp. in the act of conversion or regeneration. [C18: from New Latin *synergismus*, from Greek *sunergos*, from SYN- + *ergon* work]

syn+er+gist ('sɪnədʒɪst, sɪ'nɜ:-) *n.* **1.** a drug, muscle, etc., that increases the action of another. **2.** *Theol.* an upholder of synergism. ~*adj.* **3.** of or relating to synergism.

syn+er+gy ('sɪnədʒɪ) *n., pl.* **+gies.** another name for **synergism** (sense 1). [C19: from New Latin *synergia*, from Greek *sunergos*; see SYNERGISM] —**syn+er+gic** (sɪ'nɜ:dʒɪk) *adj.*

syn+e·sis ('sɪnɪsɪs) *n.* a grammatical construction in which the inflection or form of a word is conditioned by the meaning rather than the syntax, as for example the plural form *have* with the singular noun *group* in the sentence *the group have already assembled.* [via New Latin from Greek *sunesis* union, from *sunienai* to bring together, from SYN- + *hienai* to send]

syn+es+the+si·a (ˌsɪni:s'θi:zɪə) *n.* the usual U.S. spelling of **synaesthesia.** —**syn+es+thet+ic** (ˌsɪni:s'θɛtɪk) *adj.*

syn+ga+my ('sɪŋgəmɪ) *or* **syn+gen+e·sis** (sɪn'dʒɛnɪsɪs) *n.* other names for **sexual reproduction.** —**syn+gam+ic** (sɪŋ'gæmɪk) *or* **syn+ga+mous** ('sɪŋgəməs) *adj.*

Synge (sɪŋ) *n.* **John Mil·ling·ton.** 1871–1909, Irish playwright. His plays, marked by vivid colloquial Irish speech, include *Riders to the Sea* (1904) and *The Playboy of the Western World*, produced amidst uproar at the Abbey Theatre, Dublin, in 1907.

syn·i+ze+sis (ˌsɪnɪ'zi:sɪs) *n.* **1.** *Phonetics.* the contraction of two vowels originally belonging to separate syllables into a single syllable, without diphthongization. Compare **syneresis. 2.** *Cytology.* the contraction of chromatin towards one side of the nucleus during the prophase of meiosis. [C19: via Late Latin from Greek *sunizēsis* a collapse, from *sunizanein* to sink down, from SYN- + *hizein* to sit]

syn+kar·y+on (sɪn'kærɪˌɒn) *n. Biology.* the nucleus of a fertilized egg. [C20: New Latin, from SYN- + Greek *karuon* a nut] —**syn+ˌkar·y+'on+ic** *adj.*

syn+od ('sɪnəd, 'sɪnɒd) *n.* **1.** a local or special ecclesiastical council, esp. of a diocese, formally convened to discuss ecclesiastical affairs. **2.** *Rare.* any council, esp. for discussion. [C14: from Late Latin *synodus*, from Greek *sunodos*, from SYN- + *hodos* a way] —**'syn+od+al** *or* **syn+'od·i+cal** *adj.*

syn+od+ic (sɪ'nɒdɪk) *adj.* relating to or involving a conjunction or two successive conjunctions of the same star, planet, or satellite: *the synodic month.*

syn+od+ic month *n.* See **month** (sense 6).

syn+oe·cious, syn+e·cious (sɪ'ni:ʃəs), *or* **syn·oi+cous** (sɪ'nɔɪkəs) *adj.* (of plants) having male and female organs on the same flower or corresponding structure. [C19: SYN- + *-oecious*, from Greek *oikion* diminutive of *oikos* house]

syn+oe·kete (sɪ'ni:ki:t) *or* **syn+oe·cete** (sɪ'ni:si:t) *n.* an insect that lives in the nests of social insects, esp. ants, without receiving any attentions from the inmates. Compare **symphile.** [C20: from Greek *sunoikia* community + -ETE]

syn·o+nym ('sɪnənɪm) *n.* **1.** a word that means the same or nearly the same as another word, such as *bucket* and *pail.* **2.** a word or phrase used as another name for something, such as *Hellene* for a *Greek.* **3.** *Biology.* a taxonomic name that has been superseded or rejected. —**ˌsyn·o+'nym+ic** *or* **ˌsyn·o+'nym·i+cal** *adj.* —**ˌsyn·o+'nym·i·ty** *n.*

syn+on·y+mize *or* **syn+on·y+mise** (sɪ'nɒnɪˌmaɪz) *vb.* (*tr.*) to analyse the synonyms of or provide with synonyms.

syn+on·y+mous (sɪ'nɒnɪməs) *adj.* **1.** (often foll. by *with*) being a synonym (of). **2.** (*postpositive;* foll. by *with*) closely associated (with) or suggestive (of): *his name was synonymous with greed.* —**syn+'on·y+mous+ly** *adv.* —**syn+'on·y+mous+ness** *n.*

syn+on·y+my (sɪ'nɒnɪmɪ) *n., pl.* **+mies. 1.** the study of synonyms. **2.** the character of being synonymous; equivalence. **3.** a list or collection of synonyms, esp. one in which their meanings are discriminated. **4.** *Biology.* a collection of the synonyms of a species or group.

synop. *abbrev. for* synopsis.

syn+op+sis (sɪ'nɒpsɪs) *n., pl.* **+ses** (-si:z). a condensation or brief review of a subject; summary. [C17: via Late Latin from Greek *sunopsis*, from SYN- + *opsis* view]

syn+op+size *or* **syn+op+sise** (sɪ'nɒpsaɪz) *vb.* (*tr.*) *U.S.* variants of **epitomize.**

syn+op+tic (sɪ'nɒptɪk) *adj.* **1.** of or relating to a synopsis. **2.** (*often cap.*) *Bible.* **a.** (of the Gospels of Matthew, Mark, and Luke) presenting the narrative of Christ's life, ministry, etc. from a point of view held in common by all three, and with close similarities in content, order, etc. **b.** of, relating to, or characterizing these three Gospels. **3.** *Meteorol.* showing or concerned with the distribution of meteorological conditions over a wide area at a given time: *a synoptic chart.* **4.** *Rare.* viewing any phenomenon from the same standpoint. ~*n.* **5.** (*often cap.*) *Bible.* **a.** any of the three synoptic Gospels. **b.** any of the authors of these three Gospels. [C18: from Greek *sunoptikos*, from SYNOPSIS] —**syn+'op+ti+cal+ly** *adv.* —**syn+'op+tist** *n.*

syn·o·vi·a (saɪ'nəʊvɪə, sɪ-) *n.* a transparent viscid lubricating fluid, secreted by the membrane lining joints, tendon sheaths, etc. [C17: from New Latin, probably from SYN- + Latin *ōvum* egg] —**syn·'o·vi·al** *adj.* —**syn·'o·vi·al·ly** *adv.*

syn·o·vi·tis (ˌsaɪnəʊ'vaɪtɪs, ˌsɪn-) *n.* inflammation of the membrane surrounding a joint. —**syn·o·vit·ic** (ˌsaɪnəʊ'vɪtɪk, ˌsɪn-) *adj.*

syn·sep·al·ous (sɪn'sɛpələs) *adj.* another word for **gamosepalous.**

syn·tac·tics (sɪn'tæktɪks) *n.* (*functioning as sing.*) the branch of semiotics that deals with the formal properties of symbol systems.

syn·tag·ma (sɪn'tægmə) *or* **syn·tagm** ('sɪnˌtæm) *n., pl.* **·tag·ma·ta** (-'tægmətə) *or* **·tagms.** **1.** a syntactic unit or a word or phrase forming a syntactic unit. **2.** a systematic collection of statements or propositions. [C17: from Late Latin, from Greek, from *suntassein* to put in order; see SYNTAX] —ˌ**syn·tag·'mat·ic** *adj.*

syn·tax ('sɪntæks) *n.* **1.** the branch of linguistics that deals with the grammatical arrangement of words and morphemes in the sentences of a language or of languages in general. **2.** the totality of facts about the grammatical arrangement of words in a language. **3.** a systematic statement of the rules governing the grammatical arrangement of words and morphemes in a language. **4.** a systematic statement of the rules governing the properly formed formulas of a logical system. **5.** *Obsolete.* an orderly arrangement or system. [C17: from Late Latin *syntaxis,* from Greek *suntaxis,* from *suntassein* to put in order, from SYN- + *tassein* to arrange] —**syn·'tac·tic** *or* **syn·'tac·ti·cal** *adj.* —**syn·'tac·ti·cal·ly** *adv.*

syn·the·sis ('sɪnθɪsɪs) *n., pl.* **·ses** (-ˌsi:z). **1.** the process of combining objects or ideas into a complex whole. Compare **analysis.** **2.** the combination or whole produced by such a process. **3.** the process of producing a compound by a chemical reaction or series of reactions, usually from simpler or commonly available starting materials. **4.** *Linguistics.* the use of inflections rather than word order and function words to express the syntactic relations in a language. Compare **analysis** (sense 5). **5.** deductive reasoning from the general to the particular or from cause to effect. **6.** *Philosophy.* **a.** (in the writings of Kant) the unification of one concept with another not contained in it. Compare **analysis** (sense 7). **b.** the final stage in the Hegelian dialectic. [C17: via Latin from Greek *sunthesis,* from *suntithenai* to put together, from SYN- + *tithenai* to place] —**'syn·the·sist** *n.*

syn·the·size ('sɪnθɪˌsaɪz), **syn·the·tize** *or* **syn·the·sise, syn·the·tise** *vb.* **1.** to combine or cause to combine into a whole. **2.** (*tr.*) to produce by synthesis. —ˌ**syn·the·si·'za·tion,** ˌ**syn·the·ti·'za·tion** *or* ˌ**syn·the·si·'sa·tion,** ˌ**syn·the·ti·'sa·tion** *n.*

syn·the·siz·er ('sɪnθɪˌsaɪzə) *n.* **1.** short for **Moog synthesizer.** **2.** a person or thing that synthesizes.

syn·thet·ic (sɪn'θɛtɪk) *adj.* also **syn·thet·i·cal.** **1.** (of a substance or material) made artificially by chemical reaction. **2.** not genuine; insincere: *synthetic compassion.* **3.** denoting languages, such as Latin, whose morphology is characterized by synthesis. Compare **polysynthetic, agglutinative** (sense 2), **analytic** (sense 3). **4.** *Philosophy.* (of a proposition) having a truth value that is not determined solely by virtue of the meanings of the words, as in *all men are arrogant.* Compare **a posteriori, empirical.** ~*n.* **5.** a synthetic substance or material. [C17: from New Latin *syntheticus,* from Greek *sunthetikos* expert in putting together, from *suntithenai* to put together; see SYNTHESIS] —**syn·'thet·i·cal·ly** *adv.*

syn·thet·ic rub·ber *n.* any of various synthetic materials, similar to natural rubber, made by polymerizing unsaturated hydrocarbons, such as isoprene and butadiene.

syn·the·tism ('sɪnθɪˌtɪzəm) *n.* (*often cap.*) the symbolism of Gauguin and the Nabis, who reacted against the impressionists and realists by seeking to produce brightly coloured abstractions of their inner experience. [C19: from Greek *sunthetos* composite; see SYNTHETIC] —**'syn·the·ˌtist** *n.*

syn·ton·ic (sɪn'tɒnɪk) *adj. Psychol.* reacting to surroundings in a highly emotional way. [C20: from Greek *suntonos* in harmony with; see SYN-, TONE] —**syn·'ton·i·cal·ly** *adv.*

sy·pher ('saɪfə) *vb.* (*tr.*) to lap (a chamfered edge of one plank over that of another) in order to form a flush surface. [C19: variant of CIPHER] —**'sy·pher·ing** *n.*

syph·i·lis ('sɪfɪlɪs) *n.* a venereal disease caused by infection with the microorganism *Treponema pallidum:* characterized by an ulcerating chancre, usually on the external genitals and progressing through the lymphatic system to nearly all tissues of the body, producing serious clinical manifestations. [C18: from New Latin *Syphilis* (*sive Morbus Gallicus*) "Syphilis (or the French disease)", title of a poem (1530) by G. Fracastoro, Italian physician and poet, in which a shepherd *Syphilus* is portrayed as the first victim of the disease] —**syph·i·lit·ic** (ˌsɪfɪ'lɪtɪk) *adj.* —ˌ**syph·i·'lit·i·cal·ly** *adv.* —**'syph·i·ˌloid** *adj.*

syph·i·lol·o·gy (ˌsɪfɪ'lɒlədʒɪ) *n.* the branch of medicine concerned with the study and treatment of syphilis. —ˌ**syph·i·'lol·o·gist** *n.*

syph·i·lo·ma (ˌsɪfɪ'ləʊmə) *n., pl.* **·mas** *or* **·ma·ta** (-mətə). *Pathol.* a tumour or gumma caused by infection with syphilis. [C19: from SYPHILIS + *-oma,* as in *sarcoma*]

sy·phon ('saɪfᵊn) *n.* a variant spelling of **siphon.**

SYR *international car registration for* Syria.

Syr. *abbrev. for:* **1.** Syria. **2.** Syriac. **3.** Syrian.

Sy·ra·cuse *n.* **1.** ('saɪrəˌkju:z). a port in SW Italy, in SE Sicily on the Ionian Sea: founded in 734 B.C. by Greeks from Corinth and taken by the Romans in 212 B.C., after a siege of three years. Pop.: 118 025 (1975 est.). Italian name: **Siracusa.** **2.** ('sɪrəˌkju:s). a city in central New York State, on Lake Onondaga: site of the capital of the Iroquois Indian federation. Pop.: 184 710 (1973 est.).

Syr Dar·ya (*Russian* sɪrdarj'ja) *n.* a river in the S central Soviet Union, formed from two headstreams rising in the Tien Shan: flows generally west to the Aral Sea: the longest river in central Asia. Length: (from the source of the Naryn) 2900 km (1800 miles). Ancient name: **Jaxartes.**

Syr·i·a ('sɪrɪə) *n.* **1.** a republic in W Asia, on the Mediterranean: ruled by the Ottoman Turks (1516–1918); made a French mandate in 1920; became independent in 1944; joined Egypt in the United Arab Republic (1958–61). Language: Arabic. Religion: Muslim majority. Currency: Syrian pound. Capital: Damascus. Pop.: 6 304 685 (1970). Area: 185 180 sq. km (71 498 sq. miles). **2.** (formerly) the region between the Mediterranean, the Euphrates, the Taurus, and the Arabian Desert.

Syr·i·ac ('sɪrɪˌæk) *n.* a dialect of Aramaic spoken in Syria until about the 13th century A.D. and still in use as a liturgical language of certain Eastern churches.

Syr·i·an ('sɪrɪən) *adj.* **1.** of, relating to, or characteristic of Syria, its people, or their dialect of Arabic. **2.** *Eastern Church.* of or relating to Christians who belong to churches with Syriac liturgies. ~*n.* **3.** a native or inhabitant of Syria. **4.** *Eastern Church.* a Syrian Christian.

sy·rin·ga (sɪ'rɪŋgə) *n.* another name for **mock orange** and **lilac** (sense 1). [C17: from New Latin, from Greek *surinx* tube, alluding to the use of its hollow stems for pipes]

sy·ringe ('sɪrɪndʒ, sɪ'rɪndʒ) *n.* **1.** *Med.* an instrument, such as a hypodermic syringe or a rubber ball with a slender nozzle, for use in withdrawing or injecting fluids, cleaning wounds, etc. **2.** any similar device for injecting or extracting liquids by means of pressure or suction. ~*vb.* **3.** (*tr.*) to cleanse or inject with a syringe. [C15: from Late Latin, from Latin: SYRINX]

sy·rin·go·my·e·li·a (səˌrɪŋgəʊmaɪ'i:lɪə) *n.* a chronic progressive disease of the spinal cord in which cavities form in the grey matter: characterized by loss of the sense of pain and temperature. [C19: *syringo-,* from Greek: SYRINX + *-myelia* from Greek *muelos* marrow] —**sy·rin·go·my·el·ic** (səˌrɪŋgəʊmaɪ'ɛlɪk) *adj.*

syr·inx ('sɪrɪŋks) *n., pl.* **sy·rin·ges** (sɪ'rɪndʒi:z) *or* **syr·inx·es.** **1.** the vocal organ of a bird, which is situated in the lower part of the trachea. **2.** (in classical Greek music) a panpipe or set of panpipes. **3.** *Anatomy.* another name for the **Eustachian tube.** [C17: via Latin from Greek *surinx* pipe] —**sy·rin·ge·al** (sɪ'rɪndʒɪəl) *adj.*

Syr·inx ('sɪrɪŋks) *n. Greek myth.* a nymph who was changed into a reed to save her from the amorous pursuit of Pan. From this reed Pan then fashioned his musical pipes.

Syr·o- ('saɪrəʊ-) *combining form.* **1.** indicating Syrian and: *Syro-Lebanese.* **2.** indicating Syriac and: *Syro-Aramaic.* [from Greek *Suro-,* from *Suros* a Syrian]

syr·phid ('sɜ:fɪd) *n.* any dipterous fly of the family *Syrphidae,* typically having a coloration mimicking that of certain bees and wasps: includes the hover flies. [C19: from Greek *surphos* gnat]

Syr·tis Ma·jor ('sɜ:tɪs) *n.* a conspicuous dark region visible in the N hemisphere of Mars.

syr·up ('sɪrəp) *n.* **1.** a solution of sugar dissolved in water and often flavoured with fruit juice: used for sweetening fruit, etc. **2.** any of various thick sweet liquids prepared for cooking or table use from molasses, sugars, etc. **3.** *Informal.* cloying sentimentality. **4.** a liquid medicine containing a sugar solution for flavouring or preservation. ~*vb.* (*tr.*) **5.** to bring to the consistency of syrup. **6.** to cover, fill, or sweeten with syrup. ~Also: **sirup.** [C15: from Medieval Latin *syrupus,* from Arabic *sharāb* a drink, from *shariba* to drink] —**'syr·up-ˌlike** *adj.* —**'syr·up·y** *adj.*

sys·sar·co·sis (ˌsɪsɑ:'kəʊsɪs) *n., pl.* **·ses** (-si:z). *Anatomy.* the union or articulation of bones by muscle. [C17: from New Latin, from Greek *sussarkōsis,* from *sussarkousthai,* from SUS-SYN- + *sarkoun* to become fleshy, from *sarx* flesh] —**sys·sar·cot·ic** (ˌsɪsɑ:'kɒtɪk) *adj.*

syst. *abbrev. for* system.

sys·tal·tic (sɪ'stæltɪk) *adj.* (esp. of the action of the heart) of, relating to, or characterized by alternate contractions and dilations; pulsating. [C17: from Late Latin *systalticus,* from Greek *sustaltikos,* from *sustellein* to contract, from SYN- + *stellein* to place]

sys·tem ('sɪstəm) *n.* **1.** a group or combination of interrelated, interdependent, or interacting elements forming a collective entity; a methodical or coordinated assemblage of parts, facts, concepts, etc.: *a system of currency; the Copernican system.* **2.** any scheme of classification or arrangement: *a chronological system.* **3.** a network of communications, transportation, or distribution. **4.** a method or complex of methods: *he has a perfect system at roulette.* **5.** orderliness; an ordered manner. **6. the system.** (*often cap.*) society seen as an environment exploiting, restricting, and repressing individuals. **7.** an organism considered as a functioning entity. **8.** any of various bodily parts or structures that are anatomically or physiologically related: *the digestive system.* **9.** one's physiological or psychological constitution: *get it out of your system.* **10.** any assembly of electronic, electrical, or mechanical components with interdependent functions, usually forming a self-contained unit: *a brake system.* **11.** a group of celestial bodies that are associated as a result of natural laws, esp. gravitational attraction: *the solar system.* **12.** *Chem.* a sample of matter in which there are one or more substances in one or more phases.

See also **phase rule.** **13.** a point of view or doctrine used to interpret a branch of knowledge. **14.** *Mineralogy.* one of a group of divisions into which crystals may be placed on the basis of the lengths and inclinations of their axes. **15.** *Geology.* a stratigraphical unit for the rock strata formed during a period of geological time. It can be subdivided into series. [C17: from French *système,* from Late Latin *systēma,* from Greek *sustēma,* from SYN- + *histanai* to cause to stand] —**'sys+tem+less** *adj.*

sys+tem+at+ic (ˌsɪstɪ'mætɪk) *adj.* **1.** characterized by the use of order and planning; methodical: *a systematic administrator.* **2.** comprising or resembling a system: *systematic theology.* **3.** Also: **systematical.** *Biology.* of or relating to the taxonomic classification of organisms. —ˌ**sys+tem+'at·i·cal+ly** *adv.*

sys+tem+at+ics (ˌsɪstɪ'mætɪks) *n.* (*functioning as sing.*) the study of systems and the principles of classification and nomenclature.

sys+tem·a+tism ('sɪstɪməˌtɪzəm) *n.* **1.** the practice of classifying or systematizing. **2.** adherence to a system. **3.** a systematic classification; systematized arrangement.

sys+tem·a+tist ('sɪstɪmətɪst) *n.* **1.** a person who constructs systems. **2.** an adherent of a system. **3.** a taxonomist.

sys+tem·a+tize ('sɪstɪməˌtaɪz), **sys+tem+ize** *or* **sys+tem·a+tise, sys+tem+ise** *vb.* (*tr.*) to arrange in a system. —ˌ**sys+tem·a·ti+'za+tion,** ˌ**sys+tem·a·ti+'sa+tion** *or* ˌ**sys+tem·i·'za+tion,** ˌ**sys+tem·i·'sa+tion** *n.* —**'sys+tem·a+ˌtiz+er, 'sys+tem·a+ˌtis+er** *or* **'sys+tem+ˌiz+er, 'sys+tem+ˌis+er** *n.*

sys+tem·a+tol+o·gy (ˌsɪstɪmə'tɒlədʒɪ) *n.* the study of the nature and formation of systems.

Sys+tème In+ter+na+tio+nal d'U·ni+tés (*French* sistɛm ɛ̃tɛrnasjɔnal dyni'te) *n.* the International System of units. See **SI unit.**

sys+tem+ic (sɪ'stɛmɪk, -'stiː-) *adj.* **1.** another word for **systematic** (senses 1, 2). **2.** *Physiol.* (of a poison, disease, etc.) affecting the entire body. —**sys+'tem·i·cal+ly** *adv.*

sys+tems a·nal·y+sis *n.* the analysis of the methods involved in scientific and industrial operations, usually with a computer so that an improved system can be designed.

sys+tems en+gi+neer+ing *n.* the branch of engineering, based on systems analysis and information theory, concerned with the design of integrated systems.

sys+to+le ('sɪstəlɪ) *n.* contraction of the heart, during which blood is pumped into the aorta and the arteries that lead to the lungs. Compare **diastole.** [C16: via Late Latin from Greek *sustolē,* from *sustellein* to contract; see SYSTALTIC] —**sys+tol+ic** (sɪ'stɒlɪk) *adj.*

Syz+ran (*Russian* 'sɪzrənj) *n.* a port in the W central Soviet Union, in Kuibyshev Region on the Volga River: oil refining. Pop.: 183 000 (1975 est.).

syz·y+gy ('sɪzɪdʒɪ) *n., pl.* **+gies. 1.** either of the two positions (conjunction or opposition) of a celestial body when sun, earth, and the body lie in a straight line: *the moon is at syzygy when full.* **2.** (in classical prosody) a metrical unit of two feet. **3.** *Rare.* any pair, usually of opposites. **4.** *Zoology.* the aggregation in a mass of certain protozoans, esp. when occurring before sexual reproduction. [C17: from Late Latin *syzygia,* from Greek *suzugia,* from *suzugos* yoked together, from SYN- + *zugon* a yoke] —**sy+zyg+i·al** (sɪ'sɪdʒɪəl), **syz·y+get+ic** (ˌsɪzɪ'dʒɛtɪk), *or* **syz·y+gal** ('sɪzɪgəl) *adj.* —ˌ**syz·y+'get·i·cal+ly** *adv.*

Sza+bad+ka ('sɔbɔtkɔ) *n.* the Hungarian name for **Subotica.**

Szcze+cin (*Polish* ʃtʃɛ'tsin) *n.* a port in NW Poland, on the River Oder: the busiest Polish port and leading coal exporter; shipbuilding. Pop.: 360 500 (1974 est.). German name: **Stettin.**

Sze+chwan ('seɪ'tʃwɑːn) *n.* a province of SW China: the most populous administrative division in the country, esp. in the central Red Basin, where it is crossed by three main tributaries of the Yangtze. Capital: Chengtu. Pop.: 80 000 000 (1976 est.). Area: about 569 800 sq. km (220 000 sq. miles).

Sze+ged (*Hungarian* 'sɛgɛd) *n.* an industrial city in S Hungary, on the Tisza River. Pop.: 166 040 (1974 est.).

Szell (sɛl) *n.* **George.** 1897–1970, U.S. conductor, born in Hungary.

Sze·win·ska (*Polish* ʃɛ'vinska) *n.* **I·re·na** (i'rɛna). born 1946, Polish athlete: won the 400 metres in the 1976 Olympic Games.

Szom+bat+hely (*Hungarian* 'sombɔtˌhɛj) *n.* a city in W Hungary: site of the Roman capital of Pannonia. Pop.: 65 000 (1970).

Szy·man·ows·ki (*Polish* ˌʃɪma'nɔfski) *n.* **Ka·rol** ('karɔl). 1882–1937, Polish composer, whose works include the opera *King Roger* (1926), two violin concertos, symphonies, piano music, and songs.

T

t *or* **T** (ti:) *n., pl.* **t's, T's,** *or* **Ts. 1.** the 20th letter and 16th consonant of the modern English alphabet. **2.** a speech sound represented by this letter, usually a voiceless alveolar stop, as in *tame.* **3. a.** something shaped like a T. **b.** (*in combination*): *a T-junction.* **4. to a T.** in every detail; perfectly: *the work suited her to a T.*

t *symbol for:* **1.** ton(s). **2.** tonne(s). **3.** troy (weight). **4.** *Statistics.* distribution.

T *symbol for:* **1.** absolute temperature. **2.** tera-. **3.** *Chem.* tritium. **4.** tesla. **5.** surface tension. ~**6.** *international car registration for* Thailand.

t. *abbrev. for:* **1.** *Commerce.* tare. **2.** teaspoon(ful). **3.** temperature. **4.** *Music.* tempo. **5.** tempore. [Latin: in the time of] **6.** tenor. **7.** *Grammar.* tense. **8.** transitive.

T. *abbrev. for:* **1.** tablespoon(ful). **2.** territory. **3.** time. **4.** Tuesday.

't *contraction of* it.

ta (tɑ:) *interj. Brit. informal.* thank you.

Ta *the chemical symbol for* tantalum.

TA (in Britain) *abbrev. for* Territorial Army (now superseded by **TAVR**).

Taal[1] (tɑ:l) *n.* **the.** another name for **Afrikaans.** [Dutch: speech; see TALE]

Ta·al[2] (tɑ:'ɑ:l) *n.* an active volcano in the Philippines, on S Luzon on an island in the centre of **Lake Taal.** Height: 300 m (984 ft.). Area of lake: 243 sq. km (94 sq. miles).

taa+ta ('tata) *n. East African.* a child's word for **father.**

tab[1] (tæb) *n.* **1.** a small flap of material, esp. one on a garment for decoration or for fastening to a button. **2.** any similar flap, such as a piece of paper attached to a file for identification. **3.** a small auxiliary aerofoil on the trailing edge of a rudder, aileron, or elevator, etc., to assist in the control of the aircraft in flight. See also **trim tab. 4.** *Brit. military.* the insignia on the collar of a staff officer. **5.** *U.S.* a bill, esp. one for a meal or drinks. **6.** *Northern Brit. dialect.* a cigarette. **7. keep tabs on.** *Informal.* to keep a watchful eye on. ~*vb.* **tabs, tab+bing, tabbed. 8.** (*tr.*) to supply (files, clothing, etc.) with a tab or tabs. [C17: of unknown origin]

tab[2] (tæb) *n.* short for **tabulator** or **tablet.**

TAB *abbrev. for:* **1.** typhoid-paratyphoid A and B (vaccine). **2.** *Austral.* Totalizator Agency Board.

tab. *abbrev. for* table (list or chart).

tab·a+nid ('tæbənɪd) *n.* any stout-bodied fly of the dipterous family *Tabanidae,* the females of which have mouthparts specialized for sucking blood: includes the horseflies. [C19: from Latin *tabānus* horsefly]

tab+ard ('tæbəd) *n.* a sleeveless or short-sleeved jacket, esp. one worn by a herald, bearing a coat of arms, or by a knight over his armour. [C13: from Old French *tabart,* of uncertain origin]

tab·a+ret ('tæbərɪt) *n.* a hard-wearing fabric of silk or similar cloth with stripes of satin or moire, used esp. for upholstery. [C19: perhaps from TABBY]

Ta+bas+co[1] (tə'bæskəʊ) *n. Trademark.* a very hot red sauce made from matured capsicums.

Ta+bas+co[2] (*Spanish* ta'βasko) *n.* a state in SE Mexico, on the Gulf of Campeche: mostly flat and marshy with extensive jungles; hot and humid climate. Capital: Villahermosa. Pop.: 768 327 (1970). Area: 24 338 sq. km (9783 sq. miles).

tab+by ('tæbɪ) *adj.* **1.** (esp. of cats) brindled with dark stripes or wavy markings on a lighter background. **2.** having a wavy or striped pattern, particularly in colours of grey and brown. ~*n., pl.* **+bies. 3.** a tabby cat. **4.** any female domestic cat. **5.** a fabric with a watered pattern, esp. silk or taffeta. [C17: from Old French *tabis* silk cloth, from Arabic *al-'attabiya* literally: the quarter of (Prince) 'Attab, the part of Baghdad where the fabric was first made]

tab+er+nac+le ('tæbə,nækəl) *n.* **1.** (*often cap.*) *Old Testament.* **a.** the portable sanctuary in the form of a tent in which the ancient Israelites carried the Ark of the Covenant (Exodus 25–27). **b.** the Jewish Temple regarded as the shrine of the divine presence. **2.** a temporary boothlike structure used by Jews as a dining area on certain feast days. **3.** any place of worship that is not called a church. **4.** a small ornamented cupboard or box used for the reserved sacrament of the Eucharist. **5.** the human body regarded as the temporary dwelling of the soul. **6.** *Chiefly R.C. Church.* a canopied niche or recess forming the shrine of an icon. **7.** *Nautical.* a strong framework for holding the foot of a mast stepped on deck, allowing it to be swung down horizontally to pass under low bridges, etc. [C13: from Latin *tabernāculum* a tent, from *taberna* a hut; see TAVERN] —**,tab+er+'nac·u+lar** *adj.*

ta+bes ('teɪbi:z) *n.* **1.** a wasting of a bodily organ or part. **2.** short for **tabes dorsalis.** [C17: from Latin: a wasting away] —**ta+bet+ic** (tə'bɛtɪk) *adj.*

ta+bes+cent (tə'bɛsənt) *adj.* **1.** progressively emaciating; wasting away. **2.** of, relating to, or having tabes. [C19: from Latin *tābēscere,* from TABES] —**ta+'bes+cence** *n.*

ta+bes dor+sa+lis (dɔ:'sɑ:lɪs) *n.* a form of late syphilis that attacks the spinal cord causing degeneration of the nerve fibres, pains in the legs, paralysis of the leg muscles, acute abdominal pain, etc. Also called: **locomotor ataxia.** [New Latin, literally: tabes of the back; see TABES, DORSAL]

tab+la ('tʌblə, 'tɑ:blɑ:) *n.* a musical instrument of India consisting of a pair of drums whose pitches can be varied. [Hindu, from Arabic *tabla* drum]

tab+la+ture ('tæblətʃə) *n.* **1.** *Music.* any of a number of forms of musical notation, esp. for playing the lute, consisting of letters and signs indicating rhythm and fingering. **2.** an engraved or painted tablet or other flat surface. [C16: from French, ultimately from Latin *tabulātum* wooden floor, from *tabula* a plank]

ta+ble ('teɪbəl) *n.* **1.** a flat horizontal slab or board supported by one or more legs, on which objects may be placed. **2. a.** such a slab or board on which food is served: *we were six at table.* **b.** (*as modifier*): *table linen.* **c.** (*in combination*): *a tablecloth.* **3.** food as served in a particular household or restaurant: *a good table.* **4.** such a piece of furniture specially designed for any of various purposes: *a backgammon table; bird table.* **5. a.** a company of persons assembled for a meal, game, etc. **b.** (*as modifier*): *table talk.* **6.** any flat or level area, such as a plateau. **7.** a rectangular panel set below or above the face of a wall. **8.** *Architect.* another name for **cordon** (sense 4). **9.** an upper horizontal facet of a cut gem. **10.** *Music.* the sounding board of a violin, guitar, or similar stringed instrument. **11. a.** an arrangement of words, numbers, or signs, usually in parallel columns, to display data or relations: *a table of contents.* **b.** See **multiplication table. 12.** a tablet on which laws were inscribed by the ancient Romans, the Hebrews, etc. **13.** *Palmistry.* an area of the palm's surface bounded by four lines. **14.** *Printing.* a slab of smooth metal on which ink is rolled to its proper consistency. **15. a.** either of the two bony plates that form the inner and outer parts of the flat bones of the cranium. **b.** any thin flat plate, esp. of bone. **16. turn the tables.** to cause a complete reversal of circumstances. ~*vb.* (*tr.*) **17.** to place on a table. **18.** to submit (a bill, etc.) for consideration by a legislative body. **19.** to suspend discussion of (a bill, etc.) indefinitely or for some time. **20.** to enter or form into a list; tabulate. [C12: via Old French from Latin *tabula* a writing tablet] —**'ta+ble+ful** *n.* —**'ta+ble+less** *adj.*

tab+leau ('tæbləʊ) *n., pl.* **+leaux** (-ləʊ, -ləʊz) *or* **+leaus. 1.** See **tableau vivant. 2.** a pause during or at the end of a scene on stage when all the performers briefly freeze in position. **3.** any dramatic group or scene. [C17: from French, from Old French *tablel* a picture, diminutive of TABLE]

ta+bleau vi+vant *French.* (tablo vi'vɑ̃) *n., pl.* ***ta+bleaux vi+vants*** (tablo vi'vɑ̃). a representation of a scene, painting, sculpture, etc., by a person or group posed silent and motionless. [C19: literally: living picture]

Ta+ble Bay *n.* the large bay on which Cape Town is situated, on the SW coast of South Africa.

ta·ble+cloth ('teɪbəl,klɒθ) *n.* a cloth for covering the top of a table, esp. during meals.

ta+ble d'hôte ('tɑ:bəl 'dəʊt; *French* tabl 'do:t) *adj.* **1.** (of a meal) consisting of a set number of courses with limited choice of dishes offered at a fixed price. Compare **à la carte, prix fixe.** ~*n., pl.* **ta+bles d'hôte** ('tɑ:bəlz 'dəʊt; *French* tabl 'do:t). **2.** a table d'hôte meal or menu. [C17: from French, literally: the host's table]

ta·ble+land ('teɪbəl,lænd) *n.* flat elevated land; a plateau.

ta·ble li+cence *n.* a licence authorizing the sale of alcoholic drinks with meals only.

ta+ble mo+ney *n.* an allowance for official entertaining of visitors, clients, etc., esp. in the army.

Ta+ble Moun+tain *n.* a mountain in SW South Africa, in Cape Province overlooking Cape Town and Table Bay: flat-topped and steep-sided. Height: 1087 m (3567 ft.).

ta+ble nap+kin *n.* See **napkin** (sense 1).

ta+ble salt *n.* salt that is used at table rather than for cooking.

ta·ble+spoon ('teɪbəl,spu:n) *n.* **1.** a spoon, larger than a dessertspoon, used for serving food, etc. **2.** Also called: **ta·ble+spoon+ful.** the amount contained in such a spoon. **3.** a unit of capacity used in cooking, medicine, etc., equal to half a fluid ounce or three teaspoons.

tab+let ('tæblɪt) *n.* **1.** a pill made of a compressed powdered medicinal substance. **2.** a flattish cake of some substance, such as soap. **3.** a slab of stone, wood, etc., esp. one formerly used for inscriptions. **4. a.** a thinner rigid sheet, as of bark, ivory, etc., used for similar purposes. **b.** (*often pl.*) a set or pair of these fastened together, as in a book. **5.** a pad of writing paper. [C14: from Old French *tablete* a little table, from Latin *tabula* a board]

ta+ble ten+nis *n.* a miniature form of tennis played on a table with small bats and a light hollow ball.

ta·ble-turn·ing *n.* **1.** the movement of a table attributed by spiritualists to the power of spirits working through a group of persons placing their hands or fingers on the table top. **2.** *Often derogatory.* spiritualism in general.

ta·ble·ware ('teɪbᵊlˌwɛə) *n.* articles such as dishes, plates, knives, forks, etc., used at meals.
ta·ble wine *n.* a wine considered suitable for drinking with a meal.
tab·loid ('tæblɔɪd) *n.* a newspaper with pages about 30 cm (12 inches) by 40 cm (16 inches), usually characterized by an emphasis on photographs and a concise and often sensational style. [C20: from earlier *Tabloid,* a trademark for a medicine in tablet form]
ta·boo *or* **ta·bu** (tə'bu:) *adj.* **1.** forbidden or disapproved of; placed under a social prohibition or ban: *taboo words.* **2.** (in Polynesia and other islands of the South Pacific) marked off as simultaneously sacred and forbidden. ~*n., pl.* **·boos** *or* **·bus. 3.** any prohibition resulting from social or other conventions. **4.** ritual restriction or prohibition, esp. of something that is considered holy or unclean. ~*vb.* **5.** (*tr.*) to place under a taboo. [C18: from Tongan *tabu*]
ta·bor *or* **ta·bour** ('teɪbə) *n. Music.* a small drum used esp. in the Middle Ages, struck with one hand while the other held a three-holed pipe. See **pipe**[1] (sense 7). [C13: from Old French *tabour,* perhaps from Persian *tabīr*] —**'ta·bor·er** *or* **'ta·bour·er** *n.*
Ta·bor ('teɪbə) *n.* **Mount.** a mountain in N Israel, near Nazareth: traditionally regarded as the mountain where the Transfiguration took place. Height: 588 m (1929 ft.).
tab·o·ret *or* **tab·ou·ret** ('tæbərɪt) *n.* **1.** a low stool, originally in the shape of a drum. **2.** a frame, usually round, for stretching out cloth while it is being embroidered. **3.** Also called: **tab·o·rin, tab·ou·rin** ('tæbərɪn). a small tabor. [C17: from French *tabouret,* diminutive of TABOR]
Ta·briz (tæ'bri:z) *n.* a city in NW Iran: an ancient city, situated in a volcanic region of hot springs; university (1947); carpet manufacturing. Pop.: 510 000 (1973 est.). Ancient name: **Tauris.**
tab·u·lar ('tæbjʊlə) *adj.* **1.** arranged in systematic or table form. **2.** calculated from or by means of a table. **3.** like a table in form; flat. [C17: from Latin *tabulāris* concerning boards, from *tabula* a board] —**'tab·u·lar·ly** *adv.*
tab·u·la ra·sa ('tæbjʊlə 'rɑ:sə) *n., pl.* **tab·u·lae ra·sae** ('tæbjʊli: 'rɑ:si:). **1.** (esp. in the philosophy of Locke) the mind in its uninformed original state. **2.** an opportunity for a fresh start; clean slate. [Latin: a scraped tablet (one from which the writing has been erased)]
tab·u·late *vb.* ('tæbjʊˌleɪt). (*tr.*) **1.** Also: **tab·u·lar·ize** ('tæbjʊləˌraɪz). to set out, arrange, or write in tabular form. **2.** to form or cut with a flat surface. ~*adj.* ('tæbjʊlɪt, -ˌleɪt). **3.** having a flat surface. **4.** (of certain corals) having transverse skeletal plates. [C18: from Latin *tabula* a board] —**'tab·u·la·ble** *adj.* —**ˌtab·u·'la·tion** *n.*
tab·u·la·tor ('tæbjʊˌleɪtə) *n.* **1.** a device for setting the automatic stops that locate the column margins on a typewriter. **2.** *Computer technol.* a machine that reads data from one medium, such as punched cards, producing lists, tabulations, or totals, usually on a continuous sheet of paper. **3.** any machine that tabulates data.
tac·a·ma·hac ('tækəməˌhæk) *or* **tac·ma·hack** *n.* **1.** any of several strong-smelling resinous gums obtained from certain trees, used in making ointments, incense, etc. **2.** any tree yielding this resin, esp. the balsam poplar. [C16: from Spanish *tacamahaca,* from Nahuatl *tecomahca* aromatic resin]
tace (tæs, teɪs) *n.* a less common word for **tasset.**
ta·cet ('teɪsɛt) (of a specific instrument) not required to play during a movement or part of a movement. [C18: from Latin: it is silent, from *tacēre* to be quiet]
tache[1] (tæʃ, tɑ:ʃ) *n. Archaic.* a buckle, clasp, or hook. [C17: from Old French, of Germanic origin; compare TACK[1]]
tache[2] (tæʃ) *n. Informal.* short for **moustache.**
tach·e·o- *combining form.* variant of **tachy-.**
tach·e·om·e·ter (ˌtækɪ'ɒmɪtə) *or* **ta·chym·e·ter** *n. Surveying.* a type of theodolite designed for the rapid measurement of distances, elevations, and directions.
tach·e·om·e·try (ˌtækɪ'ɒmɪtrɪ) *or* **ta·chym·e·try** *n. Surveying.* the measurement of distance, etc., using a tacheometer. —**tach·e·o·met·ric** (ˌtækɪə'mɛtrɪk), **ˌtach·e·o·'met·ri·cal** *or* **ˌtach·y·'met·ric, ˌtach·y·'met·ri·cal** *adj.* —**ˌtach·e·o·'met·ri·cal·ly** *or* **ˌtach·y·'met·ri·cal·ly** *adv.*
tach·i·na fly ('tækɪnə) *n.* any bristly fly of the dipterous family *Tachinidae,* the larvae of which live parasitically in caterpillars, beetles, hymenopterans, and other insects. [C19: via New Latin *Tachina,* from Greek *takhinos* swift, from *takhos* fleetness]
ta·chisme ('tɑ:ʃɪzəm; *French* ta'ʃism) *n.* a type of action painting evolved in France in which haphazard dabs and blots of colour are treated as a means of instinctive or unconscious expression. [C20: French, from *tache* stain]
ta·chis·to·scope (tə'kɪstəˌskəʊp) *n.* an instrument, used mainly in experiments on perception and memory, for displaying visual images for very brief intervals, usually a fraction of a second. [C20: from Greek *takhistos* swiftest (see TACHY-) + -SCOPE] —**ta·chis·to·scop·ic** (təˌkɪstə'skɒpɪk) *adj.* —**ta·ˌchis·to·'scop·i·cal·ly** *adv.*
tach·o- *combining form.* speed: *tachograph; tachometer.* [from Greek *takhos*]
tach·o·graph ('tækəˌgrɑ:f, -ˌgræf) *n.* a tachometer that produces a graphical record (**tachogram**) of its readings, esp. a device for recording the speed of and distance covered by a heavy goods vehicle.
ta·chom·e·ter (tæ'kɒmɪtə) *n.* any device for measuring speed, esp. the rate of revolution of a shaft. Tachometers (rev counters) are often fitted to cars to indicate the number of revolutions per minute of the engine. —**tach·o·met·ric** (ˌtækə'mɛtrɪk) *or* **ˌtach·o·'met·ri·cal** *adj.* —**ˌtach·o·'met·ri·cal·ly** *adv.* —**ta·'chom·e·try** *n.*
tach·y- *or* **tacheo-** *combining form.* swift or accelerated: *tachycardia; tachygraphy; tachylyte; tachyon; tachyphylaxis.* [from Greek *takhus* swift]
tach·y·car·di·a (ˌtækɪ'kɑ:dɪə) *n. Pathol.* abnormally rapid beating of the heart, esp. over 100 beats per minute. Compare **bradycardia.** —**tach·y·car·di·ac** (ˌtækɪ'kɑ:dɪˌæk) *adj.*
ta·chyg·ra·phy (tæ'kɪgrəfɪ) *n.* shorthand, esp. as used in ancient Rome or Greece. —**ta·'chyg·ra·pher** *or* **ta·'chyg·ra·phist** *n.* —**tach·y·graph·ic** (ˌtækɪ'græfɪk) *or* **ˌtach·y·'graph·i·cal** *adj.* —**ˌtach·y·'graph·i·cal·ly** *adv.*
tach·y·lyte *or* **tach·y·lite** ('tækɪˌlaɪt) *n.* a black glassy basalt often found on the edges of intrusions of basalt. —**tach·y·lyt·ic** (ˌtækə'lɪtɪk) *or* **ˌtach·y·'lit·ic** *adj.*
ta·chym·e·ter (tæ'kɪmɪtə) *n.* another name for **tacheometer.**
ta·chym·e·try (tæ'kɪmɪtrɪ) *n.* another name for **tacheometry.**
tach·y·on ('tækɪˌɒn) *n. Physics.* a hypothetical elementary particle capable of travelling faster than the velocity of light. [C20: from TACHY- + -ON]
tach·y·phy·lax·is (ˌtækɪfɪ'læksɪs) *n.* very rapid development of tolerance or immunity to the effects of a drug.
tac·it ('tæsɪt) *adj.* **1.** implied without direct expression; understood: *a tacit agreement.* **2.** silent. **3.** created or having effect by operation of law, rather than by being directly expressed. [C17: from Latin *tacitus,* past participle of *tacēre* to be silent] —**'tac·it·ly** *adv.* —**'tac·it·ness** *n.*
tac·i·turn ('tæsɪˌtɜ:n) *adj.* habitually silent, reserved, or uncommunicative; not inclined to conversation. [C18: from Latin *taciturnus,* from *tacitus* silent, from *tacēre* to be silent] —**ˌtac·i·'tur·ni·ty** *n.* —**'tac·iˌturn·ly** *adv.*
Tac·i·tus ('tæsɪtəs) *n.* **Pub·li·us Cor·ne·lius** ('pʌblɪəs kɔ:'ni:ljəs). ?55–?120 A.D., Roman historian and orator, famous as a prose stylist. His works include the *Histories,* dealing with the period 68–96, and the *Annals,* dealing with the period 14–68.
tack[1] (tæk) *n.* **1.** a short sharp-pointed nail, usually with a flat and comparatively large head. **2.** *Brit.* a long loose temporary stitch used in dressmaking, etc. **3.** See **tailor's tack. 4.** a temporary fastening. **5.** stickiness, as of newly applied paint, varnish, etc. **6.** *Nautical.* the heading of a vessel sailing to windward, stated in terms of the side of the sail against which the wind is pressing. **7.** *Nautical.* **a.** a course sailed by a sailing vessel with the wind blowing from forward of the beam. **b.** one such course or a zigzag pattern of such courses. **8.** *Nautical.* **a.** a sheet for controlling the weather clew of a course. **b.** the weather clew itself. **9.** *Nautical.* the forward lower clew of a fore-and-aft sail. **10.** a course of action differing from some previous course: *he went off on a fresh tack.* **11. on the wrong tack.** under a false impression. ~*vb.* **12.** to secure by a tack or series of tacks. **13.** *Brit.* to sew (something) with long loose temporary stitches. **14.** (*tr.*) to attach or append: *tack this letter onto the other papers.* **15.** *Nautical.* to change the heading of (a sailing vessel) to the opposite tack. **16.** *Nautical.* to steer (a sailing vessel) on alternate tacks. **17.** (*intr.*) *Nautical.* (of a sailing vessel) to proceed on a different tack or to alternate tacks. **18.** (*intr.*) to follow a zigzag route; keep changing one's course of action. [C14 *tak* fastening, nail; related to Middle Low German *tacke* pointed instrument] —**'tack·er** *n.* —**'tack·less** *adj.*
tack[2] (tæk) *n. Informal.* food, esp. when regarded as inferior or distasteful. See also **hardtack.** [C19: of unknown origin]
tack[3] (tæk) *n.* **a.** riding harness for horses, such as saddles, bridles, etc. **b.** (*as modifier*): *the tack room.* [C20: shortened from TACKLE]
tack·et ('tækɪt) *n. Northern Brit.* a nail, esp. a hobnail. [C14: from TACK[1]]
tack ham·mer *n.* a light hammer for driving tacks.
tack·ies ('tækɪz) *pl. n., sing.* **tack·y.** *S. African informal.* tennis shoes or plimsolls. [C20: probably from TACKY[1], with reference to their nonslip rubber soles]
tack·le ('tækᵊl) *n.* **1.** any mechanical system for lifting or pulling, esp. an arrangement of ropes and pulleys designed to lift heavy weights. **2.** the equipment required for a particular occupation, etc.: *fishing tackle.* **3.** *Nautical.* the halyards and other running rigging aboard a vessel. **4.** *Sport.* a physical challenge to an opponent, as to prevent his progress with the ball. ~*vb.* **5.** (*tr.*) to undertake (a task, problem, etc.). **6.** (*tr.*) to confront (a person, esp. an opponent) with a difficult proposition. **7.** *Sport.* (esp. in football games) to challenge (an opponent) with a tackle. [C13: related to Middle Low German *takel* ship's rigging, Middle Dutch *taken* to TAKE] —**'tack·ler** *n.*
tack·y[1] *or* **tack·ey** ('tækɪ) *adj.* **tack·i·er, tack·i·est.** slightly sticky or adhesive: *the varnish was still tacky.* [C18: from TACK[1] (in the sense: stickiness)] —**'tack·i·ness** *n.*
tack·y[2] ('tækɪ) *adj.* **tack·i·er, tack·i·est.** *U.S. informal.* **1.** shabby or shoddy. **2.** ostentatious and vulgar. **3.** (of a person) eccentric; crazy. [C19: from dialect *tacky* an inferior horse, of unknown origin] —**'tack·i·ness** *n.*
tac·ma·hack ('tækməˌhæk) *n.* a variant of **tacamahac.**
Tac·na-A·ri·ca (*Spanish* 'takna a'rika) *n.* a coastal desert region of W South America, long disputed by Chile and Peru: divided in 1929 into the Peruvian department of Tacna and the Chilean department of Arica.
tac·node ('tækˌnəʊd) *n.* another name for **osculation** (sense 1). [C19: from Latin *tactus* touch (from *tangere* to touch) + NODE]

ta·co ('tɑːkəʊ) *n., pl.* ·**cos.** *Mexican cookery.* a tortilla folded into a roll with a filling and usually fried. [from Mexican Spanish]

Ta·co·ma (tə'kəʊmə) *n.* a port in W Washington, on Puget Sound: industrial centre. Pop.: 149 420 (1973 est.).

tac·o·nite ('tækəˌnaɪt) *n.* a fine-grained sedimentary rock containing magnetite, haematite, and silica, which occurs in the Lake Superior region: a low-grade iron ore. [C20: named after the *Taconic* Mountains in New England]

tact (tækt) *n.* **1.** a sense of what is fitting and considerate in dealing with others, so as to avoid giving offence or to win good will; discretion. **2.** skill or judgment in handling difficult or delicate situations; diplomacy. **3.** *Archaic.* the sense of touch. [C17: from Latin *tactus* a touching, from *tangere* to touch] —'**tact·ful** *adj.* —'**tact·ful·ly** *adv.* —'**tact·ful·ness** *n.* —'**tact·less** *adj.* —'**tact·less·ly** *adv.* —'**tact·less·ness** *n.*

tac·tic ('tæktɪk) *n.* a piece of tactics; tactical move.

-tac·tic *adj. combining form.* having a specified kind of pattern or arrangement or having an orientation determined by a specified force: *syndiotactic; phototactic.* [from Greek *taktikos* relating to order or arrangement; see TACTICS]

tac·ti·cal ('tæktɪkᵊl) *adj.* **1.** of, relating to, or employing tactics: *a tactical error.* **2.** skilful, adroit, or diplomatic: *a tactical manoeuvre.* —'**tac·ti·cal·ly** *adv.*

tac·tics ('tæktɪks) *pl. n.* **1.** (*functioning as sing.*) *Military.* the art and science of the detailed direction and control of movement or manoeuvre to achieve an aim or task. **2.** the manoeuvres used to achieve an aim or task. **3.** plans followed in order to achieve a certain aim. [C17: from New Latin *tactica,* from Greek *ta taktika* the matters of arrangement, neuter plural of *taktikos* concerning arrangement or order, from *taktos* arranged (for battle), from *tassein* to arrange] —**tac·'ti·cian** *n.*

tac·tile ('tæktaɪl) *adj.* **1.** of, relating to, affecting, or having a sense of touch: *a tactile organ; tactile stimuli.* **2.** *Now rare.* capable of being touched; tangible. [C17: from Latin *tactilis,* from *tangere* to touch] —**tac·til·i·ty** (tæk'tɪlɪtɪ) *n.*

tac·tion ('tækʃən) *n. Obsolete.* the act of touching; contact. [C17: from Latin *tactiō* a touching, from *tangere* to touch]

tac·tu·al ('tæktjʊəl) *adj.* **1.** caused by touch; causing a tactile sensation. **2.** of or relating to the tactile sense or the organs of touch. [C17: from Latin *tactus* a touching; see TACT] —'**tac·tu·al·ly** *adv.*

tad (tæd) *n. Informal, chiefly U.S.* a small boy; lad. [C20: short for TADPOLE]

Tad·mor ('tædmɔː) *n.* the biblical name for **Palmyra.**

tad·pole ('tædˌpəʊl) *n.* the aquatic larva of frogs, toads, etc., which develops from a limbless tailed form with external gills into a form with internal gills, limbs, and a reduced tail. [C15 *taddepol,* from *tadde* TOAD + *pol* head, POLL]

Ta·dzhik, Ta·djik, *or* **Ta·jik** ('tɑːdʒɪk, tɑː'dʒiːk) *n.* **1.** (*pl.* ·**dzhik,** ·**djik,** *or* ·**jik**) a member of a Persian-speaking Muslim people inhabiting Tadzhikistan and parts of Sinkiang in W China.

Ta·dzhik·i (tɑː'dʒɪkiː, -'dʒiː-) *n.* **1.** the language of the Tadzhiks, belonging to the West Iranian subbranch of the Indo-European family. ~*adj.* **2.** of or relating to the Tadzhiks or their language.

Ta·dzhik So·vi·et So·cial·ist Re·pub·lic *n.* an administrative division of the S central Soviet Union: mountainous. Capital: Dushanbe. Pop.: 2 899 602 (1970). Area: 143 100 sq. km (55 240 sq. miles). Also called: **Ta·dzhik·i·stan** (tɑːˌdʒɪkɪ'stɑːn).

tae·di·um vi·tae ('tiːdɪəm 'viːtaɪ, 'vaɪtiː) *n.* the feeling that life is boring and dull. [Latin, literally: weariness of life]

Tae·gu (tɛ'guː) *n.* a city in SE South Korea: textile and agricultural trading centre. Pop.: 1 309 454 (1975).

Tae·jon (tɛ'dʒɒn) *n.* a city in W South Korea: market centre of an agricultural region. Pop.: 506 215 (1975).

tael (teɪl) *n.* **1.** a unit of weight, used in the Far East, having various values between one to two and a half ounces. **2.** (formerly) a Chinese monetary unit equivalent in value to a tael weight of standard silver. [C16: from Portuguese, from Malay *tahil* weight, perhaps from Hindi *tolā* weight of a new rupee, from Sanskrit *tulā* weight]

ta'en (teɪn) *vb.* a poetic contraction of **taken.**

tae·ni·a *or* **te·ni·a** ('tiːnɪə) *n., pl.* ·**ni·ae** (-nɪˌiː). **1.** (in ancient Greece) a narrow fillet or headband for the hair. **2.** *Architect.* the fillet between the architrave and frieze of a Doric entablature. **3.** *Anatomy.* any bandlike structure or part. **4.** any tapeworm of the genus *Taenia,* such as *T. soleum,* a parasite of man that uses the pig as its intermediate host. [C16: via Latin from Greek *tainia* narrow strip; related to Greek *teinein* to stretch]

tae·ni·a·cide *or U.S.* **te·ni·a·cide** ('tiːnɪəˌsaɪd) *n.* a substance, esp. a drug, that kills tapeworms.

tae·ni·a·fuge *or U.S.* **te·ni·a·fuge** ('tiːnɪəˌfjuːdʒ) *n.* a substance, esp. a drug, that expels tapeworms from the body of their host.

tae·ni·a·sis *or U.S.* **te·ni·a·sis** (tiː'naɪəsɪs) *n. Pathol.* infestation with tapeworms of the genus *Taenia.*

taf·fe·ta ('tæfɪtə) *n.* **1. a.** a thin crisp lustrous plain-weave fabric of silk, rayon, etc., used esp. for women's clothes. **b.** (*as modifier*): *a taffeta petticoat.* **2.** any of various similar fabrics. [C14: from Medieval Latin *taffata,* from Persian *tāftah* spun, from *tāftan* to spin]

taff·rail ('tæfˌreɪl) *n. Nautical.* **1.** a rail at the stern or above the transom of a vessel. **2.** the upper part of the transom of a vessel, esp. a sailing vessel, often ornately decorated. [C19: changed (through influence of RAIL[1]) from earlier *tafferel,* from Dutch *taffereel* panel (hence applied to the part of a vessel decorated with carved panels), variant of *tafeleel* (unattested), from *tafel* TABLE]

taf·fy ('tæfɪ) *n., pl.* ·**fies.** **1.** *U.S.* a chewy sweet made of brown sugar or molasses and butter, boiled and then pulled so that it becomes glossy. **2.** *Chiefly U.S.* a less common term for **toffee.** [C19: perhaps from TAFIA]

Taf·fy ('tæfɪ) *n., pl.* ·**fies.** a slang word or nickname for a Welshman. [C17: from the supposed Welsh pronunciation of *Davy* (from *David,* Welsh *Dafydd*), a common Welsh Christian name]

taf·i·a *or* **taf·fi·a** ('tæfɪə) *n.* a type of rum, esp. from Guyana or the West Indies. [C18: from French, from West Indian Creole, probably from RATAFIA]

Ta·fi·lelt (tæ'fiːlɛlt) *or* **Ta·fi·la·let** (ˌtæfɪ'lɑːlɛt) *n.* an oasis in SE Morocco, the largest in the Sahara. Area: about 1300 sq. km (500 sq. miles).

Taft (tæft) *n.* **Wil·liam How·ard.** 1857–1930, U.S. statesman; 27th president of the U.S. (1909–13).

tag[1] (tæg) *n.* **1.** a piece or strip of paper, plastic, leather, etc., for attaching to something by one end as a mark or label: *a price tag.* **2.** a small piece of material hanging from or loosely attached to a part or piece. **3.** a point of metal or other hard substance at the end of a cord, lace, etc., to prevent it from fraying and to facilitate threading. **4.** an epithet or verbal appendage, the refrain of a song, the moral of a fable, etc. **5.** a brief quotation, esp. one in a foreign language: *his speech was interlarded with Horatian tags.* **6.** an ornamental flourish as at the end of a signature. **7.** the contrastingly coloured tip to an animal's tail. **8.** a matted lock of wool or hair. **9.** *Angling.* a strand of tinsel, wire, etc., tied to the body of an artificial fly. ~*vb.* **tags, tag·ging, tagged.** (*mainly tr.*) **10.** to mark with a tag. **11.** to add or append as a tag. **12.** to supply prose or blank verse with rhymes. **13.** (*intr.;* usually foll. by *on* or *along*) to trail (behind): *many small boys tagged on behind the procession.* **14.** to name or call (someone something): *they tagged him Lanky.* **15.** to cut the tags of wool or hair from (an animal). [C15: of uncertain origin; related to Swedish *tagg* point, perhaps also to TACK[1]]

tag[2] (tæg) *n.* **1.** a children's game in which one player chases the others in an attempt to catch one of them who will then become the chaser. **2.** the act of tagging one's partner in tag wrestling. **3.** (*modifier*) denoting or relating to a professional wrestling contest between two teams of two wrestlers, only one of whom may be in the ring at one time. The contestant outside the ring may enter the ring by touching his team-mate's hand while holding a rope (**tag rope**) that is attached to the corner. ~*vb.* **tags, tag·ging, tagged.** (*tr.*) **4.** to catch (another child) in the game of tag. **5.** (in tag wrestling) to touch the hand of (one's partner). [C18: perhaps from TAG[1]]

Ta·ga·log (tə'gɑːlɒg) *n., pl.* ·**logs** *or* ·**log.** **1.** a member of a people of the Philippines, living chiefly in the region around Manila. **2.** the language of this people, belonging to the Malayo-Polynesian family: the official language of the Philippines. ~*adj.* **3.** of or relating to this people or their language.

Ta·gan·rog (*Russian* təgan'rɔk) *n.* a port in the S Soviet Union, on the **Gulf of Taganrog** (an inlet of the Sea of Azov): founded in 1698 as a naval base and fortress by Peter the Great: industrial centre. Pop.: 277 000 (1975 est.).

tag end *n.* **1.** *Chiefly U.S.* the last part of something: *the tag end of the day.* **2.** a loose end of cloth, thread, etc.

tag·gers ('tægəz) *pl. n.* very thin iron or steel sheet coated with tin.

ta·glia·tel·le (ˌtæljə'tɛlɪ) *n.* a form of pasta made in narrow strips. [Italian, from *tagliare* to cut]

tag·meme ('tægmiːm) *n. Linguistics.* a class of speech elements all of which may fulfil the same grammatical role in a sentence; the minimum unit of analysis in tagmemics. [C20: from Greek *tagma* order, from *tassein* to put in order + -EME] —**tag·'mem·ic** *adj.*

tag·mem·ics (tæg'miːmɪks) *pl. n.* (*functioning as sing.*) *Linguistics.* a type of grammatical analysis based on the concept of function in sentence slots and the determination of classes of words that can fill each slot.

Ta·gore (tə'gɔː) *n.* Sir **Ra·bin·dra·nath** (rə'biːndrəˌnɑːt). 1861–1941, Indian poet and philosopher. His verse collections, written in Bengali and English, include *Gitanjali* (1910; 1912): Nobel prize for literature 1913.

Ta·gus ('teɪgəs) *n.* a river in SW Europe, rising in E central Spain and flowing west to the border with Portugal, then southwest to the Atlantic at Lisbon: the longest river of the Iberian Peninsula. Length: 1007 km (626 miles). Portuguese name: **Tejo.** Spanish name: **Tajo.**

ta·hi·na (tə'hiːnə) *n.* a paste made from sesame seeds originating in the Middle East, often used as an ingredient of houmous and other dips. [from Arabic]

Ta·hi·ti (tə'hiːtɪ) *n.* an island in the S Pacific, in the Windward group of the Society Islands: the largest and most important island in French Polynesia; became a French protectorate in 1842 and a colony in 1880. Capital: Papeete. Pop.: 84 552 (1970). Area: 1005 sq. km (388 sq. miles). —**Ta·hi·ti·an** (tə'hiːtɪən, tə'hiːʃɪən) *adj., n.*

Ta·hoe ('tɑːhəʊ, 'teɪ-) *n.* **Lake.** a lake between E California and W Nevada, in the Sierra Nevada Mountains at an altitude of 1899 m (6229 ft.). Area: about 520 sq. km (200 sq. miles).

tahr (tɑː) *n.* any of several goatlike bovid mammals of the genus *Hemitragus,* such as *H. jemlahicus* (**Himalayan tahr**), of mountainous regions of S and SW Asia, having a shaggy coat and curved horns. [from Nepali *thār*]

tah·sil (tə'siːl) *n.* an administrative division of a zila in certain states in India. [Urdu, from Arabic: collection]

tah·sil·dar (tə'siːldɑː) *n.* the officer in charge of the collection of revenues, etc., in a tahsil. [C18: via Hindi from Persian, from TAHSIL + Persian *-dār* having]

Tai (taɪ) *adj., n.* a variant spelling of **Thai.**

Tai·chung *or* **T'ai-chung** ('taɪ'tʃʊŋ) *n.* a city in the W Republic of China (Taiwan): commercial centre of an agricultural region. Pop.: 428 426 (1969 est.).

taig (teɪg) *n. Ulster dialect, often derogatory.* a Roman Catholic. [variant of the Irish name *Tadhg,* originally signifying any Irishman]

tai·ga ('taɪgə) *n.* the coniferous forests extending across much of subarctic North America and Eurasia, bordered by tundra to the north and steppe to the south. [from Russian, of Turkic origin; compare Turkish *dağ* mountain]

tail[1] (teɪl) *n.* **1.** the region of the vertebrate body that is posterior to or above the anus and contains an elongation of the vertebral column, esp. forming a flexible movable appendage. **2.** anything resembling such an appendage in form or position; the bottom, lowest, or rear part: *the tail of a shirt.* **3.** the last part or parts: *the tail of the storm.* **4.** the rear part of an aircraft including the fin, tail plane, and control surfaces; empennage. **5.** *Astronomy.* the luminous stream of gas and dust particles, up to 200 million kilometres long, driven from the head of a comet, when close to the sun, under the effect of the solar wind. **6.** the rear portion of a bomb, rocket, missile, etc., usually fitted with guiding or stabilizing vanes. **7.** a line of people or things. **8.** a long braid or tress of hair: *a ponytail; a pigtail.* **9.** a final short line in a stanza. **10.** *Informal.* a person employed to follow and spy upon another or others. **11.** an informal word for **buttocks. 12.** *Taboo slang, chiefly U.S.* **a.** the female genitals. **b.** a woman considered sexually (esp. in the phrases **piece of tail, bit of tail**). **13.** *Printing.* **a.** the margin at the foot of a page. **b.** the bottom edge of a book. **14.** the lower end of a pool or part of a stream. **15.** *Informal.* the course or track of a fleeing person or animal: *the police are on my tail.* **16.** (*modifier*) coming from or situated in the rear: *a tail wind.* **17. turn tail.** to run away; escape. **18. with one's tail between one's legs.** in a state of utter defeat or confusion. ~*vb.* **19.** to form or cause to form the tail. **20.** to remove the tail of (an animal); dock. **21.** (*tr.*) to remove the stalk of: *to top and tail the gooseberries.* **22.** (*tr.*) to connect (objects, ideas, etc.) together by or as if by the tail. **23.** (*tr.*) *Informal.* to follow stealthily. **24.** (*tr.*) *Austral.* to tend (cattle) on foot. **25.** (*intr.*) (of a vessel) to assume a specified position, as when at a mooring. **26.** (*tr.*) to build the end of (a brick, joist, etc.) into a wall or (of a brick, etc.) to have one end built into a wall. ~See also **tail off.** [Old English *tægel;* related to Old Norse *tagl* horse's tail, Gothic *tagl* hair, Old High German *zagal* tail] —**'tail·less** *adj.* —**'tail·less·ly** *adv.* —**'tail·less·ness** *n.* —**'tail-ˌlike** *adj.*

tail[2] (teɪl) *Property law.* ~*n.* **1.** the limitation of an estate or interest to a person and the heirs of his body. See also **entail.** ~*adj.* **2.** (*immediately postpositive*) (of an estate or interest) limited in this way. [C15: from Old French *taille* a division; see TAILOR, TALLY] —**'tail·less** *adj.*

tail·back ('teɪlˌbæk) *n.* a queue of traffic stretching back from an obstruction.

tail·board ('teɪlˌbɔːd) *n.* a board at the rear of a lorry, wagon, etc., that can be removed or let down on a hinge.

tail coat *n.* **1.** Also called: **tails.** a man's black coat having a horizontal cut over the hips and a tapering tail with a vertical slit up to the waist: worn as part of full evening dress. **2.** Also called: **swallow-tailed coat.** another name for **morning coat.**

tail co·vert *n.* any of the covert feathers of a bird covering the bases of the tail feathers.

tail end *n.* the last, endmost, or final part.

tail fan *n.* the fanned structure at the hind end of a lobster or related crustacean, formed from the telson and uropods.

tail gate *n.* a gate that is used to control the flow of water at the lower end of a lock. Compare **head gate.**

tail·gate ('teɪlˌgeɪt) *n.* **1.** another name (esp. U.S.) for **tailboard.** ~*vb.* **2.** *U.S.* to drive very close behind (a vehicle).

tail-heav·y *adj.* (of an aircraft) having too much weight at the rear because of overloading or poor design.

tail·ing ('teɪlɪŋ) *n.* the part of a beam, rafter, projecting brick or stone, etc., embedded in a wall.

tail·ings ('teɪlɪŋz) *pl. n.* waste left over after certain processes, such as from an ore-crushing plant or in milling grain.

taille (taɪ; *French* 'tɑːj) *n., pl.* **tailles** (taɪ, taɪz; *French* 'tɑːj). (in France before 1789) a tax levied by a king or overlord on his subjects. [C17: from French, from Old French *taillier* to shape; see TAILOR]

tail·light ('teɪlˌlaɪt) *or* **tail·lamp** *n.* the U.S. name for **rear light.**

tail off *or* **a·way** *vb.* (*adv., usually intr.*) to decrease or cause to decrease in quantity, degree, etc., esp. gradually: *his interest in collecting stamps tailed off over the years.*

tai·lor ('teɪlə) *n.* **1.** a person who makes, repairs, or alters outer garments, esp. men's wear. Related adj.: **sartorial.** ~*vb.* **2.** to cut or style (material, clothes, etc.) to satisfy certain requirements. **3.** (*tr.*) to adapt so as to make suitable for something specific: *he tailored his speech to suit a younger audience.* **4.** (*intr.*) to follow the occupation of a tailor. [C13: from Anglo-Norman *taillour,* from Old French *taillier* to cut, from Latin *tālea* a cutting; related to Greek *talis* girl of marriageable age]

tai·lor·bird ('teɪləˌbɜːd) *n.* any of several tropical Asian warblers of the genus *Orthotomus,* which build nests by sewing together large leaves using plant fibres.

tai·lor-made *adj.* **1.** made by a tailor to fit exactly: *a tailor-made suit.* **2.** perfectly meeting a particular purpose: *a girl tailor-made for him.* ~*n.* **3.** a tailor-made garment. **4.** *Slang.* a cigarette made in a factory rather than rolled by hand.

tai·lor's chalk *n.* pipeclay used by tailors and dressmakers to mark seams, darts, etc., on material.

tai·lor's-tack *n.* one of a series of loose looped stitches used to transfer markings for seams, darts, etc., from a paper pattern to material.

tail·piece ('teɪlˌpiːs) *n.* **1.** an extension or appendage that lengthens or completes something. **2.** *Printing.* a decorative design at the foot of a page or end of a chapter. **3.** *Music.* a piece of wood to which the strings of a violin, etc., are attached at their lower end. It is suspended between the taut strings and the bottom of the violin by a piece of gut or metal. **4.** Also called: **tail beam.** *Architect.* a short beam or rafter that has one end embedded in a wall.

tail·pipe ('teɪlˌpaɪp) *n.* a pipe from which the exhaust gases from an internal-combustion engine are discharged, esp. the terminal pipe of the exhaust system of a motor vehicle.

tail·plane ('teɪlˌpleɪn) *n.* a horizontal aerofoil at the tail of an aircraft to provide longitudinal stability. Also called (chiefly U.S.): **horizontal stabilizer.**

tail·race ('teɪlˌreɪs) *n.* **1.** a channel that carries water away from a waterwheel, turbine, etc. Compare **headrace. 2.** *Mining.* the channel for removing tailings in water.

tail ro·tor *n.* a small propeller fitted to the rear of a helicopter to counteract the torque reaction of the main rotor and thus prevent the body of the helicopter from rotating in an opposite direction.

tails (teɪlz) *pl. n.* **1.** an informal name for **tail coat.** ~*interj., adv.* **2.** with the reverse side of a coin uppermost: used as a call before tossing a coin. Compare **heads.**

tail·skid ('teɪlˌskɪd) *n.* **1.** a runner under the tail of an aircraft. **2.** a rear-wheel skid of a motor vehicle.

tail·spin ('teɪlˌspɪn) *n.* **1.** *Aeronautics.* another name for **spin** (sense 15). **2.** *Informal.* a state of confusion or panic.

tail·stock ('teɪlˌstɒk) *n.* a casting that slides on the bed of a lathe in alignment with the headstock and is locked in position to support the free end of workpiece.

tail wheel *n.* a wheel fitted to the rear of a vehicle, esp. the landing wheel under the tail of an aircraft.

tail·wind ('teɪlˌwɪnd) *n.* a wind blowing in the same direction as the course of an aircraft or ship. Compare **headwind.**

Tai·myr Pen·in·su·la (*Russian* taj'mɪr) *n.* a large peninsula of the N central Soviet Union, between the Kara Sea and the Laptev Sea. Also called: **Taymyr Peninsula.**

tain (teɪn) *n.* tin foil used in backing mirrors. [from French, from *étain* tin, from Old French *estain,* from Latin *stagnum* alloy of silver and lead; see STANNUM]

Tai·nan *or* **T'ai-nan** ('taɪ'næn) *n.* a city in the SW Republic of China (Taiwan): an early centre of Chinese emigration from the mainland; largest city and capital of the island (1638–1885); Chengkung University. Pop.: 461 838 (1969 est.).

Tai·na·ron ('tɛnarɔn) *n.* transliteration of the Modern Greek name for (Cape) **Matapan.**

Taine (*French* tɛn) *n.* **Hip·pol·yte A·dolphe** (ipɔlit a'dɔlf). 1828–93, French literary critic and historian. He applied determinist criteria to the study of literature, art, history, and psychology, regarding them as products of environment and race. His works include *Histoire de la littérature anglaise* (1863–64) and *Les Origines de la France contemporaine* (1875–93).

Tai·no ('taɪnəʊ) *n.* **1.** (*pl.* **·nos** *or* **·no**) a member of an extinct American Indian people of the Greater Antilles and the Bahamas. **2.** the language of this people, belonging to the Arawakan family.

taint (teɪnt) *vb.* **1.** to affect or be affected by pollution or contamination: *oil has tainted the water.* **2.** to tarnish (someone's reputation, etc.). ~*n.* **3.** a defect or flaw: *a taint on someone's reputation.* **4.** a trace of contamination or infection. [C14: (influenced by *attaint* infected, from ATTAIN) from Old French *teindre* to dye, from Latin *tingere* to dye] —**'taint·less** *adj.*

tai·pan ('taɪˌpæn) *n.* a large highly venomous elapid snake, *Oxyuranus scutellatus,* of NE Australia. [C20: from a native Australian language]

Tai·pei *or* **T'ai-pei** ('taɪ'peɪ) *n.* the capital of the Republic of China (Taiwan), at the N tip of the island: became capital in 1885; industrial centre; two universities. Pop.: 1 712 108 (1969 est.).

Tai·ping ('taɪ'pɪŋ) *n. History.* a person who supported or took part in the movement of religious mysticism and agrarian unrest in China between 1850 and 1864 (**Taiping rebellion**), which weakened the Manchu dynasty but was eventually suppressed with foreign aid. [C19: from Chinese, from *t'ai* great + *p'ing* peace]

Tai·sho (taɪ'ʃəʊ) *n.* **1.** the period of Japanese history and artistic style associated with the reign of Emperor Yoshihito (1912–26). **2.** the throne name of Yoshihito (1879–1926), emperor of Japan (1912–26).

Tai·wan ('taɪ'wɑːn) *n.* an island in SE Asia between the East China Sea and the South China Sea, off the SE coast of the People's Republic of China: the principal territory governed by the Nationalist government of China. —**ˌTai·wan·'ese** *adj., n.*

Tai·wan Strait *n.* another name for **Formosa Strait.**

Tai·yu·an *or* **T'ai-yü·an** ('taɪjuː'ɑːn) *n.* a city in N China, capital of Shansi: founded before 450 A.D.; an industrial centre, surrounded by China's largest reserves of high-grade bituminous coal. Pop.: 1 350 000 (1970 est.).

Ta·'izz (tæ'ɪz, teɪ'iːz) *n.* a town in SW Yemen: agricultural trading centre. Pop.: 80 000 (1972 est.).

taj (tɑːdʒ) *n.* a tall conical cap worn as a mark of distinction by Muslims. [via Arabic from Persian: crown, crest]

Ta·jik ('tɑːdʒɪk, tɑː'dʒiːk) *n., pl.* **·jik.** a variant spelling of **Tadzhik.**

Taj Ma·hal ('tɑːdʒ mə'hɑːl) *n.* a white marble mausoleum in central India, in Agra on the Jumna River: built (1632–43) by the emperor Shah Jahan in memory of his beloved wife, Mumtaz Mahal; regarded as the finest example of Mogul architecture.

Ta·jo ('taxo) *n.* the Spanish name for the **Tagus.**

ta·ka ('tɑːkɑː) *n.* the standard monetary unit of Bangladesh. [from Bengali]

ta·ka·he ('tɑːkəˌhiː) *n.* a very rare flightless New Zealand rail, *Notornis mantelli.* [from Maori, of imitative origin]

Tak·a·mat·su (ˌtækə'mætsuː) *n.* a port in SW Japan, on NE Shikoku on the Inland Sea. Pop.: 294 139 (1974 est.).

Ta·kao (tæ'kaʊ) *n.* the Japanese name for **Kaohsiung.**

take (teɪk) *vb.* **takes, tak·ing, took, tak·en.** (*mainly tr.*) **1.** (*also intr.*) to gain possession of (something) by force or effort. **2.** to appropriate or steal: *to take other people's belongings.* **3.** to receive or accept into a relationship with oneself: *to take a wife.* **4.** to pay for or buy. **5.** to rent or lease: *to take a flat in town.* **6.** to receive or obtain by regular payment: *we take a newspaper every day.* **7.** to obtain by competing for; win: *to take first prize.* **8.** to obtain or derive from a source: *he took his good manners from his older brother.* **9.** to assume the obligations of: *to take office.* **10.** to endure, esp. with fortitude: *to take punishment.* **11.** to adopt as a symbol of duty, obligation, etc.: *to take the veil.* **12.** to receive or react to in a specified way: *she took the news very well.* **13.** to adopt as one's own: *to take someone's part in a quarrel.* **14.** to receive and make use of: *to take advice.* **15.** to receive into the body, as by eating, inhaling, etc.: *to take a breath.* **16.** to eat, drink, etc., esp. habitually: *to take sugar in one's tea.* **17.** to have or be engaged in for one's benefit or use: *to take a rest.* **18.** to work at or study: *to take economics at college.* **19.** to make, do, or perform (an action): *to take a leap.* **20.** to make use of: *to take an opportunity.* **21.** to put into effect; adopt: *to take measures.* **22.** (*also intr.*) to make a photograph of or admit of being photographed. **23.** to act or perform: *she takes the part of the Queen.* **24.** to write down or copy: *to take notes.* **25.** to experience or feel: *to take pride in one's appearance; to take offence.* **26.** to consider, believe, or regard: *I take him to be honest.* **27.** to consider or accept as valid: *I take your point.* **28.** to hold or maintain in the mind: *his father took a dim view of his career.* **29.** to deal or contend with: *the tennis champion took her opponent's best strokes without difficulty.* **30.** to use as a particular case: *take hotels for example.* **31.** (*intr.*; often foll. by *from*) to diminish or detract: *the actor's bad performance took from the effect of the play.* **32.** to confront successfully: *the horse took the jump at the third attempt.* **33.** (*intr.*) to have or produce the intended effect; succeed: *her vaccination took; the glue is taking well.* **34.** (*intr.*) (of seeds, plants, etc.) to start growing successfully. **35.** to aim or direct: *he took a swipe at his opponent.* **36.** to deal a blow to in a specified place. **37.** *Archaic.* to have sexual intercourse with. **38.** to carry off or remove from a place. **39.** to carry along or have in one's possession: *don't forget to take your umbrella.* **40.** to convey or transport: *the train will take us out of the city.* **41.** to use as a means of transport: *I shall take the bus.* **42.** to conduct or lead: *this road takes you to the station.* **43.** to escort or accompany: *may I take you out tonight?* **44.** to bring or deliver to a state, position, etc.: *his ability took him to the forefront in his field.* **45.** to go to look for; seek: *to take cover.* **46.** to ascertain or determine by measuring, computing, etc.: *to take a pulse; take a reading from a dial.* **47.** (*intr.*) (of a mechanism) to catch or engage (a part). **48.** to put an end to; destroy: *she took her own life.* **49.** to come upon unexpectedly; discover. **50.** to contract: *he took a chill.* **51.** to affect or attack: *the fever took him one night.* **52.** (*copula*) to become suddenly or be rendered (ill): *he took sick; he was taken sick.* **53.** (*also intr.*) to absorb or become absorbed by something: *to take a polish.* **54.** (*usually passive*) to charm or captivate: *she was very taken with the puppy.* **55.** (*intr.*) to be or become popular; win favour. **56.** to require or need: *this job will take a lot of attention; that task will take all your time.* **57.** to subtract or deduct: *to take six from ten leaves four.* **58.** to hold or contain: *the suitcase won't take all your clothes.* **59.** to quote or copy: *he has taken several paragraphs from the book for his essay.* **60.** to proceed to occupy: *to take a seat.* **61.** (often foll. by *to*) to use or employ: *to take steps to ascertain the answer.* **62.** to win or capture (a trick, counter, piece, etc.). **63.** *Slang.* to cheat, deceive, or victimize. **64. take amiss.** to be annoyed or offended by. **65. take at one's word.** to believe to be true or truthful. **66. take care.** to pay attention; be heedful. **67. take care of.** to assume responsibility for; look after. **68. take chances** *or* **a chance.** to behave in a risky manner. **69. take five** (*or* **ten**). *Informal, chiefly U.S.* to take a break of five (or ten) minutes. **70. take heart.** to be encouraged. **71. take it.** *Informal.* to stand up to or endure criticism, abuse, harsh treatment, etc. **72. take one's time.** to use as much time as is needed; not rush. **73. take place.** to happen or occur. **74. take (someone's) name in vain. a.** to use a name, esp. of God, disrespectfully or irreverently. **b.** *Jocular.* to say a person's name. **75. take upon oneself.** to assume the right to do or responsibility for something. ~*n.* **76.** the act of taking. **77.** the number of quarry killed or captured on one occasion. **78.** *Informal, chiefly U.S.* the amount of anything taken, esp. money. **79.** *Films.* **a.** one of a series of recordings from which the best will be selected for general release. **b.** the process of taking one such recording. **c.** a scene or part of a scene photographed without interruption. **80.** *Informal.* **a.** any objective indication of a successful vaccination, such as a local skin reaction. **b.** a successful skin graft. **81.** *Printing.* a part of an article, story, etc., given to a compositor or keyboard operator for setting in type. **82.** *Informal.* a try or attempt. ~See also **take aback, take after, take apart, take back, take down, take for, take in, take off, take on, take out, take over, take to, take up.** [Old English *tacan,* from Old Norse *taka;* related to Gothic *tekan* to touch] —**'tak·a·ble** *or* **'take·a·ble** *adj.*

take a·back *vb.* (*tr., adv.*) to astonish or disconcert.

take af·ter *vb.* (*intr., prep.*) **1.** to resemble in appearance, character, behaviour, etc. **2.** to follow as an example.

take a·part *vb.* (*tr., adv.*) **1.** to separate (something) into component parts. **2.** to criticize or punish severely: *the reviewers took the new play apart.*

take·a·way ('teɪkəˌweɪ) *Brit.* ~*adj.* **1.** sold for consumption away from the premises on which it is prepared: *a takeaway meal.* **2.** preparing and selling food for consumption away from the premises: *a takeaway Indian restaurant.* ~*n.* **3.** a shop or restaurant that sells such food: *let's go to the Chinese takeaway.* ~U.S. word: **takeout.**

take back *vb.* (*adv., mainly tr.*) **1.** to retract or withdraw (something said, written, promised, etc.). **2.** to regain possession of. **3.** to return for exchange: *to take back a substandard garment.* **4.** (*also intr.*) *Printing.* to move (copy) to the previous line.

take down *vb.* (*tr., adv.*) **1.** to record in writing. **2.** to dismantle or tear down: *to take down an old shed.* **3.** to lower or reduce in power, arrogance, etc. (esp. in the phrase **to take down a peg**). ~*adj.* **take-down. 4.** made or intended to be disassembled.

take for *vb.* (*tr., prep.*) **1.** *Informal.* to consider or suppose to be, esp. mistakenly: *the fake coins were taken for genuine; who do you take me for?* **2. take for granted. a.** to accept or assume without question: *one takes certain amenities for granted.* **b.** to fail to appreciate the value, merit, etc., of (a person).

take-home pay *n.* the remainder of one's pay after all income tax and other compulsory deductions have been made.

take in *vb.* (*tr., adv.*) **1.** to comprehend or understand. **2.** to include or comprise: *his thesis takes in that point.* **3.** to receive into one's house in exchange for payment: *to take in washing; take in lodgers.* **4.** to make (an article of clothing, etc.) smaller by altering seams. **5.** *Informal.* to cheat or deceive. ~*n.* **take-in. 6.** *Informal.* the act or an instance of cheating or deceiving.

tak·en ('teɪkən) *vb.* **1.** the past participle of **take.** ~*adj.* **2.** (*postpositive* foll. by *with*) enthusiastically impressed (by); infatuated (with).

take off *vb.* (*adv.*) **1.** (*tr.*) to remove or discard (a garment). **2.** (*intr.*) (of an aircraft) to become airborne. **3.** *Informal.* to set out or cause to set out on a journey: *they took off for Spain.* **4.** (*tr.*) (of a disease) to prove fatal to; kill. **5.** (*tr.*) *Informal.* to mimic or imitate, esp. in an amusing or satirical manner. ~*n.* **take·off. 6.** the act or process of making an aircraft airborne. **7.** the stage of a country's economic development when rapid and sustained economic growth is first achieved. **8.** *Informal.* an act of mimicry; imitation.

take on *vb.* (*adv., mainly tr.*) **1.** to employ or hire: *to take on new workmen.* **2.** to assume or acquire: *his voice took on a plaintive note.* **3.** to agree to do; undertake: *I'll take on that job for you.* **4.** to compete against: *I will take him on at tennis.* **5.** (*intr.*) *Informal.* to exhibit great emotion, esp. of grief.

take out *vb.* (*tr., adv.*) **1.** to extract or remove. **2.** to obtain or secure (a licence, patent, etc.) from an authority. **3.** to go out with; escort: *George is taking Susan out next week.* **4.** *Bridge.* to bid a different suit from (one's partner) in order to rescue him from a difficult contract. **5.** *Austral. informal.* to win, esp. in sport: *he took out the tennis championship.* **6. take it** *or* **a lot out of.** *Informal.* to sap the energy or vitality of. **7. take out on.** *Informal.* to vent (anger, frustration, etc.) on, esp. on an innocent person. **8. take someone out of himself.** *Informal.* to make a person forget his anxieties, problems, etc. ~*adj.* **take·out. 9.** *Bridge.* of or designating a conventional informatory bid, asking one's partner to bid another suit. ~*adj., n.* **10.** an informal word (chiefly U.S.) for takeaway.

take o·ver *vb.* (*adv.*) **1.** to assume the control or management of. **2.** *Printing.* to move (copy) to the next line. ~*n.* **take·o·ver. 3.** the act of seizing or assuming power, control, etc. **4.** *Sport.* another word for **changeover** (sense 3).

tak·er ('teɪkə) *n.* a person who takes something, esp. a bet, wager, or offer of purchase.

take to *vb.* (*intr., prep.*) **1.** to make for; flee to: *to take to the hills.* **2.** to have a liking for, esp. after a short acquaintance: *I took to him straight away.* **3.** to have recourse to: *to take to the bottle.* **4. take to heart.** to regard seriously.

take up *vb.* (*adv., mainly tr.*) **1.** to adopt the study, practice, or activity of: *to take up gardening.* **2.** to shorten (a garment or part of a garment): *she took all her skirts up three inches.* **3.** to pay off (a note, mortgage, etc.). **4.** to agree to or accept (an invitation, etc.). **5.** to pursue further or resume (something): *he took up French where he left off.* **6.** to absorb (a liquid). **7.** to adopt as a protégé; act as a patron to. **8.** to occupy or fill (space or time). **9.** to interrupt, esp. in order to contradict or criticize. **10. take up on. a.** to argue or dispute with (someone): *can I take you up on two points in your talk?* **b.** to accept what is offered by (someone): *let me take you up on your invita-*

tion. **11. take up with. a.** to discuss with (someone); refer to: *to take up a fault with the manufacturers.* **b.** (*intr.*) to begin to keep company or associate with. ~*n.* **take-up. 12.** *Machinery.* the distance through which a part must move to absorb the free play in a system.

tak+in ('tɑːkiːn) *n.* a massive bovid mammal, *Budorcas taxicolor,* of mountainous regions of S Asia, having a shaggy coat, short legs, and horns that point backwards and upwards. [C19: from Mishmi]

tak+ing ('teɪkɪŋ) *adj.* **1.** charming, fascinating, or intriguing. **2.** *Informal.* infectious; catching. ~*n.* **3.** something taken. **4.** (*pl.*) receipts; earnings. —**'tak+ing+ly** *adv.* —**'tak+ing+ness** *n.*

Ta+ko+ra+di (ˌtɑːkəˈrɑːdɪ) *n.* the chief port of Ghana, in the southwest on the Gulf of Guinea: modern harbour opened in 1928. Pop.(with Sekondi): 161 071 (1970).

ta+la ('tɑːlə) *n.* the standard monetary unit of Western Samoa, divided into 100 sene.

Ta+laing (tɑːˈlaɪŋ) *n.* another name for **Mon.**

tal·a+poin ('tæləˌpɔɪn) *n.* **1.** the smallest of the guenon monkeys, *Cercopithecus talapoin,* of swampy central W African forests, having olive-green fur and slightly webbed digits. **2. a.** (in Burma and Siam) a Buddhist monk. **b.** a title of respect used in addressing such monks. [C16: from French, literally: Buddhist monk, from Portuguese *talapão,* from Mon *tala pōi* our lord; originally jocular, from the appearance of the monkey]

ta+lar·i·a (təˈlɛərɪə) *pl. n. Greek myth.* winged sandals, such as those worn by Hermes. [C16: from Latin, from *tālāris* belonging to the ankle, from *tālus* ankle]

Ta+la+ve·ra de la Rei+na (*Spanish* ˌtalaˈβera ðe la ˈreɪna) *n.* a walled town in central Spain, on the Tagus River: scene of the defeat of the French by British and Spanish forces (1809) during the Peninsular War; agricultural processing centre. Pop.: 46 412 (1970).

talc (tælk) *n. also* **tal+cum. 1.** See **talcum powder. 2.** a white, pale green, or grey soft greasy secondary mineral consisting of hydrated magnesium silicate and occurring in metamorphic rocks as micaceous flakes and as soapstone: used in the manufacture of ceramics and paints and as a filler, dusting agent, in talcum powder, etc. Formula: $Mg_3Si_4O_{10}(OH)_2$. ~*vb.* **talcs, talck+ing, talcked** *or* **talcs, talc+ing, talced. 3.** (*tr.*) to apply talc to. [C16: from Medieval Latin *talcum,* from Arabic *talq* mica, from Persian *talk*] —**'talc+ose** *or* **'tal+cous** *adj.*

Tal+ca (*Spanish* 'talka) *n.* a city in central Chile: scene of the declaration of Chilean independence (1818). Pop.: 115 130 (1975 est.).

Tal+ca+hua+no (*Spanish* ˌtalkaˈwano) *n.* a port in S central Chile, near Concepción on an inlet of the Pacific: oil refinery. Pop.: 183 591 (1975 est.).

tal+cum pow+der *n.* a powder made of purified talc, usually scented, used for perfuming the body and for absorbing excess moisture. Often shortened to **talc.**

tale (teɪl) *n.* **1.** a report, narrative, or story. **2.** one of a group of short stories connected by an overall narrative framework. **3. a.** a malicious or meddlesome rumour or piece of gossip: *to bear tales against someone.* **b.** (*in combination*): *talebearer; taleteller.* **4.** a fictitious or false statement. **5. tell tales. a.** to tell fanciful lies. **b.** to report malicious stories, trivial complaints, etc., esp. to someone in authority. **6. tell a tale.** to reveal something important. **7. tell its own tale.** to be self-evident. **8.** *Archaic.* **a.** a number; amount. **b.** computation or enumeration. **9.** an obsolete word for **talk.** [Old English *talu* list; related to Old Frisian *tele* talk, Old Saxon, Old Norse *tala* talk, number, Old High German *zala* number]

tal+ent ('tælənt) *n.* **1.** innate ability, aptitude, or faculty, esp. when unspecified; above average ability: *a talent for cooking; a child with talent.* **2.** a person or persons possessing such ability. **3.** any of various ancient units of weight and money. **4.** *Informal.* girls collectively, esp. those living in a particular place: *the local talent.* **5.** an obsolete word for **inclination.** [Old English *talente,* from Latin *talenta,* pl. of *talentum* sum of money, from Greek *talanton* unit of money or weight; in Medieval Latin the sense was extended to ability through the influence of the parable of the talents (Matthew 25:14–30)] —**'tal+ent+ed** *adj.*

tal+ent scout *n.* a person whose occupation is the search for talented artists, sportsmen, performers, etc., for engagements as professionals.

ta+ler ('tɑːlə) *n., pl.* **+ler** *or* **+lers.** a variant spelling of **thaler.**

ta+les ('teɪliːz) *n. Law.* **1.** a group of persons summoned from among those present in court or from bystanders to fill vacancies on a jury panel. **2.** the writ summoning such jurors. [C15: from Medieval Latin phrase *tālēs dē circumstantibus* such men from among the bystanders, from Latin *tālis* such] —**'ta+les+man** *n.*

Ta·li·es·in (ˌtælɪˈɛsɪn) *n.* 6th-century A.D. Welsh bard; supposed author of 12 heroic poems in the *Book of Taliesin.*

tal·i+grade ('tælɪˌgreɪd) *adj.* (of mammals) walking on the outer side of the foot. [C20: from New Latin, from Latin *tālus* ankle, heel + -GRADE]

tal·i·on ('tælɪən) *n.* the system or legal principle of making the punishment correspond to the crime; retaliation. [C15: via Old French from Latin *tāliō,* from *tālis* such]

tal·i+ped ('tælɪˌpɛd) *adj.* **1.** *Pathol.* having a club foot. ~*n.* **2.** a clubfooted person. [C19: see TALIPES]

tal·i+pes ('tælɪˌpiːz) *n.* **1.** a congenital deformity of the foot by which it is twisted in any of various positions. **2.** a technical name for **club foot.** [C19: New Latin, from Latin *tālus* ankle + *pēs* foot]

tal·i+pot *or* **tal·i+pot palm** ('tælɪˌpɒt) *n.* a palm tree, *Corypha umbraculifera,* of the East Indies, having large leaves that are used for fans, thatching houses, etc. [C17: from Bengali: palm leaf, from Sanskrit *tālī* fan palm + *pattra* leaf]

tal+is+man ('tælɪzmən) *n., pl.* **+mans. 1.** a stone or other small object, usually inscribed or carved, believed to protect the wearer from evil influences. **2.** anything thought to have magical or protective powers. [C17: via French or Spanish from Arabic *tilsam,* from Medieval Greek *telesma* ritual, from Greek: consecration, from *telein* to perform a rite, complete, from *telos* end, result] —**tal+is+man+ic** (ˌtælɪzˈmænɪk) *adj.*

talk (tɔːk) *vb.* **1.** (*intr.; often foll. by to or with*) to express one's thoughts, feelings, or desires by means of words (to); speak (to). **2.** (*intr.*) to communicate or exchange thoughts by other means: *lovers talk with their eyes.* **3.** (*intr.;* usually foll. by *about*) to exchange ideas, pleasantries, or opinions (about): *to talk about the weather.* **4.** (*intr.*) to articulate words; verbalize: *his baby can talk.* **5.** (*tr.*) to give voice to; utter: *to talk rubbish.* **6.** (*tr.*) to hold a conversation about; discuss: *to talk business.* **7.** (*intr.*) to reveal information: *the prisoner talked after torture.* **8.** (*tr.*) to know how to communicate in (a language or idiom): *he talks English.* **9.** (*intr.*) to spread rumours or gossip: *we don't want the neighbours to talk.* **10.** (*intr.*) to make sounds suggestive of talking. **11.** (*intr.*) to be effective or persuasive: *money talks.* **12. now you're talking.** *Informal.* at last you're saying something agreeable. **13. talk big.** to boast or brag. **14. talk shop.** to speak about one's work, esp. when meeting socially. **15. you can talk.** *Informal.* you don't have to worry about doing a particular thing yourself. **16. you can** *or* **can't talk.** *Informal.* you yourself are guilty of offending in the very matter you are upholding or decrying. ~*n.* **17.** a speech or lecture: *a talk on ancient Rome.* **18.** an exchange of ideas or thoughts: *a business talk with a colleague.* **19.** idle chatter, gossip, or rumour: *there has been a lot of talk about you two.* **20.** a subject of conversation; theme: *our talk was of war.* **21.** (*often pl.*) a conference, discussion, or negotiation: *talks about a settlement.* **22.** a specific manner of speaking: *children's talk.* ~See also **talk about, talk at, talk back, talk down, talk into, talk out, talk round.** [C13 *talkien* to talk; related to Old English *talu* TALE, Frisian *talken* to talk] —**'talk+a·ble** *adj.* —**ˌtalk·a+'bil+i·ty** *n.* —**'talk+er** *n.*

talk a·bout *vb.* (*intr., prep.*) **1.** to discuss. **2.** used informally and often ironically to add emphasis to a statement: *all his plays have such ridiculous plots—talk about good drama!* **3. know what one is talking about.** to have thorough or specialized knowledge.

talk at *vb.* (*intr., prep.*) to speak to (a person) in a way that indicates a response is not really wanted: *I wish he'd talk to me rather than at me.*

talk·a·tive ('tɔːkətɪv) *adj.* given to talking a great deal. —**'talk·a·tive+ly** *adv.* —**'talk·a+tive+ness** *n.*

talk back *vb.* **1.** (*intr., adv.*) to answer boldly or impudently. ~*n.* **talk+back. 2.** *Television, radio.* a system of telephone links enabling spoken directions to be given during the production of a programme.

talk down *vb.* (*adv.*) **1.** (*intr.;* often foll. by *to*) to behave (towards) in a superior or haughty manner. **2.** (*tr.*) to override (a person or argument) by continuous or loud talking. **3.** (*tr.*) to give instructions to (an aircraft) by radio to enable it to land.

talk·ie ('tɔːkɪ) *n. U.S. informal.* an early film with a soundtrack. Full name: **talking picture.**

talk+ing book *n.* a tape recording or gramophone record of a book, designed to be used by the blind.

talk·ing-to *n. Informal.* a session of criticism, as of the work or attitude of a subordinate by a person in authority.

talk in·to *vb.* (*tr., prep.*) to persuade to by talking: *I talked him into buying the house.*

talk out *vb.* (*adv.*) **1.** (*tr.*) to resolve or eliminate by talking: *they talked out their differences.* **2.** (*tr.*) *Brit.* to block (a bill, etc.) in a legislative body by lengthy discussion. **3. talk out of.** (*tr.*) to dissuade from by talking: *she was talked out of marriage.*

talk round *vb.* **1.** (*tr., adv.*) Also: **talk over.** to persuade to one's opinion: *I talked him round to buying a car.* **2.** (*intr., prep.*) to discuss the arguments relating to (a subject), esp. without coming to a conclusion: *to talk round the problem of the human condition.* **3.** (*intr., prep.*) to discuss (a subject) vaguely without considering basic facts: *they talked round the idea of moving house quite forgetting they hadn't enough money.*

talk show *n.* another name for **chat show.**

talk·y ('tɔːkɪ) *adj.* **talk+i·er, talk+i·est.** *U.S.* containing too much dialogue or inconsequential talk: *a talky novel.*

tall (tɔːl) *adj.* **1.** of more than average height. **2. a.** (*postpositive*) having a specified height: *a woman five feet tall.* **b.** (*in combination*): *a twenty-foot-tall partition.* **3.** *Informal.* exaggerated or incredible: *a tall story.* **4.** *Informal.* difficult to accomplish: *a tall order.* **5.** an archaic word for **excellent.** [C14 (in the sense: big, comely, valiant); related to Old English *getæl* prompt, Old High German *gizal* quick, Gothic *untals* foolish] —**'tall+ness** *n.*

tal+lage ('tælɪdʒ) *English history.* ~*n.* **1. a.** a tax levied by the Norman and early Angevin kings on their Crown lands and royal towns. **b.** a toll levied by a lord upon his tenants or by a feudal lord upon his vassals. ~*vb.* **2.** (*tr.*) to levy a tax; impose a tax (upon). [C13: from Old French *taillage,* from *taillier* to cut; see TAILOR]

Tal+la+has+see (ˌtæləˈhæsɪ) *n.* a city in N Florida, capital of the state: two universities. Pop.: 71 897 (1970).

tall+boy ('tɔːlˌbɔɪ) *n.* a high chest of drawers made in two sections and placed one on top of the other; chest-on-chest.

Tal·ley·rand-Pé·ri·gord ('tælɪ,rænd 'pɛrɪgɔː; *French* talɛrã peri'gɔːr) *n.* **Charles Mau·rice** (ʃarl mɔ'ris). 1754–1838, French statesman; foreign minister (1797–1807; 1814–15). He secretly negotiated with the Allies against Napoleon I from 1808 and was France's representative at the Congress of Vienna (1815).

Tal·linn *or* **Tal·lin** ('tælɪn) *n.* a port in the NW Soviet Union, capital of the Estonian SSR, on the Gulf of Finland: founded by the Danes in 1219; naval base. Pop.: 299 000 (1975 est.). German name: **Reval.**

Tal·lis ('tælɪs) *n.* **Thom·as.** ?1505–85, English composer and organist; noted for his arrangements of the liturgical music of the Church of England.

tal·lith ('tælɪθ; *Hebrew* ta'liːt) *n., pl.* **·lai·sim** (-'leɪsɪm), **·lith·es,** *or* **·li·toth** (*Hebrew* -liː'tɔt). **1.** a white shawl with fringed corners worn over the head and shoulders by Jewish males during religious services. **2.** a smaller form of this worn under the outer garment during waking hours by some Jewish males. [C17: from Hebrew *tallīt*]

tall oil *n.* any of various oily liquid mixtures obtained by acidifying the liquor resulting from the treatment of wood pulp with sodium hydroxide: it contains chiefly rosin acids and fatty acids and is used in making soaps and lubricants. [C20: partial translation of German *Tallöl,* from Swedish *tallolja,* from *tall* pine + *olja* OIL]

tal·low ('tæləʊ) *n.* **1.** a fatty substance consisting of a mixture of glycerides, including stearic, palmitic, and oleic acids and extracted chiefly from the suet of sheep and cattle: used for making soap, candles, food, etc. ~*vb.* **2.** (*tr.*) to cover or smear with tallow. [Old English *tælg,* a dye; related to Middle Low German *talch* tallow, Dutch *talk,* Icelandic *tólg*] —**'tal·low·y** *adj.*

tal·low wood *n. Austral.* a tall eucalyptus tree, *Eucalyptus microcorys,* of coastal regions, having soft fibrous bark and conical fruits and yielding a greasy timber.

tall pop·py *n. Austral. informal.* a person who has a high salary or is otherwise prominent.

tal·ly ('tælɪ) *vb.* **·lies, ·ly·ing, ·lied. 1.** (*intr.*) to correspond one with the other: *the two stories don't tally.* **2.** (*tr.*) to supply with an identifying tag. **3.** (*intr.*) to keep score. **4.** (*tr.*) *Obsolete.* to record or mark. ~*n., pl.* **·lies. 5.** any record of debit, credit, the score in a game, etc. **6.** a ticket, label, or mark, used as a means of identification, classification, etc. **7.** a counterpart or duplicate of something, such as the counterfoil of a cheque. **8.** a stick used (esp. formerly) as a record of the amount of a debt according to the notches cut in it. **9.** a notch or mark cut in or made on such a stick. **10.** a mark or number of marks used to represent a certain number in counting. [C15: from Medieval Latin *tālea,* from Latin: cutting; related to Latin *tālus* heel] —**'tal·li·er** *n.*

tal·ly-ho (,tælɪ'həʊ) *interj.* **1.** the cry of a participant at a hunt to encourage the hounds when the quarry is sighted. ~*n., pl.* **-hos. 2.** an instance of crying tally-ho. **3.** another name for a **four-in-hand** (sense 1). ~*vb.* **-hos, -ho·ing, -hoed** *or* **-ho'd. 4.** (*intr.*) to make the cry of tally-ho. [C18: perhaps from French *taïaut* cry used in hunting]

tal·ly·man ('tælɪmən) *n., pl.* **·men. 1.** a scorekeeper or recorder. **2.** *Dialect.* a travelling salesman for a firm specializing in hire-purchase. —**'tal·ly·,wom·an** *fem. n.*

Tal·mud ('tælmʊd) *n. Judaism.* **1.** the main authoritative compilation of ancient Jewish law and tradition comprising the Mishnah and the Gemara. **2.** either of two recensions of this compilation, the Palestinian Talmud of about 375 A.D., or the longer and more important Babylonian Talmud of about 500 A.D. [C16: from Hebrew *talmūdh,* literally: instruction, from *lāmadh* to learn] —**Tal·'mud·ic** *or* **Tal·'mud·i·cal** *adj.* —**'Tal·mud·ism** *n.*

Tal·mud·ist ('tælmʊdɪst) *n.* **1.** any of the writers of or contributors to the Talmud. **2.** a scholar specializing in the study of the Talmud. **3.** a person who accepts the authority of the Talmud or adheres to its teachings.

tal·on ('tælən) *n.* **1.** a sharply hooked claw, esp. of a bird of prey. **2.** anything resembling a bird's claw. **3.** the part of a lock that the key presses on when it is turned. **4.** *Piquet, etc.* the pile of cards left after the deal. **5.** *Architect.* another name for **ogee.** [C14: from Old French: heel, from Latin *tālus* heel] —**'ta·loned** *adj.*

Ta·los ('teɪlɒs) *n. Greek myth.* the nephew and apprentice of Daedalus, who surpassed his uncle as an inventor and was killed by him out of jealousy.

ta·luk ('tɑːlʊk, tɑː'lʊk), **ta·lu·ka,** *or* **ta·loo·ka** (tɑː'luːkə) *n.* (in India) **1.** a subdivision of a district; a group of several villages organized for revenue purposes. **2.** a hereditary estate. [C18: from Urdu *ta' alluk* estate, ultimately from Arabic]

ta·lus[1] ('teɪləs) *n., pl.* **·li** (-laɪ). the bone of the ankle that articulates with the leg bones to form the ankle joint. Nontechnical name: **anklebone.** [C18: from Latin: ankle]

ta·lus[2] ('teɪləs) *n., pl.* **·lus·es. 1.** *Geology.* another name for **scree. 2.** *Fortifications.* the sloping side of a wall. [C17: from French, from Latin *talūtium* slope, perhaps of Iberian origin]

tal·weg ('tɑːlvɛg) *n.* a variant spelling of **thalweg.**

tam (tæm) *n.* short for **tam-o'-shanter.**

TAM *abbrev. for* television audience measurement.

ta·ma·le (tə'mɑːlɪ) *n.* a Mexican dish made of minced meat mixed with crushed maize and seasonings, wrapped in maize husks and steamed. [C19: erroneously for *tamal,* from Mexican Spanish, from Nahuatl *tamalli*]

ta·man·du·a (,tæmən'dʊə) *or* **ta·man·du** ('tæmən,duː) *n.* a small toothless arboreal edentate mammal, *Tamandua tetradactyla,* of Central and South America, having a prehensile tail and tubular mouth specialized for feeding on termites: family *Myrmecophagidae.* Also called: **lesser anteater.** [C17: via Portuguese from Tupi: ant-trapper, from *taixi* ant + *mondê* to catch]

tam·a·rack ('tæmə,ræk) *n.* **1.** any of several North American larches, esp. *Larix laricina,* which has reddish-brown bark, bluish-green needle-like leaves, and shiny oval cones. **2.** the wood of any of these trees. [C19: from Algonquian]

ta·ma·rau *or* **ta·ma·rao** ('tæmə,raʊ) *n.* a small rare member of the cattle tribe, *Anoa mindorensis,* of lowland areas of Mindora in the Philippines. Compare **anoa.** [from Tagalog *tamaráw*]

tam·a·rin ('tæmərɪn) *n.* any of numerous small monkeys of the genera *Saguinus* (or *Leontocebus*) and *Leontideus,* of South and Central American forests; similar to the marmosets: family *Callithricidae.* [C18: via French from Galibi]

tam·a·rind ('tæmərɪnd) *or* **tam·a·rin·do** (,tæmə'rɪndəʊ) *n., pl.* **·rinds** *or* **·rin·dos. 1.** a caesalpiniaceous tropical evergreen tree, *Tamarindus indica,* having pale yellow red-streaked flowers and brown pulpy pods, each surrounded by a brittle shell. **2.** the acid fruit of this tree, used as a food and to make beverages and medicines. **3.** the wood of this tree. [C16: from Medieval Latin *tamarindus,* ultimately from Arabic *tamr hindī* Indian date, from *tamr* date + *hindī* Indian, from *Hind* India]

tam·a·risk ('tæmərɪsk) *n.* any of various ornamental trees and shrubs of the genus *Tamarix,* of the Mediterranean region and S and SE Asia, having scalelike leaves, slender branches, and feathery clusters of pink or whitish flowers: family *Tamaricaceae.* [C15: from Late Latin *tamariscus,* from Latin *tamarix*]

ta·ma·sha (tə'mɑːʃə) *n.* (in India) a show; entertainment. [C17: via Urdu from Arabic: a stroll, saunter]

Ta·ma·tave (*French* tama'taːv) *n.* a port in E Madagascar, on the Indian Ocean: the country's chief commercial centre. Pop.: 50 500 (1970 est.).

Ta·mau·li·pas (*Spanish* ,tamaʊ'lipas) *n.* a state of NE Mexico, on the Gulf of Mexico. Capital: Ciudad Victoria. Pop.: 1 456 858 (1970). Area: 79 829 sq. km (30 822 sq. miles).

tam·bac ('tæmbæk) *n.* a variant spelling of **tombac.**

Tam·bo·ra ('tæmbə,rɑː) *n.* a volcano in Indonesia, on N Sumbawa: violent eruption of 1815 reduced its height from about 4000 m (13 000 ft.) to 2850 m (9400 ft.).

tam·bour ('tæmbʊə) *n.* **1.** *Real tennis.* the sloping buttress on one side of the receiver's end of the court. **2.** a small round embroidery frame, consisting of two concentric hoops over which the fabric is stretched while being worked. **3.** embroidered work done on such a frame. **4.** a sliding door on desks, cabinets, etc., made of thin strips of wood glued side by side onto a canvas backing. **5.** *Architect.* a wall that is circular in plan, esp. one that supports a dome or one that is surrounded by a colonnade. **6.** a drum. ~*vb.* **7.** to embroider (fabric, a design) on a tambour. [C15: from French, from *tabour* TABOR]

tam·bour·a (tæm'bʊərə) *n.* an instrument with a long neck, four strings, and no frets, used in Indian music to provide a drone. [from Persian *tanbūr,* from Arabic *tunbūr*]

tam·bou·rin ('tæmbʊrɪn) *n.* **1.** an 18th-century Provençal folk dance. **2.** a piece of music composed for or in the rhythm of this dance. **3.** a small drum. [C18: from French: a little drum, from TAMBOUR]

tam·bou·rine (,tæmbə'riːn) *n. Music.* a percussion instrument consisting of a single drumhead of skin stretched over a circular wooden frame hung with pairs of metal discs that jingle when it is struck or shaken. [C16: from Middle Flemish *tamborijn* a little drum, from Old French: TAMBOURIN] —**,tam·bou·'rin·ist** *n.*

Tam·bov (*Russian* tam'bɔf) *n.* an industrial city in the W central Soviet Union: founded in 1636 as a Muscovite fort. Pop.: 257 000 (1975 est.).

Tam·bur·laine ('tæmbə,leɪn) *n.* a variant of **Tamerlane.**

tame (teɪm) *adj.* **1.** changed by man from a naturally wild state into a tractable, domesticated, or cultivated condition. **2.** (of animals) not fearful of human contact. **3.** lacking in spirit or initiative; meek or submissive: *a tame personality.* **4.** flat, insipid, or uninspiring: *a tame ending to a book.* **5.** slow-moving: *a tame current.* ~*vb.* (*tr.*) **6.** to make tame; domesticate. **7.** to break the spirit of, subdue, or curb. **8.** to tone down, soften, or mitigate. [Old English *tam;* related to Old Norse *tamr,* Old High German *zam*] —**'tam·a·ble** *or* **'tame·a·ble** *adj.* —**,tam·a·'bil·i·ty, ,tame·a·'bil·i·ty** *or* **'tam·a·ble·ness, 'tame·a·ble·ness** *n.* —**'tame·less** *adj.* —**'tame·ly** *adv.* —**'tame·ness** *n.* —**'tam·er** *n.*

Tam·er·lane ('tæmə,leɪn) *or* **Tam·bur·laine** *n.* Turkic name *Timur* (tiː'mʊə). ?1336–1405, Mongol conqueror of the area from Mongolia to the Mediterranean; ruler of Samarkand (1369–1405). He defeated the Turks at Angora (1402) and died while invading China.

Tam·il ('tæmɪl) *n., pl.* **·ils** *or* **·il. 1.** a member of a mixed Dravidian and Caucasoid people of S India and Sri Lanka. **2.** the language of this people: the state language of Madras, also spoken in Sri Lanka and elsewhere, belonging to the Dravidian family of languages. ~*adj.* **3.** of or relating to this people or their language.

Ta·mil Na·du ('tæmɪl nɑː'duː) *n.* a state of SE India, on the Coromandel Coast: reorganized in 1956 and 1960 and made smaller; consists of a coastal plain backed by hills, including the Nilgiri Hills in the west. Capital: Madras. Pop.: 41 199 168 (1971). Area: 130 357 sq. km (50 839 sq. miles). Former name (until 1968): **Madras.**

tam·is ('tæmɪ, -ɪs) *n., pl.* **·ises** (-ɪz, -ɪsɪz). a less common word for **tammy**[3].

Tam·ma·ny Hall ('tæmənɪ) *n. U.S. politics.* the central organization of the Democratic Party in New York county. Originally founded as a benevolent society (**Tammany Society**) in

1789, Tammany Hall was notorious for the corruption in city and state politics that it fostered in the 19th and early 20th centuries. Also called: **Tammany.** —'**Tam·ma·ny·ism** *n.* —'**Tam·ma·ny·ite** *n.*

Tam·mer·fors (ˌtamər'fɔrs) *n.* the Swedish name for **Tampere.**

Tam·muz *or* **Tham·muz** ('tæmu:z, -ʊz) *n.* the tenth month of the civil year and fourth of the ecclesiastical year in the Jewish calendar, falling in June and July. [from Hebrew, of Babylonian origin]

tam·my¹ ('tæmɪ) *n., pl.* **·mies.** a glazed woollen or mixed fabric, used for linings, undergarments, etc. [C17: of unknown origin]

tam·my² ('tæmɪ) *n., pl.* **·mies.** another word for **tam-o'-shanter.**

tam·my³ ('tæmɪ) *n., pl.* **·mies. 1.** Also called: **tammy cloth, tamis.** a rough-textured woollen cloth used for straining sauces, soups, etc. ~*vb.* **·mies, ·my·ing, ·mied. 2.** (*tr.*) to strain (sauce, soup, etc.) through a tammy. [C18: changed (through influence of TAMMY¹) from French *tamis*, perhaps of Celtic origin; compare Breton *tamouez* strainer]

tam-o'-shan·ter (ˌtæmə'ʃæntə) *n.* a Scottish brimless wool cap with a bobble in the centre, usually worn pulled down at one side. Also called: **tam, tammy.** [C19: named after the hero of Burns's poem *Tam O'Shanter* (1790)]

tamp¹ (tæmp) *vb.* (*tr.*) **1.** to force or pack down firmly by repeated blows. **2.** to pack sand, earth, etc. into (a drill hole) over an explosive. [C17: probably a back formation from *tampin* (obsolete variant of TAMPION), which was taken as being a present participle *tamping*]

tamp² (tæmp) *South Wales dialect.* ~*vb.* **1.** (*tr.*) to bounce (a ball). **2.** (*intr.;* usually foll. by *down*) to pour with rain. [probably special use of TAMP¹]

Tam·pa ('tæmpə) *n.* a port and resort in W Florida, on **Tampa Bay** (an arm of the Gulf of Mexico): two universities. Pop.: 275 643 (1973 est.).

tam·per¹ ('tæmpə) *vb.* (*intr.*) **1.** (usually foll. by *with*) to interfere or meddle. **2.** to use corrupt practices such as bribery or blackmail. **3.** (usually foll. by *with*) to attempt to influence or corrupt, esp. by bribery: *to tamper with the jury.* [C16: alteration of TEMPER (vb.)] —'**tam·per·er** *n.*

tam·per² ('tæmpə) *n.* **1.** a person or thing that tamps, esp. an instrument for packing down tobacco in a pipe. **2.** a casing around the core of a nuclear weapon to increase its efficiency by reflecting neutrons and delaying the expansion.

Tam·pe·re (*Finnish* 'tampɛrɛ) *n.* a city in SW Finland: the second largest town in Finland; textile manufacturing. Pop.: 164 292 (1973 est.). Swedish name: **Tammerfors.**

Tam·pi·co (*Spanish* tam'piko) *n.* a port and resort in E Mexico, in Tamaulipas on the Pánuco River: oil refining. Pop.: 222 188 (1975 est.).

tamp·ing *or* **tamp·ing mad** ('tæmpɪŋ) *adj.* (*postpositive*) *South Wales dialect.* very angry. [see TAMP¹]

tam·pi·on ('tæmpɪən) *or* **tom·pi·on** *n.* a plug placed in a gun's muzzle when the gun is not in use to keep out moisture and dust. [C15: from French: TAMPON]

tam·pon ('tæmpɒn) *n.* **1.** a plug of lint, cotton wool, cotton, etc., inserted into an open wound or body cavity to stop the flow of blood, absorb secretions, etc. ~*vb.* **2.** (*tr.*) to plug (a wound, etc.) with a tampon. [C19: via French from Old French *tapon* a little plug, from *tape* a plug, of Germanic origin] —'**tam·pon·age** *n.*

tam-tam *n.* another name for **gong** (sense 1). [from Hindi]

Tam·worth ('tæmwəθ) *n.* **1.** a market town in W central England, in SE Staffordshire. Pop.: 40 245 (1971). **2.** a city in SE Australia, in E central New South Wales: industrial centre of an agricultural region. Pop.: 25 360 (1975 est.).

tan¹ (tæn) *n.* **1.** the brown colour produced by the skin after intensive exposure to ultraviolet rays, esp. those of the sun. **2.** a light or moderate yellowish-brown colour. **3.** short for **tanbark.** ~*vb.* **tans, tan·ning, tanned. 4.** to go brown or cause to go brown after exposure to ultraviolet rays: *she tans easily.* **5.** to convert (a skin or hide) into leather by treating it with a tanning agent, such as vegetable tannins, chromium salts, fish oils, or formaldehyde. **6.** (*tr.*) *Slang.* to beat or flog. ~*adj.* **tan·ner, tan·nest. 7.** of the colour tan: *tan gloves.* **8.** used in or relating to tanning. [Old English *tannian* (unattested as infinitive, attested as *getanned*, past participle), from Medieval Latin *tannāre*, from *tannum* tanbark, perhaps of Celtic origin; compare Irish *tana* thin] —'**tan·na·ble** *adj.* —'**tan·nish** *adj.*

tan² (tæn) *n. abbrev. for* tangent (sense 2).

ta·na ('tɑ:nə) *n.* **1.** a small Madagascan lemur, *Phaner furcifer.* **2.** a large tree shrew, *Tupaia tana*, of Sumatra and Borneo. [C19: from Malay *tūpai tana* ground-squirrel]

Ta·na ('tɑ:nə) *n.* **1. Lake.** Also called: (Lake) **Tsana.** a lake in NW Ethiopia, on a plateau 1800 m (6000 ft.) high: the largest lake of Ethiopia; source of the Blue Nile. Area: 3673 sq. km (1418 sq. miles). **2.** a river in E Kenya, rising in the Aberdare Range and flowing in a wide curve east to the Indian Ocean: the longest river in Kenya. Length: 708 km (440 miles). **3.** a river in NE Norway, flowing generally northeast as part of the border between Norway and Finland to the Arctic Ocean by Tana Fjord. Length: about 320 km (200 miles). Finnish name: **Teno.**

Ta·nach *Hebrew.* (ta'nax) *n.* the Old Testament as used by Jews, divided into the Pentateuch (Torah), the Prophets, and the Hagiographa. [from Hebrew, acronym formed from *torāh* (the Pentateuch), *nebi'im* (the prophets), and *ketūbim* (the Hagiographa)]

tan·a·ger ('tænədʒə) *n.* any American songbird of the family *Thraupidae*, having a short thick bill and a brilliantly coloured male plumage. [C19: from New Latin *tanagra*, based on Tupi *tangara*]

Tan·a·gra ('tænəgrə) *n.* a town in ancient Boeotia, famous for terra-cotta figurines of the same name, first discovered in its necropolis.

Tan·a·na ('tænənɑ:) *n.* a river in central Alaska, rising in the Wrangell Mountains and flowing northwest to the Yukon River. Length: about 765 km (475 miles).

Ta·na·na·rive (*French* tanana'ri:v) *or* **An·ta·na·na·ri·vo** *n.* capital of Madagascar, on the central plateau: founded in the 17th century by a Hova chief; university (1961). Pop.: 347 466 (1971 est.).

tan·bark ('tænˌbɑ:k) *n.* the bark of certain trees, esp. the oak and hemlock, used as a source of tannin. Often shortened to **tan.**

Tan·cred ('tæŋkrɪd) *n.* died 1112, Norman hero of the First Crusade, who played a prominent part in the capture of Jerusalem (1099).

tan·dem ('tændəm) *n.* **1.** a bicycle with two sets of pedals and two saddles, arranged one behind the other for two riders. **2.** a two-wheeled carriage drawn by two horses harnessed one behind the other. **3.** a team of two horses so harnessed. **4.** any arrangement of two things in which one is placed behind the other. ~*adj.* **5.** *Brit.* used as, used in, or routed through an intermediate automatic telephone exchange: *a tandem exchange.* ~*adv.* **6.** one behind the other: *to ride tandem.* [C18: whimsical use of Latin *tandem* at length, to indicate a vehicle of elongated appearance]

Tan·djung·pri·ok *or* **Tan·jung·pri·ok** (ˌtændʒʊŋ'prɪɒk) *n.* a port in Indonesia, on the NW coast of Java adjoining the capital, Djakarta: a major shipping and distributing centre for the whole archipelago.

Tan·door·i (ˌtæn'dʊərɪ) *n.* an Indian method of cooking meat or vegetables on a spit in a clay oven. [from Urdu, from *tandoor* an oven]

tang (tæŋ) *n.* **1.** a strong taste or flavour: *the tang of the sea.* **2.** a pungent or characteristic smell: *the tang of peat fires.* **3.** a trace, touch, or hint of something: *a tang of cloves in the apple pie.* **4.** the pointed end of a tool, such as a chisel, file, knife, etc., which is fitted into a handle, shaft, or stock. [C14: from Old Norse *tangi* point; related to Danish *tange* point, spit]

Tang (tæŋ) *n.* the imperial dynasty of China from 618–907 A.D.

Tan·ga ('tæŋgə) *n.* a port in N Tanzania, on the Indian Ocean: Tanzania's second port. Pop.: 61 058 (1967).

Tan·gan·yi·ka (ˌtæŋgə'nji:kə) *n.* **1.** a former state in E Africa: became part of German East Africa in 1884; ceded to Britain as a League of Nations mandate in 1919 and as a UN trust territory in 1946; gained independence in 1961 and united with Zanzibar in 1964 as the United Republic of Tanzania. **2. Lake.** a lake in central Africa between Tanzania and Zaïre, bordering also on Burundi and Zambia, in the Great Rift Valley: the longest freshwater lake in the world. Area: 32 893 sq. km (12 700 sq. miles). Length: 676 km (420 miles). —ˌ**Tan·gan·'yi·kan** *adj., n.*

tan·ge·lo ('tændʒəˌləʊ) *n., pl.* **·los. 1.** a hybrid produced by crossing a tangerine tree with a grapefruit tree. **2.** the fruit of this hybrid, having orange acid-tasting flesh. [C20: from TANG(ERINE) + (POM)ELO]

tan·gent ('tændʒənt) *n.* **1.** a geometric line, curve, plane, or curved surface that touches another curve or surface at one point but does not intersect it. **2.** (of an angle) a trigonometric function that in a right-angled triangle is the ratio of the length of the opposite side to that of the adjacent side; the ratio of sine to cosine. Abbrev.: **tan. 3.** the straight part on a survey line between curves. **4.** *Music.* a part of the action of a clavichord consisting of a small piece of metal that strikes the string and curtails its vibrations almost immediately. **5. on** *or* **at a tangent.** on a completely different or divergent course, esp. of thought: *to go off at a tangent.* ~*adj.* **6. a.** of or involving a tangent. **b.** touching at a single point. **7.** touching. **8.** almost irrelevant. [C16: from Latin phrase *līnea tangēns* the touching line, from *tangere* to touch] —'**tan·gen·cy** *n.*

tan·gent gal·va·nom·e·ter *n.* a type of galvanometer having a vertical coil of wire with a horizontal magnetic needle at its centre. The current to be measured is passed through the coil and produces a proportional magnetic field which deflects the needle.

tan·gen·tial (tæn'dʒɛnʃəl) *adj.* **1.** of, being, relating to, or in the direction of a tangent. **2.** Also: **transverse.** *Astronomy.* (of velocity) in a direction perpendicular to the line of sight of a celestial object. Compare **radial** (sense 6). **3.** of superficial relevance only; digressive. —**tan·ˌgen·ti·'al·i·ty** *n.* —**tan·'gen·tial·ly** *or* **tan·'gen·tal·ly** *adv.*

tan·ge·rine (ˌtændʒə'ri:n) *n.* **1.** an Asian citrus tree, *Citrus reticulata*, cultivated for its small edible orange-like fruits. **2.** the fruit of this tree, having a loose rind and sweet spicy flesh. **3. a.** a reddish-orange colour. **b.** (*as adj.*): *a tangerine door.* [C19: from TANGIER]

tan·gi·ble ('tændʒəbəl) *adj.* **1.** capable of being touched or felt; having real substance: *a tangible object.* **2.** capable of being clearly grasped by the mind; substantial rather than imaginary: *tangible evidence.* **3.** having a physical existence; corporeal: *tangible property.* ~*n.* **4.** (*often pl.*) a tangible thing or asset. [C16: from Late Latin *tangibilis*, from Latin *tangere* to touch] —ˌ**tan·gi·'bil·i·ty** *or* '**tan·gi·ble·ness** *n.* —'**tan·gi·bly** *adv.*

Tan·gier (tæn'dʒɪə) *n.* a port in N Morocco, on the Strait of Gibraltar: a Phoenician trading post in the 15th century B.C.; a neutral international zone (1923–56); made the summer capital of Morocco and a free port in 1962; commercial and financial centre. Pop.: 187 994 (1971). —ˌTan+ge+ˈrine *n., adj.*

tan+gle (ˈtæŋgᵊl) *n.* **1.** a confused or complicated mass of hairs, lines, fibres, etc., knotted or coiled together. **2.** a complicated problem, condition, or situation. ~*vb.* **3.** to become or cause to become twisted together in a confused mass. **4.** (*intr.;* often foll. by *with*) to come into conflict; contend: *to tangle with the police.* **5.** (*tr.*) to involve in matters which hinder or confuse: *to tangle someone in a shady deal.* **6.** (*tr.*) to ensnare or trap, as in a net. [C14 *tangilen,* variant of *tagilen,* probably of Scandinavian origin; related to Swedish dialect *taggla* to entangle] —ˈ**tan+gle+ment** *n.* —ˈ**tan+gler** *n.* —ˈ**tan+gly** *adj.*

tan·gle+ber·ry (ˈtæŋgᵊlbərɪ, -ˌbɛrɪ) *n., pl.* **·ries.** another name for **dangleberry.**

tan+go (ˈtæŋgəʊ) *n., pl.* **+gos. 1.** a Latin-American dance in duple time, characterized by long gliding steps and sudden pauses. **2.** a piece of music composed for or in the rhythm of this dance. ~*vb.* **+goes, +go+ing, +goed. 3.** (*intr.*) to perform this dance. [C20: from American Spanish, probably of Niger-Congo origin; compare Ibibio *tamgu* to dance] —ˈ**tan+go+ist** *n.*

tan+gram (ˈtæŋgræm) *n.* a Chinese puzzle in which a square, cut into a parallelogram, a square, and five triangles, is formed into figures. [C19: perhaps from Chinese *t'ang* Chinese + -GRAM]

Tang+shan (ˈtæŋˈʃæn) *n.* an industrial city in NE China, in Hopei province. Pop.: 950 000 (1970 est.).

Tan·guy (*French* tãˈgi) *n.* **Yves** (iːv). 1900–55, U.S. surrealist painter, born in France.

tang·y (ˈtæŋɪ) *adj.* **tang·i+er, tang·i+est.** having a pungent, fresh, or briny flavour or aroma: *a tangy sea breeze.*

tanh (θæn, tænʃ) *n.* hyperbolic tangent; a hyperbolic function that is the ratio of sinh to cosh. [C20: from TAN(GENT) + H(YPERBOLIC)]

Ta+nis (ˈteɪnɪs) *n.* an ancient city located in the E part of the Nile delta: abandoned after the 6th century B.C.; at one time the capital of Egypt. Biblical name: **Zoan.**

tan+ist (ˈtænɪst) *n. History.* the heir apparent of a Celtic chieftain chosen by election during the chief's lifetime: usually the worthiest of his kin. [C16: from Irish Gaelic *tānaiste,* literally: the second person] —ˈ**tan+ist+ry** *n.*

Tan+jore (tænˈdʒɔː) *n.* the former name of **Thanjavur.**

Tan+jung+pri+ok (ˌtændʒʊŋˈprɪɒk) *n.* a variant spelling of **Tandjungpriok.**

tank (tæŋk) *n.* **1.** a large container or reservoir for the storage of liquids or gases: *tanks for storing oil.* **2. a.** an armoured combat vehicle moving on tracks and armed with guns, etc. **b.** (*as modifier*): *a tank commander; a tank brigade.* **3.** *Brit. or U.S. dialect.* a reservoir, lake, or pond. **4.** *Photog.* **a.** a light-tight container inside which a film can be processed in daylight, the solutions and rinsing waters being poured in and out without light entering. **b.** any large dish or container used for processing a number of strips or sheets of film. **5.** *Slang, chiefly U.S.* **a.** a jail. **b.** a jail cell. **6.** Also called: **tankful.** the quantity contained in a tank. **7.** *Austral.* a dam formed by excavation. ~*vb.* **8.** (*tr.*) to put or keep in a tank. **9.** (*intr.*) to move like a tank, esp. heavily and rapidly. ~See also **tank up.** [C17: from Gujarati *tānkh* artificial lake, but influenced also by Portuguese *tanque,* from *estanque* pond, from *estancar* to dam up, from Vulgar Latin *stanticāre* (unattested) to block, STANCH] —ˈ**tank+less** *adj.* —ˈ**tank+ˌlike** *adj.*

tan+ka (ˈtɑːŋkə) *n., pl.* **+kas** *or* **+ka.** a Japanese verse form consisting of five lines, the first and third having five syllables, the others seven. [C19: from Japanese, from *tan* short + *ka* verse]

tank+age (ˈtæŋkɪdʒ) *n.* **1.** the capacity or contents of a tank or tanks. **2.** the act of storing in a tank or tanks, or a fee charged for such storage. **3.** *Agriculture.* **a.** fertilizer consisting of the dried and ground residues of animal carcasses. **b.** a protein supplement feed for livestock.

tank+ard (ˈtæŋkəd) *n.* **a.** a large one-handled drinking vessel, commonly made of silver, pewter, or glass, sometimes fitted with a hinged lid. **b.** the quantity contained in a tankard. [C14: related to Middle Dutch *tankaert,* French *tanquart*]

tank en+gine *or* **lo+co+mo+tive** *n.* a steam locomotive that carries its water supply in tanks mounted around its boiler.

tank+er (ˈtæŋkə) *n.* a ship, lorry, or aeroplane designed to carry liquid in bulk, such as oil.

tank farm+ing *n.* another name for **hydroponics.** —**tank farm+er** *n.*

tank top *n.* a sleeveless upper garment with wide shoulder straps and a low neck, usually worn over a shirt, blouse, or jumper. [C20: named after *tank suits,* one-piece bathing costumes of the 1920s worn in tanks or swimming pools]

tank up *vb.* (*adv.*) *Chiefly Brit.* **1.** to fill the tank of (a vehicle) with petrol. **2.** *Slang.* to imbibe or cause to imbibe a large quantity of alcoholic drink.

tank wag+on *or esp. U.S.* **tank car** *n.* a form of railway wagon carrying a tank for the transport of liquids.

tan+nage (ˈtænɪdʒ) *n.* **1.** the act or process of tanning. **2.** a skin or hide that has been tanned.

tan+nate (ˈtæneɪt) *n.* any salt or ester of tannic acid.

Tan+nen+berg (*German* ˈtanənˌbɛrk) *n.* a village in N Poland, formerly in East Prussia: site of a decisive German victory over the Russians in 1914. Polish name: **Stębark.**

tan+ner[1] (ˈtænə) *n.* a person who tans skins and hides.

tan+ner[2] (ˈtænə) *n. Brit.* an informal word for **sixpence.** [C19: of unknown origin]

tan+ner·y (ˈtænərɪ) *n., pl.* **+ner·ies.** a place or building where skins and hides are tanned.

Tann·häu·ser (ˈtænˌhɔɪzə) *n.* 13th-century German minnesinger, commonly identified with a legendary knight who sought papal absolution after years spent in revelry with Venus. The legend forms the basis of an opera by Wagner.

tan+nic (ˈtænɪk) *adj.* of, relating to, containing, or produced from tan, tannin, or tannic acid.

tan+nin (ˈtænɪn) *n.* any of a class of yellowish or brownish solid compounds found in many plants and used as tanning agents, mordants, medical astringents, etc. Tannins are derivatives of gallic acid with the approximate formula $C_{76}H_{52}O_{46}$. Also called: **tannic acid.** [C19: from French *tanin,* from TAN]

tan+sy (ˈtænzɪ) *n., pl.* **+sies. 1.** any of numerous plants of the genus *Tanacetum,* esp. *T. vulgare,* having yellow flowers in flat-topped clusters and formerly used in medicine and for seasoning: family *Compositae* (composites). **2.** any of various similar plants. [C15: from Old French *tanesie,* from Medieval Latin *athanasia* tansy (with reference to its alleged power to prolong life), from Greek: immortality]

Tan+ta (ˈtæntə) *n.* a city in N Egypt, on the Nile delta: noted for its Muslim festivals. Pop.: 278 300 (1974 est.).

tan+ta+late (ˈtæntəˌleɪt) *n.* any of various salts of tantalic acid formed when the pentoxide of tantalum dissolves in an alkali.

tan+tal+ic (tænˈtælɪk) *adj.* of or containing tantalum, esp. in the pentavalent state.

tan+tal+ic ac+id *n.* a white gelatinous substance produced by hydrolysis of tantalic halides. It dissolves in strong bases to give tantalates.

tan+ta+lite (ˈtæntəˌlaɪt) *n.* a heavy brownish mineral consisting of a tantalum oxide of iron and manganese in orthorhombic crystalline form: it occurs in coarse granite, often with columbite, and is an ore of tantalum. Formula: $(Fe,Mn)(Ta,Nb)_2O_6$. [C19: from TANTALUM + -ITE[1]]

tan+ta+lize *or* **tan+ta+lise** (ˈtæntəˌlaɪz) *vb.* (*tr.*) to tease or make frustrated, as by tormenting with the sight of something greatly desired but inaccessible. [C16: from the punishment of TANTALUS] —ˌ**tan+ta+li+ˈza+tion** *or* ˌ**tan+ta+li+ˈsa+tion** *n.* —ˈ**tan+ta+ˌliz+er** *or* ˈ**tan+ta+ˌlis+er** *n.* —ˈ**tan+ta+ˌliz+ing+ly** *or* ˈ**tan+ta+ˌlis+ing+ly** *adv.*

tan+ta+lous (ˈtæntələs) *adj.* of or containing tantalum in the trivalent state. [C19: from TANTAL(UM) + -OUS]

tan+ta+lum (ˈtæntələm) *n.* a hard greyish-white metallic element that occurs with niobium in tantalite and columbite: used in electrolytic rectifiers and in alloys to increase hardness and chemical resistance, esp. in surgical instruments. Symbol: Ta; atomic no.: 73; atomic wt.: 180.95; valency: 2,3,4, or 5; relative density: 16.65; melting pt.: 2996°C; boiling pt.: 5425°C. [C19: named after TANTALUS, with reference to the metal's incapacity to absorb acids]

tan+ta+lus (ˈtæntələs) *n. Brit.* a case in which bottles may be locked with their contents tantalizingly visible.

Tan·ta·lus (ˈtæntələs) *n. Greek myth.* a king, the father of Pelops, punished in Hades for his misdeeds by having to stand in water that recedes when he tries to drink it and under fruit that moves away as he reaches for it.

tan+ta+mount (ˈtæntəˌmaʊnt) *adj.* (*postpositive;* foll. by *to*) as good (as); equivalent in effect (to): *his statement was tantamount to an admission of guilt.* [C17: basically from Anglo-French *tant amunter* to amount to as much, from *tant* so much + *amunter* to AMOUNT]

tan+ta+ra (ˈtæntərə, tænˈtɑːrə) *n.* a fanfare or blast, as on a trumpet or horn. [C16: from Latin *taratantara,* imitative of the sound of the tuba]

tan+tiv·y (tænˈtɪvɪ) *adv.* **1.** at full speed; rapidly. ~*n., pl.* **+tiv·ies.** *interj.* **2.** a hunting cry, esp. at full gallop. [C17: perhaps imitative of galloping hoofs]

tant mieux *French.* (tã ˈmjø) so much the better.

tan+to (ˈtæntəʊ; *Italian* ˈtanto) *adv.* too much; excessively: *allegro ma non tanto.* See **non troppo.** [C19: from Italian, from Latin *tantum* so much]

tant pis *French.* (tã ˈpi) so much the worse.

Tan+tra (ˈtæntrə, ˈtʌn-) *n. Hinduism, Buddhism.* the sacred books of Tantrism, written between the 7th and 17th centuries A.D., mainly in the form of a dialogue between Siva and his wife. [C18: from Sanskrit: warp, hence underlying principle, from *tanoti* he weaves]

Tan+trism (ˈtæntrɪzəm) *n.* **1.** a movement within Hinduism combining magical and mystical elements and with sacred writings of its own. **2.** a similar movement within Buddhism. [C18: from Sanskrit *tantra,* literally: warp, hence, doctrine] —ˈ**Tan+tric** *adj.* —ˈ**Tan+trist** *n.*

tan+trum (ˈtæntrəm) *n.* (*often pl.*) a childish fit of rage; outburst of bad temper. [C18: of unknown origin]

Tan+za+ni·a (ˌtænzəˈnɪə) *n.* a republic in E Africa, on the Indian Ocean: formed by the union of the independent states of Tanganyika and Zanzibar in 1964; a member of the Commonwealth. Exports include sisal, cotton, and coffee. Official languages: English and Swahili. Religion: Muslim, Christian, and animist. Currency: Tanzanian shilling. Capital: Dar es Salaam. Pop.: 12 313 469 (1967). Area: 945 203 sq. km (364 943 sq. miles). —ˌ**Tan+za+ˈni·an** *adj., n.*

Ta·o (ˈtɑːəʊ) *n.* (in the philosophy of Taoism) **1.** that in virtue of which all things happen or exist. **2.** the rational basis of human conduct. **3.** the course of life and its relation to eternal truth. [Chinese, literally: path, way]

Ta·o+ism (ˈtɑːəʊˌɪzəm) *n.* **1.** the philosophy of Lao-tse that advocates a simple honest life and noninterference with the course of natural events. **2.** a popular Chinese system of religion and philosophy claiming to be teachings of Lao-tse but also incorporating pantheism and sorcery. —**'Ta·o+ist** *n., adj.* —**,Ta·o+'is+tic** *adj.*

tap^{1} (tæp) *vb.* **taps, tap+ping, tapped. 1.** to strike (something) lightly and usually repeatedly: *to tap the table; to tap on the table.* **2.** to produce by striking in this way: *to tap a rhythm.* **3.** (*tr.*) to strike lightly with (something): *to tap one's finger on the desk.* **4.** (*intr.*) to walk with a tapping sound: *she tapped across the floor.* **5.** (*tr.*) to attach metal or leather reinforcing pieces to (the toe or heel of a shoe). ~*n.* **6.** a light blow or knock, or the sound made by it. **7.** the metal piece attached to the toe or heel of a shoe used for tap dancing. **8.** short for **tap dancing. 9.** *Phonetics.* the contact made between the tip of the tongue and the alveolar ridge as the tongue is flicked upwards in the execution of a flap or vibrates rapidly in the execution of a trill or roll. [C13 *tappen,* probably from Old French *taper,* of Germanic origin; related to Middle Low German *tappen* to pluck, Swedish dialect *täpa* to tap] —**'tap+pa·ble** *adj.*

tap^{2} (tæp) *n.* **1.** a valve by which a fluid flow from a pipe can be controlled by opening and closing an orifice. U.S. name: **faucet. 2.** a stopper to plug a cask or barrel and enable the contents to be drawn out in a controlled flow. **3.** a particular quality of alcoholic drink, esp. when contained in casks: *an excellent tap.* **4.** *Brit.* short for **taproom. 5.** the surgical withdrawal of fluid from a bodily cavity: *a spinal tap.* **6.** a tool for cutting female screw threads, consisting of a threaded steel cylinder with longitudinal grooves forming cutting edges. Compare **die**^{2} (sense 2). **7.** *Electronics, chiefly U.S.* a connection made at some point between the end terminals of an inductor, resistor, or some other component. Usual Brit. name: **tapping. 8.** a concealed listening or recording device connected to a telephone or telegraph wire for the purpose of obtaining information secretly. **9. on tap. a.** *Informal.* ready for immediate use. **b.** (of drinks) on draught. ~*vb.* **taps, tap+ping, tapped.** (*tr.*) **10.** to furnish with a tap. **11.** to draw off with or as if with a tap. **12.** *Brit. slang.* to ask or beg (someone) for money: *he tapped me for a fiver.* **13. a.** to connect a tap to (a telephone or telegraph wire). **b.** to listen in secret to (a telephone message, etc.) by means of a tap. **14.** to make a connection to (a pipe, drain, etc.). **15.** to cut a female screw thread in (an object or material) by use of a tap. **16.** to withdraw (fluid) from (a bodily cavity). [Old English *tæppa;* related to Old Norse *tappi* tap, Old High German *zapfo*] —**'tap+pa·ble** *adj.* —**'tap+per** *n.*

ta·pa ('tɑːpə) *n.* **1.** the inner bark of the paper mulberry. **2.** a paper-like cloth made from this in the Pacific islands. [C19: from Marquesan and Tahitian]

tap·a+der+a (,tæpə'dɛərə) *n.* the leather covering for the stirrup on an American saddle. [via American Spanish from Spanish: cover, from *tapar* to cover, of Germanic origin; compare TAMPON, TAP^{2}]

Ta+pa+jós (*Portuguese* ,tapa'ʒɔs) *n.* a river in N Brazil, rising in N central Mato Grosso and flowing northeast to the Amazon. Length: about 800 km (500 miles).

tap dance *n.* **1.** a step dance in which the performer wears shoes equipped with taps that make a rhythmic sound on the stage as he dances. ~*vb.* (*intr.*) **tap-dance. 2.** to perform a tap dance. —**'tap-,dan+cer** *n.*

tape (teɪp) *n.* **1.** a long thin strip, made of cotton, linen, etc., used for binding, fastening, etc. **2.** any long narrow strip of cellulose, paper, metal, etc., having similar uses. **3.** a string stretched across the track at the end of a race course. **4.** See **magnetic tape, ticker tape, paper tape, tape recording.** ~*vb.* (*mainly tr.*) **5.** to furnish with tapes. **6.** to bind, measure, secure, or wrap with tape. **7.** (*usually passive*) *Brit. informal.* to take stock of (a person or situation); sum up: *he's got the job taped.* **8.** (*also intr.*) Also: **tape-record.** to record (speech, music, etc.). [Old English *tæppe;* related to Old Frisian *tapia* to pull, Middle Dutch *tapen* to tear] —**'tape+,like** *adj.* —**'tap+er** *n.*

tape deck *n.* the platform supporting the spools, cassettes, or cartridges of a tape recorder, incorporating the motor or motors that drive them and the playback, recording, and erasing heads. Sometimes shortened to **deck.**

tape grass *n.* any of several submerged freshwater plants of the genus *Vallisneria,* esp. *V. spiralis,* of warm temperate regions, having ribbon-like leaves: family *Hydrocharitaceae.*

tape ma+chine *n. Stock Exchange.* a telegraphic receiving device that records current stock quotations electronically or on ticker tape. U.S. equivalent: **ticker.**

tape meas+ure *n.* a tape or length of metal marked off in inches, centimetres, etc., used principally for measuring and fitting garments. Also called (esp. U.S.): **tapeline.**

ta+per ('teɪpə) *vb.* **1.** to become or cause to become narrower towards one end: *the spire tapers to a point.* **2.** to become or cause to become smaller or less significant. ~*n.* **3.** a thin candle. **4.** a thin wooden or waxed strip for transferring a flame; spill. **5.** a narrowing. **6.** any feeble source of light. [Old English *tapor,* probably from Latin *papȳrus* PAPYRUS (from its use as a wick)] —**'ta+per+er** *n.* —**'ta+per+ing+ly** *adv.*

tape re+cord+er *n.* an electrical device used for recording sounds on magnetic tape and usually also for reproducing them, consisting of a tape deck and one or more amplifiers and loudspeakers.

tape re+cord+ing *n.* **1.** the act or process of recording on magnetic tape. **2.** the magnetized tape used in making such a recording. **3.** the speech, music, etc., so recorded.

tap+es+try ('tæpɪstrɪ) *n., pl.* **+tries. 1.** a heavy ornamental fabric, often representing a picture, used for wall hangings, furnishings, etc., and made by weaving coloured threads into a fixed warp. **2.** another word for **needlepoint.** [C15: from Old French *tapisserie* carpeting, from Old French *tapiz* carpet; see TAPIS] —**'tap+es+tried** *adj.* —**'tap·es·try-,like** *adj.*

ta+pe·tum (tə'piːtəm) *n., pl.* **·ta** (-tə). **1.** a layer of nutritive cells in the sporangia of ferns and anthers of flowering plants that surrounds developing spore cells. **2.** a membranous reflecting layer of cells in the choroid of the eye of nocturnal vertebrates. [C18: from New Latin, from Medieval Latin: covering, from Latin *tapēte* carpet, from Greek *tapēs* carpet] —**ta+'pe·tal** *adj.*

tape+worm ('teɪp,wɜːm) *n.* any parasitic ribbon-like flatworm of the class *Cestoda,* having a body divided into many egg-producing segments and lacking a mouth and gut. The adults inhabit the intestines of vertebrates. See also **echinococcus, taenia.**

tap+hole ('tæp,həʊl) *n.* a hole in a furnace for running off molten metal or slag.

tap+house ('tæp,haʊs) *n. Now rare.* an inn or bar.

tap·i·o+ca (,tæpɪ'əʊkə) *n.* a beadlike starch obtained from cassava root, used in cooking as a thickening agent, esp. in puddings. [C18: via Portuguese from Tupi *tipioca* pressed-out juice, from *tipi* residue + *ok* to squeeze out]

ta+pir ('teɪpə) *n., pl.* **+pirs** *or* **+pir.** any perissodactyl mammal of the genus *Tapirus,* such as *T. indicus* (**Malayan tapir**), of South and central America and SE Asia, having an elongated snout, three-toed hind legs, and four-toed forelegs: family *Tapiridae.* [C18: from Tupi *tapiira*]

tap+is ('tæpiː, 'tæpɪ; *French* ta'pi) *n., pl.* **tap+is. 1.** tapestry or carpeting, esp. as formerly used to cover a table in a council chamber. **2. on the tapis.** currently under consideration or discussion. [C17: from French, from Old French *tapiz,* from Greek *tapētion* rug, from *tapēs* carpet]

tap+pet ('tæpɪt) *n.* a mechanical part that reciprocates to receive or transmit intermittent motion, esp. the part of an internal-combustion engine that transmits motion from the camshaft to the push rods or valves. [C18: from TAP^{1} + -ET]

tap·pit-hen ('tæpɪt,hɛn) *n. Scot.* **1.** a hen with a crest. **2.** a pewter tankard, usually with a distinctive knob on the lid. [C18: from Scottish *tappit* topped + HEN]

tap+room ('tæp,ruːm, -,rʊm) *n.* a bar, as in a hotel or pub.

tap+root ('tæp,ruːt) *n.* the large single root of plants such as the dandelion, which grows vertically downwards and bears smaller lateral roots. —**'tap+,root·ed** *adj.*

taps (tæps) *n.* **1.** (in army camps, etc.) a signal given on a bugle, drum, etc., indicating that lights are to be put out. **2.** any similar signal, as at a military funeral.

tap+ster ('tæpstə) *n.* **1.** *Rare.* a barman. **2.** (in W Africa) a man who taps palm trees to collect and sell palm wine. [Old English *tæppestre,* feminine of *tæppere,* from *tappian* to TAP^{2}] —**'tap+stress** *fem. n.*

tap wa+ter *n.* water drawn off through taps from pipes in a house, as distinguished from distilled water, mineral water, etc.

tar^{1} (tɑː) *n.* **1.** any of various dark viscid substances obtained by the destructive distillation of organic matter such as coal, wood, or peat. **2.** another name for **coal tar.** ~*vb.* **tars, tar+ring, tarred.** (*tr.*) **3.** to coat with tar. **4. tar and feather.** to punish by smearing tar and feathers over (someone). **5. tarred with the same brush.** having the same faults. [Old English *teoru;* related to Old Frisian *tera,* Old Norse *tjara,* Middle Low German *tere* tar, Gothic *triu* tree] —**'tar+ry** *adj.* —**'tar+ri+ness** *n.*

tar^{2} (tɑː) *n.* an informal word for **seaman.** [C17: short for TARPAULIN]

Tar·a ('tærə, 'tɑːrə) *n.* a village in Co. Meath near Dublin, by the **Hill of Tara,** the historic seat of the ancient Irish kings.

Ta+ra+bu+lus el Gharb (tə'rɑːbələs ɛl 'gɑːb) *n.* transliteration of the Arabic name for **Tripoli** (Libya).

Ta+ra+bu+lus esh Sham (tə'rɑːbələs ɛʃ 'ʃæm) *n.* transliteration of the Arabic name for **Tripoli** (Lebanon).

ta+ra+did+dle ('tærə,dɪdᵊl) *n.* another spelling of **tarradiddle.**

ta+ra+ma+sa+la+ta (tə,ræməsə'lɑːtə) *n.* a creamy pale pink paté, made from the roe of grey mullet or smoked cod and served as an hors d'oeuvre. [C20: from Modern Greek, from *tarama* cod's roe]

ta+ran+tass (,tɑːrən'tæs) *n.* a large horse-drawn four-wheeled Russian carriage without springs. [C19: from Russian *tarantas,* from Kazan Tatar *taryntas*]

tar+an+tel+la (,tærən'tɛlə) *n.* **1.** a peasant dance from S Italy. **2.** a piece of music composed for or in the rhythm of this dance, in fast six-eight time. [C18: from Italian, from *Taranto* TARANTO; associated with TARANTISM]

tar+ant+ism ('tærən,tɪzəm) *n.* a nervous disorder marked by uncontrollable bodily movement, widespread in S Italy during the 15th to 17th centuries: popularly thought to be caused by the bite of a tarantula. [C17: from New Latin *tarantismus,* from TARANTO; see TARANTULA]

Ta+ran+to (tə'ræntəʊ; *Italian* 'taːranto) *n.* a port in SE Italy, in Apulia on the **Gulf of Taranto** (an inlet of the Ionian Sea): the chief city of Magna Graecia; taken by the Romans in 272 B.C. Pop.: 239 900 (1975 est.). Latin name: **Tarentum.**

ta+ran+tu+la (tə'ræntjʊlə) *n., pl.* **+las** *or* **+lae** (-,liː). **1.** any of various large hairy mostly tropical spiders of the American family *Theraphosidae.* **2.** a large hairy spider, *Lycosa tarentula* of S Europe, the bite of which was formerly thought to cause tarantism. [C16: from Medieval Latin, from Old Italian *tarantola,* from TARANTO]

Ta+ran+tu+la neb+u+la *n.* a huge bright emission nebula located in the S hemisphere in the Large Magellanic Cloud.

Ta+ra+wa (tə'rɑːwə) *n.* the capital of the Gilbert Islands, occupying a chain of islets surrounding a lagoon in the W central Pacific. Pop.: 10 616 (1968).

ta+rax+a+cum (tə'ræksəkəm) *n.* **1.** any perennial plant of the genus *Taraxacum,* such as the dandelion, having dense heads of small yellow flowers and seeds with a feathery attachment: family *Compositae* (composites). **2.** the dried root of the dandelion, used as a laxative, diuretic, and tonic. [C18: from Medieval Latin, from Arabic *tarakhshaqūn* wild chicory, perhaps of Persian origin]

Tarbes (*French* tarb) *n.* a town in SW France: noted for the breeding of Anglo-Arab horses. Pop.: 57 765 (1975).

tar+boosh, tar+bush, *or* **tar+bouche** (tɑː'buːʃ) *n.* a felt or cloth brimless cap, usually red and often with a silk tassel, worn by Muslim men. [C18: from Arabic *tarbūsh*]

tar boy *n. Austral. informal.* a boy who applies tar to the skin of sheep cut during shearing.

Tar+de+noi+si+an (ˌtɑːdə'nɔɪzɪən) *adj.* of or referring to a Mesolithic culture characterized by small flint instruments. [C20: after *Tardenois,* France, where implements were found]

tar+di+grade ('tɑːdɪˌgreɪd) *n.* **1.** any minute aquatic segmented eight-legged invertebrate of the phylum *Tardigrada,* related to the arthropods, occurring in soil, ditches, etc. Popular name: **water bear.** ~*adj.* **2.** of, relating to, or belonging to the *Tardigrada.* [C17: via Latin *tardigradus,* from *tardus* sluggish + *gradī* to walk]

tar+dy ('tɑːdɪ) *adj.* **+di+er, +di+est. 1.** occurring later than expected: *tardy retribution.* **2.** slow in progress, growth, etc.: *a tardy reader.* [C15: from Old French *tardif,* from Latin *tardus* slow] —**'tar+di+ly** *adv.* —**'tar+di+ness** *n.*

tare[1] (tɛə) *n.* **1.** any of various vetch plants, such as *Vicia hirsuta* (**hairy tare**) of Eurasia and N Africa. **2.** the seed of any of these plants. **3.** *Bible.* a troublesome weed, thought to be the darnel. [C14: of unknown origin]

tare[2] (tɛə) *n.* **1.** the weight of the wrapping or container in which goods are packed. **2.** a deduction from gross weight to compensate for this. **3.** the weight of a vehicle unladen with cargo, passengers, etc. **4.** an empty container used as a counterbalance in determining net weight. ~*vb.* **5.** (*tr.*) to weigh (a package, etc.) in order to calculate the amount of tare. [C15: from Old French: waste, from Medieval Latin *tara,* from Arabic *tarhah* something discarded, from *taraha* to reject]

Ta+ren+tum (tə'rɛntəm) *n.* the Latin name of **Taranto.**

targe (tɑːdʒ) *n.* an archaic word for **shield.** [C13: from Old French, of Germanic origin; related to Old High German *zarga* rim, frame, Old Norse *targa* shield]

tar+get ('tɑːgɪt) *n.* **1. a.** an object or area at which an archer or marksman aims, usually a round flat surface marked with concentric rings. **b.** (*as modifier*): *target practice.* **2. a.** any point or area aimed at; the object of an attack. **b.** (*as modifier*): *target area.* **3.** a fixed goal or objective: *the target for the appeal is £10 000.* **4.** a person or thing at which an action or remark is directed or the object of a person's feelings: *a target for the teacher's sarcasm.* **5.** a joint of lamb consisting of the breast and neck. **6.** *Surveying.* a marker on which sights are taken, such as the sliding marker on a levelling staff. **7.** (formerly) a small round shield. **8.** *Physics, electronics.* **a.** a substance, object, or system subjected to bombardment by electrons or other particles, or to irradiation. **b.** an electrode in a television camera tube whose surface, on which image information is stored, is scanned by the electron beam. **9.** *Electronics.* an object detected by the reflection of a radar or sonar signal, etc. ~*vb.* **10.** (*tr.*) to make a target of. [C14: from Old French *targette* a little shield, from Old French TARGE] —**'tar+get+less** *adj.*

tar+get lang+uage *n.* the language into which a text, document, etc., is translated.

tar+get man *n. Soccer.* an attacking player to whom high crosses and centres are played, esp. a tall forward.

Tar+gum ('tɑːgəm; *Hebrew* tar'gum) *n.* an Aramaic translation, usually in the form of an expanded paraphrase, of various books or sections of the Old Testament. [C16: from Aramaic: interpretation] —**Tar+gum+ic** (tɑː'guːmɪk) *or* **Tar+'gum+i+cal** *adj.* —**'Tar+gum+ist** *n.*

tar+iff ('tærɪf) *n.* **1. a.** a tax levied by a government on imports or occasionally exports for purposes of protection, support of the balance of payments, or the raising of revenue. **b.** a system or list of such taxes. **2.** any schedule of prices, fees, fares, etc. **3.** *Chiefly Brit.* **a.** a method of charging for the supply of services, esp. public services, as gas and electricity: *block tariff.* **b.** a schedule of such charges. **4.** *Chiefly Brit.* a bill of fare with prices listed; menu. ~*vb.* **5.** to set a tariff on. **6.** to set a price on according to a schedule of tariffs. [C16: from Italian *tariffa,* from Arabic *ta'rīfa* to inform] —**'tar+iff+less** *adj.*

Ta+rim ('tɑː'riːm) *n.* a river in NW China, in Sinkiang province: flows east along the N edge of the Takla Makan desert, dividing repeatedly and forming lakes among the dunes, finally disappearing in the Lop Nor depression; the chief river of Sinkiang; drains the great **Tarim Basin** between the Tien Shan and Kunlun mountain systems of central Asia, an area of about 906 500 sq. km (350 000 sq. miles). Length: 2190 km (1360 miles).

Tar+king+ton ('tɑːkɪŋtən) *n.* (**Newton**) **Booth.** 1869–1946, U.S. novelist. His works include the historical romance *Monsieur Beaucaire* (1900), tales of the Middle West, such as *The Magnificent Ambersons* (1918) and *Alice Adams* (1921), and the series featuring the character Penrod.

tar+la+tan ('tɑːlətən) *n.* an open-weave cotton fabric, used for stiffening garments. [C18: from French *tarlatane,* variant of *tarnatane* type of muslin, perhaps of Indian origin]

Tar+mac ('tɑːmæk) *n. Tradename.* (*often not cap.*) a paving material that consists of crushed stone rolled and bound with a mixture of tar and bitumen, esp. as used for a road, airport runway, etc. Full name: **Tar+mac+ad+am** (ˌtɑːmə'kædəm). See also **macadam.**

tarn (tɑːn) *n.* a small mountain lake or pool. [C14: of Scandinavian origin; related to Old Norse *tjörn* pool]

Tarn (*French* tarn) *n.* **1.** a department of S France, in Midi-Pyrénées region. Capital: Albi. Pop.: 346 775 (1975). Area: 5780 sq. km (2254 sq. miles). **2.** a river in SW France, rising in the Massif Central and flowing generally west to the Garonne River. Length: 375 km (233 miles).

tar+nal ('tɑːnəl) *U.S. dialect.* ~*adj.* **1.** (*prenominal*) damned. ~*adv.* **2.** (intensifier): *tarnal lucky!* [C18: aphetic dialect pronunciation of ETERNAL] —**'tar+nal+ly** *adv.*

tar+na+tion (tɑː'neɪʃən) *n.* a euphemism for **damnation.**

Tarn-et-Ga+ronne (*French* tar ne ga'rɔn) *n.* a department of SW France, in Midi-Pyrénées region. Capital: Montauban. Pop.: 189 547 (1975). Area: 3731 sq. km (1455 sq. miles).

tar+nish ('tɑːnɪʃ) *vb.* **1.** to lose or cause to lose the shine, esp. by exposure to air or moisture resulting in surface oxidation; discolour: *silver tarnishes quickly.* **2.** to stain or become stained; taint or spoil: *a fraud that tarnished his reputation.* ~*n.* **3.** a tarnished condition, surface, or film. [C16: from Old French *ternir* to make dull, from *terne* lustreless of Germanic origin; related to Old High German *tarnen* to conceal, Old English *dierne* hidden] —**'tar+nish+a+ble** *adj.* —**'tar+nish+er** *n.*

Tar+no+pol (tar'nɔpɔl) *n.* the Polish name for **Ternopol.**

Tar+nów (*Polish* 'tarnuf) *n.* an industrial city in SE Poland. Pop.: 89 000 (1972 est.).

ta+ro ('tɑːrəʊ) *n., pl.* **+ros. 1.** an Asian aroid plant, *Colocasia esculenta,* cultivated in the tropics for its large edible rootstock. **2.** the rootstock of this plant. ~Also called: **elephant's-ear, dasheen, eddo, Chinese eddo.** [C18: from Tahitian and Maori]

ta+rot ('tærəʊ) *n.* **1.** one of a special pack of cards, now used mainly for fortune-telling, consisting of 78 cards (4 suits of 14 cards each (the minor arcana), and 22 other cards (the major arcana)). **2.** a card in a tarot pack with distinctive symbolic design, such as the Wheel of Fortune. ~*adj.* **3.** relating to tarot cards. [C16: from French, from Old Italian *tarocco,* of unknown origin]

tarp (tɑːp) *n. Austral.* an informal word for **tarpaulin.**

tar+pan ('tɑːpæn) *n.* a European wild horse, *Equus caballus gomelini,* common in prehistoric times but now extinct. [from Kirghiz Tatar]

tar+pau+lin (tɑː'pɔːlɪn) *n.* **1.** a heavy hard-wearing waterproof fabric made of canvas or similar material coated with tar, wax, or paint, for outdoor use as a protective covering against moisture. **2.** a sheet of this fabric. **3.** a hat of or covered with this fabric, esp. a sailor's hat. **4.** a rare word for **seaman.** [C17: probably from TAR[1] + PALL[1] + -ING[1]]

Tar+pe+ia (tɑː'piːə) *n.* (in Roman legend) a vestal virgin, who betrayed Rome to the Sabines and was killed by them when she requested a reward.

Tar+pe+ian Rock (tɑː'piːən) *n.* (in ancient Rome) a cliff on the Capitoline hill from which traitors were hurled.

tar+pon ('tɑːpən) *n., pl.* **+pons** *or* **+pon. 1.** a large silvery clupeoid game fish, *Tarpon atlanticus,* of warm Atlantic waters, having a compressed body covered with large scales: family *Elopidae.* **2.** any similar related fish. [C17: perhaps from Dutch *tarpoen,* of unknown origin]

Tar+quin ('tɑːkwɪn) *n.* **1.** Latin name *Lucius Tarquinius Priscus.* fifth legendary king of Rome (616–578 B.C.). **2.** Latin name *Lucius Tarquinius Superbus.* seventh and last legendary king of Rome (534–510 B.C.).

tar+ra+did+dle ('tærəˌdɪdəl) *n.* **1.** a trifling lie. **2.** nonsense; twaddle. [of unknown origin]

tar+ra+gon ('tærəgən) *n.* **1.** an aromatic perennial plant, *Artemisia dracunculus,* of the Old World, having whitish flowers and small toothed leaves, which are used as seasoning: family *Compositae* (composites). **2.** the leaves of this plant. ~Also called: **estragon.** [C16: from Old French *targon,* from Medieval Latin *tarcon,* from Arabic *tarkhūn,* perhaps from Greek *drakontion* adderwort]

Tar+ra+go+na (*Spanish* ˌtarra'ɣona) *n.* a port in NE Spain, on the Mediterranean: one of the richest seaports of the Roman Empire; destroyed by the Moors (714). Pop.: 78 238 (1970). Latin name: **Tarraco.**

Tar+ra+sa (*Spanish* ta'rrasa) *n.* a city in NE Spain: textile centre. Pop.: 138 697 (1970).

tar+ri+ance ('tærɪəns) *n.* an archaic word for **delay.**

tar+ry ('tærɪ) *vb.* **+ries, +ry+ing, +ried. 1.** (*intr.*) to delay in coming or going; linger. **2.** (*intr.*) to remain temporarily or briefly. **3.** (*intr.*) to wait or stay. **4.** (*tr.*) *Archaic or poetic.* to await. ~*n., pl.* **+ries. 5.** *Rare.* a stay. [C14 *tarien,* of uncertain origin] —**'tar+ri+er** *n.*

tar+sal ('tɑːsəl) *adj.* **1.** of, relating to, or constituting the tarsus or tarsi. ~*n.* **2.** a tarsal bone.

Tar+shish ('tɑːʃɪʃ) *n. Old Testament.* an ancient port, mentioned in I Kings 10:22, situated in Spain or in one of the Phoenician colonies in Sardinia.

tar+si+a ('tɑːsɪə) *n.* another term for **intarsia.** [C17: from Italian, from Arabic *tarsī'*; see INTARSIA]

tar+si+er ('tɑːsɪə) *n.* any of several nocturnal arboreal prosimian primates of the genus *Tarsius,* of Indonesia and the Philippines, having huge eyes, long hind legs, and digits ending in pads to facilitate climbing: family *Tarsiidae.* [C18: from French, from *tarse* the flat of the foot; see TARSUS]

tar+so+met+a+tar+sus (ˌtɑːsəʊˌmɛtə'tɑːsəs) *n., pl.* **+si** (-saɪ). a bone in the lower part of a bird's leg consisting of the metatarsal bones and some of the tarsal bones fused together. [C19: *tarso-* from TARSUS + METATARSUS] —ˌ**tar+so+ˌmet·a+'tar+sal** *adj.*

tar+sus ('tɑːsəs) *n., pl.* **+si** (-saɪ). **1.** the bones of the ankle and heel, collectively. **2. a.** the corresponding part in other mammals and in amphibians and reptiles. **b.** another name for **tarsometatarsus. 3.** the dense connective tissue supporting the free edge of each eyelid. **4.** the part of an insect's leg that lies distal to the tibia. [C17: from New Latin, from Greek *tarsos* flat surface, instep]

Tar+sus ('tɑːsəs) *n.* **1.** a city in SE Turkey, on the Tarsus River: site of ruins of ancient Tarsus, capital of Cilicia, and birthplace of St. Paul. Pop.: 102 186 (1975). **2.** a river in SE Turkey, in Cilicia, rising in the Taurus Mountains and flowing south past Tarsus to the Mediterranean. Ancient name: **Cydnus.** Length: 153 km (95 miles).

tart[1] (tɑːt) *n.* **1.** *Chiefly Brit.* a pastry case often having no top crust, with a filling of fruit, jam, custard, etc. **2.** *Chiefly U.S.* a small open pie with a fruit filling. **3.** *Informal.* a promiscuous woman, esp. a prostitute: often a term of abuse. ~*vb.* **4.** See **tart up.** [C14: from Old French *tarte,* of uncertain origin; compare Medieval Latin *tarte;* sense 3 shortened from SWEETHEART] —'**tart·y** *adj.*

tart[2] (tɑːt) *adj.* **1.** (of a flavour, food, etc.) sour, acid, or astringent. **2.** cutting, sharp, or caustic: *a tart remark.* [Old English *teart* rough; related to Dutch *tarten* to defy, Middle High German *traz* defiance] —'**tart+ish** *adj.* —'**tart+ish+ly** *adv.* —'**tart+ly** *adv.* —'**tart+ness** *n.*

tar+tan[1] ('tɑːtᵊn) *n.* **1. a.** a design of straight lines, crossing at right angles to give a chequered appearance, esp. the distinctive design or designs associated with each Scottish clan: *the Buchanan tartan.* **b.** (*as modifier*): *a tartan kilt.* **2.** a woollen fabric or garment with this design. **3. the tartan.** Highland dress. [C16: perhaps from Old French *tertaine* linsey-woolsey, from Old Spanish *tiritaña* a fine silk fabric, from *tiritar* to rustle]

tar+tan[2] ('tɑːtᵊn) *n.* a single-masted vessel used in the Mediterranean, usually with a lateen sail. [C17: from French, perhaps from Provençal *tartana* falcon, buzzard, since a ship was frequently given the name of a bird]

tar+tar[1] ('tɑːtə) *n.* **1.** *Dentistry.* a hard crusty deposit on the teeth, consisting of food, cellular debris, and mineral salts. **2.** Also called: **argol.** a brownish-red substance consisting mainly of potassium hydrogen tartrate, present in grape juice and deposited during the fermentation of wine. [C14: from Medieval Latin *tartarum,* from Medieval Greek *tartaron*]

tar+tar[2] ('tɑːtə) *n.* (*sometimes cap.*) a fearsome or vindictive person, esp. a woman. [C16: special use of TARTAR]

Tar+tar ('tɑːtə) *n., adj.* a variant spelling of **Tatar.** —**Tar+tar+i·an** (tɑː'tɛərɪən) *or* **Tar+tar+ic** (tɑː'tærɪk) *adj.*

Tar+tar+e·an (tɑː'tɛərɪən, -'tɑːrɪ-) *adj. Literary.* of or relating to Tartarus; infernal.

tar+tar e·met+ic *n.* another name for **antimony potassium tartrate.**

tar+tar+ic (tɑː'tærɪk) *adj.* of, concerned with, containing, or derived from tartar or tartaric acid.

tar+tar+ic ac·id *n.* a colourless or white odourless crystalline water-soluble dicarboxylic acid existing in four stereoisomeric forms, the commonest being the dextrorotatory (*d*-) compound which is found in many fruits: used in soft drinks, confectionery, and baking powders and in tanning and photography. Formula: HOOCCH(OH)CH(OH)COOH.

tar+tar+ize *or* **tar+tar+ise** ('tɑːtəˌraɪz) *vb.* (*tr.*) to impregnate or treat with tartar or tartar emetic. —ˌ**tar+tar+i+'za+tion** *or* ˌ**tar+tar+i+'sa+tion** *n.*

tar+tar+ous ('tɑːtərəs) *adj.* consisting of, containing, or resembling tartar.

tar+tar sauce *n.* a mayonnaise sauce mixed with hard-boiled egg yolks, chopped herbs, capers, and gherkins. [from French *sauce tartare,* from TARTAR]

tar+tar steak *n.* a variant term for **steak tartare.**

Tar+ta+rus ('tɑːtərəs) *Greek myth.* ~*n.* **1.** an abyss under Hades where the Titans were imprisoned. **2.** a part of Hades reserved for evildoers. **3.** the underworld; Hades. **4.** a primordial god who became the father of the monster Typhon. [C16: from Latin, from Greek *Tartaros,* of obscure origin]

Tar+ta+ry ('tɑːtərɪ) *n.* a variant spelling of **Tatary.**

tart+let ('tɑːtlɪt) *n. Brit.* an individual pastry case with a filling of fruit or other sweet or savoury mixture.

tar+trate ('tɑːtreɪt) *n.* any salt or ester of tartaric acid.

tar+trat+ed ('tɑːtreɪtɪd) *adj.* being in the form of a tartrate.

Tar+tu (*Russian* 'tartu) *n.* a city in the W Soviet Union, in the SE Estonian SSR: became Russian in 1704 after successive Russian, Polish, and Swedish rule; university (1632). Pop.: 90 459 (1970). Former name (11th century until 1918): **Yurev.**

tart up *vb.* (*adv.*) *Brit. slang.* **1.** to dress and make (oneself) up in a provocative or promiscuous way. **2.** (*tr.*) to reissue or decorate in a cheap and flashy way: *to tart up a bar.*

Tar+zan ('tɑːzən) *n.* (*sometimes not cap.*) *Informal, often ironical.* a man with great physical strength, agility, and virility. [C20: after the hero of a series of stories by E. R. BURROUGHS]

Tas. *abbrev. for* Tasmania.

Ta+shi La·ma ('tɑːʃɪ 'lɑːmə) *n.* another name for the **Panchen Lama.** [from *Tashi* (*Lumpo*) name of Tibetan monastery over which this Lama presides]

Tash+kent (*Russian* taʃ'kjɛnt) *n.* a city in the S central Soviet Union, capital of the Uzbek SSR: one of the oldest and largest cities in central Asia; taken by the Russians in 1865; cotton textile manufacturing. Pop.: 1 595 000 (1975 est.).

ta+sim+e·ter (tə'sɪmɪtə) *n.* a device for measuring small temperature changes. It depends on the changes of pressure resulting from expanding or contracting solids. [C19 *tasi-,* from Greek *tasis* tension + -METER] —**tas·i+met+ric** (ˌtæsə'mɛtrɪk) *adj.* —**ta+'sim+e·try** *n.*

task (tɑːsk) *n.* **1.** a specific piece of work required to be done as a duty or chore. **2.** an unpleasant or difficult job or duty. **3.** any piece of work. **4. take to task.** to criticize or reprove. ~*vb.* (*tr.*) **5.** to assign a task to. **6.** to subject to severe strain; tax. [C13: from Old French *tasche,* from Medieval Latin *tasca,* from *taxa* tax, from Latin *taxāre* to TAX] —'**task+er** *n.* —'**task+less** *adj.*

task force *n.* **1.** a military unit formed to undertake a specific mission. **2.** any semipermanent organization set up to carry out a continuing task.

task+mas·ter ('tɑːskˌmɑːstə) *n.* a person, discipline, etc., that enforces work, esp. hard or continuous work: *his teacher is a hard taskmaster.* —'**task+ˌmis·tress** *fem. n.*

task+work ('tɑːskˌwɜːk) *n.* **1.** hard or unpleasant work. **2.** a rare word for **piecework.**

Tas+man ('tæzmən) *n.* **A·bel Jans·zoon** ('abəl 'jansuːn). 1603–59, Dutch navigator, who discovered Tasmania, New Zealand, and the Tonga and Fiji Islands (1642–43).

Tas+ma+ni·a (tæz'meɪnɪə) *n.* an island in the S Pacific, south of Australia: forms, with offshore islands, the smallest state of Australia; discovered by the Dutch explorer Tasman in 1642; used as a penal colony by the British (1803–53); mostly forested and mountainous. Capital: Hobart. Pop.: 402 800 (1976). Area: 68 332 sq. km (26 383 sq. miles). Former name (1642–1855): **Van Diemen's Land.** —**Tas+'ma+ni·an** *adj., n.*

Tas+ma+ni·an dev+il *n.* a small ferocious carnivorous marsupial, *Sarcophilus harrisi,* of Tasmania, having black fur with pale markings, strong jaws, and short legs: family *Dasyuridae.* Also called: **ursine dasyure.**

Tas+ma+ni·an wolf *or* **ti+ger** *n.* other names for **thylacine.**

Tas+man Sea *n.* the part of the Pacific between SE Australia and NW New Zealand.

tass (tæs) *or* **tas+sie** ('tæsɪ) *n. Northern Brit. dialect.* **1.** a cup, goblet, or glass. **2.** the contents of such a vessel. [C15: from Old French *tasse* cup, from Arabic *tassah* basin, from Persian *tast*]

Tass (tæs) *n.* the principal news agency of the Soviet Union. [*T*(*elegrafnoye*) *a*(*genstvo*) *S*(*ovetskovo*) *S*(*oyuza*) Telegraphic Agency of the Soviet Union]

tas+sel ('tæsᵊl) *n.* **1.** a tuft of loose threads secured by a knot or ornamental knob, used to decorate soft furnishings, clothes, etc. **2.** anything resembling this tuft, esp. the tuft of stamens at the tip of a maize inflorescence. ~*vb.* **+sels, +sel+ling, +selled** *or U.S.* **+sels, +sel+ing, +seled. 3.** (*tr.*) to adorn with a tassel or tassels. **4.** (*intr.*) (of maize) to produce stamens in a tuft. **5.** (*tr.*) to remove the tassels from. [C13: from Old French, from Vulgar Latin *tassellus* (unattested), changed from Latin *taxillus* a small die, from *tālus* gaming die] —'**tas+sel+ly** *adj.*

tas+set ('tæsɪt), **tasse** (tæs), *or* **tace** *n.* a piece of armour consisting of one or more plates fastened on to the bottom of a cuirass to protect the thigh. [C19: from French *tassette* small pouch, from Old French *tasse* purse]

Tas·sie *or* **Tas·sy** ('tæzɪ) *n. Austral. informal.* **1.** Tasmania. **2.** a native or inhabitant of Tasmania.

Tas·so (*Italian* 'tasso) *n.* **Tor·qua·to** (tor'kwaːto). 1544–95, Italian poet, noted for his pastoral idyll *Aminta* (1573) and for *Jerusalem Delivered* (1581), dealing with the First Crusade.

taste (teɪst) *n.* **1.** the sense by which the qualities and flavour of a substance are distinguished by the taste buds. **2.** the sensation experienced by means of the taste buds. **3.** the act of tasting. **4.** a small amount eaten, drunk, or tried on the tongue. **5.** a brief experience of something: *a taste of the whip.* **6.** a preference or liking for something; inclination: *to have a taste for danger.* **7.** the ability to make discerning judgments about aesthetic, artistic, and intellectual matters; discrimination: *to have taste.* **8.** judgment of aesthetic or social matters according to a generally accepted standard: *bad taste.* **9.** discretion; delicacy: *that remark lacks taste.* **10.** *Obsolete.* the act of testing. ~*vb.* **11.** to distinguish the taste of (a substance) by means of the taste buds. **12.** (*usually tr.*) to take a small amount of (a food, liquid, etc.) into the mouth, esp. in order to test the quality: *to taste the wine.* **13.** (often foll. by *of*) to have a specific flavour or taste: *the tea tastes of soap; this apple tastes sour.* **14.** (when *intr.*, usually foll. by *of*) to have an experience of (something): *to taste success.* **15.** (*tr.*) an archaic word for **enjoy. 16.** (*tr.*) *Obsolete.* to test by touching. [C13: from Old French *taster,* ultimately from Latin *taxāre* to appraise] —'**tast+a·ble** *adj.*

taste bud *n.* any of the elevated oval-shaped sensory end organs on the surface of the tongue, by means of which the sensation of taste is experienced.

taste+ful ('teɪstfʊl) *adj.* **1.** indicating good taste: *a tasteful design.* **2.** a rare word for **tasty.** —'**taste+ful+ly** *adv.* —'**taste+ful+ness** *n.*

taste+less ('teɪstlɪs) *adj.* **1.** lacking in flavour; insipid. **2.** lacking social or aesthetic taste. **3.** *Rare.* unable to taste. —'**taste+less+ly** *adv.* —'**taste+less+ness** *n.*

tast+er ('teɪstə) *n.* **1.** a person who samples food or drink for quality. **2.** any device used in tasting or sampling. **3.** a person employed, esp. formerly, to taste food and drink prepared for a king, etc., to test for poison.

tast·y ('teɪstɪ) *adj.* **tast·i+er, tast·i+est. 1.** having a pleasant flavour. 2. *Rare.* showing good taste. —'**tast·i·ly** *adv.* —'**tast·i·ness** *n.*

tat[1] (tæt) *vb.* **tats, tat·ting, tat·ted.** to make (something) by tatting. [C19: of unknown origin]

tat[2] (tæt) *n.* **1.** a ragged or tattered article or condition. **2.** a tangled mass, esp. in the hair. [C20: back formation from TATTY]

tat[3] (tæt) *n.* See **tit for tat.**

ta-ta (tæ'tɑː) *sentence substitute. Brit. informal.* goodbye; farewell. [C19: of unknown origin]

Ta·tar *or* **Tar·tar** ('tɑːtə) *n.* **1. a.** a member of a Mongoloid people who under Genghis Khan established a vast and powerful state in central Asia from the 13th century until conquered by Russia in 1552. **b.** a descendant of this people, now scattered throughout the Soviet Union but living chiefly around the middle Volga. **2.** the language or group of dialects spoken by this people, belonging to the Turkic branch of the Altaic family. ~*adj.* **3.** of, relating to, or characteristic of the Tatars. [C14: from Old French *Tartare,* from Medieval Latin *Tartarus* (associated with Latin *Tartarus* the underworld), from Persian *Tātār*] —**Ta·tar·i·an** (tɑː'tɛərɪən), **Tar·'tar·i·an** *or* **Ta·tar·ic** (tɑː'tærɪk), **Tar·'tar·ic** *adj.*

Ta·tar Au·ton·o·mous So·vi·et So·cial·ist Re·pub·lic *n.* an administrative division of the W central Soviet Union, in the RSFSR around the confluence of the Volga and Kama Rivers. Capital: Kazan. Pop.: 3 131 238 (1970). Area: 68 000 sq. km (26 250 sq. miles).

Ta·tar Strait *n.* an arm of the Pacific between the mainland of the SE Soviet Union and Sakhalin Island, linking the Sea of Japan with the Sea of Okhotsk. Length: about 560 km (350 miles). Also called: **Gulf of Tatary.**

Ta·ta·ry *or* **Tar·ta·ry** ('tɑːtərɪ) *n.* **1.** a historical region (with indefinite boundaries) in E Europe and Asia, inhabited by Bulgars until overrun by the Tatars in the mid-13th century: extended as far east as the Pacific under Genghis Khan. **2. Gulf of.** another name for the **Tatar Strait.**

Tate (teɪt) *n.* **1.** Sir **Hen·ry.** 1819–99, English sugar refiner and philanthropist; founder of the Tate Gallery in London (1897). **2. (John Orley) Al·len.** born 1899, U.S. poet and critic.

ta·ter ('teɪtə) *n.* a dialect word for **potato.**

Ta·ti (*French* ta'ti) *n.* **Jacques** (ʒak). 1908–82, French film director and comic actor, creator of the character Monsieur Hulot.

tat·ou·ay ('tætʊˌeɪ, ˌtɑːtʊ'aɪ) *n.* a large armadillo, *Cabassous tatouay,* of South America. [C16: from Spanish *tatuay,* from Guarani *tatu ai,* from *tatu* armadillo + *ai* worthless (because inedible)]

Ta·tra Moun·tains ('tɑːtrə, 'tæt-) *pl. n.* a mountain range along the border between Czechoslovakia and Poland, extending for about 64 km (40 miles): the highest range of the central Carpathians. Highest peak: Gerlachovka, 2663 m (8737 ft.). Also called: **High Tatra.**

tat·ter ('tætə) *vb.* **1.** to make or become ragged or worn to shreds. ~*n.* **2.** a torn or ragged piece, esp. of material. [C14: of Scandinavian origin; compare Icelandic *töturr* rag, Old English *tættec,* Old High German *zæter* rag]

tat·ter·de·mal·ion (ˌtætədɪ'meɪljən, -'mæl-) *n. Rare.* **a.** a person dressed in ragged clothes. **b.** (*as modifier*)*: a tatterdemalion dress.* [C17: from TATTER + *-demalion,* of uncertain origin]

tat·ter·sall ('tætəˌsɔːl) *n.* **a.** a fabric, sometimes brightly coloured, having stripes or bars in a checked or squared pattern. **b.** (*as modifier*)*: a tattersall coat.* [C19: after *Tattersall's,* a horse market in London founded by Richard *Tattersall* (died 1795), English horseman; the horse blankets at the market originally had this pattern]

tat·ting ('tætɪŋ) *n.* **1.** an intricate type of lace made by looping a thread of cotton or linen by means of a hand shuttle. **2.** the act or work of producing this. [C19: of unknown origin]

tat·tle ('tætᵊl) *vb.* **1.** (*intr.*) to gossip about another's personal matters or secrets. **2.** (*tr.*) to reveal by gossiping: *to tattle a person's secrets.* **3.** (*intr.*) to talk idly; chat. ~*n.* **4.** the act or an instance of tattling. **5.** a scandalmonger or gossip. [C15 (in the sense: to stammer, hesitate): from Middle Dutch *tatelen* to prate, of imitative origin] —'**tat·tling·ly** *adv.*

tat·tler ('tætlə) *n.* **1.** a person who tattles; gossip. **2.** any of several sandpipers of the genus *Heteroscelus,* such as *H. incanus* (**Polynesian tattler**), of Pacific coastal regions.

tat·tle·tale ('tætᵊlˌteɪl) *Chiefly U.S.* ~*n.* **1.** a scandalmonger or gossip. ~*adj.* **2.** another word for **telltale.**

tat·too[1] (tæ'tuː) *n., pl.* **·toos. 1.** (formerly) a signal by drum or bugle ordering the military to return to their quarters. **2.** a military display or pageant. **3.** any similar beating on a drum, etc. [C17: from Dutch *taptoe,* from the command *tap toe!* turn off the taps! from *tap* tap of a barrel + *toe* to shut]

tat·too[2] (tæ'tuː) *vb.* **·toos, ·too·ing, ·tooed. 1.** to make (pictures or designs) on (the skin) by pricking and staining with indelible colours. ~*n., pl.* **·toos. 2.** a design made by this process. **3.** the practice of tattooing. [C18: from Tahitian *tatau*] —**tat·'too·er** *or* **tat·'too·ist** *n.*

tat·ty ('tætɪ) *adj.* **·ti·er, ·ti·est.** *Chiefly Brit.* worn out, shabby, tawdry, or unkempt. [C16: of Scottish origin, probably related to Old English *tættec* a tatter] —'**tat·ti·ness** *n.*

tat·ty-peel·in ('tætɪ'piːlɪn) *adj. Central Scot. dialect* (esp. of speech) highfalutin, affected, or pretentious. [from *potato-peeling;* sense development obscure]

Ta·tum ('teɪtəm) *n.* **Art.** 1910–56, U.S. jazz pianist.

tau (tɔː, taʊ) *n.* the 19th letter in the Greek alphabet (Τ or τ), a consonant, transliterated as *t.* [C13: via Latin from Greek, of Semitic origin; see TAV]

tau cross *n.* a cross shaped like the Greek letter tau. Also called: **Saint Anthony's cross.**

taught (tɔːt) *vb.* the past tense or past participle of **teach.**

taunt[1] (tɔːnt) *vb.* (*tr.*) **1.** to provoke or deride with mockery, contempt, or criticism. **2.** to tease; tantalize. ~*n.* **3.** a jeering remark. **4.** *Archaic.* the object of mockery. [C16: from French phrase *tant pour tant* like for like, rejoinder] —'**taunt·er** *n.* —'**taunt·ing·ly** *adv.*

taunt[2] (tɔːnt) *adj. Nautical.* (of the mast or masts of a sailing vessel) unusually tall. [C15: of uncertain origin]

Taun·ton ('tɔːntən) *n.* a market town in SW England, in Somerset: scene of Judge Jeffreys' "Bloody Assize" (1685) after the Battle of Sedgemoor. Pop.: 37 373 (1971).

taupe (təʊp) *n.* **a.** a brownish-grey colour. **b.** (*as modifier*)*: a taupe coat.* [C20: from French, literally: mole, from Latin *talpa*]

Tau·po ('taʊpəʊ) *n.* **Lake.** a lake in New Zealand, on central North Island: the largest lake of New Zealand. Area: 616 sq. km (238 sq. miles).

Tau·rang·a (taʊ'ræŋə) *n.* a port in New Zealand, on NE North Island on the Bay of Plenty: exports dairy produce, meat, and timber. Pop.: 28 188 (1971).

tau·rine[1] ('tɔːraɪn) *adj.* of, relating to, or resembling a bull. [C17: from Latin *taurīnus,* from *taurus* a bull]

tau·rine[2] ('tɔːriːn, -rɪn) *n.* a derivative of the amino acid, cysteine, obtained from the bile of animals; 2-aminoethanesulphonic acid. Formula: $NH_2CH_2CH_2SO_3H$. [C19: from TAURO- (as in *taurocholic* acid) + -INE[2]]

tau·ro- *or before a vowel* **taur-** *combining form.* denoting a bull: *tauromachy.* [from Latin *taurus* bull, Greek *tauros*]

tau·rom·a·chy (tɔː'rɒməkɪ) *n.* the art or act of bullfighting. [C19: Greek *tauromakhia,* from TAURO- + *makhē* fight] —**tau·ro·ma·chi·an** (ˌtɔːrə'meɪkɪən) *adj.*

Tau·rus ('tɔːrəs) *n., Latin genitive* **Tau·ri** ('tɔːraɪ). **1.** *Astronomy.* a zodiacal constellation in the N hemisphere lying close to Orion and between Aries and Gemini. It contains the star Aldebaran, the star clusters Hyades and Pleiades, and the Crab Nebula. **2.** *Astrology.* **a.** Also called: the **Bull.** the second sign of the zodiac, symbol ♉, having a fixed earth classification and ruled by the planet Venus. The sun is in this sign between about April 20 and May 20. **b.** a person born when the sun is in this sign. ~*adj.* **3.** born under or characteristic of Taurus. ~Also (for senses 2b, 3): **Tau·re·an** ('tɔːrɪən, tɔː'rɪən). [C14: from Latin: bull]

Tau·rus Moun·tains *pl. n.* a mountain range in S Turkey, parallel to the Mediterranean coast: crossed by the Cilician Gates; continued in the northeast by the Anti-Taurus range. Highest peak: Kaldi Dağ, 3734 m (12 251 ft.).

taut (tɔːt) *adj.* **1.** tightly stretched; tense. **2.** showing nervous strain; stressed. **3.** *Chiefly nautical.* in good order; neat. [C14 *tought;* probably related to Old English *togian* to TOW[1]] —'**taut·ly** *adv.* —'**taut·ness** *n.*

taut·en ('tɔːtᵊn) *vb.* to make or become taut or tense.

tau·to- *or before a vowel* **taut-** *combining form.* identical or same: *tautology; tautonym.* [from Greek *tauto,* from *to auto*]

tau·tog (tɔː'tɒg) *n.* a large dark-coloured wrasse, *Tautoga onitis,* of the North American coast of the Atlantic Ocean: used as a food fish. Also called: **blackfish.** [C17: from Narragansett *tautauog,* plural of *tautau* sheepshead]

tau·tol·o·gize *or* **tau·tol·o·gise** (tɔː'tɒləˌdʒaɪz) *vb.* (*intr.*) to express oneself tautologically. —**tau·'tol·o·gist** *n.*

tau·tol·o·gy (tɔː'tɒlədʒɪ) *n., pl.* **·gies. 1.** the use of words that merely repeat elements of the meaning already conveyed, as in the sentence *Will these supplies be adequate enough?* in place of *Will these supplies be adequate?* **2.** *Logic.* a proposition that is always true whether its component terms are true or false, as in *either the sun is out or the sun is not out.* [C16: from Late Latin *tautologia,* from Greek, from *tautologos*] —**tau·to·log·i·cal,** (ˌtɔːtᵊ'lɒdʒɪkᵊl), ˌ**tau·to·'log·ic,** *or* **tau·'tol·o·gous** *adj.* —ˌ**tau·to·'log·i·cal·ly** *or* **tau·'tol·o·gous·ly** *adv.*

tau·to·mer ('tɔːtəmə) *n.* either of the two forms of a chemical compound that exhibits tautomerism.

tau·tom·er·ism (tɔː'tɒməˌrɪzəm) *n.* the ability of certain chemical compounds to exist as a mixture of two interconvertible isomers in equilibrium. See also **keto-enol tautomerism.** [C19: from TAUTO- + ISOMERISM] —**tau·to·mer·ic** (ˌtɔːtə'mɛrɪk) *adj.*

tau·to·nym ('tɔːtənɪm) *n. Biology.* a taxonomic name in which the generic and specific components are the same, as in *Rattus rattus* (black rat). —ˌ**tau·to·'nym·ic** *or* **tau·ton·y·mous** (tɔː'tɒnəməs) *adj.* —**tau·'ton·y·my** *n.*

tav *or* **taw** (tɑːv, tɑːf; *Hebrew* tav, taf) *n.* the 23rd and last letter in the Hebrew alphabet (ת), transliterated as *t* or when final *th.* [from Hebrew: cross, mark]

Ta·vel (tɑː'vɛl) *n.* a fine rosé wine produced in the Rhône valley near the small town of Tavel in S France.

tav·ern ('tævən) *n.* **1.** a less common word for **pub. 2.** *U.S.* a place licensed for the sale and consumption of alcoholic drink. [C13: from Old French *taverne,* from Latin *taberna* hut]

tav·ern·er ('tævənə) *n.* **1.** *Archaic.* a keeper of a tavern. **2.** *Obsolete.* a constant frequenter of taverns.

Tav·er·ner ('tævənə) *n.* **John.** ?1495–1545, English composer, esp. of church music.

TAVR *abbrev. for* Territorial and Army Volunteer Reserve.

taw[1] (tɔː) *n.* **1.** the line from which the players shoot in marbles. **2.** a large marble used for shooting. **3.** a game of marbles. [C18: of unknown origin]

taw[2] (tɔː) *vb.* (*tr.*) **1.** to convert (skins) into white leather by treatment with mineral salts, such as alum and salt, rather than by normal tanning processes. **2.** *Archaic or Brit. dialect.* to flog; beat. [Old English *tawian;* compare Old High German *zouwen* to prepare, Gothic *taujan* to make] —**'taw+er** *n.*

taw+dry ('tɔːdrɪ) *adj.* **+dri+er, +dri+est.** cheap, showy, and of poor quality: *tawdry jewellery.* [C16 *tawdry lace,* shortened and altered from *Seynt Audries lace,* finery sold at the fair of St. *Audrey* (Etheldrida), 7th-century queen of Northumbria and patron saint of Ely, Cambridgeshire] —**'taw+dri+ly** *adv.* —**'taw+dri+ness** *n.*

Taw·ney ('tɔːnɪ) *n.* **R(ichard) H(enry).** 1880–1962, English economic historian, born in India. His chief works are *The Acquisitive Society* (1920), *Religion and the Rise of Capitalism* (1926), and *Equality* (1931).

taw+ny *or* **taw+ney** ('tɔːnɪ) *n.* **a.** a light brown to brownish-orange colour. **b.** (*as adj.*): *tawny port.* [C14: from Old French *tané,* from *taner* to TAN] —**'taw+ni+ness** *n.*

taw+ny owl *n.* a European owl, *Strix aluco,* having a reddish-brown or grey plumage, black eyes, and a round head.

tawse *or* **taws** (tɔːz) *Rare.* ~*n.* **1.** a leather strap having one end cut into thongs, used as an instrument of punishment by a schoolmaster. ~*vb.* **2.** to punish (someone) with or as if with a tawse; whip. [C16: probably plural of obsolete *taw* strip of leather; see TAW[2]]

tax (tæks) *n.* **1.** a compulsory financial contribution imposed by a government to raise revenue, levied on the income or property of persons or organizations, on the production costs or sales prices of goods and services, etc. **2.** a heavy demand on something; strain: *a tax on our resources.* ~*vb.* (*tr.*) **3.** to levy a tax on (persons, companies, etc., or their incomes, etc.). **4.** to make heavy demands on; strain: *to tax one's intellect.* **5.** to accuse, charge, or blame: *he was taxed with the crime.* **6.** to determine (the amount legally chargeable or allowable to a party to a legal action), as by examining the solicitor's bill of costs: *to tax costs.* [C13: from Old French *taxer,* from Latin *taxāre* to appraise, from *tangere* to touch] —**'tax+er** *n.* —**'tax+ing+ly** *adv.* —**'tax+less** *adj.*

tax+a·ble ('tæksəbᵊl) *adj.* **1.** capable of being taxed; able to bear tax. **2.** subject to tax. ~*n.* **3.** *U.S.* (*often pl.*) a person, income, property, etc., that is subject to tax. —**,tax+a·'bil+i·ty** *or* **'tax+a·ble+ness** *n.* —**'tax+a·bly** *adv.*

tax·a·ceous (tæk'seɪʃəs) *adj.* of, relating to, or belonging to the *Taxaceae,* a family of coniferous trees that includes the yews. [C19: from New Latin *taxāceus,* from Latin *taxus* a yew]

tax·a·tion (tæk'seɪʃən) *n.* **1.** the act or principle of levying taxes or the condition of being taxed. **2. a.** an amount assessed as tax. **b.** a tax rate. **3.** revenue from taxes. —**tax·'a+tion+al** *adj.*

tax a·void+ance *n.* reduction or minimization of tax liability by lawful methods. Compare **tax evasion.**

tax-de·duct+i·ble *adj.* (of an expense, loss, etc.) legally deductible from income or wealth before tax assessment.

tax+eme ('tæksiːm) *n. Linguistics.* any element of speech that may differentiate one utterance from another with a different meaning, such as the occurrence of a particular phoneme, the presence of a certain intonation, or a distinctive word order. [C20: from Greek *taxis* order, arrangement + -EME] —**tax+'e·mic** *adj.*

tax e·va+sion *n.* reduction or minimization of tax liability by illegal methods. Compare **tax avoidance.**

tax-ex·empt *adj. U.S.* **1.** (of an income or property) exempt from taxation. **2.** (of an asset) earning income that is not subject to taxation.

tax ha+ven *n.* a country or state having a lower rate of taxation than elsewhere.

tax·i ('tæksɪ) *n., pl.* **tax·is** *or* **tax·ies. 1.** Also called: **cab, tax·i+cab.** a car, usually fitted with a taximeter, that may be hired to carry passengers to any specified destination. ~*vb.* **tax·ies, tax·i+ing** *or* **tax·y+ing, tax+ied. 2.** to cause (an aircraft) to move along the ground under its own power, esp. before takeoff and after landing, or (of an aircraft) to move along the ground in this way. **3.** (*intr.*) to travel in a taxi. [C20: shortened from *taximeter cab*]

tax·i·der+my ('tæksɪ,dɜːmɪ) *n.* the art or process of preparing, stuffing, and mounting animal skins so that they have a lifelike appearance. [C19: from Greek *taxis* arrangement + *-dermy,* from Greek *derma* skin] —**,tax·i+'der+mal** *or* **,tax·i+'der·mic** *adj.* —**'tax·i+,der+mist** *n.*

tax·i·me·ter ('tæksɪ,miːtə) *n.* a meter fitted to a taxi to register the fare, based on the length of the journey. [C19: from French *taximètre;* see TAX, -METER]

tax·i·plane ('tæksɪ,pleɪn) *n. U.S.* an aircraft that is available for hire.

tax+is ('tæksɪs) *n.* **1.** the movement of a cell or microorganism in a particular direction in response to an external stimulus. **2.** *Surgery.* the repositioning of a displaced organ or part by manual manipulation only. [C18: via New Latin from Greek: arrangement, from *tassein* to place in order]

-tax·is *or* **-tax·y** *n. combining form.* **1.** indicating movement towards or away from a specified stimulus: *thermotaxis.* **2.** order or arrangement: *phyllotaxis.* [from New Latin, from Greek *taxis* order] —**-tac·tic** *or* **-tax·ic** *adj. combining form.*

tax·i truck *n. Austral.* a truck with a driver that can be hired.

tax·i+way ('tæksɪ,weɪ) *n.* a marked path along which aircraft taxi to or from a runway, parking area, etc. Also called: **taxi strip, peritrack.**

tax+on ('tæksɒn) *n., pl.* **tax·a** ('tæksə). *Biology.* any taxonomic group or rank. [C20: back formation from TAXONOMY]

tax+on·o·my (tæk'sɒnəmɪ) *n.* **1. a.** the branch of biology concerned with the classification of organisms into groups based on similarities of structure, origin, etc. **b.** the practice of arranging organisms in this way. **2.** the science or practice of classification. [C19: from French *taxonomie,* from Greek *taxis* order + -NOMY] —**tax·o·nom+ic** (,tæksə'nɒmɪk) *or* **,tax·o+'nom·i·cal** *adj.* —**,tax·o+'nom·i·cal+ly** *adv.* —**tax+'on·o+mist** *or* **tax+'on·o+mer** *n.*

tax+pay·er ('tæks,peɪə) *n.* a person or organization that pays taxes or is liable to taxation. —**'tax+,pay·ing** *adj.*

tax rate *n.* the percentage of income, wealth, etc., assessed as payable in taxation.

tax re+turn *n.* a declaration of personal income made annually to the tax authorities and used as a basis for assessing an individual's liability for taxation.

tax shel+ter *n. Commerce.* a form into which business or financial activities may be organized to minimize taxation.

-tax·y *n. combining form.* variant of **-taxis.**

tay (teɪ) *n.* an Irish dialect word for **tea.**

Tay (teɪ) *n.* **1. Firth of.** the estuary of the River Tay on the North Sea coast of Scotland. Length: 40 km (25 miles). **2.** a river in central Scotland, flowing northeast through Loch Tay, then southeast to the Firth of Tay: the longest river in Scotland; noted for salmon-fishing. Length: 193 km (120 miles). **3. Loch.** a lake in central Scotland, in Tayside Region. Length: 23 km (14 miles).

Tay·lor ('teɪlə) *n.* **1. Brook.** 1685–1731, English mathematician, who laid the foundations of differential calculus. **2. E·liz·a·beth.** born 1932. U.S. film actress, born in England: films include *Butterfield 8* (1960), *Who's Afraid of Virginia Woolf?* (1966), and *Secret Ceremony* (1968). **3. Jer·e·my.** 1613–67, English cleric, best known for his devotional manuals *Holy Living* (1650) and *Holy Dying* (1651). **4. Zach·a·ry.** 1784–1850, 12th president of the U.S. (1849–50); hero of the Mexican War.

Tay·lor's se+ries *n. Maths.* an infinite sum giving the value of a function $f(z)$ in the neighbourhood of a point a in terms of the derivatives of the function evaluated at a. Under certain conditions, the series has the form $f(z) = f(a) + [f'(a)(z - a)]/1! + [f''(a)(z - a)^2]/2! + \ldots$. See also **Maclaurin's series.** [C18: named after B. TAYLOR]

Tay+myr Pen+in+su+la (taɪ'mɪə) *n.* a variant spelling of **Taimyr Peninsula.**

tay+ra ('taɪrə) *n.* a large arboreal musteline mammal, *Eira barbara,* of Central and South America, having a dark brown body and paler head. [C19: from Tupi *taira*]

Tay+side Re+gion ('teɪ,saɪd) *n.* a local government region in E Scotland: formed in 1975 from Angus, Kinross and most of Perth. Administrative centre: Dundee. Pop.: 402 180 (1976 est.). Area: 7511 sq. km (2900 sq. miles).

taz+za ('tætsə) *n.* a wine cup with a shallow bowl and a circular foot. [C19: from Italian, probably from Arabic *tassah* bowl]

Tb *the chemical symbol for* terbium.

t.b. *abbrev. for* trial balance.

T.B. *or* **t.b.** *abbrev. for:* **1.** tuberculosis. **2.** torpedo-boat.

T-bar *n.* a T-shaped wrench for use with a socket.

Tbi+li+si (dbɪ'liːsɪ) *n.* a city in the SW Soviet Union, capital of the Georgian SSR, on the Kura River: founded in 458 as capital of Georgia; taken by the Russians in 1801; university (1918). Pop.: 1 006 000 (1975 est.). Russian name: **Tiflis.**

T-bone steak *n.* a large choice steak cut from the sirloin of beef, containing a T-shaped bone.

tbs. *or* **tbsp.** *abbrev. for* tablespoon(ful).

Tc *the chemical symbol for* technetium.

TC (on cars, etc.) *abbrev. for* twin carburettors.

Tchad (tʃad) *n.* the French name for **Chad.**

Tchai·kov·sky (tʃaɪ'kɒfskɪ; *Russian* tʃɪj'kɔfskij) *n.* **Pyo·tr Il·yich** ('pjɔtᵊr ilj'jitʃ). 1840–93, Russian composer. His works, which are noted for their expressive melodies, include the *Sixth Symphony* (the *Pathétique;* 1893), ballets, esp. *Swan Lake* (1876) and *The Sleeping Beauty* (1889), and operas, including *Eugene Onegin* (1879) and *The Queen of Spades* (1890), both based on works by Pushkin.

TD, td, *or* **t.d.** *abbrev. for* touch down.

t dis+tri+bu+tion *n.* short for **student's t distribution.**

te *or* **ti** (tiː) *n. Music.* (in tonic sol-fa) the syllable used for the seventh note or subtonic of any scale. [see GAMUT]

Te *the chemical symbol for* tellurium.

tea (tiː) *n.* **1.** an evergreen shrub or small tree, *Camellia sinensis,* of tropical and subtropical Asia, having toothed leathery leaves and white fragrant flowers: family *Theaceae.* **2. a.** the dried shredded leaves of this shrub, used to make a beverage by infusion in boiling water. **b.** such a beverage, served hot or iced. **c.** (*as modifier*): *tea caddy; tea urn.* **3. a.** any of various plants that are similar to *Camellia sinensis* or are used to make a tealike beverage. **b.** any such beverage. **4.** Also called: **afternoon tea.** *Chiefly Brit.* **a.** a light meal eaten in midafternoon, usually consisting of tea and cakes, biscuits, or sandwiches. **b.** (*as modifier*): *a tea table.* **5.** Also called: **high tea.** *Brit. and Austral.* the main evening meal. **6.** *U.S.* a slang word for **marijuana.** [C17: from Chinese (Amoy) *t'e,* from Ancient Chinese *d'a*]

tea bag *n.* a small bag of paper or cloth containing tea leaves, infused in boiling water to make tea.

tea ball *n. Chiefly U.S.* a perforated metal ball filled with tea leaves and put in boiling water to make tea.

tea+ber·ry ('tiːbərɪ, -brɪ) *n., pl.* **·ries. 1.** the berry of the wintergreen (*Gaultheria procumbens*). **2.** another name for **wintergreen** (sense 1).

tea bis+cuit *n. Brit.* any of various semi-sweet biscuits.

tea+cake ('tiː,keɪk) *n. Brit.* a flat cake made from a yeast dough with raisins in it, usually eaten toasted and buttered.

tea+cart ('ti:ˌkɑ:t) *n.* a U.S. word for **tea trolley.**
teach (ti:tʃ) *vb.* **teach+es, teach+ing, taught. 1.** (*tr.; may take a clause as object or an infinitive;* often foll. by *how*) to help to learn; tell or show (how): *to teach someone to paint; to teach someone how to paint.* **2.** to give instruction or lessons in (a subject) to (a person or animal): *to teach French; to teach children; she teaches.* **3.** (*tr.; may take a clause as object or an infinitive*) to cause to learn or understand: *experience taught him that he could not be a journalist.* **4.** Also: **teach (someone) a lesson.** *Informal.* to cause (someone) to suffer the unpleasant consequences of some action or behaviour. [Old English *tǣcan;* related to *tācen* TOKEN, Old Frisian *tēken,* Old Saxon *tēkan,* Old High German *zeihhan,* Old Norse *teikn* sign] —**'teach+a·ble** *adj.*
Teach (ti:tʃ) *n.* **Ed·ward,** known as *Blackbeard.* died 1718, English pirate, active in the West Indies and on the Atlantic coast of North America.
teach+er ('ti:tʃə) *n.* **1.** a person whose occupation is teaching others, esp. children. **2.** a personified concept that teaches: *nature is a good teacher.* —**'teach+er+less** *adj.*
teach-in *n.* an informal conference, esp. on a topical subject, usually held at a university or college and involving a panel of visiting speakers, lecturers, students, etc.
teach+ing ('ti:tʃɪŋ) *n.* **1.** the art or profession of a teacher. **2.** something taught; precept.
teach+ing aid *n.* any device, object, or machine used by a teacher to clarify or enliven a subject.
teach+ing fel+low *n.* a postgraduate student who is given tuition, accommodation, expenses, etc., in return for some teaching duties. —**teach+ing fel+low+ship** *n.*
teach+ing ma+chine *n.* a machine that presents information and questions to the user, registers the answers, and indicates whether these are correct or acceptable.
tea co+sy *n.* a covering for a teapot to keep the contents hot, often having holes for the handle and spout.
tea+cup ('ti:ˌkʌp) *n.* **1.** a cup out of which tea may be drunk, larger than a coffee-cup. **2.** Also called: **tea+cup+ful.** the amount a teacup will hold, about four fluid ounces.
tea+house ('ti:ˌhaʊs) *n.* a restaurant, esp. in Japan or China, where tea and light refreshments are served.
teak (ti:k) *n.* **1.** a large verbenaceous tree, *Tectona grandis,* of the East Indies, having white flowers and yielding a valuable wood. **2.** the hard resinous yellowish-brown wood of this tree, used for furniture making, etc. **3.** any of various similar trees or their wood. **4.** a brown or yellowish-brown colour. [C17: from Portuguese *teca,* from Malayalam *tēkka*]
tea+ket·tle ('ti:ˌkɛtᵊl) *n.* a kettle for boiling water to make tea.
teal (ti:l) *n., pl.* **teals** *or* **teal. 1.** any of various small ducks, such as the Eurasian *Anas crecca* (**common teal**) that are related to the mallard and frequent ponds, lakes, and marshes. **2.** a greenish-blue colour. [C14: related to Middle Low German *tēlink,* Middle Dutch *tēling*]
tea leaf *n.* **1.** the dried leaf of the tea shrub, used to make tea. **2.** (*usually pl.*) shredded parts of these leaves, esp. after infusion.
team (ti:m) *n.* (*sometimes functioning as pl.*) **1.** a group of people organized to work together. **2.** a group of players forming one of the sides in a sporting contest. **3.** two or more animals working together to pull a vehicle or agricultural implement. **4.** such animals and the vehicle: *the coachman riding his team.* **5.** *Dialect.* a flock, herd, or brood. **6.** *Obsolete.* ancestry. ~*vb.* **7.** (when *intr.,* often foll. by *up*) to make or cause to make a team: *he teamed George with Robert.* **8.** (*tr.*) *U.S.* to drag or transport in or by a team. **9.** (*intr.*) *U.S.* to drive a team. [Old English *team* offspring; related to Old Frisian *tām* bridle, Old Norse *taumr* chain yoking animals together, Old High German *zoum* bridle]
tea-mak·er *n.* a spoon with a perforated cover used to infuse tea in a cup of boiling water. Also called (esp. Brit.): **infuser, tea egg.**
team-mate *n.* a fellow member of a team.
team spir+it *n.* willingness to cooperate as part of a team.
team+ster ('ti:mstə) *n.* **1.** a driver of a team of horses used for haulage. **2.** *U.S.* the driver of a lorry.
team teach+ing *n.* a system whereby two or more teachers pool their skills, knowledge, etc., to teach combined classes.
team+work ('ti:mˌwɜ:k) *n.* **1.** the cooperative work done by a team. **2.** the ability to work efficiently as a team.
tea+pot ('ti:ˌpɒt) *n.* a container with a lid, spout, and handle, in which tea is made and from which it is served.
tea+poy ('ti:pɔɪ) *n.* **1.** a small table or stand with a tripod base. **2.** a tea caddy on such a table or stand. [C19: from Hindi *tipāī,* from Sanskrit *tri* three + *pāda* foot; compare Persian *sīpæ* three-legged stand]
tear[1] (tɪə) *n.* **1.** a drop of the secretion of the lacrimal glands. See **tears. 2.** something shaped like a falling drop: *a tear of amber.* ~Also called: **teardrop.** [Old English *tēar,* related to Old Frisian, Old Norse *tār,* Old High German *zahar,* Greek *dakri*] —**'tear+less** *adj.*
tear[2] (tɛə) *vb.* **tears, tear+ing, tore, torn. 1.** to cause (material, paper, etc.) to come apart or (of material, etc.) to come apart; rip. **2.** (*tr.*) to make (a hole or split) in (something): *to tear a hole in a dress.* **3.** (*intr.;* often foll. by *along*) to hurry or rush: *to tear along the street.* **4.** (*tr.;* usually foll. by *away* or *from*) to remove or take by force. **5.** (when *intr.,* often foll. by *at*) to cause pain, distress, or anguish (to): *it tore at my heartstrings to see the starving child.* **6. tear one's hair.** *Informal.* to be angry, frustrated, very worried, etc. ~*n.* **7.** a hole, cut, or split. **8.** the act of tearing. **9.** a great hurry; rush. ~See also **tear away, tear down, tear into, tear off, torn.** [Old English *teran;* related to Old Saxon *terian,* Gothic *gatairan* to destroy, Old High German *zeran* to destroy] —**'tear+a·ble** *adj.* —**'tear+er** *n.*
tear a·way (tɛə) *vb.* **1.** (*tr., adv.*) to persuade (oneself or someone else) to leave: *I couldn't tear myself away from the television.* ~*n.* **tear+a·way. 2.** *Brit.* **a.** a reckless impetuous person. **b.** (*as modifier*): *a tearaway young man.*
tear down (tɛə) *vb.* (*tr., adv.*) to destroy or demolish: *to tear a wall down; to tear down an argument.*
tear duct (tɪə) *n.* the nontechnical name for **lacrimal duct.**
tear+ful ('tɪəfʊl) *adj.* **1.** about to cry. **2.** accompanying or indicative of weeping: *a tearful expression.* **3.** tending to produce tears; sad. —**'tear+ful+ly** *adv.* —**'tear+ful+ness** *n.*
tear gas (tɪə) *n.* any one of a number of gases or vapours that make the eyes smart and water, causing temporary blindness; usually dispersed from grenades and used in warfare and to control riots. Also called: **lacrimator.**
tear+ing ('tɛərɪŋ) *adj.* violent or furious (esp. in the phrase **tearing hurry** or **rush**). —**'tear+ing+ly** *adv.*
tear in·to (tɛə) *vb.* (*intr., prep.*) *Informal.* to attack vigorously and damagingly.
tear-jerk·er ('tɪəˌdʒɜ:kə) *n. Informal.* an excessively sentimental film, play, book, etc.
tear off (tɛə) *vb.* **1.** (*tr.*) to separate by tearing. **2.** (*intr., adv.*) to rush away; hurry. **3.** (*tr., adv.*) to produce in a hurry; do quickly and carelessly: *to tear off a letter.* **4. tear off a strip.** (*tr.*) *Brit. informal.* to reprimand or rebuke forcibly.
tea+room ('ti:ˌru:m, -ˌrʊm) *n.* another name for **teashop.**
tea rose *n.* **1.** any of several varieties of hybrid rose that are derived from *Rosa odorata* and have pink or yellow flowers with a scent resembling that of tea. **2. a.** a yellowish-pink colour. **b.** (*as adj.*): *tea-rose walls.*
tears (tɪəz) *pl. n.* **1.** the clear salty solution secreted by the lacrimal glands that lubricates and cleanses the surface of the eyeball and inner surface of the eyelids. **2.** a state of intense frustration (esp. in the phrase **bored to tears**). **3. in tears.** weeping. **4. without tears.** presented so as to be easily assimilated: *reading without tears.*
tear sheet (tɛə) *n.* a page in a newspaper or periodical that is cut or perforated so that it can be easily torn out.
tease (ti:z) *vb.* **1.** to annoy (someone) by deliberately offering something with the intention of delaying or withdrawing the offer. **2.** to arouse sexual desire in (someone) with no intention of satisfying it. **3.** to vex (someone) maliciously or playfully, esp. by ridicule. **4.** (*tr.*) to separate the fibres of; comb; card. **5.** (*tr.*) to raise the nap of (a fabric) with a teasel. **6.** another word (esp. U.S.) for **backcomb. 7.** (*tr.*) to loosen or pull apart (biological tissues, etc.) by delicate agitation or prodding with an instrument. ~*n.* **8.** a person or thing that teases. **9.** the act of teasing. [Old English *tǣsan;* related to Old High German *zeisan* to pick] —**'teas+er** *n.* —**'teas+ing+ly** *adv.*
tea+sel, tea+zel, *or* **tea+zle** ('ti:zəl) *n.* **1.** any of various stout biennial plants of the genus *Dipsacus,* of Eurasia and N Africa, having prickly leaves and prickly heads of yellow or purple flowers: family *Dipsacaceae.* See also **fuller's teasel. 2. a.** the prickly dried flower head of the fuller's teasel, used for teasing. **b.** any manufactured implement used for the same purpose. ~*vb.* **+sels, +sel+ling, +selled** *or U.S.* **+sels, +sel+ing, +seled. 3.** (*tr.*) to tease (a fabric). [Old English *tǣsel;* related to Old High German *zeisala* teasel, Norwegian *tīsl* undergrowth, *tīsla* to tear to bits; see TEASE] —**'tea+sel+ler** *n.*
tea ser+vice *or* **set** *n.* the china or pottery articles used in serving tea, including a teapot, cups, saucers, etc.
tea+shop ('ti:ˌʃɒp) *n. Brit.* a restaurant where tea and light refreshments are served. Also called: **tearoom.**
tea+spoon ('ti:ˌspu:n) *n.* **1.** a small spoon used for stirring tea, eating certain desserts, etc. **2.** Also called: **tea+spoon+ful** ('ti:spu:nˌfʊl). the amount contained in such a spoon. **3.** a unit of capacity used in cooking, medicine, etc., equal to about one fluid dram.
teat (ti:t) *n.* **1. a.** the nipple of a mammary gland. **b.** (in cows, etc.) any of the projections from the udder through which milk is discharged. See **nipple. 2.** something resembling a teat in shape or function, such as the rubber mouthpiece of a feeding bottle. [C13: from Old French *tete,* of Germanic origin; compare Old English *titt,* Middle High German *zitze*]
tea tow+el *or* **cloth** *n.* a towel for drying dishes and kitchen utensils. U.S. name: **dishtowel.**
tea tree *n.* any of various myrtaceous trees of the genus *Leptospermum,* of Australia and New Zealand, the leaves of which were formerly used to make tea.
tea trol+ley *n. Brit.* a trolley from which tea is served.
tea wag+on *n.* a U.S. name for **tea trolley.**
Te+bet *or* **Te+vet** ('tervəs; *Hebrew* te'vet) *n.* the fourth month of the civil year and the tenth of the ecclesiastical year in the Jewish calendar, falling in December and January. [C14: from Late Latin *tebeth,* from Hebrew *tēbhēth*]
tech. *abbrev. for:* **1.** technical. **2.** technology. **3.** *Informal.* technical college.
tech+ne+ti·um (tɛk'ni:ʃɪəm) *n.* a silvery-grey metallic element, artificially produced by bombardment of molybdenum by deuterons: used to inhibit corrosion in steel. The radioisotope **technetium-99m,** with a half-life of six hours, is used in radiotherapy. Symbol: Tc; atomic no.: 43; half-life of most stable isotope, ^{97}Tc: 2.6×10^6 years; valency: 2,4,5,6, or 7; relative density: 11.5 (approx.); melting pt.: 2200°C (approx.); boiling pt.: 5030°C. [C20: New Latin, from Greek *tekhnētos*

manmade, from *tekhnasthai* to devise artificially, from *tekhnē* skill]

tech+nic *n.* **1.** (tɛk'niːk). another word for **technique. 2.** ('tɛknɪk). another word for **technics.** [C17: from Latin *technicus,* from Greek *tekhnikos,* from *tekhnē* art, skill]

tech+ni+cal ('tɛknɪkəl) *adj.* **1.** of, relating to, or specializing in industrial, practical, or mechanical arts and applied sciences: *a technical institute.* **2.** skilled in practical and mechanical arts rather than theoretical or abstract thinking. **3.** relating to or characteristic of a particular field of activity: *the technical jargon of linguistics.* **4.** existing by virtue of a strict application of the rules or a strict interpretation of the wording: *a technical loophole in the law; a technical victory.* **5.** of, derived from, or showing technique: *technical brilliance.* **6.** (of a financial market) having prices determined by internal speculative or manipulative factors rather than by general or economic conditions. —**'tech+ni+cal+ly** *adv.* —**'tech+ni+cal+ness** *n.*

tech+ni+cal col+lege *n. Brit.* an institution for further education that provides courses in technology, art, secretarial skills, agriculture, etc.

tech+ni+cal+i·ty (ˌtɛknɪ'kælɪtɪ) *n., pl.* **·ties. 1.** a petty formal point arising from a strict interpretation of rules, etc.: *the case was dismissed on a technicality.* **2.** the state or quality of being technical. **3.** technical methods and vocabulary.

tech+ni+cal knock+out *n. Boxing.* a judgment of a knockout given when a boxer is in the referee's opinion too badly beaten to continue without risk of serious injury.

tech+ni+cal ser+geant *n.* a noncommissioned officer in the U.S. Marine Corps or Air Force ranking immediately subordinate to a master sergeant.

tech+ni+cian (tɛk'nɪʃən) *n.* **1.** a person skilled in mechanical or industrial techniques or in a particular technical field. **2.** a person employed in a laboratory, technical college, or scientific establishment to do mechanical and practical work. **3.** a person having specific artistic or mechanical skill, esp. if lacking original flair or genius.

Tech+ni+col+or ('tɛknɪˌkʌlə) *n. Trademark.* the process of producing colour film by means of superimposing synchronized films of the same scene, each of which has a different colour filter, to obtain the desired mix of colour.

tech+nics ('tɛknɪks) *n.* the study or theory of industry and industrial arts; technology.

tech+nique (tɛk'niːk) *or* **tech+nic** *n.* **1.** a practical method, skill, or art applied to a particular task. **2.** proficiency in a practical or mechanical skill. **3.** special facility; knack: *he had the technique of turning everything to his advantage.* [C19: from French, from *technique* (adj.) TECHNIC]

tech·no- *combining form.* **1.** craft or art: *technology; technography.* **2.** technological or technical: *technocracy.* [from Greek *tekhnē* skill]

tech+noc+ra+cy (tɛk'nɒkrəsɪ) *n., pl.* **+cies. 1.** a theory or system of society according to which government is controlled by scientists, engineers, and other experts. **2.** a body of such experts. **3.** a state considered to be governed or organized according to these principles. —**tech+no+crat** ('tɛknəˌkræt) *n.* —**ˌtech+no+'crat+ic** *adj.*

tech+nog+ra+phy (tɛk'nɒgrəfɪ) *n.* the study and description of the historical development of the arts and sciences in the context of their ethnic and geographical background.

technol. *abbrev. for:* **1.** technological. **2.** technology.

tech+nol+o·gy (tɛk'nɒlədʒɪ) *n., pl.* **·gies. 1.** the application of practical or mechanical sciences to industry or commerce. **2.** the methods, theory, and practices governing such application: *a highly developed technology.* **3.** the total knowledge and skills available to any human society for industry, art, science, etc. [C17: from Greek *tekhnologia* systematic treatment, from *tekhnē* art, skill] —**tech+no+log·i·cal** (ˌtɛknə'lɒdʒɪkəl) *adj.* —**ˌtech+no+'log·i·cal+ly** *adv.* —**tech+'nol·o·gist** *n.*

tech+no+struc+ture ('tɛknəʊˌstrʌktʃə) *n.* the people who control the technology of a society, such as professional administrators, experts in business management, etc.

tech·y ('tɛtʃɪ) *adj.* **tech·i+er, tech·i+est.** a variant spelling of **tetchy.** —**'tech·i+ly** *adv.* —**'tech·i+ness** *n.*

tec+ton+ic (tɛk'tɒnɪk) *adj.* **1.** denoting or relating to construction or building. **2.** *Geology.* **a.** (of landforms, rock masses, etc.) resulting from distortion of the earth's crust due to forces within it. **b.** (of processes, movements, etc.) occurring within the earth's crust and causing structural deformation. [C17: from Late Latin *tectonicus,* from Greek *tektonikos* belonging to carpentry, from *tektōn* a builder] —**tec+'ton·i+cal+ly** *adv.*

tec+ton+ics (tɛk'tɒnɪks) *n.* (*functioning as sing.*) **1.** the art and science of construction or building. **2.** the study of the processes by which the earth's surface has attained its present structure. See also **plate tectonics.**

tec+tor+i+al mem+brane (tɛk'tɔːrɪəl) *n.* the membrane in the inner ear that covers the organ of Corti. [C19: *tectorial,* from Latin *tectōrium* a covering, from *tegere* to cover]

tec+trix ('tɛktrɪks) *n., pl.* **tec+tri+ces** ('tɛktrɪˌsiːz, tɛk'traɪsiːz). *Ornithol.* (*usually pl.*) another name for **covert** (sense 7). [C19: New Latin, from Latin *tector* plasterer, from *tegere* to cover] —**tec+tri+cial** (tɛk'trɪʃəl) *adj.*

Te·cum·seh (tɪ'kʌmsə) *n.* ?1768–1813, American Indian chief of the Shawnee tribe. He attempted to unite western Indian tribes against the Whites, but was defeated at Tippecanoe (1811). He was killed while fighting for the British in the War of 1812.

ted[1] (tɛd) *vb.* **teds, ted+ding, ted+ded.** to shake out and loosen (hay), so as to dry it. [C15: from Old Norse *tethja;* related to *tad* dung, Old High German *zetten* to spread]

ted[2] (tɛd) *Informal. abbrev. for* **teddy boy.**

ted+der ('tɛdə) *n.* **1.** a machine equipped with a series of small rotating forks for tedding hay. **2.** a person who teds.

Ted·der ('tɛdə) *n.* **Ar·thur Wil·liam,** 1st Baron Tedder of Glenguin. 1890–1967, British marshal of the Royal Air Force; deputy commander under Eisenhower of the Allied Expeditionary Force (1944–45).

ted+dy bear *n.* a stuffed toy bear made from soft or fluffy material. Often shortened to **teddy.** [C20: from *Teddy,* from *Theodore,* after Theodore ROOSEVELT, who was well known as a hunter of bears]

ted+dy boy *n.* **1.** (in Britain, esp. in the mid-1950s) one of a cult of youths who wore mock Edwardian fashions, such as tight narrow trousers, pointed shoes, and long sideboards. **2.** any tough or delinquent youth. [C20: from *Teddy,* from *Edward,* referring to the Edwardian dress]

ted+dy girl *n.* a girl companion to a teddy boy.

Te De+um (ˌtiː 'diːəm) *n.* **1.** an ancient Latin hymn in rhythmic prose, sung or recited at matins in the Roman Catholic Church and in English translation at morning prayer in the Church of England and used by both Churches as an expression of thanksgiving on special occasions. **2.** a musical setting of this hymn. **3.** a service of thanksgiving in which the recital of this hymn forms a central part. [from the Latin canticle beginning *Tē Deum laudāmus,* literally: Thee, God, we praise]

te+di+ous ('tiːdɪəs) *adj.* **1.** causing fatigue or tedium; monotonous. **2.** *Obsolete.* progressing very slowly. —**'te+di+ous+ly** *adv.* —**'te+di+ous+ness** *n.*

te+di·um ('tiːdɪəm) *n.* the state of being bored or the quality of being boring; monotony. [C17: from Latin *taedium,* from *taedēre* to weary]

tee[1] (tiː) *n.* **1.** a pipe fitting in the form of a letter *T,* used to join three pipes. **2.** a metal section with a cross section in the form of a letter *T,* such as a rolled-steel joist.

tee[2] (tiː) *Golf.* ~*n.* **1.** Also called: **teeing ground.** an area, often slightly elevated, from which the first stroke of a hole is made. **2.** a support for a golf ball, usually a small wood or plastic peg, used when teeing off or in long grass, etc. ~*vb.* **tees, tee+ing, teed. 3.** (when *intr.,* often foll. by *up*) to position (the ball) ready for striking, on or as if on a tee. ~See also **tee off.** [C17 *teaz,* of unknown origin]

tee[3] (tiː) *n.* **1.** a mark used as a target in certain games such as curling and quoits. **2. to a tee.** perfectly or exactly: *that dress suits you to a tee.* [C18: perhaps from T-shaped marks, which may have originally been used in curling]

teem[1] (tiːm) *vb.* **1.** (*intr.;* usually foll. by *with*) to be prolific or abundant (in); abound (in). **2.** *Obsolete.* to bring forth (young). [Old English *tēman* to produce offspring; related to West Saxon *tīeman;* see TEAM] —**'teem+er** *n.*

teem[2] (tiːm) *vb.* **1.** (*intr.;* often foll. by *down* or *with rain*) to pour in torrents: *it's teeming down.* **2.** (*tr.*) to pour or empty out. [C15 *temen* to empty, from Old Norse *tœma;* related to Old English *tōm,* Old High German *zuomīg* empty]

teen[1] (tiːn) *adj. Chiefly U.S.* another word for **teenage.**

teen[2] (tiːn) *n. Obsolete.* affliction or woe. [Old English *tēona;* related to Old Saxon *tiono,* Old Frisian *tiona* injury]

teen+age ('tiːnˌeɪdʒ) *adj. also* **teen+aged. 1.** (*prenominal*) of or relating to the time in a person's life between the ages of 13 and 19 inclusive. ~*n.* **2.** this period of time.

teen+ag·er ('tiːnˌeɪdʒə) *n.* a person between the ages of 13 and 19 inclusive.

teens (tiːnz) *pl. n.* **1.** the years of a person's life between the ages of 13 and 19 inclusive. **2.** all the numbers that end in *-teen.*

tee+ny ('tiːnɪ) *adj.* **+ni+er, +ni+est.** extremely small; tiny. Also: **tee·ny-wee·ny** ('tiːnɪ'wiːnɪ) *or* **teen·sy-ween·sy** ('tiːnzɪ 'wiːnzɪ). [C19: variant of TINY]

tee·ny+bop·per ('tiːnɪˌbɒpə) *n. Slang.* a young teenager, usually a girl, who avidly follows fashions in clothes and pop music. [C20: *teeny,* from TEENAGE + *-bopper* see BOP[1]]

tee off *vb.* (*adv.*) **1.** *Golf.* to strike (the ball) from a tee, as when starting a hole. **2.** *Informal.* to begin; start.

tee+pee ('tiːpiː) *n.* a variant spelling of **tepee.**

Tees (tiːz) *n.* a river in N England, rising in the N Pennines and flowing southeast and east to the North Sea at Middlesbrough. Length: 113 km (70 miles).

tee shirt *n.* a variant of **T-shirt.**

Tees+side ('tiːzˌsaɪd) *n.* the industrial region around the lower Tees valley and estuary: a county borough, containing Middlesbrough, from 1968 to 1974.

tee+ter ('tiːtə) *vb.* **1.** to move or cause to move unsteadily; wobble. ~*n., vb.* **2.** another word for **seesaw.** [C19: from Middle English *titeren,* related to Old Norse *titra* to tremble, Old High German *zittarōn* to shiver]

teeth (tiːθ) *n.* **1.** the plural of **tooth. 2.** the most violent part: *the teeth of the gale.* **3.** the power to produce a desired effect: *that law has no teeth.* **4. by the skin of one's teeth.** See **skin** (sense 11). **5. get one's teeth into.** to become engrossed in. **6. in the teeth of.** in direct opposition to; against: *in the teeth of violent criticism he went ahead with his plan.* **7. to the teeth.** to the greatest possible degree: *armed to the teeth.* **8. show one's teeth.** to threaten, esp. in a defensive manner.

teethe (tiːð) *vb.* (*intr.*) to cut one's baby (deciduous) teeth.

teeth+ing ring *n.* a plastic, hard rubber, or bone ring on which babies may bite while teething.

teeth+ing trou+bles *pl. n.* the difficulties or problems that arise during the initial stages of a project, enterprise, etc.

tee+to+tal (tiː'təʊtəl) *adj.* **1.** of, relating to, or practising abstinence from alcoholic drink. **2.** *Informal.* complete. [C19: allegedly coined in 1833 by Richard Turner, English advocate of total abstinence from alcoholic liquors; probably from TOTAL, with emphatic reduplication] —**tee+'to+tal+ler** *n.* —**tee+'to+tal+ly** *adv.* —**tee+'to+tal+ism** *n.*

tee+to+tum (tiː'təʊtəm) *n. Archaic.* **1.** a spinning top bearing letters of the alphabet on its four sides. **2.** such a top used as a die in gambling games. [C18: from *T totum,* from *T* initial inscribed on one of the faces + *totum* the name of the toy, from Latin *tōtum* the whole]

tef *or* **teff** (tɛf) *n.* an annual grass, *Eragrostis abyssinica,* of NE Africa, grown for its grain. [C18: from Amharic *tēf*]

Tef+lon ('tɛflɒn) *n.* a trademark for **polytetrafluoroethylene.**

teg (tɛg) *n.* **1.** a two-year-old sheep. **2.** the fleece of a two-year-old sheep. [C16: of unknown origin]

teg+men ('tɛgmən) *n., pl.* **+mi+na** (-mənə). **1.** either of the leathery forewings of the cockroach and related insects. **2.** the delicate inner covering of a seed. **3.** any similar covering or layer. [C19: from Latin: a cover, variant of *tegimen,* from *tegere* to cover] —**'teg+mi+nal** *adj.*

Te+gu+ci+gal+pa (*Spanish* teˌɣusi'ɣalpa) *n.* the capital of Honduras, in the south on the Choluteca River: founded about 1579; university (1847). Pop.: 305 387 (1974).

teg·u+lar ('tɛgjələ) *adj.* **1.** of, relating to, or resembling a tile or tiles. **2.** *Biology.* overlapping like a series of tiles: *tegular scales.* [C18: from Latin *tēgula* a tile, from *tegere* to cover] —**'teg·u+lar+ly** *adv.*

teg·u+ment ('tɛgjʊmənt) *n.* a less common word for **integument.** [C15: from Latin *tegumentum* a covering, from *tegere* to cover] —**teg·u+men+tal** (ˌtɛgjʊ'mɛntᵊl) *or* ˌ**teg·u+'men+ta+ry** *adj.*

te-hee (tiː'hiː) *interj.* **1.** an exclamation of laughter, esp. when mocking. ~*n.* **2.** a chuckle. ~*vb.* **-hees, -hee·ing, -heed. 3.** (*intr.*) to snigger or laugh, esp. derisively. [C14: of imitative origin]

Te+he+ran (tɛə'rɑːn, -'ræn) *n.* the capital of Iran, at the foot of the Elburz Mountains: built on the site of the ancient capital Ray, destroyed by Mongols in 1220; became capital in the 1790s; three universities. Pop.: 4 002 000 (1973 est.).

Te+huan+te+pec (tə'wɑːntəˌpɛk) *n.* **Isth+mus of.** the narrowest part of S Mexico, with the Bay of Campeche on the north coast and the **Gulf of Tehuantepec** (an inlet of the Pacific) on the south coast.

Tei+de *or* **Tey+de** (*Spanish* 'teɪðe) *n.* **Pi·co de** ('piko ðe). a volcanic mountain in the Canary Islands, on Tenerife. Height: 3718 m (12 166 ft.).

te ig·i+tur *Latin.* (teɪ 'ɪdʒɪtʊə; *English* teɪ 'ɪgɪˌtʊə) *n. R.C. Church.* the first prayer of the canon of the Mass, which begins *Te igitur clementissime Pater* (*Thee, therefore, most merciful Father*).

Teil·hard de Char·din (*French* tɛjar də ʃar'dɛ̃) *n.* **Pierre** (pjɛːr). 1881–1955, French Jesuit priest, palaeontologist, and philosopher. In *The Phenomenon of Man* (1938–40), he explored the mystery of man's evolution and cites his scientific findings as proof of the existence of God.

Te·jo ('təʒu) *n.* the Portuguese name for the **Tagus.**

Te Kan·a·wa (teɪ 'kɑːnəwə) *n.* Dame **Ki·ri** ('kɪrɪ). born 1947, New Zealand operatic soprano.

tek+tite ('tɛktaɪt) *n.* any of various dark green to black glassy siliceous bodies that are thought to derive from meteorites. [C20: from Greek *tēktos* molten]

tel. *abbrev. for:* **1.** telegram. **2.** telegraph(ic). **3.** telephone.

tel- *combining form.* variant of **tele-** and **telo-** before a vowel.

te·la ('tiːlə) *n., pl.* **·lae** (-liː). *Anatomy.* any delicate tissue or weblike structure. [from New Latin, from Latin: a web]

tel+aes+the+si·a *or U.S.* **tel+es+the+si·a** ('tɛliːs'θiːzɪə) *n.* the alleged perception of events that are beyond the normal range of perceptual processes. Compare **telegnosis, clairvoyance.** —**tel+aes+thet+ic** *or U.S.* **tel+es+thet+ic** (ˌtɛlɪs'θɛtɪk) *adj.*

tel·a+mon ('tɛləmən) *n., pl.* **+mon·es** (-'məʊniːz) *or* **+mons.** a column in the form of a male figure, used to support an entablature. Also called: **atlas.** Compare **caryatid.** [C18: via Latin from Greek, from *tlēnai* to bear]

Tel·a+nai·pu+ra (ˌtɛlənaɪ'pʊərə) *n.* another name for **Djambi.**

tel+an+gi+ec+ta+sis (tɪˌlændʒɪ'ɛktəsɪs) *or* **tel+an+gi+ec+ta+si·a** (tɪˌlændʒɪɛk'teɪzɪə) *n., pl.* **+ses** (-ˌsiːz). *Pathol.* an abnormal dilation of the capillaries or terminal arteries producing blotched red spots, esp. on the face or thighs. [C19: New Latin, from Greek *telos* end + *angeion* vessel + *ektasis* dilation] —**tel+an+gi+ec+tat+ic** (tɪˌlændʒɪɛk'tætɪk) *adj.*

Tel+au·to+graph (tɛl'ɔːtəˌgræf, -ˌgrɑːf) *n. Trademark.* a telegraphic device for reproducing handwriting, drawings, etc., the movements of an electromagnetically controlled pen at one end being transmitted along a line to a similar pen at the receiving end. —**tel+ˌau·to+'graph+ic** *adj.* —**tel+au·tog+ra+phy** (ˌtɛlɔː'tɒgrəfɪ) *n.*

Tel A·viv ('tɛl ə'viːv) *n.* a city in W Israel, on the Mediterranean: the largest city and chief financial centre in Israel; incorporated with the city of Jaffa in 1950; university (1953). Pop.: 357 600 (1974 est.). Official name: **Tel A·viv-Jaf·fa** ('tɛl ə'viːv 'dʒæfə).

tel·e- *or before a vowel* **tel-** *combining form.* **1.** at or over a distance; distant: *telescope; telegony; telekinesis; telemeter.* **2.** television: *telecast.* [from Greek *tele* far]

tel·e+cast ('tɛləˌkɑːst) *vb.* **+casts, +cast+ing, +cast** *or* **+cast+ed. 1.** to broadcast (a programme) by television. ~*n.* **2.** a television broadcast. —**'tel·e+ˌcast+er** *n.*

telecomm. *abbrev. for* telecommunication(s).

tel·e+com+mu+ni+ca+tion (ˌtɛlɪkəˌmjuːnɪ'keɪʃən) *n.* the telegraphic or telephonic communication of audio or video information over a distance by means of radio waves, optical signals, etc., or along a transmission line.

tel·e+com+mu+ni+ca+tions (ˌtɛlɪkəˌmjuːnɪ'keɪʃənz) *n.* (*functioning as sing.*) the science and technology of communications by telephony, radio, television, etc.

tel+e·du ('tɛlɪˌduː) *n.* a badger, *Mydaus javanensis,* of SE Asia and Indonesia, having dark brown hair with a white stripe along the back and producing a fetid secretion from the anal glands when attacked. [C19: from Malay]

teleg. *abbrev. for:* **1.** telegram. **2.** telegraph(ic). **3.** telegraphy.

te+le+ga (tɛ'leɪgə) *n.* a rough four-wheeled cart used in Russia. [C16: from Russian]

tel·e+gen+ic (ˌtɛlɪ'dʒɛnɪk) *adj.* having or showing a pleasant television image. [C20: from TELE(VISION) + (PHOTO)GENIC] —ˌ**tel·e+'gen·i+cal+ly** *adj.*

tel+eg+no+sis (ˌtɛlə'nəʊsɪs, ˌtɛləg-) *n.* knowledge about distant events alleged to have been obtained without the use of any normal sensory mechanism. Compare **clairvoyance.** [C20: from TELE- + *-gnosis,* from Greek *gnōsis* knowledge] —**tel+eg+nos+tic** (ˌtɛlə'nɒstɪk, ˌtɛləg-) *adj.*

Te·leg·o·nus (tə'lɛgənəs) *n. Greek myth.* a son of Odysseus and Circe, who sought his father and mistakenly killed him, later marrying Odysseus' widow Penelope.

te+leg·o·ny (tɪ'lɛgənɪ) *n. Genetics.* the supposed influence of a previous sire on offspring borne by a female to other sires. —**tel+e·gon+ic** (ˌtɛlə'gɒnɪk) *or* **te+'leg·o+nous** *adj.*

tel·e+gram ('tɛləˌgræm) *n.* a communication transmitted by telegraph. See also **letter telegram, cable** (sense 5). —ˌ**tel·e+'gram+mic** *or* **tel·e+gram+mat+ic** (ˌtɛləgrə'mætɪk) *adj.*

tel·e+graph ('tɛlɪˌgræf, -ˌgrɑːf) *n.* **1. a.** a device, system, or process by which information can be transmitted over a distance, esp. using radio signals or coded electrical signals sent along a transmission line connected to a transmitting and a receiving instrument. **b.** (*as modifier*): *telegraph pole.* **2.** a message transmitted by such a device, system, or process; telegram. ~*vb.* **3.** to send a telegram to (a person or place); wire. **4.** (*tr.*) to transmit or send by telegraph. **5.** (*tr.*) *Boxing, informal.* to prepare to deliver a punch so obviously that one's opponent has ample time to avoid it. **6.** (*tr.*) to give advance notice of (anything), esp. unintentionally. **7.** (*tr.*) *Canadian informal.* to cast (votes) illegally by impersonating registered voters. —**te+leg+ra+pher** (tə'lɛgrəfə) *or* **te+'leg+ra+phist** *n.*

tel·e+graph+ic (ˌtɛlɪ'græfɪk) *adj.* **1.** used in or transmitted by telegraphy. **2.** of or relating to a telegraph. **3.** having a concise style; clipped: *telegraphic speech.* —ˌ**tel·e+'graph·i+cal+ly** *adv.*

tel·e+graph plant *n.* a small tropical Asian leguminous shrub, *Desmodium gyrans,* having small leaflets that turn in various directions during the day and droop at night.

te+leg+ra+phy (tɪ'lɛgrəfɪ) *n.* **1.** a system of telecommunications involving any process providing reproduction at a distance of written, printed, or pictorial matter. See also **facsimile** (sense 2). **2.** the skill or process of operating a telegraph.

Tel+e·gu ('tɛləguː) *n.* a variant spelling of **Telugu.**

tel·e+ki+ne+sis (ˌtɛlɪkaɪ'niːsɪs, -kɪ-) *n.* **1.** the movement of a body caused by thought or willpower without the application of a physical force. **2.** the ability to cause such movement. —**tel·e+ki+net+ic** (ˌtɛlɪkɪ'nɛtɪk) *adj.*

Te+lem·a+chus (tə'lɛməkəs) *n. Greek myth.* the son of Odysseus and Penelope, who helped his father slay his mother's suitors.

Te·le·mann (*German* 'teːləˌman) *n.* **Ge·org Phi·lipp** ('geːɔrk 'fiːlɪp). 1681–1767, German composer, noted for his prolific output.

tel·e+mark ('tɛlɪˌmɑːk) *n.* **1.** *Skiing.* a turn in which one ski is placed far forward of the other and turned gradually inwards. **2.** a step in ballroom dancing involving a heel pivot. [C20: named after *Telemark,* county in Norway]

te+lem+e·ter (tɪ'lɛmɪtə) *n.* **1.** any device for recording or measuring a distant event and transmitting the data to a receiver or observer. **2.** any device or apparatus used to measure a distance without directly comparing it with a measuring rod, etc., esp. one that depends on the measurement of angles. ~*vb.* **3.** (*tr.*) to obtain and transmit (data) from a distant source, esp. from a spacecraft. —**tel·e+met+ric** (ˌtɛlɪ'mɛtrɪk) *or* ˌ**tel·e+'met+ri+cal** *adj.* —ˌ**tel·e+'met+ri+cal+ly** *adv.*

te+lem+e·try (tɪ'lɛmɪtrɪ) *n.* **1.** the use of radio waves, telephone lines, etc., to transmit the readings of measuring instruments to a device on which the readings can be indicated or recorded. See also **radiotelemetry. 2.** the measurement of linear distance using a tellurometer.

tel+en+ceph·a+lon (ˌtɛlɛn'sɛfəˌlɒn) *n.* the cerebrum together with related parts of the hypothalamus and the third ventricle. —**tel+en+ce·phal+ic** (ˌtɛlɛnsɪ'fælɪk) *adj.*

tel·e+ol·o·gy (ˌtɛlɪ'ɒlədʒɪ, ˌtiːlɪ-) *n.* **1.** *Philosophy.* **a.** the study of the evidence of design or purpose in nature. **b.** the ultimate purpose of things, esp. natural processes. **c.** the belief that final causes exist. **2.** *Biology.* the belief that natural phenomena have a predetermined purpose and are not determined by mechanical laws. [C18: from New Latin *teleologia,* from Greek *telos* end + -LOGY] —**tel·e·o+log·i+cal** (ˌtɛlɪə'lɒdʒɪkᵊl, ˌtiːlɪ-) *or* ˌ**tel·e·o+'log+ic** *adj.* —ˌ**tel·e·o+'log·i+cal+ly** *adv.* —ˌ**tel·e+'ol·o+gism** *n.* —ˌ**tel·e+'ol·o+gist** *n.*

tel·e·ost ('tɛlɪˌɒst, 'tiːlɪ-) *n.* **1.** any bony fish of the subclass *Teleostei,* having rayed fins and a swim bladder: the group contains most of the bony fishes, including the herrings, carps, eels, cod, perches, etc. ~*adj.* **2.** of, relating to, or belonging to the *Teleostei.* [C19: from New Latin *teleosteī* (pl.) creatures having complete skeletons, from Greek *teleos* complete + *osteon* bone]

te+lep·a+thize *or* **te+lep·a+thise** (tɪ'lɛpəˌθaɪz) *vb.* (*intr.*) to practise telepathy.

te+lep·a+thy (tɪ'lɛpəθɪ) *n. Psychol.* the communication between people of thoughts, feelings, desires, etc., involving mechanisms that cannot be understood in terms of known scientific laws. Also called: **thought transference.** Compare **telegnosis, clairvoyance.** —**tel·e·path·ic** (ˌtɛlɪˈpæθɪk) *adj.* —ˌ**tel·e·ˈpath·i·cal·ly** *adv.* —**te·ˈlep·a·thist** *n.*

tel·e·phone (ˈtɛlɪˌfəʊn) *n.* **1. a.** Also called: **telephone set.** an electrical device for transmitting speech, consisting of a microphone and receiver mounted on a handset. **b.** (*as modifier*): *a telephone receiver.* **2. a.** a worldwide system of communications using telephones. The microphone in one telephone converts sound waves into electrical oscillations that are transmitted along a telephone wire or by radio to one or more distant sets, the receivers of which reconvert the incoming signal into the original sound. **b.** (*as modifier*): *a telephone exchange; a telephone call.* **3.** See **telephone box.** ~*vb.* **4.** to call or talk to (a person) by telephone. **5.** to transmit (a recorded message, radio or television programme, or other information) by telephone, using special transmitting and receiving equipment. ~Often shortened to **phone.** —ˈ**tel·e·ˌphon·er** *n.*

tel·e·phone box *n.* a soundproof enclosure from which a paid telephone call can be made. Also called: **telephone kiosk, telephone booth.**

tel·e·phone di·rec·to·ry *n.* a book listing the names, addresses, and telephone numbers of subscribers in a particular area.

tel·e·phone num·ber *n.* a set of figures identifying the telephone of a particular subscriber, and used in making connections to that telephone.

te·leph·o·nist (tɪˈlɛfənɪst) *n.* *Brit.* a person who operates a telephone switchboard. Also called (esp. U.S.): **telephone operator.**

te·leph·o·ny (tɪˈlɛfənɪ) *n.* a system of telecommunications for the transmission of speech or other sounds.

tel·e·pho·tog·ra·phy (ˌtɛlɪfəˈtɒgrəfɪ) *n.* the process or technique of photographing distant objects using a telephoto lens. —**tel·e·pho·to·graph·ic** (ˌtɛlɪˌfəʊtəˈgræfɪk) *adj.*

tel·e·pho·to lens (ˈtɛlɪˌfəʊtəʊ) *n.* a lens system that can be attached to a camera to increase the effective focal length of the camera lens and thus produce a magnified image of a distant object. See also **zoom lens.**

tel·e·play (ˈtɛlɪˌpleɪ) *n.* a play specially written or produced for television.

tel·e·print·er (ˈtɛlɪˌprɪntə) *n.* **1.** a telegraph apparatus consisting of a keyboard transmitter, which converts a typed message into coded pulses for transmission along a wire or cable, and a printing receiver, which converts incoming signals and prints out the message. U.S. name: **teletypewriter.** See also **telex, radioteletype. 2.** a network of such devices, widely used for communicating information, etc. **3.** a similar device used for direct input/output of data into a computer at a distant location.

Tel·e·ran (ˈtɛləˌræn) *n.* *Trademark.* an electronic navigational aid in which the image of a ground-based radar system is televised to aircraft in flight so that a pilot can see the position of his aircraft in relation to others. [C20: from *Tele*(*vision*) *R*(*adar*) *A*(*ir*) *N*(*avigation*)]

tel·e·scope (ˈtɛlɪˌskəʊp) *n.* **1.** an optical instrument for making distant objects appear closer by use of a combination of lenses (**refracting telescope**) or lenses and curved mirrors (**reflecting telescope**). See also **terrestrial telescope, astronomical telescope, Cassegrainian telescope, Galilean telescope, Newtonian telescope. 2.** any instrument, such as a radio telescope, for collecting, focusing, and detecting electromagnetic radiation from space. ~*vb.* **3.** to crush together or be crushed together, as in a collision: *the front of the car was telescoped by the impact.* **4.** to fit together like a set of cylinders that slide into one another, thus allowing extension and shortening. **5.** to make or become smaller or shorter: *the novel was telescoped into a short play.* [C17: from Italian *telescopio* (Galileo) or New Latin *telescopium,* literally: far-seeing instrument; see TELE-, -SCOPE]

tel·e·scop·ic (ˌtɛlɪˈskɒpɪk) *adj.* **1.** of or relating to a telescope. **2.** seen through or obtained by means of a telescope. **3.** visible only with the aid of a telescope. **4.** able to see far. **5.** having or consisting of parts that telescope: *a telescopic umbrella.* —ˌ**tel·e·ˈscop·i·cal·ly** *adv.*

tel·e·scop·ic sight *n.* a telescope mounted on a rifle, etc., used for sighting.

Tel·e·sco·pi·um (ˌtɛlɪˈskəʊpɪəm) *n., Latin genitive* **Tel·e·sco·pi·i** (ˌtɛlɪˈskəʊpɪˌaɪ). an inconspicuous constellation in the S hemisphere, close to Sagittarius and Ara. [New Latin; see TELESCOPE]

te·les·co·py (tɪˈlɛskəpɪ) *n.* the branch of astronomy concerned with the use and design of telescopes.

tel·e·script (ˈtɛlɪˌskrɪpt) *n.* a script either written or adapted for use in television.

tel·e·sis (ˈtɛlɪsɪs) *n.* the purposeful use of natural and social processes to obtain specific social goals. [C19: from Greek: event, from *telein* to fulfil, from *telos* end]

tel·e·spec·tro·scope (ˌtɛlɪˈspɛktrəˌskəʊp) *n.* a combination of a telescope and a spectroscope, used for spectroscopic analysis of radiation from stars and other celestial bodies.

tel·e·ste·re·o·scope (ˌtɛlɪˈstɪərɪəˌskəʊp, -ˈstɛrɪ-) *n.* an optical instrument for obtaining stereoscopic images of distant objects.

tel·es·the·si·a (ˌtɛliːsˈθiːzɪə) *n.* the usual U.S. spelling of **telaesthesia.** —**tel·es·thet·ic** (ˌtɛliːsˈθɛtɪk) *adj.*

te·les·tich (təˈlɛstɪk, ˈtɛlɪˌstɪk) *n.* a short poem in which the last letters of each successive line form a word. [C17: from Greek *telos* end + STICH]

tel·e·thon (ˈtɛləˌθɒn) *n.* *U.S.* a lengthy television programme to raise charity funds, etc. [C20: from TELE- + MARATHON]

tel·e·tran·scrip·tion (ˌtɛlɪtrænˈskrɪpʃən) *n.* the transcription of a television programme by means of a video tape, etc.

tel·e·tube (ˈtɛlɪˌtjuːb) *n.* short for **television tube.**

Tel·e·type (ˈtɛlɪˌtaɪp) *n.* **1.** *Trademark.* a type of teleprinter. **2.** (*sometimes not cap.*) a network of such devices, used for communicating messages, information, etc. ~*vb.* **3.** (*sometimes not cap.*) to transmit (a message) by Teletype.

Tel·e·type·set·ter (ˌtɛlɪˈtaɪpˌsɛtə, ˈtɛlɪˌtaɪp-) *n.* *Trademark, printing.* a keyboard device whose output can either be punched tape, which can be used directly to operate a line-casting machine, or be transmitted by cable or wire to operate such a machine indirectly. —ˌ**tel·e·ˈtype·ˌset·ting** *n.*

tel·e·type·writ·er (ˌtɛlɪˈtaɪpˌraɪtə, ˈtɛlɪˌtaɪp-) *n.* a U.S. name for **teleprinter.**

te·leu·to·spore (təˈluːtəˌspɔː) *n.* another name for **teliospore.** [C19: from Greek *teleutē,* from *telos* end + SPORE] —**te·ˌleu·to·ˈspor·ic** *adj.*

tel·e·vise (ˈtɛlɪˌvaɪz) *vb.* **1.** to put (a programme) on television. **2.** (*tr.*) to transmit (a programme, signal, etc.) by television.

tel·e·vi·sion (ˈtɛlɪˌvɪʒən) *n.* **1.** the system or process of producing on a distant screen a series of transient visible images, usually with an accompanying sound signal. Electrical signals, converted from optical images by a camera tube, are transmitted by UHF or VHF radio waves or by cable (**closed circuit television**) and reconverted into optical images by means of a television tube inside a television set. **2.** Also called: **television set.** a device designed to receive and convert incoming electrical signals into a series of visible images on a screen together with accompanying sound. **3.** the content, etc., of television programmes. **4.** the occupation or profession concerned with any aspect of the broadcasting of television programmes: *he's in television.* **5.** (*modifier*) of, relating to, or used in the transmission or reception of video and audio UHF or VHF radio signals: *a television transmitter.* ~Abbrev.: **TV.** —ˌ**tel·e·ˈvi·sion·al** *adj.* —ˌ**tel·e·ˈvi·sion·al·ly** *adv.* —ˌ**tel·e·ˈvi·sion·ar·y** *adj.*

tel·e·vi·sion tube *n.* a cathode-ray tube designed for the reproduction of television pictures. Sometimes shortened to **tube, teletube.** Also called: **picture tube.**

tel·e·writ·er (ˈtɛlɪˌraɪtə) *n.* a telegraphic device for reproducing handwriting by converting the manually controlled movements of a pen into signals that, after transmission, control the movements of a similar pen.

tel·ex (ˈtɛlɛks) *n.* **1.** an international telegraph service in which teleprinters are rented out to subscribers for the purpose of direct communication. **2.** a teleprinter used in such a service. **3.** a message transmitted or received by telex. ~*vb.* **4.** to transmit (a message) to (a person, office, etc.) by telex. [C20: from *tel*(*eprinter*) *ex*(*change*)]

tel·fer (ˈtɛlfə) *n.* a variant spelling of **telpher.**

tel·fer·age (ˈtɛlfərɪdʒ) *n.* a variant spelling of **telpherage.**

Tel·ford[1] (ˈtɛlfəd) *n.* a town in W central England, in Salop: designated a new town in 1963. Pop.: 79 827 (1971).

Tel·ford[2] (ˈtɛlfəd) *n.* **Thom·as.** 1757–1834, Scottish civil engineer, known esp. for his roads and such bridges as the Menai suspension bridge (1825).

tel·ic (ˈtɛlɪk) *adj.* **1.** directed or moving towards some goal; purposeful. **2.** (of a clause or phrase) expressing purpose. [C19: from Greek *telikos* final, from *telos* end]

te·li·o·spore (ˈtiːlɪəˌspɔː) *n.* any of the dark noninfective spores that are produced in each telium of the rust fungi and remain dormant during the winter. Also called: **teleutospore.** [C20: from TELIUM + SPORE]

te·li·um (ˈtiːlɪəm, ˈtɛl-) *n., pl.* **te·li·a** (ˈtiːlɪə, ˈtɛlɪə). the spore-producing body of some rust fungi in which the teliospores are formed. [C20: New Latin, from Greek *teleion,* from *teleios* complete, from *telos* end] —ˈ**te·li·al** *adj.*

tell[1] (tɛl) *vb.* **tells, tell·ing, told. 1.** (when *tr., may take a clause as object*) to let know or notify: *he told me that he would go.* **2.** (*tr.*) to order or instruct (someone to do something): *I told her to send the letter airmail.* **3.** (when *intr.,* usually foll. by *of*) to give an account or narration of (something): *she told me her troubles.* **4.** (*tr.*) to communicate by words; utter: *to tell the truth.* **5.** (*tr.*) to make known; disclose: *to tell fortunes.* **6.** (*intr.;* often foll. by *of*) to serve as an indication: *her blush told of her embarrassment.* **7.** (*tr.;* used with *can,* etc.; *may take a clause as object*) to comprehend, discover, or discern: *I can tell what is wrong.* **8.** (*tr.;* used with *can,* etc.) to distinguish or discriminate: *he couldn't tell chalk from cheese.* **9.** (*intr.*) to have or produce an impact, effect, or strain: *every step told on his bruised feet.* **10.** (*intr.;* sometimes foll. by *on*) *Informal.* to reveal secrets or gossip (about): *don't tell! she told on him.* **11.** (*tr.*) to assure: *I tell you, I've had enough!* **12.** (*tr.*) to count (votes). **13.** (*intr.*) *Brit. dialect.* to talk or chatter. **14. tell the time.** to read the time from a clock. **15. you're telling me.** *Slang.* I know that very well. [Old English *tellan;* related to Old Saxon *tellian,* Old High German *zellen* to tell, count, Old Norse *telja*] —ˈ**tell·a·ble** *adj.*

tell[2] (tɛl) *n.* a large mound resulting from the accumulation of rubbish on a long-settled site, esp. one with mudbrick buildings, particularly in the Middle East. [C19: from Arabic *tall*]

Tell (tɛl) *n.* **Wil·liam,** German name *Wilhelm Tell.* a legendary Swiss patriot, who, traditionally, lived in the early 14th century and was compelled by an Austrian governor to shoot an apple from his son's head with one shot of his crossbow. He did so without mishap.

tell a·part *vb. (tr., adv.)* to distinguish between; discern: *can you tell the twins apart?*

Tell el A·mar+na ('tɛl ɛl ə'mɑːnə) *n.* a group of ruins and rock tombs in Upper Egypt, on the Nile below Asyut: site of the capital of Amenhotep IV, built about 1375 B.C.; excavated from 1891 onwards.

tell+er ('tɛlə) *n.* **1.** the U.S. name for **bank clerk. 2.** a person appointed to count votes in a legislative body, assembly, etc. **3.** a person who tells; narrator. —**'tell+er+ˌship** *n.*

Tel·ler ('tɛlə) *n.* **Ed·ward.** born 1908, U.S. nuclear physicist, born in Hungary: a major contributor to the development of the hydrogen bomb (1952).

tell+ing ('tɛlɪŋ) *adj.* **1.** having a marked effect or impact: *a telling blow.* **2.** revealing: *a telling smile.* —**'tell+ing+ly** *adv.*

tell off *vb. (tr., adv.)* **1.** *Informal.* to reprimand; scold: *they told me off for stealing apples.* **2.** to count and dismiss: *he told off four more soldiers.*

tell+tale ('tɛlˌteɪl) *n.* **1.** a person who tells tales about others. **2. a.** an outward indication of something concealed. **b.** (*as modifier*): *a telltale paw mark.* **3.** any of various indicators or recording devices used to monitor a process, machine, etc. **4.** *Nautical.* **a.** another word for **dogvane. b.** one of a pair of light vanes mounted on the main shrouds of a sailing boat to indicate the apparent direction of the wind.

tel+lu+rate ('tɛljʊˌreɪt) *n.* any salt or ester of telluric acid.

tel+lu+ri·an (tɛ'lʊərɪən) *adj.* **1.** of or relating to the earth. ~*n.* **2.** (esp. in science fiction) an inhabitant of the earth. [C19: from Latin *tellūs* the earth]

tel+lu+ric[1] (tɛ'lʊərɪk) *adj.* **1.** of, relating to, or originating on or in the earth or soil; terrestrial. **2.** *Astronomy.* (of spectral lines or bands) observed in the spectra of celestial objects and caused by absorption of oxygen, water vapour, and carbon dioxide in the earth's atmosphere. [C19: from Latin *tellūs* the earth]

tel+lu+ric[2] (tɛ'lʊərɪk) *adj.* of or containing tellurium, esp. in a high valence state. [C20: from TELLUR(IUM) + -IC]

tel+lu+ric ac·id *n.* a white crystalline dibasic acid produced by the oxidation of tellurium by hydrogen peroxide. Formula: H_6TeO_6.

tel+lu+ride ('tɛljʊˌraɪd) *n.* any compound of tellurium, esp. one formed between tellurium and a more electropositive element or group.

tel+lu+ri+on *or* **tel+lu+ri·an** (tɛ'lʊərɪən) *n.* an instrument that shows how day and night and the seasons result from the tilt of the earth, its rotation on its axis, and its revolution around the sun. [C19: from Latin *tellūs* the earth]

tel+lu+rite ('tɛljʊˌraɪt) *n.* any salt or ester of tellurous acid.

tel+lu+ri·um (tɛ'lʊərɪəm) *n.* a brittle silvery-white nonmetallic element occurring both uncombined and in combination with metals: used in alloys of lead and copper and as a semiconductor. Symbol: Te; atomic no.: 52; atomic wt.: 127.60; valency: 2,4, or 6; relative density: 6.24; melting pt.: 449.5°C; boiling pt.: 989.8°C. [C19: New Latin, from Latin *tellūs* the earth, formed by analogy with URANIUM]

tel+lu+rize *or* **tel+lu+rise** ('tɛljəˌraɪz) *vb. (tr.)* to mix or combine with tellurium.

tel+lu+rom+e·ter (ˌtɛljʊ'rɒmɪtə) *n. Surveying.* an electronic instrument for measuring distances of up to about 30 miles that consists of two units, one at each end of the distance to be measured, between which radio waves are transmitted.

tel+lu+rous ('tɛljʊrəs, tɛ'lʊərəs) *adj.* of or containing tellurium, esp. in a low valence state.

Tel·lus ('tɛləs) *n.* the Roman goddess of the earth; protectress of marriage, fertility, and the dead.

tel+ly ('tɛlɪ) *n., pl.* **+lies.** *Informal, chiefly Brit.* short for **television.**

tel·o- *or before a vowel* **tel-** *combining form.* **1.** complete; final; perfect: *telophase.* **2.** end; at the end: *telencephalon.*

te+lom+er·i+za+tion *or* **te+lom+er·i+sa+tion** (tɛˌlɒməraɪ'zeɪʃən) *n. Chem.* polymerization in the presence of a chain transfer agent to yield a series of products of low molecular weight. [C20: from TELO- + -MER]

tel·o+phase ('tɛləˌfeɪz) *n.* **1.** the final stage of mitosis, during which the chromosomes at each end of the cell are dispersed into nuclear material and a nuclear membrane forms around the two new nuclei. See also **prophase, metaphase, anaphase. 2.** the corresponding stage of the first division of meiosis. —ˌ**tel·o+'pha+sic** *adj.*

tel+pher *or* **tel+fer** ('tɛlfə) *n.* **1.** a load-carrying car in a telpherage. **2. a.** another word for **telpherage. b.** (*as modifier*): *a telpher line; a telpher system.* ~*vb.* **3.** (*tr.*) to transport (a load) by means of a telpherage. [C19: changed from *telephore,* from TELE- + -PHORE] —**'tel+pher+ic** *or* **'tel+fer+ic** *adj.*

tel+pher+age *or* **tel+fer+age** ('tɛlfərɪdʒ) *n.* an overhead transport system in which an electrically driven truck runs along a single rail or cable, the load being suspended in a separate car beneath. Also called: **telpher line, telpher.**

tel+son ('tɛlsən) *n.* the last segment or an appendage on the last segment of the body of crustaceans and arachnids. [C19: from Greek: a boundary; probably related to *telos* end] —**tel+son+ic** (tɛl'sɒnɪk) *adj.*

Tel+star ('tɛlˌstɑː) *n.* either of two low-altitude active communications satellites launched in 1962 and 1963 by the U.S. and used in the transmission of television programmes, telephone messages, etc.

Tel·u+gu ('tɛləˌguː) *n.* **1.** a language of SE India, belonging to the Dravidian family of languages: the state language of Andhra Pradesh. **2.** (*pl.* **+gus** *or* **+gu**) a member of the people who speak this language. ~*adj.* **3.** of or relating to this people or their language.

Te+luk+be+tung *or* **Te+loek+be+toeng** (təˌlʊkbə'tʊŋ) *n.* a port in Indonesia, in S Sumatra on the Sunda Strait. Pop.: 198 986 (1971).

Te·ma ('tiːmə) *n.* a port in SE Ghana on the Atlantic: new harbour opened in 1962; oil-refining. Pop.: 26 860 (1960).

Tém+bi ('tɛmbiː) *n.* transliteration of the Modern Greek name for **Tempe.**

te+mer+i·ty (tɪ'mɛrɪtɪ) *n.* rashness or boldness. [C15: from Latin *temeritās* accident, from *temere* at random] —**tem+er+ar·i+ous** (ˌtɛmə'rɛərɪəs) *adj.*

Tem+es+vár ('tɛmɛʃˌvaːr) *n.* the Hungarian name for **Timişoara.**

Tem+ne ('tɛmnɪ, 'tɪm-) *n.* **1.** (*pl.* **+nes** *or* **+ne**) a member of a Negroid people of N Sierra Leone. **2.** the language of this people, closely related to Bantu.

temp (tɛmp) *Informal.* ~*n.* **1.** a person, esp. a typist or other office worker, employed on a temporary basis. ~*vb. (intr.)* **2.** to work as a temp.

temp. *abbrev. for:* **1.** temperate. **2.** temperature. **3.** temporary. **4.** tempore. [Latin: in the time of]

Tem+pe ('tɛmpɪ) *n.* **Vale of.** a wooded valley in E Greece, in Thessaly between the mountains Olympus and Ossa. Modern Greek name: **Témbi.**

tem+per ('tɛmpə) *n.* **1.** a frame of mind; mood or humour: *a good temper.* **2.** a sudden outburst of anger; tantrum. **3.** a tendency to exhibit uncontrolled anger; irritability. **4.** a mental condition of moderation and calm (esp. in the phrases **keep one's temper, lose one's temper, out of temper**). **5.** the degree of hardness, elasticity, or a similar property of a metal or metal object. **6.** *Archaic.* a middle course between two extremes. ~*vb. (tr.)* **7.** to make more temperate, acceptable, or suitable by adding something else; moderate: *he tempered his criticism with kindly sympathy.* **8.** to strengthen or toughen (a metal or metal article) by heat treatment, as by heating and quenching. **9.** *Music.* **a.** to adjust the frequency differences between the notes of a scale on (a keyboard instrument) in order to allow modulation into other keys. **b.** to make such an adjustment to the pitches of notes in (a scale). **10.** a rare word for **adapt. 11.** an archaic word for **mix.** [Old English *temprian* to mingle, (influenced by Old French *temprer*), from Latin *temperāre* to mix, probably from *tempus* time] —**'tem+per+a·ble** *adj.* —ˌ**tem+per+a·'bil+i·ty** *n.* —**'tem+per+er** *n.*

tem+per·a ('tɛmpərə) *n.* **1.** a painting medium for powdered pigments, consisting usually of egg yolk and water. **2. a.** any emulsion used as a painting medium, with casein, glue, wax, etc., as a base. **b.** the paint made from mixing this with pigment. **3.** the technique of painting with tempera. [C19: from Italian phrase *pingere a tempera* painting in tempera, from *temperare* to mingle; see TEMPER]

tem+per·a+ment ('tɛmpərəmənt, -prəmənt) *n.* **1.** an individual's character, disposition, and tendencies as revealed in his reactions. **2.** excitability, moodiness, or anger, esp. when displayed openly: *an actress with temperament.* **3.** the characteristic way an individual behaves, esp. towards other people. See also **character, personality. 4. a.** an adjustment made to the frequency differences between notes on a keyboard instrument to allow modulation to other keys. **b.** any of several systems of such adjustment, such as **just temperament,** a system theoretically impossible on keyboard instruments (see **just intonation), mean-tone temperament,** a system giving an approximation to natural tuning, and **equal temperament,** the system commonly used in keyboard instruments, giving a scale based on an octave divided into twelve exactly equal semitones. **5.** *Obsolete.* the characteristic way an individual behaves, viewed as the result of the influence of the four humours (blood, phlegm, yellow bile, and black bile). **6.** *Archaic.* compromise or adjustment. **7.** an obsolete word for **temperature.** [C15: from Latin *temperāmentum* a mixing in proportion, from *temperāre* to TEMPER]

tem+per·a+men+tal (ˌtɛmpərə'mɛntᵊl, -prə'mɛntᵊl) *adj.* **1.** easily upset or irritated; excitable; volatile. **2.** of, relating to, or caused by temperament. **3.** *Informal.* working erratically and inconsistently; unreliable: *a temperamental sewing machine.* —ˌ**tem+per·a+'men+tal+ly** *adv.*

tem+per+ance ('tɛmpərəns) *n.* **1.** restraint or moderation, esp. in yielding to one's appetites or desires. **2.** abstinence from alcoholic drink. [C14: from Latin *temperantia,* from *temperāre* to regulate]

tem+per+ate ('tɛmpərɪt, 'tɛmprɪt) *adj.* **1.** having a climate intermediate between tropical and polar; moderate or mild in temperature. **2.** mild in quality or character; exhibiting temperance. [C14: from Latin *temperātus*] —**'tem+per+ate+ly** *adv.* —**'tem+per+ate+ness** *n.*

tem+per+ate zone *n.* those parts of the earth's surface lying between the Arctic Circle and the tropic of Cancer and between the Antarctic Circle and the tropic of Capricorn.

tem+per·a+ture ('tɛmprɪtʃə) *n.* **1.** the degree of hotness of a body, substance, or medium; a physical property related to the average kinetic energy of the atoms or molecules of a substance. **2.** a measure of this degree of hotness, indicated on a scale that has one or more fixed reference points. **3.** *Informal.* a body temperature in excess of the normal. **4.** *Archaic.* **a.** compromise. **b.** temperament. **c.** temperance. [C16 (originally: a mingling): from Latin *temperātūra* proportion, from *temperāre* to TEMPER]

tem+per·a+ture gra+di+ent *n.* the rate of change in temperature in a given direction, esp. in altitude.

tem+per·a+ture-hu+mid·i+ty in+dex *n.* an index of the effect on human comfort of temperature and humidity levels, 65 being the highest comfortable level.

tem+pered ('tɛmpəd) *adj.* **1.** *Music.* **a.** (of a scale) having the frequency differences between notes adjusted in accordance with the system of equal temperament. See **temperament. b.** (of an interval) expanded or contracted from the state of being pure. **2.** (*in combination*) having a temper or temperament as specified: *ill-tempered.*

tem+pest ('tɛmpɪst) *n.* **1.** *Chiefly literary.* a violent wind or storm. **2.** a violent commotion, uproar, or disturbance. ~*vb.* **3.** (*tr.*) *Poetic.* to agitate or disturb violently. [C13: from Old French *tempeste,* from Latin *tempestās* storm, from *tempus* time]

tem+pes+tu+ous (tɛm'pɛstjʊəs) *adj.* **1.** of or relating to a tempest. **2.** violent or stormy: *a tempestuous love affair.* —**tem+'pes+tu+ous+ly** *adv.* —**tem+'pes+tu+ous+ness** *n.*

tem+pi ('tɛmpi:) *pl. n.* (in musical senses) the plural of **tempo.**

Tem+plar ('tɛmplə) *n.* **1.** a member of a military religious order (**Knights of the Temple of Solomon**) founded by Crusaders in Jerusalem around 1118 to defend the Holy Sepulchre and Christian pilgrims; suppressed in 1312. **2.** (*sometimes not cap.*) *Brit.* a lawyer, esp. a barrister, who lives or has chambers in the Inner or Middle Temple in London. [C13: from Medieval Latin *templārius* of the temple, from Latin *templum* TEMPLE[1]; first applied to the knightly order because their house was near the site of the Temple of Solomon]

tem+plate *or* **tem+plet** ('tɛmplɪt) *n.* **1.** a gauge or pattern, cut out in wood or metal, used in woodwork, etc., to help shape something accurately. **2.** a pattern cut out in card or plastic, used in various crafts to reproduce shapes. **3.** a short beam, made of metal, wood, or stone, that is used to spread a load, as over a doorway. **4.** *Biochem.* the molecular structure of a compound that serves as a pattern for the production of the molecular structure of another specific compound in a reaction. [C17 *templet* (later spelling influenced by PLATE), probably from French, diminutive of TEMPLE[3]]

tem+ple[1] ('tɛmpᵊl) *n.* **1.** a building or place dedicated to the worship of a deity or deities. **2.** a Mormon church. **3.** *U.S.* another name for a **synagogue. 4.** any Christian church, esp. a large or imposing one. **5.** *Theol.* any place or object regarded as a shrine where God makes himself present, esp. the body of a person who has been sanctified or saved by grace. **6.** a building regarded as the focus of an activity, interest, or practice: *a temple of the arts.* [Old English *tempel,* from Latin *templum;* probably related to Latin *tempus* TIME, Greek *temenos* sacred enclosure, literally: a place cut off, from *temnein* to cut] —**'tem+pled** *adj.* —**'tem·ple-,like** *adj.*

tem+ple[2] ('tɛmpᵊl) *n.* the region on each side of the head in front of the ear and above the cheek bone. [C14: from Old French *temple,* from Latin *tempora* the temples, from *tempus* temple of the head]

tem+ple[3] ('tɛmpᵊl) *n.* the part of a loom that keeps the cloth being woven stretched to the correct width. [C15: from French, from Latin *templum* a small timber]

Tem+ple[1] ('tɛmpᵊl) *n.* **1.** either of two buildings in London and Paris that belonged to the Templars. The one in London now houses two of the chief law societies. **2.** any of three buildings or groups of buildings erected by the Jews in ancient Jerusalem for the worship of Jehovah.

Tem·ple[2] ('tɛmpᵊl) *n.* **1.** Sir **Wil·liam.** 1628–99, English diplomat and essayist. He negotiated the Triple Alliance (1668) and the marriage of William of Orange to Mary II. **2. Wil·liam.** 1881–1944, English prelate and advocate of social reform; archbishop of Canterbury (1942–44).

Tem+ple of Ar·te·mis *n.* the large temple at Ephesus, on the W coast of Asia Minor: one of the Seven Wonders of the World.

tem+po ('tɛmpəʊ) *n., pl.* **+pos** *or* **+pi** (-pi:). **1.** the speed at which a piece or passage of music is meant to be played, usually indicated by a musical direction (**tempo marking**) or metronome marking. **2.** rate or pace. [C18: from Italian, from Latin *tempus* time]

tem+po+ral[1] ('tɛmpərəl, 'tɛmprəl) *adj.* **1.** of or relating to time. **2.** of or relating to secular as opposed to spiritual or religious affairs: *the lords spiritual and temporal.* **3.** lasting for a relatively short time. **4.** *Grammar.* of or relating to tense or the linguistic expression of time in general: *a temporal adverb.* [C14: from Latin *temporālis,* from *tempus* time] —**'tem+po+ral+ly** *adv.* —**'tem+po+ral+ness** *n.*

tem+po+ral[2] ('tɛmpərəl, 'tɛmprəl) *adj. Anatomy.* of, relating to, or near the temple or temples. [C16: from Late Latin *temporālis* belonging to the temples; see TEMPLE[2]]

tem+po+ral bone *n.* either of two compound bones forming part of the sides and base of the skull: they surround the organs of hearing.

tem+po+ral+i·ty (,tɛmpə'rælɪtɪ) *n., pl.* **·ties. 1.** the state or quality of being temporal. **2.** something temporal. **3.** (*often pl.*) a secular possession or revenue belonging to a Church, a group within the Church, or the clergy.

tem+po+ral lobe *n.* the laterally protruding portion of each cerebral hemisphere, situated below the parietal lobe and associated with sound perception and interpretation: it is thought to be the centre for memory recall.

tem+po+rar·y ('tɛmpərərɪ, 'tɛmprərɪ) *adj.* **1.** not permanent; provisional: *temporary accommodation.* **2.** lasting only a short time; transitory: *temporary relief from pain.* ~*n.* **3.** a person, esp. a secretary or other office worker, employed on a temporary basis. Often shortened to **temp.** [C16: from Latin *temporārius,* from *tempus* time] —**'tem+po+rar·i+ly** *adv.* —**'tem+po+rar·i+ness** *n.*

tem+po+rize *or* **tem+po+rise** ('tɛmpə,raɪz) *vb.* (*intr.*) **1.** to delay, act evasively, or protract a discussion, negotiation, etc., esp. in order to gain time or effect a compromise. **2.** to adapt oneself to the circumstances or occasion, as by temporary or apparent agreement. [C16: from French *temporiser,* from Medieval Latin *temporizāre,* from Latin *tempus* time] —**,tem+po+ri+'za+tion** *or* **,tem+po+ri+'sa+tion** *n.* —**'tem+po+,riz+er** *or* **'tem+po+,ris+er** *n.* —**'tem+po+,riz+ing+ly** *or* **'tem+po+,ris+ing+ly** *adv.*

tempt (tɛmpt) *vb.* (*tr.*) **1.** to attempt to persuade or entice to do something, esp. something morally wrong or unwise. **2.** to allure, invite, or attract. **3.** to give rise to a desire in (someone) to do something; dispose: *their unfriendliness tempted me to leave the party.* **4.** to risk provoking (esp. in the phrase **to tempt fate**). [C13: from Old French *tempter,* from Latin *temptāre* to test] —**'tempt+a·ble** *adj.* —**'tempt+er** *n.*

temp+ta+tion (tɛmp'teɪʃən) *n.* **1.** the act of tempting or the state of being tempted. **2.** a person or thing that tempts.

Tempt+er ('tɛmptə) *n.* **the.** Satan regarded as trying to lead men into sin.

tempt+ing ('tɛmptɪŋ) *adj.* attractive or inviting: *a tempting meal.* —**'tempt+ing+ly** *adv.*

tempt+ress ('tɛmptrɪs) *n.* a woman who sets out to allure or seduce a man or men; seductress.

tem+pu+ra ('tɛmpu:rɑ:, tɛm'pʊərə) *n.* a Japanese dish of seafood or vegetables dipped in batter and deep-fried, often at the table. [from Japanese: fried food]

tem+pus fu+git *Latin.* ('tɛmpəs 'fju:dʒɪt, -gɪt) time flies.

Te+mu+co (*Spanish* te'muko) *n.* a city in S Chile: agricultural trading centre. Pop.: 138 430 (1975 est.).

ten (tɛn) *n.* **1.** the cardinal number that is the sum of nine and one. It is the base of the decimal number system and the base of the common logarithm. See also **number** (sense 1). **2.** a numeral 10, X, etc., representing this number. **3.** something representing, represented by, or consisting of ten units, such as a playing card with ten symbols on it. **4.** Also called: **ten o'clock.** ten hours after noon or midnight. ~*determiner.* **5. a.** amounting to ten: *ten tigers.* **b.** (*as pronoun*): *to sell only ten.* ~Related adj.: **decimal.** Related prefixes: **deca-, deci-.** [Old English *tēn;* related to Old Saxon *tehan,* Old High German *zehan,* Gothic *taihun,* Latin *decem,* Greek *deka,* Sanskrit *dasa*]

ten. *Music. abbrev. for:* **1.** tenor. **2.** tenuto.

ten- *combining form.* variant of **teno-** before a vowel.

ten+a·ble ('tɛnəbᵊl) *adj.* able to be upheld, believed, maintained, or defended. [C16: from Old French, from *tenir* to hold, from Latin *tenēre*] —**,ten+a·'bil+i·ty** *or* **'ten+a·ble+ness** *n.* —**'ten+a·bly** *adv.*

ten+ace ('tɛneɪs) *n. Bridge, whist.* a holding of two nonconsecutive high cards of a suit, such as the ace and queen. [C17: from French, from Spanish *tenaza* forceps, ultimately from Latin *tenāx* holding fast, from *tenēre* to hold]

te+na+cious (tɪ'neɪʃəs) *adj.* **1.** holding or grasping firmly; forceful: *a tenacious grip.* **2.** retentive: *a tenacious memory.* **3.** stubborn or persistent: *a tenacious character.* **4.** holding together firmly; tough or cohesive: *tenacious cement.* **5.** tending to stick or adhere: *tenacious mud.* [C16: from Latin *tenāx,* from *tenēre* to hold] —**te+'na+cious+ly** *adv.* —**te+'na+cious+ness** *or* **te+nac+i·ty** (tɪ'næsɪtɪ) *n.*

te+nac·u·lum (tɪ'nækjʊləm) *n., pl.* **+la** (-lə). a surgical or dissecting instrument for grasping and holding parts, consisting of a slender hook mounted in a handle. [C17: from Late Latin, from Latin *tenēre* to hold]

te+naille (tɛ'neɪl) *n. Fortifications.* a low outwork in the main ditch between two bastions. [C16: from French, literally: tongs, from Late Latin *tenācula,* pl. of TENACULUM]

ten+an+cy ('tɛnənsɪ) *n., pl.* **+cies. 1.** the temporary possession or holding by a tenant of lands or property owned by another. **2.** the period of holding or occupying such property. **3.** the period of holding office, a position, etc. **4.** property held or occupied by a tenant.

ten+ant ('tɛnənt) *n.* **1.** a person who holds, occupies, or possesses land or property by any kind of right or title, esp. from a landlord under a lease. **2.** a person who has the use of a house, flat, etc., subject to the payment of rent. **3.** any holder or occupant. ~*vb.* **4.** (*tr.*) to hold (land or property) as a tenant. **5.** (*intr.;* foll. by *in*) *Rare.* to dwell. [C14: from Old French, literally: (one who is) holding, from *tenir* to hold, from Latin *tenēre*] —**'ten+ant+a·ble** *adj.* —**'ten+ant+less** *adj.* —**'ten·ant-,like** *adj.*

ten+ant farm+er *n.* a person who farms land rented from another, the rent usually taking the form of part of the crops grown or livestock reared.

ten·ant-in-chief *n.* (in feudal society) a tenant who held some or all of his lands directly from the king.

ten+ant+ry ('tɛnəntrɪ) *n.* **1.** tenants collectively, esp. those with the same landlord. **2.** the status or condition of being a tenant.

tench (tɛntʃ) *n.* a European freshwater cyprinid game fish, *Tinca tinca,* having a thickset dark greenish body with a barbel at each side of the mouth. [C14: from Old French *tenche,* from Late Latin *tinca*]

Ten Com+mand+ments *pl. n.* **the.** *Old Testament.* the commandments summarizing the basic obligations of man towards God and his fellow-men, delivered to Moses on Mount Sinai engraved on two tables of stone (Exodus 20:1–17). Also called: the **Decalogue.**

tend[1] (tɛnd) *vb.* (when *intr.,* usually foll. by *to* or *towards*) **1.** (when *tr., takes an infinitive*) to have a general disposition (to do something); be inclined: *children tend to prefer sweets to meat.* **2.** (*intr.*) to have or be an influence (towards a specific result); be conducive: *the party atmosphere tends to hilarity.* **3.**

(*intr.*) to go or move (in a particular direction): *to tend to the south.* [C14: from Old French *tendre,* from Latin *tendere* to stretch]

tend[2] (tɛnd) *vb.* **1.** (*tr.*) to care for: *to tend wounded soldiers.* **2.** (when *intr.*, often foll. by *on* or *to*) to attend (to): *to tend on someone's wishes.* **3.** (*tr.*) to handle or control: *to tend a fire.* **4.** (*intr.;* often foll. by *to*) *Informal, chiefly U.S.* to pay attention. [C14: variant of ATTEND]

tend+ance ('tɛndəns) *n.* **1.** *Rare.* care and attention; ministration. **2.** *Obsolete.* attendants collectively.

ten+den+cy ('tɛndənsɪ) *n., pl.* **+cies. 1.** (often foll. by *to*) an inclination, predisposition, propensity, or leaning: *she has a tendency to be frivolous; a tendency to frivolity.* **2.** the general course, purport, or drift of something, esp. a written work. [C17: from Medieval Latin *tendentia,* from Latin *tendere* to TEND[1]]

ten+den+tious *or* **ten+den+cious** (tɛn'dɛnʃəs) *adj.* having or showing an intentional tendency or bias, esp. a controversial one. [C20: from TENDENCY] **—ten+'den+tious+ly, ten+'den+cious+ly** *or* **ten+'den+tial+ly, ten+'den+cial+ly** *adv.* **—ten+'den+tious+ness** *or* **ten+'den+cious+ness** *n.*

ten+der[1] ('tɛndə) *adj.* **1.** easily broken, cut, or crushed; soft; not tough: *a tender steak.* **2.** easily damaged; vulnerable or sensitive: *a tender youth; at a tender age.* **3.** having or expressing warm and affectionate feelings: *a tender smile.* **4.** kind, merciful, or sympathetic: *a tender heart.* **5.** arousing warm feelings; touching: *a tender memory.* **6.** gentle and delicate: *a tender breeze.* **7.** requiring care in handling; ticklish: *a tender question.* **8.** painful or sore: *a tender wound.* **9.** sensitive to moral or spiritual feelings: *a tender conscience.* **10.** (*postpositive;* foll. by *of*) careful or protective: *tender of one's emotions.* **11.** (of a sailing vessel) easily keeled over by a wind; crank. Compare **stiff** (sense 10). *~vb.* **12.** (*tr.*) *Rare.* **a.** to make tender. **b.** to treat tenderly. [C13: from Old French *tendre,* from Latin *tener* delicate] **—'ten+der+ly** *adv.* **—'ten+der+ness** *n.*

ten+der[2] ('tɛndə) *vb.* (*tr.*) **1.** to give, present, or offer: *to tender one's resignation; tender a bid.* **2.** *Law.* to offer (money or goods) in settlement of a debt or claim. *~n.* **3.** the act or an instance of tendering; offer. **4.** *Commerce.* a formal offer to supply specified goods or services at a stated cost or rate. **5.** something, esp. money, used as an official medium of payment: *legal tender.* [C16: from Anglo-French *tendre,* from Latin *tendere* to extend; see TEND[1]] **—'ten+der+a·ble** *adj.* **—'ten+der+er** *n.*

ten+der[3] ('tɛndə) *n.* **1.** a small boat, such as a dinghy, towed or carried by a yacht or ship. **2.** a vehicle drawn behind a steam locomotive to carry the fuel and water. **3.** a person who tends. [C15: variant of *attender*]

ten·der+foot ('tɛndəˌfʊt) *n., pl.* **+foots** *or* **+feet. 1.** a newcomer, esp. to the mines or ranches of the southwestern U.S. **2.** (formerly) a beginner in the Scouts.

ten·der+heart·ed (ˌtɛndə'hɑːtɪd) *adj.* having a compassionate, kindly, or sensitive disposition. **—ˌten·der+'heart·ed+ly** *adv.* **—ˌten·der+'heart·ed+ness** *n.*

ten+der+ize *or* **ten+der+ise** ('tɛndəˌraɪz) *vb.* (*tr.*) to make (meat) tender by pounding it to break down the fibres, by steeping it in a marinade, or by treating it with a tenderizer. **—ˌten+der+i+'za+tion** *or* **ˌten+der+i+'sa+tion** *n.*

ten+der+iz+er *or* **ten+der+is+er** ('tɛndəˌraɪzə) *n.* a substance, such as the plant enzyme papain, rubbed onto meat to soften the fibres and make it more tender.

ten+der+loin ('tɛndəˌlɔɪn) *n.* a tender cut of pork or other meat from between the sirloin and ribs.

ten+di+nous ('tɛndɪnəs) *adj.* of, relating to, possessing, or resembling tendons; sinewy. [C17: from New Latin *tendinōsus,* from Medieval Latin *tendō* TENDON]

ten+don ('tɛndən) *n.* a cord or band of white inelastic collagenous tissue that attaches a muscle to a bone or some other part; sinew. [C16: from Medieval Latin *tendō,* from Latin *tendere* to stretch; related to Greek *tenōn* sinew]

ten+dril ('tɛndrɪl) *n.* **1.** a specialized threadlike leaf or stem that attaches climbing plants to a support by twining or adhering. **2.** something resembling a tendril, such as a wisp of hair. [C16: perhaps from Old French *tendron* tendril (confused with Old French *tendron* bud), from Medieval Latin *tendō* TENDON] **—'ten+dril+lar** *or* **'ten+dril+ous** *adj.*

Ten+e·brae ('tɛnəˌbreɪ) *n.* (*functioning as sing. or pl.*). *R.C. Church.* (formerly) the matins and lauds for Thursday, Friday, and Saturday of Holy Week, usually sung in the evenings or at night. [C17: from Latin: darkness]

ten+e·brism ('tɛnəˌbrɪzəm) *n.* (*sometimes cap.*) a school, style, or method of painting, adopted chiefly by 17th-century Spanish and Neapolitan painters, esp. Caravaggio, characterized by large areas of dark colours, usually relieved with a shaft of light. **—'ten+e·brist** *n., adj.*

ten+e·brous ('tɛnəbrəs) *or* **te+neb+ri+ous** (tə'nɛbrɪəs) *adj.* gloomy, shadowy, or dark. [C15: from Latin *tenebrōsus* from *tenebrae* darkness] **—ten+e·bros+i·ty** (ˌtɛnə'brɒsɪtɪ), **'ten+e·brous+ness,** *or* **te+'neb+ri+ous+ness** *n.*

Ten+e·dos ('tɛnɪˌdɒs) *n.* an island in the NE Aegean, near the entrance to the Dardanelles: in Greek legend the base of the Greek fleet during the siege of Troy. Modern Turkish name: **Bozcaada.**

ten+e·ment ('tɛnəmənt) *n.* **1.** Also called: **tenement building.** a large slum house divided into rooms or flats for rent. **2.** a dwelling place or residence, esp. one intended for rent. **3.** *Chiefly Brit.* a room or flat for rent. **4.** *Property law.* any form of permanent property, such as land, dwellings, offices, etc. [C14: from Medieval Latin *tenementum,* from Latin *tenēre* to hold] **—ten+e·men+tal** (ˌtɛnə'mɛntᵊl) *or* **ˌten+e·'men+ta·ry** *adj.* **—'ten+e·ment+ed** *adj.*

Ten+e·rife (ˌtɛnə'riːf; *Spanish* ˌtene'rife) *n.* a Spanish island in the Atlantic, off the NW coast of Africa: the largest of the Canary Islands; volcanic and mountainous; tourism and agriculture. Capital: Santa Cruz. Pop.: 473 971 (1970). Area: 2058 sq. km (795 sq. miles).

te+nes+mus (tɪ'nɛzməs, -'nɛs-) *n. Pathol.* an ineffective painful straining to empty the bowels or bladder. [C16: from Medieval Latin, from Latin *tēnesmos,* from Greek *teinesmos,* from *teinein* to strain] **—te+'nes+mic** *adj.*

ten+et ('tɛnɪt, 'tiːnɪt) *n.* a belief, opinion, or dogma. [C17: from Latin, literally: he (it) holds, from *tenēre* to hold]

ten+fold ('tɛnˌfəʊld) *adj.* **1.** equal to or having 10 times as many or as much: *a tenfold increase in population.* **2.** composed of 10 parts. *~adv.* **3.** by or up to 10 times as many or as much: *the population increased tenfold.*

ten-gal·lon hat *n.* (in the U.S.) a cowboy's broad-brimmed felt hat with a very high crown.

Teng Hsiao-ping ('tɛŋ sjaʊ 'pɪŋ) *n.* born 1904, Chinese Communist statesman; deputy prime minister of China since 1977, having been rehabilitated following his dismissal for the second time in 1976. A moderate and a pragmatist, he was first removed from office in 1967, during the Cultural Revolution, and was temporarily rehabilitated in 1973.

Ten+gri Khan ('tɛŋgrɪ 'kɑːn) *n.* a mountain in central Asia, on the border between the Kirghiz SSR of the Soviet Union and Sinkiang province of W China. Height: 6995 m (22 951 ft.).

Ten+gri Nor ('tɛŋgrɪ 'nɔː) *n.* another name for **Nam Tso.**

te+ni·a ('tiːnɪə) *n., pl.* **+ni·ae** (-nɪˌiː). the U.S. spelling of **taenia.**

te+ni·a+cide ('tiːnɪəˌsaɪd) *n.* the U.S. spelling of **taeniacide.**

te+ni·a+fuge ('tiːnɪəˌfjuːdʒ) *n.* the U.S. spelling of **taeniafuge.**

Ten+iers ('tɛnɪəz) *n.* **Da·vid** ('dɑːvɪt), called *the Elder,* 1582–1649, and his son **Da·vid,** called *the Younger,* 1610–90, Flemish painters.

Tenn. *abbrev. for* Tennessee.

ten+ner ('tɛnə) *n. Informal.* **1.** *Brit.* **a.** a ten-pound note. **b.** the sum of ten pounds. **2.** *U.S.* a ten-dollar bill.

Ten+nes+see (ˌtɛnɪ'siː) *n.* **1.** a state of the E central U.S.: consists of a plain in the west, rising to the Appalachians and the Cumberland Plateau in the east. Capital: Nashville. Pop.: 3 924 164 (1970). Area: 109 412 sq. km (42 244 sq. miles). Abbrevs.: **Tenn.** or (with zip code) **TN 2.** a river in the E central U.S., flowing southwest from E Tennessee into N Alabama, then west and north to the Ohio River at Paducah: the longest tributary of the Ohio; includes a series of dams and reservoirs under the Tennessee Valley Authority. Length: 1049 km (652 miles). **—ˌTen+nes+'se·an** *adj., n.*

Ten+nes+see Val+ley Au·thor+i·ty *n.* a U.S. government corporation chartered in 1933 to develop the Tennessee Valley by constructing dams, generating electricity, maintaining irrigation works, etc. Abbrev.: **TVA.**

Ten+nes+see Walk+ing Horse *n.* an American breed of horse, marked by its stamina and trained to move at a fast running walk. Often shortened to **Walking Horse.**

Ten·niel ('tɛnjəl) *n.* Sir **John.** 1820–1914, English caricaturist, noted for his illustrations to Lewis Carroll's *Alice* books and for his political cartoons in *Punch* (1851–1901).

ten+nis ('tɛnɪs) *n.* **a.** a racket game played between two players or pairs of players who hit a ball to and fro over a net on a rectangular court of grass, asphalt, clay, etc. See also **lawn tennis, real tennis, court tennis, table tennis. b.** (*as modifier*): *tennis court; tennis racket.* [C14: probably from Anglo-French *tenetz* hold (imperative), from Old French *tenir* to hold, from Latin *tenēre*]

ten+nis ball *n.* a hollow rubber ball covered with felt, used in tennis.

ten+nis el+bow *n.* a painful inflammation of the elbow caused by exertion in playing tennis and similar games.

ten+nis shoe *n.* a rubber-soled canvas shoe tied with laces.

ten+no ('tɛnəʊ) *n., pl.* **+no** *or* **+nos.** the Japanese emperor, esp. when regarded as a divine religious leader.

Ten·ny·son ('tɛnɪsᵊn) *n.* **Al·fred,** Lord Tennyson. 1809–92, English poet; poet laureate (1850–92). His poems include *The Lady of Shalott* (1832), *Morte d'Arthur* (1842), the collection *In Memoriam* (1850), *Maud* (1855), and *Idylls of the King* (1859). **—Ten+ny+so+ni·an** (ˌtɛnɪ'səʊnɪən) *adj., n.*

Te·no ('tɛnɔ) *n.* the Finnish name for **Tana** (sense 3).

ten·o- *or before a vowel* **ten-** *combining form.* tendon: *tenosynovitis.* [from Greek *tenōn*]

Te+noch+ti+tlán (tɛˌnɔːtʃtiː'tlɑːn) *n.* an ancient city and capital of the Aztec empire on the present site of Mexico City; razed by Cortés in 1521.

ten+on ('tɛnən) *n.* **1.** the projecting end of a piece of wood formed to fit into a corresponding mortise in another piece. *~vb.* (*tr.*) **2.** to form a tenon on (a piece of wood). **3.** to join with a tenon and mortise. [C15: from Old French, from *tenir* to hold, from Latin *tenēre*] **—'ten+on+er** *n.*

ten+on saw *n.* a small fine-toothed saw with a strong back, used esp. for cutting tenons.

ten+or ('tɛnə) *n.* **1.** *Music.* **a.** the male voice intermediate between alto and baritone, having a range approximately from the B a ninth below middle C to the G a fifth above it. **b.** a singer with such a voice. **c.** a saxophone, horn, recorder, etc., intermediate in compass and size between the alto and baritone or bass. **d.** (*as modifier*): *a tenor sax.* **2.** general drift of thought; purpose: *to follow the tenor of an argument.* **3. a.** (in early polyphonic music) the part singing the melody or the cantus firmus. **b.** (in four-part harmony) the second lowest part lying directly above the bass. **4.** *Changeringing.* **a.** the heaviest and lowest-pitched bell in a ring. **b.** (*as modifier*): *a tenor bell.* **5.** a settled course of progress. **6.** *Archaic.* general tendency. **7.** *Law.* **a.** the exact words of a deed, etc., as distinct from their effect. **b.** an exact copy or transcript. [C13 (originally: general meaning or sense): from Old French *tenour,* from Latin *tenor* a continuous holding to a course, from *tenēre* to hold; musical sense via Italian *tenore,* referring to the voice part that was continuous, that is, to which the melody was assigned] —**'ten+or+less** *adj.*

te+nor clef *n.* the clef that establishes middle C as being on the fourth line of the staff, used for the writing of music for the bassoon, cello, or tenor horn. See also **C clef.**

ten·o+rite ('tɛnəˌraɪt) *n.* a black mineral found in copper deposits and consisting of copper oxide in the form of either metallic scales or earthy masses. Formula: CuO. [C19: named after G. *Tenore* (died 1861), Italian botanist]

te+nor+rha+phy (tɪ'nɒrəfɪ) *n., pl.* **+phies.** *Surgery.* the union of torn or divided tendons by means of sutures.

te+not·o+my (tə'nɒtəmɪ) *n., pl.* **+mies.** surgical incision into a tendon. —**te+'not·o+mist** *n.*

ten+pen·ny ('tɛnpənɪ) *adj.* (*prenominal*) *U.S.* (of a nail) three inches in length.

ten+pin ('tɛnˌpɪn) *n.* one of the pins used in tenpin bowling.

ten+pin bowl+ing *n.* a bowling game in which heavy bowls are rolled down a long lane to knock over the ten target pins at the other end. Also called (esp. U.S.): **tenpins.**

ten+pins ('tɛnˌpɪnz) *n.* the U.S. name for **tenpin bowling.**

ten+rec ('tɛnrɛk) *n.* any small mammal, such as *Tenrec ecaudatus* (**tailless tenrec**), of the Madagascan family *Tenrecidae,* resembling hedgehogs or shrews: order *Insectivora* (insectivores). [C18: via French from Malagasy *tràndraka*]

tense[1] (tɛns) *adj.* **1.** stretched or stressed tightly; taut or rigid. **2.** under mental or emotional strain. **3.** producing mental or emotional strain: *a tense day.* **4.** (of a speech sound) pronounced with considerable muscular effort and having relatively precise accuracy of articulation and considerable duration: *in English the vowel* (iː) *in "beam" is tense.* Compare: **lax** (sense 4). ~*vb.* (often foll. by *up*) **5.** to make or become tense. [C17: from Latin *tensus* taut, from *tendere* to stretch] —**'tense+ly** *adv.* —**'tense+ness** *n.*

tense[2] (tɛns) *n. Grammar.* a category of the verb or verbal inflections, such as present, past, and future, that expresses the temporal relations between what is reported in a sentence and the time of its utterance. [C14: from Old French *tens* time, from Latin *tempus*] —**'tense+less** *adj.*

tense log+ic *n. Logic.* the study of temporal relations between propositions, usually pursued by considering the logical properties of symbols representing the tenses of natural languages.

ten+si·ble ('tɛnsəbᵊl) *adj.* capable of being stretched; tensile. —**ˌten+si·'bil+i·ty** *or* **'ten+si·ble+ness** *n.* —**'ten+si·bly** *adv.*

ten+sile ('tɛnsaɪl) *adj.* **1.** of or relating to tension. **2.** sufficiently ductile to be stretched or drawn out. **3.** *Rare.* (of musical instruments) producing sounds through the vibration of stretched strings. [C17: from New Latin *tensilis,* from Latin *tendere* to stretch] —**'ten+sile+ly** *adv.* —**ten+sil+i·ty** (tɛn'sɪlɪtɪ) *or* **'ten+sile+ness** *n.*

ten+sile strength *n.* a measure of the ability of a material to withstand a longitudinal stress, expressed as the greatest stress that the material can stand without breaking.

ten+sim+e·ter (tɛn'sɪmɪtə) *n.* a device that measures differences in vapour pressures. It is used to determine transition points by observing changes of vapour pressure with temperature. [C20: from TENSI(ON) + -METER]

ten+si+om+e·ter (ˌtɛnsɪ'ɒmɪtə) *n.* **1.** an instrument for measuring the tensile strength of a wire, beam, etc. **2.** an instrument used to compare the vapour pressures of two liquids, usually consisting of two sealed bulbs containing the liquids, each being connected to one limb of a manometer. **3.** an instrument for measuring the surface tension of a liquid, usually consisting of a sensitive balance for measuring the force needed to pull a wire ring from the surface of the liquid. **4.** an instrument for measuring the moisture content of soil.

ten+sion ('tɛnʃən) *n.* **1.** the act of stretching or the state or degree of being stretched. **2.** mental or emotional strain; stress. **3.** a situation or condition of hostility, suspense, or uneasiness. **4.** *Physics.* a force that tends to produce an elongation of a body or structure. **5.** *Physics.* **a.** voltage, electromotive force, or potential difference. **b.** (*in combination*): *high-tension; low-tension.* **6.** a device for regulating the tension in a part, string, thread, etc., as in a sewing machine. [C16: from Latin *tensiō,* from *tendere* to strain] —**'ten+sion+al** *adj.* —**'ten+sion+less** *adj.*

ten+si·ty ('tɛnsɪtɪ) *n.* a rare word for **tension** (senses 1–3).

ten+sive ('tɛnsɪv) *adj.* of or causing tension or strain.

ten+sor ('tɛnsə, -sɔː) *n.* **1.** *Anatomy.* any muscle that can cause a part to become firm or tense. **2.** *Maths.* a set of components, functions of the coordinates of any point in space, that transform linearly between coordinate systems. For three dimensional space there are 3^r components, where *r* is the rank. A tensor of zero rank is a scalar, of rank one, a vector. [C18: from New Latin, literally: a stretcher] —**ten+so+ri·al** (tɛn'sɔːrɪəl) *adj.*

ten-strike *n. Tenpin bowling.* another word for **strike** (sense 39).

tent[1] (tɛnt) *n.* **1. a.** a portable shelter of canvas, plastic, or other waterproof material supported on poles and fastened to the ground by pegs and ropes. **b.** (*as modifier*): *tent peg.* **2.** something resembling this in function or shape. ~*vb.* **3.** (*intr.*) to camp in a tent. **4.** (*tr.*) to cover with or as if with a tent or tents. **5.** (*tr.*) to provide with a tent as shelter. [C13: from Old French *tente,* from Latin *tentōrium* something stretched out, from *tendere* to stretch] —**'tent+ed** *adj.* —**'tent+less** *adj.* —**'tent+ˌlike** *adj.*

tent[2] (tɛnt) *Med.* ~*n.* **1.** a plug of soft material for insertion into a bodily canal, etc., to dilate it or maintain its patency. ~*vb.* **2.** (*tr.*) to insert such a plug into (a bodily canal, etc.). [C14 (in the sense: a probe): from Old French *tente* (n.), ultimately from Latin *temptāre* to try; see TEMPT]

tent[3] (tɛnt) *n. Obsolete.* a red table wine from Alicante, Spain. [C16: from Spanish *tinto* dark-coloured; see TINT]

tent[4] (tɛnt) *vb.* a Brit. dialect word for **attend.** —**'tent+er** *n.*

ten+ta+cle ('tɛntəkᵊl) *n.* **1.** any of various elongated flexible organs that occur near the mouth in many invertebrates and are used for feeding, grasping, etc. **2.** any of the hairs on the leaf of an insectivorous plant that are used to capture prey. **3.** something resembling a tentacle, esp. in its ability to grasp. [C18: from New Latin *tentāculum,* from Latin *tentāre,* variant of *temptāre* to feel] —**'ten+ta+cled** *adj.* —**'ten·ta·cle-ˌlike** *or* **ten+tac·u+loid** (tɛn'tækjʊˌlɔɪd) *adj.* —**ten+tac·u·lar** (tɛn'tækjʊlə) *adj.*

tent+age ('tɛntɪdʒ) *n.* **1.** tents collectively. **2.** a supply of tents or tenting equipment.

ten+ta+tion (tɛn'teɪʃən) *n.* a method of achieving the correct adjustment of a mechanical device by a series of trials. [C14: from Latin *tentātiō,* variant of *temptātiō* TEMPTATION]

ten+ta+tive ('tɛntətɪv) *adj.* **1.** provisional or experimental; conjectural. **2.** hesitant, uncertain, or cautious. [C16: from Medieval Latin *tentātīvus,* from Latin *tentāre* to test] —**'ten+ta+tive+ly** *adv.* —**'ten+ta+tive+ness** *n.*

tent cat+er+pil+lar *n.* the larva of various moths of the family *Lasiocampidae,* esp. *Malacosoma americana* of North America, which build communal webs in trees.

tent dress *n.* a very full tent-shaped dress, having no darts, waistline, etc.

ten+ter ('tɛntə) *n.* **1.** a frame on which cloth is stretched during the manufacturing process in order that it may retain its shape while drying. **2.** a person who stretches cloth on a tenter. ~*vb.* **3.** (*tr.*) to stretch (cloth) on a tenter. [C14: from Medieval Latin *tentōrium,* from Latin *tentus* stretched, from *tendere* to stretch]

ten·ter+hook ('tɛntəˌhʊk) *n.* **1.** one of a series of hooks or bent nails used to hold cloth stretched on a tenter. **2. on tenterhooks.** in a state of tension or suspense.

tenth (tɛnθ) *adj.* **1.** (*usually prenominal*) **a.** coming after the ninth in numbering or counting order, position, time, etc.; being the ordinal number of *ten:* often written 10th. **b.** (*as n.*): *see you on the tenth; tenth in line.* ~*n.* **2. a.** one of 10 approximately equal parts of something. **b.** (*as modifier*): *a tenth part.* **3.** one of 10 equal divisions of a particular measurement, etc. Related prefix: **deci-:** *decibel.* **4.** the fraction equal to one divided by ten (1/10). **5.** *Music.* **a.** an interval of one octave plus a third. **b.** one of two notes constituting such an interval in relation to the other. ~*adv.* **6.** Also: **tenthly.** after the ninth person, position, event, etc. ~ **7.** Also: **tenthly.** *sentence connector.* as the 10th point: linking what follows with the previous statements, as in a speech or argument. [C12 *tenthe,* from Old English *tēotha;* see TEN, -TH[2]]

tent stitch *n.* another term for **petit point** (sense 1).

ten·u+is ('tɛnjʊɪs) *n., pl.* **ten·u+es** ('tɛnjʊˌiːz). (in the grammar of classical Greek) any of the voiceless stops as represented by kappa, pi, or tau (k, p, t). [C17: from Latin: thin]

ten·u+ous ('tɛnjʊəs) *adj.* **1.** insignificant or flimsy: *a tenuous argument.* **2.** slim, fine, or delicate: *a tenuous thread.* **3.** diluted or rarefied in consistency or density: *a tenuous fluid.* [C16: from Latin *tenuis*] —**ten·u+i·ty** (tɛ'njuːɪtɪ) *n.* —**'ten·u+ous+ly** *adv.* —**'ten·u+ous+ness** *n.*

ten+ure ('tɛnjʊə, 'tɛnjə) *n.* **1.** the possession or holding of an office or position. **2.** the length of time an office, position, etc., lasts; term. **3.** *U.S.* the improved security status of a person after having been in the employ of the same company or institution for a specified period. **4.** *Property law.* **a.** the holding or occupying of property, esp. realty, in return for services rendered, etc. **b.** the duration of such holding or occupation. [C15: from Old French, from Medieval Latin *tenitūra,* ultimately from Latin *tenēre* to hold] —**ten·'u+ri·al** *adj.* —**ten·'u+ri+al+ly** *adv.*

te+nu+to (tɪ'njuːtəʊ) *adj., adv. Music.* (of a note) to be held for or beyond its full time value. Symbol: ¯ (written above a note). [from Italian, literally: held, from *tenere* to hold, from Latin *tenēre*]

Ten·zing Nor·gay ('tɛnsɪŋ 'nɔːgeɪ) *n.* born 1914, Nepalese mountaineer. With Sir Edmund Hillary, he was the first to reach the summit of Mount Everest (1953).

te·o+cal+li (ˌtiːəʊ'kælɪ) *n., pl.* **+lis.** any of various truncated pyramids built by the Aztecs as bases for their temples. [C17: from Nahuatl, from *teotl* god + *calli* house]

te·o+sin+te (ˌtiːəʊ'sɪntɪ) *n.* a tall Central American annual grass, *Euchlaena mexicana,* resembling maize and grown for forage in the southern U.S. [C19: from Nahuatl *teocentli,* from *teotl* god + *centli* dry ear of corn]

te+pal ('tiːpᵊl, 'tɛpᵊl) *n.* any of the subdivisions of a perianth that is not clearly differentiated into calyx and corolla. [C20: from French *tépale* changed (on analogy with *sépale* sepal) from *pétale* PETAL]

te+pee *or* **tee+pee** ('tiːpiː) *n.* a cone-shaped tent of animal skins used by certain North American Indians. [C19: from Dakota *tīpī,* from *ti* to dwell + *pi* used for]

tep+e·fy ('tɛpɪˌfaɪ) *vb.* **·fies, ·fy+ing, ·fied.** to make or become tepid. [C17: from Latin *tepēre*] —**tep+e·fac+tion** (ˌtɛpɪ'fækʃən) *n.*

teph+ra ('tɛfrə) *n. Chiefly U.S.* solid matter ejected during a volcanic eruption. [C20: Greek, literally: ashes]

teph+rite ('tɛfraɪt) *n.* a variety of basalt containing augite, nepheline, or leucite. [C17: from Greek *tephros*, from *tephra* ashes; see -ITE[1]] —**teph+rit+ic** (tɛf'rɪtɪk) *adj.*

Te+pic (*Spanish* te'pik) *n.* a city in W central Mexico, capital of Nayarit state: agricultural trading and processing centre. Pop.: 114 512 (1975 est.).

tep+id ('tɛpɪd) *adj.* **1.** slightly warm; lukewarm. **2.** relatively unenthusiastic or apathetic: *the play had a tepid reception.* [C14: from Latin *tepidus*, from *tepēre* to be lukewarm] —**te+'pid+i·ty** *or* **'tep+id+ness** *n.* —**'tep+id+ly** *adv.*

te+qui+la (tɪ'ki:lə) *n.* **1.** a spirit that is distilled in Mexico from an agave plant and forms the basis of many mixed drinks. **2.** the plant, *Agave tequilana*, from which this drink is made. [from Mexican Spanish, from *Tequila* district in Mexico]

ter. *abbrev. for:* **1.** terrace. **2.** territory.

ter- *combining form.* three, third, or three times: *tercentenary.* [from Latin *ter* thrice; related to *trēs* THREE]

ter·a- *prefix.* denoting 10^{12}: *terameter.* Symbol: T [from Greek *teras* monster]

Te+rai (tə'raɪ) *n.* **1.** (in India) a belt of marshy land at the foot of mountains, esp. at the foot of the Himalayas in Uttar Pradesh. **2.** a felt hat with a wide brim worn in subtropical regions.

ter+aph ('tɛrəf) *n., pl.* **+a·phim** (-əfɪm). *Old Testament.* any of various small household gods or images venerated by ancient Semitic peoples. (Genesis 31:19–21; I Samuel 19:13–16). [C14: from Hebrew, of uncertain origin]

ter·at- *or* **ter·a·to-** *combining form.* indicating a monster or something abnormal: *teratism; teratoid.* [from Greek *terat-*, *teras* monster, prodigy]

ter·a+tism ('tɛrəˌtɪzəm) *n.* a malformed animal or human, esp. in the fetal stage; monster.

ter·a+to+gen+ic (ˌtɛrətəʊ'dʒɛnɪk) *adj.* producing malformation in a fetus.

ter·a+toid ('tɛrəˌtɔɪd) *adj. Biology.* resembling a monster.

ter·a·tol+o·gy (ˌtɛrə'tɒlədʒɪ) *n.* **1.** the branch of biology that is concerned with the structure, development, etc., of monsters. **2.** a collection of tales about mythical or fantastic creatures, monsters, etc. —**ter·a+to+log+ic** (ˌtɛrətə'lɒdʒɪk) *or* **ˌter·a+to+'log·i·cal** *adj.* —**ˌter·a+'tol·o·gist** *n.*

ter·a·to+ma (ˌtɛrə'təʊmə) *n.* a tumour or group of tumours composed of tissue foreign to the site of growth.

ter+bi·a ('tɜ:bɪə) *n.* another name (not in technical usage) for **terbium oxide.**

ter+bi·um ('tɜ:bɪəm) *n.* a soft malleable silvery-grey element of the lanthanide series of metals, occurring in gadolinite and monazite and used in lasers and for doping solid-state devices. Symbol: Tb; atomic no.: 65; atomic wt.: 158.925; valency: 3 or 4; relative density: 8.234; melting pt.: 1360°C; boiling pt.: 3041°C. [C19: from New Latin, named after *Ytterby*, Sweden, village where it was discovered] —**'ter+bic** *adj.*

ter+bi·um met+al *n. Chem.* any of a group of related lanthanides, including terbium, europium, and gadolinium.

ter+bi·um ox+ide *n.* an amorphous white insoluble powder. Formula: Tb_2O_3. Also called: **terbia.**

Ter Borch *or* **Ter·borch** (*Dutch* tɛr 'bɔrx) *n.* **Ge·rard** ('xe:rɑrt). 1617–81, Dutch genre and portrait painter.

terce (tɜ:s) *or* **tierce** *n. Chiefly R.C. Church.* the third of the seven canonical hours of the divine office, originally fixed at the third hour of the day, about 9 a.m.

Ter·cei+ra (*Portuguese* tər'səɪrə) *n.* an island in the N Atlantic, in the Azores: NATO military air base. Pop.: 90 409 (1970). Area: 397 sq. km (153 sq. miles).

ter+cel ('tɜ:səl) *or* **tier+cel** *n.* a male falcon or hawk, esp. as used in falconry. [C14: from Old French, from Vulgar Latin *tertiolus* (unattested), from Latin *tertius* third, referring to the tradition that only one egg in three hatched a male chick]

ter+cen+te·nar·y (ˌtɜ:sɛn'ti:nərɪ) *or* **ter+cen+ten+ni·al** *adj.* **1.** of or relating to a period of 300 years. **2.** of or relating to a 300th anniversary or its celebration. ~*n.*, **+te+nar·ies** *or* **+ten+ni·als. 3.** an anniversary of 300 years or its celebration. ~Also: **tricentennial.**

ter+cet ('tɜ:sɪt, tɜ:'sɛt) *n.* a group of three lines of verse that rhyme together or are connected by rhyme with adjacent groups of three lines. [C16: from French, from Italian *terzetto*, diminutive of *terzo* third, from Latin *tertius*]

ter+e·bene ('tɛrəˌbi:n) *n.* a mixture of hydrocarbons prepared from oil of turpentine and sulphuric acid, used to make paints and varnishes and medicinally as an expectorant and antiseptic. [C19: from TEREB(INTH) + -ENE]

te+reb+ic ac·id (tɛ'rɛbɪk) *n.* a white crystalline carboxylic acid produced by the action of nitric acid on turpentine. Formula: $C_7H_{10}O_4$.

ter+e·binth ('tɛrɪbɪnθ) *n.* a small anacardiaceous tree, *Pistacia terebinthus*, of the Mediterranean region, having winged leafstalks and clusters of small flowers, and yielding a turpentine. [C14: from Latin *terebinthus*, from Greek *terebinthos* turpentine tree]

ter+e·bin+thine (ˌtɛrɪ'bɪnθaɪn) *adj.* **1.** of or relating to terebinth or related plants. **2.** of, consisting of, or resembling turpentine.

te+re+do (tə'ri:dəʊ) *n., pl.* **+dos** *or* **+di+nes** (-dɪˌni:z). any marine bivalve mollusc of the genus *Teredo*. See **shipworm.** [C17: via Latin from Greek *terēdōn* wood-boring worm; related to Greek *tetrainein* to pierce]

Ter·ence ('tɛrəns) *n.* Latin name *Publius Terentius Afer.* ?190–159 B.C., Roman comic dramatist. His six comedies, *Andria, Hecyra, Heauton Timoroumenos, Eunuchus, Phormio,* and *Adelphoe,* are based on Greek originals by Menander.

ter+eph+thal+ic ac·id (ˌtɛrɛf'θælɪk) *n.* a white crystalline water-insoluble carboxylic acid used in making polyester resins such as Terylene; 1,4-benzenedicarboxylic acid. Formula: $C_6H_4(COOH)_2$. [C20: from TEREBENE + PHTHALIC]

Te·re·sa *or* **The·re·sa** (tə'ri:zə; *Spanish* te'resa) *n.* **1. Saint,** known as *Teresa of Avila.* 1515–82, Spanish nun and mystic. She reformed the Carmelite order and founded 17 convents. Her writings include a spiritual autobiography and *The Way to Perfection.* Feast day: Oct. 15. **2. Mother.** original name *Agnes Gonxha Bojaxhiu.* born 1910, Indian Roman Catholic missionary, born in Yugoslavia of Albanian parents: noted for her work among the starving in Calcutta.

Te·resh·ko·va (*Russian* tɪrɪʃ'kɔvə) *n.* **Va·len·ti·na Vla·di·mi·rov·na** (vəlɪn'tinə vla'dimirəvnə). born 1937, Soviet cosmonaut; first woman in space (1963).

Te+re+si+na (*Portuguese* ˌtere'zina) *n.* an inland port in NE Brazil, capital of Piauí state, on the Parnaíba River: chief commercial centre of the Parnaíba valley. Pop.: 181 071 (1970). Former name: **Therezina.**

te+rete ('tɛri:t) *adj.* (esp. of plant parts) cylindrical and tapering. [C17: from Latin *teres* smooth, from *terere* to rub]

Te·re·us ('tɪərɪəs) *n. Greek myth.* a prince of Thrace, who raped Philomela, sister of his wife Procne, and was punished by being turned into a hoopoe.

ter+gi+ver+sate ('tɜ:dʒɪvəˌseɪt) *vb. (intr.)* **1.** to change sides or loyalties; apostatize. **2.** to be evasive or ambiguous; equivocate. [C17: from Latin *tergiversārī* to turn one's back, from *tergum* back + *vertere* to turn] —**ˌter+gi+ver+'sa+tion** *n.* —**'ter+gi+ver+ˌsa+tor** *or* **ter+gi+ver+sant** ('tɜ:dʒɪˌvɜ:sənt) *n.* —**ˌter+gi+'ver+sa+to·ry** *adj.*

ter+gum ('tɜ:gəm) *n., pl.* **+ga** (-gə). a cuticular plate covering the dorsal surface of a body segment of an arthropod. Compare **sternum** (sense 3). [C19: from Latin: the back] —**'ter+gal** *adj.*

ter·i+ya+ki (ˌtɛrɪ'jɑ:kɪ) *adj.* **1.** *Japanese cookery.* marinated in soy sauce and rice wine and grilled, usually over charcoal. ~*n.* **2.** a dish of meat prepared in this way. [from Japanese, from *teri* sunshine + *yaki* to broil]

term (tɜ:m) *n.* **1.** a name, expression, or word used for some particular thing, esp. in a specialized field of knowledge: *a medical term.* **2.** any word or expression. **3.** a limited period of time: *his second term of office; a prison term.* **4.** any of the divisions of the academic year during which a school, college, etc., is in session. **5.** a point in time determined for an event or for the end of a period. **6.** Also called: **full term.** the period at which childbirth is imminent. **7.** *Law.* **a.** an estate or interest in land limited to run for a specified period: *a term of years.* **b.** the duration of an estate, etc. **c.** a period of time during which sessions of courts of law are held. **d.** time allowed to a debtor to settle. **8.** *Maths.* any distinct quantity making up a fraction or proportion, or contained in a polynomial, sequence, series, etc. **9.** *Logic.* **a.** the word or phrase that forms either the subject or predicate of a proposition. **b.** any of the three subjects or predicates occurring in a syllogism. **10.** Also called: **terminal, terminus, terminal figure.** *Architect.* a sculptured post, esp. one in the form of an armless bust or an animal on the top of a square pillar. **11.** *Australian Rules football.* the usual word for **quarter** (sense 10). **12.** *Archaic.* a boundary or limit. ~*vb.* **13.** *(tr.)* to designate; call: *he was termed a thief.* [C13: from Old French *terme*, from Latin *terminus* end] —**'term+ly** *adv.*

term. *abbrev. for:* **1.** terminal. **2.** termination.

ter+ma+gant ('tɜ:məgənt) *n. Rare.* **a.** a shrewish woman; scold. **b.** (*as modifier*): *a termagant woman.* [C13: from earlier *Tervagaunt*, from Old French *Tervagan*, from Italian *Trivigante*; after an arrogant character in medieval mystery plays who was supposed to be a Moslem deity] —**'ter+ma+gan+cy** *n.* —**'ter+ma+gant+ly** *adv.*

-term·er *n.* (*in combination*) a person serving a specified length of time in prison: *a short-termer.*

ter+mi+na·ble ('tɜ:mɪnəbəl, 'tɜ:mnəbəl) *adj.* **1.** able to be terminated. **2.** terminating after a specific period or event: *a terminable annuity.* —**ˌter+mi+na·'bil+i·ty** *or* **'ter+mi+na·ble+ness** *n.* —**'ter+mi+na·bly** *adv.*

ter+mi+nal ('tɜ:mɪnəl) *adj.* **1.** of, being, or situated at an end, terminus, or boundary: *a terminal station; terminal buds.* **2.** of, relating to, or occurring after or in a term: *terminal leave; terminal examinations.* **3.** (of a disease) terminating in death: *terminal cancer.* **4.** of or relating to the storage or delivery of freight at a warehouse: *a terminal service.* ~*n.* **5.** a terminating point, part, or place. **6. a.** a point at which current enters or leaves an electrical device, such as a battery or a circuit. **b.** a conductor by which current enters or leaves at such a point. **7.** *Computer technol.* a device having input/output links with a computer but situated at a distance from the computer. **8.** *Architect.* **a.** an ornamental carving at the end of a structure. **b.** another name for **term** (sense 10). **9. a.** a point or station usually at the end of the line of a railway, serving as an important access point for passengers or freight. **b.** a less common name for **terminus. 10.** *Physiol.* **a.** the smallest arteriole before its division into capillaries. **b.** either of two veins that collect blood from the thalamus and surrounding structures and empty it into the internal cerebral vein. **c.** the portion of a bronchiole just before it subdivides into the air sacs of the lungs. [C15: from Latin *terminālis*, from *terminus* end] —**'ter+mi+nal+ly** *adv.*

ter+mi+nal ve+loc+i·ty *n.* **1.** the constant maximum velocity reached by a body falling under gravity through a fluid, esp. the atmosphere. **2.** the velocity of a missile or projectile when it reaches its target. **3.** the maximum velocity attained by a rocket, missile, or shell flying in a parabolic flight path. **4.** the maximum velocity that an aircraft can attain, as determined by its total drag.

ter+mi+nate (ˈtɜːmɪˌneɪt) *vb.* (when *intr.* often foll. by *in* or *with*) to form, be, or put an end to; conclude: *to terminate a pregnancy; their relationship terminated amicably.* [C16: from Latin *terminātus* limited, from *termināre* to set boundaries, from *terminus* end] —**ˈter+mi+na+tive** *adj.* —**ˈter+mi+na+to·ry** *adj.*

ter+mi+na+tion (ˌtɜːmɪˈneɪʃən) *n.* **1.** the act of terminating or the state of being terminated. **2.** something that terminates. **3.** a final result. —**ˌter+mi+ˈna+tion+al** *adj.*

ter+mi+na+tor (ˈtɜːmɪˌneɪtə) *n.* the line dividing the illuminated and dark part of the moon or planet.

ter+mi+nol+o·gy (ˌtɜːmɪˈnɒlədʒɪ) *n., pl.* **·gies. 1.** the body of specialized words relating to a particular subject. **2.** the study of terms. [C19: from Medieval Latin *terminus* term from Latin: end] —**ter+mi+no+log·i·cal** (ˌtɜːmɪnəˈlɒdʒɪkᵊl) *adj.* —**ˌter+mi+no+ˈlog·i·cal+ly** *adv.* —**ˌter+mi+ˈnol·o+gist** *n.*

term in+sur+ance *n.* life assurance, usually low in cost and offering no cash value, that provides for the payment of a specified sum of money only if the insured dies within a stipulated period of time.

ter+mi+nus (ˈtɜːmɪnəs) *n., pl.* **+ni** (-naɪ) *or* **+nus·es. 1.** the last or final part or point. **2.** either end of a railway, bus route, etc., or a station or town at such a point. **3.** a goal aimed for. **4.** a boundary or boundary marker. **5.** *Architect.* another name for **term** (sense 10). [C16: from Latin: end; related to Greek *termōn* boundary]

Ter·mi·nus (ˈtɜːmɪnəs) *n.* the Roman god of boundaries.

ter+mi+nus ad quem *Latin.* (ˈtɜːmɪˌnʊs æd ˈkwɛm) *n.* the aim or terminal point. [literally: the end to which]

ter+mi+nus a quo *Latin.* (ˈtɜːmɪˌnʊs ɑː ˈkwəʊ) *n.* the starting point; beginning. [literally: the end from which]

ter+mi+tar+i·um (ˌtɜːmɪˈtɛərɪəm) *n.* the nest of a termite colony. [C20: from TERMITE + -ARIUM]

ter+mite (ˈtɜːmaɪt) *n.* any whitish ant-like social insect of the order *Isoptera,* of warm and tropical regions. Some species feed on wood, causing damage to furniture, buildings, trees, etc. Also called: **white ant.** [C18: from New Latin *termitēs* white ants, pl. of *termes,* from Latin: a woodworm; related to Greek *tetrainein* to bore through] —**ter+mit+ic** (tɜːˈmɪtɪk) *adj.*

term+less (ˈtɜːmlɪs) *adj.* **1.** without limit or boundary. **2.** unconditional. **3.** an archaic word for **indescribable.**

ter+mor *or* **ter+mer** (ˈtɜːmə) *n. Property law.* a person who holds an estate for a term of years or until he dies.

terms (tɜːmz) *pl. n.* **1.** (usually specified prenominally) the actual language or mode of presentation used: *he described the project in loose terms.* **2.** conditions of an agreement: *you work here on our terms.* **3.** a sum of money paid for a service or credit; charges. **4.** (usually preceded by *on*) mutual relationship or standing: *they are on affectionate terms.* **5. bring to terms.** to cause to agree or submit. **6. in terms of.** as expressed by; regarding: *in terms of money he was no better off.* **7. come to terms.** to reach acceptance or agreement: *to come to terms with one's failings.*

terms of trade *pl. n. Economics, Brit.* the ratio of export prices to import prices. It measures a nation's trading position, which improves when export prices rise faster or fall slower than import prices.

tern[1] (tɜːn) *n.* any aquatic bird of the subfamily *Sterninae,* having a forked tail, long narrow wings, a pointed bill, and a typically black-and-white plumage: family *Laridae* (gulls, etc.), order *Charadriiformes.* [C18: from Old Norse *therna;* related to Norwegian *terna,* Swedish *tärna*]

tern[2] (tɜːn) *n.* **1.** a three-masted schooner. **2.** *Rare.* a group of three. [C14: from Old French *terne,* from Italian *terno,* from Latin *ternī* three each; related to Latin *ter* thrice, *trēs* three]

ter+na+ry (ˈtɜːnərɪ) *adj.* **1.** consisting of three or groups of three. **2.** *Maths.* **a.** (of a number system) to the base three. **b.** involving or containing three variables. **3.** (of an alloy, mixture, or chemical compound) having three different components or composed of three different elements. ~*n., pl.* **+ries. 4.** a group of three. [C14: from Latin *ternārius,* from *ternī* three each]

ter+na+ry form *n.* a musical structure consisting of two contrasting sections followed by a repetition of the first; the form *aba.* Also called: **song form.**

ter+nate (ˈtɜːnɪt, -neɪt) *adj.* **1.** (esp. of a leaf) consisting of three leaflets or other parts. **2.** (esp. of plants) having groups of three members. [C18: from New Latin *ternātus,* from Medieval Latin *ternāre* to increase threefold] —**ˈter+nate+ly** *adv.*

terne (tɜːn) *n.* **1.** Also called: **terne metal.** an alloy of lead containing tin (10–20 per cent) and antimony (1.5–2 per cent). **2.** Also called: **terne plate.** steel plate coated with this alloy. [C16: perhaps from French *terne* dull, from Old French *ternir* to TARNISH]

Ter+ni (*Italian* ˈtɛrni) *n.* an industrial city in central Italy, in Umbria: site of waterfalls created in Roman times. Pop.: 111 315 (1975 est.).

ter+ni+on (ˈtɜːnɪən) *n.* **1.** *Rare.* a group of three. **2.** *Printing.* a gathering of three sheets of paper folded once, making six leaves or 12 pages. [C16: from Latin *terniō* triad, from *ternī* three each; related to *ter* thrice]

Ter+no+pol (*Russian* tɪrˈnɔpəlj) *n.* a town in the SW Soviet Union, in the W Ukrainian SSR: formerly under Polish rule. Pop.: 120 000 (1975 est.). Polish name: **Tarnopol.**

ter·o+tech+nol+o·gy (ˌtɪərəʊtɛkˈnɒlədʒɪ, ˌtɛr-) *n.* technology concerned with the installation, efficient operation, and maintenance of equipment and machinery. [C20: from Greek *tērein* to care for + TECHNOLOGY]

ter+pene (ˈtɜːpiːn) *n.* any one of a class of unsaturated hydrocarbons, such as limonene, pinene, and the carotenes, that are found in the essential oils of many plants, esp. conifers. Their molecules contain isoprene units and have the general formula $(C_5H_8)_n$. [C19: *terp-* from obsolete *terpentine* TURPENTINE + -ENE] —**ter+ˈpe+nic** *adj.*

ter+pin+e·ol (tɜːˈpɪnɪˌɒl) *n.* a terpene alcohol with an odour of lilac, existing in three isomeric forms that occur in several essential oils. A mixture of the isomers is used as a solvent and in flavourings and perfumes. Formula: $C_{10}H_{17}OH$. [C20: from TERPENE + -INE[2] + -OL[1]]

Terp·sich·o·re (tɜːpˈsɪkərɪ) *n.* the Muse of the dance and of choral song. [C18: via Latin from Greek, from *terpsikhoros* delighting in the dance, from *terpein* to delight + *khoros* dance; see CHORUS]

Terp+si+cho+re+an (ˌtɜːpsɪkəˈrɪən, -ˈkɔːrɪən) *Often used facetiously.* ~*adj. also* **Terp+si+cho+re·al. 1.** of or relating to dancing or the art of dancing. ~*n.* **2.** a dancer.

terr. *abbrev. for:* **1.** terrace. **2.** territory.

ter+ra (ˈtɛrə) *n.* (in legal contexts) earth or land. [from Latin]

ter+ra al+ba (ˈælbə) *n.* **1.** a white finely powdered form of gypsum, used to make paints, paper, etc. **2.** any of various other white earthy substances, such as kaolin, pipeclay, and magnesia. [from Latin, literally: white earth]

ter+race (ˈtɛrəs) *n.* **1.** a horizontal flat area of ground, often one of a series in a slope. **2. a.** a row of houses, usually identical and having common dividing walls, or the street onto which they face. **b.** (*cap. when part of a street name*): *Grosvenor Terrace.* **3.** a paved area alongside a building, serving partly as a garden. **4.** a balcony or patio. **5.** the flat roof of a house built in a Spanish or Oriental style. **6.** a flat area bounded by a short steep slope formed by the down-cutting of a river or by erosion. **7.** (*usually pl.*) **a.** unroofed tiers around a football pitch on which the spectators stand. **b.** the spectators themselves. ~*vb.* (*tr.*) **8.** to make into or provide with a terrace or terraces. [C16: from Old French *terrasse,* from Old Provençal *terrassa* pile of earth, from *terra* earth, from Latin] —**ˈter+race+less** *adj.*

ter+raced house *n. Brit.* a house that is part of a terrace. U.S. name: **row house.** —**ter+raced hous+ing** *n.*

ter+ra cot+ta (ˈkɒtə) *n.* **1.** a hard unglazed brownish-red earthenware, or the clay from which it is made. **2.** something made of terra cotta, such as a sculpture. **3.** a strong reddish-brown to brownish-orange colour. ~*adj.* **4.** made of terra cotta: *a terra-cotta urn.* **5.** of the colour terra cotta: *a terra-cotta carpet.* [C18: from Italian, literally: baked earth]

ter+ra fir+ma (ˈfɜːmə) *n.* the solid earth; firm ground. [C17: from Latin]

ter+rain (ˈtɛreɪn) *n.* **1.** a piece of ground, esp. with reference to its physical character or military potential: *a rocky terrain.* **2.** a variant spelling of **terrane.** [C18: from French, ultimately from Latin *terrēnum* ground, from *terra* earth]

ter+ra in+cog+ni+ta *Latin.* (ˈtɛrə ɪnˈkɒgnɪtə) *n.* an unexplored or unknown land, region, or area for study.

Ter+ra+my+cin (ˌtɛrəˈmaɪsɪn) *n.* a trademark for **oxytetracycline.**

ter+rane *or* **ter+rain** (ˈtɛreɪn) *n.* a series of rock formations, esp. one having a prevalent type of rock. [C19: see TERRAIN]

ter+ra+pin (ˈtɛrəpɪn) *n.* any of various web-footed chelonian reptiles that live on land and in fresh water and feed on small aquatic animals: family *Emydidae.* Also called: **water tortoise.** [C17: of Algonquian origin; compare Delaware *torope* turtle]

ter+rar+i·um (tɛˈrɛərɪəm) *n., pl.* **+rar+i·ums** *or* **+rar·i·a** (-ˈrɛərɪə). a closed container in which small terrestrial animals or plants are kept. [C19: New Latin, from Latin *terra* earth]

ter+ra si+gil+la+ta (ˈtɛrə ˌsɪdʒɪˈlɑːtə) *n.* **1.** a reddish-brown clayey earth found on the Aegean island of Lemnos: formerly used as an astringent and in the making of earthenware pottery. **2.** any similar earth resembling this. **3.** earthenware pottery made from this or a similar earth, esp. Samian ware. [from Latin: sealed earth]

ter+raz+zo (tɛˈrætsəʊ) *n.* a floor or wall finish made by setting marble or other stone chips into a layer of mortar and polishing the surface. [C20: from Italian: TERRACE]

ter+rene (tɛˈriːn) *adj.* **1.** of or relating to the earth; worldly; mundane. **2.** *Rare.* of earth; earthy. ~*n.* **3.** a land. **4.** a rare word for **earth.** [C14: from Anglo-Norman, from Latin *terrēnus,* from *terra* earth] —**ter+ˈrene+ly** *adv.*

terre+plein (ˈtɛəˌpleɪn) *n.* **1.** the top of a rampart where guns are placed behind the parapet. **2.** an embankment with a level top surface. [C16: from French, from Medieval Latin phrase *terrā plēnus* filled with earth]

ter+res+tri·al (təˈrɛstrɪəl) *adj.* **1.** of or relating to the earth. **2.** of or belonging to the land as opposed to the sea or air. **3.** (of animals and plants) living or growing on the land. **4.** earthly, worldly, or mundane. ~*n.* **5.** an inhabitant of the earth. [C15: from Latin *terrestris,* from *terra* earth] —**ter+ˈres+tri+al+ly** *adv.* —**ter+ˈres+tri+al+ness** *n.*

ter+res+tri·al guid+ance *n.* a method of missile or rocket guidance in which the flight path is controlled by reference to the strength and direction of the earth's gravitational or magnetic field. Compare **inertial guidance.**

ter+res+tri·al tel·e+scope *n.* a telescope for use on earth rather than for making astronomical observations. Such telescopes contain an additional lens or prism system to produce an erect image. Compare **astronomical telescope.**

ter+ret ('tɛrɪt) *n.* **1.** either of the two metal rings on a harness saddle through which the reins are passed. **2.** the ring on a dog's collar for attaching the lead. [C15: variant of *toret,* from Old French, diminutive of *tor* loop; see TOUR]

terre-verte ('tɛə,vɜːt) *n.* **1.** a greyish-green pigment used in paints, consisting of powdered glauconite. ~*adj.* **2.** of a greyish-green colour. [C17: from French, literally: green earth]

ter+ri+ble ('tɛrəbᵊl) *adj.* **1.** very serious or extreme: *a terrible cough.* **2.** *Informal.* of poor quality; unpleasant or bad: *a terrible meal; a terrible play.* **3.** causing terror. **4.** causing awe: *the terrible nature of God.* [C15: from Latin *terribilis,* from *terrēre* to terrify] —'**ter+ri+ble+ness** *n.*

ter+ri+bly ('tɛrəblɪ) *adv.* **1.** (intensifier): *you're terribly kind.* **2.** in a terrible manner.

ter+ric·o+lous (tɛ'rɪkələs) *n.* living on or in the soil. [C19: from Latin *terricola,* from *terra* earth + *colere* to inhabit]

ter+ri+er[1] ('tɛrɪə) *n.* any of several usually small, active, and short-bodied breeds of dog, originally trained to hunt animals living underground. [C15: from Old French *chien terrier* earth dog, from Medieval Latin *terrārius* belonging to the earth, from Latin *terra* earth]

ter+ri+er[2] ('tɛrɪə) *n. English legal history.* a register or survey of land. [C15: from Old French, from Medieval Latin *terrārius* of the land, from Latin *terra* land]

Ter+ri+er ('tɛrɪə) *n. Informal.* a member of the British Army's Territorial and Volunteer Reserve.

ter+rif+ic (tə'rɪfɪk) *adj.* **1.** very great or intense: *a terrific noise.* **2.** *Informal.* very good; excellent: *a terrific singer.* **3.** very frightening. [C17: from Latin *terrificus,* from *terrēre* to frighten; see -FIC] —**ter+'rif·i·cal+ly** *adv.*

ter+ri+fy ('tɛrɪ,faɪ) *vb.* **+fies, +fy+ing, +fied.** (*tr.*) to inspire fear or dread in; frighten greatly. [C16: from Latin *terrificāre,* from *terrēre* to alarm + *facere* to cause] —'**ter+ri+,fi+er** *n.* —'**ter+ri+,fy+ing+ly** *adv.*

ter+rig+e+nous (tɛ'rɪdʒɪnəs) *adj.* **1.** of or produced by the earth. **2.** (of geological deposits) formed in the sea from material derived from the land by erosion. [C17: from Latin *terrigenus,* from *terra* earth + *gignere* to beget]

ter+rine (tɛ'riːn) *n.* **1.** an oval earthenware cooking dish with a tightly fitting lid used for patés, etc. **2.** the food cooked or served in such a dish, esp. paté. **3.** another word for **tureen.** [C18: earlier form of TUREEN]

ter+ri+to+ri+al (,tɛrɪ'tɔːrɪəl) *adj.* **1.** of or relating to a territory or territories. **2.** restricted to or owned by a particular territory: *the Indian territorial waters.* **3.** local or regional. **4.** pertaining to a territorial army, providing a reserve of trained men for use in emergency. —,**ter+ri+'to+ri+al+ly** *adv.*

Ter+ri+to+ri+al (,tɛrɪ'tɔːrɪəl) *n.* a member of a territorial army, esp. the British Army's Territorial and Volunteer Reserve.

Ter+ri+to+ri+al Ar·my *n.* (in Britain) a standing reserve army originally organized between 1907 and 1908. Full name: **Territorial and Volunteer Reserve.**

ter+ri+to+ri+al court *n.* a court in a U.S. territory with both local and federal jurisdiction.

ter+ri+to+ri+al+ism (,tɛrɪ'tɔːrɪəlɪzəm) *n.* **1.** a social system under which the predominant force in the state is the landed class. **2.** a former Protestant theory that the civil government has the right to determine the religious beliefs of the subjects of a state. —,**ter+ri+'to+ri+al+ist** *n.*

ter+ri+to+ri+al+i·ty (,tɛrɪ,tɔːrɪ'ælɪtɪ) *n.* **1.** the state or rank of being a territory. **2.** the behaviour shown by an animal when establishing and defending its territory.

ter+ri+to+ri+al+ize *or* **ter+ri+to+ri+al+ise** (,tɛrɪ'tɔːrɪə,laɪz) *vb.* (*tr.*) **1.** to make a territory of. **2.** to place on a territorial basis: *the militia was territorialized.* **3.** to enlarge (a country) by acquiring more territory. **4.** to make territorial. —,**ter+ri+,to+ri+al·i+'za+tion** *or* ,**ter+ri+,to+ri+al·i+'sa+tion** *n.*

ter+ri+to+ri+al wa·ters *pl. n.* the waters over which a nation exercises jurisdiction and control, conventionally within three miles from shore.

Ter+ri+to+ri+an (,tɛrɪ'tɔːrɪən) *n. Austral.* an inhabitant of the Northern Territory.

ter+ri+to·ry ('tɛrɪtərɪ, -trɪ) *n., pl.* **·ries. 1.** any tract of land; district. **2.** the geographical domain under the jurisdiction of a political unit, esp. of a sovereign state. **3.** the district for which an agent, etc., is responsible: *a salesman's territory.* **4.** an area inhabited and defended by an individual animal or a breeding pair of animals. **5.** an area of knowledge: *science isn't my territory.* **6.** (in football, hockey, etc.) the area defended by a team. **7.** (*often cap.*) a region of a country, esp. of a federal state, that enjoys less autonomy and a lower status than most constituent parts of the state. **8.** (*often cap.*) a protectorate or other dependency of a country. [C15: from Latin *territōrium* land surrounding a town, from *terra* land]

Ter+ri+to·ry ('tɛrɪtərɪ, -trɪ) *n.* **the.** *Austral.* See **Northern Territory.**

ter+ror ('tɛrə) *n.* **1.** great fear, panic, or dread. **2.** a person or thing that inspires great dread. **3.** *Informal.* a troublesome person or thing, esp. a child. **4.** terrorism. [C14: from Old French *terreur,* from Latin *terror,* from *terrēre* to frighten; related to Greek *trein* to run away in terror] —'**ter+ror+ful** *adj.* —'**ter+ror+less** *adj.*

ter+ror+ism ('tɛrə,rɪzəm) *n.* **1.** the act of terrorizing; systematic use of violence and intimidation to achieve some goal. **2.** the state of being terrorized. **3.** government or opposition to government by means of terror.

ter+ror+ist ('tɛrərɪst) *n.* **a.** a person who employs terror or terrorism, esp. as a political weapon. **b.** (*as modifier*): *terrorist tactics.* —,**ter+ror+'is+tic** *adj.*

ter+ror+ize *or* **ter+ror+ise** ('tɛrə,raɪz) *vb.* (*tr.*) **1.** to coerce or control by violence, fear, threats, etc. **2.** to inspire with dread; terrify. —,**ter+ror+i+'za+tion** *or* ,**ter+ror+i+'sa+tion** *n.* —'**ter+ror+,iz+er** *or* '**ter+ror+,is+er** *n.*

ter·ror-strick·en *or* **ter·ror-struck** *adj.* in a state of terror.

ter+ry ('tɛrɪ) *n., pl.* **+ries. 1.** an uncut loop in the pile of towelling or a similar fabric. **2. a.** a fabric with such a pile on both sides. **b.** (*as modifier*): *a terry towel.* [C18: perhaps variant of TERRET]

Ter·ry ('tɛrɪ) *n.* Dame **El·len.** 1847–1928, English actress, noted for her Shakespearian roles opposite Sir Henry Irving and for her correspondence with Bernard Shaw.

terse (tɜːs) *adj.* **1.** neatly brief and concise. **2.** curt; abrupt. [C17: from Latin *tersus* precise, from *tergēre* to polish] —'**terse+ly** *adv.* —'**terse+ness** *n.*

ter+tial ('tɜːʃəl) *adj., n.* another word for **tertiary** (senses 5, 6). [C19: from Latin *tertius* third, from *ter* thrice, from *trēs* three]

ter+tian ('tɜːʃən) *adj.* **1.** (of a fever or the symptoms of a disease, esp. malaria) occurring every other day. ~*n.* **2.** a tertian fever or symptoms. [C14: from Latin *febris tertiāna* fever occurring every third day, reckoned inclusively, from *tertius* third]

ter+tiar·y ('tɜːʃərɪ) *adj.* **1.** third in degree, order, etc. **2.** (of an industry) involving services as opposed to extraction or manufacture, such as transport, finance, etc. Compare **primary** (sense 8b.), **secondary** (sense 7). **3.** *R.C. Church.* of or relating to a Third Order. **4.** *Chem.* **a.** (of an organic compound) having a functional group attached to a carbon atom that is attached to three other groups. **b.** (of an amine) having three organic groups attached to a nitrogen atom. **c.** (of a salt) derived from a tribasic acid by replacement of all its acidic hydrogen atoms with metal atoms or electropositive groups. **5.** Also: **tertial.** *Ornithol, rare.* of, relating to, or designating any of the small flight feathers attached to the part of the humerus nearest to the body. ~*n., pl.* **+tiar·ies. 6.** Also called: **tertial.** *Ornithol, rare.* any of the tertiary feathers. **7.** *R.C. Church.* a member of a Third Order. [C16: from Latin *tertiārius* containing one third, from *tertius* third]

Ter+tiar·y ('tɜːʃərɪ) *adj.* **1.** of, denoting, or formed in the first period of the Cenozoic era, which lasted for 69 million years, during which mammals became dominant. ~*n.* **2. the.** the Tertiary period or rock system, divided into Palaeocene, Eocene, Oligocene, Miocene, and Pliocene epochs or series.

ter+tiar·y col+lege *n. Brit.* a college system incorporating the secondary school sixth form and vocational courses.

ter+ti·um quid ('tɜːtɪəm 'kwɪd) *n.* an unknown or indefinite thing related in some way to two known or definite things, but distinct from both: *there is either right or wrong, with no tertium quid.* [C18: from Late Latin, rendering Greek *triton ti* some third thing]

Ter·tul·li·an (tɜː'tʌlɪən) *n.* Latin name *Quintus Septimius Florens Tertullianus.* ?160–?220 A.D., Carthaginian Christian theologian, who wrote in Latin rather than Greek and originated much of Christian terminology.

Te+ruel (*Spanish* te'rwel) *n.* a city in E central Spain: 15th-century cathedral; scene of fierce fighting during the Spanish Civil War. Pop.: 21 638 (1970).

ter+va+lent (tɜː'veɪlənt) *adj. Chem.* another word for **trivalent.** —**ter+'va+len+cy** *n.*

Ter·y+lene ('tɛrə,liːn) *n. Trademark.* a synthetic polyester fibre or fabric based on terephthalic acid, characterized by lightness and crease-resistance and used for clothing, sheets, ropes, sails, etc. U.S. name (trademark): **Dacron.**

ter·za ri·ma ('tɛətsə 'riːmə) *n., pl.* **ter+ze ri·me** ('tɛətseɪ 'riːmeɪ). a verse form of Italian origin consisting of a series of tercets in which the middle line of one tercet rhymes with the first and third lines of the next. [C19: from Italian, literally: third rhyme]

ter+zet+to (tɜː'tsɛtəʊ) *n., pl.* **+tos** *or* **+ti** (-tɪ). *Music.* a trio, esp. a vocal one. [C18: Italian: trio; see TERCET]

tes+la ('tɛslə) *n.* the derived SI unit of magnetic flux density equal to a flux of 1 weber in an area of 1 square metre. Symbol: T [C20: named after Nikola TESLA]

Tes·la ('tɛslə) *n.* **Ni·ko·la** ('nɪkələ). 1857–1943, U.S. electrical engineer and inventor, born in Yugoslavia. His inventions include a transformer, generators, and dynamos.

tes·la coil *n.* a step-up transformer with an air core, used for producing high voltages at high frequencies. The secondary circuit is tuned to resonate with the primary winding. [C20: named after Nikola TESLA]

tes+sel+late ('tɛsɪ,leɪt) *vb.* **1.** (*tr.*) to construct, pave, or inlay with a mosaic of small tiles. **2.** (*intr.*) (of identical shapes) to fit together exactly: *triangles will tessellate but octagons will not.* [C18: from Latin *tessellātus* checked, from *tessella* small stone cube, from TESSERA]

tes+sel+la+tion (,tɛsɪ'leɪʃən) *n.* **1.** the act of tessellating. **2.** the form or a specimen of tessellated work.

tes+ser·a ('tɛsərə) *n., pl.* **+ser·ae** (-sə,riː). **1.** a small square tile of stone, glass, etc., used in mosaics. **2.** a die, tally, etc., used in classical times, made of bone or wood. [C17: from Latin, from Ionic Greek *tesseres* four] —'**tes+ser+al** *adj.*

tes+ser+act ('tɛsə,rækt) *n.* the four-dimensional equivalent of a cube; hypercube. [C19: from Ionic Greek *tesseres* four + *aktis* ray]

Tes·sin (tɛˈsiːn) *n.* the German name for **Ticino.**

tes·si·tu·ra (ˌtɛsɪˈtʊərə) *n. Music.* **1.** the general pitch level of a piece of vocal music: *an uncomfortably high tessitura.* **2.** the compass or range of a voice. [Italian: texture, from Latin *textura;* see TEXTURE]

test[1] (tɛst) *vb.* **1.** to ascertain (the worth, capability, or endurance) of (a person or thing) by subjection to certain examinations, etc.; try. **2.** (often foll. by *for*) to carry out an examination on (a substance, material, or system) by applying some chemical or physical procedure designed to indicate the presence of a substance or the possession of a property: *to test food for arsenic; to test for magnetization.* ~*n.* **3.** a method, practice, or examination designed to test a person or thing. **4.** a series of questions or problems designed to test a specific skill or knowledge: *an intelligence test.* **5.** a standard of judgment; criterion. **6. a.** a chemical reaction or physical procedure for testing a substance, material, etc. **b.** a chemical reagent used in such a procedure: *litmus is a test for acids.* **c.** the result of the procedure or the evidence gained from it: *the test for alcohol was positive.* **7.** *Sport.* See **test match. 8.** *Archaic.* a declaration or confirmation of truth, loyalty, etc.; oath. **9.** (*modifier*) performed as a test: *test drive; test flight.* [C14 (in the sense: vessel used in treating metals): from Latin *testum* earthen vessel] —**ˈtest·a·ble** *adj.* —ˌ**test·a·ˈbil·i·ty** *n.* —**ˈtest·ing·ly** *adv.*

test[2] (tɛst) *n.* **1.** the hard or tough outer covering of certain invertebrates and tunicates. **2.** a variant of **testa.** [C19: from Latin *testa* shell]

tes·ta (ˈtɛstə) *n., pl.* **·tae** (-tiː). a hard protective outer layer of the seeds of flowering plants; seed coat. [C18: from Latin: shell; see TEST[2]]

tes·ta·ceous (tɛˈsteɪʃəs) *adj. Biology.* **1.** of, relating to, or possessing a test or testa. **2.** of the reddish-brown colour of terra cotta. [C17: from Latin *testācens,* from TESTA]

Test Act *n.* a law passed in 1673 in England to exclude Catholics from public life by requiring all persons holding offices under the Crown, such as army officers, to take the Anglican Communion and perform other acts forbidden to a Catholic: repealed in 1828.

tes·ta·ment (ˈtɛstəmənt) *n.* **1.** *Law.* a will setting out the disposition of personal property (esp. in the phrase **last will and testament**). **2.** a proof, attestation, or tribute: *his success was a testament to his skills.* **3. a.** a covenant instituted between God and man, esp. the covenant of Moses or that instituted by Christ. **b.** a copy of either the Old or the New Testament, or of the complete Bible. [C14: from Latin: a will, from *testārī* to bear witness, from *testis* a witness] —ˌ**tes·ta·ˈmen·tal** *adj.*

Tes·ta·ment (ˈtɛstəmənt) *n.* **1.** either of the two main parts of the Bible; the Old Testament or the New Testament. **2.** the New Testament as distinct from the Old.

tes·ta·men·ta·ry (ˌtɛstəˈmɛntərɪ) *adj.* **1.** of or relating to a will or testament. **2.** derived from, bequeathed, or appointed by a will. **3.** contained or set forth in a will.

tes·tate (ˈtɛsteɪt, ˈtɛstɪt) *adj.* **1.** having left a legally valid will at death. ~*n.* **2.** a person who dies testate. ~Compare **intestate.** [C15: from Latin *testārī* to make a will; see TESTAMENT] —**tes·ta·cy** (ˈtɛstəsɪ) *n.*

tes·ta·tor (tɛˈsteɪtə) *or* (*fem.*) **tes·ta·trix** (tɛˈsteɪtrɪks) *n.* a person who makes a will, esp. one who dies testate. [C15: from Anglo-French *testatour,* from Late Latin *testātor,* from Latin *testārī* to make a will; see TESTAMENT]

test ban *n.* an agreement among nations to forgo tests of some or all types of nuclear weapons.

test-bed *n. Engineering.* an area equipped with instruments, etc., used for testing machinery, engines, etc., under working conditions.

test case *n.* a legal action that serves as a precedent in deciding similar succeeding cases.

test·er[1] (ˈtɛstə) *n.* a person or thing that tests or is used for testing.

tes·ter[2] (ˈtɛstə) *n.* (in furniture) a canopy, esp. the canopy over a four-poster bed. [C14: from Medieval Latin *testerium,* from Late Latin *testa* a skull, from Latin: shell]

tes·ter[3] (ˈtɛstə) *n.* another name for **teston** (sense 2).

tes·tes (ˈtɛstiːz) *n.* the plural of **testis.**

tes·ti·cle (ˈtɛstɪkᵊl) *n.* either of the two male reproductive glands, in most mammals enclosed within the scrotum, that produce spermatozoa and the hormone testosterone. Also called: **testis.** [C15: from Latin *testiculus,* diminutive of *testis* testicle] —**tes·tic·u·lar** (tɛˈstɪkjʊlə) *adj.*

tes·tic·u·late (tɛˈstɪkjʊlɪt) *adj. Botany.* having an oval shape: *the testiculate tubers of certain orchids.* [C18: from Late Latin *testiculātus;* see TESTICLE]

tes·ti·fy (ˈtɛstɪˌfaɪ) *vb.* **·fies, ·fy·ing, ·fied. 1.** (when *tr., may take a clause as object*) to state (something) formally as a declaration of fact: *I testify that I know nothing about him.* **2.** *Law.* to declare or give (evidence) under oath, esp. in court. **3.** (when *intr.,* often foll. by *to*) to be evidence (of); serve as witness (to): *the money testified to his good faith.* **4.** (*tr.*) to declare or acknowledge openly. [C14: from Latin *testificārī,* from *testis* witness] —ˌ**tes·ti·fi·ˈca·tion** *n.* —**ˈtes·ti·ˌfi·er** *n.*

tes·ti·mo·ni·al (ˌtɛstɪˈməʊnɪəl) *n.* **1.** a recommendation of the character, ability, etc., of a person or of the quality of a consumer product or service, esp. by a person whose opinion is valued. **2.** a formal statement of truth or fact. **3.** a tribute given for services or achievements. ~*adj.* **4.** of or relating to a testimony or testimonial.

tes·ti·mo·ny (ˈtɛstɪmənɪ) *n., pl.* **·nies. 1.** a declaration of truth or fact. **2.** *Law.* evidence given by a witness, esp. orally in court under oath or affirmation. **3.** evidence testifying to something: *her success was a testimony to her good luck.* **4.** *Old Testament.* **a.** the Ten Commandments, as inscribed on the two stone tables. **b.** the Ark of the Covenant as the receptacle of these (Exodus 25:16; 16:34). [C15: from Latin *testimōnium,* from *testis* witness]

tes·tis (ˈtɛstɪs) *n., pl.* **·tes** (-tiːz). another word for **testicle.** [C17: from Latin, literally: witness (to masculinity)]

test match *n.* (in various sports, esp. cricket) any of a series of international matches.

tes·ton (ˈtɛstən) *or* **tes·toon** (tɛˈstuːn) *n.* **1.** a French silver coin of the 16th century. **2.** Also called: **tester.** an English silver coin of the 16th century, originally worth one shilling, bearing the head of Henry VIII. [C16: from Italian *testone,* from *testa* head, from Late Latin: skull, from Latin: shell]

tes·tos·ter·one (tɛˈstɒstəˌrəʊn) *n.* a potent steroid hormone secreted mainly by the testes. It can be extracted from the testes of animals or synthesized and used to treat androgen deficiency or promote anabolis. Formula: $C_{19}H_{28}O_2$. [C20: from TESTIS + STEROL + -ONE]

test pa·per *n.* **1.** *Chem.* paper impregnated with an indicator for use in chemical tests. See also **litmus. 2.** *Brit. education.* **a.** the question sheet of a test. **b.** the paper completed by a test candidate.

test pi·lot *n.* a pilot who flies aircraft of new design to test their performance in the air.

test tube *n.* **1.** a cylindrical round-bottomed glass tube open at one end: used in scientific experiments. **2.** (*modifier*) made synthetically in, or as if in, a test tube: *a test-tube product.*

test-tube ba·by *n.* **1.** a fetus that has developed from an ovum fertilized in an artificial womb. **2.** a baby conceived by artificial insemination.

tes·tu·di·nal (tɛˈstjuːdɪnᵊl) *or* **tes·tu·di·nar·y** *adj.* of, relating to, or resembling a tortoise or turtle or the shell of either of these animals. [C19: from Latin TESTUDO]

tes·tu·do (tɛˈstjuːdəʊ) *n., pl.* **·di·nes** (-dɪˌniːz). a form of shelter used by the ancient Roman Army for protection against attack from above, consisting either of a mobile arched structure or of overlapping shields held by the soldiers over their heads. [C17: from Latin: a tortoise, from *testa* a shell]

tes·ty (ˈtɛstɪ) *adj.* **·ti·er, ·ti·est.** irritable or touchy. [C14: from Anglo-Norman *testif* headstrong, from Old French *teste* head, from Late Latin *testa* skull, from Latin: shell] —**ˈtest·i·ly** *adv.* —**ˈtest·i·ness** *n.*

te·tan·ic (təˈtænɪk) *adj.* **1.** of, relating to, or producing tetanus or the spasms of tetanus. ~*n.* **2.** a tetanic drug or agent. —**te·ˈtan·i·cal·ly** *adv.*

tet·a·nize *or* **tet·a·nise** (ˈtɛtəˌnaɪz) *vb.* (*tr.*) to induce tetanus in (a muscle); affect (a muscle) with tetanic spasms. —ˌ**tet·a·ni·ˈza·tion** *or* ˌ**tet·a·ni·ˈsa·tion** *n.*

tet·a·nus (ˈtɛtənəs) *n.* **1.** Also called: **lockjaw.** an acute infectious disease in which sustained muscular spasm, contraction, and convulsion are caused by the release of exotoxins from the bacterium, *Clostridium tetani:* infection usually occurs through a contaminated wound. **2.** *Physiol.* any tense contraction of a muscle, esp. when produced by electric shocks. [C16: via Latin from Greek *tetanos,* from *tetanos* taut, from *teinein* to stretch] —**ˈtet·a·nal** *adj.* —**ˈtet·a·ˌnoid** *adj.*

tet·a·ny (ˈtɛtənɪ) *n. Pathol.* an abnormal increase in the excitability of nerves and muscles resulting in spasms of the arms and legs, caused by a deficiency of parathyroid secretion.

te·tar·to·he·dral (tɪˌtɑːtəʊˈhiːdrəl) *adj.* (of a crystal) having one quarter of the number of faces necessary for the full symmetry of its crystal system. [C19: from Greek *tetartos* one fourth + -HEDRAL] —**te·ˌtar·to·ˈhe·dral·ly** *adv.* —**te·ˌtar·to·ˈhe·dral·ism** *or* **te·ˌtar·to·ˈhe·drism** *n.*

tetch·y (ˈtɛtʃɪ) *adj.* **tetch·i·er, tetch·i·est.** being or inclined to be cross, irritable, or touchy. [C16: probably from obsolete *tetch* defect, from Old French *tache* spot, of Germanic origin] —**ˈtetch·i·ly** *adv.* —**ˈtetch·i·ness** *n.*

tête-à-tête (ˌteɪtəˈteɪt) *n., pl.* **-têtes** *or* **-tête. 1. a.** a private conversation between two people. **b.** (*as modifier*)*: a tête-à-tête conversation.* **2.** a small sofa for two people, esp. one that is S-shaped in plan so that the sitters are almost face to face. ~*adv.* **3.** intimately; in private. [C17: from French, literally: head to head]

tête-bêche (tɛtˈbɛʃ) *adj. Philately.* (of an unseparated pair of stamps) printed so that one is reversed in relation to the other. [C19: from French, from *tête* head + *bêche,* from obsolete *béchevet* double-headed (originally of a bed)]

teth (tɛs; *Hebrew* tɛt) *n.* the ninth letter of the Hebrew alphabet (ט) transliterated as *t* and pronounced more or less like English *t* with pharyngeal articulation.

teth·er (ˈtɛðə) *n.* **1.** a restricting rope, chain, etc., by which an animal is tied to a particular spot. **2.** the range of one's endurance, etc. **3. at the end of one's tether.** distressed or exasperated to the limit of one's endurance. ~*vb.* **4.** (*tr.*) to tie or limit with or as if with a tether. [C14: from Old Norse *tjothr;* related to Middle Dutch *tūder* tether, Old High German *zeotar* pole of a wagon]

Te·thys[1] (ˈtiːθɪs, ˈtɛθ-) *n. Greek myth.* a Titaness and sea goddess, wife of Oceanus.

Te·thys[2] (ˈtiːθɪs, ˈtɛθ-) *n.* one of the ten satellites of the planet Saturn.

Te·ton Range (ˈtiːtᵊn) *pl. n.* a mountain range in the N central U.S., mainly in NW Wyoming. Highest peak: Grand Teton, 4196 m (13 766 ft.).

tet·ra ('tɛtrə) *n., pl.* ·**ra** *or* ·**ras.** any of various brightly coloured tropical freshwater fishes of the genus *Hemigrammus* and related genera: family *Characidae* (characins). [C20: short for New Latin *tetragonopterus* (former genus name), from TETRAGON + -O- + *-pterous*, from Greek *pteron* wing]

tetra- *or before a vowel* **tetr-** *combining form.* four: *tetrameter.* [from Greek]

tet·ra·ba·sic (ˌtɛtrə'beɪsɪk) *adj.* (of an acid) containing four replaceable hydrogen atoms. —**tet·ra·ba·sic·i·ty** (ˌtɛtrəbeɪ'sɪsɪtɪ) *n.*

tet·ra·brach ('tɛtrəˌbræk) *n.* (in classical prosody) a word or metrical foot composed of four short syllables (˘˘˘˘). [C19: from Greek *tetrabrakhus*, from TETRA- + *brakhus* short]

tet·ra·bran·chi·ate *adj.* (ˌtɛtrə'bræŋkɪɪt, -ˌeɪt). **1.** of, relating to, or belonging to the *Tetrabranchiata*, a former order of cephalopod molluscs having four gills and including the pearly nautilus. ~*n.* (ˌtɛtrə'bræŋkɪˌeɪt). **2.** any mollusc belonging to the *Tetrabranchiata*.

tet·ra·chlo·ride (ˌtɛtrə'klɔːraɪd) *n.* any compound that contains four chlorine atoms per molecule: *carbon tetrachloride*, CCl_4.

tet·ra·chord ('tɛtrəˌkɔːd) *n.* (in musical theory, esp. of classical Greece) any of several groups of four notes in descending order, in which the first and last notes form a perfect fourth. [C17: from Greek *tetrakhordos* four-stringed, from TETRA- + *khordē* a string] —ˌ**tet·ra**'**chor·dal** *adj.*

te·trac·id (tɛ'træsɪd) *adj.* (of a base) capable of reacting with four molecules of a monobasic acid.

tet·ra·cy·clic (ˌtɛtrə'saɪklɪk) *adj. Chem.* (of a compound) containing four rings in its molecular structure.

tet·ra·cy·cline (ˌtɛtrə'saɪklaɪn, -klɪn) *n.* an antibiotic synthesized from chlortetracycline or derived from the bacterium *Streptomyces viridifaciens:* used in treating rickettsial infections and various bacterial and viral infections. Formula: $C_{22}H_{24}N_2O_8$. [C20: from TETRA- + CYCL(IC) + -INE[2]]

tet·rad ('tɛtræd) *n.* **1.** a group or series of four. **2.** the number four. **3.** *Botany.* a group of four cells formed by meiosis from one diploid cell. **4.** *Genetics.* a four-stranded structure, formed during the pachytene stage of meiosis, consisting of paired homologous chromosomes that have each divided into two chromatids. **5.** *Chem.* an element, atom, group, or ion with a valency of four. [C17: from Greek *tetras*, from *tettares* four]

te·trad·y·mite (tɛ'trædɪˌmaɪt) *n.* a grey metallic mineral consisting of a telluride and sulphide of bismuth. Formula: Bi_2Te_2S. [C19: from Late Greek *tetradumos* fourfold, from Greek TETRA- + *didumos* double]

te·tra·dy·na·mous (ˌtɛtrə'daɪnəməs, -'dɪn-) *adj.* (of plants) having six stamens, two of which are shorter than the others. [C19: from TETRA- + Greek *dunamis* power]

tet·ra·e·thyl lead (ˌtɛtrə'iːθaɪl lɛd) *n.* a colourless oily insoluble liquid used in petrol to prevent knocking. Formula: $Pb(C_2H_5)_4$. Also called: **lead tetraethyl.**

tet·ra·gon ('tɛtrəˌgɒn) *n.* a less common name for **quadrilateral** (sense 2). [C17: from Greek *tetragōnon;* see TETRA-, -GON]

te·trag·o·nal (tɛ'trægənᵊl) *adj.* **1.** Also: **dimetric.** *Crystallog.* relating or belonging to the crystal system characterized by three mutually perpendicular axes of which only two are equal. **2.** of, relating to, or shaped like a quadrilateral. —**te**'**trag·o·nal·ly** *adv.* —**te**'**trag·o·nal·ness** *n.*

tet·ra·gram ('tɛtrəˌgræm) *n.* any word of four letters.

Tet·ra·gram·ma·ton (ˌtɛtrə'græmətᵊn) *n. Bible.* the Hebrew name for God consisting of the four consonants Y H V H (or Y H W H) and regarded by Jews as too sacred to be pronounced. It is usually transliterated as *Jehovah* or *Yahweh.* Sometimes shortened to **Tetragram.** [C14: from Greek, from *tetragrammatos* having four letters, from TETRA- + *gramma* letter]

tet·ra·he·drite (ˌtɛtrə'hiːdraɪt) *n.* a grey metallic mineral consisting of a sulphide of copper, iron, and antimony, often in the form of tetrahedral crystals: it is a source of copper. Formula: $(Cu,Fe)_{12}Sb_4S_{13}$.

tet·ra·he·dron (ˌtɛtrə'hiːdrən) *n., pl.* ·**drons** *or* ·**dra** (-drə). **1.** a solid figure having four plane faces. A **regular tetrahedron** has faces that are equilateral triangles. See also **polyhedron. 2.** any object shaped like a tetrahedron. [C16: from New Latin, from Late Greek *tetraedron;* see TETRA-, -HEDRON] —ˌ**tet·ra**'**he·dral** *adj.* —ˌ**tet·ra**'**he·dral·ly** *adv.*

te·tral·o·gy (tɛ'trælədʒɪ) *n., pl.* ·**gies. 1.** a series of four related works, as in drama or opera. **2.** (in ancient Greece) a group of four dramas, the first three tragic and the last satiric. [C17: from Greek *tetralogia;* see TETRA-, -LOGY]

te·tram·er·ous (tɛ'træmərəs) *adj.* **1.** (esp. of animals or plants) having or consisting of four parts. **2.** (of certain flowers) having parts arranged in whorls of four members. [C19: from New Latin *tetramerus*, from Greek *tetramerēs*] —**te**'**tram·er·ism** *n.*

te·tram·e·ter (tɛ'træmɪtə) *n. Prosody.* **1.** a line of verse consisting of four metrical feet. **2.** a verse composed of such lines. **3.** (in classical prosody) a line of verse composed of four dipodies.

tet·ra·me·thyl·di·ar·sine (ˌtɛtrəˌmiːθaɪldaɪ'ɑːsiːn) *n.* an oily slightly water-soluble poisonous liquid with garlic-like odour. Its derivatives are used as accelerators for rubber. Also called (not in technical usage): **cacodyl, dicacodyl.**

tet·ra·ple·gi·a (ˌtɛtrə'pliːdʒɪə) *n.* another name for **quadriplegia.**

tet·ra·ploid ('tɛtrəˌplɔɪd) *Genetics.* ~*adj.* **1.** having four times the haploid number of chromosomes in the nucleus. ~*n.* **2.** a tetraploid organism, nucleus, or cell.

tet·ra·pod ('tɛtrəˌpɒd) *n.* **1.** any vertebrate that has four limbs. **2.** Also called: **caltrop.** a device consisting of four arms radiating from a central point, each at 120° to the others, so that regardless of its position on a surface, three arms form a supporting tripod and the fourth is vertical.

te·trap·o·dy (tɛ'træpədɪ) *n., pl.* ·**dies.** *Prosody.* a metrical unit consisting of four feet. —**tet·ra·pod·ic** (ˌtɛtrə'pɒdɪk) *adj.*

te·trap·ter·ous (tɛ'træptərəs) *adj.* **1.** (of certain insects) having four wings. **2.** *Biology.* having four winglike extensions or parts. [C19: from New Latin *tetrapterus*, from *tetrapteros* from TETRA- + *pteron* wing]

te·trarch ('tɛtrɑːk) *n.* **1.** the ruler of one fourth of a country. **2.** a subordinate ruler, esp. of Syria under the Roman Empire. **3.** the commander of one of the smaller subdivisions of a Macedonian phalanx. **4.** any of four joint rulers. [C14: from Greek *tetrarkhēs;* see TETRA-, -ARCH] —**te·trarch·ate** (tɛ'trɑːˌkeɪt, -kɪt) *n.* —**te**'**trar·chic** *or* **te**'**trar·chi·cal** *adj.* —'**te·trar·chy** *n.*

tet·ra·spore ('tɛtrəˌspɔː) *n.* any of the asexual spores that are produced in groups of four in the sporangium (**tetrasporangium**) of any of the red algae. —**tet·ra·spor·ic** (ˌtɛtrə'spɒrɪk) *or* **tet·ra·spor·ous** (ˌtɛtrə'spɔːrəs, tɪ'træspərəs) *adj.*

tet·ra·stich ('tɛtrəˌstɪk) *n.* a poem, stanza, or strophe that consists of four lines. [C16: via Latin from Greek *tetrastikhon*, from TETRA- + *stikhos* row] —**tet·ra·stich·ic** (ˌtɛtrə'stɪkɪk) *or* **te·tras·ti·chal** (tɛ'træstɪkᵊl) *adj.*

te·tras·ti·chous (tɛ'træstɪkəs) *adj.* (of flowers or leaves on a stalk) arranged in four vertical rows.

tet·ra·syl·la·ble (ˌtɛtrə'sɪləbᵊl) *n.* a word of four syllables. —**tet·ra·syl·lab·ic** (ˌtɛtrəsɪ'læbɪk) *or* ˌ**tet·ra·syl**'**lab·i·cal** *adj.*

tet·ra·tom·ic (ˌtɛtrə'tɒmɪk) *adj.* composed of four atoms or having four atoms per molecule: *phosgene has tetratomic molecules.*

tet·ra·va·lent (ˌtɛtrə'veɪlənt) *adj. Chem.* **1.** having a valency of four. **2.** Also: **quadrivalent.** having four valencies. —ˌ**tet·ra**'**va·len·cy** *n.*

Te·traz·zi·ni (*Italian* ˌtetrat'tsiːni) *n.* **Lu·i·sa** (lu'iːza). 1871–1940, Italian coloratura soprano.

tet·rode ('tɛtrəʊd) *n.* **1.** an electronic valve having four electrodes, namely a cathode, control grid, screen grid, and anode. **2.** (*modifier*) (of a transistor) having two terminals on the base or gate to improve the performance at high frequencies.

te·trox·ide (tɛ'trɒksaɪd) *or* **te·trox·id** (tɛ'trɒksɪd) *n.* any oxide that contains four oxygen atoms per molecule: *osmium tetroxide*, OsO_4.

tet·ryl ('tɛtrɪl) *n.* a yellow crystalline explosive solid used in detonators; trinitrophenylmethylnitramine. Formula: $(NO_2)_3C_6H_2N(NO_2)CH_3$. Also called: **nitramine.**

tet·ter ('tɛtə) *n.* **1.** a blister or pimple. **2.** *Informal.* any of various skin eruptions, such as eczema. [Old English *teter;* related to Old High German *zitaroh*, Sanskrit *dadru*, Late Latin *derbita*]

Te·tuán (tɛ'twɑːn) *n.* a city in N Morocco: capital of Spanish Morocco (1912–56). Pop.: 139 105 (1971).

Tet·zel *or* **Te·zel** ('tɛtsᵊl) *n.* **Jo·hann** ('joːhan). ?1465–1519, German Dominican monk. His preaching on papal indulgences provoked Luther's 95 theses at Wittenberg (1517).

Teu·cer ('tjuːsə) *n. Greek myth.* **1.** a Cretan leader, who founded Troy. **2.** a son of Telemon and Hesione, who distinguished himself by his archery on the side of the Greeks in the Trojan War.

Teu·cri·an ('tjuːkrɪən) *n., adj.* another word for **Trojan.**

Teut. *abbrev. for* Teuton(ic).

Teu·to·bur·ger Wald (*German* 'tɔɪtoˌbʊrgər 'valt) *n.* a low wooded mountain range in N West Germany: possible site of the annihilation of three Roman legions by Germans under Arminius in 9 A.D.

Teu·ton ('tjuːtən) *n.* **1.** a member of an ancient Germanic people from Jutland who migrated to S Gaul in the 2nd century B.C.: annihilated by a Roman army in 102 B.C. **2.** a member of any people speaking a Germanic language, esp. a German. ~*adj.* **3.** Teutonic. [C18: from Latin *Teutonī* the Teutons, of Germanic origin]

Teu·ton·ic (tjuː'tɒnɪk) *adj.* **1.** characteristic of or relating to the German people: *Teutonic thoroughness.* **2.** of or relating to the ancient Teutons. **3.** (not used in linguistics) of or relating to the Germanic languages. ~*n.* **4.** an obsolete name for **Germanic.** —**Teu**'**ton·i·cal·ly** *adv.*

Teu·ton·ic or·der *n.* a military and religious order of German knights, priests, and serving brothers founded about 1190 during the Third Crusade, later conquering large parts of the Baltic provinces and Russia. Also called: **Teutonic Knights.**

Teu·ton·ism ('tjuːtəˌnɪzəm) *n.* **1.** a German idiom, custom, or characteristic. **2.** German society or civilization.

Teu·ton·ize *or* **Teu·ton·ise** ('tjuːtəˌnaɪz) *vb.* to make or become German or Germanic; Germanize. —ˌ**Teu·ton·i**'**za·tion** *or* ˌ**Teu·ton·i**'**sa·tion** *n.*

Te·ve·re ('teːvere) *n.* the Italian name of the **Tiber.**

Te·vet ('teɪvəs; *Hebrew* te'vet) *n.* a variant spelling of **Tebet.** [from Hebrew *tēbhēth*]

Tewkes·bur·y ('tjuːksbərɪ, -brɪ) *n.* a town in W England, in N Gloucestershire at the confluence of the Rivers Severn and Avon: scene of a decisive battle (1471) of the Wars of the Roses in which the Yorkists defeated the Lancastrians; 12th-century abbey. Pop.: 8742 (1971).

Tex. *abbrev. for:* **1.** Texan. **2.** Texas.

Tex·as ('tɛksəs) *n.* a state of the southwestern U.S., on the Gulf of Mexico: the second largest state; part of Mexico from 1821 to 1836, when it was declared an independent republic; joined the U.S. in 1845; consists chiefly of a plain, with a wide flat coastal belt rising up to the semiarid Sacramento and Davis

Mountains of the southwest; a major producer of cotton, rice, and livestock; the chief U.S. producer of oil and gas; a leading world supplier of sulphur. Capital: Austin. Pop.: 11 196 730 (1970). Area: 678 927 sq. km (262 134 sq. miles). Abbrevs.: **Tex.** or (with zip code) **TX** —'**Tex+an** *n., adj.*

Tex+as fe+ver *n.* an infectious disease of cattle caused by the protozoan *Babesia bigemina* and transmitted by the bite of a tick.

Tex+as Rang+ers *pl. n.* the state police of Texas, originally formed in the 19th century to defend outlying regions against Indians and Mexicans and to fight lawlessness.

text (tɛkst) *n.* **1.** the main body of a printed or written work as distinct from commentary, notes, illustrations, etc. **2.** the words of something printed or written. **3.** the original exact wording of a work, esp. the Bible, as distinct from a revision or translation. **4.** a short passage of the Bible used as a starting point for a sermon or adduced as proof of a doctrine. **5.** the topic or subject of a discussion or work. **6.** *Printing.* any one of several styles of letters or types. **7.** short for **textbook.** [C14: from Medieval Latin *textus* version, from Latin *textus* texture, from *texere* to compose] —'**text+less** *adj.*

text+book ('tɛkstˌbʊk) *n.* **a.** a book used as a standard source of information on a particular subject. **b.** (*as modifier*): *a textbook example.* —'**text+ˌbook+ish** *adj.*

tex+tile ('tɛkstaɪl) *n.* **1.** any fabric or cloth, esp. woven. **2.** raw material suitable to be made into cloth; fibre or yarn. ~*adj.* **3.** of or relating to fabrics or the making of fabrics. [C17: from Latin *textilis* woven, from *texere* to weave]

tex+tu+al ('tɛkstjʊəl) *adj.* **1.** of or relating to a text or texts. **2.** based on or conforming to a text. —'**tex+tu+al+ly** *adv.*

tex+tu+al crit·i+cism *n.* **1.** the scholarly study of manuscripts, esp. of the Bible, in an effort to establish the original text. **2.** literary criticism emphasizing a close analysis of the text. —**tex+tu+al crit+ic** *n.*

tex+tu+al+ism ('tɛkstjʊəˌlɪzəm) *n.* **1.** doctrinaire adherence to a text, esp. of the Bible. **2.** textual criticism, esp. of the Bible. —'**tex+tu+al+ist** *n., adj.*

tex+tu+ar·y ('tɛkstjʊərɪ) *adj.* **1.** of, relating to, or contained in a text. ~*n., pl.* **+ar·ies. 2.** a textual critic.

tex+ture ('tɛkstʃə) *n.* **1.** the surface of a material, esp. as perceived by the sense of touch: *a wall with a rough texture.* **2.** the structure, appearance, and feel of a woven fabric. **3.** the general structure and disposition of the constituent parts of something: *the texture of a cake.* **4.** the distinctive character or quality of something: *the texture of life in America.* **5.** the nature of a surface other than smooth: *woollen cloth has plenty of texture.* **6.** *Art.* the representation of the nature of a surface: *the painter caught the grainy texture of the sand.* **7. a.** music considered as the interrelationship between the horizontally presented aspects of melody and rhythm and the vertically represented aspect of harmony: *a contrapuntal texture.* **b.** the nature and quality of the instrumentation of a passage, piece, etc. ~*vb.* **8.** (*tr.*) to give a distinctive usually rough or grainy texture to. [C15: from Latin *textūra* web, from *texere* to weave] —'**tex+tur+al** *adj.* —'**tex+tur+al+ly** *adv.* —'**tex+ture+less** *adj.*

Tey+de (*Spanish* 'teɪðe) *n.* a variant spelling of **Teide.**

Te·zel ('tɛtsᵊl) *n.* a variant spelling of (Johann) **Tetzel.**

TG 1. *abbrev. for* transformational grammar. **2.** *international car registration for* Togo.

t.g. *Biology. abbrev. for* type genus.

T-group *n. Psychol.* a group that meets for educational or therapeutic purposes to study its own communication.

T.G.W.U. (in Britain) *abbrev. for* Transport and General Workers' Union.

Th *the chemical symbol for* thorium.

Th. *abbrev. for* Thursday.

-th[1] *suffix forming nouns.* **1.** (*from verbs*) indicating an action or its consequence: *growth.* **2.** (*from adjectives*) indicating a quality: *width.* [from Old English *-thu, -tho*]

-th[2] *or* **-eth** *suffix.* forming ordinal numbers: *fourth; thousandth.* [from Old English *-(o)tha, -(o)the*]

Tha·ba·na-Ntlen·ya+na (tɑː'bɑːnə ᵊn'tleɪnjənə) *n.* a mountain in Lesotho: the highest peak of the Drakensberg Mountains. Height: 3482 m (11 425 ft.). Also called: **Thadentsonyane, Thabantshonyana.**

Thack·er·ay ('θækərɪ) *n.* **Wil·liam Make·peace.** 1811–63, English novelist, born in India. His novels, originally serialized, include *Vanity Fair* (1848), *Pendennis* (1850), *Henry Esmond* (1852), and *The Newcomes* (1855).

Thad·de·us *or* **Thad·e·us** ('θædɪəs) *n. New Testament.* one of the 12 apostles (Matthew 10:3; Mark 3:18), traditionally identified with Jude.

Tha+den+tso+nya+ne (ˌtɑːdən'tsɒnjənə) *n.* another name for **Thabana-Ntlenyana.**

Thai (taɪ) *adj.* **1.** of, relating to, or characteristic of Thailand, its people, or their language. ~*n.* **2.** (*pl.* **Thais** *or* **Thai**) a native or inhabitant of Thailand. **3.** the language of Thailand, sometimes classified as belonging to the Sino-Tibetan family. ~Also called: **Siamese.**

Thai+land ('taɪˌlænd) *n.* a kingdom in SE Asia, on the Andaman Sea and the Gulf of Siam: united as a kingdom in 1350 and became a major SE Asian power; consists chiefly of a central plain around the Chao Phraya river system, mountains rising over 2400 m (8000 ft.) in the northwest, and rainforest the length of the S peninsula. Official language: Thai. Religion: mostly Hinayana Buddhist. Currency: baht. Capital: Bangkok. Pop.: 44 035 129 (1977 est.). Area: 513 998 sq. km (198 455 sq. miles). Former name (until 1939 and 1945–49): **Siam.**

Tha·ïs ('θeɪɪs) *n.* 4th century B.C., Athenian courtesan; mistress of Alexander the Great.

thal·a+men+ceph·a+lon (ˌθæləmɛn'sɛfəˌlɒn) *n., pl.* **+lons** *or* **+la** (-lə). *Anatomy.* **1.** the part of the diencephalon of the brain that includes the thalamus, pineal gland, and adjacent structures. **2.** another name for **diencephalon.** —**thal·a+men+ce·phal+ic** (ˌθæləˌmɛnsə'fælɪk) *adj.*

thal·a+mus ('θæləməs) *n., pl.* **+mi** (-ˌmaɪ). **1.** either of the two contiguous egg-shaped masses of grey matter at the base of the brain. **2.** both of these masses considered as a functional unit. **3.** the receptacle or torus of a flower. [C18: from Latin, Greek *thalamos* inner room; probably related to Greek *tholos* vault] —**tha+lam+ic** (θə'læmɪk) *adj.* —**tha+'lam+i+cal+ly** *adv.*

tha+las+sic (θə'læsɪk) *adj.* **1.** of or relating to the sea; pelagic. **2.** inhabiting or growing in the sea; marine: *thalassic fauna.* [C19: from French *thalassique*, from Greek *thalassa* sea]

thal+as+soc+ra+cy (ˌθælə'sɒkrəsɪ) *or* **thal+at+toc+ra+cy** *n.* the government of a nation having dominion over large expanses of the seas. [C19: from Attic Greek *thalassocratia*, from *thalassa* sea + -CRACY]

tha+ler *or* **ta+ler** ('tɑːlə) *n., pl.* **+ler** *or* **+lers.** a former German, Austrian, or Swiss silver coin. [from Germany; see DOLLAR]

Tha·les ('θeɪliːz) *n.* ?624–?546 B.C., Greek philosopher, mathematician, and astronomer, born in Miletus. He held that water was the origin of all things and he predicted the solar eclipse of May 28, 585 B.C.

Tha·li·a (θə'laɪə) *n. Greek myth.* **1.** the Muse of comedy and pastoral poetry. **2.** one of the three Graces. [C17: via Latin from Greek, from *thaleia* blooming]

tha+lid·o+mide (θə'lɪdəˌmaɪd) *n.* **a.** a synthetic drug formerly used as a sedative and hypnotic but withdrawn from the market when found to cause abnormalities in developing fetuses. Formula: $C_{13}H_{10}N_2O_4$. **b.** (*as modifier*): *a thalidomide baby.* [C20: from THALLIC + IMIDO- + -IMIDE]

thal+lic ('θælɪk) *adj.* of or containing thallium, esp. in the trivalent state.

thal+li·um ('θælɪəm) *n.* a soft malleable highly toxic white metallic element used as a rodent and insect poison and in low-melting glass. Its compounds are used as infrared detectors and in photoelectric cells. Symbol: Tl; atomic no.: 81; atomic wt.: 204.37; valency: 1 or 3; relative density: 11.85; melting pt.: 303.5°C; boiling pt.: 1457°C. [C19: from New Latin, from Greek *thallos* a green shoot; referring to the green line in its spectrum]

thal+lo+phyte ('θæləˌfaɪt) *n.* any plant of the group (or former division) *Thallophyta*, lacking true stems, leaves, and roots: includes the algae, fungi, lichens, and bacteria, all now regarded as separate divisions. [C19: from New Latin *thallophyta*, from Greek *thallos* a young shoot + *phuton* a plant] —**thal+lo+phyt+ic** (ˌθælə'fɪtɪk) *adj.*

thal+lous ('θæləs) *adj.* of or containing thallium, esp. in the monovalent state.

thal+lus ('θæləs) *n., pl.* **thal+li** ('θælaɪ) *or* **thal+lus·es.** the undifferentiated plant body of algae, fungi, and lichens. [C19: from Latin, from Greek *thallos* green shoot, from *thallein* to bloom] —'**thal+loid** *adj.*

thal+weg *or* **tal+weg** ('tɑːlvɛg) *n. Geography, rare.* **1.** the longitudinal outline of a riverbed from source to mouth. **2.** the line of steepest descent from any point on the land surface.

Thames *n.* **1.** (tɛmz). a river in S England, rising in the Cotswold Hills in several headstreams and flowing generally east through London to the North Sea by a large estuary. Length: 338 km (210 miles). Ancient name: **Tamesis. 2.** (teɪmz, θeɪmz). a river in SE Canada, in Ontario, flowing south to London, then southwest to Lake St. Clair. Length: 217 km (135 miles).

Tham+muz ('tæmuːz, -ʊz) *n.* a variant spelling of **Tammuz.**

than (ðæn; *unstressed* ðən) *conj.* (*coordinating*), *prep.* **1.** used to introduce the second element of a comparison, the first element of which expresses difference: *shorter than you; couldn't do otherwise than love him; he swims faster than I run.* **2.** used after adverbs such as *rather* or *sooner* to introduce a rejected alternative in an expression of preference: *rather than be imprisoned, I shall die.* **3. other than.** besides; in addition to. [Old English *thanne;* related to Old Saxon, Old High German *thanna;* see THEN]

Usage. In sentences such as *he does it far better than I, than* is usually regarded in careful usage as a conjunction governing an unexpressed verb: *he does it far better than I (do it).* The case of any pronoun therefore depends on whether it is the subject or the object of that unexpressed verb: *she likes him more than I (like him); she likes him more than (she likes) me.* However, in informal usage *than* is often treated as a preposition and any pronoun is therefore used in its objective form, so that *she likes him more than me* is ambiguous.

than·a+top+sis (ˌθænə'tɒpsɪs) *n.* a meditation on death, as in a poem. [C19: from Greek *thanatos* death + *opsis* a view]

Than·a·tos ('θænəˌtɒs) *n.* the Greek personification of death: son of Nyx, goddess of night. Roman counterpart: **Mors.** Thanatos was the name chosen by Freud to represent a universal death instinct. Compare **Eros.** —**Than·a+tot+ic** (ˌθænə'tɒtɪk) *adj.*

thane *or* **thegn** (θeɪn) *n.* **1.** (in Anglo-Saxon England) a member of an aristocratic class, ranking below an ealdorman, whose status was hereditary and who held land from the king or from another nobleman in return for certain services. **2.** (in medieval Scotland) a person of rank, often the chief of a clan, holding land from the king. [Old English *thegn;* related to Old Saxon, Old High German *thegan* thane] —**than+age** ('θeɪnɪdʒ) *n.*

Than+et ('θænɪt) *n.* **Isle of.** an island in SE England, in NE Kent, separated from the mainland by two branches of the River Stour: scene of many Norse invasions. Area: 109 sq. km (42 sq. miles).

Than+ja+vur (ˌtʌndʒəˈvʊə) *n.* a city in SE India, in E Tamil Nadu: headquarters of the earliest Protestant missions in India. Pop.: 140 547 (1971). Former name: **Tanjore.**

thank (θæŋk) *vb.* (*tr.*) **1.** to convey feelings of gratitude to. **2.** to hold responsible; *he has his creditors to thank for his bankruptcy.* **3.** used in exclamations of relief: *thank goodness; thank God.* **4. I'll thank you to.** used ironically to intensify a command, request, etc.: *I'll thank you to mind your own business.* [Old English *thancian;* related to Old Frisian *thankia,* Old Norse *thakka,* Old Saxon, Old High German *thancōn*]

thank+ful ('θæŋkfʊl) *adj.* grateful and appreciative. —**'thank+ful+ly** *adv.* —**'thank+ful+ness** *n.*

thank+less ('θæŋklɪs) *adj.* **1.** receiving no thanks or appreciation: *a thankless job.* **2.** ungrateful: *a thankless pupil.* —**'thank+less+ly** *adv.* —**'thank+less+ness** *n.*

thanks (θæŋks) *pl. n.* **1.** an expression of appreciation or gratitude or an acknowledgment of services or favours given. **2. thanks to.** because of: *thanks to him we lost the match.* ~*interj.* **3.** *Informal.* an exclamation expressing acknowledgment, gratitude, or appreciation.

thanks+giv·ing ('θæŋksˌɡɪvɪŋ) *n.* **1.** the act of giving thanks. **2. a.** an expression of thanks to God. **b.** a public act of religious observance or a celebration in acknowledgment of divine favours.

Thanks+giv·ing Day *n.* an annual day of holiday celebrated in thanksgiving to God on the fourth Thursday of November in the United States, and on the second Monday of October in Canada. Often shortened to **Thanksgiving.**

thank you *interj., n.* a conventional expression of gratitude.

Thant (θænt) *n.* U (uː). 1909–74, Burmese diplomat; secretary-general of the United Nations (1962–71).

Thap+sus ('θæpsəs) *n.* an ancient town near Carthage in North Africa: site of Caesar's victory over Pompey in 46 B.C.

thar (tɑː) *n.* a variant spelling of **tahr.**

Thar Des+ert (tɑː) *n.* a desert in NW India, mainly in NW Rajasthan state and extending into Pakistan. Area: over 260 000 sq. km (100 000 sq. miles). Also called: **Indian Desert, Great Indian Desert.**

Thá+sos ('tæsɒs) *n.* a Greek island in the N Aegean: colonized by Greeks from Paros in the 7th century B.C. as a gold-mining centre; under Turkish rule (1455–1912). Pop.: 13 316 (1971). Area: 379 sq. km (146 sq. miles).

that (ðæt; *unstressed* ðət) *determiner.* (*used before a singular n.*) **1. a.** used preceding a noun that has been mentioned at some time or is understood: *that idea of yours.* **b.** (*as pronoun*): *don't eat that; that's what I mean.* **2. a.** used preceding a noun that denotes something more remote or removed: *that dress is cheaper than this one; that building over there is for sale.* **b.** (*as pronoun*): *that is John and this is his wife; give me that.* Compare **this. 3.** used to refer to something that is familiar: *that old chap from across the street.* **4. and (all) that.** *Informal.* everything connected with the subject mentioned: *he knows a lot about building and that.* **5. at that.** (*completive-intensive*) additionally, all things considered, or nevertheless: *he's a pleasant fellow at that; I might decide to go at that.* **6. like that. a.** with ease; effortlessly: *he gave me the answer just like that.* **b.** of such a nature, character, etc.: *he paid for all our tickets—he's like that.* **7. that is. a.** to be precise. **b.** in other words. **c.** for example. **8. that's more like it.** that is better, an improvement, etc. **9. that's that.** there is no more to be done, discussed, etc. **10. with** (*or* **at**) **that.** thereupon: *with that he left the room.* ~*conj.* (*subordinating*) **11.** used to introduce a noun clause: *I believe that you'll come.* **12.** Also: **so that, in order that.** used to introduce a clause of purpose: *they fought that others might have peace.* **13.** used to introduce a clause of result: *he laughed so hard that he cried.* **14.** used to introduce a clause after an understood sentence expressing desire, indignation, or amazement: *oh, that I had never lived!* ~*adv.* **15.** used with adjectives or adverbs to reinforce the specification of a precise degree already mentioned: *go just that fast and you should be safe.* **16.** Also: **all that.** (*usually used with a negative*) *Informal.* (intensifier): *he wasn't that upset at the news.* **17.** *Brit. dialect.* (intensifier): *the cat was that weak after the fight.* ~*pron.* **18.** used to introduce a restrictive relative clause: *the book that we want.* **19.** used to introduce a clause with the verb *to be* to emphasize the extent to which the preceding noun is applicable: *genius that she is, she outwitted the computer.* [Old English *thæt;* related to Old Frisian *thet,* Old Norse, Old Saxon *that,* Old High German *daz,* Greek *to,* Latin *istud,* Sanskrit *tad*]

Usage. Precise stylists maintain a distinction between *that* and *which: that* is used as a relative pronoun in restrictive clauses and *which* in nonrestrictive clauses. In *the book that is on the table is mine,* the clause *that is on the table* is used to distinguish one particular book (the one on the table) from another or others (which may be anywhere, but not on the table). In *the book, which is on the table, is mine,* the *which* clause is merely descriptive or incidental. The more formal the level of language, the more important it is to preserve the distinction between the two relative pronouns; but in informal or colloquial usage, the words are often used interchangeably.

thatch (θætʃ) *n.* **1. a.** Also called: **thatching.** a roofing material that consists of straw, reed, etc. **b.** a roof made of such a material. **2.** anything resembling this, such as the hair of the head. **3.** Also called: **thatch palm.** any of various palms with leaves suitable for thatching. ~*vb.* **4.** to cover (a roof) with thatch. [Old English *theccan* to cover; related to *thæc* roof, Old Saxon *thekkian* to thatch, Old High German *decchen,* Old Norse *thekja*] —**'thatch+er** *n.* —**'thatch+less** *adj.* —**'thatch·y** *adj.*

That·cher ('θætʃə) *n.* **Marg·a·ret (Hilda)** (née *Roberts*). born 1925, English politician; leader of the Conservative Party since 1975; prime minister since 1979.

thau+ma+tol+o·gy (ˌθɔːməˈtɒlədʒɪ) *n.* the study of or a treatise on miracles.

thau+ma+trope ('θɔːməˌtrəʊp) *n.* a toy in which partial pictures on the two sides of a card appear to merge when the card is twirled rapidly. [C19: from THAUMATO- + -TROPE] —**thau+ma+trop·i+cal** (ˌθɔːməˈtrɒpɪkᵊl) *adj.*

thau+ma+turge ('θɔːməˌtɜːdʒ) *n. Rare.* a performer of miracles; magician. [C18: from Medieval Latin *thaumaturgus,* from Greek *thaumatourgos* miracle-working, from THAUMATO- + *-ourgos* working, from *ergon* work] —**'thau+ma+ˌtur+gy** *n.* —**ˌthau+ma+'tur+gic** *adj.*

thaw (θɔː) *vb.* **1.** to melt or cause to melt from a solid frozen state: *the snow thawed.* **2.** to become or cause to become unfrozen; defrost. **3.** to be the case that the ice or snow is melting: *it's thawing fast.* **4.** (*intr.*) to become more sociable, relaxed, or friendly. ~*n.* **5.** the act or process of thawing. **6.** a spell of relatively warm weather, causing snow or ice to melt. **7.** an increase in relaxation or friendliness. [Old English *thawian;* related to Old High German *douwen* to thaw, Old Norse *theyja* to thaw, Latin *tabēre* to waste away] —**'thaw+er** *n.* —**'thaw+less** *adj.*

Th.B. *abbrev. for* Bachelor of Theology.

Th.D. *abbrev. for* Doctor of Theology.

the[1] (*stressed or emphatic* ðiː; *unstressed before a consonant* ðə; *unstressed before a vowel* ðɪ) *determiner.* (*article*) **1.** used preceding a noun that has been previously specified: *the pain should disappear soon; the man then opened the door.* Compare: **a**[1]. **2.** used with a qualifying word or phrase to indicate a particular person, object, etc., as distinct from others: *ask the man standing outside; give me the blue one.* Compare **a**[1]. **3.** used preceding certain nouns associated with one's culture, society, or community: *to go to the doctor; listen to the news; watch the television.* **4.** used preceding present participles and adjectives when they function as nouns: *the singing is awful; the dead salute you.* **5.** used preceding titles and certain uniquely specific or proper nouns, such as place names: *the United States; the Honourable Edward Brown; the Chairman; the moon.* **6.** used preceding a qualifying adjective or noun in certain names or titles: *William the Conqueror; Edward the First.* **7.** used preceding a noun to make it refer to its class generically: *the white seal is hunted for its fur; this is good for the throat; to play the piano.* **8.** used instead of *my, your, her,* etc., with parts of the body: *take me by the hand.* **9.** (usually stressed) the best, only, or most remarkable: *Harry's is the club in this town.* **10.** used with proper nouns when qualified: *written by the young Hardy.* **11.** another word for **per,** esp. with nouns or noun phrases of cost: *fifty pence the pound.* **12.** *Often facetious or derogatory.* my; our: *the wife goes out on Thursdays.* **13.** used preceding a unit of time in phrases or titles indicating an outstanding person, event, etc.: *match of the day; housewife of the year.* [Middle English, from Old English *thē,* a demonstrative adjective that later superseded *sē* (masculine singular) and *sēo, sio* (feminine singular); related to Old Frisian *thi,* thin, Old High German *der, diu*]

the[2] (ðə, ðɪ) *adv.* **1.** (often foll. by *for*) used before comparative adjectives or adverbs for emphasis: *she looks the happier for her trip.* **2.** used correlatively before each of two comparative adjectives or adverbs to indicate equality: *the sooner you come, the better; the more I see you, the more I love you.* [Old English *thī, thȳ,* instrumental case of THE[1] and THAT; related to Old Norse *thī,* Gothic *thei*]

the- *combining form.* variant of **theo-** before a vowel.

the+a+ceous (θiːˈeɪʃəs) *adj.* of, relating to, or belonging to the *Theaceae,* a family of evergreen trees and shrubs of tropical and warm regions: includes the tea plant.

the+an+thro+pism (θiːˈænθrəˌpɪzəm) *n.* **1.** the ascription of human traits or characteristics to a god or gods. **2.** *Theol.* the doctrine of the hypostatic union of the divine and human natures in the single person of Christ. —**ˌthe+an+'throp+ic** *adj.* —**the+'an+thro+pist** *n.*

the+ar+chy ('θiːɑːkɪ) *n., pl.* **+chies.** rule or government by God or gods; theocracy. [C17: from Church Greek *thearkhia;* see THEO-, -ARCHY] —**the+'ar+chic** *adj.*

the·a+tre *or U.S.* **the·a+ter** ('θɪətə) *n.* **1. a.** a building designed for the performance of plays, operas, etc. **b.** (*as modifier*): *a theatre ticket.* **c.** (*in combination*): *a theatre-goer.* **2.** a large room or hall, usually with a raised platform and tiered seats for an audience, used for lectures, film shows, etc. **3.** Also called: **operating theatre.** a room in a hospital or other medical centre equipped for surgical operations. **4.** plays regarded collectively as a form of art. **5. the theatre.** the world of actors, theatrical companies, etc.: *the glamour of the theatre.* **6.** a setting for dramatic or important events. **7.** writing that is suitable for dramatic presentation: *a good piece of theatre.* **8.** *Austral.* the usual word for **cinema. 9.** a major area of military activity: *the theatre of operations.* **10.** a circular or semicircular open-air building with tiers of seats. [C14: from Latin *theātrum,* from Greek *theatron* place for viewing, from *theasthai* to look at; related to Greek *thauma* miracle]

the·a·tre-in-the-round *n., pl.* **the·a·tres-in-the-round. 1.** a theatre with seats arranged around a central acting area. **2.**

drama written or designed for performance in such a theatre. ~Also called: **arena theatre.**

the·a·tre of cru·el·ty *n.* a type of theatre advocated by Antonin Artaud in *Le Théâtre et son double* in which gesture, movement, sound, and symbolism are emphasized rather than language.

the·a·tre of the ab·surd *n.* drama in which normal conventions and dramatic structure are ignored or modified in order to present life as irrational or meaningless.

the·at·ri·cal (θɪˈætrɪkəl) *adj.* **1.** of or relating to the theatre or dramatic performances. **2.** exaggerated and affected in manner or behaviour; histrionic. **—the·ˌat·ri·ˈcal·i·ty** *or* **the·ˈat·ri·cal·ness** *n.* **—the·ˈat·ri·cal·ly** *adv.*

the·at·ri·cals (θɪˈætrɪkəlz) *pl. n.* dramatic performances and entertainments, esp. as given by amateurs.

the·at·rics (θɪˈætrɪks) *n.* **1.** the art of staging plays. **2.** exaggerated mannerisms or displays of emotions.

The·ba·id (ˈθiːbeɪɪd, -bɪ-) *n.* the territory around ancient Thebes in Egypt, or sometimes around Thebes in Greece.

the·ba·ine (ˈθiːbəˌiːn, θɪˈbeɪiːn, -aɪn) *n.* a poisonous white crystalline alkaloid, extracted from opium and used in medicine. Formula: $C_{19}H_{21}NO_3$. Also called: **paramorphine.** [C19: from New Latin *thebaia* opium of Thebes, (with reference to Egypt as a chief source of opium) + -INE[2]]

Thebes (θiːbz) *n.* **1.** (in ancient Greece) the chief city of Boeotia, destroyed by Alexander the Great (336 B.C.). **2.** (in ancient Egypt) a city on the Nile: at various times capital of Upper Egypt or of the entire country. **—The·ba·ic** (θɪˈbeɪɪk) *adj.* **—ˈThe·ban** *adj., n.*

the·ca (ˈθiːkə) *n., pl.* **·cae** (-siː). **1.** *Botany.* an enclosing organ, cell, or spore case, esp. the capsule of a moss. **2.** *Zoology.* a hard outer covering, such as the cup-shaped container of a coral polyp. [C17: from Latin *thēca,* from Greek *thēkē* case; related to Greek *tithenai* to place] **—ˈthe·cal** *or* **ˈthe·cate** *adj.*

the·co·dont (ˈθiːkəˌdɒnt) *adj.* **1.** (of mammals and certain reptiles) having teeth that grow in sockets. **2.** of or relating to teeth of this type. *~n.* **3.** any extinct reptile of the order *Thecodontia,* of Triassic times, having teeth set in sockets: they gave rise to the dinosaurs, crocodiles, pterodactyls, and birds. [C20: New Latin *Thecondontia,* from Greek *thēkē* case + -ODONT]

thé dan·sant *French.* (te dɑ̃ˈsɑ̃) *n., pl.* ***thés dan·sant*** (te dɑ̃ˈsɑ̃). a dance held while afternoon tea is served, popular in the 1920s and 1930s. [literally: dancing tea]

thee (ðiː) *pron.* **1.** the objective form of **thou. 2.** (*subjective*) *Rare.* refers to the person addressed: used mainly by members of the Society of Friends. [Old English *thē;* see THOU]

theft (θɛft) *n.* **1.** *Criminal law.* the dishonest taking of property belonging to another person with the intention of depriving the owner permanently of its possession. **2.** *Rare.* something stolen. [Old English *thēofth;* related to Old Norse *thȳfth,* Old Frisian *thiūvethe,* Middle Dutch *düfte;* see THIEF] **—ˈtheft·less** *adj.*

thegn (θeɪn) *n.* a variant spelling of **thane.**

the·ine (ˈθiːiːn, -ɪn) *n.* another name for **caffeine,** esp. when present in tea. [C19: from New Latin *thea* tea + -INE[2]]

their (ðɛə) *determiner.* **1.** of, belonging to, or associated in some way with them: *their finest hour; their own clothes; she tried to combat their mocking her.* **2.** belonging to or associated in some way with people in general not including the speaker or people addressed: *in many countries they wash their clothes in the river.* **3.** *Not standard.* belonging to or associated in some way with an indefinite antecedent such as *one, whoever,* or *anybody: everyone should bring their own lunch.* [C12: from Old Norse *theira* (genitive plural); see THEY, THEM]

theirs (ðɛəz) *pron.* **1.** something or someone belonging to or associated in some way with them: *theirs is difficult.* **2.** *Not standard.* something or someone belonging to or associated in some way with an indefinite antecedent such as *one, whoever,* or *anybody: everyone thinks theirs is best.* **3. of theirs.** belonging to or associated with them.

the·ism (ˈθiːɪzəm) *n.* **1.** the form of the belief in one God as the transcendent creator and ruler of the universe that does not necessarily entail further belief in divine revelation. Compare **deism. 2.** the belief in the existence of a God or gods. Compare **atheism. —ˈthe·ist** *n., adj.* **—the·ˈis·tic** *or* **the·ˈis·ti·cal** *adj.* **—the·ˈis·ti·cal·ly** *adv.*

them (ðɛm; *unstressed* ðəm) *pron.* **1.** (*objective*) refers to things or people other than the speaker or people addressed: *I'll kill them; what happened to them?* **2.** *Chiefly U.S.* a dialect word for **themselves** when used as an indirect object: *they got them a new vice president. ~determiner.* **3.** a nonstandard word for **those:** *three of them oranges.* [Old English *thǣm,* influenced by Old Norse *theim;* related to Old Frisian *thām,* Old Saxon, Old High German *thēm,* Old Norse *theimr,* Gothic *thaim*]
Usage. See at **me.**

the·mat·ic (θɪˈmætɪk) *adj.* **1.** of, relating to, or consisting of a theme or themes. **2.** denoting a vowel or other sound or sequence of sounds that occurs between the root of a word and any inflectional or derivational suffixes. **3.** of or relating to the stem or root of a word. *~n.* **4.** a thematic vowel: *'-o-' is a thematic in the combining form 'psycho-'.* **—the·ˈmat·i·cal·ly** *adv.*

theme (θiːm) *n.* **1.** an idea or topic expanded in a discourse, discussion, etc. **2.** (in literature, music, art, etc.) a unifying idea, image, or motif, repeated or developed throughout a work. **3.** *Music.* **a.** a group of notes forming a recognizable melodic unit, often used as the basis of the musical material in a composition. **4.** a short essay, esp. one set as an exercise for a student. **5.** *Grammar.* another word for **root**[1] (sense 9) or **stem**[1] (sense 9). **6.** (in the Byzantine Empire) a territorial unit consisting of several provinces under a military commander. [C13: from Latin *thema,* from Greek: deposit, from *tithenai* to lay down] **—ˈtheme·less** *adj.*

theme song *n.* **1.** a melody used, esp. in a film score, to set a mood, introduce a character, etc. **2.** another word for **signature tune.**

The·mis (ˈθiːmɪs) *n. Greek myth.* the goddess personifying justice.

The·mis·to·cles (θəˈmɪstəˌkliːz) *n.* ?527–?460 B.C., Athenian statesman, who was responsible for the Athenian victory against the Persians at Salamis (480). He was ostracized in 470.

them·selves (ðəmˈsɛlvz) *pron.* **1. a.** the reflexive form of *they* or *them.* **b.** (*intensifier*): *the team themselves voted on it.* **2.** (*preceded by a copula*) their normal or usual selves: *they don't seem themselves any more.* **3.** Also **themself.** *Not standard.* a reflexive form of an indefinite antecedent such as *one, whoever,* or *anybody: everyone has to look after themselves.*
Usage. See at **myself.**

then (ðɛn) *adv.* **1.** at that time; over that period of time. **2.** (*sentence modifier*) in that case; that being so: *then why don't you ask her? if he comes, then you'll have to leave; go on then, take it.* ~ **3.** *sentence connector.* after that; with that: *then John left the room and didn't return. ~n.* **4.** that time: *before then; from then on. ~adj.* **5.** (*prenominal*) existing, functioning, etc., at that time: *the then prime minister.* [Old English *thenne;* related to Old Saxon, Old High German *thanna;* see THAN]

the·nar (ˈθiːnɑː) *Anatomy.* *~n.* **1.** the palm of the hand. **2.** the fleshy area of the palm at the base of the thumb. *~adj.* **3.** of or relating to the palm or the region at the base of the thumb. [C17: via New Latin from Greek; related to Old High German *tenar* palm of the hand]

the·nard·ite (θɪˈnɑːdaɪt, tɪ-) *n.* a whitish vitreous mineral that consists of anhydrous sodium sulphate and occurs in saline residues. Formula: Na_2SO_4. [C19: named after Baron L. J. *Thénard* (1777–1857), French chemist; see -ITE[1]]

Thé·nard's blue (ˈteɪnɑːz, -nɑːdz) *n.* another name for **cobalt blue.** [C19: named after Baron L. J. *Thénard;* see THENARDITE]

thence (ðɛns) *adv.* **1.** from that place. **2.** Also: **thence·forth** (ˈðɛnsˈfɔːθ). from that time or event; thereafter. **3.** therefore. [C13: *thannes,* from *thanne,* from Old English *thanon;* related to Gothic *thanana,* Old Norse *thanan*]

thence·for·ward (ˈðɛnsˈfɔːwəd) *or* **thence·for·wards** *adv.* from that time or place on; thence.

the·o- *or before a vowel* **the-** *combining form.* indicating God or gods: *theology.* [from Greek *theos* god]

the·o·bro·mine (ˌθiːəʊˈbrəʊmiːn, -mɪn) *n.* a white crystalline slightly water-soluble alkaloid that occurs in many plants, such as tea and cacao: used to treat coronary heart disease and headaches. Formula: $C_7H_8N_4O_2$. See also **xanthine** (sense 2). [C18: from New Latin *theobroma* genus of trees, literally: food of the gods, from THEO- + Greek *brōma* food + -INE[2]]

the·o·cen·tric (ˌθɪəˈsɛntrɪk) *adj. Theol.* having God as the focal point of attention. **—ˌthe·o·cen·ˈtric·i·ty** *n.* **—ˌthe·o·ˈcen·trism** *or* **the·o·cen·tri·cism** (ˌθiːəʊˈsɛntrɪˌsɪzəm) *n.*

the·oc·ra·cy (θɪˈɒkrəsɪ) *n., pl.* **·cies. 1.** government by a deity or by a priesthood. **2.** a community or political unit under such government. **—ˈthe·o·ˌcrat** *n.* **—ˌthe·o·ˈcrat·ic** *or* **ˌthe·o·ˈcrat·i·cal** *adj.* **—ˌthe·o·ˈcrat·i·cal·ly** *adv.*

the·oc·ra·sy (θɪˈɒkrəsɪ) *n.* **1.** a mingling into one of deities or divine attributes previously regarded as distinct. **2.** the union of the soul with God in mysticism. [C19: from Greek *theokrasia,* from THEO- + *-krasia* from *krasis* a blending]

The·oc·ri·tus (θɪˈɒkrɪtəs) *n.* ?310–?250 B.C., Greek poet, born in Syracuse. He wrote the first pastoral poems in Greek literature and was closely imitated by Virgil. **—The·ˈoc·ri·tan** *or* **The·oc·ri·te·an** (θɪˌɒkrɪˈtiːən) *adj., n.*

the·od·i·cy (θɪˈɒdɪsɪ) *n., pl.* **·cies. 1.** the branch of theology concerned with defending the attributes of God against objections resulting from physical and moral evil. **2.** the philosophical study of God and the destiny of the soul. [C18: coined by Leibniz in French as *théodicée,* from THEO- + Greek *dikē* justice] **—the·ˌod·i·ˈce·an** *adj.*

the·od·o·lite (θɪˈɒdəˌlaɪt) *n.* a surveying instrument for measuring horizontal and vertical angles, consisting of a small tripod-mounted telescope that is free to move in both the horizontal and vertical planes. Also called (in the U.S.): **transit.** [C16: from New Latin *theodolitus,* of uncertain origin] **—the·od·o·lit·ic** (θɪˌɒdəˈlɪtɪk) *adj.*

The·o·do·ra (ˌθɪəˈdɔːrə) *n.* ?500–548 A.D., Byzantine empress; wife and counsellor of Justinian I.

The·o·do·ra·kis (*Greek* θɛoðoˈrakis) *n.* **Mikos** (ˈmikɔs). born 1925, Greek composer: wrote the music for the film *Zorba the Greek* (1965).

The·od·o·ric *or* **The·od·e·ric** (θɪˈɒdərɪk) *n.* called *the Great.* ?454–526 A.D., king of the Ostrogoths and founder of the Ostrogothic kingdom in Italy after his murder of Odoacer (493).

The·o·do·si·us I (ˌθɪəˈdəʊsɪəs) *n.* called *the Great.* ?346–395 A.D., Roman emperor of the Eastern Roman Empire (379–95) and of the Western Roman Empire (392–95).

the·og·o·ny (θɪˈɒgənɪ) *n., pl.* **·nies. 1.** the origin and descent of the gods. **2.** an account of this, often recited in epic poetry. [C17: from Greek *theogonia;* see THEO-, -GONY] **—the·o·gon·ic** (ˌθɪəˈgɒnɪk) *adj.* **—the·ˈog·o·nist** *n.*

theol. *abbrev. for:* **1.** theologian. **2.** theological. **3.** theology.

the·o·lo·gi·an (ˌθɪəˈləʊdʒɪən) *n.* a person versed in or engaged in the study of theology, esp. Christian theology.
the·o·log·i·cal (ˌθɪəˈlɒdʒɪkəl) *adj.* **1.** of, relating to, or based on theology. **2.** based on God's revelation to man of his nature, his designs, and his will. —ˌ**the·o·ˈlog·i·cal·ly** *adv.*
the·o·log·i·cal vir·tues *pl. n.* (esp. among the scholastics) those virtues that are infused into man by a special grace of God, specifically faith, hope, and charity. Compare **natural virtues.**
the·ol·o·gize *or* **the·ol·o·gise** (θɪˈɒləˌdʒaɪz) *vb.* **1.** (*intr.*) to speculate upon theological subjects, engage in theological study or discussion, or formulate theological arguments. **2.** (*tr.*) to render theological or treat from a theological point of view. —**the·ˌol·o·gi·ˈza·tion** *or* **the·ˌol·o·gi·ˈsa·tion** *n.* —**the·ˈol·o·ˌgiz·er** *or* **the·ˈol·o·ˌgis·er** *n.*
the·ol·o·gy (θɪˈɒlədʒɪ) *n., pl.* **·gies. 1.** the systematic study of the existence and nature of the divine and its relationship to and influence upon other beings. **2.** the systematic study of Christian revelation concerning God's nature and purpose, esp. through the teaching of the Church. **3.** a specific system, form, or branch of this study, esp. for those preparing for the ministry or priesthood. [C14: from Late Latin *theologia*, from Latin; see THEO-, -LOGY] —**the·ˈol·o·gist** *n.*
the·om·a·chy (θɪˈɒməkɪ) *n., pl.* **·chies.** a battle among the gods or against them. [C16: from Greek *theomakhia*, from THEO- + *makhē* battle]
the·o·man·cy (ˈθiːəʊmænsɪ) *n.* divination or prophecy by an oracle or by people directly inspired by a god.
the·o·ma·ni·a (ˌθɪəˈmeɪnɪə) *n.* religious madness, esp. when it takes the form of believing oneself to be a god. —ˌ**the·o·ˈma·ni·ac** *n.*
the·o·mor·phic (ˌθɪəˈmɔːfɪk) *adj.* of or relating to the conception or representation of man as having the form of God or a deity. [C19: from Greek *theomorphos*, from THEO- + *morphē* form] —ˌ**the·o·ˈmor·phism** *n.*
the·on·o·my (θɪˈɒnəmɪ) *n.* the state of being governed by God.
the·op·a·thy (θɪˈɒpəθɪ) *n.* religious emotion engendered by the contemplation of or meditation upon God. [C18: from THEO- + *-pathy*, from SYMPATHY] —**the·o·pa·thet·ic** (ˌθɪəpəˈθɛtɪk) *or* **the·o·path·ic** (ˌθɪəˈpæθɪk) *adj.*
the·oph·a·gy (θɪˈɒfədʒɪ) *n., pl.* **·gies.** the sacramental eating of a god.
the·oph·a·ny (θɪˈɒfənɪ) *n., pl.* **·nies.** *Theol.* a manifestation of a deity to man in a form that, though visible, is not necessarily material. [C17: from Late Latin *theophania*, from Late Greek *theophaneia*, from THEO- + *phainein* to show] —**the·o·phan·ic** (θɪəˈfænɪk) *or* **the·ˈoph·a·nous** *adj.*
The·oph·i·lus (θɪˈɒfɪləs) *n.* a conspicuous crater in the SW quadrant of the moon, over 100 kilometres in diameter.
the·o·pho·bi·a (ˌθɪəˈfəʊbɪə) *n.* morbid fear or hatred of God. —ˌ**the·o·ˈpho·bi·ˌac** *n.*
The·o·phras·tus (ˌθɪəˈfræstəs) *n.* ?372–?287 B.C., Greek Peripatetic philosopher, noted esp. for his *Characters*, a collection of sketches of moral types.
the·o·phyl·line (ˌθɪəˈfɪliːn, -ɪn; θɪˈɒfɪlɪn) *n.* a white crystalline slightly water-soluble alkaloid that is an isomer of theobromine: it occurs in plants such as tea and is used to treat heart disease and headaches. Formula: $C_7H_8N_4O_2$. See also **xanthine** (sense 2). [C19: from THEO(BROMINE) + PHYLLO- + -INE[2]]
the·or·bo (θɪˈɔːbəʊ) *n., pl.* **·bos.** *Music.* an obsolete form of the lute, having two necks, one above the other, the second neck carrying a set of unstopped sympathetic bass strings. [C17: from Italian *teorba*, probably from Venetian, variant of *tuorba* travelling bag, ultimately from Turkish *torba* bag] —**the·ˈor·bist** *n.*
the·o·rem (ˈθɪərəm) *n.* a proposition, statement, or formula, esp. one that has been or can be deduced from axioms or previously proved propositions. [C16: from Late Latin *theōrēma*, from Greek: something to be viewed, from *theōrein* to view] —**the·o·re·mat·ic** (ˌθɪərəˈmætɪk) *or* **the·o·rem·ic** (ˌθɪəˈrɛmɪk) *adj.* —ˌ**the·o·re·ˈmat·i·cal·ly** *adv.*
the·o·ret·i·cal (ˌθɪəˈrɛtɪkəl) *or* **the·o·ret·ic** *adj.* **1.** of or based on theory. **2.** lacking practical application or actual existence; hypothetical. **3.** using or dealing in theory; impractical. —ˌ**the·o·ˈret·i·cal·ly** *adv.*
the·o·re·ti·cian (ˌθɪərɪˈtɪʃən) *n.* a student or user of the theory rather than the practical aspects of a subject.
the·o·ret·ics (ˌθɪəˈrɛtɪks) *n.* (*functioning as sing. or pl.*) the theory of a particular subject.
the·o·rize *or* **the·o·rise** (ˈθɪəˌraɪz) *vb.* (*intr.*) to produce or use theories; speculate. —ˈ**the·o·rist** *n.* —ˌ**the·o·ri·ˈza·tion** *or* ˌ**the·o·ri·ˈsa·tion** *n.* —ˈ**the·o·ˌriz·er** *or* ˈ**the·o·ˌris·er** *n.*
the·o·ry (ˈθɪərɪ) *n., pl.* **·ries. 1.** a plan formulated in the mind only; speculation. **2.** a system of rules, procedures, and assumptions used to produce a result. **3.** abstract knowledge or reasoning. **4.** a set of hypotheses related by logical or mathematical arguments to explain and predict a wide variety of connected phenomena in general terms: *the theory of relativity.* **5.** a nontechnical name for **hypothesis** (sense 1). [C16: from Late Latin *theōria*, from Greek: a sight, from *theōrein* to gaze upon]
the·o·ry of games *n.* another name for **game theory.**
theos. *abbrev. for:* **1.** theosophical. **2.** theosophy.
the·os·o·phy (θɪˈɒsəfɪ) *n.* **1.** any of various religious or philosophical systems claiming to be based on or to express an intuitive insight into the divine nature. **2.** the system of beliefs of the Theosophical Society founded in 1875, claiming to be derived from the sacred writings of Brahmanism and Buddhism, but denying the existence of any personal God. [C17: from Medieval Latin *theosophia*, from Late Greek; see THEO-, -SOPHY] —**the·o·soph·ic** (ˌθɪəˈsɒfɪk) *or* ˌ**the·o·ˈsoph·i·cal** *adj.* —ˌ**the·o·ˈsoph·i·cal·ly** *adv.* —**the·ˈos·o·phism** *n.* —**the·ˈos·o·phist** *n.*
therap. *or* **therapeut.** *abbrev. for:* **1.** therapeutic. **2.** therapeutics.
ther·a·peu·tic (ˌθɛrəˈpjuːtɪk) *adj.* **1.** of or relating to the treatment of disease; curative. **2.** serving or performed to maintain health: *therapeutic abortion.* [C17: from New Latin *therapeuticus*, from Greek *therapeutikos*, from *therapeuein* to minister to, from *theraps* an attendant] —ˌ**ther·a·ˈpeu·ti·cal·ly** *adv.*
ther·a·peu·tics (ˌθɛrəˈpjuːtɪks) *n.* (*functioning as sing.*) the branch of medicine concerned with the treatment of disease.
ther·a·pist (ˈθɛrəpɪst) *n.* a person skilled in a particular type of therapy: *a physical therapist.*
the·rap·sid (θəˈræpsɪd) *n.* any extinct reptile of the order *Therapsida*, of Permian to Triassic times: considered to be the ancestors of mammals. [C20: from New Latin *Therapsida*, from Greek *theraps* attendant]
ther·a·py (ˈθɛrəpɪ) *n., pl.* **·pies. a.** the treatment of disorders or disease. **b.** (*in combination*): *physiotherapy; electrotherapy.* [C19: from New Latin *therapia*, from Greek *therapeia* attendance; see THERAPEUTIC]
Ther·a·va·da (ˌθɛrəˈvɑːdə) *n.* the southern school of Buddhism, the name preferred by Hinayana Buddhists for their doctrines. [from Pali: doctrine of the elders]
there (ðɛə) *adv.* **1.** in, at, or to that place, point, case, or respect: *we never go there; I'm afraid I disagree with you there.* ~*pron.* **2.** used as a grammatical subject with some verbs, esp. *be*, when the true subject is an indefinite or mass noun phrase following the verb as complement: *there is a girl in that office; there doesn't seem to be any water left.* ~*adj.* **3.** (*postpositive*) who or which is in that place or position: *that boy there did it.* **4. all there.** (*predicative*) having his wits about him; of normal intelligence. **5. so there.** an exclamation that usually follows a declaration of refusal or defiance: *you can't have any more, so there!* **6. there it is.** that is the state of affairs. **7. there you are. a.** an expression used when handing a person something requested or desired. **b.** an exclamation of triumph: *there you are, I knew that would happen!* ~*n.* **8.** that place: *near there; from there.* ~*interj.* **9.** an expression of sympathy, as in consoling a child. [Old English *thǣr*; related to Old Frisian *thēr*, Old Saxon, Old High German *thār*, Old Norse, Gothic *thar*]
Usage. Careful writers and speakers ensure that the verb agrees with the number of the subject in such constructions as *there is a man waiting* and *there are several people waiting.* However, where the subject is compound even careful speakers frequently use the singular as in *there is a pen and a book on the table.*
there·a·bouts (ˈðɛərəˌbaʊts) *or* **there·a·bout** *adv.* near that place, time, amount, etc.: *fifty or thereabouts.*
there·af·ter (ˌðɛərˈɑːftə) *adv.* from that time on or after that time: *thereafter, he ceased to pay attention.*
there·at (ˌðɛərˈæt) *adv. Rare.* **1.** at that point or time. **2.** for that reason.
there·by (ˌðɛəˈbaɪ, ˈðɛəˌbaɪ) *adv.* **1.** by that means; because of that. **2.** *Archaic.* by or near that place; thereabouts.
there·for (ˌðɛəˈfɔː) *adv. Archaic or law.* for this, that, or it: *he will be richer therefor.*
there·fore (ˈðɛəˌfɔː) *sentence connector.* **1.** thus; hence: used to mark an inference on the speaker's part: *those people have their umbrellas up; therefore, it must be raining.* **2.** consequently; as a result: *they heard the warning on the radio and therefore took another route.*
there·from (ˌðɛəˈfrɒm) *adv. Archaic.* from that or there: *the roads that lead therefrom.*
there·in (ˌðɛərˈɪn) *adv. Formal or law.* in or into that place, thing, etc.
there·in·af·ter (ˌðɛərɪnˈɑːftə) *adv. Formal or law.* from this point on in that document, statement, etc.
there·in·to (ˌðɛərˈɪntuː) *adv. Formal or law.* into that place, circumstance, etc.
there·of (ˌðɛərˈɒv) *adv. Formal or law.* **1.** of or concerning that or it. **2.** from or because of that.
there·on (ˌðɛərˈɒn) *adv. Archaic.* an archaic word for **thereupon.**
The·re·sa (təˈriːzə; *Spanish* teˈresa) *n.* See (Saint) **Teresa.**
Thé·rèse de Li·sieux (*French* terɛːz də liˈzjø) *n.* **Saint**, known as *the Little Flower of Jesus.* 1873–97, French Carmelite nun, noted for her autobiography, *The Story of a Soul* (1897). Feast day: Oct. 3.
there·to (ˌðɛəˈtuː) *adv.* **1.** *Formal or law.* to that or it: *the form attached thereto.* **2.** *Obsolete.* in addition to that.
there·to·fore (ˌðɛətʊˈfɔː) *adv. Formal or law.* before that time; previous to that.
there·un·der (ˌðɛərˈʌndə) *adv. Formal or law.* **1.** (in documents, etc.) below that or it; subsequently in that; thereafter. **2.** under the terms or authority of that.
there·up·on (ˌðɛərəˈpɒn) *adv.* **1.** immediately after that; at that point: *thereupon, the whole class applauded.* **2.** *Formal or law.* upon that thing, point, subject, etc.
there·with (ˌðɛəˈwɪθ, -ˈwɪð) *or* **there·with·al** *adv.* **1.** *Formal or law.* with or in addition to that. **2.** a less common word for **thereupon** (sense 1). **3.** *Archaic.* by means of or on account of that.
The·re·zi·na (*Portuguese* ˌtereˈzina) *n.* the former name of **Teresina.**
the·ri·an·throp·ic (ˌθɪərɪənˈθrɒpɪk) *adj.* **1.** (of certain mythi-

cal creatures or deities) having a partly animal, partly human form. **2.** of or relating to such creatures or deities. [C19: from Greek *thērion* wild animal + *anthrōpos* man] —**the·ri·an·thro·pism** (ˌθɪərɪˈænθrəˌpɪzəm) *n.*

the·ri·o·mor·phic (ˌθɪərɪəʊˈmɔːfɪk) *or* **the·ri·o·mor·phous** *adj.* (esp. of a deity) possessing or depicted in the form of a beast. [C19: from Greek *thēriomorphos*, from *thērion* wild animal + *morphē* shape] —**ˈthe·ri·o·ˌmorph** *n.*

therm (θɜːm) *n. Brit.* a unit of heat equal to 100 000 British thermal units. One therm is equal to $1.055\,056 \times 10^8$ joules. [C19: from Greek *thermē* heat]

ther·mae (ˈθɜːmiː) *pl. n.* public baths or hot springs, esp. in ancient Greece or Rome. [C17: from Latin, from Greek *thermai*, pl. of *thermē* heat]

therm·aes·the·si·a *or U.S.* **therm·es·the·si·a** (ˌθɜːmiːsˈθiːzɪə) *n.* sensitivity to various degrees of heat and cold.

ther·mal (ˈθɜːməl) *adj.* **1.** Also: **ther·mic.** of, relating to, caused by, or generating heat or increased temperature. **2.** hot or warm: *thermal baths; thermal spring.* ~*n.* **3.** *Meteorol.* a column of rising air caused by local unequal heating of the land surface, and used by gliders to gain height. —**ˈther·mal·ly** *adv.*

ther·mal bar·ri·er *n.* an obstacle to flight at very high speeds as a result of the heating effect of air friction. Also called **heat barrier.**

ther·mal con·duc·tiv·i·ty *n.* a measure of the ability of a substance to conduct heat, determined by the rate of heat flow between two opposite faces of a unit cube of the substance when there is unit temperature difference between them: measured in joules per second per metre per kelvin. Symbol: λ or *k*. Sometimes shortened to **conductivity.**

ther·mal ef·fi·cien·cy *n.* the ratio of the work done by a heat engine to the energy supplied to it. Compare **efficiency.**

ther·mal e·qua·tor *n.* an imaginary line round the earth running through the point on each meridian with the highest average temperature. It lies mainly to the north because of the larger landmasses and therefore greater summer heating.

ther·mal·ize *or* **ther·mal·ise** (ˈθɜːməˌlaɪz) *vb. Physics.* to undergo or cause to undergo a process in which neutrons lose energy in a moderator and become thermal neutrons.

ther·mal neu·tron *n.* a slow neutron that has a mean velocity of about 2200 metres per second, being approximately in thermal equilibrium with its moderator.

ther·mal re·ac·tor *n.* a nuclear reactor in which most of the fission is caused by thermal neutrons.

ther·mal shock *n.* a fluctuation in temperature causing stress in a material. It often results in fracture, esp. in brittle materials such as ceramics.

Ther·mi·dor *French.* (termiˈdɔːr) *n.* the month of heat: the eleventh month of the French revolutionary calendar, extending from July 20 to Aug. 18. Also called: **Fervidor.** [C19: from French, from Greek *thermē* heat + *dōron* gift]

ther·mi·on (ˈθɜːmɪən) *n. Physics.* an electron or ion emitted by a body at high temperature.

ther·mi·on·ic (ˌθɜːmɪˈɒnɪk) *adj.* of, relating to, or operated by electrons emitted from materials at high temperatures: *a thermionic valve.*

ther·mi·on·ic cur·rent *n.* an electric current produced between two electrodes as a result of electrons emitted by thermionic emission.

ther·mi·on·ic e·mis·sion *n.* the emission of electrons from very hot solids or liquids: used for producing electrons in valves, electron microscopes, x-ray tubes, etc.

ther·mi·on·ics (ˌθɜːmɪˈɒnɪks) *n.* (*functioning as sing.*) the branch of electronics concerned with the emission of electrons by hot bodies and with devices based on this effect, esp. the study and design of thermionic valves.

ther·mi·on·ic valve *or esp. U.S.* **tube** *n.* an electronic valve in which electrons are emitted from a heated rather than a cold cathode.

ther·mis·tor (θɜːˈmɪstə) *n.* a semiconductor device having a resistance that decreases rapidly with an increase in temperature. It is used for temperature measurement, to compensate for temperature variations in a circuit, etc. [C20: from THERMO- + (RES)ISTOR]

Ther·mit (ˈθɜːmɪt) *or* **Ther·mite** (ˈθɜːmaɪt) *n. Trademark.* a mixture of aluminium powder and a metal oxide, such as iron oxide, which when ignited reacts with the evolution of heat to yield aluminium oxide and molten metal: used for welding and in some types of incendiary bombs.

ther·mite pro·cess *n.* another name for **aluminothermy.**

ther·mo- *or before a vowel* **therm-** *combining form.* related to, caused by, or measuring heat: *thermodynamics; thermophile.* [from Greek *thermos* hot, *thermē* heat]

ther·mo·bar·o·graph (ˌθɜːməʊˈbærəˌɡrɑːf, -ˌɡræf) *n.* a device that simultaneously records the temperature and pressure of the atmosphere.

ther·mo·ba·rom·e·ter (ˌθɜːməʊbəˈrɒmɪtə) *n.* an apparatus that provides an accurate measurement of pressure by observation of the change in the boiling point of a fluid.

ther·mo·chem·is·try (ˌθɜːməʊˈkɛmɪstrɪ) *n.* the branch of chemistry concerned with the study and measurement of the heat evolved or absorbed during chemical reactions. —ˌ**ther·mo·ˈchem·i·cal** *adj.* —ˌ**ther·mo·ˈchem·i·cal·ly** *adv.* —ˌ**ther·mo·ˈchem·ist** *n.*

ther·mo·cline (ˈθɜːməʊˌklaɪn) *n.* a temperature gradient in a thermally stratified body of water, such as a lake.

ther·mo·cou·ple (ˈθɜːməʊˌkʌpᵊl) *n.* **1.** a device for measuring temperature consisting of a pair of wires of different metals joined at both ends. One junction is at the temperature to be measured, the second at a lower fixed temperature. The current generated in the circuit is proportional to the temperature difference. **2.** a similar device with only one junction between two dissimilar metals.

ther·mo·dy·nam·ic (ˌθɜːməʊdaɪˈnæmɪk) *or* **ther·mo·dy·nam·i·cal** *adj.* **1.** of or concerned with thermodynamics. **2.** determined by or obeying the laws of thermodynamics. —ˌ**ther·mo·dy·ˈnam·i·cal·ly** *adv.*

ther·mo·dy·nam·ic e·qui·lib·ri·um *n.* the condition of a system in which the quantities that specify its properties, such as pressure, temperature, etc., all remain unchanged. Sometimes shortened to **equilibrium.**

ther·mo·dy·nam·ics (ˌθɜːməʊdaɪˈnæmɪks) *n.* (*functioning as sing.*) the branch of physical science concerned with the interrelationship and interconversion of different forms of energy and the behaviour of systems in terms of certain basic quantities, such as pressure, temperature, etc. See also **law of thermodynamics.**

ther·mo·dy·nam·ic tem·per·a·ture *n.* the basic physical quantity used as a measure of the average thermal energy of random motion of particles in thermal equilibrium. It is measured in kelvins or degrees Celsius and defined so that the triple point of water is 273.16 kelvins. Also called: **absolute temperature.**

ther·mo·e·lec·tric (ˌθɜːməʊɪˈlɛktrɪk) *or* **ther·mo·e·lec·tri·cal** *adj.* **1.** of, relating to, used in, or operated by the conversion of heat energy to electrical energy by the Seebeck effect: *a thermoelectric thermometer.* **2.** of, relating to, used in, or operated by the conversion of electrical energy to heat energy by the Peltier effect: *a thermoelectric cooler.* —ˌ**ther·mo·e·ˈlec·tri·cal·ly** *adv.*

ther·mo·e·lec·tric ef·fect *n.* another name for the **Seebeck effect** or **Peltier effect.**

ther·mo·e·lec·tric·i·ty (ˌθɜːməʊɪlɛkˈtrɪsɪtɪ) *n.* **1.** electricity generated by a thermocouple. **2.** the study of the relationship between heat and electrical energy. See also **Seebeck effect, Peltier effect.**

ther·mo·e·lec·tron (ˌθɜːməʊɪˈlɛktrɒn) *n.* an electron emitted at high temperature, such as one produced in a thermionic valve.

ther·mo·gen·e·sis (ˌθɜːməʊˈdʒɛnɪsɪs) *n.* the production of heat by metabolic processes. —**ther·mog·e·nous** (θəˈmɒdʒɪnəs) *or* **ther·mo·ge·net·ic** (ˌθɜːməʊdʒɪˈnɛtɪk) *adj.*

ther·mo·graph (ˈθɜːməʊˌɡrɑːf, -ˌɡræf) *n.* a type of thermometer that produces a continuous record of a fluctuating temperature. The record so produced is called a **ther·mo·gram** (ˈθɜːməʊˌɡræm).

ther·mog·ra·phy (θɜːˈmɒɡrəfɪ) *n.* any writing, printing, or recording process involving the use of heat. —**ther·ˈmog·ra·pher** *n.* —**ther·mo·graph·ic** (ˌθɜːməʊˈɡræfɪk) *adj.*

ther·mo·junc·tion (ˌθɜːməʊˈdʒʌŋkʃən) *n.* a point of electrical contact between two dissimilar metals across which a voltage appears, the magnitude of which depends on the temperature of the contact and the nature of the metals. See also **Seebeck effect.**

ther·mo·la·bile (ˌθɜːməʊˈleɪbɪl) *adj.* (of certain biochemical and chemical compounds) easily decomposed or subject to a loss of characteristic properties by the action of heat: *a thermolabile enzyme.* Compare **thermostable** (sense 1).

ther·mo·lu·mi·nes·cence (ˌθɜːməʊˌluːmɪˈnɛsəns) *n.* phosphorescence of certain materials or objects as a result of heating. It is caused by pre-irradiation of the material inducing defects which are removed by the heat, the energy released appearing as light: used in archaeological dating. —ˌ**ther·mo·ˌlu·mi·ˈnes·cent** *adj.*

ther·mol·y·sis (θɜːˈmɒlɪsɪs) *n.* **1.** *Physiol.* loss of heat from the body. **2.** the dissociation of a substance as a result of heating. —**ther·mo·lyt·ic** (ˌθɜːməʊˈlɪtɪk) *adj.*

ther·mo·mag·net·ic (ˌθɜːməʊmæɡˈnɛtɪk) *n.* of or concerned with the relationship between heat and magnetism, esp. the change in temperature of a body when it is magnetized or demagnetized. Former term: **pyromagnetic.**

ther·mom·e·ter (θəˈmɒmɪtə) *n.* an instrument used to measure temperature, esp. one in which a thin column of liquid, such as mercury, expands and contracts within a graduated sealed tube. See also **clinical thermometer, gas thermometer, resistance thermometer, thermocouple, pyrometer.**

ther·mom·e·try (θəˈmɒmɪtrɪ) *n.* the branch of physics concerned with the measurement of temperature and the design and use of thermometers and pyrometers. —**ther·mo·met·ric** (ˌθɜːməˈmɛtrɪk) *or* ˌ**ther·mo·ˈmet·ri·cal** *adj.* —ˌ**ther·mo·ˈmet·ri·cal·ly** *adv.*

ther·mo·mo·tor (ˌθɜːməʊˈməʊtə) *n.* an engine that produces force from the expansion of a heated fluid.

ther·mo·nu·cle·ar (ˌθɜːməʊˈnjuːklɪə) *adj.* **1.** involving nuclear fusion: *a thermonuclear reaction.* **2.** involving thermonuclear weapons: *a thermonuclear war.*

ther·mo·nu·cle·ar bomb *n.* another name for **fusion bomb.**

ther·mo·nu·cle·ar re·ac·tion *n.* a nuclear fusion reaction occurring at a very high temperature: responsible for the energy produced in the sun, nuclear weapons, and fusion reactors. See **nuclear fusion, hydrogen bomb.**

ther·mo·phile (ˈθɜːməʊˌfaɪl) **ther·mo·phil** (ˈθɜːməʊˌfɪl) *n.* **1.** an organism, esp. a bacterium or plant, that thrives under warm conditions. ~*adj.* **2.** thriving under warm conditions. —ˌ**ther·mo·ˈphil·ic, ther·moph·i·lous** (θɜːˈmɒfɪləs) *adj.*

ther·mo·pile (ˈθɜːməʊˌpaɪl) *n.* an instrument for detecting and measuring heat radiation or for generating a thermoelectric current. It consists of a number of thermocouple junctions, usually joined together in series.

ther+mo+plas+tic (ˌθɜːməʊˈplæstɪk) *adj.* **1.** (of a material, esp. a synthetic plastic or resin) becoming soft when heated and rehardening on cooling without appreciable change of properties. Compare **thermosetting.** *~n.* **2.** a synthetic plastic or resin, such as polystyrene, with these properties. —**ther+mo+plas+tic+i+ty** (ˌθɜːməʊplæˈstɪsɪtɪ) *n.*

Ther+mop·y+lae (θəˈmɒpəˌliː) *n.* (in ancient Greece) a narrow pass between the mountains and the sea linking Locris and Thessaly: a defensible position on a traditional invasion route from N Greece; scene of a famous battle (480 B.C.) in which a Greek army under Leonidas was crushed by the Persians during their attempted conquest of Greece.

Ther+mos *or* **Ther+mos flask** (ˈθɜːməs) *n. Trademark.* a type of stoppered vacuum flask, esp. one used to keep beverages or soup hot. See also **Dewar flask.**

ther+mo+scope (ˈθɜːməˌskəʊp) *n.* a device that indicates a change in temperature, esp. one that does not measure the actual temperature. —**ther+mo+scop+ic** (ˌθɜːməˈskɒpɪk) *or* **ˌther+mo+ˈscop·i·cal** *adj.* —**ˌther+mo+ˈscop·i·cal+ly** *adv.*

ther+mo+set+ting (ˌθɜːməʊˈsɛtɪŋ) *adj.* (of a material, esp. a synthetic plastic or resin) hardening permanently after one application of heat and pressure. Thermosetting plastics, such as phenol-formaldehyde, cannot be remoulded. Compare **thermoplastic.**

ther+mo+si+phon (ˌθɜːməʊˈsaɪfən) *n.* a system in which a coolant is circulated by convection caused by a difference in density between the hot and cold portions of the liquid.

ther+mo+sphere (ˈθɜːməˌsfɪə) *n.* an atmospheric layer lying between the mesophere and the exosphere, reaching an altitude of about 400 kilometres where the temperature is over 1000°C.

ther+mo+sta+ble (ˌθɜːrməʊˈsteɪbᵊl) *adj.* **1.** (of certain chemical and biochemical compounds) capable of withstanding moderate heat without loss of characteristic properties: *a thermostable plastic.* Compare **thermolabile. 2.** not affected by high temperatures. —**ther+mo+sta+bil+i·ty** (ˌθɜːməʊstəˈbɪlɪtɪ) *n.*

ther+mo+stat (ˈθɜːməˌstæt) *n.* a device that maintains a system at a constant temperature. It often consists of a bimetallic strip that bends as it expands and contracts with temperature, thus breaking and making contact with an electrical power supply. —**ˌther+mo+ˈstat+ic** *adj.* —**ˌther+mo+ˈstat·i·cal+ly** *adv.*

ther+mo+stat+ics (ˌθɜːməˈstætɪks) *n.* (*functioning as sing.*) the branch of science concerned with thermal equilibrium.

ther+mo+tax+is (ˌθɜːməʊˈtæksɪs) *n.* the directional movement of an organism in response to the stimulus of a source of heat. —**ˌther+mo+ˈtax+ic** *adj.*

ther+mo+ten+sile (ˌθɜːməʊˈtɛnsaɪl) *adj.* of or relating to tensile strength in so far as it is affected by temperature.

ther+mo+ther·a+py (ˌθɜːməʊˈθɛrəpɪ) *n. Med.* treatment of a bodily structure or part by the application of heat.

ther+mo+tro+pism (ˌθɜːməʊˈtrəʊpɪzm) *n.* the directional growth of a plant in response to the stimulus of heat. —**ˌther+mo+ˈtrop+ic** *adj.*

-ther·my *n. combining form.* indicating heat: *diathermy.* [from New Latin *-thermia,* from Greek *thermē*] —**-ther·mic** *or* **-ther·mal** *adj. combining form.*

the+roid (ˈθɪərɔɪd) *adj.* of, relating to, or resembling a beast. [C19: from Greek *thēroeidēs,* from *thēr* wild animal; see -OID]

the+ro+pod (ˈθɪərəpɒd) *n.* any bipedal carnivorous saurischian dinosaur of the suborder *Theropoda,* having strong hind legs and grasping hands. They lived in Triassic to Cretaceous times and included tyrannosaurs and megalosaurs. [C19: from New Latin *theropoda,* from Greek *thēr* beast + *pous* foot] —**the+rop·o·dan** (θɪˈrɒpədᵊn) *n., adj.*

Ther·si·tes (θəˈsaɪtiːz) *n.* the ugliest and most evil-tongued fighter on the Greek side in the Trojan War, killed by Achilles when he mocked him.

ther+sit·i·cal (θəˈsɪtɪkᵊl) *adj. Rare.* abusive and loud.

the+sau+rus (θɪˈsɔːrəs) *n., pl.* **+ri** (-raɪ) *or* **+rus·es. 1.** a book containing systematized lists of synonyms and related words. **2.** a dictionary of selected words or topics. **3.** *Rare.* a treasury. [C18: from Latin, Greek: TREASURE]

these (ðiːz) *determiner.* **a.** the form of **this** used before a plural noun: *these men.* **b.** (*as pronoun*)*: I don't much care for these.*

The·seus (ˈθiːsɪəs) *n. Greek myth.* a hero of Attica, noted for his many great deeds, among them the slaying of the Minotaur, the conquest of the Amazons, whose queen he married, participation in the Calydonian hunt, and the search for the Golden Fleece. —**The+se·an** (θɪˈsiːən) *adj.*

the+sis (ˈθiːsɪs) *n., pl.* **+ses** (-siːz). **1.** a dissertation resulting from original research, esp. when submitted by a candidate for a degree or diploma. **2.** a theory maintained in argument. **3.** a subject for a discussion or essay. **4.** an unproved statement, esp. one put forward as a premiss in an argument. **5.** *Music.* the downbeat of a bar, as indicated in conducting. **6.** (in classical prosody) the syllable or part of a metrical foot not receiving the ictus. Compare **arsis. 7.** *Philosophy.* the first stage in the Hegelian dialectic. [C16: via Late Latin from Greek: a placing, from *tithenai* to place]

Thes·pi·an (ˈθɛspɪən) *adj.* **1.** of or relating to Thespis. **2.** of or relating to drama and the theatre; dramatic. *~n.* **3.** *Often facetious.* an actor or actress.

Thes·pis (ˈθɛspɪs) *n.* 6th-century B.C. Greek poet, regarded as the founder of tragic drama.

Thess. *Bible. abbrev. for* Thessalonians.

Thes+sa+lo+ni·an (ˌθɛsəˈləʊnɪən) *adj.* **1.** of or relating to ancient Thessalonica (modern Salonika). *~n.* **2.** an inhabitant of ancient Thessalonica.

Thes+sa+lo+ni·ans (ˌθɛsəˈləʊnɪənz) *n.* (*functioning as sing.*) either of two books of the New Testament (in full **The First and Second Epistles of Paul the Apostle to the Thessalonians**).

Thes+sa+lo+ni+ki (*Greek* ˌθesaloˈniki) *n.* a port in NE Greece, in central Macedonia at the head of the **Gulf of Salonika** (an inlet of the Aegean): capital of the Roman province of Macedonia; university (1926). Latin name: **Thessalonica.** English name: **Salonika** or **Salonica.**

Thes+sa+ly (ˈθɛsəlɪ) *n.* a region of E Central Greece, on the Aegean: an extensive fertile plain, edged with mountains. Pop.: 659 913 (1971). Area: 13 973 sq. km (5395 sq. miles). Modern Greek name: **Thes+sa+li·a** (ˌθesaˈlia). —**Thes+sa+li+an** (θɛˈseɪlɪən) *adj., n.*

the+ta (ˈθiːtə) *n.* the eighth letter of the Greek alphabet (Θ, θ), a consonant, transliterated as *th.* Compare **edh.** [C17: from Greek, of Semitic origin; compare Hebrew *tēth*]

Thet+ford Mines (ˈθɛtfəd) *n.* a city in SE Canada, in S Quebec: asbestos industry. Pop.: 22 003 (1971).

thet+ic (ˈθɛtɪk) *adj.* **1.** (in classical prosody) of, bearing, or relating to a metrical stress. **2.** positive and arbitrary; prescriptive. [C17: from Greek *thetikos,* from *thetos* laid down, from *tithenai* to place] —**ˈthet·i·cal+ly** *adv.*

The·tis (ˈθiːtɪs) *n.* one of the Nereids and mother of Achilles by Peleus.

the+ur+gy (ˈθiːˌɜːdʒɪ) *n., pl.* **+gies. 1.** *Theol.* **a.** the intervention of a divine or supernatural agency in the affairs of man. **b.** the working of miracles by such intervention. **2.** beneficent magic as taught and performed by Egyptian Neoplatonists and others. [C16: from Late Latin *theūrgia,* from Late Greek *theourgia* the practice of magic, from *theo-* THEO- + *-urgia,* from *ergon* work] —**the+ˈurg+ic** *or* **the+ˈur+gi+cal** *adj.* —**the+ˈur+gi+cal+ly** *adv.* —**ˈthe+ur+gist** *n.*

thew (θjuː) *n.* **1.** muscle, esp. if strong or well-developed. **2.** (*pl.*) muscular strength. [Old English *thēaw;* related to Old Saxon, Old High German *thau* discipline, Latin *tuērī* to observe, *tūtus* secure] —**ˈthew·y** *adj.* —**ˈthew+less** *adj.*

they (ðeɪ) *pron.* (*subjective*) **1.** refers to people or things other than the speaker or people addressed: *they fight among themselves.* **2.** refers to unspecified people or people in general not including the speaker or people addressed: *in Australia they have Christmas in the summer.* **3.** *Not standard.* refers to an indefinite antecedent such as *one, whoever,* or *anybody: if anyone objects, they can go.* **4.** an archaic word for **those:** *blessed are they that mourn.* [C12: *thei* from Old Norse *their,* masculine nominative plural, equivalent to Old English *thā*]

they'd (ðeɪd) *contraction of* they would *or* they had.

they'll (ðeɪl) *contraction of* they will *or* they shall.

they're (ðɛə, ˈðeɪə) *contraction of* they are.

they've (ðeɪv) *contraction of* they have.

T.H.I. *abbrev. for* temperature-humidity index.

thi- *combining form.* variant of **thio-.**

thi·a+mine (ˈθaɪəˌmiːn, -mɪn) *or* **thi·a+min** (ˈθaɪəmɪn) *n. Biochem.* a soluble white crystalline vitamin that occurs in the outer coat of rice and other grains. It forms part of the vitamin B complex and is essential for carbohydrate metabolism: deficiency leads to nervous disorders and to the disease beriberi. Formula: $C_{12}H_{17}ON_4SCl.H_2O$. Also called: **vitamin B_1, aneurin.** [C20: THIO- + (VIT)AMIN]

thi·a+zine (ˈθaɪəˌziːn, -ˌzaɪn) *n.* any of a group of organic compounds containing a ring system composed of four carbon atoms, a sulphur atom, and a nitrogen atom.

thi·a+zole (ˈθaɪəˌzəʊl) *or* **thi·a+zol** (ˈθaɪəˌzɒl) *n.* **1.** a colourless liquid with a pungent smell that contains a ring system composed of three carbon atoms, a sulphur atom, and a nitrogen atom. It is used in dyes and fungicides. Formula: C_3H_3NS. **2.** any of a group of compounds derived from this substance that are used in dyes.

thick (θɪk) *adj.* **1.** of relatively great extent from one surface to the other; fat, broad, or deep: *a thick slice of bread.* **2. a.** (*postpositive*) of specific fatness: *ten centimetres thick.* **b.** (*in combination*)*: a six-inch-thick wall.* **3.** having a relatively dense consistency; not transparent: *thick soup.* **4.** abundantly covered or filled: *a piano thick with dust.* **5.** impenetrable; dense: *a thick fog.* **6.** stupid, slow, or insensitive: *a thick person.* **7.** throaty or badly articulated: *a voice thick with emotion.* **8.** (of accents, etc.) pronounced. **9.** *Informal.* very friendly (esp. in the phrase **thick as thieves**). **10. a bit thick.** *Brit.* unfair or excessive. **11. a thick ear.** *Informal.* a blow on the ear delivered as punishment, in anger, etc. *~adv.* **12.** in order to produce something thick: *to slice bread thick.* **13.** profusely; in quick succession (esp. in the phrase **thick and fast**). **14. lay it on thick.** *Informal.* **a.** to exaggerate a story, statement, etc. **b.** to flatter excessively. *~n.* **15.** a thick piece or part. **16. the thick.** the most intense or active part. **17. through thick and thin.** in good times and bad. [Old English *thicce;* related to Old Saxon, Old High German *thikki,* Old Norse *thykkr*] —**ˈthick+ish** *adj.* —**ˈthick+ly** *adv.*

thick+en (ˈθɪkən) *vb.* **1.** to make or become thick or thicker: *thicken the soup by adding flour.* **2.** (*intr.*) to become more involved: *the plot thickened.* —**ˈthick+en+er** *n.*

thick+en+ing (ˈθɪkənɪŋ) *n.* **1.** something added to a liquid to thicken it. **2.** a thickened part or piece.

thick+et (ˈθɪkɪt) *n.* a dense growth of small trees, shrubs, and similar plants. [Old English *thiccet;* see THICK]

thick+head (ˈθɪkˌhɛd) *n.* **1.** a stupid or ignorant person; fool. **2.** Also called: **whistler.** any of various Australian and SE Asian songbirds of the family *Muscicapidae* (flycatchers, etc.). —ˌ**thick·'head·ed** *adj.* —ˌ**thick·'head·ed·ness** *n.*

thick-knee *n.* another name for **stone curlew.**

thick·leaf ('θɪkˌliːf) *n., pl.* **·leaves.** any of various succulent plants of the crassulaceous genus *Crassula*, having sessile or short-stalked fleshy leaves.

thick·ness ('θɪknɪs) *n.* **1.** the state or quality of being thick. **2.** the dimension through an object, as opposed to length or width. **3.** a layer of something. **4.** a thick part.

thick·set (ˌθɪk'sɛt) *adj.* **1.** stocky in build; sturdy. **2.** densely planted or placed. ~*n.* **3.** a rare word for **thicket.**

thick-skinned *adj.* insensitive to criticism or hints; not easily upset or affected.

thick-wit·ted *or* **thick-skulled** *adj.* stupid, dull, or slow to learn. —ˌ**thick-'wit·ted·ly** *adv.* —ˌ**thick-'wit·ted·ness** *n.*

thief (θiːf) *n., pl.* **thieves** (θiːvz). **1.** a person who steals something from another. **2.** *Criminal law.* a person who commits theft. [Old English *thēof;* related to Old Frisian *thiāf*, Old Saxon *thiof*, Old High German *diob*, Old Norse *thjōfr*, Gothic *thiufs*] —'**thiev·ish** *adj.* —'**thiev·ish·ly** *adv.* —'**thiev·ish·ness** *n.*

Thiers (*French* tjɛːr) *n.* **Louis A·dolphe** (lwi a'dɔlf). 1797–1877, French statesman and historian. After the Franco-Prussian war, he suppressed the Paris Commune and became first president of the Third Republic (1871–73). His policies made possible the paying off of the war indemnity exacted by Germany.

thieve (θiːv) *vb.* to steal (someone's possessions). [Old English *thēofian*, from *thēof* THIEF] —'**thiev·er·y** *n.* —'**thiev·ing·ly** *adv.*

thigh (θaɪ) *n.* **1.** the part of the leg between the hip and the knee in man. **2.** the corresponding part in other vertebrates and insects. Related adj.: **femoral.** [Old English *thēh;* related to Old Frisian *thiāch*, Old High German *dioh* thigh, Old Norse *thjō* buttock, Old Slavonic *tyku* fat]

thigh·bone ('θaɪˌbəʊn) *n.* a nontechnical name for the **femur.**

thig·mo·tax·is (ˌθɪgmə'tæksɪs) *n.* another name for **stereotaxis.** [C19: from Greek *thigma* touch + -TAXIS] —ˌ**thig·mo·'tac·tic** *adj.* —ˌ**thig·mo·'tac·ti·cal·ly** *adv.*

thig·mo·tro·pism (ˌθɪgməʊ'trəʊpɪzəm) *n.* the directional growth of a plant, in response to the stimulus of direct contact. Also called: **haptotropism, stereotropism.** [C19: from Greek *thigma* touch + -TROPISM] —ˌ**thig·mo·'trop·ic** *adj.*

thill (θɪl) *n.* another word for **shaft** (part of a horse's harness). [C14: perhaps related to Old English *thille* board, planking, Old High German *dilla* plank, Old Norse *thili*]

thim·ble ('θɪmbᵊl) *n.* **1.** a cap of metal, plastic, etc., used to protect the end of the finger when sewing. **2.** any small metal cap resembling this. **3.** *Nautical.* a loop of metal having a groove at its outer edge for a rope or cable, for lining the inside of an eye. **4.** short for **thimbleful.** [Old English *thȳmel* thumbstall, from *thūma* THUMB]

thim·ble·ful ('θɪmbᵊlˌfʊl) *n.* a very small amount, esp. of a liquid.

thim·ble·rig ('θɪmbᵊlˌrɪg) *n.* a game in which the operator rapidly moves about three inverted thimbles, one of which conceals a token, the other player betting on which thimble the token is under. —'**thim·ble·ˌrig·ger** *n.*

thim·ble·weed ('θɪmbᵊlˌwiːd) *n. U.S.* any of various plants having a thimble-shaped fruit, esp. an American anemone *Anemone virginiana* and a rudbeckia, *Rudbeckia laciniata.*

thim·ble·wit ('θɪmbᵊlˌwɪt) *n. Chiefly U.S.* a silly or dimwitted person; dunce. —'**thim·ble·ˌwit·ted** *adj.*

Thim·bu ('θɪmbuː) *or* **Thim·phu** ('θɪmfuː) *n.* the capital of Bhutan, in the west in the foothills of the E Himalayas: became the official capital in 1962. Pop.: 8000 (1969 est.).

thi·mer·o·sal (θaɪ'mɛrəˌsæl) *n.* a creamy white crystalline compound of mercury, used in solution as an antiseptic. Formula: $C_9H_9HgNaO_2S$. [C20: from THIO- + MER(CURY) + SAL(ICYLATE)]

thin (θɪn) *adj.* **thin·ner, thin·nest. 1.** of relatively small extent from one side or surface to the other; fine or narrow. **2.** slim or lean. **3.** sparsely placed; meagre: *thin hair.* **4.** of relatively low density or viscosity: *a thin liquid.* **5.** weak; poor; insufficient: *a thin disguise.* **6.** (of a photographic negative) having low density, usually insufficient to produce a satisfactory positive. **7. thin on the ground.** few in number; scarce. ~*adv.* **8.** in order to produce something thin: *to cut bread thin.* ~*vb.* **thins, thin·ning, thinned. 9.** to make or become thin or sparse. [Old English *thynne;* related to Old Frisian *thenne*, Old Saxon, Old High German *thunni*, Old Norse *thunnr*, Latin *tenuis* thin, Greek *teinein* to stretch] —'**thin·ly** *adv.* —'**thin·ness** *n.*

thine (ðaɪn) *determiner. Archaic.* **a.** (*preceding a vowel*) of, belonging to, or associated in some way with you (thou): *thine eyes.* **b.** (*as pronoun*): *thine is the greatest burden.* Compare **thy.** [Old English *thīn;* related to Old High German *dīn*, Gothic *theina*]

thin-film *adj.* (of an electronic component, device, or circuit) composed of one or more extremely thin layers of metal, semiconductor, etc., deposited on a ceramic or glass substrate: *thin-film capacitor.*

thing[1] (θɪŋ) *n.* **1.** an object, fact, affair, circumstance, or concept considered as being a separate entity. **2.** any inanimate object. **3.** an object or entity that cannot or need not be precisely named. **4.** *Informal.* a person or animal regarded as the object of pity, contempt, etc.: *you poor thing.* **5.** an event or act. **6.** a thought or statement. **7.** *Law.* any object or right that may be the subject of property (as distinguished from a person). **8.** a device, means, or instrument. **9.** (*often pl.*) a possession, article of clothing, etc. **10.** *Informal.* a mental attitude, preoccupation or obsession (esp. in the phrase **have a thing about**). **11.** an activity or mode of behaviour satisfying to one's personality (esp. in the phrase **do one's (own) thing**). **12. the thing.** the latest fashion. **13. be on to a good thing.** to be in a profitable situation or position. **14. make a thing of.** to make a fuss about; exaggerate the importance of. [Old English *thing* assembly; related to Old Norse *thing* assembly, Old High German *ding* assembly]

thing[2] (θɪŋ, tɪŋ) *n.* (*often cap.*) a law court or public assembly in the Scandinavian countries. Also: **ting**[2]. [C19: from Old Norse *thing* assembly (the same word as THING[1])]

thing-in-it·self *n.* (in the philosophy of Kant) reality regarded apart from human knowledge and perception.

thing·u·ma·bob *or* **thing·a·ma·bob** ('θɪŋəməˌbɒb) *n. Informal.* a person or thing the name of which is unknown, temporarily forgotten, or deliberately overlooked. Also: **thingumajig, thingamajig,** *or* **thingummy.** [C18: from THING[1], with humorous suffix]

think (θɪŋk) *vb.* **thinks, think·ing, thought. 1.** (*tr.; may take a clause as object*) to consider, judge, or believe: *he thinks my ideas impractical.* **2.** (*intr.;* often foll. by *about*) to exercise the mind as in order to make a decision; ponder. **3.** (*intr.*) to be capable of conscious thought: *man is the only animal that thinks.* **4.** to remember; recollect: *I can't think what his name is.* **5.** (*intr.;* foll. by *of*) to make the mental choice (of): *think of a number.* **6.** (*may take a clause as object or an infinitive*) **a.** to expect; suppose: *I didn't think to see you here.* **b.** to be considerate or aware enough (to do something): *he did not think to thank them.* **7.** (*intr.*) to focus the attention on being: *think thin; think big.* **8.** (*tr.*) to bring into or out of a specified condition by thinking: *to think away one's fears.* **9. I don't think.** *Slang.* a phrase added to an ironical statement: *you're the paragon of virtue, I don't think.* **10. think again.** to reconsider one's decision, opinion, etc. **11. a. think better of.** to change one's mind about (a course of action, decision, etc.). **b.** to have a more favourable opinion of (a person). **12. think much of.** (*usually negative*) to have a high opinion of. **13. think nothing of. a.** to regard as routine or natural. **b.** to have no compunction or hesitation about. **14. think twice.** to consider carefully before deciding (about something). ~*n.* **15.** *Informal.* a careful, open-minded assessment: *let's have a fresh think about this problem.* **16.** (*modifier*) *Informal.* characterized by or involving thinkers, thinking, or thought: *a think session.* [Old English *thencan;* related to Old Frisian *thenza*, Old Saxon *thenkian*, Old High German *denken*, Old Norse *thekkja*, Gothic *thagkjan*] —'**think·er** *n.*

think·a·ble ('θɪŋkəbᵊl) *adj.* able to be conceived or considered; possible; feasible.

think·ing ('θɪŋkɪŋ) *n.* **1.** opinion or judgment. **2.** the process of thought. ~*adj.* **3.** (*prenominal*) using or capable of using intelligent thought: *thinking people.* **4. put on one's thinking cap.** to ponder a matter or problem.

think out *or* **through** *vb.* (*tr., adv.*) to consider carefully and rationally in order to reach a conclusion.

think o·ver *vb.* (*tr., adv.*) to ponder or consider: *to think over a problem.*

think-tank *n. Informal.* a group of specialists organized by a business enterprise, governmental body, etc., and commissioned to undertake intensive study and research into specified problems.

think up *vb.* (*tr., adv.*) to invent or devise: *to think up a plan.*

thin·ner ('θɪnə) *n.* a solvent, such as turpentine, added to paint or varnish to dilute it, reduce its opacity or viscosity, or increase its penetration into the ground.

thin-skinned *adj.* sensitive to criticism or hints; easily upset or affected.

thi·o- *or before a vowel* **thi-** *combining form.* indicating that a chemical compound contains sulphur, esp. denoting that a compound is derived from a specified compound by the replacement of an oxygen atom with a sulphur atom: *thiol; thiosulphate.* [from Greek *theion* sulphur]

thi·o·al·co·hol (ˌθaɪəʊ'ælkəˌhɒl) *n.* another name for a **thiol.**

thi·o·car·ba·mide (ˌθaɪəʊ'kɑːbəˌmaɪd) *n.* another name for **thiourea.**

thi·o·cy·a·nate (ˌθaɪəʊ'saɪəˌneɪt) *n.* any salt or ester of thiocyanic acid.

thi·o·cy·an·ic ac·id (ˌθaɪəʊsaɪ'ænɪk) *n.* an unstable acid known in the form of thiocyanate salts. Formula: HSCN.

thi·o·e·ther (ˌθaɪəʊ'iːθə) *n.* any of a class of organic compounds in which a sulphur atom is bound to two hydrocarbon groups.

thi·o·fu·ran (ˌθaɪəʊ'fjʊəræn) *n.* another name for **thiophene.** [C20: from THIO- + FURAN]

thi·ol ('θaɪɒl) *n.* any of a class of sulphur-containing organic compounds with the formula RSH, where R is an organic group. Also called (not in technical usage): **mercaptan.**

thi·o·nate ('θaɪəˌneɪt) *n.* any salt or ester of thionic acid.

thi·on·ic (θaɪ'ɒnɪk) *adj.* of, relating to, or containing sulphur.

thi·o·nine ('θaɪəʊˌniːn, -ˌnaɪn) *or* **thi·o·nin** ('θaɪənɪn) *n.* **1.** a crystalline derivative of thiazine used as a violet dye to stain microscope specimens. **2.** any of a class of related dyes. [C19: by shortening, from ERGOTHIONEINE]

thi·o·nyl ('θaɪənɪl) *n.* (*modifier*) of, consisting of, or containing the divalent group SO: *a thionyl group or radical; thionyl chloride.* Also: **sulphinyl.** [C19: *thion-*, from Greek *theion* sulphur + -YL]

thi·o·pen·tone so·di·um (ˌθaɪəʊ'pɛntəʊn) *or* **thi·o·pen·tal so·di·um** *n.* a barbiturate drug used in medicine as an intravenous general anaesthetic. Formula: $C_{11}H_{17}NaN_2O_2S$. Also called: **sodium pentothal.** See also **truth drug.**

thi·o+phen ('θaɪəʊˌfɛn) *or* **thi·o+phene** ('θaɪəʊˌfi:n) *n.* a colourless liquid heterocyclic compound found in the benzene fraction of coal tar and manufactured from butane and sulphur. It has an odour resembling that of benzene and is used as a solvent and in the manufacture of dyes, pharmaceuticals, and resins. Formula: C_4H_4S. Also called: **thiofuran.**

thi·o+sin·a+mine (ˌθaɪəʊ'sɪnəˌmi:n, -sɪ'næmɪn) *n.* a white crystalline bitter-tasting compound with a slight garlic-like odour, occurring in mustard oil and used in organic synthesis; 1-allyl-2-thiourea. Formula: $CH_2{:}CHCH_2NHCSNH_2$. [C19: from THIO- + *sin-* (from Latin *sināpis* mustard) + AMINE]

thi·o+sul+phate (ˌθaɪəʊ'sʌlfeɪt) *n.* any salt of thiosulphuric acid.

thi·o+sul+phur+ic ac·id (ˌθaɪəʊsʌl'fjʊərɪk) *n.* an unstable acid known only in solutions and in the form of its salts. Formula: $H_2S_2O_3$.

thi·o+u·ra+cil (ˌθaɪəʊ'jʊərəsɪl) *n.* a white crystalline water-insoluble substance with an intensely bitter taste, used in medicine to treat hyperthyroidism; 2-thio-4-oxypyrimidine. Formula: $C_4H_4N_2OS$. [from THIO- + *uracil* (URO- + AC(ETIC) + -IL)]

thi·o+u·re·a (ˌθaɪəʊ'jʊərɪə) *n.* a white water-soluble crystalline substance with a bitter taste that forms addition compounds with metal ions and is used in photographic fixing, rubber vulcanization, and the manufacture of synthetic resins. Formula: H_2NCSNH_2.

third (θɜ:d) *adj.* (*usually prenominal*) **1. a.** coming after the second and preceding the fourth in numbering or counting order, position, time, etc.; being the ordinal number of *three:* often written 3rd. **b.** (*as n.*)*: he arrives on the third; the third got a prize.* **2.** rated, graded, or ranked below the second level. **3.** denoting the third from lowest forward ratio of a gearbox in a motor vehicle. ~*n.* **4. a.** one of three equal or nearly equal parts of an object, quantity, etc. **b.** (*as modifier*)*: a third part.* **5.** the fraction equal to one divided by three (1/3). **6.** the forward ratio above second of a gearbox in a motor vehicle. In some vehicles it is the top gear. **7. a.** the interval between one note and another three notes away from it counting inclusively along the diatonic scale. **b.** one of two notes constituting such an interval in relation to the other. See also **interval** (sense 5), **major** (sense 11a), **minor** (sense 4d). **8.** *Brit.* an honours degree of the third and usually the lowest class. Full term: **third class honours degree. 9.** (*pl.*) goods of a standard lower than that of seconds. ~*adv.* **10.** Also: **thirdly.** in the third place. ~ **11.** *sentence connector.* Also: **thirdly.** as the third point: linking what follows with the previous statements as in a speech or argument. [Old English *thirda,* variant of *thridda;* related to Old Frisian *thredda,* Old Saxon *thriddio,* Old High German *drittio,* Old Norse *thrithi,* Latin *tertius*] —'**third+ly** *adv.*

third class *n.* **1.** the class or grade next in value, quality, etc., to the second. ~*adj.* (**third-class** *when prenominal*). **2.** of the class or grade next in value, quality, etc., to the second. **3.** of or denoting the class of accommodation in a hotel, on a ship, etc., next in quality and price to the second: usually the cheapest. **4.** (in the U.S. and Canada) of or relating to a class of mail consisting largely of unsealed printed matter. **5.** *Brit.* See **third** (sense 8). ~*adv.* **6.** by third-class mail, transport, etc.

third de+gree *n. Informal.* torture or bullying, esp. used to extort confessions or information.

third-de·gree burn *n. Pathol.* See **burn**[1] (sense 19).

third di+men+sion *n.* the additional dimension by which a solid object may be distinguished from a two-dimensional drawing or picture of it or from any planar object.

third es+tate *n.* the third order or class in a country or society divided into estates, esp. for representation in a parliament; the commons, townsmen, or middle class.

third eye+lid *n.* another name for **nictitating membrane.**

third house *n. U.S.* a political lobby for a special interest.

Third In+ter+na+tion+al *n.* another name for **Comintern.**

third man *n. Cricket.* a fielding position on the off side near the boundary behind the batsman's wicket.

Third Or+der *n. R.C. Church.* a religious society of laymen affiliated to one of the religious orders and following a mitigated form of religious rule.

third par+ty *n.* **1.** a person who is involved by chance or only incidentally in a legal proceeding, agreement, or other transaction, esp. one against whom a defendant claims indemnity. ~*adj.* **2.** *Insurance.* providing protection against liability caused by accidental injury or death of other persons or damage to their property.

third per+son *n.* a grammatical category of pronouns and verbs used when referring to objects or individuals other than the speaker or his addressee or addressees.

third rail *n.* an extra rail from which an electric train picks up current by means of a sliding collector to feed power to its motors.

third-rate *adj.* not of high quality; mediocre or inferior.

third read+ing *n.* (in a legislative assembly) **1.** *Brit.* the process of discussing the committee's report on a bill. **2.** *U.S.* the final consideration of a bill.

Third Reich *n.* See **Reich**[1] (sense 4).

Third Re+pub+lic *n.* (in France) **1.** the governmental system established after the fall of Napoleon III in the Franco-Prussian War and lasting until the German occupation of 1940. **2.** the period during which this governmental system functioned (1870–1940).

third+stream ('θɜ:dˌstri:m) *adj.* **1.** (of music) combining jazz and classical elements. ~*n.* **2.** such music.

Third World *n.* the countries of Africa, Asia, and Latin America collectively, esp. when viewed as underdeveloped and as neutral in the East-West alignment.

thirl (θɜ:l) *vb.* (*tr.*) *Brit. dialect.* **a.** to bore or drill. **b.** to thrill. [Old English *thyrelian,* from *thyrel* hole; see NOSTRIL]

thirl+age ('θɜ:lɪdʒ) *n. Scot. law.* (formerly) **1.** an obligation imposed upon tenants of certain lands requiring them to have their grain ground at a specified mill. **2.** the fee paid for grinding the grain. [C16: variant of earlier *thrillage,* from *thrill,* Scottish variant of THRALL]

Thirl+mere ('θɜ:lmɪə) *n.* a lake in NW England, in Cumbria in the Lake District: provides part of Manchester's water supply. Length: 6 km (4 miles).

thirst (θɜ:st) *n.* **1.** a craving to drink, accompanied by a feeling of dryness in the mouth and throat. **2.** an eager longing, craving, or yearning: *a thirst for knowledge.* ~*vb.* (*intr.*) **3.** to feel a thirst: *to thirst for a drink; to thirst after righteousness.* [Old English *thyrstan,* from *thurst* thirst; related to Old Norse *thyrsta* to thirst, Old High German *dursten* to thirst, Latin *torrēre* to parch] —'**thirst+er** *n.*

thirst·y ('θɜ:stɪ) *adj.* **thirst·i+er, thirst·i+est. 1.** feeling a desire to drink. **2.** dry; arid: *the thirsty soil.* **3.** (foll. by *for*) feeling an eager desire: *thirsty for information.* **4.** causing thirst: *thirsty work.* —'**thirst·i+ly** *adv.* —'**thirst·i+ness** *n.*

thir+teen ('θɜ:'ti:n) *n.* **1.** the cardinal number that is the sum of ten and three and is a prime number. See also **number** (sense 1). **2.** a numeral 13, XIII, etc., representing this number. **3.** the amount or quantity that is three more than ten; baker's dozen. **4.** something represented by, representing, or consisting of 13 units. ~*determiner.* **5. a.** amounting to thirteen: *thirteen buses.* **b.** (*as pronoun*)*: thirteen of them fell.* [Old English *threotēne;* see THREE, -TEEN]

thir+teenth ('θɜ:'ti:nθ) *adj.* **1.** (*usually prenominal*) **a.** coming after the twelfth in numbering or counting order, position, time, etc.; being the ordinal number of *thirteen:* often written 13th. **b.** (*as n.*)*: Friday the thirteenth.* ~*n.* **2. a.** one of 13 equal or nearly equal parts of something. **b.** (*as modifier*)*: a thirteenth part.* **3.** the fraction equal to one divided by 13 (1/13). **4.** *Music.* **a.** an interval of one octave plus a sixth. See also **interval** (sense 5). **b.** short for **thirteenth chord.**

thir+teenth chord *n.* a chord much used in jazz and pop, consisting of a major or minor triad upon which are superimposed the seventh, ninth, eleventh, and thirteenth above the root. Often shortened to **thirteenth.**

thir+ti+eth ('θɜ:tɪɪθ) *adj.* **1.** (*usually prenominal*) **a.** being the ordinal number of *thirty* in counting order, position, time, etc.: often written 30th. **b.** (*as n.*)*: the thirtieth of the month.* ~*n.* **2. a.** one of 30 approximately equal parts of something. **b.** (*as modifier*)*: a thirtieth part.* **3.** the fraction equal to one divided by 30 (1/30).

thir+ty ('θɜ:tɪ) *n., pl.* **+ties. 1.** the cardinal number that is the product of ten and three. See also **number** (sense 1). **2.** a numeral 30, XXX, etc., representing this number. **3.** (*pl.*) the numbers 30-39, esp. the 30th to the 39th year of a person's life or of a century. **4.** the amount or quantity that is three times as big as ten. **5.** something representing, represented by, or consisting of 30 units. ~*determiner.* **6. a.** amounting to thirty: *thirty trees.* **b.** (*as pronoun*)*: thirty are broken.* [Old English *thrītig;* see THREE, -TY[1]]

Thir·ty-nine Ar+ti·cles *pl. n.* a set of formulas defining the doctrinal position of the Church of England, drawn up in the 16th century, to which the clergy are required to give general consent.

thir·ty-sec·ond note *n.* the usual U.S. name for **demisemiquaver.**

thir·ty-three *n.* a former name for **LP.**

thir·ty-two·mo (ˌθɜ:tɪ'tu:məʊ) *n., pl.* **·mos.** a book size resulting from folding a sheet of paper into 32 leaves or 64 pages. Often written: **32mo, 32°.**

Thir+ty Years' War *n.* a major conflict involving Austria, Denmark, France, Holland, Germany, Spain and Sweden that devastated central Europe, esp. large areas of Germany (1618–48). It began as a war between Protestants and Catholics but was gradually transformed into a struggle to determine whether the German emperor could assert more than nominal authority over his princely vassals.

this (ðɪs) *determiner.* (*used before a singular n.*) **1. a.** used preceding a noun referring to something or someone that is closer: distinct from **that:** *this dress is cheaper than that one; look at this picture.* **b.** (*as pronoun*)*: this is Mary and that is her boy friend; take this.* **2. a.** used preceding a noun that has just been mentioned or is understood: *this plan of yours won't work.* **b.** (*as pronoun*)*: I first saw this on Sunday.* **3. a.** used to refer to something about to be said, read, etc.: *consider this argument.* **b.** (*as pronoun*)*: listen to this.* **4. a.** the present or immediate: *this time you'll know better.* **b.** (*as pronoun*)*: before this, I was mistaken.* **5.** *Informal.* an emphatic form of **a**[1] or **the**[1]: used esp. on relating a story: *I saw this big brown bear.* **6. this and that.** various unspecified and trivial actions, matters, objects, etc. **7. this here.** *U.S., not standard.* an emphatic form of **this** (senses 1–3). **8. with** (*or* **at**) **this.** after this; thereupon. ~*adv.* **9.** used with adjectives and adverbs to specify a precise degree that is about to be mentioned: *go just this fast and you'll be safe.* [Old English *thēs, thēos, this* (masculine, feminine, neuter singular); related to Old Saxon *thit,* Old High German *diz,* Old Norse *thessi*]

This·be ('θɪzbɪ) *n.* See **Pyramus and Thisbe.**

this+tle ('θɪsəl) *n.* **1.** any of numerous plants of the genus

Cirsium, having prickly-edged leaves, pink, purple, yellow, or white dense flower heads, and feathery hairs on the seeds: family *Compositae* (composites). **2.** any of various similar or related plants, such as the star thistle. [Old English *thīstel*, related to Old Saxon, Old High German *thīstil*, Old Norse *thīstill*] —**'this+tly** *adv.*

this·tle+down ('θɪsᵊl,daʊn) *n.* **1.** the mass of feathery plumed seeds produced by a thistle. **2.** anything resembling this.

thith+er ('ðɪðə) *or* **thith+er+ward** *adv. Obsolete.* to or towards that place; in that direction. [Old English *thider*, variant of *thæder*, influenced by *hider* HITHER; related to Old Norse *thathra* there]

thith·er+to (,ðɪðə'tuː, 'ðɪðə,tuː) *adv.* until that time.

thix·o+trop+ic (,θɪksə'trɒpɪk) *adj.* (of fluids and gels) having a reduced viscosity when stress is applied, as when stirred: *thixotropic paints.* —**thix+ot+ro+py** (θɪk'sɒtrəpɪ) *n.*

tho *or* **tho'** (ðəʊ) *U.S. or poetic.* a variant spelling of **though.**

thole[1] (θəʊl) *or* **thole+pin** ('θəʊl,pɪn) *n.* a wooden pin or one of a pair, set upright in the gunwales of a rowing boat to serve as a fulcrum in rowing. [Old English *tholl*, related to Middle Low German *dolle*, Norwegian *toll*, Icelandic *thollr*]

thole[2] (θəʊl) *vb.* **1.** (*tr.*) *Northern Brit. dialect.* to put up with; bear. **2.** an archaic word for **suffer.** [Old English *tholian;* related to Old Saxon, Old High German *tholōn*, Old Norse *thola* to endure, Latin *tollere* to bear up]

tho+los ('θəʊlɒs) *n., pl.* **+loi** (-lɔɪ). a dry-stone beehive-shaped tomb associated with the Mycenaean culture of Greece in the 16th to the 12th century B.C. [C17: from Greek]

Thom·as ('tɒməs) *n.* **1.** Also called: **doubting Thomas.** one of the 12 apostles, who refused to believe in Christ's resurrection until he had seen his wounds (John 20:24–29). **2.** (*French* tɔ'mɑ). **Am·broise** (ɑ̃'brwaːz). 1811–96, French composer of light operas, including *Mignon* (1866). **3. Dyl·an (Marlais)** ('dɪlən). 1914–53, Welsh poet and essayist. His works include the prose *Portrait of the Artist as a Young Dog* (1940), the verse collection *Deaths and Entrances* (1946), and his play for voices *Under Milk Wood* (1954). **4. (Philip) Ed·ward,** pen name *Edward Eastaway.* 1878–1917, English nature poet and critic.

Thom·as à Beck·et *n.* **Saint.** See (Saint Thomas à) **Becket.**

Thom·as à Kem·pis *n.* See (Thomas à) **Kempis.**

Thom·as of Er+cel+doune ('ɜːsəl,duːn) *n.* called *Thomas the Rhymer.* ?1220–?97, Scottish seer and poet; reputed author of a poem on the Tristan legend.

Thom·as of Wood+stock *n.* 1355–97, youngest son of Edward III, who led opposition to his nephew Richard II (1386–89); arrested in 1397, he died in prison.

Tho+mism ('təʊmɪzəm) *n.* the comprehensive system of philosophy and theology developed by Saint Thomas Aquinas in the 13th century and since taught and maintained by his followers, esp. in the Dominican order. —**'Tho+mist** *n., adj.* —**Tho+'mis+tic** *or* **Tho+'mis+ti+cal** *adj.*

Thomp·son ('tɒmpsən, 'tɒmsən) *n.* **1. Ben·ja·min,** Count Rumford. 1753–1814, Anglo-American physicist, noted for his work on the nature of heat. **2. Fran·cis.** 1859–1907, English poet, best known for the mystical poem *The Hound of Heaven* (1893).

Thomp·son sub-ma·chine-gun *n. Trademark.* a .45 calibre sub-machine-gun. Also called: **Tommy gun.**

Thom·son ('tɒmsən) *n.* **1.** Sir **George Pag·et,** son of Joseph John Thomson. 1892–1975, English physicist, who discovered (1927) the diffraction of electrons by crystals: shared the Nobel prize for physics (1937). **2. James.** 1700–48, Scottish poet. He anticipated the romantics' feeling for nature in *The Seasons* (1726–30). **3. James,** pen name *B.V.* 1834–82, English poet, noted esp. for *The City of Dreadful Night* (1874), reflecting man's isolation and despair. **4.** Sir **Jo·seph John.** 1856–1940, English physicist. He discovered the electron (1897) and his work on the nature of positive rays led to the discovery of isotopes: Nobel prize for physics 1906. **5. Roy,** 1st Baron Thomson of Fleet. 1894–1976, British newspaper proprietor, born in Canada. **6.** Sir **Wil·liam.** See (1st Baron) **Kelvin.**

Thom·son ef+fect *n. Physics.* the phenomenon in which a temperature gradient along a metallic wire or strip causes an electric potential gradient to form along its length.

Thon+bu+ri (,tɒnbʊ'riː) *n.* a city in central Thailand, on the Chao Phraya River: the second largest city in Thailand and a suburb of Bangkok; the national capital (1767–82). Pop.: 627 989 (1970)

thong (θɒŋ) *n.* **1.** a thin strip of leather or other material, such as one used for lashing things together. **2.** a whip or whiplash, esp. one made of leather. **3.** *Chiefly U.S. and Austral.* the usual name for **flip-flop** (sense 5). [Old English *thwang;* related to Old High German *dwang* reins, Old Norse *thvengr* strap]

Thor (θɔː) *n. Norse myth.* the god of thunder, depicted as wielding a hammer, emblematic of the thunderbolt. [Old English *Thōr*, from Old Norse *thōrr* THUNDER]

tho+rac+ic (θɔː'ræsɪk) *or* **tho+ra+cal** ('θɔːrəkᵊl) *adj.* of, near, or relating to the thorax.

tho+rac+ic duct *n.* the major duct of the lymphatic system, beginning below the diaphragm and ascending in front of the spinal column to the base of the neck.

tho·ra·co- *or before a vowel* **tho·rac-** *combining form.* thorax: *thoracotomy.*

tho+ra+co+plas+ty ('θɔːrəkəʊ,plæstɪ) *n., pl.* **+ties. 1.** plastic surgery of the thorax. **2.** surgical removal of several ribs or a part of them to permit the collapse of a diseased lung, used in cases of pulmonary tuberculosis and bronchiectasis.

thor·a+cot·o·my (,θɔːrə'kɒtəmɪ) *n., pl.* **+mies.** surgical incision into the chest wall.

thor+ax ('θɔːræks) *n., pl.* **thor+ax·es** *or* **tho+ra+ces** ('θɔːrə,siːz, θɔː'reɪsiːz). **1.** the part of the human body enclosed by the ribs. **2.** the corresponding part in other vertebrates. **3.** the part of an insect's body between the head and abdomen, which bears the wings and legs. [C16: via Latin from Greek *thōrax* breastplate, chest]

Tho·reau ('θɔːrəʊ, θɔː'rəʊ) *n.* **Hen·ry Da·vid.** 1817–62, U.S. writer, noted esp. for *Walden, or Life in the Woods* (1854), an account of his experiment in living in solitude. A powerful social critic, his essay *Civil Disobedience* (1849) influenced such dissenters as Gandhi.

tho+ri·a ('θɔːrɪə) *n.* another name for **thorium dioxide.** [C19: THORIUM + *-a*, on the model of *magnesia*]

tho+ri·a+nite ('θɔːrɪə,naɪt) *n.* a rare black mineral consisting of thorium and uranium oxides. Formula: $ThO_2.U_3O_8$.

tho+rite ('θɔːraɪt) *n.* an orange-yellow, brownish, or black radioactive mineral consisting of thorium silicate in tetragonal crystalline form. It occurs in coarse granite and is a source of thorium. Formula: $ThSiO_4$.

tho+ri·um ('θɔːrɪəm) *n.* a soft ductile silvery-white metallic element. It is radioactive and occurs in thorite and monazite: used in gas mantles, magnesium alloys, electronic equipment, and as a nuclear power source. Symbol: Th; atomic no.: 90; atomic wt.: 232.04; half-life of most stable isotope, ^{232}Th: 1.41×10^{10} years; valency: 4; relative density: 11.72; melting pt.: 1750°C; boiling pt.: 3800°C (approx.). [C19: New Latin, from THOR + -IUM] —**'tho+ric** *adj.*

tho+ri·um di+ox+ide *n.* a heavy insoluble white powder used in incandescent mantles. Formula: ThO_2. Also called: **thoria.**

tho+ri·um se+ries *n.* a radioactive series that starts with thorium-232 and ends with lead-208.

thorn (θɔːn) *n.* **1.** a sharp pointed woody extension of a stem or leaf. Compare **prickle** (sense 1). **2. a.** any of various trees or shrubs having thorns, esp. the hawthorn. **b.** the wood of any of these plants. **3.** a Germanic character of runic origin (þ) used in Old and Modern Icelandic to represent the voiceless dental fricative sound of *th*, as in *thin, bath.* Its use in phonetics for the same purpose is now obsolete. See **theta. 4.** this same character as used in Old and Middle English as an alternative to *edh*, but indistinguishable from it in function or sound. Compare **edh. 5.** *Zoology.* any of various sharp spiny parts. **6.** a source of irritation (esp. in the phrases **a thorn in one's side** *or* **flesh**). [Old English; related to Old High German *dorn*, Old Norse *thorn*] —**'thorn+less** *adj.*

Thorn (toːrn) *n.* the German name for **Toruń.**

thorn ap+ple *n.* **1.** a poisonous solanaceous plant, *Datura stramonium*, of the N hemisphere, having white funnel-shaped flowers and spiny capsule fruits. U.S. name: **jimson weed.** See also **stramonium. 2.** any other plant of the genus *Datura*. **3.** the fruit of certain types of hawthorn.

thorn+back ('θɔːn,bæk) *n.* **1.** a European ray, *Raja clavata*, having a row of spines along the back and tail. **2.** a similar fish, *Platyrhinoidis triseriata*, of the Pacific Ocean.

thorn+bill ('θɔːn,bɪl) *n.* **1.** any of various South American hummingbirds of the genera *Chalcostigma, Ramphomicron*, etc., having a thornlike bill. **2.** Also called: **thornbill warbler.** any of various Australasian wrens of the genus *Acanthiza* and related genera: family *Muscicapidae*. **3.** any of various other birds with thornlike bills.

Thorn·dike ('θɔːn,daɪk) *n.* Dame **Syb·il.** 1882–1976, English actress.

thorn·y ('θɔːnɪ) *adj.* **thorn·i+er, thorn·i+est. 1.** bearing or covered with thorns. **2.** difficult or unpleasant: *a thorny problem.* **3.** sharp. —**'thorn·i+ly** *adv.* —**'thorn·i+ness** *n.*

tho+ron ('θɔːrɒn) *n.* a radioisotope of radon that is a decay product of thorium. Symbol: Tn or ^{220}Rn; atomic no.: 86; half-life: 54.5s. [C20: from THORIUM + -ON]

thor+ough ('θʌrə) *adj.* **1.** carried out completely and carefully: *a thorough search.* **2.** (*prenominal*) utter: *a thorough bore.* **3.** painstakingly careful: *our accountant is thorough.* [Old English *thurh;* related to Old Frisian *thruch*, Old Saxon *thuru*, Old High German *duruh;* see THROUGH] —**'thor+ough+ly** *adv.* —**'thor+ough+ness** *n.*

Thor+ough ('θʌrə) *n.* thoroughgoing policy, as adopted in England by Strafford and Laud during the reign of Charles I.

thor+ough bass (beɪs) *n.* **a.** Also called: **basso continuo, continuo.** (esp. during the baroque period) a bass part underlying a piece of concerted music. It is played on a keyboard instrument, usually supported by a cello, viola da gamba, etc. See also **figured bass. b.** (*as adj.*): *a thorough-bass part; thorough-bass technique.*

thor+ough brace *n. Chiefly U.S.* either of two strong leather straps upon which the body of certain types of carriage is supported. —**'thor·ough-,braced** *adj.*

thor·ough+bred ('θʌrə,brɛd) *adj.* **1.** purebred. ~*n.* **2.** a pedigree animal; purebred. **3.** a person regarded as being of good breeding.

Thor·ough+bred ('θʌrə,brɛd) *n.* a British breed of horse the ancestry of which can be traced to English mares and Arab sires; most often used as a racehorse.

thor·ough+fare ('θʌrə,fɛə) *n.* **1.** a road from one place to another, esp. a main road. **2.** way through, access, or passage: *no thoroughfare.*

thor·ough+go·ing ('θʌrə,gəʊɪŋ) *adj.* **1.** extremely thorough. **2.** (*usually prenominal*) absolute; complete: *thoroughgoing incompetence.* —**'thor·ough+,go·ing·ness** *n.*

thor·ough+paced ('θʌrə,peɪst) *adj.* **1.** (of a horse) showing performing ability in all paces. **2.** thoroughgoing.

thor·ough+pin ('θʌrə,pɪn) *n.* an inflammation and swelling on both sides of the hock joint of a horse affecting the sheath of the deep flexor tendon.

thor·ough+wort ('θʌrə,wɜ:t) *n.* another name for **feverwort.**

thorp *or* **thorpe** (θɔ:p) *n. Obsolete except in place names.* a small village. [Old English; related to Old Norse *thorp* village, Old High German *dorf,* Gothic *thaurp*]

Thorpe (θɔ:p) *n.* **Jer·e·my.** born 1929, British politician; leader of the Liberal party (1967–76).

Thors+havn (*Danish* 'tɔ:rshawən) *n.* the capital of the Faeroe Islands, a port on the northernmost island. Pop.: 10 726 (1970).

Thor·vald·sen *or* **Thor·wald·sen** (*Danish* 'tɔrvalsən) *n.* **Ber·tel** ('bertəl). 1770–1884, Danish neoclassical sculptor.

those (ðəuz) *determiner.* the form of **that** used before a plural noun. [Old English *thās,* plural of THIS]

Thoth (θəuθ, təut) *n.* (in Egyptian mythology) a moon deity, scribe of the gods and protector of learning and the arts.

thou[1] (ðau) *pron.* (*subjective*) **1.** *Archaic or Brit. dialect.* refers to the person addressed: used mainly in familiar address or to a younger person or inferior. **2.** (*usually cap.*) refers to God when addressed in prayer, etc. [Old English *thū;* related to Old Saxon *thū,* Old High German *du,* Old Norse *thū,* Latin *tū,* Doric Greek *tu*]

thou[2] (θau) *n., pl.* **thous** *or* **thou. 1.** one thousandth of an inch. 1 thou is equal to 0.0254 millimetre. **2.** *Informal.* short for thousand.

though (ðəu) *conj.* (*subordinating*) **1.** (sometimes preceded by *even*) despite the fact that: *though he tries hard, he always fails; poor though she is, her life is happy.* **2. as though.** as if: *he looked as though he'd seen a ghost.* ~*adv.* **3.** nevertheless; however: *he can't dance; he sings well, though.* [Old English *theah;* related to Old Frisian *thāch,* Old Saxon, Old High German *thōh* Old Norse *thō*]

thought (θɔ:t) *vb.* **1.** the past tense or past participle of **think.** ~*n.* **2.** the act or process of thinking; deliberation, meditation, or reflection. **3.** a concept, opinion, or idea. **4.** philosophical or intellectual ideas typical of a particular time or place: *German thought in the 19th century.* **5.** application of mental attention; consideration: *he gave the matter some thought.* **6.** purpose or intention: *I have no thought of giving up.* **7.** expectation: *no thought of reward.* **8.** a small amount; trifle: *you could be a thought more enthusiastic.* **9.** kindness or regard: *he has no thought for his widowed mother.* [Old English *thōht;* related to Old Frisian *thochta,* Old Saxon, Old High German *githācht*]

thought dis+or+der *n. Psychiatry.* a cognitive disorder in which the patient's thoughts or conversations are characterized by irrationality or sudden changes of subject.

thought+ful ('θɔ:tful) *adj.* **1.** considerate in the treatment of other people. **2.** showing careful thought. **3.** pensive; reflective. —**'thought+ful+ly** *adv.* —**'thought+ful+ness** *n.*

thought+less ('θɔ:tlɪs) *adj.* **1.** inconsiderate: *a thoughtless remark.* **2.** having or showing lack of thought: *a thoughtless essay.* **3.** unable to think; not having the power of thought. —**'thought+less+ly** *adv.* —**'thought+less+ness** *n.*

thought-out *adj.* conceived and developed by careful thought: *a well thought-out scheme.*

thought trans+fer+ence *n. Psychol.* another name for **telepathy.**

thou+sand ('θauzənd) *n.* **1.** the cardinal number that is the product of 10 and 100. See also **number** (sense 1). **2.** a numeral 1000, 10^3, M, etc., representing this number. **3.** (*often pl.*) a very large but unspecified number, amount, or quantity: *they are thousands of miles away.* **4.** (*pl.*) the numbers 2000–9999: *the price of the picture was in the thousands.* **5.** the amount or quantity that is one hundred times greater than ten. **6.** something represented by, representing, or consisting of 1000 units. **7.** *Maths.* the position containing a digit representing that number followed by three zeros: *in 4760, 4 is in the thousand's place.* ~*determiner.* **8. a.** amounting to a thousand: *a thousand ships.* **b.** (*as pronoun*): *a thousand is hardly enough.* **9.** amounting to 1000 times a particular scientific unit. Related prefix: **kilo-.** ~Related adj.: **millenary.** [Old English *thūsend;* related to Old Saxon *thūsind,* Old High German *thūsunt,* Old Norse *thūsund*]

Thou+sand and One Nights *n.* See **Arabian Nights' Entertainments.**

Thou+sand Guin·eas *n.,* usually written **1,000 Guin·eas.** an annual horse race, restricted to fillies, run at Newmarket since 1814. Also called: **One Thousand Guineas.**

Thou+sand Is+land dres+sing *n.* a salad dressing made from mayonnaise with ketchup, chopped gherkins, etc.

Thou+sand Is+lands *pl. n.* a group of about 1500 islands on the border between the U.S. and Canada, in the upper St. Lawrence River: administratively divided between the U.S. and Canada. —**Thou+sand Is+land** *adj.*

thou+sandth ('θauzənθ) *adj.* **1.** (*usually prenominal*) **a.** being the ordinal number of 1000 in numbering or counting order, position, time, etc. **b.** (*as n.*): *the thousandth in succession.* ~*n.* **2. a.** one of 1000 approximately equal parts of something. **b.** (*as modifier*): *a thousandth part.* **3.** one of 1000 equal divisions of a particular scientific quantity. Related prefix: **milli-:** *millivolt.* **4.** the fraction equal to one divided by 1000 (1/1000).

Thrace (θreɪs) *n.* **1.** an ancient country in the E Balkan Peninsula: successively under the Persians, Macedonians, and Romans. **2.** a region of SE Europe, corresponding to the S part of the ancient country: divided by the Maritsa River into **Western Thrace** (Greece) and **Eastern Thrace** (Turkey).

Thra+ci·an ('θreɪʃɪən) *n.* **1.** a member of an ancient Indo-European people who lived in the SE corner of the Balkan Peninsula. **2.** the ancient language spoken by this people, belonging to the Thraco-Phrygian branch of the Indo-European family: extinct by the early Middle Ages. ~*adj.* **3.** of or relating to Thrace, its inhabitants, or the extinct Thracian language.

Thra·co-Phryg·i·an (,θreɪkəu'frɪdʒɪən) *n.* **1.** a branch of the Indo-European family of languages, all members of which are extinct except for Armenian. ~*adj.* **2.** relating to or belonging to this group of languages. [from *Thraco-,* from Greek *Thraikē* Thrace; see PHRYGIAN]

thrall (θrɔ:l) *n.* **1.** Also: **thrall+dom** ('θrɔ:ldəm). the state or condition of being in the power of another person. **2.** a person who is in such a state. **3.** a person totally subject to some need, desire, appetite, etc. ~*vb.* **4.** (*tr.*) to enslave or dominate. [Old English *thrǣl* slave, from Old Norse *thrǣll*]

thrash (θræʃ) *vb.* **1.** (*tr.*) to beat soundly, as with a whip or stick. **2.** (*tr.*) to defeat totally; overwhelm. **3.** (*intr.*) to beat or plunge about in a wild manner. **4.** (*intr.*) to move the legs up and down in the water, as in certain swimming strokes. **5.** to sail (a boat) against the wind or tide or (of a boat) to sail in this way. **6.** another word for **thresh.** ~*n.* **7.** the act of thrashing; blow; beating. [Old English *threscan;* related to Old High German *dreskan,* Old Norse *thriskja*]

thrash+er[1] ('θræʃə) *n.* another name for **thresher** (the shark).

thrash+er[2] (θræʃə) *n.* any of various brown thrushlike American songbirds of the genus *Toxostoma* and related genera, having a long downward-curving bill and long tail: family *Mimidae* (mockingbirds).

thrash+ing ('θræʃɪŋ) *n.* a physical assault; flogging.

thrash out *vb.* (*tr., adv.*) to discuss fully or vehemently, esp. in order to come to a solution or agreement.

thra+son+i+cal (θrə'sɒnɪkəl) *adj. Rare.* bragging; boastful. [C16: from Latin *Thrasō* name of boastful soldier in *Eunuchus,* a play by Terence, from Greek *Thrasōn,* from *thrasus* forceful] —**thra+'son+i+cal+ly** *adv.*

thrave (θreɪv) *n. Northern Brit. dialect.* twenty-four sheaves of corn. [Old English *threfe,* of Scandinavian origin]

thrawn (θrɔ:n) *adj. Northern Brit. dialect.* **1.** crooked or twisted. **2.** stubborn. [Northern English dialect, variant of THROWN, from Old English *thrāwan* to twist about, THROW]

thread (θrɛd) *n.* **1.** a fine strand, filament or fibre of some material. **2.** a fine cord of twisted filaments, esp. of cotton, used in sewing, weaving, etc. **3.** any of the filaments of which a spider's web is made. **4.** any fine line, stream, mark, or piece: *from the air, the path was a thread of white.* **5.** a helical groove in a cylindrical hole (**female thread**), formed by a tap or lathe tool, or a helical ridge on a cylindrical bar, rod, shank, etc. (**male thread**), formed by a die or lathe tool. **6.** a very thin seam of coal or vein of ore. **7.** something acting as the continuous link or theme of a whole: *the thread of the story.* **8.** the course of an individual's life believed in Greek mythology to be spun, measured, and cut by the Fates. ~*vb.* **9.** (*tr.*) to pass (thread, film, magnetic tape, etc.) through (something): *to thread a needle; to thread cotton through a needle.* **10.** (*tr.*) to string on a thread: *she threaded the beads.* **11.** to make (one's way) through or over (something). **12.** (*tr.*) to produce a screw thread by cutting, rolling, tapping, or grinding. **13.** (*tr.*) to pervade: *hysteria threaded his account.* **14.** (of boiling syrup) to form a fine thread when poured from a spoon. [Old English *thrǣd;* related to Old Frisian *thrēd,* Old High German *drāt,* Old Norse *thrāthr* thread] —**'thread+er** *n.* —**'thread+less** *adj.* —**'thread+,like** *adj.*

thread+bare ('θrɛd,bɛə) *adj.* **1.** (of cloth, clothing, etc.) having the nap worn off so that the threads are exposed; worn out. **2.** meagre or poor: *a threadbare existence.* **3.** hackneyed: *a threadbare argument.* **4.** wearing threadbare clothes; shabby. —**'thread+,bare+ness** *n.*

thread+fin ('θrɛd,fɪn) *n., pl.* **+fin** *or* **+fins.** any spiny-finned tropical marine fish of the family *Polynemidae,* having pectoral fins consisting partly of long threadlike rays.

thread mark *n.* a mark put into paper money to prevent counterfeiting, consisting of a pattern of silk fibres.

Thread+nee·dle Street (,θrɛd'ni:dəl, 'θrɛd,ni:dəl) *n.* a street in the City of London famous for its banks, including the Bank of England, known as **The Old Lady of Threadneedle Street.**

thread+worm ('θrɛd,wɜ:m) *n.* any of various nematodes, esp. the pinworm.

thread·y ('θrɛdɪ) *adj.* **thread·i·er, thread·i·est. 1.** of, relating to, or resembling a thread or threads. **2.** *Med.* (of the pulse) barely perceptible; weak; fine. **3.** sounding thin, weak, or reedy: *a thready tenor.* —**'thread·i·ness** *n.*

threap *or* **threep** (θri:p) *vb.* (*tr.*) *Northern Brit. dialect.* **1.** to scold. **2.** to contradict. [Old English *thrēapian* to blame; related to Old Frisian *thrūwa,* Old High German *threwen,* Old Norse *threa*] —**'threap+er** *or* **'threep+er** *n.*

threat (θrɛt) *n.* **1.** a declaration of the intention to inflict harm, pain, or misery. **2.** an indication of imminent harm, danger, or pain. **3.** a person or thing that is regarded as dangerous or likely to inflict pain or misery. ~*vb.* **4.** an archaic word for **threaten.** [Old English; related to Old Norse *thraut,* Middle Low German *drōt*]

threat+en ('θrɛtən) *vb.* **1.** (*tr.*) to be a threat to. **2.** to be a menacing indication of (something); portend: *dark clouds threatened rain.* **3.** (when *tr., may take a clause as object*) to express a threat to (a person or people). —**'threat+en+er** *n.* —**'threat+en+ing+ly** *adv.*

three (θri:) *n.* **1.** the cardinal number that is the sum of two and one and is a prime number. See also **number** (sense 1). **2.** a numeral 3, III, (iii), representing this number. **3.** the amount or quantity that is one greater than two. **4.** something representing, represented by, or consisting of three units such as a playing card with three symbols on it. **5.** Also called: **three o'clock.** three hours after noon or midnight. ~*determiner.* **6. a.** amounting to three: *three ships.* **b.** (*as pronoun*): *three were killed.* ~Related adjs.: **ternary, tertiary, treble, triple.** Related prefixes: **tri-, ter-.** [Old English *thrēo;* related to Old Norse *thrīr,* Old High German *drī,* Latin *trēs,* Greek *treis*]

three-card trick *n.* a game in which players bet on which of three inverted playing cards is the queen.

three-col·our *adj.* of, relating to, or comprising a colour print or a photomechanical process in which a picture is reproduced by superimposing three prints from half-tone plates in inks corresponding to the three primary colours.

three-D *or* **3-D** *n.* a three-dimensional effect.

three-day mea+sles *n. Pathol.* an informal name for **rubella.**

three-deck·er *n.* **1. a.** anything having three levels or layers. **b.** (*as modifier*): *a three-decker sandwich.* **2.** a warship with guns on three decks.

three-di·men·sion+al, three-D, *or* **3-D** *adj.* **1.** of, having, or relating to three dimensions: *three-dimensional space.* **2.** (of a film, transparency, etc.) simulating the effect of depth by presenting slightly different views of a scene to each eye. **3.** having volume. **4.** lifelike or real.

three+fold ('θriː,fəʊld) *adj.* **1.** equal to or having three times as many or as much; triple: *a threefold decrease.* **2.** composed of three parts: *a threefold purpose.* ~*adv.* **3.** by or up to three times as many or as much.

three-four time *n. Music.* a form of simple triple time in which there are three crotchet beats to the bar, indicated by the time signature $\frac{3}{4}$. Often shortened to **three-four.** Also called (esp. U.S.): **three-quarter time.**

three-gait·ed *adj. Chiefly U.S.* (of a horse) having the three usual paces, the walk, trot, and canter.

three-leg·ged race *n.* a race in which pairs of competitors run with their adjacent legs tied together.

three-mile lim+it *n. International law.* the range of a nation's territorial waters, extending to three nautical miles from shore.

three+pen+ny bit *or* **thru+pen+ny bit** ('θrʌpnɪ, -ənɪ, 'θrɛp-) *n.* a twelve-sided British coin of nickel-brass, valued at three old pence, obsolete since 1971.

three-phase *adj.* (of an electrical system, circuit, or device) having, generating, or using three alternating voltages of the same frequency, displaced in phase by 120°.

three-piece *adj.* **1.** having three pieces, esp. (of a suit, suite, etc.) consisting of three matching parts. ~*n.* **2.** a three-piece suite, suit, etc.

three-ply *adj.* **1.** having three layers or thicknesses. **2. a.** (of knitting wool, etc.) three-stranded. **b.** (*as n.*): *the sweater was knitted in three-ply.*

three-point land+ing *n.* **1.** an aircraft landing in which the two main wheels and the nose or tail wheel all touch the ground simultaneously. **2.** a successful conclusion.

three-point turn *n.* a turn reversing the direction of motion of a motor vehicle using forward and reverse gears.

three-quar·ter *adj.* **1.** being three quarters of something: *a three-quarter turn.* **2.** being of three quarters the normal length: *a three-quarter coat.* ~*n.* **3.** *Rugby.* **a.** any of the four players between the full back and the forwards. **b.** this position. **c.** (*as modifier*): *three-quarter play.*

three-quar·ter bind+ing *n.* a bookbinding style in which the spine and much of the sides are in a different material from the rest of the covers.

three-ring cir+cus *n. U.S.* **1.** a circus with three rings in which separate performances are carried on simultaneously. **2.** a situation of confusion, characterized by a bewildering variety of events or activities.

Three Riv+ers *n.* the English name for **Trois Rivières.**

three Rs *n.* **the.** the three skills regarded as the fundamentals of education; reading, writing, and arithmetic. [from the humorous spelling *reading, 'riting,* and *'rithmetic*]

three+score ('θriː'skɔː) *determiner.* an archaic word for **sixty.**

three-six·ty *n., pl.* **·ties.** *Skateboarding.* a manoeuvre in which the rider spins the board a full turn. [C20: short for *360 degrees*]

three+some ('θriːsəm) *n.* **1.** a group of three. **2.** *Golf.* a match in which a single player playing his own ball competes against two others playing alternate strokes on the same ball. **3.** any game, etc., for three people. **4.** (*modifier*) performed by three: *a threesome game.*

three-square *adj.* having a cross section that is an equilateral triangle: *a three-square file.*

three-wheel·er *n.* a light car that has three wheels.

threm+ma+tol+o·gy (,θrɛmə'tɒlədʒɪ) *n.* the science of breeding domesticated animals and plants. [C19: from Greek *thremma* nursling + -LOGY]

thren·o·dy ('θrɛnədɪ, 'θriː-) *or* **thre+node** ('θriːnəʊd, 'θrɛn-) *n., pl.* **thren·o·dies** *or* **thre+nodes.** an ode, song, or speech of lamentation, esp. for the dead. [C17: from Greek *thrēnōidia,* from *thrēnos* dirge + *ōidē* song] —**thre+no·di·al** (θrɪ'nəʊdɪəl) *or* **thre+nod+ic** (θrɪ'nɒdɪk) *adj.* —**thren·o·dist** ('θrɛnədɪst, 'θriː-) *n.*

thre·o+nine ('θriːə,niːn, -nɪn) *n.* an amino acid, essential to man, that occurs in the hydrolysates of certain proteins; 2-amino-3-hydroxybutyric acid. Formula: $CH_3CH(OH)CH(NH_2)COOH$. [C20: *threon-,* probably from Greek *eruthron,* from *eruthros* red (see ERYTHRO-) + -INE[2]]

thresh (θrɛʃ) *vb.* **1.** to beat or rub stalks of ripe corn or a similar crop either with a hand implement or a machine to separate the grain from the husks and straw. **2.** (*tr.*) to beat or strike. **3.** (*intr.*; often foll. by *about*) to toss and turn; thrash. ~*n.* **4.** the act of threshing. [Old English *threscan;* related to Gothic *thriskan,* Old Norse *thriskja;* see THRASH] —**'thresh+er** *n.*

thresh+er ('θrɛʃə) *n.* **1.** short for **threshing machine.** **2.** Also called: **thrasher, thresher shark.** any of various large sharks of the genus *Alopias,* esp. *A. vulpinus,* occurring in tropical and temperate seas: family *Alopiidae.* They have a very long whiplike tail with which they are thought to round up the small fish on which they feed.

thresh+ing ma+chine *n.* a machine for threshing crops.

thresh+old ('θrɛʃəʊld, 'θrɛʃ,həʊld) *n.* **1.** Also called: **doorsill.** a sill, esp. one made of stone or hardwood, placed at a doorway. **2.** any doorway or entrance. **3.** the starting point of an experience, event, or venture: *on the threshold of manhood.* **4.** *Psychol.* the strength at which a stimulus is just perceived: *the threshold of pain.* **5. a.** the minimum intensity or value of a signal, etc., that will produce a response or specified effect: *a frequency threshold.* **b.** (*as modifier*): *a threshold current.* **6.** (*modifier*) designating or relating to a pay agreement, clause, etc., that raises wages to compensate for increases in the cost of living. ~Related adj.: **liminal.** [Old English *therscold;* related to Old Norse *threskoldr,* Old High German *driscubli,* Old Swedish *thriskuldi*]

thresh out *vb.* another term for **thrash out.**

threw (θruː) *vb.* the past tense of **throw.**

thrice (θraɪs) *adv.* **1.** three times. **2.** in threefold degree. **3.** *Archaic.* greatly. [Old English *thrīwa, thrīga;* see THREE]

thrift (θrɪft) *n.* **1.** wisdom and caution in the management of money. **2.** Also called: **sea pink.** any of numerous perennial plumbaginaceous low-growing plants of the genus *Armeria,* esp. *A. maritima,* of Europe, W Asia, and North America, having narrow leaves and round heads of pink or white flowers. **3.** *Rare.* vigorous thriving or growth, as of a plant. **4.** an obsolete word for **prosperity.** [C13: from Old Norse: success; see THRIVE] —**'thrift+less** *adj.* —**'thrift+less+ly** *adv.* —**'thrift+less+ness** *n.*

thrift·y ('θrɪftɪ) *adj.* **thrift·i·er, thrift·i·est.** **1.** showing thrift; economical or frugal. **2.** *Rare.* thriving or prospering. —**'thrift·i+ly** *adv.* —**'thrift·i+ness** *n.*

thrill (θrɪl) *n.* **1.** a sudden sensation of excitement and pleasure: *seeing his book for sale gave him a thrill.* **2.** a situation producing such a sensation: *it was a thrill to see Rome for the first time.* **3.** a trembling sensation caused by fear or emotional shock. **4.** *Pathol.* an abnormal slight tremor associated with a heart or vascular murmur, felt on palpation. ~*vb.* **5.** to feel or cause to feel a thrill. **6.** to tremble or cause to tremble; vibrate or quiver. [Old English *thȳrlian* to pierce, from *thyrel* hole; see NOSTRIL, THROUGH]

thrill+er ('θrɪlə) *n.* **1.** a book, film, play, etc., depicting crime, mystery, or espionage in an atmosphere of excitement and suspense. **2.** a person or thing that thrills.

thrill+ing ('θrɪlɪŋ) *adj.* **1.** very exciting or stimulating. **2.** vibrating or trembling. —**'thrill+ing+ly** *adv.*

thrips (θrɪps) *n., pl.* **thrips.** any of various small slender-bodied insects of the order *Thysanoptera,* typically having piercing mouthparts and narrow feathery wings and feeding on plant sap. Some species are serious plant pests. [C18: via New Latin from Greek: woodworm]

thrive (θraɪv) *vb.* **thrives, thriv+ing; thrived** *or* **throve; thrived** *or* **thriv+en** ('θrɪvᵊn). (*intr.*) **1.** to grow strongly and vigorously. **2.** to do well; prosper. [C13: from Old Norse *thrīfask* to grasp for oneself, reflexive of *thrīfa* to grasp, of obscure origin] —**'thriv+er** *n.* —**'thriv+ing+ly** *adv.*

thro' *or* **thro** (θruː) *prep., adv. Poetic.* variant spellings of **through.**

throat (θrəʊt) *n.* **1. a.** that part of the alimentary and respiratory tracts extending from the back of the mouth (nasopharynx) to just below the larynx. **b.** the front part of the neck. **2.** something resembling a throat, esp. in shape or function: *the throat of a chimney.* **3.** *Botany.* the gaping part of a tubular corolla or perianth. **4.** *Informal.* a sore throat. **5. cut one's (own) throat.** to bring about one's own ruin. **6. have by the throat.** to have compete control over (a person or thing). **7. jump down someone's throat.** to be quick to criticize someone. **8. ram** *or* **force (something) down someone's throat.** to insist that someone listen to or accept (something): *he rammed his own opinions down my throat.* **9. stick in one's throat.** to be difficult for one to utter or believe, esp. because of reluctance or dislike: *the accusation stuck in his throat.* ~Related adjs.: **guttural, laryngeal.** [Old English *throtu;* related to Old High German *drozza* throat, Old Norse *throti* swelling]

throat+lash ('θrəʊt,læʃ) *or* **throat+latch** *n.* the strap that holds a bridle in place, fastening under the horse's jaw.

throat mi+cro+phone *n.* a type of microphone that is held against the throat to pick up voice vibrations. Also called: **throat mike.**

throat·y ('θrəʊtɪ) *adj.* **throat·i·er, throat·i+est.** **1.** indicating a sore throat; hoarse: *a throaty cough.* **2.** of, relating to, or produced in or by the throat. **3.** deep, husky, or guttural. —**'throat·i+ly** *adv.* —**'throat·i+ness** *n.*

throb (θrɒb) *vb.* **throbs, throb+bing, throbbed.** (*intr.*) **1.** to pulsate or beat repeatedly, esp. with increased force: *to throb with pain.* **2.** (of engines, drums, etc.) to have a strong rhythmic vibration or beat. ~*n.* **3.** the act or an instance of throbbing, esp. a rapid pulsation as of the heart: *a throb of pleasure.* [C14: perhaps of imitative origin] —**'throb+bing+ly** *adv.*

throe (θrəʊ) *n. Rare.* a pang or pain. [Old English *thrāwu* threat; related to Old High German *drawa* threat, Old Norse *thrā* desire, *thrauka* to endure]

throes (θrəʊz) *pl. n.* **1.** a condition of violent pangs, pain, or convulsions: *death throes.* **2. in the throes of.** struggling with great effort with: *a country in the throes of revolution.*

throm·bin (ˈθrɒmbɪn) *n. Biochem.* an enzyme that acts on fibrinogen in blood causing it to clot.

throm·bo- *or sometimes before a vowel* **thromb-** *combining form.* indicating a blood clot: *thromboembolism.* [from Greek *thrombos* lump, clot]

throm·bo·cyte (ˈθrɒmbəˌsaɪt) *n.* another name for **platelet.** —**throm·bo·cyt·ic** (ˌθrɒmbəˈsɪtɪk) *adj.*

throm·bo·em·bo·lism (ˌθrɒmbəʊˈɛmbəˌlɪzəm) *n. Pathol.* the obstruction of a blood vessel by a thrombus that has become detached from its original site.

throm·bo·gen (ˈθrɒmbəˌdʒɛn) *n.* a protein present in blood that is essential for the formation of thrombin.

throm·bo·ki·nase (ˌθrɒmbəʊˈkaɪneɪs) *n.* another name for **thromboplastin.**

throm·bo·phle·bi·tis (ˌθrɒmbəʊflɪˈbaɪtɪs) *n.* inflammation of a vein associated with the formation of a thrombus.

throm·bo·plas·tic (ˌθrɒmbəʊˈplæstɪk) *adj.* causing or enhancing the formation of a blood clot.

throm·bo·plas·tin (ˌθrɒmbəʊˈplæstɪn) *n.* any of a group of substances that are liberated from damaged blood platelets and other tissues and convert prothrombin to thrombin. Also called: **thrombokinase.**

throm·bose (ˈθrɒmbəʊz) *vb.* to become or affect with a thrombus. [C19: back formation from THROMBOSIS]

throm·bo·sis (θrɒmˈbəʊsɪs) *n.* **1.** the formation or presence of a thrombus. **2.** *Informal.* short for **coronary thrombosis.** [C18: from New Latin, from Greek: curdling, from *thrombousthai* to clot, from *thrombos* THROMBUS] —**throm·bot·ic** (θrɒmˈbɒtɪk) *adj.*

throm·bus (ˈθrɒmbəs) *n., pl.* **·bi** (-baɪ). a clot of coagulated blood that forms within a blood vessel or inside the heart and remains at the site of its formation, often impeding the flow of blood. Compare **embolus.** [C17: from New Latin, from Greek *thrombos* lump, of obscure origin]

throne (θrəʊn) *n.* **1.** the ceremonial seat occupied by a monarch, bishop, etc. on occasions of state. **2.** the power, duties, or rank ascribed to a royal person. **3.** a person holding royal rank. **4.** (*pl.; often cap.*) the third of the nine orders into which the angels are traditionally divided in medieval angelology. ~*vb.* **5.** to place or be placed on a throne. [C13: from Old French *trone,* from Latin *thronus,* from Greek *thronos* throne] —ˈ**throne·less** *adj.*

throng (θrɒŋ) *n.* **1.** a great number of people or things crowded together. ~*vb.* **2.** to gather in or fill (a place) in large numbers; crowd. **3.** (*tr.*) to hem in (a person); jostle. ~*adj.* **4.** *Yorkshire dialect.* (*postpositive*) busy. [Old English *gethrang;* related to Old Norse *throug,* Old High German *drangōd*]

thros·tle (ˈθrɒsᵊl) *n.* **1.** a poetic name for **thrush,** esp. the song thrush. **2.** a spinning machine for wool or cotton in which the fibres are twisted and wound continuously. [Old English; related to Old Saxon *throsla,* Old Norse *thröstr,* Middle High German *drostel*]

throt·tle (ˈθrɒtᵊl) *n.* **1.** Also called: **throttle valve.** any device that controls the quantity of fuel or fuel and air mixture entering an engine. **2.** an informal or dialect word for **throat.** ~*vb.* (*tr.*) **3.** to kill or injure by squeezing the throat. **4.** to suppress: *to throttle the press.* **5.** to control or restrict (a flow of fluid) by means of a throttle valve. [C14: *throtelen,* from *throte* THROAT] —ˈ**throt·tler** *n.*

through (θru:) *prep.* **1.** going in or starting at one side and coming out or stopping at the other side of: *a path through the wood.* **2.** occupying or visiting several points scattered around in (an area). **3.** as a result of; by means of: *the thieves were captured through his vigilance.* **4.** *Chiefly U.S.* up to and including: *Monday through Friday.* **5.** during: *through the night.* **6.** at the end of; having (esp. successfully) completed. **7. through with.** having finished with (esp. when dissatisfied with). ~*adj.* **8.** (*postpositive*) having successfully completed some specified activity. **9.** (on a telephone line) connected. **10.** (*postpositive*) no longer able to function successfully in some specified capacity: *as a journalist, you're through.* **11.** (*prenominal*) (of a route, journey, etc.) continuous or unbroken: *a through train.* ~*adv.* **12.** through some specified thing, place, or period of time. **13. through and through.** thoroughly; completely. ~Also: **thro'** or **thro** (poetic), **thru** (U.S. not standard). [Old English *thurh;* related to Old Frisian *thruch,* Old Saxon *thuru,* Old High German *duruh*]

through-com·posed *adj. Music.* of or relating to a song in stanzaic form, in which different music is provided for each stanza. Compare **strophic** (sense 2).

through·ly (ˈθru:lɪ) *adv. Archaic.* thoroughly; completely.

through-oth·er *adj. Northern Brit. dialect.* untidy or dishevelled. [a literal translation of Irish Gaelic *trí n-a chéile* through each other, hence, mixed up with each other]

through·out (θru:ˈaʊt) *prep.* **1.** right through; through the whole of (a place or a period of time): *throughout the day.* ~*adv.* **2.** throughout some specified period or area.

through·put (ˈθru:ˌpʊt) *n.* the quantity of raw material processed in a given period, esp. by a computer.

through·way (ˈθru:ˌweɪ) *n. U.S.* a thoroughfare, esp. a motorway.

throve (θrəʊv) *vb.* a past tense of **thrive.**

throw (θrəʊ) *vb.* **throws, throw·ing, threw, thrown.** (*mainly tr.*) **1.** (*also intr.*) to project or cast (something) through the air, esp. with a rapid motion of the arm and wrist. **2.** (foll. by *in, on, onto,* etc.) to put or move suddenly, carelessly, or violently: *she threw her clothes onto the bed.* **3.** to bring to or cause to be in a specified state or condition, esp. suddenly or unexpectedly: *the news threw the family into a panic.* **4.** to direct or cast (a shadow, light, etc.). **5.** to project (the voice) so as to make it appear to come from other than its source. **6.** to give or hold (a party). **7.** to cause to fall or be upset; dislodge: *the horse soon threw his rider.* **8. a.** to tip (dice) out onto a flat surface. **b.** to obtain (a specified number) in this way. **9.** to shape on a potter's wheel. **10.** to move (a switch or lever) to engage or disengage a mechanism. **11.** to be subjected to (a fit). **12.** to turn (wood, etc.) on a lathe. **13.** *Informal.* to baffle or astonish; confuse: *the last question on the test paper threw me.* **14.** *Boxing.* to deliver (a punch). **15.** *Wrestling.* to hurl (an opponent) to the ground. **16.** *Informal.* to lose (a contest, fight, etc.) deliberately, esp. in boxing. **17. a.** to play (a card). **b.** to discard (a card). **18.** (of a female animal, esp. a cow) to give birth to (young). **19.** to twist or spin (filaments) into thread. **20. throw cold water on.** *Informal.* to discourage or disparage. **21. throw oneself at.** to strive actively to attract the attention or affection of. **22. throw oneself into.** to involve oneself enthusiastically in. **23. throw oneself on.** to rely entirely upon: *he threw himself on the mercy of the police.* ~*n.* **24.** the act or an instance of throwing. **25.** the distance or extent over which anything may be thrown: *a stone's throw.* **26.** *Informal.* a chance, venture, or try. **27.** an act or result of throwing dice. **28. a.** the eccentricity of a cam. **b.** the radial distance between the central axis of a crankshaft and the axis of a crankpin forming part of the shaft. **29.** *U.S.* a decorative light blanket or cover, as thrown over a chair. **30.** a sheet of fabric used for draping over an easel or unfinished painting, etc., to keep the dust off. **31.** *Geology.* the vertical displacement of rock strata at a fault. **32.** *Physics.* the deflection of a measuring instrument as a result of a sudden fluctuation. ~See also **throw about, throwaway, throwback, throw in, throw off, throw out, throw over, throw together, throw up.** [Old English *thrāwan* to turn, torment; related to Old High German *drāen* to twist, Latin *terere* to rub] —ˈ**throw·er** *n.*

throw a·bout *vb.* (*tr., adv.*) **1.** to spend (one's money) in a reckless and flaunting manner. **2. throw one's weight about.** *Informal.* to act in an authoritarian or aggressive manner.

throw·a·way (ˈθrəʊəˌweɪ) *adj.* **1.** (*prenominal*) *Chiefly Brit.* said or done incidentally, esp. for rhetorical effect; casual: *a throwaway remark.* ~*n.* **2. a.** anything that can be thrown away or discarded. **b.** (*as modifier*): *a throwaway carton.* **3.** *Chiefly U.S.* a handbill or advertisement distributed in a public place. ~*vb.* **throw a·way.** (*tr., adv.*) **4.** to get rid of; discard. **5.** to fail to make good use of; to waste: *to throw away all one's money on horses.*

throw·back (ˈθrəʊˌbæk) *n.* **1. a.** a person, animal, or plant that has the characteristics of an earlier or more primitive type. **b.** a reversion to such an organism. ~*vb.* **throw back.** (*adv.*) **2.** (*intr.*) to revert to an earlier or more primitive type. **3.** (*tr.;* foll. by *on*) to force to depend (on): *the crisis threw her back on her faith in God.*

throw in *vb.* (*tr., adv.*) **1.** to add (something extra) at no additional cost. **2.** to contribute or interpose (a remark, argument, etc.), esp. in a discussion. **3. throw in the towel** (*or* **sponge**). to give in; accept defeat. ~*n.* **throw-in. 4.** *Soccer.* the method of putting the ball into play after it has gone into touch by throwing it two-handed from behind the head to a teammate, both feet being kept on the ground.

throw·ing stick *n.* a primitive sling for shooting missiles such as javelins or spears.

thrown (θrəʊn) *vb.* the past participle of **throw.**

throw off *vb.* (*tr., adv.*) **1.** to free oneself of; discard. **2.** to produce or utter in a casual manner: *to throw off a witty remark.* **3.** to escape from or elude: *the fox rapidly threw off his pursuers.* **4.** to confuse or disconcert: *the interruption threw the young pianist off.* **5.** (often foll. by *at*) *Austral. informal.* to deride or ridicule.

throw out *vb.* (*tr., adv.*) **1.** to discard or reject. **2.** to expel or dismiss, esp. forcibly. **3.** to construct (something projecting or prominent, such as a wing of a building). **4.** to put forward or offer: *the chairman threw out a new proposal.* **5.** to utter in a casual or indirect manner: *to throw out a hint.* **6.** to confuse or disconcert: *the noise threw his concentration out.* **7.** to give off or emit. **8.** *Cricket.* (of a fielder) to put (the batsman) out by throwing the ball to hit the wicket. **9.** *Baseball.* to make a throw to a teammate who in turn puts out (a base runner).

throw o·ver *vb.* (*tr., adv.*) to forsake or abandon; jilt.

throw·ster (ˈθrəʊstə) *n.* a person who twists silk or other fibres into yarn. [C15 *throwestre,* from THROW + -STER]

throw to·geth·er *vb.* (*tr., adv.*) **1.** to assemble hurriedly. **2.** to cause to become casually acquainted.

throw up *vb.* (*adv., mainly tr.*) **1.** to give up; abandon, relinquish. **2.** to build or construct hastily. **3.** to reveal; produce: *every generation throws up its own leaders.* **4.** (*also intr.*) *Informal.* to vomit.

thru (θru:) *prep., adv., adj. U.S. not standard.* a variant spelling of **through.**

thrum[1] (θrʌm) *vb.* **thrums, thrum·ming, thrummed. 1.** to strum rhythmically but without expression on (a musical instrument). **2.** (*intr.*) to drum incessantly: *rain thrummed on the roof.* **3.** to repeat (something) monotonously. ~*n.* **4.** a repetitive strumming or recitation. [C16: of imitative origin] —ˈ**thrum·mer** *n.*

thrum[2] (θrʌm) *Textiles.* ~*n.* **1. a.** any of the unwoven ends of warp thread remaining on the loom when the web has been removed. **b.** such ends of thread collectively. **2.** a fringe or tassel of short unwoven threads. ~*vb.* **thrums, thrum+ming, thrummed. 3.** (*tr.*) to trim with thrums. [C14: from Old English; related to Old High German *drum* remnant, Dutch *dreum*]

thrush[1] (θrʌʃ) *n.* any songbird of the subfamily *Turdinae*, esp. those having a brown plumage with a spotted breast, such as the mistle thrush and song thrush: family *Muscicapidae*. Compare **water thrush.** [Old English *thrȳsce;* related to Old High German *drōsca;* see THROSTLE, THROAT]

thrush[2] (θrʌʃ) *n.* **1. a.** a fungal disease of the mouth, esp. of infants, characterized by the formation of whitish spots and caused by infection with *Candida albicans*. **b.** another word for **sprue**[2]. **2.** a softening of the frog of a horse's hoof characterized by inflammation and a thick foul discharge. [C17: related to Old Danish *törsk*, Danish *troske*]

thrust (θrʌst) *vb.* **1.** to put with force into (something); push through or against (something). **2.** to force (oneself or another) into some condition or situation. **3.** to make a stab or lunge at (a person or thing). ~*n.* **4.** a forceful drive, push, stab, or lunge. **5.** a force, esp. one that produces motion. **6. a.** a propulsive force produced by the fluid pressure or the change of momentum of the fluid in a jet engine, rocket engine, etc. **b.** a similar force produced by a propeller. **7.** a pressure that is exerted continuously by one part of an object, structure, etc., against another. **8.** *Geology.* **a.** the compressive force in the earth's crust that produces recumbent folds. **b.** See **thrust fault. 9.** *Civil engineering.* a force exerted in a downwards and outwards direction, as by an arch or a rafter. **10.** force, impetus, or drive: *a man with thrust and energy.* [C12: from Old Norse *thrysta;* related to Latin *trūdere;* see INTRUDE]

thrust+er ('θrʌstə) *n.* **1.** a person or thing that thrusts. **2.** a small rocket engine, esp. one used to correct the altitude or course of a spacecraft. Also called: **vernier rocket.**

thrust fault *n.* a fault in which the rocks on the lower side of an inclined fault plane have been displaced downwards, usually by compression; a reverse fault.

Thu·cyd·i·des (θuː'sɪdɪˌdiːz) *n.* ?460–?395 B.C., Greek historian and politician, distinguished for his *History of the Peloponnesian War.* —**Thu+ˌcyd·i·'de·an** *adj.*

thud (θʌd) *n.* **1.** a dull heavy sound: *the book fell to the ground with a thud.* **2.** a blow or fall that causes such a sound. ~*vb.* **thuds, thud+ding, thud+ded. 3.** to make or cause to make such a sound. [Old English *thyddan* to strike; related to *thoddettan* to beat, perhaps of imitative origin]

thug (θʌg) *n.* **1.** a tough and violent man, esp. a criminal. **2.** (*sometimes cap.*) (formerly) a member of an organization of robbers and assassins in India. [C19: from Hindi *thag* thief, from Sanskrit *sthaga* scoundrel, from *sthagati* to conceal] —**'thug+ger·y** *n.* —**'thug+gish** *adj.*

thug+gee (θʌ'giː) *n. History.* the methods and practices of the thugs of India. [C19: from Hindi *thagī;* see THUG]

thu+ja *or* **thu+ya** ('θuːjə) *n.* any of various coniferous trees of the genus *Thuja*, of North America and East Asia, having scalelike leaves, small cones, and an aromatic wood: family *Pinaceae*. See also **arbor vitae.** [C18: from New Latin, from Medieval Latin *thuia*, ultimately from Greek *thua* name of an African tree]

Thu+le ('θjuːlɪ) *n.* **1.** Also called: **ultima Thule.** a region believed by ancient geographers to be the northernmost land in the inhabited world: sometimes thought to have been Iceland, Norway, or one of the Shetland Islands. **2.** an Eskimo settlement in NW Greenland: a Danish trading post, founded in 1910, and U.S. air force base.

thu+li·um ('θjuːlɪəm) *n.* a malleable ductile silvery-grey element occurring principally in monazite. The radioisotope **thulium-170** is used as an electron source in portable x-ray units. Symbol: Tm; atomic no.: 69; atomic wt.: 168.93; valency: 2 or 3; relative density: 9.31; melting pt.: 1545°C; boiling pt.: 1727°C. [C19: New Latin, from THULE + -IUM]

thumb (θʌm) *n.* **1.** the first and usually shortest and thickest of the digits of the hand, composed of two short bones. Technical name: **pollex. 2.** the corresponding digit in other vertebrates. **3.** the part of a glove shaped to fit the thumb. **4.** *Architect.* another name for **ovolo. 5. all thumbs.** clumsy. **6. thumbs down.** an indication of refusal, disapproval, or negation: *he gave the thumbs down on our proposal.* **7. thumbs up.** an indication of encouragement, approval, or acceptance. **8. under someone's thumb.** at someone's mercy or command. ~*vb.* **9.** (*tr.*) to touch, mark, or move with the thumb. **10.** to attempt to obtain (a lift or ride) by signalling with the thumb. **11.** (when *intr.*, often foll. by *through*) to flip the pages of (a book, magazine, etc.) perfunctorily in order to glance at the contents. **12. thumb one's nose at.** to deride or mock, esp. by placing the thumb on the nose with fingers extended. [Old English *thūma;* related to Old Saxon *thūma*, Old High German *thūmo*, Old Norse *thumall* thumb of a glove, Latin *tumēre* to swell] —**'thumb+less** *adj.* —**'thumb+ˌlike** *adj.*

thumb in+dex *n.* **1.** a series of indentations cut into the fore edge of a book to facilitate quick reference. ~*vb.* **thumb-in·dex. 2.** (*tr.*) to furnish with a thumb index.

thumb+nail ('θʌmˌneɪl) *n.* **1.** the nail of the thumb. **2.** (*modifier*) concise and brief: *a thumbnail sketch.*

thumb+nut ('θʌmˌnʌt) *n.* a nut with projections enabling it to be turned by the thumb and forefinger; wing nut.

thumb+print ('θʌmˌprɪnt) *n.* an impression of the upper part of the thumb, used esp. for identification purposes. See **fingerprint.**

thumb+screw ('θʌmˌskruː) *n.* **1.** an instrument of torture that pinches or crushes the thumbs. **2.** a screw with projections on its head enabling it to be turned by the thumb and forefinger.

thumb+stall ('θʌmˌstɔːl) *n.* a protective sheathlike cover for the thumb.

thumb+tack ('θʌmˌtæk) *n.* the U.S. name for **drawing pin.**

Thum+mim ('θʌmɪm) *n. Old Testament.* See **Urim and Thummim.**

thump (θʌmp) *n.* **1.** the sound of a heavy solid body hitting or pounding a comparatively soft surface. **2.** a heavy blow with the hand: *he gave me a thump on the back.* ~*vb.* **3.** (*tr.*) to strike or beat heavily; pound. **4.** (*intr.*) to throb, beat, or pound violently: *his heart thumped with excitement.* [C16: related to Icelandic, Swedish dialect *dumpa* to thump; see THUD, BUMP] —**'thump+er** *n.*

thump+ing ('θʌmpɪŋ) *adj.* (*prenominal*) *Slang.* huge or excessive: *a thumping loss.* —**'thump+ing+ly** *adv.*

Thun (*German* tuːn) *n.* **1.** a town in central Switzerland, in Bern canton on Lake Thun. Pop.: 35 523 (1970). **2. Lake.** a lake in central Switzerland, formed by a widening of the Aar River. Length: about 17 km (11 miles). Width: 3 km (2 miles). German name: **Thun+er See** ('tuːnər 'zeː).

thun+der ('θʌndə) *n.* **1.** a loud cracking or deep rumbling noise caused by the rapid expansion of atmospheric gases which are suddenly heated by lightning. **2.** any loud booming sound. **3.** *Rare.* a violent threat or denunciation. **4. steal someone's thunder.** to lessen the effect of someone's idea or action by anticipating it. ~*vb.* **5.** to make (a loud sound) or utter (words) in a manner suggesting thunder. **6.** (*intr.;* with *it* as subject) to be the case that thunder is being heard. **7.** (*intr.*) to move fast and heavily: *the bus thundered downhill.* **8.** (*intr.*) to utter vehement threats or denunciation; rail. [Old English *thunor;* related to Old Saxon *thunar*, Old High German *donar*, Old Norse *thōrr;* see THOR, THURSDAY] —**'thun+der+er** *n.*

Thun+der Bay *n.* a port in central Canada, in Ontario on Lake Superior: formed in 1970 by the amalgamation of Fort William and Port Arthur; the head of the St. Lawrence Seaway for Canada. Pop.: 108 411 (1971).

thun·der+bird ('θʌndəˌbɜːd) *n.* a legendary bird that produces thunder, lightning, and rain according to the folk belief of several North American Indian peoples.

thun·der+bolt ('θʌndəˌbəʊlt) *n.* **1.** a flash of lightning accompanying thunder. **2.** the imagined agency of destruction produced by a flash of lightning. **3.** (in mythology) the destructive weapon wielded by several gods, esp. the Greek god Zeus. See also **Thor. 4.** something very startling.

thun·der+box ('θʌndəˌbɒks) *n. Slang.* **1.** a portable box-like lavatory seat that can be placed over a hole in the ground. **2.** any portable lavatory.

thun·der+clap ('θʌndəˌklæp) *n.* **1.** a loud outburst of thunder. **2.** something as violent or unexpected as a clap of thunder.

thun·der+cloud ('θʌndəˌklaʊd) *n.* **1.** a towering electrically charged cumulonimbus cloud associated with thunderstorms. **2.** anything that is threatening.

thun·der+head ('θʌndəˌhɛd) *n. Chiefly U.S.* the anvil-shaped top of a cumulonimbus cloud.

thun+der+ing ('θʌndərɪŋ) *adj.* (*prenominal*) *Slang.* very great or excessive: *a thundering idiot.* —**'thun+der+ing+ly** *adv.*

thun+der+ous ('θʌndərəs) *or* **thun+der·y** ('θʌndərɪ) *adj.* **1.** producing thunder. **2.** resembling thunder, esp. in loudness: *thunderous clapping.* —**'thun+der+ous+ly** *adv.*

thun·der+show·er ('θʌndəˌʃaʊə) *n.* a heavy shower during a thunderstorm.

thun·der+stone ('θʌndəˌstəʊn) *n.* **1.** a long tapering stone, fossil, or similar object, formerly thought to be a thunderbolt. **2.** an archaic word for **thunderbolt.**

thun·der+storm ('θʌndəˌstɔːm) *n.* a storm caused by strong rising air currents and characterized by thunder and lightning and usually heavy rain or hail.

thun·der+struck ('θʌndəˌstrʌk) *or* **thun·der+strick·en** ('θʌndəˌstrɪkən) *adj.* **1.** completely taken aback; amazed or shocked. **2.** *Rare.* struck by lightning.

thun+der·y ('θʌndərɪ) *adj.* **1.** thunderous. **2.** ominous.

Thu+ner See ('tuːnər 'zeː) *n.* the German name for (Lake) **Thun.**

Thur·ber ('θɜːbə) *n.* **James (Grover).** 1894–1961, U.S. humorist and illustrator. He contributed drawings and stories to the *New Yorker* and his books include *Is Sex Necessary?* (1929), written with E. B. White.

Thur+gau (*German* 'tuːrgaʊ) *n.* a canton of NE Switzerland, on Lake Constance: annexed by the confederated Swiss states in 1460. Capital: Frauenfeld. Pop.: 182 835 (1970). Area: 1007 sq. km (389 sq. miles). French name: **Thur+go+vie** (tyrgɔ'vi).

thu+ri+ble ('θjʊərɪbᵊl) *n.* another word for **censer.** [C15: from Latin *tūribulum* censer, from *tūs* incense]

thu+ri+fer ('θjʊərɪfə) *n.* a person appointed to carry the censer at religious ceremonies. [C19: from Latin, from *tūs* incense + *ferre* to carry]

Thu+rin+gi·a (θjʊ'rɪndʒɪə) *n.* a region of SW East Germany: a former state of central Germany (1920–45). German name: **Thür+ing+en** ('tyːrɪŋən). —**Thu+'rin+gi·an** *adj., n.*

Thu+rin+gi·an For+est *n.* a forested mountainous region in central East Germany, rising over 900 m (3000 ft.). German name: **Thür+ing+er Wald** ('tyːrɪŋər 'valt).

Thurs. *abbrev. for* Thursday.

Thurs+day ('θɜːzdɪ) *n.* the fifth day of the week; fourth day of the working week. [Old English *Thursdæg*, literally: Thor's day; related to Old High German *Donares tag;* see THOR, THUNDER, DAY]

Thurs·day Is·land *n.* an island in Torres Strait, between NE Australia and New Guinea: administratively part of Queensland, Australia. Area: 4 sq. km (1.5 sq. miles).

thus (ðʌs) *adv.* **1.** Also: **thusly.** in this manner: *do it thus.* **2.** to such a degree: *thus far and no further.* ~ **3.** *sentence connector.* therefore: *We have failed. Thus we have to take the consequences.* [Old English; related to Old Frisian, Old Saxon *thus*]

thu·ya ('θuːjə) *n.* a variant spelling of **thuja.**

thwack (θwæk) *vb.* **1.** to beat, hit, or flog, esp. with something flat. ~*n.* **2. a.** a blow with something flat. **b.** the sound made by it. ~*interj.* **3.** an exclamation imitative of this sound. [C16: of imitative origin] —**'thwack·er** *n.*

thwart (θwɔːt) *vb.* **1.** to oppose successfully or prevent; frustrate: *they thwarted the plan.* **2.** *Obsolete.* to be or move across. ~*n.* **3.** *Nautical.* **a.** a seat lying across a boat and occupied by an oarsman. **b.** a crosspiece that spreads the gunwales of a boat. ~*adj.* **4.** passing or being situated across. **5.** *Archaic.* perverse or stubborn. ~*prep., adv.* **6.** *Obsolete.* across. [C13: from Old Norse *thvert,* from *thverr* transverse; related to Old English *thweorh* crooked, Old High German *twerh* transverse] —**'thwart·ed·ly** *adv.* —**'thwart·er** *n.*

thy (ðaɪ) *determiner. (usually preceding a consonant) Archaic or Brit. dialect.* belonging to or associated in some way with you (thou): *thy goodness and mercy.* Compare **thine.** [C12: variant of THINE]

Thy·es·tes (θaɪ'ɛstiːz) *n. Greek myth.* son of Pelops and brother of Atreus, with whose wife he committed adultery. In revenge, Atreus killed Thyestes' sons and served them to their father at a banquet. —**Thy·es·te·an** *or* **Thy·es·ti·an** (θaɪ'ɛstɪən, ˌθaɪɛ'stiːən) *adj.*

thy·la·cine ('θaɪləˌsaɪn) *n.* an extinct or very rare doglike carnivorous marsupial, *Thylacinus cynocephalus,* of Tasmania, having greyish-brown fur with dark vertical stripes on the back: family *Dasyuridae.* Also called: **Tasmanian wolf.** [C19: from New Latin *thȳlacīnus,* from Greek *thulakos* pouch, sack]

thyme (taɪm) *n.* any of various small shrubs of the temperate genus *Thymus,* having a strong mintlike odour, small leaves, and white, pink, or red flowers: family *Labiatae* (labiates). [C14: from Old French *thym,* from Latin *thymum,* from Greek *thumon,* from *thuein* to make a burnt offering] —**'thym·ic** *adj.* —**'thym·y** *adj.*

thym·e·lae·a·ceous (ˌθɪmɪlɪ'eɪʃəs) *adj.* of, relating to, or belonging to the *Thymelaeaceae,* a family of trees and shrubs having tough acrid bark and simple leaves: includes spurge laurel, leatherwood, and mezereon. [C19: via New Latin, from Greek *thumelaia,* from *thumon* THYME + *elaia* olive]

-thy·mi·a *n. combining form.* indicating a certain emotional condition, mood, or state of mind: *cyclothymia.* [New Latin, from Greek *thumos* temper]

thym·ic ('θaɪmɪk) *adj.* of or relating to the thymus.

thy·mi·dine ('θaɪmɪˌdiːn) *n.* the crystalline nucleoside of thymine, found in DNA. Formula: $C_{10}H_{14}N_2O_5$. [C20: from THYM(INE) + -IDE + -INE[2]]

thy·mine ('θaɪmiːn) *n.* a white crystalline pyrimidine base found in DNA. Formula: $C_5H_6N_2O_2$. [C19: from THYMIC + -INE[2]]

thy·mol ('θaɪmɒl) *n.* a white crystalline substance with an aromatic odour, obtained from the oil of thyme and used as a fungicide, antiseptic, and anthelmintic and in perfumery and embalming; 2-isopropylphenol. Formula: $(CH_3)_2CHC_6H_3(CH_3)OH$. [C19: from THYME + -OL[2]]

thy·mus ('θaɪməs) *n., pl.* **·mus·es** *or* **·mi** (-maɪ). a glandular organ of vertebrates, consisting in man of two lobes situated below the thyroid. In early life it produces lymphocytes and is thought to influence certain immunological responses. It atrophies with age and is almost nonexistent in the adult. [C17: from New Latin, from Greek *thumos* sweetbread]

thy·ra·tron ('θaɪrəˌtrɒn) *n.* an electronic relay consisting of a gas-filled tube, usually a triode, in which a signal applied to the control grid initiates a transient anode current but subsequently loses control over it. See also **silicon controlled rectifier.** [C20: originally a trademark, from Greek *thura* door, valve + -TRON]

thy·ris·tor (θaɪ'rɪstə) *n.* another name for **silicon controlled rectifier.** [C20: from THYR(ATRON) + (TRANS)ISTOR]

thy·ro- *or before a vowel* **thyr-** *combining form.* thyroid: *thyrotropin; thyrotoxicosis; thyrotropin.*

thy·ro·cal·ci·ton·in (ˌθaɪrəʊˌkælsɪ'təʊnɪn) *n.* another name for **calcitonin.** [C20: from THYRO- + CALCITONIN]

thy·roid ('θaɪrɔɪd) *adj.* **1.** of or relating to the thyroid gland. **2.** of or relating to the largest cartilage of the larynx. ~*n.* **3.** see **thyroid gland. 4.** the powdered preparation made from the thyroid gland of certain animals, used to treat hypothyroidism. [C18: from New Latin *thyroidēs,* from Greek *thureoeidēs,* from *thureos* oblong (literally: door-shaped) shield, from *thura* door]

thy·roid·ec·to·my (ˌθaɪrɔɪ'dɛktəmɪ) *n., pl.* **·mies.** surgical removal of all or part of the thyroid gland.

thy·roid gland *n.* an endocrine gland of vertebrates, consisting in man of two lobes near the base of the neck. It secretes hormones that control metabolism and body growth.

thy·roid·i·tis (ˌθaɪrɔɪ'daɪtɪs) *n.* inflammation of the thyroid gland.

thy·roid-stim·u·lat·ing hor·mone *n.* another name for **thyrotropin.** Abbrev.: **TSH.**

thy·ro·tox·i·co·sis (ˌθaɪrəʊˌtɒksɪ'kəʊsɪs) *n.* another name for **hyperthyroidism.**

thy·ro·tro·pin (ˌθaɪrəʊ'trəʊpɪn) *or* **thy·ro·tro·phin** *n.* a glycoprotein hormone secreted by the anterior lobe of the pituitary gland: it stimulates the activity of the thyroid gland. Also called: **thyroid-stimulating hormone.** [C20: from THYRO- + -TROPE + -IN]

thy·rox·ine (θaɪ'rɒksiːn, -sɪn) *or* **thy·rox·in** (θaɪ'rɒksɪn) *n.* the principal hormone produced by the thyroid gland: it increases the metabolic rate of tissues and also controls growth, as in amphibian metamorphosis. It can be synthesized or extracted from the thyroid glands of animals and used to treat hypothyroidism. Chemical name: tetra-iodothyromine; formula: $C_{15}H_{11}I_4NO_4$. [C19: from THYRO- + OXY- + -INE[2]]

thyrse (θɜːs) *or* **thyr·sus** ('θɜːsəs) *n., pl.* **thers·es** *or* **thyr·si** ('θɜːsaɪ). *Botany.* a type of inflorescence, occurring in the lilac and grape, in which the main branch is racemose and the lateral branches cymose. [C17: from French: THYRSUS] —**'thyr·soid** *adj.*

thyr·sus ('θɜːsəs) *n., pl.* **·si** (-saɪ). **1.** *Greek myth.* a staff, usually one tipped with a pine cone, borne by Dionysus (Bacchus) and his followers. **2.** a variant spelling of **thyrse.** [C18: from Latin, from Greek *thursos* stalk]

thys·a·nu·ran (ˌθɪsə'njʊərən) *n.* **1.** any primitive wingless insect of the order *Thysanura,* which comprises the bristletails. ~*adj.* **2.** of, relating to, or belonging to the order *Thysanura.* [C19: from New Latin, from Greek *thusanos* fringe + *oura* tail] —ˌ**thys·a·'nu·rous** *adj.*

thy·self (ðaɪ'sɛlf) *pron. Archaic.* **1. a.** the reflexive form of *thou* or *thee.* **b.** (intensifier): *thou, thyself, wouldst know.* **2.** *(preceded by a copula)* your (thy) normal or usual self: *thou seemst not thyself this morning.*

ti[1] (tiː) *n. Music.* a variant spelling of **te.**

ti[2] (tiː) *n., pl.* **tis. 1.** a woody palmlike agave plant, *Cordyline terminalis,* of the East Indies, having white, mauve, or reddish flowers. The sword-shaped leaves are used for garments, fodder, thatch, etc., and the root for food and liquor. **2.** a similar and related plant, *Cordyline australis,* of New Zealand. [of Polynesian origin]

Ti *the chemical symbol for* titanium.

Ti·a Jua·na ('tɪə 'wɑːnə; *Spanish* 'tia 'xwana) *n.* a variant spelling of **Tijuana.**

Ti·a Ma·ri·a ('tɪə mə'rɪə) *n. Trademark.* a coffee-flavoured liqueur from the West Indies.

ti·ar·a (tɪ'ɑːrə) *n.* **1.** a woman's semicircular jewelled headdress for formal occasions. **2.** a high headdress worn by Persian kings in ancient times. **3.** *R.C. Church.* **a.** a headdress worn by the pope, consisting of a beehive-shaped diadem surrounded by three coronets. **b.** the office or rank of pope. [C16: via Latin from Greek, of Oriental origin] —**ti·'ar·aed** *adj.*

Ti·ber ('taɪbə) *n.* a river in central Italy, rising in the Tuscan Apennines and flowing south through Rome to the Tyrrhenian Sea: the longest river in Italy. Length: 405 km (252 miles). Ancient name: **Tiberis.** Italian name: **Tevere.**

Ti·be·ri·as (taɪ'bɪərɪˌæs) *n.* **Lake.** another name for the (Sea of) **Galilee.**

Ti·be·ri·us (taɪ'bɪərɪəs) *n.* full name *Tiberius Claudius Nero Caesar Augustus.* 42 B.C.–37 A.D., Roman emperor (14–37 A.D.). He succeeded his father-in-law Augustus after a brilliant military career. He became increasingly tyrannical.

Ti·bes·ti *or* **Ti·bes·ti Mas·sif** (tɪ'bɛstɪ) *pl. n.* a mountain range of volcanic origin in NW Chad, in the central Sahara extending for about 480 km (300 miles). Highest peak: Emi Koussi, 3415 m (11 204 ft.).

Ti·bet (tɪ'bɛt) *n.* an autonomous region of SW China: Europeans strictly excluded in the 19th century; invaded by China in 1950; rebellion (1959) against Chinese rule suppressed and the Dalai Lama fled to India; consists largely of a vast high plateau between the Himalayas and Kunlun Mountains; formerly a theocracy and the centre of Lamaism. Capital: Lhasa. Pop.: 1 400 000 (1973 est.). Area: 1 221 601 sq. km (471 660 sq. miles). Chinese name: **Sitsang.**

Ti·bet·an (tɪ'bɛtᵊn) *adj.* **1.** of, relating to, or characteristic of Tibet, its people, or their language. ~*n.* **2.** a native or inhabitant of Tibet. **3.** the language of Tibet, belonging to the Sino-Tibetan family.

Ti·bet·o-Bur·man (tɪ'bɛtəʊ'bɜːman) *n.* **1.** a branch of the Sino-Tibetan family of languages, sometimes regarded as a family in its own right. Compare **Sinitic.** ~*adj.* **2.** belonging or relating to this group of languages.

tib·i·a ('tɪbɪə) *n., pl.* **tib·i·ae** ('tɪbɪˌiː) *or* **tib·i·as. 1.** Also called: **shinbone.** the inner and thicker of the two bones of the human leg between the knee and ankle. Compare **fibula. 2.** the corresponding bone in other vertebrates. **3.** the fourth segment of an insect's leg, lying between the femur and the tarsus. [C16: from Latin: leg, pipe] —**'tib·i·al** *adj.*

tib·i·o·tar·sus (ˌtɪbɪəʊ'tɑːsəs) *n.* the bone in the leg of a bird formed by fusion of the tibia and some of the tarsal bones. [C19: from *tibio-* (combining form of TIBIA) + TARSUS]

Ti·bul·lus (tɪ'bʌləs) *n.* **Al·bi·us** ('ælbɪəs). ?54–?19 B.C., Roman elegiac poet.

Ti·bur ('taɪbə) *n.* the ancient name for **Tivoli.**

tic (tɪk) *n. Pathol.* **1.** spasmodic twitching of a particular group of muscles. **2.** See **tic douloureux.** [C19: from French, of uncertain origin; compare Italian *ticche*]

ti·cal (tɪ'kɑːl, -'kɔːl; 'tiːkᵊl) *n., pl.* **·cals** *or* **·cal. 1.** the former standard monetary unit of Thailand, replaced by the baht in 1928. **2.** a unit of weight, formerly used in Thailand, equal to about half an ounce or 14 grams. [C17: via Siamese and Portuguese from Malay *tikal* monetary unit]

tic dou·lou·reux ('tɪk ˌduːlə'ruː) *n.* a condition of momentary stabbing pain along the trigeminal nerve. Also called: **trigeminal neuralgia.** [C19: from French, literally: painful tic]

Ti+ci+no (*Italian* ti'tʃi:no) *n.* **1.** a canton in S Switzerland: predominantly Italian-speaking and Roman Catholic; mountainous. Capital: Bellinzona. Pop.: 245 458 (1970). Area: 2810 sq. km (1085 sq. miles). German name: **Tessin. 2.** a river in S central Europe, rising in S central Switzerland and flowing southeast and west to Lake Maggiore, then southeast to the River Po. Length: 248 km (154 miles).

tick[1] (tɪk) *n.* **1.** a recurrent metallic tapping or clicking sound, such as that made by a clock or watch. **2.** *Brit. informal.* a moment or instant. **3.** a mark (✓) or dash used to check off or indicate the correctness of something. ~*vb.* **4.** to produce or indicate by a recurrent tapping sound: *the clock ticked the minutes away.* **5.** (when *tr.*, often foll. by *off*) to mark or check (something, such as a list) with a tick. **6. what makes someone tick.** the basic drive or motivation of a person. ~See also **tick off, tick over.** [C13: from Low German *tikk* touch; related to Old High German *zekōn* to pluck, Norwegian *tikke* to touch]

tick[2] (tɪk) *n.* **1.** any of various small parasitic arachnids of the families *Ixodidae* (**hard ticks**) and *Argasidae,* (**soft ticks**), typically living on the skin of warm-blooded animals and feeding on the blood and tissues of their hosts: order *Acarina* (mites and ticks). See also **sheep tick** (sense 1). **2.** any of certain other arachnids of the order *Acarina.* **3.** any of certain insects of the dipterous family *Hippoboscidae* that are ectoparasitic on horses, cattle, sheep, etc., esp. the sheep ked. [Old English *ticca;* related to Middle High German *zeche* tick, Middle Irish *dega* stag beetle]

tick[3] (tɪk) *n.* **1.** the strong covering of a pillow, mattress, etc. **2.** *Informal.* short for **ticking.** [C15: probably from Middle Dutch *tīke;* related to Old High German *ziecha* pillow cover, Latin *tēca* case, Greek *thēkē*]

tick[4] (tɪk) *n. Brit. informal.* account or credit (esp. in the phrase **on tick**). [C17: shortened from TICKET]

tick-bird *n.* another name for **oxpecker.**

tick-borne ty+phus *n.* another name for **Rocky Mountain spotted fever.**

tick+er ('tɪkə) *n.* **1.** *Slang.* **a.** the heart. **b.** a watch. **2.** a person or thing that ticks. **3.** *Stock exchange.* the U.S. word for **tape machine.**

tick+er tape *n.* **1.** *Stock exchange.* a continuous paper ribbon on which a tape machine automatically prints current stock quotations. **2. ticker tape reception** (*or* **parade**). (mainly in New York) the showering of the motorcade of a distinguished politician, visiting head of state, etc., with ticker tape as a sign of welcome.

tick+et ('tɪkɪt) *n.* **1. a.** a piece of paper, cardboard, etc., showing that the holder is entitled to certain rights, such as travel on a train or bus, entry to a place of public entertainment, etc. **b.** (*modifier*) concerned with or relating to the issue, sale, or checking of tickets: *a ticket office; ticket collector.* **2.** a piece of card, cloth, etc., attached to an article showing information such as its price, size, or washing instructions. **3.** a summons served for a parking offence or violation of traffic regulations. **4.** *Informal.* the certificate of competence issued to a ship's captain or an aircraft pilot. **5.** *U.S.* the group of candidates nominated by one party in an election; slate. **6.** *Chiefly U.S.* the declared policy of a political party at an election. **7.** *Brit. informal.* a certificate of discharge from the armed forces. **8.** *Informal.* the right or appropriate thing: *that's the ticket.* **9. have (got) tickets on oneself.** *Austral. informal.* to be conceited. ~*vb.* (*tr.*) **10.** to issue or attach a ticket or tickets to. **11.** *Informal.* to earmark for a particular purpose. [C17: from Old French *etiquet,* from *estiquier* to stick on, from Middle Dutch *steken* to STICK[2]]

tick+et of leave *n.* (formerly in Britain) a permit allowing a convict (**ticket-of-leave man**) to leave prison, after serving only part of his sentence, with certain restrictions placed on him.

tick fe+ver *n.* **1.** any acute infectious febrile disease caused by the bite of an infected tick. **2.** another name for **Rocky Mountain spotted fever.**

tick+ing ('tɪkɪŋ) *n.* a strong cotton fabric, often striped, used esp. for mattress and pillow covers. [C17: from TICK[3]]

tick+le ('tɪk°l) *vb.* **1.** to touch, stroke, or poke (a person, part of the body, etc.) so as to produce pleasure, laughter, or a twitching sensation. **2.** (*tr.*) to excite pleasurably; gratify. **3.** (*tr.*) to delight or entertain (often in the phrase **tickle one's fancy**). **4.** (*intr.*) to itch or tingle. **5.** (*tr.*) to catch (a fish, esp. a trout) by grasping it with the hands and gently moving the fingers into its gills. **6. tickle pink** *or* **to death.** to please greatly: *he was tickled pink to be elected president.* ~*n.* **7.** a sensation of light stroking or itching. **8.** the act of tickling. [C14: related to Old English *tinclian,* Old High German *kizzilōn,* Old Norse *kitla,* Latin *titillāre* to TITILLATE]

tick+ler ('tɪklə) *n.* **1.** Also called: **tickler file.** *U.S.* a memorandum book or file. **2.** *Accounting, U.S.* a single-entry business journal. **3.** a person or thing that tickles. **4.** *Informal, chiefly Brit.* a difficult or delicate problem.

tick+ler coil *n.* a small inductance coil connected in series in the anode circuit of a valve and magnetically coupled to a coil in the grid circuit to provide feedback.

tick+lish ('tɪklɪʃ) *adj.* **1.** susceptible and sensitive to being tickled. **2.** delicate or difficult: *a ticklish situation.* **3.** easily upset or offended. —**'tick+lish+ly** *adv.* —**'tick+lish+ness** *n.*

tick off *vb.* (*tr., adv.*) **1.** to mark with a tick. **2.** *Informal, chiefly Brit.* to scold; reprimand.

tick o·ver *vb.* (*intr., adv.*) **1.** Also: **idle.** *Brit.* (of an engine) to run at low speed with the throttle control closed and the transmission disengaged. **2.** to run smoothly without any major changes: *keep the firm ticking over until I get back.* ~*n.* **tick-o·ver. 3.** *Brit.* **a.** the speed of an engine when it is ticking over. **b.** (*as modifier*): *tick-over speed.*

tick+tack ('tɪk,tæk) *n.* **1.** *Brit.* a system of sign language, mainly using the hands, by which bookmakers transmit their odds to each other at race courses. **2.** *U.S.* a ticking sound, as made by a clock. [from TICK[1]]

tick-tack-toe (,tɪktæk'təʊ) *or* **tick-tack-too** (,tɪktæk'tu:) *n.* the usual U.S. term for **noughts and crosses.** [C19: from TICK-TACK (meaning: an obsolete variety of backgammon)]

tick+tock ('tɪk,tɒk) *n.* **1.** a ticking sound as made by a clock. ~*vb.* **2.** (*intr.*) to make a ticking sound.

tick tre+foil *n.* any of various tropical and subtropical leguminous plants of the genus *Desmodium,* having trifoliate leaves, clusters of small purplish or white flowers, and sticky jointed seed pods, which separate into segments that cling to animals. Also called: **beggar-ticks.**

Ti+con+der+o+ga (,taɪkɒndə'rəʊgə) *n.* a village in NE New York State, on Lake George: site of Fort Ticonderoga, a strategic point in the War of American Independence.

t.i.d. (in prescriptions) *abbrev. for* ter in die. [Latin: three times a day]

tid+al ('taɪd°l) *adj.* **1.** relating to, characterized by, or affected by tides: *a tidal estuary.* **2.** dependent on the state of the tide: *a tidal ferry.* **3.** (of a glacier) reaching the sea and discharging floes or icebergs. —**'tid+al+ly** *adv.*

tid+al ba+sin *n.* a basin for vessels that is filled at high tide.

tid+al wave *n.* **1.** a nontechnical name for **tsunami. 2.** an unusually large incoming wave, often caused by high winds and spring tides. **3.** a forceful and widespread movement in public opinion, action, etc.

tid+bit ('tɪd,bɪt) *n.* the usual U.S. spelling of **titbit.**

tid+dler ('tɪdlə) *n. Brit. informal.* **1.** a very small fish or aquatic creature, esp. a stickleback, minnow, or tadpole. **2.** a small child, esp. one undersized for its age. [C19: from dialectal *tittlebat,* childish variant of STICKLEBACK, influenced by TIDDLY[1]]

tid+dly[1] ('tɪdlɪ) *Brit. adj.* small; tiny. [C19: childish variant of LITTLE]

tid+dly[2] ('tɪdlɪ) *adj. Slang, chiefly Brit.* slightly drunk. [C19 (meaning: a drink): of unknown origin]

tid·dly+winks ('tɪdlɪ,wɪŋks) *n.* a game in which players try to flick discs of plastic into a cup by pressing them sharply on the side with other larger discs. [C19: probably from TIDDLY[1] + dialect *wink,* variant of WINCH]

tide[1] (taɪd) *n.* **1.** the cyclic rise and fall of sea level caused by the gravitational pull of the sun and moon. There are usually two high tides and two low tides in each lunar day. See also **neap tide, spring tide. 2.** the current, ebb, or flow of water at a specified place resulting from these changes in level: *the tide is coming in.* **3.** See **ebb** (sense 3) and **flood** (sense 3). **4.** a widespread tendency or movement: *the tide of resentment against the government.* **5.** a critical point in time; turning point: *the tide of his fortunes.* **6.** *Northern Brit. dialect.* a fair or holiday. **7.** *Archaic except in combination.* a season or time: *Christmastide.* **8.** *Rare.* any body of mobile water, such as a stream. **9.** *Archaic.* a favourable opportunity. ~*vb.* **10.** to carry or be carried with or as if with the tide. **11.** (*intr.*) to ebb and flow like the tide. [Old English *tīd* time; related to Old High German *zīt,* Old Norse *tīthr* time] —**'tide+less** *adj.* **'tide+,like** *adj.*

tide[2] (taɪd) *vb.* (*intr.*) *Archaic.* to happen. [Old English *tīdan;* related to Old Frisian *tīdia* to proceed to, Middle Low German *tīden* to hurry, Old Norse *tītha* to desire]

tide-gauge *n.* a gauge used to measure extremes or the present level of tidal movement.

tide+land ('taɪd,lænd) *n. U.S.* land between high-water and low-water marks.

tide+mark ('taɪd,mɑ:k) *n.* **1.** a mark left by the highest or lowest point of a tide. **2.** a marker indicating the highest or lowest point reached by a tide. **3.** *Chiefly Brit.* a mark showing a level reached by a liquid: *a tidemark on the bath.* **4.** *Informal, chiefly Brit.* a dirty mark on the skin, indicating the extent to which someone has washed.

tide o·ver *vb.* (*tr.*) to help to get through (a period of difficulty, distress, etc.) *the money tided him over until he got a job.*

tide-rip *n.* another word for **riptide** (sense 1).

tide+wait·er ('taɪd,weɪtə) *n.* (formerly) a customs officer who boarded and inspected incoming ships.

tide+wat·er ('taɪd,wɔ:tə) *n.* **1.** water that advances and recedes with the tide. **2.** water that covers land that is dry at low tide. **3.** *U.S.* **a.** coastal land drained by tidal streams. **b.** (*as modifier*): *tidewater regions.*

tide+way ('taɪd,weɪ) *n.* a strong tidal current or its channel, esp. the tidal part of a river.

tid+ings ('taɪdɪŋz) *pl. n.* information or news. [Old English *tīdung;* related to Middle Low German *tīdinge* information, Old Norse *tidhendi* events; see TIDE[2]]

ti·dy ('taɪdɪ) *adj.* **+di+er, +di+est. 1.** characterized by or indicating neatness and order. **2.** *Informal.* considerable: *a tidy sum of money.* ~*vb.* **+dies, +dy+ing, +died. 3.** (when *intr.*, usually foll. by *up*) to put (things) in order; neaten. ~*n., pl.* **+dies. 4. a.** a small container in which odds and ends are kept. **b. sink tidy.** a container with holes in the bottom, kept in the sink to retain rubbish that might clog the plug hole. **5.** *Chiefly U.S.* an ornamental protective covering for the back or arms of a chair. [C13 (in the sense: timely, seasonable, excellent): from TIDE[1] + -Y[1]; related to Dutch *tijdig* timely] —**'ti+di+ly** *adv.* —**'ti+di+ness** *n.*

tie (taɪ) *vb.* **ties, ty+ing, tied. 1.** (when *tr.*, often foll. by *up*) to fasten or be fastened with string, thread, etc. **2.** to make (a knot or bow) in (something): *to tie a knot; tie a ribbon.* **3.** (*tr.*) to restrict or secure. **4.** to equal (the score) of (a competitor or fellow candidate). **5.** (*tr.*) *Informal.* to unite in marriage. **6.** *Music.* **a.** to execute (two successive notes of the same pitch) as though they formed one note of composite time value. **b.** to connect (two printed notes) with a tie. **7. fit to be tied.** *Slang.* very angry or upset. ~*n.* **8.** a bond, link, or fastening. **9.** a restriction or restraint. **10.** a string, wire, ribbon, etc., with which something is tied. **11.** a long narrow piece of material worn, esp. by men, under the collar of a shirt, tied in a knot close to the throat with the ends hanging down the front. U.S. name: **necktie. 12. a.** an equality in score, attainment, etc., in a contest. **b.** the match or competition in which such a result is attained. **13.** a structural member such as a tie beam or tie rod. **14.** *Sport, Brit.* a match or game in an eliminating competition: *a cup tie.* **15.** (*usually pl.*) a shoe fastened by means of laces. **16.** the U.S. name for **sleeper** (on a railway track). **17.** *Music.* a slur connecting two notes of the same pitch indicating that the sound is to be prolonged for their joint time value. **18.** *Surveying.* one of two measurements running from two points on a survey line to a point of detail to fix its position. **19.** *Lacemaking.* another name for **bride**². ~See also **tie in, tie up.** [Old English *tīgan* to tie; related to Old Norse *teygja* to draw, stretch out, Old English *tēon* to pull; see TUG, TOW¹, TIGHT]

tie+back ('taɪˌbæk) *n. U.S.* **a.** a length of cord, ribbon, or other fabric used for tying a curtain to one side. **b.** a curtain having such a device.

tie beam *n.* a horizontal beam that serves to prevent two other structural members from separating, esp. one that connects two corresponding rafters in a roof or roof truss.

tie+break·er ('taɪˌbreɪkə) *n. Tennis.* a method of deciding quickly the result of a set drawn at six-all, usually involving the playing of one deciding game in which each player serves alternately.

Tieck (*German* tiːk) *n.* **Lud·wig** ('luːtvɪç). 1773–1853, German romantic writer, noted esp. for his fairy tales.

tie clasp *n.* a clip, often ornamental, which holds a tie in place against a shirt. Also called: **tie clip.**

tied (taɪd) *adj. Brit.* **1.** (of a public house, etc.) obliged to sell only the beer, etc., of a particular brewery. **2.** (of a house or cottage) rented out to the tenant for as long as he is employed by the owner.

tie-dye·ing *n.* a method of dyeing textiles to produce patterns by tying sections of the cloth together so that they will not absorb the dye. —'**tie-ˌdyed** *adj.*

tie in *vb.* (*adv.*) **1.** to come or bring into a certain relationship; coordinate. ~*n.* **tie-in. 2.** a link, relationship, or coordination. **3.** publicity material, a book, tape, etc., linked to a film or broadcast programme or series. **4.** *U.S.* **a.** a sale or advertisement offering products of which a purchaser must buy one or more in addition to his purchase. **b.** an item sold or advertised in this way, esp. the extra item. **c.** (*as modifier*): *a tie-in sale.*

tie line *n.* a telephone line between two private branch exchanges or private exchanges that may or may not pass through a main exchange.

tie+man+nite ('tiːməˌnaɪt) *n.* a grey mineral consisting of mercury selenide. Formula: HgSe. [C19: named after J. C. W. F. *Tiemann* (1848–99), German scientist]

Tien Shan ('tjɛn'ʃɑːn) *n.* a great mountain system of central Asia, in the Kirghiz SSR of the Soviet Union and the Sinkiang-Uighur AR of W China, extending for about 2500 km (1500 miles). Highest peak: Pobeda Peak, 7439 m (24 406 ft.). Russian name: **Tyan-Shan.**

Tien+tsin ('tjɛn'tsɪn) *or* **T'ien-ching** ('tjɛn'tʃɪŋ) *n.* an industrial city in NE China, in Hopeh province, on the Grand Canal 51 km (32 miles) from the Yellow Sea: the third largest city in China; seat of Nankai University (1919). Pop.: 4 280 000 (1970 est.).

tie+pin ('taɪˌpɪn) *n.* an ornamental pin of various shapes used to pin the two ends of a tie to a shirt.

Tie·po·lo (*Italian* 'tjɛpolo; *English* tiː'ɛpəˌləʊ) *n.* **Gio·van·ni Bat·tis·ta** (dʒo'vanni bat'tista). 1696–1770, Italian rococo painter, esp. of frescoes as in the Residenz at Würzburg.

tier¹ (tɪə) *n.* **1.** one of a set of rows placed one above and behind the other, such as theatre seats. **2. a.** a layer or level. **b.** (*in combination*): *a three-tier cake.* **3.** a rank, order, or row. ~*vb.* **4.** to be or arrange in tiers. [C16: from Old French *tire* rank, of Germanic origin; compare Old English *tīr* embellishment]

ti·er² ('taɪə) *n.* a person or thing that ties.

tierce (tɪəs) *n.* **1.** a variant of **terce. 2.** the third of eight basic positions from which a parry or attack can be made in fencing. **3.** (tɜːs). *Piquet, etc.* a sequence of three cards in the same suit. **4.** an obsolete measure of capacity equal to 42 wine gallons. [C15: from Old French, feminine of *tiers* third, from Latin *tertius*]

tierce de Pi+car+die (*French* tjɛrs də pikar'di) *n.* another term for **Picardy third.**

tier+cel ('tɪəsəl) *n.* a variant of **tercel.**

tie rod *n.* any rod or bar designed to prevent the separation of two parts, as in a vehicle.

Tier+ra del Fue+go (*Spanish* 'tjerra ðel 'fweɣo) *n.* an archipelago at the S extremity of South America, separated from the mainland by the Strait of Magellan: the west and south belong to Chile, the east to Argentina, and several islands are disputed. Area: 73 643 sq. km (28 434 sq. miles).

tie up *vb.* (*adv.*) **1.** (*tr.*) to attach or bind securely with or as if with string, rope, etc. **2.** to moor (a vessel). **3.** (*tr.; often passive*) to engage the attentions of: *he's tied up at the moment and can't see you.* **4.** (*tr.; often passive*) to conclude (the organization of something): *the plans for the trip were tied up well in advance.* **5.** to come or bring to a complete standstill. **6.** (*tr.*) to invest or commit (funds, etc.) and so make unavailable for other uses. **7.** (*tr.*) to subject (property) to conditions that prevent sale, alienation, or other action. ~*n.* **tie-up. 8.** a link or connection. **9.** *Chiefly U.S.* a standstill. **10.** *Chiefly U.S.* an informal term for **traffic jam.**

tiff¹ (tɪf) *n.* **1.** a petty quarrel. **2.** a fit of ill humour. ~*vb.* **3.** (*intr.*) to have or be in a tiff. [C18: of unknown origin]

tiff² (tɪf) *n. Archaic.* a small draught of alcoholic drink; dram. [C18: see TIFFIN]

tif+fa+ny ('tɪfənɪ) *n., pl.* **+nies.** a sheer fine gauzy fabric. [C17: (in the sense: a fine dress worn on Twelfth Night): from Old French *tifanie,* from ecclesiastical Latin *theophania* Epiphany; see THEOPHANY]

Tif+fa+ny glass *n.* another term for **Favrile glass.** [C19: named after Louis C. *Tiffany* (1848–1933), U.S. painter and glass manufacturer]

tif+fin ('tɪfɪn) *n.* (in India) a light meal, esp. one taken at midday. [C18: probably from obsolete *tiffing,* from *tiff* to sip]

Tif+lis (tɪf'liːs) *n.* transliteration of the Russian name for **Tbilisi.**

ti+ger ('taɪgə) *n.* **1.** a large feline mammal, *Panthera tigris,* of forests in most of Asia, having a tawny yellow coat with black stripes. **2.** (*not in technical use*) any of various other animals, such as the jaguar, leopard, and thylacine. **3.** a dynamic, forceful, or cruel person. [C13: from Old French *tigre,* from Latin *tigris,* from Greek, of Iranian origin] —'**ti+ger+ish** *or* '**ti+grish** *adj.* —'**ti·ger-like** *adj.*

Ti+ger balm *n. Trademark.* (in Malaysia) a mentholated ointment widely used as a panacea.

ti+ger bee+tle *n.* any active predatory beetle of the family *Cicindelidae,* chiefly of warm dry regions, having powerful mandibles and long legs.

ti+ger cat *n.* **1.** a medium-sized feline mammal, *Felis tigrina,* of Central and South America, having a dark-striped coat. **2.** any similar feline with tiger-like markings, such as the margay.

ti+ger lil·y *n.* **1.** a lily plant, *Lilium tigrinum,* of China and Japan, cultivated for its flowers, which have black-spotted orange reflexed petals. **2.** any of various similar lilies.

ti+ger moth *n.* any of various moths of the family *Arctiidae,* esp. of the genus *Arctia,* typically having a stout body and wings conspicuously marked with stripes and spots.

ti·ger's-eye ('taɪgəzˌaɪ) *or* **ti·ger+eye** *n.* **1.** a golden brown silicified variety of crocidolite, used as an ornamental stone. **2.** a glaze resembling this, used on pottery.

ti+ger shark *n.* **1.** a voracious omnivorous requiem shark, *Galeocerdo cuvieri,* chiefly of tropical waters, having a striped or spotted body. **2.** any of certain other spotted sharks, such as *Stegostoma tigrinum,* of the Indian Ocean.

ti+ger snake *n.* a highly venomous brown-and-yellow elapid snake, *Notechis scutatus,* of Australia and Tasmania.

tight (taɪt) *adj.* **1.** stretched or drawn so as not to be loose; taut: *a tight cord.* **2.** fitting or covering in a close manner: *a tight dress.* **3.** held, made, fixed, or closed firmly and securely: *a tight knot.* **4. a.** of close and compact construction or organization, esp. so as to be impervious to water, air, etc. **b.** (*in combination*): *watertight; airtight.* **5.** unyielding or stringent: *to keep a tight hold on resources.* **6.** cramped or constricted: *a tight fit.* **7.** mean or miserly. **8.** difficult and problematic: *a tight situation.* **9.** hardly profitable: *a tight bargain.* **10.** *Economics.* **a.** (of a commodity) difficult to obtain; in excess demand. **b.** (of funds, money, etc.) difficult and expensive to borrow because of high demand or restrictive monetary policy. **c.** (of markets) characterized by excess demand or scarcity with prices tending to rise. Compare **easy** (sense 8). **11.** (of a match or game) very close or even. **12.** *Informal.* drunk. **13.** *Informal.* (of a person) showing tension. **14.** *Archaic or dialect.* neat. **15. sit tight.** to maintain one's position, stand, or opinion firmly. ~*adv.* **16.** in a close, firm, or secure way: *pull it tight.* **17. sleep tight.** to sleep soundly. [C14: probably variant of *thight,* from Old Norse *thēttr* close; related to Middle High German *dīhte* thick] —'**tight+ly** *adv.* —'**tight+ness** *n.*

tight+en ('taɪtən) *vb.* **1.** to make or become tight or tighter. **2. tighten one's belt.** to economize. —'**tight+en+er** *n.*

tight+fist·ed (ˌtaɪt'fɪstɪd) *adj.* mean; miserly.

tight+knit (ˌtaɪt'nɪt) *adj.* **1.** closely integrated: *a tightknit community.* **2.** organized carefully and concisely.

tight-lipped *adj.* **1.** reticent, secretive, or taciturn. **2.** with the lips pressed tightly together, as through anger.

tight+rope ('taɪtˌrəʊp) *n.* a rope or cable stretched taut above the ground on which acrobats walk or perform balancing feats.

tight+rope walk+er *n.* an acrobat who performs on a tightrope. —**tight+rope walk+ing** *n.*

tights (taɪts) *pl. n.* **1.** Also called (esp. U.S. and Austral.): **pantihose.** a one-piece clinging garment covering the body from the waist to the feet, worn by women in place of stockings and also by acrobats, dancers, etc. **2.** a similar garment formerly worn by men, as in the 16th century with a doublet.

tight+wad ('taɪtˌwɒd) *n. U.S. slang.* a stingy person; miser.

Tig·lath-pi·le·ser I ('tɪglæθ pɪ'liːzə, paɪ-) *n.* king of Assyria (?1116–?1093 B.C.), who extended his kingdom to the upper Euphrates and defeated the king of Babylonia.

Tig·lath-pi·le·ser III *n.* known as *Pulu.* died ?727 B.C., king of Assyria (745–727), who greatly extended his empire, subjugating Syria and Palestine.

tig+lic ac·id ('tɪglɪk) *n.* a syrupy liquid or crystalline colourless unsaturated carboxylic acid, with the *trans-* configuration, found in croton oil and used in perfumery; *trans*-2-methyl-2-butenoic acid. Formula: $CH_3CH{:}C(CH_3)COOH$. [C19 *tiglic*, from New Latin phrase *Croton tiglium* (name of the croton plant), of uncertain origin]

ti·gon ('taɪgən) *or* **tig·lon** ('tɪglɒn) *n.* the hybrid offspring of a male tiger and a female lion.

Ti·gré ('ti:greɪ) *n.* **1.** a province of N Ethiopia, bordering on Eritrea: formerly a separate kingdom. Capital: Makale. Pop.: 1 787 500 (1971 est.). Area: 65 900 sq. km (25 444 sq. miles). **2.** a language of NE Ethiopia, belonging to the SE Semitic subfamily of the Afro-Asiatic family.

ti·gress ('taɪgrɪs) *n.* **1.** a female tiger. **2.** a fierce, cruel, or wildly passionate woman.

Ti·gri·nya (tɪ'gri:njə) *n.* a language of N Ethiopia, belonging to the SE Semitic subfamily of the Afro-Asiatic family.

Ti·gris ('taɪgrɪs) *n.* a river in SW Asia, rising in E Turkey and flowing southeast through Baghdad to the Euphrates in SE Iraq, forming the delta of the Shatt-al-Arab, which flows into the Persian Gulf: part of a canal and irrigation system as early as 2400 B.C., with many ancient cities (including Nineveh) on its banks. Length: 1900 km (1180 miles).

Ti·hwa *or* **Ti·hua** ('ti:'hwɑ:) *n.* another name for **Urumchi.**

Ti·jua·na (ti:'wɑ:nə; *Spanish* ti'xhwana) *or* **Ti·a Jua·na** *n.* a city and resort in NW Mexico, in Baja California. Pop.: 386 852 (1974 est.).

tike (taɪk) *n.* a variant spelling of **tyke.**

ti·ki ('ti:kɪ) *n.* an amulet or figurine in the form of a carved representation of an ancestor, worn in some Maori cultures. [from Maori]

tik·o·loshe (ˌtɪkɒ'lɒʃ, -'lɒʃɪ) *n.* a variant of **tokoloshe.**

til (tɪl, ti:l) *n.* another name for **sesame,** esp. a variety grown in India. [C19: from Hindi, from Sanskrit *tilá* sesame]

ti·lap·i·a (tɪ'læpɪə, -'leɪ-) *n.* any mouthbrooding cichlid fish of the African freshwater genus *Tilapia:* used as food fishes. [C18: from New Latin]

Til·burg (*Dutch* 'tɪlbyrx; *English* 'tɪlbɜ:g) *n.* a city in the S Netherlands, in North Brabant: textile industries. Pop.: 152 318 (1974 est.).

til·bur·y ('tɪlbərɪ, -brɪ) *n., pl.* **·bur·ies.** a light two-wheeled horse-drawn open carriage, seating two people. [C19: probably named after the inventor]

Til·bur·y ('tɪlbərɪ, -brɪ) *n.* an area in Essex, on the River Thames: extensive docks; principal container port of the Port of London.

til·de ('tɪldə) *n.* the diacritical mark (˜) placed over a letter to indicate a palatal nasal consonant, as in Spanish *señor.* This symbol is also used in the International Phonetic Alphabet to represent any nasalized vowel. [C19: from Spanish, from Latin *titulus* title, superscription]

tile (taɪl) *n.* **1.** a flat thin slab of fired clay, rubber, linoleum, etc., usually square or rectangular and sometimes ornamental, used with others to cover a roof, floor, wall, etc. **2.** a short pipe made of earthenware, concrete, or plastic, used with others to form a drain. **3.** tiles collectively. **4.** a rectangular block used as a playing piece in mahjong and other games. **5. on the tiles.** *Informal.* on a spree, esp. of drinking or debauchery. ~*vb.* **6.** (*tr.*) to cover with tiles. [Old English *tīgele,* from Latin *tēgula;* related to German *Ziegel*] —'**til·er** *n.*

tile·fish ('taɪlˌfɪʃ) *n., pl.* **·fish** *or* **·fish·es.** a large brightly coloured deep-sea percoid food fish, *Lopholatilus chamaeleonticeps,* of warm and tropical seas, esp. the North American coast of the Atlantic: family *Branchiostegidae.*

til·i·a·ceous (ˌtɪlɪ'eɪʃəs) *adj.* of, relating to, or belonging to the *Tiliaceae,* a family of flowering plants, mostly trees and shrubs of warm and tropical regions: includes linden and jute. [C19: from Late Latin *tiliāceus,* from Latin *tilia* linden]

til·ing ('taɪlɪŋ) *n.* **1.** tiles collectively. **2.** something made of or surfaced with tiles.

till[1] (tɪl) *conj., prep.* short for **until.** Also (not standard): **'til.** [Old English *til;* related to Old Norse *til* to, Old High German *zil* goal, aim]

Usage. *Till* is a variant of *until* that is acceptable at all levels of language. *Until* is, however, often preferred at the beginning of a sentence in formal writing: *until his behaviour improves, he cannot become a member.*

till[2] (tɪl) *vb.* **1.** to cultivate and work (land) for the raising of crops. **2.** (*tr.*) another word for **plough.** [Old English *tilian* to try, obtain; related to Old Frisian *tilia* to obtain, Old Saxon *tilōn* to obtain, Old High German *zilōn* to hasten towards] —'**till·a·ble** *adj.* —'**till·er** *n.*

till[3] (tɪl) *n.* **1.** a box, case, or drawer in which money is kept, esp. in a shop. **2.** another term for **cash register.** [C15 *tylle,* of obscure origin]

till[4] (tɪl) *n.* an unstratified glacial deposit consisting of rock fragments of various sizes. The most common is boulder clay. [C17: of unknown origin]

till·age ('tɪlɪdʒ) *n.* **1.** the act, process, or art of tilling. **2.** tilled land.

til·land·si·a (tɪ'lændzɪə) *n.* any bromeliaceous epiphytic plant of the genus *Tillandsia,* such as Spanish moss, of tropical and subtropical America. [C18: New Latin, named after Elias *Tillands* (died 1693), Finno-Swedish botanist]

till·er[1] ('tɪlə) *n. Nautical.* a handle fixed to the top of a rudder-post to serve as a lever in steering it. [C15: from Anglo-French *teiler* beam of a loom, from Medieval Latin *tēlārium,* from Latin *tēla* web] —'**till·er·less** *adj.*

till·er[2] ('tɪlə) *n.* **1.** a shoot that arises from the base of the stem in grasses. **2.** a less common name for **sapling.** ~*vb.* **3.** (*intr.*) (of a plant) to produce tillers. [Old English *telgor* twig; related to Icelandic *tjalga* branch]

Til·lich ('tɪlɪk) *n.* **Paul Jo·han·nes.** 1886–1965, U.S. Protestant theologian and philosopher, born in Germany. His works include *The Courage to Be* (1952) and *Systematic Theology* (1951–63).

til·li·cum ('tɪlɪkəm) *n. North American informal.* (in the Pacific Northwest) a friend. [from Chinook Jargon, from Chinook *tlxam* kin, esp. as distinguished from chiefs]

Til·ly ('tɪlɪ) *n.* Count **Jo·han Tser·claes von** ('jo:han tsɛr'klas fɔn). 1559–1632, Flemish soldier, who commanded the army of The Catholic League (1618–32) and the imperial forces (1630–32) in the Thirty Years' War.

Til·sit ('tɪlzɪt) *n.* the former name (until 1945) of **Sovetsk.**

tilt[1] (tɪlt) *vb.* **1.** to incline or cause to incline at an angle. **2.** (*usually intr.*) to attack or overthrow (a person or people) in a tilt or joust. **3.** (when *intr.,* often foll. by *at*) to aim or thrust: *to tilt a lance.* **4.** (*tr.*) to work or forge with a tilt hammer. ~*n.* **5.** a slope or angle: *at a tilt.* **6.** the act of tilting. **7.** (esp. in medieval Europe) **a.** a jousting contest. **b.** a thrust with a lance or pole delivered during a tournament. **8.** any dispute, contest, or similar encounter. **9.** See **tilt hammer. 10. (at) full tilt.** at full speed or force. [Old English *tealtian;* related to Dutch *touteren* to totter, Norwegian *tylta* to tiptoe, *tylten* unsteady] —'**tilt·er** *n.*

tilt[2] (tɪlt) *n.* **1.** an awning or canopy, usually of canvas, for a boat, booth, etc. ~*vb.* **2.** (*tr.*) to cover or provide with a tilt. [Old English *teld;* related to Old High German *zelt* tent, Old Norse *tjald* tent]

tilth (tɪlθ) *n.* **1.** the act or process of tilling land. **2.** the condition of soil or land that has been tilled. esp. with respect to suitability for promoting plant growth. [Old English *tilthe;* see TILL[2]]

tilt ham·mer *n.* a drop hammer consisting of a heavy head moving at the end of a pivoted arm; used in forging.

tilt·yard ('tɪltˌjɑ:d) *n.* (formerly) an enclosed area for tilting.

Tim. *Bible. abbrev. for* Timothy.

Tim·a·ru ('tɪməˌru:) *n.* a port and resort in S New Zealand, on E South Island. Pop.: 28 326 (1971).

tim·bal *or* **tym·bal** ('tɪmbᵊl) *n. Music.* a type of kettledrum. [C17: from French *timbale,* from Old French *tamballe,* (associated also with *cymbale* cymbal), from Old Spanish *atabal,* from Arabic *at-tabl* the drum]

tim·bale (tæm'bɑ:l; *French* tɛ̃'bal) *n.* **1.** a mixture of meat, fish, etc. in a rich sauce, cooked in a mould lined with potato or pastry. **2.** a plain straight-sided mould in which such a dish is prepared. [C19: from French: kettledrum]

tim·ber ('tɪmbə) *n.* **1. a.** wood, esp. when regarded as a construction material. **b.** (*as modifier*): *a timber cottage.* Usual U.S. word: **lumber. 2. a.** trees collectively. **b.** *Chiefly U.S.* woodland. **3.** a piece of wood used in a structure. **4.** *Nautical.* a frame in a wooden vessel. **5.** potential material, for a post, rank, etc.: *he is managerial timber.* ~*vb.* **6.** (*tr.*) to provide with timbers. ~*interj.* **7.** a lumberjack's shouted warning when a tree is about to fall. [Old English; related to Old High German *zimbar* wood, Old Norse *timbr* timber, Latin *domus* house]

tim·bered ('tɪmbəd) *adj.* **1.** made of or containing timber or timbers. **2.** covered with trees; wooded.

tim·ber·head ('tɪmbəˌhɛd) *n. Nautical.* a timber, the top of which rises above deck level and is used as a bollard.

tim·ber hitch *n.* a knot used for tying a rope round a spar, log, etc., for haulage.

tim·ber·ing ('tɪmbərɪŋ) *n.* **1.** timbers collectively. **2.** work made of timber.

tim·ber·land ('tɪmbəˌlænd) *n. U.S.* land covered with trees grown for their timber.

tim·ber line *n.* the altitudinal or latitudinal limit of tree growth. Also called: **tree line.**

tim·ber wolf *n.* a variety of the wolf, *Canis lupus,* having a grey brindled coat and occurring in forested northern regions, esp. of North America. Also called: **grey wolf.**

tim·ber·work ('tɪmbəˌwɜ:k) *n.* a structure made of timber.

tim·ber·yard ('tɪmbəˌjɑ:d) *n. Brit.* an establishment where timber and sometimes other building materials are stored or sold. U.S. word: **lumberyard.**

tim·bre ('tɪmbə, 'tæmbə; *French* 'tɛ̃:br) *n.* **1.** *Phonetics.* the distinctive tone quality differentiating one vowel or sonant from another. **2.** *Music.* tone colour or quality of sound, esp. a specific type of tone colour. [C19: from French: note of a bell, from Old French: drum, from Medieval Greek *timbanon,* from Greek *tumpanon* drum; see TYMPANON]

tim·brel ('tɪmbrəl) *n. Chiefly biblical.* another word for **tambourine.** [C16: from Old French; see TIMBRE]

Tim·buk·tu (ˌtɪmbʌk'tu:) *n.* **1.** a town in central Mali, on the River Niger: terminus of a trans-Saharan caravan route; a great Muslim centre (14th–16th centuries). Pop.: 9000 (1967 est.). French name: **Tombouctou. 2.** any distant or outlandish place: *from here to Timbuktu.*

time (taɪm) *n.* **1. a.** the continuous passage of existence in which events pass from a state of potentiality in the future, through the present, to a state of finality in the past. **b.** (*as modifier*): *time travel.* Related adj.: **temporal. 2.** *Physics.* a quantity measuring duration, usually with reference to a periodic process such as the rotation of the earth or the vibration of electromagnetic radiation emitted from certain atoms (see **caesium clock, second**[2] (sense 1)). In classical mechanics, time is absolute in the sense that the time of an event is independent of the observer. According to the theory of relativity it depends on the observer's frame of reference.

Time is considered as a fourth coordinate required, along with three spatial coordinates, to specify an event. See **space-time continuum.** **3.** a specific point on this continuum expressed in terms of hours and minutes: *the time is four o'clock.* **4.** a system of reckoning for expressing time: *Greenwich mean time.* **5. a.** a definite and measurable portion of this continuum. **b.** (*as modifier*): *time limit.* **6. a.** an accepted period such as a day, season, etc. **b.** (*in combination*): *springtime.* **7.** an unspecified interval; a while: *I was there for a time.* **8.** (*often pl.*) a period or point marked by specific attributes or events: *the Victorian times; time for breakfast.* **9.** a sufficient interval or period: *have you got time to help me?* **10.** an instance or occasion: *I called you three times.* **11.** an occasion or period of specified quality: *have a good time; a miserable time.* **12.** the duration of human existence. **13.** the heyday of human life: *in her time she was a great star.* **14.** a suitable period or moment: *it's time I told you.* **15.** the expected interval in which something is done: *the flying time from New York to London was seven hours.* **16.** a particularly important moment, esp. childbirth or death: *her time had come.* **17.** (*pl.*) indicating a degree or amount calculated by multiplication with the number specified: *ten times three is thirty; he earns four times as much as me.* **18.** (*often pl.*) the fashions, thought, etc., of the present age (esp. in the phrases **ahead of one's time, behind the times**). **19.** *Brit.* (in bars, pubs, etc.) short for **closing time.** **20.** *Informal.* a term in jail (esp. in the phrase **do time**). **21. a.** a customary or full period of work. **b.** the rate of pay for this period. **22.** Also (esp. U.S.): **metre. a.** the system of combining beats or pulses in music into successive groupings by which the rhythm of the music is established. **b.** a specific system having a specific number of beats in each grouping or bar: *duple time.* **23.** *Music.* short for time value. **24.** *Prosody.* a unit of duration used in the measurement of poetic metre; mora. **25. against time.** in an effort to complete something in a limited period. **26. ahead of time.** before the deadline. **27. all in good time.** in due course. **28. all the time.** continuously. **29. at one time. a.** once; formerly. **b.** simultaneously. **30. at the same time. a.** simultaneously. **b.** nevertheless; however. **31. at times.** sometimes. **32. beat time.** (of a conductor, etc.) to indicate the tempo or pulse of a piece of music by waving a baton or a hand, tapping out the beats, etc. **33. before one's time.** prematurely. **34. for the time being.** for the moment; temporarily. **35. from time to time.** at intervals; occasionally. **36. gain time.** (of a timepiece) to operate too fast. **37. have no time for.** to have no patience with; not tolerate. **38. in good time. a.** early. **b.** quickly. **39. in no time.** very quickly; almost instantaneously. **40. in one's own time. a.** outside paid working hours. **b.** at one's own rate. **41. in time. a.** early or at the appointed time. **b.** *Music.* at a correct metrical or rhythmical pulse. **42. keep time.** to observe correctly the accent or rhythmical pulse of a piece of music in relation to tempo. **43. lose time.** (of a timepiece) to operate too slowly. **44. lose no time.** to do something without delay. **45. make time (with).** *U.S. informal.* to succeed in seducing. **46. in the nick of time.** at the last possible moment. **47. on time. a.** at the expected or scheduled time. **b.** *U.S.* payable in instalments. **48. pass the time of day.** to exchange casual greetings (with an acquaintance. **49. time and again.** frequently. **50. time off.** a period when one is absent from work for holidays, through sickness, etc. **51. time on.** the Austral. equivalent of **extra time. 52. time out of mind.** from time immemorial. **53. time of one's life.** a very enjoyable or memorable period of time. **54.** (*modifier*) operating automatically at or for a set time, for security or convenience: *time lock; time switch.* ~*vb.* (*tr.*) **55.** to ascertain or calculate the duration or speed of. **56.** to set a time for. **57.** to adjust to keep accurate time. **58.** to pick a suitable time for. **59.** *Sport.* to control the execution or speed of (an action, esp. a shot or stroke) so that it has its full effect at the right moment. ~*interj.* **60.** the word called out by a publican signalling that it is closing time. [Old English *tīma*; related to Old English *tīd* time, Old Norse *tīmi*, Alemanic *zīme*; see TIDE[1]]

time and a half *n.* the rate of pay equalling one and a half times the normal rate, often offered for overtime work.

time and mo·tion stud·y *n.* the analysis of industrial or work procedures to determine the most efficient methods of operation. Also: **time and motion, time study, motion study.**

time bomb *n.* a bomb containing a timing mechanism that determines the time at which it will detonate.

time cap·sule *n.* a container holding articles, documents, etc., representative of the current age, buried in the earth or in the foundations of a new building for discovery in the future.

time·card ('taɪm,kɑ:d) *n.* a card used with a time clock.

time clock *n.* a clock which records, by punching or stamping cards inserted into it, the time of arrival or departure of people, such as employees in a factory.

time con·stant *n. Electronics.* the time required for the current or voltage in a circuit to rise or fall exponentially through approximately 63 per cent of its amplitude.

time-con·sum·ing *adj.* taking up or involving a great deal of time.

time de·pos·it *n.* a bank deposit from which withdrawals may be made only after advance notice or at a specified future date. Compare **demand deposit.**

time ex·po·sure *n.* **1.** an exposure of a photographic film for a relatively long period, usually a few seconds. **2.** a photograph produced by such an exposure.

time-hon·oured *adj.* having been observed for a long time and sanctioned by custom.

time im·me·mo·ri·al *n.* **1.** the distant past beyond memory or record. **2.** *Law.* time beyond legal memory, fixed by English statute as before the reign of Richard I (1189).

time·keep·er ('taɪm,ki:pə) *n.* **1.** a person or thing that keeps or records time. **2.** an employee who maintains a record of the hours worked by the other employees. **3.** a device for indicating time; timepiece. —'**time,keep·ing** *n.*

time-lag *n.* an interval between two connected events.

time-lapse pho·tog·ra·phy *n.* the technique of recording a very slow process, such as the withering of a flower, by taking a large number of photographs on a strip of film at regular intervals. The film is then projected at normal speed.

time·less ('taɪmlɪs) *adj.* **1.** unaffected or unchanged by time; ageless. **2.** eternal. **3.** an archaic word for **untimely.** —'**time·less·ly** *adv.* —'**time·less·ness** *n.*

time loan *n.* a loan repayable before or at a specified future date. Compare **call loan.**

time·ly ('taɪmlɪ) *adj.* ·**li·er,** ·**li·est,** *adv.* **1.** at the right or an opportune or appropriate time. **2.** an archaic word for **early.** —'**time·li·ness** *n.*

time ma·chine *n.* (in science fiction) a machine in which people or objects can be transported into the past or the future.

time·ous ('taɪməs) *adj. Scot.* sufficiently early: *a timeous warning.* [C15: Scottish; see TIME, -OUS] —'**time·ous·ly** *adv.*

time-out *n. Chiefly U.S.* **1.** *Sport.* an interruption in play during which players rest, discuss tactics, or make substitutions. **2.** a break taken during working hours.

time·piece ('taɪm,pi:s) *n.* **1.** any of various devices, such as a clock, watch, or chronometer, which measure and indicate time. **2.** a device which indicates the time but does not strike or otherwise audibly mark the hours.

tim·er ('taɪmə) *n.* **1.** a device for measuring, recording, or indicating time. **2.** a switch or regulator that causes a mechanism to operate at a specific time or at predetermined intervals. **3.** a person or thing that times.

time·sav·ing ('taɪm,seɪvɪŋ) *adj.* shortening the length of time required for an operation, activity, etc. —'**time,sav·er** *n.*

time se·ries *n. Statistics.* a series of values of a variable taken in successive periods of time.

time·serv·er ('taɪm,sɜ:və) *n.* a person who compromises and changes his opinions, way of life, etc., to suit the current fashions. —'**time,serv·ing** *adj., n.*

time shar·ing *n.* **a.** a system by which users at different terminals of a computer can, due to its high speed, apparently communicate with it at the same time. Compare **batch processing. b.** (*as modifier*): *a time-sharing computer.*

time sheet *n.* a card on which are recorded the hours spent working by an employee or employees.

time sig·nal *n.* an announcement of the correct time, esp. on radio or television.

time sig·na·ture *n. Music.* a sign usually consisting of two figures, one above the other, the upper figure representing the number of beats per bar and the lower one the time value of each beat. This sign is placed after the key signature at the outset of a piece or section of a piece.

Times Square *n.* a square formed by the intersection of Broadway and Seventh Avenue in New York City, extending from 42nd to 45th Street.

time stud·y *n.* short for **time and motion study.**

time·ta·ble ('taɪm,teɪbəl) *n.* a list or table of events arranged according to the time when they take place; schedule.

time tri·al *n.* (esp. in cycling) a race in which the competitors compete against the clock over a specified course. —'**time-,tri·al·ling** *n.*

time val·ue *n. Music.* the duration of a given printed note relative to other notes in a composition or section and considered in relation to the basic tempo. Often shortened to **time.** Also called: **note value.**

time·work ('taɪm,wɜ:k) *n.* work paid for by the length of time taken, esp. by the hour or the day. Compare **piecework.** —'**time,work·er** *n.*

time·worn ('taɪm,wɔ:n) *adj.* **1.** showing the adverse effects of overlong use or of old age. **2.** hackneyed; trite.

time zone *n.* a region throughout which the same standard time is used. There are 24 time zones in the world, demarcated approximately by meridians at 15° intervals, an hour apart.

tim·id ('tɪmɪd) *adj.* **1.** easily frightened or upset, esp. by human contact; shy. **2.** indicating shyness or fear. [C16: from Latin *timidus*, from *timēre* to fear] —**ti'mid·i·ty** *or* '**tim·id·ness** *n.* —'**tim·id·ly** *adv.*

tim·ing ('taɪmɪŋ) *n.* the process or art of regulating actions or remarks in relation to others to produce the best effect, as in music, the theatre, sport, etc.

Ti·mi·şoa·ra (*Rumanian* ,timi'ʃwara) *n.* a city in W Rumania: under Turkish and later Hapsburg rule, being allotted to Rumania in 1920. Pop.: 210 520 (1974 est.). Hungarian name: **Temesvár.**

ti·moc·ra·cy (taɪ'mɒkrəsɪ) *n., pl.* ·**cies. 1.** a political unit or system in which possession of property serves as the first requirement for participation in government. **2.** a political unit or system in which love of honour is deemed the guiding principle of government. [C16: from Old French *tymocracie*, ultimately from Greek *timokratia*, from *timē* worth, honour, price + -CRACY] —**ti·mo·crat·ic** (,taɪmə'krætɪk) *or* ,**ti·mo'crat·i·cal** *adj.*

Ti·mor ('ti:mɔ:, 'taɪ-) *n.* an island in Indonesia in the Malay Archipelago, the largest and easternmost of the Lesser Sunda Islands: the east, together with an enclave on the NW coast, formed the Portuguese overseas province of Portuguese Timor until civil war in 1975 led to its annexation by Indonesia; made an Indonesian province in 1976. Area: 30 775 sq. km (11 883 sq. miles).

tim·or·ous ('tɪmərəs) *adj.* **1.** fearful or timid. **2.** indicating fear or timidity. [C15: from Old French *temoros,* from Medieval Latin *timōrōsus,* from Latin *timor* fear, from *timēre* to be afraid] —**'tim·or·ous·ly** *adv.* —**'tim·or·ous·ness** *n.*

Ti·mor Sea *n.* an arm of the Indian Ocean between Australia and Timor. Width: about 480 km (300 miles).

Ti·mo·shen·ko (ˌtɪmə'ʃɛŋkəʊ; *Russian* tima'ʃɛnkə) *n.* **Sem·yon Kon·stan·ti·no·vich** (sɪ'mjɔn kənstan'tinəvitʃ). 1895–1970, Soviet general in World War II.

Tim·o·thy ('tɪməθɪ) *n. New Testament.* **1.** a disciple of Paul, who became leader of the Christian community at Ephesus. **2.** either of the two books addressed to him (in full **The First and Second Epistles of Paul the Apostle to Timothy**), containing advice on pastoral matters.

tim·o·thy grass *or* **tim·o·thy** *n.* a perennial grass, *Phleum pratense,* of temperate regions, having erect stiff stems and cylindrical flower spikes: grown for hay and pasture. [C18: apparently named after a *Timothy Hanson,* who brought it to colonial Carolina]

Ti·mour *or* **Ti·mur** (tɪː'mʊə) *n.* See **Tamerlane.**

tim·pa·ni *or* **tym·pa·ni** ('tɪmpənɪ) *pl. n.* (*sometimes functioning as sing.*) a set of kettledrums, two or more in number. Often shortened to **timps** (informal). [from Italian, pl. of *timpano* kettledrum, from Latin: TYMPANUM] —**'tim·pa·nist** *or* **'tym·pa·nist** *n.*

tin (tɪn) *n.* **1.** a metallic element, occurring in cassiterite, that has several allotropes; the ordinary malleable silvery-white metal slowly changes below 13.2°C to a grey powder. It is used extensively in alloys, esp. bronze pewter, and as a noncorroding coating for steel. Symbol: Sn; atomic no.: 50; atomic wt.: 118.69; valency: 2 or 4; relative density: 5.75 (grey), 7.31 (white); melting pt.: 231.89°C; boiling pt.: 2270°C. **2.** Also called (esp. U.S.): **can.** an airtight sealed container of thin sheet metal, usually iron, coated with tin, used for preserving and storing food or drink. **3.** any container made of metallic tin. **4.** Also called: **tin·ful.** the contents of a tin or the amount a tin will hold. **5.** any metal regarded as cheap or flimsy. **6.** *Brit.* a loaf of bread with a rectangular shape, baked in a tin. **7.** *Slang.* money. ~*vb.* **tins, tin·ning, tinned.** (*tr.*) **8.** to put (food, etc.) into a tin or tins; preserve in a tin. **9.** to plate or coat with tin. **10.** to prepare (a metal) for soldering or brazing by applying a thin layer of solder to the surface. ~Related adjs.: **stannic, stannous.** [Old English; related to Old Norse *tin,* Old High German *zin*] —**'tin·ˌlike** *adj.*

tin·a·mou ('tɪnəˌmuː) *n.* any bird of the order *Tinamiformes* of Central and South America, having small wings, a heavy body, and an inconspicuous plumage. [C18: via French from Carib (Galibi) *tinamu*]

tin·cal ('tɪŋkᵊl) *n.* another name for **borax** (sense 1). [C17: from Malay *tingkal,* from Sanskrit *tankana*]

tin can *n.* a metal food container, esp. when empty.

tinct (tɪŋkt) *n., vb.* **1.** an obsolete word for **tint.** ~*adj.* **2.** *Poetic.* tinted or coloured. [C15: from Latin *tinctus,* from *tingere* to colour]

tinct. *abbrev. for* tincture.

tinc·to·ri·al (tɪŋk'tɔːrɪəl) *adj.* **1.** of or relating to colouring, staining, or dyeing. **2.** imbuing with colour. [C17: from Latin *tinctōrius,* from *tingere* to tinge] —**tinc·'to·ri·al·ly** *adv.*

tinc·ture ('tɪŋktʃə) *n.* **1.** *Pharmacol.* a medicinal extract in a solution of alcohol. **2.** a tint, colour, or tinge. **3.** a slight flavour, aroma, or trace. **4.** any one of the colours or either of the metals used on heraldic arms. **5.** *Obsolete.* a dye or pigment. ~*vb.* **6.** (*tr.*) to give a tint or colour to. [C14: from Latin *tinctūra* a dyeing, from *tingere* to dye]

Tin·dal *or* **Tin·dale** ('tɪndᵊl) *n.* variant spellings of (William) **Tyndale.**

tin·der ('tɪndə) *n.* **1.** dry wood or other easily combustible material used for lighting a fire. **2.** anything inflammatory or dangerous: *his speech was tinder to the demonstrators' unrest.* [Old English *tynder;* related to Old Norse *tundr,* Old High German *zuntara*] —**'tin·der·y** *adj.*

tin·der·box ('tɪndəˌbɒks) *n.* **1.** a box used formerly for holding tinder, esp. one fitted with a flint and steel. **2.** a person or thing that is particularly touchy or explosive.

tine (taɪn) *n.* **1.** a slender prong, esp. of a fork. **2.** any of the sharp terminal branches of a deer's antler. [Old English *tind;* related to Old Norse *tindr,* Old High German *zint*] —**tined** *adj.*

tin·e·a ('tɪnɪə) *n.* any fungal skin disease, esp. ringworm. [C17: from Latin: worm] —**'tin·e·al** *adj.*

tin·e·id ('tɪnɪɪd) *n.* **1.** any moth of the family *Tineidae,* which includes the clothes moths. ~*adj.* **2.** of, relating to, or belonging to the family *Tineidae.* [C19: from New Latin *Tineidae,* from Latin: TINEA]

tin·foil ('tɪn'fɔɪl) *n.* **1.** thin foil made of tin or an alloy of tin and lead. **2.** thin foil made of aluminium; used for wrapping foodstuffs.

ting[1] (tɪŋ) *n.* **1.** a high metallic sound such as that made by a small bell. ~*vb.* **2.** to make or cause to make such a sound. [C15: of imitative origin]

ting[2] (tɪŋ) *n,* (*often cap.*) a variant spelling of **thing**[2].

ting-a-ling ('tɪŋə'lɪŋ) *n.* the sound of a small bell.

tinge (tɪndʒ) *n.* **1.** a slight tint or colouring: *her hair had a tinge of grey.* **2.** any slight addition. ~*vb.* **ting·es, tinge·ing** *or* **ting·ing, tinged.** (*tr.*) **3.** to colour or tint faintly. **4.** to impart a slight trace to: *her thoughts were tinged with nostalgia.* [C15: from Latin *tingere* to colour]

tin·gle ('tɪŋgᵊl) *vb.* **1.** (*usually intr.*) to feel or cause to feel a prickling, itching, or stinging sensation of the flesh, as from a cold plunge or electric shock. ~*n.* **2.** a sensation of tingling. **3.** *Rare.* a tinkle. [C14: perhaps a variant of TINKLE] —**'tin·gler** *n.* —**'tin·gling·ly** *adv.* —**'tin·gly** *adj.*

tin god *n.* **1.** a self-important dictatorial person. **2.** a person erroneously regarded as holy or venerable.

tin hat *n. Informal.* a steel helmet worn by military personnel for protection against small metal fragments.

tin·horn ('tɪnˌhɔːn) *U.S. slang.* ~*n.* **1.** a cheap pretentious person, esp. a gambler with extravagant claims. ~*adj.* **2.** cheap and showy.

tink·er ('tɪŋkə) *n.* **1.** (esp. formerly) a travelling mender of pots and pans. **2.** a clumsy worker. **3.** a person who enjoys playing with mechanical things. **4.** any of several small mackerels that occur off the North American coast of the Atlantic. ~*vb.* **5.** (*intr.;* foll. by *with*) to play, fiddle, or meddle (with machinery, etc.), esp. while undertaking repairs. **6.** to mend (pots and pans) as a tinker. [C13 *tinkere,* perhaps from *tink* tinkle, of imitative origin] —**'tink·er·er** *n.*

tin·ker's damn *or* **cuss** *n. Slang.* the slightest heed (esp. in the phrase **not give a tinker's damn** *or* **cuss**).

tin·kle ('tɪŋkᵊl) *vb.* **1.** to ring or cause to ring with a series of high tinny sounds, like a small bell. **2.** (*tr.*) to announce or summon by such a ringing. **3.** (*intr.*) *Brit. informal.* to urinate. ~*n.* **4.** a high clear ringing sound. **5.** the act of tinkling. **6.** *Brit. informal.* a telephone call. [C14: of imitative origin] —**'tin·kling** *adj., n.* —**'tin·kly** *adj.*

tin liz·zie ('lɪzɪ) *n. Informal.* an old or decrepit car; jalopy.

tinned (tɪnd) *adj.* **1.** plated, coated, or treated with tin. **2.** *Chiefly Brit.* preserved or stored in airtight tins: *tinned soup.* **3.** coated with a layer of solder.

tinned dog *n. Slang, chiefly Austral.* tinned meat.

tin·ni·tus (tɪ'naɪtəs) *n. Pathol.* a ringing, hissing, or booming sensation in one or both ears, caused by infection of the middle or inner ear, a side effect of certain drugs, etc. [C19: from Latin, from *tinnīre* to ring]

tin·ny ('tɪnɪ) *adj.* **·ni·er, ·ni·est. 1.** of, relating to, or resembling tin. **2.** cheap, badly made, or shoddy. **3.** (of a sound) high, thin, and metallic. **4.** (of food or drink) flavoured with metal, as from a container. **5.** *Austral. informal.* lucky. ~*n.* **6.** *Austral. slang.* a can of beer. —**'tin·ni·ly** *adv.* —**'tin·ni·ness** *n.*

tin-o·pen·er *n.* a small tool for opening tins.

Tin Pan Al·ley *n.* **1.** a district in a city concerned with the production of popular music, originally a small district in New York. **2.** *Derogatory.* the strictly commercial side of show business and pop music.

tin plate *n.* **1.** thin steel sheet coated with a layer of tin that protects the steel from corrosion. ~*vb.* **tin-plate. 2.** (*tr.*) to coat (a metal or object) with a layer of tin, usually either by electroplating or by dipping in a bath of molten tin. —**'tin-ˌplat·er** *n.*

tin·pot ('tɪnˌpɒt) *adj.* (*prenominal*) *Brit. informal.* inferior, cheap, or worthless.

tin·sel ('tɪnsəl) *n.* **1.** a decoration consisting of a piece of string with thin strips of metal foil attached along its length. **2.** a yarn or fabric interwoven with strands of glittering thread. **3.** anything cheap, showy, and gaudy. ~*vb.* **·sels, ·sel·ling, ·selled** *or U.S.* **·sels, ·sel·ing, ·seled.** (*tr.*) **4.** to decorate with or as if with tinsel: *snow tinsels the trees.* **5.** to give a gaudy appearance to. [C16: from Old French *estincele* a spark, from Latin *scintilla;* compare STENCIL] —**'tin·sel-ˌlike** *adj.*

tin·smith ('tɪnˌsmɪθ) *n.* a person who works with tin or tin plate.

tin sol·dier *n.* **1.** a miniature toy soldier, usually made of lead. **2.** a person who enjoys playing at being a soldier.

tin·stone ('tɪnˌstəʊn) *n.* another name for **cassiterite.**

tint (tɪnt) *n.* **1.** a shade of a colour, esp. a pale one. **2.** a colour that is softened or desaturated by the addition of white. **3.** a tinge. **4.** a semi-permanent dye for the hair. **5.** a trace or hint: *a tint of jealousy in his voice.* **6.** *Engraving.* uniform shading, produced esp. by hatching. **7.** *Printing.* a panel of colour serving as a background to letters or other matter. ~*vb.* **8.** (*tr.*) to colour or tinge. **9.** (*tr.*) to change or influence slightly: *his answer was tinted by his prior knowledge.* **10.** (*intr.*) to acquire a tint. [C18: from earlier TINCT] —**'tint·er** *n.*

Tin·tag·el Head (tɪn'tædʒəl) *n.* a promontory in SW England, on the W coast of Cornwall: ruins of **Tintagel Castle,** legendary birthplace of King Arthur.

tin·tin·nab·u·la·tion (ˌtɪntɪˌnæbjʊ'leɪʃən) *n.* the act or an instance of the ringing or pealing of bells. —**ˌtin·tin·'nab·u·lar, ˌtin·tin·'nab·u·lar·y** *or* **ˌtin·tin·'nab·u·lous** *adj.*

tin·tin·nab·u·lum (ˌtɪntɪ'næbjʊləm) *n., pl.* **·la** (-lə). a small high-pitched bell. [C16: from Latin, from *tintinnāre* to tinkle, from *tinnīre* to ring; see TINNITUS]

tint·om·e·ter (tɪn'tɒmɪtə) *n.* another name for **colorimeter** (sense 1).

Tin·to·ret·to (ˌtɪntə'rɛtəʊ; *Italian* ˌtinto'retto) *n.* **Il** (il). original name *Jacopo Robusti.* 1518–94, Italian painter of the Venetian school. His works include *Susanna bathing* (?1550) and the fresco cycle in the Scuola di San Rocco, Venice (from 1564).

tint tool *n.* a kind of burin used in wood-engraving for carving lines of even thickness, as in hatching.

tin·type ('tɪnˌtaɪp) *n.* another name for **ferrotype** (senses 1, 2).

tin·ware ('tɪnˌwɛə) *n.* objects made of tin plate.

tin whis·tle *n.* another name for **penny whistle.**

tin·work ('tɪnˌwɜːk) *n.* objects made of tin.

tin·works ('tɪnˌwɜːks) *n.* (*functioning as sing. or pl.*) a place where tin is mined, smelted, or rolled.

ti·ny ('taɪnɪ) *adj.* **+ni+er, +ni+est.** very small; minute. [C16 *tine,* of uncertain origin] —**'ti+ni+ly** *adv.* —**'ti+ni+ness** *n.*

-tion *suffix forming nouns.* indicating state, condition, action, process, or result: *election; prohibition.* Compare **-ation, -ion.** [from Old French, from Latin *-tiō, -tiōn-*]

tip[1] (tɪp) *n.* **1.** the extreme end of something, esp. a narrow or pointed end. **2.** the top or summit. **3.** a small piece forming an extremity or end: *a metal tip on a cane.* ~*vb.* **tips, tip+ping, tipped.** (*tr.*) **4.** to adorn or mark the tip of. **5.** to form or cause to form a tip. [C15: from Old Norse *typpa;* related to Middle Low German, Middle Dutch *tip*] —**'tip+less** *adj.*

tip[2] (tɪp) *vb.* **tips, tip+ping, tipped. 1.** to tilt or cause to tilt. **2.** (*tr.; usually foll. by over or up*) to tilt or cause to tilt, so as to overturn or fall. **3.** *Brit.* to dump (rubbish, etc.). **4. tip one's hat.** to take off, raise, or touch one's hat in salutation. ~*n.* **5.** the act of tipping or the state of being tipped. **6.** *Brit.* a dump for refuse, etc. [C14: of uncertain origin; related to TOP, TOPPLE] —**'tip+pa·ble** *adj.*

tip[3] (tɪp) *n.* **1.** a payment given for services in excess of the standard charge; gratuity. **2.** a helpful hint, warning, or other piece of information. **3.** a piece of inside information, esp. in betting or investing. ~*vb.* **tips, tip+ping, tipped. 4.** to give a tip to (a person). [C18: perhaps from TIP[4]]

tip[4] (tɪp) *vb.* **tips, tip+ping, tipped.** (*tr.*) **1.** to hit or strike lightly. **2.** to hit (a ball) indirectly so that it glances off the bat in cricket. ~*n.* **3.** a light blow. **4.** a glancing hit in cricket. [C13: perhaps from Low German *tippen*]

tip and run *n.* **1.** a form of cricket in which the batsman must run if his bat touches the ball. ~*adj.* **tip-and-run. 2.** (*prenominal*) characterized by a rapid departure immediately after striking: *a tip-and-run raid.*

tip+cat ('tɪp,kæt) *n.* a game in which a short sharp-ended piece of wood (the cat) is tipped in the air with a stick.

ti·pi ('ti:pɪ) *n., pl.* **·pis.** a variant spelling of **tepee.**

tip-off *n.* **1.** a warning or hint, esp. given confidentially and based on inside information. **2.** *Basketball.* the act or an instance of putting the ball in play by a jump ball. ~*vb.* **tip off. 3.** (*tr., adv.*) to give a hint or warning to.

tip+per ('tɪpə) *n.* **1.** a person who gives or leaves a tip: *he is a generous tipper.* **2.** short for **tipper truck.**

Tip+per+ar·y (,tɪpə'rɛərɪ) *n.* a county of S Ireland, in Munster province: mountainous. County town: Clonmel. Pop.: 123 565 (1971). Area: 4255 sq. km (1643 sq. miles).

tip+per truck *or* **lor+ry** *n.* a truck or lorry the rear platform of which can be pneumatically raised at the front end to enable the load to be discharged by gravity. Also called: **dump truck, tip truck.**

tip+pet ('tɪpɪt) *n.* **1.** a woman's fur cape for the shoulders, often consisting of the whole fur of a fox, marten, etc. **2.** the long stole of Anglican clergy worn during a service. **3.** a long streamer-like part to a sleeve, hood, etc., esp. in the 16th century. [C14: perhaps from TIP[1]]

Tip+pett ('tɪpɪt) *n.* Sir **Mi·chael.** born 1905, English composer, whose works include the oratorio *A Child of Our Time* (1941) and the operas *The Midsummer Marriage* (1952), *King Priam* (1961), *The Knot Garden* (1970), and *The Ice Break* (1976).

tip+ple[1] ('tɪpᵊl) *vb.* **1.** to make a habit of taking (alcoholic drink), esp. in small quantities. ~*n.* **2.** alcoholic drink. [C15: back formation from obsolete *tippler* tapster, of unknown origin] —**'tip+pler** *n.*

tip+ple[2] ('tɪpᵊl) *n.* **1.** a device for overturning ore trucks, mine cars, etc., so that they discharge their load. **2.** a place at which such trucks are tipped and unloaded. ~*vb.* **3.** *Northern English dialect.* to fall or cause to fall. [C19: from *tipple* to overturn, from TIP[2]]

tip+pler ('tɪplə) *n.* (*sometimes cap.*) **1.** a variety of domestic pigeon bred mainly for flying. Also called: **high-flying tippler. 2.** a domestic fancy pigeon of a smaller rounder type kept mainly for exhibition. Usual name: **show tippler.** [C19: from TIPPLE[2] + -ER[1]]

tip+staff ('tɪp,stɑ:f) *n.* **1.** a court official having miscellaneous duties, mostly concerned with the maintenance of order in court. **2.** a metal-tipped staff formerly used as a symbol of office. [C16 *tipped staff;* see TIP[1], STAFF]

tip+ster ('tɪpstə) *n.* a person who sells tips on horse racing, the stock market, etc.

tip+sy ('tɪpsɪ) *adj.* **+si+er, +si+est. 1.** slightly drunk. **2.** slightly tilted or tipped; askew. [C16: from TIP[2]] —**'tip+si+ly** *adv.* —**'tip+si+ness** *n.*

tip+sy cake *n. Brit.* a kind of trifle made from a sponge cake soaked with white wine or sherry and decorated with almonds and crystallized fruit.

tip+toe ('tɪp,təʊ) *vb.* **+toes, +toe+ing, +toed.** (*intr.*) **1.** to walk with the heels off the ground and the weight supported by the ball of the foot and the toes. **2.** to walk silently or stealthily. ~*n.* **3. on tiptoe. a.** on the tips of the toes or on the ball of the foot and the toes. **b.** eagerly anticipating something. **c.** stealthily or silently. ~*adv.* **4.** on tiptoe. ~*adj.* **5.** walking or standing on tiptoe. **6.** stealthy or silent.

tip+top (,tɪp'tɒp) *adj., adv.* **1.** at the highest point of health, excellence, etc. **2.** at the topmost point. ~*n.* **3.** the best in quality. **4.** the topmost point.

tip truck *n.* another name for **tipper truck.**

tip-up *adj.* (*prenominal*) able to be turned upwards around a hinge or pivot: *a tip-up seat.*

Tip·u Sa·hib *or* **Tip·poo Sa·hib** ('tɪpu: 'sɑ:ɪb) *n.* ?1750–99, sultan of Mysore (1782–99): killed fighting the British.

TIR (on continental lorries) *abbrev. for* Transports Internationaux Routiers. [French: International Road Transport]

ti+rade (taɪ'reɪd) *n.* **1.** a long angry speech or denunciation. **2.** *Prosody, rare.* a speech or passage dealing with a single theme. [C19: from French, literally: a pulling, from Italian *tirata,* from *tirare* to pull, of uncertain origin]

Ti+ran (tɪ'rɑ:n) *n.* **Strait of.** a strait between the Gulf of Aqaba and the Red Sea. Length: 16 km (10 miles). Width: 8 km (5 miles).

Ti+ra+na (tɪ'rɑ:nə) *or* **Ti+ra+në** (*Albanian* ti'ranə) *n.* the capital of Albania, in the central part 32 km (20 miles) from the Adriatic: founded in the early 17th century by Turks; became capital in 1920; the country's largest city and industrial centre. Pop.: 171 300 (1970 est.).

tire[1] (taɪə) *vb.* **1.** (*tr.*) to reduce the energy of, esp. by exertion; weary. **2.** (*tr.; often passive*) to reduce the tolerance of; bore or irritate: *I'm tired of the children's chatter.* **3.** (*intr.*) to become wearied or bored; flag. [Old English *tēorian,* of unknown origin]

tire[2] (taɪə) *n., vb.* the U.S. spelling of **tyre.**

tire[3] (taɪə) *vb., n.* an archaic word for **attire.**

tire+less ('taɪəlɪs) *adj.* unable to be tired; indefatigable. —**'tire+less+ly** *adv.* —**'tire+less+ness** *n.*

Ti·re·si·as (taɪ'ri:sɪ,æs) *n.* a blind soothsayer of Thebes, who revealed to Oedipus that the latter had murdered his father and married his mother.

tire+some ('taɪəsəm) *adj.* boring and irritating; irksome. —**'tire+some+ly** *adv.* —**'tire+some+ness** *n.*

tire+wom·an ('taɪə,wʊmən) *n., pl.* **+wom·en.** an obsolete term for **lady's maid.**

Tîr+gu Mu+reş (*Rumanian* 'tɪrgu 'mureʃ) *n.* a city in central Rumania: manufacturing and cultural centre. Pop.: 112 779 (1974 est.).

Ti+rich Mir ('tɪərɪtʃ 'mɪə) *n.* a mountain in N Pakistan: highest peak of the Hindu Kush. Height: 7690 m (25 230 ft.).

tir+ing room *n. Archaic.* a dressing room in a theatre.

ti·ro ('taɪ,rəʊ) *n., pl.* **·ros.** a variant spelling of **tyro.**

Ti+rol (tɪ'rəʊl, 'tɪrəʊl; *German* ti'ro:l) *n.* a variant spelling of **Tyrol.** —**Tir·o+lese** (,tɪrə'li:z) *or* **Ti+ro+'le·an** *adj., n.*

Ti+ros ('taɪrəʊs) *n.* one of a series of U.S. weather satellites carrying infrared and television camera equipment for transmitting meteorological data to the earth. [C20: from T(elevision and) I(nfra-) R(ed) O(bservation) S(atellite)]

Tir+pitz (*German* 'tɪrpɪts) *n.* **Al·fred von** ('alfre:t fɔn). 1849–1930, German admiral: as secretary of state for the Imperial Navy (1897–1916), he created the modern German navy, which challenged British supremacy at sea.

Tir·so de Mo·li·na (*Spanish* 'tirso ðe mo'lina) *n.* pen name of *Gabriel Téllez.* ?1571–1648, Spanish dramatist; author of the first dramatic treatment of the Don Juan legend *El Burlador de Sevilla* (1630).

Tir·u·chi+ra+pal+li (,tɪrətʃɪrə'pʌlɪ, tɪ,ru:tʃɪ'rɑ:pəlɪ) *or* **Trich·i+nop·o+ly** *n.* an industrial city in S India, in central Tamil Nadu on the Cauvery River: dominated by a rock fortress 83 m (273 ft.) high. Pop.: 306 247 (1971).

Ti+ru+nel+vel·i (,tɪrʊ'nɛlvəlɪ) *n.* a city in S India, in Tamil Nadu: site of St. Francis Xavier's first preaching in India; textile manufacturing. Pop.: 108 498 (1971).

'tis (tɪz) *Poetic or dialect. contraction of* it is.

Ti+sa ('tisa) *n.* the Slavonic and Rumanian name for the **Tisza.**

ti+sane (tɪ'zæn) *n.* an infusion of dried or fresh leaves or flowers, as camomile. [C19: from French, from Latin *ptisana* barley water; see PTISAN]

Tish+ab b'Ab (*Hebrew* ti'ʃa bə'ab) *n. Judaism.* the ninth day of the month of Ab observed as a fast day in memory of the destruction of the First and Second Temples. Also called: **Tish+ah b'Av** ('tiʃə'bə).

Tish+ri *Hebrew.* (tɪʃ'ri:) *n.* the first month of the civil year and seventh of the ecclesiastical year in the Jewish calendar, falling in September and October. [C19: from Hebrew, from Akkadian *Tashrītu,* from *shurrū* to begin]

Ti·siph·o·ne (tɪ'sɪfənɪ) *n. Greek myth.* one of the three Furies; the others are Alecto and Megaera.

tis+sue ('tɪsju:, 'tɪʃu:) *n.* **1.** a part of an organism consisting of a large number of cells having a similar structure and function: *connective tissue; nerve tissue.* **2.** a thin piece of soft absorbent paper, usually of two or more layers, used as a disposable handkerchief, towel, etc. **3.** See **tissue paper. 4.** an interwoven series: *a tissue of lies.* **5.** a woven cloth, esp. of a light gauzy nature, originally interwoven with threads of gold or silver. ~*vb.* (*tr.*) **6.** *Rare.* to weave into tissue. **7.** to decorate or clothe with tissue or tissue paper. [C14: from Old French *tissu* woven cloth, from *tistre* to weave, from Latin *texere*]

tis+sue cul+ture *n.* **1.** the growth of small pieces of animal or plant tissue in a sterile controlled medium. **2.** the tissue produced as a result of this process.

tis+sue pa+per *n.* very thin soft delicate paper used to wrap breakable goods, as decoration, etc.

Ti+sza (*Hungarian* 'tisɔ) *n.* a river in S central Europe, rising in the W Ukrainian SSR of the Soviet Union and flowing west, forming part of the border between the Soviet Union and Rumania, then southwest across Hungary into Yugoslavia to the Danube north of Belgrade. Slavonic and Rumanian name: **Tisa.**

tit[1] (tɪt) *n.* **1.** any of numerous small active Old World songbirds of the family *Paridae* (titmice), esp. those of the genus *Parus* (bluetit, great tit, etc.). They have a short bill and feed on insects and seeds. **2.** any of various similar small birds. **3.** *Archaic or dialect.* a worthless or worn-out horse; nag. [C16: perhaps of imitative origin, applied to small animate or inanimate objects; compare Icelandic *tittr* pin]

tit² (tɪt) *n.* **1.** *Slang.* a female breast. **2.** a teat or nipple. **3.** *Derogatory.* a girl or young woman. **4.** *Taboo slang.* a despicable or unpleasant person: often used as a term of address. [Old English *titt;* related to Middle Low German *title,* Norwegian *titta*]

Tit. *Bible. abbrev. for* Titus.

ti·tan ('taɪtᵊn) *n.* a person of great strength or size.

Ti·tan¹ ('taɪtᵊn) *or (fem.)* **Ti·tan·ess** *n. Greek myth.* **1.** any of a family of primordial gods, the sons and daughters of Uranus (sky) and Gaea (earth). **2.** any of the offspring of the children of Uranus and Gaea.

Ti·tan² ('taɪtᵊn) *n.* the largest of the ten satellites of Saturn and the fourth furthest from the planet.

ti·tan·ate ('taɪtəˌneɪt) *n.* any salt or ester of titanic acid.

Ti·tan·esque (ˌtaɪtə'nɛsk) *adj.* resembling a Titan; gigantic.

ti·ta·ni·a (taɪ'teɪnɪə) *n.* another name for **titanium dioxide.**

Ti·ta·ni·a¹ (tɪ'tɑːnɪə) *n.* **1.** (in medieval folklore) the queen of the fairies and wife of Oberon. **2.** (in classical antiquity) a poetic epithet used variously to characterize Circe, Diana, Latona, or Pyrrha.

Ti·ta·ni·a² (tɪ'tɑːnɪə) *n.* the largest of the five satellites of Uranus and the second furthest from the planet.

ti·tan·ic¹ (taɪ'tænɪk) *adj.* of or containing titanium, esp. in the tetravalent state.

ti·tan·ic² (taɪ'tænɪk) *adj.* huge. **—ti·'tan·i·cal·ly** *adv.*

ti·tan·ic ac·id *n.* any of various white substances regarded as hydrated forms of titanium dioxide, typical formulas being H_4TiO_4 and H_2TiO_3.

ti·tan·ic ox·ide *n.* another name for **titanium dioxide.**

ti·tan·if·er·ous (ˌtaɪtə'nɪfərəs) *adj.* of or containing titanium; bearing titanium: *a titaniferous ore.*

Ti·tan·ism ('taɪtəˌnɪzəm) *n.* a spirit of defiance of and rebellion against authority, social convention, etc.

ti·tan·ite ('taɪtəˌnaɪt) *n.* another name for **sphene.** [C19: from German *Titanit,* so named because it contained TITANIUM]

ti·ta·ni·um (taɪ'teɪnɪəm) *n.* a strong malleable white metallic element, which is very corrosion-resistant and occurs in rutile and ilmenite. It is used in the manufacture of strong lightweight alloys, esp. aircraft parts. Symbol: Ti; atomic no.: 22; atomic wt.: 47.90; valency: 2, 3, or 4; relative density: 4.54; melting pt.: 1675°C; boiling pt.: 3620°C. [C18: New Latin; see TITAN, -IUM]

ti·ta·ni·um di·ox·ide *n.* a white insoluble powder occurring naturally as rutile and used chiefly as a pigment of high covering power and durability. Formula: TiO_2. Also called: **titanium oxide, titanic oxide, titania.**

Ti·tan·om·a·chy (ˌtaɪtə'nɒməkɪ) *n. Greek myth.* the unsuccessful revolt of the family of the Titan Iapetus against Zeus. [C19: from Greek *titanomakhia,* from TITAN + *makhē* a battle]

ti·tan·o·saur (taɪ'tænəˌsɔː) *n.* any of various herbivorous quadrupedal dinosaurs of the family *Titanosauridae,* of Jurassic and Cretaceous times: suborder *Sauropoda* (sauropods). [C19: from New Latin *Tītānosaurus,* from Greek TITAN + -SAUR]

ti·tan·o·there (taɪ'tænəˌθɪə) *n.* any of various very large horselike perissodactyl mammals of the genera *Menodus, Brontotherium,* etc., that lived in Eocene and Oligocene times in North America. See also **chalicothere.** [C19: from New Latin *Tītānotherium* giant animal, from Greek TITAN + *thēr* wild beast]

ti·tan·ous (taɪ'tænəs) *adj.* of or containing titanium, esp. in the trivalent state.

tit·bit ('tɪtˌbɪt) *or esp. U.S.* **tid·bit** *n.* **1.** a tasty small piece of food; dainty. **2.** a pleasing scrap of anything, such as scandal. [C17: perhaps from dialect *tid* tender, of obscure origin]

ti·ter ('taɪtə, 'tiː-) *n.* the usual U.S. spelling of **titre.**

tit·fer ('tɪtfə) *n. Cockney rhyming slang.* a hat. [from the phrase *tit for tat*]

tit for tat *n.* an equivalent given in return or retaliation; blow for blow. [C16: from earlier *tip for tap*]

tith·a·ble ('taɪðəbᵊl) *adj.* **1.** (until 1936) liable to pay tithes. **2.** (of property, etc.) subject to the payment of tithes.

tithe (taɪð) *n.* **1.** (*often pl.*) *Ecclesiast.* a tenth part of agricultural or other produce, personal income, or profits, contributed either voluntarily or as a tax for the support of the church or clergy or for charitable purposes. **2.** any levy, esp. of one tenth. **3.** a tenth or very small part of anything. *~vb.* **4.** (*tr.*) **a.** to exact or demand a tithe or tithes from (an individual or group). **b.** to levy a tithe upon (a crop or amount of produce, etc.). **5.** (*intr.*) to pay a tithe or tithes. [Old English *teogoth;* related to Old Frisian *tegotha,* Old Saxon *tegotho,* Old High German *zehando,* Old Norse *tīundi,* Gothic *taihunda*] **—'tith·er** *n.*

tith·ing ('taɪðɪŋ) *n. English history.* **1. a.** a tithe; tenth. **b.** the exacting or paying of tithes. **2.** a company of ten householders in the system of frankpledge. **3.** a rural division, originally regarded as a tenth of a hundred.

Ti·tho·nus (tɪ'θəʊnəs) *n. Greek myth.* the son of Laomedon of Troy who was loved by the goddess Eos. She asked that he be made immortal but forgot to ask that he be made eternally young. When he aged she turned him into a grasshopper.

ti·ti¹ ('tiːtiː) *n., pl.* **·tis.** any of several small omnivorous New World monkeys of the genus *Callicebus,* of South America, having long beautifully coloured fur and a long nonprehensile tail. [via Spanish from Aymaran, literally: little cat]

ti·ti² ('tiːtiː) *n., pl.* **·tis.** any of various evergreen shrubs or small trees of the family *Cyrillaceae* of the southern U.S., esp. the leatherwood and *Cliftonia monophyllia,* which has white or pinkish fragrant flowers. [C19: of American Indian origin]

Ti·tian ('tɪʃən) *n.* original name *Tiziano Vecellio.* ?1490–1576, Italian painter of the Venetian school, noted for his religious and mythological works, such as *Bacchus and Ariadne* (1523), and his portraits.

Ti·ti·ca·ca (*Spanish* ˌtiti'kaka) *n.* **Lake.** a lake between S Peru and W Bolivia, in the Andes: the highest large lake in the world; drained by the Desaguadero River flowing into Lake Poopó. Area: 8135 sq. km (3141 sq. miles). Altitude: 3809 m (12 497 ft.). Depth: 370 m (1214 ft.).

tit·il·late ('tɪtɪˌleɪt) *vb.* (*tr.*) **1.** to arouse, tease, interest, or excite pleasurably and often superficially. **2.** to cause a tickling or tingling sensation in, esp. by touching. [C17: from Latin *tītillāre*] **—'tit·il·ˌlat·ing·ly** *adv.* **—ˌtit·il·'la·tion** *n.* **—'tit·il·ˌla·tive** *adj.*

tit·i·vate *or* **tit·ti·vate** ('tɪtɪˌveɪt) *vb.* **1.** to smarten up (oneself or another), including making up, doing the hair, etc. **2.** to smarten up (a thing): *to titivate a restaurant.* **3.** *Rare.* another word for **titillate.** [C19: earlier *tidivate,* perhaps based on TIDY and CULTIVATE] **—ˌtit·i·'va·tion** *or* **ˌtit·ti·'va·tion** *n.* **—'tit·i·ˌva·tor** *or* **'tit·ti·ˌva·tor** *n.*

tit·lark ('tɪtˌlɑːk) *n.* another name for **pipit,** esp. the meadow pipit (*Anthus pratensis*). [C17: from TIT¹ + LARK¹]

ti·tle ('taɪtᵊl) *n.* **1.** the distinctive name of a work of art, musical or literary composition, etc. **2.** a descriptive name, caption, or heading of a section of a book, speech, etc. **3.** See **title page. 4.** a name or epithet signifying rank, office, or function. **5.** a formal designation, such as *Mr., Mrs.,* or *Miss.* **6.** an appellation designating nobility. **7.** *Films.* **a.** short for **subtitle** (sense 2). **b.** written material giving credits in a film or television programme. **8.** *Sport.* a championship. **9.** *Property law.* **a.** the legal right to possession of property, esp. real property. **b.** the basis of such right. **c.** the documentary evidence of such right: *title deeds.* **10.** *Law.* **a.** the heading or a division of a statute, book of law, etc. **b.** the heading of a suit or action at law. **11. a.** any customary or established right. **b.** a claim based on such a right. **12.** a definite spiritual charge or office in the church, without appointment to which a candidate for holy orders cannot lawfully be ordained. **13.** *R.C. Church.* a titular church. *~vb.* **14.** (*tr.*) to give a title to. [C13: from Old French, from Latin *titulus*]

ti·tled ('taɪtᵊld) *adj.* having a title: *the titled classes.*

ti·tle deed *n.* a deed or document evidencing a person's legal right or title to property, esp. real property.

ti·tle·hold·er ('taɪtᵊlˌhəʊldə) *n.* a person who holds a title, esp. a sporting championship. **—'ti·tle·ˌhold·ing** *adj.*

ti·tle page *n.* the page in a book that bears the title, author's name, publisher's imprint, date of publication, etc.

ti·tle role *n.* the role of the character after whom a play, etc., is named.

tit·man ('tɪtmən) *n., pl.* **·men.** (of pigs) the runt of a litter. [*tit-* (as in TITMOUSE) + MAN]

tit·mouse ('tɪtˌmaʊs) *n., pl.* **·mice.** (*usually pl.*) any small active songbird of the family *Paridae,* esp. those of the genus *Parus* (see **tit¹**). [C14 *titemous,* from *tite* (see TIT¹) + MOUSE]

Ti·to ('tiːtəʊ) *n.* **Mar·shal.** original name *Josip Broz.* 1892-1980, Yugoslav statesman, who led the communist guerrilla resistance to German occupation during World War II; prime minister of Yugoslavia (1945-53) and president (1953-80).

Ti·to·grad (*Serbo-Croatian* 'titɔgraːd) *n.* a city in S Yugoslavia, capital of Montenegro: under Turkish rule (1474–1878). Pop.: 54 509 (1971). Former name (until 1946): **Podgorica.**

Ti·to·ism ('tiːtəʊˌɪzəm) *n.* **1.** the variant of Communism practised by Tito, characterized by independence from the Soviet bloc and neutrality in East-West controversies, a considerable amount of decentralization, and a large degree of worker control of industries. **2.** any variant of Communism resembling Titoism. **—'Ti·to·ist** *n., adj.*

ti·trant ('taɪtrənt) *n.* the solution in a titration that is added from a burette to a measured quantity of another solution.

ti·trate ('taɪtreɪt) *vb.* (*tr.*) to measure the volume or concentration of (a solution) by titration. [C19: from French *titrer;* see TITRE] **—ti·'trat·a·ble** *adj.*

ti·tra·tion (taɪ'treɪʃən) *n.* an operation, used in volumetric analysis, in which a measured amount of one solution is added to a known quantity of another solution until the reaction between the two is complete. If the concentration of one solution is known, that of the other can be calculated.

ti·tre *or U.S.* **ti·ter** ('taɪtə, 'tiː-) *n.* **1. a.** the concentration of a solution as determined by titration. **b.** the minimum quantity of a solution required to complete a reaction in a titration. **2.** the quantity of antibody present in an organism. [C19: from French *titre* proportion of gold or silver in an alloy, from Old French *title* TITLE]

tit·ter ('tɪtə) *vb.* **1.** (*intr.*) to snigger, esp. derisively or in a suppressed way. **2.** (*tr.*) to express by tittering. *~n.* **3.** a suppressed laugh, chuckle, or snigger. [C17: of imitative origin] **—'tit·ter·er** *n.* **—'tit·ter·ing·ly** *adv.*

tit·ti·vate ('tɪtɪˌveɪt) *vb.* a less common spelling of **titivate.**

tit·tle ('tɪtᵊl) *n.* **1.** a small mark in printing or writing, esp. a diacritic. **2.** a jot; particle. [C14: from Medieval Latin *titulus* label, from Latin: TITLE]

tit·tle-tat·tle *n.* **1.** idle chat or gossip. *~vb.* **2.** (*intr.*) to chatter or gossip. **—'tit·tle-ˌtat·tler** *n.*

tit·tup ('tɪtəp) *vb.* **·tups, ·tup·ping, ·tupped** *or U.S.* **·tups, ·tup·ing, ·tuped. 1.** (*intr.*) to prance or frolic. *~n.* **2.** a caper. **3.** the sound made by high-heeled shoes. [C18 (in the sense: a horse's gallop): probably imitative]

tit·u·ba·tion (ˌtɪtjʊ'beɪʃən) *n. Pathol.* **1.** a disordered gait characterized by stumbling or staggering, often caused by a lesion of the cerebellum. **2.** Also: **lingual titubation.** stuttering or stammering. [C17: from Latin *titubātiō*, from *titubāre* to reel]

tit·u·lar ('tɪtjʊlə) *or* **tit·u·lar·y** ('tɪtjʊlərɪ) *adj.* **1.** of, relating to, or of the nature of a title. **2.** in name only. **3.** bearing a title. **4.** giving a title. **5.** *R.C. Church.* designating any of certain churches in Rome to whom cardinals or bishops are attached as their nominal incumbents. ~*n., pl.* **·lars** *or* **·lar·ies. 6.** the bearer of a title. **7.** the bearer of a nominal office. [C18: from French *titulaire*, from Latin *titulus* TITLE] —**'tit·u·lar·ly** *adv.*

Ti·tus ('taɪtəs) *n.* **1.** *New Testament.* **a.** a Greek disciple and helper of Saint Paul. **b.** the book written to him (in full **The Epistle of Paul the Apostle to Titus**), containing advice on pastoral matters. **2.** full name *Titus Flavius Sabinus Vespasianus.* ?40–81 A.D., Roman emperor (78–81 A.D.).

Ti·u ('ti:u:) *n.* (in Anglo-Saxon mythology) the god of war and the sky. Norse counterpart: **Tyr.**

Tiv (tɪv) *n.* **1.** (*pl.* **Tivs** *or* **Tiv**) a member of a negroid people of W Africa, living chiefly in the savannah of the Benue area of S Nigeria and noted by anthropologists for having no chiefs. **2.** the language of this people, belonging to the Benue-Congo branch of the Niger-Congo family.

Tiv·o·li ('tɪvəlɪ; *Italian* 'ti:voli) *n.* a town in central Italy, east of Rome: a summer resort in Roman times; contains the Renaissance Villa d'Este and the remains of Hadrian's Villa. Pop.: 41 740 (1971).

tiz·zy ('tɪzɪ) *n., pl.* **·zies.** a state of confusion, anxiety, or excitement. Also called: **tiz-woz.** [C19: of unknown origin]

Tji·re·bon *or* **Che·ri·bon** ('tʃɪərə,bɒn) *n.* a port in S central Indonesia, on N Java on the Java Sea: scene of the signing of the **Tjirebon Agreement** of Indonesian independence (1946) by the Netherlands. Pop.: 178 529 (1971).

T-junc·tion *n.* a road junction in which one road joins another at right-angles but does not cross it.

TKO *or* **T.K.O.** *Boxing. abbrev. for* technical knockout.

Tl *the chemical symbol for* thallium.

Tlax·ca·la (*Spanish* tlas'kala) *n.* **1.** a state of S central Mexico: the smallest Mexican state; formerly an Indian principality, the chief Indian ally of Cortés in the conquest of Mexico. Capital: Tlaxcala. Pop.: 420 638 (1970). Area: 3914 sq. km (1511 sq. miles). **2.** a city in E central Mexico, capital of Tlaxcala state: the church of San Francisco (founded 1521 by Cortés) is the oldest in the Americas. Pop.: 21 424 (1970). Official name: **Tlaxcala de Xicohténcatl.**

TLC *Informal. abbrev. for* tender loving care.

Tlem·cen (*French* tlɛm'sɛn) *n.* a city in NW Algeria: capital of an Arab kingdom from the 12th to the late 14th century. Pop.: 86 285 (1966).

Tlin·git ('tlɪŋgɪt) *n.* **1.** (*pl.* **·gits** *or* **·git**) a member of a seafaring group of North American Indian peoples inhabiting S Alaska. **2.** the language of these peoples, belonging to the Na-Dene phylum.

Tm *the chemical symbol for* thulium.

T. M. *abbrev. for* transcendental meditation.

T-man *n., pl.* **-men.** *U.S.* a law-enforcement agent of the U.S. Treasury.

tme·sis (tə'mi:sɪs, 'mi:sɪs) *n.* interpolation of a word or group of words between the parts of a compound word. [C16: via Latin from Greek, literally: a cutting, from *temnein* to cut]

TN *international car registration for* Tunisia.

tng. *abbrev. for* training.

TNT *n.* 2,4,6-trinitrotoluene; a yellow solid: used chiefly as a high explosive and is also an intermediate in the manufacture of dyestuffs. Formula: $CH_3C_6H_2(NO_2)_3$.

T-num·ber *or* **T num·ber** *n. Photog.* a function of the f-number of a camera lens that takes into account the amount of light actually transmitted by the lens.

to (tu:; *unstressed before vowels* tʊ; *unstressed before consonants* tə) *prep.* **1.** used to indicate the destination of the subject or object of an action: *he climbed to the top.* **2.** used to mark the indirect object of a verb in a sentence: *telling stories to children.* **3.** used to mark the infinitive of a verb: *he wanted to go.* **4.** as far as; until: *working from Monday to Friday.* **5.** used to indicate equality: *16 ounces to the pound.* **6.** against; upon; onto: *put your ear to the wall.* **7.** before the hour of: *five to four.* **8.** accompanied by: *dancing to loud music.* **9.** as compared with, as against: *the score was eight to three.* **10.** used to indicate a resulting condition: *he tore her dress to shreds; they starved to death.* **11.** a dialect word for **at:** *he's to town; where's it to.* ~*adv.* **12.** towards a fixed position, esp. (of a door) closed. [Old English *tō*; related to Old Frisian, Old Saxon *to*, Old High German *zuo*, Latin *do-* as in *dōnec* until]

Usage. In formal usage, *to* is always used with an infinitive and never omitted as in *come see the show.* The use of *and* instead of *to* (*try and come*) is very common in informal speech but is avoided by careful writers.

toad (təʊd) *n.* **1.** any anuran amphibian of the class *Bufonidae*, such as *Bufo bufo* (**common toad**) of Europe. They are similar to frogs but are more terrestrial, having a drier warty skin. **2.** any of various similar amphibians of different families. **3.** a loathsome person. [Old English *tādige*, of unknown origin; see TADPOLE] —**'toad·ish** *or* **'toad·,like** *adj.* —**'toad·ish·ness** *n.*

toad·eat·er ('təʊd,i:tə) *n.* a rare word for **toady.** [C17: originally a mountebank's assistant who would pretend to eat toads (believed to be poisonous), hence a servile flatterer, toady]

toad·fish ('təʊd,fɪʃ) *n., pl.* **·fish** *or* **·fish·es.** any spiny-finned bottom-dwelling marine fish of the family *Batrachoididae*, of tropical and temperate seas, having a flattened tapering body and a wide mouth.

toad·flax ('təʊd,flæks) *n.* any of various scrophulariaceous plants of the genus *Linaria*, esp. *L. vulgaris*, having narrow leaves and spurred two-lipped yellow-orange flowers. Also called: **butter-and-eggs.**

toad-in-the-hole *n. Brit.* a dish made of sausages baked in a batter.

toad spit *or* **spit·tle** *n.* another name for **cuckoo spit.**

toad·stone ('təʊd,stəʊn) *n.* an amygdaloidal basalt occurring in the limestone regions of Derbyshire. [C18: perhaps from a supposed resemblance to a toad's spotted skin]

toad·stool ('təʊd,stu:l) *n.* (*not in technical use*) any basidiomycetous fungus with a capped spore-producing body that is poisonous. Compare **mushroom** (sense 1a).

toad·y ('təʊdɪ) *n., pl.* **toad·ies. 1.** a person who flatters and ingratiates himself in a servile way; sycophant. **2.** *Austral.* an informal name for **toadfish.** ~*vb.* **toad·ies, toad·y·ing, toad·ied. 3.** to fawn on and flatter (someone). [C19: shortened from TOADEATER] —**'toad·y·ish** *adj.* —**'toad·y·ism** *n.*

to and fro *adj.* **to-and-fro,** *adv.* **1.** back and forth. **2.** here and there. —**to·ing and fro·ing** *n.*

toast[1] (təʊst) *n.* **1.** sliced bread browned by exposure to heat, usually under a grill, over a fire, or in a toaster. ~*vb.* **2.** (*tr.*) to brown under a grill or over a fire: *to toast cheese.* **3.** to warm or be warmed in a similar manner: *to toast one's hands by the fire.* [C14: from Old French *toster*, from Latin *tōstus* parched, baked from *torrēre* to dry with heat; see THIRST, TORRID] —**'toast·y** *adj.*

toast[2] (təʊst) *n.* **1.** a tribute or proposal of health, success, etc., given to a person or thing by a company of people and marked by raising glasses and drinking together. **2.** a person or thing honoured by such a tribute or proposal. **3.** (esp. formerly) an attractive woman to whom such tributes are frequently made: *she was the toast of the town.* ~*vb.* **4.** to propose or drink a toast to (a person or thing). [C17 (in the sense: a lady to whom the company is asked to drink): from TOAST[1], from the idea that the name of the lady would flavour the drink like a piece of spiced toast] —**'toast·er** *n.*

toast·er ('təʊstə) *n.* a device for toasting bread, usually electric, and often equipped with an automatic timer.

toast·mas·ter ('təʊst,mɑ:stə) *n.* a person who introduces after-dinner speakers, proposes or announces toasts, etc., at public or formal dinners. —**'toast·,mis·tress** *fem. n.*

Tob. *abbrev. for* Tobit.

to·bac·co (tə'bækəʊ) *n., pl.* **·cos** *or* **·coes. 1.** any of numerous solanaceous plants of the genus *Nicotiana*, having mildly narcotic properties, tapering hairy leaves, and tubular or funnel-shaped fragrant flowers. The species *N. tabacum* is cultivated as the chief source of commercial tobacco. **2.** the leaves of certain of these plants dried and prepared for snuff, chewing, or smoking. [C16: from Spanish *tabaco*, perhaps from Taino: leaves rolled for smoking, assumed by the Spaniards to be the name of the plant] —**to·'bac·co·less** *adj.*

to·bac·co mo·sa·ic vi·rus *n.* the virus that causes mosaic disease in tobacco and related plants: its discovery in 1892 provided the first evidence of the existence of viruses. Abbrev.: **TMV.**

to·bac·co·nist (tə'bækənɪst) *n. Chiefly Brit.* a person or shop that sells tobacco, cigarettes, pipes, etc.

To·ba·go (tə'beɪgəʊ) *n.* an island in the SE West Indies, northeast of Trinidad: ceded to Britain in 1814; joined with Trinidad in 1888 as a British colony; part of the independent republic of Trinidad and Tobago. Pop.: 43 000 (1970 est.). —**To·ba·go·ni·an** (,təʊbə'gəʊnɪən) *adj., n.*

-to-be *adj.* (*in combination*) about to be; future: *a mother-to-be; the president-to-be.*

To·bey ('təʊbɪ) *n.* **Mark.** 1890–1976, U.S. painter. Influenced by Chinese calligraphy, he devised a style of improvisatory abstract painting called "white writing".

To·bit ('təʊbɪt) *n. Old Testament.* **1.** a pious Jew, guided by the angel Raphael, who was released from blindness. **2.** a book of the Apocrypha relating this story.

to·bog·gan (tə'bɒgən) *n.* **1.** a light wooden frame on runners used for sliding over snow and ice. **2.** a long narrow sledge made of a thin board curved upwards and backwards at the front. ~*vb.* (*intr.*) **3.** to ride on a toboggan. [C19: from Canadian French, from Algonquian; related to Abnaki *udābāgan*] —**to·'bog·gan·er** *or* **to·'bog·gan·ist** *n.*

To·bol (*Russian* ta'bɔl) *n.* a river in the central Soviet Union, rising in the N Kazakh SSR and flowing northeast to the Irtysh River. Length: about 1300 km (800 miles).

To·bolsk (*Russian* ta'bɔljsk) *n.* a town in the central Soviet Union, at the confluence of the Irtysh and Tobol Rivers: the chief centre for the early Russian colonization of Siberia. Pop.: 49 260 (1970).

To·bruk (tə'brʊk, təʊ-) *n.* a small port in NE Libya, in E Cyrenaica on the Mediterranean coast road: scene of severe fighting in World War II, changing hands five times and finally taken by the British in 1942.

to·by jug ('təʊbɪ) *n.* a beer mug or jug typically in the form of a stout seated man wearing a three-cornered hat and smoking a pipe. Also: **toby.** [C19: from the familiar form of the Christian name *Tobias*]

To·can·tins (*Portuguese* tokã'tĩs) *n.* a river in E Brazil, rising in S central Goiás state and flowing generally north to the Pará River. Length: about 2700 km (1700 miles).

toc·ca·ta (tə'kɑ:tə) *n.* a rapid keyboard composition for organ, harpsichord, etc., dating from the baroque period, usually in a rhythmically free style. [C18: from Italian, literally: touched, from *toccare* to play (an instrument), TOUCH]

Toc H ('tɒk 'eɪtʃ) *n.* a society formed in England after World War I to fight loneliness and hate and to encourage Christian comradeship. [C20: from the obsolete telegraphic code for *T.H.*, initials of *Talbot House*, Poperinge, Belgium, the original headquarters of the society]

To·char·i·an *or* **To·khar·i·an** (tɒ'kɑːrɪən) *n.* **1.** a member of an Asian people with a complex material culture, sometimes thought to be of European origin, who lived in the Tarim Basin until overcome by the Uighurs around 800 A.D. **2.** the language of this people, known from records in a N Indian script of the 7th and 8th centuries A.D. It belongs to the Indo-European family, is regarded as forming an independent branch, and shows closer affinities with the W or European group than with the E or Indo-Iranian group. The language is recorded in two dialects, known as **Tocharian A** and **Tocharian B.** [C20: ultimately from Greek *Tokharoi*, name of uncertain origin]

to·col·o·gy *or* **to·kol·o·gy** (tɒ'kɒlədʒɪ) *n.* the branch of medicine concerned with childbirth; obstetrics. [C19: from Greek *tokos* childbirth, from *tiktein* to bear]

to·coph·er·ol (tɒ'kɒfəˌrɒl) *n.* *Biochem.* any of a group of fat-soluble alcohols that occur in wheat-germ oil, watercress, lettuce, egg yolk, etc. They are thought to be necessary for healthy human reproduction. Also called: **vitamin E.** [C20: from *toco-*, from Greek *tokos* offspring (see TOCOLOGY) + *-pher-*, from *pherein* to bear + -OL[1]]

Tocque·ville (*French* tɔk'vil; *English* 'təʊkvɪl, 'tɒk-) *n.* **A·le·xis Charles Hen·ri Mau·rice Clé·rel de** (alɛksi ʃarl ɑ̃ri mɔris kle'rɛl də). 1805–59, French politician and political writer. His chief works are *De la Démocratie en Amérique* (1835–40) and *L'Ancien Régime et la Révolution* (1856).

toc·sin ('tɒksɪn) *n.* **1.** an alarm or warning signal, esp. one sounded on a bell. **2.** an alarm bell. [C16: from French, from Old French *toquassen*, from Old Provençal *tocasenh*, from *tocar* to TOUCH + *senh* bell, from Latin *signum*]

tod[1] (tɒd) *n.* *Brit.* a unit of weight, used for wool, etc., usually equal to 28 pounds. [C15: probably related to Frisian *todde* rag, Old High German *zotta* tuft of hair]

tod[2] (tɒd) *n.* **on one's tod.** *Brit. slang.* on one's own. [C19: rhyming slang (*Tod Sloan/alone*, after Tod *Sloan*, a jockey]

tod[3] (tɒd) *n.* a northern Brit. dialect word for a **fox.** [C12: of unknown origin]

to·day (tə'deɪ) *n.* **1.** this day, as distinct from yesterday or tomorrow. **2.** the present age: *children of today.* ~*adv.* **3.** during or on this day. **4.** nowadays. [Old English *tō dæge*, literally: on this day, from TO + *dæge*, dative of *dæg* DAY]

Todd (tɒd) *n.* Baron **Al·ex·an·der Ro·ber·tus.** born 1907, Scottish chemist, noted for his research into the structure of nucleic acids: Nobel prize for chemistry 1957.

tod·dle ('tɒdᵊl) *vb.* (*intr.*) **1.** to walk with short unsteady steps, as a child does when learning to walk. **2.** (foll. by *off*) *Jocular.* to depart. **3.** (foll. by *round, over*, etc.) *Jocular.* to stroll; amble. ~*n.* **4.** the act or an instance of toddling. [C16 (Scottish and northern English): of obscure origin]

tod·dler ('tɒdlə) *n.* **1.** a young child, usually one between the ages of one and two and a half. **2.** (*modifier*) designed or suitable for a toddler: *toddler suits.*

tod·dy ('tɒdɪ) *n., pl.* **·dies.** **1.** any hot sweet drink made with whisky. **2. a.** the sap of various palm trees (**toddy** or **wine palms**), used as a beverage. **b.** the liquor prepared from this sap. **3.** (in Malaysia) a milky-white sour alcoholic drink made from fermented coconut milk, drunk chiefly by Indians. [C17: from Hindi *tārī* juice of the palmyra palm, from *tār* palmyra palm, from Sanskrit *tāra*, probably of Dravidian origin]

to-do *n., pl.* **-dos.** a commotion, fuss, or quarrel.

to·dy ('təʊdɪ) *n., pl.* **·dies.** any small bird of the family *Todidae* of the West Indies, having a red-and-green plumage and long straight bill: order *Coraciiformes* (kingfishers, etc.). [C18: from French *todier*, from Latin *todus* small bird]

toe (təʊ) *n.* **1.** any one of the digits of the foot. **2.** the corresponding part in other vertebrates. **3.** the part of a shoe, sock, etc., covering the toes. **4.** anything resembling a toe in shape or position. **5.** the front part of the head of a golf club, hockey stick, etc. **6.** the lower bearing of a vertical shaft assembly. **7.** the tip of a cam follower that engages the cam profile. **8. on one's toes.** alert. **9. tread on someone's toes.** to offend or insult a person, esp. by trespassing on his field of responsibility. ~*vb.* **toes, toe·ing, toed.** **10.** (*tr.*) to touch, kick, or mark with the toe. **11.** (*tr.*) *Golf.* to strike (the ball) with the toe of the club. **12.** (*tr.*) to drive (a nail, spike, etc.) obliquely. **13.** (*intr.*) to walk with the toes pointing in a specified direction: *to toe inwards.* **14. toe the line** *or* **mark.** to conform strictly to rules or expected behaviour. [Old English *tā*; related to Old Frisian *tāne*, Old Norse *tā*, Old High German *zēha*, Latin *digitus* finger] —**'toe·ˌlike** *adj.*

toea ('təʊɑː) *n.* a monetary unit of Papua New Guinea; one-hundredth of a kina. [from a Papuan language]

toe and heel *n.* a technique used by racing drivers while changing gear on sharp bends, in which the brake is operated by the toe (or heel) of the right foot while the heel (or toe) simultaneously operates the accelerator.

toe·cap ('təʊˌkæp) *n.* a reinforced covering for the toe of a boot or shoe.

toe crack *n.* *Vet. science.* a sand crack occurring on the forepart of the hindfoot of a horse.

toed (təʊd) *adj.* **1.** having a part resembling a toe. **2.** (of a vertical or oblique member of a timber frame) fixed by nails driven in at the foot. **3.** (*in combination*) having a toe or toes as specified: *five-toed; thick-toed.*

toe dance *n.* **1.** a dance performed on tiptoe. ~*vb.* **toe-dance. 2.** (*intr.*) *Ballet.* to dance on pointes. —**toe danc·er** *n.*

toe·hold ('təʊˌhəʊld) *n.* **1.** a small foothold to facilitate climbing. **2.** any means of gaining access, support, etc.: *the socialist party gained a toehold in the local elections.* **3.** a wrestling hold in which the opponent's toe is held and his leg twisted against the joints.

toe-in *n.* a slight forward convergence given to the wheels of motor vehicles to improve steering and equalize tyre wear.

toe·nail ('təʊˌneɪl) *n.* **1.** a thin horny translucent plate covering part of the dorsal surface of the end joint of each toe. **2.** *Carpentry.* a nail driven obliquely, as in joining one beam at right angles to another. **3.** *Printers' slang.* a parenthesis. ~*vb.* **4.** (*tr.*) *Carpentry.* to join (beams) by driving nails obliquely.

toe·y ('təʊɪ) *adj.* *Austral. slang.* **1.** (of a person) nervous or anxious. **2.** *Rare.* (of a horse) eager to race.

toff (tɒf) *n.* *Brit. slang.* a rich, well-dressed, or upper-class person, esp. a man. [C19: perhaps variant of TUFT, nickname for a commoner at Oxford University]

tof·fee *or* **tof·fy** ('tɒfɪ) *n., pl.* **·fees** *or* **·fies.** **1.** a sweet made from sugar or treacle boiled with butter, nuts, etc. **2. for toffee.** (preceded by *can't*) *Informal.* to be incompetent at a specified activity: *he can't sing for toffee.* [C19: variant of earlier TAFFY]

tof·fee-ap·ple *n.* an apple fixed on a stick and coated with a thin layer of toffee.

tof·fee-nosed *adj.* *Slang, chiefly Brit.* pretentious or supercilious; used esp. of snobbish people.

toft (tɒft) *n.* *British history.* **1.** a homestead. **2.** an entire holding, consisting of a homestead and the attached arable land. [Old English, from Old Norse *topt*]

tog (tɒg) *n.* **1.** (*usually pl.*) a garment. ~*vb.* **togs, tog·ging, togged.** **2.** (often foll. by *up* or *out*) to dress (oneself), esp. in smart clothes. [C18: probably short for obsolete cant *togemans* coat, from Latin *toga* TOGA + *-mans*, of uncertain origin]

to·ga ('təʊgə) *n.* **1.** a garment worn by citizens of ancient Rome, consisting of a piece of cloth draped around the body. **2.** the official vestment of certain offices. [C16: from Latin, related to *tegere* to cover] —**to·gaed** ('təʊgəd) *adj.*

to·ga vi·ri·lis (vɪ'raɪlɪs) *n.* (in ancient Rome) the toga assumed by a youth at the age of 14 as a symbol of manhood and citizenship. [Latin]

to·geth·er (tə'gɛðə) *adv.* **1.** with cooperation and interchange between constituent elements, members, etc.: *we worked together.* **2.** in or into contact or union with each other: *to stick papers together.* **3.** in or into one place or assembly; with each other: *the people are gathered together.* **4.** at the same time: *we left school together.* **5.** considered collectively or jointly: *all our wages put together couldn't buy that car.* **6.** continuously: *working for eight hours together.* **7.** closely, cohesively, or compactly united or held: *water will hold the dough together.* **8.** mutually or reciprocally: *to multiply seven and eight together.* **9.** *Informal.* organized: *to get things together.* **10. together with.** in addition to. [Old English *tōgædre*; related to Old Frisian *togadera*, Middle High German *gater*; see GATHER]
Usage. See at **plus.**

to·geth·er·ness (tə'gɛðənɪs) *n.* a feeling of closeness or affection from being united with other people.

tog·ger·y ('tɒgərɪ) *n.* *Informal.* clothes; togs.

tog·gle ('tɒgᵊl) *n.* **1.** a wooden peg or metal rod fixed crosswise through an eye at the end of a rope, chain, or cable, for fastening temporarily by insertion through an eye in another rope, chain, etc. **2.** a wooden or plastic bar-shaped button inserted through a loop for fastening. **3.** a pin inserted into a nautical knot to keep it secure. **4.** *Machinery.* a toggle joint or a device having such a joint. ~*vb.* **5.** (*tr.*) to supply or fasten with a toggle or toggles. [C18: of unknown origin] —**'tog·gler** *n.*

tog·gle i·ron *n.* a whaling harpoon with a pivoting barb near its head to prevent a harpooned whale pulling free. Also called: **toggle harpoon.**

tog·gle joint *n.* a device consisting of two arms pivoted at a common joint and at their outer ends and used to apply pressure by straightening the angle between the two arms.

tog·gle switch *n.* an electric switch having a projecting lever that is manipulated in a particular way to open or close a circuit.

Tog·li·at·ti (ˌtɒlɪ'ætɪ) *n.* a city in the W central Soviet Union, on the Volga River: automobile industry. Pop.: 438 000 (1975 est.). Former name (until 1964): **Stavropol.** Russian name: **Tol'yatti.**

To·go[1] ('təʊgəʊ) *n.* a republic in West Africa, on the Gulf of Guinea: became French Togoland (a League of Nations mandate) after the division of German Togoland in 1920; independent since 1960. Official language: French. Religion: animist majority. Currency: franc. Capital: Lomé. Pop.: 1 955 916 (1970). Area: 56 700 sq. km (20 900 sq. miles). —**To·go·lese** (ˌtəʊgə'liːz) *adj., n.*

To·go[2] ('təʊgəʊ) *n.* Count **Heil·ha·chi·ro** (ˌheɪhə'tʃɪərəʊ). 1847–1934, Japanese admiral, who commanded the Japanese fleet in the war with Russia (1904–05).

To·go·land ('təʊgəʊˌlænd) *n.* a former German protectorate in West Africa on the Gulf of Guinea: divided in 1922 into the League of Nations mandates of British Togoland (west) and French Togoland (east); the former joined Ghana in 1957; the latter became independent as Togo in 1960. —**'To·go·ˌland·er** *n.*

to+he+ro+a (ˌtəʊəˈrəʊə) *n.* **1.** a bivalve mollusc, *Amphidesma* (or *Semele*) *ventricosum,* of New Zealand. **2.** a greenish soup made of this. [from Maori]

toil[1] (tɔɪl) *n.* **1.** hard or exhausting work. **2.** an obsolete word for **strife.** ~*vb.* **3.** (*intr.*) to labour. **4.** (*intr.*) to progress with slow painful movements: *to toil up a hill.* **5.** (*tr.*) *Archaic.* to achieve by toil. [C13: from Anglo-French *toiler* to struggle, from Old French *toeillier* to confuse, from Latin *tudiculāre* to stir, from *tudicula* machine for bruising olives, from *tudes* a hammer, from *tundere* to beat] —**'toil+er** *n.*

toil[2] (tɔɪl) *n.* **1.** (*often pl.*) a net or snare: *the toils of fortune had ensnared him.* **2.** *Archaic.* a trap for wild beasts. [C16: from Old French *toile,* from Latin *tēla* loom]

toile (twɑːl) *n.* **1.** a transparent linen or cotton fabric. **2.** a garment of exclusive design made up in cheap cloth so that alterations and experiments can be made. [C19: from French, from Latin *tēla* a loom]

toi+let (ˈtɔɪlɪt) *n.* **1.** another word for **lavatory. 2.** the act of dressing and preparing oneself: *to make one's toilet.* **3.** a dressing table or the articles used when making one's toilet. **4.** *Rare.* costume. **5.** the cleansing of a wound, etc., after an operation or childbirth. [C16: from French *toilette* dress, from TOILE]

toi+let pa+per *or* **tis+sue** *n.* thin absorbent paper, often wound in a roll round a cardboard cylinder (**toilet roll**), used for cleaning oneself after defecation or urination.

toi+let+ry (ˈtɔɪlɪtrɪ) *n., pl.* **+ries.** an object or cosmetic used in making up, dressing, etc.

toi+let set *n.* a matching set consisting of a hairbrush, comb, mirror, and clothes brush.

toi+lette (tɔɪˈlɛt; *French* twaˈlɛt) *n. Usually literary or affected.* another word for **toilet** (sense 2). [C16: from French; see TOILET]

toi+let wa+ter *n.* a form of liquid perfume lighter than cologne. Compare **cologne.** Also called: **eau de toilette.**

toil+some (ˈtɔɪlsəm) *or* **toil+ful** *adj.* laborious. —**'toil+some+ly** *adv.* —**'toil+some+ness** *n.*

To·jo (ˈtəʊdʒəʊ) *n.* **Hi·de·ki** (ˈhiːdɛˌkiː). 1885–1948, Japanese soldier and statesman; minister of war (1940–41) and premier (1941–44); hanged as a war criminal.

to+kay (ˈtəʊkeɪ) *n.* a small gecko, *Gekko gecko,* of S and SE Asia, having a retractile claw at the tip of each digit. [from Malay *toke,* of imitative origin]

To+kay (təʊˈkeɪ) *n.* **1.** a fine sweet wine made near Tokaj, Hungary. **2.** a variety of large sweet grape used to make this wine. **3.** a similar wine made elsewhere.

to+ken (ˈtəʊkən) *n.* **1.** an indication, warning, or sign of something. **2.** a symbol or visible representation of something. **3.** something that indicates authority, proof, or authenticity. **4.** a metal or plastic disc, such as a substitute for currency for use in slot machines. **5.** a memento. **6.** a gift voucher that can be used as payment for goods of a specified value. **7.** (*modifier*) as a matter of form only; nominal: *a token increase in salary.* ~*vb.* **8.** (*tr.*) to act or serve as a warning or symbol of; betoken. [Old English *tācen;* related to Old Frisian *tēken,* Old Saxon *tēkan,* Old High German *zeihhan,* Old Norse *teikn;* see TEACH]

to+ken+ism (ˈtəʊkəˌnɪzəm) *n.* the practice of making only a token effort or doing no more than the minimum, esp. in order to comply with a law.

to+ken mon+ey *n.* coins of the regular issue having greater face value than the value of their metal content.

to+ken pay+ment *n.* a small payment made in acknowledgment of the existence of debt.

to+ken strike *n.* a brief strike intended to convey strength of feeling on a disputed issue.

to+ken vote *n.* a Parliamentary vote of money in which the amount quoted to aid discussion is not intended to be binding.

To+khar+i+an (tɒˈkɑːrɪən) *n.* a variant spelling of **Tocharian.**

tok·o·loshe (ˌtɒkɒˈlɒʃ, -ˈlɒʃɪ) *n.* (in Bantu folklore) a malevolent mythical manlike animal of short stature. Also called: **tikoloshe.** [from Xhosa *uthikoloshe*]

To·ku·ga·wa I·ye·ya·su (ˌtəʊkuːˈɡɑːwə ˌiːjeɪˈjɑːsuː) *n.* See (Tokugawa) **Iyeyasu.**

To+kyo (ˈtəʊkjəʊ, -kɪˌəʊ) *n.* the capital of Japan, a port on SE Honshu on **Tokyo Bay** (an inlet of the Pacific): the largest city in the world since the 18th century, with a conurbation of over 25 million people; major industrial centre and the chief cultural centre of Japan. Pop.: 8 640 000 (1975).

to·la (ˈtəʊlə) *n.* a unit of weight, used in India, equal to 180 ser or 180 grains. [C17: from Hindi *tolā,* from Sanskrit *tulā* scale, from *tul* to weigh]

to+lan (ˈtəʊlæn) *or* **to+lane** (ˈtəʊleɪn) *n.* a white crystalline derivative of acetylene; diphenylacetylene; diphenylethyne. Formula: $C_6H_5C{:}CC_6H_5$. [C19: from TOL(UENE) + *-an* (see -ANE)]

Tol·bert (ˈtɒlbət) *n.* **Wil·liam Rich·ard.** born 1913, Liberian statesman; president of Liberia (1971-80).

tol+booth (ˈtəʊlˌbuːθ, -ˌbuːð, ˈtɒl-) *n.* **1.** *Chiefly Scot.* a town hall or guildhall. **2.** a variant spelling of **tollbooth.**

tol+bu+ta+mide (tɒlˈbjuːtəˌmaɪd) *n.* a synthetic crystalline compound administered orally in the treatment of diabetes to lower blood glucose levels. Formula: $C_{12}H_{18}N_2O_3S$. [C20: from TOL(UYL) + BUT(YRIC ACID) + AMIDE]

told (təʊld) *vb.* **1.** the past tense or past participle of **tell.** ~*adj.* **2.** See **all told.**

tole (təʊl) *n.* enamelled or lacquered metal ware, usually gilded, popular in the 18th century. [from French *tôle* sheet metal, from French (dialect): table, from Latin *tabula* table]

To+le·do *n.* **1.** (tɒˈleɪdəʊ; *Spanish* toˈleðo). a city in central Spain, on the River Tagus: capital of Visigothic Spain, and of Castile from 1087 to 1560; famous for steel and swords since the first century. Pop.: 44 382 (1970). Ancient name: **Toletum. 2.** (təˈliːdəʊ). an inland port in NW Ohio, on Lake Erie: one of the largest coal-shipping ports in the world; transportation and industrial centre; university (1872). Pop.: 377 423 (1973 est.).

tol+er+a+ble (ˈtɒlərəbᵊl) *adj.* **1.** able to be tolerated; endurable. **2.** permissible. **3.** *Informal.* fairly good. —**'tol+er+a+ble+ness** *or* **ˌtol+er+a·'bil+i+ty** *n.* —**'tol+er+a+bly** *adv.*

tol+er+ance (ˈtɒlərəns) *n.* **1.** the state or quality of being tolerant. **2.** capacity to endure something, esp. pain or hardship. **3.** the permitted variation in some measurement or other characteristic of an object or workpiece. **4.** *Physiol.* the capacity of an organism to endure the effects of a poison or other substance, esp. when taken over a prolonged period.

tol+er+ant (ˈtɒlərənt) *adj.* **1.** able to tolerate the beliefs, actions, opinions, etc., of others. **2.** permissive. **3.** able to withstand extremes, as of heat and cold. **4.** *Med.* (of a patient) exhibiting tolerance to a drug. —**'tol+er+ant+ly** *adv.*

tol+er+ate (ˈtɒləˌreɪt) *vb.* (*tr.*) **1.** to treat with indulgence, liberality, or forbearance. **2.** to permit. **3.** to be able to bear; put up with. **4.** *Med.* to have tolerance for (a drug, poison, etc.). [C16: from Latin *tolerāre* sustain; related to THOLE[2]] —**'tol+er·a+tive** *adj.* —**'tol+er·ˌa+tor** *n.*

tol+er·a+tion (ˌtɒləˈreɪʃən) *n.* **1.** the act or practice of tolerating. **2.** freedom to hold religious opinions that differ from the established or prescribed religion of a country. —**ˌtol+er·'a+tion+ism** *n.* —**ˌtol+er·'a+tion+ist** *n.*

tol·i+dine (ˈtɒlɪˌdiːn) *n.* any of several isomeric compounds, esp. the *ortho-* isomer, which is a white or reddish crystalline substance used in the manufacture of dyes and resins. Formula: $(C_6H_3NH_2CH_3)_2$. [C19: from TOL(UENE) + -ID[3] + -INE[2]]

To+li+ma (*Spanish* toˈlima) *n.* a volcano in W Colombia, in the Andes. Height: 5215 m (17 110 ft.).

Tol·kien (ˈtɒlkiːn) *n.* **J(ohn) R(onald) R(euel).** 1892–1973, British philologist and writer, born in South Africa. He is best known for *The Hobbit* (1937) and the trilogy *The Lord of the Rings* (1954–55).

toll[1] (təʊl) *vb.* **1.** to ring or cause to ring slowly and recurrently. **2.** (*tr.*) to summon, warn, or announce by tolling. **3.** *U.S.* to decoy (game, esp. ducks). ~*n.* **4.** the act or sound of tolling. [C15: perhaps related to Old English *-tyllan,* as in *fortyllan* to attract]

toll[2] (təʊl, tɒl) *n.* **1. a.** an amount of money levied, esp. for the use of certain roads, bridges, etc., to cover the cost of maintenance. **b.** (*as modifier*): *toll road; toll bridge.* **2.** loss or damage incurred through an accident, disaster, etc.: *the war took its toll of the inhabitants.* **3.** Also called: **toll+age.** (formerly) the right to levy a toll. [Old English *toln;* related to Old Frisian *tolene,* Old High German *zol* toll, from Late Latin *telōnium* customs house, from Greek *telṓnion,* ultimately from *telos* tax]

toll+booth *or* **tol+booth** (ˈtəʊlˌbuːθ, -ˌbuːð, ˈtɒl-) *n.* a booth or kiosk at which a toll is collected.

toll call *n. Brit. obsolete.* a short-distance trunk call.

Tol·ler (*German* ˈtɔlər) *n.* **Ernst** (ɛrnst). 1893–1939, German dramatist and revolutionary, noted particularly for for his expressionist plays, esp. *Masse Mensch* (1921).

toll+gate (ˈtəʊlˌgeɪt, ˈtɒl-) *n.* a gate across a toll road or bridge at which travellers must stop and pay.

toll+house (ˈtəʊlˌhaʊs, ˈtɒl-) *n.* a small house at a tollgate occupied by a toll collector.

tol+ly *or* **tol+lie** (ˈtɒlɪ) *n., pl.* **+lies.** *S. African.* a castrated calf. [C19: from Xhosa *ithole* calf on which the horns have begun to appear]

Tol+pud+dle Mar+tyrs (ˈtɒlˌpʌdᵊl) *n.* six farmworkers sentenced to transportation for seven years in 1834 for forming a trade union in the village of Tolpuddle, Dorset.

Tol·stoy (ˈtɒlstɔɪ; *Russian* talˈstɔj) *n.* **Le·o,** Russian name *Count Lev Nikolayevich Tolstoy.* 1828–1910, Russian novelist, short-story writer, and philosopher; author of the two monumental novels *War and Peace* (1865–69) and *Anna Karenina* (1875–77). Following a spiritual crisis in 1879, he adopted a form of Christianity based on a doctrine of nonresistance to evil.

Tol+tec (ˈtɒltɛk) *n., pl.* **+tecs** *or* **+tec. 1.** a member of a Central American Indian people who dominated the valley of Mexico from their capital Tula from about 950 to 1160 A.D., when the valley was overrun by the Aztecs. ~*adj. also* **Tol+tec+an. 2.** of or relating to this people.

to+lu (tɒˈluː) *n.* an aromatic balsam obtained from a South American tree, *Myroxylon balsamum.* See **balsam** (sense 1). [C17: after *Santiago de Tolu,* Colombia, from which it was exported]

tol·u+ate (ˈtɒljʊˌeɪt) *n.* any salt or ester of any of the three isomeric forms of toluic acid. [C19: from TOLU(IC ACID) + -ATE[1]]

To+lu+ca (*Spanish* toˈluka) *n.* **1.** a city in S central Mexico, capital of Mexico state, at an altitude of 2640 m (8660 ft.). Pop.: 141 726 (1974 est.). Official name: **To+lu+ca de Ler+do** (de ˈlerðo). **2. Ne+va+do de** (neˈβaðo de). a volcano in central Mexico, in Mexico state near Toluca: crater partly filled by a lake. Height: 4577 m (15 017 ft.).

tol·u+ene (ˈtɒljʊˌiːn) *n.* a colourless volatile flammable liquid with an odour resembling that of benzene, obtained from petroleum and coal tar and used as a solvent and in the manufacture of many organic chemicals. Formula: $C_6H_5CH_3$.

[C19: from TOLU + -ENE, since it was previously obtained from tolu]

to·lu·ic ac·id (tɒ'lu:ɪk) *n.* a white crystalline derivative of toluene existing in three isomeric forms; methylbenzoic acid. The *ortho-* and *para-* isomers are used in synthetic resins and the *meta-* isomer is used as an insect repellent. Formula: $C_6H_4CH_3COOH$. [C19: from TOLU(ENE) + -IC]

to·lu·i·dine (tɒ'lju:ɪ,di:n) *n.* an amine derived from toluene existing in three isomeric forms; aminotoluene. The *ortho-* and *meta-* isomers are liquids and the *para-* isomer is a crystalline solid. All three are used in making dyes. Formula: $C_6H_4CH_3NH_2$. [C19: from TOLU(ENE) + -IDE + -INE[2]]

tol·u·ol ('tɒljʊ,ɒl) *n.* another name for **toluene.**

tol·u·yl ('tɒljʊɪl) *n.* (*modifier*) of, consisting of, or containing any of three isomeric groups $CH_3C_6H_4CO$-, derived from a toluic acid by removal of the hydroxyl group: *toluyl group or radical.* [C19: from TOLU(ENE) + -YL]

tol·yl ('tɒlɪl) *n.* **1.** (*modifier*) of, consisting of, or containing any of three isomeric groups, $CH_3C_6H_4$-, derived from toluene: *tolyl group or radical.* **2.** (*modifier*) another word for **benzyl.** Also called: *α*-**tolyl.** [C19: from TOLU (see TOLUENE) + -YL]

tom (tɒm) *n.* **a.** the male of various animals, esp. the cat. **b.** (*as modifier*): *a tom turkey.* **c.** (*in combination*): *a tomcat.* [C16: special use of the shortened form of *Thomas*, applied to any male, often implying a common or ordinary type of person, etc.]

tom·a·hawk ('tɒmə,hɔ:k) *n.* **1.** a fighting axe, with a stone or later an iron head, used by the North American Indians. **2.** *Austral.* the usual word for **hatchet.** ~*vb.* (*tr.*) *Austral. slang.* **3.** to shear (a sheep) roughly or so as to cut the skin. [C17: from Virginia Algonquian *tamahaac*]

tom·al·ley ('tɒmælɪ) *n.* the liver of a lobster, eaten as a delicacy. [C17: of Caribbean origin; compare Galibi *tumali* sauce of crab or lobster liver]

to·man (tə'mɑ:n) *n.* a gold coin formerly issued in Persia. [C16: from Persian, of Mongolian origin]

Tom and Jer·ry *n. U.S.* a hot mixed drink containing rum, brandy, egg, nutmeg, and sometimes milk.

to·ma·to (tə'mɑ:təʊ) *n., pl.* **-toes. 1.** a solanaceous plant, *Lycopersicon* (or *Lycopersicum*) *esculentum*, of South America but widely cultivated, of its red fleshy many-seeded edible fruits. **2.** the fruit of this plant, which has slightly acid-tasting flesh and is eaten in salads, as a vegetable, etc. **3.** *U.S. slang.* a girl or woman. [C17 *tomate*, from Spanish, from Nahuatl *tomatl*]

tomb (tu:m) *n.* **1.** a place, esp. a vault beneath the ground, for the burial of a corpse. **2.** a stone or other monument to the dead. **3. the tomb.** a poetic term for **death. 4.** anything serving as a burial place: *the sea was his tomb.* ~*vb.* **5.** (*tr.*) *Rare.* to place in a tomb; entomb. [C13: from Old French *tombe*, from Late Latin *tumba* burial mound, from Greek *tumbos*; related to Latin *tumēre* to swell, Middle Irish *tomm* hill] —'**tomb,like** *adj.*

tom·bac ('tɒmbæk) *or* **tam·bac** ('tæmbæk) *n.* any of various brittle alloys containing copper and zinc and sometimes tin and arsenic: used for making cheap jewellery, etc. [C17: from French, from Dutch *tombak*, from Malay *tambâga* copper, apparently from Sanskrit *tāmraka*, from *tāmra* dark coppery red]

tom·bo·la (tɒm'bəʊlə) *n. Brit.* a type of lottery, esp. at a fête, in which tickets are drawn from a revolving drum. [C19: from Italian, from *tombolare* to somersault; see TUMBLE]

tom·bo·lo ('tɒmbə,ləʊ) *n., pl.* **-los.** a narrow sand or shingle bar linking a small island with another island or the mainland. [C20: from Italian, from Latin *tumulus* mound; see TUMULUS]

Tom·bouc·tou (tɔ̃buk'tu) *n.* the French name for **Timbuktu.**

tom·boy ('tɒm,bɔɪ) *n.* a girl who acts or dresses in a boyish way, liking rough outdoor activities. —'**tom,boy·ish** *adj.* —'**tom,boy·ish·ly** *adv.* —'**tom,boy·ish·ness** *n.*

tomb·stone ('tu:m,stəʊn) *n.* another word for **gravestone.**

Tom Col·lins *n. U.S.* a long drink consisting of gin, lime or lemon juice, sugar or syrup, and soda water.

Tom, Dick, and (or) Har·ry *n.* an ordinary, undistinguished, or common person (esp. in the phrases **every Tom, Dick, and Harry; any Tom, Dick, or Harry).**

tome (təʊm) *n.* **1.** a large weighty book. **2.** one of the several volumes of a work. [C16: from French, from Latin *tomus* section of larger work, from Greek *tomos* a slice, from *temnein* to cut; related to Latin *tondēre* to shear]

-tome *n. combining form.* indicating an instrument for cutting: *osteotome.* [from Greek *tomē* a cutting, *tomos* a slice, from *temnein* to cut]

to·men·tum (tə'mɛntəm) *n., pl.* **-ta** (-tə). **1.** a feltlike covering of downy hairs on leaves and other plant parts. **2.** a network of minute blood vessels occurring in the human brain between the pia mater and cerebral cortex. [C17: New Latin, from Latin: stuffing for cushions; related to Latin *tumēre* to swell] —**to·men·tose** (tə'mɛntəʊs) *adj.*

tom·fool (,tɒm'fu:l) *n.* **a.** a fool. **b.** (*as modifier*): *tomfool ideas.* —,**tom'fool·ish** *adj.* —,**tom'fool·ish·ness** *n.*

tom·fool·er·y (,tɒm'fu:lərɪ) *n., pl.* **-er·ies. 1.** foolish behaviour. **2.** utter nonsense; rubbish.

tom·my ('tɒmɪ) *n., pl.* **-mies.** (*often cap.*) *Brit. informal.* a private in the British Army. Also: **Tommy Atkins.** [C19: originally *Thomas Atkins*, name representing typical private in specimen forms; compare TOM]

Tom·my gun *n.* an informal name for **Thompson sub-machine-gun.**

tom·my·rot ('tɒmɪ,rɒt) *n.* utter nonsense; tomfoolery.

to·mog·ra·phy (tə'mɒgrəfɪ) *n.* any of a number of techniques used to obtain an x-ray photograph of a selected plane section of the human body or some other solid object. [C20: from Greek *tomē* a cutting + -GRAPHY]

to·mor·row (tə'mɒrəʊ) *n.* **1.** the day after today. **2.** the future. ~*adv.* **3.** on the day after today. **4.** at some time in the future. [Old English *tō morgenne*, from TO (at, on) + *morgenne*, dative of *morgen* MORNING; see MORROW]

tom·pi·on ('tɒmpɪən) *n.* a variant spelling of **tampion.**

Tomsk (*Russian* tɔmsk) *n.* a city in the central Soviet Union: formerly an important gold-mining town and administrative centre for a large area of Siberia; university (1888); engineering industries. Pop.: 399 000 (1975 est.).

Tom Thumb *n.* **1. General,** stage name of *Charles Stratton*. 1838–83, U.S. midget, exhibited in P. T. Barnum's circus. **2.** a dwarf; midget. [after *Tom Thumb*, the tiny hero of several English folk tales]

tom·tit (,tɒm'tɪt) *n. Brit.* any of various tits, esp. the bluetit.

tom-tom *or* **tam-tam** *n.* **1.** a drum associated either with the American Indians or with Eastern cultures, usually beaten with the hands as a signalling instrument. **2.** a monotonous drumming or beating sound. [C17: from Hindi *tamtam*, of imitative origin]

-to·my *n. combining form.* indicating a surgical cutting of a specified part or tissue: *lobotomy.* [from Greek *-tomia*; see -TOME]

ton[1] (tʌn) *n.* **1.** Also called: **long ton.** *Brit.* a unit of weight equal to 2240 pounds or 1016.046 909 kilograms. **2.** Also called: **short ton, net ton.** *U.S.* a unit of weight equal to 2000 pounds or 907.184 kilograms. **3.** Also called: **metric ton, tonne.** a unit of weight equal to 1000 kilograms. **4.** Also called: **freight ton.** a unit of volume or weight used for charging or measuring freight in shipping. It depends on the type of material being shipped but is often taken as 40 cubic feet, 1 cubic metre, or 1000 kilograms: *freight is charged at £40 per ton of 1 cubic metre.* **5.** Also called: **measurement ton, shipping ton.** a unit of volume used in shipping freight, equal to 40 cubic feet, irrespective of the commodity shipped. **6.** Also called: **displacement ton.** a unit used for measuring the displacement of a ship, equal to 35 cubic feet of sea water or 2240 pounds. **7.** Also called: **register ton.** a unit of internal capacity of ships equal to 100 cubic feet. ~*adv.* **8. tons.** (intensifier): *the new flat is tons better than the old one.* [C14: variant of TUN]

ton[2] *French.* (tɔ̃) *n.* style, fashion, or distinction. [C18: from French, from Latin *tonus* TONE]

ton[3] (tʌn) *n. Slang, chiefly Brit.* a score or achievement of a hundred, esp. a hundred miles per hour, as on a motorcycle. [C20: special use of TON[1] applied to quantities of one hundred]

ton·al ('təʊnᵊl) *adj.* **1.** of or relating to tone. **2.** of, relating to, or utilizing the diatonic system; having an established key. Compare **atonal. 3. a.** (of an answer in a fugue) not having the same melodic intervals as the subject, so as to remain in the original key. **b.** denoting a fugue as having such an answer. Compare **real**[1] (sense 10). —'**ton·al·ly** *adv.*

to·nal·i·ty (təʊ'nælɪtɪ) *n., pl.* **-ties. 1.** *Music.* **a.** the actual or implied presence of a musical key in a composition. **b.** the system of major and minor keys prevalent in Western music since the decline of modes. Compare **atonality. 2.** the overall scheme of colours and tones in a painting.

to-name *n. Scot.* a by-name or nickname used to distinguish one person from others of the same name.

Ton·bridge ('tʌn,brɪdʒ) *n.* a market town in SE England, in SW Kent on the River Medway. Pop.: 31 006 (1971).

ton·do ('tɒndəʊ) *n., pl.* **-di** (-di:). a circular easel painting or relief carving. [C19: from Italian: a circle, shortened from *rotondo* round]

Ton Duc Thang ('tɒn 'dʊk 'θæŋ) *n.* 1888-1980, Vietnamese statesman; president of Vietnam (1976-80).

tone (təʊn) *n.* **1.** sound with reference to quality, pitch, or volume. **2.** short for **tone colour. 3.** *U.S.* another word for **note** (sense 10). **4.** (in acoustic analysis) a sound resulting from periodic or regular vibrations, composed either of a simple sinusoidal wave form (**pure tone**) or of several such wave forms superimposed upon one main one (**compound tone**). **5.** an interval of a major second; whole tone. **6.** Also called: **Gregorian tone.** any of several plainsong melodies or other chants used in the singing of psalms. **7.** *Linguistics.* any of the pitch levels or pitch contours at which a syllable may be pronounced, such as high tone, falling tone, etc. **8.** the quality or character of a sound: *a nervous tone of voice.* **9.** general aspect, quality, or style: *I didn't like the tone of his speech.* **10.** high quality or style: *to lower the tone of a place.* **11.** the quality of a given colour, as modified by mixture with white or black; shade; tint: *a tone of red.* **12.** *Physiol.* **a.** the normal tension of a muscle at rest. **b.** the natural firmness of the tissues and normal functioning of bodily organs in health. **13.** the overall effect of the colour values and gradations of light and dark in a picture. **14.** *Photog.* a colour or shade of colour, including black or grey, of a particular area on a negative or positive that can be distinguished from surrounding lighter or darker areas. ~*vb.* **15.** (*intr.*; often foll. by *with*) to be of a matching or similar tone (to): *the curtains tone with the carpet.* **16.** (*tr.*) to give a tone to or correct the tone of. **17.** (*tr.*) *Photog.* to soften or change the colour of the tones of (a photographic image) by chemical means. **18.** an archaic word for **intone.** ~See also **tone down, tone up.** [C14: from Latin *tonus*, from Greek *tonos* tension, tone, from *teinein* to stretch] —'**ton·er** *n.*

tone arm *n.* another name for **pickup** (sense 1).

tone clus·ter *n. Music.* a group of adjacent notes played simultaneously, either in an orchestral score or, on the piano, by depressing a whole set of adjacent keys.

tone col·our *n.* the quality of a musical sound that is conditioned or distinguished by the upper partials or overtones present in it. Often shortened to **tone.** See also **timbre** (sense 2).

tone con·trol *n.* a device in a radio, etc., by which the relative intensities of high and low frequencies may be varied.

tone-deaf *adj.* unable to distinguish subtle differences in musical pitch. —**tone deaf·ness** *n.*

tone down *vb.* (*adv.*) to moderate or become moderated in tone: *to tone down an argument; to tone down a bright colour.*

tone lan·guage *n.* a language, such as Chinese or certain African languages, in which differences in tone may make differences in meaning.

tone·less ('təʊnlɪs) *adj.* **1.** having no tone. **2.** lacking colour or vitality. —**'tone·less·ly** *adv.* —**'tone·less·ness** *n.*

ton·eme ('təʊni:m) *n. Linguistics.* a phoneme that is distinguished from other phoneme only by its tone. —**to·'ne·mic** *adj.* [C20: from TONE + -EME]

tone po·em *n.* another term for **symphonic poem.**

tone row *or* **se·ries** *n.* Also called: **note row.** *Music.* a group of notes having a characteristic pattern or order that forms the basis of the musical material in a serial composition, esp. one consisting of the twelve notes of the chromatic scale. See also **serialism, twelve-tone.**

to·net·ic (təʊ'nɛtɪk) *adj.* (of a language) distinguishing words semantically by distinction of tone as well as by other sounds. See **tone language.** [C20: from TONE + -ETIC, as in PHONETIC] —**to·'net·i·cal·ly** *adv.*

tone up *vb.* (*adv.*) to make or become more vigorous, healthy, etc.: *exercise tones up the muscles.*

tong[1] (tɒŋ) *vb.* (*tr.*) to gather or seize with tongs.

tong[2] (tɒŋ) *n.* (formerly) a secret society of Chinese Americans, popularly assumed to engage in criminal activities. [C20: from Chinese (Cantonese) *t'ong* meeting place]

ton·ga ('tɒŋgə) *n.* a light two-wheeled vehicle used in rural areas of India. [C19: from Hindi *tāṅgā*]

Ton·ga[1] ('tɒŋgə, 'tɒŋə) *n.* **1.** (*pl.* **·gas** *or* **ga**) a member of a Negroid people of S central Africa, living chiefly in Zambia and Rhodesia. **2.** the language of this people, belonging to the Bantu group of the Niger-Congo family.

Tong·a[2] ('tɒŋə, 'tɒŋgə) *n.* a kingdom occupying an archipelago of more than 150 volcanic and coral islands in the SW Pacific, east of Fiji: inhabited by Polynesians; became a British protectorate in 1900 and gained independence in 1970; a member of the Commonwealth. Languages: Tongan and English. Religion: Christian. Currency: pa'anga. Capital: Nuku'alofa. Pop.: 98 000 (1974 UN est.). Area: 675 sq. km (261 sq. miles). Also called: **Friendly Islands.** —**'Tong·an** *adj., n.*

tongs (tɒŋz) *pl. n.* an instrument for grasping or lifting, consisting of a hinged, sprung, or pivoted pair of arms or levers, joined at one end. Also called: **pair of tongs.** [plural of Old English *tange*; related to Old Saxon *tanga,* Old High German *zanga,* Old Norse *tong*]

tongue (tʌŋ) *n.* **1.** a movable mass of muscular tissue attached to the floor of the mouth in most vertebrates. It is the organ of taste and aids the mastication and swallowing of food. In man it plays an important part in the articulation of speech sounds. Related adj.: **lingual. 2.** an analogous organ in invertebrates. **3.** the tongue of certain animals used as food. **4.** a language, dialect, or idiom: *the English tongue.* **5.** the ability to speak: *to lose one's tongue.* **6.** a manner of speaking: *a glib tongue.* **7.** utterance or voice (esp. in the phrase **give tongue**). **8.** *Archaic.* a people or tribe, esp. one having its own language. **9.** anything which resembles a tongue in shape or function: *a tongue of flame; a tongue of the sea.* **10.** a promontory or spit of land. **11.** a flap of leather on a shoe, either for decoration or under the laces or buckles to protect the instep. **12.** *Music.* the reed of an oboe or similar instrument. **13.** the clapper of a bell. **14.** the harnessing pole of a horse-drawn vehicle. **15.** a long and narrow projection on a machine part that serves as a guide for assembly or as a securing device. **16.** a projecting strip along an edge of a board that is made to fit a corresponding groove in the edge of another board. **17. hold one's tongue.** to keep quiet. **18. on the tip of one's tongue.** about to come to mind: *her name was on the tip of his tongue.* **19. with (one's) tongue in (one's) cheek.** Also: **tongue in cheek.** with insincere or ironical intent. ~*vb.* **tongues, tongu·ing, tongued. 20.** to articulate (notes played on a wind instrument) by the process of tonguing. **21.** (*tr.*) to lick, feel, or touch with the tongue. **22.** (*tr.*) *Carpentry.* to provide (a board) with a tongue. **23.** (*intr.*) (of a piece of land) to project into a body of water. **24.** *Obsolete.* to reproach; scold. [Old English *tunge*; related to Old Saxon, Old Norse *tunga,* Old High German *zunga,* Latin *lingua*] —**'tongue·less** *adj.* —**'tongue·,like** *adj.*

tongue-and-groove joint *n.* a joint made between two boards by means of a tongue along the edge of one board that fits into a groove along the edge of the other board.

tongued (tʌŋd) *adj.* **1. a.** having a tongue or tongues. **b.** (*in combination*): *long-tongued.* **2.** (*in combination*) having a manner of speech as specified: *sharp-tongued.*

tongue-lash *vb.* (*tr.*) to reprimand severely; scold. —**'tongue-,lash·ing** *n., adj.*

tongues (tʌŋz) *n.* See **gift of tongues.**

tongue-tie *n.* a congenital condition in which the tongue has restricted mobility as the result of an abnormally short frenulum.

tongue-tied *adj.* **1.** speechless, esp. with embarrassment or shyness. **2.** having a condition of tongue-tie.

tongue twist·er *n.* a sentence or phrase that is difficult to articulate clearly and quickly, such as *Peter Piper picked a peck of pickled pepper.*

tongu·ing ('tʌŋɪŋ) *n.* a technique of articulating notes on a wind instrument. See **single-tongue, double-tongue, triple-tongue.**

ton·ic ('tɒnɪk) *n.* **1.** a medicinal preparation that improves and strengthens the functioning of the body or increases the feeling of well-being. **2.** anything that enlivens or strengthens: *his speech was a tonic to the audience.* **3.** Also called: **tonic water.** a mineral water, usually carbonated and containing quinine and often mixed with gin or other alcoholic drinks. **4.** *Music.* **a.** the first degree of a major or minor scale and the tonal centre of a piece composed in a particular key. **b.** a key or chord based on this. **5.** a stressed syllable in a word. ~*adj.* **6.** serving to enliven and invigorate: *a tonic wine.* **7.** of or relating to a tone or tones. **8.** *Music.* of or relating to the first degree of a major or minor scale. **9.** of or denoting the general effect of colour and light and shade in a picture. **10.** *Physiol.* of, relating to, characterized by, or affecting normal muscular or bodily tone: *a tonic spasm.* **11.** of or relating to stress or the main stress in a word. **12.** denoting a tone language. [C17: from New Latin *tonicus,* from Greek *tonikos* concerning tone, from *tonos* TONE] —**'ton·i·cal·ly** *adv.*

ton·ic ac·cent *n.* **1.** emphasis imparted to a note by virtue of its having a higher pitch, rather than greater stress or long duration relative to other notes. **2.** another term for **pitch accent.**

to·nic·'i·ty (təʊ'nɪsɪtɪ) *n.* **1.** the state, condition, or quality of being tonic. **2.** *Physiol.* another name for **tonus.**

ton·ic sol-fa *n.* a method of teaching music, esp. singing, used mainly in Britain, by which the syllables of a movable system of solmization are used as names for the notes of the major scale in any key. In this system *sol* is usually replaced by *so* as the name of the fifth degree. See **solmization.**

to·night (tə'naɪt) *n.* **1.** the night or evening of this present day. ~*adv.* **2.** in or during the night or evening of this day. **3.** *Obsolete or western Brit. dialect.* last night. [Old English *tōniht,* from TO (at) + NIGHT]

tonk (tɒŋk) *n. Austral. slang.* an effete or effeminate man.

ton·ka bean ('tɒŋkə) *n.* **1.** a tall leguminous tree, *Coumarouna odorata,* of tropical America, having fragrant black almond-shaped seeds. **2.** the seeds of this tree, used in the manufacture of perfumes, snuff, etc. [C18: probably from Tupi *tonka*]

Ton·kin ('tɒn'kɪn) *or* **Tong·king** *n.* **1.** a former state of N French Indochina (1883–1946), on the Gulf of Tonkin: forms the largest part of N Vietnam. **2. Gulf of.** an arm of the South China Sea, bordered by N Vietnam, the Luichow Peninsula of SW China, and Hainan Island. Length: about 500 km (300 miles).

Ton·le Sap ('tɒnlɪ 'sæp) *n.* a lake in W central Cambodia, linked with the Mekong River by the **Tonle Sap River.** Area: (dry season) about 2600 sq. km (1000 sq. miles); (rainy season) up to 24 600 sq. km (9500 sq. miles).

ton·nage *or* **tun·nage** ('tʌnɪdʒ) *n.* **1.** the capacity of a merchant ship expressed in tons, for which purpose a ton is considered as 40 cubic feet of freight or 100 cubic feet of bulk cargo, unless such an amount would weigh more than 2000 pounds in which case the actual weight is used. **2.** the weight of the cargo of a merchant ship. **3.** the total amount of shipping of a port or nation, estimated by the capacity of its ships. **4.** a duty on ships based either on their capacity or their register tonnage. [C15: from Old French, from *tonne* barrel]

tonne (tʌn) *n.* another name for **metric ton.** [from French]

ton·neau ('tɒnəʊ) *n., pl.* **·neaus** *or* **·neaux** (-nəʊ, -nəʊz). **1.** Also called: **tonneau cover. a.** a detachable cover to protect the rear part of an open car when it is not carrying passengers. **b.** a similar cover that fits over all the passenger seats, but not the driver's, in an open vehicle. **2.** *Rare.* the part of an open car in which the rear passengers sit. [C20: from French: special type of vehicle body, from Old French *tonnel* cask, from *tonne* tun]

to·nom·e·ter (təʊ'nɒmɪtə) *n.* **1.** an instrument for measuring the pitch of a sound, esp. one consisting of a set of tuning forks. **2.** any of various types of instrument for measuring pressure or tension, such as the blood pressure, vapour pressure, etc. [C18: from Greek *tonos* TONE + -METER] —**ton·o·met·ric** (,tɒnə'mɛtrɪk, ,təʊ-) *adj.* —**to·'nom·e·try** *n.*

ton·sil ('tɒnsəl) *n.* **1.** Also called: **palatine tonsil.** either of two small masses of lymphatic tissue situated one on each side of the back of the mouth. **2.** *Anatomy.* any small rounded mass of tissue, esp. lymphatic tissue. [C17: from Latin *tōnsillae* (pl.) tonsils, of uncertain origin] —**'ton·sil·lar** *or* **'ton·sil·lar·y** *adj.*

ton·sil·lec·to·my (,tɒnsɪ'lɛktəmɪ) *n., pl.* **·mies.** surgical removal of the palatine tonsils.

ton·sil·li·tis (,tɒnsɪ'laɪtɪs) *n.* inflammation of the palatine tonsils, causing enlargement, occasionally to the extent that they nearly touch one another. —**ton·sil·lit·ic** (,tɒnsɪ'lɪtɪk) *adj.*

ton·sil·lot·o·my (,tɒnsɪ'lɒtəmɪ) *n., pl.* **·mies.** surgical incision into one or both of the palatine tonsils, usually followed by removal (**tonsillectomy**).

ton·so·ri·al (tɒn'sɔ:rɪəl) *adj. Often facetious.* of or relating to barbering or hairdressing. [C19: from Latin *tōnsōrius* concerning shaving, from *tondēre* to shave]

ton·sure ('tɒnʃə) *n.* **1.** (in certain religions and monastic orders) **a.** the shaving of the head or the crown of the head only. **b.** the part of the head left bare by shaving. **c.** the state of being shaven thus. ~*vb.* **2.** (*tr.*) to shave the head of. [C14: from Latin *tōnsūra* a clipping, from *tondēre* to shave] —**'ton·sured** *adj.*

ton·tine ('tɒnti:n, tɒn'ti:n) *n.* **1. a.** an annuity scheme by which several subscribers accumulate and invest a common fund out of which they receive an annuity that increases as subscribers die until the last survivor takes the whole. **b.** the subscribers to such a scheme collectively. **c.** the share of each subscriber. **d.** the common fund accumulated. **e.** (*as modifier*): *a tontine fund.* **2.** a system of mutual life assurance by which benefits are received by those participants who survive and maintain their policies throughout a stipulated period (the **tontine period**). [C18: from French, named after Lorenzo *Tonti,* Neapolitan banker who devised the scheme]

ton-up *Brit. informal.* ~*adj.* (*prenominal*) **1.** (esp. of a motorcycle) capable of speeds of a hundred miles per hour or more. **2.** liking to travel at such speeds: *a ton-up boy.* ~*n.* **3.** a person who habitually rides at such speeds.

to·nus ('təʊnəs) *n. Physiol.* the normal tension of a muscle at rest; tone. [C19: from Latin, from Greek *tonos* TONE]

to·ny ('təʊnɪ) *adj.* **·ni·er, ·ni·est.** *U.S. informal.* stylish or distinctive; classy. [C20: from TONE]

too (tu:) *adv.* **1.** as well; in addition; also: *can I come too?* **2.** in or to an excessive degree; more than a fitting or desirable amount: *I have too many things to do.* **3.** extremely: *you're too kind.* **4.** *U.S. informal.* indeed: used to reinforce a command: *you will too do it!* [Old English *tō;* related to Old Frisian, Old Saxon *to,* Old High German *zou;* see TO]

Usage. See at **very.**

too·dle-oo (ˌtu:dᵊl'u:) *or* **too·dle-pip** *sentence substitute. Brit. informal, rare.* goodbye. [C20: perhaps imitative of the horn of a car]

took (tʊk) *vb.* the past tense of **take.**

tool (tu:l) *n.* **1. a.** an implement, such as a hammer, saw, or spade, that is used by hand. **b.** a power-driven instrument; machine tool. **c.** (*in combination*): *a toolkit.* **2.** the cutting part of such an instrument. **3. a.** any of the instruments used by a bookbinder to impress a design on a book cover. **b.** a design so impressed. **4.** anything used as a means of performing an operation or achieving an end: *he used his boss's absence as a tool for gaining influence.* **5.** a person used to perform dishonourable or unpleasant tasks for another. **6.** a necessary medium or adjunct to one's profession: *numbers are the tools of the mathematician's trade.* **7.** *Taboo slang.* another word for **penis. 8.** *Brit.* underworld slang for a **gun.** ~*vb.* **9.** to work, cut, shape, or form (something) with a tool or tools. **10.** (*tr.*) to decorate a book cover with a bookbinder's tool. **11.** (*tr.*) to furnish with tools. [Old English *tōl;* related to Old Norse *tōl* weapon, Old English *tawian* to prepare; see TAW] —**'tool·er** *n.* —**'tool·less** *adj.*

tool·ing ('tu:lɪŋ) *n.* **1.** any decorative work done with a tool, esp. a design stamped onto a book cover, piece of leatherwork, etc. **2.** the selection, provision, and setting up of tools, esp. for a machining operation.

tool-mak·er ('tu:lˌmeɪkə) *n.* a person who specializes in the production or reconditioning of precision tools, cutters, etc. —**'tool-ˌmak·ing** *n.*

tool steel *n.* any of various steels whose hardness and ability to retain a cutting edge make them suitable for use in tools for cutting wood and metal.

toon (tu:n) *n.* **1.** a large meliaceous tree, *Cedrela toona,* of the East Indies and Australia, having clusters of flowers from which a dye is obtained. **2.** the close-grained red wood of this tree, used for furniture, carvings, etc. [from Hindi *tūn,* from Sanskrit *tunna*]

toot (tu:t) *vb.* **1.** to give or cause to give (a short blast, hoot, or whistle): *to toot a horn; to toot a blast; the train tooted.* ~*n.* **2.** the sound made by or as if by a horn, whistle, etc. **3.** *U.S. slang.* a drinking spree. **4.** *Austral. slang.* a lavatory. [C16: from Middle Low German *tuten,* of imitative origin] —**'toot·er** *n.*

tooth (tu:θ) *n., pl.* **teeth** (ti:θ). **1.** any of various bonelike structures set in the jaws of most vertebrates and modified, according to the species, for biting, tearing, or chewing. Related adj.: **dental. 2.** any of various similar structures in invertebrates, occurring in the mouth or alimentary canal. **3.** anything resembling a tooth in shape, prominence, or function: *the tooth of a comb.* **4.** any of the various small indentations occurring on the margin of a leaf, petal, etc. **5.** any one of a number of uniform projections on a gear, sprocket, rack, etc., by which drive is transmitted. **6.** taste or appetite (esp. in the phrase **sweet tooth**). **7. long in the tooth.** old or ageing. **8. tooth and nail.** with ferocity and force: *we fought tooth and nail.* ~*vb.* (tu:ð, tu:θ). **9.** (*tr.*) to provide with a tooth or teeth. **10.** (*intr.*) (of two gearwheels) to engage. [Old English *tōth;* related to Old Saxon *tand,* Old High German *zand,* Old Norse *tonn,* Gothic *tunthus,* Latin *dens*] —**'tooth·less** *adj.* —**'tooth·ˌlike** *adj.*

tooth·ache ('tu:θˌeɪk) *n.* a pain in or about a tooth. Technical name: **odontalgia.**

tooth·ache tree *n.* another name for **prickly ash.**

tooth·brush ('tu:θˌbrʌʃ) *n.* a small brush, usually with a long handle, for cleaning the teeth.

toothed (tu:θt) *adj.* **a.** having a tooth or teeth. **b.** (*in combination*): *sabre-toothed; six-toothed.*

toothed whale *n.* any whale belonging to the cetacean suborder *Odontoceti,* having a single blowhole and numerous simple teeth and feeding on fish, smaller mammals, molluscs, etc.: includes dolphins and porpoises. Compare **whalebone whale.**

tooth·paste ('tu:θˌpeɪst) *n.* a paste used for cleaning the teeth, applied with a toothbrush.

tooth·pick ('tu:θˌpɪk) *n.* **1.** a small sharp sliver of wood, plastic, etc., used for extracting pieces of food from between the teeth. **2.** a slang word for **bowie knife.**

tooth pow·der *n.* a powder used for cleaning the teeth, applied with a toothbrush.

tooth shell *n.* another name for the **tusk shell.**

tooth·some ('tu:θsəm) *adj.* **1.** of delicious or appetizing appearance, flavour, or smell. **2.** attractive; alluring. —**'tooth·some·ly** *adv.* —**'tooth·some·ness** *n.*

tooth·wort ('tu:θˌwɜ:t) *n.* **1.** an orobanchaceous European plant, *Lathraea squamaria,* having scaly cream or pink stems and pinkish flowers and a rhizome covered with toothlike scales. **2.** any cruciferous North American or Eurasian plant of the genus *Dentaria,* having creeping rhizomes covered with toothlike projections. See also **crinkleroot.**

tooth·y ('tu:θɪ) *adj.* **tooth·i·er, tooth·i·est.** having or showing numerous, large, or projecting teeth: *a toothy grin.* —**'tooth·i·ly** *adv.* —**'tooth·i·ness** *n.*

too·tle[1] ('tu:tᵊl) *vb.* **1.** to toot or hoot softly or repeatedly: *the flute tootled quietly.* ~*n.* **2.** a soft hoot or series of hoots. [C19: from TOOT] —**'too·tler** *n.*

too·tle[2] ('tu:tᵊl) *Brit. informal.* ~*vb.* **1.** (*intr.*) to go, esp. by car. ~*n.* **2.** a drive, esp. a short pleasure trip. [C19: from TOOTLE[1], imitative of the horn of a car]

toots (tʊts) *or* **toot·sy** *n., pl.* **toots·es** *or* **toot·sies.** *Informal, chiefly U.S.* darling; sweetheart. [C20: perhaps related to earlier dialect *toot* worthless person, of obscure origin]

toot·sy, toot·sie ('tʊtsɪ), *or* **toot·sy-woot·sy** ('tʊtsɪ'wʊtsɪ) *n., pl.* **·sies.** a child's word for **foot.**

Too·woom·ba (tə'wʊmbə) *n.* a city in E Australia, in SE Queensland: agricultural and industrial centre. Pop.: 62 900 (1975 est.).

top[1] (tɒp) *n.* **1.** the highest or uppermost part of anything: *the top of a hill.* **2.** the most important or successful position: *to be at the top of the class; the top of the table.* **3.** the part of a plant that is above ground: *carrot tops.* **4.** a thing that forms or covers the uppermost part of anything, esp. a lid or cap: *put the top on the saucepan.* **5.** the highest degree or point: *at the top of his career.* **6.** the most important person: *he's the top of this organization.* **7.** the best or finest part of anything: *we've got the top of this year's graduates.* **8.** the loudest or highest pitch (esp. in the phrase **top of one's voice**). **9.** *Cards.* the highest card of a suit in a player's hand. **10.** *Sport.* **a.** a stroke that hits the ball above its centre. **b.** short for **topspin. 11.** a platform around the head of a lower mast of a sailing vessel, the edges of which serve to extend the topmast shrouds. **12.** *Chem.* the part of a volatile liquid mixture that distils first. **13.** a garment, esp. for a woman, that extends from the shoulders to the waist or hips. **14. blow one's top.** to lose one's temper. **15. on top of. a.** in addition to: *on top of his accident, he caught pneumonia.* **b.** *Informal.* in complete control of (a difficult situation, job, etc.). **16. off the top of one's head.** with no previous preparation; extempore. **17. over the top. a.** over the parapet or leading edge of a trench. **b.** over the limit. **18. the top of the morning.** a conventional Irish morning greeting. ~*adj.* **19.** of, relating to, serving as, or situated on the top: *the top book in a pile.* ~*vb.* **tops, top·ping, topped.** (*mainly tr.*) **20.** to form a top on (something): *to top a cake with whipped cream.* **21.** to remove the top of or from: *to top carrots.* **22.** to reach or pass the top of: *we topped the mountain.* **23.** to be at the top of: *he tops the team.* **24.** to exceed or surpass. **25.** (*also intr.*) *Sport.* **a.** to hit (a ball) above the centre. **b.** to make (a stroke) by hitting the ball in this way. **26.** *Chem.* to distil off (the most volatile part) from a liquid mixture. **27.** to add other colorants to (a dye) in order to modify the shade produced. ~See also **top off, top out, tops, top up.** [Old English *topp;* related to Old High German *zopf* plait, Old Norse *toppr* tuft]

top[2] (tɒp) *n.* **1.** a toy that is spun on its pointed base by a flick of the fingers, by pushing a handle at the top up and down, etc. **2.** anything that spins or whirls around. **3. sleep like a top.** to sleep very soundly. [Old English, of unknown origin]

top- *combining form.* variant of **topo-** before a vowel.

top·arch ('tɒpɑ:k) *n.* the ruler of a small state or realm. [C17: from Greek *toparchēs,* from *topos* a place + -ARCH] —**'top·ar·chy** *n.*

to·paz ('təʊpæz) *n.* **1.** a hard glassy mineral consisting of fluosilicate of aluminium in orthorhombic crystalline form. It is yellow, yellowish-brown, pink, or colourless, and is a valuable gemstone. Formula: $Al_2SiO_4(F,OH)_2$. **2. oriental topaz.** a yellowish-brown variety of sapphire. **3. false topaz.** another name for **citrine. 4.** either of two South American hummingbirds, *Topaza pyra* and *T. pella.* [C13: from Old French *topaze,* from Latin *topazus,* from Greek *topazos*]

to·paz·o·lite (təʊ'pæzəˌlaɪt) *n.* a yellowish-green variety of andradite garnet.

top ba·na·na *n. Slang, chiefly U.S.* **1.** the leading comedian in vaudeville, burlesque, etc. **2.** the leader; boss.

top boot *n.* a high boot, often with a decorative or contrasting upper section.

top·coat ('tɒpˌkəʊt) *n.* an outdoor coat worn over a suit, etc.

top dog *n. Informal.* the leader or chief of a group.

top-drawer *adj.* of the highest standing, esp. socially.

top-dress *vb.* (*tr.*) to spread manure or fertilizer on the surface of (land) without working it into the soil.

top dress·ing *n.* **1.** a surface application of manure or fertilizer to land. **2.** a thin layer of loose gravel that covers the top of a road surface.

tope[1] (təʊp) *vb.* to consume (alcoholic drink) as a regular habit, usually in large quantities. [C17: from French *toper* to keep an agreement, from Spanish *topar* to take a bet; probably because a wager was generally followed by a drink] —**'top·er** *n.*

tope[2] (təʊp) *n.* **1.** a small grey requiem shark, *Galeorhinus galeus,* of European coastal waters. **2.** any of various other small sharks. [C17: of uncertain origin; compare Norfolk dialect *toper* dogfish]

tope[3] (təʊp) *n.* another name for a **stupa.** [C19: from Hindi *tōp;* compare Sanskrit *stūpa* STUPA]

to·pee *or* **to·pi** ('təʊpiː, -pɪ) *n., pl.* **·pees** *or* **·pis.** another name for **pith helmet.** [C19: from Hindi *topī* hat]

To·pe·ka (tə'piːkə) *n.* a city in E central Kansas, capital of the state, on the Kansas River: university (1865). Pop.: 136 059 (1973 est.).

top-flight *adj.* of superior or excellent quality; outstanding.

top·full ('tɒp,fʊl) *adj. Rare.* full to the top.

top·gal·lant (,tɒp'gælənt; *Nautical* tə'gælənt) *n.* **1.** Also called: **topgallant mast.** a mast on a square-rigger above a topmast or an extension of a topmast. **2.** Also called: **topgallant sail.** a sail set on a yard of a topgallant mast. **3.** (*modifier*) of or relating to a topgallant.

top hat *n.* a man's hat with a tall cylindrical crown and narrow brim, often made of silk, now worn for some formal occasions. Also called: **high hat.**

top-heav·y *adj.* **1.** unstable or unbalanced through being overloaded at the top. **2.** *Finance.* (of an enterprise or its capital structure) characterized by or containing too much debt capital in relation to revenue or profit so that too little is left over for dividend distributions; overcapitalized. **3.** (of a business enterprise) having too many executives. —**,top-'heav·i·ly** *adv.* —**,top-'heav·i·ness** *n.*

To·phet *or* **To·pheth** ('təʊfɛt) *n. Old Testament.* a place in the valley immediately to the southwest of Jerusalem; the Shrine of Moloch, where human sacrifices were offered. [from Hebrew *Tōpheth*]

top-hole *interj., adj. Brit. informal.* excellent; splendid.

to·phus ('təʊfəs) *n., pl.* **·phi** (-faɪ). *Pathol.* a deposit of sodium urate in the helix of the ear or surrounding a joint: a diagnostic of advanced or chronic gout. Also called: **chalkstone.** [C16: from Latin, variant of *tōfus* TUFA, TUFF] —**to·pha·ceous** (təʊ'feɪʃəs) *adj.*

to·pi *n., pl.* **·pis. 1.** ('təʊpɪ). an antelope, *Damaliscus korrigum,* of grasslands and semideserts of Africa, having angular curved horns and an elongated muzzle. **2.** ('təʊpiː, -pɪ). another name for **pith helmet.** [C19: from Hindi: hat]

to·pi·ar·y ('təʊpɪərɪ) *adj.* **1.** of, relating to, or characterized by the trimming or training of trees or bushes into artificial decorative animal, geometric, or other shapes. ~*n., pl.* **·ar·ies. 2.** topiary work. **3.** a topiary garden. [C16: from French *topiaire,* from Latin *topia* decorative garden work, from Greek *topion* little place, from *topos* place] —**to·pi·ar·i·an** (,təʊpɪ'ɛərɪən) *adj.* —**'to·pi·a·rist** *n.*

top·ic ('tɒpɪk) *n.* **1.** a subject or theme of a speech, essay, book, etc. **2.** a subject of conversation; item of discussion. **3.** (in rhetoric, logic, etc.) a category or class of arguments or ideas which may be drawn on to furnish proofs. [C16: from Latin *topica* translating Greek *ta topika,* literally: matters relating to commonplaces, title of a treatise by Aristotle, from *topoi* pl. of *topos* place, commonplace]

top·i·cal ('tɒpɪkᵊl) *adj.* **1.** of, relating to, or constituting current affairs. **2.** relating to a particular place; local. **3.** of or relating to a topic or topics. **4.** (of a drug, ointment, etc.) for application to the body surface; local. —**top·i·cal·i·ty** (,tɒpɪ'kælɪtɪ) *n.* —**'top·i·cal·ly** *adv.*

top·ic sen·tence *n.* a sentence in a paragraph that expresses the main idea or point of the whole paragraph.

top·knot ('tɒp,nɒt) *n.* **1.** a crest, tuft, decorative bow, chignon, etc., on the top of the head. **2.** any of several European flatfishes of the genus *Zeugopterus* and related genera, esp. *Z. punctatus,* which has an oval dark brown body marked with darker blotches: family *Bothidae* (turbot, etc.).

top·less ('tɒplɪs) *adj.* **1.** having no top. **2. a.** denoting a costume which has no covering for the breasts. **b.** wearing such a costume. **3.** *Archaic.* immeasurably high. —**'top·less·ness** *n.*

top-lev·el *n.* (*modifier*) of, involving, or by those on the highest level of influence or authority: *top-level talks.*

top·loft·y ('tɒp,lɒftɪ) *adj. Informal.* haughty or pretentious. —**'top·,loft·i·ly** *adv.* —**'top·,loft·i·ness** *n.*

top·mast ('tɒp,mɑːst; *Nautical* 'tɒpməst) *n.* the mast next above a lower mast on a sailing vessel.

top·min·now ('tɒp,mɪnəʊ) *n., pl.* **·now** *or* **·nows.** any of various small American freshwater cyprinodont fishes that are either viviparous (genera *Heterandria, Gambusia,* etc.) or egg-laying (genus *Fundulus*).

top·most ('tɒp,məʊst) *adj.* highest; at or nearest the top.

top·notch ('tɒp'nɒtʃ) *adj. Informal.* excellent; superb. —**'top·'notch·er** *n.*

top·o- *or before a vowel* **top-** *combining form.* indicating place or region: *topography; topology; toponym; topotype.* [from Greek *topos* a place, commonplace]

top off *vb.* (*tr., adv.*) to finish or complete, esp. with some decisive action: *he topped off the affair by committing suicide.*

topog. *abbrev. for:* **1.** topographical. **2.** topography.

to·pog·ra·phy (tə'pɒgrəfɪ) *n., pl.* **·phies. 1.** the study or detailed description of the surface features of a region. **2.** the detailed mapping of the configuration of a region. **3.** the land forms or surface configuration of a region. **4.** the surveying of a region's surface features. **5.** the study or description of the configuration of any object. —**to·'pog·ra·pher** *n.* —**top·o·graph·ic** (,tɒpə'græfɪk) *or* **,top·o·'graph·i·cal** *adj.* —**,top·o·'graph·i·cal·ly** *adv.*

top·o·log·i·cal group *n. Maths.* a group, such as the set of all real numbers, that constitutes a topological space and in which multiplication and inversion are continuous.

top·o·log·i·cal space *n. Maths.* a set *S* with an associated family of subsets τ that is closed under set union and finite intersection. *S* and the empty set are members of τ.

to·pol·o·gy (tə'pɒlədʒɪ) *n.* **1.** the branch of mathematics concerned with generalization of the concepts of continuity, limit, etc. **2.** a branch of geometry describing the properties of a figure that are unaffected by continuous distortion, such as stretching or knotting. Former name: **analysis situs. 3.** *Maths.* a family of subsets of a given set *S,* such that *S* is a topological space. **4.** the study of the topography of a given place, esp. as far as it reflects its history. **5.** the anatomy of any specific bodily area, structure, or part. —**top·o·log·ic** (,tɒpə'lɒdʒɪk) *or* **,top·o·'log·i·cal** *adj.* —**,top·o·'log·i·cal·ly** *adv.* —**to·'pol·o·gist** *n.*

top·o·nym ('tɒpənɪm) *n.* **1.** the name of a place. **2.** any name derived from a place name.

to·pon·y·my (tə'pɒnɪmɪ) *n.* **1.** the study of place names. **2.** *Rare.* the anatomical nomenclature of bodily regions, as distinguished from that of specific organs or structures. —**top·o·nym·ic** (,tɒpə'nɪmɪk) *or* **,top·o·'nym·i·cal** *adj.*

top·os ('tɒpɒs) *n., pl.* **·oi** (-ɔɪ). a basic theme or concept, esp. a stock topic in rhetoric. [C20: Greek, literally: place]

top·o·type ('tɒpə,taɪp) *n.* a specimen plant or animal taken from an area regarded as the typical habitat.

top out *vb.* (*adv.*) to place the highest stone on (a building) or perform a ceremony on this occasion.

top·per ('tɒpə) *n.* **1.** an informal name for **top hat. 2.** a person or thing that tops. **3.** *Informal.* a remark that caps the one before. **4.** *Informal.* a good chap.

top·ping ('tɒpɪŋ) *n.* **1.** something that tops something else, esp. a sauce or garnish for food. ~*adj.* **2.** high or superior in rank, degree, etc. **3.** *Brit. slang.* excellent; splendid.

top·ping lift *n. Nautical.* a line or cable for raising the end of a boom that is away from the mast.

top·ple ('tɒpᵊl) *vb.* **1.** to tip over or cause to tip over, esp. from a height. **2.** (*intr.*) to lean precariously or totter. [C16: frequentative of TOP[1] (vb.)]

tops (tɒps) *n. Slang.* **1. the tops.** a person or thing of top quality. ~*adj.* **2.** (*postpositive*) excellent; superb.

top·sail ('tɒp,seɪl; *Nautical* 'tɒpsəl) *n.* a square sail carried on a yard set on a topmast.

top-se·cret *adj.* classified as needing the highest level of secrecy and security.

top-shell *n.* any marine gastropod mollusc of the mainly tropical Old World family *Trochidae,* having a typically brightly coloured top-shaped or conical shell.

top·side ('tɒp,saɪd) *n.* **1.** the uppermost side of anything. **2.** *Brit.* a lean cut of beef from the thigh containing no bone. **3.** (*often pl.*) **a.** the part of a ship's sides above the waterline. **b.** the parts of a ship above decks.

top·soil ('tɒp,sɔɪl) *n.* **1.** the surface layer of soil. ~*vb.* **2.** (*tr.*) to spread topsoil on (land). **3.** (*tr.*) to remove the topsoil from (land).

top·spin ('tɒp,spɪn) *n. Tennis, etc.* spin imparted to make a ball bounce or travel exceptionally far, high, or quickly, as by hitting it with a sharp forward and upward stroke. Compare **backspin.**

top·sy-tur·vy ('tɒpsɪ'tɜːvɪ) *adj.* **1.** upside down. **2.** in a state of confusion. ~*adv.* **3.** in a topsy-turvy manner. ~*n.* **4.** a topsy-turvy state. [C16: probably from *tops,* plural of TOP[1] + obsolete *tervy* to turn upside down; perhaps related to Old English *tearflian* to roll over]

top up *vb.* (*tr., adv.*) *Brit.* to raise the level of (a liquid, powder, etc.) in (a container), usually bringing it to the brim of the container: *top up the sugar in those bowls; he topped up the petrol tank before starting his journey.*

toque (təʊk) *or* **to·quet** (təʊ'keɪ) *n.* **1.** a woman's small round brimless hat, popular esp. in Edwardian times. **2.** a hat with a small brim and a pouched crown, popular in the 16th century. [C16: from French, from Old Spanish *toca* headdress, probably from Basque *tauka* hat]

tor (tɔː) *n.* **1.** a high hill, esp. a bare rocky one. **2.** *Chiefly southwestern Brit.* a prominent rock or heap of rocks, esp. on a hill. [Old English *torr,* probably of Celtic origin; compare Scottish Gaelic *torr* pile, Welsh *twr*]

To·rah ('tɔːrə; *Hebrew* tɔ'ra) *n.* **1. a.** the Pentateuch. **b.** the scroll on which this is written, used in synagogue services. **2.** the whole body of the Jewish sacred writings and tradition including oral expositions of the Law. [C16: from Hebrew: precept, from *yārāh* to instruct]

Tor·bay (,tɔː'beɪ) *n.* **1.** a resort and former county borough in SW England, in Devon, formed in 1968 by the amalgamation of Torquay with two neighbouring coastal towns. Pop.: 108 888 (1971). **2.** Also: **Tor Bay.** an inlet of the English Channel on the coast of SW England, near Torquay.

tor·bern·ite ('tɔːbə,naɪt) *n.* a green secondary mineral consisting of hydrated copper uranium phosphate in the form of square platelike crystals. Formula: $Cu(UO_2)(PO_4)_2.12H_2O$. [C19: named after *Torbern* O. Bergman (1735–84), Swedish chemist; see -ITE[1]]

torc (tɔːk) *n.* a rare spelling of **torque** (sense 1).

torch (tɔːtʃ) *n.* **1.** a small portable electric lamp powered by one or more dry batteries. U.S. word: **flashlight. 2.** a wooden or tow shaft dipped in wax or tallow and set alight. **3.** anything regarded as a source of enlightenment, guidance, etc.: *the torch of evangelism.* **4.** any apparatus that burns with a hot flame for welding, brazing, or soldering. **5. carry a torch for.** to be in love with, esp. unrequitedly. [C13: from Old French *torche* handful of twisted straw, from Vulgar Latin *torca* (unattested), from Latin *torquēre* to twist] **—'torch+,like** *adj.*

torch+bear·er ('tɔːtʃ,bɛərə) *n.* **1.** a person or thing that carries a torch. **2.** a person who leads or inspires.

tor+chère (tɔː'ʃɛə) *n.* a tall narrow stand for holding a candelabrum. [C20: from French, from *torche* TORCH]

tor+chier *or* **tor+chiere** ('tɔːtʃɪə) *n.* a standing lamp with a bowl for casting light upwards and so giving all-round indirect illumination. [C20: from TORCHÈRE]

tor+chon lace ('tɔːʃən; *French* tɔr'ʃɔ̃) *n.* a coarse linen or cotton lace with a simple openwork pattern. [C19 *torchon,* from French: a cleaning cloth, from *torcher* to wipe, from Old French *torche* bundle of straw; see TORCH]

torch song *n.* a sentimental or romantic popular song, usually sung by a woman. [C20: from the phrase *to carry a torch for (someone)*] **—torch sing+er** *n.*

torch+wood ('tɔːtʃ,wʊd) *n.* **1.** any of various rutaceous trees or shrubs of the genus *Amyris,* esp. *A. balsamifera,* of Florida and the West Indies, having hard resinous wood used for torches. **2.** any of various similar trees the wood of which is used for torches. **3.** the wood of any of these trees.

tore[1] (tɔː) *vb.* the past tense of **tear**[2].

tore[2] (tɔː) *n. Architect.* another name for **torus** (sense 1). [C17: from French, from Latin: TORUS]

tor·e·a+dor ('tɒrɪə,dɔː) *n.* a bullfighter. [C17: from Spanish, from *torear* to take part in bullfighting, from *toro* a bull, from Latin *taurus;* compare STEER[2]]

tor·e·a+dor pants *pl. n.* tight-fitting women's trousers reaching to midcalf or above the ankle.

to+re+ro (tɒ'rɛərəʊ) *n., pl.* **+ros.** a bullfighter, esp. one who fights on foot. [C18: from Spanish, from Late Latin *taurārius,* from Latin *taurus* a bull]

to+reu+tics (tə'ruːtɪks) *n. (functioning as sing. or pl.)* the art of making detailed ornamental reliefs, esp. in metal, by embossing and chasing. [C19: from Greek *toreutikos* concerning work in relief, from *toreuein* to bore through, from *toreus* tool for boring] **—to+'reu+tic** *adj.*

to·ri ('tɔːraɪ) *n.* the plural of **torus.**

tor+ic ('tɒrɪk) *adj.* of, relating to, or having the form of a torus.

tor+ic lens *n.* a lens used to correct astigmatism, having one of its surfaces shaped like part of a torus so that its focal lengths are different in different meridians.

to+ri·i ('tɔːrɪ,iː) *n., pl.* **·ri·i.** a gateway, esp. one at the entrance to a Japanese Shinto temple, constructed of two timber posts that support two horizontal beams, the upper one having upward-curving ends. [C19: from Japanese, literally: bird house, from *tori* bird + *iru* to dwell]

To+ri+no (to'riːno) *n.* the Italian name for **Turin.**

tor+ment *vb.* (tɔː'mɛnt). *(tr.)* **1.** to afflict with great pain, suffering, or anguish; torture. **2.** to tease or pester in an annoying way: *stop tormenting the dog.* ~*n.* ('tɔːmɛnt). **3.** physical or mental pain. **4.** a source of pain, worry, annoyance, etc. **5.** *Archaic.* an instrument of torture. **6.** *Archaic.* the infliction of torture. [C13: from Old French, from Latin *tormentum,* from *torquēre*] **—tor+'ment+ed+ly** *adv.* **—tor+'ment+ing+ly** *adv.*

tor+men+til ('tɔːməntɪl) *n.* a rosaceous downy perennial plant, *Potentilla erecta,* of Europe and W Asia, having serrated leaves, four-petalled yellow flowers, and an astringent root used in medicine, tanning, and dyeing. Also called: **bloodroot.** [C15: from Old French *tormentille,* from Medieval Latin *tormentilla,* from Latin *tormentum* agony; referring to its use in relieving pain; see TORMENT]

tor+men+tor *or* **tor+ment+er** (tɔː'mɛntə) *n.* **1.** a person or thing that torments. **2.** a curtain or movable piece of stage scenery at either side of the proscenium arch, used to mask lights or exits and entrances. **3.** *Films.* a panel of sound-insulating material placed outside the field of the camera to control the acoustics on the sound stage.

torn (tɔːn) *vb.* **1.** the past participle of **tear**[2]. **2. that's torn it.** *Brit. slang.* an unexpected event or circumstance has upset one's plans. ~*adj.* **3.** split or cut. **4.** divided or undecided, as in preference: *he was torn between staying and leaving.*

tor+na+do (tɔː'neɪdəʊ) *n., pl.* **+does** *or* **+dos. 1.** Also called: **cyclone** or (U.S. informal) **twister.** a violent storm with winds whirling around a small area of extremely low pressure, usually characterized by a dark funnel-shaped cloud causing damage along its path. **2.** a small but violent squall or whirlwind, such as those occurring on the West African coast. **3.** any violently active or destructive person or thing. [C16: probably alteration of Spanish *tronada* thunderstorm (from *tronar* to thunder, from Latin *tonāre*) through influence of *tornar* to turn, from Latin *tornāre* to turn in a lathe] **—tor+nad+ic** (tɔː'nædɪk) *adj.* **—tor·'na·do-,like** *adj.*

to+roid ('tɔːrɔɪd) *n.* **1.** *Geom.* a surface generated by rotating a closed plane curve about a coplanar line that does not intersect the curve. **2.** the solid enclosed by such a surface. See also **torus. —to+'roi+dal** *adj.*

To+ron+to (tə'rɒntəʊ) *n.* a city in S central Canada, capital of Ontario, on Lake Ontario: the second largest city and the major industrial centre of Canada; two universities. Pop.: 633 818 (1976 est.), with a conurbation of 2 803 101 (1976 est.). **—To+ron+'to+ni+an** *adj., n.*

to+rose ('tɔːrəʊz, tɔː'rəʊz) *or* **to+rous** ('tɔːrəs) *adj. Biology.* (of a cylindrical part) having irregular swellings; knotted. [C18: from Latin *torōsus* muscular, from *torus* a swelling] **—to+ros+i+ty** (tɔː'rɒsɪtɪ) *n.*

tor+pe+do (tɔː'piːdəʊ) *n., pl.* **+does. 1.** a cylindrical self-propelled weapon carrying explosives that is launched from aircraft, ships, or submarines and follows an underwater path to hit its target. **2.** a submarine mine. **3.** *U.S.* a firework containing gravel and a percussion cap that explodes when dashed against a hard surface. **4.** any of various electric rays of the genus *Torpedo.* ~*vb.* **5.** *(tr.)* to attack or hit (a ship, etc.) with one or a number of torpedoes. [C16: from Latin: crampfish (whose electric discharges can cause numbness), from *torpēre* to be inactive; see TORPID] **—tor·'pe·do-,like** *adj.*

tor+pe+do boat *n.* a small high-speed warship designed to carry out torpedo attacks in coastal waters.

tor·pe·do-boat de+stroy+er *n.* (formerly) a large powerful warship designed to destroy torpedo boats: a forerunner of the modern destroyer, from which the name is derived.

tor+pe+do tube *n.* the tube from which a torpedo is discharged from submarines or surface ships.

tor+pid ('tɔːpɪd) *adj.* **1.** apathetic, sluggish, or lethargic. **2.** (of a hibernating animal) dormant; having greatly reduced metabolic activity. **3.** unable to move or feel. [C17: from Latin *torpidus,* from *torpēre* to be numb, motionless] **—tor+'pid+i+ty** *or* **'tor+pid+ness** *n.* **—'tor+pid+ly** *adv.*

tor+por ('tɔːpə) *n.* a state of torpidity. [C17: from Latin: inactivity, from *torpēre* to be motionless] **—,tor+por+'if+ic** *adj.*

Tor+quay (,tɔː'kiː) *n.* a town and resort in SW England, in S Devon: administratively part of Torbay since 1968.

torque (tɔːk) *n.* **1.** a necklace or armband made of twisted metal, worn esp. by the ancient Britons and Gauls. **2.** any force or system of forces that causes or tends to cause rotation. **3.** the ability of a shaft to cause rotation. [C19: from Latin *torquēs* necklace, and *torquēre* to twist]

torque con+vert+er *n.* a hydraulic device for the smooth transmission of power in which an engine-driven impeller transmits its momentum to a fluid held in a sealed container, which in turn drives a rotor.

Tor·que·ma·da (*Spanish* ,torke'maða) *n.* **To·más de** (to'mas ðe). 1420–98, Spanish Dominican monk. As first inquisitor general of Spain (1483–98), he was responsible for the burning of some 2000 heretics.

tor+ques ('tɔːkwiːz) *n.* a distinctive band of hair, feathers, skin, or colour around the neck of an animal; a collar. [C17: from Latin: necklace, from *torquēre* to twist] **—tor+quate** ('tɔːkwɪt, -kweɪt) *adj.*

torque wrench *n.* a type of wrench with a gauge attached to indicate the torque applied to the workpiece.

torr (tɔː) *n.* a unit of pressure equal to one millimetre of mercury (133.322 newtons per square metre). [C20: named after E. TORRICELLI]

Tor+rance ('tɒrəns) *n.* a city in SW California, southwest of Los Angeles: developed rapidly with the discovery of oil. Pop.: 133 318 (1973 est.).

Tor+re del Gre+co (*Italian* 'torre del 'grɛːko) *n.* a city in SW Italy, in Campania near Vesuvius on the Bay of Naples: damaged several times by eruptions. Pop.: 91 676 (1971).

tor+re+fy *or* **tor+ri+fy** ('tɒrɪ,faɪ) *vb.* **+fies, +fy+ing, +fied.** *(tr.)* to dry (drugs, ores, etc.) by subjection to intense heat; roast. [C17: from French *torréfier,* from Latin *torrefacere,* from *torrēre* to parch + *facere* to make] **—tor+re+fac+tion** *or* **tor+ri+fac+tion** (,tɒrɪ'fækʃən) *n.*

Tor+rens ('tɒrənz) *n.* **Lake.** a shallow salt lake in E central South Australia, about 8 m (25 ft.) below sea level. Area: 5776 sq. km (2230 sq. miles).

Tor+rens ti+tle ('tɒrənz) *n. Austral.* legal title to land based on record of registration rather than on title deeds. [from Sir Robert Richard *Torrens* (1814–84), who introduced the system as premier of South Australia in 1857]

tor+rent ('tɒrənt) *n.* **1.** a fast, voluminous, or violent stream of water or other liquid. **2.** an overwhelming flow of thoughts, words, sound, etc. ~*adj.* **3.** *Rare.* like or relating to a torrent. [C17: from French, from Latin *torrēns* (n.), from *torrēns* (adj.) burning, from *torrēre* to burn]

tor+ren+tial (tɒ'rɛnʃəl, tə-) *adj.* **1.** of or relating to a torrent. **2.** pouring or flowing fast, violently, or heavily: *torrential rain.* **3.** abundant, overwhelming, or irrepressible: *torrential abuse.* **—tor+'ren+tial+ly** *adv.*

Tor+re+ón (*Spanish* ,torre'on) *n.* an industrial city in N Mexico, in Coahuila state. Pop.: 251 294 (1974 est.).

Tor+res Strait ('tɔːrɪz, 'tɒr-) *n.* a strait between NE Australia and S New Guinea, linking the Arafura Sea with the Coral Sea. Width: about 145 km (90 miles).

Tor·ri·cel·li (,tɒrɪ'tʃɛlɪ) *n.* **E·van·ge·li·sta** (e,vandʒe'lista). 1608–47, Italian physicist and mathematician, who discovered the principle of the barometer. **—,Tor+ri+'cel+li+an** *adj.*

Tor+ri+cel+li·an tube (,tɒrɪ'sɛlɪən) *n.* a vertical glass tube partly evacuated and partly filled with mercury, the height of which is used as a measure of atmospheric pressure. [C17: named after E. TORRICELLI]

Tor+ri+cel+li·an vac·u·um *n.* the vacuum at the top of a Torricellian tube. [C17: named after E. TORRICELLI]

tor+rid ('tɒrɪd) *adj.* **1.** so hot and dry as to parch or scorch. **2.** arid or parched. **3.** highly charged emotionally: *a torrid love scene.* [C16: from Latin *torridus,* from *torrēre* to scorch] **—tor+'rid+i+ty** *or* **'tor+rid+ness** *n.* **—'tor+rid+ly** *adv.*

Tor+rid Zone *n. Rare.* that part of the earth's surface lying between the tropics of Cancer and Capricorn.

tor+sade (tɔː'seɪd) *n.* an ornamental twist or twisted cord, as on hats. [C19: from French, from obsolete *tors* twisted, from Late Latin *torsus,* from Latin *torquēre* to twist]

tor·si ('tɔːsɪ) *n. Rare.* a plural of **torso.**

tor·si·bil·i·ty (ˌtɔːsə'bɪlɪtɪ) *n.* **1.** the ability to be twisted. **2.** the degree of resistance to or the capacity of recovering from being twisted.

tor·sion ('tɔːʃən) *n.* **1. a.** the twisting of a part by application of equal and opposite torques. **b.** the internal torque so produced. **2.** the act of twisting or the state of being twisted. [C15: from Old French, from medical Latin *torsiō* griping pains, from Latin *torquēre* to twist, torture] —'**tor·sion·al** *adj.* —'**tor·sion·al·ly** *adv.*

tor·sion bal·ance *n.* an instrument used to measure small forces, esp. electric or magnetic forces, by the torsion they produce in a thin wire, thread, or rod.

tor·sion bar *n.* a metal bar acting as a torsional spring, esp. as used in the suspensions of some motor vehicles.

torsk (tɔːsk) *n., pl.* **torsks** *or* **torsk.** a gadoid food fish, *Brosmius brosme,* of northern coastal waters, having a single long dorsal fin. Usual U.S. name: **cusk.** [C17: of Scandinavian origin; related to Old Norse *thorskr* codfish, Danish *torsk*]

tor·so ('tɔːsəʊ) *n., pl.* **·sos** *or* **·si** (-sɪ). **1.** the trunk of the human body. **2.** a statue of a nude human trunk, esp. without the head or limbs. **3.** something regarded as incomplete or truncated. [C18: from Italian: stalk, stump, from Latin: THYRSUS]

tort (tɔːt) *n. Law.* a civil wrong or injury arising out of an act or failure to act, independently of any contract, for which an action for damages may be brought. [C14: from Old French, from Medieval Latin *tortum,* literally: something twisted, from Latin *torquēre* to twist]

torte (tɔːt; *German* 'tɔrtə) *n.* a rich cake, originating in Austria, usually decorated or filled with cream, fruit, nuts, and jam. [C16: ultimately perhaps from Late Latin *tōrta* a round loaf, of uncertain origin]

Tor·te·lier (*French* tɔrtə'lje) *n.* **Paul** (pɔl). born 1914, French cellist and composer.

tor·tel·li·ni (ˌtɔːtə'liːnɪ) *n.* pasta cut into small rounds, folded about a filling, and boiled. [from Italian]

tort-fea·sor *n. Law.* a person guilty of tort. [C17: from Old French, literally: wrongdoer, from TORT + *faiseur,* from *faire* to do]

tor·ti·col·lis (ˌtɔːtɪ'kɒlɪs) *n. Pathol.* an abnormal position of the head, usually with the neck bent to one side, caused congenitally by contracture of muscles, muscular spasm, etc. [C19: New Latin, from Latin *tortus* twisted (from *torquēre* to twist) + *collum* neck] —ˌ**tor·ti·'col·lar** *adj.*

tor·tile ('tɔːtaɪl) *adj. Rare.* twisted or coiled. [C17: from Latin *tortilis* winding, from *tortus* twisted, from *torquēre* to twist] —**tor·til·i·ty** (tɔː'tɪlɪtɪ) *n.*

tor·til·la (tɔː'tiːə) *n. Mexican cookery.* a kind of thin pancake made from corn meal and cooked on a hot griddle until dry. [C17: from Spanish: a little cake, from *torta* a round cake, from Late Latin; see TORTE]

tor·til·lon (ˌtɔːtiː'ɒn, -'əʊn; *French* tɔrti'jɔ̃) *n.* another word for **stump** (sense 5). [from French: something twisted, from Old French *tortiller* to twist]

tor·tious ('tɔːʃəs) *adj. Law.* having the nature of or involving a tort; wrongful. [C14: from Anglo-French *torcious,* from *torcion,* literally: a twisting, from Late Latin *tortiō* torment, from Latin *torquēre* to twist; influenced in meaning by TORT] —'**tor·tious·ly** *adv.*

tor·toise ('tɔːtəs) *n.* **1.** any herbivorous terrestrial chelonian reptile of the family *Testudinidae,* of most warm regions, having a heavy dome-shaped shell and clawed limbs. **2. water tortoise.** another name for **terrapin. 3.** a slow-moving person. **4.** another word for **testudo.** ~See also **giant tortoise.** [C15: probably from Old French *tortue* (influenced by Latin *tortus* twisted), from Medieval Latin *tortūca,* from Late Latin *tartarūcha* coming from Tartarus, from Greek *tartaroukhos;* referring to the belief that the tortoise originated in the underworld]

tor·toise·shell ('tɔːtəsˌʃɛl) *n.* **1.** a horny translucent yellow-and-brown mottled substance obtained from the outer layer of the shell of the hawksbill turtle: used for making ornaments, jewellery, etc. **2.** a similar synthetic substance, esp. plastic or celluloid, now more widely used than the natural product. **3.** a breed of domestic cat, usually female, having black, cream, and brownish markings. **4.** any of several nymphalid butterflies of the genus *Nymphalis,* and related genera, having orange-brown wings with black markings. **5. tortoiseshell turtle.** another name for **hawksbill turtle. 6. a.** a yellowish-brown mottled colour. **b.** (*as adj.*): *a tortoiseshell décor.* **7.** (*modifier*) made of tortoiseshell: *a tortoiseshell comb.*

Tor·to·la (tɔː'təʊlə) *n.* an island in the NE West Indies, in the Leeward Islands group: chief island of the British Virgin Islands. Pop.: 8939 (1970). Area: 62 sq. km (24 sq. miles).

tor·to·ni (tɔː'təʊnɪ) *n.* a rich ice cream often flavoured with sherry. [from Italian: probably from the name of a 19th-century Italian caterer in Paris]

tor·tri·cid ('tɔːtrɪsɪd) *n.* **1.** any small moth of the chiefly temperate family *Tortricidae,* the larvae of which live concealed in leaves, which they roll or tie together, and are pests of fruit and forest trees: includes the codling moth. ~*adj.* **2.** of, relating to, or belonging to the family *Tortricidae.* [C19: from New Latin *Tortrīcidae,* from *tortrix,* feminine of *tortor,* literally: twister, referring to the leaf-rolling of the larvae, from *torquēre* to twist]

Tor·tu·ga (tɔː'tuːgə) *n.* an island in the West Indies, off the NW coast of Haiti: haunt of pirates in the 17th century. Area: 180 sq. km (70 sq. miles). French name: **La Tor·tue** (la tɔr'ty).

tor·tu·os·i·ty (ˌtɔːtjʊ'ɒsɪtɪ) *n., pl.* **·ties. 1.** the state or quality of being tortuous. **2.** a twist, turn, or coil.

tor·tu·ous ('tɔːtjʊəs) *adj.* **1.** twisted or winding: *a tortuous road.* **2.** devious or cunning: *a tortuous mind.* **3.** intricate. —'**tor·tu·ous·ly** *adv.* —'**tor·tu·ous·ness** *n.*

tor·ture ('tɔːtʃə) *vb.* (*tr.*) **1.** to cause extreme physical pain to, esp. in order to extract information, break resistance, etc.: *to torture prisoners.* **2.** to give mental anguish to. **3.** to twist into a grotesque form. ~*n.* **4.** physical or mental anguish. **5.** the practice of torturing a person. **6.** a cause of mental agony or worry. [C16: from Late Latin *tortūra* a twisting, from *torquēre* to twist] —'**tor·tured·ly** *adv.* —'**tor·tur·er** *n.* —'**tor·ture·some** *or* '**tor·tur·ous** *adj.* —'**tor·tur·ing·ly** *adv.* —'**tor·tur·ous·ly** *adv.*

To·ruń (*Polish* 'tɔrunj) *n.* an industrial city in N Poland, on the River Vistula: developed around a castle that was founded by the Teutonic Knights in 1230; under Prussian rule (1793–1919). Pop.: 142 000 (1974 est.). German name: **Thorn.**

to·rus ('tɔːrəs) *n., pl.* **·ri** (-raɪ). **1.** Also called: **tore.** a large convex moulding approximately semicircular in cross section, esp. one used on the base of a classical column. **2.** *Geom.* a ring-shaped surface generated by rotating a circle about a coplanar line that does not intersect the circle. Area: $4\pi^2Rr$; volume: $2\pi^2Rr^2$, where r is the radius of the circle and R is the distance from the line to the centre of the circle. **3.** *Botany.* another name for **receptacle** (sense 2). **4.** *Anatomy.* a ridge, fold, or similar linear elevation. [C16: from Latin: a swelling, of obscure origin]

To·ry ('tɔːrɪ) *n., pl.* **·ries. 1.** a member of the Conservative Party in Great Britain or Canada. **2.** a member of the English political party that opposed the exclusion of James, Duke of York from the royal succession (1679–80). Tory remained the label for subsequent major conservative interests until they gave birth to the Conservative Party in the 1830s. **3.** an American supporter of the British cause; loyalist. Compare **Whig. 4.** (*sometimes not cap.*) an ultraconservative or reactionary. **5.** (in the 17th century) an Irish Roman Catholic, esp. an outlaw who preyed upon English settlers. ~*adj.* **6.** of, characteristic of, or relating to Tories. **7.** (*sometimes not cap.*) ultraconservative or reactionary. [C17: from Irish *tōraidhe* outlaw, from Middle Irish *tōir* pursuit] —'**To·ry·ish** *adj.* —'**To·ry·ism** *n.*

Tos·ca·na (tos'kaːna) *n.* the Italian name for **Tuscany.**

Tos·ca·ni·ni (ˌtɒskə'niːnɪ) *n.* **Ar·tu·ro** (ar'tuːro). 1867–1957, Italian conductor.

tosh (tɒʃ) *n. Informal, chiefly Brit.* nonsense; rubbish. [C19: of unknown origin]

toss (tɒs) *vb.* **1.** (*tr.*) to throw lightly or with a flourish, esp. with the palm of the hand upwards. **2.** to fling or be flung about, esp. constantly or regularly in an agitated or violent way: *a ship tosses in a storm.* **3.** to discuss or put forward for discussion in an informal way. **4.** (*tr.*) (of an animal such as a horse) to throw (its rider). **5.** (*tr.*) (of an animal) to butt with the head or the horns and throw into the air: *the bull tossed the matador.* **6.** (*tr.*) to shake, agitate, or disturb. **7.** to toss up a coin with (someone) in order to decide or allot something: *I'll toss you for it; let's toss for it.* **8.** (*intr.*) to move away angrily or impatiently: *she tossed out of the room.* ~*n.* **9.** an abrupt movement. **10.** a rolling or pitching motion. **11.** the act or an instance of tossing. **12.** the act of tossing up a coin. See **toss-up. 13.** a fall from a horse or other animal. [C16: of Scandinavian origin; related to Norwegian, Swedish *tossa* to strew] —'**toss·er** *n.*

toss off *vb.* (*adv.*) **1.** (*tr.*) to perform, write, consume, etc., quickly and easily: *he tossed off a letter to Jim.* **2.** (*tr.*) to drink at one draught. **3.** *Brit. taboo.* to masturbate.

toss·pot ('tɒsˌpɒt) *n. Archaic or literary.* a habitual drinker.

toss up *vb.* (*adv.*) **1.** to spin (a coin) in the air in order to decide between alternatives by guessing which side will fall uppermost. **2.** (*tr.*) to prepare (food) quickly. ~*n.* **toss-up. 3.** an instance of tossing up a coin. **4.** *Informal.* an even chance or risk; gamble.

tot[1] (tɒt) *n.* **1.** a young child; toddler. **2.** *Chiefly Brit.* a small amount of anything. **3.** a small measure of spirits. [C18: perhaps short for *totterer;* see TOTTER]

tot[2] (tɒt) *vb.* **tots, tot·ting, tot·ted.** (usually foll. by *up*) *Chiefly Brit.* to total; add. [C17: shortened from TOTAL or from Latin *totum* all]

to·tal ('təʊtᵊl) *n.* **1.** the whole, esp. regarded as the complete sum of a number of parts. ~*adj.* **2.** complete; absolute: *the evening was a total failure; a total eclipse.* **3.** (*prenominal*) being or related to a total: *the total number of passengers.* ~*vb.* **·tals, ·tal·ling, ·talled** *or U.S.* **·tals, ·tal·ing, ·taled. 4.** (when *intr.,* sometimes foll. by *to*) to amount: *to total six pounds.* **5.** (*tr.*) to add up: *to total a list of prices.* **6.** (*tr.*) *U.S. slang.* to demolish completely. [C14: from Old French, from Medieval Latin *tōtālis,* from Latin *tōtus* all] —'**to·tal·ly** *adv.*

to·tal de·prav·i·ty *n. Chiefly Calvinist theol.* the doctrine that man's nature is totally corrupt as a result of the Fall.

to·tal e·clipse *n.* an eclipse as seen from a particular area of the earth's surface where the eclipsed body is completely hidden. Compare **annular eclipse, partial eclipse.**

to·tal in·ter·nal re·flec·tion *n. Physics.* the complete reflection of a light ray at the boundary of two media, when the ray is in the medium with greater refractive index.

to·tal·i·tar·i·an (təʊˌtælɪ'tɛərɪən) *adj.* of, denoting, relating to, or characteristic of a dictatorial one-party state that regulates every realm of life. —**to**ˌ**tal·i·'tar·i·an·ism** *n.*

to·tal·i·ty (təʊ'tælɪtɪ) *n., pl.* **·ties. 1.** the whole amount. **2.** the state of being total. **3.** the state or period of an eclipse when light from the eclipsed body is totally obscured.

to+tal·i·za+tor (ˈtəʊtəlaɪˌzeɪtə), **to+tal+iz+er** *or* **to+tal·i·sa+tor, to+tal+is+er** *n.* **1.** a system of betting on horse races in which the aggregate stake, less an administration charge and tax, is paid out to winners in proportion to their stake. **2.** the machine that records bets in this system and works out odds, pays out winnings, etc. **3.** an apparatus for registering totals, as of a particular function or measurement. ~U.S. term (for senses 1, 2): **pari-mutuel.**

to+tal+ize *or* **to+tal+ise** (ˈtəʊtəˌlaɪz) *vb.* to combine or make into a total. —ˌ**to+tal·i+ˈza+tion** *or* ˌ**to+tal·i+ˈsa+tion** *n.*

to+tal+iz+er *or* **to+tal+is+er** (ˈtəʊtəˌlaɪzə) *n.* **1.** a variant of **totalizator. 2.** *Chiefly U.S.* an adding machine.

to+tal re+call *n. Psychol.* the faculty or an instance of complete and clear recall of every detail of something.

to+tal ser·i·al+ism *or* **ser·i·al·i·sa+tion** *n.* (in some music after 1945) the use of serial techniques applied to such elements as rhythm, dynamics, and tone colour, as found in the early works of Stockhausen, Boulez, etc.

to+ta+quine (ˈtəʊtəˌkwiːn, -kwɪn) *n.* a mixture of quinine and other alkaloids derived from cinchona bark, used as a substitute for quinine in treating malaria. [C20: from New Latin *tōtaquīna,* from TOTA(L) + Spanish *quina* cinchona bark; see QUININE]

tote[1] (təʊt) *Informal.* ~*vb.* **1.** (*tr.*) to carry, convey, or drag. ~*n.* **2.** the act of or an instance of toting. **3.** something toted. [C17: of obscure origin] —**ˈtot+er** *n.*

tote[2] (təʊt) *n.* (usually preceded by *the*) *Informal.* short for **totalizator** (senses 1, 2).

tote bag *n.* a large roomy handbag or shopping bag.

to+tem (ˈtəʊtəm) *n.* **1.** (in some societies, esp. among North American Indians) an object, species of animal or plant, or natural phenomenon symbolizing a clan, family, etc., often having ritual associations. **2.** a representation of such an object. [C18: from Ojibwa *nintōtēm* mark of my family] —**to+tem+ic** (təʊˈtɛmɪk) *adj.* —**to+ˈtem·i·cal+ly** *adv.*

to+tem+ism (ˈtəʊtəˌmɪzəm) *n.* **1.** the belief in kinship of groups or individuals having a common totem. **2.** the rituals, taboos, and other practices associated with such a belief. —**ˈto+tem+ist** *n.* —ˌ**to+tem+ˈis+tic** *adj.*

to+tem pole *n.* a pole carved or painted with totemic figures set up by certain North American Indians, esp. those of the NW Pacific coast, within a village as a tribal symbol or, sometimes, in memory of a dead person.

toth+er *or* **t'oth+er** (ˈtʌðə) *Archaic or dialect.* the other. [C13 *the tother,* by mistaken division from *thet other* (*thet,* from Old English *thæt,* neuter of THE[1]]

to+ti+pal+mate (ˌtəʊtɪˈpælmɪt, -ˌmeɪt) *adj.* (of certain birds) having all four toes webbed. [C19: from Latin *tōtus* entire + *palmate,* from Latin *palmātus* shaped like a hand, from *palma* PALM[1]] —ˌ**to+ti+pal+ˈma+tion** *n.*

to+tip·o+tent (təʊˈtɪpətənt) *adj.* (of an animal cell) capable of differentiation and so forming a new individual, tissue, organ, etc. [C20: from Latin *tōtus* entire + POTENT] —**to+ˈtip·o+ten+cy** *n.*

tot+ter (ˈtɒtə) *vb.* (*intr.*) **1.** to walk or move in an unsteady manner, as from old age. **2.** to sway or shake as if about to fall. **3.** to be failing, unstable, or precarious. ~*n.* **4.** the act or an instance of tottering. [C12: perhaps from Old English *tealtrian* to waver, and Middle Dutch *touteren* to stagger] —**ˈtot+ter+er** *n.* —**ˈtot+ter·y** *adj.*

tou+can (ˈtuːkən) *n.* any tropical American arboreal fruit-eating bird of the family *Ramphastidae,* having a large brightly coloured bill with serrated edges and a bright plumage. [C16: from French, from Portuguese *tucano,* from Tupi *tucana,* probably imitative of its cry]

touch (tʌtʃ) *n.* **1.** the sense by which the texture and other qualities of objects can be experienced when they come in contact with a part of the body surface, esp. the tips of the fingers. Related adj.: **tactile. 2.** the quality of an object as perceived by this sense; feel; feeling. **3.** the act or an instance of something coming into contact with the body. **4.** a gentle push, tap, or caress. **5.** a small amount; hint: *a touch of sarcasm.* **6.** a noticeable effect; influence: *the house needed a woman's touch.* **7.** any slight stroke or mark: *with a touch of his brush he captured the scene.* **8.** characteristic manner or style: *the artist had a distinctive touch.* **9.** a detail of some work, esp. a literary or artistic work: *she added a few finishing touches to the book.* **10.** a slight attack, as of a disease: *a touch of bronchitis.* **11.** a specific ability or facility: *the champion appeared to have lost his touch.* **12.** the state of being aware of a situation or in contact with someone: *to get in touch with someone.* **13.** the state of being in physical contact. **14.** a trial or test (esp. in the phrase **put to the touch**). **15.** *Rugby, soccer, etc.* the area outside the touchlines, beyond which the ball is out of play (esp. in the phrase **in touch**). **16.** *Archaic.* **a.** an official stamp on metal indicating standard purity. **b.** the die stamp used to apply this mark. Now usually called: **hallmark. 17.** a scoring hit in competitive fencing. **18.** an estimate of the amount of gold in an alloy as obtained by use of a touchstone. **19.** the technique of fingering a keyboard instrument. **20.** the quality of the action of a keyboard instrument with regard to the relative ease with which the keys may be depressed: *this piano has a nice touch.* **21.** *Bell-ringing.* any series of changes where the permutations are fewer in number than for a peal. **22.** *Slang.* **a.** the act of asking for money as a loan or gift, often by devious means. **b.** the money received in this way. **c.** a person asked for money in this way: *he was an easy touch.* ~*vb.* **23.** (*tr.*) to cause or permit a part of the body to come into contact with. **24.** (*tr.*) to tap, feel, or strike, esp. with the hand: *don't touch the cake!* **25.** to come or cause (something) to come into contact with (something else): *their hands touched briefly; he touched the match to the fuse.* **26.** (*intr.*) to be in contact. **27.** (*tr.; usually used with a negative*) to take hold of (a person or thing), esp. in violence: *don't touch the baby!* **28.** to be adjacent to (each other): *the two properties touch.* **29.** (*tr.*) to move or disturb by handling: *someone's touched my desk.* **30.** (*tr.*) to have an effect on: *the war scarcely touched our town.* **31.** (*tr.*) to produce an emotional response in: *his sad story touched her.* **32.** (*tr.; usually used with a negative*) to partake of, eat, or drink. **33.** (*tr.; usually used with a negative*) to handle or deal with: *I wouldn't touch that business.* **34.** (when *intr.,* often foll. by *on*) to allude (to) briefly or in passing: *the speech touched on several subjects.* **35.** (*tr.*) to tinge or tint slightly: *brown hair touched with gold.* **36.** (*tr.*) to spoil or injure slightly: *blackfly touched the flowers.* **37.** (*tr.*) to mark, as with a brush or pen. **38.** (*tr.*) to compare to in quality or attainment; equal or match: *there's no-one to touch him.* **39.** (*tr.*) to reach or attain: *he touched the high point in his career.* **40.** (*intr.*) to dock or stop briefly: *the ship touches at Tenerife.* **41.** (*tr.*) *Slang.* to ask for a loan or gift of money from. **42.** *Rare.* **a.** to finger (the keys or strings of an instrument). **b.** to play (a tune, piece of music, etc.) in this way. **43.** (*tr.*) *Archaic.* to apply a stamp to (metal) indicating standard purity. ~See also **touchdown, touch off, touch up.** [C13: from Old French *tochier,* from Vulgar Latin *toccāre* (unattested) to strike, ring (a bell), probably imitative of a tapping sound] —**ˈtouch+a·ble** *adj.* —**ˈtouch+a·ble+ness** *n.* —**ˈtouch+er** *n.* —**ˈtouch+less** *adj.*

touch and go *adj.* (**touch-and-go** *when prenominal*). risky or critical: *a touch-and-go situation.*

touch+back (ˈtʌtʃˌbæk) *n. American football.* a play in which the ball is put down by a player behind his own goal line when the ball has been put across the goal line by an opponent. Compare **safety** (sense 4b.).

touch+down (ˈtʌtʃˌdaʊn) *n.* **1.** the moment at which a landing aircraft or spacecraft comes into contact with the landing surface. **2.** *Rugby.* the act of placing or touching the ball on the ground behind the goal line, as in scoring a try. **3.** *American football.* a scoring play for six points achieved by being in possession of the ball in the opponents' end zone. Abbrev.: **TD.** See also **field goal.** ~*vb.* **touch down.** (*intr., adv.*) **4.** (of a space vehicle, aircraft, etc.) to land. **5.** *Rugby.* to place the ball behind the goal line, as when scoring a try.

tou+ché (tuːˈʃeɪ) *interj.* **1.** an acknowledgment that a scoring hit has been made in a fencing competition. **2.** an acknowledgment of the striking home of a remark or the capping of a witticism. [from French, literally: touched]

touched (tʌtʃt) *adj.* (*postpositive*) **1.** moved to sympathy or emotion; affected. **2.** showing slight insanity.

touch foot+ball *n.* an informal version of football chiefly characterized by players' being touched rather than tackled.

touch+hole (ˈtʌtʃˌhəʊl) *n.* a hole in the breech of early cannon and firearms through which the charge was ignited.

touch+ing (ˈtʌtʃɪŋ) *adj.* **1.** evoking or eliciting tender feelings: *your sympathy is touching.* ~*prep.* **2.** on the subject of; relating to. —**ˈtouch+ing+ly** *adv.* —**ˈtouch+ing+ness** *n.*

touch-in goal *n. Rugby.* the area at each end of a pitch between the goal line and the dead-ball line.

touch judge *n.* one of the two linesmen in rugby.

touch+line (ˈtʌtʃˌlaɪn) *n.* either of the lines marking the side of the playing area in certain games, such as rugby.

touch+mark (ˈtʌtʃˌmɑːk) *n.* a maker's mark stamped on pewter objects.

touch-me-not *n.* any of several balsaminaceous plants of the genus *Impatiens,* esp. *I. noli-me-tangere,* having yellow spurred flowers and seed pods that burst open at a touch when ripe. Also called: **noli-me-tangere.**

touch off *vb.* (*tr., adv.*) **1.** to cause to explode, as by touching with a match. **2.** to cause (a disturbance, violence, etc.) to begin: *the marchers' action touched off riots.*

touch+stone (ˈtʌtʃˌstəʊn) *n.* **1.** a criterion or standard by which judgment is made. **2.** a hard dark siliceous stone, such as basalt or jasper, that is used to test the quality of gold and silver from the colour of the streak they produce on it.

touch sys+tem *n.* a typing system in which the fingers are trained to find the correct keys, permitting the typist to read and type copy without looking at the keyboard.

touch-type *vb.* (*intr.*) to type without having to look at the keys of the typewriter. —**ˈtouch-ˌtyp·ist** *n.*

touch up *vb.* (*tr., adv.*) **1.** to put extra or finishing touches to. **2.** to enhance, renovate, or falsify by putting extra touches to: *to touch up a photograph.* **3.** to stimulate or rouse as by a tap or light blow. **4.** *Brit. slang.* to touch or caress (someone), esp. to arouse sexual feelings. ~*n.* **touch-up. 5.** a renovation or retouching, as of a painting.

touch+wood (ˈtʌtʃˌwʊd) *n.* something, esp. dry wood or fungus material such as amadou, used as tinder. [C16: TOUCH (in the sense: to kindle) + WOOD]

touch·y (ˈtʌtʃɪ) *adj.* **touch·i+er, touch·i+est. 1.** easily upset or irritated; oversensitive. **2.** extremely risky. **3.** easily ignited. —**ˈtouch·i+ly** *adv.* —**ˈtouch·i+ness** *n.*

tough (tʌf) *adj.* **1.** strong or resilient; durable: *a tough material.* **2.** not tender: *he could not eat the tough steak.* **3.** having a great capacity for endurance; hardy and fit: *a tough mountaineer.* **4.** rough or pugnacious: *a tough gangster.* **5.** resolute or intractable: *a tough employer.* **6.** difficult or troublesome to do or deal with: *a tough problem.* **7.** *Informal, chiefly U.S.* unfortunate or unlucky: *it's tough on him.* ~*n.* **8.**

a rough, vicious, or pugnacious person. ~*adv.* **9.** *Informal.* violently, aggressively, or intractably: *to treat someone tough.* [Old English *tōh;* related to Old High German *zāhi* tough, Old Norse *tā* trodden ground in front of a house] —'**tough+ish** *adj.* —'**tough+ly** *adv.* —'**tough+ness** *n.*

tough+en ('tʌfən) *vb.* to make or become tough or tougher. —'**tough+en+er** *n.*

tough·ie ('tʌfɪ) *n. Informal, chiefly U.S.* a tough person or thing.

tough-mind·ed *adj. Chiefly U.S.* practical, unsentimental, or intractable. —ˌ**tough-'mind·ed+ly** *adv.* —ˌ**tough-'mind·ed+ness** *n.*

Toul (tu:l) *n.* a town in NE France: a leading episcopal see in the Middle Ages. Pop.: 16 832 (1975).

Tou+lon (*French* tu'lɔ̃) *n.* a fortified port and naval base in SE France, on the Mediterranean: naval arsenal developed by Henry IV and Richelieu, later fortified by Vauban. Pop.: 185 050 (1975).

Tou+louse (tu:'lu:z) *n.* a city in S France, on the Garonne River: scene of severe religious strife in the early 13th and mid-16th centuries; university (1229). Pop.: 383 176 (1975). Ancient name: **Tolosa.**

Tou·louse-Lau·trec (*French* tuluz lo'trɛk) *n.* **Hen·ri (Marie Raymond) de** (ɑ̃'ri də). 1864–1901, French painter and lithographer, noted for his paintings and posters of the life of Montmartre, Paris.

tou+pee ('tu:peɪ) *n.* **1.** a wig or hairpiece worn, esp. by men, to cover a bald or balding place. **2.** (formerly) a prominent lock on a periwig, esp. in the 18th century. [C18: apparently from French *toupet* forelock, from Old French *toup* top, of Germanic origin; see TOP[1]]

tour (tʊə) *n.* **1.** an extended voyage, usually taken for pleasure, visiting places of interest along the route. **2.** *Military.* a period of service, esp. in one place of duty. **3.** a short trip, as for inspection. **4.** a trip made by a theatre company, orchestra, etc., to perform in several different places: *a concert tour.* ~*vb.* **5.** to make a tour of (a place). [C14: from Old French: a turn, from Latin *tornus* a lathe, from Greek *tornos;* compare TURN]

tou+ra+co *or* **tu+ra+co** ('tʊərəˌkəʊ) *n., pl.* **+cos.** any brightly coloured crested arboreal African bird of the family *Musophagidae:* order *Cuculiformes* (cuckoos, etc.). [C18: of West African origin]

Tou+raine (*French* tu'rɛn) *n.* a former province of NW central France: at its height in the 16th century as an area of royal residences, esp. along the Loire. Chief town: Tours.

Tou+rane (tu:'rɑ:n) *n.* the former name of **Da Nang.**

tour+bil+lion (tʊə'bɪljən) *n.* a rare word for **whirlwind.** [C15: from French *tourbillon,* ultimately from Latin *turbō* something that spins, from *turbāre* to confuse]

Tour+coing (*French* tur'kwɛ̃) *n.* a town in NE France: textiles manufacturing. Pop.: 102 543 (1975).

tour de force *French.* (tur də 'fɔrs; *English* 'tʊə də 'fɔ:s) *n., pl.* ***tours de force*** (tur; *English* 'tʊə). a masterly or brilliant stroke, creation, effect, or accomplishment. [literally: feat of skill or strength]

Tou+ré ('tʊəreɪ) *n.* **Sé·kou** ('seɪku:). born 1922, president of the Republic of Guinea since 1958.

tour+er ('tʊərə) *n.* a large open car, usually seating a driver and four passengers. Also called (esp. U.S.): **touring car.**

tour+ing car *n.* another name (esp. U.S.) for **tourer.**

tour+ism ('tʊərɪzəm) *n.* tourist travel and the services connected with it, esp. when regarded as an industry.

tour+ist ('tʊərɪst) *n.* **1. a.** a person who travels for pleasure, usually sightseeing and staying in hotels. **b.** (*as modifier*): *tourist attractions.* **2.** a person on an excursion or sightseeing tour. **3.** Also called: **tourist class.** the lowest class of accommodation on a passenger ship. ~*adj.* **4.** of or relating to tourist accommodation. —**tour+'is+tic** *adj.*

tour+ist·y ('tʊərɪstɪ) *adj. Informal, often derogatory.* abounding in or designed for tourists.

tour+ma+line ('tʊəməˌli:n) *n.* any of a group of hard glassy minerals of variable colour consisting of complex borosilicates of aluminium with quantities of lithium, sodium, potassium, iron, and magnesium in hexagonal crystalline form: used in optical and electrical equipment. [C18: from German *Turmalin,* from Singhalese *toramalli* carnelian] —**tour+ma+lin+ic** (ˌtʊəmə'lɪnɪk) *adj.*

Tour+nai (*French* tur'nɛ) *n.* a city in W Belgium, in Hainaut province on the River Scheldt: under several different European rulers until 1814. Pop.: 32 794 (1970). Flemish name: **Doornik.**

tour+na+ment ('tʊənəmənt, 'tɔ:-, 'tɜ:-) *n.* **1.** a sporting competition in which contestants play a series of games to determine an overall winner. **2.** a meeting for athletic or other sporting contestants: *an archery tournament.* **3.** *Medieval history* **a.** (originally) a martial sport or contest in which mounted combatants fought for a prize. **b.** (later) a meeting for knightly sports and exercises. [C13: from Old French *torneiement,* from *torneier* to fight on horseback, literally: to turn, from the constant wheeling round of the combatants; see TOURNEY]

tour+ne·dos ('tʊənəˌdəʊ) *n., pl.* **·dos** (-ˌdəʊz). a thick round steak of beef cut from the fillet or undercut of sirloin. [from French, from *tourner* to TURN + *dos* back]

Tour·neur ('tɜ:nə) *n.* **Cyr·il.** ?1575–1626, English dramatist; author of *The Atheist's Tragedy* (1611) and, reputedly, of *The Revenger's Tragedy* (1607).

tour+ney ('tʊənɪ, 'tɔ:-) *Medieval history.* ~*n.* **1.** a knightly tournament. ~*vb.* **2.** (*intr.*) to engage in a tourney. [C13: from Old French *torneier,* from Vulgar Latin *tornidiāre* (unattested) to turn constantly, from Latin *tornāre* to TURN (in a lathe); see TOURNAMENT] —'**tour+ney+er** *n.*

tour+ni+quet ('tʊənɪˌkeɪ, 'tɔ:-) *n. Med.* any instrument or device for temporarily constricting an artery of the arm or leg to control bleeding. [C17: from French: device that operates by turning, from *tourner* to TURN]

Tours (*French* tu:r) *n.* a town in W central France, on the River Loire: scene of the defeat of the Arabs in 732, ending the advance of Islam in W Europe. Pop.: 145 441 (1975).

tou+sle ('taʊzᵊl) *vb.* (*tr.*) **1.** to tangle, ruffle, or disarrange. **2.** to treat roughly. ~*n.* **3.** a disorderly, tangled, or rumpled state. **4.** a dishevelled or disordered mass, esp. of hair. [C15: from Low German *tūsen* to shake; related to Old High German *zirzūsōn* to tear to pieces]

tous-les-mois (ˌtu:leɪ'mwɑ:) *n.* **1.** a large widely cultivated plant, *Canna edulis,* of the West Indies and South America, having purplish stems and leaves, bright red flowers and edible tubers: family *Cannaceae.* **2.** the tuber of this plant, used as a source of starch. [C19: from French, literally: all the months, probably an attempt to give phonetic reproduction of *tolomane,* from native West Indian name]

Tous·saint L'Ou·ver·ture (*French* tusɛ̃ luvɛr'ty:r) *n.* **Pierre Do·mi·nique** (pjɛ:r dɔmi'nik). ?1743–1803, Haitian revolutionary leader. He was made governor of the island by the French Revolutionary government (1794) and expelled the Spanish and British but when Napoleon I proclaimed the re-establishment of slavery he was arrested. He died in prison in France.

tout (taʊt) *vb.* **1.** *Informal.* to solicit (business, customers, etc.), esp. in a brazen way. **2.** (*intr.*) **a.** to spy on racehorses being trained in order to obtain information for betting purposes. **b.** to sell, or attempt to sell, such information or to take bets, esp. in public places. **3.** *Informal.* to recommend flatteringly or excessively. ~*n.* **4. a.** a person who spies on racehorses so as to obtain betting information to sell. **b.** a person who sells information obtained by such spying. **5.** *Informal.* a person who solicits business in a brazen way. [C14 (in the sense: to peer, look out): related to Old English *tȳtan* to peep out] —'**tout+er** *n.*

tout à fait *French.* (tu ta 'fɛ) *adv.* completely; absolutely.

tout court *French.* (tu 'kur) *adv.* simply; briefly.

tout de suite *French.* (tut 'swit) *adv.* at once; immediately.

tout en+sem+ble *French.* (tu tɑ̃'sɑ:bl) *adv.* **1.** everything considered; all in all. ~*n.* **2.** the total impression or effect.

tout le monde *French.* (tul 'mɔ̃:d) *n.* all the world; everyone.

tou+zle ('taʊzᵊl) *vb., n.* a rare spelling of **tousle.**

to+va+risch, to+va+rich, *or* **to+va+rish** (tə'vɑ:rɪʃ; *Russian* ta'variʃtʃ) *n.* comrade: a term of address. [from Russian]

tow[1] (təʊ) *vb.* **1.** (*tr.*) to pull or drag (a vehicle, boat, etc.), esp. by means of a rope or cable. ~*n.* **2.** the act or an instance of towing. **3.** the state of being towed (esp. in the phrases **in tow, under tow, on tow**). **4.** something towed. **5.** something used for towing. **6. in tow.** in one's charge or under one's influence. **7.** *Informal.* (in motor racing, etc.) the act of taking advantage of the slipstream of another car (esp. in the phrase **get a tow**). [Old English *togian;* related to Old Frisian *togia,* Old Norse *toga,* Old High German *zogōn*] —'**tow·a·ble** *adj.*

tow[2] (təʊ) *n.* **1.** the fibres of hemp, flax, jute, etc., in the scutched state. **2.** synthetic fibres preparatory to spinning. **3.** the coarser fibres discarded after combing. [Old English *tōw;* related to Old Saxon *tou,* Old Norse *tō* tuft of wool, Dutch *touwen* to spin] —**tow·y** *adj.*

tow+age ('təʊɪdʒ) *n.* **1.** a charge made for towing. **2.** the act of towing or the state of being towed.

to+ward *adj.* ('təʊəd). **1.** *Now rare.* in progress; afoot. **2.** *Obsolete.* about to happen; imminent. **3.** *Obsolete.* promising or favourable. ~*prep.* (tə'wɔ:d, tɔ:d). **4.** a variant of **towards.** [Old English *tōweard;* see TO, -WARD]

to+ward+ly ('təʊədlɪ) *adj. Archaic.* **1.** compliant. **2.** propitious or suitable. —'**to+ward+li+ness** *or* '**to+ward+ness** *n.*

to+wards (tə'wɔ:dz, tɔ:dz) *prep.* **1.** in the direction or vicinity of: *towards London.* **2.** with regard to: *her feelings towards me.* **3.** as a contribution or help to: *money towards a new car.* **4.** just before: *towards one o'clock.* ~Also: **toward.**

tow+bar ('təʊˌbɑ:) *n.* a rigid metal bar or frame used for towing vehicles. Compare **towrope, towline.**

tow+boat ('təʊˌbəʊt) *n.* another word for **tug** (the boat).

tow-col·oured *adj.* pale yellow; flaxen.

tow+el ('taʊəl) *n.* **1.** a square or rectangular piece of absorbent cloth or paper used for drying the body. **2.** a similar piece of cloth used for drying plates, cutlery, etc. **3. throw in the towel.** to give up completely. ~*vb.* **+els, +el+ling, +elled** *or U.S.* **+els, +el+ing, +eled. 4.** (*tr.*) to dry or wipe with a towel. **5.** (*tr.; often foll. by* up) *Austral. slang.* to assault or beat (a person). [C13: from Old French *toaille,* of Germanic origin; related to Old High German *dwahal* bath, Old Saxon *twahila* towel, Gothic *thwahan* to wash]

tow+el+ling ('taʊəlɪŋ) *n.* an absorbent fabric, esp. with a nap, used for making towels, bathrobes, etc.

tow+el rail *n.* a rail or frame in a bathroom, etc., for hanging towels on.

tow+er ('taʊə) *n.* **1.** a tall, usually square or circular structure, sometimes part of a larger building and usually built for a specific purpose: *a church tower; a conning tower.* **2.** a place of defence or retreat. **3.** a mobile structure used in medieval warfare to attack a castle, etc. **4. tower of strength.** a person who gives support, comfort, etc. ~*vb.* **5.** (*intr.*) to be or rise like a tower; loom. [C12: from Old French *tur,* from Latin *turris,* from Greek]

tow+ered ('taʊəd) *adj.* **a.** having a tower or towers. **b.** (*in combination*): *four-towered; high-towered.*
Tow+er Ham+lets *n.* a borough of Greater London, on the River Thames: contains the main part of the East End. Pop.: 146 100 (1976 est.).
tow+er+ing ('taʊərɪŋ) *adj.* **1.** very tall; lofty. **2.** outstanding, as in importance or stature. **3.** (*prenominal*) very intense: *a towering rage.* —**'tow+er+ing+ly** *adv.*
Tow+er of Lon+don *n.* a fortress in the City of London, on the River Thames: begun soon after 1066; later extended and used as a palace, the main state prison, and now as a museum containing the crown jewels.
tow-haired (təʊhɛəd) *adj.* having blond and sometimes tousled hair.
tow+head ('təʊ,hɛd) *n. Often disparaging.* **1.** a person with blond or yellowish hair. **2.** a head of such hair. [from TOW² (flax)] —**'tow+,head·ed** *adj.*
tow+hee ('taʊhɪ, 'təʊ-) *n.* any of various North American brownish-coloured sparrows of the genera *Pipilo* and *Chlorura.* [C18: imitative of its note]
tow+ing path *n.* another name for **towpath.**
tow+kay (taʊ'keɪ) *n.* sir; master: used as a form of address. [of Chinese origin]
tow+line ('təʊ,laɪn) *n.* another name for **towrope.**
town (taʊn) *n.* **1. a.** a densely populated urban area, typically smaller than a city and larger than a village, having some local powers of government and a fixed boundary. **b.** (*as modifier*): *town life.* **2.** a city, borough, or other urban area. **3.** (in the U.S.) a territorial unit of local government that is smaller than a county; township. **4.** the nearest town or commercial district. **5.** London or the chief city of an area. **6.** the inhabitants of a town. **7.** the permanent residents of a university town as opposed to the university staff and students. Compare **gown** (sense 3). **8. go to town. a.** to make supreme or unrestricted effort; go all out. **b.** *Austral. informal.* to lose one's temper. **9. on the town.** seeking out entertainments and amusements. [Old English *tūn* village; related to Old Saxon, Old Norse *tūn,* Old High German *zūn* fence, Old Irish *dūn*] —**'town+ish** *adj.* —**'town+less** *adj.*
town clerk *n.* **1.** (in Britain until 1974) the secretary and chief administrative officer of a town or city. **2.** (in the U.S.) the official who keeps the records of a town.
town cri+er *n.* (formerly) a person employed by a town to make public announcements in the streets.
town·ee (taʊ'ni:) *or U.S.* **town·ie** *or* **town·y** ('taʊnɪ) *n.* **1.** *Informal, often disparaging.* a permanent resident in a town, esp. as distinct from country dwellers or students. **2.** *Brit. Midlands dialect.* a slick and flashy male city-dweller.
town gas *n.* coal gas manufactured for domestic and industrial use.
town hall *n.* the chief building in which municipal business is transacted, often with a hall for public meetings.
town+hall clock ('taʊn,hɔ:l) *n. Brit.* another name for **moschatel.**
town house *n.* **1.** a house in an urban area, esp. a fashionable one. **2.** a person's town residence as distinct from his country residence.
town meet+ing *n. U.S.* **1.** an assembly of the inhabitants of a town. **2.** (esp. in New England) an assembly of the qualified voters of a town. Such a meeting may exercise all the powers of local government.
town plan+ning *n.* the comprehensive planning of the physical and social development of a town, including the construction of facilities. U.S. term: **city planning.**
town+scape ('taʊnskeɪp) *n.* a view of an urban scene.
Towns·hend ('taʊnzɛnd) *n.* **Pete.** born 1945, English rock guitarist and songwriter: member of The Who; writer of the rock opera *Tommy* (1969).
town+ship ('taʊnʃɪp) *n.* **1.** a small town. **2.** (in the U.S. and Canada) a territorial area, esp. a subdivision of a county: often organized as a unit of local government. **3.** (in South Africa) a planned urban settlement of Black Africans or Coloureds. Compare **location** (sense 4). **4.** *English history.* **a.** any of the local districts of a large parish, each division containing a village or small town. **b.** the particular manor or parish itself as a territorial division. **c.** the inhabitants of a township collectively.
towns+man ('taʊnzmən) *n., pl.* **+men. 1.** an inhabitant of a town. **2.** a person from the same town as oneself. —**'towns+,wom·an** *fem. n.*
towns+peo·ple ('taʊnz,pi:pᵊl) *or* **towns+folk** *n.* the inhabitants of a town; citizens.
Towns+ville ('taʊnzvɪl) *n.* a port in E Australia, in NE Queensland on the Coral Sea: centre of a vast agricultural and mining hinterland. Pop.: 82 500 (1975 est.).
tow+path ('təʊ,pɑ:θ) *n.* a path beside a canal or river, used by people or animals towing boats. Also called: **towing path.**
tow+rope ('təʊ,rəʊp) *n.* a rope or cable used for towing a vehicle or vessel. Also called: **towline.**
tow truck *n.* a U.S. name for **breakdown van.**
tox. *or* **toxicol.** *abbrev. for* toxicology.
tox-, tox·ic- *or before a consonant* **tox·o-, tox·i·co-** *combining form.* indicating poison: *toxalbumin.* [from Latin *toxicum*]
tox+ae·mi·a *or U.S.* **tox+e·mi·a** (tɒk'si:mɪə) *n.* **1.** a condition characterized by the presence of bacterial toxins in the blood. **2.** the condition in pregnancy of pre-eclampsia or eclampsia. —**tox+'ae·mic** *or U.S.* **tox+'e·mic** *adj.*
tox+al+bu+min (,tɒksæl'bju:mɪn) *n. Biochem.* any of a group of toxic albumins that occur in certain plants, such as toadstools, and in snake venom.
tox·a+phene ('tɒksə,fi:n) *n.* an amber waxy solid with a pleasant pine odour, consisting of chlorinated terpenes, esp. chlorinated camphene: used as an insecticide.
tox+ic ('tɒksɪk) *adj.* **1.** of, relating to, or caused by a toxin or poison; poisonous. **2.** harmful or deadly. [C17: from medical Latin *toxicus,* from Latin *toxicum* poison, from Greek *toxikon* (*pharmakon*) (poison) used on arrows, from *toxon* arrow] —**'tox·i·cal+ly** *adv.*
tox·i+cant ('tɒksɪkənt) *n.* **1.** a toxic substance; poison. **2.** a rare word for **intoxicant.** ~*adj.* **3.** poisonous; toxic. [C19: from Medieval Latin *toxicāre* to poison; see TOXIC]
tox+ic+i·ty (tɒk'sɪsɪtɪ) *n.* **1.** the degree of strength of a poison. **2.** the state or quality of being poisonous.
tox·i·co+gen+ic (,tɒksɪkəʊ'dʒɛnɪk) *adj.* **1.** producing toxic substances or effects. **2.** caused or produced by a toxin.
tox·i·col+o·gy (,tɒksɪ'kɒlədʒɪ) *n.* the branch of science concerned with poisons, their nature, effects, and antidotes. —**tox·i·co+log·i·cal** (,tɒksɪkə'lɒdʒɪkᵊl) *or* **,tox·i·co+'log+ic** *adj.* —**,tox·i·co+'log·i·cal·ly** *adv.* —**,tox·i+'col·o·gist** *n.*
tox·i·co+sis (,tɒksɪ'kəʊsɪs) *n.* any disease or condition caused by poisoning.
tox+in ('tɒksɪn) *or* **tok+sine** ('tɒksi:n) *n.* **1.** any of various poisonous substances produced by microorganisms that stimulate the production of neutralizing substances (antitoxins) in the body. See also **endotoxin, exotoxin. 2.** any other poisonous substance of plant or animal origin.
tox·in-an·ti·tox+in *n.* a mixture of a specific toxin and antitoxin. The diphtheria toxin-antitoxin was formerly used in the U.S. for active immunization.
tox+oid ('tɒksɔɪd) *n.* a toxin that has been treated to reduce its toxicity and is used in immunization to stimulate production of antitoxins.
tox+oph·i·lite (tɒk'sɒfɪ,laɪt) *Formal.* ~*n.* **1.** an archer. ~*adj.* **2.** of or relating to archery. [C18: from *Toxophilus,* the title of a book (1545) by Ascham, designed to mean: a lover of the bow, from Greek *toxon* bow + *philos* loving]
tox·o+plas+mo+sis (,tɒksəʊplæz'məʊsɪs) *n.* a protozoal disease characterized by jaundice, enlarged liver and spleen, and convulsions, caused by infection with *Toxoplasma gondii.* —**,tox·o+'plas+mic** *adj.*
toy (tɔɪ) *n.* **1.** an object designed to be played with. **2. a.** something that is a nonfunctioning replica of something else, esp. a miniature one. **b.** (*as modifier*): *a toy guitar.* **3.** any small thing of little value; trifle. **4. a.** something small or miniature. **b.** (*as modifier*): *a toy poodle.* ~*vb.* **5.** (*intr.;* usually foll. by *with*) to play, fiddle, or flirt. [C16 (in the sense: amorous dalliance): of uncertain origin] —**'toy+er** *n.* —**'toy+less** *adj.* —**'toy+,like** *adj.*
To+ya+ma ('təʊjɑ:,mɑ:) *n.* a city in central Japan, on W Honshu on **Toyama Bay** (an inlet of the Sea of Japan): chemical and textile centre. Pop.: 287 035 (1974 est.).
Toyn·bee ('tɔɪnbɪ) *n.* **1. Ar·nold.** 1852–83, English economist and social reformer. **2.** his nephew, **Ar·nold Jo·seph.** 1889–1975, English historian. In his chief work, *A Study of History* (1934–61), he attempted to analyse the principles determining the rise and fall of civilizations.
T.P.I. (in Britain) *abbrev. for* Town Planning Institute.
TPN *n. Biochem.* triphosphopyridine nucleotide; a former name for **NADP.**
Tpr. *abbrev. for* Trooper.
TR *international car registration for* Turkey.
tr. *abbrev. for:* **1.** transitive. **2.** translated. **3.** translator. **4.** treasurer. **5.** *Music.* trill. **6.** trustee.
tra+be·at·ed ('treɪbɪ,eɪtɪd) *or* **tra+be·ate** ('treɪbɪɪt, -,eɪt) *adj. Architect.* constructed with horizontal beams as opposed to arches. Compare **arcuate.** [C19: back formation from *trabeation,* from Latin *trabs* a beam] —**,tra+be·'a·tion** *n.*
tra+bec·u+la (trə'bɛkjʊlə) *n., pl.* **+lae** (-,li:). *Anatomy, botany.* **1.** any of various rod-shaped structures that support other organs. **2.** any of various rod-shaped cells or structures that bridge a cavity, as within the capsule of a moss. [C19: via New Latin from Latin: a little beam, from *trabs* a beam] —**tra+'bec·u·lar** *or* **tra+'bec·u·late** *adj.*
Trab+zon ('trɑ:bzɔ:n) *or* **Treb·i+zond** ('trɛbɪ,zɒnd) *n.* a port in NE Turkey, on the Black Sea: founded as a Greek colony in the 8th century B.C. at the terminus of an important trade route from central Europe to Asia. Pop.: 81 528 (1970).
tra+cass·e+rie (trə'kæsərɪ) *n.* a turmoil; annoyance. [from French, from *tracasser* to fuss about]
trace¹ (treɪs) *n.* **1.** a mark or other sign that something has been in a place; vestige. **2.** a tiny or scarcely detectable amount or characteristic. **3.** a footprint or other indication of the passage of an animal or person. **4.** any line drawn by a recording instrument or a record consisting of a number of such lines. **5.** something drawn, such as a tracing. **6.** *Chiefly U.S.* a beaten track or path. **7.** the postulated alteration in the cells of the nervous system that occurs as the result of any experience or learning. See also **memory trace, engram. 8.** *Geom.* the intersection of a surface with a coordinate plane. **9.** *Meteorol.* an amount of precipitation that is too small to be measured. **10.** *Archaic.* a way taken; route. ~*vb.* **11.** (*tr.*) to follow, discover, or ascertain the course or development of something: *to trace the history of China.* **12.** (*tr.*) to track down and find, as by following a trail. **13.** to copy (a design, map, etc.) by drawing over the lines visible through a superimposed sheet of transparent paper or other material. **14.** (*tr.;* often foll. by *out*) **a.** to draw or delineate (a plan or diagram) of:

she spent hours tracing the models one at a time. **b.** to outline or sketch (an idea, policy, etc.): *he traced out his scheme for the robbery.* **15.** (*tr.*) to decorate with tracery. **16.** (*tr.*) to imprint (a design) on cloth, etc. **17.** (usually foll. by *back*) to follow or be followed to source; date back: *his ancestors trace back to the 16th century.* **18.** *Archaic.* to make one's way over, through, or along (something). [C13: from French *tracier,* from Vulgar Latin *tractiāre* (unattested) to drag, from Latin *tractus,* from *trahere* to drag] —**'trace·a·ble** *adj.* —**,trace·a·'bil·i·ty** *or* **'trace·a·ble·ness** *n.* —**'trace·a·bly** *adv.* —**'trace·less** *adj.* —**'trace·less·ly** *adv.*

trace[2] (treɪs) *n.* **1.** either of the two side straps that connect a horse's harness to the whiffletree. **2.** *Angling.* a short piece of gut or nylon attaching a hook or fly to a line. **3. kick over the traces.** escape or defy control. [C14 *trais,* from Old French *trait,* ultimately from Latin *trahere* to drag]

trace el·e·ment *n.* any of various chemical elements that occur in very small amounts in organisms and are essential for many physiological and biochemical processes.

trac·er ('treɪsə) *n.* **1.** a person or thing that traces. **2. a.** ammunition that can be observed when in flight by the burning of chemical substances in the base of the projectile. **b.** (*as modifier*): *tracer fire.* **3.** *Med.* any radioactive isotope introduced into the body to study metabolic processes, absorption, etc., by following its progress through the body with a Geiger counter or other detector. **4.** an investigation to trace missing cargo, mail, etc.

trac·er bul·let *n.* a round of small arms ammunition containing a tracer.

trac·er·y ('treɪsərɪ) *n., pl.* **·er·ies. 1.** a pattern of interlacing ribs, esp. as used in the upper part of a Gothic window, etc. **2.** any fine pattern resembling this. —**'trac·er·ied** *adj.*

tra·che·a (trə'kiːə) *n., pl.* **·che·ae** (-'kiːiː). **1.** *Anatomy, zoology.* the membranous tube with cartilaginous rings that conveys inhaled air from the larynx to the bronchi. Nontechnical name: **windpipe. 2.** any of the tubes in insects and related animals that convey air from the spiracles to the tissues. **3.** *Botany.* another name for **vessel** (sense 5). [C16: from Medieval Latin, from Greek *trakheia,* shortened from (*artēria*) *trakheia* rough (artery), from *trakhus* rough] —**tra·'che·al** *or* **tra·'che·ate** *adj.*

tra·che·id ('treɪkɪɪd) *or* **tra·che·ide** *n. Botany.* an element of xylem tissue consisting of an elongated lignified cell with tapering ends. —**tra·che·i·dal** (trə'kiːɪdᵊl, ˌtreɪkɪ'aɪdᵊl) *adj.*

tra·che·i·tis (ˌtreɪkɪ'aɪtɪs) *n.* inflammation of the trachea.

tra·che·o- *or before a vowel* **tra·che-** *combining form.* denoting the trachea: *tracheotomy.*

tra·che·o·phyte ('treɪkɪəʊˌfaɪt) *n.* any plant that has a conducting system of xylem and phloem elements; a vascular plant.

tra·che·ost·o·my (ˌtrækɪ'ɒstəmɪ) *n., pl.* **·mies.** the surgical formation of a temporary or permanent opening into the trachea following tracheotomy.

tra·che·ot·o·my (ˌtrækɪ'ɒtəmɪ) *n., pl.* **·mies.** surgical incision into the trachea, usually performed when the upper air passage has been blocked. —**ˌtra·che·'ot·o·mist** *n.*

tra·cho·ma (trə'kəʊmə) *n.* a chronic contagious viral disease of the eye characterized by inflammation of the conjunctiva and cornea and the formation of scar tissue, caused by infection with *Chlamydia trachomatis.* [C17: from New Latin, from Greek *trakhōma* roughness, from *trakhus* rough] —**tra·chom·a·tous** (trə'kɒmətəs, -'kəʊ-) *adj.*

tra·chyte ('treɪkaɪt, 'træ-) *n.* a light-coloured fine-grained volcanic rock of rough texture consisting of feldspars with small amounts of pyroxene or amphibole. [C19: from French, from Greek *trakhutēs,* from *trakhus* rough] —**trach·y·toid** ('trækɪˌtɔɪd, 'treɪ-) *adj.*

tra·chyt·ic (trə'kɪtɪk) *adj.* (of the texture of certain igneous rocks) characterized by a parallel arrangement of crystals, which mark the flow of the lava when still molten.

trac·ing ('treɪsɪŋ) *n.* **1.** a copy made by tracing. **2.** the act of making a trace. **3.** a record made by an instrument.

trac·ing pa·per *n.* strong transparent paper used for tracing.

track (træk) *n.* **1.** the mark or trail left by something that has passed by: *the track of an animal.* **2.** any road or path affording passage, esp. a rough one. **3.** a rail or pair of parallel rails on which a vehicle, such as a locomotive, runs, esp. the rails together with the sleepers, ballast, etc., on a railway. **4.** a course of action, thought, etc.: *don't start on that track again!* **5.** a line of motion or travel, such as flight. **6.** an endless jointed metal band driven by the wheels of a vehicle such as a tank or tractor to enable it to move across rough or muddy ground. **7.** *Physics.* the path of a particle of ionizing radiation as observed in a cloud chamber, bubble chamber, or photographic emulsion. **8. a.** a course for running or racing. **b.** (*as modifier*): *track events.* **9.** *U.S.* **a.** sports performed on a track. **b.** track and field events as a whole. **10.** a path on a magnetic recording medium, esp. magnetic tape, on which information, such as music or speech, from a single input channel is recorded. **11.** Also called: **band.** any of a number of separate sections in the recording on either side of a gramophone record. **12.** the distance between the points of contact with the ground of a pair of wheels, such as the front wheels of a motor vehicle or the paired wheels of an aircraft undercarriage. **13.** a hypothetical trace made on the surface of the earth by a point directly below an aircraft in flight. **14. keep** (*or* **lose**) **track of.** to follow (or fail to follow) the passage, course, or progress of. **15. off the beaten track.** isolated; secluded. **16. off the track.** away from what is correct or true. **17. on the track of.** on the scent or trail of; pursuing. **18. the right** (*or* **wrong**) **track.** pursuing the correct (or incorrect) line of investigation, inquiry, etc. ~*vb.* **19.** to follow the trail of (a person, animal, etc.). **20.** to follow the flight path of (a satellite, spacecraft, etc.) by picking up radio or radar signals transmitted or reflected by it. **21.** *U.S. railways.* **a.** to provide with a track. **b.** to run on a track of (a certain width). **22.** (of a camera or camera-operator) to follow (a moving object) in any direction while operating. **23.** to follow a track through (a place): *to track the jungles.* **24.** (*intr.*) (of the pickup, stylus, etc., of a gramophone) to follow the groove of a record: *the pickup tracks badly.* [C15: from Old French *trac,* probably of Germanic origin; related to Middle Dutch *tracken* to pull, Middle Low German *trecken;* compare Norwegian *trakke* to trample] —**'track·a·ble** *adj.* —**'track·er** *n.*

track down *vb.* (*tr., adv.*) to find by tracking or pursuing.

track·ing sta·tion *n.* a station that can use a radio or radar beam to determine and follow the path of an object, esp. a spacecraft or satellite, in space or in the atmosphere.

track·lay·ing ('trækˌleɪɪŋ) *adj.* (of a vehicle) having an endless jointed metal band around the wheels.

track·less ('træklɪs) *adj.* **1.** having or leaving no trace or trail: *a trackless jungle.* **2.** (of a vehicle) using or having no tracks. —**'track·less·ly** *adv.* —**'track·less·ness** *n.*

track·man ('trækmən) *n., pl.* **·men.** the U.S. name for **platelayer.**

track meet *n. U.S.* an athletics meeting.

track rec·ord *n. Informal.* the past record of the accomplishments and failures of a person, business, etc.

track rod *n.* the rod connecting the two front wheels of a motor vehicle ensuring that they turn at the same angle.

tracks (træks) *pl. n.* **1.** (*sometimes sing.*) marks, such as footprints, tyre impressions, etc., left by someone or something that has passed. **2. in one's tracks.** on the very spot where one is standing (esp. in the phrase **stop in one's tracks**). **3. make tracks.** to leave or depart. **4. make tracks for.** to go or head towards.

track shoe *n.* either of a pair of light running shoes fitted with steel spikes for better grip. Also called: **spikes.**

track·suit ('trækˌsuːt, -ˌsjuːt) *n.* a warm suit worn by athletes, usually over the clothes, esp. during training.

tract[1] (trækt) *n.* **1.** an extended area, as of land. **2.** *Anatomy.* a system of organs, glands, or other tissues that has a particular function: *the digestive tract.* **3.** a bundle of nerve fibres having the same function, origin, and termination: *the optic tract.* **4.** *Archaic.* an extended period of time. [C15: from Latin *tractus* a stretching out, from *trahere* to drag]

tract[2] (trækt) *n.* a treatise or pamphlet, esp. a religious or moralistic one. [C15: from Latin *tractātus* TRACTATE]

tract[3] (trækt) *n. R.C. Church.* an anthem in some Masses. [C14: from Medieval Latin *tractus cantus* extended song; see TRACT[1]]

trac·ta·ble ('træktəbᵊl) *adj.* **1.** easily controlled or persuaded. **2.** readily worked; malleable. [C16: from Latin *tractābilis,* from *tractāre* to manage, from *trahere* to draw] —**ˌtrac·ta·'bil·i·ty** *or* **'trac·ta·ble·ness** *n.* —**'trac·ta·bly** *adv.*

Trac·tar·i·an·ism (træk'tɛərɪəˌnɪzəm) *n.* another name for the **Oxford Movement.** —**Trac·'tar·i·an** *n., adj.*

trac·tate ('træktert) *n.* a short tract; treatise. [C15: from Latin *tractātus,* from *tractāre* to handle; see TRACTABLE]

trac·tile ('træktaɪl) *adj.* capable of being drawn out; ductile. [C17: from Latin *trahere* to drag] —**trac·til·i·ty** (træk'tɪlɪtɪ) *n.*

trac·tion ('trækʃən) *n.* **1.** the act of drawing or pulling, esp. by motive power. **2.** the state of being drawn or pulled. **3.** *Med.* the application of a steady pull on a part during healing of a fractured or dislocated bone, using a system of weights and pulleys or splints. **4.** the adhesive friction between a wheel and a surface, as between a driving wheel of a motor vehicle and the road. [C17: from Medieval Latin *tractiō,* from Latin *tractus* dragged; see TRACTILE] —**'trac·tion·al** *adj.* —**trac·tive** ('træktɪv) *adj.*

trac·tion en·gine *n.* a steam-powered locomotive used, esp. formerly, for drawing heavy loads along roads or over rough ground. It usually has two large rear wheels and a rope drum for haulage purposes.

trac·tor ('træktə) *n.* **1.** a motor vehicle used to pull heavy loads, esp. farm machinery such as a plough or harvester. It usually has two large rear wheels with deeply treaded tyres. **2.** a short motor vehicle with a powerful engine and a driver's cab, used to pull a trailer, as in an articulated lorry. **3.** an aircraft with its propeller or propellers mounted in front of the engine. [C18: from Late Latin: one who pulls, from *trahere* to drag]

Tra·cy ('treɪsɪ) *n.* **Spen·cer.** 1900–67, U.S. film actor; his films include *The Power and the Glory* (1933), *Adam's Rib* (1949), and *Bad Day at Black Rock* (1955).

trad (træd) *n.* **1.** *Chiefly Brit.* traditional jazz, as revived in the 1950s. ~*adj.* **2.** short for **traditional.**

trade (treɪd) *n.* **1.** the act or an instance of buying and selling goods and services either on the domestic (wholesale and retail) markets or on the international (import, export, and entrepôt) markets. **2.** a personal occupation, esp. a craft requiring skill. **3.** the people and practices of an industry, craft, or business. **4.** exchange of one thing for something else. **5.** the regular clientele of a firm or industry. **6.** amount of custom or commercial dealings; business. **7.** a specified market or business: *the tailoring trade.* **8.** an occupation in commerce, as opposed to a profession. **9.** *Homosexual slang.* a sexual partner or sexual partners collectively. **10.** *Archaic.* a custom or habit. ~*vb.* **11.** (*tr.*) to buy and sell (commercial merchandise). **12.** to exchange (one thing) for another. **13.** (*intr.*) to engage in trade. **14.** (*intr.*) to deal or do business (with): *we trade with them regularly.* ~See also **trade-in, trade on.** [C14 (in the sense: track, hence, a regular business): related to Old Saxon *trada,* Old High German *trata* track; see TREAD] —**'trad+a·ble** *or* **'trade+a·ble** *adj.* —**'trade+less** *adj.*

trade ac+cept+ance *n. Commerce.* an accepted bill of exchange drawn on the purchaser of commodities by the seller.

trade book *or* **e·di+tion** *n.* an ordinary edition of a book sold in the normal way in shops, as opposed to a de luxe or mail-order edition.

trade cy+cle *n.* the recurrent fluctuation between boom and depression in the economic activity of a capitalist country. Also called (esp. U.S.): **business cycle.**

trade dis+count *n.* a sum or percentage deducted from the list price of a commodity allowed by a manufacturer, distributor, or wholesaler to a retailer or by one enterprise to another in the same trade.

trade gap *n.* the amount by which the value of a country's visible imports exceeds that of visible exports; an unfavourable balance of trade.

trade-in *n.* **1. a.** a used article given in part payment for the purchase of a new article. **b.** a transaction involving such part payment. **c.** the valuation put on the article traded in. **d.** (*as modifier*): *a trade-in dealer.* ~*vb.* **trade in. 2.** (*tr., adv.*) to give (a used article) as part payment for the purchase of a new article.

trade jour+nal *n.* a periodical containing new developments, discussions, etc., concerning a trade or profession.

trade-last *n. U.S. informal.* a compliment that one has heard about someone, which one offers to tell to that person in exchange for a compliment heard about oneself.

trade+mark ('treɪd,mɑːk) *n.* **1.** the name or other symbol used to identify the goods produced by a particular manufacturer or distributed by a particular dealer and to distinguish them from products associated with competing manufacturers or dealers. It is officially registered and legally protected. **2.** any distinctive sign or mark of the presence of a person or animal. ~*vb.* (*tr.*) **3.** to label with a trademark. **4.** to register as a trademark.

trade name *n.* **1.** the name used by a trade to refer to a commodity, service, etc. **2.** the name under which a commercial enterprise operates in business.

trade-off *n.* an exchange, esp. as a compromise.

trade on *vb.* (*intr., prep.*) to exploit or take advantage of: *he traded on her endless patience.*

trade plate *n.* a numberplate attached temporarily to a vehicle by a dealer, etc., before the vehicle has been registered.

trad+er ('treɪdə) *n.* **1.** a person who engages in trade; dealer; merchant. **2.** a vessel regularly employed in foreign or coastal trade. **3.** *Stock Exchange, U.S.* a member who operates mainly on his own account rather than for customers' accounts. —**'trad+er+,ship** *n.*

trad+es+can+ti·a (,trædɛs'kænʃɪə) *n.* any plant of the American genus *Tradescantia,* widely cultivated for their striped variegated leaves: family *Commelinaceae.* See also **wandering Jew, spiderwort.** [C18: New Latin, named after John *Tradescant* (1608–62), English botanist]

trade school *n.* a school or teaching unit organized by an industry or large company to provide trade training, apprentice education, and similar courses.

trade se+cret *n.* a secret formula, technique, process, etc., known and used to advantage by only one manufacturer.

trades+man ('treɪdzmən) *n., pl.* **+men. 1.** a man engaged in trade, esp. a retail dealer. **2.** a skilled worker. —**'trades+,wom·an** *fem. n.*

trades+peo·ple ('treɪdz,piːpᵊl) *or* **trades+folk** ('treɪdz,fəʊk) *pl. n. Chiefly Brit.* people engaged in trade, esp. shopkeepers.

Trades Un+ion Con+gress *n.* the major association of British trade unions, which includes all the larger unions. Abbrev.: **T.U.C.**

trade un+ion *or* **trades un+ion** *n.* an association of employees formed to improve their incomes and working conditions by collective bargaining with the employer or employer organizations. —**trade un+ion+ism** *or* **trades un+ion+ism** *n.* —**trade un+ion+ist** *or* **trades un+ion+ist** *n.*

trade wind (wɪnd) *n.* a wind blowing obliquely towards the equator either from the northeast in the N hemisphere or the southeast in the S hemisphere, approximately between latitudes 30° N and S, forming part of the planetary wind system. [C17: from *to blow trade* to blow steadily in one direction, from TRADE in the obsolete sense: a track]

trad+ing es+tate *n. Chiefly Brit.* a large area in which a number of commercial or industrial firms are situated.

trad+ing post *n.* **1.** a general store established by a trader in an unsettled or thinly populated region. **2.** *Stock Exchange.* a booth or location on an exchange floor at which a particular security is traded.

trad+ing stamp *n.* a stamp of stated value given by some retail organizations to customers, according to the value of their purchases and redeemable for articles offered on a premium list.

tra+di+tion (trə'dɪʃən) *n.* **1.** the handing down from generation to generation of the same customs, beliefs, etc., esp. by word of mouth. **2.** the body of customs, thought, practices, etc., belonging to a particular country, people, family, or institution over a relatively long period. **3.** a specific custom or practice of long standing. **4.** *Christianity.* a doctrine or body of doctrines regarded as having been established by Christ or the apostles though not contained in Scripture. **5.** (*often cap.*) *Judaism.* a body of laws regarded as having been handed down from Moses orally and only committed to writing in the 2nd century A.D. **6.** the beliefs and customs of Islam supplementing the Koran, esp. as embodied in the Sunna. **7.** *Law, chiefly Roman and Scot.* the act of formally transferring ownership of movable property; delivery. [C14: from Latin *trāditiō* a handing down, surrender, from *trādere* to give up, transmit, from TRANS- + *dāre* to give] —**tra+'di+tion+less** *adj.* —**tra+'di+tion+ist** *n.*

tra+di+tion+al (trə'dɪʃənᵊl) *adj.* **1.** of, relating to, or being a tradition. **2.** of or relating to the style of jazz originating in New Orleans, characterized by collective improvisation by a front line of trumpet, trombone, and clarinet accompanied by various rhythm instruments. —**tra+di+tion+al+i·ty** (trə,dɪʃə'nælɪtɪ) *n.* —**tra+'di+tion+al+ly** *adv.*

tra+di+tion+al+ism (trə'dɪʃənᵊ,lɪzəm) *n.* **1.** a system of philosophy in which all knowledge is thought to originate in divine revelation and to be perpetuated by tradition. **2.** adherence to tradition, esp. in religion. —**tra+'di+tion+al+ist** *n., adj.* —**tra+,di+tion+al+'is+tic** *adj.*

trad·i+tor ('trædɪtə) *n., pl.* **trad·i+to+res** (,trædɪ'tɔːriːz) *or* **trad·i+tors.** *Early Church.* a Christian who betrayed his fellow Christians at the time of the Roman persecutions. [C15: from Latin: traitor, from *trādere* to hand over]

tra+duce (trə'djuːs) *vb.* (*tr.*) to speak badly or maliciously of. [C16: from Latin *trādūcere* to lead over, transmit, disgrace, from TRANS- + *dūcere* to lead] —**tra+'duce+ment** *n.* —**tra+'duc+er** *n.* —**tra+'duc+i·ble** *adj.* —**tra+'duc+ing+ly** *adv.*

tra+du+cian+ism (trə'djuːʃə,nɪzəm) *n. Theol.* the theory that the soul is transmitted to a child in the act of generation or concomitantly with its body. Compare **creationism.** [C18: from Church Latin *trādūciānus,* from *trādux* transmission; see TRADUCE] —**tra+'du+cian+ist** *or* **tra+'du+cian** *n., adj.* —**tra+,du+cian+'is+tic** *adj.*

Tra+fal+gar (trə'fælgə; *Spanish* ,trafal'ɣar) *n.* **Cape.** a cape on the SW coast of Spain, south of Cádiz: scene of the decisive naval battle (1805) in which the French and Spanish fleets were defeated by the English under Nelson, who was mortally wounded.

traf+fic ('træfɪk) *n.* **1. a.** the vehicles coming and going in a street, town, etc. **b.** (*as modifier*): *traffic lights.* **2.** the movement of vehicles, people, etc., in a particular place or for a particular purpose: *sea traffic.* **3. a.** the business of commercial transportation by land, sea, or air. **b.** the freight, passengers, etc., transported. **4.** (usually foll. by *with*) dealings or business: *have no traffic with that man.* **5.** trade, esp. of an illicit or improper kind: *drug traffic.* **6.** the aggregate volume of messages transmitted through a communications system in a given period. **7.** *Chiefly U.S.* the number of customers patronizing a commercial establishment in a given time period. ~*vb.* **+fics, +fick+ing, +ficked.** (*intr.*) **8.** (often foll. by *in*) to carry on trade or business, esp. of an illicit kind. **9.** (usually foll. by *with*) to have dealings. [C16: from Old French *trafique,* from Old Italian *traffico,* from *trafficare* to engage in trade] —**'traf+fick+er** *n.* —**'traf+fic+less** *adj.*

traf+fi+ca+tor ('træfɪ,keɪtə) *n.* (formerly) an illuminated arm on a motor vehicle that was raised to indicate a left or right turn. Compare **indicator** (sense 3).

traf+fic cir+cle *n.* the U.S. name for **roundabout** (sense 2).

traf+fic court *n. Law.* a magistrates' court dealing with traffic offences.

traf+fic is+land *n.* another name for **island** (sense 2).

traf+fic jam *n.* a number of vehicles so obstructed that they can scarcely move. —**'traf+fic-,jammed** *adj.*

traf+fic light *or* **sig+nal** *n.* one of a set of coloured lights placed at crossroads, junctions, etc., to control the flow of traffic. A red light indicates that traffic must stop and a green light that it may go: usually an amber warning light is added between the red and the green.

traf+fic pat+tern *n.* a pattern of permitted lanes in the air around an airport to which an aircraft is restricted.

traf+fic war+den *n.* a person who is appointed to supervise road traffic and report traffic offences.

trag·a+canth ('trægə,kænθ) *n.* **1.** any of various spiny leguminous plants of the genus *Astragalus,* esp. *A. gummifer,* of Asia, having clusters of white, yellow, or purple flowers, and yielding a substance that is made into a gum. **2.** the gum obtained from any of these plants, used in the manufacture of pills and lozenges and in calico-printing. [C16: from French *tragacante,* from Latin *tragacantha* goat's thorn, from Greek *tragakantha,* from *tragos* goat + *akantha* thorn]

tra+ge·di·an (trə'dʒiːdɪən) *or* (*fem.*) **tra+ge·di+enne** (trə,dʒiːdɪ'ɛn) *n.* **1.** an actor who specializes in tragic roles. **2.** a writer of tragedy.

trag+e·dy ('trædʒɪdɪ) *n., pl.* **·dies. 1.** (esp. in classical and Renaissance drama) a play in which the protagonist, usually a man of importance and outstanding personal qualities, falls to disaster through the combination of a personal failing and circumstances with which he cannot deal. **2.** (in later drama, such as that of Ibsen) a play in which the protagonist is overcome by a combination of social and psychological circumstances. **3.** any dramatic or literary composition dealing with serious or sombre themes and ending with disaster. **4.** (in medieval literature) a literary work in which a great person falls from prosperity to disaster, often through no fault of his own. **5.** the branch of drama dealing with such themes. **6.** the unfortunate aspect of something. **7.** a shocking or sad event; disaster. ~Compare **comedy.** [C14: from Old French *tragédie,* from Latin *tragoedia,* from Greek *tragōidia,* from *tragos* goat + *ōidē* song; perhaps a reference to the goat-satyrs of Peloponnesian plays]

trag·ic ('trædʒɪk) *or* **trag·i·cal** *adj.* **1.** of, relating to, or characteristic of tragedy. **2.** mournful or pitiable: *a tragic face.* —'**trag·i·cal·ly** *adv.* —'**trag·i·cal·ness** *n.*
trag·ic flaw *n.* the failing of character in a tragic hero.
trag·ic i·ro·ny *n.* dramatic irony used to tragic effect.
trag·i·com·e·dy (ˌtrædʒɪ'kɒmɪdɪ) *n., pl.* **·dies. 1. a.** a drama in which aspects of both tragedy and comedy are found. **b.** the dramatic genre of works of this kind. **2.** an event or incident having both comic and tragic aspects. [C16: from French, ultimately from Late Latin *tragicōmoedia;* see TRAGEDY, COMEDY] —ˌ**trag·i·'com·ic** *or* ˌ**trag·i·'com·i·cal** *adj.* —ˌ**trag·i·'com·i·cal·ly** *adv.*
trag·o·pan ('trægəˌpæn) *n.* any pheasant of the genus *Tragopan,* of S and SE Asia, having a brilliant plumage and brightly coloured fleshy processes on the head. [C19: via Latin from Greek, from *tragos* goat + PAN]
tra·gus ('treɪgəs) *n., pl.* **·gi** (-dʒaɪ). **1.** the cartilaginous fleshy projection that partially covers the entrance to the external ear. **2.** any of the hairs that grow just inside this entrance. [C17: from Late Latin, from Greek *tragos* hairy projection of the ear, literally: goat] —'**tra·gal** *adj.*
Tra·herne (trə'hɜːn) *n.* **Thom·as.** 1637–74, English mystical prose writer and poet. His prose works include *Centuries of Meditations,* which was discovered in manuscript in 1896 and published in 1908.
trail (treɪl) *vb.* **1.** to drag, stream, or permit to drag or stream along a surface, esp. the ground: *her skirt trailed; she trailed her skipping rope.* **2.** to make (a track or path) through (a place): *to trail a way; to trail a jungle.* **3.** to chase, follow, or hunt (an animal or person) by following marks or tracks. **4.** (when *intr.,* often foll. by *behind*) to lag or linger behind (a person or thing). **5.** (*intr.*) (esp. of plants) to extend, hang, or droop over or along a surface. **6.** (*tr.*) to tow (a boat, caravan, etc.) behind a motor vehicle. **7.** (*tr.*) to carry (a rifle) at the full length of the right arm in a horizontal position, with the muzzle to the fore. **8.** (*intr.*) to move wearily or slowly: *we trailed through the city.* ~*n.* **9.** a print, mark, or marks made by a person, animal, or object. **10.** the act or an instance of trailing. **11.** the scent left by a moving person or animal that is followed by a hunting animal. **12.** a path, track, or road, esp. one roughly blazed. **13.** something that trails behind or trails in loops or strands. **14.** the part of a towed gun carriage and limber that connects the two when in movement and rests on the ground as a partial support when unlimbered. [C14: from Old French *trailler* to draw, tow, from Vulgar Latin *tragulāre* (unattested), from Latin *trāgula* dragnet, from *trahere* to drag; compare Middle Dutch *traghelen* to drag] —'**trail·ing·ly** *adv.* —'**trail·less** *adj.*
trail a·way *or* **off** *vb.* (*intr., adv.*) to make or become fainter, quieter, or weaker: *his voice trailed off.*
trail·blaz·er ('treɪlˌbleɪzə) *n.* **1.** a leader or pioneer in a particular field. **2.** a person who blazes a trail. —'**trail·ˌblaz·ing** *adj., n.*
trail·er ('treɪlə) *n.* **1.** a road vehicle, usually two-wheeled, towed by a motor vehicle: used for transporting boats, etc. **2.** a series of short extracts from a film, used to advertise it in a cinema or on television. **3.** a person or thing that trails. **4.** the U.S. name for **caravan** (sense 1).
trail·er truck *n.* the U.S. name for **articulated lorry.**
trail·ing ar·bu·tus *n.* a creeping evergreen ericaceous plant, *Epigaea repens,* of E North America, having clusters of fragrant pink or white flowers. Also called: **mayflower.**
trail·ing edge *n.* the rear edge of a propeller blade or aerofoil. Compare **leading edge.**
trail·ing vor·tex drag *n.* drag arising from vortices that occur behind a body moving through a gas or liquid. Former name: **induced drag.**
trail rope *n.* **1.** another name for **dragrope** (sense 2). **2.** a long rope formerly used for various military purposes, esp. to allow a vehicle, horses, or men to pull a gun carriage.
train (treɪn) *vb.* **1.** (*tr.*) to guide or teach (to do something), as by subjecting to various exercises or experiences: *to train a man to fight.* **2.** (*tr.*) to control or guide towards a specific goal: *to train a plant up a wall.* **3.** (*intr.*) to do exercises and prepare for a specific purpose: *the athlete trained for the Olympics.* **4.** (*tr.*) to improve or curb by subjecting to discipline: *to train the mind.* **5.** (*tr.*) to focus or bring to bear (on something): *to train a telescope on the moon.* ~*n.* **6. a.** a line of coaches or wagons coupled together and drawn by a railway locomotive. **b.** (*as modifier*): *a train ferry.* **7.** a sequence or series, as of events, objects, etc.: *a train of disasters.* **8.** a procession of people, vehicles, etc., travelling together, such as one carrying supplies of ammunition or equipment in support of a military operation. **9.** a series of interacting parts through which motion is transmitted: *a train of gears.* **10.** a fuse or line of gunpowder to an explosive charge, etc. **11.** something drawn along, such as the long back section of a dress that trails along the floor behind the wearer. **12.** a retinue or suite. **13.** proper order or course. [C14: from Old French *trahiner,* from Vulgar Latin *tragīnāre* (unattested) to draw; related to Latin *trahere* to drag] —'**train·a·ble** *adj.* —'**train·less** *adj.*
train·band ('treɪnˌbænd) *n.* a company of English militia from the 16th to the 18th century. [C17: altered from *trained band*]
train·bear·er ('treɪnˌbɛərə) *n.* an attendant in a procession who holds up the train of a dignitary's robe.
train·ee (treɪ'niː) *n.* **a.** a person undergoing training. **b.** (*as modifier*): *a trainee journalist.*
train·er ('treɪnə) *n.* **1.** a person who trains athletes in a sport. **2.** a piece of equipment employed in training, such as a simulated aircraft cockpit. **3.** *Horse racing.* a person who schools racehorses and prepares them for racing.
train·ing ('treɪnɪŋ) *n.* **1. a.** the process of bringing a person, etc., to an agreed standard of proficiency, etc., by practice and instruction: *training for the priesthood; physical training.* **b.** (*as modifier*): *training college.* **2. in training. a.** undergoing physical training. **b.** physically fit. **3. out of training.** physically unfit.
train spot·ter *n.* a person who collects the numbers of railway locomotives.
traipse, trapes, *or* **trapse** (treɪps) *Informal.* ~*vb.* **1.** (*intr.*) to walk heavily or tiredly. ~*n.* **2.** a long or tiring walk; trudge. [C16: of unknown origin]
trait (treɪt, treɪ) *n.* **1.** a characteristic feature or quality distinguishing a particular person or thing. **2.** *Rare.* a touch or stroke. [C16: from French, from Old French: a pulling, from Latin *tractus,* from *trahere* to drag]
trai·tor ('treɪtə) *n.* a person who is guilty of treason or treachery, in betraying friends, country, a cause or trust, etc. [C13: from Old French *traitour,* from Latin *trāditor* TRADITOR] —'**trai·tor·ous** *adj.* —'**trai·tor·ous·ly** *adv.* —'**trai·tor·ˌship** *n.* —'**trai·tress** *fem. n.*
Tra·jan ('treɪdʒən) *n.* Latin name *Marcus Ulpius Traianus.* ?53–117 A.D., Roman emperor (98–117). He extended the empire to the east and built many roads, bridges, canals, and towns.
tra·ject (trə'dʒɛkt) *vb.* (*tr.*) *Archaic.* to transport or transmit. [C17: from Latin *trājectus* cast over, from *trāicere* to throw across, from TRANS- + *iacere* to throw] —**tra·'jec·tion** *n.*
tra·jec·to·ry (trə'dʒɛktərɪ, -trɪ) *n., pl.* **·ries. 1.** the path described by an object moving in air or space, esp. the curved path of a projectile. **2.** *Geom.* a curve that cuts a family of curves or surfaces at a constant angle. —**tra·jec·tile** (trə'dʒɛktaɪl) *adj.*
tra-la *or* **tra-la-la** a set of nonsensical syllables used in humming music, esp. for a melody or refrain.
Tra·lee (trə'liː) *n.* a market town in SW Ireland, county town of Kerry, near **Tralee Bay** (an inlet of the Atlantic). Pop.: 12 287 (1971).
tram[1] (træm) *n.* **1.** Also called: **tramcar.** an electrically driven public transport vehicle that runs on rails let into the surface of the road, power usually being taken from an overhead wire. U.S. names: **streetcar, trolley car. 2.** a small vehicle on rails for carrying loads in a mine; tub. [C16 (in the sense: shaft of a cart): probably from Low German *traam* beam; compare Old Norse *thrömr,* Middle Dutch *traem* beam, tooth of a rake] —'**tram·less** *adj.*
tram[2] (træm) *n.* **1.** another name for **trammel** (sense 7). **2.** *Machinery.* a fine adjustment that ensures correct function or alignment. ~*vb.* **trams, tram·ming, trammed. 3.** (*tr.*) to adjust (a mechanism) to a fine degree of accuracy.
tram[3] (træm) *n.* (in weaving) a weft yarn of two or more twisted strands of silk. [C17: from French *trame,* from Latin *trāma;* related to Latin *trāns* across, *trāmes* footpath]
tram·line ('træmˌlaɪn) *n.* **1.** (*often pl.*) Also called: **tramway.** the tracks on which a tram runs. **2.** the route taken by a tram. **3.** (*often pl.*) the outer markings along the sides of a tennis or badminton court. **4.** (*pl.*) a set of guiding principles.
tram·mel ('træməl) *n.* **1.** (*often pl.*) a hindrance to free action or movement. **2.** Also called: **trammel net.** a fishing net in three sections, the two outer nets having a large mesh and the middle one a fine mesh. **3.** *Rare.* a fowling net. **4.** *U.S.* a fetter or shackle, esp. one used in teaching a horse to amble. **5.** a device for drawing ellipses consisting of a flat sheet of metal, plastic, or wood having a cruciform slot in which run two pegs attached to a beam. The free end of the beam describes an ellipse. **6.** (*sometimes pl.*) another name for **beam compass. 7.** Also called: **tram.** a gauge for setting up machines correctly. **8.** a device set in a fireplace to support cooking pots. ~*vb.* **·els, ·el·ling, ·elled** *or U.S.* **·els, ·el·ing, ·eled.** (*tr.*) **9.** to hinder or restrain. **10.** to catch or ensnare. **11.** to produce an accurate setting of (a machine adjustment), as with a trammel. [C14: from Old French *tramail* three-mesh net, from Late Latin *trēmaculum,* from Latin *trēs* three + *macula* hole, mesh in a net] —'**tram·mel·ler** *n.*
tram·mie ('træmɪ) *n. Austral. informal.* the conductor or driver of a tram.
tra·mon·tane (trə'mɒnteɪn) *adj. also* **trans·mon·tane. 1.** being or coming from the far side of the mountains, esp. from the other side of the Alps as seen from Italy. **2.** foreign or barbarous. **3.** (of a wind) blowing down from the mountains. ~*n.* **4.** an inhabitant of a tramontane country. **5.** Also called: **tramontana.** a cold dry wind blowing south or southwest from the mountains in Italy and the W Mediterranean. **6.** *Rare.* a foreigner or barbarian. [C16: from Italian *tramontano,* from Latin *trānsmontānus,* from TRANS- + *montānus,* from *mōns* mountain]
tramp (træmp) *vb.* **1.** (*intr.*) to walk long and far; hike. **2.** to walk heavily or firmly across or through (a place); march or trudge. **3.** (*intr.*) to wander about as a vagabond or tramp. **4.** (*intr.*) to tread or trample. ~*n.* **5.** a person who travels about on foot, usually with no permanent home, living by begging or doing casual work. **6.** a long hard walk; hike. **7.** a heavy or rhythmic step or tread. **8.** the sound of heavy treading. **9.** Also called: **tramp steamer.** a merchant ship that does not run between ports on a regular schedule but carries cargo wherever the shippers desire. **10.** *Slang, chiefly U.S.* a prostitute or promiscuous girl or woman. **11.** an iron plate on the sole of a boot. [C14: probably from Middle Low German *trampen;* compare Gothic *ana-trimpan* to press heavily upon, German

trampen to hitchhike] —**'tramp+er** *n.* —**'tramp+ish** *adj.* —**'tramp+ish+ly** *adv.* —**'tramp+ish+ness** *n.*

tram+ple ('træmpᵊl) *vb.* (when *intr.*, usually foll. by *on, upon*, or *over*) **1.** to stamp or walk roughly (on): *to trample the flowers.* **2.** to encroach (upon) so as to violate or hurt: *to trample on someone's feelings.* ~*n.* **3.** the action or sound of trampling. [C14: frequentative of TRAMP; compare Middle High German *trampeln*] —**'tram+pler** *n.*

tram+po+line ('træmpəlɪn, -ˌliːn) *n.* **1.** a tough canvas sheet suspended by springs or elasticated cords from a frame, used by acrobats, gymnasts, etc. ~*vb.* **2.** (*intr.*) to exercise on a trampoline. [C18: via Spanish from Italian *trampolino*, from *trampoli* stilts, of Germanic origin; compare TRAMPLE] —**'tram+po+lin+er** *or* **'tram+po+lin+ist** *n.*

tram+way ('træmˌweɪ) *n.* **1.** another name for **tramline** (sense 1). **2.** *Brit.* **a.** a public transportation system using trams. **b.** the company owning or running such a system. **3.** Also called (esp. U.S.): **tramroad.** a small or temporary railway for moving freight along tracks, as in a quarry.

trance (trɑːns) *n.* **1.** a hypnotic state resembling sleep. **2.** any mental state in which a person is unaware or apparently unaware of the environment, characterized by loss of voluntary movement, rigidity, and lack of sensitivity to external stimuli. **3.** a dazed or stunned state. **4.** a state of ecstasy or mystic absorption so intense as to cause a temporary loss of consciousness at the earthly level. **5.** *Spiritualism.* a state in which a medium, having temporarily lost consciousness, can supposedly be controlled by an intelligence from without as a means of communication with the dead. ~*vb.* **6.** (*tr.*) to put into or as into a trance. [C14: from Old French *transe*, from *transir* to faint, pass away, from Latin *trānsīre* to go over, from TRANS- + *īre* to go] —**'trance+ˌlike** *adj.*

tran+nie ('trænɪ) *n. Informal, chiefly Brit.* a transistor radio.

tran+quil ('træŋkwɪl) *adj.* calm, peaceful or quiet. [C17: from Latin *tranquillus*] —**'tran+quil+ly** *adv.* —**'tran+quil+ness** *n.*

tran+quil+li+ty *or U.S.* (*sometimes*) **tran+quil+i+ty** (træŋ'kwɪlɪtɪ) *n.* a state of calm or quietude.

tran+quil+lize, tran+quil+lise, *or U.S.* **tran+quil+ize** ('træŋkwɪˌlaɪz) *vb.* to make or become calm or calmer. —**ˌtran+quil+li+'za+tion** *or* **ˌtran+quil+li+'sa+tion** *n.*

tran+quil+liz+er *or* **tran+quil+lis+er** ('træŋkwɪˌlaɪzə) *n.* **1.** a drug that calms a person without affecting clarity of consciousness. **2.** anything that tranquillizes.

trans. *abbrev. for:* **1.** transaction. **2.** transferred. **3.** transitive. **4.** translated. **5.** translator. **6.** transport(ation). **7.** transparent. **8.** transpose. **9.** transverse.

trans- *or sometimes before* s- **tran-** *prefix.* **1.** across, beyond, crossing, on the other side: *transoceanic; trans-Siberian; transatlantic.* **2.** changing thoroughly: *transliterate.* **3.** transcending: *transubstantiation.* **4.** transversely: *transect.* **5.** (*often in italics*) indicating that a chemical compound has a molecular structure in which two identical groups or atoms are on opposite sides of a double bond: *trans*-butadiene. Compare **cis-** (sense 2). [from Latin *trāns* across, through, beyond]

trans+act (træn'zækt) *vb.* to do, conduct, or negotiate (business, a deal, etc.). [C16: from Latin *trānsactus*, from *trānsigere*, literally: to drive through, from TRANS- + *agere* to drive] —**trans+'ac+tor** *n.*

trans+ac+ti+nide (ˌtræns'æktɪˌnaɪd) *n.* any artificially produced element with an atomic number greater than 103. [C20: from TRANS- + ACTINIDE]

trans+ac+tion (træn'zækʃən) *n.* **1.** something that is transacted, esp. a business deal or negotiation. **2.** the act of transacting or the state of being transacted. **3.** (*pl.*) the published records of the proceedings of a society, conference, etc. —**trans+'ac+tion+al** *adj.* —**trans+'ac+tion+al+ly** *adv.*

trans+al+pine (trænz'ælpaɪn) *adj.* (*prenominal*) **1.** situated in or relating to places beyond the Alps, esp. from Italy. **2.** passing over the Alps. ~*n.* **3.** a transalpine person.

Trans+al+pine Gaul *n.* (in the ancient world) that part of Gaul northwest of the Alps.

trans+at+lan+tic (ˌtrænzət'læntɪk) *adj.* **1.** on or from the other side of the Atlantic. **2.** crossing the Atlantic.

trans+ca+lent (træns'keɪlənt) *adj. Rare.* permitting the passage of heat. [C19: TRANS- + *-calent*, from Latin *calēre* to be hot] —**trans+'ca+len+cy** *n.*

Trans+cau+ca+sia (ˌtrænskɔː'keɪzjə) *n.* a region of the SW Soviet Union, south of the Caucasus Mountains between the Black and Caspian Seas: formerly a constituent republic of the Soviet Union, divided in 1936 into the Georgian, Azerbaijan, and Armenian SSRs. —**ˌTrans+cau+'ca+sian** *adj., n.*

trans+ceiv+er (træn'siːvə) *n.* a combined radio transmitter and receiver with certain components and circuits in common but which does not allow simultaneous transmission and reception. [C20: from TRANS(MITTER) + (RE)CEIVER]

trans+cend (træn'sɛnd) *vb.* **1.** to go above or beyond (a limit, expectation, etc.), as in degree or excellence. **2.** (*tr.*) to be superior to. **3.** *Philosophy, theol.* (esp. of the Deity) to exist beyond (the material world). [C14: from Latin *trānscendere* to climb over, from TRANS- + *scandere* to climb] —**trans+'cend+ing+ly** *adv.*

trans+cend+ent (træn'sɛndənt) *adj.* **1.** exceeding or surpassing in degree or excellence. **2. a.** (in the philosophy of Kant) beyond or before experience; a priori. **b.** (of a concept) falling outside a given set of categories. **c.** beyond consciousness or direct apprehension. **3.** *Theol.* (of God) having continuous existence outside the created world. **4.** free from the limitations inherent in matter. ~*n.* **5.** *Philosophy.* a transcendent thing. —**tran+'scend+ence** *n.* —**tran+'scend+en+cy** *n.* —**tran+'scend+ent+ly** *adv.* —**tran+'scend+ent+ness** *n.*

tran+scen+den+tal (ˌtrænsɛn'dɛntᵊl) *adj.* **1.** transcendent, superior, or surpassing. **2.** (in the philosophy of Kant) **a.** (of a judgment or logical deduction) being both synthetic and a priori. **b.** of or relating to knowledge of the presuppositions of thought. **3.** *Philosophy.* beyond our experience of phenomena, although not beyond potential experience. **4.** *Philosophy.* of or relating to those theories that explain knowledge with reference to the process of knowing. **5.** *Theol.* surpassing the natural plane of reality or knowledge; supernatural or mystical. **6.** *Maths.* **a.** (of a number or quantity) real but nonalgebraic; not being a root of any polynomial with rational coefficients such as π or *e*. **b.** (of a function) not capable of expression in terms of a finite number of arithmetical operations, as sin *x*. —**ˌtran+scen+den+'tal+i+ty** *n.* —**ˌtran+scen+'den+tal+ly** *adv.*

tran+scen+den+tal+ism (ˌtrænsɛn'dɛntəˌlɪzəm) *n.* **1. a.** any system of philosophy, esp. that of Kant, holding that the key to reality lies in the critical examination of reason. **b.** any system of philosophy, esp. that of Emerson, that emphasizes intuition as a means to knowledge or the importance of the search for the divine. **2.** vague philosophical speculation. **3.** the state of being transcendental. **4.** something, such as thought or language, that is transcendental. —**ˌtran+scen+'den+tal+ist** *n., adj.*

tran+scen+den+tal med+i+ta+tion *n.* a technique, based on Hindu traditions, for relaxing and refreshing the mind and body through the silent repetition of a mantra.

trans+con+ti+nen+tal (ˌtrænzkɒntɪ'nɛntᵊl) *adj.* **1.** crossing a continent. **2.** on or from the far side of a continent. —**ˌtrans+con+ti+'nen+tal+ly** *adv.*

tran+scribe (træn'skraɪb) *vb.* (*tr.*) **1.** to write, type, or print out fully from speech, notes, etc. **2.** to make a phonetic transcription of. **3.** to transliterate or translate. **4.** to make an electrical recording of (a programme or speech) for a later broadcast. **5.** *Music.* to rewrite (a piece of music) for an instrument or medium other than that originally intended; arrange. **6.** *Computer technol.* **a.** to transfer (information) from one storage device, such as punched cards, to another, such as magnetic tape. **b.** to transfer (information) from a computer to an external storage device. **7.** (*usually passive*) *Biochem.* to convert the genetic information in (a strand of DNA) into a strand of RNA, esp. messenger RNA. See also **genetic code, translate** (sense 6). [C16: from Latin *trānscrībere*, from TRANS- + *scrībere* to write] —**tran+'scrib+a+ble** *adj.* —**tran+'scrib+er** *n.*

tran+script ('trænskrɪpt) *n.* **1.** a written, typed, or printed copy or manuscript made by transcribing. **2.** *Education, chiefly U.S.* an official record of a student's school progress and achievements. **3.** any reproduction or copy. [C13: from Latin *trānscriptum*, from *trānscrībere* to TRANSCRIBE]

tran+scrip+tion (træn'skrɪpʃən) *n.* **1.** the act or an instance of transcribing or the state of being transcribed. **2.** something transcribed. **3.** a representation in writing of the actual pronunciation of a speech sound, word, or piece of continuous text, using not a conventional orthography but a symbol or set of symbols specially designated as standing for corresponding phonetic values. —**tran+'scrip+tion+al** *or* **tran+'scrip+tive** *adj.* —**tran+'scrip+tion+al+ly** *or* **tran+'scrip+tive+ly** *adv.*

trans+cul+tur+a+tion (ˌtrænzkʌltʃʊ'reɪʃən) *n.* the introduction of foreign elements into an established culture.

trans+cur+rent (trænz'kʌrənt) *adj.* running across; transverse.

trans+duc+er (trænz'djuːsə) *n.* any device, such as a microphone or electric motor, that converts one form of energy into another. [C20: from Latin *transducere* to lead across, from TRANS- + *ducere* to lead]

trans+duc+tion (trænz'dʌkʃən) *n. Genetics.* the transfer by a bacteriophage of genetic material from one bacterium to another. [C17: from Latin *trānsductiō*, variant of *trāductiō* a leading along, from *trādūcere* to lead over; see TRADUCE]

tran+sect (træn'sɛkt) *vb.* (*tr.*) to cut or divide crossways. [C17: from Latin TRANS- + *secāre* to cut] —**tran+'sec+tion** *n.*

tran+sept ('trænsɛpt) *n.* either of the two wings of a cruciform church at right angles to the nave. [C16: from Anglo-Latin *trānseptum*, from Latin TRANS- + *saeptum* enclosure] —**tran+'sep+tal** *adj.* —**tran+'sep+tal+ly** *adv.*

trans+e+unt ('trænsɪənt) *or* **tran+si+ent** *adj. Philosophy.* (of a mental act) causing effects outside the mind. Compare **immanent** (sense 2). [C17: from Latin *trānsiēns* going over, from *trānsīre* to pass over; see TRANCE]

transf. *abbrev. for* transferred.

trans+fer *vb.* (træns'fɜː), **+fers, +fer+ring, +ferred. 1.** to change or go or cause to change or go from one thing, person, or point to another: *they transferred from the Park Hotel to the Imperial; she transferred her affections to her dog.* **2.** to change (buses, trains, etc.). **3.** *Law.* to make over (property, etc.) to another; convey. **4.** to displace (a drawing, design, etc.) from one surface to another. **5.** (of a football player, esp. a professional) to change clubs or (of a club, manager, etc.) to sell or release (a player) to another club. **6.** to leave one school, college, etc., and enrol at another. **7.** to change (the meaning of a word, etc.), esp. by metaphorical extension. ~*n.* ('trænsfɜː). **8.** the act, process, or system of transferring, or the state of being transferred. **9. a.** a person or thing that transfers or is transferred. **b.** (*as modifier*): *a transfer student.* **10.** a design or drawing that is transferred from one surface to another, as by ironing a printed design onto cloth. **11.** *Law.* the passing of title to property or other right from one person to another by act of the parties or by operation of law; conveyance. **12.** *Finance.* the act of transferring the title of ownership to shares or registered bonds in the books of the issuing enterprise. **13.** any document or form effecting or regulating a transfer. **14.**

Chiefly U.S. a ticket that allows a passenger to change routes. [C14: from Latin *trānsferre,* from TRANS- + *ferre* to carry] —**trans+'fer·a·ble** *or* **trans+'fer+ra·ble** *adj.* —**,trans+fer+a·'bil+i·ty** *n.*

trans+fer+able vote *n.* a vote that is transferred to a second candidate indicated by the voter if the first is eliminated from the ballot.

trans+fer+ase ('trænsfə,reɪs) *n.* any enzyme that catalyses the transfer of a chemical group from one substance to another.

trans+fer·ee (,trænsfə'ri:) *n.* **1.** *Property law.* a person to whom property is transferred. **2.** a person who is transferred.

trans+fer+ence ('trænsfərəns, -frəns) *n.* **1.** the act or an instance of transferring or the state of being transferred. **2.** *Psychoanal.* the redirection of attitudes and emotions towards a substitute, such as towards the analyst during therapy. —**trans+fer+en+tial** (,trænsfə'rɛnʃəl) *adj.*

trans+fer fee *n.* a sum of money paid by one football club to another for a transferred player.

trans+fer list *n.* a list of football players available for transfer.

trans+fer+or *or* **trans+fer+rer** (træns'fɜ:rə) *n. Property law.* a person who makes a transfer, as of property.

trans+fer pay+ment *n.* (*usually pl.*) money received by an individual or family from the state or other body, often a pension or unemployment benefit. It is not reckoned when calculating the national income as it is money transferred rather than paid for merchandise or a service rendered.

trans+fer+rin (træns'fɜ:rɪn) *n. Biochem.* any of a group of blood glycoproteins that transport iron. Also called: **beta globulin, siderophilin.** [C20: from TRANS- + FERRO- + -IN]

trans+fer RNA *n. Biochem.* any of several soluble forms of RNA of low molecular weight, each of which transports a specific amino acid to a ribosome during protein synthesis. Sometimes shortened to **t-RNA.** Also called: **soluble RNA.** See also **messenger RNA, genetic code.**

trans+fig·u+ra+tion (,træns,fɪgjʊ'reɪʃən) *n.* the act or an instance of transfiguring or the state of being transfigured.

Trans+fig·u+ra+tion (,træns,fɪgjʊ'reɪʃən) *n.* **1.** *New Testament.* the change in the appearance of Christ that took place before three disciples (Matthew 17:1–9). **2.** the Church festival held in commemoration of this on Aug. 6.

trans+fig+ure (træns'fɪgə) *vb.* (*usually tr.*) **1.** to change or cause to change in appearance. **2.** to become or cause to become more exalted. [C13: from Latin *trānsfigūrāre,* from TRANS- + *figūra* appearance] —**trans+'fig+ure+ment** *n.*

trans+fi+nite (træns'faɪnaɪt) *adj.* extending beyond the finite.

trans+fi+nite num+ber *n.* a cardinal or ordinal number used in the comparison of infinite sets for which several types of infinity can be classified: *the set of integers and the set of real numbers have different transfinite numbers.*

trans+fix (træns'fɪks) *vb.* **+fix·es, +fix+ing, +fixed** *or* **+fixt.** (*tr.*) **1.** to render motionless, esp. with horror or shock. **2.** to impale or fix with a sharp weapon or other device. [C16: from Latin *trānsfigere* to pierce through, from TRANS- + *figere* to thrust in] —**trans+fix+ion** (træns'fɪkʃən) *n.*

trans+form *vb.* (træns'fɔ:m). **1.** to alter or be altered radically in form, function, etc. **2.** (*tr.*) to convert (one form of energy) to another form. **3.** (*tr.*) *Maths.* to change the form of (an equation, expression, etc.) by a mathematical transformation. **4.** (*tr.*) to increase or decrease (an alternating current or voltage) using a transformer. ~*n.* ('træns,fɔ:m). **5.** *Maths.* the result of a mathematical transformation. [C14: from Latin *trānsformāre,* from TRANS- + *formāre* to FORM] —**trans+'form+a·ble** *adj.* —**trans+'form·a+tive** *adj.*

trans+for+ma+tion (,trænsfə'meɪʃən) *n.* **1.** a change or alteration, esp. a radical one. **2.** the act of transforming or the state of being transformed. **3.** *Maths.* **a.** a change in position or direction of the reference axes in a coordinate system without an alteration in their relative angle. **b.** a change in an expression or equation resulting from the substitution of one set of variables by another. **4.** *Physics.* a change in an atomic nucleus to a different nuclide as the result of the emission of either an alpha-particle or a beta-particle. Compare **transition** (sense 5). **5.** *Linguistics.* another word for **transformational rule. 6.** an apparently miraculous change in the appearance of a stage set. —**,trans+for+'ma+tion+al** *adj.*

trans+for+ma+tion+al gram+mar *n.* a grammatical description of a language making essential use of transformational rules. Such grammars are usually but not necessarily generative grammars.

trans+for+ma+tion+al rule *n. Generative grammar.* a rule that converts one phrase marker into another. Taken together, these rules, which form the **transformational component** of the grammar, convert the deep structures of sentences into their surface structures.

trans+form+er (træns'fɔ:mə) *n.* **1.** a device that transfers an alternating current from one circuit to one or more other circuits, usually with an increase (**step-up transformer**) or decrease (**step-down transformer**) of voltage. The input current is fed to a primary winding, the output being taken from a secondary winding or windings inductively linked to the primary. **2.** a person or thing that transforms.

trans+form+ism (træns'fɔ:mɪzəm) *n.* a less common word for **evolution,** esp. the theory of evolution. —**trans+'form+ist** *n.*

trans+fuse (træns'fju:z) *vb.* (*tr.*) **1.** to permeate or infuse: *a blush transfused her face.* **2. a.** to inject (blood, etc.) into a blood vessel. **b.** to give a transfusion to (a patient). **3.** *Rare.* to transfer from one vessel to another, esp. by pouring. [C15: from Latin *trānsfundere* to pour out, from TRANS- + *fundere* to pour] —**trans+'fus+er** *n.* —**trans+'fus·i·ble** *or* **trans+'fus+a·ble** *adj.* —**trans+'fu+sive** *adj.*

trans+fu+sion (træns'fju:ʒən) *n.* **1.** the act or an instance of transfusing. **2.** the injection of blood, blood plasma, etc., into the blood vessels of a patient.

trans+gress (trænz'grɛs) *vb.* **1.** to break (a law, etc.). **2.** to go beyond or overstep (a limit). [C16: from Latin *trānsgredī,* from TRANS- + *gradī* to step] —**trans+'gress+i·ble** *adj.* —**trans+'gress+ing+ly** *adv.* —**trans+'gres+sive** *adj.* —**trans+'gres+sive+ly** *adv.* —**trans+'gres+sor** *n.*

trans+gres+sion (trænz'grɛʃən) *n.* **1.** a breach of a law, etc.; sin or crime. **2.** the act or an instance of transgressing.

tran+ship (træn'ʃɪp) *vb.* **+ships, +ship+ping, +shipped.** a variant spelling of **transship.** —**tran+'ship+ment** *n.*

trans+hu+mance (træns'hju:məns) *n.* the seasonal migration of livestock to suitable grazing grounds. [C20: from French, from *transhumer* to change one's pastures, from Spanish *trashumar,* from Latin TRANS- + *humus* ground] —**trans+'hu+mant** *adj.*

tran+si+ent ('trænzɪənt) *adj.* **1.** for a short time only; temporary or transitory. **2.** *Philosophy.* a variant of **transeunt.** ~*n.* **3.** a transient person or thing. **4.** *Physics.* a brief change in the state of a system, such as a sudden short-lived oscillation in the current flowing through a circuit. [C17: from Latin *trānsiēns* going over, from *trānsīre* to pass over, from TRANS- + *īre* to go] —**'tran+si+ent+ly** *adv.* —**'tran+si+ence, 'tran+si+en+cy,** *or* **'tran+si+ent+ness** *n.*

tran+sil·i+ent (træn'sɪlɪənt) *adj.* passing quickly from one thing to another. [C19: from Latin *trānsilīre* to jump over, from TRANS- + *salīre* to leap] —**tran+'sil·i+ence** *n.*

trans+il+lu+mi+nate (,trænzɪ'lu:mɪ,neɪt) *vb.* (*tr.*) *Med.* to pass a light through the wall of (a bodily cavity, membrane, etc.) in order to detect fluid, lesions, etc. —**,trans+il+,lu+mi+'na+tion** *n.* —**,trans+il+'lu+mi+,na+tor** *n.*

tran+sis+tor (træn'zɪstə) *n.* **1.** a semiconductor device, having three or more terminals attached to electrode regions, in which current flowing between two electrodes is controlled by a voltage or current applied to one or more specified electrodes. The device is capable of amplification, etc., and has replaced the valve in most circuits since it is much smaller, more robust, and works at a much lower voltage. See also **junction transistor, field-effect transistor. 2.** *Informal.* a transistor radio. [C20: originally a trademark, from TRANSFER + RESISTOR, referring to the transfer of electric signals across a resistor]

tran+sis+tor+ize *or* **tran+sis+tor+ise** (træn'zɪstə,raɪz) *vb.* **1.** to convert (a system, device, industry, etc.) to the use or manufacture of or operation by transistors and other solid-state components. **2.** to equip (a device or circuit) with transistors and other solid-state components.

trans+it ('trænsɪt, 'trænz-) *n.* **1. a.** the passage or conveyance of goods or people. **b.** (*as modifier*): *a transit visa.* **2.** a change or transition. **3.** a route. **4.** *Astronomy.* **a.** the passage of a celestial body or satellite across the face of a relatively larger body as seen from the earth. **b.** the apparent passage of a celestial body across the meridian, caused by the earth's diurnal rotation. **5. in transit.** while being conveyed; during passage. ~*vb.* **6.** to make a transit through or over (something). **7.** *Astronomy.* to make a transit across (a celestial body or the meridian). **8.** to cause (the telescope of a surveying instrument) to turn over or (of such a telescope) to be turned over in a vertical plane so that it points in the opposite direction. [C15: from Latin *trānsitus* a going over, from *trānsīre* to pass over; see TRANSIENT] —**'tran+sit+a·ble** *adj.*

tran+sit camp *n.* a camp in which refugees, soldiers, etc., live temporarily before moving to another destination.

trans+it in+stru+ment *n.* an astronomical instrument, mounted on an E-W axis, in which the reticle of a telescope is always in the plane of the meridian. It is used to time the transit of a star, etc., across the meridian.

tran+si+tion (træn'zɪʃən) *n.* **1.** change or passage from one state or stage to another. **2.** the period of time during which something changes from one state or stage to another. **3.** *Music.* **a.** a movement from one key to another; modulation. **b.** a linking passage between two divisions in a composition; bridge. **4.** Also called: **transitional.** a style of architecture that was used in western Europe in the late 11th and early 12th century, characterized by late Romanesque forms combined with early Gothic details. **5.** *Physics.* a change in the configuration of an atomic nucleus, involving either a change in energy level resulting from the emission of a gamma-ray photon or a transformation to another element or isotope. **6.** a sentence, passage, etc., that connects a topic to one that follows or that links sections of a written work. [C16: from Latin *transitio;* see TRANSIENT] —**tran+'si+tion+al** *or* **tran+'si+tion·a+ry** *adj.* —**tran+'si+tion+al+ly** *adv.*

tran+si+tion el+e+ment *n. Chem.* any element belonging to one of three series of elements with atomic numbers between 21 and 30, 39 and 48, and 57 and 80. They have an incomplete penultimate electron shell and tend to exhibit more than one valency and to form complexes.

tran+si+tion tem+per+a+ture *n.* the temperature at which a sudden change of physical properties occurs, such as a change of phase, crystalline structure, or conductivity.

tran+si+tive ('trænsɪtɪv) *adj.* **1.** *Grammar.* **a.** denoting an occurrence of a verb when it requires a direct object or denoting a verb that customarily requires a direct object. **b.** (*as n.*): *these verbs are transitives.* **2.** *Grammar.* denoting an adjective, such as *fond,* or a noun, such as *husband,* that requires a noun phrase and cannot be used without some implicit or explicit reference to such a noun phrase. **3.** *Logic.* having the property that if one object bears a relationship to a second object that also bears the same relationship to a third object, then the first object bears this relationship to the third object: *mathematical equality is transitive, since if x = y and y = z then x = z.* ~Compare **intransitive.** [C16: from Late Latin *trānsitīvus,* from Latin *trānsitus* a going over; see TRANSIENT] —**'tran·si·tive·ly** *adv.* —**'tran·si·tive·ness** *or* **,tran·si·'tiv·i·ty** *n.*

tran·si·to·ry ('trænsɪtərɪ, -trɪ) *adj.* of short duration; transient or ephemeral. [C14: from Church Latin *trānsitōrius* passing, from Latin *trānsitus* a crossing over; see TRANSIENT] —**'tran·si·to·ri·ly** *adv.* —**'tran·si·to·ri·ness** *n.*

tran·si·to·ry ac·tion *n. Law.* an action that can be brought in any country regardless of where it originated.

trans·it the·od·o·lite *n.* a theodolite the telescope of which can be rotated completely about its horizontal axis.

Trans-Jor·dan *n.* the former name (1922–49) of **Jordan.** —**,Trans-Jor·'da·ni·an** *adj., n.*

Trans·kei (træn'skaɪ) *n.* a Bantustan in South Africa, in E Cape Province: the largest of South Africa's Bantu Homelands and the first Bantu self-governing territory (1963); became an autonomous state in 1976. Capital: Umtata. Pop.: 1 900 000 (1976 est.). Area: 42 700 sq. km (16 500 sq. miles). —**Trans·'kei·an** *adj., n.*

transl. *abbrev. for:* **1.** translated. **2.** translator.

trans·late (træns'leɪt, trænz-) *vb.* **1.** to express or be capable of being expressed in another language or dialect: *he translated Shakespeare into Afrikaans; his books translate well.* **2.** (*intr.*) to act as translator. **3.** (*tr.*) to express or explain in simple or less technical language. **4.** (*tr.*) to interpret or infer the significance of (gestures, symbols, etc.). **5.** (*tr.*) to transform or convert: *to translate hope into reality.* **6.** (*tr.; usually passive*) *Biochem.* to transform the molecular structure of (messenger RNA) into a polypeptide chain by means of the information stored in the genetic code. See also **transcribe** (sense 7). **7.** to move or carry from one place or position to another. **8.** (*tr.*) **a.** to transfer (a cleric) from one ecclesiastical office to another. **b.** to transfer (a see) from one place to another. **9.** (*tr.*) *R.C. Church.* to transfer (the body or the relics of a saint) from one resting place to another. **10.** (*tr.*) *Theol.* to transfer (a person) from one place or plane of existence to another, as from earth to heaven. **11.** *Physics.* to cause (a body) to move laterally in space without rotation or angular displacement. **12.** (*intr.*) (of an aircraft, missile, etc.) to fly or move from one position to another. **13.** (*tr.*) *Archaic.* to bring to a state of spiritual or emotional ecstasy. [C13: from Latin *trānslātus* transferred, carried over, from *trānsferre* to TRANSFER] —**trans·'lat·a·ble** *adj.* —**,trans·lat·a·'bil·i·ty** *or* **trans·'lat·a·ble·ness** *n.*

trans·la·tion (træns'leɪʃən, trænz-) *n.* **1.** something that is or has been translated, esp. a written text. **2.** the act of translating or the state of being translated. **3.** *Maths.* a transformation in which the origin of a coordinate system is moved to another position so that each axis retains the same direction. —**trans·'la·tion·al** *adj.*

trans·la·tor (træns'leɪtə, trænz-) *n.* a person or machine that translates speech or writing. —**,trans·la·'to·ri·al** *adj.*

trans·lit·er·ate (trænz'lɪtə,reɪt) *vb.* (*tr.*) to transcribe (a word, etc., in one alphabet) into corresponding letters of another alphabet: *the Greek word λογος can be transliterated as "logos".* [C19: TRANS- + *-literate,* from Latin *līttera* LETTER] —**,trans·lit·er·'a·tion** *n.* —**trans·'lit·er,a·tor** *n.*

trans·lo·cate (,trænzləʊ'keɪt) *vb.* (*tr.*) to move; displace.

trans·lo·ca·tion (,trænzləʊ'keɪʃən) *n.* **1.** *Genetics.* the transfer of one part of a chromosome to another part of the same or a different chromosome, resulting in rearrangement of the genes. **2.** *Botany.* the transport of minerals, sugars, etc., in solution within a plant. **3.** a movement from one position or place to another.

trans·lu·cent (trænz'luːsᵊnt) *adj.* allowing light to pass through partially or diffusely; semitransparent. [C16: from Latin *trānslūcēre* to shine through, from TRANS- + *lūcēre* to shine] —**trans·'lu·cence** *or* **trans·'lu·cen·cy** *n.* —**trans·'lu·cent·ly** *adv.*

trans·lu·nar (trænz'luːnə) *or* **trans·lu·nar·y** (trænz'luːnərɪ) *adj.* **1.** lying beyond the moon. Compare **cislunar. 2.** unworldly or ethereal.

trans·ma·rine (,trænzmə'riːn) *adj.* a less common word for **overseas.** [C16: from Latin *trānsmarīnus,* from TRANS- + *marīnus,* from *mare* sea]

trans·mi·grant (trænz'maɪgrənt, 'trænzmɪgrənt) *n.* **1.** an emigrant on the way to the country of immigration. ~*adj.* **2.** passing through from one place or stage to another.

trans·mi·grate (,trænzmaɪ'greɪt) *vb.* (*intr.*) **1.** to move from one place, state, or stage to another. **2.** *Theol.* (of souls) to pass from one body into another at death. —**,trans·mi·'gra·tion** *n.* —**,trans·mi·'gra·tion·al** *adj.* —**trans·'mi·gra·tive** *adj.* —**trans·'mi·gra·tor** *n.* —**trans·'mi·gra·to·ry** *adj.*

trans·mis·sion (trænz'mɪʃən) *n.* **1.** the act or process of transmitting. **2.** something that is transmitted. **3.** the extent to which a body or medium transmits light, sound, or some other form of energy. **4.** the transference of motive force or power. **5.** a system of shafts, gears, torque converters, etc., that transmits power, esp. the arrangement of such parts that transmits the power of the engine to the driving wheels of a motor vehicle. **6.** the act or process of sending a message, picture, or other information from one location to one or more other locations by means of radio waves, electrical signals, light signals, etc. **7.** a radio or television broadcast. [C17: from Latin *trānsmissiō* a sending across; see TRANSMIT] —**trans·'mis·si·ble** *adj.* —**trans·,mis·si·'bil·i·ty** *n.* —**trans·'mis·sive** *adj.* —**trans·'mis·sive·ly** *adv.* —**trans·'mis·sive·ness** *n.*

trans·mis·sion den·si·ty *n. Physics.* a measure of the extent to which a substance transmits light or other electromagnetic radiation, equal to the logarithm to base ten of the reciprocal of the transmittance. Symbol: *τ* Also called: **absorbance.** Former name: **optical density.**

trans·mis·sion line *n.* a coaxial cable, waveguide, or other system of conductors that transfers electrical signals from one location to another. Sometimes shortened to **line.**

trans·mis·siv·i·ty (,trænzmɪ'sɪvɪtɪ) *n. Physics.* a measure of the ability of a material to transmit radiation, equal to the internal transmittance of the material under conditions in which the path of the radiation has unit length.

trans·mit (trænz'mɪt) *vb.* ·**mits,** ·**mit·ting,** ·**mit·ted. 1.** (*tr.*) to pass or cause to go from one place or person to another; transfer. **2.** (*tr.*) to pass on or impart (a disease, infection, etc.). **3.** (*tr.*) to hand down to posterity. **4.** (*tr.; usually passive*) to pass (an inheritable characteristic) from parent to offspring. **5.** to allow the passage of (particles, energy, etc.): *radio waves are transmitted through the atmosphere.* **6. a.** to send out (signals) by means of radio waves or along a transmission line. **b.** to broadcast (a radio or television programme). **7.** (*tr.*) to transfer (a force, motion, power, etc.) from one part of a mechanical system to another. [C14: from Latin *trānsmittere* to send across, from TRANS- + *mittere* to send] —**trans·'mit·ta·ble** *or* **trans·'mit·ti·ble** *adj.* —**trans·'mit·tal** *n.*

trans·mit·tance (trænz'mɪtᵊns) *n.* **1.** the act of transmitting. **2.** Also called: **transmission factor.** *Physics.* a measure of the ability of anything to transmit radiation, equal to the ratio of the transmitted flux to the incident flux; the reciprocal of the opacity. For a plate of material the ratio of the flux leaving the entry surface to that reaching the exit surface is the **internal transmittance.** Symbol: *τ* Compare **reflectance, absorptance.**

trans·mit·tan·cy (trænz'mɪtᵊnsɪ) *n. Physics.* a measure of the extent to which a solution transmits radiation. It is equal to the ratio of the transmittance of the solution to the transmittance of a pure solvent of the same dimensions.

trans·mit·ter (trænz'mɪtə) *n.* **1.** a person or thing that transmits. **2.** the equipment used for generating and amplifying a radio-frequency carrier, modulating the carrier with information, and feeding it to an aerial for transmission. **3.** the microphone in a telephone that converts sound waves into audio-frequency electrical signals. **4.** a device that converts mechanical movements into coded electrical signals transmitted along a telegraph circuit. **5.** *Physiol.* a substance released by nerve endings which transmits impulses across synapses.

trans·mog·ri·fy (trænz'mɒgrɪ,faɪ) *vb.* ·**fies,** ·**fy·ing,** ·**fied.** (*tr.*) *Jocular.* to change or transform into a different shape, esp. a grotesque or bizarre one. [C17: of unknown origin] —**trans·,mog·ri·fi·'ca·tion** *n.*

trans·mon·tane (,trænzmɒn'teɪn) *adj., n.* another word for **tramontane.**

trans·mun·dane (trænz'mʌndeɪn) *adj.* beyond this world or worldly considerations.

trans·mu·ta·tion (,trænzmjuː'teɪʃən) *n.* **1.** the act or an instance of transmuting. **2.** the change of one chemical element into another by a nuclear reaction. **3.** the attempted conversion, by alchemists, of base metals into gold or silver. —**,trans·mu·'ta·tion·al** *or* **trans·'mu·ta·tive** *adj.* —**,trans·mu·'ta·tion·ist** *n., adj.*

trans·mute (trænz'mjuːt) *vb.* (*tr.*) **1.** to change the form, character, or substance of. **2.** to alter (an element, metal, etc.) by alchemy. [C15: via Old French from Latin *trānsmūtāre* to shift, from TRANS- + *mūtāre* to change] —**trans·,mut·a·'bil·i·ty** *n.* —**trans·'mut·a·ble** *adj.* —**trans·'mut·a·bly** *adv.* —**trans·'mut·er** *n.*

trans·na·tion·al (trænz'næʃənəl) *adj.* extending beyond the boundaries, interests, etc., of a single nation.

Trans-New Guin·ea phy·lum *n.* the largest grouping of the non-Austronesian languages of Papua and New Guinea and the surrounding regions. Older term: **New Guinea Macrophylum.**

trans·o·ce·an·ic (,trænz,əʊʃɪ'ænɪk) *adj.* **1.** on or from the other side of an ocean. **2.** crossing an ocean.

tran·som ('trænzəm) *n.* **1.** Also called: **traverse.** a horizontal member across a window. Compare **mullion. 2.** a horizontal member that separates a door from a window over it. **3.** the usual U.S. name for **fanlight. 4.** *Nautical.* **a.** a surface forming the stern of a vessel, either vertical or canted either forwards (**reverse transom**) or aft at the upper side. **b.** any of several transverse beams used for strengthening the stern of a vessel. [C14: earlier *traversayn,* from Old French *traversin,* from TRAVERSE] —**'tran·somed** *adj.*

tran·son·ic (træn'sɒnɪk) *adj.* of or relating to conditions when travelling at or near the speed of sound.

tran·son·ic bar·ri·er *n.* another name for **sound barrier.**

trans·pa·cif·ic (,trænzpə'sɪfɪk) *adj.* **1.** crossing the Pacific. **2.** on or from the other side of the Pacific.

trans·pa·dane ('trænzpə,deɪn, træns'peɪdeɪn) *adj.* (*prenominal*) on or from the far (or north) side of the River Po, as viewed from Rome. Compare **cispadane.** [C17: from Latin *Trānspadānus,* from TRANS- + *Padus* the River Po]

trans·par·en·cy (træns'pærənsɪ) *n., pl.* ·**cies. 1.** Also called: **trans·par·ence.** the state of being transparent. **2.** Also called: **slide.** a positive photograph on a transparent base, usually mounted in a frame or between glass plates. It can be viewed by means of a slide projector.

trans·par·ent (træns'pærənt) *adj.* **1.** permitting the uninterrupted passage of light; clear: *a window is transparent.* **2.** easy to see through, understand, or recognize; obvious. **3.** (of a substance or object) permitting the free passage of electromagnetic radiation: *a substance that is transparent to x-rays.* **4.**

candid, open, or frank. [C15: from Medieval Latin *trānspārēre* to show through, from Latin TRANS- + *pārēre* to appear] —**trans·'par·ent·ly** *adv.* —**trans·'par·ent·ness** *n.*

tran·spic·u·ous (træn'spɪkjʊəs) *adj.* a less common word for **transparent.** [C17: from Medieval Latin *trānspicuus*, from Latin *trānspicere* to look through, from TRANS- + *specere* to look] —**tran·'spic·u·ous·ly** *adv.*

trans·pierce (træns'pɪəs) *vb.* (*tr.*) to pierce through.

tran·spire (træn'spaɪə) *vb.* **1.** (*intr.*) *Informal.* to happen or occur. **2.** (*intr.*) to come to light; be known. **3.** *Physiol.* to give off or exhale (water or vapour) through the skin, a mucous membrane, etc. **4.** (of plants) to lose (water in the form of water vapour), esp. through the stomata of the leaves. [C16: from Medieval Latin *trānspīrāre*, from Latin TRANS- + *spīrāre* to breathe] —**tran·'spir·a·ble** *adj.* —**tran·spi·ra·tion** (ˌtrænspə'reɪʃən) *n.* —**tran·'spir·a·to·ry** *adj.*

Usage. It is often maintained that *transpire* should not be used to mean happen or occur, as in *the event transpired late in the evening,* and that the word is properly used to mean become known, as in *it transpired later that the thief had been caught.* The word is, however, widely used in the first sense, esp. in spoken English.

trans·plant *vb.* (træns'plɑːnt). **1.** (*tr.*) to remove or transfer (esp. a plant) from one place to another. **2.** (*intr.*) to be capable of being transplanted. **3.** *Surgery.* to transfer (an organ or tissue) from one part of the body to another or from one person or animal to another during a grafting or transplant operation. ~*n.* ('trænsˌplɑːnt). **4.** *Surgery.* **a.** the procedure involved in such a transfer. **b.** the organ or tissue transplanted. —**trans·'plant·a·ble** *adj.* —ˌ**trans·plan·'ta·tion** *n.* —**trans·'plant·er** *n.*

trans·po·lar (trænz'pəʊlə) *adj.* crossing a polar region.

tran·spond·er *or* **tran·spon·dor** (træn'spɒndə) *n.* a type of radio or radar transmitter-receiver that transmits signals automatically when it receives predetermined signals. [C20: from TRANSMITTER + RESPONDER]

trans·pon·tine (trænz'pɒntaɪn) *adj.* **1.** on or from the far side of a bridge. **2.** *Archaic.* on or from the south side of the Thames in London. [C19: TRANS- + *-pontine*, from Latin *pōns* bridge]

trans·port *vb.* (træns'pɔːt). (*tr.*) **1.** to carry or cause to go from one place to another, esp. over some distance. **2.** to deport or exile to a penal colony. **3.** (*usually passive*) to have a strong emotional effect on. ~*n.* ('trænsˌpɔːt). **4. a.** the business or system of transporting goods or people. **b.** (*as modifier*): *a modernized transport system.* **5.** *Brit.* freight vehicles generally. **6. a.** a vehicle used to transport goods or people, esp. lorries or ships used to convey troops. **b.** (*as modifier*): *a transport plane.* **7.** the act of transporting or the state of being transported. **8.** ecstasy, rapture, or any powerful emotion. **9.** a convict sentenced to be transported. [C14: from Latin *trānsportāre*, from TRANS- + *portāre* to carry] —**trans·'port·a·ble** *adj.* —ˌ**trans·port·a·'bil·i·ty** *n.* —**trans·'port·ed·ly** *adv.* —**trans·'port·er** *n.* —**trans·'port·ive** *adj.*

trans·por·ta·tion (ˌtrænspɔː'teɪʃən) *n.* **1.** a means or system of transporting. **2.** the act of transporting or the state of being transported. **3.** (esp. formerly) deportation to a penal colony. **4.** *Chiefly U.S.* a ticket or fare.

trans·port ca·fé *n. Brit.* an inexpensive eating place on a main route, used mainly by long-distance lorry drivers.

trans·port·er bridge *n.* a bridge consisting of a moving platform attached to cables, for transporting vehicles, etc., across a body of water.

trans·pose (træns'pəʊz) *vb.* **1.** (*tr.*) to alter the positions of; interchange, as words in a sentence; put into a different order. **2.** *Music.* **a.** to play (notes, music, etc.) in a different key from that originally intended. **b.** to move (a note or series of notes) upwards or downwards in pitch. **3.** (*tr.*) *Maths.* to move (a term) from one side of an equation to the other with a corresponding reversal in sign. ~*n.* **4.** *Maths.* the matrix resulting from interchanging the rows and columns of a given matrix. [C14: from Old French *transposer*, from Latin *trānspōnere* to remove, from TRANS- + *pōnere* to place] —**trans·'pos·a·ble** *adj.* —**trans·ˌpos·a·'bil·i·ty** *n.* —**trans·'pos·al** *n.* —**trans·'pos·er** *n.*

trans·pos·ing in·stru·ment *n.* a musical instrument, esp. a horn or clarinet, pitched in a key other than C major, but whose music is written down as if its basic scale were C major. A piece of music in the key of F intended to be played on a horn pitched in F is therefore written down a fourth lower than an ordinary part in that key and has the same key signature as a part written in C.

trans·po·si·tion (ˌtrænspə'zɪʃən) *n.* **1.** the act of transposing or the state of being transposed. **2.** something transposed. —ˌ**trans·po·'si·tion·al** *or* **trans·pos·i·tive** (træns'pɒsɪtɪv) *adj.*

trans·sex·u·al (trænz'sɛksjʊəl) *n.* **1.** a person who permanently acts the part of and is completely identified with the opposite sex. **2.** a person who has undergone medical and surgical procedures to alter external sexual characteristics to those of the opposite sex.

trans·sex·u·al·ism (trænz'sɛksjʊəˌlɪzəm) *n.* an abnormally strong desire to change sex.

trans·ship (træns'ʃɪp) *or* **tran·ship** *vb.* **·ships, ·ship·ping, ·shipped.** to transfer or be transferred from one vessel or vehicle to another. —**trans·'ship·ment** *or* **tran·'ship·ment** *n.*

Trans-Si·be·ri·an Rail·way *n.* a railway in the S Soviet Union, extending from Chelyabinsk in the Ural Mountains to Vladivostok on the Pacific: constructed between 1891 and 1916, making possible the settlement of sparsely inhabited regions. Length: over 6500 km (4000 miles).

tran·sub·stan·ti·ate (ˌtrænsəb'stænʃɪˌeɪt) *vb.* **1.** (*intr.*) *R.C. theol.* (of the Eucharistic bread and wine) to undergo transubstantiation. **2.** (*tr.*) to change (one substance) into another; transmute. [C16: from Medieval Latin *trānssubstantiāre*, from Latin TRANS- + *substantia* SUBSTANCE] —ˌ**tran·sub·'stan·tial** *adj.* —ˌ**tran·sub·'stan·tial·ly** *adv.*

tran·sub·stan·ti·a·tion (ˌtrænsəbˌstænʃɪ'eɪʃən) *n.* **1.** (esp. in Roman Catholic theology) **a.** the doctrine that the whole substance of the bread and wine changes into the substance of the body and blood of Christ when consecrated in the Eucharist. **b.** the mystical process by which this is believed to take place during consecration. Compare **consubstantiation. 2.** a substantial change; transmutation. —ˌ**tran·sub·ˌstan·ti·'a·tion·al·ist** *n.*

tran·su·date ('trænsʊˌdeɪt) *n.* **1.** *Physiol.* any fluid that passes through a membrane, esp. through the wall of a capillary. **2.** anything that has been transuded.

tran·sude (træn'sjuːd) *vb.* (of a fluid) to ooze or pass through interstices, pores, or small holes. [C17: from New Latin *trānsūdāre*, from Latin TRANS- + *sūdāre* to sweat] —**tran·su·da·tion** (ˌtrænsjʊ'deɪʃən) *n.* —**tran·'su·da·to·ry** *adj.*

trans·u·ran·ic (ˌtrænzjʊ'rænɪk), **trans·u·ra·ni·an** (ˌtrænzjʊ'reɪnɪən), *or* **trans·u·ra·ni·um** *adj.* **1.** (of an element) having an atomic number greater than that of uranium. **2.** of, relating to, or having the behaviour of transuranic elements. [C20: from TRANS- + *uranic*, from URANIUM]

Trans·vaal ('trænzvɑːl) *n.* a province of NE South Africa: colonized by the Boers after the Great Trek (1836); became a British colony in 1902; joined South Africa in 1910; consists mostly of a plateau sloping down from the Drakensberg in the southeast to the Limpopo River in the north; the world's chief gold producer. Capital: Pretoria. Pop.: 6 388 870 (1970). Area: 283 919 sq. km (109 621 sq. miles). —'**Trans·vaal·er** *n.* —**Trans·'vaal·i·an** *adj.*

trans·val·ue (trænz'væljuː) *vb.* **·ues, ·u·ing, ·ued.** (*tr.*) to evaluate by a principle that varies from the accepted standards. —**trans·ˌval·u·'a·tion** *n.* —**trans·'val·u·er** *n.*

trans·ver·sal (trænz'vɜːsᵊl) *n.* **1.** *Geom.* a line intersecting two or more other lines. ~*adj.* **2.** a less common word for **transverse.** —**trans·'ver·sal·ly** *adv.*

trans·verse (trænz'vɜːs) *adj.* **1.** crossing from side to side; athwart; crossways. **2.** *Geom.* denoting the axis that passes through the foci of a hyperbola. **3.** (of a flute, etc.) held almost at right angles to the player's mouth, so that the breath passes over a hole in the side to create a vibrating air column within the tube of the instrument. **4.** *Astronomy.* another word for **tangential** (sense 2). ~*n.* **5.** a transverse piece or object. [C16: from Latin *trānsversus*, from *trānsvertere* to turn across, from TRANS- + *vertere* to turn] —**trans·'verse·ly** *adv.* —**trans·'verse·ness** *n.*

trans·verse co·lon *n. Anatomy.* the part of the large intestine passing transversely in front of the liver and stomach.

trans·verse flute *n.* the normal orchestral flute, as opposed to the recorder (or **fipple flute**).

trans·verse pro·cess *n. Anatomy.* either of the projections that arise from either side of a vertebra and provide articulation for the ribs.

trans·verse wave *n.* a wave, such as an electromagnetic wave, that is propagated in a direction perpendicular to the direction of displacement of the transmitting field or medium. Compare **longitudinal wave.**

trans·ves·tite (trænz'vɛstaɪt) *n.* a person who seeks sexual pleasure from wearing clothes that are normally associated with the opposite sex. [C19: from German *Transvestit*, from TRANS- + Latin *vestītus* clothed, from *vestīre* to clothe] —**trans·'ves·tism** *or* **trans·'ves·ti·tism** *n.*

Tran·syl·va·ni·a (ˌtrænsɪl'veɪnɪə) *n.* a region of central and NW Rumania: belonged to Hungary from the 11th century until 1918; restored finally to Rumania in 1947.

Tran·syl·va·ni·an Alps (ˌtrænsɪl'veɪnɪən) *pl. n.* a mountain range in S Rumania; a SW extension of the Carpathian Mountains. Highest peak: Mount Negoiu, 2548 m (8360 ft.).

trap[1] (træp) *n.* **1.** a mechanical device or enclosed place or pit in which something, esp. an animal, is caught or penned. **2.** any device or plan for tricking a person or thing into being caught unawares. **3.** anything resembling a trap or prison. **4.** a fitting for a pipe in the form of a U-shaped or S-shaped bend that contains standing water to prevent the passage of gases. **5.** any similar device. **6.** a device that hurls clay pigeons into the air to be fired at by trapshooters. **7.** *Greyhound racing.* any one of a line of boxlike stalls in which greyhounds are enclosed before the start of a race. **8.** See **trap door. 9.** a light two-wheeled carriage. **10.** a slang word for **mouth. 11.** *Golf.* an obstacle or hazard, esp. a sand trap. **12.** (*pl.*) *Jazz slang.* percussion instruments. ~*vb.* **traps, trap·ping, trapped. 13.** to catch, take, or pen in a trap; entrap. **14.** (*tr.*) to ensnare by trickery; trick. **15.** (*tr.*) to provide (a pipe) with a trap. **16.** to set traps in (a place), esp. for animals. [Old English *træppe*; related to Middle Low German *trappe*, Medieval Latin *trappa*] —'**trap·ˌlike** *adj.*

trap[2] (træp) *n.* **1.** an obsolete word for **trappings** (sense 2). ~*vb.* **traps, trap·ping, trapped. 2.** (*tr.*; often foll. by *out*) to dress or adorn. [C11: probably from Old French *drap* cloth]

trap[3] (træp) *or* **trap·rock** *n.* **1.** any fine-grained often columnar dark igneous rock, esp. basalt. **2.** any rock in which oil or gas has accumulated. [C18: from Swedish *trappa* stair (from its steplike formation); see TRAP[1]]

trap[4] (træp) *n. Scot. dialect.* a ladder or flight of steps. [C18: probably of Low German origin; compare Dutch *trap* flight of steps]

tra+pan (trəˈpæn) *vb.* **+pans, +pan+ning, +panned,** *n.* a variant spelling of **trepan**[2]. —**tra+ˈpan+ner** *n.*

Tra+pa+ni (*Italian* ˈtraːpani) *n.* a port in S Italy, in NW Sicily: Carthaginian naval base, ceded to the Romans after the First Punic War. Pop.: 69 771 (1971).

trap door *n.* **1.** a door or flap flush with and covering an opening, esp. in a ceiling. **2.** the opening so covered.

trap-door spi+der *n.* any of various American spiders of the family *Ctenizidae* that construct a silk-lined hole in the ground closed by a hinged door of earth and silk.

trapes (treɪps) *vb., n.* a less common spelling of **traipse.**

tra+peze (trəˈpiːz) *n.* **1.** a free-swinging bar attached to two ropes, used by circus acrobats, etc. **2.** a sling like a bosun's chair at one end of a line attached to the masthead of a light racing sailing boat, used in sitting out. [C19: from French *trapèze,* from New Latin; see TRAPEZIUM]

tra+pe·zi+form (trəˈpiːzɪˌfɔːm) *adj. Rare.* shaped like a trapezium: *a trapeziform part.*

tra+pe·zi·um (trəˈpiːzɪəm) *n., pl.* **·zi·ums** *or* **·zi·a** (-zɪə). **1.** *Chiefly Brit.* a quadrilateral having two parallel sides of unequal length. Usual U.S. name: **trapezoid. 2.** *Now chiefly U.S.* a quadrilateral having neither pair of sides parallel. **3.** a small bone of the wrist near the base of the thumb. [C16: via Late Latin from Greek *trapezion,* from *trapeza* table] —**tra+ˈpe·zi·al** *adj.*

tra+pe·zi·us (trəˈpiːzɪəs) *n., pl.* **·us·es.** either of two flat triangular muscles, one covering each side of the back and shoulders, that rotate the shoulder blades. [C18: from New Latin *trapezius (musculus)* trapezium-shaped (muscle)]

tra+pe·zo+he+dron (trəˌpiːzəʊˈhiːdrən) *n., pl.* **+drons** *or* **+dra** (-drə). *Crystallog.* a crystal form in which all the crystal's faces are trapeziums. —**tra+ˌpe·zo+ˈhe+dral** *adj.*

trap+e·zoid (ˈtræpɪˌzɔɪd) *n.* **1.** a quadrilateral having neither pair of sides parallel. **2.** the usual U.S. name for **trapezium. 3.** a small bone of the wrist near the base of the index finger. [C18: from New Latin *trapezoidēs,* from Late Greek *trapezoeidēs* trapezium-shaped, from *trapeza* table]

trap+pe·an (ˈtræpɪən, trəˈpiən) *adj. Rare.* of, relating to, or consisting of igneous rock, esp. a basalt.

trap+per (ˈtræpə) *n.* a person who traps animals, esp. for their furs or skins.

trap+pings (ˈtræpɪŋz) *pl. n.* **1.** superficial additions or adornments: *the trappings of vanity.* **2.** ceremonial harness for a horse or other animal, including bridles, saddles, etc. [C16: from TRAP[2]]

Trap+pist (ˈtræpɪst) *n.* **a.** a member of a branch of the Cistercian order of Christian monks, the **Reformed Cistercians of the Strict Observance,** which originated at La Trappe in France in 1664. They are noted for their rule of silence. **b.** (*as modifier*): *a Trappist monk.*

trap+rock (ˈtræpˌrɒk) *n.* another name for **trap**[3].

traps (træps) *pl. n.* belongings; luggage. [C19: probably shortened from TRAPPINGS]

trap+shoot·ing (ˈtræpˌʃuːtɪŋ) *n.* the sport of shooting at clay pigeons thrown up by a trap. —**ˈtrap+ˌshoot·er** *n.*

tra+pun+to (trəˈpʊntəʊ) *n., pl.* **+tos.** a type of quilting that is only partly padded, in a design. [Italian, from *trapungere* to embroider, from *pungere* to prick (from Latin)]

trash[1] (træʃ) *n.* **1.** foolish ideas or talk; nonsense. **2.** *Chiefly U.S.* useless or unwanted matter or objects. **3.** a literary or artistic production of poor quality. **4.** *Chiefly U.S.* a poor or worthless person or a group of such people. **5.** bits that are broken or lopped off, esp. the trimmings from trees or plants. **6.** the dry remains of sugar cane after the juice has been extracted. **7. poor White trash.** (used derogatorily) the poor White people living in the depressed areas of the southern U.S. ~*vb.* **8.** to remove the outer leaves and branches from (growing plants, esp. sugar cane). [C16: of obscure origin; perhaps related to Norwegian *trask*] —**ˈtrash+er·y** *n.*

trash[2] (træʃ) *Archaic.* ~*vb.* **1.** (*tr.*) to restrain with or as if with a lead. ~*n.* **2.** a lead for a dog. [C17: perhaps from obsolete French *tracier* to track, TRACE[1]]

trash can *n.* a U.S. name for **dustbin.** Also called: **ash can, garbage can.**

trash farm+ing *n. U.S.* cultivation by leaving stubble, etc., on the surface of the soil to serve as a mulch.

trash·y (ˈtræʃɪ) *adj.* **trash·i+er, trash·i+est.** cheap, worthless, or badly made. —**ˈtrash·i+ly** *adv.* —**ˈtrash·i+ness** *n.*

Tra+si+mene (ˈtræzɪˌmiːn) *n.* **Lake.** a lake in central Italy, in Umbria: the largest lake in central Italy; scene of Hannibal's victory over the Romans in 217 B.C. Area: 128 sq. km (49 sq. miles). Italian name: **Trasimeno.** Also called: **(Lake) Perugia.**

trass (træs) *n.* a variety of the volcanic rock tuff, used to make a hydraulic cement. [from Dutch *tras, tarasse,* from Italian *terrazza* worthless earth; see TERRACE]

trat+to+ri+a (ˌtrætəˈrɪə) *n.* an Italian restaurant. [C19: from Italian, from *trattore* innkeeper, from French *traiteur,* from Old French *tretier* to TREAT]

trau+ma (ˈtrɔːmə) *n., pl.* **+ma+ta** (-mətə) *or* **+mas. 1.** *Psychol.* a powerful shock that may have long-lasting effects. **2.** *Pathol.* any bodily injury or wound. [C18: from Greek: a wound] —**trau+mat+ic** (trɔːˈmætɪk) *adj.* —**trau+ˈmat·i·cal+ly** *adv.*

trau+ma+tism (ˈtrɔːməˌtɪzəm) *n.* **1.** any abnormal bodily condition caused by injury, wound, or shock. **2.** (not in technical usage) another name for **trauma** (sense 2).

trau+ma+tize *or* **trau+ma+tise** (ˈtrɔːməˌtaɪz) *vb.* **1.** (*tr.*) to wound or injure (the body). **2.** to subject or be subjected to mental trauma. —**ˌtrau+ma+ti+ˈza+tion** *or* **ˌtrau+ma+ti+ˈsa+tion** *n.*

trav+ail (ˈtræveɪl) *n. Literary.* **1.** painful or excessive labour or exertion. **2.** the pangs of childbirth; labour. ~*vb.* **3.** (*intr.*) to suffer or labour painfully, esp. in childbirth. [C13: from Old French *travaillier,* from Vulgar Latin *tripaliāre* (unattested) to torture, from Late Latin *trepālium* instrument of torture, from Latin *tripālis* having three stakes, from *trēs* three + *pālus* stake]

Trav+an+core (ˌtrævənˈkɔː) *n.* a former princely state of S India which joined with Cochin in 1949 to form **Travancore-Cochin:** part of Kerala state since 1956.

trave (treɪv) *n.* **1.** a stout wooden cage in which difficult horses are shod. **2.** another name for **crossbeam. 3.** a bay formed by crossbeams. [C15: from Old French *trave* beam, from Latin *trabs*]

trav+el (ˈtrævᵊl) *vb.* **+els, +el+ling, +elled** *or U.S.* **+els, +el+ing, +eled.** (*mainly intr.*) **1.** to go, move, or journey from one place to another: *he travels to improve his mind; she travelled across France.* **2.** (*tr.*) to go, move, or journey through or across (an area, region, etc.): *he travelled the country.* **3.** to go, move, or cover a specified or unspecified distance. **4.** to go from place to place as a salesman: *to travel in textiles.* **5.** (esp. of perishable goods) to withstand a journey. **6.** (of light, sound, etc.) to be transmitted or move: *the sound travelled for miles.* **7.** to progress or advance. **8.** *Basketball.* to take an excessive number of steps while holding the ball. **9.** (of part of a mechanism) to move in a fixed predetermined path. **10.** *Informal.* to move rapidly: *that car certainly travels.* **11.** (often foll. by *with*) *Informal.* to be in the company (of); associate. ~*n.* **12. a.** the act of travelling. **b.** (*as modifier*): *a travel brochure.* Related adj.: **itinerant. 13.** (*usually pl.*) a tour or journey. **14.** the distance moved by a mechanical part, such as the stroke of a piston. **15.** movement or passage. [C14 *travaillen* to make a journey, from Old French *travaillier* to TRAVAIL]

trav+el a·gen+cy *or* **bu+reau** *n.* an agency that arranges and negotiates flights, holidays, etc., for travellers. —**trav+el a·gent** *n.*

trav+elled (ˈtrævəld) *adj.* having experienced or undergone much travelling: *a travelled urbane epicure.*

trav+el+ler (ˈtrævələ, ˈtrævlə) *n.* **1.** a person who travels, esp. habitually. **2.** See **travelling salesman. 3.** a part of a mechanism that moves in a fixed course. **4.** *Nautical.* **a.** a thimble fitted to slide freely on a rope, spar, or rod. **b.** the fixed rod on which such a thimble slides.

trav+el+ler's cheque *n.* a cheque in any of various denominations sold by a bank, etc., to the bearer, who signs it on purchase and can cash it by signing it again.

trav+el+ler's joy *n.* a ranunculaceous Old World climbing plant, *Clematis vitalba,* having white flowers and heads of feathery plumed fruits. Also called: **old man's beard.**

trav+el+ling sales+man *n.* a salesman who travels within an assigned territory in order to sell merchandise or to solicit orders for the commercial enterprise he represents by direct personal contact with customers and potential customers. Also called: **commercial traveller, traveller.**

trav+el+ling wave *n.* **a.** a wave carrying energy away from its source. **b.** (*as modifier*): *a travelling-wave aerial.*

trav+e·logue *or U.S.* (*sometimes*) **trav+e·log** (ˈtrævᵊlɒg) *n.* a film, lecture, or brochure on travels and travelling.

trav·el-sick *adj.* nauseous from riding in a moving vehicle. —**ˈtrav·el-ˌsick·ness** *n.*

trav+erse (ˈtrævɜːs, trəˈvɜːs) *vb.* **1.** to pass or go over or back and forth over (something); cross. **2.** (*tr.*) to go against; oppose; obstruct. **3.** to move or cause to move sideways or crossways. **4.** (*tr.*) to extend or reach across. **5.** to turn (an artillery gun) laterally on its pivot or mount or (of an artillery gun) to turn laterally. **6.** (*tr.*) to look over or examine carefully. **7.** (*tr.*) *Law.* to deny (an allegation of fact), as in pleading. **8.** (*intr.*) *Fencing.* to slide one's blade towards an opponent's hilt while applying pressure against his blade. **9.** *Mountaineering.* to move across (a face) horizontally. **10.** (*tr.*) *Nautical.* to brace (a yard) fore and aft. ~*n.* **11.** something being or lying across, such as a transom. **12.** a gallery or loft inside a building that crosses it. **13.** *Maths.* another name for **transversal** (sense 1). **14.** an obstruction or hindrance. **15.** *Fortifications.* a protective bank or other barrier across a trench or rampart. **16.** a railing, screen, or curtain. **17.** the act or an instance of traversing or crossing. **18.** a path or road across. **19.** *Nautical.* the zigzag course of a vessel tacking frequently. **20.** *Law.* the formal denial of a fact alleged in the opposite party's pleading. **21.** *Surveying.* a survey consisting of a series of straight lines, the length of each and the angle between them being measured. **22.** *Mountaineering.* a horizontal move across a face. ~*adj.* **23.** being or lying across; transverse. ~*adv.* **24.** an archaic word for **across.** [C14: from Old French *traverser,* from Late Latin *trānsversāre,* from Latin *trānsversus* TRANSVERSE] —**ˈtra+vers+a·ble** *adj.* —**tra+ˈvers+al** *n.* —**ˈtra+vers+er** *n.*

trav+er+tine *or* **trav+er+tin** (ˈtrævətɪn) *n.* a porous rock consisting of calcium carbonate, used for building. Also called: **calc-sinter.** [C18: from Italian *travertino* (influenced by *tra-* TRANS-), from Latin *lapis Tīburtīnus* Tiburtine stone, from *Tībur*s the district around Tibur (now Tivoli)]

trav+es+ty (ˈtrævɪstɪ) *n., pl.* **+ties. 1.** a farcical or grotesque imitation; mockery; parody. ~*vb.* **+ties, +ty+ing, +tied.** (*tr.*) **2.** to make or be a travesty of. [C17: from French *travesti* disguised, from *travestir* to disguise, from Italian *travestire,* from *tra-* TRANS- + *vestire* to clothe]

tra+vois (trəˈvɔɪ) *n., pl.* **+vois** (-ˈvɔɪz). a sled formerly used by the Plains Indians of North America, consisting of two poles joined by a frame and pulled by an animal. [from Canadian French, from French *travail* TRAVE]

trawl (trɔːl) *Sea fishing.* ~*n.* **1.** Also called: **trawl net.** a large net, usually in the shape of a sock or bag, drawn at deep levels behind special boats (trawlers). **2.** Also called: **trawl line.** a long line to which numerous shorter hooked lines are attached, suspended between buoys. See also **setline, trotline. 3.** the act of trawling. ~*vb.* **4.** to catch or try to catch (fish) with a trawl net or trawl line. **5.** (*tr.*) to drag (a trawl net) or suspend (a trawl line). ~*n., vb. Angling.* **6.** another word for **troll**[1]. [C17: from Middle Dutch *traghelen* to drag, from Latin *trāgula* dragnet; see TRAIL]

trawl+er ('trɔːlə) *n.* **1.** a vessel used for trawling. **2.** a person who trawls.

tray (treɪ) *n.* **1.** a thin flat board or plate of metal, plastic, etc., usually with a raised edge, on which things can be carried. **2.** a shallow receptacle for papers, etc., sometimes forming a drawer in a cabinet or box. [Old English *trieg;* related to Old Swedish *trö* corn measure, Old Norse *treyja* carrier, Greek *driti* tub, German *Trog* TROUGH]

tray+mobile ('treɪˌməʊbiːl) *n. Austral.* an informal word for **trolley.**

treach+er+ous ('trɛtʃərəs) *adj.* **1.** betraying or likely to betray faith or confidence. **2.** unstable, unreliable, or dangerous: *treacherous weather; treacherous ground.* —**'treach+er+ous+ly** *adv.* —**'treach+er+ous+ness** *n.*

treach+er·y ('trɛtʃərɪ) *n., pl.* **+er·ies. 1.** the act or an instance of wilful betrayal. **2.** the disposition to betray. [C13: from Old French *trecherie,* from *trechier* to cheat; compare TRICK]

trea+cle ('triːkᵊl) *n.* **1.** Also called: **black treacle.** *Brit.* a dark viscous syrup obtained during the refining of sugar. **2.** *Brit.* another name for **golden syrup. 3.** anything sweet and cloying. **4.** *Obsolete.* any of various preparations used as an antidote to poisoning. [C14: from Old French *triacle,* from Latin *thēriaca* antidote to poison; see THERIAC] —**'trea+cly** *adj.* —**'trea+cli+ness** *n.*

trea+cle mus+tard *n.* a N temperate cruciferous annual plant, *Erysimum cheiranthoides,* having small yellow flowers. It is a common weed in cultivated ground.

tread (trɛd) *vb.* **treads, tread+ing, trod, trod+den** *or* **trod. 1.** to walk or trample in, on, over, or across (something). **2.** (when *intr.,* foll. by *on*) to crush or squash by or as if by treading: *to tread grapes; to tread on a spider.* **3.** (*intr.;* sometimes foll. by *on*) to subdue or repress, as by doing injury (to): *to tread on one's inferiors.* **4.** (*tr.*) to do by walking or dancing: *to tread a tango.* **5.** (*tr.*) (of a male bird) to copulate with (a female bird). **6. tread lightly.** to proceed with delicacy or tact. **7. tread on someone's toes.** to infringe on his sphere of action, feelings, etc. **8. tread water.** to stay afloat in an upright position by moving the legs in a walking motion. ~*n.* **9.** a manner or style of walking, dancing, etc.: *a light tread.* **10.** the act of treading. **11.** the top surface of a step in a staircase. **12.** the outer part of a tyre or wheel that makes contact with the road, esp. the grooved surface of a pneumatic tyre. **13.** the part of a rail that wheels touch. **14.** the part of a shoe that is generally in contact with the ground. **15.** a rare word for **footprint.** [Old English *tredan;* related to Old Norse *trotha,* Old High German *tretan,* Swedish *träda*] —**'tread+er** *n.*

trea+dle ('trɛdᵊl) *n.* **1. a.** a rocking lever operated by the foot to drive a machine. **b.** (*as modifier*): *a treadle sewing machine.* ~*vb.* **2.** to work (a machine) with a treadle. [Old English *tredel,* from *trǣde* something firm, from *tredan* to TREAD] —**'trea+dler** *n.*

tread+mill ('trɛdˌmɪl) *n.* **1.** Also called: **tread+wheel.** (formerly) an apparatus used to produce rotation, in which the weight of men or animals climbing steps on or around the periphery of a cylinder or wheel caused it to turn. **2.** a dreary round or routine.

treas. *abbrev. for:* **1.** treasurer. **2.** treasury.

trea+son ('triːzᵊn) *n.* **1.** violation or betrayal of the allegiance that a person owes his sovereign or his country, esp. by attempting to overthrow the government; high treason. **2.** any treachery or betrayal. [C13: from Old French *traïson,* from Latin *trāditiō* a handing over; see TRADITION, TRAITOR] —**'trea+son+a+ble** *or* **'trea+son+ous** *adj.* —**'trea+son+a+ble+ness** *n.* —**'trea+son+a+bly** *adv.*

treas+ure ('trɛʒə) *n.* **1.** wealth and riches, usually hoarded, esp. in the form of money, precious metals, or gems. **2.** a thing or person that is highly prized or valued. ~*vb.* (*tr.*) **3.** to prize highly as valuable, rare, or costly. **4.** to store up and save; hoard. [C12: from Old French *tresor,* from Latin *thēsaurus* anything hoarded, from Greek *thēsauros*] —**'treas+ur+a+ble** *adj.* —**'treas+ure+less** *adj.*

treas+ure hunt *n.* a game in which players act upon successive clues and are eventually directed to a prize.

treas+ur+er ('trɛʒərə) *n.* a person appointed to look after the funds of a society, company, city, or other governing body. —**'treas+ur+er+ˌship** *n.*

Treas+ur+er ('trɛʒərə) *n.* (in the Commonwealth of Australia and each of the Australian states) the minister of finance.

treas·ure-trove *n.* **1.** *Law.* any articles, such as coins, bullion, etc., found hidden in the earth or elsewhere and of unknown ownership. **2.** anything similarly discovered that is of value. [C16: from Anglo-French *tresor trové* treasure found, from Old French *tresor* TREASURE + *trover* to find]

treas+ur·y ('trɛʒərɪ) *n., pl.* **+ur·ies. 1.** a storage place for treasure. **2.** the revenues or funds of a government, private organization, or individual. **3.** a place where funds are kept and disbursed. [C13: from Old French *tresorie,* from *tresor* TREASURE]

Treas+ur·y ('trɛʒərɪ) *n.* (in various countries) the government department in charge of finance. In Britain the Treasury is also responsible for economic strategy.

Treas+ur·y Bench *n.* (in Britain) the front bench to the right of the Speaker in the House of Commons, traditionally reserved for members of the Government.

Treas+ur·y bill *n.* a short-term noninterest-bearing obligation issued by the U.S. Treasury, payable to bearer and maturing usually in 91 days, within which it is tradable on a discount basis on the open market.

treas+ur·y bond *n.* a long-term interest-bearing bond issued by the U.S. Treasury.

treas+ur·y cer·tif·i+cate *n.* a short-term obligation issued by the U.S. Treasury, maturing in 12 months with interest payable by coupon redemption.

treas+ur·y note *n.* **1.** a note issued by the U.S. Treasury and generally receivable as legal tender for any debt. **2.** a medium-term interest-bearing obligation issued by the U.S. Treasury, maturing in from one to five years.

treat (triːt) *n.* **1.** a celebration, entertainment, gift, or feast given for or to someone and paid for by another. **2.** any delightful surprise or specially pleasant occasion. **3.** the act of treating. ~*vb.* **4.** (*tr.*) to deal with or regard in a certain manner: *she treats school as a joke.* **5.** (*tr.*) to apply treatment to: *to treat a patient for malaria.* **6.** (*tr.*) to subject to a process or to the application of a substance: *to treat photographic film with developer.* **7.** (often foll. by *to*) to provide (someone) (with) as a treat: *he treated the children to a trip to the zoo.* **8.** (*intr.;* usually foll. by *of*) *Formal.* to deal (with), as in writing or speaking. **9.** (*intr.*) *Formal.* to discuss settlement. [C13: from Old French *tretier,* from Latin *tractāre* to manage, from *trahere* to drag] —**'treat+a·ble** *adj.* —**'treat+er** *n.*

trea+tise ('triːtɪz) *n.* **1.** a formal work on a subject, esp. one that deals systematically with its principles and conclusions. **2.** an obsolete word for **narrative.** [C14: from Anglo-French *tretiz,* from Old French *tretier* to TREAT]

treat+ment ('triːtmənt) *n.* **1.** the application of medicines, surgery, psychotherapy, etc., to a patient or to a disease or symptom. **2.** the manner of handling or dealing with a person or thing, as in a literary or artistic work. **3.** the act, practice, or manner of treating. **4.** *Films.* an expansion of a script into sequence form, indicating camera angles, dialogue, etc. **5. the treatment.** *Slang.* the usual manner of dealing with a particular type of person (esp. in the phrase **give someone the (full) treatment**).

trea+ty ('triːtɪ) *n., pl.* **+ties. 1. a.** a formal agreement or contract between two or more states, such as an alliance or trade arrangement. **b.** the document in which such a contract is written. **2.** any international agreement. **3.** any pact or agreement. **4.** an agreement between two parties concerning the purchase of property at a price privately agreed between them. **5.** *Archaic.* negotiation towards an agreement. **6.** (in Canada) **a.** any of the formal agreements between Indian bands and the federal government by which the Indians surrender their land rights in return for various forms of aid. **b.** (*as modifier*): *treaty Indians; treaty money.* **7.** an obsolete word for **entreaty.** [C14: from Old French *traité,* from Medieval Latin *tractātus* treaty, from Latin: discussion, from *tractāre* to manage; see TREAT] —**'trea+ty+less** *adj.*

trea+ty port *n.* (in China, Japan, and Korea during the last half of the 19th and first half of the 20th centuries) a city, esp. a port, in which foreigners, esp. Westerners, were allowed by treaty to conduct trade.

Treb·i+zond ('trɛbɪˌzɒnd) *n.* a variant spelling of **Trabzon.**

tre+ble ('trɛbᵊl) *adj.* **1.** threefold; triple. **2.** of, relating to, or denoting a soprano voice or part or a high-pitched instrument. ~*n.* **3.** treble the amount, size, etc. **4.** a soprano voice or part or a high-pitched instrument. **5.** the highest register of a musical instrument. **6. a.** the high-frequency gain of an audio amplifier, esp. in a record player or tape recorder. **b.** a control knob on such an instrument by means of which the high-frequency gain can be increased or decreased. **7.** *Change-ringing.* the lightest and highest bell in a ring. **8. a.** the narrow inner ring on a dartboard. **b.** a hit on this ring. ~*vb.* **9.** to make or become three times as much. [C14: from Old French, from Latin *triplus* threefold, TRIPLE] —**'tre+ble+ness** *n.* —**'tre+bly** *adv.*

tre+ble chance *n.* a method of betting in football pools in which the chances of winning are related to the number of draws and the number of home and away wins forecast by the competitor.

tre+ble clef *n. Music.* the clef that establishes G a fifth above middle C as being on the second line of the staff. Symbol: 𝄞

Tre+blin+ka (trɛ'blɪŋkə) *n.* a Nazi concentration camp in central Poland, on the Bug River northeast of Warsaw: chiefly remembered as the place where the Jews of the Warsaw ghetto were put to death.

treb·u·chet ('trɛbjʊˌʃɛt) *or* **tre+buck+et** ('triːbʌkɪt) *n.* a large medieval weapon consisting of a sling on a pivoted wooden arm set in motion by the fall of a weight. [C13: from Old French, from *trebuchier* to stumble, from *tre-* TRANS- + *-buchier,* from *buc* trunk of the body, of Germanic origin; compare Old High German *būh* belly, Old English *buc*]

tre+cen+to (treɪ'tʃɛntəʊ) *n.* the 14th century, esp. with reference to Italian art and literature. [C19: shortened from Italian *mille trecento* one thousand three hundred] —**tre+'cen+tist** *n.*

tree (triː) *n.* **1.** any large woody perennial plant with a distinct trunk giving rise to branches or leaves at some distance from the ground. Related adj.: **arboreal. 2.** any plant that resembles this but has a trunk not made of wood, such as a palm tree. **3.** a wooden post, bar, etc. **4.** See **family tree, shoetree, saddletree. 5.** *Chem.* a treelike crystal growth; dendrite. **6. a.** a branching diagrammatic representation of something, such as the grammatical structure of a sentence. **b.** (*as modifier*): *a tree diagram.* **7.** an archaic word for **gallows. 8.** *Archaic.* the cross on which Christ was crucified. **9. at the top of the tree.** in the highest position of a profession, etc. **10. up a tree.** *U.S. informal.* in a difficult situation; trapped or stumped. ~*vb.* (*tr.*) **11.** to drive or force up a tree. **12.** *U.S. informal.* to force into a difficult situation. **13.** to shape or stretch (a shoe) on a shoetree. [Old English *treo;* related to Old Frisian, Old Norse *trē,* Old Saxon *trio,* Gothic *triu,* Greek *doru* wood, *drus* tree] —**'tree·less** *adj.* —**'tree·less·ness** *n.* —**'tree·,like** *adj.*

Tree (triː) *n.* Sir **Her·bert Beer·bohm.** 1853–1917, English actor and theatre manager; half brother of Max Beerbohm. He was noted for his lavish productions of Shakespeare.

tree creep·er *n.* any small songbird of the family *Certhiidae* of the N hemisphere, having a brown-and-white plumage and slender downward-curving bill. They creep up trees to feed on insects.

tree farm *n.* an area of forest in which the growth of the trees is managed on a commercial basis.

tree fern *n.* any of numerous large tropical ferns, mainly of the family *Cyatheaceae,* having a trunklike stem bearing fronds at the top.

tree frog *n.* **1.** any arboreal frog of the family *Hylidae,* chiefly of SE Asia, Australia, and America. They are strong jumpers and have long toes ending in adhesive discs, which assist in climbing. **2.** any of various other arboreal frogs of different families.

tree heath *n.* another name for **briar**[1] (sense 1).

tree·hop·per ('triː,hɒpə) *n.* any homopterous insect of the family *Membracidae,* which live among trees and other plants and typically have a large hoodlike thoracic process curving backwards over the body.

tree kan·ga·roo *n.* any of several arboreal kangaroos of the genus *Dendrolagus,* of New Guinea and N Australia, having hind and forelegs of a similar length and a long tail.

tree line *n.* another name for **timber line.**

tree mal·low *n.* a malvaceous treelike plant, *Lavatera arborea,* of rocky coastal areas of Europe and N Africa, having a woody stem, rounded leaves, and red-purple flowers.

tre·en ('triːən) *adj.* **1.** made of wood; wooden. ~*n.* **2.** another name for **treenware. 3.** the art of making treenware. [Old English *trēowen,* from *trēow* TREE]

tree·nail, tre·nail ('triːneɪl, 'trɛnᵊl), *or* **trun·nel** ('trʌnᵊl) *n.* a dowel used for pinning planks or timbers together.

tre·en·ware ('triːən,wɛə) *n.* dishes and other household utensils made of wood, as by pioneers in North America.

tree of heav·en *n.* another name for **ailanthus.**

tree of knowl·edge of good and e·vil *n. Old Testament.* the tree in the Garden of Eden bearing the forbidden fruit that Adam and Eve ate, thus incurring loss of primal innocence (Genesis 2:9; 3:2–7).

tree of life *n.* **1.** *Old Testament.* a tree in the Garden of Eden, the fruit of which had the power of conferring eternal life (Genesis 2:9; 3:22). **2.** *New Testament.* a tree in the heavenly Jerusalem, for the healing of the nations (Revelation 22:2).

tree run·ner *n. Austral.* another name for **sittella.**

tree shrew *n.* any of numerous small arboreal prosimian primates of the family *Tupaiidae,* of SE Asia, having large eyes and resembling squirrels.

tree snake *n.* any of various slender arboreal colubrid snakes of the genera *Chlorophis* (**green tree snakes**), *Chrysopelea* (**golden tree snakes**), etc.

tree spar·row *n.* **1.** a small European weaverbird, *Passer montanus,* similar to the house sparrow but having a brown head. **2.** a small North American finch, *Spizella arborea,* having a reddish-brown head, grey underparts, and brown striped back and wings.

tree sur·ger·y *n.* the treatment of damaged trees by filling cavities, applying braces, etc. —**tree sur·geon** *n.*

tree toad *n.* a less common name for **tree frog.**

tref (treɪf) *adj. Judaism.* unclean and not permitted as food. [Yiddish, from Hebrew *terēphāh,* literally: torn (i.e., animal meat torn by beasts), from *tāraf* to tear]

tre·foil ('trɛfɔɪl) *n.* **1.** any of numerous leguminous plants of the temperate genus *Trifolium,* having leaves divided into three leaflets and dense heads of small white, yellow, red, or purple flowers. **2.** any of various related plants having leaves divided into three leaflets, such as bird's-foot trefoil. **3.** a flower or leaf having three lobes. **4.** *Architect.* an ornament in the form of three arcs arranged in a circle. [C14: from Anglo-French *trifoil,* from Latin *trifolium* three-leaved herb, from TRI- + *folium* leaf] —**'tre·foiled** *adj.*

tre·ha·la (trɪ'hɑːlə) *n.* an edible sugary substance obtained from the pupal cocoon of an Asian weevil, *Larinus maculatus.* [C19: from Turkish *tīgāla,* from Persian *tīghāl*]

tre·ha·lose ('triːhə,ləʊs, -,ləʊz) *n.* a white crystalline disaccharide that occurs in yeast and certain fungi. Formula: $C_{12}H_{22}O_{11}$. [C19: from TREHALA]

treil·lage ('treɪlɪdʒ) *n.* latticework; trellis. [C17: from French, from Old French *treille* bower, from Latin *trichila;* see -AGE]

Treitsch·ke (*German* 'traɪtʃkə) *n.* **Hein·rich von** ('haɪnrɪç fɔn). 1834–96, German historian, noted for his highly nationalistic views.

trek (trɛk) *n.* **1.** a long and often difficult journey. **2.** *S. African.* a journey or stage of a journey, esp. a migration by ox wagon. ~*vb.* **treks, trek·king, trekked. 3.** (*intr.*) to make a trek. **4.** (*tr.*) *S. African.* (of an ox, etc.) to draw (a load). [C19: from Afrikaans, from Middle Dutch *trekken* to travel; related to Old Frisian *trekka*] —**'trek·ker** *n.*

trel·lis ('trɛlɪs) *n.* **1.** a structure or pattern of latticework, esp. one used to support climbing plants. **2.** an arch made of latticework. ~*vb.* (*tr.*) **3.** to interweave (strips of wood, etc.) to make a trellis. **4.** to provide or support with a trellis. [C14: from Old French *treliz* fabric of open texture, from Late Latin *trilīcius* woven with three threads, from Latin TRI- + *līcium* thread] —**'trel·lis-,like** *adj.*

trel·lis·work ('trɛlɪs,wɜːk) *n.* **a.** work or patterns of trellis; latticework. **b.** (*as modifier*): *a trelliswork fence.*

trem·a·tode ('trɛmə,təʊd, 'triː-) *n.* any parasitic flatworm of the class *Trematoda,* which includes the flukes. [C19: from New Latin *Trematoda,* from Greek *trēmatōdēs* full of holes, from *trēma* a hole]

trem·ble ('trɛmbᵊl) *vb.* (*intr.*) **1.** to vibrate with short slight movements; quiver. **2.** to shake involuntarily, as with cold or fear; shiver. **3.** to experience fear or anxiety. ~*n.* **4.** the act or an instance of trembling. [C14: from Old French *trembler,* from Medieval Latin *tremulāre,* from Latin *tremulus* quivering, from *tremere* to quake] —**'trem·bler** *n.* —**'trem·bling·ly** *adv.* —**'trem·bly** *adj.*

trem·bles ('trɛmbᵊlz) *n.* **1.** Also called: **milk sickness.** a disease of cattle and sheep characterized by muscular incoordination and tremor, caused by ingestion of white snakeroot or rayless goldenrod. **2.** a nontechnical name for **Parkinson's disease.**

trem·bling pop·lar *n.* another name for **aspen.**

tre·men·dous (trɪ'mɛndəs) *adj.* **1.** vast; huge. **2.** *Informal.* very exciting or unusual. **3.** *Informal.* (intensifier): *a tremendous help.* **4.** *Archaic.* terrible or dreadful. [C17: from Latin *tremendus* terrible, literally: that is to be trembled at, from *tremere* to quake] —**tre·'men·dous·ly** *adv.* —**tre·'men·dous·ness** *n.*

trem·o·lite ('trɛmə,laɪt) *n.* a white or pale green mineral of the amphibole group consisting of calcium magnesium silicate and used as a form of asbestos. Formula: $Ca_2(Mg,Fe)_5Si_8O_{22}(OH)_2$. [C18: from *Tremola,* name of Swiss valley where it was found + -ITE[1]]

trem·o·lo ('trɛmə,ləʊ) *n., pl.* **·los.** *Music.* **1. a.** (in playing the violin, cello, etc.) the rapid repetition of a single note produced by a quick back-and-forth movement of the bow. **b.** the rapid reiteration of two notes usually a third or greater interval apart (**fingered tremolo**). Compare **trill**[1] (sense 1). **2.** (in singing) a fluctuation in pitch. Compare **vibrato. 3.** a vocal ornament of late renaissance music consisting of the increasingly rapid reiteration of a single note. **4.** another word for **tremulant.** [C19: from Italian: quavering, from Medieval Latin *tremulāre* to TREMBLE]

trem·or ('trɛmə) *n.* **1.** an involuntary shudder or vibration, as from illness, fear, shock, etc. **2.** any trembling or quivering movement. **3.** a vibrating or trembling effect, as of sound or light. **4.** Also called: **earth tremor.** a minor earthquake. ~*vb.* (*intr.*) to tremble. [C14: from Latin: a shaking, from *tremere* to tremble, quake] —**'trem·or·less** *adj.* —**'trem·or·less·ly** *adv.* —**'trem·or·ous** *adj.*

trem·u·lant ('trɛmjʊlənt) *n. Music.* **a.** a device on an organ by which the wind stream is made to fluctuate in intensity producing a tremolo effect. **b.** a device on an electrophonic instrument designed to produce a similar effect. [C19: from Medieval Latin *tremulāre* to TREMBLE]

trem·u·lous ('trɛmjʊləs) *adj.* **1.** vibrating slightly; quavering; trembling: *a tremulous voice.* **2.** showing or characterized by fear, anxiety, excitement, etc. [C17: from Latin *tremulus* quivering, from *tremere* to shake] —**'trem·u·lous·ly** *adv.* —**'trem·u·lous·ness** *n.*

tre·nail ('triːneɪl, 'trɛnᵊl) *n.* a variant spelling of **treenail.**

trench (trɛntʃ) *n.* **1.** a deep ditch or furrow. **2.** a ditch dug as a fortification, having a parapet of the excavated earth. ~*vb.* **3.** to make a trench in (a place). **4.** (*tr.*) to fortify with a trench or trenches. **5.** to slash or be slashed. **6.** (*intr.;* foll. by *on* or *upon*) to encroach or verge. [C14: from Old French *trenche* something cut, from *trenchier* to cut, from Latin *truncāre* to cut off]

trench·ant ('trɛntʃənt) *adj.* **1.** keen or incisive: *trenchant criticism.* **2.** vigorous and effective: *a trenchant foreign policy.* **3.** distinctly defined: *a trenchant outline.* **4.** *Archaic or poetic.* sharp: *a trenchant sword.* [C14: from Old French *trenchant* cutting, from *trenchier* to cut; see TRENCH] —**'trench·an·cy** *n.* —**'trench·ant·ly** *adv.*

trench coat *n.* a belted double-breasted waterproof coat of gabardine, etc., resembling a military officer's coat.

trench·er[1] ('trɛntʃə) *n.* **1.** (esp. formerly) a wooden board on which food was served or cut. **2.** Also called: **trencher cap.** another name for **mortarboard** (sense 1). [C14 *trenchour* knife, plate for carving on, from Old French *trencheoir,* from *trenchier* to cut; see TRENCH]

trench·er[2] ('trɛntʃə) *n.* a person or thing that digs trenches.

trench·er·man ('trɛntʃəmən) *n., pl.* **·men. 1.** a person who enjoys food; hearty eater. **2.** *Archaic.* a person who sponges on others; parasite.

trench·es ('trɛntʃɪz) *pl. n.* a system of excavations used for the protection of troops, esp. those (**the Trenches**) used at the front line in World War I.

trench fe·ver *n.* an acute infectious disease characterized by fever and muscular aches and pains, caused by the microorganism *Rickettsia quintana* and transmitted by the bite of a body louse.

trench foot *n.* a form of frostbite affecting the feet of persons standing for long periods in cold water.

trench knife *n.* a double-edged steel knife for close combat.
trench mor·tar *or* **gun** *n.* a portable mortar used to shoot projectiles at a high trajectory over a short range.
trench mouth *n.* a bacterial ulcerative disease characterized by inflammation of the tonsils, gums, etc.
trench war·fare *n.* a type of warfare in which opposing armies face each other in entrenched positions.
trend (trɛnd) *n.* **1.** general tendency or direction. **2.** fashion; mode. ~*vb.* **3.** (*intr.*) to take a certain trend. [Old English *trendan* to turn; related to Middle Low German *trenden*]
trend·y ('trɛndɪ) *Brit. informal, often derogatory.* ~*adj.* **trend·i·er, trend·i·est. 1.** consciously fashionable. ~*n.* **2.** a trendy person. —**'trend·i·ly** *adv.* —**'trend·i·ness** *n.*
Treng·ga·nu (trɛŋ'gɑ:nu:) *n.* a state of Malaysia, on the E Malay Peninsula on the South China Sea: under Thai suzerainty until becoming a British protectorate in 1909; joined the Federation of Malaya in 1948; an isolated forested region; mainly agricultural. Capital: Kuala Trengganu. Pop.: 404 924 (1970). Area: 13 020 sq. km (5027 sq. miles).
Trent (trɛnt) *n.* **1.** a river in central England, rising in Staffordshire and flowing generally northeast into the Humber: the chief river of the Midlands. Length: 270 km (170 miles). **2.** Also: **Trient.** the German name for **Trento.**
trente et qua·rante (*French* trã te ka'rã:t) *n. Cards.* a gambling game played at a table specially marked in red and black for the positioning of the wagers. [C17: French, literally: thirty and forty; referring to the rule that forty is the maximum number that may be dealt and the winning colour is the one closest to thirty-one]
Tren·ti·no-Al·to A·di·ge (trɛn'ti:nəʊ 'ɑ:ltəʊ 'ɑ:dɪ,dʒeɪ) *n.* a region of N Italy: consists of the part of the Tyrol south of the Brenner Pass, ceded by Austria after World War I. Pop.: 839 025 (1971). Area: 13 613 sq. km (5256 sq. miles). Former name (until 1947): **Venezia Tridentina.**
Tren·to (*Italian* 'trɛnto) *n.* a city in N Italy, in Trentino-Alto Adige region on the Adige River: Roman military base; seat of the Council of Trent. Pop.: 91 767 (1971). Latin name: **Tridentum.** German name: **Trent.**
Tren·ton ('trɛntən) *n.* a city in W New Jersey, capital of the state, on the Delaware River: settled by English Quakers in 1679; scene of the defeat of the British by Washington (1776) during the War of American Independence. Pop.: 104 156 (1973 est.).
tre·pan[1] (trɪ'pæn) *n.* **1.** *Surgery.* an instrument resembling a carpenter's brace and bit formerly used to remove circular sections of bone from the skull. Compare **trephine. 2.** a tool for cutting out circular blanks or for making grooves around a fixed centre. **3. a.** the operation of cutting a hole with such a tool. **b.** the hole so produced. ~*vb.* **·pans, ·pan·ning, ·panned.** (*tr.*) **4.** to cut (a hole or groove) with a trepan. **5.** *Surgery.* another word for **trephine.** [C14: from Medieval Latin *trepanum* rotary saw, from Greek *trupanon* auger, from *trupan* to bore, from *trupa* a hole] —**trep·a·na·tion** (,trɛpə'neɪʃən) *n.* —**tre·'pan·ner** *n.*
tre·pan[2] (trɪ'pæn) *or* **tra·pan** (trə'pæn) *Archaic.* ~*vb.* **·pans, ·pan·ning, ·panned.** (*tr.*) **1.** to entice, ensnare, or entrap. **2.** to swindle or cheat. ~*n.* **3.** a person or thing that traps. [C17: of uncertain origin]
tre·pang (trɪ'pæŋ) *n.* any of various large sea cucumbers of tropical Oriental seas, the dried body walls of which are used as food by the Chinese. Also called: **bêche-de-mer.** [C18: from Malay *tĕripang*]
tre·phine (trɪ'fi:n) *n.* **1.** a surgical sawlike instrument for removing circular sections of bone, esp. from the skull. ~*vb.* **2.** (*tr.*) to remove a circular section of bone, esp. from the skull. ~Also called: **trepan.** [C17: from French *tréphine,* from obsolete English *trefine* TREPAN[1], allegedly from Latin *trēs fīnēs* literally: three ends; influenced also by English *trepane* TREPAN[1]] —**treph·i·na·tion** (,trɛfɪ'neɪʃən) *n.*
trep·i·da·tion (,trɛpɪ'deɪʃən) *n.* **1.** a state of fear or anxiety. **2.** a condition of quaking or palpitation, esp. one caused by anxiety. [C17: from Latin *trepidātiō,* from *trepidāre* to be in a state of alarm; compare INTREPID]
trep·o·ne·ma (,trɛpə'ni:mə) *or* **trep·o·neme** ('trɛpəni:m) *n., pl.* **·ne·mas, ·ne·ma·ta** (-mətə), *or* **·nemes.** any anaerobic spirochaete bacterium of the genus *Treponema,* such as *T. pallidum* which causes syphilis. [C19: from New Latin, from Greek *trepein* to turn + *nēma* thread] —**trep·o·nem·a·tous** (,trɛpə'nɛmətəs) *adj.*
tres·pass ('trɛspəs) *vb.* (*intr.*) **1.** (often foll. by *on* or *upon*) to go or intrude (on the property, privacy, or preserves of another) with no right or permission. **2.** *Law.* to commit trespass, esp. to enter wrongfully upon land belonging to another. **3.** *Archaic.* (often foll. by *against*) to sin or transgress. ~*n.* **4.** *Law.* **a.** any unlawful act committed with force or violence, actual or implied, which causes injury to another person, their property or rights. **b.** a wrongful entry upon another's land. **c.** an action to recover damages for such injury or wrongful entry. **5.** an intrusion on another's privacy or preserves. **6.** a sin or offence. [C13: from Old French *trespas* a passage, from *trespasser* to pass through, from *tres-* TRANS- + *passer,* ultimately from Latin *passus* a PACE] —**'tres·pass·er** *n.*
tress (trɛs) *n.* **1.** (*often pl.*) a lock of hair, esp. a long lock of woman's hair. **2.** a plait or braid of hair. ~*vb.* (*tr.*) **3.** to arrange in tresses. [C13: from Old French *trece,* of uncertain origin] —**'tress·y** *adj.*
tressed (trɛst) *adj.* (*in combination*) having a tress or tresses as specified: *gold-tressed; long-tressed.*
tres·sure ('trɛʃə, 'trɛsjʊə) *n. Heraldry.* a narrow inner border on a shield, usually decorated with fleurs-de-lis. [C14: from Old French *tressour,* from *trecier* to plait, from *trece* TRESS] —**'tres·sured** *adj.*
tres·tle ('trɛsᵊl) *n.* **1.** a framework in the form of a horizontal member supported at each end by a pair of splayed legs, used to carry scaffold boards, a table top, etc. **2. a.** a braced structural tower-like framework of timber, metal, or reinforced concrete that is used to support a bridge or ropeway. **b.** a bridge constructed of such frameworks. [C14: from Old French *trestel,* ultimately from Latin *trānstrum* TRANSOM]
tres·tle·tree ('trɛsᵊl,tri:) *n. Nautical.* either of a pair of fore-and-aft timbers fixed horizontally on opposite sides of a lower masthead to support an upper mast.
tres·tle·work ('trɛsᵊl,wɜ:k) *n.* an arrangement of trestles, esp. one that supports or makes a bridge.
tret (trɛt) *n. Commerce.* (formerly) an allowance according to weight granted to purchasers for waste due to transportation. It was calculated after deduction for tare. [C15: from Old French *trait* pull, tilt of the scale; see TRAIT]
tre·val·ly (trɪ'vælɪ) *n. Austral.* any of various marine food and game fishes of the genus *Caranx:* family *Carangidae.* [C19: probably alteration of *cavally;* see CAVALLA]
Tre·vel·yan (trɪ'vɛljən, -'vɪl-) *n.* **1. George Ma·cau·lay.** 1876–1962, English historian, noted for his *English Social History* (1944). **2.** his father, Sir **George Ot·to.** 1838–1928, English historian and biographer. His works include a biography of his uncle Lord Macaulay (1876).
Trèves (trɛ:v) *n.* the French name for **Trier.**
Tre·vi·no (trə'vi:nəʊ) *n.* **Lee.** born 1939, U.S. professional golfer: winner of the U.S. Open Championship (1968; 1971) and the British Open Championship (1971; 1972).
Tre·vi·so (*Italian* tre'vi:zo) *n.* a city in N Italy, in Veneto region: agricultural market centre. Pop.: 90 945 (1971).
trews (tru:z) *pl. n. Chiefly Brit.* close-fitting trousers, now usually for women, originally of tartan cloth and worn by certain Scottish soldiers. [C16: from Scottish Gaelic *triubhas,* from Old French *trebus;* see TROUSERS]
trey (treɪ) *n.* any card or dice throw with three spots. [C14: from Old French *treis* three, from Latin *trēs*]
T.R.H. *abbrev. for* Their Royal Highnesses.
tri- *prefix.* **1.** three or thrice: *triaxial; trigon; trisect.* **2.** occurring every three: *trimonthly.* [from Latin *trēs,* Greek *treis*]
tri·a·ble ('traɪəbᵊl) *adj.* **1. a.** liable to be tried judicially. **b.** subject to examination or determination by a court of law. **2.** *Rare.* able to be tested. —**'tri·a·ble·ness** *n.*
tri·ac·id (traɪ'æsɪd) *adj.* (of a base) capable of reacting with three molecules of a monobasic acid.
tri·ad ('traɪæd) *n.* **1.** a group of three; trio. **2.** *Chem.* an atom, element, group, or ion that has a valency of three. **3.** *Music.* a three-note chord consisting of a note and the third and fifth above it. **4.** an aphoristic literary form used in medieval Welsh and Irish literature. [C16: from Late Latin *trias,* from Greek; related to Greek *treis* three] —**tri·'ad·ic** *adj.* —**'tri·ad·ism** *n.*
Tri·ad ('traɪæd) *n.* any of several Chinese secret societies, esp. one involved in criminal activities, such as drug traffic.
tri·age ('traɪɪdʒ) *n.* the action of sorting (casualties, etc.) according to priority. [C18: from French; see TRY, -AGE]
tri·al[1] ('traɪəl, traɪl) *n.* **1. a.** the act or an instance of trying or proving; test or experiment. **b.** (*as modifier*): *a trial run.* **2.** *Law.* **a.** the judicial examination of the issues in a civil or criminal cause by a competent tribunal and the determination of these issues in accordance with the law of the land. **b.** the determination of an accused person's guilt or innocence after hearing evidence for the prosecution and for the accused and the judicial examination of the issues involved. **c.** (*as modifier*): *trial proceedings.* **3.** an effort or attempt to do something: *we had three trials at the climb.* **4.** trouble or grief. **5.** an annoying or frustrating person or thing. **6.** (*often pl.*) a competition for individuals: *sheepdog trials.* **7.** *Ceramics.* a piece of sample material used for testing the heat of a kiln and its effects. **8. on trial. a.** undergoing trial, esp. before a court of law. **b.** being tested, as before a commitment to purchase. [C16: from Anglo-French, from *trier* to TRY]
tri·al[2] ('traɪəl) *Grammar.* ~*n.* **1.** a grammatical number occurring in some languages for words in contexts where exactly three of their referents are described or referred to. **2.** (*modifier*) relating to or inflected for this number. [C19: from TRI- + -AL[1]]
tri·al and er·ror *n.* a method of discovery, solving problems, etc., based on practical experiment and experience rather than on theory: *he learnt to cook by trial and error.*
tri·al bal·ance *n. Book-keeping.* a statement of all the debit and credit balances in the ledger of a double-entry system, drawn up to test their equality.
tri·al bal·loon *n. U.S.* a tentative action or statement designed to test public opinion on a controversial matter.
tri·al by bat·tle *or* **tri·al by com·bat** *n. English history.* a method of trial introduced after the Norman Conquest. Later extended to civil disputes, the combat was waged before a judge. The parties could often employ champions, but otherwise fought in person.
tri·al court *n. Law.* the first court before which the facts of a case are decided.
tri·an·gle ('traɪ,æŋgᵊl) *n.* **1.** *Geom.* a three-sided polygon that can be classified by angle, as in an acute triangle, or by side, as in an equilateral triangle. Sum of interior angles: 180°; area: ½ base × height. **2.** any object shaped like a triangle. **3.** any situation involving three parties or points of view. See also **eternal triangle. 4.** *Music.* a percussion instrument consisting

of a sonorous metal bar bent into a triangular shape, beaten with a metal stick. **5.** a group of three. [C14: from Latin *triangulum* (n.), from *triangulus* (adj.), from TRI- + *angulus* corner] —**'tri+,an+gled** *adj.*

tri+an+gle of forc·es *n. Physics.* a triangle whose sides represent the magnitudes and directions of three forces in equilibrium.

tri+an+gu+lar (traɪ'æŋgjʊlə) *adj.* **1.** Also: **trigonal.** of, shaped like, or relating to a triangle; having three corners or sides. **2.** of or involving three participants, pieces, or units. **3.** *Maths.* having a base shaped like a triangle. —**tri+an+gu+lar+i·ty** (traɪ,æŋgjʊ'lærɪtɪ) *n.* —**tri+'an+gu+lar+ly** *adv.*

tri+an+gu+late *vb.* (traɪ'æŋgjʊ,leɪt). (*tr.*) **1. a.** to survey by the method of triangulation. **b.** to calculate trigonometrically. **2.** to divide into triangles. **3.** to make triangular. ~*adj.* (traɪ'æŋgjʊlɪt, -,leɪt). **4.** marked with or composed of triangles. —**tri+'an+gu+late+ly** *adv.*

tri+an+gu+la+tion (traɪ,æŋgjʊ'leɪʃən) *n.* **1.** a method of surveying in which an area is divided into triangles, one side (the base line) and all angles of which are measured and the lengths of the other lines calculated trigonometrically. **2.** the network of triangles so formed. **3.** the fixing of an unknown point, as in navigation, by making it one vertex of a triangle, the other two being known.

Tri+an+gu+lum (traɪ'aŋgjʊləm) *n., Latin genitive* **Tri+an+gu+li** (traɪ'æŋgjʊ,laɪ). a small triangular constellation in the N hemisphere, close to Perseus and Aries.

Tri+an+gu+lum Aus+tra+le (ɒ'streɪlɪ) *n., Latin genitive* **Tri+an+gu+li Aus+tra+lis** (ɒ'streɪlɪs). a small bright triangular constellation in the S hemisphere, lying between Ara and the Southern Cross, that contains an open star cluster. [New Latin: southern triangle]

tri+ar+chy ('traɪɑːkɪ) *n., pl.* **+chies. 1.** government by three people; a triumvirate. **2.** a country ruled by three people. **3.** an association of three territories each governed by its own ruler. **4.** any of the three such territories.

Tri+as+sic (traɪ'æsɪk) *adj.* **1.** of, denoting, or formed in the first period of the Mesozoic era that lasted for 45 million years and during which reptiles flourished. ~*n.* **2. the.** Also called: **Trias.** the Triassic period or rock system. [C19: from Latin *trias* triad, with reference to the three subdivisions]

tri+a·tom+ic (,traɪə'tɒmɪk) *adj. Chem.* having three atoms in the molecule. —**,tri+a·'tom+i+cal+ly** *adv.*

tri+ax+i·al (traɪ'æksɪəl) *adj.* having three axes.

tri·a+zine ('traɪə,ziːn, -zɪn; traɪ'æziːn, -ɪn) *or* **tri·a+zin** ('traɪəzɪn, traɪ'æzɪn) *n.* **1.** any of three azines that contain three nitrogen atoms in their molecules. Formula: $C_3H_3N_3$. **2.** any substituted derivative of any of these compounds.

tri·a+zole ('traɪə,zɒl, -,zəʊl; traɪ'æzɒl, -zəʊl) *n.* **1.** any of four heterocyclic compounds having a five-membered ring with the formula $C_2H_3N_3$. **2.** any substituted derivative of any of these compounds. —**tri·a+zol+ic** (,traɪə'zɒlɪk) *adj.*

trib+ade ('trɪbəd) *n.* a lesbian, esp. one who assumes the male role. [C17: from Latin *tribas*, from Greek *tribein* to rub] —**tri+bad+ic** (trɪ'bædɪk) *adj.* —**'trib+ad+ism** *n.*

trib+al+ism ('traɪbə,lɪzəm) *n.* **1.** the state of existing as a separate tribe or tribes. **2.** the customs and beliefs of a tribal society. **3.** loyalty to a tribe or tribal values. —**'trib+al+ist** *n., adj.* —**,trib+al+'ist+ic** *adj.*

tri+ba+sic (traɪ'beɪsɪk) *adj.* **1.** (of an acid) containing three replaceable hydrogen atoms in the molecule. **2.** (of a molecule) containing three monovalent basic atoms or groups in the molecule.

tribe (traɪb) *n.* **1.** a social division of a people, esp. of a preliterate people, defined in terms of common descent, territory, culture, etc. **2.** an ethnic or ancestral division of ancient cultures, esp. of one of the following: **a.** any of the three divisions of the ancient Romans, the Latins, Sabines, and Etruscans. **b.** one of the later political divisions of the Roman people. **c.** any of the 12 divisions of ancient Israel, each of which was named after and believed to be descended from one of the 12 patriarchs. **d.** a phyle of ancient Greece. **3.** *Informal, often jocular.* **a.** a large number of persons, animals, etc. **b.** a specific class or group of persons. **c.** a family, esp. a large one. **4.** *Biology.* a taxonomic group that is a subdivision of a subfamily. **5.** *Stockbreeding.* a strain of animals descended from a common female ancestor through the female line. [C13: from Latin *tribus*; probably related to Latin *trēs* three] —**'trib+al** *adj.* —**'trib+al+ly** *adv.* —**'tribe+less** *adj.*

tribes+man ('traɪbzmən) *n., pl.* **+men.** a member of a tribe.

trib+let ('trɪblɪt) *n.* a spindle or mandrel used in making rings, tubes, etc. [C17: from French *triboulet*, of unknown origin]

tri·bo- *combining form.* indicating friction: *triboelectricity.* [from Greek *tribein* to rub]

tri+bo+e·lec+tric+i·ty (,traɪbəʊɪlɛk'trɪsɪtɪ, -,iːlɛk-) *n.* electricity generated by friction. Also called: **frictional electricity.** —**,tri+bo+e·'lec+tric** *adj.*

tri+bol+o·gy (traɪ'bɒlədʒɪ) *n.* the study of friction, lubrication, and wear between moving surfaces.

tri+bo+lu+mi+nes+cence (,traɪbəʊ,luːmɪ'nɛsəns) *n.* luminescence produced by friction, such as the emission of light when certain crystals are crushed. —**,tri+bo+,lu+mi+'nes+cent** *adj.*

tri+brach[1] ('traɪbræk, 'trɪb-) *n. Prosody.* a metrical foot of three short syllables (˘˘˘). [C16: from Latin *tribrachys*, from Greek *tribrakhus*, from TRI- + *brakhus* short] —**tri+'brach+ic** *or* **tri+'brach+i·al** *adj.*

tri+brach[2] ('trɪbræk) *n. Archaeol.* a three-armed object, esp. a flint implement. [C19: from TRI- + Greek *brakhiōn* arm]

tri+bro+mo+eth·a+nol (traɪ,brəʊməʊ'ɛθə,nɒl) *n.* a soluble white crystalline compound with a slight aromatic odour, used as a general anaesthetic; 2,2,2-tribromoethanol. Formula: CBr_3CH_2OH.

trib·u+la+tion (,trɪbjʊ'leɪʃən) *n.* **1.** a cause of distress. **2.** a state of suffering or distress. [C13: from Old French, from Church Latin *trībulātiō*, from Latin *trībulāre* to afflict, from *trībulum* a threshing board, from *terere* to rub]

tri+bu+nal (traɪ'bjuːnᵊl, trɪ-) *n.* **1.** a court of justice or any place where justice is administered. **2.** (in England) a special court, convened by the government to inquire into a specific matter. **3.** a raised platform containing the seat of a judge or magistrate, originally that in a Roman basilica. [C16: from Latin *tribūnus* TRIBUNE[1]]

trib·u+nate ('trɪbjʊnɪt) *or* **trib+une+ship** *n.* the office or rank of a tribune.

trib+une[1] ('trɪbjuːn) *n.* **1.** (in ancient Rome) **a.** an officer elected by the plebs to protect their interests. Originally there were two of these officers but finally there were ten. **b.** a senior military officer. **2.** a person or institution that upholds public rights; champion. [C14: from Latin *tribunus*, probably from *tribus* TRIBE] —**'trib·u+nar·y** *adj.*

trib+une[2] ('trɪbjuːn) *n.* **1. a.** the apse of a Christian basilica that contains the bishop's throne. **b.** the throne itself. **2.** a gallery or raised area in a church. **3.** *Rare.* a raised platform from which a speaker may address an audience; dais. [C17: via French from Italian *tribuna*, from Medieval Latin *tribūna*, variant of Latin *tribūnal* TRIBUNAL]

trib·u+tar·y ('trɪbjʊtərɪ, -trɪ) *n., pl.* **+tar·ies. 1.** a stream, river, or glacier that feeds another larger one. **2.** a person, nation, or people that pays tribute. ~*adj.* **3.** (of a stream, etc.) feeding a larger stream. **4.** given or owed as a tribute. **5.** paying tribute. —**'trib·u+tar+i+ly** *adv.*

trib+ute ('trɪbjuːt) *n.* **1.** a gift or statement made in acknowledgement, gratitude, or admiration. **2. a.** a payment by one ruler or state to another, usually as an acknowledgment of submission. **b.** any tax levied for such a payment. **3.** (in feudal society) homage or a payment rendered by a vassal to his lord. **4.** the obligation to pay tribute. [C14: from Latin *tribūtum*, from *tribuere* to grant (originally: to distribute among the tribes), from *tribus* TRIBE]

trice[1] (traɪs) *n.* moment; instant (esp. in the phrase **in a trice).** [C15 (in the phrase *at* or *in a trice*, in the sense: at one tug): apparent substantive use of TRICE[2]]

trice[2] (traɪs) *vb.* (*tr.*, often foll. by *up*) *Nautical.* to haul up or secure. [C15: from Middle Dutch *trīsen*, from *trīse* pulley]

tri+cen+ten+ar·y (,traɪsɛn'tiːnərɪ) *or* **tri+cen+ten+ni·al** (,traɪsɛn'tɛnɪəl) *adj.* **1.** of or relating to a period of 300 years. **2.** of or relating to a 300th anniversary or its celebration. ~*n.* **3.** an anniversary of 300 years or its celebration. ~Also: **tercentenary, tercentennial.**

tri+ceps ('traɪsɛps) *n., pl.* **+ceps·es** (-sɛpsɪz) *or* **+ceps.** any muscle having three heads, esp. the one (*triceps brachii*) that extends the forearm. [C16: from Latin, from TRI- + *caput* head]

tri+cer·a+tops (traɪ'sɛrə,tɒps) *n.* any rhinoceros-like herbivorous dinosaur of the ornithischian genus *Triceratops*, of Cretaceous times, having a heavily armoured neck and three horns on the skull. [C19: from New Latin, from TRI- + Greek *kerat-*, *keras* horn + *ōps* eye]

tri+chi·a+sis (trɪ'kaɪəsɪs) *n. Pathol.* **1.** an abnormal position of the eyelashes that causes irritation when they rub against the eyeball. **2.** the presence of hairlike filaments in the urine. [C17: via Late Latin from Greek *trikhiasis*, from *thrix* a hair + -IASIS]

tri+chi+na (trɪ'kaɪnə) *n., pl.* **+nae** (-niː). a parasitic nematode worm, *Trichinella spiralis*, occurring in the intestines of pigs, rats, and man and producing larvae that form cysts in skeletal muscle. [C19: from New Latin, from Greek *trikhinos* relating to hair, from *thrix* a hair]

trich·i+nize *or* **trich·i+nise** ('trɪkɪ,naɪz) *vb.* (*tr.*) to infest (an organism) with trichinae. —**,trich·i+ni+'za+tion** *or* **,trich·i+ni+'sa+tion** *n.*

Trich·i+nop·o+ly (,trɪkɪ'nɒpəlɪ) *n.* another name for **Tiruchirapalli.**

trich·i+no+sis (,trɪkɪ'nəʊsɪs) *n.* a disease characterized by nausea, fever, diarrhoea, and swelling of the muscles, caused by ingestion of pork infected with trichina larvae. Also called: **trich·i+ni·a+sis** (,trɪkɪ'naɪəsɪs). [C19: from New Latin TRICHINA]

trich·i+nous ('trɪkɪnəs) *adj.* **1.** of, relating to, or having trichinosis. **2.** infested with trichinae.

trich+ite ('trɪkaɪt) *n.* **1.** any of various needle-shaped crystals that occur in some glassy volcanic rocks. **2.** *Botany.* any of numerous long slender crystals assumed to be present in a starch grain. —**tri+chit+ic** (trɪ'kɪtɪk) *adj.*

tri+chlo+ride (traɪ'klɔːraɪd) *n.* any compound that contains three chlorine atoms per molecule.

tri+chlo+ro+a·ce·tic ac·id (traɪ,klɔːrəʊə'siːtɪk, -'sɛtɪk) *n.* a corrosive deliquescent crystalline acid with a characteristic odour, used as a veterinary astringent and antiseptic. Formula: CCl_3COOH.

tri+chlo+ro+eth+yl+ene (traɪ,klɔːrəʊ'ɛθɪ,liːn) *or* **tri+chlor+eth+yl+ene** *n.* a volatile nonflammable mobile colourless liquid with an odour resembling that of chloroform. It is a good solvent for certain organic materials and is also an inhalation anaesthetic. Formula $CHCl{:}CCl_2$.

tri+chlo+ro+phe·nox·y+a·ce·tic ac·id (traɪ'klɔːrəʊfə,nɒksɪə'siːtɪk) *n.* an insoluble crystalline solid; 2,4,5-trichlorophenoxyacetic acid. It is a plant hormone and is used as a weedkiller. Formula: $C_8H_5Cl_3O_3$. Also called: **2,4,5-T.**

trich·o- *or before a vowel* **trich-** *combining form.* indicating hair or a part resembling hair: *trichocyst.* [from Greek *thrix* (genitive *thrikhos*) hair]

trich·o·cyst ('trɪkəˌsɪst) *n.* any of various cavities on the surface of some ciliate protozoans, each containing a sensory thread that can be ejected. —ˌ**trich·o·'cys·tic** *adj.*

trich·o·gyne ('trɪkəˌdʒaɪn, -dʒɪn) *n.* a hairlike projection of the female reproductive organs of certain algae, fungi, and lichens, which receives the male gametes before fertilization takes place. —ˌ**trich·o·'gyn·i·al** *or* ˌ**trich·o·'gyn·ic** *adj.*

trich·oid ('trɪkɔɪd) *adj. Zoology.* resembling a hair; hairlike.

tri·chol·o·gy (trɪ'kɒlədʒɪ) *n.* the branch of medicine concerned with the hair and its diseases. —**tri·'chol·o·gist** *n.*

tri·chome ('traɪkəʊm, 'trɪk-) *n.* **1.** any hairlike outgrowth from the surface of a plant. **2.** any of the threadlike structures that make up the filaments of blue-green algae. [C19: from Greek *trikhōma,* from *trikhoun* to cover with hair, from *thrix* a hair] —**tri·chom·ic** (trɪ'kɒmɪk) *adj.*

trich·o·mon·ad (ˌtrɪkəʊ'mɒnæd) *n.* any parasitic protozoan of the genus *Trichomonas,* occurring in the digestive and reproductive systems of man and animals: class *Mastigophora* (or *Flagellata*). —**trich·o·mon·a·dal** (ˌtrɪkəʊ'mɒnədəl) *or* **trich·o·mon·al** (ˌtrɪkə'mɒnᵊl, -'məʊ-; trɪ'kɒmənᵊl) *adj.*

trich·o·mo·ni·a·sis (ˌtrɪkəʊmə'naɪəsɪs) *n.* **1.** inflammation of the vagina characterized by a frothy discharge, caused by infection with parasitic protozoa (*Trichomonas vaginalis*). **2.** any infection caused by parasitic protozoa of the genus *Trichomonas.* [C19: New Latin; see TRICHOMONAD, -IASIS]

tri·chop·ter·an (traɪ'kɒptərən) *n.* **1.** any insect of the order *Trichoptera,* which comprises the caddis flies. ~*adj.* **2.** Also: **tri·chop·ter·ous** (trɪ'kɒptərəs). of, relating to, or belonging to the order *Trichoptera.* [C19: from New Latin *Trichoptera,* literally: having hairy wings, from Greek *thrix* a hair + *pteron* wing]

tri·cho·sis (trɪ'kəʊsɪs) *n.* any abnormal condition or disease of the hair. [C19: via New Latin from Greek *trikhōsis* growth of hair]

tri·chot·o·my (traɪ'kɒtəmɪ) *n., pl.* **·mies. 1.** division into three categories. **2.** *Theol.* the division of man into body, spirit, and soul. [C17: probably from New Latin *trichotomia,* from Greek *trikhotomein* to divide into three, from *trikha* triple + *temnein* to cut] —**trich·o·tom·ic** (ˌtrɪkə'tɒmɪk) *or* **tri·'chot·o·mous** *adj.* —**tri·'chot·o·mous·ly** *adv.*

tri·chro·ism ('traɪkrəʊˌɪzəm) *n.* a property of biaxial crystals as a result of which they show a perceptible difference in colour when viewed along three different axes. See **pleochroism.** [C19: from Greek *trikhroos* three-coloured, from TRI- + *khrōma* colour] —**tri·'chro·ic** *adj.*

tri·chro·mat ('traɪkrəʊˌmæt) *n.* any person with normal colour vision, who can therefore see the three primary colours.

tri·chro·mat·ic (ˌtraɪkrəʊ'mætɪk) *or* **tri·chro·mic** (traɪ'krəʊmɪk) *adj.* **1.** *Photog., printing.* involving the combination of three primary colours in the production of any colour. **2.** of, relating to, or having normal colour vision. **3.** having or involving three colours.

tri·chro·ma·tism (traɪ'krəʊməˌtɪzəm) *n.* **1.** the use or combination of three primary colours for colour reproduction in photography, printing, television, etc. **2.** *Rare.* the state of being trichromatic.

trick (trɪk) *n.* **1.** a deceitful, cunning, or underhand action or plan. **2. a.** a mischievous, malicious, or humorous action or plan; joke: *the boys are up to their tricks again.* **b.** (*as modifier*): *a trick spider.* **3.** an illusory or magical feat or device. **4.** a simple feat learned by an animal or person. **5.** an adroit or ingenious device; knack: *a trick of the trade.* **6.** a behavioural trait, habit, or mannerism. **7.** a turn or round of duty or work. **8.** *Cards.* **a.** a batch of cards containing one from each player, usually played in turn and won by the player or side that plays the card with the highest value. **b.** a card that can potentially win a trick. **9. do the trick.** *Informal.* to produce the right or desired result. **10. how's tricks?** *Slang.* how are you? ~*vb.* **11.** to defraud, deceive, or cheat (someone), esp. by means of a trick. [C15: from Old Northern French *trique,* from *trikier* to deceive, from Old French *trichier,* ultimately from Latin *trīcārī* to play tricks] —**'trick·er** *n.* —**'trick·ing·ly** *adv.* —**'trick·less** *adj.*

trick·er·y ('trɪkərɪ) *n., pl.* **·er·ies.** the practice or an instance of using tricks: *he obtained the money by trickery.*

trick·le ('trɪkᵊl) *vb.* **1.** to run or cause to run in thin or slow streams: *she trickled the sand through her fingers.* **2.** (*intr.*) to move, go, or pass gradually: *the crowd trickled away.* ~*n.* **3.** a thin, irregular, or slow flow of something. **4.** the act of trickling. [C14: perhaps of imitative origin] —**'trick·ling·ly** *adv.* —**'trick·ly** *adj.*

trick·le charg·er *n.* a small mains-operated battery charger, esp. one that delivers less than 5 amperes and is used by car owners.

trick out *or* **up** *vb. (tr., adv.)* to dress up; deck out: *tricked out in frilly dresses.*

trick·ster ('trɪkstə) *n.* a person who deceives or plays tricks.

trick·sy ('trɪksɪ) *adj.* **·si·er, ·si·est. 1.** playing tricks habitually; mischievous. **2.** crafty or difficult to deal with. **3.** *Archaic.* well-dressed; spruce; smart. —**'trick·si·ness** *n.*

trick·track ('trɪkˌtræk) *n.* a variant spelling of **trictrac.**

trick·y ('trɪkɪ) *adj.* **trick·i·er, trick·i·est. 1.** involving snags or difficulties: *a tricky job.* **2.** needing careful and tactful handling: *a tricky situation.* **3.** characterized by tricks; sly; wily: *a tricky dealer.* —**'trick·i·ly** *adv.* —**'trick·i·ness** *n.*

tri·clin·ic (traɪ'klɪnɪk) *adj.* relating to or belonging to the crystal system characterized by three unequal axes, no pair of which are perpendicular. Also: **anorthic.**

tri·clin·i·um (traɪ'klɪnɪəm) *n., pl.* **·i·a** (-ɪə). (in ancient Rome) **1.** an arrangement of three couches around a table for reclining upon while dining. **2.** a dining room, esp. one containing such an arrangement of couches. [C17: from Latin, from Greek *triklinion,* from TRI- + *klinē* a couch]

tri·col·our *or U.S.* **tri·col·or** ('trɪkələ, 'traɪˌkʌlə) *adj. also* **tri·col·oured** *or U.S.* **tri·col·ored** ('traɪˌkʌləd). **1.** having or involving three colours. ~*n.* **2.** (*often cap.*) the French national flag, having three equal vertical stripes in blue, white, and red. **3.** any flag, badge, ribbon, etc., with three colours.

tri·corn ('traɪˌkɔːn) *n. also* **tri·corne. 1.** a cocked hat with opposing brims turned back and caught in three places. **2.** an imaginary animal having three horns. ~*adj. also* **tri·cor·nered. 3.** having three horns or corners. [C18: from Latin *tricornis,* from TRI- + *cornu* HORN]

tri·cos·tate (traɪ'kɒsteɪt) *adj. Biology.* having three ribs or riblike parts: *tricostate leaves.*

tri·cot ('trɪkəʊ, 'triː-) *n.* **1.** a thin rayon or nylon fabric knitted or resembling knitting, used for dresses, etc. **2.** a type of ribbed dress fabric. [C19: from French, from *tricoter* to knit, of unknown origin]

tri·co·tine (ˌtrɪkə'tiːn, ˌtriː-) *n.* a twill-weave woollen fabric resembling gabardine. [C20: from French; see TRICOT]

tri·crot·ic (traɪ'krɒtɪk) *adj. Physiol.* (of the pulse) having a tracing characterized by three elevations with each beat. [C19: from Greek *trikrotos* having three beats, from TRI- + *krotos* a beat] —**tri·crot·ism** ('traɪkrəˌtɪzəm, 'trɪk-) *n.*

tric·trac *or* **trick·track** ('trɪkˌtræk) *n.* a game similar to backgammon. [C17: from French, imitative]

tri·cus·pid (traɪ'kʌspɪd) *Anatomy.* ~*adj. also* **tri·cus·pi·dal. 1. a.** having three points, cusps, or segments: *a tricuspid tooth; a tricuspid valve.* **b.** of or relating to such a tooth or valve. ~*n.* **2.** a tooth having three cusps.

tri·cy·cle ('traɪsɪkᵊl) *n.* **1.** a three-wheeled cycle, esp. one driven by pedals. **2.** a three-wheeler for invalids. ~*vb.* **3.** (*intr.*) to ride a tricycle. —**'tri·cy·clist** *n.*

tri·cy·clic (traɪ'saɪklɪk) *adj.* (of a chemical compound) containing three rings in the molecular structure.

tri·dac·tyl (traɪ'dæktᵊl) *or* **tri·dac·tyl·ous** *adj.* having three digits on one hand or foot.

tri·dent ('traɪdᵊnt) *n.* **1.** a three-pronged spear, originally from the East. **2.** (in Greek and Roman mythology) the three-pronged spear that the sea god Poseidon (Neptune) is represented as carrying. **3.** a three-pronged instrument, weapon, or symbol. ~*adj.* **4.** having three prongs. [C16: from Latin *tridēns* three-pronged, from TRI- + *dēns* tooth]

tri·den·tate (traɪ'dɛnteɪt) *or* **tri·den·tal** *adj. Anatomy, botany.* having three prongs, teeth, or points.

Tri·den·tine (traɪ'dɛntaɪn) *adj.* **1.** *History.* **a.** of or relating to the Council of Trent. **b.** in accord with Tridentine doctrine. ~*n.* **2.** an orthodox Roman Catholic. [C16: from Medieval Latin *Tridentīnus,* from *Tridentum* TRENT]

Tri·den·tum (traɪ'dɛntəm) *n.* the Latin name for **Trento.**

tri·di·men·sion·al (ˌtraɪdɪ'mɛnʃənᵊl, -daɪ-) *adj.* a less common word for **three-dimensional.** —ˌ**tri·di·ˌmen·sion·'al·i·ty** *n.* —ˌ**tri·di·'men·sion·al·ly** *adv.*

trid·u·um ('trɪdjʊəm, 'traɪ-) *n. R.C. Church.* a period of three days for prayer before a feast. [C19: Latin, perhaps from *triduum spatium* a space of three days]

tri·e·cious (traɪ'iːʃəs) *adj.* a variant spelling of **trioecious.**

tried (traɪd) *vb.* the past tense or past participle of **try.**

tri·en·ni·al (traɪ'ɛnɪəl) *adj.* **1.** relating to, lasting for, or occurring every three years. ~*n.* **2.** a third anniversary. **3.** a triennial period, thing, or occurrence. [C17: from TRIENNIUM] —**tri·'en·ni·al·ly** *adv.*

tri·en·ni·um (traɪ'ɛnɪəm) *n., pl.* **·ni·ums** *or* **·ni·a** (-nɪə). a period or cycle of three years. [C19: from Latin, from TRI- + *annus* a year]

Tri·ent (trɪ'ɛnt) *n.* the German name for **Trento.** Also: **Trent.**

tri·er ('traɪə) *n.* a person or thing that tries.

Trier (*German* triːr) *n.* a city in W West Germany, in the Rhineland-Palatinate on the Moselle River: one of the oldest towns of central Europe, ancient capital of a Celto-Germanic tribe (the **Treveri**); an early centre of Christianity, ruled by powerful archbishops until the 18th century; wine trade; important Roman remains. Pop.: 102 221 (1974 est.). Latin name: **Augusta Treverorum.** French name: **Trèves.**

tri·er·arch ('traɪəˌrɑːk) *n. Greek history.* **1.** a citizen responsible for fitting out a state trireme, esp. in Athens. **2.** the captain of a trireme. [C17: from Latin, from Greek *triērarkhos,* from *triērēs* equipped with three banks of oars + *arkhein* to command]

tri·er·ar·chy ('traɪəˌrɑːkɪ) *n., pl.* **·chies.** *Greek history.* **1.** the responsibility for fitting out a state trireme, esp. in Athens. **2.** the office of a trierarch. **3.** trierarchs collectively.

Tri·este (triː'ɛst; *Italian* tri'ɛste) *n.* **1.** a port in NE Italy, capital of Friuli-Venezia Giulia region, on the **Gulf of Trieste** at the head of the Adriatic Sea: under Austrian rule (1382–1918); capital of the Free Territory of Trieste (1947–54); important transit port for central Europe. Pop.: 270 641 (1975 est.). Slovene and Serbo-Croatian name: **Trst. 2. Free Territory of.** a former territory on the N Adriatic: established by the UN in 1947; most of the N part passed to Italy and the remainder to Yugoslavia in 1954.

tri·fa·cial (traɪˈfeɪʃəl) *adj.* another word for **trigeminal.**

tri·fid (ˈtraɪfɪd) *adj.* divided or split into three parts or lobes. [C18: from Latin *trifidus* from TRI- + *findere* to split]

tri·fle (ˈtraɪfᵊl) *n.* **1.** a thing of little or no value or significance. **2.** a small amount; bit: *a trifle more enthusiasm.* **3.** *Brit.* a cold dessert made with sponge cake spread with jam or fruit, soaked in wine or sherry, covered with a custard sauce and cream, and decorated. **4.** a type of pewter of medium hardness. **5.** articles made from this pewter. ~*vb.* **6.** (*intr.;* usually foll. by *with*) to deal (with) as if worthless; dally: *to trifle with a person's affections.* **7.** to waste (time) frivolously. [C13: from Old French *trufle* mockery, from *trufler* to cheat] —**'tri·fler** *n.*

tri·fling (ˈtraɪflɪŋ) *adj.* **1.** insignificant or petty. **2.** frivolous or idle. —**'tri·fling·ly** *adv.* —**'tri·fling·ness** *n.*

tri·fo·cal *adj.* (traɪˈfəʊkᵊl). **1.** having three focuses. **2.** having three focal lengths. ~*n.* (traɪˈfəʊkᵊl, ˈtraɪˌfəʊkᵊl). **3.** (*often pl.*) glasses that have trifocal lenses.

tri·fold (ˈtraɪˌfəʊld) *adj.* a less common word for **triple.**

tri·fo·li·ate (traɪˈfəʊlɪɪt, -ˌeɪt) *or* **tri·fo·li·at·ed** *adj.* having three leaves, leaflike parts, or (of a compound leaf) leaflets.

tri·fo·li·um (traɪˈfəʊlɪəm) *n.* any leguminous plant of the temperate genus *Trifolium,* having leaves divided into three leaflets and dense heads of small white, yellow, red, or purple flowers: includes the clovers and trefoils. [C17: from Latin, from TRI- + *folium* leaf]

tri·fo·ri·um (traɪˈfɔːrɪəm) *n., pl.* **·ri·a** (-rɪə). an arcade above the arches of the nave, choir, or transept of a church. [C18: from Anglo-Latin, apparently from Latin TRI- + *foris* a doorway; referring to the fact that each bay characteristically had three openings] —**tri·'fo·ri·al** *adj.*

tri·fur·cate (ˈtraɪfɜːkɪt, -ˌkeɪt) *or* **tri·fur·cat·ed** *adj.* having three branches or forks. [from Latin *trifurcus,* from TRI- + *furca* a fork] —**ˌtri·fur·'ca·tion** *n.*

trig[1] (trɪg) *Archaic or dialect.* ~*adj.* **1.** neat or spruce. ~*vb.* **trigs, trig·ging, trigged. 2.** to make or become trim or spruce. [C12 (originally: trusty): of Scandinavian origin; related to Old Norse *tryggr* true] —**'trig·ly** *adv.* —**'trig·ness** *n.*

trig[2] (trɪg) *Chiefly dialect.* ~*n.* **1.** a wedge or prop. ~*vb.* **trigs, trig·ging, trigged.** (*tr.*) **2.** to block or stop. **3.** to prop or support. [C16: probably of Scandinavian origin; compare Old Norse *tryggja* to make secure; see TRIG[1]]

trig. *abbrev. for:* **1.** trigonometry. **2.** trigonometrical.

tri·gem·i·nal (traɪˈdʒɛmɪnᵊl) *adj. Anatomy.* of or relating to the trigeminal nerve. [C19: from Latin *trigeminus* triplet, from TRI- + *geminus* twin]

tri·gem·i·nal nerve *n.* either one of the fifth pair of cranial nerves, which supply the muscles of the mandible and maxilla. Their ophthalmic branches supply the area around the orbit of the eye, the nasal cavity, and the forehead.

tri·gem·i·nal neu·ral·gia *n. Pathol.* another name for **tic douloureux.**

trig·ger (ˈtrɪgə) *n.* **1.** a small projecting lever that activates the firing mechanism of a firearm. **2.** *Machinery.* a device that releases a spring-loaded mechanism or a similar arrangement. **3.** any event that sets a course of action in motion. ~*vb.* (*tr.*) **4.** (usually foll. by *off*) to give rise (to); set (off). **5.** to fire or set in motion by or as by pulling a trigger. [C17 *tricker,* from Dutch *trekker,* from *trekken* to pull; see TREK] —**'trig·gered** *adj.* —**'trig·ger·less** *adj.*

trig·ger·fish (ˈtrɪgəˌfɪʃ) *n., pl.* **·fish** *or* **·fish·es.** any plectognath fish of the family *Balistidae,* of tropical and temperate seas. They have a compressed body with erectile spines in the first dorsal fin.

trig·ger-hap·py *adj. Informal.* **1.** tending to resort to the use of firearms or violence irresponsibly. **2.** tending to act rashly or without due consideration.

trig·ger plant *n. Austral.* any of several small grass-like plants of the genus *Stylidium,* having sensitive stamens that are erected when disturbed: family *Stylidiaceae.*

tri·glyc·er·ide (traɪˈglɪsəˌraɪd) *n.* any ester of glycerol and one or more carboxylic acids, in which each glycerol molecule has combined with three carboxylic acid molecules. Most natural fats and oils are triglycerides.

tri·glyph (ˈtraɪˌglɪf) *n. Architect.* a stone block in a Doric frieze, having three vertical channels. —**tri·'glyph·ic** *adj.*

tri·gon (ˈtraɪgɒn) *n.* **1.** (in classical Greece or Rome) a triangular harp or lyre. **2.** an archaic word for **triangle.**

trig·o·nal (ˈtrɪgənᵊl) *adj.* **1.** another word for **triangular** (sense 1). **2.** relating or belonging to the crystal system characterized by three equal axes that are equally inclined and not perpendicular to each other. Also: **rhombohedral.**

trig·o·no·met·ric func·tion *n.* **1.** Also called: **circular function.** any of a group of functions of an angle expressed as a ratio of two of the sides of a right-angled triangle containing the angle. The group includes sine, cosine, tangent, secant, cosecant, and cotangent. **2.** any function containing only sines, cosines, etc., and constants.

trig·o·nom·e·try (ˌtrɪgəˈnɒmɪtrɪ) *n.* the branch of mathematics concerned with the properties of trigonometric functions and their application to the determination of the angles and sides of triangles. Used in surveying, navigation, etc. Abbrev.: **trig.** [C17: from New Latin *trigōnometria,* from Greek *trigōnon* triangle] —**trig·o·no·met·ric** (ˌtrɪgənəˈmɛtrɪk) *or* **ˌtrig·o·no·'met·ri·cal** *adj.* —**ˌtrig·o·no·'met·ri·cal·ly** *adv.*

trig·o·nous (ˈtrɪgənəs) *adj.* (of stems, seeds, and similar parts) having a triangular cross section.

tri·graph (ˈtraɪˌgrɑːf, -ˌgræf) *n.* a combination of three letters used to represent a single speech sound or phoneme, such as *eau* in French *beau.* —**tri·graph·ic** (traɪˈgræfɪk) *adj.*

tri·he·dral (traɪˈhiːdrəl) *adj.* **1.** having or formed by three plane faces meeting at a point. ~*n.* **2.** a figure formed by the intersection of three lines in different planes.

tri·he·dron (traɪˈhiːdrən) *n., pl.* **·drons** *or* **·dra** (-drə). a figure determined by the intersection of three planes.

tri·hy·drate (traɪˈhaɪdreɪt) *n. Chem.* a substance that contains three molecules of water. —**tri·'hy·drat·ed** *adj.*

tri·hy·dric (traɪˈhaɪdrɪk) *or* **tri·hy·drox·y** (ˌtraɪhaɪˈdrɒksɪ) *adj.* (of an alcohol or similar compound) containing three hydroxyl groups.

tri·i·o·do·me·thane (ˌtraɪaɪˌəʊdəʊˈmiːθeɪn) *n.* another name for **iodoform.**

tri·i·o·do·thy·ro·nine (ˌtraɪaɪˌəʊdəʊˈθaɪrəˌniːn) *n.* an amino acid hormone that contains iodine and is secreted by the thyroid gland with thyroxine, to which it has a similar action. Formula: $C_{15}H_{12}I_3NO_4$. [C20: from TRI- + IODO- + THYRO- + -INE[2]]

trike (traɪk) *n.* **1.** short for **tricycle. 2.** short for **trichloroethylene.**

tri·lat·er·al (traɪˈlætərəl) *adj.* having three sides. —**tri·'lat·er·al·ly** *adv.*

tri·lat·er·a·tion (ˌtraɪlætəˈreɪʃən) *n.* a method of surveying in which a whole area is divided into triangles, the sides of which are measured, usually by electromagnetic distance measuring for geodetic control or by chain survey for a detailed survey.

tril·by (ˈtrɪlbɪ) *n., pl.* **·bies. 1.** *Chiefly Brit.* a man's soft felt hat with an indented crown. **2.** (*pl.*) *Slang.* feet. [C19: named after *Trilby,* the heroine of a dramatized novel (1893) of that title by George du Maurier]

tri·lem·ma (traɪˈlɛmə) *n.* **1.** a quandary posed by three alternative courses of action. **2.** an argument in which three alternatives are examined. [C17: formed on the model of DILEMMA, from TRI- + Greek *lēmma* assumption]

tri·lin·e·ar (traɪˈlɪnɪə) *adj.* consisting of, bounded by, or relating to three lines.

tri·lin·gual (traɪˈlɪŋgwəl) *adj.* **1.** able to speak three languages fluently. **2.** expressed or written in three languages. —**tri·'lin·gual·ism** *n.* —**tri·'lin·gual·ly** *adv.*

tri·lit·er·al (traɪˈlɪtərəl) *adj.* **1.** having three letters. **2.** (of a word root in Semitic languages) consisting of three consonants. ~*n.* **3.** a word root of three consonants.

tri·lith·on (traɪˈlɪθɒn, ˈtraɪlɪˌθɒn) *or* **tri·lith** (ˈtraɪlɪθ) *n.* a structure consisting of two upright stones with a third placed across the top, such as those of Stonehenge. [C18: from Greek; see TRI-, -LITH] —**tri·lith·ic** (traɪˈlɪθɪk) *adj.*

trill[1] (trɪl) *n.* **1.** *Music.* a melodic ornament consisting of a rapid alternation between a principal note and the note a whole tone or semitone above it. Symbol: *tr.* or *tr.*〰〰 (written above a note). **2.** a shrill warbling sound, esp. as made by some birds. **3.** *Phonetics.* **a.** the articulation of an (r) sound produced by holding the tip of the tongue close to the alveolar ridge, allowing the tongue to make a succession of taps against the ridge. **b.** the production of a similar effect using the uvula against the back of the tongue. ~*vb.* **4.** to sound, sing, or play (a trill or with a trill). **5.** (*tr.*) to pronounce (an (r) sound) by the production of a trill. [C17: from Italian *trillo,* from *trillare,* apparently from Middle Dutch *trillen* to vibrate]

trill[2] (trɪl) *vb., n.* an archaic or poetic word for **trickle.** [C14: probably of Scandinavian origin; related to Norwegian *trilla* to roll; see TRILL[1]]

tril·lion (ˈtrɪljən) *n.* **1.** (in Britain and Germany) the number represented as one followed by eighteen zeros (10^{18}); a million million million. U.S. word: **quintillion. 2.** (in the U.S. and France) the number represented as one followed by twelve zeros (10^{12}); a million million. Brit. word: **billion. 3.** (*often pl.*) an exceptionally large but unspecified number. ~*determiner.* **4.** (preceded by *a* or a numeral) **a.** amounting to a trillion: *a trillion stars.* **b.** (*as pronoun*): *there are three trillion.* [C17: from French, on the model of *million*] —**'tril·lionth** *n., adj.*

tril·lium (ˈtrɪljəm) *n.* any herbaceous plant of the genus *Trillium,* of Asia and North America, having a whorl of three leaves at the top of the stem with a single central white, pink, or purple three-petalled flower: family *Trilliaceae.* [C18: from New Latin, modification by Linnaeus of Swedish *trilling* triplet]

tri·lo·bate (traɪˈləʊbeɪt, ˈtraɪləˌbeɪt) *adj.* (esp. of a leaf) consisting of or having three lobes or parts.

tri·lo·bite (ˈtraɪləˌbaɪt) *n.* any extinct marine arthropod of the group *Trilobita,* abundant in Palaeozoic times, having a segmented exoskeleton divided into three parts. [C19: from New Latin *Trilobītes,* from Greek *trilobos* having three lobes; see TRI-, LOBE] —**tri·lo·bit·ic** (ˌtraɪləˈbɪtɪk) *adj.*

tri·loc·u·lar (traɪˈlɒkjələ) *adj.* (esp. of a plant ovary or anther) having or consisting of three chambers or cavities.

tril·o·gy (ˈtrɪlədʒɪ) *n., pl.* **·gies. 1.** a series of three related works, esp. in literature, etc. **2.** (in ancient Greece) a series of three tragedies performed together at the Dionysian festivals. [C19: from Greek *trilogia;* see TRI-, -LOGY]

trim (trɪm) *adj.* **trim·mer, trim·mest. 1.** neat and spruce in appearance. **2.** slim; slender. **3.** in good condition. ~*vb.* **trims, trim·ming, trimmed.** (*mainly tr.*) **4.** to put in good order, esp. by cutting or pruning. **5.** to shape and finish (timber). **6.** to adorn or decorate. **7.** (sometimes foll. by *off* or *away*) to cut so as to remove: *to trim off a branch.* **8.** to cut down to the desired size or shape: *to trim material to a pattern.* **9.** *Nautical.* **a.** (*also intr.*) to adjust the balance of (a vessel) or (of a vessel) to maintain an even balance, by distribution of ballast, cargo, etc. **b.** (*also intr.*) to adjust (a vessel's sails) to take advantage of the wind. **c.** to stow (cargo). **10.** to balance (an aircraft) before flight by adjusting the position of the load or in flight by the use of trim tabs, fuel transfer, etc. **11.** (*also intr.*) to modify (one's opinions, etc.) to suit opposing factions or for expediency. **12.** *Informal.* to thrash or beat. **13.** *Informal.* to rebuke. **14.** *Obsolete.* to furnish or equip. ~*n.* **15.** a decoration or adornment: *the trim on a shirt.* **16.** proper order or fitness; good shape: *in trim.* **17.** a haircut that neatens but does not alter the existing hairstyle. **18.** *Nautical.* **a.** the general set and appearance of a vessel. **b.** the difference between the draught of a vessel at the bow and at the stern. **c.** the fitness of a vessel. **d.** the position of a vessel's sails relative to the wind. **e.** the relative buoyancy of a submarine. **19.** dress or equipment. **20.** *U.S.* window dressing. **21.** the attitude of an aircraft in flight when the pilot allows the main control surfaces to take up their own positions. **22.** *Films.* a section of shot cut out during editing. **23.** material that is trimmed off. **24.** decorative mouldings, such as architraves, picture rails, etc. [Old English *trymman* to strengthen; related to *trum* strong, Old Irish *druma* tree, Russian *drom* thicket] —**'trim·ly** *adv.* —**'trim·ness** *n.*

tri·ma·ran ('traımə,ræn) *n.* a vessel, usually of shallow draught, with two hulls flanking the main hull. [C20: from TRI- + (CATA)MARAN]

tri·mer ('traımə) *n.* a polymer or a molecule of a polymer consisting of three identical monomers. —**tri·mer·ic** (traı'mɛrık) *adj.*

trim·er·ous ('trımərəs) *adj.* **1.** (of plants) having parts arranged in groups of three. **2.** consisting of or having three parts.

tri·mes·ter (traı'mɛstə) *n.* **1.** a period of three months. **2.** (in some U.S. universities or schools) any of the three academic sessions. [C19: from French *trimestre,* from Latin *trimēstris* of three months, from TRI- + *mēnsis* month] —**tri·'mes·tral** *or* **tri·'mes·tri·al** *adj.*

trim·e·ter ('trımıtə) *Prosody.* ~*n.* **1.** a verse line consisting of three metrical feet. ~*adj.* **2.** designating such a line.

tri·meth·a·di·one (,traımɛθə'daıəʊn) *n.* a crystalline compound with a bitter taste and camphor-like odour, used in the treatment of epilepsy. Formula: $C_6H_9NO_3$. [from TRI- + METH(YL) + DI-[1] + -ONE]

tri·met·ric (traı'mɛtrık) *or* **tri·met·ri·cal** *adj.* **1.** *Prosody.* of, relating to, or consisting of a trimeter or trimeters. **2.** *Crystallog.* another word for **orthorhombic.**

tri·met·ric pro·jec·tion *n.* a geometric projection, used in mechanical drawing, in which the three axes are at arbitrary angles, often using different linear scales.

tri·met·ro·gon (traı'mɛtrə,gɒn) *n.* **a.** a method of aerial photography for rapid topographic mapping, in which one vertical and two oblique photographs are taken simultaneously. **b.** (*as modifier*): *trimetrogon photography.* [from TRI- + *metro-,* from Greek *metron* measure + -GON]

trim·mer ('trımə) *n.* **1.** Also called: **trimmer joist.** a beam in a floor or roof structure attached to truncated joists in order to leave an opening for a staircase, chimney, etc. **2.** a machine for trimming timber. **3.** Also called: **trimming capacitor.** *Electronics.* a variable capacitor of small capacitance used for making fine adjustments, etc. **4.** a person who alters his opinions on the grounds of expediency. **5.** a person who fits out motor vehicles.

trim·ming ('trımıŋ) *n.* **1.** an extra piece used to decorate or complete. **2.** (*pl.*) additional ornaments or accompaniments: *roast turkey with all the trimmings.* **3.** (*pl.*) parts that are cut off. **4.** *Informal.* a reproof, beating, or defeat.

tri·mo·lec·u·lar (,traımə'lɛkjʊlə) *adj. Chem.* of, concerned with, formed from, or involving three molecules.

tri·month·ly (traı'mʌnθlı) *adj., adv.* every three months.

tri·morph ('traımɔ:f) *n.* **1.** a substance, esp. a mineral, that exists in three distinct forms. **2.** any of the forms in which such a structure exists.

tri·mor·phism (traı'mɔ:fızəm) *n.* **1.** *Biology.* the property exhibited by certain species of having or occurring in three different forms. **2.** the property of certain minerals of existing in three crystalline forms. —**tri·'mor·phic** *or* **tri·'mor·phous** *adj.*

trim size *n.* the size of a book or a page of a book after all excess material has been trimmed off.

trim tab *n.* a small aerofoil attached to the trailing edge of a control surface to enable the pilot to trim an aircraft.

Tri·mur·ti (trı'mʊətı) *n.* the triad of the three chief gods of later Hinduism, consisting of Brahma the Creator, Vishnu the Sustainer, and Siva the Destroyer. [from Sanskrit, from *tri* three + *mūrti* form]

Tri·na·cri·a (trı'neıkrıə, traı-) *n.* the Latin name for **Sicily.** —**Tri·'na·cri·an** *adj.*

tri·na·ry ('traınərı) *adj.* **1.** made up of three parts; ternary. **2.** going in threes. [C15: from Late Latin *trīnārius* of three sorts, from Latin *trīnī* three each, from *trēs* three]

Trin·co·ma·lee (,trıŋkəʊmə'li:) *n.* a port in NE Sri Lanka, on the **Bay of Trincomalee** (an inlet of the Bay of Bengal); British naval base until 1957. Pop.: 41 784 (1971).

trine (traın) *n.* **1.** *Astrology.* an aspect of 120° between two planets, an orb of 8° being allowed. Compare **conjunction** (sense 5), **opposition** (sense 9), **square** (sense 8). **2.** anything comprising three parts. ~*adj.* **3.** of or relating to a trine. **4.** threefold; triple. [C14: from Old French *trin,* from Latin *trīnus* triple, from *trēs* three] —**'tri·nal** *adj.*

Trin·i·dad ('trını,dæd) *n.* an island in the West Indies, off the NE coast of Venezuela: colonized by the Spanish in the 17th century and ceded to Britain in 1802; joined with Tobago in 1888 as a British colony; now part of the independent republic of Trinidad and Tobago. Pop.: 983 750 (1970 est.). —,**Trin·i·'dad·i·an** *adj., n.*

Trin·i·dad and To·ba·go *n.* an independent republic in the West Indies, occupying the two southernmost islands of the Lesser Antilles: became a British colony in 1888 and gained independence in 1962; became a republic in 1976; a member of the Commonwealth. Official language: English. Religion: Christian majority, with a large Hindu minority. Currency: Trinidad and Tobago dollar. Capital: Port-of-Spain. Combined pop.: 945 210 (1970). Area: 5128 sq. km (1980 sq. miles).

Tri·nil man ('tri:nıl) *n.* another name for **Java man.** [C20: named after the village in Java where remains were found]

Trin·i·tar·i·an (,trını'tɛərıən) *n.* **1.** a person who believes in the doctrine of the Trinity. **2.** a member of the Holy Trinity. See **Trinity** (sense 3). ~*adj.* **3.** of or relating to the doctrine of the Trinity or those who uphold it. **4.** of or relating to the Holy Trinity. —,**Trin·i·'tar·i·an·,ism** *n.*

tri·ni·tro·ben·zene (traı,naıtrəʊ'bɛnzi:n, -bɛn'zi:n) *n.* any of three explosive crystalline isomeric compounds with the formula $C_6H_3(NO_2)_3$. They are less sensitive to impact than TNT but more powerful in their explosive force.

tri·ni·tro·cre·sol (traı,naıtrəʊ'kri:sɒl) *n.* a yellow crystalline highly explosive compound. Formula: $CH_3C_6H(OH)(NO_2)_3$.

tri·ni·tro·glyc·er·in (traı,naıtrəʊ'glısərın) *n.* the full name for **nitroglycerin.**

tri·ni·tro·phe·nol (traı,naıtrəʊ'fi:nɒl) *n.* another name for **picric acid.**

tri·ni·tro·tol·u·ene (traı,naıtrəʊ'tɒljʊ,i:n) *or* **tri·ni·tro·tol·u·ol** (traı,naıtrəʊ'tɒljʊ,ɒl) *n.* the full name for **TNT.**

trin·i·ty ('trınıtı) *n., pl.* **-ties. 1.** a group of three. **2.** the state of being threefold. [C13: from Old French *trinite,* from Late Latin *trīnitās* from Latin *trīnus* triple]

Trin·i·ty ('trınıtı) *n.* **1.** Also called: **Holy Trinity, Blessed Trinity.** *Theol.* the union of three persons, the Father, Son, and Holy Ghost, in one Godhead. **2.** See **Trinity Sunday. 3. Holy Trinity.** a religious order founded in 1198.

Trin·i·ty Breth·ren *pl. n.* the members of Trinity House.

Trin·i·ty House *n.* an association that provides lighthouses, buoys, etc., around the British coast.

Trin·i·ty Sun·day *n.* the Sunday after Whit Sunday.

Trin·i·ty term *n.* the summer term at Oxford and Cambridge Universities and some other educational establishments.

trin·ket ('trıŋkıt) *n.* **1.** a small or worthless ornament or piece of jewellery. **2.** a trivial object; trifle. [C16: perhaps from earlier *trenket* little knife, via Old Northern French, from Latin *truncāre* to lop] —**'trin·ket·ry** *n.*

tri·noc·u·lar (traı'nɒkjʊlə) *adj.* of or relating to a binocular microscope having a lens for photographic recording while direct visual observation is taking place. [C20: from TRI- + (BI)NOCULAR]

tri·no·mi·al (traı'nəʊmıəl) *adj.* **1.** *Maths.* consisting of or relating to three terms. **2.** *Biology.* denoting or relating to the three-part name of an organism that incorporates its genus, species, and subspecies. ~*n.* **3.** *Maths.* a polynomial consisting of three terms, such as $ax^2 + bx + c$. **4.** *Biology.* the third word in the trinomial name of an organism, which distinguishes between subspecies. [C18: TRI- + *-nomial* on the model of *binomial*] —**tri·'no·mi·al·ly** *adv.*

tri·o ('tri:əʊ) *n., pl.* **tri·os. 1.** a group of three people or things. **2.** *Music.* **a.** a group of three singers or instrumentalists or a piece of music composed for such a group. **b.** a subordinate section in a scherzo, minuet, etc., that is contrastive in style and often in a related key. **3.** *Piquet.* three cards of the same rank. [C18: from Italian, ultimately from Latin *trēs* three; compare DUO]

tri·ode ('traıəʊd) *n.* **1.** an electronic valve having three electrodes, a cathode, an anode, and a grid, the potential of the grid controlling the flow of electrons between the cathode and anode. It is used mainly as an amplifier or oscillator but has been replaced in most circuits by the transistor. **2.** any electronic device, such as a thyratron, having three electrodes. [C20: TRI- + ELECTRODE]

tri·oe·cious *or* **tri·e·cious** (traı'i:ʃəs) *adj.* (of a plant species) having male, female, and hermaphrodite flowers in three different plants. [C18: from New Latin *trioecia,* from Greek TRI- + *oikos* house]

tri·ol ('traıɒl) *n.* any of a class of alcohols that have three hydroxyl groups per molecule. Also called: **trihydric alcohol.** [from TRI- + -OL[1]]

tri·o·le·in (traı'əʊlıın) *n.* a naturally occurring glyceride of oleic acid, found in fats and oils. Formula: $(C_{17}H_{33}COO)_3C_3H_5$. Also called: **olein.**

tri·o·let ('tri:əʊ,lɛt) *n.* a verse form of eight lines, having the first line repeated as the fourth and seventh and the second line as the eighth, rhyming a b a a a b a b. [C17: from French: a little TRIO]

tri·ose ('traıəʊz, -əʊs) *n.* a simple monosaccharide produced by the oxidation of glycerol. Formula: $CH_2OHCHOHCHO$.

tri·o so·na·ta *n.* **1.** a type of baroque composition in several movements scored for two upper parts and a bass part. **2.** a similar type of composition played on a keyboard instrument, esp. an organ.

tri·ox·ide (traı'ɒksaıd) *n.* any oxide that contains three oxygen atoms per molecule: *sulphur trioxide,* SO_3.

trip (trıp) *n.* **1.** an outward and return journey, often for a specific purpose. **2.** any tour, journey, or voyage. **3.** a false step; stumble. **4.** any slip or blunder. **5.** a light step or tread. **6.** a manoeuvre or device to cause someone to trip. **7.** Also called: **tripper.** any catch on a mechanism that acts as a switch. **8.**

Informal. a hallucinogenic drug experience. ~*vb.* **trips, trip+ping, tripped. 9.** (often foll. by *up*, or when *intr.*, by *on* or *over*) to stumble or cause to stumble. **10.** to make or cause to make a mistake or blunder. **11.** (*tr.;* often foll. by *up*) to trap or catch in a mistake. **12.** (*intr.*) to go on a short tour or journey. **13.** (*intr.*) to move or tread lightly. **14.** *Informal.* to experience the effects of LSD or any other hallucinogenic drug. **15.** to activate a mechanical trip. [C14: from Old French *triper* to tread, of Germanic origin; related to Low German *trippen* to stamp, Middle Dutch *trippen* to walk trippingly, *trepelen* to trample] —**'trip+ping+ly** *adv.*

tri+pal+mi+tin (traɪ'pælmɪtɪn) *n.* another name for **palmitin.**

tri+par+tite (traɪ'pɑːtaɪt) *adj.* **1.** divided into or composed of three parts. **2.** involving three participants. **3.** (esp. of leaves) consisting of three parts formed by divisions extending almost to the base. —**tri+'par+tite+ly** *adv.*

tri+par+ti+tion (ˌtraɪpɑː'tɪʃən) *n.* division into or among three.

tripe (traɪp) *n.* **1.** the stomach lining of an ox, cow, or other ruminant, prepared for cooking. **2.** *Informal.* something silly; rubbish. **3.** (*pl.*) *Archaic, informal.* intestines; belly. [C13: from Old French, of unknown origin]

tri+per+son+al (traɪ'pɜːsənᵊl) *adj. Theol.* (of God) existing as the Trinity. Compare **unipersonal.** —ˌ**tri+per+son+'al+i+ty** *n.*

trip+ham+mer ('trɪpˌhæmə) *n.* a power hammer that is raised or tilted by a cam and allowed to fall under gravity.

tri+phe+nyl+me+thane (traɪˌfiːnaɪl'miːθeɪn, -ˌfɛn-) *n.* a colourless crystalline solid used for the preparation of many dyes. Formula: $(C_6H_5)_3CH$.

tri+phib+i+ous (traɪ'fɪbɪəs) *adj.* (esp. of military operations) occurring on land, at sea, and in the air. [C20: from TRI- + (AM)PHIBIOUS]

triph+thong ('trɪfθɒŋ, 'trɪp-) *n.* **1.** a composite vowel sound during the articulation of which the vocal organs move from one position through a second, ending in a third. **2.** a trigraph representing a composite vowel sound such as this. [C16: via New Latin from Medieval Greek *triphthongos,* from TRI- + *phthongos* sound; compare DIPHTHONG] —**triph+'thong+al** *adj.*

triph·y+lite ('trɪfɪˌlaɪt) *n.* a bluish-grey rare mineral that consists of lithium iron phosphate in orthorhombic crystalline form and occurs in pegmatites. Formula: $LiFePO_4$. [C19: from TRI- + *phyl-*, from Greek *phulon* family + -ITE[1], referring to its three bases]

tri+pin+nate (traɪ'pɪnɪt, -eɪt) *adj.* (of a leaf) having pinnate leaflets that are bipinnately arranged. —**tri+'pin+nate+ly** *adv.*

Tri+pi+ta+ka (ˌtrɪpɪ'tɑːkə) *n. Buddhism.* the three collections of books making up the Buddhist canon of scriptures.

tripl. *abbrev. for* triplicate.

tri+plane ('traɪˌpleɪn) *n.* an aeroplane having three wings arranged one above the other.

tri+ple ('trɪpᵊl) *adj.* **1.** consisting of three parts; threefold. **2.** (of musical time or rhythm) having three beats in each bar. **3.** three times as great or as much. ~*n.* **4.** a threefold amount. **5.** a group of three. ~*vb.* **6.** to increase or become increased threefold; treble. [C16: from Latin *triplus*] —**'tri+ply** *adv.*

Tri+ple Al+li+ance *n.* **1.** the secret alliance between Germany, Austria-Hungary, and Italy formed in 1882 and lasting until 1914. **2.** the alliance of France, the Netherlands, and Britain against Spain in 1717. **3.** the alliance of England, Sweden, and the Netherlands against France in 1668.

tri+ple bond *n.* a type of chemical bond consisting of three distinct covalent bonds linking two atoms in a molecule.

Tri+ple En+tente *n.* the understanding between Britain, France, and Russia that developed between 1894 and 1907 and counterbalanced the Triple Alliance of 1882. The Entente became a formal alliance on the outbreak of World War I and was ended by the Russian Revolution in 1917.

tri+ple jump *n.* an athletic event in which the competitor has to perform successively a hop, a step, and a jump in continuous movement. Also called: **hop, step, and jump.**

tri+ple-nerved *adj.* (of a leaf) having three main veins.

tri+ple point *n. Chem.* the temperature and pressure at which the three phases of a substance are in equilibrium. The triple point of water, 273.16 K, is the basis of the definition of the kelvin.

tri+plet ('trɪplɪt) *n.* **1.** a group or set of three similar things. **2.** one of three offspring born at one birth. **3.** *Music.* a group of three notes played in a time value of two, four, etc. [C17: from TRIPLE, on the model of *doublet*]

tri+ple+tail ('trɪpᵊlˌteɪl) *n., pl.* **+tail** *or* **+tails.** any percoid fish of the family *Lobotidae,* esp. *Lobotes surinamensis,* of brackish waters of SE Asia, having tail-like dorsal and anal fins.

tri+ple-tongue *vb. Music.* to play (very quick staccato passages of notes grouped in threes) on a wind instrument by a combination of single- and double-tonguing. Compare **single-tongue, double-tongue.** —**'tri+ple-'tongu+ing** *n.*

tri+plex ('trɪplɛks) *adj.* a less common word for **triple.** [C17: from Latin *trēs* three + *-plex* -FOLD]

Tri+plex ('trɪplɛks) *n. Brit. trademark.* a laminated safety glass, as used in car windows.

trip+li+cate *adj.* ('trɪplɪkɪt). **1.** triple. ~*vb.* ('trɪplɪˌkeɪt). **2.** to multiply or be multiplied by three. ~*n.* ('trɪplɪkɪt). **3. a.** a group of three things. **b.** one of such a group. **4. in triplicate.** written out with three copies. [C15: from Latin *triplicāre* to triple, from TRIPLEX] —ˌ**trip+li+'ca+tion** *n.*

tri+plic+i+ty (trɪ'plɪsɪtɪ) *n., pl.* **+ties. 1.** a group of three things. **2.** the state of being three. **3.** *Astrology.* any of four groups, earth, air, fire, and water, each consisting of three signs of the zodiac that are thought to have something in common in their nature. [C14: from Late Latin *triplicitās,* from Latin *triplex* threefold; see TRIPLEX]

trip+lo+blas+tic (ˌtrɪpləʊ'blæstɪk) *adj.* (of all multicellular animals except coelenterates) having a body developed from all three germ layers. Compare **diploblastic.** [C19: from *triplo-* threefold (from Greek *triploos*) + -BLAST]

trip+loid ('trɪplɔɪd) *adj.* **1.** having or relating to three times the haploid number of chromosomes: *a triploid organism.* ~*n.* **2.** a triploid organism. [C19: from Greek *tripl(oos)* triple + (HAPL)OID]

tri+pod ('traɪpɒd) *n.* **1.** an adjustable and usually collapsible three-legged stand to which a camera, etc., can be attached to hold it steady. **2.** a stand or table having three legs. —**trip+o+dal** ('trɪpədᵊl) *adj.*

trip+o+dy ('trɪpədɪ) *n., pl.* **+dies.** *Prosody.* a metrical unit consisting of three feet.

trip+o+li ('trɪpəlɪ) *n.* a lightweight porous siliceous rock derived by weathering and used in a powdered form as a polish, filter, etc. [C17: named after TRIPOLI, in Libya or in Lebanon]

Trip+o+li ('trɪpəlɪ) *n.* **1.** the capital and chief port of Libya, in the northwest on the Mediterranean: founded by Phoenicians in about the 7th century B.C.; the only city that has survived of the three (Oea, Leptis Magna, and Sabratha) that formed the African Tripolis ("three cities"); fishing and manufacturing centre. Pop.: 213 506 (1964). Ancient name: **Oea.** Arabic name: **Tarabulus el Gharb. 2.** a port in N Lebanon, on the Mediterranean: the second largest town in Lebanon; taken by the Crusaders in 1109 after a siege of five years; oil-refining and manufacturing centre. Pop.: 160 000 (1973 est.). Ancient name: **Tripolis.** Arabic name: **Tarabulus esh Sham.**

Trip+o+li+ta+ni+a (ˌtrɪpəlɪ'teɪnɪə) *n.* the NW part of Libya: established as a Phoenician colony in the 7th century B.C.; taken by the Turks in 1551 and became one of the Barbary states; under Italian rule from 1912 until World War II. —ˌ**Trip+o+li+'ta+ni+an** *adj., n.*

tri+pos ('traɪpɒs) *n. Brit.* the honours degree examinations in all subjects at Cambridge University. [C16: from Latin *tripūs,* influenced by Greek noun ending *-os*]

trip+per ('trɪpə) *n.* **1.** a person who goes on a trip. **2.** *Chiefly Brit.* a tourist; excursionist. **3.** another word for **trip** (sense 7). **4. a.** any device that generates a signal causing a trip to operate. **b.** the signal so generated.

trip+pet ('trɪpɪt) *n.* any mechanism that strikes or is struck at regular intervals, as by a cam. [C15 (in the sense: a piece of wood used in a game): from *trippen* to TRIP]

trip+tane ('trɪpteɪn) *n.* a colourless highly flammable liquid alkane hydrocarbon, isomeric with heptane, used in aviation fuel; 2,2,3-trimethylbutane. Formula: $CH_3C(CH_3)_2CH(CH_3)CH_3$. [C20: shortened and altered from *trimethylbutane;* see TRI-, METHYL, BUTANE]

trip+ter+ous ('trɪptərəs) *adj.* (of fruits, seeds, etc.) having three winglike extensions or parts.

Trip+tol+e+mus (trɪp'tɒlɪməs) *n. Greek myth.* a favourite of Demeter, sent by her to teach men agriculture.

trip+tych ('trɪptɪk) *n.* **1.** a set of three pictures or panels, usually hinged so that the two wing panels fold over the larger central one: often used as an altarpiece. **2.** a set of three hinged writing tablets. [C18: from Greek *triptukhos,* from TRI- + *ptux* plate; compare DIPTYCH]

trip+tyque (trɪp'tiːk) *n.* a customs permit for the temporary importation of a motor vehicle. [from French: TRIPTYCH (referring to its three sections)]

Trip+u+ra ('trɪpʊrə) *n.* a state of NE India: formerly a princely state, ruled by the Maharajahs for over 1300 years; became a union territory in 1956 and a state in 1972; extensive jungles. Capital: Agartala. Pop.: 1 556 342 (1971). Area: 10 453 sq. km (4036 sq. miles).

trip+wire ('trɪpˌwaɪə) *n.* a wire that activates a trap, mine, etc., when tripped over.

tri+que+trous (traɪ'kwiːtrəs, -'kwɛ-) *adj.* triangular, esp. in cross section: *a triquetrous stem.* [C17: from Latin *triquetrus* having three corners]

tri+ra+di+ate (traɪ'reɪdɪɪt, -ˌeɪt) *adj. Biology.* having or consisting of three rays or radiating branches. —**tri+'ra+di+ate+ly** *adv.*

tri+reme ('traɪriːm) *n.* a galley, developed by the ancient Greeks as a warship, with three banks of oars on each side. [C17: from Latin *trirēmis,* from TRI- + *rēmus* oar]

tri+sac+cha+ride (traɪ'sækəˌraɪd) *n.* an oligosaccharide whose molecules have three linked monosaccharide molecules.

tri+sect (traɪ'sɛkt) *vb.* (*tr.*) to divide into three parts, esp. three equal parts. [C17: TRI- + *-sect* from Latin *secāre* to cut] —**tri+sec+tion** (traɪ'sɛkʃən) *n.* —**tri+'sec+tor** *n.*

tri+se+ri+al (traɪ'sɪərɪəl) *adj.* arranged in three rows or series.

tri+shaw ('traɪˌʃɔː) *n.* another name for **rickshaw** (sense 2). [C20: from TRI- + RICKSHAW]

tris+kai+dek+a+pho+bi+a (ˌtrɪskaɪˌdɛkə'fəʊbɪə) *n.* an abnormal fear of the number thirteen. [C20: from Greek *triskaideka* thirteen + -PHOBIA] —ˌ**tris+kai+dek+a+'pho+bic** *adj., n.*

tris+kel+i+on (trɪ'skɛlɪˌɒn, -ən) *or* **tris+kele** ('trɪskiːl) *n., pl.* **tri+skel+i+a** (trɪ'skɛlɪə) *or* **tris+keles.** a symbol consisting of three bent limbs or lines radiating from a centre. [C19: from Greek *triskelēs* three-legged, from TRI- + *skelos* leg]

Tris+me+gis+tus (ˌtrɪsmɪ'dʒɪstəs) *n.* See **Hermes Trismegistus.**

tris+mus ('trɪzməs) *n. Pathol.* the state or condition of being unable to open the mouth because of sustained contractions of the jaw muscles, caused by a form of tetanus. Nontechnical name: **lockjaw.** [C17: from New Latin, from Greek *trismos* a grinding] —**'tris+mic** *adj.*

tris+oc+ta+he+dron (trɪsˌɒktəˈhiːdrən) *n., pl.* **+drons** *or* **+dra** (-drə). a solid figure having 24 identical triangular faces, groups of three faces being formed on an underlying octahedron. [C19: from Greek *tris* three times + OCTAHEDRON] —**tris+ˌoc+ta+ˈhe+dral** *adj.*

tri+so+mic (traɪˈsəʊmɪk) *adj.* having one chromosome of the set represented three times in an otherwise diploid organism, cell, etc. [C20: from TRI- + (CHROMO)SOM(E) + -IC] —**tri+some** (ˈtraɪsəʊm) *n.*

Tris+tan (ˈtrɪstən) *or* **Tris+tram** *n.* (in medieval romance) the nephew of King Mark of Cornwall who fell in love with his uncle's bride, Iseult, after they mistakenly drank a love potion.

Tris+tan da Cu+nha (ˈtrɪstən də ˈkuːnjə) *n.* a group of four small volcanic islands in the S Atlantic, about halfway between South Africa and South America: comprises the main island of Tristan and the uninhabited islands of Gough, Inaccessible, and Nightingale; discovered in 1506 by the Portuguese admiral Tristão da Cunha; annexed to Britain in 1816; whole population of Tristan evacuated for two years after the volcanic eruption of 1961. Pop.: 280 (1971 est.). Area: about 100 sq. km (40 sq. miles).

triste (triːst) *or* **trist+ful** (ˈtrɪstfʊl) *adj.* an archaic word for **sad.** [from French] —**ˈtrist+ful+ly** *adv.* —**ˈtrist+ful+ness** *n.*

tri+stear+in (traɪˈstɪərɪn) *n.* another name for **stearin.**

tris+tich (ˈtrɪstɪk) *n. Prosody.* a poem, stanza, or strophe that consists of three lines. —**tris+ˈtich+ic** *adj.*

tris+ti+chous (ˈtrɪstɪkəs) *adj.* arranged in three rows, esp. (of plants) having three vertical rows of leaves.

tri+stim+u+lus val+ues (traɪˈstɪmjʊləs) *pl. n.* three values that together are used to describe a colour and are the amounts of three reference colours that can be mixed to give the same visual sensation as the colour considered. Symbol: X, Y, Z. See also **chromaticity coordinates.**

tri+sul+phide (traɪˈsʌlfaɪd) *n.* any sulphide containing three sulphur atoms per molecule.

tri+syl+la+ble (traɪˈsɪləbᵊl) *n.* a word of three syllables. —**tri+syl+lab+ic** (ˌtraɪsɪˈlæbɪk) *or* **ˌtri+syl+ˈlab+i+cal** *adj.* —**ˌtri+syl+ˈlab+i+cal+ly** *adv.*

tri+tan+o+pi+a (ˌtraɪtəˈnəʊpɪə, ˌtrɪt-) *n.* inability to see the colour blue. [C19/20: from New Latin, from Greek *tritos* third + New Latin *anopia* blindness; signifying that only two thirds of the spectrum can be distinguished] —**tri+tan+op+ic** (ˌtraɪtəˈnɒpɪk, ˌtrɪt-) *adj.*

trite (traɪt) *adj.* **1.** hackneyed; dull: *a trite comment.* **2.** *Archaic.* frayed or worn out. [C16: from Latin *trītus* worn down, from *terere* to rub] —**ˈtrite+ly** *adv.* —**ˈtrite+ness** *n.*

tri+the+ism (ˈtraɪθɪˌɪzəm) *n. Theol.* belief in three gods, esp. in the Trinity as consisting of three distinct gods. —**ˈtri+the+ist** *n., adj.* —**ˌtri+the+ˈis+tic** *or* **ˌtri+the+ˈis+ti+cal** *adj.*

trit+i+ate (ˈtrɪtɪˌeɪt) *vb.* (*tr.*) to replace normal hydrogen atoms in a compound by those of tritium. [C20: from TRITI(UM) + -ATE[1]] —**ˌtrit+i+ˈa+tion** *n.*

trit+i+ca+le (ˌtrɪtɪˈkɑːlɪ) *n.* a fertile hybrid cereal, a cross between wheat (*Triticum*) and rye (*Secale*), produced by polyploidy. [C20: from *Tritic(um)* + *(Sec)ale*]

trit+i+cum (ˈtrɪtɪkəm) *n.* any annual cereal grass of the genus *Triticum,* which includes the wheats. [C19: Latin, literally: wheat, probably from *tritum,* supine of *terere* to grind]

trit+i+um (ˈtrɪtɪəm) *n.* a radioactive isotope of hydrogen, occurring in trace amounts in natural hydrogen and produced in a nuclear reactor. Tritiated compounds are used as tracers. Symbol: T or ^{3}H; half-life: 12.5 years. [C20: New Latin, from Greek *tritos* third]

tri+ton[1] (ˈtraɪtᵊn) *n.* any of various chiefly tropical marine gastropod molluscs of the genera *Triton, Cymatium,* etc., having large beautifully-coloured spiral shells. [C16: via Latin from Greek *tritōn*]

tri+ton[2] (ˈtraɪtɒn) *n. Physics.* a nucleus of an atom of tritium, containing two neutrons and one proton. [C20: from TRIT(IUM) + -ON]

Tri+ton[1] (ˈtraɪtᵊn) *n. Greek myth.* **1.** a sea god, son of Poseidon and Amphitrite, depicted as having the upper parts of a man with a fishtail and holding a trumpet made from a conch shell. **2.** one of a class of minor sea deities.

Tri+ton[2] (ˈtraɪtᵊn) *n.* the larger of the two satellites of Neptune and the nearer to the planet. Approximate diameter: 3700 km. Compare **Nereid**[2].

tri+tone (ˈtraɪˌtəʊn) *n.* a musical interval consisting of three whole tones; augmented fourth.

trit+u+rate (ˈtrɪtjʊˌreɪt) *vb.* **1.** (*tr.*) to grind or rub into a fine powder or pulp; masticate. ~*n.* **2.** the powder or pulp resulting from this grinding. [C17: from Late Latin *trītūrāre* to thresh, from Latin *trītūra* a threshing, from *terere* to grind] —**ˈtrit+u+ra+ble** *adj.* —**ˈtrit+u+ˌra+tor** *n.*

trit+u+ra+tion (ˌtrɪtjʊˈreɪʃən) *n.* **1.** the act of triturating or the state of being triturated. **2.** *Pharmacol.* a mixture of one or more finely ground powdered drugs.

tri+umph (ˈtraɪəmf) *n.* **1.** the feeling of exultation and happiness derived from a victory or major achievement. **2.** the act or condition of being victorious; victory. **3.** (in ancient Rome) a ritual procession to the Capitoline Hill held in honour of a victorious general. **4.** *Obsolete.* a public display or celebration. **5.** *Cards.* an obsolete word for **trump.** ~*vb.* (*intr.*) **6.** (often foll. by *over*) to win a victory or control: *to triumph over one's weaknesses.* **7.** to rejoice over a victory. **8.** to celebrate a Roman triumph. [C14: from Old French *triumphe,* from Latin *triumphus,* from Old Latin *triumpus;* probably related to Greek *thriambos* Bacchic hymn] —**ˈtri+umph+er** *n.*

tri+um+phal (traɪˈʌmfəl) *adj.* **1.** celebrating a triumph: *a triumphal procession.* **2.** resembling triumph.

tri+um+phal arch *n.* an arch built to commemorate a victory.

tri+um+phant (traɪˈʌmfənt) *adj.* **1.** experiencing or displaying triumph. **2.** exultant through triumph. **3.** *Obsolete.* **a.** magnificent. **b.** triumphal. —**tri+ˈum+phant+ly** *adv.*

tri+um+vir (traɪˈʌmvə) *n., pl.* **+virs** *or* **+vi+ri** (-vɪˌriː). (esp. in ancient Rome) a member of a triumvirate. [C16: from Latin: one of three administrators, from *trium virōrum* of three men, from *trēs* three + *vir* man] —**tri+ˈum+vi+ral** *adj.*

tri+um+vi+rate (traɪˈʌmvɪrɪt) *n.* **1.** (in ancient Rome) **a.** a board of three officials jointly responsible for some task. **b.** the political alliance of Caesar, Crassus, and Pompey, formed in 60 B.C. (**First Triumvirate**). **c.** the coalition and joint rule of the Roman Empire by Antony, Lepidus, and Octavian, begun in 43 B.C. (**Second Triumvirate**). **2.** any joint rule by three men. **3.** any group of three men associated in some way. **4.** the office of a triumvir.

tri+une (ˈtraɪjuːn) *adj.* **1.** *Theol.* constituting three in one, esp. the three persons in one God of the Trinity. ~*n.* **2.** a group of three. **3.** (*often cap.*) another word for **Trinity.** [C17: TRI- + *-une,* from Latin *ūnus* one] —**tri+ˈu+ni+ty** *n.*

Tri+u+ni+tar+i+an (traɪˌjuːnɪˈtɛərɪən) *adj.* a less common word for **Trinitarian.**

tri+va+lent (traɪˈveɪlənt, ˈtrɪvələnt) *adj. Chem.* **1.** having a valency of three. **2.** having three valencies. ~Also: **tervalent.** —**tri+ˈva+len+cy** *n.*

Tri+van+drum (trɪˈvændrəm) *n.* a city in S India, capital of Kerala, on the Malabar Coast: made capital of the kingdom of Travancore in 1745; University of Kerala (1937). Pop.: 409 672 (1971).

triv+et (ˈtrɪvɪt) *n.* **1.** a stand, usually three-legged and metal, on which cooking vessels are placed over a fire. **2.** a short metal stand on which hot dishes are placed on a table. **3. as right as a trivet.** in perfect health. [Old English *trefet* (influenced by Old English *thrifēte* having three feet), from Latin *tripēs* having three feet]

triv+i+a (ˈtrɪvɪə) *pl. n.* petty details or considerations; trifles; trivialities. [from New Latin, plural of Latin *trivium* junction of three roads; for meaning, see TRIVIAL]

triv+i+al (ˈtrɪvɪəl) *adj.* **1.** of little importance; petty or frivolous: *trivial complaints.* **2.** ordinary or commonplace; trite: *trivial conversation.* **3.** *Maths.* (of the solutions of a set of homogeneous equations) having zero values for all the variables. **4.** *Biology.* denoting the specific name of an organism in binomial nomenclature. **5.** of or relating to the trivium. [C15: from Latin *triviālis* belonging to the public streets, common, from *trivium* crossroads, junction of three roads, from TRI- + *via* road] —**ˈtriv+i+al+ly** *adv.* —**ˈtriv+i+al+ness** *n.*

triv+i+al+i+ty (ˌtrɪvɪˈælɪtɪ) *n., pl.* **+ties. 1.** the state or quality of being trivial. **2.** something, such as a remark, that is trivial. ~Also called: **triv+i+al+ism** (ˈtrɪvɪəˌlɪzəm).

triv+i+al+ize *or* **triv+i+al+ise** (ˈtrɪvɪəˌlaɪz) *vb.* (*tr.*) to cause to seem trivial or more trivial; minimize: *he trivialized his injuries.* —**ˌtriv+i+al+i+ˈza+tion** *or* **ˌtriv+i+al+i+ˈsa+tion** *n.*

triv+i+um (ˈtrɪvɪəm) *n., pl.* **+i+a** (-ɪə). (in medieval learning) the lower division of the seven liberal arts, consisting of grammar, rhetoric, and logic. Compare **quadrivium.** [C19: from Medieval Latin, from Latin: crossroads; see TRIVIAL]

tri+week+ly (traɪˈwiːklɪ) *adj., adv.* **1.** every three weeks. **2.** three times a week. ~*n., pl.* **+lies. 3.** a triweekly publication.

-trix *suffix of nouns.* indicating a feminine agent, corresponding to nouns ending in *-tor: executrix.* [from Latin]

t-RNA *n. abbrev. for* **transfer RNA.**

Tro+as (ˈtrəʊæs) *n.* the region of NW Asia Minor surrounding the ancient city of Troy. Also called: **the Tro+ad** (ˈtrəʊæd).

troat (trəʊt) *vb.* (*intr.*) (of a rutting buck) to call or bellow. [C17: probably related to Old French *trout, trut,* a cry used by hunters to urge on the dogs]

Tro+bri+and Is+lands (ˈtrəʊbrɪˌænd) *pl. n.* a group of coral islands in the Solomon Sea, north of the E part of New Guinea: part of Papua New Guinea. Area: about 440 sq. km (170 sq. miles). —**Tro+bri+and Is+land+er** *n.*

tro+car (ˈtrəʊkɑː) *n.* a surgical instrument for removing fluid from bodily cavities, consisting of a puncturing device situated inside a tube. [C18: from French *trocart* literally: with three sides, from *trois* three + *carre* side]

tro+cha+ic (trəʊˈkeɪɪk) *Prosody.* ~*adj.* **1.** of, relating to, or consisting of trochees. ~*n.* **2.** another word for **trochee. 3.** a verse composed of trochees. —**tro+ˈcha+i+cal+ly** *adv.*

tro+chal (ˈtrəʊkᵊl) *adj. Zoology.* shaped like a wheel: *the trochal disc of a rotifer.* [C19: from Greek *trokhos* wheel]

tro+chan+ter (trəʊˈkæntə) *n.* **1.** any of several processes on the upper part of the vertebrate femur, to which muscles are attached. **2.** the third segment of an insect's leg. [C17: via French from Greek *trokhantēr,* from *trekhein* to run]

troche (trəʊʃ) *n. Med.* another name for **lozenge** (sense 1). [C16: from French *trochisque,* from Late Latin *trochiscus,* from Greek *trokhiskos* little wheel, from *trokhos* wheel]

tro+chee (ˈtrəʊkiː) *n. Prosody.* a metrical foot of two syllables, the first long and the second short (¯˘). Compare **iamb.** [C16: via Latin from Greek *trokhaios pous,* literally: a running foot, from *trekhein* to run]

troch+el+minth (ˈtrɒkᵊlˌmɪnθ) *n.* any invertebrate of the former taxonomic group *Trochelminthes,* which included the rotifers and gastrotrichs, now classed as separate phyla. [C19: from New Latin *trochelminthes,* from Greek *trokhos* wheel, from *trekhein* to run + HELMINTH]

troch+i+lus (ˈtrɒkɪləs) *n.* **1.** another name for **hummingbird. 2.**

any of several Old World warblers, esp. *Phylloscopus trochilus* (willow warbler). [C16: via Latin from Greek *trokhilos* name of a small Egyptian bird said by ancient writers to pick the teeth of crocodiles, from *trekhein* to run]

troch·le·a ('trɒklɪə) *n., pl.* **·le·ae** (-lɪˌiː). any bony or cartilaginous part with a grooved surface over which a bone, tendon, etc., may slide or articulate. [C17: from Latin, from Greek *trokhileia* a sheaf of pulleys; related to *trokhos* wheel, *trekhein* to run]

troch·le·ar ('trɒklɪə) *adj.* **1.** of or relating to a trochlea or trochlear nerve. **2.** *Botany.* shaped like a pulley. *~n.* **3.** See **trochlear nerve.**

troch·le·ar nerve *n.* either one of the fourth pair of cranial nerves, which supply the superior oblique muscle of the eye.

tro·choid ('trəʊkɔɪd) *n.* **1.** the curve described by a fixed point on the radius or extended radius of a circle as the circle rolls along a straight line. *~adj. also* **tro·choi·dal. 2.** rotating or capable of rotating about a central axis. **3.** *Anatomy.* (of a structure or part) resembling or functioning as a pivot or pulley. [C18: from Greek *trokhoeidēs* circular, from *trokhos* wheel] **—tro·'choi·dal·ly** *adv.*

troch·o·phore ('trɒkəˌfɔː) *or* **troch·o·sphere** *n.* the ciliated planktonic larva of many invertebrates, including polychaete worms, molluscs, and rotifers. [C19: from Greek *trokhos* wheel + -PHORE]

trod (trɒd) *vb.* the past tense of **tread.**

trod·den ('trɒdᵊn) *vb.* the past participle of **tread.**

trode (trəʊd) *vb. Archaic.* a past tense of **tread.**

trog (trɒg) *vb.* **trogs, trog·ging, trogged.** (*intr.;* often foll. by *along*) *Brit. informal.* to walk, esp. aimlessly or heavily; stroll. [C20: perhaps a blend of TRUDGE and SLOG]

trog·lo·dyte ('trɒgləˌdaɪt) *n.* **1.** a cave dweller, esp. one of the prehistoric peoples thought to have lived in caves. **2.** *Informal.* a person who lives alone and appears eccentric. [C16: via Latin from Greek *trōglodutēs* one who enters caves, from *trōglē* hole + *duein* to enter] **—trog·lo·dyt·ic** (ˌtrɒglə'dɪtɪk) *or* **ˌtrog·lo·'dyt·i·cal** *adj.*

tro·gon ('trəʊgɒn) *n.* any bird of the order *Trogoniformes* of tropical and subtropical regions of America, Africa, and Asia. They have a brilliant plumage, short hooked bill, and long tail. See also **quetzal.** [C18: from New Latin, from Greek *trōgōn,* from *trōgein* to gnaw]

troi·ka ('trɔɪkə) *n.* **1.** a Russian vehicle drawn by three horses abreast. **2.** three horses harnessed abreast. **3.** a triumvirate. [C19: from Russian, from *troe* three]

troil·ism ('trɔɪlɪzəm) *n.* sexual activity involving three people. [C20: perhaps from French *trois* three (compare MÉNAGE À TROIS) + *-l-,* as in DUALISM]

Troi·lus ('trɔɪləs, 'trəʊɪləs) *n. Greek myth.* the youngest son of King Priam and Queen Hecuba, slain at Troy. In medieval romance he is portrayed as the lover of Cressida.

Trois Ri·vières (*French* trwɑ ri'vjɛːr) *n.* a port in central Canada, in Quebec on the St. Lawrence River: one of the world's largest centres of newsprint production. Pop.: 55 869 (1971). English name: **Three Rivers.**

Tro·jan ('trəʊdʒən) *n.* **1.** a native or inhabitant of ancient Troy. **2.** a person who is hardworking and determined. *~adj.* **3.** of or relating to ancient Troy or its inhabitants.

Tro·jan Horse *n.* **1.** Also called: the **Wooden Horse.** *Greek myth.* the huge wooden hollow figure of a horse left outside Troy by the Greeks when they feigned retreat and dragged inside by the Trojans. The men concealed inside it opened the city to the final Greek assault. **2.** a trap intended to undermine an enemy.

Tro·jan War *n. Greek myth.* a war fought by the Greeks against the Trojans to avenge the abduction of Helen from her Greek husband Menelaus by Paris, son of the Trojan king. It lasted ten years and ended in the sack of Troy.

troll[1] (trəʊl) *vb.* **1.** *Angling.* **a.** to draw (a baited line, etc.) through the water, often from a boat. **b.** to fish (a stretch of water) by trolling. **c.** to fish (for) by trolling. **2.** to roll or cause to roll. **3.** *Archaic.* to sing (a refrain, chorus, etc.) or (of a refrain, etc.) to be sung in a loud hearty voice. **4.** (*intr.*) *Brit. informal.* to walk or stroll. **5.** (*intr.*) *Homosexual slang.* to stroll around looking for sexual partners; cruise. *~n.* **6.** the act or an instance of trolling. **7.** *Angling.* a bait or lure used in trolling, such as a spinner. [C14: from Old French *troller* to run about; related to Middle High German *trollen* to run with short steps] **—'troll·er** *n.*

troll[2] (trəʊl) *n.* (in Scandinavian folklore) one of a class of supernatural creatures that dwell in caves or mountains and are depicted either as dwarfs or as giants. [C19: from Old Norse: demon; related to Danish *trold*]

trol·ley ('trɒlɪ) *n.* **1.** *Brit.* a small table on castors used for conveying food, drink, etc. **2.** *Brit.* a four-wheeled cart for transporting luggage at a railway station, airport, etc., or for carrying shopping or other goods. **3.** *Brit.* See **trolley bus. 4.** *U.S.* See **trolley car. 5.** a device that collects the current from an overhead wire (**trolley wire**), third rail, etc., to drive the motor of an electric vehicle. **6.** a pulley or truck that travels along an overhead wire in order to support a suspended load. **7.** *Chiefly Brit.* a low truck running on rails, used in factories, mines, etc., and on railways. **8.** a truck, cage, or basket suspended from an overhead track or cable for carrying loads in a mine, quarry, etc. [C19: probably from TROLL[1]]

trol·ley bus *n.* an electrically driven public-transport vehicle that does not run on rails but takes its power from an overhead wire through a trolley.

trol·ley car *n.* a U.S. name for **tram**[1] (sense 1).

trol·lop ('trɒləp) *n.* **1.** a promiscuous woman, esp. a prostitute. **2.** an untidy woman; slattern. [C17: perhaps from German dialect *trolle* prostitute; perhaps related to TRULL]

Trol·lope ('trɒləp) *n.* **An·tho·ny.** 1815–82, English novelist. His most successful novels, such as *The Warden* (1855), *Barchester Towers* (1857), and *Dr. Thorne* (1858), are those in the Barsetshire series of studies of English provincial life. The Palliser series of political novels includes *Phineas Redux* (1874) and *The Prime Minister* (1876).

trom·ba ma·ri·na ('trɒmbə mə'riːnə) *n.* an obsolete viol with a long thin body and a single string. It resembled the natural trumpet in its range of notes (limited to harmonics) and its tone. [from Italian, literally: marine trumpet]

trom·bi·di·a·sis (ˌtrɒmbɪ'daɪəsɪs) *n. Pathol.* infestation with mites of the family *Trombiculidae.* [C20: New Latin, from *Trombid(ium)* genus name + -IASIS]

trom·bone (trɒm'bəʊn) *n.* **1.** a brass instrument, a low-pitched counterpart of the trumpet, consisting of a tube the effective length of which is varied by means of a U-shaped slide. The usual forms of this instrument are the **tenor trombone** (range: about two and a half octaves upwards from E) and the **bass trombone** (pitched a fourth lower). **2.** a person who plays this instrument in an orchestra. [C18: from Italian, from *tromba* a trumpet, from Old High German *trumba*] **—trom·'bon·ist** *n.*

trom·mel ('trɒməl) *n.* a revolving cylindrical sieve used to screen crushed ore. [C19: from German: a drum]

trompe (trɒmp) *n.* an apparatus for supplying the blast of air in a forge, consisting of a thin column down which water falls, drawing in air through side openings. [C19: from French, literally: trumpet]

trompe l'oeil (*French* trɔ̃p 'lœj) *n., pl.* **trompe l'oeils** (trɔ̃p 'lœj). **1.** a painting or decoration giving a convincing illusion of reality. **2.** an effect of this kind. [from French, literally: deception of the eye]

Trom·sø ('trɒmsəʊ; *Norwegian* 'trumsø) *n.* a port in N Norway, on a small island between Kvaløy and the mainland: fishing and sealing centre. Pop.: 39 145 (1970).

-tron *suffix forming nouns.* **1.** indicating a vacuum tube: *magnetron.* **2.** indicating an instrument for accelerating atomic or subatomic particles: *synchrotron.* [from Greek, suffix indicating instrument]

tro·na ('trəʊnə) *n.* a greyish mineral that consists of hydrated sodium carbonate and occurs in salt deposits. Formula: $Na_2CO_3NaHCO_32H_2O$. [C18: from Swedish, probably from Arabic *natrūn* NATRON]

Trond·heim ('trɒndˌhaɪm; *Norwegian* 'trɔnheɪm) *n.* a port in central Norway, on **Trondheim Fjord** (an inlet of the Norwegian Sea): national capital until 1380; seat of the Technical University of Norway; the second largest city in the country. Pop.: 184 039 (1974 est.). Former name (until the 16th century and from 1930 to 1931): **Nidaros.**

troop (truːp) *n.* **1.** a large group or assembly; flock: *a troop of children.* **2.** a subdivision of a cavalry regiment of about company size. **3.** (*pl.*) armed forces; soldiers. **4.** a large group of Scouts or Girl Guides comprising several patrols. **5.** an archaic spelling of **troupe.** *~vb.* **6.** (*intr.*) to gather, move, or march in or as if in a crowd. **7.** (*tr.*) *Military, chiefly Brit.* to parade (the colour or flag) ceremonially: *trooping the colour.* **8.** (*tr.*) *Brit. military slang.* to report (a serviceman) for a breach of discipline. **9.** (*intr.*) an archaic word for **consort.** [C16: from French *troupe,* from *troupeau* flock, of Germanic origin]

troop car·ri·er *n.* a vehicle, aircraft, or ship designed for the carriage of troops.

troop·er ('truːpə) *n.* **1.** a soldier in a cavalry regiment. **2.** *U.S., Austral.* a mounted policeman. **3.** *U.S.* a state policeman. **4.** a cavalry horse. **5.** *Informal, chiefly Brit.* a troopship.

troop·ship ('truːpˌʃɪp) *n.* a ship, usually a converted merchant ship, used to transport military personnel.

troost·ite ('truːstaɪt) *n.* a reddish or greyish mineral that is a variety of willemite in which some of the zinc is replaced by manganese. [C19: named after Gerard *Troost* (died 1850), U.S. geologist]

trop. *abbrev. for* tropic(al).

tro·pae·o·lin (trəʊ'piːəlɪn) *n.* any of certain yellow and orange azo dyes of complex structure. [C19: see TROPAEOLUM, -IN]

tro·pae·o·lum (trəʊ'piːələm) *n., pl.* **·lums** *or* **·la** (-lə). any garden plant of the genus *Tropaeolum,* esp. the nasturtium. [C18: from New Latin, from Latin *tropaeum* TROPHY; referring to the shield-shaped leaves and helmet-shaped flowers]

trope (trəʊp) *n.* **1.** *Rhetoric.* a word or expression used in a figurative sense. **2.** an interpolation of words or music into the plainsong settings of the Roman Catholic liturgy. [C16: from Latin *tropus* figurative use of a word, from Greek *tropos* style, turn; related to *trepein* to turn]

-trope *n. combining form.* indicating a turning towards, development in the direction of, or affinity to: *heliotrope.* [from Greek *tropos* a turn]

troph·al·lax·is (ˌtrɒfə'læksɪs) *n.* the exchange of regurgitated food that occurs between adults and larvae in colonies of social insects. [C19/20: from New Latin, from TROPHO- + Greek *allaxis* exchange, from *allassein* to change, from *allos* other] **—ˌtroph·al·'lac·tic** *adj.*

troph·ic ('trɒfɪk) *adj.* of or relating to nutrition: *the trophic levels of a food chain.* [C19: from Greek *trophikos,* from *trophē* food, from *trephein* to feed] **—'troph·i·cal·ly** *adv.*

troph·o- *or before a vowel* **troph-** *combining form.* indicating nourishment or nutrition: *trophozoite.* [from Greek *trophē* food, from *trephein* to feed]

troph·o·blast ('trɒfəˌblæst) *n.* a membrane that encloses the embryo of placental mammals, becoming attached to the uterus wall and absorbing nourishment from the uterine fluids. —ˌ**troph·o+ˈblas+tic** *adj.*

troph·o+plasm (ˈtrɒfəˌplæzəm) *n. Biology.* the cytoplasm that is involved in the nutritive processes of a cell.

troph·o+zo+ite (ˌtrɒfəˈzəʊaɪt) *n.* the form of a protozoan of the class *Sporozoa* in the feeding stage. In the malaria parasite this stage occurs in the human red blood cell. Compare **merozoite.**

tro+phy (ˈtrəʊfɪ) *n., pl.* **+phies. 1.** an object such as a silver or gold cup that is symbolic of victory in a contest, esp. a sporting contest; prize. **2.** a memento of success, esp. one taken in war or hunting. **3.** (in ancient Greece and Rome) **a.** a memorial to a victory, usually consisting of captured arms raised on the battlefield or in a public place. **b.** a representation of such a memorial. **4.** an ornamental carving that represents a group of weapons, etc. [C16: from French *trophée,* from Latin *tropaeum,* from Greek *tropaion,* from *tropē* a turning, defeat of the enemy; related to Greek *trepein* to turn]

-tro·phy *n. combining form.* indicating a certain type of nourishment or growth: *dystrophy.* [from Greek *-trophia,* from *trophē* nourishment] —**-troph·ic** *adj. combining form.*

trop+ic (ˈtrɒpɪk) *n.* **1.** (*sometimes cap.*) either of the parallel lines of latitude at about 23½°N (**tropic of Cancer**) and 23½°S (**tropic of Capricorn**) of the equator. **2. the tropics.** (*often cap.*) that part of the earth's surface between the tropics of Cancer and Capricorn; the Torrid Zone. **3.** *Astronomy.* either of the two parallel circles on the celestial sphere having the same latitudes and names as the corresponding lines on the earth. ~*adj.* **4.** a less common word for **tropical.** [C14: from Late Latin *tropicus* belonging to a turn, from Greek *tropikos,* from *tropos* a turn; from the ancient belief that the sun turned back at the solstices]

-trop·ic *adj. combining form.* turning or developing in response to a certain stimulus: *heliotropic.* [from Greek *tropos* a turn; see TROPE]

trop·i+cal (ˈtrɒpɪkᵊl) *adj.* **1.** situated in, used in, characteristic of, or relating to the tropics. **2.** (of weather) very hot, esp. when humid. **3.** *Rhetoric.* of or relating to a trope. —ˌ**trop·i+ˈcal+i·ty** *n.* —ˈ**trop·i+cal+ly** *adv.*

trop·i+cal+ize *or* **trop·i+cal+ise** (ˈtrɒpɪkᵊˌlaɪz) *vb.* (*tr.*) to adapt to tropical use, temperatures, etc. —ˌ**trop·i+cal·i+ˈza+tion** *or* ˌ**trop·i+cal·i+ˈsa+tion** *n.*

trop·i+cal year *n.* another name for **solar year.** See **year** (sense 4).

trop·ic+bird (ˈtrɒpɪkˌbɜːd) *n.* any aquatic bird of the tropical family *Phaethontidae,* having long slender tail feathers and a white plumage with black markings: order *Pelecaniformes* (pelicans, cormorants, etc.).

tro+pine (ˈtrəʊpiːn, -pɪn) *n.* a white crystalline poisonous hygroscopic alkaloid obtained by heating atropine or hyoscyamine with barium hydroxide. Formula: $C_8H_{15}NO$. [C19: shortened from ATROPINE]

tro+pism (ˈtrəʊpɪzəm) *n.* the response of an organism, esp. a plant, to an external stimulus by growth in a direction determined by the stimulus. [from Greek *tropos* a turn] —ˌ**tro+pis+ˈmat+ic** *adj.* —**tro+pis+tic** (trəʊˈpɪstɪk) *adj.*

-tro·pism *or* **-tro·py** *combining form.* indicating a tendency to turn or develop in response to a certain stimulus: *phototropism.* [from Greek *tropos* a turn]

trop·o- *combining form.* indicating change or a turning: *tropophyte.* [from Greek *tropos* a turn]

tro+pol+o·gy (trɒˈpɒlədʒɪ) *n., pl.* **·gies. 1.** *Rhetoric.* the use of figurative language in speech or writing. **2.** *Theol.* the educing of moral or figurative meanings from the Scriptures. **3.** a treatise on tropes or figures of speech. [C16: via Late Latin from Greek *tropalogia;* see TROPE, -LOGY] —ˌ**trop·o+ˈlog+ic** *or* ˌ**trop·o+ˈlog·i+cal** *adj.*

trop·o+pause (ˈtrɒpəˌpɔːz) *n. Meteorol.* the plane of discontinuity between the troposphere and the stratosphere, characterized by a sharp change in the lapse rate and varying in altitude from about 18 kilometres (11 miles) above the equator to 6 km (4 miles) at the Poles.

tro+poph·i+lous (trɒˈpɒfɪləs) *adj.* (of plants) able to adapt to seasonal changes in temperature, rainfall, etc.

trop·o+phyte (ˈtrɒpəˌfaɪt) *n.* a plant that is able to adapt to seasonal changes in temperature, rainfall, etc. —**trop·o+phyt+ic** (ˌtrɒpəˈfɪtɪk) *adj.*

trop·o+sphere (ˈtrɒpəˌsfɪə) *n.* the lowest atmospheric layer, about 18 kilometres (11 miles) thick at the equator to about 6 km (4 miles) at the Poles, in which air temperature decreases normally with height at about 6.5°C per km. Most meteorological phenomena occur in this layer.

-tro·pous *adj. combining form.* indicating a turning away: *anatropous.* [from Greek *-tropos* concerning a turn]

trop+po[1] (ˈtrɒpəʊ) *adv. Music.* too much; excessively. See **non troppo.**

trop+po[2] (ˈtrɒpəʊ) *adj. Austral. slang.* mentally affected by a tropical climate.

Tros+sachs (ˈtrɒsəks) *pl. n.* **the.** a narrow wooded valley in central Scotland, between Loch Achray and Loch Katrine: made famous by Sir Walter Scott's descriptions.

trot (trɒt) *vb.* **trots, trot+ting, trot+ted. 1.** to move or cause to move at a trot. **2.** *Angling.* to fish (a fast-moving stream or river) by using a float and weighted line that carries the baited hook just above the bottom. ~*n.* **3.** a gait of a horse or other quadruped, faster than a walk, in which diagonally opposite legs come down together. See also **jog trot, rising trot, sitting trot. 4.** a steady brisk pace. **5.** (in harness racing) a race for horses that have been trained to trot fast. **6.** *Angling.* **a.** one of the short lines attached to a trotline. **b.** the trotline. **7.** *Austral. slang.* a run of luck: *a good trot.* **8.** *Chiefly Brit.* a small child; tot. **9.** *U.S. slang.* a student's crib. **10. on the trot.** *Informal.* **a.** one after the other: *to read two books on the trot.* **b.** busy, esp. on one's feet. **11. the trots.** *Informal.* diarrhoea. [C13: from Old French *trot,* from *troter* to trot, of Germanic origin; related to Middle High German *trotten* to run]

Trot (trɒt) *n. Informal.* a follower of Trotsky; Trotskyite.

troth (trəʊθ) *n. Archaic.* **1.** a pledge or oath of fidelity, esp. a betrothal. **2.** truth (esp. in the phrase **in troth**). **3.** loyalty; fidelity. [Old English *trēowth;* related to Old High German *gitriuwida* loyalty; see TRUTH]

troth+plight (ˈtrəʊθˌplaɪt) *Archaic.* ~*n.* **1.** a betrothal. ~*vb.* **2.** (*tr.*) to betroth. ~*adj.* **3.** betrothed; engaged.

trot+line (ˈtrɒtˌlaɪn) *n. Angling.* a long line suspended across a stream, river, etc., to which shorter hooked and baited lines are attached. Compare **trawl** (sense 2). See also **setline.**

trot out *vb.* (*tr., adv.*) *Informal.* to bring forward, as for approbation or admiration, esp. repeatedly: *he trots out the same excuses every time.*

Trot·sky *or* **Trot·ski** (ˈtrɒtskɪ) *n.* **Le·on,** original name *Lev Davidovich Bronstein.* 1879–1940, Russian revolutionary and Communist theorist. He was a leader of the November Revolution (1917) and, as commissar of foreign affairs and war (1917–24), largely created the Red Army. He was ousted by Stalin after Lenin's death and deported from Russia (1929); assassinated by a Stalinist agent.

Trot+sky+ism (ˈtrɒtskɪˌɪzəm) *n.* Trotsky's theory of communism, in which he called for immediate worldwide revolution by the proletariat. —ˈ**Trot+sky+ite** *or* ˈ**Trot+sky+ist** *n., adj.*

Trot+sky+ist In+ter+na+tion+al *n.* any of several international Trotskyist organizations that have developed from the international federation of anti-Stalinist Communists founded by Trotsky in 1936.

trot+ter (ˈtrɒtə) *n.* **1.** a person or animal that trots, esp. a horse that is specially trained to trot fast. **2.** (*usually pl.*) the foot of certain animals, esp. of pigs.

tro+tyl (ˈtrəʊtɪl, -tiːl) *n.* another name for **TNT.** [C20: from (TRINI)TROT(OLUENE) + -YL]

trou+ba+dour (ˈtruːbəˌdʊə) *n.* **1.** any of a class of lyric poets who flourished principally in Provence and N Italy from the 11th to the 13th centuries, writing chiefly on courtly love in complex metric form. **2.** a singer. [C18: from French, from Old Provençal *trobador,* from *trobar* to write verses, perhaps ultimately from Latin *tropus* TROPE]

trou+ble (ˈtrʌbᵊl) *n.* **1.** a state or condition of mental distress or anxiety. **2.** a state or condition of disorder or unrest: *industrial trouble.* **3.** a condition of disease, pain, or malfunctioning: *she has liver trouble.* **4.** a cause of distress, disturbance, or pain; problem: *what is the trouble?* **5.** effort or exertion taken to do something: *he took a lot of trouble over this design.* **6.** liability to suffer punishment or misfortune (esp. in the phrase **be in trouble**): *he's in trouble with the police.* **7.** the condition of an unmarried girl who becomes pregnant (esp. in the phrase **in trouble**). ~*vb.* **8.** (*tr.*) to cause trouble to; upset, pain, or worry. **9.** (*intr.;* usually with a negative and foll. by *about*) to put oneself to inconvenience; be concerned: *don't trouble about me.* **10.** (*intr.;* usually with a negative) to take pains; exert oneself: *please don't trouble to write everything down.* **11.** (*tr.*) to cause inconvenience or discomfort to: *does this noise trouble you?* **12.** (*tr.; usually passive*) to agitate or make rough: *the seas were troubled.* **13.** (*tr.*) *Caribbean.* to interfere with: *he wouldn't like anyone to trouble his new bicycle.* [C13: from Old French *troubler,* from Vulgar Latin *turbulāre* (unattested), from Late Latin *turbidāre,* from *turbidus* confused, from *turba* commotion] —ˈ**trou+bled+ly** *adv.* —ˈ**trou+bler** *n.* —ˈ**trou+bling+ly** *adv.*

trou·ble+mak·er (ˈtrʌbᵊlˌmeɪkə) *n.* a person who makes trouble, esp. between people. —ˈ**trou·ble+ˌmak·ing** *adj., n.*

trou·ble+shoot·er (ˈtrʌbᵊlˌʃuːtə) *n. Chiefly U.S.* a person who locates the cause of trouble and removes or treats it, as in the running of a machine. —ˈ**trou·ble+ˌshoot·ing** *n., adj.*

trou+ble+some (ˈtrʌbᵊlsəm) *adj.* **1.** causing a great deal of trouble; worrying, upsetting, or annoying. **2.** characterized by violence; turbulent. **3.** *Archaic.* agitated or disturbed. —ˈ**trou+ble+some+ly** *adv.* —ˈ**trou+ble+some+ness** *n.*

trou+ble spot *n.* a place of recurring trouble, esp. of political unrest.

trou+blous (ˈtrʌbləs) *adj. Archaic or literary.* unsettled; agitated. —ˈ**trou+blous+ly** *adv.* —ˈ**trou+blous+ness** *n.*

trou-de-loup (ˌtruːdᵊˈluː) *n., pl.* **trous-de-loup** (ˌtruːdᵊˈluː). *Military.* any of a series of conical-shaped pits with a stake fixed in the centre, formerly used as protection against enemy cavalry. [C18: from French, literally: wolf's hole]

trough (trɒf) *n.* **1.** a narrow open container, esp. one in which food or water for animals is put. **2.** a narrow channel, gutter, or gulley. **3.** a narrow depression either in the land surface, ocean bed, or between two successive waves. **4.** *Meteorol.* an elongated area of low pressure, esp. an extension of a depression. Compare **ridge** (sense 6). **5.** a single or temporary low point; depression. **6.** *Physics.* the portion of a wave, such as a light wave, in which the amplitude lies below its average value. **7.** *Economics.* the lowest point or most depressed stage of the trade cycle. [Old English *trōh;* related to Old Saxon, Old Norse *trog* trough, Dutch *trügge* ladle] —ˈ**trough+ˌlike** *adj.*

trounce (traʊns) *vb.* (*tr.*) to beat or defeat utterly; thrash. [C16: of unknown origin]

troupe (truːp) *n.* **1.** a company of actors or other performers, esp. one that travels. ~*vb.* **2.** (*intr.*) (esp. of actors) to move or travel in a group. [C19: from French; see TROOP]

troup+er ('truːpə) *n.* **1.** a member of a troupe. **2.** an experienced or dependable worker or associate.

trou+pi·al ('truːpɪəl) *n.* any of various American orioles of the genus *Icterus,* esp. *I. icterus,* a bright orange-and-black South American bird. [C19: from French *troupiale,* from *troupe* flock; referring to its gregarious habits]

trouse (traʊz) *pl. n. Brit.* close-fitting breeches worn in Ireland; trews.

trou+ser ('traʊzə) *n.* (*modifier*) of or relating to trousers: *trouser buttons.*

trou+sers ('traʊzəz) *pl. n.* **1.** a garment shaped to cover the body from the waist to the ankles or knees with separate tube-shaped sections for both legs. **2. wear the trousers.** *Brit. informal.* to have control, esp. in a marriage. U.S. equivalent: **wear the pants.** [C17: from earlier *trouse,* variant of TREWS, influenced by DRAWERS] —'**trou+sered** *adj.* —'**trou+ser+less** *adj.*

trou+ser suit *n. Chiefly Brit.* a woman's suit of a jacket or top and trousers. Also called (esp. U.S.): **pant suit.**

trous+seau ('truːsəʊ) *n., pl.* **+seaux** *or* **+seaus** (-səʊz). the clothes, linen, etc., collected by a bride for her marriage. [C19: from Old French, literally: a little bundle, from *trusse* a bundle; see TRUSS]

trout (traʊt) *n., pl.* **trout** *or* **trouts. 1.** any of various game fishes of the genera *Salmo* (**brown trout,** etc.) and *Salvelinus* (**brook trout**), mostly of fresh water in northern regions: family *Salmonidae* (salmon). They resemble salmon but are smaller and spotted. **2.** any of various similar or related fishes, such as a sea trout. **3.** *Brit. informal.* a person, esp. an unattractive woman. [Old English *trūht,* from Late Latin *tructa,* from Greek *troktēs* sharp-toothed fish]

trou+vère (truː'vɛə; *French* truˈvɛːr) *or* **trou+veur** (*French* truˈvœːr) *n.* any of a group of poets of N France during the 12th and 13th centuries who composed chiefly narrative works. [C19: from French, from Old French *troveor,* from *trover* to compose; related to TROUBADOUR]

trove (trəʊv) *n.* See **treasure-trove.**

tro+ver ('trəʊvə) *n. Law.* (formerly) the act of wrongfully assuming proprietary rights over personal goods or property belonging to another. [C16: from Old French, from *trover* to find; see TROUVÈRE, TROUBADOUR]

trow (trəʊ) *vb. Archaic.* to think, believe, or trust. [Old English *treow;* related to Old Frisian *triūwe,* Old Saxon *treuwa,* Old High German *triuwa;* see TROTH, TRUE]

Trow+bridge ('trəʊˌbrɪdʒ) *n.* a market town in SW England, administrative centre of Wiltshire: woollen manufacturing. Pop.: 19 245 (1971).

trow+el ('traʊəl) *n.* **1.** any of various small hand tools having a flat metal blade attached to a handle, used for scooping or spreading plaster or similar materials. **2.** a similar tool with a curved blade used by gardeners for lifting plants, etc. ~*vb.* **+els, +el+ling, +elled** *or U.S.* **+els, +el+ing, +eled. 3.** (*tr.*) to use a trowel on (plaster, soil, etc.). [C14: from Old French *truele,* from Latin *trulla* a scoop, from *trua* a stirring spoon] —'**trow+el+ler** *n.*

Troy (trɔɪ) *n.* any of nine ancient cities in NW Asia Minor, each of which was built on the ruins of its predecessor. The seventh was the site of the Trojan War (mid-13th century B.C.). Greek name: **Ilion.** Latin name: **Ilium.**

Troyes (*French* trwa) *n.* an industrial city in NE France: became prosperous through its great fairs in the early Middle Ages. Pop.: 75 500 (1975).

troy weight *or* **troy** *n.* a system of weights used for precious metals and gemstones, based on the grain, which is identical to the avoirdupois grain. 24 grains = 1 pennyweight; 20 pennyweights = 1 (troy) ounce; 12 ounces = 1 (troy) pound. [C14: named after the city of *Troyes,* France, where it was first used]

Trst (trst) *n.* the Slovene and Serbo-Croatian name for **Trieste.**

tru+ant ('truːənt) *n.* **1.** a person who is absent without leave, esp. from school. ~*adj.* **2.** being or relating to a truant. ~*vb.* **3.** (*intr.*) to play truant. [C13: from Old French: vagabond, probably of Celtic origin; compare Welsh *truan* miserable, Old Irish *trōg* wretched] —'**tru+an+cy** *n.*

truce (truːs) *n.* **1.** an agreement to stop fighting, esp. temporarily. **2.** temporary cessation of something unpleasant. [C13: from the plural of Old English *treow* TROW; see TRUE, TRUST]

Tru+cial States ('truːʃəl) *n.* a former name (until 1971) of the **United Arab Emirates.** Also called: **Trucial Sheikdoms, Trucial Oman, Trucial Coast.**

truck[1] (trʌk) *n.* **1.** *Brit.* a vehicle for carrying freight on a railway; wagon. **2.** another name (esp. U.S.) for **lorry** (sense 1). **3.** a frame carrying two or more pairs of wheels and usually springs and brakes, attached under an end of a railway coach, etc. **4.** the swivelling frame carrying the wheels attached below the deck of a skateboard. **5.** *Nautical.* **a.** a disc-shaped block fixed to the head of a mast having sheave holes for receiving signal halyards. **b.** the head of a mast itself. **6.** any wheeled vehicle used to move goods. ~*vb.* **7.** to convey (goods) in a truck. **8.** (*intr.*) *Chiefly U.S.* to drive a truck. [C17: perhaps shortened from TRUCKLE[2]]

truck[2] (trʌk) *n.* **1.** commercial goods. **2.** dealings (esp. in the phrase **have no truck with**). **3.** commercial exchange. **4.** payment of wages in kind. **5.** miscellaneous articles. **6.** *Informal.* rubbish. **7.** *U.S.* vegetables grown for market. ~*vb.* **8.** to exchange (goods); barter. **9.** (*intr.*) to traffic or negotiate. [C13: from Old French *troquer* (unattested) to barter, equivalent to Medieval Latin *trocare,* of unknown origin]

truck+age ('trʌkɪdʒ) *n. U.S.* **1.** conveyance of cargo by truck. **2.** the charge for this.

truck+er[1] ('trʌkə) *n. U.S.* **1.** a lorry-driver. **2.** a person who arranges for the transport of goods by lorry.

truck+er[2] ('trʌkə) *n. U.S.* **1.** a market gardener. **2.** another word for **hawker**[1].

truck farm *n. U.S.* a market garden. —**truck farm+er** *n.* —**truck farm+ing** *n.*

truck·ie ('trʌkɪ) *n. Austral. informal.* a truck driver.

truck+ing[1] ('trʌkɪŋ) *n. U.S.* the transportation of goods by lorry.

truck+ing[2] ('trʌkɪŋ) *n.* **1.** the usual U.S. term for **market gardening. 2.** commercial exchange; barter.

truck+le[1] ('trʌkəl) *vb.* (*intr.;* usually foll. by *to*) to yield weakly; give in. [C17: from obsolete *truckle* to sleep in a truckle bed; see TRUCKLE[2]] —'**truck+ler** *n.*

truck+le[2] ('trʌkəl) *n.* **1.** a small wheel; caster. ~*vb.* **2.** (*intr.*) to roll on truckles. **3.** (*tr.*) to push (a piece of furniture) along on truckles. [C15 *trokel,* from Anglo-Norman *trocle,* from Latin *trochlea* sheaf of a pulley; see TROCHLEA]

truck+le bed *n.* a low bed on wheels, stored under a larger bed, used esp. formerly by a servant.

truck+load ('trʌkˌləʊd) *n.* the amount carried by a truck.

truck sys+tem *n.* a system during the early years of the Industrial Revolution of forcing workers to accept payment of wages in kind, usually to the employer's advantage.

truc·u+lent ('trʌkjʊlənt) *adj.* **1.** defiantly aggressive, sullen, or obstreperous. **2.** *Archaic.* savage, fierce, or harsh. [C16: from Latin *truculentus,* from *trux* fierce] —'**truc·u+lence** *or* '**truc·u+len+cy** *n.* —'**truc·u+lent+ly** *adv.*

Tru·deau (truː'dəʊ) *n.* **Pierre El·li·ott.** born 1919, Canadian statesman; Liberal prime minister (1968–79; since 1980).

trudge (trʌdʒ) *vb.* **1.** (*intr.*) to walk or plod heavily or wearily. **2.** (*tr.*) to pass through or over by trudging. ~*n.* **3.** a long tiring walk. [C16: of obscure origin] —'**trudg+er** *n.*

trudg+en ('trʌdʒən) *n.* a type of swimming stroke that uses overarm action, as in the crawl, and a scissors kick. [C19: named after John *Trudgen,* English swimmer, who introduced it]

true (truː) *adj.* **tru+er, tru+est. 1.** not false, fictional, or illusory; factual or factually accurate; conforming with reality. **2.** (*prenominal*) being of real or natural origin; genuine; not synthetic: *true leather.* **3. a.** unswervingly faithful and loyal to friends, a cause, etc.: *a true follower.* **b.** (*as n.*): *the loyal and the true.* **4.** faithful to a particular concept of truth, esp. of religious truth: *a true believer.* **5.** conforming to a required standard, law, or pattern: *a true aim; a true fit.* **6.** exactly in tune: *a true note.* **7.** (of a compass bearing) according to the earth's geographical rather than magnetic poles: *true north.* **8.** *Biology.* conforming to the typical structure of a designated type: *sphagnum moss is a true moss, Spanish moss is not.* **9.** *Physics.* not apparent or relative; taking into account all complicating factors: *the true expansion of a liquid takes into account the expansion of the container.* Compare **apparent** (sense 3). **10. true to life.** exactly comparable with reality. ~*n.* **11.** correct alignment (esp. in the phrases **in true, out of true**). ~*adv.* **12.** truthfully; rightly. **13.** precisely or unswervingly: *he shot true.* **14.** *Biology.* without variation from the ancestral type: *to breed true.* ~*vb.* **trues, tru+ing, trued. 15.** (*tr.*) to adjust so as to make true. [Old English *triewe;* related to Old Frisian *triūwe,* Old Saxon, Old High German *triuwi* loyal, Old Norse *tryggr;* see TROW, TRUST] —'**true+ness** *n.*

true bill *n. Criminal law.* (formerly in Britain; now only U.S.) the endorsement made on a bill of indictment by a grand jury certifying it to be supported by sufficient evidence to warrant committing the accused to trial.

true-blue *adj.* **1.** unwaveringly or staunchly loyal, esp. to a person, a cause, etc. ~*n.* **true blue. 2.** *Chiefly Brit.* a staunch royalist or conservative.

true-born *adj.* being such by birth: *a true-born Japanese.*

true lev+el *n.* a hypothetical surface that is perpendicular at every point to the plumb line, such as the mean sea level or geoid: *a still liquid surface is at true level.*

true+love ('truːˌlʌv) *n.* **1.** someone truly loved; sweetheart. **2.** another name for **herb Paris.**

true+love knot *or* **true-lov·ers' knot** *n.* a complicated bowknot that is hard to untie, symbolizing ties of love.

true rib *n.* any of the upper seven pairs of ribs in man.

true time *n.* the time shown by a sundial; solar time. When the sun is at the highest point in its daily path, the true time is exactly noon. Compare **mean time.**

Truf·faut (*French* tryˈfo) *n.* **Fran·çois** (frãˈswa). born 1932, French film director of the New Wave. His films include *Les Quatre Cents Coups* (1959), *Jules et Jim* (1961), and *Baisers volés* (1968).

truf+fle ('trʌfəl) *n.* **1.** Also called: **earthnut.** any of various edible saprophytic ascomycetous subterranean fungi of the European genus *Tuber.* They have a tuberous appearance and are regarded as a delicacy. **2.** Also called: **rum truffle.** *Chiefly Brit.* a sweet resembling this fungus in shape, flavoured with chocolate or rum. [C16: from French *truffe,* from Old Provençal *trufa,* ultimately from Latin *tūber*]

trug (trʌg) *n.* a long shallow basket for carrying flowers, fruit, etc. [C16: perhaps dialect variant of TROUGH]

tru+ism ('truːɪzəm) *n.* an obvious truth; platitude. —**tru+'is+tic** *or* **tru+'is+ti+cal** *adj.*

Tru·jil·lo (*Spanish* truˈxijo) *n.* a city in NW Peru: founded 1535; university (1824); centre of a district producing rice and sugar cane. Pop.: 240 322 (1972).

Truk Is·lands (trʌk) *pl. n.* a group of islands in the W Pacific, in the E Caroline Islands: administratively part of the U.S. Trust Territory of the Pacific Islands; consists of 11 chief islands; a major Japanese naval base during World War II. Pop.: 32 732 (1972). Area: 130 sq. km (50 sq. miles).

trull (trʌl) *n. Archaic.* a prostitute; harlot. [C16: from German *Trulle;* see TROLLOP]

tru·ly ('tru:lɪ) *adv.* **1.** in a true, just, or faithful manner. **2.** (intensifier): *a truly great man.* **3.** indeed; really. ~See also **yours truly.**

Tru·man ('tru:mən) *n.* **Har·ry S.** 1884–1972, U.S. Democratic statesman; 33rd president of the U.S. (1945–52). He approved the dropping of the two atom bombs on Japan (1945), advocated the postwar loan to Britain, and involved the U.S. in the Korean War.

tru·meau (trʊ'məʊ) *n. Architect.* a section of a wall or pillar between two openings. [from French]

trump[1] (trʌmp) *n.* **1.** Also called: **trump card. a.** any card from the suit chosen as trumps. **b.** this suit itself; trumps. **2.** Also called: **trump card.** a decisive or advantageous move, resource, action, etc. **3.** *Informal.* a fine or reliable person. ~*vb.* **4.** to play a trump card on a plain suit. **5.** (*tr.*) to outdo or surpass. ~See also **trumps, trump up.** [C16: variant of TRIUMPH] —**'trump·less** *adj.*

trump[2] (trʌmp) *Archaic or literary.* ~*n.* **1.** a trumpet or the sound produced by one. **2. the last trump.** the final trumpet call that according to the belief of some will awaken and raise the dead on the Day of Judgment. ~*vb.* **3.** (*intr.*) to produce a sound upon or as if upon the trumpet. **4.** (*tr.*) to proclaim or announce with or as if with a fanfare. [C13: from Old French *trompe,* from Old High German *trumpa* trumpet; compare TROMBONE]

trump·er·y ('trʌmpərɪ) *n., pl.* **·er·ies. 1.** foolish talk or actions. **2.** a useless or worthless article; trinket. ~*adj.* **3.** useless or worthless. [C15: from Old French *tromperie* deceit, from *tromper* to cheat]

trum·pet ('trʌmpɪt) *n.* **1.** a valved brass instrument of brilliant tone consisting of a narrow tube of cylindrical bore ending in a flared bell, normally pitched in B flat. Range: two and a half octaves upwards from F sharp on the fourth line of the bass staff. **2.** any instrument consisting of a valveless tube ending in a bell, esp. a straight instrument used for fanfares, signals, etc. **3.** a person who plays a trumpet in an orchestra. **4.** a loud sound such as that of a trumpet, esp. when made by an animal: *the trumpet of the elephants.* **5.** an eight-foot reed stop on an organ. **6.** something resembling a trumpet in shape, esp. in having a flared bell. **7.** short for **ear trumpet. 8.** *Brit.* **blow one's own trumpet.** to boast about oneself; brag. ~*vb.* **9.** to proclaim or sound loudly. [C13: from Old French *trompette* a little TRUMP[2]] —**'trum·pet-,like** *adj.*

trum·pet·er ('trʌmpɪtə) *n.* **1.** a person who plays the trumpet, esp. one whose duty it is to play fanfares, signals, etc. **2.** any of three birds of the genus *Psophia* of the forests of South America, having a rounded body, long legs, and a glossy blackish plumage: family *Psophiidae,* order *Gruiformes* (cranes, rails, etc.). **3.** (*sometimes cap.*) a breed of domestic fancy pigeon with a long ruff.

trum·pet·er swan *n.* a large swan, *Cygnus buccinator,* of W North America, having a white plumage and black bill.

trum·pet flow·er *n.* **1.** any of various plants having trumpet-shaped flowers. **2.** the flower of any of these plants.

trum·pet hon·ey·suck·le *n.* a North American honeysuckle shrub, *Lonicera sempervirens,* having orange, scarlet, or yellow trumpet-shaped flowers.

trum·pet·weed ('trʌmpɪt,wi:d) *n. U.S.* any of various eupatorium plants, esp. joe-pye weed.

trumps (trʌmps) *pl. n.* **1.** *Cards.* any one of the four suits, decided by cutting or bidding, that outranks all the other suits for the duration of a deal or game. **2. turn up trumps.** (of a person) to bring about a happy or successful conclusion (to an event, problem, etc.), esp. unexpectedly.

trump up *vb.* (*tr., adv.*) to concoct or invent (a charge, accusation, etc.) so as to deceive or implicate someone.

trun·cate *vb.* (trʌŋ'keɪt, 'trʌŋkeɪt). **1.** (*tr.*) to shorten by cutting off a part, end, or top. ~*adj.* ('trʌŋkeɪt). **2.** cut short; truncated. **3.** *Biology.* having a blunt end, as though cut off at the tip: *a truncate leaf.* [C15: from Latin *truncāre* to lop] —**'trun·cate·ly** *adv.* —**trun·'ca·tion** *n.*

trun·cat·ed ('trʌŋkeɪtɪd) *adj.* **1.** *Maths.* (of a cone, pyramid, prism, etc.) having an apex or end removed by a plane intersection that is usually nonparallel to the base. **2.** (of a crystal) having edges or corners cut off. **3.** shortened by or as if by cutting off; truncate.

trun·cheon ('trʌntʃən) *n.* **1.** *Chiefly Brit.* a short thick club or cudgel carried by a policeman. **2.** a baton of office: *a marshal's truncheon.* **3.** *Archaic.* a short club or cudgel. **4.** the shaft of a spear. ~*vb.* **5.** (*tr.*) to beat with a truncheon. [C16: from Old French *tronchon* stump, from Latin *truncus* trunk; see TRUNCATE]

trun·dle ('trʌndᵊl) *vb.* **1.** to move heavily on or as if on wheels: *the bus trundled by.* **2.** (*tr.*) *Archaic.* to rotate or spin. ~*n.* **3.** the act or an instance of trundling. **4.** a small wheel or roller. **5. a.** the pinion of a lantern. **b.** any of the bars in a lantern pinion. **6.** a small truck with low wheels. [Old English *tryndel;* related to Middle High German *trendel* disc] —**'trun·dler** *n.*

trun·dle bed *n.* a less common word for **truckle bed.**

trunk (trʌŋk) *n.* **1.** the main stem of a tree, usually thick and upright, covered with bark and having branches at some distance from the ground. **2.** a large strong case or box used to contain clothes and other personal effects when travelling and for storage. **3.** *Anatomy.* the body excluding the head, neck, and limbs; torso. **4.** the elongated prehensile nasal part of an elephant; proboscis. **5.** the U.S. name for **boot**[1] (sense 2). **6.** *Anatomy.* the main stem of a nerve, blood vessel, etc. **7.** *Nautical.* a watertight boxlike cover within a vessel with its top above the waterline, such as one used to enclose a centreboard. **8.** an enclosed duct or passageway for ventilation, etc. **9.** (*modifier*) of or relating to a main road, railway, etc., in a network: *a trunk line.* [C15: from Old French *tronc,* from Latin *truncus,* from *truncus* (adj.) lopped] —**'trunk·,ful** *n.* —**'trunk·less** *adj.*

trunk cab·in *n. Nautical.* a long relatively low cabin above the deck of a yacht.

trunk call *n. Chiefly Brit.* a long-distance telephone call.

trunk curl *n.* a physical exercise in which the body is brought into a sitting position from one of lying on the back, the legs being kept straight and in contact with the floor. Also called: **sit-up.**

trunk·fish ('trʌŋk,fɪʃ) *n., pl.* **·fish** *or* **·fish·es.** any tropical plectognath fish of the family *Ostraciidae,* having the body encased in bony plates with openings for the fins, eyes, mouth, etc. Also called: **boxfish, cowfish.**

trunk hose *n.* a man's puffed-out breeches reaching to the thighs and worn with tights in the 16th century.

trunk line *n.* **1.** a direct link between two telephone exchanges or switchboards that are a considerable distance apart. **2.** the main route or routes on a railway.

trunk road *n. Brit.* a main road, esp. one that is suitable for heavy vehicles.

trunks (trʌŋks) *pl. n.* **1.** Also called: **swimming trunks.** a man's garment worn for swimming, either fairly loose and extending from the waist to the thigh or briefer and close-fitting. **2.** shorts worn for some sports. **3.** *Chiefly Brit.* men's underpants with legs that reach midthigh.

trun·nel ('trʌnᵊl) *n.* a variant spelling of **treenail.**

trun·nion ('trʌnjən) *n.* **1.** one of a pair of coaxial projections attached to opposite sides of a container, cannon, etc., to provide a support about which it can turn in a vertical. **2.** the structure supporting such a projection. [C17: from Old French *trognon* trunk] —**'trun·nioned** *adj.*

Tru·ro ('trʊərəʊ) *n.* a market town in SW England, administrative centre of Cornwall. Pop.: 14 830 (1971).

truss (trʌs) *vb.* (*tr.*) **1.** (sometimes foll. by *up*) to tie, bind, or bundle: *to truss up a prisoner.* **2.** to fasten or bind the wings and legs of (a fowl) before cooking to keep them in place. **3.** to support or stiffen (a roof, bridge, etc.) with structural members. **4.** *Informal.* to confine (the body or a part of it) in tight clothes. **5.** *Falconry.* (of falcons) to hold (the quarry) in the stoop without letting go. **6.** *Med.* to supply or support with a truss. ~*n.* **7.** a structural framework of wood or metal, esp. one arranged in triangles, used to support a roof, bridge, etc. **8.** *Med.* a device for holding a hernia in place, typically consisting of a pad held in position by a belt. **9.** *Horticulture.* a cluster of flowers or fruit growing at the end of a single stalk. **10.** *Nautical.* a metal fitting fixed to a yard at its centre for holding it to a mast while allowing movement. **11.** *Architect.* another name for **corbel. 12.** a bundle or pack. **13.** *Chiefly Brit.* a bundle of hay or straw, esp. one having a fixed weight of 36, 56, or 60 pounds. [C13: from Old French *trousse,* from *trousser,* apparently from Vulgar Latin *torciāre* (unattested), from *torca* (unattested) a bundle, TORCH] —**'truss·er** *n.*

truss bridge *n.* a bridge that is constructed of trusses.

truss·ing ('trʌsɪŋ) *n. Engineering.* **1.** a system of trusses, esp. for strengthening or reinforcing a structure. **2.** the parts or members that form a truss.

trust (trʌst) *n.* **1.** reliance on and confidence in the truth, worth, reliability, etc., of a person or thing; faith. Related adj.: **fiducial. 2.** a group of commercial enterprises combined to monopolize and control the market for any commodity: illegal in the U.S. **3.** the obligation of someone in a responsible position: *a position of trust.* **4.** custody, charge, or care: *a child placed in my trust.* **5.** a person or thing in which confidence or faith is placed. **6.** commercial credit. **7. a.** an arrangement whereby a person to whom the legal title to property is conveyed (the trustee) holds such property for the benefit of those entitled to the beneficial interest. **b.** property that is the subject of such an arrangement. **c.** the confidence put in the trustee. Related adj.: **fiduciary. 8.** See **trust company, trust account** (sense 2). **9.** (*modifier*) of or relating to a trust or trusts: *trust property.* ~*vb.* **10.** (*tr.; may take a clause as object*) to expect, hope, or suppose: *I trust that you are well.* **11.** (when *tr., may take an infinitive;* when *intr.,* often foll. by *in* or *to*) to place confidence in (someone to do something); have faith (in); rely (upon): *I trust him to tell her.* **12.** (*tr.*) to consign for care: *the child was trusted to my care.* **13.** (*tr.*) to allow (someone to do something) with confidence in his or her good sense or honesty: *I trust my daughter to go.* **14.** (*tr.*) to extend business credit to. [C13: from Old Norse *traust;* related to Old High German *Trost* solace] —**'trust·a·ble** *adj.* —**,trust·a·'bil·i·ty** *n.* —**'trust·er** *n.*

trust ac·count *n.* **1.** Also called: **trustee account.** a savings account deposited in the name of a trustee who controls it during his lifetime, after which the balance is payable to a prenominated beneficiary. **2.** property under the control of a trustee or trustees.

trust·bust·er ('trʌst,bʌstə) *n. U.S. informal.* a person who seeks the dissolution of corporate trusts, esp. a federal official who prosecutes trusts under the antitrust laws. —**'trust·,bust·ing** *n.*

trust com·pa·ny *n.* a commercial bank or other enterprise organized to perform trustee functions. Also called: **trust corporation.**

trus+tee (trʌ'sti:) *n.* **1.** a person to whom the legal title to property is entrusted to hold or use for another's benefit. **2.** a member of a board that manages the affairs and administers the funds of an institution or organization.

trus+tee+ship (trʌ'sti:ʃɪp) *n.* **1.** the office or function of a trustee. **2. a.** the administration or government of a territory by a foreign country under the supervision of the **Trusteeship Council** of the United Nations. **b.** (*often cap.*) any such dependent territory; trust territory.

trust+ful ('trʌstfʊl) *or* **trust+ing** *adj.* characterized by a tendency or readiness to trust others. —**'trust+ful+ly** *or* **'trust+ing+ly** *adv.* —**'trust+ful+ness** *or* **'trust+ing+ness** *n.*

trust fund *n.* money, securities, etc., held in trust.

trust+less ('trʌstlɪs) *adj. Archaic or literary.* **1.** untrustworthy; deceitful. **2.** distrusting; suspicious; wary. —**'trust+less+ly** *adv.* —**'trust+less+ness** *n.*

trust ter+ri+to·ry *n.* (*sometimes cap.*) another name for a **trusteeship** (sense 2).

trust+wor·thy ('trʌst,wɜ:ðɪ) *adj.* worthy of being trusted; honest, reliable, or dependable. —**'trust+,wor·thi+ly** *adv.* —**'trust+,wor·thi+ness** *n.*

trust·y ('trʌstɪ) *adj.* **trust·i+er, trust·i+est. 1.** faithful or reliable. **2.** *Archaic.* trusting. ~*n., pl.* **trust·ies. 3.** someone who is trusted, esp. a convict to whom special privileges are granted. —**'trust·i+ly** *adv.* —**'trust·i+ness** *n.*

truth (tru:θ) *n.* **1.** the quality of being true, genuine, actual, or factual: *the truth of his statement was attested.* **2.** something that is true as opposed to false: *you did not tell me the truth.* **3.** a proven or verified fact, principle, statement, etc.: *the truths of astronomy.* **4.** a concept or system of concepts, regarded as accurately representing some aspect of the world, the universe, etc.: *the truths of ancient religions.* **5.** fidelity to a required standard or law. **6.** faithful reproduction or portrayal: *the truth of a portrait.* **7.** an obvious fact; truism; platitude. **8.** honesty, reliability, or veracity: *the truth of her nature.* **9.** accuracy, as in the setting, adjustment, or position of something, such as a mechanical instrument. **10.** the state or quality of being faithful; allegiance. ~Related adjs.: **veritable, veracious.** [Old English *triewth*; related to Old High German *gitriuwida* fidelity, Old Norse *tryggr* true] —**'truth+less** *adj.*

truth drug *or* **se+rum** *n. Informal.* any of various drugs that induce relaxation and remove inhibitions: used in treating persons with emotional problems, etc., and by some governments in interrogation.

truth+ful ('tru:θfʊl) *adj.* **1.** telling or expressing the truth; honest or candid. **2.** realistic: *a truthful portrayal of the king.* —**'truth+ful+ly** *adv.* —**'truth+ful+ness** *n.*

truth-func·tion *n. Logic.* a compound proposition, such as a conjunction or negation, the truth-value of which is always determined by the truth-values of the components with no reference to meaning.

truth set *n. Logic, maths.* the set of values that satisfy an open sentence, equation, inequality, etc., having no unique solution. Also called: **solution set.**

truth ta+ble *n.* **1.** a table, used in logic, indicating the truth-value of a compound statement for every truth-value of its component propositions. **2.** a similar table, used in transistor technology, to indicate the value of the output signal of a logic circuit for every value of input signal.

truth-val·ue *n. Logic.* either of the values, true or false, that can be determined for or accorded to a proposition.

try (traɪ) *vb.* **tries, try+ing, tried. 1.** (when *tr., may take an infinitive,* sometimes with *to* replaced by *and*) to make an effort or attempt: *he tried to climb a cliff.* **2.** (*tr.;* often foll. by *out*) to sample, test, or give experimental use to (something) in order to determine its quality, worth, etc.: *try her cheese flan.* **3.** (*tr.*) to put strain or stress on: *he tries my patience.* **4.** (*tr.; often passive*) to give pain, affliction, or vexation to: *I have been sorely tried by those children.* **5. a.** to examine and determine the issues involved in (a cause) in a court of law. **b.** to hear evidence in order to determine the guilt or innocence of (an accused). **c.** to sit as judge at the trial of (an issue or person). **6.** (*tr.*) to melt (fat, lard, etc.) in order to separate out impurities. **7.** (*tr.;* usually foll. by *out*) *Obsolete.* to extract (a material) from an ore, mixture, etc., usually by heat; refine. ~*n., pl.* **tries. 8.** an experiment or trial. **9.** an attempt or effort. **10.** *Rugby.* the act of an attacking player touching the ball down behind the opposing team's goal line, scoring four or, in Rugby League, three points. **11.** Also called: **try for a point.** *American football.* an attempt made after a touchdown to score an extra point by kicking a goal or, for two extra points, by running the ball or completing a pass across the opponents' goal line. [C13: from Old French *trier* to sort, sift, of uncertain origin]

try+ing ('traɪɪŋ) *adj.* upsetting, difficult, or annoying: *a trying day at the office.* —**'try+ing+ly** *adv.* —**'try+ing+ness** *n.*

try+ing plane *n.* a plane with a long body for planing the edges of long boards.

try+ma ('traɪmə) *n., pl.* **+ma+ta** (-mətə). *Botany.* a drupe produced by the walnut and similar plants, in which the endocarp is a hard shell and the epicarp is dehiscent. [C19: from New Latin, from Greek *truma* a hole (referring to the hollow drupe), from *truein* to wear away]

try on *vb.* (*tr., adv.*) **1.** to put on (an article of clothing) to find out whether it fits or is suitable. **2.** *Informal.* to attempt to deceive or fool (esp. in the phrase **try it on**). ~*n.* **try-on. 3.** *Brit. informal.* an action or statement made to test out a person's gullibility, tolerance, etc.

try out *vb.* (*adv.*) **1.** (*tr.*) to test or put to experimental use: *I'm going to try the new car out.* **2.** (when *intr.,* usually foll. by *for*) *U.S.* (of an athlete, actor, etc.) to undergo a test or to submit (an athlete, actor, etc.) to a test to determine suitability for a place in a team, an acting role, etc. ~*n.* **try+out. 3.** *Chiefly U.S.* a trial or test, as of an athlete or actor.

tryp·a+no+some ('trɪpənə,səʊm) *n.* any parasitic protozoan of the genus *Trypanosoma,* which lives in the blood of vertebrates, is transmitted by certain insects, and causes sleeping sickness and certain other diseases: class *Mastigophora* (or *Flagellata*). [C19: from New Latin *Trypanosoma,* from Greek *trupanon* borer + *sōma* body] —**,tryp·a+no+'so+mal** *or* **tryp·a+no+som+ic** (,trɪpənə'sɒmɪk) *adj.*

tryp·a+no+so+mi·a+sis (,trɪpənəsə'maɪəsɪs) *n.* any infection of an animal or human with a trypanosome. See also **sleeping sickness, Chagas' disease.**

try+par+sa+mide (trɪ'pɑ:səmɪd) *n.* a synthetic crystalline compound of arsenic used in the treatment of trypanosomal and other protozoan infections. Formula: $C_8H_{10}AsN_2O_4Na.\frac{1}{2}H_2O$. [C20: from a trademark]

tryp+sin ('trɪpsɪn) *n.* an enzyme occurring in pancreatic juice: it catalyses the hydrolysis of proteins to peptides and is secreted from the pancreas in the form of trypsinogen. See also **chymotrypsin.** [C19 *tryp-,* from Greek *tripsis* a rubbing, from *tribein* to rub + -IN; referring to the fact that it was originally produced by rubbing the pancreas with glycerin] —**tryp+tic** ('trɪptɪk) *adj.*

tryp+sin·o+gen (trɪp'sɪnədʒɪn) *n.* the inactive precursor of trypsin that is converted to trypsin by the enzyme enterokinase.

tryp+to+phan ('trɪptə,fæn) *n.* a sweet-tasting amino acid occurring in the seeds of some leguminous plants: it is essential for the maintenance of health. Formula: $C_{11}H_{12}N_2O_2$. [C20: from TRYPT(IC) + -O- + *-phan,* variant of -PHANE]

try+sail ('traɪ,seɪl; *Nautical* 'traɪsᵊl) *n.* a small fore-and-aft sail, triangular or square, set on the mainmast of a sailing vessel in foul weather to help keep her head to the wind. Also called: **storm trysail.**

try square *n.* a device for testing or laying out right angles, consisting of a grooved metal ruler along which a movable frame runs, one edge of the frame always being perpendicular to the ruler.

tryst (trɪst, traɪst) *Archaic or literary.* ~*n.* **1.** an appointment to meet, esp. secretly. **2.** the place of such a meeting or the meeting itself. ~*vb.* **3.** (*intr.*) to meet at or arrange a tryst. [C14: from Old French *triste* lookout post, apparently of Scandinavian origin; compare Old Norse *traust* trust] —**'tryst+er** *n.*

tsa+de ('tsɑ:di:, 'sɑ:-; *Hebrew* 'tsadi) *n.* a variant spelling of **sadhe.**

Tsa+na ('tsɑ:nə) *n.* **Lake.** another name for (**Lake**) **Tana.**

tsar *or* **czar** (zɑ:) *n.* **1.** (until 1917) the emperor of Russia. **2.** a tyrant; autocrat. **3.** *Informal.* a person in authority; leader. **4.** (formerly) any of several S Slavonic rulers, such as any of the princes of Serbia in the 14th century. [from Russian *tsar,* via Gothic *kaisar* from Latin: CAESAR] —**'tsar+dom** *or* **'czar+dom** *n.*

tsar+e·vitch *or* **czar+e·vitch** ('zɑ:rəvɪtʃ) *n.* a son of a Russian tsar, esp. the eldest son. [from Russian *tsarevich,* from TSAR + *-evich,* masculine patronymic suffix]

tsa+rev+na *or* **cza+rev+na** (zɑ:'revnə) *n.* **1.** a daughter of a Russian tsar. **2.** the wife of a Russian tsarevitch. [from Russian, from TSAR + *-evna,* feminine patronymic suffix]

tsa+ri+na, cza+ri+na (zɑ:'ri:nə) *or* **tsa+rit+sa, cza+rit+za** (zɑ:'rɪtsə) *n.* the wife of a Russian tsar; Russian empress. [from Russian, from TSAR + *-ina,* feminine suffix]

tsar+ism *or* **czar+ism** ('zɑ:rɪzəm) *n.* **1.** a system of government by a tsar, esp. in Russia until 1917. **2.** absolute rule; dictatorship. —**'tsar+ist** *or* **'czar+ist** *n., adj.*

Tsa+ri+tsyn (*Russian* tsa'ritsɪn) *n.* a former name (until 1925) of **Volgograd.**

Tse+li+no+grad (*Russian* tsəlɪna'grat) *n.* a city in the central Soviet Union, in the W Kazakh SSR. Pop.: 215 000 (1975 est.). Former name (until 1961): **Akmolinsk.**

tset+se fly *or* **tzet+ze fly** ('tsɛtsɪ) *n.* any of various bloodsucking African dipterous flies of the genus *Glossina,* which transmit the pathogens of various diseases: family *Muscidae.* [C19: via Afrikaans from Tswana]

TSH *abbrev. for* thyroid-stimulating hormone; another name for **thyrotropin.**

Tshi+lu+ba (tʃɪ'lu:bə) *n.* the language of the Luba people, used as a trade language in Zaïre. See **Luba.**

T-shirt *or* **tee-shirt** *n.* a simple sweater of knitted cotton, worn informally by men and women.

Tshom·be ('tʃɒmbɪ) *n.* **Mo·ise** (məʊ'i:z). 1919–69, Congolese statesman. He led the secession of Katanga (1960) from the newly independent Congo; forced into exile (1963) but returned (1964–65) as premier of the Congo; died in exile.

Tsi+nan ('tsi:'næn), **Chi+nan,** *or* **Chi-nan** *n.* an industrial city in NE China, capital of Shantung province: probably over 3000 years old. Pop.: 1 100 000 (1970 est.).

Tsing+hai ('tsɪŋ'haɪ), **Ching+hai,** *or* **Ch'ing-hai** *n.* **1.** a province of NW China: consists largely of mountains and high plateaus. Capital: Sining. Pop.: 2 000 000 (1967–71 est.). Area: 721 000 sq. km (278 400 sq. miles). **2.** the Chinese name for **Koko Nor.**

Tsing+tao ('tsɪŋ'taʊ), **Ching+tao,** *or* **Ch'ing-tao** *n.* a port in E China, in E Shantung province on Kiaochow Bay: developed as a naval base and fort in 1891; Shantung University (1926). Pop.: 1 300 000 (1970 est.).

Tsing+yuan ('tsɪŋ'jwɑ:n) *or* **Ch'ing-yüan** *n.* the former name of **Paoting.**

Tson+ga ('tsɒŋgə) *n.* **1.** (*pl.* **+ga** *or* **+gas**) a member of a Negroid people of S Mozambique, Swaziland, and South Africa. **2.** the language of this people, belonging to the Bantu group of the Niger-Congo family.

tso+tsi ('tsɒtsɪ, 'tsɔ:-) *n. S. African informal.* a violent usually young criminal who operates mainly in Black African townships and lives by his wits. [C20: of unknown origin; probably from a Bantu language]

tsp. *abbrev. for* teaspoon.

T-square *n.* a T-shaped ruler used in mechanical drawing, consisting of a short crosspiece, which slides along the edge of the drawing board, and a long horizontal piece: used for drawing horizontal lines and to support set squares when drawing vertical and inclined lines.

T-stop *n.* a setting of the lens aperture on a camera calibrated photometrically and assigned a T-number.

Tsu+ga+ru Strait ('tsu:gɑ:ˌru:) *n.* a channel between N Honshu and S Hokkaido islands, Japan. Width: about 30 km (20 miles).

Tsu·ka·har·a (ˌtsu:kə'hɑ:rə) *n.* **Mit·su·o** ('mɪtsu:əʊ). born 1948, Japanese gymnast: gold medallist at the 1972 and 1976 Olympic Games.

tsu+na+mi (tsʊ'nɑ:mɪ) *n.* a huge destructive wave, esp. one caused by an earthquake. Also called: **tidal wave.** [from Japanese, from *tsu* port + *nami* wave]

Tsu+shi+ma ('tsu:ʃi:ˌmɑ:) *n.* a group of five rocky islands between Japan and South Korea, in the Korean Strait: administratively part of Japan; scene of a naval defeat for the Russians (1905) during the Russo-Japanese war. Area: 698 sq. km (269 sq. miles).

tsu+tsu+ga+mu+shi dis+ease (ˌtsu:tsu:gə'mu:ʃɪ) *n.* **1.** one of the five major groups of acute infectious rickettsial diseases affecting man, common in Asia and including scrub typhus. It is caused by the microorganism *Rickettsia tsutsugamushi,* transmitted by the bite of mites. **2.** another name for **scrub typhus.** [from Japanese, from *tsutsuga* disease + *mushi* insect]

Tswa+na ('tswɑ:nə) *n.* **1.** (*pl.* **+na** *or* **+nas**) a member of a mixed Negroid and Bushman people of the Sotho group of southern Africa, living chiefly in Botswana. **2.** the language of this people, belonging to the Bantu group of the Niger-Congo family: the principal language of Botswana.

TT *international car registration for* Trinidad and Tobago.

TT *or* **T.T.** *abbrev. for:* **1.** teetotal. **2.** teetotaller. **3.** Tourist Trophy. **4.** tuberculin tested.

TTL *abbrev. for:* **1.** transistor transistor logic: a method of constructing electronic logic circuits. **2.** through-the-lens: denoting a system of light metering in cameras.

TU *or* **T.U.** *abbrev. for* trade union.

Tu. *abbrev. for* Tuesday.

Tu·a·mo·tu Ar·chi·pel·a·go (ˌtu:ə'məʊtu:) *n.* a group of about 80 coral islands in the S Pacific, in French Polynesia. Pop.: 6664 (1971). Area: 860 sq. km (332 sq. miles). Also called: **Low Archipelago, Paumotu Archipelago.**

Tua+reg ('twɑ:rɛg) *n.* **1.** (*pl.* **+reg** *or* **+regs**) a member of a nomadic Berber people of the Sahara. **2.** the dialect of Berber spoken by this people.

tu·art ('tu:ɑ:t) *n. Austral.* a eucalyptus tree, *Eucalyptus gomphocephala,* yielding a very durable light-coloured timber. [from a native Australian language]

tu·a·ta·ra (ˌtu:ə'tɑ:rə) *n.* a greenish-grey lizard-like rhynchocephalian reptile, *Sphenodon punctatus,* occurring only on certain small islands near New Zealand: it is the sole surviving member of a group common in Mesozoic times. [C19: from Maori, from *tua* back + *tara* spine]

tub (tʌb) *n.* **1.** a large open flat-bottomed container of metal or wood, used for washing, storage, etc. **2.** a small plastic or cardboard container of similar shape for ice cream, margarine, etc. **3.** Also called: **bathtub.** another word (esp. U.S.) for **bath**[1] (sense 1). **4.** Also called: **tub+ful.** the amount a tub will hold. **5.** a clumsy slow boat or ship. **6.** *Informal.* (in rowing) a heavy wide boat used for training novice oarsmen. **7. a.** Also called: **tram, hutch.** a small vehicle on rails for carrying loads in a mine. **b.** a container for lifting coal or ore up a mine shaft; skip. ~*vb.* **tubs, tub+bing, tubbed. 8.** *Brit. informal.* to wash (oneself or another) in a tub. **9.** (*tr.*) to keep or put in a tub. [C14: from Middle Dutch *tubbe*] —**'tub+ba·ble** *adj.* —**'tub+ber** *n.*

tu·ba ('tju:bə) *n., pl.* **·bas** *or* **·bae** (-bi:). **1.** a valved brass instrument of bass pitch, in which the bell points upwards and the mouthpiece projects at right angles. The tube is of conical bore and the mouthpiece cup-shaped. **2.** any other bass brass instrument such as the euphonium, helicon, etc. **3.** a powerful reed stop on an organ. **4.** a form of trumpet of ancient Rome.

tu+bal ('tju:bəl) *adj.* **1.** of or relating to a tube. **2.** of, relating to, or developing in a Fallopian tube: *a tubal pregnancy.*

Tu·bal-cain ('tju:bəlˌkeɪn) *n. Old Testament.* a son of Lamech, said in Genesis 4:22 to be the first artificer of metals.

tu+bate ('tju:beɪt) *adj.* a less common word for **tubular.**

tub+by ('tʌbɪ) *adj.* **+bi+er, +bi+est. 1.** plump. **2.** shaped like a tub. **3.** *Rare.* having little resonance. —**'tub+bi+ness** *n.*

tube (tju:b) *n.* **1.** a long hollow and typically cylindrical object, used for the passage of fluids or as a container. **2.** a collapsible cylindrical container of soft metal or plastic closed with a cap, used to hold viscous liquids or pastes. **3.** *Anatomy.* **a.** short for **Eustachian tube** or **Fallopian tube. b.** any hollow cylindrical structure. **4.** *Botany.* **a.** the lower part of a gamopetalous corolla or gamosepalous calyx, below the lobes. **b.** any other hollow structure in a plant. **5.** (*sometimes cap.*) *Brit.* **a. the tube.** Also called: **the underground.** an underground railway system, esp. that in London. U.S. equivalent: **subway. b.** the tunnels through which the railway runs. **c.** the train itself. **6.** *Electronics.* **a.** another name for **valve** (sense 3). **b.** See **electron tube, cathode-ray tube, television tube. 7.** *Slang, chiefly U.S.* a television set. **8.** *Austral. slang.* a bottle or can of beer. **9.** an archaic word for **telescope.** ~*vb.* (*tr.*) **10.** to fit or supply with a tube or tubes. **11.** to carry or convey in a tube. **12.** to shape like a tube. [C17: from Latin *tubus*] —**'tube+less** *adj.*

tube foot *n.* any of numerous tubular outgrowths of the body wall of most echinoderms that are used as organs of locomotion and respiration and to aid ingestion of food.

tube+less tyre *n.* a pneumatic tyre in which the outer casing makes an airtight seal with the rim of the wheel so that an inner tube is unnecessary.

tu+ber ('tju:bə) *n.* **1.** a fleshy underground stem (as in the potato) or root (as in the dahlia) that is an organ of vegetative reproduction and food storage. **2.** *Anatomy.* a raised area; swelling. [C17: from Latin *tūber* hump]

tu+ber+cle ('tju:bəkəl) *n.* **1.** any small rounded nodule or elevation, esp. on the skin, on a bone, or on a plant. **2.** any small rounded pathological lesion of the tissues, esp. one characteristic of tuberculosis. [C16: from Latin *tūberculum* a little swelling, diminutive of TUBER]

tu+ber+cle ba+cil+lus *n.* a rodlike Gram-positive bacterium, *Mycobacterium tuberculosis,* that causes tuberculosis: family *Mycobacteriaceae.*

tu+ber+cu+lar (tjʊ'bɜ:kjʊlə) *adj.* **1.** of, relating to, or symptomatic of tuberculosis. **2.** of or relating to a tubercle or tubercles. **3.** characterized by the presence of tubercles. ~*n.* **4.** a person with tuberculosis. —**tu+'ber+cu+lar+ly** *adv.*

tu+ber+cu+late (tjʊ'bɜ:kjʊlɪt) *adj.* covered with tubercles. —**tu+'ber+cu+late+ly** *adv.* —**tu+ˌber+cu+'la+tion** *n.*

tu+ber+cu+lin (tjʊ'bɜ:kjʊlɪn) *n.* a sterile liquid prepared from cultures of attenuated tubercle bacillus and used in the diagnosis of tuberculosis.

tu+ber+cu+lo+sis (tjʊˌbɜ:kjʊ'ləʊsɪs) *n.* a communicable disease caused by infection with the tubercle bacillus, most frequently affecting the lungs (**pulmonary tuberculosis**). Also called: **consumption, phthisis.** Abbrev.: **TB, T.B.** [C19: from New Latin; see TUBERCLE, -OSIS]

tu+ber+cu+lous (tjʊ'bɜ:kjʊləs) *adj.* of or relating to tuberculosis or tubercles; tubercular. —**tu+'ber+cu+lous+ly** *adv.*

tu+ber+ose ('tju:bəˌrəʊz) *n.* a perennial Mexican agave plant, *Polianthes tuberosa,* having a tuberous root and spikes of white fragrant lily-like flowers. [C17: from Latin *tūberōsus* full of lumps; referring to its root]

tu+ber+os+i·ty (ˌtju:bə'rɒsɪtɪ) *n., pl.* **·ties.** any protuberance on a bone, esp. for the attachment of a muscle or ligament.

tu+ber+ous ('tju:bərəs) *or* **tu+ber+ose** ('tju:bəˌrəʊs) *adj.* **1.** (of plants or their parts) forming, bearing, or resembling a tuber or tubers: *a tuberous root.* **2.** *Anatomy.* of, relating to, or having warty protuberances or tubers. [C17: from Latin *tūberōsus* full of knobs; see TUBER]

tube worm *n.* any of various polychaete worms that construct and live in a tube made of sand, lime, etc.

tu+bi+fex ('tju:bɪˌfɛks) *n., pl.* **+fex** *or* **+fex·es.** any small reddish freshwater oligochaete worm of the genus *Tubifex.* [C19: from New Latin, from Latin *tubus* tube + *facere* to make, do]

tub+ing ('tju:bɪŋ) *n.* **1.** tubes collectively. **2.** a length of tube. **3.** a system of tubes. **4.** fabric in the form of a tube, used for pillowcases and some cushions; piping.

Tub·man ('tʌbmən) *n.* **Wil·liam Va·can·a·rat Shad·rach** (və'kænəˌræt 'ʃædræk). 1895–1971, Liberian statesman; president of Liberia (1944–71).

tub-thump·er *n.* a noisy, violent, or ranting public speaker. —**'tub-ˌthump·ing** *adj., n.*

Tu+bu+ai Is+lands (ˌtu:bu:'aɪ) *pl. n.* a chain of small islands extending about 1400 km (850 miles) in the S Pacific, in French Polynesia; discovered by Captain Cook in 1777; annexed by France in 1880. Pop.: 5079 (1971). Area: 173 sq. km (67 sq. miles). Also called: **Austral Islands.**

tub·u·lar ('tju:bjʊlə) *adj.* **1.** Also: **tu+bi+form** ('tju:bɪˌfɔ:m). having the form of a tube or tubes. **2.** of or relating to a tube or tubing. —**ˌtu+bu+'lar+i·ty** *n.* —**'tu+bu+lar+ly** *adv.*

tu+bu+late *vb.* ('tju:bjʊˌleɪt). (*tr.*) **1.** to form or shape into a tube. **2.** to fit or furnish with a tube. ~*adj.* ('tju:bjʊlɪt, -ˌleɪt). **3.** a less common word for **tubular.** [C18: from Latin *tubulātus,* from *tubulus* a little pipe, from *tubus* pipe] —**ˌtu+bu+'la+tion** *n.* —**'tu+bu+ˌla+tor** *n.*

tu+bule ('tju:bju:l) *n.* any small tubular structure, esp. one in an animal, as in the kidney, testis, etc. [C17: from Latin *tubulus* a little TUBE]

tu+bu+li+flo+rous (ˌtju:bjʊlɪ'flɔ:rəs) *adj.* (of plants) having flowers or florets with tubular corollas.

tu+bu+lous ('tju:bjʊləs) *adj.* **1.** tube-shaped; tubular. **2.** characterized by or consisting of small tubes. [C17: from New Latin *tubulōsus*] —**'tu+bu+lous+ly** *adv.*

T.U.C. (in Britain) *abbrev. for* Trades Union Congress.

Tu+ca+na (tu:'kɑ:nə) *n., Latin genitive* **Tu+ca+nae** (tu:'kɑ:ni:). a faint extensive constellation in the S hemisphere close to Hydrus and Eridanus, containing most of the Small Magellanic Cloud. [probably from Tupi: toucan]

tu+chun (tu:'tʃu:n) *n.* (formerly) a Chinese military governor or war lord. [from Chinese, from *tu* to superintend + *chün* troops] —**'tu+chun+ate** *adj.* —**'tu+chun+ism** *n.*

tuck[1] (tʌk) *vb.* **1.** (*tr.*) to push or fold into a small confined space or concealed place or between two surfaces: *to tuck a* *letter into an envelope.* **2.** (*tr.*) to thrust the loose ends or sides of (something) into a confining space, so as to make neat and secure: *to tuck the sheets under the mattress.* **3.** to make a tuck or tucks in (a garment). **4.** (*usually tr.*) to draw together, contract, or pucker. ~*n.* **5.** a tucked object or part. **6.** a pleat or fold in a part of a garment, usually stitched down so as to make it a better fit or as decoration. **7.** the part of a vessel where the after ends of the planking or plating meet at the sternpost. **8.** *Brit.* **a.** an informal or schoolchild's word for **food,** esp. cakes and sweets. **b.** (*as modifier*): *a tuck box.* **9.** the action of drawing the knees up to the chest in certain dives. ~See also **tuck away, tuck in.** [C14: from Old English *tūcian* to torment; related to Middle Dutch *tucken* to tug, Old High German *zucchen* to twitch]

tuck² (tʌk) *n. Archaic.* a rapier. [C16: from French *estoc* sword, from Old French: tree trunk, sword, of Germanic origin]

tuck³ (tʌk) *Brit. dialect.* ~*n.* **1.** a touch, blow, or stroke. ~*vb.* **2.** (*tr.*) to touch or strike. **3.** (*intr.*) to throb or bump. [C16: from Middle English *tukken* to beat a drum, from Old Northern French *toquer* to TOUCH; compare TUCKET]

Tuck (tʌk) *n.* **Fri·ar.** See **Friar Tuck.**

tuck a·way *vb.* (*tr., adv.*) *Informal.* **1.** to eat (a large amount of food). **2.** to store, esp. in a place difficult to find.

tuck+er¹ ('tʌkə) *n.* **1.** a person or thing that tucks. **2.** a detachable yoke of lace, linen, etc., often white, worn over the breast, as of a low-cut dress. **3.** an attachment on a sewing machine used for making tucks at regular intervals. **4.** *Austral.* an informal word for **food.**

tuck+er² ('tʌkə) *vb.* (*tr.; often passive;* usually foll. by *out*) *Informal, chiefly U.S.* to weary or tire completely.

tuck·er-bag *or* **tuck·er+box** *n. Austral. informal.* a bag used for carrying food.

tuck+et ('tʌkɪt) *n. Archaic.* a flourish on a trumpet. [C16: from Old Northern French *toquer* to sound (on a drum)]

tuck in *vb.* (*adv.*) **1.** (*tr.*) Also: **tuck into.** to put to bed and make snug. **2.** (*tr.*) to thrust the loose ends or sides of (something) into a confining space: *tuck the blankets in.* **3.** (*intr.*) Also: **tuck into.** *Informal.* to eat, esp. heartily. ~*n.* **tuck-in. 4.** *Brit. informal.* a meal, esp. a large one.

tuck shop *n. Chiefly Brit.* a shop, esp. one in or near a school, where food such as cakes and sweets are sold.

tu+co+tu+co (ˌtu:kəʊ'tu:kəʊ) *or* **tu+cu+tu+cu** (ˌtu:ku:'tu:ku:) *n.* any of various colonial burrowing South American hystricomorph rodents of the genus *Ctenomys,* having long-clawed feet and a stocky body: family *Ctenomyidae.* [C19: of South American Indian origin]

Tuc+son ('tu:sɒn) *n.* a city in SE Arizona, at an altitude of 700m (2400 ft.): resort and seat of the University of Arizona (1891). Pop.: 307 551 (1973 est.).

Tu+cu+mán (*Spanish* ˌtuku'man) *n.* a city in NW Argentina: scene of the declaration (1816) of Argentinian independence from Spain; university (1914). Pop.: 365 757 (1970).

-tude *suffix forming nouns.* indicating state or condition: *plenitude.* [from Latin *-tūdō*]

Tu+dor ('tju:də) *n.* **1.** an English royal house descended from a Welsh squire, **O·wen Tu·dor** (died 1461), and ruling from 1485 to 1603. Monarchs of the Tudor line were Henry VII, Henry VIII, Edward VI, Mary I, and Elizabeth I. ~*adj.* **2.** denoting a style of architecture of the late perpendicular period and characterized by half-timbered houses.

Tues. *abbrev. for* Tuesday.

Tues+day ('tju:zdɪ) *n.* the third day of the week; second day of the working week. [Old English *tīwesdæg,* literally: day of Tiw, representing Latin *diēs Martis* day of Mars; compare Old Norse *týsdagr,* Old High German *zīostag;* see TIW, DAY]

tu·fa ('tju:fə) *n.* a soft porous rock consisting of calcium carbonate deposited from springs rich in lime. Also called: **calc-tufa.** [C18: from Italian *tufo,* from Late Latin *tōfus*] —**tu+fa+ceous** (tju:'feɪʃəs) *adj.*

tuff (tʌf) *n.* a hard volcanic rock consisting of consolidated fragments of erupted lava. Also called: **tufa.** [C16: from Old French *tuf,* from Italian *tufo;* see TUFA] —**tuff·a+ceous** (tʌ'feɪʃəs) *adj.*

tuf+fet ('tʌfɪt) *n.* a small mound or low seat. [C16: alteration of TUFT]

tuft (tʌft) *n.* **1.** a bunch of feathers, grass, hair, etc., held together at the base. **2.** a cluster of threads drawn tightly through upholstery, a mattress, a quilt, etc., to secure and strengthen the padding. **3.** a small clump of trees or bushes. **4.** (formerly) a gold tassel on the cap worn by titled undergraduates at English universities. **5.** a person entitled to wear such a tassel. ~*vb.* **6.** (*tr.*) to provide or decorate with a tuft or tufts. **7.** to form or be formed into tufts. **8.** to secure and strengthen (a mattress, quilt, etc.) with tufts. [C14: perhaps from Old French *tufe,* of Germanic origin; compare TOP¹] —'**tuft+er** *n.* —'**tuft·y** *adj.*

tuft+ed ('tʌftɪd) *adj.* **1.** having a tuft or tufts. **2.** (of plants or plant parts) having or consisting of one or more groups of short branches all arising at the same level.

tuft+ed duck *n.* a European lake-dwelling duck, *Aythya fuligula,* the male of which has a black plumage with white underparts and a long black drooping crest.

tug (tʌg) *vb.* **tugs, tug+ging, tugged. 1.** (when *intr.,* sometimes foll. by *at*) to pull or drag with sharp or powerful movements: *the boy tugged at the door handle.* **2.** (*tr.*) to tow (a vessel) by means of a tug. **3.** (*intr.*) to work; toil. ~*n.* **4.** a strong pull or jerk: *he gave the rope a tug.* **5.** Also called: **tugboat.** a boat with a powerful engine, used for towing barges, ships, etc. **6.** a hard struggle or fight. **7.** a less common word for **trace²** (sense 1). [C13: related to Old English *tēon* to TOW¹] —'**tug+ger** *n.*

Tu+ge+la (tu:'geɪlə) *n.* a river in E South Africa, rising in the Drakensberg where it forms the **Tugela Falls,** 856 m (2810 ft.) high, before flowing east to the Indian Ocean: scene of battles during the Zulu War (1879) and the Boer War (1899–1902). Length: about 500 km (312 miles).

tug of war *n.* **1.** a contest in which two people or teams pull opposite ends of a rope in an attempt to drag the opposition over a central line. **2.** any hard struggle, esp. between two equally matched factions.

tu+grik *or* **tu+ghrik** ('tu:ˌgri:k) *n.* the standard monetary unit of Mongolia, divided into 100 mongos. [from Mongolian]

tu·i ('tu:ɪ) *n.* a New Zealand honeyeater, *Prosthemadera novaeseelandiae,* having a glossy bluish-green plumage with white feathers at the throat: it mimics human speech and the songs of other birds. [from Maori]

Tui+ler+ies ('twi:lərɪ; *French* twil'ri) *n.* a former royal residence in Paris: begun in 1564 by Catherine de' Medici and burned in 1871 by the Commune; site of the **Tuileries Gardens** (a park near the Louvre).

tu·i·tion (tju:'ɪʃən) *n.* **1.** instruction, esp. that received in a small group or individually. **2.** the payment for instruction, esp. in colleges or universities. [C15: from Old French *tuicion,* from Latin *tuitiō* a guarding, from *tuērī* to watch over] —**tu·'i+tion+al** *or* **tu·'i+tion+ar·y** *adj.*

Tu·la (*Russian* 'tulə) *n.* an industrial city in the W central Soviet Union. Pop.: 500 000 (1975 est.).

tu+la+rae+mi·a *or U.S.* **tu+la+re·mi·a** (ˌtu:lə'ri:mɪə) *n.* an acute infectious bacterial disease of rodents, transmitted to man by infected ticks or flies or by handling contaminated flesh. It is characterized by fever, chills, and inflammation of the lymph glands. Also called: **rabbit fever.** [C19/20: from New Latin, from *Tulare,* county in California where it was first observed; see -AEMIA] —ˌ**tu+la+'rae+mic** *or* ˌ**tu+la+'re·mic** *adj.*

tu+lip ('tju:lɪp) *n.* **1.** any spring-blooming liliaceous plant of the temperate Eurasian genus *Tulipa,* having tapering bulbs, long broad pointed leaves, and single showy bell-shaped flowers. **2.** the flower or bulb of any of these plants. [C17: from New Latin *tulipa,* from Turkish *tülbend* turban, which the opened bloom was thought to resemble] —'**tu·lip-ˌlike** *adj.*

tu+lip tree *n.* **1.** Also called: **tulip poplar, yellow poplar.** a North American magnoliaceous forest tree, *Liriodendron tulipifera,* having tulip-shaped greenish-yellow flowers and long conelike fruits. **2.** any of various other trees with tulip-shaped flowers, such as the magnolia.

tu·lip+wood ('tju:lɪpˌwʊd) *n.* **1.** Also called: **white poplar, yellow poplar.** the light soft wood of the tulip tree, used in making furniture and veneer. **2.** any of several woods having stripes or streaks of colour, esp. that of *Dalbergia variabilis,* a tree of tropical South America.

Tull (tʌl) *n.* **Jeth·ro** ('dʒɛθrəʊ). 1674–1741, English agriculturalist, who invented the seed drill.

tulle (tju:l) *n.* a fine net fabric of silk, rayon, etc., used for evening dresses, as a trimming for hats, etc. [C19: from French, from *Tulle,* city in S central France, where it was first manufactured]

Tul·ly ('tʌlɪ) *n.* the former English name for (Marcus Tullius) **Cicero.**

Tul+sa ('tʌlsə) *n.* a city in NE Oklahoma, on the Arkansas River: a major oil centre; two universities. Pop.: 335 444 (1973 est.).

tum¹ (tʊm) *or* **tyum** (tjʊm) *adj. Northeast English dialect.* empty. [from Old English *tōm;* related to Old Norse *tōmr*]

tum² (tʌm) *n.* an informal or childish word for **stomach.**

tum+ble ('tʌmbᵊl) *vb.* **1.** to fall or cause to fall, esp. awkwardly, precipitately, or violently. **2.** (*intr.;* usually foll. by *about*) to roll or twist, esp. in playing: *the kittens tumbled about on the floor.* **3.** (*intr.*) to perform leaps, somersaults, etc. **4.** to go or move in a heedless or hasty way. **5.** (*tr.*) to polish (gemstones) in a tumbler. **6.** (*tr.*) to disturb, rumple, or toss around: *to tumble the bedclothes.* ~*n.* **7.** the act or an instance of tumbling. **8.** a fall or toss. **9.** an acrobatic feat, esp. a somersault. **10.** a state of confusion. **11.** a confused heap or pile: *a tumble of clothes.* [Old English *tumbian,* from Old French *tomber;* related to Old High German *tūmōn* to turn]

tum·ble-down *adj.* falling to pieces; dilapidated; crumbling.

tum·ble+home ('tʌmbᵊlˌhəʊm) *n.* the inward curvature of the upper parts of the sides of a vessel at or near the stern.

tum+bler ('tʌmblə) *n.* **1. a.** a flat-bottomed drinking glass with no handle or stem. **b.** Also called: **tum+bler+ful.** the contents or quantity such a glass holds. **2.** a person, esp. a professional entertainer, who performs somersaults and other acrobatic feats. **3.** Also called: **tumble drier, tumbler drier.** a machine that dries clothes by tumbling them in warmed air. **4.** Also called: **tumbling box.** a pivoted box or drum rotated so that the contents (usually inferior gemstones) tumble about and become smooth and polished. **5.** the part of a lock that retains or releases the bolt and is moved by the action of a key. **6.** a lever in a gunlock that receives the action of the mainspring when the trigger is pressed and thus forces the hammer forwards. **7. a.** a part that moves a gear in a train of gears into and out of engagement. **b.** a single cog or cam that transmits motion to the part with which it engages. **8.** a toy, often a doll, that is so weighted that it rocks when touched. **9.** (*often cap.*) a breed of domestic pigeon kept for exhibition or flying. The performing varieties execute backward somersaults in flight.

tum+bler gear *n.* a train of gears in which the gear-selection mechanism is operated by tumblers.

tum·ble to *vb.* (*intr., prep.*) *Informal.* to understand; become aware of: *she tumbled to his plan quickly.*

tum·ble·weed (ˈtʌmbᵊlˌwiːd) *n.* any of various densely branched western American amaranthaceous plants of the genus *Amaranthus* and related genera, esp. *A. albus.* They break off near the ground on withering and are rolled about by the wind.

tum·brel *or* **tum·bril** (ˈtʌmbrəl) *n.* **1.** a farm cart for carrying dung, esp. one that tilts backwards to deposit its load. A cart of this type was used to take condemned prisoners to the guillotine during the French Revolution. **2.** (formerly) a covered cart that accompanied artillery in order to carry ammunition, tools, etc. **3.** an obsolete word for a **ducking stool.** [C14 *tumberell* ducking stool, from Medieval Latin *tumbrellum,* from Old French *tumberel* dump-cart, from *tomber* to tumble, of Germanic origin]

tu·me·fa·ci·ent (ˌtjuːmɪˈfeɪʃɪənt) *adj.* producing or capable of producing swelling: *a tumefacient drug.* [C16: from Latin *tumefacere* to cause to swell, from *tumēre* to swell + *facere* to cause]

tu·me·fac·tion (ˌtjuːmɪˈfækʃən) *n.* **1.** the act or process of swelling. **2.** a puffy or swollen structure or part.

tu·me·fy (ˈtjuːmɪˌfaɪ) *vb.* **·fies, ·fy·ing, ·fied.** to make or become tumid; swell or puff up. [C16: from French *tumefier,* from Latin *tumefacere;* see TUMEFACIENT]

tu·mes·cent (tjuːˈmɛsənt) *adj.* swollen or becoming swollen. [C19: from Latin *tumescere* to begin to swell, from *tumēre*] —**tuˈmes·cence** *n.*

tu·mid (ˈtjuːmɪd) *adj.* **1.** (of an organ or part) enlarged or swollen. **2.** bulging or protuberant. **3.** pompous or fulsome in style: *tumid prose.* [C16: from Latin *tumidus,* from *tumēre* to swell] —**tuˈmid·i·ty** *or* **ˈtu·mid·ness** *n.* —**ˈtu·mid·ly** *adv.*

tum·my (ˈtʌmɪ) *n., pl.* **·mies.** an informal or childish word for **stomach.**

tu·mour *or U.S.* **tu·mor** (ˈtjuːmə) *n.* **1.** *Pathol.* **a.** any abnormal swelling. **b.** a mass of tissue formed by a new growth of cells, normally independent of the surrounding structures. **2.** *Obsolete.* pompous style or language. [C16: from Latin, from *tumēre* to swell] —**ˈtu·mor·ous** *or* **ˈtu·mor·al** *adj.*

tump (tʌmp) *n. Western Brit. dialect.* a small mound or clump. [C16: of unknown origin]

tump·line (ˈtʌmpˌlaɪn) *n.* (in the U.S. and Canada, esp. formerly) a leather or cloth band strung across the forehead or chest and attached to a pack or load in order to support it. Also called: **tump.** [C19: from *tump,* of Algonquian origin + LINE[1]; compare Abnaki *mádŭmbi* pack strap]

tu·mu·lar (ˈtjuːmjʊlə) *adj.* of, relating to, or like a mound.

tu·mu·lose (ˈtjuːmjʊləʊs) *or* **tu·mu·lous** (ˈtjuːmjʊləs) *adj.* **1.** abounding in small hills or mounds. **2.** being or resembling a mound. [C18: from Latin *tumulōsus,* from *tumulus* a hillock] —**tu·mu·los·i·ty** (ˌtjuːmjʊˈlɒsɪtɪ) *n.*

tu·mult (ˈtjuːmʌlt) *n.* **1.** a loud confused noise, as of a crowd; commotion. **2.** violent agitation or disturbance. **3.** great emotional or mental agitation. [C15: from Latin *tumultus,* from *tumēre* to swell up]

tu·mul·tu·ous (tjuːˈmʌltjʊəs) *adj.* **1.** uproarious, riotous, or turbulent: *a tumultuous welcome.* **2.** greatly agitated, confused, or disturbed: *a tumultuous dream.* **3.** making a loud or unruly disturbance: *tumultuous insurgents.* —**tuˈmul·tu·ous·ly** *adv.* —**tuˈmul·tu·ous·ness** *n.*

tu·mu·lus (ˈtjuːmjʊləs) *n. Archaeol.* (*no longer in technical usage*) another word for **barrow**[2]. [C17: from Latin: a hillock, from *tumēre* to swell up]

tun (tʌn) *n.* **1.** a large beer cask. **2.** a measure of capacity, usually equal to 252 wine gallons. **3.** a cask used during the manufacture of beer: *a mash tun.* ~*vb.* **tuns, tun·ning, tunned. 4.** (*tr.*) to put into or keep in tuns. [Old English *tunne;* related to Old High German, Old Norse *tunna,* Medieval Latin *tunna*]

tu·na[1] (ˈtjuːnə) *n., pl.* **·na** *or* **·nas.** another name for **tunny.** [C20: from American Spanish, from Spanish *atún,* from Arabic *tūn,* from Latin *thunnus* tunny, from Greek]

tu·na[2] (ˈtjuːnə) *n.* **1.** any of various tropical American prickly pear cacti, esp. *Opuntia tuna,* that are cultivated for their sweet edible fruits. **2.** the fruit of any of these cacti. [C16: via Spanish from Taino]

tun·a·ble *or* **tune·a·ble** (ˈtjuːnəbᵊl) *adj.* **1.** able to be tuned. **2.** *Archaic or poetic.* melodious or tuneful.

Tun·bridge Wells (ˈtʌnˌbrɪdʒ) *n.* a town and resort in SE England, in SW Kent: chalybeate spring discovered in 1606; an important social centre in the 17th and 18th centuries. Pop.: 44 506 (1971). Official name: **Royal Tunbridge Wells.**

tun·dra (ˈtʌndrə) *n.* **a.** a vast treeless zone lying between the ice cap and the timber line of North America and Eurasia and having a permanently frozen subsoil. **b.** (*as modifier*): *tundra vegetation.* [C19: from Russian, from Lapp *tundar* hill; related to Finnish *tunturi* treeless hill]

tune (tjuːn) *n.* **1.** a melody, esp. one for which harmony is not essential. **2.** the most important part in a musical texture: *the cello has the tune at that point.* **3.** the condition of producing accurately pitched notes, intervals, etc., (esp. in the phrases **in tune, out of tune**): *he can't sing in tune.* **4.** accurate correspondence of pitch and intonation between instruments (esp. in the phrases **in tune, out of tune**): *the violin is not in tune with the piano.* **5.** the correct adjustment of a radio, television, or some other electronic circuit with respect to the required frequency (esp. in the phrases **in tune, out of tune**). **6.** a frame of mind; disposition or mood. **7.** *Obsolete.* a musical sound; note. **8. call the tune.** to be in control of the proceedings. **9. change one's tune** *or* **sing another** (*or* **a different**) **tune.** to change one's mind or opinion. **10. to the tune of.** *Informal.* to the amount or extent of: *costs to the tune of a hundred pounds.* ~*vb.* **11.** to adjust (a musical instrument or a changeable part of one) to a certain pitch. **12.** to adjust (a note, etc.) so as to bring it into harmony or concord. **13.** (*tr.*) to adapt or adjust (oneself); attune: *to tune oneself to a slower life.* **14.** (*tr.;* often foll. by *up*) to make fine adjustments to (an engine, machine, etc.) to obtain optimum performance. **15.** *Electronics.* to adjust (one or more circuits) for resonance at a desired frequency. **16.** *Obsolete.* to utter (something) musically or in the form of a melody; sing. ~See also **tune in, tune up.** [C14: variant of TONE]

tune·ful (ˈtjuːnfʊl) *adj.* **1.** having a pleasant or catchy tune; melodious. **2.** producing a melody or music: *a tuneful blackbird.* —**ˈtune·ful·ly** *adv.* —**ˈtune·ful·ness** *n.*

tune in *vb.* (*adv.;* often foll. by *to*) **1.** to adjust (a radio or television) to receive (a station or programme). **2.** *Slang.* to make or become more aware, knowledgeable, etc., (about).

tune·less (ˈtjuːnlɪs) *adj.* **1.** having no melody or tune. **2.** *Chiefly poetic.* not producing or able to produce music; silent. —**ˈtune·less·ly** *adv.* —**ˈtune·less·ness** *n.*

tun·er (ˈtjuːnə) *n.* **1.** a person who tunes instruments, esp. pianos. **2.** the part of a radio or television receiver for selecting only those signals having a particular frequency.

tune·smith (ˈtjuːnˌsmɪθ) *n. Informal, chiefly U.S.* a composer of light or popular music and songs.

tune up *vb.* (*adv.*) **1.** to adjust (a musical instrument) to a particular pitch, esp. a standard one. **2.** (esp. of an orchestra or other instrumental ensemble) to tune (instruments) to a common pitch. **3.** (*tr.*) to adjust (an engine) in (a car, etc.) to improve performance. ~*n.* **tune-up. 4.** adjustments made to an engine to improve its performance.

tung oil (tʌŋ) *n.* a fast-drying oil obtained from the seeds of a central Asian euphorbiaceous tree, *Aleurites fordii,* used in paints, varnishes, etc., as a drying agent and to give a water-resistant finish. Also called: **Chinese wood oil.** [partial translation of Chinese *yu t'ung* tung tree oil, from *yu* oil + *t'ung* tung tree]

tung·state (ˈtʌŋsteɪt) *n.* a salt of tungstic acid. [C20: from TUNGST(EN) + -ATE[1]]

tung·sten (ˈtʌŋstən) *n.* a hard malleable ductile greyish-white element. It occurs principally in wolframite and scheelite and is used in lamp filaments, electrical contact points, x-ray targets, and, alloyed with steel, in high-speed cutting tools. Symbol: W; atomic no.: 74; atomic wt.: 183.85; valency: 2–6; relative density: 19.3; melting pt.: 3410°C; boiling pt.: 5927°C. Also called: **wolfram.** [C18: from Swedish *tung* heavy + *sten* STONE]

tung·sten lamp *n.* a lamp in which light is produced by a tungsten filament heated to incandescence by an electric current. The glass bulb enclosing the filament contains a low pressure of inert gas, usually argon.

tung·sten steel *n.* any of various hard steels containing tungsten (1–20 per cent) and traces of carbon. They are resistant to wear at high temperatures and are used in tools.

tung·stic (ˈtʌŋstɪk) *n.* of or containing tungsten, esp. in a high valence state. [C18: from TUNGST(EN) + -IC]

tung·stic ac·id *n.* any of various oxyacids of tungsten obtained by neutralizing alkaline solutions of tungstates. They are often polymeric substances, typical examples being H_2WO_4 (**orthotungstic acid**), $H_2W_4O_{13}$ (**metatungstic acid**), and $H_{10}W_{12}O_{14}$ (**paratungstic acid**).

tung·stite (ˈtʌŋstaɪt) *n.* a yellow earthy rare secondary mineral that consists of tungsten oxide and occurs with tungsten ores. Formula: WO_3. [C20: from TUNGST(EN) + -ITE[1]]

tung·stous (ˈtʌŋstəs) *adj.* of or containing tungsten in a low valence state.

Tung·ting *or* **Tung-t'ing** (ˌtʊŋˈtɪŋ) *n.* a lake in S China, in NE Hunan province: main outlet flows to the Yangtze; rice-growing in winter. Area: (in winter) 3900 sq. km (1500 sq. miles); (in summer) about 10 000 sq. km (4000 sq. miles).

Tun·gus (ˈtʊŋgʊs) *n.* **1.** (*pl.* **·gus·es** *or* **·gus**) a member of a Mongoloid people of E Siberia. **2.** the language of this people, closely related to Manchu, belonging to the Tungusic branch of the Altaic family.

Tun·gus·ic (tʊŋˈgʊsɪk) *n.* **1.** a branch or subfamily of the Altaic family of languages, including Tungus and Manchu. ~*adj. also* **Tun·gu·si·an. 2.** of or relating to these languages or their speakers.

Tun·gus·ka (*Russian* tunˈguskə) *n.* any of three rivers in the Soviet Union, in central Siberia, all tributaries of the Yenisei: the **Lower** (Nizhnyaya) **Tunguska,** 2690 km (1670 miles) long; the **Stony** (Podkamennaya) **Tunguska,** 1550 km (960 miles) long; the **Upper** (Verkhnyaya) **Tunguska,** which is the lower course of the Angara.

tu·nic (ˈtjuːnɪk) *n.* **1.** any of various hip-length or knee-length garments, such as the loose sleeveless garb worn in ancient Greece or Rome, the jacket of some soldiers, or a woman's hip-length garment, worn with a skirt or trousers. **2.** Also called: **tu·ni·ca.** *Anatomy, botany, zoology.* a covering, lining, or enveloping membrane of an organ or part. **3.** *Chiefly R.C. Church.* another word for **tunicle.** [Old English *tunice* (unattested except in the accusative case), from Latin *tunica*]

tu·ni·cate (ˈtjuːnɪkɪt, -ˌkeɪt) *n.* **1.** any minute primitive marine chordate animal of the subphylum *Tunicata* (or *Urochordata, Urochorda*). The adults have a saclike unsegmented body enclosed in a cellulose-like outer covering (tunic) and only the larval forms have a notochord: includes the sea squirts. See also **ascidian.** ~*adj. also* **tu·ni·cat·ed. 2.** of, relating to, or belonging to the subphylum *Tunicata.* **3.** (esp. of a bulb) having or consisting of concentric layers of tissue. [C18: from Latin *tunicātus* clad in a TUNIC]

tu·ni·cle ('tju:nɪkᵊl) *n. Chiefly R.C. Church.* the liturgical vestment worn by the subdeacon and bishops at High Mass and other religious ceremonies. [C14: from Latin *tunicula* a little TUNIC]

tun·ing ('tju:nɪŋ) *n. Music.* **1.** a set of pitches to which the open strings of a guitar, violin, etc., are tuned: *the normal tuning on a violin is G, D, A, E.* **2.** the accurate pitching of notes and intervals by a choir, orchestra, etc.; intonation.

tun·ing fork *n.* a two-pronged metal fork that when struck produces a pure note of constant specified pitch. It is used to tune musical instruments and in acoustics.

tun·ing key *n.* a small tube, open at one end and forming a keylike handle at the other, that may be placed over a wrest pin on a piano, etc., and turned so as to alter the tensions and pitch of a string.

Tu·nis ('tju:nɪs) *n.* the capital and chief port of Tunisia, in the northeast on the **Gulf of Tunis** (an inlet of the Mediterranean): dates from Carthaginian times, the ruins of ancient Carthage lying to the northeast; university (1960). Pop.: 468 997 (1966).

Tu·ni·si·a (tju:'nɪzɪə, -'nɪsɪə) *n.* a republic in N Africa, on the Mediterranean: settled by the Phoenicians in the 12th century B.C.; made a French protectorate in 1881 and gained independence in 1955. It consists chiefly of the Sahara desert in the south, a central plateau, and the Atlas Mountains in the north. Exports include petroleum, phosphates, and iron ore. Languages: Arabic and French. Religion: mostly Islam. Currency: dinar. Capital: Tunis. Pop.: 5 572 000 (1975 est.). Area: 164 150 sq. km (63 380 sq. miles). —**Tu·'ni·si·an** *adj., n.*

tun·nage ('tʌnɪdʒ) *n.* a variant spelling of **tonnage.**

tun·nel ('tʌnᵊl) *n.* **1.** an underground passageway, esp. one for trains or cars that passes under a mountain, river, or a congested urban area. **2.** any passage or channel through or under something. **3.** a dialect word for **funnel. 4.** *Obsolete.* the flue of a chimney. ~*vb.* ·**nels,** ·**nel·ling,** ·**nelled** *or U.S.* ·**nels,** ·**nel·ing,** ·**neled. 5.** (*tr.*) to make or force (a way) through or under (something): *to tunnel a hole in the wall; to tunnel the cliff.* **6.** (*intr.*; foll. by *through, under,* etc.) to make or force a way (through or under something): *he tunnelled through the bracken.* [C15: from Old French *tonel* cask, from *tonne* tun, from Medieval Latin *tonna* barrel, of Celtic origin] —**'tun·nel·ler** *n.*

tun·nel di·ode *n.* an extremely stable semiconductor diode, having a very narrow highly doped p-n junction, in which electrons travel across the junction by means of the tunnel effect. Also called: **Esaki diode.**

tun·nel dis·ease *n.* another name for **decompression sickness.**

tun·nel ef·fect *n. Physics.* the phenomenon in which an object, usually an elementary particle, tunnels through a potential barrier even though it does not have sufficient energy to surmount the barrier. It is explained by wave mechanics and is the cause of alpha decay, field emission, and certain conduction processes in semiconductors.

tun·nel vault *n.* another name for **barrel vault.**

tun·nel vi·sion *n.* **1.** a condition in which lateral vision is greatly restricted. **2.** narrowness of viewpoint resulting from concentration on a single idea, opinion, etc., to the exclusion of others.

tun·ny ('tʌnɪ) *n., pl.* ·**nies** *or* ·**ny. 1.** Also called: **tuna.** any of various large marine spiny-finned fishes of the genus *Thunnus,* esp. *T. thynnus,* chiefly of warm waters: family *Scombridae.* They have a spindle-shaped body and widely forked tail, and are important food fishes. **2.** any of various similar and related fishes. [C16: from Old French *thon,* from Old Provençal *ton,* from Latin *thunnus,* from Greek]

tup (tʌp) *n.* **1.** *Chiefly Brit.* an uncastrated male sheep; ram. **2.** the head of a piledriver or steam hammer. ~*vb.* **tups, tup·ping, tupped.** (*tr.*) **3.** to cause a ram to mate with a ewe, or (of a ram) to mate with (a ewe). **4.** *Lancashire dialect.* to butt (someone), as in a fight. [C14: of unknown origin]

Tu·pa·ma·ro (ˌtju:pə'mɑ:rə, ˌtu:-) *n., pl.* ·**ros.** any of a group of Marxist urban guerrillas in Uruguay. [C20: after *Tupac Amaru,* 18th-century Peruvian Indian who led a rebellion against the Spaniards]

tu·pe·lo ('tju:pɪˌləʊ) *n., pl.* ·**los. 1.** any of several cornaceous trees of the genus *Nyssa,* esp. *N. aquatica,* a large tree of deep swamps and rivers of the southern U.S. **2.** the light strong wood of any of these trees. [C18: from Creek *ito opilwa,* from *ito* tree + *opilwa* swamp]

Tu·pi (tu:'pi:) *n.* **1.** (*pl.* ·**pis** *or* ·**pi**) a member of a South American Indian people of Brazil and Paraguay. **2.** the language of this people, belonging to the Tupi-Guarani family. —**Tu·pi·an** *adj.*

Tu·pi-Gua·ra·ni *n.* a family of South American Indian languages spoken in Brazil, Paraguay, and certain adjacent regions. —**'Tu·pi-ˌGua·ra·'ni·an** *adj.*

tup·pence ('tʌpəns) *n. Brit.* a variant spelling of **twopence.**

tup·pen·ny ('tʌpənɪ) *adj.* a variant spelling of **twopenny.**

Tu·pun·ga·to (*Spanish* ˌtupuŋ'gato) *n.* a mountain on the border between Argentina and Chile, in the Andes. Height: 6550 m (21 484 ft.).

tuque (tu:k) *n.* (in Canada) a knitted cap with a long tapering end. [C19: from Canadian French, from French: TOQUE]

tu quo·que *Latin.* (tju: 'kwəʊkwɪ) *interj.* you likewise: a retort made by a person accused of a crime implying that the accuser is also guilty of the same crime.

tu·ra·co ('tʊərəˌkəʊ) *n., pl.* ·**cos.** a variant spelling of **touraco.**

Tu·ra·ni·an (tjʊ'reɪnɪən) *n.* **1.** a member of any of the peoples inhabiting ancient Turkestan, or their descendants. **2.** another name for **Ural-Altaic.** ~*adj.* **3.** of or relating to the Ural-Altaic languages or any of the peoples who speak them. **4.** of or relating to Turkestan or its people.

tur·ban ('tɜ:bᵊn) *n.* **1.** a man's headdress, worn esp. by Muslims, Hindus, and Sikhs, made by swathing a length of linen, silk, etc., around the head or around a caplike base. **2.** a woman's brimless hat resembling this. **3.** any headdress resembling this. [C16: from Turkish *tülbend,* from Persian *dulband*] —**'tur·baned** *adj.* —**'tur·ban-ˌlike** *adj.*

tur·ba·ry ('tɜ:bərɪ) *n., pl.* ·**ries. 1.** land where peat or turf is cut or has been cut. **2.** Also called: **common of turbary.** (in England) the legal right to cut peat for fuel on a common. [C14: from Old French *turbarie,* from Medieval Latin *turbāria,* from *turba* peat, TURF]

tur·bel·lar·i·an (ˌtɜ:bɪ'lɛərɪən) *n.* **1.** any typically aquatic free-living flatworm of the class *Turbellaria,* having a ciliated epidermis and a simple life cycle: includes the planarians. ~*adj.* **2.** of, relating to, or belonging to the class *Turbellaria.* [C19: from New Latin *Turbellāria,* from Latin *turbellae* (pl.) bustle, from *turba* brawl, referring to the swirling motion created in the water]

tur·bid ('tɜ:bɪd) *adj.* **1.** muddy or opaque, as a liquid clouded with a suspension of particles. **2.** dense, thick, or cloudy: *turbid fog.* **3.** in turmoil or confusion. [C17: from Latin *turbidus,* from *turbāre* to agitate, from *turba* crowd] —**tur·'bid·i·ty** *or* **'tur·bid·ness** *n.* —**'tur·bid·ly** *adv.*

tur·bi·dim·e·ter (ˌtɜ:bɪ'dɪmɪtə) *n.* a device that measures the turbidity of a liquid.

tur·bi·nate ('tɜ:bɪnɪt, -ˌneɪt) *or* **tur·bi·nal** ('tɜ:bɪnᵊl) *adj. also* **tur·bi·nat·ed. 1.** *Anatomy.* of or relating to any of the thin scroll-shaped bones situated on the walls of the nasal passages. **2.** shaped like a spiral or scroll. **3.** (esp. of the shells of certain molluscs) shaped like an inverted cone. ~*n.* **4.** Also called: **nasal concha.** a turbinate bone. **5.** a turbinate shell. [C17: from Latin *turbō* spinning top] —ˌ**tur·bi·'na·tion** *n.*

tur·bine ('tɜ:bɪn, -baɪn) *n.* any of various types of machine in which the kinetic energy of a moving fluid is converted into mechanical energy by causing a bladed rotor to rotate. The moving fluid may be water, steam, air, or combustion products of a fuel. See also **reaction turbine, impulse turbine, gas turbine.** [C19: from French, from Latin *turbō* whirlwind, from *turbāre* to throw into confusion]

tur·bit ('tɜ:bɪt) *n.* a crested breed of domestic pigeon. [C17: from Latin *turbō* top, with reference to the bird's shape; compare TURBOT]

tur·bo- *combining form.* of, relating to, or driven by a turbine: *turbofan.*

tur·bo·car ('tɜ:bəʊˌkɑ:) *n.* a car driven by a gas turbine.

tur·bo·charg·er ('tɜ:bəʊˌtʃɑ:dʒə) *n.* a supercharger consisting of a turbine driven by exhaust gases of an engine.

tur·bo-e·lec·tric (ˌtɜ:bəʊɪ'lɛktrɪk) *adj.* of, relating to, or using an electric generator driven by a turbine: *turbo-electric propulsion.*

tur·bo·fan (ˌtɜ:bəʊ'fæn) *n.* **1.** Also called: **high by-pass ratio engine.** a type of by-pass engine in which a large fan driven by a turbine and housed in a short duct forces air rearwards around the exhaust gases in order to increase the propulsive thrust. **2.** an aircraft driven by one or more turbofans. **3.** the ducted fan in such an engine. ~Also called (for senses 1, 2): **fanjet.**

tur·bo·gen·er·a·tor (ˌtɜ:bəʊ'dʒɛnəˌreɪtə) *n.* a large electrical generator driven by a steam turbine.

tur·bo·jet (ˌtɜ:bəʊ'dʒɛt) *n.* **1.** short for **turbojet engine. 2.** an aircraft powered by one or more turbojet engines.

tur·bo·jet en·gine *n.* a gas turbine in which the exhaust gases provide the propulsive thrust to drive an aircraft.

tur·bo·prop (ˌtɜ:bəʊ'prɒp) *n.* **1.** a gas turbine for driving an aircraft propeller. **2.** an aircraft powered by turboprops.

tur·bo·su·per·charg·er (ˌtɜ:bəʊ'su:pəˌtʃɑ:dʒə, -'sju:-) *n.* a supercharging device for an internal-combustion engine, consisting of a turbine driven by the exhaust gases.

tur·bot ('tɜ:bət) *n., pl.* ·**bot** *or* ·**bots. 1.** a European flatfish, *Scophthalmus maximus,* having a pale brown speckled scaleless body covered with tubercles: family *Bothidae.* It is highly valued as a food fish. **2.** any of various similar or related fishes. [C13: from Old French *tourbot,* from Medieval Latin *turbō,* from Latin: top, from a fancied similarity in shape; see TURBIT, TURBINE]

tur·bu·lence ('tɜ:bjʊləns) *or* **tur·bu·len·cy** *n.* **1.** a state or condition of confusion, movement, or agitation; disorder. **2.** *Meteorol.* instability in the atmosphere causing considerable gusty air currents and cumulonimbus clouds. **3.** turbulent flow in a liquid or gas.

tur·bu·lent ('tɜ:bjʊlənt) *adj.* **1.** being in a state of turbulence. **2.** wild or insubordinate; unruly. [C16: from Latin *turbulentus,* from *turba* confusion] —**'tur·bu·lent·ly** *adv.*

tur·bu·lent flow *n.* flow of a fluid in which its velocity at any point varies rapidly in an irregular manner. Compare **streamline flow.**

Tur·co ('tɜ:kəʊ) *n., pl.* ·**cos.** (formerly) an Algerian serving in the light infantry of the French army. [C19: via French from Italian: a Turk]

turd (tɜ:d) *n. Taboo.* **1.** a lump of dung; piece of excrement. **2.** *Slang.* an unpleasant or contemptible person or thing. [Old English *tord;* related to Old Norse *tordy fill* dung beetle, Dutch *tort* dung]

tur·dine ('tɜ:daɪn, -dɪn) *adj.* of, relating to, or characteristic of thrushes. [C19: from Latin *turdus* thrush]

tu·reen (tə'riːn) *n.* a large deep usually rounded dish with a cover, used for serving soups, stews, etc. [C18: from French *terrine* earthenware vessel, from *terrin* made of earthenware, from Vulgar Latin *terrīnus* (unattested) earthen, from Latin *terra* earth]

Tu·renne (*French* tyˈrɛn) *n.* **Vi·comte de,** title of *Henri de la Tour d'Auvergne.* 1611–75, French marshal. He commanded armies during the Thirty Years' War and the wars of the Fronde.

turf (tɜːf) *n., pl.* **turfs** *or* **turves** (tɜːvz). **1.** the surface layer of fields and pastures, consisting of earth containing a dense growth of grasses with their roots; sod. **2.** a piece cut from this layer, used to form lawns, verges, etc. **3. the turf. a.** a track, usually of grass or dirt, where horse races are run. **b.** horse racing as a sport or industry. **4.** *U.S. slang.* the territory claimed by a juvenile gang as its own. **5.** (in Ireland) another word for **peat.** ~*vb.* **6.** (*tr.*) to cover with pieces of turf. [Old English; related to Old Norse *torfa,* Old High German *zurba,* Sanskrit *darbha* tuft of grass]

turf ac·count·ant *n. Brit.* a formal name for a **bookmaker.**

turf·man ('tɜːfmən) *n., pl.* **·men.** *Chiefly U.S.* a person devoted to horse racing. Also called: **turfite.**

turf out *vb.* (*tr., adv.*) *Brit. informal.* to throw out or dismiss; eject: *we were turfed out of the club.*

turf·y ('tɜːfɪ) *adj.* **turf·i·er, turf·i·est. 1.** of, covered with, or resembling turf. **2.** relating to or characteristic of horse racing or persons connected with it. —**'turf·i·ness** *n.*

Tur·ge·nev (*Russian* tur'gjenɪf) *n.* **I·van Ser·ge·ye·vich** (i'van sɪr'gjejɪvitʃ). 1818–83, Russian novelist and dramatist. In *A Sportsman's Sketches* (1852) he pleaded for the abolition of serfdom. His novels, such as *Rudin* (1856) and *Fathers and Sons* (1862), are noted for their portrayal of country life and of the Russian intelligentsia. His plays include *A Month in the Country* (1890).

tur·gent ('tɜːdʒənt) *adj.* an obsolete word for **turgid.** [C15: from Latin *turgēre* to swell] —**'tur·gent·ly** *adv.*

tur·ges·cent (tɜː'dʒɛsᵊnt) *adj.* becoming or being swollen; inflated; tumid. —**tur·'ges·cence** *or* **tur·'ges·cen·cy** *n.*

tur·gid ('tɜːdʒɪd) *adj.* **1.** swollen and distended; congested. **2.** (of style or language) pompous and high-flown; bombastic. [C17: from Latin *turgidus,* from *turgēre* to swell] —**tur·'gid·i·ty** *or* **'tur·gid·ness** *n.* —**'tur·gid·ly** *adv.*

tur·gite ('tɜːdʒaɪt) *n.* a red or black mineral consisting of hydrated ferric oxide. Formula: $Fe_2O_3.nH_2O$.

tur·gor ('tɜːgə) *n.* **1.** the normal rigid state of a cell, caused by pressure of the cell contents against the cell wall or membrane. **2.** *Rare.* turgidity. [C19: from Late Latin: a swelling, from Latin *turgēre* to swell]

Tur·got (*French* tyr'go) *n.* **Anne Ro·bert Jacques** (ɑːn rɔbɛːr 'ʒɑːk). 1727–81, French economist and statesman. As controller general of finances (1774–76), he attempted to abolish feudal privileges, incurring the hostility of the aristocracy and his final dismissal.

Tu·rin ('tʊərɪn) *n.* a city in NW Italy, capital of Piedmont region, on the River Po: became capital of the Kingdom of Sardinia in 1720; first capital (1861–65) of united Italy; university (1405); a major industrial centre, producing most of Italy's cars. Pop.: 1 202 215 (1975 est.). Italian name: **Torino.**

Tu·ring ma·chine ('tjʊərɪŋ) *n.* a hypothetical universal computing machine able to modify its original instructions by reading, erasing, or writing a new symbol on a moving tape of fixed length that acts as its program. The concept was instrumental in the early development of computer systems. [C20: named after Alan Mathison *Turing* (1912–54), English mathematician]

tur·i·on ('tʊərɪən) *n.* a perennating bud produced by many aquatic plants: it detaches from the parent plant and remains dormant until the following spring. [C17: from French *turion,* from Latin *turio*]

Tu·ri·shche·va (*Russian* tu'riʃtʃəvə) *n.* **Lud·mil·la** (lʊd'mɪlə). born 1952, Soviet gymnast: world champion 1970, 1972 (at the Olympic Games), and 1974.

Turk (tɜːk) *n.* **1.** a native, inhabitant, or citizen of Turkey. **2.** a native speaker of any Turkic language, such as an inhabitant of Turkestan or the Kirghiz Steppe in the Soviet Union. **3.** a violent, brutal, or domineering person.

Turk. *abbrev. for:* **1.** Turkey. **2.** Turkish.

Tur·ke·stan *or* **Tur·ki·stan** (ˌtɜːkɪ'stɑːn) *n.* an extensive region of central Asia between Siberia in the north and Tibet, India, Afghanistan, and Iran in the south: divided into **West (Russian) Turkestan** (also called Soviet Central Asia), which includes the Turkmen, Uzbek, Tadzhik, and Kirghiz SSRs and the S part of the Kazakh SSR, and **East (Chinese) Turkestan,** consisting of the Sinkiang-Uighur AR. —ˌ**Tur·ke·'sta·ni** *adj., n.*

tur·key ('tɜːkɪ) *n., pl.* **·keys** *or* **·key. 1.** a large gallinaceous bird, *Meleagris gallopavo,* of North America, having a bare wattled head and neck and a brownish iridescent plumage. The male is brighter and has a fan-shaped tail. It is widely domesticated for its flesh. **2.** a similar and related bird, *Agriocharis ocellata* (**ocellated turkey**), of Central and N South America. **3.** *U.S. informal.* a dramatic production that fails; flop. **4.** *Slang.* (in tenpin bowling) three strikes in a row. **5.** See **cold turkey. 6. talk turkey.** *Informal, chiefly U.S.* to discuss frankly and practically. [C16: shortened from *Turkey cock* (*hen*), used at first to designate the African guinea fowl (apparently because the bird was brought through Turkish territory), later applied by mistake to the American bird]

Tur·key ('tɜːkɪ) *n.* a republic in W Asia and SE Europe, between the Black Sea, the Mediterranean, and the Aegean: one of the oldest inhabited regions of the world; the centre of the Ottoman Empire; became a republic in 1923. The major Asian part, consisting mainly of an arid plateau, is separated from European Turkey by the Bosporus, Sea of Marmara, and Dardanelles. Languages: chiefly Turkish, with Kurdish and Arabic minority languages. Religion: mostly Muslim. Currency: lira. Capital: Ankara. Pop.: 40 197 669 (1975). Area: 780 576 sq. km (301 380 sq. miles).

tur·key buz·zard *or* **vul·ture** *n.* a New World vulture, *Cathartes aura,* having a dark plumage and naked red head.

tur·key cock *n.* **1.** a male turkey. **2.** an arrogant person.

Tur·key oak *n.* an oak tree, *Quercus cerris,* of W and S Europe, with deeply lobed hairy leaves.

Tur·key red *n.* **1. a.** a moderate or bright red colour. **b.** (*as adj.*): *a Turkey-red fabric.* **2.** a cotton fabric of a bright red colour.

tur·key trot *n.* an early ragtime one-step, popular in the period of World War I.

Tur·ki ('tɜːkɪ) *adj.* **1.** of or relating to the Turkic languages, esp. those spoken in Soviet central Asia. **2.** of or relating to speakers of these languages. ~*n.* **3.** these languages collectively; Turkic, esp. Eastern Turkic.

Tur·kic ('tɜːkɪk) *n.* a branch or subfamily of the Altaic family of languages, including Turkish, Turkmen, Kirghiz, Tatar, etc., members of which are found from Turkey to NE China, esp. in Soviet central Asia.

Turk·ish ('tɜːkɪʃ) *adj.* **1.** of, relating to, or characteristic of Turkey, its people, or their language. ~*n.* **2.** the official language of Turkey, belonging to the Turkic branch of the Altaic family. See also **Osmanli.** —**'Turk·ish·ness** *n.*

Turk·ish bath *n.* **1.** a type of bath in which the bather sweats freely in a steam room, is then washed, often massaged, and has a cold plunge or shower. **2.** (*sometimes pl.*) an establishment where such a bath is obtainable.

Turk·ish cof·fee *n.* very strong black coffee made with finely ground coffee beans.

Turk·ish de·light *n.* a jelly-like sweet flavoured with flower essences, usually cut into cubes and covered in icing sugar.

Turk·ish Em·pire *n.* another name for the **Ottoman Empire.**

Turk·ish to·bac·co *n.* a fragrant dark tobacco cultivated in E Europe, esp. Turkey and Greece.

Turk·ish tow·el *n.* a rough loose-piled towel; terry towel.

Turk·ism ('tɜːkɪzəm) *n. Rare.* **1.** the culture, beliefs, and customs of the Turks. **2.** a Turkish word, fashion, etc.

Turk·men ('tɜːkmɛn) *n.* the language of the Turkomans, belonging to the Turkic branch of the Altaic family.

Turk·men So·vi·et So·cial·ist Re·pub·lic *n.* an administrative division of the S Soviet Union, on the Caspian Sea. Capital: Ashkhabad. Pop.: 2 158 880 (1970). Area: 488 100 sq. km (186 400 sq. miles). Also called: **Turk·men·i·stan** (ˌtɜːkmɛnɪ'stɑːn).

Turk·o·man ('tɜːkəmən) *or* **Turk·man** *n.* **1.** (*pl.* **·mans** *or* **·men**) a member of a formerly nomadic people of central Asia, now living chiefly in the Turkmen SSR and in NE Iran. **2.** the Turkmen language. ~*adj.* **3.** of or relating to this people or their language. [C16: from Medieval Latin *Turcomannus,* from Persian *turkumān* resembling a Turk, from *turk* Turk + *māndan* to be like]

Turks and Cai·cos Is·lands *pl. n.* a British colony in the West Indies, southeast of the Bahamas: consists of the eight **Turks Islands,** separated by the **Turks Island Passage** from the Caicos group, which has six main islands. Capital: Grand Turk. Pop.: 5675 (1970). Area: 430 sq. km (166 sq. miles).

Turk's-cap lil·y *n.* any of several cultivated lilies, such as *Lilium martagon* and *L. superbum,* that have brightly coloured flowers with reflexed petals. See also **martagon.**

Turk's-head *n.* an ornamental turban-like knot made by weaving small cord around a larger rope.

Tur·ku (*Finnish* 'turku) *n.* a city and port in SW Finland, on the Gulf of Bothnia: capital of Finland until 1812. Pop.: 160 917 (1973 est.). Swedish name: **Åbo.**

tur·mer·ic ('tɜːmərɪk) *n.* **1.** a tropical Asian zingiberaceous plant, *Curcuma longa,* having yellow flowers and an aromatic underground stem. **2.** the powdered stem of this plant, used as a condiment and as a yellow dye. **3.** any of several other plants with similar roots. [C16: from Old French *terre merite,* from Medieval Latin *terra merita,* literally: meritorious earth, name applied for obscure reasons to curcuma]

tur·mer·ic pa·per *n. Chem.* paper impregnated with turmeric used as a test for alkalis, which turn it brown, and for boric acid, which turns it reddish brown.

tur·moil ('tɜːmɔɪl) *n.* **1.** violent or confused movement; agitation; tumult. ~*vb.* **2.** *Archaic.* to make or become turbulent. [C16: perhaps from TURN + MOIL]

turn (tɜːn) *vb.* **1.** to move or cause to move around an axis: *a wheel turning; to turn a knob.* **2.** (sometimes foll. by *round*) to change or cause to change positions by moving through an arc of a circle: *he turned the chair to face the light.* **3.** to change or cause to change in course, direction, etc.: *he turned left at the main road.* **4.** (of soldiers, ships, etc.) to alter the direction of advance by changing direction simultaneously or (of a commander) to cause the direction of advance to be altered simultaneously. **5.** to go or pass to the other side of (a corner, etc.). **6.** to assume or cause to assume a rounded, curved, or folded form: *the road turns here.* **7.** to reverse or cause to reverse position. **8.** (*tr.*) to perform or do by a rotating movement: *to turn a somersault.* **9.** (*tr.*) to shape or cut a thread in (a workpiece, esp. one of metal, wood, or plastic) by rotating it on a lathe against a fixed cutting tool. **10.** (when *intr.*, foll. by *into* or *to*) to change or convert or be changed or converted: *the alchemists tried to turn base metals into gold.* **11.** (foll. by *into*) to change or cause to change in nature, character, etc.: *the frog turned into a prince.* **12.** (*copula*) to change so as to become: *he turned nasty when he heard the price.* **13.** to cause (foliage, etc.) to change colour or (of foliage, etc.) to change colour: *frost turned the trees a vivid orange.* **14.** to cause (milk, etc.) to become rancid or sour or (of milk, etc.) to become rancid or sour. **15.** to change or cause to change in subject, trend, etc.: *the conversation turned to fishing.* **16.** to direct or apply or be directed or applied: *he turned his attention to the problem.* **17.** (*intr.*; usually foll. by *to*) to appeal or apply (to) for help, advice, etc.: *she was very frightened and didn't know where to turn.* **18.** to reach, pass, or progress beyond in age, time, etc.: *she has just turned twenty.* **19.** (*tr.*) to cause or allow to go: *to turn an animal loose.* **20.** to affect or be affected with nausea: *the sight of the dead body turned his stomach.* **21.** to affect or be affected with giddiness: *my head is turning.* **22.** (*tr.*) to affect the mental or emotional stability of (esp. in the phrase **turn (someone's) head**). **23.** (*tr.*) to release from a container: *she turned the fruit into a basin.* **24.** (*tr.*) to render into another language. **25.** (usually foll. by *against* or *from*) to transfer or reverse or cause to transfer or reverse (one's loyalties, affections, etc.). **26.** (*tr.*) to bring (soil) from lower layers to the surface. **27.** to blunt (an edge) or (of an edge) to become blunted. **28.** (*tr.*) to give a graceful form to: *to turn a compliment.* **29.** (*tr.*) to reverse (a cuff, collar, etc.) in order to hide the outer worn side. **30.** (*intr.*) *U.S.* to be merchandised as specified: *shirts are turning well this week.* **31.** *Cricket.* to spin (the ball) or (of the ball) to spin. **32. turn one's hand to.** to undertake (something, esp. something practical). **33. turn tail.** *Informal.* to run away; flee. **34. turn the tables.** *Informal.* See **table** (sense 16). **35. turn the tide.** to reverse the general course of events. ~*n.* **36.** an act or instance of turning or the state of being turned or the material turned: *a turn of a rope around a bollard.* **37.** a movement of complete or partial rotation. **38.** a change or reversal of direction or position. **39.** direction or drift: *his thoughts took a new turn.* **40.** a deviation or departure from a course or tendency. **41.** the place, point, or time at which a deviation or change occurs. **42.** another word for **turning** (sense 1). **43.** the right or opportunity to do something in an agreed order or succession: *we'll take turns to play; now it's George's turn; you must not play out of turn.* **44.** a change in nature, condition, etc.: *his illness took a turn for the worse.* **45.** a period of action, work, etc. **46.** a short walk, ride, or excursion: *to take a turn in the park.* **47.** natural inclination: *he is of a speculative turn of mind; she has a turn for needlework.* **48.** distinctive form or style: *a neat turn of phrase.* **49.** requirement, need, or advantage: *to serve someone's turn.* **50.** a deed performed that helps or hinders someone: *to do an old lady a good turn.* **51.** a twist, bend, or distortion in shape. **52.** *Music.* a melodic ornament consisting of two auxiliary notes a diatonic second above and below a principal note, all four notes being rapidly executed. **53.** *Theatre, chiefly Brit.* a short theatrical act, esp. in music hall, cabaret, etc. **54.** *Stock exchange.* **a.** *Brit.* the difference between a stockjobber's bid and offer prices, representing the jobber's income. **b.** a transaction including both a purchase and a sale. **55.** a military manoeuvre in which men or ships alter their direction of advance together. **56.** *Austral. slang.* a party. **57.** *Informal.* a shock or surprise: *the bad news gave her quite a turn.* **58. at every turn.** on all sides or occasions. **59. by turns.** one after another; alternately. **60. on the turn.** *Informal.* **a.** at the point of change. **b.** about to go rancid. **61. turn and turn about.** one after another; alternately. **62. to a turn.** to the proper amount; perfectly: *cooked to a turn.* ~See also **turn against, turn away, turn down, turn in, turn off, turn on, turn out, turn over, turn to, turn up.** [Old English *tyrnian*, from Old French *torner*, from Latin *tornāre* to turn in a lathe, from *tornus* lathe, from Greek *tornos* dividers] —**'turn·a·ble** *adj.*

turn·a·bout ('tɜːnəˌbaʊt) *n.* **1.** the act of turning so as to face a different direction. **2.** a change or reversal of opinion, attitude, etc. ~Also called: **turnaround.**

turn a·gainst *vb.* (*prep.*) to change or cause to change one's attitude so as to become hostile or to retaliate.

turn·a·round ('tɜːnəˌraʊnd) *n.* **1. a.** the act or process in which a ship, aircraft, etc., unloads passengers and freight at the end of a trip and reloads for the next trip. **b.** the time taken for this act. **2.** the total time taken by a ship, aircraft, or other vehicle in a round trip. **3.** another word for **turnabout.**

turn a·way *vb.* (*adv.*) **1.** to move or cause to move in a different direction so as not to face something. **2.** (*tr.*) to refuse admittance or assistance to: *dozens of people were turned away from the hostel.*

turn bridge *n.* another name for **swing bridge.**

turn·buck·le ('tɜːnˌbʌkᵊl) *n.* an open mechanical sleeve usually having a swivel at one end and a thread at the other to enable a threaded wire or rope to be tightened.

turn·coat ('tɜːnˌkəʊt) *n.* a person who deserts one cause or party for the opposite faction; renegade.

turn·cock ('tɜːnˌkɒk) *n.* an official employed to turn on the water for the mains supply.

turn down *vb.* (*tr., adv.*) **1.** to reduce (the volume or brightness) of (something): *please turn the radio down.* **2.** to reject or refuse. **3.** to fold down (a collar, sheets on a bed, etc.). ~*adj.* **turn·down. 4.** (*prenominal*) capable of being or designed to be folded or doubled down.

turned com·ma *n. Printing.* a single inverted comma ('), esp. as used in Britain as a quotation mark.

turned pe·ri·od *n. Printing.* an inverted full stop (·), used chiefly as a decimal point.

turn·er ('tɜːnə) *n.* **1.** a person or thing that turns, esp. a person who operates a lathe. **2.** *U.S.* a member of a society of gymnasts.

Tur·ner ('tɜːnə) *n.* **Jo·seph Mal·lord Wil·liam.** 1775-1851, English landscape painter; a master of water colours. He sought to convey atmosphere by means of an innovative use of colour and gradations of light.

turn·er·y ('tɜːnərɪ) *n., pl.* **-er·ies. 1.** objects made on a lathe. **2.** Also called: **turning.** the process or skill of turning objects on a lathe. **3.** the workshop of a lathe operator.

turn in *vb.* (*adv.*) *Informal.* **1.** (*intr.*) to go to bed for the night. **2.** (*tr.*) to hand in; deliver: *to turn in an essay.* **3.** to give up or conclude (something): *we turned in the game when it began to rain.* **4.** (*tr.*) to record (a score, etc.). **5. turn in on oneself.** to withdraw or cause to withdraw from contact with others and become preoccupied with one's own problems.

turn·ing ('tɜːnɪŋ) *n.* **1.** Also called: **turn.** a road, river, or path that turns off the main way: *the fourth turning on the right.* **2.** the point where such a way turns off. **3.** a bend in a straight course. **4.** an object made on a lathe. **5.** another name for **turnery** (sense 2). **6.** (*pl.*) the waste produced in turning on a lathe.

turn·ing cir·cle *n.* the smallest circle in which a vehicle can turn.

turn·ing point *n.* **1.** a moment when the course of events is changed: *the turning point of his career.* **2.** a point at which there is a change in direction or motion, such as at a maximum or minimum point on a graph. **3.** *Surveying.* a point to which a foresight and a backsight are taken in levelling; change point.

tur·nip ('tɜːnɪp) *n.* **1.** a widely cultivated cruciferous plant, *Brassica rapa*, of the Mediterranean region, with a large yellow or white edible root. **2.** the root of this plant, which is eaten as a vegetable. **3.** any of several similar or related plants. **4. turnip cabbage.** another name for **kohlrabi.** ~Also called (for senses 1, 2): **navew.** [C16: from earlier *turnepe*, perhaps from TURN (indicating its rounded shape) + *nepe*, from Latin *nāpus* turnip; see NEEP]

turn·key ('tɜːnˌkiː) *n. Archaic.* a keeper of the keys, esp. in a prison; warder or jailer.

turn off *vb.* **1.** (*intr.*) to leave (a road, pathway, etc.). **2.** (*intr.*) (of a road, pathway, etc.) to deviate from (another road, etc.). **3.** (*tr., adv.*) to cause (something) to cease operating by turning a knob, pushing a button, etc.: *to turn off the radio.* **4.** (*tr.*) *Informal.* to cause (a person, etc.) to feel dislike or distaste for (something): *this music turns me off.* **5.** (*tr., adv.*) *Brit. informal.* to dismiss from employment. ~*n.* **turn-off. 6.** a road or other way branching off from the main thoroughfare.

turn on *vb.* **1.** (*tr., adv.*) to cause (something) to operate by turning a knob, etc.: *to turn on the light.* **2.** (*intr., prep.*) to depend or hinge on: *the success of the party turns on you.* **3.** (*prep.*) to change or cause to change one's attitude so as to become hostile or to retaliate: *the dog turned on the children.* **4.** (*tr., adv.*) *Informal.* to produce (charm, tears, etc.) suddenly or automatically. **5.** (*tr., adv.*) *Slang.* to arouse emotionally or sexually. **6.** (*intr., adv.*) *Slang.* to take or become intoxicated by drugs. **7.** (*tr., adv.*) *Slang.* to introduce (someone) to drugs.

turn out *vb.* (*adv.*) **1.** (*tr.*) to cause (something, esp. a light) to cease operating by or as if by turning a knob, etc. **2.** (*tr.*) to produce by an effort or process: *she turned out 50 units per hour.* **3.** (*tr.*) to dismiss, discharge, or expel: *the family had been turned out of their home.* **4.** (*tr.*) to clear or clean the contents of: *to turn out one's pockets.* **5.** (*copula*) to prove to be as specified, esp. against expectations: *her work turned out to be badly done.* **6.** (*tr.*) to fit as with clothes: *that woman turns her children out well.* **7.** (*intr.*) to assemble or gather: *a crowd turned out for the fair.* **8.** (of a soldier) to parade or call (a soldier) to parade. **9.** (*intr.*) *Informal.* to get out of bed. ~*n.* **turn·out. 10.** the body of people appearing together at a gathering. **11.** the quantity or amount produced. **12.** an array of clothing or equipment. **13.** the manner in which a person or thing is arrayed or equipped.

turn o·ver *vb.* (*adv.*) **1.** to change or cause to change position, esp. so as to reverse top and bottom. **2.** to start (an engine), esp. with a starting handle, or (of an engine) to start or function correctly. **3.** to shift or cause to shift position, as by rolling from side to side. **4.** (*tr.*) to deliver; transfer. **5.** (*tr.*) to consider carefully: *he turned over the problem for hours.* **6.** (*tr.*) **a.** to sell and replenish (stock in trade). **b.** to transact business and so generate gross revenue of (a specified sum). **7.** (*tr.*) to invest and recover (capital). **8.** (*tr.*) *Slang.* to rob. ~*n.* **turn·o·ver. 9. a.** the amount of business, usually expressed in terms of gross revenue, transacted during a specified period. **b.** the rate at which stock in trade is sold and replenished. **10.** a change or reversal of position. **11.** a small semicircular or triangular pastry case filled with fruit, jam, etc. **12. a.** the number of workers employed by a firm in a given period to replace those who have left. **b.** the ratio between this number and the average number of employees during the same period. **13.** *Banking.* the amount of capital funds loaned on call during a specified period. ~*adj.* **14.** (*prenominal*) able or designed to be turned or folded over: *a turnover collar.*

turn·pike ('tɜːnˌpaɪk) *n.* **1.** (between the mid-16th and late 19th centuries) **a.** gates or some other barrier set across a road to prevent passage until a toll had been paid. **b.** a road on which a turnpike was operated. **2.** an obsolete word for **turnstile. 3.** *U.S.* a motorway for use of which a toll is charged. [C15: from TURN + PIKE[2]]

turn·sole ('tɜːnˌsəʊl) *n.* **1.** any of various plants having flowers that are said to turn towards the sun. **2.** a euphorbiaceous plant, *Croton tinctoria*, of the Mediterranean region that yields a purple dye. **3.** the dye extracted from this plant. [C14: from Old French *tournesole*, from Old Italian *tornasole*, from *tornare* to TURN + *sole* sun, from Latin *sōl* sun]

turn+spit ('tɜːnˌspɪt) *n.* **1.** (formerly) a servant or small dog whose job was to turn the spit on which meat, poultry, etc., was roasting. **2.** a spit that can be so turned.

turn+stile ('tɜːnˌstaɪl) *n.* **1.** a mechanical gate or barrier with metal arms that are turned to admit one person at a time, usually in one direction only. **2.** any similar device that admits foot passengers but no large animals or vehicles.

turn+stone ('tɜːnˌstəʊn) *n.* either of two shore birds of the genus *Arenaria*, esp. *A. interpres* (**ruddy turnstone**). They are related and similar to plovers and sandpipers.

turn+ta·ble ('tɜːnˌteɪbᵊl) *n.* **1.** the circular horizontal platform that rotates a gramophone record while it is being played. **2.** a flat circular platform that can be rotated about its centre, used for turning locomotives and cars. **3.** the revolvable platform on a microscope on which specimens are examined. **4.** *Austral.* an area on a road, hill, etc., where a motor vehicle can turn round.

turn+ta·ble lad+der *n. Brit.* a power-operated extending ladder mounted on a fire engine. U.S. name: **aerial ladder.**

turn to *vb.* (*intr., adv.*) to set about a task: *we must turn to and finish our work.*

turn up *vb.* (*adv.*) **1.** (*intr.*) to arrive or appear: *he turned up late at the party.* **2.** to find or be found, esp. by accident: *his book turned up in the cupboard.* **3.** (*tr.*) to increase the flow, volume, etc., of: *to turn up the radio.* **4.** (*tr.*) *Informal.* to cause to vomit. ~*n.* **turn-up. 5.** (*often pl.*) *Brit.* the turned-up fold at the bottom of some trouser legs. U.S. name: **cuff. 6.** *Informal.* an unexpected or chance occurrence.

tur+pen+tine ('tɜːpᵊnˌtaɪn) *n.* **1.** Also called: **gum turpentine.** any of various viscous oleoresins obtained from various coniferous trees, esp. from the longleaf pine, and used as the main source of commercial turpentine. **2.** a brownish-yellow sticky viscous oleoresin that exudes from the terebinth tree. **3.** Also called: **oil of turpentine, spirits of turpentine.** a colourless flammable volatile liquid with a pungent odour, distilled from turpentine oleoresin. It is an essential oil containing a mixture of terpenes and is used as a solvent for paints and in medicine as a rubefacient and expectorant. Sometimes shortened (esp. Brit.) to **turps. 4.** Also called: **turpentine substitute, white spirit.** (*not in technical usage*) any one of a number of thinners for paints and varnishes, consisting of fractions of petroleum. Related adj.: **terebinthine.** ~*vb.* (*tr.*) **5.** to treat or saturate with turpentine. **6.** to extract crude turpentine from (trees). [C14 *terebentyne*, from Medieval Latin *terbentīna*, from Latin *terebinthīna* turpentine, from *terebinthus* the turpentine tree, TEREBINTH]

tur+pen+tine tree *n.* **1.** a tropical African leguminous tree, *Copaifera mopane*, yielding a hard dark wood and a useful resin. **2.** either of two Australian evergreen myrtaceous trees, *Syncarpia lilli* or *S. glomulifera*, that have durable wood and are sometimes planted as shade trees.

tur+peth ('tɜːpɪθ) *n.* **1.** a convolvulaceous plant, *Operculina turpethum*, of the East Indies, having roots with purgative properties. **2.** the root of this plant or the drug obtained from it. [C14: from Medieval Latin *turbithum*, ultimately from Arabic *turbid*]

Tur·pin ('tɜːpɪn) *n.* **Dick.** 1706–39, English highwayman.

tur+pi+tude ('tɜːpɪˌtjuːd) *n.* base character or action; depravity. [C15: from Latin *turpitūdō* ugliness, from *turpis* base]

turps (tɜːps) *n.* **1.** *Brit.* short for **turpentine** (sense 3). **2.** *Austral. slang.* alcoholic drink, esp. beer.

tur+quoise ('tɜːkwɔɪz, -kwɑːz) *n.* **1.** a greenish-blue fine-grained secondary mineral consisting of hydrated copper aluminium phosphate. It occurs in igneous rocks rich in aluminium and is used as a gemstone. Formula: $CuAl_6(PO_4)_4(OH)_8.4H_2O$. **2. a.** the colour of turquoise. **b.** (*as adj.*): *a turquoise dress.* [C14: from Old French *turqueise* Turkish (stone)]

tur+ret ('tʌrɪt) *n.* **1.** a small tower that projects from the wall of a building, esp. a medieval castle. **2. a.** a self-contained structure, capable of rotation, in which weapons are mounted, esp. in tanks and warships. **b.** a similar structure on an aircraft that houses one or more guns and sometimes a gunner. **3.** a tall wooden tower on wheels used formerly by besiegers to scale the walls of a fortress. **4.** a lathe part that has a number of tools projecting radially from it that, as it turns, are presented to the workpiece in succession. [C14: from Old French *torete*, from *tor* tower, from Latin *turris*]

tur+ret+ed ('tʌrɪtɪd), **tur+ric·u+late** (tʌ'rɪkjʊlɪt, -ˌleɪt), *or* **tur+ric·u+lat+ed** *adj.* **1.** having or resembling a turret or turrets. **2.** (of a gastropod shell) having the shape of a long spiral.

tur+ret lathe *n.* another name for **capstan lathe.**

tur+tle[1] ('tɜːtᵊl) *n.* **1.** any of various aquatic chelonian reptiles, esp. those of the marine family *Chelonidae*, having a flattened shell enclosing the body and flipper-like limbs adapted for swimming. **2.** *U.S.* any of the chelonian reptiles, including the tortoises and terrapins. **3.** *Nautical.* a zippered bag made as part of a spinnaker for holding the sail so that it can be set rapidly. **4. turn turtle.** to capsize. ~*vb.* **5.** (*intr.*) to catch or hunt turtles. [C17: from French *tortue* TORTOISE (influenced by TURTLE[2])] —'**tur+tler** *n.*

tur+tle[2] ('tɜːtᵊl) *n.* an archaic name for **turtledove.** [Old English *turtla*, from Latin *turtur*, of imitative origin; related to German *Turteltaube*]

tur·tle+back ('tɜːtᵊlˌbæk) *n.* **1.** an arched projection over the upper deck of a ship at the bow and sometimes at the stern for protection in heavy seas. **2.** (*now obsolete in archaeological usage*) a crude convex stone axe.

tur·tle+dove ('tɜːtᵊlˌdʌv) *n.* **1.** any of several Old World doves of the genus *Streptopelia*, having a brown plumage with speckled wings and a long dark tail. **2.** a gentle or loving person. [see TURTLE[2]]

tur·tle+neck ('tɜːtᵊlˌnɛk) *n.* **a.** a round high close-fitting neck on a sweater or the sweater itself. **b.** (*as modifier*)*: a turtleneck sweater.*

turves (tɜːvz) *n.* a plural of **turf.**

Tus+can ('tʌskən) *adj.* **1.** of or relating to Tuscany, its inhabitants, or their dialect of Italian. **2.** of, denoting, or relating to one of the five classical orders of architecture: characterized by a column with an unfluted shaft and a capital and base with mouldings but no decoration. See also **Ionic, Composite, Doric, Corinthian.** ~*n.* **3.** a native or inhabitant of Tuscany. **4.** any of the dialects of Italian spoken in Tuscany, esp. the dialect of Florence: the standard form of Italian.

Tus+ca+ny ('tʌskənɪ) *n.* a region of central Italy, on the Ligurian and Tyrrhenian Seas: corresponds roughly to ancient Etruria; a region of numerous small states in medieval times; united in the 15th and 16th centuries under Florence; united with the rest of Italy in 1861. Capital: Florence. Pop.: 3 470 915 (1971). Area: 22 990 sq. km (8876 sq. miles). Italian name: **Toscana.**

Tus+ca+ro+ra (ˌtʌskə'rɔːrə) *n.* **1.** (*pl.* **+ras** *or* **+ra**) a member of a North American Indian people formerly living in North Carolina, who later moved to New York State and joined the Iroquois. **2.** the language of this people, belonging to the Iroquoian family.

tusche (tʊʃ) *n.* a substance used in lithography for drawing the design and as a resist in silk-screen printing and lithography. [from German, from *tuschen* to touch up with colour or ink, from French *toucher* to TOUCH]

Tus+cu+lum ('tʌskjʊləm) *n.* an ancient city in Latium near Rome. —'**Tus+cu+lan** *adj.*

tush[1] (tʌʃ) *interj.* an exclamation of disapproval or contempt.

tush[2] (tʌʃ) *n. Rare.* a tusk. [Old English *tūsc;* see TUSK]

tusk (tʌsk) *n.* **1.** a pointed elongated usually paired tooth in the elephant, walrus, and certain other mammals that is specialized for fighting. **2.** the canine tooth of certain animals, esp. horses. **3.** a sharp pointed projection. **4.** Also called: **tusk tenon.** *Building trades.* a tenon shaped with an additional oblique shoulder to make a stronger joint. ~*vb.* **5.** to stab, tear, or gore with the tusks. [Old English *tūsc;* related to Old Frisian *tosk;* see TOOTH] —**tusked** *adj.* —'**tusk+ˌlike** *adj.*

tusk+er ('tʌskə) *n.* any animal with prominent tusks, esp. a wild boar or elephant.

tusk shell *n.* any of various burrowing seashore molluscs of the genus *Dentalium* and related genera that have a long narrow tubular shell open at both ends: class *Scaphopoda.* Also called: **tooth shell.**

tus+sah ('tʌsə) *or* **tus+sore** (tʊ'sɔː, 'tʌsə) *n.* **1.** a strong coarse brownish Indian silk obtained from the cocoons of an oriental saturniid silkworm, *Antheraea paphia.* **2.** a fabric woven from this silk. **3.** the silkworm producing this silk. [C17: from Hindi *tasar* shuttle, from Sanskrit *tasara* a wild silkworm]

Tus·saud (*French* ty'so) *n.* **Ma·rie** (ma'ri). 1760–1850, Swiss modeller in wax, who founded a permanent exhibition in London of historical and contemporary figures.

tus+sis ('tʌsɪs) *n.* the technical name for a **cough.** See **pertussis.** [Latin: cough] —'**tus+sal** *adj.* —'**tus+sive** *adj.*

tus+sle ('tʌsᵊl) *vb.* **1.** (*intr.*) to fight or wrestle in a vigorous way; struggle. ~*n.* **2.** a vigorous fight; scuffle; struggle. [C15: related to Old High German *zūsen;* see TOUSLE]

tus+sock ('tʌsək) *n.* a dense tuft of vegetation, esp. of grass. [C16: perhaps related to TUSK] —'**tus+sock·y** *adj.*

tus+sock grass *n. Austral.* **1.** any of several pasture grasses of the genus *Poa.* **2.** a tough grass, *Nassella trichotoma*, that is unpalatable to stock and a serious pest in overgrazed areas.

tus+sock moth *n.* any of various pale or dull-coloured moths of the family *Lymantriidae* (or *Laparidae*), the hairy caterpillars of which are pests of many trees. See also **gypsy moth, brown-tail moth, gold-tail moth.**

tut *interj.* (*pronounced as an alveolar click; spelling pron.* tʌt), *n., vb.* **tuts, tut+ting, tut+ted.** short for **tut-tut.**

Tu·tan·kha·men (ˌtuːtən'kɑːmɛn, -mən) *or* **Tu·tan·kha·mun** (ˌtuːtənkɑː'muːn) *n.* king (1361–1352 B.C.) of the 18th dynasty of Egypt. His tomb near Luxor, discovered in 1922, contained a wealth of material objects.

tu+tee (tjuː'tiː) *n.* one who is tutored, esp. in a university.

tu+te·lage ('tjuːtɪlɪdʒ) *n.* **1.** the act or office of a guardian or tutor. **2.** instruction or guidance, esp. by a tutor. **3.** the condition of being under the supervision of a guardian or tutor. [C17: from Latin *tūtēla* a caring for, from *tuērī* to watch over; compare TUITION]

tu+te·lar·y ('tjuːtɪlərɪ) *or* **tu+te·lar** ('tjuːtɪlə) *adj.* **1.** invested with the role of guardian or protector. **2.** of or relating to a guardian or guardianship. ~*n., pl.* **·lar·ies** *or* **·lars. 3.** a tutelary person, deity, or saint.

tu+ti+or+ism ('tjuːtɪəˌrɪzəm) *n.* (in Roman Catholic moral theology) the doctrine that in cases of moral doubt it is best to follow the safer course or that in agreement with the law. [C19: from Latin *tutior* safer, comparative of *tutus* safe] —'**tu+ti+or+ist** *n.*

tu+tor ('tjuːtə) *n.* **1.** a teacher, usually instructing individual pupils and often engaged privately. **2.** (at universities, colleges, etc.) a member of staff responsible for the teaching and supervision of a certain number of students. ~*vb.* **3.** to act as a tutor to (someone); instruct. **4.** (*tr.*) to act as guardian to; have care of. 5. (*intr.*) to study under a tutor. 6. (*tr.*) *Rare.* to admonish, discipline, or reprimand. [C14: from Latin: a watcher, from *tuērī* to watch over] —**'tu+tor+age** *or* **'tu+tor+ˌship** *n.*

tu+to+ri+al (tjuː'tɔːrɪəl) *n.* **1.** a period of intensive tuition given by a tutor to an individual student or to a small group of students. ~*adj.* **2.** of or relating to a tutor.

tu+to+ri+al sys+tem *n.* a system, mainly in universities, in which students receive guidance in academic or personal matters from tutors.

tut+san ('tʌtsən) *n.* a woodland shrub, *Hypericum androsaemum,* of Europe and W Asia, having yellow flowers and reddish-purple fruits: family *Hypericaceae.* See also **Saint John's wort.** [C15: from Old French *toute-saine* (unattested), literally: all healthy]

Tut+si ('tuːtsɪ) *n., pl.* **+si** *or* **+sis.** a member of a Bantu people of Rwanda.

tut+ti ('tʊtɪ) *adj., adv. Music.* to be performed by the whole orchestra, choir, etc. Compare **soli.** [C18: from Italian, pl. of *tutto* all, from Latin *tōtus*]

tut·ti-frut·ti ('tuːtɪ'fruːtɪ) *n.* **1.** an ice cream or a confection containing small pieces of candied or fresh fruits. **2.** a preserve of chopped mixed fruits, often with brandy syrup. **3.** a flavour like that of many fruits combined. ~*adj.* **4.** having such a flavour. [from Italian, literally: all the fruits]

tut-tut *interj.* (*pronounced as alveolar clicks; spelling pron.* 'tʌt'tʌt). **1.** an exclamation of mild reprimand, disapproval, or surprise. ~*vb.* **-tuts, -tut·ting, -tut·ted. 2.** (*intr.*) to express disapproval by the exclamation of "tut-tut." ~*n.* **3.** the act of tut-tutting. ~Often shortened to **tut.**

tut+ty ('tʌtɪ) *n.* finely powdered impure zinc oxide obtained from the flues of zinc-smelting furnaces and used as a polishing powder. [C14: from Old French *tutie,* from Arabic *tūtiyā,* probably from Persian, from Sanskrit *tuttha*]

tu·tu ('tuːtuː) *n.* a very short skirt worn by ballerinas, made of projecting layers of stiffened sheer material. [from French, changed from the nursery word *cucu* backside, from *cul,* from Latin *cūlus* the buttocks]

Tu+tu·i+la (ˌtuːtuː'iːlə) *n.* the largest island of American Samoa, in the SW Pacific. Chief town and port: Pago Pago. Pop.: 25 557 (1970). Area: 135 sq. km (52 sq. miles).

Tu·va Au·ton·o+mous So+vi+et So+cial+ist Re+pub+lic ('tuːvə) *n.* an administrative division of the S Soviet Union: mountainous. Capital: Kizyl. Pop.: 230 864 (1970). Area: 170 500 sq. km (65 800 sq. miles). Also called: **Tuvinian ASSR.**

Tuvalu (tuːvə'luː) *pl. n.* a group of nine coral islands in the SW Pacific: established as a British protectorate in 1892; from 1915 until 1975 they formed part of the British colony of the Gilbert and Ellice Islands; achieved full independence in 1978. Area: 24 sq. km (9.5 sq. miles). Former names: **Lagoon Islands, Ellice Islands.**

tu-whit tu-whoo (tə'wɪt tə'wuː) *interj.* an imitation or representation of the sound made by an owl.

tux+e·do (tʌk'siːdəʊ) *n., pl.* **·dos.** the usual U.S. name for **dinner jacket.** [C19: named after a country club in *Tuxedo Park,* New York]

Tux+tla Gu+tiér+rez (*Spanish* 'tustla gu'tjerres) *n.* a city in SE Mexico, capital of Chiapas state: agricultural trading centre. Pop.: 89 326 (1970).

tu+yère ('twiːɛə, 'twaɪə; *French* ty'jɛːr) *or* **twy+er** ('twaɪə) *n.* a nozzle in a blast furnace through which air is injected. [C18: from French, from *tuyau* pipe, from Old French *tuel,* probably of Germanic origin]

TV *abbrev. for* television.

TVA *abbrev. for* Tennessee Valley Authority.

Tver (*Russian* tvjerj) *n.* the former name (until 1932) of **Kalinin.**

twad+dle ('twɒdᵊl) *n.* **1.** silly, trivial, or pretentious talk or writing; nonsense. ~*vb.* **2.** to talk or write (something) in a silly or pretentious way. [C16 *twattle,* variant of *twittle* or *tittle;* see TITTLE-TATTLE] —**'twad+dler** *n.*

twain (tweɪn) *determiner, n.* an archaic word for **two.** [Old English *twēgen;* related to Old Saxon *twēne,* Old High German *zwēne,* Old Norse *tveir,* Gothic *twai*]

Twain (tweɪn) *n.* **Mark,** pen name of *Samuel Langhorne Clemens.* 1835–1910, U.S. novelist and humorist, famous for his classics *The Adventures of Tom Sawyer* (1876) and *The Adventures of Huckleberry Finn* (1885).

twang (twæŋ) *n.* **1.** a sharp ringing sound produced by or as if by the plucking of a taut string: *the twang of a guitar.* **2.** the act of plucking a string to produce such a sound. **3.** a strongly nasal quality in a person's speech, esp. in certain dialects. ~*vb.* **4.** to make or cause to make a twang: *to twang a guitar.* **5.** to strum (music, a tune, etc.): *to twang on a guitar.* **6.** to speak or utter with a sharp nasal voice. **7.** (*intr.*) to be released or move with a twang: *the arrow twanged away.* [C16: of imitative origin] —**'twang·y** *adj.*

'twas (twɒz; *unstressed* twəz) *Poetic or dialect. contraction of* it was.

twat (twæt, twɒt) *n. Taboo slang.* **1.** the female genitals. **2.** a girl or woman considered sexually. **3.** a foolish or despicable person. [of unknown origin]

twat+tle ('twɒtᵊl) *n.* a rare word for **twaddle.**

tway+blade ('tweɪˌbleɪd) *n.* any of various terrestrial orchids of the genera *Listera, Liparis, Ophrys,* etc., having a basal pair of oval unstalked leaves arranged opposite each other. [C16: translation of Medieval Latin *bifolium* having two leaves, from obsolete *tway* TWO + BLADE]

tweak (twiːk) *vb.* (*tr.*) **1.** to twist, jerk, or pinch with a sharp or sudden movement: *to tweak someone's nose.* **2.** *Motor racing slang.* to tune (a car or engine) for peak performance. ~*n.* **3.** an instance of tweaking. [Old English *twiccian;* related to Old High German *zwecchōn;* see TWITCH] —**'tweak·y** *adj.*

twee (twiː) *adj. Brit. informal.* excessively sentimental, sweet, or pretty. [C19: from *tweet,* mincing or affected pronunciation of SWEET]

tweed (twiːd) *n.* **1. a.** a thick woollen often knobbly cloth produced originally in Scotland. **b.** (*as modifier*): *a tweed coat.* **2.** (*pl.*) clothes made of this cloth, esp. a man's or woman's suit. [C19: probably from *tweel,* Scottish variant of TWILL, influenced by *Tweed,* name of Scottish river]

Tweed (twiːd) *n.* a river in SE Scotland and NE England, flowing east and forming part of the border between Scotland and England, then crossing into England to enter the North Sea at Berwick. Length: 156 km (97 miles).

Tweed+dale ('twiːdˌdeɪl) *n.* another name for **Peebles.**

Twee+dle+dum and Twee+dle+dee (ˌtwiːdᵊl'dʌm; ˌtwiːdᵊl'diː) *n.* any two persons or things that differ only slightly from each other; two of a kind. [C19: from the proverbial names of two musicians who were rivals]

Tweeds·muir ('twiːdzmjʊə) *n.* **Bar·on.** title of (John) **Buchan.**

tweed·y ('twiːdɪ) *adj.* **tweed·i+er, tweed·i·est. 1.** of, made of, or resembling tweed. **2.** showing a fondness for a hearty outdoor life, usually associated with wearers of tweeds.

'tween (twiːn) *Poetic or dialect. contraction of* between.

'tween deck *or* **decks** *n. Nautical.* a space between two continuous decks of a vessel.

tween·y ('twiːnɪ) *n., pl.* **tween·ies.** *Brit. informal, obsolete.* a maid who assists both cook and housemaid. [C19: shortened from BETWEEN (that is, a maid between cook and housemaid)]

tweet (twiːt) *interj.* **1.** (*often reiterated*) an imitation or representation of the thin chirping sound made by small or young birds. ~*vb.* **2.** (*intr.*) to make this sound. [C19: of imitative origin]

tweet+er ('twiːtə) *n.* a loudspeaker used in high-fidelity systems for the reproduction of high audio frequencies. It is usually employed in conjunction with a woofer and a crossover network. [C20: from TWEET]

tweeze (twiːz) *vb. Chiefly U.S.* to take hold of or pluck (hair, small objects, etc.) with or as if with tweezers. [C17: back formation from TWEEZERS]

twee+zers ('twiːzəz) *pl. n.* a small pincer-like instrument for handling small objects, plucking out hairs, etc. Also called: **pair of tweezers, tweezer** (esp. U.S.). [C17: plural of *tweezer* (on the model of *scissors,* etc.), from *tweeze* case of instruments, from French *étuis* cases (of instruments), from Old French *estuier* to preserve, from Vulgar Latin *studiāre* (unattested) to keep, from Latin *studēre* to care about]

twelfth (twɛlfθ) *adj.* **1.** (*usually prenominal*) **a.** coming after the eleventh in number or counting order, position, time, etc.; being the ordinal number of *twelve:* often written 12th. **b.** (*as n.*): *the twelfth of the month.* ~*n.* **2. a.** one of 12 equal or nearly equal parts of an object, quantity, measurement, etc. **b.** (*as modifier*): *a twelfth part.* **3.** the fraction equal to one divided by 12 (1/12). **4.** *Music.* **a.** an interval of one octave plus a fifth. **b.** one of two notes constituting such an interval in relation to the other. **c.** an organ stop sounding a note one octave and a fifth higher than that normally produced by the key depressed.

Twelfth Day *n.* **a.** Jan. 6, the twelfth day after Christmas and the feast of the Epiphany, formerly observed as the final day of the Christmas celebrations. **b.** (*as modifier*): *Twelfth-Day celebrations.*

twelfth man *n.* a reserve player in a cricket team.

Twelfth Night *n.* **a.** the evening of Jan. 5, the eve of Twelfth Day, formerly observed with various festal celebrations. **b.** the evening of Twelfth Day itself. **c.** (*as modifier*): *Twelfth-Night customs.*

Twelfth+tide ('twɛlfθˌtaɪd) *n.* **a.** the season of Epiphany. **b.** (*as modifier*): *the Twelfthtide celebrations.*

twelve (twɛlv) *n.* **1.** the cardinal number that is the sum of ten and two. See also **number** (sense 1). **2.** a numeral, 12, XII, etc., representing this number. **3.** something represented by, representing, or consisting of 12 units. **4.** Also called: **twelve o'clock.** noon or midnight. ~*determiner.* **5. a.** amounting to twelve: *twelve loaves.* **b.** (*as pronoun*): *twelve have arrived.* ~Related adj.: **duodecimal.** See also **dozen.** [Old English *twelf;* related to Old Frisian *twelif,* Old High German *zwelif,* Old Norse *tolf,* Gothic *twalif*]

twelve-mile lim+it *n.* the offshore boundary 12 miles from the coast claimed by some states as marking the extent of their territorial jurisdiction.

twelve+mo ('twɛlvməʊ) *n., pl.* **+mos.** *Bookbinding.* another word for **duodecimo.**

twelve+month ('twɛlvˌmʌnθ) *n. Chiefly Brit.* an archaic or dialect word for a **year.**

Twelve Ta·bles *pl. n.* **the.** the earliest code of Roman civil, criminal, and religious law, promulgated in 451–450 B.C.

twelve-tone *adj.* of, relating to, or denoting the type of serial music invented and developed by Arnold Schoenberg, which uses as musical material a tone row formed by the 12 semitones of the chromatic scale, together with its inverted and retrograde versions. The technique has been applied in various ways by different composers and usually results in music in which there are few, if any, tonal centres. See **serialism.**

twen+ti+eth ('twɛntɪɪθ) *adj.* **1.** (*usually prenominal*) **a.** coming after the nineteenth in numbering or counting order, position, time, etc.; being the ordinal number of *twenty:* often written 20th. **b.** (*as n.*): *he left on the twentieth.* ~*n.* **2. a.** one of 20 approximately equal parts of something. **b.** (*as modifier*): *a twentieth part.* **3.** the fraction that is equal to one divided by 20 (1/20).

twen·ti·eth man *n. Australian Rules football.* the second reserve player.

twen·ty ('twɛntɪ) *n., pl.* **·ties. 1.** the cardinal number that is the product of ten and two; a score. See also **number** (sense 1). **2.** a numeral, 20, XX, etc., representing this number. **3.** something representing, represented by, or consisting of 20 units. *~determiner.* **4. a.** amounting to twenty: *twenty questions.* **b.** (*as pronoun*): *to order twenty.* [Old English *twēntig;* related to Old High German *zweinzug,* German *zwanzig*]

twen·ty-one *n.* another name (esp. U.S.) for **pontoon**[2] (sense 1).

twen·ty-twen·ty *adj. Med.* having normal visual acuity: usually written 20/20.

'twere (twɜː; *unstressed* twə) *Poetic or dialect. contraction of* it were.

twerp *or* **twirp** (twɜːp) *n. Informal.* a silly, weak-minded, or contemptible person. [C20: of unknown origin]

Twi (twiː) *n.* **1.** a language of S Ghana: one of the two chief dialects of Akan. Formerly called: **Ashanti.** Compare **Fanti. 2.** (*pl.* **Twi** *or* **Twis**) a member of the Negroid people who speak this language.

twi·bill *or* **twi·bil** ('twaɪˌbɪl) *n.* **1.** a mattock with a blade shaped like an adze at one end and like an axe at the other. **2.** *Archaic.* a double-bladed battle-axe. [Old English, from *twi-* two, double + *bill* sword, BILL[3]]

twice (twaɪs) *adv.* **1.** two times; on two occasions or in two cases: *he coughed twice.* **2.** double in degree or quantity: *twice as long.* [Old English *twiwa;* related to Old Norse *tvisvar,* Middle Low German *twiges*]

twice-laid *adj.* **1.** made from strands of used rope. **2.** made from old or used material or retwisted yarn.

twice-told *adj.* hackneyed through repeated use.

Twick·en·ham ('twɪkənəm) *n.* a former town in SE England, on the River Thames: part of the Greater London borough of Richmond-upon-Thames since 1965; contains the English Rugby Football Union ground.

twid·dle ('twɪdᵊl) *vb.* **1.** (when *intr.,* often foll. by *with*) to twirl or fiddle (with), often in an idle way. **2. twiddle one's thumbs.** to do nothing; be unoccupied. **3.** (*intr.*) to turn, twirl, or rotate. **4.** (*intr.*) *Rare.* to be occupied with trifles. *~n.* **5.** an act or instance of twiddling. [C16: probably a blend of TWIRL + FIDDLE] **—'twid·dler** *n.*

twig[1] (twɪg) *n.* **1.** any small branch or shoot of a tree or other woody plant. **2.** something resembling this, esp. a minute branch of a blood vessel. [Old English *twigge;* related to Old Norse *dvika* consisting of two, Old High German *zwīg* twig, Old Danish *tvige* fork] **—'twig·ˌlike** *adj.*

twig[2] (twɪg) *vb.* **twigs, twig·ging, twigged.** *Brit. informal.* **1.** to understand (something). **2.** to find out or suddenly comprehend (something): *he hasn't twigged yet.* **3.** (*tr.*) *Rare.* to perceive (something). [C18: perhaps from Scottish Gaelic *tuig* I understand]

twig·gy ('twɪgɪ) *adj.* **·gi·er, ·gi·est. 1.** of or relating to a twig or twigs. **2.** covered with twigs. **3.** slender or fragile.

twi·light ('twaɪˌlaɪt) *n.* **1.** the soft diffused light occurring when the sun is just below the horizon, esp. following sunset. **2.** the period in which this light occurs. **3.** the period of time during which the sun is a specified angular distance below the horizon (6°, 12°, and 18° for **civil twilight, nautical twilight,** and **astronomical twilight,** respectively). **4.** any faint light. **5.** a period in which strength, importance, etc., are waning: *the twilight of his life.* **6.** (*modifier*) of or relating to twilight; dim. [C15: literally: half light (between day and night), from Old English *twi-* half + LIGHT] **—twi·lit** ('twaɪˌlɪt) *adj.*

Twi·light of the Gods *n.* another term for **Götterdämmerung** or **Ragnarök.**

twi·light sleep *n. Med.* a state of partial anaesthesia in which the patient retains a slight degree of consciousness.

twi·light zone *n.* **1.** an area of a city or town, usually surrounding the central business district, where houses have become dilapidated. **2.** the lowest level of the ocean to which light can penetrate. **3.** any indefinite or transitional condition or area.

twill (twɪl) *adj.* **1.** (in textiles) of or designating a weave in which the weft yarns are worked around two or more warp yarns to produce an effect of parallel diagonal lines or ribs. *~n.* **2.** any fabric so woven. *~vb.* **3.** (*tr.*) to weave in this fashion. [Old English *twilic* having a double thread; related to Old High German *zwilīth* twill, Latin *bilīx* two-threaded]

'twill (twɪl) *Poetic or dialect. contraction of* it will.

twin (twɪn) *n.* **1. a.** either of two persons or animals conceived at the same time. **b.** (*as modifier*): *a twin brother.* See also **identical** (sense 3), **fraternal** (sense 3). **2. a.** either of two persons or things that are identical or very similar; counterpart. **b.** (*as modifier*): *twin carburettors.* **3.** Also called: **macle.** a crystal consisting of two parts each of which has a definite orientation to the other. *~vb.* **twins, twin·ning, twinned. 4.** to pair or be paired together; couple. **5.** (*intr.*) to bear twins. **6.** (*intr.*) (of a crystal) to form into a twin. **7.** (*intr.*) *Archaic.* to be born as a twin. [Old English *twinn;* related to Old High German *zwiniling* twin, Old Norse *tvinnr* double]

twin bed *n.* one of a pair of matching single beds.

twin·ber·ry ('twɪnbərɪ, -brɪ) *n., pl.* **·ries.** another name for **partridgeberry** (sense 1).

twin bill *n. U.S.* an informal name for **double feature** or **double-header** (sense 2).

twine (twaɪn) *n.* **1.** string made by twisting together fibres of hemp, cotton, etc. **2.** the act or an instance of twining. **3.** something produced or characterized by twining. **4.** a twist, coil, or convolution. **5.** a knot, tangle, or snarl. *~vb.* **6.** (*tr.*) to twist together; interweave: *she twined the wicker to make a basket.* **7.** (*tr.*) to form by or as if by twining: *to twine a garland.* **8.** (when *intr.,* often foll. by *around*) to wind or cause to wind, esp. in spirals: *the creeper twines around the tree.* [Old English *twīn;* related to Old Frisian *twīne,* Dutch *twijn* twine, Lithuanian *dvynu* twins; see TWIN] **—'twin·er** *n.*

twin·flow·er ('twɪnˌflaʊə) *n.* an evergreen caprifoliaceous trailing shrub, *Linnaea borealis,* of North America, having round leaves, white or pink fragrant bell-shaped flowers arranged in pairs, and yellow fruits.

twinge (twɪndʒ) *n.* **1.** a sudden brief darting or stabbing pain. **2.** a sharp emotional pang: *a twinge of conscience.* *~vb.* **3.** to have or cause to have a twinge. **4.** (*tr.*) *Obsolete.* to pinch; tweak. [Old English *twengan* to pinch; related to Old High German *zwengen*]

twin·kle ('twɪŋkᵊl) *vb.* (*mainly intr.*) **1.** to emit or reflect light in a flickering manner; shine brightly and intermittently; sparkle: *twinkling stars.* **2.** (of the eyes) to sparkle, esp. with amusement or delight. **3.** *Rare.* to move about quickly. **4.** (*also tr.*) *Rare.* to wink (the eyes); blink. *~n.* **5.** an intermittent gleam of light; flickering brightness; sparkle or glimmer. **6.** an instant. **7.** a rare word for **wink.** [Old English *twinclian;* related to Middle High German *zwinken* to blink] **—'twin·kler** *n.*

twin·kling ('twɪŋklɪŋ) *or* **twink** (twɪŋk) *n.* a very short time; instant; moment. Also called: **twinkling of an eye.**

twin-lens re·flex *n.* another name for **reflex camera.**

Twins (twɪnz) *n.* **the.** the constellation Gemini, the third sign of the zodiac.

twin-screw *adj.* (of a vessel) having two propellers.

twin-set *n. Brit.* a matching jumper and cardigan.

twin town *n. Brit.* a town that has civic associations, such as reciprocal visits and cultural exchanges, with a foreign town, usually of similar size and sometimes with other similarities, as in commercial activities.

twirl (twɜːl) *vb.* **1.** to move or cause to move around rapidly and repeatedly in a circle. **2.** (*tr.*) to twist, wind, or twiddle, often idly: *she twirled her hair around her finger.* **3.** (*intr.;* often foll. by *around* or *about*) to turn suddenly to face another way: *she twirled around angrily to face him.* *~n.* **4.** an act of rotating or being rotated; whirl or twist. **5.** something wound around or twirled; coil. **6.** a written flourish or squiggle. [C16: perhaps a blend of TWIST + WHIRL] **—'twirl·er** *n.*

twirp (twɜːp) *n.* a variant spelling of **twerp.**

twist (twɪst) *vb.* **1.** to cause (one end or part) to turn or (of one end or part) to turn in the opposite direction from another; coil or spin. **2.** to distort or be distorted; change in shape. **3.** to wind or cause to wind; twine, coil, or intertwine: *to twist flowers into a wreath.* **4.** to force or be forced out of the natural form or position: *to twist one's ankle.* **5.** to change or cause to change for the worse in character, meaning, etc.; pervert: *his ideas are twisted; she twisted the statement.* **6.** to revolve or cause to revolve; rotate. **7.** (*tr.*) to wrench with a turning action: *to twist something from someone's grasp.* **8.** (*intr.*) to follow a winding course. **9.** (*intr.*) to squirm, as with pain. **10.** (*intr.*) to dance the twist. **11. twist someone's arm.** to persuade or coerce someone. *~n.* **12.** the act or an instance of twisting. **13.** something formed by or as if by twisting: *a twist of hair.* **14.** a decisive change of direction, aim, meaning, or character. **15.** (in a novel, play, etc.) an unexpected event, revelation, or other development. **16.** a bend: *a twist in the road.* **17.** a distortion of the original or natural shape or form. **18.** a jerky pull, wrench, or turn. **19.** a strange personal characteristic, esp. a bad one. **20.** a confused mess, tangle, or knot made by twisting. **21.** a twisted thread used in sewing where extra strength is needed. **22.** (in weaving) a specified direction of twisting the yarn. **23. the twist.** a modern dance popular in the 1960s, in which couples vigorously twist the hips in time to rhythmic music. **24.** a bread loaf or roll made of one or more pieces of twisted dough. **25.** a thin sliver of peel from a lemon, lime, etc., twisted and added to a drink. **26. a.** a cigar made by twisting three cigars around one another. **b.** chewing tobacco made in the form of a roll by twisting the leaves together. **27.** *Physics.* torsional deformation or shear stress or strain. **28.** *Sport, chiefly U.S.* spin given to a ball in various games, esp. baseball. **29.** the extent to which the grooves in the bore of a rifled firearm are spiralled. **30. round the twist.** *Brit. slang.* mad; eccentric. [Old English; related to German dialect *Zwist* a quarrel, Dutch *twisten* to quarrel] **—'twist·a·ble** *adj.* **—ˌtwist·a·'bil·i·ty** *n.* **—'twist·ed·ly** *adv.* **—'twist·ing·ly** *adv.*

twist drill *n.* a drill bit having two helical grooves running from the point along the shank to clear swarf and cuttings.

twist·er ('twɪstə) *n.* **1.** *Brit.* a swindling or dishonest person. **2.** a person or thing that twists, such as a device used in making ropes. **3.** *U.S.* an informal name for **tornado. 4.** a ball moving with a twisting motion.

twist grip *n.* a handlebar control in the form of a ratchet-controlled rotating grip, used on some bicycles and motorcycles as a gear-change control and on motorcycles as an accelerator.

twit[1] (twɪt) *vb.* **twits, twit·ting, twit·ted. 1.** (*tr.*) to tease, taunt, or reproach, often in jest. *~n.* **2.** *U.S. informal.* a nervous or excitable state. **3.** *Rare.* a reproach; taunt. **4.** *Rare.* the act or an instance of teasing or taunting. [Old English *ætwītan,* from *æt* against + *wītan* to accuse; related to Old High German *wīzan* to punish]

twit² (twɪt) *n. Informal, chiefly Brit.* a foolish or stupid person; idiot. [C19: from TWIT¹ (originally in the sense: a person given to twitting)]

twitch (twɪtʃ) *vb.* **1.** to move or cause to move in a jerky spasmodic way. **2.** to pull or draw (something) with a quick jerky movement. **3.** (*intr.*) to hurt with a sharp spasmodic pain. **4.** (*tr.*) *Rare.* to nip. ~*n.* **5.** a sharp jerking movement. **6.** a mental or physical twinge. **7.** a sudden muscular spasm, esp. one caused by a nervous condition. Compare **tic. 8.** a loop of cord used to control a horse by drawing it tight about its upper lip. [Old English *twiccian* to pluck; related to Old High German *zwecchōn* to pinch, Dutch *twicken*] —**'twitch+er** *n.* —**'twitch+ing+ly** *adv.*

twitch grass *n.* another name for **couch grass.** Sometimes shortened to **twitch.**

twite (twaɪt) *n.* a N European finch, *Acanthis flavirostris,* with a brown streaked plumage. [C16: imitative of its cry]

twit+ter ('twɪtə) *vb.* **1.** (*intr.*) (esp. of a bird) to utter a succession of chirping sounds. **2.** (*intr.*) to talk or move rapidly and tremulously. **3.** (*intr.*) to giggle: *her schoolmates twittered behind their desks.* **4.** (*tr.*) to utter in a chirping way. ~*n.* **5.** a twittering sound, esp. of a bird. **6.** the act of twittering. **7.** a state of nervous excitement (esp. in the phrase **in a twitter**). [C14: of imitative origin] —**'twit+ter+er** *n.* —**'twit+ter·y** *adj.*

'twixt *or* **twixt** (twɪkst) *Poetic contraction of* betwixt.

two (tu:) *n.* **1.** the cardinal number that is the sum of one and one. It is a prime number. See also **number** (sense 1). **2.** a numeral, 2, II, (ii), etc., representing this number. **3.** *Music.* the numeral 2 used as the lower figure in a time signature, indicating that the beat is measured in minims. **4.** something representing, represented by, or consisting of two units, such as a playing card with two symbols on it. **5.** Also called: **two o'clock.** two hours after noon or midnight. **6. in two.** in or into two parts: *break the bread in two.* **7. put two and two together.** to make an inference from available evidence, esp. an obvious inference. **8. that makes two of us.** the same applies to me. ~*determiner.* **9. a.** amounting to two: *two nails.* **b.** (*as pronoun*): *he bought two.* ~Related adjs.: **binary, double, dual.** Related prefixes: **di-, bi-.** [Old English *twā* (feminine); related to Old High German *zwā,* Old Norse *tvau,* Latin, Greek *duo*]

Two-and-a-half In+ter+na+tion+al *n.* another name for the **Vienna Union.**

two-bit *adj.* (*prenominal*) *U.S. slang.* worth next to nothing; cheap. [C20: from the phrase *two bits* a small sum]

two-by-four *n.* **1.** a length of untrimmed timber with a cross section that measures 2 inches by 4 inches. **2.** a trimmed timber joist with a cross section that measures 1½ inches by 3½ inches.

two-cy·cle *adj.* the U.S. word for **two-stroke.**

two-di·men+sion+al *adj.* **1.** of, having, or relating to two dimensions. **2.** having an area but no volume. **3.** lacking in depth, as characters in a literary work. **4.** (of painting or drawing) lacking the characteristics of form or depth. —**'two-di·ˌmen+sion+'al+i·ty** *n.* —**'two-di·'men+sion+al+ly** *adv.*

two-edged *adj.* **1.** having two cutting edges. **2.** (esp. of a remark) having two interpretations, such as *she looks nice when she smiles.*

two-faced *adj.* deceitful; insincere; hypocritical. —**two-fac·ed·ly** (tu:'feɪsɪdlɪ, -'feɪst-) *adv.* —**two-'fac·ed·ness** *n.*

two+fold ('tu:ˌfəʊld) *adj.* **1.** equal to twice as many or twice as much; double: *a twofold increase.* **2.** composed of two parts; dual: *a twofold reason.* ~*adv.* **3.** doubly.

two-four time *n. Music.* a form of simple duple time in which there are two crotchet beats in each bar.

two-hand·ed *adj.* **1.** requiring the use of both hands. **2.** ambidextrous. **3.** requiring the participation or cooperation of two people. —**two-'hand·ed·ly** *adv.*

two-line (*modifier*) (formerly) denoting double the normal size of printer's type: *two-line pica* (24 point).

two-name pa+per *n. U.S. finance.* a commercial paper signed by two persons both of whom accept full liability.

two-par·ty sys+tem *n.* a condition or system in which two major parties dominate a political unit.

two+pence *or* **tup+pence** ('tʌpəns) *n. Brit.* **1.** the sum of two pennies. **2.** (*used with a negative*) something of little value (in the phrase **not care** *or* **give twopence**). **3.** a former British silver coin, now only coined as Maundy money.

two+pen+ny *or* **tup+pen+ny** ('tʌpənɪ) *adj. Chiefly Brit.* **1.** Also: **twopenny-halfpenny.** cheap or tawdry. **2.** (intensifier): *a twopenny damn.* **3.** worth two pence.

two-phase *adj.* (of an electrical circuit, device, etc.) generating or using two alternating voltages of the same frequency, displaced in phase by 90°. Also: **quarter-phase.**

two-piece *adj.* **1.** consisting of two separate parts, usually matching, as of a garment. ~*n.* **2.** such an outfit.

two-ply *adj.* **1.** made of two thicknesses, layers, or strands. ~*n., pl.* **-plies. 2.** a two-ply wood, knitting yarn, etc.

two-pot scream+er *n. Austral. slang.* a person easily influenced by alcohol.

two-seat·er *n.* a vehicle providing seats for two people.

Two Sic·i·lies *n.* **the.** a former kingdom of S Italy, consisting of the kingdoms of Sicily and Naples (1061–1860).

two-sid·ed *adj.* **1.** having two sides or aspects. **2.** controversial; debatable: *a two-sided argument.*

two+some ('tu:səm) *n.* **1.** two together, esp. two people. **2.** a match between two people. **3.** (*modifier*) consisting of or played by two: *a twosome performance.*

two-spot *n.* a card with two pips; two; deuce.

two-step *n.* **1.** a ballroom dance in duple time. **2.** a piece of music composed for or in the rhythm of such a dance.

two-stroke *adj.* relating to or designating an internal-combustion engine whose piston makes two strokes for every explosion. U.S. word: **two-cycle.** Compare **four-stroke.**

Two Thou+sand Guin+eas *n., usually written* **2000 Guin+eas. the.** an annual horse race run at Newmarket since 1809.

two-time *vb. Informal.* to deceive (someone, esp. a lover) by carrying on a relationship with another. —**'two-ˌtim·er** *n.*

two-tone *adj.* **1.** of two colours or two shades of the same colour. **2.** (esp. of sirens, car horns, etc.) producing or consisting of two notes.

'twould (twʊd) *Poetic or dialect. contraction of* it would.

two-up *n. Chiefly Austral.* a gambling game in which two coins are tossed or spun. Bets are made on both coins landing with the same face uppermost.

two-way *adj.* **1.** moving, permitting movement, or operating in either of two opposite directions: *two-way traffic; a two-way valve.* **2.** involving two participants: *a two-way agreement.* **3.** involving reciprocal obligation or mutual action: *a two-way process.* **4.** (of a radio, telephone, etc.) allowing communications in two directions using both transmitting and receiving equipment.

twp (tʊp) *adj.* (*predicative*) *South Wales dialect.* stupid; daft. [Welsh]

-ty¹ *suffix of numerals.* denoting a multiple of ten: *sixty; seventy.* [from Old English *-tig* TEN]

-ty² *suffix forming nouns.* indicating state, condition, or quality: *cruelty.* [from Old French *-te, -tet,* from Latin *-tās, -tāt-;* related to Greek *-tēs*]

Tyan-Shan ('tjan'ʃan) *n.* transliteration of the Russian name for the **Tien Shan.**

Ty+burn ('taɪbɜ:n) *n.* (formerly) a place of execution in London, on the **River Tyburn** (a tributary of the Thames, now entirely below ground).

Ty·che ('taɪkɪ) *n. Greek myth.* the goddess of fortune. Roman counterpart: **Fortuna.**

tych+ism ('taɪkɪzəm) *n. Philosophy.* the theory that chance is an objective reality at work in the universe, esp. in evolutionary adaptations. [from Greek *tukhē* chance]

Ty+cho ('taɪkəʊ) *n.* a crater in the SE quadrant of the moon, 4000 metres deep and about 88 kilometres in diameter, with a central peak. It is the centre of a conspicuous system of rays. [named after Tycho BRAHE]

ty+coon (taɪ'ku:n) *n.* **1.** a business man of great wealth and power. **2.** an archaic name for a **shogun.** [C19: from Japanese *taikun,* from Chinese *ta* great + *chün* ruler]

tyke *or* **tike** (taɪk) *n.* **1.** *Informal.* a small or cheeky child: used esp. in affectionate reproof. **2.** *Northern Brit. dialect.* a dog, esp. a mongrel. **3.** *Northern Brit. dialect.* a rough ill-mannered person. **4.** Also called: **Yorkshire tyke.** *Brit. slang, often offensive.* a person from Yorkshire. **5.** *Austral. slang. offensive.* a Roman Catholic. [C14: from Old Norse *tīk* bitch]

Ty·ler ('taɪlə) *n.* **1. John.** 1790–1862, U.S. statesman; tenth president of the U.S. (1841–45). **2. Wat** (wɒt). died 1381, English leader of the Peasants' Revolt (1381).

ty+lo+pod ('taɪləʊˌpɒd) *n.* any artiodactyl mammal of the suborder *Tylopoda,* having padded, rather than hoofed, digits: includes the camels and llamas. [C19: from New Latin, from Greek *tulos* knob or *tulē* cushion + -POD]

ty+lo+sis (taɪ'ləʊsɪs) *n. Botany.* a bladder-like outgrowth from certain cells in woody tissue that extends into and blocks adjacent conducting xylem cells. [C19: from Greek *tulōsis,* from *tulos* knob or *tulē* callus + -OSIS]

tym+bal ('tɪmbᵊl) *n.* a variant spelling of **timbal.**

tym+pan ('tɪmpən) *n.* **1.** a membrane stretched over a frame or resonating cylinder, bowl, etc. **2.** *Printing.* packing interposed between the platen and the paper to be printed in order to provide an even impression. **3.** *Architect.* another name for **tympanum** (sense 3). [Old English *timpana,* from Latin; see TYMPANUM]

tym+pa+ni ('tɪmpənɪ) *pl. n.* a variant spelling of **timpani.**

tym+pan+ic (tɪm'pænɪk) *adj.* **1.** *Anatomy, architect.* of, relating to, or having a tympanum. **2.** of, relating to, or resembling a drumhead.

tym+pan+ic bone *n.* the part of the temporal bone in the mammalian skull that surrounds the auditory canal.

tym+pan+ic mem+brane *n.* the thin translucent oval membrane separating the external ear from the middle ear. It transmits vibrations produced by sound waves, via the ossicles, to the cochlea. Also called: **tympanum.** Nontechnical name: **eardrum.**

tym+pa+nist ('tɪmpənɪst) *n.* a person who plays a drum, now specifically the kettledrum.

tym+pa+ni+tes (ˌtɪmpə'naɪti:z) *n.* distention of the abdomen caused by an abnormal accumulation of gas in the intestinal or peritoneal cavity, as in peritonitis. Also called: **tympany.** [C14: from Late Latin, from Greek *tumpanitēs* concerning a drum, from *tumpanon* drum] —**tym+pa+nit+ic** (ˌtɪmpə'nɪtɪk) *adj.*

tym+pa+ni+tis (ˌtɪmpə'naɪtɪs) *n.* inflammation of the eardrum. Also called: **otitis media.**

tym+pa+num ('tɪmpənəm) *n., pl.* **+nums** *or* **+na** (-nə). **1. a.** the cavity of the middle ear. **b.** another name for **tympanic membrane. 2.** any diaphragm resembling that in the middle ear in function. **3.** Also called: **tympan.** *Architect.* **a.** the recessed space bounded by the cornices of a pediment, esp. one that is triangular in shape and ornamented. **b.** the recessed space bounded by an arch and the lintel of a doorway or window below it. **4.** *Music.* a tympan or drum. **5.** a scoop wheel for raising water. [C17: from Latin, from Greek *tumpanon* drum; related to Greek *tuptein* to beat]

tym·pa·ny ('tɪmpənɪ) *n., pl.* **·nies. 1.** another name for **tympanites. 2.** *Obsolete.* excessive pride or arrogance.

Tyn·dale, Tin·dal, *or* **Tin·dale** ('tɪndᵊl) *n.* **Wil·liam.** ?1492–1536, English Protestant and humanist, who translated the New Testament (1525), the Pentateuch (1530), and the Book of Jonah (1531) into English. He was burnt at the stake as a heretic.

Tyn·dall ('tɪndᵊl) *n.* **John.** 1820–93, Irish physicist, noted for his work on the radiation of heat by gases, the transmission of sound through the atmosphere, and the scattering of light.

Tyn·dall ef·fect *n.* the phenomenon in which light is scattered by particles of matter in its path. It enables a beam of light to become visible by illuminating dust particles, etc. [C19: named after John TYNDALL]

Tyn·dar·e·us (tɪn'dærɪəs) *n. Greek myth.* a Spartan king; the husband of Leda.

Tyne (taɪn) *n.* a river in N England, flowing east to the North Sea. Length: 48 km (30 miles).

Tyne and Wear *n.* a metropolitan county of NE England, comprising the districts of Newcastle-upon-Tyne, North Tyneside, Gateshead, South Tyneside, and Sunderland. Administrative centre: Newcastle-upon-Tyne. Pop.: 1 182 900 (1976 est.).

Tyne·mouth ('taɪn,maʊθ) *n.* a port in NE England, in Tyne and Wear at the mouth of the River Tyne: includes the port and industrial centre of North Shields; fishing, ship-repairing, and marine engineering. Pop.: 68 861 (1971).

Tyne·side ('taɪn,saɪd) *n.* the conurbation on the banks of the Tyne from Newcastle to the coast.

Tyn·wald ('tɪnwəld, 'taɪn-) *n.* **the.** the Parliament of the Isle of Man, consisting of the crown, lieutenant governor, House of Keys, and legislative council. Full name: **Tynwald Court.** [C15: from Old Norse *thingvollr* from *thing* assembly + *vollr* field]

typ., typo., *or* **typog.** *abbrev. for:* **1.** typographer. **2.** typographic(al). **3.** typography.

typ·al ('taɪpᵊl) *adj.* a rare word for **typical.**

type (taɪp) *n.* **1.** a kind, class, or category, the constituents of which share similar characteristics. **2.** a subdivision of a particular class of things or people; sort: *what type of shampoo do you use?* **3.** the general form, plan, or design distinguishing a particular group. **4.** *Informal.* a person who typifies a particular quality: *he's the administrative type.* **5.** *Informal.* a person, esp. of a specified kind: *he's a strange type.* **6. a.** a small block of metal or more rarely wood bearing a letter or character in relief for use in printing. **b.** such pieces collectively. **7.** characters printed from type; print. **8.** *Biology.* **a.** the taxonomic group the characteristics of which are used for defining the next highest group, for example *Rattus norvegicus* (brown rat) is the type species of the rat genus *Rattus.* **b.** (*as modifier*): *a type genus; a type species.* **9.** See **type specimen. 10.** the characteristic device on a coin. **11.** *Chiefly theol.* a figure, episode, or symbolic factor resembling some future reality in such a way as to foreshadow or prefigure it. **12.** *Rare.* a distinctive sign or mark. *~vb.* **13.** to write (copy) on a typewriter. **14.** (*tr.*) to be a symbol of; typify. **15.** (*tr.*) to decide the type of; clarify into a type. **16.** (*tr.*) *Med.* to determine the blood group of (a blood sample). **17.** (*tr.*) *Chiefly theol.* to foreshadow or serve as a symbol of (some future reality). [C15: from Latin *typus* figure, from Greek *tupos* image, from *tuptein* to strike]

-type *n. combining form.* **1.** type or form: *archetype.* **2.** printing type or photographic process: *collotype.* [from Latin *-typus,* from Greek *-typos,* from *tupos* TYPE]

type·bar ('taɪp,bɑː) *n.* one of the bars in a typewriter that carry the type and are operated by keys.

type·case ('taɪp,keɪs) *n.* a compartmental tray for storing printer's type.

type·cast ('taɪp,kɑːst) *vb.* **·casts, ·cast·ing, ·cast.** (*tr.*) to cast (an actor) in the same kind of role continually, esp. because of his physical appearance or previous success in such roles. —**'type·,cast·er** *n.*

type·face ('taɪp,feɪs) *n.* another name for **face** (sense 15).

type found·er *n.* a person who casts metallic printer's type. —**type found·ing** *n.* —**type found·ry** *n.*

type-high *adj.* having the height of a piece of type, standardized as 0.918 inches.

type met·al *n. Printing.* an alloy of tin, lead, and antimony, from which type is cast.

type·script ('taɪp,skrɪpt) *n.* **1.** a typed copy of a document, literary script, etc. **2.** any typewritten material.

type·set ('taɪp,sɛt) *vb.* **·sets, ·set·ting, ·set.** *Printing.* to set (textual matter) in type.

type·set·ter ('taɪp,sɛtə) *n.* **1.** a person who sets type; compositor. **2.** a typesetting machine.

type spec·i·men *n. Biology.* the original specimen from which a description of a new species is made. Also called: **holotype.**

type·write ('taɪp,raɪt) *vb.* **·writes, ·writ·ing, ·wrote, ·writ·ten.** to write by means of a typewriter; type.

type·writ·er ('taɪp,raɪtə) *n.* **1.** a keyboard machine for writing mechanically in characters resembling print. It may be operated entirely by hand (**manual typewriter**) or be powered by electricity (**electric typewriter**). **2.** *Printing.* a style of type resembling typescript.

type·writ·ing ('taɪp,raɪtɪŋ) *n.* **1.** the act or skill of using a typewriter. **2.** copy produced by a typewriter; typescript.

typh·li·tis (tɪf'laɪtɪs) *n.* **1.** inflammation of the caecum. **2.** an obsolete name for **appendicitis.** [C19: from New Latin, from Greek *tuphlon* the caecum, from *tuphlos* blind] —**typh·lit·ic** (tɪf'lɪtɪk) *adj.*

typh·lol·o·gy (tɪf'lɒlədʒɪ) *n.* the branch of science concerned with blindness and the care of the blind. [C19: from Greek *tuphlos* blind]

Ty·phoe·us (taɪ'fiːəs) *n. Greek myth.* the son of Gaea and Tartarus who had a hundred dragon heads, which spurted fire, and a bellowing many-tongued voice. He created the whirlwinds and fought with Zeus before the god hurled him beneath Mount Etna. —**Ty·'phoe·an** *adj.*

ty·pho·gen·ic (,taɪfəʊ'dʒɛnɪk) *adj.* causing typhus or typhoid fever.

ty·phoid ('taɪfɔɪd) *Pathol.* *~adj.* also **ty·phoi·dal. 1.** resembling typhus. *~n.* **2.** short for **typhoid fever.**

ty·phoid fe·ver *n.* an acute infectious disease characterized by high fever, rose-coloured spots on the chest or abdomen, abdominal pain, and occasionally intestinal bleeding. It is caused by the bacillus *Salmonella typhosa* ingested with food or water. Also called: **enteric fever.**

ty·phoi·din (taɪ'fɔɪdɪn) *n. Med.* a culture of dead typhoid bacillus for injection into the skin to test for typhoid fever.

Ty·phon ('taɪfɒn) *n. Greek myth.* a monster and one of the whirlwinds: later confused with his father Typhoeus.

ty·phoon (taɪ'fuːn) *n.* **1.** a small violent tropical storm or cyclone, esp. in the China seas and W Pacific. **2.** a violent storm of India. [C16: from Chinese *tai fung* great wind, from *tai* great + *fung* wind; influenced by Greek *tuphōn* whirlwind] —**ty·phon·ic** (taɪ'fɒnɪk) *adj.*

ty·phus ('taɪfəs) *n.* any one of a group of acute infectious rickettsial diseases characterized by high fever, skin rash, and severe headache. Also called: **typhus fever.** [C18: from New Latin *tȳphus,* from Greek *tuphos* fever; related to *tuphein* to smoke] —**'ty·phous** *adj.*

typ·i·cal ('tɪpɪkᵊl) *or* **typ·ic** *adj.* **1.** being or serving as a representative example of a particular type; characteristic: *the painting is a typical Rembrandt.* **2.** considered to be an example of some undesirable trait: *that is typical of you!* **3.** of or relating to a representative specimen or type. **4.** conforming to a type. **5.** *Biology.* having most of the characteristics of a particular taxonomic group: *a typical species of a genus.* [C17: from Medieval Latin *typicālis,* from Late Latin *typicus* figurative, from Greek *tupikos,* from *tupos* TYPE] —**'typ·i·cal·ly** *adv.* —**'typ·i·cal·ness** *or* **,typ·i·'cal·i·ty** *n.*

typ·i·fy ('tɪpɪ,faɪ) *vb.* **·fies, ·fy·ing, ·fied.** (*tr.*) **1.** to be typical of; characterize. **2.** to symbolize or represent completely, by or as if by a type. [C17: from Latin *typus* TYPE + -IFY] —**,typ·i·fi·'ca·tion** *n.* —**'typ·i·,fi·er** *n.*

typ·ist ('taɪpɪst) *n.* a person who types, esp. for a living.

ty·po ('taɪpəʊ) *n., pl.* **·pos.** *Informal.* a typographical error. Also called (Brit.): **literal.**

typo. *or* **typog.** *abbrev.* variants of **typ.**

ty·pog·ra·pher (taɪ'pɒgrəfə) *n.* **1.** a person skilled in typography. **2.** another name for **compositor.**

ty·pog·ra·phy (taɪ'pɒgrəfɪ) *n.* **1.** the art, craft, or process of composing type and printing from it. **2.** the planning, selection, and setting of type for a printed work. —**ty·po·graph·i·cal** (,taɪpə'græfɪkᵊl) *or* **,ty·po·'graph·ic** *adj.* —**,ty·po·'graph·i·cal·ly** *adv.*

ty·pol·o·gy (taɪ'pɒlədʒɪ) *n. Chiefly theol.* the doctrine or study of types or of the correspondence between them and the realities which they typify. —**ty·po·log·i·cal** (,taɪpə'lɒdʒɪkᵊl) *or* **,ty·po·'log·ic** *adj.* —**,ty·po·'log·i·cal·ly** *adv.* —**ty·'pol·o·gist** *n.*

ty·poth·e·tae (taɪ'pɒθɪ,tiː, ,taɪpə'θiːtiː) *pl. n. U.S.* printers collectively; used in the names of organized associations, as of master printers. [C19: New Latin: typesetters, from Greek *tupos* TYPE + *thetēs* one who places, from *tithenai* to place]

typw. *abbrev. for:* **1.** typewriter. **2.** typewritten.

Tyr *or* **Tyrr** (tjʊə, tɪə) *n. Norse myth.* the god of war, son of Odin. Anglo-Saxon counterpart: **Tiu.**

ty·ra·mine ('taɪrə,miːn, 'tɪ-) *n.* a colourless crystalline amine derived from phenol and found in ripe cheese, ergot, decayed animal tissue, and mistletoe and used for its sympathomimetic action; 4-hydroxyphenethylamine. Formula: $(C_2H_4NH_2)C_6H_4OH$. [C20: from TYR(OSINE) + AMINE]

ty·ran·ni·cal (tɪ'rænɪkᵊl) *or* **ty·ran·nic** *adj.* characteristic of or relating to a tyrant or to tyranny; oppressive. —**ty·'ran·ni·cal·ly** *adv.* —**ty·'ran·ni·cal·ness** *n.*

ty·ran·ni·cide (tɪ'rænɪ,saɪd) *n.* **1.** the killing of a tyrant. **2.** a person who kills a tyrant. —**tyr·,ran·ni·'cid·al** *adj.*

tyr·an·nize *or* **tyr·an·nise** ('tɪrə,naɪz) *vb.* (when *intr.,* often foll. by *over*) to rule or exercise power over (people) in a cruel or oppressive manner. —**'tyr·an·,niz·er** *or* **'tyr·an·,nis·er** *n.* —**'tyr·an·,niz·ing·ly** *or* **'tyr·an·,nis·ing·ly** *adv.*

ty·ran·no·saur (tɪ'rænə,sɔː) *or* **ty·ran·no·saur·us** (tɪ,rænə'sɔːrəs) *n.* any large carnivorous bipedal dinosaur of the genus *Tyrannosaurus,* common in North America in upper Jurassic and Cretaceous times: suborder *Theropoda* (theropods). [C19: from New Latin *Tyrannosaurus,* from Greek *turannos* TYRANT + -SAUR]

tyr·an·ny ('tɪrənɪ) *n., pl.* **·nies. 1. a.** government by a tyrant or tyrants; despotism. **b.** similarly oppressive and unjust government by more than one person. **2.** arbitrary, unreasonable, or despotic behaviour or use of authority: *the teacher's tyranny.* **3.** any harsh discipline or oppression: *the tyranny of the clock.* **4.** a political unit ruled by a tyrant. **5.** (esp. in ancient Greece) government by a usurper. **6.** a tyrannical act. [C14: from Old French *tyrannie,* from Medieval Latin *tyrannia,* from

Latin *tyrannus* TYRANT] —'**tyr+an+nous** *adj.* —'**tyr+an+nous+ly** *adv.* —'**tyr+an+nous+ness** *n.*

ty+rant ('taɪrənt) *n.* **1.** a person who governs oppressively, unjustly, and arbitrarily; despot. **2.** any person who exercises authority in a tyrannical manner. **3.** anything that exercises tyrannical influence. **4.** (esp. in ancient Greece) a ruler whose authority lacked the sanction of law or custom; usurper. [C13: from Old French *tyrant,* from Latin *tyrannus,* from Greek *turannos*]

ty+rant fly+catch·er *n.* any passerine bird of the American family *Tyrannidae.* Often shortened to **flycatcher.**

tyre *or U.S.* **tire** (taɪə) *n.* **1.** a rubber ring placed over the rim of a wheel of a road vehicle to provide traction and reduce road shocks, esp. a hollow inflated ring (**pneumatic tyre**) consisting of a reinforced outer casing enclosing an inner tube. See also **tubeless tyre, cross-ply, radial-ply. 2.** a metal band or hoop attached to the rim of a wooden cartwheel. ~*vb.* **3.** (*tr.*) to fit a tyre or tyres to (a wheel, vehicle, etc.). [C18: variant of C15 *tire,* probably from TIRE[3]]

Tyre *or* **Tyr** (taɪə) *n.* a port in S Lebanon, on the Mediterranean: founded about the 15th century B.C.; for centuries a major Phoenician seaport, famous for silks and its Tyrian purple dye; now a small market town. Pop.: 25 000 (1973 est.). Arabic name: **Sur.**

Tyr+i·an ('tɪrɪən) *n.* **1.** a native or inhabitant of ancient Tyre. **2.** short for **Tyrian purple** (sense 2). ~*adj.* **3.** of or relating to ancient Tyre.

Tyr+i·an pur+ple *n.* **1.** a deep purple dye obtained from molluscs of the genus *Murex* and highly prized in antiquity. **2. a.** a vivid purplish-red colour. **b.** (*as adj.*): *a Tyrian-purple robe.* Sometimes shortened to **Tyrian.**

ty·ro *or* **ti·ro** ('taɪrəʊ) *n., pl.* **·ros.** a novice or beginner. [C17: from Latin *tīrō* recruit] —**ty+ron+ic** *or* **ti+ron+ic** (taɪ'rɒnɪk) *adj.*

ty+ro+ci+dine (ˌtaɪrəʊ'saɪdi:n) *n.* an antibiotic that is the main constituent of tyrothricin. [C20: from TYRO(SINE) + -CID(E) + -INE[1]]

Ty+rol *or* **Ti+rol** (tɪ'rəʊl, 'tɪrəʊl; *German* ti'ro:l) *n.* a mountainous province of W Austria: passed to the Hapsburgs in 1363; S part transferred to Italy in 1919. Capital: Innsbruck. Pop.: 540 771 (1971). Area: 12 648 sq. km (4883 sq. miles). —**Ty·ro+lese** (ˌtɪrə'li:z) *or* **Ty+ro+'le·an** *adj., n.*

Ty+ro+li+enne (tɪˌrəʊlɪ'en) *n.* **1.** a gay peasant dance from the Tyrol. **2.** a song composed for or in the style of this dance, characterized by the yodel. [French: of the TYROL]

Ty+rone (tɪ'rəʊn) *n.* a county of W Northern Ireland, occupying almost a quarter of the total area of Northern Ireland. County town: Omagh. Pop.: 138 975 (1971). Area: 3266 sq. km (1260 sq. miles).

ty+ro+si+nase (ˌtaɪrəʊsɪ'neɪz, ˌtɪrəʊ-) *n.* an enzyme occurring in many organisms that is a catalyst in the conversion of tyrosine to the pigment melanin; inactivity of this enzyme results in albinism.

ty+ro+sine ('taɪrəˌsi:n, -sɪn, 'tɪrə-) *n.* an amino acid that is a precursor of the hormones adrenaline and thyroxine and of the pigment melanin. Formula: $OHC_6H_4CH_2CH(NH_2)COOH$. [C19: from Greek *turos* cheese + -INE[2]]

ty+ro+thri+cin (ˌtaɪrəʊ'θraɪsɪn) *n.* an antibiotic, obtained from the soil bacterium *Bacillus brevis,* consisting of tyrocidine and gramicidin and active against Gram-positive bacteria such as staphylococci and streptococci: applied locally for the treatment of ulcers and abscesses. [C20: from New Latin *Tyrothrix* (genus name), from Greek *turos* cheese + *thrix* hair]

Tyrr (tjʊə, tɪə) *n.* a variant spelling of **Tyr.**

Tyr+rhe+ni·an Sea (tɪ'ri:nɪən) *n.* an arm of the Mediterranean between Italy and the islands of Corsica, Sardinia, and Sicily.

tyum (tjʊm) *n. Brit. dialect.* a variant spelling of **tum**[1].

Tyu+men (*Russian* tju'mjɛnj) *n.* a port in the central Soviet Union, on the Tura River: one of the oldest Russian towns in Siberia; industrial centre with nearby oil and natural gas reserves. Pop.: 323 000 (1975 est.).

tzar (zɑ:) *n.* a variant spelling of **tsar.** —'**tzar+ism** *n.*

Tze+kung ('tsɛ'kʊŋ) *or* **Tzu-kung** ('tsu:'kʊŋ) *n.* an industrial city in W central China, in Szechwan. Pop.: 229 300 (1953).

tzet+ze fly ('tsɛtsɪ) *n.* a variant spelling of **tsetse fly.**

Tzi+gane (tsɪ'gɑ:n, sɪ-) *n.* **a.** a Gypsy, esp. a Hungarian one. **b.** (*as modifier*): *Tzigane music.* [C19: via French from Hungarian *czigány* Gypsy, of uncertain origin]

Tzu-po ('tsu:'pəʊ) *or* **Tze+po** ('tsɛ'pəʊ) *n.* a city in NE China, in Shantung province. Pop.: 850 000 (1970 est.).

U

u *or* **U** (juː) *n., pl.* **u's, U's,** *or* **Us. 1.** the 21st letter and fifth vowel of the modern English alphabet. **2.** any of several speech sounds represented by this letter, in English as in *mute, cut, hurt, sure, pull,* or *minus.* **3. a.** something shaped like a U. **b.** (*in combination*): *a U-bolt; a U-turn.*

U[1] *symbol for:* **1.** united. **2.** unionist. **3.** university. **4.** (in Britain) **a.** universal (used to describe a category of film certified as suitable for viewing by anyone). **b.** (*as modifier*): *a U film.* **5.** *Chem.* uranium. ~*adj.* **6.** *Brit. informal.* (esp. of language habits) characteristic of or appropriate to the upper class. Compare **non-U.** ~**7.** *international car registration for* Uruguay.

U[2] (uː) *n.* a Burmese title of respect for men, equivalent to *Mr.*

U. *abbrev. for:* **1.** *Maths.* union. **2.** unit. **3.** united. **4.** university. **5.** upper.

UAM *abbrev. for* underwater-to-air missile.

U.A.R. *abbrev. for* United Arab Republic.

UART (ˈjuːˌɑːt) *n. Electronics. acronym for* Universal Asynchronous Receiver Transmitter.

U·ban·gi (juːˈbæŋgɪ) *n.* **1.** a river in central Africa, flowing west and south, forming the border between Zaïre and the Central African Empire and the Republic of the Congo, into the River Congo. Length: (with the Uele) 2250 km (1400 miles). French name: **Oubangui.**

U·ban·gi-Sha·ri *n.* a former name (until 1958) of the **Central African Empire.**

Ü·ber·mensch *German.* (ˈyːbərˌmɛnʃ) *n., pl.* **·mensch·en** (-ˌmɛnʃ^{ə}n). (esp. in the writings of Nietzsche) the German word for **superman.** [literally: over-man]

u·bi·e·ty (juːˈbaɪɪtɪ) *n.* the condition of being in a particular place. [C17: from Latin *ubī* where + *-ety*, on the model of *society*]

u·biq·ui·tar·i·an (juːˌbɪkwɪˈtɛərɪən) *n.* **1.** a member of the Lutheran church who holds that Christ is no more present in the elements of the Eucharist than elsewhere, as he is present at all places at all times. ~*adj.* **2.** denoting, relating to, or holding this belief. [C17: from Latin *ubīque* everywhere; see UBIQUITOUS] —**u·ˌbiq·ui·ˈtar·i·an·ˌism** *n.*

u·biq·ui·tous (juːˈbɪkwɪtəs) *adj.* having or seeming to have the ability to be everywhere at once; omnipresent. [C14: from Latin *ubīque* everywhere, from *ubī* where] —**u·ˈbiq·ui·tous·ly** *adv.* —**u·ˈbiq·ui·ty** *or* **u·ˈbiq·ui·tous·ness** *n.*

u·bi su·pra *Latin.* (ˈuːbɪ ˈsuːprɑː) where (mentioned or cited) above.

U-boat *n.* a German submarine, esp. in World Wars I and II. [from German *U-Boot*, abbreviation for *Unterseeboot*, literally: undersea boat]

U bolt *n.* a metal bar bent into the shape of a *U* and threaded at both ends to receive securing nuts: used to secure leaf springs, ring bolts, shackles, etc.

u.c. *Printing. abbrev. for* upper case.

U.C. *abbrev. for* University College.

U·ca·ya·li (*Spanish* ˌukaˈjali) *n.* a river in E Peru, flowing north into the Marañón above Iquitos. Length: 1600 km (1000 miles).

UCCA (ˈʌkə) *n.* (in Britain) *acronym for* Universities Central Council on Admissions.

Uc·cel·lo (*Italian* utˈtʃɛllo) *n.* **Pa·o·lo** (ˈpaːolo). 1397–1475, Florentine painter noted esp. for three paintings of *The Battle of San Romano, 1432* (1456–60).

U.C.L.A. *abbrev. for* University of California at Los Angeles.

U.D.A. *or* **UDA** *abbrev. for* Ulster Defence Association.

U·dai·pur (uːˈdaɪpʊə, ˈuːdaɪˌpʊə) *n.* **1.** Also called: **Mewar.** a former state of NW India: became part of Rajasthan in 1947. **2.** a city in NW India, in S Rajasthan. Pop.: 161 278 (1971).

u·dal (ˈjuːd^{ə}l) *n. Law.* a form of freehold possession of land existing in northern Europe before the introduction of the feudal system and still used in Orkney and Shetland. [C16: Orkney and Shetland dialect, from Old Norse *othal;* related to Old English *ēthel, ōethel,* Old High German *wodal*]

U·dall (ˈjuːd^{ə}l) *or* **Uve·dale** (ˈjuːd^{ə}l, ˈjuːvˌdeɪl) *n.* **Nich·o·las.** ?1505–56, English dramatist, whose comedy *Ralph Roister Doister* (?1553), modelled on Terence and Plautus, is the earliest known English comedy.

U.D.C. (in Britain) *abbrev. for* Urban District Council.

ud·der (ˈʌdə) *n.* the large baglike mammary gland of cows, sheep, etc., having two or more teats. [Old English *ūder;* related to Old High German *ūtar*, Old Norse *jūr*, Latin *ūber*, Sanskrit *ūdhar*] —**ˈud·der-ˌlike** *adj.*

UDI *abbrev. for* Unilateral Declaration of Independence.

U·di·ne (*Italian* ˈuːdine) *n.* a city in NE Italy, in Friuli-Venezia Giulia region: partially damaged in an earthquake in 1976. Pop.: 103 868 (1975 est.).

Ud·murt Au·ton·o·mous So·vi·et So·cial·ist Re·pub·lic (ˈʊdmʊət) *n.* an administrative division of the W central Soviet Union, in the basin of the middle Kama. Capital: Izhevsk. Pop.: 1 417 675 (1970). Area: 42 100 sq. km (16 250 sq. miles). See also **Votyak.**

u·do (ˈuːdəʊ) *n., pl.* **u·dos.** a stout araliaceous perennial plant, *Aralia cordata*, of Japan and China, having berry-like black fruits and young shoots that are edible when blanched. [from Japanese]

u·dom·e·ter (juːˈdɒmɪtə) *n.* another term for **rain gauge.** [C19: from French, from Latin *ūdus* damp]

U.D.R. *abbrev. for* Ulster Defence Regiment.

Ue·le (ˈweɪlə) *n.* a river in central Africa, rising near the border between Zaïre and Uganda and flowing west to join the Bomu River and form the Ubangi River. Length: about 1100 km (700 miles).

U·fa (*Russian* uˈfa) *n.* a city in the W central Soviet Union, capital of the Bashkir ASSR: university (1957). Pop.: 895 000 (1975 est.).

UFO (*sometimes* ˈjuːfəʊ) *abbrev. for* unidentified flying object.

u·fol·o·gy (ˌjuːˈfɒlədʒɪ) *n.* the study of UFOs.

u·ga·li (uːˈgaliː) *n. E. African.* corn meal. Also called: **posho.** [from Swahili]

U·gan·da (juːˈgændə) *n.* a republic in East Africa: British protectorate established in 1894–96; gained independence in 1962 and became a republic in 1967; a member of the Commonwealth. It consists mostly of a savanna plateau with part of Lake Victoria in the southeast and mountains in the southwest, reaching 5109 m (16 763 ft.) in the Ruwenzori Range. Official language: English; Swahili, Luganda, and Luo are also widely spoken. Religion: chiefly Muslim and animist. Currency: Ugandan shilling. Capital: Kampala. Pop.: 9 548 847 (1969). Area: 235 886 sq. km (91 076 sq. miles). —**U·ˈgan·dan** *adj., n.*

U·ga·rit·ic (ˌuːgəˈrɪtɪk) *n.* **1.** an extinct Semitic language of N Syria. ~*adj.* **2.** of or relating to this language. [C19: after *Ugarit* (modern name: Ras Shamra), an ancient Syrian city-state]

U.G.C. (in Britain) *abbrev. for* University Grants Committee.

ugh (ʊx, ʊh, ʌh) *interj.* an exclamation of disgust, annoyance, or dislike.

ug·li (ˈʌglɪ) *n., pl.* **·lis** *or* **·lies.** a large juicy yellow-skinned citrus fruit of the West Indies: a cross between a tangerine, grapefruit, and orange. Also called: **ugli fruit.** [C20: probably an alteration of UGLY, referring to its wrinkled skin]

ug·li·fy (ˈʌglɪˌfaɪ) *vb.* **·fies, ·fy·ing, ·fied.** to make or become ugly or more ugly. —**ˌug·li·fi·ˈca·tion** *n.* —**ˈug·li·ˌfi·er** *n.*

ug·ly (ˈʌglɪ) *adj.* **·li·er, ·li·est. 1.** of unpleasant or unsightly appearance. **2.** repulsive, objectionable, or displeasing in any way: *war is ugly.* **3.** ominous or menacing: *an ugly situation.* **4.** bad-tempered, angry, or sullen: *an ugly mood.* [C13: from Old Norse *uggligr* dreadful, from *ugga* fear] —**ˈug·li·ly** *adv.* —**ˈug·li·ness** *n.*

ug·ly duck·ling *n.* a person or thing, initially ugly or unpromising, that changes into something beautiful or admirable.

U·gri·an (ˈuːgrɪən, ˈjuː-) *adj.* **1.** of or relating to a light-haired subdivision of the Turanian people, who include the Samoyeds, Voguls, Ostyaks, and Magyars. ~*n.* **2.** a member of this group of peoples. **3.** another word for **Ugric.** [C19: from Old Russian *Ugre* Hungarians]

U·gric (ˈuːgrɪk, ˈjuː-) *n.* **1.** one of the two branches of the Finno-Ugric family of languages, including Hungarian and some languages of NW Siberia. Compare **Finnic.** ~*adj.* **2.** of or relating to this group of languages or their speakers.

UHF *Radio. abbrev. for* ultrahigh frequency.

uh-huh *sentence substitute. Informal.* a less emphatic variant of **yes.**

uh·lan *or* **u·lan** (ˈuːlɑːn, ˈjuːlən) *n. History.* a member of a body of lancers first employed in the Polish army and later in W European armies. [C18: via German from Polish *ulan*, from Turkish *ōlan* young man]

Uh·land (*German* ˈuːlant) *n.* **Jo·hann Lud·wig** (ˈjoːhan ˈluːtvɪç). 1787–1862, German romantic poet, esp. of lyrics and ballads.

u·hu·ru (uːˈhuːruː) *n.* (esp. in E Africa) **1.** national independence. **2.** freedom. [C20: from Swahili]

Ui·gur *or* **Ui·ghur** (ˈwiːgʊə) *n.* **1.** (*pl.* **·gur** *or* **·gurs**) a member of a Mongoloid people of NW China and adjacent parts of the Soviet Union. **2.** the language of this people, belonging to the Turkic branch of the Altaic family. —**Ui·ˈgu·ri·an, Ui·ˈghu·ri·an** *or* **Ui·ˈgu·ric, Ui·ˈghu·ric** *adj.*

U·in·ta Moun·tains (juˈɪntə) *pl. n.* a mountain range in NE Utah: part of the Rocky Mountains. Highest peak: Kings Peak, 4123 m (13 528 ft.).

u·in·ta·there (juːˈɪntəˌθɪə) *n.* any of various extinct Tertiary rhinoceros-like mammals of North America, having six horny processes on the head. Also called: **dinoceras.**

uit·land·er (ˈeɪtˌlændə, -ˌlæn-, ˈɔɪt-) *n.* (*sometimes cap.*) *S. African.* a foreigner; alien. [C19: Afrikaans: outlander]

u·ja·maa vil·lage (uːdʒaˈmaː) *n.* (*sometimes cap.*) a communally organized village in Tanzania. [C20: *ujamaa*, from Swahili: brotherhood]

U·ji·ji (uːˈdʒiːdʒɪ) *n.* a town in W Tanzania, on Lake Tanganyika: a former slave and ivory centre; the place where Stanley found Livingstone in 1871. Pop.: 21 369 (1967).

Uj·jain (uːˈdʒeɪn) *n.* a city in W central India, in Madhya Pradesh: one of the seven sacred cities of the Hindus; a major agricultural trade centre. Pop.: 203 278 (1971).

U·jung Pan+dang (ˈuːdʒʊŋ pænˈdæŋ) *n.* the official name of **Makasar.**

U.K. *abbrev. for* United Kingdom.

u·kase (juːˈkeɪz) *n.* **1.** (in imperial Russia) an edict of the tsar. **2.** a rare word for **edict.** [C18: from Russian *ukaz,* from *ukazat* to command]

u·ki·yo·e (ˌuːkiːjəʊˈjeɪ) *n.* a school of Japanese painting depicting subjects from everyday life. [Japanese: genre painting]

Ukr. *abbrev. for* Ukraine.

U·krain·i·an (juːˈkreɪnɪən) *adj.* **1.** of or relating to the Ukraine, its people, or their language. ~*n.* **2.** the official language of the Ukrainian SSR: an East Slavonic language closely related to Russian. **3.** a native or inhabitant of the Ukraine. ~Formerly called: **Little Russian.**

U·krain·i·an So+vi·et So+cial+ist Re+pub+lic *n.* an administrative division of the SE Soviet Union, on the Black Sea and the Sea of Azov: the third largest constituent republic of the Soviet Union and one of the four original republics that formed the USSR in 1922; consists chiefly of lowlands; economy based on rich agriculture and mineral resources (chief Soviet producer of coal) and on the major heavy industries of the Donets Basin. Capital: Kiev. Pop.: 47 126 517 (1970). Area: 603 700 sq. km (231 990 sq. miles). Also called: **the Ukraine.**

u·ku·le·le *or* **u·ke+le·le** (ˌjuːkəˈleɪlɪ) *n.* a small four-stringed guitar, esp. of Hawaii. [C19: from Hawaiian, literally: jumping flea, from *ʻuku* flea + *lele* jumping]

u·lan (ˈuːlɑːn, ˈjuːlən) *n.* a less common spelling of **uhlan.**

U·lan Ba·tor (ʊˈlɑːn ˈbɑːtɔː) *n.* the capital of the Mongolian People's Republic, in the N central part: developed in the mid-17th century around the Da Khure monastery, residence until 1924 of successive "living Buddhas" (third in rank of Buddhist-Lamaist leaders), and main junction of caravan routes across Mongolia; university (1942); industrial and commercial centre. Pop.: 267 400 (1969). Former name (until 1924): **Urga.** Chinese name: **Kulun.**

U·lan-U·de (ʊˈlɑːn ʊˈdɛ) *n.* an industrial city in the SE Soviet Union, capital of the Buryat ASSR: an important rail junction. Pop.: 295 000 (1975 est.). Former name (until 1934): **Verkhne-Udinsk.**

Ul·bricht (*German* ˈʊlbrɪçt) *n.* **Wal·ter** (ˈvaltər). 1893-1973, East German statesman; largely responsible for the establishment and development of East German communism.

ul+cer (ˈʌlsə) *n.* **1.** a disintegration of the surface of the skin or a mucous membrane resulting in an open sore that heals very slowly. See also **peptic ulcer. 2.** a source or element of corruption or evil. [C14: from Latin *ulcus;* related to Greek *helkos* a sore]

ul+cer+ate (ˈʌlsəˌreɪt) *vb.* to make or become ulcerous.

ul+cer·a+tion (ˌʌlsəˈreɪʃən) *n.* **1.** the development or formation of an ulcer. **2.** an ulcer or an ulcerous condition.

ul+cer·a+tive (ˈʌlsəˌreɪtɪv) *adj.* of, relating to, or characterized by ulceration: *ulcerative colitis.*

ul+cer+ous (ˈʌlsərəs) *adj.* **1.** relating to, characteristic of, or characterized by an ulcer or ulcers. **2.** being or having a corrupting influence. —**ˈul+cer+ous+ly** *adv.* —**ˈul+cer+ous+ness** *n.*

-ule *suffix forming nouns.* indicating smallness: *globule.* [from Latin *-ulus,* diminutive suffix]

U·le·å+borg (ˈuːlioˌbɔrjə) *n.* the Swedish name for **Oulu.**

u·le·ma (ˈuːlɪmə) *n.* **1.** a body of Muslim scholars or religious leaders. **2.** a member of this body. [C17: from Arabic *ʼulamā* scholars, from *ʻalama* to know]

-u·lent *suffix forming adjectives.* abundant or full of: *fraudulent.* [from Latin *-ulentus*]

Ul·fi·las (ˈʊlfɪˌlæs), **Ul·fi·la** (ˈʊlfɪlə), *or* **Wul·fi·la** *n.* ?311-?382 A.D., Christian bishop of the Goths who translated the Bible from Greek into Gothic.

ul+lage (ˈʌlɪdʒ) *n.* **1.** the volume by which a liquid container falls short of being full. **2. a.** the quantity of liquid lost from a container due to leakage or evaporation. **b.** (in customs terminology) the amount of liquid remaining in a container after such loss. ~*vb.* (*tr.*) **3.** to create ullage in. **4.** to determine the amount of ullage in. **5.** to fill up ullage in. [C15: from Old French *ouillage* filling of a cask, from *ouiller* to fill a cask, from *ouil* eye, from Latin *oculus* eye] —**ˈul+laged** *adj.*

ul+lage rock+et *n.* a small hydrogen peroxide rocket engine that produces sufficient acceleration to keep propellants in their places when the main rocket is shut off.

Ulls+wa+ter (ˈʌlzˌwɔːtə) *n.* a lake in NW England, in Cumbria in the Lake District. Length: 12 km (7.5 miles).

Ulm (*German* ʊlm) *n.* an industrial city in S West Germany, in Baden-Württemberg on the Danube: a free imperial city (1155-1802). Pop.: 93 200 (1970).

ul+ma+ceous (ʌlˈmeɪʃəs) *adj.* of, relating to, or belonging to the *Ulmaceae,* a temperate and tropical family of deciduous trees and shrubs having scaly buds, simple serrated leaves, and typically winged fruits: includes the elms. [C19: via New Latin *Ulmāceae,* from Latin *ulmus* elm tree]

ul·na (ˈʌlnə) *n., pl.* **·nae** (-niː) *or* **·nas. 1.** the inner and longer of the two bones of the human forearm. **2.** the corresponding bone in other vertebrates. [C16: from Latin: elbow, ELL[1]] —**ˈul+nar** *adj.*

ul+nar nerve *n.* a nerve situated along the inner side of the arm and passing close to the surface of the skin near the elbow. See **funny bone.**

u·lot+ri+chous (juːˈlɒtrɪkəs) *adj.* having woolly or curly hair. [C19: from New Latin *Ulotrichī* (classification applied to humans having this type of hair), from Greek *oulothrix* from *oulos* curly + *thrix* hair] —**u·ˈlot+ri+chy** *n.*

Ul·pi·an (ˈʌlpɪən) *n.* Latin name *Domitius Ulpianus.* died ?228 A.D., Roman jurist, born in Phoenicia.

ul+ster (ˈʌlstə) *n.* a man's heavy double-breasted overcoat with a belt or half-belt at the back.

Ul+ster (ˈʌlstə) *n.* **1.** a former kingdom and province of N Ireland: passed to the English Crown in 1461; confiscated land given to English and Scottish Protestant settlers in the 17th century, giving rise to serious long-term conflict; partitioned in 1921 to form the six counties of Northern Ireland and the Ulster province of the Republic of Ireland. **2.** a province of the N Republic of Ireland, consisting of three counties: Cavan, Monaghan, and Donegal. Pop.: 207 204 (1971). Area: 8013 sq. km (3094 sq. miles). **3.** an informal name for **Northern Ireland.**

Ul+ster De+fence As+so+ci·a+tion *n.* (in Northern Ireland) a Protestant paramilitary organization. Abbrev.: **U.D.A.**

Ul+ster+man (ˈʌlstəmən) *n., pl.* **+men.** a native or inhabitant of Ulster. —**ˈUl+ster+ˌwo+man** *fem. n.*

ult. *abbrev. for:* **1.** ultimate(ly). **2.** Also: **ulto.** ultimo.

ul+te+ri+or (ʌlˈtɪərɪə) *adj.* **1.** lying beneath or beyond what is revealed, evident, or supposed: *ulterior motives.* **2.** succeeding, subsequent, or later. **3.** lying beyond a certain line or point. [C17: from Latin: further, from *ulter* beyond] —**ul+ˈte+ri+or+ly** *adv.*

ul+ti+ma (ˈʌltɪmə) *n.* the final syllable of a word. [from Latin: the last, feminine of *ultimus* last; see ULTIMATE]

ul+ti+mate (ˈʌltɪmɪt) *adj.* **1.** conclusive in a series or process; last; final: *an ultimate question.* **2.** the highest or most significant: *the ultimate goal.* **3.** elemental, fundamental, basic, or essential. ~*n.* **4.** the most significant, highest, furthest, or greatest thing. [C17: from Late Latin *ultimāre* to come to an end, from Latin *ultimus* last, from *ulter* distant] —**ˈul+ti+mate+ness** *n.*

ul+ti+mate con+stit·u+ent *n.* a constituent of something, such as a linguistic construction, that cannot be further subdivided in the terms of the analysis being undertaken. Compare **immediate constituent.**

ul+ti+mate+ly (ˈʌltɪmɪtlɪ) *adv.* in the end; at last; finally.

ul+ti+ma Thu+le (ˈθjuːlɪ) *n.* **1.** another name for **Thule. 2.** any distant or unknown region. **3.** a remote goal or aim. [Latin: the most distant Thule]

ul+ti+ma+tum (ˌʌltɪˈmeɪtəm) *n., pl.* **+tums** *or* **+ta** (-tə). **1.** a final communication by a party, esp. a government, setting forth conditions on which it insists, as during negotiations on some topic. **2.** any final or peremptory demand, offer, or proposal. [C18: from New Latin, neuter of *ultimatus* ULTIMATE]

ul+ti+mo (ˈʌltɪˌməʊ) *adv. Now rare except when abbreviated in formal correspondence.* in or during the previous month: *a letter of the 7th ultimo.* Abbrev.: **ult.** Compare **instant, proximo.** [C16: from Latin *ultimō* on the last]

ul·ti·mo+gen·i·ture (ˌʌltɪməʊˈdʒɛnɪtʃə) *n. Law.* **1.** a principle of inheritance whereby the youngest son succeeds to the estate of his ancestor. Compare **primogeniture. 2.** another name for **borough-English.** [C19: *ultimo-* from Latin *ultimus* last + GENITURE; compare PRIMOGENITURE]

ul+tra (ˈʌltrə) *adj.* **1.** extreme or immoderate, esp. in beliefs or opinions. ~*n.* **2.** an extremist. [C19: from Latin: beyond, from *ulter* distant]

ul·tra- *prefix.* **1.** beyond or surpassing a specified extent, range, or limit: *ultramicroscopic.* **2.** extreme or extremely: *ultramodern.* [from Latin *ultrā* beyond; see ULTRA]

ul·tra+cen+tri+fuge (ˌʌltrəˈsɛntrɪˌfjuːdʒ) *Chem.* ~*n.* **1.** a high-speed centrifuge used to separate colloidal solutions. ~*vb.* **2.** (*tr.*) to subject to the action of an ultracentrifuge. —**ul·tra+cen+trif·u+gal** (ˌʌltrəsɛnˈtrɪfjʊgᵊl, -ˌsɛntrɪˈfjuːgᵊl) *adj.* —**ˌul·tra+cen+ˈtrif·u+gal+ly** *adv.* —**ul·tra+cen+trif·u+ga+tion** (ˌʌltrəˌsɛntrɪfjʊˈgeɪʃən) *n.*

ul·tra+con+ser+va+tive (ˌʌltrəkənˈsɜːvətɪv) *adj.* **1.** highly reactionary. ~*n.* **2.** a reactionary person.

ul·tra+fiche (ˈʌltrəˌfiːʃ) *n.* a sheet of film, usually the size of a filing card, that is similar to microfiche but has a very much larger number of microcopies.

ul·tra+fil+ter (ˌʌltrəˈfɪltə) *n.* a filter with small pores used to separate very small particles from a suspension or colloidal solution. —**ul·tra+fil+tra+tion** (ˌʌltrəfɪlˈtreɪʃən) *n.*

ul·tra+high fre+quen+cy (ˈʌltrəˌhaɪ) *n.* a radio-frequency band or radio frequency lying between 3000 and 300 megahertz. Abbrev.: **UHF.**

ul·tra+ism (ˈʌltrəˌɪzəm) *n.* extreme philosophy, belief, or action. —**ˈul·tra+ist** *n., adj.* —**ˌul·tra+ˈis+tic** *adj.*

ul·tra+ma+rine (ˌʌltrəməˈriːn) *n.* **1.** a blue pigment consisting of sodium and aluminium silicates and some sodium sulphide, obtained by powdering natural lapis lazuli or made synthetically: used in paints, printing ink, plastics, etc. **2.** a vivid blue colour. ~*adj.* **3.** of the colour ultramarine. **4.** from across the seas.

ul·tra+mi+crom+e·ter (ˌʌltrəmaɪˈkrɒmɪtə) *n.* a micrometer for measuring extremely small distances.

ul·tra+mi·cro+scope (ˌʌltrəˈmaɪkrəˌskəʊp) *n.* a microscope used for studying colloids, in which the sample is illuminated from the side and colloidal particles are seen as bright points on a dark background. Also called: **dark-field microscope.**

ul·tra+mi·cro+scop+ic (ˌʌltrəˌmaɪkrəˈskɒpɪk) *adj.* **1.** too small to be seen with an optical microscope. **2.** of or relating to an ultramicroscope. —**ul·tra+mi+cros+co+py** (ˌʌltrəmaɪˈkrɒskəpɪ) *n.*

ul·tra+mod+ern (ˌʌltrəˈmɒdən) *adj.* extremely modern.

—ˌ**ul·tra**+'**mod**+**ern**+**ism** *n.* —ˌ**ul·tra**+'**mod**+**ern**+**ist** *n.* —ˌ**ul·tra**+ˌ**mod**+**ern**+'**is**+**tic** *adj.*

ul·tra+**mon·tane** (ˌʌltrəmɒn'teɪn) *adj.* **1.** on the other side of the mountains, esp. the Alps, from the speaker or writer. Compare **cismontane. 2.** of or relating to a movement in the Roman Catholic Church which favours the centralized authority and influence of the pope as opposed to local independence. Compare **cisalpine** (sense 2). ~*n.* **3.** a resident or native from beyond the mountains, esp. the Alps. **4.** a member of the ultramontane party of the Roman Catholic Church.

ul·tra+**mon·ta**+**nism** (ˌʌltrə'mɒntɪˌnɪzəm) *R.C. Church. n.* the doctrine of central papal supremacy. Compare **Gallicanism.** —ˌ**ul·tra**+'**mon·tan**+**ist** *n.*

ul·tra+**mun**+**dane** (ˌʌltrə'mʌndeɪn) *adj.* extending beyond the world, this life, or the universe.

ul·tra+**na·tion·al**+**ism** (ˌʌltrə'næʃnəˌlɪzəm) *n.* extreme devotion to one's own nation. —ˌ**ul·tra**+'**na·tion·al** *adj.* —ˌ**ul·tra**+'**na**+**tion·al**+**ist** *adj., n.* —ˌ**ul·tra**+ˌ**na·tion·al**+'**is**+**tic** *adj.*

ul·tra+**red** (ˌʌltrə'rɛd) *adj.* an obsolete word for **infrared.**

ul·tra+**short** (ˌʌltrə'ʃɔːt) *adj.* (of a radio wave) having a wavelength shorter than 10 metres.

ul·tra+**son**+**ic** (ˌʌltrə'sɒnɪk) *adj.* of, concerned with, or producing waves with the same nature as sound waves but frequencies above audio frequencies. —ˌ**ul·tra**+'**son·i**+**cal**+**ly** *adv.*

ul·tra+**son**+**ics** (ˌʌltrə'sɒnɪks) *n.* (*functioning as sing.*) the branch of physics concerned with ultrasonic waves. Also called: **supersonics.**

ul·tra+**sound** (ˌʌltrə'saʊnd) *n.* ultrasonic waves of the same nature as sound, used in cleaning metallic parts, echo sounding, medical diagnosis and therapy, etc.

ul·tra+**struc**+**ture** ('ʌltrəˌstrʌktʃə) *n.* the minute structure of an organ, tissue, or cell, as revealed by microscopy, esp. electron microscopy. —ˌ**ul·tra**+'**struc**+**tur**+**al** *adj.*

ul·tra+**vi·o**+**let** (ˌʌltrə'vaɪəlɪt) *n.* **1.** the part of the electromagnetic spectrum with wavelengths shorter than light but longer than x-rays; in the range 0.4×10^{-5} and 5×10^{-9} metres. ~*adj.* **2.** of, relating to, or consisting of radiation lying in the ultraviolet: *ultraviolet radiation.*

ul·tra vi+**res** ('vaɪriːz) *Law.* beyond the legal power or authority of a person, corporation, agent, etc. [Latin, literally: beyond strength]

ul·tra+**vi**+**rus** (ˌʌltrə'vaɪrəs) *n.* a virus small enough to pass through the panes of the finest filter.

ul·u+**late** ('juːljʊˌleɪt) *vb.* (*intr.*) to howl or wail, as with grief. [C17: from Latin *ululāre* to howl, from *ulula* screech owl] —'**ul·u**+**lant** *adj.* —ˌ**ul·u**+'**la**+**tion** *n.*

Ul+**ya**+**novsk** (*Russian* ulj'janəfsk) *n.* a city in the W central Soviet Union, on the River Volga: birthplace of Lenin (V. I. Ulyanov). Pop.: 424 000 (1975 est.). Former name: **Simbirsk.**

U·lys·ses ('juːlɪˌsiːz, juː'lɪsiːz) *n.* the Latin name of **Odysseus.**

um (ʌm, ᵊm) *interj.* a representation of a common sound made when hesitating in speech.

U·may·yad (uː'maɪjæd) *n.* a variant spelling of **Omayyad.**

um+**bel** ('ʌmbᵊl) *n.* a racemose inflorescence, characteristic of umbelliferous plants, in which the flowers arise from the same point in the main stem and have stalks of the same length, to give a cluster with the youngest flowers at the centre. [C16: from Latin *umbella* a sunshade, from *umbra* shade] —**um**+**bel**+**late** ('ʌmbɪlɪt, -ˌleɪt), **um**+**bel**+**lar** (ʌm'bɛlə), *or* '**um**+**bel**+ˌ**lat**+**ed** *adj.* —'**um**+**bel**+**late**+**ly** *adv.*

um+**bel**+**lif**+**er**+**ous** (ˌʌmbɪ'lɪfərəs) *adj.* **1.** of, relating to, or belonging to the *Umbelliferae,* a family of herbaceous plants and shrubs, typically having hollow stems, divided or compound leaves, and flowers in umbels: includes fennel, dill, parsley, carrot, celery, and parsnip. **2.** designating any other plant bearing umbels. [C17: from New Latin *umbellifer,* from Latin *umbella* sunshade + *ferre* to bear] —**um**+'**bel**+**lif**+**er** *n.*

um+**bel**+**lule** (ʌm'bɛljuːl, 'ʌmbɪˌljuːl) *n.* any of the small secondary umbels that make up a compound umbel. [C18: from New Latin *umbellula,* diminutive of Latin *umbella;* see UMBEL] —**um**+**bel**+**lu**+**late** (ʌm'bɛljʊlɪt, -ˌleɪt) *adj.*

um+**ber** ('ʌmbə) *n.* **1.** any of various natural brown earths containing ferric oxide together with lime and oxides of aluminium, manganese, and silicon. See also **burnt umber. 2.** any of the dark brown to greenish-brown colours produced by this pigment. **3.** *Obsolete.* **a.** shade or shadow. **b.** any dark, dusky, or indefinite colour. ~*adj.* **4.** of, relating to, or stained with umber.

Um·ber·to I (*Italian* um'bɛrto) *n.* 1844–1900, king of Italy (1878–1900); son of Victor Emmanuel II: assassinated at Monza.

um+**bil·i**+**cal** (ʌm'bɪlɪkᵊl, ˌʌmbɪ'laɪkᵊl) *adj.* **1.** of, relating to, or resembling the umbilicus or the umbilical cord. **2.** in the region of the umbilicus: *an umbilical hernia.* ~*n.* **3.** short for **umbilical cord.** —**um**+'**bil·i**+**cal**+**ly** *adv.*

um+**bil·i**+**cal cord** *n.* **1.** the long flexible tubelike structure connecting a fetus with the placenta: it provides a means of metabolic interchange with the mother. **2.** any flexible cord, tube, or cable used to transfer information, power, oxygen, etc., as between an astronaut walking in space and his spacecraft.

um+**bil·i**+**cate** (ʌm'bɪlɪkɪt, -ˌkeɪt) *adj.* **1.** having an umbilicus or navel. **2.** having a central depression: *an umbilicate leaf.* **3.** shaped like a navel, as some bacterial colonies.

um+**bil·i**+**ca**+**tion** (ʌmˌbɪlɪ'keɪʃən) *n.* **1.** *Biology, anatomy.* a navel-like notch or depression, as in the centre of a vesicle. **2.** the condition of being umbilicated.

um+**bil·i**+**cus** (ʌm'bɪlɪkəs, ˌʌmbɪ'laɪkəs) *n., pl.* +**bil·i**+**ci** (-'bɪlɪˌsaɪ, -bə'laɪsaɪ). **1.** *Biology.* a hollow or navel-like structure, such as the cavity at the base of a gastropod shell. **2.** *Anatomy.* a technical name for the **navel.** [C18: from Latin: navel, centre; compare Latin *umbō* shield boss, Greek *omphalos* navel] —**um**+**bil·i**+**form** (ʌm'bɪlɪˌfɔːm) *adj.*

um+**ble pie** ('ʌmbᵊl) *n.* See **humble pie** (sense 1).

um+**bles** ('ʌmbᵊlz) *pl. n.* another term for **numbles.**

um·bo ('ʌmbəʊ) *n., pl.* **um**+**bo**+**nes** (ʌm'bəʊniːz) *or* **um·bos. 1.** a small hump projecting from the centre of the cap in certain mushrooms. **2.** a hooked prominence occurring at the apex of each half of the shell of a bivalve mollusc. **3.** *Anatomy.* the slightly convex area at the centre of the outer surface of the eardrum, where the malleus is attached on the internal surface. **4.** a large projecting central boss on a shield, esp. on a Saxon shield. [C18: from Latin: boss of a shield, projecting piece] —**um**+**bo**+**nate** ('ʌmbənɪt, -ˌneɪt), **um**+**bo**+**nal** ('ʌmbənᵊl), *or* **um**+**bon**+**ic** (ʌm'bɒnɪk) *adj.*

um+**bra** ('ʌmbrə) *n., pl.* +**brae** (-briː) *or* +**bras. 1.** a region of complete shadow resulting from the total obstruction of light by an opaque object, esp. the shadow cast by the moon onto the earth during a solar eclipse. **2.** the darker inner region of a sunspot. Compare **penumbra.** [C16: from Latin: shade, shadow] —'**um**+**bral** *adj.*

um+**brage** ('ʌmbrɪdʒ) *n.* **1.** displeasure or resentment; offence (in the phrase **give** or **take umbrage**). **2.** the foliage of trees, considered as providing shade. **3.** *Rare.* shadow or shade. **4.** *Archaic.* a shadow or semblance. [C15: from Old French *umbrage,* from Latin *umbrāticus* relating to shade, from *umbra* shade, shadow]

um+**bra**+**geous** (ʌm'breɪdʒəs) *adj.* **1.** shady or shading. **2.** *Rare.* easily offended. —**um**+'**bra**+**geous**+**ly** *adv.* —**um**+'**bra**+**geous**+**ness** *n.*

um+**brel**+**la** (ʌm'brɛlə) *n.* **1.** a portable device used for protection against rain, snow, etc., and consisting of a light canopy supported on a collapsible metal frame mounted on a central rod. **2.** the flattened cone-shaped contractile body of a jellyfish or other medusa. **3.** a protective shield or screen, esp. of aircraft or gunfire. **4.** anything that has the effect of a protective screen or cover. [C17: from Italian *ombrella,* diminutive of *ombra* shade; see UMBRA] —**um**+'**brel·la**-ˌ**like** *adj.*

um+**brel**+**la bird** *n.* a black tropical American passerine bird, *Cephalopterus ornatus,* having a large overhanging crest and a long feathered wattle: family *Cotingidae* (cotingas).

um+**brel**+**la plant** *n.* an African sedge, *Cyperus alternifolius,* having large umbrella-like whorls of slender leaves: widely grown as an ornamental water plant.

um+**brel**+**la stand** *n.* an upright rack or stand for umbrellas.

um+**brel**+**la tree** *n.* **1.** a North American magnolia, *Magnolia tripetala,* having long leaves clustered into an umbrella formation at the ends of the branches and unpleasant-smelling white flowers. **2.** any of various other trees or shrubs having leaves shaped like an umbrella or growing in an umbrella-like cluster.

Um+**bri·a** ('ʌmbrɪə; *Italian* 'umbrja) *n.* a mountainous region of central Italy, in the valley of the Tiber. Pop.: 772 601 (1971). Area: 8456 sq. km (3265 sq. miles).

Um+**bri·an** ('ʌmbrɪən) *adj.* **1.** of or relating to Umbria, its inhabitants, their dialect of Italian, or the ancient language once spoken there. **2.** of or relating to a Renaissance school of painting that included Raphael. ~*n.* **3.** a native or inhabitant of Umbria. **4.** an extinct language of ancient S Italy, belonging to the Italic branch of the Indo-European family. See also **Osco-Umbrian.**

Um+**bri**+**el** ('ʌmbrɪəl) *n.* the second smallest of the five satellites of Uranus and the third nearest to the planet.

u·mi·ak *or* **oo·mi**+**ak** ('uːmɪˌæk) *n.* a large open boat made of stretched skins, used by Eskimos. [C18: from Greenland Eskimo: boat for the use of women; compare KAYAK]

um+**laut** ('ʊmlaʊt) *n.* **1.** the mark (¨) placed over a vowel in some languages, such as German, indicating modification in the quality of the vowel. Compare **dieresis. 2.** (esp. in Germanic languages) the change of a vowel within a word brought about by the assimilating influence of a vowel or semivowel in a preceding or following syllable. [C19: German, from *um* around (in the sense of changing places) + *Laut* sound]

um+**pire** ('ʌmpaɪə) *n.* **1.** an official who rules on the playing of a game, as in cricket or baseball. **2.** a person who rules on or judges disputes between contesting parties. ~*vb.* **3.** to act as umpire in (a game, dispute, or controversy). [C15: by mistaken division from *a noumpere,* from Old French *nomper* not one of a pair, from *nom-, non-* not + *per* equal, PEER] —'**um**+**pire**+ˌ**ship** *or* '**um**+**pir**+**age** *n.*

ump+**teen** (ˌʌmp'tiːn) *determiner. Informal.* **a.** very many: *umpteen things to do.* **b.** (*as pronoun*): *umpteen of them came.* [C20: from *umpty* a great deal (perhaps from *-enty* as in *twenty*) + -TEEN] —ˌ**ump**+'**teenth** *n., adj.*

ump·y ('ʌmpɪ) *n., pl.* **ump·ies.** *Austral.* an informal word for **umpire.**

Um+**ta**+**li** (ʊm'tɑːlɪ) *n.* a city in E Rhodesia, near the Mozambique border: rail and trade centre in a mining and tobacco-growing region. Pop.: 51 000 (1970 est.).

UN *or* **U.N.** *abbrev. for* United Nations.

un-[1] *prefix.* (*freely used with adjectives, participles, and their derivative adverbs and nouns: less frequently used with certain other nouns*) not; contrary to; opposite of: *uncertain; uncomplaining; unemotionally; untidiness; unbelief; unrest; untruth.* [from Old English *on-, un-;* related to Gothic *on-,* German *un-,* Latin *in-*]

un-[2] *prefix forming verbs.* **1.** denoting reversal of an action or state: *uncover; untangle.* **2.** denoting removal from, release, or deprivation: *unharness; unman; unthrone.* **3.** (intensifier): *unloose.* [from Old English *un-, on-*; related to Gothic *and-*, German *ent-*, Latin *ante*]

'un *or* **un** (ən) *pron.* a spelling of **one** intended to reflect a dialectal or informal pronunciation: *that's a big 'un.*

UNA (in Britain) *abbrev. for* United Nations Association.

un+a·bat+ed (ˌʌnəˈbeɪtɪd) *adj.* without losing any original force or violence; undiminished. —ˌ**un+a·'bat+ed+ly** *adv.*

un+a·ble (ʌnˈeɪbᵊl) *adj.* **1.** (*postpositive;* foll. by *to*) lacking the necessary power, ability, or authority (to do something); not able. **2.** *Archaic.* incompetent.

un+ac+com+mo+dat+ed (ˌʌnəˈkɒməˌdeɪtɪd) *adj.* **1.** not suitable or apt; not adapted. **2.** unprovided for.

un+ac+com+pa+nied (ˌʌnəˈkʌmpənɪd) *adj.* **1.** not accompanied. **2.** *Music.* **a.** (of an instrument) playing alone. **b.** (of music for a group of singers) without instrumental accompaniment.

un+ac+com+plished (ˌʌnəˈkɒmplɪʃt) *adj.* **1.** not accomplished or finished. **2.** lacking accomplishments.

un+ac+count+a·ble (ˌʌnəˈkaʊntəbᵊl) *adj.* **1.** allowing of no explanation; inexplicable. **2.** puzzling; extraordinary: *an unaccountable fear of hamburgers.* **3.** not accountable or answerable to. —ˌ**un+ac+'count+a·ble+ness** *or* ˌ**un+ac+ˌcount+a·'bil+i·ty** *n.* —ˌ**un+ac+'count+a·bly** *adv.*

un+ac+count·ed-for *adj.* (*usually predicative*) not understood, explained, or taken into consideration.

un+ac+cus+tomed (ˌʌnəˈkʌstəmd) *adj.* **1.** (foll. by *to*) not used (to): *unaccustomed to pain.* **2.** not familiar; strange or unusual. —ˌ**un+ac+'cus+tomed+ness** *n.*

u·na cor·da (ˈuːnə ˈkɔːdə) *adj., adv. Music.* (of the piano) to be played with the soft pedal depressed. [Italian, literally: one string; the pedal moves the mechanism so that only one string of the three tuned to each note is struck by the hammer]

un+a·dopt+ed (ˌʌnəˈdɒptɪd) *adj.* **1.** (of a child) not adopted. **2.** *Brit.* (of a road, etc.) not maintained by a local authority.

un+ad+vised (ˌʌnədˈvaɪzd) *adj.* **1.** rash or unwise. **2.** not having received advice. —**un+ad+vis+ed+ly** (ˌʌnədˈvaɪzɪdlɪ) *adv.* —ˌ**un+ad+'vis+ed+ness** *n.*

un+af+fect+ed[1] (ˌʌnəˈfɛktɪd) *adj.* unpretentious, natural, or sincere. —ˌ**un+af+'fect+ed+ly** *adv.* —ˌ**un+af+'fect+ed+ness** *n.*

un+af+fect+ed[2] (ˌʌnəˈfɛktɪd) *adj.* not affected.

U·na·las·ka Is·land (ˌuːnəˈlæskə) *n.* a large volcanic island in SW Alaska, in the Aleutian Islands. Length: 120 km (75 miles). Greatest width: about 40 km (25 miles).

un+al+ien+a·ble (ʌnˈeɪljənəbᵊl) *adj. Law.* a variant of **inalienable.**

un+al+loyed (ˌʌnəˈlɔɪd) *adj.* not mixed or intermingled with any other thing; pure: *unalloyed metal; unalloyed pleasure.*

un-A·mer·i·can *adj.* **1.** not in accordance with the aims, ideals, customs, etc., of the U.S. **2.** against the interests of the U.S. —ˌ**un-A·'mer·i·can+ism** *n.*

U·na·mu·no (*Spanish* ˌunaˈmuno) *n.* **Mi·guel de** (miˈɣel ðe). 1864–1936, Spanish philosopher and writer.

un+a+neled (ˌʌnəˈniːld) *adj. Archaic.* not having received extreme unction.

u·nan·i·mous (juːˈnænɪməs) *adj.* **1.** in complete or absolute agreement. **2.** characterized by complete agreement: *a unanimous decision.* [C17: from Latin *ūnanimus* from *ūnus* one + *animus* mind] —**u·'nan·i·mous·ly** *adv.* —**u·na+nim·i·ty** (ˌjuːnəˈnɪmɪtɪ) *or* **u·'nan·i·mous+ness** *n.*

un+an+swer+a·ble (ʌnˈɑːnsərəbᵊl) *adj.* **1.** incapable of being refuted. **2.** (of a question) not admitting of any answer. —**un+'an+swer+a·ble+ness** *n.* —**un+'an+swer+a·bly** *adv.*

un+ap+peal+a·ble (ˌʌnəˈpiːləbᵊl) *adj. Law.* (of a judgment, etc.) not capable of being appealed against. —ˌ**un+ap+'peal+a·ble+ness** *n.* —ˌ**un+ap+'peal+a·bly** *adv.*

un+ap+proach+a·ble (ˌʌnəˈprəʊtʃəbᵊl) *adj.* **1.** discouraging intimacy, friendliness, etc.; aloof. **2.** inaccessible. —ˌ**un+ap+'proach+a·ble+ness** *n.* —ˌ**un+ap+'proach+a·bly** *adv.*

un+ap+pro+pri+at+ed (ˌʌnəˈprəʊprɪˌeɪtɪd) *adj.* **1.** not set aside for specific use. **2.** *Accounting.* designating that portion of the profits of a business enterprise that is retained in the business and not withdrawn by the proprietor. **3.** (of property) not having been taken into any person's possession or control.

un+apt (ʌnˈæpt) *adj.* **1.** (*usually postpositive;* often foll. by *for*) not suitable or qualified; unfitted. **2.** mentally slow. **3.** (*postpositive; may take an infinitive*) not disposed or likely (to). —**un+'apt+ly** *adv.* —**un+'apt+ness** *n.*

un+arm (ʌnˈɑːm) *vb.* a less common word for **disarm.**

un+armed (ʌnˈɑːmd) *adj.* **1.** without weapons. **2.** (of animals and plants) having no claws, prickles, spines, thorns, or similar structures. **3.** of or relating to a projectile that does not use a detonator to initiate explosive action.

u·nar·y (ˈjuːnərɪ) *adj.* consisting of a single element or component.

un+a·shamed (ˌʌnəˈʃeɪmd) *adj.* **1.** lacking moral restraints. **2.** not embarrassed, contrite, or apologetic. —**un+a·sham+ed+ly** (ˌʌnəˈʃeɪmɪdlɪ) *adv.* —ˌ**un+a·'sham+ed+ness** *n.*

un+asked (ʌnˈɑːskt) *adj.* **1.** not requested or demanded. **2.** not invited.

un+as+sail+a·ble (ˌʌnəˈseɪləbᵊl) *adj.* **1.** able to withstand attack. **2.** undeniable or irrefutable. —ˌ**un+as+'sail+a·ble+ness** *n.* —ˌ**un+as+'sail+a·bly** *adv.*

un+as+sum+ing (ˌʌnəˈsjuːmɪŋ) *adj.* modest or unpretentious. —ˌ**un+as+'sum+ing+ly** *adv.* —ˌ**un+as+'sum+ing+ness** *n.*

un+at+tached (ˌʌnəˈtætʃt) *adj.* **1.** not connected with any specific thing, body, group, etc.; independent. **2.** not engaged or married. **3.** (of property) not seized or held as security or in satisfaction of a judgment.

un+at+tend+ed (ˌʌnəˈtɛndɪd) *adj.* **1.** not looked after or cared for. **2.** unaccompanied or alone. **3.** not listened to.

u·nau (ˈjuːnaʊ) *n.* another name for the **two-toed sloth** (see **sloth** (sense 1)). [C18: via French from Tupi]

un+a·vail+ing (ˌʌnəˈveɪlɪŋ) *adj.* useless or futile. —ˌ**un+a·'vail+ing+ly** *adv.*

un+a·void+a·ble (ˌʌnəˈvɔɪdəbᵊl) *adj.* **1.** unable to be avoided; inevitable. **2.** *Law.* not capable of being declared null and void. —ˌ**un+a·ˌvoid+a·'bil+i·ty** *or* ˌ**un+a·'void+a·ble+ness** *n.* —ˌ**un+a·'void+a·bly** *adv.*

un+a·ware (ˌʌnəˈwɛə) *adj.* **1.** (*postpositive*) not aware or conscious (of): *unaware of the danger he ran across the road.* **2.** not fully cognizant of what is going on in the world: *he's the most unaware person I've ever met.* ~*adv.* **3.** a variant of **unawares.** —ˌ**un+a·'ware+ly** *adv.* —ˌ**un+a·'ware+ness** *n.*

Usage. Careful users of English distinguish between the adjective *unaware* (to be ignorant of) and the adverb *unawares* (by surprise): *they were unaware of the danger; the danger caught them unawares.*

un+a·wares (ˌʌnəˈwɛəz) *adv.* **1.** without prior warning or plan; unexpectedly: *she caught him unawares.* **2.** without being aware of or knowing: *he lost it unawares.*

unb. *or* **unbd.** *Bookbinding. abbrev. for* unbound.

un+backed (ʌnˈbækt) *adj.* **1.** (of a book, chair, etc.) not having a back. **2.** bereft of support, esp. on a financial basis. **3.** (of a horse) **a.** not supported by bets. **b.** never having been ridden.

un+bal+ance (ʌnˈbæləns) *vb.* (*tr.*) **1.** to upset the equilibrium or balance of. **2.** to disturb the mental stability of (a person or his mind). ~*n.* **3.** imbalance or instability.

un+bal+anced (ʌnˈbælənst) *adj.* **1.** lacking balance. **2.** irrational or unsound; erratic. **3.** mentally disordered or deranged. **4.** (in double-entry book-keeping) not having total debit balances equal to total credit balances.

un+bar (ʌnˈbɑː) *vb.* **+bars, +bar+ring, +barred.** (*tr.*) **1.** to take away a bar or bars from. **2.** to unfasten bars, locks, etc., from (a door); open.

un+bat+ed (ʌnˈbeɪtɪd) *adj.* **1.** a less common spelling of **unabated.** **2.** *Archaic.* (of a sword, lance, etc.) not covered with a protective button.

un+bear+a·ble (ʌnˈbɛərəbᵊl) *adj.* not able to be borne or endured. —**un+'bear+a·ble+ness** *n.* —**un+'bear+a·bly** *adv.*

un+beat+a·ble (ʌnˈbiːtəbᵊl) *adj.* unable to be defeated or outclassed; surpassingly excellent.

ˌ**un+a·'bashed** *adj.*
ˌ**un+ab+'bre+vi+ˌat+ed** *adj.*
ˌ**un+a·'bridged** *adj.*
ˌ**un+ab+'sorbed** *adj.*
ˌ**un+ac+a+'dem+ic** *adj.*
ˌ**un+ac+'cen+ted** *adj.*
ˌ**un+ac+'cen+tu+ˌat+ed** *adj.*
ˌ**un+ac+'cep+ta+ble** *adj.*
ˌ**un+ac+'claimed** *adj.*
ˌ**un+ac+'cli+ma+ˌtized** *or* ˌ**un+ac+'cli+ma+ˌtised** *adj.*
ˌ**un+ac+'com+mo+dat+ing** *adj.*
ˌ**un+ac+'count+ed** *adj.*
ˌ**un+ac+'cred+it+ed** *adj.*
ˌ**un+ac+'knowl+edged** *adj.*
ˌ**un+ac+'quaint+ed** *adj.*
ˌ**un+ac+'quit+ted** *adj.*
un+'act+ed *adj.*
un+'ac+tion+a+ble *adj.*
un+'ac+tu+ˌat+ed *adj.*
ˌ**un+a·'dapt+a+ble** *adj.*
ˌ**un+a·'dapt+ed** *adj.*
ˌ**un+ad+'dressed** *adj.*
ˌ**un+ad+'journed** *adj.*
ˌ**un+ad+'just+a+ble** *adj.*
ˌ**un+a·'dorned** *adj.*
ˌ**un+a·'dul+ter+ˌat+ed** *adj.*
ˌ**un+ad+van+'ta+geous** *adj.*
ˌ**un+ad+'ven+tur+ous** *adj.*
ˌ**un+'ad+ver+ˌtised** *adj.*
ˌ**un+ad+'vis+a+ble** *adj.*
ˌ**un+af+'fil+i+ˌat+ed** *adj.*
ˌ**un+a·'fraid** *adj.*
ˌ**un+ag+'gres+sive** *adj.*
un+'aid+ed *adj.*
un+'aimed *adj.*
un+'aired *adj.*
ˌ**un+a·'larmed** *adj.*
ˌ**un+a·'ligned** *adj.*
ˌ**un+al+'layed** *adj.*
ˌ**un+al+'le+vi+ˌat+ed** *adj.*
ˌ**un+al+'lied** *adj.*
ˌ**un+al+'low+a+ble** *adj.*
un+'al+ter+a+ble *adj.*
un+'al+tered *adj.*
ˌ**un+am+'big+u+ous** *adj.*
ˌ**un+am+'bi+tious** *adj.*
un+'a+mi+a+ble *adj.*
un+'am+i+ca+ble *adj.*
un+'am+pli+ˌfied *adj.*
ˌ**un+a·'mused** *adj.*
un+'an+i+ˌmat+ed *adj.*
ˌ**un+an+'nounced** *adj.*
un+'an+swered *adj.*
ˌ**un+an+'tic+i+ˌpat+ed** *adj.*
ˌ**un+a·ˌpol+o+'get+ic** *adj.*
ˌ**un+ap+'par+ent** *adj.*
ˌ**un+ap+'peal+ing** *adj.*
un+'ap+pe+ˌtiz+ing *adj.*
un+'ap+pli+ca+ble *adj.*
ˌ**un+ap+'plied** *adj.*
ˌ**un+ap+'point+ed** *adj.*
ˌ**un+ap+'por+tioned** *adj.*
ˌ**un+ap+'pre+ci+ˌat+ed** *adj.*
ˌ**un+ap+'pre+ci+a+tive** *adj.*
ˌ**un+ap+pre+'hen+sive** *adj.*
ˌ**un+ap+'proved** *adj.*
un+'ar+gu+a+ble *adj.*
ˌ**un+ar+'tic+u+lat+ed** *adj.*
ˌ**un+ar+'tis+tic** *adj.*
ˌ**un+as+cer+'tain+a+ble** *adj.*
un+'as+pi+ˌrat+ed *adj.*
ˌ**un+a·'spir+ing** *adj.*
ˌ**un+as+'sailed** *adj.*
ˌ**un+as+'ser+tive** *adj.*
ˌ**un+as+'sessed** *adj.*
ˌ**un+as+'signed** *adj.*
ˌ**un+as+'sim+i+ˌlat+ed** *adj.*
ˌ**un+as+'sist+ed** *adj.*
ˌ**un+as+'sort+ed** *adj.*
ˌ**un+as+'sumed** *adj.*
ˌ**un+a·'toned** *adj.*
ˌ**un+at+'tain+a+ble** *adj.*
ˌ**un+at+'tained** *adj.*
ˌ**un+at+'tempt+ed** *adj.*
ˌ**un+at+'test+ed** *adj.*
ˌ**un+at+'trac+tive** *adj.*
ˌ**un+aus+'pi+cious** *adj.*
ˌ**un+au·'then+tic** *adj.*
ˌ**un+au·'then+ti+ˌcat+ed** *adj.*
un+'au+thor+ˌized *or* **un+'au+thor+ˌised** *adj.*
ˌ**un+a·'vail+a+ble** *adj.*
ˌ**un+a·'venged** *adj.*
ˌ**un+bap+'tized** *or* **un+bap+'tised** *adj.*

un+beat+en (ʌn'biːtᵊn) *adj.* **1.** having suffered no defeat. **2.** not worn down; untrodden. **3.** not mixed or stirred by beating: *unbeaten eggs.* **4.** not beaten or struck.

un+be+com+ing (ˌʌnbɪ'kʌmɪŋ) *adj.* **1.** unsuitable or inappropriate, esp. through being unattractive: *an unbecoming hat.* **2.** (when *postpositive,* usually foll. by *of* or an object) not proper or seemly (for): *manners unbecoming a lady.* —ˌ**un+be+'com+ing+ly** *adv.* —ˌ**un+be+'com+ing+ness** *n.*

un+be+known (ˌʌnbɪ'nəʊn) *adv.* **1.** (*sentence modifier;* foll. by *to*) Also (esp. Brit.): ˌ**un+be+'knownst.** without the knowledge (of a person): *unbeknown to him she had left the country.* ~*adj.* **2.** (*postpositive;* usually foll. by *to*) *Rare.* not known (to).

un+be+lief (ˌʌnbɪ'liːf) *n.* disbelief or rejection of belief.

un+be+liev+a+ble (ˌʌnbɪ'liːvəbᵊl) *adj.* unable to be believed; incredible or astonishing. —ˌ**un+be+ˌliev+a+'bil+i+ty** *or* ˌ**un+be+'liev+a+ble+ness** *n.* —ˌ**un+be+'liev+a+bly** *adv.*

un+be+liev+er (ˌʌnbɪ'liːvə) *n.* a person who does not believe or withholds belief, esp. in religious matters.

un+be+liev+ing (ˌʌnbɪ'liːvɪŋ) *adj.* **1.** not believing; sceptical. **2.** proceeding from or characterized by scepticism. —ˌ**un+be+'liev+ing+ly** *adv.* —ˌ**un+be+'liev+ing+ness** *n.*

un+belt (ʌn'bɛlt) *vb. (tr.)* **1.** to unbuckle the belt of (a garment, etc.). **2.** to remove (something) from a belt.

un+bend (ʌn'bɛnd) *vb.* **+bends, +bending, +bent. 1.** to release or be released from the restraints of formality and ceremony. **2.** *Informal.* to relax (the mind) or (of the mind) to become relaxed. **3.** to become or be made straightened out from an originally bent shape or position. **4.** (*tr.*) *Nautical.* **a.** to remove (a sail) from a stay, mast, yard, etc. **b.** to untie (a rope, etc.) or cast (a cable) loose. —**un+'bend+a+ble** *adj.*

un+bend+ing (ʌn'bɛndɪŋ) *adj.* **1.** rigid or inflexible. **2.** characterized by sternness or severity: *an unbending rule.* —**un+'bend+ing+ly** *adv.* —**un+'bend+ing+ness** *n.*

un+bent (ʌn'bɛnt) *vb.* **1.** the past tense or past participle of **unbend.** ~*adj.* **2.** not bent or bowed. **3.** not compelled to yield or give way by force.

un+bi+ased *or* **un+bi+assed** (ʌn'baɪəst) *adj.* having no bias or prejudice; fair or impartial. —**un+'bi+ased+ly** *or* **un+'bi+assed+ly** *adv.* —**un+'bi+ased+ness** *or* **un+'bi+assed+ness** *n.*

un+bid+den (ʌn'bɪdᵊn) *adj.* **1.** not ordered or commanded; voluntary or spontaneous. **2.** not invited or asked.

un+bind (ʌn'baɪnd) *vb.* **+binds, +bind+ing, +bound.** (*tr.*) **1.** to set free from restraining bonds or chains; release. **2.** to unfasten or make loose (a bond, tie, etc.).

un+birth+day (ˌʌn'bɜːθdeɪ) *n. Brit., jocular.* **a.** any day other than one's birthday. **b.** (*as modifier*): *an unbirthday present.*

un+blenched (ʌn'blɛntʃt) *adj. Obsolete.* undismayed.

un+blessed (ʌn'blɛst) *adj.* **1.** deprived of blessing. **2.** unhallowed, cursed, or evil. **3.** unhappy or wretched. —**un+bless+ed+ness** (ʌn'blɛsɪdnɪs) *n.*

un+blink+ing (ʌn'blɪŋkɪŋ) *adj.* **1.** without blinking. **2.** showing no visible response or emotion. **3.** not wavering through trepidation or fear. —**un+'blink+ing+ly** *adv.*

un+blown (ʌn'bləʊn) *adj.* **1.** *Archaic.* (of a flower) still in the bud. **2.** not blown.

un+blush+ing (ʌn'blʌʃɪŋ) *adj.* immodest or shameless. —**un+'blush+ing+ly** *adv.* —**un+'blush+ing+ness** *n.*

un+bolt (ʌn'bəʊlt) *vb. (tr.)* **1.** to unfasten a bolt of (a door). **2.** to undo (the nut) on a bolt.

un+bolt+ed (ʌn'bəʊltɪd) *adj.* (of grain, meal, or flour) not sifted.

un+boned (ʌn'bəʊnd) *adj.* **1.** (of meat, fish, etc.) not having had the bones removed. **2.** (of animals) having no bones.

un+bon+net (ʌn'bɒnɪt) *vb.* to remove a bonnet or hat from (one's head), esp. as a mark of respect.

un+born (ʌn'bɔːn) *adj.* **1.** not yet born or brought to birth. **2.** still to come in the future: *the unborn world.*

un+bos+om (ʌn'bʊzəm) *vb. (tr.)* to relieve (oneself) of (secrets, etc.) by telling someone. —**un+'bos+om+er** *n.*

un+bound (ʌn'baʊnd) *vb.* **1.** the past tense or past participle of **unbind.** ~*adj.* **2.** (of a book) not bound within a cover. **3.** not restrained or tied down by bonds. **4.** (of a morpheme) able to form a word by itself; free.

un+bound+ed (ʌn'baʊndɪd) *adj.* having no boundaries or limits. —**un+'bound+ed+ly** *adv.* —**un+'bound+ed+ness** *n.*

un+bowed (ʌn'baʊd) *adj.* **1.** not bowed or bent. **2.** free or unconquered.

un+brace (ʌn'breɪs) *vb. (tr.)* **1.** to remove tension or strain from; relax. **2.** to remove a brace or braces from.

un+bred (ʌn'brɛd) *adj.* **1.** a less common word for **ill-bred. 2.** not taught or instructed. **3.** *Obsolete.* not born.

un+bri+dle (ʌn'braɪdᵊl) *vb. (tr.)* **1.** to remove the bridle from (a horse). **2.** to remove all controls or restraints from.

un+bri+dled (ʌn'braɪdᵊld) *adj.* **1.** with all restraints removed. **2.** (of a horse, etc.) wearing no bridle. —**un+'bri+dled+ly** *adv.* —**un+'bri+dled+ness** *n.*

un+bro+ken (ʌn'brəʊkən) *adj.* **1.** complete or whole. **2.** continuous or incessant. **3.** undaunted in spirit. **4.** (of animals, esp. horses) not tamed; wild. **5.** not disturbed or upset: *the unbroken quiet of the afternoon.* **6.** (of a record, esp. at sport) not improved upon. **7.** (of a contract, law, etc.) not broken or infringed. —**un+'bro+ken+ly** *adv.* —**un+'bro+ken+ness** *n.*

un+bur+den (ʌn'bɜːdᵊn) *vb. (tr.)* **1.** to remove a load or burden from. **2.** to relieve or make free (one's mind, oneself, etc.) of a worry, trouble, etc., by revelation or confession. ~Archaic spelling: **un+bur+then** (ʌn'bɜːðən).

un+but+ton (ʌn'bʌtᵊn) *vb.* **1.** to undo by unfastening (the buttons) of (a garment). **2.** *Informal.* to release or relax (oneself, tension, etc.).

un+caged (ʌn'keɪdʒd) *adj.* at liberty.

un+called-for *adj.* unnecessary or unwarranted.

un+can+ny (ʌn'kænɪ) *adj.* **1.** characterized by apparently supernatural wonder, horror, etc. **2.** beyond what is normal or expected: *uncanny accuracy.* —**un+'can+ni+ly** *adv.* —**un+'can+ni+ness** *n.*

un+cap (ʌn'kæp) *vb.* **+caps, +cap+ping, +capped. 1.** (*tr.*) to remove a cap or top from (a container): *to uncap a bottle.* **2.** to remove a cap from (the head).

un+cared-for *adj.* not cared for; neglected.

un+caused (ʌn'kɔːzd) *adj. Now rare.* not brought into existence by any cause; spontaneous or natural.

un+ceas+ing (ʌn'siːsɪŋ) *adj.* not ceasing or ending. —**un+'ceas+ing+ly** *adv.* —**un+'ceas+ing+ness** *n.*

un+cer+e+mo+ni+ous (ˌʌnsɛrɪ'məʊnɪəs) *adj.* without ceremony; informal, abrupt, rude, or undignified. —ˌ**un+cer+e+'mo+ni+ous+ly** *adv.* —ˌ**un+cer+e+'mo+ni+ous+ness** *n.*

un+cer+tain (ʌn'sɜːtᵊn) *adj.* **1.** not able to be accurately known or predicted: *the issue is uncertain.* **2.** (when *postpositive,* often foll. by *of*) not sure or confident (about): *a man of uncertain opinion.* **3.** not precisely determined, established, or decided: *uncertain plans.* **4.** not to be depended upon; unreliable: *an uncertain vote.* **5.** liable to variation; changeable: *the weather is uncertain.* **6. in no uncertain terms. a.** unambiguously. **b.** forcefully. —**un+'cer+tain+ly** *adv.* —**un+'cer+tain+ness** *n.*

un+cer+tain+ty (ʌn'sɜːtᵊntɪ) *n., pl.* **+ties. 1.** Also: **un+cer+tain+ness.** the state or condition of being uncertain. **2.** an uncertain matter, contingency, etc.

un+cer+tain+ty prin+ci+ple *n.* **the.** the principle that energy and time or position and momentum, cannot both be accurately measured simultaneously. The product of their uncertainties is always greater than or equal to $h/4\pi$, where h is the Planck constant. Also called: **Heisenberg uncertainty principle, indeterminacy principle.**

un+chain (ʌn'tʃeɪn) *vb. (tr.)* **1.** to remove a chain or chains from. **2.** to set at liberty; make free.

un+chan+cy (ʌn'tʃɑːnsɪ) *adj. Scot. obsolete.* unlucky or dangerous.

un+charged (ʌn'tʃɑːdʒd) *adj.* **1.** (of land or other property) not subject to a charge. **2.** having no electric charge; neutral. **3.** *Archaic.* (of a firearm) not loaded.

un+chart+ed (ʌn'tʃɑːtɪd) *adj.* (of a physical or nonphysical region or area) not yet mapped, surveyed, or investigated: *uncharted waters; the uncharted depths of the mind.*

un+char+tered (ʌn'tʃɑːtəd) *adj.* **1.** not authorized by charter; unregulated. **2.** unauthorized, lawless, or irregular.

un+chris+tian (ʌn'krɪstʃən) *adj.* **1.** not in accordance with the principles or ethics of Christianity. **2.** non-Christian or pagan. —**un+'chris+tian+ly** *adv.*

un+church (ʌn'tʃɜːtʃ) *vb. (tr.)* **1.** to excommunicate. **2.** to remove church status from (a building).

un+ci+al ('ʌnsɪəl) *adj.* **1.** of, relating to, or written in majuscule letters, as used in Greek and Latin manuscripts of the third to ninth centuries, that resemble modern capitals, but are characterized by much greater curvature and inclination and general inequality of height. **2.** pertaining to an inch or an ounce. **3.** pertaining to the duodecimal system. ~*n.* **4.** an uncial letter or manuscript. [C17: from Late Latin *unciāles litterae* letters an inch long, from Latin *unciālis,* from *uncia* one twelfth, inch, OUNCE] —**'un+ci+al+ly** *adv.*

un+ci+form ('ʌnsɪˌfɔːm) *adj.* **1.** *Anatomy, zoology, etc.* having the shape of a hook. ~*n.* **2.** *Anatomy.* any hook-shaped structure or part, esp. a small bone of the wrist (**unciform bone**). [C18: from New Latin *unciformis,* from Latin *uncus* a hook]

un+ci+na+ri+a+sis (ˌʌnsɪnə'raɪəsɪs) *n.* the condition of being infested with hookworms; hookworm disease. [C20: via New Latin *Uncināria,* from Late Latin *uncīnus* a hook, from Latin *uncus*]

un+ci+nate ('ʌnsɪnɪt, -ˌneɪt) *adj. Biology.* **1.** shaped like a hook: *the uncinate process of the ribs of certain vertebrates.* **2.** of, relating to, or possessing uncini. [C18: from Latin *uncīnātus,* from *uncīnus* a hook, from *uncus*]

un+ci+nus (ʌn'saɪnəs) *n., pl.* **+ci+ni** (-'saɪnaɪ). *Zoology.* a small hooked structure, such as any of the hooked chaetae of certain polychaete worms. [C19: from Late Latin: hook, from Latin *uncus*]

un+cir+cum+cised (ʌn'sɜːkəmˌsaɪzd) *adj.* **1.** not circumcised. **2.** not Jewish; gentile. **3.** *Theol.* not purified.

un+cir+cum+ci+sion (ˌʌnsɜːkəm'sɪʒən) *n. Chiefly New Testament.* the state of being uncircumcised.

ˌun+be+'fit+ting *adj.*
ˌun+be+'friend+ed *adj.*
ˌun+be+'got+ten *adj.*
un+'bi+ased *adj.*
ˌun+be+'hold+en *adj.*
un+'bleached *adj.*
un+'blem+ished *adj.*
un+'block *vb.*
un+'break+a+ble *adj.*
un+'brib+a+ble *adj.*
un+'bruised *adj.*
un+'brushed *adj.*
un+'buck+le *vb.,* +les, +buck+ling, +led.
un+'budg+et+ed *adj.*
un+'built *adj.*
un+'bur+ied *adj.*
un+'cashed *adj.*
ˌun+cat+e+'gor+i+cal *adj.*
un+'caught *adj.*
un+'cel+e+ˌbrat+ed *adj.*
un+'cen+sored *adj.*
un+'cen+sured *adj.*
un+'cer+ti+ˌfied *adj.*
un+'chal+lenge+a+ble *adj.*
un+'chal+lenged *adj.*
un+'chap+er+ˌoned *adj.*
ˌun+char+ac+ter+'is+tic *adj.*
un+'char+i+ta+ble *adj.*
un+'chaste *adj.*
un+'checked *adj.*
un+'chiv+al+rous *adj.*

un+civ+il (ʌn'sɪvəl) *adj.* **1.** lacking civility or good manners. **2.** an obsolete word for **uncivilized.** —**un+ci+vil+i+ty** (ˌʌnsɪ'vɪlɪtɪ) *or* **un+'civ+il+ness** *n.* —**un+'civ+il+ly** *adv.*

un+civ·i+lized *or* **un+civ·i+lised** (ʌn'sɪvɪˌlaɪzd) *adj.* **1.** (of a tribe or people) not yet civilized, esp. preliterate. **2.** lacking culture or sophistication. —**un+civ·i+liz+ed+ly** *or* **un+civ·i+lis+ed+ly** (ʌn'sɪvɪˌlaɪzɪdlɪ) *adv.* —**un+'civ·i+ˌliz+ed+ness** *or* **un+'civ·i+ˌlis+ed+ness** *n.*

un+clad (ʌn'klæd) *adj.* having no clothes on; naked.

un+clasp (ʌn'klɑːsp) *vb.* **1.** (*tr.*) to unfasten the clasp of (something). **2.** to release one's grip (upon an object).

un+clas+si+fied (ʌn'klæsɪˌfaɪd) *adj.* **1.** not arranged in any specific order or grouping. **2.** (of information) not possessing a security classification. **3.** (of football results) not arranged in any special order or in divisions.

un+cle ('ʌŋkəl) *n.* **1.** a brother of one's father or mother. **2.** the husband of one's aunt. **3.** a term of address sometimes used by children for a male friend of their parents. **4.** *Slang.* a pawnbroker. ~Related adj.: **avuncular.** [C13: from Old French *oncle,* from Latin *avunculus;* related to Latin *avus* grandfather]

un+clean (ʌn'kliːn) *adj.* lacking moral, spiritual, ritual, or physical cleanliness. —**un+'clean+ness** *n.*

un+clean+ly[1] (ʌn'kliːnlɪ) *adv.* in an unclean manner.

un+clean+ly[2] (ʌn'klɛnlɪ) *adj.* characterized by an absence of cleanliness; unclean. —**un+'clean+li+ness** *n.*

un+clear (ʌn'klɪə) *adj.* not clear or definite; ambiguous.

Un+cle Sam *n.* a personification of the government of the United States. [C19: apparently a humorous interpretation of the letters stamped on army supply boxes during the War of 1812; *U.S.*]

Un+cle Tom *n. U.S. Informal, derogatory.* a Negro whose behaviour towards white people is regarded as obsequious and servile. [C20: after the slave who is the main character of H. B. Stowe's novel *Uncle Tom's Cabin* (1852)]

un+clog (ʌn'klɒg) *vb.* **+clogs, +clog+ging, +clogged.** (*tr.*) to remove an obstruction from (a drain, etc.).

un+close (ʌn'kləʊz) *vb.* **1.** to open or cause to open. **2.** to come or bring to light; reveal or be revealed.

un+clothe (ʌn'kləʊð) *vb.* **+clothes, +cloth+ing, +clothed** *or* **+clad.** (*tr.*) **1.** to take off garments from; strip. **2.** to uncover or lay bare.

un+co ('ʌŋkəʊ) *Scot.* ~*adj.* **+co+er, +co+est. 1.** foreign, strange, or odd. **2.** remarkable or striking. ~*adv.* **3.** very; extremely. ~*n., pl.* **+cos** *or* **+coes. 4.** a novel or remarkable person or thing. **5.** *Obsolete.* a stranger. **6.** (*pl.*) news. [C15: variant of UNCOUTH]

un+coil (ʌn'kɔɪl) *vb.* to unwind or become unwound; untwist.

un+coined (ʌn'kɔɪnd) *adj.* (of a metal) not made into coin.

un+com+fort+a·ble (ʌn'kʌmftəbəl) *adj.* **1.** not comfortable. **2.** feeling or causing discomfort or unease; disquieting. —**un+'com+fort+a·ble+ness** *n.* —**un+'com+fort+a·bly** *adv.*

un+com+mer+cial (ˌʌnkə'mɜːʃəl) *adj.* **1.** not concerned with commerce or trade. **2.** not in accordance with the aims or principles of business or trade.

un+com+mit+ted (ˌʌnkə'mɪtɪd) *adj.* not bound or pledged to a specific opinion, course of action, or cause.

un+com+mon (ʌn'kɒmən) *adj.* **1.** outside or beyond normal experience, conditions, etc.; unusual. **2.** in excess of what is normal: *an uncommon liking for honey.* ~*adv.* **3.** an archaic word for **uncommonly** (sense 2). —**un+'com+mon+ness** *n.*

un+com+mon+ly (ʌn'kɒmənlɪ) *adv.* **1.** in an uncommon or unusual manner or degree; rarely. **2.** (intensifier): *you're uncommonly friendly.*

un+com+mu+ni+ca+tive (ˌʌnkə'mjuːnɪkətɪv) *adj.* disinclined to talk or give information or opinions. —**ˌun+com+'mu+ni+ca+tive+ly** *adv.* —**ˌun+com+'mu+ni+ca+tive+ness** *n.*

un+com+pro+mis+ing (ʌn'kɒmprəˌmaɪzɪŋ) *adj.* not prepared to give ground or to compromise. —**un+'com+pro+ˌmis+ing+ly** *adv.* —**un+'com+pro+ˌmis+ing+ness** *n.*

un+con+cern (ˌʌnkən'sɜːn) *n.* apathy or indifference.

un+con+cerned (ˌʌnkən'sɜːnd) *adj.* **1.** lacking in concern or involvement. **2.** not worried; untroubled. —**un+con+cern+ed+ly** (ˌʌnkən'sɜːnɪdlɪ) *adv.* —**ˌun+con+'cern+ed+ness** *n.*

un+con+di+tion+al (ˌʌnkən'dɪʃənəl) *adj.* **1.** without conditions or limitations; total: *unconditional surrender.* **2.** *Maths.* (of an equality) true for all values of the variable: $(x+1)>x$ *is an unconditional equality.* —**ˌun+con+'di+tion+al+ly** *adv.* —**ˌun+con+'di+tion+al+ness** *or* **ˌun+con+ˌdi+tion+'al+i+ty** *n.*

un+con+di+tioned (ˌʌnkən'dɪʃənd) *adj.* **1.** *Psychol.* characterizing a response that represents an innate reflex or instinct. Compare **conditioned** (sense 1). **2.** *Metaphysics.* unrestricted by conditions; infinite; absolute. **3.** without limitations; unconditional. —**ˌun+con+'di+tioned+ness** *n.*

un+con+di+tioned re+sponse *n.* a reflex action elicited by a stimulus without the intervention of any learning process. Also called (esp. formerly): **unconditioned reflex.** Compare **conditioned response.**

un+con+form+a·ble (ˌʌnkən'fɔːməbəl) *adj.* **1.** not conformable or conforming. **2.** (of rock strata) consisting of a series of recent strata resting on different, much older rocks. —**ˌun+con+ˌform+a·'bil+i·ty** *or* **ˌun+con+'form+a·ble+ness** *n.* —**ˌun+con+'form+a·bly** *adv.*

un+con+form+i·ty (ˌʌnkən'fɔːmɪtɪ) *n., pl.* **·ties. 1.** lack of conformity. **2.** the junction between recently deposited stratified rocks and much older or folded rocks.

un+con+nect+ed (ˌʌnkə'nɛktɪd) *adj.* **1.** not linked; separate or independent. **2.** disconnected or incoherent. —**ˌun+con+'nect+ed+ly** *adv.* —**ˌun+con+'nect+ed+ness** *n.*

un+con+scion+a·ble (ʌn'kɒnʃənəbəl) *adj.* **1.** unscrupulous or unprincipled: *an unconscionable liar.* **2.** immoderate or excessive: *unconscionable demands.* —**un+'con+scion+a·ble+ness** *n.* —**un+'con+scion+a·bly** *adv.*

un+con+scious (ʌn'kɒnʃəs) *adj.* **1.** lacking normal sensory awareness of the environment; insensible. **2.** not aware of one's actions, behaviour, etc.: *unconscious of his bad manners.* **3.** characterized by lack of awareness or intention: *an unconscious blunder.* **4.** coming from or produced by the unconscious: *unconscious resentment.* ~*n.* **5.** *Psychoanal.* the part of the mind containing instincts, impulses, images, and ideas that are not available for direct examination. See also **collective unconscious.** Compare **subconscious, preconscious.** —**un+'con+scious+ly** *adv.* —**un+'con+scious+ness** *n.*

un+con+sid+ered (ˌʌnkən'sɪdəd) *adj.* **1.** not considered; disregarded. **2.** done without consideration.

un+con+sti+tu+tion+al (ˌʌnkɒnstɪ'tjuːʃənəl) *adj.* at variance with or not permitted by a constitution. —**ˌun+con+sti+ˌtu+tion+'al+i+ty** *n.*

un+con+trol+la·ble (ˌʌnkən'trəʊləbəl) *adj.* incapable of being controlled or managed. —**ˌun+con+ˌtrol+la·'bil+i·ty** *or* **ˌun+con+'trol+la·ble+ness** *n.* —**ˌun+con+'trol+la·bly** *adv.*

un+con+ven+tion+al (ˌʌnkən'vɛnʃənəl) *adj.* not conforming to accepted rules or standards. —**ˌun+con+ˌven+tion+'al+i·ty** *n.* —**ˌun+con+'ven+tion+al+ly** *adv.*

un+co+or+di+nat+ed (ˌʌnkəʊ'ɔːdɪˌneɪtɪd) *adj.* **1.** lacking order, system, or organization. **2.** (of a person, action, etc.) lacking muscular or emotional coordination.

un+cork (ʌn'kɔːk) *vb.* (*tr.*) **1.** to draw the cork from (a bottle, etc.). **2.** to release or unleash (emotions, etc.).

un+count+ed (ʌn'kaʊntɪd) *adj.* **1.** unable to be counted; innumerable. **2.** not counted.

un+cou+ple (ʌn'kʌpəl) *vb.* **1.** to disconnect or unfasten or become disconnected or unfastened. **2.** (*tr.*) to set loose; release.

un+couth (ʌn'kuːθ) *adj.* lacking in good manners, refinement, or grace. [Old English *uncūth,* from UN-[1] + *cūth* familiar; related to Old High German *kund* known, Old Norse *kunnr*] —**un+'couth+ly** *adv.* —**un+'couth+ness** *n.*

un+cov+e·nant+ed (ʌn'kʌvɪnəntɪd) *adj. Law.* **1.** not guaranteed or promised by a covenant. **2.** not in accordance with or sanctioned by a covenant.

un+cov+er (ʌn'kʌvə) *vb.* **1.** (*tr.*) to remove the cover, cap, top, etc., from. **2.** (*tr.*) to reveal or disclose: *to uncover a plot.* **3.** to take off (one's head covering), esp. as a mark of respect.

un+cov+ered (ʌn'kʌvəd) *adj.* **1.** not covered; revealed or bare. **2.** not protected by insurance, security, etc.

un+crowned (ʌn'kraʊnd) *adj.* **1.** having the power of royalty without the title. **2.** not having yet assumed the crown. **3. uncrowned king** *or* **queen.** a man or woman of high status among a certain group.

UNCTAD *abbrev. for* United Nations Commission for Trade and Development.

unc+tion ('ʌŋkʃən) *n.* **1.** *Chiefly R.C. and Eastern Churches.* the act of anointing with oil in sacramental ceremonies, in the conferring of holy orders. **2.** excessive suavity or affected charm. **3.** an ointment or unguent. **4.** anything soothing or comforting. [C14: from Latin *unctiō* an anointing, from *ungere* to anoint; see UNGUENT] —**'unc+tion+less** *adj.*

unc+tu+ous ('ʌŋktjʊəs) *adj.* **1.** slippery or greasy. **2.** affecting an oily charm. [C14: from Medieval Latin *unctuōsus,* from

---

un+'cho+sen *adj.*
un+'chris+tened *adj.*
un+'claimed *adj.*
un+'clar+i+ˌfied *adj.*
un+'cleaned *adj.*
un+'cloud+ed *adj.*
un+'clut+tered *adj.*
ˌun+col+'lect+ed *adj.*
un+'col+oured *adj.*
un+'combed *adj.*
ˌun+com+'bined *adj.*
ˌun+com+'mend+a+ble *adj.*
ˌun+com+'pan+ion+a+ble *adj.*
un+'com+pen+ˌsat+ed *adj.*
ˌun+com+'pet+i+tive *adj.*
ˌun+com+'plain+ing *adj.*
ˌun+com+'plet+ed *adj.*
ˌun+com+'pli+ant *adj.*
un+'com+pli+ˌcat+ed *adj.*
ˌun+com+pli+'men+ta+ry *adj.*
ˌun+com+'pound+ed *adj.*
ˌun+com+pre+'hend+ing *adj.*
ˌun+com+pre+'hen+si+ble *adj.*
ˌun+con+'cealed *adj.*
ˌun+con+'ced+ed *adj.*
ˌun+con+'cert+ed *adj.*
ˌun+con+'clud+ed *adj.*
ˌun+con+'demned *adj.*
ˌun+con+'densed *adj.*
ˌun+con+'du+cive *adj.*
ˌun+con+'fined *adj.*
ˌun+con+'firmed *adj.*
ˌun+con+'fused *adj.*
ˌun+con+'gen+i+al *adj.*
un+'con+quered *adj.*
ˌun+con+sci+'en+tious *adj.*
un+'con+se+ˌcrat+ed *adj.*
ˌun+con+'sent+ing *adj.*
ˌun+con+'soled *adj.*
ˌun+con+'strained *adj.*
ˌun+con+'strict+ed *adj.*
un+'con+sum+ˌmat+ed *adj.*
ˌun+con+'tam+i+ˌnat+ed *adj.*
ˌun+con+'test+ed *adj.*
ˌun+con+tra+'dict+ed *adj.*
ˌun+con+'trived *adj.*
ˌun+con+'trolled *adj.*
ˌun+con+tro+'ver+sial *adj.*
ˌun+con+'ver+sant *adj.*
ˌun+con+'vert+ed *adj.*
ˌun+con+'vinced *adj.*
ˌun+con+'vinc+ing *adj.*
un+'cooked *adj.*
ˌun+co+'op+er+a+tive *adj.*
ˌun+cor+'rect+ed *adj.*
ˌun+cor+'rob+o+ˌrat+ed *adj.*
ˌun+cor+'rupt+ed *adj.*
un+'cour+te+ous *adj.*
un+'court+ly *adj.*
ˌun+cre+'a+tive *adj.*
un+'crit+i+cal *adj.*
un+'cross *vb.*
un+'crowd+ed *adj.*
un+'crown *vb.*
un+'crys+tal+lized *or* **un+'crys+tal+ˌlised** *adj.*
un+'cul+ti+ˌvat+ed *adj.*
un+'cul+tured *adj.*

Latin *unctum* ointment, from *ungere* to anoint] —**unc·tu·os·i·ty** (ˌʌŋktjʊˈɒsɪtɪ) *or* **ˈunc·tu·ous·ness** *n.* —**ˈunc·tu·ous·ly** *adv.*

un·curl (ʌnˈkɜːl) *vb.* to move or cause to move out of a curled or rolled up position.

un·cus (ˈʌŋkəs) *n., pl.* **un·ci** (ˈʌnsaɪ). *Zoology, anatomy.* a hooked part or process, as in the human cerebrum. [C19: from Latin: hook]

un·cut (ʌnˈkʌt) *adj.* **1.** (of a book) not having the edges of its pages trimmed or slit. **2.** (of a gemstone) not cut and faceted. **3.** not abridged or shortened.

un·damped (ʌnˈdæmpt) *adj.* **1.** (of an oscillating system) having unrestricted motion; not damped. **2.** not repressed, discouraged, or subdued; undiminished.

un·daunt·ed (ʌnˈdɔːntɪd) *adj.* not put off, discouraged, or beaten. —**unˈdaunt·ed·ly** *adv.* —**unˈdaunt·ed·ness** *n.*

un·dec·a·gon (ʌnˈdɛkəˌgɒn) *n.* a polygon having eleven sides. [C18: from Latin *undecim* eleven (from *unus* one + *decem* ten) + -GON]

un·de·ceive (ˌʌndɪˈsiːv) *vb.* (*tr.*) to reveal the truth to (someone previously misled or deceived); enlighten. —ˌ**un·deˈceiv·a·ble** *adj.* —ˌ**un·deˈceiv·er** *n.*

un·de·cid·ed (ˌʌndɪˈsaɪdɪd) *adj.* **1.** not having made up one's mind. **2.** (of an issue, problem, etc.) not agreed or decided upon. —ˌ**un·deˈcid·ed·ly** *adv.* —ˌ**un·deˈcid·ed·ness** *n.*

un·de·mon·stra·tive (ˌʌndɪˈmɒnstrətɪv) *adj.* tending not to show the feelings; of a reserved nature. —ˌ**un·deˈmon·stra·tive·ly** *adv.* —ˌ**un·deˈmon·stra·tive·ness** *n.*

un·de·ni·a·ble (ˌʌndɪˈnaɪəbᵊl) *adj.* **1.** unquestionably or obviously true. **2.** of unquestionable excellence: *a man of undeniable character.* **3.** unable to be resisted or denied. —ˌ**un·deˈni·a·ble·ness** *n.* —ˌ**un·deˈni·a·bly** *adv.*

un·der (ˈʌndə) *prep.* **1.** directly below; on, to, or beneath the underside or base of: *under one's feet.* **2.** less than: *under forty years.* **3.** lower in rank than: *under a corporal.* **4.** subject to the supervision, jurisdiction, control, or influence of. **5.** subject to (conditions); in (certain circumstances). **6.** within a classification of: *a book under theology.* **7.** known by: *under an assumed name.* **8.** planted with: *a field under corn.* **9.** powered by: *under sail.* **10.** *Astrology.* during the period that the sun is in (a sign of the zodiac): *born under Aries.* ~*adv.* **11.** below; to a position underneath something. **12. one degree under.** *Informal.* off colour; ill. [Old English; related to Old Saxon, Gothic *undar,* Old High German *untar,* Old Norse *undir,* Latin *infra*]

under- *prefix.* **1.** below or beneath: *underarm; underground.* **2.** of lesser importance or lower rank: *undersecretary.* **3.** to a lesser degree than is proper; insufficient or insufficiently: *undercharge; underemployed.* **4.** indicating secrecy or deception: *underhand.*

un·der·a·chieve (ˌundərəˈtʃiːv) *vb.* (*intr.*) to fail to achieve an expected result. —ˌ**un·der·aˈchiev·er** *n.* —ˌ**un·der·aˈchieve·ment** *n.*

un·der·act (ˌʌndərˈækt) *vb. Theatre.* to play (a role) without adequate emphasis. Compare **overact.**

un·der·age (ˌʌndərˈeɪdʒ) *adj.* below the required or standard age, esp. below the legal age for voting or drinking.

un·der·arm (ˈʌndərˌɑːm) *adj.* **1.** (of a measurement) extending along the arm from wrist to armpit. **2.** *Cricket, tennis, etc.* of or denoting a style of throwing, bowling, or serving in which the hand is swung below shoulder level. **3.** below the arm. ~*adv.* **4.** in an underarm style.

un·der·bel·ly (ˈʌndəˌbɛlɪ) *n., pl.* **·lies. 1.** the part of an animal's belly nearest to the ground. **2.** a vulnerable or unprotected part, aspect, or region.

un·der·bid (ˌʌndəˈbɪd) *vb.* **·bids, ·bid·ding, ·bid. 1.** to submit a bid lower than that of (others): *Irena underbid the other dealers.* **2.** to submit an excessively low bid for. **3.** *Bridge.* to make a bid that will win fewer tricks than expected: *he underbid his hand.* —**ˈun·derˌbid·der** *n.*

un·der·bod·y (ˈʌndəˌbɒdɪ) *n., pl.* **·bod·ies.** the underpart of a body, as of an animal or motor vehicle.

un·der·bred (ˌʌndəˈbrɛd) *adj.* **1.** of impure stock; not thoroughbred. **2.** a less common word for **ill-bred.** —ˌ**un·derˈbreed·ing** *n.*

un·der·brush (ˈʌndəˌbrʌʃ) *or* **un·der·bush** *n. Chiefly U.S.* undergrowth.

un·der·buy (ˌʌndəˈbaɪ) *vb.* **·buys, ·buy·ing, ·bought. 1.** to buy (stock in trade) in amounts lower than required. **2.** (*tr.*) to buy at a price below that paid by (others). **3.** (*tr.*) to pay a price less than the true value for.

un·der·cap·i·tal·ize *or* **un·der·cap·i·tal·ise** (ˌʌndəˈkæpɪtəˌlaɪz) *vb.* to provide or issue capital for (a commercial enterprise) in an amount insufficient for efficient operation.

un·der·car·riage (ˈʌndəˌkærɪdʒ) *n.* **1.** Also called: **landing gear.** the assembly of wheels, shock absorbers, struts, etc., that supports an aircraft on the ground and enables it to take off and land. **2.** the framework that supports the body of a vehicle, carriage, etc.

un·der·cart (ˈʌndəˌkɑːt) *n. Brit., informal.* another name for **undercarriage** (sense 1).

un·der·charge (ˌʌndəˈtʃɑːdʒ) *vb.* **1.** to charge too little for. **2.** (*tr.*) to load (a gun, cannon, etc.,) with an inadequate charge. ~*n.* **3.** an insufficient charge.

un·der·clay (ˈʌndəˌkleɪ) *n.* a grey or whitish clay rock containing fossilized plant roots and occurring beneath coal seams. When used as a refractory, it is known as fireclay.

un·der·clothes (ˈʌndəˌkləʊðz) *pl. n.* a variant of **underwear.** Also: **underclothing.**

un·der·coat (ˈʌndəˌkəʊt) *n.* **1.** a coat of paint or other substance applied before the top coat. **2.** a coat worn under an overcoat. **3.** *Zoology.* another name for **underfur. 4.** the U.S. name for **underseal.** ~*vb.* **5.** (*tr.*) to apply an undercoat to (a surface).

un·der·cool (ˌʌndəˈkuːl) *vb.* a less common word for **supercool.**

un·der·cov·er (ˌʌndəˈkʌvə) *adj.* done or acting in secret: *undercover operations.*

un·der·croft (ˈʌndəˌkrɒft) *n.* an underground chamber, such as a church crypt, often with a vaulted ceiling.

un·der·cur·rent (ˈʌndəˌkʌrənt) *n.* **1.** a current that is not apparent at the surface or lies beneath another current. **2.** an opinion, emotion, etc., lying beneath apparent feeling or meaning. ~Also called: **underflow.**

un·der·cut *vb.* (ˌʌndəˈkʌt, ˈʌndəˌkʌt), **·cuts, ·cut·ting, ·cut. 1.** to charge less than (a competitor) in order to obtain trade. **2.** to cut away the under part of (something). **3.** *Golf, tennis, etc.* to hit (a ball) in such a way as to impart backspin. ~*n.* (ˈʌndəˌkʌt). **4.** the act or an instance of cutting underneath. **5.** a part that is cut away underneath. **6.** a tenderloin of beef, including the fillet. **7.** *Forestry, chiefly U.S.* a notch cut in a tree trunk, to ensure a clean break in felling. **8.** *Tennis, golf, etc.* a stroke that imparts backspin to the ball.

un·der·de·vel·op (ˌʌndədɪˈvɛləp) *vb.* (*tr.*) *Photog.* to process (a film, plate, or paper) in developer for less than the required time, or at too low a temperature, or in an exhausted solution. —ˌ**un·der·deˈvel·op·ment** *n.*

un·der·de·vel·oped (ˌʌndədɪˈvɛləpt) *adj.* **1.** immature or undersized. **2.** relating to societies in which both the surplus capital and the social organization necessary to advance are lacking. **3.** *Photog.* (of a film, plate, or print) processed in developer for less than the required time, thus lacking in contrast.

un·der·dog (ˈʌndəˌdɒg) *n.* **1.** the losing competitor in a fight or contest. **2.** a person in adversity or a position of inferiority.

un·der·done (ˌʌndəˈdʌn) *adj.* insufficiently or lightly cooked.

un·der·drain *n.* (ˈʌndəˌdreɪn). **1.** a drain buried below agricultural land. ~*vb.* (ˌʌndəˈdreɪn). **2.** to bury such drains below (agricultural land). —**ˈun·derˌdrain·age** *n.*

un·der·dressed (ˌʌndəˈdrɛst) *adj.* wearing clothes that are not elaborate or formal enough for a particular occasion.

un·der·em·ployed (ˌʌndərɪmˈplɔɪd) *adj.* not fully or adequately employed. —ˌ**un·der·emˈploy·ment** *n.*

un·der·es·ti·mate *vb.* (ˌʌndərˈɛstɪˌmeɪt). (*tr.*) **1.** to make too low an estimate of: *he underestimated the cost.* **2.** to think insufficiently highly of: *to underestimate a person.* ~*n.* (ˌʌndəˈɛstɪmɪt). **3.** too low an estimate. —ˌ**un·derˌes·tiˈma·tion** *n.*

un·der·ex·pose (ˌʌndərɪkˈspəʊz) *vb.* (*tr.*) **1.** *Photog.* to expose (a film, plate, or paper) for too short a period or with insufficient light so as not to produce the required effect. **2.** (*often passive*) to fail to subject to appropriate or expected publicity.

un·der·ex·po·sure (ˌʌndərɪkˈspəʊʒə) *n.* **1.** *Photog.* **a.** inadequate exposure to light. **b.** an underexposed negative, print, or transparency. **2.** insufficient attention or publicity.

un·der·feed *vb.* (ˌʌndəˈfiːd), **·feeds, ·feed·ing, ·fed.** (*tr.*) **1.** to give too little food to. **2.** to supply (a furnace, engine, etc.) with fuel from beneath. ~*n.* (ˈʌndəˌfiːd). **3.** an apparatus by which fuel, etc., is supplied from below.

un·der·felt (ˈʌndəˌfɛlt) *n.* thick felt laid between floorboards and carpet to increase insulation and resilience.

un·der·floor (ˈʌndəˌflɔː) *adj.* situated beneath the floor: *underfloor heating.*

un·der·flow (ˈʌndəˌfləʊ) *n.* another word for **undercurrent.**

un·der·foot (ˌʌndəˈfʊt) *adv.* **1.** underneath the feet; on the ground: *he trampled it underfoot.* **2.** in a position of subjugation or subservience.

un·der·fur (ˈʌndəˌfɜː) *n.* the layer of dense soft fur occurring beneath the outer coarser fur in certain mammals, such as the otter and seal. Also called: **undercoat.**

un·der·gar·ment (ˈʌndəˌgɑːmənt) *n.* any garment worn under the visible outer clothes, usually next to the skin.

un·der·gird (ˌʌndəˈgɜːd) *vb.* **·girds, ·gird·ing, ·gird·ed** *or* **·girt.** (*tr.*) to strengthen or reinforce by passing a rope, cable, or chain around the underside of (an object, load, etc.).

un·der·glaze (ˈʌndəˌgleɪz) *adj.* **1.** *Ceramics.* applied to pottery or porcelain before the application of glaze. ~*n.* **2.** a pigment, etc., applied in this way.

un·der·go (ˌʌndəˈgəʊ) *vb.* **·goes, ·go·ing, ·went, ·gone.** (*tr.*) to experience, endure, or sustain: *to undergo a change of feelings.* —**ˈun·derˌgo·er** *n.*

un·der·grad·u·ate (ˌʌndəˈgrædjʊɪt) *n.* a person studying in a

---

unˈcurbed *adj.*
unˈcured *adj.*
unˈcus·tom·ˌar·y *adj.*
unˈdam·aged *adj.*
unˈdat·ed *adj.*
ˌun·deˈbat·a·ble *adj.*
ˌun·deˈci·pher·a·ble *adj.*
ˌun·deˈclared *adj.*
unˈdecked *adj.*
unˈdec·o·ˌrat·ed *adj.*
ˌun·deˈfeat·ed *adj.*
ˌun·deˈfend·ed *adj.*
ˌun·deˈfiled *adj.*
ˌun·deˈfin·a·ble *adj.*
ˌun·deˈfined *adj.*
ˌun·deˈmand·ing *adj.*
ˌun·dem·oˈcrat·ic *adj.*
ˌun·deˈmon·stra·ble *adj.*
ˌun·deˈnied *adj.*
ˌun·deˈpend·a·ble *adj.*
ˌun·derˈclad *adj.*
ˈun·derˌclerk *n.*
ˌun·derˈclothed *adj.*
ˌun·derˈcook *vb.*
ˌun·derˈdo *vb.,* **·does, ·do·ing, ·did, ·done.**
ˌun·derˈeat *vb.,* **·eats, ·eat·ing, ·ate, ·eat·en.**

university for a first degree. Sometimes shortened to **undergrad.** —**ˌun·der+ˈgrad·u·ate+ˌship** *n.*

un·der+ground *adj.* (ˈʌndəˌgraʊnd), *adv.* (ˌʌndəˈgraʊnd). **1.** occurring, situated, used, or going below ground level: *an underground tunnel; an underground explosion.* **2.** secret; hidden: *underground activities.* ~*n.* (ˈʌndəˌgraʊnd). **3.** a space or region below ground level. **4. a.** a movement dedicated to overthrowing a government or occupation forces, as in the European countries occupied by the German army in World War II. **b.** (*as modifier*): *an underground group.* **5.** (often preceded by *the*) an electric passenger railway operated in underground tunnels. U.S. equivalent: **subway. 6.** (usually preceded by *the*) **a.** any avant-garde, experimental, or subversive movement in popular art, films, etc. **b.** a movement in pop music towards improvisation and experimentation. **c.** (*as modifier*): *the underground press; underground music.*

un·der+ground rail+road *n.* (*often cap.*) (in the pre-Civil War U.S.) the system established by abolitionists to aid escaping slaves.

un·der+grown (ˈʌndəˌgrəʊn, ˌʌndəˈgrəʊn) *adj.* **1.** not having the expected height. **2.** having undergrowth.

un·der+growth (ˈʌndəˌgrəʊθ) *n.* **1.** small trees, bushes, ferns, etc., growing beneath taller trees in a wood or forest. **2.** the condition of being undergrown. **3.** a growth of short fine hairs beneath longer ones; underfur.

un·der+hand (ˈʌndəˌhænd) *adj. also* **un·der+hand+ed. 1.** clandestine, deceptive, or secretive. **2.** *Sport.* another word for **underarm.** ~*adv.* **3.** in an underhand manner or style.

un·der+hand+ed (ˌʌndəˈhændɪd) *adj.* another word for **underhand** or **short-handed.** —**ˌun·der+ˈhand+ed+ly** *adv.* —**ˌun·der+ˈhand+ed+ness** *n.*

un·der+hung (ˌʌndəˈhʌŋ) *adj.* **1.** (of the lower jaw) projecting beyond the upper jaw; undershot. **2.** (of a sliding door, etc.) supported at its lower edge by a track or rail.

un·der+laid (ˌʌndəˈleɪd) *adj.* **1.** laid underneath. **2.** having an underlay or supporting layer underneath. ~*vb.* **3.** the past tense of **underlay.**

un·der+lay *vb.* (ˌʌndəˈleɪ), **+lays, +lay+ing, +laid.** (*tr.*) **1.** to place (something) under or beneath. **2.** to support by something laid beneath. **3.** to achieve the correct printing pressure all over (a forme block) or to bring (a block) up to type height by adding material, such as paper, to the appropriate areas beneath it. ~*n.* (ˈʌndəˌleɪ). **4.** a layer, lining, support, etc., laid underneath something else. **5.** *Printing.* material, such as paper, used to underlay a forme or block. **6.** felt, rubber, etc., laid beneath a carpet to increase insulation and resilience.

un·der+let (ˌʌndəˈlɛt) *vb.* **+lets, +let+ting, +let.** (*tr.*) **1.** to let for a price lower than expected or justified. **2.** a less common word for **sublet.** —**ˈun·der+ˌlet+ter** *n.*

un·der+lie (ˌʌndəˈlaɪ) *vb.* **+lies, +ly+ing, +lay, +lain.** (*tr.*) **1.** to lie or be placed under or beneath. **2.** to be the foundation, cause, or basis of: *careful planning underlies all our decisions.* **3.** *Finance.* to take priority over (another claim, liability, mortgage, etc.): *a first mortgage underlies a second.* **4.** to be the root or stem from which (a word) is derived: *"happy" underlies "happiest".* —**ˈun·der+ˌli+er** *n.*

un·der+line *vb.* (ˌʌndəˈlaɪn). (*tr.*) **1.** to put a line under. **2.** to state forcibly; emphasize or reinforce. ~*n.* (ˈʌndəˌlaɪn). **3.** a line underneath, esp. under written matter.

un·der+lin+en (ˈʌndəˌlɪnən) *n.* underclothes, esp. when made of linen.

un·der+ling (ˈʌndəlɪŋ) *n.* a person in a subordinate or subservient position; lackey.

un·der+ly+ing (ˌʌndəˈlaɪɪŋ) *adj.* **1.** concealed but detectable: *underlying guilt.* **2.** fundamental; basic. **3.** lying under. **4.** *Finance.* (of a claim, liability, etc.) taking precedence; prior.

un·der+men+tioned (ˈʌndəˌmɛnʃənd) *adj.* mentioned below or subsequently.

un·der+mine (ˌʌndəˈmaɪn) *vb.* (*tr.*) **1.** (of the sea, wind, etc.) to wear away the bottom or base of (land, cliffs, etc.). **2.** to weaken gradually or insidiously: *insults undermined her confidence.* **3.** to tunnel or dig beneath. —**ˌun·der+ˈmin+er** *n.* —**ˌun·der+ˈmin+ing+ly** *adv.*

un·der+most (ˈʌndəˌməʊst) *adj.* **1.** being the furthest under; lowest. ~*adv.* **2.** in the lowest place.

un·der+neath (ˌʌndəˈniːθ) *prep., adv.* **1.** under; beneath. ~*adj.* **2.** lower. ~*n.* **3.** a lower part, surface, etc. [Old English *underneothan,* from UNDER + *neothan* below; related to Old Danish *underneden;* see BENEATH]

un·der+nour+ish (ˌʌndəˈnʌrɪʃ) *vb.* (*tr.*) to deprive of or fail to provide nutrients essential for health and growth. —**ˌun·der+ˈnour+ish+ment** *n.*

un·der+paint+ing (ˈʌndəˌpeɪntɪŋ) *n.* the first layer in a painting, indicating the design and main areas of light and shade.

un·der+pants (ˈʌndəˌpænts) *pl. n.* a man's undergarment covering the body from the waist or hips to the top of the thighs or knees. Often shortened to **pants.**

un·der+pass (ˈʌndəˌpɑːs) *n.* **1.** a section of a road that passes under another road, railway line, etc. **2.** another word for **subway** (sense 1).

un·der+pay (ˌʌndəˈpeɪ) *vb.* **+pays, +pay+ing, +paid.** to pay (someone) insufficiently. —**ˌun·der+ˈpay+ment** *n.*

un·der+pin (ˌʌndəˈpɪn) *vb.* **+pins, +pin+ning, +pinned.** (*tr.*) **1.** to support from beneath, esp. by a prop: *to underpin a wall.* **2.** to give corroboration, strength, or support to.

un·der+pin+ning (ˈʌndəˌpɪnɪŋ) *n.* a structure, of masonry, concrete, etc., placed beneath a wall to provide support.

un·der+pin+nings (ˈʌndəˌpɪnɪŋz) *pl. n.* any supporting structure or system.

un·der+pitch vault (ˈʌndəˌpɪtʃ) *n. Architect.* a vault that is intersected by one or more vaults of lower pitch.

un·der+play (ˌʌndəˈpleɪ) *vb.* **1.** to play (a role) with restraint or subtlety. **2.** to achieve (an effect) by deliberate lack of emphasis. **3.** (*intr.*) *Cards.* to lead or follow suit with a lower card when holding a higher one.

un·der+plot (ˈʌndəˌplɒt) *n.* **1.** a subsidiary plot in a literary or dramatic work. **2.** an undercover plot.

un·der+price (ˌʌndəˈpraɪs) *vb.* (*tr.*) to price (an article for sale) at too low a level or amount.

un·der+priv·i+leged (ˌʌndəˈprɪvɪlɪdʒd) *adj.* lacking the rights and advantages of other members of society; deprived.

un·der+pro+duc+tion (ˌʌndəprəˈdʌkʃən) *n. Commerce.* production below full capacity or below demand.

un·der+proof (ˌʌndəˈpruːf) *adj.* (of a spirit) containing less than 57.1 per cent alcohol by volume.

un·der+prop (ˌʌndəˈprɒp) *vb.* **+props, +prop+ping, +propped.** (*tr.*) to prop up from beneath. —**ˈun·der+ˌprop+per** *n.*

un·der+quote (ˌʌndəˈkwəʊt) *vb.* **1.** to offer for sale (securities, goods, or services) at a price lower than the market price. **2.** (*tr.*) to quote a price lower than that quoted by (another).

un·der+rate (ˌʌndəˈreɪt) *vb.* (*tr.*) to underestimate.

un·der+score *vb.* (ˌʌndəˈskɔː). (*tr.*) **1.** to draw or score a line or mark under. **2.** to stress or reinforce. ~*n.* (ˈʌndəˌskɔː). **3.** a line drawn under written matter.

un·der+sea (ˈʌndəˌsiː) *adj., adv. also* **un·der+seas** (ˌʌndəˈsiːz). below the surface of the sea.

un·der+seal (ˈʌndəˌsiːl) *n.* **1.** *Brit.* a coating of a tar or rubber-based material applied to the underside of a motor vehicle to retard corrosion. U.S. name: **undercoat.** ~*vb.* **2.** (*tr.*) to apply a coating of underseal to (a motor vehicle).

un·der+sec+re+tar·y (ˌʌndəˈsɛkrətrɪ) *n., pl.* **+tar·ies. 1.** (in Britain) **a.** any of various senior civil servants in certain government departments. **b.** short for **undersecretary of state:** any of various high officials subordinate only to the minister in charge of a department. **2.** (in the U.S.) a high government official subordinate only to the secretary in charge of a department. —**ˌun·der+ˈsec+re+tar·y+ˌship** *n.*

un·der+sell (ˌʌndəˈsɛl) *vb.* **+sells, +sell+ing, +sold. 1.** to sell for less than the usual or expected price. **2.** (*tr.*) to sell at a price lower than that of (another seller). **3.** (*tr.*) to advertise (merchandise) with moderation or restraint. —**ˌun·der+ˈsell+er** *n.*

un·der+set (ˈʌndəˌsɛt) *n.* **1.** an ocean undercurrent. **2.** an underlying vein of ore. ~*vb.* **+sets, +set+ting, +set. 3.** (*tr.*) to support from underneath.

un·der+sexed (ˌʌndəˈsɛkst) *adj.* having weaker sex urges or responses than is considered normal.

un·der+sher+iff (ˈʌndəˌʃɛrɪf) *n.* a deputy sheriff.

un·der+shirt (ˈʌndəˌʃɜːt) *n. Chiefly U.S.* an undergarment worn under a blouse or shirt. Brit. name: **vest.**

un·der+shoot (ˌʌndəˈʃuːt) *vb.* **+shoots, +shoot+ing, +shot. 1.** (of a pilot) to cause (an aircraft) to land short of (a runway) or (of an aircraft) to land in this way. **2.** to shoot a projectile so that it falls short of (a target).

un·der+shorts (ˈʌndəˌʃɔːts) *pl. n.* another word for **shorts** (sense 2).

un·der+shot (ˈʌndəˌʃɒt) *adj.* **1.** (of the lower jaw) projecting beyond the upper jaw; underhung. **2.** (of a water wheel) driven by a flow of water that passes under the wheel rather than over it. ~Compare **overshot.**

un·der+shrub (ˈʌndəˌʃrʌb) *n.* another name for **subshrub.**

un·der+side (ˈʌndəˌsaɪd) *n.* the bottom or lower surface.

un·der+signed (ˈʌndəˌsaɪnd) *n.* **1. the.** the person or persons who have signed at the foot of a document, statement, etc. ~*adj.* **2.** having signed one's name at the foot of a document, statement, etc. **3.** (of a document) signed at the foot. **4.** signed at the foot of a document.

un·der+sized (ˌʌndəˈsaɪzd) *adj.* of less than usual size.

un·der+skirt (ˈʌndəˌskɜːt) *n.* any skirtlike garment worn under a skirt.

un·der+slung (ˌʌndəˈslʌŋ) *adj.* **1.** suspended below a supporting member, esp. (of a motor vehicle chassis) suspended below the axles. **2.** having a low centre of gravity.

un·der+soil (ˈʌndəˌsɔɪl) *n.* another word for **subsoil** (sense 1a).

un·der+stand (ˌʌndəˈstænd) *vb.* **+stands, +stand+ing, +stood. 1.** (*may take a clause as object*) to know and comprehend the nature or meaning of: *I understand you; I understand what you mean.* **2.** (*may take a clause as object*) to realize or grasp (something): *he understands your position.* **3.** (*tr.; may take a clause as object*) to assume, infer, or believe: *I understand you are thinking of marrying.* **4.** (*tr.*) to know how to translate or read: *can you understand Spanish?* **5.** (*tr.; may take a clause as object; often passive*) to accept as a condition or proviso: *it is understood that children must be kept quiet.* **6.** (*tr.*) to be sympathetic to or compatible with: *we understand each other.* [Old English *understandan;* related to Old Frisian *understonda,* Middle High German *understān* step under; see UNDER, STAND] —**ˌun·der+ˈstand+a·ble** *adj.* —**ˌun·der+ˈstand+a·bly** *adv.*

un·der+stand+ing (ˌʌndəˈstændɪŋ) *n.* **1.** the ability to learn,

---

ˌun·der+ˈed·u+ˌcat+ed adj.
ˈun·der+ˌlay+er n.
ˈun·der+ˌnamed adj.
ˌun·der+ˈpaid adj.
ˌun·der+ˌpart n.
ˌun·der+ˈpeo+pled adj.
ˌun·der+ˈpop·u+ˌlat+ed adj.
ˌun·der+ˈpow+ered adj.
ˌun·der+ˈpraise vb.
ˌun·der+pro+ˈduce vb.
ˌun·der+ˈri+pened adj.
ˈun·der+ˌserv+ant n.

judge, make decisions, etc.; intelligence or sense. **2.** personal opinion or interpretation of a subject: *my understanding of your predicament.* **3.** a mutual agreement or compact, esp. an informal or private one. **4.** *Chiefly Brit.* an unofficial engagement to be married. **5. on the understanding that.** with the condition that; providing. *~adj.* **6.** sympathetic, tolerant, or wise towards people. **7.** possessing judgment and intelligence. —ˌ**un·der·'stand·ing·ly** *adv.*

un·der·state (ˌʌndəˈsteɪt) *vb.* **1.** to state (something) in restrained terms, often to obtain an ironic effect. **2.** to state that (something, such as a number) is less than it is. —ˌ**un·der·'state·ment** *n.*

un·der·stood (ˌʌndəˈstʊd) *vb.* **1.** the past tense or past participle of **understand.** *~adj.* **2.** implied or inferred. **3.** taken for granted; assumed.

un·der·strap·per (ˈʌndəˌstræpə) *n.* a less common word for **underling.**

un·der·stud·y (ˈʌndəˌstʌdɪ) *vb.* **·stud·ies, ·stud·y·ing, ·stud·ied.** **1.** (*tr.*) to study (a role or part) so as to be able to replace the usual actor or actress if necessary. **2.** to act as understudy to (an actor or actress). *~n., pl.* **·stud·ies. 3.** an actor or actress who studies a part so as to be able to replace the usual actor or actress if necessary. **4.** anyone who is trained to take the place of another in case of need.

un·der·take (ˌʌndəˈteɪk) *vb.* **·takes, ·tak·ing, ·took, ·tak·en. 1.** (*tr.*) to contract to or commit oneself to (something) or (to do something): *to undertake a job; to undertake to deliver the goods.* **2.** (*tr.*) to attempt to; agree to start. **3.** (*tr.*) to take (someone) in charge. **4.** (*intr.; foll. by for*) *Archaic.* to make oneself responsible (for). **5.** (*tr.*) to promise. —ˌ**un·der·'tak·er** *n.*

un·der·tak·er (ˈʌndəˌteɪkə) *n.* a person whose profession is the preparation of the dead for burial or cremation and the management of funerals; funeral director.

un·der·tak·ing (ˈʌndəˌteɪkɪŋ) *n.* **1.** something undertaken; task, venture, or enterprise. **2.** an agreement to do something. **3.** the business of an undertaker.

un·der-the-coun·ter *or* **un·der-the-ta·ble** *adj.* (**under the counter** *or* **under the table** *when postpositive*). done or sold illicitly and secretly.

un·der·thrust (ˈʌndəˌθrʌst) *n. Geology.* a reverse fault in which the rocks on the lower surface of a fault plane have moved under the relatively static rocks on the upper surface. Compare **overthrust.**

un·der·tint (ˈʌndəˌtɪnt) *n.* a slight, subdued, or delicate tint.

un·der·tone (ˈʌndəˌtəʊn) *n.* **1.** a quiet or hushed tone of voice. **2.** an underlying tone or suggestion in words or actions: *his offer has undertones of dishonesty.* **3.** a pale or subdued colour.

un·der·took (ˌʌndəˈtʊk) *vb.* the past tense of **undertake.**

un·der·tow (ˈʌndəˌtəʊ) *n.* **1.** the seaward undercurrent following the breaking of a wave on the beach. **2.** any strong undercurrent flowing in a different direction from the surface current.

un·der·trick (ˈʌndəˌtrɪk) *n. Bridge.* a trick by which a declarer falls short of making his contract.

un·der·trump (ˌʌndəˈtrʌmp) *vb.* (*intr.*) *Cards.* to play a lower trump on a trick to which a higher trump has already been played.

un·der·val·ue (ˌʌndəˈvæljuː) *vb.* **·val·ues, ·val·u·ing, ·val·ued.** (*tr.*) to value at too low a level or price. —ˌ**un·der·ˌval·u·'a·tion** *n.* —ˌ**un·der·'val·u·er** *n.*

un·der·vest (ˈʌndəˌvɛst) *n. Brit.* another name for **vest** (sense 1).

un·der·wa·ter (ˈʌndəˈwɔːtə) *adj.* **1.** being, occurring, or going under the surface of the water, esp. the sea: *underwater exploration.* **2.** *Nautical.* below the water line of a vessel. *~adv.* **3.** beneath the surface of the water.

un·der way *adj.* (*postpositive*) **1.** in progress; in operation: *the show was under way.* **2.** *Nautical.* in motion in the direction headed.

un·der·wear (ˈʌndəˌwɛə) *n.* clothing worn under the outer garments, usually next to the skin. Also called: **underclothes.**

un·der·weight (ˌʌndəˈweɪt) *adj.* weighing less than is average, expected, or healthy.

un·der·went (ˌʌndəˈwɛnt) *vb.* the past tense of **undergo.**

un·der·wing (ˈʌndəˌwɪŋ) *n.* **1.** the hind wing of an insect, esp. when covered by the forewing. **2.** any of various noctuid moths, such as *Catocala nupta* (**red underwing**), in which the forewings are dull and the hind wings brightly coloured.

un·der·wood (ˈʌndəˌwʊd) *n.* a less common word for **undergrowth.**

un·der·world (ˈʌndəˌwɜːld) *n.* **1. a.** criminals and their associates considered collectively. **b.** (*as modifier*): *underworld connections.* **2.** *Greek and Roman myth.* the regions below the earth's surface regarded as the abode of the dead; Hades. **3.** the antipodes.

un·der·write (ˈʌndəˌraɪt, ˌʌndəˈraɪt) *vb.* **·writes, ·writ·ing, ·wrote, ·writ·ten.** (*tr.*) **1.** *Finance.* to undertake to purchase at an agreed price any unsold portion of (a public issue of shares, etc.). **2.** to accept financial responsibility for (a commercial project or enterprise). **3.** *Insurance.* **a.** to sign and issue (an insurance policy) thus accepting liability if specified losses occur. **b.** to insure (a property or risk). **c.** to accept liability up to (a specified amount) in an insurance policy. **4.** to write (words, a signature, etc.) beneath (other written matter); subscribe. **5.** to support or concur with (a decision, statement, etc.) by or as if by signature.

un·der·writ·er (ˈʌndəˌraɪtə) *n.* **1.** a person or enterprise that underwrites public issues of shares, bonds, etc. **2. a.** a person or enterprise that underwrites insurance policies. **b.** an employee or agent of an insurance company who assesses risks and determines the premiums payable.

un·des·cend·ed (ˌʌndɪˈsɛndɪd) *adj.* (of the testes) remaining in the abdominal cavity rather than descending to lie in the scrotum.

un·de·signed (ˌʌndɪˈzaɪnd) *adj.* **1.** (of an action) unintentional. **2.** not yet designed.

un·de·sign·ing (ˌʌndɪˈzaɪnɪŋ) *adj.* (of a person) frank; straightforward.

un·de·sir·a·ble (ˌʌndɪˈzaɪərəbᵊl) *adj.* not desirable or pleasant; objectionable. —ˌ**un·de·ˌsir·a·'bil·i·ty** *or* ˌ**un·de·'sir·a·ble·ness** *n.* —ˌ**un·de·'sir·a·bly** *adv.*

un·de·ter·mined (ˌʌndɪˈtɜːmɪnd) *adj.* **1.** not yet resolved; undecided. **2.** not known or discovered.

un·did (ʌnˈdɪd) *vb.* the past tense of **undo.**

un·dies (ˈʌndɪz) *pl. n. Informal.* women's underwear.

un·dine (ˈʌndiːn) *n.* any of various female water spirits. [C17: from New Latin *undina,* from Latin *unda* a wave]

un·di·rect·ed (ˌʌndɪˈrɛktɪd, -daɪ-) *adj.* **1.** lacking a clear purpose or objective. **2.** (of a letter, parcel, etc.) having no address.

un·dis·tin·guished (ˌʌndɪˈstɪŋgwɪʃt) *adj.* **1.** not particularly good or bad. **2.** without distinction: *undistinguished features.* **3.** *Rare.* indistinguishable.

un·dis·trib·ut·ed (ˌʌndɪsˈtrɪbjʊtɪd) *adj. Logic.* (of a term) referring only to some members of the class designated by the term, as *doctors* in *some doctors are overworked.*

un·do (ʌnˈduː) *vb.* **·does, ·do·ing, ·did, ·done.** (*mainly tr.*) **1.** (*also intr.*) to untie, unwrap, or open or become untied, unwrapped, etc. **2.** to reverse the effects of. **3.** to cause the downfall of. **4.** *Obsolete.* to explain or solve. —**un·'do·er** *n.*

un·do·ing (ʌnˈduːɪŋ) *n.* **1.** ruin; downfall. **2.** the cause of downfall: *drink was his undoing.*

un·done[1] (ʌnˈdʌn) *adj.* not done or completed; unfinished.

un·done[2] (ʌnˈdʌn) *adj.* **1.** ruined; destroyed. **2.** unfastened; untied.

un·doubt·ed (ʌnˈdaʊtɪd) *adj.* beyond doubt; certain or indisputable. —**un·'doubt·ed·ly** *adv.*

un·dreamed (ʌnˈdriːmd), *also* **un·dreamt** (ʌnˈdrɛmt). (often foll. by *of*) not thought of, conceived, or imagined.

un·dress *vb.* (ʌnˈdrɛs). **1.** to take off clothes from (oneself or another). **2.** (*tr.*) to strip of ornamentation. **3.** (*tr.*) to remove the dressing from (a wound). *~n.* (ʌnˈdrɛs). **4.** partial or complete nakedness. **5.** informal or normal working clothes or uniform. *~adj.* (ˈʌndrɛs). **6.** characterized by or requiring informal or normal working dress or uniform.

un·dressed (ʌnˈdrɛst) *adj.* **1.** partially or completely naked. **2.** (of an animal hide) not fully processed. **3.** (of food, esp. salad) not prepared with sauce or dressing.

UNDRO (ˈʌnˌdrəʊ) *n. acronym for* United Nations Disaster Relief Organization.

Und·set (*Norwegian* ˈʊnsɛt) *n.* **Sig·rid** (ˈsigri). 1882–1949, Norwegian novelist, best known for her trilogy *Kristin Lavransdatter* (1920–22): Nobel prize for literature 1928.

un·due (ʌnˈdjuː) *adj.* **1.** excessive or unwarranted. **2.** unjust, improper, or illegal. **3.** (of a debt, bond, etc.) not yet payable.

un·du·lant (ˈʌndjʊlənt) *adj. Rare.* resembling waves; undulating. —**'un·du·lance** *n.*

un·du·lant fe·ver *n.* another name for **brucellosis.**

un·du·late *vb.* (ˈʌndjʊˌleɪt). **1.** to move or cause to move in waves or as if in waves. **2.** to have or provide with a wavy form or appearance. *~adj.* (ˈʌndjʊlɪt, -ˌleɪt), *also* **un·du·lat·ed. 3.** having a wavy or rippled appearance, margin, or form: *an undulate leaf.* [C17: from Latin *undulātus,* from *unda* a wave] —**'un·du·ˌla·tor** *n.*

un·du·la·tion (ˌʌndjʊˈleɪʃən) *n.* **1.** the act or an instance of undulating. **2.** any wave or wavelike form, line, etc.

ˌ**un·der·'spend** *vb.,* **·spends, ·spend·ing, ·spent.**
ˌ**un·der·'staffed** *adj.*
ˌ**un·der·sup·'ply** *vb.,* **·plies, ·ply·ing, ·plied.**
'**un·der·ˌsur·face** *n.*
ˌ**un·der·'trained** *adj.*
ˌ**un·de·'served** *adj.*
ˌ**un·de·'serv·ing** *adj.*
ˌ**un·de·'sired** *adj.*
ˌ**un·de·'stroyed** *adj.*
ˌ**un·de·'tach·a·ble** *adj.*
ˌ**un·de·'tached** *adj.*
ˌ**un·de·'tect·ed** *adj.*
ˌ**un·de·'terred** *adj.*
ˌ**un·de·'vel·oped** *adj.*
un·'di·ag·ˌnosed *adj.*
ˌ**un·dif·fer·'en·ti·ˌat·ed** *adj.*
ˌ**un·di·'gest·ed** *adj.*
un·'dig·ni·ˌfied *adj.*
ˌ**un·di·'lut·ed** *adj.*
ˌ**un·di·'min·ished** *adj.*
un·'dimmed *adj.*
ˌ**un·dip·lo·'mat·ic** *adj.*
ˌ**un·dis·'cern·ing** *adj.*
ˌ**un·dis·'charged** *adj.*
un·'dis·ci·plined *adj.*
ˌ**un·dis·'closed** *adj.*
ˌ**un·dis·'cour·aged** *adj.*
ˌ**un·dis·'cov·ered** *adj.*
ˌ**un·dis·'crim·i·ˌnat·ing** *adj.*
ˌ**un·dis·'guised** *adj.*
ˌ**un·dis·'mayed** *adj.*
ˌ**un·dis·'posed** *adj.*
ˌ**un·dis·'put·ed** *adj.*
ˌ**un·dis·'so·ci·ˌat·ed** *adj.*
ˌ**un·dis·'solved** *adj.*
ˌ**un·dis·'tin·guish·a·ble** *adj.*
ˌ**un·dis·'tressed** *adj.*
ˌ**un·dis·'turbed** *adj.*
ˌ**un·di·'ver·si·ˌfied** *adj.*
ˌ**un·di·'vid·ed** *adj.*
un·'doc·u·ment·ed *adj.*
ˌ**un·do·'mes·ti·ˌcat·ed** *adj.*
un·'doubt·a·ble *adj.*
un·'drained *adj.*
ˌ**un·dra·'mat·ic** *adj.*
un·'draped *adj.*
un·'draw *vb.*
un·'dreamed *adj.*
un·'drink·a·ble *adj.*
un·'du·ti·ful *adj.*

un+du+la+to+ry (ˈʌndjʊlətərɪ, -trɪ) *adj.* **1.** caused by or characterized by waves or undulations. **2.** having a wavelike motion or form.

un+du+ly (ʌnˈdjuːlɪ) *adv.* **1.** immoderately; excessively. **2.** in contradiction of moral or legal standards.

un+dy+ing (ʌnˈdaɪɪŋ) *adj.* unending; eternal. —**un+ˈdy+ing+ly** *adv.*

un+earned (ʌnˈɜːnd) *adj.* **1.** not deserved. **2.** not yet earned.

un+earned in+come *n.* income from property, investment, etc., comprising rent, interest, and dividends.

un+earned in+cre+ment *n.* a rise in the market value of landed property resulting from general economic factors.

un+earth (ʌnˈɜːθ) *vb. (tr.)* **1.** to dig up out of the earth. **2.** to reveal or discover, esp. by exhaustive searching.

un+earth+ly (ʌnˈɜːθlɪ) *adj.* **1.** ghostly; eerie; weird: *unearthly screams.* **2.** heavenly; sublime: *unearthly music.* **3.** ridiculous or unreasonable (esp. in the phrase **unearthly hour**). —**un+ˈearth+li+ness** *n.*

un+eas+y (ʌnˈiːzɪ) *adj.* **1.** (of a person) anxious; apprehensive. **2.** (of a condition) precarious; uncomfortable: *an uneasy truce.* **3.** (of a thought, etc.) disturbing; disquieting. —**un+ˈeas+i+ly** *adv.* —**un+ˈeas+i+ness** *n.*

un+e+co+nom+ic (ʌnˌiːkəˈnɒmɪk, ʌnˌɛkə-) *adj.* not economic; not profitable.

UNEF (ˈjuːˌnɛf) *n. acronym for* United Nations Emergency Force.

un+em+ploy+a+ble (ˌʌnɪmˈplɔɪəbᵊl) *adj.* unable or unfit to keep a job. —**ˌun+em+ˌploy+a+ˈbil+i+ty** *n.*

un+em+ployed (ˌʌnɪmˈplɔɪd) *adj.* **1. a.** without remunerative employment; out of work. **b.** (*as collective n.* preceded by *the*): *the unemployed.* **2.** not being used; idle.

un+em+ploy+ment (ˌʌnɪmˈplɔɪmənt) *n.* **1.** the condition of being unemployed. **2.** the number of unemployed workers, often as a percentage of the total labour force.

un+em+ploy+ment ben+e+fit *n.* (in the British National Insurance scheme) a regular payment to a person who is out of work and has paid a fixed number of insurance contributions. Informal term: **dole.**

un+em+ploy+ment com+pen+sa+tion *n.* (in the U.S.) payment by a governmental agency to unemployed people.

un+e+qual (ʌnˈiːkwəl) *adj.* **1.** not equal in quantity, size, rank, value, etc. **2.** (foll. by *to*) inadequate; insufficient. **3.** not evenly balanced. **4.** (of character, quality, etc.) irregular; varying; inconsistent. **5.** (of a contest, etc.) having competitors of different ability. **6.** *Obsolete.* unjust. —**un+ˈe+qual+ly** *adv.*

un+e+qualled *or U.S.* **un+e+qualed** (ʌnˈiːkwəld) *adj.* not equalled; unparalleled or unrivalled; supreme.

un+e+quiv+o+cal (ˌʌnɪˈkwɪvəkᵊl) *adj.* not ambiguous; plain. —**ˌun+e+ˈquiv+o+cal+ly** *adv.* —**ˌun+e+ˈquiv+o+cal+ness** *n.*

un+err+ing (ʌnˈɜːrɪŋ) *adj.* **1.** not missing the mark or target. **2.** consistently accurate; certain. —**un+ˈerr+ing+ly** *adv.* —**un+ˈerr+ing+ness** *n.*

UNESCO (juːˈnɛskəʊ) *n. acronym for* United Nations Educational, Scientific, and Cultural Organization: an agency of the United Nations that sponsors programmes to promote education, communication, the arts, etc.

un+es+sen+tial (ˌʌnɪˈsɛnʃəl) *adj.* **1.** a less common word for **inessential.** ~*n.* **2.** something that is not essential. —**ˌun+es+ˈsen+tial+ly** *adv.*

un+e+ven (ʌnˈiːvən) *adj.* **1.** (of a surface, etc.) not level or flat. **2.** spasmodic or variable. **3.** not parallel, straight, or horizontal. **4.** not fairly matched: *an uneven race.* **5.** *Archaic.* not equal. **6.** *Obsolete.* unjust. —**un+ˈe+ven+ly** *adv.* —**un+ˈe+ven+ness** *n.*

un+e+vent+ful (ˌʌnɪˈvɛntfʊl) *adj.* ordinary, routine, or quiet. —**ˌun+e+ˈvent+ful+ly** *adv.* —**ˌun+e+ˈvent+ful+ness** *n.*

un+ex+am+pled (ˌʌnɪgˈzɑːmpᵊld) *adj.* without precedent or parallel.

un+ex+cep+tion+a+ble (ˌʌnɪkˈsɛpʃənəbᵊl) *adj.* beyond criticism or objection. —**ˌun+ex+ˈcep+tion+a+ble+ness** *or* **ˌun+ex+ˌcep+tion+a+ˈbil+i+ty** *n.* —**ˌun+ex+ˈcep+tion+a+bly** *adv.*

un+ex+cep+tion+al (ˌʌnɪkˈsɛpʃənᵊl) *adj.* **1.** usual, ordinary, or normal. **2.** subject to or allowing no exceptions. **3.** *Not standard.* another word for **unexceptionable.** —**ˌun+ex+ˈcep+tion+al+ly** *adv.*

un+ex+pec+ted (ˌʌnɪkˈspɛktɪd) *adj.* surprising or unforeseen. —**ˌun+ex+ˈpect+ed+ly** *adv.* —**ˌun+ex+ˈpect+ed+ness** *n.*

un+ex+pe+ri+enced (ˌʌnɪkˈspɪərɪənst) *adj.* **1.** (of a situation, sensation, fact, etc.) not having been undergone or known by experience. **2.** inexperienced.

un+ex+pressed (ˌʌnɪkˈsprɛst) *adj.* **1.** not expressed or said. **2.** understood without being expressed.

un+fail+ing (ʌnˈfeɪlɪŋ) *adj.* **1.** not failing; unflagging. **2.** continuous or unceasing. **3.** sure; certain. —**un+ˈfail+ing+ly** *adv.* —**un+ˈfail+ing+ness** *n.*

un+fair (ʌnˈfɛə) *adj.* **1.** characterized by inequality or injustice. **2.** dishonest or unethical. —**un+ˈfair+ly** *adv.* —**un+ˈfair+ness** *n.*

un+faith+ful (ʌnˈfeɪθfʊl) *adj.* **1.** not true to a promise, vow, etc. **2.** not true to a wife, husband, lover, etc., esp. in having sexual intercourse with someone else. **3.** inaccurate; inexact; unreliable; untrustworthy: *unfaithful copy.* **4.** *Obsolete.* not having religious faith; infidel. **5.** *Obsolete.* not upright; dishonest. —**un+ˈfaith+ful+ly** *adv.* —**un+ˈfaith+ful+ness** *n.*

un+fa+mil+iar (ˌʌnfəˈmɪljə) *adj.* **1.** not known or experienced; strange. **2.** (*postpositive;* foll. by *with*) not familiar. —**un+fa+mil+i+ar+i+ty** (ˌʌnfəˌmɪlɪˈærɪtɪ) *n.* —**ˌun+fa+ˈmil+iar+ly** *adv.*

un+fas+ten (ʌnˈfɑːsᵊn) *vb.* to undo, untie, or open or become undone, untied, or opened.

un+fa+thered (ʌnˈfɑːðəd) *adj.* **1.** having no known father. **2.** of unknown or uncertain origin. **3.** *Archaic.* fatherless.

un+fath+om+a+ble (ʌnˈfæðəməbᵊl) *adj.* **1.** incapable of being fathomed; immeasurable. **2.** incomprehensible. —**un+ˈfath+om+a+ble+ness** *n.* —**un+ˈfath+om+a+bly** *adv.*

un+fa+vour+a+ble *or U.S.* **un+fa+vor+a+ble** (ʌnˈfeɪvərəbᵊl, -ˈfeɪvrə-) *adj.* not favourable; adverse or inauspicious. —**un+ˈfa+vour+a+ble+ness** *or U.S.* **un+ˈfa+vor+a+ble+ness** *n.* —**un+ˈfa+vour+a+bly** *or U.S.* **un+ˈfa+vor+a+bly** *adv.*

Un+fed+er+at+ed Ma+lay States (ʌnˈfɛdəˌreɪtɪd) *pl. n.* a former group of native states in the Malay Peninsula that became British protectorates between 1885 and 1909. All except Brunei joined the Malayan Union (later Federation of Malaya) in 1946. Brunei joined the Federation of Malaysia in 1963.

un+feel+ing (ʌnˈfiːlɪŋ) *adj.* **1.** without sympathy; callous. **2.** without physical feeling or sensation. —**un+ˈfeel+ing+ly** *adv.* —**un+ˈfeel+ing+ness** *n.*

un+fet+ter (ʌnˈfɛtə) *vb. (tr.)* **1.** to release from fetters, bonds, etc. **2.** to release from restraint or inhibition.

un+fin+ished (ʌnˈfɪnɪʃt) *adj.* **1.** incomplete or imperfect. **2.** (of paint, polish, varnish, etc.) without an applied finish; rough. **3.** (of fabric) unbleached or not processed. **4.** (of fabric) with a short nap.

un+fit (ʌnˈfɪt) *adj.* **1.** (*postpositive;* often foll. by *for*) unqualified, incapable, or incompetent: *unfit for military service.* **2.** (*postpositive;* often foll. by *for*) unsuitable or inappropriate: *the ground was unfit for football.* **3.** in poor physical condition. ~*vb.* **+fits, +fit+ting, +fit+ted. 4.** (*tr.*) *Rare.* to disqualify or render unfit. —**un+ˈfit+ly** *adv.* —**un+ˈfit+ness** *n.*

un+fix (ʌnˈfɪks) *vb. (tr.)* **1.** to unfasten, detach, or loosen. **2.** to unsettle or disturb.

un+flap+pa+ble (ʌnˈflæpəbᵊl) *adj. Informal.* hard to upset; imperturbable; calm; composed. —**un+ˌflap+pa+ˈbil+i+ty** *or* **un+ˈflap+pa+ble+ness** *n.* —**un+ˈflap+pa+bly** *adv.*

un+fledged (ʌnˈflɛdʒd) *adj.* **1.** (of a young bird) not having developed adult feathers. **2.** immature and undeveloped.

un+flinch+ing (ʌnˈflɪntʃɪŋ) *adj.* not shrinking from danger, difficulty, etc. —**un+ˈflinch+ing+ly** *adv.* —**un+ˈflinch+ing+ness** *n.*

un+fold (ʌnˈfəʊld) *vb.* **1.** to open or spread out or be opened or spread out from a folded state. **2.** to reveal or be revealed: *the truth unfolds.* **3.** to develop or expand or be developed or expanded. —**un+ˈfold+er** *n.*

un+for+get+ta+ble (ˌʌnfəˈgɛtəbᵊl) *adj.* impossible to forget; highly memorable. —**ˌun+for+ˈget+ta+bly** *adv.*

un+formed (ʌnˈfɔːmd) *adj.* **1.** shapeless. **2.** immature.

un+for+tu+nate (ʌnˈfɔːtʃənɪt) *adj.* **1.** causing or attended by

---

un+ˈdyed *adj.*
un+ˈeat+a+ble *adj.*
un+ˈeat+en *adj.*
ˌun+e+co+ˈnom+ic *adj.*
ˌun+e+co+ˈnom+i+cal *adj.*
un+ˈed+i+ble *adj.*
un+ˈed+i+ˌfy+ing *adj.*
un+ˈed+it+ed *adj.*
un+ˈed+u+ca+ble *adj.*
un+ˈed+u+ˌcat+ed *adj.*
ˌun+e+ˈman+ci+ˌpat+ed *adj.*
ˌun+em+ˈbar+rassed *adj.*
ˌun+em+ˈbel+lished *adj.*
ˌun+e+ˈmo+tion+al *adj.*
ˌun+em+ˈphat+ic *adj.*
un+ˈemp+tied *adj.*
un+ˈend+ing *adj.*
ˌun+en+ˈdorsed *adj.*
ˌun+en+ˈdowed *adj.*
ˌun+en+ˈdur+a+ble *adj.*
ˌun+en+ˈforced *adj.*
ˌun+en+ˈgaged *adj.*
ˌun+en+ˈjoy+a+ble *adj.*
ˌun+en+ˈlight+ened *adj.*
un+ˈen+tered *adj.*
un+ˈen+ter+ˌpris+ing *adj.*
un+en+ter+ˈtain+ing *adj.*
ˌun+en+ˌthu+si+ˈas+tic *adj.*
un+ˈen+vi+a+ble *adj.*
ˌun+e+ˈquipped *adj.*
ˌun+es+ˈcap+a+ble *adj.*
ˌun+es+ˈcort+ed *adj.*
ˌun+es+ˈtab+lished *adj.*
un+ˈes+ti+ˌmat+ed *adj.*
un+ˈeth+i+cal *adj.*
ˌun+e+ˈvad+ed *adj.*
ˌun+ex+ˈag+ger+ˌat+ed *adj.*
ˌun+ex+ˈceed+ed *adj.*
ˌun+ex+ˈcelled *adj.*
ˌun+ex+ˈcused *adj.*
un+ˈex+e+ˌcut+ed *adj.*
un+ˈex+er+ˌcised *adj.*
ˌun+ex+ˈpe+ri+enced *adj.*
un+ˈex+pi+ˌat+ed *adj.*
ˌun+ex+ˈpired *adj.*
ˌun+ex+ˈplain+a+ble *adj.*
ˌun+ex+ˈplained *adj.*
ˌun+ex+ˈplic+it *adj.*
ˌun+ex+ˈploit+ed *adj.*
ˌun+ex+ˈplored *adj.*
ˌun+ex+ˈposed *adj.*
ˌun+ex+ˈpres+sive *adj.*
un+ˈex+pur+ˌgat+ed *adj.*
ˌun+ex+ˈtend+ed *adj.*
ˌun+ex+ˈtin+guished *adj.*
un+ˈfad+ing *adj.*
un+ˈfash+ion+a+ble *adj.*
un+ˈfath+omed *adj.*
ˌun+fa+ˈtigued *adj.*
un+ˈfa+voured *adj.*
un+ˈfea+si+ble *adj.*
un+ˈfea+tured *adj.*
un+ˈfed *adj.*
un+ˈfed+er+ˌat+ed *adj.*
un+ˈfeigned *adj.*
un+ˈfelt *adj.*
un+ˈfem+i+nine *adj.*
ˌun+fer+ˈment+ed *adj.*
un+ˈfer+ti+ˌlized *or*
un+ˈfer+ti+ˌlised *adj.*
un+ˈfilled *adj.*
un+ˈfil+tered *adj.*
un+ˈfired *adj.*
un+ˈfit+ting *adj.*
un+ˈflag+ging *adj.*
un+ˈflat+ter+ing *adj.*
un+ˈfla+voured *adj.*
ˌun+for+ˈbear+ing *adj.*
ˌun+for+ˈbid+den *adj.*
un+ˈforce+a+ble *adj.*
un+ˈforced *adj.*
ˌun+fore+ˈsee+a+ble *adj.*
ˌun+fore+ˈseen *adj.*
un+ˈfor+est+ed *adj.*
ˌun+fore+ˈtold *adj.*
ˌun+for+ˈgiv+a+ble *adj.*
ˌun+for+ˈgiv+en *adj.*
ˌun+for+ˈgiv+ing *adj.*
ˌun+for+ˈgot+ten *adj.*
un+ˈfor+mu+ˌlat+ed *adj.*
ˌun+for+ˈsak+en *adj.*
ˌun+forth+ˈcom+ing *adj.*

misfortune. **2.** unlucky, unsuccessful, or unhappy: *an unfortunate character.* **3.** regrettable or unsuitable: *an unfortunate speech.* ~*n.* **4.** an unlucky person. —**un+'for+tu+nate+ly** *adv.* —**un+'for+tu+nate+ness** *n.*

un+found+ed (ʌn'faʊndɪd) *adj.* **1.** (of ideas, allegations, etc.) baseless; groundless. **2.** not yet founded or established. —**un+'found+ed+ly** *adv.* —**un+'found+ed+ness** *n.*

un+freeze (ʌn'fri:z) *vb.* **+freez·es, +freez+ing, +froze, +fro+zen. 1.** to thaw or cause to thaw. **2.** (*tr.*) to relax governmental restrictions on (wages, prices, credit, etc.) or on the manufacture or sale of (goods, etc.).

un+friend+ed (ʌn'frɛndɪd) *adj. Now rare.* without a friend or friends; friendless.

un+friend+ly (ʌn'frɛndlɪ) *adj.* **+li+er, +li+est. 1.** not friendly; hostile. **2.** unfavourable or disagreeable. ~*adv.* **3.** *Rare.* in an unfriendly manner. —**un+'friend+li+ness** *n.*

un+frock (ʌn'frɒk) *vb.* (*tr.*) to deprive (a person in holy orders) of ecclesiastical status.

un+fruit+ful (ʌn'fru:tfʊl) *adj.* **1.** barren, unproductive, or unprofitable. **2.** failing to produce or develop into fruit. —**un+'fruit+ful+ly** *adv.* —**un+'fruit+ful+ness** *n.*

un+funded debt (ʌn'fʌndɪd) *n.* a short-term floating debt not represented by bonds.

un+furl (ʌn'fɜ:l) *vb.* to unroll, unfold, or spread out or be unrolled, unfolded, or spread out from a furled state.

un+gain+ly (ʌn'geɪnlɪ) *adj.* **+li+er, +li+est. 1.** lacking grace when moving. **2.** difficult to move or use; unwieldy. **3.** *Rare.* crude or coarse. ~*adv.* **4.** *Rare.* clumsily. —**un+'gain+li+ness** *n.*

Un·ga·ret·ti (*Italian* ˌuŋga'retti) *n.* **Giu·sep·pe** (dʒu'zɛppe). 1888–1970, Italian poet, best known for his collection of war poems *Allegria di naufragi* (1919).

Un+ga+va (ʊŋ'geɪvə, -'gɑ:-) *n.* a sparsely inhabited region of NE Canada, in N Quebec east of Hudson Bay: rich mineral resources. Area: 911 110 sq. km (351 780 sq. miles).

un+god+ly (ʌn'gɒdlɪ) *adj.* **+li+er, +li+est. 1. a.** wicked; sinful. **b.** (*as collective n.* preceded by *the*): *the ungodly.* **2.** *Informal.* unseemly; outrageous (esp. in the phrase **an ungodly hour**). —**un+'god+li+ness** *n.*

un+got+ten (ʌn'gɒtᵊn) *adj. Archaic.* not obtained or won.

un+gov+ern+a·ble (ʌn'gʌvənəbᵊl) *adj.* not able to be disciplined, restrained, etc.: *an ungovernable temper.* —**un+'gov+ern+a·ble+ness** *n.* —**un+'gov+ern+a·bly** *adv.*

un+grate+ful (ʌn'greɪtfʊl) *adj.* **1.** not grateful or thankful. **2.** unrewarding or unpleasant; thankless. **3.** (of land) failing to increase fertility in response to cultivation. —**un+'grate+ful+ly** *adv.* —**un+'grate+ful+ness** *n.*

un+grudg+ing (ʌn'grʌdʒɪŋ) *adj.* liberal; unstinted; willing: *ungrudging support.* —**un+'grudg+ing+ly** *adv.*

un+gual ('ʌŋgwəl) *or* **un+gu+lar** ('ʌŋgjʊlə) *adj.* **1.** of, relating to, or affecting the fingernails or toenails. **2.** of or relating to an unguis. [C19: from Latin *unguis* nail, claw]

un+guard+ed (ʌn'gɑ:dɪd) *adj.* **1.** unprotected; vulnerable. **2.** guileless; open; frank. **3.** incautious or careless. —**un+'guard+ed+ly** *adv.* —**un+'guard+ed+ness** *n.*

un+guent ('ʌŋgwənt) *n.* a less common name for an **ointment.** [C15: from Latin *unguentum,* from *unguere* to anoint] —**'un+guen+tar·y** *adj.*

un+guic·u+late (ʌŋ'gwɪkjʊlɪt, -ˌleɪt) *adj.* **1.** (of mammals) having claws or nails. **2.** (of petals) having a clawlike base. ~*n.* **3.** an unguiculate mammal. [C19: from New Latin *unguiculātus,* from Latin *unguiculus,* diminutive of *unguis* nail, claw]

un+gui+nous ('ʌŋgwɪnəs) *adj. Obsolete.* fatty; greasy; oily. [C17: from Latin *unguinōsus* oily, from *unguin-, unguen* a fatty substance, from *unguere* to anoint, besmear]

un+guis ('ʌŋgwɪs) *n., pl.* **+gues** (-gwi:z). **1.** a nail, claw, or hoof, or the part of the digit giving rise to it. **2.** the clawlike base of certain petals. [C18: from Latin]

un+gu+la ('ʌŋgjʊlə) *n., pl.* **+lae** (-ˌli:). **1.** *Maths.* a truncated cone, cylinder, etc. **2.** a rare word for **hoof.** [C18: from Latin: hoof, from *unguis* nail] —**'un+gu+lar** *adj.*

un+gu+late ('ʌŋgjʊlɪt, -ˌleɪt) *n.* any of a large group of mammals all of which have hooves: divided into odd-toed ungulates (see **perissodactyl**) and even-toed ungulates (see **artiodactyl**). [C19: from Late Latin *ungulātus* having hooves, from UNGULA]

un+gu+li+grade ('ʌŋgjʊlɪˌgreɪd) *adj.* (of horses, etc.) walking on hooves. [C19: from Latin *ungula* hoof + -GRADE]

un+hair (ʌn'hɛə) *vb.* to remove the hair from (a hide).

un+hal+low (ʌn'hæləʊ) *vb.* (*tr.*) *Archaic.* to desecrate.

un+hal+lowed (ʌn'hæləʊd) *adj.* **1.** not consecrated or holy: *unhallowed ground.* **2.** sinful or profane.

un+hand (ʌn'hænd) *vb.* (*tr.*) *Archaic or literary.* to release from the grasp.

un+hap+py (ʌn'hæpɪ) *adj.* **+pi+er, +pi+est. 1.** not joyful; sad or depressed. **2.** unfortunate or wretched: *an unhappy fellow.* **3.** tactless or inappropriate: *an unhappy remark.* **4.** *Archaic.* unfavourable. —**un+'hap+pi+ly** *adv.* —**un+'hap+pi+ness** *n.*

un+har+ness (ʌn'hɑ:nɪs) *vb.* (*tr.*) **1.** to remove the harness from (a horse, etc.). **2.** *Archaic.* to remove the armour from.

un+health·y (ʌn'hɛlθɪ) *adj.* **+health·i·er, +health·i·est. 1.** characterized by ill-health; sick; unwell. **2.** characteristic of, conducive to, or resulting from ill-health: *an unhealthy complexion; an unhealthy climate.* **3.** morbid or unwholesome. **4.** *Informal.* dangerous; risky. —**un+'health·i+ly** *adv.* —**un+'health·i+ness** *n.*

un+heard (ʌn'hɜ:d) *adj.* **1.** not heard; not perceived by the ear. **2.** not listened to or granted a hearing: *his warning went unheard.* **3.** *Archaic.* unheard-of.

un·heard-of *adj.* **1.** previously unknown: *an unheard-of actress.* **2.** without precedent: *an unheard-of treatment.* **3.** highly offensive: *unheard-of behaviour.*

un+helm (ʌn'hɛlm) *vb.* to remove the helmet of.

un+hes·i+tat+ing (ʌn'hɛzɪˌteɪtɪŋ) *adj.* **1.** steadfast; unwavering: *unhesitating loyalty.* **2.** without hesitation; prompt. —**un+'hes·i+ˌtat+ing+ly** *adv.*

un+hinge (ʌn'hɪndʒ) *vb.* (*tr.*) **1.** to remove (a door, etc.) from its hinges. **2.** to derange or unbalance (a person, his mind, etc.). **3.** to disrupt or unsettle (a process or state of affairs). **4.** (usually foll. by *from*) to detach or dislodge.

un+ho+ly (ʌn'həʊlɪ) *adj.* **+li+er, +li+est. 1.** not holy or sacred. **2.** immoral or depraved. **3.** *Informal.* outrageous or unnatural: *an unholy alliance.* —**un+'ho+li+ness** *n.*

un+hook (ʌn'hʊk) *vb.* **1.** (*tr.*) to remove (something) from a hook. **2.** (*tr.*) to unfasten the hook of (a dress, etc.). **3.** (*intr.*) to become unfastened or be capable of unfastening: *the dress wouldn't unhook.*

un·hoped-for *adj.* (esp. of something pleasant) not anticipated; unexpected.

un+horse (ʌn'hɔ:s) *vb.* (*tr.*) **1.** (*usually passive*) to knock or throw from a horse. **2.** to overthrow or dislodge, as from a powerful position. **3.** *Now rare.* to unharness horses from (a carriage, etc.).

un+hou+seled (ʌn'haʊzəld) *adj. Archaic.* not having received the Eucharist. [C16: from *un-* + obsolete *housel* to administer the sacrament, from Old English *hūsl* (n.), *hūslian* (vb.), of unknown origin]

un+hur+ried (ʌn'hʌrɪd) *adj.* leisurely or deliberate: *an unhurried walk.* —**un+'hur+ried+ly** *adv.*

u·ni ('ju:nɪ) *n. Austral. informal.* short for **university.**

u·ni- *combining form.* consisting of, relating to, or having only one: *unilateral; unisexual.* [from Latin *ūnus* one]

U·ni+at ('ju:nɪˌæt) *or* **U·ni+ate** ('ju:nɪɪt, -ˌeɪt) *adj.* **1.** designating any of the Eastern Churches that retain their own liturgy but submit to papal authority. ~*n.* **2.** a member of one of these Churches. [C19: from Russian *uniyat,* from Polish *unja* union, from Late Latin *ūniō;* see UNION] —**'U·ni+at+ism** *n.*

u·ni+ax+i·al (ˌju:nɪ'æksɪəl) *adj.* **1.** (esp. of plants) having an unbranched main axis. **2.** (of a crystal) having only one direction along which double refraction of light does not occur. —**ˌu·ni+'ax+i·al+ly** *adv.*

u·ni+cam+er+al (ˌju:nɪ'kæmərəl) *adj.* of or characterized by a single legislative chamber. —**ˌu·ni+'cam+er+al+ism** *n.* —**ˌu·ni+'cam+er+al+ist** *n.* —**ˌu·ni+'cam+er+al+ly** *adv.*

UNICEF ('ju:nɪˌsɛf) *n. acronym for* United Nations Children's Fund (formerly, United Nations International Children's Emergency Fund): an agency of the United Nations that administers programmes to aid education and child and maternal health in developing countries.

u·ni+cel+lu+lar (ˌju:nɪ'sɛljʊlə) *adj.* (of organisms such as protozoans and certain algae) consisting of a single cell. —**ˌu·ni+ˌcel+lu+'lar+i·ty** *n.*

u·ni+col+our *or U.S.* **u·ni+col+or** (ˌju:nɪ'kʌlə) *adj.* of one colour; monochromatic.

u·ni+corn ('ju:nɪˌkɔ:n) *n.* **1.** an imaginary creature usually depicted as a white horse with one long spiralled horn growing from its forehead. **2.** *Old Testament.* a two-horned animal, thought to be either the rhinoceros or the aurochs: (Deuteronomy 33:17): mistranslation in the Authorized Version of the original Hebrew. [C13: from Old French *unicorne,* from Latin *ūnicornis* one-horned, from *ūnus* one + *cornu* a horn]

u·ni+cos+tate (ˌju:nɪ'kɒsteɪt) *adj. Biology.* having only one rib or riblike part: *unicostate leaves.*

u·ni+cy+cle ('ju:nɪˌsaɪkᵊl) *n.* a one-wheeled vehicle driven by

---

un+'for+ti+ˌfied *adj.*
un+'fought *adj.*
un+'found *adj.*
un+'framed *adj.*
un+fre+'quent+ed *adj.*
ˌun+ful+'filled *adj.*
un+'fun+ny *adj.*
un+'fur+nished *adj.*
un+'fur+rowed *adj.*
un+'gal+lant *adj.*
un+'gath+ered *adj.*
un+'gen+er+ous *adj.*
un+'gen+tle+man+ly *adj.*
un+'gift+ed *adj.*
un+'gird *vb.,* **+girds, +gird+ing, +gird+ed** *or* **+girt.**
un+'glazed *adj.*
un+'gov+erned *adj.*
un+'grace+ful *adj.*
un+'gra+cious *adj.*
un+'grad+ed *adj.*
ˌun+gram+'mat·i+cal *adj.*
un+'grat·i+ˌfy+ing *adj.*
un+'ground+ed *adj.*
un+'grudg+ing *adj.*
un+'guid+ed *adj.*
un+'hack+neyed *adj.*
un+'hailed *adj.*
un+'ham+pered *adj.*
un+'hand·i+ˌcapped *adj.*
un+'hard+ened *adj.*
un+'harmed *adj.*
un+'harm+ful *adj.*
ˌun+har+'mo+ni+ous *adj.*
ˌun+har+'mo+ni+ous+ly *adv.*
un+'har+rowed *adj.*
un+'har+vest+ed *adj.*
un+'hatched *adj.*
un+'healed *adj.*
un+'heat+ed *adj.*
un+'heed+ed *adj.*
un+'heed+ed+ly *adv.*
un+'heed+ful *adj.*
un+'heed+ing *adj.*
un+'helped *adj.*
un+'help+ful *adj.*
un+'her+ald+ed *adj.*
ˌun+he+'ro+ic *adj.*
un+'hewn *adj.*
un+'hin+dered *adj.*
un+'hitch *vb.*
un+'hon+oured *adj.*
un+'housed *adj.*
un+'hu+man *adj.*
un+'hurt *adj.*
ˌun+hy+'gien+ic *adj.*

pedals, esp. one used in a circus, etc. Also called: **monocycle.** —**ˈu·ni·ˌcy·clist** *n.*

u·ni·di·rec·tion·al (ˌjuːnɪdɪˈrɛkʃənᵊl, -daɪ-) *adj.* having, moving in, or operating in only one direction.

UNIDO (ˌjuːˈniːdəʊ) *n. acronym for* United Nations Industrial Development Organization.

u·nif·ic (juːˈnɪfɪk) *adj. Rare.* unifying; uniting.

un·i·fied field the·o·ry *n.* any theory capable of describing in one set of equations the properties of gravitational fields, electromagnetic fields, and strong and weak nuclear interactions. No satisfactory theory has yet been found.

u·ni·fi·lar (ˌjuːnɪˈfaɪlə) *adj. Rare.* composed of, having, or using only one wire, thread, filament, etc.

u·ni·fo·li·ate (ˌjuːnɪˈfəʊlɪɪt, -ˌeɪt) *adj.* having a single leaf or leaflike part.

u·ni·fo·li·o·late (ˌjuːnɪˈfəʊlɪəˌleɪt) *adj.* (of a compound leaf) having only one leaflet.

u·ni·form (ˈjuːnɪˌfɔːm) *n.* **1.** a prescribed identifying set of clothes for the members of an organization, such as soldiers or schoolchildren. **2.** a single set of such clothes. **3.** a characteristic feature or fashion of some class or group. ~*adj.* **4.** unchanging in form, quality, quantity, etc.; regular: *a uniform surface.* **5.** identical; alike or like: *a line of uniform toys.* ~*vb.* (*tr.*) **6.** to fit out (a body of soldiers, etc.) with uniforms. **7.** to make uniform. [C16: from Latin *ūniformis,* from *ūnus* one + *forma* shape] —**ˈu·ni·ˌform·ly** *adv.* —**ˈu·ni·ˌform·ness** *n.*

u·ni·form·i·tar·i·an (ˌjuːnɪˌfɔːmɪˈtɛərɪən) *adj.* **1.** of or relating to uniformitarianism. **2.** of, characterized by, or conforming to uniformity. ~*n.* **3.** a supporter of a theory of uniformity or of uniformitarianism.

u·ni·form·i·tar·i·an·ism (ˌjuːnɪˌfɔːmɪˈtɛərɪəˌnɪzəm) *n.* the concept that geological processes, such as earthquakes and erosion, also occurred in the past and were responsible for changes in the structure of the earth.

u·ni·form·i·ty (ˌjuːnɪˈfɔːmɪtɪ) *n., pl.* **·ties. 1.** a state or condition in which everything is regular, homogeneous, or unvarying. **2.** lack of diversity or variation, esp. to the point of boredom or monotony; sameness.

u·ni·fy (ˈjuːnɪˌfaɪ) *vb.* **·fies, ·fy·ing, ·fied.** to make or become one; unite. [C16: from Medieval Latin *ūnificāre,* from Latin *ūnus* one + *facere* to make] —**ˈu·ni·ˌfi·a·ble** *adj.* —**ˌu·ni·fi·ˈca·tion** *n.* —**ˈu·ni·ˌfi·er** *n.*

u·ni·ju·gate (ˌjuːnɪˈdʒuːgɪt, -ˌgeɪt) *adj.* (of a compound leaf) having only one pair of leaflets.

u·ni·lat·er·al (ˌjuːnɪˈlætərəl) *adj.* **1.** of, having, affecting, or occurring on only one side. **2.** involving or performed by only one party of several: *unilateral disarmament.* **3.** *Law.* (of contracts, obligations, etc.) made by, affecting, or binding one party only and not involving the other party in reciprocal obligations. **4.** *Botany.* having or designating parts situated or turned to one side of an axis. **5.** *Sociol.* relating to or tracing the line of descent through ancestors of one sex only. Compare **bilateral** (sense 5). **6.** *Phonetics.* denoting an (l) sound produced on one side of the tongue only. —**ˌu·ni·ˈlat·er·al·ism** *or* **ˌu·ni·ˌlat·er·ˈal·i·ty** *n.* —**ˌu·ni·ˈlat·er·al·ly** *adv.*

U·ni·lat·er·al Dec·lar·a·tion of In·de·pend·ence *n.* a declaration of independence made by a dependent state without the assent of the protecting state. Abbrev.: **U.D.I.**

un·i·lin·gual (ˌjuːnɪˈlɪŋgwəl) *adj.* of or having only one language.

un·i·lit·er·al (ˌjuːnɪˈlɪtərəl) *adj.* consisting of one letter.

u·ni·loc·u·lar (ˌjuːnɪˈlɒkjʊlə) *adj.* (esp. of a plant ovary or anther) having or consisting of a single chamber or cavity.

U·ni·mak Is·land (ˈjuːnɪˌmæk) *n.* an island in SW Alaska, in the Aleutian Islands. Length: 113 km (70 miles).

un·im·peach·a·ble (ˌʌnɪmˈpiːtʃəbᵊl) *adj.* unquestionable as to honesty, truth, etc. —**ˌun·im·ˌpeach·a·ˈbil·i·ty** *or* **ˌun·im·ˈpeach·a·ble·ness** *n.* —**ˌun·im·ˈpeach·a·bly** *adv.*

un·im·proved (ˌʌnɪmˈpruːvd) *adj.* **1.** not improved or made better. **2.** (of land) not cleared, drained, cultivated, etc. **3.** neglected; unused: *unimproved resources.*

un·in·cor·po·ra·ted (ˌʌnɪnˈkɔːpəˌreɪtɪd) *adj.* **1.** *Law.* lacking corporate status. **2.** not unified or included.

un·in·spired (ʌnɪnˈspaɪəd) *adj.* dull or ordinary; unimaginative: *an uninspired painting.*

un·in·tel·li·gent (ˌʌnɪnˈtɛlɪdʒənt) *adj.* **1.** lacking intelligence; stupid; foolish. **2.** not endowed with a mind or intelligence. —**ˌun·in·ˈtel·li·gence** *n.* —**ˌun·in·ˈtel·li·gent·ly** *adv.*

un·in·ter·est·ed (ʌnˈɪntrɪstɪd, -tərɪs-) *adj.* **1.** indifferent; unconcerned. **2.** having no personal stake or interest. —**un·ˈin·ter·est·ed·ly** *adv.* —**un·ˈin·ter·est·ed·ness** *n.*

un·ion (ˈjuːnjən) *n.* **1.** the condition of being united, the act of uniting, or a conjunction formed by such an act. **2.** an association, alliance, or confederation of individuals or groups for a common purpose, esp. political. **3.** agreement or harmony. **4.** short for **trade union. 5.** the act or state of marriage or sexual intercourse. **6.** a device on a flag representing union, such as another flag depicted in the top left corner. **7.** a device for coupling or linking parts, such as pipes. **8.** (*often cap.*) **a.** an association of students at a university or college formed to look after the students' interests, provide facilities for recreation, etc. **b.** the building or buildings housing the facilities of such an organization. **9.** Also called: **join.** *Maths.* a set containing all members of two given sets. Symbol: ∪, as in A ∪ B. **10.** (in 19th-century England) **a.** a number of parishes united for the administration of poor relief. **b.** a workhouse supported by such a combination. **11.** *Textiles.* a piece of cloth or fabric consisting of two different kinds of yarn. **12.** (*modifier*) of or related to a union, esp. a trade union. [C15: from Church Latin *ūniō* oneness, from Latin *ūnus* one]

Un·ion (ˈjuːnjən) *n.* **the. 1. a.** the U.S., esp. during the Civil War. **b.** (*as modifier*): *Union supporters.* **2.** *Brit.* **a.** the union of the English and Scottish crowns (1603–1707). **b.** the union of England and Scotland from 1707. **c.** the political union of Great Britain and Ireland (1801–1920). **d.** the union of Great Britain and Northern Ireland from 1920. **3.** short for the **Union of South Africa.**

un·ion card *n.* a membership card for a trade union.

un·ion cat·a·logue *n.* a catalogue listing every publication held at cooperating libraries.

un·ion·ism (ˈjuːnjəˌnɪzəm) *n.* **1.** the principles of trade unions. **2.** adherence to the principles of trade unions. **3.** the principle or theory of any union.

Un·ion·ism (ˈjuːnjəˌnɪzəm) *n.* (*sometimes not cap.*) the principles or adherence to the principles of Unionists.

un·ion·ist (ˈjuːnjənɪst) *n.* **1.** a supporter or advocate of unionism or union. **2.** a member of a trade union. ~*adj.* **3.** *Chiefly Brit.* of or relating to union or unionism, esp. trade unionism. —**ˌun·ion·ˈis·tic** *adj.*

Un·ion·ist (ˈjuːnjənɪst) *n.* **1.** a member or supporter of the Unionist Party. **2.** a supporter of the U.S. federal Union, esp. during the Civil War. **3.** (*sometimes not cap.*) (before 1920) a supporter of the union of all Ireland and Great Britain. ~*adj.* **4.** of, resembling, or relating to Unionists.

Un·ion·ist Par·ty *n.* (in Northern Ireland) formerly the major Protestant political party, closely identified with Union with Britain. It formed the Northern Ireland Government from 1920 to 1972.

un·ion·ize *or* **un·ion·ise** (ˈjuːnjəˌnaɪz) *vb.* **1.** to organize (workers) into a trade union. **2.** to join or cause to join a trade union. **3.** (*tr.*) to subject to the rules or codes of a trade union. —**ˌun·ion·i·ˈza·tion** *or* **ˌun·ion·i·ˈsa·tion** *n.*

Un·ion Jack *n.* **1.** Also called: **Union flag.** the national flag of Great Britain, being a composite design composed of St. George's Cross (England), Saint Andrew's Cross (Scotland), and Saint Patrick's Cross (Ireland). **2.** (*often not caps.*) a national flag flown at the jackstaff of a vessel.

Un·ion of South Af·ri·ca *n.* the former name (1910–61) of the (Republic of) **South Africa.**

Un·ion of So·vi·et So·cial·ist Re·pub·lics *n.* the official name of the **Soviet Union.**

un·ion shop *n.* an establishment whose employment policy is governed by a contract between employer and a trade union permitting the employment of nonunion labour only on the condition that such labour joins the union within a specified time period. Compare **open shop** (sense 1), **closed shop.**

un·ion ter·ri·to·ry *n.* one of the 9 administrative territories that, with 21 states, make up the Indian Republic.

u·nip·ar·ous (juːˈnɪpərəs) *adj.* **1.** (of certain animals) producing a single offspring at each birth. **2.** (of a woman) having borne only one child. **3.** *Botany.* (of a cyme) giving rise to only one branch from each flowering stem.

u·ni·per·son·al (ˌjuːnɪˈpɜːsənᵊl) *adj.* **1.** existing in the form of only one person or being. Compare **tripersonal. 2.** (of a verb) existing or used in only one person; for example, *rain* is used only in the third person. —**ˌu·ni·ˌper·son·ˈal·i·ty** *n.*

u·ni·pla·nar (ˌjuːnɪˈpleɪnə) *adj.* situated in one plane.

u·ni·pod (ˈjuːnɪˌpɒd) *n.* a one-legged support, as for a camera.

---

un·ˈhy·phen·ˌat·ed *adj.*
ˌun·i·ˈde·al *adj.*
ˌun·i·ˈden·ti·ˌfi·a·ble *adj.*
ˌun·i·ˈden·ti·ˌfied *adj.*
ˌun·id·i·o·ˈmat·ic *adj.*
ˌun·id·i·o·ˈmat·i·cal·ly *adv.*
ˌun·il·ˈlu·mi·ˌnat·ed *adj.*
ˌun·il·ˈlu·mi·ˌnat·ing *adj.*
un·ˈil·lus·ˌtrat·ed *adj.*
un·ˈil·lus·ˌtra·tive *adj.*
ˌun·im·ˈag·i·na·ble *adj.*
ˌun·im·ˈag·i·na·bly *adv.*
ˌun·im·ˈag·i·na·tive *adj.*
ˌun·im·ˈag·i·na·tive·ly *adv.*
ˌun·im·ˈag·ined *adj.*
ˌun·im·ˈbued *adj.*
ˌun·im·ˈpaired *adj.*
ˌun·im·ˈpas·sioned *adj.*
ˌun·im·ˈped·ed *adj.*
ˌun·im·ˈpor·tant *adj.*
ˌun·im·ˈpos·ing *adj.*
ˌun·im·ˈpressed *adj.*
ˌun·im·ˈpres·sion·a·ble *adj.*
ˌun·im·ˈpres·sive *adj.*
ˌun·im·ˈpres·sive·ly *adv.*
ˌun·in·ˈclosed *adj.*
un·ˈin·cu·ˌbat·ed *adj.*
ˌun·in·ˈcum·bered *adj.*
ˌun·in·ˈdem·ni·ˌfied *adj.*
ˌun·in·ˈdorsed *adj.*
ˌun·in·ˈfect·ed *adj.*
ˌun·in·ˈflam·ma·ble *adj.*
ˌun·in·ˈflect·ed *adj.*
un·ˈin·flu·enced *adj.*
ˌun·in·flu·ˈen·tial *adj.*
ˌun·in·ˈform·a·tive *adj.*
ˌun·in·ˈformed *adj.*
ˌun·in·ˈhab·it·a·ble *adj.*
ˌun·in·ˈhab·it·ed *adj.*
ˌun·in·ˈhib·it·ed *adj.*
ˌun·in·ˈi·ti·ˌat·ed *adj.*
un·ˈin·jured *adj.*
ˌun·in·ˈquis·i·tive *adj.*
ˌun·in·ˈspir·ing *adj.*
ˌun·in·ˈspir·ing·ly *adv.*
ˌun·in·ˈstruct·ed *adj.*
ˌun·in·ˈstruc·tive *adj.*
ˌun·in·ˈsur·a·ble *adj.*
ˌun·in·ˈsured *adj.*
ˌun·in·tel·ˈlec·tu·al *adj.*
ˌun·in·ˈtel·li·gi·ble *adj.*
ˌun·in·ˈtend·ed *adj.*
ˌun·in·ˈtend·ed·ly *adv.*
ˌun·in·ˈten·tion·al *adj.*
ˌun·in·ˈten·tion·al·ly *adv.*
un·ˈin·ter·est·ing *adj.*
ˌun·in·ter·ˈrupt·ed *adj.*
ˌun·in·ˈvent·ive *adj.*
ˌun·in·ˈvest·ed *adj.*
ˌun·in·ˈves·ti·ˌgat·ed *adj.*
ˌun·in·ˈvit·ed *adj.*
ˌun·in·ˈvit·ing *adj.*
ˌun·in·ˈvit·ing·ly *adv.*
ˌun·in·ˈvoked *adj.*
ˌun·in·ˈvolved *adj.*
un·ˈi·roned *adj.*
un·ˈjoined *adj.*
un·ˈjoint·ed *adj.*

u·ni·po·lar (ˌjuːnɪˈpəʊlə) *adj.* **1.** of, concerned with, or having a single magnetic or electric pole. **2.** (of a nerve cell) having a single process. **3.** (of a transistor) utilizing charge carriers of one polarity only, as in a field-effect transistor. ~Compare **bipolar.** —**u·ni·po·lar·i·ty** (ˌjuːnɪpɒˈlærɪtɪ) *n.*

u·nique (juːˈniːk) *adj.* **1.** being the only one of a particular type; single; sole. **2.** without equal or like; unparalleled. **3.** *Informal.* very remarkable or unusual. **4.** *Maths.* leading to only one result: *the sum of two integers is unique.* [C17: via French from Latin *ūnicus* unparalleled, from *ūnus* one] —**u·ˈnique·ly** *adv.* —**u·ˈnique·ness** *n.*

Usage. Careful users of English avoid the use of comparatives or intensifiers where absolute states are concerned: *that is very exceptional* (not *very unique*); *this one comes nearer to perfection* (not *is more perfect*).

u·ni·ra·mous (ˌjuːnɪˈreɪməs) *adj.* (esp. of the appendages of crustaceans) consisting of a single branch; undivided.

u·ni·sep·tate (ˌjuːnɪˈsɛpteɪt) *adj. Biology.* having only one partition or septum: *a uniseptate fruit.*

un·i·se·ri·al (ˌjuːnɪˈsɪərɪəl) adj. in or relating to a single series.

u·ni·sex (ˈjuːnɪˌsɛks) *adj.* of or relating to clothing, a hair style, etc., that can be worn by either sex. [C20: from UNI- + SEX]

u·ni·sex·u·al (ˌjuːnɪˈsɛksjʊəl) *adj.* **1.** of or relating to one sex only. **2.** (of some organisms) having either male or female reproductive organs but not both. —**ˌu·ni·ˌsex·u·ˈal·i·ty** *n.* —**ˌu·ni·ˈsex·u·al·ly** *adv.*

u·ni·son (ˈjuːnɪsᵊn, -zᵊn) *n.* **1.** *Music.* **a.** the interval between two notes of identical pitch. **b.** (*modifier*) played or sung at the same pitch: *unison singing.* **2.** complete agreement; harmony (esp. in the phrase **in unison**). [C16: from Late Latin *ūnisonus*, from UNI- + *sonus* sound] —**u·ˈnis·o·nous, u·ˈnis·o·nal,** *or* **u·ˈnis·o·nant** *adj.*

u·nit (ˈjuːnɪt) *n.* **1.** a single undivided entity or whole. **2.** any group or individual, esp. when regarded as a basic element of a larger whole. **3.** a mechanical part or integrated assembly of parts that performs a subsidiary function: *a filter unit.* **4.** a complete system, apparatus, or establishment that performs a specific function: *a production unit.* **5. a.** a subdivision of a larger military formation. **b.** an autonomous vehicle or piece of military equipment, such as a warship, tank, lorry, etc. **6.** Also called: **unit of measurement.** a standard amount of a physical quantity, such as length, mass, energy, etc., specified multiples of which are used to express magnitudes of that physical quantity: *the second is a unit of time.* **7.** the amount of a drug, vaccine, etc., needed to produce a particular effect. **8.** Also called: **unit's place.** the digit or position immediately to the left of the decimal point. **9.** (*modifier*) having or relating to a value of one: *a unit vector.* [C16: back formation from UNITY, perhaps on the model of *digit*]

Unit. *abbrev. for* Unitarian.

u·ni·tar·i·an (ˌjuːnɪˈtɛərɪən) *n.* **1.** a supporter of unity or centralization. ~*adj.* **2.** of or relating to unity or centralization. **3.** another word for **unitary.**

U·ni·tar·i·an (ˌjuːnɪˈtɛərɪən) *n.* **1.** *Theol.* a person who believes that God is one being and rejects the doctrine of the Trinity. **2.** *Ecclesiast.* an upholder of Unitarianism, esp. a member of the Church (**Unitarian Church**) that embodies this system of belief. ~*adj.* **3.** of or relating to Unitarians or Unitarianism.

u·ni·tar·i·an·ism (ˌjuːnɪˈtɛərɪəˌnɪzəm) *n.* any unitary system, esp. of government.

U·ni·tar·i·an·ism (ˌjuːnɪˈtɛərɪəˌnɪzəm) *n.* a system of Christian belief that maintains the unipersonality of God, rejects the Trinity and the divinity of Christ, and takes reason, conscience, and character as the criteria of belief and practice.

u·ni·tar·y (ˈjuːnɪtərɪ, -trɪ) *adj.* **1.** of a unit or units. **2.** based on or characterized by unity. **3.** individual; whole. **4.** of or relating to a system of government in which all governing authority is held by the central government. Compare **federal.**

u·ni·tar·y ma·trix *n. Maths.* a square matrix that is the inverse of its Hermitian conjugate.

u·nit cell *n. Crystallog.* the smallest group of atoms, ions, or molecules that is characteristic of a particular crystal lattice.

u·nit char·ac·ter *n. Genetics.* a character inherited as a single unit and dependent on a single gene.

u·nite[1] (juːˈnaɪt) *vb.* **1.** to make or become an integrated whole or a unity; combine. **2.** to join, unify or be unified in purpose, action, beliefs, etc. **3.** to enter or cause to enter into an association or alliance. **4.** to adhere or cause to adhere; fuse. **5.** (*tr.*) to possess or display (qualities) in combination or at the same time: *he united charm with severity.* **6.** *Archaic.* to join or become joined in marriage. [C15: from Late Latin *ūnīre*, from *ūnus* one] —**u·ˈnit·er** *n.*

u·nite[2] (ˈjuːnaɪt, juːˈnaɪt) *n.* an English gold coin minted in the Stuart period, originally worth 20 shillings. [C17: from obsolete *unite* joined, alluding to the union of England and Scotland (1603)]

u·nit·ed (juːˈnaɪtɪd) *adj.* **1.** produced by two or more persons or things in combination or from their union or amalgamation: *a united effort.* **2.** in agreement. **3.** in association or alliance. —**u·ˈnit·ed·ly** *adv.* —**u·ˈnit·ed·ness** *n.*

U·nit·ed Ar·ab E·mir·ates *pl. n.* a group of seven emirates in SW Asia, on the Persian Gulf: consists of Abu Dhabi, Dubai, Sharjah, Ajman, Umm al Qaiwain, Ras el Khaimah, and Fujairah; a former British protectorate; became fully independent in 1971; consists mostly of flat desert, with mountains in the east; rich petroleum resources. Language: Arabic. Religion: Muslim. Currency: dirham. Capital: Abu Dhabi. Pop.: 220 000 (1975 UN est.). Area: 83 600 sq. km (32 300 sq. miles). Former name: **Trucial States.**

U·nit·ed Ar·ab Re·pub·lic *n.* the official name (1958–71) of **Egypt.**

U·nit·ed Ar·ab States *n.* a federation (1958–61) between the United Arab Republic and Yemen.

U·nit·ed Church of Christ *n.* a U.S. Protestant denomination formed in 1957 from the Evangelical and Reformed Church and the Congregational Christian Church.

U·nit·ed Em·pire Loy·al·ist *n. Canadian history.* any of the American colonists who settled in Canada during or after the War of American Independence because of loyalty to the British Crown. Abbrev.: **U.E.L.**

U·nit·ed King·dom *n.* a kingdom of NW Europe, consisting chiefly of the island of Great Britain together with Northern Ireland. It became the **United Kingdom of Great Britain and Northern Ireland** in 1922, after the rest of Ireland became autonomous as the Irish Free State. Primarily it is a trading nation, the chief exports being manufactured goods; joined the Common Market in January 1973. Languages: English, with Gaelic and Welsh minority languages. Religion: Christian. Currency: pound sterling. Capital: London. Pop.: 55 521 534 (1971). Area: 244 014 sq. km (94 214 sq. miles). See also **Great Britain.**

U·nit·ed Na·tions *n.* **1.** (in World War II) a coalition of 26 nations that signed a joint declaration in Jan. 1942, pledging their full resources to defeating the Axis powers. **2.** an international organization of independent states, with its headquarters in New York City, that was formed in 1945 to promote peace and international cooperation and security. Abbrev.: **UN.**

U·nit·ed Par·ty *n.* (in South Africa) formerly, the major opposition party, founded by General Smuts in 1934: disbanded 1977: the official Opposition in Parliament (1948-77). See also **Nationalist Party, Progressive Party.**

U·nit·ed Prov·inc·es *n.* **1.** a Dutch republic (1581–1795) formed by the union of the seven northern provinces of the Netherlands, which were in revolt against their suzerain, Philip II of Spain. **2.** short for **United Provinces of Agra and Oudh:** the former name of **Uttar Pradesh.**

U·nit·ed Re·formed Church *n.* (in England) a Protestant denomination formed from the union of the Presbyterian and Congregational churches in 1972.

U·nit·ed States of A·mer·i·ca *n.* a federal republic in North America consisting of 50 states: colonized principally by the English and French in the 17th century, the native Indians being gradually displaced; 13 colonies under English rule made the Declaration of Independence in 1776 and became the United States after the War of American Independence. The northern states defeated the South in the Civil War (1861–65). It consists generally of the Rocky Mountains in the west, the Great Plains in the centre, the Appalachians in the east, deserts in the southwest, and coastal lowlands and swamps in the southeast. Language: predominantly English. Religion: Christian majority. Currency: dollar. Capital: Washington, D.C. Pop.: 216 450 000 (1977 est.). Area: 9 363 405 sq. km (3 615 210 sq. miles). Often shortened to: **United States.** Abbrevs.: **U.S., U.S.A.**

u·nit fac·tor *n. Genetics.* the gene responsible for the inheritance of a unit character.

u·ni·tive (ˈjuːnɪtɪv) *adj.* **1.** tending to unite or capable of uniting. **2.** characterized by unity. —**ˈu·ni·tive·ly** *adv.*

u·nit mag·net·ic pole *n.* the strength of a magnetic pole that will repel a similar pole 1 centimetre distant from it, in a vacuum, with a force of 1 dyne.

u·nit of ac·count *n. Chiefly Brit.* a monetary denomination used for keeping accounts, making comparisons, etc., and not necessarily corresponding to any actual currency denomination. Also (esp. U.S.): **money of account.**

u·nit price *n.* a price for foodstuffs, etc., stated or shown as the cost per unit, as per pound, per kilogram, per dozen, etc.

u·nit pro·cess *n. Chemical engineering.* any of a number of standard operations, such as filtration or distillation, that are widely used in various chemical industries.

u·nit trust *n. Brit.* an investment trust that issues units for public sale, the holders of which are creditors and not shareholders with their interests represented by a trust company independent of the issuing agency.

u·ni·ty (ˈjuːnɪtɪ) *n., pl.* **·ties.** **1.** the state or quality of being one; oneness. **2.** the act, state, or quality of forming a whole from separate parts. **3.** something whole or complete that is composed of separate parts. **4.** mutual agreement; harmony or concord: *the participants were no longer in unity.* **5.** uniformity or constancy: *unity of purpose.* **6.** *Maths.* **a.** the number or numeral one. **b.** a quantity assuming the value of one: *the area of the triangle was regarded as unity.* **c.** the element of a set producing no change in a number following multiplication. **7.** the arrangement of the elements in a work of art in accordance with a single overall design or purpose. **8.** any one of the three principles of dramatic structure deriving from Aristotle's *Poetics* by which the action of a play should be limited to a single plot (unity of action), a single location (unity of place), and the events of a single day (unity of time). [C13: from Old French *unité*, from Latin *ūnitās*, from *ūnus* one]

u·nity of in·ter·est *n. Property law.* the equal interest in property held by joint tenants.

univ. *abbrev. for:* **1.** universal(ly). **2.** university.

Univ. *abbrev. for:* **1.** Universalist. **2.** University.

u·ni·va·lent (ˌjuːnɪˈveɪlənt, juːˈnɪvələnt) *adj.* **1.** (of a chromosome during meiosis) not paired with its homologue. **2.** *Chem.* another word for **monovalent.** —**ˌu·ni·ˈva·len·cy** *n.*

u·ni·valve (ˈjuːnɪˌvælv) *Zoology.* ~*adj.* **1.** relating to, designating, or possessing a mollusc shell that consists of a single piece (valve). ~*n.* **2.** a gastropod mollusc or its shell.

u·ni·ver·sal (ˌjuːnɪˈvɜːsᵊl) *adj.* **1.** of, relating to, or typical of the whole of mankind or of nature. **2.** common to, involving, or proceeding from all in a particular group. **3.** applicable to or affecting many individuals, conditions, or cases; general. **4.** existing or prevailing everywhere. **5.** applicable to or occurring throughout or relating to the universe; cosmic: *a universal constant.* **6.** (esp. of a language) capable of being used and understood by all. **7.** embracing or versed in many fields of knowledge, activity, interest, etc. **8.** *Machinery.* designed or adapted for a range of sizes, fittings, or uses. **9.** *Logic.* (of a proposition) affirming or denying something about every member of a class of objects, as in *all men are wicked.* Compare **particular** (sense 6). **10.** *Archaic.* entire; whole. ~*n.* **11.** *Philosophy.* **a.** a general term or concept or the type such a term signifies; a Platonic idea or Aristotelian form. **b.** a metaphysical entity that remains constant throughout a series of changes or changing relations. **12.** *Logic.* a universal proposition. **13.** a characteristic common to every member of a particular culture or to every human being. **14.** short for **universal joint.** —ˌ**u·ni·ˈver·sal·ness** *n.*

u·ni·ver·sal class *or* **set** *n.* (in Boolean algebra) the class containing all points and including all other classes.

u·ni·ver·sal do·nor *n.* a person who has blood of group O and whose blood may be safely transfused to persons with most other blood types.

u·ni·ver·sal·ism (ˌjuːnɪˈvɜːsəˌlɪzəm) *n.* **1.** a universal feature or characteristic. **2.** another word for **universality.**

U·ni·ver·sal·ism (ˌjuːnɪˈvɜːsəˌlɪzəm) *n. Theol.* a system of religious beliefs maintaining that all men are predestined for salvation. —ˌ**U·ni·ˈver·sal·ist** *n., adj.*

u·ni·ver·sal·ist (ˌjuːnɪˈvɜːsəlɪst) *n.* **1.** a person who has a wide range of interests, knowledge, activities, etc. ~*adj.* **2.** characterized by universality. —ˌ**u·ni·ˌver·sal·ˈis·tic** *adj.*

u·ni·ver·sal·i·ty (ˌjuːnɪvɜːˈsælɪtɪ) *n., pl.* **·ties.** the state or quality of being universal.

u·ni·ver·sal·ize *or* **u·ni·ver·sal·ise** (ˌjuːnɪˈvɜːsəˌlaɪz) *vb.* (*tr.*) to make universal. —ˌ**u·ni·ˌver·sal·i·ˈza·tion** *or* ˌ**u·ni·ˌver·sal·i·ˈsa·tion** *n.*

u·ni·ver·sal joint *or* **coup·ling** *n.* a form of coupling between two rotating shafts allowing freedom of movement in all directions.

u·ni·ver·sal·ly (ˌjuːnɪˈvɜːsəlɪ) *adv.* everywhere or in every case; without exception: *this principle applies universally.*

u·ni·ver·sal mo·tor *n.* an electric motor capable of working on either direct current or single-phase alternating current at approximately the same speed and output.

U·ni·ver·sal Soul *or* **Spir·it** *n. Hinduism.* Brahman in its aspect as the sacred syllable Om, the eternal and spiritual principle that permeates the universe.

u·ni·ver·sal time *n.* another name for **Greenwich Mean Time.**

u·ni·verse (ˈjuːnɪˌvɜːs) *n.* **1.** *Astronomy.* the aggregate of all existing matter, energy, and space. **2.** human beings collectively. **3.** a province or sphere of thought or activity. **4.** *Statistics.* another word for **population** (sense 7). [C16: from French *univers,* from Latin *ūniversum* the whole world, from *ūniversus* all together, from UNI- + *vertere* to turn]

u·ni·verse of dis·course *n. Logic.* the complete range of objects, events, attributes, relations, ideas, etc., that are expressed, assumed, or implied in a discussion.

u·ni·ver·si·ty (ˌjuːnɪˈvɜːsɪtɪ) *n., pl.* **·ties.** **1.** an institution of higher education having authority to award bachelors' and higher degrees, usually having research facilities. **2.** the buildings, members, staff, or campus of a university. [C14: from Old French *universite,* from Medieval Latin *universitās* group of scholars, from Late Latin: guild, society, body of men, from Latin: whole, totality, universe]

u·ni·vo·cal (ˌjuːnɪˈvəʊkᵊl) *adj.* **1.** unambiguous or unmistakable. ~*n.* **2.** a word or term that has only one meaning. —ˌ**u·ni·ˈvo·cal·ly** *adv.*

un·just (ʌnˈdʒʌst) *adj.* not in accordance with accepted standards of fairness or justice; unfair. —**un·ˈjust·ly** *adv.* —**un·ˈjust·ness** *n.*

un·kempt (ʌnˈkɛmpt) *adj.* **1.** (of the hair) uncombed; dishevelled. **2.** ungroomed; slovenly: *unkempt appearance.* **3.** *Archaic.* crude or coarse. [Old English *uncembed;* from UN-¹ + *cembed,* past participle of *cemban* to COMB; related to Old Saxon *kembian,* Old High German *kemben* to comb] —**un·ˈkempt·ly** *adv.* —**un·ˈkempt·ness** *n.*

un·kenned (ʌnˈkɛnd) *adj. Northern Brit. dialect.* unknown.

un·ken·nel (ʌnˈkɛnᵊl) *vb.* **·nels, ·nel·ling, ·nelled** *or U.S.* **·nels, ·nel·ing, ·neled.** (*tr.*) **1.** to release from a kennel. **2.** to drive from a hole or lair. **3.** *Rare.* to bring to light.

un·kind (ʌnˈkaɪnd) *adj.* **1.** lacking kindness; unsympathetic or cruel. **2.** *Archaic or Brit. dialect.* **a.** (of weather) unpleasant. **b.** (of soil) hard to cultivate. —**un·ˈkind·ly** *adv.* —**un·ˈkind·ness** *n.*

un·knit (ʌnˈnɪt) *vb.* **·knits, ·knit·ting, ·knit·ted** *or* **·knit.** **1.** to make or become undone, untied, or unravelled. **2.** (*tr.*) to loosen, weaken, or destroy: *to unknit an alliance.* **3.** (*tr.*) *Rare.* to smooth out (a wrinkled brow).

un·know·a·ble (ʌnˈnəʊəbᵊl) *adj.* **1.** incapable of being known or understood. **2. a.** beyond human understanding. **b.** (*as n.*): *the unknowable.* —**un·ˈknow·a·ble·ness** *or* **un·ˌknow·a·ˈbil·i·ty** *n.* —**un·ˈknow·a·bly** *adv.*

Un·know·a·ble (ʌnˈnəʊəbᵊl) *n.* **the.** *Philosophy.* the ultimate reality that underlies all phenomena but cannot be known.

un·know·ing (ʌnˈnəʊɪŋ) *adj.* **1.** not knowing; ignorant. **2.** (*postpositive;* often foll. by *of*) without knowledge or unaware (of). —**un·ˈknow·ing·ly** *adv.*

un·known (ʌnˈnəʊn) *adj.* **1.** not known, understood, or recognized. **2.** not established, identified, or discovered: *an unknown island.* **3.** not famous; undistinguished: *some unknown artist.* ~*n.* **4.** an unknown person, quantity, or thing. **5.** *Maths.* a variable whose values are solutions of a conditional equation. **6. unknown quantity.** a person or thing whose action, effect, etc., is unknown or unpredictable. —**un·ˈknown·ness** *n.*

Un·known Sol·dier *or* **War·ri·or** *n.* (in various countries) an unidentified soldier who has died in battle and for whom a tomb is established as a memorial to other unidentified dead of the nation's armed forces.

un·lace (ʌnˈleɪs) *vb.* (*tr.*) **1.** to loosen or undo the lacing of (shoes, etc.). **2.** to unfasten or remove garments, etc., of (oneself or another) by or as if by undoing lacing.

un·lade (ʌnˈleɪd) *vb.* a less common word for **unload.**

un·lash (ʌnˈlæʃ) *vb.* (*tr.*) to untie or unfasten.

un·latch (ʌnˈlætʃ) *vb.* to open or unfasten or come open or unfastened by the lifting or release of a latch.

un·law·ful (ʌnˈlɔːfʊl) *adj.* **1.** illegal. **2.** illicit; immoral: *unlawful love.* **3.** an archaic word for **illegitimate.** —**un·ˈlaw·ful·ly** *adv.* —**un·ˈlaw·ful·ness** *n.*

un·law·ful as·sem·bly *n. Law.* a meeting of three or more people with the intent of carrying out any unlawful purpose.

un·lay (ʌnˈleɪ) *vb.* **·lays, ·lay·ing, ·laid.** (*tr.*) to untwist (a rope or cable) to separate its strands.

un·lead (ʌnˈlɛd) *vb.* (*tr.*) **1.** to strip off lead. **2.** *Printing.* to remove the leads or spaces from between (lines of type).

un·lead·ed (ʌnˈlɛdɪd) *adj.* **1.** not covered or weighted with lead. **2.** *Printing.* (of lines of type, etc.) not spaced or separated with leads; solid.

un·learn (ʌnˈlɜːn) *vb.* **·learns, ·learn·ing, ·learnt** *or* **·learned** (-ˈlɜːnd). to try to forget (something learnt) or to discard (accumulated knowledge).

un·learn·ed (ʌnˈlɜːnɪd) *adj.* ignorant or untaught. —**un·ˈlearn·ed·ly** *adv.*

un·learnt (ʌnˈlɜːnt) *or* **un·learned** (ʌnˈlɜːnd) *adj.* **1.** known without being consciously learnt. **2.** not learnt or taken notice of: *unlearnt lessons.*

un·leash (ʌnˈliːʃ) *vb.* (*tr.*) **1.** to release from or as if from a leash. **2.** to free from restraint or control.

un·leav·ened (ʌnˈlɛvənd) *adj.* (of bread, biscuits, etc.) made from a dough containing no yeast or leavening.

un·less (ʌnˈlɛs) *conj.* **1.** (*subordinating*) except under the circumstances that; except on the condition that: *they'll sell it unless he hears otherwise.* ~*prep.* **2.** *Rare.* except. [C14: *onlesse,* from ON + *lesse* LESS; compare French *à moins que,* literally: at less than]

un·let·tered (ʌnˈlɛtəd) *adj.* **1.** uneducated; illiterate. **2.** not marked with letters: *an unlettered tombstone.*

un·li·censed (ʌnˈlaɪsənst) *adj.* **1.** having no licence: *an unlicensed restaurant.* **2.** without permission; unauthorized. **3.** unrestrained or lawless.

un·like (ʌnˈlaɪk) *adj.* **1.** not alike; dissimilar or unequal; different. **2.** *Archaic or northern Brit. dialect.* unlikely. ~*prep.* **3.** not like; not typical of: *unlike his father he lacks intelligence.* —**un·ˈlike·ness** *n.*

un·like·ly (ʌnˈlaɪklɪ) *adj.* not likely; improbable. —**un·ˈlike·li·ness** *or* **un·ˈlike·li·hood** *n.*

un·lim·ber (ʌnˈlɪmbə) *vb.* **1.** (*tr.*) to disengage (a gun) from its limber. **2.** to prepare (something) for use.

un·lim·it·ed (ʌnˈlɪmɪtɪd) *adj.* **1.** without limits or bounds: *unlimited knowledge.* **2.** not restricted, limited, or qualified: *unlimited power.* **3.** *Finance, Brit.* **a.** (of liability) not restricted to any unpaid portion of nominal capital invested in a business. **b.** (of a business enterprise) having owners with such unlimited liability. —**un·ˈlim·it·ed·ly** *adv.* —**un·ˈlim·it·ed·ness** *n.*

un·list·ed (ʌnˈlɪstɪd) *adj.* **1.** not entered on a list. **2.** *U.S.* (of a telephone number or telephone subscriber) not listed in a telephone directory. Brit. term **ex-directory.** **3.** (of securities) not quoted on a stock exchange.

un·live (ʌnˈlɪv) *vb.* (*tr.*) to live so as to nullify, undo, or live down (past events or times).

un·load (ʌnˈləʊd) *vb.* **1.** to remove a load or cargo from (a ship, lorry, etc.). **2.** to discharge (cargo, freight, etc.). **3.** (*tr.*) to relieve of a burden or troubles. **4.** (*tr.*) to give vent to (anxiety, troubles, etc.). **5.** (*tr.*) to get rid of or dispose of, esp. surplus goods. **6.** (*tr.*) to remove the charge of ammunition from (a firearm). —**un·ˈload·er** *n.*

un·lock (ʌnˈlɒk) *vb.* **1.** (*tr.*) to unfasten (a lock, door, etc.). **2.**

---

un·ˈjus·ti·ˌfi·a·ble *adj.*
un·ˌjus·ti·ˈfi·a·bly *adv.*
un·ˈjus·ti·ˌfied *adj.*
un·ˈkept *adj.*
un·ˈkin·dled *adj.*
un·ˈking·ly *adj., adv.*
un·ˈkissed *adj.*
un·ˈknot *vb.,* **·knots, ·knot·ting, ·knot·ted.**
un·ˈla·belled *adj.*
un·ˈla·boured *adj.*
un·ˈla·den *adj.*
un·ˈla·dy·like *adj.*
un·ˈlaid *adj.*
ˌun·la·ˈment·ed *adj.*
un·ˈleased *adj.*
un·ˈlife·ˌlike *adj.*
un·ˈlight·ed *adj.*
un·ˈlik·a·ble *adj.*
un·ˈlined *adj.*
un·ˈlink *vb.*
un·ˈlit *adj.*
un·ˈliv·a·ble *adj.*
ˌun·lo·ˈcat·ed *adj.*

(*tr.*) to open, release, or let loose. **3.** (*tr.*) to disclose or provide the key to: *unlock a puzzle.* **4.** (*intr.*) to become unlocked. —un'lock·a·ble *adj.*

un·looked-for *adj.* unexpected; unforeseen.

un+loose (ʌn'lu:s) *or* **un+loos+en** *vb.* (*tr.*) **1.** to set free; release. **2.** to loosen or relax (a hold, grip, etc.). **3.** to unfasten or untie.

un+love+ly (ʌn'lʌvlɪ) *adj.* **1.** unpleasant in appearance. **2.** unpleasant in character. —un'love+li+ness *n.*

un+luck·y (ʌn'lʌkɪ) *adj.* **1.** characterized by misfortune or failure: *an unlucky person; an unlucky chance.* **2.** ill-omened; inauspicious: *an unlucky date.* **3.** regrettable; disappointing. **4.** *Brit. dialect.* causing trouble; mischievous. —un'luck·i·ly *adv.* —un'luck·i·ness *n.*

un+made (ʌn'meɪd) *vb.* **1.** the past tense or past participle of **unmake.** ~*adj.* **2.** not yet made. **3.** existing without having been made or created. **4.** *Falconry.* another word for **unmanned** (sense 4).

un+make (ʌn'meɪk) *vb.* **+makes, +mak+ing, +made.** (*tr.*) **1.** to undo or destroy. **2.** to depose from office, rank, or authority. **3.** to alter the nature of. —un'mak+er *n.*

un+man (ʌn'mæn) *vb.* **+mans, +man+ning, +manned.** (*tr.*) **1.** to cause to lose courage or nerve. **2.** to make effeminate. **3.** to remove the men from. **4.** *Archaic.* to deprive of human qualities.

un+man+ly (ʌn'mænlɪ) *adj.* **1.** not masculine or virile. **2.** ignoble, cowardly, or dishonourable. ~*adv.* **3.** *Archaic.* in an unmanly manner. —un'man+li+ness *n.*

un+manned (ʌn'mænd) *adj.* **1.** lacking personnel or crew: *an unmanned ship.* **2.** (of aircraft, spacecraft, etc.) operated by automatic or remote control. **3.** uninhabited. **4.** *Falconry.* (of a hawk or falcon) not yet trained to accept humans.

un+man+nered (ʌn'mænəd) *adj.* **1.** without good manners; coarse; rude. **2.** not affected; without mannerisms.

un+man+ner+ly (ʌn'mænəlɪ) *adj.* **1.** lacking manners; discourteous. ~*adv.* **2.** *Archaic.* rudely; discourteously. —un'man+ner+li+ness *n.*

un+marked (ʌn'mɑ:kt) *adj.* **1.** not carrying a mark or marks. **2.** not noticed or observed.

un+mask (ʌn'mɑ:sk) *vb.* **1.** to remove (the mask or disguise) from (someone or oneself). **2.** to appear or cause to appear in true character. **3.** (*tr.*) *Military.* to make evident the presence of (weapons), either by firing or by the removal of camouflage, etc. —un'mask+er *n.*

un+mean+ing (ʌn'mi:nɪŋ) *adj.* **1.** having no meaning. **2.** showing no intelligence; vacant: *an unmeaning face.* —un'mean+ing+ly *adv.* —un'mean+ing+ness *n.*

un+meant (ʌn'mɛnt) *adj.* unintentional; accidental.

un+meas+ured (ʌn'mɛʒəd) *adj.* **1.** measureless; limitless. **2.** unrestrained; unlimited or lavish. **3.** *Music.* without bar lines and hence without a fixed pulse. —un'meas+ur+a+ble *adj.* —un'meas+ur+a+ble+ness *n.* —un'meas+ur+a+bly *adv.* —un'meas+ured+ly *adv.*

un+meet (ʌn'mi:t) *adj. Literary or archaic.* not meet; unsuitable. —un'meet+ly *adv.* —un'meet+ness *n.*

un+men+tion+a+ble (ʌn'mɛnʃənəbᵊl) *adj.* **a.** unsuitable or forbidden as a topic of conversation. **b.** (*as n.*): *the unmentionable.* —un'men+tion+a+ble+ness *n.* —un'men+tion+a+bly *adv.*

un+men+tion+a+bles (ʌn'mɛnʃənəbᵊlz) *pl. n. Chiefly humorous.* underwear.

un+mer+ci+ful (ʌn'mɜ:sɪfʊl) *adj.* **1.** showing no mercy; relentless. **2.** extreme or excessive. —un'mer+ci+ful+ly *adv.* —un'mer+ci+ful+ness *n.*

un+mind+ful (ʌn'maɪndfʊl) *adj.* (*usually postpositive* and foll. by *of*) careless, heedless, or forgetful. —un'mind+ful+ly *adv.* —un'mind+ful+ness *n.*

un+mis+tak+a+ble *or* **un+mis+take+a+ble** (ˌʌnmɪs'teɪkəbᵊl) *adj.* not mistakable; clear, obvious, or unambiguous. —ˌun+mis+'tak+a+ble+ness *or* ˌun+mis+'take+a+ble+ness *n.* —ˌun+mis+'tak+a+bly *or* ˌun+mis+'take+a+bly *adv.*

un+mit+i+gat+ed (ʌn'mɪtɪˌgeɪtɪd) *adj.* **1.** not diminished in intensity, severity, etc. **2.** (*prenominal*) (intensifier): *an unmitigated disaster.* —un'mit+i+ˌgat+ed+ly *adv.*

un+moor (ʌn'mʊə, -'mɔ:) *vb. Nautical.* **1.** to weigh the anchor or drop the mooring of (a vessel). **2.** (*tr.*) to reduce the mooring of (a vessel) to one anchor.

un+mor+al (ʌn'mɒrəl) *adj.* **1.** outside morality; amoral. —un+mo+ral+i+ty (ˌʌnmə'rælɪtɪ) *n.* —un'mor+al+ly *adv.*

un+mur+mur+ing (ʌn'mɜ:mərɪŋ) *adj.* not complaining.

un+mu+si+cal (ʌn'mju:zɪkᵊl) *adj.* **1.** not musical or harmonious. **2.** not talented in or appreciative of music. —un'mu+si+cal+ly *adv.* —un'mu+si+cal+ness *n.*

un+muz+zle (ʌn'mʌzᵊl) *vb.* (*tr.*) **1.** to take the muzzle off (a dog, etc.). **2.** to free from control or censorship.

un+named (ʌn'neɪmd) *adj.* **1.** having no name. **2.** not mentioned by name: *the culprit shall remain unnamed.*

un+nat+u+ral (ʌn'nætʃərəl, -'nætʃrəl) *adj.* **1.** contrary to nature; abnormal. **2.** not in accordance with accepted standards of behaviour or right and wrong: *unnatural love.* **3.** uncanny; supernatural: *unnatural phenomena.* **4.** affected or forced: *an unnatural manner.* **5.** inhuman or monstrous; wicked: *an unnatural crime.* **6.** *Obsolete.* illegitimate. —un'nat+u+ral+ly *adv.* —un'nat+u+ral+ness *n.*

un+nec+es+sar+y (ʌn'nɛsɪsərɪ, -ɪsrɪ) *adj.* not necessary. —un'nec+es+sar+i+ly *adv.* —un'nec+es+sar+i+ness *n.*

un+nerve (ʌn'nɜ:v) *vb.* (*tr.*) to cause to lose courage, strength, confidence, self-control, etc.

un+num+bered (ʌn'nʌmbəd) *adj.* **1.** countless; innumerable. **2.** not counted or assigned a number.

U.N.O. *abbrev. for* United Nations Organization.

un+oc+cu+pied (ʌn'ɒkjʊˌpaɪd) *adj.* **1.** (of a building) without occupants. **2.** unemployed or idle. **3.** (of an area or country) not overrun by foreign troops.

un+of+fi+cial (ˌʌnə'fɪʃəl) *adj.* **1.** not official or formal: *an unofficial engagement.* **2.** not confirmed officially: *an unofficial report.* **3.** (of a strike) not approved by the strikers' trade union. **4.** (of a medicinal drug) not listed in a pharmacopoeia. —ˌun+of+'fi+cial+ly *adv.*

un+or+gan+ized *or* **un+or+gan+ised** (ʌn'ɔ:gəˌnaɪzd) *adj.* **1.** not arranged into an organized system, structure, or unity. **2.** (of workers) not unionized. **3.** nonliving; inorganic.

un+or+tho+dox (ʌn'ɔ:θəˌdɒks) *adj.* not conventional in belief, behaviour, custom, etc. —un'or+tho+ˌdox+ly *adv.*

un+pack (ʌn'pæk) *vb.* **1.** to remove the packed contents of (a case, trunk, etc.). **2.** (*tr.*) to take (something) out of a packed container. **3.** (*tr.*) to remove a pack from; unload: *to unpack a mule.* —un'pack+er *n.*

un+paged (ʌn'peɪdʒd) *adj.* (of a book) having no page numbers.

un+paid (ʌn'peɪd) *adj.* **1.** (of a bill, debt, etc.) not yet paid. **2.** working without pay. **3.** having wages outstanding.

un+par+al+leled (ʌn'pærəˌlɛld) *adj.* unmatched; unequalled.

un+par+lia+men+ta+ry (ˌʌnpɑ:lə'mɛntərɪ, -trɪ) *adj.* not consistent with parliamentary procedure or practice. —ˌun+par+lia+'men+tar+i+ly *adv.* —ˌun+par+lia+'men+tar+i+ness *n.*

un+peg (ʌn'pɛg) *vb.* **+pegs, +peg+ging, +pegged.** (*tr.*) **1.** to remove the peg or pegs from, esp. to unfasten. **2.** to allow (prices, wages, etc.) to rise and fall freely.

un+peo+ple (ʌn'pi:pᵊl) *vb.* (*tr.*) to empty of people.

un+per+fo+rat+ed (ʌn'pɜ:fəˌreɪtɪd) *adj.* (of a stamp) not provided with perforations.

un+per+son ('ʌnpɜ:sᵊn) *n.* a person whose existence is officially denied or ignored.

un+pick (ʌn'pɪk) *vb.* (*tr.*) **1.** to undo (the stitches) of (a piece of

---

un'locked *adj.*
un'lov+a+ble *adj.*
un'loved *adj.*
un'lov+ing *adj.*
un'lu+bri+ˌcat+ed *adj.*
un'mag+ni+ˌfied *adj.*
un'man+age+a+ble *adj.*
ˌun+ma'nip+u+ˌlat+ed *adj.*
ˌun+man+u'fac+tured *adj.*
un'mar+ket+a+ble *adj.*
un'marred *adj.*
un'mar+riage+a+ble *adj.*
un'mar+ried *adj.*
un'mas+tered *adj.*
un'matched *adj.*
ˌun+ma'tured *adj.*
ˌun+me'chan+i+cal *adj.*
un'med+i+ˌcat+ed *adj.*
ˌun+me'lo+di+ous *adj.*
un'melt+ed *adj.*
un'mem+or+a+ble *adj.*
un'mem+o+ˌrized *or*
un'mem+o+ˌrised *adj.*
un'mend+ed *adj.*
un'men+tioned *adj.*
un'mer+chant+a+ble *adj.*
un'mer+it+ed *adj.*
ˌun+me'thod+i+cal *adj.*
un'met+ri+cal *adj.*
un'mil+i+ˌtar+y *adj.*
un'min+gled *adj.*
ˌun+mis'tak+en *adj.*
un'mixed *vb.*
un'mod+i+fied *adj.*
un'mod+u+ˌlat+ed *adj.*
ˌun+mo'lest+ed *adj.*
un'mo+ti+ˌvat+ed *adj.*
un'mould+ed *adj.*
un'mount+ed *adj.*
un'mourned *adj.*
un'mov+a+ble *adj.*
un'moved *adj.*
un'mov+ing *adj.*
un'mown *adj.*
un'muf+fle *vb.*
un'mys+ti+ˌfied *adj.*
un'nam+a+ble *adj.*
un'nav+i+ga+ble *adj.*
un'nav+i+ˌgat+ed *adj.*
un'need+ed *adj.*
un'need+ful *adj.*
ˌun+ne'go+ti+a+ble *adj.*
ˌun+ne'go+ti+ˌat+ed *adj.*
un'neigh+bour+ly *adj.*
un'note+ˌwor+thy *adj.*
un'no+tice+a+ble *adj.*
un'no+tice+a+bly *adv.*
un'no+ticed *adj.*
un'nur+tured *adj.*
ˌun+ob'jec+tion+a+ble *adj.*
ˌun+ob'liged *adj.*
ˌun+ob'lig+ing *adj.*
ˌun+ob'scured *adj.*
ˌun+ob'serv+ant *adj.*
ˌun+ob'served *adj.*
ˌun+ob'serv+ing *adj.*
ˌun+ob'struct+ed *adj.*
ˌun+ob'tain+a+ble *adj.*
ˌun+ob'tained *adj.*
ˌun+ob'trud+ing *adj.*
ˌun+ob'tru+sive *adj.*
ˌun+ob'tru+sive+ly *adv.*
ˌun+ob'tru+sive+ness *n.*
ˌun+of'fend+ed *adj.*
ˌun+of'fend+ing *adj.*
ˌun+of'fen+sive *adj.*
ˌun+of'fen+sive+ly *adv.*
un'of+fered *adj.*
ˌun+of'fi+cial+ly *adv.*
ˌun+of'fi+cious *adj.*
ˌun+of'fi+cious+ly *adv.*
un'o+pen *adj.*
un'o+pened *adj.*
ˌun+op'posed *adj.*
ˌun+op'pressed *adj.*
ˌun+op'pres+sive *adj.*
ˌun+op'pres+sive+ly *adv.*
ˌun+or'dained *adj.*
ˌun+o'rig+i+nal *adj.*
ˌun+or+na'men+tal *adj.*
un'or+na+ment+ed *adj.*
un'or+tho+dox+ly *adv.*
ˌun+os+ten'ta+tious *adj.*
ˌun+os+ten'ta+tious+ly *adv.*
un'owned *adj.*
un'pac+i+ˌfied *adj.*
un'paired *adj.*
un'pal+at+a+ble *adj.*
un'par+don+a+ble *adj.*
un'pas+teur+ˌized *or*
un'pas+teur+ˌised *adj.*
un'pat+ent+ed *adj.*
ˌun+pat+ri'ot+ic *adj.*
un'paved *adj.*
un'peace+ful *adj.*
un'pen+sioned *adj.*
un'pep+pered *adj.*
ˌun+per'ceived *adj.*
ˌun+per'cep+tive *adj.*
ˌun+per'fect+ed *adj.*
ˌun+per'formed *adj.*
ˌun+per'plexed *adj.*
ˌun+per'suad+ed *adj.*
ˌun+per'sua+sive *adj.*
ˌun+per'turb+a+ble *adj.*
ˌun+per'turbed *adj.*

sewing). **2.** to unravel or undo (a garment, etc.). **3.** *Obsolete.* to open (a door, lock, etc.) by picking.

un+pin (ʌnˈpɪn) *vb.* **+pins, +pin+ning, +pinned.** (*tr.*) **1.** to remove a pin or pins from. **2.** to unfasten by removing pins.

un+placed (ʌnˈpleɪst) *adj.* **1.** not given or put in a particular place. **2.** *Horse racing.* not in the first three (sometimes four) runners in a race.

un+pleas+ant (ʌnˈplɛzᵊnt) *adj.* not pleasant or agreeable. —**un+ˈpleas+ant+ly** *adv.*

un+pleas+ant+ness (ʌnˈplɛzəntnɪs) *n.* **1.** the state or quality of being unpleasant. **2.** an unpleasant event, situation, etc. **3.** a disagreement or quarrel.

un+plug (ʌnˈplʌg) *vb.* **+plugs, +plug+ging, +plugged.** (*tr.*) **1.** to disconnect (an electrical appliance) by taking the plug out of the socket. **2.** to remove a plug or obstruction from.

un+plumbed (ʌnˈplʌmd) *adj.* **1.** unfathomed; unsounded. **2.** not understood in depth. **3.** (of a building) having no plumbing.

un+pol·i·tic (ʌnˈpɒlɪtɪk) *adj.* another word for **impolitic.**

un+polled (ʌnˈpəʊld) *adj.* **1.** not included in an opinion poll. **2.** not having voted. **3.** *U.S.* not registered for an election: *unpolled votes.* **4.** *Archaic.* uncut or unshorn.

un+pop·u·lar (ʌnˈpɒpjʊlə) *adj.* not popular with an individual or group of people. —**un+pop·u·lar+i·ty** (ʌnˌpɒpjʊˈlærɪtɪ) *n.* —**un+ˈpop·u·lar+ly** *adv.*

un+prac+ti+cal (ʌnˈpræktɪkᵊl) *adj.* another word for **impractical.** —**un+ˌprac+ti+ˈcal+i·ty** *or* **un+ˈprac+ti+cal+ness** *n.* —**un+ˈprac+ti+cal+ly** *adv.*

un+prac+tised *or U.S.* **un+prac+ticed** (ʌnˈpræktɪst) *adj.* **1.** without skill, training, or experience. **2.** not used or done often or repeatedly. **3.** not yet tested.

un+prec+e·dent+ed (ʌnˈprɛsɪˌdɛntɪd) *adj.* having no precedent; unparalleled. —**un+ˈprec+e·ˌdent+ed+ly** *adv.*

un+pre+dict+a·ble (ˌʌnprɪˈdɪktəbᵊl) *adj.* not capable of being predicted; changeable. —**ˌun+pre+ˌdict+a·ˈbil+i·ty** *or* **ˌun+pre+ˈdict+a·ble+ness** *n.* —**ˌun+pre+ˈdict+a·bly** *adv.*

un+prej·u·diced (ʌnˈprɛdʒʊdɪst) *adj.* not prejudiced or biased; impartial. —**un+ˈprej·u·diced+ly** *adv.*

un+pre+med·i·tat+ed (ˌʌnprɪˈmɛdɪˌteɪtɪd) *adj.* not planned beforehand; spontaneous. —**ˌun+pre+ˈmed·i+ˌtat+ed+ly** *adv.* —**ˌun+pre+ˌmed·i·ˈta+tion** *n.*

un+pre+pared (ˌʌnprɪˈpɛəd) *adj.* **1.** having made inadequate preparations. **2.** not made ready or prepared. **3.** done without preparation; extemporaneous. —**ˌun+pre+ˈpar+ed+ly** *adv.* —**ˌun+pre+ˈpar+ed+ness** *n.*

un+priced (ʌnˈpraɪst) *adj.* **1.** having no fixed or marked price. **2.** *Poetic.* beyond price; priceless.

un+prin+ci+pled (ʌnˈprɪnsɪpᵊld) *adj.* **1.** lacking moral principles; unscrupulous. **2.** (foll. by *in*) *Archaic.* not versed in the principles of (a subject). —**un+ˈprin+ci+pled+ness** *n.*

un+print+a·ble (ʌnˈprɪntəbᵊl) *adj.* unsuitable for printing for reasons of obscenity, libel, bad taste, etc. —**un+ˈprint+a·ble+ness** *n.* —**un+ˈprint+a·bly** *adv.*

un+pro+duc+tive (ˌʌnprəˈdʌktɪv) *adj.* **1.** (often foll. by *of*) not productive of (anything). **2.** not producing goods and services with exchange value. —**ˌun+pro+ˈduc+tive+ly** *adv.* —**ˌun+pro+ˈduc+tive+ness** *n.*

un+pro+fes+sion+al (ˌʌnprəˈfɛʃənᵊl) *adj.* **1.** contrary to the accepted code of conduct of a profession. **2.** amateur. **3.** not belonging to or having the required qualifications for a profession. —**ˌun+pro+ˈfes+sion+al+ly** *adv.*

un+prof+it+a·ble (ʌnˈprɒfɪtəbᵊl) *adj.* **1.** not making a profit. **2.** not fruitful or beneficial. —**un+ˌprof+it+a·ˈbil+i·ty** *or* **un+ˈprof+it+a·ble+ness** *n.* —**un+ˈprof+it+a·bly** *adv.*

un+pro+vid+ed (ˌʌnprəˈvaɪdɪd) *adj.* (*postpositive*) **1.** (foll. by *with*) not provided or supplied. **2.** (often foll. by *for*) not prepared or ready. **3. unprovided for.** without income or means. —**ˌun+pro+ˈvid+ed+ly** *adv.*

un+qual·i+fied (ʌnˈkwɒlɪˌfaɪd) *adj.* **1.** lacking the necessary qualifications. **2.** not restricted or modified: *an unqualified criticism.* **3.** (*usually prenominal*) (intensifier): *an unqualified success.* —**un+ˈqual·i+ˌfi+a·ble** *adj.* —**un+ˈqual·i+ˌfied+ly** *adv.* —**un+ˈqual·i+ˌfied+ness** *n.*

un+ques+tion+a·ble (ʌnˈkwɛstʃənəbᵊl) *adj.* **1.** indubitable or indisputable. **2.** not admitting of exception or qualification: *an unquestionable ruling.* —**un+ˌques+tion+a·ˈbil+i·ty** *or* **un+ˈques+tion+a·ble+ness** *n.* —**un+ˈques+tion+a·bly** *adv.*

un+ques+tioned (ʌnˈkwɛstʃənd) *adj.* **1.** accepted without question. **2.** not admitting of doubt or question: *unquestioned power.* **3.** not questioned or interrogated. **4.** *Rare.* not examined or investigated.

un+qui+et (ʌnˈkwaɪət) *Chiefly literary.* ~*adj.* **1.** characterized by disorder, unrest, or tumult: *unquiet times.* **2.** anxious; uneasy. **3.** *Archaic.* noisy. ~*n.* **4.** a state of unrest. —**un+ˈqui+et+ly** *adv.* —**un+ˈqui+et+ness** *n.*

un+quote (ʌnˈkwəʊt) *interj.* **1.** an expression used parenthetically to indicate that the preceding quotation is finished. ~*vb.* **2.** to close (a quotation), esp. in printing.

un+rav+el (ʌnˈrævᵊl) *vb.* **+els, +el+ling, +elled** *or U.S.* **+els, +el+ing, +eled. 1.** (*tr.*) to reduce (something knitted or woven) to separate strands. **2.** (*tr.*) to undo or untangle (something tangled or knotted). **3.** (*tr.*) to explain or solve: *the mystery was unravelled.* **4.** (*intr.*) to become unravelled. —**un+ˈrav+el+ler** *n.* —**un+ˈrav+el+ment** *n.*

un+read (ʌnˈrɛd) *adj.* **1.** (of a book, newspaper, etc.) not yet read. **2.** (of a person) having read little. **3.** (*postpositive;* foll. by *in*) not versed (in a specified field).

un+read+a·ble (ʌnˈriːdəbᵊl) *adj.* **1.** illegible; undecipherable. **2.** difficult or tedious to read. —**un+ˌread+a·ˈbil+i·ty** *or* **un+ˈread+a·ble+ness** *n.* —**un+ˈread+a·bly** *adv.*

un+read·y (ʌnˈrɛdɪ) *adj.* **1.** not ready or prepared. **2.** slow or hesitant to see or act. **3.** *Archaic or Brit. dialect.* not dressed. —**un+ˈread·i+ly** *adv.* —**un+ˈread·i+ness** *n.*

un+re·al (ʌnˈrɪəl) *adj.* **1.** imaginary or fanciful or seemingly so: *an unreal situation.* **2.** having no actual existence or substance. **3.** insincere or artificial. —**un+ˈre+al+ly** *adv.*

un+re+al+i·ty (ˌʌnrɪˈælɪtɪ) *n.* **1.** the quality or state of being unreal, fanciful, or impractical. **2.** something that is unreal.

un+rea+son (ʌnˈriːzᵊn) *n.* **1.** irrationality or madness. **2.** something that lacks or is contrary to reason. **3.** lack of order; chaos. ~*vb.* **4.** (*tr.*) to deprive of reason.

un+rea+son+a·ble (ʌnˈriːznəbᵊl) *adj.* **1.** immoderate; excessive: *unreasonable demands.* **2.** refusing to listen to reason. **3.** lacking reason or judgment. —**un+ˈrea+son+a·ble+ness** *n.* —**un+ˈrea+son+a·bly** *adv.*

un+rea+son+a·ble be+hav+iour *n. Law.* conduct by a spouse sufficient to cause the irretrievable breakdown of a marriage.

un+rea+son+ing (ʌnˈriːzənɪŋ) *adj.* not controlled by reason; irrational. —**un+ˈrea+son+ing+ly** *adv.*

un+reck+on+a·ble (ʌnˈrɛkənəbᵊl) *adj.* incalculable; unlimited.

un+re+con+struct+ed (ˌʌnriːkənsˈtrʌktɪd) *adj. Chiefly U.S.* unwilling to accept social and economic change, as exemplified by those White Southerners who refused to accept the Reconstruction after the Civil War.

un+reeve (ʌnˈriːv) *vb.* **+reeves, +reev+ing, +rove** *or* **+reeved.** *Nautical.* to withdraw (a rope) from a block, thimble, etc.

un+re+fined (ˌʌnrɪˈfaɪnd) *adj.* **1.** (of substances such as petroleum, ores, and sugar) not processed into a pure or usable form. **2.** coarse in manners or language.

un+re+flect+ed (ˌʌnrɪˈflɛktɪd) *adj.* **1.** (foll. by *on* or *upon*) not considered. **2.** (of light, particles, etc., incident on a surface) not reflected, absorbed, or transmitted.

un+re+flec+tive (ˌʌnrɪˈflɛktɪv) *adj.* not reflective or thoughtful; rash; unthinking. —**ˌun+re+ˈflec+tive+ly** *adv.*

un+re+gen+er+ate (ˌʌnrɪˈdʒɛnərɪt) *adj. also* **un+re+gen+er+at+ed. 1.** unrepentant; unreformed. **2.** obstinately adhering to one's own views. ~*n.* **3.** an unregenerate person. —**ˌun+re+ˈgen+er+a+cy** *n.* —**ˌun+re+ˈgen+er+ate+ly** *adv.*

un+re+lent+ing (ˌʌnrɪˈlɛntɪŋ) *adj.* **1.** refusing to relent or take pity; relentless; merciless. **2.** not diminishing in determination, speed, effort, force, etc. —**ˌun+re+ˈlent+ing+ly** *adv.* —**ˌun+re+ˈlent+ing+ness** *n.*

un+re+li+gious (ˌʌnrɪˈlɪdʒəs) *adj.* **1.** another word for **irreligious. 2.** secular. —**ˌun+re+ˈli+gious+ly** *adv.*

un+re+mit+ting (ˌʌnrɪˈmɪtɪŋ) *adj.* never slackening or stopping;

ˌun+phil·o·ˈsoph·i·cal *adj.*
un+ˈpicked *adj.*
un+ˈpit+ied *adj.*
un+ˈpit·y+ing *adj.*
un+ˈplanned *adj.*
un+ˈplant+ed *adj.*
un+ˈplay+a·ble *adj.*
un+ˈplayed *adj.*
un+ˈpleas+ing *adj.*
un+ˈpledged *adj.*
un+ˈploughed *adj.*
un+ˈplucked *adj.*
ˌun+po+ˈet+ic *adj.*
un+ˈpoint+ed *adj.*
un+ˈpoised *adj.*
un+ˈpo+lar+ˌized *or* **un+ˈpo+lar+ˌised** *adj.*
un+ˈpol+ished *adj.*
ˌun+po+ˈlit·i·cal *adj.*
ˌun+pol+ˈlut+ed *adj.*
un+ˈpol+ym+er+ˌized *or* **un+ˈpol+ym+er+ˌised** *adj.*
un+ˈpop·u+ˌlat+ed *adj.*
un+ˈposed *adj.*
un+ˈprac+ti+ca·ble *adj.*
ˌun+pre+ˈdict+ed *adj.*
ˌun+pre+pos+ˈsess+ing *adj.*
ˌun+pre+ˈscribed *adj.*
ˌun+pre+ˈsent+a·ble *adj.*
ˌun+pre+ˈserved *adj.*
un+ˈpressed *adj.*
ˌun+pre+ˈsump+tu+ous *adj.*
ˌun+pre+ˈtend+ing *adj.*
ˌun+pre+ˈten+tious *adj.*
ˌun+pre+ˈvail+ing *adj.*
ˌun+ˈpro+cessed *adj.*
ˌun+pro+ˈclaimed *adj.*
ˌun+pro+ˈcur+a·ble *adj.*
ˌun+pro+ˈfessed *adj.*
ˌun+pro+ˈgres+sive *adj.*
ˌun+pro+ˈhib+it+ed *adj.*
un+ˈprom+is+ing *adj.*
un+ˈprompt+ed *adj.*
ˌun+pro+ˈnounce+a·ble *adj.*
ˌun+pro+ˈnounced *adj.*
ˌun+pro+ˈpi+tious *adj.*
ˌun+pro+ˈposed *adj.*
ˌun+pro+ˈtect+ed *adj.*
ˌun+pro+ˈtest+ing *adj.*
un+ˈproved *adj.*
un+ˈprov+en *adj.*
ˌun+pro+ˈvoked *adj.*
un+ˈpub+lished *adj.*
un+ˈpunc+tu·al *adj.*
un+ˈpun+ished *adj.*
un+ˈpu+ri+ˌfied *adj.*
un+ˈquelled *adj.*
un+ˈquenched *adj.*
un+ˈques+tion+ing *adj.*
un+ˈquot+a·ble *adj.*
un+ˈraised *adj.*
ˌun+re+al+ˈis+tic *adj.*
un+ˈre+al+ized *adj.*
un+ˈrea+soned *adj.*
ˌun+re+ˈbuked *adj.*
ˌun+re+ˈcep+tive *adj.*
ˌun+re+ˈcip+ro+cat+ed *adj.*
un+ˈreck+oned *adj.*
un+ˈrec+og+ˌniz+a·ble *or* **un+ˈrec+og+ˌnis+a·ble** *adj.*
un+ˈrec+og+ˌnized *or* **un+ˈrec+og+ˌnised** *adj.*
ˌun+rec+om+ˈmend+ed *adj.*
ˌun+rec+om+ˈpensed *adj.*
un+ˈrec+on+ˌciled *adj.*
ˌun+re+ˈcord+ed *adj.*
un+ˈrec+ti+ˌfied *adj.*
ˌun+re+ˈdeemed *adj.*
un+ˈreel *vb.*
ˌun+re+ˈflect+ing *adj.*
ˌun+re+ˈfreshed *adj.*
un+ˈreg·i+ˌment+ed *adj.*
un+ˈreg+is+tered *adj.*
un+ˈreg·u+ˌlat+ed *adj.*
ˌun+re+ˈhearsed *adj.*
ˌun+re+ˈlat+ed *adj.*
ˌun+re+ˈli+a·ble *adj.*
ˌun+re+ˈlieved *adj.*
ˌun+re+ˈmark+a·ble *adj.*
un+ˈrem+e·died *adj.*
ˌun+re+ˈmem+bered *adj.*
ˌun+re+ˈmit+ted *adj.*

unceasing; constant. —ˌ**un+re+'mit+ting+ly** *adv.* —ˌ**un+re+'mit+ting+ness** *n.*

un+re+pair (ˌʌnrɪ'pɛə) *n.* a less common word for **disrepair.** —ˌ**un+re+'paired** *adj.*

un+re+quit+ed (ˌʌnrɪ'kwaɪtɪd) *adj.* (of love, affection, etc.) not reciprocated or returned.

un+re+served (ˌʌnrɪ'zɜːvd) *adj.* **1.** without reserve; having an open manner. **2.** without reservation. **3.** not booked or bookable. —**un+re+serv+ed+ly** (ˌʌnrɪ'zɜːvɪdlɪ) *adv.* —ˌ**un+re+'serv+ed+ness** *n.*

un+rest (ʌn'rɛst) *n.* **1.** a troubled or rebellious state of discontent. **2.** an uneasy or troubled state.

un+re+strained (ˌʌnrɪ'streɪnd) *adj.* not restrained or checked; free or natural. —**un+re+strain+ed+ly** (ˌʌnrɪ'streɪnɪdlɪ) *adv.*

un+rid+dle (ʌn'rɪdᵊl) *vb.* (*tr.*) to solve or puzzle out. —**un+'rid+dler** *n.*

un+ri+fled (ʌn'raɪfᵊld) *adj.* (of a firearm or its bore) not rifled; smoothbore.

un+rig (ʌn'rɪg) *vb.* **+rigs, +rig+ging, +rigged. 1.** (*tr.*) to strip (a vessel) of standing and running rigging. **2.** *Archaic or northern Brit. dialect.* to undress (someone or oneself).

un+right+eous (ʌn'raɪtʃəs) *adj.* **1. a.** sinful; wicked. **b.** (*as n.*): *the unrighteous.* **2.** not fair or right; unjust. —**un+'right+eous+ly** *adv.* —**un+'right+eous+ness** *n.*

un+rip (ʌn'rɪp) *vb.* **+rips, +rip+ping, +ripped.** (*tr.*) **1.** to rip open. **2.** *Obsolete.* to reveal; disclose.

un+ripe (ʌn'raɪp) *or* **un+rip+ened** *adj.* **1.** not fully matured. **2.** not fully prepared or developed; not ready. **3.** *Obsolete.* premature or untimely. —**un+'ripe+ness** *n.*

un+ri+valled (ʌn'raɪvᵊld) *adj.* having no equal; matchless.

un+roll (ʌn'rəʊl) *vb.* **1.** to open out or unwind (something rolled, folded, or coiled) or (of something rolled, etc.) to become opened out or unwound. **2.** to make or become visible or apparent, esp. gradually; unfold.

un+root (ʌn'ruːt) *vb.* (*tr.*) *Chiefly U.S.* a less common word for **uproot.**

un+round+ed (ʌn'raʊndɪd) *adj. Phonetics.* articulated with the lips spread; not rounded.

un+ruf+fled (ʌn'rʌfᵊld) *adj.* **1.** unmoved; calm. **2.** still: *the unruffled seas.* —**un+'ruf+fled+ness** *n.*

un+ru+ly (ʌn'ruːlɪ) *adj.* **+li+er, +li+est.** disposed to disobedience or indiscipline. —**un+'ru+li+ness** *n.*

UNRWA ('ʌnrə) *n. acronym for* United Nations Relief and Works Agency.

un+sad+dle (ʌn'sædᵊl) *vb.* **1.** to remove the saddle from (a horse, mule, etc.). **2.** (*tr.*) to unhorse.

un+said (ʌn'sɛd) *adj.* not said or expressed; unspoken.

un+sat·u+rat+ed (ʌn'sætʃəˌreɪtɪd) *adj.* **1.** not saturated. **2.** (of a chemical compound, esp. an organic compound) containing one or more double or triple bonds and thus capable of undergoing addition reactions. **3.** (of a solution) containing less solute than a saturated solution. —ˌ**un+sat·u+'ra+tion** *n.*

un+sa+vour·y *or U.S.* **un+sa+vor·y** (ʌn'seɪvərɪ) *adj.* **1.** objectionable or distasteful: *an unsavoury character.* **2.** disagreeable in odour or taste. —**un+'sa+vour·i+ly** *or U.S.* **un+'sa+vor·i+ly** *adv.* —**un+'sa+vour·i+ness** *or U.S.* **un+'sa+vor·i+ness** *n.*

un+say (ʌn'seɪ) *vb.* **+says, +say+ing, +said.** (*tr.*) to retract or withdraw (something said or written).

un+scathed (ʌn'skeɪðd) *adj.* not harmed or injured.

un+schooled (ʌn'skuːld) *adj.* **1.** having received no training or schooling. **2.** spontaneous; natural: *unschooled talent.*

un+sci+en+tif+ic (ˌʌnsaɪən'tɪfɪk) *adj.* **1.** not consistent with the methods or principles of science, esp. lacking objectivity. **2.** ignorant of science. —ˌ**un+sci+en+'tif·i+cal+ly** *adv.*

un+scram+ble (ʌn'skræmbᵊl) *vb.* (*tr.*) **1.** *Informal.* to resolve from confusion or disorderliness. **2.** to restore (a scrambled message) to an intelligible form. —**un+'scram+bler** *n.*

un+scratched (ʌn'skrætʃt) *adj.* quite unharmed.

un+screened (ʌn'skriːnd) *adj.* **1.** not sheltered or concealed by a screen. **2.** not passed through a screen; unsifted. **3.** (of a film) not yet on show to the public. **4.** not put through a security check.

un+screw (ʌn'skruː) *vb.* **1.** (*tr.*) to draw or remove a screw from (an object). **2.** (*tr.*) to loosen (a screw, lid, etc.) by rotating continuously, usually in an anticlockwise direction. **3.** (*intr.*) (esp. of an engaged threaded part) to become loosened or separated: *the lid wouldn't unscrew.*

un+script+ed (ʌn'skrɪptɪd) *adj.* (of a speech, play, etc.) not using or based on a script.

un+scru+pu+lous (ʌn'skruːpjʊləs) *adj.* without scruples; unprincipled. —**un+'scru+pu+lous+ly** *adv.* —**un+'scru+pu+lous+ness** *or* **un+scru+pu+los+i+ty** (ʌnˌskruːpjʊ'lɒsɪtɪ) *n.*

un+seal (ʌn'siːl) *vb.* (*tr.*) **1.** to remove or break the seal of. **2.** to reveal or free (something concealed or closed as if sealed): *to unseal one's lips.* —**un+'seal+a·ble** *adj.*

un+seam (ʌn'siːm) *vb.* (*tr.*) to open or undo the seam of.

un+sea+son+a·ble (ʌn'siːzənəbᵊl) *adj.* **1.** (esp. of the weather) inappropriate for the season. **2.** untimely; inopportune. —**un+'sea+son+a·ble+ness** *n.* —**un+'sea+son+a·bly** *adv.*

un+sea+soned (ʌn'siːzənd) *adj.* **1.** (of persons) not sufficiently experienced: *unseasoned troops.* **2.** not matured or seasoned: *unseasoned timber.* **3.** (of food) not flavoured with seasoning. —**un+'sea+soned+ness** *n.*

un+seat (ʌn'siːt) *vb.* (*tr.*) **1.** to throw or displace from a seat, saddle, etc. **2.** to depose from office or position.

un+se·cured (ˌʌnsɪ'kjʊəd) *adj.* **1.** *Finance.* **a.** (of a loan, etc.) secured only against general assets and not against a specific asset. **b.** (of a creditor) having no security against a specific asset and with a claim inferior to those of secure creditors. **2.** not made secure; loose.

un+seed+ed (ʌn'siːdɪd) *adj.* (of players in various sports) not assigned to a preferential position in the preliminary rounds of a tournament.

un+seem+ly (ʌn'siːmlɪ) *adj.* **1.** not in good style or taste; unbecoming. **2.** *Obsolete.* unattractive. ~*adv.* **3.** *Rare.* in an unseemly manner. —**un+'seem+li+ness** *n.*

un+seen (ʌn'siːn) *adj.* **1.** not observed or perceived; invisible. **2.** (of passages of writing) not previously seen or prepared. ~*n.* **3.** *Chiefly Brit.* a passage, not previously seen, that is presented to students for translation.

un+self+ish (ʌn'sɛlfɪʃ) *adj.* not selfish or greedy; generous. —**un+'self+ish+ly** *adv.* —**un+'self+ish+ness** *n.*

un+set (ʌn'sɛt) *adj.* **1.** not yet solidified or firm. **2.** (of a gem) not yet in a setting. **3.** (of textual matter) not yet composed.

un+set+tle (ʌn'sɛtᵊl) *vb.* **1.** (*usually tr.*) to change or become changed from a fixed or settled condition. **2.** (*tr.*) to confuse or agitate (emotions, the mind, etc.). —**un+'set+tle+ment** *n.*

un+set+tled (ʌn'sɛtᵊld) *adj.* **1.** lacking order or stability: *an unsettled era.* **2.** unpredictable; uncertain: *an unsettled climate.* **3.** constantly changing or moving from place to place: *an unsettled life.* **4.** (of controversy, etc.) not brought to an agreed conclusion. **5.** (of debts, law cases, etc.) not disposed of. **6.** (of regions, etc.) devoid of settlers. —**un+'set+tled+ness** *n.*

un+sex (ʌn'sɛks) *vb.* (*tr.*) *Chiefly literary.* to deprive (a person) of the attributes of their sex, esp. to make a woman more callous.

un+shak+a·ble *or* **un+shake+a·ble** (ʌn'ʃeɪkəbᵊl) *adj.* (of beliefs, etc.) utterly firm and unwavering. —**un+'shak+a·ble+ness** *or* **un+'shake+a·ble+ness** *n.* —**un+'shak+a·bly** *or* **un+'shake+a·bly** *adv.*

un+shap+en (ʌn'ʃeɪpᵊn) *adj.* **1.** having no definite shape; shapeless. **2.** deformed; misshapen.

un+sheathe (ʌn'ʃiːð) *vb.* (*tr.*) to draw or pull out (something, esp. a weapon) from a sheath or other covering.

un+ship (ʌn'ʃɪp) *vb.* **+ships, +ship+ping, +shipped. 1.** to be or cause to be unloaded, discharged, or disembarked from a ship. **2.** (*tr.*) *Nautical.* to remove from a regular place: *to unship oars.*

un+sight+ed (ʌn'saɪtɪd) *adj.* **1.** not sighted. **2.** not having a clear view. **3. a.** (of a gun) not equipped with a sight. **b.** (of a shot) not aimed by means of a sight. —**un+'sight+ed+ly** *adv.*

un+sight+ly (ʌn'saɪtlɪ) *adj.* unpleasant or unattractive to look at; ugly. —**un+'sight+li+ness** *n.*

un+sized[1] (ʌn'saɪzd) *adj.* not made or sorted according to size.

un+sized[2] (ʌn'saɪzd) *adj.* (of a wall, etc.) not treated with size.

un+skil+ful *or U.S.* **un+skill+ful** (ʌn'skɪlfʊl) *adj.* **1.** lacking

---

ˌ**un+re+'morse+ful** *adj.*
ˌ**un+re+'mu+ner·a+tive** *adj.*
un+'ren+dered *adj.*
ˌ**un+re+'newed** *adj.*
ˌ**un+re+'nowned** *adj.*
un+'rent+ed *adj.*
ˌ**un+re+'pealed** *adj.*
ˌ**un+re+'peat+a·ble** *adj.*
ˌ**un+re+'pent+ant** *adj.*
ˌ**un+re+'place+a·ble** *adj.*
ˌ**un+re+'port+ed** *adj.*
ˌ**un+rep+re+'sent·a+tive** *adj.*
ˌ**un+rep+re+'sent+ed** *adj.*
ˌ**un+re+'pressed** *adj.*
ˌ**un+re+'prieved** *adj.*
ˌ**un+'rep+ri+mand+ed** *adj.*
ˌ**un+re+'proved** *adj.*
ˌ**un+re+'quest+ed** *adj.*
ˌ**un+re+'sent+ful** *adj.*
ˌ**un+re+'sist+ant** *adj.*
ˌ**un+re+'sist+ed** *adj.*
ˌ**un+re+'sist+ing** *adj.*
ˌ**un+re+'solved** *adj.*
ˌ**un+re+'spect+ful** *adj.*
un+'rest+ed *adj.*
ˌ**un+re+'strict+ed** *adj.*
ˌ**un+re+'turned** *adj.*
ˌ**un+re+'vealed** *adj.*
ˌ**un+re+'veal+ing** *adj.*
ˌ**un+re+'vised** *adj.*
ˌ**un+re+'voked** *adj.*
ˌ**un+re+'ward+ed** *adj.*
ˌ**un+re+'ward+ing** *adj.*
un+'rhymed *adj.*
un+'rhyth+mi+cal *adj.*
un+'rid+den *adj.*
un+'ri+pened *adj.*
ˌ**un+ro+'man+tic** *adj.*
un+'ruled *adj.*
un+'safe *adj.*
un+'saint+ly *adj.*
un+'sal·a+ried *adj.*
un+'sale+a·ble *adj.*
un+'salt+ed *adj.*
un+'sanc+ti+ˌfied *adj.*
un+'sanc+tioned *adj.*
un+'san·i+ˌtar·y *adj.*
un+'sat+ed *adj.*
ˌ**un+sat+is+'fac+to·ry** *adj.*
un+'sat+is+ˌfied *adj.*
un+'sat+is+fy+ing *adj.*
un+'saved *adj.*
un+'say+a·ble *adj.*
un+'scal+a·ble *adj.*
un+'scanned *adj.*
un+'scarred *adj.*
un+'scent+ed *adj.*
un+'sched+uled *adj.*
un+'schol+ar+ly *adj.*
un+'sea+ˌwor+thy *adj.*
ˌ**un+se+'clud+ed** *adj.*
un+'sec+ond+ed *adj.*
ˌ**un+se+'duced** *adj.*
un+'see+ing *adj.*
un+'seg+ment+ed *adj.*
un+'seg+re+gat+ed *adj.*
ˌ**un+se+'lect+ed** *adj.*
ˌ**un+se+'lec+tive** *adj.*
ˌ**un+self+'con+scious** *adj.*
ˌ**un+sen+ti+'men+tal** *adj.*
un+'sep·a+rat+ed *adj.*
un+'served *adj.*
un+'ser+vice+a·ble *adj.*
un+'shad+owed *adj.*
un+'shak+en *adj.*
un+'shape+ly *adj.*
un+'shared *adj.*
un+'shaved *adj.*
ˌ**un+'shav+en** *adj.*
un+'shed *adj.*
un+'shelled *adj.*
un+'shel+tered *adj.*
un+'shield+ed *adj.*
un+'shock+a·ble *adj.*
un+'shod *adj.*
un+'shrink+a·ble *adj.*
un+'signed *adj.*
un+'si+lenced *adj.*

dexterity or proficiency. **2.** (often foll. by *in*) *Obsolete.* ignorant (of). —**un+'skil+fully** *or U.S.* **un+'skill+fully** *adv.* —**un+'skil+ful+ness** *or U.S.* **un+'skill+ful+ness** *n.*

un+skilled (ʌn'skɪld) *adj.* **1.** not having or requiring any special skill or training: *unskilled workers; an unskilled job.* **2.** having or displaying no skill; inexpert: *he is quite unskilled at dancing.*

un+slaked lime (ʌn'sleɪkt) *n.* another name for **calcium oxide.**

un+sling (ʌn'slɪŋ) *vb.* **+slings, +sling+ing, +slung.** (*tr.*) **1.** to remove or release from a slung position. **2.** to remove slings from.

un+snap (ʌn'snæp) *vb.* **+snaps, +snap+ping, +snapped.** (*tr.*) to unfasten (the snap or catch) of (something).

un+snarl (ʌn'snɑːl) *vb.* (*tr.*) to free from a snarl or tangle.

un+so+cia·ble (ʌn'səʊʃəbᵊl) *or* **un+so+cial** *adj.* **1.** (of a person) disinclined to associate or fraternize with others. **2.** unconducive to social intercourse: *an unsociable neighbourhood.* **3.** *Archaic.* incompatible. —**un+ˌso+cia·'bil+i+ty** *or* **un+'so+cia+ble+ness** *n.* —**un+'so+cia·bly** *adv.*

un+so+cial (ˌʌn'səʊʃəl) *adj.* **1.** not social; antisocial. **2.** (of the hours of work of certain jobs) falling outside the normal working day.

un+so+phis+ti+cat+ed (ˌʌnsə'fɪstɪˌkeɪtɪd) *adj.* **1.** lacking experience or worldly wisdom. **2.** marked by a lack of refinement or complexity: *an unsophisticated machine.* **3.** unadulterated or genuine. —**ˌun+so+'phis+ti+ˌcat+ed+ly** *adv.* —**ˌun+so+'phis+ti+ˌcat+ed+ness** *or* **ˌun+so+ˌphis+ti+'ca+tion** *n.*

un+sound (ʌn'saʊnd) *adj.* **1.** diseased, weak, or unstable: *of unsound mind.* **2.** unreliable or fallacious: *unsound advice.* **3.** lacking solidity, strength, or firmness: *unsound foundations.* **4.** of doubtful financial or commercial viability: *an unsound enterprise.* **5.** (of fruit, timber, etc.) not in an edible or usable condition. —**un+'sound+ly** *adv.* —**un+'sound+ness** *n.*

un+spar+ing (ʌn'spɛərɪŋ) *adj.* **1.** not sparing or frugal; lavish; profuse. **2.** showing harshness or severity; unmerciful. —**un+'spar+ing+ly** *adv.* —**un+'spar+ing+ness** *n.*

un+speak (ʌn'spiːk) *vb.* **+speaks, +speak+ing, +spoke, +spo+ken.** (*tr.*) an obsolete word for **unsay.**

un+speak+a+ble (ʌn'spiːkəbᵊl) *adj.* **1.** incapable of expression in words: *unspeakable ecstasy.* **2.** indescribably bad or evil. **3.** not to be uttered: *unspeakable thoughts.* —**un+'speak+a+ble+ness** *n.* —**un+'speak+a+bly** *adv.*

un+sphere (ʌn'sfɪə) *vb.* (*tr.*) *Chiefly poetic.* to remove from (its, one's, etc.) sphere or place.

un+spoiled (ʌn'spɔɪld) *or* **un+spoilt** (ʌn'spɔɪlt) *adj.* (of a village, town, etc.) having an unaltered character.

un+spo+ken (ʌn'spəʊkən) *adj.* **1.** understood without needing to be spoken; tacit. **2.** not uttered aloud.

un+spot+ted (ʌn'spɒtɪd) *adj.* **1.** without spots or stains. **2.** (esp. of reputations) free from moral stigma or blemish. —**un+'spot+ted+ness** *n.*

un+sta+ble (ʌn'steɪbᵊl) *adj.* **1.** lacking stability, fixity, or firmness. **2.** disposed to temperamental, emotional, or psychological variability. **3.** (of a chemical compound) readily decomposing. **4.** *Physics.* **a.** (of an elementary particle) having a very short lifetime. **b.** spontaneously decomposing by nuclear decay; radioactive: *an unstable nuclide.* —**un+'sta+ble+ness** *n.* —**un+'sta+bly** *adv.*

un+stead·y (ʌn'stɛdɪ) *adj.* **1.** not securely fixed: *an unsteady foothold.* **2.** (of behaviour, etc.) lacking constancy; erratic. **3.** without regularity: *an unsteady rhythm.* **4.** (of a manner of walking, etc.) precarious or staggering, as from intoxication. ~*vb.* **+stead·ies, +stead·y+ing, +stead+ied. 5.** (*tr.*) to make unsteady. —**un+'stead·i+ly** *adv.* —**un+'stead·i+ness** *n.*

un+steel (ʌn'stiːl) *vb.* (*tr.*) to make (the heart, feelings, etc.) more gentle or compassionate.

un+step (ʌn'stɛp) *vb.* **+steps, +step+ping, +stepped.** (*tr.*) *Nautical.* to remove (a mast) from its step.

un+stick (ʌn'stɪk) *vb.* **+sticks, +stick+ing, +stuck.** (*tr.*) to free or loosen (something stuck).

un+stop (ʌn'stɒp) *vb.* **+stops, +stop+ping, +stopped.** (*tr.*) **1.** to remove the stop or stopper from. **2.** to free from any stoppage or obstruction; open. **3.** to draw out the stops on (an organ). —**un+'stop+pa·bly** *adv.*

un+stop+pa·ble (ʌn'stɒpəbᵊl) *adj.* not capable of being stopped; extremely forceful.

un+stopped (ʌn'stɒpt) *adj.* **1.** not obstructed or stopped up. **2.** *Phonetics.* denoting a speech sound for whose articulation the closure is not complete, as in the pronunciation of a vowel, fricative, or continuant. **3.** *Prosody.* (of verse) having the sense of the line carried over into the next. **4.** (of an organ pipe or a string on a musical instrument) not stopped.

un+strained (ʌn'streɪnd) *adj.* **1.** not under strain; relaxed. **2.** not cleared or separated by passing through a strainer.

un+strat·i+fied (ʌn'strætɪˌfaɪd) *adj.* (esp. of igneous rocks and rock formations) not occurring in distinct layers or strata; not stratified.

un+streamed (ˌʌn'striːmd) *adj. Brit. education.* (of children) not divided into groups or streams according to ability.

un+stressed (ʌn'strɛst) *adj.* **1.** carrying relatively little stress; unemphasized. **2.** *Phonetics.* of, relating to, or denoting the weakest accent in a word or breath group, which in some languages, such as English or German, is also associated with a reduction in vowel quality to a centralized (i) or (a). **3.** *Prosody.* (of a syllable in verse) having no stress or accent.

un+stri+at+ed (ʌn'straɪeɪtɪd) *adj.* (of muscle) composed of elongated cells that do not have striations; smooth.

un+string (ʌn'strɪŋ) *vb.* **+strings, +string+ing, +strung.** (*tr.*) **1.** to remove the strings of. **2.** (of beads, pearls, etc.) to remove or take from a string. **3.** to weaken or enfeeble emotionally (a person or his nerves).

un+striped (ʌn'straɪpt) *adj.* (esp. of smooth muscle) not having stripes; unstriated.

un+struc+tured (ʌn'strʌktʃəd) *adj.* without formal structure or systematic organization.

un+strung (ʌn'strʌŋ) *adj.* **1.** emotionally distressed; unnerved. **2.** (of a stringed instrument) with the strings detached.

un+stuck (ʌn'stʌk) *adj.* **1.** freed from being stuck, glued, fastened, etc. **2. come unstuck.** to suffer failure or disaster.

un+stud+ied (ʌn'stʌdɪd) *adj.* **1.** natural; unaffected. **2.** (foll. by *in*) without knowledge or training.

un+sub+stan+tial (ˌʌnsəb'stænʃəl) *adj.* **1.** lacking weight, strength, or firmness. **2.** (esp. of an argument) of doubtful validity. **3.** of no material existence or substance; unreal. —**ˌun+sub+ˌstan+ti+'al+i+ty** *n.* —**ˌun+sub+'stan+tial+ly** *adv.*

un+sung (ʌn'sʌŋ) *adj.* **1.** not acclaimed or honoured; *unsung deeds.* **2.** not yet sung.

un+sup+port+a+ble (ˌʌnsə'pɔːtəbᵊl) *adj.* **1.** not able to be supported. **2.** not able to be defended: *unsupportable actions.*

un+sure (ʌn'ʃʊə) *adj.* **1.** lacking assurance or self-confidence. **2.** (*usually postpositive*) without sure knowledge; uncertain: *unsure of her agreement.* **3.** precarious; insecure. **4.** not certain or reliable.

un+sus+pect+ed (ˌʌnsə'spɛktɪd) *adj.* **1.** not under suspicion. **2.** not known to exist. —**ˌun+sus+'pect+ed+ly** *adv.* —**ˌun+sus+'pect+ed+ness** *n.*

un+sus+pect+ing (ˌʌnsə'spɛktɪŋ) *adj.* disposed to trust; not suspicious; trusting. —**ˌun+sus+'pect+ing+ly** *adv.*

un+swear (ʌn'swɛə) *vb.* **+swears, +swear+ing, +swore, +sworn.** to retract or revoke (a sworn oath); abjure.

un+swerv+ing (ʌn'swɜːvɪŋ) *adj.* not turning aside; constant.

un+tan+gle (ʌn'tæŋgᵊl) *vb.* (*tr.*) **1.** to free from a tangled condition. **2.** to free from perplexity or confusion.

un+taught (ʌn'tɔːt) *adj.* **1.** without training or education. **2.** attained or achieved without instruction.

un+teach (ʌn'tiːtʃ) *vb.* **+teach·es, +teach+ing, +taught.** (*tr.*) *Rare.* **1.** to cause to disbelieve (teaching). **2.** to cause to forget (teaching).

un+ten+a+ble (ʌn'tɛnəbᵊl) *adj.* **1.** (of theories, propositions, etc.) incapable of being maintained, defended, or vindicated. **2.** unable to be maintained against attack. **3.** *Rare.* (of a house, etc.) unfit for occupation. —**un+ˌten+a·'bil+i+ty** *or* **un+'ten+a·ble+ness** *n.* —**un+'ten+a·bly** *adv.*

Un+ter den Lin+den (*German* ˌʊntər deːn 'lɪndᵊn) *n.* the main street of East Berlin, extending from the centre of the city to the Brandenburg Gate.

Un+ter+wal+den (*German* 'ʊntərˌvaldᵊn) *n.* a canton of central Switzerland, on Lake Lucerne: consists of the demicantons of **Nidwalden** (east) and **Obwalden** (west). Capitals: (Nidwalden) Stans; (Obwalden) Sarnen. Pop.: (Nidwalden) 25 634 (1970); (Obwalden) 24 509 (1970). Areas: (Nidwalden) 274 sq. km (107 sq. miles); (Obwalden) 492 sq. km (192 sq. miles).

un+think (ʌn'θɪŋk) *vb.* **+thinks, +think+ing, +thought.** (*tr.*) **1.** to reverse one's opinion about. **2.** to dispel from the mind.

un+think+a+ble (ʌn'θɪŋkəbᵊl) *adj.* **1.** not to be contemplated; out of the question. **2.** unimaginable; inconceivable. **3.** unreasonable; improbable. —**un+ˌthink+a·'bil+i+ty** *or* **un+'think+a·ble+ness** *n.* —**un+'think+a·bly** *adv.*

---

un+'sink+a+ble *adj.*
un+'smil+ing *adj.*
un+'so+cial *adj.*
un+'soiled *adj.*
un+'sold *adj.*
ˌun+so+'lic+it+ed *adj.*
un+'solv+a+ble *adj.*
un+'solved *adj.*
un+'sort+ed *adj.*
un+'sought *adj.*
un+'sown *adj.*
un+'spe+cial+ˌized *or* **un+'spe+cial+ˌised** *adj.*
ˌun+spe+'cif+ic *adj.*
un+'spec+i+ˌfied *adj.*
ˌun+spec+'tac+u+lar *adj.*
un+'spir+i+tu+al *adj.*
un+'spoiled *adj.*
un+'sport+ing *adj.*
un+'sports+man+ˌlike *adj.*
un+'stamped *adj.*
un+'stained *adj.*
un+'stand+ard+ˌized *or* **un+'stand+ard+ˌised** *adj.*
un+'stat+ed *adj.*
un+'states+man+like *adj.*
un+'stemmed *adj.*
un+'ster+ile *adj.*
un+'ster+i+ˌlized *or* **un+'ster+i+ˌlised** *adj.*
un+'stint+ed *adj.*
un+'strap *vb.,* **+straps, +strap+ping, +strapped.**
ˌun+sub+'dued *adj.*
ˌun+sub+'mis+sive *adj.*
ˌun+sub+'stan+ti+ˌat+ed *adj.*
un+'sub+tle *adj.*
ˌun+suc+'cess+ful *adj.*
un+'suit+a+ble *adj.*
un+'suit+ed *adj.*
un+'sul+lied *adj.*
un+'su+per+ˌvised *adj.*
ˌun+sup+'port+ed *adj.*
ˌun+sup+'pressed *adj.*
ˌun+sur+'mount+a+ble *adj.*
ˌun+sur+'pass+a+ble *adj.*
ˌun+sur+'passed *adj.*
ˌun+sur+'prised *adj.*
ˌun+sus+'cep+ti+ble *adj.*
ˌun+sus+'tained *adj.*
un+'swathe *vb.*
un+'swayed *adj.*
un+'sweet+ened *adj.*
ˌun+sym+'met+ri+cal *adj.*
ˌun+sym+pa+'thet+ic *adj.*
ˌun+sys+tem+'at+ic *adj.*
un+'tack *vb.*
un+'tact+ful *adj.*
un+'taint+ed *adj.*
un+'tal+ent+ed *adj.*
un+'tame+a+ble *adj.*
un+'tamed *adj.*
un+'tapped *adj.*
un+'tar+nished *adj.*
un+'tast+ed *adj.*
un+'taxed *adj.*
un+'teach+a+ble *adj.*
un+'tem+pered *adj.*
un+'tempt+ed *adj.*
un+'ten+ant+ed *adj.*
un+'tend+ed *adj.*
un+'test+ed *adj.*

un+think+ing (ʌnˈθɪŋkɪŋ) *adj.* **1.** lacking thoughtfulness; inconsiderate. **2.** heedless; inadvertent: *it was done in an unthinking moment.* **3.** not thinking or able to think. —**un+ˈthink+ing+ly** *adv.* —**un+ˈthink+ing+ness** *n.*

un+thought-of *adj.* unimaginable; inconceivable.

un+thread (ʌnˈθrɛd) *vb.* (*tr.*) **1.** to draw out the thread or threads from (a needle, etc.). **2.** to disentangle.

un+throne (ʌnˈθrəʊn) *vb.* (*tr.*) a less common word for **dethrone.**

un+ti+dy (ʌnˈtaɪdɪ) *adj.* **+di+er, +di+est. 1.** not neat; slovenly. ~*vb.* **+dies, +dy+ing, +died. 2.** (*tr.*) to make untidy. —**un+ˈti+di+ly** *adv.* —**un+ˈti+di+ness** *n.*

un+tie (ʌnˈtaɪ) *vb.* **+ties, +ty+ing, +tied. 1.** to unfasten or free (a knot or something that is tied) or (of a knot, etc.) to become unfastened. **2.** (*tr.*) to free from constraint or restriction.

un+til (ʌnˈtɪl) *conj.* (*subordinating*) **1.** up to (a time) that: *he laughed until he cried.* **2.** (*used with a negative*) before (a time or event): *until you change, you can't go out.* ~*prep.* **3.** (often preceded by *up*) in or throughout the period before: *he waited until six.* **4.** (*used with a negative*) earlier than; before: *he won't come until tomorrow.* [C13: *untill;* related to Old High German *unt* unto, until,Old Norse *und;* see TILL[1]]
Usage. See at **till.**

un+time+ly (ʌnˈtaɪmlɪ) *adj.* **1.** occurring before the expected, normal, or proper time: *an untimely death.* **2.** inappropriate to the occasion, time, or season: *his joking at the funeral was most untimely.* ~*adv.* **3.** prematurely or inopportunely. —**un+ˈtime+li+ness** *n.*

un+tit+led (ʌnˈtaɪtᵊld) *adj.* **1.** without a title: *an untitled manuscript.* **2.** having no claim or title: *an untitled usurper.*

un·to (ˈʌntuː) *prep.* an archaic word for **to.** [C13: of Scandinavian origin; see UNTIL]

un+told (ʌnˈtəʊld) *adj.* **1.** incapable of description or expression: *untold suffering.* **2.** incalculably great in number or quantity: *untold thousands.* **3.** not told.

un+touch+a·ble (ʌnˈtʌtʃəbᵊl) *adj.* **1.** lying beyond reach. **2.** above reproach, suspicion, or impeachment. **3.** unable to be touched. ~*n.* **4.** a member of the lowest class in India, whom those of the four main castes were formerly forbidden to touch. —**un+ˌtouch+a·ˈbil+i·ty** *n.*

un+touched (ʌnˈtʌtʃt) *adj.* **1.** not used, handled, touched, etc. **2.** not injured or harmed. **3.** (*postpositive*) emotionally unmoved. **4.** not changed, modified, or affected. **5.** (of food or drink) left without being consumed. **6.** not mentioned or referred to: *he left the subject untouched.*

un+to+ward (ˌʌntəˈwɔːd, ʌnˈtəʊəd) *adj.* **1.** characterized by misfortune, disaster, or annoyance. **2.** not auspicious; adverse; unfavourable. **3.** unseemly or improper. **4.** *Archaic.* refractory; perverse. **5.** *Obsolete.* awkward, ungainly, or uncouth. —**ˌun+to+ˈward+ly** *adv.* —**ˌun+to+ˈward+ness** *n.*

un+trav+elled (ʌnˈtrævᵊld) *adj.* **1.** (of persons) not having travelled widely; narrow or provincial. **2.** (of a road) never travelled over.

un+tread (ʌnˈtrɛd) *vb.* **+treads, +tread+ing, +trod, +trod+den** *or* **+trod.** (*tr.*) *Rare.* to retrace (a course, path, etc.).

un+tried (ʌnˈtraɪd) *adj.* **1.** not tried, attempted, or proved; untested. **2.** not tried by a judge or court.

un+true (ʌnˈtruː) *adj.* **1.** incorrect or false. **2.** disloyal. **3.** diverging from a rule, standard, or measure; inaccurate. —**un+ˈtrue+ness** *n.* —**un+ˈtru+ly** *adv.*

un+truss (ʌnˈtrʌs) *vb.* **1.** (*tr.*) to release from or as if from a truss; unfasten. **2.** *Obsolete.* to undress.

un+truth (ʌnˈtruːθ) *n.* **1.** the state or quality of being untrue. **2.** a statement, fact, etc., that is not true.

un+truth+ful (ʌnˈtruːθfʊl) *adj.* **1.** (of a person) given to lying. **2.** diverging from the truth; untrue. —**un+ˈtruth+ful+ly** *adv.* —**un+ˈtruth+ful+ness** *n.*

un+tuck (ʌnˈtʌk) *vb.* to become or cause to become loose or not tucked in: *to untuck the blankets.*

un+tu+tored (ʌnˈtjuːtəd) *adj.* **1.** without formal instruction or education. **2.** lacking sophistication or refinement.

un+used *adj.* **1.** (ʌnˈjuːzd). not being or never having been made use of. **2.** (ʌnˈjuːst). (*postpositive;* foll. by *to*) not accustomed or used (to something).

un+u·su·al (ʌnˈjuːʒʊəl) *adj.* out of the ordinary; uncommon; extraordinary: *an unusual design.* —**un+ˈu·su·al+ly** *adv.* —**un+ˈu·su·al+ness** *n.*

un+ut·ter·a·ble (ʌnˈʌtərəbᵊl) *adj.* **1.** incapable of being expressed in words. —**un+ˈut·ter·a·ble+ness** *n.* —**un+ˈut·ter+a·bly** *adv.*

un+val+ued (ʌnˈvæljuːd) *adj.* **1.** not appreciated or valued. **2.** not assessed or estimated as to price or valuation. **3.** *Obsolete.* of great value.

un+veil (ʌnˈveɪl) *vb.* **1.** (*tr.*) to remove the cover or shroud from, esp. in the ceremonial unveiling of a monument, etc. **2.** to remove the veil from (one's own or another person's face). **3.** (*tr.*) to make (something secret or concealed) known or public; divulge; reveal.

un+veil+ing (ʌnˈveɪlɪŋ) *n.* **1.** a ceremony involving the removal of a veil at the formal presentation of a statue, monument, etc., for the first time. **2.** the presentation of something, esp. for the first time.

un+voice (ʌnˈvɔɪs) *vb.* (*tr.*) **1.** to pronounce without vibration of the vocal cords. **2.** another word for **devoice.**

un+voiced (ʌnˈvɔɪst) *adj.* **1.** not expressed or spoken. **2.** articulated without vibration of the vocal cords; voiceless.

un+war+rant+a+ble (ʌnˈwɒrəntəbᵊl) *adj.* incapable of vindication or justification. —**un+ˈwar+rant+a+ble+ness** *n.* —**un+ˈwar+rant+a+bly** *adv.*

un+war+rant+ed (ʌnˈwɒrəntɪd) *adj.* **1.** lacking justification or authorization. **2.** another word for **unwarrantable.**

un+war·y (ʌnˈwɛərɪ) *adj.* lacking caution or prudence; not vigilant or careful. —**un+ˈwar·i·ly** *adv.* —**un+ˈwar·i+ness** *n.*

un+washed (ʌnˈwɒʃt) *adj.* **1.** not washed. ~*n.* **2. the great unwashed.** *Informal and derogatory.* the masses.

un+watched (ʌnˈwɒtʃt) *adj.* (of an automatic device, such as a beacon) not manned.

un+wea+ried (ʌnˈwɪərɪd) *adj.* **1.** not abating or tiring. **2.** not fatigued; fresh. —**un+ˈwea+ried+ly** *adv.* —**un+ˈwea+ried+ness** *n.*

un+weighed (ʌnˈweɪd) *adj.* **1.** (of quantities purchased, etc.) not measured for weight. **2.** (of statements, etc.) not carefully considered.

un+wel+come (ʌnˈwɛlkəm) *adj.* **1.** (of persons) not welcome. **2.** causing dissatisfaction or displeasure. —**un+ˈwel+come+ly** *adv.* —**un+ˈwel+come+ness** *n.*

un+well (ʌnˈwɛl) *adj.* (*postpositive*) not well; ill.

un+wept (ʌnˈwɛpt) *adj.* **1.** not wept for or lamented. **2.** *Rare.* (of tears) not shed.

un+whole+some (ʌnˈhəʊlsəm) *adj.* **1.** detrimental to physical or mental health: *an unwholesome climate.* **2.** morally harmful or depraved: *unwholesome practices.* **3.** indicative of illness, esp. in appearance. **4.** (esp. of food) of inferior quality. —**un+ˈwhole+some+ly** *adv.* —**un+ˈwhole+some+ness** *n.*

un+wield·y (ʌnˈwiːldɪ) *or* **un+wield+ly** *adj.* **1.** too heavy, large, or awkwardly shaped to be easily handled. **2.** ungainly; clumsy. —**un+ˈwield·i+ly** *or* **un+ˈwield+li+ly** *adv.* —**un+ˈwield·i+ness** *or* **un+ˈwield+li+ness** *n.*

un+willed (ʌnˈwɪld) *adj.* not intentional; involuntary.

un+will+ing (ʌnˈwɪlɪŋ) *adj.* **1.** unfavourably inclined; reluctant. **2.** performed, given, or said with reluctance. —**un+ˈwill+ing+ly** *adv.* —**un+ˈwill+ing+ness** *n.*

un+wind (ʌnˈwaɪnd) *vb.* **+winds, +wind+ing, +wound. 1.** to slacken, undo, or unravel or cause to slacken, undo, or unravel. **2.** (*tr.*) to disentangle. **3.** to make or become relaxed: *he finds it hard to unwind after a busy day at work.* —**un+ˈwind+a·ble** *adj.* —**un+ˈwind+er** *n.*

un+wink+ing (ʌnˈwɪŋkɪŋ) *adj.* vigilant; watchful.

un+wise (ʌnˈwaɪz) *adj.* lacking wisdom or prudence; foolish. —**un+ˈwise+ly** *adv.* —**un+ˈwise+ness** *n.*

un+wish (ʌnˈwɪʃ) *vb.* (*tr.*) **1.** to retract or revoke (a wish). **2.** to desire (something) not to be or take place.

un+wished (ʌnˈwɪʃt) *adj.* not desired; unwelcome.

un+wit+nessed (ʌnˈwɪtnɪst) *adj.* **1.** without the signature or attestation of a witness. **2.** not seen or observed.

un+wit+ting (ʌnˈwɪtɪŋ) *adj.* (*usually prenominal*) **1.** not knowing or conscious. **2.** not intentional; inadvertent. [Old English *unwitende,* from UN-[1] + *witting,* present participle of *witan* to know; related to Old High German *wizzan* to know, Old Norse *vita*] —**un+ˈwit+ting+ly** *adv.* —**un+ˈwit+ting+ness** *n.*

un+wont+ed (ʌnˈwəʊntɪd) *adj.* **1.** out of the ordinary; unusual. **2.** (usually foll. by *to*) *Archaic.* unaccustomed; unused. —**un+ˈwont+ed+ly** *adv.* —**un+ˈwont+ed+ness** *n.*

un+world+ly (ʌnˈwɜːldlɪ) *adj.* **1.** not concerned with material values or pursuits. **2.** lacking sophistication; naive. **3.** not of this earth or world. —**un+ˈworld+li+ness** *n.*

un+wor+thy (ʌnˈwɜːðɪ) *adj.* **1.** (often foll. by *of*) not deserving or worthy. **2.** (often foll. by *of*) beneath the level considered

---

un+ˈteth+ered *adj.*
un+ˈthanked *adj.*
ˌun+ˈthank+ful *adj.*
un+ˈthought+ful *adj.*
un+ˈtill+a·ble *adj.*
un+ˈtilled *adj.*
un+ˈtinged *adj.*
un+ˈtir+ing *adj.*
un+ˈtraced *adj.*
un+ˈtracked *adj.*
un+ˈtrac+ta·ble *adj.*
un+ˈtrained *adj.*
un+ˈtram+melled *adj.*
ˌun+trans+ˈfer+a·ble *adj.*
ˌun+trans+ˈformed *adj.*
ˌun+trans+ˈlat+a·ble *adj.*
ˌun+trans+ˈlat+ed *adj.*
un+ˈtreat+ed *adj.*
un+ˈtrod+den *adj.*
un+ˈtrou+bled *adj.*
un+ˈtrust+ˌwor+thy *adj.*
ˌun+ˈtune+ful *adj.*
un+ˈturned *adj.*
un+ˈtwine *vb.*
un+ˈtwist *vb.*
un+ˈtyp·i·cal *adj.*
un+ˈus+a·ble *adj.*
un+ˈu·ti+ˌlized *or*
un+ˈu·ti+ˌlised *adj.*
un+ˈut+tered *adj.*
un+ˈvac·ci+ˌnat+ed *adj.*
un+ˈvan+quished *adj.*
un+ˈvar+ied *adj.*
un+ˈvar+nished *adj.*
un+ˈvar·y+ing *adj.*
un+ˈven·ti+ˌlat+ed *adj.*
un+ˈver·i+ˌfi·a·ble *adj.*
un+ˈver·i+ˌfied *adj.*
un+ˈversed *adj.*
un+ˈvi+a·ble *adj.*
un+ˈvis·it·ed *adj.*
un+ˈwant+ed *adj.*
un+ˈwarmed *adj.*
un+ˈwarned *adj.*
un+ˈwa+ver+ing *adj.*
un+ˈweaned *adj.*
un+ˈwea+ry *adj.*
un+ˈwea+ry+ing *adj.*
un+ˈweave *vb.,* **+weaves, +weav+ing; +wove** *or* **+weaved; +wo+ven** *or* **+weaved.**
un+ˈwed+ded *or* +un+ˈwed *adj.*
un+ˈweed+ed *adj.*
un+ˈwished-for *adj.*
un+ˈwith+ered *adj.*
un+ˈwit+nessed *adj.*
un+ˈwood+ed *adj.*
un+ˈwork+a·ble *adj.*
un+ˈworked *adj.*
un+ˈwork+man+ˌlike *adj.*
un+ˈworn *adj.*
un+ˈwor+ried *adj.*
un+ˈwound+ed *adj.*
un+ˈyield+ing *adj.*

befitting (to): *that remark is unworthy of you.* **3.** lacking merit or value. **4.** (of treatment) not warranted or deserved. —**un+'worth·i+ly** *adv.* —**un+'worth·i+ness** *n.*

un+wound (ʌn'waʊnd) *vb.* the past tense or past participle of **unwind.**

un+wrap (ʌn'ræp) *vb.* **+wraps, +wrap+ping, +wrapped.** to remove the covering or wrapping from (something) or (of something wrapped) to have the covering come off.

un+writ+ten (ʌn'rɪtᵊn) *adj.* **1.** not printed or in writing. **2.** effective only through custom; traditional. **3.** without writing upon it.

un+writ+ten law *n.* **1.** the law based upon custom, usage, and judicial decisions, as distinguished from the enactments of a legislature, orders or decrees in writing, etc. **2. the.** the tradition that a person may avenge any insult to family integrity, as used to justify criminal acts of vengeance.

un+yoke (ʌn'jəʊk) *vb.* **1.** to release (an animal, etc.) from a yoke. **2.** (*tr.*) to set free; liberate. **3.** (*tr.*) to disconnect or separate. **4.** (*intr.*) *Archaic.* to cease working.

un+zip (ʌn'zɪp) *vb.* **+zips, +zip+ping, +zipped.** to unfasten the zip of (a garment, etc.) or (of a zip or garment with a zip) to become unfastened: *her skirt unzipped as she sat down.*

up (ʌp) *prep.* **1.** indicating movement from a lower to a higher position: *climbing up a mountain.* **2.** at a higher or further level or position in or on: *soot up the chimney; a shop up the road.* ~*adv.* **3.** (*often particle*) to an upward, higher, or erect position, esp. indicating readiness for an activity: *looking up at the stars; up and doing something.* **4.** (*particle*) indicating intensity or completion of an action: *he tore up the cheque; drink up now!* **5.** to the place referred to or where the speaker is: *the man came up and asked the way.* **6. a.** to a more important place: *up to London.* **b.** to a more northerly place: *up to Scotland.* **c.** (of a member of some British universities) to or at university. **d.** in a particular part of the country: *up north.* **7.** to appear for trial: *up before the magistrate.* **8.** having gained: *ten pounds up on the deal.* **9.** higher in price: *coffee is up again.* **10.** raised (for discussion, etc.): *the plan was up for consideration.* **11.** taught: *well up in physics.* **12.** (*functioning as imperative*) get, stand, etc., up: *up with you!* **13. up with.** (*functioning as imperative*) wanting the beginning or continuation of: *up with the monarchy!* **14. something's up.** *Informal.* something strange is happening. **15. up against. a.** touching. **b.** having to cope with: *look what we're up against now.* **16. up for.** as a candidate or applicant for: *he's up for re-election again.* **17. up to. a.** devising or scheming; occupied with: *she's up to no good.* **b.** dependent or incumbent upon: *the decision is up to you.* **c.** equal to (a challenge, etc.) or capable of (doing, etc.): *are you up to playing in the final?* **d.** aware of: *up to a person's tricks.* **e.** as far as: *up to his waist in mud.* **f.** as many as: *up to two years waiting time.* **g.** comparable with: *not up to your normal standard.* **18. up top.** *Informal.* in the head or mind. **19. up yours.** *Informal.* an expression of contempt or refusal. **20. what's up?** *Informal.* what is happening? ~*adj.* **21.** (*predicative*) of a high or higher position. **22.** (*predicative*) out of bed; awake: *the children aren't up yet.* **23.** (*prenominal*) of or relating to a train or trains to a more important place or one regarded as higher: *the up platform.* ~*vb.* **ups, up+ping, upped. 24.** (*tr.*) to increase or raise. **25.** (*intr.; foll. by* and *with a verb*) *Informal.* to do (something) suddenly, unexpectedly, etc.: *she upped and married someone else.* ~*n.* **26.** high point; good or pleasant period (esp. in the phrase **ups and downs**). **27.** *Slang.* another word (esp. U.S.) for **upper** (sense 9). **28. on the up and up. a.** trustworthy or honest. **b.** *Brit.* on the upward trend or movement: *our firm's on the up and up.* [Old English *upp;* related to Old Saxon, Old Norse *up,* Old High German *ūf,* Gothic *iup*]

U.P. *abbrev. for:* **1.** United Press. **2.** Uttar Pradesh.

up- *prefix.* up, upper, or upwards: *uproot; upmost; upthrust; upgrade; uplift.*

up-an·chor *vb.* (*intr.*) *Nautical.* to weigh anchor.

up-and-com·ing *adj.* promising continued or future success; enterprising.

up-and-down *adj.* **1.** moving, executed, or formed alternately upwards and downwards. **2.** *Chiefly U.S.* very steep; vertical. ~*adv., prep.* **up and down. 3.** backwards and forwards (along).

up-and-o·ver *adj.* (of a door, etc.) opened by being lifted and moved into a horizontal position.

up-and-un·der *n. Rugby.* a high kick forwards followed by a charge to the place where it lands.

U·pan·i+shad (u:'pʌnɪʃəd, -ˌʃæd, ju:-) *n. Hinduism.* any of a class of the Sanskrit sacred books probably composed between 400 and 200 B.C. and embodying the mystical and esoteric doctrines of ancient Hindu philosophy. [C19: from Sanskrit *upanisad* a sitting down near something, from *upa* near to + *ni* down + *sīdati* he sits] —**U·ˌpan·i+'shad+ic** *adj.*

u·pas ('ju:pəs) *n.* **1.** a large moraceous tree of Java, *Antiaria toxicaria,* having whitish bark and poisonous milky sap. **2.** the sap of this tree, used as an arrow poison. ~Also called: **antiar.** [C19: from Malay: poison]

up+beat ('ʌpˌbi:t) *n.* **1.** *Music.* **a.** an unaccented beat, esp. the last bar, **b.** the upward gesture of a conductor's baton indicating this. Compare **downbeat. 2.** an upward trend (in prosperity, etc.). ~*adj.* **3.** *Informal.* marked by cheerfulness or optimism.

up-bow ('ʌpˌbəʊ) *n.* a stroke of the bow from its tip to its nut on a stringed instrument. Compare **down-bow.**

up+braid (ʌp'breɪd) *vb.* (*tr.*) **1.** to reprove or reproach angrily. **2.** to find fault with. [Old English *upbregdan;* related to Danish *bebreide;* see UP, BRAID] —**up+'braid+er** *n.* —**up+'braid+ing** *n.* —**up+'braid+ing+ly** *adv.*

up+bring+ing ('ʌpˌbrɪŋɪŋ) *n.* the education of a person during his formative years. Also called: **bringing-up.**

up+build (ʌp'bɪld) *vb.* **+builds, +build+ing, +built.** (*tr.*) to build up; enlarge, increase, etc. —**up+'build+er** *n.*

up+cast ('ʌpˌkɑ:st) *n.* **1.** material cast or thrown up. **2.** a ventilation shaft through which air leaves a mine. Compare **downcast** (sense 3). **3.** *Geology.* (in a fault) the section of strata that has been displaced upwards. ~*adj.* **4.** directed or thrown upwards. ~*vb.* **+casts, +cast+ing, +cast. 5.** (*tr.*) to throw or cast up.

up+coun·try (ʌp'kʌntrɪ) *adj.* **1.** of or coming from the interior of a country or region. **2.** *Disparaging.* lacking the sophistication associated with city-dwellers; countrified. ~*n.* **3.** the interior part of a region or country. ~*adv.* **4.** towards, in, or into the interior part of a country or region.

up+date *vb.* (ʌp'deɪt). (*tr.*) **1.** to bring up to date. **2.** *Computer technol.* to modify (a computer instruction) so that the address number is increased each time an instruction is carried out. ~*n.* ('ʌpˌdeɪt). **3.** the act of updating or something that is updated. —**up+'dat+er** *n.*

up+draft ('ʌpˌdrɑ:ft) *n.* an upward movement of air or other gas.

up+end (ʌp'ɛnd) *vb.* **1.** to turn or set or become turned or set on end. **2.** (*tr.*) to affect or upset drastically.

up+grade *vb.* (ʌp'greɪd). (*tr.*) **1.** to assign or promote (a person or job) to a higher professional rank or position. **2.** to raise in value, importance, esteem, etc. **3.** to improve (a breed of livestock) by crossing with a better strain. ~*n.* ('ʌpˌgreɪd). **4.** *U.S.* an upward slope. **5. on the upgrade.** improving or progressing, as in importance, status, health, etc. ~*adj.* **6.** *U.S.* going or sloping upwards. ~*adv.* **7.** *U.S.* up an incline, hill, or slope. —**up+'grad+er** *n.*

up+growth ('ʌpˌgrəʊθ) *n.* **1.** the process of developing or growing upwards. **2.** a result of evolution or growth.

up+heav+al (ʌp'hi:vᵊl) *n.* **1.** a strong, sudden, or violent disturbance, as in politics, social conditions, etc. **2.** *Geology.* another word for **uplift** (sense 6).

up+heave (ʌp'hi:v) *vb.* **+heaves, +heav+ing, +heaved** *or* **+hove. 1.** to heave or rise upwards. **2.** *Geology.* to thrust (land) upwards or (of land) to be thrust upwards. **3.** (*tr.*) to disturb violently; throw into disorder.

up+held (ʌp'hɛld) *vb.* the past tense or past participle of **uphold.**

up+hill ('ʌp'hɪl) *adj.* **1.** inclining, sloping, or leading upwards. **2.** requiring arduous and protracted effort: *an uphill task.* **3.** *Rare.* located on or at a high place. ~*adv.* **4.** up an incline or slope; upwards. **5.** against difficulties. ~*n.* **6.** a rising incline; ascent.

up+hold (ʌp'həʊld) *vb.* **+holds, +hold+ing, +held.** (*tr.*) **1.** to maintain, affirm, or defend against opposition or challenge. **2.** to give moral support or inspiration to. **3.** *Rare.* to support physically. **4.** to lift up. —**up+'hold+er** *n.*

up+hol+ster (ʌp'həʊlstə) *vb.* (*tr.*) to fit (chairs, sofas, etc.) with padding, springs, webbing, and covering.

up+hol+ster+er (ʌp'həʊlstərə) *n.* a person who upholsters furniture as a profession. [C17: from *upholster* small furniture dealer; see UPHOLD, -STER, -ER[1]]

up+hol+ster·y (ʌp'həʊlstərɪ) *n., pl.* **+ster·ies. 1.** the padding, covering, etc., of a piece of furniture. **2.** the business, work, or craft of upholstering.

u·phroe ('ju:frəʊ) *n. Nautical.* a variant spelling of **euphroe.**

U.P.I. *abbrev. for* United Press International.

up+keep ('ʌpˌki:p) *n.* **1.** the act or process of keeping something in good repair, esp. over a long period; maintenance. **2.** the cost of maintenance.

up+land ('ʌplənd) *n.* **1.** an area of high or relatively high ground. ~*adj.* **2.** relating to or situated in an upland.

up+land cot+ton *n.* **1.** a tropical American cotton plant, *Gossypium hirsutum,* widely cultivated for its fibre. **2.** the fibre of this plant, or the fabric woven from it.

up+land plov+er *or* **sand+pip+er** *n.* an American sandpiper, *Bartramia longicauda,* with a short slender bill and long tail.

up+lift *vb.* (ʌp'lɪft). (*tr.*) **1.** to raise; elevate; lift up. **2.** to raise morally, spiritually, culturally, etc. ~*n.* ('ʌpˌlɪft). **3.** the act, process, or result of lifting up. **4.** the act or process of bettering moral, social or cultural conditions, etc. **5. a.** a brassiere for lifting and supporting the breasts. **b.** (*as modifier*): *an uplift bra.* **6.** the process or result of land being raised to a higher level, as during a period of mountain building. —**up+'lift+er** *n.* —**up+'lift+ment** *n.*

up-mar·ket *adj.* relating to commercial products, services, etc., that are relatively expensive and of superior quality.

up+most ('ʌpˌməʊst) *adj.* another word for **uppermost.**

U·po·lu (u:'pəʊlu:) *n.* an island in the SW central Pacific, in Western Samoa. Chief town: Apia. Area: 1114 sq. km (430 sq. miles).

up·on (ə'pɒn) *prep.* **1.** another word for **on. 2.** indicating a position reached by going up: *climb upon my knee.* **3.** imminent for: *the weekend was upon us again.*

up+per ('ʌpə) *adj.* **1.** higher or highest in relation to physical position, wealth, rank, status, etc. **2.** (*cap. when part of a name*) lying farther upstream, inland, or farther north: *the upper valley of the Loire.* **3.** (*cap. when part of a name*) *Geology, archaeol.* denoting the late part or division of a period, system, formation, etc.: *Upper Palaeolithic.* **4.** *Maths.* (of a limit or bound) greater than or equal to one or more numbers or variables. ~*n.* **5.** the higher of two objects, people, etc. **6.** the part of a shoe above the sole, covering the upper surface of the foot. **7. on one's uppers.** extremely poor; destitute. **8.** *Informal.* any tooth of the upper jaw. **9.** Also called (esp. U.S.): **up.** *Slang.* any of various drugs having a stimulant or euphoric effect. Compare **downer.**

up·per at·mo·sphere *n. Meteorol.* that part of the atmosphere above the troposphere, esp. at heights that cannot be reached by balloon.

Up·per Aus·tri·a *n.* a province of N Austria: first divided from Lower Austria in 1251. Capital: Linz. Pop.: 1 223 444 (1971). Area: 11 978 sq. km (4625 sq. miles). German name: **Oberösterreich.**

Up·per Bur·ma *n.* the inland regions of Burma, in the north of the country.

Up·per Can·a·da *n.* **1.** *History.* (from 1791–1841) the official name of the region of Canada lying southwest of the Ottawa River and north of the lower Great Lakes. Compare **Lower Canada. 2.** (esp. in E Canada) another name for **Ontario.**

up·per case *Printing.* ~*n.* **1.** the top half of a compositor's type case in which capital letters, reference marks, and accents are kept. ~*adj.* (**upper-case** *when prenominal*). **2.** of or relating to capital letters kept in this case and used in the setting or production of printed or typed matter. ~*vb.* **up·per-case. 3.** (*tr.*) to print with upper-case letters; capitalize.

up·per cham·ber *n.* another name for an **upper house.**

up·per class *n.* **1.** the class occupying the highest position in the social hierarchy, esp. the wealthy or the aristocracy. ~*adj.* (**upper-class** *when prenominal*). **2.** of or relating to the upper class. **3.** *U.S. education.* of or relating to the junior or senior classes of a college or high school.

up·per crust *n. Informal.* the upper class.

up·per·cut (ˈʌpəˌkʌt) *n.* **1.** a short swinging upward blow with the fist delivered at an opponent's chin. ~*vb.* **·cuts, ·cut·ting, ·cut. 2.** to hit (an opponent) with an uppercut.

Up·per E·gypt *n.* one of the two main administrative districts of Egypt: extends south from Cairo to the Sudan.

up·per hand *n.* **the.** the position of control; advantage (esp. in the phrases **have** *or* **get the upper hand).**

up·per house *n.* (*often cap.*) one of the two houses of a bicameral legislature. Also called: **upper chamber.** Compare **lower house.**

up·per mor·dent *n.* another name for **inverted mordent.**

up·per·most (ˈʌpəˌməʊst) *adj. also* **up·most. 1.** highest in position, power, importance, etc. ~*adv.* **2.** in or into the highest position, etc.

Up·per Pal·ae·o·lith·ic *n.* **1.** the latest of the three periods of the Palaeolithic, beginning about 40 000 B.C. and ending, in Europe, about 12 000 B.C.: characterized by the emergence of modern man, *Homo sapiens.* ~*adj.* **2.** of or relating to this period.

Up·per Pa·lat·i·nate *n.* See **Palatinate.**

Up·per Pen·in·su·la *n.* a peninsula in the northern U.S. between Lakes Superior and Michigan, constituting the N part of the state of Michigan.

up·per re·gions *pl. n.* **the.** *Chiefly literary.* the sky; heavens.

Up·per Si·le·si·a *n.* a region of SW Poland, formerly ruled by Germany: coal-mining and other heavy industry.

Up·per Tun·gus·ka *n.* See **Tunguska.**

Up·per Vol·ta *n.* an inland republic in W Africa: dominated by Mossi kingdoms (10th–19th centuries); French protectorate established in 1896; became an independent republic in 1960; consists mainly of a flat savanna plateau. Languages: French, Mossi, and African languages. Religion: mostly animist, with a Muslim minority. Currency: franc. Capital: Ouagadougou. Pop.: 6 144 013 (1975). Area: 273 200 sq. km (105 900 sq. miles).

up·per works *pl. n. Nautical.* the parts of a vessel above the waterline when fully laden.

up·pish (ˈʌpɪʃ) *adj. Brit. informal.* snobbish, arrogant, or presumptuous. [C18: from UP + -ISH] —ˈ**up·pish·ly** *adv.* —ˈ**up·pish·ness** *n.*

up·pi·ty (ˈʌpɪtɪ) *adj. Informal.* **1.** not yielding easily to persuasion or control. **2.** another word for **uppish.** [C20: humorous formation based on UP]

Upp·sa·la *or* **Up·sa·la** (ˈʌpsɑːlə) *n.* a city in E central Sweden: the royal headquarters in the 13th century; Gothic cathedral (the largest in Sweden) and Sweden's oldest university (1477). Pop.: 137 543 (1974 est.).

up·raise (ʌpˈreɪz) *vb.* (*tr.*) **1.** *Chiefly literary.* to lift up; elevate. **2.** *Archaic.* to praise; exalt. —**upˈrais·er** *n.*

up·rear (ʌpˈrɪə) *vb.* (*tr.*) to lift up; raise.

up·right (ˈʌpˌraɪt) *adj.* **1.** vertical or erect. **2.** honest, honourable, or just. ~*adv.* **3.** vertically. ~*n.* **4.** a vertical support, such as a stake or post. **5.** short for **upright piano. 6.** the state of being vertical. ~*vb.* **7.** (*tr.*) to make upright. —ˈ**upˌright·ly** *adv.* —ˈ**upˌright·ness** *n.*

up·right pi·an·o *n.* a piano in which the strings are vertically arranged. Compare **grand piano.**

up·rise *vb.* (ʌpˈraɪz), **·ris·es, ·ris·ing, ·rose, ·ris·en. 1.** (*tr.*) to rise up. ~*n.* (ˈʌpˌraɪz). **2.** another word for **rise** (senses 24, 25, 30). —**upˈris·er** *n.*

up·ris·ing (ˈʌpˌraɪzɪŋ, ʌpˈraɪzɪŋ) *n.* **1.** a revolt or rebellion. **2.** *Archaic.* an ascent.

up·riv·er (ˈʌpˈrɪvə) *adj., adv.* **1.** towards or near the source of a river. ~*n.* **2.** an area located upstream.

up·roar (ˈʌpˌrɔː) *n.* a commotion or disturbance characterized by loud noise and confusion; turmoil.

up·roar·i·ous (ʌpˈrɔːrɪəs) *adj.* **1.** causing or characterized by an uproar; tumultuous. **2.** extremely funny; hilarious. **3.** (of laughter, etc.) loud and boisterous. —**upˈroar·i·ous·ly** *adv.* —**upˈroar·i·ous·ness** *n.*

up·root (ʌpˈruːt) *vb.* (*tr.*) **1.** to pull up by or as if by the roots. **2.** to displace (a person or persons) from native or habitual surroundings. **3.** to remove or destroy utterly. —**upˈroot·ed·ness** *n.* —**upˈroot·er** *n.*

up·rouse (ʌpˈraʊz) *vb.* (*tr.*) *Rare.* to rouse or stir up; arouse.

up·rush (ˈʌpˌrʌʃ) *n.* an upward rush, as of consciousness.

up·sa·dai·sy (ˈʌpsəˈdeɪzɪ) *interj.* a variant spelling of **upsy-daisy.**

Up·sa·la (ˈʌpsɑːlə) *n.* a variant spelling of **Uppsala.**

ups and downs *pl. n.* alternating periods of good and bad fortune, high and low spirits, etc.

up·set *vb.* (ʌpˈsɛt), **·sets, ·set·ting, ·set.** (*mainly tr.*) **1.** (*also intr.*) to tip or be tipped over; overturn, capsize, or spill. **2.** to disturb the normal state, course, or stability of : *to upset the balance of nature.* **3.** to disturb mentally or emotionally. **4.** to defeat or overthrow, usually unexpectedly. **5.** to make physically ill: *seafood always upsets my stomach.* **6.** to thicken or spread (the end of a bar, rivet, etc.) by forging, hammering, or swagging. ~*n.* (ˈʌpˌsɛt). **7.** an unexpected defeat or reversal, as in a contest or plans. **8.** a disturbance or disorder of the emotions, body, etc. **9.** a tool used to upset a bar or rivet; swage. **10.** a forging or bar that has been upset in preparation for further processing. ~*adj.* (ʌpˈsɛt). **11.** overturned or capsized. **12.** emotionally or physically disturbed or distressed. **13.** disordered; confused. **14.** defeated or overthrown. [C14 (in the sense: to set up, erect; C19 in the sense: to overthrow); related to Middle High German *ūfsetzen* to put on, Middle Dutch *opzetten*] —**upˈset·ta·ble** *adj.* —**upˈset·ter** *n.* —**upˈset·ting·ly** *adv.*

up·set·ting (ʌpˈsɛtɪŋ) *n. Metallurgy.* the process of hammering the end of a heated bar of metal so that its width is increased locally, as in the manufacture of bolts.

up·shot (ˈʌpˌʃɒt) *n.* **1.** the final result; conclusion; outcome. **2.** *Archery.* the final shot in a match.

up·side (ˈʌpˌsaɪd) *n.* the upper surface or part.

up·side down *adj.* **1.** (*usually postpositive*) turned over completely; inverted. **2.** *Informal.* confused; topsy-turvy: *an upside-down world.* ~*adv.* **3.** in an inverted fashion. **4.** in a chaotic or crazy manner. [C16: variant, by folk etymology, of earlier *upsodown*] —ˌ**up·side-ˈdown·ness** *n.*

up·side-down cake *n.* a sponge cake baked with sliced fruit at the bottom, then inverted before serving.

up·sides (ˈʌpˌsaɪdz) *adv. Informal, chiefly Brit.* (foll. by *with*) equal or level (with), as through revenge or retaliation.

up·si·lon (ˈʌpsɪˌlɒn, juːpˈsaɪlən) *n.* the 20th letter in the Greek alphabet (Υ or υ) a vowel, transliterated as *y* or *u.* [C17: from Medieval Greek *u psilon* simple *u*, name adopted for graphic *u* to avoid confusion with graphic *oi*, since pronunciation was the same for both in Late Greek]

up·spring *Archaic or literary.* ~*vb.* (ʌpˈsprɪŋ), **·springs, ·spring·ing, ·sprang** *or* **·sprung, ·sprung. 1.** (*intr.*) to spring up or come into existence. ~*n.* (ˈʌpˌsprɪŋ). **2.** a leap forwards or upwards. **3.** the act of coming into existence.

up·stage (ˈʌpˈsteɪdʒ) *adv.* **1.** on, at, or to the rear of the stage. ~*adj.* **2.** of or relating to the back half of the stage. **3.** *Informal.* haughty; supercilious; aloof. ~*vb.* (*tr.*) **4.** to move upstage of (another actor), thus forcing him to turn away from the audience. **5.** *Informal.* to draw attention to oneself from (someone else); steal the show from (someone). **6.** *Informal.* to treat haughtily. ~*n.* **7.** the back half of the stage.

up·stairs (ˈʌpˈstɛəz) *adv.* **1.** up the stairs; to or on an upper floor or level. **2.** *Informal.* to or into a higher rank or office. **3.** *Informal.* in the mind: *a little weak upstairs.* **4. kick upstairs.** *Informal.* to promote to a higher rank or position, esp. one that carries less power. ~*n.* **5. a.** an upper floor or level. **b.** (*as modifier*): *an upstairs room.* **6.** *Brit. informal.* the masters of a household collectively, esp. of a large house. Compare **downstairs** (sense 3).

up·stand·ing (ʌpˈstændɪŋ) *adj.* **1.** of good character. **2.** upright and vigorous in build. **3. be upstanding.** (in a court of law) a direction to all persons present to rise to their feet before the judge enters or leaves the court. —**upˈstand·ing·ness** *n.*

up·start *n.* (ˈʌpˌstɑːt). **1. a.** a person, group, etc., that has risen suddenly to a position of power or wealth. **b.** (*as modifier*): *an upstart tyrant; an upstart family.* **2. a.** an arrogant or presumptuous person. **b.** (*as modifier*): *his upstart ambition.* ~*vb.* (ʌpˈstɑːt). **3.** (*intr.*) *Archaic.* to start up, as in surprise, etc.

up·state (ˈʌpˈsteɪt) *U.S.* ~*adj., adv.* **1.** towards, in, from, or relating to the outlying or northern sections of a state, esp. of New York State. ~*n.* **2.** the outlying, esp. northern, sections of a state. —ˈ**upˈstat·er** *n.*

up·stream (ˈʌpˈstriːm) *adv., adj.* in or towards the higher part of a stream; against the current.

up·stretched (ʌpˈstrɛtʃt) *adj.* (esp. of the arms) stretched or raised up.

up·stroke (ˈʌpˌstrəʊk) *n.* **1. a.** an upward stroke or movement, as of a pen or brush. **b.** the mark produced by such a stroke. **2.** the upward movement of a piston in a reciprocating engine.

up·surge *vb.* (ʌpˈsɜːdʒ). **1.** (*intr.*) *Chiefly literary.* to surge up. ~*n.* (ˈʌpˌsɜːdʒ). **2.** a rapid rise or swell.

up·sweep *n.* (ˈʌpˌswiːp). **1.** a curve or sweep upwards. **2.** *U.S.* an upswept hairstyle. ~*vb.* (ʌpˈswiːp), **·sweeps, ·sweep·ing, ·swept. 3.** to sweep, curve, or brush or be swept, curved, or brushed upwards.

up·swell (ʌpˈswɛl) *vb.* **·swells, ·swell·ing, ·swelled, ·swelled** *or* **·swol·len.** *Rare.* to swell up or cause to swell up.

up·swing *n.* (ˈʌpˌswɪŋ). **1.** *Economics.* a recovery period in the trade cycle. **2.** an upward swing or movement or any increase or improvement. ~*vb.* (ʌp'swɪŋ), **+swings, +swing+ing, +swung. 3.** (*intr.*) to swing or move up.

up·sy-dai·sy ('ʌpsɪ'deɪzɪ) *or* **up+sa+dai+sy** *interj.* an expression, usually of reassurance, uttered as when someone, esp. a child, stumbles or is being lifted up. [C18 *up-a-daisy*, irregularly formed from UP (adv.)]

up+take ('ʌp,teɪk) *n.* **1.** a pipe, shaft, etc., that is used to convey smoke or gases, esp. one that connects a furnace to a chimney. **2.** *Mining.* another term for **upcast** (sense 2). **3.** taking up or lifting up. **4. quick** (*or* **slow**) **on the uptake.** *Informal.* quick (or slow) to understand or learn.

up+throw ('ʌp,θrəʊ). *n.* **1.** *Geology.* the upward movement of rocks on one side of a fault plane relative to rocks on the other side. **2.** *Rare.* an upward thrust or throw; upheaval.

up+thrust ('ʌp,θrʌst) *n.* **1.** an upward push or thrust. **2.** *Geology.* a violent upheaval of the earth's surface.

up+tight (ʌp'taɪt) *adj. Slang.* **1.** displaying tense repressed nervousness, irritability, or anger. **2.** unable to give expression to one's feelings, personality, etc.

up+tilt (ʌp'tɪlt) *vb.* (*tr.*) to tilt up.

up-to-date *adj.* **a.** modern, current, or fashionable: *an up-to-date magazine.* **b.** (*predicative*): *the magazine is up to date.* —'**up-to-'date·ly** *adv.* —'**up-to-'date·ness** *n.*

up+town ('ʌp'taʊn) *U.S.* ~*adj., adv.* **1.** towards, in, or relating to some part of a town that is away from the centre. ~*n.* **2.** such a part of a town, esp. a residential part. —'**up+'town+er** *n.*

up+turn *vb.* (ʌp'tɜːn). **1.** to turn or cause to turn up, over, or upside down. **2.** (*tr.*) to create disorder. **3.** (*tr.*) to direct upwards. ~*n.* ('ʌp,tɜːn). **4.** an upward turn, trend, or improvement. **5.** an upheaval or commotion.

U.P.U. *abbrev. for* Universal Postal Union.

up+ward ('ʌpwəd) *adj.* **1.** directed or moving towards a higher point or level. ~*adv.* **2.** a variant of **upwards.** —'**up+ward+ly** *adv.* —'**up+ward+ness** *n.*

up+wards ('ʌpwədz) *or* **up+ward** *adv.* **1.** from a lower to a higher place, level, condition, etc. **2.** towards a higher level, standing, etc.

up+wind ('ʌp'wɪnd) *adv.* **1.** into or against the wind. **2.** towards or on the side where the wind is blowing; windward. ~*adj.* **3.** going against the wind: *the upwind leg of the course.* **4.** on the windward side: *the upwind side of the house has weathered.*

Ur (ɜː) *n.* an ancient city of Sumer located on a former channel of the Euphrates.

ur- *combining form.* variant of **uro-**[1] and **uro-**[2] before a vowel.

u·ra+cil ('jʊərəsɪl) *n. Biochem.* a pyrimidine present in all living cells, usually in a combined form, as in RNA. Formula: $C_4H_4N_2O_2$. [C20: from URO-[1] + ACETIC + -IL]

u·rae+mi·a *or U.S.* **u·re+mi·a** (jʊ'riːmɪə) *n. Pathol.* the accumulation of waste products, normally excreted in the urine, in the blood: causes severe headaches, vomiting, etc. Also called: **azotaemia.** —**u·'rae+mic** *or U.S.* **u·'re+mic** *adj.* [C19: from New Latin, from Greek *ouron* urine + *haima* blood]

u·rae+us (jʊ'riːəs) *n., pl.* **+us·es.** the sacred serpent represented on the headdresses of ancient Egyptian kings and gods. [C19: from New Latin, from Greek *ouraios*, from Egyptian *uro* asp]

U·ral ('jʊərəl; *Russian* u'ral) *n.* a river in the central Soviet Union, rising in the S Ural Mountains and flowing south to the Caspian Sea. Length: 2534 km (1575 miles).

U·ral-Al·ta·ic *n.* **1.** a postulated group of related languages that consists of the Altaic and Finno-Ugric families together with Samoyed, including most of the indigenous languages of the Soviet Union except Russian and Georgian, together with Turkish, Hungarian, Finnish, Mongolian, Manchu, and certain others. ~*adj.* **2.** of or relating to this group of languages, characterized by agglutination and vowel harmony.

U·ral+ic (jʊ'rælɪk) *or* **U·ra+li·an** (jʊ'reɪlɪən) *n.* **1.** a superfamily of languages consisting of the Finno-Ugric family together with Samoyed. See also **Ural-Altaic.** ~*adj.* **2.** of or relating to these languages.

u·ral+ite ('jʊərə,laɪt) *n.* an amphibole mineral, similar to hornblende, that replaces pyroxene in some igneous and metamorphic rocks. —**u·ral+it+ic** (,jʊərə'lɪtɪk) *adj.*

U·ral Moun+tains *or* **U·rals** *pl. n.* a mountain system of the Soviet Union, extending over 2000 km (1250 miles) from the Arctic Ocean towards the Aral Sea: forms part of the geographical boundary between Europe and Asia; one of the richest mineral areas in the world, with many associated major industrial centres. Highest peak: Mount Narodnaya, 1894 m (6214 ft.).

u·ra+nal·y+sis (,jʊərə'nælɪsɪs) *n., pl.* **+ses** (-,siːz) *Med.* a variant spelling of **urinalysis.**

U·ra·ni·a (jʊ'reɪnɪə) *n. Greek myth.* **1.** the Muse of astronomy. **2.** another name of **Aphrodite.** [C17: from Latin, from Greek *Ourania*, from *ouranios* heavenly, from *ouranos* heaven]

U·ra+ni·an (jʊ'reɪnɪən) *n.* **1.** a hypothetical inhabitant of the planet Uranus. ~*adj.* **2.** of, occurring on, or relating to the planet Uranus. **3.** of the heavens; celestial. **4.** relating to astronomy; astronomical. **5.** (as an epithet of Aphrodite) heavenly; spiritual. **6.** of or relating to the Muse Urania.

u·ran+ic[1] (jʊ'rænɪk) *adj.* of or containing uranium, esp. in a high valence state.

u·ran+ic[2] (jʊ'rænɪk) *adj. Obsolete.* astronomical or celestial. [C19: from Greek *ouranos* heaven]

u·ra+nide ('jʊərə,naɪd) *n.* any element having an atomic number greater than that of protactinium.

u·ran·i·nite (jʊ'rænɪ,naɪt) *n.* a blackish heavy radioactive mineral consisting of uranium oxide in cubic crystalline form together with radium, lead, helium, etc.: occurs in coarse granite. Formula: UO_2. [C19: see URANIUM, -IN, -ITE[1]]

u·ran+ism ('jʊərænɪzəm) *n.* a rare word for **homosexuality** (esp. male homosexuality). [C20: from German *Uranismus*, from Greek *ouranios* heavenly, i.e. spiritual; compare URANIAN (sense 5)]

u·ra+nite ('jʊərə,naɪt) *n.* any of various minerals containing uranium, esp. torbernite or autunite. —**u·ra+nit+ic** (,jʊərə'nɪtɪk) *adj.*

u·ra+ni·um (jʊ'reɪnɪəm) *n.* a radioactive silvery-white metallic element of the actinide series. It occurs in several minerals including pitchblende, carnotite, and autunite and is used chiefly as a source of nuclear energy by fission of the radioisotope **uranium-235.** Symbol: U; atomic no.: 92; atomic wt.: 238.03; half-life of most stable isotope, ^{238}U: 4.51×10^9 years; valency: 2-6; relative density: 18.95 (approx.); melting pt.: 1132°C; boiling pt.: 3818°C. [C18: from New Latin, from URANUS; from the fact that the element was discovered soon after the planet]

u·ra·ni·um se+ries *n. Physics.* a radioactive series that starts with uranium-238 and ends with lead-206.

u·ra·no- *combining form.* denoting the heavens: *uranography.* [from Greek *ouranos*]

u·ra+nog+ra+phy (,jʊərə'nɒgrəfɪ) *n.* the branch of astronomy concerned with the description and mapping of the stars, galaxies, etc. —,**u·ra+'nog+ra+pher** *or* ,**u·ra+'nog+ra+phist** *n.* —**u·ra+no+graph+ic** (,jʊərənə'græfɪk) *or* ,**u·ra+no+'graph·i+cal** *adj.*

u·ra+nous ('jʊərənəs) *adj.* of or containing uranium, esp. in a low valence state.

U·ra·nus[1] (jʊ'reɪnəs) *n. Greek myth.* the personification of the sky, who, as a god, ruled the universe and fathered the Titans and Cyclopes on his wife and mother Gaea (earth). He was overthrown by his son Cronus.

U·ra+nus[2] (jʊ'reɪnəs) *n.* one of the giant planets, the seventh planet from the sun, sometimes visible to the naked eye. It has five satellites and an axis of rotation almost lying in the plane of the orbit. Mean distance from sun: 2870 million km; period of revolution around sun: 84 years; period of axial rotation: 10.8 hours; diameter and mass: 3.7 and 14.5 times that of earth respectively. [C19: from Latin *Ūranus*, from Greek *Ouranos* heaven]

u·ra+nyl ('jʊərənɪl) *n.* (*modifier*) of, consisting of, or containing the divalent ion UO_2^{2+} or the group UO_2. [C19: from URANIUM + -YL] —,**u·ra+'nyl·ic** *adj.*

u·rate ('jʊəreɪt) *n.* any salt or ester of uric acid. —**u·rat+ic** (jʊ'rætɪk) *adj.*

ur+ban ('ɜːbᵊn) *adj.* **1.** of, relating to, or constituting a city or town. **2.** living in a city or town. ~Compare **rural.** [C17: from Latin *urbānus*, from *urbs* city]

Ur·ban II ('ɜːbᵊn) *n.* original name *Odo* or *Udo.* ?1042-99, French ecclesiastic; pope (1088-99). He inaugurated the First Crusade at the Council of Clermont (1095).

ur+ban blues *pl. n.* an extravert and rhythmic style of blues, usually accompanied by a band.

ur+ban dis+trict *n.* **1.** (in England and Wales from 1888 to 1974 and Northern Ireland from 1898 to 1973) an urban division of an administrative county with an elected council in charge of housing and environmental services: usually made up of one or more thickly populated areas but lacking a borough charter. **2.** (in the Republic of Ireland) any of 49 medium-sized towns with their own elected councils.

ur+bane (ɜː'beɪn) *adj.* characterized by elegance or sophistication. [C16: from Latin *urbānus* belonging to the town; see URBAN] —**ur+'bane+ly** *adv.* —**ur+'bane+ness** *n.*

ur+ban guer+ril+la *n.* a guerrilla who operates in a town or city, engaging in terrorism, kidnapping, etc.

ur+ban+ism ('ɜːbə,nɪzəm) *n. Chiefly U.S.* **1. a.** the character of city life. **b.** the study of this. **2.** a less common term for **urbanization.**

ur+ban+ite ('ɜːbə,naɪt) *n. Chiefly U.S.* a resident of an urban community; city dweller.

ur+ban+i·ty (ɜː'bænɪtɪ) *n., pl.* **·ties. 1.** the quality of being urbane. **2.** (*usually pl.*) civilities or courtesies.

ur+ban+ize *or* **ur+ban+ise** ('ɜːbə,naɪz) *vb.* (*tr.*) **1.** (*usually passive*) **a.** to make (esp. a predominantly rural area or country) more industrialized and urban. **b.** to cause the migration of an increasing proportion of (rural dwellers) into cities. **2.** *Rare.* to make urbane. —,**ur+ban·i+'zation** *or* ,**ur+ban·i+'sa+tion** *n.*

ur+ban re+new+al *n.* the process of redeveloping dilapidated or no longer functional urban areas.

ur·bi et or·bi *Latin.* ('ɜːbɪ et 'ɔːbɪ) *adv. R.C. Church.* to the city and the world: a phrase qualifying the solemn papal blessing.

U.R.C. *abbrev. for* United Reformed Church.

ur+ce·o+late ('ɜːsɪəlɪt, -,leɪt) *adj. Biology.* shaped like an urn or pitcher: *an urceolate corolla.* [C18: via New Latin *urceolātus*, from Latin *urceolus* diminutive of *urceus* a pitcher]

ur+chin ('ɜːtʃɪn) *n.* **1.** a mischievous roguish child, esp. one who is young, small, or raggedly dressed. **2.** See **sea urchin, heart urchin. 3.** an archaic or dialect name for a **hedgehog. 4.** either of the two cylinders in a carding machine that are covered with carding cloth. **5.** *Obsolete.* an elf or sprite. [C13: *urchon*, from Old French *heriçon*, from Latin *ēricius* hedgehog, from *ēr*, related to Greek *khēr* hedgehog]

urd (ɜːd) *n.* another name for **black gram** (see **gram**[2] (sense 1)).

ur·dé *or* **ur+dée** ('ɜːdeɪ, -diː, -dɪ) *adj. Heraldry.* having points; pointed. [C16 *urdee*: probably a misreading and misunderstanding of French *vidée* in the phrase *croix aiquissée et vidée* cross sharply pointed and reduced]

Ur·du ('ʊədu:, 'ɜ:-) *n.* an official language of Pakistan, also spoken in India. The script derives primarily from Persian. It belongs to the Indic branch of the Indo-European family of languages, being closely related to Hindi but containing many Arabic and Persian loan words.

-ure *suffix forming nouns.* **1.** indicating act, process, or result: *seizure.* **2.** indicating function or office: *legislature; prefecture.* [from French, from Latin *-ūra*]

u·re·a (jʊ'rɪə) *n.* a white water-soluble crystalline compound with a saline taste and often an odour of ammonia, produced by protein metabolism and excreted in urine. A synthetic form is used as a fertilizer, animal feed, and in the manufacture of synthetic resins. Formula: $CO(NH_2)_2$. [C19: from New Latin, from French *urée,* from Greek *ouron* URINE] —**u·'re·al** *or* **u·'re·ic** *adj.*

u·re·a-for·mal·de·hyde res·in *n.* any one of a class of rigid odourless synthetic materials that are made from urea and formaldehyde and are used in electrical fittings, adhesives, laminates, and finishes for textiles.

u·re·ase ('jʊərɪ,eɪs, -,eɪz) *n.* an enzyme occurring in many plants, esp. fungi, that converts urea to ammonium carbonate.

u·re·di·um (jʊ'ri:dɪəm) *or* **u·re·din·i·um** (,jʊərɪ'dɪnɪəm) *n., pl.* **·di·a** (-dɪə) *or* **·din·i·a** (-'dɪnɪə). a spore-producing body of some rust fungi in which uredospores are formed. Also called: **uredinium, uredosorus.** [C20: from New Latin, from UREDO] —**u·'re·di·al** *adj.*

u·re·do (jʊ'ri:dəʊ) *n., pl.* **u·re·di·nes** (jʊ'ri:dɪ,ni:z). a less common name for **urticaria.** [C18: from Latin: burning itch, from *ūrere* to burn]

u·re·do·so·rus (jʊ,ri:dəʊ'sɔ:rəs) *n., pl.* **·so·ri** (-'sɔ:raɪ). another word for **uredium.**

u·re·do·spore (jʊ'ri:dəʊ,spɔ:) *n.* any of the brownish spores that are produced in each uredium of the rust fungi and spread the infection between hosts.

u·re·ide ('jʊərɪ,aɪd) *n. Chem.* **1.** any of a class of organic compounds derived from urea by replacing one or more of its hydrogen atoms by organic groups. **2.** any of a class of derivatives of urea and carboxylic acids, in which one or more of the hydrogen atoms have been replaced by acyl groups: includes the cyclic ureides, such as alloxan.

u·re·mi·a (jʊ'ri:mɪə) *n.* the usual U.S. spelling of **uraemia.** —**u·'re·mic** *adj.*

-u·ret *suffix.* formerly used to form the names of binary chemical compounds. [from New Latin *-uretum*]

u·re·ter (jʊ'ri:tə) *n.* the tube that conveys urine from the kidney to the urinary bladder or cloaca. [C16: via New Latin from Greek *ourētēr,* from *ourein* to URINATE] —**u·'re·ter·al** *or* **u·re·ter·ic** (,jʊərɪ'tɛrɪk) *adj.*

u·re·thane ('jʊərɪ,θeɪn) *or* **u·re·than** ('jʊərɪ,θæn) *n.* **1.** short for **polyurethane. 2.** another name for **ethyl carbamate.** [C19: from URO-[1] + ETHYL + -ANE]

u·re·thra (jʊ'ri:θrə) *n., pl.* **·thrae** (-θri:) *or* **·thras.** the canal that in most mammals conveys urine from the bladder out of the body. In human males it also conveys semen. [C17: via Late Latin from Greek *ourēthra,* from *ourein* to URINATE] —**u·'re·thral** *adj.*

u·re·thri·tis (,jʊərɪ'θraɪtɪs) *n.* inflammation of the urethra. [C19: from New Latin, from Late Latin URETHRA] —**u·re·thrit·ic** (,jʊərɪ'θrɪtɪk) *adj.*

u·re·thro·scope (jʊ'ri:θrə,skəʊp) *n.* a medical instrument for examining the urethra. [C20: see URETHRA, -SCOPE] —**u·re·thro·scop·ic** (jʊ,ri:θrə'skɒpɪk) *adj.* —**u·re·thros·co·py** (,jʊərɪ'θrɒskəpɪ) *n.*

u·ret·ic (jʊ'rɛtɪk) *adj.* of or relating to the urine. [C19: via Late Latin from Greek *ourētikos,* from *ouron* URINE]

U·rey ('jʊərɪ) *n.* **Har·old Clay·ton.** 1893–1981, U.S. chemist, who discovered the heavy isotope of hydrogen, deuterium (1932), and worked on methods of separating uranium isotopes: Nobel prize for chemistry 1934.

Ur·fa ('ɜ:fə) *n.* a city in SE Turkey: market town. Pop.: 132 934 (1975). Ancient name: **Edessa.**

Ur·ga ('ɜ:gə) *n.* the former name (until 1924) of **Ulan Bator.**

urge (ɜ:dʒ) *vb.* **1.** (*tr.*) to plead, press, or move (someone to do something): *we urged him to surrender.* **2.** (*tr.; may take a clause as object*) to advocate or recommend earnestly and persistently; plead or insist on: *to urge the need for safety.* **3.** (*tr.*) to impel, drive, or hasten onwards: *he urged the horses on.* **4.** (*tr.*) *Archaic or literary.* to stimulate, excite, or incite. ~*n.* **5.** a strong impulse, inner drive, or yearning. [C16: from Latin *urgēre*] —**'urg·ing·ly** *adv.*

ur·gent ('ɜ:dʒənt) *adj.* **1.** requiring or compelling speedy action or attention: *the matter is urgent; an urgent message.* **2.** earnest and persistent. —**ur·gen·cy** ('ɜ:dʒənsɪ) *n.* —**'ur·gent·ly** *adv.*

urg·er ('ɜ:dʒə) *n.* **1.** a person who urges. **2.** *Austral. slang.* a person who is unwilling to take risks, speculate, etc., on his own account, esp. one who encourages others to do so.

-ur·gy *n. combining form.* indicating technology concerned with a specified material: *metallurgy.* [from Greek *-urgia,* from *ergon* WORK]

U·ri (*German* 'u:ri) *n.* one of the original three cantons of Switzerland, in the centre of the country: mainly German-speaking and Roman Catholic. Capital: Altdorf. Pop.: 34 091 (1970). Area: 1075 sq. km (415 sq. miles).

-u·ri·a *n. combining form.* indicating a diseased or abnormal condition of the urine: *dysuria; pyuria.* [from Greek *-ouria,* from *ouron* urine] —**-u·ric** *adj. combining form.*

U·ri·ah (jʊ'raɪə) *n. Old Testament.* a Hittite officer, who was killed in battle on instructions from David so that he could marry Uriah's wife Bathsheba (II Samuel 11).

u·ric ('jʊərɪk) *adj.* of, concerning, or derived from urine. [C18: from URO-[1] + -IC]

u·ric ac·id *n.* a white odourless tasteless crystalline product of protein metabolism, present in the blood and urine; 2,6,8-trihydroxypurine. Formula: $C_5H_4N_4O_3$.

ur·i·dine ('jʊərɪ,di:n) *n. Biochem.* a nucleoside present in all living cells in a combined form, esp. in RNA. [C20: from URO-[1] + -IDE + -INE[2]]

U·ri·el ('jʊərɪəl) *n.* one of the four chief angels in Jewish apocryphal writings.

U·rim and Thum·mim ('jʊərɪm; 'θʌmɪm) *n. Old Testament.* two objects probably used as oracles and carried in the breastplate of the high priest (Exodus 28:30). [C16: from Hebrew]

u·ri·nal (jʊ'raɪnᵊl, 'jʊərɪ-) *n.* **1.** a sanitary fitting, esp. one fixed to a wall, used by men for urination. **2.** a room containing urinals. **3.** any vessel for holding urine prior to its disposal.

u·ri·nal·y·sis (,jʊərɪ'nælɪsɪs) *or* **u·ra·nal·y·sis** *n., pl.* **·ses** (-,si:z). *Med.* chemical analysis of the urine to test for the presence of disease.

u·ri·nant ('jʊərɪnənt) *adj. Heraldry.* having the head downwards. [C17: from Latin *ūrīnārī* to dive]

u·ri·nar·y ('jʊərɪnərɪ) *adj.* **1.** *Anatomy.* of or relating to urine or to the organs and structures that secrete and pass urine. ~*n., pl.* **·nar·ies. 2.** a reservoir for urine. **3.** another word for **urinal.**

u·ri·nar·y blad·der *n.* a distensible membranous sac in which the urine excreted from the kidneys is stored.

u·ri·nate ('jʊərɪ,neɪt) *vb.* (*intr.*) to excrete or void urine; micturate. —,**u·ri·'na·tion** *n.* —**'u·ri·na·tive** *adj.*

u·rine ('jʊərɪn) *n.* the pale yellow slightly acid fluid excreted by the kidneys, containing waste products removed from the blood. It is stored in the urinary bladder and discharged through the urethra. [C14: via Old French from Latin *ūrīna;* related to Greek *ouron,* Latin *ūrīnāre* to plunge under water]

u·ri·nif·er·ous (,jʊərɪ'nɪfərəs) *adj.* conveying urine.

u·ri·no·gen·i·tal (,jʊərɪnəʊ'dʒɛnɪtᵊl) *adj.* another word for **urogenital** or **genitourinary.**

u·ri·nous ('jʊərɪnəs) *or* **u·ri·nose** *adj.* of, resembling, or containing urine.

Ur·mi·a ('ɜ:mɪə) *n.* **Lake.** a shallow lake in NW Iran, at an altitude of 1300 m (4250 ft.): the largest lake in Iran, varying in area from 4000–6000 sq. km (1500–2300 sq. miles) between autumn and spring.

Urm·ston ('ɜ:mstən) *n.* a town in NW England, in Greater Manchester. Pop.: 44 523 (1971).

urn (ɜ:n) *n.* **1.** a vaselike receptacle or vessel, esp. a large bulbous one with a foot. **2.** a vase used as a receptacle for the ashes of the dead. **3.** a large vessel, usually of metal, with a tap, used for making and holding tea, coffee, etc. **4.** *Botany.* the spore-producing capsule of a moss. [C14: from Latin *ūrna;* related to Latin *ūrere* to burn, *urceus* pitcher, Greek *hurkhē* jar] —**'urn,like** *adj.*

urn·field ('ɜ:n,fi:ld) *n.* **1.** a cemetery full of individual cremation urns. ~*adj.* **2.** (of a number of Bronze Age cultures) characterized by cremation in urns, which began in E Europe about the second millennium B.C. and by the seventh century B.C. had covered almost all of mainland Europe.

urn·ing ('ɜ:nɪŋ) *n.* a rare word for **homosexual** (esp. a male homosexual). [C20: from German, from URANIA (Aphrodite); compare URANISM]

u·ro-[1] *or before a vowel* **ur-** *combining form.* indicating urine or the urinary tract: *urochrome; urogenital; urolith; urology.* [from Greek *ouron* urine]

u·ro-[2] *or before a vowel* **ur-** *combining form.* indicating a tail: *urochord; uropod; urostyle.* [from Greek *oura*]

u·ro·chord ('jʊərəʊ,kɔ:d) *n.* **1.** the notochord of a larval tunicate, typically confined to the tail region. ~*n., adj.* **2.** Also: **u·ro·chor·date** (,jʊərəʊ'kɔ:deɪt). another word for **tunicate.** —,**u·ro·'chor·dal** *adj.*

u·ro·chrome ('jʊərəʊ,krəʊm) *n.* the yellowish pigment that colours urine.

u·ro·dele ('jʊərəʊ,di:l) *n.* **1.** any amphibian of the order *Urodela,* having a long body and tail and four short limbs: includes the salamanders and newts. ~*adj.* **2.** of, relating to, or belonging to the *Urodela.* [C19: from French *urodèle,* from URO-[2] + *-dèle,* from Greek *dēlos* evident]

u·ro·gen·i·tal (,jʊərəʊ'dʒɛnɪtᵊl) *or* **u·ri·no·gen·i·tal** *adj.* of or relating to the urinary and genital organs and their functions. Also: **genitourinary.**

u·ro·gen·i·tal sys·tem *or* **tract** *n. Anatomy.* the urinary tract and reproductive organs.

u·rog·e·nous (jʊ'rɒdʒɪnəs) *adj.* **1.** producing or derived from urine. **2.** involved in the secretion and excretion of urine.

u·ro·lith ('jʊərəʊlɪθ) *n. Pathol.* a calculus in the urinary tract. —,**u·ro·'lith·ic** *adj.*

u·rol·o·gy (jʊ'rɒlədʒɪ) *n.* the branch of medicine concerned with the study and treatment of diseases of the urogenital tract. —**u·ro·log·ic** (,jʊərə'lɒdʒɪk) *or* ,**u·ro·'log·i·cal** *adj.* —**u·'rol·o·gist** *n.*

u·ro·pod ('jʊərəʊ,pɒd) *n.* the paired appendage that arises from the last segment of the body in lobsters and related crustaceans and forms part of the tail fan. —**u·rop·o·dal** (jʊ'rɒpədᵊl) *or* **u·'rop·o·dous** *adj.*

u·ro·pyg·i·al gland *n.* a gland, situated at the base of the tail in most birds, that secretes oil used in preening.

u·ro·pyg·i·um (,jʊərə'pɪdʒɪəm) *n.* the hindmost part of a bird's body, from which the tail feathers grow. [C19: via New Latin

from Greek *ouropugion*, from URO-[2] + *pugē* rump] —ˌu·ro·'pyg·i·al *adj.*
u·ros·co·py (jʊ'rɒskəpɪ) *n. Med.* examination of the urine. See also **urinalysis.** —**u·ro·scop·ic** (ˌjʊərə'skɒpɪk) *adj.* —**u·'ros·co·pist** *n.*
u·ro·style ('jʊərəʊˌstaɪl) *n.* the bony rod forming the last segment of the vertebral column of frogs, toads, and related amphibians.
Ur·quhart ('ɜːkət) *n.* Sir **Thom·as.** 1611–60, Scottish author and translator of Rabelais' *Gargantua* and *Pantagruel* (1653; 1693).
Ur·sa Ma·jor ('ɜːsə 'meɪdʒə) *n., Latin genitive* **Ur·sae Ma·jor·is** ('ɜːsiː mə'dʒɔːrɪs). an extensive conspicuous constellation in the N hemisphere, visible north of latitude 40°. The seven brightest stars form the **Plough.** A line through the two brightest stars points to the Pole Star lying in **Ursa Minor.** Also called: the **Great Bear,** the **Bear.** [Latin: greater bear]
Ur·sa Mi·nor ('ɜːsə 'maɪnə) *n., Latin genitive* **Ur·sae Mi·nor·is** ('ɜːsiː mɪ'nɔːrɪs). a small faint constellation, the brightest star of which is the Pole Star, lying 1° from the true celestial pole. Also called: the **Little Bear,** the **Bear,** (U.S. only) the **Little Dipper.** [Latin: lesser bear]
ur·sine ('ɜːsaɪn) *adj.* of, relating to, or resembling a bear or bears. [C16: from Latin *ursus* a bear]
ur·sine howl·er *n.* another name for **red howler** (see **howler** (the monkey)).
Ur·spra·che *German.* ('uːrˌʃpraːxə) *n.* any hypothetical extinct and unrecorded language reconstructed from groups of related recorded languages. For example, Germanic is an Ursprache reconstructed by comparison of English, Dutch, German, the Scandinavian languages, and Gothic; Indo-European is an Ursprache reconstructed by comparison of the Germanic group, Latin, Sanskrit, etc. [from *ur-* primeval, original + *Sprache* language]
Ur·su·la ('ɜːsjʊlə) *n.* **Saint.** a legendary British princess of the fourth or fifth century A.D., said to have been martyred together with 11 000 virgins by the Huns at Cologne.
Ur·su·line ('ɜːsjʊˌlaɪn) *n.* a member of one of an order of nuns devoted to teaching in the Roman Catholic Church: founded in 1537 at Brescia. [C16: named after St. URSULA, patron saint of St. Angela Merici, who founded the order]
Ur·text *German.* ('uːrˌtɛkst) *n.* the earliest form of a text reconstructed by linguistic scholars as a basis for variants in later texts still in existence. [from *ur-* original + TEXT]
ur·ti·ca·ceous (ˌɜːtɪ'keɪʃəs) *adj.* of, relating to, or belonging to the *Urticaceae*, a family of plants, having small flowers and, in many species, stinging hairs: includes the nettles and pellitory. [C18: via New Latin from Latin *urtīca* nettle, from *ūrere* to burn]
ur·ti·car·i·a (ˌɜːtɪ'kɛərɪə) *n.* a skin condition characterized by the formation of itchy red or whitish raised patches, usually caused by an allergy. Nontechnical names: **hives, nettle rash.** [C18: from New Latin, from Latin *urtīca* nettle] —ˌ**ur·ti·'car·i·al** *or* ˌ**ur·ti·'car·i·ous** *adj.*
ur·ti·cate ('ɜːtɪˌkeɪt) *adj.* **1.** characterized by the presence of wheals. ~*vb.* **2.** to perform urtication. [C19: from Medieval Latin *urtīcāre* to sting, from Latin *urtīca* a nettle]
ur·ti·ca·tion (ˌɜːtɪ'keɪʃən) *n.* **1.** a burning or itching sensation. **2.** another name for **urticaria. 3.** a former method of producing counterirritation of the skin by beating the area with nettles.
Uru. *abbrev. for* Uruguay.
U·rua·pan (*Spanish* u'rwapan) *n.* a city in SW Mexico, in Michoacán state: agricultural trading centre. Pop.: 114 979 (1974 est.).
U·ru·guay ('jʊərəˌgwaɪ) *n.* a republic in South America, on the Atlantic: Spanish colonization began in 1624, followed by Portuguese settlement in 1680; revolted against Spanish rule in 1820 but was annexed by the Portuguese to Brazil; gained independence in 1825. It consists mainly of rolling grassy plains, low hills, and plateaus. Official language: Spanish. Religion: Roman Catholic. Currency: peso. Capital: Montevideo. Pop.: 2 763 964 (1975). Area: 182 427 sq. km (70 435 sq. miles). —ˌ**U·ru·'guay·an** *adj., n.*
U·rum·chi (uː'ruːmtʃɪ) *or* **Wu-lu-mu-ch'i** *n.* a city in NW China, capital of Sinkiang-Uighur AR: trading centre on a N route between China and the Soviet Union. Pop.: 500 000 (1970 est.). Former name: **Tihwa.**
U·run·di (ʊ'rʊndɪ) *n.* the former name (until 1962) of **Burundi.**
u·rus ('jʊərəs) *n., pl.* **u·rus·es.** another name for the **aurochs.** [C17: from *ūrus*, of Germanic origin; compare Old High German *ūr*, Old Norse *urr*, Greek *ouros* aurochs]
u·ru·shi·ol ('uːrʊʃɪˌɒl, uː'ruː-) *n.* a poisonous pale yellow liquid occurring in poison ivy and the lacquer tree. [from Japanese *urushi* lacquer + -OL[2]]
us (ʌs) *pron.* (*objective*) **1.** refers to the speaker or writer and another person or other people: *don't hurt us; to decide among us.* **2.** refers to all people or people in general: *this table shows us the tides.* **3.** an informal word for **me**: *give us a kiss!* **4.** a formal word for **me** used by editors, monarchs, etc. **5.** *Chiefly U.S.* a dialect word for **ourselves** when used as an indirect object: *we ought to get us a car.* [Old English *ūs*; related to Old High German *uns*, Old Norse *oss*, Latin *nōs*, Sanskrit *nas* we]
Usage. See at **me.**
u.s. *abbrev. for:* **1.** ubi supra. **2.** ut supra.
U.S. *abbrev. for* United States.
U/S *Informal. abbrev. for:* **1.** unserviceable. **2.** useless.
USA *international car registration for* United States of America.
U.S.A. *abbrev. for:* **1.** United States Army. **2.** United States of America.
us·a·ble *or* **use·a·ble** ('juːzəbᵊl) *adj.* able to be used. —ˌ**us·a·'bil·i·ty,** ˌ**use·a·'bil·i·ty** *or* '**us·a·ble·ness,** '**use·a·ble·ness** *n.* —'**us·a·bly** *or* '**use·a·bly** *adv.*
U.S.A.F. *abbrev. for* United States Air Force.
us·age ('juːsɪdʒ, -zɪdʒ) *n.* **1.** the act or a manner of using; use; employment. **2.** constant use, custom, or habit. **3.** something permitted or established by custom or practice. **4.** what is actually said in a language, esp. as contrasted with what is prescribed.
us·ance ('juːzəns) *n.* **1.** *Commerce.* the period of time permitted by commercial usage for the redemption of foreign bills of exchange. **2.** *Rare.* unearned income. **3.** an obsolete word for **usage, usury,** or **use.** [C14: from Old French, from Medieval Latin *ūsantia*, from *ūsāre* to USE]
use *vb.* (juːz). (*tr.*) **1.** to put into service or action; employ for a given purpose: *to use a spoon to stir with.* **2.** to make a practice or habit of employing; exercise: *he uses his brain.* **3.** to behave towards: *to use a friend well.* **4.** to behave towards in a particular way for one's own ends: *he uses people.* **5.** to consume, expend, or exhaust: *the engine uses very little oil.* **6.** *Chiefly U.S.* to partake of (alcoholic drink, drugs, etc.) or smoke (tobacco, marijuana, etc.). ~*n.* (juːs). **7.** the act of using or the state of being used: *the carpet wore out through constant use.* **8.** the ability, right, or permission to use. **9.** the occasion to use; need: *I have no use for this paper.* **10.** an instance or manner of using. **11.** usefulness; advantage: *it is of no use to complain.* **12.** custom; practice; habit: *long use has inured him to it.* **13.** the purpose for which something is used; end. **14.** *Christianity.* a distinctive form of liturgical or ritual observance, esp. one that is traditional in a Church or group of Churches. **15.** the enjoyment of property, land, etc., by occupation or by deriving revenue or other benefit from it. **16.** *Law.* the beneficial enjoyment of property the legal title to which is held by another person as trustee. **17.** *Law.* an archaic word for **trust** (sense 7). **18. have no use for. a.** to have no need of. **b.** to have a contemptuous dislike for. **19. make use of.** to employ; use. [C13: from Old French *user* to use, from Latin *ūsus* having used, from *ūtī* to use]
used (juːzd) *adj.* bought or sold second-hand: *used cars.*
used to (juːst) *adj.* **1.** made familiar with; accustomed to: *I am used to hitchhiking.* ~*vb.* (*tr.*) **2.** (*takes an infinitive or implied infinitive*) used as an auxiliary to express habitual or accustomed actions, states, etc., taking place in the past but not continuing into the present: *I don't drink these days, but I used to; I used to fish here every day.*
use·ful ('juːsfʊl) *adj.* **1.** able to be used advantageously, beneficially, or for several purposes; helpful or serviceable. **2.** *Informal.* commendable or capable: *a useful term's work.* ~*n.* **3.** *Austral. informal.* an odd-jobman or general factotum. —'**use·ful·ly** *adv.* —'**use·ful·ness** *n.*
use·less ('juːslɪs) *adj.* **1.** having no practical use or advantage. **2.** *Informal.* ineffectual, weak, or stupid: *he's useless at history.* —'**use·less·ly** *adv.* —'**use·less·ness** *n.*
us·er ('juːzə) *n.* **1.** *Law.* **a.** the continued exercise, use, or enjoyment of a right, esp. in property. **b.** a presumptive right based on long-continued use: *right of user.* **2.** (*often in combination*) a person or thing that uses: *a road-user.* **3.** *Informal.* a drug addict.
Ush·ant ('ʌʃənt) *n.* an island off the NW coast of France, at the tip of Brittany: scene of naval battles in 1778 and 1794 between France and England. Area: about 16 sq. km (6 sq. miles). French name: **Ouessant.**
Ush·as ('uːʃəs) *n.* the Hindu goddess of the dawn.
ush·er ('ʌʃə) *n.* **1.** an official who shows people to their seats, as in a church or theatre. **2.** a person who acts as doorkeeper, esp. in a court of law. **3.** (in England) a minor official charged with maintaining order in a court of law. **4.** an officer responsible for preceding persons of rank in a procession or introducing strangers at formal functions. **5.** *Brit., obsolete.* a teacher. ~*vb.* (*tr.*) **6.** to conduct or escort, esp. in a courteous or obsequious way. **7.** (usually foll. by *in*) to be a precursor or herald (of). [C14: from Old French *huissier* doorkeeper, from Vulgar Latin *ustiārius* (unattested), from Latin *ostium* door]
Ush·er ('ʌʃə) *n.* a variant spelling of (James) **Ussher.**
ush·er·ette (ˌʌʃə'rɛt) *n.* a woman assistant in a cinema, theatre, etc., who shows people to their seats.
U.S.I.A. *abbrev. for* United States Information Agency.
U.S.I.S. *abbrev. for* United States Information Service.
Usk (ʌsk) *n.* a river in SE Wales, flowing southeast and south to the Bristol Channel. Length: 113 km (70 miles).
Üs·küb ('ʊskuːb) *n.* the Turkish name (1392–1913) for **Skopje.**
Üs·kü·dar (ˌuːskuː'dɑː) *n.* a town in NW Turkey, across the Bosporus from Istanbul: formerly a terminus of caravan routes from Syria and Asia; base of the British army in the Crimean War. Former name: **Scutari.**
USM *abbrev. for* underwater-to-surface missile.
U.S.N. *abbrev. for* United States Navy.
Us·nach *or* **Us·nech** ('ʊʃnəx) *n.* (in Irish legend) the father of Naoise.
U.S.O. (in the U.S.) *abbrev. for* United Service Organization.
Us·pal·la·ta Pass (ˌuːspə'lɑːtə; *Spanish* ˌuspa'ʎata) *n.* a pass over the Andes in S South America, between Mendoza (Argentina) and Santiago (Chile). Height: 3840 m (12 600 ft.). Also called: **La Cumbre.**
us·que·baugh ('ʌskwɪˌbɔː) *n.* **1.** *Irish.* the former name for **whiskey. 2.** an Irish liqueur flavoured with coriander. [C16: from Irish Gaelic *uisce beathadh* water of life]

U.S.S. *abbrev. for:* **1.** United States Senate. **2.** United States Ship.
Ussh·er *or* **Ush·er** ('ʌʃə) *n.* **James.** 1581–1656, Irish prelate and scholar. His system of biblical chronology, which dated the creation at 4004 B.C., was for long accepted.
U.S.S.R. *abbrev. for* Union of Soviet Socialist Republics.
Us+su+ri (*Russian* ussu'ri) *n.* a river in the SE Soviet Union, flowing north, forming part of the Chinese border, to the Amur River. Length: about 800 km (500 miles).
U·sta+shi (ʊ'stɑːʃɪ) *n.* a terrorist organization of right-wing Yugoslav exiles dedicated to the overthrow of Communism in thier homeland. [from Serbo-Croatian]
Ú·stí nad La+bem (*Czech* 'uːstiː nad 'labɛm) *n.* a port in NW Czechoslovakia, on the Elbe River: textile and chemical industries. Pop.: 74 425 (1968).
Us·ti·nov ('juːstɪnɒf) *n.* **Pe·ter.** born 1921, British stage and film actor, director, dramatist, and raconteur.
Ust-Ka·me·no+gorsk (*Russian* 'ustj kəmɪna'gɔrsk) *n.* a city in the S Soviet Union, in the E Kazakh SSR: centre of a zinc-, lead-, and copper-mining area Pop.: 257 000 (1975 est.).
us+tu+la+tion (ˌʌstjʊ'leɪʃən) *n.* the act or process of searing or burning. [C17: from Late Latin *ustulāre,* from Latin *ūrere* to burn]
Ust+yurt *or* **Ust Urt** (*Russian* us'tjurt) *n.* an arid plateau of the S Soviet Union, between the Caspian and Aral seas in the SW Kazakh SSR and the Kara-Kalpak ASSR. Area: about 238 000 sq. km (92 000 sq. miles).
u·su+al ('juːʒʊəl) *adj.* **1.** of the most normal, frequent, or regular type; customary: *that's the usual sort of application to send.* ~*n.* **2.** ordinary or commonplace events (esp. in the phrase **out of the usual**). **3. the usual.** *Informal.* the habitual or usual drink, meal, etc. [C14: from Late Latin *ūsuālis* ordinary, from Latin *ūsus* USE] —**'u·su+al+ly** *adv.* —**'u·su+al+ness** *n.*
u·su+fruct ('juːsjʊˌfrʌkt) *n.* the right to use and derive profit from a piece of property belonging to another, provided the property itself remains undiminished and uninjured in any way. [C17: from Late Latin *ūsūfrūctus,* from Latin *ūsus* use + *frūctus* enjoyment] —**ˌu·su+'fruc+tu+ar·y** *n., adj.*
U·sum+bu+ra (ˌuːzəm'bʊərə) *n.* the former name of **Bujumbura.**
u·su+rer ('juːʒərə) *n.* **1.** a person who lends funds at an exorbitant rate of interest. **2.** *Obsolete.* a moneylender.
u·surp (juː'zɜːp) *vb.* to seize, take over, or appropriate (land, a throne, etc.) without authority. [C14: from Old French *usurper,* from Latin *ūsūrpāre* to take into use, probably from *ūsus* use + *rapere* to seize] —**ˌu·sur+'pa·tion** *n.* —**u·'sur+pa+tive** *or* **u·'sur+pa·to·ry** *adj.* —**u·'surp+er** *n.* —**u·'surp+ing+ly** *adv.*
u·su+ry ('juːʒərɪ) *n., pl.* **+ries. 1.** the act or practice of loaning money at an exorbitant rate of interest. **2.** an exorbitant or unlawfully high amount or rate of interest. **3.** *Obsolete.* moneylending. [C14: from Medieval Latin *ūsūria,* from Latin *ūsūra* usage, from *ūsus* USE] —**u·su+ri+ous** (juː'ʒʊərɪəs) *adj.*
U.S.W. *Radio. abbrev. for* ultrashort wave.
ut (ʌt, uːt) *Music.* **1.** the syllable used in the fixed system of solmization for the note C. **2.** the first note of a hexachord in medieval music. [C14: from Latin *ut;* see GAMUT]
U.T. *abbrev. for* universal time.
U·tah ('juːtɔː, 'juːtɑː) *n.* a state of the western U.S.: settled by Mormons in 1847; situated in the Great Basin and the Rockies, with the Great Salt Lake in the northwest. Capital: Salt Lake City. Pop.: 1 059 273 (1970). Area: 212 628 sq. km (82 096 sq. miles). Abbrevs.: **Ut.** or (with zip code) **UT** —**U·'tah+an** *adj., n.*
U·ta·ma·ro (ˌuːtə'mɑːrəʊ) *n.* **Ki·ta·ga·wa** (ˌkiːtə'gɑːwə). 1753–1806, Japanese master of painted woodcuts.
ut dict. (in prescriptions, etc.) *abbrev. for* as directed. [from Latin *ut dictum*]
ute (juːt) *n. Austral. informal.* short for **utility** (sense 5).
Ute (juːt, 'juːtɪ) *n.* **1.** (*pl.* **Utes** *or* **Ute**) a member of a North American Indian people of Utah, Colorado, and New Mexico, related to the Aztecs. **2.** the language of this people, belonging to the Shoshonean subfamily of the Uto-Aztecan family.
u·ten+sil (juː'tɛnsəl) *n.* an implement, tool, or container for practical use: *writing utensils.* [C14 *utensele,* via Old French from Latin *ūtēnsilia* necessaries, from *ūtēnsilis* available for use, from *ūtī* to use]
u+ter+ine ('juːtəˌraɪn) *adj.* **1.** of, relating to, or affecting the uterus. **2.** (of offspring) born of the same mother but not the same father: *uterine brothers.*
u·ter+us ('juːtərəs) *n., pl.* **u·ter·i** ('juːtəˌraɪ). **1.** *Anatomy.* a hollow muscular organ lying within the pelvic cavity of female mammals. It houses the developing fetus and by contractions aids in its expulsion at parturition. Nontechnical name: **womb. 2.** the corresponding organ in other animals. [C17: from Latin; compare Greek *hustera* womb, *hoderos* belly, Sanskrit *udara* belly]
Ut+gard ('ʊtgɑːd, 'uːt-) *n. Norse myth.* one of the divisions of Jotunheim, land of the giants, ruled by Utgard-Loki.
Ut·gard-Lo·ki *n. Norse myth.* the giant king of Utgard.
U Thant ('uː 'θænt) *n.* See **Thant.**
U·ther ('juːθə) *or* **U·ther Pen·drag·on** *n.* (in Arthurian legend) a king of Britain and father of Arthur.
U·ti+ca ('juːtɪkə) *n.* an ancient city on the N coast of Africa, northwest of Carthage.
u·tile ('juːtaɪl, -tɪl) *adj.* an obsolete word for **useful.** [C15: via Old French from Latin *ūtilis,* from *ūtī* to use]
u·til·i·tar·i·an (juːˌtɪlɪ'tɛərɪən) *adj.* **1.** of or relating to utilitarianism. **2.** designed for use rather than beauty. ~*n.* **3.** a person who believes in utilitarianism.
u·til·i·tar·i·an·ism (juːˌtɪlɪ'tɛərɪəˌnɪzəm) *n. Ethics.* **1.** the theory that the highest good lies in the greatest good of the greatest numbers. **2.** the theory that the criterion of virtue is utility. ~See also (John Stuart) **Mill.**
u·til+i·ty (juː'tɪlɪtɪ) *n., pl.* **·ties. 1. a.** the quality of practical use; usefulness; serviceability. **b.** (*as modifier*): *a utility fabric.* **2.** something useful. **3. a.** a public service, such as the bus system; public utility. **b.** (*as modifier*): *utility vehicle.* **4.** *Economics.* **a.** the ability of a commodity to satisfy human wants. **b.** the amount of such satisfaction. **5.** the Austral. word for **pick-up truck.** [C14: from Old French *utelite,* from Latin *ūtilitās* usefulness, from *ūtī* to use]
u·til+i·ty man *n. Chiefly U.S.* **1.** a worker who is expected to serve in any of several capacities. **2.** an actor who plays any of numerous small parts.
u·til+i·ty play+er *n. Austral., sport.* a player who is capable of playing competently in any of several positions.
u·til+i·ty room *n.* a room, esp. in a private house, used for storage, laundry, etc.
u·ti+lize *or* **u·ti+lise** ('juːtɪˌlaɪz) *vb.* (*tr.*) to make practical or worthwhile use of. —**'u·ti+ˌliz+a·ble** *or* **'u·ti+ˌlis+a·ble** *adj.* —**ˌu·ti+li+'za+tion** *or* **ˌu·ti+li+'sa+tion** *n.* —**'u·ti+ˌliz+er** *or* **'u·ti+ˌlis+er** *n.*
ut in+fra *Latin.* (ʊt 'ɪnfrɑː) as below.
u·ti pos+si+de·tis ('juːtaɪˌpɒsɪ'diːtɪs) *n. International law.* the rule that territory and other property remains in the hands of the belligerent state actually in possession at the end of a war unless otherwise provided for by treaty. [from Latin, literally: as you possess]
ut+most ('ʌtˌməʊst) *or* **ut·ter+most** *adj.* (*prenominal*) **1.** of the greatest possible degree or amount: *the utmost degree.* **2.** at the furthest limit: *the utmost town on the peninsula.* ~*n.* **3.** the greatest possible degree, extent, or amount: *he tried his utmost.* [Old English *ūtemest,* from *ūte* out + *-mest* MOST]
U·to-Az·tec·an ('juːtəʊ'æztɛkən) *n.* **1.** a family of North and Central American Indian languages including Nahuatl, Shoshone, Pima, and Ute. ~*adj.* **2.** of or relating to this family of languages or the peoples speaking them.
U·to+pi·a (juː'təʊpɪə) *n.* (*sometimes not cap.*) any real or imaginary society, place, state, etc., considered to be perfect or ideal. [C16: from New Latin *Utopia* (coined by Sir Thomas More in 1516 as the title of his book that described an imaginary island representing the perfect society), literally: no place, from Greek *ou* not + *topos* a place]
U·to+pi·an (juː'təʊpɪən) (*sometimes not cap.*) ~*adj.* **1.** of or relating to a perfect or ideal existence. ~*n.* **2.** an idealistic social reformer. —**U·'to+pi+an+ism** *n.*
u·to·pi·an so+cial+ism *n.* (*sometimes cap.*) socialism established by the peaceful surrender of the means of production by capitalists moved by moral persuasion, example, etc.: the form of socialism advocated by Robert Owen, Fichte, and others. Compare **scientific socialism.**
U·trecht (*Dutch* 'yːtrɛxt; *English* 'juːtrɛkt) *n.* **1.** a province of the W central Netherlands. Capital: Utrecht. Pop.: 838 400 (1973 est.). Area: 1362 sq. km (526 sq. miles). **2.** a city in the central Netherlands, capital of Utrecht province: scene of the signing (1579) of the **Union of Utrecht** (the foundation of the later kingdom of the Netherlands) and of the **Treaty of Utrecht** (1713), ending the War of the Spanish Succession. Pop.: 259 826 (1974 est.).
u·tri+cle ('juːtrɪkᵊl) *or* **u·tric·u+lus** (juː'trɪkjʊləs) *n., pl.* **u·tri+cles** *or* **u·tric·u·li** (juː'trɪkjʊˌlaɪ). **1.** *Anatomy.* the larger of the two parts of the membranous labyrinth of the internal ear. Compare **saccule. 2.** *Botany.* the bladder-like one-seeded indehiscent fruit of certain plants. [C18: from Latin *ūtriculus* diminutive of *ūter* bag] —**u·'tric·u+lar** *or* **u·'tric·u+late** *adj.*
u·tric·u·li·tis (juːˌtrɪkjʊ'laɪtɪs) *n.* inflammation of the inner ear.
U·tril·lo (*French* ytri'jo) *n.* **Mau·rice** (mɔ'ris). 1883–1955, French painter, noted for his Parisian street scenes.
ut su+pra *Latin.* (ʊt 'suːprɑː) as above.
Ut+tar Pra+desh ('ʊtə 'prɑːdɛʃ) *n.* a state of N India: the most populous state; originated in 1877 with the merging of Agra and Oudh as the United Provinces; augmented by the states of Rampur, Benares, and Tehri-Garhwal in 1949; lies mostly on the Upper Ganges plain but rises over 7500 m (25 000 ft.) in the Himalayas in the northwest; agricultural. Capital: Lucknow. Pop.: 88 341 144 (1971). Area: 294 364 sq. km (113 654 sq. miles).
ut+ter[1] ('ʌtə) *vb.* **1.** to give audible expression to (something): *to utter a growl.* **2.** *Criminal law.* to put into circulation (counterfeit coin, forged banknotes, etc.). **3.** (*tr.*) to make publicly known; publish: *to utter slander.* **4.** *Obsolete.* to give forth, issue, or emit. [C14: probably originally a commercial term, from Middle Dutch *ūteren* (modern Dutch *uiteren*) to make known; related to Middle Low German *ūtern* to sell, show] —**'ut+ter+a·ble** *adj.* —**'ut+ter+a·ble+ness** *n.* —**'ut+ter+er** *n.* —**'ut+ter+less** *adj.*
ut+ter[2] ('ʌtə) *adj.* (*prenominal*) (intensifier): *an utter fool; utter bliss; the utter limit.* [C15: from Old English *utera* outer, comparative of *ūte* OUT (adv.); related to Old High German *ūzaro,* Old Norse *ūtri*]
ut+ter+ance[1] ('ʌtərəns) *n.* **1.** something uttered, such as a statement. **2.** the act or power of uttering or the ability to utter.
ut+ter+ance[2] ('ʌtərəns) *n. Archaic or literary.* the bitter end (esp. in the phrase **to the utterance**). [C13: from Old French *oultrance,* from *oultrer* to carry to excess, from Latin *ultrā* beyond]
ut+ter bar+ris+ter *n. Law.* the full title of a barrister who is not a Queen's Counsel. See also **junior** (sense 6).
ut+ter+ly ('ʌtəlɪ) *adv.* (intensifier): *I'm utterly miserable.*

ut·ter+most ('ʌtə,məʊst) *adj., n.* a variant of **utmost.**

U-turn *n.* a turn made by a vehicle in the shape of a U, resulting in a reversal of direction.

U.U. *abbrev. for* Ulster Unionist.

U.V. *abbrev. for* ultraviolet.

u·va+rov+ite (u:'vɑ:rə,vaɪt) *n.* an emerald-green garnet found in chromium deposits: consists of calcium chromium silicate. Formula: $Ca_3Cr_2(SiO_4)_3$. [C19: from German *Uvarovit;* named after Count Sergei S. *Uvarov* (1785–1855), Russian author and statesman]

u·ve·a ('ju:vɪə) *n.* the part of the eyeball consisting of the iris, ciliary body, and choroid. [C16: from Medieval Latin *ūvea,* from Latin *ūva* grape] —'**u·ve·al** *or* '**u·ve·ous** *adj.*

Uve·dale ('ju:dᵊl, 'ju:v,deɪl) *n.* a variant of (Nicholas) **Udall.**

u·ve·i·tis (,ju:vɪ'aɪtɪs) *n.* inflammation of the uvea. —**u·ve·it+ic** (,ju:vɪ'ɪtɪk) *adj.*

u·vu+la ('ju:vjʊlə) *n., pl.* +**las** *or* +**lae** (-,li:). a small fleshy finger-like flap of tissue that hangs in the back of the throat and is an extension of the soft palate. [C14: from Medieval Latin, literally: a little grape, from Latin *ūva* a grape]

u·vu+lar ('ju:vjʊlə) *adj.* **1.** of or relating to the uvula. **2.** *Phonetics.* articulated with the uvula and the back of the tongue, such as the (r) sound of Parisian French. ~*n.* **3.** a uvular consonant. —'**u·vu+lar+ly** *adv.*

u·vu+li+tis (,ju:vjʊ'laɪtɪs) *n.* inflammation of the uvula.

ux. *abbrev. for* uxor. [Latin: wife]

Ux+bridge ('ʌks,brɪdʒ) *n.* a town in SE England, part of the Greater London borough of Hillingdon since 1965; chiefly residential.

Ux+mal (*Spanish* uz'mal) *n.* an ancient ruined city in SE Mexico, in Yucatán: capital of the later Maya empire.

ux·o+ri·al (ʌk'sɔ:rɪəl) *adj.* of or relating to a wife: *uxorial influence.* [C19: from Latin *uxor* wife] —**ux·'o+ri+al+ly** *adv.*

ux·o+ri+cide (ʌk'sɔ:rɪ,saɪd) *n.* **1.** the act of killing one's wife. **2.** a man who kills his wife. [C19: from Latin *uxor* wife + -CIDE] —**ux·,o+ri+'cid+al** *adj.*

ux·o+ri+ous (ʌk'sɔ:rɪəs) *adj.* excessively attached to or dependent on one's wife. [C16: from Latin *uxōrius* concerning a wife, from *uxor* wife] —**ux·'o+ri+ous+ly** *adv.* —**ux·'o+ri+ous+ness** *n.*

Uz+bek ('ʊzbɛk, 'ʌz-) *n.* **1.** (*pl.* +**beks** *or* +**bek**) a member of a Mongoloid people of Uzbekistan. **2.** the language of this people, belonging to the Turkic branch of the Altaic family.

Uz+bek So+vi+et So+cial+ist Re+pub+lic *n.* an administrative division of the SE central Soviet Union, on the Aral Sea. Capital: Tashkent. Pop.: 11 799 429 (1970). Area: 449 600 sq. km (173 546 sq. miles). Also called: **Uz+bek·i+stan** (,ʌzbɛkɪ'stɑ:n).

V

v *or* **V** (viː) *n., pl.* **v's, V's,** *or* **Vs. 1.** the 22nd letter and 17th consonant of the modern English alphabet. **2.** a speech sound represented by this letter, in English usually a voiced labio-dental fricative, as in *vote.* **3. a.** something shaped like a V. **b.** (*in combination*): *a V-neck.* See also **V-sign.**

v *symbol. for:* **1.** *Physics.* velocity. **2.** volt.

V *symbol for:* **1.** *Physics.* velocity. **2.** (in transformational grammar) verb. **3.** volume (capacity). **4.** volt. **5.** *Chem.* vanadium. **6.** luminous efficiency. **7.** victory. ~**8.** *the Roman numeral for* five. See **Roman numerals.** ~**9.** *international car registration for* Vatican City.

v. *abbrev. for:* **1.** ventral. **2.** verb. **3.** verse. **4.** version. **5.** verso. **6.** (*usually italic*) versus. **7.** very. **8.** vide [Latin: see] **9.** violin. **10.** vocative. **11.** voice. **12.** volume. **13.** von.

V. *abbrev. for:* **1.** Venerable. **2.** (in titles) Very. **3.** (in titles) Vice. **4.** Viscount.

V-1 *n.* a robot bomb invented by the Germans in World War II: used esp. to bombard London. It was propelled by a pulsejet. Also called: **doodlebug, buzzbomb.**

V-2 *n.* a rocket-powered ballistic missile invented by the Germans in World War II: used esp. to bombard London. It used ethanol as fuel and oxygen as the oxidizer.

V6 *n.* a car or internal-combustion engine having six cylinders arranged in the form of a V.

V8 *n.* a car or internal-combustion engine having eight cylinders arranged in the form of a V.

va *abbrev. for* volt-ampere.

Va. *abbrev. for* Virginia.

v.a. *abbrev. for* verb active.

V.A. *abbrev. for:* **1.** *U.S.* Veterans' Administration. **2.** Vicar Apostolic. **3.** Vice Admiral. **4.** (Order of) Victoria and Albert.

Vaal (vɑːl) *n.* a river in South Africa, rising in the Drakensberg and flowing west as the border between Transvaal and the Orange Free State, then crossing into Cape Province to the Orange River. Length: 1160 km (720 miles).

Vaa·sa (*Finnish* ˈvɑːsɑ) *n.* a port in W Finland, on the Gulf of Bothnia: the provisional capital of Finland (1918); textile industries. Pop.: 48 390 (1970). Former name: **Nikolainkaupunki.**

vac (væk) *n. Brit. informal.* short for **vacation.**

va+can+cy (ˈveɪkənsɪ) *n., pl.* **+cies. 1.** the state or condition of being vacant or unoccupied; emptiness. **2.** an unoccupied post or office: *we have a vacancy in the accounts department.* **3.** lack of thought or intelligent awareness; inanity: *an expression of vacancy on one's face.* **4.** *Physics.* a defect in a crystalline solid caused by the absence of an atom, ion, or molecule from its position in the crystal lattice. **5.** *Obsolete.* idleness or a period spent in idleness.

va+cant (ˈveɪkənt) *adj.* **1.** without any contents; empty. **2.** (*postpositive;* foll. by *of*) devoid (of something specified). **3.** having no incumbent; unoccupied: *a vacant post.* **4.** having no tenant or occupant: *a vacant house.* **5.** characterized by or resulting from lack of thought or intelligent awareness: *a vacant stare.* **6.** (of time, etc.) not allocated to any activity: *a vacant hour in one's day.* **7.** spent in idleness or inactivity: *a vacant life.* **8.** *Law.* (of an estate, etc.) having no heir or claimant. [C13: from Latin *vacāre* to be empty] —**'va+cant+ly** *adv.* —**'va+cant+ness** *n.*

va+cant pos+ses+sion *n.* ownership of an unoccupied house or property, any previous owner or tenant having departed.

va+cate (vəˈkeɪt) *vb.* (*mainly tr.*) **1.** to cause (something) to be empty, esp. by departing from or abandoning it: *to vacate a room.* **2.** (*also intr.*) to give up the tenure, possession, or occupancy of (a place, post, etc.); leave or quit. **3.** *Law.* **a.** to cancel or rescind. **b.** to make void or of no effect; annul. —**va+'cat+a+ble** *adj.*

va+ca+tion (vəˈkeɪʃən) *n.* **1.** *Chiefly Brit.* a period of the year when the law courts or universities are closed. **2.** another word (esp. U.S.) for **holiday. 3.** the act of departing from or abandoning property, etc. ~*vb.* **4.** (*intr.*) *U.S.* to take a vacation; holiday. [C14: from Latin *vacātiō* freedom, from *vacāre* to be empty] —**va+'ca+tion+less** *adj.*

va+ca+tion+ist (vəˈkeɪʃənɪst) *or* **va+ca+tion+er** (vəˈkeɪʃənə) *n.* U.S. words for **holiday-maker.**

vac+ci+nal (ˈvæksɪnəl) *adj.* of or relating to vaccine or vaccination.

vac+ci+nate (ˈvæksɪˌneɪt) *vb.* to inoculate (a person) with vaccine so as to produce immunity against a specific disease. —**'vac+ci+ˌna+tor** *n.*

vac+ci+na+tion (ˌvæksɪˈneɪʃən) *n.* **1.** the act of vaccinating. **2.** the scar left following inoculation with a vaccine.

vac+cine (ˈvæksiːn) *n. Med.* **1.** a suspension of dead, attenuated, or otherwise modified microorganisms (viruses, bacteria, or rickettsiae) for inoculation to produce immunity to a disease by stimulating the production of antibodies. **2.** a preparation of the virus of cowpox taken from infected cows and inoculated in men to produce immunity to smallpox. **3.** (*modifier*) of or relating to vaccination or vaccinia. [C18: from New Latin *variolae vaccīnae* cowpox, title of medical treatise (1798) by Edward Jenner, from Latin *vacca* a cow]

vac+cin·i·a (vækˈsɪnɪə) *n.* a technical name for **cowpox.** [C19: New Latin, from Latin *vaccīnus* of cows] —**vac+'cin+i+al** *adj.*

vache+rin *French.* (vaʃˈrɛ̃) *n.* a dessert consisting of a meringue shell filled with whipped cream, ice cream, fruit, etc.

vac+il+late (ˈvæsɪˌleɪt) *vb.* (*intr.*) **1.** to fluctuate in one's opinions; be indecisive. **2.** to sway from side to side physically; totter or waver. [C16: from Latin *vacillāre* to sway, of obscure origin] —ˌ**vac+il+'la+tion** *n.* —**'vac+il+ˌla+tor** *n.*

vac+il+lat+ing (ˈvæsɪˌleɪtɪŋ) *or* **vac+il+lant** (ˈvæsɪlənt) *adj.* inclined to waver; indecisive. —ˌ**vac+il+'lat+ing+ly** *adv.*

vac·u·a (ˈvækjʊə) *n.* a plural of **vacuum.**

va+cu+i·ty (væˈkjuːɪtɪ) *n., pl.* **·ties. 1.** the state or quality of being vacuous; emptiness. **2.** an empty space or void; vacuum. **3.** a lack or absence of something specified: *a vacuity of wind.* **4.** lack of normal intelligence or awareness; vacancy: *his stare gave an impression of complete vacuity.* **5.** something, such as a statement, saying, etc., that is inane or pointless. [C16: from Latin *vacuitās* empty space, from *vacuus* empty]

vac+u+ole (ˈvækjʊˌəʊl) *n. Biology.* a fluid-filled cavity in the cytoplasm of a cell. [C19: from French, literally: little vacuum, from Latin VACUUM] —**vac·u·o·lar** (ˌvækjʊˈəʊlə) *adj.* —**vac·u·o·late** (ˈvækjʊəlɪt, -ˌleɪt) *adj.* —**vac·u·o·la·tion** (ˌvækjʊəˈleɪʃən) *n.*

vac·u·ous (ˈvækjʊəs) *adj.* **1.** containing nothing; empty. **2.** bereft of ideas or intelligence; mindless. **3.** characterized by or resulting from vacancy of mind: *a vacuous gaze.* **4.** indulging in no useful mental or physical activity; idle. [C17: from Latin *vacuus* empty, from *vacāre* to be empty] —**'vac·u·ous+ly** *adv.* —**'vac·u·ous+ness** *n.*

vac·u·um (ˈvækjʊəm) *n., pl.* **vac·u·ums** *or* **vac·u·a** (ˈvækjʊə). **1.** a region containing no matter; free space. Compare **plenum** (sense 3). **2.** a region in which gas is present at a low pressure. **3.** the degree of exhaustion of gas within an enclosed space: *a high vacuum; a perfect vacuum.* **4.** a sense or feeling of emptiness: *his death left a vacuum in her life.* **5.** short for **vacuum cleaner. 6.** (*modifier*) of, containing, measuring, producing, or operated by a low gas pressure: *a vacuum tube; a vacuum brake.* ~*vb.* **7.** to clean (something) with a vacuum cleaner: *to vacuum a carpet.* [C16: from Latin: an empty space, from *vacuus* empty]

vac·u·um clean+er *n.* an electrical household appliance used for cleaning floors, carpets, furniture, etc., by suction. —**vac·u·um clean+ing** *n.*

vac·u·um dis+til+la+tion *n.* distillation in which the liquid distilled is enclosed at a low pressure in order to reduce its boiling point.

vac·u·um flask *n.* an insulating flask that has double walls, usually of silvered glass, with an evacuated space between them. It is used for maintaining substances at high or low temperatures. Also called: **Thermos, Dewar flask.**

vac·u·um gauge *n.* any of a number of instruments for measuring pressures below atmospheric pressure.

vac·u·um-packed *adj.* packed in an airtight container or packet under low pressure in order to maintain freshness, prevent corrosion, etc.

vac·u·um pump *n.* a pump for producing a low gas pressure.

vac·u·um tube *or* **valve** *n.* the U.S. name for **valve** (sense 3).

V.A.D. *abbrev. for* Voluntary Aid Detachment.

va·de me·cum (ˈvɑːdɪ ˈmeɪkʊm) *n.* a handbook or other aid carried on the person for immediate use when needed. [C17: from Latin, literally: go with me]

Va+do+da+ra (wəˈdəʊdərə) *n.* a city in W India, in SE Gujurat: textile manufacturing. Pop.: 467 422 (1971). Former name (until 1976): **Baroda.**

va+dose (ˈveɪdəʊs) *adj.* of, relating to, designating, or derived from water occurring above the water table: *vadose water; vadose deposits.* [C19: from Latin *vadōsus* full of shallows, from *vadum* a ford]

Va+duz (*German* faˈdʊts) *n.* the capital of Liechtenstein, in the Rhine valley: an old market town, dominated by a medieval castle, residence of the prince of Liechtenstein. Pop.: 4070 (1968 est.).

vag (væg) *Austral. informal.* ~*n.* **1.** a vagrant. **2. the vag.** the Vagrancy Act: *the police finally got him on the vag.* ~*vb.* **3.** (*tr.*) to arrest (someone) for vagrancy.

vag·a·bond (ˈvægəˌbɒnd) *n.* **1.** a person with no fixed home. **2.** an idle wandering beggar or thief. **3.** (*modifier*) of or like a vagabond; shiftless or idle. [C15: from Latin *vagābundus* wandering, from *vagārī* to roam, from *vagus* VAGUE] —**'vag·a+ˌbond+age** *n.* —**'vag·a+ˌbond+ish** *adj.* —**'vag·a+ˌbond+ism** *n.*

va+gal (ˈveɪgᵊl) *adj. Anatomy.* of, relating to, or affecting the vagus nerve: *vagal inhibition.*

va+gar·i·ous (vəˈgɛərɪəs) *adj. Rare.* characterized or caused by vagaries; irregular or erratic. —**va+'gar·i·ous+ly** *adv.*

va+gar·y (ˈveɪgərɪ, vəˈgɛərɪ) *n., pl.* **+gar·ies.** an erratic or outlandish notion or action; whim. [C16: probably from Latin *vagārī* to roam; compare Latin *vagus* VAGUE]

va+gi+na (vəˈdʒaɪnə) *n., pl.* **+nas** *or* **+nae** (-niː). **1.** the moist canal in most female mammals, including humans, that extends from the cervix of the uterus to an external opening between the labia minora. **2.** *Anatomy, biology.* any sheath or sheathlike structure, such as a leaf base that encloses a stem. [C17: from Latin: sheath] —**vag·ˈi+nal** *adj.*

vag·i+nate (ˈvædʒɪnɪt, -ˌneɪt) *adj.* (esp. of plant parts) having a vagina or sheath; sheathed: *a vaginate leaf.*

vag·i+nec+to·my (ˌvædʒɪˈnɛktəmɪ) *n.* **1.** surgical removal of all or part of the vagina. **2.** surgical removal of part of the serous sheath surrounding the testis and epididymis.

vag·i+nis+mus (ˌvædʒɪˈnɪzməs, -ˈnɪsməs) *n.* painful spasm of the vagina. [C19: from New Latin; see VAGINA, -ISM]

vag·i+ni+tis (ˌvædʒɪˈnaɪtɪs) *n.* inflammation of the vagina.

va+got·o+my (væˈgɒtəmɪ) *n., pl.* **+mies.** surgical division of the vagus nerve, performed to limit gastric secretion in patients with severe peptic ulcers. [C19: from VAG(US) + -TOMY]

va+go·to+ni·a (ˌveɪgəˈtəʊnɪə) *n.* pathological overactivity of the vagus nerve, affecting various bodily functions controlled by this nerve. [C19: from VAG(US) + *-tonia,* from Latin *tonus* tension, TONE]

va+go·trop+ic (ˌveɪgəˈtrɒpɪk) *adj. Physiol.* (of a drug, etc.) affecting the activity of the vagus nerve. [C20: from VAG(US) + -TROPIC]

va+gran+cy (ˈveɪgrənsɪ) *n., pl.* **+cies.** **1.** the state or condition of being a vagrant. **2.** the conduct or mode of living of a vagrant. **3.** *Rare.* digression in thought; mental lapse.

va+grant (ˈveɪgrənt) *n.* **1.** a person of no settled abode, income, or job; tramp. *~adj.* **2.** wandering about; nomadic. **3.** of, relating to, or characteristic of a vagrant or vagabond. **4.** moving in an erratic fashion, without aim or purpose; wayward. **5.** (of plants) showing uncontrolled or straggling growth. ~Archaic equivalent: **va+grom** (ˈveɪgrəm). [C15: probably from Old French *waucrant* (from *wancrer* to roam, of Germanic origin), but also influenced by Old French *vagant* vagabond, from Latin *vagārī* to wander] —**ˈva+grant+ly** *adv.* —**ˈva+grant+ness** *n.*

vague (veɪg) *adj.* **1.** (of statements, meaning, etc.) not explicit; imprecise: *vague promises.* **2.** not clearly perceptible or discernible; indistinct: *a vague idea; a vague shape.* **3.** not clearly or definitely established or known: *a vague rumour.* **4.** (of a person or his expression) demonstrating lack of precision or clear thinking; absent-minded. [C16: via French from Latin *vagus* wandering, of obscure origin] —**ˈvague+ly** *adv.* —**ˈvague+ness** *n.*

va+gus *or* **va+gus nerve** (ˈveɪgəs) *n., pl.* **+gi** (-dʒaɪ). the tenth cranial nerve, which supplies the heart, lungs, and viscera. [C19: from Latin *vagus* wandering]

va+hana (ˈvɑːhənə) *n. Indian myth.* a vehicle. [Hindi, from Sanskrit, from *vaha* to carry]

vail[1] (veɪl) *vb. (tr.) Obsolete.* **1.** to lower (something, such as a weapon), esp. as a sign of deference or submission. **2.** to remove (the hat, cap, etc.) as a mark of respect or meekness. [C14 *valen,* from obsolete *avalen,* from Old French *avaler* to let fall, from Latin *ad vallem* literally: to the valley, that is, down, from *ad* to + *vallis* VALLEY]

vail[2] (veɪl) *n., vb.* an archaic word for **avail.**

vail[3] (veɪl) *n., vb.* an archaic spelling of **veil.**

vain (veɪn) *adj.* **1.** inordinately proud of one's appearance, possessions, or achievements. **2.** given to ostentatious display, esp. of one's beauty. **3.** worthless. **4.** senseless or futile. *~n.* **5. in vain.** to no avail; fruitlessly. **6. take someone's name in vain.** to use the name of someone, esp. God, without due respect or reverence. [C13: via Old French from Latin *vānus*] —**ˈvain+ly** *adv.* —**ˈvain+ness** *n.*

vain+glo+ry (ˈveɪnˌglɔːrɪ) *n.* **1.** boastfulness or vanity. **2.** ostentation. —**vain+ˈglo+ri+ous** *adj.*

vair (vɛə) *n.* **1.** a fur, probably Russian squirrel, used to trim robes in the Middle Ages. **2.** one of the two principal furs used on heraldic shields, conventionally represented by white and blue skins in alternate lines. Compare **ermine** (sense 3). [C13: from Old French: of more than one colour, from Latin *varius* variegated, VARIOUS]

Vaish+na+va (ˈvɪʃnəvə) *n. Hinduism.* a member of a sect devoted to the cult of Vishnu, strongly anti-Brahminic and antipriestly in outlook and stressing devotion through image worship and simple ritual. [from Sanskrit *vaisnava* of VISHNU] —**ˈVaish+na+vism** *n.*

Vais+ya (ˈvaɪsjə, ˈvaɪʃjə) *n.* the third of the four main Hindu castes, the traders. [C18: from Sanskrit, literally: settler, from *viś* settlement]

val. *abbrev. for:* **1.** valuation. **2.** value.

Va+lais (*French* vaˈlɛ) *n.* a canton of S Switzerland: includes the entire valley of the upper Rhône and the highest peaks in Switzerland; produces a quarter of Switzerland's hydroelectricity. Capital: Sion. Pop.: 206 563 (1970). Area: 5231 sq. km (2020 sq. miles). German name: **Wallis.**

val+ance (ˈvæləns) *n.* a short piece of drapery hung along a shelf, canopy, or bed, or across a window, to hide structural detail. [C15: perhaps named after *Valence,* France, town noted for its textiles] —**ˈval+anced** *adj.*

Val+dai Hills (vɑːlˈdaɪ) *n.* a region of hills and plateaus in the NW Soviet Union, between Moscow and Leningrad. Greatest height: 346 m (1135 ft.).

Val·de·mar I (*Danish* ˈvaldəˌmar) *n.* a variant spelling of **Waldemar I.**

Val-de-Marne (*French* val də ˈmarn) *n.* a department of N France, in Île-de-France region. Capital: Créteil. Pop.: 1 222 645 (1975). Area: 244 sq. km (95 sq. miles).

Val·di·via[1] (*Spanish* balˈdiβja) *n.* a port in S Chile, on the **Valdivia River** about 19 km (12 miles) from the Pacific: developed chiefly by German settlers in the 1850s; university (1954). Pop.: 80 035 (1966 est.).

Val·di·via[2] (*Spanish* balˈdiβja) *n.* **Ped·ro de** (ˈpeðro ðe). ?1500–54, Spanish soldier; conqueror of Chile.

Val-d'Oise (*French* val ˈdwaːz) *n.* a department of N France, in Île-de-France region. Capital: Pontoise. Pop.: 847 485 (1975). Area: 1249 sq. km (487 sq. miles).

vale[1] (veɪl) *n.* a literary word for **valley.** [C13: from Old French *val,* from Latin *vallis* valley]

va·le[2] (ˈvɑːleɪ) *Latin.* farewell; goodbye.

val+e·dic+tion (ˌvælɪˈdɪkʃən) *n.* **1.** the act or an instance of saying goodbye. **2.** any valedictory statement, speech, etc. [C17: from Latin *valedīcere,* from *valē* farewell + *dīcere* to say]

val+e·dic+to·ry (ˌvælɪˈdɪktərɪ) *adj.* **1.** saying goodbye. **2.** of or relating to a farewell or an occasion of farewell. *~n., pl.* **·ries. 3.** a farewell address or speech. **4.** *U.S.* a farewell speech delivered by the most outstanding graduate.

va+lence (ˈveɪləns) *n. Chem.* **1.** another name (esp. U.S.) for **valency. 2.** the phenomenon of forming chemical bonds.

Va+lence (*French* vaˈlɑ̃ːs) *n.* a town in SE France, on the River Rhône. Pop.: 70 307 (1975).

Va+len+cia (*Spanish* baˈlenθja) *n.* **1.** a port in E Spain, capital of Valencia province, on the Mediterranean: the third largest city in Spain; capital of the Moorish kingdom of Valencia (1021–1238); university (1501). Pop.: 653 690 (1970). Latin name: **Valentia. 2.** a region and former kingdom of E Spain, on the Mediterranean. **3.** a city in N Venezuela: one of the two main industrial centres in Venezuela. Pop.: 367 171 (1971).

Va+len+ci+ennes[1] (ˌvælənsɪˈɛn) *n.* a flat bobbin lace typically having scroll and floral designs and originally made of linen, now often cotton. [named after VALENCIENNES[2], where it was originally made]

Va+len+ci+ennes[2] (*French* valɑ̃ˈsjɛn) *n.* a town in N France, on the River Escaut: a coal-mining and heavy industrial centre. Pop.: 43 202 (1975).

va+len+cy (ˈveɪlənsɪ) *or esp. U.S.* **va+lence** *n., pl.* **+cies.** *Chem.* a property of atoms or groups, equal to the number of atoms of hydrogen that the atom or group could combine with or displace in forming compounds. [C19: from Latin *valentia* strength, from *valēre* to be strong]

va+len+cy e·lec+tron *n. Chem.* an electron in the outer shell of an atom, responsible for forming chemical bonds.

Va+lens (ˈveɪlɛnz) *n.* ?328–378 A.D., emperor of the Eastern Roman Empire (364–378); appointed by his elder brother Valentinian I, emperor of the Western Empire.

val+en+tine (ˈvælənˌtaɪn) *n.* **1.** a card or gift expressing love or affection, sent, often anonymously, to one's sweetheart or satirically to a friend, on Saint Valentine's Day. **2.** a sweetheart selected for such a greeting.

Val·en·tine (ˈvælənˌtaɪn) *n.* **Saint.** 3rd-century A.D. Christian martyr, associated by historical accident with the custom of sending valentines; bishop of Terni. Feast day: Feb. 14.

Val·en·tin·i·an I (ˌvælənˈtɪnɪən) *or* **Val·en·tin·i·a·nus I** (ˌvælənˌtɪnɪˈeɪnəs) *n.* 321–375 A.D., emperor of the Western Roman Empire (364–375); appointed his brother Valens to rule the Eastern Empire.

Val·en·tin·i·an II *or* **Val·en·tin·i·a·nus II** *n.* 371–392 A.D., emperor of the Western Roman Empire (375–392), reigning jointly with his half brother Gratian until 383.

Val·en·tin·i·an III *or* **Val·en·tin·i·a·nus III** *n.* ?419–455 A.D., emperor of the Western Roman Empire (425–455). His government lost Africa to the Vandals. With Pope Leo I he issued (444) an edict giving the bishop of Rome supremacy over the provincial churches.

Val·en·ti·no (ˌvælənˈtiːnəʊ) *n.* **Ru·dolph,** original name *Rodolpho Guglielmi di Valentina d'Antonguolla.* 1895–1926, U.S. silent-film actor, born in Italy. He is famous for his romantic roles in such films as *The Sheik* (1921).

Va·ler·a (vəˈlɛərə, -ˈlɪərə) *n.* See (Eamon) **de Valera.**

va+le·ri·an (vəˈlɛərɪən) *n.* **1.** Also called: **allheal.** any of various Eurasian valerianaceous plants of the genus *Valeriana,* esp. *V. officinalis,* having small white or pinkish flowers and a medicinal root. **2.** a sedative drug made from the dried roots of *V. officinalis.* [C14: via Old French from Medieval Latin *valeriana* (*herba*) (herb) of *Valerius,* unexplained Latin personal name]

Va·le·ri·an (vəˈlɛərɪən) *n.* Latin name *Publius Licinius Valerianus.* died 260 A.D., Roman emperor (253–260): renewed persecution of the Christians; defeated by the Persians.

va+le·ri·a+na+ceous (vəˌlɪərɪəˈneɪʃəs) *adj.* of, relating to, or belonging to the *Valerianaceae,* a family of herbaceous plants having the calyx of the flower reduced to a ring of hairs: includes valerian, spikenard, and corn salad. [C19: from New Latin; see VALERIAN]

va+ler+ic (vəˈlɛrɪk, -ˈlɪərɪk) *adj.* of, relating to, or derived from valerian.

va+ler+ic ac·id *n.* another name for **pentanoic acid.**

Va·lé·ry (*French* valeˈri) *n.* **Paul** (pɔl). 1871–1945, French poet and essayist, influenced by the symbolists, esp. Mallarmé. He wrote speculative poetry, rich in imagery, as in *La Jeune Parque* (1917) and *Album de vers anciens 1890–1900* (1920).

val+et (ˈvælɪt, ˈvæleɪ) *n.* **1.** a manservant who acts as personal attendant to his employer, looking after his clothing, serving his meals, etc. French name: **valet de chambre. 2.** a manservant who attends to the requirements of patrons in a hotel, passengers on board ship, etc.; steward. [C16: from Old

French *vaslet* page, from Medieval Latin *vassus* servant; see VASSAL]

va+le+ta (vəˈliːtə) *n.* a variant spelling of **veleta.**

va+let de cham+bre *French.* (valɛ də ˈʃɑ̃ːbr) *n., pl.* ***va+lets de cham+bre*** (valɛ də ˈʃɑ̃ːbr). the full French term for **valet** (sense 1).

Va+let+ta (vəˈlɛtə) *n.* a variant spelling of **Valletta.**

val+e+tu+di+nar+i+an (ˌvælɪˌtjuːdɪˈnɛərɪən) *or* **val+e+tu+di+nar+y** (ˌvælɪˈtjuːdɪnərɪ) *n., pl.* **+nar+i+ans** *or* **+nar+ies. 1.** a person who is chronically sick; invalid. **2.** a person excessively worried about the state of his health; hypochondriac. **3.** an old person who is in good health. *~adj.* **4.** relating to, marked by, or resulting from poor health. **5.** being a valetudinarian. **6.** trying to return to a healthy state. [C18: from Latin *valētūdō* state of health, from *valēre* to be well] —ˌ**val+e+ˌtu+di+ˈnar+i+an+ism** *n.*

val+gus (ˈvælgəs) *adj. Pathol.* displaced or twisted away from the midline of the body. See **hallux valgus.** [C19: from Latin: bowlegged]

Val+hal+la (vælˈhælə), **Wal+hal+la, Val+hall,** *or* **Wal+hall** *n. Norse myth.* the great hall of Odin where warriors who die as heroes in battle dwell eternally. [C18: from Old Norse, from *valr* slain warriors + *höll* HALL]

val+iant (ˈvæljənt) *adj.* **1. a.** courageous, intrepid, or stout-hearted; brave. **2.** marked by bravery or courage: *a valiant deed.* [C14: from Old French *vaillant,* from *valoir* to be of value, from Latin *valēre* to be strong] —ˈ**val+iance, ˈval+ian+cy,** *or* ˈ**val+iant+ness** *n.* —ˈ**val+iant+ly** *adv.*

val+id (ˈvælɪd) *adj.* **1.** having some foundation; based on truth. **2.** legally acceptable: *a valid licence.* **3. a.** having legal force; effective. **b.** having legal authority; binding. **4.** having some force or cogency: *a valid point in a debate.* **5.** *Logic.* (of an inference) having premisses and a conclusion so related that if the premisses are true, the conclusion must be true: the conclusion will be false if one or more premisses are false. Compare **invalid²** (sense 2). **6.** *Archaic.* healthy or strong. [C16: from Latin *validus* robust, from *valēre* to be strong] —ˈ**val+id+ly** *adv.* —**va+lid+i+ty** (vəˈlɪdɪtɪ) *or* ˈ**val+id+ness** *n.*

val+i+date (ˈvælɪˌdeɪt) *vb.* (*tr.*) **1.** to confirm or corroborate. **2.** to give legal force or official confirmation to; declare legally valid. —ˌ**val+i+ˈda+tion** *n.* —ˌ**val+i+ˈda+to+ry** *adj.*

va+line (ˈveɪliːn, ˈvæl-) *n.* a sweet-tasting amino acid that is essential to human beings for the maintenance of health; 2-amino-3-methylbutanoic acid. Formula: $(CH_3)_2CHCH(NH_2)COOH$. [C19: from VAL(ERIC ACID) + -INE²]

va+lise (vəˈliːz) *n.* a small overnight travelling case. [C17: via French from Italian *valigia,* of unknown origin]

Val+kyr+ie, Wal+kyr+ie (vælˈkɪərɪ, ˈvælkɪərɪ)), *or* **Val+kyr** (ˈvælkɪə) *n. Norse myth.* any of the beautiful maidens who serve Odin and ride over battlefields to claim the dead heroes chosen by him or by Tyr and take them to Valhalla. [C18: from Old Norse *Valkyrja,* from *valr* slain warriors + *köri* to CHOOSE] —**Val+ˈkyr+i+an** *adj.*

Va+lla+do+lid (*Spanish* ˌbaʎaðoˈlið) *n.* **1.** a city in NW Spain: residence of the Spanish court in the 16th century; university (1346). Pop.: 236 341 (1970). **2.** the former name (until 1828) of **Morelia.**

val+la+tion (vəˈleɪʃən) *n.* **1.** the act or process of building fortifications. **2.** a wall or rampart. [C17: from Late Latin *vallātiō,* from *vallum* rampart]

val+lec+u+la (vəˈlɛkjʊlə) *n., pl.* **+lae** (-ˌliː). **1.** *Anatomy.* any of various natural depressions or crevices, such as certain fissures of the brain. **2.** *Botany.* a groove or furrow. [C19: from Late Latin: little valley, from Latin *vallis* valley] —**val+ˈlec+u+lar** *or* **val+ˈlec+u+ˌlate** *adj.*

Val+le d'A+o+sta (*Italian* ˈvalle daˈɔsta) *n.* an autonomous region of NW Italy: under many different rulers until passing to the house of Savoy in the 11th century; established as an autonomous region in 1944. Capital: Aosta. Pop.: 109 252 (1971). Area: 3263 sq. km (1260 sq. miles).

Val+let+ta *or* **Va+let+ta** (vəˈlɛtə) *n.* the capital of Malta, on the NE coast: founded by the Knights Hospitallers, after the victory over the Turks in 1565; became a major naval base after Malta's annexation by Britain (1814). Pop.: 14 049 (1974 est.).

val+ley (ˈvælɪ) *n.* **1.** a long depression in the land surface, usually containing a river, formed by erosion or by movements in the earth's crust. **2.** the broad area drained by a single river system: *the Thames valley.* **3.** any elongated depression resembling a valley. **4.** the junction of a roof slope with another or with a wall. **5.** (*modifier*) relating to or proceeding by way of a valley: *a valley railway.* [C13: from Old French *valee,* from Latin *vallis*]

Val+ley Forge *n.* an area in SE Pennsylvania, northwest of Philadelphia: winter camp (1777–78) of Washington and the American Revolutionary Army.

Val+ley of Ten Thou+sand Smokes *n.* a volcanic region of SW Alaska, formed by the massive eruption of Mount Katmai in 1912; jets of steam issue from vents up to 45 m (150 ft.) across.

Val+lom+bro+sa (*Italian* ˌvallomˈbroːsa) *n.* a village and resort in central Italy, in Tuscany region: 11th-century Benedictine monastery.

Va+lois¹ (*French* vaˈlwa) *n.* a historic region and former duchy of N France.

Va+lois² (*French* vaˈlwa) *n.* a royal house of France, ruling from 1328 to 1589.

Val+ois³ (ˈvælwɑː). Dame **Ni+nette de** (niːˈnɛt də). original name *Edris Stannus.* born 1898, British ballet dancer and choreographer, born in Ireland: a founder of the Vic-Wells Ballet Company (1931), which under her direction became the Royal Ballet (1956).

Va+lo+na (vəˈləʊnə) *n.* another name for **Vlorë.**

va+lo+ni+a (vəˈləʊnɪə) *n.* the acorn cups and unripe acorns of the Eurasian oak *Quercus aegilops,* used in tanning, dyeing, and making ink. [C18: from Italian *vallonia,* ultimately from Greek *balanos acorn*]

val+or+ize *or* **val+or+ise** (ˈvæləˌraɪz) *vb.* (*tr.*) to fix and maintain an artificial price for (a commodity) by governmental action. [C20: back formation from *valorization;* see VALOUR] —ˌ**val+or+i+ˈza+tion** *or* ˌ**val+or+i+ˈsa+tion** *n.*

val+our *or U.S.* **val+or** (ˈvælə) *n.* courage or bravery, esp. in battle. [C15: from Late Latin *valor,* from *valēre* to be strong] —ˈ**val+or+ous** *adj.* —ˈ**val+or+ous+ly** *adv.*

Val+pa+ra+í+so (*Spanish* ˌbalparaˈiso) *n.* a port in central Chile, on a wide bay of the Pacific: the second largest city and chief port of Chile; two universities. Pop.: 248 972 (1975 est.).

valse *French.* (vals) *n.* the French word, esp. used in the titles of some pieces of music, for **waltz.**

val+u+a+ble (ˈvæljʊəbᵊl) *adj.* **1.** having considerable monetary worth. **2.** of considerable importance or quality: *a valuable friend; valuable information.* **3.** able to be valued. *~n.* **4.** (*usually pl.*) a valuable article of personal property, esp. jewellery. —ˈ**val+u+a+ble+ness** *n.* —ˈ**val+u+a+bly** *adv.*

val+u+ate (ˈvæljʊˌeɪt) *vb.* (*tr.*) *U.S.* another word for **value** (senses 10, 12) or **evaluate.**

val+u+a+tion (ˌvæljʊˈeɪʃən) *n.* **1.** the act of valuing, esp. a formal assessment of the worth of property, jewellery, etc. **2.** the price arrived at by the process of valuing: *the valuation of this property is considerable; I set a high valuation on technical ability.* —ˌ**val+u+ˈa+tion+al** *adj.* —ˌ**val+u+ˈa+tion+al+ly** *adv.*

val+u+a+tor (ˈvæljʊˌeɪtə) *n.* a person who estimates the value of objects, paintings, etc.; appraiser.

val+ue (ˈvæljuː) *n.* **1.** the desirability of a thing, often in respect of some property such as usefulness or exchangeability: worth, merit, or importance. **2.** an amount, esp. a material or monetary one, considered to be a fair exchange in return for a thing; assigned valuation: *the value of the picture is £10 000.* **3.** reasonable or equivalent return; satisfaction: *value for money.* **4.** precise meaning or significance. **5.** (*pl.*) the moral principles and beliefs or accepted standards of a person or social group: *a person with old-fashioned values.* **6.** *Maths.* a particular magnitude, number, or amount: *the value of the variable was 7.* **7.** *Music.* short for **time value. 8.** (in painting, drawing, etc.) **a.** a gradation of tone from light to dark or of colour luminosity. **b.** the relation of one of these elements to another or to the whole picture. **9.** *Phonetics.* the quality or tone of the speech sound associated with a written character representing it: *"g" has the value* (dʒ) *in English "gem."* *~vb.* **+ues, +u+ing, +ued.** (*tr.*) **10.** to assess or estimate the worth, merit, or desirability of; appraise. **11.** to have a high regard for, esp. in respect of worth, usefulness, merit, etc.; esteem or prize: *to value freedom.* **12.** (foll. by *at*) to fix the financial or material worth of (a unit of currency, work of art etc.): *jewels valued at £40 000.* [C14: from Old French, from *valoir,* from Latin *valēre* to be worth, be strong] —ˈ**val+u+er** *n.*

val+ue add+ed *n.* the difference between the total revenues of a firm, industry, etc., and its total purchases from other firms, industries, etc. The aggregate of values added throughout an economy (**gross value added**) represents that economy's gross domestic product.

val+ue-add+ed tax *n. Brit.* the full name for **VAT.**

val+ued pol+i+cy *n.* an insurance policy in which the amount payable in the event of a valid claim is agreed upon between the company and policyholder when the policy is issued and is not related to the actual value of a loss. Compare **open policy.**

val+ue judg+ment *n.* a subjective assessment based on one's own code of values or that of one's class.

val+ue+less (ˈvæljʊlɪs) *adj.* having or possessing no value; worthless. —ˈ**val+ue+less+ness** *n.*

val+u+er (ˈvæljʊə) *n.* a person who assesses the monetary worth of a work of art, jewel, house, etc.; appraiser.

val+u+ta (vəˈluːtə) *n. Rare.* the value of one currency in terms of its exchange rate with another. [C20: from Italian, literally: VALUE]

val+vate (ˈvælveɪt) *adj.* **1.** furnished with a valve or valves. **2.** functioning as or resembling a valve. **3.** *Botany.* **a.** having or taking place by means of valves: *valvate dehiscence.* **b.** (of petals or sepals in the bud) having the margins touching but not overlapping.

valve (vælv) *n.* **1.** any device that shuts off, starts, regulates, or controls the flow of a fluid. **2.** *Anatomy.* a flaplike structure in a hollow organ, such as the heart, that controls the one-way passage of fluid through that organ. **3.** Also called: **tube.** an evacuated electron tube containing a cathode, anode, and, usually, one or more additional control electrodes. When a positive potential is applied to the anode, electrons emitted from the cathode are attracted to the anode, constituting a flow of current which can be controlled by a voltage applied to the grid to produce amplification, oscillation, etc. U.S. name: **vacuum tube.** See also **diode** (sense 2), **triode** (sense 1), **tetrode, pentode. 4.** *Zoology.* any of the separable pieces that make up the shell of a mollusc. **5.** *Music.* a device on some brass instruments by which the effective length of the tube may be varied to enable a chromatic scale to be produced. **6.** *Botany.* **a.** any of the several parts that make up a dry dehiscent fruit, esp. a capsule. **b.** either of the two halves of a diatom cell wall. **7.** *Archaic.* a leaf of a double door or of a folding door. [C14: from Latin *valva* a folding door] —ˈ**valve+less** *adj.* —ˈ**valve+ˌlike** *adj.*

valve gear *n.* a mechanism that operates the valves of a reciprocating engine, usually involving the use of cams, pushrods, rocker arms, etc.
valve-in-head en+gine *n.* the U.S. name for **overhead-valve engine.**
val+vu+lar ('vælvjʊlə) *adj.* **1.** of, relating to, operated by, or having a valve or valves. **2.** having the shape or function of a valve.
val+vule ('vælvju:l) *or* **valve+let** ('vælvlɪt) *n.* a small valve or a part resembling one. [C18: from New Latin *valvula,* diminutive of VALVE]
val+vu+li+tis (ˌvælvjʊ'laɪtɪs) *n.* inflammation of a bodily valve, esp. a heart valve. [C19: from VALVULE + -ITIS]
vam+brace ('væmbreɪs) *n.* a piece of armour used to protect the arm. [C14: from Anglo-French *vauntbras,* from *vaunt-* (from Old French *avant-* fore-) + *bras* arm] —**'vam+braced** *adj.*
va+moose (və'mu:s) *vb.* (*intr.*) *U.S. slang.* to leave a place hurriedly; decamp. [C19: from Spanish *vamos* let us go, from Latin *vādere* to go, walk rapidly]
vamp[1] (væmp) *Informal.* ~*n.* **1.** a seductive woman who exploits men by use of her sexual charms. ~*vb.* **2.** to exploit (a man) in the fashion of a vamp. [C20: short for VAMPIRE] —**'vamp+er** *n.* —**'vamp+ish** *adj.*
vamp[2] (væmp) *n.* **1.** something patched up to make it look new. **2.** the reworking of a theme, story, etc. **3.** an improvised accompaniment, consisting largely of chords. **4.** the front part of the upper of a shoe. ~*vb.* **5.** (*tr.*; often foll. by *up*) to give a vamp (to); make a renovation (of). **6.** to improvise (an accompaniment) to (a tune). [C13: from Old French *avantpié* the front part of a shoe (hence, something patched, etc.) from *avant-* fore- + *pié* foot, from Latin *pēs*] —**'vamp+er** *n.*
vam+pire ('væmpaɪə) *n.* **1.** (in European folklore) a corpse that rises nightly from its grave to drink the blood of the living. **2.** See **vampire bat. 3.** a person who preys mercilessly upon others, such as a blackmailer. **4.** See **vamp**[1]. **5.** *Theatre.* a trapdoor on a stage. [C18: from French, from German *Vampir,* from Magyar; perhaps related to Turkish *uber* witch, Russian *upyr* vampire] —**vam+pir+ic** (væm'pɪrɪk) *or* **vam+pir+ish** ('væmpaɪərɪʃ) *adj.*
vam+pire bat *n.* any bat, esp. *Desmodus rotundus,* of the family *Desmodontidae* of tropical regions of Central and South America, having sharp incisor and canine teeth and feeding on the blood of birds and mammals. Compare **false vampire.**
vam+pir+ism ('væmpaɪəˌrɪzəm) *n.* **1.** belief in the existence of vampires. **2.** the actions of vampires; bloodsucking. **3.** the act of preying upon or exploiting others.
van[1] (væn) *n.* **1.** short for **caravan** (sense 1). **2.** a covered motor vehicle for transporting goods, etc., by road. **3.** *Brit.* a closed railway wagon in which the guard travels, for transporting goods, mail, etc. **4.** *Brit.* See **delivery van.**
van[2] (væn) *n.* short for **vanguard.**
van[3] (væn) *n. Tennis, chiefly Brit.* **1.** short for **advantage.** Usual U.S. word: **ad. 2. van in.** an advantage scored by the server. **3. van out.** an advantage scored by the receiver.
van[4] (væn) *n.* **1.** any device for winnowing corn. **2.** an archaic or poetic word for **wing.** [C17: variant of FAN[1]]
Van (vɑ:n) *n.* **1.** a city in E Turkey, on Lake Van. Pop.: 31 010 (1965). **2. Lake.** a salt lake in E Turkey, at an altitude of 1650 m (5400 ft.): fed by melting snow and glaciers. Area: 3737 sq. km (1433 sq. miles).
van·a·date ('vænəˌdeɪt) *n.* any salt or ester of a vanadic acid.
va+nad+ic (və'nædɪk, -'neɪdɪk) *adj.* of or containing vanadium, esp. in a trivalent or pentavalent state.
va+nad+ic ac·id *n.* any one of various oxyacids of vanadium, such as H_3VO_4 **(orthovanadic acid),** HVO_4 **(metavanadic acid),** and $H_4V_2O_7$ **(pyrovanadic acid),** known chiefly in the form of their vanadate salts.
va+nad·i+nite (və'nædɪˌnaɪt) *n.* a red, yellow, or brownish mineral consisting of a chloride and vanadate of lead in hexagonal crystalline form. It results from weathering of lead ores in desert regions and is a source of vanadium. Formula: $Pb_5(VO_4)_3Cl$.
va+na·di·um (və'neɪdɪəm) *n.* a toxic silvery-white metallic element occurring chiefly in carnotite and vanadinite and used in steel alloys, high-speed tools, and as a catalyst. Symbol: V; atomic no.: 23; atomic wt.: 50.94; valency: 2–5; relative density: 6.1; melting pt.: 1890°C; boiling pt.: 3380°C. [C19: New Latin, from Old Norse *Vanadis,* epithet of the goddess Freya + -IUM]
van·a·dous ('vænədəs) *adj.* of or containing vanadium, esp. in a divalent or trivalent state.
Van Al+len belt (væn 'ælən) *n.* either of two regions of charged particles above the earth, the inner one extending from 2400 to 5600 kilometres above the earth and the outer one from 13 000 to 19 000 kilometres. The charged particles result from cosmic rays and are trapped by the earth's magnetic field. [C20: named after its discoverer, J. A. *Van Allen* (born 1914), American physicist]
va+na+spa+ti (və'næspətɪ) *n.* a hydrogenated vegetable fat commonly used in India as a substitute for butter. [C20: the Sanskrit name of a forest plant, from *vana* forest + *pati* lord]
Van·brugh ('vænbrə) *n.* Sir **John.** 1664–1726, English dramatist and baroque architect. His best-known plays are the Restoration comedies *The Relapse* (1697) and *The Provok'd Wife* (1697). As an architect, he is noted esp. for Blenheim Palace.
Van Bu·ren (væn 'bjʊərən) *n.* **Mar·tin.** 1782–1862, U.S. Democratic statesman; 8th president of the U.S. (1837–41).
Vance (væns) *n.* **Cy·rus.** born 1917, U.S. Democratic politician; secretary of state (1977–80).
Van+cou+ver[1] (væn'ku:və) *n.* **1.** an island of SW Canada, off the SW coast of British Columbia: separated from the Canadian mainland by the Strait of Georgia and Queen Charlotte Sound, and from the U.S. mainland by Juan de Fuca Strait; the largest island off the W coast of North America. Chief town: Victoria. Pop.: 380 000 (1971 est.). Area: 32 137 sq. km (12 408 sq. miles). **2.** a port in SW Canada, in SW British Columbia: Canada's chief Pacific port and third largest city. Pop.: 426 256 (1971). **3. Mount.** a mountain on the border between Canada and Alaska, in the St. Elias Mountains. Height: 4785 m (15 700 ft.).
Van·cou·ver[2] (væn'ku:və) *n.* **George.** 1757–98, English navigator, noted for his exploration of the Pacific coast of North America (1792–94).
V and A (in Britain) *abbrev. for* Victoria and Albert Museum.
van+da ('vændə) *n.* any epiphytic orchid of the E hemisphere genus *Vanda,* having white, mauve, blue, or greenish fragrant flowers. [C19: New Latin, from Hindi *vandā* mistletoe, from Sanskrit]
van+dal ('vændᵊl) *n.* **a.** a person who deliberately causes damage or destruction to personal or public property. **b.** (*as modifier*): *vandal instincts.*
Van+dal ('vændᵊl) *n.* a member of a Germanic people that raided Roman provinces in the 3rd and 4th centuries A.D. before devastating Gaul (406–409), conquering Spain and N Africa, and sacking Rome (455). —**Van+dal+ic** (væn'dælɪk) *adj.* —**'Van+dal+ism** *n.*
van+dal+ism ('vændəˌlɪzəm) *n.* the wanton or deliberate destruction caused by a vandal or an instance of such destruction. —**ˌvan+dal+'is+tic** *or* **'van+dal+ish** *adj.*
van+dal+ize *or* **van+dal+ise** ('vændəˌlaɪz) *vb.* (*tr.*) to destroy or damage (something) by an act of vandalism.
Van de Graaff gen+er+a+tor ('væn də ˌgrɑ:f) *n.* a device for producing high electrostatic potentials (up to 15 million volts), consisting of a hollow metal sphere on which a charge is accumulated from a continuous moving belt of insulating material: used in particle accelerators. [C20: named after R. J. *Van de Graaff* (1901–67), U.S. physicist]
Van·der·bilt ('vændəbɪlt) *n.* **Cor·ne·li·us,** known as *Commodore Vanderbilt.* 1794–1877, U.S. steamship and railway magnate and philanthropist.
Van der Waal's forc·es ('væn də ˌwɑ:lz) *pl. n.* weak electrostatic forces between atoms and molecules caused by transient dissymmetries in the distribution of electrons in the interacting atoms or molecules.
van der Wey·den (*Dutch* vɑn də 'wɛɪdə) *n.* **Ro·gier** (ro:'xi:r). ?1400–64, Flemish painter, esp. of religious works and portraits.
Van Die·men Gulf (væn 'di:mən) *n.* an inlet of the Timor Sea in N Australia, in the Northern Territory.
Van Die·men's Land (væn 'di:mənz) *n.* the former name (1642–1855) of **Tasmania.** —**ˌVan+de+'mo+ni+an** *n., adj.*
Van Dyck *or* **Van·dyke** (væn 'daɪk) *n.* Sir **An·tho·ny.** 1599–1641, Flemish painter; court painter to Charles I of England (1632–41). He is best known for his portraits of the aristocracy.
Van+dyke beard ('vændaɪk) *n.* a short pointed beard. Often shortened to **Vandyke.**
Van+dyke brown *n., adj.* **1. a.** a moderate brown colour. **b.** (*as adj.*): *a Vandyke-brown suit.* **2.** any of various brown pigments, usually consisting of a mixture of ferric oxide and lampblack.
Van+dyke col+lar *or* **cape** *n.* a large white collar with several very deep points. Often shortened to **Vandyke.**
vane (veɪn) *n.* **1.** Also called: **weather vane, wind vane.** a flat plate or blade of metal mounted on a vertical axis in an exposed position to indicate wind direction. **2.** any one of the flat blades or sails forming part of the wheel of a windmill. **3.** any flat or shaped plate used to direct fluid flow, esp. a stator blade in a turbine, etc. **4.** a fin or plate fitted to a projectile or missile to provide stabilization or guidance. **5.** *Ornithol.* the flat part of a feather, consisting of two rows of barbs on either side of the shaft. **6.** *Surveying.* **a.** a sight on a quadrant or compass. **b.** the movable marker on a levelling staff. [Old English *fana;* related to Old Saxon, Old High German *fano,* Old Norse *fani,* Latin *pannus* cloth] —**vaned** *adj.* —**'vane+less** *adj.*
Vane (veɪn) *n.* Sir **Hen·ry,** known as *Sir Harry Vane.* 1613–62, English Puritan statesman and colonial administrator; governor of Massachusetts (1636–37). He was executed for high treason after the Restoration.
Vä·nern (*Swedish* 'vɛ:nərn) *n.* **Lake.** a lake in SW Sweden: the largest lake in Sweden and W Europe; drains into the Kattegat. Area: 5585 sq. km (2156 sq. miles).
van Eyck (væn 'aɪk) *n.* **Jan** (jɑn). died 1441, Flemish painter; founder of the Flemish school of painting. His most famous work is the altarpiece *The Adoration of the Lamb,* in Ghent, in which he may have been assisted by his brother **Hu·bert** ('hy:bərt), died ?1426.
vang (væŋ) *n. Nautical.* **1.** a rope or tackle extended from the boom of a fore-and-aft mainsail to a deck fitting of a vessel when running, in order to keep the boom from riding up. **2.** a guy extending from the end of a gaff to the vessel's rail on each side, used for steadying the gaff. [C18: from Dutch, from *vangen* to catch]
Van Gogh (væn 'gɒx; *Dutch* vɑn 'xɔx) *n.* **Vin·cent** (vɪn'sɛnt). 1853–90, Dutch postimpressionist painter, noted for his landscapes and portraits, in which colour is used essentially for its expressive and emotive value.
van+guard ('vænˌgɑ:d) *n.* **1.** the leading division or units of an army. **2.** the leading position in any movement or field, or the people who occupy such a position: *the vanguard of modern*

literature. [C15: from Old French *avant-garde,* from *avant-* fore- + *garde* GUARD]

va+nil+la (vəˈnɪlə) *n.* **1.** any tropical climbing orchid of the genus *Vanilla,* esp. *V. plonifolia,* having spikes of large fragrant greenish-yellow flowers and long fleshy pods containing the seeds (beans). **2.** the pod or bean of certain of these plants, used to flavour food, etc. **3.** a flavouring extract prepared from vanilla beans and used in cooking. [C17: from New Latin, from Spanish *vainilla* pod, from *vaina* a sheath, from Latin *vāgīna* sheath]

va+nil+lic (vəˈnɪlɪk) *adj.* of, resembling, containing, or derived from vanilla or vanillin.

van+il+lin (ˈvænɪlɪn, vəˈnɪlɪn) *n.* a white crystalline aldehyde found in vanilla and many natural balsams and resins; 3-methoxy-4-hydroxybenzaldehyde. It is a by-product of paper manufacture and is used as a flavouring and in perfumes and pharmaceuticals. Formula: $(CH_3O)(OH)C_6H_3CHO$.

Va+nir (ˈvɑːnɪə) *n. Norse myth.* a race of ancient gods often locked in struggle with the Aesir. The most notable of them are Njord and his children Frey and Freya. [from Old Norse *Vanr* a fertility god]

van+ish (ˈvænɪʃ) *vb.* (*intr.*) **1.** to disappear, esp. suddenly or mysteriously. **2.** to cease to exist; fade away. **3.** *Maths.* to become zero. ~*n.* **4.** *Phonetics, rare.* the second and weaker of the two vowels in a falling diphthong. [C14: *vanissen,* from Old French *esvanir,* from Latin *ēvānescere* to evaporate, from *ē-* EX-[1] + *vānescere* to pass away, from *vānus* vain] —ˈ**van+ish+er** *n.* —ˈ**van+ish+ment** *n.*

van+ish+ing cream *n.* a cosmetic cream that is colourless once applied, used as a foundation for powder or as a cleansing or moisturizing cream.

van+ish+ing point *n.* **1.** the point to which parallel lines appear to converge in the rendering of perspective, usually on the horizon. **2.** a point in space or time at or beyond which something disappears or ceases to exist.

van+i+ty (ˈvænɪtɪ) *n., pl.* **·ties. 1.** the state or quality of being vain; excessive pride or conceit. **2.** ostentation occasioned by ambition or pride. **3.** an instance of being vain or something about which one is vain. **4.** the state or quality of being valueless, futile, or unreal. **5.** something that is worthless or useless. [C13: from Old French *vanité,* from Latin *vānitās* emptiness, from *vānus* empty]

van+i+ty case *or* **box** *n.* a woman's small hand case used to carry cosmetics, etc.

Van+i+ty Fair *n.* (*often not cap.*) *Literary.* the social life of a community, esp. of a great city, or the world in general, considered as symbolizing worldly frivolity.

van+i+ty u+nit *n.* a hand basin built into a wooden Formica-covered or tiled top, usually with a built-in cupboard below it. Also called (trademark): **Vanitory unit.**

van+quish (ˈvæŋkwɪʃ) *vb.* (*tr.*) **1.** to defeat or overcome in a battle, contest, etc.; conquer. **2.** to defeat or overcome in argument or debate. **3.** to conquer (an emotion). [C14: *vanquisshen,* from Old French *venquis* vanquished, from *veintre* to overcome, from Latin *vincere*] —ˈ**van+quish+a+ble** *adj.* —ˈ**van+quish+er** *n.* —ˈ**van+quish+ment** *n.*

Van·sit·tart (vænˈsɪtət) *n.* **Rob·ert Gil·bert,** 1st Baron Vansittart of Denham. 1881–1957, British diplomat and writer; a fierce opponent of Nazi Germany and of Communism.

van+tage (ˈvɑːntɪdʒ) *n.* **1.** a state, position, or opportunity affording superiority or advantage. **2.** superiority or benefit accruing from such a position, state, etc. **3.** *Tennis.* short for **advantage.** [C13: from Old French *avantage* ADVANTAGE] —ˈ**van+tage+less** *adj.*

van+tage ground *n.* a position or condition affording superiority or advantage over or as if over an opponent.

van+tage point *n.* a position or place that allows one a wide or favourable overall view of a scene or situation.

van't Hoff (*Dutch* vɑnt ˈhɔf) *n.* **Ja·co·bus Hen·dri·cus** (jaːˈkoːbys hɛnˈdriːkœs). 1852–1911, Dutch physical chemist: founded stereochemistry with his theory of the asymmetric carbon atom; the first to apply thermodynamics to chemical reactions: Nobel prize for chemistry (1901).

Va·nu·a Le·vu (vɑːˈnuːə ˈlɛvuː) *n.* the second largest island of Fiji: mountainous. Area: 5535 sq. km (2137 sq. miles).

Van·ua·tu (vænwaːˈtuː) *n.* name, since 1980, for **New Hebrides.**

Van·zet·ti (vænˈzɛtɪ) *n.* **Bar·to·lo·me·o** (ˌbartoloˈmɛːo). 1888–1927, U.S. radical agitator, born in Italy: executed with Sacco in a case that had worldwide political repercussions.

vap+id (ˈvæpɪd) *adj.* **1.** bereft of strength, sharpness, flavour, etc.; flat. **2.** boring or dull; lifeless: *vapid talk.* [C17: from Latin *vapidus;* related to *vappa* tasteless or flat wine, and perhaps to *vapor* warmth] —**va+ˈpid+i+ty** *n.* —ˈ**vap+id+ly** *adv.* —ˈ**vap+id+ness** *n.*

va+por (ˈveɪpə) *n.* the U.S. spelling of **vapour.**

va+por+es+cence (ˌveɪpəˈrɛsəns) *n.* the production or formation of vapour. —ˌ**va+por+ˈes+cent** *adj.*

va+po+ret+to (ˌveɪpəˈrɛtəʊ; *Italian* ˌvapoˈretto) *n., pl.* **·ti** (-tɪ; *Italian* -ti) *or* **·tos.** a steam-powered passenger boat, as used on the canals in Venice. [Italian, from *vapore* a steamboat]

va+por+if+ic (ˌveɪpəˈrɪfɪk) *adj.* **1.** producing, causing, or tending to produce vapour. **2.** of, concerned with, or having the nature of vapour. **3.** tending to become vapour; volatile. ~Also: **vaporous.** [C18: from New Latin *vaporificus,* from Latin *vapor* steam + *facere* to make]

va+por+im+e+ter (ˌveɪpəˈrɪmɪtə) *n.* an instrument for measuring vapour pressure, used to determine the volatility of oils or the amount of alcohol in alcoholic liquids.

va+por+ize *or* **va+por+ise** (ˈveɪpəˌraɪz) *vb.* **1.** to change or cause to change into vapour or into the gaseous state. **2.** to evaporate or disappear or cause to evaporate or disappear, esp. suddenly. **3.** (*intr.*) *Rare.* to brag. —ˈ**va+por+ˌiz+a+ble** *or* ˈ**va+por+ˌis+a+ble** *adj.* —ˌ**va+por+i+ˈza+tion** *or* ˌ**va+por+i+ˈsa+tion** *n.*

va+por+iz+er *or* **va+por+is+er** (ˈveɪpəˌraɪzə) *n.* **1.** a substance that vaporizes or a device that causes vaporization. **2.** *Med.* a device that produces steam or atomizes medication for inhalation.

va+por+ous (ˈveɪpərəs) *adj.* **1.** resembling or full of vapour. **2.** another word for **vaporific. 3.** lacking permanence or substance; ephemeral or fanciful. **4.** given to foolish imaginings. **5.** dulled or obscured by an atmosphere of vapour. —ˈ**va+por+ous+ly** *adv.* —ˈ**va+por+ous+ness** *or* **va+por+os+i+ty** (ˌveɪpəˈrɒsɪtɪ) *n.*

va+pour *or U.S.* **va+por** (ˈveɪpə) *n.* **1.** particles of moisture or other substance suspended in air and visible as clouds, smoke, etc. **2.** a gaseous substance at a temperature below its critical temperature. Compare **gas** (sense 3). **3.** a substance that is in a gaseous state at a temperature below its boiling point. **4.** *Rare.* something fanciful that lacks substance or permanence. **5. the vapours.** *Archaic.* a depressed mental condition believed originally to be the result of vaporous exhalations from the stomach. ~*vb.* **6.** to evaporate or cause to evaporate; vaporize. **7.** (*intr.*) to make vain empty boasts; brag. [C14: from Latin *vapor*] —ˈ**va+pour+a+ble** *or U.S.* ˈ**va+por+a+ble** *adj.* —ˌ**va+pour+a+ˈbil+i+ty** *or U.S.* ˌ**va+por+a+ˈbil+i+ty** *n.* —ˈ**va+pour+er** *or U.S.* ˈ**va+por+er** *n.* —ˈ**va+pour+ish** *or U.S.* ˈ**va+por+ish** *adj.* —ˈ**va+pour+less** *or U.S.* ˈ**va+por+less** *adj.* —ˈ**va·pour-ˌlike** *or U.S.* ˈ**va·por-ˌlike** *adj.* —ˈ**va+pour·y** *or U.S.* ˈ**va+por·y** *adj.*

va+pour den+si+ty *n.* the ratio of the density of a gas or vapour to that of hydrogen at the same temperature and pressure. See also **relative density.**

va+pour lock *n.* a stoppage in a pipe carrying a liquid caused by a bubble of gas, esp. such a stoppage caused by vaporization of the petrol in the pipe feeding the carburettor of an internal-combustion engine.

va+pour pres+sure *n. Physics.* the pressure exerted by a vapour, esp. that exerted by a vapour in equilibrium with its solid or liquid phase at a particular temperature.

va+pour trail *n.* a visible trail of condensed vapour left by an aircraft flying at high altitude or through supercooled air. Also called: **condensation trail, contrail.**

var (vɑː) *n.* a unit of reactive power of an alternating current, equal to the product of the current measured in amperes and the voltage measured in volts.

Var (*French* vaːr) *n.* **1.** a department of SE France, in Provence-Côte-d'Azur region. Capital: Toulon. Pop.: 643 540 (1975). Area: 6023 sq. km (2349 sq. miles). **2.** a river in SE France, flowing southeast and south to the Mediterranean near Nice. Length: about 130 km (80 miles).

VAR *abbrev. for* visual aural range.

var. *abbrev. for:* **1.** variable. **2.** variant. **3.** variation. **4.** variety. **5.** various.

va+ra (ˈvɑːrə) *n.* a unit of length used in Spain, Portugal, and South America and having different values in different localities, usually between 32 and 43 inches (about 80 to 108 centimetres). [C17: via Spanish from Latin: wooden trestle, from *vārus* crooked]

va+rac+tor (ˈvɛəˌræktə) *n.* a semiconductor diode that acts as a voltage-dependent capacitor, being operated with a reverse bias. Compare **varistor.** [C20: probably a blend based on *variable capacitor*]

Va+ra+na+si (vəˈrɑːnəsɪ) *n.* a city in NE India, in SE Uttar Pradesh on the River Ganges: probably dates from the 13th century B.C.; an early centre of Aryan philosophy and religion; a major place of pilgrimage for Hindus, Jains, Sikhs, and Buddhists, with many ghats along the Ganges; seat of the Banaras Hindi University (1916), India's leading university, and the Sanskrit University (1957). Pop.: 583 856 (1971). Former names: **Benares, Banaras.**

Va+ran+gi+an (vəˈrændʒɪən) *n.* one of the Scandinavians who invaded and settled parts of Russia and the Ukraine from the 8th to the 11th centuries, and who formed the bodyguard of the Byzantine emperor **(Varangian Guard)** in the late 10th and 11th centuries. [C18: from Medieval Latin *Varangus,* from Medieval Greek *Barangos,* from Old Norse *Væringi,* probably from *vār* pledge]

Var+dar (*Serbo-Croatian* ˈvardar) *n.* a river in S Europe, rising in SW Yugoslavia and flowing northeast, then south past Skopje into Greece, where it enters the Aegean at Thessaloníki. Length: about 320 km (200 miles).

Var·don (ˈvɑːdᵊn) *n.* **Har·ry.** 1870–1937, British golfer.

var+ec (ˈværɛk) *n.* **1.** another name for **kelp. 2.** the ash obtained from kelp. [C17: from French, from Old Norse *wrek* (unattested); see WRECK]

Va+re·se (*Italian* vaˈreːse) *n.* a historic city in N Italy, in Lombardy near Lake Varese: manufacturing centre, esp. for leather goods. Pop.: 83 150 (1971).

Va·rèse (væˈrɛːz) *n.* **Ed·gar(d)** (ɛdˈgaːr). 1885–1965, U.S. composer, born in France. His works, which combine extreme dissonance with complex rhythms and the use of electronic techniques, include *Ionisation* (1931) and *Poème électronique* (1958).

Var·gas (*Portuguese* ˈvargas) *n.* **Ge·tu·lio Dor·nel·les** (ʒeˈtulju durˈneles). 1883–1954, Brazilian statesman; president (1930–45; 1951–54).

var·i·a (ˈvɛərɪə) *pl. n.* a collection or miscellany, esp. of literary works. [Latin, neuter plural of *varius* VARIOUS]

var·i·a·ble (ˈvɛərɪəbᵊl) *adj.* **1.** liable to or capable of change:

variable weather. **2.** (of behaviour, opinions, emotions, etc.) lacking constancy; fickle. **3.** *Maths.* having a range of possible values. **4.** (of a species, characteristic, etc.) liable to deviate from the established type. **5.** (of a wind) varying its direction and intensity. **6.** (of an electrical component or device) designed so that a characteristic property, such as resistance, can be varied: *variable capacitor.* ~*n.* **7.** something that is subject to variation. **8.** *Maths.* **a.** a quantity or function that can assume any of a set of specified values. **b.** a symbol, esp. *x, y,* or *z,* representing any unspecified number, quantity, point, etc., belonging to a set. See also **dependent variable, independent variable. 9.** *Logic.* a symbol, esp. *x, y, z,* representing any member of a class of entities. **10.** *Astronomy.* See **variable star. 11.** a variable wind. **12.** (*pl.*) a region where variable winds occur. [C14: from Latin *variābilis,* changeable, from *variāre* to diversify] —ˌ**var·i·a·ˈbil·i·ty** *or* ˈ**var·i·a·ble·ness** *n.* —ˈ**var·i·a·bly** *adv.*

var·i·a·ble cost *n.* a cost that varies directly with output.

var·i·a·ble star *n.* any star that varies considerably in brightness, either irregularly or in regular periods. **Intrinsic variables,** in which the variation is a result of internal changes, include novae, supernovae, and pulsating stars. See also **eclipsing binary.**

var·i·ance (ˈvɛərɪəns) *n.* **1.** the act of varying or the quality, state, or degree of being divergent; discrepancy. **2.** an instance of diverging; dissension: *our variance on this matter should not affect our friendship.* **3. at variance. a.** (often foll. by *with*) (of facts, etc.) not in accord; conflicting. **b.** (of persons) in a state of dissension. **4.** *Statistics.* a measure of dispersion obtained by taking the mean of the squared deviations of the observed values from their mean in a frequency distribution. **5.** a difference or discrepancy between two steps in a legal proceeding, esp. between a statement in a pleading and the evidence given to support it. **6.** (in the U.S.) a licence or authority to contravene the usual rule, esp. to build contrary to the provision of a zoning code. **7.** *Chem.* the number of degrees of freedom of a system, used in the phase rule. **8.** *Accounting.* the difference between actual and standard costs of production.

var·i·ant (ˈvɛərɪənt) *adj.* **1.** liable to or displaying variation. **2.** deviating from a norm, standard, or type: *a variant spelling.* **3.** *Obsolete.* not constant; fickle. ~*n.* **4.** something that deviates or varies from a norm, standard, or type. **5.** *Statistics.* another word for **variate** (sense 1). [C14: via Old French from Latin *variāns,* from *variāre* to diversify, from *varius* VARIOUS]

var·i·ate (ˈvɛərɪɪt) *n.* **1.** *Statistics.* a random variable or a numerical value taken by it. **2.** a less common word for **variant** (sense 4). [C16: from Latin *variāre* to VARY]

var·i·a·tion (ˌvɛərɪˈeɪʃən) *n.* **1.** the act, process, condition, or result of changing or varying; diversity. **2.** an instance of varying or the amount, rate, or degree of such change. **3.** something that deviates from a standard, convention, or norm. **4.** *Music.* **a.** a repetition of a musical theme in which the rhythm, harmony, or melody are altered or embellished. **b.** (*as modifier*): *variation form.* **5.** *Biology.* **a.** a marked deviation from the typical form or function. **b.** a characteristic or an organism showing this deviation. **6.** *Astronomy.* any change in or deviation from the mean motion or orbit of a planet, satellite, etc., esp. a perturbation of the moon. **7.** another word for **magnetic declination. 8.** *Ballet.* a solo dance. **9.** *Linguistics.* any form of morphophonemic change, such as one involved in inflection, conjugation, or vowel mutation. —ˌ**var·i·ˈa·tion·al** *or* ˈ**var·i·a·tive** *adj.* —ˌ**var·i·ˈa·tion·al·ly** *or* ˈ**var·i·a·tive·ly** *adv.*

var·i·cel·la (ˌværɪˈsɛlə) *n.* the technical name for **chickenpox.** [C18: New Latin, irregular diminutive of VARIOLA] —ˌ**var·i·ˈcel·lar** *adj.*

var·i·cel·late (ˌværɪˈsɛlɪt, -eɪt) *adj.* (of certain shells) marked on the surface with small ridges. [C19: from New Latin *varicella,* diminutive of Latin *varix* dilated vein, VARIX]

var·i·cel·loid (ˌværɪˈsɛlɔɪd) *adj.* resembling chickenpox.

var·i·ces (ˈværɪˌsiːz) *pl. n.* the plural of **varix.**

var·i·co- *or before a vowel* **var·ic-** *combining form.* indicating a varix or varicose veins: *varicotomy.* [from Latin *varix, varic-* distended vein]

var·i·co·cele (ˈværɪkəʊˌsiːl) *n. Pathol.* an abnormal distension of the veins of the spermatic cord in the scrotum.

var·i·col·oured *or U.S.* **var·i·col·ored** (ˈvɛərɪˌkʌləd) *adj.* having many colours; variegated; motley.

var·i·cose (ˈværɪˌkəʊs) *adj.* of or resulting from varicose veins: *a varicose ulcer.* [C18: from Latin *varicōsus,* from VARIX]

var·i·cose veins *n.* a condition in which the superficial veins, esp. of the legs, become tortuous, knotted, and swollen: caused by a defect in the venous valves or in the venous pump that normally moves the blood out of the legs when standing for long periods.

var·i·co·sis (ˌværɪˈkəʊsɪs) *n. Pathol.* any condition characterized by distension of the veins. [C18: from New Latin, from Latin: VARIX]

var·i·cos·i·ty (ˌværɪˈkɒsɪtɪ) *n., pl.* **·ties.** *Pathol.* **1.** the state, condition, or quality of being varicose. **2.** an abnormally distended vein.

var·i·cot·o·my (ˌværɪˈkɒtəmɪ) *n., pl.* **·mies.** surgical excision of a varicose vein.

var·ied (ˈvɛərɪd) *adj.* **1.** displaying or characterized by variety; diverse. **2.** modified or altered: *the amount may be varied without notice.* **3.** varicoloured; variegated. —ˈ**var·ied·ly** *adv.* —ˈ**var·ied·ness** *n.*

var·ie·gate (ˈvɛərɪˌgeɪt) *vb.* (*tr.*) **1.** to alter the appearance of, esp. by adding different colours. **2.** to impart variety to. [C17: from Late Latin *variegāre,* from Latin *varius* diverse, VARIOUS + *agere* to make] —ˌ**var·ie·ˈga·tion** *n.*

var·ie·gat·ed (ˈvɛərɪˌgeɪtɪd) *adj.* **1.** displaying differently coloured spots, patches, streaks, etc. **2.** (of foliage or flowers) having pale patches as a result of mutation, infection, etc.

va·ri·e·tal (vəˈraɪɪtᵊl) *adj.* of, relating to, characteristic of, designating, or forming a variety, esp. a biological variety. —**va·ˈri·e·tal·ly** *adv.*

va·ri·e·ty (vəˈraɪɪtɪ) *n., pl.* **·ties. 1.** the quality or condition of being diversified or various. **2.** a collection of unlike things, esp. of the same general group; assortment. **3.** a different form or kind within a general category; sort: *varieties of behaviour.* **4.** a type of animal or plant produced by artificial breeding. **5. a.** entertainment consisting of a series of short unrelated performances or acts, such as comedy turns, songs, dances, sketches, etc. **b.** (*as modifier*): *a variety show.* [C16: from Latin *varietās,* from VARIOUS]

va·ri·e·ty meat *n. Chiefly U.S.* processed meat, such as sausage, or offal.

var·i·form (ˈvɛərɪˌfɔːm) *adj.* varying in form or shape. —ˈ**var·i·ˌform·ly** *adv.*

var·i·o- *combining form.* indicating variety or difference: *variometer.* [from Latin *varius* VARIOUS]

va·ri·o·la (vəˈraɪələ) *n.* the technical name for **smallpox.** [C18: from Medieval Latin: disease marked by little spots, from Latin *varius* spotted] —**va·ˈri·o·lar** *adj.*

va·ri·o·late (ˈvɛərɪəˌleɪt) *vb.* **1.** (*tr.*) to inoculate with the smallpox virus. ~*adj.* **2.** marked or pitted with or as if with the scars of smallpox. [C18: from VARIOLA] —ˌ**va·ri·o·ˈla·tion,** ˌ**va·ri·o·li·ˈza·tion,** *or* ˌ**va·ri·o·li·ˈsa·tion** *n.*

var·i·ole (ˈvɛərɪˌəʊl) *n.* any of the rounded masses that make up the rock variolite. [C19: from French, from Medieval Latin; see VARIOLA]

var·i·o·lite (ˈvɛərɪəˌlaɪt) *n.* any basic igneous rock containing rounded bodies (varioles) consisting of radiating crystal fibres. [C18: from VARIOLA, referring to the pock-marked appearance of the rock] —**var·i·o·lit·ic** (ˌvɛərɪəˈlɪtɪk) *adj.*

var·i·o·loid (ˈvɛərɪəˌlɔɪd) *adj.* **1.** resembling smallpox. ~*n.* **2.** a mild form of smallpox occurring in persons with partial immunity.

va·ri·o·lous (vəˈraɪələs) *adj.* relating to or resembling smallpox; variolar.

var·i·om·e·ter (ˌvɛərɪˈɒmɪtə) *n.* **1.** an instrument for measuring variations in a magnetic field, used esp. for studying the magnetic field of the earth. **2.** *Electronics.* a variable inductor consisting of a movable coil mounted inside and connected in series with a fixed coil. **3.** a sensitive rate-of-climb indicator, used mainly in gliders.

var·i·o·rum (ˌvɛərɪˈɔːrəm) *adj.* **1.** containing notes by various scholars or critics or various versions of the text: *a variorum edition.* ~*n.* **2.** an edition or text of this kind. [C18: from Latin phrase *ēditiō cum notīs variōrum* edition with the notes of various commentators]

var·i·ous (ˈvɛərɪəs) *determiner.* **1. a.** several different: *he is an authority on various subjects.* **b.** (*as pronoun;* foll. by *of*) *Not standard: various of them came.* ~*adj.* **2.** of different kinds, though often within the same general category; diverse: *various occurrences; his disguises are many and various.* **3.** (*prenominal*) relating to a collection of separate persons or things: *the various members of the club.* **4.** displaying variety; many-sided: *his various achievements are most impressive.* **5.** *Poetic.* variegated. **6.** *Obsolete.* inconstant. [C16: from Latin *varius* changing; perhaps related to Latin *vārus* crooked] —ˈ**var·i·ous·ly** *adv.* —ˈ**var·i·ous·ness** *n.*

var·is·cite (ˈværɪˌsaɪt) *n.* a green secondary mineral consisting of hydrated aluminium.

var·is·tor (vəˈrɪstə) *n.* a two-electrode semiconductor device having a voltage-dependent non-linear resistance. Compare **varactor.**

var·i·type (ˈvɛərɪˌtaɪp) *vb.* **1.** to produce (copy) on a Varityper. ~*n.* **2.** copy produced on a Varityper. —ˈ**var·i·ˌtyp·ist** *n.*

Var·i·typ·er (ˈvɛərɪˌtaɪpə) *n. Trademark.* a justifying typewriter used to produce copy in various type styles.

var·ix (ˈvɛərɪks) *n., pl.* **var·i·ces** (ˈværɪˌsiːz). *Pathol.* **a.** a tortuous dilated vein. See **varicose veins. b.** Also called: **arterial varix, varix lymphaticus.** a similar condition affecting an artery or lymphatic vessel. [C15: from Latin]

var·let (ˈvɑːlɪt) *n. Archaic.* **1.** a menial servant. **2.** a knight's page. **3.** a rascal. [C15: from Old French, variant of *vallet* VALET]

var·let·ry (ˈvɑːlɪtrɪ) *n. Archaic.* **1. the.** rabble; mob. **2.** varlets collectively.

var·mint (ˈvɑːmɪnt) *n. Informal.* an irritating or obnoxious person or animal. [C16: dialect variant of *varmin* VERMIN]

var·na (ˈvɑːnə) *n.* any of the four Hindu castes; Brahman, Kshatriya, Vaisya, or Sudra. [from Sanskrit: class]

Var·na (*Bulgarian* ˈvarna) *n.* a port in NE Bulgaria, on the Black Sea: founded by Greeks in the 6th century B.C.; under the Ottoman Turks (1391–1878). Pop.: 269 980 (1974 est.). Former name (1949–56): **Stalin.**

var·nish (ˈvɑːnɪʃ) *n.* **1.** Also called: **oil varnish.** a preparation consisting of a solvent, a drying oil, and usually resin, rubber, bitumen, etc., for application to a surface where it polymerizes to yield a hard glossy, usually transparent, coating. **2.** a similar preparation consisting of a substance, such as shellac or cellulose ester, dissolved in a volatile solvent, such as alcohol. It hardens to a film on evaporation of the solvent. See also **spirit varnish. 3.** Also called: **natural varnish.** the sap of certain trees used to produce such a coating. **4.** a smooth surface, coated with or as with varnish. **5.** an artificial, superficial, or deceptively pleasing manner, covering, etc.; veneer. **6.** *Chiefly Brit.* another word for **nail polish.** ~*vb.* (*tr.*) **7.** to cover with varnish. **8.** to give a smooth surface to, as if by painting with varnish. **9.** to impart a more attractive appearance to. **10.** to make superficially attractive. [C14: from Old French *vernis*, from Medieval Latin *veronix* sandarac, resin, from Medieval Greek *berenikē* perhaps from Greek *Berenikē*, city in Cyrenaica, Libya where varnishes were used] —**'var+nish+er** *n.*

var+nish tree *n.* any of various trees, such as the lacquer tree, yielding substances used to make varnish or lacquer.

Var·ro ('værəʊ) *n.* **Mar·cus Te·ren·ti·us** ('mɑːkəs tə'rɛntɪəs). 116–27 B.C., Roman scholar and satirist.

var+si·ty ('vɑːsɪtɪ) *n., pl.* **·ties.** *Brit. informal.* short for **university:** formerly used esp. at the universities of Oxford and Cambridge.

Var·u·na ('værʊnə, 'vʌ-) *n. Hinduism.* the ancient sky god, later the god of the waters and rain-giver. In earlier traditions he was also the all-seeing divine judge.

var+us ('vɛərəs) *adj. Pathol.* turned inwards towards the midline of the body. [C19: from Latin: crooked, bent]

varve (vɑːv) *n. Geology.* **1.** a band of sediment deposited in glacial lakes, consisting of a light layer and a dark layer deposited at different seasons. **2.** either of the layers of sediment making up this band. [C20: from Swedish *varv* layer, from *varva*, from Old Norse *hverfa* to turn]

var·y ('vɛərɪ) *vb.* **var·ies, var·y+ing, var+ied. 1.** to cause or undergo change, alteration, or modification in appearance, character, form, attribute, etc. **2.** to be different or cause to be different; be subject to change. **3.** (*tr.*) to give variety to. **4.** (*intr.*; foll. by *from*) to deviate, as from a convention, standard, norm, etc. **5.** (*intr.*) to change in accordance with another variable: *her mood varies with the weather; pressure varies directly with temperature and inversely with volume.* **6.** (*tr.*) *Music.* to modify (a theme) by the use of variation. [C14: from Latin *variāre*, from *varius* VARIOUS] —**'var·y·ing·ly** *adv.*

vas (væs) *n., pl.* **va·sa** ('veɪsə). *Anatomy, zoology.* a vessel, duct, or tube that carries a fluid. [C17: from Latin: vessel]

vas- *combining form.* variant of **vaso-** before a vowel.

Va·sa·ri (və'sɑːrɪ; *Italian* va'zaːri) *n.* **Gior·gio** ('dʒordʒo). 1511–74, Italian architect, painter, and art historian, noted for his *Lives of the Most Excellent Italian Architects, Painters, and Sculptors* (1550; 1568), a principal source for the history of Italian Renaissance art.

Vas·co da Ga·ma ('væskəʊ də 'gɑːmə) *n.* See (Vasco da) **Gama.**

vas+cu+lar ('væskjʊlə) *adj. Biology, anatomy.* of, relating to, or having vessels that conduct and circulate fluids: *a vascular bundle; the blood vascular system.* [C17: from New Latin *vāsculāris*, from Latin: VASCULUM] —**vas+cu+lar+i·ty** (ˌvæskjʊ'lærɪtɪ) *n.* —**'vas+cu+lar+ly** *adv.*

vas+cu+lar bun+dle *n.* a longitudinal strand of vascular tissue in the stems and leaves of higher plants.

vas+cu+lar·i·za+tion *or* **vas+cu+lar·i·sa+tion** (ˌvæskjʊləraɪ'zeɪʃən) *n.* the development of blood vessels in an organ or part.

vas+cu+lar ray *n.* another name for **medullary ray.**

vas+cu+lar tis+sue *n.* tissue of higher plants consisting mainly of xylem and phloem and occurring as a continuous system throughout the plant: it conducts water, mineral salts, and synthesized food substances and provides mechanical support.

vas+cu+lum ('væskjʊləm) *n., pl.* **+la** (-lə) *or* **+lums.** a metal box used by botanists in the field for carrying botanical specimens. [C19: from Latin: little vessel, from VAS]

vas de+fe+rens ('væs 'dɛfəˌrɛnz) *n., pl.* **va·sa de+fe+ren+ti·a** ('veɪsə ˌdɛfə'rɛnʃɪə). *Anatomy.* the duct within each testis that conveys spermatozoa from the epididymis to the ejaculatory duct. [C16: from New Latin, from Latin *vās* vessel + *dēferēns*, from *dēferre* to bear away]

vase (vɑːz) *n.* a vessel used as an ornament or for holding cut flowers. [C17: via French from Latin *vās* vessel]

vas+ec+to+my (væ'sɛktəmɪ) *n., pl.* **+mies.** surgical removal of all or part of the vas deferens, esp. as a method of contraception.

Vas+e·line ('væsɪˌliːn) *n.* a trademark for **petrolatum.**

Vash·ti ('væʃtaɪ) *n. Old Testament.* the wife of the Persian king Ahasuerus: deposed for refusing to display her beauty before his guests (Esther 1–2). Douay spelling: **Vas·thi.**

vas·o- *or before a vowel* **vas-** *combining form.* **1.** indicating a blood vessel: *vasodilator.* **2.** indicating the vas deferens: *vasectomy.* [from Latin *vās* vessel]

vas·o+con+stric+tor (ˌveɪzəʊkən'strɪktə) *n.* **1.** a drug, agent, or nerve that causes narrowing (**vasoconstriction**) of the walls of blood vessels. ~*adj.* **2.** causing vasoconstriction. —ˌ**vas·o+con+'stric+tive** *adj.*

vas·o+di+la+tor (ˌveɪzəʊdaɪ'leɪtə) *n.* **1.** a drug, agent, or nerve that can cause dilation (**vasodilation**) of the walls of blood vessels. ~*adj.* **2.** causing vasodilation.

vas·o+in+hib·i+tor (ˌveɪzəʊɪn'hɪbɪtə) *n.* any of a group of drugs that reduce or inhibit the action of the vasomotor nerves. —**vas·o+in+hib·i·to·ry** (ˌveɪzəʊɪn'hɪbɪtərɪ, -trɪ) *adj.*

vas·o+mo+tor (ˌveɪzəʊ'məʊtə) *adj.* (of a drug, agent, nerve, etc.) relating to or affecting the diameter of blood vessels.

vas·o+pres+sin (ˌveɪzəʊ'prɛsɪn) *n.* a polypeptide hormone secreted by the posterior lobe of the pituitary gland. It increases the reabsorption of water by the kidney tubules and increases blood pressure by constricting the arteries. Chemical name: **beta-hypophamine.** Compare **oxytocin.** [from *Vasopressin*, a trademark]

vas+sal ('væsᵊl) *n.* **1.** (in feudal society) a man who entered into a personal relationship with a lord to whom he paid homage and fealty in return for protection and often a fief. **2. a.** a person, nation, etc., in a subordinate, suppliant, or dependent position relative to another. **b.** (*as modifier*): *vassal status.* ~*adj.* **3.** of or relating to a vassal. [C14: via Old French from Medieval Latin *vassallus*, from *vassus* servant, of Celtic origin; compare Welsh *gwas* boy, Old Irish *foss* servant] —**'vas+sal+less** *adj.*

vas+sal+age ('væsəlɪdʒ) *n.* **1.** (esp. in feudal society) **a.** the condition of being a vassal or the obligations to which a vassal was liable. **b.** the relationship between a vassal and his lord. **2.** subjection, servitude, or dependence in general. **3.** *Rare.* vassals collectively.

vas+sal+ize *or* **vas+sal+ise** ('væsəˌlaɪz) *vb.* (*tr.*) to make a vassal of.

vast (vɑːst) *adj.* **1.** unusually large in size, extent, degree, or number; immense. **2.** (*prenominal*) (intensifier): *in vast haste.* ~*n.* **3. the vast.** *Chiefly poetic.* immense or boundless space. **4.** *Brit. dialect.* a very great amount or number. [C16: from Latin *vastus* deserted] —**'vas+ti·ty** *n.* —**'vast+ly** *adv.* —**'vast+ness** *n.*

Väs+ter+ås (*Swedish* ˌvɛstər'oːs) *n.* a city in central Sweden, on Lake Mälar: Sweden's largest inland port; site of several national parliaments in the 16th century. Pop.: 118 044 (1974 est.).

vas+ti+tude ('vɑːstɪˌtjuːd) *n. Rare.* **1.** the condition or quality of being vast. **2.** a vast space, expanse, extent, etc.

vast·y ('vɑːstɪ) *adj.* **vast·i·er, vast·i·est.** an archaic or poetic word for **vast.**

vat (væt) *n.* **1.** a large container for holding or storing liquids. **2.** *Chem.* a preparation of reduced vat dye. ~*vb.* **vats, vat+ting, vat+ted. 3.** (*tr.*) to place, store, or treat in a vat. [Old English *fæt*; related to Old Frisian *fet*, Old Saxon *fat*, Old Norse *fat*, Old High German *faz*]

Vat. *abbrev. for* Vatican.

VAT (*sometimes* væt) *Brit. abbrev. for* value-added tax; a tax levied on the difference between a commodity's pretax selling price per unit and its materials cost per unit.

vat dye *n.* a dye, such as indigo, that is applied by first reducing it to its leuco base, which is soluble in alkali, and then regenerating the insoluble dye by oxidation in the fibres of the material. —**'vat-ˌdyed** *adj.*

vat+ic ('vætɪk) *adj. Rare.* of, relating to, or characteristic of a prophet; oracular. [C16: from Latin *vātēs* prophet] —**va+tic·i+nal** (və'tɪsɪnᵊl) *adj.*

Vat·i+can ('vætɪkən) *n.* **1. a.** the palace of the popes in Rome and their principal residence there since 1377, which includes administrative offices, a library, museum, etc., and is attached to the basilica of St. Peter's. **b.** (*as modifier*): *the Vatican Council.* **2. a.** the authority of the Pope and the papal curia. **b.** (*as modifier*): *a Vatican edict.* [C16: from Latin *Vāticānus mons* Vatican hill, on the western bank of the Tiber, of Etruscan origin]

Vat·i+can Cit·y *n.* an independent state forming an enclave in Rome, with extraterritoriality over 12 churches and palaces in Rome: the only remaining Papal State; independence recognized by the Italian government in 1929; contains St. Peter's Basilica and Square and the Vatican; the spiritual and administrative centre of the Roman Catholic Church. Languages: Italian and Latin. Currency: lira. Pop.: 1000 (1973 est.). Area: 44 hectares (109 acres). Italian name: **Città del Vaticano.** Also called: the **Holy See.**

Vat·i+can+ism ('vætɪkəˌnɪzəm) *n. Often derogatory.* the authority and policies of the Pope and the papal curia, esp. with regard to papal infallibility.

vat·i+cide ('vætɪˌsaɪd) *n. Rare.* **a.** the murder of a prophet. **b.** a person guilty of this. [C18: from Latin *vātēs* prophet + -CIDE]

va+tic·i+nate (və'tɪsɪˌneɪt) *vb. Rare.* to foretell; prophesy. [C17: from Latin *vāticinārī* from *vātēs* prophet + *canere* to foretell] —**vat·i·ci·na+tion** (ˌvætɪsɪ'neɪʃən) *n.* —**va+'tic·i+ˌna+tor** *n.* —**va+'tic·i+na+to·ry** *adj.*

Vät+tern (*Swedish* 'vɛtərn) *n.* **Lake.** a lake in S central Sweden: the second largest lake in Sweden; linked to Lake Vänern by the Göta Canal; drains into the Baltic. Area: 1912 sq. km (738 sq. miles).

Vau·ban (*French* vo'bɑ̃) *n.* **Sé·bas·tien Le Pres·tre de** (sebastjɛ̃ lə 'prɛtr də). 1633–1707, French military engineer and marshal, who devised novel siege tactics using a series of parallel trenches.

Vau+cluse (*French* vo'klyːz) *n.* a department of SE France, in Provence—Côte-d'Azur region. Capital: Avignon. Pop.: 398 540 (1975). Area: 3578 sq. km (1395 sq. miles).

Vaud (*French* vo) *n.* a canton of SW Switzerland: mountainous in the southeast; chief Swiss producer of wine. Capital: Lausanne. Pop.: 511 851 (1970). Area: 3209 sq. km (1240 sq. miles). German name: **Waadt.**

vau+de+ville ('vəʊdəvɪl, 'vɔː-) *n.* **1.** *Chiefly U.S.* variety entertainment consisting of short acts such as acrobatic turns, song-and-dance routines, animal acts, etc., popular esp. in the early 20th century. **2.** a light or comic theatrical piece interspersed with songs and dances. [C18: from French, from *vaudevire* satirical folksong, shortened from *chanson du vau de Vire* song of the valley of Vire, a district in Normandy where this type of song flourished]

vau+de+vil+li·an (ˌvəʊdə'vɪlɪən, ˌvɔː-) *n. also* **vau+de+vil+list. 1.** a person who writes for or performs in vaudeville. ~*adj.* **2.** of, characteristic of, or relating to vaudeville.

Vau+dois ('vəʊdwɑː) *pl. n., sing.* **+dois. 1.** another name for the **Waldenses. 2.** the inhabitants of Vaud.

Vaughan (vɔːn) *n.* **Hen·ry.** 1622–95, Welsh mystic poet, best known for his *Silex Scintillans* (1650; 1655).

Vaughan Wil·liams ('vɔːn 'wɪljəmz) *n.* **Ralph.** 1872–1958, English composer, inspired by British folk songs and music of the Tudor period. He wrote operas, symphonies, hymns and choral music.

vault[1] (vɔːlt) *n.* **1.** an arched structure that forms a roof or ceiling. **2.** a room, esp. a cellar, having an arched roof down to floor level. **3.** a burial chamber, esp. when underground. **4.** a strongroom for the safe deposit and storage of valuables. **5.** an underground room or part of such a room, used for the storage of wine, food, etc. **6.** *Anatomy.* any arched or domed bodily cavity or space: *the cranial vault.* **7.** something suggestive of an arched structure, as the sky. ~*vb.* **8.** (*tr.*) to furnish with or as if with an arched roof. **9.** (*tr.*) to construct in the shape of a vault. **10.** (*intr.*) to curve, arch, or bend in the shape of a vault. [C14: *vaute,* from Old French, from Vulgar Latin *volvita* (unattested) a turn, probably from Latin *volvere* to roll] —**'vault+,like** *adj.*

vault[2] (vɔːlt) *vb.* **1.** to spring over (an object), esp. with the aid of a long pole or with the hands resting on the object. **2.** (*intr.*) to do, achieve, or attain something as if by a leap: *he vaulted to fame on the strength of his discovery.* **3.** *Dressage.* to perform or cause to perform a curvet. ~*n.* **4.** the act of vaulting. **5.** *Dressage.* a low leap; curvet. [C16: from Old French *voulter* to turn, from Italian *voltare* to turn, from Vulgar Latin *volvitāre* (unattested) to turn, leap; see VAULT[1]] —**'vault+er** *n.*

vault+ing[1] ('vɔːltɪŋ) *n.* one or more vaults in a building or such structures considered collectively.

vault+ing[2] ('vɔːltɪŋ) *adj.* **1.** (*prenominal*) excessively confident; overreaching; exaggerated: *vaulting arrogance.* **2.** (*prenominal*) used to vault: *a vaulting pole.*

vaunt (vɔːnt) *vb.* **1.** (*tr.*) to describe, praise, or display (one's success, possessions, etc.) boastfully. **2.** (*intr.*) *Rare or literary.* to use boastful language; brag. ~*n.* **3.** a boast. **4.** *Archaic.* ostentatious display. [C14: from Old French *vanter,* from Late Latin *vānitāre* to brag, from Latin *vānus* VAIN] —**'vaunt+er** *n.* —**'vaunt+ing+ly** *adv.*

vaunt-cour·i·er *n. Archaic or poetic.* a person or thing that goes in advance; forerunner; herald. [C16: from French *avant-courrier;* see AVAUNT, COURIER]

v. aux. *abbrev. for* auxiliary verb.

vav (vɔːv) *n.* the sixth letter of the Hebrew alphabet (ו) transliterated as *v* or *w.* Also called: **waw.** [from Hebrew *wāw* a hook]

vav·a·sor ('vævə,sɔː) *or* **vav·a·sour** ('vævə,sʊə) *n.* (in feudal society) the noble or knightly vassal of a baron or other vassal. Also: **vavassor.** [C13: from Old French *vavasour,* perhaps contraction of Medieval Latin *vassus vassōrum* vassal of vassals; see VASSAL]

VB (in transformational grammar) *abbrev. for* verbal constituent.

vb. *abbrev. for* verb.

V.C. *abbrev. for:* **1.** Vice Chairman. **2.** Vice Chancellor. **3.** Vice Consul. **4.** Victoria Cross. **5.** Vietcong.

VD *abbrev. for* venereal disease.

v.d. *abbrev. for* various dates.

V-Day *n.* a day nominated to celebrate victory, as in V-E Day or V-J Day in World War II.

V.D.C. *abbrev. for* Volunteer Defence Corps.

VDU *Computer technol. abbrev. for* visual display unit.

've *contraction of* have: *I've; you've.*

Ve·a+dar *Hebrew.* ('viːə,dɑː, 'veɪ-) *n. Judaism.* another term for **Adar Sheni.** [from Hebrew *va'adhar,* literally: and Adar, that is, the extra Adar]

veal (viːl) *n.* **1.** the flesh of the calf used as food. **2.** Also called: **veal calf.** a calf, esp. one bred for eating. [C14: from Old French *veel,* from Latin *vitellus* a little calf, from *vitulus* calf]

veal+er ('viːlə) *n. U.S., Austral.* another name for **veal** (sense 2).

Veb·len ('vɛblən) *n.* **Thor·stein** ('θɔːstɪn). 1857–1929, U.S. economist and social scientist, noted for his analysis of social and economic institutions. His works include *The Theory of the Leisure Class* (1899) and *The Theory of Business Enterprise* (1904).

vec+tor ('vɛktə) *n.* **1.** *Maths.* a variable quantity, such as force, that has magnitude and direction and can be resolved into components. It is represented in print by a bold italic symbol: ***F*** or $\vec{F}$. Compare **scalar** (sense 1), **tensor** (sense 2). **2.** Also called: **carrier.** *Pathol.* an organism, esp. an insect, that carries a disease-producing microorganism from one host to another, either within or on the surface of its body. **3.** the course or compass direction of an aircraft. **4.** any behavioural influence, force, or drive. ~*vb.* **5.** (*tr.*) to direct or guide (a pilot, aircraft, etc.) by directions transmitted by radio. [C18: from Latin: carrier, from *vehere* to convey] —**vec+to+ri·al** (vɛk'tɔːrɪəl) *adj.* —**vec+'to+ri+al+ly** *adv.*

vec+tor field *n.* a region of space under the influence of some vector quantity, such as magnetic field strength, in which each point can be described by a vector.

vec+tor prod+uct *n.* the product of two vectors that is itself a vector, whose magnitude is the product of the magnitudes of the given vectors and the sine of the angle between them. Its direction is perpendicular to the plane of the given vectors. Written: $\boldsymbol{A}\times\boldsymbol{B}$ or $\boldsymbol{A}\wedge\boldsymbol{B}$. Compare **scalar product.** Also called: **cross product.**

vec+tor sum *n.* a vector whose length and direction are represented by a line joining the two end points of a figure whose sides represent the lengths and directions of the given vectors. See also **resultant.**

Ve·da ('veɪdə) *n.* any or all of the most ancient sacred writings of Hinduism, esp. the Rig-Veda, Yajur-Veda, Sama-Veda, and Atharva-Veda. [C18: from Sanskrit: knowledge; related to *veda* I know] —**Ve+da+ic** (vɪ'deɪɪk) *adj.* —**Ve+da+ism** ('veɪdə,ɪzəm) *n.*

ve+da+li·a (vɪ'deɪlɪə) *n.* an Australian ladybird, *Rodolia cardinalis,* introduced elsewhere to control the scale insect *Icerya purchasi,* which is a pest of citrus fruits. [C20: from New Latin]

Ve+dan+ta (vɪ'dɑːntə, -'dæn-) *n.* one of the six main philosophical schools of Hinduism, expounding the monism regarded as implicit in the Veda in accordance with the doctrines of the Upanishads. It teaches that only Brahma has reality, while the whole phenomenal world is the outcome of illusion (maya). [C19: from Sanskrit, from VEDA + *ánta* end] —**Ve+'dan+tic** *adj.* —**Ve+'dan+tism** *n.* —**Ve+'dan+tist** *n.*

V-E Day *n.* the day marking the Allied victory in Europe in World War II (May 8, 1945).

Ved+da *or* **Ved+dah** ('vɛdə) *n.* (*pl.* **+da, +das** *or* **+dah +dahs**) a member of an aboriginal people of Sri Lanka, characterized by slender build, dark complexion, and wavy hair, noted for their Stone-Age technology. [C17: from Singhalese: hunter, of Dravidian origin]

Ved+doid ('vɛdɔɪd) *adj.* **1.** of, relating to, or resembling the Vedda. ~*n.* **2.** a Vedda. **3.** a member of a postulated prehistoric race of S Asia, having slender build, dark complexion, and wavy hair: thought to be ancestors of the Vedda.

ve+dette (vɪ'dɛt) *n.* **1.** Also called: **vedette boat.** *Naval.* a small patrol vessel. **2.** Also called: **vidette.** *Military.* a mounted sentry posted forward of a formation's position. [C17: from French, from Italian *vedetta* (influenced by *vedere* to see), from earlier *veletta,* perhaps from Spanish *vela* watch, from *velar* to keep vigil, from Latin *vigilāre*]

Ve+dic ('veɪdɪk) *adj.* **1.** of or relating to the Vedas or the ancient form of Sanskrit in which they are written. **2.** of or relating to the ancient Indo-European settlers in India, regarded as the originators of many of the traditions preserved in the Vedas. ~*n.* **3.** the classical form of Sanskrit; the language of the Vedas.

veer[1] (vɪə) *vb.* **1.** to alter direction; swing around. **2.** (*intr.*) to change from one position, opinion, etc., to another. **3.** (*intr.*) (of the wind) **a.** to change direction clockwise in the northern hemisphere and anticlockwise in the southern. **b.** *Nautical.* to blow from a direction nearer the stern. Compare **haul** (sense 5). **4.** *Nautical.* to steer (a vessel) off the wind. ~*n.* **5.** a change of course or direction. [C16: from Old French *virer,* probably of Celtic origin; compare Welsh *gwyro* to diverge] —**'veer+ing+ly** *adv.*

veer[2] (vɪə) *vb.* (*tr.;* often foll. by *out* or *away*) *Nautical.* to slacken or pay out (cable or chain). [C16: from Dutch *vieren,* from Old High German *fieren* to give direction]

veer·y ('vɪərɪ) *n., pl.* **veer·ies.** a tawny brown North American thrush, *Hylocichla fuscescens,* with a slightly spotted grey breast. [C19: probably imitative of its note]

veg (vɛdʒ) *n. Informal.* a vegetable or vegetables.

Ve·ga[1] ('viːgə) *n.* the brightest star in the constellation Lyra and one of the most conspicuous in the N hemisphere. It is part of an optical double star having a faint companion. Distance: 26 light years. [C17: from Medieval Latin, from Arabic (*al nasr*) *al wāqi,* literally: the falling (vulture), that is, the constellation Lyra]

Ve·ga[2] ('veɪgə; *Spanish* 'beɣa) *n.* See **Lope de Vega.**

ve+gan ('viːgən) *n.* a person who practises strict vegetarianism.

veg+e·ta+ble ('vɛdʒtəbᵊl) *n.* **1.** any of various herbaceous plants having parts that are used as food, such as peas, beans, cabbage, potatoes, cauliflower, and onions. **2.** *Informal.* a person who has lost control of his mental faculties, limbs, etc., as from an injury, mental disease, etc. **3. a.** a dull inactive person. **b.** (*as modifier*): *a vegetable life.* **4.** (*modifier*) consisting of or made from edible vegetables: *a vegetable diet.* **5.** (*modifier*) of, relating to, characteristic of, derived from, or consisting of plants or plant material: *vegetable oils; the vegetable kingdom.* **6.** *Rare.* any member of the plant kingdom. [C14 (adj.): from Late Latin *vegetābilis* animating, from *vegetāre* to enliven, from Latin *vegēre* to excite]

veg+e·ta+ble but+ter *n.* any of a group of vegetable fats having the consistency of butter.

veg+e·ta+ble i·vo+ry *n.* **1.** the hard whitish material obtained from the endosperm of the ivory nut: used to make buttons, ornaments, etc. **2.** another name for the **ivory nut.**

veg+e·ta+ble king+dom *n.* another name for **plant kingdom.**

veg+e·ta+ble mar+row *n.* **1.** a cucurbitaceous plant, *Cucurbita pepo,* probably native to America but widely cultivated for its oblong green striped fruit, which is eaten as a vegetable. **2.** Also called (in the U.S.): **marrow squash.** the fruit of this plant. Often shortened to **marrow.**

veg+e·ta+ble oil *n.* any of a group of oils that are esters of fatty acids and glycerol and are obtained from plants.

veg+e·ta+ble oys+ter *n.* another name for **salsify** (sense 1).

veg+e·ta+ble silk *n.* any of various silky fibres obtained from the seed pods of certain plants. See also **kapok.**

veg+e·ta+ble sponge *n.* another name for **dishcloth gourd.**

veg+e·ta+ble tal+low *n.* any of various types of tallow that are obtained from plants.

veg+e·ta+ble wax *n.* any of various waxes that occur on parts of certain plants, esp. the trunks of certain palms, and prevent loss of water from the plant.

veg+e·tal ('vɛdʒɪtᵊl) *adj.* **1.** of, relating to, or characteristic of vegetables or plant life. **2.** of or relating to processes in plants and animals that do not involve sexual reproduction; vegetative. [C15: from Late Latin *vegetāre* to quicken; see VEGETABLE]

veg·e·tar·i·an (ˌvɛdʒɪˈtɛərɪən) *n.* **1.** a person who advocates or practises vegetarianism. ~*adj.* **2.** relating to, advocating, or practising vegetarianism. **3.** *Cookery.* strictly, consisting of vegetables and fruit only, but usually including milk, cheese, eggs, etc.

veg·e·tar·i·an·ism (ˌvɛdʒɪˈtɛərɪəˌnɪzəm) *n.* the principle or practice of excluding all meat and fish, and sometimes, in the case of vegans, all animal products (such as eggs, cheese, etc.) from one's diet.

veg·e·tate (ˈvɛdʒɪˌteɪt) *vb. (intr.)* **1.** to grow like a plant; sprout. **2.** to lead a life characterized by monotony, passivity, or mental inactivity. **3.** *Pathol.* (of a wart, polyp, etc.) to develop fleshy outgrowths. [C17: from Late Latin *vegetāre* to invigorate]

veg·e·ta·tion (ˌvɛdʒɪˈteɪʃən) *n.* **1.** plant life as a whole, esp. the plant life of a particular region. **2.** the process of vegetating. **3.** *Pathol.* any abnormal growth, excrescence, etc. **4.** a vegetative existence. —ˌ**veg·e·ˈta·tion·al** *adj.*

veg·e·ta·tive (ˈvɛdʒɪtətɪv) *adj.* **1.** of, relating to, or concerned with vegetation, plant life, or plant growth. **2.** (of reproduction) characterized by asexual processes. **3.** of or relating to functions such as digestion, growth, and circulation rather than sexual reproduction. **4.** (of a style of living, etc.) dull, stagnant, unthinking, or passive. —**ˈveg·e·ˌta·tive·ly** *adv.* —**ˈveg·e·ˌta·tive·ness** *n.*

ve·he·ment (ˈviːɪmənt) *adj.* **1.** marked by intensity of feeling or conviction; emphatic. **2.** (of actions, gestures, etc.) characterized by great energy, vigour, or force; furious. [C15: from Latin *vehemēns* ardent; related to *vehere* to carry] —**ˈve·he·mence** *n.* —**ˈve·he·ment·ly** *adv.*

ve·hi·cle (ˈviːɪkᵊl) *n.* **1.** any conveyance in or by which people or objects are transported, esp. one fitted with wheels. **2.** a medium for the expression, communication, or achievement of ideas, information, power, etc. **3.** *Pharmacol.* a therapeutically inactive substance mixed with the active ingredient to give bulk to a medicine. **4.** Also called: **base.** a painting medium, such as oil, in which pigments are suspended. **5.** (in the performing arts) a play, musical composition, etc., that enables a particular performer to display his talents. **6.** a rocket excluding its payload. [C17: from Latin *vehiculum*, from *vehere* to carry] —**ve·hic·u·lar** (vɪˈhɪkjʊlə) *adj.*

Ve·ii (ˈviːjaɪ) *n.* an ancient Etruscan city, northwest of Rome: destroyed by the Romans in 396 B.C.

veil (veɪl) *n.* **1.** a piece of more or less transparent material, usually attached to a hat or headdress, used to conceal or protect a woman's face and head. **2.** part of a nun's headdress falling round the face onto the shoulders. **3.** something that covers, conceals, or separates; mask: *a veil of reticence.* **4. the veil.** the life of a nun in a religious order and the obligations entailed by it. **5. take the veil.** to become a nun. **6.** Also called: **velum.** *Botany.* a membranous structure, esp. the thin layer of cells covering a young mushroom. **7.** *Anatomy.* another word for **caul. 8.** See **humeral veil.** ~*vb.* **9.** *(tr.)* to cover, conceal, or separate with or as if with a veil. **10.** to wear or put on a veil. [C13: from Norman French *veile*, from Latin *vēla* sails, pl. of *vēlum* a covering] —**ˈveil·er** *n.* —**ˈveil·less** *adj.* —**ˈveil-ˌlike** *adj.*

veiled (veɪld) *adj.* **1.** disguised: *a veiled insult.* **2.** (of sound, tone, the voice, etc.) not distinct; muffled. —**veil·ed·ly** (ˈveɪlɪdlɪ) *adv.*

veil·ing (ˈveɪlɪŋ) *n.* a veil or the fabric used for veils.

vein (veɪn) *n.* **1.** any of the tubular vessels that convey oxygen-depleted blood to the heart. Compare **pulmonary vein, artery. 2.** any of the hollow branching tubes that form the supporting framework of an insect's wing. **3.** any of the vascular bundles of a leaf. **4.** a clearly defined mass of ore, mineral, etc., typically occurring as a thin layer in a rock fissure or between rock strata. **5.** an irregular streak of colour or alien substance in marble, wood, or other material. **6.** a natural underground watercourse. **7.** a crack or fissure. **8.** a distinctive trait or quality in speech, writing, character, etc.; strain: *a vein of humour.* **9.** a temporary disposition, attitude, or temper; mood: *the debate entered a frivolous vein.* ~*vb.* *(tr.)* **10.** to diffuse over or cause to diffuse over in streaked patterns. **11.** to fill, furnish, or mark with or as if with veins. [C13: from Old French *veine*, from Latin *vēna*] —**ˈvein·al** *adj.* —**ˈvein·less** *adj.* —**ˈvein·ˌlike** *adj.* —**ˈvein·y** *adj.*

vein·ing (ˈveɪnɪŋ) *n.* a pattern or network of veins or streaks.

vein·let (ˈveɪnlɪt) *n.* any small vein or venule.

vein·stone (ˈveɪnˌstəʊn) *n.* another word for **gangue.**

vein·ule (ˈveɪnjuːl) *n.* a less common spelling of **venule.**

vel. *Bookbinding. abbrev. for* vellum.

Ve·la (ˈviːlə) *n., Latin genitive* **Ve·lo·rum** (viːˈlɔːrəm). a constellation in the S hemisphere, close to Puppis and Carina and crossed by the Milky Way, that has four second-magnitude stars.

ve·la·men (vəˈleɪmɛn) *n., pl.* **·lam·i·na** (-ˈlæmɪnə). **1.** the thick layer of dead cells that covers the aerial roots of certain orchids and aroids and absorbs moisture from the surroundings. **2.** *Anatomy.* another word for **velum.** [C19: from Latin: a veil, from *vēlāre* to cover]

ve·lar (ˈviːlə) *adj.* **1.** of, relating to, or attached to a velum: *velar tentacles.* **2.** *Phonetics.* articulated with the soft palate and the back of the tongue, as in the sounds (k), (g), or (ŋ). [C18: from Latin *vēlāris*, from *vēlum* VEIL]

ve·lar·i·um (vɪˈlɛərɪəm) *n., pl.* **·lar·i·a** (-ˈlɛərɪə). an awning used to protect the audience in ancient Roman theatres and amphitheatres. [C19: from Latin, from *vēlāre* to cover]

ve·lar·ize *or* **ve·lar·ise** (ˈviːləˌraɪz) *vb. (tr.) Phonetics.* to pronounce or supplement the pronunciation of (a speech sound) with articulation at the soft palate, as in dark (l) in English *tall.* —ˌ**ve·lar·i·ˈza·tion** *or* ˌ**ve·lar·i·ˈsa·tion** *n.*

ve·late (ˈviːlɪt, -leɪt) *adj.* having or covered with velum.

Ve·láz·quez (*Spanish* beˈlaθkeθ) *or* **Ve·lás·quez** (*Spanish* beˈlaskeθ) *n.* **Die·go Ro·drí·guez de Sil·va y** (ˈdjeɣo roˈðriɣeθ ðe ˈsilβa i). 1599–1660, Spanish painter, remarkable for the realism of his portraits, esp. those of Philip IV of Spain and the royal household.

Vel·cro (ˈvɛlkrəʊ) *n. Trademark.* a fastening consisting of two strips of nylon fabric, one having tiny hooked threads and the other a coarse surface, that form a strong bond when pressed together.

veld *or* **veldt** (fɛlt, vɛlt) *n.* elevated open grassland in Southern Africa. Compare **pampas, prairie, steppe.** [C19: from Afrikaans, from earlier Dutch *veldt* FIELD]

veld·skoen (ˈfɛltˌskʊn, ˈvɛlt-) *n.* an ankle-length boot of soft but strong rawhide. [from Afrikaans, literally: field shoe]

ve·le·ta *or* **va·le·ta** (vəˈliːtə) *n.* a ballroom dance in triple time. [from Spanish: weather vane]

vel·i·ger (ˈvɛlɪdʒə) *n.* the free-swimming larva of many molluscs, having a rudimentary shell and a ciliated velum used for feeding and locomotion. [C19: from New Latin, from VELUM + -GER(OUS)]

ve·li·tes (ˈviːlɪˌtiːz) *pl. n.* light-armed troops in ancient Rome, drawn from the poorer classes. [C17: from Latin, pl. of *vēles* light-armed foot soldier; related to *volāre* to fly]

vel·le·i·ty (vɛˈliːɪtɪ) *n., pl.* **·ties.** *Rare.* **1.** the weakest level of desire or volition. **2.** a mere wish. [C17: from New Latin *velleitās*, from Latin *velle* to wish]

vel·li·cate (ˈvɛlɪˌkeɪt) *vb. Rare.* to twitch, pluck, or pinch. [C17: from Latin *vellicāre*, from *vellere* to tear off] —ˌ**vel·li·ˈca·tion** *n.* —**ˈvel·li·ca·tive** *adj.*

Vel·lore (vəˈlɔː) *n.* a town in SE India, in NE Tamil Nadu: medical centre. Pop.: 139 082 (1971).

vel·lum (ˈvɛləm) *n.* **1.** a fine parchment prepared from the skin of a calf, kid, or lamb. **2.** a work printed or written on vellum. **3.** a creamy coloured heavy paper resembling vellum. ~*adj.* **4.** made of or resembling vellum. **5.** (of a book) bound in vellum. [C15: from Old French *velin*, from *velin* of a calf, from *veel* VEAL]

ve·lo·ce (vɪˈləʊtʃɪ) *adj., adv. Music.* to be played rapidly. [from Italian, from Latin *vēlōx* quick]

ve·loc·i·pede (vɪˈlɒsɪˌpiːd) *n.* **1.** an early form of bicycle propelled by pushing along the ground with the feet. **2.** any early form of bicycle or tricycle. [C19: from French *vélocipède*, from Latin *vēlōx* swift + *pēs* foot] —**ve·ˈloc·i·ˌped·ist** *n.*

ve·loc·i·ty (vɪˈlɒsɪtɪ) *n., pl.* **·ties. 1.** speed of motion, action, or operation; rapidity; swiftness. **2.** *Physics.* **a.** a measure of the rate of motion of a body expressed as the rate of change of its position in a particular direction with time. It is measured in metres per second, miles per hour, etc. Symbol: ***u, v, w*** **b.** (*not in technical usage*) another word for **speed** (sense 3). [C16: from Latin *vēlōcitās*, from *vēlōx* swift; related to *volāre* to fly]

ve·loc·i·ty mod·u·la·tion *n.* the modulation in velocity of a beam of electrons or ions caused by passing the beam through a high-frequency electric field, as in a cavity resonator.

ve·lo·drome (ˈviːləˌdrəʊm, ˈvɛl-) *n.* an arena with a banked track for cycle racing. [C20: from French *vélodrome*, from *vélo-* (from Latin *vēlōx* swift) + -DROME]

ve·lours *or* **ve·lour** (vɛˈlʊə) *n.* any of various fabrics with a velvet-like finish, used for upholstery, coats, hats, etc. [C18: from Old French *velous*, from Old Provençal *velos* velvet, from Latin *villosus* shaggy, from *villus* shaggy hair; compare Latin *vellus* a fleece]

ve·lou·té (vəˈluːteɪ) *n.* a rich white sauce or soup made from stock, egg yolks, and cream. [from French, literally: velvety, from Old French *velous*; see VELOURS]

Vel·sen (*Dutch* ˈvɛlsə) *n.* a port in the W Netherlands, in North Holland at the mouth of the canal connecting Amsterdam with the North Sea: fishing and heavy industrial centre. Pop.: 66 989 (1973 est.).

ve·lum (ˈviːləm) *n., pl.* **·la** (-lə). **1.** *Zoology.* any of various membranous structures, such as the ciliated oral membrane of certain mollusc larvae or the veil-like membrane running around the rim of a jellyfish. **2.** *Anatomy.* any of various veil-like bodily structures, esp. the soft palate. **3.** *Botany.* another word for **veil** (sense 6). [C18: from Latin: veil]

ve·lure (vəˈlʊə) *n.* **1.** velvet or a similar fabric. **2.** a hatter's pad, used for smoothing silk hats. [C16: from Old French *velour*, from Old French *velous*; see VELOURS]

ve·lu·ti·nous (vəˈluːtɪnəs) *adj.* covered with short dense soft hairs: *velutinous leaves.* [C19: from New Latin *velūtīnus* like velvet]

vel·vet (ˈvɛlvɪt) *n.* **1. a.** a fabric of silk, cotton, nylon, etc., with a thick close soft usually lustrous pile. **b.** (*as modifier*): *velvet curtains.* **2.** anything with a smooth soft surface. **3. a.** smoothness; softness. **b.** (*as modifier*): *velvet skin; a velvet night.* **4.** the furry covering of the newly formed antlers of a deer. **5.** *Slang, chiefly U.S.* **a.** gambling or speculative winnings. **b.** a gain, esp. when unexpectedly high. **6. on velvet.** *Slang.* in a condition of ease, advantage, or wealth. **7. velvet glove.** gentleness or caution, often concealing strength or determination (esp. in the phrase **an iron hand in a velvet glove**). [C14: *veluet*, from Old French *veluotte*, from *velu* hairy, from Vulgar Latin *villutus* (unattested), from Latin *villus* shaggy hair] —**ˈvel·vet-ˌlike** *adj.* —**ˈvel·vet·y** *adj.*

vel·vet·een (ˌvɛlvɪˈtiːn) *n.* **1. a.** a cotton fabric resembling velvet with a short thick pile, used for clothing, etc. **b.** (*as *modifier*): *velveteen trousers.* **2.** (*pl.*) trousers made of velveteen. —ˌ**vel·vet·'eened** *adj.*

vel·vet sco·ter *n.* a European sea duck, *Melanitta fusca*, the male of which has a black plumage with white patches below the eyes and on the wings.

vel·vet stout *n.* a less common name for **black velvet.**

Vel·vet Un·der·ground *n.* **The.** U.S. avant-garde rock group in New York City (formed in 1966; disintegrated 1969–72): original lineup comprised Lou Reed (born 1944; guitar and vocals), John Cale (born 1940; bass guitar and viola), Sterling Morrison (guitar), and Maureen Tucker (drums). Their albums include *The Velvet Underground and Nico* (1967, associated with Andy Warhol), *White Light/White Heat* (1967), and *Loaded* (1970).

Ven. *abbrev. for* Venerable.

ve·na ('viːnə) *n., pl.* **·nae** (-niː). *Anatomy.* a technical word for **vein.** [C15: from Latin *vēna* VEIN]

ve·na ca·va ('keɪvə) *n., pl.* **ve·nae ca·vae** ('keɪviː). either one of the two large veins that convey oxygen-depleted blood to the heart. [Latin: hollow vein]

ve·nal ('viːnᵊl) *adj.* **1.** easily bribed or corrupted; mercenary: *a venal magistrate.* **2.** characterized by corruption: *a venal civilization.* **3.** open to purchase, esp. by bribery: *a venal contract.* [C17: from Latin *vēnālis*, from *vēnum* sale] —**ve·'nal·i·ty** *n.* —**'ve·nal·ly** *adv.*

ve·nat·ic (viː'nætɪk) *or* **ve·nat·i·cal** *adj.* **1.** of, relating to, or used in hunting. **2.** (of people) engaged in or given to hunting. [C17: from Latin *vēnāticus*, from *vēnārī* to hunt] —**ve·'nat·i·cal·ly** *adv.*

ve·na·tion (viː'neɪʃən) *n.* **1.** the arrangement of the veins in a leaf or in the wing of an insect. **2.** such veins collectively. —**ve·'na·tion·al** *adj.*

vend (vɛnd) *vb.* **1.** to sell or be sold. **2.** to sell (goods) for a living. **3.** (*tr.*) *Rare.* to utter or publish (an opinion, etc.). [C17: from Latin *vendere*, contraction of *vēnum dare* to offer for sale] —**ven·di·tion** (vɛn'dɪʃən) *n.*

Ven·da[1] ('vɛndə) *n.* **1.** (*pl.* **·da** *or* **·das**) a member of a Negroid people of southern Africa, living chiefly in the N Transvaal. **2.** the language of this people, belonging to the Bantu group of the Niger-Congo family but not easily related to any other members of the group.

Ven·da[2] ('vɛndə) *n.* a Bantustan in South Africa, consisting of three closely grouped areas in N Transvaal. Capital: Makwarela.

ven·dace ('vɛndeɪs) *n., pl.* **·dac·es** *or* **·dace.** either of two small whitefish, *Coregonus vandesius* (**Lochmaben vendace**) or ***C. gracilior*** (Cumberland vendace), occurring in lakes in Scotland and NW England respectively. See also **powan.** [C18: from New Latin *vandēsius*, from Old French *vandoise*, probably of Celtic origin]

ven·dee (vɛn'diː) *n. Chiefly law.* a person to whom something, esp. real property, is sold; buyer.

Ven·dée (*French* vɑ̃'de) *n.* a department of W France, in Pays-de-la-Loire region: scene of the **Wars of the Vendée**, a series of peasant-royalist insurrections (1793–95) against the Revolutionary government. Capital: La Roche-sur-Yon. Pop.: 461 928 (1975). Area: 7016 sq. km (2709 sq. miles).

Ven·dé·miaire *French.* (vɑ̃de'mjɛːr) *n.* the month of the grape harvest: the first month of the French Revolutionary calendar, extending from Sept. 23 to Oct. 22. [C18: from French, from Latin *vindēmia* vintage, from *vīnum* wine + *dēmere* to take away]

ven·det·ta (vɛn'dɛtə) *n.* **1.** a private feud, originally between Corsican or Sicilian families, in which the relatives of a murdered person seek vengeance by killing the murderer or some member of his family. **2.** any prolonged feud, quarrel, etc. [C19: from Italian, from Latin *vindicta*, from *vindicāre* to avenge; see VINDICATE] —**ven·'det·tist** *n.*

vend·i·ble ('vɛndəbᵊl) *adj.* **1.** saleable or marketable. **2.** *Obsolete.* venal. ~*n.* **3.** (*usually pl.*) *Rare.* a saleable object. —ˌ**vend·i·'bil·i·ty** *or* **'vend·i·ble·ness** *n.*

vend·ing ma·chine *n.* a machine that automatically dispenses consumer goods such as cigarettes, food, or petrol, when money is inserted. Also called: **automat.**

Ven·dôme (*French* vɑ̃'doːm) *n.* **Louis Jo·seph de** (lwi ʒo'zɛf də). 1654–1712, French marshal, noted for his command during the War of the Spanish Succession (1701–14).

ven·dor ('vɛndɔː) *or* **vend·er** ('vɛndə) *n.* **1.** *Chiefly law.* a person who sells something, esp. real property. **2.** another name for **vending machine.**

ven·due ('vɛndjuː) *n. U.S.* a public sale; auction. [C17: from Dutch *vendu*, from Old French *vendue* a sale, from *vendre* to sell, from Latin *vendere*]

ve·neer (vɪ'nɪə) *n.* **1.** a thin layer of wood, plastic, etc., with a decorative or fine finish that is bonded to the surface of a less expensive material, usually wood. **2.** a superficial appearance, esp. one that is pleasing: *a veneer of gentility.* **3.** any facing material that is applied to a different backing material. **4.** any one of the layers of wood that is used to form plywood. ~*vb.* (*tr.*) **5.** to cover (a surface) with a veneer. **6.** to bond together (thin layers of wood) to make plywood. **7.** to conceal (something) under a superficially pleasant surface. [C17: from German *furnieren* to veneer, from Old French *fournir* to FURNISH] —**ve·'neer·er** *n.*

ve·neer·ing (vɪ'nɪərɪŋ) *n.* **1.** material used as veneer or a veneered surface. **2.** *Rare.* a superficial show.

ven·e·nose ('vɛnɪˌnəʊs) *adj. Rare.* poisonous. [C17: from Late Latin *venēnōsus*, from Latin *venēnum* poison]

ven·e·punc·ture ('vɛnɪˌpʌŋktʃə) *n.* a variant spelling of **venipuncture.**

ven·er·a·ble ('vɛnərəbᵊl) *adj.* **1.** (esp. of a person) worthy of reverence on account of great age, religious associations, character, position, etc. **2.** (of inanimate objects) hallowed or impressive on account of historical or religious association. **3.** ancient: *venerable tomes.* **4.** *R.C. Church.* a title bestowed on a deceased person when the first stage of his canonization has been accomplished and his holiness has been recognized in a decree of the official Church. **5.** *Church of England.* a title given to an archdeacon. [C15: from Latin *venerābilis*, from *venerārī* to venerate] —ˌ**ven·er·a·'bil·i·ty** *or* **'ven·er·a·ble·ness** *n.* —**'ven·er·a·bly** *adv.*

ven·er·ate ('vɛnəˌreɪt) *vb.* (*tr.*) **1.** to hold in deep respect; revere. **2.** to honour in recognition of qualities of holiness, excellence, wisdom, etc. [C17: from Latin *venerārī*, from *venus* love] —**'ven·er·ˌa·tor** *n.*

ven·er·a·tion (ˌvɛnə'reɪʃən) *n.* **1.** a feeling or expression of awe or reverence. **2.** the act of venerating or the state of being venerated. —ˌ**ven·er·'a·tion·al** *or* **'ven·er·a·tive** *adj.* —**'ven·er·a·tive·ly** *adv.* —**'ven·er·a·tive·ness** *n.*

ve·ne·re·al (vɪ'nɪərɪəl) *adj.* **1.** of, relating to, or infected with venereal disease. **2.** (of a disease) transmitted by sexual intercourse. **3.** of, relating to, or involving the genitals. **4.** of or relating to sexual intercourse or erotic desire; aphrodisiac. [C15: from Latin *venereus* concerning sexual love, from *venus* sexual love, from VENUS[1]]

ve·ne·re·al dis·ease *n.* any of various diseases, such as syphilis or gonorrhoea, transmitted by sexual intercourse. Abbrev.: **VD**

ve·ne·re·ol·o·gy (vɪˌnɪərɪ'ɒlədʒɪ) *n.* the branch of medicine concerned with the study and treatment of venereal disease. —**ve·ˌne·re·'ol·o·gist** *n.*

ven·er·y[1] ('vɛnərɪ, 'viː-) *n. Archaic.* the pursuit of sexual gratification. [C15: from Medieval Latin *veneria*, from Latin *venus* love, VENUS[1]]

ven·er·y[2] ('vɛnərɪ, 'viː-) *n.* the art, sport, lore, or practice of hunting, esp. with hounds; the chase. [C14: from Old French *venerie*, from *vener* to hunt, from Latin *vēnārī*]

ven·e·sec·tion (ˌvɛnɪ'sɛkʃən) *n.* surgical incision into a vein. [C17: from New Latin *vēnae sectiō*, see VEIN, SECTION]

Ve·net·i (vɛ'nɛtɪ, -taɪ) *n.* **the.** (*functioning as pl.*) an ancient people who established themselves at the head of the Adriatic around 950 B.C., later becoming Roman subjects.

Ve·ne·tia (vɪ'niːʃə) *n.* **1.** the area of ancient Italy between the lower Po valley and the Alps: later a Roman province. **2.** the territorial possessions of the medieval Venetian republic that were at the head of the Adriatic and correspond to the present-day region of Veneto and a large part of Friuli-Venezia Giulia.

Ve·ne·tian (vɪ'niːʃən) *adj.* **1.** of, relating to, or characteristic of Venice or its inhabitants. ~*n.* **2.** a native or inhabitant of Venice. **3.** See **Venetian blind.** **4.** (*sometimes not cap.*) one of the tapes that join the slats of a Venetian blind. **5.** a cotton or woollen cloth used for linings.

Ve·ne·tian blind *n.* a window blind consisting of a number of horizontal slats whose angle may be altered to let in more or less light.

Ve·ne·tian glass *n.* fine ornamental glassware made in or near Venice, esp. at Murano.

Ve·ne·tian red *n.* **1.** natural or synthetic ferric oxide used as a red pigment. **2. a.** a moderate to strong reddish-brown colour. **b.** (*as adj.*): *a Venetian-red coat.*

Ve·net·ic (vɪ'nɛtɪk) *n.* an ancient language of NE Italy, usually regarded as belonging to the Italic branch of the Indo-European family. It is recorded in about 200 inscriptions and was extinct by the 2nd century A.D.

Ve·ne·to (*Italian* 'vɛːneto) *n.* a region of NE Italy on the Adriatic: mountainous in the north with a fertile plain in the south, crossed by the Rivers Po, Adige, and Piave. Capital: Venice. Pop.: 4 109 787 (1971). Area: 18 377 sq. km (7095 sq. miles). Also called: **Venezia-Euganea.**

Venez. *abbrev. for* Venezuela.

Ve·ne·zia (ve'nɛtsja) *n.* the Italian name for **Venice.**

Ve·ne·zia-E·u·ga·ne·a (*Italian* eu'gaːnea) *n.* another name for **Veneto.**

Ve·ne·zia Giu·lia (*Italian* 'dʒuːlja) *n.* a former region of NE Italy at the N end of the Adriatic: divided between Yugoslavia and Italy since World War II.

Ve·ne·zia Tri·den·ti·na (*Italian* ˌtriden'tiːna) *n.* the former name (until 1947) of **Trentino-Alto Adige.**

Ven·e·zue·la (ˌvɛnɪ'zweɪlə) *n.* **1.** a republic in South America, on the Caribbean: colonized by the Spanish in the 16th century; independence from Spain declared in 1811 and won in 1819 after a war led by Simón Bolívar. It contains Lake Maracaibo and the northernmost chains of the Andes in the northwest, the Orinoco basin in the central part, and the Guiana Highlands in the south. Exports petroleum, iron ore, and coffee. Official language: Spanish. Religion: Roman Catholic. Currency: bolívar. Capital: Caracas. Pop.: 10 721 522 (1971). Area: 912 050 sq. km (352 142 sq. miles). **2. Gulf of.** an inlet of the Caribbean in NW Venezuela: continues south as Lake Maracaibo. —ˌ**Ven·e·'zue·lan** *adj., n.*

venge (vɛndʒ) *vb.* (*tr.*) an archaic word for **avenge.** [C13: from Old French *venger*, from Latin *vindicāre*; see VINDICATE]

venge·ance ('vɛndʒəns) *n.* **1.** the act of or desire for taking revenge; retributive punishment. **2. with a vengeance.** (intensifier): *he's a coward with a vengeance.* [C13: from Old French, from *venger* to avenge, from Latin *vindicāre* to punish; see VINDICATE]

venge·ful ('vɛndʒfʊl) *adj.* **1.** desiring revenge; vindictive. **2.** characterized by or indicating a desire for revenge: *a vengeful glance.* **3.** inflicting or taking revenge: *with vengeful blows.* —'**venge·ful·ly** *adv.* —'**venge·ful·ness** *n.*

ve·ni·al ('viːnɪəl) *adj.* easily excused or forgiven: *a venial error.* [C13: via Old French from Late Latin *veniālis*, from Latin *venia* forgiveness; related to Latin *venus* love] —,**ve·ni·'al·i·ty** *or* '**ve·ni·al·ness** *n.* —'**ve·ni·al·ly** *adv.*

ve·ni·al sin *n. Theol.* a sin regarded as involving only a partial loss of grace. Compare **mortal sin.**

Ven·ice ('vɛnɪs) *n.* a port in NE Italy, capital of Veneto region, built on over 100 islands and mud flats in the **Lagoon of Venice** (an inlet of the **Gulf of Venice** at the head of the Adriatic): united under the first doge in 697 A.D.; became an independent republic and a great commercial and maritime power, defeating Genoa, the greatest rival, in 1380; contains the Grand Canal and about 170 smaller canals, providing waterways for city transport. Pop.: 365 208 (1975 est.). Italian name: **Venezia.** Related adj.: **Venetian.**

ven·in ('vɛnɪn, 'viː-) *n.* any of the poisonous constituents of animal venoms. [C20: from French *ven(in)* poison + -IN]

ven·i·punc·ture *or* **ven·e·punc·ture** ('vɛnɪ,pʌŋktʃə) *n. Med.* the puncturing of a vein, esp. to take a sample of venous blood or inject a drug.

ve·ni·re fa·ci·as (vɪ'naɪrɪ 'feɪʃɪ,æs) *n. Law.* (formerly) a writ directing a sheriff to summon suitable persons to form a jury. [C15: Latin, literally: you must make come]

ve·ni·re·man (vɪ'naɪərɪmən) *n., pl.* **·men.** (in the U.S. and formerly in England) a person summoned for jury service under a venire facias.

ven·i·son ('vɛnzən; 'vɛnɪzᵊn, -sᵊn) *n.* **1.** the flesh of a deer, used as food. **2.** *Archaic.* the flesh of any game animal used for food. [C13: from Old French *venaison*, from Latin *vēnātiō* hunting, from *vēnārī* to hunt]

Ve·ni·te (vɪ'naɪtɪ) *n.* **1.** *Ecclesiast.* the opening word of the 95th psalm, an invitatory prayer at matins. **2.** a musical setting of this. [Latin: come ye]

Ven·i·zel·os (*Greek* ,vɛni'zɛlɔs) *n.* **E·leu·the·ri·os** (ɛ,lɛfθɛ'riɔs). 1864–1936, Greek statesman, who greatly extended Greek territory: prime minister (1910–15; 1917–20; 1924; 1928–32; 1933).

Ven·lo *or* **Ven·loo** (*Dutch* 'vɛnloː) *n.* a city in the SE Netherlands, in Limburg on the Maas River. Pop.: 62 675 (1973 est.).

Venn di·a·gram (vɛn) *n. Maths, logic.* a diagram in which mathematical sets or terms of a categorical statement are represented by circles whose relative positions give the relationships between the sets or terms. [C19: named after John *Venn* (1834–1923), English logician]

ven·om ('vɛnəm) *n.* **1.** a poisonous fluid secreted by such animals as certain snakes and scorpions and usually transmitted by a bite or sting. **2.** malice; spite. **3.** *Archaic.* any kind of poison. [C13: from Old French *venim*, from Latin *venēnum* poison, love potion; related to *venus* sexual love] —'**ven·om·less** *adj.* —'**ven·om·ous** *adj.* —'**ven·om·ous·ly** *adv.* —'**ven·om·ous·ness** *n.*

ve·nose ('viːnəʊs) *adj.* **1.** having veins; venous. **2.** (of a plant) covered with veins or similar ridges. [C17: via Latin *vēnōsus*, from *vēna* a VEIN]

ve·nos·i·ty (vɪ'nɒsɪtɪ) *n.* **1.** an excessive quantity of blood in the venous system or in an organ or part. **2.** an unusually large number of blood vessels in an organ or part.

ve·nous ('viːnəs) *adj.* **1.** *Physiol.* of or relating to the blood circulating in the veins. **2.** of or relating to the veins. [C17: see VENOSE] —'**ve·nous·ly** *adv.* —'**ve·nous·ness** *n.*

vent[1] (vɛnt) *n.* **1.** a small opening for the passage or escape of fumes, liquids, etc. **2.** the shaft of a volcano or an aperture in the earth's crust through which lava and gases erupt. **3.** the external opening of the urinary or genital systems of lower vertebrates. **4.** a small aperture at the breech of old guns through which the charge was ignited. **5.** an exit, escape, or passage. **6. give vent to.** to release (an emotion, passion, idea, etc.) in an utterance or outburst. ~*vb.* (*mainly tr.*) **7.** to release or give expression or utterance to (an emotion, idea, etc.): *he vents his anger on his wife.* **8.** to provide a vent for or make vents in. **9.** to let out (steam, liquid, etc.) through a vent. [C14: from Old French *esventer* to blow out, from EX-[1] + *venter*, from Vulgar Latin *ventāre* (unattested) to be windy, from Latin *ventus* wind] —'**vent·er** *n.* —'**vent·less** *adj.*

vent[2] (vɛnt) *n.* **1.** a vertical slit at the back or both sides of a jacket. ~*vb.* **2.** (*tr.*) to make a vent or vents in (a jacket). [C15: from Old French *fente* slit, from *fendre* to split, from Latin *findere* to cleave]

vent·age ('vɛntɪdʒ) *n.* **1.** a small opening; vent. **2.** a finger hole in a musical instrument such as a recorder.

ven·tail ('vɛnteɪl) *n.* (in medieval armour) a covering for the lower part of the face. [C14: from Old French *ventaille* sluice, from *vent* wind, from Latin *ventus*]

ven·ter ('vɛntə) *n.* **1.** *Anatomy, zoology.* **a.** the belly or abdomen of vertebrates. **b.** a protuberant structure or part, such as the belly of a muscle. **c.** *Rare.* the abdominal cavity. **2.** *Botany.* the swollen basal region of an archegonium, containing the developing ovum. **3.** *Law.* the womb. **4. in venter.** *Law.* conceived but not yet born. [C16: from Latin]

ven·ti·late ('vɛntɪ,leɪt) *vb.* (*tr.*) **1.** to drive foul air out of (an enclosed area). **2.** to provide with a means of airing. **3.** to expose (a question, grievance, etc.) to public examination or discussion. **4.** *Physiol.* to oxygenate (the blood in the capillaries of the lungs. **5.** to winnow (grain). [C15: from Latin *ventilāre* to fan, from *ventulus* diminutive of *ventus* wind] —'**ven·ti·la·ble** *adj.*

ven·ti·la·tion (,vɛntɪ'leɪʃən) *n.* **1.** the act or process of ventilating or the state of being ventilated. **2.** an installation in a building that provides a supply of fresh air. —'**ven·ti·,la·tive** *adj.* —'**ven·ti·,la·to·ry** *adj.*

ven·ti·la·tor ('vɛntɪ,leɪtə) *n.* an opening or device, such as a fan, used to ventilate a room, building, etc.

Ven·tôse *French.* (vɑ̃'toːz) *n.* the windy month: the sixth month of the French Revolutionary calendar, extending from Feb. 20 to March 21. [C18: from Latin *ventōsus* full of wind, from *ventus* wind]

ven·tral ('vɛntrəl) *adj.* **1.** relating to the front part of the body; towards the belly. Compare **dorsal. 2.** of, relating to, or situated on the upper or inner side of a plant organ, esp. a leaf, that is facing the axis. [C18: from Latin *ventrālis*, from *venter* abdomen] —'**ven·tral·ly** *adv.*

ven·tral fin *n.* **1.** another name for **pelvic fin. 2.** any unpaired median fin situated on the undersurface of fishes and some other aquatic vertebrates.

ven·tri·cle ('vɛntrɪkᵊl) *n. Anatomy.* **1.** a chamber of the heart, having thick muscular walls, that receives blood from the atrium and pumps it to the arteries. **2.** any one of the four main cavities of the vertebrate brain, which contain cerebrospinal fluid. **3.** any of various other small cavities in the body. [C14: from Latin *ventriculus*, diminutive of *venter* belly]

ven·tri·cose ('vɛntrɪ,kəʊs) *adj.* **1.** *Botany, zoology, anatomy.* having a swelling on one side; unequally inflated: *the ventricose corolla of many labiate plants.* **2.** another word for **corpulent.** [C18: from New Latin *ventricōsus*, from Latin *venter* belly] —**ven·tri·cos·i·ty** (,vɛntrɪ'kɒsɪtɪ) *n.*

ven·tric·u·lar (vɛn'trɪkjʊlə) *adj.* **1.** of, relating to, involving, or constituting a ventricle. **2.** having a belly. **3.** swollen or distended; ventricose.

ven·tric·u·lus (vɛn'trɪkjʊləs) *n., pl.* **·li** (-,laɪ). **1.** *Zoology.* **a.** the midgut of an insect, where digestion takes place. **b.** the gizzard of a bird. **2.** another word for **ventricle.** [C18: from Latin, diminutive of *venter* belly]

ven·tril·o·quism (vɛn'trɪlə,kwɪzəm) *or* **ven·tril·o·quy** *n.* the art of producing vocal sounds that appear to come from another source. [C18: from Latin *venter* belly + *loquī* to speak] —**ven·tri·lo·qui·al** (,vɛntrɪ'ləʊkwɪəl) *or* **ven·tril·o·qual** (vɛn'trɪləkwəl) *adj.* —,**ven·tri·'lo·qui·al·ly** *adv.* —**ven·'tril·o·quist** *n.* —**ven·,tril·o·'quis·tic** *adj.*

ven·tril·o·quize *or* **ven·tril·o·quise** (vɛn'trɪlə,kwaɪz) *vb.* to produce (sounds) in the manner of a ventriloquist.

Ven·tris ('vɛntrɪs) *n.* **Mi·chael George Fran·cis.** 1922–56, English cryptographer, who deciphered the Linear B script, identifying it as an early form of Mycenaean Greek.

ven·ture ('vɛntʃə) *vb.* **1.** (*tr.*) to expose to danger; hazard: *he ventured his life.* **2.** (*tr.*) to brave the dangers of (something): *I'll venture the seas.* **3.** (*tr.*) to dare (to do something): *does he venture to object?* **4.** (*tr.; may take a clause as object*) to express in spite of possible refutation or criticism: *I venture that he is not that honest.* **5.** (*intr.;* often foll. by *out, forth,* etc.) to embark on a possibly hazardous journey, etc.: *to venture forth upon the high seas.* ~*n.* **6.** an undertaking that is risky or of uncertain outcome. **7. a.** a commercial undertaking characterized by risk of loss as well as opportunity for profit. **b.** the merchandise, money, or other property placed at risk in such an undertaking. **8.** something hazarded or risked in an adventure; stake. **9.** *Archaic.* chance or fortune. **10. at a venture.** at random; by chance. [C15: variant of *aventure* ADVENTURE] —'**ven·tur·er** *n.*

ven·ture cap·i·tal *n.* another name (esp. U.S.) for **risk capital.**

Ven·ture Scout *or* **Ven·tur·er** *n. Brit.* a member of the senior branch of the Scouts. Former name: **Rover.** U.S. equivalent: **Explorer.**

ven·ture·some ('vɛntʃəsəm) *or* **ven·tu·rous** ('vɛntʃərəs) *adj.* **1.** willing to take risks; daring. **2.** hazardous.

Ven·tu·ri tube (vɛn'tjʊərɪ) *n.* **1.** *Physics.* a device for measuring fluid flow, consisting of a tube so constricted that the pressure differential produced by fluid flowing through the constriction gives a measure of the rate of flow. **2.** Also called: **venturi.** a tube with a constriction used to reduce or control fluid flow, as one in the air inlet of a carburettor. [C19: named after G. B. *Venturi* (1746–1822), Italian physicist]

ven·ue ('vɛnjuː) *n.* **1.** *Law.* **a.** the place in which a cause of action arises. **b.** the place fixed for the trial of a cause. **c.** the locality from which the jurors must be summoned to try a particular cause. **2.** a meeting place. **3.** *Chiefly U.S.* a position in an argument. [C14: from Old French, from *venir* to come, from Latin *venīre*]

ven·ule ('vɛnjuːl) *n.* **1.** *Anatomy.* any of the small branches of a vein that receives oxygen-depleted blood from the capillaries and returns it to the heart via the venous system. **2.** any of the branches of a vein in an insect's wing. [C19: from Latin *vēnula* diminutive of *vēna* VEIN] —**ven·u·lar** ('vɛnjʊlə) *adj.*

Ve·nus[1] ('viːnəs) *n.* **1.** the Roman goddess of love. Greek counterpart: **Aphrodite. 2. mount of Venus.** See **mons veneris.**

Ve·nus[2] ('viːnəs) *n.* **1.** one of the inferior planets and the second nearest to the sun, visible as a bright morning or evening star. Its surface is extremely hot (over 400°C) and is completely shrouded by dense cloud consisting principally of carbon dioxide. Mean distance from sun: 108 million km; period of revolution around sun: 225 days; period of axial rotation: 244.3 days (retrograde motion); diameter and mass: 96.5 and 81.5 per cent that of earth respectively. **2.** the alchemical name for **copper.**

Ve·nus·berg ('viːnəs,bɜːg; *German* 've:nus,bɛrk) *n.* a mountain in SW East Germany: contains caverns that, according to medieval legend, housed the palace of the goddess Venus.

Ve·nu·si·an (vɪˈnju:zɪən) *adj.* **1.** of, occurring on, or relating to the planet Venus. *~n.* **2.** (in science fiction) an inhabitant of Venus.

Ve·nus's flow·er bas·ket *n.* any of several deep-sea sponges of the genus *Euplectella,* esp. *E. aspergillum,* having a skeleton composed of interwoven glassy six-rayed spicules.

Ve·nus's-fly·trap *or* **Ve·nus fly·trap** *n.* an insectivorous plant, *Dionaea muscipula,* of Carolina, having hinged two-lobed leaves that snap closed when the sensitive hairs on the surface are touched: family *Droseraceae.* See also **sundew, pitcher plant, butterwort.**

Ve·nus's-gir·dle *n.* a ctenophore, *Cestum veneris,* of warm seas, having an elongated ribbon-like body.

Ve·nus's-hair *n.* a fragile maidenhair fern, *Adiantum capillus-veneris,* of tropical and subtropical America, having fan-shaped leaves and a black stem.

Ve·nus's look·ing-glass *n.* a purple-flowered campanulaceous plant, *Legousia hybrida,* of Europe, W Asia, and N Africa.

ver. *abbrev. for:* **1.** verse. **2.** version.

ve·ra·cious (vɛˈreɪʃəs) *adj.* **1.** habitually truthful or honest. **2.** accurate; precise. [C17: from Latin *vērax,* from *vērus* true] —**veˈra·cious·ly** *adv.* —**veˈra·cious·ness** *n.*

ve·rac·i·ty (vɛˈræsɪtɪ) *n., pl.* **·ties. 1.** truthfulness or honesty, esp. when consistent or habitual. **2.** precision; accuracy. **3.** something true; a truth. [C17: from Medieval Latin *vērācitās,* from Latin *vērax;* see VERACIOUS]

Ver·a·cruz (ˌverəˈkru:z; *Spanish* ˌberaˈkrus) *n.* **1.** a state of E Mexico, on the Gulf of Mexico: consists of a hot humid coastal strip with lagoons, rising rapidly inland to the central plateau and Sierra Madre Oriental. Capital: Jalapa. Pop.: 3 815 419 (1970). Area: 72 815 sq. km (28 114 sq. miles). **2.** the chief port of Mexico, in Veracruz state on the Gulf of Mexico. Pop.: 266 255 (1974 est.).

ve·ran·da *or* **ve·ran·dah** (vəˈrændə) *n.* a porch or portico, sometimes partly enclosed, along the outside of a building. [C18: from Portuguese *varanda* railing; related to Hindi *varandā* railing] —**veˈran·daed** *or* **veˈran·dahed** *adj.*

ve·ra·tri·dine (vɪˈrætrɪˌdi:n) *n.* a yellowish-white amorphous alkaloid obtained from the seeds of sabadilla. Formula: $C_{36}H_{51}NO_{11}$. [C20: from VERATR(INE) + -ID[3] + -INE[2]]

ver·a·trine (ˈverəˌtri:n) *or* **ver·a·trin** (ˈverətrɪn) *n.* a white poisonous mixture obtained from the seeds of sabadilla, consisting of veratridine and several other alkaloids: formerly used in medicine as a counterirritant. [C19: from Latin *vērātrum* hellebore + -INE[2]]

verb (vɜ:b) *n.* **1.** (in traditional grammar) any of a large class of words in a language that serve to indicate the occurrence or performance of an action, the existence of a state or condition, etc. In English, such words as *run, make, do,* and the like are verbs. **2.** (in modern descriptive linguistic analysis) **a.** a word or group of words that functions as the predicate of a sentence or introduces the predicate. **b.** (*as modifier*): *a verb phrase.* Abbrev.: **vb.** or **v.** [C14: from Latin *verbum* a word] —**ˈverb·less** *adj.*

ver·bal (ˈvɜ:bᵊl) *adj.* **1.** of, relating to, or using words, esp. as opposed to ideas, etc.: *merely verbal concessions.* **2.** oral rather than written: *a verbal agreement.* **3.** verbatim; literal: *an almost verbal copy.* **4.** *Grammar.* of or relating to verbs or a verb. *~n.* **5.** *Grammar.* another word for **verbid.** —**ˈver·bal·ly** *adv.*

ver·bal·ism (ˈvɜ:bəˌlɪzəm) *n.* **1.** a verbal expression; phrase or word. **2.** an exaggerated emphasis on the importance of words by the uncritical acceptance of assertions in place of explanations, the use of rhetorical style, etc. **3.** a statement lacking real content, esp. a cliché.

ver·bal·ist (ˈvɜ:bəlɪst) *n.* **1.** a person who deals with words alone, rather than facts, ideas, etc. **2.** a person skilled in the use of words.

ver·bal·ize *or* **ver·bal·ise** (ˈvɜ:bəˌlaɪz) *vb.* **1.** to express (an idea, etc.) in words. **2.** to change (any word that is not a verb) into a verb or derive a verb from (any word that is not a verb). **3.** (*intr.*) to be verbose. —ˌ**ver·bal·i·ˈza·tion** *or* ˌ**ver·bal·i·ˈsa·tion** *n.* —**ˈver·balˌiz·er** *or* **ˈver·balˌis·er** *n.*

ver·bal noun *n.* a noun derived from a verb, such as *smoking* in the sentence *smoking is bad for you.*

ver·ba·tim (vɜ:ˈbeɪtɪm) *adv., adj.* using exactly the same words; word for word. [C15: from Medieval Latin: word by word, from Latin *verbum* word]

ver·be·na (vɜ:ˈbi:nə) *n.* **1.** any plant of the verbenaceous genus *Verbena,* chiefly of tropical and temperate America, having red, white, or purple fragrant flowers: much cultivated as garden plants. See also **vervain. 2.** any of various similar or related plants, esp. the lemon verbena. [C16: via Medieval Latin, from Latin: sacred bough used by the priest in religious acts, VERVAIN]

ver·be·na·ceous (ˌvɜ:bɪˈneɪʃəs) *adj.* of, relating to, or belonging to the *Verbenaceae,* a family of herbaceous and climbing plants, shrubs, and trees, mostly of warm and tropical regions, having tubular typically two-lipped flowers: includes teak, lantana, vervain, and verbena. [C19: from New Latin *Verbēnāceae,* from Medieval Latin: VERBENA]

ver·bi·age (ˈvɜ:bɪɪdʒ) *n.* **1.** the excessive and often meaningless use of words; verbosity. **2.** *Rare.* diction; wording. [C18: from French, from Old French *verbier* to chatter, from *verbe* word, from Latin *verbum*]

ver·bid (ˈvɜ:bɪd) *n. Grammar.* any nonfinite form of a verb or any nonverbal word derived from a verb: *participles, infinitives, and gerunds are all verbids.*

ver·bi·fy (ˈvɜ:bɪˌfaɪ) *vb.* **·fies, ·fy·ing, ·fied.** another word for **verbalize** (senses 2, 3). —ˌ**ver·bi·fi·ˈca·tion** *n.*

ver·bose (vɜ:ˈbəʊs) *adj.* using or containing an excess of words, so as to be pedantic or boring; prolix. [C17: from Latin *verbōsus* from *verbum* word] —**verˈbose·ly** *adv.* —**ver·bos·i·ty** (vɜ:ˈbɒsɪtɪ) *or* **verˈbose·ness** *n.*

ver·bo·ten *German.* (fɛrˈbo:tᵊn) *adj.* forbidden; prohibited.

verb phrase *n. Grammar.* a constituent of a sentence that contains the verb and any direct and indirect objects but not the subject. It is a controversial question in grammatical theory whether or not this constituent is to be identified with the predicate of the sentence. Abbrev.: **VP**

Ver·cel·li (*Italian* verˈtʃɛlli) *n.* a city in NW Italy, in Piedmont: an ancient Ligurian and later Roman city; has an outstanding library of manuscripts (notably the *Codex Vercellensis,* dating from the 10th century). Pop.: 56 494 (1971).

Ver·cin·get·o·rix (ˌvɜ:sɪnˈdʒɛtərɪks) *n.* died ?45 B.C., Gallic chieftain and hero, executed for leading a revolt against the Romans under Julius Caesar (52).

ver·dant (ˈvɜ:dᵊnt) *adj.* **1.** covered with green vegetation. **2.** (of plants, etc.) green in colour. **3.** immature or unsophisticated; green. [C16: from Old French *verdoyant,* from *verdoyer* to become green, from Old French *verd* green, from Latin *viridis,* from *virēre* to be green] —**ˈver·dan·cy** *n.* —**ˈver·dant·ly** *adv.*

verd an·tique (vɜ:d) *n.* **1.** a dark green mottled impure variety of serpentine marble. **2.** any of various similar marbles or stones. **3.** another name for **verdigris.** [C18: from French, from Italian *verde antico* ancient green]

Verde (vɜ:d) *n.* **Cape.** a cape in Senegal, near Dakar: the westernmost point of Africa.

ver·der·er (ˈvɜ:dərə) *n. English legal history.* a judicial officer responsible for the maintenance of law and order in the royal forests. [C16: from Anglo-French, from Old French *verdier,* from *verd* green, from Latin *viridis;* compare Latin *viridārium* plantation of trees]

Ver·di (ˈvɛədɪ; *Italian* ˈverdi) *n.* **Giu·sep·pe** (dʒuˈzɛppe). 1813–1901, Italian composer of operas, esp. *Rigoletto* (1851), *Il Trovatore* (1853), *La Traviata* (1853), and *Aïda* (1871).

ver·dict (ˈvɜ:dɪkt) *n.* **1.** the findings of a jury on the issues of fact submitted to it for examination and trial; judgment. **2.** any decision, judgment, or conclusion. [C13: from Medieval Latin *vērdictum,* from Latin *vērē dictum* truly spoken, from *vērus* true + *dīcere* to say]

ver·di·gris (ˈvɜ:dɪgrɪs) *n.* **1.** a green or bluish patina formed on copper, brass, or bronze and consisting of a basic salt of copper containing both copper oxide and a copper salt. **2.** a green or blue crystalline substance obtained by the action of acetic acid on copper and used as a fungicide and pigment; basic copper acetate. [C14: from Old French *vert de Grice* green of Greece]

ver·din (ˈvɜ:dɪn) *n.* a small W North American tit, *Auriparus flaviceps,* having a grey plumage with a yellow head. [French: yellowhammer]

Ver·dun (*French* vɛrˈdœ̃; *English* ˈvɛədʌn) *n.* **1.** a fortified town in NE France, on the Meuse: scene of the longest and most severe battle (1916) of World War I, in which the French repelled a powerful German offensive. Pop.: 26 927 (1975). Ancient name: **Verodunum. 2. Treaty of.** an agreement reached in 843 A.D. by three grandsons of Charlemagne, dividing his empire into an E kingdom (later Germany), a W kingdom (later France), and a middle kingdom (containing what became the Low Countries, Lorraine, Burgundy, and N Italy).

ver·dure (ˈvɜ:dʒə) *n.* **1.** flourishing green vegetation or its colour. **2.** a condition of freshness or healthy growth. [C14: from Old French *verd* green, from Latin *viridis*] —**ˈver·dured** *adj.* —**ˈver·dur·ous** *adj.*

ver·e·cund (ˈvɛrɪˌkʌnd) *adj. Rare.* shy or modest. [C16: from Latin *verēcundus* diffident, from *verērī* to fear]

Ve·ree·ni·ging (fəˈri:nɪkɪŋ, və-) *n.* a city in E South Africa, in the Transvaal: scene of the signing (1902) of the treaty ending the Boer War. Pop.: 196 357 (1970).

verge[1] (vɜ:dʒ) *n.* **1.** an edge or rim; margin. **2.** a limit beyond which something occurs; brink: *on the verge of ecstasy.* **3.** *Brit.* a grass border along a road. **4.** an enclosing line, belt, or strip. **5.** *Architect.* the edge of the roof tiles projecting over a gable. **6.** *Architect.* the shaft of a classical column. **7.** an enclosed space. **8.** *Horology.* the spindle of a balance wheel in a vertical escapement, found only in very early clocks. **9.** *English legal history.* **a.** the area encompassing the royal court that is subject to the jurisdiction of the Lord High Steward. **b.** a rod or wand carried as a symbol of office or emblem of authority, as in the Church. **c.** a rod held by a person swearing fealty to his lord on becoming a tenant, esp. of copyhold land. **10.** *Printing.* a trigger-like device for releasing the matrices on a Linotype machine. *~vb.* **11.** (*intr.;* foll. by *on*) to be near (to): *to verge on chaos.* **12.** (when *intr.,* sometimes foll. by *on*) to serve as the edge of (something): *this narrow strip verges the road.* [C15: from Old French, from Latin *virga* rod]

verge[2] (vɜ:dʒ) *vb.* (*intr.;* foll. by *to* or *towards*) to move or incline in a certain direction. [C17: from Latin *vergere*]

verge·board (ˈvɜ:dʒˌbɔ:d) *n.* another name for **bargeboard.**

ver·ger (ˈvɜ:dʒə) *n. Chiefly Church of England.* **1.** a church official who acts as caretaker and attendant, looking after the interior of a church and often the vestments and church furnishings. **2.** an official who carries the verge or rod of office before a bishop, dean, or other dignitary in ceremonies and processions. [C15: from Old French, from *verge,* from Latin *virga* rod, twig]

Ver·gil (ˈvɜ:dʒɪl) *n.* a variant spelling of **Virgil.**

ver+glas ('vɛəglɑː) *n., pl.* **+glases** (-glɑː, -glɑːz). a thin film of ice on rock. [from Old French *verre-glaz* glass-ice, from *verre* glass (from Latin *vitrum*) + *glaz* ice (from Late Latin *glacia*, from Latin *glaciēs*)]

ve+rid·i+cal (vɪ'rɪdɪkᵊl) *adj.* **1.** truthful. **2.** *Psychol.* of or relating to revelations in dreams, hallucinations, etc., that appear to be confirmed by subsequent events. [C17: from Latin *vēridicus*, from *vērus* true + *dīcere* to say] —**ve+ˌrid·i+'cal+i·ty** *n.* —**ve+'rid·i+cal+ly** *adv.*

ver·i+est ('vɛrɪɪst) *adj. Archaic.* (intensifier): *the veriest coward.*

ver·i+fi+ca+tion (ˌvɛrɪfɪ'keɪʃən) *n.* **1.** establishment of the correctness of a theory, fact, etc. **2.** evidence that provides proof of an assertion, theory, etc. **3.** *Law.* **a.** (formerly) a short affidavit at the end of a pleading stating the pleader's readiness to prove his assertions. **b.** confirmatory evidence. —**'ver·i+fi+ˌca+tive** *or* **'ver·i+fi+ˌca+to·ry** *adj.*

ver·i+fy ('vɛrɪˌfaɪ) *vb.* **+fies, +fy+ing, +fied.** (*tr.*) **1.** to prove to be true; confirm; substantiate. **2.** to check or determine the correctness or truth of by investigation, reference, etc. **3.** *Law.* to add a verification to (a pleading); substantiate or confirm (an oath). [C14: from Old French *verifier*, from Medieval Latin *vērificāre*, from Latin *vērus* true + *facere* to make] —**'ver·i+ˌfi+a·ble** *adj.* —**'ver·i+ˌfi+a·ble+ness** *n.* —**'ver·i+ˌfi+a·bly** *adv.* —**'ver·i+ˌfi+er** *n.*

ver·i+ly ('vɛrɪlɪ) *adv.* (*sentence modifier*) *Archaic.* in truth; truly: *verily, thou art a man of God.* [C13: from VERY + -LY[2]]

ver·i+sim·i+lar (ˌvɛrɪ'sɪmɪlə) *adj.* appearing to be true; probable; likely. [C17: from Latin *vērīsimilis*, from *vērus* true + *similis* like] —**ˌver·i+'sim·i+lar+ly** *adv.*

ver·i+si+mil·i+tude (ˌvɛrɪsɪ'mɪlɪˌtjuːd) *n.* **1.** the appearance or semblance of truth or reality; quality of seeming true. **2.** something that merely seems to be true or real, such as a doubtful statement. [C17: from Latin *vērisimilitūdō*, from *vērus* true + *similitūdō* SIMILITUDE]

ver+ism ('vɪərɪzəm) *n.* extreme naturalism in art or literature. [C19: from Italian *verismo*, from *vero* true, from Latin *vērus*] —**'ver+ist** *n., adj.* —**ve+'ris+tic** *adj.*

ve+ris+mo (vɛ'rɪzməʊ; *Italian* ve'rismo) *n. Music.* a school of composition that originated in Italian opera towards the end of the 19th century, drawing its themes from real life and emphasizing naturalistic elements. Its chief exponent was Puccini. [C19: from Italian; see VERISM]

ver·i+ta·ble ('vɛrɪtəbᵊl) *adj.* (*prenominal*) **1.** (intensifier; *usually qualifying a word used metaphorically*): *he's a veritable swine!* **2.** *Rare.* genuine or true; proper: *I require veritable proof.* [C15: from Old French, from *vérité* truth; see VERITY] —**'ver·i+ta·ble+ness** *n.* —**'ver·i+ta·bly** *adv.*

ver·i+ty ('vɛrɪtɪ) *n., pl.* **·ties.** **1.** the quality or state of being true, real, or correct. **2.** a true principle, statement, idea, etc.; a truth or fact. [C14: from Old French *vérité*, from Latin *vēritās*, from *vērus* true]

ver+juice ('vɜːˌdʒuːs) *n.* **1. a.** the acid juice of unripe grapes, apples, or crab apples, formerly much used in making sauces, etc. **b.** (*as modifier*): *verjuice sauce.* **2.** *Rare.* **a.** sourness or sharpness of temper, looks, etc. **b.** (*as modifier*): *a verjuice old wife.* ~*vb.* **3.** (*tr.*) *Rare.* to make sour; embitter. [C14: from Old French *vert jus* green (unripe) juice, from Old French *vert* green (from Latin *viridis*) + *jus* juice (from Latin *jūs*)]

Verkh·ne-U·dinsk (*Russian* 'vjerxnɪ u'djinsk) *n.* the former name (until 1934) of **Ulan-Ude.**

ver+kramp+te (fə'kramtə) *n.* (in South Africa) **a.** an Afrikaner Nationalist absolutely opposed to any liberalization in government policy, esp. relating to racial questions. **b.** (*as modifier*): *verkrampte politics.* Compare **verligte.** [C20: from Afrikaans (adj.), literally: restricted]

Ver+laine (*French* vɛr'lɛn) *n.* **Paul** (pɔl). 1844–96, French poet. His verse includes *Poèmes saturniens* (1866), *Fêtes galantes* (1869) and *Romances sans paroles* (1874). He was closely associated with Rimbaud and was a precursor of the symbolists.

ver+lig+te (fə'ləxtə) *n.* (in South Africa) **a.** a person of any of the white political parties who supports the more liberal trends that appear in government policy. **b.** (*as modifier*): *verligte politics.* Compare **verkrampte.** [C20: from Afrikaans (adj.), literally: enlightened]

Ver+meer (vɛə'mɪə; *Dutch* vər'meːr) *n.* **Jan** (jɑn). full name *Jan van der Meer van Delft.* 1632–75, Dutch genre painter, noted esp. for his masterly treatment of light.

ver+meil ('vɜːmeɪl) *n.* **1.** gilded silver, bronze, or other metal, used esp. in the 19th century. **2. a.** vermilion. **b.** (*as adj.*): *vermeil shoes.* [C15: from Old French, from Late Latin *vermiculus* insect (of the genus *Kermes*) or the red dye prepared from it, from Latin: little worm]

ver+mi- *combining form.* worm: *vermicide; vermiform; vermifuge.* [from Latin *vermis* worm]

ver+mi+cel+li (ˌvɜːmɪ'sɛlɪ; *Italian* ˌvermi'tʃɛlli) *n.* **1.** very fine strands of pasta, used in soups. **2.** tiny chocolate strands used to coat cakes, etc. [C17: from Italian: little worms, from *verme* a worm, from Latin *vermis*]

ver+mi+cide ('vɜːmɪˌsaɪd) *n.* any substance used to kill worms. —**ˌver+mi+'cid+al** *adj.*

ver+mic·u+lar (vɜː'mɪkjʊlə) *adj.* **1.** resembling the form, markings, motion, or tracks of worms. **2.** of or relating to worms or wormlike animals. [C17: from Medieval Latin *vermiculāris*, from Latin *vermiculus*, diminutive of *vermis* worm] —**ver+'mic·u+lar+ly** *adv.*

ver+mic·u+late *vb.* (vɜː'mɪkjʊˌleɪt). **1.** (*tr.*) to decorate with wavy or wormlike tracery or markings. ~*adj.* (vɜː'mɪkjʊlɪt, -ˌleɪt). **2.** vermicular; sinuous. **3.** worm-eaten or appearing as if worm-eaten. **4.** (of thoughts, etc.) insinuating; subtly tortuous. [C17: from Latin *vermiculātus* in the form of worms, from *vermis* worm]

ver+mic·u+la+tion (vɜːˌmɪkjʊ'leɪʃən) *n.* **1.** *Physiol.* any wormlike movement, esp. of the intestines; peristalsis. **2.** decoration consisting of wormlike carving or marks. **3.** the state of being worm-eaten.

ver+mic·u+lite (vɜː'mɪkjʊˌlaɪt) *n.* any of a group of micaceous minerals consisting mainly of hydrated silicate of magnesium, aluminium, and iron: on heating they expand and exfoliate and in this form are used in heat and sound insulation, fireproofing, and as a bedding medium for young plants. [C19: from VERMICUL(AR) + -ITE[1]]

ver+mi+form ('vɜːmɪˌfɔːm) *adj.* resembling a worm.

ver+mi+form ap+pen+dix *or* **pro+cess** *n.* a wormlike pouch extending from the lower end of the caecum in some mammals. In man it is vestigial. Also called: **appendix.**

ver+mi+fuge ('vɜːmɪˌfjuːdʒ) *n.* any drug or agent able to destroy or expel intestinal worms. Also called: **anthelminthic, anthelmintic, helminthic.** —**ver+mi+fu+gal** (ˌvɜːmɪ'fjuːgᵊl) *adj.*

ver+mil+ion *or* **ver+mil+lion** (və'mɪljən) *n.* **1. a.** a bright red to reddish-orange colour. **b.** (*as adj.*): *a vermilion car.* **2.** mercuric sulphide, esp. when used as a bright red pigment; cinnabar. [C13: from Old French *vermeillon*, from VERMEIL]

ver+min ('vɜːmɪn) *n.* **1.** (*functioning as pl.*) small animals collectively, esp. insects and rodents, that are troublesome to man, domestic animals, etc. **2.** *pl.* **+min.** an unpleasant, obnoxious, or dangerous person. [C13: from Old French *vermine*, from Latin *vermis* a worm]

ver+mi+na+tion (ˌvɜːmɪ'neɪʃən) *n.* the spreading of or infestation with vermin.

ver+mi+nous ('vɜːmɪnəs) *adj.* relating to, infested with, or suggestive of vermin. —**'ver+min+ous+ly** *adv.* —**'ver+min+ous+ness** *n.*

ver+mis ('vɜːmɪs) *n., pl.* **+mes** (-miːz). *Anatomy.* the middle lobe connecting the two halves of the cerebellum. [C19: via New Latin from Latin: worm]

ver+miv·o+rous (vɜː'mɪvərəs) *adj.* (of certain animals) feeding on worms.

Ver+mont (vɜː'mɒnt) *n.* a state in the northeastern U.S.: crossed from north to south by the Green Mountains; bounded on the east by the Connecticut River and by Lake Champlain in the northwest. Capital: Montpelier. Pop.: 444 732 (1970). Area: 2400 sq. km (9267 sq. miles). Abbrevs.: **Vt.** or (with zip code) **VT** —**Ver+'mont+er** *n.*

ver+mouth ('vɜːməθ) *n.* any of several wines containing aromatic herbs and some other flavourings. [C19: from French, from German *Wermut* WORMWOOD (absinthe)]

ver+nac·u+lar (və'nækjʊlə) *n.* **1. the.** the commonly spoken language or dialect of a particular people or place. **2.** jargon relating to a particular trade, occupation, etc.: *the vernacular of linguistics.* **3.** a vernacular term. ~*adj.* **4.** relating to, using, or in the vernacular. **5.** native to a particular place. **6.** designating or relating to the common name of an animal or plant. [C17: from Latin *vernāculus* belonging to a household slave, from *verna* household slave] —**ver+'nac·u+lar+ly** *adv.*

ver+nac·u+lar+ism (və'nækjʊləˌrɪzəm) *n.* the use of the vernacular or a term in the vernacular.

ver+nal ('vɜːnᵊl) *adj.* **1.** of or occurring in spring. **2.** *Poetic.* of or characteristic of youth; fresh. [C16: from Latin *vernālis*, from *vēr* spring] —**'ver+nal+ly** *adv.*

ver+nal e·qui+nox *n.* **1.** the time at which the sun crosses the plane of the equator towards the relevant hemisphere, making day and night of equal length. It occurs about March 21 in the N hemisphere (Sept. 23 in the S hemisphere). **2.** *Astronomy.* the point on the celestial sphere, lying in the constellation of Pisces, at which the celestial equator intersects the ecliptic.

ver+nal grass *n.* any of various Eurasian grasses of the genus *Anthoxanthum*, such as *A. odoratum* (**sweet vernal grass**), having the fragrant scent of coumarin.

ver+nal+ize *or* **ver+nal+ise** ('vɜːnəˌlaɪz) *vb.* to shorten the period between sowing and flowering in (plants), esp. by subjection of the seeds to low temperatures before planting. —**ˌver+nal·i+'za+tion** *or* **ˌver+nal·i+'sa+tion** *n.*

ver+na+tion (vɜː'neɪʃən) *n.* the way in which leaves are arranged in the bud. [C18: from New Latin *vernātiō*, from Latin *vernāre* to be springlike, from *vēr* spring]

Verne (vɜːn; *French* vɛrn) *n.* **Jules** (ʒyl). 1828–1905, French writer, esp. of science fiction, such as *Twenty Thousand Leagues under the Sea* (1870) and *Around the World in Eighty Days* (1873).

Ver+ner's law ('vɜːnəz) *n. Linguistics.* a modification of Grimm's Law accommodating some of its exceptions. It states that noninitial voiceless fricatives in Proto-Germanic occurring as a result of Grimm's law became voiced fricatives if the previous syllable had been unstressed in Proto-Indo-European. [C19: named after Karl Adolph *Verner* (1846–96), Danish philologist, who formulated it] —**Ver+ner+i+an** (vɜː'nɜərɪən) *adj.*

ver+ni+er ('vɜːnɪə) *n.* **1.** a small movable scale running parallel to the main graduated scale in certain measuring instruments, such as theodolites, used to obtain a fractional reading of one of the divisions on the main scale. **2.** an auxiliary device for making a fine adjustment to an instrument, usually by means of a fine screw thread. **3.** (*modifier*) relating to or fitted with a vernier: *a vernier scale; a vernier barometer.* [C18: named after Paul *Vernier* (1580–1637), French mathematician, who described the scale]

ver+ni+er rock+et *n.* another name for **thruster** (sense 2).

ver+nis+sage (ˌvɜːnɪˈsɑːʒ) *n.* the opening or first day of an exhibition of paintings. [French, from *vernis* VARNISH]

Ver+no+le+ninsk (*Russian* vɪrnəlɪˈnjiːnsk) *n.* the former name of **Nikolayev.**

Ver+ny (*Russian* ˈvjɛrnɪj) *n.* a former name (until 1927) of **Alma-Ata.**

Ve+ro+na (vəˈrəʊnə; *Italian* veˈroːna) *n.* a city in N Italy, in Veneto on the Adige River: strategically situated at the junction of major routes between Italy and N Europe; became a Roman colony (89 B.C.); under Austrian rule (1797–1866); many Roman remains. Pop.: 271 079 (1975 est.). —**Ver·o+nese** (ˌvɛrəˈniːz) *adj., n.*

Ver·o+nal (ˈvɛrənᵊl) *n.* a trademark for **barbitone.**

Ve·ro·ne·se (*Italian* ˌveroˈneːse) *n.* **Pa·o·lo** (ˈpaːolo), original name *Paolo Cagliari* or *Caliari.* 1528–88, Italian painter of the Venetian school. His works include *The Marriage at Cana* (1563) and *The Feast of the Levi* (1573).

ve+ron·i+ca[1] (vəˈrɒnɪkə) *n.* any scrophulariaceous plant of the genus *Veronica,* esp. the speedwells, of temperate and cold regions, having small blue, pink, or white flowers and flattened notched fruits. [C16: from Medieval Latin, perhaps from the name *Veronica*]

ve+ron·i+ca[2] (vəˈrɒnɪkə) *n. R.C. Church.* **1.** the representation of the face of Christ that, according to legend, was miraculously imprinted upon the headcloth that Saint Veronica offered him on his way to his crucifixion. **2.** the cloth itself. **3.** any similar representation of Christ's face.

ve+ron·i+ca[3] (vəˈrɒnɪkə) *n. Bullfighting.* a pass in which the matador slowly swings the cape away from the charging bull. [from Spanish, from the name *Veronica*]

Ver·ra·za·no *or* **Ver·raz·za·no** (*Italian* ˌverraˈtsaːno) *n.* **Gio·van·ni da** (dʒoˈvanni da). ?1485–?1528, Florentine navigator; the first European to sight what was to become New York (1524).

Ver·roc·chio (vəˈrəʊkɪˌəʊ; *Italian* verˈrɔkkjo) *n.* **An·dre·a del** (anˈdrɛːa del). 1435–88, Italian sculptor, painter, and goldsmith of the Florentine school: noted esp. for the equestrian statue of Bartolommeo Colleoni in Venice.

ver+ru+ca (vɛˈruːkə) *n., pl.* **+cae** (-siː) *or* **+cas. 1.** *Pathol.* a wart, esp. one growing on the hand or foot. **2.** *Biology.* a wartlike outgrowth, as in certain plants or on the skin of some animals. [C16: from Latin: wart]

ver+ru+cose (ˈvɛruˌkəʊs) *or* **ver+ru+cous** (ˈvɛrʊkəs, vɛˈruːkəs) *adj. Botany.* covered with warty processes. [C17: from Latin *verrūcōsus* full of warts, from *verrūca* a wart] —**ver+ru+cos+i·ty** (ˌvɛrʊˈkɒsɪtɪ) *n.*

vers *abbrev. for* versed sine.

Ver+sailles (vɛəˈsaɪ, -ˈseɪlz; *French* vɛrˈsɑːj) *n.* **1.** a city in N central France, near Paris: site of an elaborate royal residence built for Louis XIV; seat of the French kings (1682–1789). Pop.: 97 133 (1975). **2. Treaty of. a.** the treaty of 1919 imposed upon Germany by the Allies (except for the U.S. and the Soviet Union): the most important of the five peace treaties that concluded World War I. **b.** another name for the (Treaty of) **Paris** of 1783.

ver+sant (ˈvɜːsᵊnt) *n.* **1.** the side or slope of a mountain or mountain range. **2.** the slope of a region. [C19: from French, from *verser* to turn, from Latin *versāre*]

ver+sa+tile (ˈvɜːsəˌtaɪl) *adj.* **1.** capable of or adapted for many different uses, skills, etc. **2.** variable or changeable. **3.** *Botany.* (of an anther) attached to the filament by a small area so that it moves freely in the wind. **4.** *Zoology.* able to turn forwards and backwards: *versatile antennae.* [C17: from Latin *versātilis* moving around, from *versāre* to turn] —**ˈver+sa+tile+ly** *adv.* —**ver+sa+til+i·ty** (ˌvɜːsəˈtɪlɪtɪ) *or* **ˈver+sa+tile+ness** *n.*

vers de so+cié+té *French.* (vɛr də sɔsjeˈte) *n.* light, witty, and polished verse. [literally: society verse]

verse (vɜːs) *n.* **1.** (not in technical usage) a stanza or other short subdivision of a poem. **2.** poetry as distinct from prose. **3. a.** a series of metrical feet forming a rhythmical unit of one line. **b.** (*as modifier*): *verse line.* **4.** a specified type of metre or metrical structure: *iambic verse.* **5.** one of the series of short subsections into which most of the writings in the Bible are divided. **6.** a metrical composition; poem. ~*vb.* **7.** a rare word for **versify.** [Old English *vers,* from Latin *versus* a furrow, literally: a turning (of the plough), from *vertere* to turn]

versed (vɜːst) *adj.* (*postpositive;* foll. by *in*) thoroughly knowledgeable (about), acquainted (with), or skilled (in).

versed sine *n.* a trigonometric function equal to one minus the cosine of the specified angle. Abbrev.: **vers** [C16: from New Latin *sinus versus,* from SINE + *versus* turned, from *vertere* to turn]

ver+si+cle (ˈvɜːsɪkᵊl) *n.* **1.** a short verse. **2.** a short sentence recited or sung by the minister at a liturgical ceremony and responded to by the choir or congregation. [C14: from Latin *versiculus* a little line, from *versus* VERSE]

ver+si+col+our *or U.S.* **ver+si+col+or** (ˈvɜːsɪˌkʌlə) *adj.* of variable or various colours. [C18: from Latin *versicolor,* from *versāre* to turn + *color* COLOUR]

ver+si+cu+lar (vɜːˈsɪkjʊlə) *adj. Rare.* of, relating to, or consisting of verses or versicles.

ver+si+fi+ca+tion (ˌvɜːsɪfɪˈkeɪʃən) *n.* **1.** the technique or art of versifying. **2.** the form or metrical composition of a poem. **3.** a metrical version of a prose text.

ver+si+fy (ˈvɜːsɪˌfaɪ) *vb.* **+fies, +fy+ing, +fied.** to render (something) into metrical form or verse. [C14: from Old French *versifier,* from Latin *versificāre,* from *versus* VERSE + *facere* to make] —**ˈver+si+ˌfi+er** *n.*

ver+sion (ˈvɜːʃən, -ʒən) *n.* **1.** an account of a matter from a certain point of view, as contrasted with others: *his version of the accident is different from the policeman's.* **2.** a translation, esp. of the Bible, from one language into another. **3.** a variant form of something; type. **4.** an adaptation, as of a book or play into a film. **5.** *Med.* manual turning of a fetus to correct an irregular position within the uterus. **6.** *Pathol.* an abnormal displacement of the uterus characterized by a tilting forwards (**anteversion**), backwards (**retroversion**), or to either side (**lateroversion**). [C16: from Medieval Latin *versiō* a turning, from Latin *vertere* to turn] —**ˈver+sion+al** *adj.*

vers li+bre *French.* (vɛr ˈlibr) *n.* (in French poetry) another term for **free verse.**

ver+so (ˈvɜːsəʊ) *n., pl.* **+sos. 1. a.** the back of a sheet of printed paper. **b.** Also called: **reverso.** the left-hand pages of a book, bearing the even numbers. Compare **recto. 2.** the side of a coin opposite to the obverse; reverse. [C19: from the New Latin phrase *versō foliō* the leaf having been turned, from Latin *vertere* to turn + *folium* a leaf]

verst (vɛəst, vɜːst) *n.* a unit of length, used in Russia, equal to 1.067 kilometres (0.6629 miles). [C16: from French *verste* or German *Werst,* from Russian *versta* line]

ver+sus (ˈvɜːsəs) *prep.* **1.** (esp. in a competition or lawsuit) against; in opposition to. Abbrev.: **v** or (esp. U.S.) **vs. 2.** as opposed to; in contrast with. [C15: from Latin: turned (in the direction of), opposite, from *vertere* to turn]

vert (vɜːt) *n.* **1.** *English legal history.* **a.** the right to cut green wood in a forest. **b.** the wood itself. **2.** *Heraldry.* **a.** the colour green. **b.** (*as adj., usually postpositive*): *a table vert.* [C15: from Old French *verd,* from Latin *viridis* green, from *virēre* to grow green]

vert. *abbrev. for* vertical.

ver+te+bra (ˈvɜːtɪbrə) *n., pl.* **+brae** (-briː) *or* **+bras.** one of the bony segments of the spinal column. [C17: from Latin: joint of the spine, from *vertere* to turn] —**ˈver+te+bral** *adj.* —**ˈver+te+bral+ly** *adv.*

ver+te+bral col+umn *n.* another name for **spinal column.**

ver+te+brate (ˈvɜːtɪˌbreɪt, -brɪt) *n.* **1.** any chordate animal of the subphylum *Vertebrata,* characterized by a bony or cartilaginous skeleton and a well-developed brain: the group contains fishes, amphibians, reptiles, birds, and mammals. ~*adj.* **2.** of, relating to, or belonging to the subphylum *Vertebrata.*

ver+te+bra+tion (ˌvɜːtɪˈbreɪʃən) *n.* the formation of vertebrae or segmentation resembling vertebrae.

ver+tex (ˈvɜːtɛks) *n., pl.* **+tex·es** *or* **+ti+ces** (-tɪˌsiːz). **1.** the highest point. **2.** *Maths.* **a.** the point opposite the base of a figure. **b.** the point of intersection of two sides of a plane figure or angle. **c.** the point of intersection of a pencil of lines or three or more planes of a solid figure. **3.** *Astronomy.* a point in the sky towards which a star stream appears to move. **4.** *Anatomy.* the crown of the head. [C16: from Latin: whirlpool, from *vertere* to turn]

ver+ti+cal (ˈvɜːtɪkᵊl) *adj.* **1.** at right angles to the horizon; perpendicular; upright: *a vertical wall.* Compare **horizontal** (sense 1). **2.** extending in a perpendicular direction. **3.** at or in the vertex or zenith; directly overhead. **4.** *Economics.* of or relating to associated or consecutive, though not identical, stages of industrial activity: *vertical integration; vertical amalgamation.* **5.** of or relating to the vertex. **6.** *Anatomy.* of, relating to, or situated at the top of the head (vertex). ~*n.* **7.** a vertical plane, position, or line. **8.** a vertical post, pillar, or other structural member. [C16: from Late Latin *verticālis,* from Latin VERTEX] —**ˌver+ti+ˈcal+i·ty** *or* **ˈver+ti+cal+ness** *n.* —**ˈver+ti+cal+ly** *adv.*

ver+ti+cal an+gles *pl. n. Geom.* the pair of equal angles between a pair of intersecting lines; opposite angles.

ver+ti+cal cir+cle *n. Astronomy.* a great circle on the celestial sphere passing through the zenith and perpendicular to the horizon.

ver+ti+cal group+ing *n.* another term for **family grouping.**

ver+ti+cal mo+bil+i+ty *n. Sociol.* the process of change within a society involving the movement of individuals, groups, or classes upwards (upward mobility) or downwards (downward mobility) in terms of class, status, and power.

ver+ti+cal sta+bi+liz+er *n.* the U.S. name for **fin**[1] (sense 3a).

ver+ti+cal un+ion *n.* another name (esp. U.S.) for **industrial union.**

ver+ti+ces (ˈvɜːtɪˌsiːz) *n.* a plural of **vertex** (in technical and scientific senses only).

ver+ti+cil (ˈvɜːtɪsɪl) *n. Biology.* a circular arrangement of parts about an axis, esp. leaves around a stem. [C18: from Latin *verticillus* whorl (of a spindle), from VERTEX]

ver+ti+cil+las+ter (ˌvɜːtɪsɪˈlæstə) *n. Botany.* an inflorescence, such as that of the deadnettle, that resembles a whorl but consists of two crowded cymes on either side of the stem. [C19: from New Latin; see VERTICIL, -ASTER] —**ver+ti+cil+las+trate** (ˌvɜːtɪsɪˈlæstreɪt, -trɪt) *adj.*

ver+tic+il+late (vɜːˈtɪsɪlɪt, -ˌleɪt; ˌvɜːtɪˈsɪleɪt) *adj. Biology.* having or arranged in whorls or verticils. —**ver+ˈtic+il+ˌlate+ly** *adv.* —**ver+ˌtic+il+ˈla+tion** *n.*

ver+tig+i+nous (vɜːˈtɪdʒɪnəs) *adj.* **1.** of, relating to, or having vertigo. **2.** producing dizziness. **3.** whirling. **4.** changeable; unstable. [C17: from Latin *vertīginōsus,* from VERTIGO] —**ver+ˈtig+i+nous+ly** *adv.* —**ver+ˈtig+i+nous+ness** *n.*

ver+ti+go (ˈvɜːtɪˌgəʊ) *n., pl.* **ver+ti+goes** *or* **ver+tig+i+nes** (vɜːˈtɪdʒɪˌniːz). *Pathol.* a sensation of dizziness or abnormal motion resulting from a disorder of the sense of balance. [C16: from Latin: a whirling round, from *vertere* to turn]

ver+tu (vɜːˈtuː) *n.* a variant spelling of **virtu.**

Ver·tum·nus (vɜːˈtʌmnəs) *or* **Vor·tum·nus** *n.* a Roman god of gardens, orchards, and seasonal change. [from Latin, from *vertere* to turn, change]

Ver·u·la+mi·um (ˌvɛrʊˈleɪmɪəm) *n.* the ancient name of **Saint Albans.**

ver+vain (ˈvɜːveɪn) *n.* any of several verbenaceous plants of the genus *Verbena*, having square stems and long slender spikes of purple, blue, or white flowers. [C14: from Old French *verveine*, from Latin *verbēna* sacred bough; see VERBENA]

verve (vɜːv) *n.* **1.** great vitality, enthusiasm, and liveliness; sparkle. **2.** a rare word for **talent.** [C17: from Old French: garrulity, from Latin *verba* words, chatter]

ver+vet (ˈvɜːvɪt) *n.* a variety of a South African guenon monkey, *Cercopithecus aethiops*, having dark hair on the hands and feet and a reddish patch beneath the tail. Compare **green monkey, grivet.** [C19: from French, from *vert* green, but influenced by GRIVET]

Ver·woerd (fəˈvʊt, fɛəˈvʊət) *n.* **Hen·drik Frensch** (ˈhɛndrɪk frɛns). 1901–66, South African statesman, born in the Netherlands: prime minister of South Africa (1958 until his assassination).

ver·y (ˈvɛrɪ) *adv.* **1.** (intensifier) used to add emphasis to adjectives that are able to be graded: *very good; very tall.* ~*adj.* (*prenominal*) **2.** (intensifier) used with nouns preceded by a definite article or possessive determiner, in order to give emphasis to the significance, appropriateness or relevance of a noun in a particular context, or to give exaggerated intensity to certain nouns: *the very man I want to see; his very name struck terror; the very back of the room.* **3.** (intensifier) used in metaphors to emphasize the applicability of the image to the situation described: *he was a very lion in the fight.* **4.** *Archaic.* **a.** real or true; genuine: *the very living God.* **b.** lawful: *the very vengeance of the gods.* [C13: from Old French *verai* true, from Latin *vērax* true, from *vērus* true]

Usage. In strict usage adverbs of degree such as *very, too, quite, really,* and *extremely* are used only to qualify adjectives: *he is very happy; she is too sad.* By this rule, these words should not be used to qualify past participles that follow the verb *to be*, since they would then be technically qualifying verbs. With the exception of certain participles, such as *tired* or *disappointed*, that have come to be regarded as adjectives, all other past participles are qualified by adverbs such as *much, greatly, seriously*, or *excessively: he has been much* (not *very*) *inconvenienced; she has been excessively* (not *too*) *criticized.*

ver·y high fre+quen+cy *n.* a single radio-frequency or band lying between 300 and 30 megahertz. Abbrev.: **VHF**

Ver·y light (ˈvɛrɪ) *n.* a coloured flare fired from a special pistol (**Very pistol**) for signalling at night, esp. at sea. [C19: named after Edward W. *Very* (1852–1910), U.S. naval ordnance officer]

ver·y low fre+quen+cy *n.* a radio-frequency band or radio frequency lying between 30 and 3 kilohertz. Abbrev.: **VLF**

Ver·y Rev+er+end *n.* a title of respect for a dean.

Ve·sa·li·us (vɪˈseɪlɪəs) *n.* **An·dre·as** (anˈdreːas). 1514–64, Flemish anatomist, whose *De Humani Corporis fabrica* (1543) formed the basis of modern anatomical research and medicine.

ves·i+ca (ˈvɛsɪkə) *n., pl.* **+cae** (-ˌsiː). **1.** *Anatomy.* a technical name for **bladder** (sense 1). **2.** (in medieval sculpture and painting) an aureole in the shape of a pointed oval. [C17: from Latin: bladder, sac, blister]

ves·i+cal (ˈvɛsɪkᵊl) *adj.* of or relating to a vesica, esp. the urinary bladder.

ves·i+cant (ˈvɛsɪkənt) *or* **ves·i+ca+to·ry** (ˈvɛsɪˌkeɪtərɪ) *n., pl.* **+cants** *or* **+ca+to·ries. 1.** any substance that causes blisters, used in medicine and in chemical warfare. ~*adj.* **2.** acting as a vesicant. [C19: see VESICA]

ves·i+cate (ˈvɛsɪˌkeɪt) *vb.* to blister. [C17: from New Latin *vēsīcāre* to blister; see VESICA] —**ˌves·i+ˈca+tion** *n.*

ves·i+cle (ˈvɛsɪkᵊl) *n.* **1.** *Pathol.* **a.** any small sac or cavity, esp. one containing serous fluid. **b.** a blister. **2.** *Geology.* a rounded cavity within a rock formed during solidification by expansion of the gases present in the magma. **3.** *Botany.* a small bladder-like cavity occurring in certain seaweeds and aquatic plants. **4.** any small cavity or cell. [C16: from Latin *vēsīcula*, diminutive of VESICA] —**ve+sic·u+lar** (vɛˈsɪkjʊlə) *adj.* —**ve+ˈsic·u·lar+ly** *adv.*

ve+sic·u+late *vb.* (vɛˈsɪkjʊˌleɪt). **1.** to make (an organ or part) vesicular or (of an organ, etc.) to become vesicular. ~*adj.* (vɛˈsɪkjʊlɪt, -ˌleɪt). **2.** containing, resembling, or characterized by a vesicle or vesicles. —**ve+ˌsic·u+ˈla+tion** *n.*

Ves·pa·si·an (vɛsˈpeɪʒɪən) *n.* Latin name *Titus Flavius Sabinus Vespasianus.* 9–79 A.D., Roman emperor (69–79), who consolidated Roman rule, esp. in Britain and Germany. He began the building of the Colosseum.

ves+per (ˈvɛspə) *n.* **1.** an evening prayer, service, or hymn. **2.** an archaic word for **evening. 3.** (*modifier*) of or relating to vespers. [C14: from Latin: evening, the evening star; compare Greek *hesperos* evening; see WEST]

Ves+per (ˈvɛspə) *n.* the planet Venus, when appearing as the evening star.

ves+per+al (ˈvɛspərəl) *n. Christianity.* **1.** a liturgical book containing the prayers, psalms, and hymns used at vespers. **2.** the part of the antiphonary containing these. **3.** a cloth laid over the altar cloth between offices or services.

ves+pers (ˈvɛspəz) *n.* **1.** *Chiefly R.C. Church.* the sixth of the seven canonical hours of the divine office, originally fixed for the early evening and now often made a public service on Sundays and major feast days. **2.** another word for **Evensong.**

ves+per+til·i·o+nine (ˌvɛspəˈtɪlɪəˌnaɪn, -nɪn) *adj.* of, relating to, or belonging to the *Vespertilionidae*, a family of common and widespread bats. [C17: from Latin *vespertīliō* a bat, from *vesper* evening] —**ves+per+til·i·o+nid** (ˌvɛspəˈtɪlɪənɪd) *adj., n.*

ves+per+tine (ˈvɛspəˌtaɪn) *adj.* **1.** *Botany, zoology.* appearing, opening, or active in the evening: *vespertine flowers.* **2.** occurring in the evening or (esp. of stars) appearing or setting in the evening.

ves+pi+ar·y (ˈvɛspɪərɪ) *n., pl.* **+ar·ies.** a nest or colony of social wasps or hornets. [C19: from Latin *vespa* a wasp, on the model of *apiary*]

ves+pid (ˈvɛspɪd) *n.* **1.** any hymenopterous insect of the family *Vespidae*, including the common wasps and hornets. ~*adj.* **2.** of, relating to, or belonging to the family *Vespidae.* [C19: from New Latin *Vespidae*, from Latin *vespa* a wasp]

ves+pine (ˈvɛspaɪn) *adj.* of, relating to, or resembling a wasp or wasps. [C19: from Latin *vespa* a wasp]

Ves·puc·ci (vɛˈspuːtʃɪ) *n.* **A·me·ri·go** (ˌameˈriːgo), Latin name *Americus Vespucius.* ?1454–1512, Florentine navigator in the New World (1499–1500; 1501–02), after whom the continent of America was named.

ves+sel (ˈvɛsᵊl) *n.* **1.** any object used as a container, esp. for a liquid. **2.** a passenger or freight-carrying ship, boat, etc. **3.** an aircraft, esp. an airship. **4.** *Anatomy.* a tubular structure that transports such body fluids as blood and lymph. **5.** *Botany.* a tubular element of xylem tissue consisting of a row of cells in which the connecting cell walls have broken down. **6.** *Rare.* a person regarded as an agent or vehicle for some purpose or quality: *she was the vessel of the Lord.* [C13: from Old French *vaissel*, from Late Latin *vascellum* urn, from Latin *vās* vessel]

vest (vɛst) *n.* **1.** an undergarment covering the body from the shoulders to the hips, made of cotton, nylon, etc. U.S. equivalent: **T-shirt, undershirt. 2.** the usual U.S. and Austral. word for **waistcoat. 3.** *Obsolete.* any form of dress, esp. a long robe. ~*vb.* **4.** (*tr.;* foll. by *in*) to place or settle (power, rights, etc., in): *power was vested in the committee.* **5.** (*tr.;* foll. by *with*) to bestow or confer (on): *the company was vested with authority.* **6.** (usually foll. by *in*) to confer (a right, title, property, etc., upon) or (of a right, title, etc.) to pass to or devolve (upon). **7.** to clothe or array. **8.** (*intr.*) to put on clothes, ecclesiastical vestments, etc. [C15: from Old French *vestir* to clothe, from Latin *vestīre*, from *vestis* clothing] —**ˈvest+less** *adj.* —**ˈvest+ˌlike** *adj.*

ves+ta (ˈvɛstə) *n.* a short friction match, usually of wood.

Ves+ta[1] (ˈvɛstə) *n.* the Roman goddess of the hearth and its fire. In her temple a perpetual flame was tended by the vestal virgins. Greek counterpart: **Hestia.**

Ves+ta[2] (ˈvɛstə) *n.* the brightest of the four largest asteroids. Diameter: about 380 km (240 miles). [C19: named after the goddess; see VESTA[1]]

ves+tal (ˈvɛstᵊl) *adj.* **1.** chaste or pure; virginal. **2.** of or relating to the Roman goddess Vesta. ~*n.* **3.** a chaste woman; virgin. **4.** a rare word for **nun**[1] (sense 1).

ves+tal vir+gin *n.* (in ancient Rome) one of the four, later six, virgin priestesses whose lives were dedicated to Vesta and to maintaining the sacred fire in her temple.

vest+ed (ˈvɛstɪd) *adj. Property law.* having a present right to the immediate or future possession and enjoyment of property. Compare **contingent.**

vest+ed in+ter+est *n.* **1.** *Property law.* an existing and disposable right to the immediate or future possession and enjoyment of property. **2.** a strong personal concern in a state of affairs, system, etc., usually resulting in private gain. **3.** a person or group that has such an interest.

ves+ti+ar·y (ˈvɛstɪərɪ) *n., pl.* **+ar·ies. 1.** *Obsolete.* a room for storing clothes or dressing in, such as a vestry. ~*adj.* **2.** *Rare.* of or relating to clothes. [C17: from Late Latin *vestiārius*, from *vestis* clothing]

ves+ti+bule (ˈvɛstɪˌbjuːl) *n.* **1.** a small entrance hall or anteroom; lobby. **2.** any small bodily cavity or space at the entrance to a passage or canal. [C17: from Latin *vestibulum*] —**ves+tib·u+lar** (vɛˈstɪbjʊlə) *adj.*

ves+tige (ˈvɛstɪdʒ) *n.* **1.** a small trace, mark, or amount; hint: *a vestige of truth; no vestige of the meal.* **2.** *Biology.* an organ or part of an organism that is a small nonfunctioning remnant of a functional organ in an ancestor. [C17: via French from Latin *vestīgium* track]

ves+tig·i·al (vɛˈstɪdʒɪəl) *adj.* **1.** of, relating to, or being a vestige. **2.** (of certain organs or parts of organisms) having attained a simple structure and reduced size and function during the evolution of the species: *the vestigial pelvic girdle of a snake.* —**ves+ˈtig·i·al+ly** *adv.*

vest+ment (ˈvɛstmənt) *n.* **1.** a garment or robe, esp. one denoting office, authority, or rank. **2.** any of various ceremonial garments worn by the clergy at religious services, etc. [C13: from Old French *vestiment*, from Latin *vestīmentum* clothing, from *vestīre* to clothe] —**vest+ment+al** (vɛstˈmɛntᵊl) *adj.* —**ˈvest+ment+ed** *adj.*

vest-pock·et *n.* (*modifier*) *Chiefly U.S.* small enough to fit into a waistcoat pocket.

ves+try (ˈvɛstrɪ) *n., pl.* **+tries. 1.** a room in or attached to a church in which vestments, sacred vessels, etc., are kept. **2.** a room in or attached to some churches, used for Sunday school, meetings, etc. **3. a.** *Church of England.* a meeting of all the members of a parish or their representatives, to transact the official and administrative business of the parish. **b.** the body of members meeting for this; the parish council. **4.** *Episcopal Church, U.S.* a committee of vestrymen chosen by the congregation to manage the temporal affairs of their church. [C14: probably from Old French *vestiarie;* see VEST] —**'ves·tral** *adv.*

ves·try·man ('vɛstrɪmən) *n., pl.* **·men.** a member of a church vestry.

ves·ture ('vɛstʃə) *n.* **1.** *Archaic.* a garment or something that seems like a garment: *a vesture of cloud.* **2.** *Law.* **a.** everything except trees that grows on the land. **b.** a product of the land, such as grass, wheat, etc. ~*vb.* **3.** (*tr.*) *Archaic.* to clothe. [C14: from Old French, from *vestir,* from Latin *vestīre,* from *vestis* clothing] —**'ves·tur·al** *adj.*

ve·su·vi·an (vɪ'su:vɪən) *n.* **1.** (esp. formerly) a match for lighting cigars; fusee. **2.** another name for **vesuvianite.** [C18: (the mineral), C19 (the match): both named after VESUVIUS]

ve·su·vi·an·ite (vɪ'su:vɪəˌnaɪt) *n.* a green, brown, or yellow mineral consisting of a hydrated silicate of calcium, magnesium, iron, and aluminium: it occurs as tetragonal crystals in limestones and is used as a gemstone. Formula: $Ca_{10}Al_4(MgFe)_2Si_9O_{34}(OH)_4$. Also called: **idocrase, vesuvian.** [C19: first found in the lava of VESUVIUS]

Ve·su·vi·us (vɪ'su:vɪəs) *n.* a volcano in SW Italy, on the Bay of Naples: first recorded eruption in 79 A.D., which destroyed Pompeii, Herculaneum, and Stabiae; numerous eruptions since then. Height: (mid-1960s) 1281 m (4203 ft.). Italian name: **Ve·su·vio** (ve'zuvjo).

vet[1] (vɛt) *n.* **1.** short for **veterinary surgeon.** ~*vb.* **vets, vet·ting, vet·ted. 2.** (*tr.*) *Chiefly Brit.* to examine and appraise: *the candidates were well vetted.* **3.** to examine, treat, or cure (an animal).

vet[2] (vɛt) *n. U.S.* short for **veteran** (senses 2, 3).

vet. *abbrev. for:* **1.** veteran. **2.** veterinarian. **3.** veterinary. Also (for senses 2, 3): **veter.**

vetch (vɛtʃ) *n.* **1.** any of various climbing papilionaceous plants of the temperate genus *Vicia,* esp. *V. sativa,* having pinnate leaves, typically blue or purple flowers, and tendrils on the stems. **2.** any of various similar and related plants, such as *Lathyrus sativus,* cultivated in parts of Europe, and the kidney vetch. **3.** the beanlike fruit of any of these plants. [C14: *fecche,* from Old French *veche,* from Latin *vicia*]

vetch·ling ('vɛtʃlɪŋ) *n.* any of various papilionaceous tendril-climbing plants of the genus *Lathyrus,* esp. *L. pratensis* **(meadow vetchling),** mainly of N temperate regions, having winged or angled stems and showy flowers. See also **sweet pea.**

vet·er·an ('vɛtərən, 'vɛtrən) *n.* **1. a.** a person or thing that has given long service in some capacity. **b.** (*as modifier*): *veteran firemen.* **2. a.** a soldier who has seen considerable active service. **b.** (*as modifier*): *veteran soldier.* **3.** *U.S.* a person who has served in the military forces. **4.** See **veteran car.** [C16: from Latin *veterānus,* from *vetus* old]

vet·er·an car *n. Brit.* a car constructed before 1919, esp. one constructed before 1905. Compare **vintage car.**

Vet·er·ans Day *n.* the U.S. equivalent of **Armistice Day.**

vet·er·i·nar·i·an (ˌvɛtərɪ'nɛərɪən, ˌvɛtrɪ-) *n.* the U.S. term for **veterinary surgeon.**

vet·er·i·nar·y ('vɛtərɪnərɪ, 'vɛtrɪnrɪ) *adj.* of or relating to veterinary science. [C18: from Latin *veterīnārius* concerning draught animals, from *veterīnae* draught animals; related to *vetus* mature (hence able to bear a burden)]

vet·er·i·nar·y sci·ence *or* **med·i·cine** *n.* the branch of medicine concerned with the health of animals and the treatment of injuries or diseases that affect them.

vet·er·i·nar·y sur·geon *n. Brit.* a person skilled in the practice of veterinary medicine. U.S. term: **veterinarian.**

vet·i·ver ('vɛtɪvə) *n.* **1.** a tall hairless grass, *Vetiveria zizanioides,* of tropical and subtropical Asia, having aromatic roots and stiff long narrow ornamental leaves. **2.** the root of this plant used for making screens, mats, etc., and yielding a fragrant oil used in perfumery, medicine, etc. [C19: from French *vétiver,* from Tamil *vettivēru*]

ve·to ('vi:təʊ) *n., pl.* **·toes. 1.** the power to prevent legislation or action proposed by others; prohibition: *the presidential veto.* **2.** the exercise of this power. **3.** Also called: **veto message.** *U.S government.* a document containing the reasons why a chief executive has vetoed a measure. ~*vb.* **·toes, ·to·ing, ·toed.** (*tr.*) **4.** to refuse consent to (a proposal, esp. a government bill). **5.** to prohibit, ban, or forbid: *her parents vetoed her trip.* [C17: from Latin: I forbid, from *vetāre* to forbid] —**'ve·to·er** *n.* —**'ve·to·less** *adj.*

vex (vɛks) *vb.* (*tr.*) **1.** to anger or annoy. **2.** to confuse; worry. **3.** *Archaic.* to agitate. [C15: from Old French *vexer,* from Latin *vexāre* to jolt (in carrying), from *vehere* to convey] —**'vex·er** *n.* —**'vex·ing·ly** *adv.*

vex·a·tion (vɛk'seɪʃən) *n.* **1.** the act of vexing or the state of being vexed. **2.** something that vexes.

vex·a·tious (vɛk'seɪʃəs) *adj.* **1.** vexing or tending to vex. **2.** vexed. **3.** *Law.* (of a legal action or proceeding) instituted without sufficient grounds, esp. so as to cause annoyance or embarrassment to the defendant: *vexatious litigation.* —**vex·'a·tious·ly** *adv.* —**vex·'a·tious·ness** *n.*

vexed (vɛkst) *adj.* **1.** annoyed, confused, or agitated. **2.** much debated and discussed (esp. in the phrase **a vexed question**). —**vex·ed·ly** ('vɛksɪdlɪ) *adv.* —**'vex·ed·ness** *n.*

vex·il·lol·o·gy (ˌvɛksɪ'lɒlədʒɪ) *n.* the study and collection of information about flags. [C20: from Latin *vexillum* flag + -LOGY] —**ˌvex·il·'lol·o·gist** *n.*

vex·il·lum (vɛk'sɪləm) *n., pl.* **·la** (-lə). **1.** *Ornithol.* the vane of a feather. **2.** *Botany.* another name for **standard** (sense 15). [C18: from Latin: banner, perhaps from *vēlum* sail] —**'vex·il·lar·y** *or* **vex·'il·lar** *adj.* —**'vex·il·late** *adj.*

V.F. *abbrev. for* video frequency.

v.g. *abbrev. for* very good.

V.G. *abbrev. for* Vicar General.

VHF *or* **vhf** *Radio. abbrev. for* very high frequency.

v.i. *abbrev. for* vide infra.

V.I. *abbrev. for:* **1.** Vancouver Island. **2.** Virgin Islands.

vi·a ('vaɪə) *prep.* by way of; by means of; through: *to London via Paris.* [C18: from Latin *viā,* from *via* way]

vi·a·ble ('vaɪəbᵊl) *adj.* **1.** capable of becoming actual, useful, etc.; practicable: *a viable proposition.* **2.** (of seeds, eggs, etc.) capable of normal growth and development. **3.** (of a fetus) having reached a stage of development at which further development can occur independently of the mother. [C19: from French, from *vie* life, from Latin *vīta*] —**ˌvi·a·'bil·i·ty** *n.*

Vi·a Dol·o·ro·sa ('vi:ə ˌdɒlə'rəʊsə) *n.* **1.** the route followed by Christ from the place of his condemnation to Calvary for his crucifixion. **2.** an arduous or distressing course or experience. [Latin, literally: sorrowful road]

vi·a·duct ('vaɪəˌdʌkt) *n.* a bridge, esp. for carrying a road or railway across a valley, etc., consisting of a set of arches supported by a row of piers or towers. [C19: from Latin *via* way + *dūcere* to bring, on the model of *aqueduct*]

vi·al ('vaɪəl, vaɪl) *n.* a less common variant of **phial.** [C14: *fiole,* from Old French, from Old Provençal *fiola,* from Latin *phiala,* from Greek *phialē;* see PHIAL]

vi·a me·di·a *Latin.* ('vaɪə 'mi:dɪə) *n.* a compromise between two extremes; middle course.

vi·and ('vi:ənd, 'vaɪ-) *n.* **1.** a type of food, esp. a delicacy. **2.** (*pl.*) provisions. [C14: from Old French *viande,* ultimately from Latin *vīvenda,* things to be lived on, from *vīvere* to live]

Vi·a·reg·gio (*Italian* via'reddʒo) *n.* a town and resort in W Italy, in Tuscany on the Ligurian Sea. Pop.: 55 737 (1971).

vi·at·i·cum (vaɪ'ætɪkəm) *n., pl.* **·ca** (-kə) *or* **·cums. 1.** Holy Communion as administered to a person dying or in danger of death. **2.** *Rare.* provisions or a travel allowance for a journey. [C16: from Latin, from *viāticus* belonging to a journey, from *viāre* to travel, from *via* way]

vi·a·tor (vaɪ'eɪtɔ:) *n., pl.* **vi·a·to·res** (ˌvaɪə'tɔ:ri:z). *Rare.* a traveller. [C16: from Latin, from *viāre* to travel]

vibes (vaɪbz) *pl. n. Informal.* **1.** (esp. in jazz) short for **vibraphone. 2.** short for **vibrations.**

vib·ist ('vaɪbɪst) *n. Informal.* a person who plays a vibraphone in a jazz band or group.

Vi·borg *n.* **1.** ('vi:bɔrj). the Swedish name for **Vyborg. 2.** (*Danish* 'vibɔr). a town in N central Denmark, in Jutland: formerly a royal town and capital of Jutland. Pop.: 27 445 (1970).

vi·brac·u·lum (vaɪ'brækjʊləm) *n., pl.* **·la** (-lə). *Zoology.* any of the specialized bristle-like polyps in certain bryozoans, the actions of which prevent parasites from settling on the colony. [C19: from New Latin, from Latin *vibrāre* to brandish] —**vi·'brac·u·lar** *adj.* —**vi·'brac·u·ˌloid** *adj.*

vi·brant ('vaɪbrənt) *adj.* **1.** characterized by or exhibiting vibration; pulsating or trembling. **2.** giving an impression of vigour and activity. **3.** caused by vibration; resonant. **4.** *Phonetics.* trilled or rolled. ~*n.* **5.** a vibrant speech sound, such as a trilled (r). [C16: from Latin *vibrāre* to agitate] —**'vi·bran·cy** *n.* —**'vi·brant·ly** *adv.*

vi·bra·phone ('vaɪbrəˌfəʊn) *or esp. U.S.* **vi·bra·harp** ('vaɪbrəˌhɑ:p) *n.* a percussion instrument, used esp. in jazz, consisting of a set of metal bars placed over tubular metal resonators, which are made to vibrate electronically. —**'vi·bra·ˌphon·ist** *n.*

vi·brate (vaɪ'breɪt) *vb.* **1.** to move or cause to move back and forth rapidly; shake, quiver, or throb. **2.** to oscillate. **3.** to send out (a sound) by vibration; resonate or cause to resonate. **4.** (*intr.*) to waver. **5.** *Physics.* to produce or undergo an oscillatory or periodic process, as of an alternating current; oscillate. **6.** (*intr.*) *Rare.* to respond emotionally; thrill. [C17: from Latin *vibrāre*] —**vi·bra·tile** ('vaɪbrəˌtaɪl) *adj.* —**vi·bra·til·i·ty** (ˌvaɪbrə'tɪlɪtɪ) *n.* —**vi·'brat·ing·ly** *adv.* —**vi·'bra·tive** *or* **'vi·bra·to·ry** *adj.*

vi·bra·tion (vaɪ'breɪʃən) *n.* **1.** the act or an instance of vibrating. **2.** *Physics.* **a.** a periodic motion about an equilibrium position, such as the regular displacement of air in the propagation of sound. **b.** a single cycle of such a motion. **3.** the process or state of vibrating or being vibrated. —**vi·'bra·tion·al** *adj.* —**vi·'bra·tion·less** *adj.*

vi·bra·tions (vaɪ'breɪʃənz) *pl. n. Informal.* **1.** instinctive feelings supposedly influencing human communication. **2.** a characteristic atmosphere felt to be emanating from places or objects. ~Often shortened to **vibes.**

vi·bra·to (vɪ'brɑ:təʊ) *n., pl.* **·tos.** *Music.* **1.** a slight, rapid, and regular fluctuation in the pitch of a note produced on a stringed instrument by a shaking movement of the hand stopping the strings. **2.** an oscillatory effect produced in singing by fluctuation in breath pressure or pitch. ~Compare **tremolo.** [C19: from Italian, from Latin *vibrāre* to VIBRATE]

vi·bra·tor (vaɪ'breɪtə) *n.* **1. a.** a device for producing a vibratory motion, such as one used in massage **b.** such a device with a vibrating part or tip, used as a dildo. **2.** a device in which a vibrating conductor interrupts a circuit to produce a pulsating current from a steady current, usually so that the current can then be amplified or the voltage transformed. See also **chopper** (sense 6).

vib·ri·o ('vɪbrɪˌəʊ) *n., pl.* **·os.** any curved or spiral rodlike Gram-negative bacterium of the genus *Vibrio,* esp. the comma bacillus: family *Spirillaceae.* [C19: from New Latin, from Latin *vibrāre* to VIBRATE] —'**vib+ri+,oid** *adj.*

vi+bris+sa (vaɪ'brɪsə) *n., pl.* **+sae** (-siː). (*usually pl.*) **1.** any of the bristle-like sensitive hairs on the face of many mammals; a whisker. **2.** any of the specialized bristle-like feathers around the beak in certain insectivorous birds. [C17: from Latin, probably from *vibrāre* to shake] —**vi+'bris+sal** *adj.*

vi+bron+ic (vaɪ'brɒnɪk) *adj. Physics.* of, concerned with, or involving both electronic and vibrational energy levels: *a vibronic spectrum; a vibronic transition.* [C20: from *vibr(atory + electr)onic*]

vi+bur+num (vaɪ'bɜːnəm) *n.* **1.** any of various temperate and subtropical caprifoliaceous shrubs or trees of the genus *Viburnum,* such as the wayfaring tree, having small white flowers and berry-like red or black fruits. **2.** the dried bark of several species of this tree, sometimes used in medicine. [C18: from Latin: wayfaring tree]

Vic. *Austral. abbrev. for* Victoria (the state).

vic+ar ('vɪkə) *n.* **1.** *Church of England.* **a.** (in Britain) a clergyman appointed to act as priest of a parish. **b.** a clergyman who acts as assistant to or substitute for the rector of a parish at Communion. **c.** (in the U.S.) a clergyman in charge of a chapel. **2.** *R.C. Church.* a bishop or priest representing the pope or the ordinary of a diocese and exercising a limited jurisdiction. **3.** Also called: **lay vicar, vicar choral.** *Church of England.* a member of a cathedral choir appointed to sing certain parts of the services. **4.** a person appointed to do the work of another. [C13: from Old French *vicaire,* from Latin *vicārius* (n.) a deputy, from *vicārius* (adj.) VICARIOUS] —'**vi+car+ly** *adj.*

vic+ar+age ('vɪkərɪdʒ) *n.* **1.** the residence or benefice of a vicar. **2.** a rare word for **vicariate** (sense 1).

vic+ar ap+os+tol+ic *n. R.C. Church.* a titular bishop having jurisdiction in non-Catholic or missionary countries where the normal hierarchy has not yet been established.

vic+ar fo+rane (fɒ'reɪn) *n., pl.* **vic+ars fo+rane.** *R.C. Church.* a priest or bishop appointed by the ordinary of the diocese to exercise a limited jurisdiction in a locality at some distance from the ordinary's official see. [*forane,* from Late Latin *forāneus* in a foreign land, from Latin *forās* outside]

vic+ar gen+er+al *n., pl.* **vic+ars gen+er+al.** an official, usually a layman, appointed to assist the bishop of a diocese in discharging his administrative or judicial duties.

vi+car+i+al (vɪ'kɛərɪəl, vaɪ-) *adj.* **1.** of or relating to a vicar, vicars, or a vicariate. **2.** holding the office of a vicar. **3.** vicarious: used esp. of certain ecclesiastical powers.

vi+car+i+ate (vɪ'kɛərɪɪt, vaɪ-) *n.* **1.** Also called: **vic+ar+ship** ('vɪkə,ʃɪp). the office, rank, or authority of a vicar. **2.** the district that a vicar holds as his pastoral charge.

vi+car+i+ous (vɪ'kɛərɪəs, vaɪ-) *adj.* **1.** obtained or undergone at second hand through sympathetic participation in another's experiences. **2.** suffered, undergone, or done as the substitute for another: *vicarious punishment.* **3.** delegated: *vicarious authority.* **4.** taking the place of another. **5.** *Pathol.* (of menstrual bleeding) occurring at an abnormal site. See **endometriosis.** [C17: from Latin *vicārius* substituted, from *vicis* interchange; see VICE[3], VICISSITUDE] —**vi+'car+i+ous+ly** *adv.* —**vi+'car+i+ous+ness** *n.*

Vic+ar of Christ *n. R.C. Church.* the pope when regarded as Christ's earthly representative.

vice[1] (vaɪs) *n.* **1.** an immoral, wicked, or evil habit, action, or trait. **2.** habitual or frequent indulgence in pernicious, immoral, or degrading practices. **3.** a specific form of pernicious conduct, esp. prostitution or sexual perversion. **4.** a failing or imperfection in character, conduct, etc.: *smoking is his only vice.* **5.** *Pathol, obsolete.* any physical defect or imperfection. **6.** a bad trick or disposition, as of horses, dogs, etc. [C13: via Old French from Latin *vitium* a defect] —'**vice+less** *adj.*

vice[2] *or U.S. (often)* **vise** (vaɪs) *n.* **1.** an appliance for holding an object while work is done upon it, usually having a pair of jaws. ~*vb.* **2.** (*tr.*) to grip (something) with or as if with a vice. [C15: from Old French *vis* a screw, from Latin *vītis* vine, plant with spiralling tendrils (hence the later meaning)] —'**vice+,like** *or U.S. (often)* '**vise+,like** *adj.*

vice[3] (vaɪs) *adj.* **1. a.** (*prenominal*) serving in the place of or as a deputy for. **b.** (*in combination*): *viceroy.* ~*n.* **2.** *Informal.* a person who serves as a deputy to another. [C18: from Latin *vice,* from *vicis* interchange]

vi+ce[4] ('vaɪsɪ) *prep.* instead of; as a substitute for.

Vice (vaɪs) *n.* (in English morality plays) a character personifying a particular vice or vice in general.

vice ad+mi+ral *n.* a commissioned officer of flag rank in certain navies, junior to an admiral and senior to a rear admiral. —,**vice-'ad+mir+al+ty** *n.*

vice-chair+man *n., pl.* **+men.** a person who deputizes for a chairman and serves in his place during his absence or indisposition. —,**vice-'chair+man+,ship** *n.*

vice chan+cel+lor *n.* **1.** the chief executive or administrator at some British universities. Compare **chancellor** (sense 3). **2.** (in the U.S.) a judge in courts of equity subordinate to the chancellor. **3.** (formerly in England) a senior judge of the court of chancery who acted as assistant to the Lord Chancellor. **4.** a person serving as the deputy of a chancellor. —,**vice-'chan+cel+lor+,ship** *n.*

vice+ge+rent (,vaɪs'dʒɛrənt) *n.* **1.** a person appointed to exercise all or some of the authority of another, esp. the administrative powers of a ruler; deputy. **2.** *R.C. Church.* the pope or any other representative of God or Christ on earth, such as a bishop. ~*adj.* **3.** invested with or characterized by delegated authority. [C16: from New Latin *vicegerēns,* from VICE- + Latin *gerere* to manage] —,**vice+'ge+ral** *adj.* —,**vice+'ge+ren+cy** *n.*

vic+e+nar+y ('vɪsɪnərɪ) *adj.* **1.** relating to or consisting of 20. **2.** *Maths.* having or using a base 20. [C17 (in the sense: one who has charge over twenty persons): from Latin *vīcēnārius,* from *vīcēnī* twenty each, from *vīgintī* twenty]

vi+cen+ni+al (vɪ'sɛnɪəl) *adj.* **1.** occurring every 20 years. **2.** relating to or lasting for a period of 20 years. [C18: from Late Latin *vīcennium* period of twenty years, from Latin *vīciēs* twenty times + *-ennium,* from *annus* year]

Vi+cen+za (*Italian* vi'tʃɛntsa) *n.* a city in NE Italy, in Veneto: home of the 16th-century architect Andrea Palladio and site of some of his finest works. Pop.: 119 646 (1975 est.).

vice pres+i+dent *n.* an officer ranking immediately below a president and serving as his deputy. A vice president takes the president's place during his absence or incapacity, after his death, and in certain other circumstances. Abbrev.: **V.P.** —,**vice-'pres+i+den+cy** *n.* —,**vice-,pres+i+'den+tial** *adj.*

vice+re+gal (,vaɪs'riːgᵊl) *adj.* **1.** of or relating to a viceroy or his viceroyalty. **2.** *Chiefly Austral.* of or relating to a governor or governor general. —,**vice+'re+gal+ly** *adv.*

vice+re+gal as+sent *n. Austral.* the formal signing of an act of parliament by a governor general, by which it becomes law.

vice+reine (,vaɪs'reɪn) *n.* **1.** the wife of a viceroy. **2.** a female viceroy. [C19: from French, from VICE- + *reine* queen, from Latin *rēgīna*]

vice+roy ('vaɪsrɔɪ) *n.* a governor of a colony, country, or province who acts for and rules in the name of his sovereign or government. Related adj.: **viceregal.** [C16: from French, from VICE- + *roy* king, from Latin *rex*] —'**vice+roy+,ship** *n.*

vice+roy+al+ty (,vaɪs'rɔɪəltɪ) *n., pl.* **+ties.** **1.** the office, authority, or dignity of a viceroy. **2.** the domain governed by a viceroy. **3.** the term of office of a viceroy.

vice squad *n.* a police division to which is assigned the enforcement of gaming and prostitution laws.

vi+ce ver+sa ('vaɪsɪ 'vɜːsə) *adv.* with the order reversed; the other way around. [C17: from Latin: relations being reversed, from *vicis* change + *vertere* to turn]

Vi+chy (*French* vi'ʃi; *English* 'vɪʃɪ) *n.* a town and spa in central France, on the River Allier: seat of the collaborationist government under Marshal Pétain (1940–44); mineral waters bottled for export. Pop.: 32 251 (1975). Latin name: **Vicus Calidus.**

vi+chy+ssoise (*French* viʃi'swaːz) *n.* a thick soup made from leeks, potatoes, chicken stock, and cream, usually served chilled. [French, from (*crème*) *Vichyssoise* (*glacée*) (ice-cold cream) from Vichy]

vi+chy wa+ter *n.* **1.** (*sometimes cap.*) a natural mineral water from springs at Vichy in France, reputed to be beneficial to the health. **2.** any sparkling mineral water resembling this. ~Often shortened to **vichy.**

vic+i+nage ('vɪsɪnɪdʒ) *n. Now rare.* **1.** the residents of a particular neighbourhood. **2.** a less common word for **vicinity.** [C14: from Old French *vicenage,* from *vicin* neighbouring, from Latin *vīcīnus;* see VICINITY]

vic+i+nal ('vɪsɪnᵊl) *adj.* **1.** neighbouring. **2.** (esp. of roads) of or relating to a locality or neighbourhood. **3.** *Chem.* relating to or designating two adjacent atoms to which groups are attached in a chain. [C17: from Latin *vīcīnālis* nearby, from *vīcīnus,* from *vīcus* a neighbourhood]

vi+cin+i+ty (vɪ'sɪnɪtɪ) *n., pl.* **+ties.** **1.** a surrounding, adjacent, or nearby area; neighbourhood. **2.** the fact or condition of being close in space or relationship. [C16: from Latin *vīcīnitās,* from *vīcīnus* neighbouring, from *vīcus* village]

vi+cious ('vɪʃəs) *adj.* **1.** wicked or cruel; villainous: *a vicious thug.* **2.** characterized by violence or ferocity: *a vicious blow.* **3.** *Informal.* unpleasantly severe; harsh: *a vicious wind.* **4.** characterized by malice: *vicious lies.* **5.** (esp. of dogs, horses, etc.) ferocious or hostile; dangerous. **6.** characterized by or leading to vice. **7.** invalidated by defects; unsound: *a vicious inference.* **8.** *Obsolete.* noxious or morbid: *a vicious exhalation.* [C14: from Old French *vicieus,* from Latin *vitiōsus* full of faults, from *vitium* a defect] —'**vi+cious+ly** *adv.* —'**vi+cious+ness** *n.*

vi+cious cir+cle *n.* **1.** a situation in which an attempt to resolve one problem creates new problems that lead back to the original situation. **2.** *Logic.* **a.** an invalid form of reasoning in which a conclusion is derived from a premiss originally deduced from that same conclusion. **b.** an explanation of the meaning of a word in terms of another word originally explained by using the first word; circular definition. **3.** *Med.* a condition in which one disease or disorder causes another, which in turn aggravates the first condition.

vi+cis+si+tude (vɪ'sɪsɪ,tjuːd) *n.* **1.** variation or mutability in nature or life, esp. successive alternation from one condition or thing to another. **2.** a variation in circumstance, fortune, character, etc. [C16: from Latin *vicissitūdō,* from *vicis* change, alternation] —**vi+,cis+si+'tu+di+nar+y** *or* **vi+,cis+si+'tu+di+nous** *adj.*

Vicks+burg ('vɪks,bɜːg) *n.* a city in W Mississippi, on the Mississippi River: site of one of the most decisive campaigns (1863) of the American Civil War, in which the Confederates were besieged for nearly seven weeks before capitulating. Pop.: 25 478 (1970).

Vick+y ('vɪkɪ) *n.* professional name of *Victor Weisz.* 1913–66, British left-wing political cartoonist, born in Germany.

Vi+co ('vɪkəʊ; *Italian* 'viːko) *n.* **Gio+van+ni Bat+tis+ta** (dʒo'vanni bat'tista). 1668–1744, Italian philosopher. In *Scienza Nuova* (1721) he postulated that civilizations rise and fall in evolutionary cycles, making use of myths, poetry, and linguistics as historical evidence.

vi+comte (*French* vi'kɔ̃:t) *or* (*fem.*) **vi+com+tesse** (*French* vikɔ̃'tɛs) *n.* a French noble holding a rank corresponding to that of a British viscount or viscountess.

vic+tim ('vɪktɪm) *n.* **1.** a person or thing that suffers harm, death, etc., from another or from some adverse act, circumstance, etc.: *victims of tyranny.* **2.** a person who is tricked or swindled; dupe. **3.** a living person or animal sacrificed in a religious rite. [C15: from Latin *victima*]

vic+tim+ize *or* **vic+tim+ise** ('vɪktɪˌmaɪz) *vb.* (*tr.*) **1.** to punish or discriminate against selectively or unfairly. **2.** to make a victim of. **3.** to kill as or in a manner resembling a sacrificial victim. —ˌ**vic+tim·i+'za+tion** *or* ˌ**vic+tim·i+'sa+tion** *n.* —'**vic+tim+ˌiz+er** *or* '**vic+tim+ˌis+er** *n.*

vic+tor ('vɪktə) *n.* **1. a.** a person, nation, etc., that has defeated an adversary in war, etc. **b.** (*as modifier*): *the victor army.* **2.** the winner of any contest, conflict, or struggle. [C14: from Latin, from *vincere* to conquer]

Vic·tor Em·man·u·el II *n.* 1820–78, king of Sardinia-Piedmont (1849–78) and first king of Italy from 1861.

Vic·tor Em·man·u·el III *n.* 1869–1947, last king of Italy (1900–46): dominated after 1922 by Mussolini, whom he appointed as premier; abdicated.

vic+to+ri·a (vɪk'tɔ:rɪə) *n.* **1.** a light four-wheeled horse-drawn carriage with a folding hood, two passenger seats, and a seat in front for the driver. **2.** Also called: **victoria plum.** *Brit.* a large sweet variety of plum, red and yellow in colour. **3.** any South American giant water lily of the genus *Victoria,* having very large floating leaves and large white, red, or pink fragrant flowers: family *Euryalaceae.* [C19: all named after Queen VICTORIA]

Vic·to·ri·a[1] (vɪk'tɔ:rɪə) *n.* **1.** a state of SE Australia: part of New South Wales colony until 1851; semiarid in the northwest, with the Great Dividing Range in the centre and east and the Murray River along the N border. Capital: Melbourne. Pop.: 3 646 300 (1976). Area: 227 620 sq. km (87 884 sq. miles). **2. Lake.** Also called: **Victoria Nyanza.** a lake in East Africa, in Tanzania, Uganda, and Kenya, at an altitude of 1134 m (3720 ft.): the largest lake in Africa and second largest in the world; drained by the Victoria Nile. Area: 69 485 sq. km (26 828 sq. miles). **3.** a port in SW Canada, capital of British Columbia, on Vancouver Island: founded in 1843 by the Hudson's Bay Company; made capital of British Columbia in 1868; university (1963). Pop.: 62 761 (1971). **4.** the capital of the Seychelles, a port on NE Mahé. Pop.: 13 736 (1971). **5.** the capital of Hong Kong, on N Hong Kong Island: financial centre; university (1911). Pop.: 520 932 (1971). **6. Mount.** a mountain in SE Papua: the highest peak of the Owen Stanley Range. Height: 4073 m (13 363 ft.).

Vic·to·ri·a[2] (vɪk'tɔ:rɪə) *n.* 1819–1901, queen of Great Britain and Ireland (1837–1901) and empress of India (from 1876). She married Prince Albert of Saxe-Coburg-Gotha (1840). Her sense of vocation did much to restore the prestige of the British monarchy.

Vic·to·ri·a[3] (vɪk'tɔ:rɪə) *n.* the Roman goddess of victory. Greek counterpart: **Nike.**

Vic·to·ri·a Cross *n.* the highest decoration for gallantry in the face of the enemy awarded to the British and Commonwealth armed forces: instituted in 1856 by Queen Victoria.

Vic·to·ri·a Day *n.* the Monday preceding May 24: observed in Canada as a national holiday in commemoration of the birthday of Queen Victoria.

Vic+to+ri·a Des+ert *n.* See **Great Victoria Desert.**

Vic+to+ri·a Falls *pl. n.* a waterfall on the border between Rhodesia and Zambia, on the Zambezi River. Height: about 108 m (355 ft.). Width: about 1400 m (4500 ft.).

Vic+to+ri·a Is+land *n.* the third largest island of the Canadian Arctic: part of the Northwest Territories. Area: about 212 000 sq. km (82 000 sq. miles).

Vic+to+ri·a Land *n.* a section of Antarctica, largely in the Ross Dependency on the Ross Sea.

Vic+to+ri·an (vɪk'tɔ:rɪən) *adj.* **1.** of, relating to, or characteristic of Queen Victoria or the period of her reign. **2.** exhibiting the characteristics popularly attributed to the Victorians, esp. prudery, bigotry, or hypocrisy. **3.** denoting, relating to, or having the style of architecture used in England during the reign of Queen Victoria, characterized by massive construction and elaborate ornamentation. **4.** of or relating to Victoria (the state or any of the cities). ~*n.* **5.** a person who lived during the reign of Queen Victoria. **6.** an inhabitant of Victoria (the state or any of the cities). —**Vic+'to+ri+an+ˌism** *n.*

Vic+to+ri+a·na (vɪkˌtɔ:rɪ'ɑ:nə) *n.* objects, ornaments, etc., of the Victorian period.

Vic+to+ri·a Nile *n.* See **Nile.**

vic+to+ri+ous (vɪk'tɔ:rɪəs) *adj.* **1.** having defeated an adversary: *the victorious nations.* **2.** of, relating to, indicative of, or characterized by victory: *a victorious conclusion.* —**vic+'to+ri+ous+ly** *adv.* —**vic+'to+ri+ous+ness** *n.*

vic+to+ry ('vɪktərɪ) *n., pl.* **+ries. 1.** final and complete superiority in a war. **2.** a successful military engagement. **3.** a success attained in a contest or struggle or over an opponent, obstacle, or problem. **4.** the act of triumphing or state of having triumphed. [C14: from Old French *victorie,* from Latin *victōria,* from *vincere* to subdue]

Vic·to·ry ('vɪktərɪ) *n.* another name (in English) for the Roman goddess **Victoria** or the Greek **Nike.**

vict+ual ('vɪtᵊl) *vb.* **+uals, +ual+ling, +ualled** *or U.S.* **+uals, +ual+ing, +ualed. 1.** to supply with or obtain victuals. **2.** (*intr.*) *Rare.* (esp. of animals) to partake of victuals. [C14: from Old French *vitaille,* from Late Latin *victuālia* provisions, from Latin *victuālis* concerning food, from *victus* sustenance, from *vīvere* to live] —'**vict+ual+less** *adj.*

vict+ual+age ('vɪtəlɪdʒ) *n.* a rare word for **victuals.**

vict+ual+ler ('vɪtələ, 'vɪtlə) *n.* **1.** a supplier of victuals, as to an army; sutler. **2.** *Brit.* a licensed purveyor of spirits; innkeeper. **3.** a supply ship, esp. one carrying foodstuffs.

vict+uals ('vɪtᵊlz) *pl. n.* (*sometimes sing.*) food or provisions.

vi+cu+ña (vɪ'kju:nə) *n.* **1.** a tawny-coloured cud-chewing Andean artiodactyl mammal, *Vicugna vicugna,* similar to the llama: family *Camelidae.* **2.** the fine light wool or cloth obtained from this animal. [C17: from Spanish *vicuña,* from Quechuan *wikúña*]

vi·de ('vaɪdɪ) (used to direct a reader to a specified place in a text, another book, etc.) refer to, see (often in the phrases **vide ante** (see before), **vide infra** (see below), **vide post** (see after), **vide supra** (see above), **vide ut supra** (see as above), etc.). Abbrev.: **v., vid.** [C16: from Latin]

vi+de·li+cet (vɪ'di:lɪˌsɛt) *adv.* namely: used to specify items, examples, etc. Abbrev.: **viz.** [C15: from Latin]

vid·e·o ('vɪdɪˌəʊ) *adj.* **1.** relating to or employed in the transmission or reception of a televised image. **2.** of, concerned with, or operating at video frequencies. ~*n., pl.* **·os. 3.** the visual elements of a television broadcast. **4.** *Informal.* the quality of the visual image in a television. **5.** *U.S.* an informal name for **television.** ~Compare **audio.** [C20: from Latin *vidēre* to see, on the model of AUDIO]

vid·e·o fre+quen+cy *n.* the frequency of a signal conveying the image and synchronizing pulses in a television broadcasting system. It lies in the range from about 50 hertz to 5 megahertz.

vid·e·o+phone ('vɪdɪəˌfəʊn) *n.* a telephonic device in which there is both verbal and visual communication between parties. —**vid+e·o+phon+ic** (ˌvɪdɪə'fɒnɪk) *adj.*

vid·e·o tape *n.* **1.** magnetic tape used mainly for recording the video-frequency signals of a television programme or film for subsequent transmission. ~*vb.* **vid·e·o-tape. 2.** to record (a programme, etc.) on video tape.

vi+dette (vɪ'dɛt) *n.* a variant spelling of **vedette.**

Vi+dhan Sa+bha (vɪ'dɑ:n 'sʌbə) *n.* the legislative assembly of any of the states of India. [Hindi, from *vidhan* law + *sabha* assembly]

vid·i·con ('vɪdɪˌkɒn) *n.* a small television camera tube, used in closed-circuit television and outside broadcasts, in which incident light forms an electric charge pattern on a photoconductive surface. Scanning by a low-velocity electron beam discharges the surface, producing a current in an adjacent conducting layer. See also **plumbicon.** [C20: from VID(EO) + ICON(OSCOPE)]

vie (vaɪ) *vb.* **vies, vy+ing, vied. 1.** (*intr.;* foll. by *with* or *for*) to contend for superiority or victory (with) or strive in competition (for). **2.** (*tr.*) *Archaic.* to offer, exchange, or display in rivalry. [C15: probably from Old French *envier* to challenge, from Latin *invītāre* to INVITE] —'**vi·er** *n.* —'**vy+ing** *adj., n.* —'**vy+ing+ly** *adv.*

Vi+en+na (vɪ'ɛnə) *n.* **1.** the capital of Austria, in the northeast on the River Danube: seat of the Hapsburgs (1278–1918); residence of the Holy Roman Emperor (1558–1806); withstood sieges by Turks in 1529 and 1683; political and cultural centre in the 18th and 19th centuries, having associations with many composers; university (1365). Pop.: 1 614 841 (1971). German name: **Wien. 2.** a province of NE Austria: the smallest Austrian province. Pop.: 1 614 841 (1971). Area: 1215 sq. km (469 sq. miles).

Vi+en+na Un+ion *or* **In+ter+na+tion+al** *n.* **the.** an international conference of socialists who came together in Vienna in 1921 in an attempt to reconstruct a united International by offering an alternative to the right-wing remnant of the Second International and to the Comintern: merged into the Labour and Socialist International in 1923. Also called: **Two-and-a-half International.**

Vienne (*French* vjɛn) *n.* **1.** a department of W central France, in Poitou-Charentes region. Capital: Poitiers. Pop.: 366 530 (1975). Area: 7044 sq. km (2747 sq. miles). **2.** a town in SE France, on the River Rhône: extensive Roman remains. Pop.: 28 000 (1968 est.). Ancient name: **Vienna. 3.** a river in SW central France, flowing west and north to the Loire below Chinon. Length: over 350 km (200 miles).

Vi+en+nese (ˌvɪə'ni:z) *adj.* **1.** of, relating to, or characteristic of Vienna. ~*n., pl.* **+nese. 2.** a native or inhabitant of Vienna.

Vien+ti+ane (ˌvjɛntɪ'ɑ:n) *n.* the administrative capital of Laos, in the south near the border with Thailand: capital of the kingdom of Vientiane from 1707 until taken by the Thais in 1827. Pop.: 174 000 (1973 est.).

Vier+wald+stät+ter+see (ˌfi:r'valtʃtɛtərˌze:) *n.* the German name of (Lake) **Lucerne.**

vi et ar+mis *Latin.* ('vaɪ ɛt 'ɑ:mɪs) *n. Legal history.* a kind of trespass accompanied by force and violence. [literally: by force and arms]

Vi+et+cong (ˌvjɛt'kɒŋ) *or* **Vi·et Cong** *n.* (in the Vietnam war) **1.** the Communist-led guerrilla force and revolutionary army of South Vietnam; the armed forces of the National Liberation Front of South Vietnam. **2.** a member of these armed forces. **3.** (*modifier*) of or relating to the Vietcong or a Vietcong. [from Vietnamese *Viet Nam Cong San* Vietnamese Communist]

Vi+et+minh (ˌvjɛt'mɪn) *or* **Vi·et Minh** *n.* **1.** a Vietnamese organization led by Ho Chi Minh that first fought the Japanese and then the French (1941–54) in their attempt to achieve national independence. 2. a member or group of members of this organization, esp. in the armed forces. 3. (*modifier*) of or relating to this organization or to its members. [from Vietnamese *Viet Nam Doc Lap Dong Minh Hoi* Vietnam League of Independence]

Vi·et·nam (ˌvjɛtˈnæm) *or* **Vi·et Nam** *n.* a republic in SE Asia: an ancient empire, conquered by France in the 19th century; occupied by Japan (1940–45) when the Communist-led Viet Minh began resistance operations that were continued against restored French rule after 1945. In 1954 the country was divided along the 17th parallel, establishing North Vietnam (under the Viet Minh) and South Vietnam (under French control), the latter becoming the independent **Republic of Vietnam** in 1955. From 1959 the country was dominated by war between the Communist Viet Cong, supported by North Vietnam, and the South Vietnamese government; increasing numbers of U.S. forces were brought to the aid of the South Vietnamese army until a peace agreement (1973) led to the withdrawal of U.S. troops; further fighting led to the eventual defeat of the South Vietnamese government in March 1975 and in 1976 an elected National Assembly proclaimed the reunification of the country. Language: Vietnamese. Currency: dong. Capital: Hanoi. Pop.: 46 520 000 (1976 est.). Area: 337 870 sq. km (130 452 sq. miles). Official name: **Socialist Republic of Vietnam.**

Vi·et·nam·ese (ˌvjɛtnəˈmiːz) *adj.* 1. of, relating to, or characteristic of Vietnam, its people, or their language. ~*n., pl.* **·ese.** 2. a native or inhabitant of Vietnam. 3. the language of Vietnam, the relationships of which have not been definitely established, although it is believed by some to belong to the Mon-Khmer family.

Vi·et·nam·i·za·tion *or* **Vi·et·nam·i·sa·tion** (vɪˌɛtnəmaɪˈzeɪʃən, ˌvjɛt-) *n.* (in the Vietnam War) a U.S. government policy of transferring the tasks of fighting and directing the war to the government and forces of South Vietnam.

view (vjuː) *n.* 1. the act of seeing or observing; an inspection. 2. vision or sight, esp. range of vision: *the church is out of view.* 3. a scene, esp. of a fine tract of countryside: *the view from the top was superb.* 4. a pictorial representation of a scene, such as a photograph. 5. (*sometimes pl.*) opinion; thought: *my own view on the matter differs from yours.* 6. chance or expectation: *the policy has little view of success.* 7. (foll. by *to*) a desired end or intention: *he has a view to securing further qualifications.* 8. a general survey of a topic, subject, etc.: *a comprehensive view of Shakespearean literature.* 9. visual aspect or appearance: *they look the same in outward view.* 10. *Law.* **a.** a formal inspection by a jury of the place where an alleged crime was committed. **b.** a formal inspection of property in dispute. 11. a sight of a hunted animal before or during the chase. 12. **in view of.** taking into consideration. 13. **on view.** exhibited to the public gaze. 14. **take a dim** *or* **poor view of.** to regard (something) with disfavour or disapproval. 15. **with a view to. a.** with the intention of. **b.** in anticipation or hope of. ~*vb.* 16. (*tr.*) to look at. 17. (*tr.*) to consider in a specified manner: *they view the growth of Communism with horror.* 18. to examine or inspect carefully: *to view the accounts.* 19. (*tr.*) to survey mentally; contemplate: *to view the difficulties.* 20. to watch (television). 21. (*tr.*) to sight (a hunted animal) before or during the chase. [C15: from Old French *veue,* from *veoir* to see, from Latin *vidēre*] —**ˈview·a·ble** *adj.*

view·er (ˈvjuːə) *n.* 1. a person who views something, esp. television. 2. any optical device by means of which something is viewed, esp. one used for viewing photographic transparencies. 3. *Law.* a person appointed by a court to inspect and report upon property, etc.

view·find·er (ˈvjuːˌfaɪndə) *n.* a device on a camera, consisting of a lens system and sometimes a ground-glass screen, enabling the user to see what will be included in his photograph. Sometimes shortened to **finder.**

view hal·loo *interj.* 1. a huntsman's cry uttered when the quarry is seen breaking cover or shortly afterwards. ~*n.* 2. a shout indicating an abrupt appearance.

view·ing (ˈvjuːɪŋ) *n.* 1. the act of watching television. 2. television programmes collectively: *late-night viewing.*

view·less (ˈvjuːlɪs) *adj.* 1. (of windows, etc.) not affording a view. 2. having no opinions. 3. *Poetic.* invisible.

view·point (ˈvjuːˌpɔɪnt) *n.* 1. the mental attitude that determines a person's opinions or judgments; point of view. 2. a place from which something can be viewed.

view·y (ˈvjuːɪ) *adj.* **view·i·er, view·i·est.** *Informal, rare.* 1. having fanciful opinions or ideas; visionary. 2. characterized by ostentation; showy. —**ˈview·i·ness** *n.*

vi·ges·i·mal (vaɪˈdʒɛsɪməl) *adj.* 1. relating to or based on the number 20. 2. taking place or proceeding in intervals of 20. 3. twentieth. [C17: from Latin *vīgēsimus,* variant (influenced by *vīgintī* twenty) of *vīcēsimus* twentieth]

vig·il (ˈvɪdʒɪl) *n.* 1. a purposeful watch maintained, esp. at night, to guard, observe, pray, etc. 2. the period of such a watch. 3. *R.C. Church, Church of England.* the eve of certain major festivals, formerly observed as a night spent in prayer: often marked by fasting and abstinence and a special Mass and divine office. 4. a period of sleeplessness; insomnia. [C13: from Old French *vigile,* from Medieval Latin *vigilia* watch preceding a religious festival, from Latin: vigilance, from *vigil* alert, from *vigēre* to be lively]

vig·i·lance (ˈvɪdʒɪləns) *n.* 1. the fact, quality, or condition of being vigilant. 2. the abnormal state or condition of being unable to sleep.

vig·i·lance com·mit·tee *n.* (in the U.S.) a self-appointed body of citizens organized to maintain order, etc., where an efficient system of courts does not exist.

vig·i·lant (ˈvɪdʒɪlənt) *adj.* keenly alert to or heedful of trouble or danger, as while others are sleeping or unsuspicious. [C15: from Latin *vigilāns* keeping awake, from *vigilāre* to be watchful; see VIGIL] —**ˈvig·i·lant·ly** *adv.* —**ˈvig·i·lant·ness** *n.*

vig·i·lan·te (ˌvɪdʒɪˈlæntɪ) *n.* a member of a vigilance committee. Also called: **vigilance man.** [C19: from Spanish, from Latin *vigilāre* to keep watch]

vig·i·lan·tism (ˌvɪdʒɪˈlæntɪzəm) *n. U.S.* the methods, conduct, attitudes, etc., associated with vigilantes, esp. militancy, bigotry, or suspiciousness.

vig·il light *n. Chiefly R.C. Church.* 1. a small candle lit as an act of personal devotion before a shrine or statue, usually in a church. 2. a small lamp kept permanently burning before such a shrine or statue.

vi·gnette (vɪˈnjɛt) *n.* 1. a small illustration placed at the beginning or end of a book or chapter. 2. a short graceful literary essay or sketch. 3. a photograph, drawing, etc., with edges that are shaded off. 4. *Architect.* a carved ornamentation that has a design based upon tendrils, leaves, etc. 5. any small endearing scene, view, picture, etc. ~*vb.* (*tr.*) 6. to finish (a photograph, etc.) with a fading border in the form of a vignette. 7. **a.** to decorate with vignettes. **b.** to portray in or as in a vignette. [C18: from French, literally: little vine, from *vigne* VINE; with reference to the vine motif frequently used in embellishments to a text] —**vi·ˈgnet·tist** *n.*

vi·gnet·ting (vɪˈnjɛtɪŋ) *n.* 1. the technique of producing a photographic vignette, esp. a portrait, by progressively reducing the amount of light falling on the photographic surface towards the edges. 2. the reduction in area of a light beam passing through a camera lens as the obliquity of the beam is increased.

Vi·gno·la (*Italian* viɲˈɲɔːla) *n.* **Gia·co·mo Ba·roz·zi da** (ˈdʒaːkomo baˈrɔttsi da). 1507–73, Italian architect, whose cruciform design for Il Gesù, Rome, greatly influenced later Church architecture.

Vi·gny (*French* viˈɲi) *n.* **Al·fred Vic·tor de** (alfrɛd vikˈtɔːr də). 1797–1863, French romantic poet, novelist, and dramatist, noted for his pessimistic lyric verse *Poèmes antiques et modernes* (1826) and *Les Destinées* (1864), the novel *Cinq-Mars* (1826), and the play *Chatterton* (1835).

Vi·go (ˈviːgəʊ; *Spanish* ˈbiɣo) *n.* a port in NW Spain, in Galicia on **Vigo Bay** (an inlet of the Atlantic): site of a British and Dutch naval victory (1702) over the French and Spanish. Pop.: 197 144 (1970).

vig·or·ous (ˈvɪgərəs) *adj.* 1. endowed with bodily or mental strength or vitality; robust. 2. displaying, involving, characterized by, or performed with vigour: *vigorous growth.* —**ˈvig·or·ous·ly** *adv.* —**ˈvig·or·ous·ness** *n.*

vig·our *or U.S.* **vig·or** (ˈvɪgə) *n.* 1. exuberant and resilient strength of body or mind; vitality. 2. substantial effective energy or force: *the vigour of the tempest.* 3. forcefulness; intensity: *I was surprised by the vigour of her complaints.* 4. the capacity for survival or strong healthy growth in a plant or animal: *hybrid vigour.* 5. the most active period or stage of life, manhood, etc.; prime. 6. *Chiefly U.S.* legal force or effectiveness; validity (esp. in the phrase **in vigour**). [C14: from Old French *vigeur,* from Latin *vigor* activity, from *vigēre* to be lively]

vi·hue·la (*Spanish* biˈwela) *n.* 1. an obsolete plucked stringed instrument of Spain, related to the guitar. [from Spanish]

Vii·pu·ri (ˈviːpuri) *n.* the Finnish name for **Vyborg.**

Vi·jay·a·wa·da (ˌviːdʒaɪəˈwɑːdə) *n.* a town in SE India, in E central Andra Pradesh on the Krishna River: Hindu pilgrimage centre. Pop.:317 258 (1971). Former name: **Bezwada.**

Vi·king (ˈvaɪkɪŋ) *n.* (*sometimes not cap.*) 1. Also called: **Norseman, Northman.** any of the Danes, Norwegians, and Swedes who raided by sea most of N and W Europe from the 8th to the 11th centuries, later often settling, as in parts of Britain. 2. any sea rover, plunderer, or pirate. 3. either of two unmanned American spacecraft designed to orbit Mars. 4. (*modifier*) of, relating to, or characteristic of a Viking or Vikings: *a Viking ship.* [C19: from Old Norse *víkingr,* probably from *vík* creek, sea inlet + *-ingr* (see -ING[3]); perhaps related to Old English *wīc* camp]

vil. *abbrev. for* village.

vi·la·yet (vɪˈlɑːjɛt) *n.* a major administrative division of Turkey. [C19: from Turkish, from Arabic *wilāyat,* from *walīy* governor]

vile (vaɪl) *adj.* 1. abominably wicked; shameful or evil: *the vile development of slavery appalled them.* 2. morally despicable; ignoble: *vile accusations.* 3. disgusting to the senses or emotions; foul: *a vile smell; vile epithets.* 4. tending to humiliate or degrade: *only slaves would perform such vile tasks.* 5. unpleasant or bad: *vile weather.* 6. paltry: *a vile reward.* [C13: from Old French *vil,* from Latin *vīlis* cheap] —**ˈvile·ly** *adv.* —**ˈvile·ness** *n.*

vil·i·fy (ˈvɪlɪˌfaɪ) *vb.* **·fies, ·fy·ing, ·fied.** (*tr.*) 1. to revile with abusive or defamatory language; malign. 2. *Rare.* to make vile; debase; degrade. [C15: from Late Latin *vīlificāre,* from Latin *vīlis* worthless + *facere* to make] —**vil·i·fi·ca·tion** (ˌvɪlɪfɪˈkeɪʃən) *n.* —**ˈvil·i·ˌfi·er** *n.*

vil·i·pend (ˈvɪlɪˌpɛnd) *vb.* (*tr.*) *Rare.* 1. to treat or regard with contempt. 2. to speak slanderously or slightingly of. [C15: from Late Latin *vīlipendere,* from Latin *vīlis* worthless + *pendere* to esteem] —**ˈvil·i·ˌpend·er** *n.*

vil·la (ˈvɪlə) *n.* 1. (in ancient Rome) a country house, usually consisting of farm buildings and residential quarters around a courtyard. 2. a large and usually luxurious country residence. **3.** *Brit.* a detached or semidetached suburban house. [C17: via Italian from Latin; related to Latin *vīcus* a village] —**'vil·la+,like** *adj.*

Vi·lla ('viːə; *Spanish* 'biʎa) *n.* **Fran·cis·co** (fran'sisko), called *Pancho Villa,* original name *Doroteo Arango.* ?1877–1923, Mexican revolutionary leader.

Vil+lach (*German* 'fɪlax) *n.* a city in S central Austria, on the Drava River: nearby hot mineral springs. Pop.: 34 595 (1971).

vil+lage ('vɪlɪdʒ) *n.* **1.** a small group of houses in a country area, larger than a hamlet. **2.** the inhabitants of such a community collectively. **3.** an incorporated municipality smaller than a town in various parts of the U.S. and Canada. **4.** a group of habitats of certain animals. **5.** (*modifier*) of, relating to, or characteristic of a village: *a village green.* [C15: from Old French, from *ville* farm, from Latin: VILLA] —**'vil·lage-,like** *adj.*

vil+lage col+lege *n. Brit.* a centre, often for a group of villages, with educational and recreational facilities for the whole neighbourhood. Also called: **community college.**

vil+lag+er ('vɪlɪdʒə) *n.* **1.** an inhabitant of a village. ~*adj.* **2.** *East African.* backward, unsophisticated, or illiterate.

Vil+la+her+mo+sa (*Spanish* ,biʎaer'mosa) *n.* a town in E Mexico, capital of Tabasco state: university (1959). Pop.: 142 384 (1974 est.). Former name: **San Juan Bautista.**

vil+lain ('vɪlən) *n.* **1.** a wicked or malevolent person. **2.** (in a novel, play, film, etc.) the main evil character and antagonist to the hero. **3.** *Often jocular.* a mischievous person; rogue. **4.** *Brit. police slang.* a criminal. **5.** *History.* a variant spelling of **villein. 6.** *Obsolete.* an uncouth person; boor. [C14: from Old French *vilein* serf, from Late Latin *vīllānus* worker on a country estate, from Latin: VILLA] —**'vil+lain+ess** *fem. n.*

vil+lain+age ('vɪlənɪdʒ) *n.* a variant spelling of **villeinage.**

vil+lain+ous ('vɪlənəs) *adj.* **1.** of, like, or appropriate to a villain. **2.** very bad or disagreeable: *a villainous climate.* —**'vil+lain+ous+ly** *adv.* —**'vil+lain+ous+ness** *n.*

vil+lain·y ('vɪlənɪ) *n., pl.* **·lain·ies. 1.** conduct befitting a villain; vicious behaviour or action. **2.** an evil, abhorrent, or criminal act or deed. **3.** the fact or condition of being villainous. **4.** *English history.* a rare word for **villeinage.**

Vil·la-Lo·bos ('viːlɑː 'ləubɒs, 'vɪlə; *Portuguese* 'vila 'lobus) *n.* **Hei·tor** (ej'tor). 1887–1959, Brazilian composer, much of whose work is based on Brazilian folk tunes.

vil+la+nel+la (,vɪlə'nɛlə) *n., pl.* **+las.** a type of part song originating in Naples during the 16th century. [C16: from Italian, from *villano* rustic, from Late Latin *vīllānus;* see VILLAIN]

vil+la+nelle (,vɪlə'nɛl) *n.* a verse form of French origin consisting of 19 lines arranged in five tercets and a quatrain. The first and third lines of the first tercet recur alternately at the end of each subsequent tercet and both together at the end of the quatrain. [C16: from French, from Italian VILLANELLA]

Vil+la+no+van (,vɪlə'nəuvᵊn) *adj.* **1.** of or relating to an early Iron Age culture near Bologna, Italy, characterized by the use of bronze and the primitive use of iron. ~*n.* **2.** a member of this culture. [C19: named after the NE Italian town of *Villanova,* where the first remains of the culture were excavated in 1853]

Vil·lars (*French* vi'laːr) *n.* **Claude Louis Hec·tor de** (kloːd lwi ɛk'tɔːr də). 1653–1734, French marshal, distinguished for his command in the War of the Spanish Succession (1701–14).

vil+lat+ic (vɪ'lætɪk) *adj. Literary.* of or relating to a villa, village, or farm; rustic; rural. [C17: from Latin *vīllāticus,* from *villa* a farm]

-ville *n. Slang, chiefly U.S.* (*in combination*) a place, condition, or quality with a character as specified: *dragsville; squaresville.*

vil+lein *or* **vil+lain** ('vɪlən) *n.* (in medieval Europe) a peasant personally bound to his lord, to whom he paid dues and services, sometimes commuted to rents, in return for his land. [C14: from Old French *vilein* serf; see VILLAIN]

vil+lein+age *or* **vil+lain+age** ('vɪlənɪdʒ) *n.* (in medieval Europe) **1.** the status and condition of a villein. **2.** the tenure by which a villein held his land.

Ville·neuve (*French* vil'nœːv) *n.* **Pierre Charles Jean Bap·tiste Sil·ves·tre de** (pjɛːr ʃarl ʒɑ̃ batist sil'vɛstr də). 1763–1806, French admiral, defeated by Nelson at the Battle of Trafalgar (1805).

Ville+ur+banne (*French* vilœr'ban) *n.* a town in E France: an industrial suburb of E Lyons. Pop.: 119 438 (1975).

vil+li ('vɪlaɪ) *pl. n.* the plural of **villus.**

Vil·liers ('vɪləz, 'vɪljəz) *n.* **George.** See (Dukes of) **Buckingham.**

Vil·liers de l'Isle A·dam (*French* vilje də lil a'dɑ̃) *n.* **Au·gust, Comte de** (o'gyst, 'kɔ̃ːt də). 1838–89, French poet and dramatist; pioneer of the symbolist movement. His works include *Contes cruels* (1883) and the play *Axel* (1885).

vil+li+form ('vɪlɪ,fɔːm) *adj.* having the form of a villus or a series of villi. [C19: from New Latin *villiformis,* from Latin *villus* shaggy hair + -FORM]

Vil·lon (*French* vi'jɔ̃) *n.* **1. Fran·çois** (frɑ̃'swa). born 1431, French poet. His poems, such as those in *Le Petit Testament* (?1456) and *Le Grand Testament* (1461), are mostly ballades and rondeaus, verse forms that he revitalized. He was banished in 1463, after which nothing more was heard of him. **2. Jacques** (ʒɑːk). pseudonym of *Gaston Duchamp.* 1875–1963, French cubist painter and engraver.

vil+los+i·ty (vɪ'lɒsɪtɪ) *n., pl.* **·ties. 1.** the state of being villous. **2.** a villous coating or surface. **3.** a villus or a collection of villi.

vil+lous ('vɪləs) *adj.* **1.** (of plant parts) covered with long hairs. **2.** of, relating to, or having villi. [C14: from Latin *villōsus,* from *villus* tuft of hair] —**'vil+lous+ly** *adv.*

vil+lus ('vɪləs) *n., pl.* **vil+li** ('vɪlaɪ). (*usually pl.*) **1.** *Zoology, anatomy.* any of the numerous finger-like projections of the mucous membrane lining the small intestine of many vertebrates. **2.** any similar membranous process, such as any of those in the mammalian placenta. **3.** *Botany.* any of various hairlike outgrowths, as from the stem of a moss. [C18: from Latin: shaggy hair]

Vil+ni+us *or* **Vil+ny+us** ('vɪlnɪus) *n.* a city in the W Soviet Union, capital of the Lithuanian SSR: passed to Russia in 1795; under Polish rule (1920–39); university (1578). Pop.: 433 000 (1975 est.). Russian name: **Vil+na** ('vilna). Polish name: **Wilno.**

vim (vɪm) *n. Slang.* exuberant vigour and energy. [C19: from Latin, from *vīs;* related to Greek *is* strength]

vi+men ('vaɪmɛn) *n., pl.* **vim·i·na** ('vɪmɪnə). a long flexible shoot that occurs in certain plants. [C19: from Latin: a pliant twig, osier]

Vim·i+nal ('vɪmɪnᵊl) *n.* one of the seven hills on which ancient Rome was built. [from Latin *Vīminālis Collis* the Viminal Hill, from *vīminālis* of osiers, from *vīmen* an osier, referring to the willow grove on the hill]

vi+min+e·ous (vɪ'mɪnɪəs) *adj. Botany.* having, producing, or resembling long flexible shoots. [C17: from Latin *vīmineus* made of osiers, from *vīmen* flexible shoot]

vin- *combining form.* variant of **vini-** before a vowel.

vi·na ('viːnə) *n.* a stringed musical instrument, esp. of India, related to the sitar. [C18: from Hindi *bīnā,* from Sanskrit *vīnā*]

vi+na+ceous (vaɪ'neɪʃəs) *adj.* **1.** of, relating to, or containing wine. **2.** having a colour suggestive of red wine. [C17: from Late Latin *vīnāceus,* from Latin *vīnum* wine]

Vi·ña del Mar (*Spanish* 'biɲa ðel 'mar) *n.* a city and resort in central Chile, just north of Valparaíso on the Pacific. Pop.: 229 020 (1975 est.).

vin·ai+grette (,vɪneɪ'grɛt) *n.* **1.** Also called: **vinegarette.** a small decorative bottle or box with a perforated top, used for holding smelling salts, etc. **2.** Also called: **vinaigrette sauce.** a French dressing to which have been added chives, onions, etc., used esp. with salads. ~*adj.* **3.** served with vinaigrette. [C17: from French, from *vinaigre* VINEGAR]

vi+nasse (vɪ'næs) *n.* the residue left in a still after distilling spirits, esp. brandy. [C20: from French]

Vin+cennes (*French* vɛ̃'sɛn; *English* vɪn'sɛnz) *n.* a suburb of E Paris: 14th-century castle. Pop.: 44 467 (1975).

Vin·cent de Paul ('vɪnsənt də 'pɔːl; *French* vɛ̃sɑ̃ də 'pɔl) *n.* **Saint.** ?1581–1660, French Roman Catholic priest, who founded two charitable orders, the Lazarists (1625) and the Sisters of Charity (1634). Feast day: July 19.

Vin·cent's an+gi+na *or* **dis+ease** *n.* an ulcerative bacterial infection of the mouth, esp. involving the throat and tonsils. [C20: named after J. H. *Vincent* (died 1950), French bacteriologist]

Vin·ci ('vɪntʃɪ) *n.* See **Leonardo da Vinci.**

vin+ci·ble ('vɪnsɪbᵊl) *adj. Rare.* capable of being defeated or overcome. [C16: from Latin *vincibilis,* from *vincere* to conquer] —**,vin+ci·'bil+i·ty** *or* **'vin+ci·ble+ness** *n.*

vin+cu+lum ('vɪŋkjələm) *n., pl.* **+la** (-lə). **1.** a horizontal line drawn above a group of mathematical terms, used as a sign of aggregation in mathematical expressions, as in $\overline{x + y}$. **2.** *Anatomy.* **a.** any bandlike structure, esp. one uniting two or more parts. **b.** another name for **ligament. 3.** *Rare.* a unifying bond; tie. [C17: from Latin: bond, from *vincīre* to bind]

Vin+dhya Pra+desh ('vɪndjə) *n.* a former state of central India: merged with the reorganized Madhya Pradesh in 1956.

Vin+dhya Range *or* **Moun+tains** *n.* a mountain range in central India: separates the Ganges basin from the Deccan, marking the limits of northern and peninsular India. Greatest height: 1113 m (3651 ft.).

vin+di+ca·ble ('vɪndɪkəbᵊl) *adj.* capable of being vindicated; justifiable. —**,vin+di+ca·'bil+i·ty** *n.*

vin+di+cate ('vɪndɪ,keɪt) *vb.* (*tr.*) **1.** to clear from guilt, accusation, blame, etc., as by evidence or argument. **2.** to provide justification for: *his promotion vindicated his unconventional attitude.* **3.** to uphold, maintain, or defend (a cause, etc.): *to vindicate a claim.* **4.** *Roman law.* to bring an action to regain possession of (property) under claim of legal title. **5.** *Rare.* to claim, as for oneself or another. **6.** *Obsolete.* to take revenge on or for; punish. **7.** *Obsolete.* to set free. [C17: from Latin *vindicāre,* from *vindex* claimant] —**'vin+di+,ca+tor** *n.* —**'vin+di+,ca·to·ry** *adj.*

vin+di+ca+tion (,vɪndɪ'keɪʃən) *n.* **1.** the act of vindicating or the condition of being vindicated. **2.** a means of exoneration from an accusation. **3.** a fact, evidence, circumstance, etc., that serves to vindicate a theory or claim.

vin+dic+tive (vɪn'dɪktɪv) *adj.* **1.** disposed to seek vengeance. **2.** characterized by spite or rancour. **3.** *English law.* (of damages) in excess of the compensation due to the plaintiff and imposed in punishment of the defendant. [C17: from Latin *vindicta* revenge, from *vindicāre* to VINDICATE] —**vin+'dic+tive+ly** *adv.* —**vin+'dic+tive+ness** *n.*

vine (vaɪn) *n.* **1.** any of various plants, esp. the grapevine, having long flexible stems that creep along the ground or climb by clinging to a support by means of tendrils, leafstalks, etc. **2.** the stem of such a plant. [C13: from Old French *vine,* from Latin *vīnea* vineyard, from *vīneus* belonging to wine, from *vīnum* wine] —**vined** *adj.* —**'vine+less** *adj.* —**'vine+,like** *adj.* —**'vin·y** *adj.*

vine+dress·er ('vaɪn,drɛsə) *n.* a person who prunes, tends, or cultivates grapevines.

vin+e·gar ('vɪnɪgə) *n.* **1.** a sour-tasting liquid consisting of impure dilute acetic acid, made by oxidation of the ethyl alcohol in beer, wine, or cider. It is used as a condiment or preservative. **2.** sourness or peevishness of temper, countenance, speech, etc. **3.** *Pharmacol.* a medicinal solution in dilute acetic acid. **4.** *U.S. informal.* vitality. ~*vb.* **5.** (*tr.*) to apply vinegar to. [C13: from Old French *vinaigre*, from *vin* WINE + *aigre* sour, from Latin *acer* sharp] —**'vin·e·gar·ish** *adj.* —**'vin·e·gar-,like** *adj.* —**'vin·e·gar·y** *adj.*

vin·e·gar eel *n.* a nematode worm, *Anguillula aceti*, that feeds on the organisms that cause fermentation in vinegar and other liquids. Also called: **vinegar worm, eelworm.**

vin·e·gar·ette (,vɪnɪgə'rɛt) *n.* a variant spelling of **vinaigrette** (sense 1).

vin·e·gar fly *n.* any of various dipterous flies of the genus *Drosophila*. See **drosophila.**

vin·e·gar·roon (,vɪnɪgə'ru:n) *n.* a large whip scorpion, *Mastigoproctus giganteus*, of the southwestern U.S. and Mexico that emits a vinegary odour when alarmed. [from Mexican Spanish *vinagrón*, from Spanish *vinagre* VINEGAR]

Vine·land ('vaɪnlənd) *n.* a variant spelling of **Vinland.**

vin·er·y ('vaɪnərɪ) *n., pl.* **·er·ies. 1.** a hothouse for growing grapes. **2.** another name for a **vineyard. 3.** vines collectively.

vine·yard ('vɪnjəd) *n.* a plantation of grapevines, esp. where wine grapes are produced. [Old English *wīngeard*; see VINE, YARD²; related to Old High German *wīngart*, Old Norse *vingarthr*] —**'vine·yard·ist** *n.*

vingt-et-un *French.* (vɛ̃te'œ̃) *n.* another name for **pontoon².** [literally: twenty-one]

vin·i- *or before a vowel* **vin-** *combining form.* indicating wine: *viniculture.* [from Latin *vīnum*]

vi·nic ('vaɪnɪk, 'vɪnɪk) *adj.* of, relating to, or contained in wine. [C19: from Latin *vīnum* wine]

vin·i·cul·ture ('vɪnɪ,kʌltʃə) *n.* the process or business of growing grapes and making wine. —**,vin·i·'cul·tur·al** *adj.* —**,vin·i·'cul·tur·ist** *n.*

vi·nif·er·ous (vɪ'nɪfərəs) *adj.* wine-producing.

vi·nif·i·ca·tor ('vɪnɪfɪ,keɪtə) *n.* a condenser that collects the alcohol vapour escaping from fermenting wine. [C19: from Latin *vīnum* wine + *facere* to make]

Vin·land ('vɪnlənd) *or* **Vine·land** ('vaɪnlənd) *n.* the stretch of the E coast of North America visited by Leif Ericson and other Vikings from about 1000.

Vin·ni·tsa (*Russian* 'vinnitsə) *n.* a city in the SW Soviet Union, in the central Ukrainian SSR: passed from Polish to Russian rule in 1793. Pop.: 277 000 (1975 est.).

vi·no ('vi:nəʊ) *n., pl.* **·nos.** an informal word for **wine.** [jocular use of Italian or Spanish *vino*]

vin or·di·naire *French.* (vɛ̃ ɔrdi'nɛ:r) *n., pl.* ***vins or·di·naires*** (vɛ̃ zɔrdi'nɛ:r). cheap table wine, esp. French.

vi·nos·i·ty (vɪ'nɒsɪtɪ) *n.* the distinctive and essential quality and flavour of wine. [C17: from Late Latin *vīnōsitas*, from Latin *vīnōsus*, VINOUS]

vi·nous ('vaɪnəs) *adj.* **1.** of, relating to, or characteristic of wine. **2.** indulging in or indicative of indulgence in wine: *a vinous complexion.* [C17: from Latin *vīnōsus*, from *vīnum* WINE]

vin·tage ('vɪntɪdʒ) *n.* **1.** the wine obtained from a harvest of grapes, esp. in an outstandingly good year, referred to by the year involved, the district, or the vineyard. **2.** the harvest from which such a wine is obtained. **3. a.** the harvesting of wine grapes. **b.** the season of harvesting these grapes or for making wine. **4.** a time of origin: *a car of Edwardian vintage.* **5.** *Informal.* a group of contemporary people or objects: *a fashion of last season's vintage.* ~*adj.* **6.** (of wine) of an outstandingly good year. **7.** representative of the best and most typical: *vintage Shakespeare.* **8.** of lasting interest and importance; venerable; classic: *vintage sculpture.* **9.** old-fashioned; dated. ~*vb.* **10.** (*tr.*) to gather (grapes) or make (wine). [C15: from Old French *vendage* (influenced by *vintener* VINTNER), from Latin *vindēmia*, from *vīnum* WINE, grape + *dēmere* to take away (from *dē-* away + *emere* to take)]

vin·tage car *n. Chiefly Brit.* an old car, esp. one constructed between 1919 and 1930. Compare **veteran car.**

vin·tag·er ('vɪntɪdʒə) *n.* a grape harvester.

vint·ner ('vɪntnə) *n.* a wine merchant. [C15: from Old French *vinetier*, from Medieval Latin *vīnētārius*, from Latin *vīnētum* vineyard, from *vīnum* WINE]

vi·nyl ('vaɪnɪl) *n.* **1.** (*modifier*) of, consisting of, or containing the monovalent group of atoms CH_2CH-: *a vinyl polymer; vinyl chloride.* **2.** (*modifier*) of, consisting of, or made of a vinyl resin: *a vinyl raincoat.* **3.** any vinyl polymer, resin, or plastic, esp. PVC. [C19: from VINI- + -YL]

vi·nyl ac·e·tate *n.* a colourless volatile liquid unsaturated ester that polymerizes readily in light and is used for making polyvinyl acetate. Formula: CH_2:$CHOOCCH_3$.

vi·nyl chlo·ride *n.* a colourless flammable gaseous unsaturated compound made by the chlorination of ethylene and used as a refrigerant and in the manufacture of PVC; chloroethylene; chloroethene. Formula: CH_2:$CHCl$.

vi·nyl·i·dene (vaɪ'nɪlɪ,di:n) *n.* (*modifier*) of, consisting of, or containing the group CH_2:C: *a vinylidene group or radical; vinylidene chloride; a vinylidene resin.*

vi·nyl res·in *or* **pol·y·mer** *n.* any one of a class of thermoplastic materials, esp. PVC and polyvinyl acetate, made by polymerizing vinyl compounds.

vi·ol ('vaɪəl) *n.* any of a family of stringed musical instruments that preceded the violin family, consisting of a fretted fingerboard, a body rather like that of a violin but having a flat back and six strings, played with a curved bow. They are held between the knees when played and have a quiet yet penetrating tone; they were much played, esp. in consorts, in the 16th and 17th centuries. [C15: from Old French *viole*, from Old Provençal *viola*; see VIOLA¹]

vi·o·la¹ (vɪ'əʊlə) *n.* **1.** a bowed stringed instrument, the alto of the violin family; held beneath the chin when played. It is pitched and tuned an octave above the cello. **2.** any of various instruments of the viol family, such as the viola da gamba. [C18: from Italian *viola*, probably from Old Provençal *viola*, of uncertain origin; perhaps related to Latin *vītulārī* to rejoice]

vi·o·la² ('vaɪələ, vaɪ'əʊ-) *n.* any temperate perennial herbaceous plant of the violaceous genus *Viola*, the flowers of which have showy irregular petals, white, yellow, blue, or mauve in colour. See also **violet** (sense 1), **pansy** (sense 1). [C15: from Latin: violet]

vi·o·la·ceous (,vaɪə'leɪʃəs) *adj.* **1.** of, relating to, or belonging to the *Violaceae*, a family of herbaceous plants and shrubs including the violets and pansies. **2.** of the colour violet. [C17: from Latin *violāceus*, from *viola* VIOLET]

vi·o·la clef *n.* another term for **alto clef.**

vi·o·la da brac·ci·o (vɪ'əʊlə də 'brætʃɪ,əʊ) *n.* **1.** an old name for **viola¹** (sense 1). **2.** a type of viol held on the shoulder, from which the modern viola was developed. [from Italian, literally: viol for the arm]

vi·o·la da gam·ba (vɪ'əʊlə də 'gæmbə) *n.* the second largest and lowest member of the viol family. See **viol.** [C18: from Italian, literally: viol for the leg]

vi·o·la d'a·mo·re (vɪ'əʊlə dæ'mɔ:rɪ) *n.* an instrument of the viol family having no frets, seven strings, and a set of sympathetic strings. It was held under the chin when played. [C18: from Italian, literally: viol of love]

vi·o·late ('vaɪə,leɪt) *vb.* (*tr.*) **1.** to break, disregard, or infringe on (a law, agreement, etc.). **2.** to rape or otherwise sexually assault. **3.** to disturb rudely or improperly; break in upon. **4.** to treat irreverently or disrespectfully; outrage: *he violated a sanctuary.* **5.** *Obsolete.* to mistreat physically. ~*adj.* **6.** *Archaic.* violated or dishonoured. [C15: from Latin *violāre* to do violence to, from *vīs* strength] —**'vi·o·la·ble** *adj.* —**,vi·o·la·'bil·i·ty** *or* **'vi·o·la·ble·ness** *n.* —**'vi·o·la·bly** *adv.* —**,vi·o·'la·tion** *n.* —**'vi·o·la·tive** *adj.* —**'vi·o·,la·tor** *or* **'vi·o·,lat·er** *n.*

vi·o·lence ('vaɪələns) *n.* **1.** the exercise or an instance of physical force, usually effecting or intended to effect injuries, destruction, etc. **2.** powerful, untamed, or devastating force: *the violence of the sea.* **3.** great strength of feeling, as in language, etc.; fervour. **4.** an unjust, unwarranted, or unlawful display of force, esp. such as tends to overawe or intimidate. **5. do violence to. a.** to inflict harm upon; damage or violate: *they did violence to the prisoners.* **b.** to distort or twist the sense or intention of: *the reporters did violence to my speech.* [C13: via Old French from Latin *violentia* impetuosity, from *violentus* VIOLENT]

vi·o·lent ('vaɪələnt) *adj.* **1.** marked or caused by great physical force or violence: *a violent stab.* **2.** (of a person) tending to the use of violence, esp. in order to injure or intimidate others. **3.** marked by intensity of any kind: *a violent clash of colours.* **4.** characterized by an undue use of force; severe; harsh. **5.** caused by or displaying strong or undue mental or emotional force: *a violent tongue.* **6.** tending to distort the meaning or intent: *a violent interpretation of the text.* [C14: from Latin *violentus*, probably from *vīs* strength] —**'vi·o·lent·ly** *adv.*

vi·o·let ('vaɪəlɪt) *n.* **1.** any of various temperate perennial herbaceous plants of the violaceous genus *Viola*, such as *V. odorata* (**sweet** (or **garden**) **violet**), typically having mauve or bluish flowers with irregular showy petals. **2.** any other plant of the genus *Viola*, such as the wild pansy. **3.** any of various similar but unrelated plants, such as the African violet. **4. a.** any of a group of colours that vary in saturation but have the same purplish-blue hue. They lie at one end of the visible spectrum, next to blue; approximate wavelength range 445–390 nanometres. **b.** (*as adj.*): *a violet dress.* **5.** a dye or pigment of or producing these colours. **6.** violet clothing: *dressed in violet.* **7. shrinking violet.** *Informal.* a shy person. [C14: from Old French *violete* a little violet, from *viole*, from Latin *viola* violet] —**'vi·o·let-,like** *adj.*

vi·o·lin (,vaɪə'lɪn) *n.* a bowed stringed instrument, the highest member of the violin family, consisting of a fingerboard, a hollow wooden body with waisted sides, and a sounding board connected to the back by means of a soundpost that also supports the bridge. It has two f-shaped sound holes cut in the belly. The instrument, noted for its fine and flexible tone, is the most important of the stringed instruments. It is held under the chin when played. Range: roughly three and a half octaves upwards from G below middle C. [C16: from Italian *violino* a little viola, from VIOLA¹]

vi·o·lin·ist (,vaɪə'lɪnɪst) *n.* a person who plays the violin.

vi·ol·ist¹ (vɪ'əʊlɪst) *n. U.S.* a person who plays the viola.

vi·ol·ist² ('vaɪəlɪst) *n.* a person who plays the viol.

Viol·let-le-Duc (*French* vjɔlɛ lə 'dyk) *n.* **Eu·gène Em·ma·nuel** (øʒɛn ɛma'nɥɛl). 1814–79, French architect and leader of the Gothic revival in France, noted for his dictionary of French architecture (1854–68) and for his restoration of medieval buildings.

vi·o·lon·cel·lo (,vaɪələn'tʃɛləʊ) *n., pl.* **·los.** the full name for **cello.** [C18: from Italian, from VIOLONE + *-cello*, diminutive suffix] —**,vi·o·lon·'cel·list** *n.*

vi·o·lone ('vaɪə,ləʊn) *n.* the double-bass member of the viol family lying an octave below the viola da gamba. It corresponds to the double bass in the violin family. [C18: from Italian, from VIOLA¹ + *-one*, augmentative suffix]

V.I.P. *Informal. abbrev. for* very important person.

vi·per ('vaɪpə) *n.* **1.** any venomous Old World snake of the family *Viperidae*, esp. any of the genus *Vipera* (the adder and related forms), having hollow fangs in the upper jaw that are used to inject venom. **2.** any of various other snakes, such as the horned viper. **3.** See **pit viper**. **4.** a malicious or treacherous person. [C16: from Latin *vīpera*, perhaps from *vīvus* living + *parere* to bear, referring to a tradition that the viper was viviparous] —**'vi·per-,like** *adj.*

vi+per+ous ('vaɪpərəs) *or* **vi+per+ish** *adj.* **1.** Also: **vi+per+ine** ('vaɪpə,raɪn). of, relating to, or resembling a viper. **2.** malicious. —**'vi+per+ous+ly** *or* **'vi+per+ish+ly** *adv.*

vi+per's bu+gloss *n.* a Eurasian boraginaceous weed, *Echium vulgare*, having blue flowers and pink buds. Also called (U.S.): **blueweed,** (Austral.) **Paterson's curse.**

VIR *abbrev. for* Victoria Imperatrix Regina. [Latin: Victoria, Empress and Queen]

vi+ra+go (vɪ'rɑːgəʊ) *n., pl.* **+goes** *or* **+gos. 1.** a loud, violent, and ill-tempered woman; scold; shrew. **2.** *Archaic.* a strong, brave, or warlike woman; amazon. [Old English, from Latin: a manlike maiden, from *vir* a man] —**vi+rag·i+nous** (vɪ'rædʒɪnəs) *adj.* —**vi·'ra·go-,like** *adj.*

vi+ral ('vaɪrəl) *adj.* of, relating to, or caused by a virus.

Vir Chak+ra ('viːr 'tʃʌkrə) *n.* an award made to distinguished soldiers by the Government of India. [Hindi: *vir* brave man + *chakra* wheel]

Vir·chow (*German* 'fɪrço) *n.* **Ru·dolf Lud·wig Karl** ('ruːdɔlf 'luːtvɪç karl). 1821–1902, German pathologist, who is considered the founder of modern (cellular) pathology.

vir+e·lay ('vɪrɪ,leɪ) *n.* **1.** an old French verse form, rarely used in English, having short lines on two rhymes throughout and two opening lines recurring at intervals. **2.** any of various similar forms. [C14: from Old French *virelai*, probably from *vireli* (associated with *lai* LAY[4]), meaningless word used as a refrain]

Vi·ren ('vɪərən) *n.* **Las·se** ('læsɪ). born 1949, Finnish distance runner: winner of the 5000 metres and the 10 000 metres in the 1976 Olympic Games.

vir·e·o ('vɪrɪəʊ) *n., pl.* **vir·e·os.** any insectivorous American songbird of the family *Vireonidae*, esp. those of the genus *Vireo*, having an olive grey back with pale underparts. [C19: from Latin: a bird, probably a greenfinch; compare *virēre* to be green]

vi+res+cence (vɪ'rɛsəns) *n.* **1.** (in plants) the state of becoming green, esp. by the action of disease, etc., in parts not normally green. **2.** the condition of being or the process of becoming green. [C19: see VIRESCENT]

vi+res+cent (vɪ'rɛsənt) *adj.* greenish or becoming green. [C19: from Latin *virescere* to grow green, from *virēre* to be green]

vir+ga ('vɜːgə) *n.* (*sometimes functioning as pl.*) *Meteorol.* wisps of rain or snow, seen trailing from clouds, that evaporate before reaching the earth. [C20: from Latin: streak]

vir+gate[1] ('vɜːgɪt, -geɪt) *adj.* long, straight, and thin; rod-shaped: *virgate stems.* [C19: from Latin *virgātus* made of twigs, from *virga* a rod]

vir+gate[2] ('vɜːgɪt, -geɪt) *n. Brit.* an obsolete measure of land area, usually taken as equivalent to 30 acres. [C17: from Medieval Latin *virgāta* (*terrae*) a rod's measurement (of land), from Latin *virga* rod; the phrase is a translation of Old English *gierd landes* a yard of land]

Vir·gil *or* **Ver·gil** ('vɜːdʒɪl) *n.* Latin name *Publius Vergilius Maro.* 70–19 B.C., Roman poet, patronized by Maecenas. The *Eclogues* (42–37), ten pastoral poems, and the *Georgics* (37–30), four books on the art of farming, established Virgil as the foremost poet of his age. His masterpiece is the *Aeneid* (30–19). —**Vir+'gil+i·an** *or* **Ver+'gil+i·an** *adj.*

vir+gin ('vɜːdʒɪn) *n.* **1.** a person, esp. a woman, who has never had sexual intercourse. **2.** an unmarried woman who has taken a religious vow of chastity in order to dedicate herself totally to God. **3.** any female animal that has never mated. **4.** a female insect that produces offspring by parthenogenesis. ~*adj.* (*usually prenominal*) **5.** of, relating to, resembling, suitable for, or characteristic of a virgin or virgins; chaste. **6.** pure and natural, uncorrupted, unsullied, or untouched: *virgin purity.* **7.** not yet cultivated, explored, exploited, etc., by man: *the virgin forests.* **8.** being the first or happening for the first time. **9.** (of vegetable oils) obtained directly by the first pressing of fruits, leaves, or seeds of plants without applying heat. **10.** (of a metal) made from an ore rather than from scrap. **11.** occurring naturally in a pure and uncombined form: *virgin silver.* **12.** *Physics.* (of a neutron) not having experienced a collision. [C13: from Old French *virgine*, from Latin *virgō* virgin]

Vir+gin[1] ('vɜːdʒɪn) *n.* **1. the.** See **Virgin Mary. 2.** a statue or other artistic representation of the Virgin Mary.

Vir+gin[2] ('vɜːdʒɪn) *n.* **the.** the constellation Virgo, the sixth sign of the zodiac.

vir+gin+al[1] ('vɜːdʒɪnəl) *adj.* **1.** of, relating to, characterized by, proper to, or maintaining a state of virginity; chaste. **2.** extremely pure or fresh; untouched; undefiled. [C15: from Latin *virginālis* maidenly, from *virgō* virgin] —**'vir+gin+al+ly** *adv.*

vir+gin+al[2] ('vɜːdʒɪnəl) *n.* (*often pl.*) a smaller version of the harpsichord, but oblong in shape, having one manual and no pedals. [C16: probably from Latin *virginālis* VIRGINAL[1], perhaps because it was played largely by young ladies] —**'vir+gin+al+ist** *n.*

vir+gin birth *n.* another name for **parthenogenesis** (sense 2).

Vir+gin Birth *n.* the doctrine that Jesus Christ had no human father but was conceived solely by the direct intervention of the Holy Spirit so that Mary remained miraculously a virgin during and after his birth.

Vir·gin·i·a[1] (və'dʒɪnɪə) *n.* (*sometimes not cap.*) a type of flue-cured tobacco grown originally in Virginia.

Vir+gin·i·a[2] (və'dʒɪnɪə) *n.* a state of the eastern U.S., on the Atlantic: site of the first permanent English settlement in North America; consists of a low-lying deeply indented coast rising inland to the Piedmont plateau and the Blue Ridge Mountains. Capital: Richmond. Pop.: 4 648 494 (1970). Area: 103 030 sq. km (39 780 sq. miles). Abbrevs.: **Va.** or (with zip code) **VA** —**Vir+'gin+i·an** *adj., n.*

Vir+gin·i·a Beach *n.* a city and resort in SE Virginia, on the Atlantic. Pop.: 199 613 (1973 est.).

Vir+gin·i·a creep+er *n.* **1.** Also called (U.S.): **American ivy, woodbine.** a vitaceous woody vine, *Parthenocissus quinquefolia*, of North America, having tendrils with adhesive tips, bluish-black berry-like fruits, and compound leaves: widely planted for ornament. **2.** Also called: **Japanese ivy.** a similar related plant, *Parthenocissus tricuspidata*, of SE Asia, having trilobed leaves and purple berries. U.S. name: **Boston ivy.**

Vir+gin·i·a deer *n.* another name for **white-tailed deer.**

Vir+gin·i·a reel *n.* **1.** an American country dance. **2.** music written for or in the manner of this dance.

Vir+gin·i·a stock *n.* a Mediterranean cruciferous plant, *Malcomia maritima*, cultivated for its white and pink flowers.

Vir+gin Is+lands *pl. n.* a group of about 100 small islands (14 inhabited) in the West Indies, east of Puerto Rico: discovered by Columbus (1493); consists of the British Virgin Islands in the east and the Virgin Islands of the United States in the west and south. Area: 497 sq. km (192 sq. miles).

Vir+gin Is+lands of the U·nit+ed States *pl. n.* a territory of the U.S. in the Caribbean, consisting of islands west and south of the British Virgin Islands: purchased from Denmark in 1917 for their strategic importance. Capital: Charlotte Amalie. Pop.: 63 200 (1970). Area: 344 sq. km (133 sq. miles). Former name: **Danish West Indies.**

vir+gin+i·ty (və'dʒɪnɪtɪ) *n.* **1.** the condition or fact of being a virgin; maidenhood; chastity. **2.** the condition of being untouched, unsullied, etc.

vir+gin+i·um (və'dʒɪnɪəm) *n. Chem.* a former name for **francium.**

Vir+gin Mar·y *n.* Mary, the mother of Christ. Also called: the **Virgin.**

vir·gin's-bow·er *n.* any of several American clematis plants, esp. *Clematis virginiana*, of E North America, which has clusters of small white flowers.

vir+gin wool *n.* wool that is being processed or woven for the first time.

Vir+go ('vɜːgəʊ) *n., Latin genitive* **Vir+gi+nis** ('vɜːdʒɪnɪs). **1.** *Astronomy.* a large zodiacal constellation on the celestial equator, lying between Leo and Libra. It contains the star Spica and a cluster of several thousand galaxies, the **Virgo cluster,** lying 20 million light years away. **2. a.** Also called: the **Virgin.** *Astrology.* the sixth sign of the zodiac, symbol ♍, having a mutable earth classification and ruled by the planet Mercury. The sun is in this sign between about Aug. 23 and Sept. 22. **b.** Also called: **Vir+go·an** (vɜː'gəʊən) a person born when the sun is in this sign. ~*adj.* **3.** Also: **Virgoan.** *Astrology.* born under or characteristic of Virgo. [C14: from Latin]

vir+go in+tac+ta ('vɜːgəʊ ɪn'tæktə) *n.* a girl or woman who has not had sexual intercourse. [Latin, literally: untouched virgin]

vir+gu+late ('vɜːgjʊlɪt, -,leɪt) *adj.* rod-shaped or rodlike. [C19: from Latin *virgula* a little rod, from *virga* rod]

vir+gule ('vɜːgjuːl) *n. Printing.* another name for **solidus.** [C19: from French: comma, from Latin *virgula* a little rod, from *virga* rod]

vir·i+des+cent (,vɪrɪ'dɛsᵊnt) *adj.* greenish or tending to become green. [C19: from Late Latin *viridescere* to grow green, from Latin *viridis* green] —**,vir·i+'des+cence** *n.*

vi+rid+i+an (vɪ'rɪdɪən) *n.* a green pigment consisting of a hydrated form of chromic oxide. [C19: from Latin *viridis* green]

vi+rid+i·ty (vɪ'rɪdɪtɪ) *n.* **1.** the quality or state of being green; greenness; verdancy. **2.** innocence, youth, or freshness. [C15: from Latin *viriditās*, from *viridis* green]

vir+ile ('vɪraɪl) *adj.* **1.** of, relating to, or having the characteristics of an adult male. **2.** of or capable of copulation or procreation. **3.** strong, forceful, or vigorous. [C15: from Latin *virīlis* manly, from *vir* a man; related to Old English *wer* man and probably to Latin *vis* strength] —**vi+ril+i·ty** (vɪ'rɪlɪtɪ) *n.*

vir·i+lism ('vɪrɪ,lɪzəm) *n. Med.* the abnormal development in a woman of male secondary sex characteristics.

vi+rol+o·gy (vaɪ'rɒlədʒɪ) *n.* the branch of medicine concerned with the study of viruses and the diseases they cause. —**vi+ro+log·i+cal** (,vaɪrə'lɒdʒɪkᵊl) *adj.* —**vi+'rol·o·gist** *n.*

vir+tu *or* **ver+tu** (vɜː'tuː) *n.* **1.** a taste or love for curios or works of fine art; connoisseurship. **2.** such objects collectively. **3.** the quality of being rare, beautiful, or otherwise appealing to a connoisseur (esp. in the phrases **articles of virtu; objects of virtu**). [C18: from Italian *virtù*; see VIRTUE]

vir+tu·al ('vɜːtʃʊəl) *adj.* **1.** having the essence or effect but not the appearance or form of: *a virtual revolution.* **2.** *Physics.* being, relating to, or involving a virtual image: *a virtual focus.* **3.** *Computer technol.* of or relating to virtual storage: *virtual memory.* **4.** *Rare.* capable of producing an effect through inherent power or virtue. **5.** *Physics.* designating or relating to a particle exchanged between other particles that are interacting by a field of force: *a virtual photon.* See also **exchange force.** [C14: from Medieval Latin *virtuālis* effective, from Latin *virtūs* VIRTUE] —**,vir+tu+'al+i·ty** *n.*

vir+tu·al im+age *n.* an optical image formed by the apparent divergence of rays from a point, rather than their actual divergence from a point.

vir·tu·al·ly (ˈvɜːtʃʊəlɪ) *adv.* in effect though not in fact; practically; nearly.

vir·tu·al stor·age *n.* a computer system in which the size of the memory is effectively increased by automatically transferring sections of a program from a large capacity backing store, such as a disk, into the smaller core memory as they are required.

vir·tue (ˈvɜːtjuː, -tʃuː) *n.* **1.** the quality or practice of moral excellence or righteousness. **2.** a particular moral excellence: *the virtue of tolerance.* **3.** any of the cardinal virtues (prudence, justice, fortitude, and temperance) or theological virtues (faith, hope, and charity). **4.** any admirable quality, feature, or trait. **5.** an effective, active, or inherent power or force. **6.** chastity, esp. in women. **7. by** *or* **in virtue of.** on account of or by reason of. **8. make a virtue of necessity.** to acquiesce in doing something unpleasant with a show of grace because one must do it in any case. [C13 *vertu,* from Old French, from Latin *virtūs* manliness, courage, from *vir* man] —**ˈvir·tue·less** *adj.*

vir·tues (ˈvɜːtjuːz, -tʃuːz) *pl. n.* (*often cap.*) the fifth of the nine orders into which the angels are traditionally divided in medieval angelology.

vir·tu·o·so (ˌvɜːtjʊˈəʊzəʊ, -səʊ) *n., pl.* **·sos** *or* **·si** (-siː). **1.** a consummate master of musical technique and artistry. **2.** a person who has a masterly or dazzling skill or technique in any field of activity. **3.** a connoisseur, dilettante, or collector of art objects. **4.** *Obsolete.* a scholar or savant. **5.** (*modifier*) showing masterly skill or brilliance: *a virtuoso performance.* [C17: from Italian: skilled, from Late Latin *virtuōsus* good, virtuous; see VIRTUE] —**vir·tu·os·ic** (ˌvɜːtjʊˈɒsɪk) *adj.* —ˌ**vir·tu·ˈos·i·ty** *n.*

vir·tu·ous (ˈvɜːtʃʊəs) *adj.* **1.** characterized by or possessing virtue or moral excellence; righteous; upright. **2.** (of women) chaste or virginal. **3.** *Archaic.* efficacious; potent. —**ˈvir·tu·ous·ly** *adv.* —**ˈvir·tu·ous·ness** *n.*

vir·u·lence (ˈvɪrʊləns) *n.* **1.** the quality of being virulent. **2.** the capacity of a microorganism for causing disease.

vir·u·lent (ˈvɪrʊlənt) *adj.* **1. a.** (of a microorganism) extremely infective. **b.** (of a disease) having a rapid course and violent effect. **2.** extremely poisonous, injurious, etc.. **3.** extremely bitter, hostile, etc. [C14: from Latin *vīrulentus* full of poison, from *vīrus* poison; see VIRUS] —**ˈvir·u·lent·ly** *adv.*

vi·rus (ˈvaɪrəs) *n., pl.* **·rus·es. 1.** any of a group of submicroscopic entities consisting of a single nucleic acid surrounded by a protein coat and capable of replication only within the cells of animals and plants: many are pathogenic. **2.** *Informal.* a disease caused by a virus. **3.** any corrupting or infecting influence. [C16: from Latin: slime, poisonous liquid; related to Old English *wāse* marsh, Greek *ios* poison] —**ˈvi·rus-ˌlike** *adj.*

vis *Latin.* (vɪs) *n., pl.* ***vir·es*** (ˈvaɪriːz). power, force, or strength.

Vis. *abbrev. for* Viscount *or* Viscountess.

vi·sa (ˈviːzə) *n., pl.* **·sas. 1.** an endorsement in a passport or similar document, signifying that the document is in order and permitting its bearer to travel into or through the country of the government issuing it. **2.** any sign or signature of approval. ~*vb.* **·sas, ·sa·ing, ·saed.** (*tr.*) **3.** to enter a visa into (a passport). **4.** to endorse or ratify. [C19: via French from Latin *vīsa* things seen, from *vīsus,* past participle of *vidēre* to see]

vis·age (ˈvɪzɪdʒ) *n. Chiefly literary.* **1.** face or countenance. **2.** appearance; aspect. [C13: from Old French: aspect, from *vis* face, from Latin *vīsus* appearance, from *vidēre* to see]

-vis·aged *adj.* (*in combination*) having a visage as specified: *flat-visaged.*

Vi·sa·kha·pat·nam (vɪˌsɑːkəˈpʌtnəm) *n.* a variant spelling of **Vishakhapatnam.**

vis-à-vis (ˌviːzɑːˈviː) *prep.* **1.** in relation to; regarding. **2.** face to face with; opposite. ~*adv., adj.* **3.** face to face; opposite. ~*n., pl.* **vis-à-vis. 4.** a person or thing that is situated opposite to another. **5.** a person who corresponds to another in office, capacity, etc.; counterpart. **6.** an upholstered sofa; tête-à-tête. **7.** a type of horse-drawn carriage in which the passengers sit opposite one another. **8.** a coin having an obverse upon which two portraits appear facing each other. [C18: French, from *vis* face]

Vi·sa·yan (vɪˈsɑːjən) *or* **Bi·sa·yan** *n., pl.* **·yans** *or* **·yan. 1.** a member of the most numerous indigenous people of the Philippines. ~*adj.* **2.** of or relating to this people.

Vi·sa·yan Is·lands *pl. n.* a group of seven large and several hundred small islands in the central Philippines. Chief islands: Negros and Panay. Pop.: 9 983 251 (1970). Area: about 61 000 sq. km (23 535 sq. miles). Spanish name: **Bisayas.**

Vis·by (*Swedish* ˈviːsbyː) *n.* a port in SE Sweden, on NW Gotland Island in the Baltic: an early member of the Hanseatic League and major N European commercial centre in the Middle Ages. Pop.: 19 596 (1970).

Visc. *abbrev. for* Viscount *or* Viscountess.

vis·ca·cha *or* **viz·ca·cha** (vɪsˈkætʃə) *n.* **1.** a gregarious burrowing hystricomorph rodent, *Lagostomus maximus,* of southern South America, similar to but larger than the chinchillas: family *Chinchillidae.* **2. mountain viscacha.** another name for **mountain chinchilla** (see **chinchilla** (sense 3)). [C17: from Spanish, from Quechuan *wiskácha*]

vis·cer·a (ˈvɪsərə) *pl. n., sing.* **vis·cus** (ˈvɪskəs). **1.** *Anatomy.* the large internal organs of the body collectively, esp. those in the abdominal cavity. **2.** (less formally) the intestines; guts. [C17: from Latin: entrails, pl. of *viscus* internal organ]

vis·cer·al (ˈvɪsərəl) *adj.* **1.** of, relating to, or affecting the viscera. **2.** characterized by intuition or instinct rather than intellect. —**ˈvis·cer·al·ly** *adv.*

vis·ce·ro·mo·tor (ˈvɪsərəʊˌməʊtə) *adj. Physiol.* relating to or controlling movements of the viscera.

vis·cid (ˈvɪsɪd) *adj.* **1.** cohesive and sticky; glutinous; viscous. **2.** (esp. of a leaf) covered with a sticky substance. [C17: from Late Latin *viscidus* sticky, from Latin *viscum* mistletoe or birdlime] —**visˈcid·i·ty** *or* **ˈvis·cid·ness** *n.* —**ˈvis·cid·ly** *adv.*

vis·coid (ˈvɪskɔɪd) *or* **vis·coi·dal** (vɪsˈkɔɪdᵊl) *adj.* (of a fluid) somewhat viscous.

vis·com·e·ter (vɪsˈkɒmɪtə) *or* **vis·co·sim·e·ter** (ˌvɪskəʊˈsɪmɪtə) *n.* any device for measuring viscosity. —**vis·co·met·ric** (ˌvɪskəˈmɛtrɪk) *or* ˌ**vis·coˈmet·ri·cal** *adj.* —**visˈcom·e·try** *n.*

Vis·con·ti (*Italian* visˈkonti) *n.* **1.** the ruling family of Milan from 1277 to 1447. **2. Lu·chi·no.** 1906–76, Italian stage and film director, whose neo-realist films include *Ossessione* (1942); among his other films are *The Leopard* (1964), *Death in Venice* (1971), and *The Innocents* (1976).

vis·cose (ˈvɪskəʊs) *n.* **1. a.** a viscous orange-brown solution obtained by dissolving cellulose in sodium hydroxide and carbon disulphide. It can be converted back to cellulose by an acid, as in the manufacture of rayon and cellophane. **b.** (*as modifier*): *viscose rayon.* **2.** rayon made from this material. ~*adj.* **3.** another word for **viscous.** [C19: from Late Latin *viscōsus* full of birdlime, sticky, from *viscum* birdlime; see VISCID]

vis·cos·i·ty (vɪsˈkɒsɪtɪ) *n., pl.* **·ties. 1.** the state or property of being viscous. **2.** *Physics.* **a.** the extent to which a fluid resists a tendency to flow. **b.** Also called: **absolute viscosity.** a measure of this resistance, equal to the tangential stress on a liquid undergoing streamline flow divided by its velocity gradient. It is measured in newton seconds per metre squared. Symbol: η See also **kinematic viscosity, specific viscosity.**

vis·count (ˈvaɪkaʊnt) *n.* **1.** (in the British Isles) a nobleman ranking below an earl and above a baron. **2.** (in various countries) a son or younger brother of a count. See also **vicomte. 3.** (in medieval Europe) the deputy of a count. [C14: from Old French *visconte,* from Medieval Latin *vicecomes,* from Late Latin *vice-* VICE³ + *comes* COUNT²]

vis·count·cy (ˈvaɪkaʊntsɪ) *or* **vis·count·y** *n.* the rank or position of a viscount.

vis·count·ess (ˈvaɪkaʊntɪs) *n.* **1.** the wife or widow of a viscount. **2.** a woman who holds the rank of viscount in her own right.

vis·cous (ˈvɪskəs) *or* **vis·cose** *adj.* **1.** (of liquids) thick and sticky; viscid. **2.** having or involving viscosity. [C14: from Late Latin *viscōsus;* see VISCOSE] —**ˈvis·cous·ly** *adv.* —**ˈvis·cous·ness** *n.*

Visct. *abbrev. for* Viscount *or* Viscountess.

vis·cus (ˈvɪskəs) *n.* the singular of **viscera.**

vise (vaɪs) *n., vb. U.S.* a variant spelling of **vice².**

Vi·se·u (*Portuguese* viˈzeʊ) *n.* a city in N central Portugal: 12th-century cathedral. Pop.: 76 391 (1970).

Vi·sha·kha·pat·nam (vɪˌʃɑːkəˈpʌtnəm), **Vi·sa·kha·pat·nam,** *or* **Vi·za·ga·pa·tam** *n.* a port in E India, in NE Andhra Pradesh on the Bay of Bengal: shipbuilding and oil-refining industries. Pop.: 352 504 (1971).

Vi·shin·sky (*Russian* vɪˈʃinskij) *n.* a variant spelling of (Andrei Yanuarievich) **Vyshinsky.**

Vish·nu (ˈvɪʃnuː) *n. Hinduism.* the Pervader or Sustainer, originally a solar deity occupying a secondary place in the Hindu pantheon, later one of the three chief gods, the second member of the Trimurti, and, later still, the saviour appearing in many incarnations. [C17: from Sanskrit, literally: the one who works everywhere] —**ˈVish·nu·ism** *n.* —**ˈVish·nu·ite** *n., adj.*

vis·i·bil·i·ty (ˌvɪzɪˈbɪlɪtɪ) *n.* **1.** the condition or fact of being visible. **2.** clarity of vision or relative possibility of seeing. **3.** the range of vision: *visibility is 500 yards.*

vis·i·ble (ˈvɪzɪbᵊl) *adj.* **1.** capable of being perceived by the eye. **2.** capable of being perceived by the mind; evident: *no visible dangers.* **3.** available: *the visible resources.* **4.** (of an index or file) using a flexible display system for the contents. **5.** of or relating to the balance of trade: *visible transactions.* **6.** represented by visible symbols. ~*n.* **7.** a visible item of trade; product. [C14: from Latin *vīsibilis,* from *vidēre* to see] —**ˈvis·i·ble·ness** *n.* —**ˈvis·i·bly** *adv.*

vis·i·ble bal·ance *n.* another name for **balance of trade.**

vis·i·ble ra·di·a·tion *n.* electromagnetic radiation that causes the sensation of sight; light. It has wavelengths between about 380 and 780 nanometres.

vis·i·ble speech *n.* a system of phonetic notation invented by Alexander Melville Bell (1819–1905) that utilized symbols based on the schematic representation of the articulations used for each speech sound.

Vis·i·goth (ˈvɪzɪˌgɒθ) *n.* a member of the western group of the Goths, who were driven into the Balkans in the late 4th century A.D. Moving on, they sacked Rome (410) and established a kingdom in present-day Spain and S France that lasted until 711. [C17: from Late Latin *Visigothī* (pl.), of Germanic origin, *visi-* perhaps meaning: west] —ˌ**Vis·iˈgoth·ic** *adj.*

vi·sion (ˈvɪʒən) *n.* **1.** the act, faculty, or manner of perceiving with the eye; sight. **2.** the ability or an instance of great perception, esp. of future developments: *a man of vision.* **3.** mystical or religious experience of seeing some supernatural event, person, etc.: *the vision of St. John of the Cross.* **4.** that which is seen, esp. in such a mystical experience. **5.** (*sometimes* *pl.*) a vivid mental image produced by the imagination: *he had visions of becoming famous.* **6.** a person or thing of extraordinary beauty. *~vb.* **7.** (*tr.*) to see or show in or as if in a vision. [C13: from Latin *vīsiō* sight, from *vidēre* to see] **—'vi+sion+less** *adj.*

vi+sion+al ('vɪʒənᵊl) *adj.* of, relating to, or seen in a vision, apparition, etc. **—'vi+sion+al+ly** *adv.*

vi+sion+ar·y ('vɪʒənərɪ) *adj.* **1.** marked by vision or foresight: *a visionary leader.* **2.** incapable of being realized or effected; unrealistic. **3.** (of people) characterized by idealistic or radical ideas, esp. impractical ones. **4.** given to having visions. **5.** of, of the nature of, or seen in visions. *~n., pl.* **+ar·ies. 6.** a visionary person. **—'vi+sion+ar+i+ness** *n.*

vis+it ('vɪzɪt) *vb.* **1.** to go or come to see (a person, place, etc.). **2.** to stay with (someone) as a guest. **3.** to go or come to (an institution, place, etc.) for the purpose of inspecting or examining. **4.** (*tr.*) (of a disease, disaster, etc.) to assail; afflict. **5.** (*tr.;* foll. by *upon* or *on*) to inflict (punishment, etc.): *the judge visited his full anger upon the defendant.* **6.** (*tr.;* usually foll. by *with*) *Archaic.* to afflict or plague (with punishment, etc.). **7.** (often foll. by *with*) *U.S. informal.* to chat or converse (with someone). *~n.* **8.** the act or an instance of visiting. **9.** a stay as a guest. **10.** a professional or official call. **11.** a formal call for the purpose of inspection or examination. **12.** *International law.* the right of an officer of a belligerent state to stop and search neutral ships in war to verify their nationality and ascertain whether they carry contraband: *the right of visit and search.* **13.** *U.S. informal.* a friendly talk or chat. [C13: from Latin *vīsitāre* to go to see, from *vīsere* to examine, from *vidēre* to see] **—'vis+it+a·ble** *adj.*

vis·i+tant ('vɪzɪtənt) *n.* **1.** a supernatural being; ghost; apparition. **2.** a visitor or guest, usually from far away. **3.** a pilgrim or tourist. **4.** Also called: **visitor.** a migratory bird that is present in a particular region only at certain times: *a summer visitant.* *~adj.* **5.** *Archaic.* paying a visit; visiting. [C16: from Latin *vīsitāns* going to see, from *vīsitāre;* see VISIT]

vis+it·a·tion (ˌvɪzɪ'teɪʃən) *n.* **1.** an official call or visit for the purpose of inspecting or examining an institution, esp. such a visit made by a bishop to his diocese. **2.** a visiting of punishment or reward from heaven. **3.** any disaster or catastrophe: *a visitation of the plague.* **4.** an appearance or arrival of a supernatural being. **5.** any call or visit. **6.** *Informal.* an unduly prolonged social call. **—ˌvis+it·'a+tion+al** *adj.*

Vis+it·a·tion (ˌvɪzɪ'teɪʃən) *n.* **1. a.** the visit made by the Virgin Mary to her cousin Elizabeth (Luke 1:39–56). **b.** the Church festival commemorating this, held on July 2. **2.** a religious order of nuns, the **Order of the Visitation,** founded in 1610 and dedicated to contemplation and the cultivation of humility, gentleness, and sisterly love.

vis+it·a+to+ri·al (ˌvɪzɪtə'tɔ:rɪəl) *or* **vis·i+to+ri·al** *adj.* **1.** of, relating to, or for an official visitation or visitor. **2.** empowered to make official visitations.

vis+it+ing card *n. Brit.* a small card bearing the name and usually the address of a person, esp. for giving to business or social acquaintances. U.S. term: **calling card.**

vis+it+ing fire+man *n. U.S. informal.* a visitor whose presence is noticed because he is an important figure, a lavish spender, etc.

vis+it+ing nurse *n.* (in the U.S.) a registered nurse employed by a community, hospital, etc., to visit and nurse the sick in their homes or to promote public health.

vis+it+ing pro+fes+sor *n.* a professor invited to teach in a college or university other than his own, often in another country, for a certain period, such as a term or year.

vis·i+tor ('vɪzɪtə) *n.* **1.** a person who pays a visit; caller, guest, tourist, etc. **2.** another name for **visitant** (sense 4). **—ˌvis·i+'to+ri·al** *adj.*

Vis+lin+sky Za+liv (*Russian* vis'linski 'za:lɪf) *n.* a transliteration of the Russian name for **Vistula** (sense 2).

vis ma+jor ('vɪs 'meɪdʒə) *n:* See **force majeure.** [from Latin, literally: greater force]

vi+sor *or* **vi+zor** ('vaɪzə) *n.* **1.** a piece of armour fixed or hinged to the helmet to protect the face and furnished with slits for the eyes. **2.** another name for **peak** (on a cap). **3.** a small movable screen used as protection against glare from the sun, esp. one attached above the windscreen of a motor vehicle. **4.** *Archaic or literary.* a mask or any other means of disguise or concealment. *~vb.* **5.** (*tr.*) to cover, provide, or protect with a visor; shield. [C14: from Anglo-French *viser,* from Old French *visiere,* from *vis* face; see VISAGE] **—'vi+sored** *or* **'vi+zored** *adj.* **—'vi+sor+less** *or* **'vi+zor+less** *adj.*

vis+ta ('vɪstə) *n.* **1.** a view, esp. through a long narrow avenue of trees, buildings, etc., or such a passage or avenue itself; prospect: *a vista of arches.* **2.** a comprehensive mental view of a distant time or a lengthy series of events: *the vista of the future.* [C17: from Italian: a view, from *vedere* to see, from Latin *vidēre*] **—'vis+taed** *adj.* **—'vis+ta+less** *adj.*

VISTA ('vɪstə) *n.* (in the U.S.) *acronym for* Volunteers in Service to America: an organization of volunteers established by the Federal government to assist the poor.

Vis+tu+la ('vɪstjʊlə) *n.* **1.** a river in central and N Poland, rising in the Carpathian Mountains and flowing generally north and northwest past Warsaw and Torun, then northeast to enter the Baltic via an extensive delta region. Length: 1090 km (677 miles). Polish name: **Wisła.** German name: **Weichsel. 2. Lagoon.** a shallow lagoon on the SW coast of the Baltic Sea, between Danzig and Kalingrad, crossed by the border between Poland and the Soviet Union. German name: **Frisches Haff.** Polish name: **Wislany Zalew.** Russian name: **Vislinsky Zaliv.**

vis+u·al ('vɪʒʊəl, -zjʊ-) *adj.* **1.** of, relating to, done by, or used in seeing: *visual powers; visual steering.* **2.** another word for **optical. 3.** capable of being seen; visible. **4.** of, occurring as, or induced by a mental image. *~n.* **5.** a sketch to show the proposed layout of an advertisement, as in a newspaper. [C15: from Late Latin *vīsuālis,* from Latin *vīsus* sight, from *vidēre* to see] **—'vis·u·al+ly** *adv.*

vis·u·al aids *pl. n.* devices, such as films, slides, models, and blackboards, that display in visual form material to be understood or remembered.

vis+u·al arts *pl. n.* the arts of painting, sculpting, engraving, etc., as opposed to music, drama, and literature.

vis+u·al dis+play u·nit *n. Computer technol.* a device incorporating a cathode-ray tube that displays characters or line drawings representing data in a computer memory. It usually has a keyboard or light pen for the input of information or enquiries. Abbrev.: **VDU**

vis·u·al+ize *or* **vis·u·al+ise** ('vɪʒʊəˌlaɪz, -zjʊ-) *vb.* **1.** to form a mental image of (something incapable of being viewed or not at that moment visible). **2.** *Med.* to view by means of an x-ray the outline of (a bodily organ, structure, or part). **—ˌvis·u+al·i+'za+tion** *or* **ˌvis·u·al·i+'sa+tion** *n.* **—'vis·u·al+ˌiz+er** *or* **'vis·u+al+ˌis+er** *n.*

vis+u·al mag+ni+tude *n. Astronomy.* the magnitude of a star as determined by visual observation. Compare **photographic magnitude.**

vis+u·al pur+ple *n.* another name for **rhodopsin.**

vis+u·al vi·o+let *n.* another name for **iodopsin.**

vis+u·al yel+low *n.* another name for **retinene.**

vi·ta ('vi:tə, 'vaɪ-) *n., pl.* **vi+tae** ('vi:taɪ, 'vaɪti:). *U.S.* a less common term for **curriculum vitae.** [from Latin: life]

vi+ta+ceous (vaɪ'teɪʃəs) *adj.* of, relating to, or belonging to the *Vitaceae,* a family of tropical and subtropical flowering plants having a climbing habit and berry-like fruits: includes the grapevine and Virginia creeper. [C19: via New Latin *Vītāceae,* from Latin: vine]

vi+tal ('vaɪtᵊl) *adj.* **1.** essential to maintain life: *the lungs perform a vital function.* **2.** forceful, energetic, or lively: *a vital person.* **3.** of, relating to, having, or displaying life: *a vital organism.* **4.** indispensable or essential: *books vital to this study.* **5.** of great importance; decisive: *a vital game.* **6.** *Archaic.* influencing the course of life, esp. negatively: *a vital treachery.* *~n.* **7.** (*pl.*) **a.** the bodily organs, such as the brain, liver, heart, lungs, etc., that are necessary to maintain life. **b.** the organs of reproduction, esp. the male genitals. **8.** (*pl.*) the essential elements of anything. [C14: via Old French from Latin *vītālis* belonging to life, from *vīta* life] **—'vi+tal+ly** *adv.* **—'vi+tal+ness** *n.*

vi+tal ca+pac+i·ty *n. Physiol.* the volume of air that can be exhaled from the lungs after the deepest possible breath has been taken: a measure of lung function.

vi+tal force *n.* (esp. in early biological theory) a hypothetical force, independent of physical and chemical forces, regarded as being the causative factor of the evolution and development of living organisms.

vi+tal+ism ('vaɪtəˌlɪzəm) *n.* the doctrine that phenomena cannot be explained in purely mechanical terms because their existence depends upon a vital life-giving principle. Compare **dynamism, mechanism. —'vi+tal+ist** *n., adj.* **—ˌvi+tal+'is+tic** *adj.*

vi+tal+i·ty (vaɪ'tælɪtɪ) *n., pl.* **·ties. 1.** physical or mental vigour, energy, etc. **2.** the power or ability to continue in existence, live, or grow: *the vitality of a movement.* **3.** a less common name for **vital force.**

vi+tal+ize *or* **vi+tal+ise** ('vaɪtəˌlaɪz) *vb.* (*tr.*) to make vital, living, or alive; endow with life or vigour. **—ˌvi+tal·i+'za+tion** *or* **ˌvi+tal·i+'sa+tion** *n.* **—'vi+tal+ˌiz+er** *or* **'vi+tal+ˌis+er** *n.*

vi+tal stain+ing *n.* the technique of treating living cells and tissues with dyes that do not immediately kill them, facilitating observation under a microscope.

vi+tal sta+tis+tics *pl. n.* **1.** quantitative data concerning human life or the conditions and aspects affecting it, such as the death rate. **2.** *Informal.* the measurements of a woman's bust, waist, and hips.

vit·a+min ('vɪtəmɪn, 'vaɪ-) *n.* any of a group of substances that are essential, in small quantities, for the normal functioning of metabolism in the body. They cannot usually be synthesized in the body but they occur naturally in certain foods: insufficient supply of any particular vitamin results in a deficiency disease. [C20 *vit-* from Latin *vīta* life + *-amin* from AMINE; so named by Casimir FUNK, who believed the substances to be amines] **—ˌvit·a+'min+ic** *adj.*

vit·a+min A *n.* a fat-soluble yellow unsaturated alcohol occurring in green and yellow vegetables (esp. carrots), butter, egg yolk, and fish-liver oil (esp. halibut oil). It is essential for the prevention of night blindness and the protection of epithelial tissue. Formula: $C_{20}H_{30}O$. Also called: **vitamin A_1, retinol.**

vit·a+min A_2 *n.* a vitamin that occurs in the tissues of freshwater fish and has a function similar to that of vitamin A. Formula: $C_{20}H_{28}O$. Also called: **dehydroretinol.**

vit·a+min B *n., pl.* **B vit·a+mins.** any of the vitamins in the vitamin B complex.

vit·a+min B_1 *n.* another name for **thiamine.**

vit·a+min B_2 *n.* another name for **riboflavin.**

vit·a+min B_6 *n.* another name for **pyridoxine.**

vit·a+min B_{12} *n.* another name for **cyanocobalamin.**

vit·a+min B com+plex *n.* a large group of water-soluble vitamins occurring esp. in liver and yeast: includes thiamine, riboflavin, nicotinic acid, pyridoxine, pantothenic acid, biotin, choline, folic acid, and cyanocobalamin. Sometimes shortened to **B complex.**

vit·a·min C *n.* another name for **ascorbic acid.**

vit·a·min D *n., pl.* **D vit·a·mins.** any of the fat-soluble vitamins, including calciferol and cholecalciferol, occurring in fish-liver oils (esp. cod-liver oil), milk, butter, and eggs: used in the treatment of rickets and osteomalacia.

vit·a·min D_1 *n.* the first isolated form of vitamin D, consisting of calciferol and its precursor, lumisterol.

vit·a·min D_2 *n.* another name for **calciferol.**

vit·a·min D_3 *n.* another name for **cholecalciferol.**

vit·a·min E *n.* another name for **tocopherol.**

vit·a·min G *n.* another name (esp. U.S.) for **riboflavin.**

vit·a·min H *n.* another name (esp. U.S.) for **biotin.**

vit·a·min K *n., pl.* **K vit·a·mins.** any of the fat-soluble vitamins, including phylloquinone and the menaquinones, which are essential for the normal clotting of blood.

vit·a·min K_1 *n.* another name for **phylloquinone.**

vit·a·min K_2 *n.* another name for **menaquinone.**

vit·a·min K_3 *n.* a former name for **menadione.**

vit·a·min P *n., pl.* **P vit·a·mins.** any of a group of water-soluble crystalline substances occurring mainly in citrus fruits, blackcurrants, and rose hips: they regulate the permeability of the blood capillaries. Also called: **citrin, bioflavonoid.**

Vi+ta+phone (ˈvaɪtəˌfəʊn) *n. Trademark.* an early technique in commercial film-making in which the accompanying sound was produced by discs.

vi+ta+scope (ˈvaɪtəˌskəʊp) *n.* an early type of film projector. [C19: from Latin *vīta* life + -SCOPE]

Vi+tebsk (*Russian* ˈvitjpsk) *n.* a city in the W Soviet Union, in the Byelorussian SSR: under Russian rule since 1772. Pop.: 272 000 (1975 est.).

vi+tel+lin (vɪˈtɛlɪn) *n. Biochem.* a phosphoprotein that is the major protein in egg yolk. [C19: from VITELLUS + -IN]

vi+tel+line (vɪˈtɛlɪn, -aɪn) *adj. Zoology.* **1.** of or relating to the yolk of an egg: *the vitelline gland.* **2.** having the yellow colour of an egg yolk. [C15: from Medieval Latin *vitellīnus,* from Latin *vitellus* the yolk of an egg; see VITELLUS]

vi+tel+line mem+brane *n. Zoology.* a membrane that surrounds a fertilized ovum and prevents the entry of other spermatozoa.

vi+tel+lus (vɪˈtɛləs) *n., pl.* **+lus·es** *or* **+li** (-laɪ). *Zoology, rare.* the yolk of an egg. [C18: from Latin, literally: little calf, later: yolk of an egg, from *vitulus* calf]

vi+ti+ate (ˈvɪʃɪˌeɪt) *vb. (tr.)* **1.** to make faulty or imperfect. **2.** to debase, pervert, or corrupt. **3.** to destroy the force or legal effect of (a deed, etc.): *to vitiate a contract.* [C16: from Latin *vitiāre* to injure, from *vitium* a fault] **—ˈvi·ti·a·ble** *adj.* **—ˌvi+ti·ˈa+tion** *n.* **—ˈvi·ti·ˌa+tor** *n.*

vit·i·cul+ture (ˈvɪtɪˌkʌltʃə) *n.* **1.** the science, art, or process of cultivating grapevines. **2.** the study of grapes and the growing of grapes. [C19: *viti-,* from Latin *vītis* vine] **—ˌvit·i·ˈcul+tur+al** *adj.* **—ˌvit·i·ˈcul+tur+er** *or* **ˌvit·i·ˈcul+tur+ist** *n.*

Vi·ti Le·vu (ˈviːtiː ˈlɛvuː) *n.* the largest island of Fiji: mountainous. Chief town (and capital of the state): Suva. Area: 10 386 sq. km (4010 sq. miles).

vit·i·li·go (ˌvɪtɪˈlaɪgəʊ) *n.* another name for **leucoderma.** [C17: from Latin: a skin disease, probably from *vitium* a blemish]

Vi+to+ria (*Spanish* biˈtorja) *n.* a city in NE Spain: scene of Wellington's decisive victory (1813) over Napoleon's forces in the Peninsular War. Pop.: 136 873 (1970).

Vi+tó+ri·a (vɪˈtɔːrɪə; *Portuguese* viˈtɔrja) *n.* a port in E Brazil, capital of Espírito Santo state, on an island in the Bay of Espírito Santo. Pop.: 121 978 (1970).

vit+rain (ˈvɪtreɪn) *n.* a type of coal occurring as horizontal glassy bands of a nonsoiling friable material. [C20: from Latin *vitrum* glass + *-ain,* as in FUSAIN]

vit+re+ous (ˈvɪtrɪəs) *adj.* **1.** of, relating to, or resembling glass. **2.** made of, derived from, or containing glass. **3.** of or relating to the vitreous humour or vitreous body. [C17: from Latin *vitreus* made of glass, from *vitrum* glass; probably related to *vidēre* to see] **—ˈvit+re+ous+ly** *adv.* **—ˈvit+re+ous+ness** *or* **vit+re+os+i·ty** (ˌvɪtrɪˈɒsɪtɪ) *n.*

vit+re+ous body·y *n.* a transparent gelatinous substance, permeated by fine fibrils, that fills the interior of the eyeball between the lens and the retina.

vit+re+ous hu+mour *n.* the aqueous fluid contained within the interstices of the vitreous body.

vit+re+ous sil·i·ca *n.* another name for **silica glass.**

vi+tres+cence (vɪˈtrɛsəns) *n.* **1.** the quality or condition of being or becoming vitreous. **2.** the process of producing a glass or turning a crystalline material into glass.

vi+tres+cent (vɪˈtrɛsᵊnt) *adj.* **1.** tending to turn into glass. **2.** capable of being transformed into glass.

vit+ric (ˈvɪtrɪk) *adj.* of, relating to, resembling, or having the nature of glass; vitreous.

vit+ri+fi+ca+tion (ˌvɪtrɪfɪˈkeɪʃən) *n.* **1.** the process or act of vitrifying or the state of being vitrified. **2.** something that is or has been vitrified.

vit+ri+form (ˈvɪtrɪˌfɔːm) *adj.* having the form or appearance of glass.

vit+ri+fy (ˈvɪtrɪˌfaɪ) *vb.* **+fies, +fy+ing, +fied.** to convert or be converted into glass or a glassy substance. [C16: from French *vitrifier,* from Latin *vitrum* glass] **—ˈvit+ri+ˌfi+a·ble** *adj.* **—ˌvit+ri+ˌfi+a·ˈbil+i·ty** *n.*

vit+rine (ˈvɪtriːn) *n.* a glass display case or cabinet for works of art, curios, etc. [C19: from French, from *vitre* pane of glass, from Latin *vitrum* glass]

vit+ri+ol (ˈvɪtrɪˌɒl) *n.* **1.** another name for **sulphuric acid. 2.** any one of a number of sulphate salts, such as ferrous sulphate (**green vitriol**) or copper sulphate (**blue vitriol**). **3.** speech, writing, etc., displaying rancour, vituperation, or bitterness. *~vb.* **+ols, +ol+ing, +oled** *or* **+ols, +ol+ling, +olled.** *(tr.)* **4.** to attack or injure with or as if with vitriol. **5.** to treat with vitriol. [C14: from Medieval Latin *vitriolum,* from Late Latin *vitriolus* glassy, from Latin *vitrum* glass, referring to the glossy appearance of the sulphates]

vit+ri+ol+ic (ˌvɪtrɪˈɒlɪk) *adj.* **1.** (of a substance, esp. a strong acid) highly corrosive. **2.** severely bitter or caustic; virulent: *vitriolic criticism.*

vit+ri+ol+ize *or* **vit+ri+ol+ise** (ˈvɪtrɪəˌlaɪz) *vb. (tr.)* **1.** to convert into or treat with vitriol. **2.** to burn or injure with vitriol. **—ˌvit+ri+ol·i·ˈza+tion** *or* **ˌvit+ri+ol·i·ˈsa+tion** *n.*

Vi·tru·vi·us Pol·li·o (vɪˈtruːvɪəs ˈpɒlɪˌəʊ) *n.* **Mar·cus** (ˈmɑːkəs). 1st-century B.C., Roman architect, noted for his treatise *De architectura,* the only surviving Roman work on architectural theory and a major influence on Renaissance architects. **—Vi+ˈtru+vi·an** *adj.*

vit+ta (ˈvɪtə) *n., pl.* **+tae** (-tiː). **1.** any of numerous tubelike cavities containing oil or resin that occur in the fruits of certain plants, esp. of parsley and related plants. **2.** *Biology.* a band or stripe of colour. [C17: from Latin: headband; related to *viēre* to plait] **—ˈvit+tate** *adj.*

vit+tle (ˈvɪtᵊl) *n., vb.* an obsolete or dialect spelling of **victual.**

vi+tu+line (ˈvɪtjʊˌlaɪn, -lɪn) *adj.* of or resembling a calf or veal. [C17: from Latin *vitulīnus,* from *vitulus* a calf]

vi+tu+per+ate (vɪˈtjuːpəˌreɪt) *vb. (tr.)* to berate or rail against abusively; revile. [C16: from Latin *vituperāre* to blame, from *vitium* a defect + *parāre* to make] **—vi+ˈtu+per·ˌa+tor** *n.*

vi+tu+per·a+tion (vɪˌtjuːpəˈreɪʃən) *n.* **1.** abusive language or venomous censure. **2.** the act of vituperating. **—vi+tu+per·a+tive** (vɪˈtjuːpərətɪv, -prətɪv) *adj.* **—vi+ˈtu+per·a+tive+ly** *adv.*

vi·va[1] (ˈviːvə) *interj.* long live; up with (a specified person or thing). [C17: from Italian, literally: may (he) live! from *vivere* to live, from Latin *vīvere*]

vi·va[2] (ˈvaɪvə) *Brit.* *~n.* **1.** an oral examination. *~vb.* **+vas, +va+ing, +vaed.** *(tr.)* **2.** to examine orally. [shortened from VIVA VOCE]

vi+va+ce (vɪˈvɑːtʃɪ) *adj., adv. Music.* to be performed in a brisk lively manner. [C17: from Italian, from Latin *vīvax* long-lived, vigorous, from *vīvere* to live]

vi+va+cious (vɪˈveɪʃəs) *adj.* **1.** full of high spirits and animation; lively or vital. **2.** *Obsolete.* having or displaying tenacity of life. [C17: from Latin *vīvax* lively; see VIVACE] **—vi+ˈva+cious+ly** *adv.* **—vi+ˈva+cious+ness** *n.*

vi+vac·i·ty (vɪˈvæsɪtɪ) *n., pl.* **·ties. 1.** the quality or condition of being vivacious. **2.** *(often pl.) Rare.* a vivacious act or expression.

Vi·val·di (vɪˈvældɪ) *n.* **An·to·nio** (anˈtɔːnjo). ?1675–1741, Italian composer and violinist, noted esp. for his development of the solo concerto. His best-known work is *The Four Seasons* (1725).

vi+van+dière *French.* (vivɑ̃ˈdjɛːr) *n.* (formerly) a female sutler or victualler offering extra provisions and spirits to soldiers, esp. those of the French and British armies. [C16: see VIAND]

vi+var+i·um (vaɪˈvɛərɪəm) *n., pl.* **+i·ums** *or* **·i·a** (-ɪə). a place where live animals are kept under natural conditions for study, research, etc. [C16: from Latin: enclosure where live fish or game are kept, from *vīvus* alive]

vi·va vo·ce (ˈvaɪvə ˈvəʊtʃɪ) *adv., adj.* **1.** by word of mouth. *~n., vb.* **2.** the full form of **viva**[2]. [C16: from Medieval Latin, literally: with living voice]

vive (viːv) *interj.* long live; up with (a specified person or thing). [from French]

vi+ver+rine (vaɪˈvɛraɪn) *adj.* **1.** of, relating to, or belonging to the *Viverridae,* a family of small to medium-sized predatory mammals of Eurasia and Africa, including genets, civets and mongooses: order *Carnivora* (carnivores). *~n.* **2.** any animal belonging to the family *Viverridae.* [C19: from New Latin *viverrīnus,* from Latin *viverra* a ferret]

Viv·i·an (ˈvɪvɪən) *n.* (in Arthurian legend) the mistress of Merlin. Also called: the **Lady of the Lake.**

viv+id (ˈvɪvɪd) *adj.* **1.** (of a colour) very bright; having a very high saturation or purity; produced by a pure or almost pure colouring agent. **2.** brilliantly coloured: *vivid plumage.* **3.** conveying to the mind striking realism, freshness, or trueness to life; graphic: *a vivid account.* **4.** (of a recollection, memory, etc.) remaining distinct in the mind. **5.** (of the imagination, etc.) prolific in the formation of lifelike images. **6.** making a powerful impact on the emotions or senses: *a vivid feeling of shame.* **7.** uttered, operating, or acting with vigour: *vivid expostulations.* **8.** full of life or vitality: *a vivid personality.* [C17: from Latin *vīvidus* animated, from *vīvere* to live] **—ˈviv+id+ly** *adv.* **—ˈviv+id+ness** *n.*

viv·i·fy (ˈvɪvɪˌfaɪ) *vb.* **+fies, +fy+ing, +fied.** *(tr.)* **1.** to bring to life; animate. **2.** to make more vivid or striking. [C16: from Late Latin *vīvificāre,* from Latin *vīvus* alive + *facere* to make] **—ˌviv·i·fi·ˈca+tion** *n.* **—ˈviv·i·ˌfi+er** *n.*

vi+vip+ar+ous (vɪˈvɪpərəs) *adj.* **1.** (of most mammals) giving birth to living offspring that develop within the uterus of the mother. Compare **oviparous, ovoviviparous. 2.** (of seeds) germinating before separating from the parent plant. **3.** (of plants) producing bulbils or young plants instead of flowers. [C17: from Latin *vīviparus,* from *vīvus* alive + *parere* to bring forth] **—viv·i·par·i·ty** (ˌvɪvɪˈpærɪtɪ), **vi+ˈvip·a+rism,** *or* **vi+ˈvip·a+rous+ness** *n.* **—vi+ˈvip·a+rous+ly** *adv.*

viv·i·sect (ˈvɪvɪˌsɛkt, ˌvɪvɪˈsɛkt) *vb.* to subject (an animal) to vivisection. [C19: back formation from VIVISECTION] **—ˈviv·i+ˌsec+tor** *n.*

viv·i+sec+tion (ˌvɪvɪˈsɛkʃən) *n.* the act or practice of performing experiments on living animals, involving cutting into or dissecting the body. [C18: from *vivi-*, from Latin *vivus* living + SECTION, as in DISSECTION] —ˌviv·i·ˈsec·tion·al *adj.* —ˌviv·i·ˈsec·tion·al·ly *adv.*

viv·i·sec·tion·ist (ˌvɪvɪˈsɛkʃənɪst) *n.* **1.** a person who practises vivisection. **2.** a person who advocates the practice of vivisection as being useful or necessary to science.

vi·vo (ˈviːvəʊ) *adj., adv. Music.* (*in combination*) with life and vigour: *allegro vivo.* [Italian: lively]

vix·en (ˈvɪksən) *n.* **1.** a female fox. **2.** a quarrelsome or spiteful woman. [C15 *fixen;* related to Old English *fyxe,* feminine of FOX; compare Old High German *fuhsīn*] —**ˈvix·en·ish** *adj.* —**ˈvix·en·ish·ly** *adv.* —**ˈvix·en·ish·ness** *n.* —**ˈvix·en·ly** *adv., adj.*

Vi·yel·la (vaɪˈɛlə) *n. Trademark.* a soft fabric made of wool and cotton, used esp. for blouses and shirts.

viz. *abbrev. for* videlicet.

Vi·za·ga·pa·tam (vɪˌzægəˈpʌtəm) *n.* a variant spelling of **Vishakhapatnam.**

viz·ard (ˈvɪzəd) *n. Archaic or literary.* a means of disguise; mask; visor. —**ˈviz·ard·ed** *adj.*

viz·ca·cha (vɪsˈkætʃə) *n.* a variant spelling of **viscacha.**

vi·zier (vɪˈzɪə) *n.* a high official in certain Muslim countries, esp. in the former Ottoman Empire. Viziers served in various capacities, such as that of provincial governor or chief minister to the sultan. [C16: from Turkish *vezīr,* from Arabic *wazīr* porter, from *wazara* to bear a burden] —**vi·ˈzier·i·al** *or* **vi·ˈzir·i·al** *adj.* —**vi·ˈzier·ship** *n.*

vi·zier·ate (vɪˈzɪərɪt, -eɪt) *n.* **1.** the position, rank, or authority of a vizier. **2.** the term of office of a vizier.

vi·zor (ˈvaɪzə) *n., vb.* a variant spelling of **visor.**

vizs·la (ˈvɪʒlə) *n.* a breed of Hungarian hunting dog with a smooth rusty-gold coat.[C20: named after *Vizsla,* Hungary]

V-J Day *n.* the day marking the Allied victory over Japan in World War II (15 Aug. 1945).

v.l. *abbrev. for* variant reading. [from Latin *varia lectio*]

V.L. *abbrev. for* Vulgar Latin.

Vlaar·ding·en (*Dutch* ˈvlaːrdɪŋə) *n.* a port in the W Netherlands, in South Holland west of Rotterdam: the third largest port in the Netherlands. Pop.: 81 785 (1973 est.).

Vlach (vlɑːk) or **Wa·lach** (ˈwɑːlɒk) *n.* **1.** a member of a people scattered throughout SE Europe in the early Middle Ages, speaking a Romanic dialect. ~*adj.* **2.** of or relating to Vlachs or their dialect.

Vla·di·kav·kaz (*Russian* vlədikafˈkas) *n.* the former name (until 1944) of **Ordžhonikidze.**

Vla·di·mir[1] (*Russian* vlaˈdimir) *n.* a city in the W central Soviet Union: capital of the principality of Vladimir until the court transferred to Moscow in 1328. Pop.: 271 000 (1975 est.).

Vla·di·mir[2] (ˈvlædɪˌmɪə; *Russian* vlaˈdimir) *n.* **Saint,** called *the Great.* ?956–1015, grand prince of Kiev (980–1015); first Christian ruler of Russia. Feast day: July 15.

Vla·di·vos·tok (*Russian* vlədivasˈtɔk; *English* ˌvlædɪˈvɒstɒk) *n.* a port in the extreme SE Soviet Union, on the Sea of Japan: terminus of the Trans-Siberian Railway; the main Russian Pacific naval base since 1872 and chief Soviet port in the Far East; university (1956). Pop.: 511 000 (1975 est.).

Vla·minck (*French* vlaˈmɛ̃ːk) *n.* **Mau·rice de** (mɔˈris də). 1876–1958, French painter of the Fauve school.

vlei (fleɪ, vleɪ) *n.* **1.** *S. African.* an area of low marshy ground, esp. one that feeds a stream. **2.** *Northern U.S. dialect.* a marsh. [C19: from Afrikaans (for sense 1); from obsolete N American Dutch dialect (for sense 2): VALLEY]

VLF *or* **vlf** *Radio. abbrev. for* very low frequency.

Vlis·sing·en (ˈvlɪsɪŋə) *n.* the Dutch name for **Flushing.**

Vlo·rë (*Albanian* ˈvlorə) *or* **Vlo·në** (*Albanian* ˈvlonə) *n.* a port in SW Albania, on the **Bay of Vlorë:** under Turkish rule from 1462 until Albanian independence was declared here in 1912. Pop.: 50 000 (1970 est.). Ancient name: **Avlona.** Also called: **Valona.**

Vl·ta·va (*Czech* ˈvəltava) *n.* a river in Czechoslovakia, rising in the Bohemian Forest and flowing generally southeast and then north to the River Elbe near Melnik. Length: 434 km (270 miles). German name: **Moldau.**

V.M.D. *abbrev. for* Doctor of Veterinary Medicine. [Latin *veterinariae medicinae doctor*]

VN *international car registration for* Vietnam.

V neck *n.* a neck on a garment that comes down to a point on the throat or chest, resembling the shape of the letter 'V'. —**ˈV-ˌneck** *or* **ˈV-ˌnecked** *adj.*

V.O. *abbrev. for* very old: used to imply that a brandy or whisky is old, now often extended to port and other dessert wines.

vo. *abbrev. for* verso.

voc. *or* **vocat.** *abbrev. for* vocative.

vo·cab (ˈvəʊkæb) *n.* short for **vocabulary.**

vo·ca·ble (ˈvəʊkəbəl) *n.* **1.** any word, either written or spoken, regarded simply as a sequence of letters or spoken sounds, irrespective of its meaning. **2.** a vocal sound; vowel. ~*adj.* **3.** capable of being uttered. [C16: from Latin *vocābulum* a designation, from *vocāre* to call] —**ˈvo·ca·bly** *adv.*

vo·cab·u·lar·y (vəˈkæbjʊlərɪ) *n., pl.* **·lar·ies.** **1.** a listing, either selective or exhaustive, containing the words and phrases of a language, with meanings or translations into another language; glossary. **2.** the aggregate of words in the use or comprehension of a specified person, class, profession, etc. **3.** all the words contained in a language. **4.** a range or system of symbols, qualities, or techniques constituting a means of communication or expression, as any of the arts or crafts: *a wide vocabulary of textures and colours.* [C16: from Medieval Latin *vocābulārium,* from *vocābulārius* concerning words, from Latin *vocābulum* VOCABLE]

vo·cal (ˈvəʊkəl) *adj.* **1.** of, relating to, or designed for the voice: *vocal music.* **2.** produced or delivered by the voice: *vocal noises.* **3.** connected with an attribute or the production of the voice: *vocal organs.* **4.** frequently disposed to outspoken speech, criticism, etc.: *a vocal minority.* **5.** full of sound or voices: *a vocal assembly.* **6.** endowed with a voice. **7.** eloquent or meaningful. **8.** *Phonetics.* **a.** of or relating to a speech sound. **b.** of or relating to a voiced speech sound, esp. a vowel. ~*n.* **9.** a piece of jazz or pop music that is sung. **10.** a performance of such a piece of music. [C14: from Latin *vōcālis* possessed of a voice, from *vōx* voice] —**vo·cal·i·ty** (vəʊˈkælɪtɪ) *or* **ˈvo·cal·ness** *n.* —**ˈvo·cal·ly** *adv.*

vo·cal cords *pl. n.* either of two pairs of mucomembranous folds in the larynx. The upper pair (**false vocal cords**) are not concerned with vocal production; the lower pair (**true vocal cords** or **vocal folds**) can be made to vibrate and produce sound when air from the lungs is forced over them. See also **glottis.**

vo·cal folds *pl. n.* See **vocal cords.**

vo·cal·ic (vəʊˈkælɪk) *adj. Phonetics.* of, relating to, or containing a vowel or vowels.

vo·cal·ise (ˌvəʊkəˈliːz) *n.* a musical passage sung upon one vowel as an exercise to develop flexibility and control of pitch and tone; solfeggio.

vo·cal·ism (ˈvəʊkəˌlɪzəm) *n.* **1.** the exercise of the voice, as in singing or speaking. **2.** singing, esp. in respect to technique or skill. **3.** *Phonetics.* **a.** a voiced speech sound, esp. a vowel. **b.** a system of vowels as used in a language.

vo·cal·ist (ˈvəʊkəlɪst) *n.* a singer, esp. one who regularly appears with a jazz band or pop group.

vo·cal·ize *or* **vo·cal·ise** (ˈvəʊkəˌlaɪz) *vb.* **1.** to express with or use the voice; articulate (a speech, song, etc.). **2.** (*tr.*) to make vocal or articulate. **3.** (*tr.*) *Phonetics.* **a.** to articulate (a speech sound) with voice. **b.** to change (a consonant) into a vowel. **4.** another word for **vowelize.** **5.** (*intr.*) to sing a melody on a vowel, etc. —**ˌvo·cal·i·ˈza·tion** *or* **ˌvo·cal·i·ˈsa·tion** *n.* —**ˈvo·cal·ˌiz·er** *or* **ˈvo·cal·ˌis·er** *n.*

vo·cal score *n.* a musical score that shows voice parts in full and orchestral parts in the form of a piano transcription.

vo·ca·tion (vəʊˈkeɪʃən) *n.* **1.** a specified occupation, profession, or trade. **2. a.** a special urge, inclination, or predisposition to a particular calling or career, esp. a religious one. **b.** such a calling or career. [C15: from Latin *vocātiō* a calling, from *vocāre* to call]

vo·ca·tion·al (vəʊˈkeɪʃənəl) *adj.* **1.** of or relating to a vocation or vocations. **2.** of or relating to applied educational courses concerned with skills needed for an occupation, trade, or profession. —**vo·ˈca·tion·al·ly** *adv.*

vo·ca·tion·al guid·ance *n.* a guidance service based on psychological tests and interviews to find out what career or occupation may best suit a person.

voc·a·tive (ˈvɒkətɪv) *adj.* **1.** relating to, used in, or characterized by calling. **2.** *Grammar.* denoting a case of nouns, in some inflected languages, used when the referent of the noun is being addressed. ~*n.* **3.** *Grammar.* **a.** the vocative case. **b.** a vocative noun or speech element. [C15: from Latin phrase *vocātīvus cāsus* the calling case, from *vocāre* to call] —**ˈvoc·a·tive·ly** *adv.*

vo·ces (ˈvəʊsiːz) *n.* the plural of **vox.**

vo·cif·er·ant (vəʊˈsɪfərənt) *adj.* **1.** a less common word for **vociferous.** ~*n.* **2.** *Rare.* a vociferous person. [C17: from Latin *vōciferārī* to bawl; see VOCIFERATE] —**vo·ˈcif·er·ance** *n.*

vo·cif·er·ate (vəʊˈsɪfəˌreɪt) *vb.* to exclaim or cry out about (something) clamorously, vehemently, or insistently. [C17: from Latin *vōciferārī* to clamour, from *vōx* voice + *ferre* to bear] —**voˌcif·er·ˈa·tion** *n.* —**vo·ˈcif·er·ˌa·tor** *n.*

vo·cif·er·ous (vəʊˈsɪfərəs) *adj.* **1.** characterized by vehemence, clamour, or noisiness: *vociferous protests.* **2.** making an outcry or loud noises; clamorous: *a vociferous mob.* —**vo·ˈcif·er·ous·ly** *adv.* —**vo·ˈcif·er·ous·ness** *n.*

vod·ka (ˈvɒdkə) *n.* an alcoholic drink originating in Russia, made from grain, potatoes, etc., usually consisting only of rectified spirit and water. [C19: from Russian, diminutive of *voda* water; related to Sanskrit *udan* water, Greek *hudōr*]

voet·sek (ˈfʊtsɛk, ˈvʊt-) *interj. S. African slang.* an expletive used when chasing animals away: offensive when addressed to people. [from Afrikaans, from the phrase *voort se ek* away say I]

voets·toots *or* **voets·toets** (ˈfʊtstʊts, ˈvʊt-) *S. African.* ~*adj.* **1.** denoting a sale in which the vendor is freed from all responsibility for the condition of the goods being sold. ~*adv.* **2.** without responsibility for the condition of the goods sold. [Afrikaans, from Dutch]

Vo·gel (ˈvəʊgəl) *n.* Sir **Ju·li·us.** 1835–99, New Zealand statesman; prime minister of New Zealand (1873–75; 1876).

Vo·gel·wei·de (*German* ˈfoːgəlˌvaɪdə) *n.* See **Walther von der Vogelweide.**

vogue (vəʊg) *n.* **1.** the popular style at a specified time (esp. in the phrase **in vogue**). **2.** a period of general or popular usage or favour: *the vogue for such dances is now over.* ~*adj.* **3.** (*usually prenominal*) popular or fashionable: *a vogue word.* [C16: from French: a rowing, fashion, from Old Italian *voga,* from *vogare* to row, of unknown origin] —**ˈvogu·ish** *adj.*

Vo·gul (ˈvəʊgəl) *n.* **1.** (*pl.* **·gul** *or* **·guls**) a member of a people living in W Siberia and NE Europe. **2.** the language of this people, belonging to the Finno-Ugric family: related to Hungarian.

voice (vɔɪs) *n.* **1.** the sound made by the vibration of the vocal cords, esp. when modified by the resonant effect of the tongue and mouth. See also **speech. 2.** the natural and distinctive tone of the speech sounds characteristic of a particular person: *nobody could mistake his voice.* **3.** the condition, quality, effectiveness, or tone of such sounds: *a hysterical voice.* **4.** the musical sound of a singing voice, with respect to its quality or tone: *she has a lovely voice.* **5.** the ability to speak, sing, etc.: *he has lost his voice.* **6.** a sound resembling or suggestive of vocal utterance: *the voice of the sea; the voice of hard experience.* **7.** written or spoken expression, as of feeling, opinion, etc. (esp. in the phrase **give voice to**). **8.** a stated choice, wish, or opinion or the power or right to have an opinion heard and considered: *to give someone a voice in a decision.* **9.** an agency through which is communicated another's purpose, policy, etc.: *such groups are the voice of our enemies.* **10.** *Music.* **a.** musical notes produced by vibrations of the vocal chords at various frequencies and in certain registers: *a tenor voice.* **b.** (in harmony) an independent melodic line or part: *a fugue in five voices.* **11.** *Phonetics.* the sound characterizing the articulation of several speech sounds, including all vowels or sonants, that is produced when the vocal cords make loose contact with each other and are set in vibration by the breath as it forces its way through the glottis. **12.** *Grammar.* a category of the verb or verbal inflections that expresses whether the relation between the subject and the verb is that of agent and action, action and recipient, or some other relation. See **active** (sense 5), **passive** (sense 5), **middle** (sense 5). **13.** *Obsolete.* rumour. **14.** (foll. by *of*) *Obsolete.* fame; renown. **15. in voice.** in a condition to sing or speak well. **16. out of voice.** with the voice temporarily in a poor condition, esp. for singing. **17. with one voice.** unanimously. ~*vb.* (*tr.*) **18.** to utter in words; give expression to: *to voice a complaint.* **19.** to articulate (a speech sound) with voice. **20.** *Music.* to adjust (a wind instrument or organ pipe) so that it conforms to the correct standards of tone colour, pitch, etc. [C13: from Old French *voiz,* from Latin *vōx*] —**'voic·er** *n.*

voice box *n.* another word for the **larynx.**

voiced (vɔɪst) *adj.* **1.** declared or expressed by the voice. **2.** (*in combination*) having a voice as specified: *loud-voiced.* **3.** *Phonetics.* articulated with accompanying vibration of the vocal cords: *in English* (b) *is a voiced consonant.* Compare **voiceless.**

voice·ful ('vɔɪsfʊl) *adj. Poetic.* **1.** endowed with a voice, esp. of loud quality. **2.** full of voices. —**'voice·ful·ness** *n.*

voice-lead·ing ('vɔɪsˌliːdɪŋ) *n. U.S.* another term for **part-writing.**

voice·less ('vɔɪslɪs) *adj.* **1.** without a voice; mute. **2.** not articulated: *voiceless misery.* **3.** lacking a musical voice. **4.** silent. **5.** without the power or right to express an opinion. **6.** *Phonetics.* articulated without accompanying vibration of the vocal cords: *In English* (p) *is a voiceless consonant.* —**'voice·less·ly** *adv.* —**'voice·less·ness** *n.*

voice-o·ver *n.* the voice of an unseen commentator heard during a film, television programme, etc.

voice part *n.* a melodic line written for the voice.

voice·print ('vɔɪsˌprɪnt) *n.* a graphic representation of a person's voice recorded electronically, usually having time plotted along the horizontal axis and the frequency of the speech on the vertical axis.

voice vote *n.* a vote taken in a legislative body by calling for the ayes and the noes and estimating which faction is more numerous from the volume of the noise.

void (vɔɪd) *adj.* **1.** without contents; empty. **2.** not legally binding: *null and void.* **3.** (of an office, house, position, etc.) without an incumbent; unoccupied. **4.** (*postpositive;* foll. by *of*) destitute or devoid: *void of resources.* **5.** having no effect; useless: *all his efforts were rendered void.* **6.** (of a card suit or player) having no cards in a particular suit: *his spades were void.* ~*n.* **7.** an empty space or area: *the huge desert voids of Asia.* **8.** a feeling or condition of loneliness or deprivation: *his divorce left him in a void.* **9.** a lack of any cards in one suit: *to have a void in spades.* **10.** Also called: **counter.** the inside area of a character of type, such as the inside of an *o.* ~*vb.* (*mainly tr.*) **11.** to make ineffective or invalid. **12.** to empty (contents, etc.) or make empty of contents. **13.** (*also intr.*) to discharge the contents of (the bowels or urinary bladder). **14.** *Archaic.* to vacate (a place, room, etc.). **15.** *Obsolete.* to expel. [C13: from Old French *vuide,* from Vulgar Latin *vocītus* (unattested), from Latin *vacuus* empty, from *vacāre* to be empty] —**'void·er** *n.* —**'void·ness** *n.*

void·a·ble ('vɔɪdəbᵊl) *adj.* **1.** capable of being voided. **2.** capable of being legally annulled or made void. —**'void·a·ble·ness** *n.*

void·ance ('vɔɪdᵊns) *n.* **1.** an annulment, as of a contract. **2.** the condition of being vacant, as an office, benefice, etc. **3.** the act of voiding, ejecting, or evacuating. [C14: variant of AVOIDANCE]

void·ed ('vɔɪdɪd) *adj.* **1.** *Heraldry.* (of a design) with a hole in the centre of the same shape as the design: *a voided lozenge.* **2.** *Rare.* having a void or made void.

voile (vɔɪl; *French* vwal) *n.* a light semitransparent fabric of silk, rayon, cotton, etc., used for dresses, scarves, shirts, etc. [C19: from French: VEIL]

Voi·o·ti·a (*Greek* vjɔ'tiːa) *n.* a department of E central Greece: corresponds to ancient Boeotia and part of ancient Phocis. Pop.: 114 675 (1971). Area: 3173 sq. km (1225 sq. miles). Ancient name: **Boeotia.**

voir dire (vwɑː 'dɪə) *n. Law.* **1.** the preliminary examination on oath of a proposed witness by the judge. **2.** the oath administered to such a witness. [C17: from Old French: to speak the truth]

voix cé·leste (vwɑː sɛ'lɛst) *n.* an organ stop which produces a tremolo effect through the acoustic phenomenon of beats. [from French: heavenly voice]

Voj·vo·di·na *or* **Voi·vo·di·na** (*Serbo-Croatian* 'vɔjvɔdina) *n.* an autonomous region of NE Yugoslavia, in N Serbia: a major agricultural region. Capital: Novi Sad. Pop.: 1 935 115 (1971). Area: 22 489 sq. km (8683 sq. miles).

vol. *abbrev. for:* **1.** volcano. **2.** volume. **3.** volunteer.

Vo·lans ('vəʊlænz) *n., Latin genitive* **Vo·lan·tis** (vəʊ'læntɪs). a small constellation in the S hemisphere lying between Carina and Hydrus. [C19: from Latin, literally: flying, from *volāre* to fly]

vo·lant ('vəʊlənt) *adj.* **1.** (*usually postpositive*) *Heraldry.* in a flying position. **2.** *Rare.* flying or capable of flight. **3.** *Poetic.* moving lightly or agilely; nimble. [C16: from French: flying, from *voler* to fly, from Latin *volāre*]

Vol·a·puk *or* **Vol·a·pük** ('vɒləˌpʊk) *n.* an artificial language based on English, French, German, Latin, etc., invented in 1880 by Johann Schleyer (1831–1912). [C19: from *vol,* based on WORLD + euphonic *-a-* + *pük* speech, based on SPEAK]

vo·lar[1] ('vəʊlə) *adj. Anatomy.* of or relating to the palm of the hand or the sole of the foot. [C19: from Latin *vola* hollow of the hand, palm, sole of the foot]

vo·lar[2] ('vəʊlə) *adj. Rare.* relating to or employed in flying. [C19: from Latin *volāre* to fly]

vol·a·tile ('vɒləˌtaɪl) *adj.* **1.** (of a substance) capable of readily changing from a solid or liquid form to a vapour; having a high vapour pressure and a low boiling point. **2.** (of persons) disposed to caprice or inconstancy; fickle; mercurial. **3.** (of circumstances) liable to sudden, unpredictable, or explosive change. **4.** lasting only a short time: *volatile business interests.* **5.** *Computer technol.* (of a memory) not retaining stored information when the power supply is cut off. **6.** *Obsolete.* flying or capable of flight; volant. ~*n.* **7.** a volatile substance. **8.** *Rare.* a winged creature. [C17: from Latin *volātilis* flying, from *volāre* to fly] —**'vol·a·tile·ness** *or* **vol·a·til·i·ty** (ˌvɒlə'tɪlɪtɪ) *n.*

vol·a·tile oil *n.* another name for **essential oil.**

vol·a·tile salt *n.* another name for **sal volatile.**

vo·lat·i·lize *or* **vo·lat·i·lise** (vɒ'lætɪˌlaɪz) *vb.* to change or cause to change from a solid or liquid to a vapour. —**vo·'lat·i·ˌliz·a·ble** *or* **vo·'lat·i·ˌlis·a·ble** *adj.* —**vo·ˌlat·i·liz·'a·tion** *or* **vo·ˌlat·i·lis·'a·tion** *n.*

vol-au-vent (*French* vɔlo'vɑ̃) *n.* a very light puff pastry case filled either with a savoury mixture in a richly flavoured sauce or sometimes with fruit. [C19: from French, literally: flight in the wind]

vol·can·ic (vɒl'kænɪk) *adj.* **1.** of, relating to, produced by, or characterized by the presence of volcanoes: *a volcanic region.* **2.** suggestive of or resembling an erupting volcano: *a volcanic era.* **3.** another word for **extrusive** (sense 2). —**vol·'can·i·cal·ly** *adv.* —**vol·can·ic·i·ty** (ˌvɒlkə'nɪsɪtɪ) *n.*

vol·can·ic glass *n.* any of several glassy volcanic igneous rocks, such as obsidian and pitchstone.

vol·can·ism ('vɒlkəˌnɪzəm) *or* **vul·can·ism** *n.* those processes collectively that result in the formation of volcanoes and their products.

vol·can·ize *or* **vol·can·ise** ('vɒlkəˌnaɪz) *vb.* (*tr.*) to subject to the effects of or change by volcanic heat. —**ˌvol·can·i·'za·tion** *or* **ˌvol·can·i·'sa·tion** *n.*

vol·ca·no (vɒl'keɪnəʊ) *n., pl.* **·noes** *or* **·nos. 1.** an opening in the earth's crust from which molten lava, rock fragments, ashes, dust, and gases are ejected from below the earth's surface. **2.** a mountain formed from volcanic material ejected from a vent in a central crater. [C17: from Italian, from Latin *Volcānus* VULCAN, whose forges were believed to be responsible for volcanic rumblings]

Vol·ca·no Is·lands *pl. n.* a group of three volcanic islands in the W Pacific, about 1100 km (700 miles) south of Japan: the largest is Iwo Jima, taken by U.S. forces in 1945 and returned to Japan in 1968. Area: about 28 sq. km (11 sq. miles). Japanese name: **Kazan Retto.**

vol·can·ol·o·gy (ˌvɒlkə'nɒlədʒɪ) *or* **vul·can·ol·o·gy** *n.* the study of volcanoes and volcanic phenomena. —**vol·can·o·log·i·cal** (ˌvɒlkənə'lɒdʒɪkᵊl) *or* **ˌvul·can·o·'log·i·cal** *adj.* —**ˌvol·can·'ol·o·gist** *or* **ˌvul·can·'ol·o·gist** *n.*

vole[1] (vəʊl) *n.* any of numerous small rodents of the genus *Microtus* and related genera, mostly of Eurasia and North America and having a stocky body, short tail, and inconspicuous ears: family *Cricetidae.* See also **water vole.** [C19: short for *volemouse,* from Old Norse *vollr* field + *mus* MOUSE; related to Icelandic *vollarmus*]

vole[2] (vəʊl) *n.* (in some card games, such as écarté) the taking of all the tricks in a deal, thus scoring extra points. [C17: from French, from *voler* to fly, from Latin *volāre*]

Vol·ga ('vɒlgə) *n.* a river in the W Soviet Union, rising in the Valdai Range and flowing through a chain of small lakes to the Rybinsk Reservoir and south to the Caspian Sea through Volgograd: the longest river in Europe. Length: 3690 km (2293 miles).

Vol·go·grad (*Russian* vəlga'grat; *English* 'vɒlgəˌgræd) *n.* a port in the W central Soviet Union, on the River Volga: scene of a major engagement (1918) during the civil war and again in World War II (1942–43), in which the German forces were defeated; major industrial centre. Pop.: 900 000 (1975 est.). Former names: **Tsaritsyn** (until 1925), **Stalingrad** (1925–61).

vol·i·tant ('vɒlɪtənt) *adj.* **1.** flying or moving about rapidly. **2.** capable of flying. [C19: from Latin *volitāre* to flit, from *volāre* to fly]

vo·li·tion (və'lɪʃən) *n.* **1.** the act of exercising the will: *of one's own volition.* **2.** the faculty or capability of conscious choice, decision, and intention; the will. **3.** the resulting choice or resolution. [C17: from Medieval Latin *volitiō*, from Latin *vol-* as in *volō* I will, present stem of *velle* to wish] —**vo·'li·tion·al** *or* **vo·'li·tion·ar·y** *adj.* —**vo·'li·tion·al·ly** *adv.*

vol·i·tive ('vɒlɪtɪv) *adj.* **1.** of, relating to, or emanating from the will. **2.** *Grammar.* another word for **desiderative.**

Völk·er·wan·der·ung *German* ('fœlkərˌvandəruŋ) *n.* the migration of peoples, esp. of Germanic and Slavic peoples into S and W Europe from 2nd to 11th centuries.

Volks·lied *German.* ('fɔlksˌli:t) *n., pl.* ***·lied·er*** (-ˌli:dər). a type of popular German folk song. [literally: folk song]

vol·ley ('vɒlɪ) *n.* **1.** the simultaneous discharge of several weapons, esp. firearms. **2.** the projectiles or missiles so discharged. **3.** a burst of oaths, protests, etc., occurring simultaneously or in rapid succession. **4.** *Sport.* a stroke, shot, or kick at a moving ball before it hits the ground. Compare **half volley. 5.** *Cricket.* the flight of such a ball or the ball itself. **6.** the simultaneous explosion of several blastings of rock. ~*vb.* **7.** to discharge (weapons, etc.) in or as if in a volley or (of weapons, etc.) to be discharged. **8.** (*tr.*) to utter vehemently or sound loudly and continuously. **9.** (*tr.*) *Sport.* to strike or kick (a moving ball) before it hits the ground. **10.** (*intr.*) to issue or move rapidly or indiscriminately. [C16: from French *volée* a flight, from *voler* to fly, from Latin *volāre*] —**'vol·ley·er** *n.*

vol·ley·ball ('vɒlɪˌbɔ:l) *n.* **1.** a game in which two teams hit a large ball back and forth over a high net with their hands. **2.** the ball used in this game.

Vo·log·da (*Russian* 'vɔləgdə) *n.* an industrial city in the NW central Soviet Union. Pop.: 212 000 (1975 est.).

Vó·los (*Greek* 'vɔlɔs) *n.* a port in E Greece, in Thessaly on the **Gulf of Volos** (an inlet of the Aegean): the third largest port in Greece. Pop.: 51 290 (1971).

vo·lost ('vəulɒst) *n.* **1.** (in the Soviet Union) a rural soviet. **2.** (in tsarist Russia) a peasant community consisting of several villages or hamlets. [from Russian]

vol·plane ('vɒlˌpleɪn) *vb.* **1.** (*intr.*) (of an aircraft) to glide without engine power. ~*n.* **2.** a glide by an aircraft. [C20: from French *vol plané* a gliding flight]

vols. *abbrev. for* volumes.

Vol·sci ('vɒlski:) *n.* a warlike people of ancient Latium, subdued by Rome in the fifth and fourth centuries B.C.

Vol·sci·an ('vɒlskɪən) *n.* **1.** a member of the Volsci. **2.** the extinct language of the Volsci, closely related to Umbrian. ~*adj.* **3.** of or relating to the Volsci or their language.

Vol·sung ('vɒlsuŋ) *n.* **1.** a great hero of Norse and Germanic legend and poetry who gave his name to a race of warriors; father of Sigmund and Signy. **2.** any member of his family.

Vol·sun·ga Sa·ga ('vɒlsuŋgə) *n.* a 13th-century Icelandic saga about the family of the Volsungs and the deeds of Sigurd, related in theme and story to the Nibelungenlied.

volt[1] (vəult) *n.* the derived SI unit of electric potential; the potential difference between two points on a conductor carrying a current of 1 ampere, when the power dissipated between these points is 1 watt. Symbol: V [C19: named after Count Alessandro Volta; see VOLTA[2]]

volt[2] *or* **volte** (vɒlt) *n.* **1.** a small circle of determined size executed in dressage. **2.** a leap made in fencing to avoid an opponent's thrust. [C17: from French *volte*, from Italian *volta* a turn, ultimately from Latin *volvere* to turn]

vol·ta ('vɒltə; *Italian* 'vɔlta) *n., pl.* **·te** (*Italian* -te). **1.** a quick-moving Italian dance popular during the 16th and 17th centuries. **2.** a piece of music written for or in the rhythm of this dance, in triple time. [C17: from Italian: turn; see VOLT[2]]

Vol·ta[1] ('vɒltə) *n.* **1.** a river in W Africa, formed by the confluence of the **Black Volta** and the **White Volta** in N central Ghana: flows south to the Bight of Benin: the chief river of Ghana. Length: 480 km (300 miles); (including the Black Volta) 1600 km (1000 miles). **2. Lake.** an artificial lake in Ghana, extending 408 km (250 miles) upstream from the **Volta River Dam** on the Volta River: completed in 1966. Area: 8482 sq. km (3275 sq. miles).

Vol·ta[2] ('vəultə; *Italian* 'vɔlta) *n.* Count **A·les·san·dro** (ˌales'sandro). 1745–1827, Italian physicist after whom the volt is named. He made important contributions to the theory of current electricity and invented the voltaic pile (1800), the electrophorus (1775), and an electroscope.

volt·age ('vəultɪdʒ) *n.* an electromotive force or potential difference expressed in volts.

volt·age di·vid·er *n.* another name for a **potential divider.**

vol·ta·ic (vɒl'teɪɪk) *adj.* another word for **galvanic** (sense 1).

Vol·ta·ic (vɒl'teɪɪk) *adj.* **1.** of or relating to the Republic of Upper Volta. **2.** denoting, belonging to, or relating to the Gur group of African languages. ~*n.* **3.** this group of languages. See also **Gur.**

vol·ta·ic cell *n.* another name for **primary cell.**

vol·ta·ic cou·ple *n. Physics.* a pair of dissimilar metals in an electrolyte with a potential difference between the metals resulting from chemical action.

vol·ta·ic pile *n.* an early form of battery consisting of a pile of alternate dissimilar metals, such as zinc and copper, separated by pads moistened with an electrolyte. Also called: **galvanic pile, Volta's pile.**

Vol·taire (vɒl'tɛə, vəul-; *French* vɔl'tɛ:r) *n.* pseudonym of *François Marie Arouet.* 1694–1778, French writer, whose outspoken belief in religious, political, and social liberty made him the embodiment of the 18th-century Enlightenment. His major works include *Lettres philosophiques* (1734) and the satire *Candide* (1759). He also wrote plays, such as *Zaire* (1732), poems, and scientific studies. He suffered several periods of banishment for his radical views. —**Vol·'tair·e·an** *or* **Vol·'tair·i·an** *adj., n.*

vol·ta·ism ('vɒltəˌɪzəm) *n.* another name for **galvanism.**

vol·tam·e·ter (vɒl'tæmɪtə) *n.* another name for **coulometer.** —**vol·ta·met·ric** (ˌvɒltə'mɛtrɪk) *adj.*

volt·am·me·ter (ˌvəult'æmˌmi:tə) *n.* a dual-purpose instrument that can measure both potential difference and electric current, usually in volts and amperes respectively.

volt-am·pere *n.* a unit of electrical power in an alternating-current circuit equal to the power dissipated when an effective voltage of one volt produces an effective current of one ampere.

Vol·ta Re·don·da (*Portuguese* 'vɔlta rɛ'dõnda) *n.* a city in SE Brazil, in Rio de Janeiro state on the Paraíba River: founded in 1941; site of South America's largest steelworks. Pop.: 120 645 (1970).

volte-face ('vɒlt'fɑ:s) *n., pl.* **volte-face. 1.** a reversal, as in opinion or policy. **2.** a change of position so as to look, lie, etc., in the opposite direction. [C19: from French, from Italian *volta-faccia*, from *volta* a turn + *faccia* face]

volt·me·ter ('vəultˌmi:tə) *n.* an instrument for measuring potential difference or electromotive force.

Vol·tur·no (*Italian* vol'turno) *n.* a river in S central Italy, flowing southeast and southwest to the Tyrrhenian Sea: scene of a battle (1860) during the wars for Italian unity, in which Garibaldi defeated the Neapolitans; German line of defence during World War II. Length: 175 km (109 miles).

vol·u·ble ('vɒljub°l) *adj.* **1.** talking easily, readily, and at length; fluent. **2.** *Archaic.* easily turning or rotating, as on an axis. **3.** *Rare.* (of a plant) twining or twisting. [C16: from Latin *volūbilis* turning readily, fluent, from *volvere* to turn] —**ˌvol·u·'bil·i·ty** *or* **'vol·u·ble·ness** *n.* —**'vol·u·bly** *adv.*

vol·ume ('vɒlju:m) *n.* **1.** the magnitude of the three-dimensional space enclosed within or occupied by an object, geometric solid, etc. Symbol: *V* **2.** a large mass or quantity: *the volume of protest.* **3.** an amount or total: *the volume of exports.* **4.** fullness or intensity of tone or sound. **5.** the control on a radio, etc., for adjusting the intensity of sound. **6.** a bound collection of printed or written pages; book. **7.** any of several books either bound in an identical format or part of a series. **8.** the complete set of issues of a periodical over a specified period, esp. one year. **9.** *History.* a roll or scroll of parchment, papyrus, etc. **10. speak volumes.** to convey much significant information. ~Abbrev. (for senses 6–8): **v., vol.** [C14: from Old French *volum*, from Latin *volūmen* a roll, book, from *volvere* to roll up]

vol·umed ('vɒlju:md) *adj.* **1.** (of literary works) **a.** consisting of or being in volumes. **b.** (*in combination*): *a three-volumed history.* **2.** *Rare.* having bulk or volume. **3.** *Poetic.* forming a rounded mass.

vo·lu·me·ter (vɒ'lju:mɪtə) *n.* any instrument for measuring the volume of a solid, liquid, or gas.

vol·u·met·ric (ˌvɒlju'mɛtrɪk) *adj.* of, concerning, or using measurement by volume: *volumetric analysis.* Compare **gravimetric.** —ˌ**vol·u·'met·ri·cal·ly** *adv.* —**vo·lu·me·try** (vɒ'lju:mɪtrɪ) *n.*

vol·u·met·ric an·al·y·sis *n. Chem.* **1.** quantitative analysis of liquids or solutions by comparing the volumes that react with known volumes of standard reagents, usually by titration. Compare **gravimetric analysis. 2.** quantitative analysis of gases by volume.

vo·lu·mi·nous (və'lu:mɪnəs) *adj.* **1.** of great size, quantity, volume, or extent. **2.** (of writing) consisting of or sufficient to fill volumes. **3.** prolific in writing or speech. **4.** *Obsolete.* winding. [C17: from Late Latin *volūminōsus* full of windings, from *volūmen* VOLUME] —**vo·lu·mi·nos·i·ty** (vəˌlu:mɪ'nɒsɪtɪ) *or* **vo·'lu·mi·nous·ness** *n.* —**vo·'lu·mi·nous·ly** *adv.*

Vö·lund ('vølund) *n.* the Scandinavian name of **Wayland.**

vol·un·ta·rism ('vɒləntəˌrɪzəm) *n.* **1.** *Philosophy.* the theory that the will rather than the intellect is the ultimate principle of reality. **2.** a doctrine or system based on voluntary participation in a course of action. **3.** another name for **voluntaryism.** —**'vol·un·ta·rist** *n., adj.* —ˌ**vol·un·ta·'ris·tic** *adj.*

vol·un·tar·y ('vɒləntərɪ, -trɪ) *adj.* **1.** performed, undertaken, or brought about by free choice, willingly, or without being asked: *a voluntary donation.* **2.** (of persons) serving or acting in a specified function of one's own accord and without compulsion or promise of remuneration: *a voluntary social worker.* **3.** done by, composed of, or functioning with the aid of volunteers: *a voluntary association.* **4.** endowed with, exercising, or having the faculty of willing: *a voluntary agent.* **5.** arising from natural impulse; spontaneous: *voluntary laughter.* **6.** *Law.* **a.** acting or done without legal obligation, compulsion, or persuasion. **b.** made without payment or recompense in any form: *a voluntary conveyance.* **7.** (of the muscles of the limbs, neck, etc.) having their action controlled by the will. **8.** maintained or provided by the voluntary actions or contributions of individuals and not by the state: *voluntary schools; the voluntary system.* ~*n., pl.* **·tar·ies. 9.** *Music.* a composition or improvisation, usually for organ, played at the beginning or end of a church service. **10.** work done without compulsion. **11.** *Obsolete.* a volunteer, esp. in an army. [C14: from Latin *voluntārius*, from *voluntās* will, from *velle* to wish] —**'vol·un·tar·i·ly** *adv.* —**'vol·un·tar·i·ness** *n.*

vol·un·tar·y·ism ('vɒləntərɪˌɪzəm, -trɪ-) *or* **vol·un·ta·rism** *n.* **1.** the principle of supporting churches, schools, and various other institutions by voluntary contributions rather than with state funds. **2.** any system based on this principle. —**'vol·un·tar·y·ist** *or* **'vol·un·ta·rist** *n.*

vol·un·teer (ˌvɒlənˈtɪə) *n.* **1. a.** a person who performs or offers to perform voluntary service. **b.** (*as modifier*): *a volunteer system; volunteer advice.* **2.** a person who freely undertakes military service, esp. temporary or special service. **3.** *Law.* **a.** a person who does some act or enters into a transaction without being under any legal obligation to do so and without being promised any remuneration for his services. **b.** *Property law.* a person to whom property is transferred without his giving any valuable consideration in return, as a legatee under a will. **4. a.** a plant that grows from seed that has not been deliberately sown. **b.** (*as modifier*): *a volunteer plant.* ~*vb.* **5.** to offer (oneself or one's services) for an undertaking by choice and without request or obligation. **6.** (*tr.*) to perform, give, or communicate voluntarily: *to volunteer help; to volunteer a speech.* **7.** (*intr.*) to enlist voluntarily for military service. [C17: from French *volontaire,* from Latin *voluntārius* willing; see VOLUNTARY]

Vol·un·teers of A·mer·i·ca *n.* a religious body aimed at reform and relief of human need and resembling the Salvation Army in organization and tenets, founded in New York City in 1896 by Ballington Booth.

vo·lup·tu·ar·y (vəˈlʌptjʊərɪ) *n., pl.* **-ar·ies. 1.** a person devoted or addicted to luxury and sensual pleasures. ~*adj.* **2.** of, relating to, characterized by, or furthering sensual gratification or luxury. [C17: from Late Latin *voluptuārius* delightful, from Latin *voluptās* pleasure]

vo·lup·tu·ous (vəˈlʌptjʊəs) *adj.* **1.** relating to, characterized by, or consisting of pleasures of the body or senses; sensual. **2.** disposed, devoted, or addicted to sensual indulgence or luxurious pleasures. **3.** provocative and sexually alluring, esp. through shapeliness or fullness: *a voluptuous woman.* [C14: from Latin *voluptuōsus* full of gratification, from *voluptās* pleasure] —**vo·'lup·tu·ous·ly** *adv.* —**vo·'lup·tu·ous·ness** *or* **vo·lup·tu·os·i·ty** (vəˌlʌptjʊˈɒsɪtɪ) *n.*

vol·ute (ˈvɒljuːt, vəˈluːt) *n.* **1.** a spiral or twisting turn, form, or object; spiral; whorl. **2.** Also called: **helix.** a carved ornament, esp. as used on an Ionic capital, that has the form of a spiral scroll. **3.** any of the whorls of the spirally coiled shell of a snail or similar gastropod mollusc. **4.** any tropical marine gastropod mollusc of the family *Volutidae,* typically having a spiral shell with beautiful markings. **5.** a tangential part, resembling the volute of a snail's shell, that collects the fluids emerging from the periphery of a turbine, impeller pump, etc. ~*adj. also* **vo·lut·ed** (vəˈluːtɪd). **6.** having the form of a volute; spiral. **7.** *Machinery.* moving in a spiral path. [C17: from Latin *volūta* a spiral decoration, from *volūtus* rolled, from *volvere* to roll up]

vo·lu·tion (vəˈluːʃən) *n.* **1.** a rolling, revolving, or spiral form or motion. **2.** a whorl of a spiral gastropod shell.

vol·va (ˈvɒlvə) *n., pl.* **-vae** (-viː) *or* **-vas.** *Botany.* a cup-shaped structure that sheathes the base of the stalk of certain mushrooms. [C18: from Latin: a covering, from *volvere* to wrap] —**vol·vate** (ˈvɒlvɪt, -veɪt) *adj.*

vol·vox (ˈvɒlvɒks) *n.* any freshwater flagellate protozoan of the genus *Volvox,* occurring in colonies in the form of hollow multicellular spheres: class *Mastigophora* (or *Flagellata*). [C18: from New Latin, from Latin *volvere* to roll]

vol·vu·lus (ˈvɒlvjʊləs) *n., pl.* **-lus·es.** *Pathol.* an abnormal twisting of the intestines causing obstruction. [C17: from New Latin, from Latin *volvere* to twist]

vo·mer (ˈvəʊmə) *n.* the thin flat bone forming part of the separation between the nasal passages in mammals. [C18: from Latin: ploughshare] —**vo·mer·ine** (ˈvəʊməˌraɪn, -rɪn, ˈvɒm-) *adj.*

vom·it (ˈvɒmɪt) *vb.* **1.** to eject (the contents of the stomach) through the mouth as the result of involuntary muscular spasms of the stomach and oesophagus. **2.** to eject or be ejected forcefully; spew forth. ~*n.* **3.** the matter ejected in vomiting. **4.** the act of vomiting. **5.** a drug or agent that induces vomiting; emetic. [C14: from Latin *vomitāre* to vomit repeatedly, from *vomere* to vomit] —**'vom·it·er** *n.*

vom·i·to·ry (ˈvɒmɪtərɪ, -trɪ) *adj.* **1.** Also: **vom·i·tive** (ˈvɒmɪtɪv). causing vomiting; emetic. ~*n., pl.* **-ries. 2.** Also called: **vomitive.** a vomitory agent. **3.** *Rare.* a container for receiving vomitus. **4.** Also called: **vom·i·to·ri·um** (ˌvɒmɪˈtɔːrɪəm). a passageway in an ancient Roman amphitheatre that connects an outside entrance to a tier of seats. **5.** an opening through which matter is ejected.

vom·i·tu·ri·tion (ˌvɒmɪtjʊˈrɪʃən) *n.* the act of retching.

vom·i·tus (ˈvɒmɪtəs) *n., pl.* **-tus·es. 1.** matter that has been vomited. **2.** the act of vomiting. [Latin: a vomiting]

von Braun (vɒn ˈbraʊn, fɒn) *n.* **Wern·her.** 1912–77, U.S. rocket engineer, born in Germany, where he designed the V-2 missile used in World War II. In the U.S. he worked on the Apollo project.

von Neu·mann (vɒn ˈnjuːmən, fɒn) *n.* **John.** 1903–57, U.S. mathematician, born in Hungary. He formulated game theory and contributed to the development of the atomic bomb and to the design of high-speed computers.

von Stern·berg (vɒn ˈstɜːnˌbɜːg, ˈʃtɜːn-, fɒn) *n.* **Jo·seph.** 1894–1969, Austrian film director working in the U.S.

voo·doo (ˈvuːduː) *n., pl.* **-doos. 1.** Also called: **voodooism.** a religious cult involving witchcraft and communication by trance with ancestors and animistic deities, common among Negroes in Haiti and other Caribbean islands. **2.** a person who practises voodoo. **3.** a charm, spell, or fetish involved in voodoo worship and ritual. ~*adj.* **4.** relating to or associated with voodoo. ~*vb.* **-doos, -doo·ing, -dooed. 5.** (*tr.*) to affect by or as if by the power of voodoo. [C19: from Louisiana French *voudou,* ultimately of West African origin; compare Ewe *vodu* guardian spirit] —**'voo·doo·ist** *n.* —**ˌvoo·doo·'is·tic** *adj.*

Voor·trek·ker (ˈfʊəˌtrɛkə, ˈvʊə-) *n.* (in South Africa) **1.** one of the original Afrikaner settlers of the Transvaal and the Orange Free State who migrated from the Cape Colony in the 1830s. **2.** a member of the Afrikaner youth movement founded in 1931. [C19: from Dutch, from *voor-* FORE- + *trekken* to TREK]

vo·ra·cious (vɒˈreɪʃəs) *adj.* **1.** devouring or craving food in great quantities. **2.** very eager or unremitting in some activity: *voracious reading.* [C17: from Latin *vorāx* swallowing greedily, from *vorāre* to devour] —**vo·'ra·cious·ly** *adv.* —**vo·rac·i·ty** (vɒˈræsɪtɪ) *or* **vo·'ra·cious·ness** *n.*

Vor·arl·berg (*German* ˈfoːrarlˌbɛrk) *n.* a mountainous province of W Austria. Capital: Bregenz. Pop.: 271 473 (1971). Area: 2601 sq. km (1004 sq. miles).

Vor·la·ge *German.* (ˈfoːrlaːgə) *n. Skiing.* a position in which a skier leans forward but keeps his heels on the skis. [from *vor* before, in front of + *Lage* position, stance]

Vo·ro·nezh (*Russian* vaˈrɔnɪʃ) *n.* a city in the W central Soviet Union: engineering and chemical industries; university (1918). Pop.: 746 000 (1975 est.).

Vo·ro·shi·lov (*Russian* vərəˈʃɪləf) *n.* **Kli·ment Ye·fre·mo·vich** (ˈklimɪnt jɪˈfrjɛməvitʃ). 1881–1969, Soviet military leader; president of the Soviet Union (1953–60).

Vo·ro·shi·lov·grad (*Russian* vərəʃɪlafˈgrat) *n.* an industrial city in the SW Soviet Union, in the E Ukrainian SSR, in the Donbass mining region: established in 1795 as an iron-founding centre. Pop.: 432 000 (1975 est.). Former name (until 1935): **Lugansk.**

Vo·ro·shi·lovsk (*Russian* vəraˈʃɪləfsk) *n.* the former name of **Stavropol.**

-vo·rous *adj. combining form.* feeding on or devouring: *carnivorous.* [from Latin *-vorus;* related to *vorāre* to swallow up, DEVOUR] —**-vore** *n. combining form.*

Vor·ster (ˈfɔːstə, ˈvɔː-) *n.* **Bal·tha·zar Jo·han·nes.** born 1915, South African statesman; Nationalist prime minister 1966–78.

vor·tex (ˈvɔːtɛks) *n., pl.* **-tex·es** *or* **-ti·ces** (-tɪˌsiːz). **1.** a whirling mass or motion of liquid, gas, flame, etc., such as the spiralling movement of water around a whirlpool. **2.** any activity, situation, or way of life regarded as irresistibly engulfing. [C17: from Latin: a whirlpool; variant of VERTEX] —**vor·ti·cal** (ˈvɔːtɪkᵊl) *adj.* —**'vor·ti·cal·ly** *adv.*

vor·ti·cel·la (ˌvɔːtɪˈsɛlə) *n., pl.* **-lae** (-liː). any protozoan of the genus *Vorticella,* consisting of a goblet-shaped ciliated cell attached to the substratum by a long contractile stalk. [C18: from New Latin, literally: a little eddy, from VORTEX]

vor·ti·cism (ˈvɔːtɪˌsɪzəm) *n.* an art movement in England initiated in 1914 by Wyndham Lewis combining the techniques of cubism with the concern for the problems of the machine age evinced in futurism. [C20: referring to the "vortices" of modern life on which the movement was based] —**'vor·ti·cist** *n.*

vor·ti·cose (ˈvɔːtɪˌkəʊs) *adj. Rare.* rotating quickly; whirling. [C18: from Latin *vorticōsus,* variant of *verticōsus* full of whirlpools; see VERTEX]

vor·tig·i·nous (vɔːˈtɪdʒɪnəs) *adj.* like a vortex; vortical; whirling. [C17: variant of VERTIGINOUS]

Vor·tum·nus (vɔːˈtʌmnəs) *n.* a variant spelling of **Vertumnus.**

Vosges (*French* voːʒ) *n.* **1.** a mountain range in E France, west of the Rhine valley. Highest peak: 1423 m (4672 ft.). **2.** a department of NE France, in Lorraine region. Capital: Épinal. Pop.: 409 599 (1975). Area: 5903 sq. km (2302 sq. miles).

Vos·tok (ˈvɒstɒk) *n.* any of six manned Soviet spacecraft made to orbit the earth. **Vostok 1,** launched in April 1961, carried Yuri Gagarin, the first man in space; **Vostok 6** carried Valentina Tereshkova, the first woman in space.

vo·ta·ry (ˈvəʊtərɪ) *n., pl.* **-ries,** *also* **vo·ta·rist. 1.** *R.C. Church, Eastern Churches.* a person, such as a monk or nun, who has dedicated himself or herself to religion by taking vows. **2.** a devoted adherent of a religion, cause, leader, pursuit, etc. ~*adj.* **3.** ardently devoted to the services or worship of God, a deity, or a saint. [C16: from Latin *vōtum* a vow, from *vovēre* to vow] —**'vo·tar·ess** *or* **'vo·tress** *fem. n.*

vote (vəʊt) *n.* **1.** an indication of choice, opinion, or will on a question, such as the choosing of a candidate, by or as if by some recognized means, such as a ballot: *10 votes for Jones.* **2.** the opinion of a group of persons as determined by voting: *it was put to the vote; do not take a vote; it came to a vote.* **3.** a body of votes or voters collectively: *the Jewish vote.* **4.** the total number of votes cast: *the vote decreased at the last election.* **5.** the ticket, ballot, etc., by which a vote is expressed. **6. a.** the right to vote; franchise; suffrage. **b.** a person regarded as the embodiment of this right. **7.** a means of voting, such as a ballot. **8.** *Chiefly Brit.* a grant or other proposition to be voted upon. ~*vb.* **9.** (when *tr., takes a clause as object or an infinitive*) to express or signify (one's preference, opinion, or will) (for or against some question, etc.): *to vote by ballot; we voted that it was time to adjourn; vote for me!* **10.** (*intr.*) to declare oneself as being (something or in favour of something) by exercising one's vote: *to vote socialist.* **11.** (*tr.;* foll. by *into* or *out of,* etc.) to appoint or elect (a person to or from a particular post): *they voted him into the presidency; he was voted out of office.* **12.** to determine the condition of in a specified way by voting: *the court voted itself out of existence.* **13.** to authorize, confer, or allow by voting: *vote us a rise.* **14.** *Informal.* to declare by common opinion: *the party was voted a failure.* **15.** (*tr.*) to influence or control the voting of: *do not try to vote us!* [C15: from Latin *vōtum* a solemn promise, from *vovēre* to vow] —**'vot+a·ble** *or* **'vote+a·ble** *adj.* —**'vote+less** *adj.*

vote down *vb.* (*tr., adv.*) to decide against or defeat in a vote: *the bill was voted down.*

vot+er ('vəʊtə) *n.* a person who can or does vote.

vot+ing ma+chine *n.* (esp. in the U.S.) a machine at a polling station that voters operate to register their votes and that mechanically or electronically counts all votes cast.

vo+tive ('vəʊtɪv) *adj.* **1.** offered, given, undertaken, performed or dedicated in fulfilment of or in accordance with a vow. **2.** *R.C. Church.* optional; not prescribed; having the nature of a voluntary offering: *a votive Mass; a votive candle.* [C16: from Latin *vōtīvus* promised by a vow, from *vōtum* a vow] —**'vo+tive+ly** *adv.* —**'vo+tive+ness** *n.*

Vo+ty+ak ('vəʊtɪˌæk) *n.* **1.** (*pl.* **+aks** *or* **+ak**) a member of a Finnish people living chiefly in the Udmurt ASSR, between the Volga and the Urals. **2.** the language of this people, belonging to the Finno-Ugric family.

vouch (vaʊtʃ) *vb.* **1.** (*intr.;* usually foll. by *for*) to give personal assurance; guarantee: *I'll vouch for his safety.* **2.** (when *tr., usually takes a clause as object;* when *intr.*, usually foll. by *for*) to furnish supporting evidence (for) or function as proof (of). **3.** (*tr.*) *English legal history.* to summon (a person who had warranted title to land) to defend that title or give up land of equal value. **4.** (*tr.*) *Archaic.* to cite (authors, principles, etc.) in support of something. **5.** (*tr.*) *Obsolete.* to assert. ~*n.* **6.** *Obsolete.* the act of vouching; assertion or allegation. [C14: from Old French *vocher* to summon, ultimately from Latin *vocāre* to call]

vouch+er ('vaʊtʃə) *n.* **1.** a document serving as evidence for some claimed transaction, as the receipt or expenditure of money. **2.** *Brit.* a ticket or card serving as a substitute for cash: *a gift voucher.* **3.** a person or thing that vouches for the truth of some statement, etc. **4.** any of certain documents that various groups of British nationals born outside Britain must obtain in order to settle in Britain. **5.** *English law, obsolete.* **a.** the summoning into court of a person to warrant a title to property. **b.** the person so summoned. [C16: from Anglo-French, noun use of Old French *voucher* to summon; see VOUCH]

vouch+safe (ˌvaʊtʃ'seɪf) *vb.* (*tr.*) **1.** to give or grant or condescend to give or grant: *she vouchsafed no reply; he vouchsafed me no encouragement.* **2.** (*may take a clause as object or an infinitive*) to agree, promise, or permit, often graciously or condescendingly: *he vouchsafed to come yesterday.* **3.** *Obsolete.* **a.** to warrant as being safe. **b.** to bestow as a favour (upon). [C14 *vouchen sauf;* see VOUCH, SAFE] —**ˌvouch+'safe+ment** *n.*

vouge (vu:ʒ) *n.* a form of pike or halberd used by foot soldiers in the 14th century and later. [from Old French *voulge, vouge* (Medieval Latin *vanga*), of obscure origin]

vous+soir (vu:'swɑ:) *n.* a wedge-shaped stone or brick that is used with others to construct an arch or vault. [C18: from French, from Vulgar Latin *volsōrium* (unattested), ultimately from Latin *volvere* to turn, roll]

Vou+vray ('vəʊvreɪ; *French* vu'vrɛ) *n.* a dry white wine, which can be still, sparkling, or semisparkling, produced around Touraine in the Loire valley.

vow (vaʊ) *n.* **1.** a solemn or earnest pledge or promise binding the person making it to perform a specified act or behave in a certain way. **2.** a solemn promise made to a deity or saint, by which the promiser pledges himself to some future act, course of action, or way of life. **3. take vows.** to enter a religious order and commit oneself to its rule of life by the vows of poverty, chastity, and obedience, which may be taken for a limited period as **simple vows** or as a perpetual and still more solemn commitment as **solemn vows.** ~*vb.* **4.** (*tr.; may take a clause as object or an infinitive*) to pledge, promise, or undertake solemnly: *he vowed that he would continue; he vowed to return.* **5.** (*tr.*) to dedicate or consecrate to God, a deity, or a saint. **6.** (*tr.; usually takes a clause as object*) to assert or swear emphatically. **7.** (*intr.*) *Archaic.* to declare solemnly. [C13: from Old French *vou,* from Latin *vōtum* a solemn promise, from *vovēre* to vow] —**'vow+er** *n.* —**'vow+less** *adj.*

vow+el ('vaʊəl) *n.* **1.** *Phonetics.* a voiced speech sound whose articulation is characterized by the absence of friction-causing obstruction in the vocal tract, allowing the breath stream free passage. The timbre of a vowel is chiefly determined by the position of the tongue and the lips. **2.** a letter or character representing a vowel. [C14: from Old French *vouel,* from Latin *vocālis littera* a vowel, from *vocālis* sonorous, from *vox* a voice] —**'vow+el+less** *adj.* —**'vow·el-ˌlike** *adj.*

vow+el gra+da+tion *n.* another name for **ablaut.** See **gradation** (sense 5).

vow+el+ize *or* **vow+el+ise** ('vaʊəˌlaɪz) *vb.* (*tr.*) to mark the vowel points in (a Hebrew word or text). Also: **vocalize.** —**ˌvow+el·i+'za+tion** *or* **ˌvow+el·i+'sa+tion** *n.*

vow+el mu+ta+tion *n.* another name for **umlaut.**

vow+el point *n.* any of several marks or points placed above or below consonants, esp. those evolved for Hebrew or Arabic, in order to indicate vowel sounds.

vox (vɒks) *n., pl.* **vo+ces** ('vəʊsi:z). a voice or sound. [Latin: voice]

vox an+gel·i+ca (æn'dʒɛlɪkə) *n.* an organ stop with a soft tone, often similar to the voix céleste. [C18: from Latin: angelic voice]

vox hu+ma+na (hju:'mɑ:nə) *n.* a reed stop on an organ supposedly imitative of the human voice. [C18: from Latin: human voice]

vox po+pu+li ('pɒpjʊˌlaɪ) *n.* the voice of the people; popular or public opinion. [Latin]

voy+age ('vɔɪɪdʒ) *n.* **1.** a journey, travel, or passage, esp. one to a distant land or by sea or air. **2.** *Obsolete.* an ambitious project. ~*vb.* **3.** to travel over or traverse (something): *we will voyage to Africa.* [C13: from Old French *veiage,* from Latin *viāticum* provision for travelling, from *viāticus* concerning a journey, from *via* a way] —**'voy+ag+er** *n.*

vo+ya+geur (vwɑ:jɑ:'ʒɜ:; *French* vwaja'ʒœ:r) *n.* (in Canada) a woodsman, guide, trapper, boatman, or explorer, esp. in the North. [C19: from French: traveller, from *voyager* to VOYAGE]

vo+yeur (vwaɪ'ɜ:; *French* vwa'jœ:r) *n.* a person who obtains sexual pleasure or excitement from the observation of someone undressing, having intercourse, etc. [C20: French, literally: one who sees, from *voir* to see, from Latin *vidēre*] —**vo+'yeur+ism** *n.* —**ˌvo+yeur+'is+tic** *adj.* —**ˌvo+yeur+'is+ti+cal+ly** *adv.*

VP (in transformational grammar) *abbrev. for* verb phrase.

V.P. *or* **V.Pres.** *abbrev. for* Vice President.

V.R. *abbrev. for:* **1.** variant reading. **2.** Victoria Regina. [Latin: Queen Victoria] **3.** Volunteer Reserve.

vrai+sem+blance (ˌvreɪsɒm'blɒns; *French* vrɛsɑ̃'blɑ̃:s) *n.* verisimilitude; appearance of truth. [French, from *vrai* true + SEMBLANCE]

V. Rev. *abbrev. for* Very Reverend.

VRI *abbrev. for* Victoria Regina et Imperatrix. [Latin: Victoria, Queen and Empress]

Vries (vri:s) *n.* See (Hugo) **de Vries.**

vroom (vru:m, vrʊm) *interj.* an exclamation imitative of a car engine revving up, as for high-speed motor racing.

vs. *abbrev. for* versus.

v.s. *abbrev. for* vide supra.

V.S. *abbrev. for* Veterinary Surgeon.

V-sign *n.* **1.** (in Britain) an offensive gesture made by sticking up the index and middle fingers with the palm of the hand inwards as an indication of contempt, defiance, etc. **2.** a similar gesture with the palm outwards meaning victory or, in the U.S., peace.

V.S.O. *abbrev. for:* **1.** very superior old: used to indicate that a brandy, port, etc., is between 12 and 17 years old. **2.** (in Britain) Voluntary Service Overseas: an organization that sends young volunteers to use and teach their skills in developing countries.

V.S.O.P. *abbrev. for* very superior old pale: used to indicate that a brandy, port, etc., is between 20 and 25 years old.

Vt. *abbrev. for* Vermont.

VTOL ('vi:tɒl) *n.* **1.** vertical takeoff and landing; a system in which an aircraft can take off and land vertically. **2.** an aircraft that uses this system. Compare **STOL.**

V-type en+gine *n.* a type of internal-combustion engine having two cylinder blocks attached to a single crankcase, the angle between the two blocks forming a V.

Vuel+ta A+ba+jo (*Spanish* 'bwelta a'βaxo) *n.* a region of W Cuba: famous for its tobacco.

vug, vugg, *or* **vugh** (vʌg) *n. Mining.* a small cavity in a rock or vein, usually lined with crystals. [C19: from Cornish *vooga* cave] —**'vug+gy** *or* **'vugh·y** *adj.*

Vuil+lard (*French* vɥi'ja:r) *n.* **Jean É+douard** (ʒɑ̃ e'dwa:r). 1868–1940, French painter and lithographer.

Vul. *abbrev. for* Vulgate.

Vul+can[1] ('vʌlkən) *n.* the Roman god of fire and metal-working. Greek counterpart: **Hephaestus.** —**Vul+ca+ni·an** (vʌl'keɪnɪən) *adj.*

Vul+can[2] ('vʌlkən) *n.* a hypothetical planet once thought to lie within the orbit of Mercury. —**Vul+ca+ni·an** (vʌl'keɪnɪən) *adj.*

vul+ca+ni·an (vʌl'keɪnɪən) *adj. Geology.* **a.** of or relating to a volcanic eruption characterized by the explosive discharge of gases, fine ash, and viscous lava that hardens in the crater. **b.** a less common word for **volcanic.**

vul+can+ism ('vʌlkəˌnɪzəm) *n.* a variant spelling of **volcanism.**

vul+can+ite ('vʌlkəˌnaɪt) *n.* a hard usually black rubber produced by vulcanizing natural rubber with large amounts of sulphur. It is resistant to chemical attack: used for chemical containers, electrical insulators, etc. Also called: **ebonite.**

vul+can+ize *or* **vul+can+ise** ('vʌlkəˌnaɪz) *vb.* (*tr.*) **1.** to treat (rubber) with sulphur or sulphur compounds under heat and pressure to improve elasticity and strength or to produce a hard substance such as vulcanite. **2.** to treat (substances other than rubber) by a similar process in order to improve their properties. —**'vul+can+ˌiz+a·ble** *or* **'vul+can+ˌis+a·ble** *adj.* —**ˌvul+can·i+'za+tion** *or* **ˌvul+can·i+'sa+tion** *n.* —**'vul+can+ˌiz+er** *or* **'vul+can+ˌis+er** *n.*

vul+can+ol+o·gy (ˌvʌlkə'nɒlədʒɪ) *n.* a variant spelling of **volcanology.** —**vul+can·o+log·i+cal** (ˌvʌlkənə'lɒdʒɪkəl) *adj.* —**ˌvul+can+'ol·o+gist** *n.*

vulg. *abbrev. for* vulgar(ly).

Vulg. *abbrev. for* Vulgate.

vul+gar ('vʌlgə) *adj.* **1.** marked by lack of taste, culture, delicacy, manners, etc.: *vulgar behaviour; vulgar language.* **2.** (*often cap.; usually prenominal*) denoting a form of a language, esp. of Latin, current among common people, esp. at a period when the formal language is archaic and not in general spoken use. **3.** *Archaic.* **a.** of, relating to, or current among the great mass of common people, in contrast to the educated, cultured, or privileged; ordinary. **b.** (*as collective n.* preceded by *the*): *the vulgar.* [C14: from Latin *vulgāris* belonging to the multitude, from *vulgus* the common people] —**'vul+gar+ly** *adv.* —**'vul+gar+ness** *n.*

vul+gar frac+tion *n.* another name for **simple fraction.**

vul+gar+i+an (vʌl'gɛərɪən) *n.* a vulgar person, esp. one who is rich or has pretensions to good taste.

vul+gar+ism ('vʌlgəˌrɪzəm) *n.* **1.** a coarse, crude, or obscene expression. **2.** a word or phrase found only in the vulgar form of a language. **3.** another word for **vulgarity.**

vul+gar+i+ty (vʌl'gærɪtɪ) *n., pl.* **·ties. 1.** the condition of being vulgar; lack of good manners. **2.** a vulgar action, phrase, etc.

vul+gar+ize *or* **vul+gar+ise** ('vʌlgəˌraɪz) *vb.* (*tr.*) **1.** to make (something little known or difficult to understand) widely known or popular among the public; popularize. **2.** to make commonplace or vulgar; debase. —**ˌvul+gar+i+'za+tion** *or* **ˌvul+gar+i+'sa+tion** *n.* —**'vul+gar+ˌiz+er** *or* **'vul+gar+ˌis+er** *n.*

Vul+gar Lat+in *n.* any of the dialects of Latin spoken in the Roman Empire other than classical Latin. The Romance languages developed from them.

vul+gate ('vʌlgeɪt, -gɪt) *Rare.* ~*n.* **1.** a commonly recognized text or version. **2.** everyday or informal speech; the vernacular. ~*adj.* **3.** generally accepted; common.

Vul+gate ('vʌlgeɪt, -gɪt) *n.* **a.** (from the 13th century onwards) the fourth-century version of the Bible produced by Jerome, partly by translating the original languages, and partly by revising the earlier Latin text based on the Greek versions. **b.** (*as modifier*): *the Vulgate version.* [C17: from Medieval Latin *Vulgāta*, from Late Latin *vulgāta editiō* popular version (of the Bible), from Latin *vulgāre* to make common, from *vulgus* the common people]

vul+ner+a+ble ('vʌlnərəbᵊl) *adj.* **1.** capable of being physically or emotionally wounded or hurt. **2.** open to temptation, persuasion, censure, etc. **3.** *Military.* liable or exposed to attack. **4.** *Bridge.* (of a side who have won one game towards rubber) subject to increased bonuses or penalties. [C17: from Late Latin *vulnerābilis*, from Latin *vulnerāre* to wound, from *vulnus* a wound] —**ˌvul+ner+a+'bil+i+ty** *or* **'vul+ner+a+ble+ness** *n.* —**'vul+ner+a+bly** *adv.*

vul+ner+ar+y ('vʌlnərərɪ) *Med.* ~*adj.* **1.** of, relating to, or used to heal a wound. ~*n., pl.* **+ar+ies. 2.** a vulnerary drug or agent. [C16: from Latin *vulnerārius* belonging to wounds, from *vulnus* a wound]

Vul+pec+u+la (vʌl'pɛkjʊlə) *n., Latin genitive* **Vul+pec+u+lae** (vʌl'pɛkjʊˌliː). a faint constellation in the N hemisphere lying between Cygnus and Aquila. [C19: from Latin: a little fox, from *vulpēs* a fox]

vul+pine ('vʌlpaɪn) *adj.* **1.** Also: **vul+pec+u+lar** (vʌl'pɛkjʊlə). of, relating to, or resembling a fox. **2.** possessing the characteristics often attributed to foxes; crafty, clever, etc. [C17: from Latin *vulpīnus* foxlike, from *vulpēs* a fox]

vul+ture ('vʌltʃə) *n.* **1.** any of various very large diurnal birds of prey of the genera *Neophron, Gyps, Gypaetus*, etc., of Africa, Asia, and warm parts of Europe, typically having broad wings and soaring flight and feeding on carrion: family *Accipitridae* (hawks). See also **griffon**[1] (sense 2), **lammergeier. 2.** any similar bird of the family *Cathartidae* of North, Central, and South America. See also **condor, turkey buzzard. 3.** a person or thing that preys greedily and ruthlessly on others, esp. the helpless. [C14: from Old French *voltour*, from Latin *vultur;* perhaps related to Latin *vellere* to pluck, tear] —**'vul+ture-ˌlike** *adj.*

vul+tur+ine ('vʌltʃəˌraɪn) *adj.* **1.** of, relating to, or resembling a vulture. **2.** Also: **vul+tur+ous** ('vʌltʃərəs). rapacious, predatory, or greedy.

vul+va ('vʌlvə) *n., pl.* **+vae** (-viː) *or* **+vas.** the external genitals of human females, including the labia, mons pubis, clitoris, and the vaginal orifice. [C16: from Latin: covering, womb, matrix] —**'vul+val, 'vul+var,** *or* **vul+vate** ('vʌlveɪt) *adj.* —**vul+vi+form** ('vʌlvɪˌfɔːm) *adj.*

vul+vi+tis (vʌl'vaɪtɪs) *n.* inflammation of the vulva.

vul+vo+vag+i+ni+tis (ˌvʌlvəʊˌvædʒɪ'naɪtɪs) *n.* inflammation of the vulva and vagina or of the small glands (**vulvovaginal glands**) on either side of the lower part of the vagina.

vv. *abbrev. for:* **1.** versus. **2.** *Music.* volumes.

v.v. *abbrev. for* vice versa.

V.W. *abbrev. for* Very Worshipful.

Vyat+ka (*Russian* 'vjatkə) *n.* the former name (1780–1934) of **Kirov.**

Vy+borg (*Russian* 'vɪbərk) *n.* a port in the NW Soviet Union, at the head of **Vyborg Bay** (an inlet of the Gulf of Finland): belonged to Finland (1918–40). Pop.: 51 088 (1959). Finnish name: **Viipuri.** Swedish name: **Viborg.**

Vy·shin·sky *or* **Vi·shin·sky** (*Russian* vɪ'ʃɪnskij) *n.* **An·drei Ya·nu·ar·ye·vich** (an'drjej jənu'arjɪvitʃ). 1883–1954, Soviet jurist, statesman, and diplomat; foreign minister (1949–53). He was public prosecutor (1935–38) at the trials held to purge Stalin's rivals and was the Soviet representative at the United Nations (1945–49; 1953–54).

W

w *or* **W** (ˈdʌbəlˌjuː) *n., pl.* **w's, W's,** *or* **Ws. 1.** the 23rd letter and 18th consonant of the modern English alphabet. **2.** a speech sound represented by this letter, in English usually a bilabial semivowel, as in *web.*

W *symbol for:* **1.** watt. **2.** West. **3.** *Physics.* work. **4.** *Chem.* tungsten [from New Latin *wolframium,* from German *Wolfram*] **5.** women's (size).

w. *abbrev. for:* **1.** week. **2.** weight. **3.** width. **4.** wife. **5.** with. **6.** *Cricket.* **a.** wide. **b.** wicket.

W. *abbrev. for:* **1.** Wales. **2.** Warden. **3.** Welsh.

W.A. *abbrev. for* Western Australia.

W.A.A.A.F. *abbrev. for* Women's Auxiliary Australian Air Force.

WAAC (wæk) *n.* **1.** *acronym for* Women's Army Auxiliary Corps. **2.** Also called: **waac.** a member of this corps.

Waadt (vat) *n.* the German name for **Vaud.**

WAAF (wæf) *n.* **1.** *acronym for:* **a.** Women's Auxiliary Air Force. **b.** Women's Auxiliary Australian Air Force. **2.** Also called: **Waaf.** a member of either of these forces.

Waal (*Dutch* waːl) *n.* a river in the central Netherlands: the S branch of the Lower Rhine. Length: 84 km (52 miles).

Wa+bash (ˈwɔːbæʃ) *n.* a river in the E central U.S., rising in W Ohio and flowing west and southwest to join the Ohio River in Indiana. Length: 764 km (475 miles).

wab+ble (ˈwɒbəl) *vb., n.* a variant spelling of **wobble.** —**ˈwab+bler** *n.* —**ˈwab+bling** *adj.* —**ˈwab+bling+ly** *adv.* —**ˈwab+bly** *adj.*

Wace (weɪs) *n.* **Rob·ert.** born ?1100, Anglo-Norman poet; author of the *Roman de Brut* and *Roman de Rou.*

wack (wæk) *or* **wack+er** (ˈwækə) *n. Liverpool and English Midlands dialect.* friend; pal: used chiefly as a term of address.

wack·e (ˈwækə) *n. Obsolete.* any of various soft earthy rocks that resemble or are derived from basaltic rocks. [C18: from German: rock, gravel, basalt]

wack·y (ˈwækɪ) *adj.* **wack·i·er, wack·i·est.** *Slang.* eccentric, erratic, or unpredictable. [C19 (in dialect sense: a fool, an eccentric): from WHACK (hence, a *whacky,* a person who behaves as if he had been whacked on the head)] —**ˈwack·i·ly** *adv.* —**ˈwack·i·ness** *n.*

wad[1] (wɒd) *n.* **1.** a small mass or ball of fibrous or soft material, such as cotton wool, used esp. for packing or stuffing. **2. a.** a plug of paper, cloth, leather, etc., pressed against a charge to hold it in place in a muzzle-loading cannon. **b.** a disc of paper, felt, pasteboard, etc., used to hold in place the powder and shot in a shotgun cartridge. **3.** a roll or bundle of something, esp. of banknotes. **4.** *U.S. slang.* a large quantity, esp. of money. **5.** *Brit. dialect.* a bundle of hay or straw. ~*vb.* **wads, wad+ding, wad+ded. 6.** to form (something) into a wad. **7.** (*tr.*) to roll into a wad or bundle. **8.** (*tr.*) **a.** to hold (a charge) in place with a wad. **b.** to insert a wad into (a gun). **9.** (*tr.*) to pack or stuff with wadding; pad. [C14: from Late Latin *wadda;* related to German *Watte* cotton wool] —**ˈwad+der** *n.*

wad[2] (wɒd) *n.* a soft dark earthy amorphous material consisting of decomposed manganese minerals: occurs in damp marshy areas. [C17: of unknown origin]

Wa+dai (wɑːˈdaɪ) *n.* a former independent sultanate of NE central Africa: now the E part of Chad.

Wad+den+zee (*Dutch* ˈwɑdənˌzeː) *n.* the part of the North Sea between the Dutch mainland and the West Frisian Islands.

wad+ding (ˈwɒdɪŋ) *n.* **1. a.** any fibrous or soft substance used as padding, stuffing, etc., esp. sheets of carded cotton prepared for the purpose. **b.** a piece of this. **2.** material for wads used in cartridges or guns.

wad+dle (ˈwɒdəl) *vb.* (*intr.*) **1.** to walk with short steps, rocking slightly from side to side. ~*n.* **2.** a swaying gait or motion. [C16: probably frequentative of WADE] —**ˈwad+dler** *adj.* —**ˈwad+dling+ly** *adv.* —**ˈwad+dly** *adj.*

wad+dy (ˈwɒdɪ) *n., pl.* **+dies. 1.** a heavy wooden club used as a weapon by Australian Aborigines. ~*vb.* **+dies, +dy+ing, +died. 2.** (*tr.*) to hit with a waddy. [C19: from a native Australian language, perhaps based on English WOOD]

wade (weɪd) *vb.* **1.** to walk with the feet immersed in (water, a stream, etc.): *the girls waded the river at the ford.* **2.** (*intr.;* often foll. by *through*) to proceed with difficulty: *to wade through a book.* **3.** (*intr.;* foll. by *in* or *into*) to attack energetically. ~*n.* **4.** the act or an instance of wading. [Old English *wadan;* related to Old Frisian *wada,* Old High German *watan,* Old Norse *vatha,* Latin *vadum* FORD] —**ˈwad+a·ble** *or* **ˈwade+a·ble** *adj.*

Wade (weɪd) *n.* **Vir·gin·i·a.** born 1945, English tennis player: U.S. women's champion 1968; Wimbledon women's champion 1977.

wad+er (ˈweɪdə) *n.* **1.** a person or thing that wades. **2.** Also called: **wading bird.** any of various long-legged birds, esp. those of the order *Ciconiiformes* (herons, storks, etc.), that live near water and feed on fish, etc. **3.** a Brit. name for **shore bird.**

wad+ers (ˈweɪdəz) *pl. n.* long waterproof boots, sometimes extending to the chest like trousers, worn by anglers.

wa·di *or* **wa·dy** (ˈwɒdɪ) *n., pl.* **+dies.** a watercourse in N Africa and Arabia, dry except in the rainy season. [C19: from Arabic]

Wa·di Hal+fa (ˈwɒdɪ ˈhælfə) *n.* a town in the N Sudan that was partly submerged by Lake Nasser: an important archaeological site.

wad+mal (ˈwɒdməl) *n.* a coarse thick woollen fabric, formerly woven esp. in N Scotland, for outer garments. [C14: from Old Norse *vathmal,* from *vath* cloth + *mal* measure]

Wad Me+da+ni (wɑːd mɪˈdɑːniː) *n.* a town in the E Sudan, on the Blue Nile: headquarters of the Gezira irrigation scheme; agricultural research centre. Pop.: 110 108 (1973).

wad+set (ˈwɒdˌsɛt) *Scot. law.* ~*n.* **1.** another name for **mortgage.** ~*vb.* **+sets, +set+ting, +set+ted. 2.** (*tr.*) to pledge or mortgage. [C14: *wad,* Scottish variant of WED + SET; compare Old English *wedd settan* to deposit a pledge]

wae (weɪ) *n., interj. Northern Brit.* a dialect word for **woe.**

Wafd (wɒft) *n.* a nationalist Egyptian political party: founded in 1924 and dissolved in 1952. [Arabic: deputation] —**ˈWafd+ist** *n., adj.*

wa+fer (ˈweɪfə) *n.* **1.** a thin crisp sweetened biscuit with different flavourings, served with ice cream, etc. **2.** *Christianity.* a thin disc of unleavened bread used in the Eucharist as celebrated by the Western Church. **3.** *Pharmacol.* an envelope of rice paper enclosing a medicament. **4.** *Electronics.* a small thin slice of semiconductor material, such as silicon, that is separated into numerous individual components or circuits. **5.** a small thin disc of adhesive material used to seal letters, documents, etc. ~*vb.* **6.** (*tr.*) to seal, fasten, or attach with a wafer. [C14: from Old Northern French *waufre,* from Middle Low German *wāfel;* related to WAFFLE] —**ˈwa·fer-,like** *or* **ˈwa+fer·y** *adj.*

waff (wæf, wɑːf) *n. Northern Brit. dialect.* **1.** a gust or puff of air. **2.** a glance; glimpse. ~*vb.* **3.** to flutter or cause to flutter. [C16: Scottish and northern English variant of WAVE]

waf+fle[1] (ˈwɒfəl) *n. Chiefly U.S.* **a.** a crisp golden-brown pancake, with deep indentations on both sides. **b.** (*as modifier*): *waffle iron.* [C19: from Dutch *wafel* (earlier *wæfel*), of Germanic origin; related to Old High German *wabo* honeycomb]

waf+fle[2] (ˈwɒfəl) *Informal, chiefly Brit.* ~*vb.* **1.** (*intr.;* often foll. by *on*) to speak or write in a vague and wordy manner: *he waffled on for hours.* ~*n.* **2.** vague and wordy speech or writing. [C19: of unknown origin]

waft (wɑːft, wɒft) *vb.* **1.** to carry or be carried gently on or as if on the air or water. ~*n.* **2.** the act or an instance of wafting. **3.** something, such as a scent, carried on the air. **4.** wafting motion. **5.** Also called: **waif.** *Nautical.* (formerly) a signal flag hoisted furled to signify various messages depending on where it was flown. [C16 (in obsolete sense: to convey by ship): back formation from C15 *wafter* a convoy vessel, from Middle Dutch *wachter* guard, from *wachten* to guard; influenced by WAFF] —**ˈwaft+age** *n.*

waft+er (ˈwɑːftə, ˈwɒf-) *n.* a device that causes a draught.

waf+ture (ˈwɑːftʃə, ˈwɒf-) *n. Archaic.* **1.** the act of wafting or waving. **2.** anything that is wafted.

wag[1] (wæg) *vb.* **wags, wag+ging, wagged. 1.** to move or cause to move rapidly and repeatedly from side to side or up and down. **2.** to move (the tongue) or (of the tongue) to be moved rapidly in talking, esp. in idle gossip. **3.** to move (the finger) or (of the finger) to be moved from side to side, in or as in admonition. ~*n.* **4.** the act or an instance of wagging. [C13: from Old English *wagian* to shake; compare Old Norse *vagga* cradle]

wag[2] (wæg) *n.* a humorous or jocular person; wit. [C16: of uncertain origin] —**ˈwag+ger·y** *n.* —**ˈwag+gish** *adj.* —**ˈwag+gish+ly** *adv.* —**ˈwag+gish+ness** *n.*

WAG *international car registration for* West Africa Gambia.

wage (weɪdʒ) *n.* **1. a.** (*often pl.*) payment in return for work or services, esp. that made to workmen on a daily, hourly, weekly, or piece-work basis. Compare **salary. b.** (*as modifier*): *wage freeze.* **2.** (*pl.*) *Economics.* the portion of the national income accruing to labour as earned income, as contrasted with the unearned income accruing to capital in the form of rent, interest, and dividends. **3.** (*often pl.*) recompense, return, or yield. **4.** an obsolete word for **pledge.** ~*vb.* (*tr.*) **5.** to engage in. **6.** *Obsolete.* to pledge or wager. **7.** *Obsolete or Brit. dialect.* another word for **hire** (senses 1, 2). [C14: from Old Northern French *wagier* to pledge, from *wage,* of Germanic origin; compare Old English *weddian* to pledge, WED] —**ˈwage+less** *adj.*

wage earn+er *or U.S.* **wage work+er** *n.* **1.** a person who works for wages, esp. as distinguished from one paid a salary. **2.** the person who earns money to support a household by working.

wage-plug *n. Austral. informal, often derogatory.* a wage earner.

wa+ger (ˈweɪdʒə) *n.* **1.** an agreement or pledge to pay an amount of money as a result of the outcome of an unsettled matter. **2.** an amount staked on the outcome of such a matter or event. **3. wager of battle.** (in medieval Britain) a pledge to do battle for a cause, esp. to decide guilt or innocence by single combat. **4. wager of law.** *English legal history.* a form of trial in which the accused offered to make oath of his innocence, supported by the oaths of 11 of his neighbours declaring their belief in his statements. ~*vb.* **5.** (when *tr., may take a clause as object*) to risk or bet (something) on the outcome of an unsettled matter. **6.** (*tr.*) *History.* to pledge oneself to (battle). [C14: from Anglo-French *wageure* a pledge, from Old Northern French *wagier* to pledge; see WAGE] —'**wa·ger·er** *n.*

wage scale *n.* **1.** a schedule of wages paid to workers for various jobs in an industry, company, etc. **2.** an employer's schedule of wages.

wag·ga ('wɒgə) *n. Austral.* a blanket or bed covering made out of sacks stitched together. [C19: named after WAGGA WAGGA]

Wag·ga Wag·ga ('wɒgə 'wɒgə) *n.* a city in SE Australia, in New South Wales on the Murrumbidgee River: agricultural trading centre. Pop.: 32 510 (1975 est.).

wag·gle ('wæg°l) *vb.* **1.** to move or cause to move with a rapid shaking or wobbling motion. ~*n.* **2.** a rapid shaking or wobbling motion. [C16: frequentative of WAG] —'**wag·gling·ly** *adv.* —'**wag·gly** *adj.*

wag·gon ('wægən) *n., vb.* a variant spelling (esp. Brit.) of **wagon.**

Wag·ner ('vɑːgnə) *n.* **(Wilhelm) Ri·chard** ('rɪçart). 1813–83, German romantic composer noted chiefly for his invention of the music drama. His cycle of four such dramas *The Ring of the Nibelung* was produced at his own theatre in Bayreuth in 1876. His other operas include *Tannhäuser* (1845; revised 1861), *Tristan and Isolde* (1865), and *Parsifal* (1882).

Wag·ne·ri·an (vɑːg'nɪərɪən) *adj.* **1.** of or suggestive of the dramatic musical compositions of Richard Wagner, their massive scale, dramatic and emotional intensity, etc. **2.** denoting or relating to a singer who has a voice suitable for singing Wagner. **3.** of or relating to a big, powerful, or domineering woman: *a Wagnerian maiden.* ~*n. also* **Wag·ner·ite. 4.** a follower or disciple of the music or theories of Richard Wagner.

wag·on *or* **wag·gon** ('wægən) *n.* **1.** any of various types of wheeled vehicles, ranging from carts to lorries, esp. a vehicle with four wheels drawn by a horse, tractor, etc., and used for carrying crops, heavy loads, etc. **2.** *Brit.* a railway freight truck, esp. an open one. **3.** *U.S.* a child's four-wheeled cart. **4.** *U.S.* a police van for transporting prisoners and those arrested. **5.** *Chiefly U.S.* See **station wagon. 6.** an obsolete word for **chariot. 7. on (*or* off) the wagon.** *Informal.* abstaining (or no longer abstaining) from alcoholic drinks. ~*vb.* **8.** (*tr.*) to transport by wagon. [C16: from Dutch *wagen* WAIN] —'**wag·on·less** *or* '**wag·gon·less** *adj.*

Wag·on *or* **Wag·gon** ('wægən) *n.* **the.** another name for the Plough.

wag·on·er *or* **wag·gon·er** ('wægənə) *n.* a person who drives a wagon.

wag·on·ette *or* **wag·gon·ette** (ˌwægə'nɛt) *n.* a light four-wheeled horse-drawn vehicle with two lengthwise seats facing each other behind a crosswise driver's seat.

wa·gon-lit (*French* vagɔ̃'li) *n., pl.* **wa·gons-lits** (vagɔ̃'li). **1.** a sleeping car on a European railway. **2.** a compartment on such a car. [C19: from French, from *wagon* railway coach + *lit* bed]

wag·on·load *or* **wag·gon·load** ('wægənˌləʊd) *n.* the load that is or can be carried by a wagon.

wag·on sol·dier *n. U.S. slang.* a soldier belonging to the field artillery.

wag·on train *n.* a supply train of horses and wagons, esp. one going over rough terrain.

wag·on vault *n.* another name for **barrel vault.**

Wa·gram (*German* 'vaːgram) *n.* a village in NE Austria: scene of the defeat of the Austrians by Napoleon in 1809.

wag·tail ('wægˌteɪl) *n.* any of various passerine songbirds of the genera *Motacilla* and *Dendronanthus,* of Eurasia and Africa, having a very long tail that wags when the bird walks: family *Motacillidae.*

Wah·ha·bi *or* **Wa·ha·bi** (wə'hɑːbɪ) *n., pl.* **·bis.** a member of a strictly conservative Muslim sect founded in the 18th century with the aim of eliminating all innovations later than the 3rd century A.D. —**Wah·'ha·bism** *or* **Wa·'ha·bism** *n.*

wa·hi·ne (wɑː'hiːnɪ) *n.* (esp. in the Pacific islands) **1.** a Polynesian or Maori woman. **2.** an attractive girl, esp. one who visits beaches. [from Maori and Hawaiian]

wa·hoo[1] (wɑː'huː, 'wɑːhuː) *n., pl.* **·hoos.** an elm, *Ulmus alata,* of SE North America having twigs with winged corky edges. Also called: **winged elm.** [from Creek *ŭhawhu* cork elm]

wa·hoo[2] (wɑː'huː, 'wɑːhuː) *n., pl.* **·hoos.** an E North American shrub or small tree, *Euonymus atropurpureus,* with scarlet capsules and seeds. Also called: **burning bush.** [C19: from Dakota *wāhu* arrowwood]

wa·hoo[3] (wɑː'huː, 'wɑːhuː) *n., pl.* **·hoos.** a large fast-moving food and game fish, *Acanthocybium solandri,* of tropical seas: family *Scombridae* (mackerels and tunnies). [of unknown origin]

waif (weɪf) *n.* **1.** a person, esp. a child, who is homeless, friendless, or neglected. **2.** anything found and not claimed, the owner being unknown. **3.** *Nautical.* another name for **waft** (sense 5). **4.** *Law, obsolete.* a stolen article thrown away by a thief in his flight and forfeited to the Crown or to the lord of the manor. [C14: from Anglo-Norman, variant of Old Northern French *gaif,* of Scandinavian origin; related to Old Norse *veif* a flapping thing]

Wai·ka·to ('waɪˌkɑːtəʊ) *n.* the longest river in New Zealand, flowing northwest across North Island to the Tasman Sea. Length: 350 km (220 miles).

Wai·ki·ki ('waɪkɪˌkiː, ˌwaɪkɪ'kiː) *n.* a resort area in Hawaii, on SE Oahu: a suburb of Honolulu.

wail (weɪl) *vb.* **1.** (*intr.*) to utter a prolonged high-pitched cry, as of grief or misery. **2.** (*intr.*) to make a sound resembling such a cry: *the wind wailed in the trees.* **3.** (*tr.*) to lament, esp. with mournful sounds. ~*n.* **4.** a prolonged high-pitched mournful cry or sound. [C14: of Scandinavian origin; related to Old Norse *væla* to wail, Old English *wā* WOE] —'**wail·er** *n.* —'**wail·ful** *adj.* —'**wail·ful·ly** *adv.* —'**wail·ing·ly** *adv.*

Wail·ing Wall *n.* a wall in Jerusalem, a remnant of the temple of Herod, held sacred by Jews as a place of pilgrimage, prayer, and lamentation.

wain (weɪn) *n. Chiefly poetic.* a farm wagon or cart. [Old English *wægn;* related to Old Frisian *wein,* Old Norse *vagn*]

wain·scot ('weɪnskət) *n.* **1.** Also called: **wainscoting** *or* **wainscotting.** a lining applied to the walls of a room, esp. one of wood panelling. **2.** the lower part of the walls of a room, esp. when finished in a material different from the upper part. **3.** fine quality oak used as wainscot. ~*vb.* **4.** (*tr.*) to line (a wall of a room) with a wainscot. [C14: from Middle Low German *wagenschot,* perhaps from *wagen* WAGON + *schot* planking, related to German *Scheit* piece of wood]

wain·wright ('weɪnˌraɪt) *n.* a person who makes wagons.

waist (weɪst) *n.* **1.** *Anatomy.* the constricted part of the trunk between the ribs and hips. **2.** the part of a garment covering the waist. **3.** the middle part of an object that resembles the waist in narrowness or position. **4.** the middle part of a ship. **5.** Also called: **centre section.** the middle section of an aircraft fuselage. **6.** the constriction between the thorax and abdomen in wasps and similar insects. [C14: origin uncertain; related to Old English *wæstm* WAX[2]] —'**waist·less** *adj.*

waist·band ('weɪstˌbænd) *n.* an encircling band of material to finish and strengthen a skirt or trousers at the waist.

waist·cloth ('weɪstˌklɒθ) *n. Obsolete.* another word for **loincloth.**

waist·coat ('weɪsˌkəʊt) *n.* **1.** a man's sleeveless waistlength garment worn under a suit jacket, usually buttoning up the front. U.S. name: **vest. 2.** a man's garment worn under a doublet in the 16th century. —'**waist·ˌcoat·ed** *adj.*

waist·ed ('weɪstɪd) *adj.* **a.** having a waist or waistlike part: *a waisted air-gun pellet.* **b.** (*in combination*): *high-waisted.*

waist·line ('weɪstˌlaɪn) *n.* **1.** a line or indentation around the body at the narrowest part of the waist. **2.** the intersection of the bodice and the skirt of a dress, etc., or the level of this: *a low waistline.*

wait (weɪt) *vb.* **1.** (when *intr.,* often foll. by *for, until,* or *to*) to stay in one place or remain inactive in expectation (of something); hold oneself in readiness (for something). **2.** to delay temporarily or be temporarily delayed: *that work can wait.* **3.** (when *intr.,* usually foll. by *for*) (of things) to be in store (for a person): *success waits you in your new job.* **4.** (*intr.*) to act as a waiter or waitress. ~*n.* **5.** the act or an instance of waiting. **6.** a period of waiting. **7.** (*pl.*) *Rare.* a band of musicians who go around the streets, esp. at Christmas, singing and playing carols. **8.** an interlude or interval between two acts or scenes in a play, etc. **9. lie in wait.** to prepare an ambush (for someone). [C12: from Old French *waitier;* related to Old High German *wahtēn* to WAKE]

wait-a-bit *n.* any of various plants having sharp hooked thorns or similar appendages, esp. the greenbrier and the grapple plant.

wait·er ('weɪtə) *n.* **1.** a man whose occupation is to serve at table, as in a restaurant. **2.** a person who waits. **3.** a tray or salver on which dishes, etc., are carried.

wait·ing game *n.* the postponement of action or decision in order to gain the advantage.

wait·ing list *n.* a list of people waiting to obtain some object, treatment, status, etc.

wait·ing room *n.* a room in which people may wait, as at a railway station, doctor's or dentist's office, etc.

wait on *or* **up·on** *vb.* (*intr., prep.*) **1.** to serve at the table of. **2.** to act as an attendant or servant to. **3.** *Archaic.* to visit.

wait·ress ('weɪtrɪs) *n.* a woman who serves at table, as in a restaurant.

wait up *vb.* (*intr., adv.*) **1.** to delay going to bed in order to await some event. **2.** *Informal, chiefly U.S.* to halt and pause in order that another person may catch up.

waive (weɪv) *vb.* (*tr.*) **1.** to set aside or relinquish: *to waive one's right to something.* **2.** to refrain from enforcing or applying (a law, penalty, etc.). **3.** to defer. [C13: from Old Northern French *weyver,* from *waif* abandoned; see WAIF]

waiv·er ('weɪvə) *n.* **1.** the voluntary relinquishment, expressly or by implication, of some claim or right. **2.** the act or an instance of relinquishing a claim or right. **3.** a formal statement in writing of such relinquishment. [C17: from Old Northern French *weyver* to relinquish, WAIVE]

Waj·da (*Polish* 'vajda) *n.* **And·rei** or **And·rzej** ('andʒɛj). born 1926, Polish film director, best known for *Ashes and Diamonds* (1958).

Wa·kash·an (wɑː'kæʃən, 'wɔːkəˌʃɑːn) *n.* **1.** a family of North American Indian languages of British Columbia and Washington, including Kwakiutl and Nootka. **2.** a speaker of any of these languages.

Wa·ka·ya·ma (ˌwækə'jɑːmə) *n.* an industrial city in S Japan, on S Honshu. Pop.: 387 204 (1974 est.).

wake[1] (weɪk) *vb.* **wakes, wak·ing, woke, wok·en. 1.** (often foll. by *up*) to rouse or become roused from sleep. **2.** (often foll. by

up) to rouse or become roused from inactivity. **3.** (*intr.*; often foll. by *to* or *up to*) to become conscious or aware: *at last he woke to the situation.* **4.** (*intr.*) to be or remain awake. **5.** *Dialect.* to hold a wake over (a corpse). **6.** *Archaic or dialect.* to keep watch over. ~*n.* **7.** a watch or vigil held over the body of a dead person during the night before burial. **8.** the patronal or dedication festival of English parish churches. **9.** a solemn or ceremonial vigil. **10.** (*usually pl.*) an annual holiday in any of various towns in northern England, when the local factory or factories close, usually for a week or two weeks. **11.** *Rare.* the state of being awake. [Old English *wacian;* related to Old Frisian *wakia,* Old High German *wahtēn*] —**'wak+er** *n.*
Usage. Where there is an object and the sense is the literal one *wake* (*up*) and *waken* are the commonest forms: *I wakened him; I woke him* (*up*). Both verbs are also commonly used without an object: *I woke up. Awake* and *awaken* are preferred to other forms of *wake* where the sense is a figurative one: *he awoke to the danger.*

wake[2] (weɪk) *n.* **1.** the waves or track left by a vessel or other object moving through water. **2.** the track or path left by anything that has passed: *wrecked houses in the wake of the hurricane.* [C16: of Scandinavian origin; compare Old Norse *vaka, vök* hole cut in ice, Swedish *vak,* Danish *vaage;* perhaps related to Old Norse *vökr,* Middle Dutch *wak* wet]

Wake+field ('weɪkˌfiːld) *n.* a city in N England, administrative centre of West Yorkshire: important since medieval times as an agricultural and textile centre. Pop.: 59 650 (1971).

wake+ful ('weɪkfʊl) *adj.* **1.** unable or unwilling to sleep. **2.** sleepless. **3.** alert. —**'wake+ful+ly** *adv.* —**'wake+ful+ness** *n.*

Wake Is+land *n.* an atoll in the N central Pacific: claimed by the U.S. in 1899; developed as a civil and naval air station in the late 1930s. Area: 8 sq. km (3 sq. miles).

wake+less ('weɪklɪs) *adj.* (of sleep) deep or unbroken.

wak+en ('weɪkən) *vb.* to rouse or be roused from sleep or some other inactive state. —**'wak+en+er** *n.*
Usage. See at **wake**[1].

wake+rife ('weɪkˌraɪf) *adj. Northern Brit. dialect.* wakeful. [C15: from WAKE[1] + RIFE] —**'wake+ˌrife+ness** *n.*

wake-rob·in *n.* **1.** any of various North American herbaceous plants of the genus *Trillium,* such as *T. grandiflorum,* having a whorl of three leaves and three-petalled solitary flowers: family *Trilliaceae.* **2.** *U.S.* any of various aroid plants, esp. the cuckoopint.

wake-up *Austral. informal.* *n.* **1.** an alert or intelligent person. **2. a wake-up to.** fully alert to (a person, thing, action, etc.).

Waks·man ('wæksmən) *n.* **Sel·man A·bra·ham.** 1888–1973, U.S. microbiologist, born in Russia. He discovered streptomycin: Nobel prize for medicine 1952.

WAL *international car registration for* Sierra Leone. [from *W*(*est*) *A*(*frica*) *L*(*eone*)]

Wal. *abbrev. for* Walloon.

Wa+lach ('wɑːlɒk) *n., adj.* a variant spelling of **Vlach.**

Wa+la+chi·a *or* **Wal+la+chi·a** (wɒ'leɪkɪə) *n.* a former principality of SE Europe: a vassal state of the Ottoman Empire from the 15th century until its union with Moldavia in 1859, subsequently forming present-day Rumania. —**Wa+'la+chi·an** *or* **Wal+'la+chi·an** *n., adj.*

Wał+brzych ('vawbʒɪx) *n.* an industrial city in SW Poland. Pop.: 127 500 (1974 est.). German name: **Waldenburg.**

Wal+che+ren (*Dutch* 'wɑlxərə) *n.* an island in the SW Netherlands, in the Scheldt estuary: administratively part of Zeeland province; suffered severely in World War II, when the dykes were breached, and again in the floods of 1953. Area: 212 sq. km (82 sq. miles).

Wal·de·mar I *or* **Val·de·mar I** ('vældɪˌmɑː) *n.* called *the Great.* 1131–82, king of Denmark (1157–82). He conquered the Wends (1169), increased the territory of Denmark, and established the hereditary rule of his line.

Wal+den+burg ('valdᵊnˌbʊrk) *n.* the German name for **Wałbrzych.**

Wal+den+ses (wɒl'dɛnsiːz) *pl. n.* the members of a small sect founded as a reform movement within the Roman Catholic Church by Peter Waldo, a merchant of Lyons in the late 12th century, which in the 16th century joined the Reformation movement. Also called: **Vaudois.** —**Wal+den+si·an** (wɒl'dɛnsɪən) *n., adj.*

wald+grave ('wɔːldˌgreɪv) *n.* (in medieval Germany) an officer with jurisdiction over a royal forest. [from German *Waldgraf,* from *Wald* forest + *Graf* count]

Wald·heim (*German* 'valthaɪm) *n.* **Kurt** (kʊrt). born 1918, Austrian diplomat; secretary general of the United Nations since 1971.

Wal+dorf sal+ad ('wɔːldɔːf) *n. Chiefly U.S.* a salad of diced apples, celery, and walnuts mixed with mayonnaise. [C20: named after the *Waldorf-Astoria Hotel* in New York City]

wale[1] (weɪl) *n.* **1.** the raised mark left on the skin after the stroke of a rod or whip. **2. a.** the weave or texture of a fabric, such as the ribs in corduroy. **b.** a vertical row of stitches in knitting. Compare **course** (sense 14). **3.** *Nautical.* **a.** a ridge of planking along the rail of a ship. **b.** See **gunwale.** ~*vb.* **4.** to raise a wale or wales on by striking. **5.** to weave with a wale. [Old English *walu* WEAL; related to Old Norse *vala* knuckle, Dutch *wäle*]

wale[2] (weɪl) *Northern Brit. dialect.* ~*n.* **1.** a choice. **2.** anything chosen as the best. ~*adj.* **3.** choice. ~*vb.* **4.** (*tr.*) to choose. [C14: from Old Norse *val* choice, related to German *Wahl*]

Wa+ler ('weɪlə) *n. Chiefly Austral.* a saddle horse originating in New South Wales. [C19: from *Wales,* in *New South Wales*]

Wales (weɪlz) *n.* a principality that is part of the United Kingdom, in the west of Great Britain; conquered by the English in 1282; parliamentary union with England took place in 1536. It consists mainly of moorlands and mountains and has an economy that is chiefly agricultural, with an industrial and coal-mining area in the south. Capital: Cardiff. Pop.: 2 766 800 (1976 est.). Area: 20 767 sq. km (8018 sq. miles). Welsh name: **Cymru.**

Wa·ley ('weɪlɪ) *n.* **Ar·thur.** original name *Arthur Schloss.* 1889–1966, English orientalist, best known for his translations of Chinese poetry.

Wal+fish Bay ('wɔːlfɪʃ) *n.* a variant spelling of **Walvis Bay.**

Wal+hal+la (wæl'hælə, væl-) *n.* a variant spelling of **Valhalla.**

walk (wɔːk) *vb.* **1.** (*intr.*) to move along or travel on foot at a moderate rate; advance in such a manner that at least one foot is always on the ground. **2.** (*tr.*) to pass through, on, or over on foot, esp. habitually. **3.** (*tr.*) to cause, assist, or force to move along at a moderate rate: *to walk a dog.* **4.** (*tr.*) to escort or conduct by walking: *to walk someone home.* **5.** (*intr.*) (of ghosts, spirits, etc.) to appear or move about in visible form. **6.** (of inanimate objects) to move or cause to move in a manner that resembles walking. **7.** (*intr.*) to follow a certain course or way of life: *to walk in misery.* **8.** (*tr.*) to bring into a certain condition by walking: *I walked my shoes to shreds.* **9.** (*tr.*) to measure, survey, or examine by walking. **10.** (*intr.*) *Basketball.* to take more than two steps without passing or dribbling the ball. **11. walk the plank.** See **plank** (sense 4). **12. walk on air.** to be delighted or exhilarated. **13. walk tall.** *U.S. informal.* to have self-respect or pride. **14. walk the streets.** to be a prostitute. ~*n.* **15.** the act or an instance of walking. **16.** the distance or extent walked. **17.** a manner of walking; gait. **18.** a place set aside for walking; promenade. **19.** a chosen profession or sphere of activity (esp. in the phrase **walk of life**). **20.** a foot race in which competitors walk. **21. a.** an arrangement of trees or shrubs in widely separated rows. **b.** the space between such rows. **22.** an enclosed ground for the exercise or feeding of domestic animals, esp. horses. **23.** *Chiefly Brit.* the route covered in the course of work, as by a tradesman or postman. **24.** *Obsolete.* the section of a forest controlled by a keeper. ~See also **walk away, walk into, walk off, walk out, walkover, walk through.** [Old English *wealcan;* related to Old High German *walchan,* Sanskrit *valgati* he moves] —**'walk+a·ble** *adj.*

walk+a·bout ('wɔːkəˌbaʊt) *n.* **1.** a periodic nomadic excursion into the Australian bush made by an Aborigine. **2.** a walking tour. **3.** *Chiefly journalistic.* an occasion when celebrities, royalty, etc., walk among and meet the public.

walk a·way *vb.* (*intr., adv.*) **1.** to leave, esp. callously and disregarding someone else's distress. **2. walk away with.** to achieve or win easily.

walk+er ('wɔːkə) *n.* **1.** a person who walks. **2.** Also called: **baby walker.** a tubular frame on wheels or castors to support a baby learning to walk. **3.** a similar support for walking, often with rubber feet, for use by cripples.

walk·ie-talk·ie *or* **walk·y-talk·y** (ˌwɔːkɪ'tɔːkɪ) *n., pl.* **-talk·ies.** a small combined radio transmitter and receiver, usually operating on shortwave, that can be carried around by one person: widely used by the police, medical services, etc.

walk-in *adj.* **1.** (of a cupboard, etc.) large enough to allow a person to enter and move about in. **2.** *U.S.* (of a building or apartment) located so as to admit of direct access from the street.

walk+ing ('wɔːkɪŋ) *adj.* (of a person) considered to possess the qualities of something inanimate as specified: *he is a walking encyclopedia.*

walk+ing bass (beɪs) *n. Jazz.* a simple accompaniment played by the double bass at medium tempo, usually consisting of ascending and descending tones or semitones, one to each beat.

walk+ing del+e+gate *n.* (in the U.S.) an agent appointed by a trade union to visit branches, check whether agreements are observed, and negotiate with employers.

walk+ing fern *or* **leaf** *n.* a North American fern, *Camptosorus rhizophyllus,* having sword-shaped fronds, the tips of which take root when in contact with the ground: family *Aspleniaceae.*

walk+ing pa+pers *pl. n. Slang, chiefly U.S.* notice of dismissal.

walk+ing stick *n.* **1.** a stick or cane carried in the hand to assist walking. **2.** the usual U.S. name for **stick insect.**

walk in·to *vb.* (*intr., prep.*) to meet with unwittingly: *to walk into a trap.*

walk off *vb.* **1.** (*intr.*) to depart suddenly. **2.** (*tr., adv.*) to get rid of by walking: *to walk off an attack of depression.* **3. walk (a person) off his feet.** to make (a person) walk so fast that he is exhausted. **4. walk off with. a.** to steal. **b.** to win, esp. easily.

walk-on *n.* **1. a.** a small part in a play or theatrical entertainment, esp. one without any lines. **b.** (*as modifier*): *a walk-on part.* ~*adj.* **2.** (of an aircraft or air service) having seats to be booked immediately before departure rather than in advance.

walk out *vb.* (*intr., adv.*) **1.** to leave without explanation, esp. in anger. **2.** to go on strike. **3. walk out on.** *Informal.* to abandon or desert. **4. walk out with.** *Brit., obsolete or dialect.* to court or be courted by. ~*n.* **walk+out. 5.** a strike by workers. **6.** the act of leaving a meeting, conference, etc., as a protest.

walk+o·ver ('wɔːkˌəʊvə) *n.* **1.** *Informal.* an easy or unopposed victory. **2.** *Horse racing.* **a.** the running or walking over the course by the only contestant entered in a race at the time of starting. **b.** a race won in this way. **3.** *Skateboarding.* movement in a straight line by means of a series of half turns. ~*vb.* **walk o·ver.** (*intr., mainly prep.*) **4.** (*also adv.*) to win a race by a walkover. **5.** *Informal.* to beat (an opponent) conclusively or easily. **6.** *Informal.* to take advantage of (someone).

walk through *Theatre.* ~*vb.* **1.** (*tr.*) to act or recite (a part) in a perfunctory manner, as at a first rehearsal. ~*n.* **walk-through. 2.** a rehearsal of a part.

walk-up *n. U.S. informal.* **a.** a block of flats having no lift. **b.** (*as modifier*): *a walk-up block.*

walk+way ('wɔ:kˌweɪ) *n. Chiefly U.S.* a passage or path esp. one for walking over machinery, etc.

Wal+kyr·ie (vælˈkɪərɪ, ˈvælkɪərɪ) *n.* a variant spelling of **Valkyrie.**

wall (wɔ:l) *n.* **1. a.** a vertical construction made of stone, brick, wood, etc., with a length and height much greater than its thickness, used to enclose, divide, or support. **b.** (*as modifier*): *wall hangings.* Related adj.: **mural. 2.** (*often pl.*) a structure or rampart built to protect and surround a position or place for defensive purposes. **3.** *Anatomy.* any lining, membrane, or investing part that encloses or bounds a bodily cavity or structure: *abdominal wall.* Technical name: **paries.** Related adj.: **parietal. 4.** *Mountaineering.* a vertical or almost vertical smooth rock face. **5.** anything that suggests a wall in function or effect: *a wall of fire; a wall of prejudice.* **6. bang one's head against a brick wall.** to try to achieve something impossible. **7. drive** (*or* **push**) **to the wall.** to force into an awkward situation. **8. go to the wall.** *Informal.* to be ruined; collapse financially. **9. go** (*or* **send**) **up the wall.** *Slang.* to become (or cause to become) crazy or furious. **10. have one's back to the wall.** to be in a very difficult situation. ~*vb.* (*tr.*) **11.** to protect, provide, or confine with or as if with a wall. **12.** (often foll. by *up*) to block (an opening) with a wall. **13.** (often foll. by *in* or *up*) to seal by or within a wall or walls. [Old English *weall,* from Latin *vallum* palisade, from *vallus* stake] —**walled** *adj.* —**'wall-less** *adj.* —**'wall-ˌlike** *adj.*

wal+la+by ('wɒləbɪ) *n., pl.* **+bies** *or* **+by. 1.** any of various herbivorous marsupials of the genera *Lagorchestes* (**hare wallabies**), *Petrogale* (**rock wallabies**), *Protemnodon,* etc., of Australia and New Guinea, similar to but smaller than kangaroos: family *Macropodidae.* **2. on the wallaby (track).** *Austral. slang.* (of a person) wandering about looking for work. [C19: from native Australian *wolabā*]

Wal+la+by ('wɒləbɪ) *n., pl.* **+bies.** a member of the international Rugby Union football team of Australia.

Wal·lace ('wɒlɪs) *n.* **1. Al·fred Rus·sel.** 1823–1913, British naturalist, whose work on the theory of natural selection influenced Charles Darwin. **2. Ed·gar.** 1875–1932, English crime novelist. **3.** Sir **Rich·ard.** 1818–90, English art collector and philanthropist. His bequest to the nation forms the Wallace Collection, London. **4.** Sir **Wil·liam.** ?1272–1305, Scottish patriot, who defeated the army of Edward I of England at Stirling (1297) but was routed at Falkirk (1298) and later executed.

Wal·lace's line *n.* the hypothetical boundary between the Oriental and Australasian zoogeographical regions, which runs between the Indonesian islands of Bali and Lombok, through the Macassar Strait, and SE of the Philippines. [C20: named after A. R. WALLACE]

Wal+la·chi·a (wɒˈleɪkɪə) *n.* a variant spelling of **Walachia.**

wal+lah *or* **wal+la** ('wɒlə) *n.* (*usually in combination*) *Informal.* a person involved with or in charge of (a specified thing): *the book wallah.* [C18: from Hindi *-wālā* from Sanskrit *pāla* protector]

wal+la+roo (ˌwɒləˈru:) *n., pl.* **+roos** *or* **+roo.** a large stocky Australian kangaroo, *Macropus* (or *Osphranter*) *robustus,* of rocky regions. [C19: from native Australian *wolarū*]

Wal+la+sey ('wɒləsɪ) *n.* a town in NW England, in Merseyside on the Wirral Peninsula near the mouth of the River Mersey, opposite Liverpool. Pop.: 97 061 (1971).

wall bars *pl. n.* a series of horizontal bars attached to a wall and used in gymnastics.

wall+board ('wɔ:lˌbɔ:d) *n.* a thin board made of materials, such as compressed wood fibres or gypsum plaster, between stiff paper, and used to cover walls, partitions, etc.

wall creep+er *n.* a pink-and-grey woodpecker-like songbird, *Tichodroma muraria,* of Eurasian mountain regions: family *Sittidae* (nuthatches).

walled plain *n.* any of the largest of the lunar craters, having diameters between 50 and 300 kilometres.

Wal·len·stein (*German* 'valənʃtaɪn) *or* **Wald·stein** (*German* 'valtʃtaɪn) *n.* **Al·brecht Wen·zel Eu·se·bi·us von** ('albrɛçt 'vɛntsəl ɔɪ'ze:bɪʊs fɔn), duke of Friedland and Mecklenburg, prince of Sagan. 1583–1634, German general and statesman, born in Bohemia. As leader of the Hapsburg forces in the Thirty Years' War he won many successes until his defeat at Lützen (1632) by Gustavus Adolphus.

Wal·ler ('wɒlə) *n.* **1. Ed·mund.** 1606–87, English poet and politician, famous for his poem *Go, Lovely Rose.* **2. Thom·as,** called *Fats.* 1904–43, U.S. jazz pianist.

wal+let ('wɒlɪt) *n.* **1.** a small folding case, usually of leather, for holding paper money, documents, etc. **2.** a bag used to carry tools. **3.** *Archaic, chiefly Brit.* a rucksack or knapsack. [C14: of Germanic origin; compare Old English *weallian,* Old High German *wallōn* to roam, German *wallen* to go on a pilgrimage]

wall+eye ('wɔ:lˌaɪ) *n., pl.* **+eyes** *or* **+eye. 1.** a divergent squint. **2.** opacity of the cornea. **3.** an eye having a white or light-coloured iris. **4.** Also called: **walleyed pike.** a North American pikeperch, *Stizostedion vitreum,* valued as a food and game fish. **5.** any of various other fishes having large staring eyes. [back formation from earlier *walleyed,* from Old Norse *vagleygr,* from *vage,* perhaps: a film over the eye (compare Swedish *vagel* sty in the eye) + *-eygr* -eyed, from *auga* eye; modern form influenced by WALL] —**wall+eyed** *adj.*

wall+flow·er ('wɔ:lˌflaʊə) *n.* **1.** Also called: **gillyflower.** a cruciferous plant, *Cheiranthus cheiri,* of S Europe, grown for its clusters of yellow, orange, brown, red, or purple fragrant flowers and naturalized on old walls, cliffs, etc. **2.** any of numerous other cruciferous plants of the genera *Cheiranthus* and *Erysimum,* having orange or yellow flowers. **3.** *Informal.* a person who stays on the fringes of a dance or party on account of lacking a partner or being shy.

wal+lies ('wælɪz) *pl. n. Central Scot. urban dialect.* false teeth; dentures. [see WALLY[2]]

Wal+lis ('valɪs) *n.* the German name for **Valais.**

Wal+lis and Fu+tu+na Is+lands ('wɒlɪs; fu:'tju:nə) *pl. n.* a French overseas territory in the SW Pacific, west of Samoa. Capital: Mata-Utu. Pop.: 8546 (1969). Area: 367 sq. km (143 sq. miles).

wall knot *n.* a knot forming a knob at the end of a rope, made by unwinding the strands and weaving them together.

wall liz+ard *n.* a small mottled grey lizard, *Lacerta muralis,* of Europe, N Africa, and SW Asia: family *Lacertidae.*

wall mus+tard *n.* another name for **stinkweed** (sense 1).

Wal+loon (wɒ'lu:n) *n.* **1.** a member of a French-speaking people living chiefly in S Belgium and adjacent parts of France. Compare **Fleming**[1]. **2.** the French dialect of Belgium. ~*adj.* **3.** of, relating to, or characteristic of the Walloons or their dialect. [C16: from Old French *Wallon,* from Medieval Latin: foreigner, of Germanic origin; compare Old English *wealh* foreign, WELSH]

wal+lop ('wɒləp) *vb.* **1.** (*tr.*) *Informal.* to beat soundly; strike hard. **2.** (*tr.*) *Informal.* to defeat utterly. **3.** (*intr.*) *Dialect.* to move in a clumsy manner. **4.** (*intr.*) (of liquids) to boil violently. ~*n.* **5.** *Informal.* a hard blow. **6.** *Informal.* the ability to hit powerfully, as of a boxer. **7.** *Informal.* a forceful impression. **8.** *Brit.* a slang word for **beer.** ~*vb., n.* **9.** an obsolete word for **gallop.** [C14: from Old Northern French *waloper* to gallop, from Old French *galoper,* of unknown origin]

wal+lop+er ('wɒləpə) *n.* **1.** a person or thing that wallops. **2.** *Austral. slang.* a policeman.

wal+lop+ing ('wɒləpɪŋ) *Informal.* ~*n.* **1.** a thrashing. ~*adj.* **2.** (intensifier): *a walloping drop in sales.*

wal+low ('wɒləʊ) *vb.* (*intr.*) **1.** (esp. of certain animals) to roll about in mud, water, etc., for pleasure. **2.** to move about with difficulty. **3.** to indulge oneself in possessions, emotion, etc.: *to wallow in self-pity.* **4.** (of smoke, waves, etc.) to billow. ~*n.* **5.** the act or an instance of wallowing. **6.** a muddy place or depression where animals wallow. [Old English *wealwian* to roll (in mud); related to Latin *volvere* to turn, Greek *oulos* curly, Russian *valun* round pebble] —**'wal+low+er** *n.*

wall+pa·per ('wɔ:lˌpeɪpə) *n.* **1.** paper usually printed or embossed with designs for pasting onto walls and ceilings. ~*vb.* **2.** to cover (a surface) with wallpaper.

wall pass *n. Soccer.* a movement in which one player passes the ball to another and sprints forward to receive the quickly played return. Also called: **one-two.**

wall pel+li+to·ry *n.* See **pellitory** (sense 1).

wall pep+per *n.* a small Eurasian crassulaceous plant, *Sedum acre,* having creeping stems, yellow flowers, and acrid-tasting leaves.

wall plate *n.* a horizontal timber member placed along the top of a wall to support the ends of joists, rafters, etc., and distribute the load.

wall rock *n.* rock that is immediately adjacent to a mineral vein, fault, or igneous intrusion.

wall rock+et *n.* any of several yellow-flowered European cruciferous plants of the genus *Diplotaxis,* such as *D. muralis,* that grow on old walls and in waste places.

wall rue *n.* a delicate fern, *Asplenium ruta-muraria,* that grows in rocky crevices and walls in North America and Eurasia.

Walls+end ('wɔ:lzˌɛnd) *n.* a town in NE England, in Tyne and Wear on the River Tyne: situated at the E end of Hadrian's Wall; shipbuilding. Pop.: 45 793 (1971).

Wall Street *n.* a street in lower Manhattan, New York, where the Stock Exchange and major banks are situated, regarded as the embodiment of American finance.

wall-to-wall *adj.* (of carpeting) completely covering a floor.

wal+ly[1] ('weɪlɪ) *adj. Scot. archaic.* **1.** fine, pleasing, or splendid. **2.** robust or strong. [C16: of obscure origin]

wal+ly[2] ('wælɪ) *adj. Central Scot. urban dialect.* **1.** made of china: *a wally dog; a wally vase.* **2.** lined with ceramic tiles: *a wally street.* [from obsolete dialect *wallow* faded, adjectival use of *wallow* to fade, from Old English *wealwian*]

wal+ly[3] ('wɒlɪ) *n., pl.* **+lies.** *Slang.* a stupid person. [C20: shortened form of the given name *Walter*]

wal+nut ('wɔ:lˌnʌt) *n.* **1.** any juglandaceous deciduous tree of the genus *Juglans,* of America, SE Europe, and Asia, esp. *J. regia,* which is native to W Asia but introduced elsewhere. They have aromatic leaves and flowers in catkins and are grown for their edible nuts and for their wood. **2.** the nut of any of these trees, having a wrinkled two-lobed seed and a hard wrinkled shell. **3.** the wood of any of these trees, used in making furniture, panelling, etc. **4.** a light yellowish-brown colour. ~*adj.* **5.** made from the wood of a walnut tree: *a walnut table.* **6.** of the colour walnut. [Old English *walhhnutu,* literally: foreign nut; compare Old French *noux gauge* walnut, probably translation of Vulgar Latin phrase *nux gallica* (unattested) Gaulish (hence, foreign) nut]

Wal·pole ('wɔ:lˌpəʊl) *n.* **1. Ho·race,** 4th Earl of Orford. 1717–97,

English writer, noted for his letters and for his delight in the Gothic, as seen in his house Strawberry Hill and his novel *The Castle of Otranto* (1764). **2.** his father, Sir **Rob·ert,** 1st Earl of Orford. 1676–1745, English Whig statesman. As first lord of the Treasury and Chancellor of the Exchequer (1721–42) he was effectively Britain's first prime minister.

Wal+pur+gis Night (væl'puəgɪs) *n.* the eve of May 1, believed in German folklore to be the night of a witches' sabbath on the Brocken, in the Harz Mountains. [C19: translation of German *Walpurgisnacht,* the eve of the feast day of St. Walpurga, 8th-century abbess in Germany]

wal+rus ('wɔːlrəs, 'wɒl-) *n., pl.* **+rus·es** *or* **+rus.** a pinniped mammal, *Odobenus rosmarus,* of northern seas, having a tough thick skin, upper canine teeth enlarged as tusks, and coarse whiskers and feeding mainly on shellfish: family *Odobenidae.* [C17: probably from Dutch, from Scandinavian; compare Old Norse *hrosshvalr* (literally: horse whale) and Old English *horschwæl;* see HORSE, WHALE]

wal+rus mous+tache *n.* a long thick moustache drooping at the ends.

Wal+sall ('wɔːlsɔːl) *n.* an industrial town in central England, in the West Midlands. Pop.: 184 606 (1971).

Wal·sing·ham ('wɔːlsɪŋəm) *n.* Sir **Fran·cis.** ?1530–90, English statesman. As secretary of state (1573–90) to Elizabeth I he developed a system of domestic and foreign espionage and uncovered several plots against the Queen.

Wal·ter *n.* **1.** (*German* 'valtər). **Bru·no** ('bruːno), original name *Bruno Walter Schlesinger.* 1876–1962, U.S. conductor, born in Germany: famous for his performances of Haydn, Mozart, and Mahler. **2.** ('wɔːltə). **John.** 1739–1812, English publisher; founded *The Daily Universal Register* (1785), which in 1788 became *The Times.*

Wal+tham For+est ('wɔːlθəm) *n.* a borough of NE Greater London. Pop.: 223 700 (1976 est.).

Wal·ther von der Vo·gel·wei·de (*German* 'valtər fɔn deːr 'foːgəlˌvaɪdə) *n.* ?1170–?1230, German minnesinger, noted for his lyric verse on political and moral themes.

Wal·ton ('wɔːltən) *n.* **1. Er·nest Thom·as Sin·ton.** born 1903, Irish physicist. He succeeded in producing the first artificial transmutation of an atomic nucleus (1932) with Sir John Cockcroft, with whom he shared the Nobel prize for physics (1951). **2. I·zaak** ('aɪzək). 1593–1683, English writer, best known for *The Compleat Angler* (1653; enlarged 1676). **3.** Sir **Wil·liam (Turner).** 1902–83, English composer. His works include *Façade* (1923), a setting of satirical verses by Edith Sitwell, the *Viola Concerto* (1929), and the oratorio *Belshazzar's Feast* (1931).

waltz (wɔːls) *n.* **1.** a ballroom dance in triple time in which couples spin around as they progress round the room. **2.** a piece of music composed for or in the rhythm of this dance. *~vb.* **3.** to dance or lead (someone) in or as in a waltz: *he waltzed her off her feet.* [C18: from German *Walzer,* from Middle High German *walzen* to roll; compare WELTER] —**'waltz+er** *n.* —**'waltz+ˌlike** *adj.*

waltz Ma+til+da *vb. Austral.* See **Matilda**[1].

Wal+vis Bay ('wɔːlvɪs) *or* **Wal+fish Bay** *n.* a port in South West Africa, on the Atlantic: forms an exclave of Cape Province, South Africa, covering an area of 1124 sq. km (434 sq. miles) with its hinterland, but has been administered by South West Africa since 1922; chief port of South West Africa and rich fishing centre. Pop.: 16 490 (1961).

wam+ble ('wɒmbəl) *Dialect, chiefly Brit.* *~vb.* (*intr.*) **1.** to move unsteadily. **2.** to twist the body. **3.** to feel nausea. *~n.* **4.** an unsteady movement. **5.** a sensation of nausea. [C14 *wamelen* to feel ill, perhaps of Scandinavian origin; compare Norwegian *vamla* to stagger] —**'wam+bli+ness** *n.* —**'wam+bling+ly** *adv.* —**'wam+bly** *adj.*

wame (weɪm) *n. Northern Brit. dialect.* the belly, abdomen, or womb.

wam+pum ('wɒmpəm) *n.* **1.** formerly, money used by North American Indians, made of cylindrical shells strung or woven together, esp. white shells rather than the more valuable black or purple ones. **2.** *U.S. informal,* money or wealth. *~*Also called: **peag, peage.** [C17: short for *wampumpeag,* from Narraganset *wampompeag,* from *wampan* light + *api* string + *-ag* plural suffix]

wan (wɒn) *adj.* **wan+ner, wan+nest. 1.** unnaturally pale esp. from sickness, grief, etc. **2.** characteristic or suggestive of ill health, unhappiness, etc. **3.** (of light, stars, etc.) faint or dim. *~vb.* **wans, wan+ning, wanned. 4.** to make or become wan. [Old English *wann* dark; related to *wanian* to WANE] —**'wan+ly** *adv.* —**'wan+ness** *n.*

WAN *international car registration for* West Africa Nigeria.

Wan+chü+an *or* **Wan-ch'u·an** (ˌwæntʃʊ'ɑːn) *n.* a former name of **Changchiakow.**

wand (wɒnd) *n.* **1.** a slender supple stick or twig. **2.** a thin rod carried as a symbol of authority. **3.** a rod used by a magician, water diviner, etc. **4.** *Informal.* a conductor's baton. **5.** *Archery.* a marker used to show the distance at which the archer stands from the target. [C12: from Old Norse *vǫndr;* related to Gothic *wandus* and English WEND] —**'wand+ˌlike** *adj.*

wan+der ('wɒndə) *vb.* (*mainly intr.*) **1.** (*also tr.*) to move or travel about, in, or through (a place) without any definite purpose or destination. **2.** to proceed in an irregular course; meander. **3.** to go astray, as from a path or course. **4.** (of the mind, thoughts, etc.) to lose concentration or direction. **5.** to think or speak incoherently or illogically. *~n.* **6.** the act or an instance of wandering. [Old English *wandrian;* related to Old Frisian *wandria,* Middle Dutch, Middle High German *wanderen*] —**'wan+der+er** *n.* —**'wan+der+ing** *adj., n.* —**'wan+der+ing+ly** *adv.*

wan+der+ing al+ba+tross *n.* a large albatross, *Diomedea exulans,* having a very wide wingspan and a white plumage with black wings.

wan+der+ing Jew *n.* **1.** any of several related creeping or trailing plants of tropical America, esp. *Tradescantia fluminensis* and *Zebrina pendula:* family *Commelinaceae.* **2.** *Austral.* a similar creeping plant of the genus *Commelina.*

Wan+der+ing Jew *n.* (in medieval legend) a character condemned to roam the world eternally because he mocked Christ on the day of the Crucifixion.

Wan+der+jahr *German.* ('vandərˌjaːr) *n., pl.* **+jah+re** (-ˌjaːrə). (formerly) a year in which an apprentice travelled to improve his skills. [German, literally: wander year]

wan+der+lust ('wɒndəˌlʌst) *n.* a great desire to travel and rove about. [German, literally: wander desire]

wan+der·oo (ˌwɒndə'ruː) *n., pl.* **+der·oos.** a macaque monkey, *Macaca silenus,* of India and Sri Lanka, having black fur with a ruff of long greyish fur on each side of the face. [C17: from Singhalese *vanduru* monkeys, literally: forest-dwellers, from Sanskrit *vānara* monkey, from *vana* forest]

wan+doo ('wɒnduː) *n.* a eucalyptus tree, *Eucalyptus redunca,* of W Australia, having white bark and durable wood. [from a native Australian language]

Wands+worth ('wɒnzwəθ) *n.* a borough of S Greater London, on the River Thames. Pop.: 284 600 (1976 est.).

wane (weɪn) *vb.* (*intr.*) **1.** (of the moon) to show a gradually decreasing portion of illuminated surface, between full moon and new moon. Compare **wax**[2] (sense 2). **2.** to decrease gradually in size, strength, power, etc. **3.** to draw to a close. *~n.* **4.** a decrease, as in size, strength, power, etc. **5.** the period during which the moon wanes. **6.** the act or an instance of drawing to a close. **7.** a rounded surface or defective edge of a plank, where the bark was. **8. on the wane.** in a state of decline. [Old English *wanian* (vb.); related to *wan-,* prefix indicating privation, *wana* defect, Old Norse *vana*] —**'wan+ey** *or* **'wan·y** *adj.*

Wan+ga+nu+i (ˌwɒŋə'nuːɪ) *n.* a port in New Zealand, on SW North Island: centre for a dairy-farming and sheep-rearing district. Pop.: 35 782 (1971).

wan+gle ('wæŋgəl) *Informal.* *~vb.* **1.** (*tr.*) to use devious or illicit methods to get or achieve (something) for (oneself or another): *he wangled himself a salary increase.* **2.** to manipulate or falsify (a situation, action, etc.). *~n.* **3.** the act or an instance of wangling. [C19: originally printers' slang, perhaps a blend of WAGGLE and dialect *wankle* wavering, from Old English *wancol;* compare Old High German *wankōn* to waver] —**'wan+gler** *n.*

Wan+hsien *or* **Wan-Hsien** ('wæn'ʃjɛn) *n.* an inland port in central China, in E Szechwan province, on the Yangtze River. Pop.: 100 000 (1953 est.).

wank (wæŋk) *Taboo slang.* *~vb.* **1.** (*intr.*) to masturbate. *~n.* **2.** an instance of wanking. [of uncertain origin]

wan+kel en+gine ('wæŋkəl) *n.* a type of four-stroke internal-combustion engine without reciprocating parts. It consists of one or more approximately elliptical combustion chambers within which a curved triangular-shaped piston rotates, by the explosion of compressed gas, dividing the combustion chamber into three gastight sections. [C20: named after Felix *Wankel* (born 1902), German engineer who invented it]

wank+er *n.* **1.** *Derogatory.* a worthless fellow. **2.** *Taboo slang.* a person who wanks; masturbator.

Wan+kie ('wɑːŋkɪ) *n.* a town in W Rhodesia: coal mines. Pop.: 22 710 (1972 est.).

wan+na ('wɒnə) *vb.* a spelling of **want to** intended to reflect a dialectal or informal pronunciation: *I wanna go home.*

Wan·ne-Eick·el (*German* 'vanə 'aɪkəl) *n.* an industrial town in W West Germany, in North Rhine-Westphalia on the Rhine-Herne Canal: formed in 1926 by the merging of two townships. Pop.: 98 800 (1970).

want (wɒnt) *vb.* **1.** (*tr.*) to feel a need or longing for: *I want a new hat.* **2.** (when *tr., may take a clause as object or an infinitive*) to wish, need, or desire (something or to do something): *he wants to go home.* **3.** (*intr.;* usually used with a negative and often foll. by *for*) to be lacking or deficient (in something necessary or desirable): *the child wants for nothing.* **4.** (*tr.*) to feel the absence of: *lying on the ground makes me want my bed.* **5.** (*tr.*) to fall short by (a specified amount). **6.** (*tr.*) *Chiefly Brit.* to have need of or require (doing or being something): *your shoes want cleaning.* **7.** (*intr.*) to be destitute. **8.** (*tr.; often passive*) to seek or request the presence of: *you're wanted upstairs.* **9.** (*intr.*) to be absent. **10.** (*tr.; takes an infinitive*) *Informal.* should or ought (to do something): *you don't want to go out so late.* **11. want in** (*or* **out**). *Informal.* to wish to be included in (or excluded from) a venture. *~n.* **12.** the act or an instance of wanting. **13.** anything that is needed, desired, or lacked: *to supply someone's wants.* **14.** a lack, shortage, or absence: *for want of common sense.* **15.** the state of being in need; destitution: *the state should help those in want.* **16.** a sense of lack; craving. [C12 (vb., in the sense: it is lacking), C13 (n.): from Old Norse *vanta* to be deficient; related to Old English *wanian* to WANE] —**'want+er** *n.*

want ad *n. Informal.* a classified advertisement in a newspaper, etc., for something wanted, such as property or employment.

want+ing ('wɒntɪŋ) *adj.* (*postpositive*) **1.** lacking or absent; missing. **2.** not meeting requirements or expectations: *you have been found wanting.* *~prep.* **3.** without. **4.** *Archaic.* minus.

wan+ton ('wɒntən) *adj.* **1.** dissolute, licentious, or immoral. **2.** without motive, provocation, or justification: *wanton destruction.* **3.** maliciously and unnecessarily cruel or destructive. **4.** unrestrained: *wanton spending.* **5.** *Archaic or poetic.* playful or capricious. **6.** *Archaic.* (of vegetation, etc.) luxuriant or superabundant. ~*n.* **7.** a licentious person, esp. a woman. **8.** a playful or capricious person. ~*vb.* **9.** (*intr.*) to behave in a wanton manner. **10.** (*tr.*) to squander or waste. [C13 *wantowen* (in the obsolete sense: unmanageable, unruly): from *wan-* (prefix equivalent to UN-[1]; related to Old English *wanian* to WANE) + *-towen,* from Old English *togen* brought up, from *tēon* to bring up] —'**wan+ton+ly** *adv.* —'**wan+ton+ness** *n.*

wap+en+take ('wɒpənˌteɪk, 'wæp-) *n. English legal history.* a subdivision of certain shires or counties, esp. in the Midlands and North of England, corresponding to the hundred in other shires. [Old English *wǣpen(ge)tæc,* from Old Norse *vāpnatak,* from *vápn* WEAPON + *tak* TAKE]

wap·i+ti ('wɒpɪtɪ) *n., pl.* **+tis.** a large North American deer, *Cervus canadensis,* with large much-branched antlers. Also called: **American elk.** [C19: from Shawnee, literally: white deer, from *wap* (unattested) white; from the animal's white tail and rump]

wap+pen+shaw ('wæpənʃɔː, 'wɒp-) *n.* (formerly) a muster of clansmen in Scotland to show the chieftains that they were properly armed. [C16: from Northern English *wapen,* from Old Norse *vápn* WEAPON + *schaw* SHOW]

war (wɔː) *n.* **1.** open armed conflict between two or more parties, nations, or states. Related adj.: **belligerent. 2.** a particular armed conflict: *the 1973 war in the Middle East.* **3.** the techniques of armed conflict as a study, science, or profession. **4.** any conflict or contest: *a war of wits; the war against crime.* **5.** (*modifier*) of, relating to, resulting from, or characteristic of war: *a war hero; war damage; a war story.* **6. to have had a good war.** to have fulfilled one's potential for courageous, decisive, or heroic action or other qualities by wartime service, esp. in the armed forces. **7. in the wars.** *Informal.* (esp. of a child) hurt or knocked about, esp. as a result of quarrelling and fighting. ~*vb.* **wars, war+ring, warred. 8.** (*intr.*) to conduct a war. [C12: from Old Northern French *werre* (variant of Old French *guerre*), of Germanic origin; related to Old High German *werra*]

War. *abbrev. for* Warwickshire.

wa+ra+gi ('waragɪ, -dʒɪ) *n.* a Ugandan alcoholic drink made from bananas. [from Luganda]

Wa+ran+gal ('wʌrəŋgəl) *n.* a city in S central India, in N Andhra Pradesh: capital of a 12th century Hindu kingdom. Pop.: 207 520 (1971).

wa+ra+tah ('wɒrətə) *n. Austral.* a proteaceous shrub, *Telopea speciosissima,* having dark green leaves and large clusters of crimson flowers. [from a native Australian language]

warb (wɔːb) *n. Austral. slang.* a dirty or insignificant person. [C20: of unknown origin] —'**warb·y** *adj.*

war ba·by *n.* a child born in wartime, esp. the illegitimate child of a soldier.

War·beck ('wɔːbɛk) *n.* **Per·kin** ('pɜːkɪn). ?1474–99, Flemish impostor, pretender to the English throne. Professing to be Richard, Duke of York, he led an unsuccessful rising against Henry VII (1497) and was later executed.

War Be+tween the States *n.* the American Civil War.

war+ble[1] ('wɔːbᵊl) *vb.* **1.** to sing (words, songs, etc.) with trills, runs, and other embellishments. **2.** (*tr.*) to utter in a song. **3.** *U.S.* another word for **yodel.** ~*n.* **4.** the act or an instance of warbling. [C14: via Old French *werbler* from Germanic; compare Frankish *hwirbilōn* (unattested), Old High German *wirbil* whirlwind. See to WHIRL]

war+ble[2] ('wɔːbᵊl) *n. Vet. science.* **1.** a small lumpy abscess under the skin of cattle caused by infestation with larvae of the warble fly. **2.** a hard tumorous lump of tissue on a horse's back, caused by prolonged friction of a saddle. [C16: of uncertain origin] —'**war+bled** *adj.*

war+ble fly *n.* any of various hairy beelike dipterous flies of the genus *Hypoderma* and related genera, the larvae of which produce warbles in cattle: family *Oestridae.*

war+bler ('wɔːblə) *n.* **1.** a person or thing that warbles. **2.** any small active passerine songbird of the Old World subfamily *Sylviinae:* family *Muscicapidae.* They have a cryptic plumage and slender bill and are arboreal insectivores. **3.** Also called: **wood warbler.** any small bird of the American family *Parulidae,* similar to the Old World forms but often brightly coloured.

war bon+net *n.* a headband with trailing feathers, worn by certain North American Indian warriors as a headdress.

war bride *n.* a soldier's bride met as a result of troop movements in wartime, esp. a foreign national.

war chest *n. U.S.* a fund collected for a specific purpose, such as an election campaign.

war cor+res+pon+dent *n.* a journalist who reports on a war from the scene of action.

war crime *n.* a crime committed in wartime in violation of the accepted rules and customs of war, such as genocide, ill-treatment of prisoners of war, etc. —**war crim·i+nal** *n.*

war cry *n.* **1.** a rallying cry used by combatants in battle. **2.** a cry, slogan, etc., used to rally support for a cause.

ward (wɔːd) *n.* **1.** (in many countries) a district into which a city, town, parish, or other area is divided for administration, election of representatives, etc. **2.** a room in a hospital, esp. one for patients requiring similar kinds of care: *a maternity ward.* **3.** one of the divisions of a prison. **4.** an open space enclosed within the walls of a castle. **5.** *Law.* **a.** Also called: **ward of court.** a person, esp. a minor or one legally incapable of managing his own affairs, placed under the control or protection of a guardian or of a court. **b.** guardianship, as of a minor or legally incompetent person. **6.** the state of being under guard or in custody. **7.** a person who is under the protection or in the custody of another. **8.** a means of protection. **9. a.** an internal ridge or bar in a lock that prevents an incorrectly cut key from turning. **b.** a corresponding groove cut in a key. **10.** a less common word for **warden.** ~*vb.* **11.** (*tr.*) *Archaic.* to guard or protect. ~See also **ward off.** [Old English *weard* protector; related to Old High German *wart,* Old Saxon *ward,* Old Norse *vorthr.* See GUARD] —'**ward+less** *adj.*

Ward (wɔːd) *n.* Sir **Jo·seph George.** 1856–1930, New Zealand statesman; prime minister of New Zealand (1906–12; 1928–30).

-ward *suffix.* **1.** (*forming adjectives*) indicating direction towards: *a backward step; heavenward progress.* **2.** (*forming adverbs*) a variant and the usual U.S. form of **-wards.** [Old English *-weard* towards]

war dance *n.* **1.** a ceremonial dance performed before going to battle or after victory, esp. by certain North American Indian peoples. **2.** a dance representing warlike action.

ward+ed ('wɔːdɪd) *adj.* (of locks, keys, etc.) having wards.

war+den[1] ('wɔːdᵊn) *n.* **1.** a person who has the charge or care of something, esp. a building, or someone. **2.** *Archaic.* any of various public officials, esp. one responsible for the enforcement of certain regulations. **3.** *Chiefly U.S.* the chief officer in charge of a prison. **4.** *Brit.* the principal or president of any of various universities or colleges. **5.** See **churchwarden** (sense 1). [C13: from Old Northern French *wardein,* from *warder* to guard, of Germanic origin; see GUARD] —'**war+den+ry** *n.*

war+den[2] ('wɔːdᵊn) *n.* a variety of pear that has crisp firm flesh and is used for cooking. [C15: of obscure origin]

war+der[1] ('wɔːdə) *or (fem.)* **war+dress** *n.* **1.** *Chiefly Brit.* an officer in charge of prisoners in a jail. **2.** a person who guards or has charge of something. [C14: from Anglo-French *wardere,* from Old French *warder* to GUARD, of Germanic origin] —'**ward+er+ˌship** *n.*

war+der[2] ('wɔːdə) *n.* (formerly) a staff or truncheon carried by a ruler as an emblem of authority and used to signal his wishes or intentions. [C15: perhaps from Middle English *warden* to WARD]

ward heel+er *n. U.S. politics, disparaging.* a party worker who canvasses votes and performs chores for a political boss. Also called: **heeler.**

war+di·an case ('wɔːdɪən) *n.* a type of glass container used for housing delicate ferns and similar plants. [C19: named after N. B. *Ward* (died 1868), English botanist]

ward+mote ('wɔːdməʊt) *n. Brit.* an assembly of the citizens or liverymen of a ward. [C14: see WARD, MOOT]

ward off *vb.* (*tr., adv.*) to turn aside or repel; avert.

ward+robe ('wɔːdrəʊb) *n.* **1.** a tall closet or cupboard, with a rail or hooks on which to hang clothes. **2.** the total collection of articles of clothing belonging to one person. **3.** the collection of costumes belonging to a theatre or theatrical company. [C14: from Old Northern French *warderobe,* from *warder* to GUARD + *robe* ROBE]

ward+robe trunk *n.* a large upright rectangular travelling case, usually opening longitudinally, with one side having a hanging rail, the other having drawers or compartments.

ward+room ('wɔːdˌruːm, -ˌrʊm) *n.* **1.** the quarters assigned to the officers (except the captain) of a warship. **2.** the officers of a warship collectively, excepting the captain.

-wards *or* **-ward** *suffix forming adverbs.* indicating direction towards: *a step backwards; to sail shorewards.* Compare **-ward.** [Old English *-weardes* towards]

ward+ship ('wɔːdʃɪp) *n.* the state of being a ward.

ware[1] (wɛə) *n.* (*often in combination*) **1.** (*functioning as sing.*) articles of the same kind or material: *glassware; silverware.* **2.** porcelain or pottery of a specified type: *agateware; jasper ware.* ~See also **wares.** [Old English *waru;* related to Old Frisian *were,* Old Norse *vara,* Middle Dutch *Ware*]

ware[2] (wɛə) *Archaic.* ~*vb.* **1.** another word for **beware.** ~*adj.* **2.** another word for **wary** or **wise.** [Old English *wær;* related to Old Saxon, Old High German *giwar,* Old Norse *varr,* Gothic *war,* Latin *vereor.* See AWARE, BEWARE]

ware[3] (wɛə) *vb.* (*tr.*) *Northern Brit. dialect.* to spend or squander. [C15: of Scandinavian origin; related to Icelandic *verja*]

ware+house *n.* ('wɛəˌhaʊs). **1.** a place where goods are stored prior to their use, distribution, or sale. **2.** See **bonded warehouse. 3.** *Chiefly Brit.* a large commercial, esp. wholesale, establishment. ~*vb.* ('wɛəˌhaʊz, -ˌhaʊs). **4.** (*tr.*) to store or place in a warehouse, esp. a bonded warehouse.

ware+house+man ('wɛəˌhaʊsmən) *n., pl.* **+men.** a person who manages, is employed in, or owns a warehouse.

wares (wɛəz) *pl. n.* **1.** articles of manufacture considered as being for sale. **2.** any talent or asset regarded as a commercial or saleable commodity. **3.** *Caribbean.* earthenware.

war+fare ('wɔːˌfɛə) *n.* **1.** the act, process, or an instance of waging war. **2.** conflict, struggle, or strife.

war+fa+rin ('wɔːfərɪn) *n.* a crystalline insoluble optically active compound, used as a rodenticide and, in the form of its sodium salt, as a medical anticoagulant. Formula: $C_{19}H_{16}O_4$. [C20: from the patent owners *W(isconsin) A(lumni) R(esearch) F(oundation)* + (COUM)ARIN]

war game *n.* **1.** a notional tactical exercise for training military commanders, in which no military units are actually deployed. **2.** a game in which model soldiers are used to create battles, esp. past battles, in order to study tactics.

war+head ('wɔːˌhɛd) *n.* the part of the fore end of a missile or projectile that contains explosives.

War·hol (ˈwɔːhəʊl) *n.* **An·dy.** born ?1930, U.S. artist and film maker; one of the foremost exponents of pop art.

war+horse (ˈwɔːˌhɔːs) *n.* **1.** a horse used in battle. **2.** *Informal.* a veteran soldier, politician, or elderly person, esp. one who is aggressive.

war·i+son (ˈwærɪsən) *n.* (esp. formerly) a bugle note used as an order to a military force to attack. [C13: from Old Northern French, from *warir* to protect, of Germanic origin; compare Old English *warian* to defend]

War+ley (ˈwɔːlɪ) *n.* an industrial town in W central England, in the West Midlands: formed in 1966 by the amalgamation of Smethwick, Oldbury, and Rowley Regis. Pop.: 163 388 (1971).

war+like (ˈwɔːˌlaɪk) *adj.* **1.** of, relating to, or used in war. **2.** hostile or belligerent. **3.** fit or ready for war.

war+lock (ˈwɔːˌlɒk) *n.* **1.** a man who practises black magic; sorcerer. **2.** a fortune-teller, conjurer, or magician. [Old English *wǣrloga* oath breaker, from *wǣr* oath + *-loga* liar, from *lēogan* to LIE[1]]

war+lord (ˈwɔːˌlɔːd) *n.* a military leader of a nation or part of a nation, esp. one who is accountable to nobody when the central government is weak: *the Chinese warlords.*

warm (wɔːm) *adj.* **1.** characterized by or having a moderate degree of heat; moderately hot. **2.** maintaining or imparting heat: *a warm coat.* **3.** having or showing ready affection, kindliness, etc.: *a warm personality.* **4.** lively, vigorous, or passionate: *a warm debate.* **5.** cordial or enthusiastic; ardent: *warm support.* **6.** quickly or easily aroused: *a warm temper.* **7.** (of colours) predominantly red or yellow in tone. **8.** (of a scent, trail, etc.) recently made; strong. **9.** near to finding a hidden object or discovering or guessing facts, as in children's games. **10.** *Informal.* uncomfortable or disagreeable, esp. because of the proximity of danger. ~*vb.* **11.** (sometimes foll. by *up*) to raise or be raised in temperature; make or become warm or warmer. **12.** (when *intr.*, often foll. by *to*) to make or become excited, enthusiastic, etc., (about): *he warmed to the idea of buying a new car.* **13.** (*intr.*, often foll. by *to*) to feel affection, kindness, etc., (for someone): *I warmed to her mother from the start.* **14.** (*tr.*) *Brit.* to give a caning to: *I'll warm you in a minute.* ~*n.* **15.** *Informal.* a warm place or area: *come into the warm.* **16.** *Informal.* the act or an instance of warming or being warmed. ~See also **warm over, warm up.** [Old English *wearm;* related to Old Frisian, Old Saxon *warm,* Old Norse *varmr*] —ˈ**warm+er** *n.* —ˈ**warm+ish** *adj.* —ˈ**warm+ly** *adv.* —ˈ**warm+ness** *n.*

warm-blood·ed *adj.* **1.** ardent, impetuous, or passionate. **2.** *Zoology.* the nontechnical term for **homoiothermic.** —ˌ**warm-ˈblood·ed+ness** *n.*

warm bod·y *n. Informal, derogatory.* an employee regarded as insufficiently skilled or imaginative to undertake more than the most routine responsibilities.

war me+mo·ri·al *n.* a monument, usually an obelisk or cross, to those who died in a war, esp. those from a particular locality.

warm front *n. Meteorol.* the boundary between a warm air mass and the cold air above, which is rising at a less steep angle than at the cold front. Compare **cold front, occluded front.**

warm-heart·ed *adj.* kindly, generous, or readily sympathetic. —ˌ**warm-ˈheart·ed+ly** *adv.* —ˌ**warm-ˈheart·ed+ness** *n.*

warm+ing pan *n.* a pan, often of copper and having a long handle, filled with hot coals or hot water and formerly drawn over the sheets to warm a bed.

war+mong·er (ˈwɔːˌmʌŋgə) *n.* a person who fosters warlike ideas or advocates war. —ˈ**war+ˌmon·ger+ing** *n.*

warm o·ver *vb.* (*tr., adv.*) *U.S.* **1.** to reheat (food). **2.** to present (an idea, etc.) again, esp. without freshness or originality.

warm sec+tor *n. Meteorol.* a wedge of warm air between the warm and cold fronts of a depression, which is eventually occluded. See also **cold front, warm front.**

warmth (wɔːmθ) *n.* **1.** the state, quality, or sensation of being warm. **2.** intensity of emotion: *he denied the accusation with some warmth.* **3.** affection or cordiality.

warm up *vb.* (*adv.*) **1.** to make or become warm or warmer. **2.** (*intr.*) to exercise in preparation for and immediately before a game or contest. **3.** to run or operate (an engine, etc.) until the normal working temperature or condition is attained, or (of an engine, etc.) to undergo this process. **4.** to make or become more animated or enthusiastic: *the party warmed up when Tom came.* **5.** to reheat (already cooked food) or (of such food) to be reheated. ~*n.* **warm-up. 6.** the act or an instance of warming up.

warn (wɔːn) *vb.* **1.** to notify or make (someone) aware of danger, harm, etc. **2.** (*tr.; often takes a negative and an infinitive*) to advise or admonish (someone) as to action, conduct, etc.: *I warn you not to do that again.* **3.** (*takes a clause as object or an infinitive*) to inform (someone) in advance: *he warned them that he would arrive late.* **4.** (*tr.;* usually foll. by *away, off,* etc.) to give notice to go away, be off, etc.: *he warned the trespassers off his ground.* [Old English *wearnian;* related to Old High German *warnēn,* Old Norse *varna* to refuse] —ˈ**warn+er** *n.*

warn+ing (ˈwɔːnɪŋ) *n.* **1.** a hint, intimation, threat, etc., of harm or danger. **2.** advice to beware or desist. **3.** an archaic word for **notice** (sense 6). ~*adj.* **4.** (*prenominal*) intended or serving to warn: *a warning look.* **5.** (of the coloration of certain distasteful or poisonous animals) having conspicuous markings, which predators recognize and learn to avoid; aposematic. —ˈ**warn+ing+ly** *adv.*

War of A·mer·i·can In·de·pend·ence *n.* the conflict following the revolt of the North American colonies against British rule, particularly on the issue of taxation. Hostilities began in 1775 when British and American forces clashed at Lexington and Concord. Articles of Confederation agreed in the Continental Congress in 1777 provided for a confederacy to be known as the United States of America. The war was effectively ended with the surrender of the British at Yorktown in 1781 and peace was signed at Paris in Sept. 1783. Also called: **American Revolution** or **Revolutionary War.**

War of 1812 *n.* a war between Great Britain and the U.S., fought chiefly along the Canadian border (1812–14).

war of nerves *n.* the use of psychological tactics against an opponent, such as shattering his morale by the use of propaganda.

War of Se+ces+sion *n.* another name for the (American) **Civil War.**

War of the Aus+tri·an Suc+ces+sion *n.* the war (1740–48) fought by Austria, Britain, and the Netherlands against Prussia, France, and Spain in support of the right of succession of Maria Theresa to the Austrian throne and against the territorial aims of Prussia.

War of the Grand Al+li·ance *n.* the war (1689–97) waged by the Grand Alliance, led by Britain, the Netherlands, and Austria, against Louis XIV of France, following his invasion (1688) of the Palatinate.

War of the Span+ish Suc+ces+sion *n.* the war (1701–14) between Austria, Britain, Prussia, and the Netherlands on the one side and France, Spain, and Bavaria on the other over the disputed succession to the Spanish throne.

warp (wɔːp) *vb.* **1.** to twist or cause to twist out of shape, as from heat, damp, etc. **2.** to turn or cause to turn from a true, correct, or proper course; pervert or be perverted. **3.** (*tr.*) to prepare (yarn) as a warp. **4.** *Nautical.* to move (a vessel) by hauling on a rope fixed to a stationary object ashore or (of a vessel) to be moved thus. **5.** (*tr.*) (formerly) to curve or twist (an aircraft wing) in order to assist control in flight. **6.** (*tr.*) to flood (land) with water from which alluvial matter is deposited. ~*n.* **7.** the state or condition of being twisted out of shape. **8.** a twist, distortion, or bias. **9.** a mental or moral deviation. **10.** the yarns arranged lengthways on a loom, forming the threads through which the weft yarns are woven. **11.** the heavy threads used to reinforce the rubber in the casing of a pneumatic tyre. **12.** *Nautical.* a rope used for warping a vessel. **13.** alluvial sediment deposited by water. [Old English *wearp* a throw; related to Old High German *warf,* Old Norse *varp* throw of a dragging net, Old English *weorpan* to throw] —ˈ**warp+age** *n.* —ˈ**warp+er** *n.*

war paint *n.* **1.** painted decoration of the face and body applied by certain North American Indians before battle. **2.** *Informal.* finery or regalia. **3.** *Informal.* cosmetics.

war+path (ˈwɔːˌpɑːθ) *n.* **1.** the route taken by North American Indians on a warlike expedition. **2. on the warpath. a.** preparing to engage in battle. **b.** *Informal.* in a state of anger.

war+plane (ˈwɔːˌpleɪn) *n.* any aircraft designed for and used in warfare. Also called (U.S.): **battle plane.**

war+rant (ˈwɒrənt) *n.* **1.** anything that gives authority for an action or decision; authorization; sanction. **2.** a document that certifies or guarantees, such as a receipt, licence, or commission. **3.** *Law.* an authorization issued by a magistrate or other official allowing a constable or other officer to search or seize property, arrest a person, or perform some other specified act. **4.** (in certain armed services) the official authority for the appointment of warrant officers. ~*vb.* (*tr.*) **5.** to guarantee the quality, condition, etc., of (something). **6.** to give authority or power to. **7.** to attest to or assure the character, worthiness, etc., of. **8.** to guarantee (a purchaser of merchandise) against loss of, damage to, or misrepresentation concerning the merchandise. **9.** *Law.* to guarantee (the title to an estate or other property). **10.** to declare confidently. [C13: from Anglo-French *warrant,* variant of Old French *guarant,* from *guarantir* to guarantee, of Germanic origin; compare GUARANTY] —ˈ**war+rant+a·ble** *adj.* —ˌ**war+rant+a·ˈbil+i·ty** *n.* —ˈ**war+rant+a·bly** *adv.* —ˈ**war+rant+er** *n.* —ˈ**war+rant+less** *adj.*

war+ran+tee (ˌwɒrənˈtiː) *n.* a person to whom a warranty is given.

war+rant of+fic+er *n.* an officer in certain armed services who holds a rank between those of commissioned and noncommissioned officers.

war+ran+tor (ˈwɒrənˌtɔː) *n.* an individual or company that provides a warranty.

war+ran+ty (ˈwɒrəntɪ) *n., pl.* **+ties. 1.** *Property law.* a covenant, express or implied, by which the vendor of real property vouches for the security of the title conveyed. **2.** *Contract law.* an express or implied term in a contract collateral to the main purpose, such as an undertaking that goods contracted to be sold shall meet specified requirements as to quality, etc. **3.** *Insurance law.* an undertaking by the party insured that the facts given regarding the risk are as stated. **4.** the act of warranting. [C14: from Anglo-French *warantie,* from *warantir* to warrant, variant of Old French *guarantir;* see WARRANT]

war+ren (ˈwɒrən) *n.* **1.** a series of interconnected underground tunnels in which rabbits live. **2.** a colony of rabbits. **3.** an overcrowded area or dwelling. **4. a.** *Chiefly Brit.* an enclosed place where small game animals or birds are kept, esp. for breeding, or a part of a river or lake enclosed by nets in which fish are kept (esp. in the phrase **beasts** or **fowls of warren**). **b.** *English legal history.* a franchise permitting one to keep animals, birds, or fish in this way. [C14: from Anglo-French *warenne,* of Germanic origin; compare Old High German *werien* to preserve]

War+ren[1] ('wɒrən) *n.* a city in SE Michigan, northeast of Detroit. Pop.: 175 927 (1973 est.).

War+ren[2] ('wɒrən) *n.* **Earl.** 1891–1974, U.S. lawyer; chief justice of the U.S. (1953–69). He chaired the commission that investigated the murder of President Kennedy.

war+ren+er ('wɒrənə) *n. Obsolete.* a gamekeeper or keeper of a warren (sense 4).

war+rig+al ('wɒrɪgæl) *Austral.* ~*n.* **1.** a dingo. **2.** a wild horse. **3.** a wild Aboriginal. ~*adj.* **4.** untamed or wild. [C19: from a native Australian language]

War+ring+ton ('wɒrɪŋtən) *n.* an industrial town in NW England, in N Cheshire on the River Mersey: dates from Roman times. Pop.: 127 532 (1971).

war+ri+or ('wɒrɪə) *n.* **a.** a person engaged in, experienced in, or devoted to war. **b.** (*as modifier*): *a warrior nation.* [C13: from Old Northern *werreieor,* from *werre* WAR]

War+saw ('wɔːsɔː) *n.* the capital of Poland, in the E central part on the River Vistula: became capital at the end of the 16th century; almost completely destroyed in World War II as the main centre of the Polish resistance movement; rebuilt within about six years; university (1818); situated at the junction of important trans-European routes. Pop.: 1 400 000 (1974 est.). Polish name: **War+sza+wa** (var'ʃava).

War+saw Pact *n.* a military treaty and association of E European countries, formed in 1955, consisting of the Soviet Union, Bulgaria, Czechoslovakia, East Germany, Hungary, Poland, and Rumania.

war+ship ('wɔːʃɪp) *n.* a vessel armed, armoured, and otherwise equipped for naval warfare.

war+sle ('wɑːsəl) *n., vb. Northern Brit.* a dialect word for **wrestle.** Also: **warstle.** —**'war+sler** *n.*

Wars of the Ros·es *n.* the conflicts in England (1455–85) centred on the struggle for the throne between the house of York (symbolized by the white rose) and the house of Lancaster (of which one badge was the red rose).

wart (wɔːt) *n.* **1.** Also called: **verruca.** *Pathol.* any firm abnormal elevation of the skin caused by a virus. **2.** *Botany.* a small rounded outgrowth. [Old English *weart(e)*; related to Old High German *warza,* Old Norse *varta*] —**'wart+ed** *adj.* —**'wart+ˌlike** *adj.* —**'wart·y** *adj.*

War+ta (*Polish* 'varta) *n.* a river in Poland, flowing generally north and west across the whole W Polish Plain to the River Oder. Length: 808 km (502 miles).

Wart+burg (*German* 'vartbʊrk) *n.* a medieval castle in East Germany, in Thuringia southwest of Eisenach: residence of Luther (1521–22) when he began his German translation of the New Testament.

wart hog *n.* a wild pig, *Phacochoerus aethiopicus,* of southern and E Africa, having heavy tusks, wart-like protuberances on the face, and a mane of coarse hair.

war+time ('wɔːˌtaɪm) *n.* **a.** a period or time of war. **b.** (*as modifier*): *wartime conditions.*

war whoop *n.* the yell or howl uttered, esp. by North American Indians, while making an attack.

War+wick[1] ('wɒrɪk) *n.* a town in central England, administrative centre of Warwickshire, on the River Avon: university (1965). Pop.: 18 289 (1971).

War·wick[2] ('wɒrɪk) *n.* **Earl of,** title of *Richard Neville,* called *the Kingmaker.* 1428–71, English statesman. During the Wars of the Roses, he fought first for the Yorkists, securing the throne (1461) for Edward IV, and then for the Lancastrians, restoring Henry VI (1470). He was killed at Barnet by Edward IV.

War+wick+shire ('wɒrɪkˌʃɪə, -ʃə) *n.* a county of central England: until 1974, when the West Midlands metropolitan county was created, it contained one of the most highly industrialized regions in the world, centred on Birmingham. Administrative centre: Warwick. Pop.: 471 000 (1976 est.). Area: 2028 sq. km (783 sq. miles).

war·y ('wɛərɪ) *adj.* **war·i·er, war·i·est. 1.** watchful, cautious, or alert. **2.** characterized by caution or watchfulness. [C16: from WARE[2] + -Y[1]] —**'war·i·ly** *adv.* —**'war·i+ness** *n.*

was (wɒz; *unstressed* wəz) *vb.* (used with *I, he, she, it,* and with singular nouns) **1.** the past tense (indicative mood) of **be. 2.** *Not standard.* a form of the subjunctive mood used in place of *were,* esp. in conditional sentences: *if the film was to be with you, would you be able to process it?* [Old English *wæs,* from *wesan* to be; related to Old Frisian, Old High German *was,* Old Norse *var*]

Wa+satch Range ('wɔːsætʃ) *pl. n.* a mountain range in the W central U.S., in N Utah and SE Idaho. Highest peak: Mount Timpanogos, 3581 m (11 750 ft.).

wash (wɒʃ) *vb.* **1.** to apply water or other liquid, usually with soap, to (oneself, clothes, etc.) in order to cleanse. **2.** (*tr.;* often foll. by *away, from, off,* etc.) to remove by the application of water or other liquid and usually soap: *she washed the dirt from her clothes.* **3.** (*intr.*) to be capable of being washed without damage or loss of colour. **4.** (of an animal such as a cat) to cleanse (itself or another animal) by licking. **5.** (*tr.*) to cleanse from pollution or defilement. **6.** (*tr.*) to make wet or moist. **7.** (often foll. by *away,* etc.) to move or be moved by water: *the flood washed away the bridge.* **8.** (esp. of waves) to flow or sweep against or over (a surface or object), often with a lapping sound. **9.** to form by erosion or be eroded: *the stream washed a ravine in the hill.* **10.** (*tr.*) to apply a thin coating of paint, metal, etc., to. **11.** (*tr.*) to separate (ore, precious stones, etc.) from (gravel, earth, or sand) by immersion in water. **12.** (*intr.; usually used with a negative*) *Informal, chiefly Brit.* to admit of testing or proof: *your excuses won't wash.* **13. wash one's hands. a.** *Euphemistic.* to go to the lavatory. **b.** (usually foll. by *of*) to refuse to accept responsibility (for). ~*n.* **14.** the act or process of washing; ablution. **15.** a quantity of articles washed together. **16.** a preparation or thin liquid used as a coating or in washing: *a thin wash of paint; a hair wash.* **17.** *Med.* **a.** any medicinal or soothing lotion for application to a part of the body. **b.** (*in combination*): *an eyewash.* **18.** the flow of water, esp. waves, against a surface, or the sound made by such a flow. **19. a.** the technique of making wash drawings. **b.** See **wash drawing. 20.** the erosion of soil by the action of flowing water. **21.** a mass of alluvial material transported and deposited by flowing water. **22.** land that is habitually washed by tidal or river waters. **23.** the disturbance in the air or water produced at the rear of an aircraft, boat, or other moving object. **24.** gravel, earth, etc., from which valuable minerals may be washed. **25.** waste liquid matter or liquid refuse, esp. as fed to pigs; swill. **26.** an alcoholic liquid resembling strong beer, resulting from the fermentation of wort in the production of whisky. **27. come out in the wash.** *Informal.* to become known or apparent in the course of time. ~See also **wash down, wash out, wash up.** [Old English *wæscan, waxan;* related to Old High German *wascan;* see WATER]

Wash (wɒʃ) *n.* **the.** a shallow inlet of the North Sea on the E coast of England, between Lincolnshire and Norfolk.

Wash. *abbrev. for* Washington.

wash+a·ble ('wɒʃəbᵊl) *adj.* (esp. of fabrics or clothes) capable of being washed without deteriorating. —**ˌwash+a·'bil+i·ty** *n.*

wash-and-wear *adj.* (of fabrics, garments, etc.) requiring only light washing, short drying time, and little or no ironing.

wash+a·way ('wɒʃəˌweɪ) *n. Austral. informal.* another word for **washout.**

wash+ba·sin ('wɒʃˌbeɪsᵊn) *n.* a basin or bowl for washing the face and hands. Also called: **washbowl.**

wash+board ('wɒʃˌbɔːd) *n.* **1.** a board having a surface, usually of corrugated metal, on which clothes are scrubbed. **2.** such a board used as a rhythm instrument played with the fingers in skiffle, Country and Western music, etc. **3.** a less common U.S. word for **skirting board. 4.** *Nautical.* **a.** a vertical planklike shield fastened to the gunwales of a boat to prevent water from splashing over the side. **b.** Also called: **splashboard.** a shield under a port for the same purpose.

wash+cloth ('wɒʃˌklɒθ) *n.* the U.S. word for **flannel** (sense 4).

wash+day ('wɒʃˌdeɪ) *n.* a day on which clothes and linen are washed, often the same day each week.

wash down *vb.* (*tr., adv.*) **1.** to wash completely, esp. from top to bottom. **2.** to take drink with or after (food or another drink).

wash draw+ing *n.* a pen-and-ink drawing that has been lightly brushed over with water to soften the lines.

washed out *adj.* (**washed-out** *when prenominal*). **1.** faded or colourless. **2.** exhausted, esp. when being pale in appearance.

washed up *adj.* (**washed-up** *when prenominal*). *Informal, chiefly U.S.* **1.** no longer useful, successful, hopeful, etc.: *our hopes for the new deal are all washed up.* **2.** exhausted.

wash+er ('wɒʃə) *n.* **1.** a person or thing that washes. **2.** a flat ring or drilled disc of metal used under the head of a bolt or nut to spread the load when tightened. **3.** any flat ring of rubber, felt, metal, etc., used to provide a seal under a nut or in a tap or valve seat. **4.** See **washing machine. 5.** *Chemical engineering.* a device for cleaning or washing gases or vapours; scrubber. **6.** *Austral.* a face cloth; flannel.

wash·er·wom·an ('wɒʃəˌwʊmən), **wash+wom·an,** *or* (*masc.*) **wash·er·man** *n., pl.* **+wom·en** *or* **+men.** a person who washes clothes for a living.

wash+er·y ('wɒʃərɪ) *n.* a plant at a mine where water or other liquid is used to remove dirt from a mineral, esp. coal.

wash+in ('wɒʃɪn) *n. Aeronautics.* an increase in the angle of attack of an aircraft wing towards the wing tip. [C20: from WASH (flow) + IN]

wash+ing ('wɒʃɪŋ) *n.* **1.** articles that have been or are to be washed together on a single occasion. **2.** liquid in which an article has been washed. **3.** something, such as gold dust or metal ore, that has been obtained by washing. **4.** a thin coat of something applied in liquid form.

wash+ing ma+chine *n.* a mechanical apparatus, usually powered by electricity, for washing clothing, linens, etc.

wash+ing pow+der *n.* powdered detergent for washing fabrics.

wash+ing so·da *n.* the crystalline decahydrate of sodium carbonate, esp. when used as a cleansing agent.

Wash+ing+ton[1] ('wɒʃɪŋtən) *n.* **1.** a state of the northwestern U.S., on the Pacific: consists of the Coast Range and the Olympic Mountains in the west and the Columbia Plateau in the east. Capital: Olympia. Pop.: 3 409 169 (1970). Area: 172 416 sq. km (66 570 sq. miles). Abbrevs.: **Wash.** or (with zip code) **WA 2.** Also called: **Washington D.C.** the capital of the U.S., coextensive with the District of Columbia and situated near the E coast on the Potomac River: site chosen by President Washington in 1790; contains the White House and the Capitol; a major educational and administrative centre. Pop.: 723 000 (1974 est.). **3.** a town in Co. Durham: designated a new town in 1964; coal-mining. Pop.: 25 269 (1971). **4. Mount.** a mountain in N New Hampshire, in the White Mountains: the highest peak in the northeast U.S.; noted for extreme weather conditions. Height: 1917 m (6288 ft.). **5. Lake.** a lake in W Washington, forming the E boundary of the city of Seattle: linked by canal with Puget Sound. Length: about 32 km (20 miles). Width: 6 km (4 miles). —**Wash+ing+to+ni·an** (ˌwɒʃɪŋ'təʊnɪən) *adj., n.*

Wash·ing·ton[2] ('wɒʃɪŋtən) *n.* **1. Book·er T(aliaferro).** 1856–

1915, U.S. Negro educationalist and writer. **2. George.** 1732–99, U.S. general and statesman; first president of the U.S. (1789–97). He was appointed commander in chief of the Continental Army (1775) at the outbreak of the War of American Independence, which ended with his defeat of Cornwallis at Yorktown (1781). He presided over the convention at Philadelphia (1787) that formulated the constitution of the U.S. and elected him president.

Wash·ing·ton Is·land *n.* an island in the central Pacific, in the Line Islands: coconut plantations. Pop.: 437 (1968). Area: 13 sq. km (5 sq. miles).

Wash·ing·ton palm *n.* a palm tree, *Washingtonia filifera,* of California and Florida, having large fan-shaped leaves and small black fruits. Also called: **desert palm.**

wash·ing-up *n. Brit.* **1.** the washing of dishes, cutlery, etc., after a meal. **2.** dishes and cutlery waiting to be washed up. **3.** (*as modifier*): *a washing-up machine.*

wash out *vb.* (*adv.*) **1.** (*tr.*) to wash (the inside of something) so as to remove (dirt). **2.** Also: **wash off.** to remove or be removed by washing: *grass stains don't wash out easily.* **3.** (*tr.*) to cancel or abandon (a sporting event). ~*n.* **wash·out. 4.** *Geology.* **a.** erosion of the earth's surface by the action of running water. **b.** a narrow channel produced by this erosion. **5.** *Informal.* **a.** a total failure or disaster. **b.** an incompetent person. **6.** *Aeronautics.* a decrease in the angle of attack of an aircraft wing towards the wing tip.

wash·rag ('wɒʃˌræg) *n. U.S.* another word for **flannel** (sense 4).

wash·room ('wɒʃˌruːm, -ˌrʊm) *n.* **1.** a room, esp. in a factory or office block, in which lavatories, washbasins, etc., are situated. **2.** *U.S.* a euphemism for **lavatory.**

wash sale *n. U.S.* the illegal stock-exchange practice of buying and selling the same securities at an inflated price through a colluding broker to give the impression that the security has a strong market.

wash·stand ('wɒʃˌstænd) *n.* a piece of furniture designed to hold a basin, etc., for washing the face and hands.

wash·tub ('wɒʃˌtʌb) *n.* a tub or large container used for washing anything, esp. clothes.

wash up *vb.* (*adv.*) **1.** *Chiefly Brit.* to wash (dishes, cutlery, etc.) after a meal. **2.** (*intr.*) *U.S.* to wash one's face and hands.

wash·wom·an ('wɒʃˌwʊmən) *n., pl.* **·wom·en.** a less common word for **washerwoman.**

wash·y ('wɒʃɪ) *adj.* **wash·i·er, wash·i·est. 1.** over-diluted, watery, or weak. **2.** lacking intensity or strength. —**'wash·i·ness** *n.*

was·n't ('wɒzᵊnt) *contraction of* was not.

wasp (wɒsp) *n.* **1.** any social hymenopterous insect of the family *Vespidae,* esp. *Vespula vulgaris* (**common wasp**), typically having a black-and-yellow body and an ovipositor specialized for stinging. See also **potter wasp, hornet. 2.** any of various solitary hymenopterans, such as the digger wasp and gall wasp. [Old English *wæsp;* related to Old Saxon *waspa,* Old High German *wefsa,* Latin *vespa*] —**'wasp·ˌlike** *adj.* —**'wasp·y** *adj.* —**'wasp·i·ly** *adv.* —**'wasp·i·ness** *n.*

Wasp *or* **WASP** (wɒsp) *n. U.S., often derogatory.* a person descended from N European, usually Protestant stock, forming a group often considered the most dominant, privileged, and influential in American society. [C20: *W*(*hite*) *A*(*nglo-*) *S*(*axon*) *P*(*rotestant*)]

wasp·ish ('wɒspɪʃ) *adj.* **1.** relating to or suggestive of a wasp. **2.** easily annoyed or angered. —**'wasp·ish·ly** *adv.* —**'wasp·ish·ness** *n.*

wasp waist *n.* a very slender waist, esp. one that is tightly corseted. —**'wasp-ˌwaist·ed** *adj.*

was·sail ('wɒseɪl) *n.* **1.** (formerly) a toast or salutation made to a person at festivities. **2.** a festivity when much drinking takes place. **3.** alcoholic drink drunk at such a festivity, esp. spiced beer or mulled wine. **4.** the singing of Christmas carols, going from house to house. **5.** *Archaic.* a drinking song. ~*vb.* **6.** to drink the health of (a person) at a wassail. **7.** (*intr.*) to go from house to house singing carols at Christmas. [C13: from Old Norse *ves heill* be in good health; related to Old English *wes hāl;* see HALE[1]] —**'was·sail·er** *n.*

Was·ser·mann test *or* **re·ac·tion** ('wæsəmən; *German* 'vasərˌman) *n. Med.* a diagnostic test for syphilis. See **complement fixation test.** [C20: named after August von *Wassermann* (1866–1925), German bacteriologist]

wast (wɒst; *unstressed* wəst) *vb. Archaic or dialect.* (used with the pronoun *thou* or its relative equivalent) a singular form of the past tense (indicative mood) of **be.**

wast·age ('weɪstɪdʒ) *n.* **1.** anything lost by wear or waste. **2.** the process of wasting. **3.** reduction in size of a work force by retirement, voluntary resignation, etc. (esp. in the phrase **natural wastage**).

waste (weɪst) *vb.* **1.** (*tr.*) to use, consume, or expend thoughtlessly, carelessly, or to no avail. **2.** (*tr.*) to fail to take advantage of: *to waste an opportunity.* **3.** (when *intr.,* often foll. by *away*) to lose or cause to lose bodily strength, health, etc. **4.** to exhaust or become exhausted. **5.** (*tr.*) to ravage. **6.** (*tr.*) *U.S. slang.* to murder: *I want that guy wasted by tomorrow.* ~*n.* **7.** the act of wasting or state of being wasted. **8.** a failure to take advantage of something. **9.** anything unused or not used to full advantage. **10.** anything or anyone rejected as useless, worthless, or in excess of what is required. **11.** garbage, rubbish, or trash. **12.** a land or region that is devastated or ruined. **13.** a land or region that is wild or uncultivated. **14.** *Physiol.* **a.** the useless products of metabolism. **b.** undigestible food residue. **15.** disintegrated rock material resulting from erosion. **16.** *Law.* reduction in the value of an estate caused by act or neglect, esp. by a life-tenant. ~*adj.* **17.** rejected as useless, unwanted, or worthless. **18.** produced in excess of what is required. **19.** not cultivated, inhabited, or productive: *waste land.* **20. a.** of or denoting the useless products of metabolism. **b.** of or denoting indigestible food residue. **21.** destroyed, devastated, or ruined. **22.** designed to contain or convey waste products. **23. lay waste.** to devastate or destroy. [C13: from Anglo-French *waster,* from Latin *vastāre* to lay waste, from *vastus* empty] —**'wast·a·ble** *adj.* —**'wast·er** *n.*

waste·bas·ket ('weɪstˌbɑːskɪt) *n.* another term (esp. U.S.) for **wastepaper basket.**

waste·ful ('weɪstfʊl) *adj.* **1.** tending to waste or squander; extravagant. **2.** causing waste, destruction, or devastation. —**'waste·ful·ly** *adv.* —**'waste·ful·ness** *n.*

waste·land ('weɪstˌlænd) *n.* **1.** a barren or desolate area of land. **2.** a region, period in history, etc., that is considered spiritually, intellectually, or aesthetically barren or desolate: *American television is a cultural wasteland.*

waste lot *n. Chiefly Canadian.* a piece of waste ground in a city.

waste·pa·per ('weɪstˌpeɪpə) *n.* paper discarded after use.

waste·pa·per bas·ket *or* **bin** *n.* an open receptacle for paper and other dry litter. Usual U.S. word: **wastebasket.**

waste·weir ('weɪstˌwɪə) *n.* another name for **spillway.**

wast·ing ('weɪstɪŋ) *adj.* (*prenominal*) reducing the vitality, strength, or robustness of the body: *a wasting disease.* —**'wast·ing·ly** *adv.*

wast·ing as·set *n.* an unreplaceable business asset of limited life, such as a coal mine or an oil well.

wast·rel ('weɪstrəl) *n.* **1.** a wasteful person; spendthrift; prodigal. **2.** an idler or vagabond.

Wast Wa·ter (wɒst) *n.* a lake in NW England, in Cumbria in the Lake District. Length: 5 km (3 miles).

wat (wɑːt) *n.* a Thai Buddhist monastery or temple. [Thai, from Sanskrit *vāta* enclosure]

wa·tap (wæ'tɑːp, wɑː-) *n.* a stringy thread made by North American Indians from the roots of various conifers and used for weaving and sewing. [C18: from Canadian French, from Cree *watapiy*]

watch (wɒtʃ) *vb.* **1.** to look at or observe closely or attentively. **2.** (*intr.,* foll. by *for*) to wait attentively or expectantly. **3.** to guard or tend (something) closely or carefully. **4.** (*intr.*) to keep vigil. **5.** (*tr.*) to maintain an interest in: *to watch the progress of a child at school.* **6. watch it!** be careful! look out! ~*n.* **7. a.** a small portable timepiece, usually worn strapped to the wrist (a **wristwatch**) or in a waistcoat pocket. **b.** (*as modifier*): *a watch spring.* **8.** the act or an instance of watching. **9.** a period of vigil, esp. during the night. **10.** (formerly) one of a set of periods of any of various lengths into which the night was divided. **11.** *Nautical.* **a.** any of the four-hour periods beginning at midnight and again at noon during which part of a ship's crew are on duty. **b.** those officers and crew on duty during a specified watch. **12.** the period during which a guard is on duty. **13.** (formerly) a watchman or band of watchmen. **14. on the watch.** on the lookout; alert. ~See also **watch out.** [Old English *wæccan* (vb.), *wæcce* (n.); related to WAKE[1]]

watch·band ('wɒtʃˌbænd) *n.* a U.S. word for **watchstrap.**

watch cap *n.* a knitted navy-blue woollen cap worn by seamen in cold weather.

watch·case ('wɒtʃˌkeɪs) *n.* a protective case for a watch, generally of metal such as gold, silver, brass, or gunmetal.

watch chain *n.* a chain used for fastening a pocket watch to the clothing. See also **fob[1].**

Watch Com·mit·tee *n. Brit. history.* a local government committee composed of magistrates and representatives of the county borough council responsible for the efficiency of the local police force.

watch·dog ('wɒtʃˌdɒg) *n.* **1.** a dog trained to guard property. **2. a.** a person or group of persons that acts as a protector or guardian against inefficiency, illegal practices, etc. **b.** (*as modifier*): *a watchdog committee.*

watch·er ('wɒtʃə) *n.* **1.** a person who watches. **2.** a person who maintains a vigil at the bedside of an invalid. **3.** *U.S.* a representative of a candidate or party stationed at a poll on election day to watch out for fraud.

watch fire *n.* a fire kept burning at night as a signal or for warmth and light by a person keeping watch.

watch·ful ('wɒtʃfʊl) *adj.* **1.** vigilant or alert. **2.** *Archaic.* not sleeping. —**'watch·ful·ly** *adv.* —**'watch·ful·ness** *n.*

watch-glass *n.* **1.** a curved glass disc that covers the dial of a watch. **2.** a similarly shaped piece of glass used in laboratories for evaporating small samples of a solution, etc.

watch·mak·er ('wɒtʃˌmeɪkə) *n.* a person who makes or mends watches. —**'watch·ˌmak·ing** *n.*

watch·man ('wɒtʃmən) *n., pl.* **·men. 1.** a person employed to guard buildings or property. **2.** (formerly) a man employed to patrol or guard the streets at night.

watch night *n.* **1.** (in Protestant churches) the night of December 31, during which a service is held to mark the passing of the old year and the beginning of the new. **2.** the service held on this night.

watch out *vb.* **1.** (*intr., adv.*) to be careful or on one's guard. ~*n.* **watch·out. 2.** a less common word for **lookout** (sense 1).

watch·strap ('wɒtʃˌstræp) *n.* a strap of leather, cloth, etc., attached to a watch for fastening it around the wrist. Also called (U.S.): **watchband.**

watch·tow·er ('wɒtʃˌtaʊə) *n.* a tower on which a sentry keeps watch.

watch+word ('wɒtʃ,wɜːd) *n.* **1.** another word for **password. 2.** a rallying cry or slogan.

wa+ter ('wɔːtə) *n.* **1.** a clear colourless tasteless odourless liquid that is essential for plant and animal life and constitutes, in impure form, rain, oceans, rivers, lakes, etc. It is a neutral substance, an effective solvent for many compounds, and is used as a standard for many physical properties. Formula: H_2O. Related adj.: **aqueous.** Related combining form: **hydro-. 2. a.** any body or area of this liquid, such as a sea, lake, river, etc. **b.** (*as modifier*): *water sports; water transport; a water plant.* Related adj.: **aquatic. 3.** the surface of such a body or area: *fish swam below the water.* **4.** any form or variety of this liquid, such as rain. **5.** See **high water, low water. 6.** any of various solutions of chemical substances in water: *lithia water; ammonia water.* **7.** *Physiol.* **a.** any fluid secreted from the body, such as sweat, urine, or tears. **b.** the amniotic fluid surrounding a fetus in the womb. **8.** a wavy lustrous finish on some fabrics, esp. silk. **9.** *Archaic.* the degree of brilliance in a diamond. See also **first water. 10.** excellence, quality, or degree (in the phrase **of the first water**). **11.** *Finance.* **a.** capital stock issued without a corresponding increase in paid-up capital, so that the book value of the company's capital is not fully represented by assets or earning power. **b.** the fictitious or unrealistic asset entries that reflect such inflated book value of capital. **12.** (*modifier*) *Astrology.* of or relating to the three signs of the zodiac Cancer, Scorpio, and Pisces. Compare **air** (sense 18), **earth** (sense 1), **fire** (sense 24). **13. above the water.** *Informal.* out of trouble or difficulty, esp. financial trouble. **14. hold water.** to prove credible, logical, or consistent: *the alibi did not hold water.* **15. in deep water.** in trouble or difficulty. **16. make water. a.** to urinate. **b.** (of a boat, hull, etc.) to let in water. **17. throw** (*or* **pour**) **cold water on.** *Informal.* to discourage. **18. water under the bridge.** events that are past and done with. ~*vb.* **19.** (*tr.*) to sprinkle, moisten, or soak with water. **20.** (*tr.*; often foll. by *down*) to weaken by the addition of water. **21.** (*intr.*) (of the eyes) to fill with tears. **22.** (*intr.*) (of the mouth) to salivate, esp. in anticipation of food (esp. in the phrase **to make one's mouth water**). **23.** (*tr.*) to irrigate or provide with water: *to water the land; he watered the cattle.* **24.** (*intr.*) to drink water. **25.** (*intr.*) (of a ship, etc.) to take in a supply of water. **26.** (*tr.*) *Finance.* to raise the par value of (issued capital stock) without a corresponding increase in the real value of assets. **27.** (*tr.*) to produce a wavy lustrous finish on (fabrics, esp. silk). ~See also **water down.** [Old English *wæter*, of Germanic origin; compare Old Saxon *watar*, Old High German *wazzar*, Gothic *watō*, Old Slavonic *voda*; related to Greek *hudor*] —'**wa+ter+er** *n.* —'**wa+ter+ish** *adj.* —'**wa+ter+less** *adj.* —'**wa·ter-,like** *adj.*

wa+ter+age ('wɔːtərɪdʒ) *n. Brit.* the transportation of cargo by means of ships, or the charges for such transportation.

wa+ter back *n.* the U.S. name for **back boiler.**

wa·ter-bath *n. Chem.* a vessel containing heated water, used for heating substances.

wa+ter bear *n.* another name for a **tardigrade.**

wa+ter bed *n.* a waterproof mattress filled with water.

wa+ter bee+tle *n.* any of various beetles of the families *Dytiscidae, Hydrophilidae*, etc., that live most of the time in freshwater ponds, rivers, etc. See **whirligig beetle.**

wa+ter bird *n.* any aquatic bird, including the wading and swimming birds.

wa+ter bis+cuit *n.* a thin crisp plain biscuit, usually served with butter or cheese.

wa+ter blis+ter *n.* a blister containing watery or serous fluid, without any blood or pus.

wa+ter boat+man *n.* any of various aquatic bugs of the families *Notonectidae* and *Corixidae*, having a flattened body and oarlike legs, adapted for darting over the surface of the water.

wa·ter+borne ('wɔːtə,bɔːn) *adj.* **1.** floating or travelling on water. **2.** (of a disease, etc.) transported or transmitted by water.

wa·ter+brain ('wɔːtə,breɪn) *n. Vet. science.* another name for **gid.**

wa+ter brash *n. Pathol.* another term for **heartburn.**

wa·ter+buck ('wɔːtə,bʌk) *n.* any of various antelopes of the genus *Kobus*, esp. *K. ellipsiprymnus*, of swampy areas of Africa, having long curved ridged horns.

wa+ter buf+fa+lo *or* **ox** *n.* a member of the cattle tribe, *Bubalus bubalis*, of swampy regions of S Asia, having widely spreading back-curving horns. Domesticated forms are used as draught animals. Also called: **Asiatic buffalo, Indian buffalo, carabao.**

wa+ter bug *n.* any of various heteropterous insects adapted to living in the water or on its surface, esp. any of the family *Belostomatidae* (**giant water bugs**), of North America, India, and southern Africa, which have flattened hairy legs.

wat+er can+non *n.* an apparatus for pumping water through a nozzle at high pressure, used in quelling riots.

Wa+ter Car+ri+er *or* **Bear+er** *n.* **the.** the constellation Aquarius, the 11th sign of the zodiac.

wa+ter chest+nut *n.* **1.** Also called: **water caltrop.** a floating aquatic onagraceous plant, *Trapa natans*, of Asia, having four-pronged edible nutlike fruits. **2. Chinese water chestnut.** a Chinese cyperaceous plant, *Eleocharis tuberosa*, with an edible succulent corm. **3.** the corm of the Chinese water chestnut, used in Oriental cookery.

wa+ter chin+qua+pin *n.* a North American aquatic plant, *Nelumbo lutea*, having large umbrella-shaped leaves, pale yellow flowers, and edible nutlike seeds: family *Nelumbonaceae.* Compare **chinquapin.**

wa+ter clock *or* **glass** *n.* any of various devices for measuring time that use the escape of water as the motive force.

wa+ter clos+et *n.* **1.** a lavatory flushed by water. **2.** a small room that has a lavatory.

wa·ter+col·our *or U.S.* **wa·ter+col·or** ('wɔːtə,kʌlə) *n.* **1. a.** Also called: **pure watercolour.** water-soluble pigment, applied in transparent washes and without the admixture of white pigment in the lighter tones. **b.** any water-soluble pigment, including opaque kinds such as gouache and tempera. **2. a.** a painting done in watercolours. **b.** (*as modifier*): *a watercolour masterpiece.* **3.** the art or technique of painting with such pigments. —'**wa·ter+,col·our+ist** *or U.S.* '**wa·ter+,col·or+ist** *n.*

wa·ter-cool *vb.* (*tr.*) to cool (an engine, etc.) by a flow of water circulating in an enclosed jacket. Compare **air-cool.** —'**wa·ter-,cooled** *adj.* —'**wa·ter-,cool·ing** *adj.*

wa+ter cool+er *n.* a device for cooling and dispensing drinking water.

wa·ter+course ('wɔːtə,kɔːs) *n.* **1.** a stream, river, or canal. **2.** the channel, bed, or route along which this flows.

wa·ter+craft ('wɔːtə,krɑːft) *n.* **1.** a boat or ship or such vessels collectively. **2.** skill in handling boats or in water sports.

wa+ter crake *n.* another name for **spotted crake** and **dipper** (the bird).

wa·ter+cress ('wɔːtə,krɛs) *n.* **1.** an Old World cruciferous plant, *Rorippa nasturtium-aquaticum* (or *Nasturtium officinale*), of clear ponds and streams, having pungent leaves that are used in salads and as a garnish. **2.** any of several similar or related plants.

wa+ter cure *n.* **1.** *Med.* a nontechnical name for **hydropathy** or **hydrotherapy. 2.** *Informal.* a form of torture in which the victim is forced to drink very large amounts of water.

wa+ter cy+cle *n.* the circulation of the earth's water, in which water evaporates from the sea into the atmosphere, where it condenses and falls as rain or snow, returning to the sea by rivers or returning to the atmosphere by evapotranspiration. Also called: **hydrologic cycle.**

wa+ter di+vin+er *n. Brit.* a person able to locate the presence of water, esp. underground, with a divining rod. U.S. name: **waterfinder.**

wa+ter dog *n.* **1.** a dog trained to hunt in water. **2.** *Informal.* a dog or person who enjoys going in or on the water.

wa+ter down *vb.* (*tr., adv.*) **1.** to dilute or weaken with water. **2.** to modify or adulterate, esp. so as to omit anything harsh, unpleasant, or offensive: *to water down the truth.* —**,wa·tered-'down** *adj.*

wa·ter+fall ('wɔːtə,fɔːl) *n.* a cascade of falling water where there is a vertical or almost vertical step in a river.

wa+ter flea *n.* any of numerous minute freshwater branchiopod crustaceans of the order *Cladocera*, which swim by means of hairy branched antennae. See also **daphnia.**

Wa+ter+ford ('wɔːtəfəd) *n.* **1.** a county of S Ireland, in Munster province on the Atlantic: mountainous in the centre and in the northwest. County town: Waterford. Pop.: 77 315 (1971). Area: 1838 sq. km (710 sq. miles). **2.** a port in S Ireland, county town of Co. Waterford: famous glass industry; fishing. Pop.: 31 968 (1971).

wa·ter+fowl ('wɔːtə,faul) *n.* **1.** any aquatic freshwater bird, esp. any species of the family *Anatidae* (ducks, geese, and swans). **2.** such birds collectively.

wa·ter+front ('wɔːtə,frʌnt) *n.* the area of a town or city alongside a body of water, such as a harbour or dockyard.

wa+ter gap *n.* a deep valley in a ridge, containing a stream.

wa+ter gas *n.* a mixture of hydrogen and carbon monoxide produced by passing steam over hot carbon, used as a fuel and raw material. See also **producer gas.**

wa+ter gate *n.* **1.** a gate in a canal, etc. that can be opened or closed to control the flow of water. **2.** a gate through which access may be gained to a body of water.

Wa·ter+gate ('wɔːtə,geɪt) *n.* an incident during the 1972 U.S. presidential campaign, when a group of agents employed by the re-election organization of President Richard Nixon were caught breaking into the Democratic Party headquarters in the Watergate building, Washington, D.C. The consequent political scandal was exacerbated by attempts to conceal the fact that senior White House officials had approved the burglary, and eventually forced the resignation of President Nixon.

wa+ter gauge *n.* an instrument that indicates the presence or the quantity of water in a tank, reservoir, or boiler feed. Also called: **water glass.**

wa+ter glass *n.* **1.** a viscous syrupy solution of sodium silicate in water: used as a protective coating for cement and a preservative, esp. for eggs. **2.** another name for **water clock** or **water gauge.**

wa+ter gum *n.* **1.** any of several gum trees, esp. *Nyssa biflora* (or *tupelo*), of swampy areas of North America: family *Nyssaceae.* **2.** any of several Australian myrtaceous trees, esp. *Tristania laurina*, of swampy ground.

wa+ter gun *n.* another term (esp. U.S.) for **water pistol.**

wa+ter ham+mer *n.* a sharp concussion produced when the flow of water in a pipe is suddenly blocked.

wa+ter hem+lock *n.* another name for **cowbane** (sense 1).

wa+ter hen *n.* another name for **gallinule.**

wa+ter hole *n.* **1.** a depression, such as a pond or pool, containing water, esp. one used by animals as a drinking place. **2.** a source of drinking water in a desert.

Wa·ter·house ('wɔːtə,haus) *n.* **George Mars·den.** 1824–1906, New Zealand statesman, born in England: prime minister of New Zealand (1872–73).

wa+ter hy·a+cinth *n.* a floating aquatic plant, *Eichhornia* *crassipes,* of tropical America, having showy bluish-purple flowers and swollen leafstalks: family *Pontederiaceae.* It forms dense masses in rivers, ponds, etc., and is a serious pest in the southern U.S., Java, Australia, and parts of Africa.

wa+ter ice *n.* an ice cream made from a frozen sugar syrup flavoured with fruit juice or purée.

wa+ter+ing can *n.* a container with a handle and a spout with a perforated nozzle used to sprinkle water over plants.

wa+ter+ing place *n.* **1.** a place where drinking water for men or animals may be obtained. **2.** *Brit.* a spa. **3.** *Brit.* a seaside resort.

wa+ter+ing pot *n.* another name (U.S.) for **watering can.**

wa+ter jack+et *n.* a water-filled envelope or container surrounding a machine, engine, or part for cooling purposes, esp. the casing around the cylinder block of a pump or internal-combustion engine. Compare **air jacket.**

wa+ter jump *n.* a ditch, brook, or pond over which athletes or horses must jump in a steeplechase or similar contest.

wa+ter lev+el *n.* **1.** the level reached by the surface of a body of water. **2.** the water line of a boat or ship.

wa+ter lil·y *n.* **1.** any of various aquatic plants of the genus *Nymphaea* and related genera, of temperate and tropical regions, having large leaves and showy flowers that float on the surface of the water: family *Nymphaeaceae.* **2.** any of various similar and related plants, such as the yellow water lily.

wa+ter line *n.* **1.** a line marked at the level around a vessel's hull to which the vessel will be immersed when afloat. **2.** a line marking the level reached by a body of water.

wa+ter+logged ('wɔːtəˌlɒgd) *adj.* **1.** saturated with water. **2.** (of a vessel still afloat) having taken in so much water as to be unmanageable.

Wa+ter+loo (ˌwɔːtə'luː) *n.* **1.** a small town in central Belgium, in Brabant province south of Brussels: battle (1815) fought nearby in which British and Prussian forces under the Duke of Wellington and Blücher routed the French under Napoleon, who was thus finally defeated. Pop.: 17 764 (1970). **2.** a total or crushing defeat (esp. in the phrase **meet one's Waterloo**).

wa+ter main *n.* a principal supply pipe in an arrangement of pipes for distributing water.

wa+ter+man ('wɔːtəmən) *n., pl.* **+men.** a skilled boatman. —**'wa·ter+man+ˌship** *n.*

wa+ter+mark ('wɔːtəˌmɑːk) *n.* **1.** a distinguishing mark impressed on paper during manufacture, visible when the paper is held up to the light. **2.** another word for **water line** (sense 1). ~*vb.* (*tr.*) **3.** to mark (paper) with a watermark.

wa+ter mead+ow *n.* a meadow that remains fertile by being periodically flooded by a stream.

wa+ter+mel·on ('wɔːtəˌmɛlən) *n.* **1.** an African melon, *Citrullus vulgaris,* widely cultivated for its large edible fruit. **2.** the fruit of this plant, which has a hard green rind and sweet watery reddish flesh.

wa+ter me+ter *n.* a device for measuring the quantity or rate of water flowing through a pipe.

wa+ter mil+foil *n.* any of various pond plants of the genus *Myriophyllum,* having feathery underwater leaves and small inconspicuous flowers: family *Haloragidaceae.*

wa+ter mill *n.* a mill operated by a water wheel.

wa+ter mint *n.* a Eurasian mint plant, *Mentha aquatica,* of marshy places, having scented leaves and whorls of small flowers.

wa+ter moc+ca+sin *n.* a large dark grey venomous snake, *Agkistrodon piscivorus,* of swamps in the southern U.S.: family *Crotalidae* (pit vipers). Also called: **cottonmouth.**

wa+ter nymph *n.* **1.** any fabled nymph of the water, such as the Naiad, Nereid, or Oceanid of Greek mythology. **2.** any of various aquatic plants, esp. a water lily or a naiad.

wa+ter of crys+tal+li+za+tion *n.* water present in the crystals of certain compounds. It is chemically combined in stoichiometric amounts, usually by coordinate or hydrogen bonds, but can often be easily expelled.

wa+ter ou·zel *n.* another name for **dipper** (the bird).

wa+ter ox *n.* another term for **water buffalo.**

wa+ter part+ing *n.* another term (esp. U.S.) for **watershed** (sense 1).

wa+ter pep+per *n.* any of several polygonaceous plants of the genus *Polygonum,* esp. *P. hydropiper,* of marshy regions, having reddish stems, clusters of small greenish flowers, and acrid-tasting leaves.

wa+ter pim+per+nel *n.* another name for **brookweed.**

wa+ter pipe *n.* **1.** a pipe for water. **2.** another name for **hookah.**

wa+ter pis+tol *n.* a toy pistol that squirts a stream of water or other liquid. Also called (U.S.): **water gun.**

wa+ter plan+tain *n.* any of several marsh plants of the genus *Alisma,* esp. *A. plantago-aquatica,* of N temperate regions and Australia, having clusters of small white or pinkish flowers and broad pointed leaves: family *Alismataceae.*

wa+ter po·lo *n.* a game played in water by two teams of seven swimmers in which each side tries to throw or propel an inflated ball into the opponents' goal.

wa+ter pow+er *n.* **1.** the power latent in a dynamic or static head of water as used to drive machinery, esp. for generating electricity. **2.** a source of such power, such as a drop in the level of a river, etc. **3.** the right to the use of water for such a purpose, as possessed by a water mill.

wa+ter+proof ('wɔːtəˌpruːf) *adj.* **1.** not penetrable by water. Compare **water-repellent, water-resistant.** ~*n.* **2.** *Chiefly Brit.* a waterproof garment, esp. a raincoat. ~*vb.* (*tr.*) **3.** to make (a fabric, item of clothing, etc.) waterproof.

wa+ter purs+lane *n.* **1.** an onagraceous marsh plant, *Ludwigia palustris,* of temperate and warm regions, having reddish stems and small reddish flowers. **2.** any of several lythraceous plants of wet places that resemble purslane, such as *Peplis portular* of Europe, which has small pinkish flowers, and *Didiplis diandris* of North America, which has small greenish flowers.

wa+ter rail *n.* a large Eurasian rail, *Rallus aquaticus,* of swamps, ponds, etc., having a long red bill.

wa+ter rat *n.* **1.** any of several small amphibious rodents, esp. the water vole or the muskrat. **2.** any of various amphibious rats of the subfamily *Hydromyinae,* of New Guinea, the Philippines, and Australia. **3.** *Informal.* a person who is very fond of water sports.

wa·ter-re·pel·lent *adj.* (of fabrics or garments, etc.) having a finish that resists the absorption of water.

wa·ter-re·sis·tant *adj.* (esp. of fabrics) designed to resist but not entirely prevent the penetration of water.

wa+ter right *n.* the right to make use of a water supply, as for irrigation.

wa+ter sap+phire *n.* a deep blue variety of the mineral cordierite that occurs in Sri Lanka: used as a gemstone.

wa·ter+scape ('wɔːtəˌskeɪp) *n.* a picture, view, or representation of a body of water.

wa+ter scor+pi+on *n.* any of various long-legged aquatic insects of the heteropterous family *Nepidae,* which breathe by means of a long spinelike tube that projects from the rear of the body and penetrates the surface of the water.

wa·ter+shed ('wɔːtəˌʃɛd) *n.* **1.** the dividing line between two adjacent river systems, such as a ridge. **2.** an important period or factor that serves as a dividing line.

wa+ter shield *n.* **1.** a North American nymphaeaceous plant, *Brasenia schreberi,* with floating oval leaves and purple flowers. **2.** any of several similar and related plants of the genus *Cabomba.*

wa+ter shrew *n.* either of two small amphibious shrews, *Neomys fodiens* (**European water shrew**) or *N. anomalus* (**Mediterranean water shrew**), having a dark pelage with paler underparts.

wa·ter-sick *adj.* (of land) made infertile or uncultivable by excessive irrigation.

wa·ter+side ('wɔːtəˌsaɪd) *n.* **a.** the area of land beside a body of water. **b.** (*as modifier*): *waterside houses.*

wat·er+sid·er ('wɔːtəˌsaɪdə) *n. Austral.* a wharf labourer.

wa·ter-ski *n.* also **wa+ter ski. 1.** a type of ski used for planing or gliding over water. ~*vb.* **-skis, -ski·ing, -skied** *or* **-ski'd. 2.** (*intr.*) to ride over water on a water-ski or water-skis while holding a rope towed by a speedboat. —**'wa·ter-ˌski·er** *n.* —**'wa·ter-ˌski·ing** *n.*

wa+ter snake *n.* any of various colubrid snakes that live in or near water, esp. any of numerous harmless North American snakes of the genus *Natrix,* such as *N. sipedon.*

wa·ter-soak *vb.* (*tr.*) to soak or drench with or in water.

wa+ter sof+ten+er *n.* **1.** any substance that lessens the hardness of water, usually by precipitating or absorbing calcium and magnesium ions. **2.** a tank, apparatus, or chemical plant that is used to filter or treat water to remove chemicals that cause hardness.

wa+ter sol+dier *n.* an aquatic plant, *Stratiotes aloides,* of Europe and NW Asia, having rosettes of large leaves and large three-petalled white flowers: family *Hydrocharitaceae.*

wa+ter span+iel *n.* either of two large curly-coated breeds of spaniel (the Irish and the American), which are used for hunting waterfowl.

wa+ter spi+der *n.* a Eurasian spider, *Argyroneta aquatica,* that spins a web in the form of an air-filled chamber in which it lives submerged in streams and ponds.

wa·ter+spout ('wɔːtəˌspaʊt) *n.* **1.** *Meteorol.* **a.** a tornado or whirlwind that, when passing over water, is characterized by a column of water and mist extending between the surface and the clouds above. **b.** a sudden downpour of heavy rain. **2.** a pipe or channel through which water is discharged, esp. one used for drainage from the gutters of a roof.

wa+ter strid+er *or* **skat+er** *n.* another name for a **pond-skater.**

wa+ter sup+ply *n.* **1.** an arrangement of reservoirs, purification plant, distribution pipes, etc., for providing water to a community. **2.** the supply of treated and purified water for a community.

wa+ter sys+tem *n.* **1.** a river and all its tributaries. **2.** a system for supplying water to a community.

wa+ter ta+ble *n.* **1.** the surface of the water-saturated part of the ground, usually following approximately the contours of the overlying land surface. **2.** an offset or stringcourse that has a moulding designed to throw rainwater clear of the wall below.

wa+ter thrush *n.* either of two North American warblers, *Seiurus motacilla* or *S. noveboracensis,* having a brownish back and striped underparts and occurring near water.

wa·ter+tight ('wɔːtəˌtaɪt) *adj.* **1.** not permitting the passage of water either in or out: *a watertight boat.* **2.** without loopholes: *a watertight argument.* **3.** kept separate from other subjects or influences: *different disciplines are often thought of in watertight compartments.* —**'wa·ter+ˌtight·ness** *n.*

wa+ter tor+ture *n.* any of various forms of torture using water, esp. one in which water drips or is slowly poured onto the victim's forehead.

wa+ter tow+er ('taʊə) *n.* a reservoir or storage tank mounted on a tower-like structure so that water can be distributed at a uniform pressure.

wa+ter va+pour *n.* water in the gaseous state, esp. when due to evaporation at a temperature below the boiling point. Compare **steam.**

wa+ter vole *n.* a large amphibious vole, *Arvicola terrestris,* of Eurasian river banks: family *Cricetidae.* Also called: **water rat.**

wa+ter wag+tail *n.* another name for **pied wagtail.**

wa·ter+way ('wɔ:tə,weɪ) *n.* a river, canal, or other navigable channel used as a means of travel or transport.

wa·ter+weed ('wɔ:tə,wi:d) *n.* **1.** any of various weedy aquatic plants. **2.** another name for **pondweed** (sense 2).

wa+ter wheel *n.* **1.** a simple water-driven turbine consisting of a wheel having vanes set axially across its rim, used to drive machinery. **2.** a wheel with buckets attached to its rim for raising water from a stream, pond, etc.

wa+ter wings *pl. n.* an inflatable rubber device shaped like a pair of wings, which is placed round the front of the body and under the arms of a person learning to swim.

wa+ter witch *n.* a person who claims the ability to detect water underground by means of a divining rod.

wa·ter+works ('wɔ:tə,wɜ:ks) *n.* **1.** (*functioning as sing.*) an establishment for storing, purifying, and distributing water for community supply. **2.** (*functioning as pl.*) a display of water in movement, as in fountains. **3.** (*functioning as pl.*) *Brit. informal.* the urinary system, esp. with reference to its normal functioning: *he has trouble with his waterworks.* **4.** (*functioning as pl.*) *Slang.* crying; tears.

wa·ter+worn ('wɔ:tə,wɔ:n) *adj.* worn smooth by the action or passage of water.

wa+ter·y ('wɔ:tərɪ) *adj.* **1.** relating to, consisting of, containing, or resembling water. **2.** discharging or secreting water or a water-like fluid: *a watery wound.* **3.** tearful; weepy. **4.** insipid, thin, or weak. —**'wa+ter·i+ness** *n.*

Wat+ford ('wɒtfəd) *n.* a town in SE England, in SW Hertfordshire: printing. Pop.: 78 117 (1971).

Wat+ling Is+land ('wɒtlɪŋ) *n.* another name for **San Salvador Island.**

Wat·son ('wɒtsən) *n.* **1. James Dew·ey.** born 1928, U.S. biologist, whose contribution to the discovery of the helical structure of DNA won him a Nobel prize for medicine shared with Francis Crick and Maurice Wilkins in 1962. **2. John Broa·dus** ('brɔ:dəs). 1878–1958, U.S. psychologist; a leading exponent of behaviourism. **3. John Chris·tian.** 1867–1941, Australian statesman, born in Chile: prime minister of Australia (1904).

Wat·son-Watt ('wɒtsən,wɒt) *n.* Sir **Rob·ert Al·ex·an·der.** 1892–1973, Scottish physicist, who played a leading role in the development of radar.

watt (wɒt) *n.* the derived SI unit of power, equal to 1 joule per second; the power dissipated by a current of 1 ampere flowing across a potential difference of 1 volt. 1 watt is equivalent to 1.341×10^{-3} horsepower. Symbol: W [C19: named after J. WATT]

Watt (wɒt) *n.* **James.** 1736–1819, Scottish engineer and inventor. His fundamental improvements to the steam engine led to the widespread use of steam power in industry.

watt+age ('wɒtɪdʒ) *n.* **1.** power, esp. electric power, measured in watts. **2.** the power rating, measured in watts, of an electrical appliance.

Wat·teau ('wɒtəʊ; *French* va'to) *n.* **Jean An·toine** (ʒɑ̃ ɑ̃'twan). 1684–1721, French painter, esp. of *fêtes champêtres.*

Wat+teau back *n.* a section at the back of a woman's dress that is caught in pleats or gathers at the neck and falls unbelted to the floor.

Wat+ten+scheid (*German* 'vatᵊn,ʃaɪt) *n.* an industrial town in NW West Germany, in North Rhine-Westphalia east of Essen. Pop.: 81 200 (1970).

watt-hour *n.* a unit of energy equal to a power of one watt operating for one hour. 1 watt-hour equals 3600 joules.

wat+tle ('wɒtᵊl) *n.* **1.** a frame of rods or stakes interwoven with twigs, branches, etc., esp. when used to make fences. **2.** the material used in such a construction. **3.** a loose fold of skin, often brightly coloured, hanging from the neck or throat of certain birds, lizards, etc. **4.** any of various chiefly Australian acacia trees having spikes of small brightly coloured flowers and flexible branches, which were used by early settlers for making fences. See also **golden wattle. 5.** a southern African caesalpinaceous tree, *Peltophorum africanum,* with yellow flowers. ~*vb.* (*tr.*) **6.** to construct from wattle. **7.** to bind or frame with wattle. **8.** to weave or twist (branches, twigs, etc.) into a frame. ~*adj.* **9.** made of, formed by, or covered with wattle. [Old English *watol;* related to *wethel* wrap, Old High German *wadal,* German *Wedel*] —**'wat+tled** *adj.*

wat+tle and daub *n.* **a.** a form of wall construction consisting of interwoven twigs plastered with a mixture of clay, lime, water, and sometimes dung and chopped straw. **b.** (*as modifier*): *a wattle-and-daub hut.*

wat·tle+bird ('wɒtᵊl,bɜ:d) *n.* **1.** any of various Australian honeyeaters of the genus *Anthochaera,* such as *A. paradoxa* (**yellow wattlebird**), that have red or yellow wattles on both sides of the head. **2.** any arboreal New Zealand songbird of the family *Callaeidae,* having wattles on both sides of the bill.

watt+me·ter ('wɒt,mi:tə) *n.* a meter for measuring electric power in watts.

Watts (wɒts) *n.* **1. George Fred·er·ick.** 1817–1904, English painter and sculptor, noted esp. for his painting *Hope* (1886) and his sculpture *Physical Energy* (1904) in Kensington Gardens, London. **2. I·saac.** 1674–1748, English hymn-writer.

Wa+tu+si (wə'tu:zɪ) *or* **Wa+tut+si** (wə'tʊtsɪ) *n., pl.* **+sis** *or* **+si.** a member of a cattle-owning Negroid people of Rwanda and Burundi in Africa.

Waugh (wɔ:) *n.* **Eve·lyn (Arthur St. John).** 1903–66, English novelist. His early satirical novels include *Decline and Fall* (1928), *Vile Bodies* (1930), *A Handful of Dust* (1934), and *Scoop* (1938). His later novels include the more sombre *Brideshead Revisited* (1945) and the trilogy of World War II *Men at Arms* (1952), *Officers and Gentlemen* (1955), and *Unconditional Surrender* (1961).

waul *or* **wawl** (wɔ:l) *vb.* (*intr.*) to cry or wail plaintively like a cat.

wave (weɪv) *vb.* **1.** to move or cause to move freely to and fro: *the banner waved in the wind.* **2.** (*intr.*) to move the hand to and fro as a greeting. **3.** to signal or signify by or as if by waving something. **4.** (*tr.*) to direct to move by or as if by waving something: *he waved me on.* **5.** to form or be formed into curves, undulations, etc. **6.** (*tr.*) to give a wavy or watered appearance to (silk, etc.). **7.** (*tr.*) to set waves in (the hair). ~*n.* **8.** one of a sequence of ridges or undulations that moves across the surface of a body of a liquid, esp. the sea: created by the wind or a moving object and gravity. **9.** any undulation on or at the edge of a surface reminiscent of such a wave: *a wave across the field of corn.* **10. the waves.** the sea. **11.** anything that suggests the movement of a wave, as by a sudden rise: a crime wave. **12.** a widespread movement, that advances in a body: *a wave of settlers swept into the country.* **13.** the act or an instance of waving. **14.** *Physics.* an energy-carrying disturbance propagated through a medium or space by a progressive local displacement of the medium or a change in its physical properties, but without any overall movement of matter. See also **longitudinal wave, transverse wave. 15.** *Physics.* a graphical representation of a wave obtained by plotting the magnitude of the disturbance against time at a particular point in the medium or space; waveform. **16.** a prolonged spell of some weather condition: *a heat wave.* **17.** an undulating curve or series of curves or loose curls in the hair. **18.** an undulating pattern or finish on a fabric. [Old English *wafian* (vb.); related to Old High German *weban* to WEAVE, Old Norse *vafra;* see WAVER; C16 (n.) changed from earlier *wāwe,* probably from Old English *wǣg* motion; compare WAG[1]] —**'wave+less** *adj.* —**'wave+,like** *adj.*

wave+band ('weɪv,bænd) *n.* a range of wavelengths or frequencies used for a particular type of radio transmission.

wave-cut plat+form *n.* a flat surface at the base of a cliff formed by erosion by waves.

wave down *vb.* (*tr., adv.*) to signal with a wave to (a driver or vehicle) to stop.

wave e·qua+tion *n. Physics.* a partial differential equation describing wave motion. It has the form $\nabla^2\phi = (1/c^2) \times (\partial^2\phi/\partial t^2)$, where ∇^2 is the Laplace operator, t the time, c the velocity of propagation, and ϕ is a function characterizing the displacement of the wave.

wave+form ('weɪv,fɔ:m) *n. Physics.* the shape of the graph of a wave or oscillation obtained by plotting the value of some changing quantity against time.

wave front *n. Physics.* a surface associated with a propagating wave and passing through all points in the wave that have the same phase. It is usually perpendicular to the direction of propagation.

wave func+tion *n. Physics.* a mathematical function of position and sometimes time, used in wave mechanics to describe the state of a physical system. Symbol: ψ

wave+guide ('weɪv,gaɪd) *n. Electronics.* a solid rod of dielectric or a hollow metal tube, usually of rectangular cross section, used as a path to guide microwaves.

wave+length ('weɪv,lɛŋθ) *n.* **1.** the distance, measured in the direction of propagation, between two points of the same phase in consecutive cycles of a wave. Symbol: λ **2.** the wavelength of the carrier wave used by a particular broadcasting station. **3. on someone's** (*or* **the same**) **wavelength.** *Informal.* having similar views, feelings, or thoughts (as someone else).

wave+let ('weɪvlɪt) *n.* a small wave.

wa+vell+ite ('weɪvə,laɪt) *n.* a greyish-white, yellow, or brown mineral consisting of hydrated basic aluminium phosphate in radiating clusters of small orthorhombic crystals. Formula: $Al_3(OH)_3(PO_4)_2.5H_2O$. [C19: named after William *Wavell* (died 1829), English physician]

wave me+chan+ics *n. Physics.* the formulation of quantum mechanics in which the behaviour of systems, such as atoms, is described in terms of their wave functions.

wave+me·ter ('weɪv,mi:tə) *n.* an instrument for measuring the frequency or wavelength of radio waves.

wave num+ber *n. Physics.* the reciprocal of the wavelength of a wave. Symbol: ν, σ

wave+off ('weɪv,ɒf) *n.* a signal or instruction to an aircraft not to land.

wa+ver ('weɪvə) *vb.* (*intr.*) **1.** to be irresolute; hesitate between two possibilities. **2.** to become unsteady. **3.** to fluctuate or vary. **4.** to move back and forth or one way and another. **5.** (of light) to flicker or flash. ~*n.* **6.** the act or an instance of wavering. [C14: from Old Norse *vafra* to flicker; related to German *wabern* to move about] —**'wa+ver+er** *n.* —**'wa+ver+ing+ly** *adv.*

WAVES *or* **Waves** (weɪvz) *n. U.S. acronym for* Women Accepted for Volunteer Emergency Service: the women's reserve of the U.S. navy.

wave the·o+ry *n.* **1.** the theory proposed by Huygens that light is transmitted by waves. **2.** any theory that light or other radiation is transmitted as waves. See **electromagnetic wave.** ~Compare **corpuscular theory.**

wave train *n. Physics.* a series of waves travelling in the same direction and spaced at regular intervals.

wav·y ('weɪvɪ) *adj.* **wav·i+er, wav·i+est. 1.** abounding in or full of waves. **2.** moving or proceeding in waves or undulations. **3.** (of hair) set in or having waves and curls. **4.** unstable or wavering. —'**wav·i·ly** *adv.* —'**wav·i+ness** *n.*

waw (wɔː) *n.* another name for **vav.**

wa·wa ('wɑːˌwɑː) *n.* **1.** the sound made by a trumpet, cornet, etc., when the bell is alternately covered and uncovered: much used in jazz. **2.** an electronic attachment for an electric guitar, etc., that simulates this effect. **3.** *Canadian W coast slang.* speech; language. ~*vb.* **4.** (*intr.*) *Canadian W coast slang.* to speak. [C20: of imitative origin]

wawl (wɔːl) *vb.* a variant spelling of **waul.**

wax[1] (wæks) *n.* **1.** any of various viscous or solid materials of natural origin: characteristically lustrous, insoluble in water, and sensitive to heat, they consist largely of esters of fatty acids. **2.** any of various similar substances, such as paraffin wax or ozocerite, that have a mineral origin and consist largely of hydrocarbons. **3.** short for **beeswax** or **sealing wax. 4.** *Physiol.* another name for **cerumen. 5.** a resinous preparation used by shoemakers to rub on thread. **6. bone wax.** a mixture of wax, oil, and carbolic acid applied to the cut surface of a bone to prevent bleeding. **7.** any substance or object that is pliable or easily moulded: *he was wax in the hands of the political bosses.* **8.** (*modifier*) made of or resembling wax: *a wax figure.* **9. put on wax.** to make a gramophone record of. ~*vb.* **10.** (*tr.*) to coat, polish, etc., with wax. **11.** (*tr.*) *Informal.* to make a gramophone record of. [Old English *weax,* related to Old Saxon, Old High German *wahs,* Old Norse *vax*] —'**wax+er** *n.* —'**wax+ˌlike** *adj.*

wax[2] (wæks) *vb.* (*intr.*) **1.** to become larger, more powerful, etc. **2.** (of the moon) to show a gradually increasing portion of illuminated surface, between new moon and full moon. Compare **wane** (sense 1). **3.** *Archaic.* to become as specified: *the time waxed late.* [Old English *weaxan;* related to Old Frisian *waxa,* Old Saxon, Old High German *wahsan,* Gothic *wahsjan*]

wax[3] (wæks) *n. Informal, chiefly Brit.* a fit of rage or temper: *he's in a wax today.* [of obscure origin; perhaps from the phrase *to wax angry*]

wax bean *n. U.S.* any of certain string beans that have yellow waxy pods and are grown in the U.S.

wax+ber·ry ('wæksbərɪ, -brɪ) *n., pl.* **·ries.** the waxy fruit of the wax myrtle or the snowberry.

wax+bill ('wæksˌbɪl) *n.* any of various chiefly African finchlike weaverbirds of the genus *Estrilda* and related genera, having a brightly coloured bill and plumage.

wax+en[1] ('wæksən) *adj.* **1.** made of, treated with, or covered with wax. **2.** resembling wax in colour or texture.

wax+en[2] ('wæksən) *vb. Archaic.* a past participle of **wax**[2].

wax flow+er *n. Austral.* any of several rutaceous shrubs of the genus *Eriostemon,* having waxy pink-white five-petalled flowers.

wax in+sect *n.* any of various scale insects that secrete wax or a waxy substance, esp. the oriental species *Ceroplastes ceriferus,* which produces Chinese wax.

wax light *n.* a candle or taper of wax.

wax moth *n.* a brown pyralid moth, *Galleria mellonella,* the larvae of which feed on the combs of beehives. Also called: **honeycomb moth, bee moth.**

wax myr+tle *n.* a shrub, *Myrica cerifera,* of SE North America, having evergreen leaves and a small berry-like fruit with a waxy coating: family *Myricaceae.* Also called: **bayberry, candleberry, waxberry.**

wax palm *n.* **1.** a tall Andean palm tree, *Ceroxylon andicola,* having pinnate leaves that yield a resinous wax used in making candles. **2.** another name for **carnauba** (sense 1).

wax pa+per *n.* paper treated or coated with wax or paraffin to make it waterproof.

wax+plant ('wæksˌplɑːnt) *n.* **1.** a climbing asclepiadaceous shrub, *Hoya carnosa,* of China and Australia, having fleshy leaves and clusters of small waxy white pink-centred flowers. **2.** any of various similar plants of the genus *Hoya.*

wax tree *n.* a Japanese anacardiaceous tree, *Rhus succedanea,* having white berries that yield wax.

wax+wing ('wæksˌwɪŋ) *n.* any of several gregarious passerine songbirds of the genus *Bombycilla,* esp. *B. garrulus,* having red waxy wing tips and crested heads: family *Bombycillidae.*

wax+work ('wæksˌwɜːk) *n.* **1.** an object reproduced in wax, esp. as an ornament. **2.** a life-size lifelike figure, esp. of a famous person, reproduced in wax. **3.** (*pl.; functioning as sing. or pl.*) a museum or exhibition of wax figures or objects. —'**wax+ˌwork·er** *n.*

wax·y[1] ('wæksɪ) *adj.* **wax·i+er, wax·i+est. 1.** resembling wax in colour, appearance, or texture. **2.** made of, covered with, or abounding in wax. —'**wax·i+ly** *adv.* —'**wax·i+ness** *n.*

wax·y[2] ('wæksɪ) *adj.* **wax·i+er, wax·i+est.** *Brit. slang.* bad-tempered or irritable; angry.

way (weɪ) *n.* **1.** a manner, method, or means: *a way of life; a way of knowing.* **2.** a route or direction: *the way home.* **3. a.** a means or line of passage, such as a path or track. **b.** (*in combination*): *waterway.* **4.** space or room for movement or activity (esp. in the phrases **make way, in the way, out of the way**). **5.** distance, usually distance in general: *you've come a long way.* **6.** a passage or journey: *on the way.* **7.** characteristic style or manner: *I did it in my own way.* **8.** (*often pl.*) habits; idiosyncrasies: *he has some offensive ways.* **9.** an aspect of something; particular: *in many ways he was right.* **10. a.** a street in or leading out of a town. **b.** (*cap. when part of a street name*): *Icknield Way.* **11.** something that one wants in a determined manner (esp. in the phrases **get** *or* **have one's (own) way**). **12.** the experience or sphere in which one comes into contact with things (esp. in the phrase **come one's way**). **13.** *Informal.* a state or condition, usually financial or concerning health (esp. in the phrases **in a good** (*or* **bad**) **way**). **14.** *Informal.* the area or direction of one's home: *drop in if you're ever over my way.* **15.** movement of a ship or other vessel. **16.** a right of way in law. **17.** a guide along which something can be moved, such as the surface of a lathe along which the tailstock slides. **18.** (*pl.*) the wooden or metal tracks down which a ship slides to be launched. **19.** a course of life including experiences, conduct, etc.: *the way of sin.* **20.** *Archaic.* calling or trade. **21. by the way.** (*sentence modifier*) in passing or incidentally. **22. by way of. a.** via. **b.** serving as: *by way of introduction.* **c.** in the state or condition of: *by way of being an artist.* **23. each way.** (of a bet) laid on a horse, dog, etc., to win or gain a place. **24. give way. a.** to collapse or break down. **b.** to withdraw or yield. **25. give way to. a.** to step aside for or stop for. **b.** to give full rein to (emotions, etc.). **26. go out of one's way.** to take considerable trouble or inconvenience oneself. **27. have a way with.** to have such a manner or skill as to handle successfully. **28. have it both ways.** to enjoy two things that would normally contradict each other or be mutually exclusive. **29. in a way.** in some respects. **30. in no way.** not at all. **31. lead the way. a.** to go first. **b.** to set an example or precedent. **32. make one's way. a.** to proceed or advance. **b.** to achieve success in life. **33. no way.** *Informal.* that is impossible. **34. on the way out.** *Informal.* **a.** becoming unfashionable, obsolete, etc. **b.** dying. **35. out of the way. a.** removed or dealt with so as to be no longer a hindrance. **b.** remote. **c.** unusual and sometimes improper. **36. pay one's way.** See **pay** (sense 11). **37. see one's way (clear).** to find it possible and be willing (to do something). **38. under way.** having started moving or making progress. ~*adv.* **39.** *Informal.* **a.** at a considerable distance or extent: *way over yonder.* **b.** very far; considerably: *they're way up the mountain.* [Old English *weg;* related to Old Frisian *wei,* Old Norse *vegr,* Gothic *wigs*]

Usage. The use of *the way* for *as* in sentences such as *he does not write the way his father did* is well established in the U.S. and is common in British informal usage. Careful writers, however, prefer *as* in formal contexts.

way+bill ('weɪˌbɪl) *n.* a document attached to goods in transit specifying their nature, point of origin, and destination as well as the route to be taken and the rate to be charged.

way+far·er ('weɪˌfɛərə) *n.* a person who goes on a journey. —'**way+ˌfar·ing** *n., adj.*

way+far·ing tree *n.* a caprifoliaceous shrub, *Viburnum lantana,* of Europe and W Asia, having white flowers and berries that turn from red to black.

Way+land *or* **Way+land Smith** ('weɪlənd) *n.* a smith, artificer, and king of the elves in European folklore. Scandinavian name: **Völund.** German name: **Wieland.**

way+lay (weɪ'leɪ) *vb.* **+lays, +lay+ing, +laid.** (*tr.*) **1.** to lie in wait for and attack. **2.** to await and intercept unexpectedly. —**way+'lay+er** *n.*

Wayne (weɪn) *n.* **John,** original name *Marion Michael Morrison.* 1907-79, U.S. film actor, noted esp. for his many Westerns, which include *Stagecoach* (1939), *The Alamo* (1960), and *True Grit* (1969).

way-out *adj. Informal.* **1.** extremely unconventional or experimental; avant-garde. **2.** excellent or amazing.

-ways *suffix forming adverbs.* indicating direction or manner: *sideways.* [Old English *weges,* literally: of the way, from *weg* WAY]

ways and means *pl. n.* **1.** the revenues and methods of raising the revenues needed for the functioning of a state or other political unit. **2.** (*usually cap.*) a standing committee of the U.S. House of Representatives that supervises all financial legislation. **3.** the methods and resources for accomplishing some purpose.

way+side ('weɪˌsaɪd) *n.* **1. a.** the side or edge of a road. **b.** (*modifier*): situated by the wayside: *a wayside inn.* **2. fall by the wayside.** to cease or fail to continue doing something: *of the nine starters, three fell by the wayside.* **3. go by the wayside.** to be put aside on account of something more urgent.

way+ward ('weɪwəd) *adj.* **1.** wanting to have one's own way regardless of the wishes or good of others. **2.** capricious, erratic, or unpredictable. **3.** *Archaic.* unwelcome or unwanted. [C14: changed from *awayward* turned or turning away] —'**way+ward+ly** *adv.* —'**way+ward+ness** *n.*

way+worn ('weɪˌwɔːn) *adj. Rare.* worn or tired by travel.

wayz+goose ('weɪzˌguːs) *n.* a works outing made annually by a printing house. [C18: from earlier *waygoose,* of unknown origin]

Wa+zir+i+stan (wəˌzɪərɪ'stɑːn) *n.* a mountainous region of N Pakistan, on the border with Afghanistan.

Wb *Physics. abbrev. for* weber.

w.b. *abbrev. for:* **1.** water ballast. **2.** Also: **W/B, W.B.** waybill. **3.** westbound.

W.B.C. *abbrev. for* World Boxing Council.

w.c. *abbrev. for:* **1.** water closet. **2.** without charge.

W.C. *or* **WC** *abbrev. for:* **1.** water closet. **2.** (in London postal code) West Central.

W.C.C. *abbrev. for* World Council of Churches.

W.C.T.U. *abbrev. for* Women's Christian Temperance Union.

W.D. *abbrev. for:* **1.** War Department. **2.** Works Department.

WD *international car registration for* (Windward Islands) Dominica.

wd. *abbrev. for:* **1.** ward. **2.** wood. **3.** word.

we (wi:) *pron.* (*subjective*) **1.** refers to the speaker or writer and another person or other people: *we should go now.* **2.** refers to all people or people in general: *the planet on which we live.* **3. a.** a formal word for **I** used by editors or other writers, and formerly by monarchs. **b.** (*as n.*): *he uses the royal we in his pompous moods.* **4.** *Informal.* used instead of *you* with a tone of persuasiveness, condescension, or sarcasm: *how are we today?* [Old English *wē*, related to Old Saxon *wī*, Old High German *wir*, Old Norse *vēr*, Danish, Swedish *vi*, Sanskrit *vayam*]

W.E.A. (in Britain) *abbrev. for* Workers' Educational Association.

weak (wi:k) *adj.* **1.** lacking in physical or mental strength or force; frail or feeble. **2.** liable to yield, break, or give way: *a weak link in a chain.* **3.** lacking in resolution or firmness of character. **4.** lacking strength, power, or intensity: *a weak voice.* **5.** lacking strength in a particular part: *a team weak in defence.* **6.** lacking in conviction, persuasiveness, etc.: *a weak argument.* **7.** lacking in political or strategic strength: *a weak state.* **8.** lacking the usual, full, or desirable strength of flavour: *weak tea.* **9.** *Grammar.* **a.** denoting or belonging to a class of verbs, in certain languages including the Germanic languages, whose conjugation relies on inflectional endings rather than internal vowel gradation, as *look, looks, looking, looked.* **b.** belonging to any part-of-speech class, in any of various languages, whose inflections follow the more regular of two possible patterns. Compare **strong** (sense 13). **10.** (of a syllable) not accented or stressed. **11.** (of a fuel-air mixture) containing a relatively low proportion of fuel. Compare **rich** (sense 13). **12.** *Photog.* having low density or contrast; thin. **13.** (of an industry, market, securities, etc.) falling in price or characterized by falling prices. [Old English *wāc* soft, miserable; related to Old Saxon *wēk*, Old High German *weih*, Old Norse *veikr*] —**'weak·ish** *adj.* —**'weak·ish·ly** *adv.* —**'weak·ish·ness** *n.*

weak·en ('wi:kən) *vb.* to become or cause to become weak or weaker. —**'weak·en·er** *n.*

weak·er sex *n.* the female sex.

weak·fish ('wi:k,fɪʃ) *n., pl.* **·fish** *or* **·fish·es.** any of several sciaenid sea trouts, esp. *Cynoscion regalis*, a food and game fish of American Atlantic coastal waters.

weak in·ter·ac·tion *n. Physics.* an interaction between elementary particles that is responsible for certain decay processes, operates at distances less than about 10^{-15} metres, and is 10^{12} times weaker than the strong interaction. Compare **electromagnetic interaction, strong interaction, gravitational interaction.**

weak-kneed *adj. Informal.* yielding readily to force, persuasion, intimidation, etc. —**,weak-'kneed·ly** *adv.* —**,weak-'kneed·ness** *n.*

weak·ling ('wi:klɪŋ) *n.* a person or animal that is lacking in strength or weak in constitution or character.

weak·ly ('wi:klɪ) *adj.* **·li·er, ·li·est. 1.** sickly; feeble. ~*adv.* **2.** in a weak or feeble manner. —**'weak·li·ness** *n.*

weak-mind·ed *adj.* **1.** lacking in stability of mind or character. **2.** another word for **feeble-minded.** —**,weak-'mind·ed·ly** *adv.* —**,weak-'mind·ed·ness** *n.*

weak·ness ('wi:knɪs) *n.* **1.** the state or quality of being weak. **2.** a deficiency or failing, as in a person's character. **3.** a self-indulgent fondness or liking: *a weakness for chocolates.*

weak sis·ter *n. U.S. informal.* a person in a group who is regarded as weak or unreliable.

weak-willed *adj.* lacking strength of will.

weal[1] (wi:l) *n.* a raised mark on the surface of the body produced by a blow. Also called: **wale, welt, wheal.** [C19: variant of WALE[1], influenced in form by WHEAL]

weal[2] (wi:l) *n.* **1.** *Archaic.* prosperity or wellbeing (now esp. in the phrases **the public weal, the common weal**). **2.** *Obsolete.* the state. **3.** *Obsolete.* wealth. [Old English *wela*; related to Old Saxon *welo*, Old High German *wolo*]

weald (wi:ld) *n. Brit. archaic.* open or forested country. [Old English; related to Old Saxon, Old High German *wald*, Old Norse *vollr*, probably related to WILD]

Weald (wi:ld) *n.* **the.** a region of SE England, in Kent, Surrey, and East and West Sussex between the North Downs and the South Downs: formerly forested.

wealth (wɛlθ) *n.* **1.** a large amount of money and valuable material possessions. **2.** the state of being rich. **3.** a great profusion: *a wealth of gifts.* **4.** *Economics.* all goods and services with monetary, exchangeable, or productive value. [C13 *welthe*, from WEAL[2]; related to WELL[1]] —**'wealth·less** *adj.*

wealth tax *n.* a tax on personal property; capital levy.

wealth·y ('wɛlθɪ) *adj.* **wealth·i·er, wealth·i·est. 1.** possessing wealth; affluent; rich. **2.** of, characterized by, or relating to wealth. **3.** abounding: *wealthy in friends.* —**'wealth·i·ly** *adv.* —**'wealth·i·ness** *n.*

wean[1] (wi:n) *vb.* (*tr.*) **1.** to cause (a child or young mammal) to replace mother's milk by other nourishment. **2.** (usually foll. by *from*) to cause to desert former habits, pursuits, etc. [Old English *wenian* to accustom; related to German *gewöhnen* to get used to] —**wean·ed·ness** ('wi:nɪdnɪs, 'wi:nd-) *n.*

wean[2] (weɪn, wi:n) *n. Scot. and northern Brit. dialect.* a child; infant. [perhaps a shortened form of WEANLING, although often thought to be a contraction of *wee ane*]

wean·er ('wi:nə) *n.* **1.** a pig that has just been weaned and weighs less than 40 kg. **2.** *Austral.* a name for a lamb, pig, or calf in the year in which it has been weaned.

wean·ling ('wi:nlɪŋ) *n.* **a.** a child or young animal recently weaned. **b.** (*as modifier*): *a weanling calf.* [C16: from WEAN[1] + -LING[1]]

weap·on ('wɛpən) *n.* **1.** an object or instrument used in fighting. **2.** anything that serves to outwit or get the better of an opponent: *his power of speech was his best weapon.* **3.** any part of an animal that is used to defend itself, to attack prey, etc., such as claws, teeth, horns, or a sting. **4.** a slang word for **penis.** [Old English *wǣpen*; related to Old Norse *vápn*, Old Frisian *wēpen*, Old High German *wāffan*] —**'weap·oned** *adj.* —**'weap·on·less** *adj.*

weap·on·eer (,wɛpə'nɪə) *n.* a person associated with the use or maintenance of weapons, esp. nuclear weapons.

wea·pon·ry ('wɛpənrɪ) *n.* weapons regarded collectively.

wear[1] (wɛə) *vb.* **wears, wear·ing, wore, worn. 1.** (*tr.*) to carry or have (a garment, etc.) on one's person as clothing, ornament, etc. **2.** (*tr.*) to carry or have on one's person habitually: *she wears a lot of red.* **3.** (*tr.*) to have in one's aspect: *to wear a smile.* **4.** (*tr.*) to display, show, or fly: *a ship wears its colours.* **5.** to deteriorate or cause to deteriorate by constant use or action. **6.** to produce or be produced by constant rubbing, scraping, etc.: *to wear a hole in one's trousers.* **7.** to bring or be brought to a specified condition by constant use or action: *to wear a tyre to shreds.* **8.** (*intr.*) to submit to constant use or action in a specified way: *his suit wears well.* **9.** (*tr.*) to harass or weaken. **10.** (when *intr.*, often foll. by *on*) (of time) to pass or be passed slowly. **11.** (*tr.*) *Brit. slang.* to accept: *Larry won't wear that argument.* **12. wear ship.** to change the tack of a sailing vessel, esp. a square-rigger, by coming about so that the wind passes astern. ~*n.* **13.** the act of wearing or state of being worn. **14. a.** anything designed to be worn: *leisure wear.* **b.** (*in combination*): *nightwear.* **15.** deterioration from constant or normal use or action. **16.** the quality of resisting the effects of constant use. ~See also **wear down, wear off, wear out.** [Old English *werian*; related to Old High German *werien*, Old Norse *verja*, Gothic *vasjan*] —**'wear·er** *n.*

wear[2] (wɛə) *vb.* **wears, wear·ing, wore, worn.** *Nautical.* to tack by gybing instead of by going through stays. [C17: from earlier *weare*, of unknown origin]

We·ar (wɪə) *n.* a river in NE England, rising in NW Durham and flowing southeast then northeast to the North Sea at Sunderland. Length: 105 km (65 miles).

wear·a·ble ('wɛərəbᵊl) *adj.* **1.** suitable for wear or able to be worn. ~*n.* **2.** (*often pl.*) any garment that can be worn. —**,wear·a·'bil·i·ty** *n.*

wear and tear *n.* damage, depreciation, or loss resulting from ordinary use.

wear down *vb.* (*adv.*) **1.** to consume or be consumed by long or constant wearing, rubbing, etc. **2.** to overcome or be overcome gradually by persistent effort.

wea·ri·less ('wɪərɪlɪs) *adj.* not wearied or able to be wearied. —**'wea·ri·less·ly** *adv.*

wear·ing ('wɛərɪŋ) *adj.* causing fatigue or exhaustion; tiring. —**'wear·ing·ly** *adv.*

wea·ri·some ('wɪərɪsəm) *or* **wea·ri·ful** *adj.* causing fatigue or annoyance; tedious. —**'wea·ri·some·ly** *or* **'wea·ri·ful·ly** *adv.* —**'wea·ri·some·ness** *or* **'wea·ri·ful·ness** *n.*

wear off *vb.* (*adv.*) **1.** (*intr.*) to decrease in intensity gradually: *the pain will wear off in an hour.* **2.** to disappear or cause to disappear gradually through exposure, use, etc.: *the pattern on the ring had been worn off.*

wear out *vb.* (*adv.*) **1.** to make or become unfit or useless through wear. **2.** (*tr.*) to exhaust or tire.

wear·proof ('wɛə,pru:f) *adj.* resistant to damage from normal wear or usage.

wea·ry ('wɪərɪ) *adj.* **·ri·er, ·ri·est. 1.** tired or exhausted. **2.** causing fatigue or exhaustion. **3.** caused by or suggestive of weariness: *a weary laugh.* **4.** (*postpositive*, often foll. by *of* or *with*) discontented or bored, esp. by the long continuance of something. ~*vb.* **·ries, ·ry·ing, ·ried. 5.** to make or become weary. **6.** to make or become discontented or impatient, esp. by the long continuance of something. [Old English *wērig*; related to Old Saxon *wōrig*, Old High German *wuorag* drunk, Greek *hōrakian* to faint] —**'wea·ri·ly** *adv.* —**'wea·ri·ness** *n.* —**'wea·ry·ing·ly** *adv.*

wea·sand ('wi:zənd) *n.* a former name for the **trachea.** [Old English *wǣsend, wāsend*; related to Old Frisian *wāsenda*, Old High German *weisont* vein, Danish *vissen*]

wea·sel ('wi:zᵊl) *n., pl.* **·sel** *or* **·sels. 1.** any of various small predatory musteline mammals of the genus *Mustela* and related genera, esp. *M. nivalis* (**European weasel**), having reddish-brown fur, an elongated body and neck, and short legs. **2.** *Informal.* a sly or treacherous person. **3.** *Chiefly U.S.* a motor vehicle for use in snow, esp. one with caterpillar tracks. [Old English *weosule, wesle*; related to Old Norse *visla*, Old High German *wisula*, Middle Dutch *wesel*] —**'wea·sel·ly** *adj.*

wea·sel out *vb.* (*intr., adv.*) *Slang, chiefly U.S.* **1.** to go back on a commitment. **2.** to evade a responsibility, esp. in a despicable manner.

wea·sel words *pl. n. Informal, chiefly U.S.* intentionally evasive or misleading speech. [C20: alluding to the weasel's supposed ability to suck an egg out of its shell without seeming to break the shell] —**'wea·sel-,word·ed** *adj.*

weath·er ('wɛðə) *n.* **1. a.** the day-to-day meteorological conditions, esp. temperature, cloudiness, and rainfall, affecting a specific place. Compare **climate** (sense 1). **b.** (*modifier*): relating to the forecasting of weather: *a weather ship.* **2.** a prevailing state or condition. **3. make heavy weather. a.** (of a vessel) to roll and pitch in heavy seas. **b.** (foll. by *of*) *Informal.* to carry out with great effort or labour. **4. under the weather.** *Informal.* **a.** not in good health. **b.** intoxicated. ~*adj.* **5.** (*prenominal*) on or at the side or part towards the wind; windward: *the weather anchor.* Compare **lee** (sense 4). ~*vb.* **6.** to expose or be exposed to the action of the weather. **7.** to undergo or cause to undergo changes, such as discoloration, due to the action of the weather. **8.** (*intr.*) to withstand the action of the weather. **9.** (when *intr.* foll. by *through*) to endure (a crisis, danger, etc.). **10.** (*tr.*) to slope (a surface, such as a roof, sill, etc.) so as to throw rainwater clear. **11.** (*tr.*) to sail to the windward of: *to weather a point.* [Old English *weder;* related to Old Saxon *wedar,* Old High German *wetar,* Old Norse *vethr*] —ˌ**weath·er·a·'bil·i·ty** *n.* —'**weath·er·er** *n.*

weath·er-beat·en *adj.* **1.** showing signs of exposure to the weather. **2.** tanned or hardened by exposure to the weather.

weath·er·board ('wɛðəˌbɔːd) *n.* **1.** a timber board, with a rabbet along the front of its top edge and along the back of its lower edge, that is fixed horizontally with others to form an exterior cladding on a wall or roof. Compare **clapboard. 2.** the windward side of a vessel. **3.** Also called: **weatherboard house.** *Chiefly Austral.* a house having walls made entirely of weatherboarding.

weath·er·board·ing ('wɛðəˌbɔːdɪŋ) *n.* **1.** an area or covering of weatherboards. **2.** weatherboards collectively.

weath·er-bound *adj.* (of a vessel, aircraft, etc.) delayed by bad weather.

weath·er·cock ('wɛðəˌkɒk) *n.* **1.** a weather vane in the form of a cock. **2.** a person who is fickle or changeable. ~*vb.* **3.** (*intr.*) (of an aircraft) to turn or tend to turn into the wind.

weath·ered ('wɛðəd) *adj.* **1.** affected by exposure to the action of the weather. **2.** (of rocks and rock formations) eroded, decomposed, or otherwise altered by the action of wind, frost, heat, etc. **3.** (of a sill, roof, etc.) having a sloped surface so as to allow rainwater to run off. **4.** (of wood) artificially stained so as to appear weather-beaten.

weath·er eye *n.* **1.** the vision of a person trained to observe changes in the weather. **2.** *Informal.* an alert or observant gaze. **3. keep one's weather eye open.** to stay on the alert.

weath·er·glass ('wɛðəˌglɑːs) *n.* any of various instruments, esp. a barometer, that measure atmospheric conditions.

weath·er house *n.* a model house with human figures that enter to foretell bad weather and leave to foretell good weather.

weath·er·ing ('wɛðərɪŋ) *n.* the mechanical and chemical breakdown of rocks by the action of rain, snow, cold, etc.

weath·er·ly ('wɛðəlɪ) *adj.* (of a sailing vessel) making very little leeway when close-hauled, even in a stiff breeze. —'**weath·er·li·ness** *n.*

weath·er·man ('wɛðəˌmæn) *n., pl.* **·men. 1.** (*cap.*) *Informal.* a person who forecasts the weather, esp. one who works in a meteorological office. **2.** (*cap.*) *U.S.* a member of a militant revolutionary group.

weath·er map *n.* a synoptic chart showing weather conditions, compiled from simultaneous observations taken at various weather stations.

weath·er·proof ('wɛðəˌpruːf) *adj.* **1.** designed or able to withstand exposure to weather without deterioration. ~*vb.* **2.** (*tr.*) to render (something) weatherproof. —'**weath·er·ˌproof·ness** *n.*

weath·er sta·tion *n.* one of a network of meteorological observation posts where weather data is recorded.

weath·er strip *n.* a thin strip of compressible material, such as spring metal, felt, etc., that is fitted between the frame of a door or window and the opening part to exclude wind and rain. Also called: **weatherstripping.**

weath·er vane *n.* a vane designed to indicate the direction in which the wind is blowing.

weath·er-wise *adj.* **1.** skilful or experienced in predicting weather conditions. **2.** skilful or experienced in predicting trends in public opinion, reactions, etc.

weath·er·worn ('wɛðəˌwɔːn) *adj.* another word for **weather-beaten.**

weave (wiːv) *vb.* **weaves, weav·ing, wove** *or* **weaved; wo·ven** *or* **weaved. 1.** to form (a fabric) by interlacing (yarn, etc.), esp. on a loom. **2.** (*tr.*) to make or construct by such a process: *to weave a shawl.* **3.** (of a spider) to make (a web). **4.** (*tr.*) to construct by combining separate elements into a whole. **5.** (*tr.;* often foll. by *in, into, through,* etc.) to introduce: *to weave factual details into a fiction.* **6.** to create (a way, etc.) by moving from side to side: *to weave through a crowd.* **7. get weaving.** *Informal.* to hurry; start to do something. ~*n.* **8.** the method or pattern of weaving or the structure of a woven fabric: *a twill weave; an open weave.* [Old English *wefan;* related to Old High German *weban,* Old Norse *vefa,* Greek *hyphos,* Sanskrit *vābhis;* compare WEB, WEEVIL, WASP]

weav·er ('wiːvə) *n.* **1.** a person who weaves, esp. as a means of livelihood. **2.** short for **weaverbird.**

weav·er·bird ('wiːvəˌbɜːd) *or* **weav·er** *n.* **1.** any small Old World passerine songbird of the chiefly African family *Ploceidae,* having a short thick bill and a dull plumage and building covered nests: includes the house sparrow and whydahs. **2.** any similar bird of the family *Estrildidae,* of warm regions of the Old World: includes the waxbills, grassfinches, and Java sparrow. Also called: **weaver finch.**

weav·er's hitch *or* **knot** *n.* another name for **sheet bend.**

web (wɛb) *n.* **1.** any structure, construction, fabric, etc., formed by or as if by weaving or interweaving. **2.** a mesh of fine tough scleroprotein threads built by a spider from a liquid secreted from its spinnerets and used to trap insects. See also **cobweb** (sense 1). **3.** a similar network of threads spun by certain insect larvae, such as the silkworm. **4.** a fabric, esp. one in the process of being woven. **5.** a membrane connecting the toes of some aquatic birds or the digits of such aquatic mammals as the otter. **6.** the vane of a bird's feather. **7.** *Architect.* the surface of a ribbed vault that lies between the ribs. **8.** the central section of an I-beam or H-beam that joins the two flanges of the beam. **9.** the radial portion of a crank that connects the crankpin to the crankshaft. **10.** a thin piece of superfluous material left attached to a forging; fin. **11. a.** a continuous strip of paper as formed on a paper machine or fed from a reel into some printing presses. **b.** (*as modifier*): *web offset; a web press.* **12.** the woven edge, without pile, of some carpets. **13.** any structure, construction, etc., that is intricately formed or complex: *a web of intrigue.* ~*vb.* **webs, web·bing, webbed. 14.** (*tr.*) to cover with or as if with a web. **15.** (*tr.*) to entangle or ensnare. **16.** (*intr.*) to construct a web. [Old English *webb;* related to Old Saxon, Old High German *webbi,* Old Norse *vefr*] —'**web·less** *adj.* —'**web·ˌlike** *adj.*

Webb (wɛb) *n.* **Sid·ney (James),** Baron Passfield. 1859–1947, English economist, social historian, and Fabian socialist. He and his wife **(Martha) Be·a·trice** (*née Potter*), 1858–1943, English writer on social and economic problems, collaborated in *The History of Trade Unionism* (1894) and *English Local Government* (1906–29), helped found the London School of Economics (1895), and started the *New Statesman* (1913).

webbed (wɛbd) *adj.* **1.** (of the feet of certain animals) having the digits connected by a thin fold of skin; palmate. **2.** having, consisting of, or resembling a web.

web·bing ('wɛbɪŋ) *n.* **1.** a strong fabric of hemp, cotton, jute, etc., woven in strips and used under springs in upholstery or for straps, etc. **2.** the skin that unites the digits of a webbed foot. **3.** anything that forms a web.

web·by ('wɛbɪ) *adj.* **·bi·er, ·bi·est.** of, relating to, resembling, or consisting of a web.

we·ber ('veɪbə) *n.* the derived SI unit of magnetic flux; the flux that, when linking a circuit of one turn, produces in it an emf of 1 volt as it is reduced to zero at a uniform rate in one second. 1 weber is equivalent to 10^8 maxwells. Symbol: Wb [C20: named after W. E. WEBER]

We·ber (*German* 'veːbər) *n.* **1.** Baron **Carl Ma·ri·a Frie·drich Ernst von** (karl ma'riːa 'friːdrɪç ɛrnst fɔn). 1786–1826, German composer and conductor. His three romantic operas are *Der Freischütz* (1821), *Euryanthe* (1823), and *Oberon* (1826). **2. Ernst Hein·rich** (ɛrnst 'haɪnrɪç). 1795–1878, German physiologist and anatomist. He introduced the psychological concept of the just noticeable difference between stimuli. **3. Max** (maks). 1864–1920, German economist and sociologist, best known for *The Protestant Ethic and the Spirit of Capitalism* (1904–05). **4. Wil·helm E·du·ard** ('vɪlhɛlm 'eːdʊˌart), brother of Ernst Heinrich Weber. 1804–91, German physicist, who conducted research into electricity and magnetism.

We·bern (*German* 'veːbərn) *n.* **An·ton von** ('antoːn fɔn). 1883–1945, Austrian composer; pupil of Schoenberg, whose twelve-tone technique he adopted. His works include those for chamber ensemble, such as *Five Pieces for Orchestra* (1911–13).

web·foot ('wɛbˌfʊt) *n.* **1.** *Zoology.* a foot having the toes connected by folds of skin. **2.** *Anatomy.* a foot having an abnormal membrane connecting adjacent toes.

web-foot·ed *or* **web-toed** *adj.* (of certain animals) having webbed feet that facilitate swimming.

web spin·ner *n.* any small fragile dull-coloured typically tropical insect of the order *Embioptera,* which has biting mouthparts and constructs silken tunnels in which to live.

web·ster ('wɛbstə) *n.* an archaic word for **weaver** (sense 1). [Old English *webbestre,* from *webba* a weaver, from *webb* WEB]

Web·ster ('wɛbstə) *n.* **1. Dan·iel.** 1782–1852, U.S. politician and orator. **2. John.** ?1580–?1625, English dramatist, noted for his revenge tragedies *The White Devil* (?1612) and *The Duchess of Malfi* (?1613). **3. No·ah.** 1758–1843, U.S. lexicographer, famous for his *American Dictionary of the English Language* (1828).

web·wheel ('wɛbˌwiːl) *n.* **1.** a wheel containing a plate or web instead of spokes. **2.** a wheel of which the rim, spokes, and centre are in one piece.

wed (wɛd) *vb.* **weds, wed·ding, wed·ded** *or* **wed. 1.** to take (a person of the opposite sex) as a husband or wife; marry. **2.** (*tr.*) to join (two people) in matrimony. **3.** (*tr.*) to unite closely. [Old English *weddian;* related to Old Frisian *weddia,* Old Norse *vethja,* Gothic *wadi* pledge] —'**wed·ded** *adj.*

we'd (wiːd; *unstressed* wɪd) *contraction of* we had *or* we would.

Wed. *abbrev. for* Wednesday.

Wed·dell Sea ('wɛd^{ə}l) *n.* an arm of the S Atlantic in Antarctica.

wed·ding ('wɛdɪŋ) *n.* **1. a.** the act of marrying or the celebration of a marriage. **b.** (*as modifier*): *wedding day.* **2.** the anniversary of a marriage (in such combinations as **silver wedding** or **diamond wedding**). **3.** the combination or blending of two separate elements.

wed·ding break·fast *n.* the meal usually served after a wedding ceremony or just before the bride and bridegroom leave for their honeymoon.

wed·ding cake *n.* a rich fruit cake, with one, two, or more tiers, covered with almond paste and decorated with royal icing, which is served at a wedding reception.

wed·ding ring *n.* a band ring with parallel sides, typically of precious metal, worn to indicate married status.

We·de·kind (*German* 'veːdəˌkɪnt) *n.* **Frank.** 1864–1918, German dramatist, whose plays, such as *The Awakening of Spring*

(1891) and *Pandora's Box* (1904), bitterly satirize the sexual repressiveness of society.

wed+el+ing ('veɪdəlɪŋ) *n.* a succession of high-speed turns performed in skiing, skateboarding, etc. [from German *wedeln,* literally: to wag]

wedge (wɛdʒ) *n.* **1.** a block of solid material, esp. wood or metal, that is shaped like a narrow V in cross section and can be pushed or driven between two objects or parts of an object in order to split or secure them. **2.** any formation, structure, or substance in the shape of a wedge: *a wedge of cheese.* **3.** something such as an idea, action, etc., that tends to cause division. **4.** *Golf.* a club, a No. 10 iron with a face angle of more than 50°, used for bunker shots (**sand wedge**) or pitch shots (**pitching wedge**). **5.** a wedge-shaped extension of the high pressure area of an anticyclone, narrower than a ridge. **6.** any of the triangular characters used in cuneiform writing. **7.** (formerly) a body of troops formed in a V-shape. **8.** *Photog.* a strip of glass coated in such a way that it is clear at one end but becomes progressively more opaque towards the other end: used in making measurements of transmission density. **9. thin end of the wedge.** anything unimportant in itself that implies the start of something much larger. ~*vb.* **10.** (*tr.*) to secure with or as if with a wedge. **11.** to squeeze or be squeezed like a wedge into a narrow space. **12.** (*tr.*) to force apart or divide with or as if with a wedge. [Old English *wecg;* related to Old Saxon *weggi,* Old High German *wecki,* Old Norse *veggr* wall] —'**wedge+,like** *adj.* —'**wedg·y** *adj.*

wedge heel *n.* **1.** a raised shoe heel with the heel and sole forming a solid block. **2.** a shoe with such a heel.

wedge-tailed ea·gle *n.* a large brown Australian eagle, *Aquila audax,* having a wedge-shaped tail and a wingspan of 3 m. Also called: **eaglehawk.**

Wedg+wood ('wɛdʒwʊd) *Trademark.* ~*n.* **1. a.** pottery produced, esp. during the late 18th and early 19th centuries, at the Wedgwood factory, near Stoke-on-Trent. **b.** such pottery having applied classical decoration in white on a blue or other coloured ground. ~*adj.* **2. a.** relating to pottery made at the Wedgwood factory. **b.** characteristic of such pottery: *Wedgwood blue.* [C18: named after Josiah *Wedgwood* (1730–95), English potter]

Wedg+wood blue *n.* **a.** a pale blue or greyish-blue colour. **b.** (*as adj.*)*: a Wedgwood-blue door.*

wed+lock ('wɛdlɒk) *n.* **1.** the state of being married. **2. born** *or* **conceived out of wedlock.** born or conceived when one's parents are not legally married. [Old English *wedlāc,* from *wedd* pledge + *-lāc,* suffix denoting activity, perhaps from *lāc* game, battle (related to Gothic *laiks* dance, Old Norse *leikr*)]

Wednes+day ('wɛnzdɪ) *n.* the fourth day of the week; third day of the working week. [Old English *Wōdnes dæg* Woden's day, translation of Latin *mercurii dies* Mercury's day; related to Old Frisian *wōnsdei,* Middle Dutch *wōdensdach* (Dutch *woensdag*)]

wee[1] (wi:) *adj.* very small; tiny; minute. [C13: from Old English *wǣg* WEIGHT]

wee[2] (wi:) *Informal, chiefly Brit.* ~*n.* **1. a.** the act or an instance of urinating. **b.** urine. ~*vb.* **2.** (*intr.*) to urinate. ~Also: **wee-wee.** [of unknown origin]

weed[1] (wi:d) *n.* **1.** any plant that grows wild and profusely, esp. one that grows among cultivated plants, depriving them of space, food, etc. **2.** *Slang.* **a. the weed.** tobacco. **b.** a cigarette, often one containing marijuana. **c.** marijuana. **3.** *Informal.* a thin or unprepossessing person. **4.** an inferior horse, esp. one showing signs of weakness of constitution. ~*vb.* **5.** to remove (useless or troublesome plants) from (a garden, etc.). [Old English *weod;* related to Old Saxon *wiod,* Old High German *wiota* fern] —'**weed+er** *n.* —'**weed+less** *adj.* —'**weed+,like** *adj.*

weed[2] (wi:d) *n. Rare.* a black crepe band worn to indicate mourning. [Old English *wǣd, wēd;* related to Old Saxon *wād,* Old High German *wāt,* Old Norse *vāth*]

weed+kil·ler ('wi:d,kɪlə) *n.* a substance, usually a chemical or hormone, used for killing weeds.

weed out *vb.* (*tr., adv.*) to separate out, remove, or eliminate (anything unwanted): *to weed out troublesome students.*

weeds (wi:dz) *pl. n.* **1.** Also called: **widow's weeds.** a widow's black mourning clothes. **2.** *Obsolete.* any clothing. [pl. of WEED[2]]

weed·y ('wi:dɪ) *adj.* **weed·i·er, weed·i·est. 1.** full of or containing weeds: *weedy land.* **2.** (of a plant) resembling a weed in rapid or straggling growth. **3.** *Informal.* thin or weakly in appearance. —'**weed·i·ly** *adv.* —'**weed·i·ness** *n.*

week (wi:k) *n.* **1.** a period of seven consecutive days, esp., one beginning with Sunday. Related adj.: **hebdomadal. 2.** a period of seven consecutive days beginning from or including a specified day: *Easter week; a week from Wednesday.* **3.** the period of time within a week devoted to work. **4.** a week devoted to the celebration of a cause. ~*adv.* **5.** *Chiefly Brit.* seven days before or after a specified day: *I'll visit you Wednesday week.* [Old English *wice, wicu, wucu;* related to Old Norse *vika,* Gothic *wikō* order]

week+day ('wi:k,deɪ) *n.* any day of the week other than Sunday and, often, Saturday.

week+end *n.* (,wi:k'ɛnd). **1. a.** the end of the week, esp. the period from Friday night until the end of Sunday. **b.** (*as modifier*)*: a weekend party.* ~*vb.* ('wi:k,ɛnd). **2.** (*intr.*) *Informal.* to spend or pass a weekend.

week+end+er (,wi:k'ɛndə) *n. Austral.* a house, shack, etc., occupied only at weekends, for holidays, etc.

week+ends (,wi:k'ɛndz) *adv. Informal.* at the weekend, esp. regularly or during every weekend.

week+ly ('wi:klɪ) *adj.* **1.** happening or taking place once a week or every week. **2.** determined or calculated by the week. ~*adv.* **3.** once a week or every week. ~*n., pl.* **+lies. 4.** a newspaper or magazine issued every week.

week+night ('wi:k,naɪt) *n.* the evening or night of a weekday.

Weelkes (wi:lks) *n.* **Thom·as.** ?1575–1623, English composer of madrigals.

ween (wi:n) *vb. Archaic.* to think or imagine (something). [Old English *wēnan;* related to Old Saxon *wānian,* Gothic *wēnjan,* German *wähnen* to assume wrongly]

wee+ny ('wi:nɪ) *or* **ween+sy** ('wi:nzɪ) *adj.* **+ni+er, +ni+est** *or* **+si+er, +si+est.** *Informal.* very small; tiny. [C18: from WEE[1] with the ending *-ny* as in TINY]

wee·ny-bop·per *n. Informal.* a child of 8 to 12 years, esp. a girl, who is a keen follower of pop music. [C20: formed on the model of TEENY-BOPPER, from *weeny,* as in *teeny-weeny* very small]

weep (wi:p) *vb.* **weeps, weep+ing, wept. 1.** to shed (tears) as an expression of grief or unhappiness. **2.** (*tr.;* foll. by *out*) to utter, shedding tears. **3.** (when *intr.,* foll. by *for*) to mourn or lament (for something). **4.** to exude (drops of liquid). **5.** (*intr.*) (of a wound, etc.) to exude a watery or serous fluid. ~*n.* **6.** a spell of weeping. [Old English *wēpan;* related to Gothic *wōpjan,* Old High German *wuofan,* Old Slavonic *vabiti* to call]

weep+er ('wi:pə) *n.* **1.** a person who weeps, esp. a hired mourner. **2.** something worn as a sign of mourning. **3.** a hole through a wall, to allow water to drain away.

weep+ing ('wi:pɪŋ) *adj.* (of plants) having slender hanging branches. —'**weep+ing+ly** *adv.*

weep+ing wil+low *n.* a Chinese willow tree, *Salix babylonica,* having long hanging branches: widely planted for ornament.

weep·y ('wi:pɪ) *Informal.* ~*adj.* **weep·i·er, weep·i·est. 1.** liable or tending to weep. ~*n., pl.* **weep·ies. 2.** a romantic and sentimental film or book. —'**weep·i·ness** *n.*

wee+ver ('wi:və) *n.* any small marine percoid fish of the family *Trachinidae,* such as *Trachinus vipera* of European waters, having venomous spines around the gills and the dorsal fin. [C17: from Old Northern French *wivre* viper, ultimately from Latin *vīpera* VIPER]

wee+vil ('wi:vɪl) *n.* **1.** Also called: **snout beetle.** any beetle of the family *Curculionidae,* having an elongated snout (rostrum): they are pests, feeding on plants and plant products. See also **boll weevil. 2.** Also called: **pea** or **bean weevil.** any of various beetles of the family *Bruchidae* (or *Lariidae*), the larvae of which live in the seeds of leguminous plants. **3.** any of various similar or related beetles. [Old English *wifel;* related to Old High German *wibil;* compare Old Norse *tordȳfill* dungbeetle] —'**wee+vil·y** *adj.*

wee-wee *n., vb.* a variant of **wee**[2].

w.e.f. *abbrev. for* with effect from.

weft (wɛft) *n.* the yarn woven across the width of the fabric through the lengthwise warp yarn. Also called: **filling, woof.** [Old English, related to Old Norse *veptr;* see WEAVE]

Wehr+macht *German.* ('ve:r,maxt) *n.* the armed services of the German Third Reich from 1935 to 1945. [from *Wehr* defence + *Macht* force]

Weich·sel ('vaɪksəl) *n.* the German name for the **Vistula** (sense 1).

wei+ge+la (waɪ'gi:lə, -'dʒi:-; 'waɪgɪlə) *n.* any caprifoliaceous shrub of the Asian genus *Weigela,* having clusters of pink, purple, red, or white showy bell-shaped flowers. [C19: from New Latin, named after C. E. *Weigel* (1748–1831), German physician]

weigh[1] (weɪ) *vb.* **1.** (*tr.*) to measure the weight of. **2.** (*intr.*) to have weight or be heavy: *she weighs more than her sister.* **3.** (*tr.;* often foll. by *out*) to apportion according to weight. **4.** (*tr.*) to consider carefully: *to weigh the facts of a case.* **5.** (*intr.*) to be influential: *his words weighed little with the jury.* **6.** (*intr.;* often foll. by *on*) to be oppressive or burdensome (to). **7.** *Obsolete.* to regard or esteem. **8. weigh anchor.** to raise a vessel's anchor or (of a vessel) to have its anchor raised preparatory to departure. [Old English *wegan;* related to Old Frisian *wega,* Old Norse *vega,* Gothic *gawigan,* German *wiegen*] —'**weigh+a·ble** *adj.* —'**weigh+er** *n.*

weigh[2] (weɪ) *n.* **under weigh.** a variant spelling of **under way.** [C18: variation due to the influence of phrases such as *to weigh anchor*]

weigh+bridge ('weɪ,brɪdʒ) *n.* a machine for weighing vehicles, etc., by means of a metal plate set into a road.

weigh down *vb.* (*adv.*) to press (a person, etc.) down by or as if by weight: *his troubles weighed him down.*

weigh in *vb.* (*intr., adv.*) **1. a.** (of a boxer or wrestler) to be weighed before a bout. **b.** (of a jockey) to be weighed after, or sometimes before, a race. **2.** *Informal.* to contribute, as in a discussion, etc.: *he weighed in with a few sharp comments.* ~*n.* **weigh-in. 3.** the act of checking a competitor's weight, as in boxing, horse racing, etc.

weight (weɪt) *n.* **1.** a measure of the heaviness of an object; the amount anything weighs. **2.** *Physics.* the vertical force experienced by a mass as a result of gravitation. It equals the mass of the body multiplied by the acceleration of free fall. Its units are units of force (such as newtons or poundals) but is often given as a mass unit (kilogram or pound). Symbol: *W* **3.** a system of units used to express the weight of a substance: *troy weight.* **4.** a unit used to measure weight: *the kilogram is the weight used in SI units.* **5.** any mass or heavy object used to exert pressure or weigh down. **6.** an oppressive force: *the weight of cares.* **7.** any heavy load: *the bag was such a weight.* **8.** the main or greatest force: preponderance: *the weight of evidence.* **9.** importance, influence, or consequence:

his opinion carries weight. **10.** *Statistics.* one of a set of coefficients assigned to items of a frequency distribution that are analysed in order to represent the relative importance of the different items. **11.** *Printing.* the apparent blackness of a printed typeface. **12.** *Slang.* an amount of a drug, esp. a pound of cannabis resin. **13. pull one's weight.** *Informal.* to take one's share of responsibility. **14. throw one's weight around.** *Informal.* to act in an overauthoritarian or aggressive manner. ~*vb.* (*tr.*) **15.** to add weight to. **16.** to burden or oppress. **17.** *Statistics.* to attach a weight or weights to. **18.** to make (fabric, threads, etc.) heavier by treating with mineral substances, etc. [Old English *wiht;* related to Old Frisian, Middle Dutch *wicht,* Old Norse *vētt,* German *Gewicht*] —'**weight+er** *n.*

weight+ing ('weɪtɪŋ) *n.* an additional allowance payable in particular instances, esp. one paid to compensate for higher living costs: *a London weighting.*

weight+less+ness ('weɪtlɪsnɪs) *n.* the state or condition of having little or no weight. Weightlessness is experienced at great distances from the earth because of the reduced gravitational attraction. Also called: **zero gravity.** —'**weight+less** *adj.*

weight+lift·ing ('weɪtˌlɪftɪŋ) *n.* the sport of lifting barbells of specified weights in a prescribed manner for competition or exercise. —'**weight+ˌlift·er** *n.*

weight watch+er *n.* a person who tries to lose weight, esp. by dieting.

weight·y ('weɪtɪ) *adj.* **weight·i+er, weight·i+est. 1.** having great weight. **2.** important or momentous. **3.** causing anxiety or worry. —'**weight·i+ly** *adv.* —'**weight·i+ness** *n.*

Wei+hai *or* **Wei-hai** ('weɪ'haɪ) *n.* a port in NE China, in NE Shantung on the Yellow Sea: leased to Britain as a naval base (1898–1930). Also called: **Weihaiwei.**

Weil (*French* vaɪl) *n.* **Si·mone** (si'mɔn). 1909–43, French philosopher and mystic, whose works include *Waiting for God* (1951), *The Need for Roots* (1952), and *Notebooks* (1956).

Weill (vaɪl) *n.* **Kurt** (kʊrt). 1900–50, German composer, in the U.S. from 1935. He wrote the music for Brecht's *The Rise and Fall of the City of Mahagonny* (1927) and *The Threepenny Opera* (1928).

Wei+mar (*German* 'vaɪmar) *n.* a city in SW East Germany: a cultural centre in the 18th and early 19th centuries; scene of the adoption (1919) of the constitution of the Weimar Republic. Pop.: 63 361 (1972 est.).

Wei+mar+an+er ('vaɪməˌrɑːnə, 'waɪməˌrɑː-) *n.* an old breed of hound, having a grey usually smooth coat. [C20: named after WEIMAR, where the breed was developed]

Wei+mar Re+pub+lic *n.* the German republic that existed from 1919 to Hitler's accession to power in 1933.

weir (wɪə) *n.* **1.** a low dam that is built across a river to raise the water level, divert the water, or control its flow. **2.** a series of traps or enclosures placed in a stream to catch fish. [Old English *wer;* related to Old Norse *ver,* Old Frisian *were,* German *Wehr*]

weird (wɪəd) *adj.* **1.** suggestive of or relating to the supernatural; eerie. **2.** strange or bizarre. **3.** *Archaic.* of or relating to fate or the Fates. ~*n.* **4.** *Archaic, chiefly Scot.* **a.** fate or destiny. **b.** one of the Fates. [Old English (*ge*)*wyrd* destiny; related to *weorthan* to become, Old Norse *urthr* bane, Old Saxon *wurd;* see WORTH[2]] —'**weird+ly** *adv.* —'**weird+ness** *n.*

weir+die ('wɪədɪ) *or* **weir+do** *n., pl.* **+dies** *or* **+dos.** *Informal.* a person who behaves in a bizarre or eccentric manner.

weird sis+ters *pl. n.* **1.** another name for the **Fates. 2.** *Norse myth.* another name for the **Norns** (see **Norn**).

Weis+mann+ism ('vaɪsmənˌɪzəm) *n.* the doctrine of the continuity of the germ plasm. This theory of heredity states that all inheritable characteristics are transmitted by the reproductive cells and that characteristics acquired during the lifetime of the organism are not inherited. [C19: named after August *Weismann* (1834–1914), German biologist]

Weiss·horn ('vaɪsˌhɔːn) *n.* a mountain in S Switzerland, in the Pennine Alps. Height: 4505 m (14 781 ft.).

Weiz·mann ('waɪtsmən, 'waɪz-) *n.* **Cha·im** ('xaɪɪm). 1874–1952, Israeli statesman, born in Russia. As a leading Zionist, he was largely responsible for securing the Balfour Declaration (1917); first president of Israel (1949–52).

we·ka ('weɪkə, 'wiːkə) *n.* any flightless New Zealand rail of the genus *Gallirallus,* having a mottled brown plumage and rudimentary wings. [C19: from Maori, of imitative origin]

welch (wɛlʃ) *vb.* a variant spelling of **welsh.** —'**welch+er** *n.*

Welch[1] (wɛlʃ) *adj.* an archaic spelling of **Welsh.**

Welch[2] (wɛlʃ) *n.* **Ra·quel** ('rækɛl). born 1942, U.S. film actress, widely regarded as a sex symbol.

wel+come ('wɛlkəm) *adj.* **1.** gladly and cordially received or admitted: *a welcome guest.* **2.** bringing pleasure or gratitude: *a welcome gift.* **3.** freely permitted or invited: *you are welcome to call.* **4.** under no obligation (only in such phrases as **you're welcome** or **he's welcome,** as conventional responses to thanks). ~*sentence substitute.* **5.** an expression of cordial greeting, esp. to a person whose arrival is desired or pleasing. ~*n.* **6.** the act of greeting or receiving a person or thing; reception: *the new theory had a cool welcome.* **7. wear out one's welcome.** to come more often or stay longer than is acceptable or pleasing. ~*vb.* (*tr.*) **8.** to greet the arrival of (visitors, guests, etc.) cordially or gladly. **9.** to receive or accept, esp. gladly. [C12: changed (through influence of WELL[1]) from Old English *wilcuma* (agent noun referring to a welcome guest), *wilcume* (a greeting of welcome), from *wil* WILL[2] + *cuman* to COME] —'**wel+come+ly** *adv.* —'**wel+come+ness** *n.* —'**wel+com+er** *n.*

weld[1] (wɛld) *vb.* **1.** (*tr.*) to unite (pieces of metal or plastic) together, as by softening with heat and hammering or by fusion. **2.** to bring or admit of being brought into close association or union. ~*n.* **3.** a joint formed by welding. —'**weld+a·ble** *adj.* —ˌ**weld+a·'bil+i·ty** *n.* —'**weld+er** *or* '**wel+dor** *n.* —'**weld+less** *adj.*

weld[2] (wɛld), **wold,** *or* **woald** (wəʊld) *n.* **1.** a yellow dye obtained from the plant dyer's rocket. **2.** another name for **dyer's rocket.** [C14: from Low German; compare Middle Low German *walde, waude,* Dutch *wouw*]

Weld (wɛld) *n.* Sir **Fred·e·rick A·lo·y·sius.** 1823–91, New Zealand statesman, born in England: prime minister of New Zealand (1864–65).

wel+fare ('wɛlˌfɛə) *n.* **1.** health, happiness, prosperity, and well-being in general. **2. a.** financial and other assistance given to people in need. **b.** (*as modifier*): *welfare services.* **3.** Also called: **welfare work.** plans or work to better the social or economic conditions of various underprivileged groups. **4. the welfare.** *Informal, chiefly Brit.* the public agencies involved with giving such assistance. **5. on welfare.** *Chiefly U.S.* in receipt of financial aid from a government agency or other source. [C14: from the phrase *wel fare;* related to Old Norse *velferth,* German *Wohlfahrt;* see WELL[1], FARE]

wel+fare state *n.* **1.** a system in which the government undertakes the chief responsibility for providing for the social and economic security of its population, usually through unemployment insurance, old-age pensions, and other social-security measures. **2.** *Chiefly U.S.* a social system characterized by such policies.

wel+far+ism ('wɛlˌfɛərɪzəm) *n. U.S.* policies or attitudes associated with a welfare state.

wel+kin ('wɛlkɪn) *n. Archaic.* the sky, heavens, or upper air. [Old English *wolcen, welcen;* related to Old Frisian *wolken,* Old Saxon, Old High German *wolcan*]

Wel+kom ('wɛlkəm, 'vɛl-) *n.* a town in central South Africa, in the Orange Free State. Pop.: 131 767 (1970).

well[1] (wɛl) *adv.* **bet+ter, best. 1.** (*often used in combination*) in a satisfactory manner: *the party went very well.* **2.** (*often used in combination*) in a good, skilful, or pleasing manner: *she plays the violin well.* **3.** in a correct or careful manner: *listen well to my words.* **4.** in a comfortable or prosperous manner: *to live well.* **5.** (*usually used with auxiliaries*) suitably; fittingly: *you can't very well say that.* **6.** intimately: *I knew him well.* **7.** in a kind or favourable manner: *she speaks well of you.* **8.** to a great or considerable extent; fully: *to be well informed.* **9.** by a considerable margin: *let me know well in advance.* **10.** (preceded by *could, might,* or *may*) indeed: *you may well have to do it yourself.* **11. all very well.** used ironically to express discontent, dissent, etc. **12. as well. a.** in addition; too. **b.** (preceded by *may* or *might*) with equal effect: *you might as well come.* **13. as well as.** in addition to. **14. (just) as well.** preferable or advisable: *it would be just as well if you paid me now.* **15. leave well (enough) alone.** to refrain from interfering with something that is satisfactory. **16. well and good.** used to indicate calm acceptance, as of a decision: *if you accept my offer, well and good.* ~*adj.* (*usually postpositive*) **17.** (*when prenominal, usually used with a negative*) in good health: *I'm very well, thank you; he's not a well man.* **18.** satisfactory, agreeable, or pleasing. **19.** prudent; advisable: *it would be well to make no comment.* **20.** prosperous or comfortable. **21.** fortunate or happy: *it is well that you agreed to go.* ~*interj.* **22. a.** an expression of surprise, indignation, or reproof. **b.** an expression of anticipation in waiting for an answer or remark. ~*sentence connector.* **23.** an expression used to preface a remark, gain time, etc.: *well, I don't think I will come.* [Old English *wel;* related to Old High German *wala, wola* (German *wohl*), Old Norse *val,* Gothic *waila*]

well[2] (wɛl) *n.* **1.** a hole or shaft that is excavated, drilled, bored, or cut into the earth so as to tap a supply of water, oil, gas, etc. **2.** a natural pool where ground water comes to the surface. **3. a.** a cavity, space, or vessel used to contain a liquid. **b.** (*in combination*): *an inkwell.* **4.** an open shaft through the floors of a building, such as one used for a staircase. **5.** a deep enclosed space in a building or between buildings that is open to the sky to permit light and air to enter. **6. a.** a bulkheaded compartment built around a ship's pumps for protection and ease of access. **b.** another word for **cockpit. 7.** a perforated tank in the hold of a fishing boat for keeping caught fish alive. **8.** (in England) the open space in the centre of a law court. **9.** a source, esp. one that provides a continuous supply: *he is a well of knowledge.* ~*vb.* **10.** to flow or cause to flow upwards or outwards: *tears welled from her eyes.* [Old English *wella;* related to Old High German *wella* (German *Welle* wave), Old Norse *vella* boiling heat]

we'll (wiːl) *contraction of* we will *or* we shall.

well-ad·vised *adj.* (**well advised** *when postpositive*). **1.** acting with deliberation or reason. **2.** well thought out; considered: *a well-advised plan.*

'**well-ac·'cept·ed** *adj.*
'**well-ac·'com·plished** *adj.*
'**well-ac·'cus·tomed** *adj.*
'**well-ac·'knowl+edged** *adj.*
'**well-ac·'quaint+ed** *adj.*
'**well-'act·ed** *adj.*
'**well-a·'dapt·ed** *adj.*
'**well-ad·'just+ed** *adj.*
'**well-ad·'min·is+tered** *adj.*
'**well-'ad·ver·ˌtised** *adj.*
'**well-'aimed** *adj.*
'**well-'aired** *adj.*

Wel+land Ca+nal ('wɛlənd) *n.* a canal in S Canada, in Ontario, linking Lake Erie to Lake Ontario: part of the St. Lawrence Seaway, with eight locks. Length: 44 km (28 miles). Also called: **Welland Ship Canal.**

well-ap·point+ed *adj.* (**well appointed** *when postpositive*). well equipped or furnished; properly supplied.

well+a·way ('wɛlə'weɪ) *interj. Archaic.* woe! alas! [Old English, from *wei lā wei,* variant of *wā lā wā,* literally: woe! lo woe]

well-bal·anced *adj.* (**well balanced** *when postpositive*). **1.** having good balance or proportions. **2.** of balanced mind; sane or sensible.

well+be·ing ('wɛl'bi:ɪŋ) *n.* the condition of being contented, healthy, or successful; welfare.

well-bred *adj.* (**well bred** *when postpositive*). **1.** Also: **well-born.** of respected or noble lineage. **2.** indicating good breeding: *well-bred manners.* **3.** of good thoroughbred stock: *a well-bred spaniel.*

well-cho·sen *adj.* (**well chosen** *when postpositive*). carefully selected to produce a desired effect; apt: *a few well-chosen words may be more effective than a long speech.*

well-con·nect+ed *adj.* (**well connected** *when postpositive*). having influential or important relatives or friends.

well-dis·posed *adj.* (**well disposed** *when postpositive*). inclined to be sympathetic, kindly, or friendly: *he was never well disposed towards his relatives.*

well-done *adj.* (**well done** *when postpositive*). **1.** (of food, esp. meat) cooked thoroughly. **2.** made or accomplished satisfactorily.

Welles (wɛlz) *n.* **(George) Or·son** ('ɔ:sᵊn). born 1915, U.S. film director, actor, and producer. His *Citizen Kane* (1941) and *The Magnificent Ambersons* (1942) are regarded as film classics.

Welles·ley ('wɛlzlɪ) *n.* **1. Ar·thur.** See (1st Duke of) **Wellington. 2.** his brother, **Rich·ard Col·ley,** Marquis Wellesley. 1760–1842, British administrator. As governor general of Bengal (1797–1805) he consolidated British power in India.

Wel·lesz (*German* 'vɛlɛs) *n.* **E·gon** ('e:gɔn). 1885–1974, British composer, born in Austria.

well-fa·voured *adj.* (**well favoured** *when postpositive*). having good features; good-looking.

well-fed *adj.* (**well fed** *when postpositive*). **1.** having a nutritious diet; well nourished. **2.** plump; fat.

well-found *adj.* (**well found** *when postpositive*). furnished or supplied with all or most necessary things.

well-found·ed *adj.* (**well founded** *when postpositive*). having good grounds: *well-founded rumours.*

well-groomed *adj.* (**well groomed** *when postpositive*). **1.** (of a person) having a tidy pleasing appearance. **2.** kept tidy and neat: *a well-groomed garden.* **3.** well turned out and tended: *a well-groomed horse.*

well-ground·ed *adj.* (**well grounded** *when postpositive*). **1.** well instructed in the basic elements of a subject. **2.** another term for **well-founded.**

well+head ('wɛl,hɛd) *n.* **1.** the source of a well or stream. **2.** a source, fountainhead, or origin.

well-heeled *adj.* (**well heeled** *when postpositive*). *Slang.* rich; prosperous; wealthy.

well-hung *adj.* (**well hung** *when postpositive*). (of game) hung for a sufficient length of time.

wel+lies ('wɛlɪz) *pl. n. Brit. informal.* Wellington boots.

well in *adj.* (*postpositive*) **1.** (often foll. by *with*) *Brit. informal.* on good terms (with): *the foreman was well in with the management.* **2.** *Austral. informal.* rich; prosperous.

well-in·formed *adj.* (**well informed** *when postpositive*). **1.** having knowledge about a great variety of subjects: *he seems to be a well-informed person.* **2.** possessing reliable information on a particular subject.

Wel+ling+bor+ough ('wɛlɪŋbərə, -brə) *n.* a town in central England, in Northamptonshire. Pop.: 37 589 (1971).

Wel+ling+ton[1] ('wɛlɪŋtən) *n.* **1.** an administrative division of New Zealand, on SW North Island: chief livestock producer in New Zealand. Capital: Wellington. Pop.: 552 640 (1971). Area: 28 153 sq. km (10 870 sq. miles). **2.** the capital of New Zealand, a port on S North Island: became capital in 1865; university (1897). Pop.: 141 000 (1974 est.).

Wel·ling·ton[2] ('wɛlɪŋtən) *n.* **1st Duke of,** title of Arthur Wellesley. 1769–1852, British soldier and statesman; prime minister (1828–30). He was given command of the British forces against the French in the Peninsular War (1808–14) and routed Napoleon at Waterloo (1815).

Wel+ling+ton boots *pl. n.* **1.** Also called: **gumboots.** *Brit.* knee-length or calf-length rubber or rubberized boots, worn esp. in wet conditions. Often shortened to **wellies. 2.** military leather boots covering the front of the knee but cut away at the back to allow easier bending of the knee. [C19: named after the 1st Duke of *Wellington*]

wel+ling+ton+i·a (,wɛlɪŋ'təʊnɪə) *n.* another name for **big tree.** [C19: named after the 1st Duke of *Wellington*]

well-in·ten·tioned *adj.* (**well intentioned** *when postpositive*). having or indicating benevolent intentions, usually with unfortunate results.

well-knit *adj.* (**well knit** *when postpositive*). strong, firm, or sturdy.

well-known *adj.* (**well known** *when postpositive*). **1.** widely known; famous; celebrated. **2.** known fully or clearly.

well-man·nered *adj.* (**well mannered** *when postpositive*). having good manners; courteous; polite.

well-mean·ing *adj.* (**well meaning** *when postpositive*). having or indicating good or benevolent intentions, usually with unfortunate results.

well-nigh *adv.* nearly; almost: *it's well-nigh three o'clock.*

Usage. In strict usage, *well-nigh* is an adverb meaning *nearly* or *almost* and not a preposition meaning *near: he well-nigh cried; he was near* (not *well-nigh*) *death.*

well-off *adj.* (**well off** *when postpositive*). **1.** in a comfortable or favourable position or state. **2.** financially well provided for; moderately rich.

well-oiled *adj.* (**well oiled** *when postpositive*). *Slang.* affected by alcoholic liquor; drunk and loquacious.

well-pre·served *adj.* (**well preserved** *when postpositive*). **1.** kept in a good condition. **2.** continuing to appear youthful: *she was a well-preserved old lady.*

well-read ('wɛl'rɛd) *adj.* (**well read** *when postpositive*). having read widely and intelligently; erudite.

well-round·ed *adj.* (**well rounded** *when postpositive*). **1.** rounded in shape or well developed: *a well-rounded figure.* **2.** full, varied, and satisfying: *a well-rounded life.* **3.** well planned and balanced: *a well-rounded programme.*

Wells[1] (wɛlz) *n.* a city in SW England, in Somerset: 12th-century cathedral. Pop.: 8586 (1971).

Wells[2] (wɛlz) *n.* **H(erbert) G(eorge).** 1866–1946, English writer. His science-fiction stories include *The Time Machine* (1895), *War of the Worlds* (1898), and *The Shape of Things to Come* (1933). His novels on contemporary social questions, such as *Kipps* (1905), *Tono-Bungay* (1909), and *Ann Veronica* (1909), affected the opinions of his day. His nonfiction works include *The Outline of History* (1920).

well-spo·ken *adj.* (**well spoken** *when postpositive*). **1.** having a clear, articulate, and socially acceptable accent and way of speaking. **2.** spoken satisfactorily or pleasingly.

well+spring *n.* **1.** the source of a spring or stream; fountainhead. **2.** a source of continual or abundant supply.

well-stacked *adj.* (**well stacked** *when postpositive*). *Brit. slang.* (of a woman) of voluptuous proportions.

'well-ap·'plied *adj.*
'well-'ar·gued *adj.*
'well-'armed *adj.*
'well-ar·'ranged *adj.*
'well-as·'sort+ed *adj.*
'well-as·'sured *adj.*
'well-at·'tend+ed *adj.*
'well-at·'test+ed *adj.*
'well-at·'tired *adj.*
'well-au·'then+ti+,cat+ed *adj.*
'well-a·'ware *adj.*
'well-be·'haved *adj.*
'well-be·'loved *adj., n.*
'well-'blessed *adj.*
'well-'built *adj.*
'well-'cal·cu·,lat+ed *adj.*
'well-'clothed *adj.*
'well-'coached *adj.*
'well-'com·pen+,sat+ed *adj.*
'well-con·'cealed *adj.*
'well-con·'di·tioned *adj.*
'well-con·'duct+ed *adj.*
'well-con·'firmed *adj.*
'well-con·'sid+ered *adj.*
'well-con·'struct+ed *adj.*
'well-con·'tent+ed *adj.*
'well-con·'trolled *adj.*
'well-'cooked *adj.*
'well-'cov·ered *adj.*
'well-'cul·ti·,vat+ed *adj.*
'well-de·'fend+ed *adj.*
'well-de·'fined *adj.*
'well-'dem·on·,strat+ed *adj.*
'well-de·'scribed *adj.*
'well-de·'served *adj.*
'well-de·'vel·oped *adj.*
'well-de·'vised *adj.*
'well-di·'gest+ed *adj.*
'well-'dis·ci·plined *adj.*
'well-'doc·u·ment+ed *adj.*
'well-'dressed *adj.*
'well-'earned *adj.*
'well-'ed·u·,cat+ed *adj.*
'well-em·'ployed *adj.*
'well-en·'dowed *adj.*
'well-e·'quipped *adj.*
'well-es·'tab·lished *adj.*
'well-es·'teemed *adj.*
'well-fi·'nanced *adj.*
'well-'fin·ished *adj.*
'well-'fit·ted *adj.*
'well-'formed *adj.*
'well-'for·ti·,fied *adj.*
'well-'fought *adj.*
'well-'fur·nished *adj.*
'well-'gov·erned *adj.*
'well-'guard·ed *adj.*
'well-'han·dled *adj.*
'well-'hid·den *adj.*
'well-'housed *adj.*
'well-'il·lus·,trat+ed *adj.*
'well-in·'clined *adj.*
'well-'judged *adj.*
'well-'jus·ti·,fied *adj.*
'well-'kept *adj.*
'well-'liked *adj.*
'well-'loved *adj.*
'well-'made *adj.*
'well-'man·aged *adj.*
'well-'marked *adj.*
'well-'matched *adj.*
'well-'mer·it·ed *adj.*
'well-'mixed *adj.*
'well-'mo·ti·,vat+ed *adj.*
'well-'not·ed *adj.*
'well-'or·dered *adj.*
'well-'or·gan·,ized *adj.*
'well-'paid *adj.*
'well-'phrased *adj.*
'well-'placed *adj.*
'well-'planned *adj.*
'well-'played *adj.*
'well-'pleased *adj.*
'well-'prac·tised *adj.*
'well-pre·'pared *adj.*
'well-pro·'por+tioned *adj.*
'well-pro·'tect+ed *adj.*
'well-pro·'vid+ed *adj.*
'well-'qual·i·,fied *adj.*
'well-'rea·soned *adj.*
'well-re·'ceived *adj.*
'well-'rec·og·,nized *adj.*
'well-,rec·om·'mend+ed *adj.*
'well-re·'gard+ed *adj.*
'well-'reg·u·,lat+ed *adj.*
'well-re·'hearsed *adj.*
'well-re·'mem·bered *adj.*
'well-'rep·re·,sent+ed *adj.*
'well-re·'spect+ed *adj.*
'well-re·'viewed *adj.*
'well-'ri·pened *adj.*
'well-'sat·is·,fied *adj.*
'well-'schooled *adj.*
'well-'sea·soned *adj.*
'well-se·'cured *adj.*
'well-'shaped *adj.*
'well-'sit·u·,at+ed *adj.*
'well-'spent *adj.*

well sweep *n.* a device for raising buckets from and lowering them into a well, consisting of a long pivoted pole, the bucket being attached to one end by a long rope.
well-tem·pered *adj.* (**well tempered** *when postpositive*). (of a musical scale or instrument) conforming to the system of equal temperament. See **temperament** (sense 4).
well-thought-of *adj.* having a good reputation; respected.
well-to-do *adj.* moderately wealthy.
well-turned *adj.* (**well turned** *when postpositive*). **1.** (of a phrase, speech, etc.) apt and pleasingly sonorous. **2.** having a pleasing shape: *a well-turned leg.*
well-up·hol·stered *adj.* (**well upholstered** *when postpositive*) *Informal.* (of a person) fat.
well-wish·er *n.* a person who shows benevolence or sympathy towards a person, cause, etc. —**'well-ˌwish·ing** *adj., n.*
well-worn *adj.* (**well worn** *when postpositive*). **1.** so much used as to be affected by wear: *a well-worn coat.* **2.** used too often; hackneyed: *a well-worn phrase.*
Wels (*German* vɛls) *n.* an industrial city in N central Austria, in Upper Austria. Pop.: 47 279 (1971).
Wels+bach burn+er ('wɛlzbæk; *German* 'vɛlzbax) *n. Trademark.* a type of gaslight in which a mantle containing thorium and cerium compounds becomes incandescent when heated by a gas flame. [C19: named after Carl Auer, Baron von *Welsbach* (1858–1929), Austrian chemist, who invented it]
welsh *or* **welch** (wɛlʃ) *vb.* (*intr.*; often foll. by *on*) *Slang.* **1.** to fail to pay a gambling debt. **2.** to fail to fulfil an obligation. [C19: of unknown origin] —**'welsh+er** *or* **'welch+er** *n.*
Welsh (wɛlʃ) *adj.* **1.** of, relating to, or characteristic of Wales, its people, their Celtic language, or their dialect of English. ~*n.* **2.** a language of Wales, belonging to the S Celtic branch of the Indo-European family. Welsh shows considerable diversity between dialects. **3. the Welsh.** (*functioning as pl.*) the natives or inhabitants of Wales collectively. ~Also (rare): **Welch.** [Old English *Wēlisc, Wǣlisc;* related to *wealh* foreigner, Old High German *walahisc* (German *welsch*), Old Norse *valskr,* Latin *Volcae*]
Welsh cor+gi *n.* another name for **corgi.**
Welsh dress+er *n.* a sideboard with drawers and cupboards below and open shelves above.
Welsh harp *n.* a type of harp in which the strings are arranged in three rows, used esp. for the accompaniment of singing, improvisation on folk tunes, etc.
Welsh+man ('wɛlʃmən) *or* (*fem.*) **Welsh+wom·an** *n., pl.* **+men** *or* **+wom·en.** a native or inhabitant of Wales.
Welsh moun+tain po·ny *n.* a small sturdy but graceful breed of pony used mostly for riding, originally from Wales.
Welsh pop+py *n.* a perennial W European papaveraceous plant, *Meconopsis cambrica,* with large yellow flowers.
Welsh rab+bit *n.* a savoury dish consisting of melted cheese sometimes mixed with milk, seasonings, etc., on hot buttered toast. Also called: **Welsh rarebit, rarebit.** [C18: a fanciful coinage; *rarebit* is a later folk-etymological variant]
Welsh spring+er span+iel *n.* a red-and-white breed of spaniel slightly smaller than the English springer spaniel.
Welsh ter+ri+er *n.* a wire-haired breed of terrier with a black-and-tan coat.
welt (wɛlt) *n.* **1.** a raised or strengthened seam or edge, sewn in or on a knitted garment. **2.** another word for **weal**[1]. **3.** (in shoemaking) a strip of leather, etc., put in between the outer sole and the inner sole and upper. ~*vb.* (*tr.*) **4.** to put a welt in (a garment, etc.). **5.** to beat or flog soundly. [C15: origin unknown]
Welt+an+schau+ung *German.* ('vɛltanˌʃaʊʊŋ) *n.* a comprehensive view or personal philosophy of human life and the universe. [from *Welt* world + *Anschauung* view]
wel+ter ('wɛltə) *vb.* (*intr.*) **1.** to roll about, writhe, or wallow. **2.** (esp. of the sea) to surge, heave, or toss. **3.** to lie drenched in a liquid, esp. blood. ~*n.* **4.** a rolling motion, as of the sea. **5.** a confused mass; jumble. [C13: from Middle Low German, Middle Dutch *weltern;* related to Old High German *walzan, welzen* to roll]
wel+ter+weight ('wɛltəˌweɪt) *n.* **1. a.** a professional boxer weighing 140–147 pounds (63.5–66.5 kg). **b.** an amateur boxer weighing 63.5–67 kg (140–148 pounds). **c.** (*as modifier*): *a great welterweight era.* **2.** a wrestler in a similar weight category (usually 154–172 pounds (70–78 kg)).
Welt+po+li+tik *German.* ('vɛltpoliˌti:k) *n.* the policy of participation in world affairs. [literally: world politics]
Welt+schmerz *German.* ('vɛltˌʃmɛrts) *n.* sadness or melancholy at the evils of the world; world-weariness. [literally: world pain]
wel+witsch·i·a (wɛl'wɪtʃɪə) *n.* a gymnosperm plant, *Welwitschia mirabilis,* of arid regions of tropical and southern Africa, consisting of two large woody leaves lying on the ground with a conelike structure arising between them: order *Gnetales.* [C19: named after F. M. J. *Welwitsch* (1807–72), Portuguese botanist, born in Austria]
Wel+wyn Gar+den Cit·y ('wɛlɪn) *n.* a town in SE England, in Hertfordshire: established (1920) as a planned industrial and residential community. Pop.: 40 369 (1971).
Wem+bley ('wɛmblɪ) *n.* part of the Greater London borough of Brent: site of the English national soccer stadium.
wen[1] (wɛn) *n. Pathol.* a sebaceous cyst, esp. one occurring on the scalp. [Old English *wenn;* related to Danish dialect *van, væne,* Dutch *wenn*]
wen[2] (wɛn) *n.* a rune having the sound of Modern English *w.* [Old English *wen, wyn*]
Wen·ces·laus *or* **Wen·ces·las** ('wɛnsɪsləs) *n.* **1.** 1361–1419, Holy Roman Emperor (1378–1400) and, as **Wenceslaus IV,** king of Bohemia (1378–1419). **2. Saint,** called *Good King Wenceslaus.* ?907–929, duke of Bohemia (?925–29); patron saint of Czechoslovakia. Feast day: Sept. 28.
wench (wɛntʃ) *n.* **1.** a girl or young woman, esp. a buxom or lively one: now used facetiously. **2.** *Archaic.* a female servant. **3.** *Archaic.* a prostitute. ~*vb.* (*intr.*) **4.** *Archaic.* to frequent the company of prostitutes. [Old English *wencel* child, from *wancol* weak; related to Old High German *wanchal, wankōn*] —**'wench+er** *n.*
wend (wɛnd) *vb.* to direct (one's course or way); travel. [Old English *wendan;* related to Old High German *wenten,* Gothic *wandjan;* see WIND[2]]
Wend (wɛnd) *n.* (esp. in medieval European history) a Sorb; a member of the Slavonic people who inhabited the area between the Rivers Saale and Oder in the early Middle Ages and were conquered by Germanic invaders by the 12th century. See also **Lusatia.**
Wend+ish ('wɛndɪʃ) *adj.* **1.** of or relating to the Wends. ~*n.* **2.** the West Slavonic language of the Wends. See also **Sorbian.**
Wen+dy house ('wɛndɪ) *n.* a small model house that children can enter and play in. [C20: named after the house built for *Wendy,* the girl in J. M. Barrie's play *Peter Pan* (1904)]
wens+ley+dale ('wɛnzlɪˌdeɪl) *n.* **1.** a type of white cheese with a flaky texture. **2.** a breed of sheep with long woolly fleece. [named after *Wensleydale,* North Yorkshire]
went (wɛnt) *vb.* the past tense of **go.**
wen+tle+trap ('wɛntᵊlˌtræp) *n.* any marine gastropod mollusc of the family *Epitoniidae,* having a long pointed pale-coloured longitudinally ridged shell. [C18: from Dutch *winteltrap* spiral shell, from *wintel,* earlier *windel,* from *wenden* to wind + *trap* a step, stairs]
Went·worth ('wɛntwəθ) *n.* **Thom·as.** See (Earl of) **Strafford.**
wept (wɛpt) *vb.* the past tense or past participle of **weep.**
were (wɜ:; *unstressed* wə) *vb.* the plural form of the past tense (indicative mood) of **be** and the singular form used with *you.* It is also used as a subjunctive, esp. in conditional sentences. [Old English *wērun, wæron* past tense plural of *wesan* to be; related to Old Norse *vera,* Old Frisian *weria,* Old High German *werōn* to last]
Usage. *Were,* as a remnant of the past subjunctive in English, is used in formal contexts in clauses expressing hypotheses (*if he were to die, she would inherit everything*), suppositions contrary to fact (*if I were you, I would be careful*), and desire (*I wish he were there now*). In informal speech, however, *was* is often used instead.
we're (wɪə) *contraction of* we are.
were·n't (wɜ:nt) *contraction of* were not.
were+wolf ('wɪəˌwulf, 'wɛə-) *n., pl.* **+wolves.** a person fabled in folklore and superstition to have been changed into a wolf by being bewitched or said to be able to assume wolf form at will. [Old English *werewulf,* from *wer* man + *wulf* WOLF; related to Old High German *werwolf,* Middle Dutch *weerwolf*]
wer+gild, were+gild ('wɜ:ˌgɪld, 'wɛə-), *or* **wer+geld** ('wɜ:ˌgɛld, 'wɛə-) *n.* the price set on a man's life in successive Anglo-Saxon and Germanic law codes, to be paid as compensation by his slayer. [Old English *wergeld,* from *wer* man (related to Old Norse *ver,* Latin *vir*) + *gield* tribute (related to Gothic *gild,* Old High German *gelt* payment); see YIELD]
Wer·ner (*German* 'vɛrnər) *n.* **Al·fred** ('alfre:t). 1866–1919, Swiss chemist, born in Germany. He developed a coordination theory of the valency of inorganic complexes: Nobel prize for chemistry 1913.
wer+ner+ite ('wɜ:nəˌraɪt) *n.* another name for **scapolite.** [C19: named after A.G. *Werner* (1750–1817), German mineralogist]
wersh (wɜ:ʃ) *adj. Scot.* tasteless; insipid. [C16: perhaps alteration of dialect *wearish,* probably of Germanic origin]
wert (wɜ:t; *unstressed* wət) *vb. Archaic or dialect.* (used with the pronoun *thou* or its relative equivalent) a singular form of the past tense (indicative mood) of **be.**
We+ser (*German* 've:zər) *n.* a river in N West Germany: flows northwest to the North Sea at Bremerhaven and is linked by the Mittelland Canal to the Ems, Rhine, and Elbe waterways. Length: 477 km (196 miles).
We+ser+mün+de (*German* ˌve:zər'myndə) *n.* the former name (until 1947) of **Bremerhaven.**
Wes·ker ('wɛskə) *n.* **Ar·nold.** born 1932, English dramatist, noted for his socialist plays, such as *Roots* (1959) and *Chips With Everything* (1962).
wes+kit ('wɛskɪt) *n.* an informal word for **waistcoat.**
Wes·ley ('wɛzlɪ) *n.* **1. Charles.** 1707–88, English Methodist preacher and writer of hymns. **2.** his brother **John.** 1703–91, English preacher, who founded Methodism.
Wes+ley+an ('wɛzlɪən) *adj.* **1.** of, relating to, or deriving from

'well-'stat·ed *adj.*
'well-'stocked *adj.*
'well-'suit·ed *adj.*
'well-sup·'plied *adj.*
'well-sup·'port+ed *adj.*
'well-sus·'tained *adj.*
'well-'taught *adj.*
'well-'timed *adj.*
'well-'trained *adj.*
'well-'trav·elled *adj.*
'well-'treat·ed *adj.*
'well-'tried *adj.*
'well-'trod·den *adj.*
'well-ˌun·der·'stood *adj.*
'well-'used *adj.*
'well-'ver·i·ˌfied *adj.*
'well-'wood·ed *adj.*
'well-'word·ed *adj.*
'well-'writ·ten *adj.*
'well-'wrought *adj.*

John Wesley. **2.** of, relating to, or characterizing Methodism, esp. in its original form or as upheld by the branch of the Methodist Church known as the **Wesleyan Methodists.** ~*n.* **3.** a follower of John Wesley. **4.** a member of the Methodist Church or (formerly) of the Wesleyan Methodists. —**'Wes·ley·an·ism** *n.*

Wes·sex ('wɛsɪks) *n.* an Anglo-Saxon kingdom in S and SW England that became the most powerful English kingdom by the 10th century A.D.

west (wɛst) *n.* **1.** one of the four cardinal points of the compass, 270° clockwise from north and 180° from east. **2.** the direction along a parallel towards the sunset, at 270° clockwise from north. **3. the west.** (*often cap.*) any area lying in or towards the west. Related adjs.: **hesperian, occidental.** ~*adj.* **4.** situated in, moving towards, or facing the west. **5.** (esp. of the wind) from the west. ~*adv.* **6.** in, to, towards, or (esp. of the wind) from the west. **7. go west.** *Informal.* **a.** to be lost or destroyed irrevocably. **b.** to die. ~Abbrev.: **W.** [Old English; related to Old Norse *vestr,* Sanskrit *avástāt,* Latin *vesper* evening, Greek *hésperos*]

West[1] (wɛst) *n.* **the. 1.** the western part of the world contrasted historically and culturally with the East or Orient; the Occident. **2.** the non-Communist countries of Europe and America contrasted with the Communist states of the East. Compare **East** (sense 2). **3.** (in the U.S.) **a.** that part of the U.S. lying approximately to the west of the Mississippi. **b.** (during the Colonial period) the region outside the 13 colonies, lying mainly to the west of the Alleghenies. **4.** (in the ancient and medieval world) the Western Roman Empire and, later, the Holy Roman Empire. ~*adj.* **5. a.** of or denoting the western part of a specified country, area, etc. **b.** (*as part of a name*): *the West Coast.*

West[2] (wɛst) *n.* **1. Ben·ja·min.** 1738–1820, U.S. painter, in England from 1763. **2. Mae.** born 1892, U.S. film actress. **3.** Dame **Re·bec·ca.** pen name of *Mrs. H. M. Andrews.* born 1892, English novelist and critic.

West At·lan·tic *n.* **1.** the W part of the Atlantic Ocean, esp. the N Atlantic around North America. **2.** a branch of the Niger-Congo family of African languages, spoken in Senegal and in scattered areas eastwards, including Fulani and Wolof. ~*adj.* **3.** relating to or belonging to this group of languages.

West Ben·gal *n.* a state of E India, on the Bay of Bengal: formed in 1947 from the Hindu area of Bengal; additional territories added in 1950 (Cooch Behar), 1954 (Chandernagor), and 1956 (part of Bihar); mostly low-lying and crossed by the Hooghly River. Capital: Calcutta. Pop.: 44 312 011 (1971). Area: 87 617 sq. km (33 829 sq. miles).

West Ber·lin *n.* the part of Berlin under U.S., British, and French control. —**West Ber·lin·er** *n., adj.*

west·bound ('wɛst,baʊnd) *adj.* going or leading towards the west.

West Brom·wich ('brɒmɪdʒ, -ɪtʃ) *n.* a town in central England, in the West Midlands: coal-mining and industrial centre. Pop.: 166 626 (1971).

west by north *n.* **1.** one point on the compass north of west, 281° 15′ clockwise from north. ~*adj., adv.* **2.** in, from, or towards this direction.

west by south *n.* **1.** one point on the compass south of west, 258° 45′ clockwise from north. ~*adj., adv.* **2.** in, from, or towards this direction.

West Coast jazz *n.* a type of cool jazz displaying a soft intimate sound, regular rhythms, and a tendency to incorporate academic classical devices into jazz, such as fugue.

West Coun·try *n.* **the.** the southwest of England, esp. Cornwall, Devon, and Somerset.

West End *n.* **the.** a part of W central London containing the main shopping and entertainment areas.

west·er ('wɛstə) *vb.* **1.** (*intr.*) (of the sun, moon, or a star) to move or appear to move towards the west. ~*n.* **2.** a strong wind or storm from the west.

west·er·ing ('wɛstərɪŋ) *adj. Poetic.* moving towards the west: *the westering star.*

West·er·lies ('wɛstəlɪz) *pl. n. Meteorol.* the prevailing winds blowing from the west on the poleward sides of the horse latitudes, often bringing depressions and anticyclones.

west·er·ly ('wɛstəlɪ) *adj.* **1.** of, relating to, or situated in the west. ~*adv., adj.* **2.** towards or in the direction of the west. **3.** (esp. of the wind) from the west. ~*n., pl.* **·lies. 4.** a wind blowing from the west. —**'west·er·li·ness** *n.*

west·ern ('wɛstən) *adj.* **1.** situated in or towards or facing the west. **2.** going or directed to or towards the west. **3.** (of a wind, etc.) coming or originating from the west. **4.** native to, inhabiting, or growing in the west. **5.** *Music.* See **country-and-western.**

West·ern ('wɛstən) *adj.* **1.** of, relating to, or characteristic of the Americas and the parts of Europe not under Communist rule. **2.** of, relating to, or characteristic of the West as opposed to the Orient. **3.** of, relating to, or characteristic of the western states of the U.S. ~*n.* **4.** a film, book, etc., concerned with life in the western states of the U.S., esp. during the era of exploration and early development.

West·ern Aus·tral·i·a *n.* a state of W Australia: mostly an arid undulating plateau, with the Great Sandy Desert, Gibson Desert, and Great Victoria Desert in the interior; settlement concentrated in the southwest; rich mineral resources. Capital: Perth. Pop.: 1 144 400 (1976). Area: 2 527 636 sq. km (975 920 sq. miles).

West·ern Church *n.* **1.** the part of Christendom that derives its liturgy, discipline, and traditions principally from the patriarchate of Rome, as contrasted with the part that derives these from the other ancient patriarchates, esp. that of Constantinople. **2.** the Roman Catholic Church, sometimes together with the Anglican Communion of Churches.

west·ern·er ('wɛstənə) *n.* (*sometimes cap.*) a native or inhabitant of the west of any specific region, esp. of the western states of the U.S. or of the western hemisphere.

West·ern Ghats *pl. n.* a mountain range in W peninsular India, parallel to the Malabar coast of the Arabian Sea. Highest peak: Anai Mudi, 2695 m (8841 ft.).

west·ern hem·i·sphere *n.* (*often caps.*) **1.** that half of the globe containing the Americas, lying to the west of the Greenwich or another meridian. **2.** the lands contained in this, esp. the Americas.

west·ern hem·lock *n.* a North American coniferous evergreen tree, *Tsuga heterophylla,* having hanging branches and oblong cones: family *Pinaceae.*

Wes·tern Isles *n.* **1.** an island authority in W Scotland, consisting of the Outer Hebrides; created in 1975. Administrative centre: Stornoway. Pop.: 29 693 (1976 est.). Area: 2900 sq. km (1120 sq. miles). **2.** Also called: **Western Islands.** another name for the **Hebrides.**

west·ern·ism ('wɛstə,nɪzəm) *n.* a word, habit, practice, etc., characteristic of western people or of the American West.

west·ern·ize *or* **west·ern·ise** ('wɛstə,naɪz) *vb.* (*tr.*) to influence or make familiar with the customs, practices, etc., of the West. —**,west·ern·i·'za·tion** *or* **,west·ern·i·'sa·tion** *n.*

west·ern·most ('wɛstən,məʊst) *adj.* situated or occurring farthest west.

West·ern O·cean *n.* (formerly) another name for the **Atlantic Ocean.**

west·ern roll *n.* a technique in high-jumping in which the jumper executes a half-turn of the body to clear the bar.

West·ern Ro·man Em·pire *n.* the westernmost of the two empires created by the division of the later Roman Empire, esp. after its final severance from the Eastern Roman Empire (395 A.D.). Also called: **Western Empire.**

West·ern Sa·ha·ra *n.* a region of NW Africa, on the Atlantic: a Spanish overseas province from 1958 until 1975 when Morocco and Mauritania were left in joint control until its future was decided: mainly desert; rich phosphate deposits. Pop.: 76 425 (1970). Area: 266 000 sq. km (102 680 sq. miles). Former name (until 1975): **Spanish Sahara.**

West·ern Sa·mo·a *n.* an independent state occupying four inhabited islands and five uninhabited islands in the S Pacific archipelago of the Samoa Islands: established as a League of Nations mandate under New Zealand administration in 1920 and a UN trusteeship in 1946; gained independence in 1962 as the first fully independent Polynesian state; a member of the Commonwealth. Languages: Samoan and English. Religion: Christian. Currency: tala. Capital: Apia. Pop.: 146 635 (1971). Area: 2841 sq. km (1097 sq. miles). —**West·ern Sa·mo·an** *adj., n.*

West·fa·len (vɛst'fa:lən) *n.* the German name for **Westphalia.**

West Flan·ders *n.* a province of W Belgium: the country's chief agricultural province. Capital: Bruges. Pop.: 1 071 604 (1975 est.). Area: 3132 sq. km (1209 sq. miles).

West Ger·man·ic *n.* a subbranch of the Germanic languages that consists of English, Frisian, Dutch, Flemish, Afrikaans, Low German, German, Yiddish, and their associated dialects.

West Ger·ma·ny *n.* a republic in N central Europe, on the North Sea: established in 1949 from the zones of Germany occupied by the British, Americans, and French after the defeat of the Germans; a member of the Common Market. It consists of a low-lying plain in the north, with plateaus and uplands (including the Black Forest and the Bavarian Alps) in the centre and south. Language: German. Religion: Christian, with a slight Protestant majority. Currency: mark. Capital: Bonn. Pop.: 61 832 000 (1975 est.). Area: 248 574 sq. km (95 975 sq. miles). Official name: **Federal Republic of Germany.** See also **Germany.** —**West Ger·man** *adj., n.*

West Gla·mor·gan *n.* a county in S Wales, formed in 1974 from part of Glamorgan and the county borough of Swansea. Administrative centre: Swansea. Pop.: 371 900 (1976 est.). Area: 816 sq. km (318 sq. miles).

West Har·tle·pool ('hɑ:tlɪ,pu:l) *n.* a former town in NE England, in Cleveland: part of Hartlepool since 1967.

West In·dies ('ɪndɪz) *pl. n.* an archipelago off Central America, extending over 2400 km (1500 miles) in an arc from the peninsula of Florida to Venezuela, separating the Caribbean from the Atlantic: consists of the Greater Antilles, the Lesser Antilles, and the Bahamas; largest island is Cuba. Area: over 235 000 sq. km (91 000 sq. miles).

west·ing ('wɛstɪŋ) *n. Navigation.* movement, deviation, or distance covered in a westerly direction, esp. as expressed in the resulting difference in longitude.

West I·ri·an *n.* the W part of the island of New Guinea: formerly under Dutch rule, becoming a province of Indonesia in 1963. Capital: Djajapura. Pop.: 923 440 (1971). Area: 416 990 sq. km (161 000 sq. miles). Former names (until 1963): **Dutch New Guinea, Netherlands New Guinea.** Indonesian name: **Irian Jaya.**

West Lo·thi·an *n.* (until 1975) a county of central Scotland, now part of Lothian region.

Westm. *abbrev. for* Westminster.

West·meath (,west'mi:ð) *n.* a county of N central Ireland, in Leinster province: mostly low-lying, with many lakes and bogs. County town: Millingar. Pop.: 53 550 (1971). Area: 1764 sq. km (681 sq. miles).

West Mid·lands *n.* a metropolitan county of central England, comprising the districts of Wolverhampton, Walsall, Dudley, Sandwell, Birmingham, Solihull, and Coventry. Administrative centre: Birmingham. Pop.: 2 743 300 (1976 est.). Area: 899 sq. km (347 sq. miles).

West+min+ster ('wɛst,mɪnstə) *n.* **1.** Also called: **City of Westminster.** a borough of Greater London, on the River Thames: contains the Houses of Parliament, Westminster Abbey, and Buckingham Palace. Pop.: 216 100 (1976 est.). **2.** the Houses of Parliament at Westminster.

West+min+ster Ab+bey *n.* a Gothic church in London: site of a Benedictine monastery (1050–65); scene of the coronations of almost all English monarchs since William I.

West+mor+land ('wɛstmələnd, 'wɛsmə-) *n.* (until 1974) a county of NW England, now part of Cumbria.

west-north-west *n.* **1.** the point on the compass or the direction midway between west and northwest, 292° 30′ clockwise from north. ~*adj., adv.* **2.** in, from, or towards this direction. ~Abbrev.: **WNW**

Wes+ton stan+dard cell ('wɛstən) *n.* a primary cell used as a standard of emf, producing 1.018636 volts: consists of a mercury anode and a cadmium amalgam cathode in an electrolyte of saturated cadmium sulphate. Former name: **cadmium cell.** [C20: from a trademark]

Wes·ton-su·per-Mare ('wɛstən,su:pə'mɛə, -,sju:-) *n.* a town and resort in SW England, in SW Avon on the Bristol Channel. Pop.: 50 794 (1971).

West Pa+ki+stan *n.* the former name (until the end of 1971) of **Pakistan.**

West+pha+li·a (wɛst'feɪlɪə) *n.* a former province of NW Prussia: incorporated into the West German state of North Rhine-Westphalia in 1946. German name: **Westfalen.** —**West+'pha+li·an** *adj., n.*

West Point *n.* the U.S. Army installation in New York State that houses the U.S. Military Academy.

West Prus+sia *n.* a former province of NE Prussia, on the Baltic: assigned to Poland in 1945. German name: **West+preus+sen** ('vɛst ,prɔɪsᵊn).

West Rid+ing *n.* (until 1974) an administrative division of Yorkshire, now contained in West Yorkshire.

West Sax+on (in Anglo-Saxon England) ~*adj.* **1.** of or relating to Wessex, its inhabitants, or their dialect. ~*n.* **2.** the dialect of Old English spoken in Wessex: the chief literary dialect of Old English. See also **Anglian, Kentish. 3.** an inhabitant of Wessex.

west-south·west *n.* **1.** the point on the compass or the direction midway between southwest and west, 247° 30′ clockwise from north. ~*adj., adv.* **2.** in, from, or towards this direction. ~Abbrev.: **WSW**

West Sus+sex *n.* a county of SE England, comprising part of the former county of Sussex. Administrative centre: Chichester. Pop.: 623 400 (1976 est.). Area: 2064 sq. km (797 sq. miles).

West Vir+gin·i·a *n.* a state of the eastern U.S.: part of Virginia until the outbreak of the American Civil War (1861); consists chiefly of the Allegheny Plateau; bounded on the west by the Ohio River; coal-mining. Capital: Charleston. Pop.: 1 744 237 (1970). Area: 62 341 sq. km (24 070 sq. miles). Abbrevs.: **W. Va.** or (with zip code) **WV** —**West Vir+gin+i·an** *adj., n.*

west+ward ('wɛstwəd) *adj.* **1.** moving, facing, or situated in the west. ~*adv.* **2.** Also: **westwards.** towards the west. ~*n.* **3.** the westward part, direction, etc.; the west. —**'west+ward+ly** *adj., adv.*

West York+shire *n.* a metropolitan county of N England, comprising the districts of Bradford, Leeds, Calderdale, Kirklees, and Wakefield. Administrative centre: Wakefield. Pop.: 2 072 500 (1976 est.). Area: 2038 sq. km (787 sq. miles).

wet (wɛt) *adj.* **wet+ter, wet+test. 1.** moistened, covered, saturated, etc., with water or some other liquid. **2.** not yet dry or solid: *wet varnish.* **3.** rainy, foggy, misty, or humid: *wet weather.* **4.** employing a liquid, usually water: *a wet method of chemical analysis.* **5.** *Chiefly U.S.* characterized by or permitting the free sale of alcoholic beverages: *a wet state.* **6.** *Brit. informal.* feeble or foolish. **7. wet behind the ears.** *Informal.* immature or inexperienced. ~*n.* **8.** wetness or moisture. **9.** damp or rainy weather. **10.** *Chiefly U.S.* a person who advocates free sale of alcoholic beverages. **11.** *Brit. informal.* a feeble or foolish person. **12. the wet.** *Austral.* (in northern and central Australia) the rainy season. ~*vb.* **wets, wet+ting, wet** *or* **wet+ted. 13.** to make or become wet. **14.** to urinate on (something). **15. wet one's whistle.** *Informal.* to take a drink. [Old English *wǣt;* related to Old Frisian *wēt,* Old Norse *vātr,* Old Slavonic *vedro* bucket] —**'wet+ly** *adv.* —**'wet+ness** *n.* —**'wet+ta·'bil+i·ty** *n.* —**'wet+ta·ble** *adj.* —**'wet+ter** *n.* —**'wet+tish** *adj.*

wet-and-dry-bulb ther+mom+e·ter *n.* another name for **psychrometer.**

wet+back ('wɛt,bæk) *n. U.S. informal.* a Mexican labourer who enters the U.S. illegally.

wet blan+ket *n. Informal.* a person whose low spirits or lack of enthusiasm have a depressing effect on others.

wet-bulb ther+mom+e·ter *n.* a thermometer the bulb of which is covered by a moist muslin bag, used together with a dry-bulb thermometer to measure humidity.

wet cell *n.* a primary cell in which the electrolyte is a liquid. Compare **dry cell.**

wet dream *n.* an erotic dream accompanied by an emission of semen during or just after sleep.

wet fly *n. Angling.* **a.** an artificial fly designed to float or ride below the water surface. **b.** (*as modifier*): *wet-fly fishing.* Compare **dry fly.**

weth+er ('wɛðə) *n.* a male sheep, esp. a castrated one. [Old English *hwæther;* related to Old Frisian *hweder,* Old High German *hwedar,* Old Norse *hvatharr*]

wet look *n.* a shiny finish given to certain clothing and footwear materials, esp. plastic and leather.

wet nurse *n.* **1.** a woman hired to suckle the child of another. ~*vb.* **wet-nurse.** (*tr.*) **2.** to act as a wet nurse to (a child). **3.** *Informal.* to attend with great devotion.

wet pack *n. Med.* a hot or cold damp sheet or blanket for wrapping around a patient.

wet rot *n.* **1.** a state of decay in timber caused by various fungi, esp. *Coniophora cerebella.* **2.** any of the fungi causing this decay.

wet suit *n.* a close-fitting rubber suit used by skin divers, yachtsmen, etc., to retain body heat when they are immersed in water or sailing in cold weather.

Wet+ter+horn (*German* 'vɛtər,hɔrn) *n.* a mountain in S Switzerland, in the Bernese Alps. Height: 3701 m (12 143 ft.).

wet+ting a·gent *n. Chem.* any substance added to a liquid to lower its surface tension and thus increase its ability to spread across or penetrate into a solid.

W.E.U. *abbrev. for* Western European Union.

we've (wi:v) *contraction of* we have.

Wex+ford ('wɛksfəd) *n.* **1.** a county of SE Ireland, in Leinster province on the Irish Sea: the first Irish county to be colonized from England; mostly low-lying and fertile. County town: Wexford. Pop.: 86 351 (1971). Area: 2352 sq. km (908 sq. miles). **2.** a port in SE Ireland, county town of Co. Wexford: sacked by Oliver Cromwell in 1649. Pop.: 13 293 (1971).

Wey+mouth ('weɪməθ) *n.* a port and resort in S England, in Dorset on the English Channel: administratively part of the borough of **Weymouth and Melcombe Regis.** Pop. (with Melcombe Regis): 42 332 (1971).

w.f. *Printing. abbrev. for* wrong fount.

W.F.T.U. *abbrev. for* World Federation of Trade Unions.

WG *international car registration for* (Windward Islands) Grenada.

w.g. *or* **W.G.** *abbrev. for:* **1.** water gauge. **2.** wire gauge.

wh *or* **wh.** *abbrev. for* white.

whack (wæk) *vb.* (*tr.*) **1.** to strike with a sharp resounding blow. **2.** (*usually passive*) *Brit. informal.* to exhaust completely. ~*n.* **3.** a sharp resounding blow or the noise made by such a blow. **4.** *Informal.* a share or portion. **5.** *Informal.* a try or attempt (esp. in the phrase **have a whack at**). ~*interj.* **6.** an exclamation imitating the noise of a sharp resounding blow. [C18: perhaps a variant of THWACK, ultimately of imitative origin] —**'whack+er** *n.*

whack+ing ('wækɪŋ) *Informal, chiefly Brit.* ~*adj.* **1.** enormous. ~*adv.* **2.** (intensifier): *a whacking big lie.*

whack·o ('wækəʊ) *interj. Slang.* an exclamation of happiness, delight, etc. [C20: from WHACK]

whack off *vb.* (*intr., adv*) *Taboo slang.* to masturbate.

whack·y ('wækɪ) *adj.* **whack·i+er, whack·i+est.** *U.S. informal.* a variant spelling of **wacky.**

whale[1] (weɪl) *n., pl.* **whales** *or* **whale. 1.** any of the larger cetacean mammals, excluding dolphins, porpoises, and narwhals. They have flippers, a streamlined body, and a horizontally flattened tail and breathe through a blowhole on the top of the head. **2.** any cetacean mammal. See also **toothed whale, whalebone whale. 3. a whale of a.** *Informal.* an exceptionally large, fine, etc., example of a (person or thing): *we had a whale of a time on holiday.* [Old English *hwæl;* related to Old Saxon, Old High German *hwal,* Old Norse *hvalr,* Latin *squalus* seapig]

whale[2] (weɪl) *vb.* (*tr.*) to beat or thrash soundly. [C18: variant of WALE[1]]

whale+boat ('weɪl,bəʊt) *n.* a narrow boat from 20 to 30 feet long having a sharp prow and stern, formerly used in whaling. Also called: **whaler.**

whale+bone ('weɪl,bəʊn) *n.* **1.** Also called: **baleen.** a horny elastic material forming a series of numerous thin plates that hang from the upper jaw on either side of the palate in the toothless (whalebone) whales and strain plankton from water entering the mouth. **2.** a thin strip of this substance, used in stiffening corsets, bodices, etc.

whale+bone whale *n.* any whale belonging to the cetacean suborder *Mysticeti,* having a double blowhole and strips of whalebone between the jaws instead of teeth: includes the rorquals, right whales, and the blue whale. Compare **toothed whale.**

whale catch+er *n.* a vessel engaged in the actual harpooning of whales.

whal+er ('weɪlə) *n.* **1.** Also called (U.S.): **whale+man.** a person employed in whaling. **2.** a vessel engaged in whaling. See **factory ship, whale catcher. 3.** another word for **whaleboat. 4.** *Austral.* a nomad surviving in the bush without working.

whale shark *n.* a large spotted whalelike shark, *Rhincodon typus,* of warm seas, that feeds on plankton and small animals: family *Rhincodontidae.*

whal+ing ('weɪlɪŋ) *n.* **1.** the work or industry of hunting and processing whales for food, oil, etc. ~*adv.* **2.** *Informal.* (intensifier): *a whaling good time.*

wham (wæm) *n.* **1.** a forceful blow or impact or the sound produced by such a blow or impact. ~*interj.* **2.** an exclamation imitative of this sound. ~*vb.* **whams, wham+ming, whammed. 3.** to strike or cause to strike with great force. [C20: of imitative origin]

whang[1] (wæŋ) *vb.* **1.** to strike or be struck so as to cause a resounding noise. ~*n.* **2.** the resounding noise produced by a heavy blow. **3.** a heavy blow. [C19: of imitative origin]
whang[2] (wæŋ) *n.* **1.** a leather thong. ~*vb.* **2.** (*tr.*) to strike with or as if with a thong. [C17: variant of THONG]
Whan·ga·rei (ˌwɑːŋɑːˈreɪ) *n.* a port in New Zealand, the northernmost city of North Island: oil refinery. Pop.: 30 746 (1971).
whang·ee (wæŋˈiː) *n.* **1.** any tall woody grass of the S and SE Asian genus *Phyllostachys,* grown for its stems, which are used for bamboo canes and as a source of paper pulp. **2.** a cane or walking stick made from the stem of any of these plants. [C19: probably from Chinese (Mandarin) *huangli,* from *huang* yellow + *li* bamboo cane]
whap (wɒp) *vb.* **whaps, whap·ping, whapped,** *n.* a less common spelling of **whop.**
whare (ˈwɒrɪ) *n.* a Maori hut or dwelling place. [from Maori]
wharf (wɔːf) *n., pl.* **wharves** (wɔːvz) *or* **wharfs. 1.** a platform of timber, stone, concrete, etc., at a harbour or navigable river for the docking, loading, and unloading of ships. **2.** an obsolete word for **shore.** ~*vb.* (*tr.*) **3.** to moor or dock at a wharf. **4.** to provide or equip with a wharf or wharves. **5.** to store or unload on a wharf. [Old English *hwearf* heap; related to Old Saxon *hwarf,* Old High German *hwarb* a turn, Old Norse *hvarf* circle]
wharf·age (ˈwɔːfɪdʒ) *n.* **1.** accommodation for ships at wharves. **2.** a charge for use of a wharf. **3.** wharves collectively.
wharf·ie (ˈwɔːfɪ) *n. Austral.* a wharf labourer; docker.
wharf·in·ger (ˈwɔːfɪndʒə) *n.* an owner or manager of a wharf. [C16: probably alteration of *wharfager* (see WHARFAGE, -ER[1]); compare HARBINGER]
wharf rat *n.* **1.** any rat, usually a brown rat, that infests wharves. **2.** *Informal.* a person who haunts wharves, usually for dishonest purposes.
wharve (wɔːv) *n.* a wooden disc or wheel on a shaft serving as a flywheel or pulley. [Old English *hweorfa,* from *hweorfan* to revolve; related to Old Saxon *hwervo* axis, Old High German *hwerbo* a turn]
what (wɒt; *unstressed* wət) *determiner.* **1. a.** used with a noun in requesting further information about the identity or categorization of something: *what job does he do?* **b.** (*as pronoun*): *what is her address?* **c.** (*used in indirect questions*): *does he know what man did this? tell me what he said.* **2. a.** the (person, thing, persons, or things) that: *we photographed what animals we could see.* **b.** (*as pronoun*): *bring me what you've written; come what may.* **3.** (intensifier; used in exclamations): *what a good book!* ~*adv.* **4.** in what respect? to what degree?: *what do you care?* ~*pron.* **5.** *Not standard.* which, who, or that, when used as relative pronouns: *this is the man what I saw in the park yesterday.* **6. what about.** what do you think, know, feel, etc., concerning? **7. a.** for what purpose? why? **b.** *Informal.* a punishment (esp. in the phrase **give (a person) what for). 8. what have you.** someone, something, or somewhere unknown or unspecified: *cars, motorcycles, or what have you.* **9. what if. a.** what would happen if? **b.** what difference would it make if? **10. what matter.** what does it matter? **11. what's what.** *Informal.* the true or real state of affairs. ~*interj.* **12.** *Informal.* don't you think? don't you agree?: *splendid party, what?* [Old English *hwæt;* related to Old Frisian *whet,* Old High German *hwaz* (German *was*), Old Norse *hvatr*]
what·ev·er (wɒtˈɛvə, wət-) *pron.* **1.** everything or anything that: *do whatever he asks you to.* **2.** no matter what: *whatever he does, he is forgiven.* **3.** *Informal.* an unknown or unspecified thing or things: *take a hammer, chisel, or whatever.* **4.** an intensive form of *what,* used in questions: *whatever can he have said to upset her so much?* ~*determiner.* **5.** an intensive form of *what: use whatever tools you can get hold of.* ~*adj.* **6.** (*postpositive*) absolutely; whatsoever: *I saw no point whatever in continuing.*
what·not (ˈwɒtˌnɒt) *n.* **1.** Also called: **what-d'you-call-it.** *Informal.* a person or thing the name of which is unknown, temporarily forgotten, or deliberately overlooked. **2.** *Informal.* unspecified assorted material. **3.** a portable stand with shelves, used for displaying ornaments, etc.
what·sit (ˈwɒtsɪt), **whats·its·name,** (*masc.*) **whats·his·name,** *or* (*fem.*) **whats·her·name** *n. Informal.* a person or thing the name of which is unknown, temporarily forgotten, or deliberately overlooked.
what·so·ev·er (ˌwɒtsəʊˈɛvə) *adj.* **1.** (*postpositive*) at all: used as an intensifier with indefinite pronouns and determiners such as *none, any, no one, anybody,* etc. ~*pron.* **2.** an archaic word for **whatever.**
whaup (wɔːp) *n. Chiefly Scot.* a popular name for the **curlew.** [C16: related to Old English *huilpe,* ultimately imitative of the bird's cry; compare Low German *regenwilp* sandpiper]
wheal (wiːl) *n.* a variant spelling of **weal**[1].
wheat (wiːt) *n.* **1.** any annual or biennial grass of the genus *Triticum,* native to the Mediterranean region and W Asia but widely cultivated, having erect flower spikes and light brown grains. **2.** the grain of any of these grasses, used in making flour, pasta, etc. ~See also **emmer, durum.** [Old English *hwǣte,* related to Old Frisian, Old Saxon *hwēti,* Old High German *hweizi,* Old Norse *hveiti;* see WHITE]
wheat·ear (ˈwiːtˌɪə) *n.* any small northern songbird of the genus *Oenanthe,* esp. *O. oenanthe,* a species having a pale grey back, black wings and tail, white rump, and pale brown underparts: subfamily *Turdinae* (thrushes). [C16: back formation from *wheatears* (wrongly taken as plural), probably from WHITE + ARSE; compare Dutch *witstaart,* French *culblanc* white tail]
wheat·en (ˈwiːtᵊn) *adj.* **1.** made of the grain or flour of wheat: *wheaten bread.* **2.** of a pale yellow colour.
wheat germ *n.* the vitamin-rich embryo of the wheat kernel, which is largely removed before milling and is used in cereals, as a food supplement, etc.
wheat rust *n.* **1.** a rust fungus, *Puccinia graminis,* that attacks cereals, esp. wheat, and the barberry. **2.** the disease caused by this fungus.
Wheat·stone bridge (ˈwiːtstən) *n.* a device for measuring an unknown resistance. The unknown resistance and three known resistances are connected into a loop with a current detector connected across two opposite junctions. The other two junctions are connected to a battery and the three known resistors adjusted until the detector registers no current. [C19: named after Sir Charles *Wheatstone* (1802–75), English physicist and inventor]
wheat·worm (ˈwiːtˌwɜːm) *n.* a parasitic nematode worm, *Anguina tritici,* that forms galls in the seeds of wheat.
whee (wiː) *interj.* an exclamation of joy, thrill, etc.
whee·dle (ˈwiːdᵊl) *vb.* **1.** to persuade or try to persuade (someone) by coaxing words, flattery, etc. **2.** (*tr.*) to obtain by coaxing and flattery: *she wheedled some money out of her father.* [C17: perhaps from German *wedeln* to wag one's tail, from Old High German *wedil, wadil* tail] —**ˈwhee·dler** *n.* —**ˈwhee·dling·ly** *adv.*
wheel (wiːl) *n.* **1.** a solid disc, or a circular rim joined to a hub by radial or tangential spokes, that is mounted on a shaft about which it can turn, as in vehicles and machines. **2.** anything like a wheel in shape or function. **3.** a device consisting of or resembling a wheel or having a wheel as its principal component: *a steering wheel; a water wheel.* **4.** (usually preceded by *the*) a medieval torture consisting of a wheel to which the victim was tied and then had his limbs struck and broken by an iron bar. **5.** short for **wheel of fortune** or **potter's wheel. 6.** the act of turning. **7.** a pivoting movement of troops, ships, etc. **8.** a type of firework coiled to make it rotate when let off. **9.** a set of short rhyming lines, usually four or five in number, forming the concluding part of a stanza. Compare **bob**[2] (sense 7). 10. the disc in which the ball is spun in roulette. **11.** *U.S.* an informal word for **bicycle. 12.** *Archaic.* a refrain. **13.** *Informal, chiefly U.S.* a person of great influence (esp. in the phrase **big wheel). 14. at the wheel. a.** driving or steering a vehicle or vessel. **b.** in charge. ~*vb.* **15.** to turn or cause to turn on or as if on an axis. **16.** to move or cause to move on or as if on wheels; roll. **17.** (*tr.*) to perform with or in a circular movement. **18.** (*tr.*) to provide with a wheel or wheels. **19.** (*intr.;* often foll. by *about*) to change one's mind or opinion. **20. wheel and deal.** *Informal, chiefly U.S.* to be a free agent, esp. to advance one's own interests. [Old English *hweol, hweowol;* related to Old Norse *hvēl,* Greek *kuklos,* Middle Low German *wēl,* Dutch *wiel*] —**ˈwheel·less** *adj.*
wheel and ax·le *n.* a simple machine for raising weights in which a rope unwinding from a wheel is wound onto a cylindrical drum or shaft coaxial with or joined to the wheel to provide mechanical advantage.
wheel an·i·mal·cule *n.* another name for **rotifer.**
wheel·bar·row (ˈwiːlˌbærəʊ) *n.* **1.** a simple vehicle for carrying small loads, typically being an open container supported by a wheel at the front and two legs behind. ~*vb.* **2.** (*tr.*) to convey in a wheelbarrow.
wheel·base (ˈwiːlˌbeɪs) *n.* the distance between the front and back axles of a motor vehicle.
wheel bug *n.* a large predatory North American heteropterous insect, *Arilus cristatus,* having a semicircular thoracic projection: family *Reduviidae* (assassin bugs).
wheel·chair (ˈwiːlˌtʃɛə) *n. Med.* a special chair mounted on large wheels, for use by invalids or others for whom walking is impossible or temporarily inadvisable.
wheeled (wiːld) *adj.* **a.** having or equipped with a wheel or wheels. **b.** (*in combination*): *four-wheeled.*
wheel·er (ˈwiːlə) *n.* **1.** Also called: **wheel horse.** a horse or other draught animal nearest the wheel. **2.** (*in combination*) something equipped with a specified sort or number of wheels: *a three-wheeler.* **3.** a person or thing that wheels.
Whee·ler (ˈwiːlə) *n.* Sir (**Robert Eric**) **Mor·ti·mer.** 1890–1976, Scottish archaeologist, who did much to increase public interest in archaeology. He is noted esp. for his excavations at Mohenjo-Daro and Harappa in the Indus Valley and at Maiden Castle in Dorset.
wheel·er-deal·er *n. Informal, chiefly U.S.* a person who wheels and deals.
wheel horse *n.* **1.** another word for **wheeler. 2.** *U.S.* a person who works steadily or hard.
wheel·house (ˈwiːlˌhaʊs) *n.* another term for **pilot house.**
wheel·ie (ˈwiːlɪ) *n., pl.* **·ies.** *Skateboarding.* a manoeuvre in which either the front or back pair of wheels is raised off the ground.
wheel lock *n.* **1.** a gunlock formerly in use in which the firing mechanism was activated by sparks produced by friction between a small steel wheel and a flint. **2.** a gun having such a lock.
wheel man *n.* **1.** a cyclist. **2.** Also called: **wheelsman.** *U.S.* a helmsman.
wheel of for·tune *n.* (in mythology and literature) a revolving device spun by a deity of fate selecting random changes in the affairs of man. Often shortened to **wheel.**
wheels (wiːlz) *pl. n.* **1.** the main directing force behind an organization, movement, etc.: *the wheels of government.* **2.** an

informal word for **car.** **3. wheels within wheels.** a series of intricately connected events, plots, etc.

wheel win+dow *n.* another name for **rose window.**

wheel+work ('wi:l,wɜ:k) *n.* an arrangement of wheels in a machine, esp. a train of gears.

wheel+wright ('wi:l,raɪt) *n.* a person who makes or mends wheels as a trade.

wheen (wi:n) *determiner.* a northern Brit. dialect word for **few** or **some.** [Old English *hwēne,* instrumental of *hwōn* few, a few]

wheeze (wi:z) *vb.* **1.** to breathe or utter (something) with a rasping or whistling sound. **2.** to make or move with a noise suggestive of wheezy breathing. *~n.* **3.** a husky, rasping, or whistling sound or breathing. **4.** *Brit. slang.* a trick, idea, or plan (esp. in the phrase **good wheeze**). **5.** *Informal.* a hackneyed joke or anecdote. [C15: probably from Old Norse *hvǣsa* to hiss] —**'wheez+er** *n.* —**'wheez+ing+ly** *adv.* —**'wheez·y** *adj.* —**'wheez·i+ly** *adv.* —**'wheez·i+ness** *n.*

whelk[1] (wɛlk) *n.* any carnivorous marine gastropod mollusc of the family *Buccinidae,* of coastal waters and intertidal regions, having a strong snail-like shell. [Old English *weoloc;* related to Middle Dutch *willok,* Old Norse *vil* entrails]

whelk[2] (wɛlk) *n.* a raised lesion on the skin; wheal. [Old English *hwylca,* of obscure origin] —**'whelk·y** *adj.*

whelm (wɛlm) *vb. (tr.) Archaic.* **1.** to engulf entirely with or as if with water. **2.** another word for **overwhelm.** [C13: *whelmen* to turn over, of uncertain origin]

whelp (wɛlp) *n.* **1.** a young offspring of certain animals, esp. of a wolf or dog. **2.** *Disparaging.* a young man or youth. **3.** *Jocular.* a young child. **4.** *Nautical.* any of the ridges, parallel to the axis, on the drum of a capstan to keep a rope, cable, or chain from slipping. *~vb.* **5.** (of an animal or, disparagingly, a woman) to give birth to (young). [Old English *hwelp(a);* related to Old High German *hwelf,* Old Norse *hvelpr,* Danish *hvalp*]

when (wɛn) *adv.* **1. a.** at what time? over what period?: *when is he due?* **b.** (*used in indirect questions*): *ask him when he's due.* **2. say when.** to state when an action is to be stopped or begun, as when someone is pouring a drink. *~conj.* **3.** (*subordinating*) at a time at which; at the time at which; just as; after: *I found it easily when I started to look seriously.* **4.** although: *he drives when he might walk.* **5.** considering the fact that: *how did you pass the exam when you'd not worked for it?* *~pron.* **6.** at which (time); over which (period): *an age when men were men.* *~n.* **7.** (*usually pl.*) a question as to the time of some occurrence. [Old English *hwanne, hwænne;* related to Old High German *hwanne, hwenne,* Latin *cum*]

Usage. Care should be taken so that *when* and *where* refer explicitly to time or place, and are not used loosely to substitute for *in which* after the verb *to be: paralysis is a condition in which* (not *when* or *where*) *parts of the body cannot be moved.*

when+as (wɛn'æz) *conj.* **1.** *Archaic.* **a.** when; whenever. **b.** inasmuch as; while. **2.** *Obsolete.* whereas; although.

whence (wɛns) *Archaic or formal.* *~adv.* **1.** from what place, cause or origin? *~pron.* **2.** (*subordinating*) from what place, cause, or origin. [C13 *whannes,* adverbial genitive of Old English *hwanon;* related to Old Frisian *hwana,* Old High German *hwanan*]

Usage. Careful users of English avoid the expression *from whence,* since *whence* already means from which place: *the tradition whence* (not *from whence*) *such ideas flow.*

whence+so+ev·er (,wɛnssəʊ'ɛvə) *conj.* (*subordinating*), *adv. Archaic.* out of whatsoever place, cause, or origin.

when·e'er (wɛn'ɛə) *adv., conj.* a poetic contraction of **whenever.**

when+ev·er (wɛn'ɛvə) *conj.* **1.** (*subordinating*) at every or any time that; when: *I laugh whenever I see that.* *~adv.* also **when ev·er. 2.** no matter when: *it'll be here, whenever you decide to come for it.* **3.** *Informal.* at an unknown or unspecified time: *I'll take it if it comes today, tomorrow, or whenever.* **4.** an intensive form of *when,* used in questions: *whenever did he escape?*

when+so+ev·er (,wɛnsəʊ'ɛvə) *conj., adv. Rare.* an intensive form of **whenever.**

where (wɛə) *adv.* **1. a.** in, at, or to what place, point, or position?: *where are you going?* **b.** (*used in indirect questions*): *I don't know where they are.* *~pron.* **2.** in, at, or to which (place): *the hotel where we spent our honeymoon.* *~conj.* **3.** (*subordinating*) in the place at which: *where we live it's always raining.* *~n.* **4.** (*usually pl.*) a question as to the position, direction, or destination of something. [Old English *hwǣr, hwār(a);* related to Old Frisian *hwēr,* Old Saxon, Old High German *hwār,* Old Norse, Gothic *hvar*]

Usage. See at **when.**

where+a·bouts ('wɛərə,baʊts) *adv.* **1.** Also: **whereabout.** at what approximate location or place; where: *whereabouts are you?* **2.** *Obsolete.* about or concerning which. *~n.* **3.** (*functioning as sing.*) the place, esp. the approximate place, where a person or thing is.

where+af·ter ('wɛər,ɑ:ftə) *Archaic or formal. sentence connector.* after which.

where+as (wɛər'æz) *conj.* **1.** (*coordinating*) but on the other hand: *I like to go swimming whereas Sheila likes to sail.* *~sentence connector.* **2.** (in formal documents to begin sentences) it being the case that; since.

where+at (wɛər'æt) *Archaic.* *~adv.* **1.** at or to which place. *~sentence connector.* **2.** upon which occasion.

where+by (wɛə'baɪ) *pron.* **1.** by or because of which: *the means whereby he took his life.* *~adv.* **2.** *Archaic.* how? by what means?: *whereby does he recognize me?*

wher·e'er (wɛər'ɛə) *adv., conj.* a poetic contraction of **wherever.**

where+fore ('wɛə,fɔ:) *n.* **1.** (*usually pl.*) an explanation or reason (esp. in the phrase **the whys and wherefores**). *~adv.* **2.** *Archaic.* for what reason? why? *~sentence connector.* **3.** *Archaic or formal.* for which reason: used as an introductory word in legal preambles.

where+from (wɛə'frɒm) *Archaic.* *~adv.* **1.** from what or where? whence? *~pron.* **2.** from which place; whence.

where+in (wɛər'ɪn) *Archaic or formal.* *~adv.* **1.** in what place or respect? *~pron.* **2.** in which place, thing, etc.

where+in·to (wɛər'ɪntu:) *Archaic.* *~adv.* **1.** into what place? *~pron.* **2.** into which place.

where+of (wɛər'ɒv) *Archaic or formal.* *~adv.* **1.** of what or which person or thing? *~pron.* **2.** of which (person or thing): *the man whereof I speak is no longer alive.*

where+on (wɛər'ɒn) *Archaic.* *~adv.* **1.** on what thing or place? *~pron.* **2.** on which thing, place, etc.

where+so+ev·er (,wɛəsəʊ'ɛvə) *conj.* (*subordinating*), *adv., pron. Rare.* an intensive form of **wherever.**

where+to (wɛə'tu:) *Archaic or formal. adv.* **1.** towards what (place, end, etc.)? *~pron.* **2.** to which. *~*Also (archaic): **whereunto.**

where+u·pon (,wɛərə'pɒn) **1.** *sentence connector.* at which; at which point; upon which. *~adv.* **2.** *Archaic.* upon what?

wher+ev·er (wɛər'ɛvə) *pron.* **1.** at, in, or to every place or point which; where: *wherever she went, he would be there.* *~conj.* **2.** (*subordinating*) in, to, or at whatever place: *wherever we go the weather is always bad.* *~adv.* also **where ev·er. 3.** no matter where: *I'll find you, wherever you are.* **4.** *Informal.* at, in, or to an unknown or unspecified place: *I'll go anywhere to escape: London, Paris, or wherever.* **5.** an intensive form of *where,* used in questions: *wherever can they be?*

where+with (wɛə'wɪθ, -'wɪð) *Archaic or formal.* *~pron.* **1.** (*often foll. by an infinitive*) with or by which: *the pen wherewith I am wont to write.* **2.** something with which: *I have not wherewith to buy my bread.* *~adv.* **3.** with what? *~sentence connector.* **4.** with or after that; whereupon.

where+with+al *n.* ('wɛəwɪð,ɔ:l). **1. the wherewithal.** necessary funds, resources, or equipment (for something or to do something): *these people lack the wherewithal for a decent existence.* *~pron.* (,wɛəwɪð'ɔ:l). **2.** a less common word for **wherewith** (senses 1, 2).

wher+rit[1] ('wɛrɪt) *vb.* **1.** to worry or cause to worry. **2.** (*intr.*) to complain or moan. [perhaps from *thwert,* obsolete variant of THWART; compare WORRIT]

wher+rit[2] ('wɛrɪt) *Northern Brit. dialect.* *~vb.* **1.** (*tr.*) to strike (someone) a blow. *~n.* **2.** a blow, esp. a slap on the face; stroke. [probably of imitative origin]

wher+ry ('wɛrɪ) *n., pl.* **+ries. 1.** any of certain kinds of half-decked commercial boats, such as barges, used in Britain. **2.** a light rowing boat used in inland waters and harbours. [C15: origin unknown] —**'wher·ry+man** *n.*

whet (wɛt) *vb.* **whets, whet+ting, whet+ted.** (*tr.*) **1.** to sharpen, as by grinding or friction. **2.** to increase or enhance (the appetite, desire, etc.); stimulate. *~n.* **3.** the act of whetting. **4.** a person or thing that whets. [Old English *hwettan;* related to *hvæt* sharp, Old High German *hwezzen,* Old Norse *hvetja,* Gothic *hvatjan*] —**'whet+ter** *n.*

wheth+er ('wɛðə) *conj.* **1.** (*subordinating*) used to introduce an indirect question or a clause after a verb expressing or implying doubt or choice in order to indicate two or more alternatives, the second or last of which is introduced by *or* or *or whether: he doesn't know whether she's in Britain or whether she's gone to France.* **2.** (*subordinating;* often foll. by *or not*) used to introduce any indirect question: *he was not certain whether his friend was there or not.* **3.** (*coordinating*) another word for **either** (sense 3): *any man, whether liberal or conservative, would agree with me.* **4.** (*coordinating*) *Archaic.* used to introduce a direct question consisting of two alternatives, the second of which is introduced by *or* or *or whether: whether does he live at home or abroad.* **5. whether or no. a.** used as a conjunction as a variant of **whether** (sense 1). **b.** under any circumstances: *he will be here tomorrow, whether or no.* **6. whether...or (whether).** if on the one hand...or even if on the other hand: *you'll eat that, whether you like it or not.* *~determiner, pron.* **7.** *Obsolete.* which (of two): used in direct or indirect questions. [Old English *hwæther, hwether;* related to Old Frisian *hweder, hoder,* Old High German *hwedar,* Old Norse *hvatharr, hvarr,* Gothic *hwathar*]

whet+stone ('wɛt,stəʊn) *n.* **1.** a stone used for sharpening edged tools, knives, etc. **2.** something that sharpens.

whew (hwju:) *interj.* an exclamation or sharply exhaled breath expressing relief, surprise, delight, etc.

whey (weɪ) *n.* the watery liquid that separates from the curd when the milk is clotted, as in making cheese. [Old English *hwæg;* related to Middle Low German *wei, heie,* Dutch *hui*] —**'whey+ey, 'whey+ish,** *or* **'whey+,like** *adj.*

whey+face ('weɪ,feɪs) *n.* **1.** a pale bloodless face. **2.** a person with such a face. —**'whey+,faced** *adj.*

whf. *abbrev. for* wharf.

which (wɪtʃ) *determiner.* **1. a.** used with a noun in requesting that its referent be further specified, identified, or distinguished from the other members of a class: *which house did you want to buy?* **b.** (*as pronoun*): *which did you find?* **c.** (*used in indirect questions*): *I wondered which apples were cheaper.* **2. a.** whatever of a class; whichever: *bring which car you want.* **b.** (*as pronoun*): *choose which of the cars suits you.* *~pron.* **3.** used in relative clauses with inanimate antecedents: *the house,* *which is old, is in poor repair.* **4.** as; and that: used in relative clauses with verb phrases or sentences as their antecedents: *he died of cancer, which is what I predicted.* **5. the which.** *Archaic.* a longer form of **which,** often used as a sentence connector. [Old English *hwelc, hwilc;* related to Old High German *hwelīh* (German *welch*), Old Norse *hvelīkr*, Gothic *hvileiks*, Latin *quis, quid*]

Usage. See at **that.**

which·ev·er (wɪtʃˈɛvə) *determiner.* **1. a.** any (one, two, etc., out of several): *take whichever car you like.* **b.** (*as pronoun*): *choose whichever appeals to you.* **2. a.** no matter which (one or ones): *whichever card you pick you'll still be making a mistake.* **b.** (*as pronoun*): *it won't make any difference, whichever comes first.*

which·so·ev·er (ˌwɪtʃsəʊˈɛvə) *pron.* an archaic or formal word for **whichever.**

whick·er (ˈwɪkə) *vb.* (of a horse) to whinny or neigh; nicker. [C17: of imitative origin]

whid·ah (ˈwɪdə) *n.* a variant spelling of **whydah.**

whiff[1] (wɪf) *n.* **1.** a passing odour. **2.** a brief gentle gust of air. **3.** a single inhalation or exhalation from the mouth or nose. ~*vb.* **4.** to come, convey, or go in whiffs; puff or waft. **5.** to take in or breathe out (tobacco smoke, air, etc.). **6.** (*tr.*) to sniff or smell. **7.** (*intr.*) *Brit. slang.* to have an unpleasant smell; stink. [C16: of imitative origin] —ˈ**whiff·er** *n.*

whiff[2] (wɪf) *n. Chiefly Brit.* a narrow clinker-built skiff having outriggers, for one oarsman. [C19: special use of WHIFF[1]]

whif·fle (ˈwɪfᵊl) *vb.* **1.** (*intr.*) to think or behave in an erratic or unpredictable way. **2.** to blow or be blown fitfully or in gusts. **3.** (*intr.*) to whistle softly. [C16: frequentative of WHIFF[1]]

whif·fler[1] (ˈwɪflə) *n.* a person who whiffles.

whif·fler[2] (ˈwɪflə) *n. Archaic.* an attendant who cleared the way for a procession. [C16: from *wifle* battle-axe, from Old English *wifel,* of Germanic origin; the attendants originally carried weapons to clear the way]

whif·fle·tree (ˈwɪfᵊlˌtriː) *n.* a crossbar in a horse's harness to which the ends of the traces are attached. Also called: **whipple-tree, swingletree.**

Whig (wɪg) *n.* **1.** a member of the English political party or grouping that opposed the succession to the throne of James, Duke of York (1679–80), on the grounds that he was a Catholic. Standing for a limited monarchy, the Whigs represented the great aristocracy and the moneyed middle class for the next 80 years. In the late 18th and early 19th centuries the Whigs represented the desires of industrialists and Dissenters for political and social reform. The Whigs provided the core of the Liberal Party. **2.** (in the U.S.) a supporter of the War of American Independence. Compare **Tory. 3.** a member of the American political party that opposed the Democrats from about 1834 to 1855 and represented propertied and professional interests. **4.** a conservative member of the Liberal Party in Great Britain. **5.** a person who advocates and believes in an unrestricted laissez-faire economy. **6.** *History.* a Scottish Presbyterian, esp. one in rebellion against the Crown. ~*adj.* **7.** of, characteristic of, or relating to Whigs. [C17: probably shortened from *whiggamore,* one of a group of 17th-century Scottish rebels who joined in an attack on Edinburgh known as *the whiggamore raid;* probably from Scottish *whig* to drive (of obscure origin) + *more, mer, maire* horse, MARE] —ˈ**Whig·ger·y** *or* ˈ**Whig·gism** *n.* —ˈ**Whig·gish** *adj.* —ˈ**Whig·gish·ly** *adv.* —ˈ**Whig·gish·ness** *n.*

while (waɪl) *conj. also* **whilst** (waɪlst). **1.** (*subordinating*) at the same time that: *please light the fire while I'm cooking.* **2.** (*subordinating*) all the time that: *I stay inside while it's raining.* **3.** (*subordinating*) in spite of the fact that: *while I agree about his brilliance I still think he's rude.* **4.** (*coordinating*) whereas; and in contrast: *flats are expensive, while houses are cheap.* ~*prep.* **5.** (*used with a gerund*) during the activity of: *while walking I often whistle.* ~*prep., conj.* **6.** *Northern Brit. dialect.* another word for **until:** *you'll have to wait while Monday for these sheets; you'll never make any progress while you listen to me.* ~*n.* **7.** (*usually used in adverbial phrases*) a period or interval of time: *once in a long while.* **8.** trouble or time (esp. in the phrase **worth one's while**): *it's hardly worth your while to begin work today.* **9. the while.** at that time: *he was working the while.* [Old English *hwīl;* related to Old High German *hwīla* (German *Weile*), Gothic *hveila*, Latin *quiēs* peace, *tranquīlus* TRANQUIL]

Usage. The main sense of *while* is *during the time that.* However, many careful users of English would now accept as established the use of *while* to mean *although: while he disliked working, he was obliged to do so.* In careful usage, *while* is not used to mean *whereas* or *and: he thought that they were in Paris, whereas* (not *while*) *they had gone on to Rome; his friends went to Paris for their holiday, his brother to Rome, and* (not *while*) *his parents went to Berlin.* Careful writers try to avoid any ambiguity that may result from the possibility of two interpretations of *while* in context: *while* (*although* or *during the time that*) *his brother worked in the park, he refused to do any gardening at home.*

while a·way *vb.* (*tr., adv.*) to pass (time) idly and usually pleasantly.

whiles (waɪlz) *Archaic or dialect.* ~*adv.* **1.** at times; occasionally. ~*conj.* **2.** while; whilst.

whi·lom (ˈwaɪləm) *Archaic.* ~*adv.* **1.** formerly; once. ~*adj.* **2.** (*prenominal*) one-time; former. [Old English *hwīlum,* dative plural of *hwīl* WHILE; related to Old High German *hwīlōm,* German *weiland* of old]

whilst (waɪlst) *conj. Chiefly Brit.* another word for **while** (senses 1–4). [C13: from WHILES + *-t* as in *amidst*]

whim (wɪm) *n.* **1.** Also called: **whim-wham.** a sudden, passing, and often fanciful idea; impulsive or irrational thought. **2.** a horse-drawn winch formerly used in mining to lift ore or water. [C17: from C16 *whim-wham,* of unknown origin]

whim·brel (ˈwɪmbrəl) *n.* a small European curlew, *Numenius phaeopus,* with a striped head. [C16: from dialect *whimp* or from WHIMPER, alluding to its cry]

whim·per (ˈwɪmpə) *vb.* **1.** (*intr.*) to cry, sob, or whine softly or intermittently. **2.** to complain or say (something) in a whining plaintive way. ~*n.* **3.** a soft plaintive whine. [C16: from dialect *whimp,* of imitative origin] —ˈ**whim·per·er** *n.* —ˈ**whim·per·ing** *n.* —ˈ**whim·per·ing·ly** *adv.*

whim·si·cal (ˈwɪmzɪkᵊl) *adj.* **1.** spontaneously fanciful or playful. **2.** given to whims; capricious. **3.** quaint, unusual, or fantastic. —**whim·si·cal·i·ty** (ˌwɪmzɪˈkælɪtɪ) *n.* —ˈ**whim·si·cal·ly** *adv.* —ˈ**whim·si·cal·ness** *n.*

whim·sy *or* **whim·sey** (ˈwɪmzɪ) *n., pl.* **·sies** *or* **·seys. 1.** a capricious idea or notion. **2.** light or fanciful humour. **3.** something quaint or unusual. ~*adj.* **·si·er, ·si·est. 4.** quaint, comical, or unusual, often in a tasteless way. [C17: from WHIM; compare FLIMSY]

whin[1] (wɪn) *n.* another name for **gorse.** [C11: from Scandinavian; compare Old Danish *hvine* (*græs*), Norwegian *hvine,* Swedish *hven*]

whin[2] (wɪn) *n.* short for **whinstone.** [C14 *quin,* of obscure origin]

whin·chat (ˈwɪnˌtʃæt) *n.* an Old World songbird, *Saxicola rubetra,* having a mottled brown-and-white plumage with pale cream underparts: subfamily *Turdinae* (thrushes). [C17: from WHIN[1] + CHAT]

whine (waɪn) *n.* **1.** a long high-pitched plaintive cry or moan. **2.** a continuous high-pitched sound. **3.** a peevish complaint, esp. one repeated. ~*vb.* **4.** to make a whine or utter in a whine. [Old English *hwīnan;* related to Old Norse *hvīna,* Swedish *hvija* to scream] —ˈ**whin·er** *n.* —ˈ**whin·ing·ly** *adv.* —ˈ**whin·y** *adj.*

whinge (wɪndʒ) *vb.* (*intr.*) *Informal.* **1.** to cry in a fretful way. **2.** to complain. ~*n.* **3.** a complaint. [from a Northern variant of Old English *hwinsian* to whine; related to Old High German *winsan, winisan,* whence Middle High German *winsen*]

whin·ny (ˈwɪnɪ) *vb.* **·nies, ·ny·ing, ·nied.** (*intr.*) **1.** (of a horse) to neigh softly or gently. **2.** to make a sound resembling a neigh, such as a laugh. ~*n., pl.* **·nies. 3.** a gentle or low-pitched neigh. [C16: of imitative origin]

whin·stone (ˈwɪnˌstəʊn) *n.* any dark hard fine-grained rock, such as basalt. [C16: from WHIN[2] + STONE]

whip (wɪp) *vb.* **whips, whip·ping, whipped. 1.** to strike (a person or thing) with several strokes of a strap, rod, etc. **2.** (*tr.*) to punish by striking in this manner. **3.** (*tr.;* foll. by *out, away,* etc.) to pull, remove, etc., with sudden rapid motion: *to whip out a gun.* **4.** (*intr.,* foll. by *down, into, out of,* etc.) *Informal.* to come, go, etc., in a rapid sudden manner: *they whipped into the bar for a drink.* **5.** to strike or be struck as if by whipping: *the tempest whipped the surface of the sea.* **6.** (*tr.*) to criticize virulently. **7.** (*tr.*) to bring, train, etc., forcefully into a desired condition (esp. in the phrases **whip into line** and **whip into shape**). **8.** (*tr.*) *Informal.* to overcome or outdo: *I know when I've been whipped.* **9.** (*tr.;* often foll. by *on, out,* or *off*) to drive, urge, compel, etc., by or as if by whipping. **10.** (*tr.*) to wrap or wind (a cord, thread, etc.) around (a rope, cable, etc.) to prevent chafing or fraying. **11.** (*tr.*) *Nautical.* to hoist by means of a rope through a single pulley. **12.** (*tr.*) (in fly-fishing) to cast the fly repeatedly onto (the water) in a whipping motion. **13.** (*tr.*) (in sewing) to join, finish, or gather with whipstitch. **14.** to beat (eggs, cream, etc.) with a whisk or similar utensil to incorporate air and produce expansion. **15.** (*tr.*) to spin (a top). ~*n.* **16.** a device consisting of a lash or flexible rod attached at one end to a stiff handle and used for driving animals, inflicting corporal punishment, etc. **17.** a whipping stroke or motion. **18.** a person adept at handling a whip, as a coachman, etc. **19.** (in a legislative body) **a.** a member of a party chosen to organize and discipline the members of his faction, esp. in voting and to assist in the arrangement of the business. **b.** a call issued to members of a party, insisting with varying degrees of urgency upon their presence or loyal voting behaviour. **c.** (in the Brit. Parliament) a schedule of business sent to members of a party, indicating for which items their attendance is most important. **20.** an apparatus for hoisting, consisting of a rope, pulley, and snatch block. **21.** any of a variety of desserts made from egg whites or cream beaten stiff, sweetened, and flavoured with fruit, fruit juice, etc. **22.** See **whipper-in. 23.** a windmill vane. **24.** transient elastic movement of a structure or part, such as a shaft, when subjected to sudden loads or dynamic excitation. **25.** a percussion instrument consisting of two strips of wood, joined forming the shape of a V, and clapped loudly together. **26.** flexibility, as in the shaft of a golf club, etc. **27.** a ride in a funfair involving bumper cars that move with sudden jerks. **28.** a wrestling throw in which a wrestler seizes his opponent's arm and spins him to the floor. **29. a fair crack of the whip.** *Informal.* a fair chance or opportunity. ~See also **whip in, whip-round, whip up.** [C13: perhaps from Middle Dutch *wippen* to swing; related to Middle Dutch *wipfen* to dance, German *Wipfel* tree top] —ˈ**whip·ˌlike** *adj.* —ˈ**whip·per** *n.*

whip bird *n. Austral.* **1.** any of several birds of the genus *Psophodes,* esp. *P. olivaceus* (**eastern whip bird**) and *P. nigrogularis* (**black-throated whip bird**), having a whistle ending in a whipcrack note. **2.** any of various other birds, such as *Pachycephala pectoralis* and *P. rufiventris* (**mock whip bird**).

whip·cord (ˈwɪpˌkɔːd) *n.* **1.** a strong worsted or cotton fabric with a diagonally ribbed surface. **2.** a closely twisted hard cord used for the lashes of whips, etc.

whip graft *n. Horticulture.* a graft made by inserting a tongue cut on the sloping base of the scion into a slit on the sloping top of the stock.

whip hand *n.* (usually preceded by *the*) **1.** (in driving horses, etc.) the hand holding the whip. **2.** advantage or dominating position.

whip in *vb.* (*adv.*) **1.** (*intr.*) to perform the duties of a whipper-in to a pack of hounds. **2.** (*tr.*) *Chiefly U.S.* to keep (members of a political party, etc.) together.

whip·lash ('wɪpˌlæʃ) *n.* **1.** a quick lash or stroke of a whip or like that of a whip. **2.** *Med.* See **whiplash injury.**

whip·lash in·ju·ry *n. Med. informal.* any injury to the neck resulting from a sudden thrusting forwards and snapping back of the unsupported head. Technical name: **hyperextension-hyperflexion injury.**

whip·per-in *n., pl.* **whip·pers-in.** a person employed to assist the huntsman managing the hounds.

whip·per·snap·per ('wɪpəˌsnæpə) *n.* an insignificant but pretentious or cheeky person, often a young one. Also called: **whipster.** [C17: probably from *whipsnapper* a person who snaps whips, influenced by earlier *snippersnapper*, of obscure origin]

whip·pet ('wɪpɪt) *n.* a small slender breed of dog similar to a greyhound in appearance. [C16: of uncertain origin; perhaps based on the phrase *whip it!* move quickly!]

whip·ping ('wɪpɪŋ) *n.* **1.** a thrashing or beating with a whip or similar implement. **2.** cord or twine used for binding or lashing.

whip·ping boy *n.* a person of little importance who is blamed for the errors, incompetence, etc., of others, esp. his superiors; scapegoat. [C17: originally referring to a boy who was educated with a prince and who received punishment for any faults committed by the prince]

whip·ping cream *n.* cream that contains enough butterfat to allow it to be whipped until stiff.

whip·ple·tree ('wɪpᵊlˌtriː) *n.* a variant of **whiffletree.**

whip·poor·will ('wɪpʊˌwɪl) *n.* a nightjar, *Caprimulgus vociferus*, of North and Central America, having a dark plumage with white patches on the tail. [C18: imitative of its cry]

whip-round *Informal, chiefly Brit.* ~*n.* **1.** an impromptu collection of money. ~*vb.* **whip round. 2.** (*intr., adv.*) to make such a collection of money.

whips (wɪps) *n.* (*functioning as sing.*; foll. by *of*) *Austral. informal.* a large quantity: *I've got whips of cash at the moment.*

whip·saw ('wɪpˌsɔː) *n.* **1.** any saw with a flexible blade, such as a bandsaw. ~*vb.* **·saws, ·sawing, ·sawed, ·sawed** *or* **·sawn.** (*tr.*) **2.** to saw with a whipsaw. **3.** *U.S.* to defeat in two ways at once.

whip scor·pi·on *n.* any nonvenomous arachnid of the order *Uropygi* (or *Pedipalpi*), typically resembling a scorpion but lacking a sting. See also **vinegarroon.**

whip snake *n.* **1.** any of several long slender fast-moving nonvenomous snakes of the colubrid genus *Coluber*, such as *C. hippocrepis* (**horseshoe whipsnake**) of Eurasia. **2.** any of various other slender nonvenomous snakes, such as *Masticophis flagellum* (**coachwhip snake**) of the U.S.

whip·stall ('wɪpˌstɔːl) *n.* a stall in which an aircraft goes into a nearly vertical climb, pauses, slips backwards momentarily, and drops suddenly with its nose down.

whip·stitch ('wɪpˌstɪtʃ) *n.* **1.** a sewing stitch passing over an edge. **2.** *U.S. slang.* an instant; moment. ~*vb.* **3.** (*tr.*) to sew (an edge) using whipstitch; overcast.

whip·stock ('wɪpˌstɒk) *n.* a whip handle.

whip up *vb.* (*tr., adv.*) **1.** to excite; arouse: *to whip up a mob; to whip up discontent.* **2.** *Informal.* to prepare quickly: *to whip up a meal.*

whip·worm ('wɪpˌwɜːm) *n.* any of several parasitic nematode worms of the genus *Trichuris*, esp. *T. trichiura*, having a whiplike body and living in the intestines of mammals.

whir *or* **whirr** (wɜː) *n.* **1.** a prolonged soft swish or buzz, as of a motor working or wings flapping. **2.** a bustle or rush. ~*vb.* **whirs,** or **whirrs, whir·ring, whirred. 3.** to make or cause to make a whir. [C14: probably from Scandinavian; compare Norwegian *kvirra*, Danish *hvirre*; see WHIRL]

whirl (wɜːl) *vb.* **1.** to spin, turn, or revolve or cause to spin, turn, or revolve. **2.** (*intr.*) to turn around or away rapidly. **3.** (*intr.*) to have a spinning sensation, as from dizziness, etc. **4.** to move or drive or be moved or driven at high speed. ~*n.* **5.** the act or an instance of whirling; swift rotation or a rapid whirling movement. **6.** a condition of confusion or giddiness: *her accident left me in a whirl.* **7.** a swift round, as of events, meetings, etc. **8.** a tumult; stir. **9.** *Informal.* a brief trip, dance, etc. **10. give (something) a whirl.** *Informal.* to attempt or give a trial to (something). [C13: from Old Norse *hvirfla* to turn about; related to Old High German *wirbil* whirlwind] —'**whirl·er** *n.* —'**whirl·ing·ly** *adv.*

whirl·a·bout ('wɜːləˌbaʊt) *n.* **1.** anything that whirls around; whirligig. **2.** the act or an instance of whirling around.

whirl·i·gig ('wɜːlɪˌgɪg) *n.* **1.** any spinning toy, such as a top. **2.** another name for **merry-go-round. 3.** anything that whirls about, spins, or moves in a circular or giddy way: *the whirligig of social life.* **4.** another name for **windmill** (the toy). [C15 *whirlegigge*, from WHIRL + GIG[1]]

whirl·i·gig bee·tle *n.* any flat-bodied water beetle of the family *Gyrinidae*, which circles rapidly on the surface of the water.

whirl·pool ('wɜːlˌpuːl) *n.* **1.** a powerful circular current or vortex of water, usually produced by conflicting tidal currents or by eddying at the foot of a waterfall. **2.** something resembling a whirlpool in motion or the power to attract into its vortex.

whirl·wind ('wɜːlˌwɪnd) *n.* **1.** a column of air whirling around and towards a more or less vertical axis of low pressure, which moves along the land or ocean surface. **2. a.** a motion or course resembling this, esp. in rapidity. **b.** (*as modifier*): *a whirlwind romance.* **3.** an impetuously active person.

whirl·y·bird ('wɜːlɪˌbɜːd) *n.* an informal word for **helicopter.**

whish (wɪʃ) *n., vb.* a less common word for **swish.**

whisk (wɪsk) *vb.* **1.** (*tr.*; often foll. by *away* or *off*) to brush, sweep, or wipe off lightly. **2.** (*tr.*) to move, carry, etc., with a light or rapid sweeping motion: *the taxi whisked us to the airport.* **3.** (*intr.*) to move, go, etc., quickly and nimbly: *to whisk downstairs for a drink.* **4.** (*tr.*) to whip (eggs, cream, etc.) to a froth. ~*n.* **5.** the act of whisking. **6.** a light rapid sweeping movement or stroke. **7.** a utensil, often incorporating a coil of wires, for whipping eggs, etc. **8.** a small brush or broom. **9.** a small bunch or bundle, as of grass, straw, etc. [C14: from Old Norse *visk* wisp; related to Middle Dutch *wisch*, Old High German *wisc*]

whisk·er ('wɪskə) *n.* **1.** any of the stiff sensory hairs growing on the face of a cat, rat, or other mammal. Technical name: **vibrissa. 2.** any of the hairs growing on a person's face, esp. on the cheeks or chin. **3.** (*pl.*) a beard or that part of it growing on the sides of the face. **4.** (*pl.*) *Informal.* a moustache. **5.** Also called: **whisker boom, whisker pole.** any light spar used for extending the clews of a sail, esp. in light airs. **6.** *Chem.* a very fine filamentary crystal having greater strength than the bulk material since they are single crystals. They often show unusual electrical properties. **7.** a person or thing that whisks. **8. by a whisker.** *Informal.* by a narrow margin; only just: *he escaped death by a whisker.* —'**whisk·ered** *or* '**whisk·er·y** *adj.*

whis·key ('wɪskɪ) *n.* whisky made in the U.S. or Ireland.

whis·key sour *n.* a mixed drink of whisky and lime or lemon juice, sometimes sweetened.

whis·ky ('wɪskɪ) *n., pl.* **·kies.** a spirit made by distilling fermented cereals, which is matured and often blended. [C18: shortened from *whiskybae*, from Scottish Gaelic *uisge beatha*, literally: water of life; see USQUEBAUGH]

whis·ky mac *n. Brit.* a drink consisting of whisky and ginger wine.

whis·per ('wɪspə) *vb.* **1.** to speak or utter (something) in a soft hushed tone, esp. without vibration of the vocal cords. **2.** (*intr.*) to speak secretly or furtively, as in promoting intrigue, gossip, etc. **3.** (*intr.*) (of leaves, trees, etc.) to make a low soft rustling sound. **4.** (*tr.*) to utter or suggest secretly or privately: *to whisper treason.* ~*n.* **5.** a low soft voice: *to speak in a whisper.* **6.** something uttered in such a voice. **7.** a low soft rustling sound. **8.** a trace or suspicion. **9.** *Informal.* a rumour or secret. [Old English *hwisprian*; related to Old Norse *hvískra*, Old High German *hwispalōn*, Dutch *wispern*] —'**whis·per·er** *n.*

whis·per·ing cam·paign *n. Chiefly U.S.* the organized diffusion by word of mouth of defamatory rumours designed to discredit a person, group, etc.

whis·per·ing gal·ler·y *n.* a gallery or dome with acoustic characteristics such that a sound made at one point is audible at distant points.

whist[1] (wɪst) *n.* a card game for four in which the two sides try to win the balance of the 13 tricks: forerunner of bridge. [C17: perhaps changed from WHISK, referring to the sweeping up or whisking up of the tricks]

whist[2] (wɪst) *or* **whisht** (wɪʃt) *Archaic or dialect, esp. Scot.* ~*interj.* **1.** hush! be quiet! ~*adj.* **2.** silent or still. ~*vb.* **3.** to make or become silent.

whis·tle ('wɪsᵊl) *vb.* **1.** to produce (shrill or flutelike musical sounds), as by passing breath through a narrow constriction most easily formed by the pursed lips: *he whistled a melody.* **2.** (*tr.*) to signal, summon, or command by whistling or blowing a whistle: *the referee whistled the end of the game.* **3.** (of a kettle, train, etc.) to produce (a shrill sound) caused by the emission of steam through a small aperture. **4.** (*intr.*) to move with a whistling sound caused by rapid passage through the air. **5.** (of animals, esp. birds) to emit (a shrill sound) resembling human whistling. ~*n.* **6.** a device for making a shrill high-pitched sound by means of air or steam under pressure. **7.** a shrill sound effected by whistling. **8.** a whistling sound, as of a bird, bullet, the wind, etc. **9.** a signal, warning, command, etc., transmitted by or as if by a whistle. **10.** the act of whistling. **11.** *Music.* any pipe that is blown down its end and produces sounds on the principle of a flue pipe, usually having as a mouthpiece a fipple cut in the side. **12. wet one's whistle.** *Informal.* to take a drink. **13. blow the whistle.** (usually foll. by *on*) *U.S. informal.* **a.** to inform (on). **b.** to bring a stop (to). [Old English *hwistlian*; related to Old Norse *hvísla*]

whis·tle for *vb.* (*intr., prep.*) *Informal.* to seek or expect in vain.

whis·tler ('wɪslə) *n.* **1.** a person or thing that whistles. **2.** *Radio.* an atmospheric disturbance picked up by radio receivers, characterized by a whistling sound of decreasing pitch. It is caused by the electromagnetic radiation produced by lightning. **3.** any of various birds having a whistling call, such as certain Australian flycatchers (see **thickhead** (sense 2)) and the goldeneye. **4.** any of various North American marmots of the genus *Marmota*, esp. *M. caligata* (**hoary marmot**). **5.** *Vet. science.* a horse affected with whistling.

Whis·tler ('wɪslə) *n.* **James Ab·bott Mc·Neill.** 1834–1903, U.S. painter and etcher, living in Europe. He is best known for his sequence of nocturnes and his portraits.

whis+tle stop *n.* **1.** *U.S.* **a.** a minor railway station where trains stop only on signal. **b.** a small town having such a station. **2. a.** a brief appearance in a town, esp. by a political candidate to make a speech, shake hands, etc. **b.** (*as modifier*): *a whistle-stop tour.* ~*vb.* **whis·tle-stop, -stops, -stop·ping, -stopped. 3.** (*intr.*) to campaign for office by visiting many small towns to give short speeches.

whis+tling ('wɪslɪŋ) *n. Vet. science.* a breathing defect of horses characterized by a high-pitched sound with each intake of air. Compare **roaring** (sense 4).

whis+tling swan *n.* a white North American swan, *Cygnus columbianus,* with a black bill and straight neck. Compare **mute swan.**

whit (wɪt) *n.* (*usually used with a negative*) the smallest particle; iota; jot: *he has changed not a whit.* [C15: probably variant of WIGHT[1]]

Whit (wɪt) *n.* **1.** See **Whitsuntide.** ~*adj.* **2.** of or relating to Whitsuntide.

Whit·a·ker ('wɪtəkə) *n.* Sir **Fred·e·rick.** 1812–91, New Zealand statesman, born in England: prime minister of New Zealand (1863–64; 1882–83).

Whit+by ('wɪtbɪ) *n.* a fishing port and resort in NE England, in E North Yorkshire at the mouth of the River Esk: an important ecclesiastical centre in Anglo-Saxon times; site of an abbey founded in 656. Pop.: 12 717 (1971).

white (waɪt) *adj.* **1.** having no hue due to the reflection of all or almost all incident light. Compare **black** (sense 1). **2.** (of light, such as sunlight) consisting of all the colours of the spectrum or produced by certain mixtures of three additive primary colours, such as red, green, and blue. **3.** comparatively white or whitish-grey in colour or having parts of this colour: *white clover.* **4.** (of an animal) having pale-coloured or white skin, fur, or feathers. **5.** bloodless or pale, as from pain, emotion, etc. **6.** (of hair, a beard, etc.) silvery or grey, usually from age. **7.** benevolent or without malicious intent: *white magic.* **8.** colourless or transparent: *white glass.* **9.** capped with or accompanied by snow: *a white Christmas.* **10.** (*sometimes cap.*) counterrevolutionary, very conservative, or royalist. Compare **Red** (sense 2). **11.** blank, as an unprinted area of a page. **12.** (of wine) made from pale grapes or from black grapes separated from their skins. **13. a.** (of coffee or tea) with milk or cream. **b.** (of bread) made with white flour. **14.** *Physics.* having or characterized by a continuous distribution of energy, wavelength, or frequency: *white noise.* **15.** *Informal.* honourable or generous. **16.** (of armour) made completely of iron or steel (esp. in the phrase **white harness**). **17.** *Rare.* morally unblemished. **18.** *Rare.* (of times, seasons, etc.) auspicious; favourable. **19.** *Poetic or archaic.* having a fair complexion; blond. **20. bleed white.** to deprive slowly of resources. ~*n.* **21.** a white colour. **22.** the condition or quality of being white; whiteness. **23.** the white or lightly coloured part or area of something. **24.** (usually preceded by *the*) the viscous fluid that surrounds the yolk of a bird's egg, esp. a hen's egg; albumen. **25.** *Anatomy.* the white part (sclera) of the eyeball. **26.** any of various butterflies of the family *Pieridae,* such as *Pieris brassicae* (**large white**) and *P. rapae* (**small white**), having white wings with scanty black markings. See also **cabbage white. 27.** *Chess, draughts.* **a.** a white or light-coloured piece or square. **b.** the player playing with such pieces. **28.** anything that has or is characterized by a white colour, such as a white paint or pigment, a white cloth, a white ball in billiards. **29.** an unprinted area of a page. **30.** *Archery.* **a.** the outer ring of the target, having the lowest score. **b.** a shot or arrow hitting this ring. **31.** *Poetic.* fairness of complexion. **32. in the white.** (of wood or furniture) left unpainted or unvarnished. ~*vb.* **33.** (usually foll. by *out*) to create or leave white spaces in (printed or other matter). **34.** *Obsolete.* to make or become white. See also **white out, whites.** [Old English *hwīt;* related to Old Frisian *hwīt,* Old Saxon *hwīt,* Old Norse *hvītr,* Gothic *hveits,* Old High German *hwīz* (German *weiss*)] —'**white+ly** *adv.* —'**whit+ish** *adj.* —'**white+ness** *n.*

White[1] (waɪt) *n.* **1.** a member of the Caucasoid race. **2.** a person of European ancestry. ~*adj.* **3.** denoting or relating to a White or Whites.

White[2] (waɪt) *n.* **1. Gil·bert.** 1720–93, English clergyman and naturalist, noted for his *Natural History and Antiquities of Selborne* (1789). **2. Pat·rick (Victor Martindale).** born 1912, Australian novelist: his works include *Voss* (1957), *The Eye of the Storm* (1973), and *A Fringe of Leaves* (1976): Nobel prize for literature 1973.

white ad+mi+ral *n.* a nymphalid butterfly, *Limenitis camilla,* of Eurasia, having brown wings with white markings. See also **red admiral.**

white al+ka+li *n.* **1.** refined sodium carbonate. **2.** any of several mineral salts, esp. sodium sulphate, sodium chloride, and magnesium sulphate, that often appear on the surface of soils as a whitish layer in dry conditions.

white ant *n.* another name for **termite.**

white ar·e·a *n.* an area of land for which no specific planning proposal has been adopted.

white+bait ('waɪtˌbeɪt) *n.* **1.** the edible young of herrings, sprats, etc., cooked and eaten whole as a delicacy. **2.** any of various small silvery fishes, such as *Galaxias attenuatus* of Australia and New Zealand and *Allosmerus elongatus* of North American coastal regions of the Pacific. [C18: from its formerly having been used as bait]

white+beam ('waɪtˌbiːm) *n.* a N temperate rosaceous tree, *Sorbus aria,* having leaves that are densely hairy on the undersurface and hard timber.

white bear *n.* another name for **polar bear.**

white birch *n.* any of several birch trees with white bark, such as the silver birch of Europe and the paper birch of North America. See also **birch** (sense 1).

white blood cell *n.* a nontechnical name for **leucocyte.**

white book *n.* an official government publication in some countries.

White+boy ('waɪtbɔɪ) *n. Irish history.* a member of a secret society of violent agrarian protest, formed around 1760. [C18: adopted from the earlier use of the phrase as a term of endearment for a boy or man]

white bry·o+ny *n.* a climbing herbaceous cucurbitaceous plant, *Bryonia dioica,* of Europe and North Africa, having greenish flowers and red berries. Also called: **red bryony.** See also **black bryony, bryony.**

white+cap ('waɪtˌkæp) *n.* **1.** a wave with a white broken crest. **2.** *U.S.* a member of a vigilante organization that attempts to control a community.

white ce+dar *n.* **1.** a coniferous tree, *Chamaecyparis thyoides,* of swampy regions in North America, having scalelike leaves and boxlike cones: family *Cupressaceae.* See also **cypress**[1] (sense 2). **2.** the wood of this tree, which is used for building boats, etc. **3.** a coniferous tree, *Thuja occidentalis,* of NE North America, having scalelike leaves: family *Cupressaceae.* See also **arbor vitae. 4.** the wood of this tree, much used for telegraph poles.

White+chap·el ('waɪtˌtʃæpᵊl) *n. Billiards.* the act of potting one's opponent's white ball. [C19: slang use of *Whitechapel,* a district of London]

white clo+ver *n.* a Eurasian clover plant, *Trifolium repens,* with rounded white flower heads: cultivated as a forage plant.

white coal *n.* water, esp. when flowing and providing a potential source of usable power.

white-col·lar *adj.* of, relating to, or designating nonmanual and usually salaried workers employed in professional and clerical occupations. Compare **blue-collar.**

white cur+rant *n.* a cultivated N temperate shrub, *Ribes sativum,* having small rounded white edible berries: family *Grossulariaceae.*

white+damp ('waɪtˌdæmp) *n.* a mixture of poisonous gases, mainly carbon monoxide, occurring in coal mines. See also **afterdamp.**

whit+ed sep+ul+chre ('waɪtɪd) *n.* a hypocrite.

white dwarf *n.* one of a large class of small faint stars of enormous density (on average 10^8 kg/m^3) known to cause an Einstein shift of spectral lines. It is thought to mark the final stage in a star's evolution.

white el+e·phant *n.* **1.** a rare albino or pale grey variety of the Indian elephant, regarded as sacred in parts of S Asia. **2.** a possession that is unwanted by its owner. **3.** an elaborate venture, construction, etc., that proves useless. **4.** a rare or valuable possession the upkeep of which is very expensive.

White En+sign *n.* the ensign of the Royal Navy and the Royal Yacht Squadron, having a red cross on a white background with the Union Jack at the upper corner of the vertical edge alongside the hoist. Compare **Red Ensign.**

white-eye *n.* **1.** any songbird of the family *Zosteropidae* of Africa, Australia, and Asia, having a greenish plumage with a white ring around each eye. **2.** any of certain other birds having a white ring or patch around the eye.

white feath+er *n.* **1.** a symbol or mark of cowardice. **2. show the white feather.** to act in a cowardly manner.

White·field ('waɪtˌfiːld) *n.* **George.** 1714–70, English Methodist preacher, who separated from the Wesleys (?1741) because of his Calvinistic views.

white+fish ('waɪtˌfɪʃ) *n., pl.* **+fish** *or* **+fish·es. 1.** any herring-like salmonoid food fish of the genus *Coregonus* and family *Coregonidae,* typically of deep cold lakes of the N hemisphere, having large silvery scales and a small head. **2.** (in the Brit. fishing industry) any edible marine fish or invertebrate excluding herrings but including trout, salmon, and all shellfish.

white flag *n.* a white flag or a piece of white cloth hoisted to signify surrender or request a truce.

white flint *n.* another name for **flint** (sense 4).

white+fly ('waɪtˌflaɪ) *n., pl.* **+flies.** any hemipterous insect of the family *Aleyrodidae,* typically having a body covered with powdery wax. Many are pests of greenhouse crops.

white-foot·ed mouse *n.* any of various mice of the genus *Peromyscus,* esp. *P. leucopus,* of North and Central America, having brownish fur with white underparts: family *Cricetidae.* See also **deer mouse.**

white fox *n.* another name for **arctic fox.**

white fri+ar *n.* a Carmelite friar, so called because of the white cloak that forms part of the habit of this order.

white frost *n.* another term for **hoarfrost.**

white gold *n.* any of various white lustrous hard-wearing alloys containing gold together with platinum and palladium and sometimes smaller amounts of silver, nickel, or copper: used in jewellery.

white goods *pl. n.* **1.** household linen such as sheets, towels, tablecloths, etc. **2.** large household appliances, such as refrigerators, cookers.

white gum *n.* any of various Australian eucalyptus trees with whitish bark.

White+hall (ˌwaɪt'hɔːl) *n.* **1.** a street in London stretching from Trafalgar Square to the Houses of Parliament: site of the main government offices. **2.** the British Government or its central administration.

White·head ('waɪtˌhɛd) *n.* **Al·fred North.** 1861–1947, English

mathematician and philosopher, who collaborated with Bertrand Russell in writing *Principia Mathematica* (1910–13).
white heat *n.* **1.** intense heat or a very high temperature, characterized by emission of white light. **2.** *Informal.* a state of intense excitement or activity.
white hope *n. Informal.* a person who is expected to bring honour or glory to his group, team, etc.
white horse *n.* **1.** the outline of a horse carved into the side of a chalk hill, usually dating to the Neolithic, Bronze, or Iron Ages, such as that at Uffington, Berkshire. **2.** a wave with a white broken crest.
White+horse ('waɪtˌhɔːs) *n.* a town in NW Canada: capital of the Yukon Territory. Pop.: 11 217 (1971).
white-hot *adj.* **1.** at such a high temperature that white light is emitted. **2.** *Informal.* in a state of intense emotion.
White House *n.* **the. 1.** the official Washington residence of the president of the U.S. **2.** the U.S. presidency.
white lead (lɛd) *n.* **1.** Also called: **ceruse.** a white solid usually regarded as a mixture of lead carbonate and lead hydroxide; basic lead carbonate: used in paint and in making putty and ointments for the treatment of burns. Formula: $2PbCO_3.Pb(OH)_2$. **2.** either of two similar white pigments based on lead sulphate or lead silicate. **3.** a type of putty made by mixing white lead with boiled linseed oil.
white lead ore (lɛd) *n.* another name for **cerussite.**
white leath+er *n.* leather that has been treated with a chemical, such as alum or salt, to make it white. Also called: **whit+leath·er** ('wɪtˈlɛðə).
white leg *n.* another name for **milk leg.**
white lie *n.* a minor or unimportant lie, esp. one uttered in the interests of tact or politeness.
white light *n.* light that contains all the wavelengths of visible light at approximately equal intensities, as in sunlight or the light from white-hot solids.
white line *n.* **1.** a line or strip of white in the centre of a road to separate traffic going in different directions. **2.** *Printing.* a line of spaces without letters or other characters. **3.** a white lamination in the hoof of a horse.
white-liv·ered *adj.* **1.** lacking in spirit or courage. **2.** pallid and unhealthy in appearance.
White man's bur+den *n.* the supposed duty of the White race to bring education and Western culture to the non-White inhabitants of their colonies.
white mat+ter *n.* the whitish tissue of the brain and spinal cord, consisting mainly of myelinated nerve fibres. Technical name: **substantia alba.** Compare **grey matter.**
white meat *n.* any meat that is light in colour, such as veal or the breast of turkey. Compare **red meat.**
white met+al *n.* any of various alloys, such as Babbitt metal, used for bearings.
White Moun+tains *pl. n.* **1.** a mountain range chiefly in N New Hampshire: part of the Appalachians. Highest peak: Mount Washington, 1917 m (6288 ft.). **2.** a mountain range in E California and SW Nevada. Highest peak: White Mountain, 4342 m (14 246 ft.).
white mus+tard *n.* a Eurasian cruciferous plant, *Brassica hirta* (or *Sinapis alba*), having clusters of yellow flowers and pungent seeds from which the condiment mustard is made.
whit+en ('waɪtᵊn) *vb.* to make or become white or whiter; bleach. —**'whit+en+er** *n.* —**'whit+en+ing** *n.*
White Nile *n.* See **Nile.**
white noise *n.* sound or electrical noise that has a relatively wide continuous range of frequencies of uniform intensity.
white oak *n.* **1.** a large oak tree, *Quercus alba,* of E North America, having pale bark, leaves with rounded lobes, and heavy light-coloured wood. **2.** any of several other oaks, such as the roble.
white out *vb.* (*adv.*) **1.** (*intr.*) to lose or lack daylight visibility owing to snow or fog. **2.** (*tr.*) to create or leave white spaces in (printed or other matter). ~*n.* **white+out. 3.** a polar atmospheric condition consisting of lack of visibility and sense of distance and direction due to a uniform whiteness of a heavy cloud cover and snow-covered ground, which reflects almost all the light it receives.
white pa+per *n.* (*often caps.*) an official government report in any of a number of countries, including Britain, Australia, New Zealand, and Canada, which sets out the government's policy on a matter that is or will come before Parliament.
white pep+per *n.* a condiment, less pungent than black pepper, made from the husked dried beans of the pepper plant *Piper nigrum,* used either whole or ground.
white pine *n.* **1.** a North American coniferous tree, *Pinus strobus,* having blue-green needle-like leaves, hanging brown cones, and rough bark: family *Pinaceae.* **2.** the light-coloured wood of this tree, much used commercially.
white plague *n. Informal.* tuberculosis of the lungs.
white pop+lar *n.* **1.** Also called: **abele.** a Eurasian salicaceous tree, *Populus alba,* having leaves covered with dense silvery-white hairs. **2.** another name for **tulipwood** (sense 1).
white po+ta+to *n.* another name for **potato** (sense 1).
white pud+ding *n. Brit.* a kind of sausage made like black pudding but without pigs' blood.
white rain+bow *n.* another name for **fogbow.**
white rat *n.* a white variety of the brown rat (*Rattus norvegicus*), used extensively in scientific research.
white rose *n. English history.* a widely used emblem or badge of the House of York. See also **Wars of the Roses, red rose.**
White Rus+sia *n.* another name for the **Byelorussian Soviet Socialist Republic.**
White Rus+sian *adj., n.* another term for **Byelorussian.**
whites (waɪts) *pl. n.* **1.** household linen or cotton goods, such as sheets. **2.** white or off-white clothing, such as that worn for playing cricket. **3.** an informal name for **leucorrhoea.**
white sale *n.* a sale of household linens at reduced prices.
white sap+phire *n.* a white pure variety of corundum, used as a gemstone.
white sauce *n.* a thick sauce made from flour, butter, seasonings, and milk or stock.
White Sea *n.* an almost landlocked inlet of the Barents Sea on the coast of the NW Soviet Union. Area: 90 000 sq. km (34 700 sq. miles).
white slave *n.* a girl or woman forced or sold into prostitution. —**white slav+er·y** *n.*
white-slav·er *n.* a person who procures or forces women to become prostitutes.
white+smith ('waɪtˌsmɪθ) *n.* a person who finishes and polishes metals, particularly tin plate and galvanized iron.
white spir+it *n.* a colourless liquid obtained from petroleum and used as a substitute for turpentine.
white spruce *n.* a N North American spruce tree, *Picea glauca,* having grey bark, pale brown oblong cones, and bluish-green needle-like leaves.
white squall *n.* a violent highly localized weather disturbance at sea, in which the surface of the water is whipped to a white spray by the winds.
White su+prem·a+cy *n.* the theory or belief that White people are innately superior to people of other races. —**White su+prem·a+cist** *n., adj.*
white-tailed deer *n.* a deer, *Odocoileus virginianus,* of North America and N South America: the coat varies in colour, being typically reddish-brown in the summer, and the tail is white. Also called: **Virginia deer.**
white+thorn ('waɪtˌθɔːn) *n.* another name for **hawthorn.**
white+throat ('waɪtˌθrəʊt) *n.* either of two Old World warblers, *Sylvia communis* or *S. curruca* (**lesser whitethroat**), having a greyish-brown plumage with a white throat and underparts.
white tie *n.* **1.** a white bow tie worn as part of a man's formal evening dress. **2. a.** formal evening dress for men. **b.** (*as modifier*): *a white-tie occasion.*
white vit+ri+ol *n.* another name for **zinc sulphate.**
White Vol+ta *n.* a river in W Africa, rising in N Upper Volta and flowing southwest and south to join the Black Volta in central Ghana and form the Volta River. Length: about 885 km (550 miles).
white+wall ('waɪtˌwɔːl) *n.* a pneumatic tyre having white sidewalls.
white wal+nut *n.* another name for **butternut** (senses 1–4).
white+wash ('waɪtˌwɒʃ) *n.* **1.** a substance used for whitening walls and other surfaces, consisting of a suspension of lime or whiting in water, often with other substances, such as size, added. **2.** *Informal.* deceptive or specious words or actions intended to conceal defects, gloss over failings, etc. **3.** *Informal.* a game in which the loser fails to score. ~*vb.* (*tr.*) **4.** to cover or whiten with whitewash. **5.** *Informal.* to conceal, gloss over, or suppress. **6.** *Informal.* to defeat (someone) in a game by preventing him from scoring. —**'white+ˌwash+er** *n.*
white wa+ter *n.* **1.** a stretch of water with a broken foamy surface, as in rapids. **2.** light-coloured sea water, esp. over shoals or shallows.
white whale *n.* a small white toothed whale, *Delphinapterus leucas,* of northern waters: family *Monodontidae.* Also called: **beluga.**
white+wood ('waɪtˌwʊd) *n.* **1.** any of various trees with light-coloured wood, such as the tulip tree, basswood, and cottonwood. **2.** the wood of any of these trees.
whit+ey *or* **whit·y** ('waɪtɪ) *n. Chiefly U.S.* (used contemptuously by Negroes) a white man.
whith+er ('wɪðə) *Archaic or poetic.* ~*adv.* **1.** to what place? **2.** to what end or purpose? ~*conj.* **3.** to whatever place, purpose, etc. [Old English *hwider, hwæder;* related to Gothic *hvadrē;* modern English form influenced by HITHER]
whith·er+so+ev·er (ˌwɪðəsəʊˈɛvə) *adv., conj. Archaic or poetic.* to whichever place.
whith+er+ward ('wɪðəwəd) *adv. Archaic or poetic.* in which direction.
whit+ing[1] ('waɪtɪŋ) *n.* **1.** an important gadoid food fish, *Merlangius* (or *Gadus*) *merlangus,* of European seas, having a dark back with silvery sides and underparts. **2.** any of various similar fishes, such as *Merluccius bilinearis,* a hake of American Atlantic waters, and any of several Atlantic sciaenid fishes of the genus *Menticirrhus.* **3.** *Austral.* any of several marine food fishes of the genus *Sillago.* **4. whiting pout.** another name for **bib** (the fish). [C15: perhaps from Old English *hwītling;* related to Middle Dutch *wijting.* See WHITE, -ING[3]]
whit+ing[2] ('waɪtɪŋ) *n.* Also called: **whitening.** white chalk that has been ground and washed, used in making whitewash, metal polish, etc.
Whit·lam ('wɪtləm) *n.* **(Edward) Gough** (gɒf). born 1916, Australian Labor statesman: prime minister (1972–75).
Whit+ley Bay ('wɪtlɪ) *n.* a resort in NE England, in Tyne and Wear on the North Sea. Pop.: 37 775 (1971).
whit+low ('wɪtləʊ) *n.* any pussy inflammation of the end of a finger or toe. [C14: changed from *whitflaw,* from WHITE + FLAW[1]]
Whit·man ('wɪtmən) *n.* **Walt(er).** 1819–92, U.S. poet, whose life's work is collected in *Leaves of Grass* (1855 and subsequent enlarged editions). His poems celebrate existence and the multiple elements that make up a democratic society.

Whit Mon·day *n.* the Monday following Whit Sunday.

Whit·ney[1] ('wɪtnɪ) *n.* **Mount.** a mountain in E California: the highest peak in the Sierra Nevada Mountains and in continental U.S. (excluding Alaska). Height: 4418 m (14 495 ft.).

Whit·ney[2] ('wɪtnɪ) *n.* **1. E·li.** 1765–1825, U.S. inventor of a mechanical cotton gin (1793) and pioneer manufacturer of interchangeable parts. **2. Wil·liam Dwight.** 1827–94, U.S. philologist, noted esp. for his *Sanskrit Grammar* (1879).

Whit·sun ('wɪtsᵊn) *n.* **1.** short for **Whitsuntide.** ~*adj.* **2.** of or relating to Whit Sunday or Whitsuntide.

Whit Sun·day *n.* the seventh Sunday after Easter, observed as a feast in commemoration of the descent of the Holy Spirit on the apostles 50 days after Easter. In Scotland, it is one of the four quarter days. Also called: **Pentecost.** [Old English *hwīta sunnandæg* white Sunday, probably named after the ancient custom of wearing white robes at or after baptism]

Whit·sun·tide ('wɪtsᵊn,taɪd) *n.* the week that begins with Whit Sunday, esp. the first three days.

Whit·ting·ton ('wɪtɪŋtən) *n.* **Rich·ard,** called *Dick.* died 1423, English merchant, three times mayor of London. According to legend, he walked to London at the age of 13 with his cat and was prevented from leaving again only by the call of the church bells.

whit·tle ('wɪtᵊl) *vb.* **1.** to cut or shave strips or pieces from (wood, a stick, etc.), esp. with a knife. **2.** (*tr.*) to make or shape by paring or shaving. **3.** (*tr.; often foll. by away, down, off,* etc.) to reduce, destroy, or wear away gradually: ~*n.* **4.** *Brit. dialect.* a knife, esp. a large one. [C16: variant of C15 *thwittle* large knife, from Old English *thwitel,* from *thwītan* to cut; related to Old Norse *thveitr* cut, *thveita* to beat] —**'whit·tler** *n.*

Whit·tle ('wɪtᵊl) *n.* Sir **Frank.** born 1907, English engineer, who invented the jet engine for aircraft (1941).

whit·tlings ('wɪtlɪŋz) *pl. n.* chips or shavings whittled off from an object.

whit·y ('waɪtɪ) *n., pl.* **whit·ies 1.** *Informal.* a variant spelling of **whitey.** ~*adj.* **2. a.** whitish in colour. **b.** (*in combination*): *whity-brown.*

whiz *or* **whizz** (wɪz) *vb.* **whiz·zes, whiz·zing, whizzed. 1.** to make or cause to make a loud humming or buzzing sound. **2.** to move or cause to move with such a sound. **3.** (*intr.*) *Informal.* to move or go rapidly. ~*n.* **4.** a loud humming or buzzing sound. **5.** *Informal.* a person who is extremely skilful at some activity. [C16: of imitative origin]

whiz-bang *or* **whizz-bang** *n.* **1.** a small-calibre World War I shell that, when discharged, travelled so that when fired in a flat trajectory the sound of its flight was heard only an instant, if at all, before the sound of its explosion. ~*adj.* **2.** *Informal.* excellent or first-rate.

whiz kid, whizz kid, *or* **wiz kid** *n. Informal.* a person who is pushing, enthusiastic, and outstandingly successful for his or her age. [C20: from WHIZ, perhaps influenced by WIZARD]

wh-move·ment *n. Transformational grammar.* a rule of English that moves a relative interrogative pronoun such as *who* to the beginning of its clause.

who (hu:) *pron.* **1.** which person? what person? used in direct and indirect questions: *he can't remember who did it; who met you?* **2.** used to introduce relative clauses with antecedents referring to human beings: *the people who lived here have left.* **3.** the one or ones who; whoever: *bring who you want.* **4. who's who. a.** the identity of individual, esp. important, people: *to know who's who.* **b.** a book or list containing the names and short biographies of prominent persons. [Old English *hwā;* related to Old Saxon *hwē,* Old High German *hwer,* Gothic *hvas,* Lithuanian *kàs,* Danish *hvo*]
Usage. See at **whom.**

Who (hu:) *n.* **The.** English rock group (formed 1964): comprising Roger Daltrey (born 1944; vocals), Pete Townshend (born 1945; guitar), John Entwistle (born 1944; bass guitar), and Keith Moon (1946–78; drums). Their best known album is the rock opera *Tommy* (1969).

W.H.O. *abbrev. for* World Health Organization.

whoa (wəʊ) *interj.* a command used esp. to horses to stop or slow down. [C19: variant of HO]

who'd (hu:d) *contraction of* who had *or* who would.

who-does-what *adj.* (of a dispute, strike, etc.) relating to the separation of kinds of work performed by different trade unions.

who·dun·it *or* **who·dun·nit** (hu:'dʌnɪt) *n. Informal.* a novel, play, etc., concerned with a crime, usually murder.

who·ev·er (hu:'ɛvə) *pron.* **1.** any person who; anyone that: *whoever wants it can have it.* **2.** no matter who: *I'll come round tomorrow, whoever may be here.* **3.** an intensive form of *who,* used in questions: *whoever could have thought that?* **4.** *Informal.* an unknown or unspecified person: *give those to John, or Cathy, or whoever.*

whole (həʊl) *adj.* **1.** containing all the component parts necessary to form a total; complete: *a whole apple.* **2.** constituting the full quantity, extent, etc. **3.** uninjured or undamaged. **4.** healthy. **5.** having no fractional or decimal part; integral: *a whole number.* **6.** of, relating to, or designating a relationship established by descent from the same parents; full: *whole brothers.* **7. out of whole cloth.** *U.S. informal.* entirely without a factual basis. ~*adv.* **8.** in an undivided or unbroken piece: *to swallow a plum whole.* ~*n.* **9.** all the parts, elements, etc., of a thing. **10.** an assemblage of parts viewed together as a unit. **11.** a thing complete in itself. **12. as a whole.** considered altogether; completely. **13. on the whole. a.** taking all things into consideration. **b.** in general. [Old English *hāl, hæl;* related to Old Frisian *hāl, hēl,* Old High German *heil,* Gothic *hails;* compare HALE[1]] —**'whole·ness** *n.*

whole blood *n.* blood obtained from a donor for transfusion from which none of the elements has been removed.

whole·food ('həʊl,fu:d) *n.* (*sometimes pl.*) **a.** food that has been refined or processed as little as possible and is eaten in its natural state, such as brown rice, wholemeal flour, etc. **b.** (*as modifier*): *a wholefood restaurant.*

whole gale *n.* a wind of force ten on the Beaufort scale, seldom experienced inland.

whole·heart·ed (,həʊl'hɑ:tɪd) *adj.* done, acted, given, etc., with total sincerity, enthusiasm, or commitment. —**,whole'heart·ed·ly** *adv.* —**,whole'heart·ed·ness** *n.*

whole hog *n. Slang.* the whole or total extent (esp. in the phrase **go the whole hog**).

whole·meal ('həʊl,mi:l) *adj. Brit.* (of flour, bread, etc.) made from the entire wheat kernel. U.S. term: **whole-wheat.**

whole milk *n.* milk from which no constituent has been removed. Compare **skim milk.**

whole note *n.* the usual U.S. name for **semibreve.**

whole num·ber *n.* **1.** an integer. **2.** a natural number.

whole·sale ('həʊl,seɪl) *n.* **1.** the business of selling goods to retailers in larger quantities than they are sold to final consumers but in smaller quantities than they are purchased from manufacturers. Compare **retail** (sense 1). **2. at wholesale. a.** in large quantities. **b.** at wholesale prices. ~*adj.* **3.** of, relating to, or engaged in such business. **4.** made, done, etc., on a large scale or without discrimination. ~*adv.* **5.** on a large scale or without discrimination. ~*vb.* **6.** to sell (goods) at wholesale. —**'whole,sal·er** *n.*

whole·some ('həʊlsəm) *adj.* **1.** conducive to health or physical wellbeing. **2.** conducive to moral wellbeing. **3.** characteristic or suggestive of health or wellbeing, esp. in appearance. [C12: from WHOLE (healthy) + -SOME[1]; related to German *heilsam* healing] —**'whole·some·ly** *adv.* —**'whole·some·ness** *n.*

whole tone *or U.S.* **whole step** *n.* an interval of two semitones; a frequency difference of 200 cents in the system of equal temperament. Often shortened to **tone.**

whole-tone scale *n.* either of two scales produced by commencing on one of any two notes a chromatic semitone apart and proceeding upwards or downwards in whole tones for an octave. Such a scale, consisting of six degrees to the octave, is used by Debussy and subsequent composers.

whole-wheat *adj.* another term (esp. U.S.) for **wholemeal.**

who·lism ('həʊlɪzəm) *n.* a variant of **holism.** —**who'lis·tic** *adj.*

who'll (hu:l) *contraction of* who will *or* who shall.

whol·ly ('həʊllɪ) *adv.* **1.** completely, totally, or entirely. **2.** without exception; exclusively.

whom (hu:m) *pron.* the objective form of *who,* used when *who* is not the subject of its own clause: *whom did you say you had seen? he can't remember whom he saw.* [Old English *hwām,* dative of *hwā* WHO]
Usage. In formal English, careful writers always use *whom* when the objective form of *who* is required. In informal contexts, however, many careful speakers consider *whom* to be unnatural, esp. at the beginning of a sentence: *who were you looking for?* Careful speakers usually prefer *whom* where it closely follows a preposition: *to whom did you give it?* as contrasted with *who did you give it to?*

whom·ev·er (hu:m'ɛvə) *pron.* the objective form of *whoever: I'll hire whomever I can find.*

whoop (wu:p) *vb.* **1.** to utter (speech) with loud cries, as of enthusiasm or excitement. **2.** *Med.* to cough convulsively with a crowing sound made at each inspiration. **3.** (of certain birds) to utter (a hooting cry). **4.** (*tr.*) to urge on or call with or as if with whoops. **5.** (wʊp, wu:p). **whoop it up.** *Informal.* **a.** to indulge in a noisy celebration. **b.** to arouse enthusiasm. ~*n.* **6.** a loud cry, esp. one expressing enthusiasm or excitement. **7.** *Med.* the convulsive crowing sound made during a paroxysm of whooping cough. **8. not worth a whoop.** *Informal.* worthless. [C14: of imitative origin]

whoo·pee *Informal.* ~*interj.* (wʊ'pi:). **1.** an exclamation of joy, excitement, etc. ~*n.* ('wʊpi:). **2. make whoopee. a.** to engage in noisy merrymaking. **b.** to make love.

whoop·er *or* **whoop·er swan** ('wu:pə) *n.* a large white Old World swan, *Cygnus cygnus,* having a black bill with a yellow base and a noisy whooping cry.

whoop·ing cough ('hu:pɪŋ) *n.* an acute infectious disease characterized by coughing spasms that end with a shrill crowing sound on inspiration: caused by infection with the bacillus *Bordetella pertussis.* Technical name: **pertussis.**

whoop·ing crane *n.* a rare North American crane, *Grus americana,* having a white plumage with black wings and a red naked face.

whoops (wʊps) *interj.* an exclamation of surprise, as when a person falls over, or of apology.

whoosh *or* **woosh** (wʊʃ) *n.* **1.** a hissing or rushing sound. ~*vb.* **2.** (*intr.*) to make or move with such a sound.

whop, wop, *or* **whap** (wɒp) *Informal.* ~*vb.* **whops, whop·ping, whopped. 1.** (*tr.*) to strike, beat, or thrash. **2.** (*tr.*) to defeat utterly. **3.** (*intr.*) to drop or fall. ~*n.* **4.** a heavy blow or the sound made by such a blow. [C14: variant of *wap,* perhaps of imitative origin]

whop·per ('wɒpə) *n. Informal.* **1.** anything uncommonly large of its kind. **2.** a big lie. [C18: from WHOP]

whop·ping ('wɒpɪŋ) *adj. Informal.* uncommonly large.

whore (hɔ:) *n.* **1.** a prostitute or promiscuous woman: often a term of abuse. Related adj.: **meretricious.** ~*vb.* (*intr.*) **2.** to be or act as a prostitute. **3.** (of a man) to have promiscuous sexual relations, esp. with prostitutes. **4.** (often foll. by *after*) to seek that which is immoral, idolatrous, etc. [Old English *hōre;* related to Old Norse *hōra,* Old High German *hvora,* Latin *carus* dear] —'**whor·ish** *adj.* —'**whor·ish·ly** *adv.* —'**whor·ish·ness** *n.*

whore·dom ('hɔːdəm) *n.* **1.** the activity of whoring or state of being a whore. **2.** a biblical word for **idolatry.**

whore·house ('hɔːˌhaʊs) *n.* another word for **brothel.**

whore·mas·ter ('hɔːˌmɑːstə) *n. Archaic.* a person who consorts with or procures whores. —'**whore·ˌmas·ter·y** *n.*

whore·mong·er ('hɔːˌmʌŋgə) *n.* a person who consorts with whores; lecher. —'**whore·ˌmon·ger·y** *n.*

whore·son ('hɔːsən) *Archaic.* ~*n.* **1.** a bastard. **2.** a scoundrel; wretch. ~*adj.* **3.** vile or hateful.

whorl (wɜːl) *n.* **1.** *Botany.* a radial arrangement of three or more petals, stamens, leaves, etc., around a stem. **2.** *Zoology.* a single turn in a spiral shell. **3.** one of the basic patterns of the human fingerprint, formed by several complete circular ridges one inside another. Compare **arch**[1] (sense 4b.), **loop**[1] (sense 9a.). **4.** anything shaped like a coil. [C15: probably variant of *wherville* WHIRL, influenced by Dutch *worvel*] —**whorled** *adj.*

whor·tle·ber·ry ('wɜːtᵊlˌbɛrɪ) *n., pl.* **·ries. 1.** Also called: **bilberry, huckleberry,** and (Brit.) **blaeberry.** a small Eurasian ericaceous shrub, *Vaccinium myrtillus,* greenish-pink flowers and edible sweet blackish berries. **2.** the fruit of this shrub. **3. bog whortleberry.** a related plant, *V. uliginosum,* of mountain regions, having pink flowers and black fruits.

who's (huːz) *contraction of* who is.

whose (huːz) *determiner* **1. a.** of who? belonging to who? used in direct and indirect questions: *I told him whose fault it was; whose car is this?* **b.** (*as pronoun*): *whose is that?* **2.** of who; belonging to who; of which; belonging to which: used as a relative pronoun: *a house whose windows are broken; a man whose reputation has suffered.* [Old English *hwæs,* genitive of *hwā* WHO and *hwæt* WHAT]

who·so ('huːsəʊ) *pron.* an archaic word for **whoever.**

who·so·ev·er (ˌhuːsəʊ'ɛvə) *pron.* an archaic or formal word for **whoever.**

whr, whr., Whr, *or* **Whr.** *abbrev. for* watt-hour.

whsle. *abbrev. for* wholesale.

why (waɪ) *adv.* **1. a.** for what reason, purpose, or cause?: *why are you here?* **b.** (*used in indirect questions*): *tell me why you're here.* ~*pron.* **2.** for or because of which: *there is no reason why he shouldn't come.* ~*n., pl.* **whys. 3.** (*usually pl.*) a question as to the reason, purpose, or cause of something (esp. in the phrase **the whys and wherefores**). ~*interj.* **4.** an introductory expression of surprise, disagreement, indignation, etc.: *why, don't be silly!* [Old English *hwī;* related to Old Norse *hvī,* Gothic *hveileiks* what kind of, Latin *quī*]

Why·al·la (waɪ'ælə) *n.* a port in S South Australia, on Spencer Gulf: iron and steel and shipbuilding industries. Pop.: 33 800 (1975 est.).

whyd·ah *or* **whid·ah** ('wɪdə) *n.* any of various predominantly black African weaverbirds of the genus *Vidua* and related genera, the males of which grow very long tail feathers in the breeding season. Also called: **whydah bird, whidah bird, widow bird.** [C18: after the name of a town in Dahomey]

W.I. *abbrev. for:* **1.** West Indian. **2.** West Indies. **3.** (in Britain) Women's Institute.

Wich·i·ta ('wɪtʃɪˌtɔː) *n.* a city in S Kansas, on the Arkansas River: the largest city in the state; two universities. Pop.: 261 231 (1973 est.).

wick[1] (wɪk) *n.* **1.** a cord or band of loosely twisted or woven fibres, as in a candle, cigarette lighter, etc., that supplies fuel to a flame by capillary action. **2. get on (someone's) wick.** *Brit. slang.* to cause irritation to (a person). [Old English *weoce;* related to Old High German *wioh,* Middle Dutch *wēke* (Dutch *wiek*)] —'**wick·ing** *n.*

wick[2] (wɪk) *n. Archaic.* a village or hamlet. [Old English *wīc;* related to *-wich* in place names, Latin *vīcus,* Greek *oîkos*]

wick[3] (wɪk) *adj. Northern English dialect.* **1.** lively or active. **2.** alive or crawling: *wick with fleas.* [dialect variant of QUICK alive]

Wick (wɪk) *n.* a town in N Scotland, in the Highland region, at the head of **Wick Bay** (an inlet of the North Sea). Pop.: 7613 (1971).

wick·ed ('wɪkɪd) *adj.* **1. a.** morally bad in principle or practice. **b.** (*as collective n.* preceded by *the*): *the wicked.* **2.** mischievous or roguish, esp. in a playful way: *a wicked grin.* **3.** causing injury or harm. **4.** troublesome, unpleasant, or offensive. **5.** *Slang.* done or accomplished with great skill; masterly. [C13: from dialect *wick,* from Old English *wicca* sorcerer, *wicce* WITCH] —'**wick·ed·ly** *adv.* —'**wick·ed·ness** *n.*

wick·er ('wɪkə) *n.* **1.** a slender flexible twig or shoot, esp. of willow. **2.** short for **wickerwork.** ~*adj.* **3.** made, consisting of, or constructed from wicker. [C14: from Scandinavian; compare Swedish *viker,* Danish *viger* willow, Swedish *vika* to bend]

wick·er·work ('wɪkəˌwɜːk) *n.* **a.** a material consisting of wicker. **b.** (*as modifier*): *a wickerwork chair.*

wick·et ('wɪkɪt) *n.* **1.** a small door or gate, esp. one that is near to or part of a larger one. **2.** a small window or opening in a door, esp. one fitted with a grating or glass pane, used as a means of communication in a ticket office, bank, etc. **3.** a small sluicegate, esp. one in a canal lock gate or by a water wheel. **4.** a croquet hoop. **5. a.** *Cricket.* either of two constructions, placed 22 yards apart, consisting of three pointed stumps stuck parallel in the ground with two wooden bails resting on top, at which the batsman stands. **b.** the strip of ground between these. **c.** a batsman's turn at batting or the period during which two batsmen bat: *a third-wicket partnership.* **d.** the act or instance of a batsman being got out: *the bowler took six wickets.* **6. keep wicket.** to act as a wicketkeeper. **7. on a good, sticky, etc., wicket.** *Informal.* in an advantageous, awkward, etc., situation. [C18: from Old Northern French *wiket;* related to Old Norse *vikja* to move]

wick·et·keep·er ('wɪkɪtˌkiːpə) *n. Cricket.* the player on the fielding side positioned directly behind the wicket.

wick·et maid·en *n. Cricket.* an over in which no runs are scored with the bat and at least one wicket is taken by the bowler. See also **maiden over.**

wick·i·up, wik·i·up, *or* **wick·y·up** ('wɪkɪˌʌp) *n.* a hut used by nomadic Indians of the southwestern U.S., made of brushwood, mats, or grass and having an oval frame. [C19: from Sac, Fox, and Kickapoo *wikiyap;* compare WIGWAM]

Wick·liffe *or* **Wic·lif** ('wɪklɪf) *n.* variant spellings of (John) **Wycliffe.**

Wick·low ('wɪkləʊ) *n.* **1.** a county of E Ireland, in Leinster province on the Irish Sea: consists of a coastal strip rising inland to the **Wicklow Mountains;** mainly agricultural, with several resorts. County town: Wicklow. Pop.: 66 295 (1971). Area: 2025 sq. km (782 sq. miles). **2.** a port in E Ireland, county town of Co. Wicklow. Pop.: 37 86 (1971).

wick·thing ('wɪkˌθɪŋ) *n. Lancashire dialect.* a creeping animal, such as a woodlouse. [from WICK[3] + THING]

wic·o·py ('wɪkəpɪ) *n., pl.* **·pies.** *U.S.* any of various North American trees, shrubs, or herbaceous plants, esp. the leatherwood, various willowherbs, and the basswood. [C18: from Cree *wikupiy* inner bark, willow bark]

wid·der·shins ('wɪdəˌʃɪnz) *adv. Chiefly Scot.* a variant spelling of **withershins.**

wide (waɪd) *adj.* **1.** having a great extent from side to side. **2.** of vast size or scope; spacious or extensive. **3. a.** (*postpositive*) having a specified extent, esp. from side to side: *two yards wide.* **b.** (*in combination*): covering or extending throughout: *nationwide.* **4.** distant or remote from the desired point, mark, etc.: *your guess is wide of the mark.* **5.** (of eyes) opened fully. **6.** loose, full, or roomy: *wide trousers.* **7.** exhibiting a considerable spread, as between certain limits: *a wide variation.* **8.** *Phonetics.* another word for **lax** (sense 4) or **open** (sense 34). **9.** *Brit. slang.* unscrupulous and astute: *a wide boy.* ~*adv.* **10.** over an extensive area: *to travel far and wide.* **11.** to the full extent: *he opened the door wide.* **12.** far from the desired point, mark, etc. ~*n.* **13.** (in cricket) a bowled ball that is outside the batsman's reach and scores a run for the batting side. **14.** *Archaic or poetic.* a wide space or extent. [Old English *wīd;* related to Old Norse *vīthr,* Old High German *wīt*] —'**wide·ly** *adv.* —'**wide·ness** *n.* —'**wid·ish** *adj.*

wide-an·gle lens *n.* a lens system on a camera that can cover an angle of view of 60° or more and therefore has a fairly small focal length. See also **fish-eye lens.**

wide-a·wake *adj.* (**wide awake** *when postpositive*). **1.** fully awake. **2.** keen, alert, or observant. ~*n.* **3.** Also called: **wide-awake hat.** a hat with a low crown and very wide brim. —'**wide-a·'wake·ness** *n.*

wide-eyed *adj.* innocent or credulous.

wid·en ('waɪdᵊn) *vb.* to make or become wide or wider. —'**wid·en·er** *n.*

wide-o·pen *adj.* (**wide open** *when postpositive*). **1.** open to the full extent. **2.** (*postpositive*) exposed to attack; vulnerable. **3.** uncertain as to outcome. **4.** *U.S. informal.* (of a town or city) lax in the enforcement of certain laws, esp. those relating to the sale and consumption of alcohol, gambling, the control of vice, etc.

wide-screen *adj.* of or relating to a form of film projection in which the screen has greater width than height.

wide·spread ('waɪdˌsprɛd) *adj.* **1.** extending over a wide area. **2.** accepted by or occurring among many people.

widg·eon ('wɪdʒən) *n.* a variant spelling of **wigeon.**

Widg·e·ry ('wɪdʒərɪ) *n.* Baron **John Passmore.** 1911–81, English judge; Lord Chief Justice from 1971.

widg·et ('wɪdʒɪt) *n. Informal.* any small mechanism or device, the name of which is unknown or temporarily forgotten. [C20: changed from GADGET]

widg·ie ('wɪdʒɪ) *n. Austral. slang.* a female larrikin or bodgie. [C20: alteration of BODGIE]

Wid·nes ('wɪdnɪs) *n.* a town in NW England, in N Cheshire on the River Mersey: chemical industry. Pop.: 56 709 (1971).

wid·ow ('wɪdəʊ) *n.* **1.** a woman who has survived her husband, esp. one who has not remarried. **2.** (*usually with a modifier*) *Informal.* a woman whose husband frequently leaves her alone to indulge in a sport, etc.: *a golf widow.* **3.** *Printing.* a short line at the end of a paragraph, esp. one that occurs as the top line of a page or column. **4.** (in some card games) an additional hand or set of cards exposed on the table. ~*vb.* (*tr.; usually passive*) **5.** to cause to become a widow. **6.** to deprive of something valued or desirable. [Old English *widuwe;* related to German *Witwe,* Latin *vidua* (feminine of *viduus* deprived), Sanskrit *vidhavā*] —'**wid·ow·hood** *n.*

wid·ow bird *n.* another name for **whydah.**

wid·ow·er ('wɪdəʊə) *n.* a man whose wife has died and who has not remarried.

wid·ow's ben·e·fit *n.* (in the British National Insurance scheme) a weekly payment made to a widow.

wid·ow's cruse *n.* an endless or unfailing source of supply. [allusion to Kings 17:16]

wid+ow's mite *n.* a small contribution given by a person who has very little. [allusion to Mark 12:43]
wid+ow's peak *n.* a V-shaped point in the hairline in the middle of the forehead. [from the belief that it presaged early widowhood]
width (wɪdθ) *n.* **1.** the linear extent or measurement of something from side to side, usually being the shortest dimension or (for something fixed) the shortest horizontal dimension. **2.** the state or fact of being wide. **3.** a piece or section of something at its full extent from side to side: *a width of cloth.* **4.** the distance across a rectangular swimming bath, as opposed to its length. [C17: from WIDE + -TH[1], analogous to BREADTH]
width+wise ('wɪdθ,waɪz) *or* **width+ways** ('wɪdθ,weɪz) *adv.* in the direction of the width; from side to side.
Wi·du·kind ('vi:dʊkɪnt) *n.* a variant spelling of **Wittekind.**
Wie+land[1] ('vi:lant) *n.* the German name for **Wayland.**
Wie·land[2] (*German* 'vi:lant) *n.* **Chris·toph Mar·tin** ('krɪstɔf 'marti:n). 1733–1813, German writer, noted esp. for his verse epic *Oberon* (1780).
wield (wi:ld) *vb.* (*tr.*) **1.** to handle or use (a weapon, tool, etc.). **2.** to exert or maintain (power or authority). **3.** *Obsolete.* to rule. [Old English *wieldan, wealdan;* related to Old Norse *valda,* Old Saxon *waldan,* German *walten,* Latin *valēre* to be strong] —**'wield+a·ble** *adj.* —**'wield+er** *n.*
wield·y ('wi:ldɪ) *adj.* **wield·i+er, wield·i+est.** easily handled, used, or managed.
Wien[1] (vi:n) *n.* the German name for **Vienna.**
Wien[2] (*German* vi:n) *n.* **Wil·helm** ('vɪlhɛlm). 1864–1928, German physicist, who studied black-body radiation: Nobel prize for physics 1911.
wie+ner ('wi:nə) *or* **wie·ner+wurst** ('wi:nə,wɜ:st) *n. U.S.* a kind of smoked beef or pork sausage, similar to a frankfurter. Also called: **wienie, weenie.** [C20: shortened from German *Wiener Wurst* Viennese sausage]
Wie·ner ('wi:nə) *n.* **Nor·bert** ('nɔ:bət). 1894–1964, U.S. mathematician, who developed the concept of cybernetics.
Wie+ner Neu+stadt (*German* 'vi:nər 'nɔɪʃtat) *n.* a city in E Austria, in Lower Austria. Pop.: 34 774 (1971).
Wie+ner schnit+zel ('vi:nə 'ʃnɪtsəl) *n.* a large thin escalope of veal, coated in egg and crumbs, fried, and traditionally served with a garnish. [German: Viennese cutlet]
Wies+ba·den (*German* 'vi:sba:dᵊn) *n.* a city in W West Germany, capital of Hesse state: a spa resort since Roman times. Pop.: 252 457 (1974 est.). Latin name: **Aquae Mattiacorum.**
wife (waɪf) *n., pl.* **wives** (waɪvz). **1.** a man's partner in marriage; a married woman. Related adj.: **uxorial. 2.** an archaic or dialect word for **woman. 3. take to wife.** to marry (a woman). [Old English *wīf;* related to Old Norse *vīf* (perhaps from *vīfathr* veiled), Old High German *wīb* (German *Weib*)] —**'wife+hood** *n.* —**'wife+less** *adj.* —**'wife+like** *adj.* —**'wife+li+ness** *n.* —**'wife+ly** *adj.*
wife swap+ping *n.* **a.** the temporary exchange of wives between married couples for sexual relations. **b.** (*as modifier*): *a wife-swapping party.*
wig (wɪg) *n.* **1.** an artificial head of hair, either human or synthetic, worn to disguise baldness, as part of a theatrical or ceremonial dress, as a disguise, or for adornment. ~*vb.* **wigs, wig+ging, wigged.** (*tr.*) **2.** *Obsolete.* to furnish with a wig. **3.** *Brit. slang.* to berate severely. [C17: shortened from PERIWIG] —**wigged** *adj.* —**'wig+less** *adj.* —**'wig+,like** *adj.*
Wig. *abbrev. for* Wigtownshire.
Wig+an ('wɪgən) *n.* an industrial town in NW England, in Greater Manchester: coal-mining centre since the 14th century. Pop.: 81 258 (1971).
wig+eon *or* **widg+eon** ('wɪdʒən) *n.* **1.** a Eurasian duck, *Anas penelope,* of marshes, swamps, etc., the male of which has a reddish-brown head and chest and grey and white back and wings. **2. American wigeon.** Also called: **baldpate.** a similar bird, *Anas americana,* of North America, the male of which has a white crown. [C16: of uncertain origin]
wig+ging ('wɪgɪŋ) *n. Brit. slang.* a rebuke or reprimand.
wig+gle ('wɪgᵊl) *vb.* **1.** to move or cause to move with jerky movements, esp. from side to side. ~*n.* **2.** the act or an instance of wiggling. **3. get a wiggle on.** *Slang, chiefly U.S.* to hurry up. [C13: from Middle Low German, Middle Dutch *wiggelen*] —**'wig+gler** *n.* —**'wig+gly** *adj.*
wight[1] (waɪt) *n. Archaic.* a human being. [Old English *wiht;* related to Old Frisian *āwet* something, Old Norse *vættr* being, Gothic *waihts* thing, German *Wicht* small person]
wight[2] (waɪt) *adj. Archaic.* strong and brave; valiant. [C13: from Old Norse *vigt;* related to Old English *wīg* battle, Latin *vincere* to conquer]
Wight (waɪt) *n.* **Isle of.** an island and county of S England in the English Channel. Administrative centre: Newport. Pop.: 111 300 (1976 est.). Area: 380 sq. km (147 sq. miles).
Wig·ner ('wɪgnə) *n.* **Eu·gene Paul.** born 1902, U.S. physicist, born in Hungary. He is noted for his contributions to nuclear physics: shared the Nobel prize for physics (1963).
Wig+town ('wɪgtən) *n.* (until 1975) a county of SW Scotland, now part of Dumfries and Galloway region.
wig+wag ('wɪg,wæg) *vb.* **+wags, +wag+ging, +wagged. 1.** to move (something) back and forth. **2.** to communicate with (someone) by means of a flag semaphore. ~*n.* **3. a.** a system of communication by flag semaphore. **b.** the message signalled. [C16: from obsolete *wig,* probably short for WIGGLE + WAG] —**'wig+,wag+ger** *n.*
wig+wam ('wɪg,wæm) *n.* **1.** any dwelling of the North American Indians, esp. one made of bark, rushes, or skins spread over or enclosed by a set of arched poles lashed together. Compare **tepee. 2.** a similar structure for children. [from Abnaki and Massachuset *wīkwām,* literally: their abode]
wik·i+up ('wɪkɪ,ʌp) *n.* a variant spelling of **wickiup.**
Wil·ber·force ('wɪlbə,fɔ:s) *n.* **Wil·liam.** 1759–1833, English politician and philanthropist, whose efforts secured the abolition of the slave trade (1807) and of slavery (1833) in the British Empire.
wil+co (,wɪl'kəʊ) *interj.* an expression in signalling, telecommunications, etc., indicating that a message just received will be complied with. Compare **roger.** [C20: abbreviation for *I will comply*]
wild (waɪld) *adj.* **1.** (of animals) living independently of man; not domesticated or tame. **2.** (of plants) growing in a natural state; not cultivated. **3.** uninhabited or uncultivated; desolate: *a wild stretch of land.* **4.** living in a savage or uncivilized way: *wild tribes.* **5.** lacking restraint or control: *wild merriment.* **6.** of great violence or intensity: *a wild storm.* **7.** disorderly or chaotic: *wild thoughts; wild talk.* **8.** dishevelled; untidy: *wild hair.* **9.** in a state of extreme emotional intensity: *wild with anger.* **10.** reckless: *wild speculations.* **11.** not calculated; random: *a wild guess.* **12.** (*postpositive;* foll. by *about*) *Informal.* intensely enthusiastic or excited: *I'm wild about my new boyfriend.* **13.** (of a card, such as a joker or deuce in some games) able to be given any value the holder pleases: *jacks are wild.* ~*adv.* **14.** in a wild manner. **15. run wild. a.** to grow without cultivation or care: *the garden has run wild.* **b.** to behave without restraint: *he has let his children run wild.* ~*n.* **16.** (*often pl.*) a desolate, uncultivated, or uninhabited region. **17. the wild. a.** a free natural state of living. **b.** the wilderness. [Old English *wilde;* related to Old Saxon, Old High German *wildi,* Old Norse *villr,* Gothic *wiltheis*] —**'wild+ish** *adj.* —**'wild+ly** *adv.* —**'wild+ness** *n.*
wild boar *n.* a wild pig, *Sus scrofa,* of parts of Europe and central Asia, having a pale grey to black coat, thin legs, a narrow body, and prominent tusks.
wild bri+er *n.* another name for **wild rose.**
wild car+rot *n.* an umbelliferous plant, *Daucus carota,* of temperate regions, having clusters of white flowers and hooked fruits. Also called: **Queen Anne's lace.**
wild+cat ('waɪld,kæt) *n., pl.* **+cats** *or* **+cat. 1.** a wild European cat, *Felis silvestris,* that resembles the domestic tabby but is larger and has a bushy tail. **2.** any of various other felines, esp. of the genus *Lynx,* such as the lynx and the caracal. **3.** *U.S.* another name for **bobcat. 4.** *Informal.* a savage or aggressive person. **5.** *Chiefly U.S.* an exploratory drilling for petroleum or natural gas. **6.** *U.S.* an unsound commercial enterprise. **7.** the U.S. name for **light engine. 8.** (*modifier*) *U.S.* **a.** of or relating to an unsound business enterprise: *wildcat stock.* **b.** financially or commercially unsound: *a wildcat project.* **9.** (*modifier*) *U.S.* (of a train) running without permission or outside the timetable. ~*vb.* **+cats, +cat+ting, +cat+ted. 10.** (*intr.*) *Chiefly U.S.* to drill for petroleum or natural gas in an area having no known reserves. —**'wild+,cat+ting** *n., adj.*
wild+cat strike *n.* a strike begun by workers spontaneously or without union approval.
wild+cat+ter ('waɪld,kætə) *n. U.S. informal.* a prospector for oil or ores in areas having no proved resources.
wild cel+er·y *n.* a strongly scented umbelliferous plant, *Apium graveolens,* of temperate regions: the ancestor of cultivated celery. Archaic name: **smallage.**
wild cher+ry *n.* another name for **sweet cherry.**
wild dog *n.* another name for **dingo.**
Wilde (waɪld) *n.* **Os·car (Fingal O'Flahertie Wills).** 1854–1900, Irish writer and wit, famous for such plays as *Lady Windermere's Fan* (1892) and *The Importance of being Earnest* (1895). *The Picture of Dorian Grey* (1891) is a macabre novel about a hedonist and *The Ballad of Reading Gaol* (1898) relates to his experiences in prison while serving a two-year sentence for homosexuality.
wil+de+beest ('wɪldɪ,bi:st, 'vɪl-) *n., pl.* **+beests** *or* **+beest.** another name for **gnu.** [C19: from Afrikaans, literally: wild beast]
wil+der ('wɪldə) *vb. Archaic.* **1.** to lead or be led astray. **2.** to bewilder or become bewildered. —**'wil+der+ment** *n.*
wil+der+ness ('wɪldənɪs) *n.* **1.** a wild, uninhabited, and uncultivated region. **2.** any desolate tract or area. **3.** a confused mass or collection. **4. a voice (crying) in the wilderness.** a person, group, etc., making a suggestion or plea that is ignored. [Old English *wildēornes,* from *wildēor* wild beast (from WILD + *dēor* beast, DEER) + -NESS; related to Middle Dutch *wildernisse,* German *Wildernis*]
Wil+der+ness ('wɪldənɪs) *n.* **the.** the barren regions to the south and east of Palestine, esp. those in which the Israelites wandered before entering the Promised Land and in which Christ fasted for 40 days and nights.
wild-eyed *adj.* **1.** glaring in an angry, distracted, or wild manner. **2.** ill-conceived or totally impracticable.
wild+fire ('waɪld,faɪə) *n.* **1.** a highly flammable material, such as Greek fire, formerly used in warfare. **2. a.** a raging and uncontrollable fire. **b.** anything that is disseminated quickly (esp. in the phrase **spread like wildfire**). **3.** lightning without audible thunder. **4.** another name for **will-o'-the-wisp.**
wild flow+er *n.* **1.** any flowering plant that grows in an uncultivated state. **2.** the flower of such a plant.
wild+fowl ('waɪld,faʊl) *n.* **1.** any bird that is hunted by man, esp. any duck or similar aquatic bird. **2.** such birds collectively. —**'wild+,fowl+er** *n.* —**'wild+,fowl+ing** *adj., n.*

Wild Geese *n.* **the.** the Irish expatriates who served as professional soldiers with the Catholic powers of Europe, esp. France, from the late 17th to the early 20th centuries.

wild gin+ger *n.* a North American plant, *Asarum canadense,* having a solitary brownish flower and an aromatic root: family *Aristolochiaceae.* See also **asarabacca, asarum.**

wild-goose chase *n.* an absurd or hopeless pursuit, as of something unattainable.

wild hy·a+cinth *n.* another name for **bluebell** (sense 1).

wild in+di+go *n.* any of several North American leguminous plants of the genus *Baptisia,* esp. *B. tinctoria,* which has yellow flowers and three-lobed leaves.

wild+ing ('waɪldɪŋ) *n.* **1.** an uncultivated plant, esp. the crab apple, or a cultivated plant that has become wild. **2.** a wild animal. ~Also called: **wildling.**

wild let+tuce *n.* any of several uncultivated lettuce plants, such as *Lactuca serriola* (or *L. scariola*) of Eurasia and *L. canadensis* (**horseweed**) of North America, which grow as weeds and have yellow or blue flowers, milky juice in the stem, and prickly leaves: family *Compositae* (composites).

wild+life ('waɪldˌlaɪf) *n.* wild animals and plants collectively.

wild mus+tard *n.* another name for **charlock** (sense 1).

wild oat *n.* any of several temperate annual grasses of the genus *Avena,* esp. *A. fatua,* that grow as weeds and have long bristles on their flower spikes.

wild oats *pl. n. Slang.* the indiscretions of youth, esp. dissoluteness before settling down (esp. in the phrase **sow one's wild oats**).

wild ol+ive *n.* any of various trees or shrubs that resemble the olive tree or bear olive-like fruits, esp. the oleaster.

wild pan+sy *n.* **1.** Also called: **heartsease, love-in-idleness,** and (in the U.S.) **Johnny-jump-up.** a Eurasian violaceous plant, *Viola tricolor,* having purple, yellow, and pale mauve spurred flowers. **2.** any of various similar plants of the genus *Viola.*

wild pars+ley *n.* any of various uncultivated umbelliferous plants that resemble parsley.

wild pars+nip *n.* a strong-smelling umbelliferous plant, *Pastinaca sativa,* that has an inedible root: the ancestor of the cultivated parsnip.

wild rice *n.* another name for **Indian rice.**

wild rose *n.* any of numerous roses, such as the dogrose and sweetbrier, that grow wild and have flowers with only one whorl of petals.

wild rub+ber *n.* rubber obtained from uncultivated rubber trees.

wild rye *n.* any of various perennial grasses of the N temperate genus *Elymus,* resembling cultivated rye in having paired bristly ears or spikes and flat leaves.

wild track *n.* a soundtrack recorded other than with a synchronized picture, usually carrying sound effects, random dialogue, etc.

wild type *n. Biology.* the typical form of a species of organism resulting from breeding under natural conditions.

Wild West *n.* the western U.S. during its settlement, esp. with reference to its frontier lawlessness.

Wild West show *n. U.S.* a show or circus act presenting feats of horsemanship, shooting, etc.

wild+wood ('waɪldˌwʊd) *n. Archaic.* a wood or forest growing in a natural uncultivated state.

wile (waɪl) *n.* **1.** trickery, cunning, or craftiness. **2.** (*usually pl.*) an artful or seductive trick or ploy. ~*vb.* **3.** (*tr.*) to lure, beguile, or entice. [C12: from Old Norse *vel* craft; probably related to Old French *wile,* Old English *wīgle* magic. See GUILE]

wil+ful *or U.S.* **will+ful** ('wɪlfʊl) *adj.* **1.** intent on having one's own way; headstrong or obstinate. **2.** willed or intentional: *wilful murder.* —**'wil+ful+ly** *or U.S.* **'will+ful+ly** *adv.* —**'wil+ful+ness** *or U.S.* **'will+ful+ness** *n.*

Wil·helm I ('vɪlhɛlm) *n.* the German name of **William I** (sense 3).

Wil·helm II *n.* the German name of **William II** (sense 2).

Wil·hel·mi·na I (ˌwɪlə'miːnə; *Dutch* wɪlhɛl'miːnaː) *n.* 1880–1962, queen of the Netherlands from 1890 until her abdication (1948) in favour of her daughter Juliana.

Wil+helms+ha+ven (*German* ˌvɪlhɛlms'haːfən) *n.* a port and resort in N West Germany, in Lower Saxony: founded in 1853; was the chief German North Sea naval base until 1945; a major oil port. Pop.: 104 305 (1974 est.).

Wil+helm+stras+se (*German* 'vɪlhɛlmˌʃtraːsə) *n.* **1.** a street in the centre of Berlin, where the German foreign office and other government buildings were situated until 1945. **2.** Germany's ministry of foreign affairs until 1945.

Wilkes (wɪlks) *n.* **1. Charles.** 1798–1877, U.S. explorer of Antarctica. **2. John.** 1727–97, English politician, who was expelled from the House of Commons and outlawed for writing scurrilous articles about the government. He became a champion of parliamentary reform.

Wilkes Land *n.* a region in Antarctica south of Australia, on the Indian Ocean.

Wil·kins ('wɪlkɪnz) *n.* **1.** Sir **George Hu·bert.** 1888–1958, Australian polar explorer and aviator. **2. Mau·rice Hugh Fred·er·ick.** born 1916, British biochemist, born in New Zealand: with Crick and Watson, he shared the Nobel Prize (1962) for his work on the structure of DNA.

will[1] (wɪl) *vb. past* **would.** (takes an infinitive without *to* or an implied infinitive) used as an auxiliary. **1.** (esp. with *you, he, she, it, they,* or a noun as subject) to make the future tense. Compare **shall** (sense 1). **2.** to express resolution on the part of the speaker: *I will buy that radio if it's the last thing I do.* **3.** to indicate willingness or desire: *will you help me with this problem?* **4.** to express compulsion, as in commands: *you will report your findings to me tomorrow.* **5.** to express capacity or ability: *this rope will support a load.* **6.** to express probability or expectation on the part of the speaker: *that will be Jim telephoning.* **7.** to express customary practice or inevitability: *boys will be boys.* **8.** (*with the infinitive always implied*) to express desire: usually in polite requests: *stay if you will.* **9. what you will.** whatever you like. **10. will do.** *Informal.* a declaration of willingness to do what is requested. [Old English *willan;* related to Old Saxon *willian,* Old Norse *vilja,* Old High German *wollen,* Latin *velle* to wish, will]

Usage. See at **shall.**

will[2] (wɪl) *n.* **1.** the faculty of conscious and deliberate choice of action; volition. Related adj.: **voluntary. 2.** the act or an instance of asserting a choice. **3. a.** the declaration of a person's wishes regarding the disposal of his property after his death. **b.** a revocable instrument by which such wishes are expressed. **4.** anything decided upon or chosen, esp. by a person in authority; desire; wish. **5.** determined intention: *where there's a will there's a way.* **6.** disposition or attitude towards others: *he bears you no ill will.* **7. at will.** at one's own desire, inclination, or choice. **8. with the best will in the world.** even with the best of intentions. ~*vb.* (*mainly tr.; often takes a clause as object or an infinitive*) **9.** (*also intr.*) to exercise the faculty of volition in an attempt to accomplish (something): *he willed his wife's recovery from her illness.* **10.** to give (property) by will to a person, society, etc.: *he willed his art collection to the nation.* **11.** (*also intr.*) to order or decree: *the king wills that you shall die.* **12.** to choose or prefer: *wander where you will.* **13.** to yearn for or desire: *to will that one's friends be happy.* [Old English *willa;* related to Old Norse *vili,* Old High German *willeo* (German *Wille*), Gothic *wilja,* Old Slavonic *volja*] —**'will+er** *n.*

will+a·ble ('wɪləbəl) *adj.* able to be wished or determined by the will.

willed (wɪld) *adj.* (*in combination*) having a will as specified: *weak-willed.*

wil+lem+ite ('wɪləˌmaɪt) *n.* a secondary mineral consisting of zinc silicate in hexagonal crystalline form. It is white, colourless, or coloured by impurities and is found in veins of zinc ore. Formula: Zn_2SiO_4. [C19: from Dutch *willemit,* named after *Willem* I of the Netherlands (1772–1834)]

Wil+lem+stad (*Dutch* 'wɪləmˌstɑt) *n.* the capital of the Netherlands Antilles, a port on the SW coast of Curaçao: important for refining Venezuelan oil. Pop.: 59 586 (1964).

wil+let ('wɪlɪt) *n.* a large American shore bird, *Catoptrophorus semipalmatus,* having a long stout bill, long legs, and a grey plumage with black-and-white wings: family *Scolopacidae* (sandpipers, etc.), order *Charadriiformes.*

will+ful ('wɪlfʊl) *adj.* the U.S. spelling of **wilful.**

Wil·liam I ('wɪljəm) *n.* **1.** known as *William the Conqueror.* ?1027–1087, duke of Normandy (1035–87) and king of England (1066–87). He claimed to have been promised the English crown by Edward the Confessor, after whose death he disputed the succession of Harold II, invading England in 1066 and defeating Harold at Hastings. The conquest of England resulted in the introduction to England of many Norman customs, esp. feudalism. In 1085 he ordered the Domesday Book to be compiled. **2.** called *the Silent.* 1533–84, prince of Orange and count of Nassau: led the revolt of the Netherlands against Spain (1568–76) and became first stadholder of the United Provinces of the Netherlands (1579–84); assassinated. **3.** German name *Wilhelm.* 1797–1888, king of Prussia (1861–88) and first emperor of Germany (1871–88).

Wil·liam II *n.* **1.** called *William Rufus.* ?1056–1100, king of England (1087–1100); the son of William the Conqueror. He was killed by an arrow while hunting in the New Forest. **2.** German name *Kaiser Wilhelm.* 1859–1941, German emperor and king of Prussia (1888–1918): asserted Germany's claim to world leadership; forced to abdicate at the end of World War I.

Wil·liam III *n.* known as *William of Orange.* 1650–1702, stadholder of the Netherlands (1672–1702) and king of Great Britain and Ireland (1689–1702). He was invited by opponents of James II to accept the British throne (1688) and ruled jointly with his wife Mary II (James' daughter) until her death in 1694.

Wil·liam IV *n.* called the *Sailor King.* 1765–1837, king of Great Britain and Ireland (1830–37), succeeding his brother George IV; the third son of George III.

Wil·liam of Malmes+bur·y ('mɑːmzbərɪ, -brɪ) *n.* ?1090–?1143, English monk and chronicler, whose *Gesta regum Anglorum* and *Historia novella* are valuable sources for English history to 1142.

Wil·liams ('wɪljəmz) *n.* **1. John.** born 1941, English classical guitarist. **2. J(ohn) P(eter) R(hys).** born 1949, Welsh Rugby Union player. A fullback, he played for Wales (from 1969) and the British Lions (1971–77). **3. Ralph Vaughan.** See **Vaughan Williams. 4. Ten·nes·see.** pseudonym of *Thomas Lanier Williams.* 1912–83, U.S. dramatist. His plays include *The Glass Menagerie* (1944), *A Streetcar Named Desire* (1947), *Cat on a Hot Tin Roof* (1955), and *Night of the Iguana* (1961). **5. Wil·liam Car·los** ('kɑːləs). 1883–1963, U.S. poet, who formulated the poetic concept "no ideas but in things." His works include *Paterson* (1946–58), which explores the daily life of a man living in a modern city, and the prose work *In the American Grain* (1925).

Wil+liams+burg ('wɪljəmzˌbɜːg) *n.* a city in SE Virginia: the capital of Virginia (1693–1779); the restoration of large sections of the colonial city was begun in 1926. Pop.: 9069 (1970).

Wil·liam·son ('wɪljəmsən) *n.* **Mal·colm.** born 1931, Australian composer, living in Britain: Master of the Queen's Music since 1975. His works include operas and music for children.

Wil·liam the Con·quer·or *n.* See **William I** (sense 1).

wil·lies ('wɪlɪz) *pl. n.* **the.** *Slang.* nervousness, jitters, or fright (esp. in the phrase **give** (*or* **get**) **the willies**).

will·ing ('wɪlɪŋ) *adj.* **1.** favourably disposed or inclined; ready. **2.** cheerfully or eagerly compliant. **3.** done, given, accepted, etc., freely or voluntarily. —'**will·ing·ly** *adv.* —'**will·ing·ness** *n.*

wil·li·waw ('wɪlɪˌwɔː) *n. U.S.* **1.** a sudden strong gust of cold wind blowing offshore from a mountainous coast, as in the Strait of Magellan. **2.** a state of great turmoil. [C19: of unknown origin]

will-o'-the-wisp (ˌwɪləðə'wɪsp) *n.* **1.** Also called: **friar's lantern, ignis fatuus, jack-o'-lantern.** a pale flame or phosphorescence sometimes seen over marshy ground at night. It is believed to be due to the spontaneous combustion of methane or other hydrocarbons originating from decomposing organic matter. **2.** a person or thing that is elusive or allures and misleads. —ˌ**will-o'-the-'wisp·ish** *or* ˌ**will-o'-the-'wisp·y** *adj.*

wil·low ('wɪləʊ) *n.* **1.** any of numerous salicaceous trees and shrubs of the genus *Salix,* such as the weeping willow and osiers of N temperate regions, which have graceful flexible branches and flowers in catkins. **2.** the whitish wood of certain of these trees. **3.** something made of willow wood, such as a cricket or baseball bat. **4.** a machine having a system of revolving spikes for opening and cleaning raw textile fibres. [Old English *welig;* related to *wilige* wicker basket, Old Saxon *wilgia,* Middle High German *wilge,* Greek *helikē* willow, *helix* twisted] —'**wil·low·ish** *or* '**wil·low-**ˌ**like** *adj.*

wil·low grouse *n.* a N European grouse, *Lagopus lagopus,* with a reddish-brown plumage and white wings: now regarded as the same species as the red grouse (*L. lagopus scoticus*) of Britain.

wil·low·herb ('wɪləʊˌhɜːb) *n.* **1.** any of various temperate and arctic onagraceous plants of the genus *Epilobium,* having narrow leaves and terminal clusters of pink, purplish, or white flowers. **2.** short for **rosebay willowherb** (see **rosebay**). **3.** (*not in botanical usage*) another name for **purple loosestrife** (see **loosestrife**).

wil·low pat·tern *n.* **a.** a pattern incorporating a willow tree, river, bridge, and figures, typically in blue on a white ground, used on pottery and porcelain. **b.** (*as modifier*): *a willow-pattern plate.*

Wil·low South *n.* a city in S Alaska, about 113 km (70 miles) northwest of Anchorage: chosen as the site of the new state capital in 1976.

wil·low tit *n.* a small tit, *Parus montanus,* of marshy woods in Europe, having a greyish-brown body and dull black crown.

wil·low war·bler *n.* an Old World warbler, *Phylloscopus trochilis,* of Eurasian woodlands.

wil·low·y ('wɪləʊɪ) *adj.* **1.** slender and graceful. **2.** flexible or pliant. **3.** covered or shaded with willows.

will·pow·er ('wɪlˌpaʊə) *n.* **1.** the ability to control oneself and determine one's actions. **2.** firmness of will.

Wills (wɪlz) *n.* **Wil·liam John.** 1834–61, English explorer: Robert Burke's deputy in an expedition on which both men died after crossing Australia from North to South for the first time.

wil·ly-nil·ly ('wɪlɪ'nɪlɪ) *adv.* **1.** whether desired or not. ~*adj.* **2.** occurring or taking place whether desired or not. [Old English *wile hē, nyle hē,* literally: will he or will he not; *nyle,* from *ne* not + *willan* to WILL¹]

wil·ly wag·tail *n. Austral.* a black-and-white flycatcher, *Rhipidura leucophrys,* having white feathers over the brows.

wil·ly-wil·ly ('wɪlɪ'wɪlɪ) *n. Austral.* a tropical cyclone or duststorm. [from a native Australian language]

Wil·ming·ton ('wɪlmɪŋtən) *n.* a port in N Delaware, on the Delaware River: industrial centre. Pop.: 80 386 (1970).

Wil·no ('viːlnɔ) *n.* the Polish name for **Vilnius.**

Wil·son ('wɪlsən) *n.* **1. Al·ex·an·der.** 1766–1813, Scottish ornithologist in the U.S. **2. An·gus (Frank Johnstone).** born 1913, English writer, whose works include the collection of short stories *The Wrong Set* (1949) and the novels *Anglo-Saxon Attitudes* (1956) and *No Laughing Matter* (1967). **3. Charles Thom·son Rees.** 1869–1959, Scottish physicist, who invented the cloud chamber: shared the Nobel prize for physics (1927). **4. Ed·mund.** 1895–1972, U.S. critic, noted esp. for *Axel's Castle* (1931), a study of the symbolist movement. **5.** Sir **(James) Har·old.** born 1916, English Labour statesman; prime minister (1964–70; 1974–76). **6. Rich·ard.** 1714–82, Welsh landscape painter. **7. (Thomas) Wood·row** ('wʊdrəʊ). 1856–1924, U.S. Democratic statesman; 28th president of the U.S. (1913–21). He led the U.S. into World War I in 1917 and proposed the Fourteen Points (1918) as a basis for peace. Although he secured the formation of the League of Nations the U.S. Senate refused to support it: Nobel peace prize 1919. —**Wil·so·ni·an** (wɪl'səʊnɪən) *adj.*

Wil·son cloud cham·ber *n.* the full name for **cloud chamber.**

Wil·son's pet·rel *n.* a common storm petrel, *Oceanites oceanicus,* that breeds around Antarctica but is often seen in the Atlantic. See **storm petrel.**

Wil·son's snipe *n.* another name for **common snipe.** See **snipe** (sense 1).

wilt¹ (wɪlt) *vb.* **1.** to become or cause to become limp, flaccid, or drooping: *insufficient water makes plants wilt.* **2.** to lose or cause to lose courage, strength, etc. ~*n.* **3.** the act of wilting or state of becoming wilted. **4.** any of various plant diseases characterized by permanent wilting, usually caused by fungal parasites attacking the roots. [C17: perhaps variant of *wilk* to wither, from Middle Dutch *welken*]

wilt² (wɪlt) *vb. Archaic or dialect.* (used with the pronoun *thou* or its relative equivalent) a singular form of the present tense (indicative mood) of **will¹.**

Wil·ton ('wɪltən) *n.* a kind of carpet with a close velvet pile of cut loops.

Wilts. (wɪlts) *abbrev. for* Wiltshire.

Wilt·shire ('wɪltʃɪə, -ʃə) *n.* a county of S England, consisting mainly of chalk uplands, with Salisbury Plain in the south and the Marlborough Downs in the north; prehistoric remains (at Stonehenge and Avebury). Administrative centre: Trowbridge. Pop.: 512 800 (1976 est.). Area: 3478 sq. km (1343 sq. miles).

wil·y ('waɪlɪ) *adj.* **wil·i·er, wil·i·est.** characterized by or proceeding from wiles; sly or crafty. —'**wil·i·ness** *n.*

wim·ble ('wɪmbᵊl) *n.* **1.** any of a number of hand tools, such as a brace and bit or a gimlet, used for boring holes. ~*vb.* **2.** to bore (a hole) with or as if with a wimble. [C13: from Middle Dutch *wimmel* auger]

Wim·ble·don ('wɪmbᵊldən) *n.* part of the Greater London borough of Merton: headquarters of the All England Lawn Tennis Club since 1877 and the site of the annual international tennis championships.

wim·ple ('wɪmpᵊl) *n.* **1.** a piece of cloth draped around the head to frame the face, worn by women in the Middle Ages and still a part of the habit of some nuns. **2.** *Scot.* a curve or bend, as in a river. ~*vb.* **3.** *Rare.* to ripple or cause to ripple or undulate. **4.** (*tr.*). *Archaic.* to cover with or put a wimple on. **5.** *Archaic.* (esp. of a veil) to lie or cause to lie in folds or pleats. [Old English *wimpel;* related to Old Saxon *wimpal,* Middle Dutch *wumpel,* Middle High German *bewimpfen* to veil]

Wim·py ('wɪmpɪ) *n. Trademark.* a hamburger served in a soft bread roll.

Wims·hurst ma·chine ('wɪmzhɜːst) *n.* a type of electrostatic generator with two parallel insulating discs revolving in different directions, each being in contact with a thin metal wiper that produces a charge on the disc: usually used for demonstration purposes. [C19: named after J. *Wimshurst* (1832–1903), English engineer]

win¹ (wɪn) *vb.* **wins, win·ning, won. 1.** (*intr.*) to achieve first place in a competition. **2.** (*tr.*) to gain or receive (a prize, first place, etc.) in a competition. **3.** (*tr.*) to succeed in or gain (something) with an effort: *we won recognition.* **4. win one's spurs. a.** to achieve recognition in some field of endeavour. **b.** *History.* to be knighted. **5.** to gain victory or triumph in (a battle, argument, etc.). **6.** (*tr.*) to earn or procure (a living, etc.) by work. **7.** (*tr.*) to take possession of, esp. violently; capture: *the Germans never won Leningrad.* **8.** (when *intr.,* foll. by *out, through,* etc.) to reach with difficulty (a desired condition or position) or become free, loose, etc., with effort: *the boat won the shore; the boat won through to the shore.* **9.** (*tr.;* often foll. by *over*) to gain the support or consent of (someone): *only I can win him over!* **10.** (*tr.*) to turn someone into (a supporter, enemy, etc.): *you have just won an ally.* **11.** (*tr.*) to gain (the sympathy, loyalty, etc.) of someone. **12.** (*tr.*) to obtain (a woman, etc.) in marriage. **13.** (*tr.*) **a.** to extract (ore, coal, etc.) from a mine. **b.** to extract (metal or other minerals) from ore. **c.** to discover and make (a mineral deposit) accessible for mining. **14. you can't win.** *Informal.* an expression of resignation after an unsuccessful attempt to overcome difficulties. ~*n.* **15.** *Informal.* a success, victory, or triumph. **16.** profit; winnings. **17.** the act or fact of reaching the finishing line or post first. ~See also **win out.** [Old English *winnan;* related to Old Norse *vinna,* German *gewinnen*] —'**win·na·ble** *adj.*

win² (wɪn) *vb.* **wins, win·ning, won** *or* **winned.** (*tr.*) *Irish and Northern Brit. dialect.* **1.** to dry (grain, hay, peat, etc.) by exposure to sun and air. **2.** a less common word for **winnow.** [Old English, perhaps a variant of WINNOW]

wince¹ (wɪns) *vb.* **1.** (*intr.*) to start slightly, as with sudden pain; flinch. ~*n.* **2.** the act of wincing. [C18 (earlier (C13) meaning: to kick): via Old French *wencier, guenchir* to avoid, from Germanic; compare Old Saxon *wenkian,* Old High German *wenken*] —'**winc·er** *n.* —'**winc·ing·ly** *adv.*

wince² (wɪns) *n.* a roller for transferring pieces of cloth between dyeing vats. [C17: variant of WINCH]

win·cey ('wɪnsɪ) *n. Brit.* a plain- or twill-weave cloth, usually having a cotton or linen warp and a wool filling. [C19: of Scottish origin, probably an alteration of *woolsey* as in LINSEY-WOOLSEY]

win·cey·ette (ˌwɪnsɪ'ɛt) *n. Brit.* a plain-weave cotton fabric with slightly raised two-sided nap.

winch¹ (wɪntʃ) *n.* **1.** a windlass driven by a hand- or power-operated crank. **2.** a hand- or power-operated crank by which a machine is driven. ~*vb.* **3.** (*tr.;* often foll. by *up* or *in*) to pull (in a rope) or lift (a weight) using a winch. [Old English *wince* pulley; related to WINK] —'**winch·er** *n.*

winch² (wɪntʃ) *vb.* (*intr.*) an obsolete word for **wince¹.**

win·ches·ter ('wɪntʃɪstə) *n.* (*sometimes cap.*) a large cylindrical bottle with a narrow neck used for transporting chemicals. It contains about 2.5 litres. [after *Winchester,* Hampshire]

Win·ches·ter ('wɪntʃɪstə) *n.* a city in S England, administrative centre of Hampshire: a Romano-British town; Saxon capital of Wessex; site of **Winchester College** (1382), the oldest English public school. Pop.: 31 041 (1971).

Win·ches·ter ri·fle *n. Trademark.* a breech-loading slide-action repeating rifle with a magazine attached under the barrel. Often shortened to **Winchester.**

Winck·el·mann (*German* 'vɪŋkᵊlˌman) *n.* **Jo·hann Jo·a·chim**

('jo:han 'jo:axɪm). 1717–68, German archaeologist and art historian; one of the founders of neoclassicism.

wind[1] (wɪnd) *n.* **1.** a current of air, sometimes of considerable force, moving generally horizontally from areas of high pressure to areas of low pressure. See also **Beaufort scale.** **2.** *Chiefly poetic.* the direction from which a wind blows, usually a cardinal point of the compass. **3.** air artificially moved, as by a fan, pump, etc. **4.** any sweeping and destructive force. **5.** a trend, tendency, or force: *the winds of revolution.* **6.** *Informal.* a hint; suggestion: *we got wind that you were coming.* **7.** something deemed insubstantial: *his talk was all wind.* **8.** breath, as used in respiration or talk: *you're just wasting wind.* **9.** (often used in sports) the power to breathe normally: *his wind is weak.* See also **second wind.** **10.** *Music.* **a.** a wind instrument or wind instruments considered collectively. **b.** (*often pl.*) the musicians who play wind instruments in an orchestra. **c.** (*modifier*): of, relating to, or composed of wind instruments: *a wind ensemble.* **11.** an informal name for **flatus.** **12.** the air on which the scent of an animal is carried to hounds or on which the scent of a hunter is carried to his quarry. **13. between wind and water. a.** the part of a vessel's hull below the water line that is exposed by rolling or by wave action. **b.** any point particularly susceptible to attack or injury. **14. break wind.** to release intestinal gas through the anus. **15. get** *or* **have the wind up.** *Informal.* to become frightened. **16. have in the wind.** to be in the act of following (quarry) by scent. **17. how** *or* **which way the wind blows** *or* **lies.** what appears probable. **18. in the wind.** about to happen. **19. in the wind** *or* **three sheets in the wind.** *Informal.* intoxicated; drunk. **20. in the teeth** (*or* **eye**) **of the wind.** directly into the wind. **21. into the wind.** against the wind or upwind. **22. off the wind.** *Nautical.* away from the direction from which the wind is blowing. **23. on the wind.** *Nautical.* as near as possible to the direction from which the wind is blowing. **24. put the wind up.** *Informal.* to frighten or alarm. **25. raise the wind.** *Brit. informal.* to obtain the necessary funds. **26. sail close** *or* **near to the wind. a.** to come near the limits of danger or indecency. **b.** to live frugally or manage one's affairs economically. **27. take the wind out of someone's sails.** to destroy someone's advantage; disconcert or deflate. ~*vb.* (*tr.*) **28.** to cause (someone) to be short of breath: *the blow winded him.* **29. a.** to detect the scent of. **b.** to pursue (quarry) by following its scent. **30.** to expose to air, as in drying, ventilating, etc. [Old English *wind;* related to Old High German *wint,* Old Norse *vindr,* Gothic *winds,* Latin *ventus*] —**'wind+less** *adj.* —**'wind+less+ly** *adv.* —**'wind+less+ness** *n.*

wind[2] (waɪnd) *vb.* **winds, wind+ing, wound. 1.** (often foll. by *around, about, or upon*) to turn or coil (string, cotton, etc.) around some object or point or (of string, etc.) to be turned etc., around some object or point: *he wound a scarf around his head.* **2.** (*tr.*) to twine, cover, or wreathe by or as if by coiling, wrapping, etc.; encircle: *we wound the body in a shroud.* **3.** (*tr.;* often foll. by *up*) to tighten the spring of (a clockwork mechanism). **4.** (*tr.;* foll. by *off*) to remove by uncoiling or unwinding. **5.** (*usually intr.*) to move or cause to move in a sinuous, spiral, or circular course: *the river winds through the hills.* **6.** (*tr.*) to introduce indirectly or deviously: *he is winding his own opinions into the report.* **7.** (*tr.*) to cause to twist or revolve: *he wound the handle.* **8.** (*tr.;* usually foll. by *up* or *down*) to move by cranking: *please wind up the window.* **9.** (*tr.*) to haul, lift, or hoist (a weight, etc.) by means of a wind or windlass. **10.** (*intr.*) (of a board, etc.) to be warped or twisted. **11.** (*intr.*) *Archaic.* to proceed deviously or indirectly. ~*n.* **12.** the act of winding or state of being wound. **13.** a single turn, bend, etc.: *a wind in the river.* **14.** Also called: **winding.** a twist in a board or plank. ~See also **wind down, wind up.** [Old English *windan;* related to Old Norse *vinda,* Old High German *wintan* (German *winden*)] —**'wind+a+ble** *adj.*

wind[3] (waɪnd) *vb.* **winds, wind+ing, wind+ed** *or* **wound.** (*tr.*) *Poetic.* to blow (a note or signal) on (a horn, bugle, etc.). [C16: special use of WIND[1]]

wind+age ('wɪndɪdʒ) *n.* **1. a.** a deflection of a projectile as a result of the effect of the wind. **b.** the degree of such deflection. **c.** the extent to which it is necessary to adjust the wind gauge of a gun sight in order to compensate for such deflection. **2.** the difference between a firearm's bore and the diameter of its projectile. **3.** *Nautical.* the exposed part of the hull of a vessel responsible for wind resistance. **4.** the retarding force upon a rotating machine resulting from the drag of the air.

wind+bag ('wɪnd,bæg) *n.* **1.** *Slang.* a voluble person who has little of interest to communicate. **2.** the bag in a set of bagpipes, which provides a continuous flow of air to the pipes.

wind+blown ('wɪnd,bləʊn) *adj.* **1.** blown by the wind. **2.** (of a woman's hair style) cut short and combed to look as though it has been dishevelled by the wind. **3.** (of trees, shrubs, etc.) growing in a shape determined by the prevailing winds.

wind-borne *adj.* (esp. of plant seeds or pollen) transported by wind.

wind+bound ('wɪnd,baʊnd) *adj.* (of a sailing vessel) prevented from sailing by an unfavourable wind.

wind+break ('wɪnd,breɪk) *n.* a fence, line of trees, etc., serving as a protection from the wind by breaking its force.

wind-bro+ken *adj.* (of a horse) asthmatic or heaving.

wind+burn ('wɪnd,bɜ:n) *n.* irritation and redness of the skin caused by prolonged exposure to winds of high velocity. —**'wind+,burnt** *or* **'wind+,burned** *adj.*

wind+cheat+er ('wɪnd,tʃi:tə) *or* **wind+jam+mer** *n.* a warm jacket, usually with a close-fitting knitted neck, cuffs, and waistband. U.S. name (trademark): **Wind+break+er** ('wɪnd,breɪkə).

wind chest (wɪnd) *n.* a box in an organ in which air from the bellows is stored under pressure before being supplied to the pipes or reeds.

wind cone (wɪnd) *n.* another name for **windsock.**

wind down (waɪnd) *vb.* (*adv.*) **1.** (*tr.*) to lower or move down by cranking. **2.** (*intr.*) (of a clock spring) to become slack. **3.** (*intr.*) to diminish gradually in force or power; relax.

wind+ed ('wɪndɪd) *adj.* **1.** out of breath, as from strenuous exercise. **2.** (*in combination*) having breath or wind as specified: *broken-winded; short-winded.*

wind+er ('waɪndə) *n.* **1.** a person or device that winds, as an engine for hoisting the cages in a mine shaft or a device for winding the yarn in textile manufacture. **2.** an object, such as a bobbin, around which something is wound. **3.** a knob or key used to wind up a clock, watch, or similar mechanism. **4.** any plant that twists itself around a support. **5.** a step of a spiral staircase.

Win+der+mere ('wɪndəmɪə) *n.* **Lake.** a lake in NW England, in Cumbria in the SE part of the Lake District: the largest lake in England. Length: 17 km (10.5 miles).

wind+fall ('wɪnd,fɔ:l) *n.* **1.** a piece of unexpected good fortune, esp. financial gain. **2.** something blown down by the wind, esp. a piece of fruit. **3.** *Chiefly U.S.* a plot of land covered with trees blown down by the wind.

wind+flow+er ('wɪnd,flaʊə) *n.* any of various anemone plants, such as the wood anemone.

wind+gall ('wɪnd,gɔ:l) *n. Vet. science.* a soft swelling in the area of the fetlock joint of a horse. —**'wind+,galled** *adj.*

wind gap (wɪnd) *n.* a narrow dry valley on a mountain or ridge.

wind gauge (wɪnd) *n.* **1.** another name for **anemometer** (sense 1). **2.** a scale on a gun sight indicating the amount of deflection necessary to allow for windage. **3.** *Music.* a device for measuring the wind pressure in the bellows of an organ.

wind harp (wɪnd) *n.* a less common name for **aeolian harp.**

Wind+hoek ('wɪnt,hʊk, 'vɪnt-) *n.* the capital of South West Africa, in the centre, at an altitude of 1654 m (5428 ft.): formerly the capital of German South West Africa. Pop.: 64 095 (1970).

wind+hov+er ('wɪnd,hɒvə) *n. Brit.* a dialect name for a **kestrel.**

wind+ing ('waɪndɪŋ) *n.* **1.** a curving or sinuous course or movement. **2.** anything that has been wound or wrapped around something. **3.** a particular manner or style in which something has been wound. **4.** a curve, bend, or complete turn in wound material, a road, etc. **5.** (*often pl.*) devious thoughts or behaviour: *the tortuous windings of political argumentation.* **6.** one or more turns of wire forming a continuous coil through which an electric current can pass, as used in transformers, generators, etc. **7.** another name for **wind**[2] (sense 14). **8.** a coil of tubing in certain brass instruments, esp. the French horn. —**'wind+ing+ly** *adv.*

wind+ing sheet *n.* a sheet in which a corpse is wrapped for burial; shroud.

wind+ing stair+case *n.* another word for **spiral staircase.**

wind in+stru+ment (wɪnd) *n.* any musical instrument sounded by the breath, such as the woodwinds and brass instruments of an orchestra.

wind+jam+mer ('wɪnd,dʒæmə) *n.* **1.** a large merchant sailing ship. **2.** another name for **windcheater.**

wind+lass ('wɪndləs) *n.* **1.** a machine for raising weights by winding a rope or chain upon a barrel or drum driven by a crank, motor, etc. ~*vb.* **2.** (*tr.*) to raise or haul (a weight, etc.) by means of a windlass. [C14: from Old Norse *vindáss,* from *vinda* to WIND[2] + *ass* pole; related to Old French *guindas,* Middle Low German, Dutch *windas*]

win+dle+straw ('wɪndᵊl,strɔ:) *n. Irish and Brit. dialect.* **1.** the dried stalk of any of various grasses. **2.** anything weak or feeble, esp. a thin unhealthy person. [Old English *windelstrēaw,* from *windel* basket, from *windan* to WIND[2] + *strēaw* STRAW]

wind+mill ('wɪnd,mɪl, 'wɪn, mɪl) *n.* **1.** a machine for grinding or pumping driven by a set of adjustable vanes or sails that are caused to turn by the force of the wind. **2.** the set of vanes or sails that drives such a mill. **3.** Also called: **whirligig.** *Brit.* a toy consisting of plastic or paper vanes attached to a stick in such a manner that they revolve like the sails of a windmill. U.S. name: **pinwheel.** **4.** an imaginary opponent or evil (esp. in the phrase **tilt at** *or* **fight windmills**). **5.** a small air-driven propeller fitted to a light aircraft to drive auxiliary equipment. Compare **ram air turbine.** **6.** an informal name for **helicopter.** **7.** an informal name for **propeller** (sense 1). ~*vb.* **8.** to move or cause to move like the arms of a windmill. **9.** (*intr.*) (of an aircraft propeller, rotor of a turbine, etc.) to rotate as a result of the force of a current of air rather than under power.

win+dow ('wɪndəʊ) *n.* **1.** a light framework, made of timber, metal, or plastic, that contains glass or glazed opening frames and is placed in a wall or roof to let in light or air or to see through. Related adj.: **fenestral.** **2.** an opening in the wall or roof of a building that is provided to let in light or air or to see through. **3.** See **windowpane.** **4.** any opening or structure resembling a window in function or appearance, such as the transparent area of an envelope revealing an address within. **5.** *Astronautics.* short for **launch window.** **6.** *Physics.* a region of the spectrum in which a medium transmits electromagnetic radiation. See also **radio window.** **7.** (*modifier*): of or relating to a window or windows: *a window ledge.* ~*vb.* **8.** (*tr.*) to furnish with or as if with windows. [C13: from Old Norse *vindauga,* from *vindr* WIND[1] + *auga* EYE]

win+dow box *n.* **1.** a long narrow box, placed on or outside a windowsill, in which plants are grown. **2.** either of a pair of

vertical boxes, attached to the sides of a sash window frame, that enclose a sash cord and counterbalancing weight.
win·dow-dress·er *n.* a person employed to design and build up a display in a shop window.
win·dow-dress·ing *n.* **1.** the ornamentation of shop windows, designed to attract customers. **2.** the pleasant, showy, or false aspect of an idea, policy, etc., which is stressed to conceal the real or unpleasant nature; façade.
win·dow+pane ('wɪndəʊˌpeɪn) *n.* a sheet of glass in a window.
win+dow sash *n.* a glazed window frame, esp. one that opens.
win+dow seat *n.* **1.** a seat below a window, esp. in a bay window. **2.** a seat beside a window in a bus, train, etc.
win·dow-shop *vb.* **-shops, -shop·ping, -shopped.** (*intr.*) to look at goods in shop windows without buying them. —**'win·dow-ˌshop·per** *n.* —**'win·dow-ˌshop·ping** *n.*
win·dow+sill ('wɪndəʊˌsɪl) *n.* a sill below a window.
wind+pipe ('wɪndˌpaɪp) *n.* a nontechnical name for **trachea** (sense 1).
wind-pol·li·nat+ed *adj.* (of certain plants) pollinated by wind-borne pollen. —**'wind-ˌpol·li·'na+tion** *n.*
Wind Riv+er Range (wɪnd) *n.* a mountain range in W Wyoming: one of the highest ranges of the central Rockies. Highest peak: Gannet Peak, 4202 m (13 785 ft.).
wind rose (wɪnd) *n.* a diagram with radiating lines showing the frequency and strength of winds from each direction affecting a specific place.
wind+row ('wɪndˌrəʊ, 'wɪnˌrəʊ) *n.* **1.** a long low ridge or line of hay or a similar crop, designed to achieve the best conditions for drying or curing. **2.** a line of leaves, snow, dust, etc., swept together by the wind. ~*vb.* **3.** (*tr.*) to put (hay or a similar crop) into windrows. —**'wind+ˌrow+er** *n.*
wind+sail ('wɪndˌseɪl) *n.* **1.** a sail rigged as an air scoop over a hatch or companionway to catch breezes and divert them below. **2.** any of the vanes or sails of a windmill.
wind scale (wɪnd) *n.* a numerical scale of wind force, such as the Beaufort scale.
wind+screen ('wɪndˌskri:n) *n. Brit.* the sheet of flat or curved glass that forms a window of a motor vehicle, esp. the front window. U.S. name: **windshield.**
wind+screen wip+er *n. Brit.* an electrically operated blade with a rubber edge that wipes a windscreen clear of rain, snow, etc. U.S. name: **windshield wiper.**
wind shake (wɪnd) *n.* a crack between the annual rings in wood: caused by strong winds bending the tree trunk.
wind+shield ('wɪndˌʃi:ld) *n.* **1.** the U.S. name for **windscreen. 2.** an object designed to shield something from the wind.
wind+sock ('wɪndˌsɒk) *n.* a truncated cone of textile mounted on a mast so that it is free to rotate about a vertical axis: used, esp. at airports, to indicate the local wind direction. Also called: **air sock, drogue, wind sleeve, wind cone.**
Wind+sor[1] ('wɪnzə) *n.* **1.** a town in S England, in Berkshire on the River Thames, linked by bridge with Eton: site of **Windsor Castle,** residence of English monarchs since its founding by William the Conqueror; **Old Windsor,** royal residence in the time of Edward the Confessor, is 3 km (2 miles) southeast. Pop.: 30 065 (1971). Official name: **New Windsor. 2.** a city in SE Canada, in S Ontario on the Detroit River opposite Detroit: motor-vehicle manufacturing; university (1963). Pop.: 203 300 (1971).
Wind·sor[2] ('wɪnzə) *n.* **1.** the official name of the British royal family since 1917. **2. Duke of.** the title of **Edward VIII** from 1937.
Wind+sor chair *n.* a simple wooden chair, popular in England and America from the 18th century, usually having a shaped seat, splayed legs, and a back of many spindles.
Wind+sor knot *n.* a wide triangular knot, produced by making extra turns in tying a tie.
Wind+sor rock+er *n. U.S.* a Windsor chair on rockers.
Wind+sor tie *n.* a wide silk tie worn in a floppy bow.
wind+storm ('wɪndˌstɔ:m) *n.* a storm consisting of violent winds.
wind-suck·ing ('wɪndˌsʌkɪŋ) *n.* a harmful habit of horses in which the animal arches its neck and swallows a gulp of air. —**'wind+ˌsuck·er** *n.*
wind+swept ('wɪndˌswɛpt) *adj.* **1.** open to or swept by the wind. **2.** another word for **windblown** (sense 2).
wind tee (wɪnd) *n.* a large weather vane shaped like a *T,* located at an airfield to indicate the wind direction.
wind tun+nel (wɪnd) *n.* a chamber for testing the aerodynamic properties of aircraft, aerofoils, etc., in which a current of air can be maintained at a constant velocity.
wind up (waɪnd) *vb.* (*adv.*) **1.** to bring to or reach a conclusion: *he wound up the proceedings.* **2.** (*tr.*) to tighten the spring of (a clockwork mechanism). **3.** (*tr.; usually passive*) *Informal.* to make nervous, tense, etc.; excite: *he was all wound up before the big fight.* **4.** (*tr.*) to roll (thread, etc.) into a ball. **5.** an informal word for **liquidate** (sense 2). **6.** (*intr.*) *Informal.* to end up (in a specified state): *you'll wind up without any teeth.* **7.** (*tr.; usually passive*) to involve; entangle: *they were wound up in three different scandals.* **8.** (*tr.*) to hoist or haul up. ~*n.* **wind-up.** *Informal, chiefly U.S.* **9.** the act of concluding. **10.** the finish; end.
wind+ward ('wɪndwəd) *Chiefly nautical.* ~*adj.* **1.** of, in, or moving to the quarter from which the wind blows. **2. to windward of.** advantageously situated with respect to. ~*n.* **3.** the windward point. **4.** the side towards the wind. ~*adv.* **5.** towards the wind. ~Compare **leeward.**
Wind+ward Is+lands *pl. n.* a group of islands in the SE West Indies, in the Lesser Antilles: consists of the French Overseas Region of Martinique, the British Associated States of St. Lucia and St. Vincent, Grenada, and the Grenadines.
Wind+ward Pas+sage *n.* a strait in the West Indies, between E Cuba and NW Haiti. Width: 80 km (50 miles).
wind·y ('wɪndɪ) *adj.* **wind·i·er, wind·i·est. 1.** of, characterized by, resembling, or relating to wind; stormy. **2.** swept by or open to powerful winds. **3.** marked by or given to empty, prolonged, and often boastful speech; bombastic: *windy orations.* **4.** void of substance. **5.** an informal word for **flatulent. 6.** *Slang.* afraid; frightened; nervous. —**'wind·i+ly** *adv.* —**'wind·i+ness** *n.*
wine (waɪn) *n.* **1. a.** an alcoholic drink produced by the fermenting of grapes with water and sugar. **b.** an alcoholic drink produced in this way from other fruits, flowers, etc.: *elderberry wine.* **2. a.** a dark red colour, sometimes with a purplish tinge. **b.** (*as adj.*): *wine-coloured.* **3.** anything resembling wine in its intoxicating or invigorating effect. **4.** *Pharmacol.* fermented grape juice containing medicaments. **5. Adam's wine.** *Brit.* a dialect word for **water. 6. new wine in old bottles.** something new added to or imposed upon an old or established order. ~*vb.* **7.** (*intr.*) to drink wine. **8. wine and dine.** to entertain or be entertained with wine and fine food. [Old English *wīn,* from Latin *vīnum;* related to Greek *oinos,* of obscure origin] —**'wine+less** *adj.*
wine bar *n.* a bar in a restaurant, etc., or an establishment in which alcoholic liquor, esp. wine, is sold.
wine+bib·ber ('waɪnˌbɪbə) *n.* a person who drinks a great deal of wine. —**'wine+ˌbib·bing** *n.*
wine cel+lar *n.* **1.** a place, such as a dark cool cellar, where wine is stored. **2.** the stock of wines stored there.
wine cool+er *n.* a bucket-like vessel containing ice in which a bottle of wine is placed to be cooled.
wine gal+lon *n. Brit.* a former unit of capacity equal to 231 cubic inches.
wine+glass ('waɪnˌglɑ:s) *n.* **1.** a glass drinking vessel, typically having a small bowl on a stem, with a flared foot. **2.** Also called: **wine+glass+ful.** the amount that such a glass will hold.
wine palm *n.* any of various palm trees, the sap of which is used, esp. when fermented, as a drink. See **toddy** (sense 2). Also called: **toddy palm.**
wine+press ('waɪnˌprɛs) *n.* any equipment used for squeezing the juice from grapes in order to make wine.
win+er·y ('waɪnərɪ) *n., pl.* **+er·ies.** *Chiefly U.S.* a place where wine is made.
wine+skin ('waɪnˌskɪn) *n.* the skin of a sheep or goat sewn up and used as a holder for wine.
wing (wɪŋ) *n.* **1.** either of the modified forelimbs of a bird that are covered with large feathers and specialized for flight in most species. **2.** one of the organs of flight of an insect, consisting of a membranous outgrowth from the thorax containing a network of veins. **3.** either of the organs of flight in certain other animals, esp. the forelimb of a bat. **4. a.** a half of the main supporting aerofoil on an aircraft, confined to one side of it. **b.** the full span of the main supporting aerofoil on both sides of an aircraft. **c.** an aircraft designed as one complete wing. **d.** a position in flight formation, just to the rear and to one side of an aircraft. **5. a.** an organ or apparatus resembling a wing. **b.** *Anatomy.* any bodily structure resembling a wing: *the wings of a sphenoid bone.* Technical name: **ala. 6.** anything suggesting a wing in form, function, or position, such as a sail of a windmill or a ship. **7.** *Botany.* **a.** either of the lateral petals of a sweetpea or related flower. **b.** any of various outgrowths of a plant part, esp. the process on a wind-dispersed fruit or seed. **8.** a means or cause of flight or rapid motion; flight: *fear gave wings to his feet.* **9.** the act or manner of flying: *a bird of strong wing.* **10.** *Brit.* the part of a car body that surrounds the wheels. U.S. name: **fender. 11.** any affiliate of or subsidiary to a parent organization. **12.** *Soccer, hockey, etc.* **a.** either of the two sides of the pitch near the touchline. **b.** a player stationed in such a position; winger. **13.** a faction or group within a political party or other organization. See also **left wing, right wing. 14.** a part of a building that is subordinate to the main part. **15.** the space offstage to the right or left of the acting area in a theatre. **16. in** *or* **on the wings.** ready to step in when needed. **17.** *Fortifications.* a side connecting the main fort and an outwork. **18.** a folding panel, as of a double door or a movable partition. **19.** either of the two pieces that project fowards from the sides of some chairbacks. **20.** the U.S. name for **quarterlight. 21.** an aerodynamic device usually consisting of an aerofoil, fitted to a racing car to assist in holding it on the road at high speed. **22.** (*pl.*) an insignia in the form of stylized wings worn by a qualified aircraft pilot. **23.** any of various flattened organs or extensions in lower animals, esp. when used in locomotion. **24.** the side of a hold alongside a ship's hull. **25.** the outside angle of the cutting edge on the share and mouldboard of a plough. **26.** a jetty or dam for narrowing a channel of water. **27.** *Rare.* the feather of an arrow. **28. on the wing. a.** flying. **b.** travelling. **c.** about to leave. **29. take wing. a.** to lift off or fly away. **b.** to depart in haste. **c.** to become joyful. **30. under one's wing.** in one's care or tutelage. **31. clip (someone's) wings.** to restrict someone's freedom; discipline someone. **32. on wings.** flying or as if flying. **33. spread** *or* **stretch one's wings.** to make full use of one's abilities. ~*vb.* (*mainly tr.*) **34.** (*also intr.*) to make (one's way) swiftly on or as if on wings. **35.** to shoot or wound (a bird, person, etc.) superficially, in the wing or arm, etc. **36.** to cause to fly or move swiftly: *to wing an arrow.* **37.** to fit (an arrow) with a feather. **38.** to provide with wings. **39.** (of buildings, altars, etc.) to provide with lateral extensions. **40.** (*tr.*) *Theatre, informal.* to perform (a part) without having fully learned one's

lines. [C12: from Scandinavian; compare Old Norse *vængir* (plural), Norwegian *veng*] —'**wing+like** *adj.*

wing and wing *adv.* with sails extended on both sides by booms.

wing bow (bəʊ) *n.* a distinctive band of colour marking the wing of a domestic fowl.

wing-case *n.* the nontechnical name for **elytron.**

wing chair *n.* an easy chair having wings on each side of the back.

wing col+lar *n.* a stiff turned-up shirt collar worn with the points turned down over the tie.

wing com+mand+er *n.* an officer holding commissioned rank in certain air forces, such as the Royal Air Force: junior to a group captain and senior to a squadron leader.

wing cov+ert *n.* any of the covert feathers of the wing of a bird, occurring in distinct rows.

wing+ding ('wɪŋ,dɪŋ) *n. Slang, chiefly U.S.* **1. a.** a noisy lively party or festivity. **b.** (*as modifier*): *a real wingding party.* **2.** a real or pretended fit or seizure. [C20: of unknown origin]

wing+er ('wɪŋə) *n. Soccer, hockey, etc.* a player stationed on the wing.

wing-foot·ed *adj. Archaic.* fleet; swift.

wing+less ('wɪŋlɪs) *adj.* **1.** having no wings or vestigial wings. **2.** designating primitive insects of the subclass *Apterygota,* characterized by small size, lack of wings, and larvae resembling the adults: includes the springtails and bristletails. —'**wing+less+ness** *n.*

wing+let ('wɪŋlɪt) *n.* a small wing, esp. the bastard wing of a bird.

wing load+ing *n.* the total weight of an aircraft divided by its wing area.

wing nut *n.* a threaded nut tightened by hand by means of two flat lugs or wings projecting from the central body. Also called: **butterfly nut.**

wing+o·ver ('wɪŋ,əʊvə) *n.* a manoeuvre in which the direction of flight of an aircraft is reversed by putting it into a climbing turn until nearly stalled, the nose then being allowed to fall while continuing the turn.

wing shot *n.* **1.** a shot taken at a bird in flight. **2.** an expert at shooting birds in flight.

wing+span ('wɪŋ,spæn) *or* **wing+spread** ('wɪŋ,sprɛd) *n.* the distance between the wing tips of an aircraft, bird, etc.

wing tip *n.* the outermost edge of a wing.

wink[1] (wɪŋk) *vb.* **1.** (*intr.*) to close and open one eye quickly, deliberately, or in an exaggerated fashion to convey friendliness, etc. **2.** to close and open (an eye or the eyes) momentarily. **3.** (*tr.; foll. by away, back,* etc.) to force away (tears, etc.) by winking. **4.** (*tr.*) to signal with a wink. **5.** (*intr.*) (of a light) to gleam or flash intermittently. ~*n.* **6.** a winking movement, esp. one conveying a signal, etc., or such a signal. **7.** an interrupted flashing of light. **8.** a brief moment of time; instant. **9.** *Informal.* the smallest amount, esp. of sleep. See also **forty winks. 10. tip the wink.** *Brit. informal.* to give a hint. [Old English *wincian;* related to Old Saxon *wincon,* Old High German *winchan,* German *winken* to wave. See WENCH, WINCH]

wink[2] (wɪŋk) *n.* a disc used in the game of tiddlywinks. [C20: shortened from TIDDLYWINKS]

wink at *vb.* (*intr., prep.*) to connive at; disregard: *the authorities winked at corruption.*

Win·kel·ried (*German* 'vɪŋkəl,ri:t) *n.* **Ar·nold von** ('arnɔlt fɔn). died ?1386, Swiss hero of the battle of Sempach (1386) against the Austrians.

wink+er ('wɪŋkə) *n.* **1.** a person or thing that winks. **2.** *U.S. slang, northern Brit. dialect.* an eye, eyelash, or eyelid. **3.** another name for **blinker** (sense 1).

win+kle ('wɪŋkəl) *n.* **1.** See **periwinkle**[1]. ~*vb.* **2.** (*tr.; usually foll. by out, out of,* etc.) *Informal, chiefly Brit.* to extract or prise out.

win+kle-pick·ers *pl. n.* shoes or boots with very pointed narrow toes, popular in the mid-20th century.

Win+ne+ba+go (,wɪnɪ'beɪgəʊ) *n.* **1. Lake.** a lake in E Wisconsin, fed and drained by the Fox river: the largest lake in the state. Area: 557 sq. km (215 sq. miles). **2.** (*pl.* **+gos** *or* **+go**) a member of a North American Indian people living in Wisconsin and Nebraska. **3.** the language of this people, belonging to the Siouan family.

win+ner ('wɪnə) *n.* **1.** a person or thing that wins. **2.** *Slang.* a person or thing that seems sure to win or succeed.

win+ner's cir+cle *n.* a small area at a racecourse where winners are unsaddled after a race, and often where awards are given to their owners, trainers, or jockeys.

win+ning ('wɪnɪŋ) *adj.* **1.** (of a person, character, etc.) charming, engaging, or attractive. ~*n.* **2. a.** a shaft or seam of coal. **b.** the extraction of coal or ore from the ground. **3.** (*pl.*) money, prizes, or valuables won, esp. in gambling. —'**win+ning+ly** *adv.* —'**win+ning+ness** *n.*

win+ning gal+ler·y *n. Real tennis.* the gallery farthest from the net on either side of the court, into which any shot played wins a point.

win+ning o·pen+ing *n. Real tennis.* the grille, dedans, or winning gallery, into which any shot played wins a point.

win+ning post *n.* the post marking the finishing line on a racecourse.

Win+ni+peg ('wɪnɪ,pɛg) *n.* **1.** a city in S Canada, capital of Manitoba at the confluence of the Assiniboine and Red Rivers. Pop.: 246 246 (1971). **2. Lake.** a lake in S Canada, in Manitoba: drains through the Nelson River into Hudson Bay. Area: 23 553 sq. km (9094 sq. miles). —'**Win+ni+,peg+ger** *n.*

Win+ni+peg couch *n. Canadian.* a couch with no arms or back, opening out into a double bed.

Win+ni+pe·go+sis (,wɪnɪpə'gəʊsɪs) *n.* **Lake.** a lake in S Canada, in W Manitoba. Area: 5400 sq. km (2086 sq. miles).

win+now ('wɪnəʊ) *vb.* **1.** to separate (grain) from (chaff) by means of a wind or current of air. **2.** (*tr.*) to examine in order to select the desirable elements. **3.** (*tr.*) *Archaic.* to beat (the air) with wings. **4.** (*tr.*) *Rare.* to blow upon; fan. ~*n.* **5. a.** a device for winnowing. **b.** the act or process of winnowing. [Old English *windwian;* related to Old High German *wintōn,* Gothic *diswinthjan,* Latin *ventilāre.* See WIND[1]] —'**win+now+er** *n.*

win·o ('waɪnəʊ) *n., pl.* **·os.** *Chiefly U.S.* a person who habitually drinks wine as a means of getting drunk.

win out *vb.* (*intr., adv.*) *Informal.* to succeed or prevail as if in a contest: *sanity rarely wins out over prejudice.*

win+some ('wɪnsəm) *adj.* charming; winning; engaging: *a winsome smile.* [Old English *wynsum,* from *wynn* joy (related to Old High German *wunnia,* German *Wonne*) + *-sum* -SOME[1]] —'**win+some+ly** *adv.* —'**win+some+ness** *n.*

Win·ston-Sa·lem ('wɪnstən 'seɪləm) *n.* a city in N central North Carolina: formed in 1913 by the uniting of Salem and Winston; a major tobacco manufacturing centre. Pop.: 132 913 (1970).

win+ter ('wɪntə) *n.* **1. a.** (*sometimes cap.*) the coldest season of the year, between autumn and spring, astronomically from the December solstice to the March equinox in the N hemisphere and at the opposite time of year in the S hemisphere. **b.** (*as modifier*): *winter pasture.* **2.** the period of cold weather associated with the winter. **3.** a time of decline, decay, etc. **4.** *Chiefly poetic.* a year represented by this season: *a man of 72 winters.* Related adjs.: **hibernal, hiemal.** ~*vb.* **5.** (*intr.*) to spend the winter in a specified place. **6.** to keep or feed (farm animals, etc.) during the winter or (of farm animals) to be kept or fed during the winter. [Old English; related to Old Saxon, Old High German *wintar,* Old Norse *vetr,* Gothic *wintrus*] —'**win+ter+er** *n.* —'**win+ter+ish** *or* '**win·ter-,like** *adj.* —'**win+ter+less** *adj.*

win+ter ac·o·nite *n.* a small Old World ranunculaceous herbaceous plant, *Eranthis hyemalis,* cultivated for its yellow flowers, which appear early in spring.

win·ter+bourne ('wɪntə,bɔ:n) *n.* a stream flowing only after heavy rainfall, esp. in winter. [Old English *winterburna;* see WINTER, BURN[2]]

win+ter cher+ry *n.* **1.** a Eurasian solanaceous plant, *Physalis alkekengi,* cultivated for its ornamental inflated papery orange-red calyx. **2.** the calyx of this plant. ~See also **Chinese lantern, ground cherry.**

win·ter+feed ('wɪntə,fi:d) *vb.* **+feeds, +feed·ing, +fed.** to feed (livestock) in winter when the grazing is not rich enough.

win·ter+green ('wɪntə,gri:n) *n.* **1.** Also called: **boxberry, checkerberry, teaberry, spiceberry, partridgeberry.** any of several evergreen ericaceous shrubs of the genus *Gaultheria,* esp. *G. procumbens,* of E North America, which has white bell-shaped flowers and edible red berries. **2. oil of wintergreen.** an aromatic compound, formerly made from this and various other plants but now synthesized: used medicinally and for flavouring. **3.** any of various plants of the genus *Pyrola,* esp. *P. minor* (**common wintergreen**), of temperate and arctic regions, having rounded leaves and small pink globose flowers: family *Pyrolaceae.* Usual U.S. name: **shinleaf. 4.** any of several plants of the genera *Orthilia* and *Moneses:* family *Pyrolaceae.* **5. chickweed wintergreen.** a primulaceous plant, *Trientalis europaea,* of N Europe and N Asia, having white flowers and leaves arranged in a whorl. [C16: from Dutch *wintergroen* or German *Wintergrün;* see WINTER, GREEN]

win+ter hedge *n. West Yorkshire, south Lancashire, and Derbyshire dialect.* a clothes horse. [so called in contrast to a hedge on which clothes are dried in summer]

win+ter+ize *or* **win+ter+ise** ('wɪntə,raɪz) *vb.* (*tr.*) *U.S.* to prepare (a house, car, etc.) to withstand winter conditions. —,**win+ter+i+'za+tion** *or* ,**win+ter+i+'sa+tion** *n.*

win+ter jas+mine *n.* a jasmine shrub, *Jasminum nudiflorum,* widely cultivated for its winter-blooming yellow flowers.

win·ter+kill ('wɪntə,kɪl) *vb. Chiefly U.S.* to kill (crops or other plants) by exposure to frost, cold, etc., or (of plants) to die by this means. —'**win·ter+,kill·ing** *adj., n.*

win+ter mel+on *n.* a variety of muskmelon, *Cucumis melo inodorus,* that has sweet fruit with pale orange flesh and an unridged rind. Also called: **Persian melon.**

Win+ter O·lym+pic Games *n.* (*functioning as sing. or pl.*) an international contest of winter sports, esp. skiing, held in the year of the Olympic Games. Also called: **Winter Olympics.**

win+ter rose *n.* another name for **Christmas rose.**

win+ter sol+stice *n.* **1.** the time at which the sun is at its southernmost point in the sky (northernmost point in the S hemisphere) appearing at noon at its lowest altitude above the horizon. It occurs about December 22 (June 21 in the S hemisphere). **2.** *Astronomy.* the point on the celestial sphere, opposite the **summer solstice,** at which the ecliptic is furthest south from the celestial equator. Right ascension: 18 hours; declination: –23.5°.

win+ter sports *pl. n.* sports held in the open air on snow or ice, esp. skiing.

Win+ter+thur (*German* 'vɪntərtu:r) *n.* an industrial town in NE central Switzerland, in Zürich canton: has the largest technical college in the country. Pop.: 91 000 (1975 est.).

win·ter+time ('wɪntə,taɪm) *n.* the winter season. Also (archaic): **win·ter+tide** ('wɪntə,taɪd).

Win+ter War *n.* the war of the winter of 1939–40 between Finland and Russia after which the Finns surrendered the Karelian Isthmus to Russia.

win+ter+weight ('wɪntəˌweɪt) *adj.* (of clothes) suitable in weight for wear in the winter; relatively heavy.

win+ter wheat *n.* a type of wheat that is planted in the autumn and is harvested the following summer.

win+try ('wɪntrɪ), **win+ter·y** ('wɪntərɪ, -trɪ), *or* **win+ter+ly** *adj.* +**tri+er,** +**tri+est. 1.** (esp. of weather) of or characteristic of winter. **2.** lacking cheer or warmth; bleak. —'**win+tri+ly** *adv.* —'**win+tri+ness, 'win+ter·i+ness,** *or* '**win+ter+li+ness** *n.*

win·y ('waɪnɪ) *adj.* **win·i+er, win·i+est.** having the taste or qualities of wine, esp. in being intoxicating; heady.

winze (wɪnz) *n. Mining.* a steeply inclined shaft, as for ventilation between levels. [C18: from earlier *winds,* probably from C14 *wynde* windlass, from Middle Dutch or Middle Low German *winde;* related to Danish *vinde* pulley]

wipe (waɪp) *vb.* (*tr.*) **1.** to rub (a surface or object) lightly, esp. with (a cloth, hand, etc.), as in removing dust, water, grime, etc. **2.** (usually foll. by *off, away, from, up,* etc.) to remove by or as if by rubbing lightly: *he wiped the dirt from his hands.* **3.** to eradicate or cancel (a thought, memory, etc.). **4.** *Austral. informal.* to abandon or reject (a person). **5.** to apply (oil, etc.) by wiping. **6.** to form (a joint between two lead pipes) with solder or soft lead. **7. wipe the floor with (someone).** *Informal.* to defeat decisively. ~*n.* **8.** the act or an instance of wiping. **9.** (in film editing) an effect causing the transition from one scene to the next in which the image of the first scene appears to be wiped off the screen by that of the second. **10.** *Dialect.* a sweeping blow or stroke. **11.** *Brit. dialect.* a gibe or jeer. **12.** *Obsolete.* a slang name for **handkerchief.** [Old English *wīpian,* related to Middle Low German *wīpen, wīp* bundle (of cloth), Old High German *wīffa, wīfan* to wind, Gothic *weipan* to wreathe]

wipe out *vb.* (*adv.*) **1.** (*tr.*) to destroy completely; eradicate. **2.** (*tr.*) *Informal.* to murder or kill. **3.** (*intr.*) to fall or jump off a surfboard or skateboard. ~*n.* **wipe+out. 4.** an act or instance of wiping out. **5.** the interference of one radio signal by another so that reception is impossible.

wip+er ('waɪpə) *n.* **1.** any piece of cloth, such as handkerchief, towel, etc., used for wiping. **2.** a cam rotated to ease a part and allow it to fall under its own weight, as used in stamping machines, etc. **3.** See **windscreen wiper. 4.** *Electrical engineering.* a movable conducting arm, esp. one in a switching or selecting device, that makes contact with a row or ring of contacts.

WIPO *or* **Wipo** ('waɪpəʊ) *n. acronym for* World Intellectual Property Organization.

wire (waɪə) *n.* **1.** a slender flexible strand or rod of metal. **2.** a cable consisting of several metal strands twisted together. **3.** a flexible metallic conductor, esp. one made of copper, usually insulated, and used to carry electric current in a circuit. **4.** (*modifier*) of, relating to, or made of wire: *a wire fence; a wire stripper.* **5.** anything made of wire, such as wire netting, a barbed wire fence, etc. **6.** a long continuous wire or cable connecting points in a telephone or telegraph system. **7.** *Old-fashioned.* **a.** an informal name for **telegram** or **telegraph. b. the wire.** an informal name for **telephone. 8.** a metallic string on a guitar, piano, etc. **9.** *U.S. horse racing.* the finishing line on a racecourse. **10.** a wire-gauze screen upon which pulp is spread to form paper during the manufacturing process. **11.** anything resembling a wire, such as a hair. **12.** a snare made of wire for rabbits and similar animals. **13. down to the wire.** *Informal, chiefly U.S.* right up to the last moment. **14. get in under the wire.** *Informal, chiefly U.S.* to accomplish something with little time to spare. **15. get one's wires crossed.** *Informal.* to misunderstand. **16. pull wires.** *Chiefly U.S.* to exert influence behind the scenes, esp. through personal connections; pull strings. ~*vb.* (*mainly tr.*) **17.** (*also intr.*) to send a telegram to (a person or place). **18.** to send (news, a message, etc.) by telegraph. **19.** to equip (an electrical system, circuit, or component) with wires. **20.** to fasten or furnish with wire. **21.** to string (beads, etc.) on wire. **22.** *Croquet.* to leave (a player's ball) so that a hoop or peg lies between it and the other balls. **23.** to snare with wire. [Old English *wīr;* related to Old High German *wiara,* Old Norse *vīra,* Latin *viriae* bracelet] —'**wire+ˌlike** *adj.*

wire brush *n.* a brush having wire bristles, used for cleaning metal, esp. for removing rust.

wire cloth *n.* a mesh or netting woven from fine wire, used in window screens, strainers, etc.

wire+draw ('waɪəˌdrɔː) *vb.* +**draws,** +**draw+ing,** +**drew,** +**drawn.** to convert (metal) into wire by drawing through successively smaller dies.

wire en+tan+gle+ment *n.* a barrier or obstruction of barbed wire used in warfare.

wire-gauge *n.* **1.** a flat plate with slots in which standard wire sizes can be measured. **2.** a standard system of sizes for measuring the diameters of wires.

wire gauze *n.* a stiff meshed fabric woven of fine wires.

wire glass *n.* a sheet glass that contains a layer of reinforcing wire netting within it.

wire grass *n.* any of various grasses, such as Bermuda grass, that have tough wiry roots or rhizomes.

wire-haired *adj.* (of an animal) having a rough wiry coat.

wire+less ('waɪəlɪs) *n., vb. Chiefly Brit., old-fashioned.* another word for **radio.**

wire+less te+leg+ra+phy *n.* another name for **radiotelegraphy.**

wire+less tel+e·phone *n.* another name for **radiotelephone.** —**wire+less te+leph·o+ny** *n.*

wire+man ('waɪəmən) *n., pl.* +**men.** *Chiefly U.S.* a person who installs and maintains electric wiring, cables, etc.

wire net+ting *n.* a net made of wire, often galvanized, that is used for fencing, as a light reinforcement, etc.

wire+pull·er ('waɪəˌpʊlə) *n. Chiefly U.S.* a person who uses private or secret influence for his own ends. —'**wire+ˌpull·ing** *n.*

wir+er ('waɪərə) *n.* a person who sets or uses wires to snare rabbits and similar animals.

wire re+cord+er *n.* an early type of magnetic recorder in which sounds were recorded on a thin steel wire magnetized by an electromagnet. Compare **tape recorder.** —**wire re+cord+ing** *n.*

wire serv+ice *n. Chiefly U.S.* an agency supplying news, etc., to newspapers, radio and television stations, etc.

wire+walk·er ('waɪəˌwɔːkə) *n. Chiefly U.S.* another name for **tightrope walker.**

wire wheel *n.* **1.** a wheel in which the rim is held to the hub by wire spokes, esp. one used on a sports car. Compare **disc wheel. 2.** a power-driven rotary wire brush for scaling or burnishing.

wire wool *n.* a mass of fine wire, used esp. to clean kitchen articles.

wire+work ('waɪəˌwɜːk) *n.* **1.** functional or decorative work made of wire. **2.** objects made of wire, esp. netting. **3.** the work performed by acrobats on a tightrope.

wire+works ('waɪəˌwɜːks) *n.* (*functioning as sing. or pl.*) a factory where wire or articles of wire are made.

wire+worm ('waɪəˌwɜːm) *n.* the wormlike larva of various elaterid beetles, which feeds on the roots of many crop plants and is a serious agricultural pest.

wire-wove *adj.* **1.** of, relating to, or comprising a high-grade glazed paper, usually for writing. **2.** woven of wire.

wir+ing ('waɪərɪŋ) *n.* **1.** the network of wires used in an electrical system, device, or circuit. **2.** the quality or condition of such a network. ~*adj.* **3.** used in wiring.

wir+ra ('wɪrə) *interj. Irish.* an exclamation of sorrow or deep concern. [C19: shortened from Irish Gaelic *a Muire! O Mary!* invocation to the Virgin Mary]

Wir+ral ('wɪrəl) *n.* **the.** a peninsula in NW England between the estuaries of the Rivers Mersey and Dee.

wir·y ('waɪərɪ) *adj.* **wir·i+er, wir·i+est. 1.** (of people or animals) slender but strong in constitution. **2.** made of or resembling wire, esp. in stiffness: *wiry hair.* **3.** (of a sound) produced by or as if by a vibrating wire. —'**wir·i+ly** *adv.* —'**wir·i+ness** *n.*

wis (wɪs) *vb. Archaic.* to know or suppose (something). [C17: a form derived from IWIS, mistakenly interpreted as *I wis* I know, as if from Old English *witan* to know]

Wis. *abbrev. for* Wisconsin.

Wis+con+sin (wɪs'kɒnsɪn) *n.* **1.** a state of the N central U.S., on Lake Superior and Lake Michigan: consists of an undulating plain, with uplands in the north and west; over 168 m (550 ft.) below sea level along the shore of Lake Michigan. Capital: Madison. Pop.: 4 417 933 (1970). Area: 141 061 sq. km (54 464 sq. miles). Abbrevs.: **Wis.** or (with zip code) **WI 2.** a river in central and SW Wisconsin, flowing south and west to the Mississippi. Length: 692 km (430 miles). —**Wis+'con+sin+ˌite** *n.*

Wisd. *abbrev. for* Wisdom of Solomon.

wis+dom ('wɪzdəm) *n.* **1.** the ability or result of an ability to think and act utilizing knowledge, experience, understanding, common sense, and insight. **2.** accumulated knowledge, erudition, or enlightenment. **3.** *Archaic.* a wise saying or wise sayings or teachings. **4.** *Obsolete.* soundness of mind. ~Related adj.: **sagacious.** [Old English *wīsdōm;* see WISE[1], -DOM]

Wis+dom of Je·sus, Son of Si·rach ('saɪræk) *n.* **the.** another name for **Ecclesiasticus.**

Wis+dom of Sol·o·mon *n.* a book of the Apocrypha, probably written about 50 B.C., addressed primarily to Jews who were under the influence of Hellenistic learning.

wis+dom tooth *n.* **1.** any of the four molar teeth, one at the back of each side of the jaw, that are the last of the permanent teeth to erupt. Technical name: **third molar. 2. cut one's wisdom teeth.** to arrive at the age of discretion.

wise[1] (waɪz) *adj.* **1.** possessing, showing, or prompted by wisdom or discernment. **2.** prudent; sensible. **3.** shrewd; crafty: *a wise plan.* **4.** well-informed; erudite. **5.** aware, informed, or knowing (esp. in the phrase **none the wiser**). **6.** *Slang.* (*postpositive;* often foll. by *to*) in the know, esp. possessing inside information (about). **7.** *Archaic or Brit. dialect.* possessing powers of magic. **8.** *Slang, chiefly U.S.* cocksure or insolent. **9. be** *or* **get wise.** (often foll. by *to*) *Informal.* to be or become aware or informed (of something) or to face up (to facts). **10. put wise.** (often foll. by *to*) *Slang.* to inform or warn (of). ~*vb.* **11.** See **wise up.** [Old English *wīs*; related to Old Norse *vīss,* Gothic *weis,* German *weise*] —'**wise+ly** *adv.* —'**wise+ness** *n.*

wise[2] (waɪz) *n. Archaic.* way, manner, fashion, or respect (esp. in the phrases **any wise, in no wise**). [Old English *wīse* manner; related to Old Saxon *wīsa,* German *Weise,* Old Norse *vīsa* verse, Latin *vīsus* face]

wise[3] (waɪz) *vb.* (*tr.*) *Northern Brit. dialect.* to direct or lead. [Old English *wīsian*; related to Old Norse *vīsa,* Old Saxon *wīsōn,* German *weisen,* Old Frisian *wīsia* to turn around]

-wise *adv. combining form.* **1.** Also: **-ways.** indicating direction or manner: *clockwise; likewise.* **2.** with reference to: *profitwise; businesswise.* [Old English *-wīsan;* see WISE[2]]

Usage. The addition of *-wise* to a noun as a replacement for a lengthier phrase (such as *as far as ... is concerned*) is considered unacceptable by most careful speakers and writers: *talentwise, he's a little weak* (he's a little weak as regards talent); *the company is thriving profitwise* (as far as profits are concerned, the company is thriving).

wise·a+cre (ˈwaɪzˌeɪkə) *n.* **1.** a person who wishes to seem wise. **2.** a wise person: often used facetiously or contemptuously. [C16: from Middle Dutch *wijsseggher* soothsayer; related to Old High German *wīssaga*, German *Weissager*. See WISE[1], SAY]

wise+crack (ˈwaɪzˌkræk) *Informal.* ~*n.* **1.** a flippant jibe or sardonic remark. ~*vb.* **2.** to make a wisecrack. —ˈ**wise+ˌcrack+er** *n.*

wise guy *n. Slang.* a person who is given to making conceited, sardonic, or insolent comments.

Wise·man (ˈwaɪzmən) *n.* **Nich·o·las Pat·rick Ste·phen.** 1802–65, British cardinal; first Roman Catholic archbishop of Westminster (1850–65).

wi+sent (ˈwiːzᵊnt) *n.* another name for **European bison.** See **bison** (sense 2). [German, from Old High German *wisunt* BISON]

wise up *vb.* (*adv.*) *Slang, chiefly U.S.* (often foll. by *to*) to become or cause to become aware or informed (of).

wish (wɪʃ) *vb.* **1.** (when *tr., takes a clause as object or an infinitive;* when *intr.*, often foll. by *for*) to want or desire (something, often that which cannot be or is not the case): *I wish I lived in Italy; to wish for peace.* **2.** (*tr.*) to feel or express a desire or hope concerning the future or fortune of: *I wish you well.* **3.** (*tr.*) to desire or prefer to be as specified. **4.** (*tr.*) to greet as specified; bid: *he wished us good afternoon.* **5.** (*tr.*) *Formal.* to order politely: *I wish you to come at three o'clock.* ~*n.* **6.** the act of wishing; the expression of some desire or mental inclination: *to make a wish.* **7.** something desired or wished for: *he got his wish.* **8.** (*usually pl.*) expressed hopes or desire, esp. for someone's welfare, health, etc. **9.** (*often pl.*) *Formal.* a polite order or request. [Old English *wȳscan;* related to Old Norse *öskja*, German *wünschen*, Dutch *wenschen*] —ˈ**wish+er** *n.* —ˈ**wish+less** *adj.*

wish+bone (ˈwɪʃˌbəʊn) *n.* the V-shaped bone above the breastbone in most birds consisting of the fused clavicles; furcula. [C17: from the custom of two people breaking apart the bone after eating: the person with the longer part makes a wish]

wish+ful (ˈwɪʃfʊl) *adj.* having wishes or characterized by wishing. —ˈ**wish+ful+ly** *adv.* —ˈ**wish+ful+ness** *n.*

wish ful+fil+ment *n.* (in Freudian psychology) the mechanism involving the release of tension, brought about by re-enacting in fantasy a situation in which a goal is attained. See also **pleasure principle.**

wish+ful think+ing *n.* the erroneous belief that one's wishes are in accordance with reality. —**wish+ful think+er** *n.*

wish on *vb.* (*tr., prep.*) to hope that (someone or something) should be imposed (on someone); foist: *I wouldn't wish my wife on anyone.*

wish-wash *n. Informal.* **1.** any thin weak drink. **2.** rubbishy talk or writing.

wish·y-wash·y (ˈwɪʃɪˌwɒʃɪ) *adj. Informal.* **1.** lacking in substance, force, colour, etc. **2.** watery; thin. —ˈ**wish·y-ˌwash·i·ly** *adv.* —ˈ**wish·y-ˌwash·i·ness** *n.*

Wis+la (ˈviswa) *n.* the Polish name for **Vistula** (sense 1).

Wis+la+ny Za+lew (*Polish* viʃˈlaːni ˈzaːlɛf) *n.* the Polish name for **Vistula** (sense 2).

Wis+mar (*German* ˈvɪsmar) *n.* a port in N East Germany, on an inlet of the Baltic: shipbuilding industries. Pop.: 56 737 (1972 est.).

wisp (wɪsp) *n.* **1.** a thin, light, delicate, or fibrous piece or strand, such as a streak of smoke or a lock of hair. **2.** a small bundle, as of hay or straw. **3.** anything slender and delicate: *a wisp of a girl.* **4.** a mere suggestion or hint. **5.** a flock of birds, esp. snipe. ~*vb.* **6.** (*intr.;* often foll. by *away*) to move or act like a wisp. **7.** (*tr.*) *Chiefly Brit. dialect.* to twist into a wisp. **8.** (*tr.*) *Chiefly Brit.* to groom (a horse) with a wisp of straw, etc. [C14: variant of *wips*, of obscure origin; compare WIPE] —ˈ**wisp+ˌlike** *adj.*

wisp·y (ˈwɪspɪ) *adj.* **wisp·i+er, wisp·i+est.** wisplike; delicate, faint, light, etc. —ˈ**wisp·i·ly** *adv.* —ˈ**wisp·i+ness** *n.*

wist (wɪst) *vb. Archaic.* the past tense or past participle of **wit**[2].

wis+te+ri·a (wɪˈstɪərɪə) *n.* any twining leguminous woody vine of the genus *Wisteria*, of E Asia and North America, having blue, purple, or white flowers in large drooping clusters. [C19: from New Latin, named after Caspar *Wistar* (1761–1818), American anatomist]

wist+ful (ˈwɪstfʊl) *adj.* sadly pensive, esp. about something yearned for. —ˈ**wist+ful+ly** *adv.* —ˈ**wist+ful+ness** *n.*

wit[1] (wɪt) *n.* **1.** the talent or quality of using unexpected associations between contrasting or disparate words or ideas to make a clever humorous effect. **2.** speech or writing showing this quality. **3.** a person possessing, showing, or noted for such an ability, esp. in repartee. **4.** practical intelligence (esp. in the phrase **have the wit to**). **5.** *Northern Brit. dialect.* information or knowledge (esp. in the phrase **get wit of**). **6.** *Archaic.* mental capacity or a person possessing it. **7.** *Obsolete.* the mind or memory. [Old English *witt;* related to Old Saxon *giwitt*, Old High German *wizzi* (German *Witz*), Old Norse *vit*, Gothic *witi.* See WIT[2]]

wit[2] (wɪt) *vb.* **1.** *Archaic.* to be or become aware of (something). ~*adv.* **2. to wit.** that is to say; namely (used to introduce statements, as in legal documents. [Old English *witan;* related to Old High German *wizzan* (German *wissen*), Old Norse *vita*, Latin *vidēre* to see]

wit+an (ˈwɪtᵊn) *n.* (in Anglo-Saxon England) **1.** an assembly of higher ecclesiastics and important laymen, including king's thegns, that met to counsel the king on matters such as judicial problems. **2.** the members of this assembly. ~Also called: **witenagemot.** [Old English *witan*, plural of *wita* wise man; see WIT[2], WITNESS]

witch[1] (wɪtʃ) *n.* **1.** a person, usually female, who practises or professes to practise magic or sorcery, esp. black magic, or is believed to have dealings with the devil. **2.** an ugly or wicked old woman. **3.** a fascinating or enchanting woman. **4.** short for **water witch.** ~*vb.* **5.** (*tr.*) to cause or change by or as if by witchcraft. **6.** a less common word for **bewitch.** [Old English *wicca;* related to Middle Low German *wicken* to conjure, Swedish *vicka* to move to and fro] —ˈ**witch+ˌlike** *adj.*

witch[2] (wɪtʃ) *n.* a flatfish, *Pleuronectes* (or *Glyptocephalus*) *cynoglossus*, of N Atlantic coastal waters, having a narrow greyish-brown body marked with tiny black spots: family *Pleuronectidae* (plaice, flounders, etc.). [C19: perhaps from WITCH[1], alluding to the appearance of the fish]

witch+craft (ˈwɪtʃˌkrɑːft) *n.* **1.** the art or power of bringing magical or preternatural power to bear or the act or practice of attempting to do so. **2.** the influence of magic or sorcery. **3.** fascinating or bewitching influence or charm.

witch doc+tor *n.* **1.** Also called: **shaman, medicine man.** a man in certain societies, esp. preliterate ones, who appears to possess magical powers, used esp. to cure sickness but also to harm people. **2.** a person who seeks out or hunts witches in some African tribal cultures.

witch-elm *n.* a variant spelling of **wych-elm.**

witch+er·y (ˈwɪtʃərɪ) *n., pl.* **+er·ies. 1.** the practice of witchcraft. **2.** magical or bewitching influence or charm.

witch·es'-broom, witch+broom (ˈwɪtʃˌbruːm), *or* **witch·es'-be·som** *n.* a dense abnormal growth of shoots on a tree or other woody plant, usually caused by parasitic fungi of the genus *Taphrina.*

witch+et+ty grub (ˈwɪtʃɪtɪ) *n.* the wood-boring edible caterpillar of an Australian moth, *Xyleutes leucomochla:* family *Cossidae.* [C19 *witchetty*, from a native Australian language]

witch ha+zel *or* **wych-ha·zel** *n.* **1.** any of several trees and shrubs of the genus *Hamamelis*, esp. *H. virginiana*, of North America, having ornamental yellow flowers and medicinal properties: family *Hamamelidaceae.* **2.** an astringent medicinal solution containing an extract of the bark and leaves of *H. virginiana*, applied to treat bruises, inflammation, etc.

witch-hunt *n.* a rigorous campaign to round up or expose dissenters on the pretext of safeguarding the public welfare. —ˈ**witch-ˌhunt·er** *n.* —ˈ**witch-ˌhunt·ing** *n., adj.*

witch+ing (ˈwɪtʃɪŋ) *adj.* **1.** relating to or appropriate for witchcraft. **2.** *Now rare.* bewitching. ~*n.* **3.** witchcraft; magic. —ˈ**witch+ing+ly** *adv.*

witch+ing hour *n.* **the.** the hour at which witches are supposed to appear, usually midnight.

witch of Ag·ne·si (ɑːnˈjeɪzɪ) *n. Maths.* a plane curve, symmetrical about the *y*-axis, having the equation $x^2y = 4a^2(2a - y)$. Sometimes shortened to **witch.** [C19: named after Maria Gaetana *Agnesi* (1718–99), Italian mathematician; probably so called from the resemblance of the curve to the outline of a witch's hat]

wite (waɪt) *n.* **1.** *Northern Brit. dialect.* reproach, blame, or fault. [Old English *wīte;* related to Old Saxon *wīti*, Old High German *wīzzi*, Old Norse *vīti*]

wit+e·na+ge·mot (ˌwɪtɪnəgɪˈməʊt) *n.* another word for **witan.** [Old English *witena*, genitive plural of *wita* councillor + *gemōt* meeting, MOOT]

with (wɪð, wɪθ) *prep.* **1.** using; by means of: *he killed her with an axe.* **2.** accompanying; in the company of: *the lady you were with.* **3.** possessing; having: *a man with a red moustache.* **4.** concerning or regarding: *be patient with her.* **5.** in spite of: *with all his talents, he was still humble.* **6.** used to indicate a time or distance by which something is away from something else: *with three miles to go, he collapsed.* **7.** in a manner characterized by: *writing with abandon.* **8.** caused or prompted by: *shaking with rage.* **9.** often used with a verb indicating a reciprocal action or relation between the subject and the preposition's object: *agreeing with me; chatting with the troops.* **10. not with you.** *Informal.* not able to grasp or follow what you are saying. **11. with it.** *Informal.* **a.** fashionable; in style. **b.** comprehending what is happening or being said. **12. with that.** after that; having said or done that. [Old English; related to Old Norse *vith*, Gothic *withra*, Latin *vitricus* stepfather, Sanskrit *vitarám* wider]

with+al (wɪˈðɔːl) *adv.* **1.** *Literary.* as well; likewise. **2.** *Literary.* nevertheless. **3.** *Archaic.* therewith. ~*prep.* **4.** (*postpositive*) an archaic word for **with.** [C12: from WITH + ALL]

with+draw (wɪðˈdrɔː) *vb.* **+draws, +draw+ing, +drew, +drawn. 1.** (*tr.*) to take or draw back or away; remove. **2.** (*tr.*) to retract or recall (a statement, promise, etc.). **3.** (*intr.*) to retire or retreat: *the troops withdrew.* **4.** (*intr.;* often foll. by *from*) to back out (of) or depart (from): *he withdrew from public life.* **5.** (*intr.*) to detach oneself socially, emotionally, or mentally. [C13: from WITH (in the sense: away from) + DRAW] —**with+ˈdraw+a·ble** *adj.* —**with+ˈdraw+er** *n.*

with+draw+al (wɪðˈdrɔːəl) *n.* **1.** an act or process of withdrawing; retreat, removal, or detachment. **2.** the period a drug addict goes through following abrupt termination in the use of narcotics, usually characterized by physical and mental symptoms (**withdrawal symptoms**).

with+draw+ing room *n.* an archaic term for **drawing room.**

with+drawn (wɪðˈdrɔːn) *vb.* **1.** the past participle of **withdraw.**

~*adj.* **2.** unusually reserved, introverted, or shy. **3.** secluded or remote. —**with+'drawn+ness** *n.*
with+drew (wɪð'dru:) *vb.* the past tense of **withdraw.**
withe (wɪθ, wɪð, waɪð) *n.* **1.** a strong flexible twig, esp. of willow, suitable for binding things together; withy. **2.** a band or rope of twisted twigs or stems. **3.** a handle made of elastic material, fitted on some tools to reduce the shock during use. **4.** a wall with a thickness of half a brick, such as a leaf of a cavity wall, or a division between two chimney flues. ~*vb.* **5.** (*tr.*) to bind with withes. [Old English *withthe;* related to Old Norse *vithja,* Old High German *witta, widi,* Gothic *wida*]
with+er ('wɪðə) *vb.* **1.** (*intr.*) (esp. of a plant) to droop, wilt, or shrivel up. **2.** (*intr.; often foll. by away*) to fade or waste: *all hope withered away.* **3.** (*intr.*) to decay, decline or disintegrate. **4.** (*tr.*) to cause to wilt, fade, or lose vitality. **5.** (*tr.*) to abash, esp. with a scornful look. **6.** (*tr.*) to harm or damage. [C14: perhaps variant of WEATHER (vb.); related to German *verwittern* to decay] —**'with+ered+ness** *n.* —**'with+er+er** *n.* —**'with+er+ing+ly** *adv.*
with+er+ite ('wɪðə,raɪt) *n.* a white, grey, or yellowish mineral consisting of barium carbonate in orthorhombic crystalline form: occurs in veins of lead ore. Formula: $BaCO_3$. [C18: named after W. *Withering* (1741–99), English scientist]
with+ers ('wɪðəz) *pl. n.* the highest part of the back of a horse, behind the neck between the shoulders. [C16: short for *widersones,* from *wider* WITH + *-sones,* perhaps variant of SINEW; related to German *Widerrist,* Old English *withre* resistance]
with+er+shins ('wɪðə,ʃɪnz) *or* **wid+der+shins** *adv. Chiefly Scot.* **1.** in the direction contrary to the apparent course of the sun; anticlockwise. **2.** *Obsolete.* in a direction contrary to the usual. [C16: from Middle Low German *weddersinnes,* from Middle High German, literally: opposite course, from *wider* against + *sinnes,* genitive of *sin* course]
with+hold (wɪð'həuld) *vb.* **+holds, +hold+ing, +held. 1.** (*tr.*) to keep back; refrain from giving: *he withheld his permission.* **2.** (*tr.*) to hold back; restrain. **3.** (*tr.*) to deduct (taxes, etc.) from a salary or wages. **4.** (*intr.; usually foll. by from*) to refrain or forbear. —**with+'hold+er** *n.*
with+hold+ing tax *n. U.S.* a portion of an employee's tax liability paid directly to the government by the employer.
with+in (wɪ'ðɪn) *prep.* **1.** in; inside; enclosed or encased by. **2.** before (a period of time) has elapsed: *within a week.* **3.** not beyond the limits of; not differing by more than (a specified amount) from: *live within your means; within seconds of the world record.* ~*adv.* **4.** *Formal.* inside; internally.
with+in+doors ('wɪðɪn'dɔ:z) *adv.* an obsolete word for **indoors.**
with+out (wɪ'ðaʊt) *prep.* **1.** not having: *a traveller without much money.* **2.** not accompanied by: *he came without his wife.* **3.** not making use of: *it is not easy to undo screws without a screwdriver.* **4.** (*foll. by a present participle*) not, while not, or after not: *she can sing for two minutes without drawing breath.* **5.** *Archaic.* on the outside of: *without the city walls.* ~*adv.* **6.** *Formal.* outside; outwardly. ~*conj.* **7.** *Not standard.* unless: *don't come without you have some money.*
with+out+doors ('wɪðaʊt'dɔ:z) *adv.* an obsolete word for **outdoors.**
with+stand (wɪð'stænd) *vb.* **+stands, +stand+ing, +stood. 1.** (*tr.*) to stand up to forcefully; resist. **2.** (*intr.*) to remain firm in endurance or opposition. —**with+'stand+er** *n.*
with·y ('wɪðɪ) *n., pl.* **with·ies. 1.** a variant spelling of **withe** (senses 1, 2). **2.** a willow tree, esp. an osier. ~*adj.* **3.** (of people) tough and agile. **4.** *Rare.* resembling a withe in strength or flexibility. [Old English *wīdig*(e); related to Old Norse *vīthir,* Old High German *wīda,* Latin *vītis* vine, Sanskrit *vītika* fetter. See WITHE, WIRE]
wit+less ('wɪtlɪs) *adj.* lacking wit, intelligence, or sense; stupid. —**'wit+less+ly** *adv.* —**'wit+less+ness** *n.*
wit+ling ('wɪtlɪŋ) *n. Archaic.* a person who thinks himself witty.
wit+ness ('wɪtnɪs) *n.* **1.** a person who has seen or can give first-hand evidence of some event. **2.** a person or thing giving or serving as evidence. **3.** a person who testifies, esp. in a court of law, to events or facts within his own knowledge. **4.** a person who attests to the genuineness of a document, signature, etc., by adding his own signature. **5. bear witness. a.** to give written or oral testimony. **b.** to be evidence or proof of. ~Related adj.: **testimonial.** ~*vb.* **6.** (*tr.*) to see, be present at, or know at first hand. **7.** to give or serve as evidence (of). **8.** (*tr.*) to be the scene or setting of: *this field has witnessed a battle.* **9.** (*intr.*) to testify, esp. in a court of law, to events within a person's own knowledge. **10.** (*tr.*) to attest to the genuineness of (a document, signature, etc.) by adding one's own signature. [Old English *witnes* (meaning both *testimony* and *witness*), from *witan* to know, WIT[2] + -NESS; related to Old Norse *vitni*] —**'wit+ness+a·ble** *adj.* —**'wit+ness+er** *n.*
wit+ness box *or esp. U.S.* **wit+ness stand** *n.* the place in a court of law in which witnesses stand to give evidence.
wits (wɪts) *pl. n.* **1.** (*sometimes sing.*) the ability to reason and act, esp. quickly (esp. in the phrase **have one's wits about one**). **2.** (*sometimes sing.*) right mind, sanity (esp. in the phrase **out of one's wits**). **3. at one's wits' end.** at a loss to know how to proceed. **4. five wits.** *Obsolete.* the five senses or mental faculties. **5. live by one's wits.** to gain a livelihood by craftiness rather than by hard work.
-wit·ted *adj.* (*in combination*) having wits or intelligence as specified: *slow-witted; dim-witted.*
Wit+ten+berg (*German* 'vɪtᵊn,bɛrk; *English* 'wɪtᵊn,bɜ:g) *n.* a city in central East Germany, on the River Elbe: Martin Luther, as a philosophy teacher at Wittenberg university, began the Reformation here in 1517 by nailing his 95 theses to the doors of a church. Pop.: 47 640 (1972).
Witt·gen·stein ('vɪtgən,ʃtaɪn, -,staɪn) *n.* **Lud·wig Jo·sef Jo·hann** ('lu:tvɪç 'jo:zɛf 'jo:han). 1889–1951, British philosopher, born in Austria. After studying with Bertrand Russell, he wrote the *Tractatus Logico-Philosophicus* (1921), which explores the relationship of language to the world. In *Philosophical Investigations* (1953) he examined the various linguistic uses to which certain philosophical expressions were put. He was a major influence on logical positivism.
wit+ti+cism ('wɪtɪ,sɪzəm) *n.* a clever or witty remark. [C17: from WITTY; coined by Dryden (1677) by analogy with *criticism*]
wit+ting ('wɪtɪŋ) *adj. Rare.* **1.** deliberate; intentional: *a witting insult.* **2.** aware; knowing. —**'wit+ting+ly** *adv.*
wit+tol ('wɪtᵊl) *n. Obsolete.* a man who tolerates his wife's unfaithfulness. [C15 *wetewold,* from *witen* to know (see WIT[2]) + *-wold,* perhaps from *cokewold* CUCKOLD]
wit+ty ('wɪtɪ) *adj.* **+ti+er, +ti+est. 1.** characterized by clever humour or wit. **2.** *Archaic or Brit. dialect.* intelligent or sensible. —**'wit+ti+ly** *adv.* —**'wit+ti+ness** *n.*
Wit+wa+ters+rand (wɪt'wɔ:təz,rænd, vət'vɑ:təs,rant) *n.* a rocky ridge in NE South Africa, in S Transvaal: contains the richest gold deposits in the world, also coal and manganese; chief industrial centre is Johannesburg. Height: 1500–1800 m (5000–6000 ft.). Also called: **the Rand, the Reef.**
wive (waɪv) *vb. Archaic.* **1.** to marry (a woman). **2.** (*tr.*) to supply with a wife. [Old English *gewīfian,* from *wīf* WIFE]
wi+vern ('waɪvən) *n.* a less common spelling of **wyvern.**
wives (waɪvz) *n.* the plural of **wife.**
wiz (wɪz) *n. Informal.* a variant spelling of **whiz** (sense 5).
wiz+ard ('wɪzəd) *n.* **1.** a male witch or a man who practises or professes to practise magic or sorcery. **2.** a person who is outstandingly clever in some specified field; expert. **3.** *Obsolete.* a wise man. ~*adj.* **4.** *Informal, chiefly Brit.* superb; outstanding. **5.** of or relating to a wizard or wizardry. [C15: variant of *wissard,* from WISE[1] + -ARD] —**'wiz+ard+ly** *adj.*
wiz+ard+ry ('wɪzədrɪ) *n.* the art, skills, and practices of a wizard, sorcerer, or magician.
wiz+en[1] ('wɪzᵊn) *vb.* **1.** to make or become shrivelled. ~*adj.* **2.** a variant of **wizened.** [Old English *wisnian;* related to Old Norse *visna,* Old High German *wesanēn*]
wi+zen[2] ('wi:zᵊn) *n.* an archaic word for **weasand** (the gullet).
wiz+ened ('wɪzᵊnd) *or* **wiz+en** *adj.* shrivelled, wrinkled, or dried up, esp. with age.
wk. *abbrev. for:* **1.** (*pl.* **wks.**) week. **2.** work. **3.** weak.
wkly. *abbrev. for* weekly.
WL *international car registration for* (Windward Islands) St. Lucia.
w.l. *or* **WL** *abbrev. for* water line.
WLM *abbrev. for* women's liberation movement.
wmk. *abbrev. for* watermark.
W.M.O. *abbrev. for* World Meteorological Organization.
W.N.P. *abbrev. for* Welsh Nationalist Party.
WNW *abbrev. for* west-northwest.
wo (wəʊ) *n., pl.* **wos.** an archaic spelling of **woe.**
W.O. *abbrev. for:* **1.** War Office. **2.** Warrant Officer. **3.** wireless operator.
w/o *abbrev. for:* **1.** without. **2.** written off.
woad (wəʊd) *n.* **1.** a European cruciferous plant, *Isatis tinctoria,* formerly cultivated for its leaves, which yield a blue dye. See also **dyer's weed, dyer's rocket. 2.** the dye obtained from this plant, used esp. by the ancient Britons, as a body dye. [Old English *wād;* related to Old High German *weit;* Middle Dutch *wēd,* Latin *vitrum*]
woad+ed ('wəʊdɪd) *adj.* coloured blue with woad.
woad+wax+en ('wəʊd,wæksən) *n.* another name for **dyer's-greenweed.**
woald (wəʊld) *n.* another name for **weld**[2]**.**
wob+be+gong ('wɒbɪ,gɒŋ) *n.* any of various carpet sharks of the family *Orectolobidae,* of Australian waters, having a richly patterned brown-and-white skin. [from a native Australian language]
wob+ble ('wɒbᵊl) *vb.* **1.** (*intr.*) to move, rock, or sway unsteadily. **2.** (*intr.*) to tremble or shake: *her voice wobbled with emotion.* **3.** (*intr.*) to vacillate with indecision. **4.** (*tr.*) to cause to wobble. ~*n.* **5.** a wobbling movement, motion, or sound. ~Also: **wabble.** [C17: variant of *wabble,* from Low German *wabbeln;* related to Middle High German *wabelen* to WAVER] —**'wob+bler** *n.* —**'wob+bly** *adj.* —**'wob+bli+ness** *n.*
wob+ble board *n. Austral.* a piece of fibreboard used as a musical instrument, producing a characteristic sound when flexed.
Wob+bly ('wɒblɪ) *n., pl.* **+blies.** a member of the Industrial Workers of the World.
Wode·house ('wʊd,haʊs) *n.* Sir **P(elham) G(renville).** 1881-1975, U.S. author born in England. His humorous novels of upper-class life in England include the *Psmith* and *Jeeves* series.
Wo·den *or* **Wo·dan** ('wəʊdᵊn) *n.* the foremost Anglo-Saxon god. Norse counterpart: **Odin.** [Old English *Wōden;* related to Old Norse *Ōthinn,* Old High German *Wuotan,* German *Wotan;* see WEDNESDAY]
wodge (wɒdʒ) *n. Brit. informal.* a thick lump or chunk cut or broken off something. [C20: alteration of WEDGE]
woe (wəʊ) *n.* **1.** *Literary.* intense grief or misery. **2.** (*often pl.*) affliction or misfortune. **3. woe betide (someone).** misfortune will befall (someone): *woe betide you if you arrive late.* —*interj.* **4.** Also: **woe is me.** *Archaic.* an exclamation of sorrow or distress. [Old English *wā, wǣ;* related to Old Saxon, Old

High German *wē*, Old Norse *vei*, Gothic *wai*, Latin *vae*, Sanskrit *uvē*; see WAIL]
woe+be+gone ('wəʊbɪˌgɒn) *adj.* **1.** sorrowful or sad in appearance. **2.** *Archaic.* afflicted with woe. [C14: from a phrase such as *me is wo begon* woe has beset me]
woe+ful ('wəʊfʊl) *adj.* **1.** expressing or characterized by sorrow. **2.** bringing or causing woe. **3.** pitiful; miserable: *a woeful standard of work.* —**'woe+ful+ly** *adv.* —**'woe+ful+ness** *n.*
wog[1] (wɒg) *n. Brit. slang, derogatory.* a foreigner, esp. one who is not White. [probably from GOLLIWOG]
wog[2] (wɒg) *n. Slang, chiefly Austral.* influenza or any similar illness. [C20: of unknown origin]
wog+gle ('wɒgᵊl) *n.* the ring of leather through which a Scout neckerchief is threaded. [C20: of unknown origin]
wok (wɒk) *n.* a large metal Chinese cooking pot having a curved base like a bowl and traditionally with a wooden handle. [from Chinese (Cantonese)]
woke (wəʊk) *vb.* a past tense of **wake.**
wok+en ('wəʊkən) *vb.* a past participle of **wake.**
Wo+king ('wəʊkɪŋ) *n.* a town in S England, in central Surrey: mainly residential. Pop.: 75 771 (1971).
wold[1] (wəʊld) *n. Chiefly literary.* a tract of open rolling country, esp. upland. [Old English *weald* bush; related to Old Saxon *wald*, German *Wald* forest, Old Norse *vollr* ground; see WILD]
wold[2] (wəʊld) *n.* another name for **weld**[2].
Wolds (wəʊldz) *n.* **the.** a range of chalk hills in NE England: consists of the **Yorkshire Wolds** to the north, separated from the **Lincolnshire Wolds** by the Humber estuary.
wolf (wʊlf) *n., pl.* **wolves. 1.** a predatory canine mammal, *Canis lupus*, which hunts in packs and was formerly widespread in North America and Eurasia but is now less common. See also **timber wolf.** Related adj.: **lupine. 2.** any of several similar and related canines, such as the red wolf and the coyote (**prairie wolf**). **3.** the fur of any such animal. **4. Tasmanian wolf.** another name for the **thylacine. 5.** a voracious, grabbing, or fiercely cruel person or thing. **6.** *Informal.* a man who habitually tries to seduce women. **7.** *Informal.* the destructive larva of any of various moths and beetles. **8.** Also called: **wolf note.** *Music.* **a.** an unpleasant sound produced in some notes played on the violin, cello, etc., owing to resonant vibrations of the belly. **b.** an out-of-tune effect produced on keyboard instruments accommodated esp. to the system of mean-tone temperament. See **temperament** (sense 4). **9. cry wolf.** to give a false alarm. **10. have** *or* **hold a wolf by the ears.** to be in a desperate situation. **11. keep the wolf from the door.** to ward off starvation or privation. **12. lone wolf.** a person or animal who prefers to be alone. **13. throw to the wolves.** to abandon or deliver to destruction. **14. wolf in sheep's clothing.** a malicious person in a harmless or benevolent disguise. ~*vb.* **15.** (*tr.*; often foll. by *down*) to gulp (down). **16.** (*intr.*) to hunt wolves. [Old English *wulf*; related to Old High German *wolf*, Old Norse *ulfr*, Gothic *wulfs*, Latin *lupus* and *vulpēs* fox] —**'wolf+ish** *adj.* —**'wolf+ˌlike** *adj.*
Wolf (*German* vɔlf) *n.* **1. Frie·drich Au·gust** ('fri:drɪç 'aʊgʊst). 1759–1824, German classical scholar, who suggested that the Homeric poems, esp. the *Iliad*, are products of an oral tradition. **2. Hu·go** ('hu:go). 1860–1903, Austrian composer, esp. of songs, including the *Italienisches Liederbuch* and the *Spanisches Liederbuch*.
wolf+bane ('wʊlfˌbeɪn), **wolfs+bane,** *or* **wolf's bane** *n.* any of several poisonous N temperate plants of the ranunculaceous genus *Aconitum*, esp. *A. lycoctonum*, which has yellow hoodlike flowers.
Wolf Cub *n. Brit.* the former name for **Cub Scout.**
Wolfe (wʊlf) *n.* **1. James.** 1727–59, English soldier, who commanded the British capture of Quebec, in which he was killed. **2. Thom·as (Clayton).** 1900–38, U.S. novelist, noted for his autobiographical fiction, esp. *Look Homeward, Angel* (1929).
Wolf·en·den Re+port ('wʊlfəndən) *n.* a study produced in 1957 by the Committee on Homosexual Offences and Prostitution in Britain, which recommended that homosexual relations between consenting adults be legalized. [C20: named after Baron John *Wolfenden*, who chaired the Committee]
wolf+er ('wʊlfə) *n.* a less common spelling of **wolver.**
Wolf-Fer·ra·ri (*Italian* 'vɔlf fer'ra:ri) *n.* **Er·man·no** (er'ma:nno). 1867–1948, Italian composer born of a German father, in Germany from 1909. His works, mainly in a lyrical style, include operas, such as *The Jewels of the Madonna* (1911) and *Susanna's Secret* (1909).
Wolff+i·an bod·y ('vɒlfɪən) *n. Embryol.* another name for **mesonephros.** [C19: named after K. F. *Wolff* (1733–94), German embryologist]
wolf+fish ('wʊlfˌfɪʃ) *n., pl.* **+fish** *or* **+fish·es.** any large northern deep-sea blennioid fish of the family *Anarhichadidae*, such as *Anarhichas lupus*. They have large sharp teeth and no pelvic fins and are used as food fishes. Also called: **catfish.**
wolf+hound ('wʊlfˌhaʊnd) *n.* the largest breed of dog, used formerly to hunt wolves.
Wol·fit ('wʊlfɪt) *n.* Sir **Don·ald.** 1902–68, English stage actor and manager.
wolf+ram ('wʊlfrəm) *n.* another name for **tungsten.** [C18: from German, originally perhaps from the proper name, *Wolfram*, used pejoratively of tungsten because it was thought inferior to tin]
wolf+ram+ite ('wʊlfrəˌmaɪt) *n.* a black to reddish-brown mineral consisting of tungstates of iron and manganese in monoclinic crystalline form: it occurs mainly in quartz veins and is the chief ore of tungsten. Formula: $(Fe,Mn)WO_4$.
Wolf·ram von Esch·en·bach (*German* 'vɔlfram fən 'ɛʃᵊnˌbax) *n.* died ?1220, German poet: author of the epic *Parzival*, incorporating the story of the Grail.
Wolf-Ray·et star ('wʊlf 'reɪət) *n.* any of over 100 very hot intensely luminous stars surrounded by a rapidly expanding envelope of gas. Sometimes shortened to **W star.** [C19: named after Charles *Wolf* (1827–1918) and Georges *Rayet* (1839–1906), French astronomers]
wolfs+bane *or* **wolf's-bane** ('wʊlfsˌbeɪn) *n.* variants of **wolfbane.**
Wolfs+burg (*German* 'vɔlfsbʊrk) *n.* a city in NE West Germany, in Lower Saxony: founded in 1938; motor-vehicle industry. Pop.: 133 971 (1974 est.).
wolf spi+der *n.* any spider of the family *Lycosidae*, which chase their prey to catch it. Also called: **hunting spider.**
wolf whis+tle *n.* **1.** a whistle made by a man to express admiration of a woman's appearance. ~*vb.* **wolf-whis·tle. 2.** (when *intr.*, sometimes foll. by *at*) to make such a whistle (at someone).
wol+las+ton+ite ('wʊləstəˌnaɪt) *n.* a white or grey mineral consisting of calcium silicate in triclinic crystalline form: occurs in metamorphosed limestones. Formula: $CaSiO_3$. [C19: named after W. H. *Wollaston* (1766–1828), English physicist]
Wol+lon+gong ('wʊlənˌgɒŋ) *n.* a city in E Australia, in E New South Wales on the Pacific: an early centre of dairy farming; now a coal-mining and heavy industrial centre. Pop.: 211 240 (1975 est.).
wol+ly ('wɒlɪ) *n., pl.* **+lies.** *East London dialect.* a pickled cucumber or olive. [perhaps from OLIVE]
Wol+of ('wɒlɒf) *n.* **1.** (*pl.* **+of** *or* **+ofs**) a member of a Negroid people of W Africa living chiefly in Senegal. **2.** the language of this people, belonging to the West Atlantic branch of the Niger-Congo family.
Wol·sey ('wʊlzɪ) *n.* **Thom·as.** ?1475–1530, English cardinal and statesman; archbishop of York (1514–30); lord chancellor (1515–29). He dominated Henry VIII's foreign and domestic policies but his failure to obtain papal consent for the king's divorce from Catherine of Aragon led to his arrest for high treason (1530); he died on the journey to face trial.
wolv+er ('wʊlvə) *or* **wolf+er** *n.* a person who hunts wolves.
Wol+ver+hamp+ton (ˌwʊlvə'hæmptən) *n.* a town in W central England, in the West Midlands: iron and steel foundries. Pop.: 268 847 (1971).
wol+ver+ine ('wʊlvəˌri:n) *n.* a large musteline mammal, *Gulo gulo*, of northern forests of Eurasia and North America having dark very thick water-resistant fur. Also called: **glutton.** [C16 *wolvering*, from WOLF + -ING[3] (later altered to *-ine*)]
wolves (wʊlvz) *n.* the plural of **wolf.**
wom+an ('wʊmən) *n., pl.* **wom+en. 1.** an adult female human being. **2.** (*modifier*) female or feminine: *a woman politician; woman talk.* **3.** women collectively; womankind. **4.** (usually preceded by *the*) feminine nature or feelings: *babies bring out the woman in her.* **5.** a female servant or domestic help. **6.** a man considered as having female characteristics, such as meekness or cowardliness. **7.** *Informal.* a wife, mistress, or girlfriend. **8. the little woman.** *Informal.* one's wife. **9. woman of the streets.** a prostitute. ~*vb.* (*tr.*) **10.** *Rare.* to provide with women. **11.** *Obsolete.* to make effeminate. [Old English *wīfmann, wimman*; from WIFE + MAN (human being)] —**'wom+an+less** *adj.* —**'wom·an-ˌlike** *adj.*
wom+an+hood ('wʊmənˌhʊd) *n.* **1.** the state or quality of being a woman or being womanly. **2.** women collectively.
wom+an+ish ('wʊmənɪʃ) *adj.* **1.** having qualities or characteristics regarded as unsuitable to a strong character of either sex, esp. a man. **2.** characteristic of or suitable for a woman. —**'wom+an+ish+ly** *adv.* —**'wom+an+ish+ness** *n.*
wom+an+ize *or* **wom+an+ise** ('wʊməˌnaɪz) *vb.* **1.** (*intr.*) *Informal.* (of a man) to indulge in many casual affairs with women; philander. **2.** (*tr.*) to make effeminate. —**'wom+an+ˌiz+er** *or* **'wom+an+ˌis+er** *n.*
wom+an+kind ('wʊmənˌkaɪnd) *n.* the female members of the human race; women collectively.
wom+an+ly ('wʊmənlɪ) *adj.* **1.** possessing qualities, such as warmth, attractiveness, etc., generally regarded as typical of a woman, esp. a mature woman. **2.** characteristic of or belonging to a woman. —**'wom+an+li+ness** *n.*
womb (wu:m) *n.* **1.** the nontechnical name for **uterus. 2.** a hollow space enclosing something, esp. when dark, warm, or sheltering. **3.** a place where something is conceived: *the Near East is the womb of western civilization.* **4.** *Obsolete.* the belly. [Old English *wamb*; related to Old Norse *vomb*, Gothic *wamba*, Middle Low German *wamme*, Swedish *våmm*] —**wombed** *adj.* —**'womb+like** *adj.*
wom+bat ('wɒmbæt) *n.* either of two burrowing herbivorous Australian marsupials, *Vombatus ursinus* or *Lasiorhinus latifrons*, constituting the family *Vombatidae* (or *Phascolomidae*) and having short limbs, a heavy body, and coarse dense fur. [C18: from a native Australian language]
wom+en ('wɪmɪn) *n.* the plural of **woman.**
wom+en+folk ('wɪmɪnˌfəʊk) *or U.S.* (*sometimes*) **wom·en+folks** *pl. n.* **1.** women collectively. **2.** a group of women, esp. the female members of one's family.
Wom+en's In+sti+tute *n.* (in Commonwealth countries) a society for women interested in the problems of the home and in engaging in social activities.
Wom+en's Lib+er+a+tion *n.* a movement directed towards the removal of attitudes and practices that preserve inequalities

based upon the assumption that men are superior to women. Also called: **women's lib.**

wom·en's suf·frage *n.* the right of women to vote. See also **suffragette.**

wom·er·a ('wʊmərə) *n.* a variant spelling of **woomera.**

won[1] (wʌn) *vb.* the past tense of **win**[1].

won[2] (wɒn) *n., pl.* **won. 1.** the standard monetary unit of North Korea, divided into 100 chon. **2.** the standard monetary unit of South Korea, divided into 100 chon. ~Also called: **hwan.**

won[3] (wʌn, wʊn, wəʊn) *vb.* **·wons, ·won·ning, ·wonned.** (*intr.*) *Archaic.* to live or dwell. [Old English *wunian* to become accustomed to; related to WIN[1], WYNN]

won·der ('wʌndə) *n.* **1.** the feeling excited by something strange; a mixture of surprise, curiosity, and sometimes awe. **2.** something that causes such a feeling, such as a miracle. **3.** See **Seven Wonders of the World. 4.** (*modifier*) exciting wonder by virtue of spectacular results achieved, feats performed, etc.: *a wonder drug; a wonder horse.* **5. do** *or* **work wonders.** to achieve spectacularly fine results. **6. for a wonder.** surprisingly or amazingly. **7. nine days' wonder.** a subject that arouses general surprise or public interest for a short time. **8. no wonder.** (*sentence connector*) (I am) not surprised at all (that): *no wonder he couldn't come.* **9. small wonder.** (*sentence connector*) (I am) hardly surprised (that): *small wonder he couldn't make it tonight.* ~*vb.* (when *tr., may take a clause as object*) **10.** (when *intr.,* often foll. by *about*) to indulge in speculative inquiry, often accompanied by an element of doubt (concerning something): *I wondered about what she said; I wonder what happened.* **11.** (when *intr.,* often foll. by *at*) to be amazed (at something): *I wonder at your impudence.* [Old English *wundor;* related to Old Saxon *wundar,* Old Norse *undr,* German *Wunder*] —'**won·der·er** *n.* —'**won·der·less** *adj.*

Won·der ('wʌndə) *n.* **Stev·ie.** original name *Stephen Judkins.* born 1950, U.S. rock singer, pianist, harmonica player, and songwriter. His recordings include *Fingertips* (1963) and the albums *Music of my Mind* (1972), *Talking Book* (1972), *Innervisions* (1973), *Fulfillingness' First Finale* (1974), and *Songs in the Key of Life* (1976).

won·der·ful ('wʌndəfʊl) *adj.* **1.** exciting a feeling of wonder; marvellous or strange. **2.** extremely fine; excellent. —'**won·der·ful·ly** *adv.* —'**won·der·ful·ness** *n.*

won·der·land ('wʌndə,lænd) *n.* **1.** an imaginary land of marvels or wonders. **2.** an actual place or scene of great or strange beauty or wonder.

won·der·ment ('wʌndəmənt) *n.* **1.** rapt surprise; awe. **2.** puzzled interest; **3.** something that excites wonder.

won·der·work ('wʌndə,wɜ:k) *n.* something done or made that excites wonder; miracle or wonder. —'**won·der-,work·er** *n.* —'**won·der-,work·ing** *n., adj.*

won·drous ('wʌndrəs) *Archaic or literary.* ~*adj.* **1.** exciting wonder; marvellous. ~*adv.* **2.** (intensifier): *it is wondrous cold.* —'**won·drous·ly** *adv.* —'**won·drous·ness** *n.*

won·ga-won·ga ('wɒŋə'wɒŋə) *n.* **1.** a large Australian pigeon, *Leucosarcia melanoleuca.* **2.** an Australian evergreen vine of the genus *Pandorea* or *Tecoma,* esp. *T. australis.* [from a native Australian language]

won·ky ('wɒŋkɪ) *adj.* **·ki·er, ·ki·est.** *Brit. slang.* **1.** shaky or unsteady. **2.** not in correct alignment; askew. **3.** liable to break down or develop a fault. [C20: variant of dialect *wanky,* from Old English *wancol*]

Won·san ('wɒn'sæn) *n.* a port in SE North Korea, on the Sea of Japan: oil refineries. Pop.: 215 000 (1967 est.).

wont (wəʊnt) *adj.* **1.** (*postpositive*) accustomed (to doing something): *he was wont to come early.* ~*n.* **2.** a manner or action habitually employed by or associated with someone (often in the phrases **as is my wont, as is his wont,** etc.). ~*vb.* **3.** (when *tr., usually passive*) to become or cause to become accustomed. [Old English *gewunod,* past participle of *wunian* to be accustomed to; related to Old High German *wunēn* (German *wohnen*), Old Norse *una* to be satisfied; see WEAN, WISH, WINSOME]

won't (wəʊnt) *contraction of* will not.

wont·ed ('wəʊntɪd) *adj.* **1.** (*postpositive*) accustomed or habituated (to doing something). **2.** (*prenominal*) customary; usual: *she is in her wonted place.*

won ton ('wɒn 'tɒn) *n. Chinese cookery.* **1.** a dumpling filled with spiced minced pork, usually served in soup. **2.** soup containing such dumplings. [from Chinese (Cantonese) *wan t'an* pastry]

woo (wu:) *vb.* **woos, woo·ing, wooed. 1.** to seek the affection, favour, or love of (a woman) with a view to marriage. **2.** (*tr.*) to seek after zealously or hopefully: *to woo fame.* **3.** (*tr.*) to bring upon oneself (good or evil results) by one's own action. **4.** (*tr.*) to beg or importune (someone). [Old English *wōgian,* of obscure origin] —'**woo·er** *n.* —'**woo·ing·ly** *adv.*

wood[1] (wʊd) *n.* **1.** the hard fibrous substance consisting of xylem tissue that occurs beneath the bark in trees, shrubs, and similar plants. **2.** the trunks of trees that have been cut and prepared for use as a building material. **3.** a collection of trees, shrubs, herbs, grasses, etc., usually dominated by one or a few species of tree: usually smaller than a forest: *an oak wood.* Related adj.: **sylvan. 4.** fuel; firewood. **5.** *Golf.* **a.** a long-shafted club with a wooden head, used for driving: numbered from 1 to 5 according to size, angle of face, etc. **b.** (*as modifier*): *a wood shot.* **6.** *Tennis, etc.* the frame of a racket: *he hit a winning shot off the wood.* **7.** one of the biased wooden bowls used in the game of bowls. **8.** *Music.* short for **woodwind.** See also **woods** (sense 3). **9. a.** casks, barrels, etc., made of wood. **b. from the wood.** (of a beverage) from a wooden container rather than a metal or glass one. **10. have (got) the wood on.** *Austral. informal.* to have an advantage over. **11. out of the wood** *or* **woods.** clear of or safe from dangers or doubts: *we're not out of the woods yet.* **12. see the wood for the trees.** (*used with a negative*) to obtain a general view of a situation, problem, etc., without allowing details to cloud one's analysis: *he can't see the wood for the trees.* **13.** (*modifier*) made of, used for, employing, or handling wood: *a wood fire.* **14.** (*modifier*) dwelling in, concerning, or situated in a wood: *a wood nymph.* ~*vb.* **15.** (*tr.*) to plant a wood upon. **16.** to supply or be supplied with fuel or firewood. [Old English *widu, wudu;* related to Old High German *witu,* Old Norse *vithr*] —'**wood·less** *adj.*

wood[2] (wʊd) *adj. Obsolete.* raging or raving like a maniac. [Old English *wōd;* related to Old High German *wuot* (German *Wut*), Old Norse *ōthr,* Gothic *wōths,* Latin *vātēs* seer]

Wood (wʊd) *n.* Sir **Hen·ry (Joseph).** 1869–1944, English conductor, who founded the Promenade Concerts in London.

wood al·co·hol *n.* another name for **methanol.**

wood-and-wa·ter jo·ey *n. Austral. informal.* a person employed to carry out menial tasks. [from the biblical phrase "hewers of wood and drawers of water" (Joshua 9:21) and JOEY]

wood a·nem·o·ne *n.* any of several woodland anemone plants, esp. *Anemone quinquefolia* of E North America and *A. nemorosa* of Europe, having finely divided leaves and solitary white flowers. Also called: **windflower.**

wood ant *n.* a reddish-brown European ant, *Formica rufa,* typically living in anthills in woodlands.

wood av·ens *n.* another name for **herb bennet.**

wood·bine ('wʊ:d,baɪn) *n.* **1.** a honeysuckle, *Lonicera periclymenum,* of Europe, SW Asia, and N Africa, having fragrant yellow flowers. **2. American woodbine.** a related North American plant, *L. caprifolium.* **3.** *U.S.* another name for **Virginia creeper** (sense 1). **4.** *Austral. slang.* an Englishman.

wood block *n.* **1.** a small rectangular flat block of wood that is laid with others as a floor surface. **2.** *Music.* another word for **Chinese block.**

wood·bor·er ('wʊd,bɔ:rə) *n.* **1.** any of various beetles of the families *Anobiidae, Buprestidae,* etc., the larvae of which bore into and damage wood. **2.** any of various other unrelated invertebrates that bore into wood.

wood·carv·ing ('wʊd,kɑ:vɪŋ) *n.* **1.** the act of carving wood, esp. as an art form. **2.** a work of art produced by carving wood. —'**wood,carv·er** *n.*

wood·chat *or* **wood·chat shrike** ('wʊd,tʃæt) *n.* a songbird, *Lanius senator,* of Europe and N Africa, having a black-and-white plumage with a reddish-brown crown and a hooked bill: family *Laniidae* (shrikes).

wood·chuck ('wʊd,tʃʌk) *n.* a North American marmot, *Marmota monax,* having coarse reddish-brown fur. Also called: **ground hog.** [C17: by folk etymology from Cree *otcheck* fisher, marten]

wood coal *n.* another name for **lignite** or **charcoal.**

wood·cock ('wʊd,kɒk) *n.* **1.** an Old World game bird, *Scolopax rusticola,* resembling the snipe but larger and having shorter legs and neck: family *Scolopacidae* (sandpipers, etc.), order *Charadriiformes.* **2.** a related North American bird, *Philohela minor.* **3.** *Obsolete.* a simpleton.

wood·craft ('wʊd,krɑ:ft) *n. Chiefly U.S.* **1.** ability and experience in matters concerned with living in a wood or forest. **2.** ability or skill at woodwork, carving, etc. **3.** skill in caring for trees. —'**wood,crafts·man** *n.*

wood·cut ('wʊd,kʌt) *n.* **1.** a block of wood with a design, illustration, etc., cut along the grain, from which prints are made. **2.** a print from a woodcut.

wood·cut·ter ('wʊd,kʌtə) *n.* **1.** a person who fells trees or chops wood. **2.** a person who makes woodcuts. —'**wood,cut·ting** *n.*

wood duck *n.* a duck, *Aix sponsa,* of wooded swamps, lakes, etc., in North America, having a very brightly coloured plumage in the male.

wood·ed ('wʊdɪd) *adj.* **a.** covered with or abounding in woods or trees. **b.** (*in combination*): *a soft-wooded tree.*

wood·en ('wʊdᵊn) *adj.* **1.** made from or consisting of wood. **2.** awkward or clumsy. **3.** bereft of spirit or animation: *a wooden expression.* **4.** obstinately unyielding: *a wooden attitude.* **5.** mentally slow or dull. **6.** not highly resonant: *a wooden thud.* ~*vb.* **7.** (*tr.*) *Austral. slang.* to fell or kill (a person or animal). —'**wood·en·ly** *adv.* —'**wood·en·ness** *n.*

wood en·grav·ing *n.* **1.** the art of engraving pictures or designs on wood for printing by cutting across the grain. **2.** a block of wood so engraved or a print taken from it. —**wood en·grav·er** *n.*

wood·en·head ('wʊdᵊn,hɛd) *n. Informal.* a dull, foolish, or unintelligent person. —,**wood·en·'head·ed** *adj.* —,**wood·en·'head·ed·ness** *n.*

Wood·en Horse *n.* another name for the **Trojan Horse** (sense 1).

wood·en spoon *n.* a booby prize, esp. in sporting contests.

wood·grouse ('wʊd,graʊs) *n.* another name for **capercaillie.**

wood hy·a·cinth *n.* another name for **bluebell** (sense 1).

wood i·bis *n.* any of several storks having a downward-curved bill, esp. *Mycteria americana* of America and *Ibis ibis* of Africa.

wood·land ('wʊdlənd) *n.* **a.** land that is mostly covered with woods or dense growths of trees and shrubs. **b.** (*as modifier*): *woodland fauna.* —'**wood·land·er** *n.*

wood·lark ('wʊd,lɑ:k) *n.* an Old World lark, *Lullula arborea,* similar to but slightly smaller than the skylark.

wood lot *n.* an area restricted to the growing of trees. Also called (esp. Canadian): **bush lot.**

wood·louse ('wʊdˌlaʊs) *n., pl.* ·**lice** (-ˌlaɪs). any of various small terrestrial isopod crustaceans of the genera *Oniscus, Porcellio,* etc., which have a flattened segmented body and occur in damp habitats. See also **pill bug.**

wood·man ('wʊdmən) *n., pl.* ·**men.** **1.** a person who looks after and fells trees used for timber. **2.** another word for **woodsman.** **3.** *Obsolete.* a hunter who is knowledgeable about woods and the animals living in them.

wood·note ('wʊdˌnəʊt) *n.* a natural musical note or song, like that of a wild bird.

wood nymph *n.* one of a class of nymphs fabled to inhabit the woods, such as a dryad.

wood·peck·er ('wʊdˌpɛkə) *n.* any climbing bird of the family *Picidae,* typically having a brightly coloured plumage and strong chisel-like bill with which they bore into trees for insects: order *Piciformes.*

wood pig·eon *n.* a large Eurasian pigeon, *Columba palumbus,* having white patches on the wings and neck. Also called: **ringdove, cushat.**

wood·pile ('wʊdˌpaɪl) *n.* **1.** a pile or heap of firewood. **2.** **nigger in the woodpile.** See **nigger** (sense 3).

wood pitch *n.* the dark viscid residue left after the distillation of wood tar: used as a binder in briquettes.

wood·print ('wʊdˌprɪnt) *n.* another name for **woodcut** (sense 2).

wood pulp *n.* **1.** wood that has been ground to a fine pulp for use in making newsprint and other cheap forms of paper. **2.** finely pulped wood that has been digested by a chemical, such as caustic soda, and sometimes bleached: used in making paper.

wood rat *n.* another name for **pack rat.**

wood·ruff ('wʊdrʌf) *n.* any of several rubiaceous plants of the genus *Asperula,* esp. *A. odorata* (or *Galium odoratum*) **(sweet woodruff),** of Eurasia, which has small sweet-scented white flowers and whorls of narrow fragrant leaves used to flavour wine and liqueurs and in perfumery. [Old English *wudurofe,* from WOOD[1] + *rōfe,* related to Old High German *ruoba,* Middle Low German *rōve* (beet)root, Latin *rēpere* to creep]

wood·rush ('wʊdˌrʌʃ) *n.* any of various juncaceous plants of the genus *Luzula,* chiefly of cold and temperate regions of the N hemisphere, having grasslike leaves and small brown flowers.

woods (wʊdz) *pl. n.* **1.** closely packed trees forming a forest or wood, esp. a specific one. **2.** another word for **backwoods** (sense 2). **3.** the woodwind instruments in an orchestra. See also **wood**[1] (sense 8). **4. this (that, our,** *etc.***) neck of the woods.** this particular area or piece of territory.

Woods *n.* **Lake of the.** See **Lake of the Woods.**

wood·screw ('wʊdˌskruː) *n.* a metal screw that tapers to a point so that it can be driven into wood by a screwdriver.

Wood·ser ('wʊdzə) *n.* See **Jimmy Woodser.**

wood·shed ('wʊdˌʃɛd) *n.* a small outbuilding where firewood, garden tools, etc., are stored.

wood·si·a ('wʊdzɪə) *n.* any small fern of the genus *Woodsia,* of temperate and cold regions, having tufted rhizomes and numerous wiry fronds: family *Polypodiaceae.*

woods·man ('wʊdzmən) *n., pl.* ·**men.** a person who lives in a wood or who is skilled in woodcraft. Also called: **woodman.**

wood sor·rel *n.* a Eurasian plant, *Oxalis acetosella,* having trifoliate leaves, an underground creeping stem, and white purple-veined flowers: family *Oxalidaceae.*

wood spir·it *n. Chem.* another name for **methanol.**

wood sug·ar *n. Chem.* another name for **xylose.**

woods·y ('wʊdzɪ) *adj.* **woods·i·er, woods·i·est.** *U.S. informal.* of, reminiscent of, or connected with the woods.

wood tar *n.* any tar produced by the destructive distillation of wood: used in producing tarred cord and rope and formerly in medicine as disinfectants and antiseptics.

wood vin·e·gar *n.* another name for **pyroligneous acid.**

wood war·bler *n.* **1.** a European woodland warbler, *Phylloscopus sibilatrix,* with a dull yellow plumage. **2.** another name for the **American warbler.** See **warbler** (sense 3).

wood wasp *n.* another name for the **horntail.**

wood·wax·en ('wʊdˌwæksᵊn) *n.* another name for **dyer's-greenweed.**

wood·wind ('wʊdˌwɪnd) *Music.* ~*adj.* **1.** of, relating to, or denoting a type of wind instrument, excluding the brass instruments, formerly made of wood but now often made of metal, such as the flute or clarinet. ~*n.* **2.** (*functioning as pl.*) woodwind instruments collectively.

wood·work ('wʊdˌwɜːk) *n.* **1.** the art, craft, or skill of making things in wood; carpentry. **2.** components made of wood, such as doors, staircases, etc.

wood·work·er ('wʊdˌwɜːkə) *n.* a person who works in wood, such as a carpenter, joiner, or cabinet-maker.

wood·work·ing ('wʊdˌwɜːkɪŋ) *n.* **1.** the process of working wood. ~*adj.* **2.** of, relating to, or used in woodworking.

wood·worm ('wʊdˌwɜːm) *n.* **1.** any of various insect larvae that bore into wooden furniture, etc., esp. the larvae of the furniture beetle, *Anobium punctatum,* and the deathwatch beetle. **2.** the condition caused in wood by any of these larvae.

wood·y ('wʊdɪ) *adj.* **wood·i·er, wood·i·est.** **1.** abounding in or covered with forest or woods. **2.** connected with, belonging to, or situated in a wood. **3.** consisting of or containing wood or lignin: *woody tissue; woody stems.* **4.** resembling wood in hardness or texture. —**'wood·i·ness** *n.*

wood·y night·shade *n.* a scrambling woody Eurasian solanaceous plant, *Solanum dulcamara,* having purple flowers with recurved petals and a protruding cone of yellow anthers and producing poisonous red berry-like fruits. Also called: **bittersweet.**

woof[1] (wuːf) *n.* **1.** the crosswise yarns that fill the warp yarns in weaving; weft. **2.** a woven fabric or its texture. [Old English *ōwef,* from *ō-,* perhaps from ON, + *wef* WEB (see WEAVE); modern form influenced by WARP]

woof[2] (wʊf) *interj.* **1.** an imitation of the bark or growl of a dog. ~*vb.* **2.** (*intr.*) (of dogs) to bark or growl.

woof·er ('wuːfə) *n.* a loudspeaker used in high-fidelity systems for the reproduction of low audio frequencies.

wool (wʊl) *n.* **1.** the outer coat of sheep, yaks, etc., which consists of short curly hairs. **2.** yarn spun from the coat of sheep, etc., used in weaving, knitting, etc. **3. a.** cloth or a garment made from this yarn. **b.** (*as modifier*): *a wool dress.* **4.** any of certain fibrous materials: *glass wool; steel wool.* **5.** *Informal.* short thick curly hair. **6.** a tangled mass of soft fine hairs that occurs in certain plants. **7. dyed in the wool.** confirmed in one's beliefs or opinions. **8. lose** (*or* **keep**) **one's wool.** *Brit. informal.* to lose (or keep) one's temper. **9. pull the wool over someone's eyes.** to deceive or delude someone. [Old English *wull;* related to Old Frisian, Middle Dutch *wulle,* Old High German *wolla* (German *Wolle*), Old Norse *ull,* Latin *lāna* and *vellus* fleece] —**'wool-ˌlike** *adj.*

wool clip *n.* the total amount of wool shorn from a particular flock, or from flocks in a particular region or country, in one year.

Woolf (wʊlf) *n.* **1. Leon·ard Sid·ney.** 1880–1969, English publisher and political writer. **2.** his wife, **Vir·gin·i·a.** 1882–1941, English novelist and critic. Her novels, which include *Mrs. Dalloway* (1925), *To the Lighthouse* (1927), *The Waves* (1931), and *Between the Acts* (1941), employ such techniques as the interior monologue and stream of consciousness.

wool fat *or* **grease** *n.* another name for **lanolin.**

wool·fell ('wʊlˌfɛl) *n. Obsolete.* the skin of a sheep or similar animal with the fleece still attached.

wool·gath·er·ing ('wʊlˌgæðərɪŋ) *n.* idle or absent-minded indulgence in fantasy; daydreaming. —**'wool·ˌgath·er·er** *n.*

wool·grow·er ('wʊlˌgrəʊə) *n.* a person who keeps sheep for their wool. —**'wool·ˌgrow·ing** *n., adj.*

wool·len *or U.S.* **wool·en** ('wʊlən) *adj.* **1.** relating to or consisting partly or wholly of wool. ~*n.* **2.** (*often pl.*) a garment or piece of cloth made wholly or partly of wool, esp. a knitted one.

Wool·ley ('wʊlɪ) *n.* Sir **(Charles) Leon·ard.** 1880–1960, English archaeologist, noted for his excavations at Ur in Mesopotamia (1922–34).

wool·ly *or U.S.* (*often*) **wool·y** ('wʊlɪ) *adj.* **wool·li·er, wool·li·est.** **1.** consisting of, resembling, or having the nature of wool. **2.** covered or clothed in wool or something resembling it. **3.** lacking clarity or substance: *woolly thinking.* **4.** *Botany.* covered with long soft whitish hairs: *woolly stems.* **5.** *U.S.* recalling the rough and lawless period of the early West of America (esp. in the phrase **wild and woolly**). ~*n., pl.* ·**lies.** **6.** (*often pl.*) a garment, such as a sweater, made of wool or something similar. **7.** *Western U.S. and Austral.* (*usually pl.*) a slang word for **sheep.** —**'wool·li·ly** *adv.* —**'wool·li·ness** *n.*

wool·ly bear *n.* the caterpillar of any of various tiger moths, esp. *Arctia caja* of Europe and *Isia isabella* of North America, having a dense covering of soft hairs.

wool·ly·butt ('wʊlɪˌbʌt) *n. Austral.* any of several eucalyptus trees, esp. *Eucalyptus longifolia,* having loose fibrous bark around the base of the trunk.

wool·pack ('wʊlˌpæk) *n.* **1.** the cloth or canvas wrapping used to pack a bale of wool. **2.** a bale of wool.

wool·sack ('wʊlˌsæk) *n.* **1.** a sack containing or intended to contain wool. **2.** (in Britain) the seat of the Lord Chancellor in the House of Lords, formerly made of a large square sack of wool.

wool-sort·er's dis·ease *n.* another name for **anthrax.**

wool sta·pler *n.* a person who sorts wool into different grades or classifications. —**'wool-ˌsta·pling** *n., adj.*

Wool·worth ('wʊlwəθ) *n.* **Frank Win·field** ('wɪnˌfiːld). 1852–1919, U.S. merchant; founder of an international chain of department stores selling inexpensive goods.

woom·er·a *or* **wom·er·a** ('wʊmərə) *n. Austral.* a type of notched stick used by Australian Aborigines to increase leverage and propulsion in the throwing of a spear. [from a native Australian language]

Woom·er·a ('wʊmərə) *n.* a town in South Australia: site of the Long Range Weapons Establishment. Pop.: 4082 (1971).

Woop Woop ('wuːp ˌwuːp) *n. Austral. slang.* a jocular name for any backward or remote town or district.

woo·ra·li (wʊ'rɑːlɪ) *n.* a less common name for **curare.**

wooz·y ('wuːzɪ) *adj.* **wooz·i·er, wooz·i·est.** *Informal.* **1.** dazed or confused. **2.** experiencing dizziness, nausea, etc., as a result of drink. —**'wooz·i·ly** *adv.* —**'wooz·i·ness** *n.*

wop (wɒp) *n. Slang, derogatory.* a member of a Latin people, esp. an Italian. [C20: probably from southern Italian dialect *guappo* dandy, braggart, from Spanish *guapo*]

Worces·ter ('wʊstə) *n.* **1.** a cathedral city in W central England, on the River Severn: scene of the battle (1651) in which Charles II was defeated by Cromwell. Pop.: 73 445 (1971). **2.** an industrial city in central Massachusetts: Clark University (1887). Pop.: 170 730 (1973 est.). **3.** a town in S South Africa, in SW Cape Province. Pop.: 41 769 (1970).

Worces·ter chi·na *or* **porce·lain** *n.* porcelain articles made in Worcester (England) from 1751 in a factory that became, in 1862, the Royal Worcester Porcelain Company. Sometimes shortened to **Worcester.**

Worces+ter sauce *n.* a commercially prepared piquant sauce, made from a basis of soy sauce, with vinegar, spices, etc.

Worces+ter+shire ('wʊstəˌʃɪə, -ʃə) *n.* a former county of W central England, since 1974 part of Hereford and Worcester.

word (wɜːd) *n.* **1.** one of the units of speech or writing that native speakers of a language usually regard as the smallest isolable meaningful element of the language, although linguists would analyse these further into morphemes. **2.** an instance of vocal intercourse; chat, talk, or discussion: *to have a word with someone.* **3.** an utterance or expression, esp. a brief one: *a word of greeting.* **4.** news or information: *he sent word that he would be late.* **5.** a verbal signal for action; command: *when I give the word, fire!* **6.** an undertaking or promise: *I give you my word; he kept his word.* **7.** an autocratic decree or utterance; order: *his word must be obeyed.* **8.** a watchword or slogan, as of a political party: *the word now is "freedom."* **9.** *Computer technol.* a set of bits used to store, transmit, or operate upon an item of information in a computer, such as a program instruction. It usually consists of 32, 36, 48, or 64 bits. **10. as good as one's word.** doing what one has undertaken or promised to do. **11. at a word.** at once. **12. by word of mouth.** through the medium of human speech. **13. in a word.** briefly or in short. **14. my word! a.** an exclamation of surprise, annoyance, etc. **b.** *Austral.* an exclamation of agreement. **15. of one's word.** given to or noted for keeping one's promises: *I am a man of my word.* **16. put in a word** *or* **good word for.** to make favourable mention of (someone); recommend. **17. take someone at his** *or* **her word.** to assume that someone means, or will do, what he or she says: *when he told her to go, she took him at his word and left.* **18. take someone's word for it.** to accept or believe what someone says. **19. the last word. a.** the closing remark of a conversation or argument, esp. a remark that supposedly settles an issue. **b.** the latest or most fashionable design, make, or model: *the last word in bikinis.* **c.** the finest example (of some quality, condition, etc.); *the last word in luxury.* **20. the word.** the proper or most fitting expression: *cold is not the word for it, it's freezing!* **21. upon** *or* **on my word! a.** *Archaic.* on my honour. **b.** an exclamation of surprise, annoyance, etc. **22. word for word. a.** (of a report, transcription, etc.) using exactly the same words as those employed in the situation being reported; verbatim. **b.** translated by substituting each word in the new text for each corresponding word in the original rather than by general sense. **23. word of honour.** a promise; oath. **24.** (*modifier*) of, relating to, or consisting of words: *a word list.* ~*vb.* **25.** (*tr.*) to state in words, usually specially selected ones; phrase. **26.** (*tr.*; often foll. by *up*) *Austral. informal.* to inform or advise (a person). [Old English *word;* related to Old High German *wort,* Old Norse *orth,* Gothic *waurd,* Latin *verbum,* Sanskrit *vratá* command]

Word (wɜːd) *n.* **the. 1.** *Christianity.* the 2nd person of the Trinity. **2.** Scripture, the Bible, or the Gospels as embodying or representing divine revelation. Often called: **the Word of God.** [translation of Greek *logos,* as in John 1:1]

word+age ('wɜːdɪdʒ) *n.* words considered collectively, esp. a quantity of words.

word as+so+ci+a+tion *n.* an early method of psychoanalysis in which the patient thinks of the first word that comes into consciousness on hearing a given word. In this way it was claimed that aspects of the unconscious could be revealed before defence mechanisms intervene.

word blind+ness *n.* the nontechnical name for **alexia** and **dyslexia.** —'**word-ˌblind** *adj.*

word+book ('wɜːdˌbʊk) *n.* **1.** a book containing words, usually with their meanings. **2.** a libretto for an opera.

word+break ('wɜːdˌbreɪk) *n. Printing.* the point at which a word is divided when it runs over from one line of print to the next.

word class *n. Linguistics.* a form class in which the members are words. See **part of speech.**

word deaf+ness *n.* loss of ability to understand spoken words, esp. as the result of a cerebral lesion. Also called: **auditory aphasia.** —'**word-ˌdeaf** *adj.*

word game *n.* any game involving the formation, discovery, or alteration of a word or words.

word+ing ('wɜːdɪŋ) *n.* **1.** the way in which words are used to express a statement, report, etc., esp. a written one. **2.** the words themselves, as used in a written statement or a sign.

word+less ('wɜːdlɪs) *adj.* **1.** inarticulate or silent. **2.** *Music.* of or relating to vocal music that is not provided with an articulated text: *a wordless chorus.* —'**word+less+ly** *adv.* —'**word+less+ness** *n.*

word or+der *n.* the arrangement of words in a phrase, clause, or sentence.

word-per·fect *or U.S.* **let·ter-per·fect** *adj.* **1.** correct in every detail. **2.** (of a speech, part in a play, etc.) memorized perfectly. **3.** (of a speaker, actor, etc.) knowing one's speech, role, etc., perfectly.

word pic+ture *n.* a verbal description, esp. a vivid one.

word+play ('wɜːdˌpleɪ) *n.* verbal wit based on the meanings and ambiguities of words; puns, clever repartee, etc.

word pro+cess+ing *n.* the storage and organization of language by electronic means, esp. for business purposes.

words (wɜːdz) *pl. n.* **1.** the text of a part of an actor, etc. **2.** the text or lyrics of a song, as opposed to the music. **3.** angry speech (esp. in the phrase **have words with someone**). **4. eat one's words.** to retract a statement. **5. for words.** (preceded by *too* and an adj. or adv.) indescribably; extremely: *the play was too funny for words.* **6. have no words for.** to be incapable of describing. **7. in other words.** expressing the same idea but differently. **8. in so many words.** explicitly or precisely. **9. of many** (*or* **few**) **words.** (not) talkative. **10. put into words.** to express in speech or writing as well as thought. **11. say a few words.** to give a brief speech. **12. take the words out of one's** (*or* **someone's**) **mouth.** to say exactly what someone else was about to say. **13. words fail me.** I am too happy, sad, amazed, etc., to express my thoughts.

word square *n.* a puzzle in which the player must fill a square grid with words that read the same across as down.

word stress *n.* the stress accent on the syllables of individual words either in a sentence or in isolation.

Words·worth ('wɜːdzˌwəθ) *n.* **1. Dor·o·thy.** 1771–1855, English writer, whose *Journals* are noted esp. for their descriptions of nature. **2.** her brother **Wil·liam.** 1770–1850, English poet, whose work, celebrating nature, was greatly inspired by the Lake District, in which he spent most of his life. *Lyrical Ballads* (1798), to which Coleridge contributed, is often taken as the first example of English romantic poetry and includes his *Lines Written above Tintern Abbey.* Among his other works are *The Prelude* (completed in 1805; revised thereafter and published posthumously) and *Poems in Two Volumes* (1807), which includes *The Solitary Reaper* and *Intimations of Immortality.* —**Words+worth+i+an** (wɜːdz'wɜːðɪən) *adj., n.*

word·y ('wɜːdɪ) *adj.* **word·i+er, word·i+est. 1.** using, inclined to use, or containing an excess of words: *a wordy writer; a wordy document.* **2.** of the nature of or relating to words; verbal. —'**word·i+ly** *adv.* —'**word·i+ness** *n.*

wore (wɔː) *vb.* the past tense of **wear.**

work (wɜːk) *n.* **1.** physical or mental effort directed towards doing or making something. **2.** paid employment at a job or a trade, occupation, or profession. **3.** a duty, task, or undertaking. **4.** something done, made, etc., as a result of effort or exertion: *a work of art.* **5.** materials or tasks on which to expend effort or exertion. **6.** another word for **workmanship** (sense 3). **7.** the place, office, etc., where a person is employed. **8.** any piece of material that is undergoing a manufacturing operation or process; workpiece. **9. a.** decoration or ornamentation, esp. of a specified kind. **b.** (in combination): *wirework; woolwork.* **10.** an engineering structure such as a bridge, building, etc. **11.** *Physics.* the transfer of energy expressed as the product of a force and the distance through which its point of application moves in the direction of the force. Abbrevs.: *W, w* **12.** a structure, wall, etc., built or used as part of a fortification system. **13. at work. a.** at one's job or place of employment. **b.** in action; operating. **14. make short work of.** *Informal.* to handle or dispose of very quickly. **15.** (*modifier*) of, relating to, or used for work: *work clothes; a work permit.* ~*vb.* **16.** (*intr.*) to exert effort in order to do, make, or perform something. **17.** (*intr.*) to be employed. **18.** (*tr.*) to carry on operations, activity, etc., in (a place or area): *that salesman works the southern region.* **19.** (*tr.*) to cause to labour or toil: *he works his men hard.* **20.** to operate or cause to operate, esp. properly or effectively: *to work a lathe; that clock doesn't work.* **21.** (*tr.*) to till or cultivate (land). **22.** to handle or manipulate or be handled or manipulated: *to work dough.* **23.** to shape, form, or process or be shaped, formed, or processed: *to work copper.* **24.** to reach or cause to reach a specific condition, esp. gradually: *the rope worked loose.* **25.** (*tr.*) *Chiefly U.S.* to solve (a mathematical problem). **26.** (*intr.*) to move in agitation: *his face worked with anger.* **27.** (*tr.*; often foll. by *up*) to provoke or arouse: *to work someone into a frenzy.* **28.** (*tr.*) to effect or accomplish: *to work one's revenge.* **29.** to make (one's way) with effort: *he worked his way through the crowd.* **30.** (*tr.*) to make or decorate by hand in embroidery, tapestry, etc.: *she was working a sampler.* **31.** (*intr.*) (of a mechanism) to move in a loose or otherwise imperfect fashion. **32.** (*intr.*) (of liquids) to ferment, as in brewing. **33.** (*tr.*) *Informal.* to manipulate or exploit to one's own advantage. **34.** (*tr.*) *Informal.* to cheat or swindle. ~See also **work back, work in, work off, work on, work out, work over, works, work up.** [Old English *weorc* (n.), *wircan, wyrcan* (vb.); related to Old High German *wurchen,* German *wirken,* Old Norse *yrkja,* Gothic *waurkjan*] —'**work+less** *adj.* —'**work+less+ness** *n.*

work+a+ble ('wɜːkəbᵊl) *adj.* **1.** practicable or feasible. **2.** able to be worked. —ˌ**work+a·'bil+i+ty** *or* '**work+a+ble+ness** *n.*

work·a+day ('wɜːkəˌdeɪ) *adj.* (*usually prenominal*) **1.** being a part of general human experience; ordinary. **2.** suitable for working days; everyday or practical.

work back *vb.* (*intr., adv.*) *Austral informal.* to work overtime.

work+bag ('wɜːkˌbæg) *n.* a container for implements, tools, or materials, esp. sewing equipment. Also called: **work basket, workbox.**

work+bench ('wɜːkˌbɛntʃ) *n.* a heavy table at which work is done by a carpenter, mechanic, toolmaker, etc.

work+book ('wɜːkˌbʊk) *n.* **1.** an exercise book or textbook used for study, esp. a textbook with spaces for answers. **2.** a book of instructions for some process. **3.** a book in which is recorded all work done or planned.

work camp *n.* a camp set up for young people who voluntarily do manual work on a worthwhile project.

work+day ('wɜːkˌdeɪ) *n.* **1.** the usual U.S. term for **working day.** ~*adj.* **2.** another word for **workaday.**

worked (wɜːkt) *adj.* made or decorated with evidence of workmanship; wrought, as with embroidery or tracery.

work+er ('wɜːkə) *n.* **1.** a person or thing that works, usually at a specific job: *a good worker; a research worker.* **2.** an employee in an organization, as opposed to an employer or manager. **3.** a manual labourer or other employee working in a manufacturing or other industry. **4.** any other member of the working class. **5.** a sterile female member of a colony of bees, ants, or wasps that forages for food, cares for the larvae, etc. —ˈ**work+er+less** *adj.*

work·er-priest *n.* a Roman Catholic priest who has full-time or part-time employment in a secular job to be more closely in touch with the problems of the laity.

work+folk (ˈwɜːkˌfəʊk) *or U.S.* (*informal*) **work+folks** *pl. n.* working people, esp. labourers on a farm.

work force *n.* **1.** the total number of workers employed by a company on a specific job, project, etc. **2.** the total number of people who could be employed: *the country's work force is growing rapidly.*

work func+tion *n.* **1.** *Physics.* the minimum energy required to transfer an electron from a point within a solid to a point just outside its surface. Symbol: ϕ or Φ **2.** *Thermodynamics.* another name (not now used because of confusion with sense 1) for **Helmholtz function.**

work-hard·en *vb.* (*tr.*) to increase the strength or hardness of (a metal) by a mechanical process, such as tension, compression, or torsion. —ˈ**work-ˌhard·en+ing** *n.*

work+horse (ˈwɜːkˌhɔːs) *n.* **1.** a horse used for nonrecreational activities. **2.** *Informal.* a person who takes on the greatest amount of work in a project or job.

work+house (ˈwɜːkˌhaʊs) *n.* **1.** (formerly in England) an institution maintained at public expense where able-bodied paupers did unpaid work in return for food and accommodation. **2.** (in the U.S.) a prison for petty offenders serving short sentences at manual labour.

work in *vb.* (*adv.*) **1.** to insert or become inserted: *she worked the patch in carefully.* **2.** (*tr.*) to find space for: *I'll work this job in during the day.* ~*n.* **work-in. 3.** a form of industrial action in which a factory that is to be closed down is occupied and run by its workers.

work+ing (ˈwɜːkɪŋ) *n.* **1.** the operation or mode of operation of something. **2.** the act or process of moulding something pliable. **3.** a convulsive or jerking motion, as from excitement. **4.** (*often pl.*) a part of a mine or quarry that is being or has been worked. **5.** (*pl.*) the whole system of excavations in a mine. **6.** *Rare.* slow advance against or as if against resistance. ~*adj.* (*prenominal*) **7.** relating to or concerned with a person or thing that works: *a working man.* **8.** concerned with, used in, or suitable for work: *working clothes.* **9.** capable of being operated or used: *a working model.* **10.** sufficiently large or accurate to be useful or to accomplish a desired end: *a working majority; a working knowledge of German.* **11.** (of a theory, etc.) providing a basis, usually a temporary one, on which operations or procedures may be carried out.

work+ing cap·i·tal *n.* **1.** *Accounting.* current assets minus current liabilities. **2.** current or liquid assets. **3.** that part of the capital of a business enterprise available for operations.

work+ing class *n.* **1.** Also called: **proletariat.** the social stratum, usually of low status, that consists of those who earn wages, esp. as manual workers. Compare **lower class, middle class, upper class.** ~*adj.* **work·ing-class. 2.** of, relating to, or characteristic of the working class.

work+ing day *or esp. U.S.* **work+day** *n.* **1.** a day on which work is done, esp. for an agreed or stipulated number of hours in return for a salary or wage. **2.** the part of the day allocated to work: *a seven-hour working day.*

work+ing draw+ing *n.* a scale drawing of a part or assembly that provides a guide for manufacture.

work+ing pa+pers *pl. n.* legal documents that certain people in some countries must possess to be allowed to work.

work+ing par+ty *n.* **1.** a committee established to investigate a problem, question, etc. **2.** a group of soldiers or prisoners assigned to perform some manual task or duty.

work+ing sub+stance *or* **flu+id** *n.* the fluid, esp. water, steam, or compressed air, that operates an engine, etc.

work+ing week *or esp. U.S.* **work+week** (ˈwɜːkˌwiːk) *n.* the number of hours or days in a week actually or officially allocated to work: *a four-day working week.*

work+load (ˈwɜːkˌləʊd) *n.* the amount of work to be done, esp. in a specified period by a person, machine, etc.

work+man (ˈwɜːkmən) *n., pl.* **+men. 1.** a man who is employed in manual labour or who works an industrial machine. **2.** a craftsman of skill as specified: *a bad workman.*

work+man+like (ˈwɜːkmənˌlaɪk) *or* **work+man+ly** (ˈwɜːkmənlɪ) *adj.* appropriate to or befitting a good workman.

work+man+ship (ˈwɜːkmənˌʃɪp) *n.* **1.** the art or skill of a workman. **2.** the art or skill with which something is made or executed. **3.** the degree of art or skill exhibited in the finished product. **4.** the piece of work so produced.

work+men's com+pen+sa+tion *n.* compensation for death, injury, or accident suffered by a workman in the course of his employment and paid to him or his dependents.

work of art *n.* **1.** a piece of fine art, such as a painting or sculpture. **2.** something that may be likened to a piece of fine art, esp. in beauty, intricacy, etc.

work off *vb.* (*tr., adv.*) **1.** to get rid of or dissipate, as by effort: *he worked off some of his energy by digging the garden.* **2.** to discharge (a debt) by labour rather than payment.

work on *vb.* (*intr., prep.*) to persuade or influence or attempt to persuade or influence.

work out *vb.* (*adv.*) **1.** (*tr.*) to achieve or accomplish by effort. **2.** (*tr.*) to solve or find out by reasoning or calculation: *to work out an answer; to work out a sum.* **3.** (*tr.*) to devise or formulate: *to work out a plan.* **4.** (*intr.*) to prove satisfactory or effective: *did your plan work out?* **5.** (*intr.*) to happen as specified: *it all worked out well.* **6.** (*intr.*) to take part in physical exercise, as in training. **7.** (*tr.*) to remove all the mineral in (a mine, body of ore, etc.) that can be profitably exploited. **8.** (*intr.; often foll. by to or at*) to reach a total: *your bill works out at a pound.* **9.** (*tr.*) *Informal.* to understand the real nature of: *I shall never work you out.* ~*n.* **work-out. 10.** a session of physical exercise, esp. for training or practice.

work o·ver *vb.* **1.** (*tr., adv.*) to do again; repeat. **2.** (*intr., prep.*) to examine closely and thoroughly. **3.** (*tr., adv.*) *Slang.* to assault or thrash.

work+peo·ple (ˈwɜːkˌpiːpᵊl) *pl. n.* the working members of a population, esp. those employed in manual tasks.

work+piece (ˈwɜːkˌpiːs) *n.* a piece of metal or other material that is in the process of being worked on or made or has actually been cut or shaped by a hand tool or machine.

work+room (ˈwɜːkˌruːm, -ˌrʊm) *n.* **1.** a room in which work, usually manual labour, is done. **2.** a room in a house set aside for a hobby, such as sewing.

works (wɜːks) *pl. n.* **1.** a place where a number of people are employed, such as a factory. **2.** the sum total of a writer's or artist's achievements, esp. when considered together: *the works of Shakespeare.* **3.** the deeds of a person, esp. virtuous or moral deeds performed as religious acts: *works of charity.* **4.** the interior parts of the mechanism of a machine, etc.: *the works of a clock.* **5. in the works.** *Informal.* in preparation. **6. spanner in the works.** See **spanner** (sense 2). **7. the works.** *Slang.* **a.** full or extreme treatment. **b.** a very violent physical beating: *to give someone the works.* **8.** (*modifier*) of or denoting a racing car, etc., that is officially entered by a manufacturer in an event: *a works entry.*

works coun+cil *n. Chiefly Brit.* **1.** a council composed of both employer and employees convened to discuss matters of common interest concerning a factory, plant, business policy, etc., not covered by regular trade union agreements. **2.** a body representing the workers of a plant, factory, etc., elected to negotiate with the management about working conditions, wages, etc. ~Also called: **works committee.**

work sheet *n.* **1.** a sheet of paper used for the preliminary or rough draft of a problem, design, etc. **2.** a piece of paper recording work being planned or already in progress.

work+shop (ˈwɜːkˌʃɒp) *n.* **1.** a room or building in which manufacturing or other forms of manual work are carried on. **2.** a room in a private dwelling, school, etc., set aside for crafts. **3.** a group of people engaged in study or work on a creative project or subject: *a music workshop.*

work+shy (ˈwɜːkˌʃaɪ) *adj.* not inclined to work.

Work+sop (ˈwɜːksɒp) *n.* a mining town in N central England, in W Nottinghamshire. Pop.: 36 034 (1971).

work-study *n.* an examination of ways of finding the most efficient method of doing a job, esp. in terms of time and effort.

work+ta·ble (ˈwɜːkˌteɪbᵊl) *n.* **a.** any table at which writing, sewing, or other work may be done. **b.** (in English cabinetwork) a small elegant table fitted with sewing accessories.

work-to-rule *n.* **1.** a form of industrial action in which employees adhere strictly to all the working rules laid down by their employers, with the deliberate intention of reducing the rate of working. ~*vb.* **work to rule. 2.** (*intr.*) to decrease the rate of working by this means.

work up *vb.* (*tr., mainly adv.*) **1.** to arouse the feelings of; excite. **2.** to cause to grow or develop: *to work up a hunger.* **3.** (*also prep.*) to move or cause to move gradually upwards. **4.** to manipulate or mix into a specified object or shape. **5.** to gain knowledge of or skill at (a subject).

world (wɜːld) *n.* **1.** the earth as a planet, esp. including its inhabitants. **2.** mankind; the human race. **3.** people generally; the public: *in the eyes of the world.* **4.** social or public life: *to go out into the world.* **5.** the universe or cosmos; everything in existence. **6.** a complex united whole regarded as resembling the universe. **7.** any star or planet, esp. one that might be inhabited. **8.** (*often cap.*) a division or section of the earth, its history, or its inhabitants: *the Western World; the Ancient World; the Third World.* **9.** an area, sphere, or realm considered as a complete environment: *the animal world.* **10.** any field of human activity or way of life or those involved in it: *the world of television.* **11.** a period or state of existence: *the next world.* **12.** the total circumstances and experience of an individual that make up his life, esp. that part of it relating to happiness: *you have shattered my world.* **13.** a large amount, number, or distance: *worlds apart.* **14.** worldly or secular life, ways, or people. **15. all the world and his wife.** a large group of people of various kinds. **16. bring into the world. a.** (of a midwife, doctor, etc.) to deliver (a baby). **b.** to give birth to. **17. come into the world.** to be born. **18. dead to the world.** *Informal.* unaware of one's surroundings, esp. fast asleep or very drunk. **19. for the world.** (*used with a negative*) for any inducement, however great. **20. for all the world.** in every way; exactly. **21. give to the world.** to publish. **22. in the world.** (intensifier; *usually used with a negative*): *no-one in the world can change things.* **23. the best of both worlds.** the benefits from two different or opposed ways of life, philosophies, etc. **24. man (or woman) of the world.** a man (or woman) experienced in social or public life. **25. on top of the world.** *Informal.* exultant, elated, or very happy. **26. out of this world.** *Informal.* wonderful; excellent. **27. set the world on fire.** to be exceptionally or sensationally successful. **28. think the world of.** to be extremely fond of or hold in very high esteem. **29. world of one's own.** a state of mental detachment from other people. **30. world without end.** for ever. **31.** (*modifier*) of or concerning most or all countries; worldwide: *world politics; a world record.* **32.** (*in combination*) throughout the world:

world-famous. [Old English *w(e)orold,* from *wer* man + *ald* age, life; related to Old Frisian *warld, wrald,* Old Norse *verold,* Old High German *wealt* (German *Welt*)]

World Bank *n.* an international cooperative organization established in 1945 under the Bretton Woods Agreement to assist economic development, esp. of backward nations, by the advance of loans guaranteed by member governments. Officially called: **International Bank for Reconstruction and Development.**

World Bank Group *n.* the collective name for the International Bank for Reconstruction and Development, the International Finance Corporation, and the International Development Association, whose headquarters are all in Washington.

world-beat·er *n.* a person or thing that surpasses all others in its category; champion. —'**world-,beat·ing** *n., adj.*

World Coun+cil of Church·es *n.* the ecumenical fellowship of Churches other than the Roman Catholic Church, formally constituted at Amsterdam in 1948 for coordinated action in theological, ecclesiastical, and secular matters.

World Court *n.* another name for **International Court of Justice.**

World Cup *n.* an international association football championship competition held between 16 national teams selected through preliminary tournaments. It has been held in different countries every four years since 1930, except during World War II.

World Health Or+gan·i+za+tion *n.* an agency of the United Nations, established in 1948 with headquarters in Geneva, responsible for coordinating international health activities, aiding governments in improving health services, etc. Abbrev.: **W.H.O.**

world lan+guage *n.* **1.** a language spoken and known in many countries, such as English. **2.** a artificial language for international use, such as Esperanto.

world-line *n. Physics.* a line on a space-time path that shows the path of a body.

world+ling ('wɜːldlɪŋ) *n.* a person who is primarily concerned with worldly matters or material things.

world+ly ('wɜːldlɪ) *adj.* **+li+er, +li+est. 1.** not spiritual; mundane or temporal. **2.** Also: **worldly-minded.** absorbed in or concerned with material things or matters that are immediately relevant. **3.** Also: **worldly-wise.** versed in the ways of the world; sophisticated. **4.** *Archaic.* existing on or relating to the earth. **5.** *Obsolete.* secular; lay. ~*adv.* **6.** *Archaic.* in a worldly manner. —'**world+li+ness** *n.*

world pow+er *n.* a state that possesses sufficient power to influence events throughout the world.

World Se+ries *or* **World's Se+ries** *n. Baseball.* a best-of-seven playoff for the world championship between the two winning teams in the major leagues at the end of the season.

world-shak·ing *adj.* of enormous significance; momentous.

world-view *n.* another word for **Weltanschauung.**

World War I *n.* the war (1914–18), fought mainly in Europe and the Middle East, in which the Allies (principally France, Russia, Britain, Italy after 1915, and the U.S. after 1917) defeated the Central Powers (principally Germany, Austria-Hungary, and Turkey). The war was precipitated by the assassination of Austria's crown prince (Archduke Franz Ferdinand) at Sarajevo on June 28, 1914 and swiftly developed its major front in E France, where millions died in static trench warfare. After the October Revolution (1917) the Bolsheviks ended Russian participation in the war (Dec. 15, 1917). The exhausted Central Powers agreed to an armistice on Nov. 11, 1918 and quickly succumbed to internal revolution, before being forced to sign the Treaty of Versailles (June 28, 1919) and other treaties. Also called: **First World War, Great War.**

World War II *n.* the war (1939–45) in which the Allies (Britain and France) declared war on Germany (Sept. 3, 1939) as a result of the German invasion of Poland (Sept. 1, 1939). Italy entered the war on the side of Germany (forming the Axis) on June 10, 1940 shortly before the collapse of France (armistice signed June 22, 1940). On June 22, 1941 the Axis powers attacked the Soviet Union and on Dec. 7, 1941 the Japanese attacked the U.S. at Pearl Harbor. On Sept. 8, 1943 Italy surrendered, the war in Europe ending on May 7, 1945 with the unconditional surrender of the Germans. The Japanese capitulated on Aug. 14, 1945 as a direct result of the atom bombs dropped by the Americans on Hiroshima and Nagasaki. Also called: **Second World War.**

world-wea·ry *adj.* no longer finding pleasure in living; tired of the world. —'**world-,wea·ri·ness** *n.*

world+wide ('wɜːld'waɪd) *adj.* applying or extending throughout the world; universal.

worm (wɜːm) *n.* **1.** any of various invertebrates, esp. the annelids (earthworms, etc.), nematodes (roundworms), and flatworms, having a slender elongated body. **2.** any of various insect larvae having an elongated body, such as the silkworm and wireworm. **3.** any of various unrelated animals that resemble annelids, nematodes, etc., such as the glow-worm and shipworm. **4.** a gnawing or insinuating force or agent that torments or slowly eats away. **5.** a wretched or spineless person. **6.** anything that resembles a worm in appearance or movement. **7.** a shaft on which a helical groove has been cut, as in a gear arrangement in which such a shaft meshes with a toothed wheel. **8.** a spiral pipe cooled by air or flowing water, used as a condenser in a still. **9.** a nontechnical name for **lytta. 10.** *Anatomy.* any wormlike organ, structure, or part, such as the middle lobe of the cerebellum (*vermis cerebelli*). Technical name: **vermis.** ~*vb.* **11.** to move, act, or cause to move or act with the slow sinuous movement of a worm. **12.** (foll. by *in, into, out of,* etc.) to make (one's way) slowly and stealthily; insinuate (oneself). **13.** (*tr.;* often foll. by *out of* or *from*) to extract (information, a secret, etc.) from by persistent questioning. **14.** (*tr.*) to free from or purge of worms. **15.** (*tr.*) *Nautical.* to wind yarn around (a rope) so as to fill the spaces between the strands and render the surface smooth for parcelling and serving. [Old English *wyrm;* related to Old Frisian *wirm,* Old High German *wurm,* Old Norse *ormr,* Gothic *waurms,* Latin *vermis,* Greek *romos* woodworm] —'**worm+er** *n.* —'**worm+,like** *or* '**worm+ish** *adj.*

worm+cast ('wɜːm,kɑːst) *n.* a coil of earth or sand that has been egested by a burrowing earthworm or lugworm.

worm-eat·en *adj.* **1.** eaten into by worms: *a worm-eaten table.* **2.** decayed; rotten. **3.** old-fashioned; antiquated.

worm gear *n.* **1.** a device consisting of a threaded shaft (**worm**) that mates with a gear wheel (**worm wheel**) so that rotary motion can be transferred between two shafts at right angles to each other. **2.** Also called: **worm wheel.** a gear wheel driven by a threaded shaft or worm.

worm+hole ('wɜːm,həʊl) *n.* a hole made by a worm in timber, plants, etc. —'**worm+,holed** *adj.*

worm liz+ard *n.* any worm-like burrowing legless lizard of the family *Amphisbaenidae,* of Africa, South and Central America, and S Europe.

worms (wɜːmz) *n.* any disease or disorder, usually of the intestine, characterized by infestation with parasitic worms.

Worms (wɜːmz; *German* vɔrms) *n.* a city in S West Germany, in Rhineland-Palatinate on the Rhine: famous as the seat of imperial diets, notably that of 1521, before which Luther defended his doctrines in the presence of Charles V; river port and manufacturing centre with a large wine trade. Pop.: 77 100 (1970).

worm+seed ('wɜːm,siːd) *n.* **1.** any of various plants having seeds or other parts used in medicine to treat worm infestation, esp. an American chenopodiaceous plant, *Chenopodium anthelminticum* (or *C. ambrosioides*) (**American wormseed**), and the santonica plant. **2.** the part of any of these plants that is used as an anthelmintic.

worm's eye view *n.* a view seen from below or from a more lowly or humble point.

worm+wood ('wɜːm,wʊd) *n.* **1.** Also called: **absinthe.** any of various plants of the chiefly N temperate genus *Artemisia,* esp. *A. absinthium,* a European plant yielding a bitter extract used in making absinthe: family *Compositae* (composites). **2.** something that embitters, such as a painful experience. [C15: changed (through influence of WORM and WOOD[1]) from Old English *wormōd, wermōd;* related to Old High German *werrnuata,* German *Wermut;* see VERMOUTH]

worm·y ('wɜːmɪ) *adj.* **worm·i+er, worm·i+est. 1.** worm-infested or worm-eaten. **2.** resembling a worm in appearance, ways, or condition. **3.** (of wood) having irregular small tunnels bored into it and tracked over its surface, made either by worms or artificially. **4.** low or grovelling. —'**worm·i+ness** *n.*

worn (wɔːn) *vb.* **1.** the past participle of **wear.** ~*adj.* **2.** affected, esp. adversely, by long use or action: *a worn suit.* **3.** haggard; drawn. **4.** exhausted; spent. —'**worn+ness** *n.*

worn-out *adj.* (**worn out** *when postpositive*). **1.** worn or used until threadbare, valueless, or useless. **2.** exhausted; very weary.

wor+ri+ment ('wʌrɪmənt) *n. Informal, chiefly U.S.* anxiety or the trouble that causes it; worry.

wor+ri+some ('wʌrɪsəm) *adj.* **1.** causing worry; vexing. **2.** tending to worry. —'**wor+ri+some+ly** *adv.*

wor+rit ('wʌrɪt) *vb.* (*tr.*) *Northern Brit. dialect.* to tease or worry. [probably a variant of WORRY, but compare WHERRIT[1]]

wor+ry ('wʌrɪ) *vb.* **+ries, +ry+ing, +ried. 1.** to be or cause to be anxious or uneasy, esp. about something uncertain or potentially dangerous. **2.** (*tr.*) to disturb the peace of mind of; bother: *don't worry me with trivialities.* **3.** (*intr.;* often foll. by *along* or *through*) to proceed despite difficulties. **4.** (*intr.;* often foll. by *away*) to struggle or work: *to worry away at a problem.* **5.** (*tr.*) (of a dog, wolf, etc.) to lacerate or kill by biting, shaking, etc. **6.** (when *intr.,* foll. by *at*) to bite, tear, or gnaw (at) with the teeth: *a dog worrying a bone.* **7.** (*tr.*) to move as specified, esp. by repeated pushes: *they worried the log into the river.* **8.** (*tr.*) to touch or poke repeatedly and idly. **9.** (*tr.*) to caress, kiss, or hug vehemently. **10.** *Obsolete.* to choke or cause to choke. **11. not to worry.** *Informal.* you need not worry. ~*n.* **+ries. 12.** a state or feeling of anxiety. **13.** a person or thing that causes anxiety. **14.** an act of worrying. [Old English *wyrgan;* related to Old Frisian *wergia* to kill, Old High German *wurgen* (German *(er)würgen* to strangle), Old Norse *virgill, urga* rope]

wor+ry beads *pl. n.* a string of beads that when fingered or played with supposedly relieves nervous tension.

wor+ry+wart ('wʌrɪ,wɔːt) *n. Informal.* a person who tends to worry, esp. about insignificant matters.

worse (wɜːs) *adj.* **1.** the comparative of **bad. 2. none the worse for.** not harmed by (adverse events or circumstances). **3. the worse for wear. a.** shabby or worn. **b.** a slang term for **drunk. 4. worse luck!** *Informal.* unhappily; unfortunately. **5.** (*postpositive*) **worse off.** in a worse, esp. a worse financial, condition. ~*n.* **6.** something that is worse. **7. for the worse.** into a less desirable or inferior state or condition: *a change for the worse.* **8. go from bad to worse.** to deteriorate even more. ~*adv.* **9.** in a more severe or unpleasant manner. **10.** in a less effective or successful manner. [Old English *wiersa;* related to Old Frisian *werra,* Old High German *wirsiro,* Old Norse *verri,* Gothic *wairsiza*]

wors·en ('wɜ:sᵊn) *vb.* to grow or cause to grow worse.
wors·er ('wɜ:sə) *adj.* an archaic or nonstandard word for **worse.**
wor·ship ('wɜ:ʃɪp) *vb.* **·ships, ·ship·ping, ·shipped** *or U.S.* **·ships, ·ship·ing, ·shiped. 1.** (*tr.*) to show profound religious devotion and respect to; adore or venerate (God or any person or thing considered divine). **2.** (*tr.*) to be devoted to and full of admiration for. **3.** (*intr.*) to have or express feelings of profound adoration. **4.** (*intr.*) to attend services for worship. **5.** (*tr.*) *Obsolete.* to honour. *~n.* **6.** religious adoration or devotion. **7.** the formal expression of religious adoration; rites, prayers, etc. **8.** admiring love or devotion. **9.** *Archaic.* dignity or standing. [Old English *weorthscipe,* from WORTH + -SHIP] —**'wor·ship·a·ble** *adj.* —**'wor·ship·per** *n.* —**'wor·ship·ping·ly** *adv.*
Wor·ship ('wɜ:ʃɪp) *n. Chiefly Brit.* (preceded by *Your, His,* or *Her*) a title used to address or refer to a mayor, magistrate, or a person of similar high rank.
wor·ship·ful ('wɜ:ʃɪpfʊl) *adj.* **1.** feeling or showing reverence or adoration. **2.** (*often cap.*) *Chiefly Brit.* a title used to address or refer to various people or bodies of distinguished rank, such as mayors and certain ancient companies of the City of London. —**'wor·ship·ful·ly** *adv.* —**'wor·ship·ful·ness** *n.*
Wors·ley ('wɜ:zlɪ) *n.* a town in NW England, in Greater Manchester. Pop.: 49 873 (1971).
worst (wɜ:st) *adj.* **1.** the superlative of **bad.** *~adv.* **2.** in the most extreme or bad manner or degree. **3.** least well, suitably, or acceptably. **4.** (*in combination*) in or to the smallest degree or extent; least: *worst-loved.* *~n.* **5. the worst.** the least good or most inferior person, thing, or part in a group, narrative, etc. **6.** (often preceded by *at*) the most poor, unpleasant, or unskilled quality or condition: *television is at its worst these days.* **7.** the greatest amount of damage or wickedness of which a person or group is capable: *the invaders came and did their worst.* **8.** the weakest effort or poorest achievement that a person or group is capable of making: *the applicant did his worst at the test because he did not want the job.* **9. at worst. a.** in the least favourable interpretation or view. **b.** under the least favourable conditions. **10. if the worst comes to the worst.** if all the more desirable alternatives become impossible or if the worst possible thing happens. **11. come off worst** *or* **get the worst of it.** to enjoy the least benefit from an issue or be defeated in it. **12. give (someone) the worst of it.** to defeat (someone) soundly. *~vb.* **13.** (*tr.*) to get the advantage over; defeat or beat. [Old English *wierrest;* related to Old Frisian *wersta,* Old Saxon, Old High German *wirsisto,* Old Norse *verstr*]
wor·sted ('wʊstɪd) *n.* **1.** a closely twisted yarn or thread made from combed long-staple wool. **2.** a fabric made from this, with a hard smooth close-textured surface and no nap. **3.** (*modifier*) made of this yarn or fabric: *a worsted suit.* [C13: named after *Worstead,* a district in Norfolk]
wort (wɜ:t) *n.* **1.** (*in combination*) any of various unrelated plants, esp. ones formerly used to cure diseases: *liverwort; spleenwort.* **2.** the sweet liquid obtained from the soaked mixture of warm water and ground malt, used to make a malt liquor. [Old English *wyrt* root, related to Old High German *warz,* Gothic *waurts* root]
worth[1] (wɜ:θ) *adj.* (governing a noun with prepositional force) **1.** worthy of; meriting or justifying: *it's not worth discussing; an idea worth some thought.* **2.** having a value of: *the book is worth 30 pounds.* **3. for all one is worth.** to the utmost; to the full extent of one's powers or ability. **4. worth one's weight in gold.** extremely helpful, kind, etc. *~n.* **5.** high quality; excellence. **6.** value, price. **7.** the amount or quantity of something of a specified value: *five pounds worth of petrol.* [Old English *weorth;* related to Old Saxon, Old High German *werth* (German *Wert*), Old Norse *verthr,* Gothic *wairths*]
worth[2] (wɜ:θ) *vb.* (*intr.*) *Archaic.* to happen or betide (esp. in the phrase **woe worth the day**). [Old English *weorthan;* related to Old Frisian *wertha,* Old Saxon, Old High German *werthan* (German *werden*), Old Norse *vertha,* Gothic *wairthan,* Latin *vertere* to turn]
Worth (wɜ:θ; *French* vɔrt) *n.* **Charles Fred·e·rick.** 1825–95, French dress designer, who founded Parisian *haute couture.*
Wor·thing ('wɜ:ðɪŋ) *n.* a resort in S England, in West Sussex on the English Channel. Pop.: 88 210 (1971).
worth·less ('wɜ:θlɪs) *adj.* **1.** without practical value or usefulness. **2.** without merit; good-for-nothing. —**'worth·less·ly** *adv.* —**'worth·less·ness** *n.*
worth·while ('wɜ:θ'waɪl) *adj.* sufficiently important, rewarding, or valuable to justify time or effort spent.
wor·thy ('wɜ:ðɪ) *adj.* **·thi·er, ·thi·est. 1.** (*postpositive;* often foll. by *of* or an infinitive) having sufficient merit or value (for something or someone specified); deserving. **2.** having worth, value, or merit. *~n., pl.* **·thies. 3.** *Often facetious.* a person of distinguished character, merit, or importance. —**'wor·thi·ly** *adv.* —**'wor·thi·ness** *n.*
wot (wɒt) *vb. Archaic or dialect.* (used with *I, she, he, it,* or a singular noun) a form of the present tense (indicative mood) of **wit**[2].
Wo·tan ('vəʊtɑ:n, 'vɔ:-) *n.* the supreme god in Germanic mythology. Norse counterpart: **Odin.**
Wot·ton ('wɒtᵊn, 'wʊtᵊn) *n.* **Hen·ry.** 1568–1639, English poet.
would (wʊd; *unstressed* wəd) *vb.* (takes an infinitive without *to* or an implied infinitive) used as an auxiliary: **1.** to form the past tense or subjunctive mood of **will**[1]. **2.** (with *you, he, she, it, they,* or a noun as subject) to indicate willingness or desire in a polite manner: *would you help me, please?* **3.** to describe a past action as being accustomed or habitual: *every day we would go for walks.* **4.** I wish: *would that he were here.* **Usage.** See at **should.**
would-be *adj.* (*prenominal*) **1.** *Usually derogatory.* wanting or professing to be: *a would-be politician.* **2.** intended to be: *would-be generosity.* *~n.* **3.** *Derogatory.* a person who wants or professes to be something that he is not.
would·n't ('wʊdᵊnt) *contraction of* would not.
wouldst (wʊdst) *vb. Archaic or dialect.* (used with the pronoun *thou* or its relative equivalent) a singular form of the past tense of **will.**
Woulfe bot·tle (wʊlf) *n. Chem.* a bottle with more than one neck, used for passing gases through liquids. [C18: named after Peter *Woulfe* (?1727–1803), English chemist]
wound[1] (wu:nd) *n.* **1.** any break in the skin or an organ or part as the result of violence or a surgical incision. **2.** an injury to plant tissue. **3.** any injury or slight to the feelings or reputation. *~vb.* **4.** to inflict a wound or wounds upon (someone or something). [Old English *wund;* related to Old Frisian *wunde,* Old High German *wunta* (German *Wunde*), Old Norse *und,* Gothic *wunds*] —**'wound·a·ble** *adj.* —**'wound·er** *n.* —**'wound·ing·ly** *adv.* —**'wound·less** *adj.*
wound[2] (waʊnd) *vb.* the past tense or past participle of **wind**[2].
wound·ed ('wu:ndɪd) *adj.* **1. a.** suffering from wounds; injured, esp. in a battle or fight. **b.** (*as collective n.* preceded by *the*): *the wounded.* **2.** (of feelings) damaged or hurt.
wound·wort ('wu:nd,wɜ:t) *n.* **1.** any of various plants of the genus *Stachys,* such as *S. arvensis* (**field woundwort**), having purple, scarlet, yellow, or white flowers and formerly used for dressing wounds: family *Labiatae* (labiates). **2.** any of various other plants used in this way.
wove (wəʊv) *vb.* a past tense of **weave.**
wo·ven ('wəʊvᵊn) *vb.* a past participle of **weave.**
wove pa·per *n.* paper with a very faint mesh impressed on it by the dandy roller on the paper-making machine. Compare **laid paper.**
wow[1] (waʊ) *interj.* **1.** an exclamation of admiration, amazement, etc. *~n.* **2.** *Slang, chiefly U.S.* a person or thing that is amazingly successful, attractive, etc. *~vb.* **3.** (*tr.*) *Slang, chiefly U.S.* to arouse great enthusiasm in. [C16: originally Scottish, expressive of surprise, amazement, etc.]
wow[2] (waʊ, wəʊ) *n.* a slow variation or distortion in pitch that occurs at very low audio frequencies in sound-reproducing systems, such as a record player, usually due to variation in speed of the turntable, etc. See also **flutter** (sense 14). [C20: of imitative origin]
wow·ser ('waʊzə) *n. Austral. slang.* **1.** a fanatically puritanical person. **2.** a teetotaller. [C20: from English dialect *wow* to whine, complain]
W.P. *abbrev. for* weather permitting.
WPA (in the U.S.) *abbrev. for* Work Projects Administration or Works Progress Administration.
W.P.B. *or* **w.p.b.** *abbrev. for* waste paper basket.
W.P.C. (in Britain) *abbrev. for* woman police constable.
w.p.m. *abbrev. for* words per minute.
W.R. *abbrev. for* Western Region.
Wraac (ræk) *n.* a member of the Women's Royal Australian Army Corps.
W.R.A.A.C. *abbrev. for* Women's Royal Australian Army Corps.
W.R.A.A.F. *abbrev. for* Women's Royal Australian Air Force.
W.R.A.C. (in Britain) *abbrev. for* Women's Royal Army Corps.
wrack[1] *or* **rack** (ræk) *n.* **1.** collapse or destruction (esp. in the phrase **wrack and ruin**). **2.** something destroyed or a remnant of such. [Old English *wræc* persecution, misery; related to Gothic *wraka,* Old Norse *rāk.* Compare WRECK, WRETCH]
wrack[2] (ræk) *n.* **1.** seaweed or other marine vegetation that is floating in the sea or has been cast ashore. **2.** any of various seaweeds of the genus *Fucus,* such as *F. serratus* (**serrated wrack**). **3.** *Literary or dialect.* **a.** a wreck or piece of wreckage. **b.** a remnant or fragment of something destroyed. *~vb.* **4.** *Archaic.* to be or cause to be wrecked. [C14 (in the sense: a wrecked ship, wreckage, hence later applied to marine vegetation washed ashore): perhaps from Middle Dutch *wrak* wreckage; the term corresponds to Old English *wræc* WRACK[1]]
W.R.A.F. (in Britain) *abbrev. for* Women's Royal Air Force.
wraith (reɪθ) *n.* **1.** the apparition of a person living or thought to be alive, supposed to appear around the time of his death. **2.** a ghost or any apparition. **3.** an insubstantial copy of something. **4.** something pale, thin, and lacking in substance, such as a column of smoke. [C16: Scottish, of unknown origin] —**'wraith·,like** *adj.*
Wran (ræn) *n.* a member of the Women's Royal Australian Naval Service.
Wran·gel Is·land ('ræŋgᵊl) *n.* an island in the Arctic Ocean, off the coast of the extreme NE Soviet Union: administratively part of the Soviet Union; mountainous and mostly tundra. Area: about 7300 sq. km (2800 sq. miles).
Wran·gell ('ræŋgᵊl) *n.* **Mount.** a mountain in S Alaska, in the W Wrangell Mountains. Height: 4269 m (14 005 ft.).
Wran·gell Moun·tains *pl. n.* a mountain range in SE Alaska, extending into the Yukon, Canada. Highest peak: Mount Blackburn, 5037 m (16 523 ft.).
wran·gle ('ræŋgᵊl) *vb.* **1.** (*intr.*) to argue, esp. noisily or angrily. **2.** (*tr.*) to encourage, persuade, or obtain by argument. **3.** (*tr.*) *Western U.S.* to herd (cattle or horses). *~n.* **4.** a noisy or angry argument. [C14: from Low German *wrangeln;* related to Norwegian *vrangla*]
wran·gler ('ræŋglə) *n.* **1.** one who wrangles. **2.** *Western U.S.* a

herder; cowboy. **3.** *Brit.* (at Cambridge University) a candidate who has obtained first-class honours in part II of the mathematical tripos. Formerly, the wrangler with the highest marks was called the **senior wrangler.**

W.R.A.N.S. *abbrev. for* Women's Royal Australian Naval Service.

wrap (ræp) *vb.* **wraps, wrap·ping, wrapped.** (*mainly tr.*) **1.** to fold or wind (paper, cloth, etc.) around (a person or thing) so as to cover. **2.** (often foll. by *up*) to fold paper, etc., around to fasten securely. **3.** to surround or conceal by surrounding. **4.** to enclose, immerse, or absorb: *wrapped in sorrow.* **5.** to fold, wind, or roll up. **6.** (*intr.;* often foll. by *about, around,* etc.) to be or become wound or extended. **7.** (often foll. by *up*) Also: **rap.** *Austral. informal.* to praise (someone). ~*n.* **8.** a garment worn wrapped around the body, esp. the shoulders, such as a shawl or cloak. **9.** short for **wrapround** (sense 4). **10.** *Chiefly U.S.* wrapping or a wrapper. **11.** Also called: **rap.** *Austral. informal.* a commendation. **12. keep under wraps.** to keep secret. **13. take the wraps off.** to reveal. [C14: origin unknown]

wrap·o·ver ('ræpˌəʊvə), **wrap·a·round,** *or* **wrap·round** *adj.* **1.** (of a garment, esp. a skirt) not sewn up at one side, but worn wrapped round the body and fastened so that the open edges overlap. ~*n.* **2.** such a garment.

wrapped (ræpt) *vb.* **1.** the past participle of **wrap.** ~*adj.* **2.** Also: **rapt.** *Austral. informal.* very pleased: delighted. **3. wrapped up in.** *Informal.* **a.** completely absorbed or engrossed in. **b.** implicated or involved in.

wrap·per ('ræpə) *n.* **1.** the cover, usually of paper or cellophane, in which something is wrapped. **2.** the ripe firm tobacco leaf forming the outermost portion of a cigar and wound around its body. **3.** a loose negligee or dressing gown, esp. in the 19th century.

wrap·ping ('ræpɪŋ) *n.* the material used to wrap something.

wrap·round ('ræpˌraʊnd) *adj.* **1.** made so as to be wrapped round something: *a wrapround skirt.* **2.** surrounding, curving round, or overlapping. ~*n.* **3.** *Printing.* a flexible plate of plastic, metal, or rubber that is made flat but used wrapped round the plate cylinder of a rotary press. **4.** Also called: **outsert.** *Printing.* a separately printed sheet folded around a section for binding. Sometimes shortened to **wrap. 5.** a slip of paper folded round the dust jacket of a book to announce a price reduction, special offer, etc.

wrap up *vb.* (*adv.*) **1.** (*tr.*) to fold paper around. **2.** to put warm clothes on. **3.** (*usually imperative*) *Slang.* to be silent. **4.** (*tr.*) *Informal.* **a.** to settle the final details of. **b.** to make a summary of.

wrasse (ræs) *n.* any marine percoid fish of the family *Labridae,* of tropical and temperate seas, having thick lips, strong teeth, and usually a bright coloration: many are used as food fishes. [C17: from Cornish *wrach;* related to Welsh *gwrach* old woman]

wrath (rɒθ) *n.* **1.** angry, violent, or stern indignation. **2.** divine vengeance or retribution. **3.** *Archaic.* a fit of anger or an act resulting from anger. ~*adj.* **4.** *Obsolete.* incensed; angry. [Old English *wrǣththu;* see WROTH] —'**wrath·less** *adj.*

Wrath (rɒθ, rɔːθ) *n.* **Cape.** See **Cape Wrath.**

wrath·ful ('rɒθfʊl) *adj.* **1.** full of wrath; raging or furious. **2.** resulting from or expressing wrath. ~Also (informal): **wrath·y.** —'**wrath·ful·ly** *adv.* —'**wrath·ful·ness** *n.*

wreak (riːk) *vb.* (*tr.*) **1.** to inflict (vengeance, etc.) or to cause (chaos, etc.): *to wreak havoc on the enemy.* **2.** to express, or gratify (anger, hatred, etc.). **3.** *Archaic.* to take vengeance for. [Old English *wrecan;* related to Old Frisian *wreka,* Old High German *rehhan* (German *rächen*), Old Norse *reka,* Latin *urgēre* to push] —'**wreak·er** *n.*

wreath (riːθ) *n., pl.* **wreaths** (riːðz, riːθs). **1.** a band of flowers or foliage intertwined into a ring, usually placed on a grave as a memorial or worn on the head as a garland or a mark of honour. **2.** any circular or spiral band or formation. **3.** a spiral or circular defect appearing in porcelain and glassware. [Old English *wrǣth, wrǣd;* related to Middle Low German *wrēden* to twist. See WRITHE] —'**wreath·less** *adj.* —'**wreath·ˌlike** *adj.*

wreathe (riːð) *vb.* **1.** to form into or take the form of a wreath by intertwining or twisting together. **2.** (*tr.*) to decorate, crown, or encircle with wreaths. **3.** to move or cause to move in a twisting way: *smoke wreathed up to the ceiling.* [C16: perhaps back formation from *wrēthen,* from Old English *writhen,* past participle of *wrīthan* to WRITHE; see WREATH]

wreck (rɛk) *vb.* **1.** to involve in or suffer disaster or destruction. **2.** (*tr.*) to cause the wreck of (a ship). ~*n.* **3. a.** the accidental destruction of a ship at sea. **b.** the ship so destroyed. **4.** *Maritime law.* goods cast ashore from a wrecked vessel. **5.** a person or thing that has suffered ruin or dilapidation. **6.** Also called: **wreck·age** ('rɛkɪdʒ). the remains of something that has been destroyed. **7.** Also called: **wreck-age.** the act of wrecking or the state of being wrecked; ruin or destruction. [C13: from Scandinavian; compare Icelandic *rek.* See WRACK², WREAK]

wreck·er ('rɛkə) *n.* **1.** a person or thing that ruins or destroys. **2.** *Chiefly U.S.* a person whose job is to demolish buildings or dismantle cars. **3.** (formerly) a person who lures ships to destruction to plunder the wreckage. **4.** a U.S. name for **breakdown van.**

wreck·fish ('rɛkˌfɪʃ) *n., pl.* **·fish** *or* **·fish·es.** another name for **stone bass.** [so called because it is often found near wrecked ships]

wreck·ful ('rɛkfʊl) *adj. Poetic.* causing wreckage.

wreck·ing bar *n.* a short crowbar, forked at one end and slightly angled at the other to make a fulcrum.

Wre·kin ('riːkɪn) *n.* **1. the.** an isolated hill in the English Midlands in Salop. Height: 400 m (1335 ft.). **2. (all) round the Wrekin.** *Midland English dialect.* the long way round: *he went all round the Wrekin instead of explaining clearly.*

wren (rɛn) *n.* **1.** any small brown passerine songbird of the chiefly American family *Troglodytidae,* esp. *Troglodytes troglodytes* (**wren** in Britain, **winter wren** in the U.S.). They have a slender bill and feed on insects. **2.** any of various similar birds of the families *Muscicapidae* (Australian warblers), *Xenicidae* (New Zealand wrens), etc. [Old English *wrenna, werna;* related to Old High German *wrendo, rentilo,* Old Norse *rindill*]

Wren¹ (rɛn) *n. Informal.* (in Britain and certain other nations) a member of the Women's Royal Naval Service.

Wren² (rɛn) *n.* Sir **Chris·to·pher.** 1632–1723, English architect. He designed St. Paul's Cathedral and over 50 other London churches after the Great Fire as well as many secular buildings.

wrench (rɛntʃ) *vb.* **1.** to give (something) a sudden or violent twist or pull esp. so as to remove (something) from that to which it is attached: *to wrench a door off its hinges.* **2.** (*tr.*) to twist suddenly so as to sprain (a limb): *to wrench one's ankle.* **3.** (*tr.*) to give pain to. **4.** (*tr.*) to twist from the original meaning or purpose. **5.** (*intr.*) to make a sudden twisting motion. ~*n.* **6.** a forceful twist or pull. **7.** an injury to a limb, caused by twisting. **8.** sudden pain caused esp. by parting. **9.** a parting that is difficult or painful to make. **10.** a distorting of the original meaning or purpose. **11.** a spanner, esp. one with adjustable jaws. See also **torque wrench.** [Old English *wrencan;* related to Old High German *renken,* Lithuanian *rangyti* to twist. See WRINKLE¹]

wrest (rɛst) *vb.* (*tr.*) **1.** to take or force away by violent pulling or twisting. **2.** to seize forcibly by violent or unlawful means. **3.** to obtain by laborious effort. **4.** to distort in meaning, purpose, etc. ~*n.* **5.** the act or an instance of wresting. **6.** *Archaic.* a small key used to tune a piano or harp. [Old English *wrǣstan;* related to Old Norse *reista.* See WRITHE] —'**wrest·er** *n.*

wres·tle ('rɛsᵊl) *vb.* **1.** to fight (another person) by holding, throwing, etc., without punching with the closed fist. **2.** (*intr.*) to participate in wrestling. **3.** (when *intr.,* foll. by *with* or *against*) to fight with (a person, problem, or thing): *wrestle with one's conscience.* **4.** (*tr.*) to move laboriously, as with wrestling movements. **5.** (*tr.*) *U.S.* to throw (an animal) for branding. ~*n.* **6.** the act of wrestling. **7.** a struggle or tussle. [Old English *wrǣstlian;* related to Middle Dutch *wrastelen* (Dutch *worstelen*), Old Norse *rost* current, race] —'**wres·tler** *n.*

wres·tling ('rɛslɪŋ) *n.* any of certain sports in which the contestants fight each other according to various rules governing holds and usually forbidding blows with the closed fist. The principal object is to overcome the opponent either by throwing or pinning him to the ground or by causing him to submit. See **freestyle, Graeco-Roman, Sumo.**

wrest pin *n.* (on a piano, etc.) a pin around which one end of a string is wound: it may be turned by means of a tuning key to alter the tension of the string.

wretch (rɛtʃ) *n.* **1.** a despicable person. **2.** a person pitied for his misfortune. [Old English *wrecca;* related to Old Saxon *wrekkeo,* Old High German *reccheo* (German *Recke* warrior), Old Norse *rek(n)ingr*]

wretch·ed ('rɛtʃɪd) *adj.* **1.** in poor or pitiful circumstances. **2.** characterized by or causing misery. **3.** despicable; base. **4.** poor, inferior, or paltry. **5.** (*prenominal*) (intensifier qualifying something undesirable): *a wretched nuisance.* —'**wretch·ed·ly** *adv.* —'**wretch·ed·ness** *n.*

Wrex·ham ('rɛksəm) *n.* a town in N Wales, in SE Clwyd: seat of the Roman Catholic bishopric of Wales (except Glamorganshire); coal-mining. Pop.: 38 955 (1971).

wri·er *or* **wry·er** ('raɪə) *adj.* the comparative of **wry.**

wri·est *or* **wry·est** ('raɪɪst) *adj.* the superlative of **wry.**

wrig·gle ('rɪgᵊl) *vb.* **1.** to make or cause to make twisting movements. **2.** (*intr.*) to progress by twisting and turning. **3.** (*intr.;* foll. by *into* or *out of*) to manoeuvre oneself by clever or devious means: *wriggle out of an embarrassing situation.* ~*n.* **4.** a wriggling movement or action. **5.** a sinuous marking or course. [C15: from Middle Low German; compare Dutch *wriggelen*] —'**wrig·gler** *n.* —'**wrig·gly** *adj.*

wright (raɪt) *n.* (*now chiefly in combination*) a person who creates, builds, or repairs something specified: *a playwright; a shipwright.* [Old English *wryhta, wyrhta;* related to Old Frisian *wrichta,* Old Saxon, Old High German *wurhtio.* See WORK]

Wright (raɪt) *n.* **1. Frank Lloyd.** 1869–1959, U.S. architect, whose designs include the Imperial Hotel, Tokyo (1916), the Guggenheim Museum, New York (1943), and many private houses. His "organic architecture" sought a close relationship between buildings and their natural surroundings. **2. Jo·seph.** 1855–1930, English philologist; editor of *The English Dialect Dictionary* (1898–1905). **3. Wil·bur** (1867–1912) and his brother **Or·ville** (1871–1948), U.S. aviation pioneers, who designed and flew the first powered aircraft (1903).

wring (rɪŋ) *vb.* **wrings, wring·ing, wrung. 1.** (often foll. by *out*) to twist and compress to squeeze (a liquid) from (cloth, etc.). **2.** (*tr.*) to twist forcibly: *wring its neck.* **3.** (*tr.*) to clasp and twist (one's hands), esp. in anguish. **4.** (*tr.*) to distress: *wring one's heart.* **5.** (*tr.*) to grip (someone's hand) vigorously in greeting. **6.** (*tr.*) to obtain by or as if by forceful means: *wring information out of.* **7.** (*intr.*) to writhe with or as if with pain. **8. wringing wet.** soaking; drenched. ~*n.* **9.** an act or the process of wringing. [Old English *wringan;* related to Old

High German *ringan* (German *wringen*), Gothic *wrungō* snare. See WRANGLE, WRONG]

wring+er ('rɪŋə) *n.* a machine for drying clothes, textiles, etc., often consisting of two rollers between which the cloth is squeezed. Also called (Brit.): **mangle.**

wrin+kle[1] ('rɪŋkᵊl) *n.* **1.** a slight ridge in the smoothness of a surface, such as a crease in the skin as a result of age. ~*vb.* **2.** to make or become wrinkled, as by crumpling, creasing, or puckering. [C15: back formation from *wrinkled,* from Old English *gewrinclod,* past participle of *wrinclian* to wind around; related to Swedish *vrinka* to sprain, Lithuanian *reñgti* to twist. See WRENCH] —'**wrin+kle+less** *adj.* —'**wrin+kly** *adj.*

wrin+kle[2] ('rɪŋkᵊl) *n. Informal.* a clever or novel trick, hint, or device. [Old English *wrenc* trick; related to Middle Low German *wrank* struggle, Middle High German *ranc* sudden turn. See WRENCH]

wrist (rɪst) *n.* **1.** *Anatomy.* the joint between the forearm and the hand. Technical name: **carpus. 2.** the part of a sleeve or glove that covers the wrist. **3.** *Machinery.* **a.** See **wrist pin. b.** a joint in which a wrist pin forms the pivot. [Old English; related to Old High German, Old Norse *rist.* See WRIGGLE, WRY]

wrist+band ('rɪst,bænd) *n.* a band around the wrist, esp. one attached to a watch or forming part of a long sleeve.

wrist-drop *n.* paralysis of the extensor muscles of the wrist and fingers.

wrist+let ('rɪstlɪt) *n.* a band or bracelet worn around the wrist.

wrist+lock ('rɪst,lɒk) *n.* a wrestling hold in which a wrestler seizes his opponent's wrist and exerts pressure against the joints of his hand, arm, or shoulder.

wrist pin *n.* **1.** a cylindrical boss or pin attached to the side of a wheel parallel with the axis, esp. one forming a bearing for a crank. **2.** the U.S. name for **gudgeon pin.**

wrist+watch ('rɪst,wɒtʃ) *n.* a watch worn strapped around the wrist.

writ[1] (rɪt) *n.* **1.** a document under seal, issued in the name of the Crown or a court, commanding the person to whom it is addressed to do or refrain from doing some specified act. **2.** *Archaic.* a piece or body of writing: *Holy Writ.* [Old English; related to Old Norse *rit,* Gothic *writs* stroke, Old High German *riz* (German *Riss* a tear). See WRITE]

writ[2] (rɪt) *vb. Archaic or dialect.* a past tense or past participle of **write.**

write (raɪt) *vb.* **writes, writ+ing, wrote, writ+ten. 1.** to draw or mark (symbols, words, etc.) on a surface, usually paper, with a pen, pencil, or other instrument. **2.** to describe or record (ideas, experiences, etc.) in writing. **3.** to compose (a letter) to or correspond regularly with (a person, organization, etc.). **4.** (*tr.; may take a clause as object*) to say or communicate by letter: *he wrote that he was on his way.* **5.** (*tr.*) *Informal, chiefly U.S.* to send a letter to (a person, etc.). **6.** to write (words) in cursive as opposed to printed style. **7.** (*tr.*) to be sufficiently familiar with (a specified style, language, etc.) to use it in writing. **8.** to be the author or composer of (books, music, etc.). **9.** (*tr.*) to fill in the details for (a document, form, etc.). **10.** (*tr.*) to draw up or draft. **11.** (*tr.*) to produce by writing: *he wrote ten pages.* **12.** (*tr.*) to show clearly: *envy was written all over his face.* **13.** (*tr.*) to spell, inscribe, or entitle. **14.** (*tr.*) to ordain or prophesy: *it is written.* **15.** (*intr.*) to produce writing as specified. **16.** *Computer technol.* to record (data) in a location in a storage device, such as a drum. Compare **read**[1] (sense 16). **17.** (*tr.*) See **underwrite** (sense 3a.). ~See also **write down, write in, write off, write out, write up.** [Old English *wrītan* (originally: to scratch runes into bark); related to Old Frisian *wrīta,* Old Norse *rīta,* Old High German *rīzan* (German *reissen* to tear)] —'**writ+a+ble** *adj.*

write down *vb.* (*adv.*) **1.** (*tr.*) to set down in writing. **2.** (*tr.*) to harm or belittle by writing about (a person) in derogatory terms. **3.** (*intr.; foll. by to or for*) to write in a simplified way (to a supposedly less cultured readership). **4.** (*tr.*) *Accounting.* to decrease the book value of (an asset). ~*n.* **write-down. 5.** *Accounting.* a reduction made in the book value of an asset.

write in *vb.* **1.** (*tr.*) to insert in (a document, form, etc.) in writing. **2.** (*tr., adv.*) *U.S.* **a.** to vote for (a person not on a ballot) by writing in his name. **b.** to cast (a vote) for such a person by writing in his name. ~*n.* **write-in.** *U.S.* **3.** the voting for a person by writing his name on a ballot. **4.** a candidate or vote that has been written in. **5.** (as *modifier*): *a write-in campaign.*

write off *vb.* (*tr., adv.*) **1.** *Accounting.* **a.** to cancel (a bad debt or obsolete asset) from the accounts. **b.** to consider (a transaction, etc.) as a loss or set off (a loss) against revenues. **c.** to depreciate (an asset) by periodic charges. **d.** to charge (a specified amount) against gross profits as depreciation of an asset. **2.** to cause or acknowledge the complete loss of. ~*n.* **write-off. 3.** *Accounting.* **a.** the act of cancelling a bad debt or obsolete asset from the accounts. **b.** the bad debt or obsolete asset cancelled. **c.** the amount cancelled against gross profits, corresponding to the book value of the bad debt or obsolete asset. **4.** *Informal.* something damaged beyond repair, esp. a car.

write out *vb.* (*tr., adv.*) **1.** to put into writing or reproduce in full form in writing. **2.** to exhaust (oneself or one's creativity) by excessive writing. **3.** to remove (a character) from a television or radio series.

writ+er ('raɪtə) *n.* **1.** a person who writes books, articles, etc., esp. as an occupation. **2.** the person who has written something specified. **3.** a person who is able to write or write well. **4.** a scribe or clerk. **5.** a composer of music. **6.** a Scottish name for **solicitor. 7. writer to the signet.** (in Scotland) a lawyer who conducts cases before the Court of Session.

writ+er's cramp, pal+sy, *or* **spasm** *n.* a muscular spasm or temporary paralysis of the muscles of the thumb and first two fingers caused by prolonged writing.

write up *vb.* (*tr., adv.*) **1.** to describe fully, complete, or bring up to date in writing: *write up a diary.* **2.** to praise or bring to public notice in writing. **3.** *Accounting.* **a.** to place an excessively high value on (an asset). **b.** to increase the book value of (an asset) in order to reflect more accurately its current worth in the market. ~*n.* **write-up. 4.** a published account of something, such as a review in a newspaper or magazine. **5.** *Accounting, U.S.* **a.** an excessive or illegally high valuation of corporate assets. **b.** a raising of the book value of an asset.

writhe (raɪð) *vb.* **1.** to twist or squirm in or as if in pain. **2.** (*intr.*) to move with such motions. **3.** (*intr.*) to suffer acutely from embarrassment, revulsion, etc. ~*n.* **4.** the act or an instance of writhing. [Old English *wrīthan;* related to Old High German *rīdan,* Old Norse *rītha.* See WRATH, WREATH, WRIST, WROTH] —'**writh+er** *n.*

writh+en ('rɪðən) *Archaic or poetic.* ~*vb.* **1.** a past tense of **writhe.** ~*adj.* **2.** twisted; distorted.

writ+ing ('raɪtɪŋ) *n.* **1.** a group of letters or symbols written or marked on a surface as a means of communicating ideas by making each symbol stand for an idea, concept, or thing (see **ideogram**), by using each symbol to represent a set of sounds grouped into syllables (**syllabic writing**), or by regarding each symbol as corresponding roughly or exactly to each of the sounds in the language (**alphabetic writing**). **2.** short for **handwriting. 3.** anything expressed in letters, esp. a literary composition. **4.** the work of a writer. **5.** literary style, art, or practice. **6.** written form: *give it to me in writing.* **7.** (*modifier*): related to or used in writing: *writing ink.* **8. writing on the wall.** a sign or signs of approaching disaster.

writ+ing desk *n.* a piece of furniture with a writing surface and drawers and compartments for papers, etc.

writ+ing pa+per *n.* paper sized to take writing ink and used for letters and other manuscripts.

Writ+ings ('raɪtɪŋz) *pl. n.* **the.** another term for the **Hagiographa.**

writ of ex+e+cu+tion *n. Law.* a writ ordering that a judgment be enforced.

writ+ten ('rɪtᵊn) *vb.* **1.** the past participle of **write.** ~*adj.* **2.** taken down in writing; transcribed: *written evidence; the written word.* Compare **spoken** (sense 2).

W.R.N.S. *abbrev. for* Women's Royal Naval Service. See also **Wren**[1].

wrnt. *abbrev. for* warrant.

Wro+cław (*Polish* 'vrɔtswaf) *n.* an industrial city in SW Poland, on the River Oder: passed to Austria (1527) and to Prussia (1741); returned to Poland in 1945. Pop.: 565 000 (1974 est.). German name: **Breslau.**

wrong (rɒŋ) *adj.* **1.** not correct or truthful: *the wrong answer.* **2.** acting or judging in error: *you are wrong to think that.* **3.** (*postpositive*) immoral; bad: *it is wrong to cheat.* **4.** deviating from or unacceptable to correct or conventional laws, usage, etc. **5.** not intended or wanted: *the wrong road.* **6.** (*postpositive*) not working properly; amiss: *something is wrong with the engine.* **7.** (of a side, esp. of a fabric) intended to face the inside so as not to be seen. **8. get on the wrong side of** *or* (*U.S.*) **get in wrong with.** *Informal.* to come into disfavour with. **9. go down the wrong way.** (of food) to pass into the windpipe instead of the gullet. **10. wrong in the** (*or* **one's**) **head.** *Informal.* mad; crazy. ~*adv.* **11.** in the wrong direction or manner. **12. go wrong. a.** to turn out other than intended. **b.** to make a mistake. **c.** (of a machine, etc.) to cease to function properly. **d.** to go astray morally. **13. get wrong. a.** to fail to understand properly. **b.** to fail to provide the correct answer to. ~*n.* **14.** a bad, immoral, or unjust thing or action. **15.** *Law.* **a.** an infringement of another person's rights, rendering the offender liable to a civil action, as for breach of contract or tort: *a private wrong.* **b.** a violation of public rights and duties, affecting the community as a whole and actionable at the instance of the Crown: *a public wrong.* **16. in the wrong.** mistaken or guilty. ~*vb.* (*tr.*) **17.** to treat unjustly. **18.** to discredit, malign, or misrepresent. **19.** to seduce or violate. [Old English *wrang* injustice, from Old Norse *vrang;* see WRING] —'**wrong+er** *n.* —'**wrong+ly** *adv.* —'**wrong+ness** *n.*

wrong+do+er ('rɒŋ,duːə) *n.* a person who acts immorally or illegally. —'**wrong+,do+ing** *n.*

wrong-foot *vb.* (*tr.*) **1.** *Tennis, etc.* to play a shot in such a way so as to cause (one's opponent) to be off balance. **2.** to take by surprise so as to place in an embarrassing social position.

wrong fount *n. Printing.* an error in composition in which a type of the wrong face or size is used. Abbrev.: **wf.**

wrong+ful ('rɒŋful) *adj.* immoral, unjust, or illegal. —'**wrong+ful+ly** *adv.* —'**wrong+ful+ness** *n.*

wrong-head+ed *adj.* **1.** constantly wrong in judgment. **2.** foolishly stubborn; obstinate. —,**wrong-'head+ed+ly** *adv.* —,**wrong-'head+ed+ness** *n.*

wrong num+ber *n.* a telephone number dialled in error or the person so contacted.

wrote (rəʊt) *vb.* the past tense of **write.**

wroth (rəʊθ, rɒθ) *adj. Archaic or literary.* angry; irate. [Old English *wrāth;* related to Old Saxon *wrēth,* Old Norse *reithr,* Old High German *reid* curly haired]

wrought (rɔːt) *vb.* **1.** *Archaic.* a past tense or past participle of **work.** ~*adj.* **2.** *Metallurgy.* shaped by hammering or beating. **3.** (*often in combination*) formed, fashioned, or worked as specified: *well-wrought.* **4.** decorated or made with delicate care. [C16: variant of *worht,* from Old English *geworht,* past participle of (*ge*)*wyrcan* to WORK]

wrought i·ron *n.* **a.** a pure form of iron having a low carbon content and a fibrous microstructure. It is made by various processes and is often used for decorative work. **b.** (*as modifier*): *wrought-iron gates.*

wrought-up *or* **worked-up** *adj.* excited or agitated.

wrung (rʌŋ) *vb.* the past tense or past participle of **wring.**

W.R.V.S. *abbrev. for* Women's Royal Voluntary Service.

wry (raɪ) *adj.* **wri·er, wri·est** *or* **wry·er, wry·est. 1.** twisted, contorted, or askew. **2.** (of a facial expression) produced or characterized by contorting of the features, usually indicating dislike. **3.** dryly humorous; sardonic. **4.** warped, misdirected, or perverse. **5.** (of words, thoughts, etc.) unsuitable or wrong. ~*vb.* **wries, wry·ing, wried. 6.** (*tr.*) to twist or contort. [C16: from dialect *wry* to twist, from Old English *wrīgian* to turn; related to Old Frisian *wrīgia* to bend, Old Norse *riga* to move, Middle Low German *wrīch* bent, stubborn] —**'wry·ly** *adv.* —**'wry·ness** *n.*

wry·bill ('raɪ,bɪl) *n.* a New Zealand plover, *Anarhynchus frontalis,* having its bill deflected to one side enabling it to search for food beneath stones.

wry·neck ('raɪ,nɛk) *n.* **1.** either of two cryptically coloured Old World woodpeckers, *Jynx torquilla* or *J. ruficollis,* which do not drum on trees. **2.** another name for **torticollis. 3.** *Informal.* a person who has a twisted neck.

WS *international car registration for* Western Samoa.

W star *n.* short for **Wolf-Rayet star.**

WSW *abbrev. for* west-southwest.

wt. *abbrev. for* weight.

Wu (wu:) *n.* a group of dialects of Chinese spoken around the Yangtze delta.

Wu·chang *or* **Wu·ch'ang** ('wu:'tʃæŋ) *n.* a former city of E central China: now a part of Wuhan.

Wu·han ('wu:'hæn) *n.* a city in SE China, in Hupeh province, at the confluence of the Han and Yangtze Rivers: formed in 1950 by the union of the cities of Hanyang, Hankow, and Wuchang (the Han Cities); river port and industrial centre; university (1913). Pop.: 2 560 000 (1970 est.).

Wu·hsien ('wu:'ʃjɛn) *n.* another name for **Soochow.**

Wu·hu ('wu:'hu:) *n.* a port in E China, in E Anhwei province on the Yangtze River. Pop.: 242 100 (1953).

wul·fen·ite ('wʊlfə,naɪt) *n.* a yellow, orange, red, or grey lustrous secondary mineral consisting of lead molybdate in the form of platelike tetragonal crystals. It occurs with lead ores and is a source of molybdenum. Formula: $PbMoO_4$. [C19: from German *Wulfenit,* named after F. X. von *Wulfen* (1728–1805), Austrian mineralogist]

Wul·fi·la ('wʊlfɪlə) *n.* another name for **Ulfilas.**

Wu-lu-mu-ch'i ('wu:'lu:'mu:'tʃi:) *n.* variant of **Urumchi.**

wun·der·kind ('wʌndə,kɪnd; *German* 'vʊndər,kɪnt) *n., pl.* **·kinds** *or* **·kind·er** (*German* -,kɪndər) **1.** a child prodigy. **2.** a person who is exceptionally successful in his field while still young. [C20: German, literally: wonder child]

Wundt (*German* vʊnt) *n.* **Wil·helm Max** ('vɪlhɛlm maks). 1832–1920, German experimental psychologist.

Wup·per·tal (*German* 'vʊpərta:l) *n.* a city in W West Germany, in North Rhine-Westphalia state on the **Wupper River** (a Rhine tributary): formed in 1919 from the amalgamation of the towns of Barmen and Elberfeld and other smaller towns; textile centre. Pop.: 409 715 (1974 est.).

wurl·ey *or* **wurl·ie** ('wɜ:lɪ) *n. Austral.* an Aboriginal hut. [from a native Australian language]

Würm (vʊəm, wɜ:m) *n.* the fourth and final Pleistocene glaciation in Alpine Europe. See also **Günz, Riss, Mindel.**

wurst (wɜ:st, wʊəst, vʊəst) *n.* a large sausage, esp. of a type made in Germany, Austria, etc. [from German, literally: something rolled; related to Latin *vertere* to turn]

Würt·tem·berg ('vɜ:təm,bɜ:g; *German* 'vyrtəm,bɛrk) *n.* a former state of S Germany: made part of the West German state of Baden-Württemberg after World War II.

Würz·burg ('vɜ:ts,bɜ:g; *German* 'vyrts,bʊrk) *n.* a city in S West Germany, in NW Bavaria on the River Main: university (1582). Pop.: 113 450 (1974 est.).

wus (wʌs) *n. South Wales dialect.* a casual term of address: *fancy a drink wus?* [from Welsh *was,* variant of *gwas* servant]

Wu·sih *or* **Wu-hsi** ('wu:'si:, -ʃi:) *n.* a city in E China, in S Kiangsu province on the Grand Canal: textile industry. Pop.: 650 000 (1970 est.).

wuth·er·ing ('wʌðərɪŋ) *adj. Northern Brit. dialect.* **1.** (of a wind) blowing strongly with a roaring sound. **2.** (of a place) characterized by such a sound. [variant of *whitherin,* from *whither* blow, from Old Norse *hvithra;* related to *hvitha* squall of wind, Old English *hweothu* wind]

Wu·tsin ('wu:'tsɪn) *n.* the former name (until 1949) of **Changchow.**

WV *international car registration for* (Windward Islands) St. Vincent.

W. Va. *abbrev. for* West Virginia.

W.V.S. (in Britain) *abbrev. for* Women's Voluntary Service.

Wy·an·dotte ('waɪən,dɒt) *n.* a heavy American breed of domestic fowl with many different varieties.

Wy·att ('waɪət) *n.* **1. James.** 1746–1813, English architect; a pioneer of neo-Gothic. **2.** Sir **Thom·as.** ?1503–42, English poet at the court of Henry VIII.

wych-elm *or* **witch-elm** ('wɪtʃ,ɛlm) *n.* **1.** Eurasian elm tree, *Ulmus glabra,* having a rounded shape, longish pointed leaves, clusters of small flowers, and winged fruits. **2.** the wood of this tree. [C17: from Old English *wice* wych-elm]

Wych·er·ley ('wɪtʃəlɪ) *n.* **Wil·liam.** ?1640–1716, English dramatist. His Restoration comedies include *The Country Wife* (1675) and *The Plain Dealer* (1676).

wych-ha·zel *n.* a variant spelling of **witch hazel.**

Wyc·liffe *or* **Wyc·lif** ('wɪklɪf) *n.* **John.** ?1330–84, English religious reformer. A precursor of the Reformation, whose writings were condemned as heretical, he attacked the doctrines and abuses of the Church. He instigated the first complete translation of the Bible into English. His followers were called Lollards. Also spelt: **Wiclif, Wickliffe.** —**'Wyc·liff·ism** *or* **'Wyc·lif·ism** *n.*

Wyc·lif·fite *or* **Wyc·lif·ite** ('wɪklɪ,faɪt) *English history.* ~*n.* **1.** a follower of John Wycliffe or an adherent of his religious ideas; a Lollard. ~*adj.* **2.** of or relating to Wycliffe, his followers, or his religious ideas.

Wye (waɪ) *n.* a river in E Wales and W England, rising in Powys and flowing southeast into England, then south to the Severn estuary. Length: 210 km (130 miles).

Wyke·ham ('wɪkəm) *n.* **Wil·liam of.** 1324–1404, English prelate and statesman, who founded New College, Oxford, and Winchester College: chancellor of England (1367–71; 1389–91); bishop of Winchester (1367–1404).

wynd (waɪnd) *n. Scot.* a narrow lane or alley. [C15: from the stem of WIND[2]]

Wyo. *abbrev. for* Wyoming.

Wy·o·ming (waɪ'əʊmɪŋ) *n.* a state of the western U.S.: consists largely of ranges of the Rockies in the west and north, with part of the Great Plains in the east and several regions of hot springs. Capital: Cheyenne. Pop.: 332 416 (1970). Area: 253 597 sq. km (97 914 sq. miles). Abbrevs.: **Wyo., Wy.,** or (with zip code) **WY** —**Wy·'o·ming·,ite** *n.*

wy·vern *or* **wi·vern** ('waɪvən) *n.* a heraldic beast having a serpent's tail and a dragon's head and a body with wings and two legs. [C17: variant of earlier *wyver,* from Old French, from Latin *vīpera* VIPER]

X

x *or* **X** (ɛks) *n., pl.* **x's, X's,** *or* **Xs. 1.** the 24th letter and 19th consonant of the modern English alphabet. **2.** a speech sound sequence represented by this letter, in English pronounced as *ks* or *gz* or, in initial position, *z,* as in *xylophone.*
x *symbol for:* **1.** *Commerce, finance, etc.* ex. **2.** *Maths.* the *x*-axis or a coordinate measured along the *x*-axis in a Cartesian coordinate system. **3.** an algebraic variable.
X *symbol:* **1. a.** indicating a film that may not be publicly shown to anyone under 18. **b.** (*as modifier*)*: an X film.* **2.** denoting any unknown, unspecified, or variable factor, number, person, or thing. **3.** (on letters, cards, etc.) denoting a kiss. **4.** (on ballot papers, etc.) indicating choice. **5.** (on examination papers, etc.) indicating error. **6.** for Christ; Christian [from the form of the Greek letter khi (X), first letter of *Khristos* Christ] ~**7.** *the Roman numeral for* ten. See **Roman numerals.**
xan+thate ('zænθeɪt) *n.* any salt or ester of xanthic acid. —**xan+'tha+tion** *n.*
xan+the+in ('zænθɪɪn) *n.* the soluble part of the yellow pigment that is found in the cell sap of some flowers.
xan+thene ('zænθiːn) *n.* a yellowish crystalline heterocyclic compound used as a fungicide; benzo-1,4-pyran. Its molecular structural unit is found in many dyes, such as rhodamine and fluorosein. Formula: $CH_2(C_6H_4)_2O$.
xan+thic ('zænθɪk) *adj.* **1.** of, containing, or derived from xanthic acid. **2.** *Botany, rare.* having a yellow colour.
xan+thic ac·id *n.* any of a class of organic sulphur-containing acids with the general formula ROC(S)SH, where R is an organic group. Their salts are the xanthates.
xan+thin ('zænθɪn) *n.* any of a group of yellow or orange carotene derivatives that occur in the fruit and flowers of certain plants.
xan+thine ('zænθiːn, -θaɪn) *n.* **1.** a crystalline compound related in structure to uric acid and found in urine, blood, certain plants, and certain animal tissues. Formula: $C_5H_4N_4O_2$. **2.** any substituted derivative of xanthine, esp. one of the three pharmacologically active methylated xanthines, caffeine, theophylline, or theobromine, which act as stimulants and diuretics.
Xan·thip·pe (zæn'θɪpɪ) *or* **Xan·tip·pe** (zæn'tɪpɪ) *n.* **1.** the wife of Socrates, proverbial as a scolding and quarrelsome woman. **2.** any nagging, peevish, or irritable woman.
xan·tho- *or before a vowel* **xanth-** *combining form.* indicating yellow: *xanthophyll.* [from Greek *xanthos*]
xan+tho+chroid ('zænθəʊˌkrɔɪd) *adj. Rare.* of, relating to, or designating races having light-coloured hair and a pale complexion. [C19: New Latin *xanthochroi,* from XANTHO- + Greek *ōkhros* pale]
xan+thoch+ro+ism (zæn'θɒkrəʊˌɪzəm) *n.* a condition in certain animals, esp. aquarium goldfish, in which all skin pigments other than yellow and orange disappear. [C19: from Greek *xanthokhro*(*os*) yellow-skinned (from *xanthos* yellow + *khroia* skin) + -ISM]
xan+tho+ma (zæn'θəʊmə) *n. Pathol.* the presence in the skin of fatty yellow or brownish plaques or nodules, esp. on the eyelids, caused by a disorder of lipid metabolism.
xan+tho+phyll *or esp. U.S.* **xan+tho+phyl** ('zænθəʊfɪl) *n.* any of a group of yellow carotenoid pigments occurring in plant and animal tissue. —**ˌxan+tho+'phyll+ous** *adj.*
xan+thous ('zænθəs) *adj.* of, relating to, or designating races with yellowish hair and a light complexion.
Xan+thus ('zænθəs) *n.* the chief city of ancient Lycia in SW Asia Minor: source of some important antiquities. —**'Xan+thi·an** *adj.*
Xa·vi·er ('zeɪvɪə, 'zæv-; *Spanish* xa'βjer) *n.* **Saint Fran·cis,** known as the *Apostle of the Indies.* 1506–52, Spanish missionary, who was a founding member of the Jesuit society (1534) and later preached in Goa, Ceylon, the East Indies, and Japan. Feast day: Dec. 3.
***x*-ax·is** *n.* a reference axis, usually horizontal, of a graph or two- or three-dimensional Cartesian coordinate system along which the *x*-coordinate is measured.
X-chro·mo·some *n.* the sex chromosome that occurs in pairs in the diploid cells of the females of many animals, including humans, and as one of a pair with the Y-chromosome in those of males. Compare **Y-chromosome.**
Xe *the chemical symbol for* xenon.
xe+bec, ze+bec, *or* **ze+beck** ('ziːbɛk) *n.* a small three-masted Mediterranean vessel with both square and lateen sails, formerly used by Algerian pirates and later used for commerce. [C18: earlier *chebec* from French, ultimately from Arabic *shabbāk;* present spelling influenced by Catalan *xabec,* Spanish *xabeque* (now *jabeque*)]
Xe·na·kis (zɛ'nɑːkɪs; *Greek* ksɛ'nakis) *n.* **Yan·nis** ('janis). born 1922, Greek composer and musical theorist, born in Rumania. He is noted for his use of electronic computers in composition: his works include *ST/10-1, 080262* (1962).
xe+ni·a ('ziːnɪə) *n. Botany.* the influence of pollen upon the form of the fruit developing after pollination. [C19: from New Latin, from Greek: hospitality, from *xenos* guest] —**'xe+ni·al** *adj.*
xen·o- *or before a vowel* **xen-** *combining form.* indicating something strange, different, or foreign: *xenogamy.* [from Greek *xenos* strange]
Xe·noc·ra·tes (zɛ'nɒkrəˌtiːz) *n.* ?396–314 B.C., Greek Platonic philosopher. —**Xen·o·crat+ic** (ˌzɛnə'krætɪk) *adj.*
xen·o+cryst ('zɛnəˌkrɪst) *n.* a crystal included within an igneous rock as the magma cooled but not formed from it. [C20: from XENO- + CRYST(AL)]
xe+nog·a·my (zɛ'nɒgəmɪ) *n. Botany.* another name for **cross-fertilization.** —**xe+'nog·a·mous** *adj.*
xen·o+gen+e·sis (ˌzɛnə'dʒɛnɪsɪs) *n.* **1.** the supposed production of offspring completely unlike either parent. **2.** another name for **abiogenesis** or **alternation of generations.** —**xen·o+ge·net+ic** (ˌzɛnəʊdʒɪ'nɛtɪk) *or* **ˌxen·o+'gen+ic** *adj.*
xen·o+glos+si·a (ˌzɛnə'glɒsɪə) *n.* an ability claimed by some mediums, clairvoyants, etc., to speak a language with which they are unfamiliar. [C20: from Greek, from XENO- + Attic Greek *glossa* tongue, language]
xen·o+lith ('zɛnəlɪθ) *n.* a fragment of rock differing in origin, composition, structure, etc., from the igneous rock enclosing it. —**ˌxen·o·'lith+ic** *adj.*
xen·o+mor+phic (ˌzɛnə'mɔːfɪk) *adj.* (of a mineral constituent of an igneous rock) not having its characteristic crystal shape because of deforming pressure from adjacent minerals. —**ˌxen·o·'mor+phi+cal+ly** *adv.*
xen+on ('zɛnɒn) *n.* a colourless odourless gaseous element occurring in trace amounts in air; formerly considered inert it is now known to form compounds and is used in radio valves, stroboscopic and bactericidal lamps, and bubble chambers. Symbol: Xe; atomic no.: 54; atomic wt.: 131.30; density: 5.887 kg/m^3; melting pt.: –111.9°C; boiling pt.: –107.1°C. [C19: from Greek: something strange]
Xe·noph·a·nes (zɛ'nɒfəˌniːz) *n.* ?570–?480 B.C., Greek philosopher, noted for his monotheism and regarded as a founder of the Eleatic school.
xen·o+phile ('zɛnəˌfaɪl) *n.* a person who likes foreigners or things foreign. [C19: from Greek, from XENO- + -PHILE]
xen·o+phobe ('zɛnəˌfəʊb) *n.* a person who hates or fears foreigners or strangers.
xen·o+pho+bi·a (ˌzɛnə'fəʊbɪə) *n.* hatred or fear of foreigners or strangers or of their politics or culture. —**ˌxen·o·'pho+bic** *adj.*
Xen·o·phon ('zɛnəfən) *n.* 431–?355 B.C., Greek general and historian; a disciple of Socrates. He accompanied Cyrus the Younger against Artaxerxes II and, after Cyrus' death at Cunaxa (401), he led his army of 10 000 Greek soldiers to the Black Sea, an expedition described in his *Anabasis.* His other works include *Hellenica,* a history of Greece, and the *Memorabilia, Apology,* and *Symposium,* which contain recollections of Socrates.
xer+arch ('zɪərɑːk) *adj. Ecology.* (of a sere) having its origin in a dry habitat.
Xe+res (*Spanish* 'xeres) *n.* the former name of **Jerez.**
xe+ric ('zɪərɪk) *adj. Ecology.* of, relating to, or growing in dry conditions. —**'xe+ri+cal+ly** *adv.*
xe·ro- *or before a vowel* **xer-** *combining form.* indicating dryness: *xeroderma.* [from Greek *xēros* dry]
xe+ro+der+ma (ˌzɪərəʊ'dɜːmə) *or* **xe+ro+der+mi·a** (ˌzɪərəʊ'dɜːmɪə) *n. Pathol.* **1.** any abnormal dryness of the skin as the result of diminished secretions from the sweat or sebaceous glands. **2.** another name for **ichthyosis.** —**xe+ro+der+mat+ic** (ˌzɪərəʊdə'mætɪk) *or* **ˌxe+ro+'der+ma+tous** *adj.*
xe+rog+ra+phy (zɪ'rɒgrəfɪ) *n.* a photocopying process in which an electrostatic image is formed on a selenium plate or cylinder. The plate or cylinder is dusted with a resinous powder, which adheres to the charged regions, and the image is then transferred to a sheet of paper on which it is fixed by heating. —**xe+'rog+ra+pher** *n.* —**xe+ro+graph+ic** (ˌzɪərə'græfɪk) *adj.* —**ˌxe+ro+'graph+i+cal+ly** *adv.*
xe+ro+mor+phic (ˌzɪərə'mɔːfɪk) *adj.* (of plants or plant parts) having characteristics that serve as protection against excessive loss of water.
xe+roph+i+lous (zɪ'rɒfɪləs) *adj.* (of plants or animals) adapted for growing or living in dry surroundings. —**xe+ro+phile** ('zɪərəʊˌfaɪl) *n.* —**xe+'roph+i+ly** *n.*
xe+roph+thal+mi·a (ˌzɪərɒf'θælmɪə) *n. Pathol.* excessive dryness of the cornea and conjunctiva, caused by a deficiency of vitamin A. Also called: **xe+ro+ma** (zɪ'rəʊmə). —**ˌxe+roph+'thal+mic** *adj.*
xe+ro+phyte ('zɪərəˌfaɪt) *n.* a xerophilous plant, such as a cactus. —**xe+ro+phyt+ic** (ˌzɪərə'fɪtɪk) *adj.* —**ˌxe+ro+'phyt+i+cal+ly** *adv.* —**'xe+ro+ˌphyt+ism** *n.*
xe+ro+sere ('zɪərəˌsɪə) *n. Ecology.* a sere that originates in dry surroundings.
xe+ro+sis (zɪ'rəʊsɪs) *n. Pathol.* abnormal dryness of bodily tissues, esp. the skin, eyes, or mucous membranes. —**xe+rot+ic** (zɪ'rɒtɪk) *adj.*
Xer+ox ('zɪərɒks) *n.* **1.** *Trademark.* **a.** a xerographic copying process. **b.** a machine employing this process. **c.** a copy produced by this process. ~*vb.* **2.** to produce a copy of (a document, illustration, etc.) by this process.

Xerx·es I ('zɜ:ksi:z) *n.* ?519–465 B.C., king of Persia (485–465), who led a vast army against Greece. His forces were victorious at Thermopylae but his fleet was defeated at Salamis (480) and his army at Plataea (479).

Xho+sa ('kɔ:sə) *n.* **1.** (*pl.* **+sa** *or* **+sas**) a member of a cattle-rearing Negroid people of southern Africa, living chiefly in Cape Province of the Republic of South Africa. **2.** the language of this people, belonging to the Bantu group of the Niger-Congo family: closely related to Swazi and Zulu and characterized by several clicks in its sound system. —**'Xho+san** *adj.*

xi (zaɪ, saɪ, ksaɪ, ksi:) *n., pl.* **xis.** the 14th letter in the Greek alphabet (Ξ, ξ), a composite consonant, transliterated as *x.*

Xi·me·nes (*Spanish* xi'menes; *English* 'zɪmɪˌni:z) *n.* See (Francisco) **Jiménez de Cisneros.** Also called: **Ximenez de Cisneros.**

Xin+gú (*Portuguese* ʃiŋ'gu) *n.* a river in central Brazil, rising on the Mato Grosso plateau and flowing north to the Amazon delta, with over 650 km (400 miles) of rapids in its middle course. Length: 1932 km (1200 miles).

xiph·i- *or before a vowel* **xiph-** *combining form.* indicating a sword, esp. something shaped like or resembling a sword: *xiphisternum; xiphoid.* [from Greek *xiphos* sword]

xiph·i+ster+num (ˌzɪfɪ'stɜ:nəm) *n., pl.* **+na** (-nə). *Anatomy, zoology.* the cartilaginous process forming the lowermost part of the breastbone (sternum). Also called: **xiphoid, xiphoid process.**

xiph+oid ('zɪfɔɪd) *adj.* **1.** *Biology.* shaped like a sword. **2.** of or relating to the xiphisternum. ~*n.* **3.** Also called: **xiphoid process.** another name for **xiphisternum.**

xiph·o+su+ran (ˌzɪfə'sjʊərən) *n.* **1.** any chelicerate arthropod of the subclass *Xiphosura,* including the horseshoe crabs and many extinct forms. ~*adj.* **2.** of, relating to, or belonging to the subclass *Xiphosura.* [C19: from New Latin *Xiphosura,* irregularly from Greek *xiphos* sword + *oura* tail]

XL *abbrev. for* extra large.

X·mas ('ɛksməs, 'krɪsməs) *n. Informal.* short for **Christmas.**

Xn. *or* **Xtian.** *abbrev. for* Christian.

Xnty. *or* **Xty.** *abbrev. for* Christianity.

XP *n.* the Christian monogram made up of the Greek letters *khi* and *rho,* the first two letters of *Khristos,* the Greek form of Christ's name.

x-ra·di·a·tion *n.* another term for **x-ray.**

x-ray *or* **X-ray** *n.* **1. a.** electromagnetic radiation with wavelengths (100–0.4 nanometres) between that of ultraviolet radiation and gamma radiation. They are emitted when atoms, esp. heavy atoms, are bombarded with fast electrons. **b.** (*as modifier*): *x-ray astronomy.* **2.** a picture produced by exposing photographic film to x-rays: used in medicine as a diagnostic aid as parts of the body, such as bones, absorb x-rays and so appear as opaque areas on the picture. ~*vb.* (*tr.*) **3.** to photograph (part of the body, etc.) using x-rays. **4.** to treat or examine by means of x-rays. [C19: partial translation of German *X-Strahlen* (from *Strahl* ray), coined by W. C. RÖNTGEN in 1895]

x-ray as+tron·o+my *n.* the branch of astronomy concerned with the detection and measurement of x-rays emitted by certain celestial bodies. As x-rays are absorbed by the atmosphere, satellites and rockets are used.

x-ray crys+tal+log+ra+phy *n.* the study and practice of determining the structure of a crystal by passing a beam of x-rays through it and observing and analysing the diffraction pattern produced.

x-ray star *n.* a star that emits x-rays, as well as other types of radiation. The x-rays are detected by instruments carried in satellites and space probes.

x-ray ther·a+py *n. Med.* the therapeutic use of x-rays.

x-ray tube *n.* an evacuated tube containing a metal target onto which is directed a beam of electrons at high energy for the generation of x-rays.

Xt. *abbrev. for* Christ. [representing the initial letter (chi) and the t (tau) of Greek *Khristos*]

x-u·nit *n.* a unit of length equal to $0.100\,202 \times 10^{-12}$ metre, for expressing the wavelengths of x-rays and gamma rays.

Xu·thus ('zu:θəs) *n. Greek myth.* a son of Hellen, regarded as an ancestor of the Ionian Greeks through his son Ion.

xy+lan ('zaɪlæn) *n. Biochem.* a yellow polysaccharide consisting of xylose units: occurs in straw husks and other woody tissue.

xy+lem ('zaɪləm, -lɛm) *n.* a plant tissue that conducts water and mineral salts from the roots to all other parts, provides mechanical support, and forms the wood of trees and shrubs. It is of two types (see **protoxylem, metaxylem**), both of which are made up of vessels, tracheids, and other elements. [C19: from Greek *xulon* wood]

xy+lene ('zaɪli:n) *n.* an aromatic hydrocarbon existing in three isomeric forms, all three being colourless flammable volatile liquids used as solvents and in the manufacture of synthetic resins, dyes, and insecticides; dimethylbenzene. Formula: $C_6H_4(CH_3)_2$. Also called: **xylol.**

xy+li+dine ('zaɪlɪˌdi:n, -ˌdaɪn, 'zɪlɪ-) *n.* **1.** a mixture of six isomeric amines derived from xylene and used in dyes. Formula: $(CH_3)_2C_6H_3NH_2$. **2.** any one of these isomers.

xy·lo- *or before a vowel* **xyl-** *combining form.* **1.** indicating wood: *xylophone.* **2.** indicating xylene: *xylidine.* [from Greek *xulon* wood]

xy+lo+carp ('zaɪləˌkɑ:p) *n. Botany.* a fruit, such as a coconut, having a hard woody pericarp. —ˌ**xy+lo+'car+pous** *adj.*

xy+lo+graph ('zaɪləˌgrɑ:f, -ˌgræf) *n.* **1.** an engraving in wood. **2.** a print taken from a wood block. ~*vb.* **3.** (*tr.*) to print (a design, illustration, etc.) from a wood engraving.

xy+log+ra+phy (zaɪ'lɒgrəfɪ) *n.* the art, craft, or process of printing from wooden blocks. —**xy+'log+ra+pher** *n.* —**xy+lo+graph+ic** (ˌzaɪlə'græfɪk) *or* ˌ**xy+lo+'graph·i+cal** *adj.*

xy+loid ('zaɪlɔɪd) *adj. Botany.* of, relating to, or resembling wood; woody.

xy+lol ('zaɪlɒl) *n.* another name (not in technical usage) for **xylene.**

xy+loph·a+gous (zaɪ'lɒfəgəs) *adj.* (of certain insects, crustaceans, etc.) feeding on or living within wood.

xy+lo+phone ('zaɪləˌfəʊn) *n. Music.* a percussion instrument consisting of a set of wooden bars of graduated length. It is played with hard-headed hammers. —**xy+lo+phon+ic** (ˌzaɪlə'fɒnɪk) *adj.* —**xy+loph·o+nist** (zaɪ'lɒfənɪst) *n.*

xy+lose ('zaɪləʊz, -ləʊs) *n.* a white crystalline dextrorotatory sugar found in the form of xylan in wood and straw. It is extracted by hydrolysis with acids and used in dyeing, tanning, and in foods for diabetics. Formula: $C_5H_{10}O_5$.

xy+lot·o+mous (zaɪ'lɒtəməs) *adj.* (of certain insects, insect larvae, etc.) cutting or boring into wood.

xy+lot·o+my (zaɪ'lɒtəmɪ) *n.* the preparation of sections of wood for examination by microscope. —**xy+'lot·o+mist** *n.*

xy+lyl ('zaɪlɪl) *n.* (*modifier*) of, containing, or denoting the group of atoms $(CH_3)_2C_6H_3$-, derived from xylene.

xyst (zɪst), **xys+tus,** *or* **xys+tos** ('zɪstəs) *n.* **1.** a long portico, esp. one used in ancient Greece for athletics. **2.** (in ancient Rome) a covered garden walk or one lined with trees. [C17: from Latin *xystus,* from Greek *xustos,* literally: smoothed, polished (area), from *xuein* to scrape, make smooth]

xys+ter ('zɪstə) *n.* a surgical instrument for scraping bone; surgical rasp or file. [C17: via New Latin from Greek: tool for scraping, from *xuein* to scrape]

Y

y *or* **Y** (waɪ) *n., pl.* **y's, Y's,** *or* **Ys. 1.** the 25th letter of the modern English alphabet. **2.** a speech sound represented by this letter, in English usually a semivowel, as in *yawn*, or a vowel, as in *symbol* or *shy*. **3. a.** something shaped like a Y. **b.** (*in combination*): *a Y-cross.*
y *Maths. symbol for:* **1.** the *y*-axis or a coordinate measured along the *y*-axis in a Cartesian coordinate system. **2.** an algebraic variable.
Y *symbol for:* **1.** any unknown, unspecified, or variable factor, number, person, or thing. **2.** *Chem.* yttrium.
y. *abbrev. for:* **1.** yard. **2.** year. **3.** yen.
Y. *abbrev. for* Y.M.C.A. or Y.W.C.A.
-y[1] *or* **-ey** *suffix forming adjectives.* **1.** (*from nouns*) characterized by; consisting of; filled with; relating to; resembling: *sunny; sandy; smoky; classy.* **2.** (*from verbs*) tending to; acting or existing as specified: *leaky; shiny.* [from Old English *-ig, -ǣg*]
-y[2], **-ie,** *or* **-ey** *suffix of nouns. Informal.* **1.** denoting smallness and expressing affection and familiarity: *a doggy; a bunny; a granny; Jamie.* **2.** a person or thing concerned with or characterized by being: *a groupie; a goalie; a fatty.* [C14: from Scottish *-ie, -y,* familiar suffix occurring originally in names, as in *Jamie* (*James*)]
-y[3] *suffix forming nouns.* **1.** (*from verbs*) indicating the act of doing what is indicated by the verbal element: *inquiry.* **2.** (*esp. with combining forms of Greek, Latin, or French origin*) indicating state, condition, or quality: *geography; jealousy.* [from Old French *-ie,* from Latin *-ia*]
yab+ber ('jæbə) *Austral. informal.* ~*vb.* **1.** (*intr.*) to talk or jabber. ~*n.* **2.** talk or jabber. [C19: from a native Australian language *yabba* talk, probably influenced by JABBER]
yab+by *or* **yab+bie** ('jæbɪ) *n., pl.* **+bies.** *Austral.* any of several small freshwater crayfish: used as bait. [from a native Australian language]
Ya+blo+no+vy Moun+tains (*Russian* 'jablənəvɪj) *pl. n.* a mountain range in the SE Soviet Union, in Siberia. Highest peak: 1680 m (5512 ft.). Also called: **Ya+blo+noi Moun+tains** ('jɑːbləˌnɔɪ).
yacht (jɒt) *n.* **1.** a vessel propelled by sail or power, used esp. for pleasure cruising, racing, etc. **2.** short for **sand yacht** or **ice yacht.** ~*vb.* **3.** (*intr.*) to sail or cruise in a yacht. [C16: from obsolete Dutch *jaghte,* short for *jahtschip,* from *jagen* to chase + *schip* SHIP]
yacht+ing ('jɒtɪŋ) *n.* **a.** the sport or practice of navigating a yacht. **b.** (*as modifier*): *yachting clothes.*
yachts+man ('jɒtsmən) *or* (*fem.*) **yachts+wom·an** *n., pl.* **+men** *or* **+wom·en.** a person who sails a yacht or yachts. —**'yachts+man+ˌship** *n.*
yack (jæk) *n., vb.* a variant spelling of **yak**[2].
yack·e·ty-yak ('jækɪtɪ'jæk) *n. Slang.* noisy, continuous, and trivial talk or conversation. Sometimes shortened to **yak.**
yaf+fle ('jæfᵊl) *n.* another name for **green woodpecker.** [C18: imitative of its cry]
Ya·fo ('jɑːfɔː) *n.* transliteration of the Arabic name for **Jaffa** (sense 1).
Ya·gi aer+i·al ('jɑːgɪ, 'jægɪ) *n.* a sharply directional aerial, used esp. in television and radio astronomy, consisting of three or more elements lying parallel to each other, the principal direction of radiation being along the line of the centres. [C20: named after Hidetsugu *Yagi* (born 1886), Japanese engineer]
yah (jɑː, jɛə) *sentence substitute.* **1.** an informal word for **yes,** often used to indicate derision or contempt. ~*interj.* **2.** an exclamation of derision or disgust.
Ya+ha+ta ('jɑːhɑːˌtɑː) *n.* a variant of **Yawata.**
ya+hoo (jə'huː) *n., pl.* **+hoos.** a crude, brutish, or obscenely coarse person. [C18: from the name of a race of brutish creatures resembling men in Jonathan Swift's *Gulliver's Travels* (1726)] —**ya+'hoo+ism** *n.*
Yahr+zeit ('jɔːtsaɪt) *n. Judaism.* the anniversary of the death of a close relative, on which it is customary to kindle a light and recite the Kaddish and also, in some communities, to observe a fast. [Yiddish, from Middle High German *jārzīt* anniversary; see YEAR, TIDE[1]]
Yah+weh, Jah+weh ('jɑːweɪ) *or* **Yah+veh, Jah+veh** ('jɑːveɪ) *n. Old Testament.* the personal covenant name of God, revealed to Moses on Mount Horeb (Exodus 3); Jehovah. [from Hebrew, from YHVH, with conjectural vowels; perhaps related to *hāwāh* to be]
Yah+wism, Jah+wism ('jɑːwɪzəm) *or* **Yah+vism, Jah+vism** ('jɑːvɪzəm) *n.* the use of the name Yahweh, esp. in parts of the Old Testament, as the personal name of God.
Yah+wist, Jah+wist ('jɑːwɪst) *or* **Yah+vist, Jah+vist** ('jɑːvɪst) *n. Bible.* **the. a.** the author or authors of the earliest of four main sources or strands of tradition of which the Pentateuch is composed and in which God is called *Yahweh* throughout. **b.** (*as modifier*): *the Yahwist source.*
Yah+wis+tic, Jah+wis+tic (jɑː'wɪstɪk) *or* **Yah+vis+tic, Jah+vis+tic** (jɑː'vɪstɪk) *adj. Bible.* of or relating to Yahwism, the Yahwist, or Yahweh.
Yaj·ur-Ve·da ('jʌdʒʊə 'veɪdə) *n. Hinduism.* the second Veda, consisting of prayers and sacrificial formulas primarily for use by the priests.
yak[1] (jæk) *n.* a wild and domesticated type of cattle, *Bos grunniens,* of Tibet, having long horns and long shaggy hair. [C19: from Tibetan *gyag*]
yak[2] (jæk) *Slang.* ~*n.* **1.** noisy, continuous, and trivial talk or conversation. ~*vb.* **yaks, yak+king, yakked. 2.** (*intr.*) to chatter or talk in this way; jabber. [C20: of imitative origin]
yak+ka, yak+ker, *or* **yack+er** ('jækə) *n. Austral. informal.* work. [C19: from a native Australian language]
Ya+kut (jæ'kʊt) *n.* **1.** (*pl.* **+kuts** *or* **+kut**) a native or inhabitant of the Yakut ASSR. **2.** the language of this people, belonging to the Turkic branch of the Altaic family.
Ya+kut Au+ton+o+mous So+vi+et So+cial+ist Re+pub+lic *n.* an administrative division of the E Soviet Union, in NE Siberia on the Arctic Ocean: the coldest inhabited region of the world. Capital: Yakutsk. Pop.: 664 123 (1970). Area: 3 103 000 sq. km (1 197 760 sq. miles).
Ya+kutsk (*Russian* jɪ'kutsk) *n.* a port in the E Soviet Union, capital of the Yakut ASSR, on the Lena River. Pop.: 139 000 (1975 est.).
Yale lock (jeɪl) *n. Trademark.* a type of cylinder lock using a flat serrated key.
Yal+ta (*Russian* 'jaltə) *n.* a port and resort in the SW Soviet Union, in the S Ukrainian SSR, in the Crimea on the Black Sea: scene of a conference (1945) between Churchill, Roosevelt, and Stalin, who met to plan the final defeat and occupation of Nazi Germany. Pop.: 62 170 (1970).
Ya·lu ('jɑːˌluː) *n.* a river in E Asia, rising in N North Korea and flowing southwest to Korea Bay, forming a large part of the border between North Korea and NE China. Length: 806 km (501 miles).
yam (jæm) *n.* **1.** any of various twining plants of the genus *Dioscorea,* of tropical and subtropical regions, cultivated for their edible tubers: family *Dioscoreaceae.* **2.** the starchy tuber of any of these plants, which is eaten as a vegetable. **3.** *Southern U.S.* any of certain large varieties of sweet potato. **4.** a Scot. name for the (common) **potato.** [C17: from Portuguese *inhame,* ultimately of West African origin; compare Senegal *nyami* to eat]
Yam·a·ga·ta (ˌjæmə'gɑːtə) *n.* Prince **A·ri·to·mo** (ˌærɪ'təʊməʊ). 1838–1922, Japanese soldier and politician. As war minister (1873) and chief of staff (1878), he modernized Japan's military system. He was premier of Japan (1889–93; 1898).
Ya·ma·ni (jə'mɑːnɪ) *n.* Sheikh **Ah·med Za·ki** ('ɑːmɛd 'zɑːkɪ). born 1930, Saudi Arabian politician; minister of petroleum and natural resources since 1962.
Yam·a·shi·ta (ˌjæmə'ʃiːtə) *n.* **To·mo·yu·ki** (ˌtəʊməʊ'juːkɪ). 1885–1946, Japanese general. He commanded Japanese forces in the Malayan campaign in World War II and took Singapore (1942); captured (1945) and hanged.
ya+men ('jɑːmɛn) *n.* (in imperial China) the office or residence of a public official. [C19: from Chinese, from *ya* general's office + *mĕn* gate]
yam+mer ('jæmə) *Informal.* ~*vb.* **1.** to utter or whine in a complaining or peevish manner. **2.** to make (a complaint) loudly or persistently. **3.** (*intr.*) (esp. of an animal) to howl or wail plaintively or distressingly; yelp or yowl. ~*n.* **4.** a yammering sound, wail, or utterance. **5.** nonsense; jabber. [Old English *geōmrian* to grumble, complain; related to Old High German *iāmar* misery, lamentation, Old Norse *amra* to howl] —**'yam+mer+er** *n.*
Yang[1] (jæŋ) *n.* See **Yin and Yang.**
Yang[2] (jæŋ) *n.* **Chen Ning** ('tʃɛn 'nɪŋ). born 1922, US physicist, born in China: with Tsung-Dao Lee, he disproved the physical principle known as the conservation of parity and shared the Nobel prize for physics (1957).
Yang+tze ('jæŋksɪ, 'jæŋktsɪ) *n.* the longest river in China, rising in SE Tsinghai province and flowing east to the East China Sea near Shanghai: a major commercial waterway in one of the most densely populated areas of the world. Length: 5528 km (3434 miles). Also called: **Yangtze Kiang, Chang Kiang, Chang.**
Ya+ni+na ('jɑːnɪnə) *n.* a variant spelling of **Ioánnina.**
yank (jæŋk) *vb.* **1.** to pull, jerk, or move with a sharp movement; tug. ~*n.* **2.** a sharp jerking movement; tug. [C19: of unknown origin]
Yank (jæŋk) *n.* **1.** a slang word for an American. **2.** *U.S. informal.* short for **Yankee.**
Yan+kee ('jæŋkɪ) *or* (*informal*) **Yank** *n.* **1.** *Often disparaging.* a native or inhabitant of the U.S.; American. **2.** a native or inhabitant of New England. **3.** a native or inhabitant of the Northern U.S., esp. a Northern soldier in the Civil War. ~*adj.* **4.** of, relating to, or characteristic of Yankees. [C18: perhaps from Dutch *Jan Kees* John Cheese, nickname used derisively by Dutch settlers in New York to designate English colonists in Connecticut]
Yan+kee Doo+dle *n.* **1.** an American song, popularly regarded

as a characteristically national melody. **2.** another name for **Yankee.**

Yan+kee+ism ('jæŋkɪɪzəm) *n.* **1.** Yankee character, behaviour, or attitudes. **2.** a typical Yankee word, expression, or trait.

Ya+oun+dé *or* **Ya+un+de** (*French* jaun'de) *n.* the capital of Cameroon, in the southwest: University of Cameroon (1962). Pop.: 165 810 (1969 est.).

yap (jæp) *vb.* **yaps, yap+ping, yapped.** (*intr.*) **1.** (of a dog) to bark in quick sharp bursts; yelp. **2.** *Informal.* to talk at length in an annoying or stupid way; jabber. ~*n.* **3.** a high-pitched or sharp bark; yelp. **4.** *Slang.* annoying or stupid speech; jabber. **5.** *Slang, chiefly U.S.* a derogatory word for **mouth.** ~*interj.* **6.** (*usually reiterated*) an imitation or representation of the sound of a dog yapping or people jabbering. [C17: of imitative origin] —**'yap+per** *n.* —**'yap+ping+ly** *adv.*

Yap (jɑːp, jæp) *n.* a group of four main islands in the W Pacific, in the W Caroline Islands: administratively a district of the U.S. Trust Territory of the Pacific Islands; important Japanese naval base in World War II. Pop.: 7369 (1971). Area: 101 sq. km (39 sq. miles).

ya+pok (jə'pɒk) *n.* an amphibious nocturnal opossum, *Chironectes minimus,* of Central and South America, having dense fur and preying on shrimps, crayfish, etc. Also called: **water opossum.** [C19: named after *Oyapok,* a river flowing between French Guiana and Brazil]

ya+pon ('jɔːpᵊn) *n.* a variant spelling of **yaupon.**

Ya+pu+rá (ˌjapu'ra) *n.* the Spanish name for **Japurá.**

Ya+qui (*Spanish* 'jaki) *n.* a river in NW Mexico, rising near the border with the U.S. and flowing south to the Gulf of California. Length: about 676 km (420 miles).

yar+bor+ough ('jɑːbərə, -brə) *n. Bridge, whist.* a hand of 13 cards in which no card is higher than nine. [C19: supposed to be named after the second Earl of *Yarborough* (died 1897), who is said to have bet a thousand to one against the occurrence of such a hand]

yard[1] (jɑːd) *n.* **1.** a unit of length equal to 3 feet and defined in 1963 as exactly 0.9144 metre. Abbrev.: **yd 2.** a cylindrical wooden or hollow metal spar, tapered at the ends, slung from a mast of a square-rigged or lateen-rigged vessel and used for suspending a sail. **3.** short for **yardstick** (sense 2). [Old English *gierd* rod, twig; related to Old Frisian *jerde,* Old Saxon *gerdia,* Old High German *gertia,* Old Norse *gaddr*]

yard[2] (jɑːd) *n.* **1.** a piece of enclosed ground, usually either paved or laid with concrete and often adjoining or surrounded by a building or buildings. **2. a.** an enclosed or open area used for some commercial activity, for storage, etc.: *a railway yard.* **b.** (*in combination*): *a brickyard; a shipyard.* **3.** a U.S. word for **garden** (sense 1). **4.** an area having a network of railway tracks and sidings, used for storing rolling stock, making up trains, etc. **5.** *U.S.* the winter pasture of deer, moose, and similar animals. **6.** *Austral.* an enclosed area used to draw off part of a herd, etc. [Old English *geard;* related to Old Saxon *gard,* Old High German *gart,* Old Norse *garthr* yard, Gothic *gards* house, Old Slavonic *gradu* town, castle, Albanian *garth* hedge]

Yard (jɑːd) *n.* **the.** *Brit. informal.* short for **Scotland Yard.**

yard+age[1] ('jɑːdɪdʒ) *n.* a length measured in yards.

yard+age[2] ('jɑːdɪdʒ) *n.* **1.** the use of a railway yard in the transportation of cattle. **2.** the charge for this.

yard+arm ('jɑːdˌɑːm) *n. Nautical.* the outer end of a yard, outside the sheave holes.

yard+bird ('jɑːdˌbɜːd) *n. U.S. military.* an inexperienced, untrained, or clumsy soldier, esp. one employed on menial duties.

yard grass *n.* an Old World perennial grass, *Eleusine indica,* with prostrate leaves, growing as a troublesome weed on open ground, yards, etc. Also called: **wire grass.**

yard of ale *n.* **1.** the beer or ale contained in a narrow horn-shaped drinking glass, usually about one yard long and holding between two and three pints. **2.** such a drinking glass itself.

yard+stick ('jɑːdˌstɪk) *n.* **1.** a measure or standard used for comparison: *on what kind of yardstick is he basing his criticism?* **2.** a graduated stick, one yard long, used for measurement.

yare (jɛə) *adj.* **yar+er, yar+est. 1.** *Archaic or dialect.* ready, brisk, or eager. **2.** (of a vessel) answering swiftly to the helm; easily handled. ~*adv.* **3.** *Obsolete.* readily or eagerly. [Old English *gearu* ready; related to Old Saxon, Old High German *garo* ready, prepared, Old Norse *gorr*] —**'yare+ly** *adv.*

Yar+kand (ˌjɑː'kænd) *n.* another name for **Soche.**

Yar+mouth ('jɑːməθ) *n.* short for **Great Yarmouth.**

yar+mul+ke ('jɑːməlkə) *n. Judaism.* a man's skullcap worn at prayer, esp. by adherents of Orthodox or Conservative Judaism, and by strongly religious Jews at all times. [from Yiddish, from Ukrainian and Polish *yarmulka* cap, probably from Turkish *yağmurluk* raincoat, from *yağmur* rain]

yarn (jɑːn) *n.* **1.** a continuous twisted strand of natural or synthetic fibres, used in weaving, knitting, etc. **2.** *Informal.* a long and often involved story or account, usually telling of incredible or fantastic events. **3. spin a yarn.** *Informal.* **a.** to tell such a story. **b.** to make up or relate a series of excuses. ~*vb.* **4.** (*intr.*) to tell such a story or stories. [Old English *gearn;* related to Old High German *garn* yarn, Old Norse *görn* gut, Greek *khordē* string, gut]

yarn-dyed *adj.* (of fabric) dyed while still in yarn form, before being woven. Compare **piece-dyed.**

Ya+ro+slavl (*Russian* jɪra'slavlj) *n.* a city in the W central Soviet Union, on the River Volga: a major trading centre since early times and one of the first industrial centres in Russia; textile industries. Pop.: 568 000 (1975 est.).

yar+row ('jærəʊ) *n.* any of several plants of the genus *Achillea,* esp. *A. millefolium,* of Eurasia, having finely dissected leaves and flat clusters of white flower heads: family *Compositae* (composites). Also called: **milfoil.** See also **sneezewort.** [Old English *gearwe;* related to Old High German *garwa,* Dutch *gerwe*]

yash+mak *or* **yash+mac** ('jæʃmæk) *n.* the face veil worn by Muslim women when in public. [C19: from Arabic]

yat·a+ghan ('jætəgən) *or* **at·a+ghan** *n.* a Turkish sword with a curved single-edged blade. [C19: from Turkish *yatağan*]

yate (jeɪt) *n. Austral.* any of several small eucalyptus trees, esp. *Eucalyptus cornuta,* yielding a very hard timber. [from a native Australian language]

yauld (jɔːd, jɑːd, jɑːld) *adj. Northern Brit. dialect.* alert, sprightly, or nimble. [C18: of unknown origin]

Ya+un+de (*French* jaun'de) *n.* a variant spelling of **Yaoundé.**

yaup (jɔːp) *vb., n.* a variant spelling of **yawp.** —**'yaup+er** *n.*

yau+pon *or* **ya+pon** ('jɔːpᵊn) *n.* a southern U.S. evergreen holly shrub, *Ilex vomitoria,* with spreading branches, scarlet fruits, and oval leaves: used as a substitute for tea. [from Catawba *yopun* shrub, diminutive of *yop* tree]

yau+ti·a ('jɔːtɪə) *n.* **1.** any of several West Indian aroid plants of the genus *Xanthosoma,* such as *X. sagittifolium,* cultivated for their edible leaves and underground stems. **2.** the leaves or underground stems of these plants, which can be eaten as vegetables. [C19: American Spanish, from Taino]

Ya+va+rí (ˌjaβa'ri) *n.* the Spanish name for **Javari.**

yaw (jɔː) *vb.* **1.** (*intr.*) (of an aircraft, missile, etc.) to turn about its vertical axis. Compare **pitch**[1] (sense 10), **roll** (sense 14). **2.** (*intr.*) (of a ship, etc.) to deviate temporarily from a straight course. **3.** (*tr.*) to cause (an aircraft, ship, etc.) to yaw. ~*n.* **4.** the angular movement of an aircraft, missile, etc., about its vertical axis. **5.** the deviation of a vessel from a straight course. [C16: of unknown origin]

Ya+wa+ta ('jɑːwɑːˌtɑː) *or* **Ya+ha+ta** *n.* a former city in Japan, on N Kyushu: merged with Moji, Kokura, Tobata, and Wakamatsu in 1963 to form **Kitakyushu.**

yawl[1] (jɔːl) *n.* **1.** a two-masted sailing vessel, rigged fore-and-aft, with a large mainmast and a small mizzenmast stepped aft of the rudderpost. Compare **ketch, sloop. 2.** a ship's small boat, usually rowed by four or six oars. [C17: from Dutch *jol* or Middle Low German *jolle,* of unknown origin]

yawl[2] (jɔːl) *vb.* (*intr.*) *Brit. dialect.* to howl, weep, or scream harshly; yowl. [C14: from Low German *jaulen;* see YOWL]

yawn (jɔːn) *vb.* **1.** (*intr.*) to open the mouth wide and take in air deeply, often as in involuntary reaction to tiredness, sleepiness, or boredom. **2.** (*tr.*) to express or utter while yawning. **3.** (*intr.*) to be open wide as if threatening to engulf (someone or something): *the mine shaft yawned below.* ~*n.* **4.** the act or an instance of yawning. [Old English *gionian;* related to Old Saxon *ginōn,* Old High German *ginēn* to yawn, Old Norse *gja* gap] —**'yawn+er** *n.* —**'yawn+ing+ly** *adv.*

yawp (jɔːp) *Brit. dialect and U.S. informal.* ~*vb.* (*intr.*) **1.** to gape or yawn, esp. audibly. **2.** to shout, cry, or talk noisily; bawl. **3.** to bark, yelp, or yowl. ~*n.* **4.** a shout, bark, yelp, or cry. **5.** a noisy, foolish, or raucous utterance. [C15 *yolpen,* probably of imitative origin; see YAP, YELP] —**'yawp+er** *n.*

yaws (jɔːz) *pl. n.* an infectious nonvenereal disease of tropical climates with early symptoms resembling syphilis, characterized by red skin eruptions and, later, pain in the joints: it is caused by the spiral bacterium *Treponema pertenue.* Also called: **framboesia.** [C17: of Carib origin]

y-ax·is *n.* a reference axis, usually vertical, of a graph or two- or three-dimensional Cartesian coordinate system along which the *y*-coordinate is measured.

Yazd (jɑːzd) *or* **Yezd** *n.* a city in central Iran: a major centre of silk weaving. Pop.: 150 531 (1966).

Yb *the chemical symbol for* ytterbium.

Y-chro·mo·some *n.* the sex chromosome that occurs as one of a pair with the X-chromosome in the diploid cells of the males of many animals, including humans. Compare **X-chromosome.**

y·clept (ɪ'klɛpt) *Obsolete.* ~*vb.* **1.** a past participle of **clepe.** ~*adj.* **2.** having the name of; called. [Old English *gecleopod,* past participle of *cleopian* to call]

Y con+nec+tion *n. Electrical engineering.* a three-phase star connection.

yd *or* **yd.** *abbrev. for* yard (measure).

ye[1] (jiː, *unstressed* jɪ) *pron.* **1.** *Archaic.* refers to more than one person including the person addressed but not including the speaker. **2.** Also: **ee** (iː). *Dialect.* refers to one person addressed: *I tell ye.* [Old English *gē;* related to Dutch *gij,* Old Norse *ēr,* Gothic *jus*]

ye[2] (ðiː, *spelling pron.* jiː) *determiner.* a form of **the**[1], used as a supposed archaism, esp. in conjunction with other putative archaic spellings: *ye olde oake.* [from a misinterpretation of *the* as written in some Middle English texts. The runic letter thorn (þ, representing *th*) was incorrectly transcribed as *y* because of a resemblance in their shapes]

yea (jeɪ) *sentence substitute.* **1.** a less common word for **aye** (yes). ~*adv.* **2.** (*sentence modifier*) *Archaic or literary.* indeed; truly: *yea, though my enemies spurn me, I shall prevail.* [Old English *gēa;* related to Old Frisian *jē,* Old Saxon, Old Norse, Old High German *jā,* Gothic *jai*]

yeah (jɛə) *sentence substitute. Informal.* yes.

yean (jiːn) *vb.* (of a sheep or goat) to give birth to (offspring).

[Old English *geēanian;* related to Dutch *oonen* to bring forth young, Latin *agnus* lamb; see EWE]
yean·ling ('ji:nlɪŋ) *n.* the young of a goat or sheep.
year (jɪə) *n.* **1.** Also called: **civil year.** the period of time, the **calendar year,** containing 365 days or in a **leap year** 366 days. It is based on the Gregorian calendar, being divided into 12 calendar months, and is reckoned from January 1 to December 31. **2.** a period of twelve months from any specified date, such as one based on the four seasons. **3.** a specific period of time, usually occupying a definite part or parts of a twelve-month period, used for some particular activity: *a school year.* **4.** Also called: **astronomical year, tropical year, equinoctial year.** the period of time, the **solar year,** during which the earth makes one revolution around the sun, measured between two successive vernal equinoxes: equal to 365.242 19 days. **5.** the period of time, the **sidereal year,** during which the earth makes one revolution around the sun, measured between two successive conjunctions of a particular star: equal to 365.256 36 days. **6.** the period of time, the **lunar year,** containing 12 lunar months and equal to 354.3671 days. **7.** the period of time taken by a specified planet to complete one revolution around the sun: *the Martian year.* **8.** (*pl.*) age, esp. old age: *a man of his years should be more careful.* **9.** (*pl.*) time: *in years to come.* **10.** a group of pupils or students, who are taught or study together, divided into classes at school: *they are the best year we've ever had for history.* **11. the year dot.** *Informal.* as long ago as can be remembered. **12. year and a day.** *English law.* a period fixed by law to ensure the completion of a full year. It is applied for certain purposes, such as to determine the time within which wrecks must be claimed. **13. year in, year out.** regularly or monotonously, over a long period. ~Related adj.: **annual.** [Old English *gear;* related to Gothic *jēr,* Old Saxon, Old High German *jār,* Old Norse *ār* year, Polish *jar* springtime, Latin *hōrnus* of this year]
Usage. In writing spans of years, it is important to choose a style that avoids ambiguity. The practice adopted in this dictionary is, in four-figure dates, to specify the last two digits of the second date if it falls within the same century as the first: *1801–08; 1850–51; 1899–1901.* In writing three-figure B.C. dates, it is advisable to give both dates in full: *159–156* B.C., not *159–56* B.C. unless of course the span referred to consists of 103 years rather than three years. It is also advisable to specify B.C. or A.D. in years under 1000 unless the context makes this self-evident.
year·book ('jɪəˌbʊk) *n.* an almanac or other reference book published annually and containing details of events of the previous year.
year·ling ('jɪəlɪŋ) *n.* **1.** the young of any of various animals, including the antelope and buffalo, between one and two years of age. **2.** a thoroughbred racehorse counted for racing purposes as being one year old until the second Jan. 1 following its birth. **3. a.** a bond that is intended to mature after one year. **b.** (*as modifier*): *yearling bonds.* ~*adj.* **4.** being a year old.
year·long ('jɪə'lɒŋ) *adj.* throughout a whole year.
year·ly ('jɪəlɪ) *adj.* **1.** occurring, done, appearing, etc., once a year or every year; annual. **2.** lasting or valid for a year; annual: *a yearly subscription.* ~*adv.* **3.** once a year; annually. ~*n., pl.* **·lies. 4.** a publication, event, etc., that occurs once a year.
yearn (jɜ:n) *vb.* (*intr.*) **1.** (usually foll. by *for* or *after* or an infinitive) to have an intense desire or longing (for); hanker or pine (for). **2.** to feel tenderness or affection. [Old English *giernan;* related to Old Saxon *girnian,* Old Norse *girna,* Gothic *gairnjan,* Old High German *gerōn* to long for, Sanskrit *haryati* he likes] —'**yearn·er** *n.*
yearn·ing ('jɜ:nɪŋ) *n.* an intense or overpowering longing, desire, or need; craving. —'**yearn·ing·ly** *adv.*
year of grace *n.* any year of the Christian era, as dated from the presumed date of Christ's birth.
year-round *adj.* open, in use, operating, etc., throughout the year.
yeast (ji:st) *n.* **1.** any of various single-celled ascomycetous fungi of the genus *Saccharomyces* and related genera, which reproduce by budding and are able to ferment sugars: a rich source of vitamins of the B complex. **2.** a commercial preparation containing yeast cells and inert material such as meal that is used in raising dough for bread and for fermenting beer, whisky, etc. See also **brewers' yeast. 3.** a preparation containing yeast cells, used to treat diseases caused by vitamin B deficiency. **4.** froth or foam, esp. on beer. ~*vb.* **5.** (*intr.*) to froth or foam. [Old English *giest;* related to Old Norse *jostr,* Old High German *jesan,* Swedish *esa,* Norwegian *asa,* Sanskrit *yasati*] —'**yeast·less** *adj.* —'**yeast·ˌlike** *adj.*
yeast cake *n. Chiefly U.S.* living yeast cells compressed with a little starch into a small cake, suitable for use in baking or brewing.
yeast·y ('ji:stɪ) *adj.* **yeast·i·er, yeast·i·est. 1.** of, resembling, or containing yeast. **2.** fermenting or causing fermentation. **3.** tasting of or like yeast. **4.** insubstantial or frivolous. **5.** restless, agitated, or unsettled. **6.** covered with or containing froth or foam. —'**yeast·i·ly** *adv.* —'**yeast·i·ness** *n.*
Yeats (jeɪts) *n.* **W(illiam) B(utler).** 1865–1939, Irish poet and dramatist. His collections of verse include *Responsibilities* (1914), *The Tower* (1928), and *The Winding Stair* (1929). Among his plays are *The Countess Cathleen* (1892; 1912) and *Cathleen ni Houlihan* (1902); he was a founder of the Irish National Theatre Company at the Abbey Theatre in Dublin. He won the Nobel prize for literature (1923).
yegg (jɛg) *n. Slang, chiefly U.S.* a burglar or safe-breaker. [C20: perhaps from the surname of a burglar]
Yeisk, Yeysk, *or* **Eisk** (*Russian* jejsk) *n.* a port and resort in the SW Soviet Union, on the Sea of Azov. Pop.: 64 418 (1970).
Ye·ka·te·rin·burg *or* **E·ka·te·rin·burg** (*Russian* jɪkətɪrim'burk) *n.* the former name (until 1924) of **Sverdlovsk.**
Ye·ka·te·ri·no·dar *or* **E·ka·te·ri·no·dar** (*Russian* jɪkətɪrina'dar) *n.* the former name (until 1920) of **Krasnodar.**
Ye·ka·te·ri·no·slav *or* **E·ka·te·ri·no·slav** (*Russian* jɪkətɪrina'slaf) *n.* the former name (1787–96, 1802–1926) of **Dnepropetrovsk.**
yeld (jɛld) *adj. Northern Brit. dialect.* **1.** (of an animal) barren or too young to bear young. **2.** (of a cow) not yielding milk. [Old English *gelde* barren; related to GELD[1]]
Ye·li·sa·vet·grad *or* **E·li·sa·vet·grad** (*Russian* jɪliza'vjɛtgrət) *n.* the former name (until 1924) of **Kirovograd.**
Ye·li·sa·vet·pol *or* **E·li·sa·vet·pol** (*Russian* jɪliza'vjɛtpəlj) *n.* the former name (until 1920) of **Kirovabad.**
Yelizaveta Petrovna *n.* See **Elizabeth**[2] (sense 3).
yelk (jɛlk) *n.* a dialect word for **yolk** (of an egg).
yell (jɛl) *vb.* **1.** to shout, scream, cheer, or utter in a loud or piercing way. ~*n.* **2.** a loud piercing inarticulate cry, as of pain, anger, or fear. **3.** *U.S.* a rhythmic cry of words or syllables, used in cheering in unison. [Old English *giellan;* related to Old Saxon *gellon,* Old High German *gellan,* Old Norse *gjalla;* see NIGHTINGALE] —'**yell·er** *n.*
yel·low ('jɛləʊ) *n.* **1.** any of a group of colours that vary in saturation but have the same hue. They lie in the approximate wavelength range 585–575 nanometres. Yellow is the complementary colour of blue and with cyan and magenta forms a set of primary colours. Related adj.: **xanthous. 2.** a pigment or dye of or producing these colours. **3.** yellow cloth or clothing: *dressed in yellow.* **4.** the yolk of an egg. **5.** a yellow ball in snooker, etc. ~*adj.* **6.** of the colour yellow. **7.** yellowish in colour or having parts or marks that are yellowish: *yellow jasmine.* **8.** having a yellowish skin; Mongoloid. **9.** *Informal.* cowardly or afraid. **10.** offensively sensational, as a cheap newspaper (esp. in the phrase **yellow press**). ~*vb.* **11.** to make or become yellow. [Old English *geolu;* related to Old Saxon, Old High German *gelo,* Old Norse *gulr,* Latin *helvus*] —'**yel·low·ish** *adj.* —'**yel·low·ness** *n.* —'**yel·low·y** *adj.*
yel·low·bark ('jɛləʊˌbɑ:k) *n.* another name for **calisaya.**
yel·low-bel·ly *n., pl.* **·lies.** a slang word for **coward.** —'**yel·low-ˌbel·lied** *adj.*
yel·low bel·ly *n. Austral.* any of several freshwater food fishes with yellow underparts.
yel·low bile *n. Archaic.* one of the four bodily humours, choler.
yel·low·bird ('jɛləʊˌbɜ:d) *n.* any of various birds having a yellow plumage, such as the American goldfinch.
yel·low cake *n. Canadian informal.* a uranium ore.
yel·low-dog con·tract *n. U.S.* a contract with an employer, now illegal, in which an employee agreed not to join a trade union during his employment.
yel·low fe·ver *n.* an acute infectious disease of tropical and subtropical climates, characterized by fever, haemorrhages, vomiting of blood, and jaundice: caused by a virus transmitted by the bite of a female mosquito of the species *Aedes aegypti.* Also called: **yellow jack, black vomit.**
yel·low·ham·mer ('jɛləʊˌhæmə) *n.* **1.** a European bunting, *Emberiza citrinella,* having a yellowish head and body and brown streaked wings and tail. **2.** *U.S.* an informal name for the **yellow-shafted flicker,** an American woodpecker (see **flicker**[2]).
yel·low jack *n.* **1.** *Pathol.* another name for **yellow fever. 2.** a yellow flag hoisted on a ship to warn of disease, etc. **3.** any of certain large yellowish carangid food fishes, esp. *Caranx bartholomaei,* of warm and tropical Atlantic waters.
yel·low jack·et *n. U.S.* any of several social wasps of the genus *Vespa,* having yellow markings on the body.
yel·low jas·mine *n.* a climbing shrub, *Gelsemium sempervirens,* of the southeastern U.S., having fragrant funnel-shaped yellow flowers: family *Loganiaceae.* See also **gelsemium.**
yel·low jour·nal·ism *n.* the type of journalism that relies on sensationalism and lurid exaggeration to attract readers. [C19: perhaps shortened from the phrase *Yellow Kid journalism,* referring to the *Yellow Kid,* a cartoon (1895) in the *New York World,* a newspaper having a reputation for sensationalism]
Yel·low·knife ('jɛləʊˌnaɪf) *n.* a city in N Canada, capital of the Northwest Territories on the Great Slave Lake. Pop.: 6122 (1971).
yel·low·legs ('jɛləʊˌlɛgz) *n.* either of two North American sandpipers, *Tringa melanoleuca* (or *Totanus melanoleucus*) (**greater yellowlegs**) or *T. flavipes* (**lesser yellowlegs**), having bright yellow legs.
yel·low line *n. Brit.* a yellow line painted along the edge of a road indicating waiting restrictions.
yel·low met·al *n.* **1.** a type of brass having about 60 per cent copper and 40 per cent zinc. **2.** another name for **gold.**
yel·low pag·es *pl. n.* a classified telephone directory or section of a directory that lists subscribers by the business or service provided.
yel·low per·il *n.* the power or alleged power of Asiatic peoples, esp. the Chinese, to threaten or destroy the supremacy of White or Western civilization.
yel·low pop·lar *n.* another name for **tulip tree** (sense 1) or **tulipwood** (sense 1).
Yel·low Riv·er *n.* the second longest river in China, rising in

SE Tsinghai and flowing east, south, and east again to the Gulf of Pohai south of Tientsin; it has changed its course several times in recorded history. Length: about 4350 km (2700 miles). Chinese name: **Hwang Ho.**

yel+lows ('jɛləʊz) *pl. n.* **1.** any of various fungal or viral diseases of plants, characterized by yellowish discoloration and stunting. **2.** *Vet. science.* another name for **jaundice.**

Yel+low Sea *n.* a shallow arm of the Pacific between Korea and NE China. Area: about 466 200 sq. km (180 000 sq. miles). Chinese name: **Hwang Hai.**

yel+low spot *n. Anatomy.* another name for **macula lutea.**

Yel·low+stone ('jɛləʊˌstəʊn) *n.* a river rising in N Wyoming and flowing north through Yellowstone National Park, then east to the Missouri. Length: 1080 km (671 miles).

Yel·low+stone Falls *pl. n.* a waterfall in NW Wyoming, in Yellowstone National Park on the Yellowstone River.

Yel·low+stone Na+tion+al Park *n.* a national park in the NW central U.S., mostly in NW Wyoming: the oldest and largest national park in the U.S., containing unusual geological formations and geysers. Area: 8956 sq. km (3458 sq. miles).

yel+low streak *n.* a cowardly or weak trait, characteristic, or flaw in a person's nature.

yel·low+tail ('jɛləʊˌteɪl) *n., pl.* **+tails** *or* **+tail. 1.** a carangid game fish, *Seriola dorsalis,* of coastal waters of S California and Mexico, having a yellow tail fin. **2.** any of various similar fishes.

yel+low wa+ter lil·y *n.* an aquatic nymphaeaceous plant, *Nuphar lutea,* of Europe and N Asia, having floating heart-shaped leaves and yellow flowers. Also called: **brandy bottle.**

yel·low+weed ('jɛləʊˌwi:d) *n.* any of various yellow-flowered plants, such as the ragwort in Europe and some species of goldenrod in the U.S.

yel·low+wood ('jɛləʊˌwʊd) *n.* **1.** Also called (U.S.): **gopherwood.** any of several leguminous trees of the genus *Cladrastis,* esp. *C. lutea,* of the southeastern U.S., having clusters of white flowers and yellow wood yielding a yellow dye. **2.** Also called: **West Indian satinwood.** a rutaceous tree, *Zanthoxylum flavum,* of the West Indies, with smooth hard wood. **3.** any of several other trees with yellow wood, esp. *Podocarpus falcatus,* a conifer of southern Africa: family *Podocarpaceae.* **4.** the wood of any of these trees.

yelp (jɛlp) *vb.* **1.** (esp. of a dog) to utter a sharp or high-pitched cry or bark, often indicating pain. *~n.* **2.** a sharp or high-pitched cry or bark. [Old English *gielpan* to boast; related to Low German *galpen* to croak, Danish *gylpe* to croak] **—'yelp+er** *n.*

Yem+en ('jɛmən) *n.* a republic in SW Arabia, on the Red Sea: declared a republic in 1962; consists of part of the Red Sea rift valley, with arid coastal lowlands, rising to fertile upland valleys and mountains, and the Great Sandy Desert in the east. Language: Arabic. Religion: Muslim. Currency: riyal. Capital: Sanaa. Pop.: 5 237 893 (1975). Area: 195 000 sq. km (75 290 sq. miles). Official name: **Yemen Arab Republic. —'Yem+e·ni** *adj., n.*

yen[1] (jɛn) *n., pl.* **yen.** the standard monetary unit of Japan, divided into 100 sen. [C19: from Japanese *en,* from Chinese *yüan* circular object, dollar]

yen[2] (jɛn) *Informal.* *~n.* **1.** a passionate, ardent, or intense longing or desire. *~vb.* **yens, yen+ning, yenned. 2.** (*intr.*) to yearn. [perhaps from Chinese (Cantonese) *yăn* a craving, addiction]

Yen+an ('jɛn'æn) *n.* a city in NE China, in N Shensi province: political and military capital of the Chinese Communists (1935–49). Pop.: 45 000 (1971 est.). Also called: **Fushih.**

Ye+ni+sei *or* **Ye+ni+sey** (ˌjɛnɪ'seɪ; *Russian* jɪni'sjej) *n.* a river in the central Soviet Union, in central Siberia, formed by the confluence of two headstreams in the Tuva ASSR: flows west and north to the Arctic Ocean; the largest river in volume in the Soviet Union. Length: 4129 km (2566 miles).

Yen+tai *or* **Yen-t'ai** ('jɛn'taɪ) *n.* a port in E China, in NE Shantung. Pop.: 140 000 (1958 est.). Also called: **Chefoo.**

yeo+man ('jəʊmən) *n., pl.* **+men. 1.** *History.* **a.** a member of a class of small freeholders of common birth who cultivated their own land. **b.** an assistant or other subordinate to an official, such as a sheriff, or to a craftsman or trader. **c.** an attendant or lesser official in a royal or noble household. **2.** (in Britain) another name for **yeoman of the guard. 3.** (*modifier*) characteristic of or relating to a yeoman. [C15: perhaps from *yongman* young man]

yeo+man+ly ('jəʊmənlɪ) *adj.* **1.** of, relating to, or like a yeoman. **2.** having the virtues attributed to yeomen, such as staunchness, loyalty, and courage. *~adv.* **3.** in a yeomanly manner, as in being brave, staunch, or loyal.

yeo+man of the guard *n.* a member of the bodyguard (**Yeomen of the Guard**) of the English monarch. This unit was founded in 1485 and now retains ceremonial functions only.

yeo+man+ry ('jəʊmənrɪ) *n.* **1.** yeomen collectively. **2.** (in Britain) a volunteer cavalry force, organized in 1761 for home defence: merged into the Territorial Army in 1907.

yep (jɛp) *sentence substitute.* an informal word for **yes.**

yer+ba *or* **yer+ba ma·té** ('jɛəbə, 'jɜ:bə) *n.* another name for **maté.** [from Spanish *yerba maté* herb maté]

Ye+re+van (*Russian* jɪrɪ'van) *n.* an industrial city in the SW Soviet Union, capital of the Armenian SSR: founded in the 8th century B.C.; a main focus of trade routes since ancient times; university. Pop.: 899 000 (1975 est.). Also called: **Erevan** or **Erivan.**

Yer·wa-Mai·du·gu+ri ('jɜ:wəˌmaɪdʊ'gu:rɪ) *n.* another name for **Maiduguri.**

yes (jɛs) *sentence substitute.* **1.** used to express acknowledgment, affirmation, consent, agreement, or approval or to answer when one is addressed. **2.** used, often with interrogative intonation, to signal someone to speak or keep speaking, enter a room, or do something. *~adv.* **3.** (*sentence modifier*) used to emphasize a positive statement, esp. when disagreeing: *yes I can.* *~n.* **4.** an answer or vote of *yes.* **5.** (*often pl.*) a person who votes in the affirmative. ~Compare **no**[1]. [Old English *gēse,* from *iā sīe* may it be; see YEA]

ye+shi+va (jə'ʃi:və; *Hebrew* jə'ʃi:va) *n., pl.* **+vahs** *or* **+voth** (*Hebrew* -vɔt). **1.** a traditional Jewish school devoted chiefly to the study of rabbinic literature and the Talmud. **2.** a school run by Orthodox Jews for children of elementary school age, providing both religious and secular instruction. [from Hebrew *yĕshībhāh* a sitting, seat, hence, an academy]

Ye+şil Ir+mak (jɛ'ʃi:l ɪə'mɑ:k) *n.* a river in N Turkey, flowing northwest to the Black Sea. Length: 418 km (260 miles). Ancient name: **Iris.**

Ye+şil+köy (ˌjɛʃi:l'kɔɪ) *n.* the Turkish name for **San Stefano.**

yes man *n.* a servile, submissive, or acquiescent subordinate, assistant, or associate; sycophant.

yes+ter ('jɛstə) *adj. Archaic.* of or relating to yesterday: *yester sun.* Also: **yes+tern** ('jɛstən). [Old English *geostror;* related to Old High German *gestaron,* Gothic *gistra,* Old Norse *ī gǣr*]

yes·ter- *prefix.* **1.** indicating the day before today: *yesterday.* **2.** indicating a period of time before the present one: *yesteryear.* [Old English *geostran;* compare German *gestern,* Latin *hesternus* of yesterday]

yes+ter+day ('jɛstəˌdɪ, -ˌdeɪ) *n.* **1.** the day immediately preceding today. **2.** (*often pl.*) the recent past. *~adv.* **3.** on or during the day before today. **4.** in the recent past.

yes+ter+year ('jɛstəˌjɪə) *Formal or literary.* *~n.* **1.** last year or the past in general. *~adv.* **2.** during last year or the past in general.

yes+treen (jɛ'stri:n) *adv. Scot.* yesterday evening. [C14: from YEST(E)R- + E(V)EN[2]]

yet (jɛt) **1.** *sentence connector.* nevertheless; still; in spite of that: *I want to and yet I haven't the courage; she is strange yet kind.* *~adv.* **2.** (*usually used with a negative or interrogative*) so far; up until then or now: *they're not home yet; is it teatime yet?* **3.** (often preceded by *just; usually used with a negative*) now (as contrasted with later): *we can't stop yet.* **4.** (*often used with a comparative*) even; still: *yet more potatoes for sale; yet another problem family.* **5.** eventually, in spite of everything: *we'll convince him yet.* **6. as yet.** so far; up until then or now. [Old English *gēta;* related to Old Frisian *jēta*]

yet·i ('jɛtɪ) *n.* another term for **abominable snowman.** [C20: from Tibetan]

Yev·tu·shen·ko (ˌjɛvtu:'ʃɛŋkəʊ; *Russian* jɪftu'ʃɛnkə) *n.* **Yev·ge·ny A·le·ksan·dro·vich** (jɪv'gjenij alɪ'ksandrəvitʃ). born 1933, Soviet poet. His often outspoken poetry includes *Babi Yar* (1962) and *Bratsk Station* (1966).

yew (ju:) *n.* **1.** any coniferous tree of the genus *Taxus,* of the Old World and North America, esp. *T. baccata,* having flattened needle-like leaves, fine-grained elastic wood, and cuplike red waxy cones resembling berries: family *Taxaceae.* **2.** the wood of any of these trees, used to make bows for archery. **3.** *Archery.* a bow made of yew. [Old English *īw;* related to Old High German *īwa,* Old Norse *ȳr* yew, Latin *ūva* grape, Russian *iva* willow]

Yezd (jɛzd) *n.* a variant spelling of **Yazd.**

Y·gerne (i:'geən) *n.* a variant spelling of **Igraine.**

Ygg+dra+sil, Yg+dra+sil, *or* **Ig+dra+sil** ('ɪgdrəsɪl) *n. Norse myth.* the ash tree that was thought to overshadow the whole world, binding together earth, heaven, and hell with its roots and branches. [Old Norse (probably meaning: Uggr's horse), from *Uggr* a name of Odin, from *yggr, uggr* frightful + *drasill* horse, of obscure origin]

Y.H.A. (in Britain) *abbrev. for* Youth Hostels Association.

YHVH, YHWH, JHVH, *or* **JHWH** *Old Testament.* the letters of the **Tetragrammaton.** See also **Yahweh, Jehovah.**

yid (jɪd) *n. Slang.* a derogatory word for a Jew. [C20: probably from *Yiddish,* from Middle High German *Jude* JEW]

Yid+dish ('jɪdɪʃ) *n.* a language spoken as a vernacular by Jews in Europe and elsewhere by Jewish emigrants, usually written in the Hebrew alphabet. Historically, it is a dialect of High German with an admixture of words of Hebrew, Romance, and Slavonic origin, developed in central and E Europe during the Middle Ages. [C19: from German *jüdisch,* from *Jude* JEW]

yield (ji:ld) *vb.* **1.** to give forth or supply (a product, result, etc.), esp. by cultivation, labour, etc.; produce or bear. **2.** (*tr.*) to furnish as a return: *the shares yielded three per cent.* **3.** (*tr.;* often foll. by *up*) to surrender or relinquish, esp. as a result of force, persuasion, etc. **4.** (*intr.;* sometimes foll. by *to*) to give way, submit, or surrender, as through force or persuasion: *she yielded to his superior knowledge.* **5.** (*intr.;* often foll. by *to*) to agree; comply; assent: *he eventually yielded to their request for money.* **6.** (*tr.*) to grant or allow; concede: *to yield right of way.* **7.** (*tr.*) *Obsolete.* to pay or repay: *God yield thee!* *~n.* **8.** the result, product, or amount yielded. **9.** the profit or return, as from an investment or tax. **10.** the annual income provided by an investment, usually expressed as a percentage of its cost or of its current value: *the yield on these shares is 15 per cent at today's market value.* **11.** the energy released by the explosion of a nuclear weapon. **12.** *Chem.* the quantity of a specified product obtained in a reaction or series of reactions, usually expressed as a percentage of the quantity that is theoretically obtainable. [Old English *gieldan;* related to Old Frisian *jelda,* Old High German *geltan,* Old Norse *gjalda,* Gothic *gildan*] **—'yield+a·ble** *adj.* **—'yield+er** *n.*

yield·ing ('ji:ldɪŋ) *adj.* **1.** compliant, submissive, or flexible. **2.** pliable or soft: *a yielding material.* —'**yield·ing·ly** *adv.* —'**yield·ing·ness** *n.*

yield point *n.* the stress at which certain materials, such as steel, suffer a large elongation that is independent of the applied load. Also called: **yield stress, yield strength.**

yike (jaɪk) *Austral. informal.* ~*n.* **1.** an argument, squabble, or fight. ~*vb.* **2.** to argue, squabble, or fight. [origin unknown]

Yin and Yang (jɪn) *n.* two complementary principles of Chinese philosophy: Yin is negative, dark, and feminine, Yang positive, bright, and masculine. Their interaction is thought to maintain the harmony of the universe and to influence everything within it. [from Chinese (Peking) *yin* dark + *yang* bright]

Yin·chuan, Yin-ch'uan, *or* **Yin·chwan** ('jɪn'tʃwɑ:n) *n.* a city in N central China, capital of the Ningsia Hui AR, on the Yellow River. Pop.: 90 000 (1957 est.).

Ying·kow *or* **Ying-k'ou** ('jɪŋ'kaʊ) *n.* a port in NE China, in SW Liaoning province: a major shipping centre for Manchuria. Pop.: 131 400 (1953).

yip·pee (jɪ'pi:) *interj.* an exclamation of joy, pleasure, anticipation, etc.

yirr (jɜ:) *vb.* (*intr.*) *Brit. dialect, chiefly Scot.* to snarl, growl, or yell. [C18: perhaps from Old English *georran, gyrran* to growl, of imitative origin]

-yl *suffix of nouns.* (in chemistry) indicating a group or radical: *methyl; carbonyl.* [from Greek *hulē* wood, matter]

y·lang-y·lang *or* **i·lang-i·lang** ('i:læŋ'i:læŋ) *n.* **1.** an aromatic Asian tree, *Cananga odorata* (or *Canangium odoratum*), with fragrant greenish-yellow flowers yielding a volatile oil: family *Annonaceae.* **2.** the oil obtained from this tree, used in perfumery. [C19: from Tagalog *ilang-ilang*]

y·lem ('aɪləm) *n.* the original matter from which the basic elements are said to have been formed following the explosion postulated in the big bang theory of cosmology. [Middle English, from Old French *ilem,* from Latin *hȳlē* stuff, matter, from Greek *hulē*; see HYLE]

Y-lev·el *n. Surveying.* a level mounted on a Y-shaped support that can be rotated.

Y.M.C.A. *abbrev. for* Young Men's Christian Association.

Y.M.H.A. *abbrev. for* Young Men's Hebrew Association.

Y·mir ('i:mɪə) *or* **Y·mer** ('i:mə) *n. Norse myth.* the first being and forefather of the giants. He was slain by Odin and his brothers, who made the earth from his flesh, the water from his blood, and the sky from his skull.

-yne *suffix forming nouns.* denoting an organic chemical containing a triple bond: *alkyne.* [alteration of -INE²]

yob (jɒb) *or* **yob·bo** ('jɒbəʊ) *n., pl.* **yobs** *or* **yob·bos.** *Brit. slang.* an aggressive and surly youth, esp. a teenager. [C19: perhaps back slang for BOY]

yod *or* **yodh** (jʊd) *n.* the tenth letter in the Hebrew alphabet (י), transliterated as *y.* [C18: from Hebrew, literally: hand]

yo·del ('jəʊdᵊl) *n.* **1.** an effect produced in singing by an abrupt change of register from the chest voice to falsetto, esp. in popular folk songs of the Swiss Alps. ~*vb.* **·dels, ·del·ling, ·delled** *or U.S.* **·dels, ·del·ing, ·deled. 2.** to sing (a song) in which a yodel is used. [C19: from German *jodeln,* of imitative origin] —'**yo·del·ler** *n.*

yo·dle ('jəʊdᵊl) *n.* a variant spelling of **yodel.** —'**yo·dler** *n.*

yo·ga ('jəʊgə) *n.* (*often cap.*) **1.** a Hindu system of philosophy aiming at the mystical union of the self with the Supreme Being in a state of complete awareness and tranquillity through certain physical and mental exercises. **2.** any method by which such awareness and tranquillity are attained, esp. a course of related exercises and postures designed to promote physical and spiritual wellbeing. [C19: from Sanskrit: a yoking, union, from *yunakti* he yokes] —**yo·gic** ('jəʊgɪk) *adj.* —'**yo·gism** *n.*

yogh (jɒg) *n.* **1.** a character (ʒ) used in Old and Middle English to represent a palatal fricative very close to the semivowel sound of Modern English *y,* as in Old English *ʒeong* (young). **2.** this same character as used in Middle English for both the voiced and voiceless palatal fricatives; when final or in a closed syllable in medial position the sound approached that of German *ch* in *ich,* as in *knyʒt* (knight). After the 14th century this symbol became the modern consonantal (semivocalic) *y* when initial or commencing a syllable, and though no longer pronounced in medial position it is preserved in many words by a modern *gh,* as in *thought.* [C14: perhaps from *yok* YOKE, referring to the letter's shape]

yo·ghurt *or* **yo·gurt** ('jɒgət) *n.* a thick custard-like food prepared from milk that has been curdled by bacteria, often sweetened and flavoured with fruit, chocolate, etc. [C19: from Turkish *yoğurt*]

yo·gi ('jəʊgɪ) *n., pl.* **·gis** *or* **·gin** (-gɪn). a person who is a master of yoga. —**yo·gi·ni** (jəʊ'gi:ni:) *fem. n.*

yo-heave-ho (ˌjəʊhi:v'həʊ) *interj.* a cry formerly used by sailors while pulling or lifting together in rhythm.

yo·him·bine (jəʊ'hɪmbi:n) *n.* an alkaloid found in the bark of the tree *Corynanthe yohimbe.* It is used in medicine as an adrenergic blocking agent. Formula: $C_{21}H_{26}N_2O_3$. [C19: from Bantu *yohimbé* a tropical African tree + -INE¹]

yo-ho-ho *interj.* **1.** an exclamation to call attention. **2.** another word for **yo-heave-ho.**

yoicks (haɪk; *spelling pron.* jɔɪks) *interj.* a cry used by huntsmen to urge on the hounds to the fox.

yoke (jəʊk) *n., pl.* **yokes** *or* **yoke. 1.** a wooden frame, usually consisting of a bar with an oxbow or similar collar-like piece at either end, for attaching to the necks of a pair of draught animals, esp. oxen, so that they can be worked as a team. **2.** something resembling a yoke in form or function, such as a frame fitting over a person's shoulders for carrying buckets suspended at either end. **3.** an immense oppressive force or burden: *under the yoke of a tyrant.* **4.** a pair of oxen or other draught animals joined together by a yoke. **5.** a part, esp. one of relatively thick cross section, that secures two or more components so that they move together. **6.** a crosshead that transmits the drive of an opposed piston engine from the upper of a pair of linked pistons to the crankshaft through a connecting rod. **7.** *Nautical.* a crossbar fixed athwartships to the head of a rudderpost in a small boat, to which are attached ropes or cables for steering. **8.** a Y-shaped cable, rope, or chain, used for holding, towing, etc. **9.** a fitted part of a garment, esp. around the neck, shoulders, and chest or around the hips, to which a gathered, pleated, flared, or unfitted part is attached. **10.** (in the ancient world) a symbolic reconstruction of a yoke, consisting of two upright spears with a third lashed across them, under which conquered enemies were compelled to march, esp. in Rome. **11.** a mark, token, or symbol of slavery, subjection, or suffering. **12.** *Now rare.* a link, tie, or bond: *the yoke of love.* **13.** *Brit. dialect.* a period of steady work, esp. the time during which a ploughman and his team work at a stretch. ~*vb.* **14.** (*tr.*) to secure or harness (a draught animal) to a (plough, vehicle, etc.) by means of a yoke. **15.** to join or be joined by means of a yoke; couple, unite, or link. **16.** (*tr.*) *Obsolete.* to oppress, burden, or enslave. [Old English *geoc;* related to Old High German *ioh,* Old Norse *ok,* Gothic *juk,* Latin *iugum,* Sanskrit *yugam*] —'**yoke·less** *adj.*

yo·kel ('jəʊkᵊl) *n. Disparaging.* (used chiefly by townspeople) a person who lives in the country, esp. one who is simple and old-fashioned. [C19: perhaps from dialect *yokel* green woodpecker, yellowhammer] —'**yo·kel·ish** *adj.*

Yo·ko·ha·ma (ˌjəʊkəʊ'hɑ:mə) *n.* a port in central Japan, on SE Honshu on Tokyo Bay: a major port and the country's third largest city situated in the largest and most populous industrial region of Japan. Pop.: 2 620 000 (1975).

Yo·la ('jəʊlə) *n.* a market town in E Nigeria, capital of Gongola state. Pop.: 8 573 (1963).

yolk (jəʊk) *n.* **1.** the substance in an animal ovum consisting of protein and fat that nourishes the developing embryo. **2.** a greasy substance secreted by the skin of a sheep and present in the fleece. [Old English *geoloca,* from *geolu* YELLOW] —'**yolk·less** *adj.* —'**yolk·y** *adj.*

yolk sac *n. Zoology.* **1.** the membranous sac that is attached to the ventral surface of the embryos of birds, reptiles, and some fishes and contains yolk. **2.** the corresponding part in the embryo of mammals, which contains no yolk.

Yom Kip·pur (jɒm 'kɪpə; *Hebrew* jɔm ki'pur) *n.* an annual Jewish holiday celebrated on Tishri 10 as a day of fasting, on which prayers of penitence are recited in the synagogue throughout the day. Also called: **Day of Atonement.** [from Hebrew, from *yōm* day + *kippūr* atonement]

Yom Kip·pur War *n.* a war in which Egypt and Syria launched a joint surprise attack on Israel on the Jewish festival of Yom Kippur (Oct. 6, 1973). It ended with a ceasefire (Oct. 25, 1973), Syrian forces having been repulsed, Egypt having reoccupied a belt of the Sinai desert on the E bank of the Suez Canal, and Israel having established a salient on the W bank.

yomp (jɒmp) *vb.* to walk or trek laboriously, esp. heavily laden and over difficult terrain. [C20: military slang, of uncertain origin]

yon (jɒn) *or* **yond** (jɒnd) *determiner.* **1.** *Chiefly Northern Brit.* **a.** an archaic or dialect word for **that:** *yon man.* **b.** (*as pronoun*): *yon's a fool.* ~ **2.** variants of **yonder.** [Old English *geon;* related to Old Frisian *jen,* Old High German *jenēr,* Old Norse *enn,* Gothic *jains*]

yon·der ('jɒndə) *adv.* **1.** at, in, or to that relatively distant place; over there. ~*determiner.* **2.** being at a distance, either within view or as if within view: *yonder valleys.* [C13: from Old English *geond* yond; related to Old Saxon *jendra,* Old High German *jenēr,* Gothic *jaind*]

yo·ni ('jəʊnɪ) *n. Hinduism.* **1.** the female genitalia, regarded as a divine symbol of sexual pleasure and matrix of generation and the visible form of Sakti. **2.** an image of these as an object of worship. [C18: from Sanskrit, literally: vulva, womb]

Yon·kers ('jɒŋkəz) *n.* a city in SE New York State, near New York City on the Hudson River. Pop.: 195 542 (1973 est.).

Yonne (*French* jɔn) *n.* **1.** a department of N central France, in Burgundy region. Capital: Auxerre. Pop.: 297 851 (1975). Area: 7461 sq. km (2910 sq. miles). **2.** a river in N France, flowing generally northwest to the Seine at Montereau. Length: 290 km (180 miles).

yon·nie ('jɒnɪ) *n. Austral., children's slang.* a stone. [from a native Australian language]

yoo-hoo ('ju:ˌhu:) *interj.* a call to attract a person's attention.

yore (jɔ:) *n.* **1.** time long past (now only in the phrase **of yore**). ~*adv.* **2.** *Obsolete.* in the past; long ago. [Old English *geāra,* genitive plural of *gēar* YEAR; see HOUR]

york (jɔ:k) *vb.* (*tr.*) *Cricket.* to bowl or try to bowl (a batsman) by pitching the ball under or just beyond the bat. [C19: back formation from YORKER]

York¹ (jɔ:k) *n.* **1.** a walled city in NE England, in North Yorkshire, on the River Ouse: the military capital of Roman Britain; capital of the N archiepiscopal province of Britain since 625, with a cathedral (the Minster) begun in 1154; noted for its cycle of medieval mystery plays; university (1963). Pop.: 104 513 (1971). Latin name: **Eboracum. 2. Cape.** a cape in NE Australia, in Queensland at the N tip of Cape York Peninsula, extending into Torres Strait: the northernmost point of Australia.

York² (jɔ:k) *n.* **1.** the English royal house, a branch of the

Plantagenet line, that reigned from 1461 to 1485. **2. Al·vin C(ullum).** 1887–1964, U.S. soldier and hero of World War I.

Yorke Pen+in+su+la (jɔ:k) *n.* a peninsula in South Australia, between Spencer Gulf and St. Vincent Gulf: mainly agricultural with several coastal resorts.

york+er (jɔ:kə) *n. Cricket.* a ball bowled so as to pitch just under or just beyond the bat. [C19: probably named after the *Yorkshire* County Cricket Club]

York+ist ('jɔ:kɪst) *English history* ~*n.* **1.** a member or adherent of the royal house of York, esp. during the wars of the Roses. ~*adj.* **2.** of, belonging to, or relating to the supporters or members of the house of York.

Yorks. (jɔ:ks) *abbrev. for* Yorkshire.

York+shire ('jɔ:kʃɪə, -ʃə) *n.* a former county of N England: it was the largest English county, divided administratively into East, West, and North Ridings. In 1974 it was much reduced in size and divided into North, West, and South Yorkshire.

York+shire Dales *pl. n.* the valleys of the rivers flowing from the Pennines in W Yorkshire: chiefly Airedale, Ribbledale, Teesdale, Swaledale, Nidderdale, Wharfedale, and Wensleydale; tourist area. Also called: **the Dales.**

York+shire pud+ding *n. Chiefly Brit.* a light puffy baked pudding made from a batter of flour, eggs, and milk, traditionally served with roast beef.

York+shire ter+ri+er *n.* a very small breed of terrier with a long straight glossy coat.

York+town ('jɔ:kˌtaʊn) *n.* a village in SE Virginia: scene of the surrender (1781) of the British under Cornwallis to the Americans under Washington at the end of the War of American Independence.

Yo+ru+ba ('jɒrʊbə) *n.* **1.** (*pl.* **+bas** *or* **+ba**) a member of a Negroid people of W Africa, living chiefly in the coastal regions of SW Nigeria: noted for their former city states and complex material culture, particularly as evidenced in their music, art, and sculpture. **2.** the language of this people, belonging to the Kwa branch of the Niger-Congo family. —**'Yo+ru+ban** *adj.*

Yo+sem·i+te Falls (jəʊ'sɛmɪtɪ) *pl. n.* a series of waterfalls in central California, in the Yosemite National Park, with a total drop of 770 m (2525 ft.): includes the **Upper Yosemite Falls,** 436 m (1430 ft.) high, and the **Lower Yosemite Falls,** 98 m (320 ft.) high.

Yo+sem·i+te Na+tion+al Park *n.* a national park in central California, in the Sierra Nevada Mountains: contains the **Yosemite Valley,** at an altitude of about 1200 m (4000 ft.), with sheer walls rising about another 1200 m (4000 ft.). Area: 3061 sq. km (1182 sq. miles).

Yo·shi·hi·to (ˌjɒʃɪ'hi:təʊ) *n.* See **Taisho.**

Yosh·kar-O·la (*Russian* jaʃ'kar a'la) *n.* a city in the W Soviet Union, capital of the Mari ASSR. Pop.: 202 000 (1975 est.).

you (ju:; *unstressed* jʊ) *pron.* (*subjective or objective*) **1.** refers to the person addressed or to more than one person including the person or persons addressed but not including the speaker: *you know better; the culprit is among you.* **2.** Also: **one.** refers to an unspecified person or people in general: *you can't tell the boys from the girls.* **3.** *Chiefly U.S.* a dialect word for **yourself** or **yourselves** when used as an indirect object: *you should get you a wife now.* ~*n.* **4.** *Informal.* the personality of the person being addressed or something that expresses it: *that hat isn't really you.* **5. you know what** *or* **who.** a thing or person that the speaker cannot or does not want to specify. [Old English *ēow,* dative and accusative of *gē* YE[1]; related to Old Saxon *eu,* Old High German *iu,* Gothic *izwis*]
Usage. See at **me.**

you-all a U.S., esp. Southern, word for **you,** esp. when addressing more than one person.

you'd (ju:d; *unstressed* jʊd) *contraction of* you had *or* you would.

you'll (ju:l; *unstressed* jʊl) *contraction of* you will *or* you shall.

young (jʌŋ) *adj.* **young+er** ('jʌŋgə), **young+est** ('jʌŋgɪst). **1. a.** having lived, existed, or been made or known for a relatively short time: *a young man; a young movement; a young country.* **b.** (*as collective n.;* preceded by *the*): *the young.* **2.** youthful or having qualities associated with youth; vigorous or lively: *she's very young for her age.* **3.** of or relating to youth: *in my young days.* **4.** having been established or introduced for a relatively short time: *a young member.* **5.** in an early stage of progress or development; not far advanced: *the day was young.* **6.** *Geography.* **a.** (of mountains) formed in the Alpine orogeny and still usually rugged in outline. **b.** another term for **youthful** (sense 4). **7.** (*often cap.*) of or relating to a rejuvenated group or movement or one claiming to represent the younger members of the population, esp. one adhering to a political ideology: *Young England; Young Socialists.* ~*n.* **8.** (*functioning as pl.*) offspring, esp. young animals: *a rabbit with her young.* **9. with young.** (of animals) pregnant. [Old English *geong;* related to Old Saxon, Old High German *iung,* Old Norse *ungr,* Latin *iuvenis,* Sanskrit *yuvan*] —**'young+ish** *adj.*

Young (jʌŋ) *n.* **1. Brig·ham.** 1801–77, U.S. Mormon leader, who led the Mormon migration to Utah and founded Salt Lake City (1847). **2. Ed·ward.** 1683–1765, English poet and dramatist, noted for his *Night Thoughts on Life, Death, and Immortality* (1742–45). **3. Thom·as.** 1773–1829, English physicist, physician, and Egyptologist. He helped to establish the wave theory of light by his experiments on optical interference and assisted in the decipherment of the Rosetta Stone.

young+ber·ry ('jʌŋbərɪ, -brɪ) *n., pl.* **·ries. 1.** a trailing bramble of the southwestern U.S. that is a hybrid of a blackberry and dewberry with large sweet dark purple fruits. **2.** the fruit of this plant.

young blood *n.* young, fresh, or vigorous new people, ideas, attitudes, etc.

Young Ire+land *n.* a movement or party of Irish patriots in the 1840s who split with Daniel O'Connell because they favoured a more violent policy than that which he promoted.

young la·dy *n.* a girlfriend; sweetheart.

young+ling ('jʌŋlɪŋ) *n.* **1.** *Literary.* **a.** a young person, animal, or plant. **b.** (*as modifier*): *a youngling brood.* **2.** *Rare.* a beginner; novice. [Old English *geongling*]

young man *n.* a boyfriend; sweetheart.

Young Pre+tend+er *n.* See (Charles Edward) **Stuart.**

Young's mod·u+lus *n.* a modulus of elasticity, applicable to the stretching of a wire etc., equal to the ratio of the applied load per unit area of cross section to the increase in length per unit length. Symbol: *E*

young+ster ('jʌŋstə) *n.* **1.** a young person; child or youth. **2.** a young animal, esp. a horse.

Youngs+town ('jʌŋzˌtaʊn) *n.* a city in NE Ohio: a major centre of steel production: university (1908). Pop.: 133 452 (1973 est.).

Young Turk *n.* **1.** a progressive, revolutionary, or rebellious member of an organization, political party, etc., esp. one agitating for radical reform. **2.** a member of an abortive reform movement in the Ottoman Empire, originally made up of exiles in W Europe who advocated liberal reforms. The movement fell under the domination of young Turkish army officers of a nationalist bent, who wielded great influence in the government between 1908 and 1918.

youn+ker ('jʌŋkə) *n.* **1.** *Archaic or literary.* a young man; lad. **2.** *Obsolete.* a young gentleman or knight. [C16: from Dutch *jonker,* from Middle Dutch *jonc* YOUNG]

your (jɔ:, jʊə; *unstressed* jə) *determiner.* **1.** of, belonging to, or associated with you: *your nose; your house; your first taste of freedom.* **2.** belonging to or associated with an unspecified person or people in general: *the path is on your left heading north; this lotion is for your head only.* **3.** *Informal.* used to indicate all things or people of a certain type: *your part-time worker is a problem.* **4. your actual.** *Brit. informal.* (intensifier): *here is your actual automatic tin-opener.* [Old English *eower,* genitive of *gē* YE[1]; related to Old Frisian *jūwe,* Old Saxon *euwa,* Old High German *iuwēr*]

you're (jʊə, jɔ:; *unstressed* jə) *contraction of* you are.

yours (jɔ:z, jʊəz) *pron.* **1.** something or someone belonging to or associated in some way with you: *I've eaten yours.* **2.** your family: *greetings to you and yours.* **3.** used in conventional closing phrases at the end of a letter: *yours sincerely, yours faithfully.* **4. of yours.** belonging to or associated with you. **5. what's yours?** *Jocular.* what would you like to drink?

your+self (jɔ:'sɛlf jʊə-) *pron., pl.* **+selves. 1. a.** the reflexive form of *you.* **b.** (intensifier): *you yourself control your destiny.* **2.** (*preceded by a copula*) your normal or usual self: *you're not yourself these days.*
Usage. See at **myself.**

yours tru+ly *pron.* an informal term for *I, myself,* or *me.* [from the conventional closing phrase used at the end of letters]

youth (ju:θ) *n., pl.* **youths** (ju:ðz). **1.** the quality or condition of being young, immature, or inexperienced: *his youth told against him in the contest.* **2.** the period between childhood and maturity, esp. adolescence and early manhood. **3.** the freshness, vigour, or vitality characteristic of young people: *youth shone out from her face.* **4.** any period of early development: *the project was in its youth.* **5.** a young person, esp. a young man or boy. **6.** young people collectively: *youth everywhere is rising in revolt.* [Old English *geogoth;* related to Old Frisian *jogethe,* Old High German *iugund,* Gothic *junda,* Latin *juventus*] —**'youth+less** *adj.*

youth club *n.* a centre providing leisure activities for young people, often associated with a church or community centre.

youth+ful ('ju:θfʊl) *adj.* **1.** of, relating to, possessing, or characteristic of youth. **2.** fresh, vigorous, or active: *he's surprisingly youthful for his age.* **3.** in an early stage of development: *a youthful culture.* **4.** Also: **young.** (of a river, valley, or land surface) in the early stage of the cycle of erosion, characterized by steep slopes, lack of flood plains, and V-shaped valleys. Compare **mature** (sense 6), **old** (sense 18). —**'youth+ful+ly** *adv.* —**'youth+ful+ness** *n.*

youth hos+tel *n.* one of a chain of inexpensive lodging places for young people travelling cheaply. Often shortened to **hostel.**

you've (ju:v; *unstressed* jʊv) *contraction of* you have.

yowl (jaʊl) *vb.* **1.** to express with or produce a loud mournful wail or cry; howl. ~*n.* **2.** a loud mournful cry; wail or howl. [C13: from Old Norse *gaula;* related to German *jaulen;* see YAWL] —**'yowl+er** *n.*

yo-yo ('jəʊjəʊ) *n., pl.* **-yos. 1.** a toy consisting of a spool attached to a string, the end of which is held while it is repeatedly spun out and reeled in. **2.** *U.S. slang.* a stupid person, esp. one who is easily manipulated. [C20: originally a trademark for this type of toy]

Y·pres (*French* 'ipr) *n.* a town in W Belgium, in W Flanders province near the border with France: scene of many sieges and battles, esp. in World War I, when it was completely destroyed. Pop.: 20 825 (1970). Flemish name: **Ieper.**

Yp·si·lan·ti (ˌɪpsɪ'læntɪ) *or* **Hyp·si·lan·tis, Hyp·si·lan·tes** (*Greek* ˌipsi'landis) *n.* **1. A·le·xan·der** (ˌalek'sander). 1792–1828, Greek patriot, who led an unsuccessful revolt against the Turks (1821). **2.** his brother, **De·met·ri·os** (ðimitri'ɔs). 1793–1832, Greek revolutionary leader; commander in chief of Greek forces (1828–30) during the war of independence.

Y·quem (iː'kɛm) *n.* a French vineyard of the Sauternes area of Bordeaux that produces a sweet white table wine. Also called: **Château d'Yquem.**
yr. *abbrev. for:* 1. (*pl.* **yrs.**) year. 2. younger. 3. your.
yrs. *abbrev. for:* 1. years. 2. yours.
Y·ser (*French* i'zɛːr) *n.* a river in NW central Europe, rising in N France and flowing through SW Belgium to the North Sea: scene of battles in World War I. Length: 77 km (48 miles).
Y·seult (ɪ'suːlt) *n.* a variant spelling of **Iseult.**
Ys+sel ('aɪsᵊl) *n.* a variant spelling of **IJssel.**
Yt *the former chemical symbol for* yttrium (now **Y**).
Y.T. *abbrev. for* Yukon Territory.
yt+ter+bi·a (ɪ'tɜːbɪə) *n.* another name for **ytterbium oxide.** [C19: New Latin, named after *Ytterby,* Swedish quarry where it was discovered]
yt+ter+bite (ɪ'tɜːbaɪt) *n.* another name for **gadolinite.**
yt+ter+bi·um (ɪ'tɜːbɪəm) *n.* a soft malleable silvery element of the lanthanide series of metals that occurs in monazite and is used to improve the mechanical properties of steel. Symbol: Yb; atomic no.: 70; atomic wt.: 173.04; valency: 2 or 3; relative density: 6.97 or 6.54; melting pt.: 824°C; boiling pt.: 1193°C. [C19: New Latin; see YTTERBIA]
yt+ter+bi·um ox+ide *n.* a colourless weakly basic hygroscopic substance used in certain alloys and ceramics. Formula: Yb_2O_3. Also called: **ytterbia.**
yt+tri·a ('ɪtrɪə) *n.* another name for **yttrium oxide.** [C19: New Latin, named after *Ytterby;* see YTTERBIA]
yt+trif+er+ous (ɪ'trɪfərəs) *adj.* containing or yielding yttrium.
yt+tri·um ('ɪtrɪəm) *n.* a silvery metallic element occurring in monazite and gadolinite and used in various alloys, in lasers, and as a catalyst. Symbol: Y; atomic no.: 39; atomic wt.: 88.90; valency: 3; relative density: 4.46; melting pt.: 1523°C; boiling pt.: 3337°C. [C19: New Latin; see YTTERBIA] —**'yt+tric** *adj.*
yt+tri·um met+al *n. Chem.* any one of a group of elements including yttrium and the related lanthanides holmium, erbium, thulium, ytterbium, and lutecium.
yt+tri·um ox+ide *n.* a colourless or white insoluble solid used mainly in incandescent mantles. Formula: Y_2O_3. Also called: **yttria.**
YU *international car registration for* Yugoslavia.
yu·an ('juː'æn) *n., pl.* **·an. 1.** the standard monetary unit of the People's Republic of China, divided into 100 fen. **2.** the former name for **dollar** (sense 2). [from Chinese *yüan* round object; see YEN[1]]
Yü·an[1] ('juː'æn) *n.* **1.** the imperial dynasty of China from 1279 to 1368. *~adj.* **2.** of or relating to the Chinese porcelain produced during the Yüan dynasty, characterized by the appearance of under-glaze blue-and-white ware.
Yü·an[2] ('juː'æn) *or* **Yü·en** *n.* a river in SE central China, rising in central Kweichow province and flowing northeast to Lake Tungting. Length: about 800 km (500 miles).
Yu+ca+tán (ˌjuːkə'tɑːn); *Spanish* ˌjuka'tan) *n.* **1.** a state of SE Mexico, occupying the N part of the Yucatán peninsula. Capital: Mérida. Pop.: 758 355 (1970). Area: 43 379 sq. km (16 749 sq. miles). **2.** a peninsula of Central America between the Gulf of Mexico and the Caribbean, including the Mexican states of Campeche, Yucatán, and Quintana Roo, and part of Belize: a centre of Mayan civilization from about 100 B.C. to the 18th century. Area: about 181 300 sq. km (70 000 sq. miles).
Yu+ca+tán Chan+nel *n.* a channel between W Cuba and the Yucatán Peninsula.
yuc+ca ('jʌkə) *n.* any of several liliaceous plants of the genus *Yucca,* of tropical and subtropical America, having stiff lancelike leaves and spikes of white flowers. See also **Adam's-needle, Spanish bayonet.** [C16: from American Spanish *yuca,* ultimately from an American Indian word]
Yü·en ('juː'ɛn) *n.* a variant of **Yüan**[2].
Yu·ga ('jʊgə) *n.* (in Hindu cosmology) one of the four ages of mankind, together lasting over 4 million years and marked by a progressive decline in the vitality and morals of men. [C18: from Sanskrit: yoke, race of men, era; see YOKE]
Yugo. *abbrev. for* Yugoslavia.
Yu+go+slav *or* **Ju+go+slav** ('juːgəʊˌslɑːv) *n.* **1.** a native, inhabitant, or citizen of Yugoslavia. **2.** (not in technical use) another name for **Serbo-Croatian** (the language). *~adj.* **3.** of, relating to, or characteristic of Yugoslavia or its people.
Yu+go+sla+vi·a *or* **Ju+go+sla+vi·a** (ˌjuːgəʊ'slɑːvɪə) *n.* a federal republic in SE Europe, on the Adriatic: established in 1918 from the independent states of Macedonia and Montenegro, and regions that until World War I had belonged to Austria-Hungary (Croatia, Slovenia, and Bosnia and Herzegovina); the name was changed from Kingdom of Serbs, Croats, and Slovenes to Yugoslavia in 1929; German invasion of 1941–44 was resisted chiefly by a Communist group led by Tito, who declared a people's republic in 1945; a socialist federal republic was declared in 1963. It is mainly mountainous and rugged, rising over 2700m (9000 ft.) in the Julian Alps, with the fertile Danube-Sava Basin in the northeast. Languages: Serbo-Croatian, Slovene, and Macedonian. Currency: dinar. Capital: Belgrade. Pop.: 21 352 000 (1975 est.). Area: 255 804 sq. km (98 766 sq. miles). —ˌ**Yu+go+'sla+vi·an** *or* ˌ**Ju+go+'sla+vi·an** *adj., n.*
yuk (jʌk) *Slang, chiefly U.S.* *~interj.* **1.** an exclamation indicating contempt, dislike, or disgust. *~n.* **2.** Also: **yuk-yuk.** a loud laugh or an imitation of one. —**'yuk+ky** *adj.*
Yu·ka·wa (juː'kɑːwə) *n.* **Hi·de·ki** ('hiːdɛkɪ). 1907–81, Japanese nuclear physicist, who predicted (1935) the existence of mesons: Nobel prize for physics 1949.
Yu+kon ('juːkɒn) *n.* **the.** a territory of NW Canada, on the Beaufort Sea: arctic and mountainous, reaching 6050 m (19 850 ft.) at Mount Logan, Canada's highest peak; mineral resources. Capital: Whitehorse. Pop.: 21 836 (1976). Area: 536 327 sq. km (207 076 sq. miles). —**'Yu+kon+er** *n.*
Yu+kon Riv+er *n.* a river in NW North America, rising in NW Canada on the border between the Yukon Territory and British Columbia: flows northwest into Alaska, U.S., and then southwest to the Bering Sea; navigable for about 2850 km (1775 miles) to Whitehorse. Length: 3185 km (1979 miles).
yu+lan ('juːlæn) *n.* a Chinese magnolia, *Magnolia denudata,* that is often cultivated for its showy white flowers. [C19: from Chinese, from *yu* a gem + *lan* plant]
yule (juːl) *n.* (*sometimes cap.*) *Literary, archaic, or dialect.* **a.** Christmas, the Christmas season, or Christmas festivities. **b.** (*in combination*): *yuletide.* [Old English *geōla* originally a name of a pagan feast lasting 12 days; related to Old Norse *jōl* Swedish *jul,* Gothic *jiuleis*]
yule log *n.* a large log of wood traditionally used as the foundation of a fire in the hearth at Christmas.
Yu+man ('juːmən) *n.* **1.** a family of North American Indian languages spoken chiefly in Arizona, California, and Mexico. *~adj.* **2.** relating to or belonging to this family of languages.
yum+my ('jʌmɪ) *Slang.* *~interj.* **1.** Also: **yum-yum.** an exclamation indicating pleasure or delight, as in anticipation of delicious food. *~adj.* **+mi+er, +mi+est. 2.** delicious, delightful, or attractive. [C20: from *yum-yum,* of imitative origin]
Yün+nan (juː'næn) *n.* a province of SW China: consists mainly of a plateau broken in the southeast by the Red and Black Rivers, with mountains in the west, rising over 5500 m (18 000 ft.); large deposits of tin, lead, zinc, and coal. Capital: Kunming. Pop.: 28 000 000 (1976 est.). Area: 436 200 sq. km (168 400 sq. miles).
yup (jʌp) *sentence substitute.* an informal word for **yes.**
Yur+ev (*Russian* 'jurjɪf) *n.* the former name (11th century until 1918) of **Tartu.**
yurt (jʊət) *n.* a circular tent consisting of a framework of poles covered with felt or skins, used by Mongolian and Turkic nomads of E and central Asia. [from Russian *yurta,* of Turkic origin; compare Turkish *yurt* abode, home]
Yu+zov+ka (*Russian* 'juzəfkə) *n.* a former name (1872 until after the Revolution) of **Donetsk.**
YV *international car registration for* Venezuela.
Yve+lines (*French* i'vlin) *n.* a department of N France, in Île de France region. Capital: Versailles. Pop.: 1 099 416 (1975). Area: 2271 sq. km (886 sq. miles).
Y.W.C.A. *abbrev. for* Young Women's Christian Association.
Y.W.H.A. *abbrev. for* Young Women's Hebrew Association.
y·wis (ɪ'wɪs) *adv.* a variant spelling of **iwis.**

Z

z or **Z** (zɛd; *U.S.* zi:) *n., pl.* **z's, Z's,** *or* **Zs. 1.** the 26th and last letter and the 20th consonant of the modern English alphabet. **2.** a speech sound represented by this letter, in English usually a voiced alveolar fricative, as in *zip.* **3. a.** something shaped like a Z. **b.** (*in combination*): *a Z-bend in a road.*

z *Maths. symbol for:* **1.** the *z*-axis or a coordinate measured along the *z*-axis in a Cartesian or cylindrical coordinate system. **2.** an algebraic variable.

Z *symbol for:* **1.** any unknown, variable, or unspecified factor, number, person, or thing. **2.** *Chem.* atomic number. **3.** *Physics.* impedance. **4.** zone. ~ **5.** *international car registration for* Zambia.

z. *abbrev. for:* **1.** zero. **2.** zone.

ZA *international car registration for* South Africa. [from Afrikaans *Zuid Afrika*]

Zaan+dam ('za:ndam) *n.* a town in the W Netherlands, in North Holland: an important shipbuilding centre in the 17th century; timber industry. Pop.: 69 000 (1971 est.).

za+ba+glio+ne (ˌzæbəˈljəʊnɪ) *n.* a light foamy dessert made of egg yolks, sugar, and marsala, whipped together and served hot in a glass. [Italian; probably related to Late Latin *sabaia* Illyrian drink made from grain]

Za+brze (*Polish* 'zabʒɛ) *n.* a city in SW Poland: under Prussian rule from 1742 until 1921, when it passed to Germany; restored to Poland in 1945; industrial centre in a coal-mining region. Pop.: 201 600 (1974 est.). German name: **Hindenburg.**

Za+ca+te+cas (*Spanish* ˌsakaˈtekas) *n.* **1.** a state of N central Mexico, on the central plateau: rich mineral resources. Capital: Zacatecas. Pop.: 951 462 (1970). Area: 75 040 sq. km (28 973 sq. miles). **2.** a city in N central Mexico, capital of Zacatecas state: silver mines. Pop.: 56 829 (1970).

Zach·a·ri·as (ˌzækəˈraɪəs), **Zach·a·ri·ah** (ˌzækəˈraɪə), *or* **Zach·a·ry** ('zækərɪ) *n. New Testament.* John the Baptist's father, who underwent a temporary period of dumbness for his lack of faith (Luke 1).

Za+cyn+thus (zəˈsɪnθəs, -ˈkɪn-) *n.* the Latin name for **Zante.**

zaf+fer *or* **zaf+fre** ('zæfə) *n.* impure cobalt oxide, used to impart a blue colour to enamels. [C17: from Italian *zaffera;* perhaps related to Latin *sapphīrus* SAPPHIRE]

Zag·a·zig ('zægəˌzɪg) *or* **Zaq·a·ziq** *n.* a city in NE Egypt, in the Nile Delta: major cotton market. Pop.: 195 100 (1974 est.).

Za+greb ('zɑ:grɛb) *n.* a city in NW Yugoslavia, capital of the republic of Croatia; university (1874); industrial centre. Pop.: 566 224 (1971). German name: **Agram.**

Zag·re·us ('zægrɪəs) *n. Greek myth.* a young god whose cult came from Crete to Greece, where he was identified with Dionysus. The son of Zeus by either Demeter or Persephone, he was killed by the Titans at the behest of Hera.

Zag+ros Moun+tains ('zægrɒs) *pl. n.* a mountain range in S Iran: has Iran's main oilfields in its W central foothills. Highest peak: Zard Kuh, 4548 m (14 920 ft.).

zai+bat+su ('zaɪbætˈsu:) *n.* (*functioning as sing. or pl.*) the group or combine comprising a few wealthy families that controls industry, business, and finance in Japan. [from Japanese, from *zai* wealth, from Chinese *ts'ai* + *batsu* family, person of influence, from Chinese *fa*]

za+ïre (zɑ:ˈɪə) *n., pl.* **+ïre.** the standard monetary unit of Zaïre.

Za+ïre (zɑ:ˈɪə) *n.* **1.** a republic in S central Africa, with a narrow strip of land along the Congo estuary leading to the Atlantic in the west: Congo Free State established in 1885, with Leopold II of Belgium as absolute monarch; became the Belgian Congo colony in 1908; gained independence in 1960, followed by civil war and the secession of Katanga (until 1963). It consists chiefly of the Congo basin, with large areas of dense tropical forest and marshes, and the Mitumba highlands reaching over 5000 m (16 000 ft.) in the east. Official language: French. Religion: Christian and animist. Currency: zaïre. Capital: Kinshasa. Pop.: 24 222 000 (1974 est.). Area: 2 344 116 sq. km (905 063 sq. miles). Former names: **Congo Free State** (1885–1908), **Belgian Congo** (1908–60), **(Democratic Republic of the) Congo** (1960–71), **Congo-Kinshasa. 2.** the Zaïrese name (since 1971) for the (River) **Congo.** —ˌ**Za+ïr+'ese** *adj., n.*

Zá+kin+thos ('zakinˌθɔs) *n.* transliteration of the Modern Greek name for **Zante.**

za+kus+ki *or* **za+kous+ki** (zæˈkʊskɪ) *pl. n., sing.* **+ka** (-kə). *Russian cookery.* hors d'oeuvres, consisting of tiny open sandwiches spread with caviar, smoked sausage, etc., or a cold dish such as radishes in sour cream, all usually served with vodka.

Za+ma ('zɑ:mə) *n.* the name of several ancient cities in N Africa, including the one near the site of Scipio's decisive defeat of Hannibal (202 B.C.).

Zam+be+zi *or* **Zam+be+se** (zæmˈbi:zɪ) *n.* a river in S central and E Africa, rising in NW Zambia and flowing across E Angola back into Zambia, continuing south to the Caprivi Strip of South West Africa, and then east through Rhodesia and Mozambique to the Indian Ocean: the fourth longest river in Africa. Length: 2740 km (1700 miles). —**Zam+'be+zi·an** *adj.*

Zam+bi·a ('zæmbɪə) *n.* a republic in central Africa: an early site of human settlement; controlled by the British South Africa Company by 1900 and unified as Northern Rhodesia in 1911; made a British protectorate in 1924; part of the Central African Federation (1953–63), gaining independence within the Commonwealth in 1964; important mineral exports, esp. copper. Official language: English. Religion: mostly animist. Currency: kwacha. Capital: Lusaka. Pop.: 4 056 995 (1969). Area: 752 617 sq. km (290 587 sq. miles). Former name (until 1964): **Northern Rhodesia.** —**'Zam+bi·an** *adj., n.*

Zam+bo+an+ga (ˌzæmbəʊˈæŋgə) *n.* a port in the Philippines, on SW Mindanao on Basilan Strait: founded by the Spanish in 1635; tourist centre, with fisheries. Pop.: 240 066 (1975 est.).

Za·men·hof (*Polish* 'zamɛnxɔf) *n.* **Laz·a·rus Lud·wig** (laˈzarus ˈludvik). 1859–1917, Polish oculist; invented Esperanto.

za+mi·a ('zeɪmɪə) *n.* any cycadaceous plant of the genus *Zamia,* of tropical and subtropical America, having a short thick trunk, palmlike leaves, and short stout cones. [C19: from New Latin, from Latin *zamiae,* erroneous reading of phrase *nucēs azāniae* pine cones, probably from Greek *azainein* to dry up]

za+min·dar *or* **ze+min·dar** (zəmi:nˈdɑ:) *n.* (in India) the owner of an agricultural estate. [via Hindi from Persian: landholder, from *zamīn* land + *-dār* holder]

za+min·dar·i *or* **ze+min·dar·i** (zəmi:nˈdɑ:rɪ) *n., pl.* **·is.** (in India) a large agricultural estate.

Za+mo+ra (*Spanish* θaˈmora) *n.* a city in NW central Spain, on the Douro River. Pop.: 49 029 (1970).

Zan+te ('zæntɪ) *n.* an island in the Ionian Sea, off the W coast of Greece: southernmost of the Ionian Islands; traditionally belonged to Ulysses, king of Ithaca. Pop.: 30 187 (1971). Area: 402 sq. km (155 sq. miles). Latin name: **Zacynthus.** Ancient Greek name: **Zakynthos.** Modern Greek name: **Zákinthos.**

zan+thox·y+lum (zænˈθɒksɪləm) *n.* any rutaceous shrub or tree of the genus *Zanthoxylum,* of temperate and subtropical E Asia and North America: includes the prickly ash and the West Indian yellowwood (or satinwood). [C19 *zantho-* variant of XANTHO- + Greek *xulon* wood]

ZANU ('zɑ:nu:) *n. acronym for* Zimbabwe African National Union.

za·ny ('zeɪnɪ) *adj.* **·ni·er, ·ni·est. 1.** comical in an endearing way; imaginatively funny or comical, esp. in behaviour. ~*n., pl.* **·nies. 2.** a clown or buffoon, esp. one in old comedies who imitated other performers with ludicrous effect. **3.** a ludicrous or foolish person. [C16: from Italian *zanni,* from dialect (Venice and Lombardy) *Zanni,* nickname for *Giovanni* John; one of the traditional names for a clown] —**'za+ni·ly** *adv.* —**'za+ni+ness** *n.* —**'za+ny+ism** *n.*

Zan+zi+bar (ˌzænzɪˈbɑ:) *n.* an island in the Indian Ocean, off the E coast of Africa: settled by Persians and Arabs from the 7th century onwards; became a flourishing trading centre for ivory, slaves, and cloves; made a British protectorate in 1890, becoming independent within the Commonwealth in 1963 and a republic in 1964; joined with Tanganyika in 1964 to form the United Republic of Tanzania. Pop.: 68 490 (1967). —ˌ**Zan+zi+'ba+ri** *adj., n.*

zap (zæp) *Slang.* ~*vb.* **zaps, zap+ping, zapped. 1.** (*tr.*) to attack, kill, or destroy, as with a sudden bombardment. **2.** (*intr.*) to move quickly; rush. ~*n.* **3.** energy, vigour, or pep. ~*interj.* **4.** an exclamation used to express sudden or swift action.

Za·pa·ta (zəˈpɑ:tə *Spanish* saˈpata) *n.* **Em·i·lia·no** (ˌemiˈljano). ?1877–1919, Mexican guerrilla leader.

za+pa+te·a+do *Spanish.* (ˌθapateˈaðo) *n., pl.* **+dos** (-ðos). a Spanish dance with stamping and very fast footwork. [from *zapatear* to tap with the shoe, from *zapato* shoe]

Za+po+rozh+ye (*Russian* zəpaˈrɔʒjɛ) *n.* a city in the SW Soviet Union, in the Ukrainian SSR on the Dnieper River: developed as a major industrial centre after the construction (1932) of the Dnieper hydroelectric station. Pop.: 744 000 (1975 est.). Former name (until 1921): **Aleksandrovsk.**

Za+po+tec ('zɑ:pəˌtɛk) *n.* **1.** (*pl.* **+tecs** *or* **+tec**) Also called: **Zap·o·tec·an** (ˌzæpəʊˈtɛkən, ˌzɑ:-). any member of a large tribe of central American Indians inhabiting S Mexico, esp. the Mexican state of Oaxaca. **2.** the group of languages spoken by this people. **3.** Also: **Zapotecan.** of or relating to this people or their language. [from Spanish *Zapoteca,* from Nahuatl *Tzapoteca,* literally: people of the land of the sapodillas, from *tzapotl* sapodilla]

Zap·pa ('zæpə) *n.* **Frank.** born 1940, U.S. rock musician and producer: founder and only permanent member of the large amorphous group the Mothers, also called Mothers of Invention. His recordings include *Freak out* (1966), *Reuben and the Jets* (1968), and *Hot Rats* (1969).

ZAPU ('zæpu:) *n. acronym for* Zimbabwe African People's Union.

Zaq·a+ziq ('zækəˌzɪk) *n.* a variant spelling of **Zagazig.**

Za+ra+go+za (*Spanish* ˌθaraˈɣoθa) *n.* a city in NE Spain, on the River Ebro: Roman colony established 25 B.C.; under Moorish rule (714–1118); capital of Aragon (12th–15th centuries); twice besieged by the French during the Peninsular War and captured (1809); university (1474). Pop.: 479 845 (1970). Pre-Roman name: **Salduba.** Latin name: **Caesaraugusta.** English name: **Saragossa.**

Zar·a·thus·tra (ˌzærəˈθuːstrə) *n.* the Avestan name of **Zoroaster.** —ˌ**Zar·a**+ˈ**thus**+**tri·an** *or* ˌ**Zar·a**+ˈ**thus**+**tric** *adj., n.*

zar·a+**tite** (ˈzærəˌtaɪt) *n.* a green amorphous mineral consisting of hydrated nickel carbonate. Formula: $NiCO_3.2Ni(OH)_2.4H_2O$. [C19: from Spanish *zaratita*, named after G. *Zárate*, 19th-century Spaniard]

za+**re·ba** *or* **za**+**ree**+**ba** (zəˈriːbə) *n.* (in northern E Africa, esp. formerly) **1.** a stockade or enclosure of thorn bushes around a village or campsite. **2.** the area so protected or enclosed. [C19: from Arabic *zarībah* cattlepen, from *zarb* sheepfold]

zarf (zɑːf) *n.* (esp. in the Middle East) a holder, usually ornamental, for a hot coffee cup. [from Arabic: container, sheath]

Zar+**ga** *or* **Sar**+**ka** (ˈzɑːkə) *n.* the second largest town in Jordan, northeast of Amman. Pop.: 226 000 (1974 est.).

Za+**ri·a** (ˈzɑːrɪə) *n.* a city in N central Nigeria: former capital of a Hausa state; agricultural trading centre; university (1962). Pop.: 224 000 (1975 est.).

zar+**zue**+**la** (zɑːˈzweɪlə) *n.* **1.** a type of Spanish vaudeville or operetta, usually satirical in nature. **2.** a seafood stew. [from Spanish, from *La Zarzuela*, name of the palace near Madrid where such vaudeville was first performed (1629)]

za+**stru**+**ga** (zəˈstruːgə, zæ-) *n.* a variant spelling of **sastruga.**

Zá·to·pek (*Czech* ˈzaːtɔpɛk) *n.* **Em·il** (ˈemil). born 1922, Czech runner; winner of the 5000 and 10 000 metres' races and the Marathon at the 1952 Olympic Games in Helsinki.

z-ax·is *n.* a reference axis of a three-dimensional Cartesian coordinate system along which the *z*-coordinate is measured.

za+**yin** (ˈzɑːjɪn) *n.* the seventh letter of the Hebrew alphabet (ז), transliterated as *z.* [from Hebrew, literally: weapon]

Z chart *n. Statistics.* a chart often used in industry and constructed by plotting on it three series: monthly, weekly, or daily data, the moving annual total, and the cumulative total dating from the beginning of the current year.

zeal (ziːl) *n.* fervent or enthusiastic devotion, often extreme or fanatical in nature, as to a religious movement, political cause, ideal, or aspiration. [C14: from Late Latin *zēlus*, from Greek *zēlos*]

Zea+**land** (ˈziːlənd) *n.* the English name for **Sjælland.**

zeal+**ot** (ˈzɛlət) *n.* an immoderate, fanatical, or extremely zealous adherent to a cause, esp. a religious one. [C16: from Late Latin *zēlōtēs*, from Greek, from *zēloun* to be zealous, from *zēlos* ZEAL]

Zeal+**ot** (ˈzɛlət) *n.* any of the members of an extreme Jewish sect or political party that resisted all aspects of Roman rule in Palestine in the 1st century A.D.

zeal+**ot**+**ry** (ˈzɛlətrɪ) *n.* extreme or excessive zeal or devotion.

zeal+**ous** (ˈzɛləs) *adj.* filled with or inspired by intense enthusiasm or zeal; ardent; fervent. —ˈ**zeal**+**ous**+**ly** *adv.* —ˈ**zeal**+**ous**+**ness** *n.*

Ze·a·mi or **Se·a·mi** (siːˈɑːmɪ) *n.* **Mo·to·ki·yo** (ˌməʊtəʊˈkiːəʊ). 1363–1443, Japanese dramatist, regarded as the greatest figure in the history of No drama.

ze+**bec** *or* **ze**+**beck** (ˈziːbɛk) *n.* variant spellings of **xebec.**

Zeb·e·dee (ˈzɛbɪdɪ) *n. New Testament.* the father of the apostles James and John (Matthew 4:21).

zeb+**ra** (ˈzɛbrə; *U.S.* ˈziːbrə) *n., pl.* +**ras** *or* +**ra.** any of several mammals of the horse family (*Equidae*), such as *Equus burchelli* (the **common zebra**), of southern and eastern Africa, having distinctive black-and-white striped hides. [C16: via Italian from Old Spanish: wild ass, probably from Vulgar Latin *eciferus* (unattested) wild horse, from Latin *equiferus*, from *equus* horse + *ferus* wild] —ˈ**zeb·ra**-ˌ**like** *or* **ze**+**bra**+**ic** (zɪˈbreɪɪk) *adj.* —**ze**+**brine** (ˈziːbraɪn, ˈzɛb-) *or* ˈ**ze**+**broid** *adj.*

zeb+**ra cross**+**ing** *n. Brit.* a pedestrian crossing marked on a road by broad alternate black and white stripes. Once on the crossing the pedestrian has right of way.

zeb+**ra finch** *n.* any of various Australasian songbirds with zebra-like markings, such as the grassfinch *Poephila castanotis.*

zeb·ra+**wood** (ˈzɛbrəˌwʊd, ˈziː-) *n.* **1.** a tree, *Connarus guianensis*, of tropical America, Asia, and Africa, yielding striped hardwood used in cabinetwork: family *Connaraceae.* **2.** any of various other trees or shrubs having striped wood. **3.** the wood of any of these trees.

ze·bu (ˈziːbuː) *n.* a domesticated ox, *Bos indicus*, having a humped back, long horns, and a large dewlap: used in India and E Asia as a draught animal. [C18: from French *zébu*, perhaps of Tibetan origin]

Zeb·u·lun (ˈzɛbjʊlən, zəˈbjuː-) *n. Old Testament.* **1.** the sixth son whom Leah bore to Jacob: one of the 12 patriarchs of Israel (Genesis 30:20). **2.** the tribe descended from him. **3.** the territory of this tribe, lying in lower Galilee to the north of Mount Carmel and to the east of the coastal plain. Douay spelling: **Zab·u·lon** (ˈzæbjʊlən, zəˈbjuː-).

zec+**chi**+**no** (zɛˈkiːnəʊ) *n., pl.* +**ni** (-nɪ). another word for **sequin** (the coin). [C18: from Italian; see SEQUIN]

Zech. *Bible. abbrev. for* Zechariah.

Zech·a·ri·ah (ˌzɛkəˈraɪə) *n.* **1.** *Old Testament.* **a.** a Hebrew prophet of the late 6th century B.C. **b.** the book containing his oracles, which are chiefly concerned with the renewal of Israel after the exile as a national, religious, and messianic community with the restored Temple and rebuilt Jerusalem as its centre. Douay spelling: **Zach·a·ri·as. 2.** a variant spelling of **Zachariah.**

zed (zɛd) *n.* the Brit. spoken form of the letter *z.* U.S. word: **zee.** [C15: from Old French *zede*, via Late Latin from Greek *zēta*]

Zed·e·ki·ah (ˌzɛdəˈkaɪə) *n. Old Testament.* the last king of Judah, who died in captivity at Babylon. Douay spelling: **Sed·e·ci·as** (ˌsɛdəˈkaɪəs).

zed+**o**+**ar·y** (ˈzɛdəʊərɪ) *n.* the dried rhizome of the tropical Asian plant *Curcuma zedoaria*, used as a stimulant and a condiment: family *Zingiberaceae.* [C15: from Medieval Latin *zedoaria*, from Arabic *zadwār*, of Persian origin]

zee (ziː) *n.* the U.S. word for **zed** (letter *z*).

Zee+**brug**+**ge** (*Flemish* ˈzeːbryxə; *English* ˈziːˌbrʊgə) *n.* a port in NW Belgium, in W Flanders on the North Sea: linked by canal with Bruges; German submarine base in World War I.

Zee+**land** (*Dutch* ˈzeːlɑnt; *English* ˈziːlənd) *n.* a province of the SW Netherlands: consists of a small area on the mainland together with a number of islands in the Scheldt estuary; mostly below sea level. Capital: Middelburg. Pop.: 319 300 (1973 est.). Area: 2700 sq. km (1042 sq. miles). —ˈ**Zee**+**land**+**er** *n.*

Zee+**man ef**+**fect** (ˈziːmən) *n.* the splitting of a spectral line of a substance into several closely spaced lines when the substance is placed in a magnetic field. [C20: named after Pieter *Zeeman* (1865–1943), Dutch physicist]

Zef·fi·rel·li (*Italian* dzɛffiˈrɛlli) *n.* **Fran·co** (ˈfraŋko). born 1923, Italian stage and film director and designer, noted esp. for his work in opera.

ze·in (ˈziːɪn) *n.* a protein of the prolamine group occurring in maize and used in the manufacture of plastics, paper coatings, adhesives, etc. [C19: from New Latin *zēa* maize, from Latin: a kind of grain, from Greek *zeia* barley]

Zeist (zaɪst; *Dutch* zɛjst) *n.* a city in the central Netherlands, near Utrecht. Pop.: 57 155 (1973 est.).

Zeit*+*geist *German.* (ˈtsaɪtˌgaɪst) *n.* the spirit, attitude, or general outlook of a specific time or period, esp. as it is reflected in literature, philosophy, etc. [German, literally: time spirit; see TIDE[1], GHOST]

ze+**min**+**dar** (zəmiːnˈdɑː) *n.* a variant spelling of **zamindar.**

zem+**stvo** (ˈzɛmstvəʊ; *Russian* ˈzjɛmstvə) *n., pl.* +**stvos.** (in tsarist Russia) an elective provincial or district council established in most provinces of Russia by Alexander II in 1864 as part of his reform policy. [C19: from Russian, from *zemlya* land; related to Latin *humus* earth, Greek *khamai* on the ground]

Zen (zɛn) *Buddhism.* ~*n.* **1.** a Japanese school, of 12th-century Chinese origin, teaching that contemplation of one's essential nature to the exclusion of all else is the only way of achieving pure enlightenment. **2.** (*modifier*) of or relating to this school: *Zen Buddhism.* [from Japanese, from Chinese *ch'an* religious meditation, from Pali *jhāna*, from Sanskrit *dhyāna*] —ˈ**Zen**+**ic** *adj.* —ˈ**Zen**+**ist** *n.*

ze+**na**+**na** (zɛˈnɑːnə) *n.* (in the East, esp. in Muslim and Hindu homes) part of a house reserved for the women and girls of a household. [C18: from Hindi *zanāna*, from Persian, from *zan* woman]

Zend (zɛnd) *n.* **1.** a former name for **Avestan. 2.** short for **Zend-Avesta. 3.** an exposition of the Avesta in the Middle Persian language (Pahlavi). [C18: from Persian *zand* commentary, exposition; used specifically of the Middle Persian commentary on the Avesta, hence of the language of the Avesta itself] —ˈ**Zend**+**ic** *adj.*

Zend-A·ves·ta (ˌzɛndəˈvɛstə) *n.* the Avesta together with the traditional interpretative commentary known as the Zend, esp. as preserved in the Avestan language among the Parsees. [from Avestan, representing *Avesta'-va-zend* Avesta with interpretation] —**Zend-A·ves·ta**+**ic** (ˌzɛndəvɛsˈteɪɪk) *adj.*

Ze+**ner di**+**ode** (ˈziːnə) *n.* a semiconductor diode that exhibits a sharp increase in reverse current at a well-defined reverse voltage: used as a voltage regulator. [C20: named after C. M. *Zener* (born 1905), U.S. physicist]

zen+**ith** (ˈzɛnɪθ; *U.S.* ˈziːnɪθ) *n.* **1.** *Astronomy.* the point on the celestial sphere vertically above an observer. **2.** the highest point; peak; acme: *the zenith of someone's achievements.* ~Compare **nadir.** [C17: from French *cenith*, from Medieval Latin, from Old Spanish *zenit*, based on Arabic *samt*, as in *samt arrās* path over one's head, from *samt* way, path + *al* the + *rās* head] —ˈ**zen**+**ith**+**al** *adj.*

zen+**ith**+**al pro**+**jec**+**tion** *n.* a type of map projection in which part of the earth's surface is projected onto a plane tangential to it, either at one of the poles (**polar zenithal**), at the equator (**equatorial zenithal**), or between (**oblique zenithal**).

Ze·no·bi·a (zɪˈnəʊbɪə) *n.* 3rd-century A.D. queen of Palmyra (?267–272), who was captured by the Roman emperor Aurelian.

Ze+**no of Ci·ti·um** (ˈziːnəʊ əv ˈsɪtɪəm) *n.* ?336–?264 B.C., Greek philosopher, who founded the Stoic school in Athens.

Ze+**no of E·lea** *n.* ?490–?430 B.C., Greek Eleatic philosopher; disciple of Parmenides. He defended the belief that motion and change are illusions in a series of paradoxical arguments, of which the best known is that of Achilles and the tortoise.

ze·o+**lite** (ˈziːəˌlaɪt) *n.* **1.** any of a large group of glassy secondary minerals consisting of hydrated aluminium silicates of calcium, sodium, or potassium: formed in cavities in lava flows and plutonic rocks. **2.** any of a class of similar synthetic materials used in ion exchange and as selective absorbents. See **molecular sieve.** [C18 *zeo-*, from Greek *zein* to boil + -LITE; from the swelling up that occurs under the blowpipe] —**ze·o·lit**+**ic** (ˌziːəˈlɪtɪk) *adj.*

Zeph. *Bible. abbrev. for* Zephaniah.

Zeph·a·ni·ah (ˌzɛfəˈnaɪə) *n. Old Testament.* **1.** a Hebrew prophet of the late 7th century B.C. **2.** the book containing his oracles, which are chiefly concerned with the approaching judgment by God upon the sinners of Judah. Douay spelling: **Soph·o·ni·as** (ˌsɒfəˈnaɪəs).

zeph+yr (ˈzɛfə) *n.* **1.** a soft or gentle breeze. **2.** any of several delicate soft yarns, fabrics, or garments, usually of wool. [C16: from Latin *zephyrus*, from Greek *zephuros* the west wind; probably related to Greek *zophos* darkness, west]

Zeph·y·rus (ˈzɛfərəs) *n. Greek myth.* the god of the west wind.

zep+pe+lin (ˈzɛpəlɪn) *n.* (*sometimes cap.*) a large cylindrical rigid airship designed to carry passengers, bombs, etc. [C20: named after Count von ZEPPELIN]

Zep·pe·lin (*German* ˈtsɛpəˌliːn) *n.* Count **Fer·di·nand von** (ˈfɛrdinant fɔn). 1838–1917, German aeronautical pioneer, who designed and manufactured airships (zeppelins).

Zer+matt (*German* tsɛrˈmat) *n.* a village and resort in S Switzerland, in Valais canton at the foot of the Matterhorn: not accessible by car. Pop.: 3101 (1970).

ze·ro (ˈzɪərəʊ) *n., pl.* **·ros** *or* **·roes. 1.** the symbol 0, indicating an absence of quantity or magnitude; nought. Former name: **cipher. 2.** the integer denoted by the symbol 0; nought. **3.** the ordinal number between +1 and -1. **4.** nothing; nil. **5.** a person or thing of no significance; nonentity. **6.** the lowest point or degree: *his prospects were put at zero.* **7.** the line or point on a scale of measurement from which the graduations commence. **8. a.** the temperature, pressure, etc., that registers a reading of zero on a scale. **b.** the value of a variable, such as temperature, obtained under specified conditions. **9.** a gunsight setting in which accurate allowance has been made for both windage and elevation for a specified range. **10.** *Maths.* **a.** the cardinal number of a set with no members. **b.** the identity element of addition. **11.** *Linguistics.* **a.** an allomorph with no phonetic realization, as the plural marker of English *sheep.* **b.** (*as modifier*): *a zero form.* ~*adj.* **12.** having no measurable quantity, magnitude, etc. **13.** *Meteorol.* **a.** (of a cloud ceiling) limiting visibility to 15 metres (50 feet) or less. **b.** (of horizontal visibility) limited to 50 metres (165 feet) or less. ~*vb.* **·roes, +ro+ing, +roed. 14.** (*tr.*) to adjust (an instrument, apparatus, etc.) so as to read zero or a position taken as zero. ~*determiner.* **15.** *Informal, chiefly U.S.* no (thing) at all: *this job has zero interest.* [C17: from Italian, from Medieval Latin *zephirum*, from Arabic *sifr* empty, CIPHER]

ze·ro grav+i·ty *n.* the state or condition of weightlessness.

ze·ro graz+ing *n.* a type of dairy farming in which the cattle are fed with cut grass.

ze·ro hour *n.* **1.** *Military.* the time set for the start of an attack or the initial stage of an operation. **2.** *Informal.* a critical time, esp. at the commencement of an action.

ze·ro in *vb.* (*adv.*) **1.** (often foll. by *on*) to bring (a weapon) to bear (on a target), as while firing repeatedly. **2.** (*intr.;* foll. by *on*) *Informal.* to bring one's attention to bear (on a problem, etc.). **3.** (*intr.;* foll. by *on*) *Informal.* to converge (upon): *the police zeroed in on the site of the crime.*

ze·ro-ra·ted *adj.* denoting goods on which the buyer pays no value-added tax although the seller can claim back any tax he has paid.

ze·roth (ˈzɪərəʊθ) *adj.* denoting a term in a series that precedes the term otherwise regarded as the first term. [C20: from ZERO + -TH[2]]

zest (zɛst) *n.* **1.** invigorating or keen excitement or enjoyment: *a zest for living.* **2.** added interest, flavour, or charm; piquancy: *her presence gave zest to the occasion.* **3.** something added to give flavour or relish. **4.** the peel or skin of an orange or lemon, used as flavouring in drinks, etc. ~*vb.* **5.** (*tr.*) to give flavour, interest, or piquancy to. [C17: from French *zeste* peel of citrous fruits used as flavouring, of unknown origin] **—ˈzest+ful** *adj.* **—ˈzest+ful+ly** *adv.* **—ˈzest+ful+ness** *n.* **—ˈzest+less**

ze·ta (ˈziːtə) *n.* the sixth letter in the Greek alphabet (Z, ζ), a consonant, transliterated as *z.* [from Greek, of Semitic origin; compare Hebrew *sādhē*]

Ze·ta (ˈziːtə) *n.* (*foll. by the genitive case of a specified constellation*) the sixth brightest star in a constellation: *Zeta Tauri.*

ZETA (ˈziːtə) *n.* a torus-shaped apparatus used for research on controlled thermonuclear reactions and plasma physics. [C20: from *z(ero)-e(nergy) t(hermonuclear) a(pparatus)*]

Zet+land (ˈzɛtlənd) *n.* the official name (until 1974) of **Shetland.**

zeug+ma (ˈzjuːgmə) *n.* a figure of speech in which a word is used to modify or govern two or more words although appropriate to only one of them or making a different sense with each, as in the sentence *Mr. Pickwick took his hat and his leave* (Charles Dickens). [C16: via Latin from Greek: a yoking, from *zeugnunai* to yoke] **—zeug+mat+ic** (zjuːgˈmætɪk) *adj.* **—zeug+ˈmat·i·cal·ly** *adv.*

Zeus (zjuːs) *n.* the supreme god of the ancient Greeks, who became ruler of gods and men after he dethroned his father Cronus and defeated the Titans. He was the husband of his sister Hera and father by her and others of many gods, demigods, and mortals. He wielded thunderbolts and ruled the heavens, while his brothers Poseidon and Hades ruled the sea and underworld respectively. Roman counterpart: **Jupiter.**

Zeux·is (ˈzjuːksɪs) *n.* late 5th-century B.C. Greek painter, noted for the verisimilitude of his works.

Zhao Zi Yang (tʃaʊ ziː ˈjɑːŋ) *n.* born 1920, Chinese Communist politician; prime minister of China from 1981.

Zhda+nov (*Russian* ˈʒdanəf) *n.* a port in the SW Soviet Union, in the SE Ukrainian SSR near the Sea of Azov: industrial centre. Pop.: 459 000 (1975 est.). Former name (until 1948): **Mariupol.**

Zhi+to+mir (*Russian* ʒɪˈtɔmir) *n.* a city in the SW Soviet Union, in the central Ukrainian SSR. Pop.: 219 000 (1975 est.).

Zhiv·kov (*Bulgarian* ˈʒifkof) *n.* **To·dor** (ˈtɔdor). born 1911, Bulgarian statesman and party leader; prime minister (1962–71); head of state since 1971.

zho (zəʊ) *n., pl.* **zhos** *or* **zho.** a variant spelling of **zo.**

Zhu·kov (*Russian* ˈʒukəf) *n.* **Ge·or·gi Kon·stan·ti·no·vich** (gɪˈɔrgij kənstanˈtinəvitʃ). 1896–1974, Soviet marshal. In World War II, he led the offensives that broke the sieges of Stalingrad and Leningrad (1942–43) and later captured Warsaw and Berlin; minister of defence (1955–57).

Zi·a ul Haq (ˈzɪə ʊl ˈhak) *n.* born 1924, Pakistani general; chief martial law administrator of Pakistan since 1977, following the overthrow of Z. A. Bhutto by a military coup.

Zi·aur Rah·man (ˈziːaʊə ˈraxman) *n.* born 1936, Bangladesh general and statesman; president of Bangladesh (1977–81).

zib+el+ine (ˈzɪbəˌlaɪn, -lɪn) *n.* **1.** a sable or the fur of this animal. **2.** a thick cloth made of wool or other animal hair, having a long nap and a dull sheen. ~*adj.* **3.** of, relating to, or resembling a sable. [C16: from French, from Old Italian *zibellino,* ultimately of Slavonic origin; compare SABLE]

zib+et (ˈzɪbɪt) *n.* a large civet, *Viverra zibetha,* of S and SE Asia, having tawny fur marked with black spots and stripes. [C16: from Medieval Latin *zibethum,* from Arabic *zabād* CIVET]

Zieg·feld (ˈziːgˌfɛld) *n.* **Flor·enz** (ˈflɒrənz). 1869–1932, U.S. theatrical producer, noted for his series of extravagant revues (1907–31), known as the Ziegfeld Follies.

Zieg·ler cat·a+lyst (ˈziːglə) *n.* any of a group of catalysts, such as titanium trichloride ($TiCl_3$) and aluminium alkyl ($Al(CH_3)_3$), that produce stereospecific polymers. [C20: named after Carl *Ziegler* (1898–1973), German chemist]

ziff (zɪf) *n. Austral. informal.* a beard. [C20: of unknown origin]

zig+gu+rat (ˈzɪgʊˌræt), **zik+ku+rat,** *or* **zik·u+rat** (ˈzɪkʊˌræt) *n.* a type of rectangular temple tower or tiered mound erected by the Sumerians, Akkadians, and Babylonians in Mesopotamia. The tower of Babel is thought to be one of these. [C19: from Assyrian *ziqqurati* summit, height]

zig+zag (ˈzɪgˌzæg) *n.* **1.** a line or course characterized by sharp turns in alternating directions. **2.** one of the series of such turns. **3.** something having the form of a zigzag. ~*adj.* **4.** (*usually prenominal*) formed in or proceeding in a zigzag. ~*vb.* **+zags, +zag+ging, +zagged. 5.** to proceed or cause to proceed in a zigzag. **6.** (*tr.*) to form into a zigzag. [C18: from French, from German *zickzack,* from *Zacke* point, jagged projection; see TACK[1]] **—ˈzig+ˌzag+ged+ness** *n.*

zig+zag+ger (ˈzɪgˌzægə) *n.* **1.** a person or thing that zigzags. **2.** an attachment on a sewing machine for sewing zigzag stitches, as for joining two pieces of material.

zi·la, zil+la, *or* **zil+lah** (ˈzɪlɑː) *n.* an administrative district in India. [C19: from Hindi *dilah* division, from Arabic *dil'* part]

zi·la pa+ri+shad (ˈpʌrɪʃəd) *n.* a district council in India. [Hindi, from *zila'* district (from Arabic *dil'* part) + *parishad* assembly, council]

zilch (zɪltʃ) *U.S. slang.* nothing. [C20: of uncertain origin]

zil+lion (ˈzɪljən) *Informal.* ~*n., pl.* **+lions** *or* **+lion. 1.** (*often pl.*) an extremely large but unspecified number, quantity, or amount: *zillions of flies in this camp.* ~*determiner.* **2. a.** amounting to a zillion: *a zillion different problems.* **b.** (*as pronoun*): *I found a zillion under the sink.*

Zil·pah (ˈzɪlpə) *n. Old Testament.* Leah's maidservant, who bore Gad and Asher to Jacob (Genesis 30:10–13).

Zim+ba+bwe (zɪmˈbɑːbwɪ, -weɪ) *n.* **1.** a republic in Southern Africa: became independent in 1980 after a guerrilla war and ceasefire monitored by Commonwealth forces: Official language: English. Capital: Harare. Pop.: 6 100 000 (1974 est.). Area: 390 624 sq. km (150 820 sq. miles). Former name (1964–80) **Rhodesia. 2.** a ruined fortified settlement in Zimbabwe, which at its height, in the 15th century, was probably the capital of an empire covering SE Africa. **—Zim+ˈba·bwe·an** *adj., n.*

zinc (zɪŋk) *n.* **1.** a brittle bluish-white metallic element that becomes coated with a corrosion-resistant layer in moist air and occurs chiefly in sphalerite and smithsonite. It is a constituent of several alloys, esp. brass and nickel-silver, and is used in die-casting, galvanizing metals, and in battery electrodes. Symbol: Zn; atomic no.: 30; atomic wt.: 65.37; valency: 2; relative density: 7.133; melting pt.: 419.58°C; boiling pt.: 907°C. **2.** *Informal.* corrugated galvanized iron. [C17: from German *Zink,* perhaps from *Zinke* prong, from its jagged appearance in the furnace] **—ˈzinc+ic, ˈzinc+ous,** *or* **ˈzinc+oid** *adj.* **—ˈzinck·y, ˈzinc·y,** *or* **ˈzink·y** *adj.*

zin+cate (ˈzɪŋkeɪt) *n.* any of a class of salts derived from the amphoteric hydroxide of zinc, $Zn(OH)_2$, often thought of as the acid H_2ZnO_2.

zinc blende *n.* another name for **sphalerite.**

zinc chlo+ride *n.* a white odourless soluble poisonous granular solid used in manufacturing parchment paper and vulcanized fibre and in preserving wood. It is also a soldering flux, embalming agent, and a medical astringent and antiseptic. Formula: $ZnCl_2$ Also called: **butter of zinc.**

zinc+if+er+ous (zɪŋˈkɪfərəs) *adj.* containing or yielding zinc.

zinc+ite (ˈzɪŋkaɪt) *n.* a red or yellow mineral consisting of zinc oxide in hexagonal crystalline form. It occurs in metamorphosed limestone. Formula: ZnO.

zinck+en+ite (ˈzɪŋkəˌnaɪt) *n.* a variant spelling of **zinkenite.**

zin+co+graph (ˈzɪŋkəˌgrɑːf, -ˌgræf) *n.* **1.** a printing plate made by zincography. **2.** a print taken from such a plate.

zin+cog+ra+phy (zɪŋˈkɒgrəfɪ) *n.* the art or process of engraving zinc to form a printing plate. —zin·'cog·ra·pher *n.* —zin·co·graph·ic (ˌzɪŋkəˈgræfɪk) *or* ˌzin·co·'graph·i·cal *adj.*

zinc oint·ment *n.* a medicinal ointment consisting of zinc oxide, petrolatum, and paraffin, used to treat certain skin diseases.

zinc ox·ide *n.* a white insoluble powder used as a pigment in paints (**zinc white** or **Chinese white**), cosmetics, glass, and printing inks. It is an antiseptic and astringent and is used in making zinc ointment. Formula: ZnO. Also called: **flowers of zinc, philosopher's wool.**

zinc sul·phate *n.* a colourless soluble crystalline substance usually existing as the heptahydrate or monohydrate: used as a mordant, in preserving wood and skins, and in the electrodeposition of zinc. Formula: $ZnSO_4$. Also called: **white vitriol, zinc vitriol.**

zinc white *n.* another name for **Chinese white.**

zin·da·bad (ˈzɪndɑːˌbɑːd) *vb.* (*tr.*) *Indian.* long live: used as part of a slogan in India, Pakistan, etc. Compare **murdabad.** [Hindi, from Persian]

Zin·fan·del (ˈzɪnfənˌdɛl) *n.* a Californian wine grape originally transplanted from Europe and producing a quick-maturing fruity red wine. [C19: of unknown origin]

zing (zɪŋ) *n. Informal.* **1.** a short high-pitched buzzing sound, as of a bullet or vibrating string. **2.** vitality; zest. ~*vb.* **3.** (*intr.*) to make or move with or as if with a high-pitched buzzing sound. [C20: of imitative origin] —ˈ**zing·y** *adj.*

zin·ga·ro (ˈtsiŋgaˌro) *or* (*fem.*) ***zin·ga·ra*** (ˈtsiŋgaˌra) *Italian.* *n., pl.* ***·ri*** (-ˌri) *or* ***·re*** (-ˌre). an Italian Gypsy. [C16: ultimately from Greek *Athinganoi* name of an oriental people]

zin·gi·ber·a·ceous (ˌzɪndʒɪbəˈreɪʃəs) *adj.* of, relating to, or belonging to the *Zingiberaceae,* a family of tropical aromatic plants that typically have fleshy rhizomes and flowers in spikes or clusters: includes ginger and the plants yielding arrowroot and turmeric. [C19: via New Latin from *zingiber* GINGER]

zin·jan·thro·pus (zɪnˈdʒænθrəpəs) *n.* a type of australopithecine, *Australopithecus boisei* (formerly *Zinjanthropus boisei*), remains of which were discovered in the Olduvai Gorge in Tanzania in 1959. [C20: New Latin, from Arabic *Zinj* East Africa + Greek *anthrōpos* man]

zin·ken·ite *or* **zinck·en·ite** (ˈzɪŋkəˌnaɪt) *n.* a steel-grey metallic mineral consisting of a sulphide of lead and antimony. Formula: $PbSb_2S_4$. [C19: named after J. K. L. *Zincken* (1790–1862), German mineralogist]

zin·ni·a (ˈzɪnɪə) *n.* any annual or perennial plant of the genus *Zinnia,* of tropical and subtropical America, having solitary heads of brightly coloured flowers: family *Compositae* (composites).

Zi·nov·ievsk (*Russian* ziˈnɔvjɪfsk) *n.* a former name (1924–36) for **Kirovograd.**

Zin·zen·dorf (*German* ˈtsɪntsənˌdɔrf) *n.* Count **Ni·ko·la·us Lud·wig von** (ˈniːkolaʊs ˈluːtvɪç fɔn). 1700–60, German religious reformer, who organized the Moravian Church.

Zi·on (ˈzaɪən) *or* **Si·on** *n.* **1.** the hill on which the city of Jerusalem stands. **2.** *Judaism.* **a.** the ancient Israelites of the Bible. **b.** the modern Jewish nation. **c.** Israel as the national home of the Jewish people. **3.** *Christianity.* heaven regarded as the city of God and the final abode of his elect. **4.** any form of social organization, way of life, or life after death regarded as an ultimate goal. **5. a.** a religious community or its site, regarded as chosen by God and under his special protection. **b.** an ideal theocratic community, esp. any of the Christian Churches regarded as such a community.

Zi·on·ism (ˈzaɪəˌnɪzəm) *n.* **1.** a political movement for the establishment and support of a national homeland for Jews in Palestine, now concerned chiefly with the development of the modern state of Israel. **2.** a policy or movement for Jews to return to Palestine from the Diaspora. —ˈ**Zi·on·ist** *n., adj.* —ˌ**Zi·on·ˈis·tic** *adj.*

zip (zɪp) *n.* **1. a.** Also called: **zip fastener.** a fastening device operating by means of two parallel rows of metal or plastic teeth on either side of a closure that are interlocked by a sliding tab. U.S. term: **zipper. b.** (*modifier*) having or equipped with such a device: *a zip bag.* **2.** a short sharp whizzing sound, as of a passing bullet. **3.** *Informal.* energy; vigour; vitality. ~*vb.* **zips, zip·ping, zipped. 4.** (*tr.;* often foll. by *up*) to fasten (clothing, etc.) with a zip. **5.** (*intr.*) to move with a zip: *the bullet zipped past.* **6.** (*intr.;* often foll. by *along, through,* etc.) to hurry; rush: *they zipped through town.*

Zi·pan·gu (zɪˈpæŋguː) *n.* Marco Polo's name for **Cipango.**

zip code *n.* the U.S. equivalent of **postcode.** [C20: from *zone improvement plan*]

zip gun *n. U.S. slang.* a crude homemade pistol, esp. one powered by a spring or rubber band.

zip·per (ˈzɪpə) *n.* the U.S. word for **zip** (sense 1a.).

zip·py (ˈzɪpɪ) *adj.* **·pi·er, ·pi·est.** *Informal.* full of energy; lively.

zirc·al·loy (zɜːkˈælɔɪ) *n.* an alloy of zirconium containing small amounts of tin, chromium, and nickel. It is used in pressurized-water reactors.

zir·con (ˈzɜːkɒn) *n.* a reddish-brown, grey, green, blue, or colourless hard mineral consisting of zirconium silicate in tetragonal crystalline form with hafnium and some rare earths as impurities. It occurs principally in igneous rocks and is an important source of zirconium, zirconia, and hafnia: it is used as a gemstone and a refractory. Formula: $ZrSiO_4$. [C18: from German *Zirkon,* from French *jargon,* via Italian and Arabic, from Persian *zargūn* golden]

zir·co·ni·a (zɜːˈkəʊnɪə) *n.* another name (not in technical usage) for **zirconium oxide.**

zir·co·ni·um (zɜːˈkəʊnɪəm) *n.* a greyish-white metallic element, occurring chiefly in zircon, that is exceptionally corrosion-resistant and has low neutron absorption. It is used as a coating in nuclear and chemical plants, as a deoxidizer in steel, and alloyed with niobium in superconductive magnets. Symbol: Zr; atomic no.: 40; atomic wt.: 91.22; valency: 2, 3, or 4; relative density: 6.51; melting pt.: 1852°C; boiling pt.: 4377°C. [C19: from New Latin; see ZIRCON] —**zir·con·ic** (zɜːˈkɒnɪk) *adj.*

zir·co·ni·um ox·ide *n.* a white amorphous powder that is insoluble in water and highly refractory, used as a pigment for paints, a catalyst, and an abrasive. Formula: ZrO_2. Also called: **zirconia.**

Zis·ka (ˈzɪskə) *or* **Žiž·ka** (*Czech* ˈʒiʃka) *n.* **Jan** (jan). ?1370–1424, Bohemian soldier, who successfully led the Hussite rebellion (1420–24) against emperor Sigismund.

zith·er (ˈzɪðə) *n.* a plucked musical instrument consisting of numerous strings stretched over a resonating box, a few of which may be stopped on a fretted fingerboard. [C19: from German, from Latin *cithara,* from Greek *kithara*] —ˈ**zith·er·ist** *n.*

zi·zith (ˈtsɪtsɪs, tsiːˈtsiːt) *n.* (*functioning as sing. or pl.*) *Judaism.* the tassels or fringes of thread attached to the four corners of the tallith. [from Hebrew *sīsīth*]

Zla·to·ust (*Russian* zlətaˈust) *n.* a town in the central Soviet Union, on the Ay river: one of the chief metallurgical centres of the Urals. Pop.: 191 000 (1975 est.).

zlo·ty (ˈzlɒtɪ) *n., pl.* **·tys** *or* **·ty.** the standard monetary unit of Poland, divided into 100 groszy. [from Polish: golden, from *zlyoto* gold; related to Russian *zoloto* gold]

Zn *the chemical symbol for* zinc.

zo, zho, *or* **dzo** (zəʊ) *n., pl.* **zos, zhos, dzos** *or* **zo, zho, dzo.** a Tibetan breed of cattle, developed by crossing the yak with common cattle. [C20: from Tibetan]

zo- *combining form.* variant of **zoo-** before a vowel.

zo·a (ˈzəʊə) *n.* the plural of **zoon.**

-zo·a *suffix forming plural proper nouns.* indicating groups of animal organisms: *Protozoa.* [from New Latin, from Greek *zōia,* plural of *zōion* animal, living being]

zo·ae·a (zəʊˈiːə) *n., pl.* **zo·ae·ae** (zəʊˈiːiː) *or* **zo·ae·as.** a variant spelling of **zoea.**

Zo·an (ˈzəʊæn) *n.* the Biblical name for **Tanis.**

zod. *abbrev. for* zodiac.

zo·di·ac (ˈzəʊdɪˌæk) *n.* **1.** an imaginary belt extending 8° either side of the ecliptic, which contains the 12 **zodiacal constellations** and within which the moon and planets appear to move. It is divided into 12 equal areas, called **signs of the zodiac,** each named after the constellation in which it once lay. **2.** *Astrology.* a diagram, usually circular, representing this belt and showing the symbols, illustrations, etc., associated with each of the 12 signs of the zodiac, used to predict the future. **3.** *Rare.* a complete circuit; circle. [C14: from Old French *zodiaque,* from Latin *zōdiacus,* from Greek *zōidiakos* (*kuklos*) (circle) of signs, from *zōidion* animal sign, carved figure, from *zōion* animal] —**zo·di·a·cal** (zəʊˈdaɪəkəl) *adj.*

zo·di·a·cal con·stel·la·tion *n.* any of the 12 constellations after which the signs of the zodiac are named: Aries, Taurus, Gemini, Cancer, Leo, Virgo, Libra, Scorpio, Sagittarius, Capricorn, Aquarius, or Pisces.

zo·di·a·cal light *n.* a very faint cone of light in the sky, visible in the east just before sunrise and in the west just after sunset. It is probably due to the reflection of sunlight from cosmic dust in the plane of the ecliptic.

zo·e·a *or* **zo·ae·a** (zəʊˈiːə) *n., pl.* **zo·e·ae, zo·ae·ae** (zəʊˈiːiː) *or* **zo·e·as, zo·ae·as.** the free-swimming larva of a crab or related crustacean, which has well-developed abdominal appendages and may bear one or more spines. [C20: New Latin, from Greek *zōē* life]

Zof·fa·ny (ˈzɒfənɪ) *n.* **John** *or* **Jo·hann** ?1733–1810, British painter, esp. of portraits; born in Germany.

Zo·har (ˈzəʊhɑː) *n. Judaism.* a mystical work, consisting of a commentary on parts of the Pentateuch and the Hagiographa, probably composed in the second century A.D.

zois·ite (ˈzɔɪˌsaɪt) *n.* a grey, brown, or pink mineral consisting of hydrated calcium aluminium silicate in orthorhombic crystalline form. Formula: $Ca_2Al_3(SiO_4)_3(OH)$. [C19: from German *Zoisit;* named after Baron Sigismund *Zois* von Edelstein (1747–1819), Slovenian nobleman; see -ITE[1]]

Zo·la (ˈzəʊlə; *French* zɔˈla) *n.* **É·mile** (eˈmil). 1840–1902, French novelist and critic; chief exponent of naturalism. In *Les Rougon-Macquart* (1871–93), a cycle of 20 novels, he explains the behaviour of his characters in terms of their heredity: it includes *L'Assommoir* (1877), *Nana* (1880), *Germinal* (1885), and *La Terre* (1887). He is also noted for his defence of Dreyfus in his pamphlet *J'accuse* (1898).

Zoll·ver·ein *German.* (ˈtsɔlfɛrˌaɪn) *n.* the customs union of German states organized in the early 1830s under Prussian auspices. [C19: from *Zoll* tax, TOLL[2] + *Verein* union]

Zom·ba (ˈzɒmbə) *n.* a city in S Malawi: the capital of Malawi until 1971. Pop.: 20 000 (1970 est.).

zom·bie *or* **zom·bi** (ˈzɒmbɪ) *n., pl.* **·bies** *or* **·bis. 1.** a person who is or appears to be lifeless, apathetic, or totally lacking in independent judgment; automaton. **2.** a supernatural spirit that reanimates a dead body. **3.** a corpse brought to life in this manner. **4.** the snake god of voodoo cults in the West Indies, esp. Haiti, and in scattered areas of the southern U.S. **5.** the python god revered in parts of West Africa. [from Kongo *zumbi* good-luck fetish] —ˈ**zom·bi·ism** *n.*

zon+al ('zəʊnᵊl) *or* **zon·a+ry** ('zəʊnərɪ) *adj.* of, relating to, or of the nature of a zone. —**'zon+al+ly** *adv.*

zon+al soil *n.* soil having a profile determined mainly by the local climate and vegetation. Compare **azonal soil, intrazonal soil.**

zon+ate ('zəʊneɪt) *or* **zo+nat+ed** *adj.* marked with, divided into, or arranged in zones.

zo+na+tion (zəʊ'neɪʃən) *n.* arrangement in zones; zonate formation.

Zond (zɒnd) *n.* any of a series of unmanned Soviet spacecraft, first launched in 1964 as interplanetary space probes, the most successful of which, **Zond 3,** sent back photographs of the hidden side of the moon in 1965.

zone (zəʊn) *n.* **1.** a region, area, or section characterized by some distinctive feature or quality. **2.** a sphere of thought, disagreement, argument, etc. **3.** an area subject to a particular political, military, or government function, use, or jurisdiction: *a demilitarized zone.* **4.** (*often cap.*) *Geography.* one of the divisions of the earth's surface, esp. divided into latitudinal belts according to temperature. See **Torrid Zone, Frigid Zone, Temperate Zone. 5.** *Geology.* a distinctive layer or region of rock, characterized by particular fossils, metamorphism, structural deformity, etc. **6.** *Ecology.* an area, esp. a belt of land, having a particular flora and fauna determined by the prevailing environmental conditions. **7.** *Maths.* a portion of a sphere between two parallel planes intersecting the sphere. **8.** *Archaic or literary.* a girdle or belt. ~*vb.* (*tr.*) **9.** to divide into zones, as for different use, jurisdiction, activities, etc. **10.** to designate as a zone. **11.** to mark with or divide into zones. [C15: from Latin *zōna* girdle, climatic zone, from Greek *zōnē*]

zone re+fin+ing *n.* a technique for producing solids of extreme purity, esp. for use in semiconductors. The material, in the form of a bar, is melted in one small region that is passed along the solid. Impurities concentrate in the melt and are moved to the end of the bar.

zone+time ('zəʊn,taɪm) *n.* the standard time of the time zone in which a ship is located at sea, each zone extending 7½° to each side of a meridian.

zonked (zɒŋkt) *adj. Slang.* highly intoxicated from drugs or alcohol. [C20: of imitative origin]

zon+ule ('zɒnju:l) *n.* a small zone, band, or area. [C19: from New Latin *zōnula* a little ZONE] —**zon·u+lar** ('zɒnjʊlə) *adj.*

zoo (zu:) *n., pl.* **zoos.** a place where live animals are kept, studied, bred, and exhibited to the public. Formal term: **zoological garden.** [C19: shortened from *zoological gardens* (originally applied to those in London)]

zo·o- *or before a vowel* **zo-** *combining form.* indicating animals: *zooplankton.* [from Greek *zōion* animal]

zo·o+chem+is+try (,zəʊə'kɛmɪstrɪ) *n.* the branch of biochemistry that is concerned with the constituents of an animal's body. —**,zo·o+'chem·i+cal** *adj.*

zo·o+chore ('zəʊə,kɔ:) *n.* a plant the spores or seeds of which are dispersed by animals.

zo·o+ge·og+ra+phy (,zəʊədʒɪ'ɒgrəfɪ) *n.* the branch of zoology concerned with the geographical distribution of animals. —**,zo·o+ge·'og+ra+pher** *n.* —**zo·o+ge·o+graph+ic** (,zəʊə,dʒɪə'græfɪk) *or* **,zo·o+,ge·o+'graph·i+cal** *adj.* —**,zo·o+,ge·o+'graph·i+cal+ly** *adv.*

zo·o+gloe·a (,zəʊə'gli:ə) *n.* a mass of bacteria adhering together by a jelly-like substance derived from their cell walls. [C19: ZOO- + New Latin *gloea* glue, from Greek *gloia*] —**,zo·o+'gloe·al** *adj.*

zo+og+ra+phy (zəʊ'ɒgrəfɪ) *n.* the branch of zoology concerned with the description of animals. —**zo+'og+ra+pher** *n.* —**zo·o+graph+ic** (,zəʊə'græfɪk) *or* **,zo·o+'graph·i+cal** *adj.*

zo+oid ('zəʊɔɪd) *n.* **1.** any independent animal body, such as an individual of a coelenterate colony. **2.** a motile cell or body, such as a gamete, produced by an organism.

zool. *abbrev. for:* **1.** zoological. **2.** zoology.

zo+ol·a+try (zəʊ'ɒlətrɪ) *n.* **1.** (esp. in ancient or primitive religions) the worship of animals as the incarnations of certain deities, symbols of particular qualities or natural forces, etc. **2.** extreme or excessive devotion to animals, particularly domestic pets. —**zo+'ol+at+er** *n.* —**zo+'ol·a+trous** *adj.*

zo·o+log·i+cal gar+den *n.* the formal term for **zoo.**

zo+ol+o·gy (zəʊ'ɒlədʒɪ, zu:-) *n., pl.* **·gies. 1.** the study of animals, including their classification, structure, physiology, and history. **2.** the biological characteristics of a particular animal or animal group. **3.** the fauna characteristic of a particular region. **4.** a book, treatise, etc., dealing with any aspect of the study of animals. —**zo·o+log·i+cal** (,zəʊə'lɒdʒɪkᵊl, ,zu:ə-) *adj.* —**zo+'ol·o+gist** *n.*

zoom (zu:m) *vb.* **1.** to make or cause to make a continuous buzzing or humming sound. **2.** to move or cause to move with such a sound. **3.** (*intr.*) to move very rapidly; rush: *we zoomed through town.* **4.** to cause (an aircraft) to climb briefly at an unusually steep angle, or (of an aircraft) to climb in this way. **5.** (*intr.*) (of prices) to rise rapidly. ~*n.* **6.** the sound or act of zooming. **7.** See **zoom lens.**

zo+om+e·try (zəʊ'ɒmɪtrɪ) *n.* the branch of zoology concerned with the relative length or size of the different parts of an animal or animals. —**zo·o+met+ric** (,zəʊə'mɛtrɪk) *or* **,zo·o+'met+ri+cal** *adj.*

zoom in *or* **out** *vb.* (*intr., adv.*) *Photog., films, television.* to rapidly increase or decrease the magnification of the image of a distant object by means of a zoom lens.

zoom lens *n.* a lens system that allows the focal length of a camera lens to be varied continuously without altering the sharpness of the image. See also **telephoto lens.**

zo·o+mor+phism (,zəʊə'mɔ:fɪzəm) *n.* **1.** the conception or representation of deities in the form of animals. **2.** the use of animal forms or symbols in art, literature, etc. —**,zo·o+'mor+phic** *adj.*

zo·on ('zəʊɒn) *n., pl.* **zo·a** ('zəʊə) *or* **zo·ons.** a less common term for **zooid** (sense 1). [C19: from New Latin, from Greek *zōion* animal; related to Greek *zōē* life] —**zo+'on+al** *adj.*

-zo·on *n. combining form.* indicating an individual animal or an independently moving entity derived from an animal: *spermatozoon.* [from Greek *zōion* animal]

zo+on·o+sis (zəʊ'ɒnəsɪs, ,zəʊə'nəʊsɪs) *n., pl.* **+ses** (-si:z). *Pathol.* any infection or disease that is transmitted to man from lower vertebrates.

zo+oph·a+gous (zəʊ'ɒfəgəs) *adj.* feeding on animals.

zo·o+phile ('zəʊə,faɪl) *n.* a person who is devoted to animals and their protection from practices such as vivisection. —**zo·o+phil+ic** (,zəʊə'fɪlɪk) *adj.*

zo·o+phil·i·a (,zəʊə'fɪlɪə) *n.* a morbid condition in which a person has a sexual attraction for animals; bestiality.

zo+oph·i+lism (zəʊ'ɒfɪ,lɪzəm) *n.* the tendency to be emotionally attached to animals.

zo+oph·i+lous (zəʊ'ɒfɪləs) *adj.* **1.** (of plants) pollinated by animals. **2.** of, characterized by, or relating to zoophilism.

zo·o+pho·bi·a (,zəʊə'fəʊbɪə) *n.* an unusual or morbid dread of animals. —**zo+oph·o+bous** (zəʊ'ɒfəbəs) *adj.*

zo·o+phyte ('zəʊə,faɪt) *n.* any animal resembling a plant, such as a sea anemone. —**zo·o+phyt+ic** (,zəʊə'fɪtɪk) *or* **,zo·o+'phyt·i+cal** *adj.*

zo·o+plank+ton (,zəʊə'plæŋktən) *n.* the animal constituent of plankton, which consists mainly of small crustaceans and fish larvae. Compare **phytoplankton.**

zo·o+plas+ty ('zəʊə,plæstɪ) *n.* the surgical transplantation to man of animal tissues. —**,zo·o+'plas+tic** *adj.*

zo·o+sperm ('zəʊə,spɜ:m) *n.* another word for **spermatozoon.** —**zo·o+sper+mat+ic** (,zəʊəspɜ:'mætɪk) *adj.*

zo·o+spo+ran+gi·um (,zəʊəspɔ:'rændʒɪəm) *n., pl.* **+gi·a** (-dʒɪə). *Botany.* a sporangium that produces zoospores. —**,zo·o+spo+'ran+gi·al** *adj.*

zo·o+spore ('zəʊə,spɔ:) *n.* **1.** an asexual spore of some algae and fungi that moves by means of flagella. **2.** one of several spores produced in a saclike body (sporocyst) by some parasitic protozoans. —**,zo·o+'spor+ic** *or* **zo+os+por+ous** (zəʊ'ɒspərəs, ,zəʊə'spɔ:rəs) *adj.*

zo+os+ter+ol (zəʊ'ɒstə,rɒl) *n.* any of a group of animal sterols, such as cholesterol.

zo·o+tech+nics (,zəʊə'tɛknɪks) *n.* the science concerned with the domestication and breeding of animals.

zo+ot·o+my (zəʊ'ɒtəmɪ) *n.* the branch of zoology concerned with the dissection and anatomy of animals. —**zo·o+tom+ic** (,zəʊə'tɒmɪk) *or* **,zo·o+'tom·i+cal** *adj.* —**,zo·o+'tom·i+cal+ly** *adv.* —**zo+'ot·o+mist** *n.*

zo·o+tox+in (,zəʊə'tɒksɪn) *n.* a toxin, such as snake venom, that is produced by an animal. Compare **phytotoxin.** —**,zo·o+'tox+ic** *adj.*

zoot suit (zu:t) *n. Slang.* a man's suit consisting of baggy trousers with very tapered bottoms and a long jacket with wide padded shoulders, popular esp. in the U.S. in the 1940s. —**'zoot-,suit·er** *n.*

zo+ril+la (zə'rɪlə) *or* **zo+rille** (zə'rɪl) *n.* a skunklike African musteline mammal, *Ictonyx striatus,* having a long black-and-white coat. [C18: from French, from Spanish *zorrillo* a little fox, from *zorro* fox]

Zorn (*Swedish* so:rn) *n.* **An·ders Le·on·hard** ('andərs 'le:ɔnard). 1860–1920, Swedish painter and etcher, esp. of impressionist portraits and landscapes.

Zor·o·as·ter (,zɒrəʊ'æstə) *n.* Avestan name **Zarathustra.** ?628–?551 B.C., Persian prophet; founder of Zoroastrianism.

Zo+ro+as+tri·an (,zɒrəʊ'æstrɪən) *adj.* **1.** of or relating to Zoroastrianism or Zoroaster. ~*n.* **2.** a follower of Zoroaster or adherent of Zoroastrianism: in modern times a Gabar or a Parsee.

Zo+ro+as+tri+an+ism (,zɒrəʊ'æstrɪən,ɪzəm) *or* **Zo+ro+as+trism** *n.* the dualistic religion founded by the Persian prophet Zoroaster in the late 7th or early 6th centuries B.C. and set forth in the sacred writings of the Zend-Avesta. It is based on the concept of a continuous struggle between Ormazd (or Ahura Mazda), the god of creation, light, and goodness, and his arch enemy, Ahriman, the spirit of evil and darkness, and it includes a highly developed ethical code. Also called: **Mazdaism.**

Zor·ri·lla y Mo·ral (*Spanish* θor'riʎa i mo'ral) *n.* **Jo·sé** (xo'se). 1817–93, Spanish poet and dramatist, noted for his romantic plays based on national legends, esp. *Don Juan Tenorio* (1844).

zos+ter ('zɒstə) *n. Pathol.* short for **herpes zoster.** [C18: from Latin: shingles, from Greek *zōstēr* girdle]

Zou+ave (zu:'ɑ:v, zwɑ:v) *n.* **1.** (formerly) a member of a body of French infantry composed of Algerian recruits noted for their dash, hardiness, and colourful uniforms. **2.** a member of any body of soldiers wearing a similar uniform or otherwise modelled on the French Zouaves, esp. a volunteer in such a unit of the Union Army in the American Civil War. [C19: from French, from *Zwāwa,* tribal name in Algeria]

Zoug (zug) *n.* the French name for **Zug.**

zounds (zaʊndz) *or* **swounds** (zwaʊndz, zaʊndz) *interj. Archaic.* a mild oath indicating surprise, indignation, etc. [C16: euphemistic shortening of *God's wounds*]

zoy+si·a ('zɔɪzɪə) *n.* any creeping perennial grass of the genus *Zoysia,* of warm dry regions, having short stiffly pointed leaves: often used for lawns. [C19: from New Latin, named after Karl von *Zois* (d. 1800), German botanist]

Z.P.G. *abbrev. for* zero population growth.
Zr *the chemical symbol for* zirconium.
Zsig·mon·dy (*German* 'ʃɪgmɔndi) *n.* **Ri·chard A·dolf** ('rɪçart 'a:dɔlf). 1865–1929, German chemist, born in Austria, noted for his work on colloidal particles and, with H. Siedentopf, his introduction (1903) of the ultramicroscope: Nobel prize for chemistry 1925.
zuc+chet+to (tsu:'kɛtəʊ, su:-, zu:-) *n., pl.* **+tos.** *R.C. Church.* a small round skullcap worn by certain ecclesiastics and varying in colour according to the rank of the wearer, the Pope wearing white, cardinals red, bishops violet, and others black. [C19: from Italian, from *zucca* a gourd, head, from Late Latin *cucutia* gourd, probably from Latin *cucurbita*]
zuc+chi+ni (tsu:'ki:nɪ, zu:-) *n., pl.* **+ni** *or* **+nis.** the U.S. name for **courgette.** [Italian, pl. of *zucchino* a little gourd, from *zucca* gourd; see ZUCCHETTO]
Zug (*German* tsu:k) *n.* **1.** a canton of N central Switzerland: the smallest Swiss canton; mainly German-speaking and Roman Catholic; joined the Swiss Confederation in 1352. Capital: Zug. Pop.: 67 996 (1970). Area: 239 sq. km (92 sq. miles). **2.** a town in N central Switzerland, the capital of Zug canton, on Lake Zug. Pop.: 22 972 (1970). **3. Lake.** a lake in N central Switzerland, in Zug and Schwyz cantons. Area: 39 sq. km (15 sq. miles). French name: **Zoug.**
zug+zwang (*German* 'tsu:ktsvaŋ) *Chess.* ~*n.* **1.** a position in which one player can move only with loss or severe disadvantage. ~*vb.* **2.** (*tr.*) to manoeuvre (one's opponent) into a zugzwang. [from German, from *Zug* a pull, tug + *Zwang* force, compulsion]
Zui+der Zee *or* **Zuy+der Zee** ('zaɪdə 'zi:; *Dutch* 'zœɪdər 'ze:) *n.* a former inlet of the North Sea in the N coast of the Netherlands: sealed off from the sea by a dam in 1932, dividing it into the Waddenzee and the freshwater IJsselmeer, with several large areas under reclamation.
Zuid+hol+land (zœɪt'hɔlɑnt) *n.* the Dutch name for **South Holland.**
Zu·lu ('zu:lʊ -lu:) *n.* **1.** (*pl.* **+lus** *or* **+lu**) a member of a tall Negroid people of SE Africa, living chiefly in N Natal, who became dominant during the 19th century due to a warrior-clan system organized by the powerful leader, Tchaka. **2.** the language of this people, belonging to the Bantu group of the Niger-Congo family, closely related to Swazi and Xhosa.
Zu+lu+land ('zu:lʊ,lænd, 'zu:lu:-) *n.* a region of South Africa, in NE Natal on the Indian Ocean; partly corresponds to Kwazulu bantustan. Chief town: Eshowe. Pop.: 2 105 509 (1970). Area: 26 838 sq. km (10 362 sq. miles).
Zun+gar+i·a (zʊŋ'gɛərɪə) *n.* a variant spelling of **Dzungaria.**
Zu·ñi ('zu:nji:, 'su:-) *n.* **1.** (*pl.* **·ñis** *or* **·ñi**) a member of a North American Indian people of W New Mexico. **2.** the language of this people, of no known relationship. —**'Zu+ñi·an** *adj., n.*
Zur·ba·rán (*Spanish* ,θurβa'ran) *n.* **Fran·cis·co de** (fran'θisko ðe). 1598–1664, Spanish Baroque painter, esp. of religious subjects.
Zü+rich ('zjʊərɪk; *German* 'tsy:rɪç) *n.* **1.** a canton of NE Switzerland: mainly Protestant and German-speaking. Capital: Zürich. Pop.: 1 107 788 (1970). Area: 1 729 sq. km (668 sq. miles). **2.** a city in NE Switzerland, the capital of Zürich canton, on Lake Zürich: the largest town and industrial centre in Switzerland; centre of the Swiss Reformation; financial centre. Pop.: 396 300 (1975 est.). **3. Lake.** a lake in N Switzerland, mostly in Zürich canton. Area: 89 sq. km (34 sq. miles).
Zuy+der Zee ('zaɪdə 'zi:; *Dutch* 'zœɪdər 'ze:) *n.* a variant spelling of **Zuider Zee.**
Zweig (*German* tsvaɪk) *n.* **1. Ar·nold** ('arnɔlt). 1887–1968, German novelist, famous for his realistic war novel *The Case of Sergeant Grischa* (1927). **2. Ste·fan** ('ʃtɛfan). 1881–1942, Austrian novelist, dramatist, essayist, and poet.
Zwick·au (*German* 'tsvɪkaʊ) *n.* a city in S East Germany: Anabaptist movement founded here (1521); coal-mining and industrial centre. Pop.: 122 604 (1975 est.).
zwie+back ('zwaɪ,bæk, 'zwi:-; *German* 'tsvi:bak) *n.* a small type of rusk, which has been baked first as a loaf, then sliced and toasted, usually bought ready-made. [German: twice-baked]
Zwing·li (*German* 'tsvɪŋli) *n.* **Ul·rich** ('ʊlrɪç) *or* **Hul·dreich** ('hʊltraɪç). 1484–1531, Swiss leader of the Reformation, based in Zurich. He denied the Eucharistic presence, holding that the Communion was merely a commemoration of Christ's death.
Zwing·li·an ('zwɪŋglɪən, 'swɪŋ-, 'tsvɪŋ-) *n.* **1.** an upholder of the religious doctrines or movement of Zwingli. ~*adj.* **2.** of or relating to Zwingli, his religious movement, or his doctrines, esp. his interpretation of the Eucharist. —**'Zwing+li+an+ism** *n.* —**'Zwing+li+an+ist** *n.*
zwit+ter·i+on ('tsvɪtər,aɪən) *n. Chem.* an ion that carries both a positive and a negative charge. [C20: from German *Zwitter* mongrel + ION] —**zwit+ter·i+on+ic** (,tsvɪtəraɪ'ɒnɪk) *adj.*
Zwol+le (*Dutch* 'zwɔlə) *n.* a town in the central Netherlands, capital of Overijssel province. Pop.: 77 122 (1973 est.).
Zwor·y·kin ('zwɔ:rɪkɪn) *n.* **Vla·di·mir Kos·ma** ('vlædɪmɪə 'kɒsmə). 1889–1982, U.S. physicist and television pioneer, born in Russia. He developed the first practical television camera.
zyg·a+poph·y+sis (,zɪgə'pɒfɪsɪs, ,zaɪgə-) *n., pl.* **+ses** (-,si:z). *Anatomy, zoology.* one of several processes on a vertebra that articulates with the corresponding process on an adjacent vertebra. —**zyg+ap·o+phys+e·al** *or* **zig+ap·o+phys+i·al** (,zɪgæpə'fɪzɪəl) *adj.*
zy·go- *or before a vowel* **zyg-** *combining form.* indicating a pair or a union: *zygodactyl; zygospore.* [from Greek *zugon* yoke]
zy+go+dac+tyl (,zaɪgəʊ'dæktɪl, ,zɪgə-) *adj. also* **zy+go+dac+ty+lous. 1.** (of the feet of certain birds) having the first and fourth toes directed backwards and the second and third forwards. ~*n.* **2.** a zygodactyl bird. ~Compare **heterodactyl.** —**,zy+go+'dac+tyl+ism** *n.*
zy+go+ma (zaɪ'gəʊmə, zɪ-) *n., pl.* **+ma+ta** (-mətə). another name for **zygomatic arch.** [C17: via New Latin from Greek, from *zugon* yoke] —**zy+go+mat+ic** (,zaɪgəʊ'mætɪk, ,zɪg-) *adj.*
zy+go+mat+ic arch *n.* the slender arch of bone that forms a bridge between the cheekbone and the temporal bone on each side of the skull of mammals. Also called: **zygoma.**
zy+go+mat+ic bone *n.* either of two bones, one on each side of the skull, that form part of the side wall of the eye socket and part of the zygomatic arch; cheekbone. Also called: **malar, malar bone.**
zy+go+mat+ic pro+cess *n.* a slender bony process of the temporal bone that forms part of the zygomatic arch.
zy+go+mor+phic (,zaɪgəʊ'mɔ:fɪk, ,zɪg-) *or* **zy+go+mor+phous** *adj.* (of a flower) capable of being cut in only one plane so that the two halves are mirror images. See also **actinomorphic.** —**,zy+go+'mor+phism** *or* **'zy+go+,mor+phy** *n.*
zy+go+phyl+la+ceous (,zaɪgəʊfɪ'leɪʃəs, ,zɪg-) *adj.* of, relating to, or belonging to the *Zygophyllaceae,* an Old World family of flowering plants having pinnate leaves and capsules as fruits: includes the bean caper and guaiacum.
zy+go+phyte ('zaɪgəʊ,faɪt, 'zɪg-) *n.* a plant, such as an alga, that reproduces by means of zygospores.
zy+go+sis (zaɪ'gəʊsɪs, zɪ-) *n. Biology.* another name for **conjugation.** —**zy+gose** ('zaɪgəʊs, 'zɪg-) *adj.*
zy+go+spore ('zaɪgəʊ,spɔ:, 'zɪg-) *n.* a thick-walled sexual spore formed from the zygote of some fungi and algae. —**,zy+go+'spor+ic** *adj.*
zy+gote ('zaɪgəʊt, 'zɪg-) *n.* **1.** the cell resulting from the union of an ovum and a spermatozoon. **2.** the organism that develops from such a cell. [C19: from Greek *zugōtos* yoked, from *zugoun* to yoke] —**zy+got+ic** (zaɪ'gɒtɪk, zɪ-) *adj.* —**zy+'got·i+cal+ly** *adv.*
zy+go+tene ('zaɪgə,ti:n, 'zɪg-) *n.* the second stage of the prophase of meiosis, during which homologous chromosomes become associated in pairs (bivalents).
zy+mase ('zaɪmeɪs) *n.* a mixture of enzymes that is obtained as an extract from yeast and ferments sugars.
zy·mo- *or before a vowel* **zym-** *combining form.* indicating fermentation: *zymology.* [from Greek *zumē* leaven]
zy+mo+gen ('zaɪməʊ,dʒɛn) *n. Biochem.* any of a group of compounds that are inactive precursors of enzymes and are activated by a kinase.
zy+mo+gen+e·sis (,zaɪməʊ'dʒɛnɪsɪs) *n.* the conversion of a zymogen into an enzyme.
zy+mo+gen+ic (,zaɪməʊ'dʒɛnɪk) *adj.* **1.** of, or relating to a zymogen. **2.** capable of causing zymogenesis.
zy+mol+o·gy (zaɪ'mɒlədʒɪ) *n.* the chemistry of fermentation. —**zy+mo+log+ic** (,zaɪməʊ'lɒdʒɪk) *or* **,zy+mo+'log·i+cal** *adj.* —**zy+'mol·o+gist** *n.*
zy+mol·y+sis (zaɪ'mɒlɪsɪs) *n.* the process of fermentation. Also called: **zymosis.** —**zy+mo+lyt+ic** (,zaɪməʊ'lɪtɪk) *adj.*
zy+mom+e+ter (zaɪ'mɒmɪtə) *n.* an instrument for estimating the degree of fermentation.
zy+mo+sis (zaɪ'məʊsɪs) *n., pl.* **+ses** (-si:z). **1.** *Med.* **a.** any infectious disease. **b.** the developmental process or spread of such a disease. **2.** another name for **zymolysis.**
zy+mot+ic (zaɪ'mɒtɪk) *adj.* **1.** of, relating to, or causing fermentation. **2.** relating to or caused by infection; denoting or relating to an infectious disease. —**zy+'mot·i+cal+ly** *adv.*
zy+mur+gy ('zaɪmɜ:dʒɪ) *n.* the branch of chemistry concerned with fermentation processes in brewing, etc.
Zyr+i+an ('zɪrɪən) *n.* **1.** the language of the people of the Komi ASSR, belonging to the Finno-Ugric family; Komi. ~*adj.* **2.** of or relating to this language or its speakers.

TABLES OF WEIGHTS AND MEASURES

THE METRIC SYSTEM

Linear Measure

		1 millimetre	=	0.039 37	inch
10 millimetres	=	1 centimetre	=	0.3937	inch
10 decimetres	=	1 metre	=	39.37	inches or 3.2808 feet
		1 kilometre	=	0.621	mile or 3280.8 feet

Square Measure

		1 square millimetre	=	0.001 55	square inch
100 square millimetres	=	1 square centimetre	=	0.154 99	square inch
100 square decimetres	=	1 square metre	=	1549.9	square inches or 1.196 square yards
100 square hectometres	=	1 square kilometre	=	0.386	square mile or 247.1 acres

Land Measure

100 centiares	=	1 are	=	119.6	square yards
100 ares	=	1 hectare	=	2.471	acres
100 hectares	=	1 square kilometre	=	0.386	square mile or 247.1 acres

Volume Measure

1000 cubic millimetres	=	1 cubic centimetre	=	0.061 02	cubic inch
1000 cubic centimetres	=	1 cubic decimetre (1 litre)	=	61.023	cubic inches or 0.0353 cubic foot
1000 cubic decimetres	=	1 cubic metre	=	35.314	cubic feet or 1.308 cubic yards

Weights

10 decigrammes	=	1 gram	=	15.432	grains or 0.035 274 ounce (avdp.)
10 hectogrammes	=	1 kilogram	=	2.2046	pounds
10 quintals	=	1 metric ton	=	2204.6	pounds

THE IMPERIAL SYSTEM

Linear Measure

1 mil	=	0.001 inch	=	0.0254	millimetre
1 inch	=	1000 mils	=	2.54	centimetres
12 inches	=	1 foot	=	0.3048	metre
3 feet	=	1 yard	=	0.9144	metre
5½ yards or 16½ feet	=	1 rod (or pole or perch)	=	5.029	metres
40 rods	=	1 furlong	=	201.168	metres
8 furlongs or 1760 yards or 5280 feet	=	1 (statute) mile	=	1.6093	kilometres

Square Measure

		1 square inch	=	6.452	square centimetres
144 square inches	=	1 square foot	=	929.03	square centimetres
9 square feet	=	1 square yard	=	0.8361	square metre
30¼ square yards	=	1 square rod (or square pole or square perch)	=	25.292	square metres
160 square rods or 4840 square yards or 43 560 square feet	=	1 acre	=	0.4047	hectare
640 acres	=	1 square mile	=	259.00	hectares or 2.590 square kilometres

Cubic Measure

		1 cubic inch	=	16.387	cubic centimetres
1728 cubic inches	=	1 cubic foot	=	0.0283	cubic metre
27 cubic feet	=	1 cubic yard	=	0.7646	cubic metre

Nautical Measure

6 feet = 1 fathom = 1.829 metres

100 fathoms = 1 cable's length

(In the Royal Navy, 608 feet, or 185.319 metres = 1 cable's length)

10 cables' length = 1 international nautical mile = 1.852 kilometres (exactly)

1 international nautical mile = 1.150 779 statute miles

(the length of a minute of longitude at the equator)

60 nautical miles = *1 degree of a great circle of the earth*

= 69.047 statute miles